Film Guide

Penguin Books

The first edition of the *Time Out Film Guide*, edited by Tom Milne, was published in 1989, to mark *Time Out* magazine's twenty-first birthday. Since 1968 *Time Out* has grown from a flimsy fortnightly broadsheet to become a London institution. The magazine has chronicled every kind of event in the city and development in culture – in art, music, clubs, dance, theatre, TV and film, in high art and on the streets.

The previews, reviews and interviews from *Time Out*'s pages constitute a very special record of the movements, currents or crazes in cinema over the past 30 years, whether in Hollywood, France or Hong Kong. This material – reviews written on the actual release or re-release of each film – is the core of the annual *Time Out Film Guide*, together with many reviews from eras not covered in the magazine and a significant number of feature films released straight to video.

The seventh edition of the *Film Guide*, in addition to some 530 extra reviews (with enriched coverage, once again, of Asian cinema), contains the results of our international readers' poll to find world cinema's Top One Hundred films,

expanded indexes, and an updated appendix for the chief prizewinners at the Academy Awards and the BAFTA ceremonies, plus those from the Cannes, Berlin and Venice film festivals. The 1999 *Film Guide* also contains *Time Out* magazine's Top One Hundred Poll marking the Centenary of Cinema.

John Pym, who took over the editorship of the *Film Guide* in 1994, was born in north London in 1947 and spent many childhood afternoons in the shilling seats of the Tolmer, the Everyman and the Odeon Muswell Hill. He was educated in England and America and began reviewing films for *Time Out* in 1975 before joining the British Film Institute for a 13-year spell on the *Monthly Film Bulletin* and *Sight and Sound*. He has written four books on the cinema, including a history of Channel 4 TV's 'Film on Four', and has made independent documentary films on, among others, the reclusive American author Evan Connell and the film-makers James Ivory and Ismail Merchant. He lives in Kent and has a regular front-row seat at the Plaza, Oxted.

Edited and designed by
Time Out Guides Ltd
Universal House
251 Tottenham Court Road
London W1P OAB
Tel +44 (0)171 813 3000
Fax +44 (0)171 813 6001
E-mail guides@timeout.co.uk
http://www.timeout.co.uk

Editor editions 4–7 John Pym
Editor editions 1–3 Tom Milne
Consultant Editor Geoff Andrew

Managing Editor Peter Fiennes

Art Director John Oakey
Art Editor Mandy Martin
Designers Benjamin de Lotz, Scott Moore,
Lucy Grant, Paul Mansfield
Scanning/Imaging Chris Quinn
Picture Editor Kerri Miles
Picture Researcher Emma Tremlett
Illustrations David Lyttleton
Lauren Bacall photography The Kobal Collection

Publisher Tony Elliott
Managing Director Mike Hardwick
Financial Director Kevin Ellis

The Editors wish to thank the following for advice and
assistance:
Derek Adams, Tom Charity and Wally Hammond of
the Time Out film section; Chris Bohn, Bob Baker and
Tony Rayns; Bob Mastrangelo and Michael Walker;
Simon Chappell and Miranda Wildi; Sarah Guy, Nicholas
Royle and Caroline Taverne; Geoffrey Macnab and
Trevor Johnston; Celia, William and Martha Pym; Tom
Milne and Markku Salmi.

Film Guide

Edited by John Pym

Seventh Edition 1999

Penguin Books

PENGUIN BOOKS

Published by the Penguin Group
Penguin Books Ltd, 27 Wrights Lane, London W8 5TZ, England
Penguin Putnam Inc, 375 Hudson Street, New York, New York 10014, USA
Penguin Books Australia Ltd, Ringwood, Victoria, Australia
Penguin Books Canada Ltd, 10 Alcorn Avenue, Toronto, Ontario, Canada M4V 3B2
Penguin Books (NZ) Ltd, Private Bag 102902, NSMC, Auckland , New Zealand

Penguin Books Ltd, Registered Offices: Harmondsworth, Middlesex, England

First published 1989
Second edition 1991
Third edition 1993
Fourth Edition 1995
Fifth edition 1996
Sixth edition 1997
Seventh edition 1998
10 9 8 7 6 5 4 3 2 1

Copyright © Time Out Group, 1989, 1991, 1993, 1995, 1996, 1997, 1998
All rights reserved

The moral right of the author has been asserted

Printed in England by Clays Ltd, St Ives plc

Contents

List of Contributors

This guide is a compilation of reviews published in *Time Out* magazine's Film and TV columns since 1968. The reviews have been selected and edited by the editors. Individual reviewers can be identified by their initials, listed here, and printed at the end of each entry. Where no initials are given after an entry the identity of the reviewer is no longer known.

AB	Anne Billson	DAt	Don Atyeo	JPi	Jim Pines
AC	Al Clark	DC	David Curtis	JPy	John Pym
ACh	Anita Chaudhuri	DD	Deke Dusinberre	JR	Jonathan Rosenbaum
AG	Anton Gill	DJ	DH Joseph	JRo	Jonathan Romney
AH	Amanda Hopkinson	DJe	David Jenkins	JS	Jennifer Selway
AJ	Alkarim Jivani	DMcG	David McGillivray	JW	John Wyver
AM	Angela Mason	DMacp	Don Macpherson	JWi	Judith Williamson
AMac	Angus MacKinnon	DP	David Pirie	JWil	Julia Williams
AN	Andrew Nickolds	DPe	Don Peretta	KG	Keith Griffiths
AO	Alistair Owen	DPer	David Perry	KJ	Kevin Jackson
AP	Andrew Pulver	DR	Don Ranvaud	KM	Karen McLuskey
AR	Allen Robertson	DRo	David Rose	LC	Laura Connelly
AS	Allan T Sutherland	DS	Deborah Steels	LD	Laura Lee Davies
ASh	Andrew Shields	DSi	Diana Simmonds	LF	Lizzie Francke
AT	Archie Tait	DT	David Thompson	LH	Liz Heron
ATu	Adrian Turner	DW	Dominic Wells	LM	Lynda Myles
BB	Belkis Bhegani	EP	Elaine Paterson	LMu	Lisa Mullen
BBa	Bob Baker	EPe	Emma Perry	LQ	Leonard Quart
BC	Brian Case	EPr	Edward W Proctor	LR	Len Richmond
BD	Bruce Dessau	FD	Frances Dickinson	LS	Lindsay Shapero
BG	Brian Glasser	FF	Fiona Ferguson	LU	Lisa Ubsdell
BP	Brian Priestley	FL	Frances Lass	LW	Lesley Weeks
BPa	Beverly Pagram	FM	Fiona Morrow	MA	Martyn Auty
CA	Chris Auty	GA	Geoff Andrew	MB	Mike Bygrave
CAub	Crispin Aubrey	GAd	Gilbert Adair	MBo	Mihir Bose
CB	Colin Booth	GB	Geoff Brown	MC	Mark Cordery
CG	Carl Gardner	GD	Giovanni Dadomo	MG	Michael Griffiths
CGi	Chris Gilders	GM	Geoffrey Macnab	MH	Matthew Hoffman
CL	Chris Lloyd	GO	Grainne O'Kelly	MHo	Mark Hosenball
CM	Colette Maude	GS	Gerry Sandford	MHoy	Martin Hoyle
CO'S	Catriona O'Shaughnessy	GSa	Geoff Samuel	MK	Mark Kermode
		HH	Helen Hawkins	MM	Mandy Merck
CO'Su	Charlotte O'Sullivan	HK	Helen Van Kruyssen	MO'P	Michael O'Pray
CPa	Claire Pajaczkowska	HM	Helen MacKintosh	MP	Mike Phillips
CPe	Chris Petit	HR	Helen Rose	MPa	Myles Palmer
CPea	Chris Peachment	IA	Isabelle Appio	MPe	Mal Peachey
CR	Cynthia Rose	IB	Ian Birch	MPl	Martin Plimmer
CS	Colin Shearman	IC	Ian Christie	MPo	Mike Poole
CSi	Clancy Sigal	JB	Jerome Burne	MS	Mark Sanderson
CW	Chris Wicking	JBa	Jane Bartlett	MSu	Martin Sutton
DA	Derek Adams	JC	John Collis	MV	Micheline Victor (now Wandor)
		JCh	James Christopher		
		JCl	Jane Clarke	MW	Mark Williams
		JCo	John Conquest	NA	Nigel Algar
		JCoh	Joyce Cohen	NAn	Nigel Andrews
		JD	Jan Dawson	NB	Nick Bradshaw
		JdeG	Jessica de Grazia	NC	Nick Coleman
		JDuC	John Du Cane	NF	Nigel Floyd
		JE	Jane Edwardes	NFe	Nigel Ferguson
		JF	John Ford	NJ	Nicolas Joy
		JG	John Gill	NK	Naseem Khan
		JGl	Joanne Glasbey	NKe	Nigel Kendall
		JK	Jeff Katz	NR	Nick Roddick
		JM	Jo Creed-Miles	NRo	Nicholas Royle
		JMo	John Morrish	OM	Olivia Maxwell
		JMu	Jan Murray	PB	Peter Ball
		JO'C	John O'Connell	PBu	Pat Butcher
		JP	John Preston	PBur	Paul Burston

PH	Phil Hardy
PHo	Pierre Hodgson
PK	Paul Kerr
PM	Paul Moffat
PP	Peter Paphides
PT	Paul Taylor
RB	Ruth Baumgarten
RC	Richard Combs
RD	Raymond Durgnat
RDo	Ray Douglas
RG	Richard Greenleaf
RI	Robert Irwin
RK	Rachel Kirkby
RM	Rod McShane
RMy	Robert Murphy
RP	Roger Parsons
RR	Richard Rayner
RS	Rupert Smith
RW	Richard White
RY	Robert Yates
SC	Sandy Craig
SCu	Simon Cunliffe
SF	Simon Field
SFe	Suzi Feay
SFr	Sophie Frank
SFra	Susannah Frankel
SG	W Stephen Gilbert
SGa	Simon Garfield
SGo	Steven Goldman
SGr	Steve Grant
SH	Simon Hartog
SHi	Susan Hill
SJ	Steve Jenkins
SJo	Sheila Johnston
SK	Sarah Kent
SM	Scott Meek
SMac	Suzie Mackenzie
SMcA	Sarah McAlister
SP	Steve Pinder
SPr	Steve Proctor
SW	Steve Woolley
SWo	Sue Woodman
TC	Tim Clark
TCh	Tom Charity
TE	Tony Elliott
TJ	Trevor Johnston
TM	Tom Milne
TP	Tim Pulleine
TR	Tony Rayns
TRi	Tim Rivers
VG	Verina Glaessner
WH	Wally Hammond
WSG	WS Grant
WW	Winslow Wong
YS	Yvette Sitten

Foreword

by Geoff Andrew

As the years go by and the *Time Out Film Guide* becomes ever more widely recognised as one of the most valuable movie reference books on the market, it seems increasingly unnecessary to point out what we hope, intend and believe to be its virtues. Plenty has already been written elsewhere praising the concise, informed reviews; the usefulness of the various appendices and indexes; the lively, forthright writing; and the unusually wide range of movies covered – in dealing not only with the English-language mainstream but with foreign-language fare, experimental and avant-garde movies, documentary and animation, the book goes far beyond the remit of supposedly similar guides. And as I look back over the past year, this last aspect appears to have become ever more important.

Like it or not, both our cinema screens and the mass of media coverage now devoted to the cinema are increasingly dominated by the Hollywood mainstream. With the rise of the multiplexes and the decline of art house and repertory venues, the range of films on offer to cinema-goers is getting narrower by the month; at the same time, so obsessed are the vast majority of magazines and newspapers, television and radio programmes with covering big budgets, box-office performance, stars, scandals, gimmicks and gossip that there's very little serious attention paid to anything unlikely to qualify as a hit or an 'event-movie', whatever its standing in terms of cinematic artistry. And, quite frankly, far too many American blockbusters, quality-wise, are dismal disappointments.

This, as the whole world knows, has been the year of *Titanic*. Disregarding the ethical questions surrounding its elephantine budget, and the kudos James Cameron and Co have gleaned from its extraordinary success, one may still ask whether the film is actually good. Certainly, it's impressive on a technical level – it *should* be, with all that time, energy and money spent on special effects. Artistically, however, it's a very different story: the cliché-packed script managed simultaneously to be primitive, naive and formulaic; the acting served up risible caricatures and stereotypes; and the 'uplifting' coda to the soppy central love story was both mawkish and an insult to those who died in the disaster. Not that *Titanic* was by any means the worst blockbuster of the year: *Deep Impact* and *Godzilla*, for example, made Cameron's film look quite sophisticated by comparison.

Of course, there are still very good studio films being made (*The Truman Show*, *LA Confidential*, *Midnight in the Garden of Good and Evil*, for example), but even away from the action spectaculars, it's generally most profitable – if you prefer American films to have a heart, mind and soul – to seek out lower-budget and/or independent fare, whether it be *Jackie Brown*, *The Big Lebowski*, *Henry Fool*, *Happiness* or (my favourite American movie of the last year) *The Apostle*. Or, of course (and *this*, I'd argue, is where the *Time Out Film Guide* is streets ahead of the competition), you could look beyond America altogether. And I don't just mean to Britain – though, despite several severe disappointments, the country has continued in its all-too-recent tradition of producing a number of extremely fine films, including *My Name Is Joe*, *Love Is the Devil*, *Love and Death on Long Island* and (this, admittedly, by an American auteur) *Velvet Goldmine*.

Though you might not know it from what's on at your local or in your paper, cinema continues to thrive around the world, creatively if not economically. True, Europe – with the predictable exception of France – has still not managed to pull itself out of the doldrums, while many of the Far Eastern industries, which caused such excitement only a few years ago, now face serious problems. But there are still original, stimulating, exciting movies emerging from all over the globe, and I for one would argue that many of the world's very finest working directors – the real *maîtres du cinéma* – do not speak the same language (in several senses of the phrase) as Hollywood: how else should we regard the likes of Theo Angelopoulos, Youssef Chahine, Hou Hsiao-hsien, Abbas Kiarostami, Takeshi Kitano, Eric Rohmer, Jan Svankmajer, the Taviani Brothers or Wong Kar-Wai? There are, of course, many others I might mention who because of their nationality have never received the recognition they deserve, and that, sadly, is unlikely to change, however much we may complain about the imaginatively impoverished fodder that swamps our screens. At least, however, this book, in aiming to cover the full range of features that play in London (including one-off repertory and festival screenings), also recognises that out there, beyond the much-hyped mainstream, there remains something of value.

Key to the Guide

Titles are filed in directory order (ignoring word divisions). Thus: *Dance of the Vampires/Dancers/Dances with Wolves.*

American and other English-language films are listed under their original titles, followed in parentheses by their alternative American or British release titles, where different titles have been used. Thus: *Fortune Cookie, The (aka Meet Whiplash Willie).* Alternative titles are cross-referenced.

Foreign-language films are listed under their English title, with the original-language title following in parentheses. Exception to this rule is made where the film is commonly referred to under its original title; where a film has never been released with an English title; or where it is known under different titles in Britain and the USA. In these cases, to avoid confusion, the film is listed under its original title, with cross-references from the alternative English titles.

Following the title(s), each entry lists (in parentheses) the name of the director, the date of the film and the country of origin; and then the leading members of the cast; the running time; the annotation 'b/w' if the film is in black-and-white, 'b/w & col' if it has one or more sequences in colour. No annotation after the running time means the film is in colour.

The date given is normally the registration date, not the release date (which may or may not be the same, depending on whether release of a film was delayed). The **country of origin** indicates where a film's producers were based, not where it was made (see below). The **running time** given is that of the longest known version (many release prints are, of course, cut for one reason or another). Since many films are circulated in different versions in different countries, recorded running times are at best approximate.

In the case of silent films, which may be projected at different speeds (from 24 to 16 frames per second) for optimum effect, the length given is the footage (where known). To calculate the length of a film projected at 24 fps, divide the footage by 90; at 20 fps, by 75; at 16 fps, by 60.

The critics' initials (see page vi) follow at the end of each review.

Abbreviations for producer countries

The following abbreviations, given after the director's name and the date below the title, are used for the countries of origin of films listed in the Guide. This refers specifically to the country or countries in which companies or organizations taking part in and providing finance for a production were officially registered at the time.

Alg	Algeria	Leb	Lebanon
Arg	Argentina	Mex	Mexico
Arm	Armenia (post-1991)	Mor	Morocco
		Moz	Mozambique
Aus	Austria	Neth	The Netherlands
Aust	Australia	Nic	Nicaragua
Bel	Belgium	Nor	Norway
Bol	Bolivia	NZ	New Zealand
Braz	Brazil	Pak	Pakistan
Bulg	Bulgaria	Pan	Panama
Can	Canada	Phil	Philippines
Col	Colombia	Pol	Poland
CR	Costa Rica	Port	Portugal
Cur	Curaçao	Rus	Russia (post-1991)
Cyp	Cyprus		
Czech	Czechoslovakia	SAf	South Africa
Den	Denmark	Sen	Senegal
Dom	Dominican Republic	SKor	South Korea
		Sp	Spain
EGer	East Germany	Swe	Sweden
El S	El Salvador	Switz	Switzerland
Fin	Finland	Tai	Taiwan
Fr	France	Thai	Thailand
GB	Great Britain and Northern Ireland	Trin	Trinidad
		Tun	Tunisia
		Tur	Turkey
Ger	Germany (pre-1945 and post-1990)	UAR	United Arab Republic
		Uru	Uruguay
HK	Hong Kong	US	United States of America
Hun	Hungary		
Ice	Iceland	USSR	Union of Soviet Socialist Republics
Ind	India		
Indon	Indonesia		
Ire	Ireland	Ven	Venezuela
Isr	Israel	WGer	West Germany
It	Italy	Yugo	Yugoslavia
Ivory C	Ivory Coast	Zam	Zambia
Jam	Jamaica	Zim	Zimbabwe
Jap	Japan		

In addition, films produced in the most-represented countries (other than Britain and the USA) are listed separately in the following sections: Australia (Appendix 16); Canada (Appendix 17); France (Appendix 18); Germany (Appendix 19); Italy (Appendix 20); and Japan (Appendix 21). These lists cover all films involving producers based in these countries, including co-productions. Films produced elsewhere are listed under the name of the country in the General Subject Index.

The Readers' Top One Hundred

In the sixth edition of the Guide we invited readers to submit lists of their all-time Top Ten films. Your response was substantial. Readers wrote to us from all parts of the United Kingdom, as well as from the United States, Canada, Ireland, Denmark, Spain, France, Italy, Switzerland, Norway and Hong Kong – nominating in all more than 1,000 films.

We offered a collection of video classics to the compilers of the first five lists drawn from a hat, but most of you (judging from the letters and comments accompanying many of your Top Tens) seem to have participated less in anticipation of a prize, and more for the sheer pleasure (or pleasurable frustration) of the exercise – and in several cases, first and foremost, to set the record straight as far as *Time Out*'s 1995 Cinema Centenary Poll of film-makers, actors, programmers and critics was concerned.

Here, then, is your poll, expanded by force of numbers from a Top Ten to a Top One Hundred. Hollywood dominates the list, with American films (just over half the total) outstripping their nearest rivals by a ratio of more than three to one.

The league table of countries is: United States, 59 (all figures including co-productions); Great Britain, 17; France, 15; Italy, six; Germany, Japan, Poland and the Soviet Union, each with three; and Algeria, Denmark, Hong Kong, New Zealand and Spain, each with one. The earliest film in the poll is *Battleship Potemkin* (1925), and the most recent films *The Full Monty* and *LA Confidential* (1997). There are two silent movies in the list; six from the 1930s, 15 from the '40s; and 14 each from the four decades from 1950 to 1989. Twenty-three films from the 1990s made it into the top hundred.

Martin Scorsese – the most popular director – has five films in the top one hundred, followed by Alfred Hitchcock with four.

Krzysztof Kieslowski, Sergio Leone, Orson Welles and Billy Wilder each have three films; and Woody Allen, Joel Coen, Francis Ford Coppola, Victor Fleming, Milos Forman, Howard Hawks, Stanley Kubrick, Akira Kurosawa, David Lean, Powell and Pressburger, Nicolas Roeg and Wim Wenders each have two. Fifty-four other directors are represented by one film each.

Participants in the poll (and in the Centenary poll of 1995 which follows it) were each given 40 points. If they stipulated that their choices weren't in order of preference, each movie received 4 points. For those who nominated their selection in preferential order, the first choice received 7 points, the second 6, third 5, fourth 4, and fifth to tenth 3 each. Points for split/equal choices were divided appropriately. The aim of this points system was simple: to reward preferred films without pretending, say, that a number one favourite was 10 times as popular as a tenth choice, as a '10 down to 1' points system would have reflected.

The competition winners, each of whom received 20 videos from the BFI's Connoisseur list, were Kerry Beckley, Sue Johnson, Graham Barrick, Margaret Thornborogh and Michael Howard. With thanks to you all.

> **The readers' top 100 films are marked in the text with this logo (100)**

1. The Godfather *223 points*
(Francis Ford Coppola, 1971/74/90, US – Centenary poll No. 2)
Disregarding the ambitious but botched third instalment, this is not only one of the cinema's great gangster sagas but a gloriously detailed – if romanticised – historical look at the ethics of American business, family values and food consumption (all that pasta!). For once, Part II (singled

out by a number of readers) was superior to the original, though the whole thing – a model of Hollywood craftsmanship – was instrumental in igniting several careers: De Niro, Pacino, Duvall, Caan. Brando's finest hour, the mannerisms and mouth full of cottonwool notwithstanding.

2. Casablanca *199*
(Michael Curtiz, 1942, US – Cent. No. 80=)
Made in the year when the outcome of the war hung precariously in the balance, this was, and is, popular cinema par excellence – achingly nostalgic, clear cut, ruthlessly well plotted – and a film which has triumphantly withstood the test of time. Bogart, the laconic club owner, and Bergman the girl he left in Paris, and for whom he still feels tenderness and more … Who can forget Rains, Henreid, Lorre, Greenstreet, Veidt, Dooley Wilson, Marcel Dalio and SZ Sakall; and who will not rise (in their mind at least) for the singing of 'The Marseillaise'?

3. Citizen Kane *192*
(Orson Welles, 1941, US – Cent. No. 1)
The most influential talkie ever, this poignant, witty account of the multifarious contradictions in one man's life (a news tycoon based on William Randolph Hearst, who effectively banned the movie for years) takes delirious delight in exploiting the film medium to its full. Rewarding, too, as a prophetic autobiography by its 25-year-old writer/director; most intriguing, however, is that there's actually no one around to hear Kane mutter 'Rosebud', the enigmatic word that sets the film's search-for-meaning story going. So is everything we see and hear really the dying man's dream?

4. Blade Runner *168*
(Ridley Scott, 1982/91, US – Cent. No. 60=)

2019: a Chandlertown odyssey, adapted from Philip K Dick's novel *Do Androids Dream of Electric Sheep?*, in which Harrison Ford hunts down human robot killers, both repulsive and seductive. A seminal sci-fi movie whose reputation has grown since the release of the restored Director's Cut in 1991 (polled separately by a number of readers): simultaneously bleak and glittering, with a bold and extraordinarily evocative production design.

5. Vertigo *163.5*
(Alfred Hitchcock, 1958, US – Cent. No. 4)
The master of suspense at his least concerned with suspense, proffering an unprecedentedly bleak vision of human love: namely, of how we try to mould others' personalities and looks according to our own (diseased) desires. An unsettling, dreamy tale of irrational obsession, much loved by the Hitchcock imitators – and *the* great Jimmy Stewart performance.

6. Apocalypse Now *162*
(Francis Ford Coppola, 1979, US – Cent. No. 17)
Orson Welles abandoned plans to film Conrad's *Heart of Darkness* and made *Kane* instead. In the early '70s Francis Coppola returned to the idea, with George Lucas down to direct on location in the middle of the Vietnam conflict. Eventually Coppola grasped the reins himself, and the project mushroomed into this spectacular, hallucinatory phantasmagoria of war.

7. Some Like It Hot *160*
(Billy Wilder, 1959, US – Cent. No. 23=)
The greatest farce from the talkies' most consistently funny and biting film-maker. Anyone who would argue with that should submit themselves to this glorious transvestite chase movie in which edgy jazz musicians Lemmon and Curtis witness the St Valentine's Day massacre, join an all-women band, are troubled by romance, both available and simultaneously impossible, and find dime-flipping George Raft and his heavies breathing ominously down their necks … and not forgetting Marilyn and her heart-stopping gowns.

8. Taxi Driver *128*
(Martin Scorsese, 1976, US – Cent. No. 23=)

The best alien movie ever made? De Niro's space capsule is a checker cab, while New York at night is on the outer limits of another world. This remains a profoundly troubling essay on violence and insanity; its images burn in the mind, twenty years on, and will probably still burn twenty years hence when most of the extreme, mocking mayhem of the cinema of the '90s is long forgotten. For the cinephile, De Niro's Travis Bickle subconsciously informs all the great actor's subsequent performances: there is the spring, waiting to uncoil …

9. 2001: A Space Odyssey *123*
(Stanley Kubrick, 1968, US – Cent. No. 37=)
Still, triumphantly – exasperatingly – the most spectacular and magisterial space movie of all time. Just what it means (from the prehistoric ape tossing up a bone, through the black monolith, to the vast human foetus) is unclear. Here, however, is the lurking, unambiguous danger of the rogue computer: a prophetic warning – as we await the effect of the millennium bug – more than thirty years before the event.

10. It's a Wonderful Life *118.5*
(Frank Capra, 1946, US – Cent. No. 28=)
Never was divine intervention so urgently needed as on the Christmas night James Stewart – personifying a man who judged himself a failure – stood on the ledge of a snowy bridge and contemplated suicide. A film designed to grab your cockles and warm them till they smoulder.

11. GoodFellas *109*
(Martin Scorsese, 1990, US)
Another Mob picture: De Niro and Scorsese again, both in top form. Liotta, eyes on fire, is the unblooded youngster who aspires to be a big time 'family' member. A fast, violent, stylish portrait of the Italian American underworld from the mid- '50s to the late '70s. Screen murder has rarely been committed with such cocky assurance, or contemplated with such sang froid.

12. North by Northwest *102*
(Alfred Hitchcock, 1959, US – Cent. No. 17=)
'What's the *O* for?' 'Nothing,'

replies Cary Grant's Roger O Thornhill, revealing the redemptive moral strain that underlies this admirably light-hearted romantic thriller. It's not just magnificent set-pieces (most notably the attack by a crop-duster's plane and the chase on Mt Rushmore), but a sly, witty satire on the shallow ethics of modern advertising man.

13. Pulp Fiction *101*
(Quentin Tarantino, 1994, US)
The most recent film in the top fifteen had, inevitably, to be a Tarantino movie – just as, had this poll been conducted in the '60s, it would have had to be a cutting-edge Godard. Three up-to-the-minute stories, full of effing and blinding and pop cultural references, and lashings of Grand Guignol violence (and more), executed with that breezy, exhilarating confidence which says look at me – and keep looking.

14. Seven Samurai *100*
(Akira Kurosawa, 1954, Jap – Cent. No. 5)
An epic Western in eastern garb, with a genuinely Homeric sense of character, nature and physicality, plagiarised to far less effect by *The Magnificent Seven*. Kurosawa himself, of course, meant it partly as a tribute to Ford, though Jack probably never filmed action – let alone mud and rain – quite so well. Even Mifune, as unrestrained energy incarnate, is overshadowed by Takashi Shimura's paragon of threatened, ancient wisdom.

15. The Third Man *95*
(Carol Reed, 1948, GB – Cent. No. 49=)
Dang-gadang-gadang … and Welles' Lime is less than cordial. Pulp writer Cotten chases the shadow of his old friend, now gone to the bad, through a devastated Vienna still shell-shocked by the war. This cool, perfect adaptation of Grahame Greene's novel is photographed in black and white by Robert Krasker: the ferris wheel, the boy with a ball, the kitten and the polished shoes, the fingers through the grating.

16. Lawrence of Arabia *90*
(David Lean, 1962, GB – Cent. No. 6)
Much admired by the likes of Spielberg for its sumptuous desert imagery and its slick editing (the match and the sun), and more recently for its romanticised view

of its enigmatic hero. The rot, probably, set in here for Lean, but there's no denying its visual elegance or its vaunting ambition.

— Raging Bull *90*
(Martin Scorsese, 1980, US – Cent. No. 7)
Often lauded as the finest movie of the '80s, this biopic of boxing champ Jake La Motta is less about physical violence in the ring (though that's depicted, in stunning monochrome, with superbly visceral energy) than about the emotional violence of marital and family relationships, particularly as perpetrated by brute, inarticulate males.

18. Gone With the Wind *86*
(Victor Fleming, 1939, US – Cent. No. 42=)
Scarlett O'Hara's getting of wisdom. What more can be said about this much loved, much discussed, legendary blockbuster from Margaret Mitchell's novel. It epitomises pre-war Hollywood at its most ambitious: respectable middlebrow entertainment on a huge polished platter. Acted to the hilt by all concerned, spectacular and then some, an evergreen classic. The tears flow on cue, every time.

19. A Matter of Life and Death *84*
(Michael Powell/Emeric Pressburger, 1946, GB – Cent. No. 13=)
Though partly a propaganda piece aimed at improving Anglo-American relations, this beautifully bizarre romantic fantasy, in which love conquers death at a celestial court, is also a cheeky display of Powell and Pressburger's contempt for the grim homilies of the British 'documentary boys'. The second Bill and Ted movie may have paid dubious homage to the Stairway to Heaven, but this really is absurd material made utterly enthralling by wit and endless invention.

20. Schindler's List *83*
(Steven Spielberg, 1994, US – Cent. No. 49=)
Spielberg's most grown-up film, a noble account – photographed in grainy black and white, and not sparing the viewer from matter-of-fact horrors – of the wartime work of Oskar Schindler, the ambiguous, unknowable man who saved the lives of 1,100 Polish Jews by employing them in his factory. A Hollywood film, of course, for both good (marvellously edited,

effortlessly well acted) and bad (sentimentality creeps in at the end), but one made with unassailable conviction.

21. Rear Window *82*
(Alfred Hitchcock, 1954, US – Cent. No. 26=)
Masterly voyeuristic thriller with James Stewart as the man who sees too much.

— The Searchers *82*
(John Ford, 1956, US – Cent. No. 20=)
The pioneer spirit gives way to the demands of family, community, and civilisation. A heartbreaker.

23. Les Enfants du Paradis *77*
(Marcel Carné, 1945, Fr – Cent. No. 13=)
France's answer to the Occupation: a tribute to the life of the mind and the sovereignty of the heart.

24. Chinatown *76*
(Roman Polanski, 1974, US – Cent. No. 19)
Nicholson inhabits the skin of down-at-heel private eye Jake Gittes in this silky *film noir*.

25. Manhattan *75*
(Woody Allen, 1979, US)
Allen's relaxed, uncomplicated, rhapsodic love affair with New York.

26. Star Wars *74*
(George Lucas, 1977, US)
No drop yet in the voltage.

— Withnail & I *74*
(Bruce Robinson, 1986, GB)
A gloriously funny British comedy, about two no-hope actors, with a cult status that won't stop growing.

28. Singin' in the Rain *73*
(Stanley Donen/Gene Kelly, 1952, US – Cent. No. 57=)
Kelly gets his trousers wet as the movies learn to talk. Great satire, great music, great dance.

29. The Night of the Hunter *72*
(Charles Laughton, 1955, US – Cent. No. 11)
A magical Depression-era fable in which murderous rogue preacher Mitchum and stout-hearted angel Gish battle for the souls of two innocent children, overseen by the stars and God's small creatures.

— Psycho *72*
(Alfred Hitchcock, 1960, US)
The mild mannerd motel keeper; the shower curtain and the shadow of the knife; the wig; the mummy – scream and scream again.

— The Wild Bunch *72*
(Sam Peckinpah, 1969, US – Cent. No. 22)
The Western bites the dust and Peckinpah sounds this ecstatic, slo-mo death rattle. Bill Holden, Ernie Borgnine, Robert Ryan and Warren Oates go along for the ride.

32. The Shawshank Redemption *69*
(Frank Darabont, 1994, US)
Tim Robbins, unjustly jailed for murder, takes time to execute his very satisfying revenge.

33. Three Colours: Red *68*
(Krzysztof Kieslowski, 1994, Fr/Pol/Switz – Cent. No. 85=)
Kieslowski's valedictory trilogy culminates in wise affirmation: a classic for tomorrow.

34. The Big Sleep *67*
(Howard Hawks, 1946, US)
Marlowe mixes it with the Sternwoods and you'll never, ever figure out exactly who did what to whom.

35. One Flew Over the Cuckoo's Nest *66*
(Milos Forman, 1975, US)
Breaking out of the asylum – and ex-hippies are rooting for the inmates all the way.

36. Paris, Texas *65.5*
(Wim Wenders, 1984, WGer/Fr/GB)
Harry Dean Stanton emerges from the desert and heads for home: an achingly sad German-American masterpiece.

37. Blue Velvet *63*
(David Lynch, 1986, US – Cent. No. 60=)
Middle America under the microscope – and it's freak city, daddy-o. Surrealist Lynch hits his peak.

38. Tokyo Story *61*
(Yasujiro Ozu, 1953, Jap – Cent. No. 9)
Philosophical calm in the face of inescapable hardship reigns supreme in this moving exploration of the gulf between parents and children.

39. The Deer Hunter *57*
(Michael Cimino, 1978, US)
Still America's most controversial (and affecting) movie about the US experience of the Vietnam War.

— Three Colours: Blue *57*
(Krzysztof Kieslowski, 1993, Fr)
What happens when the nerve

fails on the brink of suicide? The first part of Kieslowski's magisterial trilogy.

41. Once Upon a Time in the West 56
(Sergio Leone, 1968, It – Cent. No. 32=)
The horse opera as myth; a magnificent, baroque costume picture written in the dust.

42. The Piano 55
(Jane Campion, 1993, NZ/Fr – Cent. No. 40=)
Brontë-like melodrama: a mute wife, a clueless husband, and a naked, tattooed Harvey Keitel.

43. Double Indemnity 50
(Billy Wilder, 1944, US – Cent. No. 72=)
Sexual dominance, guilt, suspicion and insurance fraud define a generic mood of dark pessimism.
— Once Upon a Time in America 50
(Sergio Leone, 1983, US – Cent. No. 36)
A mature meditation on time, honour and brotherhood, and another gangster epic on a grand scale.

45. L'Atalante 49
(Jean Vigo, 1934, Fr – Cent. No. 10)
One of the cinema's very greatest (unsentimental) romances, set on a Seine barge skippered by the imperishable Michel Simon, about the pitfalls of marriage and possessive relationships.

46. Aliens 48
(James Cameron, 1986, US – Cent. No. 88=)
Monstrous hi-tech mayhem to the max as Sigourney goes gunning.

47. Dr Strangelove 46
(Stanley Kubrick, 1964, GB – Cent. No. 57=)
This is how the world ends, with a bang and Peter Sellers in three roles.
— Performance 46
(Nicolas Roeg/Donald Cammell, 1970, GB – Cent. No. 28=)
Sixties psychological psychedelia from jigsaw-makers Roeg and Cammell.

49. Wings of Desire 45.5
(Wim Wenders, 1987, WGer/Fr)
The angels are listening – and falling in love.

50. Brazil 44
(Terry Gilliam, 1985, GB)
A terrifying comic view of the future: anarchic, inventive,

visually arresting – and sometimes in danger of being hoist by its own petard.
— The Double Life of Véronique 44
(Krzysztof Kieslowski, 1991, Pol)
Véronique/Veronika: a mesmerising study of affinity and spiritual disquiet.

52. The Maltese Falcon 43
(John Huston, 1941, US)
The chase for Hammett's black bird, and the vanity of human wishes – greed in particular.

53. La Règle du Jeu 42
(Jean Renoir, 1939, Fr – Cent. No. 3)
The daddy of all those 'weekend gathering in a country house' movies, and among much else a celebration of life as living theatre.
— The Wizard of Oz 42
(Victor Fleming, 1939, US)
The red shoes, the yellow brick road …

55. Fargo 40
(Joel Coen, 1995, US)
Pregnant police chief Frances McDormand sees off the black hats in a marvellous deadpan thriller about a kidnap that goes spectacularly wrong.

56. Don't Look Now 39
(Nicolas Roeg, 1973, GB – Cent. No. 88=)
Wintry Venetian chronicle of a death foretold.

57. Touch of Evil 38
(Orson Welles, 1958, US – Cent. No. 8)
Proof that post-*Kane* Welles was not a downward spiral, this flamboyant exercise in baroque *film noir* begins with the cinema's most exhilarating and complex opening-shot ever.

58. Annie Hall 37
(Woody Allen, 1977, US)
Well, la-di-dah – and Diane Keaton sets a fashion for waistcoats and baggy pants. Plus the escaping lobsters.
— Cinema Paradiso 37
(Giuseppe Tornatore, 1988, It/Fr)
A childhood to die for … ?
— LA Confidential 37
(Curtis Hanson, 1997, US)
A Veronica Lake lookalike trapped in a web of male desires.
— The English Patient 37
(Anthony Minghella, 1996, US)
A dying man in a Tuscan monastery lets his memories wander.

62. The Apartment 36
(Billy Wilder, 1960, US)

The perils of ingratiation, or why *not* to lend your pad to a philandering boss.
— The Magnificent Ambersons 36
(Orson Welles, 1942, US – Cent. No. 15=)
RKO hacked it down to what Welles saw as a travesty of his original gently ironic elegy for a lost America. A masterpiece, none the less.
— Un Coeur en hiver 36
(Claude Sautet, 1991, Fr)
A troubling study of a *ménage à trois*, complex and effectively underplayed.

65. Jules and Jim 35
(François Truffaut, 1961, Fr)
The swooningly romantic whirlwind of love and friendship. Why one adored French movies (and Jeanne Moreau) in the '60s.
— Reservoir Dogs 35
(Quentin Tarantino, 1991, US)
The heist gone wrong, '90s-style. Tarantino lands a straight left – smack on a glass jaw.

67. High Noon 34
(Fred Zinnemann, 1952, US)
'Oh, don't forsake me …' Marshal Coop does his duty while his Quaker bride waits. A classic old-school Western.

68. Mean Streets 33
(Martin Scorsese, 1973, US – Cent. No. 32=)
The first time Scorsese really showed what he had in him: Catholic turmoil, masochistic machismo, a love of rock'n'roll and a genius for motion pictures.
— The Good, the Bad and the Ugly 33
(Sergio Leone, 1966, It)
Splashy, excessive, cynical US Civil War yarn, with lashings of hot spaghetti sauce.

70. His Girl Friday 32
(Howard Hawks, 1940, US)
Hecht and MacArthur's *Front Page* given a brilliant twist by turning Hildy Johnson into Walter Burns' ex-wife. Cary Grant vs. Rosalind Russell, the repartee was never faster or funnier.
— Mirror 32
(Andrei Tarkovsky, 1974, USSR – Cent. No. 88=)
Archive footage and shimmering forests create an autobiographical cine-poem, a beautiful enigma.
— The Usual Suspects 32
(Bryan Singer, 1995, US)
Labyrinthine ultra-modern thriller, satisfyingly clever.

— **Trainspotting** *32*
(Danny Boyle, 1995, GB)
A novel Edinburgh drug story.
74. Chungking Express *31*
(Wong Kar-Wai, 1994, HK)
Two lovelorn Hong Kong cops,
two interlinked stories – speedy,
wry, sympathetic and very catchy.
— **Seven** *31*
(David Fincher, 1995, US)
Impressively nasty thriller
featuring a couple of mismatched
cops, a cunning serial killer and
the Seven Deadly Sins.

76. The Sound of Music *30*
(Robert Wise, 1965, US)
The cloud of fascism and the
singing nanny.
— **The Thing from Another
World** *30*
(Christian Nyby, 1951, US)
A lonely group of scientists in the
Antarctic, a flying saucer, and the
… Forget the *X Files*, this is the
real thing.
— **Battleship Potemkin** *30*
(Sergei Eisenstein, 1925, USSR –
Cent. No. 28=)
Eisenstein raises the Red Flag and
determines the future of film
montage.

79. Amadeus *29*
(Milos Forman, 1984, US – Cent.
No. 88=)
Worra lorra Mozza while Hulce
composes himself for Shaffer's
portrait of genius.
— **The Age of Innocence** *29*
(Martin Scorsese, 1993, US)
Scorsese and Edith Wharton: a
surprising, bravura marriage.
— **The Seventh Seal** *29*
(Ingmar Bergman, 1956, Swe –
Cent. No. 88=)
Death and knight von Sydow play
chess in a portentous medieval fable.

**82. Kind Hearts and
Corronets** *28*
(Robert Hamer, 1949, GB – Cent.
No. 88=)
The English art of murder:
Guinness snuffs it eight times in
Ealing's blackest comedy.
— **The Cook, the Thief, His
Wife & Her Lover** *28*
(Peter Greenaway, 1989, GB/Fr)
Tasty cannibal drama, for those
with the stomach.
— **The General** *28*
(Buster Keaton/Clyde Bruckman,
1926, US – Cent. No. 31)
Buster right on track in the finest
silent comedy of them all.

85. La Dolce Vita *27*
(Federico Fellini, 1960, It – Cent.
No. 20=)

Fellini's magnum opus begins with
the ascension of Christ – by
helicopter – and then dives straight
into the gutter press, as
Mastroianni's *paparazzo* hack gets
a taste for the 'sweet life'.
— **Miller's Crossing** *27*
(Joel Coen, 1990, US)
Convoluted Prohibition-era thriller
with all the trimmings. The Coens'
tribute to the genre, with Finney
as the spider at the centre of the
web.
— **The Battle of Algiers** *27*
(Gillo Pontecorvo, 1965, It/Alg –
Cent. No. 48)
Unflinching near-documentary
chronicle of a guerilla campaign,
too true to ignore.
— **Top Hat** *27*
(Mark Sandrich, 1935, US)
Fred and Ginger: who could ask
for anything more?

89. My Life as a Dog *26*
(Lasse Hallström, 1985, Swe)
A bitter-sweet evocation of a boy's
experiences in the rural Sweden of
the '50s.
— **The Full Monty** *26*
(Peter Cattaneo, 1997, US/GB)
The Sheffield strippers take it
away.

91. Black Narcissus *25*
(Michael Powell/Emeric
Pressburger, 1946, GB – Cent.
No. 72=)
The Archers get themselves to a
nunnery in a tense, erotic,
Himalayan pressure-cooker.
— **Halloween** *25*
(John Carpenter, 1978, US)
The corpse won't lie down, of
course.
— **Letter from an Unknown
Woman** *25*
(Max Ophuls, 1948, US – Cent.
No. 42=)
Unrequited Joan Fontaine suffers
exquisitely in this glittering,
irresistible fable of doomed love.
— **M** *25*
(Fritz Lang, 1931, Ger)
Based on a real life manhunt for a
childkiller; Lorre chills to the bone.
— **Ran** *25*
(Akira Kurosawa, 1985, Fr/Jap –
Cent. No. 80=)
A samurai *King Lear*: film-making
on a huge, colour-coded canvas.
— **Secret & Lies** *25*
(Mike Leigh, 1995, GB)
Successful middle-class black
optometrist finds her long-lost
natural mother, a boozy white
woman with a particularly trying
family. Then the fireworks.

97. A Bout de Souffle *24*
(Jean-Luc Godard, 1959, Fr – Cent.
No. 32=)
Godard's breathless reinvention of
the cinema; the flagship of the
nouvelle vague.
— **Andrei Rublev** *24*
(Andrei Tarkovsky, 1966, USSR)
Tarkovsky, never less than
enigmatic, and a 15th century
Russian icon painter.
— **L'Avventura** *24*
(Michelangelo Antonioni, 1960, It –
Cent. No. 88=)
An unsolved disappearance sparks
this modernist monument to
bourgeois malaise.
— **Delicatessen** *24*
(Jean-Pierre Jeunet/Marc Caro,
1990, Fr)
An ex-clown falls for the daughter
of a butcher who trades in human
flesh. Can a group of subterranean
vegetarian fanatics save him?
— **Great Expectations** *24*
(David Lean, 1946, GB)
The gold standard of Dickens'
adaptations.
— **The Remains of the Day** *24*
(James Ivory, 1993, US)
The butler, the stately home, the
housekeeper – and a failure to
connect.

Centenary Top One Hundred

In 1995, to mark the Centenary of Cinema, *Time Out* polled a host of directors, producers, actors, programmers and critics to find out what they felt had been the high points of that last 100 years. Each person was asked to name their top ten films. The resulting list, drawn up from this poll, was first published in the fourth edition of the *Time Out Film Guide*. The scoring system was the same as the one used for the Readers' Top One Hundred.

> The top 100 films are marked in the text with this logo 100

1. Citizen Kane *111 points*
(Orson Welles, 1941, US)

2. The Godfather *101*
(Francis Ford Coppola, 1971/74/90, US)

3. La Règle du Jeu *77*
(Jean Renoir, 1939, Fr)

4. Vertigo *73*
(Alfred Hitchcock, 1958, US)

5. Seven Samurai *63*
(Akira Kurosawa, 1954, Jap)

6. Lawrence of Arabia *60*
(David Lean, 1962, GB)

7. Raging Bull *58*
(Martin Scorsese, 1980, US)

8. Touch of Evil *55*
(Orson Welles, 1958, US)

9. Tokyo Story *50*
(Yasujiro Ozu, 1953, Jap)

10. L'Atalante *49*
(Jean Vigo, 1934, Fr)

11. The Night of the Hunter *47*
(Charles Laughton, 1955, US)

12. The Conformist *46*
(Bernardo Bertolucci, 1969, It/Fr/WGer)

13. Les Enfants du Paradis *41*
(Marcel Carné, 1945, Fr)
— A Matter of Life and Death *41*
(Michael Powell/Emeric Pressburger, 1946, GB)
15. 8½ *37*
(Federico Fellini, 1963, It)
— The Magnificent Ambersons *37*
(Orson Welles, 1942, US)

17. Apocalypse Now *36*
(Francis Ford Coppola, 1979, US)
— North by Northwest *36*
(Alfred Hitchcock, 1959, US)

19. Chinatown *32*
(Roman Polanski, 1974, US)

20. La Dolce Vita *31*
(Federico Fellini, 1960, It)
— The Searchers *31*
(John Ford, 1956, US)

22. The Wild Bunch *30*
(Sam Peckinpah, 1969, US)

23. The Life and Death of Colonel Blimp *29*
(Michael Powell/Emeric Pressburger, 1943, GB)
— Some Like It Hot *29*
(Billy Wilder, 1959, US)
— Taxi Driver *29*
(Martin Scorsese, 1976, US)

26. Napoléon *28*
(Abel Gance, 1927, Fr)
— Rear Window *28*
(Alfred Hitchcock, 1954, US)

28. Battleship Potemkin *26*
(Sergei Eisenstein, 1925, USSR)
— It's a Wonderful Life *26*
(Frank Capra, 1946, US)
— Performance *26*
(Nicolas Roeg/Donald Cammell, 1970, GB)

31. The General *25*
(Buster Keaton/Clyde Bruckman, 1926, US)

32. A Bout de Souffle *24*
(Jean-Luc Godard, 1959, Fr)
— Mean Streets *24*
(Martin Scorsese, 1973, US)
— Once Upon a Time in the West *24*
(Sergio Leone, 1968, It)
— Rio Bravo *24*
(Howard Hawks, 1959, US)
36. Once Upon a Time in America *23*
(Sergio Leone, 1983, US)

37. All About Eve *22*
(Joseph L Mankiewicz, 1950, US)
— My Darling Clementine *22*
(John Ford, 1946, US)
— 2001: A Space Odyssey *22*
(Stanley Kubrick, 1968, US)

40. The Piano *21*
(Jane Campion, 1993, NZ/Fr)
— Pierrot le Fou *21*
(Jean-Luc Godard, 1965, Fr/It)

42. Bringing Up Baby *20*
(Howard Hawks, 1938, US)
— The 400 Blows *20*
(François Truffaut, 1959, Fr)
— Gone With the Wind *20*
(Victor Fleming, 1939, US)
— The Lady Eve *20*
(Preston Sturges, 1941, US)
— Last Year in Marienbad *20*
(Alain Resnais, 1961, Fr)
— Letter from an Unknown Woman *20*
(Max Ophuls, 1948, US)

48. The Battle of Algiers *19*
(Gillo Pontecorvo, 1965, It/Alg)

49. The Gold Rush *18*
(Charles Chaplin, 1925, US)
— La Grande Illusion *18*
(Jean Renoir, 1937, Fr)
— Une Partie de Campagne *18*
(Jean Renoir, 1936, Fr)
— The Philadelphia Story *18*
(George Cukor, 1940, US)
— Pickpocket *18*
(Robert Bresson, 1959, Fr)
— Schindler's List *18*
(Steven Spielberg, 1994, US)
— The Shining *18*
(Stanley Kubrick, 1980, GB)
— The Third Man *18*
(Carol Reed, 1948, GB)
57. Dr Strangelove *17*
(Stanley Kubrick, 1964, GB)
— The Reckless Moment *17*
(Max Ophuls, 1949, US)

— Singin' in the Rain *17*
(Stanley Donen/Gene Kelly, 1952, US)
60. Blade Runner *16*
(Ridley Scott, 1982, US)
— Blue Velvet *16*
(David Lynch, 1986, US)
— Pather Panchali *16*
(Satyajit Ray, 1955, Ind)
— Le Samourai *16*
(Jean-Pierre Melville, 1967, Fr)
— Sans Soleil (Sunless) *16*
(Chris Marker, 1983, Fr)
— Sweet Smell of Success *16*
(Alexander Mackendrick, 1957, US)

66. Amarcord *15*
(Federico Fellini, 1973, It/Fr)
— Greed *15*
(Erich von Stroheim, 1923, US)
— The Passion of Joan of Arc *15*
(Carl Theodor Dreyer, 1928, Fr)
— Persona *15*
(Ingmar Bergman, 1966, Swe)
— Rashomon *15*
(Akira Kurosawa, 1951, Jap)
— The Treasure of the Sierra Madre *15*
(John Huston, 1948, US)

72. All That Heaven Allows *14*
(Douglas Sirk, 1955, US)
— Black Narcissus *14*
(Michael Powell/Emeric Pressburger, 1946, GB)
— Double Indemnity *14*
(Billy Wilder, 1944, US)
— Intolerance *14*
(DW Griffith, 1916, US)
— Notorious *14*
(Alfred Hitchcock, 1946, US)
— Out of the Past *14*
(Jacques Tourneur, 1947, US)
— The Red Shoes *14*
(Michael Powell/Emeric Pressburger, 1948, GB)
— Sunset Boulevard *14*
(Billy Wilder, 1951, US)

80. Casablanca *13*
(Michael Curtiz, 1942, US)
— City Lights *13*
(Charles Chaplin, 1931, US)
— Ran *13*
(Akira Kurosawa, 1985, Fr/Jap)
— The Spirit of the Beehive *13*
(Victor Erice, 1973, Sp)
— Sunrise *13*
(FW Murnau, 1927, US)

85. The Killing of a Chinese Bookie *12*
(John Cassavetes, 1976, US)
— Ordet (The Word) *12*
(Carl Theodor Dreyer, 1954, Den)
— Three Colours: Red *12*
(Krzysztof Kieslowski, 1994, Fr/Pol/Switz)

88. Aliens *11*
(James Cameron, 1986, US)
— Amadeus *11*
(Milos Forman, 1984, US)
— L'Avventura *11*
(Michelangelo Antonioni, 1960, It)
— Badlands *11*
(Terrence Malick, 1973, US)
— Barry Lyndon *11*
(Stanley Kubrick, 1975, GB)
— The Bridge on the River Kwai *11*
(David Lean, 1957, GB)
— The Colour of Pomegranates *11*
(Sergo Paradjanov, 1969, USSR)
— Don't Look Now *11*
(Nicolas Roeg, 1973, GB)
— Earth *11*
(Alexander Dovzhenko, 1930, USSR)
— Fanny and Alexander *11*
(Ingmar Bergman, 1982, Swe)
— La Jetée *11*
(Chris Marker, 1962, Fr)
— Kind Hearts and Coronets *11*
(Robert Hamer, 1949, GB)
— The Man Who Fell to Earth *11*
(Nicolas Roeg, 1976, US)
— Mirror *11*
(Andrei Tarkovsky, 1974, USSR)
— Pandora's Box *11*
(GW Pabst, 1928, Ger)
— The Quiet Man *11*
(John Ford, 1952, US)
— Sansho Dayu *11*
(Kenji Mizoguchi, 1954, Jap)
— The Seventh Seal *11*
(Ingmar Bergman, 1956, Swe)
— Ugetsu Monogatari *11*
(Kenji Mizoguchi, 1953, Jap)
— West Side Story *11*
(Robert Wise/Jerome Robbins, 1961, US)

End Credits
Obituaries 1997–98

This is a selection only of those connected with movie-making who died between June 1997 and June 1998. The fact that most of them are men can be charged to the capriciousness of fate and the policies and traditions that have prevailed in the various film industries.

Three Hollywood superstars with two of them dying on consecutive days ... Even if you're nearly 60, **James Stewart**, **Robert Mitchum** and **Frank Sinatra** were operating in the background of your entire life. Mitchum and Sinatra, at their most characteristic, shared a similar persona: the free spirit, unimpressed by authority and tough enough to take the consequences. Particularly as exemplified by Mitchum, this was an image that provided solace for at least three generations of civil servants in pullovers and timid teachers fretting about their marking. On the other hand, many came to value most Mitchum's eccentric or anomalous roles: the murderously fixated preacher in *The Night of the Hunter*, the dim hood in *The Friends of Eddie Coyle*. When last encountered (in Jarmusch's *Dead Man*) he was playing a demented tycoon, given to conversing with a stuffed bear, a gratifyingly unexpected exit piece. Stewart was even more various. If he was often the conformist compared to Mitchum's misfit, his most effective moments came when the good natured bumbling gave way to rage and panic. If one had to summarise Stewart with a phrase, 'the fragility of self-control' might do as well as most. *Mr Smith Goes to Washington*, *It's a Wonderful Life*, *The Man from Laramie*, *Vertigo* ... the litany of masterworks is burned into any cinephile's consciousness.

Sinatra died while the Cannes film festival was in progress. '*Frank Sinatra n'est plus*' was a stark French headline, which may not have detained for long the majority of the product salespersons buzzing around, but

certainly transfixed a few elderly critics. The compilers of all the tribute programmes had a wealth of material to pick from, but it was noticeable that few omitted a well known passage from the 1954 *Young at Heart*: the scene is a crowded bar, general hubbub, and nobody paying much attention, as he sits at a piano on a slightly raised dais, aching his way through 'One for My Baby'. The heroine (Doris Day) enters, watches and listens, adoringly. The essential Sinatra seems contained in the elements of that small sequence – although it doesn't solve the mystery of why he kept naming his production companies after English counties.

The distinction between a star and a superstar is not just a matter of intensity but also of duration. **Alice Faye**'s popularity, though enormous, lasted for only a few years, say 1938 to 1943, when she drew the crowds in a succession of Fox musicals. Her rendition of 'No Love, No Nothing' (in *The Gang's All Here*) may not be significant and expressive in the way of the Sinatra number, but still deserves a privileged place in any anthology of torch songs, of WWII-related material, or just of favourite moments generally. Although **Maureen O'Sullivan**'s career extended across six decades, she was essentially a creature of the '30s, the prettily dimpled younger sister/daughter for whose happiness father figures throughout MGM-land were expected to sacrifice all. But chiefly, of course, she was Jane to Johnny Weissmuller's Tarzan.

The list of stars surviving from the silent era shortens. **Billie Dove** died, the pseudonym carefully devised to cater for the Victorian tastes and assumptions which still prevailed, as the titles of some of her vehicles (*The Heart of a Follies Girl*, *Painted Angel*) also attest. It was the big sayonara for **Toshiro Mifune**, perhaps the closest the East has come to a durable, export strength attraction

in, say, the Mitchum class. Foreigners undoubtedly had only a partial idea of his versatility since in general it was his sword-slashing, bone-snapping Kurosawa roles (*Seven Samurai*, *Yojimbo*, *Red Beard*) that played on the international scene. Phonetics ruled out much of a career in the West, with *Hell in the Pacific* the most interesting of his few sallies in that direction.

Of the semi-stars, the reliables and endurables, one notes the passing of **Burgess Meredith**, whose George in *Of Mice and Men* had the distinction, if that's the word, of being translated into a Tex Avery cartoon character, and who enjoyed a late boost to his career with Stallone's *Rocky* franchise. The understated best of him is to be found alongside Mitchum in Wellman's *The Story of GI Joe*, one of the few wartime war films which can be watched without making allowances; he sometimes turns up in showbiz memoirs and published diaries (including Christopher Isherwood's), usually drunk and behaving disgracefully. **Brian Keith**, with his crumpled features and body like a sack of potatoes, played heavies in his early years (*Nightfall*) before mellowing into a comedian and the prototype Disney dad; his line in *Nickelodeon*, 'I guess I'll be leaving now, the room's on fire,' would make a good epitaph.

Lean **Lloyd Bridges** took longer to incorporate the comic into his tough guy persona, from *The Sound of Fury* to *Airplane!*; his credits as father (Beau, Jeff) are arguably at least as significant as those in his actual filmography. **Gene Evans** was Samuel Fuller's idea of a tough guy, barrel-shaped, stogie jammed in his face, the acme of gruff. But he always seemed more natural as a victim, for example being skinned alive in *Nevada Smith*. Also appearing in the foothills of that cast list was **Josephine Hutchinson**, who tended to exemplify integrity (scientist's wife in *The Story of Louis Pasteur*, headmaster's wife in the 1940 *Tom Brown's Schooldays*), thereby ensuring it would come as no surprise when Hitchcock cast her as the blandly mendacious 'house-owner' in *North by Northwest*.

Such is life, that audiences always take to their hearts actors with a knack for embodying the despicable; perhaps we suspect they're our secret biographers. **J.T. Walsh** mostly played shiftless, spineless characters, often the hero's boss (*Good Morning Vietnam*), in which case the hero was in big trouble. He might occasionally be sympathetic in a feeble sort of way (*A Few Good Men*), recalling baby-faced **Richard Jaeckel**, the fool kid who gunned down Gregory Peck at the end of *The Gunfighter*. Jaeckel himself expired memorably in *Sometimes a Great Notion*, taking a whole reel to succumb to rising floodwater. **Jeanette Nolan** was unpleasant on two big occasions: as Lady Macbeth in Orson Welles' 1948 version of the play; and as the devious widow of a corrupt cop in Fritz Lang's *The Big Heat*.

Jack (*Hawaii Five-O*) **Lord** had a few good roles, notably for Anthony Mann (*God's Little Acre, Man of the West*) but he was only ever going to be a small-screen star, such was the scale of his personality. And the comedian **Red Skelton**, who visually seemed to comprise an assembly of acute angles – Red passed on, perhaps too much of a grotesque to find acceptance as a major star rather than as comic relief.

The unenviable label 'male starlet' attached to **Gene Raymond** at the start of his career, and persisted so long as his blond, bland good looks did likewise. He was in one or two interesting movies (*Zoo in Budapest, The Locket*) but the phrase 'in spite of' – seldom 'thanks to' – usually stood in front of his name. **John Derek** was even prettier than Gene Raymond, and was a minor '50s fixture (see *Run for Cover*) before turning photographer and director of movies showcasing first one wife (Ursula Andress) then another (Bo Derek).

There was a clutch of casualties among those good old, bad old British faces, from that generation of supporting players whose predominance lasted, say, between Potsdam and Profumo. One can imagine a movie which accommodated all of them, though such a work would probably be too ignominious to be recorded in these pages, even if it existed. This would be 'the little picture', playing before a late Bogart or an early Paul Newman. The hero walks into a nightclub. Behind the bar is **Michael Balfour**, cocktail shaker in his chubby mitt, about to serve one too many to stringy, lugubrious **Billy Shine**. The head waiter, **Michael Ward**, flutters nearby, so effete as to make Kenneth Williams look as butch as Aldo Ray. Ramrod-spined, regimentally moustached **Richard Vernon** is the police inspector who drops in to warn the hero to lay off and leave things to the Yard. The sinister club owner is **Ferdy Mayne**, all-purpose foreigner, whose provenance could turn out to be anywhere between Cairo and Transylvania. He may have a discarded girlfriend, eyes flashing fire, and that will be **Rosalie Crutchley**. Meanwhile, the reason our hero is having to treat with all these ominous characters is sitting outside in the car: his leading lady, **Lana Morris**, cute, amiable, classless and well used to hanging

'I guess I'll be leaving now, the room's on fire'

around while the action proceeds elsewhere.

Some of the succeeding wave of British character people also disappeared. **Daniel Massey** was a scaled down version of his father, the alp-like Raymond, and may be designated as primarily a stage player, cinematically contributing a cameo here (as Noël Coward in *Star!*), an episode in a horror portmanteau there. **Brian Glover** was in the grunt-and-grapple game until induced to appear in *Kes*, thereafter becoming an irrepressible part of the scene, with his distinctive voice and wrestler's grasp of showmanship; **James Villiers**, six foot-plus of superciliousness, played characters just begging to be taken down a peg, as per *King and Country*, *Otley*; **Richard Warwick** was a more affable representative of the upper crust, in *If...* and *Sebastiane*. Warwick was one of a number who left the scene much too early. There was also **Chris Farley**, in direct line of descent from the Three Stooges and Abbott-Costello, deriving humour from the obtuse and the destructive (see, or not, *Tommy Boy, Black Sheep*). **Simon de la Brosse** was a Rohmer discovery (*Pauline à la Plage*), subsequently appearing in movies by Sautet, Téchiné and Claude Miller (*La Petite Voleuse*). He killed himself, aged 32. **Stephen Archibald**, who died in obscurity, was the protagonist of Bill Douglas's trilogy, his pinched, desperate features a token of all kinds of deprivation. Is it sentimental to predict that when our times have become one with the age of the stovepipe hat, and the likes of Keanu Reeves and Tom Cruise long been consigned to the discard, then wee Stephen will still be piercing the emotions of discerning students of the era? In any case, not a destiny likely to befall the shade of **David Warbeck**, who was a dead ringer for Jack Nicholson and a favourite in Fulci (*The Beyond*) and Fulci-esque horrors.

And we lost **Olga Georges-Picot**, gorgeous and refined in *Je t'aime, Je t'aime* and *Love and Death*, given to excursions into semi-porn, albeit occasionally with an artistic alibi. Amateurs of such matters will long recall the scene in Robbe-Grillet's *Glissements Progressifs du Plaisir*, in which she and a girlfriend amuse themselves with a carton of eggs and a bottle of red wine.

Samuel Fuller died, to widespread lamentation. The abrasive roughneck of the 1950s (the decade of his best, most characteristic movies for which, at the time, few could find a good word) had somehow transmuted into an unassailable icon, representing hard-won experience, enthusiasm and probity; he had become 'Sam'. A sense of diminishment could be felt: he had allowed himself to be regarded as lovable. Fortunately the films remain, in all their confusing, often disagreeable contrariness.

On the evidence of *Ososhiki*, with its coolly amused sketches of events following a death in the family, **Juzo Itami** had a commendably relaxed attitude towards life's big stuff. It came as a shock therefore to learn that he had taken a header off a ten-storey car park, following private upheavals which would have had many of his western colleagues smirking across the front pages of the tabloids – a further reminder perhaps of the space between the artist and the art.

Shirley Clarke's *The Connection* is, along with *Bob Roberts*, one of the few movies to consist entirely of pastiche. There was conjecture a few years later that Shirley was having us on again with *Portrait of Jason* or, if she wasn't, that Jason was having her on, with his rambling tales of sexual triumph and misadventure. Duuh, what is truth anyhow, man? A number of obscure dance documentaries also form part of a career which, *Ornette* notwithstanding, can barely be said to have made it out of the '60s.

That a cinematic facility runs freer and more promiscuously in France than almost anywhere else is demonstrated by the way in which specialists in various of the natural sciences, bio-ecologists and so on, have tended to express themselves as readily on film as on the printed page. Three of these left-handed cineastes departed recently. **Jacques-Yves Cousteau**, oceanographer, was the star among them, although his first film for the general public – *Le Monde du Silence*, made in 1956 with Louis Malle – seems today quite comically non-PC with its merry cries of 'A la cuisine!' as another exotic and probably rare specimen of marine life flounders on the deck – reminding us that Cousteau was, in all his aspects, a Frenchman. Not a claim that would be made about **Haroun Tazieff**, who certainly made French films, but was actually born in Poland of partly Moslem parentage, brought up in Belgium and, as a rugby fan, perfectly at home in Twickenham. Primarily he was a vulcanologist, or is it volcanologist, anyway – taken in all – an absolute one-off. His *Les Rendez-vous du Diable* was a film society favourite in the early '60s, while for *Le Volcan Interdit* he collaborated with the estimable Chris Marker. And it was announced that **Pierre-Dominique Gaisseau**, ethnologist, had died; his *Le Ciel, la Boue* (*The Sky Above, The Mud Below*) won a 1961 Oscar for best feature documentary.

James Algar's movies were frequent Oscar winners, too, though being a Disney employee, it was usually not he but Uncle Walt who strode forth to accept the statuette. Algar's work is anthologised in *The Best of Walt Disney's True Life Adventures*, with its square-dancing scorpions, and similar anthropomorphic gems. The Dutchman **Bert Haanstra** was also primarily a documentarist and occasional Oscar winner. His studies of reflections in canals, of glassblowers, zoos and such were either gentle, humorous and humanist or tame, simplistic and condescending, according to taste and temperament. Mind you, Haanstra was a wild and crazy documentarist compared to the unswervingly party-line **Santiago Alvarez**, whose movies were mostly devoted to acclaiming his President (*Mi hermano Fidel*), attacking the USA (*La Guerra Necesaria*) and generally affirming the orthodoxy.

Harold French was probably born in 1897 (though sources disagree) in which case he just made it into triple figures; ex-West End actor, director of respectable literary adaptations for the movies

A horror entitled They Saved Hitler's Brain ...

(Maugham, Rattigan), he was also responsible for the doom laden *The Man Who Watched Trains Go By*, a key British *noir*. **Carlo Ludovico Bragaglia** did even better in terms of longevity, dying at 103. You may not be familiar with Carlo, but one doesn't need to be much of a linguist to understand the titles of his most characteristic movies (*La Cortigiana di Babilonia*, *Gli Amori di Ercole*) nor much by way of a sophisticate to take their measure.

Pilar Miró had a long way to go before her centenary loomed, but in her lifetime she had exercised considerable influence on Spanish cinema, as director (*Gary Cooper, Who Art in Heaven*) and administrator (of the state film school ICAA and of Televisión Española). **Riccardo Franco** (nephew of Jesus Franco) started his directing career with a bang, getting himself arrested for the alleged subversions in *El Desastre de Annual* (1970). Latterly he became most active as a documentarist for Spanish televison.

Claudio Gora was able to maintain in tandem an identity as a director and a separate one as actor, though in neither capacity did he achieve much recognition outside of Italy. In Britain, **Maurice Hatton** slouched off the set; his *Praise Marx and Pass the Ammunition* represents an aspect of '60s cinema, seeming torn between wishing to amuse its audience and to scold them.

Hollywood directors: Fuller, of course. Also **George Schaefer**, who was sort of a Hollywood director, when he wasn't working on Broadway or directing prestige television specials. His movies were an alternation of the defiantly uncommercial (*An Enemy of the People*) and the opposite (*Doctors' Wives*). **David Bradley** also just about qualifies as Hollywood, having been under contract to MGM at one point. History records him as a director of curios and aberrations, for example his 16mm efforts (*Peer Gynt, Julius Caesar*) shot in Illinois with a youthful Charlton Heston, and, years later, a Stanley Cortez-photographed, Ed Wood-esque horror picture entitled *They Saved Hitler's Brain*.

Gene Fowler Jr would perhaps be more appropriately included among the production artists noted later, since his most prestigious credits were those as editor (on films by Wellman, Fuller and Fritz Lang). But he did direct a handful of movies, including *I Was a Teenage Werewolf* and *I Married a Monster from Outer Space*, feeble and forgettable things in themselves, but persisting in the memory and in the history books, thanks to those artfully awful titles. **Leslie Stevens** died, his distinction of being the only director to have shot a film in Esperanto (*Incubus*, 1961) still intact. He accumulated an odd set of credits, as both director and writer, and it has to be taken on trust that there was only one Leslie Stevens, not two or three, and that the man who scripted *The Left Handed Gun* was indeed the same one who wrote *Return to the Blue Lagoon*.

Finally, **Hy Averback**, a name for gag writers to have fun with – and Averback was indeed primarily a humorist, at first voicing Disney cartoon characters, then moving on to direct vehicles for the likes of Peter Sellers and Doris Day, as well as absolutely miles of TV McClouds, Columbos and Rockfords.

It's difficult to know whom to single out among the cohorts of writers, cinematographers, film editors, composers, art directors and production folk generally who have slipped away during the past year or so. These are the artists in effect abolished by auteur principles, so that when we say of *The Lady Vanishes*, 'Hitchcock cuts from …' we negate the contribution of **Alfred Roome**; or when we write of *The Magnificent Ambersons*, 'Welles frames his shot so that …' we ignore the lavish talents of **Stanley Cortez**; and when we observe of *Fires Were Started* that 'Jennings has constructed his sets to convey …' we overlook the artistry of **Edward Carrick**.

The period seems to have been a specially perilous one for film editors. Apart from Roome and Gene Fowler Jr, we have lost **William Reynolds**, who cut Kazan's *Wild River* to such unexpectedly gentle and romantic effect, and who later shaped the mountain of footage Coppola shot for *The Godfather*. The most distinguished credits in **Peter Taylor**'s CV were *The Bridge on the River Kwai* and *This Sporting Life*, the latter with its cut from the dentist's chair to the coalface, a crude idea, redeemed in the timing. And there was **Sidney Cole** who, apart from his editing room assignments for the likes of Carol Reed and Thorold Dickinson, maintained a secondary career as producer (at Ealing and for early television) and then even a third one as livener-up and general mover and shaker for the Association of Cine Technicians, as the union was then called.

Stanley Cortez and **Charles B. Lang** were perhaps the most distinguished and certainly the most venerable of the departed cameramen. Besides *Ambersons*, Cortez was associated with the creation of the disturbing dream worlds of *Secret Beyond the Door*, *The Night of the Hunter*, *Shock Corridor*. Lang was a director of photography ever since silent days, and his filmography testifies to an impressive versatility, whether working in black and white (the soft, romantic look in *Peter Ibbetson*, the hard, big city glitter of *Some Like It Hot*) or in colour (the delicately rain washed Paris of *Charade*, the blazing light south of the border in *The Magnificent Seven*).

Dietrich Lohmann, effectively only in mid-career when he died, graduated or, if you prefer, retrogressed from the photography of early work by Herzog, Reitz, Fassbinder and Syberberg to that of big budget productions like his final credit, the Spielberg spectacular *Deep Impact*. From all the images left us by **Arthur Ibbetson**, one might pick out those of two adolescent girls in the north country: Hayley Mills, among the cheerlessly monochrome winterscapes of *Whistle Down the Wind*, and Jenny Agutter, briskly arranging matters on a sunny Yorkshire branchline in *The Railway Children*.

Linwood G. Dunn made his name as the wizard of the optical printer. As head of RKO's photographic effects department, he had ample opportunity to refine and extend the possibilities of that critical piece of technology: *King Kong*, *Bringing Up Baby*, *The*

Incubus, the only film in Esperanto intact

Hunchback of Notre Dame … but above all, *Citizen Kane*. It has been estimated that fifty per cent of *Kane* was printed optically and if, say, some of its transitions from miniatures to live action now look a little crude, there's no doubt that the film's celebrated boldness, the impression it gives of rising above constraints, is thanks in part to Dunn's unflagging ingenuity. He later worked on the original TV *Star Trek*.

As for producers, there can be little argument that it was the loss of **Anatole Dauman** that was most widely and grievously felt. His company Argos Films, formed in the early '50s, backed movies by Resnais, Marker, Bresson, Godard, Oshima, Wenders, Tarkovsky … Maybe some of his productions would still have been made elsewhere, had he decided to go into some other line of business but, even so, it's painful to imagine world cinema without Anatole Dauman.

The composer **Edwin Astley** was most noted for his television work, including the Richard Greene *Robin Hood* series of the 1950s. But he also scored a number of big screen titles, including the Peter Sellers fantasy *The Mouse That Roared* and Hammer's 1962 *Phantom of the Opera*, for which Astley had to contrive some fake turn-of-the-century arias.

Thomas Narcejac followed, at last, his old writing partner Pierre Boileau, who had passed on years earlier. Together, B-N spun a succession of creepy yarns which provided the basis for, notably, Clouzot's *Les Diaboliques* and Hitchcock's *Vertigo*. These two stories plus B-N's original screenplay for Franju's *Pleins Feux sur l'Assassin* constitute an unofficial trilogy, offering three variations on the narrative ploy whereby a character whom we're assured is dead seems, nevertheless, still to be moving about somewhere. (Solutions, respectively: not dead at all/someone dead, but not who we think/yes, really dead this time.)

Cockney fabulist **Wolf Mankowitz** and pillar of the establishment Sir **Ronald Millar** make an unlikely pairing of British scriptwriters – although it was for his facility as a speechwriter (for Prime Minister Thatcher) rather than for his work on the likes of the 1954 *Rose Marie* that Millar found himself in line for a knighthood. Earlier, he had been a playwright (*Frieda*, filmed by Basil Dearden) and had spent several years in Hollywood, with MGM. Mankowitz was known primarily for his tales of London life, ranging between Petticoat Lane (*A Kid for Two Farthings*), Soho (*Expresso Bongo*) and Fleet Street (*The Day the Earth Caught Fire*). One should also perhaps add the novelist **Hammond Innes**, whose outdoor adventure yarns provided manly things to do for the likes of Dirk Bogarde (*Campbell's Kingdom*) and Charlton Heston (*The Wreck of the Mary Deare*).

A bunch of American writers went to their reward. Neither **Harold Robbins** nor **James A. Michener** did much direct work for the movies. They wouldn't have had the time, their literary outputs consisting of melodramas bulky enough to sustain the traveller through a journey from *Hawaii* to *The Bridges at Toko-Ri*, to invoke a couple of Michener's filmed epics. Robbins probably matched him for wordage published, but unlike Michener was too much of a hooligan to be in line for a Pulitzer. His boxing novel *A Stone for Danny Fisher* was Presley-ised into *King Creole*, numbers replacing bouts, and he even provided material (*The Lonely Lady*) for Pia Zadora, a name that already seems as much a part of the past as that of Elinor Glyn.

Both **Paul Jarrico** and **Millard Lampell** were formed in the US Communist Party of the 1930s and wrecked by the blacklist of the 1950s. Jarrico was perhaps the more dynamic, being 'named' no less that 14 times during the House Un-American Activities hearings, though in retrospect anyone who co-scripted a film called *Song of Russia* was asking to end up in the doghouse. Out of his time of adversity came *Salt of the Earth*, on which he is credited as producer; a little later in a poignant volte face, post-Hungary '56, Jarrico wrote of the realisation 'that all the terrible things our enemies had been saying about us were true, and that we had been defending indefensible things.' Lampell, though associated with the stage as much as the screen, was obliged to follow Jarrico and the rest into exile, out of which came perhaps his most distinguished cinematic credit, on Losey's *Blind Date* – though some might sooner assign that distinction to the lyrics he wrote for the ballads punctuating Milestone's *A Walk in the Sun*. ('It was just a little walk in the warm Italian sun, / But it was not an easy thing …')

Anyone devising categories quickly runs upon the uncategorisable – the eccentric, the anomalous and the downright singular. All of the following have something of those qualities about them – one fears there was trouble in paradise if they all ascended Powell and Pressburger's celestial escalator as part of the same consignment.

Vittorio Mussolini was certainly unique or at least in a unique position, being the son of *Il Duce*, to implement his cinematic brainwaves. He elected to function as writer and producer, to what effect can be gauged by the silence which usually ensues when you challenge someone to name three Italian movies from the 1930s. Or two. Or one. He leaves us at least

with a conversational divertissement: what would you do if you were movie-struck and your doting poppa was also the country's fascist dictator?

'"You're right, Peter," grinned Anthony Quinn, dipping his tortilla into his guacamole.' That was **Peter Noble**, in his persona of bon vivant, man-about-town and showbiz gossip-monger for such publications as *What's On in London* and *Screen International*. However, he was also the compiler of a series of impressively informative *British Film Yearbooks*, post-war and into the '50s, the author of books on Welles and von Stroheim and in general the prototype film buff. The cliché about a particular death marking the end of an era seemed somehow apt for this in many ways endearing throwback to a more illusioned, less abrasive time.

(And speaking of buffs, a big parenthesis here to note the

Too much of a hooligan to be in line for a Pulitzer

demise of *Films in Review*. Latterly, *FIR* became a perfectly unremarkable periodical, full of severely factual articles bearing on the lost highways and forgotten byways of movie history. But back in the '50s and '60s, it was the assertive voice of the cinematic American right, with such critics as Flavia Wharton and Tatiana Balkoff Drowne peering balefully at each month's batch of new movies for signs of such tendencies as socialism, effeminacy, artistic ambition. Still, a trawl through the back issues nets some unexpected oddities, including a 1954 review of *Dial M for Murder* by one Steve Sondheim and a 1955 letter from Luis Buñuel indignantly denying any inclination to sadism. *Caramba* – the very idea! In the present context, of course, it should be borne in mind that magazines, unlike people, can always be resurrected.)

Then there was **William**

Burroughs, who was certainly the most … though in other respects perhaps the least … and in any case the epitome of whatever it was he represented. During his years in the UK, Burroughs devised, to use the vaguest term available, a number of cinematic oddities, including *Towers Open Fire*, partly shot in the boardroom of the British Film Institute's old Dean Street offices. Cronenberg's adaptation of *The Naked Lunch*, peculiar as it is, actually seems the most mainstream movie with which Burroughs was associated.

Lotti Huber was a nightclub entertainer of part-Jewish extraction in 1930s Berlin. Nearly half a century later, after brushing against some of the rougher parts of the century's history, she encountered Rosa von Praunheim, who featured her in a succession of his movies. Thus did Lotti Huber find herself, well into her seventies and against all the odds, translated into that dubious commodity, a gay icon.

It is only in movie-related obituaries that the death of **Dodi Fayed** is noted and not that of any other occupant of the car which slammed into the thirteenth column of the Pont de l'Alma underpass. Dodi executive produced a grab bag of British and international movies, swapping cheques with the likes of David Puttnam (*Chariots of Fire*) and Steven Spielberg (*Hook*). His other enduring legacy is likely to be via the plurality of fictional reconstructions of that notorious night, stretching into the next century as far as the eye can see, and featuring actors as yet unborn.

Harrison Marks – this is for nostalgic Brits only – was a minor fantasy figure for adolescent males in the late '50s/early '60s, with his cigarette holder, his Vandyke, the quantities of nude models strewn about his studio. His glossy booklets of smutty snaps were eventually superseded by raunchier fare, and Harrison went into the movies, where his talents as a director proved impossible to understate. However and at least, *Naked as Nature Intended* may be the only movie with the word 'Intended' in its title, while *Come Play with Me* is probably the only soft porn movie to bear the credit 'Starring Irene Handl'. Another end of another era.

STAN MAPPERLEY

James ALGAR
11 Jun 12 – 27 Feb 98

Santiago ALVAREZ
8 Mar 19 – 20 May 98

Stephen ARCHIBALD
5 May 59 – 24 Mar 98

Edwin ASTLEY
12 Apr 22 – 19 May 98

Hy AVERBACK
1920 – Oct 97

Michael BALFOUR
1918 – 24 Oct 97

David BRADLEY
1920 – Dec 97

Carlo Ludovico BRAGAGLIA
8 Jul 1894 – 4 Jan 98

Lloyd BRIDGES
15 Jan 13 – 10 Mar 98

William BURROUGHS
5 Feb 14 – 2 Aug 97

Edward CARRICK
3 Jan 05 – 21 Jan 98

Shirley CLARKE
1919 or '25 – 23 Sep 97

Sidney COLE
31 Oct 08 – 25 Jan 98

Stanley CORTEZ
4 Nov 08 – 23 Dec 97

Jacques-Yves COUSTEAU
11 Jun 10 – 24 Jun 97

Rosalie CRUTCHLEY
4 Jan 21 – 27 Jul 97

Anatole DAUMAN
7 Feb 25 – 8 Apr 98

Linwood G. DUNN
1904 – May 98

Simon DE LA BROSSE
1965 – 17 Apr 98

John DEREK
12 Aug 26 – 22 May 98

Billie DOVE
14 May 00 – 31 Dec 97

Gene EVANS
11 Jul 22 – 1 Apr 98

Chris FARLEY
15 Feb 64 – 18 Dec 97

Alice FAYE
5 May 15 – 9 May 98

Dodi FAYED
15 Apr 55 – 31 Aug 97

FILMS IN REVIEW
1950 –1997

Gene FOWLER Jr
1917 – 11 May 98

Riccardo FRANCO
25 Apr 49 – 21 May 98

Harold FRENCH
23 Apr 1897 or 1900 – 19 Oct 97

Samuel FULLER
12 Aug 11 – 31 Oct 97

Pierre-Dominique GAISSEAU
1921 – Oct 97

Olga GEORGES-PICOT
1944 – 19 Jun 97

Brian GLOVER
2 Apr 34 – 24 Jul 97

Claudio GORA
27 Jul 13 – 13 Mar 98

Bert HAANSTRA
31 May 16 – 23 Oct 97

Maurice HATTON
1938 – 25 Oct 97

Lotti HUBER
16 Oct 12 – 31 May 98

Josephine HUTCHINSON
12 Oct 1898 – 4 Jun 98

Arthur IBBETSON
8 Sep.22 – 19 Oct 97

Hammond INNES
15 Jul 13 – 10 Jun 98

Juzo ITAMI
1933 – 21 Dec 97

Richard JAECKEL
10 Oct 96 – 14 Jun 97

Paul JARRICO
12 Jan 15 – 28 Oct 97

Brian KEITH
14 Nov 21 – 24 Jun 97

Millard LAMPELL
10 Jan 19 – 3 Oct 97

Charles B. LANG
27 May 02 – 3 Apr 98

Dietrich LOHMANN
1943 – Nov 97

Jack LORD
30 Dec 28 –21 Jan 98

Wolf MANKOWITZ
7 Nov 24 – 20 May 98

Harrison MARKS
1926 – 27 Jun 97

Daniel MASSEY
10 Oct 33 – 26 Mar 98

Ferdy MAYNE
1916 – 30 Jan 98

Burgess MEREDITH
16 Nov 08 – 10 Sep 97

James A. MICHENER
3 Feb 07 – 16 Oct 97

Toshiro MIFUNE
1 Apr 20 – 23 Dec 97

Ronald MILLAR
12 Nov 19 – 16 Apr 98

Pilar MIRÓ
20 Apr 40 – 19 Oct 97

Robert MITCHUM
6 Aug 17 – 1 Jul 97

Lana MORRIS
11 Mar 30 – 27 May 98

Vittorio MUSSOLINI
27 Dec 16 – 12 Jun 97

Thomas NARCEJAC
3 Jul 08 – 7 Jun 98

Peter NOBLE
18 Jun 17 – 16 Aug 97

Jeanette NOLAN
30 Dec 11 – 5 Jun 98

Maureen O'SULLIVAN
17 May 11 –23 Jun 98

Gene RAYMOND
3 Aug 08 – 3 May 98

William REYNOLDS
14 Jun 10 – 16 Jul 97

Harold ROBBINS
1 May 12 – 14 Oct 97

Alfred ROOME
22 Dec 08 – 19 Nov 97

George SCHAEFER
16 Dec 20 – Sep 97

Billy SHINE
20 Oct 11 – 24 Jul 97

Red SKELTON
18 Jul 13 – 16 Sep 97

Frank SINATRA
12 Dec 15 – 14 May 98

Leslie STEVENS
3 Feb 24 – 24 Apr 98

James STEWART
20 May 08 – 2 Jul 97

Peter TAYLOR
28 Feb 22 – 17 Dec 97

Haroun TAZIEFF
11 May 14 – 2 Feb 98

Richard VERNON
7 Mar 25 – 4 Dec 97

James VILLIERS
29 Sep 33 – 19 Jan 97

J.T. WALSH
1 Mar 42 – 27 Feb 98

Michael WARD
9 Apr 15 – 8 Nov 97

David WARBECK
17 Nov 41 – 23 Jul 97

Richard WARWICK
24 Apr 45 – 16 Dec 97

a

The Adventures of Baron Munchausen

a

ABBA The Movie
(Lasse Hallström, 1977, Swe/Aust) ABBA,
Robert Hughexs, Tom Oliver, Bruce Barry.
95 min.
Unashamed and supremely slick commercial for
the group, maintaining a gentle air of self-parody while at the same time being a celebration of
all the various apparatuses which make a merchandising phenomenon like ABBA possible.
The narrative, without which the film would
mostly consist of footage of the band on stage,
follows ABBA through an Australian tour pursued by a Sydney deejay. If the idea's spread a
bit thin, it's occasionally handled with a humour
and panache worthy of Dick Lester's Beatles'
movies or ABBA's own Phil Spector/Brian
Wilson-inspired studio craftsmanship. RM

Abbott and Costello
Meet Frankenstein
(aka Abbott and Costello
Meet the Ghosts)
(Charles T Barton, 1948, US) Bud Abbott, Lou
Costello, Bela Lugosi, Lon Chaney Jr, Glenn
Strange, Lenore Aubert.
92 min. b/w.
First and possibly the best of the horror spoofs
indulged in by this comic duo. Not that it is particularly funny, but showing a surprising respect
for Universal tradition in the matter of its monsters, it at least looks remarkably good.
Graceless imitations of Laurel and Hardy (never
revealing the deep-rooted affection for each other
beneath the exasperations, which made Stan and
Ollie so well-beloved) and of the Marx Brothers
(although their verbal routines never even begin
to scale the same heights of surrealist fantasy).
They nevertheless made 35 movies between One
Night in the Tropics (1940) and Dance With Me,
Henry (1956). TM

Abdication, The
(Anthony Harvey, 1974, GB) Peter Finch, Liv
Ullmann, Cyril Cusack, Paul Rogers, Graham
Crowden, Michael Dunn.
103 min.
Cold Scandinavian obsession drives Queen
Christina to relinquish her throne, convert to
Catholicism and seek the warmer climate of
Rome, where she pours out her heart to Cardinal
Peter Finch ('It seems strange to call somebody
father'). As an exploration of private spaces in the
lives of public people (who, through circumstance
or choice, are committed to celibacy), psychological insight is too often sacrificed for the sake of
verbal swordplay. It ends up skirting perilously
close to superior cliché ('Are we not the world's
strangest couple?'). At least Garbo, playing the
same role in Mamoulian's Queen Christina, conspired with her audience against the rest of the
film. One wishes for something like that here: it
all seems so remote.

Abduction
(Joseph Zito, 1975, US) Judith-Marie Bergman,
David Pendleton, Gregory Rozakis, Leif
Erickson, Dorothy Malone, Lawrence Tierney.
100 min.
Low-budget, quasi-documentary thriller about the
kidnapping of a tycoon's daughter by a revolutionary cell. Despite disclaimers in the titles and
despite being based on a novel (Black Abductors
by Harrison James) written before the event, it's
obviously modelled on the Patty Hearst kidnapping. Not bad at suggesting the girl's moral and
political confusion, but it founders on its own confusion of styles, methods and aims. RG

Abel
(Alex van Warmerdam, 1985, Neth) Alex van
Warmerdam, Olga Zuiderhoek, Henri Garcin,
Loes Luca, Annet Malherbe.
103 min.
Abel is a spoilt, possibly retarded, certainly
eccentric 31-year-old mummy's boy whose suffocating relationship with his mother is balanced
by the constant torment which father and son
inflict on each other. A final rift occurs over a TV
set (father refuses to have one, mother and son
smuggle a set into the loft), and Abel is booted
out into the streets. Father finds solace at an
establishment called 'Naked Girls', where he
picks up Zus (the voluptuous Malherbe) but Abel
also stumbles upon Zus, is seduced, and shares

her bohemian lifestyle... Van Warmerdam, who
also stars as gormless Abel, directs with brash,
colourful simplicity, evidently on a minute budget. The film is self-consciously quirky, and
while some of the non-stop visual jokes hit the
right note of irrational oddness, others are silly
and contrived. But at least it has a distinctive
flavour, and some scenes display a flair for social
satire. Wittily comic or tiresome, according to
taste. SFe

Abenteuer des Werner
Holt, Die
see Adventures of Werner Holt, The

Abgeschminkt
see Making Up

Abismos de pasión
(Cumbres borrascosas/
Wuthering Heights)
(Luis Buñuel, 1953, Mex) Jorge Mistral,
Irasema Dilian, Lilia Prado, Ernesto Alonso,
Luis Aceves Castañeda.
90 min. b/w.
While it's certainly true that Emily Bronte's
classic novel appealed strongly to the
Surrealists, with the love between Heathcliff and
Cathy an almost textbook case of l'amour fou,
it must be said that much of Buñuel's adaptation is surprisingly lifeless, a fact perhaps attrib-
utable largely to the severe shortcomings of his
lead actors. Despite impressive use of arid locations, and numerous Buñuelian 'touches' depicting man's capacity for cruelty and violence, it's
only in the final moments, when
Alejandro/Heathcliff, consumed with passion,
breaks into Catarina's funeral vault for one more
kiss, that the director appears fully engaged
with his material. GA

Abominable Dr Phibes, The
(Robert Fuest, 1971, GB) Vincent Price, Joseph
Cotten, Virginia North, Hugh Griffith, Terry-
Thomas, Aubrey Woods.
94 min.
Cult camp horror, with Price in fine fettle as a
disfigured composer devising murders based on
the ten curses of Pharaoh to avenge himself on
the doctors who let his wife die on the operating
table. Often amusing, occasionally sickening,
always impressive for the imaginative Art Deco
sets, it's pretty flatly directed, despite memorable images like the opening shot of Price
hunched as manically as the Phantom of the
Opera over a Hammond organ in a black plastic cowl. GA

Abominable Snowman, The
(Val Guest, 1957, GB) Forrest Tucker, Peter
Cushing, Maureen Connell, Richard Wattis,
Robert Brown.
90 min. b/w.
Hammer's botch of Nigel Kneale's teleplay The
Creature, about an expedition to the Himalayas.
Tucker wants to exploit the Yeti, so gets killed;
Cushing doesn't, so is allowed to live. The crea-
tures, glimpsed just briefly in their gorilla suits,
are hardly worth the dreary trip. TM

A Bout de Souffle 100 (100)
(Breathless)
(Jean-Luc Godard, 1959, Fr) Jean-Paul
Belmondo, Jean Seberg, Daniel Boulanger,
Jean-Pierre Melville, Van Doude.
90 min. b/w.
Godard's first feature spins a pastiche with
pathos as joyrider Belmondo shoots a cop, chases friends and debts across a night-time Paris,
and falls in love with a literary lady. Seberg
quotes books and ideas and names; Belmondo
measures his profile against Bogart's, pawns a
stolen car, and talks his girlfriend into a cash
loan 'just till midday'. The camera lavishes
black-and-white love on Paris, strolling up the
Champs-Elysées, edging across café terraces,
sweeping over the rooftop skyline, Mozart mixing with cool jazz riffs in the night air. The ultimate night-time film noir noir noir...until
Belmondo pulls his own eyelids shut when he
dies. More than any other, this was the film
which epitomised the iconoclasm of the early
Nouvelle Vague, not least in its insolent use of
the jump-cut. CA

About Last Night...
(Edward Zwick, 1986, US) Rob Lowe, Demi
Moore, James Belushi, Elizabeth Perkins,
George DiCenzo.
113 min.
Danny is a restaurant supplies salesman. He
meets Debbie, an advertising art director. They
bonk. She moves in with him. They argue. They
split up. That's it. Surprisingly, About Last
Night... is not dull, due to the razor-sharp writing
at its source, David Mamet's play Sexual
Perversity in Chicago. There are the usual
attempts at 'opening out', consisting of the lovers
roaming the beach, buying balloons etc. to the
requisite disco-dunk of the soundtrack album,
and the original ending has been considerably
sweetened. But Mamet explores all the wince-
making awfulness of sexual clichés, all the wisecracking self-consciousness of individuals unable
to articulate what's really on their minds, all the
petty quirks of men who don't like Tampax wrap-
pers cluttering up their bathrooms, and all the
foibles of females who pretend not to be brandishing their pregnancy-testing kits. AB

About Love, Tokyo
(Ai ni tsuite, Tokyo)
(Mitsuo Yanagimachi, 1992, Jap) Wu Xiao
Tong, Asuka Okasaka, Hiroshi Fujioka.
110 min.
A scummy, indefensible picture from a once-
important director. Yanagimachi's weakness has
always been his uncritical fetishisation of macho
bad boys, from the bike gang in Black Emperor
to the murderous lumberjack in Fire Festival; his
heroes this time are Mainland Chinese students
in Tokyo's answer to Stepney, and he sees them
(with only a figleaf of detachment) as amoral,
foul-mouthed misogynists slipping easily into the
city's underworld of crime, gambling, violence
and commercial sex. Whatever his intentions, the
view of immigrant behaviour and attitudes
chimes neatly with the prejudices of the Japanese
Right; so it's fortunate that the visual style is as
squalid as the screenplay, making the film a completely repulsive experience. TR

About Mrs Leslie
(Daniel Mann, 1954, US) Shirley Booth, Robert
Ryan, Alex Nicol, Marjie Millar, Eilene
Janssen, Henry Morgan.
104 min. b/w.
In one of her rare film roles, Shirley Booth is perfectly cast as the cheerfully competent, middle-aged
owner of a Beverly Hills boarding-house, sympathetic – but not indulgent – to the various problems
of her roomers. Flashbacks reveal her bitter-sweet
past when, as a night-club singer, she found happiness with a mysterious, lonely tycoon (Ryan) who
is able to spare only six weeks a year away from
business pressures to be with her. At first resentful when she discovers that he is trapped by a marriage contracted for social and material advantage
when he was young and ambitious, she learns to
be grateful for what she has. It's soap, of course,
especially given that Booth's story is lent a happy
ending, as it were, by two roomers who turn their
backs on the rat race for fame and fortune, electing
instead to settle humbly for each other. But it's
scripted with wit, insight and no small dash of acerbity (by Ketti Frings from a novel by Vina Delmar),
while Booth and Ryan give terrific performances.
Their (on the face of it) unlikely pairing lends the
film a distinctly offbeat flavour. TM

Above Suspicion
(Richard Thorpe, 1943, US) Joan Crawford,
Fred MacMurray, Conrad Veidt, Basil
Rathbone, Reginald Owen.
90 min. b/w.
Brisk and lightly likeable spy thriller, with
MacMurray and Crawford as newly-weds on hon-
eymoon in Europe (hence the title), persuaded by
Britain to do a bit of spying. Rathbone con-
tributes his characteristic flair as the Nazi villain,
and the whole thing gallops along in pleasant,
undemanding and totally incredible fashion. GA

Above the Law (aka Nico)
(Andrew Davis, 1988, US) Steven Seagal, Pam
Grier, Henry Silva, Ron Dean, Daniel Faraldo,
Sharon Stone.
99 min.
Chicago cop Nico is an Italian immigrant, an aiki-
do Black Belt, fluent in several languages, an ex-

CIA operative with 'Nam experience, a fine husband and father, and possessed of the brains and brawn to back him up in his fight for what he believes is right. *Phew!* The plot concerns a Secret Service attempt to assassinate a senator about to blow the whistle on an undercover drugs trafficking/political destabilisation gimmick, and detours via scenes of a bombed church, 'Nam torture flashbacks, and numerous scraps and car chases. Through this scattergun proliferation strides Nico (Seagal in his debut) like a holy mixture of Bruce Lee, Clint Eastwood, John Wayne and Jon Miller. This he does with considerable élan. Davis' direction is *Miami Vice*-tight, though with frequent attempts at humour: this, together with the caricature psycho-baddie (Silva), and the mixture of spectacular, bone-crunchingly realistic violence with a stab at topical socio-political commentary, makes for a *very* uncertain tone. MC

Above the Rim

(Jeff Pollack, 1994, US) Duane Martin, Leon, Tupac Shakur, David Bailey, Tonya Pinkins, Marlon Wayans, Bernie Mac.
98 min.
Forsaking teamwork to impress a university scout, high-school basketball star Kyle-Lee Watson (Martin) succeeds in alienating teammates and coach. The only person he impresses is his friend Bugaloo (Wayans), who introduces him to drug-dealer Birdie (Shakur). Seduced by the promise of fame and fortune, Kyle abandons the school squad to run instead with the Birdmen in the upcoming street basketball tournament. It's unclear if this is a realistic depiction of black youth culture, but it's certainly a moral one. A formula script, but a mobile camera, pulsing rap soundtrack and a game cast whip up the necessary fizz. AO

Above Us the Earth

(Karl Francis, 1977, GB) Windsor Rees, Gwen Francis, Michael Foot, Neil Kinnock, Joe Gormley.
85 min.
At times inclined to substitute special pleading for analytical fact, but extremely refreshing as a study of Welsh miners and their environment, especially given the alacrity with which the British cinema has usually retreated to defensive stereotypes to characterise the working class. Documentary footage concerning the closure of Ogilvie Colliery in 1975 and the miners' attitude towards this is intercut with staged sequences of the decline and death of an old miner from lung disease. The subject is sombre and its treatment reflective, as well it might be when the director, himself a miner's son, had to mortgage his home to help complete the film. SM

Above Us the Waves

(Ralph Thomas, 1955, GB) John Mills, John Gregson, Donald Sinden, James Robertson Justice, Michael Medwin, OE Hasse.
99 min. b/w.
Lamentable World War II heroics, told in muddled, would-be semi-documentary style, with the 'Tirpitz' sunk in a flood of stiff upper lips. Mills is the commander sending his midget submarines out into the studio tank. TM

Abraham Valley (Vale Abraão)

(Manoel de Oliveira, 1993, Port/Fr/Switz) Mário Barroso, Leonor Silveira, Cecile Sanz de Alba, Luis Miguel Cintra, Rui de Carvalho, Luis Lima Barreto.
189 min.
This Portuguese adaptation of Madame Bovary – or rather a poetic meditation on the novel by Augustina Bessa-Luis – is encased in a hypnotic atmosphere, both melancholic and tranquil. Ema (Silveira), orphaned at six, house-bound till 14, grows up in a bourgeois family in the unchanging vine-terraced Duoro valley. She's slightly lame, but possesses a beauty which is 'exuberant and therefore dangerous'. Despite a taste for luxury, she marries a doctor who depends on her 'like a worm on soil'. She's twice unfaithful, but her only close bond is with a mute servant. In a world where 'the pleasures of hypocrisy exceed those of love', her spirit must die. Subtle, elegant, enigmatic, this movie by the veteran Oliveira exercises a powerful grip. Oliveira's style is hard to categorise (the director began making films in 1931): the timelessness of the modern-day setting, where the Lotuses and

Maseratis seem so incongruous, is reminiscent of Resnais, but the languorous acting echoes the satiric irony of late Buñuel and the secretive minimalism of Bresson. WH

Abschied vom Falschen Paradies

see Farewell to False Paradise

Abschied von Gestern

see Yesterday Girl

Absence of Malice

(Sydney Pollack, 1981, US) Paul Newman, Sally Field, Bob Balaban, Melinda Dillon, Luther Adler, Barry Primus.
116 min.
Impeccably liberal in its orientation to 'issues' – the power and responsibilities of the press, the impact of misinformation – this avoids the excesses of Stanley Kramer-like telegraphy, only to come up looking aesthetically wet. It's not just a reliance on star casting to sugar the pill as reporter Field picks up a malicious crime squad 'leak' and smears innocent Newman. Sheer worthy dullness comes closer to describing the problem. For all the smokescreen convolutions of legalistic conspiracy and juxtapositions of ethics, 'professionalism', public interest and private morality, we're basically presented with two attractive victims on the same hook who will inevitably spar their way past one of democracy's little hiccups. PT

Absolute Beginners

(Julien Temple, 1986, GB) Eddie O'Connell, Patsy Kensit, David Bowie, James Fox, Ray Davies.
108 min.
This musical taken from Colin MacInnes' book about life on the edge in the Soho and Notting Hill of 1958 is a thing of bits and shards. A pair of flyweight leads are counterbalanced by some lurid casting (including Lionel Blair as a pederast tin pan alley king, Alan Freeman's clueless trendspotter, Steven Berkoff's usual Fascist rant, and Bowie, whose face at last is taking on character). Clearly a nightmare to edit, the narrative stutters into life only occasionally. Charm is everywhere, humour thin; and the soundtrack is very contemporary for a movie which in the pre-publicity boasted of its jazz origins. The whole film is an example of the strange influence of pop promo mentality on cinema. All that noise, all that energy, so little governing thought. CPea

Absolute Power

(Clint Eastwood, 1996, US) Clint Eastwood, Gene Hackman, Ed Harris, Laura Linney, Scott Glenn, Dennis Haysbert, Judy Davis, EG Marshall.
121 min.
When ultra-secretive master burglar Luther Whitney (Eastwood) breaks into the mansion of a politically influential millionaire (Marshall), he's surprised by the arrival of the owner's wife and the discovery (he's hiding in a closet behind a two-way mirror) that she's carrying on with the US President (Hackman). Worse, after their drunken shenanigans turn nasty, Whitney witnesses both a murder and a cover-up. He's soon being chased by the cops (Harris) and the president's aides. Surely the best defence is attack. This light, part-comic Hitchcockian thriller, scripted by William Goldman from a novel by Daniel Baldacci, doesn't rank with Eastwood's best work as actor/director, but it's nevertheless solidly enjoyable. The script may lack even a shading of political analysis or comment, but it's hard to take against a contemporary Hollywood movie which forefronts a cowardly, cynical, philandering president. GA

Absolution (aka Murder by Confession)

(Anthony Page, 1978, GB) Richard Burton, Dominic Guard, Dai Bradley, Andrew Keir, Billy Connolly.
95 min.
A hoary old Gothic thriller from the pen of Anthony Shaffer which should surprise nobody familiar with the plot twists wrought in *Sleuth* and *Deathtrap*. Burton as the humourless teacher-priest in a

Catholic boarding school oozes fleshly torment as his prize pupil (Guard) develops a malicious rebellious streak, indulged in by a cunning manipulation of the inviolable privacy of the confessional. But, as always with Shaffer, things are not what they seem, and the last act revelations about the mystery of the missing pupil (Bradley as a grotesquely pimply cripple) tumble tediously out. RM

Abyss, The

(James Cameron, 1989, US) Ed Harris, Mary Elizabeth Mastrantonio, Michael Biehn, Leo Burmester, Todd Graf, John Bedford Lloyd, JC Quinn, Kimberley Scott.
140 min.
James Cameron's follow-up to *Aliens* abandons deep space for the spacey deep, and hits rock bottom as the submarine genre meets *Close Encounters*. A nuclear sub crashes on the floor of the Atlantic, and the motley crew of an underwater station attached to an oil rig investigate. Inevitably problems mount: a hurricane rages above, a loony marine is on the loose, and cap'n Ed Harris is forced to work with his estranged wife (Mastrantonio), who we're continually told is an utter bitch but who is actually characterised as a perfectly reasonable, efficient engineer. Moreover, there's *something out there* – though from the first glimpse of flashing lights cruising the deep, anyone who knows their Spielberg will guess the presence is benign. After a relatively gripping start, Cameron's *folie de grandeur* rapidly sinks into cliché, absurdity and hyperbole; a collapsing crane contributes one pleasingly extended chain of disasters, but the rest of this overlong concoction is scuppered by dire dialogue, histrionic performances and maudlin sentimentality. GA

Abyss: Special Edition, The

(James Cameron, 1992, US) Ed Harris, Mary Elizabeth Mastrantonio, Michael Biehn.
171 min.
This is no more the 'director's cut' than the original, over which Cameron had full control; it simply incorporates footage deemed gratuitous first time round. The abyss is death, of course, and in particular the spectre of nuclear war. A sub founders on the Atlantic floor. The team of an underwater drilling rig checks out the wreck. Meanwhile, topside, a storm is blowing, and the superpowers rerun the Cuban missile crisis. Sam Goldwyn once prayed for a movie that began with a hurricane and built to a climax. This is it. The first 90 minutes are as good as anything Cameron has done: hi-tech, blue-collar film-making; tense, brittle, on-the-knuckle. The last hour-and-a-bit is increasingly OTT, sentimental and unconvincing. The new footage doesn't change much, but aggravates the problem of the climax, which now resembles *Explorers* played straight. The impression remains of a talented director drowning in the shallows of his deepest thoughts. TCh

Accattone

(Pier Paolo Pasolini, 1961, It) Franco Citti, Franca Pasut, Roberto Scaringella, Adriana Asti.
120 min. b/w
The seamy side of the sub-proletariat of Rome, a world of prostitutes, layabouts and petty thieves in which Franco Citti's Accattone, not quite making the grade as a pimp, finds himself trapped between the alternatives of working for starvation wages, or trying – with the police already on his tail – for easy pickings as a thief. Treating a social milieu Pasolini knew at first hand, his first film as a director was misunderstood by many critics when it was first released as a return to the canons of Italian neo-realism of the '40s and '50s. In fact, its editing style, use of close-ups, dialogue in the Romanesco vernacular – not to mention the Bach score – all betray an originality much more of a piece with Pasolini's later work than with neo-realism. And the character of Accattone himself, self-destructive and conscious of his situation within a class from which he cannot escape, embodies many of the contradictions in Pasolini's lifetime of coming to terms with Marxism and Catholicism. RM

Acceptable Levels

(John Davies, 1983, GB) Andrew Rashleigh, Kay Adshead, Sally McCafferty, Roisina Brown, George Shane.
100 min.

A British TV crew assemble in Belfast to make a documentary, one of a series about children in Britain. Immured within their barricade of script, cameras and determined objectivity, they eye the disorder in which their child-subject lives for possible locations without really *seeing* anything until another child is killed by a rubber bullet. Compromises are made, images junked, ideals sacrificed to professionalism. The contrasts between crew and subject are well pointed, and the ironies, suitably loaded, trip one another domino-like. FD

Accident
(Joseph Losey, 1967, GB) Dirk Bogarde, Stanley Baker, Jacqueline Sassard, Michael York, Vivien Merchant, Delphine Seyrig, Ann Firbank.
105 min.
A stunningly confident, oblique study of six people (three men, two wives, one girl) and the way they tear each other to pieces emotionally amid the droning calm of an Oxford summer as urbanity is ruffled by an accident that begins to send out lazy tendrils of hostility and suspicion (the performances are superb all round). With Losey's camera taking its cue for reticence from Pinter's script, *Accident* is an eminently civilised film, sometimes criticised for distilling a bland classicism out of the baroque provocations that made Losey's work from *The Criminal* to *The Servant* so excitingly unpredictable to watch. But what surprises is the extent to which, in discovering the real pain and the areas of darkness lurking beneath the surface of these donnish lives, Losey in fact reverts to the mood and methods of his early American masterpiece, *The Prowler*. TM

Accidental Hero
(Stephen Frears, 1992, US) Dustin Hoffman, Geena Davis, Andy Garcia, Joan Cusack, Kevin J O'Connor, Maury Chaykin, Stephen Tobolowsky, Tom Arnold.
118 min.
When Bernie (Hoffman), a cynical petty criminal, finds himself reluctantly saving passengers from a crashed plane, little does he realise that his momentarily selfless actions will change lives, including his own. For one thing, a survivor – star TV reporter Gale Gayley (Davis) sets up a search for the anonymous 'angel of flight 204', with the result that John Bubber (Garcia) – a charismatic Vietvet down-and-out – usurps the real hero's place in the hearts of the public. For another, since Bernie's toils delayed a visit to his estranged wife (Cusack) and young son, he's in the doghouse... Intelligently written but clumsily executed, Frears' comedy-drama is frustratingly uneven. Besides a smattering of good gags, David Webb Peoples' script touches on numerous intriguing questions (notably, what constitutes heroism?) while piling irony upon irony. But while Garcia waxes credibly sincere, Hoffman hams, and Davis simply looks lost: small wonder, given Frears' leaden direction, which contrives to scupper suspense *and* comedy through sluggish pacing and misguided camera placement. GA

Accidental Legend (Fei Tian)
(Wang Shaudi, 1996, Tai) René Liu, Niu Chenze, Chang Shih, Miao Tien, Wei Su, Ge Hsiao-Bin.
120 min.
Splendidly anarchic first feature from a well-known TV director/screenwriter, this is a prime mix of adventure, comedy, satire and fantasy shot on spectacular locations in NW China and inspired by the long history of peasant revolts in the late-imperial era. At least three strands of storyline are intertwined, the main one centred on two boy thieves from a village of outcasts who unwittingly bring the wrath of the regional authorities down on their community. It all revolves around the authenticity (or otherwise) of gold, superstitions, good government and redeemer myths; sorting the real from the fake, Wang concludes, is not always as easy as it seems. TR

Accidental Tourist, The
(Lawrence Kasdan, 1988, US). William Hurt, Kathleen Turner, Geena Davis, Amy Wright, David Ogden Stiers, Ed Begley Jr.
121 min.
In this subtly-modulated romantic comedy-drama, Hurt plays a travel writer, separated from

his wife (Turner) after the death of their young son, who returns to the bosom of his home-loving family when he breaks his leg. Enter wacky dog-trainer Davis, whose spontaneity disrupts Hurt's muffled life-style. That Davis has a sickly son complicates things, as does Hurt's publisher's interest in his sister Rose; and when Hurt's repentant wife tries to rekindle their marriage, he must make a choice. The screenplay by Kasdan and Frank Gelati achieves numerous shifts of tone within a compressed emotional range, while the ensemble cast responds equally well to the comic and tragic elements. Hurt excels as the writer, Davis exudes loopy charm, and Turner is brilliant as the anaesthetising wife. Even those who blew hot and cold over the slickness of *Body Heat* and *The Big Chill* should warm to Kasdan's most emotionally complex film to date. NF

Acción Mutante
(Alex de la Iglesia, 1993, Sp) Antonio Resines, Frédérique Feder, Alex Angulo, Juan Viadas, Karra Elejalde.
94 min.
The year is 2012 and a terrorist group, Mutant Action, is hitting back at the beauty industry and the media's focus on physical perfection. 'We don't want to smell good or lose weight!' snarls Ramón (Resines), his deformed face half covered by a leather mask. They infiltrate the society wedding of bread heiress Patricia (Feder), and just when it all looks likes a satire on terrestrial follies, take off for outer space demanding 10 million ecus in ransom for the chick. On the mining planet Axturias, peopled by sex offenders, the plot falls off, along with most of Feder's clothes. Director de la Iglesia likes tacky music, political incorrectness and TV send-ups. He is a Basque, and with some straining this could be read as a comment on his violent compatriots and their relationship with Spain. But more telling is the influence of comics, the love of the individual frame at the expense of overall coherence. SFe

Accompagnatrice, L'
(The Accompanist)
(Claude Miller, 1992, Fr) Richard Bohringer, Elena Safonova, Romane Bohringer, Bernard Verley, Samuel Labarthe.
111 min.
Ever get the feeling that life is passing you by? That's how it is for 20-year-old Sophie (Bohringer) as she reaches womanhood in Occupied Paris. Brought up in tenement-block poverty by her single mother, Sophie is ecstatic when she lands a job as piano accompanist to gifted singer Irène Brice (Safonova), becoming her devoted employee and companion. Taken into the wealthy home she shares with husband Charles (Bohringer *père*), Sophie soon learns that Irène is having an affair, and the young girl enthusiastically enmeshes herself in the household's drama as a way of filling the void at the heart of her own existence. Claude Miller is a master of the lingering close-up and the subtlest nuances of character. This is essentially a film about the inner life, and the cast all deliver highly complex performances. Sophie is revealed in her fragility and passion; there's also the jealousy and bitterness she feels in her role as accompanist to the true players of life. Safonova meanwhile illuminates the absolute joy of being given a celestial voice. JBa

Accompanist, The
see Accompagnatrice, L'

Accumulator 1
(Jan Sverak, 1994, Czech Republic) Petr Forman, Edita Brychta, Zdenek Sverak.
102 min.
Despite its strong designs and evident ambitions, this bizarre blend of sci-fi thriller, romance and comedy is too incoherent – indeed, too obscure – to succeed as anything other than a curiosity. It has something to do with the vampiric, energy-draining powers of TV (or is that of voyeurism in general?); it's probably an allegory about complacency, enthusiasm and commitment – though it's hard to say for sure. GA

Accused, The
(Jonathan Kaplan, 1988, US). Kelly McGillis, Jodie Foster, Bernie Coulson, Leo Rossi, Ann Hearn, Carmen Argenziano, Steve Antin.
111 min.

A young waitress, clothes ripped, bruised, runs screaming from a bar. Sarah Tobias (Foster, excellent) has been gang-raped, and her case is taken on by cool and efficient Deputy DA Kathryn Murphy (McGillis). When Murphy makes a deal with the accused men to reduce the charge to reckless endangerment, Sarah is enraged; and Murphy, beginning to feel the pangs of guilt, decides to prosecute the men who did not take part in the rape but encouraged the others. Surrounded by a storm of controversy – mostly generated by the inclusion of the explicit, some say exploitative, gang-rape scene – the film was written and directed by men, and produced by the Jaffe-Lansing *Fatal Attraction* stable, which hasn't helped its cause. And though it does make a clear stand on vital social and legal questions, one is left feeling distinctly uneasy at the inclusion of the scene. IA

Ace High
see Quattro dell'Ave Maria, I

Ace in the Hole
(aka The Big Carnival)
(Billy Wilder, 1951, US) Kirk Douglas, Jan Sterling, Robert Arthur, Porter Hall, Frank Cady, Richard Benedict, Ray Teal.
112 min. b/w.
Wilder ran into charges of bad taste with this acid tale of reporter Chuck Tatum (Douglas), resentfully stagnating in a New Mexico backwater after being repeatedly fired from jobs in the big time, who sees a chance to manufacture a scoop when a man is trapped by a rockfall. The sheriff, calculating the publicity value to his forthcoming election campaign, agrees to spin out the rescue operation; Tatum builds his story into a nationwide sensation; and as thrill seekers, media hounds, and profiteers turn the site into a gaudy carnival, the victim quietly dies. As a diatribe against all that is worst in human nature, it has moments in pure vitriol ('Kneeling bags my nylons', snaps Sterling as the victim's wife when invited to be photographed praying for her husband's safety), even though the last reel goes rather astray in comeuppance time. TM

Aces High
(Jack Gold, 1976, GB/Fr) Malcolm McDowell, Christopher Plummer, Simon Ward, Peter Firth, John Gielgud, Trevor Howard, Ray Milland.
114 min.
Transposition of RC Sherriff's play *Journey's End* from the trenches into the air. Off the ground the film is entertainingly cinematic (photography by Peter Allwork from Roger Corman's *The Red Baron*): the aerial battles, combining comic strip close-ups with long shots, produce a cumulative intensity that achieves the right degree of awe and horror. But on the ground the script fails to provide much more than a routine account of a young flier's brief active service. The film offers some perspective on the officer/public school product, and deals well with negatives – suppressed emotions, solitariness – but falls apart over such 'positive' clichés as the rural interlude, the brothel visit, and subsequent sexual initiation. Disappointing when you consider writer Howard Barker's stage work and Gold's TV achievements. CPe

Ace Ventura, Pet Detective
(Tom Shadyac, 1993, US) Jim Carrey, Sean Young, Courteny Cox, Tone Loc, Dan Marino, Noble Willingham, Troy Evans.
86 min.
The tale of a bumbling sleuth who specialises in finding other people's lost animals. When the emblem of the Miami Dolphins – one 'Snowflake' – is stolen on the eve of the Superbowl, our man is called in, stays one step ahead of the local police, gets the dolphin and uncovers an unfeasibly wicked plot into the bargain. In the title role is Carrey, known and loved in the States for his manic humour on the comedy show *In Living Color*. Familiarity with the character is, one assumes, why American audiences found this *Naked Gun* rip-off funny. Desperate stuff. NKe

Ace Ventura –
When Nature Calls
(Steve Oedekerk, 1995, US) Jim Carrey, Ian McNeice, Simon Callow, Maynard Eziashi, Bob Gunton, Sophie Okonedo, Tommy Davidson.
93 min.

Topographically speaking, this sequel to Carrey's 1993 hit starts off on a high (when the pet detective fails to save a racoon, he retreats to a Tibetan mountain monastery) but from then on it's all downhill. Ventura is persuaded by a Brit diplomat (McNeice) to make tracks to an obscure African nation, where the Consul (Callow) persuades him to hunt down a stolen Great White Bat, the dowry in an inter-tribal marriage which will stop the Wachati and the Wachootoo fighting each other. Trouble is, Ventura hates bats, and even more bat guano, staple of the Wachatis' economy and cuisine. Crass. GA

Acque di Primavera
see Torrents of Spring

Across 110th Street
(Barry Shear, 1972, US) Anthony Quinn, Yaphet Kotto, Anthony Franciosa, Paul Benjamin, Ed Bernard, Antonio Fargas.
102 min.
Unremittingly violent account of a pair of New York cops (one black, one white) assigned to track down three Harlem robbers-cum-murderers. Familiar crime movie characterisations, but as directed by Shear, who made the highly impressive *Todd Killings*, it's a gutsy affair, given a distinct lift by the Harlem locations; and between the bouts of physical aggression, there are occasional moments of insight into the fraught relationship between Quinn and Kotto. GA

Across the Pacific
(John Huston, 1942, US) Humphrey Bogart, Mary Astor, Sydney Greenstreet, Victor Sen Yung, Charles Halton.
97 min. b/w.
Slow to begin, this accelerates into a fine, *noir*-ish thriller, set on the eve of Pearl Harbour and pitting Bogart against Jap spies plotting to destroy the Panama Canal with aerial torpedoes. Featuring the same irresistible mixture of darkness, double-cross and quirky humour as *The Maltese Falcon*, it again boasts – in addition to some superbly laconic intimations of violence – the inimitable Greenstreet, at his silkiest as a turncoat given to justifying his treachery by discoursing on the arts of judo and the *haiku*. But the real delight is the wisecracking relationship between Bogart and Astor, who put a brilliant switch on their earlier romantic partnership – though still teased by a note of doubt – into the Nick and Nora charades of *The Thin Man*. The absurd, flag-waving finale was added by Vincent Sherman after Huston, mobilised before completing the film, maliciously left Bogart in a tight corner from which only Superman could reasonably hope to escape. TM

Across the Sea of Time: A New York Adventure
(Steven Low, 1997, US) Peter Reznik, John McDonough, Donald Trump.
51 min.
A young Russian immigrant wanders the streets of the Big Apple, retracing the footsteps of his grandfather, guided by letters and photos from eight decades earlier. A terribly dull IMAX venture. Only that old 3D standby the rollercoaster ride gives much sense of vertigo, the rest is perversely static. TCh

Across the Wide Missouri
(William A Wellman, 1951, US) Clark Gable, Ricardo Montalban, John Hodiak, Adolphe Menjou, Maria Elena Marques, J Carrol Naish, Jack Holt.
78 min.
Though subjected to brutal studio cutting which largely wrecked it, an impressive Western set in Colorado in the 1820s and anticipating *Jeremiah Johnson* in its celebration of the rumbustiously idyllic life of the early fur trappers, which ended in bloodshed with the Indians aroused by the coming of greedy civilisation. Shot almost entirely on location, it's worth seeing for the landscapes alone. TM

Action for Slander
(Tim Whelan, 1937, GB) Clive Brook, Ann Todd, Margaretta Scott, Ronald Squire, Arthur Margetson.
83 min. b/w.
Upright stuff with Brook, the quintessential Englishman, being spitefully accused of cheating at cards by the husband of a woman with whom

Brook is infatuated. He may be a bounder but he's not a cad, and he insists (at the cost of his good name and his army career) on proving it in court. Ann Todd (as his wife) does a passable imitation of a volcano about to blow, and Margaretta Scott has a ball as the 'other woman'. It's sincere enough but rather leaden. MA

Action in the North Atlantic
(Lloyd Bacon, 1943, US) Humphrey Bogart, Raymond Massey, Alan Hale, Julie Bishop, Ruth Gordon, Sam Levene, Dane Clark.
127 min. b/w.
Tough, pacy tribute to the American Merchant Marine, with a convoy en route to Russian waters being attacked on all sides by Nazi submarines and aircraft. The rather fine special effects of explosions and fires tend to overshadow characterisation (the crew of the main ship are the usual mix of ethnic stereotypes), while the blatantly propagandist nature of the film means that the enemy are portrayed as vicious, inhuman, smiling sadists. But the performances are strong, and there is considerable curiosity value. The merchant seamen's union was Communist-controlled at the time, and fellow-travelling John Howard Lawson conceived his script in terms of Soviet cinema, with *Battleship Potemkin* as a model (and characteristic montages executed by Don Siegel). GA

Action Jackson
(Craig R Baxley, 1988, US) Carl Weathers, Craig T Nelson, Vanity, Sharon Stone, Thomas F Wilson, Bill Duke.
96 min.
Sometime stunt co-ordinator Baxley directs this feebly-scripted, sporadically-exciting crime pic like a showpiece for his former speciality. He fills the screen with spectacular deaths, metal-crunching car chases, and more explosions than you could shake a stick of dynamite at. In between, Weathers (in his first lead role) gets a walk-on part as Action Jackson, a disgraced cop settling old scores with ruthless businessman Dellaplane (Nelson). A few years back, Dellaplane lost Jackson his stripes, his gun, and his wife, but now Jackson has linked him to some aggressive union-busting professional hitmen. Weathers looks distinctly uncomfortable whenever the action gives way to reams of plot exposition, anti-drugs sermons, and embarrassing romantic interludes, which is often. Fans of state-of-the-art destruction would seem to be the target audience. NF

Act of Vengeance (aka Rape Squad/The Violator)
(Bob Kelljan, 1974, US) Jo Ann Harris, Peter Brown, Jennifer Lee, Lisa Morre, Connie Strickland, Patricia Estrin, Lada Edmund Jr, Steve Kanaly.
90 min.
Not as uninteresting as the title(s) might suggest, this deals with the negative reactions encountered by rape victims, and the tactics resorted to by a group who band themselves together as a 'rape squad', giving help and advice to other victims. Perhaps inevitably, the film becomes crippled by the demands of its exploitation format (the group seeking revenge against a particular rapist). It is further hamstrung by very obvious cuts, which may well serve to mute the male potency fantasy lurking around the edges, but also tend to make the women's revenge tactics seem singularly perfunctory. Nevertheless, the film boasts an interesting script (co-written by Betty Conklin) which puts the women's case more clearly and resonantly than you might expect, and entertains between times by building their sexual taunts somewhat in the style of a Shirelles chorus. VG

Actor's Revenge, An (Yukinojo Henge)
(Kon Ichikawa, 1963, Jap) Kazuo Hasegawa, Fujiko Yamamoto, Ayako Wakao, Ganjiri Nakamura.
113 min.
Yukinojo, a female impersonator in a Kabuki theatre troupe, takes revenge on the three nobles who forced his parents to commit suicide. Maintaining his female role offstage, he pursues his vendetta by playing out a false courtship, and by turning his enemies against each other. A film of phenomenal all-round accomplishment, with daringly stylised visuals. Nothing is more astonishing than the twin performances of Kazuo Hasegawa as both Yukinojo and the thief who befriends him, Yomitaro – especially when you learn that Hasegawa had already played the dual role in Kinugasa's version of the story, made nearly thirty years earlier. TR

Actress (Ruan Ling Yu)
(Stanley Kwan, 1991, HK) Maggie Cheung, Tony Leung, Shin Hong, Carina Lau.
146 min.
This film picks up where Kwan's *Rouge* left off, measuring people of present-day Hong Kong against their forebears of the 1930s and charting both the gains and losses of 'progress'. The forebears in question are the Shanghai film-makers who gave Chinese cinema its golden age; the film centres on the great proto-feminist actress Ruan Lingyu, who was hounded to suicide by gossip tabloids at the age of 25. The present-day participants are Kwan himself and his cast and crew, seen interviewing veterans from the 1930s, looking at clips from Ruan's surviving films, and discussing their own work. Nothing like an orthodox biopic, the result is tender, vivid and almost overwhelmingly moving. TR

Actress, The
(George Cukor, 1953, US) Spencer Tracy, Jean Simmons, Teresa Wright, Anthony Perkins, Mary Wickes.
91 min. b/w.
Based on Ruth Gordon's autobiographical play *Years Ago*, chronicling her youthful experiences as a would-be actress in New England just before World War II (Gordon, with her husband Garson Kanin, wrote many screenplays for Cukor, including this one), *The Actress* is a remarkable domestic comedy. The centre of the film is not so much Jean Simmons' Broadway hopes, but rather the slow growth to understanding of her father (Tracy), who in the course of the film re-lives his own youthful hopes, and for the first time realises the compromises he made for a settled, comfortable life. Beautiful performances. PH

Actresses (Actrius)
(Ventura Pons, 1996, Sp) Núria Espert, Rosa Maria Sardà, Anna Lizaran, Mercè Pons.
88 min.
Three middle-aged actresses, former disciples of a legendary diva, reunite to mull over their loves, lives, differences and similarities. This Catalan feature, from a play by JM Benet i Jornet, is unimaginatively directed and betrays its stage origins at every turn. It also looks as if made for TV. Solid but less than remarkable performances. GA

Acts of Love
see Carried Away

Adalen '31
(Bo Widerberg, 1969, Swe) Peter Schildt, Kerstin Tidelius, Roland Hedlund, Stefan Feierbach.
115 min.
Attempting to blend the sombre themes of *Raven's End* with the (superficial) lyricism of *Elvira Madigan*, Widerberg, in his depiction of a protracted strike at a paper mill in Sweden in 1931, to convey either the political context behind the strike or the developing political consciousness of the strikers. A beautiful, empty film. PH

Adam's Rib
(George Cukor, 1949, US) Katharine Hepburn, Spencer Tracy, Judy Holliday, Tom Ewell, David Wayne, Jean Hagen.
101 min. b/w.
Delightful Cukor comedy in which Hepburn and Tracy are husband-and-wife lawyers engaged in a battle of the sexes as they respectively defend and prosecute a dumb blonde (the inimitable Holliday) accused of shooting her two-timing husband with intent to kill. If Hepburn's feminist arguments are a little on the wild side and too easily bounced off Tracy's paternalistic chauvinism, the script by the Kanins so bristles with wit that it scarcely matters. And in a film in which everybody is acting – a point neatly stressed by the stylised staginess of Cukor's direction – the performances (not least from Wayne and Hagen) are matchless. TM

Addams Family, The

(Barry Sonnenfeld, 1991, US) Anjelica Huston, Raúl Julia, Christopher Lloyd, Dan Hedaya, Elizabeth Wilson, Judith Malina, Carel Struycken, Dana Ivey, Paul Benedict, Christina Ricci, Jimmy Workman.
100 min.
'Unhappy, darling?' Gomez asks his wife. 'Totally' replies Morticia with a blissful smile. This behavioural inversion is the key, indeed the only, gag of the film. But for a one-joke movie, this adaptation of the TV series based on the *New Yorker* cartoons still summons up enough laughs. The chief pleasure is in the casting: Huston was born to play cadaverously glamorous Morticia; Julia buckles a goodly swash as her duelling, devoted husband; and Lloyd is so good as Fester that you feel the film was written as a star vehicle for him. But then Fester alone is allowed any development – is he really an impostor after the family fortune? – and it's hard to care what happens to the rest. Even the film's glorious look is second-hand (you can tell that visual effects supervisor Alan Munro worked on *Beetlejuice*), with the Coen brothers' cinematographer Barry Sonnenfeld setting a cracking pace in his directorial debut, but suggesting that Tim Burton might have given the film the edge it lacks. Ooky the Addamses may be, subversive they ain't; it plays like a paean to the nuclear family. DW

Addams Family Values

(Barry Sonnenfeld, 1993, US) Anjelica Huston, Raul Julia, Christopher Lloyd, Joan Cusack, Carol Kane, Christina Ricci, Jimmy Workman.
94 min.
Gomez and Morticia (Julia and Huston) have a baby, Pubert. As sequels go, this is passable: no more coherent than the episodic first instalment, but with enough sick humour to satisfy the mildly depraved. Wednesday (Ricci) and Pugsley (Workman) use a guillotine in a playfully attempt to lop off the new branch of the family tree. Pubert survives. But Uncle Fester (Lloyd) looks like falling into the clutches of the new nanny, Debbie Jellinsky (Cusack), an ample-bosomed black widow with an eye on the family fortune. NF

Addicted to Love

(Griffin Dunne, 1997, US) Matthew Broderick, Meg Ryan, Kelly Preston, Tcheky Karyo, Maureen Stapleton, Nesbitt Blaisdell, Richard Dreyfuss.
100 min.
A romantic comedy without the romance. Small town astrologer Broderick is dumped by girlfriend Preston. He follows her to New York, takes the apartment opposite (she's already moved in with French chef Karyo), and fixes up a sophisticated camera obscura so he can watch them on his sitting room wall. Enter punky black-leather biker Ryan as the chef's spurned squeeze. She's got it worse than Matthew. Together, they mike up the lovers for the full audio-visual experience, then plot revenge. These obsessives would seem to offer scope for dark, edgy humour – until, that is, you cast such overweeningly cute stars as Broderick and Ryan. Meg should give up the hardboiled masquerade and go back to being the lovable ditz she really is. The set-up's way too slow, but first-time director Dunne contrives a couple of maliciously farcical revenge sequences. TCh

Addiction, The

(Abel Ferrara, 1994, US) Lili Taylor, Christopher Walken, Annabella Sciorra, Edie Falco, Paul Calderon, Fredro Starr, Robert Castle.
82 min. b/w.
Chronologically, this precedes *The Funeral* by about a year. Both were scripted by Nicolas St John after the death of his son. Both were shot quickly, on limited budgets, by much the same crew, and feature Walken and Sciorra, and a Catholic priest, Father Robert Castle. Finally, both are philosophical/religious ruminations, in genre form, on the nature of sin and redemption. *The Funeral*, though, is the far more accessible, even conventional drama. By contrast, this is one wild, weird, wired movie, the kind that really shouldn't be seen before midnight. Taylor is commanding as New York philosophy student Kathleen Conklin. Dragged into a back alley, she's vamped by Sciorra's voluptuous Casanova. Soon she starts obsessing on images of My Lai and the Holocaust, name-dropping Nietzsche, Sartre and Heidegger, and taking a syringe to a vagrant's artery for a late-night snack. Shot in b/w, with an effectively murky jungle/funk/rap score, this is the vampire movie we've been waiting for: a reactionary urban-horror flick that truly has the ailing pulse of the time. AIDS and drug addiction are points of reference, but they're symptoms, not the cause. Ferrara's chiaroscuro imagery is as striking as anything in Coppola's *Dracula*, while the voice-over narration often recalls *Apocalypse Now*. Scary, funny, magnificently risible, this could be the most pretentious B-movie ever – and I mean that as a compliment. TCh

Addition, L' (The Patsy)

(Denis Amar, 1984, Fr) Richard Berry, Richard Bohringer, Victoria Abril, Farid Chopel.
87 min.
Berry is an actor whose short stay in jail goes wrong when he is innocently involved in a breakout. One of the guards (Bohringer) gets his knee shot off, and vengefully hounds Berry through a further prison sentence, playing sado-masochistic cat-and-mouse games spiced with a little homophobia. The psychological thriller in which the victim needs the torturer as much as vice versa is familiar territory, but any game which can only reach a sudden death resolution is always good value. Unfortunately, what the film would propose as a happy ending for the hero is in fact the point when his troubles are just beginning. CPea

Address Unknown

(William Cameron Menzies, 1944, US) Paul Lukas, Morris Carnovsky, KT Stevens, Peter Van Eyck, Carl Esmond, Mady Christians.
72 min. b/w.
Based on a novella by Kressman Taylor which sensationally exposed the Nazi threat back in 1938, this gets somewhat tangled in a Jacobean revenge plot about two old friends in San Francisco whose children plan to marry. One (Lukas) returns to Germany with the other's daughter, and, falling under the spell of Nazism, fails to intervene when she is persecuted as a Jew. Lukas' portrayal of a man haunted by guilt, and cracking when a series of anonymous letters bring him under suspicion himself, almost edges the film into *noir* territory. It's often heavy-handed, but fascinating for the way Menzies (abetted by Rudolph Maté's lighting and expressionist touches) designs the film as though he had *Things to Come* in mind. Hollywood almost invariably dwarfed its soulless Nazis within vast chambers dominated by monstrous portraits of *Der Führer*, but the syndrome never ran riot quite so headily as here. TM

Adieu Bonaparte (Al-wedaa ya Bonaparte)

(Youssef Chahine, 1984, Egypt/Fr) Michel Piccoli, Mohsen Mohiedine, Mohsena Tewfik, Patrice Chéreau.
120 min.
Chahine's account of Napoleon's Egyptian campaign of 1798 is idiosyncratic, sprawling, wicked. It offers an oblique comment on Egypt's place in the world today, but typically chooses to focus on affairs of the heart, seeing international relations in terms of emotional exploitation and sexual attraction. Louis Caffarelli (Piccoli), a one-legged homosexual, arrives with Bonaparte's scientific expedition and falls in love with two Arab brothers, one for his body, the other for his mind. The film's strong gay interest is clinched by Chéreau's brilliant performance as Napoleon. Chahine is too wise to blame anyone for what happened in Egypt: he reaches for new notions of cooperation. TR

Adjuster, The

(Atom Egoyan, 1991, Can) Elias Koteas, Arsinée Khanjian, Maury Chaykin, Gabrielle Rose, Jennifer Dale, David Hemblen, Rose Sarkisyan.
102 min.
An insurance adjuster (Koteas) arrives at the scene of a fire and takes the burned-out owner-occupier in hand. 'You may not feel it,' he tells her, 'but you're in a state of shock'. Egoyan's characters are always at a remove from the world, emotionally numb, psychically dislocated. He's fascinated by parallax and discrepancy, the gap between image and reality. Noah – the adjuster – tries to help his clients reproduce their material effects so that the clients can be exactly as they were before. Scrupulously poring over photographs for clues, he places a value on everything; and part of the special relationship he establishes with his clients is having sex with them... *The Adjuster* might almost be the third instalment in a trilogy which began with *Family Viewing* and *Speaking Parts*. It's his richest, most expansive film to date, an engrossing, deadpan tragicomedy, evocatively shot in CinemaScope, with surprisingly affecting performances from Koteas and Chaykin in particular. TCh

Admirable Crichton, The

(Lewis Gilbert, 1957, GB) Kenneth More, Diane Cilento, Cecil Parker, Sally Ann Howes, Martita Hunt, Jack Watling, Peter Graves.
93 min.
JM Barrie's comic war-horse trotted out again for More's resourceful butler to teach his shipwrecked betters the ropes of surviving with grace. It actually worked better as a musical in the 1934 Hollywood version, *We're Not Dressing*, with Bing Crosby, Carole Lombard, and Burns and Allen. PT

Adolf Hitler – My Part in His Downfall

(Norman Cohen, 1972, GB) Jim Dale, Arthur Lowe, Bill Maynard, Tony Selby, Windsor Davies, Spike Milligan.
102 min.
A clever scripting job by Johnny Byrne, some enjoyable acting, and a very real evocation of what it must have been like for an ordinary bunch of young men suddenly to be required to turn into soldiers, make this adaptation of Spike Milligan's novel a much better prospect than it might seem. The story is based on embroidered fact and takes Spike from the time he received his World War II call-up papers to the moment of embarking to tackle the Hun. In many ways the film looks like a classy *Carry On*, a feeling strengthened by the casting of Dale as Milligan (with Milligan playing his own father), though overlaid by the zaniness and compassion of Milligan's humour. The comedy is occasionally given bite by credible moments of sudden tragedy. JC

Adoption (Örökbefogadás)

(Márta Mészáros, 1975, Hun) Kati Berek, Laszlo Szabo, Gyongyver Vigh.
89 min. b/w.
Unmomentous portrait of a woman in middle-age, whose unsatisfactory romance with a married man and involvement with a delinquent girl from a nearby remand home lead her to consider adopting a child. It's a welcome change to find such a character as the subject of a movie, especially when she's as well played as she is by Kati Berek. But the direction stays locked in the hoariest 'social realist' tradition and constantly verges on cliché. TR

A Double Tour (Leda/Web of Passion)

(Claude Chabrol, 1959, Fr/It) Madeleine Robinson, Jacques Dacqmine, Jean-Paul Belmondo, Bernadette Lafont, Antonella Lualdi, André Jocelyn, Jeanne Valérie, Mario David, Laszlo Szabo.
110 min (release version: 87 min).
Chabrol's third film, greeted at the time as a Hitchcock pastiche, now looks like pure Chabrol: his first demolition job on the bourgeois family as internal tensions – father (Dacqmine) is indulging a clandestine affair, mother (Robinson) worries what the neighbours will think, daughter (Valérie) struggles with her inhibitions, and son (Jocelyn) quietly strangles on his mother's apron-strings – finally succumb to spontaneous combustion. Belmondo is fun as the uncouth, outrageously *déclassé* interloper who serves as a catalyst, goading both father and daughter into an open acknowledgment of their sexual needs, but he seems to have come from another, more overt movie, at odds with the subtly detailed (and beautifully acted) portrait of social repressions and malaises. Seen in the light of Chabrol's later work, the film has gained considerably in stature. Best of several stunning scenes is the climactic murder of the mistress (Lualdi), a fragile china doll

who comes gift-wrapped in a Japanese-style house. Glacial, almost serene in its inevitability, this chilling sequence reveals the first glimpses of the Fritz Lang influence later to flower in Chabrol's work. TM

Adrenalin – Fear the Rush
(Albert Pyun, 1995, US) Natasha Henstridge, Christophe Lambert, Norbert Weisser, Elizabeth Barondes, Craig Davis.
76 min.
This effluent from the bowels of Hollywood is right down there with Lambert's worst. It's set in a post-apocalyptic urban Wild West landscape, a quarantine camp for immigrants to the US where Henstridge's police officer joins a SWAT-team operation to clear a killer from the estate. Shown only in extra close-up, the killer has bloodshot eyes, bloody fangs, braces, jeans and bovver boots. He also has a large knife, some virulent disease, a taste for coppers' flesh and a facility for taking out whole teams of armed police. Cheap *Alien* out-takes with a dumb underground Hannibal Lecter. NB

Adrift (Hrst Plná Vody)
(Ján Kadár, 1969, Czech/US) Rade Markovic, Milena Dravic, Paula Pritchett, Josef Kroner.
108 min.
About a fisherman's obsession for a girl he has rescued from the river. The story is not developed analytically enough to justify the extremely arty pretensions of the film's form, and the music often seems to be trying to turn it into a comedy. VG

Adult Fun
(James Scott, 1972, GB) Peter Marinker, Deborah Norton, Judy Liebert, Roger Booth.
102 min.
The influenza of Italian and French assaults on narrative film-making (during the '50s and '60s) eventually spread to Britain (in the '70s); and one of the more interesting cases is this rather opaque film. It looks very Godard-like in its combination and parody of genres (potboiler fiction, documentary, pseudo-documentary) and in its action-packed plot which pivots on underworld crime as a young stockbroker suffering from feelings of alienation becomes nightmarishly involved, Graham Greene style, in industrial espionage. Scott got one step ahead of Godard, however, in the complex mixing of the soundtrack so that words do not merely accompany the image, but must be problematically deciphered against it. DD

Advance to the Rear
(George Marshall, 1964, US) Glenn Ford, Stella Stevens, Melvyn Douglas, Jim Backus, Joan Blondell, Andrew Prine.
97 min. b/w.
Yes, it does sound like some sub-*Carry On* lark, but the title actually masks a rather jolly comedy Western. Col Douglas and Capt Ford are members of a Union cavalry troop so inept that Gen Backus has sent them West by riverboat rather than risk losing the Civil War. Their new mission sees them more interested in professional lady Stevens, but the accident-prone twosome still manage to cover themselves in glory in this romp with a decided anti-military tone. It's not exactly *M*A*S*H* out West, but fun none the less. TJ

Adventure for Two
see Demi-Paradise, The

Adventure in Baltimore
(aka Bachelor Bait)
(Richard Wallace, 1949, US) Shirley Temple, John Agar, Robert Young, Albert Sharpe, Josephine Hutchinson.
89 min. b/w.
Despite hopefully provocative re-titling for British release, a very tepid comedy set in 1905. Temple plays a young woman upsetting family and social conventions when she turns to painting 'scandalous' portraits and becomes a suffragette (finally settling, of course, for domestic bliss). GA

Adventure of Sherlock Holmes' Smarter Brother, The
(Gene Wilder, 1975, US) Gene Wilder, Madeline Kahn, Marty Feldman, Dom DeLuise, Leo McKern, Roy Kinnear, John Le Mesurier, Douglas Wilmer, Thorley Walters.
91 min.

'Sheer luck,' Sigerson Holmes derisively tags his more famous older brother. Sherlock nevertheless delegates a blackmail case involving a soubrette (Kahn) to young Sigi (Wilder),while he himself concentrates on the more pressing investigation of the theft of state documents from the Foreign Secretary. The cases become entangled, however, when it transpires that the soubrette's father is the Foreign Secretary (Le Mesurier) and that her fiancé, the opera singer Gambetti (DeLuise), wants to obtain papers in papa's safe. Writer/director Wilder spins a very tangled tale, and production designer Terry Marsh has gone to town on the excessively cluttered 1890s sets, but there's a magnificent on-stage climax, when, during a production of *The Masked Ball*, documents are due to change hands and the drugged chorus progressively collapses. Hit and miss, with plums picked from all chapters of the comic handbook, and plenty of innocent lavatory humour. Kahn and DeLuise shine among the strong ensemble. JPy

Adventurers, The
(Lewis Gilbert, 1970, US) Bekim Fehmiu, Alan Badel, Candice Bergen, Ernest Borgnine, Leigh Taylor-Young, Fernando Rey, Charles Aznavour, Olivia de Havilland.
171 min.
Revolutionary politics in a fictitious South American state seen through the eyes of Harold Robbins. Or in other words, the usual mixture of sex, fast cars and drugs with a few 'Eh gringos' and 'Viva la Revoluciones' thrown in for good measure. A really bad movie made even worse by the appearance of 'actor extraordinaire' Rossano Brazzi in a cameo role. PH

Adventures in Babysitting
(aka A Night on the Town)
(Chris Columbus, 1987, US) Elisabeth Shue, Maia Brewton, Keith Coogan, Anthony Rapp, Calvin Levels, Vincent Philip D'Onofrio, Penelope Ann Miller.
102 min.
While babysitting the neighbours' brats, 17-year-old Chris (Shue) gets an SOS call from her chubby chum Brenda (Miller), who has run away from home and is stranded at a downtown bus depot. Bundling her charges into the family Chevy, Chris sets off on a rescue mission, and ends up running the gauntlet of big city perils in a belaboured spinning-out of a weak storyline. The central issue is how the babysitters will explain away to doting parents the death, disfigurement or molestation of randy adolescents Brad and Daryl and nine-year-old Sara (a goofball of cute), should the batty lorry driver, gangsters or prostitutes they encounter have their evil way. If this family fodder is functional, it's due largely to its production design and cinematography, which endow the city of Chicago with an effectively menacing aspect. EP

Adventures of a Brown Man in Search of Civilization
(James Ivory, 1971, GB) Nirad C Chaudhuri, Richard Macrory.
54 min.
Born in a village in East Bengal in 1897, the scholar Nirad Chaudhuri has been a lifelong enemy of received wisdom, especially Indian received wisdom. In the early '70s, he was in England researching a book on the German-born British Sanskrit scholar Max Müller. James Ivory took time out, shortly after finishing his fourth Indian feature film, *Bombay Talkie*, to observe Chaudhuri in Oxford and London dressing up in a velvet party coat with lace cuffs, commanding a dinner party, dominating a seminar, and laying down the law on every subject under the sun. The servants of the British Raj, to whose memory this diminutive gadfly dedicated his best-known book, *Autobiography of an Unknown Indian*, once behaved with a similar sort of unabashed self-assurance. JPy

Adventures of a Gnome Named Gnorm
see Gnome Named Gnorm, A

Adventures of a Private Eye
(Stanley Long, 1977, GB) Christopher Neil, Suzy Kendall, Harry H Corbett, Fred Emney, Liz Fraser, Irene Handl.
96 min.
Surprising, really, that this rock-bottom British 'sex' comedy wasn't called *Adventures of a*

Private Dick – that's about the level of the humour. A plot that isn't even worth mentioning, much playing to camera, plodding scenes and dreary gags make the whole thing instantly forgettable. Stanley Long's mercifully brief series, following in the naughty farce wake of the *Carry On* films, began and ended equally limply with *Adventures of a Taxi Driver* (1975) and *Adventures of a Plumber's Mate* (1978). CPe

Adventures of Baron Munchausen, The
(Terry Gilliam, 1988, GB/WGer). John Neville, Sarah Polley, Eric Idle, Charles McKeown, Winston Dennis, Jack Purvis, Valentina Cortese, Oliver Reed, Jonathan Pryce, Bill Paterson, Robin Williams, Sting.
126 min.
The tall tales of the legendary 18th century Baron Munchausen would seem perfect subject matter for Gilliam's fertile imagination; indeed, despite production problems, the film is an engaging and dottily fantastic spectacular. The Baron (Neville) and his superhuman colleagues are rather colourless creations, but the characters they encounter during their odyssey – mafioso-like King of the Moon (Williams), love-lorn Vulcan (Reed) – are vivid and funny. Still more bizarre is the look of the film: an island transformed into a monstrous fish, a balloon sewn from underwear sailing over a war-torn city, a ship rippling through a desert strewn with statuary. But this third part of Gilliam's trilogy, about 'the triumph of imagination over rationality' and lighter in tone than *Brazil*, hardly warrants serious analysis. More of its budget should have been spent on the script – there are jarring leaps in the narrative – but it's good, intelligent fun, and occasionally truly surprising. GA

Adventures of Baron Munchhausen, The (Münchhausen)
(Josef von Baky, 1943, Ger) Hans Albers, Brigitte Horney, Wilhelm Bendow, Michael Bohnen, Kathe Haack.
103 min.
A spectacular film fantasy, based on the legendary exploits of the fictional Baron Münchhausen, this escapist extravaganza (which was commissioned by Nazi propaganda minister Joseph Goebbels) is simply an excuse for a series of surreal episodes: the Baron's adventures take him from the opulent court of Catherine the Great, via a Turkish sultan's harem and Venice's Grand Canal, to the surreal landscape of the moon. NF

Adventures of Barry McKenzie, The
(Bruce Beresford, 1972, Aust) Barry Crocker, Barry Humphries, Peter Cook, Spike Milligan, Dick Bentley, Dennis Price.
114 min.
Unappealing spinoff from the *Private Eye* comic strip, chronicling the adventures, with and without his Aunt Edna, of a loud-mouthed, sex-crazed innocent from Oz newly arrived in Earl's Court. The odd amusing incident, but mostly spoiled by sheer repetitiveness and the unmodulated top-of-the voice vulgarity sought at all costs. VG

Adventures of Buckaroo Banzai Across the 8th Dimension, The
(WD Richter, 1984, US) Peter Weller, Ellen Barkin, John Lithgow, Jeff Goldblum, Christopher Lloyd.
102 min.
Banzai – comic-book superhero, neurosurgeon, pop star, mystic, nuclear physicist and teenage heartthrob – is testing a new jet-propelled Ford Fiesta when he crashes into one side of a mountain to exit miraculously unharmed from the other. Evil Black Lectoids from Planet 10 have been exiled within the rock, and Buck accidentally releases a few, leaving him the only one who can save the Earth from destruction. His allies include a New Jersey cowboy-brain-surgeon (Goldblum) and a six-foot extra-terrestrial rasta; their chief enemy, evil Dr Lizardo (Lithgow). Richter's comic genre hybrid comes complete with its own mythology, and team of established superheroes, and is curiously appealing. SGo.

Adventures of Captain Marvel, The (aka The Return of Captain Marvel)

(William Witney/John English, 1941, US) Tom Tyler, Frank Coghlan Jr, Harry Worth, Louise Currie, William Benedict.
12 episode serial. b/w.
Captain Marvel was one of the greatest of comic strip characters until DC publications, creators of Superman, sued his publishers for plagarism and wiped him off the news-stands in the '50s. He was revived later by DC themselves, but when this vintage serial was put together he was at the height of his fame and glory. Young Billy Batson, who changes into superhero Captain Marvel on uttering the magic 'Shazam', here ventures to Siam to ensure that the secrets of the Scorpion Dynasty, violated from the tomb, are not put to wicked use (naturally by a master-mind intent on world domination). Fun. DP

Adventures of Don Juan (aka The New Adventures of Don Juan)

(Vincent Sherman, 1948, US) Errol Flynn, Viveca Lindfors, Robert Douglas, Alan Hale, Ann Rutherford, Raymond Burr.
110 min.
Flynn's last swashbuckler, and – surprisingly – not half bad, even though the climactic duel with Robert Douglas had to be completed with doubles for both actors. A lavish, elegant tale of the fencing-master who trades on the queen's susceptibility to prevent Spain from raising a second Armada, it has gorgeous colour camerawork (Elwood Bredell) and a nice line in mocking wit. TM

Adventures of Ford Fairlane, The

(Renny Harlin, 1990, US) Andrew Dice Clay, Wayne Newton, Priscilla Presley, Morris Day, Lauren Holly, Maddie Corman, Gilbert Gottfried, Vince Neil.
106 min.
A poorly streamlined vehicle for America's prime exponent of the Comedy of Hate, Andrew Dice Clay, this expensively empty action comedy is as much fun as a car crash. Shortly after Heavy Metal superstar Bobby Black (Vince Neil of Motley Crue) gets fried alive on stage, 'rock'n'roll detective' Ford Fairlane (Clay) is hired by rich bitch Colleen (Presley) to find bubble-headed groupie Zuzu Petals (Corman). When 'shock jock' Johnny Crunch (Gottfried) also gets his plug pulled, Ford starts looking for someone with lots of juice. That's it on the plot level, so the rest is padded out with Ford playing rock'n'roll (badly), driving flash cars, cracking wise, talking dirty to women, or standing around like a spare dick at a wedding while Die Hard 2 director Harlin smashes up cars, blows up buildings, and mistimes every comic scene. Worse still is the Diceman's cynical attempt to soften his bad boy image; he still comes over as a racist, homophobic, sexist asshole who mistakes sentimentality for true feeling. NF

Adventures of Frontier Fremont, The (aka Spirit of the Wild)

(Richard Friedenberg, 1976, US) Dan Haggerty, Denver Pyle, Tony Miratti, Norman Goodman, Teri Hernandez.
96 min.
Mountain-man Jacob Fremont (a wimpy Jeremiah Johnson for juniors) attempts to find harmony in nature, sporting a bushy beard, conversing endlessly ('Best thing Ah ever dun was ter lose mah gun') with the local Indians, and clearing evil crit-tur-killin' trappers off his mountain. Predatory adult animals he scares off merely with his shout (or is it Haggerty's acting?). This idealised, ecologically-sound, pastoral adventure seems to please young kids; but you grown-ups'd be plumb crazy to mosey along to see it. GA

Adventures of Gerard, The

(Jerzy Skolimowski, 1970, GB/It/Switz) Peter McEnery, Claudia Cardinale, Eli Wallach, Jack Hawkins, Mark Burns, John Neville.
91 min.
A film from Skolimowski's period of exile into the clutches of international co-production. Like his eminently Nabokovian King, Queen, Knave,

it suffers from the semi-dubbing of an 'English version', with voices and bodies sometimes coming apart. But excused by commerce from the need to be serious, Skolimowski gives free rein to his fantasy in a careering period charade which makes amiable mockery of military glory. McEnery is perfect as Conan Doyle's dashing French hussar, prancing through Napoleon's Peninsular campaign with one hand on hip and the other courting disasters averted only by his sublime insouciance. Not all the gags work, but enough do to make this something of a welcome – and exquisitely photographed – treat. TM

Adventures of Goopy and Bagha, The (Goopy Gyne Bagha Byne)

(Satyajit Ray, 1968, Ind) Tapen Chatterjee, Robi Ghose, Santosh Dutt, Durgadas Bannerjee.
132 min. b/w & col.
Ray's 'fairytale for adults', based on a story by his own grandfather about the travels of two outcast musicians who are granted three wishes by the King of the Ghosts, has many attractions. There's much bizarre wit, some delightful songs, and (especially in the pantomime-style transformation scenes and magical manifestations) a sense of wide-eyed wonder so important to this kind of fantasy. But as its picaresque structure stretches further and further into the two-hours-plus running time (it was cut by 14 minutes for British release), even the favourably disposed may get the fidgets. GB

Adventures of Hambone and Hillie, The

see Hambone and Hillie

Adventures of Huck Finn, The

(Stephen Sommers, 1993, US) Elijah Wood, Courtney B Vance, Robbie Coltrane, Jason Robards, Ron Perlman, Dana Ivey, James Gammon.
108 min.
This Disney movie has Huck as cheeky but resourceful artful dodger – which softens the hard times and produces an efficient but unexceptional adventure side-stepping the moral dimension and pathos of Twain's original story. The film has a Gothic beginning, but that's perhaps chiefly a nod to modern horror, and is soon dropped as Huck (Wood) takes to the raft with the runaway Jim (Vance) for his unsentimental education on the Mississippi. The Grangerford/Shepherdson feud is glossed over, and it's only with the arrival of Robards' 'King' and Coltrane's 'Duke' that things begin to liven up. WH

Adventures of Huckleberry Finn, The

(Michael Curtiz, 1960, US) Tony Randall, Eddie Hodges, Archie Moore, Patty McCormack, Neville Brand, Buster Keaton.
107 min.
Fourth screen version of the Twain classic, made by a very tired and under-inspired Curtiz, but featuring light-heavyweight boxing champ Moore as Jim, and the great Keaton as a lion-tamer among the veteran supporting cast (which includes Andy Devine, John Carradine, Sterling Holloway, Finlay Currie, Judy Canova and Royal Dano). PT

Adventures of Huckleberry Finn, The

see Huckleberry Finn

Adventures of Mark Twain, The

(Irving Rapper, 1944, US) Fredric March, Alexis Smith, Donald Crisp, Alan Hale, C Aubrey Smith, John Carradine.
130 min. b/w.
Some soggy moments, but on the whole one of the best of the Warner biopics: solidly stylish, well acted, and with some superb camerawork from Sol Polito (especially in the riverboat sequences). It's romanticised, of course, but reasonably accurate since Twain's career (as printer, river pilot, prospector, newspaper editor, bankrupt and international lecture tourist, among other things) was colourful enough to satisfy even Hollywood. Better when it's lighthearted (the delightful jumping-frog sequence) than when it's solemn (Twain's encounter with the assembled lions of American literature). TM

Adventures of Mark Twain, The

(Will Vinton, 1985, US) voices: James Whitmore, Michele Mariana, Gary King, Chris Ritchie.
90 min.
Kids will probably adore the colourful clay figures and spectacular action sequences in this technically remarkable animated feature, but its relentless imagination will be best appreciated by adults. Born in 1835 (year of a visit by Halley's Comet), Twain prepares for death and reunion with his late wife by steering a bizarre balloon to meet the comet on its next appearance. En route, stowaways Huck Finn, Tom Sawyer and Becky Thatcher listen to the writer's fantastic fables as Vinton's sophisticated claymation puts characters and locations through strange metamorphoses to sometimes alarming, always amusing effect. Behind the laughs and lovely visuals, however, lies an astute acknowledgment of the author's embittered duality: the kindly Southern patrician is shadowed by a darker double, and for once the Twain shall meet – at the moment of death. In paying tribute to a man of originality, compassion and intelligence, Vinton has adopted those very qualities himself. GA

Adventures of Michael Strogoff, The (aka The Soldier and the Lady/ Michael Strogoff)

(George Nicholls Jr, 1937, US) Anton Walbrook, Elizabeth Allan, Akim Tamiroff, Margot Grahame.
85 min. b/w.
RKO's cannibalisation of the exteriors from a 1936 German adaptation of Jules Verne's historical romp, directed by Richard Eichberg (Der Kurier des Zaren) and simultaneously filmed in French. Appearing in all three versions, Walbrook is suitably dashing as the envoy galloping across the Steppes to prevent a Tartar uprising, getting blinded (well, not really), falling in love and fighting a duel to the death with the evil Tamiroff. Quite fun, though saddled with silly dialogue of the 'I must get to Omsk' variety. TM

Adventures of Milo and Otis, The (Koneko Monogatari)

(Masanori Hata, 1986, Jap)
76 min.
This film's international appeal (big success in the United States) was probably boosted by the fact that neither Milo nor Otis speak during the course of the picture (no subtitles or dubbing problems here). Milo, you see, is a cat, Otis a dog. After playing havoc with the other farm animals, the pesky pair go down to the river, where Milo is whisked away in a box. Stout-hearted Otis follows down the bank, but cannot keep up with the current. All kinds of fraught encounters ensue before the pals are reunited – and I drifted off myself. A live-action feature, it scores high on the cute-ometer, what with narrator Dudley Moore working himself into a frolicsome frenzy, a singalong signature tune, and more animals than you'll find at Whipsnade. The Japanese original ran for 90 minutes. TCh

Adventures of PC 49, The

(Godfrey Grayson, 1949, GB) Hugh Latimer, Patricia Cutts, John Penrose, Pat Nye, Annette Simmonds.
67 min. b/w.
Rousing little low-budget movie, a lighthearted look at the perils a London bobby faces when he witnesses a truck robbery and comes up against the dreaded Rossini gang of Manchester. Truly British stuff, based on a radio series, complete with colourful criminal slang and seamy, if hardly menacing, low-life. GA

Adventures of Pinocchio, The

(Steve Barron, 1996, GB/Fr/Ger/Czech Republic/US) Martin Landau, Jonathan Taylor Thomas, Bebe Neuwirth, Rob Schneider, Udo Kier, Geneviève Bujold, Dawn French, Griff Rhys Jones, John Sessions.
94 min.
Landau, as the lonely puppeteer Gepetto, tries his best to bring some heart to this live action version of the rich dark fantasy, and though the effects (digital technology and Jim Henson's Creature Shop) don't always seamlessly integrate Pinocchio with his surroundings, the decorative period detail still gives a strong flavour of Carlo Collodi's imag-

ination. The film starts well with jaunty knockabout fun as the animated Pinocchio runs rings round teacher Sessions and baker's missus Dawn French, but then comes the point where it looks as though someone got cold feet. Just when you think you're about to get a solidly traditional rendering, bets are hedged by wheeling on a computer-generated cricket sounding like a sixth-rate Woody Allen, ginger-coiffed comic baddie Schneider, and a dreadfully out-of-place MOR rock ballad from Brian May. Enjoyably extravagant wickedness from Kier's rival marionette-master and tempter of naughty little boys. TJ

Adventures of Priscilla Queen of the Desert, The

(Stephan Elliott, 1994, Aust) Terence Stamp, Hugo Weaving, Guy Pearce, Bill Hunter, Sarah Chadwick, Mark Holmes, Julia Cortez.
103 min.
This brash, liberating and poignant road movie follows three drag queens as they travel in a silver bus – 'Priscilla' – from Sydney to a gig in Alice Springs. 'Les Girls' are Bernadette, an ageing transsexual (Stamp), sharp-tongued Felicia (Pearce) and sensitive-flower Mitzi (Weaver), and this celebration of camp takes them where no lip-synching queens have ever been before. Unlike the bus, the film never gets bogged down, driven forward inexorably by naff disco tunes and crackling dialogue. Most impressive is the Fellini-esque panache writer/director Elliott brings to the visuals, isolating the extravagantly dressed figures in astonishing, orange-tinted landscapes and staging the production numbers like a frustrated director of musicals. Excellent, anchoring performances. Hard not to be swept along. NF

Adventures of Quentin Durward, The (aka Quentin Durward)

(Richard Thorpe, 1955, GB) Robert Taylor, Kay Kendall, Robert Morley, Alec Clunes, Marius Goring, George Cole, Ernest Thesiger, Wilfrid Hyde-White.
101 min.
If you want to be picky, Taylor is too mature to be playing Walter Scott's dashing young gallant, sent from Scotland to press his aged uncle's suit for the hand of the Duke of Burgundy's pretty ward, and winning her himself after her recalcitrance to an arranged marriage occasions much politicking. Otherwise an enjoyable costume romance, colourfully done with a dash of humour, some nice Gothic touches, and the châteaux de la Loire looking really splendid as a setting. The predominantly English cast, with Clunes outstanding as the Duke of Burgundy, make the most of what is often Scott's dialogue, and the climactic duel in a blazing belltower (with the contestants doing Tarzan acts on the ropes) is terrific. TM

Adventures of Robin Hood, The

(Michael Curtiz/William Keighley, 1938, US) Errol Flynn, Olivia de Havilland, Basil Rathbone, Claude Rains, Eugene Pallette, Alan Hale.
105 min.
One of the few great adventure movies that you can pretend you are treating the kids to when you are really treating yourself: the kind of Hollywood film to which *Star Wars* pays tribute, and one of the best examples of what large studio resources could produce. Glorious colour, sumptuous sets, and a brilliantly choreographed climactic sword fight between Flynn and Rathbone: the stuff of which Saturday matinee dreams were made. SM

Adventures of Robinson Crusoe

see Robinson Crusoe

Adventures of Sadie, The

see Our Girl Friday

Adventures of Sherlock Holmes, The

(Alfred Werker, 1939, US) Basil Rathbone, Nigel Bruce, Ida Lupino, George Zucco, Alan Marshal, Henry Stephenson.
85 min. b/w.

Second in the Rathbone/Bruce series, after which it shifted from Fox to Universal, modern dress, and wartime uplift. The deer-stalkered one is here up against arch-enemy Moriarty, who has fiendish plans to commit that most heinous of all crimes: the theft of the Crown Jewels. Lightly likeable and beautifully mounted, the film succeeds thanks to some witty dialogue (Holmes to Moriarty: 'You've a magnificent brain. I'd like to present it pickled in alcohol to the London Medical Society'), and to nicely nuanced performances from Rathbone, Bruce and (as Moriarty) Zucco. GA

Adventures of Tom Sawyer, The

(Norman Taurog, 1938, US) Tommy Kelly, Jackie Moran, Ann Gillis, May Robson, Walter Brennan, Victor Jory.
91 min.
Extraordinarily handsome to look at, with exquisite Technicolor camerawork by Wong Howe and some imaginative designs (especially the cave sequence) by William Cameron Menzies. Has its longueurs, but it does capture the sense of a lazy Mississippi summer and much of the spirit of the book, with Jory making a superbly villainous Injun Joe. TM

Adventures of Werner Holt, The (Die Abenteuer des Werner Holt)

(Joachim Kunert, 1963, EGer) Klaus-Peter Thiele, Manfred Karge, Arno Wyzniewski, Günter Junghans, Peter Reusse.
164 min. b/w.
Adaptation of an autobiographical novel by Dieter Noll which sets out to tell it like it was for a young man growing up in Nazi Germany. Painstakingly worthy but excruciatingly long, and hopelessly naive in its characterisation of a hero symbolically torn since childhood between two friends, one who enjoys beating people up, the other preferring such weedy intellectual pursuits as piano-playing. Small surprise when, at long last, our hero wakes up to the truth about concentration camps while serving on the Eastern front, and becomes disaffected from Nazism. TM

Adventuress, The

see I See a Dark Stranger

Adversary, The (Pratidwandi)

(Satyajit Ray, 1970, Ind) Dhritiman Chatterjee, Indiri Devi, Debraj Roy, Krishna Bose.
110 min. b/w.
This opens and closes with the same scene: an unemployed ex-student waiting for a job interview with some fifty others in a crowded corridor. In between, Ray takes us on a lightning excursion through the preoccupations of disenchanted urban Indian youth. Taking in concern for the underprivileged, distaste for rich hippies, hangovers of the old puritanical morality, emergent Marxism, the ground he tries to cover is almost too much; and when the hero marches into the interview room in the final scene to attack the complacent officials, it's more a dramatic device than a resolution of his conflicts. Even so, Ray's observation of human behaviour is as acute as ever, with the young man's hang-ups constantly emphasised by the gap between his actions and his dreams. CAub

Advise and Consent

(Otto Preminger, 1962, US) Don Murray, Charles Laughton, Walter Pidgeon, Lew Ayres, Franchot Tone, Henry Fonda, Gene Tierney, Peter Lawford, Burgess Meredith.
139 min. b/w.
A companion piece to Anatomy of a Murder and The Cardinal, tackling Washington politics with the best-selling mixture of sophistication and evasion characteristic of Preminger in his 'problem picture' mood. More McCarthy than Watergate, the exposé of political barter and blackmail not unnaturally looks a little quaint now, but still grips like a vice thanks to the skill with which Preminger's stunning mise en scène absorbs documentary detail. A decided bonus is the fact that the need to let every viewpoint have its say gives a starry cast opportunities gratefully grabbed all round. TM

Affair, The

(Paul Seed, 1995, GB) Kerry Fox, Courtney B Vance, Leland Gantt, Ciaran Hinds.
105 min.
An efficiently performed but finally rather dull (and very televisual) study of a neglected historical subject: the reception of black GIs in Britain during WWII. The racist slurs and aggression which the soldiers endure come less from the rural, middle-class Brits, and more from their white American counterparts; indeed, Fox, whose husband is off in Europe, even goes so far as to contemplate, guiltily, an affair with the impeccably well-mannered Vance. Things turn horribly, though predictably sour. GA

Affair, The

(Gilbert Cates, 1973, US) Natalie Wood, Robert Wagner, Bruce Davison, Kent Smith.
92 min.
For a while it seems that Cates might just pull off this modest little film, originally made for TV. Wood stars as a successful songwriter crippled by polio as a girl, with Wagner, a grey-suited straight man from her father's world of lawyers and businessmen, trying to strike up an affair with her. The predictable parallels drawn between her crippled body and emotional life are acceptable enough, because Cates handles her initial lack of interest in Wagner very sensitively, and the dialogue by Barbara Turner is exceptionally good. But about half way through, round about the time she loses her virginity (at 32), the situation runs awry. Up till then, trendy dress and soft focus visuals had been excusable because Cates handles his actors so well. Now the dialogue lapses into folksiness, then into cliché, leaving nothing but the inevitable broken glass, slashed wrists, and older but wiser body recuperating in a hospital bed. RM

Affaire du Courrier de Lyon, L'

(Maurice Lehmann/Claude Autant-Lara, 1937, Fr) Pierre Blanchar, Dita Parlo, Charles Dullin, Jean Tissier, Dorville, Jacques Copeau, Pierre Alcover.
103 min. b/w.
This *affaire* has been troubling the French for 200 years. In 1796 the Lyons mail coach was held up and its two drivers butchered. Five suspects were quickly arrested, condemned and guillotined, though the involvement of one of them, Lesurques, was far from clear. As impossible to believe in his guilt as in his innocence, according to one commentator, though the film-makers have no doubt. Lesurques is shown as the victim of a chance resemblance (Blanchar in a double role), and the parallels between this and Hitchcock's *The Wrong Man* are striking, with Dita Parlo touching in the thankless Vera Miles role. Lehmann being a stage director, Autant-Lara was assigned to handle the cinema, in theory. At any rate, the melodramatic and the factual are kept roughly in balance, so you can't be sure, for instance, if it really did rain on the executions. Rumour has it that an uncredited Jacques Prévert wrote the dialogue. BBa

Affairs of Annabel, The

(Ben Stoloff, 1938, US) Lucille Ball, Jack Oakie, Ruth Donnelly, Bradley Page, Thurston Hall, Fritz Feld.
68 min. b/w.
Keen to cash in on the considerable comic talents of their up-and-coming Lucille Ball, RKO intended to set her up in a series. This, the first, sees her as a movie actress in need of publicity whose resourceful press agent (Oakie) contrives to have her imprisoned as a stunt. Fast, undemanding and bright, but only one more in the series followed: *Annabel Takes a Tour* (1938). GA

Affairs of Cellini, The

(Gregory La Cava, 1934, US) Fredric March, Constance Bennett, Fay Wray, Frank Morgan, Jessie Ralph, Louis Calhern.
80 min. b/w.
Costume romp in 16th century Florence, with March as the roguish artist who switches his amorous attentions from his model (Wray) to a married duchess (Bennett), whose husband (Morgan) is meantime pursuing the model. Mildly

diverting in a rather tiresome, bedroom farcical way, but entirely forgettable aside from Charles Rosher's attractive camerawork. TM

Affair to Remember, An
(Leo McCarey, 1957, US) Cary Grant, Deborah Kerr, Cathleen Nesbitt, Richard Denning, Neva Patterson.
115 min.
Remake of McCarey's own *Love Affair* of 1939, with Grant and Kerr taking over from Charles Boyer and Irene Dunne in this comedy drama about a shipboard romance between a wealthy playboy and an ex-chanteuse. Entertaining enough while the action's still afloat, the plot later gets bogged down in soapy clichés when the characters debark in New York, agreeing to separate and test their love before they marry. Boyer's romantic gravity is much missed in the second half. GA

Affiche Rouge, L'
(Frank Cassenti, 1976, Fr) Pierre Clémenti, Anicée Alvina, Maya Wodeska, Laszlo Szabo.
90 min.
Blood-red posters featuring portraits of wanted 'terrorists' decorated street walls in occupied France during World War II, and this account of how twenty-three foreigners working for the Resistance were caught and executed dramatises one of the heroic myths of the Occupation. But Cassenti adopts a radically different perspective from the humanist 'honesty' of *L'Armée des Ombres* or even *Lacombe Lucien*, and instead attempts a Marxist analysis of the myth and what it means, historically, to re-enact it. As it moves from one level of representation to another with a Brechtian approach to performance, the film occasionally obscures its aims but never fails to challenge the way we receive history in the cinema. MA

Affinità Elettive, Le
see Elective Affinities

Affliction
(Paul Schrader, 1997, US) Nick Nolte, Sissy Spacek, James Coburn, Willem Defoe, Mary Beth Hurt, Jim True.
114 min.
Schrader's sensitive but rather dull adaptation of Russell Banks' novel is set in a visually entrancing snowy, small town landscape and concerns mixed-up families beset by physical and emotional abuse. Nolte's his usual reliable self as the cop haunted by his relationship with his father (Coburn in a rare but welcome reappearance); Dafoe, however, as Nolte's brother, looks a little lost and awkward; and the narrative's too unfocused and low key really to engage the heart or mind. GA

Afraid of the Dark
(Mark Peploe, 1991, GB/Fr) James Fox, Fanny Ardant, Paul McGann, Clare Holman, Robert Stephens, Susan Wooldridge, Ben Keyworth, David Thewlis.
92 min.
11-year-old Lucas (Keyworth) is worried that his mother (Ardant) will fall victim to a psychopath who is terrorising West London with a series of razor attacks on blind women. Holding little faith in the abilities of his father (Fox) as a policeman on the case, the boy begins to suspect those around him... Screenwriter Peploe's debut as director is an ingenious psychological thriller that attempts to delve inside the dark recesses of the mind of its pre-pubescent protagonist. To some extent, it succeeds, thanks partly to genuinely touching playing from Keyworth, partly to a script that contrives to endow what is essentially a very simple plot with a wealth of Freudian symbols, cinematic references and narrative twists. It was probably more satisfying on paper than in its finished form, however: several of the performances in the first half are (perhaps deliberately) somewhat stilted, and there's a faint academicism at work which militates against real suspense. GA

Africa Addio
(Africa Blood and Guts)
(Gualtiero Jacopetti/Franco Prosperi, 1965, It)
122 min.
Purporting to be a dispassionate documentary about the 'birth struggles' of an Africa freeing itself from Colonialism, this was banned all over the continent except for South Africa, where it played to packed houses. Atrocity after atrocity is shown, with no real concern to analyse the context. It's all very interesting, but as one might expect from the team that produced the notorious *Mondo Cane*, the motives are undeniably exploitative.

African Elephant, The
(aka King Elephant)
(Simon Trevor, 1971, US) narrator: David Wayne.
92 min.
Wild-life adventures often work like Disney cartoons – they're most successful when the animals, the heroes, are humanised to the point of being excessively charming. This documentary, which was shot in East Africa, works along these lines, especially in the way it describes the matriarchy of the elephant world and the idiosyncrasies of other socially rejected creatures. In fact the commentary written by Alan Landsburg is so full of humanly innuendos that one begins to suspect a heavy 'people' message; and it would be fair to simply dismiss the film for being into disguised (and dishonest) 'noble savagery'. Still, there's some fine photography, and some delicate observations which make this film a trillion times better than any zoo. JPi

African Queen, The
(John Huston, 1951, US/GB) Katharine Hepburn, Humphrey Bogart, Robert Morley, Peter Bull.
105 min.
Impossible to deny this film's entertainment value, even if it's hardly the great classic it's often claimed to be. Bogart, hammier than usual and thus managing to win an Oscar, is the gin-swigging, cussing river trader who helps prim missionary Hepburn to escape the Germans in East Africa during World War I. Their trying odyssey downriver, of course, gradually sees the two incompatibles falling in love, with the as always detached Bogart finally discovering commitment and attacking a German gunboat. A witty script by James Agee (from CS Forester's novel) and fine colour photography by Jack Cardiff help to counteract the basically contrived and implausible nature of the story. GA

Africa – Texas Style
(Andrew Marton, 1967, GB) Hugh O'Brien, John Mills, Nigel Green, Tom Nardini, Adrienne Corri, Ronald Howard.
109 min.
Virtually a pilot movie for Ivan Tors' short-lived TV series *Cowboys in Africa*, this kiddie-market entry spiced its copious wild life footage with a slim yarn about a Kenyan settler hiring a pair of Texans to help run his game 'ranch'. PT

After Dark, My Sweet
(James Foley, 1990, US) Jason Patric, Rachel Ward, Bruce Dern, George Dickerson, James Cotton.
111 min.
James (*At Close Range*) Foley demonstrates again his affinity for the climate of mundane evil, this time Jim Thompson's random world, where all the characters play with crooked cues. Ex-boxer and drifter Collie (Patric) seems just punchy enough to recruit as the muscle in a child kidnapping, but turns out unpredictable; and Uncle Bud (Dern) and Fay (Ward) have a testing time keeping up with his mood swings. Nobody trusts anybody, and they're right. Dern, always awkward, has matured into a showpiece of behavioural hairpin bends. Excellent. BC

Afterglow
(Alan Rudolph, 1997, US) Nick Nolte, Julie Christie, Lara Flynn Boyle, Jonny Lee Miller, Jay Underwood, Domini Blythe, Yves Corbeil.
114 min.
As ever, Rudolph's subject is love cross-wired. Nolte is 'Lucky Mann', a fix-it man ready, willing and able to screw away from home with the tacit consent of his wife Phyllis (Christie), a retired B-movie actress. This ageing couple can't conceal the cracks in their marriage caused by the disappearance of their only daughter some years ago. A yuppie couple represent their mirror image: Marianne (Boyle) desperately wants to have a baby, but Jeffrey (Miller) refuses to have sex. As Marianne puts Lucky to work in the spare bedroom and Jeffrey chats up Phyl, each character in turn steps through the looking glass. The film begins with a man teetering on the edge and ends in a howl of anguish – and Tom Waits' aching 'Somewhere'. In between, Rudolph's taste for monologue and metaphorical conceit may prove too arch or theatrical for some, but when he zooms in slowly on Nolte's crumpled, leonine dignity or Christie's pained, still luminous smile, he achieves a singular nakedness. If the younger couple don't achieve the same resonance, they bring a welcome off-kilter energy to the mix. This rakes over the ashes, the inflections and infractions of an unhappy, still loving, marriage with a memorable, plaintive grace. TCh

After Hours
(Martin Scorsese, 1985, US) Griffin Dunne, Rosanna Arquette, Verna Bloom, Linda Fiorentino, Teri Garr, John Heard.
97 min.
A quiet New York computer programmer (Dunne) travels downtown to SoHo for a vaguely arranged date. Losing his taxi fare en route is only the first of the night's many increasingly menacing situations, with neurotic New Yorkers all apparently determined to prevent his returning home alive. Scorsese's screwball comedy is perhaps his most frightening picture to date as Dunne slowly but inexorably sinks into a whirlpool of mad and murderous emotions; but a tight and witty script and perfectly tuned performances, perilously balanced between normality and insanity, keep the laughs flowing, while the direction is as polished and energetic as ever. Only the nagging undercurrents of misogyny leave a sour taste in what is otherwise inventive film-making of the first order. GA

Afternoon Breezes
(Kazetachi no Gogo)
(Hitoshi Yazaki, 1980, Jap) Setsuko Aya, Naomi Ito, Hiroshi Sugita, Mari Atake.
105 min. b/w.
This first feature by the director of *March Comes in Like a Lion* was a seminal film for Japan's emerging independent cinema in the early 1980s. A young woman falls insanely in love with her flatmate. Unable to voice her feelings, she tries to disrupt the other woman's existing love life by seducing her boyfriend – only to find herself pregnant by him. Filmed (almost entirely in longshots) with remarkable delicacy and restraint, it gets inside the mind of a manic obsessive with near-hallucinatory intensity. TR

After Office Hours
(Robert Z Leonard, 1935, US) Clark Gable, Constance Bennett, Stuart Erwin, Billie Burke, Harvey Stephens, Henry Travers.
75 min. b/w.
Standard Depression era plot, with Gable overdoing the brashness as a working newspaperman who resents the socialite (Bennett) he assumes to be slumming when she joins the paper's staff. Their love-hate affair, conducted in pretty flat wisecracks, comes to a head when a friend of hers is murdered and he tracks down the killer. Fine Charles Rosher camerawork, otherwise unremarkable. TM

After the Fox
(Caccia alla Volpe)
(Vittorio De Sica, 1966, It/US) Peter Sellers, Britt Ekland, Lidia Brazzi, Victor Mature, Paolo Stoppa, Akim Tamiroff, Martin Balsam.
103 min.
Try to imagine a comic farce co-scripted by one of the founding fathers of Italian neo-realism, Cesare Zavattini, and a wisecracking Jewish playwright, Neil Simon. Pretty funny, yes? No! Ill-fated international co-production isn't in it: we are talking turkey here as master criminal The Fox (Sellers) escapes from jail into streets full of excitable Italians, executes a gold bullion robbery, and saves his sister's honour. Marginally enlivened by Mature's witty self-mockery as a beefcake movie star fretting over his fading charms. NF

After the Thin Man
(WS Van Dyke, 1936, US) William Powell, Myrna Loy, James Stewart, Elissa Landi, Joseph Calleia.
113 min. b/w.

Surprisingly successful sequel to the delightful, Dashiell Hammett-based comedy-mystery, *The Thin Man*, with Powell and Loy as charmingly witty as ever as the bibulous sophisticates Nick and Nora Charles, revelling in sparkling dialogue as they solve a murder. Notionally based on a story by Hammett, the plot is ingenious enough, though the then up-and-coming Stewart now seems uncomfortable cast as the culprit. After this the series grew distinctly thin, though Powell and Loy continued to give good value: Another *Thin Man* (1939), *Shadow of the Thin Man* (1941), *The Thin Man Goes Home* (1944), *Song of the Thin Man* (1947). TM

Against All Odds
(Taylor Hackford, 1984, US) Rachel Ward, Jeff Bridges, James Woods, Alex Karras, Jane Greer, Richard Widmark, Swoosie Kurtz.
128 min.
This places itself in much the same category as Jim McBride's *Breathless* – a glossy remake of an old and much loved classic, in this case Jacques Tourneur's 1947 *noir* thriller *Out of the Past* – and once again it is best to forget the original. Bridges is a fading football star with an iffy shoulder and friends in low places. When one of them, the owner of an iniquitous night club (Woods), sends him off to Mexico to recover an errant girlfriend, the problem of finding her, and the problem of the small murder she commits, pale beside the problem of coming back to admit they've fallen in love. There are *longueurs*; there are also compensations, however: pointed performances from Woods and Greer, passion on a Mexican beach, and as in *Breathless*, LA never looked so beautiful. CPea

Against the Wind
(Charles Crichton, 1948, GB) Robert Beatty, Simone Signoret, Jack Warner, Gordon Jackson, Paul Dupuis, John Slater.
96 min. b/w.
Above-average Ealing thriller, with a mixture of British and Belgian agents helping the resistance movement in occupied Europe during World War II. A little implausible, but backed by some semi-documentary training scenes before the group (in a plot remarkably similar to that of *13 Rue Madeleine*) set off on their mission with a traitor (Warner, cast against type) among them. Crichton, taking a break from comedy along with scriptwriter TEB Clarke, turns in some tense moments, and Signoret adds a touch of style in a pre-*L'Armée des Ombres* bout of heroism. GA

Agantuk
see Stranger, The

Agatha
(Michael Apted, 1978, US) Dustin Hoffman, Vanessa Redgrave, Timothy Dalton, Helen Morse, Celia Gregory.
105 min.
The premise is superb: the (real) mystery of Agatha Christie's ten-day disappearance in 1926, during the much-reported disintegration of her marriage. The film, though, only partly fulfills its promise, despite a sensitive script and Vanessa Redgrave's excellent, introverted performance. Period re-creation – of the hotels, railway stations, dress – is almost *too* perfect, with production values tending to distract attention from the situation's intrinsic interest; and a brooding plotline is weakened by slapstick secondary characters and by Hoffman's jaunty pastiche of a performance as an arrogant American newspaperman who finds and falls in love with Agatha in the spa town of Harrogate. Though undercut by a last scene redolent of *Brief Encounter*, the brilliant, suspended twist in the central story – with its ingenious perception that one may write murder 'stories' to stave off the prospect of one's own death – remains memorable. CA

Age d'Or, L'
(Luis Buñuel, 1930, Fr) Gaston Modot, Lya Lys, Max Ernst, Pierre Prévert.
60 min. b/w.
'Our sexual desire has to be seen as the product of centuries of repressive and emasculating Catholicism...it is always coloured by the sweet secret sense of sin,' mused Buñuel in his autobiography *My Last Breath*. One might describe *L'Age d'Or* as 60 minutes of *coitus interruptus*, a scabrous essay on Eros and civilisation, wherein a couple is constantly prised apart from furious love-making by the police, high society and,

above all, the Church. Financed by the Vicomte de Noailles, a dream patron who loyally pronounced the film exquisite and delicious, even as right-wing extremists were pelting it with ink and stink bombs, this is a jagged memento of that Golden Age before directors forgot the art of filming erotica (the celebrated toe-sucking is sexier by far than almost anything since), the revolutionary avant-garde lost its sense of humour, and surrealism itself fell prey to advertising-agency chic. SJo

Agency (aka Mind Games)
(George Kaczender, 1981, Can) Robert Mitchum, Lee Majors, Valerie Perrine, Saul Rubinek, Alexandra Stewart, Anthony Parr.
94 min.
An advertising agency is taken over by a political group, who inject subliminal messages into their commercials. Any potential in this idea was overlooked by Kaczender, whose dull, plodding style is a turn-off, while Lee Majors makes a blank hero. For the real dope on subliminals, see *Videodrome* or *They Live*. TCh

Age of Consent
(Michael Powell, 1969, Aust) James Mason, Helen Mirren, Jack MacGowran, Frank Thring.
103 min.
Not quite Powell's last film, since he followed it with *The Boy Who Turned Yellow* for the Children's Film Foundation, and his revised version of *The Edge of the World*; but it is a last return to his favourite theme of the artist taking stock of his life, which he treats with new mellowness while exploiting '60s liberality to give it a direct erotic dimension. Mason plays a commercially successful painter who retires from New York City to the Great Barrier Reef; his creative drive is re-awakened when he finds there an innocent but physically mature teenager, whom he strips and paints at the first opportunity. The emotional and psychological results of the encounter are followed through with exemplary seriousness and wit, in some way anticipating the themes and visuals of Nicolas Roeg's *Walkabout*. There are some nervous insertions of redundant comic relief, but not enough to shatter the prevailing mood: brilliant sunlight illuminating all the unmomentous ins and outs of a human passion. TR

Age of Cosimo de Medici, The (L'Età di Cosimo de Medici)
(Roberto Rossellini, 1973, It) Marcello Di Falco, Virginio Gazzolo, Adriano Amidei Migliano.
225 min.
Rossellini's trilogy portraying the eruption of Renaissance Florence was originally made for TV (Part One: *The Exile of Cosimo de Medici*; Part Two: *The Power of Cosimo de Medici*; Part Three: *Leon Battista Alberti*). Cosimo's rise to power, his exile and return, are related in scenes of austere beauty which animate the economic, legal, military, religious and aesthetic structures of a 15th century city state. Cosimo, the artists, the merchants, the tax-collectors and the priests are all vivid Renaissance men, yet men understood not in an individual psychological frame, but in a historical materialist one. Certain sequences force a complete reappraisal of screen history: an explanation of the tax system, a discussion about architecture, an election to the ruling council, open up ways of seeing the past to which British television obstinately remains largely blind. The revealed world is both patently artificial and startlingly real. Rossellini's restless camera analyses and interrogates the continually stimulating debates about power and freewill. And the greatest achievement is the trilogy's final section, focusing on scholar and artist Leon Battista Alberti. Through him we understand the emergence of the humanist consciousness; through him we recognise the birth of our culture. JW

Age of Innocence, The (100)
(Martin Scorsese, 1993, US) Daniel Day-Lewis, Michelle Pfeiffer, Winona Rider, Richard E Grant, Alec McCowen, Geraldine Chaplin, Mary Beth Hurt, Miriam Margolyes, Alexis Smith, Michael Gough, Robert Sean Leonard.
138 min.
Scorsese's magnificent film, taken from Edith Wharton's novel, is set in 1870s New York and centres on lawyer Newland Archer (Day-Lewis), whose plans to wed the impeccably connected May Welland (Rider) are upset by his love for

her unconventional cousin, the Countess Olenska (Pfeiffer). The performances are excellent, while the director employs all the tools of his trade to bring his characters and situations vividly to life; from the start, it's clear from the speedy cutting and sumptuous mise-en-scène that Scorsese and his team are intent on drawing us into the heart of Archer's perceptions and the world around him (this is, most certainly, an expressionist film). Decor reflects and oppresses characters; posture, gesture and glance (like the witty, ironic narration) convey not only individual psychology but the ideals of an entire, etiquette-obsessed elite. Everything here serves to express an erotic fervour, imprisoned by unbending social rituals designed to preserve the status quo in favour of a self-appointed aristocracy. Scorsese's most poignantly moving film. GA

Aggression
see Agression, L'

Aggro Seizeman
(James Mannas/Brian Stuart-Young, 1975, Guyana) Gordon Case, Martha Gonsalves, Pauline McKenzie, Oscar Edwards.
110 min.
Uneasy balance of late-adolescent trauma, comedy thriller and romance 'Aggro' is the hero's nickname (ie, he's rough), 'Seizeman' his occupation, meaning he repossesses goods from punters who haven't kept up their hire purchase, usually without informing his victims. His girl's parents think he's a creep, she's not so sure, and the 'seizures' are mostly meant to have us rolling in the aisles until we discover why the chip is on his shoulder. Unfortunately this is one rebel who's missing not only a cause but also a script, director, editor and any competent fellow actors. GD

Agnes of God
(Norman Jewison, 1985, US) Jane Fonda, Anne Bancroft, Meg Tilly, Anne Pitoniak, Winston Rekert.
98 min.
When Agnes, a young novice, gives birth to a baby later found strangled, a court psychiatrist (Fonda) is despatched to the convent to discover whether the girl (who claims to remember neither conception nor pregnancy) is fit to stand trial. Fonda, a chain-smoking lapsed Catholic, is determined to find the answer within the girl's subconscious; the worldly Mother Superior (Bancroft) believes a miracle might have taken place. Thus (based on a play) the obvious and slightly spurious battle between science and faith. Splendidly shot by Sven Nykvist and with excellent performances, it's an agreeable puzzle which doesn't, thank heaven, come up with a solution to the meaning of life. JE

Agony (Agonia)
(Elem Klimov, 1975, USSR) Alexei Petrenko, Velta Linei, Alisa Freindlikh, Anatoly Romashin.
148 min. b/w & col.
Headily melodramatic and overlong biopic of Rasputin, from the director of *Come and See* and *Farewell*, to which this is immeasurably inferior. The central performance by Petrenko is at best vivid and energetic, at worst mannered and over-the-top, while the whole thing, fitted out with political asides and historical footnotes, comes across as disjointed claptrap, notable only for having broken certain taboos of silence about the infamous charlatan in his native country. Obviously well-intentioned, it's nevertheless often virtually unwatchable. GA

Agony and the Ecstasy, The
(Carol Reed, 1965, US/It) Charlton Heston, Rex Harrison, Diane Cilento, Harry Andrews, Alberto Lupo, Adolfo Celi, Venantino Venantini, John Stacy, Fausto Tozzi, Maxine Audley, Tomas Milian.
139 min.
Chuck paints the Sistine Chapel while Pope Rex looks up and wonders when it will be finished. The conflict between artist and sponsor often leads to some fine and even witty interplay, though the extremely dubious love affair and the pallid battle sequences make the film lose focus. Heston is good in the role – he looks less like Michelangelo than Michelangelo's statue of Moses – and the way that Reed conveys the actual painting is impressive. The original version included a 15-minute prologue, with music by

Jerry Goldsmith, which toured the world's museums so that audiences might not muddle this Michelangelo with another. ATu

Agression, L' (Aggression)

(Gérard Pirès, 1975, Fr/It) Jean-Louis Trintignant, Catherine Deneuve, Claude Brasseur, Milena Vukotic.
101 min.
A French motorcycle picture which, though based on John Buell's novel *The Shrewsdale Exit*, transcends the limitations of imitating the American genre, and offers in its place a sustained attack on French middle class values. Trintignant goes on a trail of revenge after the rape and murder of his wife and daughter; bourgeois dream disintegrates into nightmare, but the seeds of destruction are shown to be internal. Deneuve, as Trintignant's sister-in-law, provides the film's emotional core with a fine performance, the film's presence questioning male assumptions, even when her lines don't. CPe

Aguirre, Wrath of God (Aguirre, der Zorn Gottes)

(Werner Herzog, 1972, WGer) Klaus Kinski, Cecilia Rivera, Ruy Guerra, Helena Rojo, Del Negro.
95 min.
As in *Even Dwarfs Started Small*, the exposition of Herzog's film about the crazy, megalomaniac dream of the Spanish Conquistadors is both functional and extremely concentrated: each scene and each detail is honed down to its salient features. On this level, the film effectively pre-empts analysis by analysing itself as it proceeds, admitting no ambiguity. Yet at the same time, Herzog's flair for charged explosive imagery has never had freer rein, and the film is rich in oneiric moments. The extraordinary, beautiful opening scene illustrates the ambivalence. In long shot, the image of the conquistadors descending the Andes pass brims with poetic resonances: the men are situated between the peaks and the valleys, between conquered land and unexplored forests, between 'heaven' and 'earth', shrouded in mists. In close-up, the procession picking its way down the narrow path is presented and defined with specific accuracy: all the leading characters are introduced, the social hierarchy is sketched (the slave porters in chains, the women carried in chairs), and the twin poles of the expedition's ideology are signified through the loads it carries (a large Madonna figure and an even larger cannon). Neither 'reading' of the action contradicts the other: they are, rather, mutually illuminating. TR

A-Haunting We Will Go

(Alfred Werker, 1942, US) Stan Laurel, Oliver Hardy, Dante the Magician, John Shelton, Sheila Ryan, Elisha Cook Jr.
68 min. b/w.
Not, frankly, one of Laurel and Hardy's better features. The pair are as likeable as ever as down-and-outs hired to deliver a coffin (containing not a corpse but a live gangster) which becomes mixed up with a magician's stage props when they act as his stooges. With pauses for Dante's stage illusions, the plot drags. TM

Ah Kam (A-Jin/aka The Stuntwoman)

(Ann Hui, 1996, HK) Michelle Khan (aka Michelle Yeoh), Samo Hung, Jimmy Wong, Kent Cheng, Man Hoi, Richard Ng.
95 min.
Surprisingly unvarnished tribute to the unsung women and men who perform stunts in Hong Kong movies. Bond-girl-to-be Michelle Khan (who actually did break into movies doing stunts) plays Ah Kam, an immigrant from Mainland China who braves her way into movie work, bungles an affair with a businessman and winds up confronting the triad gangsters who have killed her mentor (Hung). Not one of Hui's personal films, but transparently sincere. Khan did her own stunts and broke a leg during production. TR

Ah Ying (Banbianren)

(Allen Fong, 1982, HK) Hui So-Ying, Peter Wang, Hui Pui, Yao Lin-Shum, Shu Kei, Charles Ng.
104 min.
Allen Fong invents Chinese docu-drama, taking Hui So-Ying out of her job on her parents' fish market stall and following her progress in acting classes; in the background, her family acts out its real-life domestic strains and crises. Fong based the character of Ah Ying's drama teacher Cheung on his late friend Koh Wu (Peter Wang's performance is a creditable impersonation), who spent years trying but failing to raise money for a film in Hong Kong. It adds up to a wry panorama of everyday dreams and aspirations, often – but not always – doomed to be dashed. TR

Aigle à Deux Têtes, L' (The Eagle Has Two Heads/ Eagle With Two Heads)

(Jean Cocteau, 1948, Fr) Edwige Feuillère, Jean Marais, Sylvia Monfort, Jean Debucourt, Jacques Varennes, Yvonne de Bray.
99 min. b/w.
One of Cocteau's more conventional films, based on his own play, with Marais as a poet/anarchist out to assassinate a 19th century Queen. But when she lays eyes on the ragged poet, it is, alas, love at first sight. He is the spitting image of her deceased husband, the King. When the emerging world of the bourgeoisie closes in (in the form of a corrupt Republican official), the couple has no other escape but death. Very Romantic, very Cocteau, and surprisingly, after 40 years, still very moving.

Ailsa

(Paddy Breathnach, 1994, Ire) Brendan Coyle, Andrea Irvine, Juliette Grouber.
75 min.
Young married Dubliner Miles (Coyle) is a genealogist – he traces family trees. When a young American (Grouber) moves into a neighbouring flat, Miles becomes obsessed with her, even stealing her mail, though he hasn't the courage to introduce himself. Structured in flashbacks by award-winning novelist Joseph O'Connor, with tracts of voice-over narration, this mood piece feels uncomfortably like an illustrated novella. First-time director Breathnach does well enough, but he might be more sparing with the blue filter next time. TCh

Ai No Corrida (L'Empire des Sens/The Realm of the Senses/In the Realm of the Senses)

(Nagisa Oshima, 1976, Fr/Jap) Tatsuya Fuji, Eiko Matsuda, Aoi Nakajima, Meika Seri.
105 min.
Oshima's erotic masterpiece, which attracted some unsavoury attention for its hardcore elements, should be seen in the context of his other films. The central couple are archetypal Oshima outsiders, turning their backs on the militarist realities of 1936 and plunging into an erotic world of their own, created and sustained by their own fantasies of hyper-virility and hyper-arousal. The film celebrates their passion, steadfastly confronting even its most alarming implications. But it's also the most involving (and hence disturbing) film about voyeurism since *Rear Window*. As ever, Oshima broaches taboos not in a spirit of adolescent daring, but in the knowledge that the most deep-rooted taboos are personal, not social. TR

Ain't Misbehavin'

(Peter Neal/Anthony Stern, 1974, GB)
85 min. b/w.
Fairly intriguing collage of cinematic ephemera from the early part of this century: newsreels, blue films, fashion shorts, *What the Butler Saw* material, and glimpses of Fats Waller, George Formby, Nat King Cole, Sophie Tucker and other performers. Some of the material is fascinating, and put together in such a way that it brings home how little there is to distinguish between respectable Hollywood and its underbelly. When the film goes out for laughs, on the other hand, the results are dire in the extreme. It is this way the movie porn of the '30s and '40s is as much a revelation as reading about Victorian England via the author of *My Secret Life*. It doesn't need amplification. DP

Air America

(Roger Spottiswoode, 1990, US) Mel Gibson, Robert Downey Jr, Nancy Travis, Ken Jenkins, David Marshall Grant, Lane Smith, Art La Fleur, Burt Kwouk, Tim Thomerson.
118 min.
Goooood morning, Vietnam – again? Actually, the fly boys in Spottiswoode's megabudget action comedy are just over the border in Laos, but the song remains the same: innocent and not-so-innocent Americans caught up in a war they don't understand. Crazy pilot Gibson is employed by the CIA to transport humanitarian aid and heroin, the latter intended to finance the local anti-Communist warlord's private army. Despite the black comic tone, it is impossible to identify with Gibson's cynical, selfish loner whose lucrative sideline is gun-running. That leaves the uncharismatic, ineffectual Downey holding the conscience ticket – as the wide-eyed new boy whose efforts to expose such nefarious activities cause the faeces to hit the propeller – and a huge hole in the middle of the picture. Somewhere amid the *M*A*S*H*-style lunacy, magnificent flying sequences and expertly choreographed stunts, a serious political movie is struggling to make itself heard. Mostly, however, this contentious counterpoint is reduced to background noise, drowned out by maniacal laughter, deafening explosions and a slew of late-'60s pop songs. NF

Air de Famille, Un

(Cédric Klapisch, 1996, Fr) Jean-Pierre Bacri, Jean-Pierre Darroussin, Catherine Frot, Agnès Jaoui, Claire Maurier, Wladimir Yordanoff, Sophie Simon, Cédric Klapisch.
110 min.
In a French provincial town, Henri Menard (Bacri) runs the old family restaurant where the clan convenes every Friday night. This Friday, everyone's ego is in for a bruising. A subtle, breezy comedy of manners, Klapisch's follow-up to *When the Cat's Away…* may not have quite the novelty and charm of that work, but otherwise it's a fresh and unassuming treat. Based on Bacri and Jaoui's award-winning play, the film avoids staginess, less through studied adjustment, than by naturalistic observation, delicately turned characterisation and confident performances. Pity, however, about the 'silent' dreamy flashbacks. NB

Air Force

(Howard Hawks, 1943, US) John Garfield, John Ridgely, George Tobias, Harry Carey, Edward S Brophy, Arthur Kennedy, Gig Young.
124 min. b/w.
Hawks' 'contribution to the war effort', for all its then topical anti-Japanese propaganda, now comes across as a typical Hawksian examination of the isolated, all-male group, here the crew of an American B-17 Bomber operating in the Pacific shortly after Pearl Harbor. As so often, the predominant themes are self-respect, loyalty, professionalism, and the problems of integration facing the newcomer/outsider, in this case cynical rear-gunner Garfield. Rather like a bleak version of the director's earlier *Only Angels Have Wings*, it's an unusually moving example of the 'why-we-fight' genre, with genuinely horrific scenes of widespread destruction alternating with more intimate, introspective scenes depicting the tensions between the various vividly characterised members of the crew. GA

Air Force One

(Wolfgang Petersen, 1997, US) Harrison Ford, Gary Oldman, Glenn Close, Wendy Crewson, Paul Guilfoyle, William H Macy, Dean Stockwell, Jürgen Prochnow.
124 min.
Kazakhstani terrorists hijack Air Force One, the presidential 747, and the leader of the Free World puts his life on the line to rescue family and staff, then wrests control of the plane from maniac beardie Oldman. The early suspense stuff inside the plane is competently done. Ford (in Jack Ryan mode) hides in the bowels of the jet and draws on his own resources to work out the next move. Meanwhile, back at the White House, Vice-President Close runs the joint as political vultures jostle for position. Imagine *Die Hard in a Jumbo* plus action highlights from *Airport 1975*. TJ

Airheads

(Michael Lehmann, 1994, US) Brendan Fraser, Steve Buscemi, Adam Sandler, Chris Farley, Joe Mantegna, Michael McKean.
92 min.
Rightly despairing of ever landing a record deal, Los Angeles rockers The Lone Rangers infiltrate their favourite radio station with a demo tape and

water pistols. Matters get out of control, and before they know it, Chazz (Fraser), Rex (Buscemi) and Pip (Sandler) are holding the entire station hostage, live on KPPX. The exposition is such a drag, it seems impossible that the movie won't improve once the hostage situation develops. But despite the presence of such worthies as Mantegna as a disillusioned DJ and McKean as the unctuous station manager, it never does. About airheads, and for them too. TCh

Airplane!
(Jim Abrahams/David Zucker/Jerry Zucker, 1980, US) Robert Hays, Julie Hagerty, Peter Graves, Robert Stack, Lloyd Bridges, Leslie Nielsen, Kareem Abdul-Jabaar.
87 min.
Zapping every disaster movie cliché with the cartoon subtlety of *Mad* magazine may only be cannibal glee, but it prompts enough convulsions of laughter in this wacky spoof from the *Kentucky Fried Movie* team for you not to notice their dead hand at work. Imagine the same old '50s airplane yarn: pilots poisoned, passengers panic, while a traumatised war-hero lands the jalopy. It should be disastrous. But psycho ground controllers (Stack and Bridges), laff-a-second pace, and bludgeoning innuendo make this the acceptable face of the locker-room satire. DMacp

Airplane II The Sequel
(Ken Finkleman, 1982, US) Robert Hays, Julie Hagerty, Lloyd Bridges, Peter Graves, Raymond Burr, Chuck Connors, Rip Torn, William Shatner.
84 min.
Granted the producers wanted to repeat their success, but taking the same stars and copying the same jokes merely makes for a thin rehash. The doomed aircraft is now a moon-bound space shuttle departing on its maiden voyage from a commercial terminal with the usual bunch of loonies and loopies on board. Although Graves' paedophiliac pilot hasn't been sacrificed, nearly all the other dodgy bits have been replaced – to little avail – by a sprinkling of self-parodic guest stars such as Burr, Connors and Shatner. FL

Airport
(George Seaton, 1969, US) Burt Lancaster, Dean Martin, Jean Seberg, Jacqueline Bisset, George Kennedy, Helen Hayes, Van Heflin, Maureen Stapleton, Dana Wynter, Barry Nelson, Lloyd Nolan.
137 min.
The first in the ghastly series spawned by Arthur Hailey's bestseller, this is the one about the mad bomber on the Rome flight, plus the statutory collection of cardboard characters with pop-up problems. Lancaster is the harassed airport manager trying to cope, in addition to the aforesaid autodestruct passenger, with snow-bound flying conditions, a wife talking divorce, an affair with another employee (Seberg), and a brother-in-law (Martin) who is not only piloting the threatened aircraft but has contrived to impregnate the stewardess (Bisset). With clichés fairly running riot, the efficient cast, at least, is a mercy. TM

Airport 1975
(Jack Smight, 1974, US) Charlton Heston, Karen Black, George Kennedy, Efrem Zimbalist Jr, Susan Clark, Gloria Swanson, Linda Blair, Dana Andrews, Sid Caesar, Myrna Loy, Nancy Olson, Martha Scott.
107 min.
A ridiculous sequel, bad enough to be enjoyable, what with its jumbo jet crammed full of Hollywood celebs – Gloria Swanson, Myrna Loy, Sid Caesar, even Linda Blair (as a teenager being rushed to a kidney transplant) who looks like she is going to vomit over two nuns. Suddenly there is a mid-air collision, and the jumbo has grown a private two-seater aircraft like a facial wart. With the pilot blinded and the co-pilot killed, only stewardess Karen Black is left in the cockpit, until her lover Chuck Heston plays Tarzan by being lowered from a helicopter to save the day. Just routine procedure for any old airline nowadays. ATu

Airport '77
(Jerry Jameson, 1977, US) Jack Lemmon, Lee Grant, Brenda Vaccaro, Joseph Cotten, James Stewart, Olivia de Havilland, Darren McGavin, Christopher Lee.
114 min.
Disaster movie in which a converted luxury airliner laden with guests and art treasures is hijacked by terrorists and crashes into the sea near an oil-rig. The survivors then spend their time trying to overact their way out of the claustrophobic script, which threatens a death even more slow and painful than suffocation or drowning. NF

Airport '80 The Concorde (aka The Concorde – Airport '79)
(David Lowell Rich, 1979, US) Alain Delon, Susan Blakely, Robert Wagner, Sylvia Kristel, George Kennedy, Eddie Albert, Bibi Andersson, Martha Raye.
123 min.
A deafening sonic yawn signs off this desperate finale to Universal's Arthur Hailey-inspired quartet of in-flight entertainments. A goodwill Washington-to-Moscow Concorde flight to celebrate the 1980 Olympics takes on its own heavy layer of irony, while the hazards of evasive action and depressurisation parallel the general drop in hysteria value, with even the passengers less problem-stricken than usual. An arms dealer taking disproportionate steps to cover his tracks is the cause of all cartoonish fuss. PT

Air Up There, The
(Paul M Glaser, 1993, US) Kevin Bacon, Charles Gitonga Maina, Yolanda Vazquez, Winston Ntshona, Mabutho 'Kid' Sithole, Sean McCann, Dennis Patrick.
107 min.
An American basketball coach talent-scouting among Kenyan tribesmen – you'd expect standard fish-out-of-water culture-clash stuff, in which the natives teach the coach as much as he teaches them, leading to a rousing we-play-as-brothers climax. Sure enough, that's exactly what you get. Give or take the odd spot of predictable arrogance, however, it's a good-humoured, good-hearted film. Bacon is the quintessential smirking and swaggering thirty-something at whom the elders initially poke fun, but to whom they eventually owe a debt of gratitude. Only in Hollywood could a single game of basketball solve a violent territorial dispute. AO

A.K.
(Chris Marker, 1985, Fr/Jap)
75 min.
A documentary shot on the black volcanic ash at the foot of Mount Fuji, where Akira Kurosawa was filming *Ran*. While Marker makes it clear why Kurosawa has earned the title 'Sensei' (master), this is not a vapid piece of hero worship. He explores some of Kurosawa's obsessions, but it is the minutiae that really attract Marker's eye: a squad of extras adjusting the fastenings of their samurai armour can expand into large speculations on the nature of film-making. Indeed it is this ability to move from the small to the very large without slick metaphor that makes this more than an expert companion to a great film, and a work of art in its own right. CPea

Akenfield
(Peter Hall, 1974, GB) Garrow Shand, Peggy Cole, Barbara Tilney, Lyn Brooks, Ida Page.
98 min.
A fitfully engaging oddity, adapted by Ronald Blythe from his own study of everyday life, past and present, in a Suffolk farming village. The use of non-professional actors is for the most part effective in a sub-Loachian kind of way, but the intercutting between the largely prosaic lives of Akenfield's contemporary inhabitants, and the harsher but seemingly more lyrical existence of their Edwardian forebears, makes for some fairly simplistic contrasts. That said, Ivan Strasberg's lush, soft-focus landscape photography – especially when accompanied by the lilting pastoral strains of Tippett's 'Fantasia Concertante on a Theme of Corelli' – imbues the past with a not unappealing romantic aura. GA

Akira
(Katsuhiro Otomo, 1987, Jap) voices: Mitsuo Iwata, Nozomu Sasaki, Mami Koyama.
124 min.
In 2019, some 31 years after the destruction of Tokyo in WWIII, the rebuilt city is in chaos. Pill-popping biker gangs wage deadly warfare; ter-
rorism and riots by the unemployed are common; martial law holds sway; and the masses, duped by the leaders of fanatical religious cults, await a second coming by the legendary Akira. But would this eponymous hero be sufficiently powerful to overcome Tetsuo, a young biker with telekinetic powers who threatens to lead the world towards apocalypse? Reworked from his own hugely successful comic strip, Otomo's first excursion into movies features some of the most mind-blowing animation ever seen. Even if the human characters are flatly two-dimensional, the metropolis itself is a wondrous jumble of highways, slums, skyscrapers and labyrinthine passages, while the drawings imitate (exaggerate?) the pyrotechnical zooms, dollies and close-ups of live action camerawork to exhilarating effect. Artwork apart, the admirably complex plot is imaginative and serious. An impressive achievement, often suggesting a weird expressionist blend of *2001*, *The Warriors*, *Blade Runner* and *Forbidden Planet*. GA

Akira Kurosawa's Dreams
(Akira Kurosawa, 1990, US) Chishu Ryu, Mieko Harada, Mitsuko Baisho, Chosuke Ikariya, Akira Terao, Martin Scorsese.
119 min.
Depicting, rather indulgently, a number of dreams vaguely intended to reflect Kurosawa's life and abiding obsessions, this is – to be frank – regrettably embarrassing. Its eight episodes, moving from childhood through war to a terror of nuclear pollution, are wholly devoid of narrative drive. Kurosawa's penchant for metaphor leads to risibly misguided and inadequate clichés: life's vicissitudes seen as a long mountain trek through a blizzard, the guilty aftermath of war as dark at the end of a tunnel, scientific fervour as a lemmings' leap into the abyss. Not a little reactionary, the film's main achievement is to show a once impressive director quite out of touch both with the world and with developments in cinema. Much of it is like a moron's guide to the Green manifesto, transforming serious issues into banal trivia, while George Lucas' Industrial Light and Magic supply surprisingly shoddy visual effects. Only during a final procession does the old Kurosawa magic get a brief look-in, but by then the hackneyed moralising and dramatic languor have ensured that, despite the well-meaning message, it's hard to care. GA

Akseli and Elina
see Täällä Pohjantähden alla

Aladdin
(John Musker/Ron Clements, 1992, US) voices: Scott Weinger, Robin Williams, Linda Larkin, Jonathan Freeman, Gilbert Gottfried.
90 min.
The most successful animated feature ever, and it's easy to see why. Visually, it's a treat, a perfect marriage of hi-tech graphics and the traditional Disney virtue of strong characterisation and colour. The script crackles with wit and life. Williams' Genie is matched by Freeman's malevolent Jafar, and by Gottfried as Jafar's wise-cracking parrot Iago. The only disappointments are the wet Aladdin and his sweetheart Jasmine and five rather ordinary original songs. NKe

Alambrista!
(Robert M Young, 1977, US) Domingo Ambriz, Trinidad Silva, Linda Gillin, Ned Beatty.
110 min.
Young's first feature. Functioning here as writer, director and cameraman, he spent over a year living among Mexican wet-backs in the US Southwest to discover what it actually feels like working illegally, and in voluntary exile, for a society barely conscious of your existence, far less your rights. His discoveries, though nothing new, remain disturbing: workers housed and transported in sub-animal conditions, slowly bled of their dignity and culture. Yet for all his righteous indignation, *Alambrista!* fails to ignite. The fictional characters through whom he dramatises his observations appear too stereotyped, caught in as many clichés as the film is trying to fight. JD

Alamo, The
(John Wayne, 1960, US) John Wayne, Richard Widmark, Laurence Harvey, Richard Boone, Frankie Avalon, Linda Cristal, Chill Wills.

192 min.
An elephantine, historically inaccurate, stridently patriotic tribute to the handful of Texans who faced assault by 7,000 Mexican baddies. Not helped any by Avalon's vocal efforts, but occasional good patches are probably accountable to uncredited help from John Ford, while 2nd unit director Cliff Lyons certainly contributed the excellent climactic battle (which is a long, long time a-coming). TM

Alamo Bay
(Louis Malle, 1985, US) Amy Madigan, Ed Harris, Ho Nguyen, Donald Moffat, Truyer V Tran, Rudy Young, Cynthia Carle.
99 min.
Malle is not normally noted for his toughness, but tackling racial prejudice head on results in one of his most compelling films. Dinh, a cheerful young Vietnamese, arrives in the Texan port to become an all-American fisherman. His reception varies from one sympathetic veteran ('good-looking women, dynamite drugs!') to the violent Shang (Harris), an embittered local with an ever-increasing family, a failing business, and a long-standing love affair with Glory (Madigan). While the conflict leads inexorably into the revival of the Ku Klux Klan, Glory's untameable obsession for Shang is cruelly tested by the surrounding tensions. Malle makes this splintering of interests a virtue by his casting of the wonderful Madigan, who adapts her forthright style (remember *Streets of Fire?*) to create one of the richest female characters in contemporary American cinema. She's teamed here with real-life husband Harris, and their scenes together really *seethe*. DT

Albero degli Zoccoli, L'
see Tree of Wooden Clogs, The

Albert, RN
(aka Break to Freedom)
(Lewis Gilbert, 1953, GB) Anthony Steel, Jack Warner, Robert Beatty, Anton Diffring, William Sylvester, Guy Middleton.
88 min. b/w.
Stolidly unimaginative World War II prison escape movie, with a dummy used as cover for head counts. The characters are dreadfully stereotypical, with the plot revolving unconvincingly around the fact that Steel, originator of the plan, is reluctant to make the break himself because he's fallen in love with a pen pal and is worried about actually meeting her. But at least the action sticks to the camp and avoids resorting to flashbacks. TM

Albino Alligator
(Kevin Spacey, 1996, US/Fr) Matt Dillon, Faye Dunaway, Gary Sinise, William Fichtner, Viggo Mortensen, Skeet Ulrich, M Emmet Walsh, Joe Mantegna.
97 min.
Three fugitive New Orleans crims make a former speakeasy their bolthole, slowly realising there's no back exit. Dillon takes charge, since a collision en route has injured brother Sinise – and the trigger finger of tight-coiled Fichtner could leap at any moment. Hostess Dunaway tries to calm nerves, enigmatic quaffer Mortensen may know more than he's letting on, and teenager Ulrich looks doomed as the boys get rolling on their negotiating tactics. A regulation stand-off, but Spacey (in his directorial debut) makes intelligent use of the single location, and the performers take care of the rest. Dillon exudes befuddled authority as he gets in deeper than he'd really like, while mama-fixated Fichtner adds the pepper, and Dunaway skilfully plays up the kidnapper/victim relationship. Regrettably, everything's a bit vacuum-packed. TJ

Al Capone
(Richard Wilson, 1959, US) Rod Steiger, Fay Spain, Murvyn Vye, James Gregory, Nehemiah Persoff, Martin Balsam.
105 min. b/w.
One of the better gangster biopics, with a sure, painstaking sense of period and a general reluctance to whitewash its brutal hero, the film nevertheless stands or falls according to how you feel about Steiger. In what is undeniably his film, he gives a magnetic performance so full of detail and mannerisms that one could accuse it of arrogance, were it not so entirely appropriate for the char-

acter of Capone. Also to be recommended are Lucien Ballard's superb monochrome camerawork and Wilson's unhurried, unsentimental direction.

Alchemist, The
(Charles Band, 1981, US) Robert Ginty, Lucinda Dooling, John Sanderford, Viola Kate Stimpson, Robert Glaudini.
84 min.
One of a host of movies sold on the back of the ultra-gross(ing) *The Exterminator*. The connection here is Ginty, a potato-head mumbler with a passing resemblance to Lon Chaney Jr. So too, its familiar plot owes much to the werewolf genre. Ginty is the victim of a century-old curse that keeps him young but means he goes on the blood-trail nightly (sans make-up: costly stuff, hair). Its other debt (Chaney again) is to Mummy movies, with a reincarnated lover drawn into the plot in a battered but still handsome red-and-white Plymouth that's a ringer for Stephen King's 'Christine'. The auto and some amusingly inept demons – whack 'em with a tire iron, they're out for the count – must be considered the highspots in this spectacularly low-energy multi-pastiche. GD

Alchemy
(Suzanne Myers, 1996, US) Rya Kihlstedt, Jeff Webster, DV de Vincentis, Marian Quinn, Maggie Estep, Erica Chahoy, Jessica Stone.
96 min.
A distinguished and original indie debut which describes scenes from the life of an artist (Kihlstedt, excellent) who makes small boxes filled with meticulously arranged found objects, and also transcribes Russian fairy tales. Organised in three loose sections – titled charity, faith and hope – it's a delicate, meditative, 'mood' piece, which takes its heroine on a painful journey from loss to restoration of 'her pure heart'. Consciously feminist in tone, the film is filled with scenes of highly composed, occasionally magical, always sensitive, and often humorous appeal. Shot with Terence Davies-like attention to detail in brown or blue duotones by Tami Reiker. WH

Al Corazón
see To the Heart

Al di là delle nuvole
see Beyond the Clouds

Alexander Nevsky
(Sergei Eisenstein, 1938, USSR) Nikolai Cherkassov, Nikolai Okhlopkov, Alexandr Abrikosov, Dmitri Orlov.
111 min. b/w.
Eisenstein's first project to reach completion in nearly ten years, *Alexander Nevsky* is widely regarded as an artistic and political disaster, despite its wide international popularity. Conceived as a kind of nationalist epic (and approved as such by Stalin), it resurrects the 13th century hero Nevsky as an almost mythic guardian of the Russian heritage, and celebrates his victories against the Teutonic invaders; it was read as an anti-Nazi film during the war. It's easy to see why the mixture of religiosity, caricature and bold aestheticism has pleased many of the people some of the time. It's main interest now is that it cleared the way for the infinitely richer and more complex achievement of *Ivan the Terrible*. TR

Alexander the Great
(Robert Rossen, 1956, US) Richard Burton, Fredric March, Claire Bloom, Danielle Darrieux, Barry Jones, Stanley Baker, Harry Andrews, Peter Cushing.
141 min.
A sprawling, misbegotten epic that undercuts its serious intent by constantly declaiming it, and fails to strike a balance between spectacle and speechifying. Burton's Alexander, with his hatred and fear of father figures, comes in for some heavy-handed cod-Freud analysis as he sweeps across Europe and Asia in search of glory. PT

Alexander the Great
(O Megalexandros)
(Theo Angelopoulos, 1980, Greece/It) Omero Antonutti, Eva Kotanidou, Grigoris Evangelatos, Michalis Yannatos.

230 min.
A tale of socialism first deformed and then destroyed by an authoritarian leader, set in Greece a few years after the Paris Commune. Its Alexander is a bandit who became a popular folk hero. Following his escape from prison, he kidnaps some English aristocrats and demands as ransom that the rich local landowners hand over their property to the peasants. When a commune is set up, socialist ideals are betrayed by internal struggles as Italian anarchists, agrarian communists and radical extremists jostle for supremacy. A relentless demonstration of stylistic brilliance, it leaves one wondering why the parable is not more challenging and its point less predictable. SH

Alexandre (Alexandre le Bienheureux)
(Yves Robert, 1967, Fr) Philippe Noiret, Françoise Brion, Marlène Jobert, Paul le Person, Jean Carmet.
96 min.
Very strange movie about a farmer who goes to bed for a couple of months after his nagging wife's death; and how the villagers, who feel that he isn't living up to his status as a landowner, try to wake him up and end up falling asleep themselves; and how he almost meets his match, someone equally slothful. In fact the film makes an interesting companion piece to Nelly Kaplan's *La Fiancée du Pirate*, except that her heroine here becomes the deceitful chief baddy: the male dropout's only way of survival is to avoid alluring ladies who entice him into conformity. Pretty strongly anti-women. Has some antics with a trained dog.

Alexandria Encore (Eskendereya kaman we kaman)
(Youssef Chahine, 1990, Egypt/Fr) Yousra, Youssef Chahine, Hussein Fahmy, Amr Abdel Guelil.
101 min.
The third in a loose trilogy by Egypt's most widely respected director that began with *Alexandria Why?* in 1979. This takes as its starting point an argument between a film-maker (played by Chahine himself) and his favourite actor, an argument that precipitates the director into an 8½-style creative crisis and inspires the director to re-evaluate his work and his world. It's an exhilaratingly imaginative and sophisticated movie, embracing a number of themes and styles (including some marvellous musical sequences), beautifully shot and performed. TCh

Alex & the Gypsy
(John Korty, 1976, US) Jack Lemmon, Genevieve Bujold, James Woods, Gino Ardito, Robert Emhardt.
99 min.
Lemmon blusters for all he's worth, but to no effect, in this tale of a disenchanted California bail-bondsman called upon to post an immense surety for his former mistress, a sultry wind-blown gypsy (Bujold), who finds herself in the slammer awaiting sentence for the attempted murder of her oafish husband. Although patently striving for something tougher, Korty's direction achieves little more than a succession of bravura romantic flourishes. Whatever statement was intended about a couple of losers given a last chance to opt out of the system (for some sort of hazy nomadic existence) is lost in the half-hearted jokiness. JPy

Alex in Wonderland
(Paul Mazursky, 1970, US) Donald Sutherland, Ellen Burstyn, Meg Mazursky, Glenna Sergent, Viola Spolin, Federico Fellini, Jeanne Moreau, Paul Mazursky.
109 min.
Dr Mazursky's *1.5*. Having made a box-office killing with his directing debut *Bob & Carol & Ted & Alice*, Mazursky found he was Hollywood flavour of the month and, given virtual carte blanche, didn't know how to follow his success. His financially disastrous solution to the problem was to make a movie about his own predicament: Sutherland plays a self-obsessed director whose dreams of transcending the kind of Tinseltown escapism that made his first film a hit throw him into self-indulgent doubt. Should he make a movie

about racism, revolution or pollution, or buy a better house? Mazursky's most deliberately 'arty' film lacks the ironic wit of his finest work, his awe of the freedom allowed the top European directors giving rise to a cameo for Fellini himself, who turns up to console Alex in his somewhat privileged quandary. But the performances are strong, Laszlo Kovacs's camerawork is impressively dreamlike, and it's an intriguing, if deeply flawed, study of the ambitions of a Hollywood hack who fancies himself an artist. GA

Alfie
(Lewis Gilbert, 1966, GB) Michael Caine, Shelley Winters, Millicent Martin, Julia Foster, Jane Asher, Shirley Anne Field, Vivien Merchant.
114 min.
Given the full swinging London mod movie treatment of the day, Bill Naughton's funny and rather moving play emerges as a terribly dated (and one might add, terribly misogynist) account of a Cockney lecher's selfish seduction and abuse of a series of compliant females. Of course he gets his comeuppance, in an ending that has all the moral weight and sincerity of a DeMille sex'n'-sawdust spectacular. Good performances though. GA

Alfie Darling
(Ken Hughes, 1975, GB) Alan Price, Jill Townsend, Paul Copley, Joan Collins, Sheila White, Annie Ross, Hannah Gordon, Rula Lenska.
102 min.
In what looks like developing into an EEC movie, Price shows those M'zelles what a British leg-over is all about. But back home, this belated sequel to *Alfie* switches to the Americanisation of the Cockney skirt-chaser (Pontiac, Marlboros, etc) in a desperate bid to prove that the Affluent Society is still available, even to the working class. As for the 'birds', it's a matter of showing what those middle class dollies really want. In its efforts to sell a lifestyle, the film comes really unstuck when Alfie falls in love with hard-to-get Townsend. No one, it seems, can deal with the emotions involved: the film looks increasingly like an advert with no product to sell. CPe

Alfredo Alfredo
(Pietro Germi, 1971, It/Fr) Dustin Hoffman, Stefania Sandrelli, Carla Gravina, Clara Colosimo, Daniele Patella.
110 min.
Snails are both faster and funnier than this limp little man vs big women sex comedy, which manages to waste not only Hoffman but also Sandrelli, a fine caricaturist of the Italian female (see *The Conformist*): their subtleties of characterisation are all but steamrollered by vile mid-Atlantic dubbing. The end result is exactly the kind of mediocrity Woody Allen parodied so beautifully in *Everything You Always Wanted to Know About Sex*. GD

Algiers
(John Cromwell, 1938, US) Charles Boyer, Sigrid Gurie, Hedy Lamarr, Joseph Calleia, Gene Lockhart, Alan Hale.
95 min. b/w.
The Hollywood remake of the Jean Gabin classic, *Pépé le Moko*, and usually compared unfavourably. Certainly there is little tension or grit in this version of the story of the supercrook who pines for Paris and is lured from the safety of the Casbah for love of a beautiful woman. Instead, there is a fantastic opulence in the black-and-white photography (by James Wong Howe), and a totally aestheticised style of acting from Boyer and Lamarr in particular. Lamarr is extraordinarily sultry (especially with her indefinable accent), and the overall effect is as if producer Walter Wanger was trying to imitate Von Sternberg's work at Paramount with Dietrich. DT

Alias Bulldog Drummond
see Bulldog Jack

Alias Nick Beal (aka The Contact Man)
(John Farrow, 1949, US) Ray Milland, Thomas Mitchell, Audrey Totter, George Macready, Fred Clark.
93 min. b/w.

An undeservedly neglected film which should rank high on the list of Farrow's best. Starting out as a political thriller, almost imperceptibly it turns into fantasy, a variation on the Faust legend with honest, conscientious politician Mitchell falling under the spell of old Nick Beal (Milland) and turning into a ruthless, power-hungry monster. Working with his regular writer Jonathan Latimer, Farrow has a model screenplay of precision and construction, and adds to it careful detail, allusion and suggestion. Best of all is his visual coup of never having Milland walk into a scene: the camera continually discovers him as it or a character moves, and suddenly *there* he is when seconds ago he was nowhere. Sadly, there's a sellout religioso ending, which lessens the overall power of the suggestion of some all-pervasive, satanic evil. CW

Alice
(Jan Svankmajer, 1988, Switz) Kristina Kohoutova.
85 min.
Nobody who has seen even one of Svankmajer's shorts is likely to doubt that the Czech surrealist would make the definitive version of Lewis Carroll's *Alice's Adventures in Wonderland*. For no other film-maker – and that includes David Lynch – is so consistently inventive in his ability to marry pure, startling nonsense with rigorous logic, black wit with piercing psychological insights. Here, as always, Svankmajer's methods are hugely enjoyable in their perversity: Alice (the only human in a feature debut populated by a fantastic array of superbly animated puppets) not only changes size, but actually becomes her own doll; when the White Rabbit loses his stuffing, he simply secures his gaping chest with a safety-pin and eats the sawdust. Eggs crack to reveal skulls. Rolls sprout nails. Steaks crawl. A wonderland, indeed, imbued with a grotesque, cruel, and menacing dream-logic at once distinctively Svankmajer's and true to the spirit of Carroll. GA

Alice
(Woody Allen, 1990, US) Mia Farrow, William Hurt, Joe Mantegna, Alec Baldwin, Judy Davis, Blythe Danner, Bernadette Peters, Keye Luke, Cybill Shepherd, Julie Kavner, Gwen Verdon, Patrick O'Neal, Bob Balaban, James Toback.
106 min.
Allen's eponymous heroine (Farrow) – a devoted housewife burdened with existential angst and neuroses – is suddenly plunged into mid-life crisis when she falls for nice guy saxophonist Joe (Mantegna). Is he really a worthy rival to her successful but workaholic husband (Hurt)? How do her repressed rebellious impulses square with her Catholic roots and her family? And what of her Chinese acupuncturist-hypnotist's warning that it's her heart, not her back, that ails her, and his herbal prescription that renders her invisible so that she can spy on her lover, husband and friends? Allen's renewed semi-comic exploration of the upper-crust New York psyche displays many of his worst traits, and then some. It's hard to care much about the pallid Alice's anxieties, and the silly whimsy of the fantasy interludes sits uneasily within what remains, essentially, a naturalistic comic style. A scattering of fine one-liners, but one can't help wishing that Allen would investigate pastures new. GA

Alice Adams
(George Stevens, 1935, US) Katharine Hepburn, Fred MacMurray, Fred Stone, Evelyn Venable, Frank Albertson, Hedda Hopper.
99 min. b/w.
Hepburn is magnificent as the small-town social climber, although the script so softens Booth Tarkington's novel that she emerges throughout as a Persil-white heroine tarnished only by a little adolescent foolishness. With Tarkington's acidly observed social satire on Midwestern attitudes carefully ironed out by the Hollywood machine, little remains beyond a glowingly nostalgic slice of Americana. But Stevens fills the gap with some brilliant set pieces, including the exemplary scene-setting of the opening sequence, the society ball at which Hepburn is reduced to endless subterfuge to mask her gauche unease, and the ghastly dinner party at which all her social pretensions finally collapse under pressure from a heatwave. TM

Alice Doesn't Live Here Anymore
(Martin Scorsese, 1974, US) Ellen Burstyn, Kris Kristofferson, Billy Green Bush, Diane Ladd, Lelia Goldoni, Alfred Lutter.
112 min.
Although the ending is a bit of a cop out from a feminist point of view, Scorsese's warm and witty blending of the road movie with the conventions of the women's weepie is a delight. Burstyn is excellent as the eponymous heroine who, following the death of a husband she barely loved, sets off for the Monterey of her childhood with hopes of reviving her abandoned singing career. Her encounters, and those of her precociously witty 12-year old son, are observed with great generosity and a raw realism, while Scorsese typically makes wonderful use of music to underline character and situation. Bitter-sweet and very charming. GA

Alice in the Cities (Alice in den Städten)
(Wim Wenders, 1974, WGer) Rüdiger Vogeler, Yella Rottländer, Elisabeth Kreuzer, Edda Köchl.
110 min. b/w.
A photo-journalist travels across the United States on an abortive assignment, and finds himself returning to Germany (via Amsterdam) encumbered by an independent-minded nine-year-old girl. Wenders approaches his subject with telling obliqueness, taking it – and us – continually by surprise, allowing his themes to surface gracefully from the tale, documenting and questioning the seductive overlay of American culture. VG

Alice in Wonderland
(Norman Z McLeod, 1933, US) Charlotte Henry, Gary Cooper, WC Fields, Cary Grant, Edward Everett Horton, Edna May Oliver, Charles Ruggles.
77 min. b/w.
Curiouser and curiouser and that's not the half of it. With Cary Grant as the Mock Turtle, Gary Cooper as the White Knight and WC Fields as Humpty Dumpty, great things might be expected, but something went disastrously wrong in the pot. Most of the blame must rest with McLeod, whose incredibly cackhanded direction piles on the whimsy by the bucket-load and can't come to grips with the absurdity at all. Carroll may not have envisaged Alice as being totally unsullied by the ways of the world, but as played by Charlotte Henry she's as pert a piece of jailbait as ever fell down a rabbit-hole. Even the backdrops look as if they'd been lifted from Donald McGill postcards. JP.

Alice in Wonderland
(Dallas Bower/Lou Bunin, 1951, US/Fr/GB) Carol Marsh, Stephen Murray, Pamela Brown, Felix Aylmer, Ernest Milton.
83 min.
Bunin, puppetoonist extraordinaire, encountered many frustrations during his lengthy battle to bring his Carroll to the screen (the quaint live action prologue is directed by Bower). First he came up against Technicolor, who refused to handle the processing, thus forcing him to use inferior Ansco Color. Then he was drummed off the screen for daring to release his film in the same year as Disney's all-American version. And finally, Bunin discovered that he sailed too close to the satirical winds by identifying an imperious Queen Victoria (Brown) with the off-with-his-head Queen of Hearts, thus keeping the film out of Britain. Bunin employs a diverting combination of actors and puppets against a simple Klee-like background: purists will enjoy moaning at the songs while acknowledging that elsewhere he maintains the sharpness of the original. JE

Alice's Adventures in Wonderland
(William Sterling, 1972, GB) Fiona Fullerton, Michael Crawford, Robert Helpmann, Michael Hordern, Spike Milligan, Flora Robson, Ralph Richardson, Peter Sellers.
101 min.
A confectionery version of Carroll, lumbered with an unmemorable 'Curiouser and Curiouser' and other ditties by John Barry. The bevy of stars doesn't help.

Alice's Restaurant

(Arthur Penn, 1969, US) Arlo Guthrie, Pat Quinn, James Broderick, Michael McClanathan, William Obanhein.
111 min.

Brilliantly visualised, Arlo Guthrie's very funny 20-minute talking blues – about how, fined $50 for being a litterbug, he was subsequently rejected for service in Vietnam as an unrehabilitated criminal – is retained as the centrepiece of a film which expands into a sort of chronicle of Arlo's hippy wanderings through rural America. The context is different, but the reference point powerfully echoed throughout is his father Woody Guthrie's experience as the troubadour of the dying Dustbowl during the American Depression of the '30s, with the ballad this time asking what went wrong with the dropout dream of the '60s. Criticised at the time for a certain opportunism, Penn's lyrical vision of the end of an era looks increasingly apt in the perspective of passing time. TM

Alien

(Ridley Scott, 1979, GB) Tom Skerritt, Sigourney Weaver, Veronica Cartwright, Harry Dean Stanton, John Hurt, Yaphet Kotto.
117 min.

In the wake of the huge commercial success of Alien, almost all attention has perversely focused on the provenance of the script (was it a rip-off of It, the Terror from Beyond Space? Of Van Vogt's fiction? Was former John Carpenter collaborator Dan O'Bannon sold out by producers Walter Hill and David Giler's rewrites?). But the limited strengths of its staple sci-fi horrors – crew of commercial spacecraft menaced by stowaway monster – always derived from either the offhand organic/Freudian resonances of its design or the purely (brilliantly) manipulative editing and pacing of its above-average shock quota. Intimations of a big-budget Dark Star fade early, and notions of Weaver as a Hawksian woman rarely develop beyond her resourceful reaction to jeopardy. At least Scott has no time to dawdle over redundant futuristic effects in the fashion that scuttles his later Blade Runner. PT

Aliens 100 (100)

(James Cameron, 1986, US) Sigourney Weaver, Carrie Henn, Michael Diehn, Paul Reiser, Lance Henriksen, Bill Paxton.
137 min.

After a s-l-o-w build-up, Cameron scores a bulls-eye with a sequel which manages to be more thrilling than Alien (but less gory). Ripley (Weaver) survives 57 years of deep space sleep, only to be sent back, at the head of a Marine Combat Patrol, to the original Alien planet, where a load of colonials have mysteriously gone AWOL No prizes for guessing what will happen: it's Marines versus Aliens, lots of them, with some added refinements such as Ripley's newly discovered maternal instinct, and another one of those androids being sneakily passed off as an ordinary crew member. One helluva roller-coaster ride. AB

Alien³

(David Fincher, 1992, US) Sigourney Weaver, Charles S Dutton, Charles Dance, Paul McGann, Brian Glover, Ralph Brown, Danny Webb.
115 min.

Aliens, a great action movie, cheapened the original by replacing one hyper-intelligent, indestructible monster with an army of gormless critters. This third entry has only one creature, but unfortunately it's just as gormless. When Ripley (Weaver) crash-lands on a prison planet full of hard-nut slap-heads, they haven't seen a woman in years. Discovering that there's an alien loose, Ripley asks the warden to break out the guns, and can't believe it when she is told there aren't any. Nor can we. Good acting has salvaged many a poor script in the past, but not here. Dance is slaughtered in the first act, as is the regulation bastard warden (Glover), leaving only Sigourney, impressive as ever, and a motley cast of extras. Though wasteful of the expensive sets, Fincher's tight close-ups do add to the sense of claustrophobic panic. DW

Alien Nation

(Graham Baker, 1988, US) James Caan, Mandy Patinkin, Terence Stamp, Kevin Major Howard, Leslie Bevins, Peter Jason.
90 min.

Patinkin plays a member of an alien community which, having crash-landed in the Mojave Desert some years earlier, has now established itself in California. The aliens are called 'newcomers' by those who like them, 'slags' by those who don't. Hard-nosed cop Caan is one who doesn't, since his partner got blown away by a newcomer robbery gang; he nevertheless volunteers to take on the inexperienced Patinkin as his partner, figuring to use the alien's inside knowledge to find the killer. Their investigations lead to ruthless businessman Stamp, another newcomer who seems to be the brains behind a drugs operation. Played hard and fast, the film might just have worked, but the decision to soft-pedal the violence merely emphasises the obviousness of the liberal point-scoring (parallels with Vietnamese or Nicaraguan refugees are so facile as to be crass). Worthy, predictable, and dull. NF

Alien Resurrection

(Jean-Pierre Jeunet, 1997, US) Sigourney Weaver, Winona Ryder, Dominique Pinon, Ron Perlman, Michael Wincott, Kim Flowers, Dan Hedaya, JE Freeman, Brad Dourif.
109 min.

Two hundred years after her suicide, Ellen Ripley's cloned by scientists intent on nurturing the alien foetus inside her. The new Ripley couldn't care less – she's dead already – but goes along for the ride when Call (Ryder) and a band of marooned space pirates fight the inevitable rearguard action. In outline, the resilient Alien movies may be little more than slasher movies in space, yet equipped with strong, imaginative directors, each has proved distinctive and surprisingly resonant. Jeunet, the series' supreme fantasist, plunges deep into the nightmarish genetic whirlpool concocted by screenwriter Joss Whedon. After an ominous, memorably ghoulish opening, however, the Frenchman can't disguise a lack of engagement with the action sequences. The laziest stuff is all linear, mechanical business, much of it concerning Ryder, inadequate in a role designed simply to guarantee the teenage male fan-base. With her deep-freeze intensity and sinewy self-sufficiency, Weaver needs no such back-up. Choking as she comes face to face with earlier, aborted clones, grappling with residual maternal feelings towards the monsters she's long since left behind, Ripley Mk II is a terrifyingly ambivalent millennial saviour, more frightening than a score of aliens. TCh

Alien Thunder (aka Dan Candy's Law)

(Claude Fournier, 1973, Can) Donald Sutherland, Chief Dan George, Kevin McCarthy, Jean Duceppe, Jack Creely.
90 min.

Traditionally obsessive pursuit movie, with Sutherland living up to the Mounties' motto as he tracks an Indian murder suspect across both the impressive landscape and the cultural divide. Québécois director Fournier was formerly a vérité documentarist with both the National Film Board and the New York-based Leacock/Pennebaker axis. PT

Alive

(Frank Marshall, 1992, US) Ethan Hawke, Vincent Spano, Josh Hamilton, Bruce Ramsay, John Haymes Newton, David Kriegel, Kevin Breznahan, John Malkovich.
127 min.

1972: a plane crashes in the Andes. Despite subzero temperatures and scarce supplies, the survivors hold out for a rescue party. On the eighth day, they hear a radio report: they've been given up for dead. Little by little, the unthinkable becomes unavoidable. If they are to survive, they must cannibalise the corpses frozen in ice. In adapting Piers Paul Read's account of the Andes air disaster, Marshall and screenwriter John Patrick Shanley address any moral squeamishness head-on: in this do-or-die situation, they insist, the greater sin would be to die. It's not quite fair to say that this is the first tasteful cannibalism picture (the crash itself is a tour de force, and the camera never shies away from the meat of the matter), but this spiritual disaster movie does sometimes feel like a papal injunction. Within 30 seconds we're in the presence of God – or at least bearded John Malkovich is musing to that effect. Rosaries, prayers and carols are never far away after that,

and over the end credits Aaron Neville lets fly with Ave Maria. Skilfully crafted and doggedly performed, the film pushes too hard and too far; it strives for the inspirational but falls well short of inspired. TCh

Alive and Kicking (aka Indian Summer)

(Nancy Meckler, 1996, GB) Jason Flemyng, Antony Sher, Dorothy Tutin, Anthony Higgins, Bill Nighy, Philip Voss, Diane Parish.
99 min.

Tonio (Flemyng) is the leading light of the Ballet Luna, and probably the last: with its ranks decimated by AIDS, and Luna (Tutin) going down with Alzheimer's, the company is in an advanced stage of disrepair. Offered the lead in a valedictory production of an old success, 'Indian Summer', Tonio throws himself into the part. It could be the chance of a lifetime, because he too has AIDS; then again, perhaps the hard work is also an evasion – isolated, confused and emotionally disoriented, he's already accepted the virus as a death sentence on his love life. Then he meets Jack (Sher), HIV-negative, but interested, despite Tonio's rebuffs. How better to extend one's horizons than a relationship with a dumpy, balding older man who can't dance? This remains solidly in the tradition of gritty British realism, resolutely unglamorous and looking always rather TV-bound. However, Martin Sherman's script, adapted from his stage play, is cogent and witty, and steers clear of the downbeat worthiness of the AIDS-drama ghetto towards the more invigorating realms of contemporary gay courtship. NB

All About Eve 100

(Joseph L Mankiewicz, 1950 US) Bette Davis, Anne Baxter, George Sanders, Celeste Holm, Thelma Ritter, Marilyn Monroe.
138 min.

Davis plays the successful actress, ageing and fundamentally insecure, who employs Baxter in exchange for her flattery. From there the scheming Baxter connives her way to the top at the expense of her employer, who realises what is happening but is powerless to do anything. Mankiewicz's bitchy screenplay makes the most of the situation, being both witty and intelligent. The young Monroe gets to have a stairway entrance (introduced by cynical critic Sanders as a 'graduate of the Copacabana school of acting').

All At Sea

See Barnacle Bill

All Creatures Great and Small

(Claude Whatham, 1974, GB) Simon Ward, Anthony Hopkins, Lisa Harrow, Brian Stirner, Freddie Jones, TP McKenna, Brenda Bruce.
92 min.

Complacently 'charming' compendium of incidentals from the early years of vet James Herriot's Yorkshire tenure. Herriot's books later found a natural home in a TV series. PT

All Dogs Go to Heaven

(Don Bluth, 1989, Eire) voices: Burt Reynolds, Vic Tayback, Judith Barsi, Dom De Luise, Loni Anderson.
85 min.

This animated feature from Bluth, who left Disney in 1979 to develop his own inimitably kinetic brand of animation, is a seriously flawed piece shot through with teasing glimpses of excellence. After escaping from a New Orleans dog pound, German Shepherd Charlie B Barkin (voice by Burt Reynolds) and psychotic side kick Itchy (De Luise) high-tail it to ex-partner Carface (Tayback), a casino-owning pit bull. Double-crossed by Carface, finding himself at the pearly gates without a good deed to his name, Charlie tricks his way back to earth, and liberates a young girl from Carface, who uses her ability to talk to animals to predict race-winners. The usual rompery ensues, as Charlie and Itchy exploit, then grow to love, the multi-lingual cutie. The most obvious disappointment is the songs (courtesy of Charles Strouse and TJ Kuenster), which are strikingly unmemorable, a situation worsened by Reynolds' vocal inadequacies. More worryingly, something seems to have gone seriously wrong in the editing, so that the establishment of character and scene is frequently confused. The animation is fine, but flashy visuals hardly paste over the gaping inconsistencies. MK

Allegro Non Troppo

(Bruno Bozzetto, 1977, It)
85 min.
An animated feature parodying *Fantasia* which is sufficiently inventive to hold its own. By sticking to short popular classics and allowing different animators to interpret each one, what it loses in thematic unity and sustained trajectory it makes up for in wit, variety and even, once or twice, a fine controlling intelligence. Occasionally *kitsch* intrudes, and the interpretations remain too single-mindedly literal to allow impressionistic flights that the music might deserve, but overall very amiable, quirky fun. *Allegro*, in fact, but *non troppo*. CPea

All Fall Down

(John Frankenheimer, 1962, US) Warren Beatty, Eva Marie Saint, Karl Malden, Angela Lansbury, Brandon de Wilde.
110 min. b/w.
Drawling his way round William Inge's dialogue with methodical surliness while lumbered with a Christian name – Berry-Berry – which sounds more like a disease, Beatty is the epitome of itchy, preening 'rebellion' in this marvellously silly hothouse melodrama of familial angst. In the '50s there would have been a toss-up over James Leo Herlihy's source novel becoming either a Kazan movie or a Golden Age tele-drama, but MGM accommodated that decade's slow fade by letting TV graduate Frankenheimer direct it as if remaking *East of Eden*. Lansbury and Malden head the gallery of grotesques, while de Wilde's young eyes gradually narrow in disillusion over older brother Beatty's posturing antics. PT

All I Desire

(Douglas Sirk, 1953, US) Barbara Stanwyck, Richard Carlson, Lyle Bettger, Maureen O'Sullivan, Lori Nelson.
79 min. b/w.
There are things wrong with *All I Desire*, but Sirk isn't responsible for them. It didn't need the forced 'happy ending' for a start, and it should clearly have been made in colour. But Hollywood producers were even more stupid in 1953 than they are now, and directors didn't often get their way. Sirk was less compromised than most, because his strategy was a kind of 'hidden' subversion of genres like musicals and weepies: appearing to deliver the producer's goods, and simultaneously undercutting them. Here, the excellent Stanwyck plays an actress who hasn't made the grade, returning to the small-town family she walked out on after a scandalous affair with a local stud. She moves from one 'imitation of life' to another: from life-on-the-run in showbiz to life-under-wraps in Hicksville, Wisconsin. Sirk's delineation of the manners and 'morality' of bourgeois middle America is devastating; and the precision with which he dissects the repressions, jealousies and joys that permeate a family has never been rivalled. TR

Alligator

(Lewis Teague, 1980, US) Robert Forster, Robin Riker, Michael Gazzo, Dean Jagger, Perry Lang, Henry Silva, Jack Carter.
94 min.
Ramon, the eponymous star, is flushed down the pan as a baby, grows to an inordinate size by feeding on the corpses of pets used in hormone experiments (plus the odd sewer worker), and finally hits the streets looking for food and action. The basic angle to John Sayles' script (dubious scientific research leading to a dangerous freak of nature) is a reworking of his 1978 *Piranha*, but the sense of humour, narrative economy and attention to character are as sharp and fresh as you could wish. No prizes for guessing that Ramon finally devours the shady hand that unwittingly fed him, or that the cop on his tail literally blows the lid off his own guilt problems, but Sayles and Teague never stint on incidental pleasures. The result is an effective and unpretentious treat. SJ

Alligator Eyes

(John Feldman, 1990, US) Annabelle Larsen, Roger Cabler, Allen McCullough, Mary McLaine.
90 min.

Three old college friends, Lance, Robbie and Marjorie, go on a driving holiday together. Everything goes smoothly – Lance and Marjorie reviving their youthful affair, Robbie rediscovering the bottle – until they pick up a beautiful blind hitchhiker, Pauline. Using her blindness and her body, Pauline drives a wedge between the three buddies, and then draws them into her obsessive quest to find the man who murdered her parents. An impressive psycho-thriller, and although the pace flags at times, the central enigma of Pauline's motivation is enough to keep you guessing. NKe

All I Want for Christmas

(Robert Lieberman, 1991, US) Leslie Nielsen, Lauren Bacall, Harley Jane Kozak, Jamey Sheridan, Ethan Randall, Kevin Nealon, Thora Birch, Amy Oberer.
92 min.
Take one street-wise adolescent (Randall), an infuriatingly precocious younger sister (Birch), a wish for Santa to bring their divorced parents back together, and stir. Throw in a couple of big names, like Lauren Bacall as Granny and Leslie Nielsen as Santa; add juvenile love interest, and *voilà!*, the perfect Christmas turkey. This is family fare for the '90s at its most shameless and formulaic. What makes the film so nauseating is not that it's badly acted or made, but that its motives are presented with such sledgehammer subtlety that even the youngest children would feel insulted by it. NKe

All Men Are Mortal

(Ate de Jong, 1995, GB/Neth/Fr) Irène Jacob, Stephen Rea, Colin Salmon, Marianne Sägebrecht, Maggie O'Neill, Steve Nicolson, Chiara Mastroianni.
91 min.
WWII is over and Regina (Jacob) is the uncrowned queen of the Parisian stage, her avant-garde Hamlet the toast of the town. It's not enough: she lusts after immortality. Thus she falls under the spell of Fosca (Rea), an anti-social derelict who claims to be 700 years old. Could she live forever in his memory? Whatever its own merits, Simone de Beauvoir's 1946 novel emerges as a pretentious farrago in this clumsily literal Dutch English-language production. As a romance, it never gets close to the heart. Quite what the narcissistic Regina sees in the near-comatose Fosca is impossible to divine – and his own motives are no clearer. In any case, we don't care about either of them. Nor are Fosca's low-budget flashbacks to centuries past particularly impressive; any con-man worth his salt could contrive his supposedly death-defying stunts. Rea is terrible, morosely confining his acting to the eyebrows and up, but at least he's supposed to be mired in ennui – Fosca has seen it all – whereas Jacob is stuck with the thankless role of Europe's greatest actress, and in English. Perhaps Kieslowski might have made us believe it, but de Jong (*Drop Dead Fred*) is not quite in that league. TCh

All My Good Countrymen (Vsichni Dobri Rodaci/aka All Good Citizens)

(Voytech Jasny, 1968, Czech) Radoslav Brozobohaty, Vlastimil Brodsky, Vladimir Mensik, Draholslava Hofman.
126 min.
Jasny, a leading light in the new wave of Czech film-makers since the late '50s, won best director at Cannes in 1969 for this kaleidoscopic portrait of a Moldavian village over the twenty-odd years since the end of WWII. The significant deaths of sundry community members throughout that time punctuate a bitter-sweet, affectionate and pointed picture of a life many Czechs would have recognised. A key film from the 'Prague Spring', it was banned in Czechoslovakia soon after the news broke of its Cannes award. TJ

Allnighter, The

(Tamar Simon Hoffs, 1987, US) Susanna Hoffs, Dedee Pfeiffer, Joan Cusack, Michael Ontkean, John Terlesky, Pam Grier.
108 min.
Dreary, misconceived sorority drama, charting the romantic adventures of its three female leads as student days come to an end. Hoffs the director is mother of Hoffs the star, but this particular project could have done with a lot more family planning. GM

All Night Long

(Jean-Claude Tramont, 1981, US) Gene Hackman, Barbra Streisand, Diane Ladd, Dennis Quaid, William Daniels.
88 min.
Intermittently engaging comedy, with Hackman as a frustrated executive who chucks up his job and family after meeting a kooky suburban sexpot (Streisand, natch), hopefully setting up his own workshop in a converted warehouse. Its dropout theme is rather too tritely familiar to generate much enthusiasm. TM

All Night Long

see Toute une Nuit

All of Me

(Carl Reiner, 1984, US) Steve Martin, Lily Tomlin, Victoria Tennant, Madolyn Smith, Dana Elcar, Jason Bernard.
93 min.
When wealthy heiress Tomlin dies, something goes awry with her guru's transcendental arrangements and her soul passes into Martin, or at least into one half of his body. The gag of gender-switching is not new, but here for the first time is an internal sex war on numerous levels, not the least being a woman discovering the extreme peculiarities that constitute male behaviour. Martin is his usual combination of flat cynicism and crazed childishness, indulging in some inspired Jerry Lewis-like clowning with his arms and legs hopelessly out of synch. And there are gems from a blind black sax player (Bernard). CPea

Allonsanfan

(Paolo Taviani/Vittorio Taviani, 1974, It) Marcello Mastroianni, Lea Massari, Mimsy Farmer, Laura Betti, Bruno Cirino.
111 min.
A film with an even greater thrust of excitement than the Tavianis' subsequent *Padre Padrone*. Mastroianni, at his most convincingly dissolute, plays a spineless aristocrat who wanders through Italy in 1816 trying to rub out his past association with a radical group, without daring to tell them he's lost their faith in Napoleonic revolution. The tangled and sumptuously melodramatic plot allows the Tavianis to lay into left-wing idealism and gullibility without departing from their own commitment for a second. Ennio Morricone's score tops a rousing and passionate entertainment. TR

All Over Me

(Alex Sichel, 1997, US) Alison Folland, Tara Subkoff, Cole Hauser, Wilson Cruz, Pat Briggs, Leisha Hailey.
90 min.
A sincere rites-of-passage movie from two first-timers (Alex Sichel directing, and sister Sylvia writing). Fifteen-year-old Claude (Folland) is loyal to her better-looking best friend Ellen (Subkoff, affecting), despite the latter's self-destructive, sex 'n' drug liaison with aggressive homophobic arsehole Mark (Hauser), who may have been involved in the sadistic murder of a gay Hell's Kitchen neighbour. It's the last day of school and as adult life beckons unenticingly, the girls' intimacy crosses over to the sexual. Music scene debutantes (Briggs from Psychotica, Hailey from the Murmurs as Claude's lesbian friend) perform impressively, but Folland is the stand-out. She doesn't overplay her teenage confusion, carries scenes with expressive looks when the script – the film's big let-down – lapses, and gears up credibly when her character's courage and assertiveness come into play. Joe DeSalvo shoots the interiors and NY streets in harmony with the movie's desultory mood, and there's a sensitive score by Miki Navazio. WH

All Quiet on the Western Front

(Lewis Milestone, 1930, US) Lew Ayres, Louis Wolheim, John Wray, Slim Summerville, Russell Gleason, Ben Alexander.
138 min. b/w.
Based on Erich Maria Remarque's pacifist novel and renowned as *the* classic anti-war movie – it details the slow but steady extermination of a group of idealistic young German soldiers in World War I – the film's strength now derives less from its admittedly powerful but highly sim-

plistic utterances about war as waste, than from a generally excellent set of performances (Ayres especially) and an almost total reluctance to follow normal plot structure. It is in fact the often relentless depiction of unflagging warfare and suffering that eventually pummels one into *feeling*, rather than understanding, the film's message. GA

All Quiet on the Western Front

(Delbert Mann, 1980, US/GB) Richard Thomas, Ernest Borgnine, Donald Pleasence, Ian Holm, Patricia Neal.
158 min.
A horrible instance of international packaging (past-master Lew Grade naturally got a finger in the pie) that has all the excitement of a financial balance sheet. Remarque's classic novel resists the attempts, signposted by the American presence of Thomas and Borgnine in the World War I German trenches, to make it 'relevant' to post-Vietnam. The desperate substitution of a twittering bird for the famous butterfly at the climax marks the extent to which the 1930 version remains a Milestone around director Delbert Mann's neck. Originally shown on American TV in three segments – though made as a feature film – it was cut by almost half-an-hour for release in Britain. PT

All-Round Reduced Personality – Redupers, The (Die allseitig reduzierte Persönlichkeit – Redupers)

(Helke Sander, 1977, WGer) Helke Sander, Joachim Baumann, Andrea Malkowsky, Ronny Tanner.
98 min. b/w.
Directing her first feature from her own script, Sander – a founder of the German Women's movement – also stars as an unmarried mother and freelance photographer in West Berlin, obsessed with interpreting both The Wall which separates her from the well-rounded socialists back East, and the equally divisive social structures which prevent her from uniting her different abilities in a single coherent life. A brilliant achievement: personal, political, witty, sad and rigorously dialectical. JD.

All's Fair

(Rocky Lane, 1989, US) George Segal, Sally Kellerman, Robert Carradine, Jennifer Edwards, Lou Ferrigno.
89 min.
A dreary unfunny mess that follows a group of businessmen's wives who organise mock war games at the weekend to show their high-powered husbands they know a thing about the competitive spirit too. It didn't make it to UK cinemas, fortunately, but there is a surprise happy ending (see *Flirting with Disaster*). TJ

All Stars

(Jean van de Velde, 1997, Neth) Anthonie Kamerling, Danny de Munck, Paul Muller, Isa Hoes.
112 min.
Every week, come rain or shine, seven childhood friends, now in their late 20s, play football. Their Sunday get-togethers are threatened by the pressures of work and relationships, but they're determined to finish their 500th match before disbanding. This amiable rites-of-passage yarn, a hit in Holland, captures both the immaturity and idealism of its soccer-crazy characters. Although they don't want to grow up, adult responsibilities are crowding in. There's a wry, self-deprecating humour to the storytelling. The screenplay touches all the usual bases – one player is gay, one has a pregnant girlfriend, another has a disabled father – but sensitive direction combined with engaging performances from a cast of well-known Dutch TV actors ensures a freshness and delicacy which most sports movies miss by a mile. GM

All That Heaven Allows `100`

(Douglas Sirk, 1955, US) Jane Wyman, Rock Hudson, Agnes Moorehead, Conrad Nagel, Virginia Grey, Charles Drake.
89 min.
On the surface a glossy tearjerker about the problems besetting a love affair between an attractive middle class widow and her younger, 'bohemian' gardener, Sirk's film is in fact a scathing attack on all those facets of the American Dream widely held dear. Wealth produces snobbery and intolerance; family togetherness creates xenophobia and the cult of the dead; cosy kindness can be stultifyingly patronising; and materialism results in alienation from natural feelings. Beneath the stunningly lovely visuals – all expressionist colours, reflections, and frames-within-frames, used to produce a precise symbolism – lies a kernel of terrifying despair created by lives dedicated to respectability and security, given its most harrowing expression when Wyman, having given up her affair with Hudson in order to protect her children from gossip, is presented with a television set as a replacement companion. Hardly surprising that Fassbinder chose to remake the film as *Fear Eats the Soul*. GA

All That Jazz

(Bob Fosse, 1979, US) Roy Scheider, Jessica Lange, Ann Reinking, Leland Palmer, Cliff Gorman.
123 min.
Apparently Bob Fosse thought it 'foolish' to call *All That Jazz* self-indulgent. But he did direct, choreograph and co-write this musical comedy; it's about his life; it's very pleased with itself. As translated onto screen, his story has been created in the cutting-room and have lost any sense of fun; Fellini-esque moments add little but pretension; and scenes of a real open-heart operation, alternating with footage of a symbolic Angel of Death in veil and white gloves, fail even in terms of the surreal. HM

All That Money Can Buy (aka The Devil and Daniel Webster/Daniel and the Devil)

(William Dieterle, 1941, US) Walter Huston, Edward Arnold, James Craig, Jane Darwell, Gene Lockhart, Simone Simon, Anne Shirley.
112 min. b/w.
A fascinating version of the Faust legend adapted from Stephen Vincent Benet's short story. Craig is the poor New Hampshire farmer in the 1840s driven to such straits that he swears he'd sell his soul for two cents, and up pops Mr Scratch (Huston in a wonderful personification of the devil of New England folklore). A rapid rise to fame and fortune follows, with Mr Scratch's handmaiden (the delightful Simon) temptingly on hand. Things get a little portentously patriotic when the seven years are up, Craig elects to have the famous orator/politican Daniel Webster (Arnold) defend him against Mr Scratch's claim for his soul, and Mr Scratch counters by summoning famous villains from history as judge and jury. But it all looks terrific, directed by Dieterle in his best expressionist mood, with superb sets (Van Nest Polglase), score (Bernard Herrmann), camerawork (the great Joe August), and a township that looks as if it came straight out of a Grant Wood painting. *Daniel and the Devil* is a cut version running 85 mins. TM

All the King's Men

(Robert Rossen, 1949, US) Broderick Crawford, Joanne Dru, John Ireland, Mercedes McCambridge, John Derek, Shepperd Strudwick, Anne Seymour.
109 min. b/w.
A fine adaptation of Robert Penn Warren's Pulitzer novel, chronicling the rise and fall of Southern demagogue Willie Stark (Crawford), a thinly disguised portrait of Huey Long, the Louisiana state governor and US senator whose career – a fine record of civic improvment turned to ashes by an uncontrollable greed for power – was ended by assassination in 1935. The thesis is basically that power corrupts, with Stark presented as a man who starts out with a burning sense of purpose and a defiant honesty. Rossen, however, injects a note of ambiguity early on (a scene where Willie impatiently shrugs off his wife's dream of the great and good things he is destined to accomplish); and the doubt as to what he is *really* after is beautifully orchestrated by being filtered through the eyes of the press agent (Ireland) who serves as the film's narrator, and whose admiration for Stark gradually becomes tempered by understanding. Given that Stark's relationship with his son builds latterly to some overheated melodrama, the first half of the film is by far the best, but Rossen retains his grip throughout; and the performances (Crawford, Ireland and McCambridge especially) are superb. TM

All the Marbles (aka The California Dolls)

(Robert Aldrich, 1981, US) Peter Falk, Vicki Frederick, Laurene Landon, Burt Young, Tracy Reed, Richard Jaeckel.
113 min.
Aldrich's last film, a sad summation of his attempts to gauge his contemporary audience, turns out an intermittently hilarious but generally compromised mix of '50s introspection and '70s grand-standing (last pulled off coherently in *The Mean Machine*). With Falk as manager of a female tag wrestling duo, graduating via broad road movie conventions from the steel town small halls to the MGM Grand Hotel in Reno for a championship bout, it slips in and out of styles and stylisations as if trying on each for size or for laughs, maintaining a tenuous integrity only through its director's self-deprecating self-consciousness. PT

All the President's Men

(Alan J Pakula, 1976, US) Dustin Hoffman, Robert Redford, Jack Warden, Martin Balsam, Hal Holbrook, Jason Robards.
138 min.
Inevitably softened by hints of self-congratulation concerning the success of Woodward and Bernstein's uncovering of the Watergate affair, Pakula's film is nevertheless remarkably intelligent, working both as an effective thriller (even though we know the outcome of their investigations) and as a virtually abstract charting of the dark corridors of corruption and power. Pakula's visual set-ups are often extraordinary, contrasting the light of the *Washington Post* newsroom with the shadows in which hides star informant Deep Throat, and dramatically engulfing Hoffman and Redford in monumental buildings to stress the enormity of their task. GA

All the Right Moves

(Michael Chapman, 1983, US) Tom Cruise, Craig T Nelson, Lea Thompson, Charles Cioffi, Christopher Penn, Paul Carafotes.
91 min.
Passable teen/sports movie, with a youthful Tom Cruise gunning for a football scholarship to get out of the grey Pennsylvania milltown where he lives. Chapman – who is better known as a cinematographer – aims for naturalism and sometimes gets it from his young cast (Lea Thompson makes a strong impression for once), but the script draws too heavily on the crowd-pleasing tactics of *An Officer and a Gentleman* and its ilk to stand apart. TCh

All This and Heaven Too

(Anatole Litvak, 1940, US) Charles Boyer, Bette Davis, Barbara O'Neil, Virginia Weidler, Jeffrey Lynn, Henry Daniell.
143 min. b/w.
Davis in relatively subdued form as a governess accused of having an affair with a married nobleman (Boyer) in 19th century France, and of aiding and abetting in the murder of his neurotically jealous wife (O'Neil). Telling her innocent story in flashback to a class of American schoolchildren who have recognised her as a notorious woman, she is eventually rewarded by their sympathy and understanding. Adapted from a bestseller by Rachel Field: a pretty long, gloomy haul, though lavishly mounted (with photography by Ernest Haller) and sensitively acted. GA

All This and Money Too

see Love Is a Ball

All This and World War II

(Susan Winslow, 1976, US) The Bee Gees, Bryan Ferry, David Essex, Peter Gabriel, Frankie Laine, Status Quo.
88 min. b/w & col.
Unbelievably stupid idea of setting archive footage of the years before and during World War II to the music of the Beatles, performed by an insane assortment of singers accompanied by the

London Symphony Orchestra and the Royal Philharmonic. The connections made ('The Fool on the Hill' accompanying shots of Hitler at his mountain retreat in Berchtesgaden) are crushingly crass. GA

All Through the Night

(Vincent Sherman, 1942, US) Humphrey Bogart, Conrad Veidt, Peter Lorre, Judith Anderson, Karen Verne, William Demarest.
107 min. b/w.
Lively if unremarkable Warners comedy thriller with Bogart as a wisecracking New York gambler taking on Veidt's Nazi fifth columnists, who are planning to sabotage a battleship anchored in the harbour. Shades of Runyon in the brisk banter as Bogart rallies his underworld troops, and strong acting from a superb cast (that goes on to include Jane Darwell, Jackie Gleason, Phil Silvers, Frank McHugh, Barton MacLane and Martin Kosleck) make it more than watchable, though both propaganda and direction are less than inspired. GA

All Visitors Must Be Announced

(Dree Andrea, 1996, Neth)
78 min.
This profile of three New York City doormen admits us to a shadowy, purgatorial world. The doormen are gatekeepers for the rich folk of the apartment blocks they look after. They check the mail, receive parcels, allow pizza deliveries, and sometimes even help their married clients with illicit affairs. Unfortunately, the qualities which suit the doormen to their job – they're stoical, phlegmatic types – don't make them exciting subjects for a film. Despite the observational detail, the documentary is short on the adrenalin you might expect from a film set in the heart of the city. GM

Alma Gitana

see Gypsy Soul

Almonds and Raisins

(Russ Karel, 1983, GB)
90 min. b/w.
When *The Jazz Singer* broke the sound barrier in 1927, Jewish immigrants in New York were astounded to hear the Jewish hero talking to his momma in English rather than Yiddish; but they could identify with the tragedy of Jolson's singer realising the American dream only by going off with a shiksa and sacrificing his racial identity. Post-talkie and pre-World War II, about 300 Yiddish movies were made: Manhattan-set melodramas, nostalgic tales of the old stetl, even a Western. With sherry-ripe voice-over purred by Orson Welles, this compilation stitches together snips from such meisterworks as *Mottl der Operator*, *Where Is My Child?* and *Uncle Moses*, intercut with talking heads of some of the participants. Like scenes from a soap opera awash with sentimental strings, reality rubs shoulders with schmaltz. A fascinating peek into the rituals and obsessions of a close-knit culture. AB

Almost an Angel

(John Cornell, 1990, US) Paul Hogan, Elias Koteas, Linda Kozlowski, Doreen Lang, Robert Sutton, Travis Venable, Douglas Seale, Ruth Warshawsky, Parley Baer, Ben Slack, Charlton Heston.
95 min.
Saving a youngster from a road accident, rough-diamond ex-con Terry Dean (Hogan) is knocked into oblivion. He hallucinates an audience with God (Heston), who refuses him entry to paradise on the grounds that he's a scumbag, sending him back to earth as a probationary angel. So far so good, as Hogan runs through his innocent abroad routine, calling God 'your honour', holding up foodstores for the poor, and attempting to fathom the extent of his imagined angelic powers ('I'm bullet-proof', he tells a bemused clergyman, 'but I can't fly yet'). Things take a nosedive, however, when he teams up with irritating do-gooder Rose (Kozlowski) and her invalid brother (Koteas), and Hogan's script ploughs into the realms of pseudo-serious philosophising. Aided and abetted by Cornell's limp direction, a hideously self-congratulatory catalogue of 'tender' set pieces ensues, revealing that Hogan is (surprise, surprise) the most wonderful, loving, caring person alive – or indeed dead. Almost a turkey. MK

Almost Perfect Affair, An

(Michael Ritchie, 1979, US) Keith Carradine, Monica Vitti, Raf Vallone, Christian De Sica, Dick Anthony Williams.
93 min.
Ritchie's last 'personal' (and, for that matter, interesting) movie before he went blandly commercial is, like his early work, a study in the ethics of competitive rivalry. Carradine (as fine as ever) plays a self-centred independent American film-maker who meets with cute Vitti during the Cannes Film Festival. How honest are his proclamations of love? Hard to tell, given that she is the wealthy ex-actress wife of Italian producer Vallone. A strangely disenchanted romantic comedy, the film impresses with its strong performances and its ambivalent attitude towards the emotional deceptions of its lovers, while there's a bonus for buffs in the in-jokes and documentary cameo-shots of various directors caught on location along the Croisette. GA

Almost Summer

(Martin Davidson, 1977, US) Bruno Kirby, Lee Purcell, John Friedrich, Didi Conn, Thomas Carter, Tim Matheson.
89 min.
Funny but airtight tale of student electioneering and crushes in Beach Boy/Beach Baby land, contemporary in setting but as backward-looking as *The Lords of Flatbush* (which Davidson co-directed). It's the same old 'Is There Life After High School?', lubricated by mesmerising visions of material privilege - sunshine, wheels, and no parents in sight. The performances are assured, the cutting slick, the whole story runs along with compulsive familiarity: Italian-style hustler runs an unknown candidate against super-popular ball-busting cheerleader. We gawp at harsh political realities (side order of irony here), naked ambition is eventually outclassed by immense personal integrity, and everyone gets partners at the prom. RP

Almost You

(Adam Brooks, 1984, US) Brooke Adams, Griffin Dunne, Karen Young, Marty Watt, Christine Estabrook, Josh Mostel.
97 min.
Erica (Adams) and Alex (Dunne) have reached a marital crisis, and when Erica breaks her hip, fickle, confused Alex finds himself attracted to her young nurse, Lisa. The tension is further aggravated by Lisa's actor-lover, whose fears impel him to introduce himself, incognito, to Alex with unexpected results. Brooks' first feature distinguishes itself from superficially similar romantic comedies by its tough, unsentimental tone. Though generous towards his characters' various anxieties and foibles, Brooks never shies away from their blinkered selfishness, or from the very real unhappiness caused by Alex's philandering ways. At the same time, the sense of pain is offset by often gorgeously observed comic moments. Assured and deliciously performed. GA

Aloha, Bobby and Rose

(Floyd Mutrux, 1975, US) Paul LeMat, Dianne Hull, Tim McIntire, Leigh French, Martine Bartlett, Robert Carradine.
89 min.
The same compulsive electric landscape of California as *American Graffiti*, but now it's a decade later and the snakes have got into the garden: LeMat (from *Graffiti*) and Hull play two disappointed fugitives from the '60s on the run after an accidental shooting. Mutrux achieves the same kind of dizzying skating-rink effect that Lucas managed in the earlier film, and gives it a vicious added edge by some unexpected juxtapositions: 'Locomotion' by Little Eva punctuates a terrifying slow-motion car accident. As the movie develops, the couple resemble human pinballs sliding back and forth among the cruelly compulsive lights and sounds. With little characterisation or depth, the plot doesn't finally add up to much more than a coda to *Graffiti*, but a sharply effective one. DP

Aloha Summer

(Tommy Lee Wallace, 1988, US) Chris Makepeace, Yuji Okumoto, Don Michael Paul, Tia Carrere, Andy Bumatai, Lorie Griffin.
98 min.
This predictable rites-of-passage picture, directed by a John Carpenter associate and set in the summer of '59 (the year Hawaii joined the US), follows Makepeace and the gang as they square up to the glorious local surf, confront racial prejudice, and overcome their timidity in the face of bikini-clad womenfolk (including future *Wayne's World* siren Tia Carrere). *Big Wednesday* it ain't. TJ

Aloma of the South Seas

(Alfred Santell, 1941, US) Dorothy Lamour, Jon Hall, Lynne Overman, Philip Reed, Katherine DeMille.
77 min.
Grin-and-bear-it melodrama of the Tropical Paradise variety, dismissed as routine nonsense even at the time. Lamour and Hall, reunited from Ford's *The Hurricane* four years earlier, mouth some unbelievable dialogue in aid of a story which manages to include the obligatory cataclysm (a volcano erupting) as part of the action. DMcG

Alone in the Dark

(Jack Sholder, 1982, US) Jack Palance, Donald Pleasence, Martin Landau, Dwight Schultz, Erland Van Lidth, Deborah Hedwall.
93 min.
'I guess I just prefer psychopaths...' smiles bug-eyed Donald Pleasence, director of the fashionably liberal 'Haven' mental institute. We've already seen what the psychopaths think of *him* in a pre-credit nightmare: he hangs his victims by the ankles and splits their personalities with a meat-cleaver through the crotch. There's a sharp sense of humour at work in this school-of-Carpenter siege movie, even if, for all its ironic observations on madness in American society, it never cuts free of genre routine. A citywide black-out lets out the 370lb child molester, crazed preacher, military hardnut and faceless 'nose-bleed killer,' to put the wimpish assistant director and his family through the suspense grinder; but with the strength of the cast (Landau, Palance) on the *outside*, the siege machine seems to have slipped a gear. RP

Alone on the Pacific (Taiheiyo Hitoribotchi)

(Kon Ichikawa, 1963, Jap) Yujiro Ishihara, Kinuyo Tanaka, Masayuki Mori, Ruriko Asaoko.
104 min.
Shot with Ichikawa's characteristically picturesque feel for the wide expanses of the 'Scope screen, this account of a yachtsman's solo trans-Pacific expedition – based on the real-life 94-day trip from Osaka to San Francisco undertaken by Kenichi Horie in 1962 – alleviates the potential tedium of its story by means of flashback inserts recalling the sailor's conflicts with a stern and disapproving family. Storms, sharks and solitude imperil his voyage, but the real drama is psychological and spiritual: the film is ultimately a celebration of Horie's determination to free himself from a society devoted to conformism and the negation of the needs of the individual. GA

Along Came Jones

(Stuart Heisler, 1945, US) Gary Cooper, Loretta Young, Dan Duryea, William Demarest, Frank Sully, Don Costello, Walter Sande, Russell Simpson, Willard Robertson, Ray Teal.
90 min. b/w.
Produced by Cooper himself, this comedy Western typecasts him as a mild-mannered wandering cowboy, given to bursts of song and hopelessly butter-fingered with a gun, who is mistaken for a dangerous outlaw (Duryea). Tickled by the respect that now attends him, Cooper soon finds himself in trouble, being manipulated by Duryea's childhood sweetheart (Young) until she has a change of heart, while assorted people try to kill him, bring him to justice, or beat him up in the hope of hijacking his loot. Scripted by Nunnally Johnson from a novel by Alan LeMay, the film demonstrates Johnson's belief that the writer is the *auteur* in cinema (the title even announces 'Nunnally Johnson's *Along Came Jones*'). Alas for illusions, but Stuart Heisler is clearly hamstrung by having to adhere to a muddled script which cries out for pruning, with more visualisation and less verbiage. The three stars do their thing adequately, but their supposed emotional cross-purposes come to grief on the strictly two-dimensional characterisations. Frequent resort to back-projected landscapes doesn't help, either. TM

Alors voilà,
see So there,

Alphabet Murders, The
(Frank Tashlin, 1965, GB) Tony Randall, Anita Ekberg, Robert Morley, Maurice Denham, Sheila Allen, Guy Rolfe.
90 min. b/w.
Adapted from *The A.B.C. Murders*, this won't please Agatha Christie purists, with Tashlin's cool eye for the grotesque appropriately spoofing a Hercule Poirot adventure in which the famous detective has to track down a lunatic who murders his victims alphabetically. Randall plays Poirot for laughs, but did he have any choice with both Morley and Ekberg around? DMacp

Alpha Caper, The (aka Inside Job)
(Robert Michael Lewis, 1973, US) Henry Fonda, Leonard Nimoy, James McEachin, Larry Hagman, Elena Verdugo, John Marley, Noah Beery.
85 min.
Senior citizen Fonda, forced to retire early from his job as parole officer, takes his revenge on the city officials by using his inside knowlege to rip off a mammoth gold shipment while it is being moved to a new depository. The film's success relies on the audience's complicity and the neatness of the robbery, plus a couple of good sequences thrown in as a bonus: a funeral next to a noisy freeway, an excruciating retirement party. Fonda's accomplices are rather Three Stoogish (though Larry Hagman's special cinematic special effects man is a nice idea), and the film too often betrays the limitations of its made-for-TV budget. Apart from an absurd epilogue, an undemandingly enjoyable support. CPe

Alphaville (Alphaville, Une Etrange Aventure de Lemmy Caution)
(Jean-Luc Godard, 1965, Fr/It) Eddie Constantine, Anna Karina, Howard Vernon, Akim Tamiroff, Laszlo Szabo.
98 min. b/w.
One of Godard's most sheerly enjoyable movies, a dazzling amalgam of *film noir* and science fiction in which tough gumshoe Lemmy Caution turns inter-galactic agent to re-enact the legend of Orpheus and Eurydice in conquering Alpha 60, the strange automated city from which such concepts as love and tenderness have been banished. As in Antonioni's *The Red Desert* (made the previous year), Godard's theme is alienation in a technological society, but his shotgun marriage between the poetry of legend and the irreverence of strip cartoons takes the film into entirely idiosyncratic areas. Not the least astonishing thing is the way Raoul Coutard's camera turns contemporary Paris into an icily dehumanised city of the future. TM

Alpine Fire (Höhenfeuer)
(Fredi M Murer, 1985, Switz) Thomas Nock, Johanna Lier, Dorothea Moritz, Rolf Illig, Tilli Breidenbach.
117 min.
The impact of Murer's film springs directly from its method: scrupulously detailed and naturalistic observation of a quite extraordinary reality. A family of four lives and farms in isolation near the top of a Swiss Alp. Their chief problem is a slightly retarded deaf-mute who is fast coming into puberty. In the time-honoured cure for frustrations, the father sets his son to building stone walls, as he himself did in his youth. But the boy's case is more extreme: he takes off up the mountain and builds his own small empire of fortresses, towers and phallic monuments. And when his teenage sister comes to bring him food, she stays the night with him... Murer's triumph is that he provides all the information without spelling anything out: he lets us discover these people and their relationships gradually. The tension between vision and voyeurism echoes the space between the tightness of the family and huge expanses of landscape they inhabit, pushing the film into the Surrealist key in which it finds its sublime, elegiac climax. TR

Al-Risalah (The Message/ Mohammad, Messenger of God)
(Moustapha Akkad, 1976, Leb) Anthony Quinn, Irene Papas, Michael Ansara, Johnny Sekka, Michael Forest, Damien Thomas.
182 min.
An epic which trades on the conventions of the Hollywood Christpic without quite living up to DeMille vulgarity. The historical parallels of the ascendancy of Islam with early Christianity are heavily stressed throughout: a persecuted minority gradually emerging victorious with large-scale conversions ; ideals of religious toleration; slave, female, and even camel liberation. Mohammad doesn't appear, and as a subjective presence (when he's there, the characters address the camera) he's mostly effective, sometimes clumsy as a narrative device. There's some fine widescreen desert location shooting, and a couple of fairish battles. All in all, a fair piece of Arab PR. RM

Alsino and the Condor (Alsino y el Condor)
(Miguel Littin, 1982, Nic/Cuba/Mex/CR) Alan Esquivel, Dean Stockwell, Carmen Bunster, Alejandro Parodi.
89 min.
Set against the almost unbelievable brutality of an internecine guerilla war (Nicaragua, 1979), a young boy's dream to fly like the birds seems almost commonplace. In his dreams Alsino can fly, but when he wakes up everything is somehow different. The delightful Esquivel brings to the title role a fragile passion around which the Chilean film-maker Littin conjures an archetypal South American world of enchantment (the grandmother and her chest of secrets, the prostitute and the bird man, familiar from the writings of García Márquez and others) which can absorb intrusive realities as easily as the ever-present verdant jungle. FD

Altered States
(Ken Russell, 1980, US) William Hurt, Blair Brown, Bob Balaban, Charles Haid, Thaao Penghlis.
102 min.
Based on a novel and a disowned script by the late Paddy Chayefsky, Russell's noisily grandiose swipe at psychedelia embellishes what is no more than the cosily familiar story of the obsessive Scientist Who Goes Too Far and Unwittingly Unleashes, etc. Harvard clever-dick (played with almost unconvincing solemnity by Hurt) blows his sensory deprivation experiments (with a little help from his friends and hallucinogenic drugs), and starts to regress – spectacularly – until he looks in serious danger of being sucked in down the cosmic lavatory pan into the big zilch. JS

Alternative Miss World, The
(Richard Gayor, 1980, GB) Andrew Logan, Divine, Luciana Martinez.
90 min.
Documentary about the 1978 final of this drag contest, a monumental folly inaugurated in 1972 by Andrew Logan. Director Gayor charts each step in the proceedings with sycophantic relish, from the marquee being erected on Clapham Common to the walk-around itself. But if you enjoy gossip column vitriol, showbiz decadence, and a particularly vacuous brand of performance art, this is your experience. IB

Alvin Purple
(Tim Burstall, 1973, Aust) Graeme Blundell, Abigail, Lynette Curran, Christine Amor, Dina Mann.
97 min.
Comedy about the sexual adventures of a clumsy, ordinary youth who nevertheless has a way with girls. It's pretty much what you'd expect from an Australian cinema enjoying its first phase of liberal censorship: an adolescent insistence on outraging 'decency' with a display of sundry organs, tits and bums; a story that could well have been written as they were going along; and jokes comprising a barrage of appalling *double entendres*. Ponderous at every level. CPe

Always
(Henry Jaglom, 1985, US) Patrice Townsend, Henry Jaglom, Joanna Frank, Alan Rachins, Bob Rafelson, Michael Emil, André Gregory.
105 min.
This is not only the story of the break-up of director Jaglom's marriage, it's also an undisguised attempt to put it back together again. Using the camera as a kind of confessional, he begins by telling how his ex-wife Townsend left him. Two years later, they meet on the eve of their divorce, and chew over what went wrong as friends arrive for a Fourth of July party. He plays himself, Townsend plays herself, and most of the cast are their real-life friends. Slow to start, and intermittently tedious until the house guests begin to arrive, the film is an honest look at a particular kind of contemporary Califorian relationship. Audiences will have no problem relating to the universal desire for love and affection, nor in identifying with Jaglom's predicament. What they might find difficult is actually liking any of the characters involved. CB

Always
(Steven Spielberg, 1989, US) Richard Dreyfuss, Holly Hunter, John Goodman, Brad Johnson, Audrey Hepburn, Roberts Blossom, Keith Davis, Ed Van Nuys.
123 min.
Spielberg here updates the plot of the WWII movie *A Guy Named Joe*, replacing fighter pilots with firefighters. Pilot Pete (Dreyfuss) and dispatcher Dorinda (Hunter) are a loving couple who share a dangerous profession. Dorinda's worst fears are confirmed when Pete dies a fiery death, but unseen to the human eye he reemerges on earth as a guiding spirit to a novice pilot (Johnson). Divested of wartime significance, this process is rationalised as for reasons of spiritual growth (the afterlife appears distinctly New Age as a green glade inhabited by a tranquil Audrey Hepburn). After an unpromising beginning, which conveys the couple's tediously arrogant exchanges, the film gathers force in its examination of grief and longing. Pete must oversee Dorinda's burgeoning affair with his trainee; she must overcome deep-seated despair at her lover's death. The bizarre nature of the conflict never lapses into absurdity, thanks largely to sound casting and a strong supporting performance from the ever-dependable John Goodman. Spielberg's confident direction is particularly effective in the aerial sequences, but he gets carried away in an overblown conclusion. CM

Always for Pleasure
(Les Blank, 1978, US) 'Kid Thomas', Valentine, Professor Longhair, The Wild Tchoupitoulas, Art Ryder's Electric Street Band, Harold Dejan's Olympian Jazz Band.
58 min.
Les Blank continues to map the USA's rich heritage of regional cultures, bringing to New Orleans street parades, jazz funerals, and the Mardi Gras itself, the same kind of effusively enthusiastic documentary sensibility that has turned portraits of the lifestyles surrounding blues, Cajun, and Tex-Mex music into full-blooded celebrations. Good-time film-making, ethnography with rhythm: the title says all you need to know about Blank's unique movie on the tributaries of rock'n'roll. PT

Alzire, or the New Continent (Alzire, oder der neue Kontinent)
(Thomas Koerfer, 1978, Switz) Rüdiger Vogeler, Verena Buss, François Simon, Roger Jendly.
97 min.
Koerfer made an extremely impressive debut with *Death of the Flea Circus Director*, a genuinely Brechtian entertainment, and then promptly fell into the trap of making prettified political historiography in his second feature *The Assistant*. He hauls himself back into the real world impressively with this film, which has odd twinges of Tanner-esque liberal conscience-stroking, but mainly reconciles its politics and its fiction interestingly. It deals with a ramshackle group of actors who struggle to resurrect a Voltaire play about the conquistadors. Their internal problems and their campaign for subsidy from the Swiss authorities are counterpointed with glimpses of Voltaire and Rousseau, still hammer-and-tonging each other after all these years. TR

Ama

(Kwesi Owusu/Kwate Nee-Owoo, 1991, GB)
Thomas Baptiste, Anima Misa, Roger
Griffiths, Nii Oma Hunter, Joy Elias-Rilwan,
Georgina Ackerman.
100 min.
This sets out to explore the themes and aesthetics of African cinema and traditional Akan storytelling in the context of contemporary Britain.
Babs Ababio (Baptiste) is a middle-aged
Ghanaian living in a London suburb with his
wife, boxer son Joe, and 12-year-old daughter
Ama (Ackerman). On a visit to the countryside,
Ama has a spiritual experience, from which she
brings away a golden floppy disc. She learns its
contents at the office cleaned by her mother. It's
a double warning from her ancestors: Babs will
die unless he returns to his homeland, Joe will be
paralysed if he boxes again. The women are
shocked, the men too stubborn to listen... *Ama* is
nothing less than an Afrocentric art film.
Unfortunately, for all its ambition and the
warmth of its playing, it works intermittently at
best. Ploddingly shot and eccentrically scripted,
it hits on a magical realism that is neither magical nor realistic. TCh

Amadeus ⁜⁜⁜

(Milos Forman, 1984, US) F Murray Abraham,
Tom Hulce, Elizabeth Berridge, Simon Callow,
Roy Dotrice.
160 min.
Antonio Salieri, one of the most competent composers of his age, finds himself in competition
with Mozart. This turns him into a hate-filled
monster whose only aim in life is to ruin his more
talented colleague. None the less Salieri emerges
as the more tragic and sympathetic character,
partly because he alone, of all his contemporaries,
can appreciate this almost perfect music, and –
more importantly, perhaps – because he speaks
up for all of us whose talents fall short of our
desires. The entire cast speaks in horribly intrusive American accents, but Forman makes some
perceptive connections between Mozart's life and
work. CS

Amant, L'
see Lover, The

Amantes
see Lovers

Amants, Les (The Lovers)

(Louis Malle, 1959, Fr) Jeanne Moreau, Alain
Cuny, José-Luis de Villalonga, Jean-Marc Bory.
88 min. b/w.
In Malle's second feature, he continued his association with new star Moreau in an (at the time)
controversial study of bourgeois emptiness and
sexual yearnings. She plays a chic, high society
wife with money, a daughter, smart friends and
a casual lover. Then one night, she makes passionate love with a young student of a few hours
acquaintance, and leaves it all for a new life. If
it now looks too much like an angry young sensualist's movie, the combination of highly pleasurable body language, Brahms on the
soundtrack, and the ravishing, velvety monochrome photography of Henri Decaë proves
hard to resist. The film established Moreau's
screen persona - commanding, wilful, sultry -
but it marked the stylistically-conscious Malle
apart from his more tearaway *nouvelle vague*
colleagues. DT

Amants de Vérone, Les
(The Lovers of Verona)

(André Cayatte, 1948, Fr) Pierre Brasseur,
Serge Reggiani, Anouk Aimée, Martine Carol,
Louis Salou, Marcel Dalio.
110 min. b/w.
Scripted, like *Les Enfants du Paradis*, by Jacques
Prévert, this is another homage to the acting profession. However, lacking the historical perspective of the earlier film, Cayatte's handling of the
story of two stand-ins for the stars of a film version of 'Romeo and Juliet', who slowly become the
roles they play, quickly degenerates into a simple tale of young love, despite beautiful sets and
atmospheric camerawork. Though set in Italy,
with the Fascist past contributing to the troubles
of the star-crossed lovers, it is interesting in retrospect as an indication of the mood of the post-
war, pre-New Wave French cinema. PH

Amants du Pont-Neuf, Les

(Léos Carax, 1991, Fr) Juliette Binoche, Denis
Lavant, Klaus-Michael Gruber, Daniel Buain,
Marion Statens, Edith Scob.
126 min.
Following a spell in a hostel for the homeless
after he is injured by a hit-and-run driver, fire-
eater Alex (Lavant) returns to his open-air home
on Paris's oldest bridge. There, besides his
drugs supplier Hans (Gruber), he finds a new
tenant: Michèle (Binoche), a middle-class art student who has taken to the streets for as long as
her failing sight holds. Tentatively, Alex and
Michèle embark on a drunken, anarchic, mutually healing affair – but she is haunted both by
the prospect of blindness and by a previous,
painful romance, while he is increasingly consumed by jealousy. Set against the extravagant
backdrop of France's bicentennial shenanigans,
Carax's tale of *amour fou* is even bolder than
Boy Meets Girl and *Mauvais Sang*. It's filled
with ecstatic imagery which manages not to jar
after the gritty realism of the early scenes, and
constitutes a heady anthem to abstracted, mad
passion: at once a modern fairy tale and a
cinephile's *folie de grandeur*, frequently exhilarating but never wholly free of pretentiousness.
GA

Amarcord ⁜⁜⁜

(Federico Fellini, 1973, It/Fr) Puppela Maggio,
Magali Noël, Armando Brancia, Ciccio
Ingrassia.
123 min.
Fellini at his ripest and loudest recreates a fan-
tasy-vision of his home town during the fascist
period. With generous helpings of soap opera and
burlesque, he generally gets his better effects by
orchestrating his colourful cast of characters
around the town square, on a boat outing, or at a
festive wedding. When he narrows his focus
down to individual groups, he usually limits himself to corny bathroom and bedroom jokes, which
produce the desired titters but little else. But
despite the ups and downs, it's still Fellini, which
has become an identifiable substance like salami
or pepperoni that can be sliced into at any point,
yielding pretty much the same general consistency and flavour. JR

Amateur

(Hal Hartley, 1994, Fr/GB) Isabelle Huppert,
Martin Donovan, Elina Löwensohn, Damian
Young, Chuck Montgomery, David Simonds.
105 min.
Hal Hartley's movie – his most accessible and
entertaining to date – starts with a man
(Donovan) waking in a New York gutter, head
bloodied, memory gone. Who is he? How did
he get there? Was he a kindly soul, or a violent man linked to the Mob? Certainly for
Isabelle (Huppert), an ex-nun and would-be
pornographer, who lets him recuperate in her
apartment, the latter seems to be true, particularly when a porn star (Löwensohn), a crazed
accountant and two hitmen begin to intrude
on their lives. A delightfully stylish and
skewed picture of sex, violence and love in
contemporary America, the film wears its
more serious concerns (guilt, responsibility,
exploitation, redemption) admirably lightly.
Huppert is especially good, conjuring up a
canny blend of hilarious melancholy and
unexpected eroticism which, incidentally, provides the film-maker with his most poignant
portrait yet of an ill-starred love affair. As
ever, Hartley regulars do sterling service,
while fine camerawork and plangent music
add to the movie's more sensual pleasures.
Enjoy. GA

Amateur, The

(Charles Jarrott, 1981, US) John Savage,
Christopher Plummer, Marthe Keller, Arthur
Hill, Nicholas Campbell, John Marley.
112 min.
From a compelling opening with all the sensational detachment of photojournalism - the random execution of a woman hostage by
international terrorists - this turns into a lumbering vehicle for woolly idealism, trite moralising, and gung-ho action as the dead woman's
boyfriend (a computer technologist) blackmails
his CIA employers into helping avenge the murder. Stock characterisation and dreadful dialogue
scarcely aid credibility. FD

Amazing Captain Nemo, The
(aka The Return of Captain
Nemo)

(Alex March, 1978, US) Jose Ferrer, Burgess
Meredith, Tom Hallick, Burr DeBenning,
Lynda Day George, Mel Ferrer, Horst
Buchholz.
103 min.
There's no peace for some fictional characters.
Just as Sherlock Holmes was given an extra lease
of life in the '40s to fight off the Nazi threat, so
Jules Verne's ascetic sea captain reappears (in a
feature cobbled from the TV series) in the form
of a white-bearded Ferrer and saves the free
world (ie America) from Meredith's mad
Professor Cunningham. You can gauge the level
of this appallingly witless nonsense by the names
given to the weapons Cunningham unleashes in
between sucking his spectacles and patting his
robot minions. They include 'delta beams', 'Z-
rays' and the horrendous 'Doomsday machine' –
this with seven writers credited, including Robert
Bloch. GB

Amazing Colossal
Man, The

(Bert I Gordon, 1957, US) Glenn Langan, Cathy
Downs, James Seay, Larry Thor.
80 min. b/w.
King Kong for the atomic age: US Army Colonel
Manning (MAN-ing) is exposed to radiation during a nuclear bomb test, mutates into a giant, and
is finally hunted down by his own army in this
ferocious cold-war fable, which spins Korea, the
army's obsessive secrecy, and America's post-
war growth into one fantastic whole. Above-average special effects are mixed with
quasi-documentary footage: armies on the move,
test houses under nuclear attack, the colonel's
skin shredding before our eyes under the blast.
A film of uncertain politics and scathing cynicism, in which a Bible is shown shrinking to
unreadable size in the giant's hand, and whose
climax features an attack on Las Vegas, dream-
city of the New America. CA

Amazing Doctor
Clitterhouse, The

(Anatole Litvak, 1938, US) Edward G
Robinson, Claire Trevor, Humphrey Bogart,
Allen Jenkins, Donald Crisp, Gale Page, Maxie
Rosenbloom.
87 min. b/w.
John Huston, at the outset of his screenwriting
career, helped to transfer Barre Lyndon's British
play from St John's Wood to Park Avenue. It's an
amusing anecdote about a psychiatrist whose
research for a book on the criminal psyche leads
him to burglary and murder (very *House of
Games*). The characterisations are all a bit heavy-
handed, but the denouement is a doozy, with the
doc in the dock desperately pleading the validity
of his work, even though that would make him
responsible for his actions in the eyes of the law.
TCh

Amazing Grace and Chuck
(aka Silent Voice)

(Mike Newell, 1987, US) Alex English, Joshua
Zuehlke, Gregory Peck, Jamie Lee Curtis,
William L Petersen, Frances Conroy.
115 min.
The concept that a 12-year-old Little League
pitcher from small-town Montana could force the
US and Soviet leaders to their knees, abjuring
nuclear weapons, would seem to indicate that
writer/producer David Field had been dropped
on his head. He must have remained persuasive,
however, since he got Newell to direct, and Peck
and Jamie Lee Curtis to star. Chuck (Zuehlke)
despairs after going on a school trip to a
Minuteman missile silo, and gives up baseball in
protest. Six-foot-seven basketball ace Amazing
Grace Smith (English) reads the item in the press
and comes out in sympathy, followed by most of
the world's sportsmen, who move into Amazing's
barn to coordinate the campaign. President Peck
is seldom off Chuck's lawn, confessing that 'this
job of mine can get a bit lonely', and offering limited reductions; but the button won't budge.
Puerile. BC

Amazing Mr Beecham, The

see Chiltern Hundreds, The.

Amazing Mr Blunden, The

(Lionel Jeffries, 1972, GB) Laurence Naismith, Lynne Frederick, Garry Miller, Rosalyn Landor, Marc Granger, Diana Dors, James Villiers.
99 min.
A fine adaptation of Antonia Barber's novel *The Ghosts*, which begins with a quiet nostalgia reminiscent of Jeffries' earlier *The Railway Children*: a cosy suburban house, a death, and then the miraculous translation of a widowed mother and her children to a cottage in the country. The translator is a friendly ghost (Naismith), and in the crumbling old mansion where their mother is now caretaker, James and Lucy are drawn into a strange adventure where they find themselves going back 100 years to save another brother and sister from being hounded to death for their money. Handled with that sense of enchanted stillness which is one of Jeffries' great gifts as a director, the apparitions, the apprehensions, and the atmosphere of brooding menace about the house are exquisitely done. TM

Amazing Stories

(Steven Spielberg/William Dear/Robert Zemeckis, 1987, US) Kevin Costner, Casey Siemaszko, Tom Harrison, Bronson Pinchot, Christopher Lloyd, Scott Coffey, Mary Stuart Masterson.
110 min.
Three short stories based in '50s comic book lore. Spielberg's World War II yarn of a doomed cartoonist saved through the power of imagination is the worst by far: it begins as pulp and sinks into pure slush. The second segment, in which a horror actor dressed as a mummy is mistaken by rednecks for the real thing, is almost worth the price of admission alone: directed by Dear with the speed, flash and wit of *Raiders*-era Spielberg. The Zemeckis contribution is a heavy-handed but enjoyable spoof, with two pupils terrorised by a headless English teacher spouting Shakespeare. There's salt enough to the popcorn, but as with Romero's *Creepshow*, the whole is never more than the sum of its parts. DW

Amazonia: Voices from the Rainforest (Amazonia: Vozes da Floresto)

(Monti Aguirre/Glenn Switkes, 1991, Braz/US/Col)
70 min.
This independent documentary offers a quick runthrough of the history of the Amazon over the last 500 years or so, and reiterates the urgent ecological message that our complicity in the deforestation of this area is tantamount to suicide, but its real focus is the testimony of the local inhabitants. Of an estimated 800 tribes indigenous to Brazil, only 80 remain today. Increasingly, the Indians are presenting their case to the world media, and for the first time, those old adversaries the rubber trappers and the farmers are uniting against the government. *Amazonia* is a bit scrappy, but a salutary film all the same. TCh

Amazons, The (Le Guerriere dal Seno Nuda)

(Terence Young, 1973, It/Fr) Alena Johnston, Sabine Sun, Rosanna Yanni, Helga Line.
91 min.
A silly male chauvinist rewrite of the Amazon myth, specialising in bare-breasted wrestling matches and blood-and-guts action fodder, with occasional anachronisms that are meant to be funny. The sets are half-decent, and Alena Johnston has an exceptionally luscious body: too bad the dubbers gave her such a grating voice to go with it. JR

Amazon Women on the Moon

(John Landis/Joe Dante/Robert K Weiss/Carl Gottlieb/Peter Horton, 1987, US) Rosanna Arquette, Ralph Bellamy, Carrie Fisher, Griffin Dunne, Steve Guttenberg.
84 min. b/w & col.
A formless compendium of sketches very loosely parodying late-night American television. The tone veers from slapstick (the predictable but delightfully over-the-top opening sketch about the perils of condo-life) through stodgy satire (the excesses of computer dating) to smutty silliness (*Video Date*). The overall result, unsurprisingly, is patchy in the extreme. Weiss' title piece – frag-

ments guying the portentous scripts, wooden acting and non-existent budgets of Z-grade '50s sci-fi movies – is obvious but occasionally spot-on with its appalling sets and repetitive use of the same bit of landscape; Dante's *Critics Corner*, in which a pair of TV reviewers turn from movies like *Winter of My Despondency* to real lives, is pleasantly dark; and Landis' own *Blacks Without Soul*, featuring singing dork Don Simmons, who 'turned a personal affliction into a career', is a gem of brevity and precision. Slim pickings. GA

Ambassador, The

(J Lee Thompson, 1984, US) Robert Mitchum, Ellen Burstyn, Rock Hudson, Fabio Testi, Donald Pleasence, Heli Goldenberg, Michal Bat-Adam.
95 min.
The American ambassador to Israel (Mitchum) is placed in a compromising position when his wife (Burstyn) is filmed *in flagrante delicto* with a PLO leader (Testi). Resisting attempts at blackmail, Mitchum instead uses his wife's lover's influence to set up a meeting between Palestinian and Israeli students. But the success of Mitchum's personal peace initiative is threatened by the fanatical terrorist faction SEIKA, who are determined to frustrate all attempts to negotiate a peaceful settlement. Thompson handles the cumbersome mechanics of this Cannon-financed political pot-boiler ('suggested' by Elmore Leonard's novel *52 Pick-Up*) with a singular lack of style, displacing the violence on to the mad terrorists and fudging all the major political issues. Rock Hudson plays Mitchum's sidekick in what was to be his last feature film. NF

Ambulance, The

(Larry Cohen, 1990, US) Eric Roberts, James Earl Jones, Megan Gallagher, Richard Bright, Janine Turner, Eric Braeden, Red Buttons.
95 min.
New York comic book artist Josh Baker (Roberts) sees a young woman collapse in the street and rushes to help her. As an ambulance arrives and whisks her away, Josh catches something about Cheryl (Gallagher), diabetes, and St Francis hospital. But when he enquires there, they have no record of her having been admitted... Once again Larry Cohen transforms a familiar and benign object into something mysterious and frightening. He keeps things light and pacy, eschewing *Coma*-style medical horror in favour of a sharp comic mystery. Great supporting performances, too, from James Earl Jones as a gum-chewing cop, and Red Buttons as an ex–press photographer with a smart line in cheap patter. NF

Ambushers, The

(Henry Levin, 1967, US) Dean Martin, Senta Berger, Janice Rule, James Gregory, Albert Salmi, Kurt Kasznar.
102 min.
Dire Dino vehicle, his third appearance as superagent Matt Helm (after *The Silencers* and *Murderers' Row*), this time attempting to save the first US flying saucer from sabotage. The tongues of all concerned are firmly in cheek, as well they might be, given the awful script – but the humour is never less than indulgent.

America, America (aka The Anatolian Smile)

(Elia Kazan, 1963, US) Stathis Giallelis, Frank Wolff, Harry Davis, Elena Karam, Estelle Hemsley, Lou Antonio, John Marley.
177 min. b/w.
Shot by Haskell Wexler in a stark black-and-white deliberately designed to lend the film the feel of documentary, Kazan's epic was based on his own novel, and inspired by the journey his uncle made from a Turkish peasant village, via Constantinople, to New York. For once in his career, the director employed little-known actors, with a welcome loss of theatricality; indeed, the entire movie benefits from its authenticity, the geographical, historical and emotional, and may be seen as one of the peaks of Kazan's career. Certainly, it is one of the finest movies to deal with the plight of those thousands of immigrants who travelled in steerage to Ellis Island at the turn of the century. GA

America – From Hitler to M-X

(Joan Harvey, 1982, US)
95 min. b/w & col.

Despite Joan Harvey's provocative thesis – that US finance capital was deeply implicated in the Nazi armaments industry, and is involved again in today's nuclear escalation – her documentary has little of the polemical agit-prop of its companion in the nuclear controversy stakes, *The Atomic Café*. Instead, it's a painstakingly detailed compilation of archive material, investigative reportage, and masses of interviews – with ex-uranium miners, Navajos, many now critically ill; with scientists; with top military and intelligence brass – used to quietly convincing effect. SJo

Americana

(David Carradine, 1981, US) David Carradine, Barbara Hershey, Michael Greene, Arnold Herzstein, Sandy Ignon.
93 min.
In his independent movie, shot in 1973 with post-production work undertaken sporadically over the next seven years, Carradine plays a Vietnam veteran (no traumatised psycho, thankfully), who drifts into a small Kansas township and decides to stay on to repair a disused, dilapidated merry-go-round in the face of uncomprehending hostility from the locals. Clearly intended as an allegory both on middle American morality and on man's need for faith, it works largely due to the unsentimental depiction of the rural community, and to the fact that the potentially portentous plot never overwhelms the film's quiet atmosphere and observation. The only drawbacks, in fact, are some silly '60s style camera flourishes and the needless inclusion of Carradine's beloved Hershey, who keeps turning up wordlessly as some sort of elfin nature girl. GA

American Blue Note (aka Fakebook)

(Ralph Toporoff, 1989, US) Peter MacNicol, Carl Capotorto, Tim Guinee, Bill Christopher-Myers, Jonathan Walker, Charlotte D'Amboise.
97 min.
Low-key but sincere jazz movie follows the crisis of confidence of '60s saxman MacNicol as he realises that strolling through the standards with his quintet for weddings and local gigs isn't getting him any closer to his dreams of the big time. The movie lacks the big-name involvement of '*Round Midnight* or *Bird*, but has an acute eye for the everyday dilemmas of the working musician. TJ

American Boy

(Martin Scorsese, 1977, US) Steven Prince, Martin Scorsese, George Memmoli, Mardik Martin.
55 min.
A documentary about Steven Prince, the fever-eyed gun salesman in *Taxi Driver* (Scorsese's friend and associate since 1968), who emerges as a hip bore in a floral shirt, and dangerous to boot. A manic raconteur, his stories about working as a roadie for the old whiner Neil Young yield some intriguing anecdotage, but when he gets worked up about killing people with his Magnum, doubts about Scorsese's stance creep in: it looks suspiciously like another demonstration of his awe of violence that makes some of *Taxi Driver* look immature. CPea

American Buffalo

(Michael Corrente, 1995, US/UK) Dustin Hoffman, Sean Nelson, Dennis Franz.
87 min.
'Action talks and bullshit walks,' Don (Franz) tells his errand boy Bobby (Nelson) at the start of David Mamet's adaptation of his own play. Unfortunately, action isn't on the agenda. Talking, on the other hand, we get a-plenty. Talking about business, money, character, ethics. And this being Mamet, we get a lot of it twice. Don's working a scam with Bobby – they plan to steal a rare coin collection – but he reckons without the help of his poker buddy Teach (Hoffman), a seedy, paranoid waster, who inveigles himself into the scheme at Bobby's expense. In the theatre, this is doubtless riveting, but it's no surprise that it took two decades to make the transfer to the screen. The action's confined to Don's junk shop, and such plot as there is sneaks in by the back door about an hour into the proceedings. No complaints about the cast. Hoffman plays Teach like Ratso Rizzo twenty years on. He's good value, but Franz really nails the emotional core, painful-

ly reconciling himself to his own flaws under the brutal tutelage of his 'friend'. Solid but stifled. TCh

American Dream, An (aka See You in Hell, Darling)

(Robert Gist, 1966, US) Stuart Whitman, Janet Leigh, Eleanor Parker, Barry Sullivan, Lloyd Nolan, Murray Hamilton.
103 min.
Somewhat messy adaptation of Norman Mailer's novel, with Whitman as the ruthless TV commentator who implies that the cops are in the pay of the Mob, only to find himself winding up on a murder charge. Would-be nightmarish, it's merely tediously violent. Parker as Whitman's embittered and alcoholic ex-wife, brings the thing to life in her scenes, but otherwise it's a long haul. GA

American Dreamer

(Rick Rosenthal, 1984, US) JoBeth Williams, Tom Conti, Giancarlo Giannini, Coral Browne, James Staley.
105 min.
Housewife Williams enters a writing competition, wins a week in Paris, and escapes from miserable husband and boring existence. After a knock on the head, she wakes up convinced she is the debonair heroine of her fantasies, and – hey, presto! – gets stuck into real-life intrigues, falls in love, etc. If you can suspend disbelief, this basically dippy story is actually quite appealing. It's not helped, though, by curiously varied performances: Conti's Englishman in Paris seems faintly embarrassed, while Giannini's villain just looks bored. But it has some amusing moments, despite slushy dialogue and a yukky happy ending. GO

American Flyers

(John Badham, 1985, US) Kevin Costner, David Grant, Rae Dawn Chong, Alexandra Paul, Janice Rule.
114 min.
A pleasant, straight-down-the-road, cliché-ridden ride with two brothers (Costner and Grant) battling against a hysterical mother, a potentially fatal inheritance (cerebral aneurism), fraternal rivalry and fear of flying, and finally teaming up one last time for the gruelling 'Hell of the West' bicycle race in Golden Colorado. Badham and scriptwriter Steve Tesich keep the syrup and scenery flowing along nicely, and there's always Chong and Paul to lead the cheers. WH

American Friend, The (Der Amerikanische Freund)

(Wim Wenders, 1977, WGer/Fr) Dennis Hopper, Bruno Ganz, Gérard Blain, Lisa Kreuzer, Nicholas Ray, Samuel Fuller.
123 min.
Superb adaptation of Patricia Highsmith's novel Ripley's Game, with Hopper as her amiably cynical hero, asked to find a non-professional for a killing or two, and – in echo of Strangers on a Train – drawing an innocent family man (Ganz) into the game by persuading him that the blood disease he is suffering from is not merely incurable but terminal. Good Highsmith, it's even better Wenders, with Ripley, an American expatriate in Germany, first seen keeping a rendezvous with a dead man, then confiding his disorientation to a tape recorder ('There is nothing to fear but fear itself...I know less and less about who I am or who anybody else is'). Ripley, in other words, becomes the quintessential Wenders hero, the loner travelling through alien lands in quest of himself, of friendship, of some meaning to life. Emerging enviously from his solitude to wonder at the radiating warmth of Ganz' family circle, he is irresistibly attracted; but he is also condemned by his own self-disgust to approach only someone on whom he can already smell the scent of death, and by destroying whom he can complete his drive to self-destruction. TM

American Friends

(Tristram Powell, 1991, GB) Michael Palin, Trini Alvarado, Connie Booth, Bryan Pringle, Fred Pearson, Alfred Molina, Robert Eddison, Alun Armstrong.
95 min.
It's 1861, and Caroline Hartley (Booth) is holidaying in Switzerland with her 18-year-old ward

Elinor (Alvarado). While out walking, the impressionable teen spies bookish Oxford don Francis Ashby (Palin) through her telescope (both a literal and figurative device: as she attempts to draw Ashby out, the film focuses on what Palin has described as 'fragments of life'). From that moment on, their destinies are linked, but the gulf in their ages (he's 46) and backgrounds provides endless hurdles. This was a personal project for co-writer and star Palin, inspired by his great-grandfather's diaries. The restrained interplay and gentle gibes at English mores are precisely balanced against the forces of intellectual and emotional change, and the mood is subtle, conveying both regret and expectation in equal measure. A film of small pleasures. CM

American Gigolo

(Paul Schrader, 1980, US) Richard Gere, Lauren Hutton, Hector Elizondo, Nina Van Pallandt, Bill Duke.
117 min.
Fascinating but botched attempt to update and translate Bresson's Pickpocket to contemporary California. Gere is the highly paid gigolo who finds himself suspected of murdering one of the women he has serviced; Hutton the rich, married woman who falls for him. Part thriller, part portrait of American malaise, it finally comes to focus on Gere's inability to get in touch with his own feelings, and therein lies the Bressonian theme of redemption. Unfortunately, the film is so determinedly stylish (Gere's costumes, Giorgio Moroder's soundtrack, John Bailey's noir-inflected camerawork), and the performances generally so vacuous (only Elizondo's detective really breathes), that it all becomes something of an academic, if entertaining, exercise that fails to stir the emotions. GA

American Graffiti

(George Lucas, 1973, US) Richard Dreyfuss, Candy Clark, Ronny Howard, Paul LeMat, Cindy Williams, Harrison Ford.
110 min.
The film that launched a thousand careers. 'Star Wars' inventor Lucas got together a bunch of young actors who later went on to make it big in one way or another, and used them to populate his celluloid memoirs of what it was like cruising the strip back in small-town California '62. Too full of incident to reflect a typical night in reality, it's nevertheless funny, perceptive, pepped up by a great soundtrack, and also something of a text-book lesson in parallel editing as it follows a multitude of adolescents through their various adventures with sex, booze, music and cars. Its enormous success guaranteed a surfeit of imitations, only a few of which (Big Wednesday, Diner) match its glowing, controlled nostalgia. GA

American Guerilla in the Philippines (aka I Shall Return)

(Fritz Lang, 1950, US) Tyrone Power, Micheline Presle, Tom Ewell, Bob Patten, Jack Elam, Tommy Cook.
105 min.
Lang seems only moderately involved in this WWII flagwaver-after-the-fact, though he rouses himself for the challenge of shooting on the actual locations involved. Power and Ewell are US sailors who get caught up in the Japanese invasion and throw in their lot with the local resistance. It's not a terrible movie, but eliminating the romance with planter's wife Presle and sprucing up the script (from an Ira Wolfert novel) might have made more of it. TJ

American Heart

(Martin Bell, 1992, US) Jeff Bridges, Edward Furlong, Lucinda Jenney, Don Harvey, Tracey Tyla Kapisky.
114 min.
For his first feature Martin Bell returns to the terrain of his acclaimed 1984 BBC documentary Streetwise – a mournful portrait of runaway kids living hand-to-mouth in downtown Seattle. Ironically, this looks grimy and drab compared to its predecessor's vivid urgency; at the same time, the feature gives more coherent expression to the downbeat romanticism which sometimes felt unduly manipulative in the non-fiction film. Bridges is Jack Kelson, a middleweight ex-con trying to go straight; he hopes to save enough money to go to Alaska, but life isn't made any

easier by his teenage son Nick's decision to stick by him no matter what. With dirty ponytail and battle-scar tattoos, Jack makes no bones about being out for himself: he kicks his son out of bed and then out of the apartment when he brings a woman to their bare room late at night. It's a credible, minimalist performance, and the sad-faced Furlong responds well as his son. Compassionate; moving; heavy-going. TCh

American Hot Wax

(Floyd Mutrux, 1977, US) Tim McIntire, Fran Drescher, Jay Leno, Laraine Newman.
91 min.
The early history of rock'n'roll seen through the eyes of its mentor, the New York disc jockey Alan Freed (played by McIntire), who was eventually run out of town as a payola scapegoat. With this subject, plus Chuck Berry and Jerry Lee Lewis (among others) in the cast, it seems hard to imagine any film going wrong. But American Hot Wax badly lacks a hard narrative core, and it makes no attempt to discipline its performers into an even approximate re-creation of their '50s acts. The result is an only occasionally moving ragbag, with a really disappointing final concert which conveys little of the raw energy of the period. DP

American in Paris, An

(Vincente Minnelli, 1951, US) Gene Kelly, Leslie Caron, Oscar Levant, Nina Foch, Georges Guetary.
113 min.
A musical both ludicrously overpraised (especially in Hollywood) and underrated. The script is admittedly lax, while the Gershwin numbers defer to too many contradictory performing styles (Levant and Guetary) and can be patronisingly twee (Kelly with the children in 'I Got Rhythm'). But there are ecstatic moments, like Kelly's jazz eruption into the ballet as Toulouse-Lautrec's Chocolat, his pas-de-deux with Caron on the river-bank, his solo to 'S Wonderful'. And finally of course there is the climactic American in Paris ballet, which places dancers against backdrops pastiched from the paintings of Dufy, Renoir, Utrillo, Rousseau, Van Gogh, Manet and Toulouse-Lautrec. There are those who describe this as vulgar or pretentious, forgetting that the story is about Kelly as a frustrated artist. The sequence, besides being colourful, invigorating, ambitious, is also entirely appropriate to Minnelli's interest in his characters' emotions. To criticise this merging of form with content, of style with meaning – especially in a film-maker whose principal desire seems to have been to excite the senses – seems unwarranted. GA

Americanization of Emily, The

(Arthur Hiller, 1964, US) James Garner, Julie Andrews, Melvyn Douglas, James Coburn, Joyce Grenfell, Keenan Wynn.
117 min. b/w.
A decidedly black comedy. Andrews is the British war widow who falls for Garner's cowardly marine, who is scheduled (For the Good of the Service) to be the first man to die in the course of the Normandy landings. In one fell swoop, writer Paddy Chayevsky celebrates American hedonism (as the prim Ms Andrews learns to have fun) and attacks the puritan conscience that turns fun into cynicism. The result is Hospital without the gore: witty despite Hiller's direction. PH

American Madness

(Frank Capra, 1932, US) Walter Huston, Pat O'Brien, Kay Johnson, Constance Cummings, Gavin Gordon, Arthur Hoyt, Robert E O'Conner.
81 min. b/w.
Huston, the joshing, principled New York bank manager, Tom Dickson, animates this sermon (scripted by Robert Riskin) by sheer force of personality: a Depression-era bank-run is halted by the little people who rally to Dickson's defence and shame the selfish plutocrats on the bank's board. Huston's rough-hewn character is matched by a wonderfully sophisticated and seductive performance by Johnson, as the manager's somewhat neglected wife. She unwittingly abets her husband's discomfort by allowing herself to be wooed by the chief cashier (Gordon), who's been forced into dishonesty by his gam-

bling debts. Beautifully shot by Joseph Walker, with several striking expressionistic touches, this breathtaking film from Capra's golden period with Harry Cohn's Columbia is notable among much else for its vivid depiction of how a bank operates and for a tremendous climax in which a sea of desperate depositors clamour for their cash. JPy

American Ninja
(aka American Warrior)
(Sam Firstenberg, 1985, US) Michael Dudikoff, Steve James, Judie Aronson, Guich Koock.
95 min.
Joe, new to a US Army base in the Philippines, squints a lot and goes round the island zapping foreign types who steal Army weaponry for their own devious political purposes. He's a top-grade Ninja, which allows him to catch arrows in midflight, look serious, spout cod-Zen aphorisms, and don a natty black designer boilersuit and mask before kicking the shit out of thousands of Oriental Ninjas. This flaccid fiasco fails not merely due to the endless series of clichés and questionable political attitudes on view, but also because the script, direction and performances are so risibly inept. GA

Americano, The
(William Castle, 1954, US) Glenn Ford, Frank Lovejoy, Cesar Romero, Ursula Thiess, Abbe Lane, Rodolfo Hoyos.
85 mins.
Ponderously dreary Western made before Castle decided to ape Hitchcock. Ford delivers three prize bulls in Brazil, finding the buyer mysteriously murdered and tangling with bandits amid exotic scenery. TM

American Pictures
(Amerikanske Billeder)
(Jacob Holdt, 1981, Den)
280 min. b/w.
For five years Jacob Holdt, a former Danish palace guard, hitchhiked around the United States, selling his blood twice a week to buy film for his camera. The result is this vast collection of stills, linked by Holdt's narrative and occasional interviews as he trudges through a land raddled by racial persecution, bigotry, chronic poverty and the enduring legacy of slavery. Here is America with its pants down: utter hopelessness in the land of plenty. By turns indignant, self-righteous, sympathetic and, occasionally, leadenly aphoristic – 'You can learn more about society from a black prostitute in a night than you can from ten universities' – this nevertheless adds up to a rare and moving indictment of the conditions that cause and foster racialism. JP

American President, The
(Rob Reiner, 1995, US) Michael Douglas, Annette Bening, Michael J Fox, Martin Sheen, Richard Dreyfuss, David Paymer, Anna Deavere Smith, Samantha Ma mthis.
114 min.
Part romantic comedy, part Capra-corny political drama, this movie exudes so much sympathy, it sweats. Douglas's eminently decent, recently widowed Democratic President, 'Andy' Shepherd, is so squeaky-clean, his faults seem like the blemishes that make the perfect face. Why, the film asks, shouldn't the leader of the free world be free to form relationships like any Joe Doe? Because it's an election year, say his aides (reliable Chief of Staff Sheen, policy adviser and conscience-figure Fox, realist in-house pollster Paymer), and what's more, right-wing Presidential hopeful Dreyfuss will use any alliance to kebab his *cojones*. Aaron Sorkin's script goes light on the duplicity and corruption of office. This President's worst dilemma is being caught between mutually exclusive noble options (gun restriction law or green legislation) and the pressure of time. Bening's Sydney Wade, the environmental lobbyist Shepherd sets out to woo, is straight out of the Jean Arthur school of klutzy charm, without a diploma. An animated *Hello!* magazine spread: mildly diverting. WH

American Romance, An
(King Vidor, 1944, US) Brian Donlevy, Ann Richards, Walter Abel, John Qualen, Stephen McNally, Ray Teal, Jackie 'Butch' Jenkins.
151 min.

Vidor's major contribution to the war effort, a huge dynastic saga (reduced by MGM to 122 minutes) that charts the progress of a Czech immigrant (Donlevy) from his arrival on Ellis Island in 1898 to the wartime conversion of his car factory to aircraft production. The fifty-year span takes in everything from '30s union-bashing to the career of the son who becomes a great musician, and adds up to the acceptable face of right wing social history. No other American director ever matched Vidor's sense of personal struggle, or the muscular poetry he found to express it. TR

American Roulette
(Maurice Hatton, 1987, GB/Aust) Andy Garcia, Kitty Aldridge, Robert Stephens, Al Matthews, Susannah York.
102 min.
A depressingly botched political thriller from Hatton and producer Verity Lambert. Andy Garcia – who'd committed to the script just before his *Untouchables* breakthrough – is Carlos, an implausible South American poet in London. He is also a president in exile, and a target for assassination, though how and why this came to be remains a mystery for a good while. Hatton seems to be angling for an old-fashioned romantic intrigue, with chummy British secret agents, the odd suspense set-piece, and bumbling Soviet spies for comic relief. What he gets is a wayward, muddled mess. TCh

American Soldier, The
(Der Amerikanische Soldat)
(Rainer Werner Fassbinder, 1970, WGer) Karl Scheydt, Elga Sorbas, Jan George, Margarethe von Trotta, Kurt Raab.
80 min. b/w.
Far from Vietnam, indeed. Fassbinder's American soldier is actually a German, who comes home to roost as a hired killer in the Munich underworld. The miasma into which he sinks involves an ageing rent-boy whose time is up, a roving porn-shark-cum-supergrass called Magdalena Fuller, a mother with a pinball machine in her living-room, and a two-timing moll called Rosa von Praunheim. There is no attempt at plausibility, just a relentless insistence on mood (manic depressive) and behaviour patterns (ex-*film noir*). The gangsters in Fassbinder's earlier movies were sad, pale shadows of their American prototypes; by this time, they've become full-fledged Neuroses. In other words, this film marks a decisive step towards 'real' Fassbinder: the absurdity of its world of second-hand experience invests every cliché with a meaning it never had before. TR

American Stories (Histoires d'Amérique: Food, Family and Philosophy)
(Chantal Akerman, 1989, Fr/Bel) Eszter Balint, Stefan Balint, Sharon Diskin, Victor Talmadge, Mark Amitin, Kirk Baltz, George Bartenieff.
95 min.
Chantal Akerman used to make great 'minimalist' movies in which very little yielded a lot. here, sadly, she takes a lot and reduces it to a small pile of mush. The film opens with a fatuous (because completely ahistorical) evocation of the Manhattan skyline as a 'mythic' palace of dreams, and then launches into an interminable anthology of monologues and sketches about the Jewish immigrant experience, most of them played out in an open-air restaurant under the Williamsburg Bridge. The most ancient Jewish jokes are retold with agonising pedantry, and interspersed with ghetto sob stories, refugee memories, tales of persecution and pub-theatre-type recitations. Most of the material apparently comes from Isaac Bashevis Singer, but that's no excuse. Jewish culture was never this dull or maudlin. TR

American Success Company, The (aka Success)
(William Richert, 1979, US) Jeff Bridges, Belinda Bauer, Ned Beatty, Steven Keats, Bianca Jagger, John Glover.
94 min.
Scripted by Richert (of *Winter Kills* fame) from a story by Larry Cohen, this black comedy is a delightfully offbeat satire both on capitalism and on macho posing. Bridges is excellent as the

wimpy rich boy, disillusioned with wife and family business, who determines to change his life by taking on a completely new second identity as a cold, callous, misogynistic, semi-criminal type. Loosely structured and often verging on the farcical, it misses as often as it hits, but the performances are superb, and Richert manages to keep the excesses of the script nicely under control. Disarmingly unAmerican in tone and message, it was perhaps not surprisingly shot abroad in Germany. GA

American Tail, An
(Don Bluth, 1986, US)
80 min.
An animated feature set towards the end of the last century, this is a tale of persecuted Russian mice – the Mouskowitzes – travelling to America in search of a cat-free life. Inevitably, young Feivel is separated from his family and left to wander the mean streets of the Big Apple, encountering corrupt Irish-American politicians from Tammany Hall, streetwise Italian-American guttersnipes, and friendly French pigeons. For all its state-of-the-art animation techniques, Spielberg's production remains resolutely conservative: visually it's virtually indistinguishable from Walt at his wimpiest. GA

American Tail: Fievel Goes West, An
(Phil Nibbelink/Simon Wells, 1991, US) voices: Phillip Glasser, James Stewart, Nehemiah Persoff, Amy Irving, John Cleese, Dom DeLuise.
75 min.
When you're a cat-harassed, down-and-out mouse, holed up in the streets of New York, there's only one thing to do: head West, where prosperity beckons and cats and mice live in loving harmony. Or so the Mousekewitz family is led to believe by feline fiend Cat R Waul. Miles better than the overrated *American Tail*, this laugh-packed sequel boasts all the classic elements so often missing from modern cartoon features: a straightforward zip-zang-boom storyline, clearly etched characters with instantly identifiable flaws, tip-top voice-overs by well-chosen celebrities, and oodles of elasticated slapstick. There are moments of the goo which marred Don Bluth's original, but in general the sentimentality is kept to a minimum as Fievel and his fat-cat friend Tiger prepare to kick ass. MK

American Tickler or The Winner of 10 Academy Awards (aka Draws)
(Chuck Vincent, 1976, US) Joan Sumner, WP Dremak, Marlow Ferguson, Jeff Alin.
77 min.
Little more than a series of sketches taking satirical swipes at well-hammered American institutions, this hodge-podge leaves almost everything to be desired. A runaway giant penis (offscreen) is lured into New York's Lincoln Tunnel; 'Jews!' yells a distraught father, his child seemingly menaced, as a bearded man in a black coat emerges from the sea. Chuck Vincent, his taste for nudity and sexual high jinks apparently dulled by having directed a string of porn movies, appears not to have lost an unamusing propensity for fevered tastelessness. JPy

American Tragedy, An
(Josef von Sternberg, 1931, US) Phillips Holmes, Sylvia Sidney, Frances Dee, Irving Pichel, Frederick Burton, Claire McDowell.
96 min. b/w.
Faced with Sternberg's distillation of his undeniably great but unreadably turgid novel – about a social climber who murders a factory girl when her pregnancy threatens his romance with a wealthy socialite – Dreiser sued Paramount. Not surprisingly he lost, since Sternberg uses dialogue and situations drawn directly from the book (following it much more closely than the later *A Place in the Sun*: a travesty where the socialite sticks to the social climber even unto the death cell). Where Sternberg does 'betray' Dreiser is in suggesting (with water omnipresent as a subtle Freudian motif) that sexual desire is perhaps more responsible than social circumstance for what happens. As a result, the second half of the film devoted to the trial – crucial to Dreiser but of no interest to Sternberg – is drearily

expendable. But the first half, deftly sketching the hero's dreams and lonely frustrations as he struggles to shake off his bleak mission background and the dreary monotony of factory life, deserves to rank with Sternberg's best work. TM

American Warrior
see American Ninja

American Way, The (aka Riders of the Storm)
(Maurice Phillips, 1986, GB) Dennis Hopper, Michael J Pollard, Eugene Lipinski, James Aubrey, Nigel Pegram.
104 min.
High above America in a re-equipped bomber that serves as an anarchic pirate TV station, a motley crew of renegade Viet vets await amnesty from the authorities; but their captain (Hopper) cherishes his outlaw status, and jumps at the chance to wage a sabotage-and-smear campaign against a right-wing, female, war-mongering Presidential candidate. The lame suspense centres around whether S&M TV can expose her before the Pentagon blasts their hi-tech home out of the skies. There are a few endearingly naive swipes at Establishment hypocrisy, but the caricatures are far too broad to constitute biting satire, political or otherwise. The celebration of rebellious rock mores is dated and embarrassing; the haywire narrative reflects Maurice Phillips' pop-promo background. Only the dependable Hopper, giving with the crazed visionary hippy once again, offers real wit or conviction, and even he is indulged. Little more than a well-intentioned oddity. GA

American Werewolf in London, An
(John Landis, 1981, GB) David Naughton, Jenny Agutter, Griffin Dunne, John Woodvine, Brian Glover, Lila Kaye.
97 min.
Delirious amalgam of guffaws'n'gore, with two American hitchhikers attacked by a wolf on the Yorkshire Moors. One of them dies. The other recuperates in a London hospital, but finds that his fast-decaying friend keeps popping up to warn him about the upcoming full moon. Landis takes affectionate swipes at such British institutions as the pub ('The Slaughtered Lamb'), the sleazy smut cinema (full of zombies) and Piccadilly Circus, which is devastated in a Blues Brotherly car-wreck climax. Special effects wizard Rick Baker's man-into-wolf transformation is extraordinary, and never has the music of Creedence Clearwater Revival been put to better use. AB

American Werewolf in Paris, An
(Anthony Waller, 1997, US/Luxembourg/Fr/ GB) Tom Everett Scott, Julie Delpy, Vince Vieluf, Phil Buckman, Julie Bowen, Pierre Cosso, Tom Novembre.
103 min.
Forget Landis's fondly remembered jape, *An American Werewolf in London* (1981), this is a cash-in title. Scott (Hanks' alter ego in *That Thing You Do*) is about to make a midnight bungee-jump from the Eiffel Tower when a wan, tearful Delpy throws herself off. Seconds later, he's fallen for her and she's at the end of his tether. Too bad she has so many skeletons in her closet (including both parents). Waller's *Mute Witness* indicated he had the necessary credentials, but the most frightening thing about this effort is how unfunny it is. TCh

Amérique des autres, L'
see Someone Else's America

Amiche, Le (The Girlfriends)
(Michelangelo Antonioni, 1955, It) Eleonora Rossi Drago, Valentina Cortese, Gabriele Ferzetti, Yvonne Furneaux, Franco Fabrizi, Madeleine Fischer.
104 min. b/w.
Though seldom seen now, Antonioni's fourth feature is one of his greatest films, in which diverse plot strands, character psychology, and a masterful control of the camera are perfectly fused. Drawn from Pavese, the story begins when local-girl-made-good Clelia returns to Turin to open a

fashion salon, and finds the girl in the hotel room next to her has attempted suicide. This introduces Clelia to a new set of friends, whose various amorous problems become the focus of interest. With two bravura set pieces – a picnic by the sea that foreshadows *L'Avventura*, and a troubled tea party – Antonioni's intensity and grip, and his vivid portrayal of feminine anxiety in particular, make for a film that has barely dated at all. DT

Ami de Mon Amie, L'
see My Girlfriend's Boyfriend

Amiga, La
see Girlfriend, The

Amigomio
(Jeanine Meerapfel/Alcides Chiesa, 1993, Arg) Daniel Kuzniecka, Diego Mesaglio, Mario Adorf.
115 min.
An intelligent, if meandering tale, set during the military dictatorship, of a man who leaves Argentina for Ecuador with his young son when his estranged wife, who is involved in the leftist underground, 'disappears'; en route through Bolivia, they encounter corruption, superstition, con artists and further political turmoil. Vague parallels with the flight of the man's parents from Nazi Germany do not help, but the performances and assured direction hold the film together. GA

Amin, the Rise and Fall (aka Rise and Fall of Idi Amin)
(Sharad Patel, 1980, GB/Kenya) Joseph Olita, Geoffrey Keen, Denis Hills, Leonard Trolley, Andre Maranne, Diane Mercer.
101 min.
The music, the stilted acting, the plethora of hardware, all suggest that this reconstruction of Idi Amin's path to dictatorship might have been inspired by the puppet antics of TV's 'Thunderbirds' series. True, the sickening truth of Amin's regime in Uganda should not be forgotten; but this testimony, like its subject, will probably just take its quiet leave. FD

Amir
(John Baily, 1986, GB) Amir Mohammed.
52 min.
The makers of the Mercedes Sosa documentary, *Será Posible el Sur*, should take a peek at this portrait of Amir Mohammed, an Afghan refugee now living in poverty in Pakistan, who subsists on the income derived from the music he plays at Muslim weddings and functions. The music itself is a joy; but the film is also admirably lucid and informative, placing Amir's music in a clearly defined socio-political context, and letting Amir and his colleagues speak for themselves. No sycophantic pap here: the objectionable aspects of the culture on view (not one woman appears on screen, for example) are never glossed over, though the eponymous subject emerges with dignity indeed. GA

Ami retrouvé, L'
see Reunion

Amistad
(Steven Spielberg, 1997, US) Morgan Freeman, Nigel Hawthorne, Anthony Hopkins, Djimon Hounsou, Matthew McConaughey, David Paymer, Pete Postlethwaite, Stellan Skarsgård, Razaaq Adoti, Anna Paquin, Tomas Milian.
155 min.
For all its good intentions, Spielberg's fact-based film about African slaves fighting for their lives and freedom in 1830s America falls short of *Schindler's List*. Except for the overkill of the seizure of the Spanish ship (*La Amistad*) transporting the slaves to the New World, and a flashback of Africans being sent to a watery grave, it registers chiefly as upmarket, visually bland TV drama. As the fate of the 53 slaves charged with murder is determined in the courts, the politically and philosophically diverse factions are laboriously established: the Abolitionists (Freeman and Skarsgård); their initially dispassionate young lawyer (McConaughey); the pro-slavery attorney (Postlethwaite); President Van Buren (Hawthorne), keen to appease the South, Spain's teenage Queen Isabella, and an electorate about to vote; and former President John Quincy Adams

(Hopkins), a curmudgeonly eccentric who eventually emerges from retirement to argue for brave, unbending Cinque (Hounsou) and the other defendants. In short, a wordy courtroom drama which seldom progresses beyond ciphers, stereotypes and salutary slogans. GA

Amityville Horror, The
(Stuart Rosenberg, 1979, US) James Brolin, Margot Kidder, Rod Steiger, Don Stroud, Murray Hamilton, John Larch.
118 min.
First of three tall tales spun out of Jay Anson's supposedly factually-based bestseller. Family moves into reputedly haunted Long Island house: cue for bad smells, slamming doors, and a horrible sense of *déjà vu* as the movie churns out numerous post-*Exorcist* clichés. Tautly directed, but the thin material, and a dreadfully hammy priest from Steiger, effectively wreck what little suspense remains. GA

Amityville II: The Possession
(Damiano Damiani, 1982, US) James Olson, Burt Young, Rutanya Alda, Jack Magner, Andrew Prine, Diane Franklin.
105 min.
Prequel to *The Amityville Horror* which begins in much the same way, except that the tenants arriving here are presented as jerks: noisy, working class Italian Catholics who don't deserve to live in a Long Island WASP mansion, even one where blood comes out of the kitchen taps from time to time. And clearly we are not meant to care when the eldest boy (Magner), who has been contacted by a demon on his Walkman and is gradually acquiring the rotten teeth and gooseberry eyes of the possessed, wastes the entire family. Awful. JS

Amityville 3-D (aka Amityville: The Demon)
(Richard Fleischer, 1983, US) Tony Roberts, Tess Harper, Robert Joy, Candy Clark, John Beal.
105 min.
What with its history of butchery and the Gateway to Hell lying next to the fusebox in the basement, you wonder why anyone in their right mind would go anywhere near this house. Somehow, the Evil Force manages to creep, *Omen*-style, all the way into town where it mucks about with a lift to see off some tell-tale photographs. Both the house and its special effects are pathetic by *Poltergeist* standards; sensitive viewers will probably find the pink frisbee hurled in their faces (courtesy of 3-D) a far more disturbing phenomenon than a swarm of bluebottles and the odd spot of green ectoplasm. AB

Amleto di Meno, Un
see One Hamlet Less

Amnesia
(Gonzalo Justiniano, 1994, Chile) Julio Jung, Nelson Villagra, Pedro Vicuna, Marcelo Osorio.
90 min.
Stylised farcical tragedy about the cost of forgetting the pre-'democracy' dictatorship. A one-time soldier of the 'Devil's Route Battalion' comes across his sadistic former sergeant in the streets of Valparaiso and contemplates revenge. This quiet, melancholic film uses a nightmare-like flashback structure, expressionistic sound effects, surreal colour photography, wide lenses, lonely night-time locations and heightened naturalistic performances to weave a compassionate examination of the fallacy (as the sergeant puts it) that 'time erases everything'. WH

Amongst Friends
(Rob Weiss, 1992, US) Steve Parlavecchio, Joseph Lindsey, Patrick McGaw, Mira Sorvino, Chris Santos.
87 min.
In the well-off Long Island suburbs of Five Towns, three teens act the musketeers of petty crime. But when a drugs bust puts one of them in jail for two years, the seeds of betrayal are sown. Writer/director Weiss's first feature attempts to relocate the themes and characters of *Mean Streets* to a relatively unfamiliar milieu. The bond of friendship, however, is insufficiently established to make us greatly care when it disintegrates. GA

a

Among the Living

(Stuart Heisler, 1941, US) Albert Dekker, Susan Hayward, Frances Farmer, Harry Carey, Gordon Jones.
68 min. b/w.

A gripping piece of Southern gothic, with Albert Dekker (excellent) as identical twins. John, sent away to school as a boy, returns home after 25 years for his father's funeral, and is horrified to learn that his brother Paul is not dead as everybody thought, but shut away in the family mansion, driven insane by his father's cruelty to his mother when he was still a boy. In a nicely grisly touch, echoed in a later murder, the body of Paul's keeper is found with his hands placed over his ears (shutting out the mother's screams that Paul still hears); and in a wonderfully touching sequence, Paul goes walkabout in town, tasting freedom with the same joyous innocence as Frankenstein's monster when he first comes alive. But the violence underlying everyday life sparks a new crisis in him; the two people who know his story try to duck responsibility to preserve their own reputations; and soon the town is in the grip of lynch-fever. Script (Lester Cole/Garrett Fort), camera (Theodor Sparkuhl) and direction all conspire beautifully to keep the screws turned tight. TM

Amor Brujo, El

see Love Bewitched, A

Amore, L'

(Roberto Rossellini, 1948, It) Anna Magnani, Federico Fellini.
79 min. b/w.

Rossellini's two-part showcase for Magnani's operatic excess. In *The Miracle*, she plays a retarded goatherd who confuses her seducer with St Joseph and her illegitimate child with a new Messiah; in *The Human Voice* (based on Cocteau's play), a middle-aged bourgeoise abandoned by her lover and clinging tenaciously to the telephone as if to a lifebuoy. Basically, the first is claptrap, the second reeks of greasepaint, but the demented virtuosity of their interpreter carries all before it. GAd

Amore Molesto, L'

(Mario Martone, 1995, It) Anna Bonaiuto, Angela Luce, Gianni Cajafa.
104 min.

Neapolitan thriller in which Anna Bonaiuto returns home to investigate the suspicious death of her 70-year-old mother (her near-naked body was found washed up on a beach). She delves into her own memory for clues about her relationship with her parent and the various men in her life. Writer/director Martone uses a *noir* mystery as an intriguing framework for the exploration of feminist, Freudian and social concerns, and thanks to his firm control of mood, it mostly works. Adventurous and unexpectedly engrossing. GA

Amorosa

(Mai Zetterling, 1986, Swe) Stina Ekblad, Erland Josephson, Philip Zandén, Peter Schildt, Lena T Hansson.
117 min.

In this Swedish art movie set in Venice, Agnes von Krusenstjerna is first seen being transported to the local asylum in a straitjacket, her career as Sweden's reviled writer of eroticism over, the history of her neurosis about to unfold. Born into the aristocracy, von K rebelled against the etiquette that was her family's foil for homosexuality, incest and insanity, jilting her noble fiancé for David Sprengel, an older man with a reputation as a lecher. Sprengel took over Agnes' life, managing her money, revising her books, and administering morphine to curb increasing fits of anxiety. There are echoes of Bergman in the themes and look of the film – beautifully shot colour-coded landscapes representing youthful summers contrast with weighty interiors for adult anguish – but Zetterling has none of the master's restraint. There's little sense of context, and we don't learn much about the author's work. Too full of its own importance, the film is completely over the top. EP

Amour à Mort, L'

(Alain Resnais, 1984, Fr) Sabine Azéma, Fanny Ardant, Pierre Arditi, André Dussollier, Jean Dasté.
93 min.

Azéma and Arditi are star-crossed lovers. When Arditi is 'resurrected' from a mysterious, fatal collapse, their love is intensified but confounded by his medical and spiritual status: is he a dead man? Has he been resurrected from an afterlife he doesn't believe in? Did he dream it? Cleric friends (Ardant and Dussollier) are enlisted to solve the conundrum, only to find their own beliefs compromised. It's shot in short, oddly stylised scenes, punctuated by mysterious footage of drifting plankton (make of that what you will). Both a discourse on love, life and belief, and a tale of extreme romantic love, it looks to be Resnais' most straightforward film to date. But there's a suspect, often humorous archness about it, to suggest he may be playing one of his biggest intellectual tricks yet. JG

Amour de Swann, Un

see Swann in Love

Amour en Fuite, L'

see Love on the Run

Amour Fou, L'

(Jacques Rivette, 1968, Fr) Bulle Ogier, Jean-Pierre Kalfon, Josée Destoop, Michèle Moretti, André S Labarthe.
252 min. b/w.

Rivette's claim to the status of a key innovator in contemporary cinema began with this film; it marks the beginning of his distrust of the mechanisms of fiction. A theatre director (Kalfon) mounts a production of Racine's *Andromache* starring his wife (Ogier), under the mechanical eyes of a TV documentary unit. Wife cracks under the strain and withdraws; director's former mistress takes the part. The field is thus cleared for confrontations between husband and wife, between theatre and TV, between ordered passion and mad love. All confrontations duly occur (plus a clash between 16mm filmstock for the theatre scenes and 35mm for the rest), at a length that exceeds all obvious expectation – and thus begins to reach areas that conventional movies don't touch. Finally, even the pretentious title is justified by the shattering, improvised ending, which sees Kalfon and Ogier demolish each other and their apartment. TR

Amour, l'Après-midi, L'

see Love in the Afternoon

Amour par terre, L' (Love on the Ground)

(Jacques Rivette, 1984, Fr) Geraldine Chaplin, Jane Birkin, André Dussollier, Jean-Pierre Kalfon, Laszlo Szabo, Facundo Bo, Sandra Montaigu.
127 min.

Chaplin and Birkin are actresses taken up by an enigmatic playwright (Kalfon) and installed in his fabulous suburban mansion in order to perform a play (whose last act is still unknown) for one of his house parties. With the agency of a magician and clairvoyant, melodrama gradually seeps into both life and the rehearsals of fiction; the *affaires* promoted between playwright, magician and actresses lead to premonitions, hallucination, jealousy and dark secrets, all of them threaded into a weird finale of reconciliation. As with *Céline and Julie*, the concern here is less with the contrast between fiction and reality, more with the invention of a magical realm from which reality is rigorously excluded: enchantment is discovered not from fairytale, but within life itself. Rivette creates a unique world and language, answerable finally only to himself. CPea

Amsterdam Kill, The

(Robert Clouse, 1977, HK) Robert Mitchum, Bradford Dillman, Richard Egan, Leslie Nielsen, Keye Luke.
132 min.

Dim attempt to re-establish Hong Kong's international reputation. Mitchum plays a discredited agent who acts as liaison between ageing Triad boss who wants out and the US Drug Enforcement Agency. Results are predictably bloody, but with no one thinking beyond set pieces and international locations, the film quickly stagnates in its own violence. CPe

Amsterdamned

(Dick Maas, 1988, Neth) Huub Stapel, Monique Van de Ven, Serge-Henri Valcke, Tanneke Hartsuiker, Wim Zomer, Hidde Maas, Lou Landré, Tatum Dagelet.
113 min.

Having unleashed a killer elevator on us in *The Lift*, Dick Maas here comes up with the authentically crazy notion of a psycho-diver. By prowling (paddling?) the hundreds of canals which traverse the Dutch capital, our wetsuit wacko easily escapes detection, and can engage concurrently in his two favourite sports: diving and murder. Much of the pleasure derives from the outrageous set pieces the film wrings from a familiar formula. Aside from the eccentric psychopath, we have the divorced cop and his obnoxious kid, the bungling sidekick, the blatantly obvious suspect, and the woman relegated to an 'ooh, aargh' role. Yet Maas has talent to burn: snappy dialogue (he wrote the screenplay); brooding *Jaws*-type atmospherics (and music); and stylish execution(s). Like Dario Argento's early slasher thrillers, as a murder mystery it is frankly naff (there is at least one red herring too many); but as a spectacle it is fascinatingly gruesome. Maas murder may not be to everyone's taste, but those who take to tomato ketchup with relish – this one's for you. TCh

Amy Foster (aka Swept from the Sea – The Story of Amy Foster)

(Beeban Kidron, 1997, GB/US/Fr) Vincent Perez, Rachel Weisz, Ian McKellen, Joss Ackland, Kathy Bates, Tom Bell, Zoë Wanamaker, Tony Haygarth.
113 min.

Amy (Weisz) is a Cornish servant girl, shunned by her parents, and animated only by the sight of the sea and the treasures it sweeps into her arms. A Ukrainian ship is wrecked and Amy assumes possession of Yanko (Perez), the sole survivor. He's happy with the arrangement, but Amy's community is against the match. She is a woman both behind the times and ahead of them: an unwitting revolutionary who manages to undo the punitive logic of 'civilised' society. Kidron's direction is alternately flat and glossily overwrought; the sets jar; and Tim Willocks' screenplay has drained Joseph Conrad's story of its tortuous peculiarity. This could be any TV friendly costume drama, complete with hair-centric stars and dodgy accents. CO'Su

Anaconda

(Luis Llosa, 1997, US/Braz) Jennifer Lopez, Ice Cube, Jon Voight, Eric Stoltz, Jonathan Hyde, Owen Wilson, Kari Wuhrer.
89 min.

A seven-strong documentary film crew, sailing the mighty Amazon in search of a lost tribe, pick up stranded cruiser Voight. Before long he's telling them of his encounter with the elusive Shirishama tribe, and guiding them down unfamiliar tributaries. He's also beginning to act strangely, and worse, the direction in which they're heading is home to a 40ft man-eating snake. And then there were six, five, four… Voight, permanently OTT, wears a fixed scowl and tries a funny accent. The plot, meanwhile, meanders more than the river, through a series of time-filling false alarms before we get down to the big signposted main course. One never questions the realism of the remarkable animatronic and computer-generated effects, but it's hard to credit a snake that screams. DA

Anastasia

(Anatole Litvak, 1956, GB) Ingrid Bergman, Yul Brynner, Helen Hayes, Akim Tamiroff, Martita Hunt, Felix Aylmer, Ivan Desny, Serge Pitoeff.
105 min.

Paris, 1928: When White Russian general Brynner picks out amnesiac peasant Bergman to claim she's the daughter of the murdered Tsar, little does he know how well she'll stand up to a grilling at the hands of Hayes' formidable Empress Dowager. Glossy 'Scope historical puzzler (from the play by Marcelle Maurette and Guy Bolton) with Oscar-winning Bergman on regal form in her first Hollywood picture after her European adventure with Rossellini. TJ

Anastasia

(Don Bluth/Gary Goldman, 1997, US) voices: Meg Ryan, John Cusack, Kelsey Grammer, Christopher Lloyd, Bernadette Peters, Angela Lansbury.
94 min.
This engaging love story is free of candy flavoured characters (though not some execrable songs), and the animation's a ten-fold improvement on Bluth's recent offerings (*The Pebble and the Penguin*, etc). This being a children's film, the story of the legendary disappearance of the Romanov princess has been altered to accommodate mad magician Rasputin (voiced by Lloyd), who instigates public revolt by casting a spell on the entire royal family. As destructive forces rage in the streets of 1917 St Petersburg, panic sweeps the Imperial Palace and the royal family flees. Ten years later, confused orphan Anya (Ryan) wanders the same streets, unsure of her identity and dogged by memories of a privileged childhood. Enter con-man Dimitri (Cusack), who starts by exploiting 'Anastasia', and ends by falling in love with her. Bluth has rediscovered the ingredients of quality mainstream animation: depth and movement are more in evidence, and the action sequences are expertly staged, notably a harrowing train crash. DA

Anatahan

see Saga of Anatahan, The

Anatolian Smile, The

see America, America

Anatomy of a Murder

(Otto Preminger, 1959, US) James Stewart, Ben Gazzara, Lee Remick, Eve Arden, Arthur O'Connell, George C Scott.
160 min. b/w.
One of Preminger's most compelling and perfectly realised films (with a terrific Duke Ellington score). A long, detailed account of the efforts of a smalltown lawyer (Stewart) to defend an army sergeant (Gazzara) accused of murdering the bartender who, it is claimed, raped his wife (Remick), it's remarkable for the cool, crystal clear direction, concentrating on the mechanical processes and professional performances guiding the trial, and for the superb acting. Chilling, ironic and sceptical, it is far less confident in the law than most courtroom dramas, which makes one suspect that it was this probing cynicism rather than the 'daring' use of words that caused controversy at the time of release. GA

Anchoress

(Chris Newby, 1993, GB/Bel) Natalie Morse, Eugene Bervoets, Peter Postlethwaite, Toyah Wilcox, Annette Badland, Veronica Quilligan.
107 min. b/w.
This directorial debut convinces in its exploration of spiritual ferment, but fumbles the task of assembling a coherent narrative. In a remote medieval community, an illiterate peasant (Morse) becomes obsessed with the local chapel's statue of the Virgin, and, pronounced a holy anchoress, is walled up in the building with the object of her passion. With only a small window to the world, the girl creates a rich interior domain for herself, but in the process becomes something of a tourist attraction and starts to long for freedom. The film is most powerful during the cell-bound mid-section, contrasting the heroine's innocence with the machinations of Church and State. Aided by lustrous b/w cinematography, Newby delineates the textures of her pastoral surroundings to hallucinatory effect. TJ

Anchors Aweigh

(George Sidney, 1944, US) Gene Kelly, Frank Sinatra, Kathryn Grayson, José Iturbi, Dean Stockwell, Sharon McManus.
140 min.
Something of a precursor to *On the Town*, with Kelly and Sinatra as sailors rushing round town (in this case Hollywood) and anxious to score with women. Thunderously patriotic (the navy is wonderful) and sentimental (kids are wonderful), it's heavily dependent on Kelly's charm and Sinatra's supposed little-boy appeal, the combination of which fuels the running gags and almost saves the scenes with Grayson. The best item is Kelly's dance with Jerry, of 'Tom and Jerry'; otherwise, in a so-so score, Kelly has his first number with a child, and Sinatra sings 'I Fall in Love Too Easily' like he means it. SG

Anderson Tapes, The

(Sidney Lumet, 1971, US) Sean Connery, Dyan Cannon, Martin Balsam, Ralph Meeker, Alan King, Christopher Walken.
99 min.
Watchable but curiously muffled thriller in which Connery masterminds a plan to rob an entire apartment block, unaware that everybody involved is under surveillance by somebody or other. The ironies never really focus, and Lumet's hesitant direction undermines the tension. TM

And God Created Woman

see Et Dieu Créa la Femme

And God Created Woman

(Roger Vadim, 1987, US) Rebecca De Mornay, Vincent Spano, Frank Langella, Donovan Leitch, Judith Chapman.
98 min.
Vadim's update of his sensational 1956 debut offers a completely new scenario, but even so a sense of *déjà vu* prevails. Following a failed escape attempt, prisoner De Mornay is advised by slimy would-be governor Langella to slip out the back door, by marrying a solid member of the community; she therefore makes a deal with hunky carpenter Spano, with whom she has already enjoyed a close encounter in the prison gym. She gets her freedom, Langella gets some useful publicity, and Spano gets $5,000 plus someone to look after him, his teenage brother, and his five-year-old son while De Mornay lives out her 12-month parole. But De Mornay's no nookie rule provokes emotional friction, while she prefers practising with her newly-formed rock band to playing domestic slave. Nevertheless, the couple survive their spats, not to mention Langella's shifty manoeuvring, to resolve their differences in a corny fairytale ending. Were it not for the fleshy couplings which punctuate the slim storyline, Vadim's flimsy moral tale would simply blow away. NF

...and justice for all

(Norman Jewison, 1979, US) Al Pacino, Jack Warden, John Forsythe, Lee Strasberg, Christine Lahti, Sam Levene.
119 min.
...and justice for all aims to do for the American judicial system what *All the President's Men* did for the presidency, and if Jewison had only maintained the tone of the superb original screenplay (by Valerie Curtin and Barry Levinson), he might have succeeded. The script's view of the behind-the-scenes wheeling and dealing in the criminal courts is both fascinating and horrifying: it employs a series of sharply observed episodes to expose a mountain of lies, chicanery, corruption and legalised sadism as Pacino's attorney battles to save various clients from the terrifying whims of the system. But, almost as if he were scared of becoming too serious, Jewison alternates some incredibly powerful moments with breezy farce, and also proceeds to drown the whole thing under a sub-disco score. The result is a bit like finding lumps of condensed milk in your gravy. DP

And Life Goes On... (Zendegi Va Digar Hich...)

(Abbas Kiarostami, 1992, Iran) Farhad Kheradmand, Buba Bayour.
108 min.
Despite its narrative simplicity, this is more complex than Abbas Kiarostami's earlier film, *Where Is My Friend's House?* (1987). Learning that the region in which he shot *Where Is...* has been devastated by an earthquake, the director (played by an actor) leaves Tehran, along with his son, to see whether his actors, especially the boy who played Ahmed, have survived. Quitting the clogged main road for perilous mountain routes, he's happy to discuss with various locals the details of the disaster, and its meaning (has God abandoned them?) – but will he reach his destination? Straddling the divide between fiction and documentary with graceful ease, this is both a subtle study in the ethics of film-making, and a compassionate (but never mawkish or depressing) portrait of courage and determination in the face of overwhelming grief and hardship. GA

And Now for Something Completely Different

(Ian Macnaughton, 1971, GB) Graham Chapman, John Cleese, Terry Gilliam, Eric Idle, Terry Jones, Michael Palin.
88 min.
Hardly very different, since this first outing for *Monty Python* on the big screen consists of a rehash of TV sketches hopefully aimed at the American market. All good stuff, though, and notably featuring 'The Upper Class Twit of the Year Race', 'Hell's Grannies' and 'The Townswomen's Guild Reconstruction of Pearl Harbor'. TM

And Now My Love (Toute une Vie)

(Claude Lelouch, 1974, Fr/It) Marthe Keller, André Dussollier, Charles Denner, Carla Gravina, Charles Gérard, Gilbert Bécaud.
150 min.
A film so defiantly sentimental and implausible that its emotional indulgence almost seems avant-garde as it presents the glossy interplay of various cultural/historical/emotional threads that finally cause a millionairess and a film-maker to fall in love at first sight. It is always stylistically dazzling, but the feelings and the characters are so shallow that they could almost be part of some satire on the French bourgeoisie. The fact that it is clearly autobiographical makes the whole thing even more remarkable. Cut by nearly thirty minutes for English and American release: the mind boggles. DP

...And Now the Screaming Starts! (aka Fengriffen)

(Roy Ward Baker, 1973, GB) Peter Cushing, Herbert Lom, Patrick Magee, Stephanie Beacham, Ian Ogilvy.
91 min.
Disastrous feature from omnibus specialists Amicus. It's sins-of-the-fathers time again, with a disembodied hand avenging the rape of a servant's bride by an ancestral member of the Fengriffen household. The sufferers of the curse are Ogilvy and his pregnant bride Beacham, but fortunately Dr Pope (Cushing) is on hand to explain all. The film might more accurately have been called 'The Screaming Never Stops', because Beacham screeches incessantly throughout, an effect more wearing than suspenseful. NF

And Now Tomorrow

(Irving Pichel, 1944, US) Alan Ladd, Loretta Young, Susan Hayward, Barry Sullivan, Beulah Bondi, Cecil Kellaway.
85 min. b/w.
Young, left deaf by meningitis, is cured by Dr Ladd with an untried serum. She's a socialite, he's from the wrong side of the tracks, but they settle their differences by falling in love. Romantic twaddle, co-scripted by Raymond Chandler, though his touch is evident only in the briefly laconic scene of Ladd's first encounter with Young in a diner. TM

Andre

(George Miller, 1994, US) Keith Carradine, Tina Majorino, Chelsea Field, Keith Szarabajka, Shane Meier, Aidan Pendleton, Shirley Broderick, Andrea Libman.
95 min.
Andre is an abandoned new-born seal discovered by Maine harbour master Harry Whitney (Carradine) and his seven-year-old daughter Toni (Majorino). With the help of Mum (Field), they nurse the creature to healthy adulthood. When Andre masters the art of balancing balls and dressing in Hawaiian shirts, Dad seizes the chance to attract the attention of the national press. But he's not counted on Billy Baker (Szarabajka), an ignorant seal-hating fisherman. Andre is not naturally winning, and the human characters don't seem to be giving body and soul to the enterprise. Undemanding. WH

Andrei Rublev (100)

(Andrei Tarkovsky, 1966, USSR) Anatoly Solonitsyn, Ivan Lapikov, Nikolai Grinko, Nikolai Sergeyev, Irma Rausch.
185 min. b/w & col.
The complete version (39 minutes longer than the print originally released) 'explains' no more than

the cut version, but at least Tarkovsky's mysteries and enigmas are now intact. Rublev was a minor icon-painter of the early 1400s. Tarkovsky re-imagines him as a Christ-like cypher for the sufferings of a divided Russia under the Tartar invaders: a troubled visionary reduced to years of silence by the horrors that he witnesses, who finally rediscovers the will to speak – and to paint. The film offers eight imaginary episodes from Rublev's life: the most brilliant coup is the story of a beardless boy saving his own life by pretending that he knows how to cast a giant bell – and finding that he can do it. This boy's blind faith rekindles Rublev's confidence in himself and his people, leading the film into its blazing climax: a montage of details from Rublev's surviving icons. TR

Androcles and the Lion

(Chester Erskine, 1952, US) Jean Simmons, Victor Mature, Alan Young, Maurice Evans, Elsa Lanchester, Robert Newton.
98 min. b/w.
Producer-elect to Bernard Shaw for *Pygmalion, Major Barbara* and *Caesar and Cleopatra*, Gabriel Pascal foundered in Hollywood with this pompously stagebound and unhappily cast spectacular which simply ambles through the play. The original casting of Harpo Marx as Androcles (he was fired by Howard Hughes after five weeks' shooting) might have been really something. TM

Android

(Aaron Lipstadt, 1982, US) Klaus Kinski, Don Opper, Brie Howard, Norbert Weisser, Crofton Hardester, Kendra Kirchner.
80 min.
Built to succeed in Roger Corman's exploitation labs, this is a remarkably skilful first feature; its space-locked power struggles are in the same perilous future as *Blade Runner*, but a witty script and concise action supplant the flash and portent of megablocks sets. Kinski is Dr Daniel, illegally engaged in advanced android research, while his less advanced android assistant Max (Opper) zaps space invaders and teaches himself the history of an Earth he's never seen with rock'n'roll and sex instruction tapes. The abrupt arrival of three fugitive convicts brings the woman Daniel needs to activate his Cassandra project, and begins a dangerous sentimental education for Max, since – unlike the characters in his pet video of Capra's *It's a Wonderful Life* – these men and women seem doomed to conflict. The result is an enjoyable genre film which never loses its sense of humour, and manages an upbeat ending instead of smoke, symbols and angst. RP

Andromeda Strain, The

(Robert Wise, 1970, US) Arthur Hill, David Wayne, James Olson, Kate Reid, Paula Kelly.
131 min.
Soon after this fair-to-middling adaptation of his sci-fi novel, Michael Crichton took to directing his own scripts. No connection necessarily, but Wise does rather plod through the plot, so that when his scientists finally make the connection between the micro-thing from outer space and a secret bacteriologial warfare project, it seems high time indeed. After a splendidly traditional opening sequence, the message about the dangers of scientific research begins to loom ponderously large, with banks of super-computers dedicated to science fact but the dialogue ('Good God, it's *growing!*') still mired in fiction. TM

And Soon the Darkness

(Robert Fuest, 1970, GB) Pamela Franklin, Michele Dotrice, Sandor Eles, John Nettleton, Clare Kelly.
99 min.
Unappealing women-in-peril thriller, scripted by Brian Clemens and centred on a young nurse (Franklin) whose holiday companion (Dotrice) is savagely murdered by a sex maniac on a lonely country road as they cycle through France. Predictable, implausible, and not a little nasty.

And the Band Played On

(Roger Spottiswoode, 1993, US) Matthew Modine, Alan Alda, Glenn Headly, Lily Tomlin, Nathalie Baye, Ian McKellen, Richard Gere, Anjelica Huston, Steve Martin.
141 min.
So keen were the makers of this adaptation of Randy Shilts' best-seller to bombard us with the facts and figures of the history of AIDS that they forgot to offer a properly dramatic human framework to make us care fully about the characters. The all-star film (from HBO Pictures) covers the early years of research: by 1980, a handful of medics had begun investigating the AIDS virus, but, despite the escalation of the numbers of those infected or dead, politicians denied them adequate funding. Meanwhile, bigots spoke of a gay plague, scientists fought for the kudos of being first to identify the virus, and disagreements beset San Francisco's gays over the closure of the bathhouses. The film, quite rightly, deals with these issues; trouble is they make for a disjointed, clichéd narrative, with Modine's honest, visionary boffin striving to make public the Truth against all odds. GA

...And the Moon Dances (Bulan Tertusuk Ilalang)

(Garin Nugroho, 1995, Indonesia) Ki Sutarman, Patna Paquita, Norman Wibowo, Wiwiek Handawiyah, Pramana Padmodarmaya.
125 min.
A young man and woman, both from troubled backgrounds, come to Surakarta to study under Waluyo, a master of traditional Javanese arts. The boy, Ilalang, wants to write music but seems trapped in memories of childhood traumas; the girl, Bulan (= Moon), is simply trying to find herself. The suppressed violence which haunts their lives – which, the film implies, may be endemic in Indonesian society – surfaces when their master dies in an accidental fire. Nugroho's exquisite film doesn't tell a story so much as it explores ambiguities of mood, texture, light and meaning. There's nothing folksy or 'Third World' about this daringly modernist film which uses a rich sound design to point up submerged emotional truths. TR

And Then There Were None (aka Ten Little Niggers)

(René Clair, 1945, US) Walter Huston, Roland Young, Louis Hayward, June Duprez, Barry Fitzgerald, C Aubrey Smith, Judith Anderson, Mischa Auer.
97 min. b/w.
Often overrated version of Agatha Christie's play in which a group of people with no discernible connections are invited to a remote island mansion by an unknown host, only to be murdered one by one. The macabre humour is the best thing about the movie, with the suspense rarely tightening the screws and some of the performances (Fitzgerald in particular) tending towards cartoonish caricature. Enjoyable, though, which is more than can be said for the 1965 (as *Ten Little Indians*) and 1974 remakes. GA

And There Were None (aka Ten Little Indians)

(Peter Collinson, 1974, GB) Oliver Reed, Richard Attenborough, Elke Sommer, Gert Fröbe, Adolfo Celi, Stéphane Audran, Charles Aznavour, Herbert Lom.
98 min.
Glossily bland tax-shelter travesty of Agatha Christie's play, shot partly as an advert for upmarket tourism in the Shah's Iran, and featuring the disembodied voice of Orson Welles as the most palatable of its international cameos. Aznavour inevitably manages a song before he becomes the first of ten assembled strangers to receive retribution for a past murder. PT

...and the pursuit of happiness

(Louis Malle, 1986, US)
80 min.
A companion piece to *God's Country*, in which Malle continues his exploration of America. The theme is immigrants, starting with a lone Rumanian touring Texas on foot in homage to his adoptive home. Success stories follow, among them a whole string of bright kids winning acceptance at Ivy League universities, at MIT, as America's first immigrant astronaut. Then there is the other side of the coin: black residents driven to violent resentment on a housing development in Houston when Vietnamese start displacing them (they have more money, say the blacks; because the blacks are lazy, say the Vietnamese). The pervasive fear – of homes and jobs put at risk by immigrants – surfaces most openly in a vivid survey of the wetback problem, with so many now arriving in quest of illegal employment that all they find is illegal unemployment. A characteristically generous film, marginally less involving than *God's Country* only because the emotional ambivalence of the earlier film (where Malle fell haplessly in love with a community that invites political contempt) is lacking here. TM

And There Was Jazz (Eyl Jazz)

(Feliks Falk, 1981, Pol) Jerzy Gudejko, Andrzej Chicklowski, Jacek Strzemzalski, Kazimierz Wysota.
100 min.
A product of the 'X' film unit under Andrzej Wajda: one of the 'missing ten' films, banned at the time for their unsympathetic view of life in Poland. It follows the efforts to keep together, and to find venues for gigs, of a group of young, mainly 'middle class' (traditional) jazz buffs and musicians. The period is the years leading up to, and immediately following, Stalin's death in 1953: jazz is seen by the authorities as 'Western bourgeois immoralism', and the only music officially sanctioned is either martial music or dire folk songs. This group prefer listening to Charlie Parker on the Voice of America, setting up crazy jam sessions in attics etc, but their energy is finally sapped by the revelations that follow the deaths, first of 'Uncle Joe' and then, tragically, one of their company. Falk offers no searing cultural or political analysis here, but an informative and likeable depiction of growing up under Stalin's dark shadow. WH

And the Ship Sails On (E la Nave Va)

(Federico Fellini, 1983, It/Fr) Freddie Jones, Barbara Jefford, Victor Poletti, Peter Cellier, Elisa Mainardi.
132 min.
Here we go again: the Italian *buffo* happily constructing his own world of elaborate grotesquerie in a studio far away from the problems of the real world. This time it is a marvellous ship, full of opera stars who set sail on the eve of WWI to bury one of their number. And as usual there are the anecdotes of droll inconsequence and pleasure – a symphony played on wine glasses, the divas serenading the stokers. When the boat picks up some refugees from the first flickerings of the war, a re-found social conscience seems about to edge in, only to be handled with the man's monumental off-handedness. But while Fellini may simply observe the chattering of his clowns and have absolutely nothing to say himself, it still (as usual) adds up to marginal doodlings which are unique, curious, ingratiatingly charming, and quietly nostalgic for the last great and peaceful age in Europe. CPea

And Woman...Was Created

see Et Dieu Créa la Femme

And Women Shall Weep

(John Lemont, 1959, GB) Ruth Dunning, Max Butterfield, Gillian Vaughan, Richard O'Sullivan.
65 min. b/w.
Truly terrible cautionary tale about juvenile delinquency, with a frantically overpitched performance from Ruth Dunning as the widowed mum who hands her elder son (Butterfield) over to the police to prevent the younger one (O'Sullivan) from going the same way. TM

Andy Warhol's Bad

(Jed Johnson, 1976, US) Carroll Baker, Perry King, Susan Tyrrell, Stefania Cassini, Cyrinda Foxe.
109 min.
If ever a movie set out to live up to its title... Baker runs a home electrolysis parlour as a front for a dial-a-murder organisation: she puts her clients in touch with lethal girls who will assassinate unwanted offspring, relatives and other enemies. The New York streets are already so full of violence that the crimes pass virtually unnoticed, but the movie makes a point of lingering over its sadistic details; everything is as grotesque as possible. At the same time, it's played as much as possible like American TV soap opera, complete with its repetitions and stretches of tedium. The

main plot centres on Perry King and whether he'll be cold enough to kill an autistic child. In terms of its own frames of reference, the movie is competent enough to almost transcend criticism, but its humour proved way too sick for most English critics. TR

Andy Warhol's Dracula
see Blood for Dracula

Angel
(Ernst Lubitsch, 1937, US) Marlene Dietrich, Herbert Marshall, Melvyn Douglas, Edward Everett Horton, Ernest Cossart.
98 min. b/w.
While the servants gossip below stairs, Dietrich flirts enigmatically between her suave English diplomat husband (Marshall) and a beguiling American old flame (Douglas). Characteristically dry Lubitsch sophistication, not much liked at the time but since hailed by enthusiasts as one of his masterpieces. To the less committed, Dietrich – caressingly photographed by Charles Lang in a manner that doesn't quite make the Sternberg grade – bats her eyelashes once too often and twice too coyly. TM

Angel
(Neil Jordan, 1982, Eire) Veronica Quilligan, Stephen Rea, Alan Devlin, Peter Caffrey, Honor Heffernan.
92 min.
An apocalyptic voyage into violence triggered by a chilling sectarian double murder of which Danny, a sax player in a rock showband, becomes first witness and subsequently avenger. The movie bristles with visual ironies, downbeat humour, upbeat action, and is powered by a sequence of chance encounters as Stephen Rea's Danny, like Lee Marvin in Point Blank, picks up the trail of the killers and, swapping his sax for a gun, pursues them through the towns and countryside of Armagh. Ostensibly a naturalistic thriller, but reaching beyond to hyper-realism and surrealism, Angel carries subtle echoes of Buñuel and the early Scorsese films (Who's That Knocking at My Door?, Mean Streets), but remains uniquely true to its time and place – contemporary Ireland. A stunning debut from an esteemed novelist. MA

Angel
(Robert Vincent O'Neil, 1983, US) Cliff Gorman, Donna Wilkes, Susan Tyrrell, Dick Shawn, Rory Calhoun, John Diehl.
93 min.
Producer Sandy Howard appears to have stumbled on an insatiable American appetite for stories of sweet young girls who trade their sneakers for stiletto heels at sundown and cruise the street for clients. This is his second movie on the subject in a year, and has made even more money than its predecessor Vice Squad. But in the true tradition of such exploitation, the posters are a thousand times more suggestive than anything in the films. Much of it is played for comedy of an innocuous if tedious kind, and it's left to the psycho dredged up from Taxi Driver to provide the more repulsive moments. DP

Angela
(Rebecca Miller, 1994, US) Miranda Stuart-Rhyne, Charlotte Blythe, Anna Thomson.
99 min.
Ambitious but uneven indie US debut about two girls and their reaction to their mother's mental and emotional volatility and their father's increasing resort to the church as a provider of stability; the titular elder girl entertains visions of a punitive devil, and decides to purify the family of sin. An imaginative attempt to get into a young girl's mind, not unlike Ann Turner's Celia, but one which suffers from languid pacing and some rather overt poeticism. GA

Angel at My Table, An
(Jane Campion, 1990, NZ) Kerry Fox, Karen Fergusson, Alexia Keogh, KJ Wilson, Colin McColl, Martyn Sanderson, William Brandt, Peter Dennett.
158 min.
Though adapted for television from three volumes of autobiography by New Zealand writer Janet Frame, Campion's film is both wholly cinematic and true to her own preoccupations. Her

subject is the privations and anxieties of childhood and adolescence, the weird absurdity of ordinary life, and the disconcertingly thin line between normality and madness, all depicted with an unsentimental honesty that veers abruptly (but never jarringly) between naturalism and surrealism, comedy and tragedy. As the introverted Frame – a plain, bubble-haired redhead born into a poor, close-knit family in 1924 – progresses through school, college and erroneously diagnosed schizophrenia towards final liberation as a respected writer, Campion deploys a wealth of economically observed details to explore her heroine's passionate, deceptively placid perceptions of the world. There are none of the usual artist-biopic clichés here. Frame, as embodied by three uncannily-matched actresses, is bright but intensely, awkwardly passive, and inhabits a chaotic, arbitrary universe. Watching her hard, slow struggle for self-respect, happiness and peace becomes a profoundly moving, strangely affirmative experience. GA

Angel Baby
(Paul Wendkos, 1960, US) George Hamilton, Mercedes McCambridge, Salomé Jens, Joan Blondell, Henry Jones, Burt Reynolds.
97 min. b/w.
Travelling evangelist shows get the once-over in this modestly intriguing exposé, with newcomer Salomé Jens as the mute girl Jenny Brooks who throws herself at itinerant preacher Paul Strand (Hamilton), whom she believes responsible for restoring her voice. Her subsequent exploitation (as the testifying 'Angel Baby') soon gives cause for doubt that he's for real. Reynolds (minus moustache) made his film bow as the girl's best pal. The script skilfully adapted from the novel Jenny Angel by Elsie Oaks Barbour is set against the telling background of the the poverty-stricken farms of the American South. Evocative low-key camerawork from Haskell Wexler, and a first-rate performance from Mercedes McCambridge as the preacher's obsessive wife. TJ

Angel Baby
(Michael Rymer, 1995, Aust) John Lynch, Jacqueline McKenzie, Colin Friels.
105 min.
A problematic but intense romance develops between Harry (Lynch) and Kate (McKenzie), who meet at a day-clinic for the psychologically disturbed. Family, friends and shrinks are happy about the relationship at first, but when Kate announces she's pregnant, concern grows over whether the couple can cope. True to tradition, Rymer strives to ensure that our sympathies lie with his optimistic outsiders rather than with the more conventionally settled. Happily, however, tendencies towards fairytale whimsy are mostly held in check by crisp visuals, an imaginative use of music, and down-to-earth performances. It's a sensitive, witty film, with an oddly benign take on the effects of watching TV quiz shows, and admirably ambivalent about the causes of the lovers' troubles. GA

Angel City
(Jon Jost, 1977, US) Robert Glaudini, Winifred Golden, Pierce Del Rue, Kathleen Kramer.
70 min.
American independent Jon Jost must be tired of being compared with Godard, but there's no denying that his Angel City does for Los Angeles some of what Alphaville did for Paris. Both movies use private eye characters to investigate more than mere murder: Jost's Frank Goya ('like the painter') is hired to check out the death of a Hollywood starlet, and winds up identifying the villains as illusionism and monopoly capitalism. The movie is structured as a kind of countdown in twelve numbered sections, ranging in theme and tone from satire of Hollywood to American 'visionary' poetry. Interesting stuff. TR

Angel Dust
(Sogo Ishii, 1994, Jap) Kaho Minami, Takeshi Wakamatsu, Etsushi Toyokawa, Ryoko Takizawa, Masayuki Shionoya, Yukio Yamato.
116 min.
This psycho-thriller about urban paranoia (from the director of Crazy Family) suggests terrifyingly that the millennium is already with us. At 6 pm each Monday a killer strikes on the Tokyo

metro, silently injecting his female victim. In shades of Manhunter, an expert in abnormal criminal cases (Minami) is brought in to try to enter his mind; she intuits that the perpetrator can sense the feeling of isolation and self-destructiveness in people. The trail leads to the HQ of the Ultimate Truth Church, in the shadow of Mt Fuji, a centre for rumoured reverse brainwashing. Beautifully acted, superbly shot, this erotic, enigmatic film has the compulsiveness of Gilliam's Brazil mixed with the darkness of Lang's M. Quite how many levels it works on is up to your own sympathies – or should that be empathies? The film is an uncanny pre-echo of 1995's Aum Shinrikyo's metro gas attack. WH

Angel Dust
(Poussière d'Ange)
(Edouard Niermans, 1987, Fr) Bernard Giraudeau, Fanny Bastien, Fanny Cottençon, Michel Aumont, Jean-Pierre Sentier, Gérard Blain.
95 min.
For Inspector Blount (Giraudeau), life is pretty confusing. His wife has left him. Murder investigations reveal that the victims have been sent dead rats. And then he becomes obsessed with an angelic waif (Bastien) with a callous disregard for the truth. With Blount suddenly immersed in a whirlpool of hidden pasts and shifting identities, the film resembles the layer-peeling methods of the admittedly superior One Deadly Summer. The elliptical noir plot allows plenty of space for offbeat comedy and generous characterisation, and Blount himself emerges as a truly sympathetic, if flawed, hero. If the final denouement is less than startling, there are more than enough digressions, twists and hints of Catholic symbolism to hold the interest. GA

Angel Face
(Otto Preminger, 1952, US) Robert Mitchum, Jean Simmons, Herbert Marshall, Mona Freeman, Leon Ames, Barbara O'Neil.
90 min. b/w.
Superb Freudian crime thriller, noir-inflected in theme but shot by and large in crisp, bright drawing-rooms. Mitchum is the archetypal noir-hero confronted with a devious femme fatale; as an ambulance driver who becomes so infatuated with the outwardly angelic Simmons that he moves in as her family's chauffeur and can't bring himself to admit that she is trying to murder her mother, he gives one of his most restrained and lyrical performances, perfectly offset by Simmons' demonic ingenue. Preminger, as it were, flattens the melodramatics of the story with typically cool clarity, emphasising its psychological complexities and allowing the occasional incursions of violence to emerge with shocking matter-of-factness. GA

Angel Heart
(Alan Parker, 1987 , US) Mickey Rourke, Robert De Niro, Lisa Bonet, Charlotte Rampling, Stocker Fontelieu, Brownie McGhee.
113 min.
A first-person Faustian detective novel presents quite a problem to the screenwriter, and Parker's alterations to William Hjortsberg's Falling Angel slacken the cunning weave of strands. Private eye Harry Angel (Rourke) is hired by the mysterious and malevolent Louis Cyphre (De Niro) to find a missing crooner who dabbled in the occult; but Angel's leads all wind up dead in a series of ritual murders. The supernatural is rendered in standard props (steam from a New York grating, silent nuns, the ominous motif of the clanking ceiling fan), and the information encoded in Angel's dreams emerges in the standard approved fashion. There isn't much imagination at work, but – damagingly – there is the disastrous quirkiness of a Coney island beach scene for winter sunbathers, while a copulation scene featuring writhing bodies and a ceiling pouring blood overwhelms the final horror of the detective's situation. BC

Angelic Conversation, The
(Derek Jarman, 1985, GB) Paul Reynolds, Phillip Williamson.
81 min.
Jarman's setting for twelve Shakespeare sonnets has no narrative as such, and the only dialogue is Judi Dench's reading of the poems. Yet even

though it dispenses with such conventions, it remains a hypnotically beautiful film. Its textured, stop-frame tableaux of caves, rocks, water, and figures in strange and terrible landscapes throw up myriad painterly similarities: the lesser religious nightmares of a Bosch or Brueghel, Victorian landscape of the 'Gordale Scar school'. Very romantic. JG

Angel in Exile
(Allan Dwan/Philip Ford, 1948, US) John Carroll, Adele Mara, Thomas Gomez, Barton MacLane, Alfonso Bedoya, Grant Withers.
90 min. b/w.
Low-budget drama about an ex-con who travels to Mexico to regain his hidden loot of gold, only to undergo a character transformation under the influence of a good woman and the local peasants who acclaim him as a saint. Carroll makes a wooden lead, but the supporting cast and Dwan's fluency with narrative (Ford took over direction for a week while he was ill) make it just about watchable. GA

Angel Levine, The
(Ján Kadár, 1970, US) Zero Mostel, Harry Belafonte, Ida Kaminska, Milo O'Shea, Eli Wallach, Anne Jackson.
105 min.
Unappealing whimsy, based on a Bernard Malamud short story, about an elderly Jewish tailor (Mostel) plagued by a bad back, a sick wife, and a business destroyed by fire, who suddenly finds an angel in his kitchen offering to help. The angel (Belafonte) is not only black but Jewish, allowing for some treacly platitudes about racial togetherness. Directed with discretion, some humour, and a soggy performance from Mostel. TM

Angel of Vengeance
see Ms .45

Angelo My Love
(Robert Duvall, 1982, US) Angelo Evans, Michael Evans, Ruthie Evans, Debbie Evans, Steve 'Patalay' Tsigonoff, Katerina Ribraka.
116 min.
The genesis of this film occurred when Duvall overheard an eight-year-old boy on a New York street having a lover's tiff with an adult woman and saying, 'If you don't love me no more, Patricia, I swear I'm gonna go back to Philadelphia'. The ardent boy turned out to be a member of NY's little-known gypsy community, and Duvall personally financed this dramatised film about their lives, using one of his favourite films, Ken Loach's Kes, as a model. The thrust of the story depends upon the rites of passage of this boy into an early adulthood, the possession of an important gypsy ring stolen by some less scrupulous members of the clan, and the eventual necessity for Angelo to choose which world, the gypsy or the wider one, he wishes to inhabit. But the film's chief joy is its patient, unobtrusive observation of a culture miles out of synch with surrounding modern America. CPea

Angelos
(Yorgos Katakouzinos, 1982, Greece) Michalis Maniatis, Dionisis Xanthos, Katerina Chelmi, Maria Alkaiou.
126 min.
Angelos is shy, tender, and gay, the product of a wretched family life (drunkard dad, ex-whore mom, crippled sister). When he meets a brashly confident macho marine, he therefore makes his bid for freedom and sets up a cosily domesticated flat with his lover, only to be sent out on the streets as a transvestite prostitute, with shame, humiliation, violence and death as the inevitable result. The sad-to-be-gay stance, so reminiscent of Nighthawks, is reinforced by the humourless central performance, while Katakouzinos' direction is frankly dull. GA

Angels
see Angels in the Outfield

Angels and Insects
(Philip Haas, 1995, GB/US) Mark Rylance, Patsy Kensit, Saskia Wickham, Kristin Scott Thomas, Annette Badland, Jeremy Kemp, Chris Larkin, Douglas Henshall, Anna Massey.
117 min.
A Victorian explorer-cum-naturalist, William Adamson (Rylance), who's returned from the Amazon in financial straits, arrives at the country estate of his patron, amateur entomologist Harald Alabaster (Kemp), who not only lends a surprisingly sympathetic ear to Adamson's interest in Darwin's theories on natural selection, but even looks kindly on the scientist's courtship of his daughter Eugenie (Kensit). Nevertheless, soon after their marriage, the newcomer has reason to feel unease: Alabaster's boorish son Edgar (Henshall) openly considers him too low-born for his sister, while Eugenia herself veers confusingly between brazen sexual passion and lengthy periods of locking him out of her boudoir. Happily, however, Adamson has an ally in Matty Crompton (Scott Thomas), a likewise impoverished dependant of the Alabasters, who shares his interest in insects and the discoveries of the age. Haas's intriguing adaptation of a novella by AS Byatt is not your average period drama. For one thing, the costumes, designs, music and camerawork steer clear of naturalism, highlighting both the modernity of the approach and the notion of humans as creatures to be observed dispassionately. Despite some uneven pacing and variability in performance, this is a work of clarity, ambition and intelligence. GA

Angels From Hell
(Bruce Kessler, 1968, US) Tom Stern, Arlene Martel, Ted Markland, Stephen Oliver, Paul Bertoya.
86 min.
Routine motorcycle gang movie, violent and gory, with spurious references to Vietnam thrown in by way of an excuse.

Angels in the Outfield
(aka Angels)
(William Dear, 1995, US) Danny Glover, Brenda Fricker, Ben Johnson, Joseph Gordon-Levitt, Christopher Lloyd, Tony Danza.
102 min.
Amiable remake of the 1951 MGM fantasy of the same title about divine intervention rescuing a down-at-heel Major League baseball team. Much bat-and-ball activity, as young Gordon-Levitt's hope for a family reunion to extricate him from the care of kindly foster mum Fricker comes to depend on an equally unlikely upturn in fortunes for local also-rans the California Angels. Soon, Lloyd's angelic helpers are improving matters on the diamond, gruff manager Glover gets convinced the kid's some kind of mascot, and even long-suffering owner Johnson starts believing that this year his boys might just go all the way. Thus the scene is set for much digital image manipulation, a plethora of think-positive platitudes and a narrative line of blinding predictability; disappointing in the circumstances, given a hard-working cast, major production values and well-staged on-field action. Fans should enjoy it; parents won't suffer too much. TJ

Angels One Five
(George More O'Ferrall, 1952, GB) Jack Hawkins, John Gregson, Michael Denison, Andrew Osborn, Veronica Hurst, Dulcie Gray.
98 min. b/w.
An unromantic view of Britain's air war, with a heavy emphasis on the mysteries of the control room. TV pioneer O'Ferrall (Murder in the Cathedral in 1936) brings to bear his WWII experience at Fighter Command HQ to depict a nervy, uncertain Battle of Britain. This slice-of-life realism reveals a world where heroism, pragmatism and fear are inextricably entwined, and easily ridiculed stiff-upper-lip restraint is a necessary defence against panic and despair. RMy

Angels Over Broadway
(Ben Hecht/Lee Garmes, 1940, US) Douglas Fairbanks Jr, Rita Hayworth, Thomas Mitchell, John Qualen, George Watts.
80 min. b/w.
A characteristically slick (if moralising) script by Hecht and fine camerawork from Garmes can't quite prevent tedium setting in as the excellent cast play a group of moral down-and-outs (embezzler, con-man, dancer, disillusioned playwright) who see the light and discover that life is worth living during a night's gambling in a New York café. The problem lies less in the pacing – as one would expect with Hecht, it moves along quickly enough – than in the incursions of uplifting sentiment into the generally downbeat proceedings. GA

Angels Wash Their Faces, The
(Ray Enright, 1939, US) Ann Sheridan, Ronald Reagan, Frankie Thomas, Dead End Kids, Bonita Granville, Margaret Hamilton, Marjorie Main, Eduardo Ciannelli, Henry O'Neill.
84 min. b/w.
Quickie sequel to the classic Warners melodrama Angels with Dirty Faces. Minus gangster Cagney and priest Pat O'Brien, it has to content itself with Sheridan's hand-wringing over young brother Thomas and his involvement with the Dead End Kids (stars of the first film and later to land a movie series of their own). A young Ronald Reagan crops up as a kindly lawyer's son and resident romance angle. TJ

Angels With Dirty Faces
(Michael Curtiz, 1938, US) James Cagney, Pat O'Brien, Humphrey Bogart, Ann Sheridan, George Bancroft, The Dead End Kids.
97 min. b/w.
A gutsy, rousing blend of gangster thriller and social comment, Curtiz' brisk film follows the lives of two slum kids who take different paths into adulthood: Cagney becomes a violent hood, O'Brien a priest. Problems arise when the local street gang – played by the Dead End Kids – come to admire Cagney for his toughness, and O'Brien has to try (the ending is hauntingly ambiguous) to persuade his former pal to pretend to be terrified as he's led to the electric chair. Great performances all round, and enough pace, shadowy camerawork and snappy dialogue to make this one of Warners' most memorable '30s dramas, despite the moralising air. GA

Angel Who Pawned Her Harp, The
(Alan Bromly, 1954, GB) Diane Cilento, Felix Aylmer, Jerry Desmonde, Joe Linnane, Sheila Sweet, Alfie Bass.
76 min. b/w.
A whimsical fantasy from Group 3, the low-budget production offshoot of the British Film Production Fund which operated under John Grierson and John Baxter to provide 'quality' second feature material and act as a training ground for emergent film-makers. Cilento is the heavenly visitor to Islington, dispensing good deeds from a pawnshop base, amidst an already nostalgic evocation of Cockney community life. PT

Anger Magick Lantern Cycle, The
(Kenneth Anger, 1947-1980, US)
151 min.
The anthology of Anger's nine released films is the most coherent (and remarkable) body of work produced by any American 'underground' film-maker. All the films are ritualistic in form and content; the later ones refer directly to the 'magick' of Anger's professed idol, Aleister Crowley. Anger's most obvious aesthetic forefathers are Eisenstein and Cocteau. Fireworks (1947, 14 min) and its inverse twin Eaux d'artifice (i.e. Waterworks, 1953, 13 min) show wish-fulfilment quests, the first successful (a lonely, masochistic boy survives a heart-stopping beating to earn himself a male lover), the second not (a crinolined dwarf cruises the dark gods of a water garden but isn't picked up). Puce Moment (1949, 6 min) salutes 1920s Hollywood, when stars were magic. In Rabbits' Moon (1950/79, 7 min), Harlequin snares Pierrot with a magic lantern image of Columbine, an illusion which kills him. Inauguration of the Pleasure Dome (1954/66, 38 min) shows a fancy dress party at which a beautiful boy is violated by intoxicated guests; the host grows stronger by subsuming everything that happens. Scorpio Rising (1964, 29 min) is an exhaustive tour of the death-wish in Western culture with a legendary rock'n'roll soundtrack; the word is made flesh in the person of Thanatos. In Kustom Kar Kommandos (1964, 3 min) a Kalifornian beach bum caresses his hot rod. Invocation of My Demon Brother (1969, 11 min) shows Crowleyan and other rituals; a god of light is born from the union of opposites. And Lucifer Rising (1980, 30 min), which features Marianne Faithfull and Donald Cammell among others, invokes Egyptian and Celtic myth (and flying saucers) to conjure the rise of Anger's own dream lover. TR

Anges du Péché, Les

(Robert Bresson, 1943, Fr) Renée Faure, Jany
Holt, Sylvie, Mila Parély, Marie-Hélène Dasté,
Louis Seigner.
96 min. b/w.
One of the most astonishing film debuts ever,
made while France was still under Nazi occupation. Bresson chose an apparently timeless subject: the way that people affect each other's
destinies. Based on the real convent of the Sisters
of Béthany, a secluded order of nuns are minutely observed in their rehabilitation of women from
prison. If the salvation is tangibly close to a
Resistance adventure, it is the simple human confrontations that fascinate Bresson – the consuming desire of secure, bourgeois-born Anne-Marie
to save the unrepentant Thérèse, wrongly imprisoned for the sake of her criminal lover.
Concentrated dialogue (with a little help from
Jean Giraudoux) and moulded monochrome photography by Philippe Agostini contribute to an
outstanding film. Rarely have the seemingly
opposite worlds of the spiritual and the erotic
received such sublime, ennobling treatment. DT

Angie

(Martha Coolidge, 1994, US) Geena Davis,
Stephen Rea, James Gandolfini, Aida Turturro,
Philip Bosco, Jenny O'Hara, Michael Rispoli.
108 min.
Angie (Davis) is a working-class Italian from
Bensonhurst, New York, who idolises her 'free-
spirited' mother whom she hasn't seen since she
was three, loves her devoted father (Bosco), and
loathes her fussy stepmother (O'Hara). At first
the only sign that she feels constricted by
plumber boyfriend Vinnie (Gandolfini) is her
sudden interest in art; then she discovers she's
pregnant, goes to a gallery, and picks up Irish
chancer Noel (Rea). Even her best friend Tina
(Turturro) thinks she's crazy when she drops
Vinnie, but her affair with Noel is a fairy-tale
romance – until unforeseen crises force her to
reassess her life. For the first hour, this adaptation of Avra Wing's novel delivers: you're carried
along by the quirky romance, sharp dialogue, and
the jokes about gynaecology and vibrators. But
then, in the last half hour, there's a change of
direction and events take an unpersuasive turn
towards tragedy – a great pity, since, as a spirited comedy, the film had a lot going for it. CO'S

Angi Vera

(Pal Gabor, 1978, Hun) Veronika Pap, Erzsi
Pasztor, Eva Szabo, Tamas Dunai.
96 min.
Set in 1948 in Stalinist Hungary, *Angi Vera* tells
the story of a bold, innocent girl sent on a course
to improve her standing in the Party. As Gabor's
camera circles, a silent witness to the emotional and moral dilemmas that surface in the group
and particularly Vera herself, we gradually discover the susceptibility which turns her from
apparently brave idealist to seemingly wilful
liar, trading her integrity (and betraying her
love) for a place in the only system which has
taken an interest in her. It's a very humanist film
which successfully blends melodrama, morals
and political comment. It also looks tremendous.
HM

Angry Silence, The

(Guy Green, 1960, GB) Richard Attenborough,
Pier Angeli, Michael Craig, Bernard Lee,
Geoffrey Keen, Alfred Burke, Oliver Reed.
95 min. b/w.
A strange mixture of melodramatic union-bashing and sharp, penetrating observations on working-class life. The villains are phantoms of an
ill-informed imagination, but Attenborough's
lone-wolf worker, holding out against an unofficial strike, is vivid and well thought out. The realism of his life with fading Italian bride (Angeli)
and womanising lodger (Craig) is superbly
realised, and hardly seems to belong to the same
film as the leering Teddy boys who act as union
heavies and the steely-eyed agitator (Burke)
whose machinations control the fate of the sheep-
like workers. As Attenborough's jaunty individualism is transmuted into paranoid hysteria, the
intrusion of tragic melodrama into what looked
like a realist social problem film becomes more
satisfying. With the villains scattered and the
hero blinded for daring to take on the world single-handed, one emerges, like the workers, suitably chastened. RMy

Angst

(Judy Menczel, 1993, Aust) Deb Filler, 'Austen
Tayshus', Moshe Waldoks.
56 min.
This documentary looks at three Jewish comedians, whose fathers were in concentration camps.
It doesn't sound like a barrel of laughs, yet the
mixture of tragedy and comedy makes for a stimulating film. Character comic Deb Filler recalls
how her school friends used to think her dad's tattoo was his telephone number; 'Austen Tayshus'
muses on the conflict between assimilating and
retaining his history; and Moshe Waldoks poses
the profound question – if Jewish parents want
all their children to be doctors, how did so many
turn out to be comics? BD

Angst

see Schizophrenia

Angst essen Seele auf

see Fear Eats the Soul

Anguish (Angustia)

(JJ Bigas Luna, 1987, Sp) Zelda Rubenstein,
Michael Lerner, Talia Paul, Angel Jove.
89 min. Video
A strikingly original, intricately constructed, and
extremely gruesome horror film about a mother-
fixated opthalmologist's assistant with an
unhealthy interest in eyeballs. 'Soon' says his
diminutive mother (Rubenstein), 'all the eyes in
the city will be ours' – and she means it. Using
creepily effective ultra close-ups and a clever
Chinese box structure, Luna introduces another
level of voyeuristic disturbance by allowing the
events in this film-within-the-film to spill out into
the auditorium (it's a case of who's watching who
when?), where a teenage girl in the audience is
becoming increasingly disturbed by the twitchy
antics of a popcorn-eating man. The execution
doesn't always match the boldness of the conception, but this post-modern shocker intelligently exploits the notion that horror is in the eye
of the beholder. NF

Angus

(Patrick Read Johnson, 1995, US) Charlie
Talbert, George C Scott, Kathy Bates, Chris
Owen, James Van Der Beek, Rita Moreno,
Ariana Richards.
90 min.
Angus is a fat kid. As we know, fat kids have it
rough: there's always some school-favourite out
there, looking to further his own vainglory at
your expense; some golden Rick Sanford (Van
Der Beek), goading you, spreading scurrilities,
running your over-sized underwear up the flag-
pole. Angus (Talbert) has it so bad he's applying
to move school, but there's a more pressing problem when Rick rigs the election for the Winter
Ball King and Queen, sending the unballetic
Angus out to an embarrassingly public dance
with the one and only Melissa Lefevre (Richards).
Basic, yes, but for a teen message movie, this is
surprisingly fun, and so sweetly good-natured it
feels churlish to sneer. Partly that's because the
film adopts such an unassuming profile: there's
little preachiness or sentimentalism. If you're a
tubby adolescent with girl trouble or a self-esteem
problem, and in need of some sensible and reassuring escapism, this may be the one for you. NB

Animal Crackers

(Victor Heerman, 1930, US) The Marx
Brothers, Margaret Dumont, Lillian Roth,
Louis Sorin, Robert Greig.
98 min. b/w.
The Marx Brothers' second film and one of their
best, satirising the rich at play as they infiltrate
a society party and beome involved with a stolen
painting. Groucho is Captain Spaulding the
explorer, the art expert is Abey the Fishmonger,
Chico and Harpo have trouble with a flash, and
Groucho insults the beautiful Ms Dumont. GA

Animal Farm

(John Halas/Joy Batchelor, 1954, GB) voices:
Gordon Heath, Maurice Denham.
75 min.
Produced and directed by Halas and Batchelor,
Britain's first feature length animation sticks to
the letter of Orwell's 'memorable fable' on the
hopes and failures of the Soviet revolution, using
an avuncular narrator (Gordon Heath) and ced-

ing all the (infrequent and largely inarticulate)
character voices to Maurice Denham, rather than
attempting to get under the skin of the piece.
Consequently, the film feels more like an illustrated audio book (or study aid) than a fully
fledged movie: an intellectual experience, not an
emotional one. TCh

Animal Love

see Tierische Liebe

Animals Film, The

(Victor Schonfeld/Myriam Alaux, 1981,
GB/US)
136 min.
Who cares about cruelty to animals? You should,
suggests this documentary narrated by Julie
Christie, not just cranks and misty-eyed pet-
lovers with more sentiment than sense, because
it's a basic political issue as much as a moral/emo-
tional one. Animal abuse means mega-profits for
factory farming and pharmaceutics, but the final
appeal is to naked self-interest rather than compassion: when life is held cheap, it's a small step
from mutilating pigs in H-bomb tests today to
annihilating people tomorrow. The film uses
expressive montage to drive its points home with
a raw and blistering anger that can't fail to move,
even if you don't always entirely agree (or care to
watch the screen). SJo

Animalympics

(Steven Lisberger, 1979, US)
80 min.
Conceived in 1976 as a 7-minute parody of the
media coverage aroused by the Olympic Games,
this animated film eventually turned up 73 merciless minutes longer. Using an assortment of animals and an armoury of terrible puns to run
national stereotypes into the ground, it might
have been tedious-but-funny. Actually it's just
tedious, with a shampoo-commercial soundtrack
from songsmith Graham Gouldman. CR

Anita

(Torgny Wickman, 1973, Swe) Christina
Lindberg, Stellan Skarsgård, Michael David,
Danièle Vlaminck, Per Mattson.
96 min.
Swedish sex film, ludicrous and melancholy, in
which Skarsgård plays a psychiatrist, an advocate of 'rational-emotive' therapy, whoever that
may be, who eventually goes to bed with, and satisfies, his 17-year-old 'nymphomaniac' patient
Anita (Lindberg). At the close, Anita's parents,
having finally lost patience with their promiscuous daughter, change the front-door locks and
have an orgy of their own. Watching this, Anita
realises she is at last free. A muddled left-over
from the Swinging '60s. JPy

Anita: Dances of Vice
(Anita: Tänze des Lasters)

(Rosa von Praunheim, 1987, WGer) Lotti
Huber, Ina Blum, Mikael Honesseau, Tillmann
Lehnert, Marion Kutschke.
87 min. b/w & col.
On a dirty grey street in Berlin, a crowd gathers
round an eccentric old woman who is performing
a strip-tease. Dragged off to a psychiatric hospital,
she demands cocaine instead of thorazine, tries to
seduce everyone in sight, and insists that she is the
legendary dancer Anita Berber, darling of the
decadent '20s. Suddenly, in true *Wizard of Oz* style,
the film departs from monochrome reality into the
colour-drenched world of the woman's fantasies,
a wildly exaggerated evocation of Weimar Berlin
filmed in full-blown expressionist style. The young
Anita (Blum) and her partner Droste (Honesseau)
set out to be the most perverse people in the world,
develop a reputation for pornographic stage performances, and have sex with anything that
moves. Inevitably, both come to bad ends: Droste
arrested for fraud, Anita dying of TB. The identity of the old woman (Huber) is never certain. Her
belief in her own fantasy is unshakeable; and von
Praunheim's film, visually astounding and performed with hilarious conviction, is an exhilarating testament to the power of the imagination. RS

Ankur (The Seedling)

(Shyam Benegal, 1974, Ind) Anant Nag,
Mirza Qadir Ali Baig, Shabana Azmi,
Priya Tendulka.
131 min.

Benegal's first narrative feature mostly recalls the modest realism of Satyajit Ray. The story is of a reluctant young rural landlord attracted to a servant whom he eventually seduces and takes as his mistress. It clearly intends some measure of social protest against an impossibly rigid caste system, the subjection of women, and traditional ruling class privilege; and if the seduction is coyly shown, the sexual nature of the relationship is at least spoken about surprisingly candidly for an Indian film. RM

Anna

(Yurek Bogayevicz, 1987, US) Sally Kirkland, Robert Fields, Paulina Porizkova, Larry Pine, Steven Gilborn.
100 min.
Much-loved '60s Czech movie star Anna (Kirkland), imprisoned for criticising the authorities, is banished to the US. There her refugee spouse spurns her to make TV commercials. Now she's just a 'resting' actress. After an audition, she befriends fellow-immigrant Krystyna (the beautiful Porizkova), who has a photo of Anna clutched in her hand. Anna takes Krystyna home, and so begins the age-old tale of master and pupil. As soon as Krystyna has her teeth done, she lands a director in the Hamptons. Bigger and better roles follow, while Anna is attacked by the green-eyed monster. What price Hollywood? A must for those who adore all things theatrical, and a maybe for those who don't. Bogayevicz's superbly acted film is for the most part an amiable study of ageing and exile. Its low-key kookiness is reminiscent of Jarmusch; its final descent into mawkish melodrama is not. MS

Anna and the King of Siam

(John Cromwell, 1946, US) Irene Dunne, Rex Harrison, Linda Darnell, Gale Sondergaard, Lee J Cobb.
128 min. b/w.
A lavish entertainment based on the real-life experiences of English governess Margaret Langdon, who arrived in Siam in 1862 to teach the King's 67 children. Sumptuous sets, exceptional photography (Arthur Miller), and some crisp verbal exchanges between the strong-willed King of Thailand and his new employee give Cromwell's light comedy the edge over the later musical version of the same story, The King and I, starring Yul Brynner and Deborah Kerr. NF

Annabelle partagée

(Francesca Comencini, 1990, Fr) Delphine Zingg, François Marthouret, Jean-Claude Adelin, Florence Thomassin, Dominique Régnier.
80 min.
It's over almost before it has begun, but you can't help noticing the close-up of an erect penis in the first few seconds; nor, despite a timely pull of focus, its subsequent discharge. This is the first and last coup in what proves to be a tedious example of the French Art Film. Annabelle (Zingg) is a 25-year-old dance student living in Paris. The obtuse angle in an Eternal Triangle, she vacillates between two lovers, the youthful Luca (Adelin) and Richard (Marthouret), an architect her father's age. The writer-director approaches this tiresome situation from an oblique, feminine perspective, but there's no insight; the film is studiously humourless, explicitly unerotic, and alienatingly disengaged. When Annabelle complains that she feels colourless, one can only agree – Mlle Zingg doesn't live up to her billing. Surely it's only in (bad) art movies that people lounge around naked staring at empty spaces, assuring a lover ad nauseam that 'I want you to death'. Numbing intellectual masturbation. TCh

Anna Christie

(Clarence Brown, 1930, US) Greta Garbo, Charles Bickford, George F Marion, Marie Dressler, James T Mack, Lee Phelps.
90 min. b/w.
Garbo Talks. So, unfortunately, does everyone else (following an evocation of the foggy wharfside, marvellously lit by William Daniels), carefully enunciating Eugene O'Neill's quaint attempts at ethnic speech patterns for a good twenty minutes before Garbo makes her appearance as the prostitute wearily seeking haven on her father's barge (and there finding love with a young seaman). As soon as she makes her entry,

hovering in the saloon doorway trailing an almost visibly murky past, one knows one is in safe hands. Even then it is several minutes before she is allowed to risk her memorable first line: 'Gimme a whisky with a ginger ale on the side. And don't be stingy, baby'. She's terrific, but she gets little support from O'Neill's play (a conventional romance tarted up with pseudo poetics) or the rest of the cast (with the exception of Dressler's gin-soaked harridan). TM

Anna Karenina

(Clarence Brown, 1935, US) Greta Garbo, Fredric March, Basil Rathbone, Maureen O'Sullivan, Freddie Bartholomew.
95 min. b/w.
Surprisingly, this mixture of MGM gloss, the aloof Garbo, and the labyrinthine Tolstoy works like a charm: visually and emotionally the most rarefied of Garbo's '30s films, with William Daniels' radiant photography preventing decorative blossoms, vines, banquet tables and riding-habits from congealing into the usual dull display of studio extravagance, and the dappled sunlight providing an ingenious background for Garbo's finely tortured passions. Rathbone, as usual, is enjoyably villainous as the husband; a drastically barbered March is less at ease as the lover; but the only real blot is provided by Freddie Bartholomew as the heroine's darling child, looking and sounding the way sickly chocolate tastes. GB

Anna Karenina

(Julien Duvivier, 1947, GB) Vivien Leigh, Ralph Richardson, Kieron Moore, Sally Ann Howes, Martita Hunt, Niall MacGinnis, Marie Lohr.
139 min.
Visually opulent but lifeless Korda production which reduces Tolstoy's novel to a routine triangle situation. Leigh and Moore make a vacant duo, with Richardson's Karenin a bundle of theatrical mannerisms. TM

Anna Karenina (aka Leo Tolstoy's Anna Karenina)

(Bernard Rose, 1997, US) Sophie Marceau, Sean Bean, Alfred Molina, Mia Kirshner, James Fox, Fiona Shaw, Danny Huston, Phyllida Law.
108 min. ·
With the authentic backdrop of imperial Russia at his disposal, writer/director Rose luxuriates in Viscontian sumptuousness, but marble and gold leaf do not by themselves a movie make. Both Marceau's Anna and Bean's Vronsky seem tentative in the extreme, especially towards each other. We don't believe their grand passion for a moment, and without much emotional involvement to usher us along, the philosophical progress of Molina's narrator is abandoned in favour of the sixth form inanities packing Rose's turgid script. Tchaikovsky's 'Pathétique' swells every time anyone so much as coughs. TJ

Anna Pavlova

see Pavlova – A Woman for All Time

Anne and Muriel

see Deux Anglaises et le Continent, Les

Anne Devlin

(Pat Murphy, 1984, Eire) Brid Brennan, Bosco Hogan, Des McAleer, Gillian Hackett, David Kelly.
121 min.
Loosely based on the journals of Anne Devlin, Murphy's second feature (following Maeve) shows how, at the start of the 19th century, the daughter of an Irish peasant farmer becomes a collaborator with the rebel leader Robert Emmet, and proves to be stronger than any man. The fight for Irish independence is equated with the struggle for female emancipation, with the military conflict occurring off-camera, concentrating attention on the battle Anne wages at home. This restraint is maintained throughout: Murphy demonstrates rather than remonstrates. With the beauty of the Vermeer-like interiors and the towering performance of Brid Brennan compensating for the somewhat slow pace, Anne Devlin is a powerful, compassionate, and ultimately persuasive film. MS

Année Dernière à Marienbad, L' (Last Year in Marienbad) 100

(Alain Resnais, 1961, Fr/It) Delphine Seyrig, Giorgio Albertazzi, Sacha Pitoeff, Françoise Bertin.
94 min. b/w.
Something of a key film in the development of concepts of cinematic modernism, simply because – with a script by nouveau roman iconoclast Alain Robbe-Grillet – it sets up a puzzle that is never resolved: a man meets a woman in a rambling hotel and believes he may have had an affair with her the previous year at Marienbad – or did he? Or was it somewhere else? Deliberately scrambling chronology to the point where past, present and future become meaningless, Resnais creates a vaguely unsettling mood by means of stylish composition, long, smooth tracking shots along the hotel's deserted corridors, and strangely detached performances. Obscure, oneiric, it's either some sort of masterpiece or meaningless twaddle. GA

Anne of Green Gables

(George Nicholls Jr, 1934, US) Anne Shirley, Tom Brown, OP Heggie, Helen Westley, Charley Grapewin, Sara Haden.
79 min. b/w.
A passable adaptation of LM Montgomery's children's classic, beginning well with the placidly fraught arrival in a backwoods town of the orphan girl whose horrified adoptive parents instantly protest that they actually ordered a boy (the atmosphere helped no end by Heggie's lovely performance as the henpecked husband who slyly – and mutely – rebels in her favour). After that the plot begins to develop galloping consumption in order to get everything in, while simultaneously sliding into sentimentality. A further hazard is the lead performance by former child star Dawn O'Day (who adopted the professional name of Anne Shirley after the character she enacts here): much too knowingly sophisticated in playing the wilfully imaginative child, she makes one feel that what the dear thing really rates is a sound thrashing. TM

Anne of the Indies

(Jacques Tourneur, 1951, US) Jean Peters, Louis Jourdan, Debra Paget, Herbert Marshall, Thomas Gomez, James Robertson Justice.
81 min.
Pretty much of a swashbuckling potboiler aside from the switch of having Peters, spirited but not entirely convincing, as the bloodthirsty (but she has her reasons) pirate chief. Not one of Tourneur's better films, although he does give it some of the same colourful bounce as The Flame and the Arrow. TM

Anne of the Thousand Days

(Charles Jarrott, 1969, GB) Richard Burton, Genevieve Bujold, Irene Papas, Anthony Quayle, John Colicos, Michael Hordern.
146 min.
Interminable plod through the story of Henry the Eighth and Anne Boleyn, sticking mainly to domestic trivia with dialogue to match. The few attempts at pageantry founder in an uneasy mixture of real locations and stagy sets, with the odd appalling painted backdrop thrown in. Burton plays throughout on a monotonous note of bluff ferocity, while Bujold remains sweetly vacuous. TM

Anne Trister

(Lea Pool, 1985, Can/Switz) Albane Guilhe, Louise Marleau, Lucie Laurier, Hugues Quester.
115 min.
Melancholy, well-observed chronicle of a painter's self-discovery. After the death of her father, Guilhe gives up art studies in her native Switzerland and moves to Quebec, sharing an apartment with child psychologist friend Marleau, but spending much time in a nearby studio confronting her emotional upheavals through work on a huge mural. Pool's understated style captures the artistic process on the wing and isn't too heavy-handed in detailing Guilhe's growing feelings for her expat host. An impressive achievement on a minor scale. TJ

Annie

(John Huston, 1981, US) Albert Finney, Aileen Quinn, Carol Burnett, Ann Reinking, Bernadette Peters, Tim Curry.
128 min.

The mystery about Huston's $60m screen adaptation of the hit stage musical – an entirely ordinary and comparatively unspectacular musical fable in which perky orphan Annie (Quinn) wins the heart of mean millionaire Daddy Warbucks (Finney) – is how it could possibly have cost so much. The songs never take off into anything very much, the whole atmosphere (apart from the climax) is distinctly stagebound, and Huston merely reveals why he had never before in his long career been hired to make a musical. DP

Annie Get Your Gun
(George Sidney, 1950, US) Betty Hutton, Howard Keel, Louis Calhern, Edward Arnold, Keenan Wynn, J Carrol Naish.
107 min.
It was to have been Judy Garland directed by the tasteful Charles Walters, but the lady was in one of her problem patches, and this version of Irving Berlin's barn-storming musical (a bit old-fashioned even when it appeared in 1946) finally emerged with vastly different personnel. In some ways Hutton and Sidney make a better team: they share a streak of vulgarity five miles wide, and the character of the gun-toting Annie Oakley offers Hutton ample opportunity to do 'what comes naturally', as the song has it. She screams, capers around, fires lots of bullets, and generally lets off sufficient energy to see one through the coldest winter. If you sit towards the back of the cinema, and don't mind leaving your aesthetic scruples with the usherette, you can be guaranteed an enjoyably rowdy, gaudy time. GB

Annie Hall (100)
(Woody Allen, 1977, US) Woody Allen, Diane Keaton, Tony Roberts, Carol Kane, Paul Simon, Shelley Duvall, Janet Margolin.
93 min.
These were the days when Allen was still a comedian who happened to make films, rather than the comic film-maker he became (Don't believe it? Then read film editor Ralph Rosenblum's account of the film's chaotic creation in the cutting-room, in his book *When the Shooting Stops*). The movie is therefore little more than a series of shrewd but disjointed anecdotes dealing with Allen's usual self-obsessive hangups and fashionable metropolitan pastimes: existential dread, masturbation, coke-sniffing, movie-going, psychoanalysis, etc. The one-liners are razor-sharp, the observations of Manhattanite manners as keen as mustard, and some of the romantic stuff even quite touching. If you can forgive the fact that it's a ragbag of half-digested intellectual ideas dressed up with trendy intellectual references, you should have a good laugh. NF

Annie Oakley
(George Stevens, 1935,US) Barbara Stanwyck, Preston Foster, Melvyn Douglas, Moroni Olsen, Pert Kelton.
88 min. b/w.
Stanwyck's first Western (of sorts), aptly described as *Annie Get Your Gun* without the songs. Not strong on fact, and inclined to string out the tiresome twists that attend the crackshot lady's rivalry/romance with the resident sharpshooter (Foster) when she joins Buffalo Bill's Wild West Show. But Stevens turns it into a nice piece of nostalgic Americana, and Stanwyck is great. TM

Annie's Coming Out
(Gil Brealey, 1984, Aust) Angela Punch McGregor, Drew Forsythe, Tina Arhondis, Liddy Clark, Mark Butler.
93 min.
Annie is stuck in a 'state garbage bin', where the staff see her as little more than a vegetable to be fed and clothed. Smitten with the drooling exterior of a cerebral palsy sufferer, she is in fact highly intelligent, and it's only thanks to the devotion of a bright young psychiatric assistant that she learns to read and write her way out of mental solitary confinement. But the biggest struggle is against society's sweep-it-under-the-carpet attitude, typified by the hospital's attempts to discredit the assistant as a neurotic meddler. A film taken from a true story which raises disturbing questions, it also comes complete with heavily loaded soundtrack and readymade emotions which, as usual, underestimate the ability of viewers to empathise with the central character. AB

Anniversary, The
(Roy Ward Baker, 1967, GB) Bette Davis, Sheila Hancock, Jack Hedley, James Cossins, Christian Roberts.
95 min.
High camp black comedy from Hammer, with one-eyed momma Davis glorying in her shrill domestic tyranny over three helpless sons. Stagy evidence that Davis never really got over *What Ever Happened to Baby Jane?*, but she still had enough industrial clout to get the original director, Alvin Rakoff, fired after a week's shooting. PT

Anno Uno
see Italy: Year One

A Nos Amours
see To Our Loves

Another Country
(Marek Kanievska, 1984, GB) Rupert Everett, Colin Firth, Michael Jenn, Robert Addie, Anna Massey.
90 min.
In Julian Mitchell's adaptation of his own award-winning play (a naive and romanticised exploration of how ruling-class attitudes in the '30s were shaped), we are asked to believe that a brilliant young homosexual (modelled on Guy Burgess) turns eastwards to communism and the USSR when he is passed over for election to an exclusive prefects' society at his public school. Where the original play was long and more meditative, making suspension of disbelief at least possible, here it just seems like nonsense. There are compensations: Kanievska successfully overcomes the theatrical origins, and Everett turns in an electric performance. As for the rest, the film persuades you that the past is indeed another country, while offering an unreliable guide to its landscape. RR

Another Dawn
(William Dieterle, 1937, US) Errol Flynn, Kay Francis, Ian Hunter, Frieda Inescort, Mary Forbes, Herbert Mundin.
73 min. b/w.
Flynn and Dieterle picked the short straw when the assignments were being handed out at the studio that week, for this African colonial melodrama wherein spouse Francis finds herself torn between husband Hunter and British army officer Flynn is flimsy fare indeed. Footnote: whenever a Warners movie of the '30s featured a cinema marquee in the background, the stock title *Another Dawn* was invariably featured. TJ

Another 48 HRS
(Walter Hill, 1990, US) Eddie Murphy, Nick Nolte, Brion James, Kevin Tighe, Ed O'Ross, David Anthony Marshall, Andrew Divoff, Bernie Casey.
96 min.
The key words here are lazy and contrived. In this pointless sequel to *48 HRS*, we get a tired replay of the classic redneck bar scene, and a desperate attempt to revive the antagonism (minus its crucial racial element) between San Francisco cop Nolte and fast-talking ex-con Murphy. The plot contortions necessary to achieve this are absurd: Nolte faces a manslaughter charge, while the resentful Murphy is about to be released after seven years in the slammer. Only when a pair of vicious bikers blow up his car does Murphy agree to team up with the gruff cop again. The sole innovation is Nolte's obsession with the mysterious Iceman, a criminal kingpin he alone believes exists. Hill's action scenes are par for the course, with plenty of shotgun slayings, vehicle chases and bodies crashing through windows. There is a certain residual pleasure, too, in Hill's atavistic efforts to introduce Western elements into an urban crime thriller, with one of the gun-toting bikers, Willie Hickok (geddit?), saying 'We're the only real outlaws left'. NF

Another Girl, Another Planet
(Michael Almereyda, 1992, US) Nic Ratner, Elina Löwensohn, Barry Sherman.
56 min. b/w.
Writer/director Almereyda shot his near-feature on a Fisher-Price PXL 2000 camera, a discontinued 'toy' that's been taken up by several American indie film-makers and artists for its unique visual qualities and marginal costs. The

ghostly monochrome works best on an intimate scale, giving this East Village, New York, chamber drama a dreamy intensity, as its boho participants float through a late-night haze of romantic pessimism. Nic (Ratner) is married, Bill (Sherman) determinedly single; they live on different floors in the same block, pursuing the mysteries of love, sex and the sway of feminine caprice. Evocative score. Leaves an impression. TJ

Another Lonely Hitman (Shin Kanashiki Hitman)
(Rokuro Mochizuki, 1995, Jap) Ryo Ishibashi, Asami Sawaki, Tatsuzo Yamada, Kazuhiko Kanayama, Yukio Yamanouchi.
105 min.
This moody Osaka blues gives a new tonality and impact to the generic tale of a hitman coming out of jail and finding everything changed. Ex-rocker Ishibashi plays Tachibana, who carries out a shattering, heroin-charged hit in the opening moments and serves a 10-year term for it. Discharged, he's disgusted to find the yakuza world he knows overrun by junk and so begins a doomed mission to clean it (and a new girlfriend) up. Mochizuki shoots the film as slow-burn drama interspersed with moments of intense violence; the images are as cool as the performances. The screenplay's from a novel by Yukio Yamanouchi, former lawyer to Japan's biggest yakuza gang, who does a cameo as a slimy bank manager welshing on a golf course deal. TR

Another Man, Another Woman
see Autre Homme une Autre Chance, Un

Another Mother (De Nieuwe Moeder)
(Paula van der Oest, 1996, Neth) Arijs Adamsons, Janis Reinis, Peteris Liepins, Anneke Blok, Geert de Jong, Theu Boermans.
95 min.
Van der Oest's refugee road movie follows a Latvian father and son as they uproot from their homeland in search of a new family life in the Netherlands. Moon-faced 10-year-old Elvis has given up on talk since his mother died. Yuris, the boy's father, snatches him from hospital and the pair wing and pray their way across the Dutch countryside in search of Yuris' one-time penfriend, and long-lost first love, Marie. There's a surprising amount packed into this superficially unassuming film: a generous-spirited overview that crosses borders, generations and life styles, ending on a note of hard-won, bitter-sweet optimism. A subtle and quietly touching contribution to Europe's burgeoning cinema of post-Cold War upheaval. NB

Another Shore
(Charles Crichton, 1948, GB) Robert Beatty, Moira Lister, Stanley Holloway, Michael Medwin, Dermot Kelly.
91 min. b/w.
Patchy and characteristically whimsical Ealing comedy, set in an unconvincingly observed Dublin, about an Irish customs clerk with dreams of moving to a South Sea paradise. An encounter with a wealthy alchoholic (Holloway) offers him his chance, but he is forced to give it up for the sake of love. Beatty is miscast as the feckless dreamer, and the whole thing is too slim to sustain interest. GA

Another Stakeout
(John Badham, 1993, US) Richard Dreyfuss, Emilio Estevez, Rosie O'Donnell, Dennis Farina, Marcia Strassman, Madeleine Stowe, Cathy Moriarty.
108 min.
Amiable bantering Seattle PD duo Dreyfuss and Estevez keep tabs on a wealthy crime couple (Farina and Strassman) suspected of sheltering a fugitive state's witness, linchpin in a major mob investigation. This time, the catch is that brassy, inexperienced DA O'Donnell has come along for the ride, determined that the three officers should pose as a vacationing family to maintain cover. There are explosions, car chases, a climactic shoot-out, and a comic dog. Comedy and suspense sensibly packaged; but very old hat. TJ

Another Time, Another Place
(Lewis Allen, 1958, GB) Lana Turner, Sean
Connery, Barry Sullivan, Glynis Johns,
Sidney James.
95 min. b/w.
Dreary tosh with Turner as an American journalist falling in love with a married British war
correspondent (Connery) during WWII. He's
killed in action, and she sets off to Cornwall to
comfort his family, in order to stave off her own
breakdown. Yucky Muck. GA

Another Time, Another Place
(Michael Radford, 1983, GB) Phyllis Logan,
Giovanni Mauriello, Denise Coffey, Tom
Watson, Gian Luca Favilla.
102 min.
Set in rural Scotland during the final year of
WWII, the boldly-explored concerns of Radford's
debut feature are with desire and desperation,
passion and imprisonment. With a classically
simple metaphor of liberation and constraint at
its heart – the relationship between a trio of
Italian POWs and a girl stifling in a barren environment of loveless labour – the film widens its
focus on crossed cultures and connections into a
productive interrogation of both the narrative
and formal seductions of foreign-ness. Cast, shot
and cut with startling effectiveness, and confidently carving its own sometimes quirky path
between those territories already staked out by
Bill Douglas and Bill Forsyth, the film emerges
as a generous delight, almost exotically moving.
PT

Another Way
(Egymásra nézve)
(Karoly Makk, 1982, Hun) Jadwiga Jankowksa-
Cieslak, Grazyna Szapolowska, Jozef Kroner,
Gabor Reviczky.
109 min.
Opening and closing – in a circular flashback
movement – on the classic cold war cliché of the
corpse by the mist-enshrouded watchtower, this
film cunningly undercuts expectations aroused
by its 1958 Hungarian setting. For the body
belongs to a female reporter punished for loving
Truth, Freedom and Beauty – in the form of other
women. Probing the interface of professional and
sexual integrity, Makk troublingly links 'deviant'
lesbianism with a commitment to impeccably
democratic ideals. Not just a film of Big Themes,
though: the love scenes sail close to the wind,
steering an unsteady course between voyeurism
and candour. SJo

Another Woman
(Woody Allen, 1988, US) Gena Rowlands, Mia
Farrow, Ian Holm, Blythe Danner, Gene
Hackman, Betty Buckley, Martha Plimpton,
John Houseman, Sandy Dennis, David Ogden
Stiers, Philip Bosco, Harris Yulin.
84 min.
A reflective drama about a college professor in
her fifties. On sabbatical to write a book on
German philosophy, Marion (Rowlands) rents an
apartment for the necessary solitude. There she
starts overhearing sessions in the psychologist's
office next door, in particular the disclosures of
Hope (Farrow), who has cause to question her
marriage, the meaning of life and death, etc.
Marion gets to thinking, and is appalled to realise
that so many assumptions about her own life and
marriage are largely unfounded: in her desire for
a controlled existence, she has evaded the emotional truth about relationships with her best
friend (Dennis), brother (Yulin) and husband
(Holm). The film shows a refinement and development of recurrent Allen themes, particularly in
the characterisation of what is arguably his most
complex female character to date. But in choosing a stylised approach, Allen too often obscures
points in overstatement and intellectual posturing. Where the film gains considerable momentum and richness is in the marvellous
performances: Rowlands' perfectly pitched
approach to a demanding role is particularly
stunning. CM

Another You
(Maurice Phillips, 1991, US) Gene Wilder,
Richard Pryor, Mercedes Ruehl, Stephen Lang,
Vanessa Williams.
98 min.
The comic duo have both seen better days. In this
fairly desperate romp con-man Pryor takes pathological liar Wilder under his wing after he's
released from a sanatorium into the LA equivalent of 'care in the community'. Ruehl and Lang
supply what plot there is (it involves a missing
brewery magnate), but Pryor's health problems
(the onset of multiple sclerosis some 5 years previously) have sapped his energy and much of his
old gumption. (Peter Bogdanovich was replaced
as director.) TJ

Antonia's Line (Antonia)
(Marleen Gorris, 1995, Neth/Bel/GB) Willeke
van Ammelrooy, Els Dottermans, Dora van
der Groen, Veerle van Overloop.
102 min.
A vibrant saga, from the firebrand writer/direc-
tor of A Question of Silence, combining feminist rigour with an involving dynastic
narrative. At 85, Antonia's reached her last day
on earth, a moment to reflect on the last five
decades since returning to her native village in
Holland after WWII – years which have seen
her raise daughter Danielle, make a life on the
farm for herself and a small community of society's flotsam and jetsam, and part from the
world a richly experienced grandmother.
Judicious character development whisks us
through the generations, but with ample compassion for the women's struggle against the
farming patriarchy, and a voice for the innocent
victims of male sexual abuse, no one in the sizeable ensemble cast ever seems left out. Solid
performances and a leavening of absurd
humour, but a touch airless. TJ

Anou Banou or the Daughters of Utopia (Anou Banou oder die Töchter der Utopie)
(Edna Politi, 1983, WGer)
85 min.
In this documentary, six Israeli women, now in
their seventies, recall their roles in the founding
of a nation that was to be a refuge for a battered
people and a light to the world. Socialism, feminism, agricultural self-reliance were to be combined in the desert of Palestine; shibboleths were
abandoned by a new generation of Jews that
would think everything out anew. Now the young
women of those days sit bemused in homes and
gardens, more splendid than any they had ever
imagined for themselves, and try to trace how
their ideals seeped away. Intelligent use is made
of archive footage, conversation and interviews
to produce a witty, and affecting, memorial to yet
another promised land. MH

A Nous la Liberté
(Freedom for Us)
(René Clair, 1931, Fr) Raymond Cordy, Henri
Marchand, Rolla France, Germaine Aussey,
Paul Olivier.
97 min. b/w.
With its barrel-organ score and mechanistic
choreography (rather than direction) of actors,
this jolly satire on automation may be dated, but
no more so now than in its own time. Though it
pales in comparison with the anarchic, even scatological, vulgarity of Chaplin's Modern Times,
which it influenced, it's well worth a look today
as simultaneously vindicating Clair's former high
reputation and his subsequent expulsion from
most critical pantheons. GAd

A Nous les Petites Anglaises!
(Michel Lang, 1976, Fr) Rémi Laurent,
Stéphane Hillel, Véronique Delbourg,
Sophie Barjac.
112 min.
A larky, strung-out tale of two Parisian youths
in Ramsgate struggling to lose their virginity
rather than improve their English. The fun, a
good deal of it at the expense of the boys' boorish, blancmange-eating hosts, is all very well for
those with an appetite for sexy adolescent cuteness; but writer/director Lang might have taken
more trouble to avoid getting the period (1959) so
ineptly wrong. No latter-day 400 Blows, it might
well be a hazy chapter in someone's autobiography: arriving in Ramsgate after dark, one of the
boys (the future cinéaste Lang?) remarks of a
churchyard that it reminds him of the opening of
Moonfleet. JPy

Ansiktet
(The Face/The Magician)
(Ingmar Bergman, 1958, US) Max Von Sydow,
Ingrid Thulin, Gunnar Björnstrand, Ake
Fridell, Naima Wifstrand, Bibi Andersson,
Bengt Ekerot, Erland Josephson.
103 min. b/w.
Widely underrated, probably because of its
strong comic elements and a tour-de-force scene
derived from horror movie conventions,
Bergman's chilling exploration of charlatanism
is in fact one of his most genuinely enjoyable
films. Von Sydow is the 19th century magi-
cian/mesmerist Volger, on the run with his troupe
from debts and charges of blasphemy, whose diabolical talents are put to the test by the cynical
rationalist Dr Vergerus (Björnstrand); their clash
results in humiliation, doubt, and death. Much of
the film is devoted to wittily ironic sideswipes at
bourgeois hypocrisy; more forceful, however, is
the way Bergman transforms Volger's ultimately futile act of revenge into a sequence of nightmarish suspense. GA

Antagonists, The
see Masada

Anthony Adverse
(Mervyn LeRoy, 1936, US) Fredric March,
Olivia de Havilland, Gale Sondergaard,
Edmund Gwenn, Claude Rains, Anita Louise,
Donald Woods, Louis Hayward, Akim
Tamiroff.
141 min. b/w.
An early stab at the swashbuckler from Warner
Brothers, which proved popular at the time but has-
n't improved with age. A deluxe period production,
adapted from Hervey Allen's doorstop novel about
'the adventures of a soul in quest of ultimate truth',
it meanders along with its gallant hero through
France, Africa, the Americas and countless contrivances, with little sense of discrimination or
structure. Although there are plenty of welcome
faces in the cast, March isn't one of them: he hasn't
the dash or the zest of an adventurer, and the film
quickly becomes arduous to sit through. TCh

Antichrist, The
see Anticristo, L'

Anticristo, L'
(The Antichrist/The Tempter)
(Alberto De Martino, 1974, It) Carla Gravina,
Mel Ferrer, Arthur Kennedy, George
Coulouris, Alida Valli.
112 min.
An Exorcist rip-off to go with The Devil Within
Her. This has got the lot, though the vomit is of
a darker green than in Devil Within Her, less
lumpy than in The Exorcist. Plus a few plot variations: girl becomes cripple, cripple becomes reincarnated burned witch, devil impregnates witch,
witch does blow-job on goat. The cosmopolitan
cast must have been selected from Spotlight with
a pin, and the dubbing is evil. AN

Antonio das Mortes
(O Dragão da Maldade contra o Santo Guerreiro)
(Glauber Rocha, 1969, Braz) Mauricio do Valle,
Odete Lara, Hugo Carvana, Othon Bastos.
95 min.
Rocha's sequel to his own Black God, White Devil
returns to the Brazilian Sertao in the period after
1940, the key year in which the last of the canga-
ceiro bandits was killed. The legendary 'warrior
saint' Antonio is now the central character, and
the movie celebrates his turn against the military
regime that hires him, offering his righteous fight
as a model for all revolutionary resistance. This
time, though, Rocha completely rejects the elements of realism that made his earlier films particularly obscure: the movie is styled and paced
like a Leone Western, and is as flamboyantly
operatic as a Jancsó parable. Interestingly, the
lack of direct historical references makes the
result all the more venomously agitational. TR

Antony and Cleopatra
(Charlton Heston, 1972, Switz/Sp/GB) Charlton
Heston, Hildegard Neil, Eric Porter, John
Castle, Fernando Rey, Freddie Jones.
160 min.

Shakespeare's play directed with hopeless stodginess, contriving to damp down all the fires (romantic, poetic, histrionic) to a sort of shabby naturalism, and very nearly irretrievably sunk by Hildegard Neil's petulant Cleopatra, a suburban schoolmarm having a fling on the Nile. On the credit side, the verse is very capably and clearly spoken; Heston gives an intelligently *sotto voce* reading of Antony as an old lion moth-eaten at the edges but still with a few roars in him; and there are excellent performances from Porter (Enobarbus) and Castle (Octavius). TM

Any Wednesday (aka Bachelor Girl Apartment)

(Robert Ellis Miller, 1966, US) Jane Fonda, Jason Robards, Dean Jones, Rosemary Murphy, Ann Prentiss.
109 min.
Limp adaptation of a stage farce in which Robards is the wealthy businessman with a roving eye, Fonda the girl on whose flat he may be found any Wednesday, and Jones the clean-living boy who means marriage. Complications and misunderstandings are permutated to the point of screaming boredom. TM

Any Which Way You Can

(Buddy Van Horn, 1980, US) Clint Eastwood, Sondra Locke, Ruth Gordon, Geoffrey Lewis, William Smith, Harry Guardino.
116 min.
Eastwood at his least appealing in a poor sequel to the already disappointing redneck comedy of *Every Which Way But Loose*. The story is similarly thin – trucker Eastwood, accompanied by his orang-utan buddy Clyde, gets involved in repetitive brawls with sundry unsavoury brutes – while the humour is far too broad and the direction plodding. GA

Anzio

see Sbarco di Anzio, Lo

Apache

(Robert Aldrich, 1954, US) Burt Lancaster, Jean Peters, John McIntire, John Dehner, Charles Bronson.
87 min.
Aldrich's first Western is a fine, muscular piece anticipating *Ulzana's Raid* in its acceptance of the alien nature of the Apache. Set in 1886, it opens with a superbly staged skirmish in which, with Geronimo having already surrendered, one of his braves (Lancaster) launches a fresh attack and is captured, but denied the death he sought: 'You're not a warrior now, you're just a whipped Indian'. What follows, as Lancaster is forced to adapt, is very much of the '50s in its view of the alienated Indian; but the Apache's odyssey is delineated with considerable complexity, alternately confirming and challenging his distrust of the white man's ways. Sadly, the logic of the film, with the Apache eventually stranded between two worlds, was compromised by interference which imposed an upbeat ending instead of accepting the inevitability of the Apache's death. Originally, after conducting his one-man war and then abandoning it, Lancaster was to have been shot needlessly in the back by Federal troops. TM

Apache Drums

(Hugo Fregonese, 1951, US) Stephen McNally, Coleen Gray, Arthur Shields, Willard Parker, James Griffith, Armando Silvestre.
75 min.
A modest but unusually effective B Western about a small township overrun by *Mescalero* Apaches when a warning from the gambler expelled earlier by the mayor goes unheeded. Beautifully staged by Fregonese, especially the climactic attack on the church where the survivors make their stand, with painted Apaches erupting through the high windows like demons from hell. Val Lewton's last production, it is full of touches instantly recognisable from his RKO series: the subtle ambivalence undermining attitudes and ethical principles, the generous stance against racism, the concern for childhood (the gambler distracts the frightened kids with an exhibition of sleight-of-hand), the love of traditional songs (the kids led into a chorus of 'Oranges and Lemons'; the minister countering the Apache chanting by launching into 'The Men of Harlech'). TM

Apartment, The (100)

(Billy Wilder, 1960, US) Jack Lemmon, Shirley MacLaine, Fred MacMurray, Ray Walston, Jack Kruschen, Edie Adams.
125 min. b/w.
Diamond-sharp satire with a brilliant performance from Lemmon as the insurance clerk who forges ahead in the rat race by lending his apartment out to philandering senior executives, only to outsmart himself when the girl of his dreams is brought there by his boss. Full of sly bits of business (MacLaine admitting to three affairs but betrayed by fingers unconsciously announcing four), and with its jaundiced vision leavened by a tender sympathy for the frailty of human motives. Even the cop-out ending (boy forgives girl and all's well) is rather moving, given the delicate skill with which Lemmon and MacLaine commute between comedy and pathos. TM

Apartment Zero

(Martin Donovan, 1989, GB) Colin Firth, Hart Bochner, Dora Bryan, Liz Smith, Fabrizio Bentivoglio, James Telfer, Mirella D'Angelo, Juan Vitali.
125 min.
No film that begins with the end of *Touch of Evil* can be all bad, but it won't win any prizes for humility either. Adrian (Firth) runs a struggling rep cinema in Buenos Aires. Empty houses oblige him to take a lodger, Jack Carney (Bochner). Carney is as laid-back and friendly as Adrian is repressed and paranoid, and soon insinuates himself into the life of the apartment block, his killer charm seducing young and old, male and female alike. He's Adrian's fantasy and his nemesis, for neither man is what he seems. Up to this point the movie comes on like Polanski's *The Tenant* buggered by Losey's *The Servant*: a heady A to Z of male melodrama with existential pretensions and film-buff iconography. Then a dose of political realism lurches us into violent thriller territory. The result is largely unconvincing; the dialogue sounds like translation, and the direction also has an affected air, An extraordinary over-emphasis on extreme close-up abandons Bochner in particular to no man's land. Donovan clearly believes he has another James Dean on his hands, but the curling lip and arched brow more often suggest Presley's *Blue Hawaii* period. TCh

Apocalypse Now 100 (100)

(Francis Coppola, 1979, US) Martin Sheen, Robert Duvall, Marlon Brando, Frederic Forrest, Dennis Hopper, Albert Hall, Larry Fishburne, Sam Bottoms.
153 min.
Film-as-opera, as spectacular as its plot is simple: Vietnam in mid-war, and a dazed American captain (Sheen) is sent up a long river to assassinate a renegade colonel (Brando) who is waging a brutal, unsanctioned war in Cambodia. Burdened by excessive respect for its source novel (Conrad's *Heart of Darkness)*, this is a film of great effects (a flaming bridge, Wagnerian air strikes) and considerable pretension (quotes from TS Eliot !?). The casting of Brando is perhaps the acid-test: brilliant as movie-making, but it turns Vietnam into a vast trip, into a War of the Imagination. CA

Apollo 13

(Ron Howard, 1995, US) Tom Hanks, Kevin Bacon, Bill Paxton, Ed Harris, Gary Sinise, Kathleen Quinlan, Mary Kate Schellhardt, Emily Ann Lloyd.
140 min.
Two hundred thousand miles from home, the Apollo 13 astronauts, Jim Lovell (Hanks, highly effective), Fred Haise (Paxton) and Jack Swigert (Bacon, great fun), find that a leaking fuel tank has made a moon landing impossible. Worse, the power drops so low, and the toxic gas levels rise so high, that the mission controllers in Houston fear they may lose their first astronauts in space. Not with Harris's Gene Krantz in charge, they won't! That the rest of the story is a matter of record (they lived) is part of the problem and the interest of the film. Ron Howard's spectacular (arguably reactionary) mega-hit about the 1970 moon-shot sticks so faithfully to the version of events related in Lovell's book *Lost Moon*, that this may qualify as the most expensive drama-doc ever made. Certainly, the suspense is missing. As a result, Howard has to rig it: the tension comes from communication breakdown, the falling-out among the crew, and the battle on the

ground between the boffins and the armed services. Sure, there are thrills and spills: the adrenaline rush of the well-mounted Saturn launch; the too-strange-not-to-be-true trajectory realignment as Bacon goes to manual; the race to fabricate a new filter from spare parts. Nevertheless, the film's low on dramatic scenes; furthermore, for a 'space movie', both the special effects and photography are surprisingly pedestrian. Where it scores is in subtly restating traditional notions of male heroism. WH

Apostle, The

(Robert Duvall, 1997, US) Robert Duvall, Farrah Fawcett, Todd Allen, Miranda Richardson, June Carter Cash, Billy Bob Thornton.
134 min.
Duvall's second feature as writer/director charts the backroad to redemption travelled by Pentecostal preacher Sonny Dewey, after he takes a drunken swipe with a baseball bat at his wife Jesse's lover. Fearing imprisonment, he leaves Texas, ditches his car and his identity, and ends up in a small, poor, largely black Louisiana town, where – as 'the Apostle EF' – he sets about building himself a new church and a new life. This is far more than a beautifully observed character study and an authentic, respectful portrait of the South; it's also a thrilling, insightful, uncommonly honest study of religious experience. For while Sonny (Duvall, seldom off screen) is prone to womanising, violent anger and the odd argument with the Lord, and while his preaching style is not without its showbiz tropes, he genuinely believes. Accordingly, the film never patronises or caricatures him, his flock or their faith. The secret of the movie's emotional power lies in Duvall's unforced, witty, profoundly humane brand of realism, and in the intoxicating energy of the church gatherings. GA

Appaloosa, The (aka Southwest to Sonora)

(Sidney J Furie, 1966, US) Marlon Brando, Anjanette Comer, John Saxon, Rafael Campos, Miriam Colon, Emilio Fernandez, Alex Montoya, Frank Silvera.
98 min.
Brando, virtually repeating his morose, vengeance-driven characterisation from *One-Eyed Jacks*, plays a lone wanderer who rides back to his home town with some hard-earned cash and a valuable Appaloosa stallion, planning to fulfil his dream of settling down. But a crazy Mexican bandit (Saxon) first humiliates him, then steals the horse, sparking a protracted running duel which allows Brando his regulation bout of suffering (after losing an arm-wrestling match, and paying the penalty of being stung by a scorpion). Being the good guy – you know this because he is kind to Mexican peasants – Brando comes out on top in the end. The film has its moments, but is rendered virtually unwatchable by Furie's mania for weirdly mannered camera angles (you spend half the time peering round, over or under obstacles behind which the action is strategically placed) and enormous, pointless close-ups. TM

Appartement, L'

(Gilles Mimouni, 1996, Fr/Sp/It) Vincent Cassel, Monica Bellucci, Jean-Philippe Ecoffey, Romane Bohringer, Sandrine Kiberlain, Olivier Granier.
116 min.
A chance encounter in a Paris café puts young exec Max (Cassel) on the trail of the girl he loved and lost. He bids goodbye to his fiancée, pretends to go on a business trip, and sets off in search of the elusive Lisa (Bellucci). Flashbacks and reminiscences with his best pal (Ecoffey) reveal the story of a passionate near-thing, while the present is complicated by the enigmatic Alice (Bohringer, simmering). The double narrative melding past and present is managed with nonchalant grace, and a leavening sense of its own ridiculousness. Hitchcock echoes through this realm of obsession, voyeurism and desire. Moreover, writer/director Mimouni toys pleasurably with the tricks of celluloid illusion: masks, mirrors and colour-coding deliver a self-consciously heightened experience almost woozy with its own playfulness. A smart, sexy, and effortlessly cool first feature. TJ

Appât, L' (The Bait)

(Bertrand Tavernier, 1995, Fr) Marie Gillain, Olivier Sitruk, Bruno Putzulu, Richard Berry, Philippe Duclos, Marie Ravel.
116 min.

In most respects, Nathalie (Gillain) is like any other 18-year-old Parisian shopgirl: just attractive enough to do a little modelling, devoted to her boyfriend Eric (Sitruk), and bright enough to keep both of them afloat. But her means of making extra cash (chatting up rich businessmen in bars) isn't enough to fulfil their dream of going to America. So when Eric suggests they do a robbery or two, using Nathalie's promises of sex to get to her various 'acquaintances', she reluctantly agrees. But the best laid plans… Tavernier has always seemed most comfortable when dealing with ordinary people in extraordinary situations, and this proves an intriguing antidote to the slick, quick-paced thrillers favoured by Hollywood. It's not that easy a movie to watch – some of it is slow, the three main characters are not very sympathetic, and the violence (while not graphic by American standards) derives from a callousness that is quite sickening – but its quiet assurance and unsentimental intelligence makes for engrossing viewing. GA

Appel du Silence, L'

(Léon Poirier, 1936, Fr) Jean Yonnel, Pierre de Guingand, Jacqueline Francell, Suzanne Bianchetti.
102 min. b/w.

Through a scheme sponsored by the Catholic Church, 100,000 of the faithful each stumped up a few francs to finance this movie, said sum eventually to be deductible at the box office. (The idea was instantly copied by the workers' CGT to make Renoir's La Marseillaise.) The result was a hero-worshipping account of the life of Charles de Foucauld, soldier, explorer, missionary ('the hermit of the Sahara'), killed by Arab rebels in 1916. The plodding Poirier's tableaux are notable only for their wholesale issue-dodging and the suppression of everything even slightly contentious to do with colonialism, race, religion and sex. BBa

Applause

(Rouben Mamoulian, 1929, US) Helen Morgan, Joan Peers, Fuller Mellish Jr, Henry Wadsworth, Jack Cameron, Dorothy Cumming.
82 min. b/w.

Despite being both Mamoulian's debut for the cinema and a very early talkie, this deeply affecting tale of Stella Dallas-style maternal self-sacrifice transcends its sentimental shortcomings through the fluency of direction that was to become Mamoulian's trademark. As Helen Morgan's ageing burlesque queen steadily progresses towards giving up everything – even her life – for her convent-educated daughter (Peers), Mamoulian pulls out all the stops, employing unusually mobile expressionist camerawork to convey a wealth of detail in his portrait of the seedy backstage realities of the vaudeville world. Pacy, concise and innovative, the film also benefits from a truly magnificent performance from torch-singer Morgan. GA

Apple, The

(Samira Makhmalbaf, 1998, Iran) Massoumeh Naderi, Zahra Naderi, Ghorbanali Naderi, Azizeh Mohamadi.
85 min.

Directed by the 18-year-old daughter of Mohsen Makhmalbaf (who wrote and edited this film), this tells the story of two gauche, innocent girls suddenly let loose on the streets of Tehran (by a pleasingly determined social worker) after being kept locked indoors for twelve years by their impoverished, elderly father and their blind, deeply insecure mother. Like so many Iranian films about children, it's simplicity itself in terms of its narrative, but cute charm is effectively offset by the harsh, unsentimental portrait of family life based on inflexibly strict, finally self-serving traditions. It's a witty, gentle but often surprisingly acerbic little movie, slowly working its way towards a quite devastating final shot which underlines the need for an open heart and mind. GA

Apple Dumpling Gang, The

(Norman Tokar, 1974, US) Bill Bixby, Susan Clark, Don Knotts, David Wayne, Slim Pickens.
100 min.

A comparatively attractive Disney comedy, set in Californ-i-ay in the 1870s, about a professional gambler lumbered with three orphaned children. The traditional ingredients of homely moralising, sentimentality and raucous slapstick are used sparingly, the dialogue is fairly bright, some visual gags are neatly executed, even Knotts is bearable, and Susan Clark makes an auspicious Disney debut as the Calamity Jane-type heroine. GB

Appointment in Honduras

(Jacques Tourneur, 1953, US) Glenn Ford, Ann Sheridan, Zachary Scott, Rodolfo Acosta, Jack Elam, Ric Roman, Rico Aloniz.
79 min.

A lurid jungle adventure, complete with crocodiles, piranhas, vampire bats, ants and a puma. Ford is an American planter with an urgent rendezvous in Honduras to deliver money to the former President, ousted in a coup. When the ship's captain refuses to dock because revolution is brewing, Ford frees five Nicaraguan criminals being shipped home to jail, hijacks a lifeboat with their help, and takes along a married couple (Scott, Sheridan) as hostages. Mainly because he alone knows the jungle, Ford has an edge on everyone else, and predictably wins Sheridan over from the cowardly Scott. With fine camerawork (Joseph Biroc), good performances, and a script that weaves a shallow but surprisingly complex tangle of lies and loyalties, Tourneur keeps things moving along briskly and enjoyably. His choreography of the showdown, a running fight through jungle and village, is particularly skilful. TM

Appointment With Death

(Michael Winner, 1988, US) Peter Ustinov, Lauren Bacall, Carrie Fisher, John Gielgud, Piper Laurie, Hayley Mills, Jenny Seagrove, David Soul.
102 min.

Winner's tongue-in-cheek direction overplays the clichés: even Hercule Poirot (Ustinov) seems to have lost respect for his profession. Agatha Christie's story concerns a stepmother (Laurie) who cheats her adopted family out of the proceeds of their father's will; to distract their attention, she arranges a family cruise to Palestine, where the old bag is bumped off and various well-met stiff upper Britishers lengthen the list of suspects. Much is made of period (the '30s), picture-postcard settings, and a host of stars, some of them already veterans of Christie adaptations, others probably doomed to a similar tale in the future. For all the glitter and gloss that Golan and Globus can buy, the film suffers from a mind-numbing inertia, its acting anal retentive, its scene-shifts stagy. EP

Appointment with Venus (aka Island Rescue)

(Ralph Thomas, 1951, GB) David Niven, Glynis Johns, George Coulouris, Kenneth More, Patric Doonan, Noel Purcell, Bernard Lee.
89 min. b/w.

Leaden, would-be whimsical Rank comedy about a World War II British commando raid to rescue the pregnant prize-winning cow of the title from a Nazi-occupied minor Channel isle and secure its valuable breeding strain. A mere moment's meditation on the ramifications of a narrative about generic superiority (albeit bovine) should convince you that you'd be deeply offended if you were daft enough to see it. PT

Apprenticeship of Duddy Kravitz, The

(Ted Kotcheff, 1974, Can) Richard Dreyfuss, Micheline Lanctôt, Jack Warden, Randy Quaid, Joseph Wiseman, Denholm Elliott.
121 min.

Adaptation of Mordecai Richler's serio-comic novel about a whizz-kid's no-pause-for-thought dash for the top, with Dreyfuss playing Duddy like the kid we were all at school with who was already working on his first ulcer, confirming his earlier promise in Dillinger and American Graffiti. Set in the Jewish community of 1948 Montreal, the film has everybody parading their obsessions up front in a manner that too often makes for easy pigeon-holing (voice-of-conscience grandfather, torn Christian girlfriend, etc). Such characterisation serves the film's comic

intentions better than its message, most notably in the performances of Denholm Elliott as the drunken English film director requisitioned by Duddy to film Bar Mitzvahs, and Randy Quaid as an innocent simpleton. CPe

Apprentis, Les

(Pierre Salvadori, 1995, Fr) François Cluzet, Guillaume Depardieu, Judith Henry, Claire Laroche, Philippe Girard, Bernard Yerles, Marie Trintignant.
98 min.

Salvadori's follow-up to his eccentric debut Wild Target is another droll comedy of manners that milks humour from a story of outsiders. Here – more properly insiders, given the time they spend in the flat – they are two no-hopers, Antoine (Cluzet in po-faced, mildly hysteric form) and Fred (gangling Depardieu), thrown together when they find themselves permanently taking temporary residence in the vacated Paris apartment of a mutual friend. The older Antoine, an aspirant writer without a whole idea, is neurotic, ditzy and incredulous; Fred, a likeable, half-dressed slouch, is more phlegmatic. Theirs is not a marriage of true minds, more a coupling of convenience – strictly heterosexual, of course – until the going gets tough, and Antoine comes close to losing his mind. Salvadori has the confidence to gear down from the frenetic farce of the earlier movie to a laid-back observational style more suited to his odd couple's languorous misadventures. Cluzet makes a fine curmudgeon, a facial register of woe; and Depardieu (who won a César for his performance) is a seductive naïf. Marie Vermillard's script pushes too hard for significance and pathos at the end, and the film misses the gravity lent by Jean Rochefort to Wild Target, but it's a genuinely winning light comedy. WH

Après l'Amour

(Diane Kurys, 1992, Fr) Isabelle Huppert, Bernard Giraudeau, Hippolyte Girardot, Lio.
105 min.

Thirty-year-old novelist Lola (Huppert) is involved with two men: David (Giraudeau), an architect, and Tom (Girardot), a guitarist. Both are unhappily married with kids. Lola tries to maintain her independence, to conduct her affairs on her own terms, but age is catching up with her, and her freedom is an illusion of sorts, perhaps just a subtler form of entrapment. And after love, there is punishment. You may not agree with Kurys' thesis, but it's sincere. Her mise-en-scène gains in immediacy and spontaneity, and the acting is surprisingly forceful, given that the characters are mostly ineffectual. Finally, however, the narrow perspective doesn't square with the movie's pretensions to art: one longs for more dangerous liaisons, and when Kurys tries to reach out towards other people, other lives, the film loses its definition. TCh

Aprile

(Nanni Moretti, 1998, It) Nanni Moretti, Silvia Nono, Pietro Moretti, Silvio Orlando, Daniele Luchetti.
78 min.

More explicitly political than Dear Diary, this again occupies that intriguing territory between reality and fiction as it celebrates both the birth of Moretti's son and (with some reservations) the long awaited triumph of the Left in Italy. Once again, too, it's heartfelt, eccentric and often very funny, as Moretti shares his anxieties and joys, likes and dislikes, incidentally including his own manifest shortcomings (paranoia, hysteria, self-centredness, indecision). Simultaneously sharp and gentle, rambling and to the point, it stealthily leads us into an ever stranger personal world, so that by the finale, extraordinary images of the film crew (with Moretti in cape, motorbike helmet and shades) swaying to the rhythms of a musical sequence about a Trotskyist pastry chef (!) seem perfectly normal. GA

April Fools, The

(Stuart Rosenberg, 1969, US) Jack Lemmon, Catherine Deneuve, Peter Lawford, Jack Weston, Myrna Loy, Charles Boyer.
95 min.

Despite the cast, a dire romantic comedy, with Lemmon as a New York stockbroker grasping at extra-marital bliss in the shape of a married Frenchwoman. It looks as though Rosenberg had taken a crash course in Lelouch chic before making it. TM

Apu Trilogy, The

see Pather Panchali

Arabesque

(Stanley Donen, 1966, US) Gregory Peck,
Sophia Loren, Alan Badel, Kieron Moore, Carl
Duering, George Coulouris.
105 min.
Espionage thriller in which Peck is an American
professor adrift in a tourist-eye England, coping
with mysterious hieroglyphs, sinister Arabs, and
an ambiguous Loren. Much flashier than Donen's
earlier *Charade* (also scripted by Peter Stone,
alias Pierre Marton) and very sub-Hitchcock. TM

Arabian Adventure

(Kevin Connor, 1979, GB) Christopher Lee,
Oliver Tobias, Emma Samms, Milo O'Shea,
Mickey Rooney, Puneet Sira, John
Ratzenberger, Shane Rimmer, Peter Cushing.
98 min.
Lavishly mounted Arabian Nights fantasy
including the usual magic carpets, evil caliphs,
cheeky beggar boys and comely princesses, but
lacking the requisite invention and fizz. Tobias
is the heroic prince whose task it is to retrieve the
legendary Rose of Elil, defeat dictator Lee and
win the hand of fair Emma Samms. Crisply photographed by Alan Hume, and in terms of effects
and model work an improvement on director
Connor's earlier lost-world pictures. TJ

Arabian Nights (Il Fiore delle Mille e una Notte)

(Pier Paolo Pasolini, 1974, It/Fr) Ninetto
Davoli, Ines Pellegrina, Franco Citti.
130 min.
If *The Decameron* represented an intense vision
behind its humourous facade, and *The
Canterbury Tales* – the trilogy's weak point – a
loss of ground amid a welter of sexual exhibitionism, the *Arabian Nights* emerges as a wonderfully relaxed and open puzzle of interlinked
tales dedicated to the multiplicity of truth. It
yields an engrossing array of mysterious, profound and liberating moments. The tales revolve
around slaves and kings, demons, love, betrayal,
loss and atonement. Zumurrud (Pellegrina), a
slave turned monarch, after her 'drag' wedding,
amid delightfully conspiratorial laughter, reveals
her true sexual identity to her diminutive (and
equally delighted) bride. Shot on location in North
Africa, the film has rarely been seen in Britain
after its release in 1975 by United Artists – in an
insanely dubbed version, ludicrously cut by the
censor. VG

Arachnophobia

(Frank Marshall, 1990, US) Jeff Daniels, Harley
Jane Kozak, John Goodman, Julian Sands,
Stuart Pankin, Brian McNamara, Mark L.
Taylor, Henry Jones, Mary Carver.
109 min.
Dr Ross Jennings (Daniels), his wife (Kozak) and
their two children uproot from the urban sprawl
to a picturesque Californian small town. But the
locals are distrustful of the city slickers – feelings
compounded when the new doctor's patients start
dropping dead. A poisonous spider, accidentally
imported from the Venezuelan rain forests, has
also taken up residence, and its deadly offspring
are making house calls outside surgery hours.
For his directorial debut, long-time Spielberg producer Frank Marshall has crammed the screen
with plenty of knee-jerk thrills interlaced with
black humour. Subtlety of characterisation is secondary to the antics of the 'little vampires', with
victims conveniently earmarked (gluttons, a jock
and an unshaven whinger receive painful lessons
in social rejection), and John Goodman easily
upstaging his co-stars in a glorious appearance
as a bull-headed pest controller. Designed to
reduce the audience to a squirming mass, the film
yields plenty of grisly pleasures. CM

Archangel

(Guy Maddin, 1990, Can) Kyle McCulloch,
Kathy Marykuca, Sarah Neville, Ari Cohen,
Michael Gottli.
90 min. b/w.
WWI. Deep in Russian snows, peg-leg Canadian soldier Boles, pining for his lost Iris, is billeted in
Archangel with the family of the lovely Danchuk;
but the addled Boles ignores Danchuk's feelings for
him in favour of mysterious Veronkha, whom he

mistakes for Iris, although she is really the spurned
wife of a faithless Belgian aviator... Confused? No
matter; so are the characters in this absurdist melodrama. Maddin's second feature is pitched
straighter than *Tales from the Gimli Hospital*, but
is every bit as inspired and patchy. Pastiche remains
to the fore, with Maddin's acute sense of camp more
historically motivated than before. Complete with
hieratic '20s-style acting, the film is an extravagant
mélange of *All Quiet on the Western Front*,
Eisenstein and DeMille, all the more impressive for
its cut-price *mise en scène*. The war scenes are
extraordinary, although thrown in far too liberally;
even better are the daft tableaux vivants which
seem to comprise Archangel's only entertainment.
JRo

Arch of Triumph

(Lewis Milestone, 1948, US) Charles Boyer,
Ingrid Bergman, Charles Laughton, Louis
Calhern, Roman Bohen.
120 min. b/w.
Like Milestone's *All Quiet on the Western Front*,
this was based on a novel by Erich Maria
Remarque (disastrously bowdlerised on the way
to the screen). Boyer is an Austrian refugee who
hits Paris in 1938 and has a doomed affair with
suicidal doxy Bergman, while Laughton lurks as
the sinister Gestapo menace. Gloomy melodrama,
woodenly directed, and too self-conscious to provoke much snuffling into paper tissues. AB

Ardilla Roja, La

see Red Squirrel, The

Arena, The

(Steve Carver. 1973, US) Pam Grier, Margaret
Markov, Lucretia Love, Paul Muller,
Daniel Vargas.
83 min.
High camp from Roger Corman's New World
Pictures, with the ancient Romans setting their
women slaves to fight in the arena. Fetishistic costumes and nudity are carefully harnessed to the
portrait of a decadent society keeping the mob suppressed by letting them vent their feelings on blood
sports. Enjoyable to watch the actresses getting
their tongues round lines like 'O Guards! Do you
mean to say we have to satisfy their animal lust?'

Are You Being Served?

(Bob Kellett, 1977, GB) John Inman, Mollie
Sugden, Frank Thornton, Trevor Bannister,
Wendy Richard, Arthur English.
95 min.
Woefully unfunny and extremely objectionable
big-screen spin-off from the woefully unfunny
and extremely objectionable TV sitcom series set
in a none too realistic department store. Crap of
the lowest order as the staff of Grace Brothers'
clothing department go on holiday to the Costa
Plonka. GA

Are You Dying, Young Man?

see Beast in the Cellar, The

Argent, L'

(Marcel L'Herbier, 1928, Fr) Pierre Alcover,
Alfred Abel, Brigitte Helm, Mary Glory,
Raymond Rouleau, Antonin Artaud, Jules
Berry, Yvette Guilbert.
195 min. b/w.
One of the great silent movies: a superlative adaptation of Zola's novel about warfare in the world
of international finance when one tycoon sets out
to ruin another. Full of delicate metaphorical touches, the film has an intricate narrative fluidity that
never betrays its origins in a densely plotted novel.
What chiefly amazes, though, is the extreme
sophistication of L'Herbier's visual approach: vast
architectural sets dwarf the humans scurrying in
frenzied quest of fame and fortune; scenes in echoing corridors leading to the bank anticipate
Antonioni as people come and go between massive pillars, aware of each other and of conflicting
interests, but never quite connecting; strange, gliding movements of the camera, constantly zeroing
in to isolate the private motivations of a character,
or withdrawing to reorientate the context, to make
new connections, to suggest wider implications.
Deliberate mystification is one of L'Herbier's tools.
One scene, an unmistakable premonition of *Last
Year in Marienbad*, has the camera travelling sinuously through halls and corridors before discovering a benign old gentleman – the *eminence grise*,

we realise, behind a Stock Exchange collapse –
feeding his lapdog. Not for nothing did Resnais
acknowledge his debt to L'Herbier. TM

Argent, L' (Money)

(Robert Bresson, 1983, Switz/Fr) Christian
Patey, Sylvie van den Elsen, Michel Briguet,
Caroline Lang.
84 min.
A single 500 franc forged note changes hands as
a schoolboy prank; and with remorseless logic,
an innocent is led down the path to becoming an
axe-murderer. Taken from a Tolstoy short story,
this is a return to the extremes of crime and punishment that Bresson last used in *Pickpocket;* and
as in that film, crime is a model of redemption and
prison a metaphor for the soul. True to a taste for
Catholic paradox, the murderer may or may not
'find' himself through his acts; the family is axed
in the name of spiritual release; and most powerful of all, Evil is not demeaned by any vacuous
sociological explanation. Filming with his usual
tranquil, austere feeling for the miraculous,
Bresson still manages to make most other film-
makers appear hysterical over-reachers; at nearly 80, his power to renew our faith in cinema is
as firm as one could wish for. Gold, pure. CPea

Argie

(Jorge Blanco, 1985, GB) Jorge Blanco,
Christine Plisson, Christine von Schreitter,
Ella Blanco.
75 min.
A film whose main attraction is its wild premise:
a drunken Argentinian no-hoper, settled in Britain
at the time of the Falklands, decides he should
declare war on the UK and opts for the rape of a
barmaid as his martial overture. Unfortunately
she turns out to be only too willing, and they team
up together to vent their dissatisfaction on the rest
of the world. It has a certain crude charm, rather
like finger-painting. CPea

Argent de Poche, L' (Small Change)

(François Truffaut, 1976, Fr) Geory
Desmouceaux, Philippe Goldmann, Jean-
François Stévenin, Virginie Thévenet,
Marcel Berbert.
105 min.
That critics hailed Truffaut's film about children
as 'delightful' and 'enchanting' is a fair indication
of its gross sentimentality. An initial sequence
showing pupils arriving for school in a small
French provincial town serves as the linking device
for a series of unrelated episodes involving individual children and their families, ranging from the
inconsequential to the downright mawkish. There's
not a snotty nose in sight, just endless well-
scrubbed faces into whose mouths Truffaut frequently puts lines of quite nauseating cuteness:
'Gregory went BOOM!' burbles the toddler who has
fallen – unscathed, alas – from a ninth floor window. And most winsome of all is Julien (Goldmann),
the doe-eyed welfare case whom a school medical
reveals to have been beaten up by his parents: presumably this film's intended audience would have
difficulty feeling sorry for an *unattractive* child. AS

Argent des Autres, L' (Other People's Money)

(Christian de Chalonge, 1978, Fr) Jean-Louis
Trintignant, Claude Brasseur, Catherine
Deneuve, Michel Serrault, Juliet Berto,
Umberto Orsini.
105 min.
This Prix Delluc winner is a surprisingly compulsive microcosmic political thriller, delving into
the labyrinthine world of banking and high-finan-
cial manipulation. The astute casting of that
perennial victim Trintignant – made the scapegoat for a scandal the bank is hushing up, he
explores the system in his determination to fight
back – points the cinematic connection with the
more overtly violent, equally ghastly worlds of
Costa Gravas and Yves Boisset. PT

Aria

(Nicolas Roeg/Charles Sturridge/Jean-Luc
Godard/Julien Temple/Bruce Beresford/Robert
Altman/Franc Roddam/Ken Russell/Derek
Jarman/Bill Bryden, 1987, GB) John Hurt,
Theresa Russell, Julie Hagerty, Linzi Drew,
Tilda Swinton.
89 min.

Ten directors, ten arias. Don Boyd's opera omnibus was bound to be hit-and-miss. Bryden's linking passages, and the Sturridge and Beresford sections, miss; Jarman's and Temple's are largely about Super 8 and Steadicam respectively. Roddam's *Tristan and Isolde*, like Temple's *Rigoletto*, is the work of a Brit thrilled by the neon tackiness of America, and determinedly candid in its sex and violence. Russell's *Turandot* comes on like a decorative episode of the *The Twilight Zone*. The Godard undoubtedly makes the most waves, being far out and featuring bodybuilders and nubile cleaning ladies: infuriatingly preposterous or light years ahead, its use of sound is astonishingly effective. Roeg's marvellous opener will stir memories of *The Eagle Has Two Heads*, *The Third Man*, and most things Ruritanian down Zenda way. Altman's typically droll decision to film the response, to a performed aria, of an audience of Hogarthian bedlamites, provides a mesmerising parallel activity which fans of Free Jazz drumming will find no difficulty in following. BC

Ariel

(Aki Kaurismäki, 1988, Fin) Turo Pajala, Susanna Haavisto, Matti Pellonpää, Eetu Hilkamo, Erkki Pajala, Matti Jaaranen, Hannu Viholainen.
72 min.
It begins like a road movie. When the local mine is closed, Taisto (Turo Pajala) takes his redundancy pay and his father's parting gift – a snow-white Cadillac convertible – and sets off across Finland headed nowhere in particular. Soon relieved of his money, he drifts into a few days work on the docks, and then into a relationship with Irmeli (Haavisto) and her young son. In a similarly abstracted manner the film goes through the motions of social realism, and subsequently the conventions of the prison drama, but retains the stripped-down style and cool existentialism of the road movie long after the Cadillac is sold and the journey is waylaid. With restraint worthy of Bresson, Kaurismäki defuses the dramatics, but explodes our preconceptions. Fades to black punctuate scenes of immaculate simplicity, photographed impeccably by Timo Salminen. There is an obvious affinity, too, with Jim Jarmusch's work; the prevailing gloom is undercut by the music, kitsch pop and Finnish tango, and a sense of humour dry as a Buñelian martini. TCh

Arise, My Love

(Mitchell Leisen, 1940, US) Claudette Colbert, Ray Milland, Walter Abel, George Zucco, Dennis O'Keefe.
113 min. b/w.
Like *To Be or Not To Be*, a film that defies bad taste with a starkly low-key opening in a Spanish jail where Milland awaits the firing-squad for his part in the Civil War, but walks bemusedly out into the arms of Colbert, a stranger (and aspiring reporter) claiming him as her husband and successful in an appeal for clemency. What follows, set in Hollywood's dreamy notion of springtime in Paris as the Nazi boot relentlessly crushes Europe, is romantic comedy at its most brilliant, scripted by Brackett and Wilder with a nice line in sexual innuendo and cynical irreverence. Inspiration flags latterly, though, as the groundwork is laid for a message to democracy. Even Brackett and Wilder can't quite get away with the notion of adapting the lines quoted earlier from 'The Song of Solomon' ('Arise, my love, my fair one, come away') as a rousing appeal to America ('Arise, my love, arise, be strong'). TM

Aristocats, The

(Wolfgang Reitherman, 1970, US) voices: Hermione Baddeley, Roddy Maude-Roxby, Eva Gabor.
79 min.
The last of the Disney animated features conceived under the great Walt's perfectionist reign of terror, this 1970 Technicolor classic marks the move towards the less labour-intensive ink-and-wash cell design which followed. The ersatz Parisian atmosphere, circa 1910, is a wonder. Maurice Chevalier may have made the theme song familiar, but the voice cast boasts a fine array of ex-pats: spinster cat-lover Mme Bonfamille is Hermione Baddeley; the conniving butler – the cad who casts her cats into the countryside to inherit her wealth – is Roddy Maude-Roxby; her beloved cat Duchess the

seductive Eva Gabor. As Scatman Crothers has it: 'Everybody's picking up the feline beat, 'cos everything else is ob-so-lete!' Purr-fect. WH

Arizona Dreaming

(Emir Kusturica, 1993, Fr/Former Yugo) Johnny Depp, Jerry Lewis, Faye Dunaway, Lili Taylor.
135 min.
The first 'American' film by the director of *Time of the Gypsies* is every bit as bizarre and imaginative as his earlier work, although it's also maddeningly indulgent and erratic. Depp is persuaded to leave his job counting fish (!) to attend uncle Jerry Lewis's wedding in the Midwest; there he becomes embroiled in the lives of Taylor and her crazy mother, Dunaway, and invents a flying machine. A curate's egg with more than its share of longueurs, but its comically surreal viewpoint is infectious (an aspiring actor's *pièce de résistance* turns out to be the crop-dusting scene from *North by Northwest*). TCh

Arm, The (aka The Big Town)

(Ben Bolt, 1987, US) Matt Dillon, Diane Lane, Tommy Lee Jones, Bruce Dern, Lee Grant, Tom Skerritt.
110 min.
Gambler JC Cullen (Dillon) meets Hooker, a retired diceman in his Indiana hometown, who urges him to chance his arm in Chicago, and gives him his lucky dollar and an introduction to a husband and wife team (Dern and Grant) who have the action sewn up. He shoots dice for them for percentages, but itches to crack the big game in the back room of the strip club run by badman Cole (Jones). Torn between good girl Aggie and Cole's conniving stripper wife (Lane), JC has to discover the things that are meaningful and enduring the hard way. Just about the only pleasure in this formula effort is matching up memories of Rip Torn in *The Cincinnati Kid* with Bruce Dern. Edward G and McQ still have the only game in town. BC

Armed and Dangerous

(Mark L Lester, 1986, US) John Candy, Eugene Levy, Robert Loggia, Kenneth McMillan, Meg Ryan, Brion James, Don Stroud, Steve Railsback, Jonathan Banks.
88 min.
Given the potential of the very reasonable cast, one might expect rather more than is delivered by this dim comedy-thriller about a couple of idiots (Candy and Levy) who take jobs with a security firm and end up involved with the Mob (led by Loggia). Pap of the lowest order. BC

Armeé des Ombres, L' (The Army in the Shadows)

(Jean-Pierre Melville, 1969, Fr/It) Lino Ventura, Paul Meurisse, Simone Signoret, Jean-Pierre Cassel, Claude Mann, Christian Barbier, Serge Reggiani.
140 min.
Melville's tribute to the French Resistance in World War II was a project he nurtured for 25 years, and is the summit of both his own work and his collaboration with the actor Ventura. The film was wrongly criticised for introducing the codes of the French gangster film to the sentimental heroics of the Resistance, because it was the former that borrowed and sustained the myths and rituals of the latter in the first place. Melville's style here has a quite outstanding hallucinatory quality entirely appropriate to its subject of lives and memories that are forced underground for too long. It is, in a way, the stoic alternative to Cocteau's *Orphée*, a film whose suspense derives from a state where any moment may be the moment of death. CPe

Armored Attack

see North Star, The

Armored Car Robbery

(Richard Fleischer, 1950, US) Charles McGraw, Adele Jergens, William Talman, Steve Brodie, Douglas Fowley.
68 min. b/w.
The caper movie has since succumbed to over-familiarity and over-elaboration, but this one – pointing the way to *The Asphalt Jungle* and *The Killing* – is a model of its kind. Almost documentary in its account of the heist that goes

wrong and the police procedures that are set in motion, making excellent use of LA locations, it relies on superb high contrast lighting to meld reality into the characteristic *noir* look. Vivid characterisations, too, from Talman as the vicious mastermind, Jergens as a sleazy stripper playing games, and McGraw as the steely cop out to avenge the death of his partner. TM

Armour of God, The (Long Xiong Hu Di)

(Jackie Chan, 1986, HK) Jackie Chan, Alan Tam, Rosamund Kwan, Lola Forner.
88 min.
Since jumping into Bruce Lee's shoes, Chan has produced a furious fistful of Hong Kong-set action pics, low on plot but high on jinks and Chan's brand of self-deprecating humour. Here he strays far from home, and much of the magic evaporates with bigger budgets and the European locations which adventurer 'Asian Hawk' (Chan) and his pop star foil (Tam) pass through in their crazy quest for some relics of Crusader's armour, ending up outside Zagreb to take on a motley fraternity of malevolent troglodyte monks led by a Grand Wizard sporting Bela Lugosi's cloak. What pleasures the action sequences offer are negated by the ludicrous dubbing and half-hour tracts of tedium. WH

Army in the Shadows, The

see Armée des Ombres, L'

Army of Darkness: The Medieval Dead

(Sam Raimi, 1992, US) Bruce Campbell, Embeth Davidtz, Marcus Gilbert, Sam Raimi.
90 min.
A calculated tilt at the cross-over mainstream audience, this second sequel eschews the hardcore horror of *The Evil Dead* and the splatter comedy of *Evil Dead II*, in favour of a swashbuckling comedy. Catapulted back in time, chainsaw-wielding hero Ash (Campbell) joins forces with the inhabitants of a besieged castle – and damsel in distress Sheila (Davidtz) – in their battle against an army of skeleton Deadites. With its stop-motion effects and knockabout humour, this plays more like a Ray Harryhausen version of *El Cid* than a horror movie, with plenty of slapstick but very little gore. NF

Army of Lovers or Revolt of the Perverts (Armee der Liebenden oder Revolte der Perversen)

(Rosa von Praunheim, 1979, WGer)
98 min.
A vacuous gay liberation documentary which rapidly breaks down into a stream of talking heads – from a celebration of the anniversary of gay revolt in San Francisco to interviews with gay Nazis, gay porn movie stars and others. Politically it seems suspect; and the crew clearly enjoyed making it a lot more than an audience will enjoy watching it. CA

Arnelo Affair, The

(Arch Oboler, 1947, US) John Hodiak, George Murphy, Frances Gifford, Dean Stockwell, Eve Arden.
86 min. b/w.
Arch Oboler earned himself a footnote in cinema history when he directed the first-ever 3-D feature, *Bwana Devil*, in 1952. Unfortunately, this earlier effort is two or three dimensions short of a decent thriller. Bored young wife is strangely drawn to her attorney husband's charismatic, nightclub-owning client, but soon discovers he's a murderer, and she's somehow implicated in his crime. GM

Arnold

(Georg Fenady, 1973, US) Stella Stevens, Roddy McDowall, Elsa Lanchester, Shani Wallis, Farley Granger, Victor Buono.
100 min.
A thoroughly inept black comedy/horror send-up about a wealthy man who arranges for his mistress to go through a wedding ceremony with his corpse after his death. Arnold's will also entangles a number of other members of the family,

who make supposedly gruesome exits via acid-laced cleansing cream, a shrinking suit, etc. The plot itself isn't so bad; it's the relentlessly chirpy American humour trowelled over everything, the impossible ballad, and the way the performers pause in delivery as if waiting for laughter, that really makes *Arnold* unbearable. VG

Around the World in 80 Days
(Michael Anderson, 1956, US) David Niven, Cantinflas, Shirley MacLaine, Robert Newton.
167 min.
Mike Todd's inflation of Jules Verne, with Niven as Phileas Fogg and the Mexican comedian Cantinflas as Passepartout, becomes an interminable travelogue interspersed with sketches in which star-spotting affords some relief (there are cameos from hordes of luminaries ranging from Dietrich and Beatrice Lillie to Keaton and Sinatra). Some nice period touches, but the best bit comes courtesy of Méliès, whose 'Trip to the Moon' is used at the beginning. TM

Arousers, The
see Sweet Kill

Arp Statue, The
(Alan Sekers, 1971, GB) Mel Lamb, François Hugo, Monique Hugo, James L Fox.
70 min. b/w.
A rather silly tale about a model who has her arm eaten by a lion and suffers subsequent crisis, with lots of ponderous-pretentious references to Arp's statues. The use of stills to tell the story is handled well enough.

Arrangement, The
(Elia Kazan, 1969, US) Kirk Douglas, Faye Dunaway, Deborah Kerr, Richard Boone, Hume Cronyn.
125 min.
Having been absent from the screen since *America, America* (1963), Kazan returned with this glossy account of middle-age crack-up based on his own glossy, Harold Robbins-ish novel. Douglas plays an advertising executive who suddenly clues into the emptiness of his existence and drives serenely under a truck – there after driving his family up the wall as he follows his failed suicide attempt with the kind of high jinks that had earlier served Britain's Angry Young Men in cocking a snook at society. It all seems very forced in Kazan's case, where it isn't simply glib and indulgent (as in Douglas' sybaritic fling with Dunaway's liberated lady ad exec). GA

Arrival, The
(David Twohy, 1996, US) Charlie Sheen, Ron Silver, Teri Polo, Lindsay Crouse, Richard Schiff.
120 min.
An alien-landing thriller dedicated to the proposition that even if extra-terrestrials are the scurvy planet-swiping scumbags we suspect – well, it's not as if we're keeping the place in such good nick ourselves. Sheen's a NASA boffin convinced an audio signal he's picked up is an alien transmission. Unfortunately, when he informs his boss, he finds himself on the wrong side of a mandatory personnel cutback – with apologies, of course, but we know no one as smooth as Silver can be trusted. Sure enough, after rigging up his neighbours' satellite dishes to his computer, meeting a scientist in Mexico investigating global-warming, and breaking into a secret energy installation in the jungle, Charlie finds things go deeper than anyone could've imagined. This risible hokum cashes in on TV's *The X Files* and invasion mania, but what it lacks in sophistication (everything), it partly makes up for in sheer gall. NB

Arrivederci Millwall
(Charles McDougall, 1989, GB) Kevin O'Donohue, Sidney Cole, Peter McNamara, Tim Keen.
50 min.
Originally shown on TV in a cut form. Scripted by Nick Perry, it's not a 'football film', but rather an examination of the lives of a group of 'hardcore' Millwall supporters as they prepare for England's World Cup match in Bilbao in 1982. With the build-up and subsequent 'victory' in the Falklands as a backdrop, the gang's bigoted, nationalistic views and love of violence are exacerbated after the death, in the conflict, of their leader's brother. *Sun*

readers to a man, they take an overdose of jingoism on board the ferry for Spain, where they indulge in loutish behaviour and are subsequently imprisoned. But on release, Billy's desire to avenge his brother's death ('All dagoes are the same') backfires when he steals a pistol and accidentally kills a friend. The violence is neither condoned nor glamorised, serving merely to reinforce the futility of war and aggression in all its guises. A depressing film, none the less. GBa

Arsenal Stadium Mystery, The
(Thorold Dickinson, 1939, GB) Leslie Banks, Greta Gynt, Esmond Knight, Ian MacLean, Brian Worth, Wyndham Goldie, Anthony Bushell.
84 min. b/w.
More entertainment than you'd get from a Saturday afternoon at Highbury these days, this vintage thriller works Arsenal's 1938 Championship side into a murder mystery that has Slade of the Yard (Banks) pacing the marble halls in search of the killer of an opposition player, nobbled during a friendly. PT

Arsene Lupin
(Jack Conway, 1932, US) John Barrymore, Lionel Barrymore, Karen Morley, Tully Marshall, John Miljan, Henry Armetta.
84 min. b/w.
The first time the Barrymore brothers had appeared together, John as the titled French cracksman manoeuvring Lionel's prefect of police into becoming chief suspect for his exploits (which include stealing the Mona Lisa). Very dated and sluggishly directed, but John Barrymore is fun. TM

Arsenic and Old Lace
(Frank Capra, 1942, US) Cary Grant, Priscilla Lane, Raymond Massey, Peter Lorre, Josephine Hull, Jean Adair, John Alexander.
118 min. b/w.
Joseph Kesselring's black comedy about two quaint spinsters with the murderous capabilities of Venus Flycatchers comes across as dusty but gentle entertainment. As transferred to the screen by Capra, it's dusty but ferocious, with rampant overacting and little sense of comic timing. Cary Grant, doing enough double-takes to dislocate his eyeballs for life, gives a particularly horrible performance. Best value is given by Massey and Lorre (playing two wandering criminals), who don't struggle to get laughs and just act macabre. It's all weird, but not wonderful. GB

Arsonist, The (Kaki Bakar)
(U-Wei Bin Haji Saari, 1994, Malaysia) Khalid Salleh, Ngasrizal Ngasri, Kuswadinata, Anwar Idris, Azizah Mahzan.
70 min.
A very impressive transposition of William Faulkner's story *Barn Burning* to rural Malaysia, this centres on an embittered worker-for-hire who uses arson as his weapon to attack those who exploit or cheat him, but doesn't hesitate to bully his own family into submission. As the spare drama unfolds, attention focuses on the man's youngest son (Ngasri), whose instinct is to rebel against his tyrannical father but who has been more influenced by him than he realises. Everything here from the dialogue and performances to the lighting represents a break with the traditions of Malay movie melodrama. TR

Art for Teachers of Children
(Jennifer Montgomery, 1995, US) Duncan Hannah, Caitlin Grace McDonnell.
82 min. b/w.
Clinical-sounding title notwithstanding, Montgomery's autobiographical recollection of an illicit adolescent relationship is a courageous, incendiary and contentious exploration of attitudes to under-age sexuality. Now professor of film at a New York art school, Montgomery, who wrote, directed, shot and edited the film, was spurred to distil her experiences when pressured by the FBI in 1989 to testify against an alleged child pornographer. Montgomery was one of his photographic subjects, and her film is pitched as a fictionalised 'boarding school melodrama', charting the brief liaison that develops after 14-year-old Jennifer (poet Caitlin Grace McDonnell) poses for dorm counsellor, art teacher and aspiring photographer John (NY

painter Hannah). Filmed in grainy b/w with an amateur cast, the piece has all the formal impetus of an industrial training documentary. A problem, however, is that while Montgomery has earned the right to explore her own experiences, as soon as this material appears in public its specificity evaporates, prompting the risk that it might be read as a tacit endorsement of under-age sex. TJ

Arthur
(Steve Gordon, 1981, US) Dudley Moore, Liza Minnelli, John Gielgud, Geraldine Fitzgerald, Jill Eikenberry.
97 min.
Overrated one-joke comedy which indulges Moore's perpetual drunk act as his wastrel playboy attempts to mend his ways in order to get his hands on an inheritance and a blushing bride. Some of the lines are funny, but how can one applaud a movie which relies so heavily on the novelty value of Gielgud as a bitter butler pronouncing profanities in a posh accent? GA

Arthur 2: On the Rocks
(Bud Yorkin, 1988, US) Dudley Moore, Liza Minnelli, John Gielgud, Geraldine Fitzgerald, Stephen Elliot, Paul Benedict, Cynthia Sikes, Jack Gilford.
113 min.
Multi-millionaire sot Arthur (Moore) and an ex-shopgirl Linda (Minnelli), now married five years, are sans child but happy. He's still rolling around town regaling the pofaced populace with a stale repertoire of pranks, drinking champers in the bath, laughing at his own jokes. Linda is still putting up with the shit. So far, so formula. Arthur's vindictive would-be-father-in-law (Elliot) engineers a takeover coup, leaving Arthur penniless. Linda waitresses, but Arthur can't tie his own shoelaces, so he's soon hitting rock bottom. That blows the adoption plans and sets up the emotional crisis. Worst of all, Gielgud's vitriolic British butler Hobson is dead; his replacement (Benedict) is no match, so Hobson has to be resurrected, via Arthur's hallucinations, to provide homilies and set Arthur back on the path to a happy ending. As funny as a cerebral haemorrhage. WH

Artistes at the Top of the Big Top: Disorientated (Die Artisten in der Zirkuskuppel: ratlos)
(Alexander Kluge, 1968, WGer) Hannelore Hoger, Siegfried Graue, Alfred Edel, Bernd Holtz, Eva Oertel.
103 min. b/w & col.
Kluge's second feature is a brilliant marriage of abstract ideas and concrete images. The daughter of a trapeze artist dreams of revolutionising the circus, but comes up against reality in all its forms: the Moscow cultural chief, the capitalists who have the power but not the will to change, and her elephants – who after all remain circus elephants. Part political essay on utopia and how to achieve it, part fiction, part a 'mondo bizarro' of circus life, it's a real rarity. And, of course, it's part of the film's task to deal with such disorientating impossibilities. The circus performers – a man wrestling with a crocodile, the lion tamer, the elephants standing on their hands – would surely agree. DMacp

Artists and Models
(Frank Tashlin, 1955, US) Dean Martin, Jerry Lewis, Shirley MacLaine, Dorothy Malone, Eddie Mayehoff, Eva Gabor, Anita Ekberg, Jack Elam.
109 min.
Martin and Lewis play New York bohemians, sidetracked from their artistic aspirations by Lewis' obsession with comic strips, which leads into some mild satire on their dangerously violent content as well as a daft plot involving state secrets. Tashlin's splashy use of colour, and strong contributions from the female leads (including Anita Ekberg in a cameo), help to give the film its wacky, over-heated edge. There's even the suggestion that Lewis' backward manners are the result of a childhood spent reading comics – so now we know. DT

Art of Love, The
(Norman Jewison, 1965, US) James Garner, Dick Van Dyke, Elke Sommer, Angie Dickinson, Ethel Merman.
99 min.

A weird comedy, set in Paris and mounted with the gloss characteristic of Ross Hunter productions, in which a struggling writer (Garner) incites his equally struggling artist friend (Van Dyke) to increase the value of his work by faking suicide. The script's few good ideas are soon flogged to death, although it all becomes interestingly tasteless towards the end when Van Dyke, nursing amorous and other grudges while in hiding, has Garner arrested for his 'murder' and saved only when his head is on the guillotine. Sommer and Dickinson give performances much too charming to be wasted on this loutish pair. DMcG

Art Pepper: Notes from a Jazz Survivor

(Don McGlynn, 1982, US)
49 min.
In this moving documentary souvenir of the man and his music, Art Pepper speaks frankly and unsentimentally about his tortured history – his fight against heroin addiction, prison stretches, chaotic emotional affairs, bouts of depression – and still proclaims his love of life. And this rings true whenever he lifts his sax to his lips. Whether in a tight, funky blues, a plaintive Parker-ish ballad that fragments into Dolphy-like wailings, or a fast bebop shuffle, Pepper blows with an intense joy, power and passion. Avoiding adulation, this is an intelligent epitaph to a brave, restless and remarkable man. GA

Ascendancy

(Edward Bennett, 1982, GB) Julie Covington, Ian Charleson, John Phillips, Susan Engel, Philip Locke.
85 min.
This continues the BFI Production Department's concern with Northern Ireland (Cross and Passion, Maeve) while clearly also intended to reach the art house audience hooked by The Draughtsman's Contract. A history lesson, around the exploitation of Irish sectarian differences in the interests of the British ruling class of 1920, is therefore rendered as costume drama. The spectator's stand-in here is Julie Covington, whose emotional/physical paralysis, occasioned by the death of her brother in World War I, gives way to an awareness of the Trouble outside. Unfortunately, and symptomatically, she functions as an obvious symbol but carries little dramatic weight (despite an excellent performance). The result seems unlikely to provoke or enlighten audiences. SJ

Ascending Scale (Arohan)

(Shyam Benegal, 1982, Ind) Om Puri, Victor Banerjee, Noni Ganguly, Rajen Tarafdar, Gita Sen.
147 min.
As an agit-prop tract, designed to instruct the Indian peasant sharecropper in legal rights that are still under abuse from landowners despite government legislation, this rings loud and clear. For the Western viewer, running in at 147 minutes, it may seem to thump its tub a little too simplistically, despite stunning cinematography and some fine sequences. TM

Ascenseur pour l'Echafaud (Frantic/Lift to the Scaffold)

(Louis Malle, 1957, Fr) Maurice Ronet,Jeanne Moreau, Georges Poujouly, Lino Ventura, Yori Bertin, Ivan Petrovich, Charles Denner.
92 min. b/w.
Malle's first feature, a straightforward but classy thriller about an ex-paratrooper's attempt to dispose of his mistress' tycoon husband in a perfect murder. It became associated with the early excitements of the nouvelle vague mainly through the performances of Ronet (playing a prototype of the disgruntled Vietnam veteran) and Moreau (who does some moody solo wandering in the streets searching for her missing lover). The ingenious plot, using a malfunctioning lift as its deus-ex-machina, has one carefully plotted murder conjure another as its shadow image. But the cement holding the film together is really the splendid jazz score improvised by Miles Davis. TM

Ascent, The (Voskhozhdenie)

(Larissa Shepitko, 1976, USSR) Boris Plotnikov, Vladimir Gostjuchin, Sergei Yakovlev, Ludmila Polyakova.
105 min. b/w.

An extraordinary, gruelling account of the partisans' fight against the Nazis in German-occupied Belorussia, The Ascent reflects the Russian obsession with the horrors of the Great Patriotic War, but unusually is both steeped in religious symbolism and ready to acknowledge the existence of the less than great Russian collaborator. The true battle is not with the Nazis, who hover in the background as mere extras, but between the Russian Nazi investigator and Sotnikov, the captured partisan who finds the spiritual strength to go to his death unbeaten. With its many references to the Crucifixion, the story takes on heroic proportions glorifying the sufferings of the martyr and his influence on future generations. A remarkable piece of work, not least for being filmed in black-and-white against a vast, bleak expanse of snow. SJo

As Good As It Gets

(James L Brooks, 1997, US) Jack Nicholson, Helen Hunt, Greg Kinnear, Cuba Gooding Jr, Skeet Ulrich, Shirley Knight.
138 min.
New York romantic novelist Melvin Udall (Nicholson) doesn't live up to his writing: an obsessive-compulsive, he's given to insulting whoever he meets. Melvin lowers his defences, however, after he's lumbered with the dog belonging to his neighbour Simon (Kinnear), a gay artist recuperating from a mugging, and after he decides to lure Carol (Hunt), a waitress at his local diner, back to work by offering to pay for her young son's treatment for asthma. So begins Melvin's unwitting progress towards something resembling normal behaviour. The film may be more ambitious and sophisticated than most Hollywood comedy-dramas, but for all the delight it takes in Melvin's outrageous sarcasm, it never quite eschews cornball cliché. Nicholson gives a committed, credible, typically charismatic performance, and the rest of the cast lends able support. The trouble lies in the rambling narrative, Brooks' cautious direction and the cosy tone which renders the whole thing reminiscent of an extended sitcom. GA

Ashanti

(Richard Fleischer, 1979, Switz) Michael Caine, Omar Sharif, Peter Ustinov, Rex Harrison, Beverly Johnson, William Holden.
117 min.
Faced with a dire script about the kidnapping of an Afro-American doctor into a trans-Sahara slave caravan, Fleischer opts for functional anonymity. Would that his cast had done likewise: all seem determined on self-parody in an otherwise humourless context, with Ustinov essaying a disastrous funny-voice act as the Arab slaver, and Caine, as the doctor's pursuing husband, looking totally uninterested. His recalcitrant camel remains the perfect image of and for a clapped-out primitive 'star vehicle'. PT

Ashes and Diamonds (Popiól i Diament)

(Andrzej Wajda, 1958, Pol) Zbigniew Cybulski, Ewa Krzyzanowska, Adam Pawlikowski, Bogumil Kobiela.
104 min.b/w.
The last of Wajda's unplanned trilogy about the legacy of World War II on his generation, following A Generation (1954) and Kanal (1956), Ashes and Diamonds is also the most flamboyant, and features the iconic figure of Cybulski, frequently cited as the 'Polish James Dean', who died in an accident in 1967. The time is the first days of peace, though from Cybulski's dark glasses the mood could be a decade on. He plays a young fighter waiting to assassinate a recently appointed communist official in a small Polish town. But a burgeoning love affair with a hotel barmaid leads him to question the value of this continual struggle. Wajda's way is the sweet smell of excess, but some scenes remain powerfully memorable – the lighting of drinks on the bar, the upturned Christ in a bombed church, and Cybulski's prolonged death agonies at the close. DT

Ashes of Time (Dong Xie Xi Du)

(Wong Kar-Wai, 1994, HK) Leslie Cheung, Brigitte Lin, Tony Leung Ka-Fai, Tony Leung Chiu-Wai, Maggie Cheung, Carina Lau, Jacky Cheung, Charlie Young.
95 min.
An all-star cast, Chris Doyle's extraordinary cinematography and innovative action sequences

choreographed by Samo Hung were not enough to turn Wong Kar-Wai's most ambitious movie from an art house triumph into a commercial success. Wong takes characters from a famous martial arts novel (Jin Yong's The Eagle-Shooting Heroes) and deposits them in the middle of a vast desert to work through their various obsessions and manias: set in the eye of an off-screen storm, it's a tender group portrait of fallible people crawling from the wreckage of their lives. At its emotional core is Brigitte Lin playing a self dangerously divided between Yin and Yang. TR

Ashik Kerib

(Dodo Abashidze/Sergo Parajanov, 1988, USSR) Yuri Mgoyan, Veronika Metonidze, Levan Natroshvili, Sofiko Chiaureli.
78 min.
In a period of the undefined past, Ashik Kerib is a wandering minstrel, a lute player and singer, who falls for a rich merchant's daughter, is spurned by the father (minstrels are poor functionaries), and is despatched, to wander for 1001 nights, but not before he's made the girl promise not to marry till his return. True to Paradjanov's unique method, the ensuing episodic tale of his meetings, experiences, difficulties and growth are told in a blaze of visually splendid 'tableaux vivants' and miraculous images and symbols (doves, swans, pomegranates), intercut with religious iconic works and artefacts, and overlaid with song and poetry. The source is a short story by poet Mikhail Lermontov, but the interpretation, though grounded in the world of ethnic cultural references of the Turkish (Muslim) Azerbaijani peoples, is free, open, sensual and personal. There are coded messages of the tribulations of the artist here, and also a playful, mischievous comedic tone that allays any feeling of self-absorbtion on the director's part. Astonishing. WH

Ash Wednesday

(Larry Peerce, 1973, US) Elizabeth Taylor, Henry Fonda, Helmut Berger, Keith Baxter, Maurice Teynac.
99 min.
Liz, aged 55, sagging and wrinkled in a carefully cosmetic sort of way, secretly undergoes a face and body lift in an attempt to rejuvenate herself and her marriage. In what is little more than a homage to Taylor's face, the film spends a good deal of time looking at her reflection in the mirror and endorsing her Martini ad lifestyle up to the hilt.

As in Heaven (Svo a Jördu sem á Himni)

(Kristín Jóhannesdóttir, 1992, Ice) Alfrun H Ornolfsdóttir, Pierre Vaneck, Tinna Gunnlaugsdóttir.
124 min.
The imagination of a young girl, living in a remote Icelandic fishing community in the late '30s, is so imbued with traditional superstition that she dreams herself back into the fourteenth century in order to fend off a family curse. Rather like a Nordic amalgam of Spirit of the Beehive and Venus Peter, this is a good-looking film that makes fine use of a harsh, dramatic landscape; but the adult performances, at least, tend towards the histrionic, and the whole is rather too self-consciously mysterious and slowly paced for its own good. GA

Ask Any Girl

(Charles Walters, 1959, US) David Niven, Shirley MacLaine, Gig Young, Rod Taylor, Jim Backus, Elisabeth Fraser, Claire Taylor.
101 min.
MGM laid on the Fifth Avenue gloss for this obvious but not unpleasing comic romance in which Pennsylvanian hick Shirley MacLaine (very appealing in one of her first major roles) comes to New York City, beats off a queue of menfolk, and then enlists the help of suave David Niven in winning the affections of his Lothario brother Gig Young. It doesn't take X-ray vision to figure out who she's gonna end up with, but these folks know how to make the time pass amiably enough. Adapted by George Wells from the novel by Winifred Wolfe, and shot in 'Scope. TJ

Asking for Trouble

(Oswald Mitchell, 1942, GB) Max Miller, Carol Lynne, Mark Lester, Wilfrid Hyde-White, Aubrey Mallalieu.
81 min. b/w.

The Cheeky Chappie is his usual brash self as a fishmonger (bookie on the side) who finds himself helping a damsel in distress by masquerading obnoxiously as Captain Fortescue from Africa, whom her father wants her to marry. Fast-talking but not very funny. TM

As Long as You're Healthy
see Tant qu'on a la Santé

Aspern
(Eduardo de Gregorio, 1981, Port) Jean Sorel, Bulle Ogier, Alida Valli, Ana Marta, Teresa Madruga.
96 min.
A film of limpid clarity adapted from Henry James' The Aspern Papers, with present-day Lisbon smoothly substituting for 19th century Venice, and terrific performances from Valli and Ogier as the old lady and the spinster niece under siege from a writer determined to lay his hands on a fabulous manuscript entrusted to their keeping. Although the finer Jamesian ironies are compromised by an added subplot designed to allow the writer to explain his motivations, the central theme is subtly orchestrated as the two women fight to preserve their private feelings and memories from being made public. De Gregorio's obsession with time, memory and the sinister emanations from old dark houses (cf. his own Sérail, his scripts for Celine and Julie Go Boating and The Spider's Strategy) is made all the more effective here by his use of an abrupt editing style in disruptive counterpoint to the brooding atmosphere. TM

Asphaltflimmern
see Flickering Roads

Asphalt Jungle, The
(John Huston, 1950, US) Sterling Hayden, Louis Calhern, Jean Hagen, Sam Jaffe, James Whitmore, John McIntire, Marilyn Monroe.
112 min. b/w.
A classic heist movie, and one of Huston's finest, this adaptation of WR Burnett's novel in which a gang of thieves falls apart after attempting a daring robbery is a taut, unsentimental study in character and relative morality. Beautifully shot by Harold Rosson, played to perfection by a less than starry cast, and directed in admirably forthright fashion by Huston, it has spawned countless imitations, few of which even remotely approach the intelligence and detail of the original. Re-made as The Badlanders (1958), Cairo (1963) and Cool Breeze (1972). GA

Asphalt Night (Asphaltnacht)
(Peter Fratzscher, 1980, WGer) Gerd Udo Heinemann, Thomas Davis, Monika Rack, Gaby Helene Ruthmann.
90 min.
Two musicians, a punk and a '60s leftover, find uneasy romance during a night in Berlin. The encounter inspires the older one to complete his masterpiece, a hideous piece of bombast about 'the kids of 1984' (sic). Strictly for people who missed out on punk's heyday but needed to be reassured, after the event, that it wouldn't hurt them. A film whose seductive visual surface can't hide its reactionary musical soul. SJ

Asphyx, The
(aka Horror of Death)
(Peter Newbrook, 1972, GB) Robert Stephens, Robert Powell, Jane Lapotaire, Alex Scott, Ralph Arliss, Fiona Walker.
99 min.
A person's 'asphyx' is his spirit of death, which can be attracted at the moment of dying and trapped, conferring immortality on the subject. This promising notion, combined with intriguing glimpses into Victorian psychical research and a strong cast, get the film off to a good start. Sadly, it soon degenerates into formula and farce, with Stephens' theatrical delivery adding the mortal blow. DP

Assam Garden, The
(Mary McMurray, 1985, GB) Deborah Kerr, Madhur Jaffrey, Alec McCowen, Zia Mohyeddin.
90 min.
Though very much a two-hander and marred by

the restraint that the film itself castigates, this is an often affecting study of two women – the widow of a colonial bigwig, cherishing memories of her privileged years in India, and the elderly Indian immigrant who to some extent penetrates the English woman's loneliness by forcefully offering friendship. It's a discreet and subtle movie, gradually scratching away at Kerr's veneer of happiness to reveal a core of frustration and resentment. Both the camera, prowling around the gorgeous garden that the women tend together, and Kerr's carefully controlled performance, suggest further depths of dissatisfaction. Far from original, but engaging. GA

Assassin
(Peter Crane, 1973, GB) Ian Hendry, Edward Judd, Frank Windsor, Ray Brooks, Verna Harvey.
83 min.
Charting the familiar area of spyland double-cross and disillusion, directed with much heavy 'style', this is lifted out of the run-of-the-mill by Hendry's haunting, evocative performance as the isolated, disillusioned hired killer.

Assassin, The
see Point of No Return

Assassination
(Peter Hunt, 1986, US) Charles Bronson, Jill Ireland, Stephen Elliott, Jan Gan Boyd, Randy Brooks, Eric Stern.
88 min.
Dispirited action movie with baggy-faced Bronson, as a federal agent assigned to protect the newly instated first lady (code name One Mama), grappling listlessly with a script that gives him lines like 'The yacht was definitely blown up premeditatively'. One Mama (Ireland) doesn't hold much truck with security ('I am not going to be coerced by your chauvinistic rules'), but is forced to eat her words when it becomes clear that someone is trying to kill her. The plot, with the two going into hiding together and the sexual tension between them brewing, shambles along as predictably as a dot-to-dot quiz. EP

Assassination Bureau, The
(Basil Dearden, 1968, GB) Oliver Reed, Diana Rigg, Telly Savalas, Curd Jürgens, Philippe Noiret, Warren Mitchell, Beryl Reid, Clive Revill.
110 min.
None too witty black comedy, loosely based on Stevenson's unfinished novel and set in the first decade of this century. Rigg is the journalist who uncovers a secret organisation of professional killers, and manages to fight it with the help of its leader (Reed), who falls in love with her. Amid all the heavy caricaturing and the funereal pace, only Geoffrey Unsworth's photography of the Venetian scenes is of note. GA

Assassination of Trotsky, The
(Joseph Losey, 1972, Fr/It/GB) Richard Burton, Alain Delon, Romy Schneider, Valentina Cortese, Giorgio Albertazzi, Duilio Del Prete, Jean Desailly.
103 min.
Unhistorical evocation of Trotsky's last couple of months in exile in Mexico before the Stalinist agents got to him. Burton as Trotsky is set up very deliberately as a dry, pedantic figure, and his ideas accordingly shrink in importance. Delon, too, as the enigmatic assassin, seems like an unfinished character until the brilliantly shot scene where he watches a bullfight. From there Losey's on his own, fascinatedly turning this key historical event into a Secret Ceremony. We're so starved of hard information that one can only wish for more. VG

Assassin Habite au 21, L'
(The Murderer Lives at
Number 21)
(Henri-Georges Clouzot, 1942, Fr) Pierre Fresnay, Suzy Delair, Jean Tissier, Pierre Larquey, Noël Roquevert.
83 min. b/w.
Clouzot's first feature, an engaging serio-comic thriller, with Fresnay as a whimsical police inspector who poses as a pastor to infiltrate the boarding-house where a Jack the Ripper killer is

hiding out. The moderately ingenious mystery is boosted by the fantastical characterisations, and there are nice touches of black humour (like the toy working models of the killer made by one of the suspects). TM

Assassin of the Tsar
(Tsareubiitsa)
(Karen Shakhnazarov, 1991, GB/Rus) Malcolm McDowell, Oleg Yankovsky, Armen Dzhigarkhanyan.
104 min.
Mental patient Timofeyev (McDowell, twitchy and grizzled) is convinced that he assassinated Tsar Alexander II in 1881, and that he also led the firing squad that executed Nicholas II and his family in 1918. Dr Smirnov (Yankovsky) concludes that the only way to treat Timofeyev is to enter his fantasies, and so he starts playing Tsar to his patient's executioner. Before long, present and past are blurring together and we're on a full-dress reconstruction of the last weeks of the Romanov dynasty. About halfway through this lugubrious Anglo-Russian co-production, it dawns that the film is bending over backwards to avoid being seen as just another costume-drama plod through the Kremlin's secret files. Big mistake. The historical scenes are actually credible, dignified and rather watchable, whereas the implied parallel with the collapse of the USSR doesn't begin to cohere. And the whole mental-hospital framework is a hugely tautologous way of saying that these are unhealed wounds from the past. Hard to recommend except as an oddity. TR

Assassin(s)
(Mathieu Kassovitz, 1997, Fr) Michel Serrault, Mathieu Kassovitz, Mehdi Benoufa.
134 min.
Kassovitz's follow-up to La Haine is a disappointing misfire. Jobless petty criminal Kassovitz is taken up by ageing hitman Serrault, who'd like to see his perverse code of ethics carried on into an increasingly amoral world. So far, so implausible, but once teenager Benoufa takes to their murderous world like a duck to water, and Kassovitz the writer/director starts blaming the increase in violence on watching too much TV, it's hard not to object to the facile, conservative moralising and sledge-hammer dramaturgy. The actors are indulged, the ethical stance is duplicitous (given the relish the film displays in mounting scenes of horrific violence), and the overall result is extremely tedious. GA

Assassins
(Richard Donner, 1995, US) Sylvester Stallone, Antonio Banderas, Julianne Moore, Anatoly Davydov, Muse Watson, Stephen Kahan, Kelly Rowan.
133 min.
An unusually serious, almost sombre thriller from the versatile action producer Joel Silver in which Stallone's a jaded assassin haunted by the past but unable to face the future. As Robert Rath, he gives his best performance for some time, abandoning the self-mockery of Demolition Man and the risible muscle-flexing of The Specialist in favour of a more contained stillness. If only director Donner had inspired Banderas with the same confidence in this essentially generic, but involving scenario; as Miguel Bain, however, an upstart obsessed with inheriting Rath's position as the world's number-one assassin, he's horribly embarrassing, acting throughout like a St Vitus Dance sufferer on amphetamines. Plotwise, things are straightforward. Julianne Moore has unwittingly acquired a computer disk containing dangerously incriminating information, Stallone's hired to kill her, but is having a mid-life career crisis, the bad guys and Interpol are slaughtering everything that moves, and Banderas is the joker in the pack. Between the hits, car chases and gunfire, there are numerous quiet scenes in darkened rooms in which Sly and Moore discover an affinity in their loneliness. NF

Assault, The (De Aanslag)
(Fons Rademakers, 1986, Neth) Derek De Lint, Marc Van Uchelen, Monique Van De Ven, John Kraaykamp, Huub Van Der Lubbe.
148 min.
One fateful night in a quiet Dutch street during the German occupation, a collaborator is shot by the Resistance. Fearing reprisals if the body is found outside their house, a couple of burghers park the

corpse outside the neighbours', with the result that the family is executed. The only survivor is 12-year-old Anton, and these traumatic events determine the course of his life over the next 30 years, leaving him numb to the march of history and troubled by flashbacks. Anton's exorcism is a long haul, awash with madeleine cakes and intimations of the randomness of things. Rademakers never quite reconciles the needs of the psychological detective story with those of biography, settling finally for a divinity which shapes our ends, but raises interesting moral questions along the way. BC

Assault on a Queen
(Jack Donohue, 1966, US) Frank Sinatra, Virna Lisi, Anthony Franciosa, Alf Kjellin, Errol John, Richard Conte.
106 min.
Silly nonsense about a group of adventurers who salvage a sunken U-Boat and use it to hijack the Queen Mary. A sad travesty which muddies the clean lines of Jack Finney's novel. TM

Assault on Precinct 13
(John Carpenter, 1976, US) Austin Stoker, Darwin Joston, Laurie Zimmer, Martin West, Tony Burton, Charles Cyphers, Nancy Loomis.
91 min.
Just as *Dark Star* undercut the solemnity of space movies like *2001* with hilarious astronaut situation comedy, Carpenter's second feature borrows the conventions of protagonists in jeopardy from *Night of the Living Dead* to produce one of the most effective exploitation movies of the decade. The gimmick is cops and cons besieged in an abandoned LA police station by a group of kamikaze urban guerillas. Carpenter scrupulously avoids any overt socio-political pretensions, playing it instead for laughs and suspense in perfectly balanced proportions. The result is a thriller inspired by a buff's admiration for Ford and Hawks (particularly *Rio Bravo*), with action sequences comparable to anything in Siegel or Fuller. It's sheer delight from beginning to end. RM

Associate, The
(Donald Petrie, 1996, US) Whoopi Goldberg, Tim Daly, Diane Wiest, Eli Wallach.
113 min.
Passed over for promotion, financial consultant Laurel Ayers (Goldberg) strikes out on her own. Prospective clients turn her down; they're impressed to a man, they say, but their partners will never support them. Thus Laurel forges Mr Robert S Cutty, a white man whose acumen, elusiveness and impressively masculine personal effects enchant Wall Street and kick start Ayers Cutty's business ventures. Then Bob Cutty gets out of hand. He takes all the praise, attracts media attention and even turns out to be an absent father. A righteous populist comedy, with some dark tinges to the element of fairy story; but also a standard Whoopi-cushion – a plot for kids, puerile characterisation, and sentimentality hammered home by the score. NB

As Tears Go By
(Wangjiao Jiamen)
(Wong Kar-Wai, 1988, HK) Andy Lau, Jacky Cheung, Maggie Cheung, Alex Man.
94 min.
A Hong Kong remake of *Mean Streets* (with emphasis on the violence and the love story, but nothing on Catholicism), this was the first feature from Wong Kar-Wai, recently [1995] established as the great romantic of the Asian avant-garde. It's more generic than either the gorgeous *Days of Being Wild* or *Chungking Express*, and less interesting, but it's clearly the work of a gifted film-maker, highly atmospheric with a number of exciting set-pieces (there's a deliriously kitschy romantic montage set to the Mandarin cover of Berlin's 'Take My Breath Away'). If it fails, ultimately, it's because the relationship between the rational gangster Lau and the impetuous Jacky Cheung never really rings true. A cut above the usual HK action melodrama all the same. TCh

Asterix and the Big Fight
(Le Coup de Menhir)
(Philippe Grimond, 1989, Fr/WGer) voices: Bill Oddie, Bernard Bresslaw, Ron Moody, Sheila Hancock, Peter Hawkins, Brian Blessed, Michael Elphick, Andrew Sachs, Tim Brooke-Taylor.
81 min.

The sixth animated Asterix feature. Yet again the gall of the indomitable Gauls rises against the superior forces of the Roman Empire. In the only village left to be captured, Asterix and Obelix, plus faithful canine accomplice Dogmatix, are the fighters maintaining freedom against the legionnaires and their collaborators, including a surly trickster who passes himself off as a soothsayer. Unfortunately, due to an over-enthusiastic Obelix, the village druid Getafix is out of action and unable to provide the magic brew which will give the superhuman strength Asterix relies on. Magic animation and a familiarly reassuring cast of English voices contribute to an engaging film. JGl

Asterix Conquers America
(Asterix in Amerika)
(Gerhard Hahn, 1994, Ger) voices: John Rye, Craig Charles, Howard Lew Lewis.
84 min.
For those late for the news from the Gallic Wars, the French village of Asterix and Obelix is still holding out, but Caesar's disguised henchman, unable to steal village 'supplier' Getafix's recipe for their magic potion, catapults him over the edge of the flat Earth, straight into the pipe-smoking clutches of the Native Americans. The formula (for this seventh installment) is still basically the same: a good-natured punch-up heavy rescue-adventure, with Roman puns for the adults. The racism is still universally applied: massive rubber-lipped blacks on the palm island; Roman legionnaires with 'Mama Mia' accents from Italian ice-cream ads; and, interestingly, upper-crust Brits as galley-slaves rowing in competition like Edwardian varsity blues. The animation, however, is good; and while it's low on the musical count, it all rushes by too fast to notice. WH

Asterix in Amerika
see Asterix Conquers America

Asterix in Britain
(Astérix chez les Brétons)
(Pino Van Lamsweerde, 1986, Fr) voices: Jack Beaber, Bill Kearns, Graham Bushnell, Gordon Heath.
89 min.
Asterix and Obelix are once more called upon to lay waste the Romans in this third animated feature to be lifted from the marvellous text and drawings of Goscinny and Uderzo's books. It's 50 BC, and the Romans have just invaded British shores. The Brits, however, seem more interested in their daily cuppa than fisticuffs. But one little village, still holding fort against the invaders, do call on the plucky Gauls, who come to their aid replete with a barrel of their strength-giving and intoxicating magic potion. Apart from some questionable editing and the use of slightly watered-down colours, the film stays true to the original characters. Youngsters will no doubt enjoy it, but true fans may prefer to stick with the pun-riddled books. DA

Asthenic Syndrome, The
(Asteniceskij Sindrom)
(Kira Muratova, 1989, USSR) Sergei Popov, Olga Antonova, Natalja Busko.
153 min. b/w & col.
Muratova's literally ungodly film is the most recommendable hard-to-sit-through movie of the year. It starts out in monochrome, telling the story of a woman who goes to pieces after her husband's funeral, but that turns out to be a film-within-the-film (one which empties the theatre at a preview, moreover) which prefaces an extended collage of 'fear and loathing' scenes from Russian life. Asthenia is blind aggression masking underlying weakness, and Muratova sees it as pervading her society; not only in hooliganism, vandalism and crime, but also in male-female and teacher-pupil relations, and virtually everyone's attitude to life. Not an incisive, organised movie like her long-banned *Short Meetings*, but equally distinctive and memorable. TR

Astonished Heart, The
(Terence Fisher/ Anthony Darnborough, 1949, GB) Noël Coward, Celia Johnson, Margaret Leighton, Joyce Carey.
89 min. b/w.
Intriguingly schematic account (based on Coward's own playlet) of a psychiatrist's sexual

obsession with a good-time girl (Leighton), and the effect it has on his devoted, self-denying, sexless wife (Johnson) as it ultimately drives him to self-destruct by throwing himself off a high building. In its way it crystallises and criticises the conventional attitudes towards sex prevalent throughout British cinema in the immediate postwar period, and which Fisher was to turn upside-down in his vampire movies, where the neurotic female altruism represented here by Celia Johnson is transformed by the cathartic presence of Dracula into ravening sexuality. DP

Astragale, L'
(Guy Casaril, 1968, Fr/WGer) Marlène Jobert, Horst Buchholz, Magali Noël, Claude Génia, Georges Géret, Jean-Pierre Moulin.
102 min.
Jobert plays (rather well) a juvenile delinquent who decides she can't take it when her lesbian cellmate is released from jail. So she escapes, breaking her astragalus (an ankle-bone) in the process: a metaphor for her crippled life as she hobbles around on crutches, goes on the streets to support herself, suffers agonies of jealousy when her boyfriend (Buchholz, supplanting the lesbian) starts disappearing for long periods, and lives in constant terror of being trapped by the police. It is presumably meant to be all about solitude and the prisons of the mind, but Guy Casaril's flabbily uninspired direction succeeds only in making one wish Bresson had taken over. TM

Asya's Happiness (Istoriya
Asi Klyachinoi, Kotoraya
Lyubila, da nie vshla zamuzh)
(Andrei Mikhalkov-Konchalovsky, 1967, USSR) Iya Savvina, Lyubov Sokolova, Alexander Surin, Gennady Yegorychev, Ivan Petrov.
98 min. b/w.
Shot in 1966 and subsequently banned for some 20 years, this is far superior to Konchalovsky's later work in America. Basically about a group of villagers working a collective farm, and partly focused on the options open to the lame, pregnant but proud Asya, it is an oblique, touching portrait of a remote community that is both poor and apparently forgotten by the Soviet authorities. Most of the time, the outside world barely intrudes (there is talk of Vietnam, distant tanks rumble); the farm-folk spend their non-working hours gossiping, drinking, reminiscing and, in the case of a selfish layabout and a visiting gypsy, jealously quarrelling over Asya. But plot is of less importance than atmosphere – it was probably the unglamourous vision of village life that incurred official wrath – and the fluid, even virtuoso direction. The black-and-white camerawork is very lyrical, the acting (by a cast largely made up of local non-professionals) lends the film a quiet emotional integrity, and the shifts in tone – from long contemplative shots of landscape and faces to rapidly cut, *vérité*-style sequences of joyous communal dancing and singing – are effortlessly smooth. Rarely has such a vivid, plausible sense of daily life been conveyed by a Soviet director. GA

Asylum
(Roy Ward Baker, 1972, GB) Patrick Magee, Robert Powell, Geoffrey Bayldon, Barbara Parkins, Peter Cushing, Barry Morse, Britt Ekland, Charlotte Rampling, Herbert Lom.
88 min.
The fourth Amicus horror omnibus, comprising four Robert Bloch stories, set in an asylum and boasting a fairly ingenious framing device whereby the glowering director (Magee) sets a young psychiatrist applying for a job (Powell) the task of discovering which of the patients is a former colleague gone mad. Cheerfully gruesome (especially the last tale involving Lom and a murderous manikin), but done without much wit or style. TM

As You Desire Me
(George Fitzmaurice, 1932, US) Greta Garbo, Melvyn Douglas, Erich Von Stroheim, Owen Moore, Hedda Hopper.
71 min. b/w.
Garbo in one of her archetypally enigmatic roles as a Budapest cabaret entertainer, an amnesia victim who may or may not be the wife Douglas has long believed dead, but in any case falls for

him while her 'protector' Stroheim fumes malevolently. Don't expect to find too much of
Pirandello's play, but Garbo (sporting a peroxide
wig some of the time) brings a real erotic undertow to the love scenes, while Stroheim is terrific
as the demonically sadistic writer trying to model
her as one of his own creations. TM

As You Like It
(Christine Edzard, 1992, GB) Cyril Cusack,
James Fox, Don Henderson, Miriam
Margolyes, Emma Croft, Griff Rhys Jones,
Andrew Tiernan, Celia Bannerman.
117 min.
In Edzard's modern-dress version of
Shakespeare's comedy, the forest is an urban
wasteland, the exiled Duke lords it over a group
of down-and-outs, and Orlando versifies with an
aerosol can. After the scrupulous period detail of
her earlier work, this is a surprise, and the conceit weighs heavily on the entire production,
putting text against context. The Duke's court
appears to be a defunct town hall (with the
acoustics of a swimming-pool). Andrew Tiernan
plays both Orlando and his brother Oliver – but
never in the same frame. Emma Croft is Rosalind,
caparisoned like a man (and countless modern
women) in jeans and sweater: if there be truth in
sight, her Ganymede can make no sense. Both are
swamped by their lines, and even Griff Rhys
Jones' Touchstone makes heavy weather of the
Bard's tortuous wit. It is easy to believe Edzard's
claim that 'the film made itself...we just let the
play do its own thing'. The wonder is that they
bothered to put film in the camera, for sadly this
is Shakespeare *sans* teeth, eyes, taste, *sans* everything. TCh

Atalante, L' 100 (100)
(Jean Vigo, 1934, Fr) Michel Simon, Jean Dasté,
Dita Parlo, Louis Lefebvre, Gilles Margaritis.
89 min. b/w.
Mesmeric movie mutilated by Gaumont distributors on its first release, but subsequently
restored to the form its devoted maker (the avant
garde-ish son of an anarchist) intended. Not a lot
happens: a sailor and his young bride share a
barge home with an old eccentric, fall out, and fall
in love again. But the aesthetic appeal lies in the
tension between surface realism (the hardships
of working class life on the canals) and the delicate surrealism of the landscapes (desolate
Parisian suburbs bestraddled by pylons) and of
the justly celebrated sequence where the sailor
searches for his lost love. MA

Atame!
see Tie Me Up! Tie Me Down!

At Close Range
(James Foley, 1985, US) Sean Penn,
Christopher Walken, Mary Stuart
Masterson, Christopher Penn, Millie
Perkins, Eileen Ryan.
115 min.
After young Penn is thrown out by his stepfather,
he encounters his real father (Walken), who
impresses the lad with his life as a successful outlaw in the Pennsylvania backwoods. He trains up
the boy in stealing anything that moves, and life
seems very jolly and fulfilled in a hillbilly sort of
way. Then Walken is slowly revealed to the boy's
eyes as a murderer and rapist; and when the boy
and his friends decide to blow the whistle, the
guns are turned inwards on the family. Foley has
opted for a mixture of documentary 'realism' and
set pieces which have clearly escaped from over-
lit pop promos. Mingle this with Penn and
Walken going heavily over the top in usual
Method fashion, and the brew is less than intoxicating. CPea

At First Sight
see Coup de Foudre

At Gunpoint (aka Gunpoint)
(Alfred Werker, 1955, US) Fred MacMurray,
Dorothy Malone, Walter Brennan, Skip
Homeier, Whit Bissell, Jack Lambert, John
Qualen, Irving Bacon.
81 min.
MacMurray plays a storekeeper who, more by
accident than marksmanship, shoots the leader
of a gang robbing the town bank. From there on,
this Western turns into a cross between *High

Noon and *The Man Who Shot Liberty Valance*,
with the townsfolk proudly boosting MacMurray
as a hero, then – as the rest of the gang come for
revenge – leaving him to stand alone. The first
half is quite gripping, with excellent performances from MacMurray and the ever-dependable Walter Brennan (with teeth), as the
hard-drinking, cynical doctor who remains the
hero's sole but over-age ally. Latterly, though,
Daniel B Ullman's script develops a case of creeping sententiousness, tending to speechify about
civic conscience and the American Way, and
throwing in an absurdly contrived upbeat ending. TM

Atlantic Adventure
(Albert Rogell, 1935, US) Nancy Carroll, Lloyd
Nolan, Harry Langdon, Arthur Hohl, Robert
Middlemass, EE Clive.
68 min. b/w.
Bracing little second-feature in which dashing
reporter Lloyd Nolan is fired from the paper when
he keeps a date with his fiancée rather than cover
the murder of the DA. He's tipped off that the
killer is fleeing to Europe on an ocean liner, so he
joins him for the voyage, hoping to put his career
back on track. It's a little sad to see Harry
Langdon, one of the top comics of the 1920s, providing the light relief as Nolan's photographer,
but the old-timer still knows how to get a laugh.
GM

Atlantic City
(aka Atlantic City U.S.A.)
(Louis Malle, 1980, Can/Fr) Burt Lancaster,
Susan Sarandon, Kate Reid, Michel Piccoli,
Hollis McLaren, Robert Joy.
105 min.
Eclectic, pacy and hard to categorise, it's part
crime thriller, part love story, part fairytale, and
part a gentle, generous examination of certain
dying aspects of American culture. Lancaster
turns in the performance of his career as the ageing petty crook, running a numbers racket,
indulging in nostalgic delusions about his past
experiences in the Big Time with Capone et al,
and finally getting a chance to discover true self-
respect when he gets involved with a young
hippy who's stolen a stash of coke from the mob.
Between the gripping and beautifully staged
action sequences, Malle contrasts the rather sad
and slightly seedy lives of various loners with
their romantic dreams of success, wealth and
fame, while never treating his characters with
condescension or contempt. Witty, warm, but
never sentimental, it also benefits from being set
in the fading glories of the resort town of the title:
grand seaside facades behind which lie more
mundane realities, surrounded by decay and
demolition. GA

At Long Last Love
(Peter Bogdanovich, 1975, US) Burt Reynolds,
Cybill Shepherd, Madeline Kahn, Duilio Del
Prete, Eileen Brennan, John Hillerman,
Mildred Natwick.
118 min.
Everybody hated Bogdanovich's homage, a triv-
ial story slotted round some Cole Porter songs.
It's an indulgent movie – Peter and Cybill having
a lark with their friends – but it's also a neat parody of '30s musicals, with sets nodding to Van
Nest Polglase, Hillerman taking the Eric Blore
part with unerring restraint, Reynolds hamming
away as if he's Cary Grant crossed with
Muhammad Ali, the much-maligned Cybill
Shepherd an icy honey-blonde in the Tracy Lord
tradition (the Grace Kelly, not the Katharine
Hepburn version). Better still, the brittle, clipped
world of Porter's songs is perfectly evoked. It
may be a movie we'll come back to later and find
we all like it. SG

Atomic Café, The
(Kevin Rafferty/Jayne Loader/Pierce Rafferty,
1982, US)
89 min. b/w.
A compilation of film clips from the late '40s and
'50s, chronicling America's attempts to make the
nuclear bomb an acceptable part of its cultural
life. The material evidently took years to unearth,
and most of it is fascinating by any standards.
But like so many compilations, this emerges as
much less than the sum of its parts. For one thing,
the sheer bizarreness of the cultural phenomenon
it displays utterly swamps some weak attempts

at humour in the editing. For another, the film
fails to offer even the barest social context for its
material, as if atomic madness was an isolated
phenomenon unrelated to the whole constellation
of '50s paranoia from McCarthyism to UFOs. DP

Atomic Man, The
see Timeslip

A Toute Vitesse (Full Speed)
(Gaël Morel, 1996, Fr) Elodie Bouchez,
Stéphane Rideau, Pascal Cervo, Meziane
Bardadi.
85 min.
Morel came to film-goers' attention with his performance in *Les Roseaux sauvages* (as, indeed,
did the very able Bouchez), and his directorial
debut is clearly influenced by Téchiné's film. A
rather unfocused, often overly elliptical study of
a group of young French provincials – some from
north Africa – falling in and out with each other,
the film's hardly the most original account of
teenage loyalties, ambitions and hedonism, but
like other French films of recent years, it does
attempt to treat both racism and homosexuality
with some frankness. The performances, too, are
strong; a pity, though, that the film finally
plunges into melodramatic contrivance. GA

At Play in the
Fields of the Lord
(Hector Babenco, 1991, US) Tom Berenger,
John Lithgow, Daryl Hannah, Aidan Quinn,
Tom Waits, Kathy Bates, Stenio Garcia,
Nelson Xavier.
186 min.
Babenco's ambitious eco-movie, co-scripted with
Jean-Claude Carrière, condenses Peter Matthiessen's lengthy novel embracing greed, disloyalty
and religious conflict in the Amazon rainforest.
Martin Quarrier (Quinn) strives to understand the
very culture he seeks to change: when he arrives
to convert Niaruna tribesmen, clashes with his
repressive wife (Bates) and dogmatic fellow-mis-
sionary Huben (Lithgow) foreshadow terrible violence. His despair is more discreetly matched by
that of Huben's wife (Hannah, weak in a sketchy
role), but overshadowed by that of Lewis Moon
(Berenger), a part-Cheyenne mercenary who
throws in his lot with the Niaruna. The film
boasts a sense of conviction and wonderful natural spectacle, but lacks drive. There are also
awkward lunges in tone, most evident in Bates'
swift decent into madness, and the casting is
problematic. Lithgow, Bates and Waits (as
Moon's low-life partner) are all excellent, but
Quinn's heart-throb status jars with the requirements of his role. CM

At Sundance
(Michael Almereyda/Amy Hobby, 1995, US)
Robert Redford, Danny Boyle, Richard
Linklater, Atom Egoyan, James Mangold,
Whit Stillman, James Gray, Nick Gomez, Abel
Ferrara, Larry Gross, Todd Haynes.
71 min.
'What are your feelings about the broad future of
the movies?' That's the poser for a couple of dozen
film-makers, caught in Almereyda's pixel camera lens at the 1995 Sundance film festival. Fans
of American independent cinema will enjoy this
glimpse of such unlikely heroes as James
Mangold, Whit Stillman and James Gray, but the
endless parade of talking heads speculating
rather haphazardly is of marginal interest.
There's a scary double act by Nick Gomez and
Abel Ferrara. Scriptwriter Larry Gross quotes
Gramsci ('the pessimism of the inteligence and
the optimism of the will'), but it's Todd Haynes
who hits the bull's eye when he claims to be
'guardedly pessimistic'. TCh

Attack!
(Robert Aldrich, 1956, US) Jack Palance, Eddie
Albert, Lee Marvin, Robert Strauss, Richard
Jaeckel, Buddy Ebsen, Peter Van Eyck.
107 min. b/w.
Often described as hysterical, this is in fact a brilliant predecessor to Kubrick's *Paths of Glory*
using a fictional slant on World War II's Battle
of the Bulge – the cowardice of a CO (Albert),
resulting in heavy casualties, is studiously
ignored by superiors with an eye to his father's
political pull – to express a virulent disgust not
so much with war itself as with the systems of

privilege and self-interest which perpetuate its disasters. Where Kubrick analyses, Aldrich *attacks*; and his images, crowding a young officer driven almost to psychosis by his entrapment in the machine of privilege (a magnificent performance from Palance), have precisely the same hallucinatingly twisted quality as the war-torn landscapes in which they take shape. TM

Attack of the 50 Foot Woman

(Nathan Juran, 1958, US) Allison Hayes, William Hudson, Yvette Vickers, Roy Gordon, George Douglas.
65 min. b/w.
Delirious pre-feminist horror movie about a rejected woman who suffers a dose of extra-terrestrial gigantism and finally rampages into town to twist her husband round one little finger (literally!). The special effects are dire, but the film's psycho-pathology is fascinating, and the lines have to be heard to be believed ('Put him down, Mrs Archer...'). Perfect late night indulgence. DP

Attack of the 50ft Woman

(Christopher Guest, 1994, US) Daryl Hannah, Daniel Baldwin, William Windom, Frances Fisher, Christi Conaway, Paul Benedict, O'Neal Compton, Victoria Haas.
89 min.
Searching for her errant husband one evening, Nancy Archer (Hannah) is zapped by a UFO. Although neither her husband Harry (Baldwin) nor her tycoon father (Windom) believe her story, it soon becomes transparently obvious that something extraordinary has happened: she experiences such rapid personal growth that she has to move out to the barn. This HBO remake of a notable example of '50s schlock substitutes knowing camp tackiness and post-feminist truisms for the authentic proto-feminist vulgarity of the original; but both versions are essentially about a whacking 50ft metaphor. The special effects are superior, but not a lot; and characterisation and development are still disappointingly sketchy. Of course the sexists get all the best lines. Appalled when big Nancy comes on to him, Harry pipes up: 'What do you expect me to do – buy a wetsuit and flashlight?' TCh

Attack of the Killer Tomatoes

(John DeBello, 1978, US) Sharon Taylor, David Miller, George Wilson, Jack Riley.
87 min.
One-joke spoof on that B movie staple of the '50s, monstrously enlarged scientific mutations. The big red ones have their way with corrupt politicians and (via bloody Bloody Marys) housewife tipplers, while the pastiche '50s soundtrack croons 'I know I'm gonna miss her, a tomato ate my sister'. CR

Attack of the Puppet People

(Bert I Gordon, 1958, US) John Agar, June Kenny, John Hoyt, Michael Mark, Marlene Willis.
79 min. b/w.
Having already cashed in on the success of *The Incredible Shrinking Man* by rushing out (on the principle of opposites) *The Amazing Colossal Man*, producer/director Gordon went the whole hog with this tale of a lonely doll-maker (Hoyt) given to miniaturising human beings. Unsurprisingly, it's a poor second cousin to the Richard Matheson/Jack Arnold mini-classic, with poor characterisation beaten only by penny-pinching special effects, reaching a nadir with some truly laughable back projection when a couple of the unwilling little people take to the pre-dawn LA streets. Nevertheless, this is still plenty of fun, from its pseudo-science ('You know how a projector works, enlarging an image...' begins Zer Nutsy Puppeteer) to one of the shrunken gals launching reluctantly into the pop pastiche 'I'm Your Living Doll'. GD

Attentat, L' (Plot)

(Yves Boisset, 1972, Fr/It/WGer) Jean-Louis Trintignant, Michel Piccoli, Gian Maria Volonté, Jean Seberg, François Périer, Philippe Noiret, Michel Bouquet.
124 min.
Glossy style conflicts with content (political intrigue expanding on the known facts of the Ben Barka affair) as Boisset indicts the CIA, the media, the law, and the French political system

in a tale of an all-out conspiracy to rid France of an exiled socialist who is planning to return to his own country to set up a revolutionary government, and who becomes an embarrassment to the establishment. Strong performances from an excellent cast, Morricone's music, and a script by Jorge Semprun – who wrote Costa-Gavras' *Z* – make it a polished entertainment rather than a truly political film. GA

At the Circus

(Edward Buzzell, 1939, US) The Marx Brothers, Margaret Dumont, Eve Arden, Nat Pendleton, Kenny Baker, Fritz Feld.
87 min. b/w.
Definitely sub-standard Marxism as the brothers set about saving a circus from bankruptcy. Nice moments (much ado with badges, Groucho singing 'Lydia the Tattooed Lady', and the endless insulting repartee with Dumont), but the whole thing is rather tired and over-familiar.

At the Earth's Core

(Kevin Connor, 1976, GB) Doug McClure, Peter Cushing, Caroline Munro, Cy Grant, Godfrey James.
90 min.
Sequel to (and improvement on) *The Land That Time Forgot*. Cushing and McClure go Edgar Rice Burrowing in their mechanical mole and end up in an exotic underworld where hokey special effects run riot around buxotic maidens like Caroline Munro. Daft stuff, but the telepathic crow-creatures are impressive, and there's enough idiocy to keep even the most avid corn-collectors happy. AB

Attic, The

see Blackout

Attica

(Cinda Firestone, 1973, US)
79 min. b/w & col.
A documentary which reveals, among other things, that the American prison is run as an industry along capitalist lines: it has to maintain the same number of inmates in order to function properly. The film centres on the conditions and events that led up to the prisoners' rebellion in Attica State Penitentiary in 1971 which ended with the death of 43 people, some of whom, as this film shows, were actually murdered after the 'restoration of order'. A sobering and trenchant film.

Attila '74

(Michael Cacoyannis, 1975, Greece)
103 min.
Cacoyannis' documentary 'testimony' is a passionate massing of evidence and accusation concerning the Turkish invasion of Cyprus in 1974 that finally raises more questions than it answers, particularly about the mechanics and motivations of international power politics. The film's presiding spirit is Archbishop Makarios, shown wandering impishly at one point among the ruins of his palace while a voice on post-coup radio declares him dead, and much of the film is made up of an extended interview with him. An *Eoka B* man quotes Alexander the Great on the Gordian Knot. Puppet President Nicos Sampson, in many ways the affair's most intriguing stooge, speaks volubly but unintelligibly. And there's a vast chorus of dispossessed Greeks, mostly women, voicing personal distress, confusion and hysteria – especially the latter, for Cacoyannis is at all points longer on emotion than political analysis, which does his issue a disservice. VG

Attracta

(Kieran Hickey, 1983, Ire) Wendy Hiller, Kate Thompson, Joe McPartland, John Kavanagh, Kate Flynn, Deirdre Donnelly.
55 min.
Redemption and the pain of a wasted life are the disturbing themes of this adaptation of William Trevor's short story. An ageing spinster teacher, Attracta, fastidiously played by Wendy Hiller, cracks under the strain when she realises too late her failure to teach generations of Irish pupils that good can come out of the most horrific sectarian violence. Very moving, with a manic performance from McPartland as a warped Protestant.

Auberge Rouge, L' (The Red Inn)

(Claude Autant-Lara, 1951, Fr) Fernandel, Julien Carette, Françoise Rosay, Marie-Claire Olivia, Didier d'Yd, Lud Germain, Grégoire Aslan, Nane Germon.
110 min. b/w.
A successfully weird little tale about a 19th century inn located in the Ardèche with a history of disappearing guests, Autant-Lara's studio snowbound black comedy is chiefly remembered now as one of the better vehicles for moose-faced Fernandel. As a gluttonous monk privy to the special service offered by the innkeeper's wife (Rosay), he is the key to saving the latest visitors from oblivion at the risk of breaking the secrecy of the confessional. The script by Aurenche and Bost has their famed polish and irony, as well as a stream of anti-clerical jibes, and is played to the hilt by an expert cast. DT

Audience, The (L'Udienza)

(Marco Ferreri, 1971, It) Ugo Tognazzi, Michel Piccoli, Alain Cary, Enzo Jannacci, Claudia Cardinale, Vittorio Gassman.
114 min.
A laboured satire of Vatican bureaucracy, this tells a would-be Kafkaesque story of a supplicant's vain attempts to get to the Pope. Only the devoutest Catholics will be able to stay awake to be outraged. As usual, Ferreri avoids the clichés of 'realism', but his mixture of high gloss, caricature, and studied seriousness is even less adequate here than in *The Last Woman*. TR

Audrey Rose

(Robert Wise, 1977, US) Anthony Hopkins, Marsha Mason, John Beck, Susan Swift, Norman Lloyd, John Hillerman.
113 min.
About reincarnation, with Hopkins persuading Mason and Beck that their daughter may be his dead child returned to life, but not one in the long line of demonic kiddie pics. Wise's film is overlong, sometimes over-emphatic, and it has a staggeringly misjudged ending. But it's also notable for centering on the emotional plight of the paranormal malarkey. It is ultimately, in fact, a strikingly sober portrait of the incompatibilities of marriage, filmed with an attention to 'style' and design that is positively old-fashioned. TR

August

(Anthony Hopkins, 1995, GB) Anthony Hopkins, Leslie Phillips, Kate Burton, Gawn Grainger, Rhian Morgan, Menna Trussler, Rhoda Lewis, Hugh Lloyd.
94 min.
Louis Malle took Uncle Vanya to New York's 42nd Street, Michael Blakemore transplanted him to Australia in *Country Life*, and now Hopkins has brought him, via Julian Mitchell's capable adaptation, to late Victorian Wales. This directorial debut, however, leaves much to be desired. As Vanya, Hopkins indulges himself something rotten. Gentleman farmer Ieuan Davies scampers, larks, and generally behaves like a spoilt ham, but at least he's having fun. The other players barely get the measure of a film which veers from sentimental, philosophical interludes, à la Merchant Ivory, to rambunctious (unfunny) farce. Hopkins appears clueless when it comes to the camera. From time to time, he dispatches it on intrepid, ill-advised excursions around the cast with what can only be called missionary zeal. Elsewhere, he toys with depth of field and overlapping sound, but with equally unbecoming results. TCh

Augustine of Hippo (Agostino di Ippone)

(Roberto Rossellini, 1972, It) Dary Berkani, Virgilio Gazzolo, Cesare Barbetti.
120 min.
By concentrating on supremely important questions in a cool, apparently artless way, Rossellini's film (made for TV) forces a very dramatic tension. The life of Saint Augustine during the decadence of the Roman Empire becomes the axis for debates on politics and power, morality and conscience: how can a state survive with Christian morals? From this seemingly impossible (and un-filmable) brief, Rossellini achieves moments of devastating clarity. DMacp

August in the Water (Mizu no Naka no Hachigatsu)

(Sogo Ishii, 1995, Jap) Rena Komine, Shinsuke Aoki, Masaaki Takarai, Naho Toda, Reiko Matsuo.
117 min.
After the appearance of a new black hole and the fall to earth of two meteorites, a city in Fukuoka suffers both a major drought and an epidemic of a strange disease which causes human inner organs to petrify. A boy working on the languages of fish starts dating a girl with the makings of a diving champion. But she nearly dies in a mysterious diving accident and emerges from hospital somehow changed, knowing that she has to find one of the meteors. The extraordinary climax brings it all together: the drought, the water, the flesh, the stone. Touches the parts ordinary acid doesn't reach. TR

Au Hasard, Balthazar (Balthazar)

(Robert Bresson, 1966, Fr/Swe) Anne Wiazemsky, François Lafarge, Philippe Asselin, Nathalie Joyaut.
95 mins. b/w.
Animal as saint: Bresson's stark, enigmatic parable, a donkey (named after one of the Three Wise Men) is both a witness to and the victim of mankind's cruelty, stupidity – and love. Taking his lack of faith in theatrical acting to its logical limit, Bresson perversely places the mute beast centre-screen as he passes from owner to owner, giving rides, heaving agricultural machinery, and receiving beatings and caresses in a coolly observed landscape of poverty and folly. The effect could not be more different from that of other films (Disney's say, or *Jaws*) that centre around animals; Balthazar's death during a smuggling expedition, amidst a field of sheep, is both lyrical and entirely devoid of maudlin sentiment. Imbued with a dry, ironic sense of humour, the film is perhaps the director's most perfectly realised, and certainly his most moving. GA

Au loin s'en vont les nuages

see Drifting Clouds

Au Nom de la Loi

(Maurice Tourneur, 1931, Fr) Charles Vanel, Marcelle Chantal, Gabriel Gabrio, Jean Marchant, Jean Dax.
85 min. b/w.
Men in big hats gather round The Chief to hear the word. Whether they're cops or robbers is irrelevant; it's equally unimportant why the same guys are now creeping up a stairway in single file, just before tommy gun bullets stud the wall in a chiaroscuro firefight (plenty of oscuro, not a lot of chiaro). Here is a genre in the process of fine-tuning its own imagery via the tale of a tough young *flic* lured to cocaine-soaked destruction by a soulless femme fatale. Catalogue, in other words under *noir*, antecedents of. But it's not the real thing, not quite yet, because the rhythms are all wrong, especially the cutting. This goes like a train, so Warner-esque you'd hardly be surprised if Cagney and Pat O'Brien appeared in gendarme outfits. BBa

Auntie Mame

(Morton Da Costa, 1958, US) Rosalind Russell, Forrest Tucker, Coral Browne, Fred Clark, Roger Smith, Patric Knowles, Peggy Cass, Joanna Barnes, Pippa Scott.
143 min.
Later adapted into a Broadway musical (and one of the all-time dire movies with Lucille Ball), this is the first screen version of Patrick Dennis's novel, set during the inter-war years when the larger-than-life Mame adopts a young orphan and shows the littl'un exactly how to have a high old time of it. Sadly, the movie's loud, lumpen and hellishly over-extended, notwithstanding Russell's force-of-nature star turn. TJ

Aunt Julia and the Scriptwriter

see Tune in Tomorrow

Au Pair Girls

(Val Guest, 1972, GB) Gabrielle Drake, Astrid Frank, Nancie Wait, Me Me Lay, Richard O'Sullivan, John Le Mesurier.
86 min.
Feeble attempt to do what the Germans do. And if German sex films are bad, at least they're better than efforts like this, involving four au pairs on the loose in England.

Au Revoir (Tot Ziens)

(Heddy Honigmann, 1995, Neth) Johanna Ter Steege, Guy Van Sande, Els Dottermans.
114 min.
A woman (Ter Steege) catches the eye of a young man (Van Sande) on the skating rink. Later, by chance, they end up cycling alongside each other. The man follows her home, and within ten minutes they're fucking on the carpet. 'Just like the 1,000-metre sprint,' the man gasps afterwards. 'You're Belgian!' she exclaims, breaking into an uncontrollable fit of giggles. Worse, he's married. Honigmann's intense relationship-drama is a mite televisual, but it doesn't pull any punches, and the performances are the real McCoy. TCh

Au Revoir les Enfants

(Louis Malle, 1987, Fr/WGer) Gaspard Manesse, Raphael Fejtö, Francine Racette, Stanislas Carré de Malberg, Philippe Morier-Genoud.
104 min.
Plotwise Malle's autobiographical film, set in a Carmelite convent school in 1944, is simplicity itself: 12-year-old Julien doesn't understand why new boy Jean Bonnet – real name, he later learns is Kippelstein – is bullied by the other pupils and protected by the teachers. Only with the arrival of the Gestapo does he see the full implications of Jean's 'difference'. If the outcome of this sombre, lovingly detailed film is unsurprising, its emotional power remains undeniable, precisely because Malle never sentimentalises his material (neither boy is particularly loveable, nor is their friendship free of petty rivalries and cruelty). Instead, he creates an authentic mood of unspoken suspicions and everyday secrecy, drawing upon performances, decor, even nature itself to paint a wintry portrait of childhood on the brink of horrific discovery. The film's quiet integrity finally depends on his avoidance of heroic cliché and stylistic bombast, and on the unindulgent generosity extended towards his characters. GA

Au revoir, mon amour (He Rijun Zai Lai)

(Tony Au, 1991, HK) Anita Mui, Tony Leung, Hidekazu Akai.
126 min.
Tony Au's over-designed melodrama is a vehicle for *Rouge* star Anita Mui, set (like the much less interesting *Kawashima Yoshiko*) amid the Sino-Japanese conflicts of the 1930s. Here she plays a night-club singer torn between the Chinese guerrilla who once abandoned her and a humane Japanese officer. It's one of those movies in which the script's determination to provide a murder or explosion every few minutes allows no space for character development or emotional depth. The ending in post-war Japan is the only scene in the whole two hours that isn't numbingly obvious. TR

Aurora Encounter, The

(Jim McCullough Sr, 1985, US) Jack Elam, Peter Brown, Carol Bagdasarian, Mindy Smith, Mickey Hays, Dottie West, Spanky McFarland.
90 min.
Ever desperate to find that new miracle formula, the producers of this concoction have come up with *ET* drops in on *The Little House on the Prairie*. In a spaceship that resembles an antiquated vacuum cleaner, a particularly ugsome midget scarifies the denizens of Aurora before discovering a predilection for beer, checkers and cigars. Soon after rescuing some silly children from the local caves, the alien prangs his vessel and dies. Or does he? For small children this variation of a threadbare theme will have a certain charm, but adults are advised to watch it on video with a finger on the fast-forward button. MS

Aus einem deutschen Leben

see Death Is My Trade

Austerlitz (aka The Battle of Austerlitz)

(Abel Gance, 1959, Fr/It/Liechtenstein/Yug) Claudia Cardinale, Martine Carol, Leslie Caron, Vittorio De Sica, Jean Marais, Ettore Manni, Pierre Mondy, Jean Mercure, Jack Palance, Orson Welles.
123 min.
Silent-cinema genius he may well have been, but by this time in his career Abel Gance was creatively a shadow of his former self. It was a bold idea of the Salkinds to hire him for this chronicle of Bonaparte's famous victory over the Austro-Prussian army, but the result, for all its lavish scale and roster of stars, is a turgid bore. The original cut ran 166 minutes. TJ

Austin Powers: International Man of Mystery

(Jay Roach, 1997, US) Mike Myers, Elizabeth Hurley, Robert Wagner, Michael York, Mimi Rogers, Fabiana Udenio, Neil Mullarkey, Burt Bacharach, Carrie Fisher, Christian Slater.
96 min.
The psychedelic era's silliest secret agent is resurrected in a world that's moved on three decades. Myers (star and writer) gets so much of the detail right, it's easy to take his resourcefulness for granted. Everything, from Austin's velvet frock coats and frilly shirts, to the casting (Hurley's slinky sidekick Vanessa Kensington, scheming henchman Wagner, and York's Basil Exposition, the Ministry Man who explains the plot), and cred soundtrack (Burt Bacharach turns up in person), demonstrates how much the creator of *Wayne's World* enjoyed doing his homework. Someone, however, should have weeded out the dud gags and dissuaded Myers from playing the villain as well. Overall, though, it would take a stone face not to crumple at Austin's dodgy catchphrases and irrepressible sexual desperation. 'Shall we shag now, or shag later?' Soon, baby, soon. TJ

Australia

(Jean-Jacques Andrien, 1989, Fr/Bel/Switz) Jeremy Irons, Fanny Ardant, Tchéky Karyo, Agnès Sorel.
118 min.
A period romance that attempts, unsuccessfully, to explore the blocked sensibilities of the Belgian bourgeoisie in a particular time and place (1955, Verviers, once preeminently a wool city), this quickly becomes suffocated by dramatic inertia, irrelevance and wool. Edouard Pierson (Irons, sporting two execrable accents: phony English and awesomely deliberate French) is a Belgian living, in self-imposed exile, in Southern Australia with his 12-year-old daughter, buying and selling wool for export; his Indonesian wife, met when he was a war pilot, is dead, and the daughter is a secret from his family, presumably because they might disapprove. When the wool-processing business run by brother Julien (Karyo) runs into trouble, he returns home alone, and initiates a difficult affair with a well-married country girl (Ardant, always a class act) in London and misty Verviers. Things change, and the past must be put behind. The film often looks great, but Andrien (who lives in Verviers) has clearly let his documentary instincts run riot. Wool pops up all the time, in bales, out of bales, on factory floors, felt, bought, sold and discussed. The result is inoffensive, but woolly. WH

Author! Author!

(Arthur Hiller, 1982, US) Al Pacino, Dyan Cannon, Tuesday Weld, Bob Dishy, Bob Elliott.
109 min.
It improves, so sit out the opening credits and the frightful theme song advising that home is where there's 'always milk and cookies and a friend'. An I-Love-New-York movie that takes its pick from *Kramer vs Kramer*, it stars Pacino as a Broadway writer left by his wife to care for the shared children of several marriages while completing his latest play. Pacino can do you a volatile, middle class intellectual with one hand behind his back, and along with his streetwise brood has all the best and funniest lines. But the women lose out. Weld's role is simply the necessary evil to prove the point that men are people too. And Cannon is, in her hairy, furry, woolly way, radiantly two-dimensional. JS

Autobiography of a Princess

(James Ivory, 1975,GB) James Mason, Madhur Jaffrey.
59 min.
Imperial India seen through old home movies of court life as they are watched by the besotted, blinkered daughter-in-exile of a Maharajah and the latter's former English tutor, who still meet once a year in London for tea. The film explores the gradually revealed tensions and similarities between the two as they both gravitate towards the memory of her father, the magnetic and domineering Maharajah. Her unswerving loyalty to the past empire is answered by his mounting indignation at its monstrosities and his own weaknesses. Yet nothing really happens because the two draw a veil over their true emotions, and over the true nature of the dark scandals merely hinted at (apart from one clumsy flashback). A refined, ironic exercise whose brittleness is effectively countered by Mason's playing. CPe

Autobiography of Miss Jane Pittman, The

(John Korty, 1973, US) Cicely Tyson, Michael Murphy, Richard A Dysart, Katherine Helmond.
110 min.
Originally made for TV, this fictional recounting of the 110 years lived by one one black woman in Louisiana has a deceptively natural ring to it: what better way to reflect the range of American black experience? What greater challenge than limiting that experience to the life of one woman (ranging from Civil War to Civil Rights Movement), which has to serve as history, myth, personal story, commentary and newsreel all at once? Aiming for the stars, the film hits a magazine spread by Norman Rockwell, and obstinately stays there: a respectable enough achievement in its way, but one that ultimately dims the mind as it stirs up the emotions. JR

Autobus

see Aux Yeux du monde

Autour de Minuit

see 'Round Midnight

Autre Homme une Autre Chance, Un (Another Man, Another Woman/Another Man, Another Chance)

(Claude Lelouch, 1977, Fr) James Caan, Genevieve Bujold, Francis Huster, Jennifer Warren, Susan Tyrrell.
132 min.
Lelouch's soap opera Western proves yet again that a man (Caan as a horse doctor) and a woman (Bujold as a French immigrant) will eventually find love and happiness, no matter what contrivances, colour filters or saccharine music the master puts in their way. What other Western accompanies shots of the hero on horseback with the opening chords of Beethoven's Fifth? Who but Lelouch would compound a bilingual script of disarming coyness, peppered with current phrases ('Have a nice day') and historical pin-pointers ('It's too bad there's still no way to print pictures in a newspaper')? Not much dramatic interest, but the curiosity value is colossal. GB

Autumn Afternoon, An (Samma no aji)

(Yasujiro Ozu, 1962, Jap) Chishu Ryu, Shima Iwashita, Shinichiro Mikami, Keiji Sada, Mariko Okada.
113 min.
A widower (Ryu) arranges for his loyal daughter (Iwashita) to be wed, and tries to drown his sorrows in sake and drunken comradeship. Given the homogeneity of Ozu's work, perhaps it is meretricious to dwell on the fact that this was his final film. Still, its sweet, mellow air is all the more moving seen in that light, and it is clearly the testament of an old man. It's also worth noting that the film-maker's mother died in the course of the shooting: Ozu had lived with her all his life. Only this film and Good Morning were made in colour, but Ozu applies it here with great care and precision, another mark of his sublime philosophical and cinematic continuity (incidentally, note how red and silver motifs recur throughout the picture). TCh

Autumn Crocus

(Basil Dean, 1934, GB) Fay Compton, Ivor Novello, Esme Church, Jack Hawkins, George Zucco.
85 min. b/w.
Despite the skimpy story and makeshift construction – the Alpine location stuff was shot by Carol Reed without the cast – this adaptation of Dodie Smith's first play emerges as a rich evocation of the hopes and dreams of the '30s. Meandering between farce, fairytale and doomed romance, the film gently explores the Cinderella story of an ageing schoolmistress who discovers her Prince is a happily married man. Compton, emanating an intensely wistful beauty, progresses convincingly from virginal exuberance to a sad knowledge that fantasy is best left as fantasy. The presence of slyly camp Novello, looking like an overgrown boy scout in his Tyrolean lederhosen, and an array of grubbily eccentric character actors (Hawkins unrecognisable as a sex-obsessed psychiatrist) obviates the danger of maudlin sentimentality. RMy

Autumn Leaves

(Robert Aldrich, 1956, US) Joan Crawford, Cliff Robertson, Vera Miles, Lorne Greene, Ruth Donnelly, Shepperd Strudwick.
108 min. b/w.
A seemingly eccentric, but in fact characteristic, Aldrich film: cutting a radical cinematic swathe through weepie material. It rattles both psychological skeletons and the skeleton of psychology as Crawford's middle-aged spinster and Robertson's seductive young liar rush first into marriage and then at each other's throats. An 'extraordinary combination of domestic Guignol and elephantised soap opera', as Richard Combs has described it. PT

Autumn Moon (Qiuyue)

(Clara Law, 1992, HK/Jap) Masatoshi Nagase, Li Pui Wai, Choi siu Wan.
108 min.
Clara Law's limpid, understated movie justifies its own poetic title by minimising plot and avoiding melodramatics; it's the flip-side of the slam-bang heroics that dominate Hong Kong cinema. An aimless Japanese private eye (Nagase, the Elvis fan from Mystery Train) catches the current autumnal mood of Hong Kong when he runs into a schoolgirl in the grip of her first crush and her dying grandmother; he has a brief sexual fling with an old flame from Japan, but nothing much else happens. The movie sees Hong Kong as a technopolis on a par with Tokyo, but regrets the waning of Chinese social and cultural traditions, and ponders the city's future in the run-up to 1997. The Brits, chasteningly, have no part to play in the film's equation. TR

Autumn Sonata (Herbstsonate)

(Ingmar Bergman, 1978, WGer) Ingrid Bergman, Liv Ullmann, Lena Nyman, Halver Björk, Gunnar Björnstrand.
92 min.
Now about these women...Mother (concert pianist Bergman) and daughter (parson's wife Ullmann) come face to face after seven years to touch, cry and whisper – and to confront and confess – in an atmosphere pregnant with death and disease, shame and silence. Routine obsessions, routine hysteria; maybe even a routine masterpiece. Of course Bergman's actresses suffer superbly in microscopic close-up, but the nagging doubt persists as to whether this is incisive psychodrama or just those old nordic blues again. PT

Aux Yeux du monde (Autobus)

(Eric Rochant, 1991, Fr) Yvan Attal, Charlotte Gainsbourg, Kristin Scott-Thomas, Marc Berman, Renan Mazeas, David Burstzein.
98 min.
Desperate to impress his long-distance girlfriend (Gainsbourg), Bruno (Attal) hijacks a school bus and, at gunpoint, forces the driver, kids and teacher (Scott-Thomas) to accompany him on his long, wayward odyssey to the girl's home. Panic ensues, but the infants strike up a relationship of sorts with their often befuddled captor, while the teacher remains firm but understanding. The cops, how ever, are less forgiving... Like Hippo in Rochant's earlier World Without Pity, Bruno is less an angry young man than sorely in need of attention. Rochant and Attal (astonishingly good in his first lead role) certainly make him sympathetic, but never gloss over his ludicrous braggadocio or his fundamental wrong-headedness about his beloved's feelings. What makes the film so engrossing is its complexity, with a simple road thriller plot enormously enhanced by subtle performances, a telling use of landscape and psychological details, and an assured control of mood, which shifts effortlessly between manic comedy, taut suspense and more contemplative moments. GA

Avalanche

(Corey Allen, 1978, US) Rock Hudson, Mia Farrow, Robert Forster, Jeanette Nolan, Rick Moses, Barry Primus.
91 min.
In which Hudson, as icy and mountainous as the landscape, leads a cast of generally unpleasant leisure-seekers to the belated realisation that the wages of sin is getting dumped-on by white polystyrene. The inhabitants of the wonderful world of winter sports, predictably too engrossed in sexual and commercial intrigue to heed weather warnings, undergo a semi-slapstick series of snowy effects before performing pathetic rescue dramas. Pretty lacklustre for a Roger Corman production, but as (unconscious?) disaster movie parody it's entertaining enough. GA

Avalanche Express

(Mark Robson, 1979, Eire) Lee Marvin, Robert Shaw, Linda Evans, Maximilian Schell, Mike Connors, Horst Buchholz.
88 min.
Formulary East-West spy saga involving a KGB defector, a biological warfare programme, and running battles on the transcontinental express. Hammily acted and obviously subject to cobbling after both Robson and Shaw died before the film was completed, it's awful but given a certain fascination by the disjunctive editing style which reduces Abraham Polonsky's script to an abstraction, and which it is tempting to ascribe to Monte Hellman (called upon for 'post-production services' after Robson's death). TM

Avalon

(Barry Levinson, 1990, US) Armin Müller-Stahl, Elizabeth Perkins, Joan Plowright, Kevin Pollak, Aidan Quinn, Leo Fuchs, Eve Gordon, Lou Jacobi, Elijah Wood, Ronald Guttman.
128 min.
Levinson returns to Baltimore, home of Diner and Tin Men, for this semi-autobiographical voyage into family history. Sam Krichinsky (Müller-Stahl), arriving in America from the Old Country on July 4, 1914, wanders awestruck against a night sky alive with firecrackers. He is joined by his brothers, who acquire jobs, produce children, and reside in a row-house neighbourhood. The sprawling story eventually traces four generations; changing circumstances and wider social influences are reflected in the way family circle meetings give way to internal divisions and personal ambitions. It's a shamelessly sentimental interpretation of history, with television ushering in a generation which has lost the art of communication and the ability to care. Against this blinkered vision, even Levinson's confident direction and ability to capture the absurdities and rhythms of everyday speech fail to provide sufficient compensation. CM

Avanti!

(Billy Wilder, 1972, US) Jack Lemmon, Juliet Mills, Clive Revill, Edward Andrews.
144 min.
A sunny black comedy about a stuffy American who meets an overweight Englishwoman on the tourist paradise of Ischia. Each has come to claim the body of a deceased parent – his father, her mother – only to discover that the dead pair were lovers and to find history inexorably repeating itself. The humour (derived largely from unstereotypical national stereotypes, plus the inexhaustible confusion over luggage, hotel accommodations and bureaucratic red tape) is sometimes a little leisurely, while the camera has a tendency to linger over the travelogue scenery. But any longueurs are more than made up for by the same strangely moving undercurrent of tenderness that Wilder brought to The Private Life of Sherlock Holmes. Marvellous performances from Lemmon and Mills. TM

Avenger, The

see Texas, Addio

Avenir d'Emilie, L'

see Future of Emily, The

Aventure Malgache

(Alfred Hitchcock, 1944, GB) The Molière
Players.
31 min. b/w.
The lesser of two French-language propaganda
shorts made by Hitchcock in 1944 for the British
Ministry of Information (see *Bon Voyage*),
Aventure Malgache is a laboured attempt to
dramatise the internal conflicts between the
Gaullists, Pétainists and Vichyites in the French
colonies. Welwyn Garden City stands in for
Madagascar. In the event, these tensions proved
so sensitive that the film was never exhibited.
The plot concerns the rivalry between a corrupt
Vichyite police chief and a lawyer who masterminds the local Resistance. Imaginative touches
and a characteristically droll denouement. TCh

Aventures de Rabbi Jacob, Les

see Mad Adventures of 'Rabbi' Jacob, The

Aveu, L' (The Confession)

(Costa-Gavras, 1970, Fr/It) Yves Montand,
Simone Signoret, Gabriele Ferzetti, Michel
Vitold, Jean Bouise, Laszlo Szabo.
160 min.
The problem with Costa-Gavras movies is that
they seem to feed off rather than inform the left-
liberal sentiments they espouse. Thus in *L'Aveu*,
an actual case history, we get no context beyond
'here is an example of the evils of Stalinism'.
Instead we are offered the simple perspective of
the suffering of Arthur London (Montand), a
Czech party official (and his wife, Signoret), who
is faced in 1951 with the problem of whether to
confess to things he didn't do for the sake of the
party. The result is a film which blurs as many
issues as it raises. Cut by over 20 minutes for distribution in both Britain and America. PH

Aviator's Wife, The (La Femme de l'Aviateur)

(Eric Rohmer, 1980, Fr) Philippe Marlaud,
Marie Rivière, Anne-Laure Meury, Mathieu
Carrière, Fabrice Luchini.
106 min.
The first in Rohmer's series *Comédies et
Proverbes*, this gentle comedy laced with pain is
a delight from start to finish. Erroneously assuming that his more experienced girlfriend is being
unfaithful, a young student decides to investigate
the identity of the man he sees leaving her room
early one morning. Following the man through
Paris, he meets up with a pert schoolgirl, obviously attracted but bemused by his actions, who
offers to help in his ludicrous detection. The
whole thing would remain at the level of whimsical farce, were it not for Rohmer's emphasis on
the very real pain, confusion and wasted attempts
at happiness underlying the complicated
intrigues of the characters. As always, Rohmer
makes clear the enormous gulf between feelings
and words, intention and effect. The result is a
hilarious, wonderfully bitter-sweet acknowleg-
ment of the chasms between people trying desperately to understand and be understood. GA

Avventura, L' (The Adventure)

(Michelangelo Antonioni, 1960, It) Monica
Vitti, Gabriele Ferzetti, Lea Massari,
Dominique Blanchar, Renzo Ricci, James
Addams.
145 min. b/w.
Though once compared to *Psycho*, made the same
year and also about a couple searching for a
woman who mysteriously disappears after featuring heavily in the opening reel, Antonioni's film
could not be more dissimilar in tone and effect.
Slow, taciturn and coldly elegant in its visual evocation of alienated, isolated figures in a barren
Sicilian landscape, the film concerns itself less
with how and why the girl vanished from a group
of bored and wealthy socialites on holiday, than
with the desultory nature of the romance
embarked upon by her lover and her best friend
while they half-heartedly look for her. If it once

seemed the ultimate in arty, intellectually chic
movie-making, the film now looks all too studied
and remote a portrait of emotional sterility. GA

Awakening, The

(Mike Newell, 1980, GB) Charlton Heston,
Susannah York, Jill Townsend, Stephanie
Zimbalist, Patrick Drury.
105 min.
The opening section of this glossy, boringly shot
mummy drama, loosely based on Bram Stoker's
novel *The Jewel of Seven Stars*, is packed with
cheapo Freudian parallels between an archaeologist's obsession with the tomb of an Egyptian
princess, and his jealous wife's pregnancy (much
intercutting between the ancient doors being thrust
open and the graphic hospital birth). Though crude,
this tack might have proved interesting, but the rest
is part ineffective horror, part coyly underplayed
element of incest as the archaeologist's daughter
(aged 18) becomes the reincarnated princess and
evil forces are unleashed on the world. JWi

Awakenings

(Penny Marshall, 1990, US) Robert De Niro,
Robin Williams, Julie Kavner, Ruth Nelson,
John Heard, Penelope Ann Miller, Alice
Drummond, Judith Malina, Dexter Gordon.
121 min.
With Robin Williams as neurologist Oliver Sacks
– here Dr Sayer – and De Niro as Leonard Lowe,
the most afflicted Parkinson's case on the ward,
we are deep in *Rain Man* territory (a terrain
notable for its squashiness) in another homage to
catatonia. The patients, frozen in what Pinter
called 'A Kind of Alaska' in his play about the
case, have been sealed off for decades. The good
doctor treats them with L-Dopa, despite official
hostility (Heard), with miraculous results. We
don't get the euphoric explosions of libido detailed
in Ry Cooder's 'What Makes Granny Run', nor do
we get the depressions you might expect from all
those wasted years. We do get Dr Sayer and
Leonard relating, and – briefly – Leonard's diffident romance with a visitor (Miller) before he
reverts. Dexter Gordon, one of the patients, was
actually dying and looks it, which is something of
a visual bring-down for the phony charades.
Penny Marshall presses all the easy buttons,
Williams bumbles loveably, and De Niro shakes
his chassis to bits. Dramatically, it's a twin-tub,
with a big slot on top to pour in the caring. BC

Away All Boats

(Joseph Pevney, 1956, US) Jeff Chandler,
George Nader, Julie Adams, Lex Barker, Keith
Andes, Richard Boone, David Janssen, Frank
Faylen, Clint Eastwood.
114 min.
Standard-issue WWII action picture (from a novel
by Kenneth M Dodson) follows a US Navy transport boat as Capt Chandler and his inexperienced
crew see a good deal of wide-screen combat in the
Pacific. Competently staged, though the (post-
war) flagwaving is as trite as the characterisation. A young Clint Eastwood appears some way
down the cast list. TJ

Awfully Big Adventure, An

(Mike Newell, 1994, GB) Alan Rickman, Hugh
Grant, Georgina Cates, Alun Armstrong, Peter
Firth, Prunella Scales, Rita Tushingham,
Edward Petherbridge, Nicola Pagett, Carol
Drinkwater, Clive Merrison.
112 min.
Newell's follow-up to *Four Weddings and a
Funeral* offers many subtle if somewhat sombre
pleasures. Charles Wood's adaptation of Beryl
Bainbridge's novel about backstage theatrical life
in postwar Liverpool evokes the period's dusty
oppressiveness and moral hypocrisies. Cates
gives a luminous performance as the starstruck
trainee stagehand Stella; and Grant is cast effectively against type as Meredith Potter, the company's cruel, manipulative director who vies for
Stella's innocent soul with Rickman's suave,
haunted leading man PL O'Hara. When O'Hara
is called back to reprise his acclaimed Captain
Hook, a complex web of past and present entanglements begins to unravel. Newell's handling of
the exterior scenes has a slightly cursory air, but
his sharp dramatic focus draws the best from an
exceptional ensemble cast. With its flawed characters and disturbingly dark centre, this fragile
gem of a movie sparkles with intelligence and
glows with feeling. NF

Awful Truth, The

(Leo McCarey, 1937, US) Cary Grant, Irene
Dunne, Ralph Bellamy, Alexander D'Arcy,
Cecil Cunningham.
92 min. b/w.
Zappy, sophisticated screwball comedy with
Grant and Dunne displaying perfect timing as the
husband and wife who get divorced and then,
after enjoying quick flings with a cabaret artiste
and an oil tycoon respectively, decide to get
together again. A routine story perhaps, but
McCarey transforms it , through his customary
affection for his characters and taut pacing, into
delightfully effective entertainment. The erotically teasing ending, with a black cat obstinately barring the communicating bedroom door
which the *almost* un-estranged couple are praying will open, has a delicacy of touch that
Lubitsch rarely managed. GA

A.W.O.L.

(Sheldon Lettich, 1990, US) Jean-Claude Van
Damme, Harrison Page, Deborah Rennard,
Lisa Pelikan, Ashley Johnson, Brian
Thompson.
108 min.
This fight movie, despite its faults, is a considerable improvement on the cynical *Kickboxer*,
Cyborg, etc. With Van Damme deserting from the
Foreign Legion when his brother is fatally injured
in an LA drug feud, the exposition suggests a
revenge story, but in fact events follow an altogether livelier course: the AWOL legionnaire
resolves to help his destitute sister-in-law and
niece by making fast money the best way he can,
as a bare-knuckle fighter. Making something of
the character's immigrant status, the film-makers establish a commendably downtown perspective; the *really* seedy characters are the
wealthy gamblers who get off on the bloody gladiatorial matches. This is a B-movie, crude in execution, with gimmicky set pieces, risibly
caricatured villains, and overblown sentimentality. But Van Damme is beginning to come good
on his promise; in particular, his friendship with
the wonderful Harrison Page, as his hustling
guide and mentor, bears the fruit of a more
human action-movie, one that's almost worth getting excited about. TCh

Ay! Carmela

(Carlos Saura, 1990, Sp/It) Carmen Maura,
Andres Pajares, Gabino Diego, Maurizio De
Razza, Miguel A Rellan, Edward Zentara.
103 min.
Saura's work has so often made tacit reference to
the Spanish Civil War that one might reasonably
expect this, his most direct look at the conflict to
date, to be one of his more heartfelt efforts. It concerns a raggedy but enthusiastic cabaret trio –
lusty Carmela (Maura), husband Paulino
(Pajares), and their hapless, mute dogsbody
(Diego) – who, in 1938, decide to take a break
from entertaining Republicans on the Aragon
front and retreat to a less beleaguered Valencia.
But (surprise, surprise), lost after a foggy
overnight drive, they find themselves behind
enemy lines, where their only hope of escaping
imprisonment or execution is to take fidelity to
Franco, and stage a show for his troops with
lyrics and gags doctored accordingly. As political cinema, this exceedingly broad 'tragi-comedy' falls flat on its face, never moving beyond
simplistic polarities and a concept of history as
sentimental as it is falsely heroic. As drama, too,
it fails to transcend maudlin stereotypes (both
national and sexual), while its origins as a stage
play are all too obvious, and the performances
given to grotesque overstatement. GA

b

The Big Lebowski

Babar: The Movie

(Alan Bunce, 1989, Can/Fr) voices: Gordon Pinsent, Elizabeth Hanna, Lisa Yamanaka, Marsha Moreau.
76 min.
Initial delight that Laurent de Brunhoff's elegant, courtly and very European cartoons have been rescued from the elephants' graveyard soon turns to horror: this Americanises both characters and setting beyond recognition. The premise is a staple of successful kids' movies from *Bambi* to *ET*: separation from Mommy. Babar, boy king of the elephants, must help Celeste rescue mother from the evil rhinoceros Rataxas, picking up help on the way: Zephir the monkey and a vegetarian crocodile. Somehow the precocious pachyderm overcomes all odds, indulges in some Indiana Jones-style swashbuckling, and single-handedly defeats the rhino army before his decadent and bureaucratic generals can muster so much as one soldier. Hooray! The odd good wisecrack and a cracking pace help gloss over flat and unimaginative animation, and teeny tots will adore it. DW

Baba Yaga – The Devil Witch (Baba Yaga)

(Corrado Farina, 1973, It/Fr) Carroll Baker, George Eastman, Isabelle de Funès, Ely Galleani.
90 min.
Mixture of sex and horror based on the comic strips of Guido Crepax, whose main character Valentina (played by Louis de Funès' niece Isabelle), famous fashion photographer and clothes-fetishist, gets involved in those weird adventures which all hot-blooded males are supposed to dream about. Here she meets up with lesbian witch Baba Yaga (Baker), who lures her into a murky old house with snakes, rusty sewing machines, and a bottomless pit concealed under the carpet. Followers of Crepax will find only a few moments which recall the master's style. The rest (though Farina claimed that scenes of political relevance were removed by the producers) can be safely left to connoisseurs of handsomely photographed, high class trash. GB

Babe

(Chris Noonan, 1995, Aust) James Cromwell, Magda Szubanski, Zoe Burton, Paul Goddard; voices: Christine Cavanaugh, Miriam Margoyles, Roscoe Lee Browne.
92 min.
Degree of difficulty apart – and difficulty involved making an entire farmyard of real animals talk – the merits of *Babe* are those of Dick King-Smith's classic, *The Sheep-Pig*. Piglet Babe beats the slaughterhouse and is adopted by a sheepdog who coaches him in the art of rounding up sheep. Taciturn farmer Hoggett (Cromwell) wonderingly goes along with this apprenticeship, and is gratified when Babe wins the rosette at the trials. Babe's secret is politeness which gets better results than barking, and raises lots of laughs. Charming, eccentric and very amusing. BC

Babe, The

(Arthur Hiller, 1991, US) John Goodman, Kelly McGillis, Trini Alvarado, Bruce Boxleitner, Peter Donat, James Cromwell, JC Quinn, Joe Ragno.
115 min.
A biopic of Babe Ruth, the sultan of swat and baseball's Don Bradman. Goodman gives a splendid performance as the fat-boy genius who loved life and single-handedly rescued the USA's summer sporting obsession between the wars after the Chicago White Sox scandal of 1919. Alvarado and McGillis provide strong support in a film which shows Ruth in warts-and-all mode: a boy abandoned to the priests aged seven as uncontrollable and incorrigible; a man who ate and drank like a pig, fought with fans and officials, cheated on his wife, but had a touching generosity, kindness and insecurity that stemmed from his hideous childhood. Surprisingly interesting, even if you don't know a home run from a stolen base. SGr

Bab El-Oued City

(Merzak Allouache, 1994, Alg/Fr) Nadia Kaci, Hassan Abdou, Nadia Samir, Mohamed Ourdache.
93 min.
Frustrated by the confines of Muslim society, and angered by the religious propaganda blaring across the casbah, Boualem (Abdou) rashly steals a loudspeaker rigged up by the militants. Once they discover the culprits, the fundamentalists are determined to make an example of him. A fascinating portrait of life in contemporary Algeria – the smuggling, hypocrisy and widespread intimidation – but one that doesn't really deliver in the story department; it's cryptic to the point of impenetrability, but, paradoxically, dully predictable. TCh

Babes in Arms

(Busby Berkeley, 1939, US) Mickey Rooney, Judy Garland, Charles Winninger, Guy Kibbee, June Preisser.
96 min. b/w.
First of the Garland-Rooney musicals, clothing a tired plot (old vaudevillians can't cope with competition from the movies, but their putting-on-a-show youngsters emphatically can) with much charm, energy and, mercifully, no Busby Berkeley chorine patterns. Sadly, one of Rodgers and Hart's best scores was mostly shed on the way to the screen, possibly considered too sophisticated for high school junketings. But the replacement numbers, including some old minstrel show favourites, have an appropriately nostalgic quality. *Babes in Arms* was followed by *Strike Up the Band* (1940), *Babes on Broadway* (1941) and *Girl Crazy* (1943). TM

Babes on Broadway

(Busby Berkeley, 1941, US) Mickey Rooney, Judy Garland, Virginia Weidler, Ray McDonald, Richard Quine, Fay Bainter.
118 min. b/w.
Perhaps the best of the Garland-Rooney musicals, only momentarily marred by some sentimentality about British war orphans. Following the usual putting-on-a-show formula, it features an unusually rich and varied collection of numbers, and gives Rooney a rare opportunity to show off his talent for impersonation. Minnelli got his first taste of direction on Garland's solos, in particular the 'Ghost Theatre' sequence. TM

Babette's Feast (Babettes Gaestebud)

(Gabriel Axel, 1987, Den) Stéphane Audran, Jean-Philipe Lafont, Gudmar Wivesson, Jarl Kulle, Bibi Andersson, Bodil Kjer, Birgitte Federspiel.
103 min.
Why, in the 1870s, would a Parisienne (Audran), an acclaimed chef, be working for a pittance for two elderly sisters supervising a remote religious community on Denmark's windswept Jutland coast? The unlikely answer to that question may be found in Axel's superb adaptation of Isak Dinesen's very funny short story, a bizarre, magical concoction, seasoned to literally mouthwatering effect. The ingredients are marvellous locations, crisp photography, and an excellent cast. Axel never overstates the opposition between the villagers' God-fearing asceticism and Babette's feats of gastronomic wizardry, preferring instead a gently comic portrait of lives defined by pious austerity. It's a tale of self-sacrifice, thwarted ambitions, and lost love, but sheer sensuous joy suffuses the screen when Babette performs her own special miracle for one last supper. Axel, too, is surely an alchemist; compared to most literary adaptations, this is the word made flesh. GA

Baby, The

(Ted Post, 1973, US) Anjanette Comer, Ruth Roman, Marianne Hill, Suzanne Zenor.
102 min.
What starts out as a seemingly realist study of the relationship between social worker Comer and the dysfunctional family presided over by Roman develops into a full-blown horror movie. Comer has a consuming interest in 'Baby', a man with the mind of a child, and, convinced that Roman and her sisters are bent on murder, abducts Baby. An unusual chiller, well directed by co-scripter Ted (*Magnum Force*) Post. NF

Baby Blue Marine

(John Hancock, 1976, US) Jan-Michael Vincent, Glynnis O'Connor, Katherine Helmond, Dana Elcar, Bert Remsen, Richard Gere, Art Lund, Michael Conrad.
90 min.
Stodgily directed effort that rates high on curiosity value. Ostensibly dealing with WWII traumas, the film in fact attempts a weirdly fascinating washing away of post-Vietnam guilt. Vincent, then cornering the market in all-American clean-cut heroes, is the dubious choice for the part of the reject marine who finds himself playing war hero to an eager small-town audience. VG

Baby Boom

(Charles Shyer, 1987, US) Diane Keaton, Harold Ramis, Sam Wanamaker, James Spader, Pat Hingle, Britt Leach, Sam Shepard.
111 min.
A working woman's fantasy, mixing cute in both the business acumen and coochy-coo varieties. Keaton (uneasily neurotic and capable), a thrusting NY advertising exec, inherits a relative's toddler, and is forced suddenly into a crash course in adoption, diapers, child-care, and a re-examination of her own feelings. Puritan would-be adopters present a fearsome option; her lover (Ramis) finds the disruption unacceptable and leaves; her boss (Wanamaker) forgets a partnership offer. What's a wealthy single parent to do? Take the tiny tot to leafy upstate Smallsville, and make with the chequered aprons and homemade victuals. It's played like a '40s comedy; heartwarming, sentimental, simplistic. Sickeningly calculated. WH

Baby Doll

(Elia Kazan, 1956, US) Carroll Baker, Karl Malden, Eli Wallach, Mildred Dunnock, Lonny Chapman, Rip Torn.
114 min. b/w.
Based by Tennessee Williams on two of his one-act plays, this is arguably one of Kazan's least ambitious and most successfully realised movies. Essentially a black comedy about a bizarre and cruel romantic triangle, it concerns the intrusion of Wallach's cunning Sicilian businessman into the ramshackle Deep South lives of boor Malden and his immature nymphet wife Baker. Inevitably, flirtation, seduction and jealousy are the result. Condemned by the Legion of Decency upon release, its erotic content now seems tame indeed; but the grotesquely caricatured performances and the evocation of the baking, dusty, indolent homestead make for witty and compelling viewing. GA

Baby Face

(Alfred E Green, 1933, US) Barbara Stanwyck, George Brent, Donald Cook, Henry Kolker, Douglas Dumbrille, Margaret Lindsay, John Wayne.
70 min. b/w.
Directed with more pace than style, but what matter with Stanwyck in peak form? Starting out as a barmaid in dad's speakeasy in the Pittsburgh slums, she moves to New York when he dies, and calculatingly climbs man by man from basement to penthouse. For all the moralising which has her pre-Hayes Code golddigging lead through fraught paths to true love, the character probably grew into the Phyllis Dietrichson of *Double Indemnity*. TM

Baby Face Morgan

(Arthur Dreifuss, 1942, US) Richard Cromwell, Mary Carlisle, Robert Armstrong, Chick Chandler, Warren Hymer, Vince Barnett.
60 min. b/w.
Very minor crime caper from the PRC stable, where they turned 'em out even cheaper and quicker than sister company Monogram Pictures, leading light on Hollywood's so-called Poverty Row. This one's about a mobster's son who's made the director of a dodgy insurance company by his dad's old partners in crime. In the midst of the ensuing tedium you may develop the suspicion that it was conceived as a comedy. Grim all the same. TJ

Baby Face Nelson

(Don Siegel, 1957, US) Mickey Rooney, Carolyn Jones, Cedric Hardwicke, Ted De Corsia, Emile Meyer, Leo Gordon, Jack Elam.
85 min. b/w.
One of Siegel's most vigorous crime-thrillers, and a key study of the gangster as psychotic. Rooney is surprisingly and superbly cast as the Depression desperado increasingly unable to control his outbursts of irrational violence, while the supporting cast – including Gordon as John Dillinger – is expertly deployed. But it is the sheer pace and economy of Siegel's direction that lend

the film its anarchic energy; recreation of period is almost ignored in favour of an emphasis on actions exemplifying the anti-hero's sexually-insecure neuroses. A superior example of the way B-movie conventions may be transcended by wit and a fertile imagination. GA

Baby It's You
(John Sayles, 1982, US) Rosanna Arquette, Vincent Spano, Joanna Merlin, Jack Davidson, Nick Ferrari.
104 min.
High school in New Jersey, 1966: she's en route for college and WASPdom, he's more concerned with miming to Sinatra and curling his lip the right amount at the teachers. As usual Sayles invests his subject with great care, and breaks with tradition by pursuing the pair into post-school life: the effects of hippy culture on her, of real life (washing up in Miami) on him. There is no easy moralising, nor any patronising of the characters; their reunion is as moving and hopeless as was their first love. Arquette and Spano hit exactly the right note; and having had *Return of the Secaucus Seven* recycled by *The Big Chill*, Sayles now outdoes the Chill with his own soundtrack (uniting Sinatra, Springsteen, Shirelles). CPea

Babylon
(Franco Rosso, 1980, GB) Brinsley Forde, Karl Howman, Trevor Laird, Brian Bovell, Victor Romero Evans.
95 min.
Although *Babylon* shows what it's like to be young, black and working class in Britain, the final product turns dramatised documentary into a breathless helter-skelter. Rather than force the social and political issues, Rosso lets them emerge and gather momentum through the everyday experience of his central character Blue (sensitively played by Forde). A series of increasingly provocative incidents finally polarise Blue and lead to uncompromising confrontation. Although the script runs out of steam by the end, the sharp use of location, the meticulous detailing of black culture, the uniformly excellent performances and stimulating soundtrack command attention. IB

Babylon: la paura e la migliore amica dell'uomo
see Lies to Live by (Babylon)

Baby of Mâcon, The
(Peter Greenaway, 1993, GB/Neth/Fr/Ger) Julia Ormond, Ralph Fiennes, Philip Stone, Jonathan Lacey, Don Henderson, Celia Gregory.
122 min.
Set halfway through the 17th century, Greenaway's film follows a church play performed for the benefit of the young aristocrat Cosimo (Lacey). In the play, a grotesque old woman gives birth to a beautiful baby boy. The child's older sister (Ormond) is quick to exploit the situation, selling blessings from the baby, and even claiming she's the true mother by virgin birth. However, when she attempts to seduce the bishop's son (Fiennes), the Church exacts a terrible revenge. An agnostic's vision of the Nativity, *The Baby of Mâcon* is an elaborate desecration of Catholic iconography, and a merciless assault on superstition and religion. Greenaway breaks down the barriers between the play and the outside world, the actors and their audience, so that the performance itself becomes just another corrupt religious ritual. The film is repetitive, cold and misanthropic; everyone here is a fraud, a cynic or a simpleton; even the baby proves malign. TCh

Baby's Day Out
(Patrick Read Johnson, 1994, US) Joe Mantegna, Lara Flynn Boyle, Joe Pantoliano, Brian Haley, John Neville, Eddie Bracken.
99 min.
Say what you like about *Home Alone* creator John Hughes, he knows how to pen a formula picture. Though heir to a fortune, Baby Bink has never had his picture in the paper, a situation his mother (Boyle) intends to rectify. But the photographers are three bungling kidnappers (led by Mantegna), who make off with the sprog and demand a tidy ransom. The baby soon escapes, proceeding to duplicate the trip round the big city described in his favourite book, as he takes in a department store, a zoo, and finally a building

site. The abductors, meanwhile, suffer humiliation as they attempt to recapture him. Cartoon crude, but quite lively. NF

Baby – Secret of the Lost Legend
(BWL Norton, 1985, US) William Katt, Sean Young, Patrick McGoohan, Julian Fellowes.
95 min.
McGoohan is a nasty, glory-seeking crypto-zoologist following up rumours of a brontosaurus family living deep in the Congo. His persistent assistant (Young) decides to venture into the bush herself when he dismisses her discovery of a set of bones. Then follow standard chases up and down the jungle, plus brushes with natives and soldiers, as the adversaries and their allies try to steal the creatures off each other. The bronts are brilliant, while snappy dialogue keeps the film from sinking into the absurd. Undemanding Disney family entertainment. DPe

Babysitter, The
(Guy Ferland, 1995, US) Alicia Silverstone, JT Walsh, Lois Chiles, George Segal.
85 min.
Although sent it straight to video on both sides of the Atlantic and packaged like a thousand other titillating thrillers ('Obsession is a Dangerous State of Mind,' indeed), *The Babysitter* turns out to be something a little different. Written and directed by one Guy Ferland, it's based on a story by Robert Coover, and remains true to Coover's teasing comedy of rampant sexual fantasy, that peculiar brand of esoteric erotica which deconstructionists call their own. Silverstone is the innocent babysitter who unwittingly works all the men in her life (the puberulent brat in her charge, his dad, a boyfriend, and his scheming mate) into paroxysms of polymorphous lust. The fantasy sequences grow a mite tedious – most of them centre on Alicia taking a bath – and the movie shies away from anything *too* dirty, but Walsh and Chiles have fun as the boozy parents whose marriage is on the rocks, while the true/false plotting keeps you guessing. TCh

Baby the Rain Must Fall
(Robert Mulligan, 1964, US) Steve McQueen, Lee Remick, Don Murray, Paul Fix, Josephine Hutchinson, Ruth White, Charles Watts, Kimberly Block.
93 min. b/w.
Horton Foote adapted his play *The Traveling Lady* for this vaguely literary tale of small town Texas folk, one of the string of well-meaning but amorphous pictures (*To Kill A Mockingbird* was the best) turned out by Mulligan and producing partner Alan Pakula throughout the '60s. McQueen is slightly ill-at-ease as a rebellious rockabilly singer trying to stay on the right side of the law after his release on parole, lip-synching unconvincingly on the bandstand, and unable to invest his characteristically spare acting style with the psychological insights that would enable the audience to 'read' his self-destructive character. Remick is typically radiant in a typically thankless role as the doormat wife. The impressive high-contrast b/w camerawork is by Ernest Laszlo. TJ

Baby Tramp
see Butterfly

Bachelor Bait
see Adventure in Baltimore

Bachelor Girl Apartment
see Any Wednesday

Bachelor Mother
(Garson Kanin, 1939, US) Ginger Rogers, David Niven, Charles Coburn, Frank Albertson, Ernest Truex.
81 min. b/w.
Rogers is superb as the brassy lady from the Bronx in this comedy of mistaken identity and parenthood, in which a young shopgirl is forced by her employers (Coburn as the department store owner, Niven as his urbanely flustered, eligible son) into becoming foster-mother to an abandoned child. It's a hilarious, snappy, loose-jointed comedy in the best Hollywood tradition, but the script and direction by Kanin have an intelligence and

sense of irony which raise provocative question after provocative question – about the role of women as workers, mothers, and mistresses; about male hypocrisy. A salutary reminder that Sirk wasn't the only 'subversive' to burrow his way into the woodwork of tinsel city. CA

Bachelor Party
(Neal Israel, 1984, US) Tom Hanks, Tawny Kitaen, Adrian Zmed, George Grizzard, Barbara Stuart, William Tepper.
105 min.
A quintet of fun-loving stags round up a lot of chicks, drugs, booze, tits and bums for some terminal whoops-a-daisy. But Hanks (last seen making a big *Splash*) lends a touch of comic class as the prospective groom who struggles to remain faithful to his beloved girlfriend (Kitaen). AB

Bachelor Party, The
(Delbert Mann, 1957, US) Don Murray, EG Marshall, Jack Warden, Patricia Smith, Carolyn Jones.
93 min. b/w.
Based on Paddy Chayefsky's highly successful TV play (itself a follow-up to *Marty*), this is a story about a debauch among office workers that sours as the night wears on. Praised in its day for its ensemble acting and acute analysis of middle-class anxieties, it now looks rather drab and dated. MA

Back Alley Princes (Malu Xiao Yingxiong)
(Lo Wei, 1972, HK) Shangkuan Ling Feng, Samuel Hui, Angela Mao, Tien Feng.
100 min.
A socially conscious comedy which may not handle its gags with much subtlety, but does manage to portray, with deliberate casualness, life lived on the edge of desperation in Hong Kong as it charts the supposedly carefree lives of two jaunty street kids (one of whom is a girl dressed as a boy) who stage minor con-jobs for a living. The fringes of the action are littered with the activities of small-time gamblers, pimps and hustlers, while the world of bar hostesses and sexual profiteering is shown without recourse to histrionics. VG

Backbeat
(Iain Softley, 1993, GB) Sheryl Lee, Stephen Dorff, Ian Hart, Gary Bakewell, Chris O'Neill, Scot Williams, Wolf Kahler.
100 min.
Lively, light-hearted and long on period detail, this portrait of the pre-stardom Beatles focuses on the relationship of Lennon, his pal and 'fifth Beatle' Stuart Sutcliffe, and Astrid Kirchherr, the Hamburg photographer partly responsible for creating the band's mop-top image, with whom Sutcliffe fell in love. There's not much story – the lads' experience in Hamburg at the start of the '60s, their disagreements, their acquisition of a loyal club following, and Sutcliffe's appointment with death – so that the film depends for effect on atmosphere, performance and panache. Happily, it largely succeeds in each respect. Much of the credit must go to Hart, whose Lennon is convincingly acerbic, rebellious and petty. Dorff is adequately cool, good looking and Scousey as Sutcliffe; the other Beatles are played by fair lookalikes; and only Lee's vapid Astrid disappoints. The music is loud and raw, but nevertheless evokes the excitement it generated. GA

Back Door to Hell
(Monte Hellman, 1964, US/Phil) Jimmie Rodgers, Jack Nicholson, John Hackett, Annabelle Huggins, Conrad Maga.
68 min. b/w.
A war movie shot for around three bucks in the Philippines and seemingly pitched at the sub-drive-in market. However, followers of Hellman should be able to discern traces of the futility that dominated subsequent films like *The Shooting* and *Two Lane Blacktop*. The script throws in much talk to disguise the fact that the budget couldn't accommodate more battle scenes, and amuses itself by giving a younger and greener Nicholson lines like 'You're the kinda guy who'd call Mahatma Gandhi a rabble-rouser'. CPe

Backdraft
(Ron Howard, 1991, US) Kurt Russell, William Baldwin, Robert De Niro, Donald Sutherland,

Jennifer Jason Leigh, Scott Glenn, Rebecca De Mornay, Jason Gedrick, JT Walsh.
136 min.
Being a fireman is just like belonging to a football team, or so screenwriter Gregory Widen would have us believe. 'You dropped the ball, you split the team up,' says scornful firefighter Stephen McCaffrey (Russell) to his rookie brother (Baldwin). As though sibling rivalry was not enough, Widen (an ex-firefighter) lumbers the plot with unnecessary complications and obvious confrontations: an investigator (De Niro) is on the trail of a skilful arsonist, the squabbling brothers have troubled romances. Ron Howard creates some promo-style sequences that would look more at home in a Gillette advert, but he does a superb job with the ultra-realistic effects. The fire sequences are stunning, and the buildup to them, complete with blaring sirens and bellowed conversations, has an aggressive immediacy. CM

Backfire

(Gilbert Cates, 1987, US) Karen Allen, Keith Carradine, Jeff Fahey, Bernie Casey, Dean Paul Martin, Virginia Capers, Dinah Manoff.
91 min.
Vietnam rears its head again in this who's-haunting-who thriller about a wealthy shell-shocked veteran, Donny (Fahey), whom his wife Mara (Allen) hopes, with the help of her kindled old flame (Martin) and some gruesome special effects, to drive to suicide. The plot backfires, and she's left with a catatonic husband whose fortune she forfeits to his devoted sister (Manoff) if she puts him in an institution. Suddenly it's Mara's turn to worry about things going bump in the night. Is she cracking up, is Donny faking his catatonia, is the sister trying to get her hands on the dough, or are the weird happenings linked to the arrival of an enigmatic stranger (Carradine)? Lacking the narrative assurance to exploit its switchback plottings, this would-be Hitchcockian mystery ends up floundering in the shallows. Only Carradine's nicely judged performance escapes the formulaic straitjacket. NF

Back from Eternity

(John Farrow, 1956, US) Robert Ryan, Anita Ekberg, Rod Steiger, Gene Barry, Phyllis Kirk, Keith Andes, Beulah Bondi, Cameron Prud'homme, Fred Clark.
97 min. b/w.
Despite a typically fine, tormented performance from Ryan as the drunken pilot, Farrow's remake of his own Five Came Back loses out to its predecessor, partly because (without adding anything of note) it takes significantly longer to tell its tale of crashed air passengers fending off headhunters in the Amazon jungle, partly because the stereotype characters and situations had by now lost their freshness. Steiger, over-acting, is no match for the original's Joseph Calleia; Ekberg is purely ornamental; and the voluntary self-sacrifice of elderly professor Prud'homme and his scared but loving wife (Bondi) carries less weight than in the earlier film. Tense in parts, but largely formulaic. GA

Background to Danger

(Raoul Walsh, 1943, US) George Raft, Brenda Marshall, Sydney Greenstreet, Peter Lorre, Osa Massen, Kurt Katch.
80 min. b/w.
Maybe not up there with the best of Walsh's action pics, but still an efficient and entertaining WWII spy thriller. Raft is the American agent travelling to Turkey to prevent the country from allying itself with the Nazis, and encountering that colourful pair, Greenstreet (a Nazi) and Lorre (his Turkish opponent) en route. A bit too light to be a really good espionage drama – the genre works best when presenting a bleak world of betrayal and doubt – but Walsh keeps it moving along at a cracking pace, while the script (adapted by WR Burnett from Eric Ambler's novel) is vivid and sharp. GA

Back in the USSR

(Deran Sarafian, 1992, US) Frank Whaley, Natalya Negoda, Roman Polanski, Andrew Divof, Dey Young, Brian Blessed.
87 min.
Yarn about a much-stolen Russian icon, made by Corman protégé Deran Sarafian, in which

Polanski features as a black marketeer with a violent sense of humour: too farcical to be a thriller; too brutal to be a comedy; and insufficiently surefooted to be a comedy-thriller. AO

Backlash

(Bill Bennett, 1986, Aust) David Argue, Gia Carides, Lydia Miller, Brian Syron, Anne Smith, Don Smith.
90 min.
Two cops drive an Aboriginal barmaid (Miller), accused of castrating her over-attentive boss with garden shears, across country to face trial. Argue is a cynical, aggressive, seen-it-all type, Caridis a rookie policewoman with starry-eyed notions about law enforcement and an increasing sympathy for their prisoner. The tensions within the group create a shifting pattern of alliances, especially when an ill-advised short cut leaves them stranded miles from anywhere. Here, the freewheeling narrative gives way to more static psychodrama. And who is the mysterious man who tracks them by day and disturbs their sleep with anguished cries by night? Former documentarist Bennett makes good use of the sun-parched landscape and improvised dialogue, while his unobtrusive camera style allows the actors ample scope to explore the drama and humour of a scenario laced with social comment. If this loosely coiled road movie doesn't always generate the kind of excitement suggested by the title, it does have a sting in its tail. NF

Back of Beyond

(Michael Robertson, 1995, Aust) Paul Mercurio, Dee Smart, Rebekah Elmaloglou, Colin Friels, John Polson.
85 min.
Blaming himself for the death of his sister, a traumatised mechanic (Mercurio) has all but given up on the lonely outback petrol station where he lives, but when a trio of jewel thieves break down in the vicinity, he's enlisted in emergency repair work at gunpoint. Gangsters holed up in a desert outpost in the company of an honest man: the set-up's at least as old as The Petrified Forest (1936), and though director Robertson has a few tricks up his sleeve, these are so blatantly signposted you could see them coming with your eyes shut. Friels plays the key thug, his Aryan dye job and hairnet insufficient to prevent his girl (newcomer Smart) from drifting to Mercurio's side. It's easy to understand Friels' consternation – what does she see in this sullen, monosyllabic pretty boy? He looks cute in his overalls, perhaps, but corpses have more personality. The B-movie dialogue doesn't extend to irony ('You've gotta find your purpose,' we're earnestly informed), while the director's pseudo-mystic mumbo-jumbo is strictly skin deep. TCh

Back Roads

(Martin Ritt, 1981, US) Sally Field, Tommy Lee Jones, David Keith, Miriam Colon, Michael Gazzo, M Emmet Walsh.
95 min.
Pleasantly old-fashioned romantic comedy in which two losers meet cute – he's a broken-down boxer, she a hooker angrily throwing him out after belatedly realising he's broke – then set off on a road movie odyssey through picturesque redneck locations in search of a new life. Very good on local colour but a bit sugary in its attitude to the central relationship, it would have been better taking a bleaker cue from Tommy Lee Jones' admirably dry performance. TM

Backroads

(Phillip Noyce, 1977, Aust) Gary Foley, Bill Hunter, Zac Martin, Terry Camilleri, Julie McGregor.
59 min.
An Aussie male duo, one redneck dropout white, the other a young black, steal a car and joyride their way across the outback of New South Wales before coming to the inevitable end of all good movie outlaws. Very much the result of a collaborative tension between director Noyce and his black lead actor (Foley), Backroads is an outstanding road movie to stand beside the very best American examples of the genre. Often brilliantly funny, it manages to be both completely commercial and a scathing depiction of one of the world's most racist societies. RM

Back-Room Boy

(Herbert Mason, 1942, GB) Arthur Askey, Moore Marriott, Graham Moffatt, Googie Withers, Vera Francis, Joyce Howard.
82 min. b/w.
Askey's an incompetent young meteorologist sent to a remote Orkney lighthouse, where he somehow rumbles a Nazi spy ring. This is typical Will Hay and the Crazy Gang territory: chaotic, childish, and much improved by the mugging of Hay's old sidekicks, Marriott and Moffatt. Co-writer Val Guest recycles many of the situations and jokes he patented in Oh, Mr Porter! and The Frozen Limits. Derivative but fun. GM

Back Street

(John M Stahl, 1932, US) Irene Dunne, John Boles, George Meeker, ZaSu Pitts, Arlette Duncan, June Clyde.
89 min. b/w.
Fine adaptation of Fannie Hurst's tearjerking novel about a girl (Dunne) who falls in love with a man engaged to be married. An accident prevents her from pursuing the romance; he marries; and when they meet again after some years, she becomes his mistress. Soon realising the demi-paradise that awaits her alone in 'the back street' of his life, she tries to break away, only to find that the desperate need created by their love for each other makes this impossible; and remaining loyal for the rest of her life, she calmly accepts all the heartbreak and humiliation that follows. Stahl counters the danger of sentimentality by maintaining an even, beautifully controlled monotone (very moving in its quietude) that establishes a discreet distance between his camera and the excesses of the plot. One thinks, oddly, of Ozu and Dreyer as the characters find themselves quietly swept away by currents over which they have no control. TM

Back Street

(Robert Stevenson, 1941, US) Charles Boyer, Margaret Sullavan, Richard Carlson, Frank McHugh, Tim Holt.
89 min. b/w.
While John M Stahl's 1932 version of Fannie Hurst's tearjerking romantic novel achieved the emotional charge later associated with the best of Douglas Sirk's work, this careful, well acted remake seldom ignites the explosive emotions. Sullavan is the self-annihilating mistress who lives for twenty years in shabby rooms, while her lover (Boyer) goes on with his comfortable married life. Remade, to lushly unhappy effect, in a Ross Hunter production directed by David Miller in 1961, with Susan Hayward and John Gavin. NF

Back to Back, Face to Face (Bei kao Bei, Lian dui Lian)

(Huang Jianxin, 1994, HK/China) Niu Zhenhua, Lei Gesheng, Li Qiang, Ju Hao.
138 min.
Huang Jianxin has been getting away with the sharpest political satire in China ever since he made The Black Cannon Incident, largely because he leaves viewers free to draw their own conclusions about the absurd situations he explores in his movies. This time, he dissects a power struggle for control of a cultural centre: Wang (comedian Niu Zhenhua), its vice-president, assumes his political skills and connections make him a shoo-in for the top job, but the local cultural bureau chief has other ideas. This is a combination of darkish comedy with the appeal of an on-going soap opera. Its core is acid: here is a perfect microcosm of the way the political process works in China, with barely a whisper of exaggeration. TR

Back to Bataan

(Edward Dmytryk, 1945, US) John Wayne, Anthony Quinn, Beulah Bondi, Lawrence Tierney, Paul Fix, Fely Franquelli, Richard Loo, Philip Ahn.
95 min. b/w.
Big John is the cowboy in colonel's clothing organising guerrilla attacks against the Japanese in the Philippines while waiting for the main forces to arrive. Designed as a tribute to the Filipino resistance, it's fast, vigorous and quite exciting, but marred by incessant flag-waving, the usual racist depiction of the enemy, and some atrocious sentimentality (featuring not only a heroic small boy, but Quinn's Filipino sweetheart, who becomes a sort of Tokyo Rose for the Japs while passing information on the side). GA

Back to School

(Alan Metter, 1986, US) Rodney Dangerfield, Sally Kellerman, Burt Young, Keith Gordon, Robert Downey Jr.
97 min.

The campus comedy comes of age. At last, instead of the usual brattish jocks and nerds, we have a protagonist old enough to have a son at college, which is where Dangerfield's self-made millionaire ends up after bribing the authorities with his promises of the moolah for a new Business Administration block. Sidestepping such trivial matters as work (a thesis on Kurt Vonnegut to write it himself), he distributes largesse, gives good parties, and seduces the Eng Lit teacher while his son struggles in his shadow. There are fairly crass showdowns between teachers and pupil, between father and son. But the film belongs to Dangerfield; a loveable, vulgar comedian who refuses to recognise the virtues of standing still, delivers his every bit of dialogue as though it were a punchline, but who can stumble through a bit of Dylan Thomas as though he really meant it. AB

Back to the Future

(Robert Zemeckis, 1985, US) Michael J Fox, Christopher Lloyd, Lea Thompson, Crispin Glover, Thomas F Wilson, Claudia Wells.
116 min.

Teenager Marty McFly's dad is a hideous wimp, his mother a dipso, so he befriends mad scientist Dr. Brown (Lloyd). In a DeLorean time machine they travel back to 1955, the year his parents met in high school. But at that age, mom rather fancies her offspring more than his prospective father. Zemeckis takes obvious pleasure in solving not just the technical but also the emotional problems of time travel: how to avoid incest, how to unite your parents in order that you will be born, how to return to the future when both the car and the professor have blown a fuse, and above all how to avoid tampering with history. If this all sounds schematic, it shouldn't: the movie has all the benign good nature of a Frank Capra. CPea

Back to the Future Part II

(Robert Zemeckis, 1989, US) Michael J Fox, Christopher Lloyd, Lea Thompson, Thomas F Wilson, Harry Waters Jr, Charles Fleischer, Joe Flaherty, Elizabeth Shue, James Tolkan.
108 min.

No sooner has Marty McFly (Fox) returned to 1985, than Doc Brown (Lloyd) turns up to whisk him and perfunctory romantic interest Jennifer (Shue) off to 2015, in order to prevent grown-up Marty's kids going to jail. Meanwhile, mean old man Biff Tannen (Wilson) picks up an almanac of sports results, borrows the DeLorean, and heads back to the '50s to make himself rich and turn Hill valley into hell on earth. With Bob Gale, Zemeckis has fashioned a script whose complex twists, ironies and paradoxes amply compensate for the somewhat juvenile nature of the action itself. Kids will love the wham-bang-wallop, but adults will probably be more concerned with trying to fathom exactly what is going on, how and why. It's impressive entertainment, and best of all, it never degenerates into Spielbergian sentimentality: you can laugh, be thrilled *and* think without feeling embarrassed. GA

Back to the Future Part III

(Robert Zemeckis, 1989, US) Michael J Fox, Christopher Lloyd, Mary Steenburgen, Thomas F Wilson, Lea Thompson, Elisabeth Shue, Matt Clark, Richard Dysart, Harry Carey Jr, Dub Taylor.
119 min.

In this exuberant final instalment of the time-travelling trilogy, with Doc (Lloyd) happily settled in 1885, Marty (Fox) realises he must go back when he learns that Doc faces death at the hands of villainous Mad Dog Tannen (Wilson) in Hill Valley, a bustling gold rush town. Marty's arrival, coinciding with an Indian charge, involves an explosive fusion of history and modern technology, with damage to the DeLorean. As Doc and Marty hastily try to assemble transport home, there comes an even more complicated development: Doc falls for a schoolmarm (Steenburgen). The resulting movie is affectionate, innovative, and vaguely lunatic. With Marty's experience of the past filtered through a lifetime of watching Westerns on TV, he struts around as though he'd

wandered onto the set of a Sergio Leone movie. Western conventions are gleefully challenged, and with the camera gliding and swooping over the action (though visual pyrotechnics never obscure the emotional core), Zemeckis and writer Bob Gale – insisting that this is the final outing – bring off an audacious marriage of genres to grand and enjoyable effect. CM

Bad and the Beautiful, The

(Vincente Minnelli, 1952, US) Kirk Douglas, Lana Turner, Barry Sullivan, Dick Powell, Gloria Grahame, Walter Pidgeon, Gilbert Roland.
118 min. b/w.

Hollywood on Hollywood: the ambitions, the dreams, the successes, the heartbreaks, all much as you'd expect. But Minnelli brings a tougher eye to his story of a young producer's meteoric rise and fall than most directors would have done, and the copious references to actual people/movies/events anchor the melodrama in a spirit not unlike that of *Sunset Boulevard*. It's constructed as a series of three long flashbacks: the careers of a writer, a star and a director, all 'made' by producer Kirk Douglas and all disowning him now that they've reached their pinnacles of success. Fascinating as a companion piece to *Two Weeks in Another Town*, which resumes the themes and some of the characters a decade later. TR

Bad Behaviour

(Les Blair, 1992, GB) Stephen Rea, Sinead Cusack, Philip Jackson, Claire Higgins, Phil Daniels, Saira Todd, Mary Jo Randle.
103 min.

Les Blair's improvised feature is the sort of film Mike Leigh might have made if he liked people. It shares the same pleasing regard for the textures of the everyday, but gone is the malign tendency towards futile caricature; instead, this Kentish Town slice-of-life chimes with affection for its characters as they shamble their way through middle-class mid-life crisis. Gerry (Rea) is a North London council planning officer wrestling with a local permanent site for travellers. His wife Ellie (Cusack) looks after the kids and does a part-time stint in a bookshop. He's from Belfast, she's from Dublin, and even at home their heads seem to be in different places, but a chance entanglement with a building-trade scammerchant (Leigh regular Philip Jackson), the contrasting fortunes of Claire Higgins' insecure single mum, and an office romance-that-never-was has the effect of making them realise how close and interdependent they really are. TJ

Bad Blood

(Chuck Vincent, 1989, US) Gregory Patrick, Ruth Raymond, Linda Blair, Troy Donahue, Carolyn Van Bellinghen, Christina Veronica.
104 min.

Study the following plot synopsis: strapping young thing Ted finds that his mummy isn't his real mother, that in fact he was stolen from his real mother by his real father, who then had his brains blown out by his real mother's real father. Got that? Good. Now when Ted goes to visit his real mom with his real wife, things start to get complicated, because mommy thinks her son is actually her deceased husband, thus making her her own son's wife. Problems arise from the fact that Ted already has a real wife (in the form of the magnificent Linda Blair), so mom has to stiff her daughter-in-law in order to become her own daughter-in-law, so that she can have sex with her dead husband. Now answer the following questions: 1) How much of a bad time did the movie's writer probably have during potty training? 2) How long will it be before the above plot is reproduced in either *Neighbours* or *Dallas*? 3) How can you explain sitting through this to your friends? MK

Bad Boy Bubby

(Rolf de Heer, 1993, Aust/It) Nicholas Hope, Claire Benito, Ralph Cotterill, Carmel Johnson, Sid Brisbane, Nikki Price.
114 min.

Rolf de Heer's film is pretty much a weirdo. It begins in the sordid flat which 35-year-old Bubby (Hope) shares with his corpulent, incestuously demanding mum; since she insists the outside world is poisoned by gas, the only creatures he knows are the cat he torments and the cockroaches he eats. Then his long-lost dad turns up: jeal-

ous that he's been usurped in his mother's affections, Bubby deals with the situation the only way he knows how and, with a mixture of fear and curiosity, leaves the slum. The following adventures are somewhat predictable; but at the same time the world into which the innocent hero is cast has a singular loneliness and desolation. The film's attitude to misfits is admirable, but it's hard not to feel slightly uneasy about the use of real handicapped people in the later scenes. That said, this proficient film is never less than intriguing. It may be muddled, but one can't deny its ambitions, or the integrity of Hope's performance. GA

Bad Boys

(Rick Rosenthal, 1983, US) Sean Penn, Reni Santoni, Jim Moody, Eric Gurry, Esai Morales.
123 min.

O'Brien and Brennan are tough teenage hoodlums who try to heist a load of drugs from rival Moreno and his gang. Brennan gets blasted; O'Brien mows down Moreno's kid brother and winds up in the Correctional shithouse. Will he realise the futility of his macho existence? Will he succumb to the challenge of a psyched-up Moreno, dumped in the very same bin for his brutal revenge-rape of O'Brien's girl? The characters are all stock, and the essential crudity is emphasised by hack editing, bad bruise make-up, and fortissimo violence (a welter of sickening splats and ketchup-sodden thunks). But what it lacks in delicacy, it makes up with tightly-strung tension, while Penn is sullen, unattractive and irresistible as O'Brien, all fucked up and teetering on the thin edge of his nerves. AB

Bad Boys

(Michael Bay, 1995, US) Martin Lawrence, Will Smith, Téa Leoni, Tchéky Karyo, Theresa Randle.
118 min.

Marcus is married and steady, Mike a lone wolf. Then, for reasons too unreasonable to explain, Marcus has to pass himself off as fellow drugbuster Mike in order to babysit a sassy murder witness (Leoni) in the latter's bachelor pad, while Mike makes himself at home with his buddy's partner. As long as it's taking pot shots at macho attitudes, there's plenty of comic play in this set-up, happily exploited by the snappy, charismatic pairing of Smith and Lawrence. Unfortunately, the movie is a couple of rewrites short of 'developed', and the thriller configurations are stale. TCh

Bad Company

(Robert Benton, 1972, US) Jeff Bridges, Barry Brown, Jim Davis, David Huddleston, John Savage, Ed Lauter.
93 min.

Benton's first film, a Western good enough to make everything he has done since seem disappointing by comparison. Set in 1863, with Union troops scouring the countryside for reluctant recruits who scurry about dressed as girls, it offers Vietnam parallels for the asking, but is really more concerned with the old mythologies as the innocent young hero sets off in best Horatio Alger fashion to seek safety, fame and fortune out West. Wandering through a land of russet melancholy (superb camerawork by Gordon Willis), he and the ragtail gang of youths he falls in with find themselves light years away from the myth of the heroic West. A few inhabitants scratch a miserable existence on chicken farms. The gunfighters are sordid, petty crooks who hit and run. Everybody else seems to be coming or going, cursing the ill luck which brought them to this wilderness. And virtue, as the young man discovers to his cost, is the first thing to go west. Elegantly and engagingly funny, it is filmed with a loving care for period detail which gives the images the feel of animated tintypes. TM

Bad Day at Black Rock

(John Sturges, 1954, US) Spencer Tracy, Robert Ryan, Anne Francis, Dean Jagger, Walter Brennan, Ernest Borgnine, Lee Marvin.
81 min.

Occasionally flabby but generally impressive thriller in which one-armed war-veteran Tracy gets off a train to encounter a desert town full of aggressive types clearly hiding a secret (involving land-grabbing and murder: Hollywood's first acknowledgment of America's less than honourable treatment of its Japanese citizens during World War II). Nicely put together by Sturges, its suspense derives largely from the excellent performances and imaginative use of the 'Scope frame by cameraman William C Mellor. GA

Badge 373

(Howard W Koch, 1973, US) Robert Duvall, Verna Bloom, Henry Darrow, Eddie Egan, Felipe Luciano, Tina Cristiana.
116 min.
An attempt to out-Dirty Harry that has none of the flair of Siegel's film. Ryan (Duvall), a mean Irish cop who spends his life battling against spics and spades, finds himself suspended for having pushed a guy off a roof when in fact he fell. He hands in his badge but fights on alone, finding a cesspool (the film's definition) of gun-running to Puerto Rico and demos plastered with 'Free Puerto Rico' banners. Koch both produced and directed this ham-fistedly unpleasant film.

Bad Girls

(Jonathan Kaplan, 1994, US) Madeleine Stowe, Mary Stuart Masterson, Andie MacDowell, Drew Barrymore, James LeGros, Robert Loggia, Dermot Mulroney.
93 min.
This cowgirl opus may aspire to frontier feminism, but its stale stereotypes, hackneyed plotting and fashion-conscious sensibility is more in the tradition of Howard Hughes' campfire kitsch. Discriminated against by the law, four prostitutes flee for their lives. Cody (Stowe) is the leader, a tough, sharp-shooting 'honky-tonk harlot'; Eileen (MacDowell) a Southern gentlewoman by predilection, an outlaw by destiny; Anita (Masterson) an impoverished widow; and Lilly (Barrymore, the best of them) a hard-riding, hard-drinking tomboy. There's no depth here, and precious little surface. Things move at a fair gallop, but the last 45 minutes simply rehash kidnap scenarios with one character after another. TCh

Bad Influence

(Curtis Hanson, 1990, US) Rob Lowe, James Spader, Lisa Zane, Tony Maggio, Marcia Cross, Kathleen Wilhoite.
100 min.
Michael Boll (Spader) is up against a rival at work, his fiancée is boring, and he suffers mysterious stomach ailments. So when he meets smoothie Alex (Lowe), a man-about-town of independent means, he's nipping out of his hi-tech flat and into hi-tech discos before you can say 'Faust'. Work improves, sex gets kinkier. Exhausted but satisfied, Michael accepts the fact that his new friend filmed him bonking, but knows things are going too far when he falls over a dead body in his apartment...This vacuous exploration of the perils of greed lacks the intelligence and perspective to work on a subversive level. Hanson indulges in extremely obvious symbolism, and despite attempts to convey Michael's inner conflict, the dangers remain resolutely external. 'I didn't make you do anything that wasn't in you already' says Alex to his protégé. Yawn. CM

Badlanders, The

(Delmer Daves, 1958, US) Alan Ladd, Ernest Borgnine, Katy Jurado, Anthony Caruso, Claire Kelly, Nehemiah Persoff.
83 min.
Turn-of-the-century Nevada and ex-cons Ladd and Borgnine plan a major heist on a goldmine, but aren't sure whether they can trust each other enough to stick with the complex plan they've devised to reclaim the property that's rightfully theirs. A virtual remake of The Asphalt Jungle, it has CinemaScope and an amiable rough-house humour, but you'd certainly never prefer it to the Huston film. TJ

Badlands 100

(Terrence Malick, 1974, US) Martin Sheen, Sissy Spacek, Warren Oates, Ramon Bieri, Alan Vint, Gary Littlejohn.
94 min.
One of the most impressive directorial debuts ever. On the surface, it's merely another rural-gangster movie in the tradition of Bonnie and Clyde, with its young 'innocents' – a James Dean-lookalike garbage collector and his magazine-addict girlfriend – first killing her father when he objects to their relationship, then going on a seemingly gratuitous homicidal spree across the Dakota Badlands. But what distinguishes the

film, beyond the superb performances of Sheen and Spacek, the use of music, and the luminous camerawork by Tak Fujimoto, is Malick's unusual attitude towards psychological motivation: the dialogue tells us one thing, the images another, and Spacek's beautifully artless narration, couched in terms borrowed from the mindless media mags she's forever reading, yet another. This complex perspective on an otherwise simple plot, developed even further in Malick's subsequent Days of Heaven, manages to reveal so much while making nothing explicit, and at the same time seems perfectly to evoke the world of '50s suburbia in which it is set. GA

Bad Lieutenant

(Abel Ferrara, 1992, US) Harvey Keitel, Victor Argo, Paul Calderone, Leonard Thomas, Robin Burrows, Frankie Thorn, Victoria Bastel, Paul Hipp.
96 min.
Keitel is the depraved and corrupt New York cop of the title. Hooked on crack, heroin and alcohol, he's up to his eyeballs in debt and staking his life on the Dodgers – and they're starting to lose. Perversely, the appalling rape of a nun proffers salvation: a $50,000 reward to find the perpetrator. The film isn't so much a thriller as a slice of (low-)life. The script is cut to the bone, the set-ups have a vérité feel, while the editing mimics real time in long, nearly unwatchable sequences in which Keitel shoots up, or masturbates before two teenage girls. Ferrara allows his star to dictate the pace, and is rewarded with a performance of extraordinary, terrifying honesty. This is an actor laying himself bare before the camera/confessor. Astonishingly, Ferrara ups the ante. Out of degradation, he pulls redemption. It is a jarring stroke, and will divide audiences who have stayed with the film this far. It seems to me that Ferrara is an artist of the profane; his Catholicism looks suspiciously like a Scorsese hand-me-down. In this exploitation/art movie, it may just be that the truth is in the sleaze. TCh

Bad Lord Byron, The

(David Macdonald, 1948, GB) Dennis Price, Mai Zetterling, Joan Greenwood, Linden Travers, Sonia Holm, Raymond Lovell.
85 min. b/w.
Not as bad as its reputation would suggest, since it is well acted and stylishly shot, but the script is undeniably silly. Starting with Byron (Price) dying in Greece, it cuts to a celestial trial at which the women in his life appear to give evidence, their stories being seen in flashback. The fatuous point is to determine whether Byron is a great poet and fighter for liberty or a bad, evil rake. Very basic stuff, historically inaccurate and not made any more convincing by the eventual revelation that the judge is Byron himself (though his lines have hitherto been delivered by someone else). TM

Bad Man's River
(El Hombre del Rio Malo)

(Eugenio Martin, 1971, Sp/It/Fr) Lee Van Cleef, James Mason, Gina Lollobrigida, Simon Andreu, Diana Lorys.
100 min.
It took Van Cleef so long to become a star that latterly it seemed he'd accept any project which would have his name at the top. This jokey, old-fashioned Western – where his outlaw is variously bamboozled by a widow on the make (Lollobrigida) and by a revolutionary (Mason) into agreeing to blow up the Mexican army arsenal – is so out of touch that you expect Stubby Kaye to appear and sing a song. it attempts to appear modish by freezing frames with annoying irrelevance. For undemanding six-year-olds.

Bad News Bears, The

(Michael Ritchie, 1976, US) Walter Matthau, Tatum O'Neal, Vic Morrow, Jackie Earle Haley, Alfred Lutter, Joyce Van Patten.
103 min.
Amiably engrossing satire on the 'win ethic' that offers a take-it-or-leave-it approach to its serious points about enforcing precociousness on kids, but consistently delights with its panoramic comic invention. Drunken slob Matthau (perfect) coaches an abysmally inept Little League baseball team that sniffs unaccustomed success when joined by street-smart girl pitcher O'Neal, and a windmill tilt at the championship ensues. Two sequels never came close to repeating its pleasures. PT

Bad News Bears in Breaking Training, The

(Michael Pressman, 1977, US) William Devane, Clifton James, Jackie Earle Haley, Jimmy Baio, Chris Barnes, Alfred Lutter.
100 min.
Bad news indeed. A quite ghastly sequel to The Bad News Bears in which the subject's incipient sentimentality has been left to run riot, with all charm, humour and believability lost in the process. GB

Bad News Bears Go to Japan, The

(John Berry, 1978, US) Tony Curtis, Jackie Earle Hayley, Tomisaburo Wayakama, George Wyner, Lonny Chapman.
91 min.
Third and last in the Bad News series, with Curtis as a Hollywood hustler trying to make a buck exploiting the sad sack little league baseballers, but suffering the obligatory change of heart. Dire. TM

Bad Seed, The

(Mervyn LeRoy, 1956, US) Patty McCormack, Nancy Kelly, Henry Jones, Eileen Heckart, Evelyn Varden, William Hopper.
129 min. b/w.
8-year old Rhoda is a real cutie, never scuffs her shoes, sends all the adults into paroxysms of icky adoration. If only they knew...for Rhoda is the descendant of a coldblooded multiple murderess. Phooey to factors such as environment and upbringing, blood will out! Rhoda's already got a fix on little Claude, who won the coveted Gold Medal for Penmanship, and she's not overfond of Leroy the retarded handyman. A smash hit on the stage, The Bad Seed seems to have been lifted intact from proscenium to projection; the players emote with grand gestures which would be visible from the back seats in the stalls; and the psychology is a hoot. AB

Bad Sleep Well, The (Warui Yatsu Hodo Yoko Nemuru)

(Akira Kurosawa, 1960, Jap) Toshiro Mifune, Takeshi Kato, Masayuki Mori, Takashi Shimura, Kyoko Kagawa.
151 min. b/w.
Kurosawa's first venture for his own short-lived production company, a revenge tragedy (employee of big housing corporation marries the boss' daughter while simultaneously seeking the truth of his father's 'suicide') which attempts to indict the corruptions that go hand-in-hand with big business, ultimately hinting that even the government cannot be said to have clean hands. Freed from immediate box-office pressures, Kurosawa rather loaded the film on the side of social significance, while neglecting to capitalise on the noir aspects that underlie it. Even so, his use of the 'scope screen is masterly, suggesting right from the opening sequence – a wedding at which the cake is a replica of the company offices, and the crippled bride has obviously had a groom bought from among daddy's employees – a boardroom table across which manipulations gradually unfold. Exported in a 135-minute version. TM

Bad Taste

(Peter Jackson, 1987, NZ) Terry Potter, Pete O'Herne, Craig Smith, Mike Minett, Peter Jackson, Doug Wren.
92 min.
When a small New Zealand town is overrun by man-eating space aliens, it's left to gawky Derek (Jackson) and the Alien Investigation Defence Service (spot the horrible pun) to deal with them. Within the opening five minutes, one such extraterrestrial has half his head blown off. Derek himself suffers the indignity of having a cat-flap incorporated into the back of his skull, whence fall large amounts of brain matter, some of it to be replaced with assorted bowel matter. Made over four years on an incredibly low budget, the film has its moments, though ironically most of the best jokes have nothing to do with the gore: some terrifically banal conversations pass between the members of the AIDS team, and there are a few fine sequences of Three Stooges-type slapstick. Things hot up in the last 20 minutes, when Peter Jackson stops chucking intestines around and gets some serious hardware under way – we're talking rocket launchers

and big chainsaws, equipment essential to the success of any movie. Indeed, a climatic rebirth-by-chainsaw scene almost makes it all worthwhile, though you may have had to visit the bathroom once or twice in the wait. MK

Bad Timing
(Nicolas Roeg, 1980, GB) Art Garfunkel, Theresa Russell, Harvey Keitel, Denholm Elliott, Daniel Massey, Dana Gillespie.
123 min.
One of Roeg's most complex and elusive movies, building a thousand-piece jigsaw from its apparently simple story of a consuming passion between two Americans in Vienna. Seen in flashback through the prism of the girl's attempted suicide, their affair expands into a labyrinthine enquiry on memory and guilt as Theresa Russell's cold psychoanalyst lover (Garfunkel) himself falls victim to the cooler and crueller investigations of the detective assigned to her case (Keitel in visionary form as the policeman turned father-confessor). But where *Don't Look Now* sustained its Gothic intensity with human intimacy, this film seems a case-example of how more could have been achieved with less editing, less ingenuity, less even of the bravura intelligence with which Roeg at one point matches Freud with Stalin as guilt-ridden spymasters. CA/DMacp

Bagdad Café
(aka Out of Rosenheim)
(Percy Adlon, 1987, WGer) Marianne Sägebrecht, CCH Pounder, Jack Palance, Christine Kauffman, Monica Calhoun, Darron Flagg, George Aquilar.
91 min.
A radiant, oddball comedy-drama about the relationship that develops between a fat Bavarian tourist (Sägebrecht), an irritable black truckstop owner (Pounder), and a weirdo artist (Palance, smiling and delightful, in bandana and snakeskin boots), set in the dusty Arizona desert land of lonesome motels beloved of Sam Shepard. Sägebrecht, her husband ditched along the way, arrives sweatily out of the yellow haze, absurdly decked out in buttoned-up suit, green felt hat and feather, high heels and suitcase; gradually she transforms, and is transformed by, the lives of a motley band of misfits who inhabit a dilapidated diner exotically named 'The Bagdad Café'. A wish-fulfilling fable about culture-clash and the melting-pot, it's also firmly grounded in telling and cinematically original observations. Adlon's method is at once intimate, quirky and affirmative: precise evocation of place, expressive colours, and a slow build-up of characters, allow him to raise the film effortlessly into realms of fantasy, shafted with magic and moments of epiphany. WH

Baie des Anges, La
(Bay of Angels)
(Jacques Demy, 1962, Fr) Jeanne Moreau, Claude Mann, Paul Guers, Henri Nassiet.
85 min. b/w.
Demy's second feature has a ravishing Jeanne Moreau, ash-blonde for the occasion and dressed all in white, as a compulsive gambler who doesn't care what happens to her so long as she has a chip to start her on the roulette tables. Ostensibly the subject is gambling, but the real theme is seduction – with Moreau casting a spell on Mann that turns him every which way – and this is above all a visually seductive film. Shot mainly inside the casinos and on the sunstruck promenades of Nice and Monte Carlo, it is conceived as a dazzling symphony in black and white. Moreau's performance is magnificent, but it's really Jean Rabier's camera which turns the whole film into an expression of sheer joy – not only in life and love, but things. Iron bedsteads make arabesques against white walls; a little jeweller's shop becomes a paradise of strange ornamental clocks; a series of angled mirrors echo the heroine as she runs down a corridor into her lover's arms; roulette wheels spin to a triumphant musical accompaniment; and over it all hangs an aura of brilliant sunshine. TM

Baisers Volés
(Stolen Kisses)
(François Truffaut, 1968, Fr) Jean-Pierre Léaud, Delphine Seyrig, Claude Jade, Michel Lonsdale, Harry Max, André Falcon, Claire Duhamel.
91 min.

A persuasively charming comedy (the third instalment of the Antoine Doinel saga), in which Léaud wanders into a job as a private detective and falls hopelessly and idealistically in love with a client's wife. The film is comprised of several flawlessly observed episodes, and Paris has never looked so nice or its inhabitants so whimsically attractive. Dedicated to Henri Langlois, the head of the Paris Cinémathèque who was nearly sacked by De Gaulle, it was made at the time of the political upheavals of 1968 in which Truffaut was directly involved. But the film itself betrays an amazing serenity in such troubled times, transforming the anxiety and pain into a sad lyricism. DP

Bait, The
see Appât, L'

Baker's Bread
(Das Brot des Bäckers)
(Erwin Keusch, 1976, WGer) Günter Lamprecht, Bernd Tauber, Maria Lucca, Silvia Reize, Anita Lochner.
122 min.
A minor key, low-budget delight with an appropriate 'small is beautiful' theme: an elaborately naturalistic account of a young baker's progress through apprenticeship and adolescence. Laced with an almost documentary insistence on the precise art of 'real' bread-making, and with a Brechtian presentation of competitive capitalism, it makes surprisingly compelling cinema from such an unlikely subject. PT

Baker's Wife, The
see Femme du Boulanger, La

Bal, Le
(Ettore Scola, 1982, Fr/It/Alg) Le Troupe du Théâtre du Campagnol.
112 min.
Scola's wordless musical-dance extravaganza traces the life of a ballroom from 1936 to the present. While couples meet, steal kisses, and separate, events in the world outside are echoed in their mimetic rituals and groupings; for the film is clearly intended as a historical and political allegory. Instead of offering any insights into France's shifting character, it relies largely on the audience's smug recognition of supposedly 'significant' cultural symbols. Fatuous stuff, really, especially when several references are anachronistic. A strong cast struggles valiantly against Felliniesque stereotypes to convey the gaucheries of human coupling. But in a movie aiming for something more ambitious, that's simply not enough. GA

Balalaika
(Reinhold Schunzel, 1939, US) Nelson Eddy, Ilona Massey, Charles Ruggles, Frank Morgan, Lionel Atwill, C Aubrey Smith.
102 min. b/w.
Draggy MGM operetta, raising some involuntary horse laughs with its notion of the Russian revolution as Bolshevik wench falls for stout Cossack. Just as you're dozing off to sleep, the bovine Eddy launches into 'The Volga Boatman's Song'. TM

Balance, La
(Bob Swaim, 1982, Fr) Nathalie Baye, Philippe Léotard, Richard Berry, Christophe Malavoy, Jean-Paul Connart, Maurice Ronet.
102 min.
The mean, cobbled streets of the Belleville quartier in Paris yield up another story of love, money and death, and all the requisite shootouts, car chases and lowlife infighting are delivered with great verve and pace: but what really distinguishes this excellent thriller is Swaim's strength on the emotional front. The flics set up a pimp (Léotard) to be a new informer ('balance') by leaning on the whore he very much loves (Baye); the loyalties become more and more crossed until betrayal is the only means to salvation. Léotard is superb as the crook with a heart of glass; Baye at last breaks out of her nun's habits and gives us a tart with the strength of ten; Berry is the sympatico cop. They order these things better in France. CPea

Balkanisateur (Balkanisater)
(Sotiris Goritsas, 1997, Greece/Bulg/Switz) Stelios Mainas, Giota Festa.
98 min.

Average road movie/adventure, with two strapped-for-cash Salonikans driving through Yugoslavia, Bulgaria and Switzerland on a currency scam, enriched by telling observation and uningratiating but engaging performances. Fotis is the footloose and fancy free womaniser, Stavros the married, more educated, sensible one. Notable scenes include a pick-up at a kitschy Sofia dance hall as, afterwards at the woman's flat, Stavros refuses to make love, perturbed by the grandmother's knitting and the peering kids outside; and a meal in Belgrade, where the two men are moved by the humanising hospitality of a group of disparan Greeks. The film may have a conventional heart, but it tries hard to avoid easy targets. WH

Ballad in Blue
(aka Blues for Lovers)
(Paul Henreid, 1964, GB) Ray Charles, Mary Peach, Tom Bell, Dawn Addams.
88 min. b/w.
'You're always trying to get me discovered – as if I were some new Italian restaurant': Tom Bell's composer/nightclub pianist gets the one good line in this combination of concert movie and sentimental B picture. Charles doesn't play himself off-stage too convincingly, and a cloying story of how he helps a little blind boy into the arms of a Paris specialist ('Is there a chance, doctor?' etc) doesn't help. Admirers of the man's music – about thirty percent of the movie is concert footage – will find the in-between tedium tolerable, although director Henreid could hardly get a gig with *Top of the Pops* on the evidence here. GD

Ballad of a Soldier
(Ballada o Soldate)
(Grigori Chukhrai, 1959, USSR) Vladimir Ivashov, Shanna Prokhorenko, Antonina Maximova, Nikolai Kruchkov, Ievgeni Urbanski.
89 min. b/w.
This picaresque tale was a great classic of postwar Soviet Realism – but don't let that put you off. Ivashov makes a touching figure as the teenage WWII combatant who wins four days' leave as a reward for an act of courage against the Nazis, heads off home to repair his old mother's leaking roof, yet finds himself constantly waylaid on his journey by people who need his help. Chukhrai's film may come from the stylistically more conservative wing of the Russian cinema, but its careful detail and underlying emotional clout are never in doubt. TJ

Ballad of Cable Hogue, The
(Sam Peckinpah, 1970, US) Jason Robards, Stella Stevens, David Warner, Strother Martin, Slim Pickens, LQ Jones, RG Armstrong.
121 min.
A strange and fascinating Western from the man renowned for the blood baths of *The Wild Bunch* and *Straw Dogs*. In gentler vein than usual, he portrays the efforts of a prospector, robbed and left to die in the desert, to turn a waterhole into a personal oasis, and to take revenge on the men who betrayed him. Hogue is possibly Peckinpah's most likeable hero, and the film benefits from Robards' wry performance, as well as from the unusual mixture of comedy, action, romance, nostalgic elegy, and even song. The tone is uneven, but it's a touching and original portrait of a man trying to go it alone in the world, with tragically ironic results. GA

Ballad of Gregorio Cortez,
The (aka Gregorio Cortez)
(Robert M Young, 1982, US) Edward James Olmos, James Gammon, Tom Bower, Bruce McGill, Brion James, Alan Vint.
105 min.
Set at the turn of the century, this is based on a Mexican ballad about one of the most famous manhunts in Texas history. A young Mexican farmhand kills a sheriff in self-defence, and lights out for the border with the Texas Rangers in hot pursuit. From such tawdry incidents do heroic legends grow as news of the slaying speeds down the telegraph. The longer he evades capture, the more inflated becomes the myth, and the more ironic the backlash that finally descends on the hapless, determinedly non-heroic Cortez. Beautifully shot and directed with great understatement, the result is a film of considerable poignancy and compassion. JP

Ballad of Joe Hill, The
see Joe Hill

Ballad of Josie, The
(Andrew V McLaglen, 1967, US) Doris Day, Peter Graves, George Kennedy, Andy Devine, William Talman.
102 min.
Doris Day leads the fight for women's rights on the prairie, doing a kind of Lysistrata act to end a range war in turn-of-the-century Wyoming. A comedy Western with ideas, but lumberingly scripted and even more laboriously directed. TM

Ballad of Little Jo, The
(Maggie Greenwald, 1993, US) Suzy Amis, Bo Hopkins, Ian McKellen, David Chung, Carrie Snodgress, Rene Auberjonois.
121 min.
Maggie Greenwald's third film is inspired by the true story of a woman who in 1866 passed herself off as a man to survive the masculine brutishness of the American frontier. Expelled from her well-to-do New York home, for a pre-marital affair, Josephine Monaghan (Amis) heads West, and, taking refuge in trousers, cutting her hair and scarring her face, becomes 'Little Jo'. This is relatively unexplored terrain, and the film gets much mileage and fun out of the sex-role reversal, especially upon the arrival of Jo's lover and servant, the long-haired Tinman Wong (Chung), who sews and bakes apple pie. The mud and desperation of the frontier is vividly rendered, but the film is marred by a lack of emotional drama. JBa

Ballad of Narayama, The (Narayama Bushi-ko)
(Shohei Imamura, 1983, Jap) Ken Ogata, Sumiko Sakamoto, Tonpei Hidari, Takejo Aki, Shoichi Ozawa.
130 min.
A remote village in the foothills of a great mountain, sometime in the past. A widow is approaching her 70th birthday – the age at which village law says she must go up to the mountain to die. She faces this prospect with surprising equanimity, but there are some things she wants to take care of first: to find a good new wife for her widowed eldest son, to help her runtish second son get laid for the first and only time in his life, to take her brattish eldest grandson down several pegs. The process whereby she sets about these tasks, while preparing herself serenely for her own death, amounts to a story of her personal fulfilment the like of which the cinema has rarely seen. Her society is one that is in most ways the antithesis of our own. Imamura realises this vision with shocking humour and immediacy, and then challenges us to say whether this fictitious community is more or less humane than ours. Awe-inspiring. TR

Ballad of the Sad Café, The
(Simon Callow, 1990, US) Vanessa Redgrave, Keith Carradine, Cork Hubbert, Rod Steiger, Austin Pendleton.
101 min.
Callow makes his debut as a director with enormously difficult material: a strange and fantastical novella, written by the young Carson McCullers, about a barren, hayseed Georgia community. The tone is always a grainy Southern realism teetering on the edge of lunacy; and, given that the central characters are a giantess, a dwarf, and a redneck recidivist who makes the town's meat go bad, one can see the problem. Like Sartre's Huis Clos, this is a story of triple-unrequited passion in which fairytale and myth come to the fore, partly because (even as played by the superb Redgrave and Carradine) the main combatants are hardly made of the usual sympathetic stuff that passionate sagas need. Instead, Callow has cleverly created a company style that can encompass everyone from stand-up comedian Hubbert as the perky dwarf, Steiger as the local preacher, and Carradine, the ultimate rangy screen professional, as badman Marvin Macy. But despite traces of the English accent, it's Ms Redgrave who steals the show; the finale in which she and Carradine engage in a bloody fist-fight makes Liam Neeson's bit of bother in The Big Man look like handbags at dawn. SGr

Ballet Black
(Stephen Dwoskin, 1986, GB)
83 min.
Though now nothing but historic footnote, Ballets Nègres was Europe's first all-black dance ensemble, which had its debut in London in April 1946, and its final performances in 1952. During those six years, Ballets Nègres opened doors and broke down barriers with its vibrant celebrations of Caribbean cultures. This film attempts to assemble all the scanty available documentation on the company. Lengthy sequences are jigged together from still photographs, or feature contemporary dancers trying to reconstruct one of the company's major creations. As director/ writer/photographer/editor, Dwoskin should have made more choices. Had he selectively edited down his footage, the result would have been twice as compelling. As it stands, Ballet Black moves at a creeping, magisterial pace. Reverent, much too reverent. AR

Ball of Fire
(Howard Hawks, 1942, US) Gary Cooper, Barbara Stanwyck, Oscar Homolka, Richard Haydn, SZ Sakall, Dana Andrews, Dan Duryea.
111 min. b/w.
Marvellous performance from Stanwyck, all snap, crackle and pop as the brassy nightclub entertainer Sugarpuss O'Shea who seeks refuge with seven crusty old professors (plus Cooper) to escape unwelcome attentions from a gangster, and whose vocabulary (not to mention charms) excite delighted wonderment in the professors since they have just reached 'Slang' in the encyclopaedia they are compiling. Rather surprisingly, Hawks slightly muffs the sequence in which the gangster and his aides get their comeuppance; otherwise his handling of the sparkling Brackett-Wilder script and its subversions of Snow White and the Seven Dwarfs is pure joy. TM

Ballon d'Or, Le (The Golden Ball)
(Cheik Doukouré, 1993, Guinea/Fr) Aboucar Sidiki Sumah, Agnès Soral, Habib Hammoud, Salif Keita.
100 min.
This deceptively light comedy-drama follows the unsentimental education of village boy Bandian (fresh-faced Sumah), a diminutive teenager mad-keen on football and hopeful of great things in the euphoric atmosphere of Cameroon's unprecedented challenge in the 1990 World Cup. Doukouré traces the condition of the boy's life in scenes that lose no power through their low-key integration into the narrative. Bandian's mother languishes ill for lack of care, and he is forced to rely on the Médecins sans Frontières centre run by doctor Isabelle (Soral); nor are the boy's skills helped by having to play with what look like coconut shells. As Bandian moves to the big city and comes under the sway of both businessman Béchir, and football manager Karim (Malian soccer star Keita), who wants to nurture Bandian's talents for the good of African football, the metaphorical resonances threaten to drown out the drama, but the gusto and vitality of the playing, the vibrancy of the photography and the sympathy of the direction pull it through. WH

Balthazar
see Au Hasard, Balthazar

Baltimore Bullet, The
(Robert Ellis Miller, 1980, US) James Coburn, Omar Sharif, Ronee Blakley, Bruce Boxleitner, Jack O'Halloran, Calvin Lockhart.
103 min.
Pool-hustling saga which borrows its basic situation from The Hustler, much of its detail (including a New Orleans jazz funeral) from The Cincinnati Kid, and never comes within striking distance of either film. It's passable enough thanks to Coburn and Sharif (both grinning as toothily as Burt Lancaster), but meanders aimlessly through some lamentable direction and a silly gangster subplot. TM

Balto
(Simon Wells, 1995, US/GB) Miriam Margolyes, Lola Bates-Campbell; voices: Kevin Bacon, Bob Hoskins, Bridget Fonda, Phil Collins, Jim Cummings.
77 min.
The true story of a 1925 sled team's 'serum run' across Alaska, and its husky hero Balto. Whereas Disney would have pillaged the facts for its own exacting purposes, the makers of this half-hearted animated feature let the story ramble on with a minimum of second-hand plotting and characterisation. Balto being the archetypal dog-from-the-wrong-side-of-the-tracks, when diphtheria strikes Nome, his services aren't required for the team that must fetch the life-saving anti-toxin. Injustice is compounded by the team being led by the purebreed Steele, vain, scheming, town favourite and Balto's rival for the beautiful Jenna. The one notable spin on the story is that Balto's half-wolf. As you'd expect, we start with the old boy having internalised prejudices about his lack of pedigree; only when he's stuck down a canyon does he realise the advantages of his make-up. Mismatched TV-standard animation styles (plus some one-dimensional live action inserts); a Hoskins-voiced Russian émigré goose (fun); and a pair of comic-relief polar bears (Collins-voiced, and not fun). Probably insufficient for any but the least demanding kids. NB

Bamba, La
(Luis Valdez, 1986, US) Lou Diamond Phillips, Esai Morales, Rosana De Soto, Danielle von Zerneck, Elizabeth Peña.
108 min.
An enjoyable if slightly innocuous biopic based on the brief life and short-lived fame of teen rock-'n'roll idol Richie Valens ('La Bamba'). You know the kind of thing: poor but talented kid, spotted playing in local band by LA record producer, enjoys all too brief a spell of fame before dying tragically young. Plus the usual background stuff: hard-pressed but cheerful mother struggling to make ends meet, no-good brother always in trouble, girlfriend's father objecting to her dating a kid who sings 'jungle music'. The musical side of things is handled surprisingly well. Phillips mimes convincingly to Los Lobos' admirably faithful cover versions of the songs, and there's a show-stealing rendition of Jackie Wilson's 'Lonely Teardrops' by Howard Huntsberry. NF

Bambi
(David Hand, 1942, US)
72 min.
From Disney's richest period, interleaving splendid animation with vulgar Americana. Babycham images occupy only a fraction of the running time in this tale of the adventures of a fawn; the rest is a strikingly impressionistic version of life in the forest and the meadow. Silhouette, panorama, and the cod use of classical music recall the best moments of Fantasia, while the animals are all given irresistible human traits: Bambi, Flower the skunk, and Thumper the rabbit ('Watchya doin' hibernatin'?) are like members of one of Mickey Rooney's gangs. AN

Bamboo Gods and Iron Men
(Cesar Gallardo, 1973, Phil/US) James Iglehart, Shirley Washington, Chiquito, Marissa Delgado.
96 min.
Uninspiring if innocuous offshoot of the kung-fu genre, made in the Philippines. The story revolves around some hokum about a false-bottomed Buddha in which is concealed the secret of the centuries – how to dominate the world. Supposedly novel twists are wrung on the situation by making the tourist couple who are drawn into the bizarre situation rich, young and black (genial performances, incidentally, from Iglehart and Washington). The humour is misjudged, and if the Philippine locations bring a little freshness to the film, it remains one of those efforts which an audience watches in disbelief. VG

Banana Ridge
(Walter C Mycroft, 1941, GB) Robertson Hare, Alfred Drayton, Isabel Jeans, Nova Pilbeam, Dulcie Gray.
87 min. b/w.
Veteran farceur Ben Travers had a hand in adapting his own play, set on a Malaysian rubber plantation, in which returning adventuress Isabel Jeans claims that either haughty Hare or self-regarding Drayton is actually the father of her twenty-something son. Ructions ensue, but decidedly creaky ructions. TJ

Bananas
(Woody Allen, 1971, US) Woody Allen, Louise Lasser, Carlos Montalban, Jacobo Morales, Rene Enriquez.
81 min.

Allen's second feature, a tribute to the Marx Brothers' *Duck Soup*, is a wonderfully incoherent series of one-liners centred around a puny New York Jew's unwitting and unwilling involvement in a South American revolution. The revolutionary party's new policies are an absurd comment on the corruption of power, especially when everyone is informed that the official, non-decadent language of the country will be Swedish. GA

Bande à part (The Outsiders/Band of Outsiders)
(Jean-Luc Godard, 1964, Fr) Anna Karina, Claude Brasseur, Sami Frey, Louisa Colpeyn, Chantal Darget, Ernest Menzer.
95 min. b/w.
Godard at his most off-the-cuff takes a '*Série Noire*' thriller (*Fool's Gold* by Dolores Hitchens) and spins a fast and loose tale that continues his love affairs with Hollywood and with actress Anna Karina. Karina at her most naive is taken up by two self-conscious toughs ('The little suburban cousins of Belmondo in *A Bout de Souffle*', is how Godard described them), and they try to learn English, do extravagant mimes of the death of Billy the Kid, execute some neat dance steps, run around the Louvre at high speed, and rob Karina's aunt with disastrous consequences. One of Godard's most open and enjoyable films. CPe

Bandido!
(Richard Fleischer, 1956, US) Robert Mitchum, Gilbert Roland, Zachary Scott, Ursula Thiess, Rodolfo Acosta, Henry Brandon.
92 min.
Routine plot about the Yankee soldier of fortune playing both sides as he does a spot of gun-running in revolutionary Mexico, but ending up with his heart in the right place. But the direction and performances (Mitchum and Roland especially) are excellent. TM

Bandit, The (Eskiya)
(Yavuz Turgul, 1996, Tur) Sener Sen, Sermin Sen, Ugur Yücel.
128 min.
This leisurely action film spreads its tale of honour, corruption, solidarity and betrayal over a broad canvas. Sener Sen's ancient bandit, sole survivor of his gang after 35 years in jail, returns to a land that no longer remembers his legendary exploits. Back in the hill country, he finds his hunting grounds under a reservoir and his community vanished. He returns to Istanbul to seek out past accomplices – specifically best pal Mahmud, who, he learns, betrayed him all those years ago to win Keje (Sermin Sen), love of both their lives. The director mirrors the bandit's temporal and emotional displacement in his ironic uprooting of old genre codes, playfully transposing elements of mythic and American cinema into Turkey's contemporary urban reality. He films modern Istanbul like the location for a Western, and takes time out for wry and discursive asides. Warm, accessible and socially engaged. NB

Bandit of Sherwood Forest, The
(George Sherman/Henry Levin, 1946, US) Cornel Wilde, Anita Louise, Jill Esmond, Edgar Buchanan, Henry Daniell, George Macready.
86 min.
Very creditable swashbucklery with Wilde, a fencer of Olympic standard, looking much more at home as Robin Hood Junior than as Frederic ('You must stop this polonaise jangle') Chopin in *A Song to Remember*. If the dialogue is imbecillic, the villainy is splendid and Tony Gaudio's Technicolor camerawork very lush. TM

Bandit Queen
(Shekhar Kapur, 1994, Ind/GB) Seema Biswas, Nirmal Pandey, Manoj Bajpai, Rajesh Vivek, Raghuvir Yadav, Govind Namdeo.
120 min.
A low-caste woman who fought back, Phoolan Devi became a social outcast from her village in Uttar Pradesh when she refused to submit quietly to rape, and a folk hero when she led a group of bandits in a series of bloody raids against the higher-caste Thakurs, climaxing in the notorious Behmai massacre. This as recently as 1983 – when she finally surrendered to the authorities on her own terms. Harrowingly graphic in its treatment of violence, the film fell foul of the Indian censors and of Devi herself, but Western audiences are likely to be impressed by how director Shekhar Kapur neither sensationalises nor sermonises. The focus is squarely on Phoolan – played with blistering intensity by Seema Biswas – but Kapur doesn't glorify her, or her increasingly traumatic acts of vengeance. Instead, there's a searing anger running through the film, at the oppression of women and at the caste-system which keeps everyone in place. TCh

Band of Outsiders
see Bande à part

Band of the Hand
(Paul Michael Glaser, 1986, US) Stephen Lang, Michael Carmine, Lauren Holly, John Cameron Mitchell, Daniele Quinn, Leon Robinson, Al Shannon.
110 min.
The story of a group of Miami Vice Guys turned Miami Nice Guys (sort of). Five uncontrollable teenage delinquents are dumped in the heart of the Florida Everglades where they meet Joe Tiger, a 'Nam vet turned social worker who's traded in his greens for the black Japanese designer equivalent. Joe doesn't say much, but from his allegorical one-liners we understand that he has wisdom of a profound nature to impart. The boys' education starts in the jungle, where they learn to survive or die, and ends in the urban jungle where they apply new-found self-esteem and Joe's terrorist techniques to a vigilante crusade against the entire Miami gangland. Crudely directed by Glaser, crassly acted and irresponsibly anarchistic. EP

Bandolero!
(Andrew V McLaglen, 1968, US) James Stewart, Dean Martin, Raquel Welch, George Kennedy, Andrew Prine, Will Geer, Clint Ritchie, Denver Pyle, Tom Heaton, Harry Carey Jr, Dub Taylor.
106 min.
An affably unpretentious Western, particularly attractive in its lazily offbeat opening as Stewart arrives in town to find the flophouse full because of an impending hanging, meets the hangman while luxuriating in the open-air bathhouse, waylays him for a lugubrious lecture on the secrets of the trade, and returns in the hangman's top hat and frock coat to compliment the sheriff (Kennedy) on the magnificence of his five-man gallows. Calmly staging a last-minute rescue of the condemned gang headed by his brother (Martin), he equally calmly robs the bank they failed to breach before, with the sheriff now safely in pursuit of his vanishing prisoners. A spirited chase of course ensues, with Raquel Welch as hostage, a troublesome faction in the gang, and hordes of bloodthirsty bandoleros in wait across the Mexican border. Script and direction both flag latterly, but the admirable cast keeps things going. TM

Band Wagon, The
(Vincente Minnelli, 1953, US) Fred Astaire, Jack Buchanan, Cyd Charisse, Oscar Levant, Ninette Fabray.
112 min.
One of Minnelli's best musicals, with an ingenious book which has Buchanan as a highbrow producer trying to turn Astaire's comeback show into an art house 'Faust', while Astaire and Charisse are meantime resolving the problem of whether their dancing styles can meld into a partnership. More importantly, it parades a stream of brilliant Howard Dietz-Arthur Schwartz numbers. Astaire is superlative in several items, notably 'By Myself' (a solitary introspection which opens the show with a purr), 'A Shine on Your Shoes', and (with Charisse) the gorgeous 'Dancing in the Dark'. So he can be forgiven for trying to do a Gene Kelly in the 'Girl Hunt' ballet (a parody of Mickey Spillane sleaze more notable for Michael Kidd's choreography and Charisse's startlingly sinuous femme fatale). All this and witty dialogue too. A treat. TM

Bang
see Big Bang Theory, The

Bang! You're Dead (aka Game of Danger)
(Lance Comfort, 1954, GB) Jack Warner, Derek Farr, Veronica Hurst, Michael Medwin, Gordon Harker, Anthony Richmond.
88 min. b/w.
Strange little movie about a young boy who kills a man by mistake with a gun he thought was a toy. As the police hunt goes up, with an innocent man coming under suspicion, the film can't make up its mind whether it's a thriller or a piece of social conscience, but the performance of the boy (Richmond) lends it charm. GA

Banjo on My Knee
(John Cromwell, 1936, US) Barbara Stanwyck, Joel McCrea, Helen Westley, Walter Brennan, Buddy Ebsen, Walter Catlett, Tony Martin, Katherine DeMille.
96 min. b/w.
Stanwyck carries this episodic Southern saga virtually single-handed, striking out for New Orleans on her own when Mississippi riverman McCrea does a runner after their nuptials – mistakenly believing he's accidentally killed a man during the reception. Needless to say, it all ends happily, but by a roundabout route. Undemanding. TJ

Bank Dick, The
(Eddie Cline, 1940, US) WC Fields, Cora Witherspoon, Una Merkel, Evelyn Del Rio, Jessie Ralph, Grady Sutton, Franklin Pangborn.
74 min. b/w.
By far the best of Fields' last comedies, with the great man trundling through an impeccably loony scenario of his own devising. As Egbert Souse, he does a spot of film direction, foils bank bandits, drinks in the Black Pussy Café, and marries his daughter to the gormless Og Oggilby (Grady Sutton in his greatest role). Totally ramshackle and marvellous. GB

Bank Holiday
(Carol Reed, 1938, GB) Margaret Lockwood, Hugh Williams, John Lodge, Kathleen Harrison, Wally Patch, Rene Ray, Wilfrid Lawson.
86 min. b/w.
Comedy-drama about an August bank holiday at the seaside. Though it lacks the guts and vitality of *Millions Like Us* and *Holiday Camp* as similarly populist epics, Reed's film, in its gentle mockery of the hopes and dreams of its 'ordinary' protagonists, is unique. Lockwood, not yet a wicked lady, needs an alibi of conscientious do-gooding to mask her desire, but at least it enables her to refuse to fulfil the fantasies of her office-boy fiancé. The film's real delights, though, come from the superb working-class character acting, particularly Kathleen Harrison, resplendent in beach pyjamas, defying her Cockney caricature of a husband by dancing with a college boy, and Wilfrid Lawson, lighting up the whole film with his suggestion of undreamed of worlds of eccentricity within a sleepy Sussex station sergeant. RMy

Bank Shot
(Gower Champion, 1974, US) George C Scott, Joanna Cassidy, Sorrell Booke, Clifton James, G Wood, Bob Balaban.
83 min.
It would be nice to say that ex-MGM choreographer Champion came up with a goodie in this adaptation of Donald Westlake's novel about an escaped con (Scott) who steals an entire (mobile) bank. But despite sundry excellent ideas and the odd touch of magic (a scene shot in silhouette; Scott swimming out to sea at the end), *Bank Shot* is one of those caper films that start all stops out and have nowhere to go. Potentially good gags get lost in the rush: the jailbreak accomplished in a bulldozer; the arrival of the stolen bank in a senior citizens' mobile home park – nothing is as funny as it should be. VG

Bantsuma: The Life and Times of Tsumasaburo Bando (Bantsuma: Bando Tsumasaburo no Shogai)
(Shunsui Matsuda, 1980, Jap) Tsumasaburo Bando, Takahiro Tamura, Shizuko Mori, Daisuke Ito.
91 min.

A splendid cine-history documentary about the career of the great movie actor Bando Tsumasaburo (the contraction 'Bantsuma' was his popular nickname). He started out in the 1920s as a faintly radical samurai star, turned into a gung-ho action hero in the '30s, and brought his time to an end in the '50s with mellower roles. The interest of this compilation is that the clips from the silent movies are shown complete with music and *benshi* commentary, as they were seen at the time. The narration is written by Japan's foremost critic, Tadao Sato, who also conducted the interviews with Bantsuma's colleagues and relatives. TR

BAPS

(Robert Townsend, 1997, US) Halle Berry, Natalie Desselle, Martin Landau, Ian Richardson, Troy Beyer, Luigi Amodeo.
93 min.
A fish-out-of-water comedy in which 'Black American Princesses' Berry and Desselle play daft but lovable Georgia belles with dreams of Hollywood glory. Following a ridiculous pop video audition, they're brought to Landau's Beverly Hills mansion by his scheming nephew, who hopes thereby to grab the old-timer's fortune. You can see how the black, modern-day Pygmalion-type story could work, just, but not with this heap of cabbage leaves for a script, and not with such desperately goofy acting from Berry and Desselle. On first encountering a bidet, the girls can't turn off the tap, so they get very wet – that's the level of humour. Landau provides a wide and knowing smile. Richardson is easier as the stuffy butler, over-acting in more taciturn style than the other loudmouths. NB

Barabbas (Barabba)

(Richard Fleischer, 1961, It) Anthony Quinn, Vittorio Gassman, Silvana Mangano, Jack Palance, Arthur Kennedy, Norman Wooland, Valentina Cortese, Harry Andrews, Katy Jurado, Ernest Borgnine.
144 min.
One of the most stylish and successful epics to emerge from the Hollywood-on-the-Tiber phase of film history. Quinn plays the legendary thief whose spiritual/physical journey begins at the Crucifixion and ends in the Roman arena, with a period in the sulphur mines in between. The unexpected quality owes everything to Christopher Fry's highly literate dialogue and Fleischer's very considerable abilities as a director of action. DP

Baraka

(Ron Fricke, 1992, US)
96 min.
Technically, a wow. *Koyaanisqatsi* cinematographer Fricke offers more wordless eco-spectacle. With startling depth and luminosity, a tumble of images whirls the viewer on a world tour: ancient temples and ethnic rites, unfolding landscapes and teeming cities. Japanese snow monkeys; Angkor Wat; Grand Central Station; Auschwitz; a chicken processing plant; Mecca; the changing skies over Utah. Fricke has been there. That's the problem. Any one sequence might work powerfully in its own right, but string them together with a musical overlay and the banality of the connections becomes apparent. TJ

Barbarella

(Roger Vadim, 1967, Fr/It) Jane Fonda, John Phillip Law, Anita Pallenberg, Milo O'Shea, David Hemmings, Marcel Marceau, Ugo Tognazzi.
98 min.
Vadim kicks off his adaptation of Jean-Claude Forest's 'adult' comic strip by stripping Fonda starkers. From there on it's typically vacuous titillation as Barbarella takes off for the mysterious planet Sorgo in 40,000 AD, there to survive attack by perambulating dolls with vampire fangs, receive her sexual initiation from a hairy primitive, fall in love with a blind angel, be whisked off to an alarming Lesbian encounter with the tyrannical Black Queen, etc. But Terry Southern's dialogue occasionally sparkles, and the imaginative designs, as shot by Claude Renoir, look really splendid. TM

Barbarosa

(Fred Schepisi, 1982, US) Willie Nelson, Gary Busey, Gilbert Roland, Isela Vega, Danny De La Paz, George Voskovec.
90 min.

Testifying to the timelessness of the Western genre through both its ballad form and its circular narrative about the functions of legend, this is also blessed with perfect casting: Nelson and Busey as the grizzled border-country gringo and the raw German-American farmboy, both outcasts in a vast, spartan, Texan terrain – the one a resigned wanderer whose invincibility sustains a 30-year old blood feud with the family that fears his name, the other accidentally apprenticed to this mythical menace. Transplanted Australian director Schepisi confidently threads his own route through Peckinpah territory (a Mexican patriarch demanding honour; a graveyard resurrection), less concerned with Peckinpah's gothic haunting than with teasing dark, absurd ironies from the symbiosis of sworn enemies. PT

Barbary Coast

(Howard Hawks, 1935, US) Miriam Hopkins, Edward G Robinson, Joel McCrea, Walter Brennan, Frank Craven, Brian Donlevy, Harry Carey.
90 min. b/w.
Perhaps not one of Hawks' greatest films, but none the less interesting. Set in the isolating fog and mist that immediately removes turn-of-the-century San Francisco from time and space, it deals with the competition between nightclub owner Robinson and prospector McCrea for Miriam Hopkins' dancer. Though the Hecht-MacArthur script is surprisingly poetic and derring-do, Hawks' direction is typically matter-of-fact. PH

Barb Wire

(David Hogan, 1995, US) Pamela Anderson Lee, Temuera Morrison, Jack Noseworthy, Victoria Rowell, Xander Berkeley, Steve Railsback, Udo Kier.
98 min.
Hogan's credits include second unit direction of the diabolical *Batman Forever*, plus numerous pop videos. No coincidence, then, that this awful action-adventure should employ similar production principles: waste land sets, rusty warehouses, plenty of fireworks, and orange filters to depict the dying skyline of a futuristic America ravaged by its second civil war. The year's 2017, the place Steel Harbor, home to a raggle-taggle society of misfits and the legendary Hammerhead Bar and Grille, owned by the eponymous heroine, a stiletto-toed, heavy-leather blonde with a penchant for roughing it. Before long, former freedom-fighter Barb (Anderson Lee) is roped into helping some old resistance colleagues find a pair of contact lenses which will enable a government employee, who alone knows about her bosses' plans for biological warfare, to flee the country. Mean, nasty and looking not unlike Nazi extras from *Kelly's Heroes*, the Congressional Directorate always seem to be one step ahead…until Barb gets serious and tools up for a showdown. To be fair, Anderson Lee cuts a fair dash as a cartoon-style heroine (acting aside). But the film's haphazardly edited, lacks narrative clout, and rambles on to a ludicrously extended conclusion. DA

Barcelona

(Whit Stillman, 1994, US) Taylor Nichols, Chris Eigeman, Tushka Bergen, Mira Sorvino, Pep Munné, Hellena Schmied.
101 min.
Writer/director Stillman again casts an affectionate eye on the foibles of preppy young Americans, this time two cousins all at sea in the sexual, moral and political whirl of a changing Old World. It's the 'last decade of the Cold War'. Ted (Nichols) is a young, serious-minded car-company executive getting over a failed affair, his recovery hardly helped when Fred (Eigeman) – a brash naval officer – turns up uninvited to stay in his Barcelona flat. When Fred starts 'borrowing' money from his host and meddling in his encounters with various girls, tensions between the pair come to a boil. An incisive comedy of misplaced American manners, this is for the most part a very funny portrait of immaturity deceived by its own ignorance and blinkered obstinacy. Agreed, it's harder to like or care about Ted and Fred as much as their younger (and therefore more forgivably deluded) counterparts in Stillman's earlier *Metropolitan*, and the story's sudden shift into life-and-death melodrama in the final reel is a little clumsy. But the film looks good, the performances are sharp and droll, and there's more than enough originality here to confirm Stillman as a distinctive, beguiling talent. GA

Barefoot Contessa, The

(Joseph L Mankiewicz, 1954, US) Ava Gardner, Humphrey Bogart, Edmond O'Brien, Marius Goring, Rossano Brazzi, Warren Stevens, Valentina Cortese.
128 min.
Like *The Bad and the Beautiful*, this starts with a funeral, then moves into flashback with three different guides to the scandalous life of a movie queen who started in the Spanish slums and liked to keep her feet in the dirt. Not as incisive as Minnelli's film, but still a heady Mankiewicz brew of Hollywood trash and wit. Also something of a *film à clef*, in which the millionaire producer is Howard Hughes, there are disguised caricatures (Farouk, the Duke of Windsor), and the Contessa herself is a tactful mixture (mostly Rita Hayworth). TM

Barefoot in the Park

(Gene Saks, 1967, US) Robert Redford, Jane Fonda, Mildred Natwick, Charles Boyer.
105 min.
Disposable Neil Simon comedy about newlyweds coping with their unheated walkup apartment, a flighty mother-in-law, and a romantically disreputable neighbour. Sprightly dialogue, nice performances. TM

Barfly

(Barbet Schroeder, 1987, US) MickeyRourke, Faye Dunaway, Alice Krige, JC Quinn, Frank Stallone, Jack Nance, Sandy Martin.
100 min.
Rourke plays one Henry Chimaski, habitué of the Golden Horn, a '40s down-town LA dive where no iceman cometh, but one day battered princess Wanda (Dunaway) does. A few hard days' nights in Wanda's flat has the two barflies abandoning their tentative move towards a mutual expression of need in favour of rejoining the death-wish trail. Chimaski is as articulate as a lorry, so the arrival of 'beautiful' literary agent Tully (Krige) in pursuit of his genius and punchy charm comes as a surprise; his refusal of her largesse is merely a chance to show Integrity. Schroeder's direction of Charles Bukowski's script is consistent with the film's throwaway mood, stresses the upbeat, and mercifully eschews seriousness, cleverly relying on Robby Müller's efficient colour photography to create atmosphere. WH

Bargee, The

(Duncan Wood, 1964, GB) Harry H Corbett, Hugh Griffith, Eric Sykes, Ronnie Barker, Julia Foster, Miriam Karlin, Eric Barker.
106 min.
Leaden comedy about a Casanova of the canals, scripted by Ray Galton and Alan Simpson but failing to match the flavour of their TV hit, *Steptoe and Son*. TM

Bari-Zogon

(Fumiki Watanabe, 1996, Jap) Fumiki Watanabe, Ryu Sasaki, Gaetano Tanaka, Makoto Akiyama.
114 min.
The title means 'Abusive Language' – a recurrent element in Watanabe's guerilla approach to indie production, which is generally rooted in his real-life investigations of personal problems and miscarriages of justice and distinguished by his un-Japanese refusal to go along with group-think. Here he reopens a case classed as 'accidental death' – a 26-year-old guy who froze to death in a cesspit – and dramatises what he believes really happened: the boy was silenced for voicing fears about the safety of nuclear power plants and refusing to go along with a related cover-up in the local mayor's election campaign. Watanabe predictably fails to get straight answers from the people involved in the case, but he puts up a persuasive argument. TR

Barkleys of Broadway, The

(Charles Walters, 1949, US) Fred Astaire, Ginger Rogers, Oscar Levant, Billie Burke, Gale Robbins.
109 min.
Originally planned by MGM as an Astaire-Garland follow-up to *Easter Parade*, but Judy dropped out, thus opening the door for one last Fred'n'Ginger movie, ten years after their previous work together. It's a pretty flat affair, with a

thin story about a married dancing couple splitting up when the woman decides to take up a straight acting career. But it does, of course, have its moments: Fred cavorting with 'Shoes with Wings On', and a happy ending accompanied by 'They Can't Take That Away from Me'. GA

Barnabo of the Mountains (Barnabo delle Montagne)
(Mario Brenta, 1994, Fr/It/Switz) Marco Pauletti, Duilio Fontana, Carlo Caserotti, Antonio Vecellio, Angelo Chiesura, Alessandra Milan.
125 min.
In the years after the Great War, high in the Dolomites, conflict rages between forest-rangers and gun-toting poachers. Enter soft-spoken Barnabo (Pauletti), a new ranger, whose nerve gives way during an operation to track down the gang that killed the station commander. Dismissed, the young man repairs to the solace of a peasant household, but when he receives a letter from his former superior, the call of the peaks and the chance to right old wrongs is too strong to resist. With its spare dialogue, meditative pacing and expressive use of Schubert's chamber music, this slow, rather beautiful piece is very much a European Art Movie writ large. You'll look elsewhere for snappy one-liners, but in its own way this mesmeric work has rare restorative powers. A gentle giant. TJ

Barnacle Bill (aka All At Sea)
(Charles Crichton, 1957, GB) Alec Guinness, Irene Browne, Percy Herbert, Maurice Denham, Victor Maddern, Lionel Jeffries.
87 min. b/w.
Belated addition to the Ealing comedy cycle, with Guinness as the scion of a long line of seadogs who switches to commanding a pier because he gets seasick. Much too stereotypical, with laboured jokes about bureaucracy as efforts are made to turn the pier into an entertainments centre. In a nod to *Kind Hearts and Coronets*, Guinness also plays his ancestors. TM

Baron Fantôme, Le (The Phantom Baron)
(Serge de Poligny, 1943, Fr) Jany Holt, Odette Joyeux, Alain Cuny, Gabrielle Dorziat, Claude Sainval, Jean Cocteau.
100 min. b/w.
A film to delight those with a taste for the slightly rarefied pleasures of a French Gothic-pastoral plot featuring a vanishing nobleman (played by Cocteau, who also served as dialogue-writer), a tumbledown castle, hidden treasure, two pairs of sparkling lovers, a gamekeeper posing as the Dauphin...and much, much more. Making light of the distinction between fantasy and reality, the kaleidoscopic tale weaves through the gradations of French society in the 1830s. Distinguished by several impeccable classical performances, Dior costumes, ravishing filtered photography and a tone of benign whimsicality, this represents the cinema of fantasy as its best and most compelling. JPy

Barquero
(Gordon Douglas, 1970, US) Lee Van Cleef, Warren Oates, Forrest Tucker, Kerwin Mathews, Mariette Hartley, Armando Silvestre, John Davis Chandler.
114 min.
Uneasy derivative of the spaghetti Western's blood and guts, but with a certain fascination to its cat-and-mouse conflict between Van Cleef, as a ferryman who despises the townsfolk he serves, and Oates as the leader of an outlaw band trying to escape across the river. Terrific interplay from Oates as the drug-fuddled psychopath plagued by bouts of Hamlet-like indecision, good ones from Van Cleef and Tucker. TM

Barravento
(Glauber Rocha, 1962, Braz) Antonio Sampaio, Luiza Maranhão, Aldo Teixeira, Lucy Carvalho.
72 min. b/w.
Rocha's first film, a denunciation of exploitation and the superstition that helps maintain it; an exploration of 'macumba', the mixture of Christianity and African tribal religion whose superstition aids the successful subjugation and exploitation of the fishermen in the Bahia province.

Barren Lives (Vidas Secas)
(Nelson Pereira Dos Santos, 1963, Braz) Atila Jório, Maria Ribeiro, Orlando Macedo.
135 min. b/w.
Dealing with the plight of the very poor in Northeastern Brazil, this centres on a family that has been forced by drought to wander through the desert seeking some kind of work to keep them from starving. A brief respite when the man finds a job as a cattle-herder is shattered by a further drought, a disastrous gambling session, and a beating-up by the police for having insulted an officer. The film moves slowly, with a type of minimalism that emphasises the oppressive fatefulness of the family's existence: a strong comment against the landowners, priests and police, whose individualism perpetuates a needless suffering. JDuC

Barretts of Wimpole Street, The
(Sidney Franklin, 1934, US) Norma Shearer, Fredric March, Charles Laughton, Maureen O'Sullivan, Katherine Alexander, Una O'Connor.
110 min. b/w.
Slow, deliberate, dull, and Irving Thalberg's favourite director, Franklin fittingly turned to production after Thalberg's death in 1936. This MGM prestige version of the love of Elizabeth Barrett (Shearer) and Robert Browning (March) is, as one would expect, high on production values and low on atmosphere and excitement. Even Laughton as Elizabeth's demented father does little to raise the spirits. All of which is rather surprising considering Franklin's obvious attachment to the project. In 1957, he returned briefly to directing, after a twenty year absence, with another version, once again with the producer's wife (Jennifer Jones/Selznick this time) as Elizabeth. PH

Barrier (Bariera)
(Jerzy Skolimowski, 1966, Pol) Jan Nowicki, Joanna Szczerbic, Tadeusz Lomnicki, Zdzislaw Maklakiewicz.
83 min. b/w.
Skolimowski's third film and one of his best, an extraordinary fusion of fantasy and documentary that adds up to a bleakly disenchanted look at the Polish here-and-now. It begins with images of strange, indefinable menace that resolve themselves into one of those ritualistic Polish games (like the one in *Knife in the Water*) being played by medical students. The winner, grabbing the piggy-bank containing the spoils (no communal ownership for him) and brandishing a sabre (sole legacy of his father), sets out into streets illuminated by the ubiquitous candles of Easter, seeking the good life in a society that proves to be haunted by the oppressive weight of past glories, peopled by old age, death, disillusionment and hordes of commuters scurrying past the huge, blank new buildings. He ends clinging precariously to the front of a rattletrap tram ('There are romantic impulses left in our cynical generation') driven by the quizzical blonde he meets, loses and finally finds again as his only spark of hope. With its startling imagery and bizarre landscapes, *Barrier* is that rare bird, a genuinely surrealist film. TM

Barry Lyndon `100`
(Stanley Kubrick, 1975, GB) Ryan O'Neal, Marisa Berenson, Patrick Magee, Hardy Krüger, Steven Berkoff, Gay Hamilton, Marie Kean.
187 min.
A triumph of technique over any human content that takes Thackeray's hero and traces his rise and fall through the armies and high societies of 18th century Europe. Given the singular lack of drama, perspective or insight, the way the film looks becomes its only defence. But the constant array of waxworks figures against lavish backdrops finally vulgarises the visual sumptuousness. CPe

Bartleby
(Anthony Friedmann, 1970, GB) Paul Scofield, John McEnery, Thorley Walters, Colin Jeavons, Raymond Mason.
79 min.
Made largely thanks to Paul Scofield's support, this was much vaunted in its day as an example of what could be done by a British independent cinema. What it actually does is betray Herman

Melville's enigmatic story (about a clerk's passive withdrawal from his office responsibilities) by updating it to present-day London and anchoring its mysterious ambiguities in all-too-prosaic realities. And it vividly illustrates the pitfalls of film-making divorced from any real social, political or aesthetic context. TR

Barton Fink
(Joel Coen, 1991, US) John Turturro, John Goodman, Judy Davis, Michael Lerner, John Mahoney, Tony Shalhoub, Jon Polito, Steve Buscemi, David Warrilow.
116 min.
In 1941, the well-meaning, vaguely leftist Broadway playwright of the title (Turturro) tries to settle into a rancid Hollywood hotel room to write his first script for eccentric mogul Jack Lipnick (Lerner). Trouble is, it's a Wallace Beery wrestling pic, and he develops a severe case of writer's block. His only hope, it seems, is to take inspiration from a fellow writer's 'secretary' (Davis) and from his insurance salesman neighbour (Goodman), welcomed by Fink as a living paradigm of the 'Common Man'. The tortuous narrative twists that have always marked the Coens' work here inform the entire structure of the movie. As it suddenly shifts gear from its bizarre blend of brooding psychodrama and screwball satire, the film accelerates into a Gothic fantasy as outrageous as it is terrifying. Somehow everything coheres, thanks to the Coens' superb writing and assured direction, and a roster of marvellous performances. The result works on numerous levels, thrilling the mind, ears and eyes, and racking the nerves. GA

Bas-Fonds, Les (The Lower Depths)
(Jean Renoir, 1936, Fr) Louis Jouvet, Jean Gabin, Suzy Prim, Vladimir Sokoloff, Junie Astor, Robert Le Vigan, Camille Bert, Jany Holt.
90 min. b/w.
The location of Renoir's adaptation of Maxim Gorki's play is not identified, but from the distinctive acting styles the feel is very French, with the enclosed world of a studio-built courtyard suggesting the dark side to his earlier success, *Le Crime de Monsieur Lange*. But rather than building on a feeling of community, the characters assembled – among them an actor, a drunk, a fallen baron – exist more as individuals looking for a way to escape. Gabin and Jouvet are their usual glorious selves, though the tendency towards pessimism makes this one of Renoir's less rewarding films. DT

Basic Instinct
(Paul Verhoeven, 1992, US) Michael Douglas, Sharon Stone, George Dzundza, Jeanne Tripplehorn, Denis Arndt, Leilani Sarelle, Bruce A Young, Chelcie Ross, Dorothy Malone, Stephen Tobolowsky.
128 min.
Nick Curran (Douglas) is a cop on the edge. Investigated for an over-zealous approach to his work, saddled with a drink and relationships problem, he becomes slowly embroiled with the case, then with the suspect, when a former rock star is found murdered at the climax of some bondage-style sex. Catherine Tramell (Stone), an ultra-clever, ultra-rich author and bisexual free spirit, is at the core of all the basic instinct paraded in the film. One scene in which she teases and bosses a roomful of hard law enforcement men is probably the best illustration of post-feminism in action that Hollywood has offered. Yet the film's depiction of not one but several bisexual women with murky, murderous pasts has angered activists, and does illustrate that sensitivity is not always the strong suit of Verhoeven or scriptwriter Joe Eszterhas. But if you like things unrestrained, hard, adult and off-the-rails, then Douglas and Stone are superb, and George Dzundza (as sidekick Gus) delivers another classic hard-boiled cameo. SGr

Basic Training
(Frederick Wiseman, 1971, US)
89 min. b/w.
A companion piece to Wiseman's earlier *High School*, this is another bleak *cinéma vérité* study of institutional indoctrination: in this case, the US Army. Filmed at the Fort Knox training centre, Kentucky, it follows a group of new recruits from induction and orientation through to the

regimented discipline of the graduation ceremony (prior to shipping out to Vietnam). Beneath the austere 'objectivity' of Wiseman's camera, the editing implicitly emphasises the perpetual process of dehumanisation intrinsic to the system, and finds a focal point of sorts in the maladjusted Private Hickman, whose inability to fit in leads to a suicide attempt. Hickman is a skinny precursor to Stanley Kubrick's Gomer Pyle, and the first half of *Full Metal Jacket* borrows significantly from *Basic Training*. TCh

Basilischi, I
see Lizards, The

Basil the Great Mouse Detective
see Great Mouse Detective, The

Basketball Diaries, The
(Scott Kalvert, 1995, US) Leonardo DiCaprio, Ernie Hudson, Mark Wahlberg, James Madio, Lorraine Bracco, Roy Cooper.
102 min.
Jim Carroll (DiCaprio) plays basketball for his NY Catholic boys school, sniffs cleaning fluid with pals Mickey (Wahlberg) and Pedro (Madio), and writes about his life in an exercise book he carries in his back pocket. When he gets into heroin, he still keeps up the diary, transcribing the dirt in his life to eloquent hipster prose. Half-heartedly updated from the late '60s, Kalvert's adaptation faithfully tracks Carroll's descent into the realms of addiction, but fails to shed much light on the impulses which take him there. Like most drug movies, it fails to translate the highs to the screen, but dwells long and hard on the lows. Carroll's book was distinguished by the language, closer to Hubert Selby than Adrian Mole. We get snatches of this in voice-over, but not enough to make it integral to the film, which twists the material into just another cautionary tale with homophobic underpinnings. The angel-faced DiCaprio is a gifted actor, but he lacks the authority and physical presence to keep us with him. TCh

Basket Case
(Frank Henenlotter, 1981, US) Kevin Van Hentenryck, Terri Susan Smith, Beverly Bonner, Robert Vogel, Diana Browne.
91 min.
A freak-show revenge plot that puts small ugly creatures like ET and Ewoks back where they belong: in baskets. Much of the suspense lies in the question: what is in the basket? It eats junk food in quantity, flaps its little lid, belches, and goes walkabout with deadly effect. Its custodian is a painfully fresh-faced nerd strangely adrift among the big-city low-life; and the secret of the wicker world is soon revealed to be the victim of extremely prejudicial surgery by a nympho doctor and desperate veterinarian. In a flashback, the nerd rescued his brother from a black plastic bag; now is the hour of their revenge...Same old gore and poignancy, but some garish characters and the nightmare quality of the New York hotel give it more low budget charm than it deserves. RP

Basket Case 2
(Frank Henenlotter, 1989, US) Kevin Van Hentenryck, Annie Ross, Kathryn Meisle, Heather Rattray.
89 mins.
With its prominent coupling motif, this sleazy romp would have perhaps been better entitled 'Bride of Basket Case'. After surviving a near-fatal fall from a New York tenement building, Duane Bradley (Van Hentenryck) and his twisted brother Belial find sanctuary from prying public eyes in the home of philanthropic granny Ruth (Ross), who presides over a menagerie of mutant misfits. While the brothers discover love is a many-splendoured thing, scheming journalist Marcie Elliot traces them to their new home, causing the normally amiable aberrations to turn nasty. Henenlotter's sequel to his shoestring-budget horror classic is an inconsistent affair which mixes comedy, shock and boredom in roughly equal proportions. Lacking the gritty, grainy quality of its predecessor, *Basket Case 2* finds itself overstretched in its ambitious attempts to parody (or perhaps honour) Tod Browning's seminal *Freaks*, despite the impressive efforts of make-up artist Gabe Bartalos. However, the gra-

tuitous unpleasantry is present, correct, and (unsurprisingly) sexual, and the occasional snappy one-liner is welcome. MK

Basquiat
(Julian Schnabel, 1996, US) Jeffrey Wright, Christopher Walken, Dennis Hopper, David Bowie, Gary Oldman, Benico Del Toro, Parker Posey, Elina Löwensohn, Paul Bartel, Courtney Love, Tatum O'Neal, Willem Dafoe.
107 min.
He was a 19-year-old black graffiti artist who became the darling of the '80s New York art scene, then self-destructed at the age of 27. The film directed by the Basquiat's old friend and rival Julian Schnabel announces itself as an insiders' view, with a soundtrack reportedly cobbled together from Basquiat's record collection (Tom Waits, Iggy Pop, Charlie Parker) and a cult clique of a cast (Bowie as Warhol, Hopper as the Swiss dealer Bruno Bischofberger); but it actually tells us little about the artist, the impulses behind his art, or what drove him to his death. Wright is supremely self-possessed in the title role, but Schnabel allows him to sail through life oblivious to anything save his talent. One scene with Christopher Walken, however, hits home. He's an intrusive journalist who asks Basquiat all the right questions, about colour, celebrity, and the true value of art. They don't speak the same language, but even if we only get half-answers, it's fascinating to see Basquiat's unease when he's really being pressed. Otherwise, this is just another tale of the perils of stardom overlaid with kitsch symbolism. TCh

Bataan
(Tay Garnett, 1943, US) Robert Taylor, George Murphy, Thomas Mitchell, Lloyd Nolan, Robert Walker, Lee Bowman, Desi Arnaz, Barry Nelson.
114 min. b/w.
Not exactly a gung ho WWII movie, since even Hollywood had to acknowledge American setbacks in the Pacific campaign at this stage of the war, but still contriving to have its scratch patrol of thirteen men (entrusted with a suicidal rearguard action) wipe out half the Japanese army while being decimated to tunes of glory. The ending, with the last survivor (Taylor, naturally) still firing defiantly on the advancing yellow hordes, hardly needed the closing title commending the heroism ('Their spirit will lead us back to Bataan'). So much for the realism much vaunted at the time, but – clearly modelled on *The Lost Patrol* – the film is beautifully paced by Garnett and boasts a sterling cast. TM

Bataille de San Sebastian, La
see Guns for San Sebastian

Bataille des Dix Millions, La
see Battle of the Ten Million, The

Bataille du Rail, La (Battle of the Rails)
(René Clément, 1946, Fr) Antoine Laurent, Desagneux, Leroy, Redon, Pauléon.
87 min. b/w.
The French neo-realist 'movement' began and ended with this film, whose innovations were developed neither in Clément's nor the national cinema. A semi-documentary study of World War II resistance among Breton railwaymen, using non-professional actors and natural locations, it's compromised by the director's periodic recourse to affirmative, audience-rousing set pieces, but achieves overall a sobriety that is oddly modern, even 'Bressonian' in tone. GAd

Bath House
see Oksutan

Batman
(Leslie Martinson, 1966, US) Adam West, Burt Ward, Lee Meriwether, Burgess Meredith, Cesar Romero, Frank Gorshin, Alan Napier, Neil Hamilton, Reginald Denny, Sterling Holloway.
105 min.
This spin-off from the camp '60s TV series is bolstered with all the major baddies: The Penguin (Meredith), Joker (Romero), Riddler (Gorshin) and Catwoman (Meriwether). With a flip script by Lorenzo Semple Jr, it has a few

inspired slapstick sequences (West trying desperately to dispose of a bomb without blowing up nuns, children or animals), but the emphatic senselessness gradually becomes tiresome. More surprisingly, the production work is by and large excellent. Nelson Riddle's musical cues are fun, and the design still looks sleek today – I'd choose Adam West's Batmobile over Michael Keaton's any day. TCh

Batman
(Tim Burton, 1989, US) Michael Keaton, Jack Nicholson, Kim Basinger, Robert Wuhl, Pat Hingle, Billy Dee Williams, Michael Gough, Jack Palance, Jerry Hall, Tracey Walter.
121 min.
In everything but its commercial success, *Batman* most resembles Lynch's *Dune*: plotless, unfocused, barely held together by mind-blowing sets, gadgets and costumes, and by director Burton's visual flair. It begins with promising angles – is Batman crazed vigilante or hero? Will journos Vicki Vale (Basinger) and Alex Knox (Wuhl) win the Pulitzer for discovering him? Why does Bruce Wayne spend millions dressing up as a bat? – but all are abandoned half-way through for a straight slugging match between Good and Evil. Cackling, dancing, killing for sheer humour value and hogging the best one-liners, Nicholson's Joker makes *The Witches of Eastwick* seem restrained and pulls off the greatest criminal coup of the decade: stealing a whole movie. Though Keaton is a perfect Bruce Wayne, at the heart of the film, where a *noir*-ish, psychologically disturbed Batman should be, there are only a small actor and a couple of stunt doubles in an inflexible rubber suit. Basinger's role, on the other hand, is over-inflated, presumably in order to prove by her presence, as with Aunt Harriet in the '60s series, that there's nothing kinky about a hero who likes to dress up in cape and leathers. In the end, one's reaction to Burton's blockbuster is little more than that of the Joker to Batman: 'Where did he get those wonderful toys?'. DW.

Batman Returns
(Tim Burton, 1992, US) Michael Keaton, Danny DeVito, Michelle Pfeiffer, Christopher Walken, Michael Gough, Michael Murphy, Cristi Conaway, Andrew Bryniarski, Pat Hingle, Vincent Schiavelli.
126 min.
Bigger, louder, more relentlessly action-packed than its predecessor, *Batman Returns* batters its audience into submission. The main problems are both the lack of story and the wealth of superfluous detail in the dialogue that is sometimes barely intelligible. Precisely what the villains – Catwoman (Pfeiffer), the Penguin (DeVito) and property developer Max Shreck (Walken) – are up to, and why, is often unclear, save that they're all on some sort of power trip. Catwoman's schizophrenia, never properly explored, seems a scriptwriter's cop-out; the Penguin is merely unrepelled for being consigned to the sewers at birth; and Shreck is simply a corrupt, murderous tycoon posing as Gotham's leading philanthropist. Even the epically conceived and impressively executed set pieces become wearisome after a while. If you're satisfied with stars in funny costumes playing shallow characters involved in an obscure battle to the death, fine; but if huge sets, special effects and a blaring score are not enough, it's a long haul. GA

Batman Forever
(Joel Schumacher, 1995, US) Val Kilmer, Jim Carrey, Tommy Lee Jones, Nicole Kidman, Chris O'Donnell, Michael Gough, Pat Hingle, Drew Barrymore, Debi Mazar, Rene Auberjonois.
121 min.
The second sequel to Tim Burton's 1989 blockbuster makes its predecessors appear models of subtlety and coherence. In theory the film marks a new lease of life for the caped crusader (new star, new faces, new director); in practice everything about *Forever* feels stale and self-conscious. Kilmer is a more sensual Bruce Wayne than Michael Keaton, but if anything his remodelled body-tight Batsuit proves even more of a strait-jacket. As in *Returns*, our hero has to fight for screen time with not one, but two scene-stealing villains, Jones's (wasted) Harvey Two-Face and Carrey's Riddler, plus the love interest, Kidman's

ludicrously perverse shrink Dr Meridian. As if that's not enough, he's been stuck with a partner-in-crimebusting, O'Donnell's butch young Robin, obviously designed to broaden the demographics (the queer styling even runs to a fetishistic close-up of the Bat-butt). The perfunctory plot concerns the Riddler's mass-marketing of a televisual brain drain. TCh

Batman & Robin
(Joel Schumacher, 1997, US) George Clooney, Arnold Schwarzenegger, Uma Thurman, Chris O'Donnell, Alicia Silverstone, Pat Hingle.
125 min.
The fourth Bat-flick finds this juvenile franchise running on empty. Oozing insincerity and perplexed paternalism, Clooney plays Batman as an irrelevant bystander. Screenwriter Akiva Goldman sets up a 'revenge of nature' theme, with Schwarzenegger's lumpen Mr Freeze croaking interminable 'cool' puns ('Tchill'), and Thurman vamping as eco-terrorist Poison Ivy, but soon falls back on recycling random Batpieces with scant rhyme or reason. Robin, the blandly obnoxious O'Donnell, meets his match in Silverstone's unintentionally hilarious Oxbridge biker chick, but Batgirl is just another doll looking for a merchandising tie-in. TCh

Battaglia di Maratona, La
see Giant of Marathon, The

Batteries Not Included
(Matthew Robbins, 1987, US) Hume Cronyn, Jessica Tandy, Frank Mc Rae, Elizabeth Peña, Michael Carmine, Dennis Boutsikaris.
106 min.
At the heart of this Spielberg production is a clever idea: pocket-sized flying saucers with heavy-lidded flashlights. Unfortunately, the schmaltzy tale that accompanies them would make you puke. Elderly couple Faye and Frank (Tandy and Cronyn) are respectively loco and feisty. Their New York brownstone is threatened with demolition, so Frank prays for a miracle, which arrives in the form of little creatures from another planet. They take up residence in the tenement, where they show an amazing propensity for mending things that are damaged – bye-bye suspense. Robbins' handling of the human element is as sickly and soggy as a dunked doughnut, and the script makes gonks out of its characters. But the flirting frisbee scenes are pretty neat. EP

Battle Beneath the Earth
(Montgomery Tully, 1967, GB) Kerwin Mathews, Viviane Ventura, Robert Ayres, Martin Benson, Peter Arne.
91 min.
A hilarious example of Reds-under-the-bed literalism, Battle Beneath the Earth takes for its starting point the notion that Chinese troops are burrowing their way under America as part of a devilish plan to conquer the bastion of Western Democracy. Sadly, the film itself is neither as naive nor as adventurous as its premise. PH

Battle Beyond the Stars
(Jimmy T Murakami, 1980, US) Richard Thomas, Robert Vaughn, John Saxon, George Peppard, Darlanne Fluegel, Sybil Danning, Sam Jaffe.
103 min.
Scripted by John Sayles, Battle Beyond the Stars rips off all sorts of nice genre items (including a feisty-talking computer and a Russ Meyer-ish Valkyrie) with shameless abandon, the best being the plot of The Magnificent Seven. Like its model, the fun comes in the gathering of the samurai: there's even the black-clad Robert Vaughn, who reprises his twitchy mercenary, exuding the awful solitude of deep space and just looking for a way to go out in style. The last quarter will please only space invader freaks, but any movie which has the line 'Have you never seen a Valkyrie go down?' surely cannot be wholly devoid of cultural merit. CPea

Battle for Anzio, The
see Sbarco di Anzio, Lo

Battle for the Planet of the Apes
(J Lee Thompson, 1973, US) Natalie Trundy,

Roddy McDowall, Claude Akins, Severn Darden, Lew Ayres, John Huston.
92 min.
The fifth offshoot from Pierre Boulle's novel, last and worst of the 'Ape' series. It's hampered by a banal script which, bringing the story full circle by way of an uninteresting struggle between warlike gorillas, peaceful chimps and underground mutants, seems reluctant to use the potentials for astute comic strip philosophy that all the other films revelled in for a greater or lesser extent.

Battleground
(William Wellman, 1949, US) Van Johnson, John Hodiak, Ricardo Montalban, George Murphy, Marshall Thompson, Jerome Courtland, Denise Darcel, Don Taylor, Richard Jaeckel, James Whitmore, Leon Ames, James Arness.
118 min. b/w.
A serious and frequently powerful re-enactment of WWII's Battle of the Bulge that centres on a platoon virtually lost in a blanket of fog in the harsh Ardennes winter, convincingly recreated on the back lot. It may well have been an influence on several Vietnam movies – notably Platoon and Hamburger Hill – in its unglamorous portrait of men in war. A major battle was also fought behind the scenes. It was the pet project of Dore Schary, MGM's newly arrived left wing production chief, who had the backing of MGM's president Nick Schenck in New York, but not Louis B Mayer, who hated the script and thought the film would be a disaster. Schary won the day (the film was a huge commercial success and was nominated for all the major Oscars), and Mayer's days were numbered. He was toppled in a coup led by Schary a year later. ATu

Battle Hell
see Yangtse Incident

Battle Hymn
(Douglas Sirk, 1956, US) Rock Hudson, Martha Hyer, Anna Kashfi, Dan Duryea, Don DeFore, Jock Mahoney, Alan Hale, James Edwards, Philip Ahn, Carl Benton Reid.
108 min.
Hudson plays a preacher who trains fighter pilots in Korea. Problem is, he is plagued with guilt for bombing a German orphanage during WWII, and sure enough a bunch of orphaned Orientals show up wanting shelter from Commie attacks. Pure sentimental slop, with accompanying choral music. Apparently based on a true story; the biggest joke is that Hudson's character is a certain Colonel Hess. ATu

Battle of Algiers, The (La Battaglia di Algeri) [100] (100)
(Gillo Pontecorvo, 1965, Alg/It) Jean Martin, Yacef Saadi, Brahim Haggiag, Tommaso Neri.
135 min. b/w.
The prototype for all the mainstream political cinema of the '70s, from Rosi to Costa-Gavras. It relegates the actual liberation of Algeria to an epilogue, and focuses instead on a specific phase of the Algerian guerrilla struggle against the French, the years between 1954 (when the FLN regrouped, recruited new members, and tackled the problem of organised crime in the Casbah) and 1957 (when French paratroopers under Colonel Mathieu launched a systematic – and largely successful – attack on the FLN from the roots up). Some fifteen minutes were cut from prints shown in both Britain and America, removing the more graphic sequences of French torture methods, but it seems clear that even these would not have altered the film's scrupulous balance. Pontecorvo refuses to caricature the French or glamorise the Algerians: instead he sketches the way a guerrilla movement is organised and the way a colonial force sets about decimating it. There's a minimum of verbal rhetoric: the urgent images and Ennio Morricone's thunderous score spell out the underlying political sympathies. TR

Battle of Austerlitz, The
see Austerlitz

Battle of Britain
(Guy Hamilton, 1969, GB) Laurence Olivier, Michael Caine, Robert Shaw, Christopher Plummer, Susannah York, Ian McShane,

Kenneth More, Trevor Howard, Ralph Richardson, Michael Redgrave.
131 min.
Dull, all-star treatment of a potentially stirring historical event, notable mainly for its lengthy, boring and far too numerous dogfight sequences, the tediousness of which is matched by the dialogue which the unfortunate actors are forced to deliver whenever they are grounded. NF

Battle of Chile, The (Batalla de Chile)
(Patricio Guzman, 1973-8, Chile) Part I: 'The Insurrection of the Bourgeoisie; Part 2: 'The Coup d'Etat'; Part 3: 'The Power of the People'.
106/99/97 min. b/w.
Not only the best films about Allende and the coup d'etat, but among the best documentary films ever made, changing our concepts of political documentary within a framework accessible to the widest audience. The films (which form a unity) are committed, analytical and chronological, allowing the participants in history to explain it. The result is of an extraordinary passion. SM

Battle of Midway, The
see Midway

Battle of the Bulge
(Ken Annakin, 1965, US) Henry Fonda, Robert Shaw, Robert Ryan, Dana Andrews, George Montgomery, Ty Hardin, Pier Angeli.
163 min.
Though writer/producer Milton Sperling dubbed his company United States Pictures after he'd seen World War II service in the Marines, the war movies he subsequently backed were notable for their avoidance of either gung-ho excess or 'war-is-hell' blandness. Both Joseph H Lewis' Retreat, Hell! and Fuller's Merrill's Marauders are riven with contradictory impulses about heroism, duty, futility and necessity; and, if finally the epic logistics of this sprawling Cinerama spectacular submerge the sparkier points of the Philip Yordan/Sperling script, Battle of the Bulge is no simplistic flag-waver or exorcism either. Shaw's panzer commander takes on various Allied stars in games of strategic cat-and-mouse, both lucidly and dispassionately observed, during the German counter-offensive in the Ardennes in late 1944. PT

Battle of the River Plate, The (aka Pursuit of the Graf Spee)
(Michael Powell, Emeric Pressburger, 1956, GB) John Gregson, Anthony Quayle, Peter Finch, Ian Hunter, Bernard Lee, Patrick McNee, Douglas Wilmer, Christopher Lee.
119 min.
Powell and Pressburger's final collaboration as The Archers was also, perhaps, their dullest. Certainly it's a pretty routine account of the British attempt to capture of the German battleship Graf Spee in Montevideo harbour in '39, even if it is sharply shot by Chris Challis and reasonably acted by a superior cast. Admittedly, the stiff-upper-lip factor is relatively low, and the Germans are not the usual sadistic two-dimensional villains, but those in search of the baroque romanticism usually prevalent in the team's work will be sorely disappointed. GA

Battle of the Sexes, The
(Charles Crichton, 1959, GB) Peter Sellers, Constance Cummings, Robert Morley, Donald Pleasence, Ernest Thesiger, Jameson Clark.
84 min. b/w.
The tone shifts uncertainly between facile farce and sharp satire in this sub-Ealing comedy (based on James Thurber's The Catbird Seat) about an accountant (Sellers) who plots the murder of the female efficiency expert (Cummings) who has disrupted the comfortable regime of a traditionally-run Edinburgh tweed cloth factory. Its view of women's place in the business world is unlikely to find favour with feminists and enlightened fellow travellers. NF

Battle of the Ten Million, The (La Bataille des Dix Millions)
(Chris Marker, 1970, Fr/Bel/Cuba).
58 min. b/w.
Clear, informative, well-argued account of the revolution in Cuba, looked at through the documentation of a single facet: Castro's attempt to

raise the 1970 sugar harvest from 42 million tons to an all-time high of ten million. Beneath the level of narrative it presents an unclichéd view of the implications of revolution.

Battle of the Villa Fiorita, The

(Delmer Daves, 1964, GB) Maureen O'Hara, Rossano Brazzi, Richard Todd, Phyllis Calvert, Martin Stephens, Olivia Hussey.
111 min.
Lushly silly soap opera about a diplomat's wife who runs off to romantic Italy with a widowed concert pianist. Even Daves and his swooping crane can do nothing to stem the tiresomeness when the children of both parties turn up to do battle for respectability. TM

Battleship Potemkin 100 (100) (Bronenosets Potyomkin)

(Sergei Eisenstein, 1925, USSR) Alexander Antonov, Vladimir Barsky, Grigori Alexandrov, Mikhail Gomorov, Beatrice Vitoldi.
5,709 ft. b/w.
What more can be said about *Potemkin* – the celebrated re-creation, in documentary style, of the key events of the failed 1905 Kronstadt revolution against Tsarist oppression – re-issued (in 1998) in a new print, with music by Shostakovich replacing Meisel's original score. It exemplifies, we know, Eisenstein's fascination with 'montage' (the use of dialectical forms of editing to create meaning) and 'typage' (non-actors cast for physical characteristics). This, however, is propaganda, just as much as art, and looking back after more than 70 years there's something cold, academic, even manipulative about the meticulous compositions, schematic characterisations and complex choreography of massed movement. It lacks the genuinely fiery passion of Eisenstein's earlier *Strike*, not to mention the lyricism of Dovzhenko or the perky wit of Vertov. Edward Tissé's camerawork remains impressive, and there's no doubt that the whole is a technical tour de force, but the obsession with forces of power, as opposed to individual experience, is ultimately oppressive. GA

Battlestar Galactica

(Richard A Colla, 1978, US) Lorne Greene, Richard L Hatch, Dirk Benedict, Maren Jensen, Ray Milland, John Colicos, Lew Ayres.
125 min.
Feature cobbled from the American TV series, complete with shots and effects repeated ad nauseam. Similar in plot and costume to *Star Wars*, but at heart a traditional space Western with less emphasis on droids and more on shootouts. Some good special effects, but with strictly tele-standard acting, straightforward space opera plot, grandiose sentiment and slushy love interest, it's really only meat for genre fans. DP

Battling Butler

(Buster Keaton, 1926, US) Buster Keaton, Sally O'Neil, Snitz Edwards, Walter James, Bud Fine.
7 reels. b/w.
Charming comedy in which Buster, a scion of the idle rich, has to make good his supposed prowess as a prizefighter (a mistake occasioned by an unfortunate coincidence of names) in order to win the hand of a mountain girl. The first half is delightfully inventive as Keaton takes to the mountains in his Rolls for a hilariously feckless hunting trip. A slight drop in temperature latterly, despite some very funny business during the training scenes and the pseudo-championship bout, but the final grudge fight (when Buster realises how the real boxer has tricked him) is a little too nasty for comfort. TM

Bat 21

(Peter Markle, 1988, US) Gene Hackman, Danny Glover, Jerry Reed, David Marshall Grant, Clayton Rohner, Erich Anderson.
105 min.
An unsatisfactory mix of low-key heroics, buddy-buddy humour, and anti-war sentiment, this downbeat Vietnam pic has reconnaissance expert Hackman (codename Bat 21) – a career colonel with no frontline experience – struggling to survive in a jungle crawling with North Vietnamese troops after ejecting from his plane. Making radio contact with spotter pilot Glover (codename Birddog), he maps out a coded route to a rendezvous. Cue for a cross-country hike punctuated

by brushes with NVA patrols, a machete-wielding peasant, and an ambiguously angelic Vietnamese child. Certain scenes achieve a genuine tension, as when Hackman has to watch a captured chopper pilot sent into a waterlogged minefield by NVA soldiers; but this is immediately undercut by a retaliatory bombing raid that destroys a camouflaged NVA hideout, regardless of civilian casualties. Like the film as a whole, such scenes elicit sympathy more for the tacitly guilty Hackman than for the innocent victims. NF

Bat Whispers, The

(Roland West, 1930, US) Chester Morris, Una Merkel, Maud Eburne, William Bakewell, Gustav von Seyffertitz.
88 min. b/w.
A talkie remake of West's silent *The Bat*, adapted from a hugely popular Broadway whodunit. The creaky plot, about a super-thief hiding out in an old dark house and terrifying its inhabitants, is virtually incomprehensible, a non-stop succession of spooky clichés strung together with scant regard for logic or motivation; while attempts to inject humour – centred largely around an hysterical housemaid – are often embarrassingly unfunny. Fascinating, however, is West's unusual visual sense: all enormous shadows, overhead shots, and (for the time) a surprisingly mobile camera. Remade, ineffectually, in 1958 as *The Bat*. GA

Bawdy Adventures of Tom Jones, The

(Cliff Owen, 1975, GB) Nicky Henson, Trevor Howard, Terry-Thomas, Arthur Lowe, Georgia Brown, Joan Collins, William Mervyn.
93 min.
Many distinguished names who should have known better lend themselves to this smutty musical version of Henry Fielding's tale. CPe

Baxter!

(Lionel Jeffries, 1972, GB) Patricia Neal, Jean-Pierre Cassel, Britt Ekland, Lynn Carlin, Scott Jacoby.
105 min.
Jeffries' second film treats that most treacherous of subjects: the emotional deprivations of childhood. Reginald Rose's cliché-oriented script notwithstanding, Jeffries emerges successful from the project, neither wallowing in melodrama nor seeking social significance where none is to be found. Scott Jacoby is masterful as the emotionally disturbed 12-year-old caught between two worlds, California and London, and helped by an odd collection of friends. PH

Bayan Ko: My Own Country (Bayan Ko – Kapit Sa Patalim)

(Lino Brocka, 1984, Phil/Fr) Phillip Salvador, Gina Alajar, Claudia Zobel, Carmi Martin.
108 min.
Made under the noses of the Marcos censors in the thick of Manila's social and political turmoil, this is based on two news stories from 1980. It centres on a brawny, sympathetic Manila print-shop worker, whose political naivety lands him on the wrong side during a strike, and whose anger and frustration finally drive him into crime. Shot with the urgency of newsreel, the film is a brilliantly topical thriller, and an admirable act of civil disobedience. If ever a film caught the spirit of its time, this is it. TR

Bay Boy, The

(Daniel Petrie, 1984, Can/Fr) Liv Ullmann, Kiefer Sutherland, Peter Donat, Allan Scarfe, Mathieu Carrière.
107 min.
The trouble with this attractively photographed story of the pangs of adolescence, set against the background of a dismal mining town on the coast of Nova Scotia in 1937, is that it is too busy. So much happens to the young hero that he barely has time to react to one event before he has to be ready for the next: murder, homo-and heterosexual advances, first love, torn loyalties, loss of virginity. Thus experience changes no one, and the spectator gets little out of it. Redeeming features are some excellent performances, and two brilliantly directed seduction scenes. AG

Bay of Angels

see Baie des Anges, La

Beach Blanket Bingo

(William Asher, 1965, US) Frankie Avalon, Annette Funicello, Linda Evans, Paul Lynde, Don Rickles, Marta Kristen, Buster Keaton.
98 min.
More seafront fluff from the AIP stable, with Annette mad at Frankie for fancying starlet Evans (decades before her *Dynasty* fame) and mounting a rescue mission when she's kidnapped by a biker gang. Madhouse plot elements thrown into the mix include a passing mermaid, abrasive comic Don Rickles as the owner of a sky-diving club, and Buster Keaton as a leching old beachcomber, gamely taking falls as he chases after bikini-ed youth. Pretty dumb really, but at least it knows it, and for the record, they never actually play bingo, with beach blankets or anything else. TJ

Beachcomber, The

see Vessel of Wrath

Beachcomber, The

(Muriel Box, 1954, GB) Robert Newton, Glynis Johns, Donald Sinden, Paul Rogers, Donald Pleasence, Michael Hordern.
90 min.
Lamentable version of the Somerset Maugham story about a drunken beach bum and a prissy missionary lady, previously filmed as *Vessel of Wrath* with Charles Laughton and Elsa Lanchester. Just to add to the hammy indignities, a silly *Androcles and the Lion* role has been dreamed up for an elephant. TM

Beaches

(Garry Marshall, 1988, US) Bette Midler, Barbara Hershey, John Heard, Spalding Gray, Lainie Kazan, James Read.
123 min.
CC and Hillary first meet under the boardwalk in Atlantic City. CC is a vulgar, would-be singer, Hillary a beautiful, poor little rich girl. As they grow up into Midler and Hershey, they keep their relationship alive by writing letters. Then one day Hillary turns up in New York and becomes CC's flatmate. Hillary sleeps with theatre director Heard; CC marries him. Marshall's slick and stylish flick follows the ups and downs of their marriages and careers, but because CC becomes a star, the pace is sabotaged by several Midler numbers. Even so, Midler carries the movie: nearly all the giggles are due to her cosmic skills. Two-thirds of the way through, a funny film turns tragic with the utterance of a single word, *virus*, which means that Hershey has to start gasping and preparing for death. But even though tear-jerking has never been so blatant, your tears of laughter are replaced, God damn it, by tears of grief. MS

Beach of the War Gods (Zhan Shen Tan)

(Wang Yu, 1973, HK) Wang Yu, Lung Fei, Tien Yeh, Hsueh Han, Tsao Chien.
100 min.
Simplistic dialogue with all the subtlety of a WWII comic book mars this visually exciting effort which replays *The Magnificent Seven* on an epic scale against the background of invasion-raddled China at the end of the Ming dynasty. Wang Yu – the original one-armed swordsman – who wrote, directed and stars in the film, shows skill in shaping individual shots and keeping the project (which took three years to complete) afloat with some superb torchlit battles.

Beach Red

(Cornel Wilde, 1967, US) Cornel Wilde, Burr De Benning, Patrick Wolfe, Rip Torn, Jaime Sanchez, Jean Wallace, Genki Koyama.
105 min.
Wilde's neglected WWII movie is an allegory about the futility and the carnage of Vietnam. Set in the Pacific, it details a probably suicidal mission to take a Japanese-held island. The movie is massively and harrowingly brutal, almost like a horror movie, with severed limbs washing up on the beach. Although Wilde deals exclusively in pacifist clichés, the film has a genuine primitive power; in fact, it's the equal of anything made by Fuller. ATu

Beads of One Rosary, The (Paciorki Jednego Rózanca)

(Kazimierz Kutz, 1979, Pol) Augustyn Halotta, Marta Straszna, Jan Bogdol, Ewa Wisniewska.
111 min.
The hero is a retired miner who stubbornly refuses to vacate his home for a new high-rise block. Everyone else has gone, but the old man remains, a last outpost defending tradition, family and freedom. And just to complicate matters, he is stoutly backed by his son, a bead from the same rosary. The relevance to the Gdansk strikes of 1980 is obvious; and an ironic ending, demonstrating the crafty compromises which can undermine rebellion, is a bitter footnote to the Polish situation. An impressive film, therefore, full of dogged humanist spirit, but also lumbering along in flat, documentary style, emerging a little like a cross between Ealing comedy and Italian neo-realism. TM

Bean

(Mel Smith, 1997, GB) Rowan Atkinson, Peter MacNicol, Pamela Reed, Harris Yulin, Burt Reynolds, Larry Drake, John Mills, Peter Egan, Peter Capaldi.
90 min.
Rowan Atkinson's TV series *Mr Bean* enjoyed worldwide syndication, and this feature revamps the familiar material: the coffee joke, the tongue-shaving sequence, the falling-asleep-on-head joke, and the exploding air-sick-bag (very graphic). Mr Bean, a security guard at the National Gallery in London, is selected to travel to California as the gallery's representative at the unveiling of 'Whistler's Mother'. His host (MacNicol) is expecting London's finest art scholar. The jokes have a variable strike rate, and there are times when you feel that everyone's just treading water before the next big set-piece. Still, Atkinson's on peak form, witness the hilarious but risky public loo gag. The theme – a strange man in a strange land – is quite amusing too. It's just that, well, it's all a bit of a yawn. DA

Bear, The (L'Ours)

(Jean-Jacques Annaud, 1988, Fr) Tchéky Karyo, Jack Wallace, André Lacombe.
98 min.
In *Quest for Fire*, Annaud tried to explore our primal emotions by delving into pre-history; here he attempts much the same thing, although this time it's not our ancestors but the beasts with whom we share the planet that are intended to shed light on our deepest instincts. At the turn of the century in British Columbia, a young kodiak bear, suddenly orphaned, takes up with a massive wounded grizzly. Inevitably, the cub undergoes the usual rites of passage, his awareness of death enhanced by a couple of hunters determinedly tracking his adoptive dad. Despite the enormous and very evident technical expertise involved in making the film, Annaud never manages to dispel memories of those Disney features in which animal behaviour was presented in human terms. This being the '80s, there's sex'n'violence (baby bear sees daddy bear getting it on with a local floozie bear; a clash with trappers ends in vivid realistic gore), not to mention an uplifting ecological finale. Otherwise, it's simply a ripping yarn, too prone to anthropomorphism to work successfully as a proper study either of ursine behaviour or of our own relationship to their world. GA

Bear Island

(Don Sharp, 1979, Can/GB) Donald Sutherland, Vanessa Redgrave, Richard Widmark, Christopher Lee, Barbara Parkins, Lloyd Bridges.
118 min.
Despite a better cast than most Alistair MacLean adaptations and an interesting Arctic story about Cold War struggles to dominate the globe by weather control, this fast becomes a dodo with such elements as a former U-Boat base, most of the cast's suspiciously Nazi pasts, and an array of Teutonic accents clearly destined to play a large part in the story. Faced with such silliness, the writers panic and abandon exposition for slug-out set pieces, loud bangs and noisy chases. Left stranded, the cast must have drawn straws for lines like 'This is no place for scientists who can't control themselves'. CPe.

Bearskin

(Ann Guedes/Eduardo Guedes, 1989, GB/Port) Tom Waits, Damon Lowry, Julia Britton, Isabel Ruth, Charlotte Coleman, Bill Paterson, Ian Dury, Alex Norton.
95 min.
If you can accept the idea of a Portuguese city standing in for London, you may just have no problem with the other weirdness dished up in this arty 'urban fairytale'. On the run from hoodlums, Lowry dons a bear-suit and prowls around Waits's Punch and Judy show; Bill Paterson as a guardian angel is a mite easier to accept than some of the film's other self-indulgent peculiarities. NF

Beast, The

see Bête, La

Beast, The (aka The Beast of War)

(Kevin Reynolds, 1988, US/Isr) George Dzundza, Jason Patric, Steven Bauer, Stephen Baldwin, Don Harvey, Frick Avari, Kabir Bedi.
109 min.
Filmed on extraordinary desert locations in Israel, this superior war movie effortlessly fuses the moral complexity of scriptwriter William Mastrosimone's original stage play with the visual spectacle and narrative drive of a full-blown cinema feature. During the second year of the Soviet invasion of Afghanistan, a Soviet tank razes an Afghan village to the ground, before becoming lost in the aptly named Valley of the Jackal. Vengeful Afghan rebels track and circle the wounded beast, taking bites out of its tough metal hide in an effort to expose the soft flesh inside. The action is tough and gripping, while the quieter scenes explore the adversaries' contrasting, sometimes self-contradictory, attitudes towards the conflict. Mark Isham's spare electronic score is an added bonus. NF

Beast from Haunted Cave

(Monte Hellman, 1959, US) Michael Forest, Sheila Carol, Frank Wolff, Wally Campo, Chris Robinson.
75 min. b/w.
Routine programmer made for Roger Corman in which gangsters holed up in a ski lodge tangle with the thing in the cave. Hellman's first film, but there's nothing to distinguish it from any other grade Z horror pic of the '50s. DP

Beast from 20,000 Fathoms, The

(Eugène Lourié, 1953, US) Paul Christian, Paula Raymond, Cecil Kellaway, Kenneth Tobey, Donald Woods, Lee Van Cleef.
80 min. b/w.
Freed from the Arctic ice by atomic blasts, one of Ray Harryhausen's most loveable prehistoric beasts trundles down the US coast to stomp New York, before going out in a blaze of glory at Coney Island funfair (thereby starting a stampede of similar monsters, including Godzilla). Quite what Jean Renoir made of his regular art director's switch to monster-movie auteur (*The Colossus of New York*, *The Giant Behemoth* and *Gorgo* followed) isn't recorded, but Lourié was merely one of a long line of designers to turn sci-fi director, alongside the likes of Harry Horner (*Red Planet Mars*), William Juran (*Attack of the 50 Foot Woman*), and William Cameron Menzies (*Invaders from Mars*). PT

Beast in the Cellar, The (aka Are You Dying, Young Man?)

(James Kelly, 1970, GB) Beryl Reid, Flora Robson, Tessa Wyatt, John Hamill, TP McKenna.
101 min.
Weird sisters in rural England with something in the cellar and lots of friendly army officers popping by to see that they're OK as murder spreads. Familiar stuff with the addition of a bit of nastiness and gore; very average.

Beastmaster, The

(Don Coscarelli, 1982, US) Marc Singer, Tanya Roberts, Rip Torn, John Amos, Josh Milrad.
118 min.
Rehash of *Conan the Barbarian*, with another hunk-of-the-month in a leather thong, a crisp smile, and a Buck's Fizz haircut. He also has a posse of animal friends to highlight his exis-

tential aloneness: a panther is his strength, an eagle his eyes, and two possums to handle the rest. Sorcery, ham, various hordes and polystyrene sets stalk the land (looks like Apache country), with the routine of swordfights, narrow escapes and ancient prophecies occasionally enlivened by flashes of sicko – a living eyeball ring, fluorescent blood – from the director who brought you the disgusting horror *Phantasm*. RP

Beast Must Die, The

(Paul Annett, 1974, GB) Calvin Lockhart, Peter Cushing, Charles Gray, Anton Diffring, Marlene Clark.
93 min.
The Amicus studio is better known for omnibus horror films like *Torture Garden* and *Tales from the Crypt*, and this flaccid feature suggests they would have done better to stick to that winning formula. Rich eccentric Lockhart invites a group of guests to his country mansion to discover which of them is a werewolf: a standard country house-mystery, in fact, with werewolf substituted for murderer. Worse still, the film employs an awkward device whereby the audience is also invited to wade through the shoals of red herrings to guess the werewolf's identity for themselves. NF

Beast of War, The

see Beast, The

Beast With Five Fingers, The

(Robert Florey, 1946, US) Peter Lorre, Victor Francen, Robert Alda, Andrea King, J Carrol Naish, Charles Dingle.
88 min. b/w.
Effective supernatural thriller in which a famous pianist (Francen) who has suffered a stroke ekes out his last days in an Italian Gothic mansion, surrounded by grasping relatives. When he finally dies, leaving his fortune to a young niece, the other relatives are well pissed off; so too is secretary Lorre, who wanted not only the old man's loot but also access to his library of books on the occult. Then the dead man's severed hand starts tinkling the ivories, dislodging books, and crawling around the terrified Lorre. The fudged ending imposed by the studio deflates much of the mystery, but the animated hand, creepy piano music, and Lorre's eye-popping performance are all memorable. Fans of Sam Raimi's *Evil Dead II* will note the derivation of that film's hilarious disembodied hand sequence. NF

Beat Girl (aka Wild for Kicks)

(Edmond T Gréville, 1960, GB) Gillian Hills, David Farrar, Noelle Adam, Christopher Lee, Adam Faith, Shirley Anne Field.
85 min. b/w.
Hills is the resentful teenager, daughter of a middle class father remarried to a gorgeous 'woman with a past', who decides to rebel by playing jukebox records and mixing with Beatniks. Fascinating partly for the sheer prurience of its content and for Adam Faith's first film appearance.

Beat Street

(Stan Lathan, 1984, US) Rae Dawn Chong, Guy Davis, Jon Chardiet, Leon W Grant, Saundra Santiago.
106 min.
The Bopsical breaks not-so-new ground in this, a hip-hop hupdate of *Saturday Night Fever* which trades Brooklyn for the Bronx and mixes its ethnics, but otherwise revolves in the same old grooves. The story is a load of old cobblers and the gushy grand finale tries in vain to spin some deep sociological significance from the phenomena of breaking, rapping and burning, but there are zesty musical interludes with the traditional street rumble ousted by tribal war dancing. AB.

Beat the Devil

(John Huston, 1954, US) Humphrey Bogart, Jennifer Jones, Gina Lollobrigida, Robert Morley, Peter Lorre, Ivor Barnard.
100 min. b/w.
In this offbeat spoof of *Maltese Falcon* - type thrillers, an ill-assorted group of travellers are en route to the African coast, where they each plan to stake a claim to a plot of uranium-rich

land. Truman Capote's absurdly talky script is stuffed with in-jokes and bizarre characters, but is seldom as clever as it thinks it is. Despite slack plotting and a complete lack of suspense, the film has achieved an undeserved cult status. NF

Beau Geste
(William A Wellman, 1939, US) Gary Cooper, Ray Milland, Robert Preston, Brian Donlevy, J Carrol Naish, Susan Hayward, Heather Thatcher, Albert Dekker, Broderick Crawford.
120 min. b/w.
The finest of three screen versions of PC Wren's tale of heroism in the French Foreign Legion (the others were made in 1926 and 1966, the latter a travesty). Pictorially ravishing, it features a memorable opening with a fort garrisoned by corpses, and the high adventure tone carries on from there. Cooper is suitably strong in his usual taciturn and gentle way as 'Beau', eldest of the three brothers who join the Legion to cover the mysterious 'theft' of a valuable jewel, but it is really Donlevy who leaves the most lasting impression as the sadistic Legion sergeant. Boys' Own stuff, maybe, but fun. GA

Beau James
(Melville Shavelson, 1957, US) Bob Hope, Vera Miles, Paul Douglas, Alexis Smith, Darren McGavin.
105 min.
Lightly likeable but awkward attempt by Hope to sustain a more dramatic role than usual in a romanticised biopic of Jimmy Walker, the not altogether honest mayor of New York during the roaring '20s. Good period atmosphere and a few charming guest appearances from Jimmy Durante, Jack Benny and others, but it's all very slight. GA

Beaumarchais
(Beaumarchais l'insolent)
(Edouard Molinaro, 1996, Fr) Fabrice Luchini, Manuel Blanc, Sandrine Kiberlain, Michel Serrault, Jacques Weber, Michel Piccoli, Jean-Claude Brialy, Murray Head, Dominique Besnehard.
100 min.
None too subtle in borrowing the boisterous but lyrical mood and certain dramatic elements from both Les Enfants du Paradis and Cyrano de Bergerac, this costume romp soons runs out of steam. It starts, in 1770s Paris, with the playwright Beaumarchais taking on a young friend of Voltaire as his secretary and, it transpires, his conscience. The bustling crowds, the lively word play, the solid camerawork and designs, and the overall theatricality bode well. As the episodic narrative proceeds, however, outlining the insolent hero's multifarious talents (scourge of the nobility and champion of the people; unrepentant womaniser; arms dealer, spy, supporter of American independence; dramaturgical iconoclast), the film meanders and rapidly becomes a series of decorous, undifferentiated historical tableaux inhabited by venerables of the French acting world. That said, Luchini gives Beaumarchais an exquisite, mellifluous air of arrogance and irony, notably offset by Sandrine Kiberlain as his devout wife. GA

Beau Mariage, Le
(A Good Marriage)
(Eric Rohmer, 1981, Fr) Béatrice Romand, André Dussollier, Arielle Dombasle, Huguette Faget, Thamila Mezbah.
97 min.
The second in Rohmer's series of 'Comedies and Proverbs' tells the cautionary tale of a girl who impulsively decides to marry, picks out a suitable mate in the conviction that he finds her equally eligible, and then suffers agonies of humiliation when she discovers that he does not. Funny, touching and beautifully acted, it is acutely exact both psychologically and socially, not least in the way the troubled heroine shuttles between the busy highways of Paris and the ancient cobbled streets of Le Mans, with the different settings ironically reflecting the paradox that this paragon of women's lib chooses to see liberation as allowing her to live like a Victorian lady of leisure. TM.

Beau-père
see Stepfather

Beau Serge, Le
(Claude Chabrol, 1958, FR) Gérard Blain, Jean-Claude Brialy, Michèle Meritz, Bernadette Lafone, Jeanne Perez, Claude Cerval.
97 min. b/w.
Chabrol's first film – one of the first manifestations of the Nouvelle Vague – is about a young student (Brialy) who returns to his native village to convalesce from an illness, finds that his childhood friend and hero (Blain) has become a hopeless drunk, and attempts to reclaim him at the cost of his own health. As mirror images of each other, the two men reflect the interest in Hitchcockian themes of transference later elaborated in Chabrol's work, but here expressed rather too overtly in terms of Christian allegory (a transference not so much of guilt as of redemption). Shot entirely on location in the village of Sardent (where Chabrol spent much of his childhood), it presents a bleak, beautifully observed picture of provincial life, later revisited to even more stunning effect in Le Boucher. TM

Beauté du Diable, La
(Beauty and the Devil)
(René Clair, 1949, Fr/It) Michel Simon, Gérard Philippe, Nicole Besnard, Simone Valère, Carlo Ninchi, Paolo Stoppa, Raymond Cordy.
96 min. b/w.
In spite/because of what must have seemed impeccable credentials – Clair, the two leads, a screenplay by the dramatist Armand Salacrou, and nostalgic, Méliès-inspired sets by Barsacq – this version of the Faust legend is a turgidly literary cocktail of escapist fantasy and Sartrean engagement, which could not even plead the excuse of Carné's comparable Les Visiteurs du Soir of having been filmed during the Occupation. GAd

Beauté Volée
see Stealing Beauty

Beauties of the Night
see Belles de nuit, Les

Beautiful Blonde from Bashful Bend, The
(Preston Sturges, 1949, US) Betty Grable, Rudy Vallee, Cesar Romero, Olga San Juan, Sterling Holloway, Hugh Herbert, El Brendel.
77 min.
Fast-moving and witty spoof of Western conventions from one of Hollywood's finest writer/directors of comedy. Grable is the crackshot chanteuse hiding from the law as a schoolmarm (after accidentally shooting a judge in the rear when two-timed by her lover Romero) and getting involved in the numerous shootouts between the local townsmen. It relies a little too much on zany slapstick, but the dialogue is sharp and the Technicolor photography by Harry Jackson adds a pleasant gloss. GA

Beautiful Dreamers
(John Harrison, 1990, Can) Colm Feore, Rip Torn, Wendel Meldrum, Sheila McCarthy, Colin Fox, David Gardner, Marsha Moreau, Tom McCamus.
108 min.
In 1880, progressive doctor Maurice Bucke invited American poet Walt Whitman to London, Ontario, where he was superintendent of the mental asylum. Whitman, whose brother was mentally ill, was a source of spiritual enlightenment for the doctor: they formed a lifelong friendship, and Bucke eventually went on to write the poet's biography. Writer-director Harrison uses these facts to develop a tale primarily of emotional rediscovery and sexual awakening. Bucke (Feore) finds his strait-laced wife (Meldrum) antagonistic to Whitman, until she too throws convention aside and goes skinny-dipping with the guys. Where the film drags is in its earnest attempt to convey the doctor's euphoric response to Whitman's message: applying the tone of Bucke's writings to the screen doesn't always make for credible exchanges. More involving are the scenes within the asylum which indicate the value of compassionate treatment, and Torn's glorious performance as Whitman. CM

Beautiful Girls
(Ted Demme, 1996, US) Timothy Hutton, Michael Rapaport, Matt Dillon, Noah

Emmerich, Annabeth Gish, Lauren Holly, Uma Thurman, Mira Sorvino, Natalie Portman, Martha Plimpton, Rosie O'Donnell, Max Perlich.
113 min.
A bunch of guys share beer and bewilderment over the course of a wintry reunion weekend. They talk sports and missed chances, but it's women they obsess about: the ones that got away, and the ones that won't let them get away with a thing. Willie (Hutton) is back home alone, contemplating marriage like it's a slow death sentence. His buddies Birdman (Dillon), Paul (Rapaport) and Kev (Perlich) aren't much help: they're hopelessly stuck on the beauty myth. And then he meets this amazing woman (Portman) – too bad she's just 13. With this cast, the title's no misnomer, but the point of view basically belongs to the unreconstructed male. Women may be unimpressed, but men will squirm with recognition. The sensibility's very Diner, and rather smart-alecky, but this is a picture worth listening to. You don't have to check your brain at the box-office, just your PC sensibilities. TCh

Beautiful Mystery – Legend of Big Horn (Utsukushiki Nazo: Kyokon Densetsu)
(Genji Nakamura, 1983, Jap) Nagamoto Tatuya, Shiyuto Kei, Yamashina Kaoru, Osugi Ren.
60 min.
Scripted by Rokuro Mochizuki, Nakamura's film dramatises the gay bar legends about Yukio Mishima and his private army. Aspiring muscle queen Shinohara is recruited into the 'militia' run by famous writer/demagogue Mitani and whisked off to boot camp, where his roommate buggers him at the first opportunity. He soon overcomes his prim objections and relaxes into the gruelling regimen of gay orgies – only to oversleep and and miss his leader's attempted coup d'état. This ribald, highly entertaining film was Japan's first gay exploitation feature. Amazing that it was made at a time when discussion of Mishima's sexuality was a virtual taboo in Japan. TR

Beautiful People
(Jamie Uys, 1974, SAf)
93 min.
Abysmally anthropomorphic wild-life documentary which persists in lumbering its poor subjects with the attributes of people ('The jackal is a slob', etc).

Beautiful Thing
(Hettie MacDonald, 1995, GB) Glen Berry, Linda Henry, Scott Neal, Tameka Empson, Ben Daniels, Meera Syal.
91 min.
A real winner this, from producer Tony Garnett and Channel 4: an 'urban fairytale' set in darkest Thamesmead, South London. Jamie (Berry) is in love with next-door neighbour Ste (Neal), but he's terrified his mum will find out, and Ste has plenty of troubles of his own. It may sound like a feelgood movie, but throw in the timeless tunes of Mama Cass, a funny romantic screenplay by Jonathan Harvey (skillfully adapting his own play), and a formidable performance from Linda Henry as Jamie's independent-minded mother, and you have the likeliest gay crossover hit since My Beautiful Laundrette. TCh

Beauty and the Beast
see Belle et la Bête, La.

Beauty and the Beast
(Fielder Cook, 1976, US) George C Scott, Trish Van Devere, Virginia McKenna, Bernard Lee, Michael Harbour.
91 min.
Made for TV but theatrically released, this retelling of the Perrault fairytale falls flat on its face by comparison with Cocteau's marvellous La Belle et la Bête. Cook introduces us to the Beast's castle by way of a distorting lens that promptly robs it of any magic whatsoever; its interiors remind one of nothing so much as a slightly seedy stately home in which things have a tiresome habit of appearing and disappearing. Even more dispiritingly, Scott's Beast, turned into a snouty pig with tusks and a waistline to match, has been robbed of the heady eroticism Jean Marais brought to the part. Small wonder that Belle (Van

Devere), behaving like a callow coed with a beady eye for the material benefits provided by magic, keeps inventing little games of hide-and-seek and suchlike to keep her suitor occupied. TM

Beauty and the Beast

(Gary Trousdale/Kirk Wise, 1991, US) voices: Paige O'Hara, Robby Benson, Richard White, Jerry Orbach, David Ogden Stiers, Angela Lansbury.
84 min.
Disney animation enters the '90s, embraces the stunning technical advances of computer-generated imagery, and updates the traditional dependent heroine. Belle, besides representing a move away from the usual Barbie Doll looks, is resourceful, bookish, and vigorous in resisting the chauvinist advances of Gaston, the character who turns out to bear the true mark of the beast. Gaston was based on LA's Medallion Man narcissists, and is well and truly lampooned in the barroom waltz. Beast, based on a menagerie of brooding buffalo, bear, boar and gorilla, learns to master his temper, and his growing relationship with Belle is infinitely touching. His bewitched castle is enlivened by an antic household including a candelabra with the panache of a French maître d', a neurotic clock, and a mother-and-son teapot and cup. The six musical numbers either reveal character or push the action, with 'Be Our Guest' an outstanding example of cartoon choreography. Dazzlingly good. BC

Beauty and the Devil
see Beauté du Diable, La.

Beauty Jungle, The

(Val Guest, 1964, GB) Ian Hendry, Janette Scott, Ronald Fraser, Edmund Purdom, Jean Claudio, Kay Walsh, Norman Bird, Tommy Trinder.
114 min.
Typist Janette Scott signs up for a beauty contest and before long she's wearing the 'Miss Globe' crown and sash in this vapid would-be exposé. The path to the gutter is, however, as swift as it is predictable. Shot in 'Scope with guest appearances by, among others, Sid James, Sterling Moss and the Duchess of Bedford. TJ

Beavis and Butt-head Do America

(Mike Judge, 1996, US) voices: Mike Judge, Robert Stack, Cloris Leachman, Eric Bogosian, Bruce Willis, Demi Moore.
81 min.
Beavis and Butt-head are the no-brain buddies who laugh like worried sheep and move as gracefully as ironing boards. From their rightful place – in front of the TV and on it – the sedentary duo have been forced on to the celluloid highway. The point is, barring the loss of the naff music videos, nothing much about Mike Judge's creation has changed. Under the happy delusion that someone will pay them to have sex with a beautiful chick, the pair get caught up in an international spy ring, with all roads leading to the White House and much classic American scenery studiously ignored in favour of obsessive word play. This can pall after a while, yet what holds the interest is the attention to character, with B&B the latest incarnation of the Odd Couple. Beavis can't handle caffeine and hates the idea of flying. He's a '90s icon, but a jibbering fit on a plane highlights his acute discomfort with modernity. The pair are also all at sea in pioneer country. In the film's finest moment, when the boys meet up with their roadie fathers in the desert, the cry from the heart is: 'We need a 7-Eleven!' Without a TV, they have no rightful place and only mind-altering substances can restore equilibrium. With most mainstream US movies rabidly anti-drugs, this is a strikingly contrary message, rammed home by a splendid Butthole Surfers' song, which even the sober happy-clappy ending can't erase. CO'Su

Because of That War (Biglal Hamilkhama Hahi)

(Orna Ben-Dor Niv, 1988, Isr) Yehuda Poliker, Jacko Poliker, Yaakov Gilad, Halina Gilad.
90 min.
An affecting 'talking heads' documentary which traces the stories of four Israelies: Yehuda Poliker and Yaakov Gilad, two rock musicians bound together not only by their music, but also by their common experience as the offspring of survivors of the Nazi extermination camps; and those survivors themselves – Yehuda's father Jacko (from Salonika, taken to Treblinka), and Yaakov's mother Halina (from Warsaw, taken to Auschwitz as a teenager). The film is punctuated by renderings of songs, both live and studio performances, which reflect the traumas of dealing with the aftermath of the Holocaust, and some of which use the work of Halina, a writer and poet. It is a thoughtful and thought-provoking film which, despite the harrowing sequences (Jacko breaking down recalling the death of one of his brothers – his whole family was wiped out; Halina describing, in a lengthy sentence with a group of students, her experience of the camps and the 'death march') maintains a considerable control, which allows space for difficulties and ambivalences to be expressed without losing sympathy for its witnesses. As much is said here on what it means to live so continuously and intimately with death, loss and guilt, as is understood, unspoken, about the need for love. WH

Beck

(Jacob Bijl, 1992, Neth/Bel) Jan Decleir, Els Dottermans, Warre Borgmans, Jakob Beks.
100 min.
When chief inspector Beck returns to work upon recovery from a shooting incident, he is asked to look into the case of an apparent suicide; colleagues, meanwhile, are investigating a series of robberies. But both cases merge when single mother Monita is asked to act as a courier for an unscrupulous photographer... This modest, competent thriller works effectively as a police procedural; but more interestingly, with studious detachment, it explores how far chance determines one's destiny. CM

Becky Sharp

(Rouben Mamoulian, 1935, US) Miriam Hopkins, Cedric Hardwicke, Nigel Bruce, Frances Dee, Alan Mowbray, GP Huntley Jr, Billie Burke.
84 min.
So much has been made of the fact that this was the first feature to be shot in three-strip Technicolor that it's often forgotten just how marvellous a film it actually is. A sophisticated, witty, and beautifully economical adaptation of Thackeray's Vanity Fair as it charts its cunning heroine's meteoric rise in society, it rightly and explicitly treats her entirely amoral manipulation of sympathetic women and besotted men as an on-going performance of immense versatility. But the colour is supremely important, in that Mamoulian uses costume, decor and lighting to precise symbolic effect, most memorably, perhaps, in the famous ballroom sequence on the eve of Waterloo when, as battle is announced, the pastel gowns are suddenly replaced by the crimson cloaks of soldiers rushing to war. Its enormously funny script might nevertheless seem precious, even stilted, were it not for the excellence of the performances, of which Miriam Hopkins' Becky is merely the most dazzling. GA

Bed and Board
see Domicile Conjugal.

Bedazzled

(Stanley Donen, 1967, GB) Peter Cook, Dudley Moore, Eleanor Bron, Michael Bates, Raquel Welch.
103 min.
Pete and Dud's update of the Faust legend is a hit-and-myth affair in which diminutive cook Dud, finding his love for waitress Eleanor Bron unrequited, attempts suicide and is offered seven wishes in return for his soul by the devilish Pete. Good fun sometimes but a little too sketchy, with a plot that is almost as threadbare as the outfit worn by the voluptuous Raquel Welch in her cameo role as one of the Seven Deadly Sins – need one add which?

Bedevil

(Tracey Moffatt, 1993, Aust) Lex Marinos, Tracey Moffatt, Diana Davidson, Jack Charles.
90 min.
The brash '60s-style credits are promising, but what follows doesn't live up to the expectations raised by Moffatt's shorts. This trilogy of vaguely supernatural tales may look striking – it was shot, very noticeably, in the studio, for control of colour and camera movement – but the 'elliptical' stories remain bafflingly obscure. To put it kindly: pretentious as hell. GA

Bedford Incident, The

(James B Harris, 1965, GB) Richard Widmark, Sidney Poitier, James MacArthur, Eric Portman, Martin Balsam, Wally Cox, Phil Brown, Donald Sutherland.
102 min. b/w.
Harris, Stanley Kubrick's former producer, here came up with his own Dr Strangelove variant, muting the black humour but just as incisively diagnosing nuclear insanity, as Widmark's super-patriot warship captain hunts a Soviet sub in Arctic waters, justifying his brinkmanship to Poitier's junketing journalist (along to do a story) and a sorely tried crew. PT

Bedknobs and Broomsticks

(Robert Stevenson, 1971, US) Angela Lansbury, David Tomlinson, Roddy McDowall, Sam Jaffe, Cindy O'Callaghan, Roy Smart.
117 min.
Disney comedy about an apprentice witch in good old cutesy-pie England, helped by three kids in making a contribution to the war effort. Never boring, and has a well-animated soccer match with animals. Must all films for kids be so shoddy, though? The music is appalling.

Bedlam

(Mark Robson, 1946, US) Boris Karloff, Anna Lee, Billy House, Richard Fraser, Glenn Vernon, Ian Wolfe, Jason Robards Sr.
79 min. b/w.
Even Val Lewton's staunchest fans don't claim Bedlam as one of his most successful productions, but its tale of the celebrated 18th century madhouse is both intelligently written and admirably acted. Its major pretension is also its greatest weakness: the design is scrupulously modelled on Hogarth prints, and the aestheticism finally swamps most of the gusto in the plot. Robson's notably unpoetic direction doesn't help, either; yet few Hollywood films ever had such ambition. TR

Bed of Roses

(Michael Goldenberg, 1996, US) Christian Slater, Mary Stuart Masterson, Pamela Segall, Josh Brolin, Brian Tarantina.
88 min.
Lisa (Masterson), an industrious New York investment banker, learns in quick succession of the deaths of her father Stanley and goldfish Melville. Next day she receives a lavish bouquet via deliveryman Lewis (Slater). Despite her best efforts, the sender's identity remains a mystery, until she wakes up one night to see Lewis staring longingly at her apartment window. It's a modestly engaging set-up, but once love has blossomed, what's to keep our attention? There's a well-signposted consideration of the discrepancies betwixt fantasy and reality, more talked about than enacted. As for the basic story-line, the characters are too anodyne to keep us involved in their repetitive cycle of break-ups and reconciliations; Slater especially, in the more passive role, is almost terminally nice. Humdrum. NB

Bedroom Window, The

(Curtis Hanson, 1987, US) Elizabeth McGovern, Steve Guttenberg, Isabelle Huppert, Paul Shenar, Carl Lumbly, Wallace Shawn, Brad Greenquist.
113 min.
Terry Lambert (Guttenberg) is not a bright man. Having just bonked his boss' wife Sylvia (Huppert), he gets up to take a leak. While he is in the bathroom, the rich bitch witnesses an assault on a young woman (McGovern) from the bedroom window, and scares the attacker off. The next day, the corpse of a woman is found in a dumpster a few blocks away. Because Terry wants to do the right thing, and his affair with Sylvia must remain secret, he tells the cops that he saw the attack. So when the accused is released due to lack of evidence, the boys in blue start leaning on Terry...Writer/director Hanson has created a plausible thriller with several neat twists; but the last half-hour, while never quite losing its grip, degenerates into pure flapdoodle, with McGovern coming to the rescue by using herself as bait to trap the real sicko. MS

Bed Sitting Room, The

(Richard Lester, 1969, GB) Ralph Richardson, Rita Tushingham, Michael Hordern, Arthur Lowe, Mona Washbourne, Peter Cook, Dudley Moore, Spike Milligan.
91 min.
Surreal after-the-bomb comedy (adapted from the play by Spike Milligan and John Antrobus) that suffers from being too hit-and-miss, despite flashes of brilliance and some dazzling photography. However, if time as we know it will cease after the bomb, then the film offers an adequate representation of temporal dislocation: its non-plot frequently makes the 91 minutes seem interminable. CPe

Bee Keeper, The
(O Melissokomos)

(Theodore Angelopoulos, 1986, Greece/Fr) Marcello Mastroianni, Nadia Mourouzi, Serge Reggiani, Jenny Roussea.
122 min.
Angelopoulos' odyssey of a middle-aged man in the grip of terminal emptiness has a stately pace and a shortage of event or information that are a lot to take. It's always raining, usually evening, and the settings are mainly petrol stations and sad rooming houses in Greek tank towns. Spyros (Mastroianni) resigns his job as a schoolmaster, leaves his wife, and drives off with his beehives to follow the pollen route. A teenage hitchhiker (Mourouzi) attaches herself, bumming fags and food, and even using his room to score with a passing soldier. Spyros remains uncomplaining, wordless and lifeless throughout. They finally get it on in a neglected cinema, which not only fails to buck up his ideas, but appears to confirm his disenchantment, because the next day he surrenders to death by bee-sting. A muffled, deeply interior film. BC

Beethoven

(Brian Levant, 1992, US) Charles Grodin, Bonnie Hunt, Dean Jones, Nicholle Tom, Christopher Castille, Oliver Platt, Stanley Tucci, David Duchovny.
87 min.
Sounds horrible: a comedy about a big shaggy dog which wins the love of a suburban family by destroying their home. Things start out badly when baby Beethoven (a St Bernard so named for his musicality) piddles on a pet shop patron before the credits are finished. Mercifully, the excrement gags are soon exhausted and things take a turn for the better, thanks largely to the sublimely sour-faced antics of Charles Grodin as dad, a neurotic dog-hater who markets air-fresheners for a living. Elevated from the doldrums of Digby-esque sentimentality by a surprisingly bouncy script, the film is also redeemed by regular interludes of acerbic dialogue and a brace of fine supporting performances (notably David Duchovny as a slimy yuppie git who says 'Ciao, bello!' and criticises the cappuccino). MK

Beethoven's 2nd

(Rod Daniel, 1993, US) Charles Grodin, Bonnie Hunt, Debi Mazar, Nicholle Tom, Christopher Castile, Sarah Rose Karr, Jeff Corey, Beethoven.
89 min.
Daniel's hit Beethoven sequel builds on the high slobber and house-destruct factor of the earlier film by adding aahhh! appeal in the shape of four puppies. The soulful St Bernard – now secure in the household of persuadable grump Grodin and supermum Hunt – finds a pedigree chum in Sissy, owned by evil stack-heeled Mazar. The plot follows the dogs' romance, passes discreetly over the sex, and has Grodin's three brats engaging in benign subterfuge, hiding the fruits of the union from daddy in the basement cupboard. Then the evil stack-heeled one wants Sissy back in some palaver over an emotional tug-of-love divorce settlement. Then she wants to sell the offspring for profit! Then...It's a shaggy-dog story, targeted at children and the softer cinemagoer, but amiable enough not to offend the hard-boiled. WH

Beetlejuice

(Tim Burton, 1988, US) Michael Keaton, Alec Baldwin, Geena Davis, Jeffrey Jones, Winona Ryder, Catherine O'Hara, Glenn Shadix, Sylvia Sidney, Annie McEnroe.
92 min.
This ghost story from the haunters' perspective (co-scripted by Michael McDowell) provides some of the most surprisingly enjoyable viewing in years. The drearily happy Maitlands (Baldwin and Davis) drive into the river, come up dead, and return to their beloved, quaint house as spooks intent on despatching the hideous New York yuppie family which had usurped their property. The humour unfolds as the horrible Deetzes (Jones and O'Hara) fill the house with revolting avant-garde art, bulldozers, and camp interior designers spitting venom; while only their mournful teenage daughter (Ryder) seems either aware of or in tune with the ghostly couple, whose failure to shine in the scare stakes finally drags them into the arms of the gunslinger-exorcist Betelgeuse (Keaton), a kind of OTT demonic Clint Eastwood of the underworld (who rids houses of unwanted humans). Off-the wall humour and some sensational sight gags make the movie, maddeningly disjointed though it sometimes is, a truly astonishing piece of work. SGr

Before and After

(Barbet Schroeder, 1996, US) Meryl Streep, Liam Neeson, Edward Furlong, Julia Weldon, Alfred Molina, Daniel von Bargen, John Heard, Larry Pine, Wesley Addy.
108 min.
A director who still thinks like a producer, Barbet Schroeder has a way of making decent, intelligent, rather boring films (Reversal of Fortune, Kiss of Death), but this is simply more mediocre than most: a fraught family drama which never really hits home. When a local teenager turns up dead, Ben and Carolyn Ryan (Neeson and Streep) have no inkling that their lives will be affected. Even when son Jacob (Furlong) runs off, Carolyn can't believe he's done anything wrong; but a police inquiry soon persuades Ben otherwise, and he angrily destroys incriminating evidence, a course of adamant non-cooperation which horrifies his wife and daughter. Plenty of dramatic meat here, but the talky screenplay by Ted (Silence of the Lambs) Tally, from the book by Rosellen Brown, soon forgoes any semblance of suspense in favour of supposedly subtle character study and a thorny ethical conundrum: what price truth when your own flesh and blood faces life behind bars? While the script pays brief lip service to class questions, the movie runs away from guilt as surely as young Jacob. Streep has virtually nothing to play with, while Neeson's bullish chauvinism is indulged right up to a phoney prison-scene showdown. It's not a stupid film, exactly, but badly made, stagnant, humourless, and sorely lacking in authentic human behaviour. TCh

Before and After Sex
(Prima e Dopo l'Amore ...
Un Grido d'Allarme)

(Giovanni Crisci, 1972, It) Farid Bendali, Franco Jamonte, Leonora Vivaldi, Richard Melville.
91 min.
Unappetising and repressive film that presumably attempts to act as a Trojan horse by infiltrating a dire warning about syphilis through the medium of a sexploitation piece. It fails primarily through doing nothing to explain the disease in rational, helpful terms, and everything to play on panic and mystification. VG

Before Dawn

(Irving Pichel, 1933, US) Stuart Erwin, Warner Oland, Dorothy Wilson, Dudley Digges, Jane Darwell.
60 min. b/w.
RKO cheapie based on Edgar Wallace's Death Watch, with Wilson as the pretty spiritualist involved in the unmasking of a murderer. Set in an old dark house where loot lies hidden, it's watchable (with a nicely sinister performance from Oland), but pretty routine when one recalls that Pichel made The Most Dangerous Game a year earlier. TM

Before Dawn (Di Ba Zhan)

(Clarence Ford, i.e. Fok Yiu-Leung, 1983, HK) Deannie Ip, Lau Dan, Loletta Lee, Ku Feng, Wong Sue-Kei, Leung Saan.
88 min.
Ah Po, aged 17, has been spoiled all his life by his mother, a nightclub dancer dumped by his father and a succession of other men. He considers himself straight but one night's service as a rent boy

leaves him implicated in a series of murders of gay men – which are actually being carried out by the bent cop who is charged with investigating them. Fok's hysterical, barely coherent melodrama throws in everything from kitchen sink realism to forced-sodomy fantasies with fluttering doves but centres on the chasm between adults and kids. It had the distinction of being the first Hong Kong feature to imagine a gay subculture and broach the possibility of its protagonist's sexual ambivalence. No 'positive images', but it was a cult favourite in underground gay circles in the unliberated '80s. TR

Before Hindsight

(Jonathan Lewis, 1977, GB) James Cameron, Edgar Anstey, George Elvin, Leslie Mitchell, Ivor Montagu, Jonathan Dimbleby.
78 min. b/w & col.
Newsreels from the '30s constitute the bulk of this fascinating documentary, clearly illustrating that the public was fed an extremely biased view of events: straight propaganda, the stricture to provide entertainment, and the attempt to be objective all contributing to this. Lewis and producer Elizabeth Taylor-Mead have constructed their argument well, but it is Jonathan Dimbleby's brief comments towards the end that contain the crucial lesson: forty years on, the same forces work to distort our view of Northern Ireland. The film only indicates this to be the case, but it is precise and coherent enough to make the point with considerable force. JW

Before I Hang

(Nick Grinde, 1940, US) Boris Karloff, Evelyn Keyes, Bruce Bennett, Edward Van Sloan, Pedro de Cordoba.
71 min. b/w.
Karloff brings his usual injection of class to this middling B-pic about a scientist working in the field of rejuvenation through blood plasma treatment, which comes in handy when he's sentenced to death for a mercy killing and is able to rejuvenate himself behind bars to escape the sentence. The catch is, of course, that he's had to use the blood of a convicted murderer – definitely not a good idea, as any genre buff knows. TJ

Before Stonewall

(Greta Schiller/Robert Rosenberg, 1984, US)
87 min. b/w & col.
Films like Word Is Out and The Times of Harvey Milk have done valuable lesbian and gay archaeology, but none so well as this documentary. Mixing present-day footage with older material mined from Hollywood newsreel and home movie, it achieves a near-perfect balance between historical and political perspectives, and sometimes unconsciously hilarious archive footage. Its politics are sensible, the life stories touching, warm and funny, and the archive stuff camper than Butlin's empire. JG

Before Sunrise

(Richard Linklater, 1995, US) Ethan Hawke, Julie Delpy, Andrea Eckert, Hanno Pöschl.
101 min.
Céline (Delpy), an easy-going Parisian, is on her way back from Budapest to study at the Sorbonne; Jesse (Hawke), a young American, is at the end of a Eurorail tour. They meet on a train just outside Vienna; by the time they reach the station, they've hit it off well enough for Jesse to propose that Céline spend the next 14 hours wandering the city with him, until his flight leaves for the States. Intrigued, she accepts. So begins an unexpected adventure of the heart. What's magical about Linklater's entrancing movie is the way he and his actors manage to convey the emotional truths that underlie all the talk as the potential lovers test each other's opinions and commitment. Funny, poignant and perceptive, this is a brilliant gem. GA

Before the Nickelodeon:
The Early Cinema of
Edwin S Porter

(Charles Musser, 1982, US)
60 min. b/w & col.
Edwin S Porter's contribution to the history of the movies is enormous. At a time when most filmmakers were content with crude one-take shorts of straightforward dramatic design, Porter was already experimenting with editing his stories to include different points of view and various trick

special effects which he may have learned from Méliès. His Western *The Great Train Robbery* (1902) set the stamp on what was to become Hollywood's greatest genre, and was the most popular film until *The Birth of a Nation* (1915), directed by DW Griffith, an actor who was given his first movie break by Porter.Musser's enchanting piece of movie archaeology traces the life of this key figure, with plenty of clips from his greatest hits, a commentary from Blanche Sweet (the Griffith star), and just the right note of amused genuflection to a master. Also included, complete, are four of Porter's short films. CPea

Before the Rain (Pred Dozdot)

(Milcho Manchevski, 1994, Macedonia/GB/Fr) Rade Serbedzija, Katrin Cartlidge, Grégoire Colin, Labina Mitevska, Jay Villiers, Phyllida Law.
113 min.
A solemn triptych that transports us from the ethnic tensions of Macedonia to the urban strife of London, and back again. In 'Words', we see a monk break his vow of silence to shelter an Albanian girl from a lynch mob; in 'Faces', Anne (Cartlidge), an English picture-editor, refuses to accompany her photographer lover Aleksandar (Serbedzija) to the village where he grew up, and tells her estranged husband that she's pregnant; while in part three, 'Pictures', Aleksandar returns home for the first time in 20 years, and struggles to make sense of the madness infesting his country. As a director, Manchevski is still finding his feet. The tragic portents of the first story are heavily signalled, and the attempt to convey the rhythm of London life in nervy edits is unconvincing, but the boldness of the conception sees him through. Flawed, certainly, and a little infatuated with its own tragic aura, but a brave, compelling work which repays serious attention. TCh

Before the Revolution (Prima della Rivoluzione)

(Bernardo Bertolucci, 1964, It) Francesco Barilli, Adriana Asti, Allen Midgette, Morando Morandini, Domenico Alpi.
112 min. b/w.
In all of Bertolucci's movies, there's a central conflict between the 'radical' impulses and a pessimistic (and/or willing) capitulation to the mainstream of bourgeois society and culture. It's a contradiction that takes on juggernaut proportions in '1900', but it stands as a major source of tension and interest in many of the earlier films. Both *Before the Revolution* (Bertolucci's second feature) and *Partner* try to examine it head-on. *Revolution* is about a middle-class 20-year old who 'discovers' Marxism and tries – for a while – to change his life; *Partner* is an exuberant response to the student riots of '68, with Pierre Clémenti as a timid drama student confronting his own anarchic revolutionary alter ego. The first is mostly 'classical' in style, while the second is aggressively 'new wave', but both are full of interruptions and digressions: they throw out ideas and allusions (usually to other movies) with reckless enthusiasm, and they remain invaluable aids to an understanding of the '60s. TR

Before Winter Comes

(J Lee Thompson, 1968, GB) David Niven, Topol, Anna Karina, John Hurt, Ori Levy, Anthony Quayle, John Collin.
107 min.
Towards the end of WWII, Major Niven has the difficult task of deciding the fate of displaced persons: send them to the Free World, or to Russia? His job is made rather easier when co-star Topol arrives, a valued linguist who claims to be a Yugoslav refugee but is in fact a Russian deserter. Scripted by Andrew Sinclair from a short story by Frederick L Keefe, it's impeccably humanistic, unusually contrived and incredibly dull. It should have been a comedy or a musical. ATu

Beggars of Life

(William A Wellman, 1928, US) Louise Brooks, Richard Arlen, Wallace Beery, Edgar Washington.
7,504 ft. b/w.
If it weren't for two of its lead performances, this would be a simple period curiosity, one of Hollywood's first sympathetic portraits of life on the run from the police. A vagrant falls in with a young woman wanted for murder: the two of

them seek refuge with a group of hoboes, but find their own kind as hostile as the rest of society. Wellman sketches the hobo mentality with a fine economy, but cannot deliver the pace and suspense that the plot demands. Hence the importance of the players. Beery, entering with a pilfered beer-barrel on his shoulder, offers an extravagantly randy, bullying and sentimental performance as Oklahoma Red, leader of the hoboes. Despite his excellence, though, all eyes are on the 22-year-old Louise Brooks, who was about to leave for Germany to star in *Pandora's Box*. As the movie opens, she has just shot her adoptive father, who tried to rape her. She flees in boy's clothes, tough and vulnerable in equal proportions. The camera loves her, and she rewards it with a performance that radiates inner life. TR

Beggar's Opera, The

(Peter Brook, 1952, GB) Laurence Olivier, Dorothy Tutin, Stanley Holloway, Daphne Anderson, Hugh Griffith, Sandra Dorne, Yvonne Furneaux, George Devine, Laurence Naismith, Athene Seyler, George Rose, Kenneth Williams.
94 min.
A commercial disaster, Peter Brook's first movie has gradually grown in stature as more people have discovered its delights. John Gay's original concoction satirised the conventions of Italian opera and dumped them into Merrie England's morass of highwaymen, whores and hangmen. The movie, with the music adapted by Arthur Bliss, and the script adapted by Dennis Cannan and Christopher Fry, sets out to send up what was already partly a send-up; and Brook, of course, was the ideal director, committed to radical theatre and disrespectful (or innocent) of cinematic forms. He has trouble when dialogue gives way to song (though even here one might call this a Brechtian device, as in *The Threepenny Opera*), but gets performances from Olivier (as the swashbuckling MacHeath) and Tutin (as Polly Peachum) of such mellifluous exuberance that the cracks are neatly sealed. ATu

Begging the Ring

(Colin Gregg, 1978, GB) Danny Simpson, Jon Croft, Janette Legge, Kenneth Midwood.
55 min.
Typical attempt at social realism by the independent team of Gregg and writer Hugh Stoddart. An investigation of a family's dilemma when the 18-year-old son, trained by his ambitious father for the local wrestling championships, receives his call-up papers for WWI, its failure derives not only from the limitations of the realist, semi-documentary style (Gregg fails to tease out the knotty problems of enforced conscription clearly; but also from the difficulty of following some of the Cornish dialect; and, most noticeably, from the awkward insertion of an intellectual-outsider, commenting chorus-fashion with lines like 'We're all wrestling with the angel of darkness, lad'. GA

Beginning, The (Nachalo)

(Gleb Panfilov, 1970, USSR) Inna Churikova, Leonid Kuravlev, Valentin Telichkina, Yuri Klepikov.
90 min. b/w.
About a girl who works in a factory, spends her spare time acting in a local drama group, and is discovered by a film director looking for an unknown to play Joan of Arc in his next movie, *The Beginning* avoids all the clichés you'd expect from a plot like this, souping the whole thing up by interweaving segments from the 'Joan' film with sequences around the girl's life. This is Panfilov's second film, and he has obviously absorbed his fair share of Bergman, Bresson, Forman and Godard, but generally without allowing their influence to get in the way. The film also says something about the manufacturing of stereotypes. At the end the girl is unemployed, doing the agency rounds before going back to where she came from, while the camera lingers on an impossibly glamorous poster of her outside a cinema.

Beguiled, The

(Don Siegel, 1970, US) Clint Eastwood, Geraldine Page, Elizabeth Hartman, Jo Ann Harris, Darleen Carr, Mae Mercer.
109 min.
Combining the conventions of both Western and

Grand Guignol chiller, and often directed as if it were an art movie, this is one of Siegel and Eastwood's strangest – and most beguiling – collaborations. Eastwood is the Yankee soldier, who after being wounded during the Civil War, takes refuge in an isolated Southern seminary for young women. Shut away from the world, the women project their romantic fantasies onto him, and he responds with callous, male manipulation. But jealousy and resentment raise their heads, and he finds himself in a world of brutal revenge. Beautifully shot by Bruce Surtees, carefully paced, it's a haunting, elegant work that seems to have influenced the troubled sexuality of Eastwood's own *Play Misty for Me* and *Tightrope*. GA

Béguines, The

see Rempart des Béguines, Le

Behind Convent Walls (L'Interno di un Convento)

(Walerian Borowczyk, 1977, It) Ligia Branice, Marina Pierro, Gabriella Giaccobe, Loredana Martinez.
95 min.
Borowczyk has fetishised prostitution (*The Streetwalker*) and bestiality (*The Beast*), so turning out this pastiche of sex-movie staple (the convent as a sexual greenhouse) can't have been too challenging. The film's pace is too slow, and interest in detail overwhelms the narrative. But this waywardness allows some unusual inflexions: masturbation as a real centre of interest, Christ as a laughable sex-martyr. Ultimately the convent-as-haven is exploded: patriarchy intrudes to deliver punishment, and the tale ends (?) with the murder of the abbess and multiple suicide by the nuns. CA

Behindert

see Hindered

Behind the Iron Curtain

see Iron Curtain, The

Behind the Rent Strike

(Nicholas Broomfield, 1974, GB)
50 min.
Brilliant documentary attempt to understand the 14 months rent strike by the people of Kirkby New Town, near Liverpool, which started just before Christmas in 1973. An analysis of the social conditions is preceded by an interview between the film-maker and an extremely shrewd working-class housewife who debunks this and all other investigations by the media as just another form of bourgeois masturbation. This in itself makes a complacent viewing, which might normally act as an appeaser to liberal conscience, impossible. RM

Beijing Bastards (Beijing Zazhong)

(Zhang Yuan, 1993, HK/China) Cui Jian, Li Wei, Wu Lala.
95 min.
This is a film without precedent in Chinese cinema: a seemingly free-form portrait of rock-generation kids in the city, its own quest for a structure mirroring their search 'for something to help them live'. One broken relationship provides the overall frame (a young guy named Karzi searches for the pregnant girlfriend who has left him), but half a dozen other characters also clamour for the film's attention, chief among them Cui Jian, China's rock pioneer, who plays himself and contributes several songs. Zhang Yuan has an acute feel for street-level realities, and gets very close to these kids blowing their lives on drink, dope and petty squabbles. Not exactly a blank generation, but they sure do look lost. TR

Beim jodeln juckt die Lederhose

see There's No Sex Like Snow Sex

Being at Home with Claude

(Jean Beaudin, 1992, Can) Roy Dupuis, Jacques Godin, Jean-François Pichette, Gaston Lepage, Hugo Dubé.
85 min. b/w & col.
Adapted from René-Daniel Dubois' controversial stage hit, this is everything Gregg Araki's *The*

Living End was hyped up to be, but fell sorely short of. Queer criminality meets aching romanticism in a daring, moving illustration of Wilde's maxim 'each man kills the thing he loves'. Opening with an explosive sequence in which a man is literally fucked to death, the mystery of the film is not whodunit, but why. A hustler (Dupuis) confesses to the murder, but the law, in the shape of a nameless police inspector (Godin) requires a motive. What follows is an extended dialogue between a gay outlaw and the voice of a shocked society. The prospect of 85 minutes in the company of two characters enclosed in a single set might not sound like such a thrilling ride, but there's more drama to be found contained in these four walls than on the run through all Araki's wide-angle landscapes. The lead performances are superb, Beaudin's direction is tighter than a rent boy's vest, and if the opening scene doesn't leave you gasping, you're probably already dead. PBur

Being Human
(Bill Forsyth, 1994, US) Robin Williams, John Turturro, Anna Galiena, Vincent D'Onofrio, Hector Elizondo, Lizzy McInerny, Ewan McGregor; voice: Theresa Russell.
122 min.
Forsyth's most ambitious film disappeared after its disastrous US opening. Warners sat on it for a year, trying to figure out a recut which would make sense. They eventually gave the film back to the director who added Russell's voice-over narration as a sign of good faith. It's a difficult picture to get a handle on (five stories spanning 6,000 years): in each tale, Williams plays a human being (sic), Hector – a caveman, Roman slave, medieval traveller, 17th century aristocrat, and finally a contemporary New Yorker. The stories are low-key and deliberately anti-climactic, but they coalesce into a tender, contemplative whole that's profound and moving. While Hector may not be reincarnated, exactly, each story feeds on what has gone before, so that after losing his family in the Bronze Age, he's separated from them in every other tale. Other motifs recur: fear and anxiety, superstition and sacrifice; the nature of partnership, how men treat women (and other men) as chattels; the significance of water-crossings; the need and difficulty of filling other men's shoes; the abused integrity of a name. The studio was probably right: there is no general audience for this mid-life crisis of a movie, but it's singular and fascinating all the same. TCh

Being There
(Hal Ashby, 1979, US) Peter Sellers, Shirley MacLaine, Melvyn Douglas, Jack Warden, Richard Dysart, Richard Basehart.
130 min.
Sellers' performance – as the innocent neuter figure who rises accidentally to political power on the strength of vacant homilies – is remarkable. But Ashby's direction is marred by the same softness that made *The Last Detail* and *Coming Home* so morally bland. What emerges in the end is a strange ambiguity of attitude to the American political system and a hollow humour about cultural values. The cinema of cynicism, really. CA

Bel Ami
(Willi Forst, 1939, Ger) Willi Forst, Johannes Riemann, Olga Tschechowa, Lizzi Waldmüller, Hilde Hildebrandt.
102 min. b/w.
'Bubblier than champagne and lighter than the air of Paris' has been the verdict of French critics on the co-scenarist, director and star of *Bel Ami*. In the congenial role of Maupassant's irresistible womaniser, who uses his charm to get to the top, the Viennese Forst managed to resurrect the frivolous light-heartedness of a waltzing never-never land in the shape of turn-of-the-century Paris. A delightful parade of Germany's most forceful female stars as Bel Ami's victims(?), and satirical comments on bourgeois parliamentarianism and the free press make it doubly interesting to watch, considering its market was Nazi Germany in 1939. RB

Believe in Me
(Stuart Hagmann, 1971, US) Michael Sarrazin, Jacqueline Bisset, Jon Cypher, Allen Garfield, Kurt Dodenhoff.
90 min.
Hagmann, of, *The Strawberry Statement* shows

the same concern here to isolate his audience from his subject by glossy technique. The story tracks a sensitive young doctor driven to speed by the strain of watching kids die daily in his ward. He meets Bisset, turns her on, brings her down, etc. A pernicious film that trades on deliberate confusion of values, and glamorises mainlining as effectively as a tube ad.

Believers, The
(John Schlesinger, 1987, US) Martin Sheen, Helen Shaver, Harley Cross, Robert Loggia, Elizabeth Wilson, Harris Yulin, Lee Richardson, Richard Masur, Jimmy Smits.
114 min.
There's a shocking start: due to a dodgy coffee machine, Cal Jamison's wife ends up frying over spilt milk. To get over their loss, Cal (Sheen), a trick cyclist for cops, and his 7-year-old son move to New York, where they become involved with the age-old religion Santeria, which worships African spirits in the shape of Christian saints. As one little boy after another dies a grisly death – sacrificed, it turns out, in return for perpetual parental gratification – the ever more ridiculous plot encompasses auto-suggestion, voodoo, and not-so-special effects. It's not at all scary, but there's one good bit where this bubo on a woman's cheek bursts open and all these itsy-bitsy spiders scurry out. The real mystery is what Schlesinger and Sheen are doing making this schlock. MS

Bella Vita, La
see Living It Up

Bellboy, The
(Jerry Lewis, 1960, US) Jerry Lewis, Alex Gerry, Bob Clayton, Sonny Sand, Herkie Styles, Milton Berle, Walter Winchell.
72 min. b/w.
For his first venture into direction, Lewis forsook the saccharine plotlines of his previous work for a film of sketches based on the character of a bumbling bellboy at the Fontainebleau Hotel in Miami. The result, each scene working like a fully achieved comic short, boasts more hits than miss-es, including such superbly timed gags as the speedy assembling of chairs in a hall and the relapse of a hopeless diet-watcher, as well as guest appearances by Walter Winchell, Milton Berle and 'Jerry Lewis' (revealingly irascible). Lewis even throws in a tribute to his great mentor, Stan Laurel. Perhaps to the relief of many, Lewis (in his bellboy character) remains entirely mute for most of the movie. DT

Belle
(André Delvaux, 1973, Bel/Fr) Jean-Luc Bideau, Danièle Delorme, Adriana Bogdan, Roger Coggio, René Hainaux.
93 min.
Delvaux again reveals his preoccupation with illusion and reality. Mathieu (Bideau) is a successful academic and family man until, profoundly threatened by his daughter's imminent marriage, he retreats into a barren landscape inhabited by a beautiful, silent stranger (Delorme). What develops is a love story turned surreal thriller, an investigation of the male ego and sexual paranoia. However, overlong and with some very obvious symbolism (a dull wasteland for isolation; windblown grass for sexual fulfilment; guns, trains and furs for good measure), the film is visually disappointing and fails to sustain its interesting ideas. HM

Belle de Jour
(Luis Buñuel, 1967, Fr/It) Catherine Deneuve, Jean Sorel, Michel Piccoli, Genevieve Page, Francisco Rabal, Pierre Clémenti, Georges Marchal.
100 min.
Buñuel's cool, elegant version of Joseph Kessel's novel is an amoral comedy of manners. Beautiful, bored and bourgeoise Séverine, married to a surgeon, decides to while away her afternoons by working in a high-class whorehouse, where she encounters a variety of characters – a Chinaman with a strangely erotic box, a depraved Duke, and a gangster with gold teeth, with whom she falls in love. Or does she? Allowing us no indication of what is real, what is not, Buñuel constructs both a clear portrait of the bourgeoisie as degenerate, dishonest and directionless, and an unhysterical depiction of Deneuve's inner fantasy life, where

she entertains dreams of humiliation galore. For a film about such a potentially sensationalist subject, it's remarkably discreet and chaste. GA

Belle Epoque
(Fernando Trueba, 1992, Sp) Fernando Fernán Gómez, Jorge Sanz, Maribel Verdú, Ariadna Gil, Miriam Diaz-Aroca, Mary Carmen Ramirez.
109 min.
Provincial Spain, 1931, Elderly artist Manolo (Gómez) shelters a young deserter from the royalist army. Fernando (Sanz) is happy to accept, especially when he sets eyes on Manolo's four daughters. To his surprise, the bugle boy is seduced by each in turn, but even in this rural backwater the etiquette of love is more sophisticated than he appreciates. Trueba's rich, sunny film harks back to the sort of pastoral idyll that only exists in romances. Despite the conventional farce structure, it's never quite the straight male fantasy you might imagine. There's a marvellous cameo by Mary Carmen Ramirez as Manolo's operatically inclined wife; but all the women are marvellous. Somehow the film's wistful and ironic leanings are embodied in Gómez's bemused patriarch: a self-confessed libertine who can only make love to his wife. Ultimately the movie's too flirtatious to be for real – but you might indulge yourself this once. TCh

Belle Equipe, La
(Julien Duvivier, 1936, Fr) Jean Gabin, Viviane Romance, Charles Vanel, Raymond Aimos, Charpin, Raymond Cordy.
94 min. b/w.
An amiable group of misfits living together in destitution win a sweepstake, and with their pooled resources decide to turn a derelict old building on the Marne embankment into a café-concert. With its pervasive odour of fried sausages and bicycle tyres, the gruff voices of Gabin, Vanel et al, and an authentic whiff of the Popular Front (dispersed all too soon by a mixture of wanderlust and woman-lust among the five), this minor 'classic' – once intended for Renoir – is a Cartier-Bresson photograph teased into life. GAd

Belle et la Bête, La (Beauty and the Beast)
(Jean Cocteau, 1946, Fr) Jean Marais, Josette Day, Marcel André, Mila Parély, Michel Auclair, Nane Germon.
100 min. (cut to 92). b/w.
Cocteau's fairytale set standards in fantasy which few other film-makers have reached. Despite the Vermeer-like compositions, he has some trouble capturing the right tone for the 'realistic' scenes, but the sequences in the enchanted castle – wonderfully designed by Christian Bérard complete with fantastic living statuary, and dignified by a Beast at once ferocious, erotic and genuinely tragic – are pure magic. René Clément is credited as co-director, but had very little to do with the *mise en scène*. TM

Belle Fille comme moi, Une (A Gorgeous Bird Like Me/Such a Gorgeous Kid Like Me)
(François Truffaut, 1972, Fr) Bernadette Lafont, Claude Brasseur, Charles Denner, Guy Marchand, André Dussollier, Philippe Léotard, Anne Kreis.
98 min.
Truffaut's weakest movie, a black comedy which totally misfires. Lafont languishes in prison and relates to a sociologist (Dussollier) her life of crime, which begins with patricide (at the age of nine) and goes down from there. While there is nothing objectionable about the story – she is a real slut and the men are an awful lot who get their just deserts, thus sidestepping charges of misogyny – Truffaut miscalculates the tone. He was normally the most civilised of directors, but this is a loud and crude film. ATu

Belle Noiseuse, La
(Jacques Rivette, 1991, Fr) Michel Piccoli, Jane Birkin, Emmanuelle Béart, David Bursztein, Marianne Denicourt, Gilles Arbona.
239 min.
Confronting the issue of creativity with honesty

and insight, Rivette's loose adaptation of Balzac's short story 'The Unknown Masterpiece' is for the most part hypnotically fascinating. Hidden away with wife Liz (Birkin) in their rambling Languedoc mansion, Edouard Frenhofer (Piccoli) has painted next to nothing for years; but when a friend introduces painter Nicolas (Bursztein) and his lover Marianne (Béart), Frenhofer is so taken with the girl that he asks her to pose for a masterpiece he abandoned a decade earlier. So begins a battle of wills waged between the artist, his recalcitrant model, her increasingly jealous lover, a wife wary of his motives, and his own self-doubt. Firmly anchored by a strong cast, the relationships are explored in exhaustive detail, so that the tensions arising, as the painter's cauterising work proceeds, are convincing throughout. (Rather less plausible is the suggestion that Frenhofer is a genius, since the canvases we see – painted by the off-screen hand of Bernard Dufour – are hardly wonderful.) As impeccably shot as its subject deserves, the film is more accessible than most of Rivette's work, with characteristically playful passing nods to the relationship between life and performance. GA

Belle Noiseuse – Divertimento, La

(Jacques Rivette, 1991, Fr) Michel Piccoli, Jane Birkin, Emmanuelle Béart, David Bursztein, Marianne Denicourt, Gilles Arbona.
126 min.
Rivette here remodels La Belle Noiseuse into another film entirely, using alternative takes, recutting to a much brisker rhythm, and bookending it with a discreetly but crucially different beginning and ending. The lengthy close-ups of painter Bernard Dufour's hand in action have gone; so have most of the agonising sittings in which Piccoli tries to wring out of Béart the realisation of his ideal masterpiece. This makes for a less tangible sense of painting's material nature, and makes more of a mystery out of the artist-model relationship; the emphasis shifts radically on to Piccoli's wife (Birkin), who now sees the sittings from outside, much as we do. It's a lighter film, but by no means slighter, more like the difference between a Henry James short story and an extended performance piece. JRo

Belle of New York, The

(Charles Walters, 1952, US) Fred Astaire, Vera-Ellen, Marjorie Main, Keenan Wynn, Alice Pearce.
82 min.
Classically simple Arthur Freed musical with Vera-Ellen in the unlikely guise of a high-kicking 'Daughter of the Right' who proves capable of moving from primness to flamboyant sauciness with remarkable efficacy, while her doll-like dancing is overshadowed but never overawed by Astaire's light-footed zaniness. The plot – dissolute playboy seeks redemption in the arms of purer-than-the-driven-snow maiden – is merely the minimal requirement for an escape into fantasy. If it isn't quite on the level of Minnelli's jagged surrealism, the film's central conceit – that those truly in love can walk on air – allows for some spectacular special effects as the lovers levitate up and away over the star-spangled roofs of New York. RMy

Belles de nuit, Les (Beauties of the Night/Night Beauties)

(René Clair, 1952, Fr/It) Gérard Philipe, Martine Carol, Gina Lollobrigida, Magali Vendeuil, Raymond Bussières, Raymond Cordy, Paolo Stoppa.
89 min. b/w.
Clair's engaging fantasy stars Philipe as a frustrated young composer who escapes from poverty, noise and failure into dreams of la belle époque, where his music is the talk of the Paris Opéra, and a lovely married woman (Carol, in reality mother of one of his pupils) melts in his arms. But old men lamenting, first that the real belle époque was 1830, then 1789, drive his dreams back in time to military conquest and an exotic princess (Lollobrigida, in reality the cashier in the local café), then to revolutionary fervour and the love of a pretty aristocrat (Vendeuil, in reality the girl next door). At the risk of seeming scrappy (a risk not always avoided), his fantasies obey dream logic by arbitrarily chopping, changing and melting into each other; but they are often witty (nightmarishly, his opera turns into a symphony for

motor horns, pneumatic drills and vacuum cleaners), and they borrow an overall structure from Griffith and Intolerance (building to simultaneous perils from a jealous husband's duelling pistol, from harem scimitars, and from the guillotine). The trouble with the film is that its reality, pretty much duplicating the cosily antiquated world of Le Million, is in itself a dream: all too predictably, love and success await the dreamer. TM

Belles of St Trinian's, The

(Frank Launder, 1954, GB) Alastair Sim, Joyce Grenfell, Hermione Baddeley, George Cole, Joan Sims, Beryl Reid, Betty Ann Davies.
91 min. b/w.
First in the highly enjoyable if hardly sophisticated series of Launder and Gilliat comedies based on Ronald Searle's cartoons about unruly brats and incompetent staff at a seedy girls' school. Predictable, perhaps, but it's hard to resist the performances of Cole as a conniving spiv and Sim (in drag) as the bumbling headmistress. GA

Bell from Hell, The

see Campana del Infierno, La

Bellissima

(Luchino Visconti, 1951, It) Anna Magnani, Walter Chiari, Tina Apicella, Gastone Renzelli, Alessandro Blasetti.
113 min. b/w.
A curiously sentimental satire on Cinecittà Film Studios, in which half of Rome's adoring mothers stridently cajole their untalented offspring into a studio child-star competition. It rivals most Hollywood-on-Hollywood movies in ironic entertainment value, but the abiding memory is of Magnani at full throttle contributing to quite the noisiest film ever made. PT

Bellman and True

(Richard Loncraine, 1987, GB) Bernard Hill, Derek Newark, Richard Hope, Ken Bones, Frances Tomelty, Kieran O'Brien.
122 min.
There are kiss-off points in Loncraine's caper thriller – notably a silky Mister Big who calls his victim 'Dear Heart' while the muscle brandishes a Stanley knife – but the complexity of the characters more than compensates. More crucially, the balance of the film is off in the telling, and after a gabbled scene-setter, we spend too long bogged down in an empty mansion with alcoholic computer expert Hiller (Hill), his small stepson (O'Brien), and Mr Big (Hope), as pressure is put on Hiller to hack into a bank's security system and take out the alarms. The villainy braces up with the appearance of Guv'nor (Newark), whose threats are convincing enough to cause Hiller an involuntary evacuation, and the actual robbery powers along on a nice mixture of humour and tension, topped by a getaway containing a memorably tight squeeze. Hill is grimly anxious as the reluctant pawn, and his bedtime story sessions with the boy are suitably transparent. Nice try. BC

Bells Are Ringing

(Vincente Minnelli, 1960, US) Judy Holliday, Dean Martin, Fred Clark, Eddie Foy Jr, Frank Gorshin.
127 min.
Minnelli's last musical before On a Clear Day You Can See Forever, and like it a curate's egg. The two stars are a pleasure to behold, particularly the genially dizzy Holliday, a telephone answering-service operator who can't help involving herself in the lives and hopes of her clients. And old Mr Nonchalance Martin sidles through his part as a doubting, drunken playwright with his customary charm. But their material just isn't up to the mark: Betty Comden and Adolph Green's script involves much jaded satire of jaded topics like Method acting, pop music and smart parties, while Jule Styne's infrequent songs don't really get the bells ringing. Something is also wrong with Minnelli's presentation, for the action tends to hang inside the 'scope frame looking theatrical and inert; even the location stuff seems phony. GB

Bells Go Down, The

(Basil Dearden, 1943, GB) Tommy Trinder, James Mason, Beatrice Varley, Philip Friend, Mervyn Johns, William Hartnell.
90 min. b/w.

Uncomfortable war effort from Ealing, semi-documentary in intent but getting bogged down in silly histrionics as one auxiliary fireman has to work on a blazing warehouse while his own home burns, and another perishes in an attempt to save his hated chief while his wife has a baby in the blitz. Horribly patronising in its view of the humble doing their bit for Britain (even the crook turns up trumps), and knocked sideways as a tribute to the Auxiliary Fire Service by Humphrey Jennings' Fires Were Started, coincidentally released the same month. TM

Bells of St Mary's, The

(Leo McCarey, 1945, US) Bing Crosby, Ingrid Bergman, Henry Travers, William Gargan, Ruth Donnelly.
126 min. b/w.
Rambling, embarrassingly winsome sequel to Going My Way, with Crosby's crooning priest transferred to a rundown parish where Barry Fitzgerald's roguish twinkle is replaced by Bergman's wholesome (but roguish) nun. TM

Belly of an Architect, The

(Peter Greenaway, 1987, GB/It) Brian Dennehy, Chloe Webb, Lambert Wilson, Sergio Fantoni, Stefania Casini.
118 min.
When middle-aged American architect Stourley Kracklite (Dennehy) visits Rome to oversee an exhibition in tribute to an 18th century predecessor, Boullée, his grand ambitions founder in a morass of disease, doubt and intrigue. Is his pregnant wife (Webb) having an affair with the insidiously reptilian Caspasian (Wilson), himself possibly plotting to steal the kudos for the exhibition? Is she even poisoning him, thus causing debilitating cramps in Kracklite's up-ended dome of a stomach? The story is decorated in the usual Greenaway style; visual and symbolic rhymes galore produce a quizzical and quirky meditation on a multitude of themes. But where the film perhaps wins out over Greenaway's earlier movies is in its admission of feeling. The exquisitely framed images, the allusive script, the droll witticisms are counterbalanced by Dennehy's literally enormous performance, which threatens to tear the film's formal symmetries to vividly memorable shreds. GA

Beloved Enemy

(HC Potter, 1936, US) Merle Oberon, Brian Aherne, Karen Morley, Theodore Von Eltz, Henry Stephenson, Jerome Cowan, David Niven, Donald Crisp.
86 min. b/w.
Sam Goldwyn turned the Irish Troubles of 1921 into the backdrop for a tale of doomed love. Oberon's the daughter of a stuffy English civil servant sent to Dublin, Aherne a fiery rebel leader, but the drawstrings of romance bind them together in this hokey tale of passion, duty, betrayal, etc. First-time director Henry Codman Potter was later to find fame with Hellzapoppin', which gives some idea where his talents lay. Not here, in other words. TJ

Beloved Infidel

(Henry King, 1959, US) Gregory Peck, Deborah Kerr, Eddie Albert, Philip Ober, Herbert Rudley, John Sutton, Karin Booth.
123 min.
An adaptation of the book by journalist Sheilah Graham about her affair with the permanently sozzled F Scott Fitzgerald during his ill-fated last days as a '30s Hollywood screenwriter. This is a great artist's life as grimly self-conscious soap opera. Peck and Kerr are awkwardly stiff, burdened by literary history. Vaguely caustic attitude towards Tinseltown mores; and notable 'Scope photography from Leon Shamroy. TJ

Below the Belt

(Robert Fowler, 1980, US) Regina Baff, John C Becher, Jane O'Brien, Mildred Burke, James Gammon, Shirley Stoler, Dolph Sweet.
98 min.
A cheapo independent precursor of Aldrich's California Dolls, adapting road movie clichés to the women's wrestling circuit, which lacks – if you'll excuse the expression – the balls of classic exploitation. Baff (cast as virtually the same waif she patented as truckers' moll Janice for Joseph Strick) quits the urban dead-end for an apprenticeship of grappling gigs in the Southern States,

learning the ropes before inevitably bringing an old pro favourite to her knees and the crowd to its feet. PT

Belstone Fox, The

(James Hill, 1973, GB) Eric Porter, Rachel Roberts, Jeremy Kemp, Bill Travers, Dennis Waterman.
103 min.
A dismayingly literal and unimaginative version of David Rook's novel *Ballad of the Belstone Fox*, a simple country tale of fox-hunting and the havoc wrought upon an ageing huntsman through his moment of kindness in nurturing a young fox cub.

Ben

(Phil Karlson, 1972, US) Lee Harcourt Montgomery, Joseph Campanella, Arthur O'Connell, Rosemary Murphy, Meredith Baxter.
94 min.
Small boy with heart condition finds (to music) that 'he has a friend in Ben', which is more than the audience is likely to have. Carried on from *Willard* and its wonder rat. The rats next door make their presence known, and Ben leads them to a safer life in the drain, helped by this same small boy (with heart condition). The whole nature-rising-against-man fable becomes a kind of sub-Disney tale. Ben himself is a sleek well-trained creature. Can't say the same for those who dreamed up the project.

Bend of the River (aka Where the River Bends)

(Anthony Mann, 1952, US) James Stewart, Julia Adams, Arthur Kennedy, Rock Hudson, Lori Nelson, Jay C Flippen, Harry Morgan, Stepin Fetchit.
91 min.
Mann's finest Western casts Stewart as a wagon train leader, guiding a group of settlers through Indian country to the Oregon Territory. Stewart is a man haunted by a secret, his violent past as a Missouri border raider – a past which catches up with him when another former raider (Kennedy) joins the wagon train. The two men are paralleled throughout, Kennedy representing the old violence which may yet erupt in the reformed Stewart, and the whole film is concerned with the testing of Stewart's capacity for change. Continually provoked by his spiky relationship with Kennedy, Stewart is a man who must clarify and reaffirm his new relationship with a peaceful society. Lighthearted comedy, majestic scenery, and superbly handled action are fused into a unifying moral vision which, though it deals with abstractions, always expresses itself through visible actions and tangible symbols. NF

Beneath the Planet of the Apes

(Ted Post, 1970, US) James Franciscus, Charlton Heston, Kim Hunter, Maurice Evans, Victor Buono.
84 min.
Beneath the planet of the apes is discovered an older civilisation: a tribe of mutant humans living in the ruins of New York and now maniacally worshipping an atom bomb. This first sequel to *Planet of the Apes* isn't bad, but already shows the way the original conception was to degenerate into routine comic strip adventure. TM

Beneath the 12-Mile Reef

(Robert D. Webb, 1953, US) Robert Wagner, Terry Moore, Gilbert Roland, J Carrol Naish, Richard Boone, Peter Graves.
102 min.
Wagner and Moore replay Romeo and Juliet in Tarpon Springs, Florida, with rival sponge fishermen standing in for the Montagues and Capulets. One of the earliest CinemaScope pictures, it looks better than it ought to, and Bernard Herrmann provides an eerie score. But it's best remembered for the incredibly young Robert Wagner scrapping with an octopus (you won't get that in staged Shakespeare). TCh

Beneath the Valley of the Ultra Vixens

(Russ Meyer, 1979, US) Francesca 'Kitten' Natividad, Anne Marie, Ken Kerr, June Mack, Russ Meyer.
93 min.

Delirious proof that Meyer deserves to be considered as one of America's foremost satirists. His use of ludicrously pneumatic female 'stars' has come to seem less like simple soft-core titillation and more a turning of their over-endowed bodies into a grand metaphor for Female sexual appetite, the central nightmare of the all-American Male psyche. Less subversive than his earlier work; still hilarious, though.

Benefit of the Doubt

(Jonathan Heap, 1993, US/Ger) Donald Sutherland, Amy Irving, Rider Strong, Christopher McDonald, Graham Greene, Theodore Bikel.
91 min.
Paroled wife-murderer (Sutherland) returns to eye-pleasing Cottonwood, Arizona, to haunt his daughter Karen (Irving), 22 years after her testimony put him in jail. He insinuates his way into her life by doting on her 11-year-old son (Strong). While father Frank remains ambiguous, this is mildly unsettling; once he goes loco and killing or terrorising everyone in sight, it loses all credibility. Most contrived. NF

Bengazi

(John Brahm, 1955, US) Richard Conte, Victor McLaglen, Richard Carlson, Mala Powers, Richard Erdman, Hillary Brooke.
78 min. b/w.
A risibly dud script never gives Brahm's stylish direction or Joseph Biroc's fine camerawork a chance to make anything of this adventure set in postwar Bengazi. Conte and McLaglen, unscrupulous co-owners of a seedy café (shades of *Casablanca*), set out for a desert oasis to hijack a cache of gold, only to find themselves surrounded by hostile Bedouins (shades of *The Lost Patrol*). Also trapped are a pursuing police chief (Carlson) and McLaglen's anxious daughter (Powers), a colleen fresh from the Dublin convent: cue for both bad boys to outdo each other in heroic self-sacrifice. Conte is excellent, but McLaglen as usual overdoes his loveable Irish rogue bit, while Carlson ('I'm thinkin' of the wee village in Scotland where I was born') offers one of the screen's most excruciating accents. TM

Ben-Hur

(Fred Niblo, 1925, US) Ramon Novarro, May McAvoy, Francis X Bushman.
145 min. b/w & col.
Despite the numerous disasters encountered during its production in Italy and Hollywood, MGM's spectacular about a Jew's conflicts with the authority of the Roman Empire remains one of the most impressive silent epics, largely thanks to the sheer scale of its conception and to the execution of its several set pieces (most notably the famed chariot race). The print under review, refurbished by Kevin Brownlow and David Gill for the 'Thames Silents' series with a new score by Carl Davis, has the added delight of a careful restoration of the several Technicolor sequences. GA

Ben-Hur

(William Wyler, 1959, US) Charlton Heston, Jack Hawkins, Haya Harareet, Stephen Boyd, Hugh Griffith, Martha Scott, Sam Jaffe, Finlay Currie.
217 min.
Although a bit like a four-hour Sunday school lesson, 'Ben-Hur' is not without its compensations, above all, of course, the chariot race (which was directed not by Wyler but by Andrew Marton, and it shows). The rest is made interesting by the most sexually ambivalent characters sporting togas this side of *Satyricon*. When not fondling phallic substitutes, Heston and Boyd gaze admiringly into each other's eyes, but when they fall out - well, hell hath no fury like a closet queen scorned. Heston ends up naked in the galleys where he's rowing and Jack Hawkins is commanding; one look at Chuck's rippling muscles, and Hawkins adopts him. Heston goes back for revenge on Boyd, who's lying around in the baths with his men looking like they're auditioning for *Sebastiane*. Along the way, an unbilled Jesus performs miracles for Ben's kinsfolk, which are convincing enough to convert him. The movie could be trying to say that for some people religion is an escape from their sexuality, but it seems unlikely. SM

Benji

(Joe Camp, 1974, US) Peter Breck, Edgar Buchanan, Terry Carter, Christopher Connelly.
86 min.
Big-grossing film in the States, about the life'n'love of a stray mongrel, told from the dog's point of view. Against the novelty of the canine stunts one has to balance some terribly variable acting, poor lighting, and spotty photography. Attendant adults will probably find it a long haul. A sequel ensued, *For the Love of Benji* (1977).

Benny and Joon

(Jeremiah Chechik, 1993, US) Johnny Depp, Mary Stuart Masterson, Aidan Quinn, Julianne Moore, Oliver Platt, CCH Pounder.
99 min.
Another one flies over the cuckoo's nest in this soft-hearted romantic three-hander. Joon (Masterson) plays cooky – sorry, severely emotionally unstable. She's a vegetarian painter in airy print dresses and bobby sox. Sam (Depp) is a kind of gentle man-child fantasy creation, who expresses himself through Chaplin and Keaton mime routines. Piggy-in-the-middle is Quinn's blue-collar straight man, Joon's together brother Benny, who looks after her at home, just managing to keep her from being institutionalised. He refuses to bless Sam and Joon's marriage of true minds…It's acted out in the secondary emotional register of the glass menagerie: whimsical, delicate, idiosyncratic, barmy. WH

Benny's Video

(Michael Haneke, 1992, Aus) Arno Frisch, Angela Winkler, Ulrich Mühe.
105 min.
An unsettling if not entirely successful social-cum-psychological drama. Benny – a well-off 14-year-old whose none too warmly affectionate parents have bought him an amazing array of video equipment – has become so desensitised to reality by watching endless violent images on the small screen that he ends up killing an almost total stranger. So far, so unremarkable; but his remorseless, *Psycho*-style reaction to the deed, his mute 'confession' to his parents via video, and their reaction in turn, are quietly chilling. As a study in the complex relationship between violence and cinema, it's an unsensational alternative to *Henry: Portrait of a Serial Killer* and *Man Bites Dog*. GA

Bent

(Sean Mathias, 1996, GB/US/Japan) Lothaire Bluteau, Clive Owen, Brian Webber, Ian McKellen, Mick Jagger, Jude Law, Suzanne Bertish, Rupert Graves, Charlie Watts.
116 min.
Fassbinder and Costa-Gavras both wanted to film Martin Sherman's 1979 play about gay persecution under the Nazis, but it was theatre director Mathias who finally got it on screen. In this visually daring adaptation a ruined power station on the Clyde stands in for '30s Berlin, and Dachau is represented by a disused cement factory outside Tring. Owen and Bluteau are the gay men, Max and Horst, who trace a line between these points. Leaving the decadent nightlife over which Jagger's club owner, Greta, holds court, the two eventually meet in line at the concentration camp. Horst wears the homosexual's pink triangle and Max has been trying to pass as a Jew. That way, he reckons, he's not quite the lowest of the low. Although Sherman's ranking of the gays as even more oppressed than the Jewish prisoners seems unnecessary, the anger behind his screenplay is never in doubt. Life on the run keeps the first half moving, but it's hard to connect with the performers when Owen and Bluteau are dwarfed by the post-industrial surroundings. TJ

Benvenuta

(André Delvaux, 1983, Bel/Fr/It) Fanny Ardant, Vittorio Gassman, Françoise Fabian, Mathieu Carrière, Claire Wauthion.
106 min.
A film about fictions, their fascination, and the processes by which they are created. A young screenwriter visits a famous novelist, seeking background for a script based on the scandalous love story she published twenty years before. As they talk, two romances are rhymed: one, from the novel as remembered by her and imagined by him, is strange, exalted, melodramatic (played by Gassman and Ardant); the other is shy, tender,

hesitant as the two writers (Fabian, Carrière) warm to their collaboration. Meanwhile, conjured out of the network of memories, cross references, musical and visual analogies, an entirely different story gradually emerges. Working through subtle Jamesian nuance, it's not an easy film but an immensely rewarding one. TM

Bequest to the Nation (aka The Nelson Affair)

(James Cellan Jones, 1973, GB) Glenda Jackson, Peter Finch, Michael Jayston, Anthony Quayle, Margaret Leighton, Dominic Guard.
116 min.
Terence Rattigan's adaptation of his own play in which Finch (Nelson) and Jackson (Lady Hamilton) attempt to take the lid off a relationship which 'changed the course of British history'. Histrionics apart, you come out wondering whether it really matters.

Berdel

(Atif Yilmaz, 1990, Tur) Türkan Soray, Tarik Akan, Mine Cayiroglv.
83 min.
Yilmaz' powerful film starts with Hikmet the Supermarket, a travelling purveyor of essential goods to this rural clime of Turkey, shouting 'Quinine for men! Condoms for women!' Meanwhile, Hanim (Soray), wife to Ömer (Akan), is giving birth to her fifth girl – a disaster in this patriarchal community – and Ömer is wandering the coffee-houses in a terminal state of anxiety. He must have a boy. Nobody's happy, least of all Hanim's daughter Beyaz (Cayiroglv). It is she who will be forced to become the second wife of an older man so that her father may himself take a second wife and avoid the dowry – the custom of 'Berdel'. This moving and finely acted drama describes the tragic implications of these events with compassion, restraint and a close attention to detail; and in so doing, paints a forceful portrait of a society painfully entering the modern world. WH

Berlin Affair, The (Interno Berlinele)

(Liliana Cavani, 1985, It/WGer) Gudrun Landgrebe, Kevin McNally, Mio Takaki, Hanns Zischler, Massimo Girotti, Philippe Leroy.
121 min.
Cavani's monumentally dull opus has little to offer even the raincoat trade. Darling Lili is back among the kinky Nazis (remember Charlotte and Dirk smearing each other with jam in The Night Porter?). This time it's Berlin, 1938, where bored diplomat's wife Louise joins an art class and encounters the sensuous Mitsuko, daughter of the Japanese ambassador. Soon they're fumbling away inside each other's kimonos, until Louise's ambitious hubby discovers the awful truth. Filmed with a curious kind of glazed indifference, never has sex every which way seemed so boring, interminable and *unnecessary*. DT

Berlin Alexanderplatz

(Rainer Werner Fassbinder, 1979/80, WGer) Günter Lamprecht, Hanna Schygulla, Barbara Sukowa.
15 hr. 30 min.
This shattering adaptation of Alfred Döblin's masterpiece – made for TV in 13 episodes with a two-hour epilogue – offers a level-headed account of protagonist Biberkopf's key weakness: his quasi-sexual infatuation with the psychotic pimp Reinhold. Aided by great design, cinematography, and, not least, performances, Fassbinder tells the story surprisingly naturalistically. Then in the epilogue, he offers a disturbing meditation on his own fantasies about Biberkopf. This phantasmagoria is Fassbinder's most daring act of self-exposure: a movie time-bomb that forces you to rethink the series as a whole. The work of a genuine master with nothing left to lose or hide. TR

Berlin Express

(Jacques Tourneur, 1948, US) Merle Oberon, Robert Ryan, Paul Lukas, Charles Korvin, Robert Coote.
87 min. b/w.
Four representatives of the Occupying Powers join forces to aid a 'good' German with an unspecified plan to unify his country in the immediate aftermath of WWII. Minor stuff, if diverting enough in its absurdity (Oberon pick-

ing her way through the rubble of Berlin in a series of Orry-Kelly gowns). But the train itself whisks the narrative along, and Tourneur's unflinching stare at postwar devastation owes less to any documentary pretensions that to an almost Langian beadiness of eye. GAd

Berlin Jerusalem

(Amos Gitai, 1989, Fr) Lisa Kreuzer, Rivka Neuman, Markus Stockhausen, Benjamin Lévy, Vernon Dobtcheff, Bernard Eisenschitz.
89 min.
By telling the story of two historical pioneers reclaimed from the amber of Israeli mythology, Gitai explores nothing less than the journey to the Promised Land, the Zionist dream made reality. Else Lasker-Schüler (Kreuzer) is a German expressionist poet, Tania Shocat (Neuman) a Russian socialist activist. In a boldly conceptualised Berlin, Tania takes leave of Else and sets off for the Holy Land, where she participates in one of the original agricultural collectives. Meanwhile, as Hitler rises to power, Else finds herself a stranger in her own land; she too must take the road from Berlin to Jerusalem. In a sense, both women are revolutionaries – Else in art, Tania in politics – and Gitai juxtaposes their different perspectives on life, adopting a relevant style for each. In Berlin (actually Paris), master cinematographer Henri Alékan visualises a blue-black city with explicit references to expressionism; in Tania's story, the arid landscape and low-key drama are photographed realistically by Nurith Aviv. If this subtle and restrained film struggles to accommodate Else's flamboyant personality, it nevertheless climaxes with her, amid a shattering sonic barrage of death and destruction that brings it bang up to date. 'There is lamentation in the world/As if God had died/And we are in his cemetery'. TCh

Berlin Report

(Park Kwang-Su, 1991, SKor) Ahn Song-Gi, Kang Soo-Yeon, Moon Sung-Kuen.
100 min.
Shot entirely in Europe, much of it on trans-continental autoroutes, Park's weird political allegory doesn't manage to say much about the prospects or perils of Korean reunification but it sort of delivers as a mystery thriller. Raised in France by foster parents, a Korean brother and sister have gone separate ways. The boy, an artist and socialist, has vanished into East Germany; the girl has sunk into a reclusive silence since the unexplained death of her adoptive father. Ahn plays a Paris-based journalist who sets out to break the girl's silence by locating her brother – just after the Berlin Wall has come down. Stylishly shot, decently acted, intriguing. TR

Bermuda Triangle, The

(Richard Friedenberg, 1978, US) Brad Crandall, Donald Albee, Lin Berlitz, Vickery Turner.
94 min.
This speculative grab-bag spends most of its running time in dull, badly acted reconstructions of boats, planes and people disappearing in a welter of tacky special effects, and then wheels in the loony fringe psychics, conspiracy theorists and UFO freaks for a decidedly 'unbalanced' appraisal of the Triangle's enigma. It makes The Island look plausible. PT

Bermude: La Fossa Maledetta

see Sharks' Cave, The

Bernadette

(Jean Delannoy, 1988, Fr) Sydney Penny, Jean-Marc Bory, Philippe Rondest, Arlette Didier, Roland Lesaffre, Michel Duchaussoy.
119 min.
Veteran director Delannoy keeps things simple in his account of the peasant girl who claimed to have seen a vision at Lourdes. Bernadette lives with her family in appalling poverty, suffers from asthma, and is a slow learner, unable to grasp the intricacies of the catechism. One day a lady in white bathed in a heavenly glow appears in a grotto (the first of 17 such sightings). The peasant community believes her unhesitatingly, but official bodies sceptically search for scientific explanations or even political conspiracies. There's no doubting Delannoy's allegiance: he takes time to establish Bernadette's goodness and

humility, painting as insipid a character as is usual for cinematic saints, while Sydney Penny brings to the part a naive allure. Long takes and Francis Lai's haunting music set a solemn tone that hints at big implications, but spirituality finally swamps the facts, and at two hours, this small story seems overstretched. EP

Bernie

(Albert Dupontel, 1996, Fr) Albert Dupontel, Claude Perron, Roland Blanche, Hélène Vincent, Roland Bertin.
87 min.
Released from an institution 30 years after his parents dumped him down a garbage chute, Bernie Noel (Dupontel) finds a Paris apartment, buys a video camera, and sets about tracking down his folks. His tenuous grip on reality isn't improved by contact with the world at large; he leaves a trail of corpses and headless budgies in his wake. To complain that a black comedy is tasteless and offensive is probably to miss the point, but there it is. The violence against women of all ages is particularly grating. A hit in France. TCh

Bert Rigby, You're a Fool

(Carl Reiner, 1989, US) Robert Lindsay, Anne Bancroft, Corbin Bernsen, Robbie Coltrane, Cathryn Bradshaw, Jackie Gayle, Bruno Kirby, Liz Smith.
94 min.
Reiner scripted this musical after seeing Robert Lindsay's acclaimed stage performance in Me and My Girl. Such is the apparent admiration, all perspective has been lost. Details from Lindsay's own life are loosely incorporated into the plot, which becomes progressively inflated and thus – paradoxically – a thoroughly inadequate showcase for the star's more intimate style. Striking miner Bert Rigby (Lindsay) enlivens his humdrum life with impersonations of Kelly and Astaire. When an amateur talent show comes to town, Bert's bungled rendition of 'Isn't It Romantic' proves a huge hit, and sets the chirpy singer-dancer on the road to Hollywood. Stock characters litter his progress: manipulative agent (Coltrane), producer's frustrated wife (Bancroft), pretentious TV commercials director (Kirby), egocentric movie star (Bernsen). Certainly the performances aren't at fault, but it's difficult to imagine what sort of audience has been targeted for this bizarre hybrid of cinematic styles. One thing's for sure: a musical it ain't. Even the numbers reviving Cole Porter, Noël Coward and Irving Berlin fail to light up the screen; along with the star, they're hopelessly misused. CM

Best Age, The (Nejkrasnejsi Vek)

(Jaroslav Papousek, 1968, Czech) Hana Brejchová, Vera Kresadlová, Ladislava Jakim, Jan Stöckl.
80 min. b/w.
One of those pleasingly elliptical Czech comedies which flourished briefly during the '60s, never quite confronting their subjects head on, and in not doing so managing to speak volumes about the foibles of humanity. Querulous old men queue up for the privilege of adding a few pence to their pensions by acting as models at an art school; callow young students ponder the mysteries of death behind the tired old skulls they are set to sculpt; and a strange, yearning discontent permeates the air, with each age group firmly convinced that the other has the best of things. It's very slight, but although Papousek hasn't quite the same infallible command of timing as a film like Milos Forman's A Blonde in Love, he does extract very much the same flavour of dry, deadpan humour from his sidelong view of the human comedy. TM

Best Boy

(Ira Wohl, 1979, US) Philip Wohl, Max Wohl, Pearl Wohl, Ira Wohl.
111 min.
About the director's cousin, Philly, who's 52, says he's 16, and actually has the mental age of a five-year-old. When Wohl started filming, it was because he'd convinced Philly's protective, elderly parents that they had to help their son towards greater independence. The result is in part a sensitive record of that three year process, in a film which never preaches but almost incidentally points out what help is available, where it works and where it falls short. It's also a tale of the love,

guilt and stoicism of Philly's parents, and despite moments of real sorrow, the final impression left by the film is one of optimism – in the way it discovers dignity in ordinary people, an infectious sense of humour in adversity, and the songs in the heart of a mentally disabled man. HM

Best Defence
(Willard Huyck, 1984, US) Dudley Moore, Eddie Murphy, Kate Capshaw, George Dzundza, Helen Shaver.
94 min.
Dud is an industrial engineer who is struggling to perfect his DYP Gyro for the XM10 Annihilator Tank, 'the latest super-weapon in America's arsenal'. Eddie plays an army lieutenant who is putting the finished product through its trial run in Kuwait. The action switches back and forth as though some idiot were fooling with the remote control and chopping between TV channels. Dud gets involved with the KGB, the FBI, and his lady boss. Eddie says 'shit' a lot. Everyone throws a wobbly whenever the script gets too awful for words, which is often. AB

Best Foot Forward
(Edward Buzzell, 1943, US) Lucille Ball, William Gaxton, Tommy Dix, Virginia Weidler, Nancy Walker, June Allyson, Gloria De Haven, Chill Wills.
95 min.
A breezy but bland adaptation of the Broadway musical, with Lucille Ball as a movie star called Lucille Ball who, as a publicity stunt designed to revive a flagging career, accepts an invitation from a star-struck cadet (Dix) to attend a prom at his military academy. Much farcical ado ensues since the star's presence has to be kept secret from the authorities and the cadet's regular girlfriend (Weidler), while Ball herself is not pleased at having to garner publicity while remaining incognito. Buzzell's direction is laboured, and the merely passable musical numbers are staged by Charles Walters with surprisingly little flair. Harry James, providing the brash big band swing for the prom, manages to squeeze in his flashy rendition of 'Flight of the Bumble Bee' (not much cop there for the dancers on the floor). TM

Best Friends
(Norman Jewison, 1982, US) Burt Reynolds, Goldie Hawn, Jessica Tandy, Barnard Hughes, Audra Lindley, Keenan Wynn.
116 min.
Screenwriters Barry Levinson and Valerie Curtin present a semi-autobiographical study of two people who have lived together successfully for years, but find that the act of marriage virtually destroys their relationship. Hawn and Reynolds play two screenwriters who keep the ceremony secret from everyone except their parents, but still find the pressures almost too much to bear. The script is sharply written, while Jewison is a lot more sensitive to the material than he was on that earlier Levinson-Curtin effort, And Justice For All. But though engaging and agreeable, the film is never wildly funny. DP

Best Hotel on Skid Row
(Christine Choy/Renee Tajima, 1990, US)
47 min.
In the City of Angels, Skid Row covers 50 square blocks. This rather scattershot documentary introduces us to the residents of the Madison Hotel ($8.20 a night): drunks, drug addicts, the walking wounded. Charles Bukowski's w(h)iney voice-over and music by Tom Waits, Coltrane et al threaten to romanticise the film, and at times it does feel like an old Disney travelogue gone badly off course, but gradually the lives of these people take over. Billy hasn't left the fifth floor in two months. He pays Adam to run his errands. Adam, he explains, can't talk – lung cancer – can't read or write, he's 'in a world of trouble'. They all are. TCh

Best Intentions, The (Den Goda Viljan)
(Bille August, 1992, Swe) Samuel Fröler, Pernilla August, Max von Sydow, Ghita Norby, Lennart Hjulström, Mona Malm, Anita Björk.
181 min.
Ingmar Bergman's Fanny and Alexander mined his childhood for inspiration; next came the auto-biography, The Magic Lantern; and now, his

screenplay recounting his parents' courtship and early days of marriage preceding his birth. But the joy which finally infused the earlier film is lacking in this much bleaker affair. Henrik Bergman (Fröler) is an impoverished theology student when he meets spoiled, rich Anna (Pernilla August). Instantly attracted, the couple spend the next two years battling parental obstruction; once together, their problems really begin... Bille August has space to develop relationships and explore the emotional nuances which lead to numerous confrontations; with cinematographer Jörgen Persson, he conveys a firm sense of oppressive natural forces; and the film boasts impeccable performances (von Sydow is splendid as Anna's father). But with a running time of three hours, this weighty drama tests the most patient soul. CM

Best Little Whorehouse in Texas, The
(Colin Higgins, 1982, US) Burt Reynolds, Dolly Parton, Dom DeLuise, Charles Durning, Robert Mandan, Lois Nettleton.
114 min.
The brothel as soul of the community, charitable institution, or social therapy on a par with raffia work? This musical avoids sensitive issues like the clap, settling for stock tarts-with-hearts, loyal regulars, virginal jocks, and an outraged clean-up-the-state prude (DeLuise) of monstrously miscamped proportions. Clumsy chorus-lining, a penchant for ostrich plumes, and a tinny musical sameness betray the film's stage origins. One good number: Durning's Governor tripping a neat political 'Sidestep'. But the dialogue is Texas crude, the sentiment Bible Belt coy, and the songs conveyor-belt Broadway: stale air on a G-string. AM

Best Man, The
(Franklin Schaffner, 1964, US) Henry Fonda, Cliff Robertson, Edie Adams, Margaret Leighton, Ann Sothern, Kevin McCarthy, Lee Tracy, Shelley Berman.
104 min. b/w.
Presidential politics may loom larger and darker since Watergate, but this disenchanted peek behind the scenes of an American election still bites, thanks to a Gore Vidal script (based on his own play) which dissects with gleeful cynicism the machinery of tub-thumping, image-building and chicanery that goes into motion as rival presidential candidates (Fonda the nice liberal, Robertson the nasty extremist) fight to cut each other's throats. Memorable lines galore, like the Southern senator's all-purpose reply to awkward questions about how many integrated schools there are in his state ('None, thank God, but we're making remarkable progress'), and a whole string of brilliant performances. TM

Best of the Best
(Bob Radler, 1989, US) Eric Roberts, James Earl Jones, Louise Fletcher, Sally Kirkland, Christopher Penn, Phillip Rhee, John P Ryan, John Dye, David Agresta, Simon Rhee.
100 min.
'No women, no alcohol, no drugs. You will eat, drink and shit competition' warns coach James Earl Jones, pretty much summing up the attraction of this particular 'entertainment'. The perfunctory plot concerns the selection and training of a five-man US karate team to take on the formidable Koreans. This might have made an interesting documentary, but the film-makers opt instead for hokey drama. The squad includes Penn's two-dimensional red-neck Travis Bickley (!), Roberts as a comparatively enlightened old hand, and Phillip Rhee as the young hopeful with the obligatory revenge motif. This surprisingly heavyweight cast – Louise Fletcher and Sally Kirkland lend spiritual support – manages to lower itself to the exploitation level material without apparent strain; indeed the performances are all truly atrocious. After much fist-clenching, the movie closes to a draw – a small mercy to be grateful for, though kamikaze kids inclined to stay the course will probably be disappointed by the shallow rhetoric. TCh

Best of the Best 2
(Robert Radler, 1992, US) Eric Roberts, Phillip Rhee, Christopher Penn, Wayne Newton, Ralph Moeller, Meg Foster, Edan Gross.
100 min.
Three years ago, Roberts, Rhee and a surpris-

ingly mercenary supporting cast enacted the Olympian efforts of the US karate team against the mighty Koreans; but this effort, less sequel than cast reunion, jettisons the comparatively ascetic demands of the sports movie formula for the more demonstratively decadent pleasures of action-melodrama. Newton invites a select group of high-rollers to the Las Vegas Colosseum's nightly no-rules blood bout, where our horizontally-challenged pair vow to avenge the death of their team-mate (Penn). Radler's contemporary gladiator movie is little more than a crude pastiche: no matter that its prime role models come from sci-fi (Rollerball, The Running Man), at least it musters the courage of its shameless contrivance. TCh

Best of Times, The
(Roger Spottiswoode, 1986, US) Robin Williams, Kurt Russell, Pamela Reed, Holly Palance, Donald Moffat, Margaret Whitton, M. Emmet Walsh, RG Armstrong, Donovan Scott.
104 min.
At 9.22pm on November 15, 1972, Jack Dundee (Williams) dropped a catch in a game of American football and caused his team, the Taft Rockets, to lose to the rival town of Bakersfield. Thirteen years later he is still haunted by his error, which is hardly surprising considering that no one will let him forget it. Prompted by the friendly neighbourhood whore, Dundee decides to stage a rematch, and persuades his buddy, quarterback Russell, to help him. When their wives find out, they chuck them out, so both men have more than just their reputations to regain. Though it does have its moments, the result is never as funny as it should be. Williams and Russell, although fine individually, don't spark off each other as a comic duo should, and the ending is so predictable it's almost unexpected. MS

Best of Walt Disney's True Life Adventures, The
(James Algar, 1975, US)
89 min.
True life? The 'adventures' in this compilation are about as true to life as those ads with cats wearing bow-ties and sheep sauntering by washing-machines. Disney's field photographers procured fine and rare footage, only to have it dolled up with jokey editing, cute music, and a patronising commentary: scorpions doing a barn dance, polar bears rolling down ice-caps by mistake, ducks slipping on a frozen pond, and Skinny the bravado squirrel demonstrating his bravado. The final image consists of a skyful of birds: you expect them to form the words 'The End', but they never do. GB

Best Revenge
(John Trent, 1983, Can) John Heard, Levon Helm, Alberta Watson, Stephen McHattie, Moses Znaimer, John Rhys-Davies.
96 min.
This trundles along tracks well oiled by the likes of Midnight Express. Heard is the small-time drug runner forced – the baddies are holding his buddy by the balls until he delivers the goods – to hotfoot it over to Morocco to take a puff of the stuff before shipping it back. There follows much back-stabbing and bribery, police brutality and cruelty to cars; and the xenophobia is given an added twist by having the token Mustapha Nice-Guy played by a Welshman (Rhys-Davies reprising his friendly foreigner role from Raiders of the Lost Ark). AB

Best Seller
(John Flynn, 1987, US) James Woods, Brian Dennehy, Victoria Tennant, Allison Balson, Paul Shenar, George Coe.
95 min.
This Larry Cohen-scripted thriller reworks the old idea of the symbiotic relationship between cop and killer, adding a new twist. LA Detective Meechum (Dennehy) is a burnt-out wreck whose sideline as a crime novelist has dried up since his wife's death. Sleazy, amoral hit-man Cleve (Woods) steps out of Meechum's past and offers him the dirt on his ex-boss, major league criminal turned legitimate corporation boss Madlock. The deal is that Meechum gets to write again and Cleve gets to be the hero of a hard-hitting exposé of Madlock's bloodstained past. Tough action,

hardboiled dialogue and a tightly constructed script keep the action brisk and bloody, while the jaundiced sideswipes at American capitalism are laced with cynicism. Sadly, the potentially explosive confrontation between Dennehy and Woods never quite lives up to expectations; but Flynn's lean direction achieves a gritty B movie edge as the sparks fly and Dennehy moves towards a grudging respect for his manic alter ego. NF

Best Shot
see Hoosiers

Best Things in Life Are Free, The
(Michael Curtiz, 1956, US) Gordon MacRae, Dan Dailey, Ernest Borgnine, Sheree North, Murvyn Vye, Tommy Noonan, Tony Galento.
104 min.
One of the very best of the musical biopics (of the DeSylva/Henderson/Brown songwriting team): a strangely neglected film, perhaps because the superb string of numbers are mostly 'thrown away' on delightfully modest, off-the-cuff renditions, either by Sheree North or by the songwriters themselves (with Borgnine keeping his end up admirably). The two big production numbers are gems: 'Black Bottom' done as a spirited gangster movie parody, and 'Birth of the Blues' as a brilliantly evocative, mostly all-black mood piece. Even the plot is livelier than usual, centering on DeSylva's defection from the team to try his hand as a Hollywood producer. A lot can be forgiven, in any case, for its maliciously illustrated anecdote about how the trio, regally ordered to write a song for Al Jolson (who wasn't above neglecting to pay), concocted one so trashily treacly that nobody could sing it. Jolson was thrilled. The song: 'Sonny Boy'. TM

Best Way to Walk, The (La Meilleure Façon de Marcher/ aka The Best Way)
(Claude Miller, 1976, Fr) Patrick Dewaere, Patrick Bauchitey, Christine Pascal, Claude Piéplu, Michel Blanc.
86 min.
A film about getting off on the 'right' foot. Dealing with the confusions of adolescent sexuality, it's less about groping one's way towards adulthood than about the search for sexual identity. Set in 1960 in a boys' summer camp, it traces the ambiguous relationship between two camp monitors. Claude Miller, Truffaut's former assistant, handles the contrasts of his script with assurance, especially those between group conformity and private individual feelings. Only at the end does his touch falter, because until then his perception of emotional nuances effectively masks the stereotypical equations he makes between sex, class and, to a lesser extent, politics. But overall it's a highly assured first feature. CPe

Best Years of Our Lives, The
(William Wyler, 1946, US) Fredric March, Myrna Loy, Dana Andrews, Teresa Wright, Virginia Mayo, Harold Russell, Hoagy Carmichael.
172 min. b/w.
Overlong, perhaps, but this tender and occasionally tough look at the plight of returning war veterans is one of Wyler's best films. Robert Sherwood's script is thorough without falling into undue sentimentality or bombast, the performances throughout are splendid (including that of Russell, an amateur actor who was himself an amputee), and Gregg Toland's masterly camerawork serves as a textbook on the proper use of deep focus. Maybe not the masterpiece it would like to be, but a model of fine Hollywoood craftsmanship all the same. GA

Bête, La (The Beast)
(Walerian Borowczyk, 1975, Fr) Sirpa Lane, Lisbeth Hummel, Elisabeth Kahson, Pierre Benedetti, Marcel Dalio.
102 min.
Once upon a time, in the eighteenth century, a beast lived in the woods of an aristocratic estate. And this beast, possessed of a giant phallus and an insatiable lust, set upon the beautiful young lady of the house. But the lady was of an even greater sexual appetite, and laid the beast to eternal rest. Two centuries later, the tale of the beast would return in the dreams of an American

heiress contracted to carry the male descendant of the same crumbling aristocratic family... Borowczyk's all-out assault on social conventions and repressed desires, an outrageously ironic blend of French farce and surrealist poetry, can be seen as signposting both the peak of his sexual fables (*Blanche, Immoral Tales*) and his subsequent decline into ephemeral soft porn. Its shameless shuffling of equine couplings, pederastic priests and priapic black manservants earns it *nul points* for political correctness. But seen from its own amoral perspective, aided by Borowczyk's remarkable sense of framing and rhythm, *La Bête* is that rare achievement, a truly erotic film. DT

Bête Humaine, La (The Human Beast/Judas Was a Woman)
(Jean Renoir, 1938, Fr) Jean Gabin, Simone Simon, Fernand Ledoux, Julien Carette, Blanchette Brunoy, Jean Renoir.
99 min. b/w.
Stunning images of trains and railway lines as a metaphor for the blind, immutable forces that drive human passions to destruction. Superb performances from Gabin, Simon and Ledoux as the classic tragic love triangle. The deterministic principles of Zola's novel, replaced by destiny in Lang's remake *Human Desire*, are slightly muffled here. But given the overwhelming tenderness and brutality of Renoir's vision, it hardly matters that the hero's compulsion to kill, the result of hereditary alcoholism, is left half-explained. TM

Betrayal
(David Jones, 1982, GB) Jeremy Irons, Ben Kingsley, Patricia Hodge, Avril Elgar.
95 min.
Stagy adaptation by Pinter of his own theatrical success about a determinedly upper-middle class romantic triangle between Kingsley's publisher, wife Hodge, and glacial lover Irons. Hodge is fine, Kingsley tries his best, and Irons is as tight-assed as ever. But it's all so uncinematic as to make one wonder why it was ever made in the first place. GA

Betrayed
see When Strangers Marry

Betrayed
(Costa-Gavras, 1988, US) Debra Winger, Tom Berenger, John Heard, Betsy Blair, John Mahoney, Ted Levine, Jeffrey DeMunn.
127 min.
After the Chicago killing of a controversial radio talk-show host by right wing extremists, FBI agent Winger goes undercover to investigate prime suspect Berenger. A widowed family man farmer, he's as clean-living and charming as they come; inevitably she falls for him, uncertain of his guilt until he takes her hunting by night...for human prey. Winger wants out, but when her boss and ex-lover (Heard) refuses the request, she finds herself involved in a white supremacist conspiracy against blacks, Jews and gays, and living with a man she detests and fears. If the forte of Costa-Gavras' political thriller is its acting, that only underlines the flaws in Joe *Jagged Edge* Eszterhas' murky, often contrived script. The racist sentiments and deeds on view are plausible; it's the plot details that suspend disbelief (why for instance, doesn't Berenger notice Winger's deceptions earlier?). The film has its fair share of chilling moments, and its determination to expose the moral sickness infesting the Midwest's conservative heartlands is admirable. But Winger's emotional dilemma is clumsily sketched, leaving the film relying for suspense on a handful of set pieces; and that isn't quite enough. GA

Betsy, The
(Daniel Petrie, 1978, US) Laurence Olivier, Robert Duvall, Katharine Ross, Tommy Lee Jones, Jane Alexander, Lesley-Anne Down.
125 min.
Power struggles in the motor industry are personified by young Tommy Lee Jones, who should be dynamic but lacks the energy of a suburban second-hand car salesman, and old Laurence Olivier. But not even decades as a 'great actor' allow Olivier to invest dialogue like 'Never shit a shitter' with feeling, so he plays with his American accent instead. All the sex is

so discreet that the movie never allows itself to get as trashy as a Harold Robbins bestseller should be. SM

Betsy's Wedding
(Alan Alda, 1990, US) Alan Alda, Molly Ringwald, Madeline Kahn, Joe Pesci, Ally Sheedy, Burt Young, Anthony LaPaglia, Joey Bishop, Catherine O'Hara, Julie Bovasso.
94 min.
When fashion student Betsy (Ringwald) visits her parents in the West Hamptons, she announces to dad and mom – motormouth Italian-American architect Eddie (Alda) and talkative American-American Lola (Kahn) – that she's gonna marry straight WASP Jake: it's Betsy's last word on the matter. Mom wants the wedding Jewish; financially-overstretched Dad, despite killing looks from his wife, wins a verbal poker game with the wealthy in-laws and gets to foot the bill. Plans are laid for a reception tent larger than the Yankee Stadium, and the invitation list takes on telephone book proportions. Betsy and Jake are tempted to call the whole thing off. Alda's foray into the wedding movie may lack the acerbity of Minnelli or the cinematic competence of Altman, but it's a warm, wordy, middlebrow crowd-pleaser. Alda's skill is with witty, fast-talking patter and in coaxing fine performances from his actors (playing an extended family of gently caricatured New York types). The values are bollocks, but the film is fun. WH

Better Late Than Never
(Bryan Forbes, 1983, GB) David Niven, Art Carney, Maggie Smith, Lionel Jeffries, Kimberly Partridge.
95 min.
Forbes seemed to have hit rock bottom with the ghastly *International Velvet*. But he found even more abject depths with this comedy about a moppet and two elderly parties scrabbling to claim (illegitimate) grandpaternity, initially because there's a fortune involved, but then love... TM

Better Tomorrow, A (Yingxiong Bense)
(John Woo, 1986, HK) Chow Yun-Fat, Leslie Cheung, Ti Lung, Emily Chu, Waise Lee, Tian Feng.
95 min.
Woo's career was at its nadir when Tsui Hark brought him into Film Workshop and proposed this 'remake' of Patrick Lung's 1967 movie *Story of a Discharged Prisoner* (also called *Yingxiong Bense* – 'The Nature of Heroes' – in Chinese). It's known that Tsui 'helped out' with the direction and editing, but the focus on codes of honour between men and wildly hyperbolic gunplay is 100 per cent Woo. Sung (Ti Lung) and Lee (Chow), traffickers in forged banknotes, are set up for a bust. Sung serves time in Taiwan while the wounded Lee hits the skids in Hong Kong. Three years later they team up to revenge themselves on their betrayer. Matters are complicated by Sung's brother Kit (Cheung, hilariously miscast in a macho role), a cop who blames Sung for the death of their father. Floridly romantic and serenely excessive (men shot a dozen times don't die, guns never need reloading), it has the bravado of a minor classic. TR

Better Tomorrow II, A (Yingxiong Bense II)
(John Woo, 1987, HK) Chow Yun-Fat, Leslie Cheung, Ti Lung, Dean Shek, Emily Chu.
104 min.
Chuffed by the success of *A Better Tomorrow*, Woo wanted to go straight on to *The Killer* and *Bullet in the Head*. But Tsui Hark insisted on a sequel, and came up with a storyline to press his point. The result is not 'the worst film ever made' (as Woo has been heard to describe it), but it's clear that his heart wasn't in it. The plot is a virtual rerun of the first one: ex-hoods and cops team up to beat ruthless counterfeiting racketeers by any means necessary. Since the Mark Lee character was killed off last time, it was necessary to invent Ken Lee, a twin brother in New York, to bring back Chow Yun-Fat – who (not surprisingly in the circumstances) treats the whole thing as a joke. There are odd flashes of Woo's talent, but the endless cross-cutting between characters generates no tension and the vast

expenditure of (mostly ineffective) bullets and grenades looks more like *Death Wish* than a sign of visionary excess. TR

Betty Blue (37°2 le Matin)
(Jean-Jacques Beineix, 1986, Fr) Béatrice Dalle, Jean-Hugues Anglade, Consuelo De Haviland, Gérard Darmon, Clementine Celarié.
121 min.
Betty (Dalle) is in her boyfriend Zorg's (Anglade) beach house, bonking his brains out first thing in the morning. They do a lot of that. Then she discovers his notebooks in which he has been scribbling his novel (he does a lot of that), promptly burns down the house and forces him to go to Paris in search of fame with her. Here they team up with another wiggy couple who run a pizza joint, and they do a lot of funny things. This mid-section provides the film's humorous and good-natured antics. From there, the couple move to the south, and finally dissolve to a sad attack of *amour fou*. Full of comic asides, the whole thing is all rather wonderful in the traditional Gallic way. The fullness of life, while not exactly celebrated, is certainly lived through; mostly without clothes on. CPea

Betty Blue (37°2 le Matin)
(Jean-Jacques Beineix, 1986, Fr) Béatrice Dalle, Jean-Hugues Anglade, Consuelo De Haviland, Gérard Darmon, Clementine Celarié.
183 min.
Beineix's basic story – the obsessive passion of Betty and Zorg and her descent into madness – remains the same in this 'director's cut', it just takes longer. Most of the restored sections simply add to Beineix's musings on the nature of obsession: there's a mattress-hating binman, a drunken olive salesman, and a detective who, like Zorg, is a frustrated writer, and who, like Betty, wants to kill all publishers. The problem with all this light relief is that it unbalances the rest of the film. Whereas in the shorter cut Eddy and Lisa played a crucial role, by the time this version finishes you've forgotten they ever existed. Granted, the reintroduction of a long child-kidnapping scene and a security guard robbery slows down the advance of Betty's illness, which in the original turned her from wild lover to crazed demon overnight. Otherwise, though, Beineix's determination to tell the full story results in a bum-numbing and often downright dull three hours. NKe

Betty Boop Follies, The
(Dave Fleischer, 1972, US)
93 min.
A random collection of fourteen cartoons featuring the cartoon vamp created by Max Fleischer, the only real rival of the Disney and Ub Iwerks team in American animation of the early '30s. The mini-skirted and gartered Betty resembles the dumb broad sex-object satirised by Wilder in *Some Like It Hot*, but it's difficult to see why the Hayes Office considered the character too risqué. Fleischer's style at times borders on surrealism, the animation feeding off the rhythms of the soundtrack popular jazz music. The cartoons, originally in black-and-white, have been brightly coloured electronically. RM

Betty's Brood
(Mick McConnell, 1991, GB) Marjory McCavigan, Diane Kurys, Eileen Cumming.
70 min.
Though certainly a little rough-and-ready (particularly in the editing), this *very* low-budget feature, made for just £2000 by the Gorbals Unemployed Workers' Centre, gets by on an intelligent script and naturalistic performances of great conviction from an almost entirely non-professional cast. A look at life in contemporary Britain, as evidenced by the Gorbals, it tells of one family's attempts to deal with death, drug addiction, disease and the threat of dissolution. Very much in the Loach/Amber mould, but none the worse for that. GA

Between Friends
(Donald Shebib, 1973, Can) Michael Parks, Bonnie Bedelia, Chuck Shamata, Henry Beckman, Hugh Webster.
90 min.
After days of youthful glory in the '60s as a surfboard champion, a young Californian (Parks) drifts into petty crime. Teaming up in Toronto with an old friend (Shamata), his girl (Bedelia), and her father (Beckman), he plans the big robbery. The tensions among the group, sparked by the inevitable attraction between Parks and Bedelia, gradually emerge and take over. Laconic and low-keyed, set in a decaying winter. CPe

Between Heaven and Hell
(Richard Fleischer, 1956, US) Robert Wagner, Terry Moore, Broderick Crawford, Buddy Ebsen, Robert Keith, LQ Jones.
89 min. b/w.
Haughty Southern gentleman Wagner is forced to buck up his ideas when he's sent to the Pacific campaign during WWII and finds himself in the 'suicide' platoon commanded by the psychotic Crawford. Needless to say, Wagner's reforming snob learns all about humanity and humility in the tough times that follow. Fleischer keeps his head down, knits the action together, and tries not to let the worthy sentiments saturate the proceedings entirely. TJ

Between the Lines
(Joan Micklin Silver, 1977, US) John Heard, Lindsay Crouse, Jeff Goldblum, Jill Eikenberry, Bruno Kirby, Gwen Welles, Michael J Pollard.
101 min.
An odd film. Ostensibly an examination (and celebration?) of the counter-culture from within, in the form of the story of trials and tribulations of the staff of the *Back Bay Mainline* (a Boston fringe paper) as the '60s edge into the '70s, *Between the Lines* is soon revealed to be an unabashedly Hollywoodian paean to journalism and the free drink. The various reporters ache for fame and brood about the commercialisation of their craft with cynical detachment. That said, Silver's penny plain direction is surprisingly effective. An odd film. PH

Between Wars
(Michael Thornhill, 1974, Aust) Corin Redgrave, Arthur Dignam, Judy Morris, Patricia Leehy, Gunter Meisner.
100 min.
The story of an Australian doctor between the wars. Ostensibly the subject is the young war surgeon's early exposure to the theories of Freud, through to his eventual disillusioned settlement in a comfortable Sydney psychiatric practice. But the real concern is with the texture of Australian social life (in its broadest possible terms) between the wars. Thornhill's direction of the actors is low-key enough to allow the repressive nature of Australian life to emerge from a meticulously controlled *mise en scène*. RM

Beverly Hillbillies, The
(Penelope Spheeris, 1993, US) Lily Tomlin, Dabney Coleman, Rob Schneider, Cloris Leachman, Zsa Zsa Gabor, Buddy Ebsen, Dolly Parton.
93 min.
Savour the music and lyrics from the original TV series – it's one of the highlights of this lamentable half-hour sit-com masquerading as a movie. Rich bumpkin family takes over Hollywood mansion and evil scheming couple try to cheat them of their wealth. No unexpected twists; very few jokes; not much talent. After the glory that was *Wayne's World*, director Spheeris should be ashamed of herself. NKe

Beverly Hills Brats
(Dimitri Sotirakis, 1989, US) Martin Sheen, Peter Billingsley, Burt Young, Terry Moore, Ramon Estevez.
90 min.
Teenager Billingsley is at home alone in his folks' ritzy Hollywood pad when burglar Young breaks in and the pair hatch a plan to make the kid's parents sit up and take notice of him, while the latter pockets a bob or two for himself. Sometimes the movie goes for satire, sometimes it goes for sentiment, either way it's difficult to care. TJ

Beverly Hills Cop
(Martin Brest, 1984, US) Eddie Murphy, Judge Reinhold, John Ashton, Lisa Eilbacher, Ronny Cox, Steven Berkoff.
105 min.
Constructed purely to allow Murphy full rein, the movie leads with its strongest card: Murphy as a cop, black, dirty, fast, on a case of stolen Marlboros in Detroit. When he begins unofficially to investigate the death of a friend, the trail leads him to Beverly Hills. The only black comic who doesn't make white audiences feel guilty expertly steps into the gaping holes left specifically for him in the film, but the connecting stuff is just bagatelle. CPea

Beverly Hills Cop II
(Tony Scott, 1987, US) Eddie Murphy, Judge Reinhold, Jürgen Prochnow, Ronny Cox, John Ashton, Brigitte Nielsen, Allen Garfield, Dean Stockwell.
103 min.
Whatever was fresh and funny about Murphy's Detroit street cop in the original has disappeared: all of his fast-talking con-man impersonations are uniformly yammering and repetitive. Called off a credit card case in Detroit to help his old LA buddies solve The Alphabet Crimes, Murphy is soon on the track of an illegal arms dealer (Prochnow) and his Bondish hit-lady (Nielsen). Scott's direction is a mixmaster without a compass. Depressing. BC

Beverly Hills Cop III
(John Landis, 1994, US) Eddie Murphy, Judge Reinhold, Hector Elizondo, Theresa Randle, Jon Tenney, Joey Travolta.
104 min.
After a colleague is murdered Detroit cop Axel Foley (Murphy) tracks the killers to – you guessed it! – Beverly Hills. The best screenwriter Steven de Souza can do by way of novelty is to locate the action in an LA amusement park, Wonder World. This is an incredibly cheap looking production. You can see the joins in the matte work; and hear the joins in the dialogue, huge chunks of clumsy exposition in what should be a straightforward thriller. There are germs of interest – America's theme-park culture and obsession with weapons – but on the whole Landis aims for the obvious. TCh

Beverly Hills Nightmare
see Bone

Beware, My Lovely
(Harry Horner, 1952, US) Ida Lupino, Robert Ryan, Taylor Holmes, Barbara Whiting, OZ Whitehead.
77 min. b/w.
Not uninteresting woman in jeopardy thriller, worth a look for Lupino and Ryan: she as a lonely war widow, he as the itinerant handyman who suddenly goes funny, locks her up, and alternates unpredictable moods of tenderness and violence. Let down by broodingly sluggish direction (production designer Horner's debut) and by a script which gets bogged down in repetitive action instead of exploring the characters. The deliberately anticlimactic ending should have been much more effective than it is. TM

Beware of a Holy Whore (Warnung vor einer heiligen Nutte)
(Rainer Werner Fassbinder, 1970, WGer) Lou Castel, Hanna Schygulla, Eddie Constantine, Rainer Werner Fassbinder, Ulli Lommel.
103 min.
A film about film-making with roots in Fassbinder's unhappy experience shooting *Whity* in Spain. A German unit stalled by financial and technical problems, lethargically brooding in a Spanish hotel, is finally galvanised by the arrival of the manic director (Castel) and laconic star (Constantine) into a frenzy of activity which ends – the film they are making is a denunciation of state-sanctioned violence – in a concerted attack on the director. Tediously self-indulgent yet fascinating, it works better in its exploration of sexual frustrations than in its thesis that cinema should not be allowed to remain 'a holy whore of entertainment'. TM

Beware! the Blob (aka Son of Blob)
(Larry Hagman, 1972, US) Robert Walker, Gwynne Gilford, Godfrey Cambridge, Richard Stahl, Robert Webb, Carol Lynley, Shelley Berman, Burgess Meredith, Gerrit Graham, Larry Hagman.
88 min.
A tongue-in-cheek sequel to *The Blob* (around the time of the spin-off hit single by The Five Blobs which went: 'It creeps, it crawls, it slithers up the walls'), this is Mary Martin's son's only director-

ial effort, and he plays a cameo part as a hobo. The best moment occurs when the Blob (what *is* it made of?) takes over a bowling alley, then an ice-skating rink. For the rest, assorted guest stars are trundled on to do unfunny turns before getting eaten. CR

Bewegte Mann, Der (The Most Desired Man/ Maybe...Maybe Not)

(Sönke Wortmann, 1994, Ger) Til Schweiger, Katja Riemann, Joachim Król, Rufus Beck, Armin Rohde, Nico van der Knapp.
94 min.
Doro (Riemann) catches boyfriend Axel (Schweiger) in flagrante and kicks him out; he winds up sharing a place with gay acquaintance Norbert (Król) but, after learning she's pregnant, she begins to suspect there's something going on between her ex and his new flatmate. By way of proof, she finds Norbert naked in the wardrobe. Preening cross-dresser Walter (Beck) and sad-faced Norbert offer us a choice of gay stereotypes, but director Wortmann has nothing but sympathy for their pangs of lust for the leading man, and even suggests that *his* desires are a lot less straight and narrow than he'd care to admit. Unfortunately, just when you think the film's turned all liberating and subversive, it wheels on a brazenly throwaway finale and, disappointingly, ends up endorsing the heterosexual coupledom it's been trying to undercut. Billed as the most successful German comedy of all time. Moderately diverting. TJ

Beyond, The (....E Tu Vivrai nel Terrore! L'Aldila)

(Lucio Fulci, 1981, It) Katherine McColl, David Warbeck, Sarah Keller, Antoine Saint John.
88 min.
A shamelessly artless horror movie whose senseless story – a girl inherits a spooky, seedy hotel which just happens to have one of the Seven Doors of Hell in its cellar – is merely an excuse for a poorly connected series of sadistic tableaux of torture and gore. Suspense takes second place to repulsion as faces melt into bubbling, psychedelic disfigurements, crumbling zombies appear everywhere for no apparent reason other than to crumble a little more, and characters sporting strange green contact lenses stare ominously into the camera. GA

Beyond a Reasonable Doubt

(Fritz Lang, 1956, US) Dana Andrews, Joan Fontaine, Sidney Blackmer, Barbara Nichols, Philip Bourneuf.
80 min. b/w.
Lang's most austere film, reducing the characters to pawns arbitrarily shifted in demonstration of a fascinating theorem. Andrews plays a writer who plans, with the cooperation of a newspaper publisher, to discredit the concept of capital punishment: by deliberately implicating himself as a murderer, he will prove the ease with which circumstantial evidence can lead to wrongful conviction. But after he is duly convicted, the publisher (his sole confidant) is accidentally killed and evidence of the plan destroyed. Despite the ingenious/ingenuous twist that ensues, the film is not concerned with innocence or guilt but with demonstrating that justice, finally, lies in the hand of fate. Not a forthcoming film, but one which repays attention. TM

Beyond Bedlam

(Vadim Jean, 1993, GB) Craig Fairbrass, Elizabeth Hurley, Keith Allen, Anita Dobson, Jesse Birdsall, Georgina Hale, Craig Kelly.
89 min.
Jean's second feature (after Leon the Pig Farmer) is pitched somewhere between a psychological thriller and an out-and-out horror movie. In his cell, thanks to Dr Hurley's mind-control drug experiments, 'Bone Man' Allen amuses himself as a dream-invading serial killer. Alerted by a string of suicides at the block of flats where Hurley lives, cynical cop Fairbrass soon realises that she's been experimenting on herself too. Sucked into a dream world where reality and illusion blur, Fairbrass must confront not only his old criminal nemesis, but the guilty memories lurking in his unconscious. The film ends with a brutal punch-up in which Fairbrass finally faces the seemingly indestructible Allen. Like the film

as a whole, this scene is skilfully shot, creatively designed and well edited – but it also undermines the story's premise, that the killer's power now lies in his ability to manipulate the unconscious rather then to punish the flesh. NF

Beyond Evil (Al di là Bene e del Male)

(Liliana Cavani, 1977, It/Fr/WGer) Dominique Sanda, Robert Powell, Erland Josephson, Virna Lisi, Philippe Leroy, Umberto Orsini.
127 min.
Cavani's biopic tracing the relationship between Friedrich Nietzsche (Josephson), minor writer Paul Rée (Powell), and Lou Salomé (Sanda), successful novelist and later student of Freud. Its celebration of a 'pure' and passionate friendship committed to Nietzsche's ideas (of a life transcending ethics) is given a handsome Cinecittà period production. But Cavani's curious dramatic conceit that the writings of the Superman himself can be injected into flesh-and-blood historical characters – as dialogue, as models for outrageous social behaviour – finally ends up as ambiguous, sensationalistic and overblown as its true precursor, Ken Russell's *Women in Love*, a film to which *Beyond Evil*, to pu it politely, more than pays homage. RM

Beyond Rangoon

(John Boorman, 1995, US) Patricia Arquette, U Aung Ko, Frances McDormand, Spalding Gray.
100 min.
1988: Profoundly scarred by the deaths of her husband and son, American doctor Patricia Arquette remains largely unmoved by what she sees around her in Burma, until she is suddenly thrown into the midst of the conflict between the ruling fascist regime and the dissident democracy movement, incarnated here by the wise old tour guide U Aung Ko. While it's hard, finally, to care much about Arquette's road to redemption (especially given her flat and unappealing performance), and while some of the mystical/philosophical homilies advanced by the screenplay simply sound banal, there's no denying Boorman's commitment to the cause of freedom, nor his assured handling of the scenes depicting the larger chaos of a beautiful land torn apart by violence. Illuminating fare. GA

Beyond Reasonable Doubt

(John Laing, 1980, NZ) David Hemmings, John Hargreaves, Tony Barry, Martyn Sanderson, Grant Tilly, Diana Rowan.
127 min.
'You wouldn't want me to confess to something I didn't do, would you?...Would you?' But that's just what Inspector David Hemmings does want in this true tale of Rough Justice Down Under, based on a controversial court case involving a New Zealand farmer charged with a double killing, which occupied the country's courts from 1970 till the Prime Minister's pardon in 1979. This modest but enjoyable film wears its pessimistic *noir* trappings well: cops who believe everyone's got something to hide, everybody's guilty, and rigging evidence and jury lists accordingly; the wife who almost cracks under the strain; most of all, the lack of faith in the truism that justice will out. RM

Beyond Silence (Jenseits der Stille)

(Caroline Link, 1996, Ger) Sylvie Testud, Tatjana Trieb, Howie Seago, Emmanuelle Laborit.
110 min.
A study of living with deafness, which approaches the disability through the eyes and ears of someone who can see and hear. Young Lara (Trieb) can hear fine, but both her parents are deaf, and thus somewhat reliant on her – provoking small frictions, with her stubborn-minded father in particular. Given a clarinet by her aunt, Lara takes it up eagerly, defiantly, and successfully. Cut (mid-performance) to Lara as a young adult (Testud). Her aunt now suggests she move to music college in Berlin. Thanks to rich characterisation (wonderfully acted by all concerned, the Laras especially) and Caroline Link's impressively controlled direction, the film's possessed of a quiet beauty. It tails off toward the close, but still there are some scenes to cherish (how about a deaf church congregation sign singing in unison). NB

Beyond the Blue Horizon

(Alfred Santell, 1942, US) Dorothy Lamour, Richard Denning, Jack Haley, Patricia Morison, Walter Abel.
76 min.
Silly stuff indeed, but OK if you like the lady in the sarong's jungle epics, especially since this is slightly more tongue-in-cheek than most. Here she's an heiress to a fortune, ignorant of her wealth because she's lived on an exotic island since childhood. But then she's rescued, true love calls, and intrigue beckons. GA

Beyond the Clouds (Par-delà les Nuages/Al di là delle nuvole/Jenseits der Wolken)

(Michelangelo Antonioni, 1995, Fr/It/Ger) John Malkovich, Vincent Perez, Sophie Marceau, Irène Jacob, Chiara Caselli, Peter Weller, Fanny Ardant.
115 min.
Antonioni's first film in ten years, and it's like he's never been away. This is European art cinema as it used to be known: composed, stately, meditative, in every sense formal. (Modernism looks better than ever, now it's so old fashioned.) The film tells four stories – four potential films in the mind of director Malkovich (the linking material is by Wim Wenders) – in Italian, English, French, music and silence. Four brief encounters are imbued with concerted philosophical and spiritual gravitas by the grace and patience of the camera: 'I only discovered reality when I began to photograph it,' muses Malkovich. Antonioni has always been one to exercise his metaphoric *droit de seigneur*, and women may feel uncomfortable with the intensity of the director's gaze here, but it makes for entrancing cinema. TCh

Beyond the Door

see Chi Sei?

Beyond the Door (Oltrela Porta)

(Liliana Cavani, 1982, It) Marcello Mastroianni, Eleonora Giorgi, Tom Berenger, Michel Piccoli, Paolo Bonetti.
116 min.
There is something to be said for Liliana Cavani, but it is difficult to remember what it is. The cruelty of her *Night Porter* was ruined by sentimentality, and *Beyond Good and Evil* managed to conflate Nietzsche *and* Robert Powell in a ménage à trois. *Beyond the Door* is the usual mix of cheapjack sentiment, cutprice Freudian familial relations, and a baffled cast running way over boiling point. Giorgi (a madonna face) keeps her stepfather Mastroianni (or *maybe* he's her father) in a Moroccan prison after faking evidence against him over her mother's death, so that she can keep her claws on his body, which she desires far more than the American oilman (Berenger, looking like a young Paul Newman) who desires her like mad but can't understand what's going on here. Un peu tortueuse, hein? There are some dinky touristique scenes in the brothels of Marrakesh, that mosaic city which caters to the devices and desires of your heart; but it should all have been made in hardcore by Robert Damiano (*Behind the Green Door*). CPea

Beyond the Forest

(King Vidor, 1949, US) Bette Davis, Joseph Cotten, David Brian, Ruth Roman, Dona Drake, Regis Toomey, Minor Watson.
96 min. b/w.
Rosa Moline (Davis) is a twelve o'clock girl in a nine o'clock town. Loyalton is the burg in question, and Rosa doesn't like it one bit: 'What a dump...like sitting in a coffin and waiting to be carried out!' Her personal rebellion takes the form of adultery, miscarriage and murder, in King Vidor's most demented film from his most frenzied period, immediately after *Duel in the Sun* and *The Fountainhead* and before *Ruby Gentry*. Davis, done up for all the world like Jennifer Jones, is too old for the part, but gives it her all (she used the film for her own rebellion, escaping a Warner Bros contract that still had ten years to run). She's like a caricature of herself, and the movie, too, is soap gone into lather. Laugh it off, by all means, but American melodrama at this pitch of alienation is quite fascinating. TCh

Beyond the Limit

see Honorary Consul, The

Beyond the Poseidon Adventure

(Irwin Allen, 1979, US) Michael Caine, Sally Field, Telly Savalas, Peter Boyle, Jack Warden, Shirley Knight, Shirley Jones, Karl Malden.
122 min.
After the disaster of *The Poseidon Adventure*, the Salvage Operation. It provides the thinnest of excuses for rerunning the 'dramas' of the night before, but it doesn't do anything to salvage the venerable formula. This time it's the ship that sinks. JCR

Beyond Therapy

(Robert Altman, 1986, US) Julie Hagerty, Jeff Goldblum, Glenda Jackson, Tom Conti, Christopher Guest, Genevieve Page, Cris Campion.
93 min.
Having dealt with computer dating in the insanely neglected *A Perfect Couple*, Altman turns his attention to Lonely Hearts subscribers in a film that merges the romantic merry-go-round antics of *La Ronde* with the clamorous, overflowing narrative tactics of *Nashville*. Based on a stage play – though you wouldn't know it – the movie commences in a ritzy French restaurant where goofy Goldblum meets nutsy nice girl Hagerty; he's bisexual, she's scared stiff of virtually everything. On the fringes of their frantic, stop-go love affair jabbers a gaggle of eccentric lovers, mothers and shrinks. Besides their evidently loose grip on sanity, the members of this group share a desire for a protector. Altman's brash, broad satire retains the ability to touch the heart, evincing a very real sense of pain in certain otherwise contrived scenes. Stunningly designed and shot, it's a weird and sometimes wonderful excursion into New York neurotica that will offend, disturb and intrigue. GA

Beyond the Stars (aka Personal Choice)

(David Saperstein, 1989, US) Christian Slater, Martin Sheen, Sharon Stone, F Murray Abraham, Robert Foxworth, Olivia d'Abo.
87 min.
An expensive cast assembles for this dreary and cliché-intensive chronicle of would-be astronaut Slater's loss of innocence when he meets up with old hand Sheen, a man who's been up there, done it, and suffered a hefty dose of radiation poisoning for his troubles. TJ

Beyond the Valley of the Dolls

(Russ Meyer, 1970, US) Dolly Read, Cynthia Myers, Marcia McBroom, John La Zar, Michael Blodgett.
109 min.
With his first movie for a major studio, Meyer simply did what he'd been doing for years, only bigger and better. That's to say, he turned the homely story of an all-girl rock band's rise to fame under their transsexual manager into a delirious comedy melodrama, soused in self-parody but spiked with dope, sex and thrills. TR

Beyond the Walls (Me'Achorei Hasoragim)

(Uri Barbash, 1984, Isr) Arnon Zadok, Muhamad Bakri, Hilel Ne'eman, Assi Dayan, Boaz Sharaabi.
103 min.
Prison as a metaphor for society at large: there are the rulers/jailers and the ruled/prisoners; the governors play a game of divide and rule with the governed in order to ensure their dominance. *Beyond the Walls* hammers home this cliché in an Israeli prison, where the authorities are ugly sadists and the prisoners' leaders – both Arab and Jew – tall, handsome figures of heroic moral stature. The enduring impression is not the liberal homiletics, however, but rather the unremitting beastliness of the prisoners' lives: a foul stew of humiliation, beatings and homosexual rape. Still, if you like your politics simplistic and your movies brutal – as apparently do the judges who awarded this film the International Critics Prize at the 1984 Venice Festival – you might enjoy the touching details, good character performances, and overall enthusiasm that embellish this thin allegory. MH

B.F.'s Daughter

(Robert Z Leonard, 1948, US) Barbara Stanwyck, Charles Coburn, Van Heflin, Richard Hart, Spring Byington, Keenan Wynn, Margaret Lindsay.
108 min. b/w.
Stanwyck weds poor pinko prof Heflin, then surprises him by giving him a mansion and revealing that her dad is actually millionaire Coburn. This trite social comedy makes a real mess of a then-admired novel by JP Marquand. Nobody's finest hour. TJ

Bhaji on the Beach

(Gurinder Chadha, 1993, GB) Kim Vithana, Jimmi Harkishin, Sarita Khajuria, Mo Sesay, Lalita Ahmed, Zohra Segal, Peter Cellier.
101 min.
A group of Asian 'sisters' go on a women's trip to Blackpool, only to be pursued and confronted by their menfolk. Plot and motivation are both contrived, but once the story gets going, first-time director Gurinder Chadha extracts maximum fun from her sedate matrons and wild teenagers let loose in a working-class holiday hell; she is, in fact, as comfortable with the bhaji as the beach. Segal is wonderfully wrong-headed as chief of the censorious aunties, and Ahmed delightful as the wistful shopkeeper Asha, who meets a camp old English actor (Cellier) and cavorts with him in Bollywood daydreams. The men - the stage villains of the piece - do the best they can. SFe

Bhowani Junction

(George Cukor, 1956, GB) Ava Gardner, Stewart Granger, Francis Matthews, Bill Travers, Abraham Sofaer, Marne Maitland, Freda Jackson.
110 min.
Cukor's abiding interest in both the predicament of women in a male-dominated society and the problems of role-playing are given their most explicitly political expression in this marvellous melodrama set in India during the last gasps of British colonialism. Focusing on an Anglo-Indian girl torn apart by her feelings for three men – an English soldier, an Indian, and another Anglo-Indian – it's one of those rare films that successfully and intelligently combine personal and political issues, in that Gardner's status as a woman without a recognised racial/national idenity dramatically embodies widely conflicting cultural and political ideas. As such, it's very much an intimate epic, drawing an unsentimental portrait of a society in transition, and a vivid, moving account of its heroine's tragic dilemma. Beautiful to look at, and perfectly acted throughout. GA

Bhumika

see Role, The

Bible...In the Beginning, The (La Bibbia)

(John Huston, 1966, It/US) Michael Parks, Ulla Bergryd, Richard Harris, John Huston, Stephen Boyd, George C Scott, Ava Gardner, Peter O'Toole.
175 min.
Turgid account of Old Testament events from the Creation to Abraham's sacrifice of Isaac. Huston himself adds a touch of life as Noah, and the Tower of Babel scene is fairly well done, but overall it's a long haul which manages to suggest that places like Eden and Sodom weren't much fun at all. GA

Biches, Les (The Does)

(Claude Chabrol, 1968, Fr/It) Stéphane Audran, Jacqueline Sassard, Jean-Louis Trintignant, Nane Germon, Henri Attal, Dominique Verdi, Serge Bento.
99 min.
The film with which Chabrol returned to 'serious' film-making after his series of delightful thriller/espionage spoofs, this was also the film in which he began transferring his allegiance from baroque Hitchcockery to the bleak geometry of Lang. A calm, exquisite study, set in an autumnal Riviera, of the permutational affairs of one man and two women which lead to obsession, madness and despair. Each sequence is like a question-mark adding new doubts and hypotheses to the circular (as opposed to triangular) relationship as a rich lady of lesbian leanings (Audran) picks up

an impoverished girl (Sassard), and whisks her off to her St Tropez villa. There, much to the distress of her benefactress, the girl embarks on an affair with a handsome young architect (Trintignant), only to find in her turn that architect and lesbian lady are in the throes of a mutual passion. Impeccably performed, often bizarrely funny, the film winds, with brilliant clarity, through a maze of shadowy emotions to a splendidly Grand-Guignolesque ending. TM

Bicycle Thieves (Ladri di Biciclette)

(Vittorio De Sica, 1948, It) Lamberto Maggiorani, Enzo Staiola, Lianella Carell, Gino Saltamerenda.
90 min. b/w.
A working class Italian, out of work for some time, has the bicycle stolen which he needs for a new job; he and his son wander round Rome looking for it. Often hailed as an all-time classic, *Bicycle Thieves* tries to turn a simple story into a meditation on the human condition, but its greatest achievement is in bringing the lives of ordinary Italian people to the screen. However, like so many of the films grouped together under the heading of Italian neo-realism, its grainy monochrome images and simple storyline never delve beneath the surface of the characters' lives to reveal the social mechanisms at work there. It is as if, just by portraying the events unobtrusively, De Sica imagines that they will yield up their essential truth by a process of revelation - a very appropriate image for a strain of liberal humanism strongly influenced by Catholicism. Observant and sympathetic it is, politically perceptive it is not. NF

Biddy

(Christine Edzard, 1983, GB) Celia Bannerman, Sam Ghazoros, Patricia Napier, John Dalby.
85 min.
A meticulously realised, perfectly nostalgic picture whose subject is a Victorian nurserymaid. Biddy's voice, decorated equally with passages from English literature and pithy homilies, runs on and on (all other voices are surreal noises-off) marshalling the forces of the nursery and the pattern of her charges' lives. She revels, Mrs Tiggy-Winkle-like, in mending, clean linen and the laying of tea, happiest when 'everything is in its proper place, everything is in order'. But even as this spare, deliberately wrought film so carefully points and extolls the virtues of Biddy and those many others like her, it is apparent that what is really being celebrated is the paraphernalia of these lives. The sewing-boxes, the button-hooks, the pieces of treen and piles of handworked lace, these are the real stars of the film. FD

Bidone, Il (The Swindlers)

(Federico Fellini, 1955, It/Fr) Broderick Crawford, Giulietta Masina, Richard Basehart, Franco Fabrizi, Alberto De Amicis.
114 min. b/w.
A pair of provincial con-men (Crawford and Basehart) pose as priests to swindle ignorant peasant farmers, but what begins as comedy turns sour, cruel, and finally tragic. Characteristically, Fellini stacks the pack with a final victim of great facial beauty, palsied legs and obscurantist belief, after which it is only a matter of time before bad Brod receives his comeuppance on a stony hillside. Most of Fellini's preoccupations are present, but in 1955 had not yet blown the obligation to tell a story off-course. BC

Big

(Penny Marshall, 1988, US) Tom Hanks, Elizabeth Perkins, Robert Loggia, John Heard, Jared Rushton, David Moscow, Jon Lovitz.
104 min.
It's no fun being in your early teens, especially if you're none too tall. So thinks Josh Baskin, having been denied a ride on a fairyground suppoop. But neither is being a kid in a grown-up body so hot, as Josh discovers after a carnival wishing-machine grants the change overnight. What do you do when Mom doesn't recognise you, and thinks you're your own abductor? How do you get a job when you can't drive and have no social security number? And when you do find work with a toy-design company, how do you cope with board meetings, office rivalries, and swish staff parties? Marshall's movie may be a mite predictable, but it's genuinely funny, thanks partly to Hanks' engagingly gauche and gangly performance as

the overgrown Josh, and partly to a script that steers admirably clear of gross innuendo. Much of the humour derives from Josh's inability to comprehend adult life; much of its charm from the way his forthright innocence steadily revitalises those around him. Admittedly, this latter theme makes for an ending oozing with saccharine sentiment; but until then Marshall, Hanks, and his co-stars seldom put a foot wrong. GA

Bigamist, The
(Ida Lupino, 1953, US) Edmond O'Brien, Ida Lupino, Joan Fontaine, Edmund Gwenn, Jane Darwell, Kenneth Tobey.
80 min. b/w.
One of Lupino's sympathetic little problem pictures. Its weakness, perhaps, is that in trying to avoid the obvious of making a whipping-boy of the bigamous husband, it creates characters who are a shade too good to be true. But the three lead performances are terrific, movingly illuminating the impasse whereby O'Brien's travelling salesman finds himself in love with two women – Fontaine as the outgoing career-woman who can't have children, Lupino as the quiet home-lover who has borne him a child – each of whom brings him something the other can't. The complex issues are sketched in with both tact and compassion. TM

Big Bad Mama
(Steve Carver, 1974, US) Angie Dickinson, William Shatner, Tom Skerritt, Susan Sennett, Robbie Lee, Noble Willingham, Dick Miller.
85 min.
Roger Corman's production, following up on his own Bloody Mama, is something of a delight. Although covering the familiar ground of bank robbing during the Depression, the film persistently and boisterously treads its own path. Dickinson and her two daughters, the one practised beyond her years, the other pretty dumb, move through rural and small-town America selling bootleg liquor, picking up men, robbing banks, and kidnapping rich daughters, arguing that if Ford, Rockefeller, Capone and the rest can have a slice of the cake, why can't they? The ribald script, pausing occasionally for insight, sets up various wayward characters (most of them hot for Mama and her girls) and indulges a capacity for ménages à trois.

Big Banana Feet
(Murray Grigor/Patrick Higson, 1976, GB)
77 min.
The paradoxical fascination with showbiz exhibited by cinéma-vérité film-makers continues unabated. And this record of Billy Connolly's 1975 Irish tour survives inevitable comparisons with Pennebaker, Graef and the Maysles, largely because its subject is caught at the peak of his form, and because Connolly remains resolutely immune to standard showbiz poses; offstage he effortlessly extends his wit to the grotesqueries of touring. A thoroughly entertaining film. PT

Big Bang, The
(James Toback, 1989, US)
81 min.
James Toback has his own theory about the universe to set against Genesis and the Big Bang: 'It all started with the orgasmic explosion of God,' he announces with revelatory fervour at the beginning of this film, which starts with his pitch to independent financier Joe Kanter: it's got no script, no actors, no story, just a bunch of people talking about their lives and beliefs. And this is what we get: a gangster who had a bit part in GoodFellas explains that the best day of his life was when he fell out of love; a basketball star momentarily lays aside his macho bluff to reveal how his wife committed suicide. Movie jock Don Simpson is opaque, Auschwitz survivor Barbara Traub reflective, and no, painter Charles Lassiter couldn't kill even in self-defence, he's more the victim type. Toback asks the big questions, and elicits honest, thoughtful responses from his 19 subjects. His quietly composed picture engages right from its exuberant, staccato opening to a subtle, affecting coda. Sex, love, life, death and the whole damn thing...TCh

Big Bang, The (Le Big Bang)
(Picha, 1987, Fr/Bel)
90 min.
A far cry from Raymond Briggs' nuclear warning, Picha's 'adult cartoon' combines both readings of

its title in what '60s counter-culture would probably have mistaken for Swiftian satire. Following the Bomb, Planet Earth has polarised into two nations, both deficient in the standard number of limbs and sexual characteristics. All the men, who have their arses blown off, are gay and live in an American-Soviet zone, while the multi-breasted women live in Vaginia. A fourth world war threatens, and only Fred, the last possible superhero, can avert it. The final conflict is fought out by a megaton tit and a megaton prick. It is all determinedly gross, with something to offend everyone. BC

Big Bang Theory, The (aka Bang)
(Ash, 1995, US) Darling Narita, Peter Greene, Everlast, Michael Arturo, James Sharpe, Luis Guizar, Art Cruz.
100 min.
A bad day in Los Angeles: get up, lose your apartment, go to a film audition (plus casting couch), get arrested by a cop who'll release you only if you give him head. So far, so demeaning. The Girl (with no name) handcuffs the officer to a tree, takes his uniform and motorbike - and checks out how all that power feels by patrolling the local environs, whereupon various subdivisions of hell break loose. Written and directed by a young LA Brat named Ash, this is defiantly independent film-making, shot guerilla-style, fast and without permits. The vérité ambience is less affected than usual, and a genuine sense of recalcitrant rage distinguishes the film from the fraudulent nonsense of Falling Down. Things improve after a shaky start, and Narita delivers a gutsy performance as the Girl. Ash, however, shows little idea of how each narrative appendix fits into his half-formed overall design. NB

Big Bankroll, The
see King of the Roaring 20's – The Story of Arnold Rothstein

Big Blockade, The
(Charles Frend, 1942, GB) Leslie Banks, Michael Redgrave, Will Hay, John Stuart, John Mills, Bernard Miles, Robert Morley.
73 min. b/w.
Like Next of Kin, this was expanded by Ealing from what had been planned as a propaganda short explaining the work of the Ministry of Economic Warfare. Much more didactic than Dickinson's film, and much less well directed, it's strictly a museum piece. TM

Big Blue, The
(Luc Besson, 1988, US) Rosanna Arquette, Jean-Marc Barr, Jean Reno, Paul Shenar, Sergio Castellitto, Jean Bouise, Griffin Dunne.
119 min.
The action centres on the rivalry between freedivers Barr and Reno – they dive deep without an aqualung – which begins when they are little boys. The first time you see someone plunging into alien blackness is exciting, but the novelty soon wears off. The first half-hour is the best part of the movie. Going through her usual kooky routine, Arquette plays a New York insurance agent who encounters Barr in Peru, and is captivated by his wide-eyed innocence (which others might describe as bovine stupidity). Her sole purpose seems to be to reassure the audience that there is nothing funny going on between best buddies Barr, who talks to dolphins, and Reno, a macho mother's boy (a performance of much comic credibility). The ending is the worst part of the movie: Barr rejects the pregnant Arquette in favour of going under one last time to become a dolphinman. Such bathos reeks of cod-Camus. What lies in between is a series of CinemaScopic swathes of blue seas and white cliffs. Besson's film is exactly like his hero: very pretty but very silly. MS

Big Boss, The (Tangshan Daxiong/aka Fists of Fury)
(Lo Wei, 1971, HK) Bruce Lee, Maria Yi, James Tien, Nora Miao.
100 min.
Lee had been a child star in Hong Kong movies of the 1950s; this crudely made but highly enjoyable revenge drama marked his return to Hong Kong (after his failure to escape stereotyped bit-parts in the US) and launched a worldwide fashion for 'kung fu' movies. Cheng (Lee) arrives in Thailand to join relatives working in an ice-pack-

ing plant. When he learns that the place is a front for heroin smuggling, he reveals his martial prowess and takes on the villainous boss (Han Yingjie, also the film's martial arts choreographer) in a frighteningly intense duel to the death. The mix of authentic martial arts skills, cartoonlike violence, righteous anger and filial piety (Cheng never forgets his promises to dear old mum, back in Hong Kong) struck a chord with audiences everywhere in a way rarely seen since the heyday of the James Dean cult, making Lee a global star overnight. TR

Big Brawl, The
(Robert Clouse, 1980, US) Jackie Chan, José Ferrer, Kristine De Bell, Mako, Ron Max, David S Sheiner.
105 min.
No prizes for sophistication, but a much less botched job than Enter the Dragon. The first half, at least, is an adequate showcase for the not inconsiderable talents of Jackie Chan (trained in a Cantonese Opera school, he is less a martial artist than a highly skilled and inventive acrobat, with a sharp sense of physical comedy). The thinly motivated plot (involving Mafiosi, kidnapping, and a brawl tournament in '30s Texas) is as implausible, sexist and naive as an average Hong Kong movie, but Chan gets enough of his own way to emerge radiating charm and to perform a few genuinely amazing stunts. TR

Big Business
(Jim Abrahams, 1988, US) Bette Midler, Lily Tomlin, Fred Ward, Edward Herrman, Michele Placido, Daniel Gerroll, Barry Primus, Michael Gross.
98 min.
Two sets of identical twins, one of each having been accidentally swapped at birth by a shortsighted nurse, are finally, and confusingly, reunited years later in New York. You get the picture, they check into the same hotel, and spend the whole film rushing from room to room, being mistaken for each other by an assortment of bellboys, conspiratorial executives, and conniving Italian businessmen. Midler gets to play her vulgar, trashy self twice over, Tomlin introduces a little comic variety as the gutsy blue collar worker and the drippy sister, and Abrahams handles the mechanical plot with skill, if not style. The frenetic fun reduces everyone to a cipher; it's difficult to care about any of them. NF

Big Bus, The
(James Frawley, 1976, US) Joseph Bologna, Stockard Channing, John Beck, Rene Auberjonois, Ned Beatty, José Ferrer, Ruth Gordon.
89 min.
Frawley's experience directing the Monkees serves him well in timing the one-liners which make up this engaging parody of the airport disaster movie. The maiden voyage of the first nuclear-powered bus – dogged by cannibalistic bus driver, saboteur from the oil companies, and ecstatically stereotyped passengers rediscovering God, sex and will to live in moments of crisis – is really very funny even if the film never gets anywhere. TM

Big Carnival, The
see Ace in the Hole

Big Chill, The
(Lawrence Kasdan, 1983, US) Tom Berenger, Glenn Close, Jeff Goldblum, William Hurt, Kevin Kline, Mary Kay Place, Meg Tilly, JoBeth Williams.
105 min.
A funeral reunites a group of friends from the idealistic '60s who have gone their separate ways in the pragmatic '80s. Over the weekend they eat a lot, argue, go jogging, try to bed one another, and reminisce endlessly to the accompaniment of a host of '60s greats on the soundtrack. However, the script deftly avoids the twin pitfalls of solemnity or sentimentality which threaten such a scenario; instead it's perceptive, affectionate and often very funny. JB

Big Circus, The
(Joseph M Newman, 1959, US) Victor Mature, Red Buttons, Rhonda Fleming, Kathryn Grant, Vincent Price, Peter Lorre.
108 min.

Hitchcock's old scriptwriter from *Blackmail*, Charles Bennett, worked on the screenplay of this pleasing big-top melodrama. Circus owner Mature is left bankrupt when his erstwhile partners walk out on him. He begs a bank loan and puts the show back on the road. But somebody is out to get him. The story is straggly but there are plenty of incidental pleasures: Peter Lorre does a turn as a clown, and matters close with a walk across Niagara Falls. GM

Big City, The
see Mahanagar

Big Clock, The
(John Farrow, 1948, US) Ray Milland, Charles Laughton, Maureen O'Sullivan, George Macready, Rita Johnson, Elsa Lanchester.
95 min. b/w.
Excellent *noir* thriller in which crime-journalist Milland, innocently involved with a girl subsequently murdered by his megalomaniac boss Laughton, is then commissioned by Laughton to find the culprit. When he himself becomes the framed suspect, the trap seems closed....With strong performances (especially Laughton as the gross, sexually insecure tycoon, confident in his ability to control the law through his wealth and status), the film also delights through Farrow's evocative direction: the newspaper conglomerate's enormous clock indicating not only the race against time but also the inhumanly inflexible world in which the action takes place; the phallic ornament with which the impotent murderer kills his mocking mistress; and John Seitz's marvellous high contrast photography, portraying a world of isolation in which nothing is as it seems. The source novel by Kenneth Fearing was remade, much altered, as *No Way Out* (1986). GA

Big Combo, The
(Joseph H Lewis, 1955, US) Cornel Wilde, Richard Conte, Jean Wallace, Brian Donlevy, Lee Van Cleef, Earl Holliman.
89 min. b/w.
Terrific gangster movie, although – despite the syndicate shenanigans promised by the title – it's more of a *film noir* focusing on the private, obsessional duel between Wilde's cop and Conte's gangster, each variously haunted by a woman and virtually becoming the other's alter ego during the course of their deadly vendetta. A film structured by viciousness and pain (amplified by two peculiarly hideous torture scenes involving a hearing aid), it's a dark night of several souls perfectly visualised in John Alton's extraordinary camerawork. Even better than Lewis' earlier – and remarkable – *Gun Crazy*. TM

Big Country, The
(William Wyler, 1958, US) Gregory Peck, Burl Ives, Jean Simmons, Charlton Heston, Carroll Baker, Charles Bickford, Chuck Connors.
166 min.
One of those Big Westerns - feuding families with rival patriarchs back on the farm - which aren't so much epic as long. Finely crafted, though, with some marvellous camerawork (Franz Planer), an outstanding performance from Heston, and a vague message about violence predictably underscored by a marathon fist-fight between Peck and Heston. TM

Big Deal at Dodge City
see Big Hand for the Little Lady, A

Big Deal on Madonna Street
see Soliti Ignoti, I

Big Easy, The
(Jim McBride, 1986, US) Dennis Quaid, Ellen Barkin, Ned Beatty, Ebbe Roe Smith, John Goodman, Lisa Jane Persky.
101 min.
Lieutenant Remy McSwain of Homicide (Quaid) comes from a long line of venal cops, and although he does little more than run red lights, eat on the cuff in restaurants, and subscribe to the mildly extortionate Widows and Orphans Fund, he is not about to blow the whistle on his 'family's' fancier deals. Crusading Assistant DA Anne Osborne (Barkin) soon locks horns with him in and out of bed, but it takes a multiple murder and heroin scam to make him face up to his own corruption. You might take issue with the

ratio of romance to detection, and to the toy alligator he cuddles in bed, but there is a gusto to the movie and a rush of incidental delights. Highly enjoyable. BC

Big Fella
(James Elder Wills, 1937, GB) Paul Robeson, Eldon Grant, Elisabeth Welch, Marcelle Rogez, Roy Emerton, James Hayter.
73 min. b/w.
Sentimental tosh leavened only by the easy-going acting and powerful singing of its star. Robeson plays a Marseilles layabout hired by a wealthy English couple to find their missing son; when he finally discovers the boy's whereabouts, the latter prefers to stay with Robeson rather than return to Mater and Pater. A comedy drama that fails to tug the heartstrings or tickle the funnybone. GA

Big Fix, The
(Jeremy Paul Kagan, 1978, US) Richard Dreyfuss, Susan Anspach, Bonnie Bedelia, John Lithgow, Ofelia Medina, Nicholas Coster.
108 min.
Much underrated wry thriller with a nice sense of its own scale and an occasionally tough way with eccentricity, in which Dreyfuss' sort-of-private-eye ('a would-be marxist gumshoe') finds nostalgia for an activist past turning sour as an unlikely rightist backlash violently hits a Californian gubernatorial election campaign, and his counter-culture quipping has to be put on hold. A more characteristically quirky work from the oddball Kagan than *The Chosen*. PT

Bigfoot and the Hendersons
see Harry and the Hendersons

Bigger Splash, A
(Jack Hazan, 1974, GB) David Hockney, Peter Schlesinger, Celia Birtwell, Mo McDermott, Henry Geldzahler.
105 min.
Elegantly framed improvisation around the lifestyle of painter David Hockney and friends. Like its protagonists, the film's main preoccupations are composition and style, which often leaves it unquestioningly reflecting their vapid antics.

Bigger Than Life
(Nicholas Ray, 1956, US) James Mason, Barbara Rush, Walter Matthau, Robert Simon, Roland Winters.
95 min.
Mason's furrowed brow and brooding presence have rarely (never?) been used to better effect: 30 years on, his performance as the mild schoolteacher who is prescribed the wonder drug cortisone and becomes a raving megalomaniac addict remains profoundly disturbing. Suburbia is haunted by psychosis; family life torn apart by Oedipal bloodlust. Ray's direction (in 'Scope and Eastman Colour) is as moving as ever - delicate compositions and fluid camerawork contradicted by the image of weak men locked into obsessive self-destruction. At every level the banal props of '50s prosperity are turned into symbols of suffocation and trauma, from the X-ray machine used to diagnose Mason's 'disease' to the bathroom cabinet mirror shattering under a desperate blow. Trashed on first release, resurrected by Truffaut and Godard, lovingly imitated by Wim Wenders (in *American Friend*): this is *Rebel Without a Cause* for the grown-up world. CA

Big Girls Don't Cry...They Get Even (aka Stepkids)
(Joan Micklin Silver, 1992, US) Griffin Dunne, Dan Futterman, Patricia Kalember, Jenny Lewis, Ben Savage, Adrienne Shelly, David Strathairn, Trenton Teigen, Margaret Whitton, Hillary Wolf.
104 min.
Precocious adolescent Laura (Wolf), who remonstrates straight to camera and consoles herself from a miniature book of quotes (Thoreau, etc), is related to half of California through multiple marriages. Fed up, she is the hub of this entirely predictable ensemble piece. There are those with whom she lives: couture-obsessed mom (Whitton) and her clone stepdaughter; pint-sized 'GI Joe' stepbrother (Teigen); neglectful stepdad (Strathairn). And those with whom she doesn't, including estranged man-child dad (Dunne, excellent as usual), temporarily shacked up with a win-

some air-head hippy (Shelly), and favourite step-brother Josh (Futterman). The extended family finally all meet up in a wood cabin by a lake for a *Big Chill*-out, awaiting Laura's return from an attempted runaway. Directed by numbers, this continues a sad decline which has taken Joan Micklin Silver from *Hester Street* through *Loverboy* to this. WH

Biggles
(John Hough, 1986, GB) Neil Dickson, Alex Hyde-White, Fiona Hutchinson, Peter Cushing, Marcus Gilbert, William Hootkins.
92 min.
Sci-fi! Special effects! Disco dogfights! Americans! It is not generally known that time slippage was a very common thing in the World War I trenches. But it was. And Biggles did it, looping the temporal loop in tandem with his so-called Time Twin, an American fast-food entrepreneur of the '80s called Jim. Their lives are inextricably interwoven 'twixt trench and many of London's modern tourist landmarks. Biggles and Jim abseil off Tower Bridge before nicking a state-of-the-science helicopter, whirly-birding it back into 1917 to clobber the Huns' fiendish Sensurround machine. Biggles! Boggles! Buggles! Bunkum! AB

Big Hand For the Little Lady, A (aka Big Deal at Dodge City)
(Fielder Cook, 1966, US) Henry Fonda, Joanne Woodward, Jason Robards, Charles Bickford, Burgess Meredith, Kevin McCarthy, Paul Ford, Robert Middleton.
96 min.
A superb cast makes up for indifferent direction in this engaging O Henryish yarn about a marathon poker game (in Laredo, despite the British release title) and the little lady who uses her feminine wiles to scoop the pot. To be fair to Cook, this started life as a 48-minute teleplay by Sidney Carroll; the rest he has to pad out with close-ups and irrelevancies. TM

Big Heat, The
(Fritz Lang, 1953, US) Glenn Ford, Gloria Grahame, Jocelyn Brando, Lee Marvin, Carolyn Jones, Alexander Scourby.
90 min. b/w.
Homicide Sgt Dave Bannion (Ford), a seemingly wholesome family man, investigates a fellow officer's suicide. Lifting the lid off the garbage can, he uncovers a world where megalomaniac crime bosses, police commissioners and city councillors share the same poker table, and all opposition is put on the payroll. Pulled off the case and suspended from duty, personal tragedy and a growing contempt for his peers lead him into a vengeful vendetta that equates his actions with those of his enemies. Lang strips down William P McGivern's novel to essentials, giving the story a narrative drive as efficient and powerful as a handgun. The dialogue is functional. Every shot is composed with economy and exactitude, no act gratuitous. The most celebrated scene, where Marvin's psychopathic gangster mutilates his moll Grahame's face with scalding coffee, is remarkable in that you never see him do it; the contract killings are also sex murders, but again unseen. Bannion's redemption comes as he (and we) are moved by the courage of others; a crippled woman gives him a lead, a band of old army chums protect his daughter, and finally Grahame, in whose retributive act lies his purgation. WH

Big Hit, The
(Che-Kirk Wong, 1998, US) Mark Wahlberg, Lou Diamond Phillips, Christina Applegate, Avery Brooks, China Chow, Elliott Gould.
91 min.
Wong's first US feature (he's credited by a bizarre Anglicisation of his Chinese name, Wong Chi-Keung) is only marginally slicker and more sophisticated than his HK movies, but a whole lot more anonymous. Melvin Smiley (Wahlberg, mostly fully clothed) is a sweet natured hitman, great at his job but too naive to realise that everyone around him is ripping him off. His boss Cisco (Phillips, in live-action cartoon mode) kidnaps an heiress for ransom, unaware that her dad has just gone bankrupt and that his own boss (Brooks) is the girl's godfather. Melvin is blamed for the mistake, and winds up hiding the victim (newcomer Chow, sparky) from both the cops and his own gang. Not as funny or exciting as it thinks it is, this

lurches from violent set pieces in the John Woo vein (Woo is an executive producer) to extended sit-com scenes, and fails to tie up its loose ends by demolishing a video-rental barn for the finale. Despite some homoerotic locker-room stuff at the beginning, it all feels very 'corporate'. TR

Big Jake

(George Sherman, 1971, US) John Wayne, Richard Boone, Maureen O'Hara, Patrick Wayne, Chris Mitchum, Bobby Vinton, Bruce Cabot, Glenn Corbett, Harry Carey Jr. 110 min.
Duke in one of his latter-day vehicles (a bit of a jalopy, actually) as cattle baron Big Jake, who goes gunning after the baddies when they kidnap Little Jake. A queasy combination of classic Wayne oat opera and happy jalopy jokiness à la *Butch Cassidy and the Sundance Kid*. AB

Big Job, The

(Gerald Thomas, 1965, GB) Sidney James, Sylvia Syms, Dick Emery, Joan Sims, Lance Percival, Jim Dale, Deryck Guyler. 88 min. b/w.
Director, screenwriter (Talbot Rothwell), producer (Peter Rogers) and the familiar cast ensure that this 'unoffical' Carry On reproduces the familiar formula of its virtually institutionalised predecessors. Here Sid's hapless gang emerge from jail fifteen years after the eponymous disaster, and attempt to recover their hidden loot from the grounds of a police station that has sprung up on the site. PT

Big Knife, The

(Robert Aldrich, 1955, US) Jack Palance, Ida Lupino, Shelley Winters, Rod Steiger, Everett Sloane, Jean Hagen, Wendell Corey, Wesley Addy. 111 min. b/w.
Hollywood on Hollywood: 'They louse you up, and then they call you a louse'. Aldrich coaxes independent, intense performances from Clifford Odets' wordy and stagebound script, which is left to wrestle with its own rather precious liberal conscience while Aldrich concentrates upon what interests him more: the problems of survival and redemption. Undoubtedly daring in its day, *The Big Knife* remains intelligent and literate, but saved from 'safety' by Palance and Steiger's obviously mutual loathing. Palance's performance as the cracking star shows that he once had a great capacity for suffering, and Steiger's hammy outrageousness (playing a mixture of studio bosses Cohn and Mayer) has never been so adroitly exploited. CPe

Big Lebowski, The

(Joel Coen, 1998, US/GB) Jeff Bridges, John Goodman, Julianne Moore, Steve Buscemi, David Huddleston, Philip Seymour Hoffman, Tara Reid, Peter Stomare, John Turturro, David Thewlis, Ben Gazzara, Sam Elliott. 117 min.
This comic update of the world crystallised by Raymond Chandler charts the disastrous involvement of laidback dopehead Jeff 'the Dude' Lebowski (Bridges) in a kidnapping case involving the wife of his millionaire namesake (Huddleston). The Dude is hired as bagman and of course finds himself increasingly at risk as he makes his way about an LA populated by the rich, strange and dangerous. Nor do his bowling buddies help: Donny (Buscemi) is frankly several pins short of a strike; while Walter (Goodman), a crazed, irascible Viet vet, is so determined to stand his (and the Dude's) ground that he causes more trouble than he solves. Immensely inventive and entertaining, the film may not have the enigmatic elegance or emotional resonance of *Barton Fink* or *Fargo*, but it's still a prime example of the Coens' effortless brand of stylistic and storytelling brilliance. Thanks to Roger Deakins' gleaming camerawork, T-Bone Burnett's eclectic soundtrack selection and the Coens' typically pithy dialogue, it looks and sounds wonderful. Moreover, far from being shallow pastiche, it's actually about something: what it means to be a man, to be a friend, and to be a 'hero' for a particular time and place. GA

Big Lift, The

(George Seaton, 1950, US) Montgomery Clift, Paul Douglas, Cornell Borchers, Bruni Lobell, OE Hasse. 120 min. b/w.

Filming in Germany against the backdrop of the Berlin Airlift adds an extra element of historical interest to this social-conscience picture exploring differing American attitudes to the former enemy five years after the war. Clift is good value as the young idealist airman who discovers that girlfriend Borchers has been lying to him about her past, while radio operator Douglas, soured by his experiences during combat, can barely disguise his xenophobia, even though he's going out with attractive fraulein Lobell. TJ

Big Man, The

(David Leland, 1990, GB) Liam Neeson, Joanne Whalley-Kilmer, Billy Connolly, Ian Bannen, Maurice Roëves, Kenny Ireland, John Beattie, Amanda Walker. 116 min.
By adhering to the classic fight-movie formula of beleaguered pugilist vs manipulative crime boss in this adaptation of William McIlvanney's novel, Leland and scriptwriter Don Macpherson have made one of Britain's finest existential thrillers in ages. When unemployed Scottish miner Danny Scoular (Neeson) agrees to fight a one-off bare-knuckle bout, he not only risks losing his wife (Whalley-Kilmer) and kids, but enters a hellish domain lorded over by ruthless Glasgow gang boss Matt Mason (Bannen). The tortuous, taciturn script centres on questions of integrity, courage, commitment and betrayal; and the mood of corruption, paranoia and violence is palpable throughout, thanks in no small measure to excellent performances from Neeson and Bannen. There are minor flaws, but as a portrait of one man's desperate struggle to survive against all odds, the film is tough, taut and intelligently critical of the man's world it depicts. GA

Big Meat Eater

(Chris Windsor, 1982, Can) George Dawson, Big Miller, Andrew Gillies, Stephen Dimopoulous, Georgina Hegedos. 82 min.
Who's that man? It's Bob Sanderson, the friendly neighbourhood butcher strutting his stuff through the streets of small-town Burquitlam. And who's that fat Turk who makes fillets out of Mayor Rigatoni's fingers before stowing the corpse in Bob's deep freeze? That's Abdulla, psychopath, dogsbody and dab hand at growling out a musical number like 'Baghdad Boogie'. For this is that rare treat, a singalong sci-fi exposé made on a budget that would barely keep Marlon Brando in beef-steak. The story is so much fricassé of *Plan 9*; too endearing and eccentric to be dismissed as trash, too smart to be described as camp, this may not be prime celluloid cut, but it's certainly best quality hamburger for the fast film set. AB

Big Mouth, The

(Jerry Lewis, 1967, US) Jerry Lewis, Harold J Stone, Susan Bay, Buddy Lester, Del Moore. 107 min.
A prime example of a comic genius on the border line between comedy and tragedy, Lewis is the double of a wanted diamond smuggler in this intricate, machine-like movie. Frustrating and embarrassing, it's one of the few children's films to treat paranoia seriously and humorously at the same time. DMacp

Big Night, The

(Joseph Losey, 1951, US) John Barrymore Jr, Preston Foster, Howland Chamberlain, Howard St John, Dorothy Comingore, Joan Lorring, Philip Bourneuf. 75 min. b/w.
Losey's last American film before his European exile opens on a note strikingly reminiscent of 'The Killers': a sensitive 17-year-old boy (Barrymore) watches in shattered disbelief as the father he hero-worships (Foster) tamely submits to a brutal thrashing at the hands of a crippled sports reporter (St John). Then, wandering with vengeful gun through a seedy nighttown inferno of bars, boxing-rings and nightclubs, he gradually discovers why in a process of growing up. Intense, sharply characterised, brilliantly shot by Hal Mohr, it works extremely well even though Losey subsequently objected to the chronological narrative imposed by producer Philip Waxman: 'It had been planned in a frame of flashback'. TM

Big Night

(Campbell Scott/Stanley Tucci, 1995, US) Stanley Tucci, Tony Shalhoub, Isabella Rossellini, Ian Holm, Minnie Driver, Allison Janney, Marc Anthony, Campbell Scott. 108 min.
New Jersey, the late '50s: Italian immigrants Primo and Secondo Pilaggi (Shalhoub and Tucci) are struggling to make a go of their restaurant, The Paradise. While Primo is a master chef with a near-mystical faith in the traditional food of the old country – too subtle for the locals, who'd rather dine down the street at the glitzy Americanised eatery owned by the flamboyant Pascal (Holm) – Secondo tactfully suggests his older brother offer a few compromises on the menu before the bank forecloses. Ironically, potential salvation comes from Pascal, who promises that, as a publicity stunt, he'll get his friend, the crooner Louis Prima, to visit The Paradise. It's their last chance, and the brothers prepare a banquet no one will ever forget. Directed by actors Tucci and Scott, and written by Tucci with his cousin Joseph Tropiano, this beautifully acted film is a modest but big-hearted delight. Focusing firmly on mood, character and situation, it finds time not only for a generous, balanced appraisal of the brothers' relationship, but for a wealth of other deftly drawn personalities. Much is made of the big night and its preparation, with mouth-watering results, but it's the long, final shot of an omelette being cooked and eaten that best characterises the film's prime virtues: simple, unpretentious, to the point, and warmly human. GA

Big Parade, The

(King Vidor, 1925, US) John Gilbert, Renée Adorée, Hobart Bosworth, Claire Adams, Robert Ober, Tom O'Brien, Karl Dane. 12, 550 ft. b/w & col.
Time has not dealt altogether kindly with Vidor's silent blockbuster which, like *All Quiet on the Western Front* five years later, made both art and box-office out of the disillusionments of WWI. Too much of it is plain embarrassing: the buddy humour which scriptwriter Laurence Stallings carries over from *What Price Glory?*; the snatches of all-American whimsy (French girl introduced to the mysteries of chewing gum; the sentimentality of the hero's return minus a leg but plus superimpositions showing his mother remembering him as a child falling and grazing his knee. Yet even if it romanticises the true horrors beyond all recognition, there is undeniable power in Vidor's vision of a doughboy's episodic odyssey through the vast landscape of war. One is never left in any doubt that he was, even then, a major talent. TM

Big Parade, The (Da Yuebing)

(Chen Kaige, 1986, China) Wang Xueqi, Sun Chun, Lu Lei, Wu Ruofu, Guan Qiang. 103 min.
Chen sees his follow-up to *Yellow Earth* as a metaphor for life in China today: the need to overcome personal frustrations and failings for the common good. It also works extremely well simply as a film about men under stress. Four hundred-odd volunteers, many of the fresh recruits still in their teens, come to a training camp for eight months of intensive drilling. Some of them will win places in China's National Day parade. The film focuses on four of the young squaddies and two of the officers, looking at the ways they bond and split apart, but also at their most intimate feelings; their sense of physical inadequacy, for instance, or their hypocrisy in presenting an exterior they know to be false. It's surprisingly humane and moving. As in *Yellow Earth*, Zhang Yimou's photography lifts the drama into another dimension; there are images here whose power and grace burn themselves into the mind. TR

Big Picture, The

(Christopher Guest, 1988, US) Kevin Bacon, Emily Longstreth, JT Walsh, Jennifer Jason Leigh, Martin Short, Michael McKean, Kim Miyori, Teri Hatcher, Tracy Brooks Swope, Elliott Gould, Roddy McDowall, John Cleese, Eddie Albert. 101 min.
Actor-turned-director Guest presents a comic cautionary tale about a young film school graduate (Bacon) seduced into the compromises necessary to make his first big picture – a

snowbound country-house drama that almost ends up as a teen comedy called 'Beach Nuts'. Bacon is engagingly naive as the starstruck director whose artistic pretensions are whittled away by a slimy studio exec (Walsh). He also becomes increasingly estranged from homely girlfriend (Longstreth) and best pal cinematographer (McKean), and carnal temptation comes in the heavenly form of a TV starlet (Hatcher) who sees him as a ticket to big screen fame. The movie references may strike some as in-jokey, but Guest's likeable film has enough jaundiced sideswipes and lighter chuckles to see it through its slacker spells. Even so, an increasing sense of bitterness creeps in, emphasised by a series of cameos: loopy Jennifer Jason Leigh, an Irish John Cleese, judge Roddy McDowall, and spaced-out agent Martin Short (whose contribution alone is worth the price of admission). NF

Big Red One, The
(Samuel Fuller, 1980, US) Lee Marvin, Mark Hamill, Robert Carradine, Bobby DiCicco, Kelly Ward.
113 min.
In outline, a chronicle of the movements of a squad from the 1st US Infantry Division through WWII, from a beach-head assault in North Africa to the liberation of a concentration camp in Czechoslovakia. The sergeant is played by Marvin, and four young riflemen are the only members of his squad who survive the war with him; one of them (Carradine) is Fuller's surrogate - because this is Fuller telling his own story, synthesising every thought he ever had about the experience of warfare. No heroics, no anti-heroics, no 'drama' to speak of; instead a racy description of incidents from a great war correspondent, married with a Bressonian concentration on feelings of isolation and dislocation. Visually and philosophically, it's Fuller's equivalent of Kurosawa's Kagemusha, although Fuller's film is more complex, more absurd and more haunted. TR

Big Shot, The
(Lewis Seiler, 1942, US) Humphrey Bogart, Irene Manning, Richard Travis, Susan Peters, Stanley Ridges, Minor Watson, Chick Chandler, Howard da Silva.
82 min. b/w.
Tired gangster movie covering much the same ground as the infinitely superior High Sierra from the previous year. Bogart is fine as the three-time loser trying to go straight, framed back into jail, and breaking out again to meet his doom, but the film goes downhill around him. TM

Big Silence, The (Il Grande Silenzio)
(Sergio Corbucci, 1969, Fr/It) Jean-Louis Trintignant, Klaus Kinski, Vonetta McGee.
115 min.
While Django remains the erratic Corbucci's best picture, this slightly later spaghetti Western does well by an inventive set-up, which has unusually heavy snowfalls on the US-Mexican border bringing various outlaws down from the mountains, where Kinski's ruthless bounty hunter is waiting for them. Trintignant is 'Silenzio', the mute gunfighter determined to stop the carnage, and between the bullets there's engaging stuff from the two stars and an unmistakable chill in the air. TJ

Big Sky, The
(Howard Hawks, 1952, US) Kirk Douglas, Dewey Martin, Steve Geray, Elizabeth Threatt, Arthur Hunnicutt, Buddy Baer.
122 min. b/w.
While not up to the standard of Hawks' best Westerns (Red River, Rio Bravo), still an evergreen delight. Douglas and Martin are the two Kentuckians who join a pioneering trading expedition up the Missouri River to buy furs from the Blackfoot Indians. Problems are many, what with the dangers of the landscape and the hostility of certain Indians. But Hawks is less concerned with the adventurous aspect of the odyssey than with the relationship between the two men, who slowly discover a deep mutual respect, only to have it threatened by their both loving the same woman (an Indian they capture as a hostage against trouble). Episodic, rambling and very amiable, with a nice line in black humour (most evident in the marvellous sequence where Douglas has his finger amputated, only to lose it in the undergrowth). First shown in a 140-minute version. GA

Big Sleep, The (100)
(Howard Hawks, 1946, US) Humphrey Bogart, Lauren Bacall, John Ridgely, Martha Vickers, Dorothy Malone, Regis Toomey, Elisha Cook Jr.
114 min. b/w.
One of the finest mainstream noir-thrillers ever made. As Bogart's Marlowe gets involved with the Sternwood family's many problems (drugs, blackmail, nymphomania and murder), Hawks never allows the plot to get in the way of his real interest: the growing love, based on remarkably explicit sexual attraction, between Bogie and Bacall, and the way that emotion causes both of them to modify their initial positions regarding the criminal goings-on. In fact, the story is virtually incomprehensible at points, but who cares when the sultry mood, the incredibly witty and memorable script, and the performances are so impeccable? GA

Big Sleep, The
(Michael Winner, 1978, GB) Robert Mitchum, Sarah Miles, Richard Boone, Candy Clark, Joan Collins, Edward Fox, John Mills, James Stewart, Oliver Reed.
99 min.
The residue of Chandler in Winner's remake of The Big Sleep might just con audiences unfamiliar with the novels and who haven't seen the 1946 Hawks/Bogart version. Otherwise, it's on very shaky ground indeed. Spuriously relocated in London (Winner's facility with luxurious location set pieces is anything but masterful), and with Marlowe dressed by Savile Row (Mitchum seems to sleepwalk through the part), the film sorely lacks any of the seediness and menace which made the 1973 remake of Farewell My Lovely at least watchable. Winner's insistence as a director on making everything as explicit as possible is often stultifying beyond belief. RM

Big Steal, The
(Don Siegel, 1949, US) Robert Mitchum, Jane Greer, William Bendix, Ramon Novarro, Patric Knowles.
71 min. b/w.
Reuniting the team of Mitchum, Greer and ace-scriptwriter Daniel Mainwaring after the classic noir-romance Out of the Past, this takes a typical thriller situation (for that matter, a common Siegel motif: society's outsider up against authority) and turns it into a fast-moving, witty parody. Mitchum is the GI framed for a payroll robbery, on the run from dumb officer Bendix, falling in love with the delectable Greer, and in pursuit of the real culprit. Dialogue sparkles, the Mexican locations are atmospherically shot by Harry Wild, and Siegel handles the action with characteristic pace and vigour. The numerous plot twists are in themselves an exhilaratingly tongue-in-cheek exaggeration of noir conventions, while remaining central to the excitement of the film. Vigorous, playful stuff. GA

Big Steal, The
(Nadia Tass, 1990, Aust) Ben Mendelsohn, Claudia Karvan, Steve Bisley, Marshall Napier, Damon Herriman, Angelo D'Angelo.
100 min.
Australian teen Danny (Mendelsohn) craves only two things from life: a Jaguar and fellow-student Joanna (Karvan). He's working class, she's not, so Danny convinces himself that she will only go out with him if he possesses the dream car. Cue large debts and a spiralling nightmare with shady car-dealer Gordon Farkas (Bisley), setting the scene for a ruined date and desperate revenge. In this unevenly paced film, the directing-writing team of Tass and David Parker have retained some of the absurdity of their earlier Malcolm. The film eventually veers off into slapstick: a shame, because the prolonged chase scenes detract from the offbeat view of suburbia and peer pressure which lifts this above more mundane offerings in the genre. Mendelsohn's combination of vulnerability and bravado is a consistent delight. CM

Big Store, The
(Charles Riesner, 1941, US) The Marx Brothers, Tony Martin, Virginia Grey, Margaret Dumont, Douglas Dumbrille, Virginia O'Brien, Henry Armetta.
80 min. b/w.

Kitsch wins over comedy in the Marx Brothers' last MGM film, which remains in the mind mainly because of the amazingly awful 'Tenement Symphony', in which Tony Martin and a screen full of sparkling urchins warble a lyric of the finest drivel: 'The songs of the ghetto inspired the allegretto'. Nothing the Marx Brothers do is funnier than this, though Harpo and Chico's musical bits are livelier than usual. Dumont is prominently featured and totally mishandled, Groucho seems half asleep, and the plot (centred on a department store) doesn't bear thinking about. GB

Big Street, The
(Irving Reis, 1942, US) Henry Fonda, Lucille Ball, Ray Collins, Sam Levene, Eugene Pallette, Agnes Moorehead, Barton MacLane.
88 min. b/w.
Adapted from a story by Damon Runyon ('Little Pinks'), this captures much of his low-life spirit and colourful vernacular, but occasionally spoils it all by wallowing in unnecessary sentimentality. Busboy Fonda idolises nightclub chanteuse Ball so much that when she's crippled by her gangster friend, he devotes himself to her well-being, even to the extent of pushing her wheelchair to Florida. Most appealing are the performances by the likes of Pallette, Collins and Levene, although Ball, in a rare straight role, is stunning as the hard-as-nails, embittered exploiter of Fonda's affections. GA

Big Swap, The
(Niall Johnson, 1997, GB) Antony Edridge, Sorcha Brooks, Richard Cherry, Julie-Ann Gillitt, Kevin Howarth, Alison Egan, Mark Caven, Clarke Hayes, Jackie Sawiris.
122 min.
An adult British movie about sex and its role in modern relationships. Five comfortably off, thirty-something couples decide one weekend to try, just for fun, partner swapping. The group embraces diverse characteristics – shy, candid, cautious, adventurous, sensitive, misogynist, closet lesbian, man dependent – without ever offering one rounded human being. Notwithstanding a few lame attempts at humour, the film is dreadfully earnest in its remorseless attempts to touch on every imaginable insecurity, jealousy, anxiety, need and sexual proclivity. GA

Big Time
(Chris Blum, 1988, US) Tom Waits, Michael Blair, Ralph Carney, Greg Cohen, Marc Ribot, Willy Schwarz.
87 min.
This magnificent movie, filmed on a set consisting of a red-and-black checked floor and neon light boxes, cross-cut with scenes shot around the theatre, sees Waits adopt a variety of guises; the pencil-moustached ticket-seller who 'dreams the film', a sit-down comedian in stained white tuxedo and glitter-flecked face – sort of Victor Borge from Hell – and more or less straight troubadour. The music is from 'Frank's Wild Years', 'Rain Dogs' and 'Swordfishtrombones'. Musical, visual, and verbal puns abound; elements of vaudeville, burlesque, and soulful balladry are orchestrated by what is evidently, for all the downbeat, offbeat imagery, a fantastically energetic imagination. A concert film unlike any other, owing something to the work of '40s fashion photographer/jazz film-maker Djon (Jammin the Blues) Mili, and with no shots of an audience at all. MC

Big Top Pee-Wee
(Randal Kleiser, 1986, US) Paul Reubens, Penelope Ann Miller, Kris Kristofferson, Valeria Golino, Susan Tyrrell, Albert Henderson, Kevin Peter Hall, Kenneth Tobey.
90 min.
This second feature from minor-comedian-cum-notorious-cult-figure Paul Reubens (alias Pee-Wee Herman) isn't in the same class as Pee-Wee's Big Adventure, but still provides plenty of prize pickings for kids, kooks and academics. Pee-Wee is down on the farm with his talking pig Vincent when a circus pitches tent in the adjacent field. Soon our hero is convinced there's sawdust in his veins. So are we, because comedians don't come much stranger than Pee-Wee. You'd think twice about taking candy from this baby, but his deadpan perversity is both funny peculiar and funny ha-ha. TCh

Big Town, The

see Arm, The

Big Trail, The

(Raoul Walsh, 1930, US) John Wayne, Marguerite Churchill, El Brendel, Tully Marshall, Ward Bond, Tyrone Power Sr.
125 min. b/w.
Walsh's epic Western led the way in cinema history as the film that made bit-part actor Marion Morrison into leading man John Wayne (though it needed Ford's *Stagecoach* to revive his career a decade later). Originally made simultaneously in normal 35mm and a short-lived 70mm process called 'Grandeur', it has recently been restored to its spectacular wide-screen glory. The saga of a wagon trail, the film is more striking now for its wide shots - vast landscapes, wagons being hauled up impossibly steep cliffs - than for the knock-about humour of the character scenes. DT

Big Trouble

(John Cassavetes, 1986, US) Peter Falk, Alan Arkin, Beverly D'Angelo, Charles Durning, Paul Dooley, Robert Stack, Valerie Curtin.
93 min.
Presumably directed as a favour to old buddy Falk, Cassavetes' last film is a far cry from the glories of *Gloria*, *Husbands*, *Shadows* and the rest. Indeed, it's absolutely unrecognisable as his work, being a conventionally glossy spoof thriller in which insurance salesman Arkin, desperate for finance to send his musical triplets through Yale, agrees to forge a double indemnity policy on Falk's life for his third wife D'Angelo. Sounds familiar? For the first third, this is a comic reshuffle of moments from Wilder and Chandler's classic *Double Indemnity*, but then out come the wacky surprises in a chaotically inventive mish-mash of black neurotic humour. Never hysterically funny but scattered with pleasingly OTT moments and throwaway lines, it looks as if Cassavetes merely wanted a).to prove he could make a blandly stylish commercial piece, and b) to make the cash. GA

Big Trouble in Little China

(John Carpenter, 1986, US) Kurt Russell, Kim Cattrall, Dennis Dun, James Hong, Victor Wong, Kate Burton.
100 min.
'Ready, Jack?' asks Kurt Russell's Chinese buddy before another fraught round of mayhem beneath the streets of San Francisco's Chinatown. 'I was born ready', comes back the growled response; and it is this level of conscious self-mockery which saves the John Wayne posturing and genre high kicks from being just another climber on the *Raiders of the Lost Ark* band wagon. Russell is the T-shirted bozo trucker, who only has to fire his gun into the ceiling for the plaster to fall on his head. Down the mean catacombs and underground streams of Chinatown he goes, in search of something or other and encountering every Chinese cliché known to man: devil women, 900-year-old sages, water tortures, black magic monsters. The icing on all this cake is a load of kung-fuey, which in spite of three nifty warlords who come equipped with their own static electricity and interesting hats, isn't really up to the mark established in the meanest of Hong Kong martial arts movies. Carpenter has always been a skilful genre mechanic, breathing life into old forms; if he stubs his toes up against the bamboo curtain this time, there is still more enjoyable sly humour than in most slug-fests. CPea

Big Wednesday

(John Milius, 1978, US) Jan-Michael Vincent, William Katt, Gary Busey, Patti D'Arbanville, Lee Purcell, Sam Melville.
119 min.
A personal elegy (and a celebration of traditional values) that follows three male friends over a decade of surfing - the '60s - under the gradual encroachment of external considerations: age, the war, responsibility. Misguided occasionally, suspect even, it represents the painful growing-up of the beach/youth movie; possibly one of the best American films of the '70s. CPe

Big Wheels and Sailor

(Doug Aitken, 1979, GB) Nigel Humphries, Julian Curry, Sheila Reid, Dominic Letts, Glen Cunningham.
55 min.
Lively, innocent and highly characteristic Children's Film Foundation offering in which the 'Big Wheels' of a decidedly well-spoken truck-driver (plus two kids) is hijacked by 'Mother', the cigar-smoking owner of a cab company (Reid), slit-eyed and hissingly dismissive of her incompetent 'children'. Plenty of wheezing hydraulic breaks, junior motorbike rough-riding, and chasing over teetering industrial structures. No less implausible than *Teenage Mutant Ninja Turtles*, but from a different age. JPy

Big Zapper

(Lindsay Shonteff, 1973, GB) Linda Malowe, Richard Monette, Gary Hope, Sean Hewitt, Jack May.
94 min.
Imagine TV's *The Avengers* yoked to a British sex movie, add some conscious efforts to imitate Hong Kong kung-fu movies, and you have some idea of this lamentable enterprise. Totally raddled effort devoid of any finer judgment or humour.

Bike Boy

(Paul Morrissey/Andy Warhol, 1967, US) Joe Spencer, Viva, Bridgit Polk, Ingrid Superstar, Ed Hood.
96 min.
The idea in this one was to take a typical American stud (Spencer, never seen before or since) and place him in 'situations' with experienced Warhol actresses. How did he acquit himself? Impassively. The funniest things are the finale, which has Viva racing to get the guy to drop his pants before the film runs out, and the added prologue, with Spencer showing off his scrumptious physique in the shower, included in order to step up the film's nudity quotient. TR

Bilitis

(David Hamilton, 1976, Fr) Patti D'Arbanville, Mona Kristensen, Bernard Giraudeau, Mathieu Carrière, Gilles Kohler.
95 min.
The source for this debilitatingly tasteful tosh is the *Chansons de Bilitis* by Pierre Louys. Surprisingly, a strong hint of Louys' erotic spirit survives, transmitted mainly through the effective playing and poise of the two leading characters. But it needs much more than a strong hint to counteract Hamilton's fey and phony style. GB

Bill & Ted's Excellent Adventure

(Stephen Herek, 1988, US) Keanu Reeves, Alex Winter, George Carlin, Terry Camilleri, Bernie Casey, Dan Shor, Robert V Barron.
89 min.
Bill (Winter) and Ted (Reeves) are cool dudes, but to their teacher, they're high school no-hopers. They fantasise about forming a rock band called 'Wyld Stallyns'; one day they'll pull themselves together and learn how to play guitar. Unless he achieves the seemingly impossible and passes a history presentation, Ted will be shipped off to military school; end of friendship! A figure from the future (Carlin) appears in the nick of time, providing a time-travelling phone booth. The two jump in and out of different epochs, collecting historical figures (from Socrates to Billy the Kid) and confronting them with West Coast culture. This is extremely silly, good natured, superficial stuff; a lot depends on whether you take to Bill and Ted's unique lingo (which contorts surfers' expressions) and their gormless behaviour. The funniest scenes involve Napoleon (Camilleri) adrift in Southern California: pompous and power-hungry, he devours the menu in an ice-cream parlour and hogs the rides in a waterslide park. CM

Bill & Ted's Bogus Journey

(Peter Hewitt, 1991, US) Alex Winter, Keanu Reeves, George Carlin, Joss Ackland, William Sadler, Pam Grier, Sarah Trigger, Amy Stock-Poynton, Jeff Miller, David Carrera.
93 min.
The Utopia created in *Bill & Ted's Excellent Adventure* is threatened by two robot Doppelgängers of the meat-headed, mop-topped duo. These two Terminators travel back in time to present-day San Dimas, California, and swiftly despatch the real Bill & Ted. But death is only the beginning... The first Bill & Ted movie remained a minor cult in Britain, but this far more

cinematic sequel deserves a wider audience. Winter (Bill) and Reeves (Ted) make a comic pairing to rival Laurel and Hardy, blundering through life – and the afterlife – with an endearing naivety (when the Grim Reaper promises them their lives if they beat him at chess, they suggest a game of Battleships). The eventual triumph of US junk culture is somewhat offensive, even if prophetic, and there are a few naff ideas; but for those who appreciate dude-speak and bozo humour, this is a very funny film. DW

Billion Dollar Brain

(Ken Russell, 1967, GB) Michael Caine, Karl Malden, Françoise Dorléac, Oscar Homolka, Ed Begley, Guy Doleman, Vladek Sheybal.
111 min.
One of Russell's most enjoyable movies, completely free of the pretentious bombast that has become his trademark, so that its meaning is embodied in the narrative rather than imposed on it with a directorial sledgehammer. This was the third and last of Caine's appearances as Len Deighton's Harry Palmer, dominated by Russell's skill and visual flair. The plot is a particularly good one about a fascist Texan general called Midwinter (Begley) who plans the invasion of Russia with the aid of a computer and his own private army (the computer has a screen personality almost as distinctive and pleasing as Hal's in *2001*). In an excellent supporting cast, Homolka is outstanding as the Russian general who collaborates with Palmer to prevent the war, and Russell ingeniously constructs the invasion as a parody of the famous ice-breaking sequence in Eisenstein's *Alexander Nevsky*. DP

Bill of Divorcement, A

(George Cukor, 1932, US) John Barrymore, Katharine Hepburn, Billie Burke, David Manners, Henry Stephenson, Elizabeth Patterson.
70 min. b/w.
Skilfully canned version of Clemence Dane's terribly dated problem play about a shellshocked WWI veteran (possibly suffering from hereditary insanity) who returns from the asylum after 15 years to find his wife planning divorce and his daughter a stranger. Full of strangled sentiments and easy options, with a rather too carefully studied performance by Barrymore. But fascinating to see Hepburn's raw-boned talent already at work in her first film, and Cukor already responding to it. Remade in 1940 with Adolphe Menjou and Maureen O'Hara. TM

Billy Bathgate

(Robert Benton, 1991, US) Dustin Hoffman, Nicole Kidman, Loren Dean, Bruce Willis, Steven Hill, Steve Buscemi, Billy Jaye, John Costelloe, Tim Jerome, Stanley Tucci.
107 min.
Despite a Tom Stoppard script and diligent direction, EL Doctorow's novel about a youngster's experience of the life and times of Dutch Schultz seldom takes off as a movie. An early scene, in which the gangster (Hoffman) sees 16-year-old Billy (Dean) juggling balls high above the street on a railway bridge, catches the magic realism of the novel, but little else does. Schultz, past his peak and awaiting trial, is a changeable mixture of the kindly and the murderous, but Hoffman's performance seems to be based on Arturo Ui, and his voice sounds as if it has been dredged up from the river, along with the corpse of Bo (Willis), first encountered with his feet in a bucket of cement. Dutch's mistress (Kidman), a society woman slumming, takes a shine to Billy, and their affair provides some necessary development to relationships within the gang. The best performance comes from Steven Hill as Otto, the gangster's faithful retainer, and although Dean is OK as the kid with luck, the role of talisman doesn't play on film. BC

Billy Budd

(Peter Ustinov, 1962, GB) Robert Ryan, Peter Ustinov, Terence Stamp, Melvyn Douglas, Paul Rogers, John Neville, Ronald Lewis, David McCallum.
125 min. b/w.
Ustinov directs this adaptation of Melville's last work in uncharacteristically serious vein. There is a decided shift in emphasis from Melville's allegory of absolute good and evil to a poignant examination of the blindness of justice and law.

The angelic Billy is played by a blond Stamp in his first film role; Ustinov himself is Man-o-War Captain Vere, forced to try the naif Billy for the accidental murder of master-at-arms Claggart; and Ryan's performance as the evil Claggart, a role he had long coveted, is staggeringly authoritative, right up to the smile on his face as he dies knowing Billy will hang for his murder. There are many powerful scenes unspoilt by attempts from Ustinov to be cinematic; in fact his self-effacing direction allows the actors to give uniformly sincere performances. Only marginally spoiled by such visual conceits as the lurching ship representing the tilting scales of justice during Vere's debate on whether Billy should hang. RM

Billy Jack

(TC Frank, ie Tom Laughlin, 1971, US) Tom Laughlin, Delores Taylor, Clark Howat, Bert Freed, Julie Webb, Kenneth Tobey.
113 min.
One of the most significant American films of the '70s, not because it's good – it's terrible – but because of the way in which producer/writer/director/star Laughlin marketed it. After it flopped when first distributed through Warners, Laughlin sued the company for nonfulfilment of their contract - a step few independent producers have ever taken - and then independently distributed it across America, carefully balancing promotional expenditure in accordance with daily examinations of the film's local box-office returns. This marketing of the film, as though it were a rock record rather than a film, produced a bonanza for Laughlin and subsequently set the pattern for the intensive promotions of selective films to their 'natural' markets. The film itself is a down market youth pic with Laughlin as the half-breed Vietnam veteran who stands up for America's misunderstood youth and operates a sort of one-man Countryside Commission. PH

Billy Liar!

(John Schlesinger, 1963, GB) Tom Courtenay, Julie Christie, Wilfred Pickles, Mona Washbourne, Ethel Griffies, Finlay Currie, Rodney Bewes, Helen Fraser.
98 min. b/w.
Courtenay as the undertaker's clerk in a dull Northern town who escapes, Walter Mitty-like, into fantasy, scripted by Keith Waterhouse from his own novel (and the play he adapted from it with Willis Hall). Made three years later than *Saturday Night and Sunday Morning*, this is already in a different world. The back-to-backs are being torn down to make way for high-rise flats and supermarkets, gritty realism blossoms into flamboyant fantasy, and the feminine is now represented by kookie 'swinging '60s' Christie. A warm, witty, sensitive film: whatever happened later, something stirred in British cinema in the '60s. RMy

Billy Rose's Jumbo (aka Jumbo)

(Charles Walters, 1962, US) Doris Day, Stephen Boyd, Jimmy Durante, Martha Raye, Dean Jagger.
125 min.
'Oh my God! There she is' screams Ignatius Reilly, the film buff who loves to fan his pet hates in John Kennedy Toole's *A Confederacy of Dunces*. She, of course, is Doris Day, here involved in the direst of circus plots ('What degenerate produced this abortion?' asks the indignant Reilly; answer, Hecht and McArthur). A former choreographer and a fine hand at musicals (*Good News, Easter Parade, Summer Stock*), Walters almost makes up for the three-ring vulgarities with some beautifully staged Rodgers and Hart numbers, although the best of them (the opening sequence) clearly reveals the hand of Busby Berkeley, credited as 2nd unit director. TM

Billy the Kid

(David Miller, 1941, US) Robert Taylor, Brian Donlevy, Ian Hunter, Mary Howard, Gene Lockhart, Lon Chaney Jr.
95 min.
As a studio, MGM was never very happy on the range – indeed this main units rarely got out there, staying in front of process screens and depending on 2nd units. This a typically lumbering brew, with Taylor as an unlikely Billy Bonney; but then the film has little to do with 'myth', let alone any of the 'reality' behind it. Of interest only as proof of how important it was for Ford to discover Monument Valley. CW

Billy the Kid and the Green Baize Vampire

(Alan Clarke, 1985, GB) Phil Daniels, Alun Armstrong, Bruce Payne, Louise Gold, Eve Ferret, Don Henderson.
93 min.
So utterly crazed in conception and so defiantly weird in execution that one can't help harbouring a sneaking *something* for it. A very simple story of the challenge and run-up to the final snooker showdown between the reigning champion (Armstrong) and the would-be contender (Daniels) is confined in a nondescript studio-built breeze-block nightmare interior of dark labyrinthine corridors, featureless rooms and odd pool parlours. A musical, it rattles along in its own funny way to the final grudge match filmed in great swooping takes on a louma crane. It has a kind of balls-out courage. One can certainly see why, but they don't make many films like this. CPea

Billy the Kid vs. Dracula

(William Beaudine, 1965, US) Chuck Courtney, John Carradine, Melinda Plowman, Virginia Christine, Harry Carey Jr.
89 min.
Billy has made an honest Kid of himself around Betty Bentley's Bar-B Ranch until Carradine's Count Dracula enters the plot, posing as Betty's prodigal uncle. An unlikely combination of prairie chases and deftly-wielded crucifixes ensues in what *may* be intended as a campy spoof. CR

Billy Two Hats

(Ted Kotcheff, 1973, GB) Gregory Peck, Desi Arnaz Jr, Jack Warden, Sian Barbara Allen, David Huddleston.
99 min.
Given that it was scripted by Alan Sharp, who wrote Penn's wonderful *Night Moves* and Aldrich's *Ulzana's Raid*, a disappointing attempt to merge serious statements about racial prejudice with a Western pursuit story. Peck is miscast as the ageing Scots outlaw who befriends a half-breed Indian (Arnaz), only to be hounded after a bank raid by Warden's ruthless, bigoted sheriff. Shot in Israel, it looks like Kotcheff was more interested in the scenery than in the characters. GA

Biloxi Blues

(Mike Nichols, 1987, US) Matthew Broderick, Christopher Walken, Matt Mulhern, Corey Parker, Markus Flanagan, Casey Siemaszko, Michael Dolan, Penelope Ann Miller, Park Overall.
107 min.
As predictable as *Brighton Beach Memoirs*, Neil Simon's army reminiscences (adapted from his own play) interest – if at all – through the appropriateness of the playing. It's the ethnic mixture as usual at boot camp, from Jewish intellectual (Parker) to dumb, bullying Polack (Mulhern). Again our narrator is wry, sensitive would-be writer Broderick, so we hear the cues and cadences of Simon's Broadway plays. The new recruits have standard issue hilarious-style problems – route marching, press-ups, food, the local brothel – but most of all they have psychotic, cruel-to-be-kind drill sergeant Walken, who longs to be included in their banal bunkhouse fantasy quizzes, but not the sodomy in the showers, of course. Why Walken plays him so dulcet and limp is beyond comprehension. Suffice it to say it is suicidally against the grain. BC

Bim

(Hugh A Robertson, 1974, Trinidad) Ralph J Maharaj, Anand Maharaj, Hamilton Parris, Wilbert Holder, Joseph Gilbert.
102 min.
Set in colonial Trinidad of the '40s, and using the racial conflict between Indian sugar-cutters and black Trinidadians as the dramatic spring (centred on a *Harder They Come*- type fugitive outlaw protagonist), *Bim* continually throws up intriguing facets of the social texture. Best is the casual acceptance of violence (if not fear or pain) as a fact of life; worst is the treatment of the avuncular British godparents of independence, looking for all the world as if there were no past of colonial exploitation to answer for. RM

Bingo

(Matthew Robbins, 1991, US) Cindy Williams, David Rasche, Robert J Steinmiller Jr, David French, Kurt Fuller, Joe Guzaldo, Glenn Shadix.
87 min.
Canine caper in which a mutt forsakes the circus for the company of a boy whose parents have warned him he can't have a dog. Unsuitable for grown-ups. TJ

Bingo Long Travelling All-Stars & Motor Kings, The

(John Badham, 1976, US) Billy Dee Williams, James Earl Jones, Richard Pryor, Rico Dawson, Jophery Brown.
111 min.
After two disasters (*Lady Sings the Blues*, *Mahogany*), Motown's affair with the cinema produced this over-glossy but attractive period comedy (the setting is 1939, with music to match) about a group of black baseball players trying to make the big time. Excellent performances, but the best thing about it is the sharp, sceptically witty script by Hal Barwood and Matthew Robbins (of *The Sugarland Express*) which teases one or two old sores (notably the black man's recipe for success in a white world: be a clown). TM

Bird

(Clint Eastwood, 1988, US) Forest Whitaker, Diane Venora, Michael Zelniker, Samuel E Wright, Keith David, Michael McGuire, James Handy, Diane Salinger.
160 min.
Eastwood's Bird is bravely the Bird of the jazz faithful, with few concessions. Most of the exaggerations and telescopings of place and time will offend only the discographical mentality. The treatment of narcotics, race, and racism is matter-of-fact, nor is the sense of period insisted upon as it was in The Cotton Club; above all, brave beyond the call of duty, the director trusts the music, tricky old bebop. Music properly dominates the biopic, explaining Chan's long-suffering love for Bird and Bird's whole outlook on the world. The way the narrative leaps back and forth in time parallels the neurotic speed of uptake in bebop itself. Whitaker looks as if he's really playing, indicates the protean nature of the genius, and grabs the part of a lifetime with both hands. Venora's Chan is a miracle. The progression from the Chan of the courtship days,, with her hip, sassy dancer's walk, to the set face and shoulders of the common-law wife, tells a touching story of betrayed dreams. At last American cinema has done black music proud. Unforgettable. BC

Birdcage, The

(Mike Nichols, 1996, US) Robin Williams, Gene Hackman, Nathan Lane, Dianne Wiest, Dan Futterman, Calista Flockhart, Hank Azaria, Christine Baranski.
119 min.
Anodyne Hollywood remake of the 1978 gay farce *La Cage aux Folles*. Homely Armand (Williams) and drag queen Albert (Lane) are thrown into a flap by the imminent arrival of Armand's son Val (Futterman), his fiancée Barbara (Flockhart), and her parents, bigoted Senator Keeley (Hackman) and his well-meaning wife Louise (Wiest). While Albert sulks and minces, Armand removes the soft furnishings and objets d'art. But from the moment their lisping Hispanic houseman Agador (Azaria) trips in on high heels, the edifice of lies starts to totter. Williams' unusually restrained performance is his best for years, Hackman again reveals his under-used gift for comedy, and the build-up to the hysterical finale is dotted with slick flourishes. Lane's squealing Albert, on the other hand, is a test. Director Nichols and scriptwriter Elaine May obviously see this as a satire on moralistic, right-wing Republicanism. In fact, it doesn't so much champion diversity as celebrate conformity, stressing the gay and straight characters' shared investment in the idea of 'family', however that mutable institution may now be defined. NF

Bird Man of Alcatraz

(John Frankenheimer, 1961, US) Burt Lancaster, Karl Malden, Thelma Ritter, Betty Field, Neville Brand, Edmond O'Brien.
148 min. b/w.

Striking performance by Lancaster in this factually based story of a double killer, sentenced to life in solitary, who gets hooked on birds after rescuing a fledgling sparrow, and gradually turns himself into a noted ornithologist. Despite some embarrassing sociological trimmings and an overwrought Ritter as mom fighting for her boy, a likeable film, particularly in its observation of the evolving relationship between the anti-social prisoner and the hostile warder (Brand, excellent) from whom he is forced to beg favours. TM

Bird Now

(Marc Huraux, 1987, Bel/Fr) Chan Parker, Doris Parker, Bill Miles, Dizzy Gillespie, Walter Bishop Jr, Lester Bowie, Henry Threadgill.
90 min.
Huraux's semi-documentary purports to view the phenomenon of Charlie Parker through the cityscapes of New York, but often looks like footage in search of a peg. Wouldn't Kansas City have been more germane to the subject, since Bird was formed before he hit the Apple? The interviews with the bebop veterans are intermittently informative but largely over-familiar, though the real Chan and the rarer Doris are a find. Henry Threadgill comes over as a pretentious twit. A ragbag premise. BC

Bird on a Wire

(John Badham, 1990, US) Mel Gibson, Goldie Hawn, David Carradine, Bill Duke, Stephen Tobolowsky, Joan Severance, Harry Caesar, Jeff Corey.
111 min.
Beware films which boast hybrid classifications like action-romantic comedy and credit three screenwriters (one per genre?). This formulaic offering teams Gibson and Hawn – a love match made in casting heaven – as ex-lovers, reunited after years apart, who find themselves on the run from vengeful criminals. Rick (Gibson), hiding under the Federal Witness Protection Program, changes identities and jobs like most people change socks; Marianne (Hawn) is a lawyer who, in taking up Rick's dangerous life-style, bears the permanent expression of a kid on a rollercoaster. Within the first half-hour, we've met the baddies (led by a taciturn Carradine), heard Rick and Marianne's teasing banter, and experienced the thrills of a shootout and car chase. As for what follows, this drearily repetitious film offers more of the same with variations in backdrop, all directed in perfunctory fashion by Badham. It does have a nice '60s soundtrack; shame about the rest. CM

Bird People in China, The (Chugoku no Chojin)

(Takashi Miike, 1998, Jap) Masahiro Motoko, Renji Ishibashi, Mako, Wang Lili.
118 min.
Very different from Miike's gangster movies but equally rooted in his obvious passion for all things Chinese, this 'adult fairytale' sends two ill-matched Japanese men on a mission to investigate a seam of jade in a remote area of Yunnan (China's deep south-west). Wada (Motoko) is a lily-livered company man; Ujiie (Ishibashi) is a bad mannered, foul mouthed and latently psychotic yakuza who muscles in on the trip because Wada's firm owes money to his gang. The perilous quest takes up the first half of the film, but the second is something else again: both men fall under the spell of the village and Wada grows fascinated by the (mysteriously blue-eyed) girl who claims to be teaching the local children to fly. Pitched somewhere between King of the Children and Mad Max: Beyond Thunderdome, the film's mix of adventure-comedy and magic realism confirms Miike as a genuinely innovative talent. TR

Birds, The

(Alfred Hitchcock, 1963, US) Tippi Hedren, Rod Taylor, Suzanne Pleshette, Jessica Tandy, Ruth McDevitt, Veronica Cartwright, Ethel Griffies, Charles McGraw.
119 min.
'The Birds Is Coming' the advance posters twittered ungrammatically but with justifiable excitement. With death dropping blandly out of a clear sky – its menace magnified into apocalypse from the crop-dusting scene in North by Northwest – this is Hitchcock at his best. Full of subterranean

hints as to the ways in which people cage each other, it's fierce and Freudian as well as great cinematic fun, with ample fodder for the amateur psychologist following up on Hitch's tortuous involvement with his leading ladies. TM

Birds and the Bees, The

(Norman Taurog, 1956, US) George Gobel, Mitzi Gaynor, David Niven, Reginald Gardiner.
94 min.
Flat remake of The Lady Eve in which the humour relies more heavily on crude slapstick. Gaynor is no Barbara Stanwyck, and Gobel (in the Henry Fonda part) was here making what was to be the start of a very short-lived film career. DMcG

Bird's Singing, The (Para Recibir el Canto de los Pájaros)

(Jorge Sanjines, 1995, Bol) Guido Arce, Marcelo Guzman, Reynaldo Yujra, Geraldine Chaplin.
97 min.
A heavy-handed allegory by a veteran Bolivian film-maker about the racism endemic in his country and the more universal inability to learn from history. It opens with masked conquistadors (the harquebus angels) lined against the Andean altiplano skyline, as a mainly mestizo film crew track up the hill like Aguirre's invading army in Herzog's Wrath of God. Thus begins a series of broad parallels, culminating in a siege, whereby the crew, assailed by the Indian community (who have refused to be in their historical movie), almost resort to the use of the ancient harquebuses in their possession. The song of the title refers to the birds of the Indians' annual music festival: the crew shoot them for sport. Beautiful scenery. WH

Bird with the Crystal Plumage, The

see L'Uccello Dalle Piume di Cristallo

Birdy

(Alan Parker, 1984, US) Matthew Modine, Nicolas Cage, John Harkins, Sandy Baron, Karen Young, Bruno Kirby.
120 min.
A trifle self-indulgent – well, it is directed by Alan Parker – but never boring, this tells of the strange, trusting friendship between Birdy (Modine), an introverted teenager whose ideal companion is one of his pet birds, and his protective mate Al (Cage). Their relationship is explored both through flashback, larking about at school and fighting as Vietnam conscripts, and in the present: interned in an army mental hospital, the lonely Birdy appears to believe that he has actually turned into one of his own feathered pets. A military doctor has sent for Al in the hope that he can bring his pal back to his senses. But is he mad? Or can genuine freedom exist only in someone's head? You come away convinced that all that RD Laing stuff about the integrity of mad people ought not to be consigned to the dustbin of the '60s after all. CS

Birth, The

see Piravi

Birthday Party, The

(William Friedkin, 1968, GB) Robert Shaw, Patrick Magee, Dandy Nichols, Sydney Tafler, Moultrie Kelsall, Helen Fraser.
127 min.
Film version of Pinter's first full-length play, a rather unsubtle and flashy piece of seaside gothic in which a scruffy, stay-at-home boarding-house lodger is terrorised by two sinister visitors: rather clever inversions of the stereotypic stage Jew and Irishman. Seems long and fussy, partly the fault of both play and director, but some marvellous performances (Nichols creating her Silly Moo character, Tafler superb as the anecdotal Goldberg) make it worth seeing. SGr

Birth of a Nation, The

(DW Griffith, 1915, US) Lillian Gish, Mae Marsh, Henry Walthall, Miriam Cooper, Mary Alden, Ralph Lewis, Raoul Walsh.
13,058 ft. b/w.
Based on the Rev. Thomas Dixon Jr's deliriously racist The Clansman, a melodramatic novel about the American Civil War and its aftermath,

Griffith's film is remarkable for its technical innovations and for the truly epic feel created by the carefully orchestrated, swirling masses of figures in the battle scenes. It's also remarkable for having had no written scenario, costumes that were made by Lillian Gish's mother, battle scenes that were shot in a day, and a cost that meant Griffith had nothing left but the shirt on his back. The biggest challenge the film provided for its audiences is perhaps to decide when 'ground-breaking, dedicated, serious cinematic art' must be reviled as politically reprehensible. The film's explicit glorification of the Ku Klux Klan has never tempered with time. MSu

Birth of a Nation, The (Die Geburt der Nation)

(Klaus Wyborny, 1973, WGer) Christoph Hemmerling, Peter Flak, Nick Busch, Hannes Hatje.
70 min. b/w & col.
Authentically 'New' German Cinema, and, simultaneously, an archaeology of narrative film itself, Wyborny's avant-garde landmark defines cinema as a 'nation' that has perversely acquired rulers, laws and hierarchies before it has even been physically mapped out. At first appearing to spin an elementary yarn of social organisation (the predictably fraught establishment of a rudimentary commune in the Moroccan desert of 1911) in the 'authoritative' film language of DW Griffith, Wyborny proceeds to break down that language to its constituent elements and produce fragmentary hints of alternatives. Structural filmmaking of a rare wit and accessibility results, with flashes of appropriate absurdity (like the sudden intrusion of Randy Newman's 'Lonely at the Top') highlighting the redundancy of closed systems, whether social or cinematic. PT

Birth of the Blues

(Victor Schertzinger, 1941, US) Bing Crosby, Mary Martin, Brian Donlevy, Carolyn Lee, Eddie 'Rochester' Anderson.
86 min. b/w.
Blues schmuse: if you believe in Bing as the father of New Orleans jazz (well, of the first white Dixieland band, anyway), you'll believe anything. Sappy story with token blacks, Jack Teagarden, and some terrific tunes like 'Tiger Rag' and 'Melancholy Baby'. AB

Bis ans Ende der Welt

see Until the End of the World

Bisexual (Les Onze Mille Verges)

(Eric Lipmann, 1975, Fr/It) Yves-Marie Maurin, Florence Cayrol, Nathalie Zeiger, Jenny Arasse.
98 min.
This better-than-average sex film is based on Guillaume Apollinaire's erotic novel of the same title. Narrative development is largely jettisoned in favour of films-within films, Freudian slips, and Surrealist elements of nightmare. The direction, though, remains sadly unimaginative. CPe

Bishop's Story, The

(Bob Quinn, 1993, Ire) Donal McCann, Maggie Fegan, Ray McBride, Paedar Lamb.
82 min. b/w.
In this deliberate b/w homage to the silent era, a bishop (McCann) relates to a fellow priest (McBride) at a Roman Catholic retreat the story of how as a young man in a coastal village in the West of Ireland he fell in love with a girl (Fegan). The flashbacks which make up the body of the film are printed in sepia and shot in a style reminiscent of Flaherty and Sjöström. It's a nostalgic, memorable piece, from the veteran Bob Quinn, not so much for the resigned mood of the storyteller, as for the deeply moving imagery – a collie running up a hill; the white-clothed ankle of a girl; the dancing torches of a midnight search party; the expressive, weather-beaten faces of the villagers. The dialogue is in Gaelic, post-synched and quiet, as if heard from down the tunnel of memory. WH

Bishop's Wife, The

(Henry Koster, 1947, US) Cary Grant, Loretta Young, David Niven, Monty Woolley, Gladys Cooper, Elsa Lanchester, James Gleason.
108 min. b/w.

b

Pleasant enough Goldwyn-produced whimsy, cashing in on the success of '40s angelic fantasies such as *Here Comes Mr Jordan* and *It's a Wonderful Life*. Angel Grant responds to a bishop's plea for help after his devotion to his plans for a new cathedral has alienated him from family and parishioners. Cary's charm works as successfully upon audiences as it does upon the film's characters, and his relaxed wit plus Loretta Young's delicate loveliness makes for a frothily touching comedy. GA

Bitch, The
(Gerry O'Hara, 1979, GB) Joan Collins, Michael Coby, Kenneth Haigh, Ian Hendry, Carolyn Seymour, Mark Burns.
94 min.
Dreadful sequel to *The Stud* from the Collins sisters, cynically predicated on the supposed desire of the depressed masses to glimpse the Mayfair disco-culture high-life they otherwise can't afford. JS

Bite the Bullet
(Richard Brooks, 1975, US) Gene Hackman, Candice Bergen, James Coburn, Ben Johnson, Ian Bannen, Jan-Michael Vincent, Paul Stewart.
131 min.
A straining think-piece on Western/American morality and values, Brooks' would-be epic charts a 700-mile horse race as a simplistic graph of courage, caring and callousness, with Hackman and Coburn emerging as *Professional*-like pillars of integrity from a meltingly macho proving ground. Any random thought ever committed to paper about the intrinsic 'messages' of the Western genre here turns up as a line of speechifying dialogue: the result is a folly stultified by its own seriousness. PT

Bit of Scarlet, A
(Andrea Weiss, 1996, GB)
75 min.
This documentary, a companion piece to *The Celluloid Closet*, examines gay and lesbian cinematic representation (or non-representation) in mainstream British cinema and TV. Basically, it's a clipfest, with Andrea Weiss and Stuart Marshall's tart narration spoken by Ian McKellen, which trawls the sound era from the Rathbone/Bruce pairing in *The Hound of the Baskervilles* (1939), through the recidivist belles of St Trinian's, the *Carry On* movies, Dirk Bogarde in *Victim* and Malcolm McDowell in *If...*, to Terence Davies and the present. Serious but light, the film presents a provocative, more or less orthodox gay reading, broken down into chapters and using mock 'rules' of behaviour to ironic effect. The participation of various archives (including Britain's NFTVA) is a plus: the shot, for instance, of Kathleen Byron's glare at fellow nun Deborah Kerr in *Black Narcissus* wouldn't seem half so powerful or erotic if it weren't shown in a plush Technicolor print. WH

Bits and Pieces
(Il cielo è sempre più blu)
(Antonello Grimaldi, 1996, It) Enrico Lo Verso, Asia Argento, Dario Argento, Gabriele Salvatores, Monica Bellucci, Daniele Lucchetti.
110 min.
This kaleidoscopic portrait of Rome is peppered with small, intriguing pleasures and leaves a strangely lasting impression. Whether it adds up to an essay on the mind's ability to comprehend something so vast as a city (or the world for the matter) is a moot point. The myriad separate (if slowly relating) scenes offer much droll, mysterious and uniquely Roman amusement. It's one of those idiosyncratic movies that turn up once in a while, usually by people like Otar Iosseliani or Nanni Moretti. Among the throng, Romans and film buffs will spot any number of cameos (Dario Argento, Gabriele Salvatores). WH

Bitter Cane
(Jacques Arcelin, 1983, US)
74 min.
Haiti was first colonised by the French, who turned the island into a giant coffee plantation. In 1804, it witnessed the world's first successful slave revolution. The US Marines arrived in 1915, introduced American capital investment, shifted the economy towards producing crops and products for export, and set up the first in a series of

puppet dictators to protect their interests. And, aside from a brief hiccough under Papa Doc Duvalier, that's the way it's been ever since. This history is outlined eloquently and succinctly in Arcelin's documentary, shot clandestinely in Haiti in collaboration with the Mouvement Haitien de Libération. The film avoids all the pitfalls of agit-prop rhetoric; its only (forgivable) weakness is that it gets emotionally carried away by some of its ghastly human testimonies. TR

Bitteren Tränen der Petra von Kant, Die
see Bitter Tears of Petra von Kant, The

Bitter Harvest
(Peter Graham Scott, 1963, GB) Janet Munro, John Stride, Anne Cunningham, Alan Badel, Vanda Godsell, Norman Bird, Terence Alexander.
96 min.
A tepid sex drama, one of a number of tedious and supposedly 'realistic' British films that attempted to cash in on the success of *Saturday Night and Sunday Morning* etc. in the early '60s. Janet Munro is the Welsh village girl who becomes caught up in the vice-ridden world of the big city. DP

Bitter Moon (Lunes de fiel)
(Roman Polanski, 1992, Fr/GB) Hugh Grant, Kristin Scott-Thomas, Emmanuelle Seigner, Peter Coyote, Victor Bannerjee, Sophie Patel, Stockard Channing, Patrick Albenque.
139 min.
Like Polanski's debut feature *Knife in the Water*, this is set partly on a boat, and charts the shifts in power between characters performing complex sexual/emotional manoeuvres. Nigel (Grant) and Fiona (Scott-Thomas), a wealthy English couple on a second honeymoon, meet Oscar (Coyote) and Mimi (Seigner) on a Mediterranean cruise. The wheelchair-bound Oscar is determined to regale Nigel with a lurid tale of his awful love for Mimi, and exploits her charms to ensure that Nigel hears the story to its bitter end. Characteristically, Polanski treats this slightly protracted tale of erotic obsession partly as deeply ironic black comedy. But there's also real seriousness in the way the film condenses a whole range of feelings into one crazed, cruel relationship and its effect on another couple, so that it becomes both a grotesque portrait of love's variety and a queasy commentary on the perverse pleasures we derive from the suffering of others. Rich and darkly disturbing, it's also wickedly entertaining. GA

Bitter Rice (Riso Amaro)
(Giuseppe De Santis, 1948, It) Silvana Mangano, Vittorio Gassman, Raf Vallone, Doris Dowling, Lia Corelli.
108 min. b/w.
Intended as a hard-hitting social critique of the exploitation of rice-field workers in the Po Valley, this was much criticised at the time for compromising its neo-realism by sugaring the bleak message with some souped-up sex and violence. Actually it all seems very mild now, but De Santis' bold camera style and superb handling of crowd movement are well worth a look. TM

Bitter Sweet
(WS Van Dyke, 1940, US) Jeanette MacDonald, Nelson Eddy, George Sanders, Felix Bressart, Lynne Carver, Ian Hunter, Fay Holden, Sig Ruman.
92 min.
Second screen version of the Noël Coward operetta (adapted by Lesser Samuels) about young love in turn-of-the-century Vienna. MacDonald pips, squeaks and chirps in her melodious fashion as the red-cheeked English rose who elopes to Austria. Eddy is her music teacher and sweetheart. Shot in best MGM Technicolor, the film looks a treat, but there's no disguising the flimsy, winsome storyline. GM

Bitter Tea of General Yen, The
(Frank Capra, 1933, US) Barbara Stanwyck, Nils Asther, Gavin Gordon, Toshia Mori, Richard Loo, Walter Connolly.
89 mins. b/w.

Light years away from the homespun, small-town Capracorn for which the director is best known, this exotic, erotic melodrama is by far his finest achievement. Stanwyck, subtly radiant, is the American missionary in Shanghai who is abducted by a highly sophisticated Chinese warlord (Asther); like the film itself, she is both fascinated and repelled by the prospect of miscegenation. Where Capra's other films are largely stolid, prosaic and talky, this is sensuous and profoundly cinematic, perhaps most notably in a sequence in which Stanwyck dreams of her seduction by a forceful Asther. Odd, but oddly moving. GA

Bitter Tears of Petra von Kant, The (Die Bitteren Tränen der Petra von Kant)
(Rainer Werner Fassbinder, 1972, WGer) Margit Carstensen, Hanna Schygulla, Irm Hermann, Katrin Schaake, Eva Mattes.
124 min.
If *Fear Eats the Soul* used Emmi and Ali's improbable relationship as a key to deep-set patterns of social prejudice and fear, then the slightly earlier *Bitter Tears* sketches the currents of dominance and submission that lie beneath the surface of any human relationship. This time, the focus is gay rather than straight: fashion designer Petra (once widowed, once divorced) develops a fiercely possessive crush on her model Karin, and, as soon as the one-sided affair reaches its necessary end, starts wallowing in theatrical self-pity. Coldly described, the set and costume design and the hothouse atmosphere represent so much high-camp gloss; but once again this careful stylisation enables Fassbinder to balance between parody of an emotional stance and intense commitment to it. He films in long, elegant takes, completely at the service of his all-female cast, who are uniformly sensational. TR

Bitter Victory (Amère Victoire)
(Nicholas Ray, 1957, Fr) Richard Burton, Curd Jürgens, Ruth Roman, Raymond Pellegrin, Nigel Green, Christopher Lee, Anthony Bushell.
100 min. b/w.
The title tells all. Though Jürgens and Burton lead a successful World War II assault on Rommel's desert headquarters (for which Jürgens is undeservedly decorated), in the course of the raid both men are broken. Jürgens falls prey to indecision and cowardice brought on by his envy of the seeming ease with which Burton handles both the military situation and his personal affairs (including a past liaison with Jürgens' wife), while Burton's romantic veneer is shattered by the conflicting emotions he discovers within himself. The resulting personal anguish, summed up in Burton's blank delivery of the line 'I kill the living and save the dead', seeps into the very grain of Ray's magisterial black-and-white 'Scope set-ups. PH.

Bix
(Brigitte Berman, 1981, Can) Mary Louise Shoemaker, Hoagy Carmichael, Bill Challis, Esten Spurrier, Artie Shaw.
116 min. b/w & col.
A documentary in which the legendary jazz cornettist Bix Beiderbecke, who blew his one chance to get on film (*The King of Jazz*) through his ultimately fatal alcoholism, is brought to life with interviews and well-chosen records though he died over fifty years ago. Overlong towards the end but beautiful to look at, the pastel tones on the new material blending with black-and-white archive still and movie footage, which instead of distancing the music even further places it vividly in its period. BP

Bizarre, Bizarre
see Drôle de Drame

Black and Silver
(William Raban/Marilyn Raban,1981, GB) Marilyn Raban, Jessica Bennett, Lily Dragalla, Juliette Tully, Roger Tully.
75 min. b/w & col.
This radical reworking of an Oscar Wilde tale (*The Birthday of the Infanta*) based on Velasquez' painting 'Las Meninas', marked the Rabans' first venture into 'experimental narrative' territory. A film of often glacial beauty and formal dexterity,

it is also, in its continually looping themes of duplicity, self-deception and loss, a subtle and intuitive essay on the nature of film itself. One of the more successful films from the avant-garde, and for its imagery alone well worth seeing. MO'P

Black and White in Color (La Victoire en Chantant)

(Jean-Jacques Annaud, 1976 (Fr/Switz/Ivory Coast) Jean Carmet, Jacques Dufilho, Catherine Rouvel, Jacques Spiesser,Dora Doll.
100 min.
It would be difficult to imagine how this supposedly liberal satire on colonialism and racism could be more offensive. Set in the Ivory Coast French colony of 1915, it concentrates on the disruption caused to a sleepy French community by the belated news of the outbreak of World War I. Pricking the pretensions of characters stirred by patriotism as they mobilise the natives into battle against the neighbouring German community, writer/director Annaud unfortunately also manages to reinforce some of the worst racist and sexist stereotypes (funny, gullible niggers; giggly, busty women), and couch the whole thing in a broad, farcical style of comic acting familiar from the French cinema of the '30s. RM

Black Angel

(Roy William Neill, 1946, US) Dan Duryea, June Vincent, Peter Lorre, Broderick Crawford, Wallace Ford, Constance Dowling.
80 min. b/w.
Not exactly a pristine Cornell Woolrich adaptation, since the brooding subjectivism (so lovingly preserved in a real poverty row quickie like *Fear in the Night*) has been partly pruned to leave a moody thriller along the lines of *Phantom Lady*, beautifully crafted with the sort of unpretentious skill Neill brought to the Rathbone-Bruce Sherlock Holmes series. The authentic tang of *noir* is lent by Duryea, superb in (for once) a sympathetic role as the tormented musician with the faithless wife who finds the solution to the mystery of her murder surfacing through the alcoholic haze of his memory. Lovely supporting cast too. TM

Blackbeard's Ghost

(Robert Stevenson, 1967, US) Peter Ustinov, Dean Jones, Suzanne Pleshette, Elsa Lanchester, Joby Baker, Michael Conrad.
107 min.
A typically larky Disney film, heavily over-directed and under-written, in which the ghost of a fearsome pirate is summoned from limbo (where he is condemned to wander until he manages to do one good deed). His task is to save a bevy of poor old ladies – his proud descendants, collectively known as the Daughters of Blackbeard, and running an inn dedicated to his memory – from eviction by developers who have a gambling-joint in mind. Ustinov has his moments as the ghostly pirate, but seems to have got bogged down in an imitation of Peter Cook's inimitably peculiar Cockney whine – which Peter Cook does so much better. TM

Blackbeard the Pirate

(Raoul Walsh 1952, US) Robert Newton, Linda Darnell, Keith Andes, William Bendix, Torin Thatcher, Richard Egan, Alan Mowbray.
99 min.
Despite the combination of Walsh, Darnell and Bendix, a mediocre swashbuckler with Sir Henry Morgan (Thatcher) swishing about on the high seas in pursuit of the deadly Blackbeard (Newton, overdoing the ham, as usual). At best, colourful; at worst, drearily predictable. GA

Black Beauty

(Caroline Thompson, 1994, GB/US) Sean Bean, David Thewlis, Jim Carter, Peter Davison, Alun Armstrong, John McEnery, Eleanor Bron, Peter Cook, Adrian Ross Magenty.
88 min.
This version slow-burns with an old-fashioned sense of injustice. The story is told from Black Beauty's point of view (voice, Alan Cumming), and it's a Dickensian catalogue of conscience-pricking social and class conditions. Directing her first feature, screenwriter Caroline Thompson adopts a level-headed tone, avoiding the twin traps of sentimentality and sermonising. The film is shot with a good eye for scenery and com-

position, and Thompson shows total commitment to the story. But what can a horse do to engage the emotions? On the whole, it's just an undramatic working life, enlivened somewhat by David Thewlis' performance as a cabman, the most fully realised character among a gallery of quick-sketch ciphers. WH

Black Belt Jones

(Robert Clouse, 1973, US) Jim Kelly, Gloria Hendry, Malik Carter, Scatman Crothers, Alan Weeks.
87 min.
The crew from *Enter the Dragon* strike again with the irritating tendency to cram in every feasible plot variation, confusing good with more and bigger. Where the film diverges from its Chinese forebears is in making its hero not just one of the karate students whose school is threatened – here by a collusion between civic developers and Mafia money men – but a rich outsider in the employ of the US government, thus losing whatever subversive qualities the Chinese originals contain. VG.

Black Bird, The

(David Giler, 1975, US) George Segal, Stéphane Audran, Lionel Stander, Lee Patrick, Elisha Cook, Signe Hasso, John Abbott .
98 min.
Giler's first film, a parody-sequel to John Huston's *The Maltese Falcon*, has Segal as Bogie's inept son, Sam Spade Jr, bumbling about present-day San Francisco, harried by father's blowsy secretary (Lee Patrick, from the original) and pursued by Elisha Cook, three murderous Hawaiians, and a crazy dwarf. Giler's earnest screenplay scrupulously updates the Hammett novel: Audran plays the daughter of the late General Kemidov who, you may remember, was the last legitimate owner of the priceless black bird. However, despite a strong cast which pulls together several sharply written episodes, as a whole the movie fails to top the wry tone of Huston's classic or to produce a surprise denouement equal to the impact of Mary Astor's treachery. JPy

Blackboard Jungle, The

(Richard Brooks, 1955, US) Glenn Ford, Anne Francis, Vic Morrow, Louis Calhern, Sidney Poitier, Richard Kiley.
101 min. b/w.
This was the movie which featured 'Rock Around the Clock' over the credits and had Teds ripping up the seats on its first release in Britain. But this notoriety gives a false impression of the film. It's based on Evan Hunter's moralistic bestseller about a young New York teacher at a tough school, and is very worthy in its intentions. Highlights include Vic Morrow as a confused knife-wielding delinquent, but the studied pseudo-documentary atmosphere never quite convinces.

Blackboard Massacre

see Massacre at Central High

Black Book, The

see Reign of Terror

Black Bounty Killer, The

see Boss Nigger

Black Bunch, The (aka Jungle Sex)

(Henning Schellerup, 1972, US) Gladys Bunker, Betty Barton, Yvonne, Marshall Breedson, Evan Renshaw, Kurt Horst.
67 min.
Four African village women, sole survivors of a mercenary massacre, swear vengeance. They join an unsavoury party of bounty hunters on the trail of a millionaire's kidnapped son. The women seduce the bounty hunters but fail to obtain their weapons. The mercenaries harry the party; a pouch of diamonds is introduced into the script; and almost everybody ends up dead. Shoddy and reprehensible. JPy

Black Caesar (aka The Godfather of Harlem)

(Larry Cohen, 1973, US) Fred Williamson, D'Urville Martin, Gloria Hendry, Art Lund, Val Avery, Minnie Gentry, Julius W Harris.
96 min.

Retitled for release in Britain, although *Black Caesar* gives a more accurate indication of the film's theme of the hero as over-reacher. James Brown belts out 'Ain't It Cool to Be a Boss' as Williamson decides to take over Harlem's crime from the whites, ostensibly to give the blacks a better deal. In doing so, he ends up a white man's nigger, abandoning all that he has intended to destroy, and losing his girl into the bargain. Unfortunately it all remains too crude to convince one of its better intentions. What survives is a chase with the wounded Williamson riding taxi through snarled-up streets, his pursuers on foot; an extraordinary wish-fulfilment fantasy where a white middle class party (albeit of gangsters) is mown down; and an ending that caters for the inevitable sequel 'Hell Up in Harlem'. CPe

Black Cannon Incident, The (Heipao Shijian)

(Huang Jianxin, 1985, China/WGer) Liu Zifeng, Gerhard Olschewski, Gao Ming, Wang Yi, Yang Yazhou.
99 min.
An inoffensive engineer comes under suspicion of industrial espionage. The Security Bureau finds plenty to worry over in his file: raised as a Catholic, never married, he'd had a mysterious argument with a visiting expert from Germany. And so he's packed off to the maintenance depot (where, of course, there is nothing to do) while a pea-brained investigation is launched. Take the resulting chaos as comedy or tragedy; either way, there's no doubt the Chinese ruling class comes in for an unsparing hammering. What's more, the film's political daring is matched by a torrent of bright ideas in the plotting, design and colour-control departments. TR

Black Cat, The

(Albert S Rogell, 1941, US) Basil Rathbone, Broderick Crawford, Bela Lugosi, Hugh Herbert, Gale Sondergaard, Anne Gwynne, Gladys Cooper.
70 min. b/w.
Undistinguished comedy-chiller involving the familiar routine of old dark house, reading of a will, assorted murders. Nothing to do with Poe's story except for some business involving cats, it's worth watching mainly for the admirable Stanley Cortez camerawork. Alan Ladd has a small role as Rathbone's son. TM

Black Cat, The (aka House of Doom)

(Edgar G Ulmer, 1934, US) Boris Karloff, Bela Lugosi, David Manners, Jacqueline Wells, Lucille Lund.
65 min. b/w.
Written and directed by Ulmer, most obscure of all the German émigrés in Hollywood, *The Black Cat* owes nothing at all to the Poe short story but everything to the splendours of the German-American expressionist fantasy tradition. Virtually plotless, it describes the sadistic, guilt-ridden clash between Karloff and Lugosi, enemies from WWI; the Karloff character was reputedly inspired by Aleister Crowley. The arena of combat is Karloff's futuristic mansion, built on the site of a concentration camp; enthralling design and camerawork conjure disquiet from the smallest detail or gesture; the classic highpoint is the game of chess for the life of the heroine. Sumptuously subversive ... one of the very best horror movies Universal ever made. TR

Black Cauldron, The

(Ted Berman/Richard Rich, 1985, US)
80 min.
The long-touted magnum opus – an animated feature – supposed to revive Disney's flagging fortunes. Ostensibly a sinister sword and sorcery epic, it comes across as a major disappointment. Of course there's the statutuory naughty, cute furry animal to keep the very small children happy, but the rest of us kiddies walk out wondering when Jiminy Cricket is going to dust off his whistle. As usual it is technically excellent, but the charm, characterisation and sheer good humour that made features like *Pinocchio* and *Jungle Book* so enjoyable are sadly absent. DPe

Black Christmas

(Bob Clark, 1974, Can) Olivia Hussey, Keir
Dullea, Margot Kidder, Andrea Martin, John
Saxon, Marian Waldman.
97 min.
Just who is making all those obscene phone calls
and murdering the inmates of a sorority house
before the girls go off on their Christmas holidays? A vague knowledge of the cast's previous
experience will provide the answer, but for all
one's accurate guesswork, the film still manages
a good slice of old-fashioned suspense. CPe

Black Diamond Rush

(Kurt Miller/Peter Speek, 1993, US)
100 min.
Writer/narrator Warren Miller has been making
ski films in the US for more than 40 years.
In this documentary, a clutch of bold American
skiers and snow-boarders (prone to pulling faces
for the camera) search out slopes far removed
from the manicured motorways populated by the
rest of us. After a while the mountains tend to
merge, and the high-speed wipe-outs begin to
lose their bone-crunching impact. Breathtaking
camerawork. ASh

Black Eagle

(Eric Karson, 1988, US) Sho Kosugi, Jean-
Claude Van Damme, Doran Clark, Bruce
French, Vladimir Skomarovsky.
104 min.
Codename Black Eagle (Kosugi) is summoned to
Malta to thwart KGB plans to steal a sunken
laser device. And, barring sundry explosions,
killings, a subplot in which his two children are
kidnapped, and a car chase (visibly at 33 mph)
through the streets of Malta, that's about it.
Directed without flair, this is a movie that defies
easy classification: it's either a spy thriller without glamour, gadgets, or twists, or a martial arts
movie with only two real fights; and if the script
ever had a good line, it's fumbled somewhere
between the Russian and Japanese accents. The
only difference between this and countless other
low-budget action movies is that the hero is not
macho: he's thin, doesn't screw around, and even
fails to defeat the KGB's balletic kung-fu king
(Van Damme). In fact, he does nothing of any
interest at all: refile under codename Black
Turkey. DW

Black Emanuelle
(Emanuelle Nera)

(Adalberto Albertini, 1976, It) Laura Gemser,
Karin Schubert, Angelo Infanti, Isabelle
Marchall, Venantino Venantini, Gabriele Tinti.
96 min.
'They're a peaceful tribe, but when they get carried away with their rites nothing can stop them',
Emanuelle is warned as she totes her Nikon
through the bush in search of the origins of
African civilisation. And you can bet she finds
more than she bargained for. Her journey is one
of inner discovery too – is she a lesbian, as beach
and poolside scenes would seem to testify? Does
she prefer it with white men or black? And what
of the hockey team who finish the film by raping her on the night train through Nairobi? Crude
symbolism, with the couplings shot as dully as
the travelogue stuff. AN

Black Eye

(Jack Arnold, 1973, US) Fred Williamson,
Rosemary Forsyth, Teresa Graves, Floy Dean,
Richard Anderson, Cyril Delevanti.
97 min.
Not a bad stab at all at turning out a private eye
film in the Chandler mould around a black investigator called Stone, played not brilliantly but
well enough by Williamson. The Southern
Californian environment is sketched in well, a
superficially bland jungle populated by eccentric
mystics, phony Godmongers, smooth society
women, and a seemingly eclectically chosen
array of corpses. Having Stone too out-of-pock-
et to afford an office but operating out of a neighbourhood bar is also a nice touch. And several of
the women characters remain firmly in the mind.
Unexpected place to find the director of The
Creature from the Black Lagoon. VG

Black Flowers for the Bride

see Something for Everyone.

Black Fox

(Louis Clyde Stoumen, 1962, US)
89 min. b/w.
A documentary produced by Jack Le Vien and
narrated by Marlene Dietrich, this semi-allegorical account of Adolf Hitler's rise and fall offers
no surprises but reiterates some interesting
points. Selected factual details of his career are
projected against the backcloth of Goethe's
adaptation of the fable of Reynard the Fox – 'who
some would say was a liar, a thief and a murderer – but often spoke of God'. Hitler is placed
firmly and intelligently in his historical context,
and is shown to be as much a product of his time
(the world recession, Versailles, the foundering
of the German democratic experiment) as of his
personal genius. In other words, the German people and the world got the dictator they deserved,
and the German people at least were glad to have
him. FD

Black Fury

(Michael Curtiz, 1935, US) Paul Muni, Karen
Morley, William Gargan, Barton MacLane,
John Qualen, J Carrol Naish, Mae Marsh, Akim
Tamiroff, Vince Barnett.
92 min. b/w.
'Torn from the front-page headlines', this strike
drama is a good example of the extent to which
Warner Bros was the proletarian studio: it plays
with political dynamite while preaching conciliation and moderation. Fielding a Polish accent
only Meryl Streep could understand, Muni is Joe
Radek, an easy-going miner whose popularity
among his workmates makes him the perfect
dupe for a labour agitator planted by strike-
breaking racketeers. Something of a buffoon,
Radek finds himself leading a walk-out which
wrecks the delicate relations between union and
management, who are compelled to bring in
scabs and industrial police. These last are the real
villains of the piece – not the bosses – but at least
there is no question that the heroes are the
'bohunks', immigrant workers whose harsh living and working conditions are vividly recreated
in Warner's specially constructed 'Coal Town', an
impressive complex of wooden shacks, drills and
mineshafts. Inspired by the case of Mike
Shemanski, a Pittsburgh miner murdered by
three company policemen, it is hardly surprising
that the film was censored in some states and
banned outright in Pennsylvania itself. TCh

Black Girl (Une Noire de ...)

(Ousmane Sembene, 1966, Sen) Mbissine
Therese Diop, Anne-Marie Selinek
Robert Fontaine.
55 min. b/w.
Originally intended to be feature length,
Sembene's third film tells of the destruction of a
young woman who leaves to work as a maid in
Antibes. Sembene, who abandoned the novel for
film, who trained in Moscow with Donskoi, and
whose commitment to African cinema was in
part provoked by the racism of Leni Riefenstahl's
Olympiad, has here contrived a masterful if not
entirely flawless rendering of the key themes in
Francophone African cinema. It is an essential
step in his project to 'totally Africanise the style
and conception of my cinema'. SH

Black God, White Devil (Deus
e o Diabo na Terra do Sol)

(Glauber Rocha, 1964, Braz) Yona Magalhaes,
Geraldo Del Rey, Othon Bastos, Mauricio de
Valle, Lidio Silva.
110 min. b/w.
Rocha's first major film introduced most of the
methods, themes and even characters that were
developed five years later in his Antonio das
Mortes. Set in the drought-plagued Brazilian
Sertao in 1940, it explores the climate of superstition, physical and spiritual terrorism and fear that
gripped the country: the central characters,
Manuel and Rosa, move credulously from allegiance to allegiance until they finally learn that the
land belongs not to god or the devil, but to the people themselves. The film's success here doubtless
reflects the 'exoticism' of its style, somewhere
between folk ballad and contemporary myth, since
the references to Brazilian history and culture are
pervasive and fairly opaque to the uninitiated. But
Rocha's project is fundamentally political, and
completely unambiguous: he faces up to the contradictions of his country in an effort to understand, to crush mystiques, and to improve. TR

Black Gunn

(Robert Hartford-Davis, 1972, US) Jim Brown,
Martin Landau, Brenda Sykes, Luciana
Paluzzi, Vida Blue, Stephen McNally, Keefe
Brasselle.
98 min.
Hartford-Davis crucifies Jim Brown (figuratively
speaking) by directing this tale of a black capitalist avenging his brother's death with startling
lack of inspiration. The modulation of the pimp
image, however, after the explicitness of Superfly,
is a wonder to behold. Collectors only.

Black Hand, The

(Richard Thorpe, 1949, US) Gene Kelly, J
Carrol Naish, Teresa Celli, Marc Lawrence,
Frank Puglia.
93 min. b/w.
Kelly in a rare dramatic role is an Italian-
American out for revenge on the Black Hand, the
Mafia-like organisation of extortionists who
murdered his lawyer father. Training in the law
himself, he enlists the help of New York police
inspector Naish, who makes a courageous trip to
Sicily to retrieve the information they need to
crack the organisation. Although the two Irish-
American leads aren't ideally cast, they both give
a decent account of themselves in an unusual,
neatly plotted little thriller. TJ

Black Hole, The

(Gary Nelson, 1979, US) Maximilian Schell,
Anthony Perkins, Robert Forster, Joseph
Bottoms, Yvette Mimieux, Ernest Borgnine.
98 min.
Disney's most ambitious and costly production
to date – about a spaceship crew which encounters a Black Hole and a long-lost madman – and
if looks were everything you could hardly fault
it. The company's effects team have excelled
themselves in the creation of spectacular settings
and holograms, but the script reads as though
they simply ordered up a melange of Forbidden
Planet and 20,000 Leagues Under the Sea (with
a little bit of R2D2 on the side). Next time around
they ought to pension off a few designers to pay
for a decent screenplay. DP

Black Holes, The (I Buchi
Neri)

(Pappi Corsicato, 1995, It) Iaia Forte, Vincenzo
Peluso, Marinella Anaclerio.
92 min.
Some may claim Corsicato as a Neapolitan
Almodóvar, but this tale of the offbeat relationship
between a roadside hooker and an enigmatic, idle,
sexually ambivalent hunk visiting his hometown
for his mother's funeral, is too inconsequential to
hold the attention. Much of it is a none-too-witty
kitsch pastiche of '60s B-movies, though heaven
knows where the mystical whimsy about chickens
and epiphanies fits in. The hero resembles Keanu
Reeves in a bleach-blond wig. GA

Black Holiday
(La Villeggiatura)

(Marco Leto, 1973, It) Adalberto Maria Merli,
Adolfo Celi, Milena Vukotic, John Steiner,
Roberto Herlitzka.
112 min. b/w.
Set in Fascist Italy and focused around the internment of a young professor of law on a prison
island, Black Holiday maintains an impressive
ideological urgency and relevance. Inspector
Rizzuto (Celi, excellent) attempts to 'contain' and
control the renegade teacher through the most
telling, 'civilised' and classist of methods, by
wrapping him in privileges. And the professor
(Merli), class-bound but initially blind to the
implications of the fact, begins to succumb. The
parameters of middle class compromise are very
clearly drawn. The precision is admirable, the
images spare; and if the hero of the film is the
inarticulate Communist who dislocates the professor's essential complacency, its heart can be
perceived in the owlish anarchist who remains
rousingly defiant to the end. VG

Black Jack

(Kenneth Loach, 1979, GB) Stephen Hirst,
Louise Cooper, Jean Franval, Phil Askham, Pat
Wallis.
110 min.
An amiable adaptation of the classic kids' novel
by Leon Garfield, which tells the adventures of a

boy on the road in brutal, colourful 1750s England. Loach shoots the film with characteristic sensitivity (and scrupulous period realism), but his unwillingness to face the challenges of social history, and his failure to capture the magical spirit of the novel, let him down. CA

Black Joy

(Anthony Simmons, 1977, GB) Norman Beaton, Trevor Thomas, Floella Benjamin, Oscar James.
109 min.
A comedy of social manners which manages a fair penetration of Brixton realities and immigrant culture despite its predictable format: survival of the fittest in a jungle of squatters, hookers, urchins and conmen. The ending lacks music, but most of the film has a pace and energy not often seen in British movies. TR

Black Knight, The

(Tay Garnett, 1954, GB/US) Alan Ladd, Patricia Medina, Andre Morell, Harry Andrews, Peter Cushing, Anthony Bushell, Patrick Troughton.
85 min.
Low-budget Arthurian antics featuring vengeful armourer Ladd's specially scaled-down sword and very little cinematic sorcery. Erratic veteran Garnett coasts through the second-hand motions of a hastily concocted patchwork script. PT

Blackmail

(Alfred Hitchcock, 1929, GB) Anny Ondra, John Longden, Sara Allgood, Donald Calthrop, Cyril Ritchard, Charles Paton.
85 min. b/w.
Blackmail marked Hitchcock's first use of sound, and it remains famous for its innovations in that area. But it's now more stimulating for its experiment with narrative structure: an efficient, impersonal police investigation that elides into a messy, personal story of attempted rape, murder in self-defence, blackmail and chase to the death. TR

Blackmail

(HC Potter, 1939, US) Edward G Robinson, Ruth Hussey, Gene Lockhart, Guinn Williams, John Wray, Arthur Hohl, Bobs Watson.
81 min. b/w.
Robinson is excellent as a fugitive from a chain gang, convicted of a crime he didn't commit, who nine years later has become a pillar of society with wife, child and enviable reputation as an oilwell troubleshooter. Lockhart is even better as the blackmailer, oozing sleazy, scalp-crawling bonhomie, who confesses that *he* committed the crime, plausibly claims to be anxious to set the record straight, and engineers a scam which puts Robinson back on the chain gang. Potter handles the sharply shifting moods very well: the authentic excitement of the oil-rig fire at the beginning; the *ordinariness* of the family background and the blackmailer's scenes; the dark, brooding brutality (mental as much as physical) of the chain gang sequences. Much of the film's edge is guaranteed by a fine script from David Hertz and William Ludwig, which cleverly paces its action to a parabola between two oil fires (the first a blaze of glory for Robinson, the second his season in hell). Pity about the totally duff upbeat ending. TM

Black Marble, The

(Harold Becker, 1980, US) Robert Foxworth, Paul Prentiss, Harry Dean Stanton, Barbara Babcock, John Hancock, James Woods.
113 min.
Repeat teaming for Becker and Joseph Wambaugh after *The Onion Field*, mining the latter's usual preoccupation in an adaptation of his novel about a cop driven to drink by the pressures of his job, but pulling himself together when he is teamed with policewoman Prentiss as his new partner. Sound in most departments and with an excellent cast, but not all that interesting. TM

Black Moon

(Louis Malle, 1975, Fr) Cathryn Harrison, Thérèse Giehse, Alexandra Stewart, Joe Dallesandro.
101 min.
Malle's weird surrealist fantasy updates *Alice in Wonderland* into a future society where men and women are engaged in deadly combat, seemingly coexistent with an alternative comradeship of talking rats and enchanted unicorns. Malle offers no explanation for his heroine's visionary odyssey through a world in which all history runs parallel with all realities. Yet a logic is there, even if its reference point is jabberwocky. A black moon, in astrological terms, refers to the time of chaos that preludes some cataclysmic change. And like Malle's other films around this time, *Black Moon* hopefully posits a social revolution in which such outmoded concepts as innocence and sin will appear in new guises. TM

Black Moon Rising

(Harley Cokliss, 1985, US) Tommy Lee Jones, Linda Hamilton, Robert Vaughn, Richard Jaeckel, Lee Ving, Bubba Smith.
100 min.
Pulling a quick theft of a dodgy company's computer cassette for the Government, Jones then finds himself pursued by both company and Government, and hides the merchandise in the back of a passing car. The car can do an improbable 350 mph. Unfortunately it is stolen by a gang, so his task is to penetrate the impregnable lair of Vaughn's carnapping set-up. It all gets off to a cracking start, only to dwindle very rapidly into thin and predictable variations on the formulaic ploys. And Vaughn gives his usual performance of perfect menace, which suggests that he should be about to engage in world domination, not just nicking motors. CPea

Black Narcissus 100 (100)

(Michael Powell/Emeric Pressburger, 1946, GB) Deborah Kerr, Sabu, David Farrar, Flora Robson, Kathleen Byron, Jean Simmons, Jenny Laird, Esmond Knight.
100 min.
Interesting to compare with another version of a Rumer Godden story, Renoir's *The River*, in that whereas Renoir shot on location in India and created an almost documentary feel to his film, Powell refused to go to the Himalayas and shot at Pinewood, coming up with a heady melodrama that treats India as a state of mind rather than a real country. A group of nuns launch a tough, isolated existence in a mountain convent, and find themselves psychologically disturbed by all manner of physical phenomena: extremes of weather and temperature, illness, a local agent's naked thighs, a young prince's perfume purchased, ironically, at London's Army and Navy stores. As temptation draws the women away from their vocation, they fall prey to doubt, jealousy and madness. Powell's use of colour, design and music was never so perfectly in tune with the emotional complexities of Pressburger's script, their talents combining to create one of Britain's great cinematic masterpieces, a marvellous evocation of hysteria and repression, and incidentally one of the few genuinely erotic films ever to emerge from these sexually staid isles. GA

Black Night

see Lumière Noire

Black on White (Mustaa Valkoisella)

(Jörn Donner, 1967, Fin) Jörn Donner, Kristiina Halkola, Liisamaija Laaksonen.
95 min.
A simple triangle affair, shot in stunning colour, which somehow contrives to make capital out of its own banality. Nothing much happens, but a great deal is revealed about the illusion of happiness, as a young businessman (well played by Donner himself) breaks up his 'perfect' marriage to pursue a short-lived affair with a flighty young secretary (Halkola). He manoeuvres to get her away on an imaginary business trip; he begins to get caught up in a tissue of lies both at home and at the office; and he watches helplessly as the girl gradually drifts indifferently away, leaving him forlornly dogging her footsteps. With quiet, unobtrusive compassion, always revealing more than is said, Donner records the hell on earth of man's quest for happiness. TM

Black Orchid, The

(Martin Ritt, 1959, US) Sophia Loren, Anthony Quinn, Ina Balin, Jimmie Baird, Mark Richman, Naomi Stevens, Frank Puglia.
96 min. b/w.
A seriously bad tearjerker. Loren's life is in ruins

– her gangster husband has died, her son has become James Dean – until she meets up with nice widower Mr Quinn, who shows her his farm and daughter. Cue for the daughter to go round the twist at the thought of Loren as a stepmother. One in a long line of clinkers (except for the masterly *Hud*) from Ritt, and a first script by composer Joseph Stefano, who got his act together with his next picture, which was *Psycho*. ATu

Black Orpheus (Orfeu Negro)

(Marcel Camus, 1959, Fr/It/Braz) Breno Mello, Marpessa Dawn, Adhemar Da Silva, Lourdes De Oliveira, Lea Garcia.
106 min.
In recreating the Orpheus legend in Rio de Janeiro with an all black cast, Camus celebrates not only the universality of the story, but the exoticism and poetry of Brazil and her culture. Orpheus, a charismatic trolley car conductor and star of one of the Carnival's Samba schools, is betrothed to the wonderfully brassy Mira but in love with Eurydice. Pursued by Death and the vengeful Mira, the doomed lovers weave their way through a carnival-mad Rio that seethes and strains towards the sweaty release of Carnival night. Although certain of the more sentimental scenes seem rather dated, the relentless – almost abstract – onslaught of colour, noise and frenetic movement stands up very well, compelling one towards the visual splendour of the inevitably poignant ending. FD

Blackout

see Contraband

Blackout (aka The Attic)

(Doug Adams, 1988, US) Carol Lynley, Gail O'Grady, Michael Keys Hall, Joseph Gian, Deena Freeman, Joanna Miles.
91 min.
Years after the mysterious disappearance of her father, plucky runaway Caroline Boyle (O'Grady) receives a letter from him requesting that she return for a family reunion. Intrigued, she goes home, to be met by her unwelcoming mother (Lynley) and a strange new boyfriend. Confused, she embarks on a fact-finding mission which, via many a knife-wielding flashback, eventually leads her to the attic...A cheaply made psychological thriller, scripted by Joseph Stefano, this certainly has its fair share of claret, but is strictly fodder for slasher fans. DA

Blackout, The

(Abel Ferrara, 1997, US/Fr) Matthew Modine, Claudia Schiffer, Béatrice Dalle, Sarah Lassez, Dennis Hopper.
98 min.
So incoherent, sloppy and determinedly sleazy that it looks like self-parody, Ferrara's psychodrama tells of a movie star (Modine) heavily into drugs and booze. Ignoring girlfriend Dalle's objections to his lifestyle, he ODs and blacks out; 18 months later, cleaned up and living quietly with Schiffer, he's nevertheless haunted by fantasies that he may have murdered Dalle. Neither the pretentious dialogue nor the sudden shifts in character (particularly that of Hopper's crazed director) makes sense; and the visuals are often pitifully voyeuristic in their emphasis on female flesh and all-round degeneracy. GA

Black Panther, The

(Ian Merrick, 1977, GB) Donald Sumpter, Debbie Farrington, Marjorie Yates, Sylvia O'Donnell, Andrew Burt.
98 min.
Based on the case of Donald Neilson, who killed three sub-postmasters and 17-year-old heiress Lesley Whittle, this dull but earnest movie bends over backwards not to exploit its subject. But strained realism and an obsession with facts permit little insight and even less drama. The film does little more than plod after the central character on his criminal rounds.

Black Pirate, The

(Albert Parker, 1926, US) Douglas Fairbanks, Billie Dove, Donald Crisp, Anders Randolf, Tempe Pigott.
8,312 ft.
Alongside Keaton and Gene Kelly, Fairbanks was perhaps the most gracefully athletic mover in the history of the movies, and *The Black Pirate* per-

fectly captures his relaxed, exuberant optimism. A pacy tale of romance and revenge on the high seas, it sees Doug swashing his buckle with unsurpassed ease: the daring stunts are breathtakingly stylish (none more so than the celebrated descent down a sail on the point of a dagger), while scenes like the shoal of soldiers swimming underwater to invade the pirate ship are shot through with a poetic beauty. An added bonus is that the film was shot in two-strip Technicolor, a lovely pastel process that defies description. GA

Black Rain

(Ridley Scott, 1989, US) Michael Douglas, Andy Garcia, Ken Takakura, Kate Capshaw, Yusaku Matsuda, Shigeru Koyama, John Spencer.
125 min.
Dishonoured detective Nick Conklin (Douglas) and easygoing partner Charlie Vincent (Garcia) escort a desperately ruthless *yakuza* from New York to Osaka. When he is snatched from under their noses, they join forces with the Japanese police to recover their man. Most of the interplay is between Conklin, under investigation back home, and his Japanese colleague Matsumoto (Takakura), who upholds group loyalty over the American's individualism. 'You must have patience', Conklin is warned by his Japanese hosts. 'Fuck patience', he retorts, and goes about cutting corners. Their quarry belongs to a counterfeiting ring which schemes to infiltrate the American economy – Japanese revenge, it would seem, for losing the war (black rain refers to radioactive fallout after Hiroshima and Nagasaki). Tiresome gags abound at the expense of the uptight Japanese detective, with Conklin revelling in language misunderstandings, and prejudices are aired until some sort of reconciliation is reached – *after* Matsumoto has adopted vigilante methods. Obvious stuff. CM

Black Rain (Kuroi Ame)

(Shohei Imamura, 1989, Jap) Yoshiko Tanaka, Kazuo Kitamura, Etsuko Ichihara, Shoichi Ozawa.
123 min. b/w.
On an August morning in 1945, the inhabitants of Hiroshima set out for another day at work. In minutes a sudden flash reduces the city to a nightmarish furnace strewn with rubble, crumbling corpses and charred survivors. Presently, this gut churningly graphic opening switches to what appears to be a rural idyll some five years later; in a small village, a family who escaped have settled down in an attempt to regain some sense of purpose in life. But radiation sickness takes its toll, and the bulk of Imamura's emotionally serious domestic drama charts the inexorable decay of the entire social, psychological and moral fabric of a community. Rarely does the film preach, and only the repeated rantings of a demented army veteran – so OTT as to be unintentionally comic – break the consistently understated mood. But despite the largely sensitive depiction of waste, suffering and despair, the often ponderous pacing and the script's solemnity tend to work against emotional involvement. Grimly compelling viewing, but perhaps a little too determinedly gloomy for its own good. GA

Black Rainbow

(Mike Hodges, 1989, GB) Rosanna Arquette, Jason Robards, Tom Hulce, Mark Joy, Ron Rosenthal, John Bennes, Linda Pierce, Olek Krupa.
103 min.
Spiritualist Martha Travis (Arquette) puts the recently bereaved in touch with their loved ones, reassuring them of a happy hereafter; but when she develops the gift – or rather curse – of prophecy, she becomes the disembodied witness to a brutal killing, and the hit-man's next target. As she fights to convince her drunken father (Robards) and a sceptical journalist (Hulce) that her powers are real, the rainbow colours of her visions are painted black, and she slips towards madness and despair...Writer-director Hughes has coaxed superbly understated performances from his cast, even down to the suburban black-gloved assassin who commutes to killings after kissing his wife and kids. The pacing, too, is tight and restrained, building slowly so that the climax, when it comes, packs a real wallop (though he can't resist an ambiguous coda). The result is Hodges' best film since his debut with *Get Carter*.

a psychological thriller with a brain and a heart, which challenges the audience to explore their assumptions about reality, religion and the supernatural. DW

Black Republic (Keduldo Urichorum)

(Park Kwang-Su, 1990, SKor) Moon Sung-Keun, Shim Hye-jin, Park Joong-hoon.
100 min.
Park Kwang-Su is the foremost director of the New Korean Cinema, and this is the best of his three features to date. Soon after the brutal suppression of the Kwangju Uprising in 1980, a student activist on the wanted list hides out in a dying mining town near the North Korean border. Very little happens in plot terms, but his edgy relationships with others (a prostitute who's also on the run from something in her past, a mother-fixated thug who turns out to be the spoiled son of the town's last employer) give the film all the grip of a hard-boiled thriller. It adds up to a persuasive account of the terrible state of South Korean society a decade ago (and by implication, still). TR

Black Rider, The

(Wolf Rilla, 1954, GB) Jimmy Hanley, Rona Anderson, Leslie Dwyer, Lionel Jeffries, Beatrice Varley, Kenneth Connor.
66 min. b/w.
Workaday British support feature from years gone by in which tyro reporter Hanley and the chaps from the local motorcycle club investigate the apparent haunting of a nearby castle. Could it possibly have something to do with the nefarious activities of a bunch of smugglers? Director Wolf Rilla was in more genuinely spooky territory six years later with *Village of the Damned*. TJ

Black River

(Kevin Lucas, 1993, Aust) Maroochy Barambah, John Pringle, James Bonnefin, Clive Birch, The Bangarra Dance Theatre.
60 min.
This is a bold transfer of a Sydney Metropolitan Opera production (words by journalist Julianne Schultz, music by brother Andrew) inspired by a human rights enquiry into the fractious state of race relations in a small outback town. The action centres on an angry Aboriginal woman Miriam (mezzo Barambah), who's come to the local jail after her son's suspicious death in custody and finds herself thrown together with a judge on a fact-finding visit (baritone Pringle), the village drunk (tenor Bonnefin) and a surprisingly easy-going cop (bass Birch) – all marooned in the cells as the waters of a flash flood rise around them. The score builds in intensity as Barambah recounts centuries of her people's oppression. Piercing the innermost conflicts of the Australian psyche, all this might mean more on home ground, but to an outsider the result plays rather like a high art music video. The blending of realist and supernatural elements is ambitious, but the relative compactness of the material hardly allows convincing characterisation to emerge. A genuine curio, if not an unqualified success. TJ

Black Robe

(Bruce Beresford, 1991, Can/Aust) Lothaire Bluteau, Aden Young, Sandrine Holt, August Schellenberg, Tantoo Cardinal, Billy Two Rivers, Lawrence Bayne.
100 min.
Brian Moore here adapts his own savage, elegiac novel about the Jesuit mission to 'reap souls' among the Iroquois in 1630s Quebec. The film details the harrowing canoe trip undertaken in intense cold by idealistic Father Laforgue (Bluteau), a young carpenter named Daniel (Young) and a band of Algonquin Indians, way up into Huron territory to reach a disease-stricken outpost. It's a Conradian journey into the heart of darkness. Laforgue's mind and body are assaulted by privation, doubt, sexual arousal and horror, which sends him into faith-destroying anguish, with worse to come. The film is essentially illustrative, and Moore's screenplay understandably softens the text somewhat, but it still contains shocking scenes of torture and murder. What distinguishes the result is the brutal, clear-eyed honesty with which the Native American (and the missionary) culture is represented. Beautifully shot, too. WH

Black Room, The

(Roy William Neill, 1935, US) Boris Karloff, Marian Marsh, Robert Allen, Katherine DeMille, Thurston Hall.
67 min. b/w.
Moodily stylish Gothic melodrama, with Karloff in a dual role as twins fulfilling a family curse. Solid rather than distinguished (striking sets but too many rhubarbing villagers), although Karloff's performance is outstanding, especially in a subtle pantomime sequence where the bad twin rehearses his transformation into the brother he has killed. TM

Black Sabbath (I Tre Volti della Paura)

(Mario Bava, 1963, It/Fr) Boris Karloff, Susy Andersen, Mark Damon, Michèle Mercier, Lidia Alfonsi, Jacqueline Pierreux, Milly Monti.
99 min.
Vintage Bava in which Karloff introduces three adaptations from famous tales of the supernatural (and also stars in the last): *The Drop of Water* by Chekhov, *The Telephone* by Howard Snyder, and *The Wurdalak* by Tolstoy. Pictorially it's amazing, and even the script and dubbing are way above average. If only Amicus, who subsequently cornered the horror omnibus market, had taken heed they might have got some ideas as to what can be done with the format. DP

Blacks Britannica

(David Koff, 1978, US)
57 min.
Of all the films which have so far been made about the black community in Britain, this one comes closest to telling it how it is. The thesis is that the black community in Britain is the most oppressed section of an oppressed working class. The fact that young blacks reject their decreed role in the country's social and economic structure has meant that the state has been obliged to use a number of devices to reinforce its intentions, including the police, the judiciary, the media and the schools. The whole picture is linked by a number of interviews with activists in the black community, which means that the picture which emerges is an authentic black view of affairs. British TV could have, and should have, done this years ago. MP

Black Shack Alley (Rue Cases Nègres)

(Euzhan Palcy, 1983, Fr) Garry Cadenat, Darling Legitimus, Douta Seck, Joby Bernabé, Francisco Charles.
106 min.
Palcy's first feature is set in her native Martinique of the '30s: an eleven-year old boy lives in a shanty row (Rue Cases Nègres) in the middle of the back-breaking regime of the sugar cane plantations. Thanks to the selfless devotion of his grandmother, and the spiritual awakening offered by an ancient mentor, whose father was an African slave, he prospers at school, and manages to escape the grinding round of poverty by dint of education. Shot in ochre hues, with a remarkable polish, the movie never allows itself the easy route of angry misery, but actively engages its themes with optimism and its characters with love. The old people, especially, are treated with great dignity, while the boy's slow awakening to a poetic understanding of his condition is imbued with potent, primitive magic. CPea

Black Sheep

(Penelope Spheeris, 1996, US) Chris Farley, David Spade, Tim Matheson, Christine Ebersole, Gary Busey, Grant Hershov, Timothy Carhart, Bruce McGill.
87 min.
In freefall since *Wayne's World*, Penelope Spheeris's career has descended halfway down the deep-sea Marianas Trench, whence comes this soggy comedy, guaranteed to induce the bends. It features Farley and Spade, the director's co-fugitives from *Saturday Night Live* (previously paired in *Tommy Boy*), and revolves around the gubernatorial candidacy of Al Donnelly (Matheson). Al's riding high in the polls against the unscrupulous incumbent (Ebersole), which is why his campaign can't afford the damaging presence of brother Mike (Farley), a sweet but self-destructive oaf. Mike's packed off with some guy called Steve (Spade) to

an isolated cabin, where the duo perform incompetent slapstick. Mike slips and falls down a hill; a big boulder rolls on to the hut; Mike, trying to use his mobile phone, walks into a tree. NB

Black Sheep of Whitehall, The

(Will Hay/Basil Dearden, 1941, GB) Will Hay, John Mills, Basil Sydney, Felix Aylmer, Henry Hewitt, Thora Hird.
80 min. b/w.
The traditional Hay formula – his seedy correspondence course lecturer is mistaken for an economics expert kidnapped by spies, allowing him to indulge in much pretence and buffoonery, and to end up in a manic chase – is inserted into a predictably patriotic plot about plucky little Brits outwitting the Nazi villains. Funny in parts. GA

Blacksnake (aka Slaves)

(Russ Meyer, 1973, US) Anouska Hempel, David Warbeck, Percy Herbert, Milton McCollin, Thomas Baptiste, Bernard Boston.
82 min.
A gorgeous mix of sex, violence, social comment, and film parody, set in the Caribbean in 1853, with Hempel as the whip-wielding plantation mistress taking black slaves as studs until they finally revolt. Catch the super sermon by a crucified rebel (complete with choral backing), and Meyer's final eulogy to racial harmony (ie. miscegenation). Makes even *Mandingo* look serious.

Black Snow (Ben Ming Nian)

(Xie Fei, 1989, China) Jiang Wen, Cheng Lin, Yue Hong, Liu Xiaoning, Cai Hongxing, Lui Bin.
107 min.
This was adapted by young writer Liu Heng from his own short story about an ex-con trying to go straight in the back alleys of Beijing, but finding himself dragged down by the crime and violence he encounters. Film-school teacher Xie Fei keeps it all very low-key, but has no obvious point of view about the characters or the material. What brings the film to life is the writing (realistic to a fault, but very sharply observed), and the superb central performance of Jiang Wen, previously seen in films like *Red Sorghum* and *Hibiscus Town*. Jiang really is in the class of Gary Oldman: a young actor capable of inhabiting a role in a way that makes his smallest gesture count. TR

Black Stallion, The

(Carroll Ballard, 1979, US) Kelly Reno, Mickey Rooney, Teri Garr, Clarence Muse, Hoyt Axton, Michael Higgins.
117 min.
Walter Farley's classic tale has been adapted with amazing facility by Ballard and executive producer Coppola. Even though its essential features (shipwrecked child, desert island, magical stallion, '40s New York) represented appalling production problems, the film jettisons most of the cuteness implicit in its theme and handles the material with dream-like clarity. A magnificently well-crafted movie. DP.

Black Stallion Returns, The

(Robert Dalva, 1983, US) Kelly Reno, Vincent Spano, Allen Garfield, Woody Strode, Ferly Mayne, Teri Garr.
103 min.
Fun follow-up to *The Black Stallion* (which Dalva edited), with the horse stolen by enigmatic Arabs, and a determined Alec Ramsay (now the archetypal '50s teenager) stowing away on a plane bound for Casablanca, landing in the very middle of a sticky web of tribal rivalries and desert traditions. As in the original, the character of Alec distinguishes the film: he's resourceful, single-minded, but it is perhaps his very ordinariness that matters. FD

Black Sunday

see Maschera del Demonio, La

Black Sunday

(John Frankenheimer, 1976, US) Robert Shaw, Bruce Dern, Marthe Keller, Fritz Weaver, Steven Keats, Bekim Fehmiu, Michael V Gazzo, William Daniels.
143 min.
Black September terrorists attempt to wipe out a US football crowd by hijacking the TV blimp.

Besides some good suspense sequences, Frankenheimer tries to utilise his well-known skill with actors to open up all sides of the issue. Unfortunately, all the major characters have a whiff of Hollywood artifice, largely because (as has happened too often before in his career) Frankenheimer gets carried away by their verbosity. But perhaps any Hollywood film giving the Palestinian case an airing deserves to be welcomed. DP

Black Swan, The

(Henry King, 1942, US) Tyrone Power, Maureen O'Hara, Laird Cregar, Thomas Mitchell, George Sanders, Anthony Quinn, George Zucco, Fortunio Bonanova.
85 min.
A splendidly overripe swashbuckler, with Power as an adventurer who lends a sword to his old comrade Henry Morgan (Cregar) when he is appointed governor of Jamaica, seconding his bid to rid the Caribbean of buccaneers, in the process wooing and winning O'Hara's feisty damsel in distress, daughter of the former governor (Zucco). Sanders is the villain of the piece, one Captain Leech, an unreformed pirate with a brazen red hairpiece and the beard to go with it. Excitingly staged, boldly photographed in Technicolor, and boasting a flamboyant cast, this is a classic of its type. TCh

Black Tent, The

(Brian Desmond Hurst, 1956, GB) Anthony Steel, Donald Sinden, Anna Maria Sandri, Andre Morell, Donald Pleasence, Michael Craig, Anton Diffring.
93 min.
WWII romance mystery (scripted by Robin Maugham and Bryan Forbes) has the folk at the ancestral seat worried when son and heir Steel fails to return home from the North African campaign. Brother Sinden is packed off to discover that he's fallen for a sheikh's daughter and thrown in his lot with the bedouin. Director Hurst and a stiff cast manage to flatten the interest out of potentially intriguing material. TJ

Black Torment, The

(Robert Hartford-Davis, 1964, GB) John Turner, Heather Sears, Ann Lynn, Peter Arne, Francis de Wolff, Edina Ronay, Joseph Tomelty, Raymond Huntley.
85 min.
Occasionally effective ghost chiller, detailing an 18th century aristocrat's investigations into a series of hauntings that follow his first wife's suicide. The explanation, when it comes, its both rational and unsurprising, but the general mood of the piece carries it through despite atrocious direction. GA

Black Wax

(Robert Mugge, 1982, GB/US) Gil Scott-Heron and the Midnight Band.
79 min.
Admirers of the special blend of tight jazzy funk and intelligently political lyrics that is the hallmark of singer/composer/poet Gil Scott-Heron will find much to enjoy in this engaging documentary. A mixture of coolly shot concert footage and scenes of Scott-Heron taking us on an 'alternative' tour of Washington while pronouncing on politics, poetry and prejudice, the film displays both the man's exhilarating musical eclecticism and his sharply ironic, often cynical vision of an America torn apart by fear, loathing and misguided ideals. Highly watchable and listenable material. GA.

Black Widow

(Nunnally Johnson, 1954, US) Van Heflin, George Raft, Gene Tierney, Ginger Rogers, Reginald Gardiner, Peggy Ann Garner, Otto Kruger.
95 min.
An adaptation of Patrick Quentin's fine thriller which starts promisingly with Heflin's distinguished Broadway producer, meeting a sweetly aspiring young playwright (Garner), helplessly bemused when (actually vampirishly ambitious) she virtually takes over his apartment on the excuse that the surroundings are conducive to inspiration. When she is subsequently found murdered there and he becomes the prime suspect, the film degenerates into a routine whodunnit. Worth seeing for the fine cast, Raft

(dreary as ever as the investigating cop) and Rogers (unexpectedly overdoing it as a bitchy actress) excepted. TM

Black Widow

(Bob Rafelson, 1987, US) Debra Winger, Theresa Russell, Sami Frey, Dennis Hopper, Nicol Williamson, Diane Ladd.
102 min.
From its opening shot – Theresa Russell's split reflection in a make-up mirror – both the theme and the over-schematic symbolism of Rafelson's thriller are immediately apparent. For Russell plays a homicidal psychopath whose killings of various wealthy husbands are investigated by a Justice Department workaholic (Winger), who slowly but surely becomes a kind of mirror-image of her Protean prey. The story and treatment are familiar from '40s *noir* thrillers, but it's clear that Rafelson is attempting something more than mere homage. Disappointingly, the femme fatale – apparently in love with her husbands even as she plans their demise – is presented as somehow more female, fulfilled and complete than the career woman, who in turn eventually discovers both dress sense and the joy of sex with her opposite's next victim-to-be. There are things to enjoy – committed performances, Conrad Hall's elegant camerawork, a script that becomes pleasurably tortuous towards the end – but the film finally offers far less than meets the eye. GA

Black Windmill, The

(Don Siegel, 1974, US) Michael Caine, Joseph O'Connor, Donald Pleasence, John Vernon, Janet Suzman, Delphine Seyrig, Joss Ackland, Clive Revill.
106 min.
Although received with critical disappointment, mainly because Siegel had forsaken his exploration of American mythology and violence for what seemed to be a rather old-fashioned British thriller, there is in fact a lot to enjoy in *The Black Windmill*. It's a very playful piece at the expense of the British stiff-upper lip, made with a discerning American's eye for London. The plot is a shaggy dog story (with just the right degree of nightmarishness) revolving around intelligence agent Caine's single-handed attempts to retrieve his kidnapped son. Though by no means a perfect film, it is a much more coherent work than it is given credit, held together by Siegel's exuberant eye for the incongruous. CPe

Blacula

(William Crain, 1972, US) William Marshall, Vonetta McGee, Denise Nicholas, Thalmus Rasulala, Gordon Pinsent, Charles Macaulay.
93 min.
Disappointing black horror movie which followed in the successful wake of *Shaft*. The script by Joan Torres and Raymond Koenig seems to be the real problem: apart from a garbled opening in which Blacula is vampirised while trying to liberate his people, the plot simply turns away from all the obvious political/social/sexual implications, even on the level of action. Instead, Blacula becomes a less than impressive lovesick vampire chasing his reincarnated wife through LA (one of the dullest plot mechanisms of all), and the film remains a lifeless reworking of heroes versus vampires with soul music and a couple of good gags. Not a particularly promising debut for Crain, whose TV background is all too obvious in the cramped over-emphatic style. DP.

Blade, The (Dao)

(Tsui Hark, 1995, HK) Wing Zhao, Xiong Xinxin, Su Tsui-Yu, Wai Tin-Chi. Chan Ho, Valerie Chow.
104 min.
Nominally a remake of the old Shaw Brothers/ Wang Yu *One-Armed Boxer*, this is actually a (not very) original story: a young man discovers belatedly that he should be out avenging the father he never knew, loses an arm while rescuing a girl from kidnappers, and trains himself to overcome his handicap so as to confront the worst of the bad guys in the final reel. As rife with continuity errors and other signs of haste as most latter-day Tsui Hark movies, this is chiefly notable for its emphasis on naked male flesh; the girl's first-person voice-over is there to deflect suspicions of homo-eroticism. TR

Blade Runner

(Ridley Scott, 1982, US) Harrison Ford, Rutger Hauer, Sean Young, Edward James Olmos, M Emmet Walsh, Daryl Hannah.
117 min.
An ambitious and expensive adaptation of one of Philip K Dick's best novels (*Do Androids Dream of Electric Sheep?*), with Ford as the cop in 2019 Los Angeles whose job is hunting mutinous androids that have escaped from the off-world colonies. The script has some superb scenes, notably between Ford and the (android) femme fatale Young, while Scott succeeds beautifully in portraying the LA of the future as a cross between a Hong Kong street-market and a decaying 200-storey Metropolis. But something has gone badly wrong with the dramatic structure: the hero's voice-over and the ending feel as if they've strayed in from another movie, and the android villains are neither menacing nor sympathetic, when ideally they should have been both. This leaves Scott's picturesque violence looking dull and exploitative. DP

Blade Runner – The Director's Cut

(Ridley Scott, 1982/1991, US) Harrison Ford, Rutger Hauer, Sean Young, Edward James Olmos, M Emmet Walsh, Daryl Hannah.
112 min.
More notable for what's been removed than for what's been added, this restored version of Scott's seminal sci-fi movie makes it clear that all its former faults were introduced by nervous studio executives, who thought the narrative too confusing, the ending too bleak. Gone is the redundant *noir*-style voice-over by Harrison Ford's blade runner (the plot makes more sense without it). Gone, too, the obviously tacked-on happy ending in which Ford and the replicant (Young) flew off into the sunset (which contradicted what we already knew about the replicant's built-in obsolescence). With one crucial exception, the effect of the restorations is less radical, although the extended romantic scenes between Ford and Young do flesh out their relationship. More cryptically, Ford's restored 'unicorn dream' is echoed later by an origami figure left by police chief Bryant's right-hand man Gaff (Olmos) – possibly hinting that Ford himself is a replicant. Perhaps this, too, like Young's treasured childhood memories, is just an implant. In its earlier incarnation, the film was a flawed masterpiece; in Scott's restored version, it is, quite simply, a masterpiece. NF

Blaise Pascal

(Roberto Rossellini, 1972, Fr/It) Pierre Arditi, Rita Forzano.
131 min.
A thrilling, intense chronicle analysing the thought and development of 'a very boring man who never made love in his life' (Rossellini). The 17th century scientist and philosopher struggles with a society which believes in witchcraft and ridicules his discovery of the vacuum. Notions of both are made concrete as the film illustrates Pascal painfully pushing Europe towards Enlightenment. Discoursing with Descartes, he explains the necessity of limits to reason for the existence of God. And the 20th century audience *understands*, recognising a world explored with extraordinary lucidity and simplicity. Faith grapples with empiricism, reason routs superstition, and with every frame, Rossellini reinvents the historical biography. JW

Blame It On Rio

(Stanley Donen, 1984, US) Michael Caine, Joseph Bologna, Valerie Harper, Michelle Johnson, Demi Moore.
100 min.
Two middle-aged businessmen (Caine and Bologna) take a holiday in Rio without their wives but with their teenage daughters. When Bologna's daughter, a pyrogenic half-pint with the subtle approach of a heat-seeking missile, homes in on Caine, the result is a very predictable sort of French farcing about. Aside from a good exchange rate of one-liners, the chief feeling left by the movie (a remake of Claude Berri's *Un Moment d'Egarement*) is of a thin, cynical calculation. Sole reason to catch it would be to monitor one more step of Caine's increasing excellence as middle age overtakes him. CPea

Blame It on the Bellboy

(Mark Herman, 1992, GB) Dudley Moore, Bryan Brown, Richard Griffiths, Andreas Katsulas, Patsy Kensit, Alison Steadman, Penelope Wilton, Bronson Pinchot, Lindsay Anderson.
78 min.
Confusion over a name by a bellboy (Pinchot) in a Venetian hotel leads to lots of Benny Hill-style sexual innuendo, torture of the wrong man by the Mafia, and a hitman unable to work out who he's to hit. Meek Melvyn (Moore) is visiting Venice to buy a property for his boss, but falls into the hands of villainous Scarpa (Katsulas). Estate agent Caroline (Kensit) is mistaken for a sure bonk by porky Maurice (Griffiths), whose wife (Steadman) turns up unexpectedly. Only Bryan Brown (the hitman) and Penelope Wilton (the girl Maurice expected to meet) manage to do anything with their roles, even though she's cast as a Mickey Spillane fan. Mark Herman wrote as well as directed this leaden farce. BC

Blanche

(Walerian Borowczyk, 1971, Fr) Ligia Branice, Michel Simon, Lawrence Trimble, Jacques Perrin, Georges Wilson, Denise Peronne.
92 min.
In this remarkable film, Borowczyk, through his commitment to ambiguity (notably in his framing, which forever denies the foreground/background opposition) and his belief in almost entomological observation, transforms his 13th century characters – a foolish old Baron, an over-proud King, a lecherous page and a stupidly handsome lover, all of whom are in love with and/or lust after the simple Blanche, the Baron's young wife – into tragic figures caught up in a dance of death over which they have no control. In exactly the same way, the castle and its decor, photographed by Borowczyk as though it were living and its inhabitants were mere dolls for the most part, is seen as the backdrop to a happy fairytale, and at the same time as the root of all evil, as rooms and bizarre machines are opened and set in motion. PH

Blanche Fury

(Marc Allégret, 1948, GB) Valerie Hobson, Stewart Granger, Walter Fitzgerald, Michael Gough, Maurice Denham, Sybilla Binder, Edward Lexy.
95 min.
A strikingly designed Victorian melodrama, produced by Cineguild, which had made David Lean's two Dickens adaptations and was now trying to get into the Gainsborough market. Hobson plays a poor-relation governess who marries a widowed cousin and falls in love with Granger, a bastard who believes he has been disinherited. What makes the film rather distinctive is its eagerness to kill off the cast, whose acting is too lightweight for the material. ATu

Blank Check (aka Blank Cheque)

(Rupert Wainwright, 1994, US) Brian Bonsall, Karen Duffy, James Rebhorn, Jayne Atkinson, Michael Faustino, Miguel Ferrer.
93 min.
Neglected by his parents in favour of his older brother, 11-year-old Preston (Bonsall) wants money and his own house for his birthday. His wish is granted when crook Quigley (Ferrer) drives over his bike, since damages consist of a blank cheque; but when Preston fills in the amount as $1 million, he gets more than he bargained for, bringing both Quigley and the FBI down on top of him. A Disney feature from a first-time British director: inauspicious. AO

Blaze

(Ron Shelton, 1989, US) Paul Newman, Lolita Davidovich, Jerry Hardin, Gailard Sartain, Jeffrey DeMunn, Garland Bunting, Richard Jenkins, Brandon Smith, Jay Chevalier.
117 min.
In the late '50s, Louisiana governor Earl K Long (brother of Huey) scandalised voters when news broke of his affair with stripper Blaze Starr. In what is essentially a vehicle for Paul Newman, Long comes over as gangling eccentric and political visionary: he keeps his boots on while love-making, and at a time of entrenched prejudice approves voting rights for blacks. While opponents plot his abduction, supporters applaud his outspokenness. The film's overall tone is light, and against this Newman cuts an imposing, vigorous figure. But Ron Shelton's script is inconsistent. Co-star Davidovich attempts a sympathetic rendering of Blaze Starr, but her role is underdeveloped; given that the central relationship prevails over the political agenda, it's an oversight which leaves dialogue one-sided and often toothless. Considering the awareness of post-Watergate audiences, it's not enough merely to portray a gutsy, glitzy couple who both, by Starr's definition, work in 'showbiz'. The film has a certain candour, but it would have been enhanced by a less superficial approach. CM

Blazing Guns (Uomo avvisato mezzo ammazzato...parola di Spirito Santo)

(Anthony Ascott, 1972, It/Sp) Gianni Garko, Pilar Velasquez, Paul Stevens, Chris Huerta, Polda Bendandi, George Rigaud.
91 min.
Gory (and excremental) spaghetti Western about a goldmine won in a poker game and the trouble it causes in revolution-torn Mexico. The white-cloaked protagonist, Harold 'Holy Ghost' (Garko), owner of a dove named 'Eagle', is a pretty unconvincing avenging angel. JPy

Blazing Saddles

(Mel Brooks, 1974, US) Cleavon Little, Gene Wilder, Slim Pickens, Harvey Korman, Madeline Kahn, Mel Brooks, David Huddleston.
93 min.
'Oh Lord', says the preacher in a suitably grave voice, 'do we have the strength to carry out this task in one night, or are we just jerking off?' Maybe Mel Brooks should have asked himself that question about this movie. The screenplay is credited to five writers, and it shows in the confused melange of styles. There are some lovely touches, and a score of lines like the preacher's which start pompous and end crude; or the contrast between picture – archetypal white-haired old lady – and words – 'Up yours, Nigger!' But if part is delightful, a larger part proves that there is more corn in Hollywood than Oklahoma, and a lot is just Hollywood jerking off. PB

Blazing Sun

see Plein Soleil

Bleak Moments

(Mike Leigh, 1971, GB) Anne Raitt, Sarah Stephenson, Eric Allan, Joolia Cappleman, Mike Bradwell.
111 min.
A girl left at home with her mentally retarded sister tries to work out her own communication problems. She fails with a well-meaning teacher, especially in a Chinese restaurant where the only other diner gobbles down his food in contrasting extravagance, and also with a long-haired would-be guitarist, who buries his head in his own silence. Says a lot about repressed feelings, with none of the social propaganda of Ken Loach's *Family Life*. The bleak moments are everywhere, and pretty harrowing.

Blended

see Métisse

Blind Alley

(Charles Vidor, 1939, US) Chester Morris, Ralph Bellamy, Ann Dvorak, Joan Perry, Melville Cooper, Rose Stradner, Marc Lawrence.
71 min. b/w.
Interesting but somewhat ramshackle chunk of Freudiana adapted from a stage play, in which an escaped convict (Morris) and his associates hold a remote household hostage while waiting for their getaway transport. The house happens to belong to a psychiatrist (Bellamy), and the process by which he gradually asserts his dominance, realising that the convict is a compulsive killer who is afraid he's going mad, is persuasively done; the miracle analysis he achieves within hours (programming the killer so that he can no longer pull the trigger), is ludicrous, to say the least. The best sequence details the killer's recurring nightmare of cowering

b

from a relentless shower of blood under a perforated umbrella, simply but very effectively staged in negative; and throughout, Lucien Ballard's deep focus compositions enhance the otherwise routine tensions. Remade in 1948 as *The Dark Past*. TM

Blind Alley (Mienai)

(Go Riju, 1985, Jap) Koji Sano, Asao Kobayashi, Go Riju.
58 min.
A sort of documentary by a bright young actor-director (he plays the young Mishima in Paul Schrader's *Mishima*), shot on video and transferred to 16 mm film. Riju starts out talking about his own inability to feel political commitment and his uncertainties about cinema, then stumbles on an inarticulate and reclusive young truck-driver and decides to make a film about him. The film records their encounters over a period of weeks, with Riju driven into a frenzy of frustration by the boy's passivity and lack of interest in 'important' questions, until they finally come to blows. This is funny and surprisingly engrossing – and a surprise ending rockets it into another dimension entirely. TR

Blind Chance (Przypadek)

(Krzysztof Kieslowski, 1982, Pol) Boguslaw Linda, Tadeusz Lomnicki, Zbigniew Zapasiewicz, Boguslawa Pawelec.
122 min.
Kieslowski's film was originally suppressed under Martial Law for its gloomy political prognosis. It offers three quite distinct possibilities for Poland's future by having a former medical student running to catch a train from Lodz to Warsaw. First, he catches the train, meets an old-style Stalinist, and joins the Party. Second, he misses the train, gets arrested, and is jailed with dissident students. Lastly, he misses the train again, gets married, and settles down to sexy and apolitical bliss. A fourth story, in which Poland throws out the Communist Party, was presumably unthinkable in 1982... ATu

Blind Corner

(Lance Comfort, 1963, GB) William Sylvester, Barbara Shelley, Elizabeth Shepherd, Alex Davion, Mark Eden, Ronnie Carroll.
80 min. b/w.
An unassuming but occasionally effective second feature thriller which is marred by some phony characterisation. Sylvester plays a blind pop music composer, with Shelley as his apparently loving wife who plans to murder him and go off with her lover. Of interest chiefly to admirers of Barbara *Cat Girl* Shelley or Elizabeth *Ligeia* Shepherd.

Blind Date

(Nico Mastorakis, 1984, US) Joseph Bottoms, Kirstie Alley, James Daughton, Lana Clarkson, Keir Dullea.
99 min.
Bottoms becomes traumatically blind after witnessing his object of desire with another man, and so has a computer embedded in his brain. The resulting dayglow vision turns the world into one huge video game inside his head; but the picture quality isn't good enough to enable him to see the face of the killer who is carving up the women of Athens with a scalpel. Unfortunately not enough is made of this blurring of the interface between man and machine; and the key concept of voyeurism is kept strictly on the exploitative level. The rest of the film (shot in Greece) is largely composed of women in slashed blouses or wet bikinis undergoing humiliation. It needs the kind of nasty thoughtfulness of a De Palma behind it; but it just comes out a Babycham picture in a Moet bottle. CPea

Blind Date

(Blake Edwards, 1987, US) Kim Basinger, Bruce Willis, John Larroquette, William Daniels, George Coe, Mark Blum.
95 min.
Walter (Willis) needs a date for that all-important business dinner, but the lady his brother fixes him up with should carry a blue-touch-paper warning. Nadia (Basinger) can't drink without going ape. She loses him his job, wrecks his car, and inadvertently sets her insanely jealous ex-boyfriend David (Larroquette) on his

case. Most of the set pieces are predictable in this formula comedy, though there is a sprinkling of chuckles in the sight gags. BC

Blind Date
(aka Chance Meeting)

(Joseph Losey, 1959, GB) Hardy Krüger, Stanley Baker, Micheline Presle, Robert Flemyng, Gordon Jackson, John Van Eyssen, Jack MacGowran.
95 min. b/w.
Made four years before the Profumo affair gave such scandals a real-life significance, Losey's thriller – based on Leigh Howard's novel – deals with the murder of a diplomat's French mistress (Presle), and the pressures on a cynical cop (Baker) to pin the case on her other lover (Krüger), a Dutch artist from the lower classes. Although the script is dramatically weak, Losey's precise view of the characters in terms of class conflict and erotic obsession gives the film an edge absent in the work of most resident British directors of the period. DT

Blindfold

(Philip Dunne, 1965, US) Rock Hudson, Claudia Cardinale, Guy Stockwell, Jack Warden, Brad Dexter.
102 min.
A wryly self-mocking spy thriller coating a convoluted international plot and stock genre characters (psychologist, mad scientist, security chief, et al) in the requisite '60s gloss. The final film as director of former Fox contract writer (*How Green Was My Valley*, *Forever Amber*, *The Robe* etc) Dunne. PT

Blind Fury

(Phillip Noyce, 1989, US) Rutger Hauer, Terrance O'Quinn, Brandon Call, Noble Willingham, Lisa Blount, Nick Cassavetes, Rick Overton, Randall 'Tex' Cobb, Meg Foster, Sho Kosugi.
86 min.
Like many a damaged hero, Nick Parker (Hauer) is a Vietvet, but his experiences left him blind, not batty. A credits sequence shows how the stricken Parker was rescued from the battlefield by gentle Vietnamese and taught some nifty (if not downright supernatural) sword skills. He also (Rambo, please note) learns tolerance, self-restraint and compassion. Pair him with a cute menaced kid whose mum has been offed by the Mob, and whose dad (O'Quinn) is Parker's long-lost army pal, and you have a New Man with a Mission. Hauer's Parker, shambling, shrewd and powerful, is humorous and appealing, and Noyce skilfully orchestrates a hilarious army of gurning baddies. It thunders along admirably, if rather unbelievably, and to counter the sickly moments with the cute kid (Call), there's plenty of pleasurable ass-kicking. SFe

Blind Husbands

(Erich von Stroheim, 1918, US) Erich von Stroheim, Gibson Gowland, Sam de Grasse, Francilla Billington, Fay Holderness.
8 reels. b/w.
Stroheim's first film as director (he also wrote, starred in, and designed the sets for it). Apart from the naturalistic acting styles from all the principals, *Blind Husbands* is not particularly remarkable in itself; but it adequately signposts many of the aspects of Stroheim's later work which make him unique. Stroheim himself plays the aristocratic officer attempting to seduce the neglected wife of a young American on holiday in the Austro-Italian Alps. It's a moral tale, as simplistic as it sounds, but what makes it distinctive is the use of design and the characters' personal mannerisms as fully functional elements of the director's overall moral purpose. RM

Blindman

(Ferdinando Baldi, 1971, US/It) Tony Anthony, Ringo Starr, Agneta Eckemyr, Lloyd Batista, Magda Konopka.
105 min.
Alternately amusing and embarrassing sub-Leone Western, with a blind pudgy-faced hero who can nevertheless shoot straight and enjoys a psychic understanding with his horse. Despite some striking widescreen photography, the hero and the silly plot, involving his attempts to regain fifty stolen mail order brides, relegates it to passable viewing for a local double bill, but that's about all.

Blind Spot
(Die Reise nach Lyon)

(Claudia von Alemann, 1980, WGer) Rebecca Pauly, Jean Badin, Denise Péron, Sarah Stern.
111 min.
Flora Tristan was a 19th century utopian socialist feminist, notorious in her day, now largely forgotten. A young historian (Pauly) leaves husband and child to seek traces of Tristan in contemporary Lyons. Disillusioned with the records-and-monuments methods of historians, she roams the streets recording sounds Tristan may have heard. A film about the impossibility of knowing the past; the camera looks and looks but only yields implacably closed images. Sound's the thing, and in the final, long-held shot of the woman ecstatically playing her violin, the film's complex and compelling themes come together. JR

Blink

(Michael Apted, 1994, US) Madeleine Stowe, Aidan Quinn, James Remar, Peter Friedman, Bruce A Young, Laurie Metcalf.
106 min.
Suddenly, after 20-odd years of living in darkness, Emma Brody has seen too much – or has she? Well, you can join the dots to complete Apted's thriller from the blurb, except for the question bit at the end. That's the hook. Retroactive vision is a rare phenomenon which accompanies the early stages of restored sight, involving flashbacks and, for the purposes of movies, lots and lots of computer-generated effects. Emma (Stowe), a folk fiddle player, suffers from the above, which makes her an unreliable murder witness. Who believes her? The murderer for one, and the coarse cop Hallstrom (Quinn) for another, and it isn't long before he becomes someone to watch over her. The handling of both plot and romance is muddled, and the film is largely fuelled by Stowe's tough, independent characterisation. She plays against the sentimentality inherent in her predicament, but isn't consistently helped by either script or sugary compositions. Fairly functional time-passer, but it would've passed anyway. BC

Bliss

(Ray Lawrence, 1985, Aust) Barry Otto, Lynette Curran, Helen Jones, Gia Carides, Miles Buchanan, Jeff Truman.
112 min.
Lawrence's adaptation of Peter Carey's novel in no way pants after American prototypes. Part surrealist comedy and part mid-life crisis drama, its madcap energy and anarchic intelligence put it in a class of its own. Harry Joy (Otto), rich advertising executive, is loved by everyone except his wife, who is having an affair with his partner and best friend. Harry only discovers this after a four-minute clinical death from a heart attack, when he begins to see his life in perspective: his marriage is in ruins, his son swaps drugs for sex from his daughter, all around him people are dying of cancer, and his wife has him committed to an asylum. Then into his life steps the young and beautiful Honey (Jones), and the sweet-toothed Harry falls in love as she beckons him into the bush and a back-to-nature idyll. Witty and profoundly enjoyable. CB

Bliss of Mrs Blossom, The

(Joseph McGrath, 1968, GB) Shirley MacLaine, Richard Attenborough, James Booth, Freddie Jones, William Rushton, Bob Monkhouse.
93 min.
Coarse comedy which looks a little like Joe Orton gone disastrously wrong (actually it's based on a play by Alec Coppel) as Attenbor-ough's downtrodden brassière manufacturer dreams of being an orchestra conductor, his wife secretly instals a lover in the attic, and an effeminate detective prowls in quest of a crime. Any sparks in the script or performances are ruthlessly extinguished by atrocious direction. TM

Blithe Spirit

(David Lean, 1945, GB) Rex Harrison, Constance Cummings, Kay Hammond, Margaret Rutherford, Hugh Wakefield, Joyce Carey.
96 min.
A classy adaptation of Noël Coward's successful stage play, in which the wedded bliss of cynical remarried novelist Harrison is threatened

by the mischievous ghost of his first wife (Hammond), who appears at a seance presided over by Rutherford's eccentric medium and proceeds to bother his none-too-amused second wife (Cummings). Nifty special effects for the time, and plenty of Coward's inimitable wit and repartee. NF

Blob, The

(Irwin S Yeaworth Jr, 1958, US) Steve McQueen, Anita Corseaut, Earl Rowe, Olin Howlin.
86 min.
Arriving from outer space (for which read Russia), a large ball of interstellar snot terrorises a small American town by eating everything in sight. McQueen turns in a commendable performance as the (not so) young rebel without a car, who attempts to alert his townsfolk to the threat of the amorphous alien, demonstrating in the process that tearaway teens can still be steadfast, loyal and true when the shit comes down. Despite producer Jack Harris' pooh-poohing of the 'political subtext' theory, rampant Commie-phobia pervades as the ever-redder blob sucks the life-blood out of every sacred American institution, climaxing in a truly marvellous scene in which the enemy within devours an entire diner, over easy, with a side salad and fries to go. MK

Blob, The

(Chuck Russell, 1988, US) Shawnee Smith, Donovan Leitch, Ricky Paull Goldin, Kevin Dillon, Billy Beck, Candy Clark, Del Close.
95 min.
This reworking of the 1958 cheapie clearly illustrates one thing: that no increase in budget and no amount of state-of-the-art special effects can compensate for a slim B-movie plot. After a meteorite crashes to earth, the amorphous Blob slimes its way through the small town of Arborville, ingesting en route a varied diet of dogs, groping couples, cinema patrons, and other disposable teens. The gelatinous monster slides from one set piece to the next more smoothly than the stop-start plot, which (as in the original) consists largely of the efforts of cheerleader Smith and rebellious biker Dillon to alert sceptical adults to the alien threat. More successful is the film's main innovation, a government conspiracy subplot in which a biological containment team seal off the town and put the monster's potential as a weapon above the safety of the townspeople. It's the effects that carry the day, however with the sluggish, oozing blob of the original now a clear pink amoebic predator that lashes out sticky tendrils and digests its victims in full view. NF

Blockade

(William Dieterle, 1938, US) Henry Fonda, Madeleine Carroll, Leo Carrillo, Reginald Denny, John Halliday, Vladimir Sokoloff.
85 min. b/w.
Classic example of Hollywood easing its conscience about the Spanish Civil War (never identified by name) while carefully hedging its bets. Scripted by John Howard Lawson (later one of the Hollywood Ten), it's littered with pseudo-echoes of Soviet movies as Fonda's peasant rabbits on about his love of the soil, while Carroll does the Dietrich bit as a spy suffering romance and a change of heart. Totally spurious, though well shot (Rudolph Maté) and directed, it ends in cringing embarrassment with Fonda making an appeal to camera for the world to stop this war. TM

Blockheads

(John G Blystone, 1938, US) Stan Laurel, Oliver Hardy, Billy Gilbert, Patricia Ellis, James Finlayson, Minna Gombell.
57 min. b/w.
Planned as the last Laurel & Hardy film (which fortunately turned out not to be the case), this remains one of their best features. From its opening sequence– Stan guarding the front, twenty years after the end of World War I hostilities — through the chance re-meeting of Stan and a horribly domesticated Ollie, to the climax of disaster caused by Stan's good intentions, *Blockheads* (co-scripted by Harry Langdon) is a triumphant exploration of the quality and kind of relationship between Stan and Ollie that underlies their best comedy. PH

Blockhouse, The

(Clive Rees, 1973, GB) Peter Sellers, Charles Aznavour, Per Oscarsson, Peter Vaughn, Alfred Lynch, Jeremy Kemp.
92 min.
A group of slave workers, drafted by the Nazis to help construct their coastal defences in 1944, are sealed underground during an Allied naval bombardment. They find huge stores of food, but candles to last only so long. The slow dying of their light provides the film with its meagre dramatic impetus, as one by one they are done in by boredom, illness, jealousy. Incongruous casting lends piquancy to their fate, but like them the film seems designed for terminal obscurity. RC

Blonde Ambition

(John Amero/Lem Amero, 1980, US) Suzy Mandel, Dory Devon, Eric Edwards, George Payne, Kurt Mann, Jamie Gillis.
81 min.
A bawdy rip-off of *Gentlemen Prefer Blondes* from the porn circuit. The storytelling is paltry, most of the acting aboriginal, but there is a pyrogenic half-pint in the shape of Mandel, who has all the dumb-puckering ingenuousness of the early Monroe. At the drop of a champagne glass, she is rending her garments and preparing to break the seventh commandment with some humdinger in a stetson, only the infuriating cuts for the British market (six minutes gone) coming between her and you and the fun. There is also evidence of a certain crude humour at work: an amorous version of *Gone With the Wind* ('The Yankees are coming!') being directed by Jamie Gillis, NY porn star. And the bizarre spectacle of someone's front room transformed into a skating rink for a set piece of troilism on ice, yet. CPea

Blonde Fist

(Frank Clarke, 1991, GB) Margi Clarke, Carroll Baker, Ken Hutchinson, Sharon Power, Angela Clarke, Lewis Bester, Gary Mavers.
102 min. b/w & col.
A pugnacious but misbegotten celebration of working-class values, Clarke's directorial debut (he wrote *Letter to Brezhnev*) is a sad disappointment. Ronnie (Margi Clarke) is an embodiment of female working-class strengths. She also has a deadly right fist, inherited from her bare-knuckle fighter father, which lands her in gaol for assaulting her husband's girlfriend, and later – after she's escaped to America in search of her father – gives her a chance to make some desperately needed money on the female boxing circuit. The film starts intriguingly, with a black-and-white sequence set in the late '50s, in which dad (Hutchinson) fights round the back while mum gives birth. But as we move into colour and modern times, it falls apart: ploddingly paced and cliché-filled. WH

Blonde in Love, A

see *Lásky Jedné Plavovlásky*

Blonde Venus

(Josef von Sternberg, 1932, US) Marlene Dietrich, Herbert Marshall, Cary Grant, Sidney Toler, Dickie Moore.
97 min. b/w.
With characteristic exaggeration, Sternberg himself wrote off *Blonde Venus* as a disaster. He made it (under protest) in response to studio pressure for another Dietrich vehicle, and seems to have attempted to work a number of autobiographical elements into its sprawling extremes of glamour and squalor. The film is certainly a mess at one level, with damaging fluctuations in tone and pace, and some ropey supporting performances, but it remains enough of a visual triumph to earn its place in the series of Dietrich movies. Dietrich is here not only married but also a mother, forced into a career as a nightclub singer to pay for her husband's medical fees, and then lured into an affair with playboy Grant. Her misadventures (including a flight into seedy hotels in the Deep South) are a bizarre mixture of fairytale and social-realist drama, snapping into sharpest focus when she performs the legendary 'Hot Voodoo' number while emerging from a gorilla-skin. TR

Blondie

(Frank Strayer, 1938, US) Penny Singleton, Arthur Lake, Gene Lockhart, Ann Doran, Larry Simms, Jonathan Hale.
69 min. b/w.

First in the series based on Chic Young';s comic strip about the bumbling Dagwood Bumstead and his dizzy blonde wife (who wore the pants, but pretended not to). Popular at the time, brightly and breezily done, it ran to twenty-seven sequels ending in 1950, during which time Baby Dumpling (played throughout by Simms) grew up to become the adolescent Alexander. A prototype of the average TV sitcom today. TM

Blood and Concrete

(Jeffrey Reiner, 1990, US) Billy Zane, Jennifer Beals, Darren McGavin, James Le Gros, Nicholas Worth, William Bastiani.
99 min.
A black comic cocktail of '50s B *film noir* and post-modern irony, with a bitter twist. Small-time criminal Joey Turks (Zane) stumbles into a scam involving an addictive aphrodisiac drug, Libido, then hooks up with damaged romantic Mona (Beals). Veteran cop Hank Dick (McGavin), meanwhile, wants to settle a long-standing score with the package's real owner, criminal big-shot Spuntz, whose gay psycho hoodlum Lance (Le Gros) has become Joey's shadow. Jim Thompson might have recognised the survival ethic and scuzzy characters, but this is soft-boiled pastiche rather than hard-boiled parody. NF

Blood and Sand

(Fred Niblo, 1922, US) Rudolph Valentino, Nita Naldi, Lila Lee, George Field, Walter Long.
7,100 ft. b/w.
Matador Valentino and vamp Naldi tango this rise-and-fall *corrida* melodrama towards the realm of the senses. But Niblo's prosaic direction is at odds with the Iberian exotica, and it is left to the odd inventions of June Mathis' script, and the bullfight sequences constructed by editor Dorothy Arzner, to add anything to the curiosity value of the Great Lover's work. PT

Blood and Sand

(Rouben Mamoulian, 1941, US) Tyrone Power, Linda Darnell, Rita Hayworth, Laird Cregar, Anthony Quinn, J Carrol Naish, John Carradine, Alla Nazimova.
123 min.
One of *the* great colour films (with Mamoulian taking the inspiration for his lush visuals from Spanish masters like Goya, Velasquez and El Greco), this is melodramatic romance of the first order. The story is hardly a stunner, taken from Ibañez and telling of a young man's rags-to-riches rise as a matador, only to fall under the spell of Hayworth's aristocratic temptress, who lures him away from virginal childhood sweetheart Darnell. What makes the film so enjoyable is the sheer elegance of the execution, with Mamoulian's sense of rhythm, the rich Technicolor, and Richard Day's sets conjuring up an imaginary Spain of the heart, poignant location of love in the shadows and death in the afternoon. GA

Blood and Wine

(Bob Rafelson, 1996, US/GB) Jack Nicholson, Michael Caine, Stephen Dorff, Jennifer Lopez, Judy Davis, Harold Perrineau Jr, Robyn Peterson.
100 min.
The theft of a $1m diamond necklace from a wine dealer's wealthy client is merely the generic hook for Rafelson's insidious character study, which teams Nicholson's over-reaching vintner with Caine's terminally seedy safe cracker. As in *The Postman Always Rings Twice*, the crime itself proves deceptively easy; it's the ensuing complications that expose the subtly shifting alliances, the sly deceptions and the murky motives. With his crudely dyed black hair and big talk, the has-been Caine's professional competence is as shaky as his health, and everything is complicated by Nicholson and his unwitting son Dorff's mutual lust for the inside connection, the client's sexy, manipulative nanny, Jennifer Lopez. An engrossing thriller – and one sparkling with intelligence, with the surprising twists grounded in credible human behaviour. NF

Bloodbath at the House of Death

(Ray Cameron, 1983, GB) Kenny Everett, Pamela Stephenson, Vincent Price, Gareth Hunt, John Fortune, Sheila Steafel.
92 min.

Headstone Manor saw the disappearance of 18 souls in 18 grisly ways, which the locals have variously put down to some dodgy monkey business, visitors from outer space, or fast food excess. Ten years on, strong radiation readings bring the one-legged Dr Mandeville (Everett) to do some paranormal research, and the carnage begins. The spoofings of so many genre films in a barrage of visual gags quickly becomes predictable; only Sheila Steafel's *Carrie* sketch is done with any imagination. FL

Blood Beach

(Jeffrey Bloom, 1980, US) David Huffman, Mariana Hill, John Saxon, Otis Young, Stefan Gierasch, Burt Young.
89 min.
Bringing the fear of the thing that may lurk under the water and nibble your toes one step further inland, *Blood Beach* locates its murderous monster under the sand. Its debt to *Jaws* is implicit from the setting (seaside town loses tourists and trade) to the music (subterranean bass rumbles signal monster's approach), but the bad-taste jokes and the light-hearted approach inspire laughter, not the thrill of fear. Good, cheap B-movie fun.

Blood Beast from Outer Space

see Night Caller, The

Blood Beast Terror, The (aka The Vampire Beast Craves Blood)

(Vernon Sewell, 1967, GB) Peter Cushing, Robert Flemyng, Wanda Ventham, Vanessa Howard, David Griffin, Roy Hudd.
88 min.
Tacky, indifferently acted horrors involving a weremoth (Ventham, who metamorphoses into a giant death's head) loose in rural England. Flemyng is the loony entomologist, Cushing the cop investigating a series of murders. TM

Bloodbrothers

(Robert Mulligan, 1978, US) Paul Sorvino, Tony Lo Bianco, Richard Gere, Lelia Goldoni, Yvonne Wilder, Kenneth McMillan.
116 min.
A ludicrously overblown soap opera set in Italian Brooklyn which races from childhood anorexia to adolescent sexual trauma via wife-battering. Gere, as the pretty school-leaver who wants to be a social worker but comes up against his father's hard-hat ambitions, is fine, but his sensitive performance is simply mangled by the movie's muddled glorification of the macho ethos. Mulligan recut the film to 98 minutes for TV.

Blood Brothers, The (Cia Ma/aka Chinese Vengeance)

(Chang Cheh, 1973, HK) David Chiang, Ti Lung, Chen Kuan Tai, Ching Li.
117 min.
Visually rich and one of Chang Cheh's most satisfying efforts, a heady mixture of heroism, fatalism and sensuality. The slow unravelling of the relationship between the three 'blood brothers' of very different character – the noble knight (Ti Lung), the fraught avenger (David Chiang) and the loose, 'innocent' victim (Chen Kuan Tai) – fits well with the rigorous ethical structure that is glimpsed from time to time beneath the exotic surface trappings of dynastic China. There is also bold use of superimposition and collage. VG

Blood for Dracula (Dracula Vuole Vivere: Cerca Sangue di Vergine!)

(Paul Morrissey, 1973, It/Fr) Joe Dallesandro, Udo Kier, Maxime McKendry, Vittorio De Sica, Milena Vukotic, Roman Polanski.
103 min.
The time-honoured myth refracted through the lens of New York lifestyle. Dracula (Kier) becomes just another junkie searching for his fix, having quit Romania on a quest for the virgin blood that he desperately needs in Catholic Italy. Little Joe, as per, hunkers around after anything in skirts, looks puzzled, and spouts neo-Marxist claptrap. The deadpan dialogue is improved no

end by wayward dialectic from De Sica, incomprehensible as an Italian with four sexy daughters. Often startlingly beautiful to look at. CPea

Blood from the Mummy's Tomb

(Seth Holt/Michael Carreras, 1971, GB) Andrew Keir, Valerie Leon, James Villiers, Hugh Burden, George Coulouris, Rosalie Crutchley.
94 min.
An adaptation of Bram Stoker's *Jewel of the Seven Stars*, scripted by former *TO* contributor Chis Wicking, and directed by cult horror-merchant Holt (who sadly died during production, leaving Carreras to finish it off). A stylish addition to the mummy genre, with members of an expedition which brought a mummy back to Britain suddenly kicking the bucket years later, and the expedition leader's daughter being possessed by the ancient princess. One of the better late efforts from Hammer. GA

Bloodhounds of Broadway

(Howard Brookner, 1989, US) Madonna, Jennifer Grey, Rutger Hauer, Matt Dillon, Randy Quaid, Julie Hagerty, Josef Sommer.
93 min.
An American Playhouse production of a '20s musical pastiche based on four Damon Runyon stories, featuring Madonna as a nightclub singer, Hauer as a gangster, Dillon as a gambler, Quaid as a hapless swain, Grey as 'Lovely Lou', and Hagerty as a society dame. Actually, the performances aren't too bad – even Madonna's, although her squeaky disco voice is manifestly unsuited to period crooning. But even the all-star cast can't impose order or interest on the ludicrous and mystifyingly convoluted plot. Madonna's confession that she wants to drop being a jazz baby and retire to a 'quarter-acre in Newark' to raise babies and chickens might just be worth your attention. But ultimately the film delivers its own epitaph: 'The Brain is dead'. I'm afraid so. SFe

Blood In Blood Out

see Bound by Honor

Bloodline (aka Sidney Sheldon's Bloodline)

(Terence Young, 1979, US/WGer) Audrey Hepburn, Ben Gazzara, James Mason, Claudia Mori, Irene Papas, Michelle Phillips, Maurice Ronet, Romy Schneider, Omar Sharif.
127 min.
Boardroom fun and games and lots of soap opera antics occur when Hepburn takes over the family multi-million, multi-national company after dad gets bumped off. Like Sheldon's *The Other Side of Midnight*, it's expensive, old-fashioned and overlong.

Blood Money (aka The Stranger and the Gunfighter)

(Antonio Margheriti, 1974, HK/It/Sp/US) Lee Van Cleef, Lo Lieh, Karen Yeh, Julian Ugarte.
107 min.
Ludicrous Chinese/Italian Western, shot in Spain on mostly American money, teaming up a bemused Lee Van Cleef with an embarrassed Lo *King Boxer* Lieh. The vulgar plot centres on a treasure map tattooed in segments on female buttocks; the action scenes are uniformly buggered up by the director. TR

Blood Oath

(Stephen Wallace, 1990, Aust) Bryan Brown, George Takei, Terry O'Quinn, John Bach, Toshi Shioya, John Clarke, Tetsu Watanabe, Deborah Unger, John Polson, Jason Donovan.
108 min.
Ambon Island, Indonesia, 1946: dejected Japanese PoWs lead members of the Australian Army Legal Corps to a hidden clearing where scores of Australian PoWs were executed by prison camp guards. What follows is run-of-the-mill courtroom drama as Captain Robert Cooper (Brown, predictably curt), the hard-line prosecutor assigned to the war crimes case, questions suspects: Vice-Admiral Baron Takahashi (Takei, impressive), his sadistic underling Captain Ikeuchi (Watanabe), and a young Japanese signals officer (Shioya). The result may be of historical interest to those unfamiliar with some of

the lesser-known details of WWII, and goes some way towards highlighting cultural differences and opposing views of war. Jason Donovan makes his big screen debut: two minutes and the immortal line, 'Do you need anything?'. Quite. DA

Blood of a Poet, The,

see Sang d'un Poète, Le

Blood of Doctor Jekyll, The

see Docteur Jekyll et les Femmes

Blood of Hussain, The

(Jamil Dehlavi, 1980, GB/Pak) Salmaan Peerzada, Kika Markham, Durriya Kazi, Kabuli Baba.
112 min.
A startling premonition and damning indictment of General Zia's Pakistan, this is nonetheless the very antithesis of crude agit-prop. The eruption of a white stallion from beneath the red desert earth strikingly exemplifies writer/director Dehlavi's accessible use of mythical metaphor to underpin his fiction of contemporary rebellion and martyrdom; and such visual coups abound as he interrogates notions of power and responsibility in the family and the state. PT

Blood of the Condor (Yawar Mallku)

(Jorge Sanjines, 1969, Bol) Marcelino Yanahuaya, Benedicta Mendoza Huanca, Vicente Salinas.
74 min. b/w.
About a conflict between the Peace Corps and a local tribe in Bolivia , used to dramatise the racism latent in 'Western Aid' programmes. The Peace Corps were discovered to be practising sterilisation on Indian women without their knowledge. Sanjines' film explores the implications of this policy.

Blood of the Dragon (Satsujinken 2)

(Shigehiro Ozawa, 1974, Jap) Shinichi Chiba, Yoko Ichiji, Masafumi Suzuki, Kaoru Nakajima.
88 min.
From the same unarmed combat series as *Kung Fu Street Fighter* (qv. since the same general remarks apply). Chiba again stars as Terry Tsuguri, with a lot of flashbacks to the earlier film. But new linking material includes at least one devastating fight scene: an all-but-naked Tsuguri fighting off an ambush in a sauna. TR

Blood of the Vampire

(Henry Cass, 1958, GB) Donald Wolfit, Barbara Shelley, Vincent Ball, Victor Maddern, William Devlin, Andrew Faulds, John Le Mesurier.
85 min.
The barnstorming Wolfit as a mad doctor returning to life after execution, taking control of a lunatic asylum (which comes complete with torture dungeon, useful for chastising the recalcitrant Shelley and her lover), and using the patients as a blood bank for his vampirism. As produced by Baker and Berman, never a guarantee of anything very much, it's lusty but not exactly subtle, with one or two florid colour effects. TM

Blood on Satan's Claw

see Satan's Skin

Blood on the Moon

(Robert Wise, 1948, US) Robert Mitchum, Barbara Bel Geddes, Robert Preston, Walter Brennan, Tom Tyler, Harry Carey Jr.
88 min. b/w.
A bevy of late '40s RKO talent, including ace cameraman Nick Musuraca, combine to make an intriguing *noir* Western. A complex tale of duplicity and split loyalties is played out against a *noir* backdrop of low-ceilinged bars and rain-soaked windswept darkness. Mitchum delivers his customarily immaculate, stoned performance as a reluctant hired gun duped into heading a trumped-up homesteaders' revolt, and Bel Geddes plays the spunky cowgirl who engages him in erotic gun-play. NA

Blood on the Streets

see Borsalino & Co.,

Blood on the Sun

(Frank Lloyd, 1945, US) James Cagney, Sylvia Sidney, Wallace Ford, Rosemary DeCamp, John Emery, Robert Armstrong.
98 min. b/w.

Based on fact but a typical Cagney actioner for which, playing a newspaperman in Japan during the late '20s who uncovers a dastardly plot to conquer the world, he added martial arts skills to his usual two-fisted armoury. Marred by crude Jap-baiting propaganda and a silly romantic complication (Sidney as a Chinese American spy) but fun. TM

Blood Red

(Peter Masterson, 1988, US) Eric Roberts, Giancarlo Giannini, Dennis Hopper, Burt Young, Carlin Glynn, Lara Harris, Elias Koteas, Marc Lawrence, Frank Campanella, Aldo Ray, Susan Anspach, Julia Roberts.
91 min.

This liberal quasi-Western is like the Jesse James story updated by the right-on, socially-minded Sundance Institute. Eric Roberts plays the no-good son of a 19th century immigrant Sicilian wine-grower whose livelihood is threatened by the railroad which a ruthless Irish carpetbagger (Hopper) plans to drive through the vineyards. After his father is killed, Roberts takes the law into his own hands, becoming an outlaw and rallying the hitherto pacifist Sicilians to the cause. What started as a sincere social drama suddenly explodes into a fully-fledged Western, with plenty of fisticuffs and gunplay. Julia Roberts stands around in the background looking pretty, with only a dozen or so lines. NF

Blood Red Roses

(John McGrath, 1986, GB) Elizabeth MacLennan, James Grant, Gregor Fisher, Dawn Archibald, Louise Beattie, Amanda Walker, Julie Graham.
150 min.

Originally a stage play and reverting to TV after its theatrical screening, John McGrath's feminist saga is what might be termed a curate's scotch egg. In parts it's moving, funny and warm, in others (notably much of the last third) it's mind-numbingly boring, self-righteous and over-prone to the use of that terrible short-cut of having its characters reacting to world events (the Falklands, the Miners' Strike, Thatcher's victories) on TV. Its story is that of one woman, Bessie Gordon, moving from Highland childhood to Glasgow, where she works in an engineering factory, marries the shop steward, becomes politicised, alienated from her sexist-but-leftist hubby, and ends up still optimistic, independent, divorced and recovering from her (deserved?) reputation as a red wrecker in '86. There are some brilliant moments, but the pace is often achingly slow, the dice overloaded in obvious directions, and nothing is helped by the abrupt switch of actresses as Bessie ages from the charming Louise Beattie to the hectoring Elizabeth MacLennan. SGr

Blood Reincarnation
(Yin-yang Jieh)

(Ding Shanxi, 1974, HK) Yang Qun, Tang Baoyun, Suzy Mang, Henry Yue Young, Dean Shek.
99 min.

An anthology of three ghost/horror stories, each of them something of a tour de force. The first is gutsy and visceral: a wronged woman returns to haunt the couple who killed her while the wife is in labour. The second is played for black laughs: a drowned husband gets his revenge on his wife and her lover by haunting them as a water spirit (amazing scenes when the lover can't stop drinking, and then can't stop peeing). And the third is sad and elegiac: an unjustly executed acupuncturist uses a 'blood reincarnation' spell to live on as a spirit in order to complete his medical text-book. Horror movie fans will emerge rejuvenated. TR

Blood Relatives
(Liens de Sang)

(Claude Chabrol, 1977, Can/Fr) Donald Sutherland, Aude Landry, Lisa Langlois, Laurent Malet, Stéphane Audran, Donald Pleasence, David Hemmings.
100 min.

Uneasy and only partly successful thriller, taken from one of Ed McBain's 87th Precinct novels, with Sutherland overshadowing the rest of the cast as the detective investigating the assault and murder of a young girl in Montreal. The result is pretty much par for the Chabrol course, with the girl's family – a hive of incest that provides the chief suspects – pictured as a typically degenerate example of the bourgeoisie. But it's mainly rather wooden, and shot in a flat television style; only towards the end do suspense and the director's full talent really take hold. GA

Blood River
(Dio Perdona...Io No!)

(Giuseppe Colizzi, 1967, It/Sp) Terence Hill, Bud Spencer, Frank Wolff, Gina Rovere, José Manuel Martin.
115 min.

Stock spaghetti Western, predating the much wittier 'Trinity' series featuring the same stars. A brilliant opening sequence has a train, apparently empty, pull into an isolated station decked out with a welcoming band and all; gradually it is revealed that the carriage is a sea of corpses with only one man left alive. The rest of the plot, told in flashback without much dash, involves a gambling duel with a gun loaded with blanks, a gold robbery, an insurance investigator, a fight to the death.

Blood Simple

(Joel Coen, 1983, US) John Getz, Frances McDormand, Dan Hedaya, M Emmet Walsh, Samm-Art Williams, Deborah Neumann.
99 min.

Hugely enjoyable *film noir* in which a Texan bar-owner hires a seedy private eye, first to spy on his wife, then to kill her and her lover. Instead, the eye (a marvellous performance from Walsh), having collected his fee, executes a variation on the contract. Whereupon things take off in a maelstrom of misunderstanding that spreads guilt and fear like a plague through the characters, and escalates a nightmarish terror (premature burial, murder by battery, crucifying impalement) that owes some debt to the horror comic. A remarkably assured debut for Coen, formerly assistant editor on *The Evil Dead*. TM

Blood Sisters
see Sisters

Bloodsport

(Newt Arnold, 1987, US) Jean-Claude Van Damme, Donald Gibb, Leah Ayres, Norman Burton, Forest Whitaker, Roy Chiao, Philip Chan, Bolo Yeung.
92 min.

Sporting the charisma of a lobotomised newt, hunky US Defense Intelligence agent Van Damme goes AWOL and turns up in Hong Kong, where he bumps into mountain man Gibb who, like Van Damme, is there to take part in a secret international martial arts competition. They become good buddies. This gives Van Damme extra reason to get riled when he eventually faces Yeung in the final, since this murderous, cheating inscrutable, yellow-bellied Korean villain has stomped all over his friend's head in the semis. Journalist Ayres tags along to provide a modicum of hero worship and heterosexuality. Forest Whitaker's cameo adds plumage to what is otherwise a well-plucked turkey, humourless and plagued by a script full of stilted mumbo-jumbo. SCu

Blood Ties
(Il Cugino Americano)

(Giacomo Battiato, 1986, It) Brad Davis, Tony Lo Bianco, Vincent Spano, Barbara De Rossi, Arnoldo Foà, Delia Boccardo,
120 min.

Snivelling punk Spano is a coke-snorting American mafioso. Lo Bianco is a Sicilian judge putting the heat on Palermo's drug-trafficking mobsters. And good guy Davis, who 'owes' the Mafia, is a respectable New England academic 'persuaded' by Spano to fly to the old country, wheedle his way into cousin Lo Bianco's affections, and kill him, in return for the life of his kidnapped father. The film (a feature carved out of a 4-hour TV series, and cut by a further 22 minutes for release in Britain) is a collection of Coppola-derived clichés. The action consists of repeated macho standoffs and routine car chases, the women are disposable chattels, and the

performances range from the wooden set-jaw squinting of Davis to the effulgent Method mannerisms of Spano at his most sweatily unappealing, with little in between. Lo Bianco alone reveals true class. GA

Blood Virgin, The
see Symptons

Blood Wedding
see Noces Rouges, Les

Blood Wedding
(Bodas de Sangre)

(Carlos Saura, 1981, Sp) Antonio Gades, Cristina Hoyos, Juan Antonio Jiménez, Pilar Cárdenas, Carmen Villena.
71 min.

Choreographed by Gades from a play by Lorca, with Saura recording not the polished final production but a day-lit dress rehearsal in a bare studio with no scenery and minimal props. This visual austerity accentuates gesture, ceremony and convention, in both the ballet itself (a drama of outraged honour and revenge) and the dancers' parallel, ritual preparations for performance. Saura uses cinematic effects sparingly, at dramatic highpoints (in particular the climactic knife-fight, filmed in a vertiginous circular tracking shot) which draw the viewer from beyond the metaphorical footlights into the very heart of passion and desire. Dance-lovers will need no further encouragement, but it's seductive enough to fascinate even balletophobes. SJo

Bloody Fists, The
(Dangkou Tan)

(Ng Sze-Yuen, 1972, HK) Chen Xing, Henry Yue Young, Chen Kuan-Tai, Lindy Lam, Liu Daqian
100 min.

A lively example of the work of Chinese filmmakers outside the major studios, with a good portrait of collective villainy led by Chen Kuan Tai, evocatively kitted out in flowing mane, black mask, and black gloves which conceal equally blackened hands (due to the 'iron fist' martial arts technique). Matters are helped, too, by stylish visuals and the care taken to provide adequate motivation for the usual conflict of interests between the Chinese and the Japanese.VG

Bloody Kids

(Stephen Frears, 1979, GB) Derrick O'Connor, Gary Holton, Richard Thomas, Peter Clark, Gwynneth Strong, Caroline Embling, Jack Douglas.
91 min.

Night time on the streets of Southend, and a dazzled 11-year-old schoolboy wanders through the floodlit aftermath of an auto accident, transfixed by the chaos with which the grown-ups can hardly cope. He teams up with his 11-year-old mate and the two stage their own happening, a knife-fight that goes slightly wrong and puts one in hospital and the other on the run through the night. School hasn't a clue, the hospital is a ringing void, the cops don't know where to begin, and the only ones left in Thatcherite Britain with any energy are the kids, with nothing to do except bugger about. Frears' film (scripted by Stephen Poliakoff and originally made for TV) has dark humour, a taste for the surreal aspects of this crashed world, and a head-on energy which leaves most contemporary offerings on the state-of-the-nation looking distinctly lame. CPea

Bloody Mama

(Roger Corman, 1970, US) Shelley Winters, Pat Hingle, Don Stroud, Bruce Dern, Diane Varsi, Robert De Niro, Robert Walden, Clint Kimbrough.
90 min.

'The family that *slays* together stays together', ran the ads. Immersed in Freudian motifs, Corman's foray into rural gangsterdom makes no bones about its anti-social anti-heroes: the Barker clan are blatantly public enemies. A prologue sees young Kate Barker raped by her brothers; 'Blood's thicker than water' says her Pa. It's advice she clings to. Cutting to the Depression years, Corman finds Ma Barker abandoning her weak husband and taking her brood off on a brutal crime spree. This family unit comprises a sadist, a homosexual, a junkie (De Niro, sniffing glue like there's no tomorrow) and a lady-killer, and it's held together by incest and murder. Despite such sleazy subject matter, the cast is outstanding, dominated by a fierce Shelley Winters, and Corman pulls no punches, delivering a searing Jacobean tragedy of a gangster movie. TCh

Bloody Morning
(Xuese Qingchen)
(Li Shaohong, 1990, China) Hu Yajie, Kong Lin, Zhao Jun, Wang Guangquan.
100 min.
Finally unbanned by China's political thaw, this is the finest movie made in China since the Beijing massacre. Fifth-generation woman director Li Shaohong has freely adapted the García Márquez novel *Chronicle of a Death Foretold* to produce a truly shocking account of the consequences of poverty and backwardness in a North China village. In her version, the victim of the all-too-preventable killing is not a wealthy man but the village teacher, the only intellectual in a community of peasants. The build-up to the crime, explored in a web of flashbacks, turns out to hinge on the inner rage of a 36-year-old male virgin and on the puritanical stance of traditional village society; but what Li ultimately lays bare is the psyche of a people for whom existence means no more than survival. TR

Bloomfield (aka The Hero)
(Richard Harris, 1969, GB) Richard Harris, Romy Schneider, Kim Burfield, Maurice Kaufmann, Yossi Yadin.
95 min.
Harris, directing himself (an embarrassing debut in that department) as an ageing Israeli soccer star, has a row with his plump sculptress girlfriend (Schneider). 'Give eet up!' she begs. 'You don't understand. They need me' he says, miming exasperation. There's even a clock ticking in the background. All this plus potted music and long shots of architecture and desertscapes. *Bloomfield* never approaches even the energy level of those hilariously dated commercials which send you scurrying to the ice-cream girl as a hero-worshipping kid hovers and Harris is offered a car to throw the game. Hanging up by your nipples may be masochism, but this is suicide. MPa

Blossoms in the Dust
(Mervyn LeRoy, 1941, US) Greer Garson, Walter Pidgeon, Felix Bressart, Marsha Hunt, Fay Holden, Samuel S Hinds.
100 min.
Glossy biopic of Edna Gladney, a childless Texan lady who channelled her frustration into taking up the cause of illegitimate children and running foster homes. Pretty Technicolor, but the tear-jerking is shameless. TM

Blossom Time
(Paul L Stein, 1934, GB) Richard Tauber, Jane Baxter, Carl Esmond, Athene Seyler, Paul Graetz, Charles Carson.
91 min. b/w.
Where Hitchcock's near contemporary *Waltzes from Vienna* relied on poorly worked-out gimmicks and the rather irrelevant talents of Jessie Matthews, Stein's Berlin/Hollywood apprenticeship enabled him to produce a classic musical biopic. Purists may sneer at the representation of Franz Schubert as a popular singer/songwriter, but Tauber's voice is magnificent and his minimally melodramatic acting fits perfectly this Ruritanian world where a fire-eating, snuff-sniffing duchess stands in the path of true love. The story may be flimsy, but the way Stein deftly moves it forward to its wedding-ritual finale is superb. RMy

Blow for Blow
see Coup pour Coup

Blown Away
(Stephen Hopkins, 1994, US) Jeff Bridges, Tommy Lee Jones, Suzy Amis, Lloyd Bridges, Forest Whitaker, Stephi Lineburg.
121 min.
This action-thriller is a tense, effective bomb-fest; technically high-powered and unsophisticated enough in narrative and cultural terms to raise more than the odd laugh. Boston, it seems, has a bomb problem, with a disposal squad larger than

the London Met. Dove (Bridges) is its maverick expert, of the breed who are mad, brave and cool, who crack jokes as the seconds tick away and vomit later in alleys, unseen. He's on the point of jacking it in for marriage and surrogate fatherhood when a spate of blasts are caused by ex-IRA loon Gaerity (Jones). The explosions dog Dove's path and he scents a 'this-time-it's-personal' scenario. Bridges walks through the bravura sequences and his père (Lloyd), as Dove's 'dad', does the funniest pixie American-Irishman. Jones, as ever, is menace incarnate. WH

Blow Out
(Brian De Palma, 1981, US) John Travolta, Nancy Allen, John Lithgow, Dennis Franz, John Aquino, Peter Boyden.
108 min.
The recipe for this is two parts Antonioni's *Blow-Up* to one part Coppola's *The Conversation*: mix well and garnish with stars Travolta and Allen. Sound man Travolta witnesses what may or may not be murder. Can he prove the US Presidential aspirant's car crash was no accident? Will happy hooker Allen stay alive long enough to help him? Where Antonioni's images made you think, De Palma's merely make you blink, and the baroque plot confuses as often as it frightens. Still, plenty of style, a modicum of thrills, and a suitably s(l)ick ending. Collectors of character performances will enjoy Lithgow's right-wing nut. MB

Blow-Out (La Grande Bouffe)
(Marco Ferreri, 1973, Fr/It) Marcello Mastroianni, Ugo Tognazzi, Michel Piccoli, Philippe Noiret, Andrea Ferreol.
133 min.
Sade's *120 Days of Sodom* reworked, with few of the resonances and none of the rigour of Pasolini's *Salo*. Four men immure themselves in a mansion for protracted orgies of eating and screwing: their excesses make for a colourful social satire, but when the tone turns sombre it looks awkwardly as if Ferreri was trying for something more. TR

Blow to the Heart
(Colpire al Cuore)
(Gianni Amelio, 1982, It) Jean-Louis Trintignant, Laura Morante, Fausto Rossi, Sonia Gessner, Vanni Corbellini.
105 min.
A middle-aged professor flirts with the Red Brigade, more for the frisson it brings than through any great political commitment. His inquisitive, priggish adolescent son watches with mounting disgust and determines to bring him to justice. At first the pace is stultifyingly slow. Amelio seems determined to excise any tension he creates by constantly undercutting the narrative with long (very long) reflective scenes. Gradually, though, the rhythm begins to establish itself as Trintignant (excellent as always) realises he's being outmanoeuvred by his son, whom he continues to dote on. A curiously bewitching movie, originally made for TV. JP

Blow-Up
(Michelangelo Antonioni, 1966, GB) David Hemmings, Vanessa Redgrave, Peter Bowles, Sarah Miles, John Castle, Jane Birkin, Gillian Hills, Julian Chagrin.
111 min.
As often with Antonioni, a film riddled with moments of brilliance and scuppered by infuriating pretensions; full of longueurs, it works neither as a portrait of Swinging London, nor as a *bona fide* thriller. But as it establishes its metaphysical mystery – Hemmings' vacuously trendy photographer discovers a purpose to his life when he enlarges a picture that may or may not prove that a murder has taken place – it does become strangely gripping, questioning the maxim that the camera never lies, and settling into a virtually abstract examination of subjectivity and perception. Deep stuff, then, though the surrounding dross – sex'n'fashion'n'rock'n'roll – makes it pretty hard to watch. Still, at least Carlo Di Palma's camerawork leavens the brew. GA

Blue
(Silvio Narizzano, 1968, US) Terence Stamp, Joanna Pettet, Karl Malden, Ricardo Montalban, Anthony Costello, Joe De Santis, Stathis Giallelis.
113 min.

A grotesque, pretension-ridden Western which falls flat on its face with a ponderous yarn about a white boy, raised by Mexican bandits, who returns to civilisation with a war-whoop and a chip on his shoulder the size of Brooklyn Bridge about which side he belongs to. Terence Stamp struggles unavailingly against the ludicrous dialogue, and some fine landscape photography by Stanley Cortez is wrecked by a penchant for gaudy filters and even gaudier sunsets. TM

Blue
(Derek Jarman, 1993, GB) voice: Nigel Terry.
76 min.
The screen is a perfect blue throughout as Derek Jarman faces up to AIDS, the loss of loved ones, the breakdown of the body, blindness, his own approaching fall into the void. The film embodies the spiritual transcendence which Cyril Collard sought to convey in the last reel of his anguished melodrama *Savage Nights*, crucially in the serene contemplation of the screen itself, but also in Jarman's beautiful poetry. Extracts from the film-maker's diary supply an ironic commentary on the 'progress' of his illness so that the movie becomes a juxtaposition between the finite and the infinite, the sublime and the ridiculous. Greatly helped by Simon Fisher Turner's soundtrack. Moving beyond words. TCh

Blue Angel, The
(Der blaue Engel)
(Josef von Sternberg, 1930, Ger) Emil Jannings, Marlene Dietrich, Kurt Gerron, Rosa Valetti, Hans Albers, Eduard von Winterstein.
108 min. b/w.
Lola, star at the sleaziest nightclub in screen history, meets, seduces and ultimately destroys the upright bourgeois schoolteacher, Professor Rath. A tragedy? A comedy? It's actually a surprisingly complex morality play: a celebration of Lola's sexuality (it was Dietrich's first major role) and an ironic observation of Rath's repression and masochism (Jannings never suffered more or better). The film looks and sounds its age, but remains enthralling. Sternberg shot English and German versions simultaneously. TR

Bluebeard
(Edgar G Ulmer, 1944, US) Jean Parker, John Carradine, Nils Asther, Ludwig Stossel, Iris Adrian.
73 min. b/w.
Ulmer (Murnau's one time art director and assistant) is the most subterranean of all directors, and here turns out a triumph of mind, eye and talent over the matter handed him by a PRC budget. Carradine is the turn-of-the-century painter, part-time puppeteer and pathological killer in some spellbinding schizophrenic sleaze. CW

Bluebeard's Castle
(Michael Powell, 1964, WGer) Norman Foster, Anna Raquel Sartre.
60 min.
An intriguing rarity for Powell completists, this straightforward performance film of Bartok's opera was shot only after the score had already been recorded in Zagreb. As a result, Powell was free to indulge himself with the look of the film, so long-term collaborator Hein Heckroth went to town on the cobwebby gauzes and nets. And indeed, it does look terrific, if rather too busy, a brooding tapestry of browns, blues and greys. That said, it's inevitably of limited interest only, and finally something of a footnote from (two of) the men behind *The Red Shoes* and *The Tales of Hoffman*. GA

Bluebeard's Eighth Wife
(Ernst Lubitsch, 1938, US) Claudette Colbert, Gary Cooper, David Niven, Edward Everett Horton, Elizabeth Patterson, Herman Bing, Franklin Pangborn.
85 min. b/w.
The film in which Brackett and Wilder supposedly perfected the Hollywood ploy of 'meeting cute' with a Riviera department store scene where Coop wants to buy pyjama tops and Colbert the bottoms. Otherwise a sporadically funny, somewhat contrived comedy, with Lubitsch softening the script's acidity (thereby giving the wrong sort of discomfort to the closing scenes in a lunatic asylum), and Cooper miscast as a playboy millionaire who has divorced seven wives and has a comeuppance coming up from the eighth. TM

Blue Belle

(Massimo Dallamano, 1975, GB/It) Annie Belle, Charles Fawcett, Felicity Devonshire, Ciro Ippolito, Maria Rohm.
87 min.
This Harry Alan Towers film has nothing to offer except some widescreen Chinese locations (much beloved of Towers, who also produced the *Fu Manchu* series) and a variety of sexual venues: art gallery, riding stables, Tibetan monastery. Otherwise it's 'Convent-bred Emanuelle 3 Goes East' as Eponymous Annie meets up with Felicity Devonshire – looking as though she's on a modelling trip for *The Sun* – and they both strip off a lot. A Jane Birkin-type song plays endlessly in the background. Someone says 'There is a Chinese legend – when you throw in lead, you can fish out gold'. Not here. AN

Blue Bird, The

(George Cukor, 1976, US/USSR) Elizabeth Taylor, Jane Fonda, Ava Gardner, Cicely Tyson, Will Geer, Robert Morley, George Cole, Harry Andrews.
99 min.
Forget the alluring cast (incorporating some Russian dancers for the ballet sequences), this is a desperately pedestrian, hideously glitzy version of Maeterlinck's delicate fantasy about two kids and their quest for the blue bird of happiness. You'd never believe in a month of Sundays that Cukor directed it. TM

Blue Black Permanent

(Margaret Tait, 1992, GB) Celia Imrie, Jack Shepherd, Gerda Stevenson, James Fleet, Sean Scanlan, Hilary Maclean.
86 min.
A first feature from veteran avant-garde filmmaker Tait, a septuagenarian Orcadian. A work of extraordinary emotion, the film takes the form of a remembrance, with troubled Edinburgh photographer Barbara (Imrie) attempting to tell her boyfriend (Shepherd) the story – sketched in flashback – of her mother Greta (Stevenson), who died in the sea off Orkney when Barbara was nine, some 40 years earlier, leaving her guilty and confused. This is about the struggle to give shape and meaning to life, and it's rare to see a film that attempts to do this so directly. The presiding spirit (and imagery) is that of the sea: its intimations of mystery, overwhelming elemental and impersonal forces, rhythm and eventual balm. But Tait also seems miraculously to invest the ordinary (scenes are simply and unostentatiously shot) with equal mystery, cutting to a close-up of a pebble beach, not a face, at moments of revelation. Even the awkwardness of the present-day scenes with Imrie and Shepherd, as they wander in their car or through the streets, she talking, he listening, seems surreal. A film that strikes deep chords. WH

Blue Chips

(William Friedkin, 1994, US) Nick Nolte, Mary McDonnell, JT Walsh, Shaquille O'Neal, Alfre Woodard, Ed O'Neill, Bob Cousy, Anfernee 'Penny' Hardaway, Matt Nover, Larry Bird, Lou Gossett Jr.
101 min.
This hard-hitting college basketball drama (unreleased in UK cinemas) marks a notable return to form for William Friedkin. The movie has parallels with the documentary *Hoop Dreams*: both use the fate of promising young players to criticise capitalist structures. Heading an exceptionally strong cast, Nolte is magnificent as the team coach Pete Bell: a wounded, angry bear of a man. He loves the game, but under pressure from the college authorities to produce a winning team, he's tempted to bend the rules, to bribe three youngsters to sign for Western Uni. The pithy script is by Ron (*White Men Can't Jump*) Shelton, and Friedkin gets in so close to the games you feel on court yourself. Highly recommended. TCh

Blue City

(Michelle Manning, 1986, US) Judd Nelson, Ally Sheedy, David Caruso, Paul Winfield, Scott Wilson, Anita Morris.
83 min.
An addition to the sub-genre of Hollywood movies that involves fashionable youth striking aggressive postures, riding motorcycles, smashing up bars, and getting a good beating to the sound of loud rock music. Wild boy Nelson returns to his home town to find that his father, the slightly crooked ex-mayor, has been bumped off by persons unknown. Aided by his best chum (who can't walk properly) and his best chum's sister, he embarks on the unlikely programme of harassing the local heavies, with a view to obtaining a lead. The inevitable final shootout reveals all and justice is seen to be done. Fast, stylish, but the formula palled ages back and it hardly does justice to the Ross Macdonald novel on which it is based. DPe

Blue Collar

(Paul Schrader, 1978, US) Richard Pryor, Harvey Keitel, Yaphet Kotto, Ed Begley Jr, Harry Bellaver, George Memmoli, Lucy Saroyan.
114 min.
Very probably the most clear-sighted movie ever made about the ways that shopfloor workers get fucked over by 'the system'. Three guys (two black, one Polack) work on the production line in a Detroit automobile factory. One day they figure their union does them no more favours than their bosses. They pull a clumsy robbery at union HQ, and get no more than some suspicious documents that point to union links with organised crime. Suddenly they're out of their league: violence, paranoia, rivalry and recrimination erupt around them. This movie was directed and co-written by a theology graduate. TR

Blue Dahlia, The

(George Marshall, 1946, US) Alan Ladd, Veronica Lake, William Bendix, Howard Da Silva, Hugh Beaumont, Doris Dowling.
98 min. b/w.
Ladd's returning war veteran stalks stoically down these mean streets once more in search of the killer of his wife (Dowling), a faithless floozie undeserving of his concern. Raymond Chandler's script never quite recovers from the Navy Department's objection to having Ladd's war-wounded buddy Bendix, wandering around with a steel plate in his head and intermittent amnesia, turn out to have done the killing (out of outraged loyalty to his friend, then blanking it out in his memory). The plot rewrite involves one or two arbitrary connections and a much less satisfactory conclusion. A fine hardboiled thriller for all that, with excellent dialogue and performances, and much more apt direction from Marshall than one might expect. TM

Blue Denim (aka Blue Jeans)

(Philip Dunne, 1959, US) Carol Lynley, Brandon de Wilde, Macdonald Carey, Marsha Hunt, Warren Berlinger, Roberta Shore.
89 min. b/w.
A controversial film in its time, this now looks hilariously banal. It's a prototype youth movie about kids who Go Too Far, with Lynley and de Wilde having to face the consequences of her pregnancy. The backstreet abortionist is naturally presented as the summit of all depravity, and the pair seem idiotically naive by present standards, but it does carry '50s atmosphere and the performances (Lynley especially) aren't too bad. But unlike Nicholas Ray's *Rebel Without a Cause*, there is no attempt here to come within a thousand miles of the real problems of adolescence. DP

Blue Exile, The (Mavi Sürgün)

(Erden Kiral, 1993, Tur/Ger/Greece) Can Togay, Hanna Schygulla, özay Fecht.
113 min.
This ambitious co-production, based on Cevat Sakir's autobiographical novel *The Fishermen of Helicarnassus* (*Mavi Sürgün*), describes the author's six-month journey in 1925 from Ankara to exile in the SW fishing port that is now Bodrum, where he was to serve the second half of a sentence for writing about WWI deserters. Kiral uses the epic journey as a poetic meditation on the writer's life, and also on memory, history and the meaning of life. Replete with quotes from Dante and mysterious dark episodes (such as one on a train in which Schygulla's 'Levant Marie' reminds the exile of his first wife), it's an enigmatic confusing drama, but one which often succeeds in triggering 'the unbearable smell of the past'. WH

Blue Eyes of Yonta, The (Udju Azul di Yonta)

(Flora Gomes, 1992, Guinea-Bissau/Port) Maysa Marta, António Simão Mendes, Bia Gomes.
90 min.
Only the second film to emerge from Guinea-Bissau, this is an engaging domestic drama about Yonta, a young girl in love with Vicente, an older man home from the war. Vicente has other fish to fry – literally, a consignment of them to be sold – but Yonta has a secret admirer, whose florid declarations of passion are, to her embarrassment, getting read out in the local disco. Kid brother Amilcar just stands back and revels in the flying sparks. Stylistically, it's low-key, apart from the remarkable final tracking shot that comes as a genial surprise. Thanks to the diversity of the narrative, and the real presence of its leads, this state-of-Guinea domestic drama comes across as something more than *Neighbours* with Creole dialogue. JRo

Blue Fin

(Carl Schultz, 1978, Aust) Greg Rowe, Hardy Krüger, John Jarrett, Elspeth Ballantyne, Liddy Clarke.
90 min. b/w.
Boy's adventure material from the *Storm Boy* stable, with Rowe this time the son of tuna-fishing captain Kruger, eventually disproving his father's estimation of his unsuitability as a sailor by saving his boat and his life. The early fishing scenes are fascinating on a quasi-documentary level, but the yarn itself is too slight and predictable, even down to its routine tragedies and satirical digs at landlubbing poms. PT

Blue Gardenia, The

(Fritz Lang, 1953, US) Anne Baxter, Richard Conte, Ann Sothern, Raymond Burr, Jeff Donnell, Richard Erdman, Nat 'King' Cole.
90 min.
Relatively minor but still gripping *film noir*, in which Baxter, jilted by her soldier fiancé, goes on a blind date with Burr, gets drunk...and awakes to discover that the pushy playboy has been murdered, quite possibly by herself. The story, which continues with news-reporter Conte's attempts first to get the killer to come forward and then to clear Baxter's name, is not altogether original, but Lang, his cast, and cameraman Nic Musuraca manage to inject the proceedings with a grimly compelling atmosphere. And the title? It's the name of the nightclub where Baxter's fateful encounter with Burr occurs, and where Nat King Cole contributes a welcome musical cameo. GA

Blue Hawaii

(Norman Taurog, 1961, US) Elvis Presley, Joan Blackman, Angela Lansbury, Roland Winters, Nancy Walters, Iris Adrian.
101 min.
Presley escapes the *GI Blues* and takes a job with a Hawaii tourist agency in this innocuous star vehicle/holiday brochure. Lots of scenery and one tolerable song, 'Can't Help Falling in Love'. NF

Blue Heat

see Last of the Finest, The

Blue Ice

(Russell Mulcahy, 1992, US) Michael Caine, Sean Young, Ian Holm, Bobby Short, Alun Armstrong, Sam Kelly, Jack Shepherd, Phillip Davis, Patricia Hayes, Alan MacNaughtan, Bob Hoskins.
105 min.
It is a testament to Caine's screen presence that, as an ex-MI6 agent turned jazz club-owner, he almost single-handedly carries this routine thriller. Young is glamorously sexy as the US ambassador's wife whose passionate advances embroil Caine once more in the dangerous world of espionage, while director Mulcahy tempers his flashy visual style and unobtrusively propels the narrative forward. Ageing romantic Caine falls hard for Young, and agrees to help find an ex-lover who, she claims, is threatening to tell the tabloids about their torrid affair. But when Caine and a friendly copper track her old flame to a seedy hotel, the bodies start piling up and Caine finds himself on the wrong end of a murder investigation. You don't need a billion dollar brain

to discern the echoes of Caine's Harry Palmer character. So despite a promising set-up, not even Caine can dispel an air of desperate atavism. NF

Blue in the Face
(Wayne Wang/Paul Auster, 1995, US) Harvey Keitel, Roseanne, Michael J Fox, Lily Tomlin, Giancarlo Esposito, Mel Gorham, Jared Harris, Madonna, Mira Sorvino, Victor Argo, Lou Reed, Jim Jarmusch, RuPaul.
89 min.
Wang and Auster had so many ideas and incidents left over from *Smoke* that they knocked out this mostly improvised feature in one week after finishing the shoot of the other film. Prior commitments prevented most of the *Smoke* cast from sticking around, so this centres on Keitel's Auggie Wren and makes his tobacco store the centre of a freewheeling Brooklyn universe. Roseanne barges in as the semi-detached wife of the owner, Lily Tomlin hangs around as the bag lady, Fox intercepts passers-by with a questionnaire, Jim Jarmusch buys what he says will be his last packet of cigarettes and Madonna drops in to sing a telegram. It's hit and miss, of course, but its slacker charm perfectly complements the dovetailed plotting of *Smoke*. A celebration of loose ends that will have you thinking of a move to Brooklyn. TR

Blue Jean Cop
see Shakedown

Blue Jeans
see Blue Denim

Blue Juice
(Carl Prechezer, 1995, GB) Sean Pertwee, Catherine Zeta Jones, Steven Mackintosh, Ewan McGregor, Peter Gunn, Heathcote Williams.
98 min.
Fast approaching 30, JC (Pertwee) is torn – between his love for Chloe (Jones) and his obsession with surfing; between travelling the globe with his girl and staying in Cornwall with old mates down from London. In short, JC is worried about getting old. British surfing movies might not be everyone's cup of tea, but this is a droll feature debut revelling in odd juxtapositions and riding along with enough flair to distract from its shortcomings. GA

Blue Kite, The (Lan Fengzheng)
(Tian Zhuangzhuang, 1992, HK/China) Yi Tian, Zhang Wenyao, Chen Xiaoman, Lu Liping.
138 min.
About the experiences of a Beijing family – seen largely through the eyes of its youngest member, Tietou – between 1953 and 1967, Tian's epic domestic drama is a direct, honest account of how Mao's policies affected the lives of ordinary people. While the steadily darkening tale makes for a film at least partly about death and absence, it focuses not on those who are exiled or die, but on those left behind. Tian's method is understatement, with the result that the trials faced by Shujuan (Lu Liping), her brothers and sister, her three husbands and her son Tietou become all the more plausible and affecting. There's an immense amount of telling detail, and Tian manages to express both sympathy and righteous anger without once resorting to bombast or sentimentality. A masterly blend of the personal and the political. GA

Blue Knight, The
(Robert Butler, 1973, US) William Holden, Lee Remick, Joe Santos, Eileen Brennan, Emile Meyer, Sam Elliott.
103 min.
Feature cut-down of US TV's first ever mini-series (originally aired over four nights in November 1973), perhaps now less interesting as a digest of a fair LAPD drama (covering the lead-up to veteran cop Holden's retirement from the force) than for its intriguingly tentacular influence over subsequent developments in US police representation, primarily exerted via creative personnel Butler, E Jack Neuman and Joseph Wambaugh. The quality anthology series *Police Story* was the first result, supervised by writer Neuman and shadowed by cop-turned-novelist Wambaugh who, as that series began spinning off its own variants,

moved his awareness of law'n'order contradictions and his own brand of special pleading to the big screen (*The Onion Field, The Black Marble*). Butler, after playing shy of the cop genre for some time, then re-emerged to establish the particular radical texture of the opening series of *Hill Street Blues*. Seminal stuff. PT

Blue Lagoon, The
(Frank Launder, 1949, GB) Jean Simmons, Donald Houston, Susan Stranks, Peter Jones, Noel Purcell, James Hayter, Cyril Cusack.
103 min.
Previously an unrealised Carol Reed project, and subsequently a risibly coy teen-sex tease from Randal Kleiser, H de Vere Stacpoole's novel was first filmed by Launder and Gilliat's Individual Pictures, who utilised Technicolor for the first time and split their schedule between Fiji and Pinewood. Stranks and Jones are the child castaways who mature into Simmons and Houston's supposedly unsocialised adolescent lovers on a Pacific paradise. Audiences flocked, as they have since, at the mere promise. PT

Blue Lagoon, The
(Randal Kleiser, 1980, US) Brooke Shields, Christopher Atkins, Leo McKern, William Daniels, Elva Josephson, Glenn Kohan.
104 min.
This remake of the H de Vere Stacpoole novel about two shipwrecked kids growing up on a desert island was hyped as being about 'natural love'; but apart from 'doing it in the open air', there is nothing natural about two kids (unfettered by the bonds of society from their early years) subscribing to marriage and traditional role-playing. The only thing blue about the movie is the sea, and the way you'll feel after wasting your time on this dose of 'tasteful', TV commercial-style, nudity. FF

Blue Lamp, The
(Basil Dearden, 1949, GB) Jack Warner, Jimmy Hanley, Dirk Bogarde, Peggy Evans, Patric Doonan, Robert Flemyng, Bernard Lee, Meredith Edwards, Gladys Henson.
84 min. b/w.
The film that spawned George Dixon, of 'Dock Green' fame, here presented as the perfect friendly bobby, teaching new recruit Hanley the rules of the game, until half way through he is shot and killed by Bogarde's reckless delinquent. Thereafter the film details the search for the killer, but it's less interesting as a thriller than as a cosy, rosy depiction of both the police and the society in which they function, ever ready to help the bobbies in their quest for justice. Very, very British, and not a patch on its far tougher, darker Hollywood counterparts. GA

Blue Max, The
(John Guillermin, 1966, GB) George Peppard, James Mason, Ursula Andress, Jeremy Kemp, Karl Michael Vogler.
155 min.
Guillermin has made rather a career of the sort of film which is remembered for its special effects and pyrotechnical action sequences, usually in a context of unashamed banality. *The Blue Max* deserves plaudits for its WWI dogfight sequences, but the human drama (overweeningly ambitious pilot scuppers himself by playing footsy with his superior's wife) never gets off the ground, despite the novelty of its involving German airmen (on which score it was later wiped out of the skies by Roger Corman's *The Red Baron*). GA

Blue Moon (Lan Yue)
(Ko I-cheng, 1997, Tai) Tarcy Su, Leon Dai, David Wang, Chang Han, Teddy Lo.
99 min.
In Godard's words, this is a film with a beginning, a middle and an end – but not necessarily in that order. It's a fascinating experiment: five reels – each centred on the tangled relationship between a divorced author, a volatile film producer and a determinedly free spirited young woman, all involved at some point or another with gun toting hoods – which may be shown in any order. The arrangement I saw definitely worked, since the themes of chance, predestination, choice and indecision were well to the fore. Witty, perceptive and consistently intriguing. GA

Blue Mountains (Golubye Gory Ely Nepravdopodobnaya Istoria)
(Eldar Shengelaya, 1983, USSR) R Giorgobiani, V Kakhniashvili, T Chirgadze, I Sakvarelidze.
97 min.
Transcending its status as a somewhat overfamiliar allegorical satire on the shortcomings of bureaucracy, this most enjoyable Russian comedy becomes, through richly detailed observation, a wicked, winning farce about universal human foibles. Detailing a year in the life of a chaotic, literally crumbling publishing house as viewed through the initially hopeful eyes of a young writer, it quickly establishes a vivid tapestry of eccentrics, layabouts, liggers, obsessives, and incompetents, all too preoccupied with their own ludicrously personal concerns ever to get *anything* done. The realism of the beginning gradually yields to spiralling fantasy, surreal and revealing in the Buñuel style; the strangely formal repetitive narrative only serves to underline the hilarious absurdity of the imaginative script, while the dark, 'meaningful' currents beneath the brightly sparkling surface are clear but never laboured. GA

Blue Movie
(Andy Warhol, 1968, US) Viva, Louis Waldon.
133 min.
A totally inoffensive introduction to a fairly natural and often witty couple learning to improvise a bantering fuck for the camera. The sex is no stronger than the light and pretty blue in which it's photographed. No doubt it's the very naturalness of it which some find so disturbing; there's no attempt to get in the way of our straight appreciation of the camera's appreciation of their having some offhand fun one lazy sunny day. It's worth seeing, if only as a strong reminder of the enormous dishonesty and guilt-coyness with which sex is normally dealt with in the commercial cinema. JDuC

Blue Murder at St Trinian's
(Frank Launder, 1957, GB) Alastair Sim, George Cole, Joyce Grenfell, Terry-Thomas, Lionel Jeffries, Judith Furse, Sabrina.
86 min. b/w.
Jewel thief Jeffries is forced to masquerade as a St Trinian's mistress while the school is making a Grand Tour of Europe. Inventive situations utilising a classic British blend of comedy and crime make it the best (if you like this sort of thing) in the series which followed *The Belles of St Trinian's*. With all the regulars, plus Terry-Thomas and the legendary Sabrina as a big schoolgirl. DMcG

Blue Notes and Exiled Voices
(Imruh Bakari, 1991, GB)
52 min.
An informative, well-made documentary from the Ceddo workshop about the experience of exile of the generations of black South African musicians who have emigrated to Britain since the mid-'50s. It's a mixture of talking head interviews, archive footage, stills and well-integrated performances – from the Mervyn Africa Quintet, the Brotherhood of Breath, and the Hugh Masakela Band (which ends the film with a deeply expressive rendition of 'Healing'). The interviewees came over in different waves: Masakela as a reaction to the 1960 Sharpeville massacre, for instance, and many others to join their already exiled friends; many stayed – like Pinise Saul – after London shows such as *King Kong* and *Ipi Tombi*. Mervyn Africa describes the stresses – SA was never out of their hearts – and how too many of his fellow musicians have died young. The film sheds additional light on the pervasive tragic effects of apartheid. WH

Blue Peter, The (aka Navy Heroes)
(Wolf Rilla, 1955, GB) Kieron Moore, Greta Gynt, Sarah Lawson, Mervyn Johns, Harry Fowler, Anthony Newley, Vincent Ball.
94 min.
Basically a new recruits army drama transposed to an Outward Bound camp for sea cadets, with nervy Korean vet Moore subsuming his own problems beneath those of his young charges, including Fowler and Newley. Flatly directed by the man who sounds more like a Japanese movie

monster; acted with apparent conviction by Moore, who himself subsequently directed several Catholic-backed documentaries. PT

Blues Brothers, The

(John Landis, 1980, US) John Belushi, Dan Aykroyd, Kathleen Freeman, James Brown, Henry Gibson, John Landis, Frank Oz.
133 min.
A dispiriting indulgence, Landis' $27 million whoopee cushion embodies the current well-meaning but directionless predicament of the Rolling Stone generation. Belushi and Aykroyd evolved the fraternal idea (spivvy white kids obsessed with R & B) when it tackled real prejudices with a liberating directness. Now that incisiveness is blunted and the energy funnelled into extravagant spectacle. What should have been an epic, surreal romp through the America of Howard Johnsons, turns out like a grandiose TV variety show stuffed to the gills with dislocated cameo appearances. They're either pointless (Twiggy, Carrie Fisher) or come close to being patronising (Ray Charles, James Brown, Aretha Franklin, Cab Calloway). IB

Blues Brothers 2000

(John Landis, 1998, US) Dan Aykroyd, John Goodman, Joe Morton,., J Evan Bonifant, Aretha Franklin, James Brown, BB King, Steve Cropper.
123 min.
In 1980 John Landis' rhythm 'n' blues demolition derby was slated by critics (see above) and written off as a box office flop. It became a cult hit, and must now be counted a popular classic. Eighteen years since his last public engagement, Elwood Blues (Aykroyd) is broke and all but washed up. Despite the death of his brother Jake (John Belushi), he decides to put the band back together for one last throw of the dice. This isn't a sequel, it's a remake. Some ingredients have been substituted, but it's the same recipe of R & B and comic overkill. As before, the best thing is the music: Aretha Franklin, Sam Moore, James Brown. The rest is stale, cynical and hamfisted. TCh

Blues entre les Dents, Le

see Blues Under the Skin

Blues for Lovers

see Ballad in Blue

Blue Skies

(Stuart Heisler, 1946, US) Bing Crosby, Fred Astaire, Joan Caulfield, Billy de Wolfe, Olga San Juan.
104 min.
Unusually lavish Paramount musical with a generous quota of 21 Irving Berlin songs (only four of them new). Negligible backstage plot, but the numbers are fine (even if Crosby does groan his tiresomely soulful way through 'White Christmas' and 'How Deep is the Ocean), with a particularly spirited Carmen Miranda-ish rendering of 'Heat Wave' by Olga San Juan. High spot is undoubtedly Astaire's great interpretation of 'Puttin' on the Ritz' accompanied, courtesy of trick photography, by a chorus line of Astaires each doing a solo act. TM

Blue Sky

(Tony Richardson, 1994, US) Tommy Lee Jones, Jessica Lange, Powers Boothe, Carrie Snodgress, Amy Locane, Anna Klemp, Chris O'Donnell, Mitchell Ryan.
101 min.
Hank (Jones) is besotted with his sexy, manic-depressive wife Carly (Oscar-winner Lange) to the extent that their daughters (Locane and Klemp) more or less raise themselves. He's an Army scientist researching levels of radiation after '60s nuclear tests in the desert, and official pressure on him to massage his readings gets heavier after a pair of cowboys stray into the fall-out. But the real drama here is his marriage, neatly delineated by Carly sashaying about like Marilyn on Jones Beach, half-naked under a gauze scarf, and later breaking down in public as she sees their sordid quarters on camp. She's infantile, a fantasist dreaming of Hollywood, and easy prey for the horny commanding officer (Boothe). In this portrait of a complex, painful, dependent relationship, the two leads deliver their blazing best, helped by an intelligent, unsparing script. BC

Blue Steel

(Kathryn Bigelow, 1990, US) Jamie Lee Curtis, Ron Silver, Clancy Brown, Elizabeth Pena, Louise Fletcher, Philip Bosco, Kevin Dunn.
102 min.
On her first day of active duty, rookie NY cop Megan Turner (Curtis) surprises a supermarket robber and blows him away. Suspended for shooting an unarmed suspect (his gun has mysteriously disappeared), Megan is later seduced by charming commodities-broker Eugene Hunt (Silver). Then dead bodies start turning up all over town, killed with bullets fired from her gun and etched with her name. Detective Nick Mann (Brown) takes Megan under his wing, but even when Hunt virtually confesses to the crimes, the disturbing cat-and-mouse games have just begun. Curtis gives her most complex performance to date as the reckless Megan, whose obsessive behaviour and over-reactions have more to do with turning the tables on violent men than balancing the scales of justice. Short on plausibility but preserving the psycho-sexual ambiguities throughout, Bigelow's seductively stylish, wildly fetishistic thriller is proof that a woman can enter a traditionally male world and, like Megan, beat men at their own game. NF

Blues Under the Skin
(Le Blues entre les Dents)

(Robert Manthoulis, 1972, Fr) Amelia Cortez, Onike Lee, Roland Sanchez, BB King, Brownie McGhee, Sonny Terry, Mance Lipscomb, Furry Lewis.
88 min.
A mixture of documentary and fiction that alternates between bluesmen – from those on the chain gangs right up to BB King – singing and talking about their work, and a classic blues story set in Harlem about a girl who quits her man. The mixture is not a wholly comfortable one, the story and the acting of the young couple being too self-conscious to stand up to the naturalness of the bluesmen themselves. But the music survives on its own, and Amelia Cortez, a real old blues lady playing the mother-in-law, holds the story together with her reminiscences.

Blue Sunshine

(Jeff Lieberman, 1977, US) Zalman King, Deborah Winters, Mark Goddard, Robert Walden, Charles Siebert.
95 min.
An intriguing premise: what if a certain species of LSD, a decade later, should begin to have an unexpected effect on its users' chromosomes? All over an American city, isolated individuals inexplicably slaughter their loved ones before going on the rampage. The film has a phenomenal opening, and makes the most of its plot possibilities, but the police's continual arrival at the scene of murder just in time to implicate the investigative hero will put a strain on any audience's credulity. Exploitation of a superior kind, none the less. DP

Blue Thunder

(John Badham, 1982, US) Roy Scheider, Warren Oates, Candy Clark, Daniel Stern, Paul Roebling, David S Sheiner, Malcolm McDowell.
110 min.
'Blue Thunder' is a souped-up helicopter, equipped with all mod audio-visual cons, computers and cannons. Scheider, as the astro-cop assigned to pilot it (suffering sporadically from the dreaded Nam Flashback Disease), finds that its function is more sinister than a mere anti-terrorist tactic for the 1984 Olympics. There are limits to the scope of human drama playable within the confines of a cockpit, so we get a ground-level conspiracy and a couple of car chases thrown in for filler, but of course the high spot of the movie proves to be all loopy aerodynamics over the LA skyline. It would be a moderately thrilling, hi-tech Whirlybirds if the film didn't founder on its central paradox: touting its chunk of hardware as the Eighth Wonder of the World, while purporting to condemn the militaristic omnipotence and invasion of privacy that its very existence would imply. AB

Blue Tiger

(Norberto Barba, 1994, US) Virginia Madsen, Toru Nakamura, Ryo Ishibashi, Harry Dean Stanton.
88 min.
A directorial debut which takes a formula, straight-to-video screenplay and gives it a huge shot of adrenaline in the heart. It's the familiar exploitation story of a single mother who takes up arms when her child is killed in a mob shootout, but with gleaming cinematography, tight editing and top-notch performances across the board, this is worth a detour. Barba has an eye for detail (a new tattoo bleeding through Madsen's blouse) and a special way with action sequences – could John Woo be replacing David Lynch as the American indies' spiritual mentor for the mid-'90s? TCh

Blue Velvet 100 (100)

(David Lynch, 1986, US) Kyle MacLachlan, Isabella Rossellini, Dennis Hopper, Laura Dern, Hope Lange, Dean Stockwell, George Dickerson.
120 min.
Jeffrey (MacLachlan) is the contemporary knight in slightly tarnished armour, a shy and adolescent inhabitant of Lumberton, USA. After discovering a severed ear in an overgrown backlot, he embarks upon an investigation that leads him into a hellish netherworld, where he observes – and comes to participate in – a terrifying sado-masochistic relationship between damsel-in-distress Dorothy (Rossellini) and mad mobster Frank Booth (Hopper). Grafting on to this story his own idiosyncratic preoccupations, Lynch creates a visually stunning, convincingly coherent portrait of a nightmarish substratum to conventional, respectable society. The seamless blending of beauty and horror is remarkable – although many will be profoundly disturbed by Lynch's vision of male-female relationships, centred as it is on Dorothy's psychopathic hunger for violence – the terror very real, and the sheer wealth of imagination virtually unequalled in recent cinema. GA

Blue Villa, The
(Un bruit qui rend fou)

(Alain Robbe-Grillet/Dimitri de Clerq, 1995, Belg/Fr/Switz) Fred Ward, Arielle Dombasle, Charles Tordjman, Sandrine Le Berre, Dimitri Poulikakos.
100 min.
Perhaps the French title – Un bruit qui rend fou (a maddening noise) – evokes more accurately the particular qualities of Robbe-Grillet's movie. As in Last Year in Marienbad and L'Immortelle, the writer/director can't simply let a story unfold, but worries away at it with question after question, hypothesis after hypothesis. Thus, when a Mediterranean island is revisited by Frank (Ward), a sailor said to have drowned a year earlier when he fled after allegedly killing 16-year-old Santa, we're unsure not only whether he's a ghost, but whether the girl is actually dead or hidden in a bordello, the Blue Villa, run by a shady chanteuse (Dombasle). We're unsure whether Frank's return is for real, or something imagined by Santa's father, a screenwriter (Tordjman), whom, naturally, the police chief suspects of being behind the crime, if it ever happened. Despite the longueurs, fans of Ruiz, Greenaway or Welles' Confidential Report may find much to enjoy. Nevertheless, just as the whiff of sexual perversity now seems both dubious and dated, so the film's arch artifice seems strangely out of touch with current film-making concerns. GA

Blue Water, White Death

(Peter Gimbel/James Lipscomb, 1971, US).
99 min.
A pre-Jaws documentary on the search by a team of cameramen/divers for the Great White Shark. Still surprisingly unclichéd; a film definitely to get your teeth into.

Blume in Love

(Paul Mazursky, 1973, US) George Segal, Susan Anspach, Kris Kristofferson, Marsha Mason, Shelley Winters, Paul Mazursky.
116 min.
As Willie & Phil demonstrated conclusively, Mazursky's exposure to European art cinema (Jules et Jim) must have come at an impressionable age. Almost all the affectedly ampersanded characters of his rollcall filmography (Bob & Carol & Ted & the rest) are adrift in the emotional flux of infinitely permutated relationships, and there's only so much mileage to be gained from

glossing the '50s Hollywood sex comedy with 'sophisticatedly' ambivalent light satire. Here the never-ending game of musical beds is played by divorce lawyer Segal, ex-wife Anspach, and assorted lovers Mason and Kristofferson, with Venice the cultural postcard backdrop. PT

Blush (Hongfen)

(Li Shaohong, 1995, HK/China) Wang Ji, Wang Zhiwen, He Saifei.
115 min.
Based on a story by Su Tong (original author of *Raise the Red Lantern*), this explores the contrasted but linked fates of two Suzhou prostitutes in the years after the communist victory in 1949. Neither adapts to 'New China': one marries a former client, imagining he'll bring back the good times, and the other finds herself pregnant in a Buddhist nunnery. Li's previous films blended spot-on social realism with sharp psychological insights; here she adds a knowingly decadent languor to the mix, producing a Chinese 'women's movie' like no other. TR

Blutigen Geier von Alaska, Die

see Hellhounds of Alaska, The

B. Must Die (Hay que Matar a B)

(José Luis Borau, 1973, Sp/Switz) Burgess Meredith, Stéphane Audran, Patricia Neal,Darren McGavin.
102 min.
Somewhere in South America, there's a country on the brink of chaos, a no-hope Hungarian recruited as an unwilling hit man, a popular politician called B.... A simple, no frills thriller with an international cast and a rather bland international taste. The plot ticks over efficiently enough, and could be seen as a covert fable on fascist Spain, but it's mainly surprising as a conspicuous contrast to the later, much more poetic/fantastical 'new wave' Spanish cinema. SJo

BMX Bandits

(Brian Trenchard-Smith, 1983,Aust) David Argue, John Ley, Nicole Kidman, Angelo D'Angelo, James Lugton.
90 min.
Two teenage boy BMXers gang up with a young supermarket girl after an unexpected meeting with one of her trolleys. While oyster-catching to raise readies for the bike repairs, they stumble on a stash of illegal walkie-talkies intended for use in a bank job, which leads to a slapstick bike/car chase, culminating in a mass rally of young bikers. Obviously made on a TV budget, the plot is weedy, and the film is saved only by some neat stunts and the splendour of the Australian landscape. DA

Bo's Bolero

see Bolero

Boardwalk

(Stephen Verona, 1979, US) Ruth Gordon, Lee Strasberg, Janet Leigh, Joe Silver, Eddie Barth, Merwin Goldsmith, Kim Delgado.
100 min.
Disappointing after Verona's earlier *Lords of Flatbush*, this tale of elderly Strasberg and Gordon, a loving couple living on Coney Island, standing up to the marauding, mugging youth gangs that forever threaten them, is smug, sentimental, and more than a mite objectionable in some of its implications. *Death Wish* meets *On Golden Pond* – eminently avoidable. GA

Boat, The (Das Boot)

(Wolfgang Petersen, 1981, WGer) Jürgen, Prochnow, Herbert Grönemeyer, Klaus Wennemann, Hubertus Bengsch, Martin Semmelrogge.
149 min.
This belongs to that least enticing of genres, the submarine movie. Yet, despite a narrative almost wholly confined to the cramped interior of a U-boat patrolling the Atlantic, it isn't hard to understand why Germany's most expensive film ever became an international hit. Apart from the fact that, like *Chariots of Fire*, it exploits a contemporary soft spot for nostalgic, non-sectarian

patriotism, Petersen's shooting style displays a breathtaking, if impersonal and faintly academic, virtuosity comparable to that of Lean or Coppola. As the brilliantly deployed Steadicam whizzes through the sweaty clutter of the vessel's living quarters, the film's unfailing (and paradoxical) sense of spectacle is rendered even more dynamic by appearing about to burst at the seams of its own claustrophobia. A pity, then, that its ironies on the futility of warfare prove trite beyond belief. GAd

Boat: The Director's Cut, The (Das Boot)

(Wolfgang Petersen, 1981, WGer) Jürgen, Prochnow, Herbert Grönemeyer, Klaus Wennemann, Hubertus Bengsch, Martin Semmelrogge.
209 min.
Restored footage from the original German TV version brings this portrait of life on a WWII U-boat close to three and a half hours. As captain Prochnow and his crew hunt British convoys in the North Atlantic, it's hard to think of any other film that makes the experience of combat so palpable. Although the bursts of action are appropriately visceral and the travails of sinking to the ocean floor unbelievably tense, what makes the film so powerful is the space it gives to characterisation. We get to know these people, and thus care desperately about their survival. Perhaps Petersen's script dissociates them to easily from the Nazi cause, but it's clear that these so-called 'Grey Wolves' (all volunteers, most of whom never returned) were the true mavericks of the German war machine. TJ

Boatman

(Gianfranco Rosi, 1993, It)
56 min. b/w.
Excellent look at life on and around the Ganges at Benares, where the dead are cremated, buried or dumped, according to caste or wealth, and the living come to mourn, worship, bathe, gawp and ply their trades. Besides the non-judgmental tone, what impresses about this documentary is the way it balances the many contradictions in the teeming lives it reveals, and the way poetry is combined with wit. There's understanding here (though Rosi never pretends to be other than an outsider); the only pity is that it's not in colour. GA

Boatman (Ang Bangkero)

(Tikoy Aguiluz, 1984, Phil) Ronnie Lazaro, Sarsi Emmanuelle.
115 min.
A gauche young boatman from the sticks makes his way to the Big City, finds work in live sex shows, and winds up starring in soft-porn movies with two women fighting over his body offscreen. The London Festival described this spineless and exploitative mess as 'audacious', clearly forgetting that Lino Brocka covered very similar ground with very much more integrity ten years earlier, when martial law was still in force. At best this is embarrassing, at worst it's amateur night in Manila. TR

Bob & Carol & Ted & Alice

(Paul Mazursky, 1969, US) Natalie Wood, Robert Culp, Elliott Gould, Dyan Cannon, Horst Ebersberg.
105 min.
All frightfully modern for the late '60s, and consequently dated as hell for these cynical, herpes-ridden times, this is one of those comedies about so-called sexually liberated couples coming clean with each other and dabbling in group therapy and wife-swapping. A quaint, amusing look at American morals. AB

Bobby Deerfield

(Sydney Pollack, 1977, US) Al Pacino, Marthe Keller, Anny Duperey, Walter McGinn, Romolo Valli.
123 min.
A classic example of a Hollywood director being struck down by a lethal 'art' attack as soon as he sets foot in Europe. Pacino's cripplingly introverted racing driver falls in love with dying heiress. Although Pollack at times seems to be struggling to avoid the obvious pitfalls, he ultimately wallows in all of them, making the characters and settings into something very like a prolonged Martini ad. DP

Bob le Flambeur (Bob the Gambler)

(Jean-Pierre Melville, 1955, Fr) Roger Duchesne, Isabelle Corey, Daniel Cauchy, Guy Decomble, André Garret, Claude Cerval, Simone Paris, Howard Vernon.
100 min. b/w.
The cable car leads us down from the 'heaven' of the Sacré Coeur in Montmartre to the 'hell' of Pigalle, and as the neon is extinguished for another dawn, a weary Bob the Gambler treads his way home from the tables. Melville's 'love letter to Paris' is shot, like all good city films, between the hours of dusk and dawn, and is a loving recreation of all that is wonderful about the dark American city thrillers of the '30s and '40s. What doubles the pleasure, however, is that in spite of the heist, the double-crosses and the sudden death, it is still remarkably light in tone: an underworld comedy of manners. The courtly Monsieur Bob may wear a trenchcoat and fedora, but he rescues young ladies adrift in the milieu, remains loyal to his friend *l'inspecteur*, and gives the impression of wanting to rob the casino, not to assuage his gambling fever, but simply so that he can perform a robbery in dinner jacket. A wonderful movie with all the formal beauty, finesse and treacherous allure of green baize. CPea

Bobo, The

(Robert Parrish, 1967, GB) Peter Sellers, Britt Ekland, Rossano Brazzi, Adolfo Celi, Hattie Jacques, Ferdy Mayne, Kenneth Griffith, John Wells.
103 min.
A sourly unfunny comedy, set in Spain (local colour has the characters lisping when talking about Barthelona), with Sellers as a singing matador and Ekland as a gold-digging floozie. The ghastly plot calls for the impoverished Sellers to seduce the mercenary Ekland within three days to win a bet (his prize, the contract he yearns for as a professional crooner). He does so, at great length. Inevitably but improbably, the pair fall in love; and an even ghastlier finale has Ekland discovering the truth, Sellers performing a noble act of self-sacrifice, and bitter-sweetness reigning on the screen. Even more embarrassing than Sellers' efforts to be funny is the realisation that he is trying to be moving too. TM

Bob Roberts

(Tim Robbins, 1992, US) Tim Robbins, Giancarlo Esposito, Alan Rickman, Ray Wise, Brian Murray, Gore Vidal, Rebecca Jenkins, Susan Sarandon, David Strathairn, John Cusack, James Spader, Peter Gallagher.
104 min.
Bob Roberts (Robbins, in his first film as writer/director) is a senatorial candidate in Pennsylvania in 1990. As a successful folk-singer, he knows how to use easy sentiment and emotive words to win support for his reactionary manifesto; as a self-made millionaire who took against a '60s childhood spent in a hippy commune, he is the living embodiment of the materialistic message he preaches; and he knows how to conduct a ruthless smear campaign against his rival, incumbent Democrat Senator Paiste (Vidal). Presenting itself as a documentary, *Bob Roberts* is not merely a satirical fictional biopic, but a wry exploration of the relationship between political reality and manufactured image, showing how far contemporary politics has been reduced by the media to the level of easy-to-handle entertainment. It does have flaws, but its confidence and courage in going against the grain of an increasingly conservative America are impressive. GA

Bob's Weekend

(Jevon O'Neill, 1996, GB) Bruce Jones, Charlotte Jones, Ricky Tomlinson, Brian Glover, Anna Jaskolka.
93 min.
Likeable realist-tinged fantasy adventure by debut director (and co-writer) O'Neill: the last journey of a sacked security guard (Bruce Jones) who high-tails to Blackpool to end it all after discovering his wife's infidelity. This diffident, dictionary-reading man buys a Bolivian admiral's uniform (the Bolivians' have a land-locked cardboard navy, he's told) and pile of Encyclopedia Britannicas. He's intent on jumping off the pier thus laden, until a pretty student gets interested in his case. WH

Bob the Gambler

see Bob le Flambeur

Boca a Boca

see Mouth to Mouth

Boccaccio '70

(Federico Fellini/Mario Monicelli/Vittorio de Sica/Luchino Visconti, 1961, It) Anita Ekberg, Sophia Loren, Romy Schneider.
210 mins.
Probably the best remembered of that exasperating sub-genre, the portmanteau film, largely because the directors concerned (the undisputed heavyweights of their time) let rip in their most vulgar styles in an attempt to recapture the spirit of Boccaccio. The filmettes also reveal a startling fear of women in general. Fellini's episode concerns an outsize Ekberg who steps out of a billboard poster to torment an ineffectual puritan; while Visconti delivered a vicious tale of a beautiful young wife (a stunning performance by Schneider) who takes revenge on her husband by making him pay for her body. De Sica and Monicelli went for broader, more traditional comedic effect – less pretentious, but perhaps inevitably in this company, less memorable. DT

Bodas de Sangre

see Blood Wedding

Boda secreta

see Secret Wedding

Bodies, Rest & Motion

(Michael Steinberg, 1993, US) Phoebe Cates, Bridget Fonda, Tim Roth, Eric Stoltz, Alicia Witt.
94 min.
Roger Hedden's adaptation of his own play charts the reverberations of a collision between four young dead-enders in an Arizona desert town. Selfish, nihilistic TV salesman Nick (Roth) is determined to head for Bute, Montana; Beth (Fonda), his current partner, is altogether less restless, while Carol (Cates) – friend to both and Nick's former (?) lover – seems to want them around. Into this unappealing ménage stumbles Sid (Stoltz), a decorator come to paint Nick and Beth's house for the next tenant, a banal doper with the hots for Beth. A laid-back look at youthful rootlessness which never really catches fire. GA

Bodo (Baodao Dameng)

(Huang Ming-Chuan, 1993, Tai) Bodo, Tsai Yi, Shi Nanhua, Huang Hongbin, Huang Zhiqi, Lin Wenyi, Wang Yiyan.
80 min.
Highly imaginative – not to say seriously hallucinatory – indie feature in which Huang sets out to exorcise Taiwan's problems with militarism, past and present. The chief setting is a southern garrison, first line of defence against invaders from the sea – who never come. Boredom, inactivity and tropical torpor take their toll and, as usual, the sleep of reason begets monsters: dangerous games, dark desires and nightmarish fantasies which afflict everyone from the kids doing military service, to the deserters living rough, and the pretty, vacant locals. Bodo, incidentally, is the Taiwanese-dialect nickname for Taiwan; it means 'Treasure Island'. TR

Body and Soul

(Robert Rossen, 1947, US) John Garfield, Lilli Palmer, Hazel Brooks, Anne Revere, William Conrad, Joseph Pevney, Canada Lee.
104 min. b/w.
With its mean streets and gritty performances, its ringside corruption and low-life integrity, *Body and Soul* looks like a formula '40s boxing movie: the story of a (Jewish) East Side kid who makes good in the ring, forsakes his love for a nightclub floozie, and comes up against the Mob and his own conscience when he has to take a dive. But the single word which dominates the script is 'money', and it soon emerges that this is a socialist morality on Capital and the Little Man – not surprising, given the collaboration of Rossen, Polonsky (script) and Garfield, all of whom tangled with the HUAC anti-Communist hearings (Polonsky was blacklisted as a result). A curious mixture: European intelligence in an American frame, social criticism disguised as

noir anxiety (the whole film is cast as one long pre-fight flashback). But Garfield's bullish performance saves the movie from its stagy moments and episodic script. CA

Body and Soul

(George Bowers, 1981, US) Leon Isaac Kennedy, Jayne Kennedy, Muhammad Ali, Michael Gazzo, Perry Lang, Kim Hamilton, Gilbert Lewis.
122 min.
With great predecessors like *The Set-Up*, *Fat City* and *Raging Bull*, it's hard to see how this travesty (rather than remake) of the Rossen/ Polonsky original could be so agonisingly awful. Sketchily skipping through the predictable vacillations of its boxer-hero's career, the film's plastic performances, saccharine sentiments, inept fight scenes, and sexist fantasy all vie for the honour of pummelling the audience into mindless shock. Garbage. GA

Body Bags

(John Carpenter/Tobe Hooper, 1993, US) Stacy Keach, Mark Hamill, Robert Carradine, David Warner, David Naughton, Alex Datcher, Sheena Easton, Deborah Harry, Roger Corman, Sam Raimi, Wes Craven, John Agar, John Carpenter, Tobe Hooper.
93 min.
With its trio of warmed-over stories (a killer eye, some killer hair, even a boring old serial killer), this is an attempt by a pair of one-time horror auteurs to emulate the successful *Tales from the Crypt* formula, only now it's nowhere near as happening. Not content with exposing his directorial shortcomings in two of the segments (Hooper directs the third in equally average fashion), Carpenter also inflicts a half-assed imitation of Michael Keaton's *Betelgeuse* on his audience as he presents all three parts from a morgue. Made for cable with many has-beens from hell. AO

Body Count

(Robert Patton-Spruill, 1997, US/GB) David Caruso, Linda Fiorentino, John Leguizamo, Ving Rhames, Donnie Wahlberg, Forest Whitaker.
84 min.
Slow-drawling Crane (Whitaker) invites sleazy two-time loser Pike (Rhames) to join a wild card Puerto Rican (Leguizamo), a racist psycho (Caruso), and a half-brain (Wahlberg) in a Boston art gallery heist. A guard is shot, Crane's gunned down by the law, and as the carload of villains escapes to rendezvous with the fence, the paranoia and bickering kicks straight in – and that's before they pick up dame-in-distress Fiorentino, who adds sexual rivalry to the deadly brew. The director seems unsure whether this is a violent thriller or a *Ladykillers*-style black comedy, so goes for both with disconcerting consequences. Peppered with darkly humorous set-pieces, the script is laced with elaborate non sequiturs. WH

Body Double

(Brian De Palma, 1984, US) Craig Wasson, Melanie Griffith, Gregg Henry, Deborah Shelton, Guy Boyd, Dennis Franz.
114 min.
De Palma actually has the gall to combine the plots from both *Vertigo* and *Rear Window* in one big voyeur-fest and pull it off with a certain sly efficiency. Struggling actor Wasson is fired from his role as a punk vampire because of claustrophobia. While flat-sitting for a friend, he spends his hours glued to the telescope watching an interesting lady opposite. But who is the scarred Indian, coming at her with a power drill? And why is he so obviously wearing a mask? Unblinking tosh of this order needs to be put on the protected list. CPea

Bodyguard, The

(Mick Jackson, 1992, US) Kevin Costner, Whitney Houston, Gary Kemp, Bill Cobbs, Ralph Waite, Tomas Arana, Michele Lamar Richards.
129 min.
Whitney Houston's screen debut sees her as famous singer/actress Rachel Marron. Bodyguard Frank Farmer (Costner) turns up at her mansion, ready to protect her in the wake of a series of death threats, but he encounters resentments as the Oscar-nominated megastar insists on following a demanding schedule in the run-up to the awards. Is the killer her slimy press

agent (Kemp), the loon who keeps a shrine to her in his locker, or dodgy bodyguard Greg (Arana) with the strange squint and roving hands? Farmer and Marron fall in love and escape to the lakeside home of his dad (Waite); but even there danger lurks. Jackson's showy technique does little to lighten the over-earnest heroics and ponderous references to samurai, which are punctuated by assorted numbers and costume changes for Houston. Lawrence Kasdan, it seems, mulled over the first draft of his screenplay twenty years ago; it should have been left to languish in development purgatory. CM

Body Heat

(Lawrence Kasdan, 1981, US) William Hurt, Kathleen Turner, Richard Crenna, Ted Danson, JA Preston, Mickey Rourke.
113 min.
Hot and sticky, though never less than sumptuously deodorised, this is a neon-shaded contemporary *noir* romance: all lust, greed, murder, duplicity and betrayal. As credulously myopic lawyer Ned and slinky femme fatale Matty progress from dirty talk to dirty deeds (a disposable husband, a contestable will), there's the pleasure of unravelling a confidently dense yarn for its own sake, alongside the incongruous experience of finding yellowing pulp fiction classily rebound, or hearing a '40s standard of romantic unease re-recorded with digital precision. Whether the movie-movie cleverness becomes as stifling as the atmosphere Kasdan casts over his sunstruck night people is all down to personal taste, but there's no denying the narrative confidence that brings the film to its unfashionably certain double-whammy conclusion. PT

Body in the Forest, A (Cuerpo en el Bosque)

(Joaquín Jordá, 1996, Sp) Rossy de Palma, Núria Prims, Ricard Borràs, Pep Molina, Joan Masdeu, Julieta Serrano.
91 min.
Catalonia: four men on a boar hunt discover the remains of a girl, Montse. The corpse is cut up and daubed 'whore' in blood. The Civil Guard send in an outside investigator, Lt Cifuentes (Rossy de Palma). Ignoring the local policeman, who focuses on the centuries of ill fate that have befallen the girl's family, Cifuentes interviews Montse's last few acquaintances, treating them with mounting contempt as she reconstructs events. Occasionally we hear the girl's voice, winding its way through the film's staggered flashback structure. Writer/director Jordá has an elliptical way with film grammar, and plays similar insouciant games with the audience's identification. Rather than an unreliable narrator, it's the protagonist who proves, well, ethically double-jointed. The film works as an enjoyably overheated investigative thriller, but also as a bleak indictment of a community where superstition and bigotry conceal a contemporary culture of callous opportunism. NB

Body Melt

(Philip Brophy, 1993, Aust) Gerard Kennedy, Andrew Daddo, Ian Smith, Vince Gill, Regina Gaigalas.
84 min.
A vitamin drink delivered free to residents of idyllic housing development Pebbles Court provokes a series of ghastly body mutations. Two investigating cops trace the trouble to the futuristic 'health farm' of Dr Carrera (Smith) where guests are being used for crazed experiments. Despite its preoccupations – exploding stomachs, elongating tongues, etc – this mordant debut feature is in fact less a splatterfest than a consumerist satire. It's overlaid with black humour and takes swipes at health fads, body building, soap operas and the false utopia of suburban living. NF

Body of Evidence

(Uli Edel, 1992, US) Madonna, Willem Dafoe, Joe Mantegna, Anne Archer, Jürgen Prochnow, Julianne Moore, Frank Langella.
101 min.
Whatever aims Uli (*Last Exit to Brooklyn*) Edel set out with, this turned into a tributary to *Sex* as soon as Madonna came aboard. She plays a dominatrix, and what she gets up to with her defence attorney (Dafoe) is what will pull audiences, rather than the courtroom debate. As a child, she

confides, she observed that the strawberries one had to wade through thorns to reach were the sweetest, after which she introduces Dafoe to SM. Enumerating these strawberries, we get the following. She drips hot candle-wax on to his body, registering a consensual moment before dripping it on to his dick. She rummages in his flies in a crowded lift. He muff-dives her in an underground car park. She has a wank. There's bondage, buggery, and a clothes-ripping chase up the stairs. Apart from that, there's a bit of verbal back-and-forth in court between the DA (Mantegna) and defence about whether she used her body as a lethal weapon to kill her millionaire lover and inherit; a brace of shifty witnesses (Archer and Prochnow); no tension; and Portland, Oregon in the rain. BC

Body Parts
(Eric Red, 1991, US) Jeff Fahey, Lindsay Duncan, Kim Delaney, Zakes Mokae, Brad Dourif, John Walsh, Paul Benevictor.
88 min.
Director Eric Red, screenwriter of *The Hitcher*, gives a grungy new spin to a familiar genre theme in this tacky but vigorous mad doctor movie. Fahey's a criminal psychologist who has a new arm grafted on by doc Duncan, but after his behaviour turns erratic, he discovers that the limb in question once belonged to an executed killer – and that there are other recipients of the deceased slayer's bits and pieces also going haywire around town. Dourif's an artist who received the killer's left arm: in the old days he used to execute tepid watercolours of Cape Cod; now he hurls paint at the canvas with the intensity of Jackson Pollock on a bad day. Loosely based on *Choice Cuts*, by the French team Narcejac and Boileau, whose novels inspired *Vertigo* and *Les Diaboliques*. TJ

Body Rock
(Marcelo Epstein, 1984, US) Lorenzo Lamas, Vicki Frederick, Cameron Dye, Michelle Nicastro, Ray Sharkey.
94 min.
A breakdancing morality tale. Chilly D (Lamas), a singer/dancer from downtown New York, becomes the darling of a trendy niterie. He snubs his pals, throws over his nice girlfriend for a high-living rich bitch, and gets his comeuppance, before honest poverty and spontaneous street culture triumph over capricious uptown exploitation at a hijacked 'Rapstravaganza' event. Drearily reminiscent of a souped-up Marcel Marceau. GA

Body Snatcher, The
(Robert Wise, 1945, US) Boris Karloff, Bela Lugosi, Henry Daniell, Edith Atwater, Russell Wade, Rita Corday, Sharyn Moffett, Donna Lee.
78 min. b/w.
Not one of the really top-notch Val Lewton productions: unlike Jacques Tourneur, Wise could never control Lewton's tendency to stuff every scene to the hilt with bookish period detail and fusty dialogue. But this adaptation of the old Burke and Hare business (Based on a Robert Louis Stevenson story) is still great entertainment, with Karloff, Lugosi and Daniell (Hollywood's greatest sourpuss) leaving no dead body unturned in 19th century Edinburgh. Lewton's Edinburgh is predictably full of cobbles, clip-clopping horses, street singers and other atmospheric bric-à-brac – all very nice, but they do slow proceedings down. However, the film accelerates to great effect towards the end. GB

Body Snatchers
(Abel Ferrara, 1994, US) Gabrielle Anwar, Meg Tilly, Forest Whitaker, Terry Kinnelly, Billy Wirth.
87 min.
This remake of the classic '50s paranoia movie, Don Siegel's *Invasion of the Body Snatchers*, is evidence that the end of the Cold War hasn't dispelled fears of creeping authoritarianism and loss of individuality. The story is relocated to a southern military base – a more credible breeding ground for insurgency than the San Francisco of Phil Kaufman's chilling 1978 version – with disaffected teenager Anwar at the centre of the drama. At first this seems like a sop to Hollywood fashion, but in fact it's a switch which lends an intriguing perspective as the nuclear family approaches meltdown. Tilly (and her body dou-

ble) are excellent as the teenager's stepmom; and there's a good tight script from Stuart Gordon, Dennis Paoli and long-time Ferrara collaborator Nicholas St John. This slick, polished film is a change of pace for Ferrara, but fans of his more abrasively challenging work are unlikely to feel short-changed – 'I always loved *Martian* movies,' Ferrara has said. 'I used to dress up as a Martian when I was a kid and go out and terrify the neighbours…' TCh

Body Stealers, The (aka Thin Air/Invasion of the Body Stealers)
(Gerry Levy, 1969, GB/US) George Sanders, Maurice Evans, Patrick Allen, Neil Connery, Hilary Dwyer, Robert Flemyng, Lorna Wilde, Allan Cuthbertson.
91 min.
Parachutists testing new gear are taken over by aliens after descending through a strange red cloud. Gen Sanders orders US Air Force special investigator Allen to come up with some answers. A threadbare Anglo-American enterprise, with too much vapid chat and too little action, ending very feebly (in a British sort of way) with alien girl Lorna Wilde coming over to our side and Allen agreeing to find volunteers to boost her planet's diminishing population. TJ

Boesman and Lena
(Ross Devenish, 1973, SAf) Athol Fugard, Yvonne Bryceland, Sandy Tubé.
102 min.
A sour film about down-and-out coloured people trying to scrabble an existence in South Africa. When the government bulldozers move in, Boesman and Lena set out on the road. There's little story, beyond the separate reactions of each of them to an old, sick Kaffir who comes to their fire. What it's about is simply the situation of dereliction, of being without homes, roots, dignity. And although there are faults in the film – it still smells heavily of the stage for which it was originally written by Athol Fugard – enough of that feeling still comes through to make it valid. NK

Bof!
(Claude Faraldo, 1971, Fr) Marie Dubois, Julian Negulesco, Paul Crauchet, Marie-Hélène Breillat, Marie Mergey, Mamadiou Diop.
94 min.
Social fantasy about a young French worker whose father decides to murder his melancholy wife and set up a free-wheeling commune with his son and daughter-in-law. The film has considerable humour and charm, but in illustrating this engaging interpersonal revolution, Faraldo has to skate over so many psychological and social obstacles that the film finally ends up Utopian rather than fantastic, wish fulfilment rather than satire. DP

Bofors Gun, The
(Jack Gold, 1968, GB) Nicol Williamson, Ian Holm, David Warner, Richard O'Callaghan, Barry Jackson, Donald Gee, John Thaw, Peter Vaughan, Barbara Jefford.
105 min.
A British army camp in Occupied Germany, 1954. John McGrath's adaptation of his own play perfectly captures the tang of the barrack room in all its brutish, scarifyingly jocular destructiveness as he sets up a classic situation. A young National Serviceman (Warner), obvious officer material, nervously prepares to exercise authority for the first time as corporal of the guard; facing him are six old hands, eager to slope off, probing for signs of weakness. Basically, the conflict is between authority and responsibility. Warner is responsible, all right, but the authority is all in the hands of the drunken, totally irresponsible Irishman (Williamson) who goads his man like a matador tormenting a bull. If the explosive climax is a shade too melodramatic to be entirely convincing, the performances are first-rate, and Gold (his debut feature) directs with precise, self-effacing control. TM

Bogey Man, The (Kummatty)
(G Aravindan, 1980, Ind) Ramunni, Master Ashokan, Vilasini.
90 min.
A little myth, a little magic, folklore and folksongs combine in this story of an Indian Pied Piper's

visit to a small village, and the dusty band of children he befriends there. Though sometimes slow, what makes the film so beguiling is its conviction and lack of condescension in depicting a world where fact and fantasy collide. FF

Bohème, La
(Luigi Comencini, 1988, Fr/It) Barbara Hendricks, Luca Canonici, Angela Maria Blasi, Gino Quilico, Richard Cowan, Francesco Ellera D'Artegna.
107 min.
In adapting the story of Puccini's opera, Comencini has created a cogent, perceptive, and often illuminating visual narrative. In the opening scenes, Mimi (Hendricks) overhears the boisterous bohemians in the attic above, and later, knowing Rodolfo (Canonici, sung by José Carreras) has been left alone, initiates a meeting by knocking on his door, pretending her candle has gone out. It makes sense, although the aura of twinkling lights that surrounds her during his passionate outpourings in 'Che gelida manina!' is unfortunate. But that is Comencini's only trespass into outright kitsch. Other variations on the storyline are perfectly acceptable: musicians of the Café Momus accompany Musetta (Blasi) in 'Quando men vo soletta'; the introduction of a silent, older admirer in the third act deftly explains Marcello's outrage; while Mimi's 'Addio' is beautifully observed. James Conlon conducts the Orchestre National de France with passion in his gut. Don't forget the tissues...OM

Bohemian Life
see Vie de Bohème, La

Boiling Point
(James B Harris, 1993, US) Dennis Hopper, Wesley Snipes, Viggo Mortensen, Valerie Perrine, Lolita Davidovich, Tony Lo Bianco, Seymour Cassel.
92 min.
A slow-burning study of a Treasury agent and a con-artist separated by the law but united by their need for love. Fresh out of jail, doper conman Red Diamond (Hopper) teams up with psychotic sidekick Ronnie (Mortensen) to raise the $50,000 he owes a Mafia boss. But the 'buyer' Ronnie kills during a funny-money transaction is the partner of Treasury agent Jimmy Mercer (Snipes), who swears revenge. From then on, Red and Jimmy's lives run in parallel, the two men passing and repassing each other until their paths finally cross. Director Harris's strength is his ability to flesh out routine crime scenarios with credibly motivated characters, adding emotional depth and texture to familiar generic pleasures. That said, Snipes never quite finds the measure of his role; so, despite Hopper's unusually funny and warm performance, the final impression is tepid. NF

Boiling Point (3–4x Jugatsu/San tai Yon x Jugatsu)
(Takeshi Kitano, 1990, Jap) Masahiko Ono, Yuriko Ishida, Takahito Iguchi, Minoru Iizuka, Makoto Ashikawa, Hisashi Igawa, Takeshi Kitano.
96 min.
Diffident, dreamy, dim-witted Masaki hasn't a lot going for him. Moreover, he habitually misreads a situation, so that when he hits out at a dissatisfied customer who's quite clearly a yakuza, he gets his boss into big trouble with the Mob. Fortunately, there's help in the form of his ex-yakuza pal Takashi, who takes on the hoods but who, after being beaten up, is forced to ask the hapless Masaki to go buy him a gun in Okinawa. There the boy falls in with the nastiest gangster of 'em all: the drunken, sadistic, conspicuously crazy Uehara, played by the film's writer/director Kitano. Ono's gormless protagonist and Kitano's charismatic but despicable psycho are particularly memorable comic creations. The funniest film to date from a key '90s film-maker. GA

Bolero
(Wesley Ruggles, 1934, US) George Raft, Carole Lombard, Sally Rand, Gertrude Michael, Ray Milland, William Frawley.
85 min. b/w.
Ravel's mesmeric theme provides the inspiration

for this largely undistinguished tale of an exhibition dancer's rise to fame and fortune. Raft at his most wooden (from the waist up), Lombard at her most decorative (all over), a dumb script, and much early '30s decolletage (before the Hayes Code was strictly enforced). RM

Bolero

see Uns et les autres, Les

Bolero (aka Bo's Bolero)

(John Derek, 1984, US) Bo Derek, George Kennedy, Andrea Occhipinti, Ana Obregon, Greg Bensen.
104 min.
With ruddy cheeks glowing and ripe bazoomas bouncing, Bo is a breathtaking vision of womanhood. In a triumph of creative casting, husband John has her as a fresh-faced virgin straight out of school, who runs around throwing her maidenhead at any old Valentino type. Bo's first beau falls asleep licking honey from her quivering navel, but her second is more forthcoming. 'Do *everything* to me', pleads Bo, but the bullfighter wisely ignores such niceties as foreplay and scores a hole in one, shortly before being bored in the groin by an irate bull. But Bo is a simple girl at heart, and only realists, puritans and most other sections of society would suggest that she is totally without charm and possesses an IQ slightly below her chest measurement. AB

Bolshe Vita (Bolse Vita)

(Ibolya Fekete, 1995, Hun) Yuri Fomichev, Igor Chernievich, Alexei Serebriakov, Agnes Máhr, Helen Baxendale, Caroline Loncq.
97 min.
This first feature is a mellow high of a trip through that fleeting moment after the overthrow of the Soviet empire, 'when Eastern Europe was happy,' flush with optimism and self-determination, before darker forces again asserted their control. From the Bolshe Vita – a bohemian club in Budapest and point of convergence, like the city itself, for pilgrims and wayfarers from all directions – the film follows a diverse and divergent troupe of characters through a tender, melancholic, unsentimental and very funny celebration of this evanescent period of openness and freedom. Rough around the edges, but if it seems rambling and uneventful, that's because writer/director Fekete understands that life's memorable moments aren't about what you did so much as who you were with. NB

Bolwieser
(The Stationmaster's Wife)

(Rainer Werner Fassbinder, 1977, WGer) Kurt Raab, Elisabeth Trissenaar, Bernhard Helfrich, Karl-Heinz von Hassel, Udo Kier.
111 min.
Marvellous performance from Trissenaar – justifiably compared to Garbo and Dietrich – as the enigmatically errant wife of a provincial stationmaster, doting but hardly of the stallion breed. In mood, something of a cross between *Fear of Fear* and *Chinese Roulette* as Fassbinder continues his Sirkian task of exploring the cheerless grey world of petit bourgeois morality (the time is just after the First World War), highlighting a series of melodramatic sexual betrayals in order to dissect (with surprising compassion) the tissue of lies and deceptions that makes them inevitable while simultaneously keeping society going (towards the fascism that clearly lies just ahead). A feature drawn from the original 2-part, 200 minute TV film. TM

Bombay Our City
(Hamara shaher)

(Anand Patwardhan, 1985, Ind)
82 min.
Double-deckers and Victorian Gothic are ironically glimpsed past Bombay's shanty-towns. Unforgettable images of brutality (the police sporadically demolish the huts, beat the inhabitants, destroy their possessions and livelihood) jostle the resigned: a girl recalls her teenage brother, shot by the police. 'Nothing remains. I do my work. When I think of my brother, I keep quiet'. An untouchable gratefully describes his 'good municipal job': unblocking open gutters, carting off the filth. The Advertising Club discusses improving the police's image. A cripple hobbles through floods on a peg-leg that turns out to be

his limb, withered to a stick. Shot over three years, this is documentary to make you angry; for once, not with the British. MHoy

Bombay Talkie

(James Ivory, 1970, Ind) Shashi Kapoor, Jennifer Kendal, Zia Mohyeddin, Aparna Sen, Utpal Dutt.
105 min.
Misjudged attempt at examining the popular Indian cinema while trying to reach both its audience and a wider international one. American writer arrives in Bombay, starts affair with film star, and slights would-be-poet – with tragic consequences. With the playing not quite satire, not quite straight, the compromises leap from every frame. Gentle and pleasing in a perverse way, but entirely insubstantial. JW

Bombsight Stolen

see Cottage to Let

Bone (aka Dial Rat
for Terror/Beverly Hills
Nightmare)

(Larry Cohen, 1972, US) Andrew Duggan, Joyce Van Patten, Yaphet Kotto, Jeannie Berlin, Casey King.
92 min.
Cohen's first feature is a strange black comedy with Kotto as a reluctant rapist confronting a smart couple in their home, and finally colluding with the wife against the husband. Cohen himself says he was attempting 'something like Joe Orton's work', and although it's pretentious in places, the Orton themes are not hard to spot. Critic Robin Wood went so far as to call it 'one of the most remarkable debuts in American cinema'. DP

Bonfire of the Vanities, The

(Brian De Palma, 1990, US) Tom Hanks, Bruce Willis, Melanie Griffith, Kim Cattrall, Saul Rubinek, Morgan Freeman, F Murray Abraham, John Hancock, Kevin Dunn, Clifton James, André Gregory, Robert Stephens.
125 min.
De Palma's film of Tom Wolfe's dark, hilarious magnum opus bombed in the States – amid charges of racism – and it's easy to see why. It's norra lorra laffs. Wolfe's book about the inhabitants of the Big Bad Apple has a Dickensian scope and a Faustian dynamic: 'What shall it profit a man, if he gain the whole, but lose his soul?' His view of an ethnic pressure-cooker society is ironic and caustic but even-handed. In the movie, simplification and scaling down – plus significant changes in ethnicity – lose the balance. In a twin-track movie, we watch dipso journo Peter Fallow (Willis) – who narrates – rise as adulterous Wall Street trader Sherman McCoy (Hanks) falls. Fallow is put onto a story: a poor Bronx black is a near-fatal hit-and-run casualty. The car turns out to be McCoy's Mercedes – scoop! – and the jackals descend. What De Palma delivers is merely a mediocre yuppy nightmare movie, stylistically flashy but with little pace, bite or pathos. As usual with De Palma, the woman gets shafted (here Griffith as McCoy's mistress). If anything, it's a Hanks 'little boy lost' movie, more in the *Big* tradition than The Big Tradition. WH

Bongo Man

(Stefan Paul, 1981, WGer) Jimmy Cliff and the Oneness Band, Miriam Makeba, Barbara Jones, Nadine Sullivan, Bob Marley and the Wailers.
93 min.
Having to wait ten years before seeing Jimmy Cliff on film again after *The Harder They Come* was bad enough; having to watch him witlessly lionised is rubbing salt into the wounds. As if director Paul had got his artistic needle stuck, *Bongo Man* is little more than a repeat of his *Reggae Sunsplash* formula: sliced up concert footage and interviews over which a narrator/commentator intones lines like 'politicans divide, musicians unite'. Not that it doesn't have its moments as Cliff is followed through a series of concerts, walkabouts and rasta raps set against the politically volatile atmosphere of 1980's Jamaican elections; most of them spring from the thirteen or so resonant reggae anthems and the odd bit of wit in the face of 'babilan'. But overall it's a sprawling muddy mess of a movie. FL

Bonheur, Le (Happiness)

(Agnès Varda, 1965, Fr) Jean-Claude Drouot, Claire Drouot, Sandrine Drouot, Olivier Drouot, Marie-France Boyer.
79 min.
The sheer visual elegance and romantic splendour of Varda's film aroused the kind of critical suspicions that quite rightly surround *Un Homme et une Femme*. But although the sexual politics of its plot (about a man trying to love two women) may seem stilted, the film retains two huge advantages. In the first place, Varda is trying to explore on film the kind of romantic areas that have so often (and so wrongly) been the exclusive province of male directors. And in the second, the overwhelming beauty of the movie's surface is not so much used to glamorise its characters as to illuminate their own dream worlds. DP

Bonheur est dans le pré, Le

(Etienne Chatiliez, 1995, Fr) Michel Serrault, Eddy Mitchell, Sabine Azéma, Carmen Maura, François Morel, Jean Bosquet, Eric Cantona.
106 min.
Francis (Serrault) is undergoing a late-life crisis – the workers at his Paris factory are on strike, his imbecile wife Nicole (Azéma) and daughter are as insensitive as always, and his best friend Gérard (Mitchell) has misremembered his birthday – and the easiest solution seems to be a heart attack. Nope, try again. As he watches a plaintive TV show with his gawping family, his face suddenly appears accompanying a piece on a woman (Maura) looking for her long-lost husband. He's hesitant, but hey-ho, it's off to the South we go: a change of scene, good weather, food, wine, love, a new life. Thereafter we make a gentle approach-landing on to a firm ground of lower-middlebrow escapism. A well-adorned buddy movie, with a faint whiff of misogyny. NB

Bonjour Tristesse

(Otto Preminger, 1958, US) Deborah Kerr, David Niven, Jean Seberg, Mylène Demongeot, Geoffrey Horne, Juliette Greco, Martita Hunt, Jean Kent.
94 min. b/w & col.
The flirtation with incest at the centre of this adaptation of Françoise Sagan's novel is tame by modern standards, but the evil scheming of Seberg as the daughter set on separating her father and his mistress is still forceful. But is it 'evil' scheming? Preminger's cool, detached camera scuttles between a wintry black-and-white present and Technicolor flashbacks to summer on the Riviera to provide the necessary evidence, but leaves us, the audience, to draw the conclusions. PH

Bonne Année, La
(Happy New Year)

(Claude Lelouch, 1973, Fr/It) Lino Ventura, Françoise Fabian, Charles Gérard, André Falcon, Silvano Tranquilli, Claude Mann.
115 min.
Un Homme et une Femme revisited seven years on (with different leads). Ventura plays an ageing thief, pulling a diamond job in Cannes and falling for Fabian's elegant antique-dealer. The robbery is slickly done, but treatment of the affair is less certain. Opening with a clip from *Un Homme et une Femme*, the film by implication yearns nostalgically for the relative simplicity and certainty of that relationship. The present couple have become less sure but more knowing. Twice divorced, she feels obliged to take lovers while he's in prison; he looks far from convinced by their final reconcilation. But any exploration of such cynicism is largely dissipated by the surfeit of Gallic charm, with Lelouch's camera fidgeting away as he bolsters up his story with a layer of chic, some pat phrase-making, and a lot of modish references. Ventura's presence nevertheless lends weight.

Bonnes Femmes, Les
(The Girls)

(Claude Chabrol, 1960, Fr/It) Bernadette Lafont, Stéphane Audran, Clothilde Joano, Lucile Saint-Simon, Claude Berri, Mario David.
102 min. b/w.
Guilt, complicity, bourgeois aspirations and murder: Chabrol's fourth feature clearly illuminates his abiding interests, even as it achieves a dazzling formal complexity in its arrangement of a series of events charting the dreams of a better

life entertained by four Parisian shopgirls desperate to escape the daily monotony of their existence. One longs for success in the music halls, one the staid security of marriage, another a good time and little else; and the last, seeking romance, is the most vulnerable...At once a detailed portrait of Parisian life and an ironic, witty study of human foibles, the film remains emotionally affecting thanks to Chabrol's unsentimental compassion for his subjects. GA

Bonnie and Clyde
(Arthur Penn, 1967, US) Warren Beatty, Faye Dunaway, Michael J Pollard, Gene Hackman, Estelle Parsons, Denver Pyle, Dub Taylor, Gene Wilder.
111 min.
Reclaiming the American gangster movie after it had been stolen by the *Nouvelle Vague*, Penn's film was so successful (and so imitated) that it inevitably met with some grudging devaluation. But it's still great: half comic fairytale, half brutal fact, it reflects the essential ambiguity of its heroes (faithfully copied from history and the real-life Barrow gang which terrorised the American South in the early '30s) by treading a no man's land suspended between reality and fantasy. With its weird landscape of dusty, derelict towns and verdant highways, stunningly shot by Burnett Guffey in muted tones of green and gold, it has the true quality of folk legend. TM

Bonnie Scotland
(James W Horne, 1935, US) Stan Laurel, Oliver Hardy, Anne Grey, David Torrence, James Finlayson, June Lang.
80 min. b/w.
Little to do with life north of the border, since this parody of *Lives of a Bengal Lancer* sees the darling duo travelling from America to Scotland to collect an inheritance, and thereafter enlisting (accidentally, natch) with the army to serve in India. Not one of the pair's funniest features – which are almost all inferior to the shorts, anyway – but there are a few memorable moments, not least when they improvise one of their little dances while supposedly cleaning up the parade-ground. GA

Bon Voyage
(Alfred Hitchcock, 1944, GB) John Blythe, The Molière Players.
26 min. b/w.
In 1944 Hitchcock made two British shorts – *Bon Voyage* and *Aventure Malgache* – for the Ministry of Information; they were shot in French and intended exclusively as propaganda for liberated French territories. *Bon Voyage*, from an idea by Arthur Calder-Marshall, unfolds through flashbacks. A Scottish RAF officer (with an Etonian burr) is debriefed in London after his escape through Occupied France. Hitch is right at home with the man-on-the-run scenario, but what's most interesting is the cleverly structured shift in perspective, from the subjective testimony of the officer to the overview afforded by his superiors. Essential viewing for completists, but not, perhaps, for others. TCh

Bonzesse, La
(François Jouffa, 1974, Fr) Sylvie Meyer, Bernard Verley, Olga Valery, Christine Aurel, Bernard Tixier.
103 min.
An astonishingly uncoordinated sex film with a false air of seriousness: the title, meaning 'The Priestess', refers to a spurious ending which sees plucky Sylvie Meyer hoof off to Katmandu to get her head together and shaved. Ostensibly a detailed account of the techniques and mechanics of prostitution – Meyer is a philosophy student who supplements her grant, gains insight, and gets laid simultaneously – it's enjoyable enough so long as it sticks to the minutiae (bidets, poor pervs in crocodile suits, business chat in the brothel kitchen). But then it lurches out into the world of admen and nightclubs, and is conventionally angled towards the sex scenes. There's also a strange subplot about a servant who keeps a poster for *The Servant* on his wall. Uncensored, it might have made more sense. AN

Boogie Man Will Get You, The
(Lew Landers, 1942, US) Boris Karloff, Peter Lorre, Jeff Donnell, Larry Parks, Maxie Rosenbloom, Frank Puglia, Don Beddoe.
66 min. b/w.

Irresistibly ramshackle horror spoof, with Karloff – abetted by a puckish Lorre, who's the town mayor, police chief, estate agent and everything else – as a mad scientist busily at work in the basement of a house let to newlyweds, trying to help the war effort by creating a superman out of raw materials obtained by bumping off the living. Often crudely farcical but still surprisingly inventive, and the cast (Lorre especially) do wonders. TM

Boogie Nights
(Paul Thomas Anderson, 1997, US) Mark Wahlberg, Burt Reynolds, Julianne Moore, Don Cheadle, Heather Graham, Alfred Molina, Philip Baker Hall, Nicole Ari Parker, Luis Guzman, William H Macy, Phil Hoffman.
156 min.
Anderson's second feature – a dazzling, highly confident, atmospherically original and refreshingly non-prurient take on the LA porn movie community – may not be a '90s *Citizen Kane*, as some claim, but in terms of sweep, ambition and precocious cinematic competence, it heralds the arrival of a new talent. Charting the rise and fall of well-endowed teenage ingénu Dirk Diggler (Wahlberg), from dishwasher to subcultural skin-flick superstar, and back to washed-out junkie, the film is less a cautionary tale than a free-wheeling, talent-showcasing homage to the glitter, tack and kitsch excesses of the drug-fuelled late '70s and the hangover '80s. The sense of homage/pastiche goes further still: if the rambling ensemble construction derives from *Nashville*, the swooping long takes and whiplash pans come courtesy of Scorsese. But it's the music that calls the tune with the energetic soul and disco records of the period dictating the editing, pacing and the slightly sleazy, morally neutral tone. This is style condescending magnificently to content, but what stiffens this unashamedly exhibitionist muscle's muscles are the 'family' of beautifully judged performances, from Reynolds' stand-out as porn-king auteur/father figure, to Moore's superb cokehead survivor-star and Macy's humiliated cuckold, right down to Hoffman's gut-wrenching gay crew member. WH

Book of Love
(Robert Shaye, 1990, US) Chris Young, Keith Coogan, Aeryk Egan, Josie Bissett, Tricia Lee Fisher, Danny Nucci, John Cameron Mitchell, Michael McKean.
87 min.
Adapted by William Kotzwinkle from his novel *Jack in the Box*, this tale of young lust in the '50s utilises all the usual period memorabilia: good-looking cars, better-looking hairstyles, psychotically uptight parents, and the obligatory Greatest Hits soundtrack. Against this formulaic backdrop, Shaye offers vignettes of hyper-hormonal teen torment, from whackin' off in class to being buggered with a candle on a Merry Ranger camp outing. 'I suppose it's time for another dick-measuring contest,' opines one poor sap when all other forms of entertainment seem exhausted. Unlike so many first-fumbling '50s movies, however, this one tempers its scrotal obsessions with a sense of naive wide-eyed delight, for which credit is largely due to the fresh-faced cast (Chris Young in particular). Hardly *American Graffiti*, but way above the inanities of *Lemon Popsicle*. MK

Boom
(Joseph Losey, 1968, GB) Elizabeth Taylor, Richard Burton, Noël Coward, Joanna Shimkus, Michael Dunn, Romolo Valli, Veronica Wells.
113 min.
A typically heady serio-comic brew, adapted by Tennessee Williams from his own playlet *The Milk Train Doesn't Stop Here Any More*, in which an ageing beauty, awaiting death immured in her fortress home, finds fanciful comfort in the attentions of a wandering poet, known as the Angel of Death because he has a knack of being in at the kill when rich women die. Clearly written for an older woman and younger man, it gets Burton and Taylor, comfortably matched, making nonsense of theme and relationships, and giving monotonously unsubtle performances (she screeches, he glooms). The setting, not a fading Southern mansion but a bleakly beautiful Mediterranean island, also seems peculiarly alien to the atmosphere of hothouse decadence. Still, Losey and cameraman Douglas Slocombe make it *look* gorgeous in a pile-up of baroque detail; at

times it almost seems as though it might blossom wittily into a chronicle of the declining years of Modesty Blaise. TM

Boomerang
(Elia Kazan, 1947, US) Dana Andrews, Jane Wyatt, Lee J Cobb, Arthur Kennedy, Sam Levene, Ed Begley, Karl Malden.
88 min. b/w.
Kazan's third film, a semi-documentary thriller loaded with social conscience (it was produced by Louis de Rochemont, the man behind *The March of Time*). Shot on location in a small New England town, it follows State Attorney Andrews' attempts to prove that a tramp (Kennedy) accused of murdering an elderly priest may, despite the town's prejudices, be innocent. The unemphatic presentation of details, the use of locations, and strong performances from a largely non-professional supporting cast, lend the film authenticity and power. But as Kazan himself later stated: 'There is a dramatic trick in it; it turns out there is a villain, and at a certain point the author uncovers him... Actually civic corruption is much more widespread. It is much more complex, and I know that now'. GA

Boomerang
(Reginald Hudlin, 1992, US) Eddie Murphy, Robin Givens, Halle Berry, David Alan Grier, Martin Lawrence, Grace Jones, Geoffrey Holder, Eartha Kitt, Tisha Campbell, Melvin Van Peebles.
117 min.
Patchy sex comedy about an irresistible ad-man who meets his match after feeling what it's like to be a sex object. It's hard not to wonder at Eddie Murphy's seemingly limitless egotism, which allows him to waltz through a movie in which he not only 'comes' on camera but is described as having 'the best ass' in the world. Not that there isn't a lot to laugh at: one scene where Murphy's shy pal is embarrassed by his horny, sassy parents is a side-splitter. The film is far too slick to be ineffective, but its attempts to play with the sex-war theme are often unbelievably crass. Mike Tyson's ex-wife Givens gives an understandably convincing performance as a ball-buster, and it's good to see a black-based film *not* concerned with guns, drugs and dem dere pigs. SGr

Boomerang (Comme un Boomerang)
(José Giovanni, 1976, Fr/It) Alain Delon, Carla Gravina, Suzanne Flon, Dora Doll, Charles Vanel.
90 min.
A good *série noire* novelist, Giovanni took less happily to film-making, and does little right with this melodrama-plus-message produced by Delon as a vehicle for Delon. The latter plays a prominent businessman attempting to save his son, who killed a cop while turned on at a wild party. But the truth of his own criminal past emerges, the son decides to emulate dad by busting out, and predictable complications bolster the argument against hysterical media campaigns demanding the death penalty. The general air of cliché is sealed by the inevitable final freeze-frame as Delon and son, trying to escape on foot across the border, make it and/or are nailed by a pursuing helicopter. TM

Boom Town
(Jack Conway, 1940, US) Clark Gable, Spencer Tracy, Claudette Colbert, Hedy Lamarr, Frank Morgan, Lionel Atwill, Chill Wills.
116 min. b/w.
All the clichés as two buddies tangle over romance while undergoing ups and downs in the oil business. The cast keep things going as Gable wins Colbert, Tracy is decent about it, then Lamarr hoves in view... TM

Boon, The (Kondura)
(Shyam Benegal, 1978, Ind) Vanishree, Anant Nag, Smita Patil, Satyadev Dubey, Amrish Puri.
132 min.
The boon bestowed on the self-pitying black sheep of a rural Indian family by a gnarled deity is a decidedly mixed blessing: a magic root guaranteeing power at the price of celibacy, and bringing knowledge at the price of tragedy. Benegal's delineation – hardly revelatory – of the

community's hopeless subjection to the mutually reinforcing tyranny of religious superstition and the local landowner is similarly a mixed bag of fantasy and realism; its intricately established humanist dilemma is undermined by caricatured villainy. PT

Boost, The

(Harold Becker, 1988, US) James Woods, Sean Young, John Kapelos, Steven Hill, Kelle Kerr, John Rothman, Amanda Blake.
95 min.
A well-crafted, hard-hitting look at an ideal marriage torn apart by personal insecurity, material greed and designer drugs. After years of frustration, Woods meets a sympathetic Californian businessman (Hill), who soon has him selling tax-shelter real estate investments as if his life depended on it. The market is wiped out overnight. Woods is left with no job and a lot of bills. He still has his beautiful wife (Young), but his fragile self-respect is shattered. Offered a little 'boost' by a pal, Woods snorts coke for the first time, instantly dispelling despair but also tapping into an already dangerously addictive personality. The addiction scenario is standard stuff: stress and temptation followed by steep decline, short-lived clean up, and final tragic lapse. The real fascination, though, is the sense that Woods is a disaster waiting to happen, a hollow man constantly on the verge of implosion. The approach here is slightly too monotone and distanced, curiously at odds with Woods' compulsively energetic performance. NF

Boot, Das

see Boat, The

Bootleggers

(Charles B Pierce, 1974, US) Slim Pickens, Paul Koslo, Dennis Fimple, Jaclyn Smith, Seamon Glass, Daryle Ann Lindley.
115 min.
Any film which actually stars Slim Pickens can't be all good, and *Bootleggers* isn't remotely good. It's a thuddingly dull yarn about two Arkansas roisterers and their feud with a neighbouring family. The actors show an understandable reluctance to give their dialogue any life ('I gotta do what I gotta do' is the most notable chestnut), and director Pierce (whose name proliferates over the credits to an unseemly degree) stages events with a dramatic ineptness and visual crudity usually consigned to rock-bottom porno. GB

Booty Call

(Jeff Pollack, 1997, US) Jamie Foxx, Tommy Davidson, Vivica A Fox, Tamala Jones, Scott LaRose, Ric Young, Art Malik.
79 min.
A teen friendly sitcom stretched to cinema length. Two soul brothers want to score before the night's out: bland Rushon (Davidson) with his demure girl Nikki (Jones), and big mouth Bunz (Jamie Foxx) with her classy, but wild best friend, Lysterine (Vivica A Fox). The hip-hop soundtrack may be full of new tunes, but racial stereotypes abound and the battle of the sexes strikes a wretchedly familiar note. As in: Woman with moustache, she scary. Woman in fussy lingerie, she sexy! Or: Men will do anything to get sex, but clever women use it as a bargaining chip. Very occasionally, there's a surreal sparkle. 'You go to a club and a girl looks great,' Bunz explains. 'Come high noon, there's a sea donkey climbing into your car!' But don't hold your breath. CO'Su

Bopha!

(Morgan Freeman, 1993, US) Danny Glover, Alfre Woodard, Malcolm McDowell, Marius Weyers, Maynard Eziashi, Malick Bowens.
120 min.
After *Cry Freedom*, *A Dry White Season* and *The Power of One*, it's good to see a Hollywood movie about apartheid-era South Africa that comes from a black perspective. Adapted from a play by Percy Mtwa, Freeman's directorial debut is the involving and complex study of a proud black policeman (Glover) who believes he's doing right by upholding the rule of white law. His life is about to crumble around him when his son takes part in the protest against schooling in Afrikaans, and a hardline Special Branch officer (McDowell) is brought in to snuff out the agitation. Video release only in Britain. TJ

Border, The

(Tony Richardson, 1981, US) Jack Nicholson, Harvey Keitel, Valerie Perrine, Warren Oates, Elpidia Carrillo, Dirk Blocker.
108 min.
A Tex-Mex stew that looks to have all the right spicy ingredients, but emerges under gringo chef Richardson as not exactly indigestible, merely flavourless. Limping home late and lost amid numerous exposés of tragedy and corruption along America's chain-link southern frontier, it simply hands us Nicholson moodily scratching his conscience as a patrolman pitying the poor immigrants (one young wetback madonna in particular), and going up against his superiors' smuggling operation. PT

Border Incident

(Anthony Mann, 1949, US) Ricardo Montalban, George Murphy, Howard da Silva, James Mitchell, Arnold Moss, Alfonso Bedoya, Teresa Celli, Charles McGraw.
96 min. b/w.
Conventional script about two immigration service agents who join hands across the border to smash a murderous racket exploiting cheap Mexican labour. Lifted right out of the rut by John Alton's camerawork, which helps Mann to transform routine heroics into the stuff of *film noir*. However well-trodden its path, the film shines bright by comparison with Tony Richardson's later *The Border*, which treated a similar subject with twice the ambition and half the conviction. TM

Borderline

(Jerrold Freedman, 1980, US) Charles Bronson, Bruno Kirby, Bert Remsen, Michael Lerner, Kenneth McMillan, Ed Harris.
105 min.
Entirely bland actioner, with Bronson as the laconic border patrolman on the track of the bad guys bringing illegal immigrants in. Only Tak Fujimoto's typically professional camerawork offers any interest. GA

Border Shootout

(CJ McIntyre, 1990, US) Cody Glenn, Jeff Kaake, Glenn Ford, Lizabeth Rohovit, Michael Horse, Russell Todd, Michael Ansara.
110 min.
Another Elmore Leonard novel bites the dust, this time in a poor latter-day Western in which greenhorn rancher Cody Glenn is appointed sheriff of a frontier town which has grown impatient with veteran lawman Glenn Ford. Unfortunately, the town council don't make it easy for themselves by deciding to hang a couple of cattle rustlers, thus pitching retribution down on everyone's head. TJ

Bordertown

(Archie Mayo, 1934, US) Paul Muni, Bette Davis, Margaret Lindsay, Eugene Pallette, Robert Barrat, Soledad Jimenez.
90 min. b/w.
Muni, in one of his careful ethnic portraits, plays a streetwise Mexican from the LA ghetto who graduates from night school as a lawyer after five tough years, only to be disbarred when he loses his temper and first court case – against a pretty socialite (Lindsay) charged with drunken driving – because influence and legal skills are stacked against him. Disillusioned, he heads across the border to make money, convinced that nothing else matters in the Land of Opportunity; and does so by working his way up from bouncer to partner in Pallette's Tijuana night-club, in the process becoming an object of desire to Pallette's bored wife (Davis, incandescent in a sketchy part). Misreading his lack of interest, she clears the decks by murdering her husband; then, driven insane by guilt, she tries (but fails) to frame him for the murder. Muni, now affluent, meanwhile takes up with his dream girl, the socialite from his court case, who is happy to flirt while slumming in Tijuana, but laughs him off ('You belong to a different tribe, savage') when he proposes marriage. Beautifully shot by Tony Gaudio, well acted, grippingly directed, the film makes acutely acerbic points about privilege and prejudice; but typically of Warners in its social conscience mode, settles in the end for the status quo. The Mexican decides to go 'back where I belong, with my own people', and the message is clear: had he respected the principles of apartheid, he'd have earned himself a gold star. TM

Born for Glory

see Forever England

Born in East L.A.

(Cheech Marin, 1987, US) Cheech Marin, Daniel Stern, Paul Rodriguez, Jan-Michael Vincent, Kamala Lopez, Alma Martinez, Tony Plana.
87 min.
Minus his old smoking partner Tommy Chong, writer/director/star Cheech Marin obviously put a lot into this story of a third generation Hispanic American who's unwittingly dumped back in Tijuana by US immigration authorities, doesn't speak a word of Spanish, and spends the rest of the movie trying to get back Stateside. The result is a well-meaning bore, which isn't sure whether to play it for laughs or to make a serious point, and ends up missing out on both fronts. Based on a routine Marin built around Bruce Springsteen's 'Born in the USA'. TJ

Born in Flames

(Lizzie Borden, 1983, US) Honey, Adele Bertei, Jeanne Satterfield, Flo Kennedy, Pat Murphy, Kathryn Bigelow, Becky Johnston.
80 min.
'The right to violence is like the right to pee: you've gotta have the right place and the right time'. The time: the near future. The place: New York, ten years after a peaceful revolution has recreated all men equal. All men, leaving the women to mouth their discontent: like Adele (Satterfield) as a member of the militant women's army; like Honey, beautiful and black, presenter for the pirate Phoenix radio; or Isabel (Bertei), who performs nightly on Radio Ragazza. Borden charts the explosive coming together of the women as they forge their own liberation, handling her story with audacity and making even the driest argument crackle with humour, while the more poignant moments burn with a fierce white heat. FD

Born Losers, The

(TC Frank, ie Tom Laughlin, 1967, US) Tom Laughlin, Elizabeth James, Jane Russell, Jeremy Slate, Paul Bruce, William Wellman Jr.
114 min.
Unprepossessing meet-violence-with-vengeance movie in which Hell's Angels terrorise a California town, rape teenagers, and receive their comeuppance from a taciturn halfbreed Vietnam veteran. Of interest only to cult buffs as the home movie which launched Laughlin's money-spinning 'Billy Jack' series. Laughlin subsequently cut much of the copious violence, but could do nothing to improve the rock-bottom acting and production values. JPy

Born of Fire
(aka The Master Musician)

(Jamil Dehlavi, 1986, GB) Peter Firth, Suzan Crowley, Stefan Kalipha, Oh-Tee, Nabil Shaban.
84 min.
A virtuoso English flautist (Firth) is lured to Turkey to confront a seductive djinn and a naked devil in order to learn the secret of his father's death. The story, which starts quite sensibly in the Wigmore Hall, London, becomes increasingly cocooned in impenetrable mysticism. Strikingly weird mountain locations of jagged caves and calcified rock pools, but the whole concoction's decidedly rum. JPy

Born on the Fourth of July

(Oliver Stone, 1989, US) Tom Cruise, Kyra Sedgwick, Raymond J Barry, Willem Dafoe, Jerry Levine, Frank Whaley.
144 min.
Broadening the sweep of *Platoon*, this is a more ambitious, accomplished film about Vietnam, but not because it treads the now familiar path from innocence to enlightenment. Rather, its strength stems from the intense depiction of a man stripped of dignity and sexuality as a result of appalling injuries. Based on the experiences of veteran Ron Kovic (who co-scripted, with Stone, this adaptation of his book), the film encompasses two decades. From an upright, Catholic background, Kovic (Cruise) emerges ready to kill Commies. After being wounded, he ends up in the veterans' hospital back home – a hellish place short on funds and sentiment. Starting the slow

process of re-education, from the confines of a wheelchair he begins active participation in the anti-war movement. Cruise's performance is a powerful, credible interpretation; but Stone can't resist sermonising, particularly when he overplays Kovic's tortured attempts at catharsis after he accidentally shoots a fellow soldier. Idyllic childhood scenes signpost all too clearly the ensuing nightmare. But things progressively improve, the sheer scope of the action accomodating the more vigorous approach applied to later sequences. A compelling, elegiac film, particularly encouraging after the simplified morality of *Platoon*. CM

Born to Be Bad

(Nicholas Ray, 1950, US) Joan Fontaine, Robert Ryan, Zachary Scott, Joan Leslie, Mel Ferrer.
94 min. b/w.
While far from being one of Ray's finest films – he himself was decidedly unhappy with the basic material – this is still a highly watchable bitchy melodrama. Fontaine is admirably cast as the deceitful, ambitous go-getter dying to get her claws into a rich husband and playing off various suitors against one another; her customary 'nice' image is undermined throughout, exposing the wiles that may underlie traditional 'feminine innocence', and at the same time revealing that men gullible enough to believe in such sweetly simpering pleasantry deserve what they get. A pretty predictable story, in fact, but directed by Ray with great attention to emotional states and telling camera compositions (all those staircases!). GA

Born to Boogie

(Ringo Starr, 1972, GB) Marc Bolan, T. Rex, Ringo Starr, Elton John.
The inevitable mixture of concert footage (Empire Pool, Wembley, 1972) and would-be surrealist horseplay. Even more gruesome than you might fear, despite Elton John's energetic rendition of 'Tutti Frutti'.

Born to Dance

(Roy Del Ruth, 1936, US) Eleanor Powell, James Stewart, Virginia Bruce, Una Merkel, Sid Silvers, Frances Langford, Raymond Walburn, Buddy Ebsen, Alan Dinehart, Reginald Gardiner.
105 min. b/w.
Planned as a revue with Cole Porter numbers, this evolved into a full-fledged musical with *On the Town* plot: three sailors on shore leave (Stewart, Silvers, Ebsen) become involved with a trio of girls (Powell, Merkel, Langford). Reminders of the original conception surface in a series of specialty acts – a ballroom dance duo, comic monologues for store floor-walker and switchboard girl, a Chaplinesque mime by a cop with a yen to be an orchestra conductor – which are surprisingly good and cleverly integrated with the main action, concerning Stewart's efforts to resolve a romantic misunderstanding with Powell and to secure her big break as a dancer. The grand finale is one of Powell's rather mechanical tap numbers, complete with spectacular chorus, on the foredeck of a battleship, but she comes up with much more inventive routines to 'Rap Tap on Wood' and 'Easy to Love' (the latter in rapturous response to a crooning Stewart in moonlit Central Park). Cole Porter's excellent score also includes 'I've Got You Under My Skin', and a delightful Gilbert & Sullivan pastiche for Raymond Walburn's gallant captain and his crew. TM

Born to Kill
(aka Lady of Deceit)

(Robert Wise, 1947, US) Claire Trevor, Lawrence Tierney, Walter Slezak, Philip Terry, Audrey Long, Elisha Cook Jr, Isabel Jewell, Esther Howard.
92 min. b/w.
A touch of the old mutilated ecstasy, this. One of the B movies that Wise directed before his career took off, it's an unthrilling *noir* thriller about a psychopathic slum kid (Tierney) marrying into wealth, and his relationship on the side with a woman (Trevor) who gets her kicks from living dangerously. Not a frame of it is convincing at the intended level, but it is consistently fascinating in its relentless emphasis on cruelty, degradation and duplicity – and the scene in which a lurid description of two corpses provokes paroxysms of lust in Tierney and Trevor is a classic of its kind. It also boasts Slezak as a rotundly philo-

sophical (and corrupt) gumshoe, Elisha Cook as the usual fall-guy with a viciousness all his own, and a lot of surprising 'dirty' talk for the period. The pervasive misogyny is given some engagingly fresh angles too. TR

Born Yesterday

(George Cukor, 1950, US) Judy Holliday, William Holden, Broderick Crawford, Howard St John, Frank Otto, Larry Oliver.
103 min. b/w.
Despite the tendency of Garson Kanin's play to go all dewy-eyed in its celebration of American democratic ideals, Cukor's screen version is still a delight. The story – rehashed later in 'The Girl Can't Help It' – concerns the apparently dumb chorus-girl mistress of a ruthless tycoon-cum-gangster; the big shot decides she should become more sophisticated and knowledgeable (purely for the sake of appearances), and employs Holden to give her a few lessons. But the plan backfires, both because she falls for the teacher and because her education turns her against her brutish lover's rather dubious moral practices. A very simple idea, but enlivened by a sharp, witty script, and by Cukor's effortless handling of the brilliant performances: especially fine are Holliday as the dumb blonde who makes good, and Crawford as the confused sugar-daddy, nowhere more so than in the marvellous scene where her mindless singing disturbs his concentration over a game of gin rummy. Magic. GA

Born Yesterday

(Luis Mandoki, 1993, US) Melanie Griffith, John Goodman, Don Johnson, Edward Herrmann, Max Perlich, Michael Ensign.
100 min.
The triumphant trio of Holliday, Holden and Crawford in Cukor's 1950 version of Garson Kanin's sharp stage comedy is a hard act to follow. Ironically, however, in this once-more-with-out-feeling remake, sketchily updated to the '90s, Griffith's performance in the not-so-dumb broad role is closer in some ways to Kanin's conception than Holliday's. Kanin wanted to play on opposites, requiring gangster Harry's moll to be a clean slate on which the not-so-smart journo (Johnson), hired by Harry to give her class, could write. Where Holliday was always too sophisticated a butterfly right from the off, Griffith's copycat performance starts dumb – but then never takes wing. WH

Borrowed Life, A (Duo-sang)

(Wu Nianzhen, 1994, Tai) Tsai Chen-Nan, Tsai Chiou-Feng, Fu Jun, Peng Wan-Chun.
165 min.
Taiwan's foremost scriptwriter turned director to make this sprawling and highly resonant autobiographical film. Spanning the years from his childhood in the 1950s to the present, it centres on his often difficult relationship with his father, a coal miner turned gold miner who considered himself Japanese rather than Chinese and never fulfilled his role as head of the family. Wu not only uses his own story as a yardstick for the social, cultural and economic changes Taiwan has seen over four decades, but offers an indelible picture of the mining community in which he grew up. Regrettably, the protracted closing scenes flirt with the clichés of melodrama. TR

Borrower, The

(John McNaughton, 1989, US) Rae Dawn Chong, Don Gordon, Tom Towles, Antonio Fargas, Neil Giuntoli, Larry Pennell, Tony Amendola, Pam Gordon.
97 min.
McNaughton's second movie (following *Henry: Portrait of a Serial Killer*) is a low-budget sci-fi shocker about an Earth-bound, 'genetically devolved' alien whose modus operandi is not unlike the host-seeking creature in *The Hidden*, only messier. Instead of invading a human body, the mutating monster simply rips the head off some unsuspecting Earthling, squishes it down on its shoulders, and goes about its business. Meanwhile, smart-mouthed female cop Chong is chasing an escaped psycho, the two plot threads coming together when the killer and the headhunter meet up and form a gruesome, deadly composite. *Henry* it ain't, but this black comic gore fest has its moments, the best of which are reminiscent of Stuart Gordon's *Re-Animator*. NF

Borrowers, The

(Peter Hewitt, 1997, GB) John Goodman, Jim Broadbent, Mark Williams, Celia Imrie, Hugh Laurie, Ruby Wax, Flora Newbigin.
87 min.
The nice Lender family don't realise they have Borrowers nestling under the floorboards and living off domestic scraps. Digital technology brings the tiny folk of Mary Norton's children's books to life as never before. Scampering round the kitchen, Arietty Borrower (Newbigin) is almost locked in the freezer when the lure of ice-cream proves too strong. Mum and dad (Imrie and Broadbent, a terrific team) administer a scolding, but this little fracas is as nothing compared to the upheaval that's to follow. The Lenders' great aunt, owner of the house, has died, and since lawyer Ocious Potter (Goodman) can find no will, he's announced his intention to demolish the place. Exemplary entertainment. TJ

Borsalino

(Jacques Deray, 1970, Fr/It) Jean-Paul Belmondo, Alain Delon, Michel Bouquet, Catherine Rouvel, Corinne Marchand, Françoise Christophe, Julien Guiomar.
126 min.
Competent but stereotypical performances from the two stars as small-time hoodlums working their way up in the Marseilles underworld of the '30s. Fairly basic as a gangster pastiche, despite its nods to Hawks, Melville, et al; but not unenjoyable thanks to its loudly stressed period detail and Claude Bolling's jolly score for mechanical piano. TM

Borsalino & Co
(Blood on the Streets)

(Jacques Deray, 1974, Fr/It/WGer) Alain Delon, Catherine Rouvel, Riccardo Cucciolla, Reinhardt Kolldehoff, Daniel Ivernel.
91 min.
Produced by Delon primarily, it seems, as a showcase for himself (his wardrobe is prodigious), this takes up the story of the underworld struggle for the supremacy of Marseilles in the '30s where the immeasurably superior *Borsalino* left off. Delon's brutality is presented as somehow less reprehensible than that of Mafia capo Cucciolla (who aims to promote Fascism through heroin) because he is sustained by the love of Rouvel's golden-hearted tart (the violins are almost audible). Delon's overblown reprise of Gene Hackman's drug addiction in *French Connection II* effectively tips the movie into the realm of hackneyed but not altogether unenjoyable fantasy. JPy

Bosna!

(Bernard-Henri Lévy/Alain Ferrari, 1994, Fr)
117 min.
This two-hour essay-reportage goes behind Bosnian lines to show horrors and hear testimonies that will never reach the TV news; it makes incisive use of archive footage to back up its argument. In the future, the directors assert, no one will be able to plead ignorance as happened with the Holocaust. Bernard-Henri Lévy is a writer, philosopher and art critic, and his voice-over narration is prone to a rhetorical excess that can only be described as 'very French'. But the accuracy – and urgency – of his polemic is undeniable. The Bosnians are fighting fascism, their own localised version of the Spanish Civil War or WWII, against empire-building, book-burning neo-Hitlers named Milosevic and Karadzic. Pitched somewhere between Orwell and Robert Fisk, *Bosna!* is cultured, humane and carefully reasoned – but above all angry. TR

Boss Nigger (aka The Black Bounty Killer)

(Jack Arnold, 1974, US) Fred Williamson, D'Urville Martin, RG Armstrong, William Smith, Carmen Hayworth, Barbara Leigh.
92 min.
Williamson parodies his own star image from numerous violent black movies in this cod Western which he wrote for his own production company. Bounty hunter Williamson, self-appointed sheriff of terrorised San Miguel, having outsmarted the cowardly white mayor and extricated himself from romance with an orphaned black girl and a nubile Boston schoolmarm, despatches villainous William Smith with a sawn-off rifle. Cobbled together as though made for TV, this is an enter-

taining mix of clichéd lines delivered straightfaced and an invigorating dose of old-fashioned bloodless violence. Despite moments of glutinous sentimentality, an interesting and intermittently amusing black picture. JPy

Bostonians, The

(James Ivory, 1984, GB) Christopher Reeve, Vanessa Redgrave, Madeleine Potter, Jessica Tandy, Nancy Marchand, Wesley Addy, Linda Hunt.
122 min.
Ruth Prawer Jhabvala's finely honed script cuts through both Henry James' cynicism and the dense jungle of his prose to reveal a story of unexpected passion, a love triangle set against the early stirrings of the suffragette movement in late 19th century Boston. The core of the film is the battle between shy, intense proto-feminist and struggling, reactionary lawyer for the love, and allegiance, of a young girl who also happens to be a formidably gifted orator. At times too decorous, too slow for its own good, it is given guts by intense, acutely observed performances from Reeve and Redgrave. RR

Boston Kickout

(Paul Hills, 1995, GB) John Simm, Emer McCourt, Marc Warren, Nathan Valente.
110 min.
For disillusioned teenager Phil (Simm) and his three closest pals, 'coming of age' in Stevenage in the late '70s is no picnic. New Town utopianism has given way to an alienated reality of unemployment, violence, crime, alcoholism and drug abuse. The performances are heartfelt, if a little uneven, with Valente's skinhead nutter threatening to steal the show. Shrewdly observed, full of incident and unafraid of emotion. NF

Boston Strangler, The

(Richard Fleischer, 1968, US) Tony Curtis, Henry Fonda, George Kennedy, Mike Kellin, Hurd Hatfield, Murray Hamilton, Jeff Corey, Sally Kellerman.
120 min.
A nasty case of multiple schizophrenia. Not only are the images tiresomely fragmented by the then fashionable split-screen technique, but the character of Albert DeSalvo, self-confessed perpetrator of 11 stranglings, has been tailored into a straightforward case of split personality, so that we may weep sympathetically as we watch a happy family man being gradually forced to face the crimes committed by his other self without his conscious knowledge. Curtis gives a careful performance, but can breathe little life into this expurgated cliché. Boston in panic (split-screen images of old ladies gossiping on one side of the screen while a corpse awaits detection on the other) is not exactly compulsive. And the interrogation scenes are interminable. Nice stuff around the middle, though, when the stones turned over by the police during their investigations reveal a fine collection of pallid, squirming perverts. TM

Botany Bay

(John Farrow, 1952, US) Alan Ladd, James Mason, Patricia Medina, Cedric Hardwicke, Jonathan Harris, Murray Matheson.
94 min.
Floggings and keelhaulings as Ladd, a medical student condemned to transportation on the first British convict ship bound for Australia in 1787, suffers stoically while Mason's captain sneers sadistically and Medina hovers prettily. Even dumber when Australia is reached, aborigines attack, and plague breaks out. Farrow and Ladd, with Howard da Silva in the Mason role, had already tackled a similar yarn much more creditably with *Two Years Before the Mast*. TM

Both Sides of the Street
(La Contre-allée)

(Isabel Sébastian, 1991, Fr) Caroline Cellier, Jennifer Covillault, Jacqueline Maillan.
83 min.
Lilas and Marie are the unlikeliest of friends – one a prostitute, the other a young virgin – but their relationship prompts Lilas' discovery of maternal urges, while Marie learns to embrace her sexuality. Meanwhile, playboy Pierre is on hand to offer advice to his young friend. Writer/director Sébastian tones down sensa-

tionalism, but she also strips the film of credibility; some sequences prove titillating, and the characters remain woefully two-dimensional. Superficial and unaffecting. CM

Boucher, Le (The Butcher)

(Claude Chabrol, 1969, Fr/It) Stéphane Audran, Jean Yanne, Antonio Passalia, Mario Beccaria, Pasquale Ferone, Roger Rudel.
94 min.
Classically simple but relentlessly probing thriller, set in a French village shadowed by the presence of a compulsive killer. Some lovely Hitchcockian games, like the strange ketchup that drips onto a picnic hamburger from a clifftop where the latest victim has been claimed. But also more secretive pointers to social circumstance and the 'exchange of guilt' as Audran's starchy schoolmistress finds herself irresistibly drawn to the ex-army butcher she suspects of being the killer: the fact, for instance, that alongside the killer as he keeps vigil outside the schoolhouse, a war memorial stands sentinel with its reminder of society's dead and maimed. With this film Chabrol came full circle back to his first, echoing not only the minutely detailed provincial landscape of *Le Beau Serge* but its theme of redemption. The impasse here, a strangely moving tragedy, is that there is no way for the terrified teacher, bred to civilised restraints, to understand that her primeval butcher may have been reclaimed by his love for her. TM

Boudu Sauvé des Eaux
(Boudu Saved from Drowning)

(Jean Renoir, 1932, Fr) Michel Simon, Charles Grandval, Marcelle Hainia, Séverine Lerczinska, Jean Dasté, Max Dalban Jacques Becker.
87 min. b/w.
Boudu, a scrofulous, anarchic tramp, is saved from a watery suicide by the well-intentioned but irredeemably bourgeois bookseller Lestingois, and repays his favour by becoming the most morally, socially, sexually and philosophically disruptive house-guest of all time. Renoir's most Buñuelesque movie remains as fresh and 'scandalous' as it must have been in 1932, a delicious clash of manners between the unregenerate tramp with bizarre principles of his own and the ultra-proper middle class household where the principles are showing signs of tarnish. Michel Simon's outrageous performance as Boudu, and Renoir's 'liberated' location camerawork are still wholly seductive. TR

Boulangère de Monceau, La

(Eric Rohmer, 1962, Fr) Barbet Schroeder, Michèle Girardon, Claudine Soubrier, Michel Mardore.
26 min.
Before he shot any of them, Rohmer announced the titles of his 'Six Moral Tales', the series that would occupy him for the next decade and make the French critic and academic an international name as a writer/director. Shot in 16mm and never released theatrically, this fledgling effort (though Rohmer had already made his first feature *Le Signe du Lion* in 1959) is narrated by Bertrand Tavernier and follows the fortunes of a student, Barbet Schroeder, who returns each day to the spot where he fell in love with a girl he met in the street. On the way though, there's a bakery where he stops for his daily cakes, and a very alluring young lady behind the counter. TJ

Boule de Suif

(Christian-Jaque, 1945, Fr) Micheline Presle, Louis Salou, Alfred Adam, Jean Brochard.
103 min. b/w.
'We've been betrayed,' snarls the bedraggled soldier, arriving with news of Sedan and the surrender of the Prussians. But for 1870, read 1940. This was hustled into production after the Liberation and while the war was still in progress, an instant response to the trauma of defeat and occupation. Two de Maupassant stories are harnessed together for an account of a coach journey across a landscape dominated by fear, compromise and humiliation. With its not very hidden agenda the film can only elicit concern for its characters as representative types rather than individuals. But the moral climax is exemplary, with plucky hooker Presle spitting on a Prussian cur – no genteel miming of the act, either, but a great

messy oyster, delivered full face. You can even now sense the straining towards catharsis, and if the film's first audiences were still capable of cheering, then cheer they probably did. BBa

Boulevard Nights

(Michael Pressman, 1979, US) Richard Yniguez, Danny de la Paz, Marta DuBois, James Victor, Betty Carvalho.
102 min.
An unexceptional cocktail of traditional underdog ingredients: gangland rivalry, James Dean-type angst, and some simplistic social comment – poverty Mexican-American style, where the only entertainment comes from cruising custom cars and protecting territorial rights. The downtrodden side of LA is well shot, and Danny de la Paz is excellent as the non-conforming youngster. But that's not enough to save the film or provide it with an identity of its own.

Bound

(Andy Wachowski/Larry Wachowski, 1996, US) Jennifer Tilly, Gina Gershon, Joe Pantoliano, John P Ryan, Christopher Meloni, Richard C Sarafian.
109 min.
Chicago: when hood's moll Violet (Tilly) and ex-con Corky (Gershon) size each other up across a corridor, things soon get plenty biblical. They're made up, they've made out, and now Violet wants to make off with Corky and $2m that hubby's laundering for his boss. Lusty lesbian leads, looting lots of lolly! One of the most blatantly calculated, artistically bankrupt Hollywood calling-cards in ages, this by-the-numbers neo-*noir* has one gimmick – dyke desire – and no ideas. Circumstantial evidence against the Wachowskis points to fraternal band-wagoning, deliberate marketing to both icon-starved lesbian audiences and the dirty-mac brigade, and cynical courting of lascivious media hype. NB

Bound and Gagged:
A Love Story

(Daniel B Appleby, 1992, US) Ginger Lynn Allen, Elizabeth Saltarrelli, Karen Black, Mary Ella Ross, Chris Denton, Chris Mulkey.
94 min.
A first feature less about sex than emotional baggage – the real ties that bind. Leslie (Allen) seeks refuge from brutal Steve (Mulkey) in the arms of another woman, Elizabeth (Saltarrelli). But Elizabeth also resorts to force. Helped by suicidal Cliff (Denton), she kidnaps Leslie after the latter refuses to divorce her husband. A black comic road movie and a rather paternalistic post-feminist parable, this might have worked better with a more consistent tone. Director Appleby is uncomfortable with stereotypes, and Denton's running suicide-gag is misjudged. On the other hand, the tug-of-love between the besotted, powerful Elizabeth and the weak, resistant Leslie is more confidently handled – with both actresses making the most of meaty roles. TCh

Bound by Honor
(aka Blood In Blood Out)

(Taylor Hackford, 1992, US) Damian Chapa, Jesse Borrego, Benjamin Bratt, Enrique Castillo, Victor Rivers.
180 min.
Few films justify three-hour running times, and, despite solid performances, this epic tale of a Chicano sub-culture isn't one of them. Certainly, there are moments of powerful physical and emotional violence as half-caste hero Miklo (Chapa) attempts to consolidate his gangland heritage. Convicted of a shooting, Miklo rises to prominence within prison walls, while his former accomplices on the outside turn variously to drug abuse and law enforcement. What bond can remain between the blood brothers when circumstances divide them so dramatically? Clearly a labour of love for director Hackford, the film oozes integrity and is heavy with the stench of an authentic milieu; but forceful set-pieces and astute cultural observations are lost amid a sea of confusing (and eventually dull) stand-offs between warring gangs. MK

Bound for Glory

(Hal Ashby, 1976, US) David Carradine, Ronny Cox, Melinda Dillon, Gail Strickland, John Lehne, Randy Quaid.
148 min.

Ashby forsakes the bleak satire of *The Last Detail* and *Shampoo* for an overlong, sentimental and lifeless biopic of Woody Guthrie. The film glosses the legendary folksinger-cum-hobo into a beatific eccentric who mimics the actions of others more than forges a radical lifestyle. Within these confines, Carradine's studious underplaying is impressive, and Haskell Wexler's Oscar-winning photography evokes a lyrical sense of atmosphere and location. IB

Bounty, The
(Roger Donaldson, 1984, GB) Mel Gibson, Anthony Hopkins, Laurence Olivier, Edward Fox, Daniel Day-Lewis, Bernard Hill, Philip Davis.
133 min.
Definitely not a remake of the MGM classic, but a Robert Bolt-scripted meditation on the conflict between Bligh's puritanism and Christian's surrender to Polynesian paganism. The floggings and sadism are thus kept to a minimum, with Hopkins' Bligh emerging less as a hissable villain than as a credibly sympathetic but flawed character. It's all a brave try, though Gibson is perhaps not up to the demands of a Christian's progress from naive rating to self-loathing exile, and Donaldson's direction often verges on the stolid. GA

Bowery, The
(Raoul Walsh, 1933, US) Wallace Beery, George Raft, Jackie Cooper, Fay Wray, Pert Kelton, Herman Bing, George Walsh, Harold Huber, Lillian Harmer.
90 min. b/w.
A cheerfully colourful portrayal of New York City low-life during the 1880s (or Gay Nineties, as a title declares), not long on historical accuracy, despite token appearances by John L Sullivan (Walsh) and Carrie Nation (Harmer), and a reconstruction of Steve Brodie's famous jump off the Brooklyn Bridge for a bet in 1888. Basically, it's a sentimentally rumbustious buddy movie in which gambler Brodie (Raft) and saloon-owner Chuck Connors (Beery) indulge in furious rivalry for the title of 'King of the Bowery', as well as for the affections of pretty Lucy Calhoun (Wray) and a pouting streetwise moppet (Cooper). It's entertaining enough in its raucous way, but marred by a complacently racist attitude to the Chinese community. TM

Bowery to Broadway
(Charles Lamont, 1944, US) Jack Oakie, Donald Cook, Maria Montez, Susanna Foster, Turhan Bey, Louise Albritton, Andy Devine.
94 min. b/w.
Patchy (and worse) musical set in the naughty nineties, with Oakie and Cook as rival impresarios climbing from beergarden to Broadway. Montez is awful as an exotic European star, Foster not much better doing her operetta bit. But the period numbers are bright, and there is one delightful song-and-dance routine from Donald O'Connor and Peggy Ryan. TM

Boxcar Bertha
(Martin Scorsese, 1972, US) Barbara Hershey, David Carradine, Barry Primus, Bernie Casey, John Carradine.
97 min.
Superior formula stuff, injected with a rare degree of life by enthusiastic direction that occasionally tries for virtuosity and succeeds, and by a neat performance from Hershey that avoids the yawning traps in the script (built-in sex sequences, the she-loved-her-man theme in general). She plays Bertha, the Arkansas farm girl who hits the road, with the right degree of matter-of-factness and a lot of humour. The film traces the alienation of Bertha, a trade unionist she meets, a black friend of his, and a small-time Yankee conman – slipping into crime, stealing from the railroad bosses, and sending part of the haul back to the railway union. Produced by Cormans Roger and Julie, from the memoirs of the real Bertha Thompson. VG

Boxer, The
(Shuji Terayama, 1977, Jap) Kentaro Shimizu, Bunta Sugawara, Masumi Harukawa, Yoko Natsuki.
94 min.
Terayama has here brilliantly fused the elements of his previous film and theatre work – surreal-

ism, a sense of the essential anarchy of relationships, and a flair for startling and beautiful images – with a compulsively exciting Hollywood-style narrative about a young man's relentless ambition to be a champion boxer. The film synthesises these seemingly disparate approaches while allowing them separate existences, and through this evokes not only a poetic vision of modern industrial Tokyo and the fading dreams of the city's losers, but also a tense and realistic portrayal of the sheer brutality of the world of boxing, in its inexorable attraction and its heroic despair. SM

Boxer, The
(Jim Sheridan, 1997, Ire/GB/US) Daniel Day-Lewis, Emily Watson, Brian Cox, Ken Stott, Gerard McSorley, Eleanor Methven, Ciaran Fitzgerald.
114 min.
Danny Flynn (Day-Lewis) returns to Belfast after 14 years in prison for IRA activity. He's an outcast, castigated by a former boxing colleague Ike (Stott) for having wasted his talents; by old flame Maggie (Watson), now married to a jailed terrorist, for the ruin of their relationship; and by Republican militants for having renounced violence outside the ring. Despite the disapproval of Maggie's son and father (Cox), a peace-seeking Republican leader who views the resumption of their affair as personally and politically dangerous, Danny and Maggie find themselves drawn together again. Moreover, Danny teams with Ike to set up a gym where training and bouts ignore the sectarian divide. But even love and the most modest projects can fall foul of ingrained prejudice. This may not offer a hugely original take on the Troubles, but it does deliver dramatically. Day-Lewis, taciturn and strong-willed, is as persuasive as ever, while Stott and Cox offer strong support. While Sheridan (who co-wrote) weighs in with gutsy, gritty direction, shooting the fight scenes with panache and cutting sharply throughout for suspense and pace. Politically, too, it's sensitive and sensible. GA

Boxing Helena
(Jennifer Chambers Lynch, 1992, US) Julian Sands, Sherilyn Fenn, Art Garfunkel, Bill Paxton.
105 min.
Fenn is the free-spirited Helena, unfortunate object of surgeon Sands' sexual obsession. His courtship only invites scorn – but, when Helena is hit by a car outside his family mansion, the doc sees a chance to cut her down to size. Lynch in her first stab at directing tries for the black-comic, blue velvet knife-edge between surrealism and perversity, but the results – neither graphic, nor gruesome – are simply incongruous. Grotesquely misconceived. TCh

Box of Moon Light
(Tom DiCillo, 1996, US) John Turturro, Sam Rockwell, Catherine Keener, Lisa Blount, Annie Corley.
112 min.
After DiCillo's delicious *Living in Oblivion*, this comes as a disappointment. Turturro's on form as the straitlaced, clock-watching, by-the-book construction foreman who cracks up when a job is cancelled and goes looking for a happy-holiday lake from his youth. Fair enough, but when he falls in with Rockwell, a half-crazed hippy kid into self-sufficient country life and irresponsible behaviour, you know Turturro's in for a trite lesson in living. Not as funny, deep or original as it would like to be, although things pick up with yet another fine turn from Catherine Keener. GA

Boy (Shonen)
(Nagisa Oshima, 1969, Jap) Tetsue Abe, Fumio Watanabe, Akiko Koyama, Tsuyoshi Kinoshita.
97 min.
It came from a Japanese newspaper story: a down-and-out family were making their young son fake road accidents in order to blackmail motorists for 'hospital fees'. Oshima starts from character studies of the members of the family as outsiders in Japanese society: the lazy, facilely embittered father, the tackily glamorous mother longing for her stepson's love, the 10-year-old boy hopelessly confused about his role as the family breadwinner. With characteristic tender roughness, Oshima then develops this extraordi-

nary story into an open-ended question about the truth of appearances, centering on the boy's own fantasies about his sci-fi hero. A key film in the struggle for a modern, political cinema. TR

Boy and His Dog, A
(LQ Jones, 1974, US) Don Johnson, Susanne Benton, Jason Robards, Alvy Moore, Helene Winston, Charles McGraw.
89 min.
Based on Harlan Ellison's novella, this covers familiar territory – vigorously and imaginatively – as feuding clans of scavengers prowl the desolate American landscape left by a nuclear holocaust. What lifts things right out of the rut is the cynical commentary provided by the hero's dog, communicating telepathically (in voice-off admirably spoken by Tim McIntire) and kicking the daylights out of all those boy-and-his-dog yarns (canine values win out, for example, when with barely a qualm the hero consigns his girl to serve as dogfood). The second half, venturing underground to find Middle America miraculously preserved but rapidly dying, is less good. Jones' debut as a director nevertheless has a distinctive tang, as affably unprincipled as the series of villains he played for Sam Peckinpah. TM

Boy Called Charlie Brown, A
see Boy Named Charlie Brown, A

Boy Called Hate, A
(Mitch Marcus, 1995, US) Scott Caan, Missy Crider, James Caan, Adam Beach, Elliott Gould.
95 min.
Extravagantly praised in some quarters ('there haven't been many better US studies in adolescent ennui since Jonathan Kaplan's equally uncompromising *Over the Edge*,' according to *Sight and Sound*), this direct-to-video debut isn't worth getting too worked up about. The very familiar tale has Caan Jr as a misunderstood kid who takes off through the Midwest with a tearaway gal (Crider) after putting a bullet in the man who was attacking her. It's photographed with some élan, but Marcus's own script is mired in cliché, to the point where our runaways are inducted into Native American lore by a wild Indian (Beach) who seems to have strayed from the Oliver Stone reservation. Scott Caan is a bit of a pudding, but at least Crider gives good attitude. TCh

Boy Friend, The
(Ken Russell, 1971, GB) Twiggy, Christopher Gable, Barbara Windsor, Moyra Fraser, Bryan Pringle, Max Adrian, Catherine Wilmer, Vladek Sheybal, Tommy Tune.
125 min.
Sandy Wilson's delightfully lightweight musical is given the unnecessary avoirdupois that seems unavoidable with Russell. Some things work beautifully: Tommy Tune's deliriously leggy Charleston, the bathing beauty inanities of 'Sur la Plage', almost everything Twiggy does as the wide-eyed ingenue. But there are also some bloated Busby Berkeley pastiches which clash horribly with Wilson's mock-Twenties score. Consistency was never Russell's strong point. TM

Boyfriends
(Neil Hunter/Tom Hunsinger, 1996, GB) James Dreyfus, Mark Sands, Andrew Ableson, Michael Urwin, David Coffey, Darren Petrucci, Michael McGrath, Russell Higgs.
81 min.
This low-budget first feature takes a wry look at the ideals, desires and neuroses of a bunch of mostly middle-class gay men who come together for a country weekend. Tetchy video documentarist Paul (Dreyfus) and passive Ben (Sands) have decided to end their five-year relationship; after just three months, romantic Matt (Urwin) reckons he's met Mr Right in Owen (Ableson), who's wary of the suggestion that they move in together; meanwhile, social-worker Will (Coffey) brings along young, working-class Adam (Petrucci), yet to succumb to emotional or sexual commitment. Attraction, betrayal, jealousy and misunderstanding run their course. The performances are on the whole convincing, while every so often the petty, ratty tensions, coupled with lines of acerbic wit, hint at a more complex scenario of genuine pain and confusion. GA

Boy from Mercury, The

(Martin Duffy, 1996, GB/Fr/Ire) Rita Tushingham, Tom Courtenay, Hugh O'Conor, James Hickey, Ian McElhinney.
87 min.
Writer/director Duffy's semi-autobiographical first feature breathes life into the rites-of-passage movie, mostly by respecting the scale and nature of childhood experience. Set in Dublin sometime between the Sputnik going up and Gagarin going round, it concerns an eight-year-old, James Cronin (Hickey), who becomes convinced that he and his dog are Mercurians with special powers. His doting mother (Tushingham) is as acquiescent as his brother and schoolmates are derisive: her forbearance is based on concern – and maybe guilt – following her husband's death. As the boy's delusions persist, uncle Tony (Courtenay), a gentle, almost foolish man wedded to his scooter, is called in. An opening quote from Terence Davies' *The Long Day Closes* proves an affectionate homage not a stylistic introduction. Thereafter Duffy settles down to his own narrative style: one of gradually beguiling understatement. The early '60s era of Bakelite and pinafores is unobtrusively caught by cinematographer Seamus Deasy. Courtenay's turn errs on the side of mannerism, but otherwise Hickey's unfussy playing has fine support. A sweetheart of a movie. WH

Boy Is Ten Feet Tall, A

see Sammy Going South

Boy Meets Girl

(Lloyd Bacon, 1938, US) James Cagney, Pat O'Brien, Marie Wilson, Ralph Bellamy, Frank McHugh, Dick Foran, Ronald Reagan.
86 min. b/w.
Not as sharp a satire on Hollywood as Kaufman and Hart's *Once in a Lifetime*, but a lively jibe all the same, with Cagney and O'Brien striking sparks off each other as the slap-happy screenwriters who decide to take their revenge on producer Bellamy and an arrogant cowboy star (Foran) by cooking up an ingenious, if unlikely, script for their next movie. Fast, funny and none too demanding. GA

Boy Meets Girl

(Léos Carax, 1984, Fr) Denis Lavant, Mireille Perrier, Carroll Brooks, Elie Poicard, Maïté Nahyr, Christian Cloarec.
104 min. b/w.
Shy young Alex wanders the dark Parisian streets gazing in confusion at the passers-by. Meanwhile Mireille is being given the brush-off by her live-in lover. Eventually, their paths cross as if by destiny; in the meantime, numerous other loners have wandered in and out of Carax's meandering, moody narrative. Easy but unfair to fault Carax's first feature when he has conjured up a persuasively poetic atmosphere for his meditation on the failings of human intercourse. Credit must go to Jean-Yves Escoffier's astonishing black-and-white camerawork, and to the largely wordless, eloquent performances. Finally, however, the film's greatest coup is its creation of a Parisian purgatory of lost souls, bathed eternally in night. Absurd humour counteracts the morbid philosophising, while the alternately surreal and expressionist imagery is reminiscent of silent cinema at its most elegant. GA

Boy Named Charlie Brown, A (aka A Boy Called Charlie Brown)

(Bill Melendez, 1969, US)
86 min.
An animated feature derived from the cartoon strip. Very flat animation, occasionally carelessly painted, with the characters often 'out of tune' with the style of the background. Schulz's script maintains much of the irony of the strips, but the injections of whimsy put its appeal uneasily between adults and children. Snoopy has some beautiful moments, though.

Boys

(Stacy Cochran, 1995, US) Winona Ryder, Lukas Haas, John C Reilly, James LeGros, Skeet Ulrich, Chris Cooper, Bill Sage.
86 min.
Scholarship student at an all-male boarding school, John Baker (Haas) is under pressure from his ambitious dad, but feels gnawing restlessness at the prospect of another term. But while he can't wait for his life to begin, dissolute twenty-something Patty Vare (Ryder) probably wishes she could rewind hers a little. It's the morning after the night before, the police are at the door talking about a stolen car, and she may already have reached the wreckage stage herself. Horse-riding provides a few hours' distraction, but a fall leaves her prone on the ground and, soon, an unwitting, forbidden guest in John's dorm. From such circumstances springs a hesitant if unlikely attraction that fulfils a need in each, but which might take some explaining to the outside world. Writer/director Cochran is stronger on capturing the texture surrounding her characters' converging experiences than making much of it when they do get together. Most striking is the background detail at the boys' school, where the unfolding girl-in-the-room crisis hits a properly complex note of panic, excitement, embarrassment and yearning. TJ

Boys from Brazil, The

(Franklin J Schaffner, 1978, US) Gregory Peck, Laurence Olivier, James Mason, Lilli Palmer, Uta Hagen, Steven Guttenberg, Denholm Elliot, Rosemary Harris, John Dehner.
125 min.
Ira Levin's novel was so obviously devised for the cinema that it reads more like a script. Its premise was ingenious: why has a Nazi hit team from South America begun a systematic slaughter of innocuous middle-aged professional men all over Europe? The answer should have made a great thriller, but the film is sunk by a series of preposterous performances. There are more phony German accents than in a prep school version of *Colditz*, and Levin's expert plotting is buried beneath an avalanche of lines like 'Vat are we goink to do?'. Easy answer. DP

Boys in Blue, The

(Val Guest, 1983, GB) Bobby Ball, Tommy Cannon, Suzanne Danielle, Roy Kinnear, Eric Sykes, Jack Douglas, Edward Judd, Arthur English.
91 min.
This is matriarch humour, strayed from the bosom of clubland; only a Lancashire mother can truly appreciate the feature-length witless babble of Cannon and Ball dressed as bobbies. Cannon has the brain cell, Ball has the catchphrase ('Rock on, Tommy'); they both talk about pulling birds and going to the pictures, repeating each other's lines endlessly, thereby requiring only half a script. Which is all they get; it's about country coppers whose station is under threat until Big Crime turns up on their doorstep. To complete the picture of the typical British film comedy cashing in on TV success, just look at the cast list, halve the budget you first thought of, and add a gratuitous advert for British Leyland. RP

Boys in Company C, The

(Sidney J Furie, 1977, HK) Stan Shaw, Michael Lembeck, James Canning, Craig Wasson, Andrew Stevens, Noble Willingham.
128 min.
Gruelling yet humorous look at a bunch of marines through training and posting to Vietnam in 1968, this turns every war film cliché upside down: transistor radios grind out rock music over the life-and-death patrols, and the GIs behave less like soldiers than shambling tourists. DP

Boys Next Door, The

(Penelope Spheeris, 1985, US) Maxwell Caulfield, Charlie Sheen, Patti D'Arbanville, Christopher McDonald, Hank Garrett, Paul C Dancer.
91 min.
When Bo and Roy, 18-year-olds fresh from school and seemingly normal, decide to hit LA for one last fling before settling into factory jobs, neither they nor the audience are prepared for their sudden descent into committing a series of brutal, apparently motiveless murders. Whereas Spheers' *Suburbia* was weakened by sentimentalising its disaffected punk heroes, her second feature presents a tougher and more balanced view of teen violence; while we're allowed a glimmer of understanding into the murderers' feelings, we never indulge them with misplaced sympathies: these boys are *monsters*. GA

Boy Soldier

(Karl Francis, 1986, GB) Richard Lynch, Bernard Latham, Dafydd Hywel, James Donnelly, WJ Phillips, Timothy Lyn.
100 min.
When Wil Thomas, tired of unemployment and a nagging mother, enlists in a Welsh army regiment for a stretch in Belfast, he makes friends, falls in love, and shapes up as an efficient cog in the military machine. Suddenly, however, there's a shooting, and Wil is imprisoned for murder. The complex but lucid account of his political education is performed partly in Welsh, no nationalist gimmick but a dramatically essential device. For the boy's resort to his native tongue not only signifies his growing solidarity with the 'enemy'; it also serves as a vital strategy of self-defence in his war with the English officers. The occasionally needless fragmentation of the narrative at times weakens the film's emotional punch, while the almost universal depiction of Wil's would-be moral guardians as corrupt and hypocritical brutes might seem overemphatic. But it's a brave, sincere and intelligent movie, forcefully grasping a thorny subject all too often handled with kid gloves. GA

Boys on the Side

(Herbert Ross, 1995, US) Whoopi Goldberg, Mary-Louise Parker, Drew Barrymore, Matthew McConaughey, James Remar, Estelle Parsons.
117 min.
Goldberg's in her element here as Jane, a lesbian singer with attitude to spare who shares a cross-country drive first with Robin (Parker) and then with wild-child Holly (Barrymore). On the road, this female buddy-movie plays like a camper *Thelma and Louise* (rescued from her abusive boyfriend, Holly finds herself on the run when his corpse turns up on the front pages); it changes gears abruptly at the halfway mark, when Robin goes down with an AIDS-related illness. This tender, ticklish chicks' flick pushes a good many emotional buttons, but resists at least some of the easier options. TCh

Boys Will Be Boys

(William Beaudine, 1935, GB) Will Hay, Gordon Harker, Claude Dampier, Jimmy Hanley, Davy Burnaby, Norma Varden.
75 min. b/w.
Typically hectic Hay farce in which, thanks to a bit of crookery, he graduates from prison teacher to headmaster of a decidedly unorthodox school. Underhand dealing and batty backchat galore, lorded over by its garrulous star and the marvellous Harker. GA

Boy Who Could Fly, The

Nick Castle, 1986, US) Lucy Deakins, Jay Underwood, Bonnie Bedelia, Fred Savage, Colleen Dewhurst, Fred Gwynne, Mindy Cohen.
114 min.
With such a promising premise, it's a shame that *The Boy Who Could Fly* so quickly descends into Disneyland. Milly (Deakins) is the new kid on the block. The boy next door is Eric (Underwood), an autistic child who spends his days perched on a bedroom windowsill with arms outstretched in dreams of flight. The two outsiders are at once drawn to one another, and a sympathetic teacher (Dewhurst) plays upon their developing relationship, hoping to reintegrate Eric into the classroom and prevent the authorities from institutionalising him. As the adults close in, the young dreamers are chased on to the school roof, with nowhere to turn but up or down. Director Castle gets lost in fantasy, spoiling a promising portrait with some heavy-handed emotional manipulation and an escapist conclusion. SGo

Boy Who Cried Bitch, The

(Juan José Campanella, 1990, US) Harley Cross, Karen Young, Dennis Boutsikaris, Adrien Brody, Gene Canfield, Moira Kelly.
105 min.
An unevenly pitched, resolutely sincere adaptation by scriptwriter Catherine May Levin of her novel about a delinquent 12-year-old boy whose guilt-ridden mother is forced by an emotional war of attrition to commit her potentially violent son to a series of unsuitable psychiatric institutions. Although Cross, as the delinquent boy, and Young as his long-suffering mother, lend a pow-

erful conviction to their demanding roles, Campanella's aimlessly roaming camera and elliptical scene transitions are curiously at odds with the predominantly naturalistic tone. NF

Boy Who Had Everything, The

(Stephen Wallace, 1984, Aust) Jason Connery, Diane Cilento, Laura Williams, Lewis Fitz-Gerald, Ian Gilmour.
94 min.
Chariots of Fire, ocker-style, with its over-achieving hero caught between mother, a brassy blonde parvenue, and alma mater, a pretentious private college with sadistic humiliation rites. Wallace bodges around the early '60s context and his golden boy's Oedipal inclinations, and understandably there's an awkwardness here in the performances of real-life mother and son Cilento and Connery, who evinces little of father Sean's cruel charisma or acting ability. SJo

Boy with Green Hair, The

(Joseph Losey, 1948, US) Dean Stockwell, Pat O'Brien, Robert Ryan, Barbara Hale, Samuel S Hinds, Walter Catlett.
82 min.
Imagine a cosy Disney feature crossed with an allegory on war and racism, and you have some idea of the bizarre flavour of Losey's first feature. A rather simplistic symbolic tale about a war-orphan whose hair turns green in protest against his plight, only to be rejected by friends and strangers alike, it's muddled, awkward, pretentious, and often downright embarrassing. But the very fact that it is so ridiculous, with absurd moments like the garrulous old grandfather (O'Brien) singing silly songs, lends it a certain offbeat charm. GA

Boyz N the Hood

(John Singleton, 1991, US) Larry Fishburne, Cuba Gooding Jr, Ice Cube, Morris Chestnut, Nia Long, Tyra Ferrell, Angela Bassett.
112 min.
South Central LA, 1984: anxious that her son will fall prey to the drug-related violence of the local gangs, ten-year-old Tre Styles' mother hands the boy over to her estranged husband, Furious (Fishburne). Seven years later, his father's strict lessons in the art of taking responsibility have ensured Tre's moral strength, black pride and rigorous self-discipline; but in a community ravaged by crack, poverty, police harassment and guns, it's hard to stay true to one's principles when life-long friends are shot at and revenge is called for. If the coming-of-age story is in itself hardly original, and the speeches are sometimes a mite preachy, writer/director Singleton (his debut) mounts his arguments forcefully and clearly. But what makes the film so affecting is the no-nonsense direction and Singleton's sure, specific sense of the rewards and hardships of community; in this, he is lent excellent support from a fine cast. GA

Brady Bunch Movie, The

(Betty Thomas, 1995, US) Shelley Long, Gary Cole, Christopher Daniel Barnes, Christine Taylor, Michael McKean, Jean Smart, Henriette Mantel, Paul Sutera, Jennifer Elise Cox, Jesse Lee.
89 min.
An anodyne family-values sitcom, *The Brady Bunch* ran from 1969 to 1974, and somehow reflected the Nixon presidency without mentioning drugs, Vietnam or Watergate. Two decades later, how relevant can the Brady Bunch be? The screenwriters' answer, subverting the original, is simply to plonk the family in the middle of contemporary LA. All around is greed, apathy and dog-eat-dog, but the Brady home remains a haven of cheesy smiles and moral certitude. Director Thomas (once Sgt Lucy Bates of *Hill Street Blues*) has recreated '70s sitcom-land with the kind of unerring attention to detail Merchant-Ivory lavish on a society ball, and she's drawn hilariously synthetic performances from a shrewdly cloned cast. TCh

Brain Damage

(Frank Henenlotter, 1987, US) Rick Herbst, Gordon MacDonald, Jennifer Lowry, Theo Barnes, Lucille Saint-Peter, Vicki Darnell.
86 min.
Escaping from a nice old Jewish couple unwilling to cater for his unusual dietary needs, the phallic Elmer, a parasitic creature, fastens on to Brian (Herbst) as a more promising victim. By tapping into the back of Brian's neck, Elmer blue-rinses his brain with a euphoria-inducing liquid. Brian thinks he can handle it, but it's addictive, and pretty soon he's helping Elmer to obtain his preferred food, human brains. While it would win few prizes for narrative sophistication and visual imagination – the euphoric hallucinations seem to have strayed from a '60s LSD movie – *Brain Damage* does display a commendable social conscience in deploring the perils of mindbending substances. By way of aversion therapy, it presents gruesome scenes like that in which Brian pulls a bloody string of mental floss from out of his left ear. Similarly, the most disgusting scene will deter impressionable young women from performing the act of fellatio for life. There are some nice comic moments though; in fact relying as heavily on its disquieting black humour as on images of physical disgust, the whole thing works far better as comedy than horror. NF

Braindead

(Peter Jackson, 1992, NZ) Timothy Balme, Diana Peñalver, Elizabeth Moody, Ian Watkin, Brenda Kendall.
104 min.
Peter Jackson's zombiefest follow-up to *Bad Taste*, set in suburbia in the late '50s, is 'a slapstick comedy with blood and guts instead of custard pies'. When 25-year-old virgin Lionel (Balme) falls for the lovely Paquita (Peñalver), he provokes his domineering mother's jealousy. Soon after, a toxic nip from a Sumatran rat-monkey at the local zoo transforms Lionel's mother – through several putrescent stages – into a hideous, pustulant monster with a craving for human flesh. The finale, in which Lionel reduces a horde of flesh-eaters to a mulch of blood, flesh and offal with the aid of a flymo, is probably the goriest scene ever. NF

Brain Machine, The

(Ken Hughes, 1955, GB) Patrick Barr, Elizabeth Allan, Maxwell Reed, Russell Napier, Gibb McLaughlin, Vanda Godsell.
83 min. b/w.
When the reading on psychiatrist Allan's electro-encephalograph indicates that amnesiac hospital patient Reed is none other than a dangerous psychopath she'd previously tested, the patient in question kidnaps the doctor and threatens her life – leaving medic huusband Barr racing against time to track down the villain's hide-out. Pacy little British B-pic which finds an interesting early techno angle on a pretty familiar storyline. TJ

Brainscan

(John Flynn, 1994, US) Edward Furlong, Frank Langella, T Ryder Smith, Amy Hargreaves, Jamie Marsh, Victor Ertmanis.
95 min.
The titular computer game, 'the ultimate experience in inter-active horror', gets a little too real for high-school misfit Michael (Furlong) in this dumb hi-tech horror movie. While playing Brainscan and seeing through the eyes of a killer, Michael breaks into a suburban house, grabs a kitchen knife, climbs the stairs and stabs to death a sleeping, middle-aged man. Next day, he learns that a middle-aged man has been murdered in his quiet suburban neighbourhood. Was it real or was it virtual reality? 'Reality, unreality, what's the difference?' asks the cadaverous Trickster (Smith), who emerges from the screen as the personification of the game's malevolent electrical impulses. Director Flynn presents the dogged investigation by smoothly insinuating detective Hayden (Langella) with some style; but he seems much less interested in the fantastic elements, the self-conscious in-jokes and lacklustre visual effects. NF

Brainstorm

(Douglas Trumbull, 1983, US) Christopher Walken, Natalie Wood, Louise Fletcher, Cliff Robertson, Jordan Christopher, Donald Hotton.
106 min.
On paper, with its fascinating premise – a helmet-like device to enable people to experience other people's experiences – this has a lot going for it. On screen, however, it's an interesting and ambitious package that doesn't quite work. Use of the device is limited to the obvious, like sex and racing cars, or to the impossibly mystical, which fails to crack the old problem that hell is always more vivid than heaven. The drama comes from the battle between the mad scientist (Walken) who wants the device to benefit mankind, and the mysterious men in dark suits who want to keep it all under wraps for the military. As a thriller it's a bit soft, as sci-fi it's a bit simple. JB

Brainwaves

(Ulli Lommel, 1982, US) Keir Dullea, Suzanna Love, Tony Curtis, Vera Miles, Percy Rodrigues, Paul Willson.
80 min.
Ulli Lommel graduated from playing twitchers and fruitcakes in Fassbinder movies by directing *Tenderness of the Wolves*, a touching account of a gay paedophile butcher. He then decamped to Hollywood to essay a career pitched somewhere between Dennis Hopper and Paul Morrissey. Mostly he made no-budget schlock, like this ludicrously straightfaced 'thriller' about brainwave transplants. A black hole for fading stars in which Dr Curtis kindly operates on the heroine (Love) who is in a coma after suffering a traumatic blow to the brain. The donor is a murder victim, unexpectedly supplying not only motor reflexes but memories, so that the poor recipient is soon being stalked herself. ATu

Bramble Bush, The

(Daniel Petrie, 1959, US) Richard Burton, Barbara Rush, Jack Carson, Angie Dickinson.
105 min.
Alcohol, adultery and euthanasia loom large in this glossy version of Charles Mergendahl's sub-*Peyton Place* novel about a New England doctor going home to Cape Cod and falling for his dying friend's wife. One of Burton's take the money and run performances. TM

Bram Stoker's Dracula

see Dracula

Branches of the Tree (Shakha Proshakha)

(Satyajit Ray, 1990, Ind/Fr) Ajit Banerjee, Maradan Banerjee, Lily Charraborty, Soumitra Chatterjee, Mamata Shankar.
120 min.
A sombre family drama occasioned by the heart attack of a venerable businessman and philanthropist, who lives with his senile father and mentally disturbed son, but derives hope and a measure of satisfaction from his other three sons, successful men instilled with his principles of hard work and integrity. The family dutifully gathers at his bedside and awaits some sign of recovery; but old resentments cloud the air as first one son, then another, admit that their father's values are no longer tenable in a modern society where corruption distinguishes winners from losers. Ray stressed that the scenario for this, his second film since his serious coronary problems, was written 25 years ago and should not be taken as autobiographical. For all that, it is evidently an old man's film. With a single principal setting, and long passages of unwieldy exposition or earnest sermonising, the script might have been intended for the stage; and although it reclaims some of the ground lost in *An Enemy of the People*, Ray's functional, inelegant *mise en scène* provides little embellishment. TCh

Branded to Kill (Koroshi No Rakuin)

(Seijun Suzuki, 1966, Jap) Jo Shishido.
91 min. b/w.
The film that got Suzuki fired by Nikkatsu, and it's not hard to see why. It starts almost straightforwardly as a bluesy gangster thriller in pared-down Melville mould. But as 'number three killer' Shishido (a Suzuki regular) moves from some beautifully staged hits to perverse obsession with an ultra cool femme fatale and a set-to with 'number one killer', the weirder the film becomes. Just as Shishido cracks up and enters a surreal nightmare world, so Suzuki breaks the film down into a bizarre but beguiling chain of absurdist, OTT, barely related elements. It looks a little like golden-age Godard (but far more stylish). The climax, oddly reminiscent of *Point Blank* (made the same year), shows how much further Suzuki was prepared to push even than Boorman, let alone Hollywood. Occasionally mystifying, but always witty, inventive and dazzling to look at. GA

Brandy Ashore
see Green Grow the Rushes

Brannigan
(Douglas Hickox, 1975, GB) John Wayne, Richard Attenborough, Judy Geeson, Mel Ferrer, John Vernon, Daniel Pilon, John Stride.
111 min.
Wayne playing national monument (in the guise of a Chicago cop) is exported to London to get his man and take in the sights. What follows is flatly predictable: some grousing about wearing neckties in the Garrick Club; tedious 'language' problems; relentless use of tourist locations and some jokey fisticuffs in a pub brawl that's geared solely for the American market. CPe

Brasher Doubloon, The
(aka The High Window)
(John Brahm, 1946, US) George Montgomery, Nancy Guild, Florence Bates, Fritz Kortner, Conrad Janis, Roy Roberts, Marvin Miller, Houseley Stevenson.
72 min. b/w.
Usually shrugged aside as a negligible Chandler adaptation, but Brahm has other fish to fry. The tone is set by the opening shot of an old dark house as Philip Marlowe's offscreen voice complains about the wind blowing eternally off the Mojave. That wind continues throughout, stirring the mood of malaise as swaying branches set shadows flickering in dim-lit rooms where the heroine is being slowly driven mad. The opening interview, with the marvellously malevolent Florence Bates easily outgunning General Sternwood in flesh-crawling unease, challenges *The Big Sleep* on its own ground. The middle stretches, with Kortner outstanding in the Lorre role, produce as vivid a set of grotesques as *The Maltese Falcon*. But what keeps the last third afloat owes less to Chandler or Hammett than to the sense of brooding Gothic melodrama in which Brahm specialised. Forget Philip Marlowe, enjoy a fine companion piece to *The Lodger*, *Guest in the House*, *Hanover Square* and *The Locket*. TM

Brassed Off
(Mark Herman,1996, GB/US) Pete Postlethwaite, Ewan McGregor, Tara Fitzgerald, Stephen Tompkinson, Jim Carter, Philip Jackson, Stephen Moore.
107 min.
This is an angry, tragic film, which softens you up with a few off-the-peg stereotypes and colloquial laughs and then rams them back down your throat. Postlethwaite is Danny, the devoted leader of the Grimley Colliery Band. Music is so important to him, he barely notices that the pit's on the verge of closure, and can't begin to understand why members like Andy (McGregor), Harry (Carter) and even his own son, Phil (Tompkinson), are finding it hard to cough up their subs. Matters come to a head with the band competing in the national championships and the miners voting for voluntary redundancy. Writer/director Herman pulls off a popular, proletarian comedy which might actually appeal to the people it's about. He uses comic shorthand – not all the relationships are as developed as they might be – but captures a credible sense of the tensions within the community at large, and the devastating impact of the pit closures. He's not shy about laying the blame, either. Tompkinson, Postlethwaite and Carter are stand-outs in an impressive ensemble cast, but for many, the brass band music will come as the real revelation. TCh

Brass Monkey, The
(aka Lucky Mascot)
(Thornton Freeland, 1948, GB) Carroll Levis, Carole Landis, Herbert Lom, Avril Angers, Ernest Thesiger, Terry-Thomas.
84 min. b/w.
Radio personality Levis, who hosted a long-running talent-spotting show on Radio Luxembourg, made an unlikely transition to the big screen in this ramshackle support feature that sat on the shelf for three years before its eventual release in 1951. Levis more or less plays himself, implicated in Buddhist connoisseur Thesiger's search for a trio of valuable brass monkeys, with villainous Lom under suspicion of theft. A curio, but not really a collectible. TJ

Brass Target
(John Hough, 1978, US) Sophia Loren, John Cassavetes, George Kennedy, Robert Vaughn, Patrick McGoohan, Bruce Davison, Edward Herrmann, Max von Sydow.
111 min.
Mining the profitable vein of *Day of the Jackal*, this tale of conspiracy and assassination has General Patton murdered by subordinates involved in a vast gold heist. The movie goes for several targets – historical significance, murky intrigue, Bond-style techno-glamour – but misses them all. Loren, as the woman with a past, drifts in and out of a defiantly labyrinthine plot which reaches rock bottom with the revelation that Patton's adjutant's mistress' ex-husband was (maybe) a Nazi cabinet minister. Pretty thin. CA

Bravados, The
(Henry King, 1958, US) Gregory Peck, Stephen Boyd, Albert Salmi, Henry Silva, Lee Van Cleef, Joan Collins, Joe De Rita, Andrew Duggan, George Voskovec, Gene Evans.
98 min.
Nine years after the impressive *Twelve O'Clock High*, eight after the magnificent *The Gunfighter*, King and Peck teamed up again for this revenge Western. For a while, it looks as though the magic is going to work again, as Peck rides grimly into a small town, announces that his purpose is to watch four outlaws hang, and – when they contrive to escape – outrides the posse to exterminate the outlaws one by one. Ironically, although guilty of similar crimes, the quartet (Boyd, Salmi, Van Cleef and Silva) turn out to be not guilty of the rape/murder of Peck's wife. Cue for a crisis of conscience which is worked out in perfunctory religious terms, with Joan Collins conveniently on hand as an image of salvation. With good performances and excellent 'Scope camerawork from Leon Shamroy, the action sequences are fine, but the religious motifs are as maudlin as *The Song of Bernadette*. TM

Brave, The
(Johnny Depp, 1997, US) Johnny Depp, Marlon Brando, Elpidia Carrillo, Marshall Bell.
123 min.
Depp's directorial debut is a *folie de grandeur*. There's nothing intrinsically wrong with the story, in which Depp, a Latin or Native American – it's unclear which – living with his wife and kids in a shanty town next to a garbage dump, decides to help his family escape poverty by being paid a fortune for his own death. But after the scenes in which he makes his deal with Brando – a snuff-movie producer? (again it's unclear) – the film goes seriously off the rails as it forsakes glum realism for maudlin sentiment and whimsical, symbolic fantasy (Depp gets back in touch with his kids and builds a fairground for the other dispossessed). Besides the implausibilities, the direction has two fatal flaws: it's both tediously slow and hugely narcissistic as the camera focuses repeatedly on Depp's bandana'd head and rippling torso. GA

Brave Don't Cry, The
(Philip Leacock, 1952, GB) John Gregson, Meg Buchanan, John Rae, Fulton Mackay, Andrew Weir, Russell Waters, Jameson Clark.
90 min. b/w.
By rights a title like this should herald some high-flown best-seller garbage, but in fact this is quite a decent little film from the short-lived Group 3 venture, produced by John Grierson and John Baxter: a semi-documentary reenactment of the 1950 Knockshinnoch mine disaster in Scotland. Sober, careful, making excellent use of locations and a cast drawn largely from the Glasgow Citizens' Theatre, it is only occasionally inclined to over-emote. TM

Braveheart
(Mel Gibson, 1995, US) Mel Gibson, Sophie Marceau, Patrick McGoohan, Catherine McCormack, Alun Armstrong, Ian Bannen, Brendan Gleeson, James Cosmo.
177 min.
Scotland at the end of the 13th century: William Wallace (Gibson) purposes to free his country from the tyranny of Edward Longshanks (McGoohan). From the opening shots, swirling through the mists o' time over snowy peaks and silvery lochs, to the final torture scenes in which disembowelment provokes only a brave grimace,

Gibson's epic offers a stew of Hollywood clichés. Political analysis is not on the menu; this is a tale of heroes 'n' villains, pure and simplistic. The Sassenachs are rude stereotypes, while the Scots are either macho hunks or, should they be aristos, dour quislings. The battle scenes are staged effectively, but for the most part this is a vehicle for Gibson, graduating from cocky *Lethal Weapon* register to something more one-dimensional and rhetorically solemn. Pure hokum. GA

Brave Little Toaster, The
(Jerry Rees, 1987, US) voices: Jon Lovitz, Tim Stack, Timothy E Day, Thurl Ravenscroft, Deanna Oliver, Phil Hartman.
90 min.
This gem of an adventure, from a novel by Thomas M Disch, is essentially *The Incredible Journey* with five animated electrical appliances (toaster, lamp, vacuum-cleaner, electric blanket and portable radio) that are not so much live as *alive!* Abandoned by their 'master', a spotty kid who moves off with parents to the big city, the plucky quintet are left with no option but to up cables and set off into the wild blue yonder. A winning combination of inventive characters, amusing dialogue, excellent voice-overs, likeable tunes (courtesy of former Beach Boys collaborator Van Dyke Parks), and first-rate animation. Indeed, one of the most enchanting animated films since *The Snowman*. A volt from the blue. DA

Brazil (100)
(Terry Gilliam, 1985, GB) Jonathan Pryce, Robert De Niro, Katherine Helmond, Ian Holm, Bob Hoskins, Michael Palin, Ian Richardson.
142 min.
Fortunately the story of an alternative future is realised with such visual imagination and sparky humour that it's only half way through that the plot's weaknesses become apparent. Like *1984*, it looks forward from the '40s to a vast urban society ruled by an oppressive bureaucracy that has developed primitive valve computers. Pryce plays a worker in the all-powerful Ministry of Information, and the best moments arise when his flat's central heating system becomes a kind of spiritual battleground between guerrilla engineer De Niro and his state opposite number Hoskins. Here Gilliam fuses terror and comedy with real brilliance; elsewhere the plot's gaping holes reduce the film to a glittering novelty. DP

Bread and Chocolate
(Pane e Cioccolata)
(Franco Brusati, 1973, It) Nino Manfredi, Anna Karina, Johnny Dorelli, Paolo Turco, Ugo D'Alessio.
112 min.
Production-line Italian comedy only slightly helped by the tragi-comic skills of Nino Manfredi, as a guest-worker in oh-so-clean Switzerland desperately trying to break into the Aryan leisure culture. Brusati fatally miscalculates this comedy of failure, despising his protagonist, confusing pathos with camp. Almost as sad, the sublime Karina is thrown away in a sort of EEC cameo (as a Greek exile on the run). Good acting, dreadful everything else. CA

Break The
see Further Gesture, A

Breakdance
see Breakin'

Breakdown
(Jonathan Mostow, 1997, US) Kurt Russell, JT Walsh, Kathleen Quinlan, MC Gainey, Jack Noseworthy, Rex Linn.
93 min.
East Coast sophisticate Russell drives across the Southwest with wife Quinlan in a new Jeep. Breaking down in the middle of nowhere, he stays with the vehicle while Quinlan accepts a lift from trucker Walsh to the nearest phone. The thing is, Kurt gets the jeep going again, and by the time he's caught up with the truck, Kathleen has vanished and JT claims he must have the wrong fella – he's never seen him before in his life. There's not much fuel in the tank, but co-writer/director Mostow keeps this belated *Duel* retread streamlined and reasonably efficient. But it has no real credibility except for the gritty conviction of the stars, especially the late JT Walsh, oozing his sin-

gularly malevolent bonhomie. Mostow makes the most of the deserted truckstop landscapes but rehashes all the paranoid Hollywood clichés about the dangers lurking behind the gap-toothed smiles of Middle America – and caps it all with an insultingly brutal OTT ending. TCh

Breaker Morant

(Bruce Beresford, 1979, Aust) Edward Woodward, Jack Thompson, John Waters, Bryan Brown, Charles Tingwell, Terence Donovan, Lewis Fitz-Gerald.
107 min.
Three lieutenants (Woodward, Brown, Fitz-Gerald), members of an Australian platoon fighting in the Boer War, are court-martialled for murdering Boer prisoners and a German missionary, and Jack Thompson steps in to try to prove their innocence. It's a 'Paths of Glory' situation, complete with righteous anger at the expedient conniving authorities, distinguished by some strong courtroom scenes and an overwhelming pessimism. If it hardly breaks any new ground either formally or politically, it's nevertheless a moving and highly professional affair, in which Brown and Thompson give particularly good performances. GA

Breakfast at Tiffany's

(Blake Edwards, 1961, US) Audrey Hepburn, George Peppard, Patricia Neal, Buddy Ebsen, Mickey Rooney, John McGiver, Martin Balsam.
115 min.
Bowdlerised but pleasant enough adaptation, by George Axelrod, of Truman Capote's novel, with Hepburn rather too winsome as the Manhattan callgirl Holly Golightly, who has an on-off relationship with Peppard's writer, himself juggling an affair with a (Neal) wealthy patroness. The party scenes and intimations of hipness now look dated, and it's all rather too sugary for its own good (Henry Mancini's award-winning 'Moon River' being symptomatic); but taken as a shallow fairytale it has a certain charm. GA

Breakfast Club, The

(John Hughes, 1984, US) Emilio Estevez, Paul Gleason, Anthony Michael Hall, John Kapelos, Judd Nelson, Molly Ringwald, Ally Sheedy.
97 min.
Take five American teenagers – a deb, a punk, a jock, a swot and a nut – and thrust them into the enforced intimacy of a Saturday's detention at high school for a contrived set piece of ensemble acting in which the characters drone on about themselves and their puerile problems en route to emerging as fully paid-up members of the Me Generation. After dodging their supervising teacher, puffing at a joint, losing their inhibitions and dissolving into tears, they neatly conclude that their parents are to blame for everything. Pah. Characters who beef about not being taken seriously as real people would cut more ice were they not merely clothes-horses for crudely defined teen tribalism and strings of social clichés. The Big Chill served up again for the Simple-Minded set. AB

Breakheart Pass

(Tom Gries, 1975, US) Charles Bronson, Ben Johnson, Jill Ireland, Richard Crenna, Charles Durning, Archie Moore, Ed Lauter.
94 min.
Pretty typical Alistair MacLean adventure with all the usual failings: minimal characterisation, terrible dialogue, too much plot, and too little real, inherent dynamism as opposed to weightily set up action pieces. This one manages to combine a basic Ten Little Indians plot with murder on a train à la Orient Express, set in the old West. VG

Breakin' (aka Breakdance)

(Joel Silberg, 1984, US) Lucinda Dickey, Adolfo 'Shabba-Doo' Quinones, Michael 'Boogaloo-Shrimp' Chambers, Ben Lokey.
90 min.
A vehicle for the astonishing form of 'breaking' in which athletic types perform as if they were having a molar drilled without novocaine while being simultaneously kneecapped...all to that disco beat. On the athletic level alone it trashes Flashdance into the boards, and the film's three heroes, Dickey, Shabba-Doo and Boogaloo-Shrimp (Oscars all round, just for the names) are all spellbinding; the soundtrack is also a treat, and the storyline, if lame (boy meets girl, sticks

two fingers up at the dance establishment, and still wins prestigious audition) is peppered with enough modern motifs to suspend disbelief. DS

Breaking Away

(Peter Yates, 1979, US) Dennis Christopher, Dennis Quaid, Daniel Stern, Jackie Earle Haley, Barbara Barrie, Paul Dooley, Robyn Douglass.
101 min.
Class conflict and small town chauvinism are the subject of Yates' ingenious youth movie, a film which intrigues as much by its portait of working-class America bitterly opposed to the affluent society as by its large measure of lovingly-crafted fantasy. Hero Dave (Christopher) and his mates try to win the annual 'Little Indy' team cycle race in their home town (Bloomington, Indiana), as a gesture of defiance to the richly privileged college boys. Scripted by Steve Tesich, it's Yates' best film since The Friends of Eddie Coyle and displays the kind of unsentimental optimism that went out of fashion with Hawks. DP

Breaking Glass

(Brian Gibson, 1980, GB) Phil Daniels, Hazel O'Connor, Jon Finch, Jonathan Pryce, Peter-Hugo Daly.
104 min.
Super-cynical first feature by ex-TV director Gibson. Its version of punk London in the '80s is a bizarre mix of Big Brother fantasy and shallow realism, with rock singer Kate (O'Connor) making it to rock star and losing her marbles on the way. The Glenn Miller Story meets Rude Boy.

Breaking In

(Bill Forsyth, 1989, US) Burt Reynolds, Casey Siemaszko, Sheila Kelley, Lorraine Toussaint, Albert Salmi, Harry Carey, Maury Chaykin, Stephen Tobolowsky.
94 min.
Forsyth's second American picture (the first actually shot in the States) is a gentle comedy about a couple of guys who happen to break into the same house at the same time. Mike (Reynolds) is an old-time pro, but Ernie (Siemaszko) is a kid, only in it for thrills. Declaring he'd sooner have a partner than a witness, Mike sets about showing Ernie the ropes. Despite the caper movie framework, John Sayles' screenplay is not as far from That Sinking Feeling as you might think. Forsyth has a rare talent for locating the comic in the real world. His heroes and heroines never quite fit in, and who can blame them? There's something funny going on: a guard dog more inquisitive than aggressive, a Christian hostel with thousands of dollars in its safe, a poetic prostitute who muses, 'What would I do with your balls were they mine?'. Reynolds reminds one of the easy charm he commands when he doesn't force it, and young gun Siemaszko is marvellous as a likeable schmuck who wants only to belong; together they're poignant and very funny. A subtle, masterly film, a series of life lessons which never ducks the moral ironies, no less precious for their simplicity. TCh

Breaking Point

(Bob Clark, 1976, Can) Bo Svenson, Robert Culp, Belinda J Montgomery, Stephen Young, John Colicos, Linda Sorenson.
92 min.
Canadian version of Death Wish. If the thrust of the film is a rising curve of violence, Clark's direction is far less certain, with the result that odd touches in the script suggest the film has aspirations which are never fulfilled. Instead stock resolutions abound. PH

Breaking Point, The

(Michael Curtiz, 1950, US) John Garfield, Patricia Neal, Phyllis Thaxter, Juano Hernandez, Wallace Ford.
97 min.
Hawks messed around with Hemingway and made To Have and Have Not (1944); six years later Curtiz played it straighter and wound up with this thoroughly competent smuggling drama, which, without Bogey and Bacall on board, has faded into the celluloid woodwork. Garfield works hard though as the Southern California boat-owner who puts himself in danger when he agrees to take on illegal cargo to pay his debts, and even if you know and love the Hawks' movie there's still much to intrigue here. (Don Siegel directed a third version, The Gun Runners, with Audie Murphy in 1958.) TJ

Breaking Point, The (aka The Great Armored Car Swindle)

(Lance Comfort, 1960, GB) Peter Reynolds, Dermot Walsh, Joanna Dunham, Lisa Gastoni, Brian Cobby.
59 min. b/w.
Humdrum, mercifully brief British thriller adapted by producer Peter Lambert from a not-bad novel by Laurence Meynell: matters revolve around attempts to flood a small Middle Eastern country, Lalvadore, with counterfeit notes. The story, too, has a flat, forged feel. GM

Breaking the Sound Barrier

see Sound Barrier, The

Breaking the Waves

(Lars von Trier, 1996, Den/Swe/Fr/Neth/Nor) Emily Watson, Stellan Skarsgård, Katrin Cartlidge, Jean-Marc Barr, Adrian Rawlins, Jonathan Hackett, Sandra Voe.
159 min.
The '70s, North-West Scotland: despite opposition from the Calvinist community in which she lives, Bess (Watson) is sufficiently sure God looks kindly on her love for oil-rig worker Jan (Skarsgård) that she marries him. When he returns to the rig, however, she can barely tolerate his absence, and prays for his return – which he does, paralysed and perhaps brain-damaged by an accident. Distraught that his wife's brief sexual bliss is over, Jan suggests she take lovers and describe her liaisons afterwards, so they might still enjoy sex by proxy. Bess consents reluctantly – until, that is, she comes to believe that the sacrifices she's making will restore Jan's health, or at least save his life. Meanwhile, the villagers ostracise her as a whore. This epic melodrama about love, faith, suffering and redemption is emotionally overwhelming. Its raw power is assured not only by the forthright performances and the increasingly cruel, violent events of the last hour, but by Robby Müller's edgily realist 'Scope camerawork. It's a rapt movie, and so wrapped up in its own harrowing dynamics that it finally, perhaps, goes too far in subjecting its selfless heroine to pain and indignity; is this sympathy or sadism? That said, it's a remarkable achievement for all concerned, with Katrin Cartlidge, as Bess's widowed sister-in-law, sharing the acting laurels with the radiant Emily Watson, and writer/director Lars von Trier building the emotional and dramatic intensity with consummate skill. GA

Breaking Up

(Robert Greenwald, 1996, US) Russell Crowe, Salma Hayek, Abraham Alvarez.
89 min.
Steve (Crowe) and Monica (Hayek) keep breaking up. Nothing can stop them. They try to make a clean break by getting married, but it doesn't work. Almost the only other thing in the lives of this pair is the camera, with which, admittedly, they have a healthy interaction, inviting it over for dinner, into the shower, or, when apart, gregariously telling it about their feelings. There's hardly any sign of work, friends, family, and no suggestion that social or professional influences inform a relationship. And there's no attempt at rounded storytelling, or any insight into this self-contradictory love affair – merely a skin-deep litany of symptoms. NB

Break of Dawn

(Isaac Artenstein, 1988, US/Mex) Oscar Chavez, Maria Rojo, Peter Henry Schroeder.
115 min.
A fairly workmanlike movie, but the fascinating subject matter intrigues. Mexican actor and singer Oscar Chavez stars as Pedro J Gonzalez, the first Spanish-speaking radio star to make it in the US.His career ended prematurely in the 1930s when his outspoken comments on the forced deportation of Mexican immigrants were met by a vindictive response from a publicity-seeking DA. Unjustly convicted of the rape of an underage girl and sentenced to 50 years in San Quentin, his plight mobilised the Mexican-American community in the fight to clear his name. TJ

Breakout

(Tom Gries, 1975, US) Charles Bronson, Robert Duvall, Jill Ireland, Randy Quaid, Sheree North, Emilio Fernandez, Alan Vint.
96 min.
A routinely spectacular adventure, set in Mexican

border country and featuring Bronson as the mastermind behind a series of attempts to spring a framed man from jail. It offers little of substance beyond some fancy stunts, a number of obvious plagiarisms (*Chinatown*, *Charley Varrick*, *Thunderbolt and Lightfoot*), and a strong support cast who deserved better.

Break to Freedom
see Albert RN

Breathless
(Jim McBride, 1983, US) Richard Gere, Valerie Kaprisky, William Tepper, John P Ryan, Art Metrano, Robert Dunn.
100 min.
Neither straight remake nor looser homage to Godard's *A Bout de Souffle*; better by far to just enjoy it on its own terms when it turns out at least three parts better than anyone predicted. Gere is the rockabilly punk living permanently on the edge, on the run from a cop-killing, and certain of at least two things: how to steal cars and his obsession with his girl. Together they conduct a fugitive romance across LA, a common enough idea from Hollywood (*Gun Crazy* is a motif) but one which is burning with a rarely seen passion. The breathless shooting style lingers forever on Gere's pumping, preening narcissism, which leaves you in no doubt that the true romance is not between boy and girl, but between Gere and camera. The film's other star is LA, which is filmed as a series of dazzling pop art backdrops – cultural vacancy and hedonism, yoked together by violence: a city for the '80s. A wanton, playful film, belying the stated despair by its boiling energy. CPea

Breathless
see A Bout de Souffle

Breezy
(Clint Eastwood, 1973, US) William Holden, Kay Lenz, Roger C Carmel, Marj Dusay, Joan Hotchkis, Jamie Smith Jackson.
107 min.
Eastwood has often been noted for his sudden, surprising and adventurous switches in direction, but none of them (not even *Tightrope*) is quite as extraordinary as this. For one thing he does not appear in it himself (well, only in a Hitchcock-style shot); for another, the subject matter is hardly what one would associate with 'Dirty Harry'. A middle-aged real-estate broker meets a hippy hitchhiker less than half his age. They fall in love. A project full of pitfalls, all of which Eastwood, remarkably, manages to avoid. The film is sentimental only in that its characters, being human and in love, are sentimental; otherwise the script (by Jo Heims, who also wrote *Play Misty For Me*) and direction clearly chart the many obstacles facing the pair in terms of age, background, ideals and so on. It's performed beautifully, laced with a quietly ironic wit, and quite lovely to look at. GA

Breve Vacanza, Una
see Brief Vacation, A

Brewster McCloud
(Robert Altman, 1970, US) Bud Cort, Sally Kellerman, Michael Murphy, Shelley Duvall, William Windom, Rene Auberjonois, Stacy Keach, John Schuck.
105 min.
Though it bears more than a few traces of the forced outrageousness that marked Doran William Cannon's previous screenplay, for Preminger's lamentable comedy *Skidoo*, Altman's unexpected follow-up to *M.A.S.H.* is pitched fairly successfully between escapist fantasy and satirical comment on the same. Cort is the Icarus figure attempting to become airborne in the Houston Astrodome, Kellerman the sort of guardian angel who appears to have wandered in from a Dennis Potter play, and Murphy the cop mulling connections between bird shit and murder. PT

Brewster's Millions
(Allan Dwan, 1945, US) Dennis O'Keefe, Helen Walker, Eddie 'Rochester' Anderson, June Havoc, Gail Patrick, Mischa Auer.
79 min. b/w.
The fifth adaptation of the perennial play about a young man (here an ex-GI, engagingly played by O'Keefe) who stands to inherit seven million dollars provided he can get rid of one million (in

secret, no giving it away) within a couple of months. No masterpiece but really quite inventive, it was one of three breathless farces directed by Dwan during the '40s (the other two, marginally superior, were *Up in Mabel's Room* and *Getting Gertie's Garter*). TM

Brewster's Millions
(Walter Hill, 1985, US) Richard Pryor, John Candy, Lonette McKee, Stephen Collins, Jerry Orbach, Pat Hingle, Hume Cronyn.
101 min.
Hill's first attempt at straight comedy is less than happy. Pryor is the pitcher for the Hackensack Bulls baseball team, suddenly left $300 million in a will. But he first has to spend 30 million in a month without revealing the wheeze and ending up with no assets. The ideas here aren't nearly up to the scratch that writers Herschel Weingrod and Timothy Harris established in *Trading Places*. That the story has been filmed successfully seven times previously might have sounded warning bells that a more modernist treatment was called for than simply updating the amount involved to take inflation into account. CPea

Bribe, The
(Robert Z Leonard, 1949, US) Robert Taylor, Ava Gardner, Charles Laughton, Vincent Price, John Hodiak.
98 min. b/w.
Price and Laughton make a formidable pair of heavies in this otherwise feeble thriller shot on a cheaply rigged-up corner of the MGM backlot. Taylor isn't up to moral dilemma as a US government agent sent to crack illicit aircraft engine trading in the Caribbean, yet tempted by a lucrative cash offer and the irresistible charm of café chanteuse Gardner. TJ

Bridal Path, The
(Frank Launder, 1959, GB) Bill Travers, Fiona Clyne, George Cole, Gordon Jackson, Dilys Laye, Duncan Macrae, Charlotte Mitchell, Bernadette O'Farrell.
95 min.
Travers donned a kilt and spruced up his braw bricht accent one more time for this Launder and Gilliat frolic (from a novel by Nigel Tranter), in which a cheery Hebridean islander, Ewan McEwan, is despatched to the mainland to search for a wife. Along the way, he gets himself mistaken for a notorious salmon poacher. In the end, however, he's allowed to marry his island sweetheart (Fiona Clyne), who turns out not to be his cousin after all (the island Elders had been worried about inbreeding). Everything's handled very decorously (this being 1959), but the jokes are a bit thin, and the Technicolor landscape (photographed by Arthur Ibbetson) is laid on rather thick. TJ

Bride, The
(Franc Roddam, 1985, GB) Sting, Jennifer Beals, Anthony Higgins, Clancy Brown, David Rappaport, Geraldine Page, Alexei Sayle, Quentin Crisp.
119 min.
A monster movie with a difference: Roddam's update of the classic *The Bride of Frankenstein* is not so much a movie, more a monster. Sting looks like he's smelt something rotten (the script?) as Baron Frankenstein, he with other people's bits in his mitts, a man determined to create the perfect bride for his less than perfect monster. Uncertain in tone, uneasy in conception, preposterous as a love story and possessing all the horror of an advert for Holsten Pils, this is perhaps the silliest film of the year. RR

Bride of Frankenstein, The
(James Whale, 1935, US) Boris Karloff, Colin Clive, Valerie Hobson, Ernest Thesiger, Elsa Lanchester, Una O'Connor, Dwight Frye.
80 min. b/w.
Tremendous sequel to Whale's own original, with a clever prologue between Byron and Mary Shelley setting the scene for the revival of both Frankenstein and his monster. Thereafter Thesiger's loony Dr Praetorius arrives on the scene, complete with miniaturised humans, and tries to persuade the good doctor to have another go at creating life, this time in the form of a female companion for Karloff. What distinguishes the film is less its horror content, which is admittedly low, than the macabre humour

and sense of parody. Strong on atmosphere, Gothic sets and expressionist camerawork, it is – along with *The Old Dark House*, Whale's most perfectly realised movie, a delight from start to finish. GA

Bride of Vengeance
(Mitchell Leisen, 1949, US) Paulette Goddard, John Lund, Macdonald Carey, Raymond Burr, John Sutton, Albert Dekker.
91 min. b/w.
In this poker-faced absurdity the Duke of Ferrara adopts the Zorro gambit, pretending to be a fop, so the Borgias won't suspect he means to fight them with the enormous cannon he's building in his cellar. This business of the cannon ('Jupiter') is the sort of dream one of Freud's more humorous patients might have made up, though it's of a piece with the extraordinary men's costumes, designed by Leisen himself; with the nude male statuary discreetly decorating the ducal estate; and with Paulette Goddard's demonstrations of passionate agitation, not least when she first claps eyes on Jupiter. Otherwise, Lucrezia and Cesare are on form ('Remove his tongue and an arm'), suggesting the idea of incest as clearly as Paramount would then permit. Traces of Leisen's intermittently fastidious directorial personality remain, though the notion of fastidious camp may be too paradoxical to sustain. BBa

Brides of Dracula, The
(Terence Fisher, 1960, GB) Peter Cushing, David Peel, Martita Hunt, Yvonne Monlaur, Miles Malleson, Mona Washbourne, Freda Jackson.
85 min.
Patchy but striking, and directed with Fisher's usual flair. Not really a sequel to Hammer's *Dracula*, since Christopher Lee refused to repeat his role, it has Peel as a youthful and somewhat pallid relative who is kept locked up (though thoughtfully provided with suitable victims) by a fond mamma, but escapes to get within biting distance of an academy for young ladies. Hunt (the mother) and Jackson (a crazed retainer) are fun. TM

Brides of Fu Manchu, The
(Don Sharp, 1966, GB) Christopher Lee, Douglas Wilmer, Marie Versini, Heinz Drache, Howard Marion Crawford, Tsai Chin.
91 min.
This was the second of the two movies that the talented Sharp made for producer Harry Alan Towers in the Fu Manchu series, based on Sax Rohmer's vintage yellow bogeyman. Although nothing like as stylish as its predecessor, *The Face of Fu Manchu*, it manages to get quite a lot of fun out of a Bondish plot in which the evil doctor (played with as much sinister menace as ever by Christopher Lee) kidnaps a dozen girls so as to force key relatives to develop a deadly new energy ray. DP

Bride Wore Black, The
(La Mariée était en Noir)
(François Truffaut, 1967, Fr/It) Jeanne Moreau, Claude Rich, Jean-Claude Brialy, Michel Bouquet, Michel Lonsdale, Charles Denner, Daniel Boulanger, Alexandra Stewart.
107 min.
Truffaut has stated that this elegant detective thriller, based (like his *Mississippi Mermaid*) on a novel by Cornell Woolrich, was an attempt to reconcile his two cinematic idols, Alfred Hitchcock and Jean Renoir. It's about Julie Kohler (Moreau), whose husband is inexplicably shot dead on the church steps after their wedding. Truffaut follows Julie's systematic and deadly revenge with a light, idyllic style as she ruthlessly hunts and kills her victims (by methods which include pushing the first over a balcony, poisoning the next, and suffocating the third). Perhaps the mixture of crime fiction and Renoir never quite jells, but it's all highly entertaining, and Hitchcock buffs will enjoy picking out the many echoes (of *Marnie* especially). DP

Bridge, The
(Sydney MacCartney, 1990, GB) Saskia Reeves, David O'Hara, Joss Ackland, Rosemary Harris, Anthony Higgins, Geraldine James.
102 min.
Another of those parasol and starched linen Vic-

wardian costumers of TV drama dimensions, this time the account of an impossible romantic liaison between a beautiful and sensitive married mother (Reeves) and the youthful Impressionist painter Philip Wilson Steer (O'Hara). Based on the novel by Maggie Hemingway, the film takes its mood from a Steer painting: an enigmatic depiction of a lone woman on a remote Suffolk bridge. Despite being well acted (especially by Reeves), well scripted, finely shot by David Tattersall, and directed with discretion and sensitivity, the result is enervatingly familiar and too tastefully corseted in propriety to arouse the least passion. The working classes, of course, are the ones who don't have sunlight artistically highlighting their despairing faces. WH

Bridge at Remagen, The

(John Guillermin, 1968, US) George Segal, Robert Vaughn, Ben Gazzara, Bradford Dillman, EG Marshall, Peter Van Eyck, Matt Clark.
116 min.
Cliché runs riot in this WWII yarn, where much ado about a bridge that nobody wants spells that old war-is-madness message trumpeted by *The Bridge on the River Kwai*. Segal, Gazzara and some fine camerawork by Stanley Cortez more or less save the day. TM

Bridge on the River Kwai, The [100]

(David Lean, 1957, GB) William Holden, Alec Guinness, Jack Hawkins, Sessue Hayakawa, James Donald, Andre Morell.
161 min.
A classic example of a film that fudges the issues it raises: Guinness restores the morale of British PoWs by building a bridge which it transpires is of military value to the Japanese, and then attempts to thwart Hawkins and Holden's destruction of it – or does he? etc. The film's success also marked the end of Lean as a director and the beginnings of American-financed 'British' films. PH

Bridges at Toko-Ri, The

(Mark Robson, 1954, US) William Holden, Grace Kelly, Fredric March, Mickey Rooney, Robert Strauss, Charles McGraw, Earl Holliman.
103 min.
Big-budget adaptation of James Michener's Korean war novel, making some noises about the essential futility of the conflict but concluding that the bridges must be bombed to stop the spread of Communism. Competent, well acted and with some excellent aerial special effects, but flawed by mawkish sentimentality in orchestrating its nobility of self-sacrifice theme. Holden is the WWII pilot, now married and established in a civilian career, who resents being recalled to risk his life in a forgotten war; Rooney (sporting a non-regulation green silk topper) and Strauss are on hand to provide the other-ranks humour. TM

Bridges of Madison County, The

(Clint Eastwood, 1995, US) Clint Eastwood, Meryl Streep, Annie Corley, Victor Slezak, Jim Haynie.
135 min.
When the daughter and son of the late Francesca Johnson (Streep) return home to Madison County, Iowa, to oversee the funeral arrangements, they're shocked to learn that their mother wished to have her ashes scattered from the Roseman Bridge, not buried beside their father. Worse, they find Francesca's diary, relating how, in '65 while they were off with dad on a visit to Illinois, she met and fell for *National Geographic* photographer Robert Kincaid (Eastwood): an affair which was to affect her entire life. Immaculately performed, and assembled with wit and sensitivity, this is one of the most satisfying weepies in years. Indeed, it's hard to imagine anyone but Eastwood doing such a fine job of adapting Robert James Waller's best-seller for the screen. Typically, his clean, pared direction, coupled with Richard LaGravenese's mostly no-frills script, ensures that the film avoids sentimentality even as the two lovers rush to embrace it. GA

Bridge Too Far, A

(Richard Attenborough, 1977, GB) Dirk Bogarde, James Caan, Michael Caine, Sean Connery, Edward Fox, Elliott Gould, Gene Hackman, Anthony Hopkins, Laurence Olivier, Robert Redford.
175 min.
Attenborough's trumpeted entry into the all-time blockbuster stakes (based on the book by Cornelius Ryan) is noisy and protracted and has a name cast list as long as your arm. Bogarde, as the ranking officer-actor, presides over the execution of Montgomery's bold plan to seize six Dutch bridges. It turns out to be an overworked, very old and very tired warhorse. Glossy, ponderous, predictable. JPy

Brief Ecstasy

(Edmond T Gréville, 1937, GB) Paul Lukas, Linden Travers, Hugh Williams, Marie Ney, Renee Gadd.
71 min. b/w.
A remarkable film, thematically not dissimilar to *Brief Encounter*, except that lust is given a fair crack of the whip. A strong erotic undertow runs through the witty opening scene: in the exchange of covert glances as Williams comes into a snack bar where Travers is having coffee; in the 'accidental' pawing of her person as he mops the coffee he has spilt; in the over-pitched fury with which she slaps him. His subsequent apology accepted, a superb montage (soft music, silhouettes, champagne, whispered exchanges) heralds a brief night of ecstasy, after which he announces his imminent departure for India. Five years later, he returns to find her the beloved wife of a distinguished, much older scientist (Lukas), and desire is reborn. The excellent script plays fair by all the characters (one scene has Lukas start skipping gaily upstairs to bed in his wife's wake, only to pause, puffing, before he makes it). And Travers' inner struggle, no becoming yes then no again as she realises what she means to her husband, is beautifully detailed in both performance and Gréville's expressionist-tinged direction, which makes it clear that her choice of love is made at the bitter cost of the other thing. TM

Brief Encounter

(David Lean, 1945, GB) Celia Johnson, Trevor Howard, Stanley Holloway, Joyce Carey, Cyril Raymond, Valentine Dyall.
86 min. b/w.
Much beloved, but still exemplary in demonstrating exactly what is wrong with so much of British cinema. OK, so after the war people weren't as quick to jump into bed with other people's spouses as they are now (or were before AIDS), nor were they as open about it. But the stiff-lipped restraint that marks and mars this piece about mild extra-marital petting pertains not merely to the depiction of physical attraction and activity but, more importantly, to the emotions. Much ado about nothing, really, with a classy veneer of sugary romanticism added in the use of Rachmaninov on the soundtrack. GA

Brief Vacation, A (Una Breve Vacanza)

(Vittorio De Sica, 1973, It/Sp) Florinda Bolkan, Renato Salvatori, Daniel Quenaud, José Maria Prada, Teresa Gimpera.
112 min.
De Sica and Zavattini administer the last rites over the corpse of neo-realism in this travesty which starts with one of those vociferous Italian domestic squabbles, but soon switches to masturbatory fantasy with a gushy celebration of romance in a mountain TB sanatorium. Bolkan, as the working-class housewife drudging to feed a thankless family who is sent to the clinic at the government's expense, deserves better. TM

Brigadoon

(Vincente Minnelli, 1954, US) Gene Kelly, Van Johnson, Cyd Charisse, Elaine Stewart, Barry Jones, Hugh Laing.
108 min.
A classic – if not *the* classic – Minnelli musical, *Brigadoon* is an explicit statement about (and partial criticism of) the notion that an artist only lives through his art, preferring its reality to the world's. The film begins with a disenchanted Kelly in flight from 'civilised' New York, lost in

the Scottish Highlands and stumbling on the legendary village of Brigadoon which only appears for one day each century. There he meets the love of his life Fiona (Charisse), only to discover both the truth about Brigadoon and that some of its inhabitants want the real life he is fleeing from, even though it will destroy Brigadoon. Disillusioned when the villagers kill the would-be escapees, Kelly leaves. But in New York, amidst the chaos of modern living, he discovers he is yearning for Fiona and Brigadoon. He returns to Scotland where his faith (and Fiona's love) conjures up Brigadoon. This time he settles there, accepting that the price of happiness is to live but one day a century. As this description of the film makes clear, it (and Minnelli's musicals in general) is escapist to say the least. However, Minnelli's musicals must be seen alongside his dramas which examine the other side of the coin, the problems of confronting reality, rather than evading it or constructing one's own. PH

Brigand of Kandahar, The

(John Gilling, 1965, GB) Ronald Lewis, Oliver Reed, Yvonne Romain, Duncan Lamont, Glyn Houston, Catherine Woodville.
81 min.
Minor 'Cinema of Empire' episode from the erratic Gilling, who found his happiest niche with Hammer (who produced this) but in their horror mode. India in 1850 provides the backdrop (supposedly, at least, since papier mâché rocks and rural England are much in evidence) for a routine military adventure, with a half-caste officer (Lewis) facing court-martial for cowardice as the natives indicate their restlessness in time-honoured style. PT

Brigands

(Otar Iosseliani, 1996, Fr) Amiran Amiranachvili, Dato Gogibedachvili, Guio Tzintsadze, Nino Ordjonikidze.
128 min.
More properly, 'Brigands, Chapter VII', this mournful, over-long, virtually dialogue-free account of man's inhumanity to man cuts between the centuries, from the recent civil war in Georgia to medieval feuding and Stalinist torture chambers, using the same group of actors in each setting. The film's deadpan tone is eloquence itself, but there's no narrative momentum when everything is so clearly hopeless. TCh

Brigham Young – Frontiersman

(Henry Hathaway, 1940, US) Tyrone Power, Linda Darnell, Dean Jagger, Brian Donlevy, John Carradine, Jane Darwell, Mary Astor, Vincent Price.
114 min. b/w.
Jagger plays the title role of the 1840s Mormon leader who leads his flock all the way from Illinois to Utah, where they go on to found the teetotalling Salt Lake City. The wide-open Western epic style is somewhat diluted by the encroachment of soppy stuff between romantic leads Power and Darnell, but there is an amusing little scene in which a plague of crop-crunching locusts is devoured by gulls. Young's 17 wives were reduced, for reasons of propriety, to four. AB

Brighter Summer Day, A (Guling Jie Shaonian Sha Ren Shijian)

(Edward Yang, 1991, Tai) Zhang Zhen, Lisa Yang, Zhang Guozhu.
237 min.
Slow, elliptical, and for the most part understated, Yang's masterly account of growing up in Taiwan at the start of the '60s is as visually elegant as his own *Taipei Story* and *The Terroriser*, and as epic in scope as Hou Xiaoxian's *City of Sadness* (which Yang produced). On the surface, it's about one boy's involvement in gang rivalry and violence (on which level, it's often a little obscure, so numerous are the characters) and his experience of young love. On a deeper level, however, it's about a society in transition and in search of an identity, forever aware of its isolation from mainland China, and increasingly prey to Americanisation. The measured pace may be off-putting, but stay with it – the accumulated wealth of detail invests the unexpected final scenes with enormous, shocking power. GA

Bright Lights, Big City

(James Bridges, 1988, US) Michael J Fox, Kiefer Sutherland, Phoebe Cates, Swoosie Kurtz, Frances Sternhagen, Tracy Pollan, John Houseman, Jason Robards, Dianne Wiest.
107 min.

It's hard to care much about Jamie Conway, an aspiring novelist who is dissipating his substance in New York on cocaine and parties: Fox hasn't the range to play anguish, so the explanatory voice-over is less a survival from the best-selling novel than a necessity. Why is he doing this to himself? It's a cry for help, of course, and there's a lengthy monologue at a concerned colleague's apartment that brings any dramatic thrust to a stop. Jamie's wife (Cates) has left him, and his beloved mother (Wiest) has died of cancer, so he clings to bad influences like Tad the Lad (Sutherland). 'The Bolivian Marching Powder' finally gives him a nose-bleed, which forces him to take stock of his soul, and in a risible piece of symbolism, he trades his shades for a loaf of bread like Mother use to bake. Some telling cameos, however: Robards as a boozy bore who once hobnobbed with the greats of American Lit; Houseman as an etymological pedant; Wiest in a wonderfully moving death-bed scene. BC

Brightness

see Yeelen.

Brighton Beach Memoirs

(Gene Saks, 1986, US) Blythe Danner, Bob Dishy, Brian Drillinger, Stacey Glick, Judith Ivey, Jonathan Silverman.
110 min.

Neil Simon's autobiographical play, a Jewish *Dear Octopus*, makes for mildly diverting comedy in overexposed terrain. 15-year-old Eugene (Silverman) is the tour guide of his Brooklyn household, staring into the camera and commentating. His adolescent fantasies of sex and baseball are continually interrupted by his mother (Danner), who keeps him running errands. Danner does what she can with the stereotype between cooking, tidying and *kvetching*, while dad (Dishy) overworks, worries about Hitler, and denies that he's a saint. All social life revolves around the liver-and-cabbage, all unsocial life around the bathroom. All grievances come to a head dramatically, but blood is the rap you can't beat. BC

Brighton Rock

(John Boulting, 1947, GB) Richard Attenborough, Carol Marsh, Hermione Baddeley, William Hartnell, Harcourt Williams, Alan Wheatley.
92 min. b/w.

Thanks to a marvellous source in Graham Greene's novel, one of the finest British thrillers ever. Attenborough puts in his most memorable performance (with the possible exception of his Christie in *10 Rillington Place*) as Pinky, the psychopathic and murderous leader of a Brighton gang working the racetrack, who courts and marries a waitress (witness to one of his crimes) in order to keep her silent. Beautifully shot by Harry Waxman, it's perhaps the nearest thing to a British *noir* thriller, and as David Thomson has written, has the authentic 'tang of fish and chips'. And the ending is less a happy cop-out than a climax of superb irony. GA

Brighton Strangler, The

(Max Nosseck, 1945, US) John Loder, June Duprez, Michael St Angel, Miles Mander, Rose Hobart, Gilbert Emery, Rex Evans, Ian Wolfe.
67 min. b/w.

Good old amnesia gets a none too convincing outing as Loder, star of a play called *The Brighton Strangler* in London's West End, gets hit on the head when the theatre is bombed in an airraid on closing night, and revives – presumed killed – under the impression that he is the character he played for 300 performances. Ingenious plotting gets him to Brighton in circumstances similar enough to the play to keep him on the rails; and the script is ruthless enough to have him bring off a couple of garrottings before reality catches up with him. Nosseck keeps things moving along smoothly enough, despite an irritating penchant for little 'mood' montages (generally when Loder's mind stutters between fiction and reality); but the credibility quotient, already low, is not improved by studio sets and backdrops which make what is supposedly happening in real life look very much like theatrical artifice. TM

Brilliant Lies

(Richard Franklin, 1996, Aust) Gia Carides, Anthony LaPaglia, Zoe Carides, Ray Barrett, Michael Veitch.
94 min.

Franklin's adaptation of David Williamson's play about sexual harassment in the workplace is a huge improvement on his abysmal *Hotel Sorrento*, but still suffers from staginess. Centred on the accusations of flirty, money-grabbing Gia Carides against slimy, misogynist boss LaPaglia, the script delves into a range of heavily conflicting attitudes (to sexual politics, family relationships, honesty, ethics), remaining sensitive throughout to male paranoia and female resentment. Motivation and resolution, finally, are a little pat, but the sturdy performances flesh out the schematic scenario and, clumsy flashbacks aside, Franklin directs with a fair sense of irony and immediacy. GA

Brimstone and Treacle

(Richard Loncraine, 1982, GB) Sting, Denholm Elliott, Joan Plowright, Suzanna Hamilton, Benjamin Whitrow, Dudley Sutton.
87 min.

Into the musty atmosphere of the Bates' suburban household comes incubus/angel figure Martin Taylor (a pleasing performance from Sting in a role which conveniently requires the star to be *seen* to be acting). Posing as a friend of their recently brain-damaged child, the narcissistic Taylor charms the prayer-trusting, light-brained mother (Plowright) and challenges the lustfully guilt-ridden father (Elliott), while doing dirty deeds to their daughter in the front room. The quality and ambiguities of good and evil get a thorough, if predictable going-over as Taylor manoeuvres around the parents like a clay-footed Pan. Betrayed by an over-familiar plotline (Orton's *Entertaining Mr Sloane* and Pasolini's *Theorem* for a start) it also suffers from a mild case of stagebounditis as a TV play transferred to the big screen. Otherwise very watchable, thanks to a trio of superb performances, and confident, well-paced direction which only goes overboard in the fantasy sequences. FL

Bringing Up Baby [100]

(Howard Hawks, 1938, US) Cary Grant, Katharine Hepburn, Charles Ruggles, May Robson, Barry Fitzgerald, Walter Catlett.
102 min. b/w.

One of the finest screwball comedies ever, with Grant – a dry, nervous, conventional palaeontologist – meeting up with madcap socialite Hepburn and undergoing the destruction of his career, marriage, sanity and sexual identity. The catalyst in the process is Baby, a leopard that causes chaos wherever he goes, and finally awakens Grant to the attractions of irresponsible insanity. Fast, furious and very, very funny. GA

Bring Me the Head of Alfredo Garcia

(Sam Peckinpah, 1974, US/Mex) Warren Oates, Isela Vega, Gig Young, Robert Webber, Helmut Dantine, Emilio Fernandez, Kris Kristofferson.
112 min.

After the deathwish of *Pat Garrett and Billy the Kid*, it's logical that the spirit of a dead man should dominate its successor. And for a director so preoccupied with male virility, it's hardly surprising that Peckinpah has made a film primarily about impotence: Oates, a washed-up American barroom pianist, hunts for the head of the stud Garcia and for his own machismo through a contemporary Mexico that reflects Peckinpah's continuing love affair with that country. There's no suspense; what happens is as predictable as it is inevitable. Peckinpah has structured a slow, almost meditative film out of carefully fashioned images that weave inextricable links between sex, death, music and violence. CPe

Bring Me the Head of Mavis Davis

(John Henderson, 1997, GB) Rik Mayall, Jane Horrocks, Danny John-Miles Pickup, Philip Martin-Brown, Heathcote Williams.
99 min.

Marty Starr (Mayall) is a bullying record producer. In 1980, Marty discovered mousy Mavis Davis (Horrocks), and threw her back to the world as glamorous Marla Dorland. Now he's in trouble: Marla's sales aren't flourishing and she wants out of the contract. But debt-ridden, disaster-prone Marty has a plan: an early death would be the perfect end to Marla's career, and the rebirth of his. Horrocks seems unaware that this is not some ditzy ad, but the unforgiving big screen; her warbling is neither bad enough to be entertaining, nor good enough to engross. As for Mayall, he never stops being Mayall, and thus deserves every cheap line he gets. The sterling presence of Aiello as a mobster only adds to the embarrassing sense of resources being frenetically whooshed down the drain. CO'Su

Bring On the Night

(Michael Apted, 1985, US) Sting, Omar Hakim, Darryl Jones, Kenny Kirkland, Branford Marsalis, Miles Copeland.
97 min.

One of the more intelligent, slick and witty shots at the bronzed, big-named rockumentary. Tracing the 'Dream of the Blue Turtles' live project from press conference through rehearsals to the first night in Paris, we get about two-thirds music and one-third chat, both elements varying greatly in quality. Sting, though central, is seldom as colourful or revealing as jazz-rooted band members Marsalis, Kirkland or Hakim. Things are also a little too clean and easy throughout, but then there's always the music – never jazz, of course, but at its best tuneful, highly politicised rock in the hands of some of the most talented musicians in the world. SGa

Brink of Hell

see Toward the Unknown

Brink's Job, The

(William Friedkin, 1978, US) Peter Falk, Peter Boyle, Allen Garfield, Warren Oates, Gena Rowlands, Paul Sorvino.
103 min.

Despite Friedkin's strong track record – *The French Connection*, *The Exorcist* – this is a comedy thriller as lacking in skill, direction or wit as it's possible to imagine. Falk, as the leader of a gang of fools engaged in a multi-million dollar heist, hams his way anxiously through a plot full of childish hiccups, with only Warren Oates (as a weak, tormented accomplice) injecting even a minimum of conviction. CA

Britannia Hospital

(Lindsay Anderson, 1982, GB) Leonard Rossiter, Graham Crowden, Joan Plowright, Jill Bennett, Marsha Hunt, Malcolm McDowell, Fulton Mackay.
116 min.

It's not merely the rather obvious and all-embracing metaphor of a chaotic and run-down hospital standing in for Britain that is the problem with Anderson's vitriolic attempt at a comedy on the state of the nation; what is perhaps more annoying, finally, is his general tone, that of a cynical old sourpuss with an enormous chip on his shoulder and little – if any – sympathy for anybody. As the caricatures of authoritarians, strikers, media hacks and so on go through the nightmarish events surrounding a royal visit to the hospital on its 500th anniversary, one can't help feeling that so much contempt on the director's part only hides a lack of commitment and focus; the result is less neo-Swiftian satire than a 'Carry On Down the Drain, Britain' with pretensions to deep significance. GA

British Sounds

(Jean-Luc Godard, 1969, GB)
52 min.

The film that was made for and then banned from London Weekend TV. Essentially a documentary, it's a genuine political artefact in which Godard contrives to assault the British sensibility with a series of images and provocations (the slogans flashed on the screen are sometimes humorous and always to the point). The parts where people just talk really work; when Ford Dagenham workers discuss the company-employee situation, the effect is simple and uncluttered but devastatingly effective. Sometimes, however, the control vanishes – the sequence with Essex students making posters, for instance – and this confirms the impression that revolution in Britain will only come from the industrial army who need it, not the middle class academics who play it. TE

Broadcast News

(James L Brooks, 1987, US) William Hurt, Albert Brooks, Holly Hunter, Jack Nicholson, Robert Prosky, Lois Chiles, Joan Cusack, Peter Hackes.
132 min.
Writer/director Brooks is knowing about the wisecracks, back-stabbings, political shifts, and innate decencies of the media game, and underpinning what is a charming, protean love-triangle is a serious statement about the function, value, and direction of television news. Aaron Altman (Albert Brooks) is brave, decent, witty, committed, and hopelessly in love with his Mensa-plus producer Jane Craig (Hunter, magnificent), a skilful but personally unfulfilled member of their Washington bureau. Enter Hurt's Tom Grunick, irresistable to women and station executives alike. Aaron is exceptional, but Tom has the looks and presentation to please corporate media America. He just can't grasp or weigh facts. So who gets the jobs, and who gets Jane? Brooks' script has some superb set pieces, crackles with furious one-liners, and mirrors fact. Though a little soft-centred, and closing with a too open-ended postscript, it confirms all the camaraderies and care beyond and behind the pressures and pratfalls, and manages to knock rivals in Yuppie-tography like *Wall Street* and *Fatal Attraction* sideways. SGr

Broadway

(William A Seiter, 1942, US) George Raft, Pat O'Brien, Janet Blair, Broderick Crawford, Marjorie Rambeau, SZ Sakall.
91 min. b/w.
The George Abbott and Philip Dunning play (first filmed by Paul Fejos in 1929) reshaped as a vehicle for Raft who, playing himself, recalls his days as a nightclub dancer and his association with Prohibition racketeers. He gets to tango and to tangle with a tough gangster (Crawford) over his girl. But studded with songs and all a bit hackneyed, it's more a curiosity than anything else. TM

Broadway Bill (aka Strictly Confidential)

(Frank Capra, 1934, US) Warner Baxter, Myrna Loy, Walter Connolly, Helen Vinson, Douglas Dumbrille, Raymond Walburn, Lynne Overman, Clarence Muse, Margaret Hamilton, Frankie Darro, Ward Bond.
104 min. b/w.
Scripted by Robert Riskin from a story by Mark Hellinger, this is an early sample of Capracorn, with Connolly as a tyrannical tycoon who uses his three sons-in-law as yes men. One of the three (Baxter) rebels, tells Connolly he is a shark preying on small businesses, and goes back to his earlier life on the racetrack, hoping to make a champion of his horse Broadway Bill. His wife (Vinson) turns her back on him, but her rebellious younger sister (Loy) delightedly abets him. Complications ensue, since the horse won't run unless its rooster pal is on hand, conmanship is required to raise the Derby entrance fee, and the fix proves to be on. Gallant Broadway Bill nevertheless wins (though his heart bursts with the effort), justifying the faith of all the small-time punters who had bet on him. Baxter is consoled by his realisation that Loy loves him, and the chastened Connolly (surprise, surprise) gives his empire back to the little people. Ethically dubious and mostly tedious, it was remade by Capra as *Riding High* in 1950, re-using some of the racetrack footage. TM

Broadway Bound

(Paul Bogart, 1991, US) Anne Bancroft, Hume Cronyn, Corey Parker, Jonathan Silverman, Jerry Orbach, Michele Lee, Marilyn Cooper.
94 min.
Made as a TV movie, the last part of Neil Simon's autobiographical trilogy – following *Brighton Beach Memoirs* and *Biloxi Blues* – is also the nadir. All together now – let my people go! This Jewish family seems to have been with us as long as the Archers, with Momma (Bancroft) cooking, Poppa (Orbach) kvetching, Granddad (Cronyn) complaining, the boys (Parker and Silverman) spoiled and getting ahead, and typicality ruling unchallenged for the first half. A little drama is injected when the boys, trying out as radio script writers, put their own family on the air, which pisses off Poppa in a big way. Momma and Poppa and the boys go their separate ways; Momma

remembers dancing as a teenager with George Raft. That's it. Bancroft does her considerable best with a squashy role, but the marvellous Cronyn is stuck with an unbudgeable garden gnome. Barely endurable. BC

Broadway Danny Rose

(Woody Allen, 1984, US) Woody Allen, Mia Farrow, Nick Apollo Forte, Sandy Baron, Corbett Monica, Jackie Gayle, Morty Gunty, Milton Berle.
84 min. b/w.
Admittedly slighter than its immediate predecessor *Zelig*, this is still a delightful comedy that sees Allen as a no-hope theatrical agent (his clients include balloon twisters, wine-glass players and bird trainers, who *all* leave him when the Big Time beckons) who acts as beard for an adulterous, unmusical crooner on his books, and gets involved with a brassy Mafia widow (Farrow, unrecognisable). The jokes are firmly embedded in plot and characterisation, and the film, shot by Gordon Willis in harsh black-and-white, looks terrific; but what makes it work so well is the unsentimental warmth pervading every frame. GA

Broadway Melody of 1936

(Roy Del Ruth, 1935, US) Eleanor Powell, Robert Taylor, Jack Benny, Una Merkel, Sid Silvers, Buddy Ebsen, Vilma Ebsen.
102 min. b/w.
'She put 'em down like a man, no ricky-ticky-sissy stuff with Ellie,' Fred Astaire once observed of Eleanor Powell, a dancer he admired enormously. She blazes through this otherwise routine (if very luxurious) MGM musical. Moss Hart's contrived story (unaccountably nominated for an Oscar) casts her as a struggling actress who pretends to be a famous French star in order to land the plum role in Robert Taylor's forthcoming Broadway extravaganza. Comedian Jack Benny, in a role modelled on newsman Walter Winchell, plays a columnist with a grudge against Taylor. And yes, as always in these backstage musicals, everything comes right on the night. GM

Broken Arrow

(Delmer Daves, 1950, US) James Stewart, Jeff Chandler, Debra Paget, Will Geer, Jay Silverheels, Arthur Hunnicutt.
93 min.
The Western that launched the be-nice-to-the-Indian cycle of the '50s now looks a little on the self-consciously liberal side, making something of a meal of its plea for racial tolerance and peaceful coexistence, as Stewart's army scout and Chandler's Cochise strive to bring peace to the Apache. A little awkward, too, in its bows to convention while trying to present an authentic picture of the Indian way of life (lots of Apache extras, but the leads are played by white actors; the Apache language rendered into 'poetic' English). A fine film all the same, despite the compromised ending, quite beautifully shot by Ernest Palmer. TM

Broken Arrow

(John Woo, 1996, US) John Travolta, Christian Slater, Samantha Mathis, Delroy Lindo, Bob Gunton, Frank Whaley, Howie Long.
86 min.
There are no rough edges in Woo's second Hollywood outing. Working with more money than on his first (the unhappy *Hard Target*), a better cast and a script by Graham Yost (*Speed*), the director has fashioned a high-powered, streamlined, comfortably ludicrous entertainment in which bomber pilots Travolta and Slater go *mano-a-mano* in the Arizona desert, with two hot nuclear warheads between them. If movies were censored for implausiblility, this would be deemed unfit for public viewing. It's incredible in both senses of the word. You're never bored in a Woo movie: he's the kind of stylist who does everything to the max. Mostly what he does is action, and this script is tailor-made: a series of superb set-pieces in which a nuclear explosion is far from the climax. If the movie feels more callous than *Speed*, that's partly because Slater and spunky park ranger Mathis lack the warmth of Reeves and Bullock, but the charismatically crazy Travolta has the measure of it. This is just what Hollywood wanted of John Woo: more bang for the buck. The scary part is, where does he go from here? TCh

Broken Arrow 29

(Dina Hecht, 1986, GB) The people of Palomares and Villaricos.
72 min.
In January 1966, a US B-52 carrying four nuclear bombs crashed near the Spanish villages of Palomares and Villaricos. Dina Hecht returned to the scene of the crime and subsequent cover-up twenty years later, using a classified US Defence Department report as her guide. Though the Americans don't come up smelling like anything particularly fragrant (despite some archive footage showing the former US ambassador bathing in the now 'decontaminated' sea), Hecht does not engage in a melodramatic plutonium slinging match. Most interesting is her examination of the local politicians and their use of the incident, the small seaside villages serving as a microcosm of the national government's inability – and seeming lack of real desire – to effect change in Spain. SGo

Broken Blossoms

(DW Griffith, 1919, US) Lillian Gish, Richard Barthelmess, Donald Crisp, Arthur Howard, Edward Peil, George Beranger, Norman Selby.
6,013 ft. b/w.
There is a marvellous moment when Barthelmess, as the gentle Chinese who offers Gish shelter from her brutal father, gathers an imaginary spray of moondust to sprinkle on her hair as she huddles in bed. But for all that he is making a fervent plea for tolerance, Griffith is careful to let the hint of romance go no further: miscegenation has no place in his hoarily traditional melodrama of waifs and strays and the villains who make them so. This is in fact Griffith at his best and worst. On the debit side, some risibly highfalutin titles, some naive attempts to impose wider contexts on what is essentially a fragile short story (already stretched dangerously thin) and a monotonously simplistic view of the drunken prizefighter father's brutality. Very much on the credit side, though, are stretches of pure Griffith poetry, marvellous use of light and shadow in cameraman Billy Bitzer's evocation of foggy Limehouse, and a truly unforgettable performance from Gish. TM

Broken Blossoms

(John Brahm, 1936, GB) Dolly Haas, Emlyn Williams, Arthur Margetson, Gibb McLaughlin, Donald Calthrop, Ernest Sefton, Jerry Verno.
78 min. b/w.
A pale shadow of Griffith's film, with Haas struggling vainly to emulate the limpid Lillian Gish, and Williams (who also scripted) coming a ludicrous cropper compared to the marvellously expressive passivity of Richard Barthelmess' Chinaman. With no performances to speak of, the whole rickety structure collapses like a pricked balloon. Very pleasing to the eye, all the same, with Brahm giving the whole thing a moody veneer of UFA expressionism. TM

Broken Branches (Naeil ui Hyahae Hurunun Kang)

(Park Jae-Ho, 1995, SKor) Kim Ye-Ryung, Lee Hong-Sung, Lee Dae-Yun, Lee In-Chul, An Hae-Sook.
96 min.
The first 'gay movie' ever made in Korea, a country more homophobic than most, spans the years from 1955 to the present, rhyming the country's social and political changes with the fortunes of one extended family. Each of the three chapters marks a phase in the breakdown of the traditional Confucian-patriarchal family; the tone gradually shifts from tragedy to comedy. Most attention has been focused on the third chapter, in which the narrator comes out as gay and describes the joys and miseries of his affair with a married man. Let down by some dodgy performances in minor roles and some spasms of melodrama, but the overall scope is impressive for an indie feature – and the candour and sincerity are piercing. TR

Broken Butterfly

see Butterfly

Broken English

(Gregor Nicholas, 1996, NZ) Rade Serbedzija, Aleksandra Vujcic, Julian Arahanga, Marton Csokas, Madeline McNamara.
92 min.

An ethnic drama set in Auckland: violent Croatian immigrant (Serbedzija) is unhappy when daughter Nina (Aleksandra Vujcic, overflowing with sensual vitality) falls for fellow restaurant worker Eddie (Arahanga). Eddie, a Maori, hot foots it home; Nina's battened in her room. The future looks grim. This first feature is prone to over-emphatic contrasts: from the Croatians' Independence Day feast, for example, the camera travels to the Maori feast over the fence like an equal opportunities arbiter. And stylistically, there's an element of schizophrenia: painting a kinetic ad-style gloss over sombre realism tends to trivialise the director's evident concern to escape the confines of conventional drama. That said, the film gets by on its energy and self-belief. Arahanga has an easy, uningratiating charm, and Serbedzija, a bit of a cartoon bastard as written, gives a discomforting power to his role. (The music includes so-called 'Croatian Barbecue Songs' and work from the Taokotaianga Cultural Group.) WH

Broken Glass

(David Thacker, 1996, GB) Mandy Patinkin, Henry Goodman, Margot Leicester, Elizabeth McGovern, Julia Swift, Ed Bishop.
96 min.
Arthur Miller's greatest work may be well behind him, but this strikes with the dramatic power of a sledgehammer. Young Vic director David Thacker and playwright David Holman (the co-adaptors) have made a gripping movie out of the play. The troubled matter of Jewish identity is the subject, and the ramifications take in everything from society to marriage. Sylvia (Leicester) reads about Nazi Party attacks on Jews in Berlin and is struck down with hysterical paralysis. Her husband Gellburg (Goodman) sends for a specialist (Patinkin) who begins to uncover the unlovely facts about their marriage, a union entered into for everyone's sake but hers. Fear has brought them to this state and, thanks to faultless playing and exemplary writing, the tragedy becomes universal. BC

Broken Harvest

(Maurice O'Callaghan, 1994, Ire) Colin Lane, Marian Quinn, Niall O'Brien, Darren McHugh.
97 min.
A lyrical but relatively unsentimental tale of the tensions that beset Ireland for years after the Civil War. Focused on local rivalries, particularly between two men who fell out over a woman and over political differences, the film is good on the conflicting impulses of hating and forgiving, forgetting and remembering, but less certain in its execution: visuals, editing and story are a shade obvious, the acting a little unsure. GA

Broken Lance

(Edward Dmytryk, 1954, US) Spencer Tracy, Robert Wagner, Jean Peters, Richard Widmark, Katy Jurado, Earl Holliman, Hugh O'Brien.
96 min.
Internecine family struggles, hijacked from Mankiewicz's excellent House of Strangers to provide a gripping if hardly original Western. Tracy is the Lear-like patriarch dismayed to discover that filial strife and betrayal is threatening his cattle empire. Strong performances, ably augmented by Joe McDonald's lovely 'Scope camerawork.

Broken Mirrors
(Gebroken Spiegels)

(Marleen Gorris, 1984, Neth) Lineke Rijxman, Henriette Tol, Edda Barends, Coby Stunnenberg, Carla Hardy.
116 min.
Humour, the currency of Dutch director Gorris' first feminist thriller, A Question of Silence, is exchanged in her second for the much darker coinage of horror. A murderer is at large: a well-dressed businessman who incarcerates his victims, chains and starves them, and documents their death amid their filth with instamatic snaps. Meanwhile, in another part of town, a woman joins a brothel. These two simple strands of plot come together within the film, and are united by a single theme: that women's suffering is basic to man's pleasure. A film directed by a duller dog than Gorris would remain just this: a bleak message wagged by a compelling tale. But Gorris' talent as a director is to mobilise ideas to grip an audience, with characters that fill us with com-

passion and respect and allow us to derive a guilty pleasure from this very special film about the ordinary pain of others. FD

Broken Noses

(Bruce Weber, 1987, US) Andy Minsker.
77 min. b/w & col.
Black-and-white pix of male models in Calvin Klein knickers – that's photographer Bruce Weber. Or is it? His first feature, an experimental documentary in mono and colour, breaks the mould. It follows boxing lightweight Andy Minsker, a ringer for Chet Baker, round Portland, Oregon: he talks to camera, engages parents and friends in tense, hearty conversation, and hangs out with his adopted gang, the tough kids he trains in his Mt Scott boxing club. Weber's eye is insistent and very subtle, and what emerges from a somewhat mawkish tale is deeply engaging. The unstable foundations of faux machismo gently rock his various encounters, and truth leaks out: his separated parents, for instance, unwittingly delineate a nasty family tableau from his youth when they get enthusiastic about the need for stern but fair discipline. Weber leaves joins showing and takes risks: a colour sequence of Minsker in a rose garden reluctantly reading from Richard II works against all odds. Throughout, the sounds of such as Gerry Mulligan, Julie London, and Chet Baker overlay these curiously tender images. TC

Bronco Billy

(Clint Eastwood, 1980, US) Clint Eastwood, Sondra Locke, Geoffrey Lewis, Scatman Crothers, Bill McKinney, Sam Bottoms, Dan Vadis, Sierra Pecheur, Woodrow Parfrey, Hank Worden.
119 min.
A disarming movie, standing somewhere between a comic, contemporary version of The Outlaw Josey Wales (bunch of no-hopers finding fulfilment together) and Frank Capra (good 'little people', runaway heiress, scheming Eastern bureaucrats). Basically, it's the charming tale of a New Jersey shoe-salesman who fantasises about being a cowboy, and takes a group of assorted weirdos on the road with a travelling show. Not a lot to it in terms of plot, but Eastwood manages to both undermine and celebrate his character's fantasy life, while offering a few gentle swipes at contemporary America (the Stars and Stripes tent sewn together by mental hospital inmates). Fragile, fresh, and miles away from his hard-nosed cop thrillers, it's the sort of film only he would, and could, make. GA

Bronco Bullfrog

(Barney Platts-Mills, 1970, GB) Del Walker, Anne Gooding, Sam Shepherd, Roy Haywood, Freda Shepherd.
86 min. b/w.
This healthy antidote to the 'classless' swinging '60s was made for £17,000, a major achievement in itself. What one least expects from the subject – the drift into aimless petty crime and misdemeanours of a trio of working class youths in London's East End – is the dominant mood of shyness that gives the film much of its effect. This can be attributed mainly to a cast of non-professionals unconcerned with showing off by 'acting', and to Platts -Mills' understated storyline and direction. Bronco Bullfrog's true subject is the mediocrity of British life, but at exactly the points where one begins to fear a customary excess of bathos, the film discovers its sense of humour. As such, its feelings are truer to its subject than later, more vaunted youth pictures like Quadrophenia. CPe

Bronx Tale, A

(Robert De Niro, 1993, US) Robert De Niro, Chazz Palminteri, Lillo Brancato, Francis Capra, Taral Hicks, Joe Pesci.
121 min.
De Niro takes a confident stab at familiar material in his first film as director. He plays an unassuming bus driver, a straight-arrow good father, appalled when son Calogero (Capra at 9, Brancato at 17) falls under the influence of local wiseguy Sonny. The first hour or so, set in 1960, is a delight. De Niro knows the flavour inside out. He gets the music right, the speech rhythms and the faces – and a largely unknown cast does wonders. Despite a charismatic performance from Chazz Palminteri (author of the play from which the

film is drawn), Sonny is, however, just too good to be true: a Mafia kingpin, who comes on more like a radical priest, steering young 'C' away from racism, sexism and guns. When the scene switches to 1968, problems become more pronounced: C falls for a black girl (Hicks), and has to chose between his crazy pals and his own heart. Not an unalloyed success, but the performances and youthful vigour make up for the somewhat clumsy structure. TCh

Bronx Warriors (1990 I Guerrieri del Bronx)

(Enzo G Castellari, 1982, It) Vic Morrow, Christopher Connolly, Fred Williamson, Mark Gregory, Stefania Girolami.
84 min.
Interleaving script pages from The Warriors and Escape from New York has proved a cheap departure for Italian schlock-merchants. Here, we're offered the Bronx of 1990, surrendered to the gangs, but now invaded by freelance psychopath Morrow, hired to liberate a runaway heiress (happily slumming as a biker's moll until kidnapped by rival sickies) from across the river, but more intent on wiping out all scummy life in his former habitat. Muddy, muddled and moronic: heavily censored ultra-violence, interval-style ice-cream score, insultingly perfunctory climax and all. Next from the Cinecittà carbon factory – Mad Mario 3?.PT

Brood, The

(David Cronenberg, 1979, Can) Oliver Reed, Samantha Eggar, Art Hindle, Cindy Hinds, Nuala Fitzgerald, Henry Beckman.
91 min.
Despite its protestations to the contrary, Cronenberg's films are epics of sexual anxiety boasting an almost Calvinistic focus on the human body as the centre of evil: a strain of sexual rabies in Rabid; slug-like parasites (curiously resembling faeces) in Shivers. In The Brood the threat seems initially more exterior (and so less threatening), with deranged patients from the sinister 'Institute of Psychoplasmics' on release, and small mutant murderers leaping out from behind doors and out of cupboards. But the source of the mayhem, it transpires, is Samantha Eggar, an improbably psychotic mother, busy unleashing hatred on her husband (and on Family Life generally). It's a strong theme, unfortunately undercut by faulty pacing and odd lapses in the tension. Still worth seeing for its latently political story and its gory special effects. CA

Brother and Sister
(Ani Imoto/aka Mon and Ino)

(Tadashi Imai, 1976, Jap) Kumiko Akiyoshi, Masao Kusakari, Kimiko Ikegami, Shuji Otaki, Natsuko Kahara.
98 min.
Refreshing to be given the opportunity to see a Japanese film that is neither 'high art', nor period dramatics or grinding social realism. Imai is not always in total control of his subject – the reaction of a Japanese family to the pregnancy of one of two unmarried daughters – but the directness and charm of his unassuming approach make this a film well worth seeing. Excellent performances, too, from Kahara as the mother, Akiyoshi and Ikegame as the sisters. VG

Brother, Can You Spare a Dime?

(Philippe Mora, 1975, GB)
109 min. b/w.
A maddening mixture, with fascinating material put to often questionable uses, this compilation film tries to chronicle the history of America from the Wall Street Crash to Pearl Harbor, using only contemporary newsreels and Hollywood features (without commentary) to tell the story. Extracts from movies are strung together to make James Cagney an all-purpose hero (setting jauntily out in life with his sweetheart, surviving the train crash wrought by King Kong, joining the queue of hungry unemployed, getting rich quick as a mobster, etc); meanwhile, newsreels offer starker visions of the Depression and the political manoeuvrings behind the scenes (including the insidious, fascistic appeal of 'a strong man to put things right'). Beautifully put together to the ironic accompaniment of songs from Bessie Smith,

Billie Holiday, Woody Guthrie and others, the film is highly entertaining but also highly specious. Not only because it misrepresents the material (dubbing new sound, deliberately blurring the distinction between fiction and newsreel), but because it imposes a frivolous, one-dimensional interpretation that often obscures the real implications of the period. TM

Brother from Another Planet, The

(John Sayles, 1984, US) Joe Morton, Tom Wright, Caroline Aaron, Herbert Newsome, Dee Dee Bridgewater, Darryl Edwards.
108 min.
A mute, black extra-terrestrial fetches up in Harlem to be greeted first with bewildered hostility, then with a certain casual friendliness. The slim, episodic, but thoroughly enjoyable story shoots off like a firework in numerous directions: droll comedy among a group of cheery, bleary barflies; unforced intimations of a streetwise messiah as Bro's peculiar powers put paid to a drugs ring; delicate insights into Harlem's social mores, wrapped up in unpretentious fashion without a trace of stereotyping. Central to the film's deft balancing act between shaggy dog humour and something just a little more serious is Morton's expressive performance as the alien, though the rest of the cast also plays admirably. GA

Brotherhood, The

(Martin Ritt, 1968, US) Kirk Douglas, Alex Cord, Irene Papas, Luther Adler, Susan Strasberg, Murray Hamilton, Eduardo Ciannelli, Joe De Santis.
98 min.
Douglas, dressed up in droopy moustache and dyed hair, plays a board member of the New York Syndicate who has nostalgic memories of how much better things were done in the old Mafia days. Not surprisingly, he falls foul of the syndicate, flees into retirement in Sicily, and confronts the man sent to kill him – none other than the younger brother (Cord) he raised with selfless devotion. Ritt can do very little with the breast-beating which attends this tale of brotherly love and self-sacrifice. It therefore wends its way, slowly and stolidly, to the bitter end, pausing to allow Luther Adler to brighten things up briefly as a plump, greasy and rather engaging stool pigeon-turned respectable. TM

Brotherly Love

see Country Dance

Brother Orchid

(Lloyd Bacon, 1940, US) Edward G Robinson, Ann Sothern, Humphrey Bogart, Donald Crisp, Ralph Bellamy, Allen Jenkins, Charles D Brown.
91 min. b/w.
Racketeer Robinson, Little John Sarto, takes time out from a life of crime, but when he returns to the fray, he discovers Bogart's now running the old gang and his presence is no longer required. Brother Superior Crisp's monastery provides unlikely sanctuary in this enjoyable, though not unpredictable star comedy made when Bogie's career hadn't yet peaked and he was still doing second-string roles, like tough Jack Buck here. TJ

Brothers and Sisters

(Richard Woolley, 1980, GB) Carolyn Pickles, Sam Dale, Robert East, Jennifer Armitage, Elizabeth Bennett.
101 min.
Prompted by the terrible murders of 'The Yorkshire Ripper' (and made before he was caught), this examination of contemporary sexual politics and violence is too simplistic by half. After a prostitute is murdered, two brothers (one apparently right wing, one left) are suspected, and the film investigates their attitudes towards women as police proceedings continue. Despite its obvious sincerity and ambitions, the film is wrecked by its half-hearted adherence to the thriller format (neither implicating its audience in the sadistic impulses behind voyeurism and film-watching, nor denying them that excitement by avoiding thriller-style scenes), by its schematic approach towards characterisation, and by its complacent sense

of male guilt, simply asserting (in too direct a way) that all men are responsible for violence towards women. GA

Brothers in Law

(Roy Boulting, 1956, GB) Ian Carmichael, Richard Attenborough, Terry-Thomas, Jill Adams, Miles Malleson, Irene Handl, John Le Mesurier, Leslie Phillips, Kenneth Griffith.
94 min. b/w.
This Boulting brothers comedy (from a novel by Henry Cecil) about the absurdities of the British legal system chugs along amiably but lacks real satirical bite. The usual gallery of eccentric British character actors are out in force (Malleson the absent-minded pupil master, Terry-Thomas the court-hardened swindler), giving their usual mannered but doughty performances. Carmichael is the innocent abroad, a newly qualified barrister exposed to the baffling rituals and bizarre antics of his peers. GM

Brothers in Trouble

(Udayan Prasad, 1995, GB) Om Puri, Angeline Ball, Pavan Malhotra, Pravesh Kumar, Ahsen Bhatti.
102 min.
Illegal Pakistani immigrants, packed into a London house in the 1960s, work non-stop in abysmal conditions to send paltry sums home to their families. The arrival of Mary (Ball, proving The Commitments was no fluke) introduces a spark of humanity into their miserable existence, but also ultimately destroys it. This over-long film, a BBC production with German and Italian backing, is at its best when concentrating on the relationship between the newest immigrant Amir (Malhotra) and the studious Sakib (Kumar), but the pace is uneven and the final scene badly misjudged. FM

Brothers Karamazov, The

(Richard Brooks, 1958, US) Yul Brynner, Claire Bloom, Richard Basehart, Lee J Cobb, Maria Schell, Albert Salmi, William Shatner.
146 min.
Painstaking attempt to reduce Dostoievsky's novel to manageable proportions, retaining most of the major episodes but contriving to miss the point – the tortuous quest for God – by giving one brother (Brynner) the star role whereas all four should contribute equally to the theme. Very uncertain in period and atmosphere, and saddled with some terrible performances. TM

Brothers Karamazov, The (Bratya Karamazovy)

(Ivan Pyriev, 1968, USSR) Mikhail Ulianov, Lionella Pyrieva, Kirill Lavrov, Andrei Myahkov, Marc Prudkin, Leonela Skirda.
220 min.
Given essentially theatrical performances, Dostoievsky's tale – of the tensions and ties between three sons of a divisive father –comes across as akin to Grand Soap Opera, while the brown-rich Soviet colour stock, the wooden buildings and the 19th century outfits lend an aura reminiscent of '50s Gothic Westerns. Most of the characters are delightfully sozzled, brooding deeply over thoughts of murderous passion or hopes of saintly redemption, and lamenting things like, 'Beauty is terrible! A clash of good and evil fought out on the battlefield of the human heart!' This refers to the effect good-time girl Grusha has on old Karamazov and his son Dimitri. It's Dimitri's jealousy, and his resentment at getting the short straw with an inheritance, that sparks tragic events. Through the misery these events bring, Dimitri and his two brothers are finally united – in guilt. And there's a twist! Overlong, but fun. WH

Brothers McMullen, The

(Edward Burns, 1995, US) Jack Mulcahy, Edward Burns, Mike McGlone, Connie Britton, Edward Burns, Maxine Bahns, Elizabeth P McKay.
108 min.
Burns' engaging first feature is a witty romantic comedy about God, sex and commitment in Long Island, New York. The brothers are: Jack (Mulcahy), happily married and about to fall into a reckless affair; Barry (Burns himself), a bachelor who may just have got the woman of his

dreams; and Patrick (McGlone), a devoutly Catholic graduate whose Jewish girlfriend has their whole future mapped out. Circumstances bring the three together again under one roof, where they pool their guilt, bafflement and indecision. Burns wrote and directed the film on a shoestring, but if his stamping ground is determinedly working-class Irish-American, the tone is closer to the gentle Uptown ironies of Woody Allen than to Hal Hartley or Jim Jarmusch. Macho pride is the font of most of the comedy, and it's only in the rather pat conclusion that the clan work out an uneasy rapprochement with their female partners. Burns is hardly the most innovative talent to have emerged this year, but he's found plenty of comic mileage in his own backyard. TCh

Brother Sun, Sister Moon (Fratello Sole, Sorella Luna)

(Franco Zeffirelli, 1972, It/GB) Graham Faulkner, Judi Bowker, Leigh Lawson, Kenneth Cranham, Lee Montague, Valentina Cortese, Alec Guinness.
122 min.
Hello flowers, hello sky: the life of St Francis of Assisi, viewed as a wimpy hippy by the unspeakably daft Zeffirelli, wandering through soft focus landscapes accompanied by the strains of Donovan. Avoid at all costs. GA

Browning Version, The

(Anthony Asquith, 1951, GB) Michael Redgrave, Jean Kent, Nigel Patrick, Ronald Howard, Wilfrid Hyde-White, Brian Smith.
90 min. b/w.
A careful adaptation of Terence Rattigan's play – in effect a re-run of Goodbye Mr Chips seen through dark-tinted glasses – which draws what little venom the original had by adding an absurdly sentimental coda. Worth watching for Redgrave's powerfully detailed performance as the schoolmaster who has masked his feelings of inadequacy by turning into a petty tyrant over the years, and whose facade is disastrously breached by a small act of kindness from one of the boys. But the rest of the characters are strictly cardboard. TM

Browning Version, The

(Mike Figgis, 1994, GB) Albert Finney, Greta Scacchi, Matthew Modine, Julian Sands, Bern Silverstone.
97 min.
Considered dispassionately, Figgis' lavish update of Terence Rattigan's play must be judged redundant, even meaningless, as an account of contemporary British manners. However much Ronald Harwood's screenplay tries to 'modernise' things, the story belongs inescapably to a different world with different social mores. That said, as Crocker-Harris, the buttoned-up classics teacher (Finney), faces an enforced retirement, not to mention rumours that his wife Laura (Scacchi) might be having an affair with his friend, the chemistry teacher Frank Hunter (Modine), the film contrives, despite its conspicuous faults, to work surprisingly well as a full-blown weepie. Most of the credit must go to Finney, whose quiet but overwhelmingly moving performance lends the film an emotional truth its heritage trimmings hardly deserve. GA

Brubaker

(Stuart Rosenberg, 1980, US) Robert Redford, Yaphet Kotto, Jane Alexander,Murray Hamilton, David Keith, Morgan Freeman.
130 min.
Redford is Brubaker, all gritty integrity and inner resolve as the new warden of a Southern prison farm, who arrives disguised as a prisoner so that he may better expose the mugging, raping and murdering cesspit he discovers. By its attribution of every evil to simple human greed, the melodrama remains hamfisted; while Rosenberg's direction (the original director, Bob Rafelson was fired for thumping the producer) signals 'realism' with crude denim-blue tints in every image. After two hours and ten minutes one is left only with a numbing awareness of Redford's charmless charm, the macho image unable (unlike Eastwood or Reynolds) to even contemplate self-irony. CA

Bruce Lee Story, The

see Dragon Dies Hard, The

Bruce Lee: The Man, The Myth (Li Xiaolong Chuanqi/aka Bruce Lee – True Story)

(Wu Szu-Yuen, 1976, HK) Bruce Li, Unicorn Chan, Liang Shao-Sung, Ch'en Chien-Po.
104 min.
Numbingly unimaginative and exploitative biography. Would you trust a film that opens on a '70s street scene and captions it 'Hong Kong 1958'?

Bruit qui rend fou, Un
see Blue Villa, The

Brute, The

(Gerry O'Hara, 1976, GB) Sarah Douglas, Julian Glover, Bruce Robinson, Jenny Twigge, Suzanne Stone, Peter Bull.
90 min.
Crazy collision of sensationalism and social concern makes this wife-battering study seem more like a horror movie – which is both endearing and disturbing. CW

Brute, The
see Bruto, El

Brute Force

(Jules Dassin, 1947, US) Burt Lancaster, Hume Cronyn, Charles Bickford, Sam Levene, Whit Bissell, John Hoyt, Art Smith, Howard Duff, Yvonne De Carlo, Ann Blyth, Ella Raines.
98 min. b/w.
Despite a loss of temperature through the flashbacks which let in some female interest, this is one of Dassin's best films. Less coherent than Siegel's *Riot in Cell Block 11* in its challenge to prison conditions, it draws on WWII experience to draw a powerful analogy between the prison (where Cronyn's sadistic chief guard beats up prisoners to the strains of Wagner) and a fascist state. With brutality breeding brutality in this world which the dialogue (script by Richard Brooks) defines as an existentialist hell from which there is no escape, *Brute Force* was a notably violent film in its day. The scene in which an informer is herded by blow-torches to execution in a steam press still chills. TM

Bruto, El (The Brute)

(Luis Buñuel, 1952, Mex) Pedro Armendariz, Katy Jurado,Rosita Arenas, Andres Soler.
83 min. b/w.
One of the fascinating melodramas Buñuel made during his early years in Mexico. The landlord of a block of tenements tries to throw his tenants out to make way for a luxurious new house for himself and his mistress. To implement this, he hires a 'strong and devoted' slaughterhouse worker, and talks him into eliminating the community's leading resisters. Unusually, the film concentrates not on the heroic resistance of the tenants but on El Bruto himself, and his growing awareness of the iniquities of the paternalistic order he is helping. Buñuel sharpens the political edge by having El Bruto discover that his boss is also his natural father. The images are powerful, not to say – in a nightime chase sequence – magnetic, and the character of the reliable worker-cum-hired 'brute', who discovers who his real enemies are, unforgettable.

Brutti, sporchi e cattivi (Ugly, Dirty and Bad/Ugly, Dirty and Mean/Down and Dirty)

(Ettore Scola, 1976, It) Nino Manfredi, Francesco Anniballi, Maria Bosco, Franco Merli, Ettore Garofolo, Alfredo D'Ippolito.
115 min.
Scola picked up the best director prize at Cannes for this grim comedy about a large, degenerate family living in a shanty town on the outskirts of Rome. Manfredi is the pathetic and monstrous one-eyed patriarch Giacinto, consumed with fear that his bundle of insurance money (a million lire!) will be stolen by his scheming relatives. They would too! Scola by no means romanticises the poor (drinking, thieving and copulation is about all they're interested in), but in this environment it's hard to see how it could be otherwise. Depressing

and funny at the same time: cross *Bicycle Thieves* and *Steptoe and Son* and you're in the right vicinity. TCh

Brylcreem Boys, The

(Terence Ryan, 1995, GB) Bill Campbell, William McNamara, Angus MacFadyen, John Gordon Sinclair, Gabriel Byrne, Jean Butler.
106 min.
WWII, neutral Ireland: German and Allied soldiers share the same prison camps. The potentially rewarding premise is wasted in a whimsical comedy that resorts to predictable plot twists and character development, to national stereotyping, and to the convention of having two guys on different sides fall for the same girl. Byrne does his best as the camp commander, but the dice are loaded. GA

BS I Love You

(Steven Hillard Stern, 1970, US) Peter Kastner, Joanna Cameron, Louise Sorel, Gary Burghoff, Joanna Barnes.
98 min.
'BS' is revealed during the credits to stand for 'bullshit', which is an indication of the desperately trendy nature of the film. Kastner, star of *You're a Big Boy Now*, plays a similar character a few years on, an adman beset by women. Some good gags, but forget it.

Buccaneer, The

(Anthony Quinn, 1958, US) Yul Brynner, Charlton Heston, Claire Bloom, Charles Boyer, Inger Stevens, EG Marshall, Henry Hull.
121 min.
Lavish spectacle produced for DeMille (who had directed his own version in 1938, and whose last production this was), misfiring lamely in its attempt to make swashbuckling entertainment out of the historical fact of pirate Jean Lafitte's patriotic assistance in fighting the Battle of New Orleans in 1815. Very stodgy. TM

Buchanan Rides Alone

(Budd Boetticher, 1958, US) Randolph Scott, Craig Stevens, Barry Kelley, Tol Avery, Peter Whitney, Manuel Rojas, LQ Jones, Joe De Santis, Roy Jenson.
78 min.
Randolph Scott rides into a small border town, becomes innocently involved in a killing (Mexican youth of wealthy family avenges the rape of his sister), and is escorted out again at gunpoint with his life spared but his money-belt emptied. Being Scott, he naturally turns right around to recover his money, in the process stoutly righting assorted wrongs without ever really knowing what is going on as Charles Lang's script drives with admirable lucidity through a morass of enigmatic loyalties and abruptly shifting partnerships, mainly involving the frenzied efforts of the three corrupt brothers who run the town to doublecross each other for profit by alternatively hanging, ransoming or kidnapping the Mexican youth. A minor film compared to *The Tall T* or *Ride Lonesome*, maybe, but foregrounding the poker-faced sense of absurdity that lurks never far below the surface through the entire Boetticher/Scott series, it is still a marvel of economical craftsmanship. TM

Buchi Neri
see Black Holes, The

Büchse der Pandora, Die
see Pandora's Box

Buck and the Preacher

(Sidney Poitier, 1971, US) Sidney Poitier, Harry Belafonte, Ruby Dee, Cameron Mitchell, Denny Miller, Nita Talbot.
103 min.
Poitier's first film as director has an excellent subject which is rather reminiscent of Ford's *Wagon Master*: the long, hard trek through the wilderness, harassed by marauding white nightriders all the way, of a group of Negro slaves freed after the end of the Civil War. It is pleasant enough, but somehow – despite excellent performances by Poitier (the intrepid wagonmaster) and Belafonte (a roguish preacher) – it never quite clicks. Nice, though, to see the Indians riding to the rescue instead of the Cavalry. TM

Bucket of Blood, A

(Roger Corman, 1959, US) Dick Miller, Barboura Morris, Anthony Carbone, Julian Burton, Ed Nelson, John Brinkley.
66 min. b/w.
Corman's first full-blooded horror comedy was put in a class of its own by Charles Griffith's unusually witty script. Walter, hapless waiter in a Greenwich Village hangout, yearns to be as famous as the poets and musicians he serves endless coffee to. After a lucky break (straight out of Poe), he begins to make it as a prolific sculptor of gruesome corpses...Not surprisingly, the parody of the 'beat scene' (including a hilarious caricature of Allen Ginsberg) is closer to the truth than those attempted in many mainstream movies.

Buck Rogers in the 25th Century

(Daniel Haller, 1979, US) Gil Gerard, Pamela Hensley, Erin Gray, Henry Silva, Tim O'Connor, Joseph Wiseman.
89 min.
The way space jock and cosmic smartass Buck Rogers does his thing, launched into the 25th century from 1987, the audience will soon twig that he's been deep-frozen for at least 30 years longer than the script lets on: his humour is pure *Playboy* 50s. Same for the sexual rivalry between Good and Bad: the competent but prudish Captain Wilma Deering ('Commander of the Earth's Defences') and languorous but evil Princess Ardala ('With a man like you, I could defy my father'). In homage to Buck's cartoon strip origins, blonde Deering wears crisp and manly uniform, while the dark Princess sports barbarian gear right out of *Conan* by *Barbarella*. At best, the formula works like vintage Bond (explicitly so in the title sequence). But too much time is wasted with stale *Star Wars* plagiarisms, including the screen's dullest robot. Better to have made more of the best urban gang for some time: nuclear mutants roaming what's left of Chicago. CR

Bucktown

(Arthur Marks, 1975, US) Fred Williamson, Pam Grier, Thalmus Rasulala, Tony King, Bernie Hamilton, Art Lund.
94 min.
Reactionary vengeance movie, blaxploitation style. Having effortlessly wiped out the entire corrupt white police department of Buchanan (known as Bucktown to the police grafters) to avenge his brother, Williamson's super ghetto-black Duke Johnson falls for the uncharacteristically simpering Pam Grier and opts for a life of macho domestic bliss. But not before he has disposed of all his former street buddies (who have taken over the graft) in a finale of massive retribution. JPy

Buddha Bless America (Taiping Tianguo)

(Wu Nianzhen, 1996, Tai) Lin Cheng-Sheng, Jiang Shuna, Yang Congxian.
125 min.
The second feature by Taiwan's pre-eminent scriptwriter is a wonderfully wry comedy with undertones of melancholy. In the late '60s, a remote village in southern Taiwan is chosen as the site for some US Army war games; the villagers, promised compensation for the damage to their homes and crops, are resettled in the schoolhouse while the smartest local entrepreneur builds a temporary nightclub to keeps the GIs entertained. Against the backdrop, the smartest guy in the community (played by Lin, himself a distinguished director) fights a losing battle to maintain his dignity and honour. Wise, worldly and only gently anti-American. TR

Buddha's Lock (Tian Pusa)

(Yim Ho, 1987, HK/China) John X Heart, Zhang Lutong, Yan Bide, Sun Feihu, Wei Zongwan, Steve Horowitz.
96 min.
This has a fascinating subject, based on fact: the arrest and enslavement of a crashed American airman by a backward tribe of the Yi people in central Sichuan during WWII. Unfortunately, it also has a script (by a Mainland Chinese writer) that has no real idea how to set up or develop characters, and constantly lets ethnographic elements get in the way of the narrative. The result is a strange

b

mixture of excellence and hopeless misjudgements, never quite strong enough to overcome the handicap of a weak performance from the main America actor. At its best, it plays like an early Herzog movie: an assault on the very concept of human dignity in primitive, elemental landscapes. TR

Buddies
(Arthur J Bressan Jr, 1985, US) Geoff Edholm, David Schachter, Billy Lux, David Rose, Libby Saines, Damon Hairston, Tracy Vivat.
79 min.
An angry film, but it's a quiet, calm, insistent kind of anger which is all the more effective for its undestatement. The action is based in New York, and set around a dying AIDS patient and his 'buddy', a voluntary counsellor/visitor sent by the local gay centre. Edholm acts with intensity and conviction as the dying man railing against a government and a system that rejects him; Schachter is weaker and less believable as his buddy, though he improves as the film progresses, until by the end, as he parades outside the White House, his character and commitment are fully realised. It's a clever film, a good campaigning and educational piece, moving, funny, depressing and yet ultimately uplifting in its acknowledgment that people were beginning to realise that something had to be done, and were willing to commit themselves to doing it. The US government is seen as the ultimate villain, and mankind as the victim of a problem which can only be fought by more research, action and government money. MG

Buddy Buddy
(Billy Wilder, 1981, US) Jack Lemmon, Walter Matthau, Paula Prentiss, Klaus Kinski, Dana Elcar, Miles Chapin.
96 min.
After failing to set the box-office on fire with such sublime achievements of the '70s as *The Private Life of Sherlock Holmes* and *Fedora*, Wilder was understandably playing safe this time around. One is therefore less inclined to condemn than to overlook this farce about a hardboiled hit man and the suicidal pest next door (previously filmed by Edouard Molinaro in 1973 as *L'Emmerdeur*). What makes it even easier to ignore is that it looks so little like a Wilder film. There is some byplay with doubles, disguises and mistaken identity, but the rest is all bland Panavision, dreary back projection, and laboured dialogue. RC

Buddy Holly Story, The
(Steve Rash, 1978, US) Gary Busey, Don Stroud, Charles Martin Smith, Conrad Janis, William Jordan, Maria Richwine.
114 min.
Fine biopic which showcases a brilliant performance by Busey as Holly, and conveys a real, raw feeling for the music. The opening sequence, for example – a roller-rink gig to a stunned Hicksville audience – was done 'live' and it shows. Streets ahead of most rock celluloid. CA

Buddy's Song
(Claude Whatham, 1990, GB) Roger Daltrey, Chesney Hawkes, Sharon Duce, Michael Elphick, Douglas Hodge, Paul McKenzie, James Aubrey, Liza Walker.
106 min.
Not quite a British musical, more a *Minder*-ish comedy-drama with songs. Daltrey plays Terry, a superannuated Teddy Boy ducking and diving on the fringes of the criminal world, who gets landed with some stolen property and ends up in jail. Meanwhile his wife Carol (Duce) decides to better herself by taking an interest in computers and having it off with her boss, leaving son Buddy (Hawkes) sufficiently perturbed to pick up a guitar and sing some New Town blues. Dad, now out of jail, wants to make him a star. Sadly, he's the all-time nightmare parent: he fails to resurrect his marriage, build a new life, or steer his boy's talents in the right direction. The usual teenage rock-band incidents pile up alarmingly, but Hawkes greets triumph and disaster alike with the same sullen depressed-adolescent expression (perhaps because the loathsome 'Lite Rock' songs he's been given make him sound like a secular Cliff Richard). Daltrey's central performance, on the other hand, is fearless and compelling. JMo

Buena Vida, La
see Good Life, The

Buenos Aires Vice Versa
(Alejandro Agresti, 1996, Arg) Vera Fogwill, Fernan Miras, Mirta Busnelli, Nicolas Pauls, Carlos Roffe.
122 min.
Agresti returned home from Europe to film this colourful, deceptively casual kaleidoscopic look at life in contemporary Buenos Aires: a city, as the various fragmented stories show, where the past – particularly in the form of absent (i.e. 'disappeared') families – exerts a strong, even tragic influence on the present. If that sounds heavy and obvious, the film has the same steadily intoxicating blend of passion and wit, romance and melancholy, meditation and vitality as the Astor Piazzolla tangos argued over in one café scene. And the characters, from a young woman hired to shoot a video of city life by a reclusive old couple, to a shunned woman who bellows at her ex when he's on the TV, and a kid who lives on the streets, are as engaging and easy to watch as the relaxed but vibrant camerawork. GA

Buffalo Bill and the Indians, or Sitting Bull's History Lesson
(Robert Altman, 1976, US) Paul Newman, Joel Grey, Burt Lancaster, Kevin McCarthy, Harvey Keitel, Allan Nichols, Geraldine Chaplin, Will Sampson.
123 min.
Altman's continuing fascination with the lunatic reality underlying America's popular myths finds an obvious subject in Buffalo Bill. William F Cody was a nonentity who utilised the heroic Western image of 'Buffalo Bill' to create a capitalist showbiz enterprise grossing a million a year. With typical fast-paced wit, Altman focuses on Cody's blinkered, scatter-brained retinue, contrasting their alcoholic self-deception with the mystical reality and strength of the Indians destroyed in their grand distortion of history. Some of it comes off well, and Newman is superb. But the film shows tiresome signs of its origins as a stage play (by Arthur Kopit), and the good moments aren't quite enough to make up for its overall predictability. DP

Buffet Froid
(Bertrand Blier, 1979, Fr) Gérard Depardieu, Bernard Blier, Jean Carmet, Genevieve Page, Denise Gence, Carole Bouquet, Michel Serrault.
95 min.
Rigorously absurd contemporary *film noir* which presents every character, incident and situation known to the genre, but none of the customary explanations, motivations or consequences. A blackly surreal procession of amoral and/or illegal acts proceed haphazardly from Depardieu's discovery of his lost penknife embedded in a dying Métro traveller, and his subsequent alliance with his wife's murderer and a police inspector, producing a cherishably Buñuelian depiction of the far-from-discreet crimes of the bourgeoisie. PT

Buffy the Vampire Slayer
(Fran Rubel Kuzui, 1992, US) Kristy Swanson, Donald Sutherland, Paul Reubens, Rutger Hauer, Luke Perry, Michele Abrams, Hilary Swank, Candy Clark.
94 min.
Buffy (Swanson) and her vacuous valley-girl pals are, like, *rilly* irritating: they have a keen fashion sense and an imaginative line in vapid chat, but they're in desperate need of a reality check. Enter creepy old Merrick (Sutherland), who tells Buffy her weird dreams are the result of her being The Chosen One, the Slayer. So off they wander to a moonlit cemetery, where a recently fanged victim emerges from a fresh grave, and Buffy instinctively stabs him through the heart. But what will her pals say? Should she skip cheerleading practice? 'The world is under threat from the legions of the Undead, and you're worried about the Seniors' Dance', gasps exasperated hunk Pike (Perry), who's smitten but can't believe her attitude. Unfocused stuff, pitched at undemanding teenagers. Swanson can't act but moves well, while Hauer is far too louche to be a scary vampire villain. NF

Bug
(Jeannot Szwarc, 1975, US) Bradford Dillman, Joanna Miles, Richard Gilliland, Jamie Smith Jackson, Alan Fudge, Jesse Vint.
101 min.
Basically a mad scientist story enlivened by eco-subtexts, in which horrible self-combusting cockroaches are thrown up from beneath the earth's crust during an earthquake, only to commence setting fire to everyone and everything they touch; meanwhile Dillman's hermit-like scientist investigates, analyses, and comes to play God. Therein lies the film's interest: biblical and religious images (heads aflame with tongues of fire, winged demons) hold sway right from the film's opening, set effectively in a remote desert church, to establish a schlock-horror allegory on the creation myth. Tacky in parts – as one might expect from producer William Castle (his last film; he also co-scripted) – and occasionally lacking in plot logic, it's nevertheless an imaginative little B thriller that manages to be genuinely suspenseful. GA

Bugis Street
(Yonfan, 1994, Singapore) Hiep Thi Le, Michael Lam, Benedict Goh, Greg-O, Ernest, Gerald Chen.
101 min.
Before the ultimate nanny state tidied away all signs of 'dirt', Bugis Street was Singapore's centre for transvestite hookers. This movie, by a Hong Kong fashion photographer turned director, is a fey evocation of those days, centred on the imaginary Sin-Sin Hotel, crammed to the rafters with she-males and their drunken sailor pick-ups. There's no plot; the film explores its world through the eyes of the newly arrived maid (Le, from Oliver Stone's *Heaven & Earth*), an innocent who winds up learning all she'll ever need to know about eye-liner, falsies, penises and putting a brave face on things. Better as censor-bait than as drama, but it contains several powerful direct-to-camera monologues by real life drag queens. TR

Bugles in the Afternoon
(Roy Rowland, 1952, US) Ray Milland, Helena Carter, Hugh Marlowe, Forrest Tucker, Barton MacLane, George Reeves, James Millican, Gertrude Michael.
85 min.
Derived from an Ernest Haycox Western, this begins well, with unusually cool, composed performances from Carter (as the heroine) and Michael (a striking cameo as a saloon girl). Milland, cashiered from the army after running a fellow officer through with his sabre (for pressing his attentions on Milland's fiancée, it eventually emerges), enlists as a private in the frontier cavalry, only to find the same officer (Marlowe) installed as his commanding officer and getting up to his old tricks again. Though Daniel Mainwaring and Harry Brown provide some good scenes and intelligent dialogue, the plot works too hard to prove Marlowe a double-dyed villain, cheerfully sacrificing lives if only Milland's can be one of them, and ending in absurdity as the pair work up to their grudge fight while the Sioux are busy massacring everybody in sight at the Little Big Horn. A pity, because Rowland directs with a fine control of mood and pace, and there are sterling performances from Milland and Tucker to add to those by the two women. TM

Bugsy
(Barry Levinson, 1991, US) Warren Beatty, Annette Bening, Harvey Keitel, Ben Kingsley, Elliott Gould, Joe Mantegna, Richard Sarafian, Bebe Neuwirth, Wendy Phillips, Robert Beltran, James Toback.
136 min.
Sent by Meyer Lansky and Lucky Luciano to take care of West Coast business, the womanising Benjamin 'Bugsy' Siegel (Beatty) settles down to a life of Hollywood glitz. His fraught affair with starlet Virginia Hill (Bening), which places great strain on Siegel's otherwise happy marriage, is only one of the psychopathically violent mobster's obsessions. For his dreams, too, of building a casino-hotel in Las Vegas. But Bugsy's twin passions put him at risk: his extravagance with Mob money and his high profile turn the crime barons against him... One can, of course, remain sceptical about the film's unabashedly romantic portrait of Siegel (though Beatty is truly unsettling when called on to come up with murderous rage), but its virtues

are many: Bugsy's risible efforts at self-improvement through language; a farcical *tour de force* where he juggles a daughter's birthday meal, phone calls from Virginia and a business meeting; mad plans to kill Mussolini; brutal humiliations meted out to disloyal wiseguys. With a sparklingly witty script (James Toback), classy direction and terrific performances all round, Beatty's return to the fray is his best movie since *McCabe and Mrs Miller*. GA

Bugsy Malone
(Alan Parker, 1976, GB) Scott Baio, Jodie Foster, Florrie Dugger, John Cassisi, Martin Lev.
93 min.
Novelty gangster pic with an entire cast of children who use guns which fire ice cream. Adults may be diverted by the affectionate pastiche of old gangster movies and by Paul Williams' pleasant Nilsson-like song'n'dance numbers. CPe

Build My Gallows High
see Out of the Past

Bulldog Drummond
(F Richard Jones, 1929, US) Ronald Colman, Joan Bennett, Montagu Love, Lilyan Tashman, Claud Allister, Lawrence Grant.
89 min. b/w.
No less than thirteen different actors have impersonated Sapper's perennially gentlemanly hero in films, ranging from Carlyle Blackwell in 1922 to Richard Johnson in 1966 and 1968. In theory, at least, Colman is perfect casting, well able to cope with both the suavity and the built-in humour, and his talkie debut (with its Chandlerian plot about a girl trying to rescue her uncle from a sanitorium where he is being coerced into signing away his fortune) was a huge success at the time. If the pre-Bond formula and the military clubman hero prove a little jaded now, there is compensation in the careful Goldwyn packaging: direction by a graduate of the Sennett school, sets by William Cameron Menzies, low-key camerawork from Gregg Toland. TM

Bulldog Drummond Comes Back
(Louis King, 1937, US) John Howard, John Barrymore, Louise Campbell, Reginald Denny, EE Clive, J Carrol Naish, John Sutton.
64 min. b/w.
Second – and perhaps the best – in Paramount's *Bulldog Drummond* series, with Howard taking over the lead from Ray Milland (whose star was rising). It boasts a waspishly nasty villain (Naish), and the Holmesian revenge plot, complete with clues in rhyming couplets, is considerably enhanced by Barrymore as a Scotland Yard detective with an irresistible flair for disguises. Then on the downgrade, Barrymore belies his demotion to a B movie series with a performance of witty relish, at one point grumbling (as he removes an unduly adhesive putty nose) 'To think that I should ever descend to being an actor!' The series, featuring Howard throughout, continued with *Bulldog Drummond's Peril*, *Bulldog Drummond's Revenge*, *Bulldog Drummond in Africa* (1938), *Arrest Bulldog Drummond*, *Bulldog Drummond's Secret Police* and *Bulldog Drummond's Bride* (1939). TM

Bulldog Drummond Escapes
(James Hogan, 1937, US) Ray Milland, Heather Angel, Reginald Denny, Porter Hall, Sir Guy Standing, EE Clive, Walter Kingsford.
65 min. b/w.
First in Paramount's series of B movies devoted to 'Sapper' HC McNeile's British ex-army officer with a taste for adventure. A fine if familiarly atmospheric opening as our hero, driving through the inescapable English fog, is hailed by a damsel in distress, has his car stolen from under his nose, and finds a corpse lurking in the marshes. Thereafter the scene shifts to a country mansion complete with the usual equipment ranging from shifty butler to secret passages, and everything begins to creak audibly. TM

Bulldog Jack (aka Alias Bulldog Drummond)
(Walter Forde, 1935, GB) Jack Hulbert, Fay Wray, Ralph Richardson, Claude Hulbert, Paul Graetz, Gibb McLaughlin, Athol Fleming.
72 min. b/w.

Sleuthing send-up from Michael Balcon's Gaumont with Jack Hulbert masquerading as the famous English detective in order to track down criminal mastermind Richardson, who's been snaffling gems from the British Museum. A jolly jape, and comedy man Forde slings together a cracking climactic chase through the London underground. TJ

Bull Durham
(Ron Shelton, 1988, US) Kevin Costner, Susan Sarandon, Tim Robbins, Trey Wilson, Robert Wuhl, William O'Leary, David Neidorf, Danny Gans, Tom Silardi, Max Patkin.
108 min.
Less a baseball movie than a romantic comedy based around the sacred diamond. Each season, Annie (Sarandon) – devout believer in the Church of Baseball – favours one member of the Durham Bulls minor league team with her patented instruction in the subtle arts of baseball and love-making. Selecting young acolyte Ebby (Robbins), she initiates him into the secret of 'breathing through your eyelids', encourages him to wear a suspender belt while pitching, and ties him to a bed to read him extracts from Whitman's erotic poem 'I Sing the Body Electric'. The seasoned Crash (Costner) meanwhile grooms the youngster for a shot at the major league, concentrating on his fast but undisciplined pitching, because he throws like he fucks, all over the place. Paradoxically, writer/director Shelton's intimate knowledge of baseball allows him to convey the feel of the game, its esoteric mythology and quirky superstitions, without losing sight of the real issue: when will Annie and Crash get it together? The film's delicious charge stems not from a rush towards a big game climax, but from the aching pleasure of Crash and Annie's potential consummation. Exuding easy charm, Costner confirms his status as *the* romantic leading man of the late '80s; Sarandon is sexier reading Emily Dickinson's poems fully clothed than most actresses would be writhing naked on a bed; together, they are indeed the bodies electric. Marvellous stuff. NF

Bullet for the General, A (¿Quién sabe?)
(Damiano Damiani, 1966, It) Gian Maria Volonté, Klaus Kinski, Martine Beswick, Lou Castel, Jaime Fernández, Andrea Checchi.
135 min.
A spaghetti Western on a par with Leone's. It shares Volonté and Kinski with *For a Few Dollars More*, and Luis Bacalov's haunting score was 'supervised' by Ennio Morricone, but the politics are more radical than anything Leone stood for (it ends with a ringing call to arms: 'Don't buy bread, buy dynamite!'). Lou Castel plays a tight-lipped gringo who insinuates himself into Volonté's gang of Mexican bandits on the fringes of the revolution. The film charts the peculiar friendship between these two blinkered mercenaries, and Volonté's belated arrival at a political consciousness. This intelligent, compelling reversal of the archetypal Hollywood schema (in which an American star lends his gun to the peasants' cause) was scripted by Franco Solinas, who also contributed to Rosi's *Salvatore Giuliano*, Costa-Gavras' *State of Siege*, Pontecorvo's *Battle of Algiers* and *Queimada!*. TCh

Bullet in the Head (Diexue Jietou)
(John Woo, 1990, HK) Tony Leung, Jacky Cheung, Waise Lee, Simon Yam, Fennie Yuen.
136 min.
Highly ambitious Vietnam epic about the dehumanising effects of greed and repression. Ben (Leung) grows up in the Hong Kong slums in the late '60s with best friends Paul (Waise Lee) and Frank (Cheung). Fleeing to Saigon after a fight with a gangster, the three attempt to profit from the war, smuggling first penicillin, then gold. Their enterprise comes at a heavy price. Paul becomes obsessed with the gold, and after capture by the Vietcong, they are forced to choose between murder or death. The governing metaphor is spelled out in the title: Woo recreates the infamous news photo of a Vietnamese executed by a gun to his head, ups the ante on the Russian roulette sequence in *The Deer Hunter*, and puts his own macabre spin on Peckinpah's *Bring Me the Head of Alfredo*

Garcia. The early sequences play like one of Woo's gangster films, with their heroic rhetorical imagery, slow motion, dissolves and freeze frames, but the director tightens the screw when the action shifts to Vietnam. Sometimes incoherent, over-pitched or simply painful to watch, this is Woo's most personal and political morality tale – a substantial movie all but consumed in the flames of its own madness. TCh

Bulletproof
(Steve Carver, 1987, US) Gary Busey, Darlanne Fluegel, Henry Silva, Thalmus Rasulala, LQ Jones, René Enriquez, Mills Watson, RG Armstrong.
94 min.
In order to flush out Communist guerillas gathering near the Mexican/US border, the CIA use a prototype super-tank as bait, and lure former Special Forces agent Frank 'Bulletproof' McBain (Busey) out of retirement. One of the 'expendable' US soldiers captured at the same time is McBain's ex-lover (Fluegel). The terrorists are a motley rabble: Arab rapists, Mexican toy soldiers, and Nicaraguan sadists with a strong line in priest-slapping, nun-wasting and church-burning – atheistic Commies and racial stereotypes to a man. The Russkies, for whom the stolen tank is destined, are icy killers armed with a flimsy-looking helicopter gunship and AK47s that don't shoot straight. The excellent Busey is here wasted in a comic-strip hero role which taxes only his muscles and lopsided grin; Fluegel, meanwhile, scowls attractively while never quite pulling off her tough-girl act. Awkward slo-mo flashbacks and cheapskate production values add technical insult to artistic injury, and the whole thing is reminiscent of early Chuck Norris. NF

Bullets or Ballots
(William Keighley, 1936, US) Edward G Robinson, Joan Blondell, Barton MacLane, Humphrey Bogart, Frank McHugh, Joseph King, Richard Purcell, George E Stone.
70 min. b/w.
Dark Warners gangster film scripted by Seton I Miller (*G-Men*) and directed at a fair lick by studio journeyman Keighley. The war on crime won't easily be won. Robinson's on the side of the law for the first time, and relishes it. He's a New York cop who goes undercover to bust a racket. The machine guns keep rattling, Blondell reprises her sassy siren routine, and Bogart snarls away as the gangster Nick 'Bugs' Fenner. Both Bogey and Robinson go down at the close. GM

Bullets Over Broadway
(Woody Allen, 1994, US) John Cusack, Jack Warden, Chazz Palminteri, Tony Sirico, Joe Viterelli, Dianne Wiest, Jim Broadbent, Jennifer Tilly, Mary-Louise Parker, Tracey Ullman, Rob Reiner, Harvey Fierstein.
99 min.
Set in the Runyonesque New York of the Jazz Age, when artists rubbed shoulders with gangsters at speakeasies, this is the story of idealistic young playwright David Shayne (Cusack). With backing from mob boss Nick Valenti (Viterelli), Shayne can direct his new work on Broadway, and even attract stars of the magnitude of Helen Sinclair (Wiest) and Warner Purcell (Broadbent). There's just one catch: Valenti insists that his flapper girlfriend Olive (Tilly) play a leading role. Not only is she terrible, she comes with a shadow, Nick's bodyguard Cheech (Palminteri), who oversees the rehearsals with barely concealed impatience. A merciless satire on the pretensions, hypocrisies and indulgences of theatre folk, this is Allen's fizziest piece in years. It's propped up by two fiercely competitive caricatures from Tilly and Wiest, who completely and appropriately overshadow Cusack's approximation of the inexperienced author. It must be said that this is scarcely new ground, and that the staging is sometimes clumsy, but just when you wonder how much life is left in these stereotypes, Allen pulls off a doozy of a dramatic switch which takes the farce to unexpected, dizzy heights. No! Don't speak! See it! TCh

Bullet Train, The (Shinkansen Daibakuha)
(Junya Sato, 1975, Jap) Ken Takakura, Shinichi Chiba, Akira Oda, Kei Yamamoto, Fumio Watanabe.
89 min.

A terrific central concept: a bomb is planted on one of Japan's 200 mph Shinkansen expresses, primed to explode as soon as the train slows to a certain speed. Savour it, because it's virtually all there is; the clumsy plotting, low-octane direction and muffled performances certainly don't add up to much of a movie. All that's required from Ken Takakura (as the chief bomber) is his presence, which he delivers adequately. Maybe the original Japanese version (running at 155 minutes) made more of the political undercurrents, but all that's left here are glimmerings of suspense in the final half-hour. TR

Bullfighter and the Lady, The

(Budd Boetticher, 1950, US) Robert Stack, Gilbert Roland, Joy Page, Katy Jurado, Virginia Grey, John Hubbard.
124 min. b/w.
Produced by John Wayne, and shorn down to 87 minutes by John Ford for a release print that surely must have had more dramatic bite than the complete version, this sees Boetticher getting far too close to the subject of his beloved bullfighting for the film's good. Stack is the arrogant American film-maker who, on a trip to Mexico, enlists Roland's champion toreador to pass on his skills. Inevitably, there must be death in the afternoon – not to mention many hard lessons in the Latin sense of honour – before Stack grows up enough to become a true man and great artist. Dire continuity and shifts in point of view, endless didactic sequences extolling the bullfighter's grace, and generally wooden performances result in a surprising fiasco of almost unbearable tedium. GA

Bullitt

(Peter Yates, 1968, US) Steve McQueen, Robert Vaughn, Jacqueline Bisset, Don Gordon, Robert Duvall, Simon Oakland, Norman Fell, Carl Reindel.
114 min.
A thriller which begins, as it means to go on, with a bang. Only minutes after the preliminaries are over, a door bursts open, a shotgun is fired, and the victim is blasted clean off the bed into the wall behind him. The plot, concerning the battle of wits between an honest cop and an ambitious politician for possession of the key witness in a Mafia exposé, is serviceable but nothing special. But the action sequences are brilliant, done without trickery in real locations (including a great car chase which spawned a thousand imitations) to lend an extraordinary sense of immediacy to the shenanigans and gunfights. TM

Bullseye!

(Michael Winner, 1990, US) Michael Caine, Roger Moore, Sally Kirkland, Deborah Barrymore, Lee Patterson, Mark Burns, Derren Nesbitt.
92 min.
In Winner's frantic and seriously unfunny comedy, Caine and Moore play a couple of recently reunited colourful conmen, respectively donkey-jacketed Sid and suave Gerald. What they have in common is severe cash-flow problems and remarkable resemblances to two dishonest scientists – Dr Hicklar (Caine), a Yank, and Sir John Bavistock (Moore), a nob – whom they see on the box talking guardedly about their potentially invaluable experiments in initiating cold fusion in a test-tube. Sid and Gerald bone up on their respective accents – Caine's American accent is funny – don cunning disguises, and assume the roles of Hicklar and Bavistock in order to perpetrate a heist. The whole thing then spirals off into total chaos with an all-nonsense plot about selling the plans to the highest bidder, involving gunfights on the Orient Express, double-crosses, and a visit to every stately home in Britain. No actor comes out unscathed from this stinker. Menahem Golan produced. WH

Bullshot

(Dick Clement, 1983, GB) Alan Shearman, Diz White, Ron House, Frances Tomelty, Michael Aldridge.
88 min.
A movie based on a stage spoof of Sapper McNeile's Bulldog Drummond secret agent stories, and from almost the first five minutes of exploding test-tubes and pratfalls and false wigs, it's obvious that what might have worked in the theatre is all wrong for the screen. It's not simply that banana-skin jokes look a bit ridiculous

when we're used to modern stuntwork. By now films like *Superman* and *Raiders of the Lost Ark* have also shown that it's quite possible to take pulp heroes, and make the audience care for them without resorting to the banality of all-out camp. This basic disability is all the more regrettable since the film is very handsomely mounted and performed with gusto. DP

Bulto, El (Excess Baggage)

(Gabriel Retes, 1992, Mex) Gabriel Retes, Hector Bonilla, Lourdes Elizarraras.
114 min.
A radical photo-journalist is knocked down by a Government riot control squad ('The Hawks') in 1971, is put into a coma, and finally awakes 20 years later. The household he re-enters – which includes the son and daughter he never knew he had, his wife has remarried – has moved into the modern world, with its Nintendos, Walkmans, and shifted political and social perspectives. 'El Bulto' ('The Lump', as they have referred to him) has to learn to walk again and to live in the present. Director Retes finely calibrates his re-entry from his 'space capsule', and in so doing makes many acute points about the history of social and political change for the Mexico City middle-class intelligentsia. WH

Bundle of Joy

(Norman Taurog, 1956, US) Debbie Reynolds, Eddie Fisher, Adolphe Menjou, Tommy Noonan, Una Merkel, Melville Cooper.
98 min.
Lame remake of *Bachelor Mother* with songs. As the shopgirl who finds an abandoned baby, and by looking after it prompts a sacndal when everyone thinks it's hers, Reynolds is cute but lacks the sparky vivacity of Ginger Rogers, while Fisher is simply no match for David Niven. GA

Bunny Caper, The

see Sex Play

Bunny Lake is Missing

(Otto Preminger, 1965, GB) Keir Dullea, Carol Lynley, Laurence Olivier, Martita Hunt, Noël Coward, Lucie Mannheim, Adrienne Corri, Anna Massey, Finlay Currie, Clive Revill.
107 min. b/w.
A middling thriller scripted by John and Penelope Mortimer (from Evelyn Piper's novel) in which weary Inspector Olivier cruises a cameo-strewn London in search of Lynley's mislaid (and just possibly non-existent) child, and Preminger characteristically nags away at the minor-key ambiguities as if the investigation were philosophical rather than criminal. A brief appearance by The Zombies places the time of the season quite neatly, though London doesn't so much swing as creak eerily. PT

Bunny O'Hare

(Gerd Oswald, 1971, US) Bette Davis, Ernest Borgnine, Jack Cassidy, Joan Delaney, Jay Robinson, John Astin.
92 min.
Embarrassingly unfunny caper in which Davis and Borgnine masquerade as hippies to commit a series of 'social revenge' bank robberies. Davis, supported by Oswald, understandably sued producers AIP for post-production tampering which ineptly stressed the knockabout aspects. TM

Buona Sera, Mrs Campbell

(Melvin Frank, 1968, US) Gina Lollobrigida, Phil Silvers, Telly Savalas, Peter Lawford, Shelley Winters, Lee Grant, Janet Margolin.
113 min.
Lollobrigida as an unmarried Italian mum (the Mrs Campbell derives from a soup can) whose deception – she has been enjoying child support from three different US airmen since World War II – is threatened by a squadron reunion. Formulary but mildly amusing until it gravitates to sentimentality. TM

'burbs, The

(Joe Dante, 1988, US) Tom Hanks, Bruce Dern, Carrie Fisher, Rick Ducommun, Corey Feldman, Wendy Schaal, Henry Gibson, Brother Theodore, Courtney Gains, Gale Gordon, Dick Miller, Robert Picardo.
102 min.
When Ray Peterson (Hanks) opts to take his

vacation at home in Hinckley Hills – the epitome of suburban conformism – he soon becomes infected by his neighbours' paranoia over the Klopeks, new arrivals to the scuzziest house in the street. Okay, they're ugly, they keep a dog called Landru, dig up the garden by night, and have a noisy basement; but are they *really* 'neighbours from hell'? After all, Ray's pals are pretty weird: Mark (Dern) is a rabid militarist, Art (Ducommun) is obsessed with macabre murders, and Ricky (Feldman) is a thrill-crazy Heavy Metal freak. Joe Dante's manic black satire portrays the investigations of this quartet of eternal adolescents into the Klopeks' admittedly unusual lifestyle with enormous glee, revelling in OTT behaviour and absurd dialogue, and tossing out film parodies with reckless abandon. Characteristically, Dante's nonchalant attitude towards plot structure makes for erratic pacing (the last half hour does flag), but that's part and parcel of his breathless, anarchic style. It's *very* silly, of course, but Hanks' fine timing is matched by a strong supporting cast, and thanks to Dante's wicked, comic-strip view of the world, the movie achieves an admirably wacky consistency as it debunks American mores and movie clichés, from Hitchcock and Leone to Michael Winner and Tobe Hooper. GA

Burden of Dreams

(Les Blank, 1982, US) Werner Herzog, Klaus Kinski, Claudia Cardinale, Jason Robards, Mick Jagger.
95 min.
Blank's special brand of ethnographic film documentary finds a curiously appropriate subject in that weirdest of all capsule cultures: the on-location film crew. Blank chronicles Herzog's notorious and near-disastrous filming of his epic *Fitzcarraldo* in the face of a temperamental cast (including at various stages Mick Jagger, Jason Robards and Kinski), Amazon locations, the local populace, and the fates in general. Blank's footage, which at times must have looked like being the only cinematic record that would come out of the jungle, clarifies many of the rumours about the shooting, and also takes on a crazy life of its own as the Amazon tributary becomes a blackly comic shit creek of (off camera) tribal skirmishes. But ultimately it's left to us to decide where Herzog could or should have drawn the line. PT

Bureau of Missing Persons

(Roy Del Ruth, 1933, US) Pat O'Brien, Bette Davis, Lewis Stone, Glenda Farrell, Allen Jenkins, Hugh Herbert, Ruth Donnelly, Alan Dinehart.
75 min. b/w.
Not a Davis vehicle, since she only appears halfway through, playing a girl wanted for murder. Based on a book by former police captain John Ayres, it cross-breeds an attempt to document the range of work covered by the NY Missing Persons Bureau (a number of unconnected cases are developed in parallel) and a healthily cynical vein of macabre humour. With Del Ruth directing at screwball pace, things sometimes get a little too jokey; but at its best, in noting the obsessive quirks developed by officers, it has some claim to be considered an ancestor of *Hill Street Blues*. TM

Buried Alive

(Gerard Kikoine, 1990, US) Robert Vaughn, Donald Pleasence, Karen Witter, John Carradine, Nia Long.
91 min.
Bits of several Edgar Allan Poe stories make up this schlock offering, shot on the cheap in South Africa. It's set in a school for delinquent young ladies (cue shower scene), where new teacher Karen Witter is about to connect the shock disappearance of several pupils with the nefarious activities of mad doctor Vaughn. A sad checkout for John Carradine in his final role. TJ

Burglar

(Hugh Wilson, 1987, US) Whoopi Goldberg, Bob Goldthwait, GW Bailey, Lesley Ann Warren, James Handy, John Goodman.
102 min.
A fairly grim work-out for Whoopi Goldberg as a likeable cat burglar who witnesses a murder then turns amateur 'tec to nail the culprit before she's charged with the crime herself. Memorable one-liners in short supply. TJ

Burglar (Vzlomshchik)

(Valery Ogorodnikov, 1987, USSR) Oleg Elykomov, Konstantin Kinchev, Yuri Tsapnik,Svetlana Gaitan, Polina Petrenko.
89 min.
With a brother dedicated to punk rock stardom at any cost and a drunken father who chases skirt between robotic dancing lessons from the TV, young Senka stands as much chance of nurture as the hero of Truffaut's *400 Blows*. The amazing thing about Ogorodnikov's film is that it was made in Russia. Clearly, plenty of Soviet teenies share the nihilistic feelings of their Western counterparts, and the extensive footage of safety-pin chic at concerts perhaps points to a sound export instinct on the director's part. Senka's brother Kostya is under pressure from Howmuch, a very heavy rocker, to steal a synthesiser from the Community Centre, so to protect him Senka steals it himself. The story occupies little more space than the music, but the performances are splendid enough to lodge Senka's predicament in the heart. BC

Burglars, The (Le Casse)

(Henri Verneuil, 1971, Fr/It) Jean-Paul Belmondo, Omar Sharif, Dyan Cannon, Robert Hossein, Nicole Calfan, Renato Salvatori.
120 min.
Fine *film noir* material (David Goodis' novel *The Burglar*, previously filmed as Paul Wendkos' impressive debut in 1956), but here it suffers an overdose of sunshine and multi-national production values to emerge as just another glossy heist replete with sparring jewel thief and detective. PT

Burke and Hare

(Vernon Sewell, 1971, GB) Derren Nesbitt, Glynn Edwards, Harry Andrews, Dee Shenderey, Yootha Joyce, Françoise Pascal.
91 min.
Vacillating between melodrama and bathos, this moves uneasily from one unfulfilled promise to another, dogged from first image to last by an overwhelming mediocrity. The film attempts a historical reconstruction of the murderous activities of the infamous bodysnatchers, with a concurrent reinterpretation of the economic and sexual contexts of the Edinburgh of the 1820s within which they operated. Needless to say, the sexuality is prudish, coarse and vicarious in the 'Carry On' style, and the attempts at horror are unconvincing in the extreme. JDuC

Burmese Harp, The (Biruma no Tategoto)

(Kon Ichikawa, 1956, Jap) Shoji Yasui, Rentaro Mikuni, Tatsuya Mihashi.
116 min. b/w.
Lyrical and rather ostentatiously humanist, Ichikawa's film tells of a Japanese soldier in Burma, so appalled by the bloody carnage of war that he refuses to return home after his country's defeat, and stays on, garbed as a Buddhist monk, to bury the dead. If the film was clearly a sincere castigation of the militarist fervour that swept Japan during the war, it nevertheless suffers from its rather deliberate heart-warming tone and a too leisurely pace that tends to over-emphasise moments of pathos. That said, it is hard not to be swayed by the pacifist sentiments. GA

Burn!

see Queimada!

Burning, The

(Tony Maylam, 1980, US) Brian Matthews, Leah Ayres, Brian Backer, Larry Joshua, Jason Alexander, Lou David.
91 min.
In the tradition of such horror pix as *Halloween* and *Friday the 13th*, this portrays the gruesome extermination of a group of charmless adolescents by a bogey man. This time it's a hulk of burnt flesh wielding garden shears and terrorising a summer camp; and true to cycle, it's the teenage girls who are the chief victims of both the murderer's savage cuts and the camera's leering gaze. Presented as provocative teasers, they're despatched while the mini-machos laugh, lust, bully, build rafts and, finally become heroes. Suspensewise, it's proficient enough, but familiarity with this sort of stuff can breed contempt. GA

Burning an Illusion

(Menelik Shabazz, 1981, GB) Cassie McFarlane, Victor Romero, Beverley Martin, Angela Wynter, Malcolm Fredericks.
111 min.
A young British-born black woman is forced into encounters with sexism and racism in her attempt to negotiate some kind of future in a community where patriarchal power often erupts into street violence. As the heroine finds herself drawn into black militancy and feminism, a good chance is missed to develop the character of her more passive friend who wants no truck with 'Africa'. An important film for Britain in 1981, nevertheless, though in need of cutting to sharpen its edge. MA

Burning Hills, The

(Stuart Heisler, 1956, US) Tab Hunter, Natalie Wood, Skip Homeier, Eduard Franz, Earl Holliman, Claude Akins, Ray Teal, Frank Puglia.
94 min.
A stock revenge Western, nicely shot in 'Scope by Ted McCord. When his brother is murdered, Trace Jordan (Hunter) confronts the local cattle baron, Sutton (Teal), knowing that he has had settlers killed before in his determination to keep the whole range to himself. Both men are wounded after Sutton denies it and draws his gun; but with the aid of a feisty half-Mexican girl (Wood) whose father was one of the settlers killed, Jordan manages to get away, eventually outwitting a posse of pursuing gunmen led by Sutton's vicious son (Homeier). Heisler keeps the single-minded action admirably taut, while the script, based on a novel by Louis L'Amour, tries (without much success) to ring a few changes by detailing some uncertain loyalties among the characters. A less bland hero than Tab Hunter might have helped; Natalie Wood, though miscast, is not at all bad. TM

Burning Life

(Peter Welz, 1994, Ger) Maria Schrader, Anna Thalbach, Max Tidof.
105 min.
This strangely dated road movie (very loosely in the *Thelma and Louise* mould) sees two women go on a bank robbing spree along the backroads of post-Wall East Germany, pursued by a showman/fakir in a hippie van, and assorted fascistic cops in leathers. The 'chicks', one a frustrated history teacher maddened by her father's suicide, the other a frustrated cabaret-style chanteuse (she gets to do an embarrassing microphone caressing number) sport the complete range of guns, specs and threads from the renta-cool catalogue. Audaciously unoriginal. WH

Burning Memory (Resism)

(Yossi Somer, 1988, Isr) Danny Roth, Shmuel Edelman, Pauli Reshef, Etty Ankri, Alon Oliarchick, Renven Dayan.
93 min.
Writer/director Somer poured experience gained as a paramedic during the Israeli-Lebanese conflict into this impassioned first feature. Roth goes through it as the shell-shocked soldier treated to a course of military-style psychotherapy, the object being to get him back in the field as soon as possible. It's not exactly a polished effort, but Somer knows the milieu and we're never in doubt where his sympathies lie. TJ

Burning Paradise (Huoshao Honglian Si)

(Ringo Lam, 1993, HK) Willie Chi, Carmen Lee, Cheng Dong, Yang Sheng, KK Huang, Lin Quan.
104 min.
A box office disaster in Hong Kong and straight-to-video in Britain, this finds Lam working with a cast of unknowns in Mainland China, trying to freshen up an often-told story first filmed in Shanghai in 1928. (Tsui Hark, doyen of remaking/remodelling jobs, served as producer.) Fong Sai-Yuk (Chi) is one of many Shaolin monks arrested for fomenting anti-Manchu resistance and imprisoned in the Red Lotus Temple. Lam's big idea is to see the prison as a literal hell, governed by a depraved psychotic whose project is to create the Anti-Buddha; the best scenes pursue this dark vision, which extends to presenting the Shaolin hero Hong Xiguan (Yang) as an apparent traitor. Some of the acrobatic fights do seem grimly anarchic, but the endless booby

traps grow tiresome and the film's 'dark side' is undercut by feeble elements of humour and romance. As a genre piece: too little, too late. TR

Burning Secret

(Andrew Birkin, 1988, GB/US) David Eberts, Faye Dunaway, Klaus Maria Brandauer, Ian Richardson, John Nettleton.
107 min.
Based on a short story by Stefan Zweig, set in post-World War I Austria. Asthmatic Edmund (Eberts) is the 12-year-old son of an American diplomat. In an attempt to cure his wheezing, his mother (Dunaway) takes him to stay in a remote mountain spa where he falls under the spell of the Baron (Brandauer), who fills his head with stories of his war exploits. What Edmund doesn't know is that the Baron is only using him to reach his mother. Of course, it all ends in tears. Snowbound Marienbad looks splendid, Brandauer oozes his usual sinister charm, and Dunaway is at her most haughtily haunted. The well-meaning sensitivity is seriously weakened, though, by the way Edmund's asthma appears to be caused by telepathy: before his mother has had a chance to become breathless in the Baron's bed, the boy's lungs have already collapsed in sympathy, leaving the audience gasping for air. It isn't meant to be funny – this is a tale about adult cruelty and the tragic loss of childhood innocence – but the end quotation from Goethe's *Erl King* has all the crashing finality of a coffin-lid. MS

Burnt by the Sun (Utomlennye sointsem/ Soleil trompeur)

(Nikita Mikhalkov, 1994, Rus/Fr) Nikita Mikhalkov, Ingeborga Dapkounaite, Nadia Mikhalkov, Oleg Menchikov, Andre Oumansky.
134 min.
A summer's day at a dacha in Stalinist Russia, 1936. A hero of the Revolution, Kotov (director Mikhalkov), basks in the affection of his wife Maroussia (Dapkounaite) and their daughter Nadia (Nadia Mikhalkov), but his cosy world is disturbed by the arrival of Dimitri (Menchikov), Maroussia's first love. In the course of a day, Dimitri charms the household with his bravado and good looks, but Kotov grows uneasy as the reason for Dimitri's presence emerges. This is a careful, telling portrait of a community blinded by its illusions. For most of its running time, the film seems to follow suit: it's a placid, languorous country-house comedy far removed from the realities of the Stalinist terror. This is a masquerade, however. Dimitri's first appearance isn't quite the idle jape it first seems, while Kotov's dacha really is some kind of madhouse. Mikhalkov is a quintessentially Russian director: awkwardly, theatrically expansive, somewhat lugubrious even in the midst of an idyll, but unafraid of ideas and complexity. His own performance is impeccable, and the scenes with his daughter Nadia achieve a rare poignancy. TCh

Burnt Offerings

(Dan Curtis, 1976, US) Karen Black, Oliver Reed, Burgess Meredith, Eileen Heckart, Lee Montgomery, Dub Taylor, Bette Davis.
115 min.
The current minor boom in American horror films has two notable features: the single-minded concentration on the nuclear family as a point of attack, and the consistent rejection of happy endings. This tale of a family taking a spooky old mansion for the summer would be strictly formula stuff were it not for these elements; but veteran Eugène Lourié's art direction helps. DP

Burn, Witch, Burn!

see Night of the Eagle

Burra Sahib

(Nick Gifford, 1975, GB)
55 min.
Taken together with its companion piece *General Sahib* (Nick Gifford, 1976), this forms an unforgettable documentary portrait of curious lives from the days of the Raj. The first deals with Gifford's three uncles, all Boer expatriates, who run a taxidermy business in India. With patient elaboration, a picture of a time-warped Imperial past emerges alongside the personal details. Sepia photographs of polo and pig-sticking compare with Uncle Joubert's contemporary sporting life

– duck-shooting or fishing from the same hide coracle that he has used for forty years. Few words, the images speak for themselves. 'General Sahib' follows the daily duties of a retired Major-General (MC) from the Indian Army who runs a hospital for lepers, mental cases and children – poor creatures who have lost their bodies and minds and wander in the other world of sickness. The bristling, leonine General is also seen visiting his old military barracks at Poona, and indulging in a chukka of polo. His manner does not change, he still has a word for everyone. A slightly unnerving reminder that compassion is not necessarily excluded from the military cast of mind, although its expression may appear rather odd. Two great portraits of anachronism. CPea

Business Affair, A
(Charlotte Brandstrom, 1993, GB/Fr/Ger/Sp) Christopher Walken, Jonathan Pryce, Carole Bouquet, Sheila Hancock, Tom Wilkinson, Anna Manahan.
102 min.
Carole Bouquet is a floor-walking model and would-be writer caught between two contrasting but equally self-absorbed men in this well-written romantic comedy with a gently feminist undertow. While nursing her novelist husband through a chronic bout of writer's block, she is seduced by the brash charm of her publisher. Sold short by both men, Bouquet eventually opts for a literary identity of her own. Greatly helped by Pryce's atypically unsympathetic performance and Walken's easy charm, writer William Stadiem and director Brandstrom cut to the intellectual root, if not the emotional heart, of this ill-fated triangle of ambition and desire. Ultimately, perhaps, slightly too modest to attract the thoughtful art-house audience it's aimed at. NF

Business As Usual
(Lezli-An Barrett, 1987, GB) Glenda Jackson, John Thaw, Cathy Tyson, Mark McGann, Eamon Boland, James Hazeldine.
89 min.
When Babs (Jackson, uncharacteristically warm), manageress of a Liverpool fashion store, confronts the area manager (Boland) about his indecent advances towards one of her staff (Tyson), she is promptly sacked. The incident exacerbates existing friction at home between her unemployed ex-shop steward husband (Thaw) and her left-wing son (McGann), who quarrel over tactics for fighting her unfair dismissal. An accomplished first feature, this is no strident feminist sermon, the main theme being Babs' awakening to an untapped inner strength and confidence. Barrett's unsensational approach, offset by the raw indignation piercingly communicated by a superb cast, puts sexual intimidation powerfully in perspective as part of what is, for many, a broader everyday campaign. EP

Bus Riley's Back in Town
(Harvey Hart, 1965, US) Michael Parks, Ann-Margret, Jocelyn Brando, Janet Margolin, Kim Darby, Brad Dexter, Mimsy Farmer.
93 min.
Universal, attempting to cash in on the success of the French New Wave in the States, set up two films starring Michael Parks, of which this was the second, and allowed the directors comparative studio freedom. Although romantic and heavy-handed, Hart's piece is a well-intentioned study of small-town life in America, centred round Parks as a hellraiser back from the navy and determined to mend his ways. A handful of jobs later and he's serving as a stud to Ann-Margret before sinking into suitable obscurity, married and contemplating work in a garage. When Universal saw the poor returns from *Wild Seed*, the first film, they intervened, shot extra footage involving Ann-Margret, and demanded so many cuts that scriptwriter William Inge removed his name from the credits: probably no great loss, since the script was the weakest aspect of the whole thing. But it did set back the career of a promising director a good few years. DP

Bus Stop
(Joshua Logan, 1956, US) Marilyn Monroe, Don Murray, Betty Field, Arthur O'Connell, Eileen Heckart, Hope Lange, Hans Conried.
96 min.
Although it's not explicitly a musical, *Bus Stop* is certainly a product of that imagination which says the best things in life are free, and if you don't have a dream how you gonna have a dream come true. Once that's understood, it's easier to go beyond the bizarre misogyny and stilted theatricality of the plot in which a naive, loud-mouthed cowboy (Murray) tries to kidnap a saloon singer from the Ozarks played by Monroe. Apart from her engaging performance, the film's real interest lies in the unpleasant nature of its subtext: equations of poverty with personal unworthiness, and the uneasiness of an implicitly homosexual focus on Murray. CR

Buster
(David Green, 1988, GB) Phil Collins, Julie Walters, Larry Lamb, Stephanie Lawrence, Ellen Beaven, Michael Attwell, Sheila Hancock, Anthony Quayle.
102 min.
This is a love story, not a crime adventure. When Buster Edwards (Collins) receives his share of the 1963 Great Train Robbery, he doesn't know what to do with it except spend it. Soon he and his wife June (Walters) are stuck in Acapulco, down to £20,000. June who can't bear to be without chips, rain, and bingo, takes their darling daughter Nicky back to the Elephant and Castle, and Buster, though he knows he'll get nicked, soon follows. We're invited to view Edwards as the archetypal cheeky Cockney, to condone his crimes, and commiserate when he gets his comeuppance: character development, moral perspective, and cinematic style are out of the question. The re-enactment of the heist, for instance, has no place for the iron bar used to 'persuade' the engine driver. There are a couple of good moments – the Edwards family emerging into the Mexican sun swathed in winter coats, the massive police presence at the inevitable arrest – while Collins and Waters make the most of seriously underwritten roles. MS

Buster and Billie
(Daniel Petrie, 1973, US) Jan-Michael Vincent, Joan Goodfellow, Pamela Sue Martin, Clifton James, Robert Englund.
100 min.
An attempt to come to grips with repressed adolescent sexuality in backwoods Georgia by way of the touching relationship that develops between the high school's clean-cut good-looker and the dumb ugly duckling who gets used for the boys' gang bangs. The handling of the aggression that inevitably disrupts the idyllic affair is adequate, but the film falls down over its attempts to give credibility to the central relationship. Meticulous period (1948) detail. CPe

Busting
(Peter Hyams, 1973, US) Elliott Gould, Robert Blake, Allen Garfield, Antonio Fargas, Michael Lerner, Ivor Francis, William Sylvester, Logan Ramsey.
92 min.
Slick and often witty cop thriller, with Gould and Blake in fine form as the vice-squad detectives going it alone in the face of apathy and corruption among their superiors in their attempts to clean up LA. Cynical and rather too determinedly hip, it nevertheless entertains – thanks to some good action sequences and firm control of atmosphere – and, as Hyams' first feature, presages the delights to come in *Capricorn One* and *Outland*. GA

Bustin' Loose
(Oz Scott, 1981, US) Richard Pryor, Cicely Tyson, Angel Ramirez, Jimmy Hughes, Edwin DeLeon.
94 min.
A remarkable change of direction for the subsequently self-immolating Pryor, whose biting stand-up barrage had put him in the Lenny Bruce class of hard-core comic satire. A 'warm-hearted comedy' involving a bunch of orphan kids promises neither a rewarding evening nor the best use of Pryor's considerable talent. However, in spite of an impractically pat 'happy ending' and liberal spoonfuls of sugar, we are kept some way from Walt Disney territory. Some of the set pieces, notably Pryor's encounter with the Ku Klux Klan, are beautifully achieved; the sentimentality is usually effective, and protected by a hard edge of fast-rap comedy; the kids are bearable. The plotting is sloppy at times and this is undoubtedly a minor film, but its rewards are surprising. JC

Butch and Sundance: The Early Days
(Richard Lester, 1979, US) William Katt, Tom Berenger, Jeff Corey, John Schuck, Michael C Gwynne, Peter Weller, Brian Dennehy, Jill Eikenberry.
112 min.
As a star-less 'prequel' to the Goldman/Hill, Redford/Newman moneyspinner, this was always a commercial no-hoper, but early signposted ambitions to dig beneath its predecessor's ingratiating lyricism don't really pan out either. Allan Burns' script contents itself with episodic variations on its model, while notions of a myth in-the-making hang a little too heavily on the self-conscious dialogue, and Lester merely pumps up the quirk quotient. PT

Butch Cassidy and the Sundance Kid
(George Roy Hill, 1969, US) Paul Newman, Robert Redford, Katharine Ross, Strother Martin, Henry Jones, Jeff Corey, Cloris Leachman, Ted Cassidy.
110 min.
You could do worse than catch Redford and Newman in one of the funniest if slightest Westerns of recent years. Unashamedly escapist, it rips off most of its plot (from pursuit to final shootout) and much of its visual style from Peckinpah's *The Wild Bunch*, and even parodies *Jules and Jim*. It's slightly the worse for some of the borrowings, but the script is often hilarious, Newman and Redford making the best use of it when they get to parry dialogue with each other (eg, during the pursuit). It is much better and funnier than the *The Sting* precisely because it allows the two stars to play off each other. RM

Butcher, The
see Boucher, Le

Butcher Boy, The
(Neil Jordan, 1997, US) Stephen Rea, Fiona Shaw, Eamonn Owens, Alan Boyle, Niall Buggy, Brendan Gleeson, Gerard McSorley, Ardal O'Hanlon, Milo O'Shea, Sinéad O'Connor, Aisling O'Sullivan.
110 min.
Set in an Irish town in the early '60s, Jordan's film of Patrick McCabe's novel centres on troubled teen Francie Brady (Owens), a lippy lad who withdraws from family strife – dad (Rea) is almost permanently drunk, mum (O'Sullivan) sliding towards insanity – into fantasies inspired by comics, sci-fi movies and TV shows, and into blood brother pacts with best pal Joe (Boyle). His renown as an ill-mannered hothead, however, is such that he's denied access to his friend. Moreover, after a spell in a church-run remand home, he returns to find his family in tatters. This consistently surprising, even shocking work moves from sly social comedy to something more darkly disturbing as Francie's sense of control begins to crumble. Though the movie sometimes looks as if the authentic Irish wit, colour and blarney has been filtered through the sensibility of a Buñuel or Polanski, Jordan never allows the surreal/expressionist aspects to dominate. GA

Butcher's Wife, The
(Terry Hughes, 1991, US) Demi Moore, Jeff Daniels, George Dzundza, Mary Steenburgen, Frances McDormand, Margaret Colin, Miriam Margolyes.
105 min.
Lovelorn psychic Marina (Moore) wafts about her North Carolina look-out tower, putting all her considerable mental energies into finding Mr Right. Tell-tale signs indicate a lover is on his way, and before you can say crystal ball, the tide washes up portly New York butcher Leo (Dzundza). Is this fate, or did Leo simply make a wrong turn at the last island? Within days they're married and setting up home in Greenwich Village, where Marina starts dishing out clairvoyant advice with the pork chops, a development which pleases everyone but Leo and psychiatrist Dr Alex Tremor (Daniels). Moore sports blonde hair and – less convincingly – a Southern accent, but these are the only elements which jar in this hugely engaging romantic comedy. Hughes' direction and crisp visuals turn studio artifice into something altogether magical. CM

Butley
(Harold Pinter, 1973, US/GB/Can) Alan Bates, Jessica Tandy, Richard O'Callaghan, Susan Engel, Michael Byrne, Georgina Hale.
130 min.
One of the American Film Theatre series of filmed plays, which racked up a considerable amount of transcribed contemporary drama in the early '70s before the experiment dried up in the face of audience indifference. Simon Gray's account of an academic with rather too much wit, acerbity and withering honesty than is good for him follows a predictable course, in which one is allowed to enjoy Butley's lacerations of those around him until the play shows its moral side by revealing Butley to be a hopelessly self-deceived bastard who has cut himself to pieces in the process. A tour de force, as these things are evidently stacked to be, for Alan Bates. GA

Buttane, Le
see Whores, The

Buttercup Chain, The
(Robert Ellis Miller, 1970, GB) Hywel Bennett, Leigh Taylor-Young, Jane Asher, Sven-Bertil Taube, Clive Revill, Roy Dotrice, Michael Elphick.
95 min.
Awesomely arty tosh in which Bennett and Asher play the children of identical twins. In love but inhibited from making love with each other, they console themselves with an American girl who drives on the wrong side of the road (Taylor-Young) and a Swede called Fred who swims in the nude (Taube). Resolutely globe-trotting from one tourist attraction to the next, the camera follows the quartet to Spain, Sweden and Italy as they pair off into various combinations, meanwhile suffering self-inflicted torments. Miller's fulsome direction very nearly puts even Lelouch in the shade. TM

Butterfield 8
(Daniel Mann, 1960, US) Elizabeth Taylor, Laurence Harvey, Eddie Fisher, Betty Field, Dina Merrill, Mildred Dunnock.
109 min.
Once thought of as racy and adventurous in its treatment of sex, this turgid nonsense about a high-class whore with love in her heart has dated atrociously. Taylor hams away and Harvey in his debonair mood is distinctly unappealing, while the overall effect is too excruciating even to be unintentionally funny. GA

Butterflies Are Free
(Milton Katselas, 1972, US) Goldie Hawn, Edward Albert, Eileen Heckart, Michael Glasser, Mike Warren.
109 min.
A piece of (barely) stage-adapted nonsense, scripted by Leonard Gershe from his own play, about blind-boy-meets-emotionally-immature girl and how his mum brings them together. With some funny lines from Goldie Hawn and little else.

Butterfly
(Matt Cimber, 1981, US) Stacy Keach, Pia Zadora, Orson Welles, Lois Nettleton, Edward Albert, Stuart Whitman, Ed McMahon, June Lockhart, James Franciscus.
108 min.
A blatant vehicle for much-hyped sex symbol Zadora, who looks less like a backwoods baby doll than an ageing Barbie doll, and whose millionaire husband funded the film. Co-starring Keach as the long-lost Daddy who can't keep his hands off her, this is less an adaptation of James M Cain's novel than a grotesque parody of Tennessee Williams, and by the time the plot reaches its incest trial climax it is close to open farce, despite a pleasing cameo from Welles as the judge. DP

Butterfly (Broken Butterfly/ Baby Tramp)
(Joseph W Sarno, 1972, Switz) Marie Forsa, Harry Reems, Rob Everett, Zoe.
86 min.
Intriguing title, but don't be tempted: it's the same old slop with a young and pure country girl running away from her auntie's farm ('I must find out what lies on the other side of our fields') and discovering a disgusting new life in Munich. The chief perverter is played by Harry Reems, later to appear in *Deep Throat*. Sarno's direction has a slight plodding charm, and the foreigners in the cast speak deliciously wayward English. GB

Butterfly and Flowers (Peesua lae dokmai)
(Euthana Mukdasanit, 1985, Thai) Suriya Yaovasang, Vasana Pholyiem, Suchow Phongvilai.
126 min.
An exceptionally beautiful movie set among Thailand's Muslim minority in villages near the Malaysian border, and centering on a bright teenage kid forced to drop out of school and support his family by turning small-time smuggler. Impossible to convey its qualities without falling back on turn-off words like 'charm' and 'sensitivity', but the fact is that it succeeds in evoking the trials, terrors and excitements of childhood with an immediacy that's both sweet *and* tough. There's an eye-opening blend of universal and local elements: trouble with punks at a rock concert, daredevil feats on the roof of a moving train. And it offers the joy of seeing a director in full control of his medium. TR

Butterfly Ball, The
(Tony Klinger, 1976, GB) Glenn Hughes, Eddie Hardin, Roger Glover, Earl Jordan, Mickey Lee Soule, Twiggy.
87 min.
One of the worst of the spate of rock extravaganzas churned out around this time. The core, with linking commentary by Vincent Price, is a live performance at the Albert Hall of the music Roger Glove scored for William Plomer's book (an adaptation of a 19th century fairytale), which is embroidered with 'imaginative' sequences meant to highlight the different songs. Klinger, who wrote, produced and directed this dinosaur, shows absolutely no insight into the visual presentation of hard rock or fantasy fiction. The imaginative sequences employ the most hackneyed of rock movie clichés, mushroom clouds, some Walt Disney wild life, a masked magician, and an *Alice in Wonderland* tea party. The only hint of life emerges in a brief animation sequence, which returns to Alan Aldridge's illustrations for the book. The music is equally arthritic. Devastatingly boring. IB

Butterfly Effect, The (El Efecto Mariposa)
(Fernando Colomo, 1995, Sp/Fr/GB) María Barranco, Coque Malla, Rosa María Sardá, James Fleet, Peter Sullivan, Cécile Pallas, José María Pau.
109 min.
Fernando Colomo, the Spanish producer/director best known for *Skyline*, based on his experiences in New York, transfers his gently satirical gaze to London. Straitlaced Luis (Malla) enrols in a summer course at the London School of Economics. Soon after he finds lodgings in a Camberwell council flat with untidy *Star Trek* fanatic Oswald (Fleet), their neighbour, Luis's free-spirited aunt Olivia (Barranco), has a bust-up with her philandering actor partner (Sullivan). Luis offers comfort, but, when his mum (Sardá) asked her younger sister to shake him out of his conservative ways, was an affair what she had in mind? The movie's scores on its vitality and because Colomo has an evident feel for London life, especially as experienced by foreigners. Less successful is the ambitious attempt to relate Chaos Theory (direct-to-camera explanations) to human personalities, emotions and behaviour, and the predictable half-hearted celebration of 'liberated' ethics in an otherwise conventional romance. GA

Butterfly Kiss
(Michael Winterbottom, 1994, GB) Amanda Plummer, Saskia Reeves, Kathy Jamieson, Des McAleer, Lisa Jane Riley.
88 min.
When punky weirdo Eunice wanders into a service-station in search of a friend, the dowdy girl at the counter, Miriam, is so drawn to the belligerent vagrant that she takes her home. That night, to Miriam's bemusement, Eunice strips off to reveal a bruised, chained, pierced body and seduces her; the next morning, however, finding her guest gone, Miriam feels impelled to head off in pursuit, a move that will draw her into Eunice's brutal world of seedy sexual encounters and habitual murder. This bleak, provocative debut is at once emphatically English and clearly indebted to American crime and road movies. It's an odd, unsettling little movie, graced with an uneven but authentically raw performance from Plummer as the ranting sociopath and a subtler, sometimes touching turn from Reeves as her beguiled accomplice/would-be redeemer. GA

Butterfly Murders, The (Die Bian)
(Tsui Hark, 1979, HK) Liu Zhaoming, Michelle Mee, Huang Shutang,Zhang Guozhu.
88 min.
A dazzling movie from the vanguard of the 'new wave' in Hong Kong Chinese cinema. Swarms of killer butterflies lay siege to a medieval castle while, inside, the scholar-hero unravels a tangle of secret identities, arcane plots and cruel inventions. Enough plot ideas and visual flair to sustain a dozen average 'thrillers'. Here making his debut, Tsui does what Corman would have done, had he been Chinese and had a million butterflies to play with. TR

...But Then, She's Betty Carter
(Michelle D Parkerson, 1980, US) Betty Carter, Lionel Hampton.
53 min.
A profile of Betty 'Bebop' Carter, intercutting interview material with footage from a public concert sponsored by Howard University at the Cranston Auditorium. Roughly slapped together in a manner not entirely inappropriate to the lady's brash personality and scat-singing style, the numbers tend to be truncated by conversations which reveal remarkably little. Even Lionel Hampton, in a guest spot, seems infected by the air of self-congratulation. TM

By Candlelight
(James Whale, 1933, US) Paul Lukas, Elissa Landi, Nils Asther, Dorothy Revier, Lawrence Grant.
70 min. b/w.
A dazzling display of romantic confidence trickery which takes on Lubitsch in his own territory. Convinced that he too can be a Casanova, a butler (Lukas) seizes his chance when his aristocratic employer (Asther) goes underground to avoid an importunate mistress, but discovers that upstairs and downstairs aren't quite the same thing. Delightful in its complications and malicious social implictions, the whole film – designed as a theatrical charade in which the butler casts himself above his station – fairly glitters with wit. TM

Bye-Bye Babushka
(Rebecca Feig, 1997, US)
80 min. b/w & col.
Rebecca Feig and her co-producer/camerman, Mitchell Rosenbaum, spent two years in Russia during the shooting of this empathetic documentary about the daily lives of a handful of Russian grandmothers. 'We are not women, we are horses.' The women, some in their eighties or nineties, are still working – simply to survive. In the cities they must scrape together the money for food, in the country they break their backs on scraps of land. War, revolution and toil have taken away most of their children. They are together, alone, with a combined stoicism and spirit which is humbling. FM

Bye Bye Birdie
(George Sidney, 1963, US) Ann-Margret, J anet Leigh, Dick Van Dyke, Bobby Rydell, Maureen Stapleton, Jesse Pearson, Paul Lynde, Ed Sullivan.
112 min.
One of the more unsung '60s musicals, this is a big, splashy, Broadway-derived mix of boisterous rock'n'roll satire and breezy showbiz formulas. Hip-swivelling singing idol Conrad Birdie (Pearson in a juicy send-up of Elvis-style narcissism) gets drafted into the army, but not before his managers ('oldsters' Leigh and Van Dyke) arrange for him to bestow a last, symbolic kiss on one lucky Middle American Miss (Ann-Margret). Released just months before Kennedy's assassination, this enjoyable timepiece is notable today for its peppy score, energetic

b

dancing, and for having made a star of the extremely nubile Ann-Margret, 22 passing for 16. Her fresh, wholesome eroticism fairly bursts off the screen. DJ

Bye Bye Blues

(Anne Wheeler, 1989, Can) Michael Ontkean, Rebecca Jenkins, Luke Reilly, Stuart Margolin, Wayne Robson, Robyn Stevan, Leon Pownall.
117 min.
When WWII breaks out, the idyllic colonial existence of Daisy Cooper (Jenkins) and her husband Teddy (Ontkean) is destroyed: a doctor, he is transferred from India to Singapore, while she returns to Canada and the demands of prying neighbours and parochial constraints. But seizing an opportunity to make extra cash singing and playing piano for a dance band, she falls under the spell of Max (Reilly), a rakish trombone player. Will she wait dutifully for Teddy, or dump the kids with relatives and hit the road? Unimaginative direction makes too much use of hackneyed conventions: rain-spattered windows, lonely silhouettes in the night, Max playing a pensive tune beneath a flickering hotel sign. Such techniques are a little like the plot: you've seen it all before. CM

Bye Bye Braverman

(Sidney Lumet, 1968, US) George Segal, Jack Warden, Joseph Wiseman, Sorrell Booke, Jessica Walter, Phyllis Nweman, Zohra Lampert, Godfrey Cambridge.
109 min.
One of Lumet's New York movies, based on Wallace Markfield's acidly funny novel *To an Early Grave*, about four literary mediocrities driving around in search of a friend's funeral (the eponymous Braverman, a lionised success), meanwhile giving vent to their spleen in conversations haunted by middle-age, failure and death. Unreleased in Britain, perhaps because of its 'doubtful' taste (at one point the four find themselves hilariously stalled at the wrong funeral), it's a little unfocused but bristles with Jewish wit and fine performances. TM

Bye Bye Brazil

(Carlos Diegues, 1979, Braz/Fr) Betty Faria, José Wilker, Fabio Junior, Zaira Zambelli.
110 min.
About a group of travelling players and their adventures on the road, this is designed as a fairytale with social asides. It wears its Brazilian charm heavily on its sleeve, but its picture of social changes is so resolutely apolitical – and its tale so commercially upbeat – that finally it leaves only the impression of a series of friendly and not very perceptive postcards. SM

Bye Bye Love

(Sam Weisman, 1994, US) Matthew Modine, Randy Quaid, Paul Reiser, Janeane Garofalo, Amy Brenneman, Eliza Dushku, Lindsay Crouse, Rob Reiner.
106 min.
This anodyne domestic caper is one of those movies where you keep waiting for the ad breaks. The star power is strictly middle-ranking: an ill-at-ease Modine is recently divorced womaniser Dave; remarkably chummy Quaid is recently divorced Vic, stuck in blind-date purgatory; and Reiser is Donny, also recently divorced but still in love with his ex-wife. All three have kids, all three have custody during one weekend of meticulously organised fun and extra-curricular romantic intrigue. It's hard to be much concerned about these plastic people and their travails. Even so, you have to admit a certain grudging admiration for the way the slick construction and the stream of mildly amusing one-liners keep you watching despite yourself. TJ

By Nightfall (Verso sera)

(Francesca Archibugi, 1990, It) Marcello Mastroianni, Sandrine Bonnaire.
99 min.
Archibugi returns to the family strife of her previous *Mignon Has Left* for this drama about a university professor (Mastroianni) whose life is turned upside-down when his young granddaughter and her free-wheeling mother (Bonnaire) take up residence in his house. He is forced to re-examine rigid priorities, but newfound affections prove more difficult to comprehend. Some scenes strain towards didacticism,

but these are tempered by touching performances and the film's gentle exploration of love's restorative qualities. CM

By the Law (Dura Lex)

(Lev Kuleshov, 1926, USSR) Alexandra Khokhlova, Sergei Komarov, Vladimir Fogel, Pyotr Galadzhez.
5, 489 ft. b/w.
The least expensive Russian feature ever made, which cut its production costs by isolating in a log cabin the three main characters (one of them played by the ravishing Khokhlova – incredibly considered 'not attractive enough' for commercial purposes). A prospector is smitten with a murderous case of gold fever, and his companions' strict adherence to the Law is swamped by roaring storms and raging floods. Adapted from a short story by Jack London and set in Alaska, the film has an atmosphere of claustrophobic hysteria so strong that it comes as something of a shock to see a picture of Queen Victoria pinned to the wall in an impromptu trial scene. Silent films like this don't need soundtracks to make their noise: you can hear the screaming in your head. AB

By the Light of the Silvery Moon

(David Butler, 1952, US) Doris Day, Gordon MacRae, Leon Ames, Rosemary DeCamp, Mary Wickes, Billy Gray.
102 min.
Harmless sequel to *On Moonlight Bay*, which left Day and MacRae on the brink of marriage at the end of World War I. Manufactured delays for the wedding provide a tiresomely thin plot, but leaves more time for comedy involving young brother, who becomes convinced that dad is romancing a French actress. The gaps are plugged by another batch of nostalgic songs like 'If You Were the Only Girl in the World' and 'Be My Little Bumble Bee'. TM

By the Sword

(Jeremy Paul Kagan, 1991, US) Eric Roberts, F Murray Abraham, Chris Rydell, Mia Sara.
91 min.
Inevitably reminiscent of *Amadeus*, what with Abraham playing Max Suba, an ex-fencing star faced with a younger, more brilliant exponent of the art (compare 'You are the best composer known to me' with 'You're the best fencer I've ever known'). Just like in *Amadeus*, Abraham gets to flash that sinister smile – both sets of teeth showing – and cry 'Maestro!'. Roberts is an unbelievably mannered actor, but as Villard, he's playing an unbelievably mannered man, 'a freak who thinks he's living in the fourteenth century,' as one of the students complains. Villard runs a viciously competitive Salle (fencing school), and Suba, 25 years in the slammer, turns up to try for an instructor's post. Sternly repulsed ('One must learn, before one teaches'), he accepts a job as janitor. After many shots of him practising with a duster, a paint brush and a french stick, he begins to teach, but his gentle, philosophical style clashes with the Maestro's macho technique. A deeper secret links the two men, spelled out in nightmarish flashback, and there's an inevitable showdown. Right down to the painful fencing-to-disco-music routine, this is embarrassingly fab. SFe

Bwana

(Imanol Uribe, 1995, Sp) Andrés Pajares, Maria Barranco, Emilio Buale, Alejandro Martinez, Andrea Granero, Miguel del Arco.
87 min.
This begins promisingly, as a broad comedy about a taxi driver and his family stranded on a remote beach with an enigmatic, non-Spanish-speaking black man. The authority of Pajares' bullying yet ineffectual father is repeatedly undercut by his wife, Barranco's sly mockery, his fractious children's unruly behaviour, and the dignified stillness of Buale's iconic black man. However, with the subsequent arrival of three skinhead neo-Nazis, Basque director Uribe's broken-backed film suddenly becomes a facile social allegory about everyday racism. NF

C

Cinema Paradiso

C

Cabaret

(Bob Fosse, 1972, US) Liza Minnelli, Michael
York, Helmut Griem, Joel Grey, Fritz Wepper,
Marisa Berenson.
123 min.
A maddening mixture, this adaptation of John
Kander's fine musical based on Christopher
Isherwood's Berlin stories. Superbly choreographed by Fosse, the cabaret numbers evoke the
Berlin of 1931 – city of gaiety and perversion, of
champagne and Nazi propaganda – so vividly
that only an idiot could fail to perceive that something is rotten in the state of Weimar. Doubling
as director, Fosse unfortunately feels the need to
put the boot in with some crude cross-cutting (eg
from a man being beaten up by Nazis in the street
to the leering faces of the cabaret performers)
which lands the film in a queasy morass of overstatement. TM

Cabinet of Dr Caligari, The (Das Kabinett des Dr Caligari)

(Robert Wiene, 1919, Ger) Werner Krauss,
Conrad Veidt, Lil Dagover, Friedrich Feher,
Hans Heinz von Twardowski.
5,587 ft. b/w.
Undoubtedly one of the most exciting and
inspired horror movies ever made. The story is
a classic sampling of expressionist paranoia
about a hypnotist who uses a somnambulist to
do his murders, full of the gloom and fear that
prevailed in Germany as it emerged from WWI.
There are plenty of extremely boring sociolog-
ical/critical accounts of the film; best to avoid
them and enjoy the film's extraordinary use of
painted light and Veidt's marvellous performance. Incidentally, the influence of *Caligari* on
the cinema is much more problematic than
some historians suppose. Thematically it has
rarely been copied, and the style only really
infiltrated in dream sequences and other odd
devices. DP

Cabin in the Sky

(Vincente Minnelli, 1943, US) Eddie
'Rochester' Anderson, Lena Horne, Ethel
Waters, Louis Armstrong, Rex Ingram,
Duke Ellington.
100 min. b/w.
One can easily criticise this all-black musical
(Minnelli's first feature) for falling prey to the
same 'Uncle Tom' stereotyping that characterised
Green Pastures, but there's no denying both the
compassion with which Minnelli treats his characters and the immense cinematic talent on view.
The gorgeous dreamlike sets and consummate
control of the fantastic atmosphere that imbues
the story (an idle, poverty-stricken farmer dreams
of being sent to Hell upon dying) are already well
developed. And the cast are magnificent, delivering the lovely Harold Arlen score with style and
power. GA

Cable Guy, The

(Ben Stiller, 1996, US) Jim Carrey, Matthew
Broderick, Leslie Mann, Jack Black, Diane
Baker, George Segal, Ben Stiller, Eric Roberts,
Janeane Garofalo.
96 min.
A twisted and often nasty black comedy. When
naive suburbanite Broderick asks Carrey's over-
eager Cable Guy to give him a few extra channels
for free, he has no idea he's inviting the wired-up
plugster into his life. Newly separated from his
girlfriend, Broderick is sucked into his socially
inept pal's deranged fantasy world, the result of
a lonely boyhood spent watching TV. Carrey's
whirlwind comic energy is too spontaneous and
elusive to be contained by Lou Holtz Jr's initially
unsettling script. Also, Stiller's erratic direction
fails to establish a consistent tone, so that obvious, crowd pleasing set-pieces alternate with
creepy, disturbing weirdness. Compare, for
instance, Carrey's typically berserk karaoke rendition of Jefferson Airplane's 'Somebody to Love?'
with the nightmarish sequence in a kitschy
Arthurian theme restaurant, where he and
Broderick quaff ale and gnaw chicken before
fighting, virtually to the death, with swords, axes,
maces and jousting lances. Nevertheless, because
it dares to expose the dark side of Carrey's persona, and to take chances at this pivotal stage in
his meteoric career, Stiller's film ranks as an honourable failure. NF

Caboblanco

(J Lee Thompson, 1980, US) Charles Bronson,
Jason Robards, Dominique Sanda, Fernando
Rey, Simon MacCorkindale, Camilla Sparv,
Gilbert Roland.
87 min.
Appalling rehash of *Casablanca*, with Bronson as
the expat living on the coast of Peru after the war
and coming into conflict with Nazis over treasure
at the bottom of the sea. Indescribably inept. GA

Cactus

(Paul Cox, 1986, Aust) Isabelle Huppert,
Robert Menzies, Norman Kaye, Monica
Maughan, Banduk Marika.
96 min. b/w.
Separated from her husband, partially blinded in a
car crash, Colo (Huppert) takes refuge in friendship
with Robert (Menzies), himself completely blind
since birth. Love blooms...Given the subject matter,
Cox's bitter-sweet romance might have been pure
soap; but thanks to superior performances and
Cox's strangely detached tone, sentimentality is
held at bay. This is due partly to his characteristically elevated concerns – occasionally stilted
'telling' dialogue suggests that he views blindness
as a perversely privileged path towards self-awareness – and partly to his seeming determination to
become the Australian *auteur sans pareil*: the
flower symbolism, the use of classical music, and
the flickery flashbacks are all familiar from his earlier *Lonely Hearts, Man of Flowers* and *My First
Wife*. It's an often over-schematic movie that holds
the attention through its extreme elegance, the camera slowly prowling to explore a luscious Eden-like
landscape that Huppert is increasingly unable to
see. Best, however, are the film's apparently most
inconsequential moments – a tipsy birthday party
peopled by elderly eccentrics, a stormy cactus-
growers' committee meeting – which exude a vitality and humour to carefully counterpoint the
solemnity of the story proper. GA

Cactus Jack

see Villain, The

Cadaveri Eccellenti

see Illustrious Corpses

Caddie

(Donald Crombie, 1976, Aust) Helen Morse,
Takis Emmanuel, Kirrily Nolan, Jacki Weaver,
Jack Thompson, Lynette Curran, Melissa Jaffer.
106 min.
An intelligent script, based on an anonymous
autobiography, and charting the struggles of an
independent woman in Depression-era Australia,
gets an unfortunate sentimentalising gloss from
Crombie's direction, which attempts to realign
essentially tough-minded material with the
prevalent trend to retro prettiness. Morse is fine
as the abandoned wife who becomes a barmaid
to support herself and her two kids, though her
retention of plucky charm under her 'deviate' circumstances rings a little too good to be true. PT

Caddyshack

(Harold Ramis, 1980, US) Chevy Chase,
Rodney Dangerfield, Ted Knight, Michael
O'Keefe, Bill Murray, Sarah Holcomb, Scott
Colomby, Cindy Morgan.
98 min.
If you're still at the age when farting and nose-pick-
ing seem funny, then *Caddyshack* should knock
you dead. Buried deep – very deep – beneath the
rising tide of effluent is a pleasant enough story of
a kind about trying to make it to the top as a caddy
while yet remaining human; a movie which could
have done for golf what *Breaking Away* did for
cycling. Instead it allows a string of resistible TV
comics (Chase excepted) to mug through an atrocious chain of lame-brained set pieces, the least vulgar of which involves a turd in a swimming pool.
Going a bit far? Well, then someone eats it. And
then someone sits in a pile of vomit. And then...it
just gets worse. CPea

Cadillac Man

(Roger Donaldson, 1990, US) Robin Williams,
Tim Robbins, Pamela Reed, Fran Drescher,
Zack Norman, Annabella Sciorra, Lori Petty,
Paul Guilfoyle.
97 min.
Robin Williams' role here as ruthless, womanising
auto-salesman Joey O'Brien seems at first ideally
suited to his motormouth persona. When the company secretary's jealous, machine gun-toting husband Larry (Robbins) roars into the showroom,
takes everyone hostage, and demands to know the
identity of his wife's lover, Joey's quick-fire patter
undergoes the ultimate road test: as a SWAT team,
TV crews and spectators gather outside, he tries
to stop Larry shooting or blowing up the hostages.
To his credit, Robbins more than holds his own,
his credibly unhinged husband alternating
between frustrated ranting, nervy panic and childlike vulnerability. Very soon, however, the film
swerves violently into overpitched farce, then
plummets into irksome, *Good Morning, Vietnam*-
style sentimentality. While he's lying through his
teeth or improvising a sales pitch that might save
his skin, Williams is funny and convincing; but
once he starts getting dewy-eyed and sincere, flesh-
crawling embarrassment takes over. NF

Caesar and Cleopatra

(Gabriel Pascal, 1945, GB) Claude Rains,
Vivien Leigh, Cecil Parker, Stewart Granger,
Flora Robson, Francis L Sullivan, Basil
Sydney, Ernest Thesiger.
138 min.
Lavish but frequently dull and theatrical adaptation of Bernard Shaw's play about imperial
romance up the Nile. Some of the wit survives
despite being swamped by the spectacle, the
Technicolor photography (by a number of cameramen) is eye-catching, and Rains turns in his
usual sturdy performance. But it's all something
of an overwrought folly. GA

Cafe au Lait

see Métisse

Café Flesh

(Rinse Dream, 1982, US) Pia Snow, Kevin Jay,
Marie Sharp, Andrew Nichols.
76 min.
Terminal sleaze territory, but with 'plot' and 'performances' a cut above the average slice of hardcore. The setting is a post-apocalyptic future
where 99 per cent of the populace is Sex Negative,
unable to indulge in any form of rumpy-pumpy
because it makes them retch. Surrogate kicks are
available, via voyeurism, at 'Café Flesh', where
the unfortunate Negatives stare dead-eyed, much
like any audience of pornoflick punters, as superstud Johnny Rico gets his rocks off. AB

Cage aux Folles, La (Birds of a Feather)

(Edouard Molinaro, 1978, Fr/It) Michel Serrault,
Ugo Tognazzi, Michel Galabru, Claire Maurier,
Rémi Laurent, Benny Luke, Carmen Scarpitta.
91 min.
Barefoot black butler can't decide whether he's a
Pearl Bailey or Paul Robeson. Father of the family has a teenage son for a heterosexual fling, and
'mother' is a drag star. Between them they make
John Inman look like Richard Harris. But the son
wants to marry the daughter of a morality campaigner, and the in-laws must meet...High camp
and farce are acquired tastes, but even those who
usually resist should find amusement in the last
act's mounting hysteria. Although theatrical, it
remains very funny, and uses the overt stereotyping with great sympathy. SM

Cage aux Folles II, La

(Edouard Molinaro, 1980, Fr/It) Michel
Serrault, Ugo Tognazzi, Marcel Bozzuffi, Paola
Borbini, Giovanni Vettorazzo, Glauco Onorato,
Michel Galabru.
99 min.
This time round, Renato (still phlegmatic and long-
suffering) and Albin (still squawking like a constipated parrot) find themselves on the run from the
macho world of spy rings, counter-espionage, and
all manner of things that go wrong on the night.
It's a finely timed and often hilarious airy-fairy
farce, full of ironies with so many twists that they
make Chubby Checker look like a slide rule. FL

Cage aux Folles III: The Wedding, La

(Georges Lautner, 1985, Fr/It) Michel Serrault,
Ugo Tognazzi, Michel Galabru, Antonella
Interlenghi, Benny Luke, Saverio Vallone,
Stéphane Audran.
91 min.

Time Out Film Guide **129**

The huge success of the original rested on Mr and Mrs Popcorn's delighted discovery that, deep down, all those raving queers were very wonderful human beings just like them, while hipper viewers savoured its sly send-up of sexual stereotypes. Fat chance of either happening in this silly farrago of a second sequel, wherein Serrault's flamboyant drag artiste (his ample form, encased in a black-and-yellow striped leotard, bringing new meaning to the term Queen Bee) must sire a child to inherit a fortune. Serrault is too, too outré as the shrieking Zaza, Tognazzi approaches rigor mortis as his straightman, and Lautner (taking over from Edouard Molinaro) directs with zero comic flair. SJo

Caged

(John Cromwell, 1949, US) Eleanor Parker, Agnes Moorehead, Ellen Corby, Hope Emerson, Jan Sterling, Jane Darwell.
96 min. b/w.
Writer Virginia Kellogg spent time behind bars to research this women-in-prison saga, which gained Parker an Oscar nomination as the teenager who's jailed for a crime committed by her man, has his baby while she's inside, and winds up a hard case. Agnes Moorehead's the concerned warden, Emerson the sadistic bull-dyke guard, staples of a genre which started here and has the likes of *Prisoner Cell Block H* and *Bare Behind Bars* to answer for. TJ

Caged Heat

(Jonathan Demme, 1974, US) Juanita Brown, Roberta Collins, Erica Gavin, Ella Reid, Lynda Gold, Warren Miller, Barbara Steele, Toby Carr Rafelson.
83 min.
The US drive-in audience's taste for renegade women has thrown up some pretty bizarre movies, but few more distinctive than Demme's directorial debut. It starts out as a bare-knuckled women's prison pic and turns into a 'girl gang' rampage, by way of a lot of witty feminist gags and the incursion of what William Burroughs would call a 'technological psychiatry' theme. A percussive, Velvet-y score by John Cale and several casting surprises (including the long-absent Barbara Steele) help keep both pace and interest high. It's no more than passable as a thriller, but the density of invention and energy in other respects is enough to shame a dozen contemporary major studio movies. TR

Cage of Gold

(Basil Dearden, 1950, GB) Jean Simmons, David Farrar, James Donald, Madeleine Lebeau, Herbert Lom, Bernard Lee, Gladys Henson.
83 min. b/w.
Middling Ealing thriller which sees Simmons marrying the caddish Farrar, only to be deserted when he discovers she has no money. Then, when she marries her childhood sweetheart, believing Farrar dead, he returns to blackmail her. It takes far too long to get going, and even during the melodramatic climax, never really convinces. Nicely shot, though, by Douglas Slocombe. GA

Cahill – US Marshal

(Andrew V McLaglen, 1973, US) John Wayne, George Kennedy, Gary Grimes, Neville Brand, Marie Windsor, Harry Carey Jr.
103 min.
Wayne, running to fat and covered in pancake, finds that even he has trouble with his kids in this rather slow Western. Seventeen-year-old Danny and little Billy Joe Cahill collude with a gang to rob a bank...all on account of Big Daddy's been out huntin' villains and neglecting them.

Caine Mutiny, The

(Edward Dmytryk, 1954, US) Humphrey Bogart, Jose Ferrer, Van Johnson, Robert Francis, Fred MacMurray, EG Marshall, Lee Marvin, Claude Akins.
125 min.
Having aligned himself with producer Stanley Kramer after naming names during the HUAC witch-hunt trials, Dmytryk opted for ever more turgidly serious subject matter. This, the last and perhaps the best of his films for Kramer, was an adaptation of Herman Wouk's Pulitzer Prizewinning novel about the court martial carried out against peacetime naval destroyer officers Francis and Johnson after they have mutinied

against Bogart's Captain Queeg, who panics during a storm. Bogie's considerable charisma is visibly weakened by his tired appearance, and the strong cast is never really allowed full rein by Dmytryk, whose abiding concern that fair play be seen to be done, with regard to all the characters' various motivations, makes for a stodgily liberal courtroom drama. GA

Cairo Road

(David Macdonald, 1950, GB) Eric Portman, Laurence Harvey, Maria Mauban, Camelia, Harold Lang, Coco Aslan, Karel Stepanek, John Gregson, Peter Jones.
95 min.
Britain's Anti-Narcotics Bureau takes the fight against the dope smugglers to the Egyptian capital in this workaday thriller, whose makers actually took the trouble to go to Cairo and Port Said to shoot it. Twenty-something Harvey makes an early appearance as Inspector Portman's bumbling, keen-as-mustard assistant. TJ

Cal

(Pat O'Connor, 1984, GB) Helen Mirren, John Lynch, Donal McCann, John Kavanagh, Ray McAnally, Stevan Rimkus, Catherine Gibson.
102 min.
Too sensitive for the abattoir where his father works and with no stomach for the IRA driving jobs he is pressured into, Cal tries to dodge the Protestant gangs that roam his predominantly Loyalist estates and yearns after the local librarian. That he should have driven the car carrying the gunman who killed her husband, entails a familiar pattern of love laced with guilt and doomed to founder in the great divide. Bernard MacLaverty's fine script keeps the action batting along and the focus narrow, concentrating on the human tragedy rather than plugging any partisan line. The symbolism is thrashed just a little hard at times, but on the whole it's a most impressive debut from O'Connor, strongly acted all round. JP

Calamity Jane

(David Butler, 1953, US) Doris Day, Howard Keel, Allyn McLerie, Philip Carey, Gale Robbins.
101 min.
OhtheDeadwoodStageiscomin'upoverthehill (fortissimo). Doris, bless her, belts her heart out as the pistol-packin' tomboy who has to clean up her act when she falls for Wild Bill Hickok. Much spunkier than *Annie Get Your Gun*, with better tunes (from Sammy Fain). AB

Calcutta

(John Farrow, 1947, US) Alan Ladd, Gail Russell, William Bendix, June Duprez, Lowell Gilmore.
83 min. b/w.
Although shot entirely in the black hole of the backlot, this is a seasoned programmer with hard-living pilot Ladd, a mainstay of the Calcutta-Chungking air route, braving the bazaars of the Indian city in search of his best pal's killer. Evidence points to the Chalgani Club and Ms Russell. TJ

Calendar

(Atom Egoyan, 1993, Can/Arm/Ger) Atom Egoyan, Arsinée Khanjian, Ashot Adamian.
75 min.
After photographing a series of churches in his native Armenia for a calendar commission, a man looks back on the trip to retrace the disintegration of his relationship with his then partner. In Canada, a year later, the glossy prints look down from the walls on his loneliness, while his ex's occasional telephone calls go miserably unanswered. A certain piquancy (for those in the know) is gained from the Armenian-born Egoyan's casting of himself as the lovelorn lensman and spouse Khanjian as the woman he left behind. Egoyan filters his customary themes – the difficulties of personal communication, the relationship between emotional lives and video technology – in a film which incisively balances metaphor and awkward realism, while shuttling nimbly through time and space, between celluloid and video formats. TJ

California Dolls, The

see All the Marbles

California Man

see Encino Man

California Split

(Robert Altman, 1974, US) Elliott Gould, George Segal, Ann Prentiss, Gwen Welles, Edward Walsh, Joseph Walsh, Bert Remsen, Jeff Goldblum.
109 min.
Gould and Segal on some wild casino sprees in Los Angeles and Reno, speeding through a compulsive night world of frenzied overlapping chatter. Like Hawks, Altman feels rather than thinks his way into a subject, with a special interest in how people relate to one another in moments of crisis. In the process he shows more of what's happening in America than most newsreels, coaxes jazzy and inventive performances out of his actors (Prentiss and Welles are particular treats), and asks for a comparable amount of creative improvisation from his audience while busily hopping from one distraction to the next. JR

California Suite

(Herbert Ross, 1978, US) Alan Alda, Michael Caine, Bill Cosby, Jane Fonda, Walter Matthau, Elaine May, Richard Pryor, Maggie Smith.
103 min.
Quick and varied comedy, highly suited to Neil Simon's machine-gun gag-writing. The four sketches about guests in a Hollywood hotel range from out-and-out banana peel slapstick (Cosby and Pryor) to tragi-comedy of a superior kind (Fonda). Inevitably Fonda provides the film with its centre, giving another performance of unnerving sureness. Also on the credit side is a bedroom farce of epic proportions from Matthau and May. The other vignettes are a bit glum. DP

Caligula

(Tinto Brass, 1979, US/It) Malcolm McDowell, Teresa Ann Savoy, Guido Mannari, John Gielgud, Peter O'Toole, Helen Mirren.
160 min.
Nobody wanted anything to do with *Caligula*: Gore Vidal didn't want his name on it, producer Bob Guccione of *Penthouse* didn't want the Italian director to finish it (then didn't want reviewers to see it), the stars didn't want to be associated with it. The appealing idea of a raging loony who has the power to pursue his little whims has attracted and sunk better talents than these. Indeed, dotted throughout there are glimpses of what might have been: Caligula enquiring of an ebbing Gielgud what it's like to die, a death machine that operates like a combine harvester, some exotic sets in Italo-barbaric style. But all in all it's a dreary shambles, directed by Brass *toto drosso con abandimento*. CPea

Callan

(Don Sharp, 1974, GB) Edward Woodward, Eric Porter, Carl Mohner, Catherine Schell, Peter Egan, Russell Hunter, Kenneth Griffith, Veronica Lang.
106 min.
If any TV spin-off should work, it's *Callan*, a descendant of Michael Caine's Harry Palmer, a loner, a technician who finds conscience clogging the wheels and his actions reverberating within an ever more disillusioning environment. In fact the film is solid rather than inspired, disastrously taking a good third of its running-time to establish its authority over the big screen. Apart from one brilliant cat-and-mouse game played in cars, most of the ideas seem to remain firmly in the admittedly strong script. Callan has even been awarded a Magnum à la Dirty Harry, and a tricksily filmed 'iron fist' technique to rival Lo Lieh's. VG

Callejon de los Milagros, El

see Midaq Alley

Calle Mayor (The Love Maker/Main Street)

(Juan Antonio Bardem, 1956, Sp/Fr) Betsy Blair, José Suárez, Yves Massard, René Blancard, Dora Doll, Lila Kedrova.
95 min. b/w.
Calle Mayor is adapted from a classic novel of Spanish provincial life by Carlos Arniches, which had previously been filmed in the '30s. Bardem's version of this bitter tale of a woman's oppres-

sion was made at the height of Francoism, and had to carry an unconvincing foreword claiming that the story could happen 'anywhere'. When a group of idle young men decide as a joke that one of them should seduce an unmarried woman in her mid-30s, she becomes smitten by him, and the situation turns sourly serious. Bardem's neo-realist pretensions look a trifle thin now, but the film's portrait of a town riddled with prejudice and hypocrisy still packs a weighty punch. The central performance by the un-Spanish seeming Betsy Blair is especially touching. DT

Call Harry Crown
see 99 and 44/100% Dead

Calling All Cats
see 6.5 Special

Call Me
(Sollace Mitchell, 1987, US) Patricia Charbonneau, Stephen McHattie, Boyd Gaines, Sam Freed, Steve Buscemi, Patti D'Arbanville, John Seitz, David Strathairn.
98 min.
Anna's boyfriend Alex (Freed) is a supercilious nerd who fits in his fucking around his work and the evening news. When Anna (Charbonneau) starts receiving velvet-voiced phone calls exhorting her to dress sexily and meet in a downtown New York bar, she is intrigued and complies, believing the caller to be Alex. There follows a wonderfully uncomfortable scene when she waits in a sleazy drinking hole surrounded by looming off-cue characters, but Alex doesn't show. In the loo, she earwigs a brutal killing, thus becoming a risk to an organised crime syndicate. Meanwhile the mysterious calls continue, and she finds herself drawn to someone who, besides alerting her to the erotic potential of oranges, expresses concern for her safety...While Mitchell's directing debut is not slick, it is highly enjoyable, and should do for Jaffa what *Last Tango* did for butter. EP

Call Northside 777
(Henry Hathaway, 1948, US) James Stewart, Richard Conte, Lee J Cobb, Helen Walker, Betty Garde, Moroni Olsen, EG Marshall.
111 min. b/w.
One of the most impressive of Fox's semi-documentary *noir* thrillers shot on location (here Chicago), this sees Stewart as a hard-boiled newspaper reporter latching on to a 'human interest' story of a woman slaving away for years to save the money which may help free her son from prison, and then setting out to prove the man innocent of murder. Besides the generally strong performances and Joe MacDonald's fine monochrome camera-work, what finally impresses about the film is Stewart's gradual development from sceptical scoop-hunter to a committed crusader for justice. Add to that the suggestion that the police are less than willing to be proved wrong in their conviction of Conte (it was a cop that he allegedly killed), and you have an absorbingly intelligent thriller. GA

Call of the Wild, The
(Ken Annakin, 1972, GB/WGer/Sp/It/Fr) Charlton Heston, Michèle Mercier, Raimund Harmstorf, George Eastman, Maria Rohm.
105 min.
Jack London's Yukon yarn of an alsatian sled-dog and his master has been filmed three times. The 1935 William Wellman version compensated for a tame adaptation by the presence of Clark Gable and Loretta Young; the 1976 telemovie benefited from a tougher James (*Deliverance*) Dickey script; all this has to boast is dreaded multi-national packager Harry Alan Towers, who was still mining the same seam of fool's gold in 1979 with the tax-sheltered *Klondike Fever*. At least Canadian money ensured the right locations for that; here Norwegian snowscapes substitute. PT

Caluga o Menta
(Gonzalo Justiniano, 1990, Chile) Mauricio Vega, Aldo Parodi, Patricia Riva de Neira, David Olguiser, Luis Alarlon.
100 min.
An effectively gritty account of the nihilistic existence led by a selection of petty criminals, druggies, down-and-outs and prostitutes living on the margins of Chilean society. There's nothing particularly original or insightful about its portrait of disaffected youth, but the actors have talent and the right faces, and Justiniano directs his rambling story with a good sense of economy and detail. GA

Came a Hot Friday
(Ian Mune, 1984, NZ) Peter Bland, Phillip Gordon, Billy T James, Michael Lawrence, Marshall Napier, Don Selwyn.
101 min.
A splendidly engaging Kiwi comic Western set in 1949 and based on the novel by the highly regarded novelist Ronald Hugh Morrieson. Two con-men who make a tidy if perilous living from scamming village bookmakers descend on a one-lamb town just as the local club-owner is committing a spot of arson and murder for the insurance money. After falling out with both clubman and bookie, the merry pranksters meet up with a bizarre Maori who lives in the woods and thinks he's a Mexican bandit, endure much violence, sexual chicanery and sundry perils, and don't end up with the gold. It's sometimes too chirpy and bumptious, and has a hideous soundtrack, but it holds one and cheers the parts that even mint sauce cannot reach. SGr

Camelot
(Joshua Logan, 1967, US) Richard Harris, Vanessa Redgrave, Franco Nero, David Hemmings, Lionel Jeffries, Laurence Naismith, Estelle Winwood.
181 min.
This thuddingly dull musical (all false eyelashes and kohl) drowns the Arthurian legend in a sea of pink blancmange and leaves one desperately scanning the horizon for flotsam. All hands lost. Can the actors possibly be taking this farrago seriously? One looks in vain for their private signals to indicate the contrary. Redgrave, to her lasting embarrassment, one suspects, plays Guenevere with absolute sincerity, even when singing 'Where Are the Simple Joys of Maidenhood?' The men's vocal mannerisms make them sound as though they're on the far end of a long-distance telephone. CPe

Camels Are Coming, The
(Tim Whelan, 1934, GB) Jack Hulbert, Anna Lee, Hartley Power, Harold Huth, Allan Jeayes.
80 min. b/w.
This wobbly Gainsborough vehicle, produced by Michael Balcon, sends Hulbert of the Camel Corps on an Egyptian drug trafficking investigation; he faces hostile tribesmen and an extremely disobliging 'ship of the desert'. TJ

Camera Buff (Amator)
(Krzysztof Kieslowski, 1979, Pol) Jerzy Stuhr, Malgorzata Zabkowska, Ewa Pokas, Stefan Czyzewski, Jerzy Nowak.
112 min.
Fairly impressive account of an amateur moviemaker who progresses from home movies, via the factory film club, to documentaries of a more political kind. But in improving his technique and his status as a film-maker, he lays himself open to criticism and censorship from the local authorities, and so begins the ideological battle – artistic expression vs political oppression – of Kieslowski's satire. It's not as funny as some critics would have it, and the basic theme is hardly original in Eastern European cinema, but the evocation of the hero's passion for movies, and Stuhr's central performance, manage to make it intelligent entertainment. GA

Camera: Je, The
(Babette Mangolte, 1977, US)
88 min.
This self-portrait of the artist in 1976/77 achieved through subjective camera technique, is actually a kind of diptych. On one side, a photographic session with a series of interesting subjects, some relaxed, some tense and reluctant, whose encounters with the camera emerge as a power struggle, a remorseless battle of wills. On the other, an interminable tour through New York on a clear winter's day, snapping random images of street corners and skyscrapers. Designed to set up a number of dichotomies (people/ cityscapes, interior/exterior, stasis/movement, flatness/depth of field), it all has a sort of satisfying symmetry, but doesn't entirely escape degenerating into a sterile academic exercise. SJo

Cameraman, The
(Edward Sedgewick, 1928, US) Buster Keaton, Marceline Day, Harry Gribbon, Harold Goodwin, Sidney Bracy.
8 reels. b/w.
Keaton's first feature after moving to MGM. That this meant the eventual sacrifice of his career can be seen in the story – Keaton becomes an MGM newsreel camera-man in order to get the girl, who works in the MGM office – and the first half of the film, a series of gags (collapsing bed, reflextesting, mixed-up bathing suits) second-hand enough to have come out of *Nickelodeon*. But the final sequences make up for this disappointment: Keaton gets involved in a Tong war and (inadvertently) with an organ-grinder's monkey. He shoots exclusive footage, but the monkey steals the film. Keaton returns with an empty camera and is kicked out. Gloomily he goes to the beach. His girl is in a boating accident. Forsaking his camera, he rescues her. The monkey keeps the camera rolling. Keaton gets the girl, and back at MGM, it's the greatest news film they've ever seen...shot by the monkey. A delightful piece of film-making within-a-film which is both an insight into Keaton's own logic, and also, alas, a sort of epitaph. AN

Cameron's Closet
(Armand Mastroianni, 1987, US) Cotter Smith, Mel Harris, Scott Curtis, Chuck McCann, Leigh McCloskey, Kim Lankford, Gary Hudson, Tab Hunter.
87 min.
If nothing else, this muddled horror pic contains so many diverse elements that you can't help wondering what Mastroianni might throw in next. Here, in no particular order, are telekinetic mayhem, psychic premonitions, wigged-out scientists, disconnected dream sequences, a female shrink, a Mayan fetish doll, the now obligatory running down corridors, and an evil, cupboard-dwelling monster which can only be summoned by the innocent mind of a child. Curtis plays a young boy whose exceptional psychic powers have been allowed to run out of control by his scientist father (Hunter) and the latter's assistant (McCann). As a result, Cameron's fertile imagination has conjured up a red-eyed monster which lives in the closet (*any* closet) and tends to do nasty things to anyone he doesn't much like. With its mix of mawkish family stuff and graphic mutilations, this is one closet you'll be happy to come out of. NF

Camila
(Maria Luisa Bemberg, 1984, Arg/Sp) Susu Pecoraro, Imanol Arias, Hector Alterio, Elena Tasisto, Carlos Muñoz.
105 min.
Described by the director as 'a passionate woman's intellectual and sexual seduction of a man she found morally desirable', this is the true story of the doomed amours of a young socialite from the beau monde of Buenos Aires and her Jesuit priest. The historical background (the Rosas dictatorship, 1847) is left somewhat sketchy, and Bemberg, a 62-year-old feminist who made her first film at 58, evidences an over-fondness for the Laura Ashley school of costume drama, all starched petticoats and soft-focus cinematography. But, presided over by an unholy trinity of Church, State and family, Susu Pecoraro as Camila conducts her romance with proper abandon and a vibrant intelligence that burns bright and true amid the frilly period fashions. SJo

Camilla
(Deepa Mehta, 1993, Can/GB) Jessica Tandy, Bridget Fonda, Elias Koteas, Maury Chaykin, Graham Greene, Hume Cronyn, Atom Egoyan.
95 min.
Freda Lopez (Fonda), an aspiring songwriter, is going nowhere fast with her career, and her marriage has lost its sparkle; she and her graphic-artist husband (Koteas) take a vacation on Peabo Island, in the Deep South, in the hope of re-energising their lives. Freda forms a close friendship with Camilla (Tandy), eccentric owner of their beach home, who enjoys launching into a fantasy world concerning her own past career as a classical violinist. The pair hit the road and bond, each inspiring the other to unfold her life that little bit more fully. A feel-good romantic comedy which wears its heart a little too obviously on its sleeve. JBa

Camille

(Ray Smallwood, 1922, US) Alla Nazimova, Rudolph Valentino.
5,600 ft. b/w.
Typically cockeyed Hollywoodian notion of how to approach Art, from self-styled exoticist Nazimova. Pointlessly updating Dumas' tale of the tubercular Mlle Gautier's doomed romance with her too socially respectable lover to 1920s Paris, the movie is all Style and no substance: art deco sets (designed by Rudy's later wife Natacha Rambova), hammy histrionics from Nazimova, and not a camera movement in sight. A pity, then, that the initially subdued Valentino's rather impressive performance is allowed to degenerate into overstatement, and then to disappear, as Alla indulges in interminable death throes. GA

Camille

(George Cukor, 1936, US) Greta Garbo, Robert Taylor, Lionel Barrymore, Elizabeth Allan, Henry Daniell, Laura Hope Crews.
108 min. b/w.
MGM's high camp 'funereal' decor, the judicious adaptation of Dumas' play, Cukor's gay sensibility in directing women, and William Daniels' atmospheric photography – all these made *Camille* Garbo's most popular film. Her aura of self-knowledge, inner calm and strength of purpose intermeshed finely with elements of the production to produce a tragedy of love-as-renunciation which was closer in spirit to *Hedda Gabler* than to Dumas. As Roland Barthes says of the character: 'Marguerite is aware of her alienation, that is to say she sees reality as alienation...she knows herself to be an object but cannot think of any destination for herself other than that of ornament in the museum of the masters'. The camera's reliance upon 'The Face' of Garbo was never more obvious than in the final shot of the film. It is through the face that death is signalled, in a long-held close-up of Camille's last few moments that fades into darkness on the point of her demise. MSu

Camille Claudel

(Bruno Nuytten, 1988, Fr) Isabelle Adjani, Gérard Depardieu, Alain Cuny, Laurent Gréville, Philippe Clévenot, Katrine Boorman, Danielle Lebrun, Madeleine Robinson.
174 min.
Paris 1885: by night, a sculptress fills a suitcase with clay from a workman's trench. Such is the intense dedication of Camille Claudel (Adjani), whose desire to win favourable patronage from Rodin (Depardieu) drives her into a disastrous affair with that womanising egotist, thus alienating her family (including poet Paul). As ever in movies about artistic genius, a break-up sends Camille round the bend – a surefire guarantee of prolific productivity, the inevitable neglect of which, by a blinkered bourgeois intelligentsia, pushes her into ever more manic creativity and misery. Nuytten's film would seem far less banal if it were half the length; at almost three hours, we are simply left with trite ideas about artistic inspiration, and a glossy costumer that makes all too predictable points about the ambivalent nature of insanity, the importance of status and money in the art world, and the position of women in a male-dominated society. GA

Camille without Camellias

see Signora senza camelie, La

Camisards, Les

(René Allio, 1972, Fr) Philippe Clevennot, Jacques Debary, Gérard Desarthe, Dominique Labourier, François Marthouret, Rufus, Hubert Gignoux.
120 min.
Set in the Cévannes region of France in the 18th century, *Les Camisards* is about a band of Huguenot rebels who turn their anger at the repressive tactics of a Catholic state into active confrontation (burning churches, hanging informers, guerilla tactics against the army). When it first appeared at the London Film Festival in 1972, it was described as 'Brechtian, distanced, cool rather than emotional and romantic'. True, but it sometimes falls *beteeen* the stools of an all-out costume drama and a political film about repression. It has fine moments though. The rebels roam about a lazy summer countryside, egged on by religious fanatic

Abraham Mazel (Desarthe), occasionally meeting the incompetent state troopers in miniature pitched battles. As the red-jacketed soldiers fall to their knees to fire, the camisards respond by singing a song of solidarity: enough to make your heart beat a little faster.

Cammina Cammina

(Ermanno Olmi, 1983, It) Alberto Fumagalli, Antonio Cucciarrè, Eligio Martellacci, Renzo Samminiatesi.
155 min.
Directed, produced, written, photographed and edited all by Ermanno Olmi, this vast film follows the ramblings of a ragged caravan across an Africa that looks suspiciously like Lower Tuscany. After a deal of time it becomes apparent that these are the Magi, following yonder star, while clad in ethnic sacking. Olmi treats the whole escapade with a delightful irreverence, which apparently has not amused the Vatican.

Campana del Infierno, La (The Bell of Hell/The Bell from Hell)

(Claudio Guerin Hill, 1973, Sp/Fr) Renaud Verley, Viveca Lindfors, Alfredo Mayo, Maribel Martin.
106 min.
On the whole a reasonably thought out baroque tale about a young man whose aunt is trying to get him certified in order to collect his inheritance. In return, he plans elaborate revenge against her and her three beautiful daughters. The complexities of the central character are well handled, and there's enough evidence to suggest that some care went into the film's making. So even when the plot flags, it remains good to look at (a mixture of Buñuel and Roger Corman), apart from some graphic scenes in an abattoir. Lindfors is excellent as the aunt. In a tragic irony, the director jumped or fell to his death from the bell-tower after shooting was completed. CPea.

Campsite Massacre

see Final Terror, The

Camp Thiaroye (Camp de Thiaroye)

(Ousmane Sembene/Thierno Faty Sow, 1987, Sen/Tun/Alg) Ibrahima Sane, Sigiri Bakara, Gustave Sorgho, Camara Med Donsogho.
152 min.
In 1939, young men in French African colonies were recruited to fight the 'World's' war in Europe. Five years later, some returned to Camp Thiaroye to await back pay and demobbing. Tension between men and officers, complaints about chow, a misadventure in a brothel: staples of the basic training and/or prison camp genre are all present and correct. But although the influence of years in France is apparent (he fought in WWII himself), Sembene's is an African sensibility; and the after-effects of the culture clash (literal and metamorphical) precipitated by Hitler is but one of the themes in a subtle and moving picture. Through a series of everyday incidents, we gradually reduce the extent of the French (white) officers' racism; the hypocritical games they play seem ironic at first, but lead to a shameful and bloody end. This, in microcosm, is a story of colonialism, told from the receiving end and taken to a radical conclusion. Sembene and Sow have made what is not only a humane, passionate film, but an honest and vital memorial to those men who died, after the war, at Camp Thiaroye. TCh

Canadian Bacon

(Michael Moore, 1995, US) Alan Alda, John Candy, Kevin Pollak, Rhea Perlman, Bill Nunn, Rip Torn, GD Spradlin, James Belushi.
95 min.
Moore took a mischievous but pointed look at American mores in *Roger & Me* and in his small-screen series *TV Nation*. This satirical sideswipe at the Land of the Free is, however, a stifferoonie. The plot has one joke: hard-pressed US President Alda, a fumbling liberal in the Clinton tradition, needs a war, or something, to up his ratings and win a second term, but after the end of the Cold War there are no enemies left – so the White House staff decide to take on the evil empire to the north, *Canada!* Dismal days. TJ

Canadians, The

(Burt Kennedy, 1961, US) Robert Ryan, John Dehner, Torin Thatcher, John Sutton, Teresa Stratas.
85 min.
Kennedy's first feature, a Western about the Sioux flight to Canada following the death of Custer at Little Big Horn, running into trouble with a rancher (Dehner), but kept to the straight and narrow by Ryan's Mountie. Despite Ryan's performance, a completely inferior film, with a trite script constantly slanted by the presence of Brooklyn opera singer Teresa Stratas as a squaw. DP

Canal Zone

(Frederick Wiseman, 1977, US)
175 min. b/w.
First of a disappointing trilogy of Wiseman documentaries on export versions of Americana (followed by the military sketches of 'Sinai Field Mission' and 'Manoeuvre'), in which the pettily formal rituals of life around the Panama Canal are registered as if the politically sensitive zone had no social, economic, cultural or geographic identity beyond its backdrop function as a bicentennial home from home. Unilluminating and, at nearly three hours, deadly boring. PT

Can-Can

(Walter Lang, 1960, US) Frank Sinatra, Shirley MacLaine, Maurice Chevalier, Louis Jourdan, Juliet Prowse.
131 min.
Sinatra is the lawyer who defends the aesthetic merits of the can-can in the Paris of the 1890s in this vulgar and gaudy version of the Cole Porter musical. MacLaine and Prowse provide the dancing, while Jourdan and Chevalier inject Hollywood's idea of Gallic charm. The film has a small place in cinema history for being savaged by Nikita Khrushchev in the course of his visit to America. Terrible. PH

Candidate, The

(Michael Ritchie, 1972, US) Robert Redford, Peter Boyle, Don Porter, Allen Garfield, Karen Carlson, Quinn Redeker, Melvyn Douglas.
110 min.
Ritchie and Redford's follow-up to *Downhill Racer* is one of the more intelligent films to have been made about political machinations in America. Redford plays an idealistic young lawyer, concerned with grass roots issues, refusing to play the media games that are so much part of the political campaign he becomes involved in, and determined to do and say exactly what he feels. But gradually the desire for the power by which he can implement his ideas leads him into fatal compromise. A fairly obvious story, perhaps, but one that is helped enormously both by Ritchie's reluctance to move away from simulated realism into melodramatic plotting, and by his customary generosity, clear-eyed and unsentimental, towards his characters. And the trap of blaming the inexorable move towards compromise and sellout either on a lone individual (which would suggest that otherwise everything would be all right) or on the system (a vague concept which would excuse the protagonist) is carefully avoided. Rather, the symbiotic relationships into which Redford and his agents, publicists and colleagues willingly, if reluctantly, allow themselves to fall, make for a far more thorough depiction of the seductive nature of power. GA

Candido Erotico

(Claudio De Molinis, 1978, It) Lilli Carati, Mircha Carven, Maria Baxa, Ajita Wilson.
95 min.
Another immaculate conception from Cinecitta's booming 'Vatican' stable, a solemn rehearsal of soft-core rituals: troilism, voyeurism, snide cracks at women's liberation. The glossy young gigolo-hero fucks mother for her money and daughter for lurv, but on the Catholic fun-first-pay-later principle ends up both married *and* impotent. Oedipus + hip guilt = yuk! CA

Candleshoe

(Norman Tokar, 1977, US) David Niven, Helen Hayes, Jodie Foster, Leo McKern, Veronica Quilligan, Ian Sharrock.
101 min.
Comedy-adventure with a hit-and-miss list of Disney ingredients: street-smart (formerly 'spunky') Jodie Foster, Uncle David Niven wear-

ing eccentric disguises, sweet Ms Hayes, winsome orphans, a slapstick climax. Candleshoe is the stately Warwicks manor occupied by Lady Gwendolyn, her butler and her multi-racial brood. The problem of its upkeep would be solved by the discovery of the treasure buried by a pirate ancestor; Foster, the delinquent double of Hayes' long-lost granddaughter is imported by the villains to find it first. AN

Candy

(Christian Marquand, 1968, US/It/Fr) Ewa Aulin, Marlon Brando, Richard Burton, James Coburn, Walter Matthau, Charles Aznavour, John Huston, John Astin, Elsa Martinelli, Ringo Starr.
124 min.
As adapted by Buck Henry, Terry Southern's genuinely, wickedly funny novel – a Candide-style sex satire, about a naive American teenage girl whose innocence automatically provokes the men she meets to feverish, rapacious lust – is neither erotic nor funny. Aulin, besides being unable to act, can't manage an American accent; her various sexual encounters are ludicrously over-long; and quite what the film is meant to be satirising remains obscure throughout. Indeed, it's a typically undisciplined example of late '60s movie-making, dependent on a bland series of caricature cameos from decent actors who should have known better. Burton's Dylan Thomas parody alleviates the tedium temporarily, but Marquand simply doesn't seem to know what directing is all about; the overall effect is profoundly exhausting. GA

Candyman

(Bernard Rose, 1992, US) Virginia Madsen, Tony Todd, Xander Berkeley, Kasi Lemmons, DeJuan Guy, Vanessa Williams.
98 min.
This faithful, scary and visually imaginative adaptation of Clive Barker's story 'The Forbidden' casts Madsen as a Chicago doctoral student researching an urban myth about a hookhanded killer called Candyman. A series of murders in the city's run-down projects are linked with stories about a figure who appears when you say his name five times in front of a mirror. But are the frightened residents and elaborate graffiti proof that Candyman exists, or simply evidence of their wish to believe in the bogeyman? Following up on Paperhouse, Rose stages the suspense and horror with skill and panache, making this one of the best sustained horror movies for some years. NF

Candyman 2:
Farewell to the Flesh

(Bill Condon, 1995, US) Tony Todd, Kelly Rowan, Timothy Carhart, Veronica Cartwright, William O'Leary, Bill Nunn, Matt Clark.
94 min.
Candyman was the best Clive Barker adaptation to date. This follow-up is a travesty of both its literary source and the original film. The only logical sequel would have been 'Candywoman', centred on Virginia Madsen's transformed character. Instead, we have a tedious, fright-free prequel featuring Todd's vanquished Candyman. Director Condon and his writers have misunderstood the myth, which holds that the legendary hook-handed killer exists only in the spaces between the many stories about him; there can, therefore, be no definitive account of his origins. Most of this film, however, is spent explaining how, after the Civil War, Daniel Robataille, the artistic son of a black slave, fell in love with a landowner's daughter, made her pregnant and was punished for his sins. All of which we already knew, and little of which is relevant to a modern-day story about New Orleans schoolteacher Annie Tarrant (Rowan), whose father was slashed to death some years ago. Now Annie is intrigued by her pupil Matthew's obsessive drawings, all of which depict a tall black figure being pursued by a vengeful white mob. Atrocious. NF

Candy Mountain

(Robert Frank/Rudy Wurlitzer, 1987, Switz/Fr/Can) Kevin J O'Connor, Harris Yulin, Tom Waits, Bulle Ogier, Roberts Blossom, Leon Redbone, Dr John, Rita MacNeil, Joe Strummer, Laurie Metcalf, Jayne Eastwood, Kazuko Oshima.
92 min.

A witty anti-road-movie with a subplot on the nature of the artist. Julius (O'Connor, who looks streetwise but plays with aching vunerability) is young, broke, and dreams of rock star fame and fortune. He lands a job with a dodgy band and an assignment to track down Elmore Silk (Yulin), a reclusive, masterly maker of acoustic guitars. Things don't go well: Julius loses his girl and car at the first gas station. From then on, his search is determined by providence and a host of (perfectly cast) off-the-wall characters – a glamorous Frenchwoman (Ogier) stuck out in the middle of the prairies, a father and son laying down the law in barely inhabited North Canada, a woman who kidnaps him for company. As Silk's plaid-clad brother, Tom Waits rasps credibility into the script, telling Julius to 'play golf instead of travelling without knowing where you're going': so begins a steady undermining of the road as a symbol of freedom. The journey ends in Nova Scotia with our James Dean-ish hero humbled by the road but not quite broken. It's left to Elmore Silk to hammer the nail in the coffin of his ideals. Not beat and not downbeat, the general message is a reaffirmation of life after Kerouac. EP

Candy Stripe Nurses

(Allan Holleb, 1974, US) Candice Rialson, Robin Mattson, Maria Rojo, Kimberly Hyde, Roger Cruz, Rick Gates, Rod Haase, Dick Miller.
80 min.
A terrific pulp B feature which relates the adventures of three such renegade 'stripers' (young orderlies) who variously cure the ailments, physical and spiritual, of a Chicano wrongly accused of masterminding a robbery, a self-consumed rock star in an advanced state of doped lethargy, and a basketball player hooked on rippling muscles and amphetamines. Holleb keeps the pace exuberantly frenetic, darting from genuine pathos to quality Cheech and Chong styled humour within the comic strip framework. Particularly effective are the performances which, apart from an excessive parody of the rock star, stay on the restrained side of caricature. In addition, numerous sharply observed details, a tight and spicy script, a splendidly brash punk rock score, and good use of location (including loudly coloured street graffiti and a labyrinthine car repairs yard) make this New World production fairly essential viewing for devotees of exploitation movies. IB

Cane Toads –
An Unnatural History

(Mark Lewis, 1987, Aust) narrators: Stephanie Lewis, Paul Johnstone.
46 min.
Optimistically imported into Australia to curb the destructive sugar cane beetle in 1935 –'Now we've got these cane grubs by the balls!' – the cane toad proved useless. Worse, it bred at an astonishing rate, choked the billabongs, ate everything including ping-pong balls, emitted toxins to the touch, and possessed a sex drive so strong that it would mate with mud. 'They're a bit of a rough bunch', comments one of the numerous and hilarious interviewees. But in some areas of Queensland, the cane toad is regarded with reverence and even affection –'They're mates' – and statues have been erected to the warty oversized amphibian. Little girls put little frocks on them and put them in little beds; junkies smoke them and hallucinate; a citizen impersonated one on the highway and was fined. The most curious nature film since The Hellstrom Chronicle. BC

Cannery Row

(David S Ward, 1982, US) Nick Nolte, Debra Winger, Audra Lindley, Frank McRae, M Emmet Walsh.
120 min.
Based on John Steinbeck's novel about a skid row community full of lovable tramps and prostitutes. Nolte is the ex-baseball star turned marine biologist whose life is changed by the love of a good woman, Winger. Sentimental comedies must walk a fine line between mawkishness and insipidity: although this one slips off the wire occasionally, a strong script, careful treatment and some spirited performances keep it aloft. John Huston serves as narrator. MH

Cannibal (Ultimo
Mondo Cannibale)

(Ruggero Deodato, 1976, It) Massimo Foschi, Me Me Lay, Ivan Rassimov, Sheik Razak Shikur.
92 min.
An oil prospector is captured in a remote Philippine rain forest by a tribe of stone age cannibals, and imprisoned until rescued by the inevitable lustful lady cannibal. Cheapo exploitation director Deodato takes his 'true story' plot, average exploiter rituals and distinctly paunchy hero far too seriously for the film not to be laughable despite its two strong ingredients: excellent cro-magnon acting and a surprising amount of 'frank' (because anthropological?) male nudity. CA

Cannibals, The (I Cannibali)

(Liliana Cavani, 1969, It) Britt Ekland, Pierre Clémenti, Tomas Milian, Francesco Leonetti, Delia Boccardo.
87 min.
Made directly after Galileo, whose strengths Cavani enlarges and develops, this also postulates a primacy of human and emotional response over the nihilism of The Night Porter (made four years later). In this modern day reworking of Antigone, Cavani's striking visual sense illuminates her subject sufficiently to overcome doubts about some of the '60s conceits. Where she manages to evoke her Fascist state as exceptionally normal, the film works exceptionally well; where she obsessively indulges in hyperbolic scenes of Fascist ritual, it all but scuttles itself. VG

Cannibal Women in the
Avocado Jungle of Death
(aka Piranha Women in the
Avocado Jungle of Death)

(JD Athens, 1988, US) Shannon Tweed, Bill Maher, Barry Primus, Adrienne Barbeau, Karen Mistal, Brett Stimely.
90 min.
Following a military failure, ethno-historian Margaret Hunt (Tweed) is sent by the CIA into the Avocado Jungle to track down eminent radical feminist Dr Kurtz, a former chat-show personality turned man-eating Piranha Woman. Aided only by dong-headed guide Maher (not so much a walking erection as a semi-ambulant willy) and the vacuous Bunny, a student whose idea of a good time involves licorice ropes, Hunt sets off into the heart of trashiness where she encounters The Donahews, a tribe of emasculated men who shower her with gifts of handmade pot-holders, and a splinter tribe of women who hate the Piranha's penchant for eating men with guacamole dip (they opt for clam dip themselves). Amid a plethora of 'garbage genre' movies which fail to fulfil the promise of their titles, this is something of a relief, aided by a genuinely funny script, a tip-top performance from Maher, and film trivia aplenty for those who want it. MK

Cannonball (aka Carquake)

(Paul Bartel, 1976, US/HK) David Carradine, Bill McKinney, Veronica Hamel, Gerrit Graham, Robert Carradine, Belinda Balaski, Judy Canova.
93 min.
In many ways this is the film Bartel wanted Death Race 2000 to be. Once again starring David Carradine and constructed around another Trans-American race, it is both better and worse. The comedy cut from Death Race by producer Roger Corman – here guesting as the DA who tries to ban the race – is now present with a vengeance: Gerrit Graham's would-be country singer and a marvellous comic-strip pile-up of cars provide the film's highlights. That said, Cannonball lacks its predecessor's dramatic tension, and by the middle of the film Bartel's disregard for narrative in favour of a series of jokes leaves no dramatic resolution. The movie also features a number of in-joke guest appearances, including (in addition to Corman and Bartel himself) Martin Scorsese, Jonathan Kaplan, Joe Dante, Allan Arkush and Sylvester Stallone. PH

Cannonball Run, The

(Hal Needham, 1980, US) Burt Reynolds, Roger Moore, Farrah Fawcett, Dom DeLuise, Dean Martin, Sammy Davis Jr, Jack Elam, Adrienne Barbeau, Jackie Chan, Peter Fonda.
95 min.

Stars' home movie, with Burt Reynolds and the gang having a terrific time with the camera and each other. Looks like something knocked off on rest days from *Smokey and the Bandit II*. The last five minutes, when they show out-takes of flubbed lines etc, are hysterical. The rest is strictly for those willing to pay for a series of TV chat show performances. MB

Cannonball Run II
(Hal Needham, 1983, US) Burt Reynolds, Dom DeLuise, Dean Martin, Sammy Davis Jr, Marilu Henner, Telly Savalas, Shirley MacLaine, Ricardo Montalban, Henry Silva, Frank Sinatra, Sid Caesar, Jackie Chan, Jack Elam.
108 min.
Cannonball Baker set the first New York to LA road record back in the '20s with a time of 60 hours for the 3,000 miles. When Congress effectively castrated the big-engined muscle cars of the '60s with smog emission laws and a blanket 55mph speed limit, Brock Yates, a motoring journalist, inaugurated the highly illegal 'Cannonball Baker Sea-to-Shining-Sea Memorial Trophy Dash' in 1971. US Grand Prix star Dan Gurney brought the time down to 35 hrs 54 mins, and Hollywood stuntman Needham once took part in a camouflaged ambulance, went on to make the first *Cannonball Run*, a lot of money, and then this sequel, in which the old Hollywood 'Rat Pack' of Sinatra, Martin, Davis and MacLaine are reunited for the first time since *Ocean's 11* (1960). There are nun jokes, mafia jokes, big breast jokes, karate jokes, *Jaws* jokes, more big breasts. It's a long ride. CPea

Can She Bake a Cherry Pie?
(Henry Jaglom, 1983, US) Karen Black, Michael Emil, Michael Margotta, Frances Fisher, Martin Harvey Friedberg.
90 min.
This takes Jaglom one step further in cornering the US market in the lost and the lonely, with a personal style that is pure innocent delight. Emil is the sort of middle-aged baldy who combs the few remaining strands over his dome, wears socks under his sandals, and spends his time busking his way through endless free-form monologues about his tottering love-life. Crossing over his shambling rhetoric is Black, giving the performance of her career, as an unfocused kook who hasn't a clue what she wants but is fairly certain that she's being followed by her ex-husband. The film is essentially a plotless reverie of lyrical whimsy encircling the usual New York crazies in a slow waltz. There is more than a little magic abroad: Orson Welles (in footage borrowed from Jaglom's own *A Safe Place*) tries to make some very large animals disappear; Black can sing a mean blues. It ought to fall apart in its own cheerful indulgence, leaving all concerned with egg on their faces; but somehow it's all done with such a loopy benevolence that it emerges as the damn nicest film since Astaire stopped dancing. CPea

Cantata of Chile (Cantata de Chile)
(Humberto Solás, 1976, Cuba) Nelson Villagra, Shenda Román, Eric Heresmann, Alfredo Tornquist, Leonardo Perucci
119 min.
A stylised fresco of constant class struggle interfacing the mythic dimensions of a reconstruction of the 1907 Iquique massacre, when 3,600 Latin American workers died following strikes in the British-owned nitrate mines. A fervent, inspirational hymn to resistance and solidarity, the film encodes its political analysis in its montage of sounds and images, which occasionally overwhelm in their emotive intensity (unfortunately so in a couple of passages of excruciating violence). In part it recalls Jancsó, and is in some way the film Bertolucci would have liked to have made of *1900*, vindicating the epic spectacle as a progressive form. PT

Can't Buy Me Love
(Steve Rash, 1987, US) Patrick Dempsey, Amanda Peterson, Courtney Gains, Tina Caspary, Seth Green, Sharon Farrell, Dennis Dugan.
94 min.
Ronald Miller (Dempsey) is a nerd who wants to be in with the cool clique: the elite jocks and cheerleaders of your average American co-ed high school. Miller pays cheerleading princess (Peterson) to step out with him for a month; the ploy works, and pretty soon Ronald has gained a whole new wardrobe and a whole new attitude. So cool does he become that he fails to notice the real warm feelings that the lovely Cindy has developed for him; so when their time is up, he drops her as planned and begins to work his way through her friends. The director has a feel for this shopping-with-Mummy's-plastic milieu, but the theme of peer group pressure and the almost universal human need for acceptance is compromised by a script of very Californian piety. Otherwise a slight but not unenjoyable movie. MC

Canterbury Tale, A
(Michael Powell/Emeric Pressburger, 1944, GB) Eric Portman, Sheila Sim, Sgt John Sweet, Dennis Price, Esmond Knight, Hay Petrie, George Merritt, Edward Rigby.
124 min. b/w.
Michael Powell's extraordinary film proceeds from the faintly bizarre story of three characters (a land girl, a British sergeant and a US sergeant) who, arriving by the same train in a small Kent village, make friends and set out to unmask the mysterious 'glue man' who pours glue on to the hair of girls out late at night with servicemen. But the film shows a sharp awareness of the tensions underlying a country community in wartime – from rural resentment of the influx of outsiders to more long-term fears of the decay of a traditional social order. An assertion of stability to counterbalance these is provided by Powell's almost mystical sense of historical continuity, epitomised by Canterbury Cathedral and the Pilgrims' Way as captured in Erwin Hillier's lyrical photography. Though infuriatingly difficult to categorise, the film is bold, inventive, stimulating and extremely entertaining. AS

Canterbury Tales, The (I Racconti di Canterbury)
(Pier Paolo Pasolini, 1971, It/Fr) Pier Paolo Pasolini, Laura Betti, Franco Citti, Ninetto Davoli, Hugh Griffith, Derek Deadman, Jenny Runacre.
109 min.
Like *The Decameron*, a broad canvas on which is writ large and bawdy the life of the people. We are again plummeted into a world of lecherous ladies, ugly old husbands, willing and ready pages, ending with a superb final fling in a gaudy red Sicilian hell, accompanied by a salvo of farts. As usual Pasolini creates visual magic where other directors would never see beyond the banal, and the humour is as rich as ever; but there is a distinct feeling of strain, not to say waste, about this film. The best tales are of course the blacker ones: Franco Citti as the Devil, in the Friar's tale, blackmailing sexual offenders; or the Steward's tale, a neat variation on one of the hoariest sex gags around.

Can't Help Singing
(Frank Ryan, 1944, US) Deanna Durbin, Robert Paige, Akim Tamiroff, David Bruce, Ray Collins, Thomas Gomez.
89 min.
Lively Technicolor musical bearing more than a slight resemblance to *Oklahoma*, with a grown-up Durbin as the girl travelling against her father's wishes to meet her fiancé in California but falling for another man instead. A spirited score by Jerome Kern and EY Harburg, plus some fine location photography, allow a strong supporting cast to display its talents. GA

Can't Stop the Music
(Nancy Walker, 1980, US) The Village People, Valerie Perrine, Bruce Jenner, Steve Guttenberg, Tammy Grimes, June Havoc, Barbara Rush.
124 min.
The big joke in this disco-musical is having gay butch stereotypes of both sexes carry on as if they were straight. Six dopey members of the Village People, all with bursting flies, fall for Valerie Perrine (who has a just-platonic relationship with her male room-mate), while the Lesbian advertising agent swoons into the arms of a man. It follows that most of the dialogue is gay in-jokes, with the odd music biz joke for variety. A wretchedly sub-standard score from Jacques Morali and production numbers of exceptional tackiness round things off. Oh, and yes, there is fun in the showers in the 'YMCA' number. TR

Can You Keep It Up for a Week?
(Jim Atkinson, 1974, GB) Jeremy Bulloch, Jill Damas, Neil Hallett, Richard O'Sullivan, Sue Longhurst.
94 min.
Embarrassing British sex comedy, featuring Jeremy Bulloch (late of the Billy Bunter TV series) and – God help him – Richard O'Sullivan. The solitary laugh comes in the credits at the end: 'The producers acknowledge the assistance of the management of the Holiday Inn hotels at Swiss Cottage and Heathrow in making this film'. Surprising that it took as long as 12 days to shoot...mind you, it was quite a trek out to the airport in those days before the Piccadilly Line extension was complete. AN

Cape Fear
(J Lee Thompson, 1961, US) Gregory Peck, Robert Mitchum, Polly Bergen, Lori Martin, Martin Balsam, Jack Kruschen, Telly Savalas, Barrie Chase.
105 min. b/w.
An irredeemable criminal exacts his revenge on the family of a lawyer who put him away. This supremely nasty thriller – originally severely cut by the British censor – boasts great credentials: a source in John D MacDonald's novel *The Executioners*, Mitchum as the sadistic villain (a bare-chested variant on his *Night of the Hunter* role), Peck as the epitome of threatened righteousness, seedy locations in the Southern bayous, and whooping music by Bernard Herrmann. If director Thompson isn't quite skilful enough to give the film its final touch of class (many of the shocks are just too planned), the relentlessness of the story and Mitchum's tangibly sordid presence guarantee the viewer's quivering attention. DT

Cape Fear
(Martin Scorsese, 1991, US) Robert De Niro, Nick Nolte, Jessica Lange, Juliette Lewis, Joe Don Baker, Robert Mitchum, Gregory Peck, Martin Balsam, Illeana Douglas.
128 min.
While one can't deny the technical bravura of this remake of J Lee Thompson's 1961 thriller, it's hard not to feel that Scorsese is selling himself short. Max Cady (De Niro) – the manic, bible-quoting rapist who sets out to wreak sadistic revenge on the family of defence attorney Sam Bowden (Nolte), who suppressed evidence that might have kept him out of jail – comes over less as a credible human being or as Scorsese's 'malignant spirit' of the Bowdens guilt, more as a virtually indestructible monstrosity. Likewise, the Bowdens' newly acquired 'sins' – flirtations with adultery for Sam, unforgiving neuroses for his wife (Lange), nascent interest in sex for his daughter (Lewis) – neither deserve the punishment the film inflicts on them, nor lend substance to the conceit that the family must embrace the violent nemesis Cady represents if it is to find redemption. Except for Lewis and a typically solid turn by Baker, the performances are largely unimaginative in this overblown horror-schlocker. GA

Caper of the Golden Bulls, The (aka Carnival of Thieves)
(Russell Rouse, 1966, US) Stephen Boyd, Yvette Mimieux, Giovanna Ralli, Walter Slezak, Vito Scotti.
105 min.
Abominable caper movie in which a jewel robbery is planned to occur (cue for much gaudy local colour) during the festival of bulls at Pamplona. So manaically dreary that even the ever-reliable Walter Slezak can do nothing to save it. TM

Cape Town Affair, The
(Robert D Webb, 1967, US/SAf) James Brolin, Jacqueline Bisset, Claire Trevor, Jon Whiteley.
103 min.
Horrendously unworthy remake of Fuller's clas-

sic *Pickup on South Street*, with the action switched to South Africa. Brolin takes over Richard Widmark's role as the pickpocket stealing a girl's handbag, only to discover in it microfilm which leads them both into espionage and murder. GA

Capitaine Fracasse, Le

(Abel Gance, 1942, Fr) Fernand Gravey, Assia Noris, Jean Weber, Jean Fleur.
95 min. b/w.
Forget *Napoleon* and its vaulting ambition. Directed with bare competence, this is a limp adaptation of Théophile Gautier's historical fantasy (one of the source books of camp) about a penniless baron who joins a group of travelling players after falling for the *ingénue*. Both the theatrical and the swashbuckling larks remain dispiritingly lifeless. TM

Capitano, Il

(Jan Troell, 1991, Swe/Fin/Ger/Den) Antti Reini, Maria Heiskanen, Berto Marklund.
110 min.
Jan Troell's plodding tale of a punkish teenage couple thieving their way across Finland suffers from memories of Malick's *Badlands*. The girl wants out after the boy kills her rabbits, but can't break the spell of the tyrannical psycho who winds up becoming a family. All we know about him is generic: he watches Sid Vicious doing 'My Way' on the motel TV, likes car crash video games, and cuts the cards to determine their destination. Inordinately slow, with endlessly similar highways and little faith in the audience's uptake. Unsensational. BC

Capone

(Steve Carver, 1975, US) Ben Gazzara, Susan Blakely, Harry Guardino, John Cassavetes, Sylvester Stallone, Frank Campanella, Royal Dano, Dick Miller.
101 min.
The failure of Corman's *St Valentine's Day Massacre* apparently led to his quitting directing. So quite why he produced this lavish though palpably inferior version of the Capone story remains something of a mystery. Tracing the rise and fall of its hero from Union Street punk to syphilitic madman, *Capone* begins well enough as a resolutely profane alternative to Corman's version ('Give you five grand? I wouldn't piss up your arse if you were on fire'), and emphasises well enough that in an amoral world of 'free enterprise' gangsters are merely less hypocritical than anyone else. But as the complex internecine warfare unfolds (with good emphasis on the nationalities involved), the script becomes increasingly schematic, finally degenerating into one endless shoot-out. CPe

Caporal Epinglé, Le
(The Elusive Corporal/
The Vanishing Corporal)

(Jean Renoir, 1962, Fr) Jean-Pierre Cassel, Claude Brasseur, Claude Rich, OE Hasse, Jean Carmet, Mario David, Jacques Jouanneau.
106 min. b/w.
A deceptively slight tale of the attempts by three Frenchmen to escape from a Nazi prison camp during World War II, this late addition to Renoir's impressively wide-ranging oeuvre is nevertheless suffused with the same warm and generous humanism as the great *Règle du Jeu* or *Grande Illusion*. Though the whole thing is played as a comedy, the scenes in the prison camp display Renoir's characteristically sharp eye for regional and class differences, even under the yoke of common suffering. The final parting on the bridge in Paris is a scene which will ring loud and true for anyone with the slightest sense of the value of freedom and friendship. NF

Caprice

(Frank Tashlin, 1967, US) Doris Day, Richard Harris, Ray Walston, Jack Kruschen, Lilia Skala.
98 min.
Characteristically dotty Tashlin comedy about industrial espionage. Incoherently scripted, heavily miscast (Day and Harris hardly add up to a Jerry Lewis), with its few bright moments bogged down in a wearisome spoof of the then fashionable spy cycle. TM

Capricious Summer
(Rozmarné Leto)

(Jiří Menzel, 1968, Czech) Rudolf Hrušínsky, Vlastimil Brodský, František Rehák, Jiří Menzel, Jana Drchalová.
75 min.
Menzel's second feature is adapted from a novel by Vladislav Vancura, rated alongside *The Good Soldier Schweik* as one of the twin masterpieces of Czech comic literature. Some of the dialogue's subtler social and philosophical relevance may prove elusive, but it hardly matters as three middle-aged friends – priest, retired army officer, and owner of the bathing-station – enjoy some end-of-season bathing in a small provincial watering-place, meanwhile discoursing desultorily on their favourite topics (philosophy, strategy, and fleshly pleasures). Suddenly, like a visitation from another planet, a caravan arrives, bringing a sad, stick-like showman who sets up in the village square. His tacky little tightrope-and-conjuring show is suddenly illuminated by real magic when his wife appears, a delicate, honey-haired vision of beauty in black mask and yellow dress. From that moment, with its glimpse of something lost and forgotten, a kind of autumnal madness invades the trio, until the caravan moves on, leaving them brooding again as the sun goes down on their last Indian summer of romance. Menzel's evocation of place and mood, of soft summer days threatened by winter, of regret for lost youth and opportunity, of hope for things to come, is perfection. TM

Capricorn One

(Peter Hyams, 1977, US) Elliott Gould, James Brolin, Brenda Vaccaro, Sam Waterston, OJ Simpson, Hal Holbrook, Karen Black, Telly Savalas.
124 min.
The premise of *Capricorn One* is so intrinsically arresting that it almost saves the film from the sheer incompetence of its script: as a breathless public stands by for the first American flight to Mars, the astronauts are bundled away to a desert location where NASA intends to secretly simulate the whole thing for the TV networks of the world. For a while the film makes the most of the surrealism of this eerie conceit with some effective juxtapositions of illusion and reality as the spacemen play kiddy-cars in their clandestine studio. But pretty soon the project gets bogged down in innumerable difficulties, not helped by the awfulness of most of the dialogue. The climactic introduction of Telly Savalas in a crop-dusting plane must rank as one of the most desperate measures to save a thriller since William Castle hung luminous skeletons from the cinema roof. DP

Captain Blood

(Michael Curtiz, 1935, US) Errol Flynn, Olivia de Havilland, Basil Rathbone, Lionel Atwill, Ross Alexander, Guy Kibbee, Henry Stephenson, Robert Barrat.
99 min. b/w.
The movie that launched both Flynn and the '30s cycle of swashbucklers. Conceived by Warner Brothers as a rival to MGM's *Mutiny on the Bounty*, it's a straightforward adaptation of Sabatini's adventure novel about a young doctor who starts as a deportee, succeeds as a pirate, and winds up as Governor of Jamaica, with Olivia de Havilland on his arm. Less florid sword-play than in later movies, but the formula is all there. RG

Captain Boycott

(Frank Launder, 1947, GB) Stewart Granger, Kathleen Ryan, Cecil Parker, Mervyn Johns, Noel Purcell, Niall MacGinnis, Alastair Sim, Robert Donat.
93 min. b/w.
Lively and intelligent historical drama about the peaceful but spirited battles (in the 19th century) between Irish landowners (led by Boycott, whose name became a synonym for ostracism) and the farmers he tries to evict. Pretty good on period reconstruction, and enlivened no end by a classy cast. GA

Captain Horatio
Hornblower R.N.

(Raoul Walsh, 1951, GB) Gregory Peck, Virginia Mayo, Robert Beatty, Denis O'Dea, Terence Morgan, James Robertson Justice.
117 min.
CS Forester's seafaring epic of the 19th century adapted as a surging tribute to 'bravery', to long-gone 'leaders', and as much a study of the heroic spirit as an action romp. Peck is Hornblower, Mayo the initially ill-fated love interest, and Walsh seems more interested in their inner life and emotional vulnerability, which makes for an oddly limpid (but often quite beautiful) and non-dynamic work from such a primal force. CW

Captain January

(David Butler, 1936, US) Shirley Temple, Guy Kibbee, Slim Summerville, Buddy Ebsen, June Lang.
75 min. b/w.
Miss Curly Top, here named Star (yuk!), is orphaned in a shipwreck, brought up by an old lighthouse keeper, hounded by the education authorities, and dazzling in her scholastic prowess. Oh yes, she sings and dances too. Sticky going. TM

Captain Johnno

(Mario Andreacchio, 1988, Aust) Damien Walters, John Waters, Joe Petruzzi, Michele Fawdon, Rebecca Sykes.
100 min.
A children's tale which illustrates silent life in a world dripping with sound. Quaint, moving, and often humorous, it centres on partially-deaf 12-year-old Johnno (Walters, himself deaf). The setting is a small coastal town where Johnno spends every available moment skin-diving – anything to take his mind off a clumsy, uncaring father (Waters) and taunting classmates. Only his mother (Fawdon) and sister (Sykes) marginally understand his closed world, and new depression comes with his sister's imminent departure for boarding school. Cue the arrival of Italian migrant Tony (Petruzzi) – equally ridiculed for his lack of English – and the start of a close friendship. When father plans his enrolment in a special school, however, Johnno ups and runs…Waters and Fawdon excepted, the performances are quite excellent (Petruzzi especially), and for low-budget film-making, it really drums the message home. DA

Captain Kronos –
Vampire Hunter

(Brian Clemens, 1972, GB) Horst Janson, John Carson, John Cater, Shane Briant, Caroline Munro, Ian Hendry.
91 min.
Even by latter-day Hammer standards, writer-director Clemens transfuses movie vampire lore outrageously, and introduces conventions from a host of other pulp forms. Kronos is an unmistakably Germanic comic strip hero with a crusading zeal for his profession (Stan Lee out of Lang's *Siegfried*). By medieval standards he's distinctly cosmopolitan – carries a samurai sword, smokes dope, meditates; is accompanied on his travels by the scholarly Hieronymous Grost as he rescues distressed damsels from pillory or despatches bullies in Falstaffian taverns. Though Clemens manages sly quotes from the likes of *Nosferatu* and *The Seventh Seal*, the film has absolutely no pretensions beyond being a thoroughly endearing entertainment, and succeeds admirably despite the pastiche of incongruous conventions. RM

Captain Nemo and
the Underwater City

(James Hill, 1969, GB) Robert Ryan, Chuck Connors, Nanette Newman, John Turner, Luciana Paluzzi, Bill Fraser.
106 min.
Jules Verne's Nemo and his undersea kingdom had been the inspiration for numerous special effects work-outs in Hollywood since the silent days, but here it was the MGM-British contingent who were charged with topping the splendours of Disney's *20,000 Leagues Under the Sea*, with a recycled yarn of a shipwrecked sextet rescued and then held captive by the venerable captain of the *Nautilus*. Nicely naïve stuff. PT

Captain Ron

(Thom Eberhardt, 1992, US) Kurt Russell, Martin Short, Mary Kay Place, Meadow Sisto, Benjamin Salisbury, Paul Anka.
100 min.
Would-be seadog Short inherits old boat and sets sail for adventure in the Caribbean only to have soz-

zled captain Russell land the whole crew in deep trouble. Queasy ocean-going comedy, not helped by Kurt's Robert Newton impersonation. TJ

Captains Courageous
(Victor Fleming, 1937, US) Spencer Tracy, Lionel Barrymore, Freddie Bartholomew, Mickey Rooney, Melvyn Douglas, John Carradine.
116 min. b/w.
Archetypal MGM family fodder, with rich brat Bartholomew falling overboard from an ocean liner, and getting saved by Portuguese fisherman Tracy, who knocks the stuffing out of the spoilt kid and teaches him a few of the less luxurious lessons of life. Based on a Kipling story, it's hardly great art, but it passes the time. GA

Captain's Paradise, The
(Anthony Kimmins, 1953, GB) Alec Guinness, Celia Johnson, Yvonne De Carlo, Charles Goldner, Miles Malleson.
89 min. b/w.
Lightly likeable farce about a ferryboat captain whose enviable life with two wives – one in Tangier, one in Gibraltar – inevitably begins to come unstuck. Not exactly sophisticated, it benefits from restrained, civilised performances from an excellent cast. GA

Captain's Table, The
(Jack Lee, 1958, GB) John Gregson, Peggy Cummins, Donald Sinden, Nadia Gray, Maurice Denham, Richard Wattis.
89 min.
Cargo ship skipper Gregson, having his boorish horizons rapidly widened when he takes command of an ocean liner, is the fulcrum of this class satire co-written by Bryan Forbes. Peggy Cummins, never in British films offered a challenge remotely comparable to that she accepted in *Gun Crazy*, plays one of the shipboard rivals for a status-weighted seat at Gregson's side. PT

Captain Stirrick
(Colin Finbow, 1982, GB) Julian Silvester, Jason Kemp, Toby Robertson, Christopher Donkin.
90 min.
The ballad of *Captain Stirrick* (produced by the Children's Film Unit), to be sung to the tune of 'Oranges and Lemons': Victorian children sit locked up in prison/Telling tales of adventure to keep up their spirits/The newest among them tells a story in his turn/'Bout Captain Stirrick, and his bold gang of kids/Who pick pockets and purses to trade for their supper/At a fair out at Smithfield Captain Ned meets misfortune/Betrayed by his temper and a friend he's arrested/So much for the plot. The real charm of this film/Is it's the work of children, on both sides of the camera/Dickensian horror and Grange Hill type heroes/Plus rarefied humour, may be too much for parents/For kids it's a treat, it'll keep 'em off the streets. FD

Captive
(Paul Mayersberg, 1985, GB/Fr) Irina Brook, Oliver Reed, Xavier Deluc, Corinne Dacla, Hiro Arai.
98 min.
Mayersberg's first feature is as richly allusive and as teasingly multi-layered as his scripts for Roeg, *The Man Who Fell to Earth* and *Eureka*. The basis is a Patti Hearst-style tale of an heiress, kept more or less secluded in a castle by her doting tycoon father, who is kidnapped by terrorists from equally privileged backgrounds and subjected to a mixture of brain-washing tortures and love until she comes to recognise the sham of her life. It's a film about change, about discovery of self and the rejection of received values. But it is also a fairy-tale, a nightmare, an operatic fantasy (the music is marvellous) in which unreality holds sway right from the spellbinding opening evocation of a turreted castle in the moonlight. Thereafter, as the princess is rescued from her ogre-father by the young Japanese terrorist who sets up as her Prince Charming, a complex weave of parallels and mirror images illuminates the path of her discovery that she has escaped one captivity merely to fall into another. Stunningly shot and with a knockout performance from Oliver Reed, it's as strange and magical a movie about childhood as *Les Enfants Terribles*. TM

Captive City, The
(Robert Wise, 1952, US) John Forsythe, Joan Camden, Harold J Kennedy, Marjorie Crosland, Ray Teal, Martin Milner.
90 min. b/w.
Crime melodrama with crusading small-town newspaper editor Forsythe exposing organised crime, despite collusion of corrupt police force and Mafia threats against his life. The earnest plot is nothing to write home about, but the effective use of documentary-style location shooting and deep-focus photography was innovatory for its day. NF

Captive du Désert, La (Captive of the Desert)
(Raymond Depardon, 1990, Fr) Sandrine Bonnaire, Dobi Kor, Fadi Taha, Dobi Wachink, Badel Barka.
101 min.
Based on the experience of political kidnappee Françoise Claustre, Depardon's rigorously understated film is short on event but long on presence. The story is rudimentary – a woman lives in captivity with a desert tribe, makes a desultory escape attempt, and is finally released – but the film is extraordinary in its ability to evoke her experience, with its total dislocation of space and time, and above all its fundamental monotony. The image of the desert here is worlds apart from the spuriously mystical dunescape of *The Sheltering Sky*. Depardon's own photography depicts a very material place with its own timetable and demands, the wilderness unfolding prosaically across the screen like some austere colour-field canvas. Acquainting us intimately with the life of the tribe, but without ever coming across as an ethnological document, the film's observation of minutiae is quite transfixing. JRo

Captive Heart, The
(Basil Dearden, 1946, GB) Michael Redgrave, Mervyn Johns, Basil Radford, Jack Warner, Jimmy Hanley, Rachel Kempson, Gordon Jackson.
108 min. b/w.
Decent, plodding attempt to tell it like it was in a German prisoner of war camp, which still manages to deal almost exclusively in stereotypes (every part comfortably tailored to a familiar character actor) and to wave a flag or two (what with rousing choruses of 'Roll Out the Barrel' drowning out the nasty propaganda emitted by the camp loudspeakers). Redgrave almost makes something of his character as a Czech prisoner who assumes a dead Englishman's identity and is forced for his own protection to write love letters to the widow. But with credibility barely enhanced by establishing shots filmed in occupied Germany, even he is finally swamped by the soap-opera atmosphere. TM

Captive of the Desert
see Captive du Désert, La

Captives
(Angela Pope, 1994, GB) Tim Roth, Julia Ormond, Keith Allen, Richard Hawley, Jeff Nuttall, Bill Moody, Peter Capaldi, Siobhan Redmond, Annette Badland.
100 min.
Rachel (Ormond) is a dentist who works part-time at an unnamed London prison. An inmate, Philip (Roth), slips her a note asking her to visit him, and she does. They agree to meet in a nearby cafe when Philip's on day-release, and end up making love in the lavatory, but their affair cannot remain secret for long. It's a mark of director Pope's assurance, and the conviction of the performers, that this somewhat far-fetched set-up doesn't overshadow the proceedings. Gripping and economical, this is a romance shot like a thriller. Ormond throws herself into the role, giving a tremendously honest, passionate performance, well matched by a surprisingly sexy Roth. Inevitably, perhaps, the claustrophobia takes on some negative connotations (the film was made for the BBC and that shows round the edges); but at least Pope has the measure of her material: a truly dangerous love story. TCh

Car, The
(Elliot Silverstein, 1977, US) James Brolin, Kathleen Lloyd, John Marley, RG Armstrong, Ronny Cox, John Rubinstein.
98 min.

A demonic black limousine, with no driver behind its tinted windows, races around exterminating the inhabitants of a small Californian town. Interminably drawn out, with some good special effects but its characters hauled straight out of the cracker-barrel, it has nowhere near the same minatory charge as Spielberg's *Duel*. TM

Carabiniers, Les (The Riflemen/The Soldiers)
(Jean-Luc Godard, 1963, Fr/It) Marino Masè, Albert Juross, Geneviève Galéa, Catherine Ribéro.
80 min. b/w.
Godard's strangest movie, based on a political play and nurtured along as a project by Rossellini. Two moronic thugs (with ironically 'classical' names) join up as soldiers and pillage the world in a global war; they return home to their equally moronic wives and display their spoils. Godard juxtaposes their mindless exploits with extensive archive footage of warfare. His presentation of the sheer idiocy of war admits moments of grotesque humour (one of the soldiers sees his first-ever movie and tries to enter the screen), but it's mostly a cold and pitiless vision. Perhaps the most usefully extreme film of its kind ever made. TR

Caravaggio
(Derek Jarman, 1986, GB) Nigel Terry, Sean Bean, Tilda Swinton, Nigel Davenport, Robbie Coltrane.
93 min.
As Caravaggio (excellently played by Terry) lies dying at Porto Ercole in 1610, his mind drifts back over a short life of extraordinary passion: his relationship with his model, Ranuccio Thomasoni, who posed perhaps as the muscular assassin in so many 'martyrdom' pictures, and the other apex in the triangle, Lena, who is Ranuccio's mistress and Caravaggio's model for the Magdalene and the dead Virgin. Jarman proposes a murderous intensity as the mainspring for both Caravaggio's love life and for his furious painting, and it certainly carries great weight of conviction. For all the melodrama of the story, however, he has elected a style of grave serenity, composed of looks and glances, long silences in shaded rooms, sudden eruptions of blood. It all works miraculously well, even the conscious use of anachronisms and the street sounds of contemporary Italy. CPea

Caravan of Courage
see Ewok Adventure, The

Caravans
(James Fargo, 1978, US/Iran) Anthony Quinn, Michael Sarrazin, Jennifer O'Neill, Christopher Lee, Joseph Cotten, Barry Sullivan.
123 min.
Quicksand, thirst and sadism: the movies have always traded to good effect on the romantic allure of the Middle East, from Valentino to Peter O'Toole. Unfortunately, this slice of epic schlock has all the seductive power of a syphilitic camel. Lacking enough guts to go for the stops-out treatment suggested by its story-line – the diplomatic pursuit of an American woman gone native – it stutters off into liberal apologetics for Islam's quainter customs (summary executions, their polite reverence for women, and so on). The second half picks up the right note with Slocombe's atmospheric photography of Bedouin thundering around ancient Lost Cities; but Zorba the Arab inevitably spoils it all with spontaneous ethnic dancing of appalling jollity. No great sheiks. CPea

Caravan to Vaccares
(Geoffrey Reeve, 1974, GB/Fr) Charlotte Rampling, David Birney, Michel Lonsdale, Michael Bryant, Serge Marquand.
98 min.
The voices form the most attractive part of this film, which suggests that Alistair MacLean's story would have been better as a radio serial. The plot revolves around a Hungarian professor (Bryant) fleeing ze East vor America vher he can develop hiz infention vor everyvon. With irritatingly smart-ass observations like 'Did you ever see a gypsy wearing Gucci shoes?', it all cries out for a sense of irony that only Lonsdale's performance starts to exploit. Rampling and Birney prove totally incapable of forming a convincing

relationship. He makes little of his boorish American hero on the loose and often out of his depth in Europe, while she, looking sadly lost, instead of putting him in his place, climbs into his bed, an event that must go down as one of the most implausible screen moments of the year. CPe

Carbon Copy
(Michael Schultz, 1981, US) George Segal, Susan Saint James, Jack Warden, Dick Martin, Denzel Washington, Paul Winfield.
91 min.
Feeble race comedy, recalling the witlessness and offensiveness of *The Watermelon Man*, in which a secretly Jewish man (Segal secretly Jewish?) makes it big in WASP America until his illegitimate black son shows up and shows him up. Director Schultz is still best known for his funky *Car Wash*, but this marks his decline into MOR movie-making. *Carbon Copy* looks very good, but style doesn't make up for narrative weakness. MA

Card, The (aka The Promoter)
(Ronald Neame, 1952, GB) Alec Guinness, Glynis Johns, Petula Clark, Valerie Hobson, Edward Chapman, George Devine.
91 min. b/w.
Complacent class-based British comedy, adapted by Eric Ambler from one of Arnold Bennett's Potteries-set novels, charting Guinness' rags-to-riches rise to provincial power with no hint of the sourness underlying the later, ostensibly similar, *Room at the Top*, and even less of the prickly probing of the social texture sustaining a Guinness comedy like *The Man in the White Suit*. PT

Cardinal, The
(Otto Preminger, 1963, US) Tom Tryon, Romy Schneider, Carol Lynley, Maggie McNamara, John Saxon, John Huston, Dorothy Gish, Burgess Meredith, Cecil Kellaway, Robert Morse, Ossie Davis.
175 min.
Interminable trials of an Irish-American boy from seminary to cardinal's hat, taking in some twenty years of history and every problem known to Catholic conscience, from religious intermarriage and abortion to the Ku Klux Klan and the Nazi menace by way of the role of the Man of God. Risible script based on a doorstop novel by Henry Morton Robinson, but handled by Preminger with tremendous panache; worth seeing just for the incredible skill and flair with which he stages the action and moves the camera. TM

Card of Fate
see Grand Jeu, Le

Care Bears Movie, The
(Arna Selznick, 1985, US) voices of Mickey Rooney, Jackie Burroughs, Georgia Engel, Sunny Besen Thrasher, Harry Dean Stanton.
76 min.
Animated feature about Kim and Jason, two warm and loving children for whom the Care Bears find parents; Nicholas, of spunkier stuff, tries to take over the world at the behest of an evil green face before he is brainwashed by the Care Bears' cant, 'Friends – that's what it's all about!' Only cynical children armed with jumbo-sized sick-bags and hand grenades should be allowed within earshot of this appallingly animated hippy-speak decked out in pastel shades of puke. AB

Care Bears Adventure in Wonderland!, The
(Raymond Jafelice, 1987, Can) voices: Bob Dermer, Eva Almos, Dan Hennessy, Jim Henshaw, Colin Fox.
75 min.
The Princess of Wonderland has been kidnapped by an evil wizard, so the White Rabbit teams up with a little girl named Alice and (ahem!) the Care Bears to save her. Hemlock to Lewis Carroll fans. TJ

Career
(Joseph Anthony, 1959, US) Dean Martin, Shirley MacLaine, Anthony Franciosa, Carolyn Jones, Joan Blackman.
105 min. b/w.
Well-acted version of a Broadway success (by James Lee), has Franciosa in his pre-exploitation days as an aspiring actor going through tough times in New York theatreland. Martin's a big-head director, MacLaine the protagonist's drink-sodden spouse. Low-key throughout, it also lacks punch. TJ

Career Girls
(Mike Leigh, 1997, GB) Katrin Cartlidge, Lynda Steadman, Mark Benton, Kate Byers, Andy Serkis, Joe Tucker, Margo Stanley, Michael Healy.
87 min.
Leigh reverts to type: good news for anyone who feared our harshest caricaturist might be losing his edge, not so good for those who felt *Secrets & Lies* represented a personal breakthrough in its emotional maturity, dramatic coherence and overriding compassion. Presumably, even its admirers would acknowledge that this is a less ambitious piece than its predecessor. The film mirrors Leigh's own development in two contrasting time frames. In the present, Hannah (Cartlidge) and Annie (Steadman) are composed, self-assured young women making their way in society. Ten years earlier, as student flatmates, they were a bundle of nervous tics, inflamed allergies and shrill neuroses. Leigh's eye for detail is precise, but the hysterical, mannered antics of the flashbacks are over-pitched and alienating. Cartlidge, particularly, seems to have angst in her pants. The present tense material comes as some relief, then, with its prevailing mood of calm introspection, the actresses delicately adumbrating the hesitant intimacy of old friends after a long separation. Yet Leigh is at a loss to develop this situation. They drop in on a sexist yuppie for a spot of tired, knee-jerk 'satire', encounter a smarmy estate agent who fails to recognise them with their clothes on, and finally they meet Ricky (Benton), a massive, stammering wreck of a man who may just represent the conscience of this thin, disappointing film. TCh

Carefree
(Mark Sandrich, 1938, US) Fred Astaire, Ginger Rogers, Ralph Bellamy, Luella Gear, Jack Carson, Franklin Pangborn.
85 min. b/w.
Last but one of the RKO Astaire-Rogers series, *Carefree* is the one in which Ginger falls for Fred (rather than the other way round), Fred dances and drives golf-balls at the same time (the title number – it's said the balls fell in a very tight group bang in the middle of the fairway), Ralph Bellamy socks Ginger in the jaw, and Fred and Ginger perform what has been called 'the kiss of the century'. Not quite as unrelievedly marvellous as the earlier films, *Carefree* is short on length and numbers (Berlin's 'Change Partners' is its all-time hit) and on funny supporters and lines. But there can be few better ways of passing the time than watching Fred's psychiatrist hypnotizing Ginger's pert patient, or the pair of them doing 'The Yam'. SG

Careful
(Guy Maddin, 1992, Can) Gosia Dobrowolska, Kyle McCulloch, Sarah Neville, Paul Cox.
100 min.
It's then that Guy Maddin, the brilliant Winnipeg fabulist who gave us *Tales from the Gimli Hospital* and *Archangel*, was rescued from cult obscurity. Hopefully, this darkly idiosyncratic gem will do the trick. In the 19th century Alpine town of Tolzbad, the puritanical townspeople tread and speak softly, for fear of bringing down an avalanche. But beneath this soft blanket of repression lurk incestuous desires, unspoken fears, and the ever-present threat of violent death. A postmodern silent melodrama, its wry inter-titles and colour-tinted images hark back to, and yet cruelly dissect, a lost 'innocence'. Uniquely weird, subtly macabre, and utterly compelling. NF

Careful, He Might Hear You
(Carl Schultz, 1983, Aust) Wendy Hughes, Robyn Nevin, Nicholas Gledhill, John Hargreaves, Geraldine Turner.
116 min.
Schultz presents a knee-high view of the world in this tug-of-love drama, set in the depression, between two sisters fighting for custody of their orphan nephew. Vanessa (Hughes) wants him in order to relive her fantasies about his father; she is rich, snobbish and beautiful, while Lila (Nevin) – poor, kind and asthmatic – is so prim she speaks of his mother being with 'God's angels'. The law settles for Vanessa's wealth, but the film's sympathies lie all too obviously with honest Lila. Sumner Locke Elliott's novel is ill-served by this adaptation: beautiful to look at, it's still a superficial, Gothic costume drama with a romantic score which pounds out the significance of every gesture. JE.

Careful, Soft Shoulder
(Oliver HP Garrett, 1942, US) Virginia Bruce, James Ellison, Aubrey Mather, Sheila Ryan, Ralph Byrd, Sigurd Tor.
69 min. b/w.
Sole directorial credit rung up by screenwriter Garrett (*City Streets*, *Duel in the Sun*, *Dead Reckoning*), this is only a B movie, but one which brings freshness and a touch of reality to tired genre conventions. Set in Washington, it's about a bored socialite, paid a retainer to hang around political and social circles displaying the latest fashions, who gets more than she bargained for when a conversational gambit that she wouldn't mind being a spy is taken seriously by a Nazi (played by the portly Mather in the blandly avuncular Greenstreet manner). Most of it is wise-crackingly light-hearted, gradually shading into Hitchcock territory with a climactic fight in a deserted mill. But the point is that the story is casually told in flashback by the heroine, still offhand and joking about the whole thing, and thereby underlining Garrett's charge of dilettantism about the war (even after Pearl Harbor) aimed against the Washington upper crust at all levels. TM

Care of the Spitfire Grill
see Spitfire Grill, The

Caretaker, The (aka The Guest)
(Clive Donner, 1963, GB) Donald Pleasence, Alan Bates, Robert Shaw.
105 min. b/w.
Donner's version of Pinter's funniest and most famous play is creditably straight and subdued. Avoiding cinematic intrusions, he allows three of the greatest stage interpretations of Pinter's characters to speak for themselves. Pleasence gives so strong a performance as Davies the tramp that he has never quite been able to escape from it since. Bates and Shaw are both far more restrained than their subsequent careers would lead you to expect. It's rare for a film to rely so heavily on its actors and still be worth watching. DP

Carey Treatment, The
(Blake Edwards, 1972, US) James Coburn, Jennifer O'Neill, Skye Aubrey, Pat Hingle, Elizabeth Allen, Dan O'Herlihy.
101 min.
A bizarre predecessor to *Coma* (in fact based on a pseudonymous novel by Michael Crichton), this hospital thriller sees pathologist Coburn attempting to unravel deaths occurring in connection with abortions and drug pilfering. Oddly balanced between straightforward thriller and semi-parody (towards the end, the body count rises ridiculously), and structured around a nicely complex plot, it nevertheless never examines any of the issues it toys with, and is saddled with incredibly shallow characterisations (O'Neill especially). But for all its faults, at least it's better than the mess of most of Edwards' later efforts. GA

Carla's Song
(Ken Loach, 1996, GB/Ger/Sp) Robert Carlyle, Oyanka Cabezas, Scott Glenn, Salvador Espinoza, Louise Goodall, Richard Loza. Gary Lewis.
125 min.
George (Carlyle), a Glaswegian bus driver, is headstrong and goofy enough to steal his sweetheart away on a diversion around Loch Lomond in his double-decker. The object of his affection, Carla (Cabezas), is a refugee from Central America. Alerted to her suicidal tendencies, George persuades Carla to return with him to Central America, so that she can confront the ghosts of her past, and resolve her relationship with the mysterious Antonio. The year's 1987, and he has no idea what life's really like in a war zone. A film of two halves, this has all Loach's virtues and failings, and in that order. The first hour is sharp and funny, tender and real. George's courtship of an exotic stranger whose pain he can only dimly

comprehend rings very true. His attention makes things harder for her, and he's in over his head well before they touch down in Managua. But here the film loses its feet. The focus shifts from foreground to background. George becomes a passive witness – an audience identification figure whose political re-education fits surprisingly neatly into the liberal Hollywood tradition of *Missing* and *Under Fire*. Fair enough, but Loach never looks very comfortable with this formula, Carla is lost in the shuffle, and screenwriter Paul Laverty's belated attempts to graft some suspense on to the proceedings are half-cocked and under-plotted. TCh

Carlito's Way
(Brian De Palma, 1993, US) Al Pacino, Sean Penn, Penelope Ann Miller, John Leguizamo, Ingrid Rogers, Luis Guzman, Viggo Mortensen, Paul Mazursky.
145 min.
A fairly straightforward '30s-style gangster tragedy about a man doomed to an early grave by his society and his own code. Carlito (Pacino) wants out of the rackets, but to get there he has to 'play Bogart', running a discotheque, and even then he can't escape his friends – lover Miller and lawyer Penn. Just as Carlito can't reconcile who he is and where he came from, so Brian De Palma can't quite craft an anonymous mainstream movie. The picture comes alive in its set-pieces, most notably in the climax at Grand Central Station. It runs long and is ultimately not much more than a showpiece, but Pacino looks every inch a movie star, and De Palma provides a timely reminder of just how impoverished the Hollywood lexicon has become since the glory days of the '70s. TCh

Carlota Joaquina, Princess of Brazil
(Carla Camurati, 1995, Braz) Marieta Severo, Marco Nanini, Ludmila Dayer.
101 min.
This first feature is like an historically accurate *Carry On* without the camp. In 1785, Carlota (Severo) is married, aged ten, to Portugal's Prince João (Nanini), later Dom João VI. Come 1808 and the Napoleonic invasion, and the Portuguese court relocates to Brazil, its largest colony, at the scheming behest of their English allies, where it remains until 1821. Dom João is a docile, bumbling, sometime idiot who just about manages to run a kingdom; Carlota whiles away her hours having numerous men and babies. The aim may be bawdy comedy, but it ain't funny. All this would be fairly inoffensive, but for the film's flashback structure. In an apparent sop to the international market, the tale is narrated in stultifyingly drawn-out English to a ten-year-old on a Scottish beach: 'She had lots of lovers. L-o-t-s of them. And she could eat any one of them like a crazy animal.' NB

Carmen
(Cecil B DeMille, 1915, US) Geraldine Farrar, William Reid, Pedro de Cordoba, Horace B Carpenter.
77 min. b/w (tinted).
Farrar caught the eye of Jesse Lasky when she sang Carmen at the Met in 1914, and he subsequently persuaded her to collaborate with DeMille on this scaled down version of the opera. The print under review (from George Eastman House) has been restored and tinted to DeMille's specifications: the ethereal blue of the opening sequence with the smugglers on a California hillside is notably striking. It's topped with a montage of stills and some historical notes, and tailed with a number of imperfect recordings of Farrar herself. The result, regrettably, despite the academic documentation, is frankly a mess. There are repeated shots of a breached, theatrical wall, and even the bullfight, staged in Los Angeles 'by special arrangement', is an anti-climax by DeMille standards (where are the 20,000 extras?). Furthermore, to add to the sense of hodge-podge, some modern non-synched arias and duets have been added. All the hand-to-hand fights, however, are staged with that uniquely cheerful, silent screen gusto. JPy

Carmen
(Carlos Saura, 1983, Sp) Antonio Gades, Laura del Sol, Paco de Lucia, Cristina Hoyos, Juan Antonio Jimenez.
101 min.

Saura's *Carmen* is a Spaniard's examination of the story which did for Spain what the Hovis ads did for Yorkshire. Like his earlier *Blood Wedding*, it explores the legend through various forms of popular Spanish dance and folksong, entirely transposing Bizet's music. The result is as visually exhilarating as the earlier film, but far more complex in its ambitions and achievements. Mingling dance rehearsals with sexual encounters, real fights with choreographed rumbles, and producing a hilarious pastiche of the dreadful 'March of the Toreadors', *Carmen* is both a new kind of musical and marvellous cinema. NR

Carmen
(Francesco Rosi, 1984, Fr/It) Julia Migenes-Johnson, Placido Domingo, Ruggero Raimondi, Faith Esham.
152 min.
Cameraman Pasqualino De Santis' muted colours provide a suitable frame for Rosi's mixed realistic and balletic treatment of Bizet's opera, which climaxes in the symbolically red-clad Carmen goading her maddened victim into murder on the sun-baked sand. Lorin Maazel, heading the Orchestre National de France, conducts a musically first-rate performance; both leading men are, well, mature, but Domingo's bemused passion as the simple soldier is underpinned by magnificent burnished tones. The warm-voiced Carmen, Migenes-Johnson, fleetingly resembling a de-beaked Streisand, recalls a Broadway background in her engaging bump-and-grind concept of sexuality – a reminder that *Carmen* is simply the best musical ever written. Hugely enjoyable for opera buff and non-buff alike. MHoy

Carmen Jones
(Otto Preminger, 1954, US) Dorothy Dandridge, Harry Belafonte, Pearl Bailey, Olga James, Roy Glenn, Diahann Carroll, Brock Peters.
105 min.
Prosper Mérimée's fine old tale of high passions and low morals gets re-upholstered Hollywood-style in Preminger's all-black musical. The cigarette-maker with a rose instead of a fag between her teeth is transformed into Dandridge's parachute factory worker, whose romance with GI Joe (Belafonte) is interrupted by Harlem's equivalent of the toreador – a boxer. Given such a lushly familiar score as Bizet's, the dis, dats and deys with which Oscar Hammerstein liberally sprinkles his lyrics seem oddly fey, even when handled by the competent voices of Marilyn Horne and Laverne Hutchinson. The somewhat heavy-handed direction and the ultimately two-dimensional characters leave you admiring the workmanship without plucking at the necessary emotional/romantic heart-strings. FL

Carmen Miranda: Bananas Is My Business
(Helena Solberg, 1994, Braz/US) Cynthia Adler, Eric Barreto, Leticia Monte.
92 min.
Ae ae ae…at 92 minutes this is more than most people will ever want to know about the Brazilian samba star with the tutti-frutti gimmick. She is clearly a very personal obsession for director/narrator Solberg, though the most interesting material here relates to Miranda's role as a national symbol for Brazilians, and as the embodiment of Roosevelt's Good Neighbor policy during WWII. The exuberant personality comes through loud and clear, but once she made it in Hollywood, Carmen never varied her act, and it's all too obvious why she was crushed under the weight of all those bananas before she reached 50. TCh

Carmin profond
see Deep Crimson

Carnal Knowledge
(Mike Nichols, 1971, US) Jack Nicholson, Candice Bergen, Arthur Garfunkel, Ann-Margret, Rita Moreno, Cynthia O'Neal, Carol Kane.
97 min.
As a slice of familiar Feiffer cynicism, tracing the arid sex life of two contrasting males from eager college days to drained middle age, this was

never quite the major assault on sexism and male chauvinism it set itself up to be. For one thing, Nichols directs with his usual mixture of theatricality and artiness, so that parts (the fumbling triangular courtship at the beginning; the incandescent vulnerability of Ann-Margret; the bleak squalor of Nicholson's slide-show lecture on his conquests) are much better than the whole. For another, Feiffer's arrows, despite some neatly barbed dialogue, mostly seem to fall short of the target. TM

Carné
(Gaspar Noé, 1991, Fr) Philippe Nahon, Blandine Lenoir, Frankye Pain, Hélène Testud.
40 min.
The raw power of this disturbing study of an alienated Parisian horsemeat butcher's over-protective, potentially incestuous relationship with his pubescent daughter is contained only by its meticulously framed CinemaScope images. Black humour plays a part too, as Philippe Nahon's coarse, prejudiced butcher tries to cope with the cruel vagaries of life. Noé's bleak social vision is reminiscent of early Fassbinder, but his powerful, visceral imagery is all his own. NF

Carne Trémula
see Live Flesh

Carnival in Flanders
see Kermesse Héroique, La

Carnival of Souls
(Herk Harvey, 1962, US) Candace Hilligoss, Frances Feist, Sidney Berger, Art Ellison, Stan Levitt, Herk Harvey.
81 min. b/w.
The only survivor when a car plunges into a river, Mary Henry (Hilligoss) emerges on to a sandbank like a sodden sleepwalker. Shortly afterwards, en route to Utah to take up a job as a church organist, Mary is frightened by a ghostly apparition, a white-faced man whose repeated appearances seem mysteriously connected with an abandoned carnival pavilion. Other strange episodes, during which Mary seems to become invisible and inaudible to those around her, exacerbate her feeling that she has no place in this world. With its striking black-and-white compositions, disorienting dream sequences and eerie atmosphere, this has the feel of a silent German expressionist movie. Unfortunately, so does some of the acting, which suffers from exaggerated facial expressions and bizarre gesturing. But the mesmerising power of the carnival and dance-hall sequences far outweighs the corniness of the awkward intimate scenes; and as Mary, caught in limbo between this world and the next, dances to the discordant carnival music of time, the subsequent work of George Romero and David Lynch comes constantly to mind. NF

Carnival of Thieves
see Caper of the Golden Bulls, The

Carny
(Robert Kaylor, 1980, US) Gary Busey, Jodie Foster, Robbie Robertson, Meg Foster, Kenneth McMillan, Elisha Cook, Bill McKinney, Bert Remsen.
106 min.
A long-cherished project of writer-director Kaylor (hitherto best remembered for *Roller Derby*), packaged on the strength of former Band-leader Robertson's enthusiastic involvement, this caused much unease among its backers with its dark tone and manic moodiness. Set amid the greasepaint and behind-the-canvas graft of a travelling carnival, it features Robertson as the resident con-artist and all-purpose fixer; Busey as the crazed bozo, goading the punters into taking pot-shots at his perch above a water-tank; and Jodie Foster as the runaway who threatens to split their strange bond. The road movie/buddy movie situations and emotions gain an intriguing perverse edge from the setting, with its genuine freaks and sideshow illusionism, as well as from Alex North's wonderfully unsettling score and Harry Stradling's dark cinematography. Better on electric, eccentric ambience than for its final rush of plotting, but such risk-taking movies are a welcome rarity. PT

Caro Diario
see Dear Diary

Carousel
(Henry King, 1956, US) Gordon MacRae, Shirley Jones, Cameron Mitchell, Barbara Ruick, Claramae Turner, Gene Lockhart, Robert Rounseville.
128 min.
Ferenc Molnar's play *Liliom* had already been filmed by Fritz Lang (in France) and Frank Borzage (in Hollywood) when Rodgers and Hammerstein adapted it for their Broadway musical, and here Henry King is content to defer to his betters and simply stand back while the schmaltzy material is overwhelmed by Fox opulence. MacRae is the former fairground barker given celestial leave to visit his loved ones on earth for a day, and incidentally revealing the source of a million Kop anthems with 'You'll Never Walk Alone'. PT

Carquake
see Cannonball

Carrie
(William Wyler, 1952, US) Jennifer Jones, Laurence Olivier, Miriam Hopkins, Eddie Albert, Ray Teal, Barry Kelley.
118 min. b/w.
No relation whatever to De Palma's schlock-horror shocker, but a typically grave Wyler adaptation of Theodore Dreiser's dry novel of social criticism, *Sister Carrie*. Depicting the sliding scales of love and money in turn-of-the-century Chicago, the film has Olivier sinking further and further towards ruin with every helping hand he offers to aspiring, ambitious actress Jones. PT

Carrie
(Brian De Palma, 1976, US) Sissy Spacek, Piper Laurie, Amy Irving, William Katt, John Travolta, Nancy Allen.
98 min.
Unlike other Hollywood virtuosos, De Palma's central inspiration remains unashamedly the horror film and its thundering techniques of emotional manipulation. *Carrie* is almost an amalgamation of *The Exorcist* and *American Graffiti*, with Spacek as a religious maniac's daughter whose experience of puberty is so harrowing that it develops paranormal aspects. De Palma's ability to combine the romantic and the horrific has never been so pulverising. Here he contrives a wild juxtaposition of Carrie's freakish inner turmoil with the dreamy cruisin' mentality of her high-school colleagues. The style and imagery are strictly primary in the Freudian sense: menstrual blood and spotless ball dresses, Cinderella dressed up for the abattoir. But the fierce sympathy it extends to its unfashionable central character puts the film a million miles above the contemporary line in sick exploitation. DP

Carried Away
(aka Acts of Love)
(Bruno Barreto, 1995, US) Dennis Hopper, Amy Locane, Amy Irving, Julie Harris, Gary Busey, Hal Holbrook.
109 min.
A backwoods Texas schoolteacher (Hopper), nearing retirement, is transformed by a relationship with a new 17-year-old pupil (Locane): dodgy territory, given that this is based on a novella by Jim Harrison, author of such 'manly' pseudo-Lawrentian works as *Wolf* and *Legends of the Fall*. Hopper's Joseph Svenden is a likeable, honourable man, consumed by phlegmatic inertia: he describes himself as 'a mediocre teacher', with reluctant plans to return to farming if his small school closes; still lives in the old farm with his dying Ma (Harris); and walks crouched over a stick since a tractor accident. He reacts at first with an almost distant attitude to the forceful, knowing advances of the girl. The movie gets interesting not with his hay-barn sexual encounters, nor when he gazes at her naked form as she does a brazen (and ridiculous) Lady Godiva act, but in later scenes, such as when Joseph talks quietly in a bar with his doctor friend (Holbrook) of his lack of concern at the community's disapproval. Busey is good and authoritative as the girl's menacing father. Hackneyed but dignified. WH

Carrière de Suzanne, La
(Suzanne's Profession)
(Eric Rohmer, 1963, Fr) Catherine Sée, Philippe Beuzin, Christian Charrière, Diane Wilkinson, Jean-Claude Biette, Patrick Bauchau, Jean-Louis Comolli.
52 min.
The second of the 'Six Moral Tales', and more substantial than the first (*La Boulangère de Monceau*): here the focus is on two young men, Beuzen and Charrière, who take advantage of Catherine Sée's ethereal Suzanne to bum drinks and food off her, but the crunch comes when it's revealed which one she's actually interested in. Although the resources are relatively modest, Rohmer's elegant wordplay and his exquisite attunement to the vagaries of the human psyche are evident even at this early stage in the director's career. TJ

Carrington
(Christopher Hampton, 1995, GB) Emma Thompson, Jonathan Pryce, Steven Waddington, Rufus Sewell, Samuel West.
123 min.
Hampton's solidly performed directorial debut is a tasteful account of the intense, bizarre relationship between the effete author Lytton Strachey (Pryce, particularly good) and the young painter Dora Carrington (Thompson). This devout but chiefly spiritual affair, which eventually drove Carrington into the arms of other members of the bohemian set, should have made for an intriguing, if ironic, study of exploratory eroticism at odds with conventional morals. Instead, Hampton falls into the usual 'heritage movie' traps: the sex scenes are so timid they appear voyeuristic; the seasons in graceful rural England seem always to be late spring or early summer; and in general there's a sense not of a film but of an illustrated book. The few good lines come from Strachey; though you'd hardly know he was a writer, or Carrington an artist, so little attention is paid to their work. GA

Carrington VC
(aka Court Martial)
(Anthony Asquith, 1954, GB) David Niven, Margaret Leighton, Noelle Middleton, Maurice Denham, Laurence Naismith, Mark Dignam, Victor Maddern, Allan Cuthbertson.
106 min. b/w.
Dorothy and Campbell Christie's stage success was the sort of trusted material to which British stalwart Asquith often turned his skills, and here the result's a typically well-acted courtroom drama lacking only the last ounce of sheer cinematic flair. Niven proves a little more involved than usual as a hard-up army officer, egged on by his unscrupulous wife Leighton, who determines to take the money owed him from the battery safe, then finds himself before a court-martial when his superiors refuse to speak up for him. TJ

Carrosse d'Or, Le
see Golden Coach, The

Carry Greenham Home
(Beeban Kidron/Amanda Richardson, 1983, GB)
69 min.
You don't have to be a woman to watch this documentary by National Film School students, but it certainly helps. Seven months spent sharing the experiences of the peace protesters at Greenham Common has produced a faithful picture, but rarely a compelling one. It is moving to witness the bleak conditions in which the women continue their fight, and solidarity has a way of making you want to participate in its victories. But protests get nowhere by being innocuous, and the film's virtue – it's unflinching honesty – brings about its defects: a bland directorial eye, an assumption that they have your sympathies, and if they don't, they're not worth having. To maintain its momentum, the peace movement needs to make constant inroads on the flagging public consciousness. SMac

Carry Me Back
(John Reid, 1983, NZ) Grant Tilly, Kelly Johnson, Dorothy McKegg.
90 min.
South Island brothers Arthur and Jimmy (Tilly and Johnson) persuade their father to travel to the North Island for the first time in his life to attend a rugby international, but the excitement of an All Blacks victory proves too much for the old guy and his sons are left with a body to transport back to home turf. Cue ferry strikes, stolen vans and inclement weather as the dark comedy turns into a Kiwi variant of *Weekend at Bernie's*.

Carry On Admiral
(aka The Ship Was Loaded)
(Val Guest, 1957, GB) David Tomlinson, Brian Reece, Peggy Cummins, Eunice Gayson, AE Matthews.
82 min. b/w.
Adaptation of an antiquated stage farce by Ian Hay and Stephen King-Hall, about a drunken mix-up which results in a sea-going naval officer (Reece) and a parliamentary private secretary (Tomlinson) inadvertently switching places and duties. Not in the *Carry On* series, though the larks are as witless. TM

Carry On Columbus
(Gerald Thomas, 1992, GB) Jim Dale, Peter Richardson, Alexei Sayle, Sara Crowe, Bernard Cribbins, Julian Clary, Richard Wilson, Keith Allen, Nigel Planer, Rik Mayall, Tony Slattery, Maureen Lipman, Jon Pertwee, Leslie Phillips, June Whitfield, Larry Miller, Jack Douglas.
91 min.
Whatever affection one had for the *Carry On* films died with Sid James for most moviegoers. None of the new crew of Sayle, Richardson, Mayall and Planer is remotely endearing in their awfulness, which goes double for camp Clary. Jim Dale in the title role is anonymous under his cow-pat beret. In fact, the only comedian worth a fart is Larry Miller, playing a cigar-chewing Brooklynite Red Indian chief, though the routines in the New World resemble outtakes from Abbott and Costello. Of course, it's meant to be awful. Gerald Thomas can rest assured that his film looks terrible at all times, while the jokes are puerile and either telegraphed or botched. BC

Carry On Sergeant
(Gerald Thomas, 1958, GB) William Hartnell, Bob Monkhouse, Shirley Eaton, Eric Barker, Dora Bryan, Bill Owen, Kenneth Connor, Kenneth Williams, Charles Hawtrey.
83 min. b/w.
Although not planned as such (it was based on an RF Delderfield play, *The Bull Boys*), this waggish army farce, with Hartnell as the roaring sergeant coping with his National Service awkward squad, became the granddaddy of the *Carry On* series. Built around a resident comic team (notably Sid James, Kenneth Williams, Joan Sims and Charles Hawtrey), with occasional guests of the calibre of Frankie Howerd and Phil Silvers, the series notched up 28 titles from *Carry On Nurse* (1959) to *Carry on Emmanuelle* (1978), all produced by Peter Rogers and directed by Gerald Thomas, mostly written by Talbot Rothwell. Slapdash in conception and execution, the films nominally satirised British customs and institutions or other movie genres, but soon became bogged down in a preoccupation with tits and bums, celebrated in a non-stop flow of innuendo and excruciating puns. The earlier films (*Carry On Cleo*, 1964, being one of the best) had their moments; but the routines became increasingly mechanical, and the jokes increasingly laboured (sample from *Carry On Dick*, 1974: 'As soon as I got into her room, she asked me to bath with her' –'Perhaps she wanted to show you the delights of that fair city'). Paul Taylor neatly summed up the whole phenomenon in a comment on *Carry On Up the Khyber* (1968): 'The sun obstinately refusing to set on a British comedy empire founded on such fearsome mythologies as what a Highlander (from the 3rd Foot and Mouth, naturally) wears under his kilt. Prodigiously awful in the tradition of "it may be rubbish, but it's English rubbish".'

Carson City
(Andre De Toth, 1952, US) Randolph Scott, Lucille Norman, Raymond Massey, Richard Webb, James Millican.
87 min.
Stock Western plot about the laying of railroad lines to forestall raids on the stage-coach carrying gold from the mines, with Scott contracting to build a tunnel through a mountain, and the villainous Massey (mine boss doubling as thief, his

hold-ups hallmarked by the champagne suppers he lays out on the scene for his victims) doing his damnedest to stop him. Not exactly distinguished, but very neatly directed, nicely shot in colour, and with a beautifully judged performance from Scott as the foot-loose mining engineer who takes things very much as they come, but who, once laconically committed, stays committed. TM

Cars That Ate Paris, The

(Peter Weir, 1974, Aust) Terry Camilleri, John Meillon, Melissa Jaffa, Kevin Miles, Max Gillies.
91 min.
Taking his cue from the novels of JG Ballard, Weir (his first feature) chronicles a mutated Australian township which survives by cannibalising the vehicles of unwary travellers and leaving the occupants either dead or 'vegies' for medical experimentation; consequently the town's currency consists of tyres, radios and other highway flotsam. The tone is beautifully sustained throughout, hovering just on the right side of conviction, with superbly understated comic performances from Camilleri and Meillon (the latter as a cosmically impotent mayor). Several genres are deftly skirted, including the increasingly familiar sub-horror theme of an isolated psychopathic community, but the plot never gets bogged down in formula. DP

Car Trouble

(David Green, 1985, GB) Julie Walters, Ian Charleson, Vincenzo Ricotta, Stratford Johns, Hazel O'Connor.
93 min.
Walters (who seems to be getting more unlovably vulgar with each role she plays) and Charleson are a couple of embarrassing caricatures who have just celebrated nine years of marriage. She borrows his brand-new E-Type Jag for an extra-marital bonking session with a greasy car salesman. A minor prang induces vaginismus and locks them together *in flagrante*. Firemen are forced to cut the car in half. It is the sort of hoary old urban myth on which people base brain-damaging short films, but here it is stretched to feature length with wince-making 'jokes' about women drivers, suburbia and knobs. One might have said that the plot would have been improved by the introduction of an axe-wielding maniac, except that there already is an axe-wielding maniac and he doesn't improve it at all. AB

Carve Her Name with Pride

(Lewis Gilbert, 1958, GB) Virginia McKenna, Paul Scofield, Jack Warner, Maurice Ronet, Denise Grey, Billie Whitelaw, Sydney Tafler.
119 min. b/w.
Gilbert and co-writer Vernon Harris had already sanctified Douglas Bader on film in *Reach for the Sky* when they turned here to the biography of allied spy Violette Szabo for more inspirational wartime heroism, greyly mapping her martyrdom in France as an illustration that the stiff upper lip can be inculcated even in a foreign woman if the training's true Brit. PT

Car Wash

(Michael Schultz, 1976, US) Franklyn Ajaye, Antonio Fargas, Richard Pryor, Ivan Dixon, Sully Boyar, Tracy Reed.
97 min.
An amazingly sprightly account of a day in the life of a car wash, demonstrating that work is a four-letter word (especially if you happen to be black or underprivileged), and concerned partly with the variety of excretory messes that have to be dealt with, partly with the flights of ribald fancy indulged in by the employees in an effort to while away the hours till closing time. The remarkable thing is the way characters, jokes and meaning are dovetailed into a single rhythmic flow that makes the film look like TV's *Laugh-In* redesigned as a Minnelli musical. Highly enjoyable. TM

Casablanca 100 (100)

(Michael Curtiz, 1942, US) Humphrey Bogart, Ingrid Bergman, Claude Rains, Paul Henreid, Sydney Greenstreet, Peter Lorre, Conrad Veidt, Dooley Wilson, Marcel Dalio, SZ Sakall.
102 min. b/w.
Once a movie becomes as adulated as *Casablanca*, it is difficult to know how to begin to approach it, except by saying that at least 70 per cent of its cult reputation is deserved. This was Bogart's

greatest type role, as the battered, laconic owner of a nightclub who meets a girl (Bergman) he left behind in Paris and still loves. The whole thing has an intense wartime nostalgia that tempts one to describe it as the sophisticated American version of Britain's naïve *Brief Encounter*, but it has dated far less than Lean's film and is altogether a much more accomplished piece of cinema. There are some great supporting performances, and much of the dialogue has become history. DP

Casa de Bernarda Alba, La
see House of Bernada Alba, The

Casa del sorriso, La
see House of Smiles

Casanova's Big Night

(Norman Z McLeod, 1954, US) Bob Hope, Joan Fontaine, Audrey Dalton, Basil Rathbone, Vincent Price, Hugh Marlowe.
86 min.
Laborious costume parody in which Hope, as a humble tailor induced to impersonate Casanova while the latter flees his creditors, mechanically gags his way through his usual role as a craven braggart. Worth watching mainly for the unusually strong supporting cast, which reads on down the credits to include John Carradine, Lon Chaney Jr, Primo Carnera and Raymond Burr. TM

Casanova '70

(Mario Monicelli, 1965, It/Fr) Marcello Mastroianni, Virna Lisi, Michèle Mercier, Enrico Maria Salerno, Marisa Mell, Guido Alberti.
113 min.
One of Carlo Ponti's numerous internationalist assaults on the American box-office, exploiting Mastroianni's currency as the Latin lover with a light comedy that has him fetishising dangerous romance to the extent that he can only perform under pressure. Six writers provide what seems like a joke apiece, and Marco *Blow-Out* Ferreri lends his considerable presence as actor when he might have been more profitably employed as director. PT

Casey's Shadow

(Martin Ritt, 1977, US) Walter Matthau, Alexis Smith, Robert Webber, Murray Hamilton, Andrew E Rubin, Michael Hershewe.
116 min.
This tale of a small boy's substitution of a horse for his mother boasts several features which put it furlongs out in front of gush like *The Champ*: Ritt's solid feel for the milieu of the Louisiana horse-tracks, an interesting amount of the off-track dealings, but most of all Matthau's acidic performance as the boy's father, a Cajun no-hoper bucking for the big time, which always rescues the film when sentimentality threatens. Seems a shame to keep slagging off Ritt for his liberalism when he can turn in something as well-crafted and unpretentious as this. Nice New Orleans score, too. CPea

C.A.S.H.
see Whiffs

Cash McCall

(Joseph Pevney, 1960, US) James Garner, Natalie Wood, Nina Foch, Dean Jagger, EG Marshall, Otto Kruger.
102 min.
Virtually anonymous Warners soft soap about business community 'values', with Garner's whizz-kid financial maverick slowing down long enough to romance Wood and inadvisedly bail out her father (Jagger). The final screenplay credit for veteran melodramatist Lenore Coffee, adapting the novel by Cameron *Executive Suite* Hawley. PT

Cash on Demand

(Quentin Lawrence, 1961, GB) Peter Cushing, Andre Morell, Richard Vernon, Barry Lowe, Norman Bird, Edith Sharpe.
66 min. b/w.
Small-scale crime drama with Cushing as the fussy, by-the-book manager of a provincial bank who is made an unwilling accomplice to robbery by smooth-talking thief Morell. Though the menace is confined to the verbal game-playing, it is none the less tangibly present, making this a tense little thriller. NF

Casino

(Martin Scorsese, 1995, US) Robert De Niro, Joe Pesci, Sharon Stone, James Woods, Don Rickles, Alan King.
178 min.
Scorsese's movie is technically impressive. There's even something inherently fascinating about the subject – the way Las Vegas, and the organised criminals who run it, have changed over the last couple of decades. What's wrong is the approach: virtuosity seems almost to have become an end in itself, and, as the film charts the experiences of Sam 'Ace' Rothstein (De Niro), a gambler the Mob places in charge of the Tangiers casino, Scorsese's dazzling, kinetic technique calls attention to itself so persistently that story and characters retreat into the background. Not that there's much story, anyway. The first two hours are so heavily video-overed, so bereft of narrative drive, that the film initially resembles some bizarre, hyper-glossy drama-doc. Eventually, some semblance of plot seeps into the last hour, about Ace's disastrous dealings with his ex-hooker wife Ginger (Stone, fine in an under-written role) and with the uncontrollably volatile mobster Nicky (Pesci), but even that's like a tired rerun of *GoodFellas*. The result, sadly, is that contradiction in terms, a dull Scorsese movie. GA

Casino Royale

(John Huston/Ken Hughes/Val Guest/Robert Parrish/Joe McGrath/Richard Talmadge, 1967, GB) David Niven, Peter Sellers, Woody Allen, Deborah Kerr, Orson Welles, Ursula Andress, Joanna Pettet, William Holden, Charles Boyer.
131 min.
Awful spoof-Bond adventure, with Niven heading an all-star cast as 007 and trying desperately to wring some laughs out of a terrible script as he's called out of retirement to battle against SMERSH. Even less amusing than the more 'serious' Bond films. GA

Caso Mattei, Il
see Mattei Affair, The

Casper

(Brad Silberling, 1995, US) Christina Ricci, Bill Pullman, Cathy Moriarty, Eric Idle, Chauncey Leopardi, Amy Brenneman.
100 min.
Lonely guy he may be, but the incorporeal, 'living-impaired' kid of the title occupies a haunted manor like Xanadu, remodelled by Gaudi in expansive mood. The set design, however, merely disguises what is in fact an intimate and likeable picture. As a part-animated live-action movie, it harks back to less frenetic kids' fare from the '60s like *Bedknobs and Broomsticks*, rather than, say, the 'toon-laden *Roger Rabbit*. In fact, despite the sophistication of the computer-generated special effects, Casper and the house's three ghostly stooges are the only non-'fleshies'; for the rest, the priest's neck twists *Death Becomes Her*-style, there's some gentle fun with objects (coffee poured horizontally), and whirlwinds released by screams. The plot's perfunctory: Casper's a lonely channel-hopper who falls for the daughter (Ricci) of ghost therapist Dr Harvey (a winning, soft-centred Pullman), who's employed to exorcise the house – which contains treasure – by scheming Carrigan (Moriarty) and her dozy helpmate Dibs (Idle, playing his usual annoying English twit). WH

Casque d'Or (Golden Marie)

(Jacques Becker, 1952, Fr) Simone Signoret, Serge Reggiani, Claude Dauphin, Raymond Bussières, Gaston Modot, Paul Barge.
96 min. b/w.
There is a deceptive simplicity to Becker's work which may explain why, alone among the major film-makers, he has never quite achieved due recognition. This elegant masterwork is a glowingly nostalgic evocation of the Paris of the Impressionists, focusing on the apache underworld and an ill-starred romance that ends on the scaffold, with an elusive density, a probing awareness of emotional complexities, which reminds one that Becker was once Renoir's assistant. Not his equal, perhaps, but the relationship is inescapable in the texture of the movies themselves. Signoret, as voluptuously sensual as a Rubens painting, has never been more stunning than as the Golden Marie of the English title; and she is perfectly partnered by Reggiani, seemingly carved out of

mahogany yet revealing an ineffable grace in movement, as the honest carpenter who defies the malevolent apache leader (Dauphin) to claim her. Along with *Letter from an Unknown Woman*, one of the great movie romances. TM

Cassandra Crossing, The
(George Pan Cosmatos, 1976, GB/It/WGer) Sophia Loren, Richard Harris, Ava Gardner, Burt Lancaster, Martin Sheen, Ingrid Thulin, Lee Strasberg, John Phillip Law, Lionel Stander.
129 min.
Dire thriller about the dangers of bacteriological research, with an international rag-bag of stars mouthing dialogue of supreme banality as an intercontinental express is summarily rerouted to a former concentration camp after passengers are exposed to a deadly pneumonic plague virus as a result of an abortive terrorist raid on the International Health Organisation in Geneva. Naturally a bridge *en route* is crumbling, and just to add a turn of the screw to the histrionics, one of the passengers happens to be an ex-inmate of the concentration camp. Unbelievable tosh. TM

Cast a Dark Shadow
(Lewis Gilbert, 1955, GB) Dirk Bogarde, Margaret Lockwood, Kay Walsh, Kathleen Harrison, Mona Washbourne, Robert Flemyng.
82 min. b/w.
Well performed woman-in-peril thriller, with Bogarde as the murderous fortune-hunting estate agent who, having already done away with one wife only to discover he's inherited nothing, turns to marrying wealthy ex-barmaid Lockwood. Gilbert unfortunately fails to exact enough tension, but it's still watchable. GA

Cast a Deadly Spell
see Lovecraft

Casta Diva
(Eric de Kuyper, 1982, Neth) Jack Post, Emile Poppe, Ben Kentenis, Paul Verstraten, Walter Nuyens, Gerard Lemaître.
107 min. b/w.
A series of set pieces observing men (and sometimes men watching men): single, lengthy takes from static camera set-ups; an almost total absence of the spoken word; the radiant clarity of black-and-white images. As a celebration of the male form, Eric de Kuyper's first feature is not without its longueurs, but it has a wit and a consistency which both fascinates and impresses. For some, the final flurry of bravura camerawork breaks the tone, but in its own way it's quite ravishing. SM

Cast a Giant Shadow
(Melville Shavelson, 1965, US) Kirk Douglas, Senta Berger, Angie Dickinson, Luther Adler, Yul Brynner, John Wayne, Frank Sinatra, James Donald.
141 min.
Another spectacular in the wake of *Exodus* about the founding of Israel. A highly romanticised fiction about Colonel Mickey Marcus, real-life hero of the Arab-Israeli war, it's riddled with clichés and more than a bit silly, but efficiently staged. TM

Castaway
(Nicolas Roeg, 1986, GB) Oliver Reed, Amanda Donohue, Georgina Hale, Frances Barber.
120 min.
Given the material he began with – Lucy Irvine's rambling, disconnected, soapy saga of love turned sour in a Pacific paradise – Roeg has produced a remarkably straightforward narrative which, while encapsulating all his previous obsessions and themes (strangers in strange lands, love and hate and the whole damn thing), irons out all the wrinkles and time warps which were the hallmarks of his earlier works. In fact, what we get is surprisingly plain sailing through the Blue Lagoon. Gerald (Reed) is a beer-bellied mcp ('Give me a woman that can cook, sew and put up a tent') who advertises for an island soulmate and winds up with Lucy (Donohue), a frustrated London Inland Revenue clerk up for a voyage of self-discovery. Forced into a marriage of convenience, this ill-matched, ill-equipped couple rapidly becomes a non-item when the Tuin island paradise is reached – she refuses to put out, he refuses to put up the shelter, both refuse to face reality. In fact it's a lifetime of marriage – courtship, estrangement, understanding and separation – condensed into a single year. All of which makes for less than comfortable viewing, but real life rarely is, be it in Tuin or Tooting. DAt.

Castle, The
(Rob Sitch, 1997, Aust) Michael Caton, Anne Tenney, Stephen Curry, Sophie Lee, Anthony Simcoe.
82 min.
Forget the rudimentary visual style, the Capra-esque plot (against all odds, a family battles the fat cats who slap a compulsory purchase order on their far from prepossessing home), and the very slight possibility that the film could be an allegory about governmental attitudes towards Aboriginal land. This Oz comedy is terrifically funny from start to finish, largely because the relentlessly optimistic Kerrigans are not just the usual wacky eccentrics beloved by cinema – they're downright moronic, under-achievers in almost every imaginable way. (We've heard of stories with unreliable narrators – but cretinous?) Crucially, however, Sitch and his team present them in a sufficiently sympathetic light to make us care about their fate – that is, providing there's time for such considerations between the virtually non-stop laughs. Bonzer indeed. GA

Castle Keep
(Sydney Pollack, 1969, US) Burt Lancaster, Patrick O'Neal, Jean-Pierre Aumont, Peter Falk, Al Freeman Jr, Scott Wilson, Astrid Heeren, Tony Bill, Bruce Dern.
107 min.
An eccentric endgame allegory based on William Eastlake's novel, critically culted in France but a commercial disaster everywhere, Pollack's war movie contrasts two sets of civilised values (American/European) as Lancaster's platoon fights to hold a medieval castle and its treasures against the German advance, and finds both too retrogressively dogmatic in the face of the holocaust. An ill-moment attempt at likewise fusing an American action genre with Euro art-house 'ideas' ('I didn't intend for people to believe that the castle really existed.'), Pollack's folly remains an intriguing curio in spite of its pretensions. Shot in Yugoslavia by Henri Decae, with similar sterling French support from art director Max Douy and composer Michel Legrand. PT

Castle on the Hudson
(aka Years Without Days)
(Anatole Litvak, 1940, US) John Garfield, Ann Sheridan, Pat O'Brien, Burgess Meredith, Jerome Cowan, Henry O'Neill.
77 min. b/w.
Garfield's again made to suffer, this time as an arrogant petty hood who takes the heat when his girlfriend kills a corrupt lawyer. As ever, he brings bravado and pathos in equal measure to a tailor-made role. Pat O'Brien's the righteous prison warder determined to bring him to heel. As usual in Warner Bros pics of the time, there are plenty of swipes at the iniquities of the system. A remake of *20,000 Years in Sing-Sing*. GM

Casual Relations
(Mark Rappaport, 1973, US) Sis Smith, Mel Austin, Paula Barra, Peter Campus.
80 min.
Rappaport's début feature was an object lesson in turning the limitations of a poverty-row budget to advantage. Various lonely New York neurotics live out their isolated fantasies, fed by cathode-ray glare and memories of movies. It's all pretty funny. A shrink like Lacan might call it a revision of the psychotic subject; the Walker Brothers called their version *In My Room*. TR

Casual Sex?
(Genevieve Robert, 1988, US) Lea Thompson, Victoria Jackson, Stephen Shellen, Jerry Levine, Andrew Dice Clay, Mary Gross.
97 min.
A sex comedy from the female perspective. Originally a three-song sketch by Wendy Goldman and Judy Toll, it was then worked up into a play, and finally a screenplay, reflecting the new AIDS consciousness. Stacy and Melissa re-evaluate their sexual attitudes, and decide to holiday at an upmarket health spa, where potential partners should at least be in good nick. After a variety of sketchy farcical/romantic complications, the movie settles for a rather sentimental epilogue, but it remains surprisingly engaging. The biggest shock is Andrew Dice Clay – the comedian you love to boycott – whose 'Vin-Man' character gets laughs transforming himself from a macho beast to a caring, sharing New Man via the 'Pretend You're Sensitive Handbook'. TCh

Casualties of War
(Brian De Palma, 1989, US) Michael J Fox, Sean Penn, Don Harvey, John C Reilly, John Leguizamo, Thuy Thu Le, Erik King, Ving Rhames, Dale Dye.
113 min.
De Palma is not a director one looks to for conscience, and his track record on the issue of rape has been innocent of moral debate. It's odd to find him dealing with both, and the non-sensationalist approach seems to have taken a toll on his energies: *Casualties of War* is dull. Sgt Meserve (Penn) kidnaps a Vietnamese girl to service his squad during a dangerous reconnaisance mission, and only the rookie Eriksson (Fox) opposes him. The quarrel is as static as their characters – Meserve plain nasty, Eriksson a model of decency. They shout at each other lots; when Eriksson reports the crime, Meserve tries to blow him up in the latrine. The official reaction – what's a crime in wartime? – only comes to life when Lt Reilly (Rhames) explains what injustice means to a black Southerner. David Rabe's screenplay is disappointing in the light of his brilliant *Streamers*, and the conclusion in which Eriksson achieves catharsis back home with a Vietnamese girl on a campus is preposterously corny. BC

Cat, The
see Chat, Le

Cat and the Canary, The
(Paul Leni, 1927, US) Laura LaPlante, Creighton Hale, Lucien Littlefield, Flora Finch, Arthur Edmund Carewe, Tully Marshall.
86 min. b/w.
Paul Leni was the first of the great German expressionist directors to split to Hollywood, and this adaptation of John Willard's stage thriller was his American début. It's the definitive 'haunted house' movie, with the cast gathered for the midnight reading of a bizarre will in a mansion where a maniac is on the loose. Since the plot creaks as much as all the secret passageways, Leni wisely plays it mainly for laughs, but his prowling, Murnau-like camera-work generates a frisson or two on the way. It is, in fact, hugely entertaining, and Laura LaPlante makes a charming victim. TR

Cat and the Canary, The
(Elliott Nugent, 1939, US) Bob Hope, Paulette Goddard, Gale Sondergaard, John Beal, Douglass Montgomery, George Zucco.
72 min. b/w.
A remake of Paul Leni's 1927 *Old Dark House* classic, this was Hope's first really big success. The tale of a group of characters gathered for a reading of a will, with spooky goings-on galore, it's a perfect vehicle for Hope's bluff, cowardly persona. Predictable, but surprisingly atmospheric (Sondergaard helps no end) and often very funny. GA

Cat and the Canary, The
(Radley Metzger, 1979, GB) Honor Blackman, Michael Callan, Edward Fox, Wendy Hiller, Olivia Hussey, Beatrix Lehmann, Carol Lynley, Daniel Massey, Peter McEnery, Wilfrid Hyde-White.
98 min.
From the thunderstorm to the old dark house in which no item of furniture can be trusted not to conceal a secret passage, predictability is the keynote to this fifth remake of John Willard's play. It's obvious from the start whodunit; so the cast are much given to eye-rolling and chilling smiles, either to throw one off the scent or to disguise their embarrassment, for this adaptation is so turgidly faithful that one expects the entire lot (mauled bodies and all) to take a bow as the credits roll. FF

Cat Ballou
(Elliot Silverstein, 1965, US) Jane Fonda, Lee Marvin, Michael Callan, Dwayne Hickman, Nat King Cole, Stubby Kaye, Tom Nardini, John Marley.
96 min.

Western parody, tinged with melancholy for the good old days, in which prim Fonda returns home from school to find her rancher father under threat of eviction or worse, and hires a once-famous gunfighter (Marvin) – who proves to be a drunken bum – as protection against the dreaded hired gunman with the tin nose (also Marvin). The film presents such a mixture of comedy styles that the more lumpen slapstick routines, and the cosy musical interludes from Nat King Cole and Stubby Kaye, may lull you into overlooking some brilliant throwaways. Marvin is consistently brilliant, but the film is patchy. PG

Catch-22
(Mike Nichols, 1970, US) Alan Arkin, Martin Balsam, Richard Benjamin, Anthony Perkins, Orson Welles, Jon Voight, Art Garfunkel, Jack Gilford, Buck Henry, Bob Newhart, Paula Prentiss, Martin Sheen.
122 min.
Faced with the impossibility of filming Joseph Heller's marvellous novel (the ultimate World War II *purgatorio*), Nichols simply arranges a series of brilliantly funny set pieces around the recurring nightmare that haunts Yossarian (Arkin), the bomber pilot determined to fly no more missions because everyone is trying to murder him out there. Though the vertiginously absurdist logic of the book is hopelessly fractured, some of it does filter through (the mostly superb performances are a great help). Nichols unfortunately grafts on a Meaningful Statement by way of a ponderous Fellini-ish sequence in which Yossarian, on leave in Rome, finds himself wandering the seventh circle of hell. TM

Cat Chaser
(Abel Ferrara, 1988, US) Peter Weller, Kelly McGillis, Charles Durning, Frederic Forrest, Tomas Milian, Juan Fernandez, Kelly Jo Minter, Phil Leeds.
90 min. & col.
Co-scripted by Elmore Leonard from his own novel, starting out with black-and-white footage of war-torn Santo Domingo before jumping to the palmless tat of a Florida motel, this is a typical Leonard brew: extreme passion and violence interspersed with mature characterisations, wit, and a non-judgemental attitude. Weller leads a splendid cast as George Moran, a laid-back motelier who dreams about his paratrooper past and about the wife (McGillis) of a particularly sadistic Dominican ex-police chief (Milian)who has a thing about testicles and garden shears. On the way, from quirky opening to woozily abrupt climax, we pick up low-life and hustler, big-wig and flunky, as George finds himself tangling not only with the powerful hubby but with the wonderfully decrepit, ruthless figure of Jiggs Scully, played by Charles Durning as if *Blood Simple* had collided with *The Killers*. Jiggs isn't after the lady (perish the thought) but the *generalissimo's* loot. Both Durning and Forrest, as a boozy drifter, excel in a gripping thriller marred only by some precious and unrevealing voice-overs presumably meant to remind us that Leonard is nearer to Hammett and Chandler than *Miami Vice*. SGr

Catchfire
(Alan Smithee, ie Dennis Hopper, 1989, US) Dennis Hopper, Jodie Foster, John Turturro, Joe Pesci, Fred Ward, Dean Stockwell, Vincent Price, Charlie Sheen, Julie Adams, Bob Dylan.
99 min.
Dennis Hopper, denying directorial responsibility behind the traditional Alan Smithee credit, has certainly lost a fair amount of plot logic in the editing. Judging by the lady trucker who discusses genital symbolism in Georgia O'Keefe, he may have been shorn of larky digressions too, as well as the odd guest, though Dylan's walk-on survives. It's a picaresque charade about hit-man Milo (Hopper) who falls for his hit, artist Anne (Foster), kidnaps her and dodges the mob (Price, Pesci, Stockwell) who commissioned him. He has deep, inarticulate feelings of love, despite his underwear fetish and an unfortunate jump-start with rape. Quite why Anne reciprocates has got lost in the wash. Hiding out in the hills, she encourages him to rescue a lamb from a crevasse, but we've already been hipped to his heart since he plays solitary saxophone. Hopper plays a variant on Nicholson in *Prizzi's Honor*, and a finale at the San Pedro oil refinery falls far short of

White Heat. The nicest idea is the way Milo traces his quarry through her mind, to find her thinking up slogans in an ad agency. BC

Catch Me a Spy (aka To Catch a Spy)
(Dick Clement, 1971, GB/Fr/US) Kirk Douglas, Marlène Jobert, Trevor Howard, Tom Courtenay, Patrick Mower, Bernadette Lafont, Bernard Blier, Sacha Pitoeff, Richard Pearson.
94 min.
Dim comedy thriller written by Clement and La Frenais, concerning complex intrigues in the world of Anglo-Russian espionage. Filmed largely in Knightsbridge, with brief outings to Bucharest and the Scottish Highlands for limp action scenes, it also manages to waste a marvellous cast, most notably Lafont (Nelly Kaplan's *Fiancée du Pirate*) and veteran actor Blier (Bertrand's dad). AB

Catch My Soul
(Patrick McGoohan, 1973, US) Richie Havens, Lance LeGault, Season Hubley, Tony Joe White, Susan Tyrrell.
95 min.
Lame attempt to film Jack Good's rock opera version of Shakespeare's *Othello*, a folly which started life on the stage. Hampered all the way by McGoohan's languorous direction, which lets each appalling moment of this uncomfortable hybrid of grade-school Shakespeare and grade-school religion sink wincingly in.

Catch Us If You Can (aka Having a Wild Weekend)
(John Boorman, 1965, GB) The Dave Clark Five, Barbara Ferris, David Lodge, Robin Bailey, Yootha Joyce, Clive Swift.
91 min. b/w.
With this envisaged as a cash-in on the Beatles films, Boorman and playwright Peter Nichols were given a free hand, so long as the group and songs were interwoven into a 'musical'. Taking a landscape Boorman knew from his BBC documentary days – Bath and the west – he was able, in his first feature, to create a cockeyed vision of Britain through the attempt of angry young Clark and determinedly kooky Ferris to escape the fake world of advertising. The film doesn't always avoid glibness in its hedonistic aspirations and obvious satire, but Boorman's passionate eye and his circumscribing of the band's evident lack of acting talent remain impressive. DT

Cat From Outer Space, The
(Norman Tokar, 1978, US) Ken Berry, Sandy Duncan, Harry Morgan, Roddy McDowall, McLean Stevenson, Hans Conried.
103 min.
Disney contribution to the 'we are not alone' syndrome. Billed as a 'Close Encounter of the Furred Kind', it concerns the plight of extra-terrestrial talking cat Jake, when his giant ladybird craft crash-lands on Earth. Despite Jake's paranormal powers, he has to enlist some local boffins to assist in a little spaceship maintenance. Ranged against them is the mighty US Army, and a megalomaniac villain (straight out of *Goldfinger*) bent on collaring the cat. Routine hi-jinks ensue, mixing strangely with ecology consciousness-raising, pseudo-scientific jargon, and everyday telekinesis. FF

Cat Girl
(Alfred Shaughnessy, 1957, GB) Barbara Shelley, Robert Ayres, Kay Callard, Paddy Webster, Ernest Milton, Jack May.
76 min. b/w.
Barbara Shelley's first horror film, an extraordinary British pastiche of Jacques Tourneur's *Cat People*, in which she plays a victimised and sexually repressed middle class woman who is suddenly able to channel her repressed emotion and sensuality into a ghostly cheetah which begins by savaging her husband. Tedious in places, and with an obviously low budget, it's still fascinating to witness the Ealing drawing-room tradition merge into that of an RKO-type horror film. DP

Catherine and Co. (Catherine et Cie)
(Michel Boisrond, 1975, Fr/It) Jane Birkin, Patrick Dewaere, Jean-Pierre Aumont, Vittorio Caprioli, Jean-Claude Brialy.
99 min.

Not hot enough to be a sexploiter, but not sophisticated enough to be anything better, this never quite finds its feet. Birkin plays a Manchester girl who comes to Paris for some ooh-la-la and ultimately sets up a corporation to accomplish it. She flaunts herself with complete self-confidence, an effect that would be totally horrible if her personality weren't so disarming. The starry actors around her are utterly wasted. GB

Catherine the Great
(Paul Czinner, 1934, GB) Elisabeth Bergner, Douglas Fairbanks Jr, Flora Robson, Gerald du Maurier, Irene Vanbrugh, Griffith Jones.
95 min. b/w.
Korda's expensive follow-up to *The Private Life of Henry VIII* fared badly against Sternberg's extravaganza *The Scarlet Empress*. Dietrich's siren attractions proved irresistible, and two Catherines in one year was too much for most audiences. Hungarian director Czinner has little of Sternberg's visual flair, but he is well served by Vincent Korda's sets and elicits marvellous performances from his players. Robson, even at 32, has the haggard authority of an old woman; Fairbanks descends into madness with a minimum of cliché; and Bergner, in her first English film, dispenses with her little-girl grotesqueries and is dazzling in her progress from lovelorn child to indomitable empress. RMy

Catholic Boys
see Heaven Help Us

Cathy's Child
(Donald Crombie, 1978, Aust) Michele Fawdon, Alan Cassell, Bryan Brown, Arthur Dignam.
85 min.
A turgid tabloid heart-warmer from the director of *Caddie*, in which a hard-drinking hack rediscovers his social concern when he follows a tug-of-love saga through to its happy end. Soft centred for all its crusading zeal against bureaucracy and the baby export trade, it fudges even its rare portrait of the exiled Greek community with its constant recourse to tear-jerk melodramatics. PT

Cathy's Curse (Cauchemars)
(Eddy Matalon, 1976, Fr/Can) Alan Scarfe, Randi Allen, Beverley Murray, Roy Witham, Mary Morter.
91 min.
One of the many movies puffing along hopefully in the wake of *The Exorcist*. The script places a lot of emphasis on 'possession' special effects, which quite laughably fail to deliver. The direction between these 'climactic' scenes is amateurish. All of which wastes a potentially interesting idea: Cathy's possession begins with a rejection of her female identity. VG

Catlow
(Sam Wanamaker, 1971, GB) Yul Brynner, Richard Crenna, Leonard Nimoy, Daliah Lavi, Jo Ann Pflug, Jeff Corey, Bessie Love.
101 min.
Lowbrow Western shot in Spain, with genial performances from Brynner and Crenna as the roguish outlaw and upright sheriff who remain buddies while trying to do each other down, simultaneously coping with waterless deserts, Mexican soldiers, assorted brands of Indians, and a wildcat girl (Lavi, excellent). Wanamaker's direction, unfortunately, is basic stodge. TM

Cat on a Hot Tin Roof
(Richard Brooks, 1958, US) Elizabeth Taylor, Paul Newman, Burl Ives, Judith Anderson, Jack Carson, Madeleine Sherwood.
108 min.
Overheated melodrama, based on Tennessee Williams' play about frustration, greed, lust and impotence wreaking havoc among a wealthy Southern family. Taylor overdoes it as the nagging wife of neurotic Newman, uncertain about his sexuality; Carson connives for the favours of his dying father, hoping to inherit; and Ives is magnificently patriarchal as Big Daddy, ruling the roost with an ego the size of his stomach. As so often with adaptations of Williams, it frequently errs on the side of overstatement and pretension, but still remains immensely enjoyable as a piece of cod-Freudian codswallop. GA

C appears top right

Cat o' Nine Tails, The
(Il Gatto a Nove Code)

(Dario Argento, 1971, It/WGer/Fr) Karl
Malden, James Franciscus, Catherine Spaak,
Cinzia De Carolis, Carlo Alighiero.
112 min.
Typically over-the-top murder mystery from
Argento, neglecting its rather straightforward
plot about a series of killings connected with a
genetics research institute in favour of gruesome
set pieces, bravura camera-work and set design
(one character has some truly amazing wallpaper, seemingly spattered with blood), heavy symbolism, and a strong sound-track by Ennio
Morricone. Reason doesn't come into it; gorgeous,
grisly style is all. GA

Cat People

(Jacques Tourneur, 1942, US) Simone Simon,
Kent Smith, Tom Conway, Jane Randolph,
Elizabeth Russell, Jack Holt, Alan Napier.
73 min. b/w.
First in the wondrous series of B movies in which
Val Lewton elaborated his principle of horrors
imagined rather than seen, with a superbly judged
performance from Simon as the young wife
ambivalently haunted by sexual frigidity and by
a fear that she is metamorphosing into a panther.
With its chilling set pieces directed to perfection
by Tourneur, it knocks Paul Schrader's remake
for six, not least because of the care subtly taken
to imbue its cat people (Simon, Russell) with feline mannerisms. Its sober psychological basis is barely shaken by the studio's insistence on introducing, as a stock horror movie ploy, a shot of a black
panther during one crucial scene. TM

Cat People

(Paul Schrader, 1982, US) Nastassja Kinski,
Malcolm McDowell, John Heard, Annette
O'Toole, Ruby Dee, Ed Begley Jr.
118 min.
Beauty is the beast in Schrader's erotic update of
RKO's 1942 horror classic. Kinski's ambivalently bewildered Irena, subject to feline metamorphosis when aroused, is the deadly composite of
sex-kitten and *femme fatale*: the virgin who literally develops claws (and more) in bed. Caught
between her similarly cursed brother's pleas for
incest, and her zoo-keeper boy-friend's ostensibly
more natural desires, she's ironically caged as
much by current notions of psycho-sexual 'liberation' as by the bars which await her. The seductively exotic surface of this mythically
underpinned fantasy might be offset for some by
much graphic gore, but if you can buy the romantic metaphors for the primitivisms of sexual
obsession, the film delivers down the line. PT

Cat's Eye

(Lewis Teague, 1984, US) Drew Barrymore,
James Woods, Alan King, Kenneth McMillan,
Robert Hays, Candy Clark.
94 min.
Two short stories and an original screenplayette
by Stephen King, linked by a stray catalyst
pussyfooting to the rescue of Barrymore, who is
being menaced by a toothy troll which patters out
of the woodwork every night. *En route* in this
episode, the moggy is catapulted into two other
adventures: one about a 'firm' employing
unorthodox methods to persuade its clients to
quit smoking, the other about a mobster getting
a high-rise out of the discomfiture of his wife's
lover. This is King in a skittenish mode, liable to
induce catalepsy, but there is one sequence to
treasure when the wonderful Woods, suffering
from nicotine withdrawal, undergoes fag-filled
hallucinations. AB

Cat's-Paw, The

(Sam Taylor, 1934, US) Harold Lloyd, Una
Merkel, George Barbier, Grace Bradley, Alan
Dinehart.
100 min. b/w.
Ezekiel Cobb (Lloyd), the only son of missionar-
ies posted to rural China in 1914, returns to
Stockport, California, in 1934 to find 'a mother for
his children'. He has a letter of introduction to the
head of the mission, but the man turns out to be
the cat's paw of local tough guys – the man regularly put up against the corrupt mayor of
Stockport. During the current mayoral election
the cat's paw dies, and Ezekiel agrees to stand in
his place, providing he's guaranteed non-election.

He is, of course, elected. A ponderous vehicle, for
the naive, exact Lloyd (spouting fortune cookie
aphorisms), distinguished only by an extended
finale in which Ezekiel rounds up the black hats
in a dungeon and forces them to confess their
crimes by decapitating two of them (with the help
of huge Chinese swordsmen) and parading the
corpses, complete with bleeding necks and the
heads in bowls on their chests. Sixty years on,
political incorrectness, in terms of Oriental stereotypes, doesn't come much more incorrect than
this. Una Merkel plays the love interest, Petunia
Pratt, with a certain dry irony. JPy

Cattle Annie
and Little Britches

(Lamont Johnson, 1980, US) Burt Lancaster,
John Savage, Rod Steiger, Diane Lane,
Amanda Plummer, Scott Glenn.
98 min.
Uninspired Western about a couple of teenage
girls who join the Doolin-Dalton gang, and take
to the outlaw life like ducks to water. Highly
derivative in its playing with themes about a-
changing times and a-shrinking frontiers, it is
also plagued by one of those awful cheerful banjo
sound-tracks that should have been abandoned
back in the days of *Bonnie and Clyde* and *Butch
Cassidy*. GA

Cattle Queen of Montana

(Allan Dwan, 1954, US) Barbara Stanwyck,
Ronald Reagan, Gene Evans, Lance Fuller,
Anthony Caruso, Jack Elam, Chubby Johnson,
Morris Ankrum.
88 min.
Despite promising credentials – not just Dwan
and Stanwyck, but John Alton on camera – this
RKO Western is pretty much a non-starter. The
first half is efficient but predictable as Stanwyck
and her dad (Ankrum), arriving in Montana after
driving a herd up from Texas, are ambushed by
a band of renegade Blackfeet secretly in the pay
of a would-be cattle baron (Evans) who wants the
land on which they plan to build a ranch.
Befriended by the Blackfoot chief's college-edu-
cated son (Fuller) after her father is killed,
Stanwyck stubbornly determines to stay put,
though warned off by Evans' hired gunslinger
(Reagan, obviously destined to turn good guy).
Thereafter, the script starts going in circles, producing plenty of incident (mainly Evans trying
to provoke an Indian war, Fuller stoutly fighting
for peace) but losing any sense of dramatic
progress. Though accused of being an Indian
lover, Stanwyck naturally entertains no yearnings for her gallant Blackfoot, but settles for
Reagan (working undercover for the army) in
what must be one of the most perfunctory love
affairs in Western history. TM

Cauchemars

see Cathy's Curse

Caught

(Max Ophüls, 1949, US) Barbara Bel Geddes,
Robert Ryan, James Mason, Frank Ferguson,
Curt Bois, Natalie Schafer.
88 min. b/w.
A key American melodrama: draw a line between
Citizen Kane and *Written on the Wind*, and you'll
find Ophuls' *noir* classic at the heady mid-point.
A car-hop Cinderella (Bel Geddes) chases a fashion-plate, charm-school dream; a childishly megalomaniac millionaire (Ryan) marries her to spite
his analyst. Ophuls holds back his camera to
frame the sour domestic nightmare, but gloriously equates motion with emotion when Bel
Geddes takes solace with James Mason's virtuous doctor. The alluring web of hearts and dollars has rarely looked so deadly, and only the
studio spared us the sight of the kill. PT

Caught Looking

(Constantine Giannaris, 1991, GB)
35 min. b/w & col.
Commissioned for Channel 4's lesbian and gay
series *Out*, this was deemed inappropriate for the
mid-evening time slot, which cannot have come
as a great shock to Giannaris: with its explicit sex
scenes, playful annexation of risqué fantasies,
and a tone that veers from weary self-disgust to
the enthusiastically debauched, the film positively courts controversy. A man logs on to an
inter-active virtual-reality computer game. He has

four options, each with a different seduction scenario and a cast of available pick-ups. The first
takes place in a (black-and-white) 1940s-style
waterfront hotel, another harks back to '50s 'classical' homoerotica (strangely Jarmanesque, this),
another zeroes in on cottage trade. It's an original, sly exercise in perversion and subversion,
wittily scripted by Paul Hallam, and directed with
exquisite poise. TCh

Cause for Alarm!

(Tay Garnett, 1951, US) Loretta Young, Barry
Sullivan, Bruce Cowling, Margalo Gillmore,
Irving Bacon, Don Haggerty, Richard Anderson.
74 min. b/w.
A not uninteresting attempt at a suburban *film
noir*, with Loretta Young as a housewife whose
bed-ridden ex-serviceman husband (Sullivan),
consumed with totally unfounded jealousy, concocts a fiendish revenge plot. Having planted evidence indicating that she and her supposed lover
were conspiring to poison him, he then proposes
to shoot her, but dies of a heart attack. Although
rather too fluttery for comfort, Young gives a good
account of the woman's panic-stricken dilemma
as, left alone with a corpse in the house and her
every move adding to the web of suspicious circumstances, she desperately battles red tape to
retrieve an incriminating letter posted to the DA.
Unfortunately, the script throws in some heavy-
handed exposition (notably a 'meeting cute' scene
designed to shed light on Sullivan's mental state),
betrays its MGM origins by a tiresome insistence
on family values (a moppet next door stands in
for the child the heroine yearns for), and contrives
a risibly arbitrary happy ending. TM

Cavafy (Cavafis)

(Iannis Smaragdis, 1997, Greece/Fr) Dimitris
Katalifos, Vassilis Diamandopoulos.
90 min.
A bio-pic of the great (gay) Greek Alexandrian poet,
related with discretion and evident admiration and
shot with glissando camera movement and dark,
often night-time, hues by cinematographer Nikos
Emaragous. The film begins at Cavafy's death bed
in 1933, and the episodes – from the waltzes in
grand houses in the 1880s to later penury – are told
as dream reverie. Cavafy, a passionate, but lonely,
secretive and often strangely uncommunicative
man, is quoted: 'I've brought to Art desires and sensations, things half-glimpsed, unfulfilled love
affairs…' and that's what we're shown. Vangelis,
to whom the film is dedicated, provides the emotional if occasionally trivialising score. WH

Cavalcade

(Frank Lloyd, 1933, US) Clive Brook, Diana
Wynyard, Herbert Mundin, Frank Lawton,
Ursula Jeans, Margaret Lindsay, Una
O'Connor, Billy Bevan.
110 min. b/w.
Snobbery, sentimentality and jingoism run riot
in Noël Coward's pageant of life as experienced
by an 'ordinary' British family (and their comic
relief servants) from Boer War and death of the
dear old queen to date. Nary a tear-jerking trick
is missed (our family loses one son to the Titanic,
the other to World War I), and the strangulation
is compounded by the staginess since the film, at
Coward's insistence, slavishly followed the Drury
Lane production. The interpolated war footage
was the work of William Cameron Menzies. TM

Caza, La (The Hunt)

(Carlos Saura, 1965, Sp) Ismael Merlo, Alfredo
Mayo, José Maria Prada, Fernando Sanchez,
Emilio Guiterrez Caba, Violeta Garcia.
87 min. b/w.
La Caza manages, with very little reading
between the lines, a remarkably overt condemnation of Spain's presiding spirit. Three middle-
aged men and a youth embark on a day's rabbit
hunting. They take with them the trappings of
material success, and their prattle places them
alongside the status quo. Petty vanities and jealousies lie close to the surface, but it is a deeper-
felt, more inarticulate sense of guilt that grows to
dominate. Where they hunt had been a battleground during the war (and still contains its rotting corpses), half the rabbits they kill are
diseased. And as the sun gets hotter, the stare of
the camera becomes more relentless, burning into
the flesh of ageing men who twitch and grunt in
their sleep. Feverish sexuality (linked by implication to repressive politics), outbursts of violence

and a sense of foreboding all contribute to the group's self-destruction. Although over-emphatic in its editing, seldom has a film been informed with such crystal hatred for its characters. CPe

CB4
(Tamra Davis, 1993, US) Chris Rock, Allen Payne, Deezer D, Chris Elliott, Phil Hartman.
89 min.
A sometimes gross, no-pose-barred rap-culture satire. CB4, aka Cell Block 4, are a trio of hip-hopping young-bloods stage-named Stab Master Arson, Mad Mike and MC Gusto, the last Afrocentric played by the splendid co-writer Chris Rock, who provides most of the threesome's music. CB4 is not, however, in the Spinal Tap league, lacking that film's merciless detail and consistency. But in parts it is hugely, monstrously funny; and with guest cameos from the likes of Ice T, Ice Cube, basketball's Shaquille O'Neal, Eazy E and Flavor Flav, and a first-rate soundtrack from Public Enemy, the Beastie Boys, PM Dawn, MC Ren and CB4 themselves, it will be an undoubted winner with the people who count. SGr

Cease Fire
(David Nutter, 1985, US) Don Johnson, Lisa Blount, Robert F Lyons, Richard Chavez, Rick Richards.
98 min.
Tormented by his experiences in Vietnam, Tim (Johnson) finds it increasingly difficult to adjust to everyday life and vents his frustration on his family. The traumatic and insidious aftermath of the 'suckers' war' is a serious subject, but that does not prevent this spasmodic film from being silly. Not only are the war scenes laughable, but there is also a hilarious episode when the flaky veteran reverts to jungle tactics in his own living-room. Lots of acting but little action; worthy but not worth watching. MS

Cecilia, La
(Jean-Louis Comolli, 1975, It/Fr) Massimo Foschi, Maria Carta, Vittorio Mezzogiorno, Biagio Pelligra, Giancarlo Pannese.
105 min.
Intelligent and stimulating, La Cecilia is based on the story of the colony set up in Brazil in 1890 by a group of Italian anarchists. The colony lasted about three years, and Comolli's account, drawing on original sources, examines its development and eventual collapse. Documenting both external pressures and internal tensions, the film lucidly considers what kind of political organisation is needed in a supposedly collective situation, and the kind of obstacles that occur. Comolli creates no villains to pin the blame on; the fact that one can retain emotional solidarity with the colonists makes the immediate relevance of the questions raised all the more apparent and thought-provoking. AS

Ceddo
(Ousmane Sembene, 1976, Sen) Tabara N'diaye, Alioune Fall, Moustapha Yade, Mamadou N'diaye Diagne.
117 min.
Banned in Senegal on an absurd technicality which is merely the tip of an iceberg of threats posed by a film which picks at the scab of many of Senegal's current sores. The story concerns an 18th century Senegalese village where the Christian and Islamic faiths are vying with each other and the older African traditions for adherents and power. The Ceddo ('outsiders') who do not wish to be converted take the desperate step of kidnapping the chief's daughter. Within this spare plot, Sembene raises issues of obvious pertinence to modern Senegal, such as the tension between spiritual and temporal power, Princess Dior's renunciation of her role of victim to take decisive action, and village leaders who are only too willing to betray their Africanness to maintain the status quo. Beneath the patina of universally comprehensible motifs lie peculiarly African symbols and meanings which will prove largely inaccessible to an English audience. Still, some of the homilies with which the film is riddled are universally pertinent: 'A man who wears trousers full of fat should not approach the fire'. FD

Ceiling Zero
(Howard Hawks, 1935, US) James Cagney, Pat O'Brien, June Travis, Stuart Erwin, Isabel Jewell, Barton MacLane.
95 min. b/w.

Something of a try-out for the later Only Angels Have Wings, this adaptation of a stage-play about mail pilots braving not only the elements but their own failing powers may suffer from a certain claustrophobic theatricality of setting, but Hawks keeps both his abiding interests (the tensions and loyalties within an enclosed group, the need for professionalism and a responsibility towards others) and his brisk narrative style to the fore. Cagney is superb as the devil-may-care flier whose womanising imperils the whole operation; O'Brien supplies solid support as the boss who ensures Cagney's belated redemption. Less complex and lyrical than Angels, but more than enough to go on with. GA

Cela s'appelle l'Aurore
(Luis Buñuel, 1955, Fr/It) Georges Marchal, Lucia Bosé, Nelly Borgeaud, Gianni Esposito, Julien Bertheau, Gaston Modot.
102 min. b/w.
Highly rated by the director himself, but poorly received and subsequently rarely shown, this is actually a beautifully made parable about commitment, and curiously one of Buñuel's most moving films. The setting is Corsica, where a sympathetic company doctor (Marchal) hides a sacked worker (Esposito) who has murdered their boss in revenge for the death of his sick wife. Typically for Buñuel, he offers no traditional moral structure, but a wealth of complex characters, including a police chief (Bertheau) who dislikes torture, decorates his office with Dali's 'Crucifixion', and reads Claudel. DT

Celebration, The (Festen)
(Thomas Vinterberg, 1998, Den) Henning Moritzen, Ulrich Thomsen, Thomas Bo Larsen, Paprika Steen, Birthe Neumann.
105 min.
Family and friends gather to celebrate the 60th birthday of a wealthy patriarch: after the eldest son, invited to offer a few words in tribute to his recently deceased sister, starts making increasingly serious 'jokes' about his father's recently deceased sister, starts making increasingly serious 'jokes' about his father's horrendously abusive treatment of the family, tensions mount until all hell breaks loose. Played mostly as black anti-bourgeois comedy, this is thoroughly entertaining but rather less outrageous, substantial and original than it thinks it is; imagine Buñuel making a foray into the world of Fanny and Alexander, edited by someone determined to impress the younger members of the audience (the style, dictated partly by the back-to-basics 'Dogma 95' manifesto, is somewhat tricksy), and you're elsewhere there. Reservations apart, however, it's an assured, admirably abrasive little movie which never outstays its welcome. GA

Céleste
(Percy Adlon, 1981, WGer) Eva Mattes, Jürgen Arndt, Norbert Wartha, Wolf Euba.
106 min.
An ambitious attempt to film a biography of literature's most celebrated autobiographer, Céleste is based on the published memoirs of Céleste Albaret, housekeeper to Marcel Proust from 1914 until his death in 1922. If the movie is only partially successful in making the Proust story cinematic, it may be because, apart from some bold jump-cuts and fastidious camera-work that parallels the writer's sense of precision, Adlon fails to sustain a visual rhetoric that approximates the Proustian style. And although Céleste (finely portrayed by Eva Mattes, matching a peasant woman's restraint and good humour to the dandy's tyranny and dependency) provides the source material, the film's true subject is inescapably Proust himself – his writing, his illness, his occasional sorties into a moribund artistic demi-monde. Yet the man remains elusive, almost as if he had died with the 19th century, so that all Céleste was nursing was a 'memory' of Proust. It is this 'emptiness' and Céleste's apparent devotion to it that makes the film at best a half-satisfying experience. MA

Celestine, Maid at Your Service (Célestine, Bonne à Tout Faire)
(Clifford Brown, ie. Jesus Franco, 1974, Fr) Lina Romay, Howard Vernon, Jean-Pierre Granet, Pamela Stanford, Olivier Mathot.
84 min.
An object lesson in how potentially liberating

material (the nominal source is Octave Mirbeau's Diary of a Chambermaid) can be manhandled into heavy-handed voyeurism treading an unresolved line between the Pasolini-inspired bawdy romp and Buñuelian subversion. Celestine, fleeing a brothel after a police raid, finds herself in a stately home full of promisingly wan-looking sexual repressives she makes it her task to liberate, while still serving the needs of her fellow-workers (male and female). The print under review is rendered unwatchable by terrible dubbing. VG

Celia
(Ann Turner, 1988, Aust) Rebecca Smart, Nicholas Eade, Mary-Anne Fahey, Margaret Ricketts, Victoria Longley, Alexander Hutchinson, Adrian Mitchell, Callie Gray, Martin Sharman.
103 min.
A subtly affecting rites-of-passage drama, set in Melbourne in 1957 and charting one summer in the life of nine-year-old Celia (a wonderful performance from Rebecca Smart).Thematic and structural faults expose writer/director Turner's inexperience in her debut: episodes are awkwardly linked, steam runs short towards the end, tenuous links are drawn between political paranoia and legislative attempts to curb an explosion in the rabbit population. But the film beautifully explores the fear which so often informs childhood perception, and focuses on accompanying defensive rituals; superstition (parental discipline is avenged with voodoo) and gang rivalry. The arid Australian landscape is at once banal and mysterious; the hideous creatures stalking Celia's favourite fiction are as real to her as the taunts of an obnoxious cousin. Her imagination is misunderstood by her father, but Celia finds – to his dismay – that the new Communist neighbours encourage flights of fancy and her questionning mind. The central characterisation is the film's strength, striking just the right balance between apprehension and wonder. CM

Céline and Julie Go Boating (Céline et Julie Vont en Bateau: Phantom Ladies Over Paris)
(Jacques Rivette, 1974, Fr) Juliet Berto, Dominique Labourier, Bulle Ogier, Marie-France Pisier, Barbet Schroeder.
192 min.
Favourite films are always the hardest to describe. There are the two pairs of actresses, Berto/Labourier and Ogier/Pisier.The first play a magician and a librarian who meet in Montmartre and wind up sharing the same flat, bed, fiancé, clothes, identity and imagination; the other two are the Phantom Ladies Over Paris, whom Céline and Julie either invent or stumble upon (or both) in a haunted house, along with a man and a child. There's also Rivette's love of cinema – the movies he cherishes– and the childishness of his and our and Céline and Julie's rapt attention as we embark on an adventure together, experiencing a collective form of narrative rape, all spinning a tale that's spinning us. It's scary, evocative, exhilarating and essential. JR

Cellar, The
(Kevin S Tenney, 1988, US) Patrick Kilpatrick, Chris Miller, Suzanne Savoy, Ford Rainey.
90 min.
Totally pedestrian, directionless dirge concerning a house built upon Indian land whose cellar is home to a living, breathing folk-devil. With over half the running-time spent establishing the existence of the beast in question, the final arrival of a man in a rubber suit walking on all fours is irritatingly laughable. This is really an innocuous Saturday morning kids' movie, complete with a young hero whose father gets angry when his son screams about 'monsters', but who finally realises the error of his ways: 'I was afraid you wouldn't love me if you thought that I was scared,' he opines as the whole family indulges in a wholesome hug. Pass me that bucket, I'm gonna throw up. MK

Celluloid Closet, The
(Rob Epstein/Jeffrey Friedman, 1995, US) Tom Hanks, Shirley MacLaine, Gore Vidal, Susan Sarandon, Harvey Fierstein, Armistead Maupin, Richard Dyer, Tony Curtis, Whoopi Goldberg, Antonio Fargas.
101 min.

A witty, touching study of Hollywood's (mostly on screen) treatment of homosexuality. Epstein and Friedman approach the question chronologically and by type, with astringent comments from an array of unusual suspects, including Gore Vidal (hilarious on how Stephen Boyd played up the gay subtext in *Ben-Hur*, while Heston obliviously rendered his Francis X Bushman impersonation), Tom Hanks, Shirley MacLaine, Armistead Maupin, Richard Dyer and Harvey Fierstein ('I'd rather have visibility than nothing'). There's no great radical agenda here, just an honest assessment of lives relegated to the shadows of the screen. The montage of homophobic slurs from mainstream contemporary movies is especially telling. TCh

Cement Garden, The

(Andrew Birkin, 1992, GB/Ger/Fr) Charlotte Gainsbourg, Andrew Robertson, Ned Birkin, Alice Coulthard, Sinead Cusack.
105 min.
The film begins with an appropriate oedipal image: surly, spotty, 15-year-old Jack (Robertson) masturbates in front of a mirror, while out in the garden his father keels over and dies. Later, when their mother follows suit, Jack and his older, more pragmatic sister Julie (Gainsbourg) adopt a quasi-parental attitude to their younger siblings. Unusually, they bury Mum in the basement, lest as orphans they be taken into care. Jack longs jealously for Julie. Birkin's film of Ian McEwan's novel soon settles into a claustrophobic mood, the sweltering summer matching the overheated adolescent emotions. Gainsbourg and Coulthard (as sister Sue) give fine performances, the former balanced between bossy provocation and vulnerability; and Birkin keeps it all in line by avoiding sensationalism and showing a tender understanding of youthful confusion. An unusually sensitive and, dare one say, cinematic Brit Lit adaptation. GA

Cemetery Girls

see Velvet Vampire, The

Centennial Summer

(Otto Preminger, 1946, US) Jeanne Crain, Cornel Wilde, Linda Darnell, William Eythe, Walter Brennan, Constance Bennett, Dorothy Gish.
102 min.
An attempt to recapture the family nostalgia of Minnelli's *Meet Me in St Louis*, made two years earlier, this light musical comedy centres on the Great Exposition of 1876. Sisters Crain and Darnell both drool over dashing Frenchman Cornel Wilde, to the sound of tunes from Oscar Hammerstein II and Jerome Kern, who died shortly before the picture was completed. Director Preminger – best remembered now, perhaps, for such adult pictures as *Anatomy of a Murder* – did a more than adequate job.

Central Do Brasil

(Walter Salles, 1998, Braz) Fernanda Montenegro, Vincius De Oliveira, Marilia Pera.
115 min.
Dora (Montenegro) is a retired schoolteacher eking out an existence by writing letters for illiterate passers-by in Rio's busiest railway station. She never bothers posting the letters. Josue (De Oliveira) is the nine-year-old son of one of the women she deceives. When his mother is killed, Josue is left alone in the big city. Dora takes pity on the boy and reluctantly joins him on an epic cross-country journey in search of his father. Part travelogue, part neo-realist fable, the film works so well because the director refuses to play up the sentimentality. Both the boy and the older woman are hardened and cynical. Only very slowly does their mutual distrust break down. GM

Century

(Stephen Poliakoff, 1993, GB) Charles Dance, Clive Owen, Miranda Richardson, Robert Stephens, Joan Hickson, Lena Headey.
112 min.
Poliakoff's film finds the seeds of two of the 20th century's big ideas present on the cusp of 1900 – eugenics, which led to the Holocaust, and the emancipation of women. Thus Professor Mandry (Dance) sterilises the poor without their consent, and Clara (Richardson) demands con-

trol over her own life and no marriage-knot in her relationship with idealistic young doctor Paul Reisner (Owen). But if the plot structure is pleasing, the pacing is not, and the stand-off between the Prof and Doc stalls so badly that it takes an Ealing caricature, philanthropist Joan Hickson, to kick-start the drama again. Paul becomes the Prof's star pupil at the research hospital, hankers after lab assistant Clara, crosses the Prof, turns to Clara for solace, and when he discovers the sterilisation programme, pulls the plug on the entire institution. Dance is elitist arrogance to a nicety, Richardson appropriately spiky, and Stephens turns up in an impersonation of Owen's Romanian Jewish father. A big theme that got away. BC

C'era una Volta

see Cinderella – Italian Style

Cercle Rouge, Le

see Red Circle, The

Cérémonie, La
(A Judgement in Stone)

(Claude Chabrol, 1995, Fr) Sandrine Bonnaire, Isabelle Huppert, Jean-Pierre Cassel, Jacqueline Bisset, Virginie Ledoyen, Valentin Merlet, Julien Roquefort, Dominique Frot.
112 min.
When Catherine (Bisset) takes on Sophie (Bonnaire) as housekeeper, her family's impressed by Sophie's aura of quiet responsibility, even though they're not convinced she knows how to serve dinner correctly. Snobbish but liberal, they nevertheless treat her generously. Only when she starts to consort with postmistress Jeanne (Huppert), a gossip whom husband Georges (Cassel) suspects of opening the family mail, do they find real cause for complaint. But by then the women have a secret bond which excludes them from the safe cosseted world of Sophie's employers. Chabrol's adaptation of Ruth Rendell's *A Judgement in Stone* benefits from the director's immaculate sense of social and psychological detail. The film's strong points are not mystery, suspense or even surprise, but Chabrol's flair for characterisation, careful pacing and solid evocation of bourgeois complacency and anti-bourgeois hatred creates a palpable sense of unease that fully justifies the shockingly violent finale. Ledoyen, the daughter of the household, is a discovery; Bisset returns to form; and Huppert, unusually vivacious, is terrific. GA

Ceremony, The (Gishiki)

(Nagisa Oshima, 1971, Jap) Kenzo Kawarazaki, Atsuo Nakamura, Akiko Koyama, Atsoku Kaku, Kiyoshi Tsuchiya.
121 min.
A thinly disguised commentary on Japan's postwar history, using ceremonial family gatherings (mainly weddings and funerals) as a key to the changes in Japanese society: individual characters represent specific political factions, just as events in the narrative mirror the twists and turns in the country's domestic and foreign policies. However dense the allegory, though, Oshima keeps it very accessible to his audience by stressing individuals' feelings as much as ceremonies; their dreams, aspirations, frustrations and agonies are all too familiar. A significant political film for the time. TR

César

(Marcel Pagnol, 1936, Fr) Raimu, Pierre Fresnay, Orane Demazis, André Fouché, Fernand Charpin, Edouard Delmont.
121 min. b/w.
Pagnol himself clambered into the director's chair for the final instalment of his trilogy (taking over from Alexander Korda, who directed *Marius*, and Marc Allégret who made *Fanny*), and things move at a slower, more theatrical pace – luckily entirely suited to events, which are full of remembrances of things past and regrets at the passing of time. A new character stands in the spotlight: Césariot, son of Marius and Fanny, who has to learn the awful truth about his parentage. This is the trilogy's least funny, most affecting, part. 'What a pity that there aren't more of them,' an anonymous critic sighed when it was reissued in 1951; today the modest charms and graces of the Pagnol trilogy seem more precious than ever. GB

César and Rosalie
(César et Rosalie)

(Claude Sautet, 1972, Fr/It/WGer) Yves Montand, Romy Schneider, Sami Frey, Umberto Orsini, Eva Maria Meincke, Isabelle Huppert.
105 min.
One of Sautet's supposedly realistic accounts of French middle-class life, in which a divorcée and her ageing lover battle through an eternal triangle situation with all the romantic agony of *Love Story*, *César and Rosalie* (Lelouch by any other name) is saved from colour supplement chic only by sympathetic performances from Schneider and Montand. TM

C'est arrivé près de chez vous

see Man Bites Dog

C'est la Vie

see La Baule-les pins

C'est la Vie, Ma Cherie
(Xin Buliao Qing)

(Derek Yee ie Yee Tung-shing, 1993, HK) Anita Yuen, Lau Ching-wan, Carina Lau, Sylvia Chang.
105 min.
Grade-A weepie about a rapturous but doomed affair between a jaded jazz musician and a young woman with health problems who sings in the night market. Just as you're recovering from the shock of a Hong Kong movie made with sincerity, credible emotions, a coherent script and a truly joyous use of music, director Derek Yee delivers an emotional knockout that would make a stone weep. A triumph for independent production (no Hong Kong major wanted to touch it), it made a star of the wonderful Anita Yuen and swept the board at the 1994 HK Film Awards. TR

Cet Obscur Objet du Désir

see That Obscure Object of Desire

Ceux qui m'aiment prendront le train

see Those Who Love Me Will Take the Train

Chac

(Rolando Klein, 1976, Mex/US) Pablo Cacha Balan, Alonso Mendez Tom.
95 min.
Indian villagers are led by charismatic Man of Mountains over a South American lake, through a jungle, across a waterfall and down a cavern to collect a bucket of water used in an elaborate ceremony to the rain-god Chac. Punctuated with unsubtitled Mayan hieroglyphics and the occasional supernatural special effect, *Chac* is probably primarily of interest to students of anthropology. The narrative consists mostly of unrelieved trekking, and remains resolutely free of drama despite a last-minute murder and some initial falling-about comedy involving an ineffective drunken shaman. JPy

Cha-Cha for the Fugitive, A
(Gei Taowangzhe de Qiaqia)

(Wang Tsai-Sheng, 1997, Tai) Julien Chen, Lu Hsin-Yu, Chen Jie-Yi, Liu Shen-Hsin, Ho Tzong-Shian.
85 min.
Hard to say if the frenetic visuals are a reaction against most other Taiwanese cinema or merely a reflection of the director's own background in advertising. Either way, this chaotic, enervating first feature has a core of authentic emotion and commitment which makes it impossible to shrug off. A young male dancer with avant-garde leanings dreams of escaping to join a (male) lover in New York, works nights in a sleazy club and spends days failing to relate to his girlfriend in his studio atop a grungy apartment block. His confused thoughts about Taiwan, materialism, corrupt politicians and murderous gangsters hit the screen in shards of splintered imagery. Wang, who wrote, designed and shot the film, as well as directing, doesn't always avoid cliché, but he's definitely on to something real. TR

Chacun cherche son chat

see When the Cat's Away...

Chad Hanna

(Henry King, 1940, US) Henry Fonda, Dorothy
Lamour, Linda Darnell, Guy Kibbee, John
Carradine, Jane Darwell.
86 min.
A thin and hardly engrossing story – country boy
Fonda joins an upstate New York circus in the
1840s, and falls in love first with bareback rider
Lamour, then with runaway Darnell – is decked
out by King with lovingly atmospheric details.
Attractive to look at, but little more.

Chain, The

(Jack Gold, 1984, GB) Bernard Hill, Leo
McKern, Billie Whitelaw, Phyllis Logan,
Warren Mitchell, Maurice Denham, Anna
Massey.
100 min.
Tracing seven interconnected house moves all
scheduled for the same day, this borrows its circular storyline from *La Ronde* while swapping
that film's continental obsession with sex for the
peculiarly British ones of property and class. The
strengths of this old-fashioned, rather parochial
picture lie in writer Jack Rosenthal's ear for the
absurd undercurrents of everyday speech, and the
solid cast of character actors. But its weak
links are the grand philosophical pretensions
that have each household standing for one of the
Seven Deadly Sins, and Mitchell's genial
removal man musing benignly on the Great
Chain of Being. SJo

Chain of Desire

(Temistocles Lopez, 1992, US) Linda
Fiorentino, Elias Koteas, Angel Aviles, Patrick
Bauchau, Malcolm McDowell, Seymour Cassel.
107 min.
Max Ophuls' version of Schnitzler's *La Ronde*
epitomised – for all time – world-weary
Viennese decadence. The temptations of a
remake are obvious. Sex is never off the menu;
and what's more, given that the lovers don't
stick around, subtleties of characterisation can
be dispensed with. Wasting an intriguing cast,
this Big Apple bonkfest drags us on yet another spin on the crotch-level merry-go-round. But
when the most noteworthy elements are dire
songs and shallow gestures to the spectre of
AIDS, the ride's a dull one. Flaccid in every
respect. TJ

Chain Reaction, The

(Ian Barry, 1980, Aust) Steve Bisley, Arna-
Maria Winchester, Ross Thompson, Ralph
Cotterill, Hugh Keays-Byrne.
92 min.
A conspiracy thriller based around the increasingly familiar theme of nuclear contamination
and corporate cover-up, *Chain Reaction* neatly
illustrates the strengths and weaknesses of popular Australian cinema. Its opening is pacy and
visually assured, with an effective series of chases and shocks. But once it's necessary to introduce some characters, the script becomes
intensely awkward and the whole plot begins to
lose its bearings. Only the trappings of apocalypse (radiation suits, zombie-like guards) retain
any of the intended impact. DP

Challenge, The

(John Frankenheimer, 1982, US) Scott Glenn,
Toshiro Mifune, Donna Kei Benz, Atsuo
Nakamura, Calvin Jung.
116 min.
Kung-fu action thriller set in Tokyo which pits
the samurai tradition of honourable combat
against the new westernised Japan of guns and
super-capitalism. The elaborate combat will
please fans, but anyone not much engaged by
martial arts as a genre will soon find themselves
pretty bored despite the script's occasional
ironies. *The Yakuza* did it all so much better. DP

Chamber, The

(James Foley, 1996, US) Gene Hackman, Faye
Dunaway, Chris O'Donnell, Lela Rochon,
Robert Prosky, Raymond Barry, Harve
Presnell.
113 min.
Opus V from the John Grisham production line is
grey, humourless and unimaginative. Alleged

killer Sam Cayhill (Hackman) has been on death
row in Mississippi since 1967. Now he has a
month to live. Sam himself isn't putting much
effort into his defence, but legal greenhorn Adam
Hill (O'Donnell) can do that. Adam is Sam's
grandson, and despite Sam's brush-offs, the
young lawyer suspects the black sheep of the
family is taking the fall for a racist conspiracy.
The occasionally murky character, turning up
with some revelation to get things moving, is a
relief from O'Donnell's blandness and his earnest
delivery of Grisham's lifeless dialogue. NB

Chamber of Horrors

(Hy Averback, 1966, US) Patrick O'Neal,
Cesare Danova, Wilfrid Hyde-White, Laura
Devon, Patrice Wymore, Philip Bourneuf,
Wayne Rogers, Suzy Parker.
100 min.
Pilot for a TV series based on *House of Wax* and
intended to feature Danova and Hyde-White as
owners of a wax museum who dabble in criminol-
ogy. Judged too gruesome for TV (O'Neal, as the
Baltimore Strangler, hacks off his own manacled
hand in escaping from the police, later ends up
impaled on a hook), it was expanded into a feature,
with a *Fear Flasher* and *Horror Horn* as silly gimmicks. Tacky stuff, but it has its luridly bizarre
moments and a nice performance from O'Neal as
the seemingly indestructible homicidal maniac. TM

Chambre Verte, La
(The Green Room)

(François Truffaut, 1978, Fr) François
Truffaut, Nathalie Baye, Jean Dasté, Jean-
Pierre Moulin, Antoine Vitez.
94 min.
Adapted from two Henry James short stories,
The Green Room stars Truffaut himself as an
ageing provincial journalist on a failing periodical, solitary despite his housekeeper and (inexplicably) deaf-mute child, as he looks back from
the late 1920s at the two traumas that have
shaped his life – the massacre of World War I
in which he lost most of his friends and acquaintances, and the death of his beloved wife. A
story full of Gothic promise. The similar binding of personal and historical events, of obsessively remembered love and morbid longing for
death, were elements that pulsed vitally – if sentimentally – in the earlier *Jules et Jim*. And the
failure of *Chambre Verte* is technically all too
simple. Truffaut's lack of range as an actor is
not helped by the script's purple prose. But one
suspects the real problems to be much larger:
the human face in this film has become clouded
and curiously vague – neither direct enough to
stand for itself (as it did in the earlier films), nor
sufficiently eloquent to carry as much metaphysical baggage as the script implies. Truffaut
has made more than his share of maverick and
self-critical films; his later retreat into period
pieces and production values becomes all the
more regrettable. CA

Chameleon Street

(Wendell B Harris Jr, 1991, US) Wendell B
Harris Jr, Angela Leslie, Amina Fakir.
95 min.
Virtually a lost film, this picked up a prize at the
Sundance festival and earned some critical raves,
but when Warners acquired the rights with a
view to remaking it, they didn't bother to dis-
tribute the shoestring original – according to the
writer/director/star, they actively suppressed it
(it's never been released in the UK, even on video).
It's flawed but often brilliant, one of the most
provocative and adventurous American movies
of the '90s. Harris is Douglas Street, a kind of professional black Zelig, who successfully passes
himself off as a reporter, an exchange student, a
lawyer and even a surgeon without any relevant
qualifications. Formally adventurous, very
funny, and deeply sour. Incredibly, it's based on
a true story. TCh

Champ, The

(Franco Zeffirelli, 1979, US) Jon Voight, Faye
Dunaway, Ricky Schroder, Jack Warden,
Arthur Hill, Strother Martin, Joan Blondell,
Elisha Cook.
122 min.
Syrupy schlock from perhaps the most sentimental of all Italian directors, a pointless update
of King Vidor's 30's weepie about a former champion boxer's attempts to hang on to his doting

son when his estranged wife reappears on the
scene. An all too real and common dilemma treated in tediously glossy fashion. GA

Champagne

(Alfred Hitchcock, 1928, GB) Betty Balfour,
Gordon Harker, Ferdinand von Alten, Jack
Trevor, Jean Bradin, Marcel Vibert.
7,830 ft. b/w.
Hitchcock's five not very happy years at Elstree
produced a crop of ten films, most of which are
now unfairly neglected. Saddled with a clichéd
story from studio rival Walter Mycroft and an
ebullient, assertive star, he still managed to
imbue this light romantic melodrama with an air
of sinister menace. The champagne-drinking
sophisticate who clouds the destiny of millionaire's daughter Balfour more than makes up for
the weak 'cake-hound' hero, and Balfour herself
proves remarkably adept at parodying her lost-
little-girl image. Hitchcock's sly blend of fantasy,
game-playing and frightening lechery, and his
continually inventive visuals, make for an
intriguing exploration of '20s high-life. RMy

Champagne Charlie

(Alberto Cavalcanti, 1944, GB) Tommy
Trinder, Stanley Holloway, Betty Warren,
Austin Trevor, Jean Kent, Guy Middleton.
107 min. b/w.
Never did Cavalcanti's misspent avant-garde
youth fuse more fascinatingly with his mature
flair for melodrama than in this entrancingly flamboyant celebration of the English music hall.
Trinder's slyly innocent rendering of 'Everything
will be lovely when the pigs begin to fly' is interrupted by a riot and a pair of bizarre female jug-
glers, Holloway's Great Vance has a luminous
vitality which verges on the surreal, and Warren's
larger-than-life Bessie Bellwood subversively
drowns aristocratic disdain in a sea of sensuous
vulgarity. The atmosphere of cosy communality
that permeates the film leaves little room for the
grim poverty which surrounded the real music
halls, but Cavalcanti happily sacrifices realism to
create a monument to popular culture. RMy

Champagne Murders, The
(Le Scandale)

(Claude Chabrol, 1967, Fr) Anthony Perkins,
Maurice Ronet, Stéphane Audran, Yvonne
Furneaux, Suzanne Lloyd, Christa Lang.
107 min.
The most striking feature of Chabrol's glossy
murder mystery is the totally incomprehensible
plot, revolving around rivalry for the rights to a
family champagne firm: Perkins has said that he
took his part solely in order to figure out whodunit. Rather like a pop *Huis Clos*, it turns out that
all four parties in the bourgeois household are as
intolerable as each other, but who strangled whom
and why remains opaque. Made by Chabrol's regular team, it's relentlessly stylish. TR

Champion

(Mark Robson, 1949, US) Kirk Douglas,
Marilyn Maxwell, Arthur Kennedy, Ruth
Roman, Lola Albright.
90 min. b/w.
Given a punchy performance from Douglas and
skilful direction, this tale of a boxer's ruthless
drive to the top is flashily effective. But it's mostly wind and piss, with the vicious hero of Ring
Lardner's story now conventionally excused (he
stomps on people because he had an underprivileged childhood and wants to take care of ma).
The *Set-Up*, made the same year, is infinitely
superior. TM

Champion, The

see Shanghai Lil

Champions

(John Irwin, 1983, GB) John Hurt, Edward
Woodward, Ben Johnson, Jan Francis, Peter
Barkworth, Ann Bell, Judy Parfitt,
Alison Steadman.
115 min.
Into those purple areas where fiction quails to go,
Real Life occasionally ventures unabashed. Once
launched on its grimly portentous way (in Great
Medical Clichés of the Movies, 'That's a nasty
cough' has finally been usurped by 'What does
your doctor say about that swelling?'), the story of
jockey Bob Champion (Hurt), his fight against can-

cer, and his subsequent ride to glory in the Grand National, steers a careful path between celebration of courage and avoidance of hagiography. Indeed, Champion is portrayed in distinctly unflattering terms: stubborn, bloody-minded, and a rotter to his long-standing girl-friend. It's all efficiently done, and the slow-motion climax can scarcely fail to stuff the requisite frog down the gullet. Nevertheless, one can't help wishing that a director of Irvin's calibre would tackle more testing material than this. JP

Champions
see Mighty Ducks, The

Chance, History, Art...
(James Scott, 1979, GB) Anne Bean, John McKeon, Rita Donagh, Stuart Brisley, Jamie Reid, Jimmy Boyle, Lusha Kellgren.
50 min.
Glaswegian convict Jimmy Boyle pedals a stationary bicycle opposite his prison mural of a disappearing horizon; Sex Pistols designer Jamie Reid offers hints on rip-off art; James Scott's anthology of interviews salutes the practitioners of surrealism (rather than those who mummify it) in an entertainingly provocative film. DMacp

Chance Meeting
see Blind Date

Chance of a Lifetime
(Bernard Miles, 1950, GB) Basil Radford, Bernard Miles, Niall MacGinnis, Geoffrey Keen, Kenneth More, Josephine Wilson, Julien Mitchell.
89 min. b/w.
Amiable little film about a small engineering works turning out agricultural equipment whose owner, irritated by disagreements with his workers, stalks out leaving them to get on with it. An independent's answer to the Ealing comedies, it tries (reasonably successfully) to keep its feet more firmly on the ground with locations in a real factory and plausible characters. TM

Chances Are
(Emile Ardolino, 1989, US) Cybill Shepherd, Robert Downey Jr, Ryan O'Neal, Mary Stuart Masterson, Christopher McDonald, Josef Sommer.
108 min.
This went direct to video in Britain, but as latter-day Hollywood romantic comedies go, it has a bit more style than you might expect. Downey displays a surprising lightness of touch as the teenager who visits his girlfriend's house and gradually comes to the complex oedipal realisation that he himself may be the reincarnated spirit of her mother's late husband. Don't you just hate it when that happens. TJ

Chanel Solitaire
(George Kaczender, 1981, Fr/GB) Marie-France Pisier, Timothy Dalton, Rutger Hauer, Karen Black, Brigitte Fossey.
124 min.
Madame Chanel changed the way all women dressed and deserves a better biopic than this. Not that exquisite Pisier is subjected to hours of make-up to achieve the withered beldame of later years. The film simply ends in the '20s, by which time Chanel had made it. But how? When Pisier isn't pouting 'adorably', she's occasionally discovered pinning something, but there's no sign of the hard work that created a huge business empire. Chanel's world apparently revolved round men, and all her intuitive genius is unfortunately attributed to their influence: the bobbed hair is created in pique, and the trademark pearls are a reconciliation gift. A Lesbian affair is treated as an aberration. Worst thing in the film is Dalton as the twit lover. Best thing is a sweaty, corseted Black as a member of the demi-monde. Otherwise, chaps, save your money and put it towards that little black dress. JS

Changeling, The
see Middleton's Changeling

Changeling, The
(Peter Medak, 1979, Can) George C Scott, Trish Van Devere, Melvyn Douglas, John Colicos, Jean Marsh, Barry Morse.
109 min.
Murdered by his father 70 years ago, the outraged spirit of a small boy makes it known through his haunting of Scott, a lonely composer, that his real grudge is not against the killer but The Changeling (now an elderly senator), who took his place and inherited his fortune. In an atmosphere that resembles the electrocardiogram of a corpse, the administration of shocks (murderous wheelchairs, mysterious bangings and firebolts) becomes risible rather than disturbing. And the leaps made by Scott's agile mind in identifying both victim and usurper leave logic and credence on the starting block. FF

Change of Seasons, A
(Richard Lang, 1980, US) Shirley MacLaine, Anthony Hopkins, Bo Derek, Michael Brandon, Mary Beth Hurt.
102 min.
Another dull round of middle-class shagging which, twelve years on from Bob & Carol & Ted & Alice, still thinks that talking up front about adultery is somehow both daringly honest and funny. Glib trappings (skiing in Vermont, frolics in the hot tub) and witless dialogue sink everything except for the perky intelligence of MacLaine, who clearly deserves better than this, and Derek, who doesn't. Kitsch without conviction, schlock without end. CPea

Chan Is Missing
(Wayne Wang, 1981, US) Wood Moy, Marc Hayashi, Laureen Chew, Judi Nihei, Peter Wang.
80 min. b/w.
A raunchy, sprawling and completely unpredictable panorama of the Chinese-American experience, which opens with Hong Kong pop star Sam Hui's Cantonese version of 'Rock Around the Clock' on the sound-track (he has turned it into a kind of inflation blues, lamenting the rising cost of rice). The plot, such as it is, kicks off with the disappearance of one Chan Hung; the problem is that he had $4,000 in his pocket, belonging to Jo and Steve, two Chinese cab-drivers. Their search for Chan takes them to the heart of the fortune cookie: the tensions between Chinese and American identity (especially when there's a generation gap, as there is between Jo and Steve), the chasm between ABCs (American-Born Chinese) and FOBs (Fresh Off the Boats), the clashes between PRC patriots and renegade Taiwan loyalists...It is sometimes wildly comic, sometimes melancholy, sometimes suspenseful and often strangely touching. The missing Chan – almost certainly a descendant of Charlie Chan, but also a cypher for 'CHinese-americAN' – never turns up, although the missing money does. But the search is the thing, and it goes round all the Chinatown corners you never dared explore for yourself. TR

Chant of Jimmie Blacksmith, The
(Fred Schepisi, 1978, Aust) Tommy Lewis, Freddy Reynolds, Ray Barrett, Jack Thompson, Angela Punch, Steve Dodds.
122 min.
Fine adaptation of Thomas Keneally's novel about a half-caste caught between his aboriginal heritage and his mission-bred belief that he has a stake in white society. The setting is New South Wales on the eve of federation between the Australian states in 1900, and when Jimmie discovers the truth of this brave new world ('You'll still have the same rights – none'), he declares war in an orgy of murder. A little too leisurely in its eye for landscapes, but a film of real power. TM

Chantons sous l'Occupation
(André Halimi, 1976, Fr)
94 min. b/w.
Brimming with torch songs, boulevard ballads and kitsch dance routines, Halimi's exhaustive documentary compilation is a chronicle of the wartime entertainment scene in Paris, featuring most of the famous names of the period, from Jean Cocteau to Maurice Chevalier. All good French joie de vivre...except that Halimi's deadly serious purpose is to expose how eagerly French showbiz collaborated with the Nazis in preserving a public image of 'normality' under the Occupation. Following outraged protests in France, Halimi reportedly added footage showing entertainers who didn't fraternise with the Germans or who actively worked with the Resistance; but his indictment doubtless remains scathing. TR

Chaplin
(Richard Attenborough, 1992, GB) Robert Downey Jr, Dan Aykroyd, Geraldine Chaplin, Kevin Dunn, Anthony Hopkins, Milla Jovovich, Moira Kelly, Kevin Kline, Diana Lane, Penelope Ann Miller, Paul Rhys, John Thaw, Marisa Tomei, Nancy Travis, James Woods, Bill Paterson.
145 min. b/w & col.
Attenborough's very traditional biopic is a disappointment. Going for the whole life has meant an even, plodding, surface treatment, and using the device of an old Chaplin reminiscing to the publisher of his autobiography (Hopkins) lends it an air of Desert Island Discs. The one imaginative stroke misfires: Chaplin's trademark bowler and cane magically presenting themselves to him in the props room like refugees from Industrial Light & Magic. The one conspicuous bit of mise en scène – Chaplin and Fairbanks (Kline) clambering about on the Hollywood sign (Hollywoodland: yes, they've done their research) – could have come from a commercial. Downey has captured the idealism and the melancholy, but not the sentimentality of the comic. He has also mastered the pratfalls and the balletics, and there are dazzling demonstrations when he does the drunk in the theatre box and the first impromptu audition for Sennett (Aykroyd), but he isn't funny. This is underlined when clips of the real thing are shown. A bit of a beached whale. BC

Chapman Report, The
(George Cukor, 1962, US) Efrem Zimbalist Jr, Shelley Winters, Jane Fonda, Claire Bloom, Glynis Johns, Ray Danton, Ty Hardin, Andrew Duggan.
125 min.
Cukor at home among the women again, chicly cosseting a quartet of suburbanites as their schematically stereotyped sex lives (frigid Fonda, nympho Bloom, etc) come under the sensationalist investigative eye of Kinsey-style research. With four writers adapting the Irving Wallace novel and numerous hands cutting the result, it's something of a mess; but it's none the less an intriguing staging-post between Little Women and Rich and Famous. PT

Chapter Two
(Robert Moore, 1979, US) James Caan, Marsha Mason, Joseph Bologna, Valerie Harper, Alan Fudge.
126 min.
The success of Neil Simon movies is dispiriting evidence that most people still watch with their ears. 'Seen one, seen 'em all' quite literally applies to his static exercises in theatrical smart-talk and unfailing wit-under-pressure. Chapter Two is no exception: Caan and Mason indulge in a two-hour session of repartee-swapping and painful coming to terms with each other's sense of humour and loss (she's just divorced, his wife has just died). Director Moore's ambitions stretch little farther than keeping his actors in frame and earshot, though he occasionally follows them out of chic apartments to chic NY cultural landmarks. The rest is words, words, words – the regular Broadway takeaway. PT

Character
see Karakter

Charade
(Stanley Donen, 1953, US) Cary Grant, Audrey Hepburn, Walter Matthau, James Coburn, George Kennedy.
113 min.
Donen's typically slick comedy thriller, ingeniously scripted by Peter Stone, is a mammoth audience teaser, with a small cast of characters, bursting with multiple identities, caught up in a complicated hunt for a fortune in gold coins seemingly secreted by Hepburn's murdered husband. Grant imparts his ineffable charm, Kennedy (with metal hand) provides comic brutality, while Hepburn is elegantly fraught. There are also smart Parisian settings and smart Mancini music. The result has a chic rating of at least 180; and while hardly as sturdy or provoking an entertainment as North by Northwest, say, it remains an entertainment. GB

Charge at Feather River, The

(Gordon Douglas, 1953, US) Guy Madison, Frank Lovejoy, Vera Miles, Helen Westcott, Dick Wesson.
96 min.
Western originally in 3-D, with the usual hail of arrows and tomahawks hurled at the audience, and here more inventively augmented by a stream of tobacco juice (aimed at a rattlesnake). Actually, directed with great drive and beautifully shot by Peverell Marley, it's much better than you might expect, even though the script (two sisters captured by Cheyennes are rescued five years later, one by force since she has married a chief) serves mainly as an excuse for non-stop Indian fighting. TM

Charge of the Light Brigade, The

(Michael Curtiz, 1936, US) Errol Flynn, Olivia de Havilland, Patric Knowles, Nigel Bruce, David Niven, Henry Stephenson, Donald Crisp.
116 min. b/w.
So-so attempt to repeat the success of *Lives of a Bengal Lancer*, with rousing action on the North-West Frontier embedded in much romantic attitudinising from Flynn and Knowles as brothers in love with the same girl. Switching belatedly to the Crimea, the plot finally justifies the title with a bizarre – but beautifully shot – account of the famous charge (the wicked Rajah causing all the trouble in India, it seems, was in command of the Russian guns). TM

Charge of the Light Brigade, The

(Tony Richardson, 1968, GB) Trevor Howard, Vanessa Redgrave, John Gielgud, Harry Andrews, Jill Bennett, David Hemmings, Peter Bowles, Mark Burns, Howard Marion Crawford, Mark Dignam, Alan Dobie, Willoughby Goddard, TP McKenna, Corin Redgrave, Norman Rossington, Helen Cherry, Rachel Kempson, Donald Wolfit.
141 min.
Richardson's shapeless, hapless epic, starring half the British acting profession – the other half having said 'no' or dropped out – in which some stylish touches and a potentially persuasive treatment get buried by the evidence of production difficulties of every conceivable kind. Ironic that, after three years of catastrophes, the animated title sequence by Richard Williams should remain the most memorable element. SG

Chariots of Fire

(Hugh Hudson, 1981, GB) Ben Cross, Ian Charleson, Nigel Havers, Cheryl Campbell, Ian Holm, John Gielgud.
123 min.
Gosh, aren't the British remarkable? They win Olympic races despite running in slow motion, they castigate old conservatives while revelling in patriotic claptrap, they win Oscars galore while making crappy films. OK, so some of the acting's all right, but really this is an overblown piece of self-congratulatory emotional manipulation perfectly suited for Thatcherite liberals. Pap. And *Greystoke* is no better. GA

Chariots of the Gods (Erinnerungen an die Zukunft)

(Harald Reinl, 1969, WGer)
98 min.
Based on Erich von Däniken's books, and heavily cut on release in Britain. A travelogue of 'evidence' that Blue Meanies from deep space got here before us and took time out to knock up the Pyramids, the Easter Island heads and Centre Point. For flat-earthers, people who walk round ladders and get killed by juggernaut lorries, and all those who lie awake fretting about things that go bump and get cut by 46 minutes in the night.

Charles and Lucie (Charles et Lucie)

(Nelly Kaplan, 1979, Fr) Daniel Ceccaldi, Ginette Garcin, Georges Claisse, Nelly Kaplan, Jean-Marie Proslier.
98 min.
Whimsical but totally enjoyable romantic comedy from the impressive if erratic Kaplan (*La Fiancée du Pirate, Néa*). An elderly couple – a layabout junk merchant and a charlady – take a gamble on gaining fortune and happiness, and find themselves swindled; penniless and pursued by the law through the South of France, they are thrown back on their wits for survival, and finally find their menopausal dissatisfaction with one another replaced by a rebirth of love. Sounds sentimental? It is, but Kaplan's ironic humour, and almost surreal sense of absurdity in her outlandish sequence of narrative events, make for a delightfully off-beat and touching film. GA

Charles Dead or Alive (Charles Mort ou Vif)

(Alain Tanner, 1970, Switz) François Simon, Marcel Robert, Marie-Claire Dufour, Maya Simon, André Schmidt.
93 min.
Like *The Salamander*, Tanner's first feature takes one person's life and examines it within an environment of ideas as much as within a physical environment. Charles is a rich industrialist in complacent old Switzerland who reaches a crisis point in his life – one marked by a television interview he gives – and walks out. He settles in with a youngish couple (she the daughter of a judge, he a sign painter),and his daughter, a member of a revolutionary student group, visits them. It's an isolated community, one at odds with society at large, 'caught in a structure' as Charles says, 'that they can't accept'. As in *The Salamander*, Tanner uses the mechanics of New Wave film-making, but freshly, and is close enough to the unheroic realities of daily life in sad, materialistic, authoritarian Europe to make his film a rewarding experience.

Charles Dickens' David Copperfield

(Don Arioli, 1993, US) voices: Julian Lennon, Michael York, Kelly LeBrock, Sheena Easton, Joseph Marcell, Andrew Martin.
90 min.
The great *Bildungsroman* is animated and set in the mouse community of a cheese factory. Not exactly a tiny tot's best introduction to the Inimitable.

Charles Mingus: Triumph of the Underdog

(Don McGlynn, 1997, US) Charles Mingus, Eric Dolphy, Gunther Schuller, Sue Mingus, Dannie Richmond, Celia Mingus, John Handy, Jimmy Knepper, Wynton Marsalis, Snookie Young, Eddie Bert, Dorian Mingus.
78 min.
Mingus was one of the great jazz composers and bassists; the blend of lyricism, intelligence, soul and fire in his music was also, by all accounts, painfully present in his personality, though this fascinating documentary, complete with rare clips and interviews with those who knew, played and lived with him, tends to soft pedal his more abrasively volatile side. That said, there are treats galore, perhaps most notably footage of Mingus duetting with the equally magnificent Eric Dolphy in 1964 and performing 'Pithecanthropus Erectus' in 1970. GA

Charley-One-Eye

(Don Chaffey, 1972, GB) Richard Roundtree, Roy Thinnes, Nigel Davenport, Jill Pearson, Aldo Sambrell.
107 min.
Undeniable tendencies to symbolic overkill and messy over-statement mar this Civil War Western polemic on the dispossessed. But Chaffey copes well with the Spanish desert locations, and draws excellent performances from Roundtree and Thinnes as the black Union Army deserter and the Indian outcast who find common ground in oppression (eventually personified by Davenport's ruthless bounty-hunter). VG

Charley Varrick

(Don Siegel, 1973, US) Walter Matthau, Joe Don Baker, Felicia Farr, Andy Robinson, John Vernon, Sheree North, Benson Fong, Norman Fell.
111 min.
Marvellous, toughly eccentric thriller which confirmed that Siegel had more responses to '70s paranoia than a mere Magnum blast, and decisively removed Matthau from the wasteland of Neil Simon wit. Varrick, 'the last of the independents', unwittingly hits a Mafia payroll; staying alive means outwitting Molly (Baker), the Mafia's freak-killer hitman. The defensive odyssey is through sunlit *noir* territory, populated exclusively with cherishably individuated oddballs. Clever, but never cold. PT

Charlie Bubbles

(Albert Finney, 1967, GB) Albert Finney, Billie Whitelaw, Colin Blakely, Liza Minnelli, Peter Sallis, Timothy Garland, Richard Pearson.
89 min.
Finney's sole film to date as director, a *cause célèbre* in its day because it was refused a circuit release, is something of a curio, a movie with a tone and taste all its own. Charlie is a successful writer run dry (Shelagh Delaney, who wrote the script, hasn't exactly been a cataract since 1968). He fools without relish with a pal in a restaurant, watches his female menials on his domestic closed circuit, goes north dutifully to his ex-wife and son, is too tired to care about a come-on from Liza-with-a-Zee en route. The coda, which looked a resonant little fantasy then, may well come across as a thunderous cop-out now. SG

Charlie Chan and the Curse of the Dragon Queen

(Clive Donner, 1980, US) Peter Ustinov, Lee Grant, Angie Dickinson, Richard Hatch, Brian Keith, Roddy McDowall, Rachel Roberts.
97 min.
A blandoid pastiche in which Ustinov plays the inscrutable detective who has an adoring half-Jewish *klutz* of a grandson, who in turn has an adoring halfwit doll of a girl-friend. Farce, chase sequences and one-liners all fall mirthlessly through the bottomless plot, which has something to do with convoluted family shenanigans, and the whole mess cost a staggering $9 million. Confucius say: 'High time comedies got act together, this one fall apart at scanty seams.' HM

Charlie Chan at the Opera

(H Bruce Humberstone, 1936, US) Warner Oland, Keye Luke, Boris Karloff, Charlotte Henry, Thomas Beck, William Demarest.
66 min. b/w.
One of the best in the series featuring Earl Derr Biggers' Chinese detective with the taste for Holmesian deduction and Confucian pearls of wisdom (often acidly apt: 'Bad alibi like dead fish; can't stand test of time'). This was Oland's thirteenth appearance in the role, and the earlier serial-style plotting had given way to subtler whodunitry, here given a considerable boost by atmospheric backstage settings and the inimitable Karloff, who provides a wonderfully sinister red herring as an escaped lunatic, once a famous baritone supposedly burned to death in a fire and vengefully prowling around. Oland – plump, enigmatic, presiding with a barely suppressed air of secret mockery – wasn't the first Charlie Chan (the part had been played once each by George Kuwa, Kamayama Sojin and EL Park between 1926 and 1929); but taking over in 1931 (*Charlie Chan Carries On*) for a run of 16 films, he invariably lent a touch of distinction to the series. Taking over after Oland's death for *Charlie Chan in Honolulu* (1938), Sidney Toler was competent but much less subtle, although the series maintained its standards. Particularly good are *Charlie Chan at Treasure Island* (1939), a spiritedly eerie affair involving murder and blackmail at the San Francisco Fair, where assorted magicians and psychics (one of whom reads the killer's mind to save Charlie's life) get into the act; and the weirdly Gothic *Castle in the Desert* (1942), featuring murder by poison in a Mojave Desert castle built by an eccentric recluse who wears a mask to hide a facial disfigurement and whose wife happens to be a descendant of the Borgias. Toler made 22 films in the series, which began going downhill when Monogram took it over for *Charlie Chan in the Secret Service* (1944). The last six entries (1947-49), with Roland Winters taking over from Toler, are real Poverty Row quickies.

Charlotte (La Jeune Fille Assassinée)

(Roger Vadim, 1974, Fr/It/WGer) Sirpa Lane, Michel Duchaussoy, Mathieu Carrière, Roger Vadim, Alexandre Astruc.
103 min.
Vadim's piece of characteristically humourless comic-strip sexism uses the hoary literary

device of revivifying its ex-heroine by patching together a multi-faceted biography from all her previous lovers. It's a predictable chain of *haute-couture* bunk-ups until a wayward play-boy takes '*le petit mort*' a shade literally and strangles her at the point of orgasm: she comes and goes. Unlike Damiano's (hardcore) *Story of Joanna* or Roeg's *Bad Timing*, Vadim's film hasn't got the imagination to cope with the large-scale metaphysical implications surrounding sexuality and death. But at least he does have the nerve to confront his fantasies. Where else can you see someone wanking over a Madonna and Child in the Pitti Palace gallery to the strains of Tubular Bells? Or a modern - dress version of Watteau's *The Swing*? Or a pederast film critic quoting Gide in Highgate cemetery? CPea

Charlotte's Web

(Charles A Nichols/Iwao Takamoto, 1972, US) voices of Debbie Reynolds, Henry Gibson, Paul Lynde, Agnes Moorehead.
96 min.
Innocuous animated fare (with songs) from Hanna-Barbera, based on EB White's fantasy. About a runt pig who, with some help from unexpected friends, sidesteps the bacon pan forever.

Charme Discret de la Bourgeoisie, Le

see Discreet Charm of the Bourgeoisie, The

Charro!

(Charles Marquis Warren, 1969, US) Elvis Presley, Ina Balin, Barbara Werle, Lynn Kellogg, Victor French, James Sikking.
98 min.
Turgid Western with Presley (singing only over the titles) wandering expressionlessly through a stock plot as a reformed outlaw framed by his former buddies. All but unwatchable. TM

Chartreuse de Parme, La

(Christian-Jaque, 1947, Fr) Gérard Philipe, Louis Salou, Renée Faure, Maria Casarès, Louis Seigner, Tullio Carminati.
170 min. b/w.
Fabrizio, Stendhal's hero, contrives to be present at the Battle of Waterloo without really seeing it, which is much the same as Christian-Jaque blithely turning a great novel into a routine swashbuckling vehicle for his willowy leading man. It demonstrates to what degree French *cinéma de qualité* was rather a matter of 'quantity', demanding a complacent accumulation of production values in lieu of the slightest vision or intelligence. GAd

Charulata (The Lonely Wife)

(Satyajit Ray, 1964, Ind) Soumitra Chatterjee, Madhabi Mukherjee, Sailen Mukherjee, Shyamal Ghoshal, Geetali Roy.
124 min. b/w.
A wonderfully Jamesian study of Victorian India in which a neglected wife, on the point of breaking through to self-awareness, begins to perceive male dominion as a hollow façade of beards, braces and boredom. Immensely funny (with the dialogue peppered by solemn anglicisms and toasts to Gladstone and the Liberals), but also elegant and gracefully moving as the heroine flirts with romance and domestic tragedy on her way to becoming the New Woman. Certainly one of Ray's best films, with a superb music score of his own composition. TM

Chase, The

(Arthur Penn, 1965, US) Marlon Brando, Jane Fonda, Robert Redford, EG Marshall, Angie Dickinson, Janice Rule, James Fox, Miriam Hopkins, Robert Duvall.
133 min.
Terror in a Texas town as a prison escapee (Redford), returning home to seek shelter and justice, stirs up a cesspit of hatred, corruption, guilt, lust and racial prejudice. Lillian Hellman's script, based on a novel/play by Horton Foote but emerging as a sort of updated and expanded *Little Foxes*, sometimes fringes absurdity in trying to indict practically everybody in town as a secret sinner, and in its stagy contrivance (the refugee just happens by on the night of a convention when temperatures are running drunkenly high). But it does manage to weave a credible pattern out of the tan-gled loyalties and enmities, which Penn's direction takes by the scruff and shakes into a firework display of controlled violence. Terrific performances too, although Brando (undergoing his statutory beating up as the sheriff caught in the middle) rather overdoes the broody bit. TM

Chase, The

(Adam Rifkin, 1994, US) Charlie Sheen, Kristy Swanson, Ray Wise, Josh Mostel, Wayne Grace, Rocky Carroll, Henry Rollins, Cary Elwes.
94 min.
Jack Hammond (Sheen), an escaped, falsely convicted bank-robber, jump starts his romance with unhappy heiress Natalie (Swanson) by abducting her from a gas station. The daughter of Dalton Voss (Wise), the Donald Trump of California, she's none too pleased – even less so when father offers a paltry ransom and turns her live-on-TV kidnap into a travelling media circus. As the ill-matched couple settle their differences and get better acquainted, the growing convoy of cop cars and outside-broadcast vans nears the Mexican border and freedom…or, perhaps, a dead end. Swanson displays fine dental work and a synthetic 'attitude', mostly whining on about what a drag it is to be rich, so only rock'n'roll hardman Henry Rollins, as a standard-issue cop and blasé star of 'reality TV', makes any lasting impression. Unroadworthy. NF

Chase a Crooked Shadow

(Michael Anderson, 1957, GB) Richard Todd, Anne Baxter, Herbert Lom, Alexander Knox, Faith Brook.
87 min. b/w.
Hitchcockian thriller with Baxter as an heiress seemingly the victim of a conspiracy of terror involving the family jewels and someone (Todd) turning up claiming to be her supposedly dead brother. Passably suspenseful, but lacking Hitchcock's plausibility (especially the tricksy ending) and saddled with a dreary performance from the dreary Todd. TM

Chasers

(Dennis Hopper, 1994, US) Tom Berenger, William McNamara, Erika Eleniak, Dean Stockwell, Gary Busey, Seymour Cassel, Marilu Henner, Dennis Hopper.
101 min.
Dennis Hopper's film is a lightweight affair, but amiable enough. It's the story of two naval shore-patrolmen – by-the-book hardass Berenger and slick young McNamara – ordered to escort a prisoner cross-country on the Fourth of July. The catch is the prisoner's a she: Eleniak of *Baywatch* fame. Saddled with such a tired script and a sorely unprepossessing star as McNamara, Hopper amuses himself by doodling in the margins: he's got a wonderful eye for authentic pop-art Americana, truck-stop culture and crazy golf landscapes. He also has a lot of cool friends willing to put in a day's work for the heck of it. Nothing essential, then, but not a total loss either. TCh

Chasing Amy

(Kevin Smith, 1996, US) Ben Affleck, Joey Lauren Adams, Jason Lee, Dwight Ewell, Jason Mewes, Kevin Smith.
113 min.
Banky (Lee) and Holden (Affleck) are beginning to make a name for themselves as creators of the cult comic book 'Bluntman & Chronic', but their partnership is threatened when Holden falls for fellow artist Alyssa (Adams). For one thing, Banky – whose attitude to women is at best neanderthal, at worst blatantly misogynist – is jealously proprietorial about his buddy; for another, Alyssa already has a girlfriend. Though Smith's directing talent remains rudimentary, as a writer he's progressed from the basic schtick-and-gags routine of *Clerks*, his gleefully un-PC debut. Again, there's plenty of profanity, but the film scores in its exploration of the social and psychological implications of Alyssa's increasingly tender feelings for Holden. The script moves beyond Smith's customary cataloguing of male adolescent ignorance and idiocy to offer sharp insights into the romanticism and pragmatism, pride and double standards that define the tangled threesome. GA

Chasing Dreams

(Caleb Lindsay, 1994, GB) Ian Prince, Luke Shaw, Adam Russ, Dominic Knutton.
83 min.
Something of a gem, writer/director Lindsay's micro-budget independent feature is low on big sets (why worry, if you've got London available), but big on individuality and quirky sensibility. It comes on like a mongrel blend of Jarmusch and Mike Leigh as it traces the lives of a trio of likeable, ever-hopeful non-achievers. Ex-borstal boy Alex tries to make a go of it buying and fixing-up rust-bucket 'motors'; Pat and Dave are struggling with an album (there's an hilarious set-piece with the producer of 'Lucky Records'): all chase girls with a staggering lack of success. Throughout Lindsay shows a real affection for his characters. Often the film is exquisitely inconsequential and disconsolate; it's always stylistically interesting (filters and all); and the ending is great. WH

Chasing the Deer

(Graham Holloway, 1994, GB) Brian Blessed, Iain Cuthbertson, Dominique Carrara, Jake D'Arcy, Dominic Borrelli.
105 min.
This bold local production, subtitled 'A Story of the '45', was financed by small investors. The result, regrettably, is not a patch on what Peter Watkins did with a small TV budget in *Culloden*. A handful of beardies in kilts skirl about in the mist of a smoke machine…The best thing in this truly lamentable account of Bonnie Prince Charlie's doomed attempt to regain his throne is bellowing Brian Blessed as an English officer leading a regiment of loyalist Scots. BC

Chat, Le (The Cat)

(Pierre Granier-Deferre, 1970, Fr) Simone Signoret, Jean Gabin, Annie Cordy.
88 min.
In this anaemic adaptation of a characteristically sour and sweaty Simenon novel, a long-married couple is sucked into a triangular sado-masochistic relationship with a cat, on which the husband lavishes the suffocating possessive affection he once devoted to his once-beautiful, now alcoholically bloated, spouse. Simenon, however, invested her eventual killing of the pet with all the neurotic squalor of a *crime passionnel*; here, given the mutual malignity of Gabin and Signoret, one simply wonders how the cat managed to survive so long. GAd

Château de ma mère, Le (My Mother's Castle)

(Yves Robert, 1990, Fr) Philippe Caubère, Nathalie Roussell, Didier Pain, Thérèse Liotard, Julie Timmerman, Paul Crauchet, Jean Rochefort, Jean Carmet, Georges Wilson.
98 min.
Unsurprisingly, this sequel to *La Gloire de mon père*, adapted from the second volume of Marcel Pagnol's autobiography, is very similar in tone (though mercifully more sparing with the music). Your attitude to it depends on whether you viewed the first film as a touching evocation of a Provence childhood, or as a tedious travelogue drowning in sentiment. The storyline is enlivened early on by a disillusioning encounter between young Marcel and a most pretentious girl whose father (vividly played by the wonderful Rochefort) is an absinthe-crazed would-be poet who speaks in rhyming couplets *à la* Cyrano. From there on, the tone darkens, with Marcel's father persuaded away from the path of rectitude; and before long the narrator is rounding things off with a solemn roll-call of the dear departed. The coda, in which the adult Pagnol conjures up a vision of his mother as she was in his childhood, is very moving. JMo

Chato's Land

(Michael Winner, 1971, GB) Charles Bronson, Jack Palance, Richard Basehart, James Whitmore, Richard Jordan, Simon Oakland, Roddy McMillan.
110 min.
Bronson and Winner united in their usual sledgehammer style as Charlie plays a half-breed Apache hunted for murder, and Palance leads a posse in pursuit. They rape his wife, and the Indian plots and wastes their downfall. There are attempts in Gerald Wilson's script to say something about racism and violence, and some critics have even suggested parallels with the disastrous American involvement in Vietnam; but in Winner's hands, it's just a rag-bag of muddled clichés. GA

Chattahoochee

(Mick Jackson, 1989, US) Gary Oldman, Dennis Hopper, Frances McDormand, Pamela Reed, Ned Beatty, M Emmet Walsh, William De Acutis, Lee Wilkof.
97 min.
Florida, 1955. After sniping at his neighbours, Korean war vet Foley (Oldman), depressed by debts, unsuccessfully turns the gun on himself. Committed to the maximum-security Chattahoochee hospital for the criminally insane, he finds himself trapped in a nightmare world of squalor, humiliation and sadism. Life's hell; even his wife (McDormand) deserts him while he's inside. But with help from friends – including his sister (Reed) and Hopper's melancholy rapist – Foley gens up on the law and fights the good fight against institutionalised inhumanity. Coming on like a cross between *Midnight Express*, *One Flew Over the Cuckoo's Nest* and *The Birdman of Alcatraz*, Jackson's well-meaning but clichéd film staggers towards a predictable climax. Hopper simply does what comes easy, Oldman yields to twitchy histrionics, and it's left to Reed to supply a touch of restraint in a small, relatively thankless part. GA

Che!

(Richard Fleischer, 1969, US) Omar Sharif, Jack Palance, Cesare Danova, Robert Loggia, Woody Strode, Barbara Luna, Frank Silvera.
96 min.
One of the bizarre products of Hollywood's brief flirtation with revolution in the '60s, a fence-sitting but occasionally amusing account of Guevara's career. Remarkable for its eccentric casting of Palance as an amphetamine-popping Castro.

Cheap Detective, The

(Robert Moore, 1978, US) Peter Falk, Ann-Margret, Eileen Brennan, James Coco, Dom DeLuise, Stockard Channing, John Houseman, Louise Fletcher, Phil Silvers, Sid Caesar, Madeline Kahn.
92 min.
Neil Simon-scripted spoof of films based on Chandler/Hammett private eye novels, with *Casablanca* thrown in for bad measure. Designed as a follow-up to the scarcely more successful *Murder by Death*, it's the usual collection of quick-fire one-liners punctuated by huge wads of unfunny padding. Buffs may amuse themselves by noting obvious references to *The Maltese Falcon*, *The Big Sleep*, *Farewell My Lovely* and the like. *The Cheap Idea* might have been a better title. NF

Cheaper by the Dozen

(Walter Lang, 1950, US) Clifton Webb, Myrna Loy, Jeanne Crain, Edgar Buchanan, Barbara Bates, Mildred Natwick.
85 min.
Webb's spinsterish acidity, so effective in *Laura* and *The Razor's Edge*, was amusing enough when he was elevated to stardom as the waspish baby-sitter in *Sitting Pretty*. But by the time he came to play this paterfamilias of the '20s who organises his twelve children along the same efficiency lines as his business, the act was wearing distinctly thin (and suffering from spots of sentimentality). Only one sequence really takes off, with the delightfully bemused Natwick trying to recruit the mother of twelve as a lecturer on birth control. TM

Cheap Shots

(Jeff Ureles/Jerry Stoeffhaas, 1988, US) Louis Zorich, David Patrick Kelly, Marie Louise Wilson, Clarke Gordon, Patience Moore.
92 min.
Middle-aged Latin loser Louie (Zorich) owns a run-down motel, is penniless, fed up with domestic chores, his obnoxious wife, continual promises of help from her wheelchair-bound father, and life in general. Hardly surprising, then, that Louie's eyes should stray in the direction of a blonde guest who arrives with a male companion: a voyeuristic urge shared by young resident Arnold (Kelly). The two decide to instal a newly-acquired video-camera in the couple's cottage in the hope of recording some frisky action, but what they eventually witness is something they rather wish they hadn't... Ureles and Stoeffhaas extract some marvellous performances from an unknown cast, the result being a fine blend of Tati-esque humour, household drama, and mild eroticism, with occasional unexpected dollops of suspenders, sorry, suspense. DA

Checking Out

(David Leland, 1988, GB) Jeff Daniels, Melanie Mayron, Michael Tucker, Kathleen York, Ann Magnuson, Allan Havey, Jo Harvey Allen, Ian Wolfe, Billy Beck, John Durbin, Felton Perry.
95 min.
You suspect from the first fantasy sequence – hero Ray Macklin (Daniels) in his grave – that things are going to be wild, wacky, raucous and asprawl, and by the time you reach the final fantasy of Heaven as a Howard Hughes desert motel with George Harrison pushing broom, you know it. This 'light-hearted', heavy-handed skit on hypochondria in the suburbs is a miscalculation from start to finish. Macklin's life starts to go wrong when his best friend dies of a heart attack in his prime. Heck, this could happen to him, and he becomes increasingly hysterical and dishevelled, pestering doctors and loading up the household with personal oxygen supplies and pulse monitors until his wife (Mayron) can endure no more of it. There's no real structure to the film, and incidents and meetings – the orgy in the car, or the weirdo junk-food millionaire, for example – are the screenwriter's version of builder's rubble. Desperately unfunny. BC

Cheech & Chong's Next Movie (aka High Encounters of the Ultimate Kind)

(Thomas Chong, 1980, US) Richard 'Cheech' Marin, Thomas Chong, Evelyn Guerrero, Betty Kennedy, Sy Kramer, Rikki Marin.
99 min.
For a comedy double-act who make their money out of people stoned beyond discrimination, Cheech and Chong are probably better than we deserve. This free-wheeling sequel to their first feature, *Up in Smoke*, has the duo sharing a precarious state of independence in time-warp California. Cheech, the Chicano, charms foxy ladies with his smart line in dirty talk ('I'm serving tube steak covered in underwear. I hope she hasn't eaten yet'). Chong, the dead hippy, deals dope to himself and stays at home awaiting legalisation of the magic weed and laying down Richter-scale solos on his guitar. The plot is, er, like an irrelevant hassle, and the observations on sub-culture work better than the slapstick paced for the brains of the wasted, but there are enough of these – especially a welfare office freak show – to serve as a reminder of how good the high times can be. RP

Cheer, Boys, Cheer

(Walter Forde, 1939, GB) Nova Pilbeam, Edmund Gwenn, Jimmy O'Dea, CV France, Peter Coke, Moore Marriott, Graham Moffatt, Alexander Knox.
85 min. b/w.
The film Charles Barr saw both as an allegory for Ealing's own history and a remarkable precursor of the later Ealing comedies. Unfortunately, Gwenn's fascist brewer (busily trying to take over his rival) is left disappointingly one-dimensional, and the romantic sub-plot wavers precariously as Pilbeam pulls out all the stops to deal with two horribly miscast suitors. As compensation, though, much of the film takes off into glorious comedy as Moore Marriott and Graham Moffatt – surely the most enduring comics of the period – anarchically disrupt each scene they appear in. RMy

Cheetah

(Jeff Blyth, 1989, US) Keith Coogan, Lucy Deakins, Collin Mothupi, Timothy Landfield, Breon Gorman.
84 min.
Disney offering (unreleased in UK cinemas) which sends Californian teenagers Coogan and Deakins to Kenya for a stay in the bush with their parents; there they befriend a Masai boy and look after an abandoned baby cheetah. Decent and old-fashioned. TJ

Chelsea Girls

(Andy Warhol, 1967, US) Nico, Ari, Bob 'Ondine' Olivio, Ingrid Superstar, Mario Montez, Marie Menken, Bridget Polk.
215 min. b/w & col.
Bits of this shambling mess gave us a big buzz way back when Wendy Arthole flamboyantly (but minimally) gratified curiosity about the then new decadence, while soupcan aesthetic theory glorified its many hours of brain-crushing tat. It's alive while nutty naturals like Menken and Ondine perform. The other 85 per cent is wallpaper, the concept pompous, and zomboidal. View'n doze. RD

Chemins de l'Exil, Les

see Roads of Exile, The

Chère Louise (Louise)

(Philippe de Broca, 1972, Fr/It) Jeanne Moreau, Julian Negulesco, Didi Perego, Yves Robert.
105 min.
Moreau is the spinsterly divorcée, taking up a new post as a schoolteacher after the death of her mother, who befriends and then seduces a young, out-of-work Italian in this surprisingly unsentimental, even detached film. However, where in de Broca's comedies the wit of his direction and the speed of his narration are the film's major virtues, here his would-be stylishness has the effect of highlighting rather than camouflaging the thinness of his material. PH

Cherry 2000

(Steve DeJarnatt, 1988, US) Melanie Griffith, Ben Johnson, Harry Carey Jr, Tim Thomerson, Pamela Gidley, Jennifer Mayo.
93 min.
After a minimal release in the US this tilt at cultish sci-fi wnet straight to video in the UK. Its a post-apocalyptic adventure, from the director of *Miracle Mile*, that plays like a jauntier version of *Mad Max*. Griffith sports bright red hair as the eponymous heroine, a female mercenary charged with breaking into the villains' robot-packed warehouse; and much of the action takes place in striking desert landscapes. Plus marks for the presence of the old-timers, but overall it's a walk on the mild side. TJ

Chess Players, The (Shatranj ke Khilari)

(Satyajit Ray, 1977, Ind) Sanjeev Kumar, Saeed Jaffrey, Amjad Khan, Richard Attenborough, Shabana Azmi.
129 min.
The short-story irony of two nawabs playing interminable games of chess while their domestic domains crumble, and of a king wrapped up in his aesthetic pursuits while his territory is threatened by British expansionism, is decked out opulently enough (notably a lavish recreation of 1856 Lucknow); but it pales beside that of Ray's inability to distinguish a historical film from a mere costume drama. This has its moments as a gentle comedy, with Saeed Jaffrey in good form, but its nudging metaphors on queens and pawns provide a facile analysis of colonial politics. PT

Cheval d'Orgueil, Le (The Proud Ones)

(Claude Chabrol, 1980, Fr) Jacques Dufilho, Bernadette Lesache, François Cluzet, Ronan Hubert.
118 min.
This impressionistic account of peasant life in Brittany around the time of World War I is a reminder that Chabrol began his career with a bleak portrayal of the provinces in *Le Beau Serge*. This is a much rosier picture, attractively – perhaps too attractively – shot by Jean Rabier. Stressing the poverty, it caresses the eye with picturesque interiors worthy of any model village, while the peasants decked out in their national costumes look like delegates to a folk-lore congress. Hardly another Tree of Wooden Clogs, but it does have charm, sparks of Chabrol clownery, and plenty of intriguing information about superstitions and customs. One problem is that the autobiographical book by Pierre Jakez Hélias on which it is based has obviously been too severely truncated. In the latter half, particularly, attempts to get to grips with the social and cultural implications of being Breton emerge with curious muddlement. TM

Cheyenne Autumn

(John Ford, 1964, US) Richard Widmark, Carroll Baker, Karl Malden, Sal Mineo, Edward G Robinson, James Stewart, Dolores del Rio, Ricardo Montalban. Gilbert Roland, Arthur Kennedy.
170 min.
Making amends for his less than sensitive treat-

ment of the Indians in his earlier movies, Ford came up with a sprawling epic illustrating the callous disregard with which the US government treated the Cheyenne in the 1880s, uprooting them from the Yellowstone and resettling them in distant Oklahoma without proper provisions for survival. Over-long, often clichéd and uneven (there are comic interludes complete with cameo performances), but still imbued with moments of true poetry, thanks largely to William Clothier's magnificent Panavision landscapes. GA

Cheyenne Social Club, The

(Gene Kelly, 1970, US) James Stewart, Henry Fonda, Shirley Jones, Sue Ane Langdon, Elaine Devry, Robert Middleton, Arch Johnson.
102 min.
Leisurely comedy Western in which Stewart and Fonda, respectively an honest cowpuncher who inherits a brothel and the garrulous friend looking on as he struggles with his moral indignation, cope with their new status as businessmen, their increasing involvement with luscious employees, and the assortment of bad guys who force gunfights on them. Directed very much as it comes by Kelly and utterly undistinguished, but an object lesson by two old masters in the art of conjuring laughs out of nothing. TM

Chicago Joe and the Showgirl

(Bernard Rose, 1989, GB) Kiefer Sutherland, Emily Lloyd, Patsy Kensit, Keith Allen, Liz Fraser, Alexandra Pigg, John Lahr, Harry Fowler, Harry Jones.
103 min.
It's ironic that each scene seems inspired by movies, rather than life, when the film purports to show wartime England as it was. This cine-literacy may not be writer David Yallop's fault, but the script is hackneyed too, despite the story's (factually-based) potential. In 1944, an American GI (Sutherland) and a local showgirl (Lloyd) met in a Hammersmith café; a week later they were arrested for murder. Nobody ever knew the reason for their crime spree, and Yallop, none too originally, attributes their deeds to a naive faith in movie myth born of economic and cultural deprivation. The film skims the surface of its themes, and it's all poorly executed. Lloyd, like a 12- rather than 18-year-old, offers further evidence of her shortcomings, and Sutherland has no real part to play. Worse still is the 'direction'. Scenes go on far too long; the symbolism is thumpingly obvious; lighting, sets and dodgy London topography all evoke a video-neverworld. GA

Chicken and Duck Talk (Ji tong ya jiang)

(Clifton Ko, 1988, HK) Michael Hui, Sylvia Chang, Ricky Hui, Lawrence Ng.
97 min.
Cantonese comedy generally doesn't travel too well, but Michael Hui's comeback movie (he made a series of Tashlin-esque classics in the '70s) would be a riot in any context. Hui plays the stingy, stupid and backward-looking proprietor of a traditional duck restaurant; his meagre turnover plummets when a bright new fast-food chicken joint opens across the street. He frantically tries to stop his resentful staff from defecting, while dreaming up stunts to win back lost customers; the plot is garnished with everything from inspired slapstick to mother-in-law jokes. You could read it as a sardonic commentary on China's often farcical struggle to 'modernise' – except that you'd be laughing too much to think through the parallels. TR

Chienne, La

(Jean Renoir, 1931, Fr) Michel Simon, Janie Marèze, Georges Flamant, Madeleine Bérubet, Gaillard, Jean Gehret.
100 min. b/w.
M Legrand (Simon), a mild-mannered, middle-aged cashier, uses painting as a means of expression, of escape from his shrewish wife and the tedium of his job. After an accidental encounter with femme fatale Lulu (Marèze), he falls madly in love, setting her up in a flat which he fills with his paintings. Lulu, who loves only her pimp Dédé (Flamant), uses Legrand as a milch-cow, and when his money runs short, starts selling his paintings as her own (with the Sunday painter ironically unaware that his work is now much sought after). Freeing himself finally from his wife, Legrand arrives at the flat, only to realise

that Lulu is still bedding Dédé...Renoir's first great talkie has been described as 'an insignificant little melodrama, given unexpected vigour and depth by a sense of momentary occasion in the filming'. That is, a glorious experiment in, and exploration of, the nature of cinema. Wonderfully moving, with great performances. Remade by Fritz Lang as Scarlet Street. WH

Chiens, Les (The Dogs)

(Alain Jessua, 1978, Fr/Tahiti) Gérard Depardieu, Victor Lanoux, Nicole Calfan, Pierre Vernier, Gérard Séty.
99 min.
A doctor becomes increasingly disturbed by the number of bite wounds he is treating. The town is a vile new creation in which street crime is rampant, racism abounds, and the local bourgeoisie have taken to keeping Alsatians for pets. But as in Shock Treatment (shown here as Doctor in the Nude), Jessua is adept at intimating a large political conspiracy from his thriller elements. The finger here seems to point back to Depardieu, who is the local dog-trainer but who when pressed goes a little Fascist around the gills and starts spouting Nietzsche. Considerable ambiguity is lent to it all by the conversion of the doctor's liberal girl-friend from a rape victim into a dog-toting vigilante. There is also the spectre of France's colonial past in the shape of black gastarbeiter. A worthwhile, thoughtful film which deals with its large themes with surprising complexity. CPea

Chikamatsu Monogatari (The Crucified Lovers)

(Kenji Mizoguchi, 1954, Jap) Kazuo Hasegawa, Kyoko Kagawa, Yoko Minamida, Eitaro Shindo, Sakae Ozawa.
102 min. b/w.
Straightforward adaptation of a famous kabuki/bunraku play by 16th century master Chikamatsu Monzaemon, about a couple compromised by circumstances who become illicit lovers – and pay the price their society demands. Distinctly pedantic in tone and style compared with Sansho Dayu. TR

Childhood of Maxim Gorki, The (Detstvo Gorkovo)

(Mark Donskoi, 1938, USSR) Alexei Lyarsky, Varvara Massalitinova, Mikhail Troianovski, Daniil Sagal, J Alexieva.
100 min. b/w.
Donskoi's Gorki Trilogy, completed by My Apprenticeship (1939, 98 min, b/w) and My Universities (1940, 104 min, b/w) is still widely revered as one of the all-time humanist classics, and it's true that the films' expert balance between guileless simplicity and rustic mythmaking (seen to best advantage in Childhood) does give them a quality not often found outside the work of John Ford. But it's interesting to note that Donskoi's direction couldn't lie further from the mainstream of Russian film culture. Not only is he not very concerned about montage, but his concern with the lyricism of individual images leads him to neglect continuity of almost any sort: at one level, the films play like an anthology of continuity errors. That said, though, all three films do contain images of great strength in the Dovzhenko tradition. And Donskoi's handling of his actors (always encouraging them to play up to emotion, never shy of excess or sentimentality) certainly has the courage of its convictions. TR

Child Is Waiting, A

(John Cassavetes, 1963, US) Burt Lancaster, Judy Garland, Gena Rowlands, Steven Hill, Bruce Ritchey, Paul Stewart, Lawrence Tierney.
102 min. b/w.
Disowned by Cassavetes after producer Stanley Kramer edited it against his wishes and made it more sentimental than intended, this is none the less a very affecting study of the plight of mentally retarded children. Shot in semi-documentary style and using (with the exception of Ritchey, the film's central 'case history') actual retarded children, the movie concerns a new teacher (Garland) whose excessive concern with Ritchey's predicament brings her into conflict with her boss (Lancaster). As ever, Cassavetes elicits magnificent performances from his cast, making especially fine use of Garland's tremulous emotionalism, although the occasional drifts into

didacticism (the script was by Abby Mann, who wrote Judgment at Nuremberg and Ship of Fools) entail the sort of special pleading Cassavetes was keen to avoid. Flawed but fascinating. GA

Child of Divorce

(Richard Fleischer, 1946, US) Sharyn Moffett, Regis Toomey, Madge Meredith, Walter Reed, Doris Merrick, Ann Carter, Una O'Connor.
62 min. b/w.
Fleischer's modest first feature, about a child's reaction to divorce, is a beauty. Lillie Hayward's script, based on a play (Wednesday's Child by Leopold L Atlas), avoids all the pitfalls of special pleading. Both parents (Toomey and Meredith) want what is best for the child; their new partners are genuine in their desire to become friends; but the child herself, partly because of innocent teasing at school, mainly because she just can't understand, remains obstinately unaccommodating. The only solution, therefore, is boarding school: not some Dickensian horror, but a gracious, spacious place in the country boasting every amenity a child could desire. And there, in a nakedly moving final sequence, the child learns, under the sympathetic tutelage of a new friend who has been through the mill, what to expect: a time when presents come thick and fast; a time when visits grow fewer and fewer; and then, just the long, long wait to grow up. Fleischer puts scarcely a foot wrong, and the kids (Sharyn Moffett as the unhappy child, Ann Carter as her friend) are astonishing. TM

Children of a Lesser God

(Randa Haines, 1986, US) William Hurt, Marlee Matlin, Piper Laurie, Philip Bosco, Allison Gompf.
119 min.
Those whom we set free we cannot hope to own. That's the message of Mark Medoff's stage hit, which he and Hesper Anderson have adapted for the screen in a way which opens out its dimensions without ever clouding its intentions or enervating its tensions. Hurt is James, a likeably unorthodox teacher of the hearing-impaired, who becomes attracted to Sarah (Matlin, a stunning début), a pupil who left the school with little more than a large chip on her shoulder and a knowledge that sex doesn't require too much of a conversational manner. Their relationship is both a genuinely touching love story and a clever gloss on the barriers and extensions of language. It also contains a truly didactic other-dimension which points out some very salutary things about our often unintentional slights towards the deaf, without being either a simple sob or an issue story. SGr

Children of Lumière, The

see Enfants de Lumière, Les

Children of Nature (Börn Náttúrunnar)

(Fridrik Thór Fridriksson, 1991, Ice) Gsli Halldorsson, Valgerdur Dan, Hallmar Sigurdsson.
85 min.
A worthy film about the elderly – in the style of a road movie with docu-drama trimmings. The protagonist is a taciturn widower (Halldorsson) brought up in the savage northern fjords and mountains, which he abandoned for a lonely sheep farmer's life in the verdant southern pastures. The film starts with him – having shot his old dog – quitting his shack and paying an unannounced visit to his married daughter and family in Reykjavik. They quickly move him into an old people's home, where he meets a fiery old flame. Sympathetic tone but sketchy characters. WH

Children of Paradise

see Enfants du Paradis, Les

Children of Theatre Street, The

(Robert Dornheim/Earle Mack, 1977, US) Students and faculty of the Vaganova Choreographic Institute.
100 min.
An affectionate, respectful documentary about the Kirov Ballet School in Leningrad, full of interesting stuff about the school's history, selection of pupils, and teaching techniques. Enjoyable for kids and balletomanes who get misty-eyed over a single grand jeté. JS

Children of the Corn

(Fritz Kiersch, 1984, US) Peter Horton, Linda Hamilton, RG Armstrong, John Franklin, Courtney Gains, Robby Kiger.
92 min.

The pre-credits sequence shows all the adults in a small-town coffee-bar being poisoned or hacked to bits by horrible children who seem to have got their Bible hopelessly confused with *The Golden Bough*. This gambit, though amusing, neatly removes all elements of surprise from the rest of the film, so that when a post-teen couple strays into the Nebraskan cornstalks to ominous choral rumblings, the tension is of the Look Behind You variety, instead of Where Do You Suppose All The Over-18s Are, Eh? Yet another yarn from Stephen (arentcha sick of him?) King is spun out to less than the sum of his text: much hue and cry provides the padding as the hero is pursued back and forth by scythe-wielding youngsters. A late lurch from *Lord of the Fly*-ish mass psychosis to silly supernatural SPFX topples the film into total cornetto. AB

Children of the Damned

(Anton M Leader, 1963, GB) Ian Hendry, Alan Badel, Barbara Ferris, Alfred Burke, Sheila Allen, Ralph Michael, Martin Miller.
90 min. b/w.

A fairly intriguing and atmospheric exercise in science fiction, made as a sequel to *Village of the Damned* (an adaptation of John Wyndham's novel *The Midwich Cuckoos*). About a race of superchildren who (in the eyes of the authorities, at any rate) threaten to take over the world, it has some good moments, though its surreal beginning promises a generation war of apocalyptic dimensions that is never delivered, and the film finally falls into some unconvincing liberal moralising (one of the persisting curses of SF in the cinema). DP

Child's Play

(Sidney Lumet, 1972, US) James Mason, Robert Preston, Beau Bridges, Ronald Weyand, Charles White, David Rounds.
100 min.

Atrocious nonsense set in a Catholic boarding school for boys where melodramatic goings-on suggest that the devil lurks in the person of jolly Joe Dobbs, popular English master and probably closet queen (Preston, looking uncomfortable in a role originally slated for Marlon Brando). With Robert Marasco's play creaking at every joint, not even Mason's carefully tortured performance (he's the master the boys all love to hate, nursing a mum dying of cancer and a drawerful of girlie magazines) can rouse much interest. TM

Child's Play (Kinderspiel)

(Wolfgang Becker, 1992, Ger) Jonas Kipp, Oliver Bröcker, Burghart Klaussner, Angelika Bartsch, Matthias Friedrich.
107 min.

This picture of working-class life as seen through the eyes of a depressed child (Kipp) is depressing indeed. Senile Granny spends much of her time on the toilet; Dad is a child-batterer; the lad's contemporaries are bullies; and the only bit of radiance that comes his way is spying on a naked girl through the bathroom keyhole. BC

Child's Play

(Tom Holland, 1988, US) Catherine Hicks, Chris Sarandon, Alex Vincent, Brad Dourif, Dinah Manoff, Tommy Swerdlow.
87 min.

Faced with the prospect of a movie about a killer doll, you might be forgiven some scepticism; but Holland demonstrates how a well-written script and taut direction can triumph over the silliest premise. When Hicks buys her six-year-old son a talking doll called Chucky for his birthday, she has no idea it's possessed by the malevolent spirit of psychopath Dourif, whom Chicago cop Sarandon blew away in a shootout the day before. So when her babysitting friend (Manoff) takes a dive from her apartment window and the kid says the doll did it, he gets a ticket for the funny farm. Sarandon doesn't buy it either, until vengeful Chucky tries to strangle him while he's driving. Holland's sure handling of the suspense and shock moments lends the film a sharp and scary edge. NF

Child's Play 2

(John Lafia, 1990, US) Alex Vincent, Jenny Agutter, Gerrit Graham, Christine Elise, Grace Zabriskie, Peter Haskell.
84 min.

This perfunctory sequel finds the soul of serial killer Charles Lee Ray (voice by Brad Dourif) *still* trapped in the body of a Chucky doll, *still* vainly trying to usurp the more desirable body of sprightly young Andy (Vincent). Conveniently reconstructed from the frazzled ashes of Part One, souped-up Chucky traces Andy to the home of his newly acquired foster parents (Agutter and Graham), spending an inordinate amount of time jumping out of confined spaces, shouting 'Fuck you, bitch!', and slaughtering Andy's nearest and dearest. Since the gaff has long been blown (we know Chucky is alive from the outset), the original's menacing tension is entirely absent. Lafia attempts to compensate by relying heavily on Kevin Yagher's advanced doll animations, but articulated facial features, however clever, are no substitute for thrills. Only in the highly orchestrated, surprisingly gory climax, wherein Chucky's plastic form takes on the sins of the flesh, is there a spark of originality. MK

Child Under a Leaf (aka Love Child)

(George Bloomfield, 1974, Can) Dyan Cannon, Donald Pilon, Joseph Campanella, Albert S Waxman, Micheline Lanctôt.
88 min.

You've surely seen the prizewinning 'drink and drive' ad where a couple leave a cinema – she muttering that she doesn't know why they make them so sad – and go and get legless before crashing? This might well have been the film they saw: it's a formula two Kleenex movie, and enough to drive anyone to drink. Dyan Cannon is married to the sort of man who'd kill her pet poodle (he does), but she has a beautiful relationship with artist Donald Pilon, who's the father of her new-born child, and they phone each other every day, and regularly zoom off in matching white sports cars for lyrical lovemaking in the fields, and agonise over the husband's violent tendencies. Director Bloomfield's own script veers off into ever more embarrassing melodrama, but his efforts are hardly necessary: Francis Lai's superlush score tells the whole sorry story. PT

Chilsu and Mansu (Chilsu oa Mansu)

(Park Kwang-Su, 1988, SKor) Ahn Song-Gi, Park Joong-Hun, Bae Chong-Okk.
109 min.

Park's first film begins like a buddy movie – it's the story of two billboard painters: Chilsu is a youthful romantic and a bit of a dreamer; Mansu is older, quieter and hard-drinking. The tone shifts subtly with the progress of Chilsu's courtship of a pretty student, and gradually this portrait of a generation obsessed with Western culture takes on a political dimension: when the two friends stand atop one of their own billboards, discussing their frustration with the fledgling democracy down below them, the police mistakenly assume they are staging a protest, with potentially dangerous implications. An estimable film, funny, provocative and very well acted. TCh

Chiltern Hundreds, The (aka The Amazing Mr Beecham)

(John Paddy Carstairs, 1949, GB) Cecil Parker, AE Matthews, David Tomlinson, Marjorie Fielding, Joyce Carey, Lana Morris, Helen Backlin.
84 min. b/w.

Adaptation of William Douglas Home's drawing-room comedy about a shocked butler (Parker) who puts up for election as Tory candidate when the young master (Tomlinson) proposes to run for Labour and marry the parlourmaid. Needless to say the conservative proprieties are observed at the end, and it all emerges more as domestic farce than political satire, but excellent performances (Parker, Fielding and Matthews in particular) make it really rather engaging. TM

Chimes at Midnight (Campanadas a Medianoche)

(Orson Welles, 1966, Sp/Switz) Orson Welles, Keith Baxter, John Gielgud, Margaret

Rutherford, Jeanne Moreau, Norman Rodway, Marina Vlady, Alan Webb, Fernando Rey.
119 min. b/w.

The mongrel heritage of *Chimes at Midnight* is hard to credit, given the intensely personal reading of English history and literature that emerges from an incongruous Spanish/Swiss co-production of a life of Falstaff culled from five Shakespearean texts and Holinshed's *Chronicles*. Infused with a politically acute nostalgia for Merrie England, this elegiac tragi-comedy comes over as uncompromisingly modern entertainment, from its playful ruptures of traditional film grammar to its characterisation of Falstaff as hero at the crossroads of history, a spiritual and thematic precursor of Peckinpah's Cable Hogue. Welles waddles through the foreground with an eye on his own problems of patronage, while behind the camera he conjures a dark masterpiece, shot through with slapstick and sorrow. Magic. PT

China Clipper

(Ray Enright, 1936, US) Pat O'Brien, Beverly Roberts, Ross Alexander, Humphrey Bogart.
85 min. b/w.

Warner Bros salutes American technology and enterprise in this humdrum but engaging drama about one of the early heroes of aviation. O'Brien, the most solemn star on the lot (he was generally cast as cop or priest), is the hero, an industrious businessman determined to build up a Transpacific air route. Like all such success stories, this one begins in failure. But doughty O'Brien tries and tries again until his vision is made reality. If he neglects his wife and family, that's only because he is in pursuit of the American dream – nothing must stand between him and his manifest destiny. GM

China Girl

(Abel Ferrara, 1987, US) James Russo, Richard Panebianco, Sari Chang, David Caruso, Russell Wong, Joey Chin.
90 min.

This superior exploitation picture is a tough, stylish but often painfully misjudged reworking of *Romeo and Juliet*, with rival teenage gangs battling it out, sparked by the inter racial love affair between an Italian (Panebianco) and a Chinese girl (Chang). Ferrara makes excellent use of the Chinatown and Little Italy locations, and delivers the choreographed violence with his usual muscular panache, but his handling of the younger, inexperienced actors is distinctly dodgy. The major strength of the script is its accommodation of three generations: the elders and their aspiring sons are seen to conspire against the warring youngsters, putting money before family. But the bitter taste of this radical undercurrent is ultimately drowned out by saccharine sentiment and histrionic overkill. NF

China Is Near (La Cina è vicina)

(Marco Bellocchio, 1967, It) Paulo Graziosi, Glauco Mauri, Elda Tattoli, Daniela Surina, Pierluigi Aprà.
95 min. b/w.

A stinging political satire which bears the same bizarre hallmarks as *Fists in the Pocket*. Once again the protagonists are a family, and once again they live a secret life as mysteriously inaccessible as that of the epileptics in Bellocchio's earlier film. But this time they are out in the world, with older brother busily pursuing a political career, younger brother touting for Mao in hopes of ruining his brother, and sister squatting at home indulging lazy love affairs. They are upper middle class and the world is theirs; but the day of reckoning is at hand, and in a brilliantly funny series of sexual encounters, elder brother and sister find themselves bemusedly trapped into marriage by a pair of working class secretaries on the make. A dazzling and curiously foreboding comedy of manners, it shares with Godard's *La Chinoise* a sense of May 1968 just around the corner. TM

China Moon

(John Bailey, 1994, US) Ed Harris, Madeleine Stowe, Charles Dance, Benicio Del Toro, Pruitt Taylor Vince, Roger Aaron Brown, Patricia Healy.
99 min.

Directed by cinematographer John Bailey, and produced by Kevin Costner's TIG company, this neo-*noir* thriller set in Florida is classier than most UK video premieres, but hardly anything to write home about. The set-up's familiar from *Double Indemnity* and a thousand-and-one other movies: the wife of an abusive millionaire seduces a cop (Harris), and the next thing he knows he's dumping Mr Money's bullet-ridden body in a remote, moonlit lake and watching his whole life go under. The denouement at least produces a novel twist, which it would be churlish to discuss, though that lake would probably be easier to swallow. It's diverting enough, however, with strong performances all round, and it's interesting to see the divine Benicio Del Toro (Fenster in *The Usual Suspects*) in another role, as Harris's partner. No, he doesn't use that voice. TCh

China 9, Liberty 37
(Monte Hellman, 1977, It) Warren Oates, Fabio Testi, Jenny Agutter, Sam Peckinpah, Isabel Mestres, Franco Interlenghi.
102 min.
Hellman's seriously absurdist streak happily finds a comically absurd parallel within the stereotyped framework of the European Western: he revels in the sheer gratuitousness of traditional character-types and plot mechanisms to produce an uproarious genre critique. Fabio Testi, a gunslinger in a Tom Mix hat, alternately stalks, befriends, and is stalked by Warren Oates, holding out against the advancing railroad with his trusty rifle and his less-than-trusty Anglo-Irish wife (Agutter). PT

China Seas
(Tay Garnett, 1935, US) Jean Harlow, Clark Gable, Wallace Beery, Lewis Stone, Rosalind Russell, Robert Benchley.
90 min. b/w.
An implausible but enjoyable tale of sexual rivalry and modern-day piracy aboard a ship *en route* to Hong Kong, this reunites Gable and Harlow, so effective together in the earlier *Red Dust*. The script by James Kevin McGuinness and Jules Furthman (who wrote such exotic masterpieces as *Morocco* and *Only Angels Have Wings*) is tailor-made for its stars, providing Gable with some suitably gruff heroics as the ship's captain, and plenty of snappy innuendo with the remarkable Harlow. It's a typical MGM production – glossy, romantic and far removed from reality – but Garnett keeps the pace going well enough to suspend disbelief. GA

China Syndrome, The
(James Bridges, 1978, US) Jane Fonda, Jack Lemmon, Michael Douglas, Scott Brady, James Hampton, Peter Donat, Wilford Brimley.
122 min.
Largely successful attempt to merge politics with Hollywood mainstream, as Fonda and Douglas play TV news-reporters latching on to a nuclear power scare about falsification and negligence of safety regulations. All a bit too earnest, despite the seriousness of the subject, with Fonda setting her jaw and stepping into father's footsteps as Tinseltown's very own protector of humanity; but it's tightly scripted and directed, and genuinely tense in places. GA

Chinatown 100 (100)
(Roman Polanski, 1974, US) Jack Nicholson, Faye Dunaway, John Huston, Perry Lopez, John Hillerman, Darrell Zwerling, Diane Ladd.
131 min.
Classic detective film, with Nicholson's JJ Gittes moving through the familiar world of the Forties *film noir* uncovering a plot whose enigma lies as much within the people he encounters as within the mystery itself. Gittes' peculiar vulnerability is closer to Chandler's concept of Philip Marlowe than many screen Marlowes, and the sense of time and place (the formation of LA in the '30s) is very strong. Directed by Polanski in bravura style, it is undoubtedly one of the great films of the '70s.

Chinese Box
(Wayne Wang, 1997, US/HK/Fr) Jeremy Irons, Gong Li, Maggie Cheung, Michael Hui, Ruben Blades.
110 min.
Designed to reflect the 'drama' of the hand over of Hong Kong, Wang's semi-improvised movie was partly scuppered by the fact that nothing striking happened when China reclaimed its 'Special

Administrative Region' on 1 July 1997. But it's hard to imagine that the film would have worked out better if there'd been riots on the streets, despite the big names (Theroux, Carrière) on the credits. Irons plays a foreign correspondent dying in synch with the British administration, obsessed with both Gong Li (manager of a chic bar/cheap hooker – evidently representing China) and Maggie Cheung (a go-getting hustler – evidently representing the confused spirit of HK). Ludicrously contrived incidents are garnished with desultory dialogue; the underlying prostitution and slaughterhouse metaphors were wrung dry last time Wang tackled the city of his birth, in *Life Is Cheap*. Maybe Wang has lived too long in California; the average tourist with a camcorder would see the city more clearly than this. TR

Chinese Boxes
(Christopher Petit, 1984, WGer) Will Patton, Gottfried John, Adelheid Arndt, Robbie Coltrane, Beate Jensen.
87 min.
Langdon Marsh (an expatriate American played with the charm of early Nicholson by Patton) is trapped in a ghostly, neon-streaked Berlin after the sudden deaths of his heroin-smuggling associate and a teenage girl. A bar-owner friend and a mysterious 'customs' man (Coltrane performing an Orson Welles cameo ahead of his years) both offer Marsh a way out, but only as a pawn in their duplicitous, gun-toting game. With an excess of plot staving off any safe resolution, the reduction of character psychology to a guiltless state of wonder proves a virtue. Despite the contingencies of low-budget filming – bold colour camera-work and blatant post-synchronisation – there is more fun to be had here than in the current British infatuation for the 'Laura Ashley school of film-making'. DT

Chinese Connection, The (Quan Ji/aka Duel of Fists)
(Chang Cheh, 1971, HK) David Chiang, Ti Lung, Li Ching, Lan Ying.
86 min.
A film from the Shaw Brothers' reliable action unit of director Chang Cheh (obviously relieved to be away from costume heroics) and acting duo Ti Lung and David Chiang, that turns out to be one of the funniest and most invigorating of their output: a spoofy foray into the gangster-controlled world of Thai boxing (it was partly shot in Bangkok), mock heroism, and a sub-Pimpernel search for a missing brother. Good use is made of locations, the ringside boxing sequences, and some well-handled street fighting. VG

Chinese Ghost Story, A (Qiannü Youhun)
(Ching Siu-Tung, 1987, HK) Leslie Cheung, Wang Zuxian, Wu Ma, Liu Zhaoming.
95 min.
A big hit in Hong Kong, credited to a young director of mildly inventive martial arts films, but showing all the signs of having been gazumped by producer Tsui Hark, director of cult hits *The Butterfly Murders* and *Zu: Warriors from the Magic Mountain*. Many of the ideas and visuals are swiped from recent horror movies like *The Evil Dead*. The storyline is a Ming Dynasty chestnut about a wandering scholar who falls in love with a glamorous female ghost, only to find the hordes of hell on his tail. Low points include the scenes in town, with market stallholders endlessly rhubarbing warnings about not going near the old house on the lake. High points include the special effects and a rap version of the opening words of 'Tzu's *Tao Te Ching* by a Taoist priest (Wu Ma, himself a director of some talent). TR

Chinese Ghost Story II, A (Qiannü Youhun zhi Renjian Dao)
(Ching Siu-Tung, 1990, HK) Leslie Cheung, Wang Hsu Hsien, Michelle Li, Wu Ma, Jacky Cheung.
104 min.
Very much the same formula as last time around: high style, low comedy, classy special effects, rap renditions of classical Taoist poetry, and so on. But the huge international success of the first film has given everyone involved new energy and confidence; sheerly as a ride on a ghost train, the sequel beats the original. The array of demonic

foes includes the decomposing corpse of a giant, a lord of hell who poses as the Buddha, and a climactic monster from a William Burroughs nightmare. The only real regret is that the irascible Taoist swordsman (played by Wu Ma) doesn't show up until the last reel. TR

Chinese Roulette (Chinesisches Roulette)
(Rainer Werner Fassbinder, 1976, WGer/Fr) Margit Carstensen, Andrea Schober, Ulli Lommel, Anna Karina, Macha Méril, Alexander Allerson.
86 min.
Made after Fassbinder disbanded his 'stock company' of actors, *Chinese Roulette* is quite different from his earlier bourgeois satires. The script is boldly non-naturalistic: a crippled girl connives to get herself, both her parents and their respective lovers to a country house all at the same time, for a weekend of intense embarrassments. And the style, all double reflections and shifting points of view, suspends the cast like flies in an amber of deceptions, neuroses and panics. The humour fits the cruelty as a boot fits a groin. TR

Chinese Vengeance
see Blood Brothers, The

Chino
see Valdez il Messosangue

Chinoise, La (La Chinoise, ou plutôt à la Chinoise)
(Jean-Luc Godard, 1967, Fr) Anne Wiazemsky, Jean-Pierre Léaud, Michel Sémeniako, Juliet Berto, Lex de Bruijn, Omar Diop, Francis Jeanson.
90 min.
Godard's brilliant dialectical farce, distinctly disquieting as well as gratingly funny, in which five Parisian students, members of a Maoist cell, discuss the implications of the Chinese cultural revolution and the chances of using terrorism to effect a similar upheaval in the West. Dazzlingly designed as a collage of slogans and poster images, it was widely attacked at the time for playing with politics. But Godard was well aware what he was doing creating these 'Robinson Crusoes with Marxism as their Man Friday', and his film stands as a prophetic and remarkably acute analysis of the impulse behind the events of May 1968 in all their desperate sincerity and impossible naïveté. TM

Chi Sei? (Beyond the Door/Devil Within Her)
(Oliver Hellman ie. Sonia Assonitis, 1974, It)Juliet Mills, Richard Johnson, Gabriele Lavia, Barbara Fiorini, Elizabeth Turner.
109 min.
Ludicrous bastard offspring of *The Exorcist* and *Rosemary's Baby* filmed in English. All-American mum Juliet Mills becomes the victim of a diabolic immaculate conception so that the devil's advocate can take up residence in the baby. Little does he know... IB

Chisum
(Andrew V McLaglen, 1970, US) John Wayne, Forrest Tucker, Christopher George, Ben Johnson, Glenn Corbett, Bruce Cabot, Andrew Prine, Patric Knowles, Richard Jaeckel.
110 min.
The range wars, Wayne-style; and a piece of Western revisionism to compare with *The Green Berets* for its articulation of the Duke's right-wing ethos. John Chisum here is on the side of the angels, with both Pat Garrett and Billy the Kid riding for him against capitalist competition. No mention of Chisum's own expansionist, monopolistic approach to the land; no mention of his subsequent hiring of the ageing Garrett to kill Billy. Enjoy veteran William Clothier's superb cinematography and wait for the next re-run of Peckinpah's version in *Pat Garrett and Billy the Kid*. PT

Chitty Chitty Bang Bang
(Ken Hughes, 1968, GB) Dick Van Dyke, Sally Ann Howes, Lionel Jeffries, Anna Quayle, Benny Hill, James Robertson Justice, Gert Fröbe, Robert Helpmann.
145 min.
Nauseatingly cute musical whimsy about an

inventor (creations courtesy of Rowland Emmett) and his wonderful magic car. Ken Adam's sets are inventive, but the special effects are shoddy, the songs instantly forgettable, and the leisurely length an exquisite torture. TM

Chocolat
(Claire Denis, 1988, Fr) Issach de Bankolé, Giulia Boschi, François Cluzet, Cécile Ducasse, Jean-Claude Adelin, Kenneth Cranham, Emmet Judson Williamson, Mireille Perrier.
105 min.
A young woman called France (Perrier; Ducasse as a child) returns to the Cameroons, where she recalls (in one long flashback) her childhood as the daughter of a district governor of French West Africa. This idyllic existence is shattered when a plane prangs near her home, forcing the stranded passengers to stay with her parents. The motley crew – all demonstrating various aspects of empire-building – include a white plantation owner and his black concubine, a newly-wed couple on their first visit to the dark continent, and an ex-priest (Adelin) full of Rousseau-esque ideals who turns out to be the worst of the lot. It is his influence that destroys France's friendship with the houseboy (de Bankolé), and prompts her mother (Boschi) to make a pass at the servant. In her amazingly assured debut, Clare Denis draws out the implications of the action with great subtlety. She makes the most of the exotic location, and elicits strong performances from all her cast. Abdullah Ibrahim's excellent score enhances the atmosphere of repression and frustration. MS

Chocolate Soldier, The
(Roy Del Ruth, 1941, US) Nelson Eddy, Rise Stevens, Nigel Bruce, Florence Bates.
102 min. b/w.
Confusingly, not the Oscar Strauss operetta based on Shaw's *Arms and the Man*, but an operetta using some of the Strauss songs to decorate (because Shaw wanted too much money) Molnar's play *The Guardsman*. About a singing duo, with the husband arranging a backfiring plot to test his wife's fidelity, it is pleasant enough (though lethargic) if you can stand that sort of thing and the bovine Eddy. TM

Chocolate War, The
(Keith Gordon, 1988, US) John Glover, Ilan Mitchell-Smith, Wally Ward, Bud Cort, Adam Baldwin, Jenny Wright, Doug Hutchinson.
103 min.
Having co-written, co-produced and starred in an outstanding independent film – Mark Romanek's *Static* – Keith Gordon made his directorial debut with this perfectly controlled study of teen tyranny. Every year the pupils of a strict Catholic boys' school are cajoled into selling boxes of chocolates to raise funds for their ailing alma mater. Morale is all-important, so when quiet new boy Jerry (Mitchell-Smith) refuses to participate, the school's principal, Brother Leon (Glover), uses the Vigils (a sadistic elite who terrorise their fellow pupils by giving them devilishly difficult 'assignments' to perform) to bring the rebel into line. But even when the full force of the Vigils is unleashed against him, Jerry continues to resist. A lovingly crafted and superbly acted attack on what Fassbinder used to call 'quiet fascism', this is smooth and rich, but with a delightfully bitter aftertaste. NF

Choice of Weapons, A
see Trial by Combat

Choirboys, The
(Robert Aldrich, 1977, US) Charles Durning, Lou Gossett, Perry King, Tim McIntire, Randy Quaid, Don Stroud, James Woods, Robert Webber, Burt Young, Charles Haid.
120 min.
Sadly, this adaptation of Joseph Wambaugh's bestseller about the LA police plumps entirely for grossly inflating the vulgar 'playfulness' of the dozen-or-so cops in their on and off duty hours, while ignoring the fact that the humour has to be seen in counterpoint to the frightening descriptions of urban horror which the police confront daily. The book's humour was the ribald and understandable explosion of a safety valve; here it is merely an offensive display of stereotyping, sexism and patronising insincerity. A travestied misrepresentation and a notably complete failure. SM

Choke Canyon
(aka On Dangerous Ground)
(Chuck Bail, 1986, US) Stephen Collins, Janet Julian, Lance Henriksen, Bo Svenson, Victoria Racimo, Nicholas Pryor, Robert Hoy, Walter Robles.
94 min.
An agreeable piece of hokum in which a young physicist tries to convert sound waves into a usable form of energy. He believes that the spirits of Choke Canyon and Halley's Comet can help him (I'd advise a trick cyclist). His efforts bring him into conflict with the ruthless Pilgrim Corporation – a nuclear combine – and into the arms of Pilgrim's breathless but beautiful daughter. There are numerous stunts, some of which are quite interesting, and a batty climax in which the comet outshines them all. MS

Choose Me
(Alan Rudolph, 1984, US) Keith Carradine, Genevieve Bujold, Lesley Ann Warren, Rae Dawn Chong, Patrick Bauchau, John Larroquette.
106 min.
Rudolph here brings his variation on the kaleidoscopic Altman style to perfection with a marvellous gloss on *La Ronde* set in a Los Angeles bar that seems real but serves as a neon-lit dream world where everyone – not least Bujold's agony aunt, solving other people's problems but herself suffering untold miseries of sexual frustration – sooner or later tunes up in quest of the partner who will bring emotional fulfilment, only to discover that it isn't necessarily there just for the asking. Often very funny as well as gorgeous to look at in its ineffable blend of realism and rhapsody, it comes on a little like a free jazz improvisation on the vulnerability of the human heart to the ecstasies and disenchantments that attend it in permanent orbit. TM

Chorus Line, A
(Richard Attenborough, 1985, US) Michael Douglas, Alyson Reed, Terrence Mann, Michael Blevins, Yamil Borges, Jan Gan Boyd.
118 min.
Michael Bennett's 1975 Broadway hit was a triumph of edgy nerve and steamroller energy. Attenborough's film version is anything but. The grit and drive of the original have been dissipated into studiously unkempt glitz as empty as plasticised pop. A group of dancers (auditioning for a new show) are put through the hoops of humiliation by the director (Douglas), a mild-mannered sadist who delves into their private parts with voyeuristic enthusiasm, but Attenborough and screenwriter Arnold Schulman fail to justify this guy's nasty Citizen Kane megalomania. It's too corny and unbelievable for words. AR

Chorus of Disapproval, A
(Michael Winner, 1988, GB) Anthony Hopkins, Jeremy Irons, Richard Briers, Gareth Hunt, Patsy Kensit, Alexandra Pigg, Prunella Scales, Jenny Seagrove, Pete Lee-Wilson, Barbara Ferris, Lionel Jeffries, Sylvia Syms.
99 min.
Once upon a time there was a stage comedy called *A Chorus of Disapproval*, a clever, multilateral saga about a production of John Gay's *The Beggars Opera* by a local amateur dramatic society, crawling with a modern suburban version of the twisters, shysters and adulterers presented by Gay with such *brio*. Enter Michael Winner, to take Alan Ayckbourn's vibrant original, ruin its point and its structure, and pour the cold porridge of his filmic imagination all over it. Now we have a great series of visual plugs for the charming seaside town of Scarborough, a very few moments when the humour and poignancy of the original escape unscathed, and a Rolls Royce cast of British actors who, except for Hopkins' ferociously frustrated Dafydd Ap Llewellyn and fine cameos from Briers and Jeffries, can't cope with either the heavily truncated script or Winner's cloddish, half-baked direction. SGr

Chosen, The
see Holocaust 2000

Chosen, The
(Jeremy Paul Kagan, 1981, US) Maximilian Schell, Rod Steiger, Robby Benson, Barry Miller, Hildy Brooks, Val Avery.
108 min.

A worthy but irretrievably dull homily (based on the novel by Chaim Potok) about the conflict between adolescent friendship – two Jewish boys, one orthodox and Zionist, the other a Hasidic – and filial devotion within the demands of the faith. This is post-war New York, and The Issue is the founding of the Jewish state in Palestine, a little-known piece of history but here uncomfortably yoked to a story of heartfelt human relationships, and topped off by Steiger's most mannered performance ever as the Hasidic rabbi. Whispering into his patriarch's beard and rolling his eyes heavenward, Steiger milks the role you suspect he has longed for ever since The *Pawnbroker*, and director Kagan makes little attempt to hold the ham in check. MA

Chosen One, The (Ishanou)
(Aribam Syam Sharma, 1989, Ind) Kiranmala, Tomba, Manbi.
91 min.
Sharma's film is almost un-Indian in its rapid pacing and tight narrative focus, but it couldn't be more culturally specific in subject. It's set in the Manipur Valley in NE India, and centres on the unique Maibi cult that flourishes in the area. Maibi are women who suddenly respond to some higher call, abandon their normal lives, and join the cult under a guru. The film explores one (fictional) case: a young woman named Tampha who deserts her husband and child and disappears into the cult. Sharma asks all the awkward questions. What does it mean to a mother to abandon her family? And what can a man do when he loses his wife to an impenetrable cult? The film doesn't pretend to explain the cult, but looks at its social repercussions through clear and searching eyes. TR

Choses de la Vie, Les
(The Things of Life)
(Claude Sautet, 1969, Fr/It) Michel Piccoli, Romy Schneider, Lea Massari, Gérard Lartigau, Jean Bouise.
89 min.
A not uninteresting attempt to make a film about ordinary, everyday minutiae, with Piccoli as an average sensual man, vaguely torn between a demanding mistress (Schneider) and an ex-wife (Massari) to whom he still feels bound. Quietly and deftly, Sautet sketches in the portrait of a man gradually becoming aware that he is coming to a crossroads in his life. But since the opening sequence reveals that he is shortly to die in a car crash, his attempt to make some decision about his life is much ado about nothing – which is precisely the point of the film. Difficult to make a film about banality without being boring in the process, but Sautet all but pulls it off, thanks to a beautifully understated performance from Piccoli which manages to extract a whole lifetime of meaning from a simple gesture like lighting a cigarette, and to illuminate the film's meticulously detailed naturalistic surface. TM

Christiane F. (Christiane F. wir Kinder vom Bahnhof Zoo)
(Ulrich Edel, 1981, WGer) Natja Brunckhorst, Thomas Haustein, Jens Kuphal, Rainer Wölk.
131 min.
A European box-office phenomenon on the strength of aghast multi-media exposure for the true confessions tale of a 13-year-old girl turned hooker to support her heroin habit. As Awful Warnings go, it's way above the *Reefer Madness* class, though its lurid drama-doc sheen – and insistent use of David Bowie's *Heroes* – create some ambivalent tensions between medium and message. Finally, the film's very relentlessness (whether calculated or naive) ensures a 'correct' gut reaction to the spectacle of a near-zomboid alternation of fix and hustle: there's only so much cautionary misery you want rubbed into your face, and this fruitfully goes beyond. Cursory on causes, but devastating on effects. PT

Christine
(John Carpenter, 1983, US) Keith Gordon, John Stockwell, Alexandra Paul, Robert Prosky, Harry Dean Stanton, Christine Belford.
110 min.
Carpenter and novelist Stephen King share not merely a taste for genre horror but a love of '50s teenage culture; and although set in the present, *Christine* reflects the second taste far more effectively than the first. It concerns a demonic 1958

Plymouth Fury which not only suffocates its victims to blasts of Larry Williams' 'Boney Moronie', but also reconstitutes itself before the naked eye like some fetishistic amoeba, incidentally transforming its puny owner from a pimply nonentity into one of the baddest boys on the block. All of this works rather well as black comedy. But from the horror perspective, Carpenter is only the latest in a long line of film-makers who've been seduced by King's sheer plausibility as a writer. Off the page, a 1958 Plymouth is no more scary than the St Bernard which romped through *Cujo*. DP

Christine Jorgensen Story, The

(Irving Rapper, 1970, US) John Hansen, Joan Tompkins, Quinn Redeker, John W Himes, Ellen Clark.
98 min.
A well-meaning if somewhat sanctimonious piece of claptrap about the first man to undergo a sex-change operation (in 1952). Although attempting a serious and sympathetic treatment of its subject, it confronts few of the real issues involved, and actor Hansen proves incapable of tackling the female part of his role. DP

Christmas Carol, A

(Clive Donner, 1984, GB) George C Scott, Frank Finlay, Angela Pleasance, Edward Woodward, Michael Carter, David Warner, Susannah York, Anthony Walters, Roger Rees.
101 min.
The only character in Dickens' sentimental tale who never stuck in one's craw was the pre-reformation Scrooge, and so it seems exactly right that Donner's movie should rest entirely on the solid shoulders of George C Scott. His intelligence and quickness at last give us a Scrooge of many dimensions; a man of tortured and forbidding nobility, made cruel by uncaring parentage and a malign fate, rather than the usual thin miser. The fact that he is also one of nature's monetarists does not go unnoticed. As to the rest: Shrewsbury looks well enough under snow; one can enjoy the urge to kick away the crutch of a more than usually repellent Tiny Tim; and only Roger Rees (as Scrooge's nephew) suggests that goodness might be vertebrate. CPea

Christmas Holiday

(Robert Siodmak, 1944, US) Deanna Durbin, Gene Kelly, Gale Sondergaard, Gladys George, Richard Whorf, Dean Harens, David Bruce.
93 min. b/w.
Scripted by Herman Mankiewicz from Somerset Maugham's novel about a young woman whose illusions come a cropper when she realises that the wealthy charmer she married is a mother-fixated wastrel, this might have been one of Siodmak's best and blackest *noirs* had Deanna Durbin not baulked at portraying a prostitute. Opting for compromise, she appears as a New Orleans nightclub hostess, which makes rather a nonsense of the second half of the plot when the husband, jailed for murder, escapes with the intention of killing her because of 'what she has become'. It also undermines the sense of guilty responsibility for his fate which prompted her claim, as he offers to kill her, that she deliberately hit bottom so that she too should have her prison. A fascinating film nevertheless, tainted with a brooding sense of malaise, and with fine performances from Kelly and Sondergaard which dovetail the suppressed hints of homosexuality and incest. TM

Christmas in August (Pal-Wol ui Christmas)

(Hur Jin-Ho, 1998, SKor) Han Suk-Kyu, Shim Eun-Ha, Shin Ku, Oh Ji-Hae.
97 min.
A likeable, understated movie about facing up to death, from a first time director. Jung-Won (Han, Korea's coolest young actor) is a pro photographer with his own shop in a suburb of Seoul; only he and his immediate relatives know that he has just a few months to live. Nothing 'dramatic' happens. He runs into his childhood sweetheart and regrets that her life hasn't worked out better. He goes to a friend's funeral. He makes a point of seeing other old friends. And he develops a slightly abrasive friendship with a young woman traffic warden, which leaves her wanting to know him better and not understanding why he isn't 'there' for her. Hur conjures up quotidian rhythms very plausibly,

and draws fine performances from his whole cast. It was the last film shot by the great Yoo Young-Kil, to whose memory it's dedicated. TR

Christmas in July

(Preston Sturges, 1940, US) Dick Powell, Ellen Drew, Raymond Walburn, William Demarest, Franklin Pangborn, Ernest Truex.
67 min. b/w.
Minor but delightful Sturges comedy (his second film) about a go-getting clerk who is tricked into believing his truly lousy slogan dreamed up for a contest has won him $25,000, learning the truth only when he has spent the money on credit buying goodies all round. The satire on big business, advertising and the success ethic doesn't amount to much, but the Sturges stock company is rampant, and there is a terrific slapstick escalation when the storeowners, busting in on the ongoing neighbourhood party to repossess their goods, provoke a custard-pie riot (but with fish). TM

Christmas Story, A

(Bob Clark, 1983, US) Melinda Dillon, Darren McGavin, Peter Billingsley, Ian Petrella, Scott Schwartz.
98 min.
Surely everyone remembers how they felt, at primary school, when a literary masterpiece came back marked with a mere C+? This and many other such crimes perpetrated by the adult world on the inhabitants of kid-dom are exposed in this nostalgic mock-epic tale of young Ralphie's quest to ensure that presents assembled under the tree on Christmas morning include a much-coveted BB air-rifle. Delightfully entertaining, with a wryly amusing narration to keep the adults in the audience smirking. DPe

Christopher Columbus

(David MacDonald, 1948, GB) Fredric March, Florence Eldridge, Francis L Sullivan, Linden Travers, Kathleen Ryan, Derek Bond, James Robertson Justice.
104 min.
Gainsborough's flailing attempts to add 'class' and international prestige to their more interestingly low-key 'domestic' output resulted in this expensively mounted dodo, elegantly consigned to the scrapheap of film history by contemporary critic Richard Winnington with the withering opinion that it 'contrives with something like genius neither to inform, excite, entertain, titillate or engage the eye'. PT

Christopher Columbus: The Discovery

(John Glen, 1992, US) Marlon Brando, Tom Selleck, George Corraface, Rachel Ward, Robert Davi, Catherine Zeta Jones, Oliver Cotton, Benicio Del Toro, Mathieu Carrière.
121 min.
Who needs *Carry On Columbus* when you can have the real thing? It's hard to fathom the minds of people who could make this kind of tripe. The film is wretched in most respects (Robert Davi is a ruggedly good Martin Pinzon), but even fine writers like Louis Macneice and Richard Nelson have been stumped by the intractability of the Columbus story: he came, he saw, he went home. It's boring enough crossing the Atlantic on British Airways, never mind months in a wooden hulk surrounded by exiles from the RSC and the National. Selleck looks suitably embarrassed as King Ferdinand of Aragon, Ward is a head-girl Isabella of Castille, Jones is Columbus' bit on the (quay)side, an unknown Greek with designer stubble (Corraface) is Columbus, and Brando is a completely barmy Torquemada. Solid gold shit. SGr

Christopher Strong

(Dorothy Arzner, 1933, US) Katharine Hepburn, Colin Clive, Billie Burke, Helen Chandler, Ralph Forbes, Irene Browne, Jack LaRue.
77 min. b/w.
Early Hollywood movies (re)claimed for feminist film history sometimes require complex analysis to explain their relevance, but this teaming of Arzner and Hepburn is absolutely central to an understanding of women's place within classical Hollywood. Hepburn plays pioneer aviatrix Cynthia Darrington, courted by Christopher Strong (though why the title should bear his

name and not hers is a mystery). She plays him along but independently pursues her career, telling Strong 'Don't ever stop me doing what I want', only to fall into typical Hollywood compromise and find herself pregnant by her (married) lover in the last reel. Suicide is offered as the only way out, but even in her dying moments (a high-altitude record-breaking flight) she rebels against society's required sacrifice and tries to replace her oxygen mask. Fascinating precisely for the vacillation of its central (female) character, and for the way in which aviation (itself a uniquely 20th century activity virtually closed to women) is used as a metaphor for film-making and women's attempts to gain a foothold in that male-dominated territory. MA

Christ Stopped at Eboli (Cristo si è Fermato a Eboli)

(Francesco Rosi, 1979, It/Fr) Gian Maria Volonté, Paolo Bonacelli, Alain Cuny, Lea Massari, Irene Papas, François Simon.
155 min.
This adaptation of Carlo Levi's autobiographical book awkwardly bridges the space between Rosi's justly celebrated political dossier thrillers (*The Mattei Affair, Lucky Luciano, Illustrious Corpses*) and his more recent *Three Brothers*, and has to be counted a major disappointment. Covering the period of Levi's Fascist-imposed exile to the southern Italian region of Lucania in the '30s, Rosi ditches analysis to allow the desolate landscapes and faces of a remote peasant culture (seen as somehow beyond ideology) to tell their own tale. An unfortunate tendency to sentimentalise mars even this limited schema, though, and Volonté's suitably humbled Levi is even followed around by a Disneyesque dog. PT

Chronicle of a Death Foretold (Cronaca di una Morte Annunciata)

(Francesco Rosi, 1987, It/Fr) Rupert Everett, Ornella Muti, Gian Maria Volonté, Irene Papas, Lucia Bosé, Alain Cuny.
110 min.
Rosi's adaptation of Garcia Márquez's novel is an absorbing and unusual murder mystery set within a tiny South American community. A wealthy and mysterious stranger (Everett, cringingly affected) chooses a local girl (Muti) as his wife. No virgin, she is returned to her family on the wedding night, and the brothers determine to kill her previous lover. They brag their intentions around the village, yet no one intervenes. The tale is narrated, through interviews and flashbacks, by the dead man's best friend, returned home after a long absence to find the villagers still nursing their guilt. The simple facts hold no answers; the real clues lie in a web of tradition and centuries-old conditioning. The omnipresent Catholicism, the empty macho stances of the men, the strains of violence underlying strong familial bonds: these propel the action, giving the film an almost mystical aura. Although occasionally so languorously photographed that it almost grinds to a halt, the film is ultimately memorable. EP

Chronicle of a Love Affair

see Cronaca di un Amore

Chronicle of Anna Magdalena Bach (Chronik der Anna Magdalena Bach)

(Jean-Marie Straub, 1968, It/WGer) Gustav Leonhardt, Christiane Lang, Paolo Carlini, Ernst Castelli.
93 min. b/w.
'A film about the past which is lucid can help people of the present to achieve that necessary lucidity.' Straub's account of Bach is nothing if not lucid: it documents the last 27 years of its subject's life (through the mediating eyes of his wife) principally in terms of his music. The music itself obviates any need for a 'drama' to present Bach; Straub celebrates its range and complexity while showing it always in performance, to emphasise the nature of Bach's work as musician/conductor. A narration (compiled from contemporary sources) sets the man in his economic and social context. With his minimalist's sensitivity to nuance and inflection, Straub eschews pointless cutting and camera movement. The beautiful result has the air of a crystal-clear meditation. TR

Chronicle of a Summer

see Chronique d'un Eté

Chronique d'un Eté (Chronicle of a Summer)

(Jean Rouch/Edgar Morin, 1961, Fr) Jean Rouch, Edgar Morin, Marceline, Marilù, Angélo.
90 min. b/w.
The notion of a domestically-based 'ethnological study' dates at least from Montesquieu's *Lettres persanes*. But what distinguishes this attempt by Rouch and the sociologist Edgar Morin to 'bottle' the climate of Paris circa 1960 is their camera's candid assumption of its own disruptively active presence: interviewees are introduced to each other, form groups, and may well (in one case) have got married after shooting was over. In an interesting epilogue, Rouch invites them all to comment on his footage. GAd

Chu Chin Chow

(Walter Forde, 1934, GB) George Robey, Fritz Kortner, Anna May Wong, John Garrick, Pearl Argyle, Francis L Sullivan.
103 min. b/w.
This jolly celebration of Oriental brutality confounds all expectations of restraint and respectability in pre-war British cinema. Blood-curdling murders, scantily-clad slave-girls, and an atmosphere of delicious terror induced by the ever-present threat of being boiled in oil, fed to the dogs or cut into tiny pieces by the magnetically vindictive villain, come as something of a shock even though they're all part of an unabashedly English pantomime tradition. Filmed with verve and audacity and a lavishness completely untypical of the small Gainsborough Studios, the result is a gutsy melodramatic piece of popular cinema. RMy

Chuka

(Gordon Douglas, 1967, US) Rod Taylor, John Mills, Ernest Borgnine, Luciana Paluzzi, James Whitmore, Louis Hayward, Angela Dorian.
105 min.
A Western, passably well handled by Gordon Douglas, but scripted (by Richard Jessup from his own novel) along such well-beaten tracks that you can almost sing along to it. Rod Taylor is the roving gunfighter who understands that the Indians are on the warpath only because they're hungry; John Mills is the army officer stubbornly insisting on doing things by the book; the company at the fort he commands, because he has a Fatal Flaw, is composed exclusively of drunks, card-sharps and cut-throats; and of course there is a long-lost love (Paluzzi) conveniently turning up to cover the romantic angle. A cliché is found for every occasion, except perhaps the end, when everybody (with the possible exception of Taylor) gets killed off in the Indian attack. TM

Chump at Oxford, A

(Alfred Goulding, 1939, US) Stan Laurel, Oliver Hardy, Wilfred Lucas, Forrester Harvey, James Finlayson, Anita Garvin, Peter Cushing.
63 min. b/w.
Not so much a parody of the nonsensically moralising *A Yank at Oxford* as an amiable shaggy-dog romp through the usual Laurel and Hardy routines. It doesn't really matter very much that it takes place at Oxford University (this is not exactly a biting social satire); rather it's the usual collection of slow but delightful set pieces in which the duo are confused by the niceties of normal civilised behaviour. The best moments see Stan and Ollie chaotically in service as butler and maid, and Stan's marvellous transformation, by amnesia, into an aristocratic twit. GA

Chungking Express (Chongqing Senlin) (100)

(Wong Kar-Wai, 1994, HK) Brigitte Lin, Tony Leung, Faye Wang.
97 min.
Wong Kar-Wai's movie tells two loosely inter-linked stories, both about lovelorn cops who get involved with women who are wrong for them. In the first, Takeshi Kaneshiro tries to pick up Brigitte Lin in a late-night bar, unaware she's a big-time heroin smuggler who's spent the evening hunting down some absconding drug couriers. In the second, the boyish Faye Wang (a star is born!) gets a crush on Tony Leung and starts breaking into his apartment to redecorate it while he's out. This is what Godard movies were once like: fast, hand-held, funny and very, very catchy. The year's zingiest visit to Heartbreak Hotel. TR

Chuquiago

(Antonio Equino, 1977, Bol) Néstor Yujra, Edmundo Villarroel, David Santalla, Tatiana Aponte.
86 min.
Equino uses the old neo-realist ploy of overlapping four separate stories, each dealing with a person from a different social stratum, to illustrate the shaping forces, economic and political, of the four lives. A rural Indian boy is sold to a market stallholder in La Paz; a *cholo* boy turns to petty crime; a petit-bourgeois civil servant dies on his Friday night respite from the daily grind; a rich student is torn between radicalism and her family's wishes. She opts for safety, and is the film's final, most obvious, example of its main topic: the political compromises, knowing and unknowing, by which we undo ourselves. CPea

Ciao! Manhattan

(John Palmer/David Weisman, 1972, US) Édie Sedgwick, Wesley Hayes, Isabel Jewell, Jane Holzer, Viva, Roger Vadim.
92 min. b/w & col.
Two attempts at a movie spliced uneasily into one. A sort of mystery thriller shot in black-and-white and set in New York in the 1960s with Sedgwick, Holzer, Viva and other 'superstars' of the era, is combined with a colour study of the very deranged and desperate Edie in 1971, living out her last days (she died at 28 soon after the shooting) in her parents' house in California. The result is a mess. On the other hand, the ensuing confusion is in keeping with Edie's own disordered existence in her increasing drug dependency, and the contrasts (and continuities) between the '70s woman with the swollen silicon breasts and the elfin magnetic personality of the '60s are deeply disturbing. MH

Cible émouvante (Wild Target)

(Pierre Salvadori, 1993, Fr) Jean Rochefort, Marie Trintignant, Guillaume Depardieu, Patachou, Charlie Nelson, Wladimir Yordanoff.
88 min.
Victor (Rochefort) is a middle-aged hit-man and a self-improver who keeps a fastidiously ordered life. When a naive young messenger (Depardieu) accidentally mixes himself up in Victor's affairs, he keeps him, trains him up, and softens up; enough, at least, to balk at his next assignment (Trintignant), a wanton fellow rogue, art forger and thief. And thus the three are forced to team up to top the man who ordered her killed. Salvadori's debut feature, which he also wrote, is a winning well-directed combination of deadpan black farce, knowing genre comedy and wistful romantic triangle. Anchoring the film is another of Rochefort's superb portrayals of the haut bourgeois whose very inscrutability and repression engender sympathy and amusement in equal portion. As his dignity is eroded in a knockabout farce around the streets of Paris, his emotions begin to unbutton. This situation comedy is fine, but the film's bid for pathos fails, amid side-swipes at sexual manners only the French will ken. But it ends with such ridiculous symmetry that you'll forgive it. WH

Ciclone, Il

see Cyclone, The

Ciel est à nous, Le

see Shooting Stars

Cielo è sempre più blu, Il

see Bits and Pieces

Cimarron

(Anthony Mann, 1960, US) Glenn Ford, Maria Schell, Anne Baxter, Arthur O'Connell, Russ Tamblyn, Mercedes McCambridge, David Opatoshu.
147 min.
This second screen version of Edna Ferber's frontier saga (1890–1915) marks the transitional point between Mann's '50s cycle of Westerns and the expansive epics which occupied his final years. Ford's hero is a man set on lighting out of Oklahoma territory, but so ambiguous is his relationship with spouse Schell that the producer added new clarifying material without the director's permission. Occasionally spectacular, mostly baggy. TJ

Cina è vicina, La

see China Is Near

Cincinnati Kid, The

(Norman Jewison, 1965, US) Steve McQueen, Edward G Robinson, Karl Malden, Tuesday Weld, Ann-Margret, Joan Blondell, Rip Torn, Jack Weston.
113 min.
With Jewison replacing Peckinpah as director, nowhere near as strong as it might have been, but Ring Lardner and Terry Southern's script, taken from Richard Jessup's novel about poker-sharks meeting for a big game in '30s New Orleans, is a vivid character study in the tradition of the not dissimilar *The Hustler*. Marvellous performances throughout ensure interest. GA

Cinderella

(Wilfred Jackson, 1949, US)
74 min.
From the first tumescent AAaaooooo of the chorus and plig plig of the harp, this is bang-on course Disney animation. Once you get past the 'storybook' framing and the information that 'a dream is a wish the heart makes' – eat lead, Sigmund – it is played for laughs all the way. Furry creature value is high, and there is an extra-wicked stepmother who is the stuff of infant nightmares. The prince is as wooden as Letraset, and the real moral dramas, battles between good and evil, social conditioning, hygiene, procreation etc. take place among poor Cinders' allies, the mice, and the complacently vicious cat Lucifer. The set pieces, all transformation scenes of some kind, will probably be familiar, the mouse voices rising to operatic heights as they sweatshop together a ball gown in under three minutes. As usual, everything is slightly glossy, soppy and hearty, yet not a string is left untwanged. RP

Cinderella – Italian Style (C'era una Volta)

(Francesco Rosi,1967, It/Fr) Sophia Loren, Omar Sharif, Dolores Del Rio, Georges Wilson, Leslie French, Carlo Pisacane.
103 min.
This extraordinary fairy-tale couldn't be further from a film like *The Mattei Affair* but it's none the less informed by the same intelligence that Rosi brings to his directly political work. It deals with all its whimsical elements (from Loren to a flying monk) in a wholly non-whimsical way, introduces a strongish undertone of class-consciousness into its comedy, and pushes its plot recklessly into the bizarre. TR

Cinderella Liberty

(Mark Rydell, 1973, US) James Caan, Eli Wallach, Marsha Mason, Kirk Calloway, Burt Young, Allyn Ann McLerie.
117 min.
Uneven semi-comic look at a sailor's romantic adventures while ashore in Seattle, falling in with pool-hustling hooker Mason and her delinquent mulatto son. Based like *The Last Detail* on a novel by Darryl Ponicsan, it starts off well enough, with the offbeat atmosphere and characterisation reminiscent of Altman (Rydell had played Marty Augustine in *The Long Goodbye*), but things steadily turn to mush as crusty exteriors crack to reveal hearts of gold. GA

Cinderfella

(Frank Tashlin, 1960, US) Jerry Lewis, Ed Wynn, Judith Anderson, Anna Maria Alberghetti, Henry Silva, Robert Hutton, Count Basie.
91 min.
In a contemporary updating of the fairytale, Lewis plays a male Cinderella, treated as an all-purpose servant by his wicked stepmother and her two greedy sons in a vast mansion belonging to his late father. A hidden secret fortune, a fairy godfather, and a visiting foreign princess com-

plete the mixture; but despite some extremely lavish set design and the occasional good sight gag, the overall effect is glutinous in the extreme. For hardcore fans and soft-centred infants only. DT

Cinema Cinema
(Krishna Shah, 1979, Fr/US) Hema Malini, Amitabh Bachchan, Dharmendra, Zeenat Aman.
138 min.
Subtitled *That's Entertainment – Indian Style*, this is basically a compilation film, substituting Indian epics for MGM musicals. As such, despite the coy introductory comments by well-fed stars, the uncertain grasp of film history, and the interchangeability of most of the extracts, it is not without interest as a helping of 'Madras Curry' (the staple Bombay diet of lavish melodramas packed to inordinate length with interminable songs, dances and comic interludes). Unfortunately it also has semi-sociological pretensions, and assembles a dismal collection of stereotypes (supposedly watching the extracts in a sleazy cinema) in an attempt to demonstrate the screen/audience relationship. Their reactions are, quite literally, the pits. TM

Cinema of Unease
(Sam Neill/Judy Rymer, 1995, GB/NZ)
52 min.
Neill has been closely involved with New Zealand film-making since it started going places 20 years ago, and his take on this 'uniquely dark and strange film industry' makes for one of the most interesting films in the BFI's 'Century of Cinema' series. He uses clips from movies set in the '50s and '60s (*Heavenly Creatures, An Angel at My Table*) to evoke the strangeness of his own childhood experiences, and goes on to suggest that there's something about the country's landscape which breeds madness and dysfunction, especially in would-be macho men. Maybe Neill overplays NZ's struggle to break away from British cultural domination, but his celebration of the recent arrival of new voices (Maoris, women, gays) provides a genuinely upbeat punchline. TR

Cinema Paradiso (100)
(Nuovo Cinema Paradiso)
(Giuseppe Tornatore, 1988, It/Fr) Phillipe Noiret, Jacques Perrin, Salvatore Cascio, Mario Leonardi, Agnese Nano, Leopoldo Trieste, Nicolo Di Pinto.
155 min. b/w & col.
A successful movie director in his 40s, Salvatore returns home to Sicily after hearing of the death of Alfredo, ex-projectionist at the eponymous village cinema. The greater part of Tornatore's film is a flashback to Salvatore's WWII childhood and adolescence when, obsessed by movies, he is befriended by the wise and gruffly benevolent Alfredo (Noiret), the local priest censors kissing scenes, the whole village is wowed by *Rome, Open City*, a fire caused by nitrate stock blinds Alfredo, and just as Salvatore is shooting his first home movie he falls in love. Warmly nostalgic without (for the most part) falling foul of Felliniesque caricature, the film is too emotionally manipulative for its own good, Noiret's typically professional performance notwithstanding. Alfredo's mystic sagacity is implausible, and the infant Salvatore (Cascio) is too cutely precocious by half. The politics and history, too, are simplified (partly, perhaps, by a 30 minute pruning for export release). But the final montage of censored clips, hoarded by the boy and rediscovered in adult life, is a sweet hymn to the romance of cinema. GA

Cinema Paradiso: The Special Edition (Nuovo Cinema Paradiso)
(Giuseppe Tornatore, 1989, It/Fr) Philippe Noiret, Jacques Perrin, Salvatore Cascio, Mario Leonardi, Agnese Nano, Leopoldo Trieste, Nicolo Di Pinto, Brigitte Fossey.
175 min. b/w & col.
This is no mere cash-in, but director Tornatore's original cut, which flopped so badly on its Italian release, was withdrawn, trimmed to 123 minutes, and entered at the 1989 Cannes festival. The rest is cinematic history. Ironically, however, the two-hour version is substantially inferior to the expansive, roundly satisfying original. Largely unaltered is the nostalgic chronicle of Salvatore, a Sicilian

youngster's formative relationship with his local movie house and its wise projectionist; still enshrined are the affectionate performances of Cascio and Noiret. The reinstated material follows the much older Salvatore (Perrin) on his traumatic return home, shows what happens when he meets up with his never-forgotten teenage paramour (the previously excised Brigitte Fossey), and alters the tone of the film, darkening it considerably. Here we experience a catalogue of loss, betrayal and regret which renders the paean to celluloid romance a more complex finale, bitter-sweet yet ineffably emotive. A masterpiece restored, Tornatore's film is, literally, a revelation. TJ

Cinq et la Peau
see Five and the Skin

Cinquième Elément, Le
see Fifth Element, The

Cinquième saison
see Season Five

Circle of Danger
(Jacques Tourneur, 1951, GB) Ray Milland, Patricia Roc, Marius Goring, Hugh Sinclair, Naughton Wayne, Dora Bryan.
86 min. b/w.
An underrated film-maker whose best work (*I Walked with a Zombie, Build My Gallows High*) truly reached the heights, Jacques Tourneur came to Britain for the first time to put together this military conspiracy thriller, adapted by Philip Macdonald from his own novel. It's one of his more routine assignments, however, as Milland returns from the States to investigate his younger brother's death – although the authorities maintain he was killed in action, the testimony of some of his platoon's survivors suggests a very different course of events. Good camerawork by Ossie Morris and fascinating use of the Scottish and Welsh locations. TJ

Circle of Deceit (Die Fälschung)
(Volker Schlöndorff, 1981, WGer/Fr) Bruno Ganz, Hanna Schygulla, Jerzy Skolimowski, Gila von Weitershausen, Jean Carmet.
109 min.
It's the classic front-line story: Ganz's German war correspondent goes off to Beirut to cover the Lebanese war, and while there suffers a crisis of conscience about whether he should passively observe or actively intervene. So far, so straightforward, except that Schlöndorff actually made his film in Beirut, yards away from the real carnage, which not only gives it an immediacy and power missing from, say, *Missing* or *Under Fire*, but also questions our whole experience of, and attitude towards, 'the pornography of violence' as portrayed by the news media. To complicate things further, Polish director Skolimowski is on hand, playing Ganz's photographer who casually (an)aesthetises the corpses around him as he wanders the streets. A brave film full of danger, and all the more disturbing and provocative for that. GA

Circle of Friends
(Pat O'Connor, 1995, Ire/US) Chris O'Donnell, Minnie Driver, Geraldine O'Rawe, Alan Cumming, Saffron Burrows, Colin Firth, Mick Lally, Ciaran Hands.
102 min.
Maeve Binchy's novel, adapted by Andrew Davies, whisks us back to rural Ireland, 1957, for a rites-of-passage tale – with the Roman Catholic Church lurking as usual in the wings. Benny (Driver) and her Knockglen chums go to college in Dublin, where she's enraptured by rugby player Jack Foley (O'Donnell), creditable, despite the knitwear) and is dithering about just how fully to give herself when the plot intervenes. Courtesy of father's fatal heart attack, Benny's landed back home and faced with the unwelcome advances of repellent-but-persistent Sean, the prospective shop-owner her parents have long wanted her to marry. The fizzing dialogue gets all the little details right, but the plot's nothing new (cue unwanted pregnancy and Firth's stuffy Anglophile Protestant) and the lingering shots of hibernian greenery aim straight for mid-Atlantic bland-out. While Cumming's turn as the oleaginous Sean offers bravura overstatement, it hardly belongs in the same picture as Minnie Driver's

fresh, immensely appealing Benny, one of those rare feature debuts whose palpable inner fire transcends the workaday material. TJ

Circle of Gold
(Uday Bhattacharya, 1988, GB) narrator: Uday Bhattacharya.
52 min.
A first film made almost single-handedly on a tiny budget, this is an admirably ambitious stab at the documentary-essay form familiar from films like Chris Marker's *Sunless*. A brazenly personal response to Calcutta, it attempts to delve beyond the facile notions the West entertains about the city ('an example of wretched over-population'), and combines vivid visuals with a narration that plunges fearlessly into economics, politics, religion, sociology and philosophy. At times the verbal text is too densely literary and abstract, making its often tortuous theses somewhat opaque, but the collision of images and words is generally provocative and telling. Adverts, movie clips, comic strips, stills of the director's mother, footage of religious ritual and street life merge into a complex web of ideas that are neither hackneyed nor obvious. A tantalising effort. GA

Circle of Iron
see Silent Flute, The

Circle of Two
(Jules Dassin, 1980, Can) Richard Burton, Tatum O'Neal, Nuala Fitzgerald, Robin Gammell, Patricia Collins.
105 min.
Sarah (O'Neal) is fifteen going on sixteen, and lives at home. Dad's an Egyptologist; Mom refuses to acknowledge any generation gap; boy-friend wants to get her into the sack, but she refuses. Dodging him one day she meets Ashley (Burton), a once-chic artist who's currently light on inspiration. He might be sixty but he's hunky in that experienced way, and he has a Bohemian haven in the country where he plays Vivaldi. The pair get literary and have intense chats in which Sarah tries the difference between the Sistine Chapel and Burger Kings. Sarah tries the physical, but Ashley sagely demurs. Mom and Dad are horrified by the liaison (bye-bye wet liberalism) and imprison her until she sees sense. But Sarah's having none of that...Preposterous serial syrup which should shame everyone involved. IB

Circuito Chiuso
see Closed Circuit

Circumstance, The (La Circonstanza)
(Ermanno Olmi, 1974, It) Ada Savelli, Gaetano Porro, Raffaella Bianchi, Mario Sireci.
92 min.
The bourgeois family Olmi observes here is caught in a process of disintegration that hardly requires the promptings of a languid summer's minor crisis. A motor-cycle crash, a business reorganisation seminar, and a childbirth represent the unlikely-seeming dramatic punctuation in Olmi's mosaic portrait of minimal domestic communication; while the director himself adopts an uncharacteristically elliptical structure and a rare stridency to capture both the frenetic tail-chasing and tentative adaptations to change which criss-cross the dead institutional centre. If the criticism is muted, it's because for Olmi, every new circumstance offers at least a new option. PT

Circus, The
(Charles Chaplin, 1928, US) Charlie Chaplin, Merna Kennedy, Allan Garcia, Harry Crocker, Henry Bergman.
6,700 ft. b/w.
Placing screen clowns within congenial environments (as with *The Marx Brothers at the Circus*) is one of the best ways to produce a bummer, but Chaplin manages to work a miracle, exploiting the various circus activities to richly comic effect. Charlie is chased through a hall of mirrors and trapped in a lion's cage; the climax comes when he battles along a tightrope hampered by falling trousers and a clinging monkey. The set pieces are linked, none too neatly, by a framing story of disappointed love. GB

Circus Boys
(Nijusseiki Shonen Dokuhon)

(Kaizo Hayashi, 1989, Jap) Hiroshi Mikami,
Moe Kamura, Ken Shu, Michiro Akiyoshi.
106 min. b/w.
The Japanese title translates as 'The Boy's Own
Book of the 20th Century', which gives a good
idea of the way it hovers on the brink of allegory
without ever quite freezing into pretentiousness.
Shot in glittering monochrome, it contrasts the
paths of two brothers from a circus family: one
stays with the circus and tries to renew it, while
the other leaves to become a roaming con-man
and quack doctor. Between one man's idealism
and the other's cynicism, Hayashi traverses a
magical terrain of the mind and reaches a conclusion not far off the sublime. TR

Circus of Fear
(aka Psycho-Circus)

(John Moxey, 1966, GB) Leo Genn, Christopher
Lee, Anthony Newlands, Klaus Kinski, Suzy
Kendall, Cecil Parker, Victor Maddern,
Maurice Kaufmann.
83 min. b/w.
Rarely seen shocker, released in the US as *Psycho-
Circus*. Genn plays a dogged, elderly detective
investigating an armoured truck robbery. All the
evidence points to a local circus, but other suspects include a masked lion tamer (Lee), a jittery
knife-thrower (Kaufmann) and various other
clowns. Worse, the corpses are beginning to stack
up. The film-makers never seem quite sure
whether they're making a thriller or a horror pic.
No wonder Genn looks so confused. GM

Circus of Horrors

(Sidney Hayers, 1960, GB) Anton Diffring,
Erika Remberg, Yvonne Monlaur, Donald ,
Jane Hylton, Kenneth Griffith, Yvonne
Romain.
91 min.
A somewhat tacky pendant to *Peeping Tom*, featuring Diffring as a plastic surgeon obsessed by
female disfigurement. Obliged to flee after a cosmetic operation goes horribly wrong, he takes to
running a travelling circus with his refurbished
beauties as performers; there, tangled motives of
jealousy and revenge stir up an outlandish bloodbath in which most of the cast are eliminated one
by one (incidentally gratifying the sensation-
seeking circus audience with a knife-throwing
accident, a nosedive from the big top, and a mauling by lion's jaws). Perhaps inspired by *Les Yeux
sans Visage*, it misses out on Franju's wild poetry but is undeniably bizarre and bloody. TM

Cisco Kid and the Lady, The

(Herbert I Leeds, 1939, US) Cesar Romero,
Marjorie Weaver, Chris-Pin Martin, George
Montgomery, Robert Barrat, Virginia Field,
Harry Green, Ward Bond.
74 min. b/w.
The first of six films in which Cesar Romero took
over the O Henry character – now more insouciant
lover than ruthless outlaw – from Warner Baxter.
Intent on some horse rustling, the Kid finds himself falling heir to an orphaned baby and part of a
map to a gold mine, for which the villain (Barrat)
had murdered the baby's prospector father. Falling
for the new schoolteacher (Weaver), who helps him
look after the baby he now regards as his son, the
Kid is not displeased when her tight-assed fiancé
(Montgomery) misunderstands the situation on
arriving from the East. However, realising in the
process of routing the villain that the young couple still love each other, the Kid promotes a marriage at gunpoint, presents them with baby and
gold mine, and rides off into the sunset with the
saloon girl (Field) he intends to marry – to someone else. Unexpectedly, the result has a shaggy-
dog charm, with free-wheeling sequences
(except from the appallingly inept Montgomery)
and several sequences benefiting from their air of
having been semi-improvised. TM

Cisco Pike

(Bill L Norton, 1972, US) Kris Kristofferson,
Karen Black, Gene Hackman, Harry Dean
Stanton, Viva, Joy Bang, Roscoe Lee Brown,
Antonio Fargas.
94 min.
Kristofferson gets the title role in his first movie
and turns in one of his best performances, as the
fading rocker hanging around the LA music

scene in the hope of a comeback, but scraping a
living as a small time drug dealer. Hackman, on
a run of strong pictures at the time, is the conniving cop on his case, who blackmails him into
offloading one hundred kilos of marijuana inside
three days – or else. Kristofferson conveys the
myopic exhilaration of a string of minor scores
with the tensile, empty conviction of a man only
just holding desperation at bay. TJ

Citadel, The

(King Vidor, 1938, GB) Robert Donat, Rosalind
Russell, Ralph Richardson, Cecil Parker, Rex
Harrison, Emlyn Williams.
110 min. b/w.
Solidly impressive adaptation of AJ Cronin's
novel about an idealistic young doctor who, disillusioned by the hostility he encounters while
trying to improve slum conditions in the Welsh
mining valleys, takes up a Mayfair practice and
finds his principles steadily eroded. Sweetened
with a happy ending, it's still an effective piece
of work, thanks to Donat's typically sturdy performance and Vidor's powerful direction. GA

Citadel, The (El Kalaa)

(Mohamed Chouikh, 1988, Alg) Khaled Barkat,
Djillali Ain-Tedeles, Fettouma Ousliha, Momo,
Fatima Belhadj.
98 min.
A sombre portrait of life in a remote Algerian village, with much of the troubled humanity that
distinguishes films like the Tavianis' *Padre
Padrone*. Through a number of characters – in
particular, a rich wool merchant's three wives,
and Kaddour (Barkat), an unmarried orphan,
shepherd and dogsbody the merchant has adopted – Chouikh dramatises his outrage at the
destructive, outmoded workings of the polyga-
mous Muslim marital laws. While the merchant
wants to take a fourth wife, the orphan, deemed
ineligible for marriage because of his poverty,
falls for a married woman. When the community's male elders discover this forbidden liaison,
they demand that the merchant find Kaddour a
bride within 24 hours to save the village's honour. The film uses powerful, often poetic images
to illuminate the iniquities and hypocrisy that
produce explosive tensions within the community. But the characterisations are too thin –
Chouikh relies heavily on faces – and the sympathies too wide and opaque for the film to work
as drama. The result is distanced and confusing,
like watching people through a window. WH

Cité des enfants perdus, La
(The City of Lost Children)

(Jean-Pierre Jeunet/Marc Caro, 1995, Fr)
Ron Perlman, Daniel Emilfork, Judith Vittet,
Dominique Pinon, Jean-Claude Dreyfus,
Marc Caro.
112 min.
A child smiles delightedly in his toy-filled room
as Santa emerges from the chimney-piece, but joy
turns to terror as the bearded visitor is followed
by more of the same; cut to a man screaming in
a laboratory where, unable to dream himself, he
has stolen the nightmare of a kidnapped orphan.
The opening of another of Jeunet and Caro's forays into the *fantastique* is the perfect introduction to what's essentially a hugely inventive
blend of dream, fairytale and myth, and to a
strange, sinister sea-girt world that functions
according to its own crazy logic. After his infant
brother is abducted by a gang of semi-robotic
Cyclops, kindly strong-man One (Perlman) sets
off on a search that will unite him with feisty 9-
year-old orphan Miette (Vittet) and lead him to
the sea-rig laboratory inhabited by the evil Krank
(Emilfork), his six cloned brothers (Pinon), their
diminutive 'mother', and Uncle Irvin, a sardonic
brain floating in a fish tank. Extraordinary. GA

Citizen Cohn

(Frank Pierson, 1992, US) James Woods, Joe
Don Baker, Pat Hingle, Joseph Bologna,
Frederic Forrest, Lee Grant, Josef Sommer,
Tovah Feldshuh, Allen Garfield.
115 min.
In this hard-hitting biopic, rента-scumbag Woods
plays Roy Cohn, known during the Communist
witch-hunts of the '50s as 'Joe McCarthy's strong
right hand'. On his sickbed, dying of AIDS, Cohn
is haunted by the ghosts of those he persecuted as
a result of his own twisted self-loathing – many of
them Jews (like the Rosenbergs) or gays (like him-

self) – while reflecting on his headline-grabbing victories and behind-the-scenes defeats that 'I had to
fight someone to stay strong'. Adapted from
Nicholas von Hoffman's biography, the film
emphasises Cohn's obsession with loyalty, a lesson
learned early from his mother and one which (when
he pulled strings to get his rich kid lover out of the
army) was to sow the seeds of his destruction. The
dialogue-heavy script and claustrophobic, over-
dressed interiors betray the film's cable TV origins,
but the direction is admirably controlled and the
acting first rate, notably Baker's McCarthy and
Grant as Cohn's domineering mother. NF

Citizen Kane 🎬100 (100)

(Orson Welles, 1941, US) Orson Welles, Joseph
Cotten, Everett Sloane, Dorothy Comingore,
Agnes Moorehead, Ray Collins, Paul Stewart,
George Coulouris, Ruth Warrick.
119 min. b/w.
The source book of Orson Welles, and still a marvellous movie. Thematically less resonant than
some of Welles' later meditations on the nature
of power, perhaps, but still absolutely riveting as
an investigation of a citizen – newspaper tycoon
William Randolph Hearst by any other name –
under suspicion of having soured the American
Dream. Its imagery (not forgetting the oppressive
ceilings) as Welles delightedly explores his mastery of a new vocabulary, still amazes and
delights, from the opening shot of the forbidding
gates of Xanadu to the last glimpse of the vanishing Rosebud (tarnished, maybe, but still a
potent symbol). A film that gets better with each
renewed acquaintance. TM

Citizen Langlois

(Edgardo Cozarinsky, 1995, Fr) Henri
Langlois, Lotte Eisner, Marie Epstein, Mary
Meerson, François Truffaut, Eric Rohmer,
Georges Franju, Jonas Mekas, Allen Ginsberg.
67 min. b&w & col.
Cozarinsky's documentary portrait of Henri
Langlois, the great film historian, archivist and co-
founder (with Georges Franju, seen interviewed
here) of the Cinémathèque Française, is respectful,
informative but never hagiographic. Langlois had
an importance unthinkable in Britain – the French
government's attempt to dismiss him from the
Cinémathèque was one of the key events in the ferment of 1968 – and his progress from amateur collector to *nouvelle vague* hero and friend of the stars
is related with wit and sensitivity, complete with
clips from some of the movies he rescued, fascinating interviews and home-movies (Langlois with
Mekas and Ginsberg!). GA

Citizens Band

(Jonathan Demme, 1977, US) Paul LeMat,
Candy Clark, Ann Wedgeworth, Marcia Rodd,
Charles Napier, Roberts Blossom.
98 min.
As in *Melvin and Howard*, Demme's genuine
curiosity about the eccentricities hidden within
the most seemingly ordinary of American lives
ensures a largely engaging slab of cinematic
graffiti. The populace of script-writer Paul
Brickman's small town includes a hooker on
wheels, a cattle-truck-driving bigamist whose
two wives meet up by accident, and at the centre,
the excellent LeMat as a CB vigilante clobbering
misusers of the airwaves, his chief misery being
a hopeless attachment to a near-gaga father who
only comes to life at his radio mike. The film uses
the CB craze as a metaphor for lack of human
communication, and proceeds in a somewhat
elliptical manner, but the alternation of moments
of black humour and funny-sad incidents lends
it a considerable charm. RM

City After Dark

see Manila by Night

City Beneath the Sea

(Budd Boetticher, 1953, US) Robert Ryan,
Anthony Quinn, Mala Powers, Suzan Ball,
Karel Stepanek, Lalo Rios.
87 min.
Well below average from Boetticher, whose series
of Westerns with Randolph Scott and *The Rise
and Fall of Legs Diamond* display a simple but
effective B movie intensity. This is far more routine, with Ryan and Quinn as deep-sea divers
falling out over sunken treasure. Strong performances from the leads, but little else to hold the
interest. GA

C

City Farm
(John Davies/Robert Smith, 1978, GB) Peter J Rome, Rosie Tennent, Andy Greenhouse, Chris Charles, Pam Hemmingway.
90 min.
The reunion of a sister and two brothers provides Davies and Smith with the basis for an experimentation with, and partial dislocation of, traditional narrative structures. *City Farm* has been compared to a crossword puzzle, but the precision necessary in crossword design is certainly lacking from the film's final shape. A sympathetic tone and worthy ambition do not finally disguise a lack of control over material and direction. SM

City Girl
(aka Our Daily Bread)
(FW Murnau, 1928, US) Charles Farrell, Mary Duncan, David Torrence, Ivan Linow, Guinn Williams.
67 min. b/w.
Murnau's final Hollywood film is widely underrated, no doubt because Fox cut it against his wishes and turned the original silent film into a poorly synchronised part-talkie. Nonetheless, the director's visual talents remain evident in the soft lighting and the pastoral landscapes, and the film is of more than passing interest. As in the superior *Sunrise*, Murnau is concerned with the difference between urban and rural life: a wheat-farmer's son marries a waitress who longs to escape the city, but the old man, suspicious of her fidelity, rejects her, turning against his son. If the plot sounds vaguely familiar, that may be because Malick's *Days of Heaven* trod somewhat similar ground. GA

City Hall
(Harold Becker, 1996, US) Al Pacino, John Cusack, Bridget Fonda, Danny Aiello, Martin Landau, David Paymer, Tony Franciosa.
111 min.
Al Pacino is John Pappas, the best Mayor New York never had. We know because he comes on like Elmer Gantry at every large public gathering, funerals a speciality. But are we're meant to admire his caring-sharing Democrat rabble-rousing? When not being a liberal-conscience drama, or perhaps a political satire (Pappas has presidential ambitions), the film, written by Ken Lipper and Paul Schrader, busies itself being an investigative thriller. Peppy young political strategist Cusack (Pacino's right-hand man) and Detectives' Endowment Association attorney Fonda race for the dark truth behind a Brooklyn street shooting that left a police detective, a small-time mobster and an innocent black child bleeding to death. Confused? The producers obviously were. Five screenwriters are credited, and the end product, despite moments of individual quality from an able cast, pulls in at least as many different directions. There's some attempt to probe the grindings of the Democrat Party machine; there's also a long hard look at the day-to-day workings of the Probation Office. All of this is moderately absorbing, and somehow, somewhere the movie does care; it's just that the notion of corruption being endemic in the US system ain't hot news. TJ

City Heat
(Richard Benjamin, 1984, US) Clint Eastwood, Burt Reynolds, Jane Alexander, Madeline Kahn, Rip Torn, Richard Roundtree, Tony Lo Bianco.
97 min.
Kansas City in the early '30s: prohibition, mob rule and jumping jazz-joints. Taking on the might of competing gangs are cop Eastwood and seedy shamus Reynolds, themselves immersed in some pretty ridiculous rivalry since Burt gave up the Department for independent business. This is not only a pleasantly nostalgic mixture of mobster-movie and *noir* thriller; it is also Eastwood's funniest comedy in years. While Reynolds indulges in his usual cheery blend of bluster and craven cowardice, Clint stealthily outdoes him with self-parodic image-knocking; after his lone-ranger walk down a bullet-ridden city street mad with bloody mayhem, his haloed heroics will never seem the same again. It's certainly not a subtle movie, but with memorable performances, ludicrously over-the-top one-liners and amiable zaniness, it qualifies as a lot of fun. GA

City Lights 100
(Charles Chaplin, 1931, US) Charlie Chaplin, Virginia Cherrill, Florence Lee, Harry Myers, Allan Garcia, Hank Mann.
87 min. b/w.
With its plot focusing on Charlie's love for a blind flower-seller and his attempts to get enough money to pay for an eye operation, *City Lights* edges dangerously close to the weepie wonderland of *Magnificent Obsession* and other lace-handkerchief jobs. This horrid fate is narrowly avoided by bracing doses of slapstick (the heroine unravels Charlie's vest thinking it's her ball of wool) and Chaplin's supreme delicacy in conveying all shades of human feeling. Matters aren't helped by the film's structure, which is as tattered and baggy as the tramp's trousers. But there are plenty of great moments, and the occasional comic use of sound (despite its date, the film is silent) is beautifully judged. GB

City of Angels
(Brad Silberling, 1998, US/Ger) Nicolas Cage, Meg Ryan, Dennis Franz, André Braugher, Colm Feore, Robin Bartlett.
114 min.
A Hollywood remake of *Wings of Desire*, directed by the man who gave us *Casper*. The mind boggles. But elegant direction, luscious camerawork, a mostly unsentimental script, and sterling performances from the stars turns this into be an honourable effort – at least until the last 20 minutes, when the movie goes spectacularly off the rails. Seth (Cage, charismatic) is one of many angels who wander LA listening in to people's thoughts, trying to allay their anxieties, and, when death rears its head, leading them 'home'. He sees heart surgeon Maggie (Ryan) fighting to save a patient: when she fails, he's struck by her sadness, guilt and sense of confusion, and – already wondering what it would be like to experience taste, smell, touch, tears and transient joy – falls so in love that he begins to make himself visible to her. This is funnier than Wenders' version, and it also succeeds in visualising LA as a magical city while dealing intelligently with the themes of mortality, sacrifice, free will, and the mixed blessings of the human condition. GA

City of Fear
(Irving Lerner, 1958, US) Vince Edwards, John Archer, Patricia Blair, Steven Ritch, Lyle Talbot, Joe Mell, Sherwood Price.
75 min. b/w.
Pacy Columbia B-picture from a film-maker who did pretty well on the barest of resources and later won praise from Martin Scorsese (who also hired him as co-editor on *New York, New York*). Edwards escapes from prison with a sealed canister he believes contains $1m worth of heroin. In fact he's toting radioactive cobalt that could contaminate the whole city. The premise is more exciting than the execution, but the movie's strong on seedy atmosphere (notable b/w camerawork from Lucien Ballard) and there's an excellent jazz-tinged score from Jerry Goldsmith. TJ

City of Hope
(John Sayles, 1991, US) Vincent Spano, Joe Morton, Tony Lo Bianco, Barbara Williams, Stephen Mendillo, Chris Cooper, Charlie Yanko, Jace Alexander, Todd Graff, Scott Tiler, John Sayles, David Strathairn, Kevin Tighe, Maggie Renzi, Josh Mostel, Lawrence Tierney, Angela Bassett, Anthony John Denison.
130 min.
Building contractor Joe (Lo Biancо) is up to his neck in the scratch-my-back ethics of corrupt property developers and politicians. Son Nick (Spano) has been tempted into petty crime. Idealistic councilman Wynn (Morton) is torn between professional ambition and loyalty to local blacks, who accuse him of having sold them down the line. Black teenagers Tito and Desmond are so fed up with being hassled by racist cops that they mug a college professor... These are only a few of the characters and stories that colour Sayles' masterly account of the everyday workings of a contemporary New Jersey city: a genuinely epic, politically astute, profoundly humanist and dramatically gripping study of the conflicts, compromises and power plays that define life in any community on the verge of economic breakdown. As ever, much enjoyment may be had from both the complex,

interwoven threads of Sayles' script and the powerful, naturalistic performances. What really impresses, however, is the confidence of Sayles' fluid direction. GA

City of Industry
(John Irvin, 1996, US) Harvey Keitel, Stephen Dorff, Famke Janssen, Timothy Hutton.
97 min.
A derivative, mostly dull contemporary crime movie in which a heist goes wrong and the survivors fight to the death. Wary, honourable, world-weary thief Roy Egan (Keitel) is out for revenge against semi-psychotic, untrustworthy upstart Skip Kovich (Dorff), who betrayed his fellow gang members – including Roy's brother Lee (Hutton) – after a daring diamond snatch. True to formula, the relationship of Roy and the widow of another victim of Skip's deceit (Janssen, not without appeal) shifts from mutually cool to respectful and tender. GA

City of Joy
(Roland Joffé, 1992, GB/Fr) Patrick Swayze, Om Puri, Pauline Collins, Shabana Azmi, Ayesha Dharker, Santu Chowdhury, Imran Badsah Khan, Art Malik.
135 min.
East and West learn from each other, and it's an interminable seminar. In Calcutta, the fortunes of rickshaw man Hasari (Puri) and American dropout doctor Max (Swayze) intertwine, but the acting styles are so divergent that they may as well be in different films. Max is selfish and suicidally sick of life, while Hasari has to fight for the daily bread to support his family; but Max learns how to care again after delivering a baby, while Hasari learns how to embrace American can-do and reject his Asian acceptance of the system. Together, they stand up to the razor-wielding bad guy (Malik). Presiding over the City of Joy school and clinic is Irish Joan (Collins), pushy, practical, and derived from other movies. It's very old-fashioned stuff, with the impoverished Indian slum-dwellers working like cheerful chipmunks to build a better clinic, and a climactic monsoon on hand to bring out the best in everybody. BC

City of Lost Children, The
see Cité des enfants perdus, La

City of Lost Souls (Stadt der Verlorenen Seelen)
(Rosa von Praunheim, ie. Holger Mischwitzki, 1983, WGer) Angie Stardust, Jayne County, Lorraine Muthke, Wolfgang Schumacher.
94 min.
Rosa von Praunheim's fictionalised account of the lives of his expatriate American acquaintances in Berlin. On the surface, a deranged comedy caper; sympathetically observed TVs and TSs, bizarre cabaret artistes, prostitutes, gays, straights, blacks and whites thriving in adversity in a Berlin of hallucinogenic fast-food outlets, lunatic self-improvement cults, cartooned nightclub life and immigration-squad raids. But behind the laughter there are numerous pointed comments on modern-day Germany, on fascism and on sexual, social, political and geographical statelessness. Heavy stuff – but von Praunheim ends up celebrating his friends' lives in a funny, startling and mocking 'punk' musical that even finds time for a Broadway-style happy ending. Jayne County's rise to Iron Curtain pop stardom is debilitatingly funny, and the whole might be described as a Rocky Horror *Gastarbeiter* Problem. JG

City of Pirates
(La Ville des Pirates)
(Raúl Ruiz, 1983, Fr/Port) Hugues Quester, Anne Alvaro, Melvil Fouquad, André Engel, Duarte De Almeida.
121 min.
Forget the pirates – there aren't any in Ruiz's provocative fairy-tale. But there is a lost boy, who has already massacred his family before he seduces his Wendy, in the shape of a downtrodden servant girl, and transports her to her Neverland (there isn't a city either). If Ruiz's 'free transcription' of *Peter Pan* sounds more like a subtitled *Friday the 13th*, it's because he takes the sexual undercurrent of children's literature as seriously as Angela Carter. The atmosphere is magical, perversely playful and macabre: in a moment of pure, surreal poetry, the boy-murderer sails a fleet of burning paper

boats on a tide of his victim's blood. What really distinguishes this is a gripping performance by Alvaro as the haunted lover-cum-mother, and the images that are the very stuff of nightmares. IC

City of Sadness, A
(Beiqing Chengshi)

(Hou Xiaoxian, 1989, Tai) Tony Leung, Xin Shu-fen, Li T'ien-lu, Kao Chieh, Ikuyo Nakamura.
158 min.
Loaded with detail and elliptically structured to let viewers make their own connections, Hou's film spans four fateful years of transition in Taiwan, from the defeat of the Japanese colonialists in WWII, when the island was returned to China, to the retreat to Taiwan of Chiang Kai-Shek's Nationalists at the end of the civil war in 1949. The period is shown from the perspective of a single family: a virtually senile widower, his sons (one missing presumed dead, one a gangster, one a deaf-mute photographer, the fourth a former translator for the Japanese) and their wives. As always with Hou, the human dimension is paramount – this is no history lesson – but it's clear that he is reaching for a sense of Taiwan's identity through the family's affairs. Given the panoramic sweep – which focuses particularly on the underworld and the political underground – Hou turns in a masterpiece of small gestures and massive resonance; once you surrender to its spell, the obscurities vanish. TR

City of the Living Dead
see Paura nella Città dei Morti Viventi

City of Women
(La Città delle Donne)

(Federico Fellini, 1980, It/Fr) Marcello Mastroianni, Anna Prucnal, Bernice Stegers, Iole Silvani, Donatella Damiani, Ettore Manni.
139 min.
Will Fellini ever learn to count beyond eight and a half? As Snaporaz (a discreetly ageing Mastroianni, still the alter egoist and flattering mirror image of his director) dozes off in a train to be whisked through a nightmare of ultra-militant feminism, here we are again on that familiar gaudy treadmill of Barnum and ballet, circus and comic strip. Yet if much of it verges on self-parody, a few of the set pieces are superb (the Women's Lib congress, every word of which, swears Fellini, was taken verbatim from feminist literature; the homage to the communal masturbatorium the cinema used to be). In his martyrdom, Snaporaz becomes hardly less poignant a creation than Ophüls' Lola Montès; and only a pinchpenny soul could denigrate the generosity, the sheer fertility of the Maestro's invention in this curate's egg by Fabergé. GAd

City on Fire
(Longhu Fengyun)

(Ringo Lam, 1987, HK) Chow Yun Fat, Danny Lee, Sun Yueh, Roy Cheung.
110 min.
The inspiration for *Reservoir Dogs*, this 1987 crime movie is a good example of the thriller HK-style ('style' being the operative word). Social and psychological nuance is out. Designer shades are in. Hong Kong's biggest movie star, Chow Yun Fat (*The Killer*, *A Better Tomorrow*, *Hard-Boiled*) is the epitome of *Esquire* cool, more playful than Clint, more intense than Mel, much better looking than Arnie or Sly. Here he's an undercover cop, Ko Chow, who works his way into a gang of jewel thieves at the cost of his fiancée and, perhaps, his own integrity. This is straight-cut, fashion-plate pulp. Tarantino fans will note the familiarity of the set-up. In fact, *Reservoir Dogs* is an elaboration on the the climax of Ringo Lam's film: after the heist goes wrong, the gang hole up in a warehouse, where bullets and recriminations start to fly. There's none of Tarantino's formal inventiveness, none of the finesse or the wit, just a gut-wrenching dramatic situation ready to explode. TCh

City on Fire

(Alvin Rakoff, 1979, Can/US) Barry Newman, Susan Clark, Shelley Winters, Leslie Nielsen, James Franciscus, Ava Gardner, Henry Fonda.
106 min.
Thoroughly routine disaster movie, about the sweaty travails of a fire-fighting team squirting around a huge inferno after an explosion at an oil-refinery. To make matters worse, there's a hos-

pital in the middle of the holocaust, with babies to deliver and emergency ops to complete. Fonda purses his lips, and the rest of the cast scream, emote and generally irritate. GA

City Slickers

(Ron Underwood, 1991, US) Billy Crystal, Daniel Stern, Bruno Kirby, Patricia Wettig, Helen Slater, Jack Palance, Josh Mostel, David Paymer, Noble Willingham, Tracey Walter.
114 min.
You've seen it all before: pals approaching mid-life crisis explore the Great Outdoors, rethink values, and by trail's end vow never to complain about putting out the trash. Three married men – bewildered Mitch (Crystal), playboy Ed (Kirby) and unfaithful Phil (Stern) – are pitted against the rigours of a 200-mile cattle drive led by cowpoke Curly (Palance), so tough he lights matches on his face. Crystal's self-pitying character starts out promisingly – an early highlight being his lecture on ageing to schoolchildren – but the constant rapid-fire quips become increasingly predictable. CM

City Slickers II:
The Legend of Curly's Gold

(Paul Weiland, 1994, US) Billy Crystal, Daniel Stern, Jon Lovitz, Jack Palance, Patricia Wettig, Pruitt Taylor Vince, Josh Mostel.
116 min.
The original offered an easy-going spin on the fish-out-of-water routine, packing its three suburban menopausal males off into the dusty yonder to be licked into shape by life on the range. This time the chaps head into the desert with a treasure map in the their hands and greed in their hearts. What follows is a jolly blend of zippy dialogue, Western-type action, and lots of spot-on humour about guys being guys together. TJ

City Streets

(Rouben Mamoulian, 1931, US) Gary Cooper, Sylvia Sidney, Paul Lukas, Guy Kibbee, William Boyd, Wynne Gibson, Stanley Fields.
82 min. b/w.
Strikingly stylised bootlegging yarn, more romance than gangster movie, said to have been an Al Capone favourite because the gang boss (Lukas), far from rampaging Cagney-style with machine-gun in the streets, is always careful to be seen to have clean hands: all deaths take place discreetly off-screen, and a contract to kill drawn up in an offhand line of dialogue ('I'd be willing to do business with you, if anything happened to Blackie') is equally elliptically sealed when the other party lights his cigar, looks at the match, and then pensively snuffs it out. Mamoulian sometimes over-stresses the visual and aural symbolism he experiments with in support of these ellipses, but creates a wonderfully evocative, low-key atmosphere not dissimilar to Sternberg's *Underworld* with terrific camerawork from Lee Garmes, and fine performances from Cooper and Sidney as the young lovers enmeshed in the rackets. TM

City Under the Sea
(aka War Gods of the Deep)

(Jacques Tourneur, 1965, GB/US) Vincent Price, David Tomlinson, Tab Hunter, Susan Hart, John , Henry Oscar.
84 min.
Tacky Jules Verne-ish adventure inspired by Poe's poem 'The City in the Sea', with Price as The Captain (obviously kin to Nemo) kidnapping a girl he takes to be the reincarnation of his dead wife and bringing her to the lost city of Lyonesse under the sea. A sad disappointment as Tourneur's last film, with occasional imaginative touches (but surprisingly little atmosphere) and a dismal cast (Price excepted), although the narrative keeps going perkily enough. TM

Claire's Knee
(Le Genou de Claire)

(Eric Rohmer, 1970, Fr) Jean-Claude Brialy, Aurora Cornu, Béatrice Romand, Laurence de Monaghan, Michèle Montel, Fabrice Luchini.
106 min.
The fifth and most accessible of Rohmer's six 'moral tales', *Claire's Knee* is the story of the temptation of an affianced diplomat (Brialy) while on holiday, and its successful suppression. The film was rapturously received as a cinematic equivalent to Jane Austen at the time of its orig-

inal release. The comparison is apt, though a better one would be with Joseph L Mankiewicz, a director of similarly literate, talky, classically structured movies, but none the less misses the point. For Brialy is no throwback to the 19th century but rather a Martian, a visitor to this planet discovering the values of his own culture through surveying those of the people he finds himself among, and finally retreating back home. If this makes Rohmer sound like a poet of bourgeois repression (just as Chabrol can be seen as a poet of bourgeois excess), one must also add that the film's self-reflexive structure makes it both more exciting and more ambiguous than such a description allows for. PH

Clairvoyant, The

(Maurice Elvey, 1935, GB) Claude Rains, Fay Wray, Jane Baxter, Ben Field, Athole Stewart, Mary Clare, Felix Aylmer.
80 min. b/w.
Enjoyable if unremarkable thriller about a phoney music-hall clairvoyant who suddenly discovers that he has genuine prescience in the presence of a girl (Baxter). Things get fraught when his wife (Wray) disapproves of his involvement, even more so when he predicts a tunnel disaster, it takes place (the authorities wouldn't listen), and he is blamed for causing it by having spread panic. Rains lends a touch of credibility to the far-fetched plot. GA

Clando (Clandestine)

(Jean Marie Téno, 1996, Cameroon) Paulin Fodouop, Caroline Redl, Henriette Fenda, Joseph Momo, Guillaume Nana.
98 min.
After an enigmatic opening, this political/psychological drama turns into an arresting portrait of a life thrown into turmoil by the pernicious actions of corrupt authorities. After computer programmer Anatole (Fodouop) is arrested and tortured for helping an anti-government group print leaflets, he becomes impotent both sexually and socially, reduced to working illegally as an unlicensed cab-driver (*clando*); in an attempt to improve his lot, he leaves Cameroon for Cologne, where the life of an exile is a little easier. Occasionally slow and rather clumsily acted, the film nevertheless offers insights into questions of freedom, activism, apathy and responsibility, and as a bonus features a marvellously seductive jazz blues score. GA

Clan of the Cave Bear, The

(Michael Chapman, 1985, US) Daryl Hannah, Pamela Reed, James Remar, Thomas G Waites, John Doolittle, Curtis Armstrong.
98 min.
Adopted by the Neanderthal *Clan of the Cave Bear*, Cro-Magnon Hannah (taking a giant evolutionary leap forward from her previous incarnation in *Splash*) is maligned for her ability to count beyond ten, dexterity with weapons, and disdain for the males' primitive seduction rites (a fist thumped in the palm of the hand as prelude to some vigorous rutting). In the end this primeval feminist rejects miscegenation with nasty, brutish Stone Age bozos, stalking off into the sunset in search of an appropriately Aryan mate. Devotees of John Sayles' witty, literate screenplays will be disappointed by the repartee of subtitled grunts, while beneath the film's apparent plea for tolerance lies the offensive (if quite possibly true) assumption that tall, tanned Californian blondes represent the highest form of human life. Based on a fat novel by Jean Auel (who subsequently sued the producers), this is *Reader's Digest* prehistory, though at least director Chapman (cameraman on *Raging Bull*) makes sure the murky caves look nice. SJo

Clara's Heart

(Robert Mulligan, 1988, US) Whoopi Goldberg, Michael Ontkean, Kathleen Quinlan, Neil Patrick Harris, Spalding Gray, Beverly Todd.
108 min.
When Clara (Goldberg) come to America from Jamaica to keep house for an irritating white middle class couple (Ontkean and Quinlan), all does not look well to the couple's little boy: after all Clara is black, cooks weird food, and 'talks funny'. Nevertheless, when his parents' marriage begins to crumble, young David turns to the newcomer, and soon learns that she is the most wonderful human being alive. In no time at all he's 'speaking her language' and generally getting to grips with the real world, while his parents disappear

even further up their psychological backsides. Mulligan's adaptation of Joseph Olshan's novel doesn't merely flirt with pathos, it positively marries it. There are moments of genuinely touching comedy; Spalding Gray's nauseatingly condescending psychotherapist is spot on; and Whoopi Goldberg, admirable as always, fights a losing battle against a script which forces her to deliver the most appalling imitation of patois since C Thomas Howell in 'Soul Man'. MK

Clarence and Angel
(Robert Gardner, 1980, US) Darren Brown, Mark Cardova, Izola Armstrong, Christine Campbell, Janice Jenkins.
75 min.
Clarence, a near-illiterate black teenager, picks up the knack of reading from Angel, a Puerto Rican live wire, during daily sessions together in the school corridor to which both are exiled for misbehaviour. Though lent a superficial 'marginality' by its use of non-professional performers, playground scat songs and dialogue of such authentic (and indecipherable) Harlemese as to give the layman the impression of overhearing rather than hearing it, the film's message – that the resilience of childhood will always win through against the odds – recalls the reactionary softie humanism of a Saroyan. An unassuming little film, nevertheless, touching and droll, and boasting in Cardova (as Angel) a born performer whose flawless timing and diminutive sex appeal suggest that he might grow up to become the American cinema's first Puerto Rican heart-throb. GAd.

Clarence, the Cross-Eyed Lion
(Andrew Marton, 1965, US) Marshall Thompson, Betsy Drake, Cheryl Miller, Richard Hayden, Alan Caillou.
98 min.
Clarence is a myopic beast who has difficulty focusing on his prey, Thompson is the animal behaviourist who tries to set his vision straight. There are also poachers closing in on the local gorillas. This was the movie which spawned the TV series *Daktari*. Director Marton (once Lubitsch's editor) efficiently blends the human drama with African wildlife footage. GM

Clash By Night
(Fritz Lang, 1952, US) Barbara Stanwyck, Paul Douglas, Robert Ryan, Marilyn Monroe, Keith Andes, J Carroll Naish.
105 min. b/w.
Clifford Odets' original play was a hoary item of Broadway neo-realism in the Arthur Miller vein: a 'mature' study of a cynical woman's adultery with an equally cynical man. Lang and his producer Jerry Wald transposed the setting from Staten Island to a small fishing village, and had the brilliant idea of grounding the characters in a documentary on the community industry, giving them a substance never intrinsic in the script. What follows is a very Langian picture of the dangerous undercurrents in emotional relationships, excellently acted by the three principals, interestingly counterpointed by Marilyn Monroe (in her first major role) and Keith Andes as uninhibited young lovers. TR

Clash of the Ash
(Fergus Tighe, 1987, Ire) William Heffernan, Vincent Murphy, Gina Moxley, Michael McAuliffe.
50 min.
Phil (Heffernan) is in his final year at secondary school. On top of the pressures exerted by the adults around him – from his mother to study and do well at his exams, his father to take a job at the local garage, and his hurling trainer to prove himself on the field – there's the frustration of small-town life with its limited social outlets and air of claustrophobia. Phil's smouldering restlessness pervades this evenly paced and sensitively portrayed slice of provincial life, which manages to tell its yarn with a great deal of humour and compassion. GS

Clash of the Titans
(Desmond Davis, 1981, GB) Harry Hamlin, Judi Bowker, Laurence Olivier, Claire Bloom, Maggie Smith, Burgess Meredith, Ursula Andress, Flora Robson.
118 min.

Old-style monster-and-mythology movie, made with the entrancing splendour of Ray Harryhausen's visual effects (the Pegasus flights) and the occasional cynicism which results from under-using and abusing a star cast. Perseus (Hamlin) and Andromeda (Bowker) are as boringly lovely as classical hero/ines should be, and even the scaly Kraken looks too dazed to bite Bowker in half. JS

Class
(Lewis John Carlino, 1983, US) Jacqueline Bisset, Rob Lowe, Andrew McCarthy, Cliff Robertson, Stuart Margolin, John Cusack.
98 min.
Another of those mildly titillating high-school films, soulless and self-satisfied, realising the youthful fantasy of being initiated into the joys of sex by an older woman. Uncritically portraying a group of materialistic pupils (at an expensive academy) for whom education is merely a passport to success, politics don't exist, poverty sucks, and women's panties are collected like trophies, the film has Jonathan and Skip as a couple of pretty little room-mates. Unacceptably still a virgin, Jonathan is packed off to Chicago to bed his first woman, unwittingly meets Skip's 38-year-old mother (Bisset), and is seduced in a glass elevator. Naturally the older, unhappy woman is dumped in favour of male buddyness. JE

Class Action
(Michael Apted, 1990, US) Gene Hackman, Mary Elizabeth Mastrantonio, Colin Friels, Joanna Merlin, Larry Fishburne, Donald Moffat, Jan Rubes, Matt Clark, Fred Dalton Thompson.
109 min.
Maggie Ward (Mastrantonio) may have followed her father into the law, but she embodies the kind of values he despises and is embittered about her long-suffering mother. Daddy (the ever reliable Hackman) is a flamboyant civil liberties lawyer who has spent his life championing the underdog and pursuing extra-marital affairs. When a class action lawsuit comes along, involving injured drivers and a car manufacturer accused of producing dangerous vehicles, guess which lawyers decide to take up opposing sides? Apted builds up a combative atmosphere both in and out of the courtroom, but the studied contrivances which work so well before the judge appear more strained during the emotional confrontations, which ambitiously attempt to redress all wrongs. Worthy stuff, most effective during the courtroom theatricals. CM

Class of '44
(Paul Bogart, 1973, US) Gary Grimes, Jerry Houser, Oliver Conant, William Atherton, Sam Bottoms, Deborah Winters.
95 min.
Little Benjy (remember him?) joins the Marines 'cos of their tradition, while Hermie and Oscy go to college in this follow-up to Robert Mulligan's *Summer of '42*. Looking back to a fat, happy America, from a European point of view very much secure at the end of the rainbow during World War II, it has Oscy thrown out of college for pimping off a 32-year-old whore he installs in his room, while Hermie has girl trouble, feels guilty about not fighting, and is faced with the death of a father he never really knew. A serious analysis of the period might have been interesting, but *Class of '44* just opts for clichés and nostalgia in equal doses.

Class of Miss MacMichael, The
(Silvio Narizzano, 1978, GB) Glenda Jackson, Oliver Reed, Michael Murphy, Rosalind Cash, John Standing, Riba Akabusi, Phil Daniels.
99 min.
Reed, as the neo-fascist headmaster of a school for delinquents, parodies his boorish film persona to the point of farce, alternately strutting around like a boiled turkey or oiling his way with the school's visitors, while Jackson goes at her role of committed teacher/lone befriender of kids with jaw-forward heartiness. Add to this conflict in styles the film's confused intentions – black comedy, the horrific realities of reform schools, a sentimental belief that understanding will overcome – and you have a mess. HM

Class of 1984
(Mark L Lester, 1981, Can) Perry King, Merrie Lynn Ross, Timothy Van Patten, Roddy McDowall, Stefan Arngrim, Michael Fox.
98 min.
A stomping reworking of *The Blackboard Jungle* for the '80s, with Perry King – in the part of the well-meaning teacher originally played by Glenn Ford – faced with a bunch of delinquents who make Ford's sulky juveniles look quite angelic by comparison: psychos, pushers and hookers throng the class of '84 carrying a fancy range of weaponry which somehow escapes the metal detector in the hall. And ultimately King wins through not by patience or insight or understanding, but by something more old-fashioned, like ramming them with cars and smashing their brains out on the concrete. While there can be no doubt that in true tabloid style *Class of 1984* feeds on everything it is condemning, as an energetic comic strip it has considerable fascination. DP

Class of Nuke 'Em High
(Richard W Haines/Samuel Weil, 1986, US) Janelle Brady, Gilbert Brenton, Robert Prichard, RL Ryan, James Nugent Vernon.
85 min.
Yet another mutant movie genre: the Blackboard Jungle meets the hardcore splatter eco-horror, and it's all played, with sub-Animal House humour, for very cheap yucks. Tromaville High School gets leaked on by the near-by nuclear power plant. Clean-cut preppies turn into violent, perverted creeps. Nerds turn homicidal and froth up green stuff. Contaminated joints turn their smokers into sex maniacs, and pre-marital bonking leads to miscarried slime monsters with teeth and tendrils. Lacks any redeeming features whatsoever, which lends it a certain cachet. AB

Class Relations (Klassenverhältnisse)
(Jean-Marie Straub/Danièle Huillet, 1983, WGer/Fr) Christian Heinisch, Reinald Schnell, Anna Schnell, Klaus Traube, Mario Adorf.
127 min. b/w.
The Straubs always base their movies on existing texts (novels, poems, essays, plays or operas), choosing material, they say, that 'resists' them in some way. The idea is that their films become battlegrounds where the original author's words are confronted by the rigorous materialism of the Straubs' approach to film-making. In this case the source is Kafka's last novel *Amerika*, and the problem is that it doesn't yield much of a skirmish. This is the closest the Straubs have ever come to a straightforward literary adaptation: young Karl Rossman, newly arrived in a very German America, moves through a series of brutal encounters that destroy his 'New World' idealism and educate him in the verities of power and class difference. This is not to say that the film plays like a BBC 'classic serial', but the axeing of the book's philosophical speculations leaves the Straubs plodding rather than soaring through Kafka's political undercurrents. The stark images none the less have the 'minimalist' beauty that drives some viewers to distraction. TR

Claudine
(John Berry, 1974, US) Diahann Carroll, James Earl Jones, Lawrence Hinton-Jacobs, Tamu, David Kruger.
92 min.
Black welfare comedy with a catch in its throat that has a beautiful mother of six trying to get her man as well as cope with domestic problems like a militant son and pregnant daughter. Meanwhile her man (a garbage collector) wins the kids over by preaching the virtues of savvy and education. Most of the humour is aware of the blacks' place at the bottom of the heap, and the stream of welfare gags occasionally hit home; but mostly the film is dogged by its middle-of-the road comedy format and its refusal to trade in anything but stereotypes.

Clay Pigeon, The
(Richard Fleischer, 1949, US) Bill Williams, Barbara Hale, Richard Loo, Richard Quine, Frank Fenton, Martha Hyer.
63 min. b/w.
Williams as an ex-PoW suffering from amnesia (that favourite standby of the *film noir*) and setting out to establish his innocence after being accused of treason and responsibility for the

death of a friend in a Jap camp. Directed by Fleischer with tight, spare energy, although the implausible script and bland leading performances (with Hale as the dead friend's wife, initially hostile but soon losing her heart) make it much inferior to *The Narrow Margin*. TM

Clean and Sober

(Glenn Gordon Caron, 1988, US) Michael Keaton, Kathy Baker, Morgan Freeman, M Emmet Walsh, Tate Donovan, Luca Bercovici, Ben Piazza, Henry Judd Baker.
124 min.
A film about addiction and redemption which avoids the usual sensationalism. Daryl Poynter (Keaton) doesn't realise how bad he is until he wakes up to find his date dead of an overdose in bed beside him, and embezzlement charges brewing up at his real estate firm. Drink and drugs have eroded all sense of responsibility, and rather than face the music, he takes refuge in a chemical dependency centre without any intention of toeing the line. It takes some tough talk from the councillor (Freeman, excellent) and the shock of enforced abstinence to shape him up. A supportive romance with fellow inmate Charlie (Kathy Baker) nose-dives abruptly, and his rehabilitation is ultimately down to character. The film doesn't cheat at all – Keaton's Poynter is a dislikeable proposition, always ready with a contemptuous crack, his pzazz verging on panic. The cold turkey sequence is devoid of Elmer Bernstein's brass, and the end is no more dramatic than an admission of answerability. A level look at a common problem. BC

Clean, Shaven

(Lodge Kerrigan, 1993, US) Peter Greene, Molly Castelloe, Megan Owen, Robert Albert, Jennifer MacDonald.
80 min.
Kerrigan's feature debut is an edgy, engrossing, intelligent study of schizophrenia, formulated as an impressionistically fragmented variation of the hunter/hunted road thriller. Right from the start, we can see that Peter Winter (Greene) is falling apart at the seams; his reaction to a small girl bouncing a ball against his car, coupled with reports of murder on the radio, suggest that he's probably also homicidal. At any rate, he sets off across a bleak landscape, visiting his far-from-welcoming mother and searching for the daughter whose company he's been denied; meanwhile, a detective is on his trail, checking out murder locations and contacting Winter's estranged wife for clues as to his likely whereabouts and intentions. What lifts the film out of the rut is its use of expressionistic sound design (there's little dialogue, let alone plot) and occasionally disturbing images to reveal Winter's wretched, hallucinatory perceptions of the world around him; few movie portraits of the paranoid experience have been so detailed or, for that matter, so harrowing. GA

Clean Slate
(Coup de Torchon)

(Bertrand Tavernier, 1981, Fr) Philippe Noiret, Isabelle Huppert, Jean-Pierre Marielle, Stéphane Audran, Eddy Mitchell, Guy Marchand.
128 min.
Purists may object to Tavernier's treatment of Jim Thompson's excellent if sordid and sadistic thriller, *Pop.1280*, but this eccentric, darkly comic look at a series of bizarre murders is stylish, well-crafted, and thoroughly entertaining. Transferring the action from the American Deep South to French West Africa in the late '30s, Tavernier elicits a characteristically colourful performance from Noiret as the manic but outwardly easy going slob of a cop who initiates a private vendetta against the town's more obnoxious citizens by resorting to murder. Strange insights into the effects of racism and the complicity of its victims, embellished with black wit and an elegant visual sense. GA

Clear and Present Danger

(Phillip Noyce, 1994, US) Harrison Ford, Willem Dafoe, Anne Archer, Henry Czerny, Donald Moffat, Harris Yulin, Joaquim de Almeida, Dean Jones, Hope Lange.
141 min.
This third, dispiriting screen outing for Tom Clancy's CIA operative Jack Ryan has Ford's rugged protagonist promoted to Deputy Director and swiftly finding himself out of his depth on two

fronts: negotiating the treacherous corridors of high office, at the same time as presidential initiative demands improved results in his war against Colombia's drug barons. The elements of the plot can be ticked off: an auto-pilot star; better playing in the subsidiary roles; and a grim determination throughout to impress us with the number of locations, aircraft and warships at the production's disposal. There's a glimmer of interest in the film's ideological contortions, but as a commercial action thriller this is inflated and sluggish. TJ

Cléo de 5 à 7
(Cleo from 5 to 7)

(Agnès Varda, 1961, Fr/It) Corinne Marchand, Antoine Bourseiller, Dorothée Blanck, Dominique Davray, Michel Legrand.
90 min. b/w & col.
If much of Varda's airy cinema has not lasted well, this classic 'two hours in the life of' still casts a sympathetic spell. Successful pop singer Cleo (Marchand), depressed by the imminent arrival of a doctor's report that could be very serious, quits her secluded, protected world for the Parisian streets and eventually meets up with a young soldier (Bourseiller), finding an unexpected intimacy and renewed hope. The fluid, whited-out photography gives the film a genuine grace, and the music session midway with Michel Legrand is a real joy. There is also a brief burlesque movie, featuring (among others) Godard, Karina and Eddie Constantine. Not every minute is as spirited as Varda would like us to believe, but in the cinema of enchantment this ranks pretty high. DT

Cleopatra

(Cecil B DeMille, 1934, US) Claudette Colbert, Warren William, Henry Wilcoxon, Gertrude Michael, Joseph Schildkraut, C Aubrey Smith.
98 min. b/w.
Archly silly, but quite fun if you go for DeMille's po-faced blend of titillation and uplift. When you get tired of watching the scantily-clad cuties who seem to go into their dance every few minutes, there are some glitteringly opulent Hans Dreier sets: the burnished barge is a masterpiece of bordello art. TM

Cleopatra

(Joseph L Mankiewicz, 1963, US) Elizabeth Taylor, Richard Burton, Rex Harrison, Roddy McDowall, Cesare Danova, Hume Cronyn, Robert Stephens, Kenneth Haigh, George Cole.
243 min.
A mess, as you might expect from the disastrous series of stoppages and personnel changes that dogged production. Mankiewicz does his best with a script worked on by so many writers that it never hits any recognisable tone, but the effect is of acres of dreary spectacle (lacking even DeMille's amusing vulgarity) gradually swamping the cast. Harrison, doing his waspish don act as Caesar, alone rises above mediocrity. GA

Cleopatra Jones

(Jack Starrett, 1973, US) Tamara Dobson, Bernie Casey, Brenda Sykes, Antonio Fargas, Bill McKinney, Dan Frazer, Shelley Winters.
89 min.
Blaxploitation product in which six-foot-two Agent Tamara Dobson wages war on drugs, rednecks and other social evils. Luckily Starrett played it for laughs: the film stands or falls by the flamboyant comic-strip style of its Cat Woman heroine. VG

Cleopatra Jones and the
Casino of Gold

(Chuck Bail, 1975, US/HK) Tamara Dobson, Stella Stevens, Tanny, Norman Fell, Albert Popwell.
96 min.
This lame follow-up to the less than brilliant Cleopatra Jones has its black special agent combating drug rings in Hong Kong hand-in-glove with the local special branch. Mechanically scripted, incoherently put together. VG

Clerks

(Kevin Smith, 1993, US) Brian O'Halloran, Jeff Anderson, Marilyn Ghigliotti, Lisa Spoonauer.
90 min.
Shot in a New Jersey convenience store for $27,575, this talky, scabrous and very funny first

feature is a bargain-price comedy. Store clerk Dante (O'Halloran) and his pal Randal (Anderson), who minds the adjacent video shop, use the gaps between awkward customers to discuss their career trajectories, the ending of *Return of the Jedi*, the oral excesses of Dante's current girlfriend, and the impending nuptials of his highschool ex. If it's fancy packaging you want, forget it; if scuzzy talk and laugh-out-loud humour are your bag, check this out. NF

Client, The

(Joel Schumacher, 1994, US) Tommy Lee Jones, Susan Sarandon, Mary-Louise Parker, Anthony LaPaglia, JT Walsh, Brad Renfro, Will Patton.
121 min.
When two young brothers find themselves reluctant witnesses to a suicide, at least 11-year-old Mark knows enough to realise that his terrifying conversation with the man immediately before his death will attract the attention of the legal authorities – the Feds, no less, headed by prosecutor Foltrigg (Jones); but he probably didn't expect to hear from the Mob. Trouble is, Mark (Renfro) knows too much. But while lawyer Reggie Love (Sarandon) is canny, caring and tough enough to do her best for the boy, is he man enough to reciprocate her trust? And can the pair of them fend off ruthless law-enforcement types and near-psychotic hitmen? Slick, solid and saddled throughout with hackneyed motivation and implausible moments, Schumacher's film is both the best adaptation of a John Grisham novel to date, and a surprisingly suspenseful slice of escapist entertainment. Efficient fun, no more, no less. GA

Cliffhanger

(Renny Harlin, 1993, US) Sylvester Stallone, John Lithgow, Michael Rooker, Janine Turner, Rex Linn.
112 min.
There are some things a man just can't walk around. When Gabe Walker (Stallone) fails to stop a girl falling to her death, his nerve is broken and he leaves the Rocky Mountain Rescue Team and his lover Jessie (Turner). But a chance for redemption arises when he and now vengeful colleague Tucker (Rooker) are duped into 'rescuing' a motley gang of villains who have lost three stolen Treasury coffers in an air crash in the high peaks. Director Harlin makes the most of the scenery, but seldom manages to induce a tingling sense of vertigo. Fun for the undemanding, but Stallone's 'comeback' should have been much tighter. GA

Climax (Ich – das Abenteuer
heute eine Frau zu sein)

(Roswitha vom Bruck, 1972, WGer) Renate Carol, Frank Glaubrecht, Ingo Baerow, B ert Hochschwarzer.
89 min.
Husband Karl is none too good in bed, so Monika's GP advocates masturbation. Friend suggests, 'You'd better get a lover. After all, you can't keep masturbating all your life,' and there's the GP waiting to transport her to full awareness to the accompaniment of a wavering trumpet solo. Not that much to indicate that *Climax* was the first sex film to be directed by a woman. Vom Bruck makes a few jokes at the expense of an expectant male audience, but fights a losing battle against the banality of the acting and a script which comes up with such remarks as 'Any man who makes love to you once would never let you get away,' and so tries to compensate by handling the whole thing with a certain Teutonic relentlessness. CPe

Clinic, The

(David Stevens, 1982, Aust) Chris Haywood, Simon Burke, Gerda Nicolson, Rona McLeod, Suzanne Roylance.
92 min.
An Australian comedy about the clap is bound to produce premature conclusions. In fact, this is a million kangaroo hops from the chundering humour of Barry McKenzie and similarly broad Ozports. If it weren't for the obviously still taboo nature of the subject matter, the film would be an excellent TV series pilot, a medical cousin to *Barney Miller*. Strong playing from the amiable Haywood as the harassed gay doctor in charge, Burke as his potentially rednecked student trainee. The laughter is infectious, and there aren't too many herpes jokes. GD

Cloak and Dagger

(Fritz Lang, 1946, US) Gary Cooper, Lilli Palmer, Robert Alda, Vladimir Sokoloff, Helene Thimig, J Edward Bromberg.
106 min. b/w.
Tolerably exciting, but despite some electric moments (the shockingly casual execution of Thimig, a brutal fight in an alley conducted in death like silence), a conventional World War II espionage thriller and far from Lang at his best. Cooper, morosely miscast as a scientist serving with the OSS, spends most of the time trotting round Europe ensuring that the Nazis don't get the atom bomb and that he gets the girl. The version shot by Lang was considerably more doom-laden, carrying on in a lengthy coda to suggest that Nazi scientists had found the secret of atomic power, and escaped with it to Argentina or parts unknown. Then Warners got into the act, and cut for the happy ending. TM

Clock, The
(aka Under the Clock)

(Vincente Minnelli, 1945, US) Judy Garland, Robert Walker, James Gleason, Keenan Wynn, Lucille Gleason, Marshall Thompson.
90 min. b/w.
Minnelli's charming tale of office girl Garland and soldier Walker (on a two-day leave) meeting at New York's Penn Station and plunging into a whirlwind romance and marriage. Though it might seem a little too heart-warming for modern tastes, it is beautifully designed (with impressive studio sets) and performed, GA

Clockers

(Spike Lee, 1995, US) Harvey Keitel, Mekhi Phifer, Delroy Lindo, John Turturro, Isaiah Washington, Keith David, Pee Wee Love.
128 min.
Strike (Phifer) deals crack from the benches in front of the Brooklyn tenement where he grew up. Rodney (Lindo) has his protégé earmarked for big things, but he has to be blooded first: murder is Rodney's only insurance. Strike listens, but when his intended victim turns up dead, it's Strike's straight-arrow brother Victor (Washington) who confesses to the crime. Rodney isn't happy. That goes double for detective Klein (Keitel) who, unlike his partner Mazilli (Turturro), refuses to accept they've put away the real killer. Spike Lee's adaptation of Richard Price's novel cuts back on the cops' perspective but retains the essential overview of a society trapped in a cycle of despair. In an apparent reaction against the plethora of flashy 'hood' movies his success helped spawn, Lee has toned down the snap of his montage, muted his saturated mise-en-scène in favour of streetlight chiaroscuro, and co-opted jerky, handheld zooms from cinéma vérité. Scored largely to plaintive soul tracks (Seal, Marc Dorsey), the result is a more sober, mournful and meditative expressionism than you'd expect. That's not to say the film isn't suspenseful, but the director's distaste for the inner city's gun culture is clear to see. Superbly acted. TCh

Clockmaker, The

see Horloger de St Paul, L'

Clockwise

(Christopher Morahan, 1985, GB) John Cleese, Alison Steadman, Sharon Maiden, Stephen Moore, Chip Sweeney, Penelope Wilton, Joan Hickson.
96 min.
Clock-watching comprehensive headmaster Mr Stimpson (Cleese) momentarily boards the wrong train when he sets out for a Headmasters' Conference in Norwich; the result, a never-ending nightmare as he's forced to hijack one of his sixth-formers, complete with her parents' car, and to travel hell-for-leather across the Midlands countryside. Much of Michael Frayn's original screenplay might seem like routine farce, were it not for the furious pace and level of invention in terms of both plot and dialogue. But what finally makes it consistently amusing is, of course, Cleese. GA

Clockwork Mice

(Vadim Jean, 1994, GB) Ian Hart, Catherine Russell, Joseph Gordon-Levitt, John Alderton, Ruaidhri Conroy, Claire Skinner, Art Malik, James Bolam.
100 min.

A novice teacher, Steve (Hart), arrives at a special-needs school just in time to see one of his charges hurtling along a high-wire and dive bombing kamikaze-style some poor teacher's 2CV. Such 'spirited' behaviour turns out to be par for the course at a school, where survival depends on a certain amount of laissez-faire. Steve's thankless attempts to instill a sense of poetry in the kids look doomed, but when he challenges charismatic ne'er-do-well Conrad (Conroy) to a cross-country run he captures the imagination of the school. The film takes 'difficult' raw material and puts it to the service of middlebrow feelgood entertainment. It mostly soft-pedals the trauma of emotional violence and plays the physical variety for (admittedly black) comedy. Hart is a tremendously vigorous, alert screen presence, and Conroy's bruised sensitivity is equally expressive. Prettily photographed and handled with considerable assurance, the film runs up a head of steam, but not much more. TCh

Clockwork Orange, A

(Stanley Kubrick, 1971, GB) Malcolm McDowell, Patrick Magee, Michael Bates, Warren Clarke, John Clive, Adrienne Corri, Carl Duering.
136 min.
Kubrick's film exploited the current debate on the validity of aversion therapy in the context of a working lad's freedom to choose violence as his form of self-expression. A sexless, inhuman film, whose power derives from a ruthless subordination of its content to the demands of telling a good story. A glossy, action-packed ritual which is fun to watch but superficial to think about.

Clonus

see Parts: The Clonus Horror

Closed Circuit
(Circuito Chiuso)

(Giuliano Montaldo, 1978, It) Flavio Bucci, Aurore Clément, Ettore Manni, Brizzio Montinaro, Giuliano Gemma, William Berger.
105 min.
The central idea of Closed Circuit – an audience watches a spaghetti Western in a cinema; as it finishes the gunman on screen shoots and a member of the audience drops dead with a bullet hole in his chest – is just fine. Sadly, the film proceeds to dissipate its generic thriller elements in stodgy Italian stereotyping and overplaying, while never quite having the courage to fully develop its philosophical pretensions about the spectator and the screen. Unable to resolve its dilemma, it opts for an unsatisfying mish-mash of half-baked notions and presents it as a climax. SM

Close Encounters
of the Third Kind

(Steven Spielberg, 1977, US) Richard Dreyfuss, François Truffaut, Teri Garr, Melinda Dillon, Bob Balaban, Warren Kemmerling.
135 min.
Close Encounters takes the favoured dream of every UFO enthusiast (that the US government has been operating a cover-up) and turns it into a majestic and finally unprecedented adventure story. As early references to The Ten Commandments and Chuck Jones's Warner cartoons show, the film seems less concerned with science fiction than with recapturing the wonder of a child's first experience of the cinema, and the surprising thing is that Spielberg moves into this territory so effectively. There are some awkward touches (Truffaut never ceases to be Truffaut, while some of the comedy scenes are a little overplayed), but they're small price to pay for the first film in years to give its audiences a tingle of shocked emotion that is not entirely based either on fear or on suspense. DP

Close Encounters of the
Third Kind – Special Edition

(Steven Spielberg, 1977/80) Richard Dreyfuss, François Truffaut, Teri Garr, Bob Balaban, Warren Kemmerling.
132 min.
The years since 1977 have shrunk Star Wars, but Close Encounters looks more classic than ever, an insane burst of cinematic optimism which somehow combines Disney and '50s SF and the imagery of junk food into the most persuasive (if arrested) version of the American dream yet accomplished.

Now Spielberg has added some new special effects, but more importantly, he has cut and altered the central section concerning Dreyfuss' obsession with the image of Devil's Tower, Wyoming. These scenes, formerly hysterical and unconvincing, are now more potent, leaving Truffaut's slightly mannered performance as one of the film's few awkward areas. It is now also easier, following Spielberg's 1941, to see why Close Encounters works so well: the child's bedroom scene where all the toys come alive has more adrenalin in it than a dozen demolitions. DP

Closely Observed Trains
(Ostre Sledované Vlaky)

(Jiri Menzel, 1966, Czech) Václav Neckár, Jitka Bendova, Vladimir Valenta, Josef Somr.
92 min. b/w.
A real charmer from the heyday of the Czech New Wave, set during the German occupation but totally immersed in the pubescent problems of a youth (as uncannily reminiscent of Buster Keaton as the boy in Olmi's Il Posto) taking up his first job as an apprentice railway platform guard with the firmly anti-social resolve to do as little work as possible while others slave. Wonderfully funny observation of the sleepy little backwater depot where nothing ever happens, and he maintains his resolve while hero-worshipping a philandering older guard (who whiles away the time by rubber-stamping the hindquarters of a delighted girl), avoiding the station-master (who emerges now and again to cry Sodom and Gomorrah before returning to his pigeons), and carrying on an unconsummated flirtation with the conductress of a passing train. The Resistance beckons, but ejaculatio praecox is still his most pressing problem. An airy pointilliste comedy, but it celebrates a whole universe of frustration, eroticism, adventure and romance. TM

Close My Eyes

(Stephen Poliakoff, 1991, GB) Alan Rickman, Clive Owen, Saskia Reeves, Karl Johnson, Lesley Sharp, Kate Gartside, Karen Knight.
108 min.
Poliakoff's second film as a director marks a distinct change in tone from his rather more languid earlier pieces. It begins in a café full of signals of decay – a ketchup squirter has a rotten tooth inside – and moves forward in time and affluence as brother and sister Richard and Natalie (Owen and Reeves), parted in childhood by divorce, reunite one blistering summer for a torrid, incestuous affair. 'Being single – it's not as simple as it used to be,' declares Richard to his sister one riverside evening. Given that he's rogering her, not only helping her to cheat on husband Rickman (a superbly dynamic performance) but also putting off a visit to his boss who's dying of AIDS, this is some understatement. Despite its obsession with covering up Owen's cock, this is steamy and passionate stuff. As well as the forbidden love theme, the film is also about the end of the '80s, and is full of intelligent insights into physical and moral decay, contrasting the squalor and bathos of the city with the cloistered joys of suburban greenery. SGr

Close Shave, A

(Nick Park, 1995, GB)
30 min.
Park's claymation film follows an Ealing-esque comedy-with-sinister-undertones scenario. The adventure centres on the case of the disappearing sheep. Northern gadget-meister Wallace and his hound Gromit have taken up window-cleaning, and it isn't long before Wallace is swept off his feet by the owner of the local wool shop, Wendolene Ramsbottom. Amateur sleuth Gromit, meanwhile, investigates the mysterious movements of her shifty-looking dog, Preston. Extremely engaging, very funny and perfectly paced (plus nods to Batman and The Terminator). DA

Closet Land

(Radha Bharadwaj, 1991, US) Madeleine Stowe, Alan Rickman.
89 min.
This highly stylised drama is resolutely theatrical: with the exception of fleeting flashbacks and fantasy sequences, the action is confined to one austere interior, and revolves around a political interrogation. Stowe plays a bewildered, nameless children's author taken from her bed in the

middle of the night to face questioning by a government official (Rickman). She stands accused of 'subliminal indoctrination' in her book 'Closet Land', which explores the liberating force of the imagination. But subversion is far from the writer's mind: under torture, her creations are shown to provide redemption from her traumatised childhood. Writer/director Bharadwaj's debut offers appropriately brutal, intense exchanges, with Rickman's commanding performance quite overshadowing Stowe. But such a stage-bound project demands a stronger script, while the lack of identifiable names and political targets compromises a powerful subject. CM

Close to Eden
(Sidney Lumet, 1992, US) Melanie Griffith, Eric Thal, John Pankow, Tracy Pollan, Lee Richardson, Mia Sara.
109 min.
Detective Emily Eden (Griffith), already chastised for using excessive force, is assigned to investigate the disappearance of a Hasidic jeweller and a fortune in diamonds; when, after finding his corpse in the ceiling of his own office, she concludes that he knew his killer, with the permission of the Rebbe she goes undercover in the Hasidic community. Cue culture clash, romantic yearnings for improbably sensitive Rebbe-to-be Ariel (Thal), and a steadily growing disenchantment with the harsh ways of her own Gentile world. All too obviously influenced by *Witness*, the film fails on all counts. The lackadaisical plotting is frequently implausible, and the depiction of Hasidic warmth and integrity is not only embarrassingly rose-tinted but objectionable in its implied endorsement of the archaically subservient position of women. GA

Close to the Wind (Oss Emellan)
(Stellan Olsson, 1969, Swe) Per Oscarsson, Bärbel Oscarsson, Lina Oscarsson, Boman Oscarsson, Maria Oscarsson, Beppe Wolgers.
110 min.
Effectively low-key realism in a naturalistic account of a none-too-successful artist and sculptor who comes into conflict with society at large when his only patrons – a bureaucratic committee commissioning work for a company's centenary – subtly but steadily alter his original conception. It's all pretty thin, and stands or falls by its performances (largely amateur, including Oscarsson's own family), but it does have a certain charm that is never ingratiating. GA

Close-Up (Namayeh Nazdik)
(Abbas Kiarostami, 1989, Iran) Hossain Sabzian, Mohsen Makhmalbaf, Hossain Farazmand, Abdolfazl Ahankhah.
93 min.
Kiarostami's masterpiece is a rich, multi-layered but beautifully forthright film in which Sabzian (playing himself – a movie fanatic – in a story based on fact) pretends to a middle-class family likewise interested in cinema that he is film director Makhmalbaf (who also appears as himself). As the film alternates between scenes of Sabzian's trial for fraud and reconstructions of his encounters with the family and of a journalist's attempts to discover the truth, Kiarostami constructs a complex (but never complicated) series of interwoven narratives to interrogate notions of fiction and documentary, appearance and reality, truth and falsehood. It's enormously intelligent stuff, witty, poignant and thoroughly engrossing, and ends with one of the sharpest, funniest deconstructions of film form ever shot. Absolutely wonderful. GA

Closing Numbers
(Stephen Whittaker, 1993, GB) Tim Woodward, Jane Asher, Frank Mills, Hazel Douglas, Jamie Glover, Patrick Pearson, Nigel Charnock.
95 min.
A comfortable family is thrown in turmoil by infidelity and the spectre of HIV in this Channel 4 movie. Jane Asher's the housewife whose routine existence is ruptured by the shock discovery of husband Woodward's on-going affair with a male lover (Pearson), who in turn is understandably shaken up by caring for his close friend Charnock as he suffers through the advanced stages of full-blown AIDS. Scriptwriter David Cook (who wrote C4's opening night film *Walter*) brings his customary sensitivity to bear on the subject matter,

and all concerned tackle their roles with dedication – not least dancer Nigel Charnock in a typically self-lacerating role – but the scale is still one of middle-class chamber drama, however tough-minded and concerned. TJ

Cloud-capped Star (Meghe Dhaka Tara)
(Ritwik Ghatak, 1960, Ind) Supriya Choudhury, Anil Chatterjee, Bijon Bhattacharya, Guita De, Gita Ghatak, Dwiju Bhawal, Niranjan Roy.
127 min. b/w.
The Bengali writer/director Ritwik Ghatak has been acclaimed as the most important Indian filmmaker after Satyajit Ray. The first part of a trilogy that included *E Flat* and *Subarnarekha*, this is a dark melodrama, set in Calcutta in the late '50s, in which Nita (Choudhury) struggles to keep her refugee family afloat and together. Her father, a teacher, earns a pittance; her elder brother dreams of becoming a famous singer; a younger brother is forced to abandon his studies and work in a factory; and her mother hopes that Sanat, the young scientist her eldest daughter loves, will transfer his affections to the younger Guita. For Western viewers it's perhaps most easily approached as a bitter critique of harsh social and economic conditions, particularly those arising from the 1947 Partition of East Bengal. More interesting cinematically, however, is Ghatak's inventive, not quite naturalistic treatment of the story: in order to underline or undercut certain elements in terms of narrative, theme and characterisation, the performances, images, music and, most especially, sound are given almost expressionist nuances. GA

Clouded Yellow, The
(Ralph Thomas, 1950, GB) Jean Simmons, Trevor Howard, Barry Jones, Sonia Desdel, Maxwell Reed, Kenneth More, Geoffrey Keen, Andre Morell, Richard Wattis.
96 min. b/w.
Eric Ambler had a hand in the script for this unsurprising, but watchable sub-Hitchcock British thriller, which has Howard as a former spy getting himself into hot water after he goes off to catalogue the butterfly collection of the eccentric Jones. When Simmons, his new employer's daughter, is accused of murdering the handyman who's molested her, Howard spirits the girl away and sets about hunting the real killer. TJ

Clown Must Laugh, A
see Pagliacci

Clowns, The (I Clowns)
(Federico Fellini, 1970, It/Fr/WGer) Riccardo Billi, Tino Scotti, Fanfulla, Carlo Rizzo, Freddo Pistoni.
92 min.
Fellini's documentary celebration of the dying art of the clown is his best film in years. As overtly personal as his autobiographical *Roma*, it has little of the self-indulgence of that film, mainly because of Fellini's relentless pursuit of his elusive subject. Made for the RAI TV company, it includes much interview material with once-famous clowns now long forgotten; reconstructions of scenes from Fellini's own childhood, attempting to explain his obsessive fascination with the circus; and a final tribute to the clowns themselves, a slapstick funeral staged in a circus ring. The final image in this funeral sequence, with pathetic trumpet music across an empty ring, is memorably touching. DP

Club, The
(Bruce Beresford, 1980, Aust) Frank Wilson, Harold Hopkins, Jack Thompson, Alan Cassell, Graham Kennedy.
99 min.
The Australian cinema in noisy rather than nostalgic mood, indulging a series of lusty bawling bouts (interspersed with *Match of the Day* views of Aussie rules football and its supporters) in a caustic look at the power struggles threatening to disrupt a Melbourne club. Based on a play by David Williamson (who scripted *Don's Party* for Beresford), it's all predictable stuff, but vigorously performed. TM

Club, The (Wuting)
(Kirk Wong, 1981, HK) Chan Wai-Man, Tsui Siu-Keung, Mabel Kwong, Miyai Haru.
90 min.

This first feature by a young Hong Kong director is an ultra-violent Triad thriller about gang warfare in the sleazier back streets of Kowloon. Characters (macho men and exploited women) are as stereotyped as they come, but plus factors include very stylish visuals, a couple of interesting performances, and a considerable sense of humour. RG

Clubbed to Death
(Yolande Zauberman, 1997, Fr/Port/Neth) Elodie Bouchez, Roschdy Zem, Béatrice Dalle, Richard Courcet, Alex Descas, Gérald Thomassin, Julie Bataille.
88 min.
Lola (Bouchez) falls asleep on a bus and wakes up at the end of the line, in the Parisian 'burbs. She wanders into a cavernous techno club – a barrage of sound and strobing lights – where someone slips her a pill. She becomes involved with a French Arab, Emir (Zem), and returns the next day to look for him in this strange, alien, nocturnal world. The film all but dispenses with dialogue: atmosphere is everything in this minimalist foray into exotic youth culture. This may be full of fascinating insights for sheltered over-40s (if they're interested), but the club scene is hardly uncharted territory for the rest of us. There's something deeply old fashioned about what passes for narrative here, and little else to hold the attention – a tab might relieve the tedium. TCh

Club de Femmes
(Jacques Deval, 1936, Fr) Danielle Darrieux, Valentine Tessier, Josette Day, Eve Francis, Elise Argal.
91 min. b/w.
This French farce suggests that *mesdemoiselles* who sleep around are redeemable, cops a peep at one-and-a-half pairs of breasts, and turns up an unmistakeable lesbian character. Set in a chastely run hotel for women, it traces the fortunes of various young residents of burgeoning sexual impulses: representing the dark side of female sexuality are a student lured into prostitution by the devious hotel telephone operator, and a bookish beauty who kills to avenge a crime against her beloved. But the tale of the spirited dancer (Darrieux), who smuggles her fiancé into the hotel and ends up pregnant, overrides the film's more serious implications to arrive at conclusions of Hollywood-style wholesomeness. Playful, energetic, and sustaining a high level of female hysteria, the movie is certainly camp, often riotously funny, and nostalgically enjoyable, but don't expect feminist leanings just because a lesbian's around. EP

Clue
(Jonathan Lynn, 1985, US) Eileen Brennan, Tim Curry, Madeline Kahn, Christopher Lloyd, Michael McKean, Lesley Ann Warren.
87 min.
The biggest mystery is why anyone should adapt Waddington's Cluedo board game for the screen in the first place. It is New England in 1954, and *Clue* posits a cast of characters only marginally more fleshed out than their plastic counterparts, stuck with a butler in an old dark house as guests of a Mr Boddy who is blackmailing them all and duly gets offed. The corpse count mounts, the lights go on and off, everyone runs from room to room. The plot looks as though it had been devised by dice-throwing. All concerned should go directly to jail. AB

Clueless
(Amy Heckerling, 1995, US) Alicia Silverstone, Stacey Dash, Brittany Murphy, Paul Rudd, Donald Faison, Elisa Donovan, Wallace Shawn, Twink Caplan, Dan Hedaya.
98 min.
Heckerling still appears to edit her movies by random select, and, despite reference to Jane Austen's *Emma*, her narrative is anorexic; but this satiric portrait of California rich kids has plenty of charm and wit, and a winning central performance from Silverstone. Cher, 15, is a designer mall rat with a world view several sizes narrower than her vanity mirror, but a heart as big as her dad's bank account. During a typically unexacting term at Beverly Hills High, Cher adopts newcomer Tai (Murphy) and teaches her how to be a 'Betty' (a she-babe), falls for a 'Baldwin' (a he-babe), and learns that "tis a far, far better thing, when you do stuff for other peo-

ple.' There's something downright perverse about the romantic fade-out Heckerling engineers between Cher and her stepbrother, and the philanthropic message is almost as superficial as the rampant materialism which precedes it, but Silverstone makes Cher's insularity appealingly innocent (even in the midst of crisis, she can't resist checking out the latest fashion lines), and an attempted seduction scene is sweetly hopeless. TCh

Cluny Brown
(Ernst Lubitsch, 1946, US) Charles Boyer, Jennifer Jones, Peter Lawford, Reginald Gardiner, Reginald Owen, Richard Haydn.
100 min. b/w.
Lubitsch's last film and one of his most engaging comedies, with Jones and Boyer surprisingly well-teamed as the plumber's niece (later housemaid) and the Czech refugee who throw English society into a tizzy with their disregard for conventions, while simultaneously allowing Lubitsch to take a few digs at well-meaning liberals. The satire, though taking in snobbery upstairs, downstairs and in the middle classes, doesn't exactly bite, but is given a jolly run around by a cast comprising most of Hollywood's British stalwarts from Sir C Aubrey Smith to Sara Allgood and Una O'Connor. TM

Coal Miner's Daughter
(Michael Apted, 1980, US) Sissy Spacek, Tommy Lee Jones, Levon Helm, Phyllis Boyens, Beverly D'Angelo.
124 min.
Beautifully acted (with Spacek winning an Oscar) rags-to-riches biopic of Country & Western singer Loretta Lynn, here working her way from the Kentucky coalfields, via the Grand Ol' Opry, to superstardom. For all the modern gloss, what with poverty and nervous breakdowns it's still highly conventional stuff, but lovingly constructed to produce unremarkable but heart-warming entertainment. GA

Coast to Coast
(Joseph Sargent, 1980, US) Dyan Cannon, Robert Blake, Quinn Redeker, Michael Lerner, Maxine Stuart.
94 min.
Cannon's husband is trying to get her declared insane. She clobbers her shrink with a bust of Freud and escapes from the fruitcake farm to hitch a cross-continental ride with a long-distance lorry-driver (Blake). Performances apart, the road movie that develops has its ups and downs, mostly downs. AB

Coast to Coast
(Sandy Johnson, 1986, GB) Lenny Henry, John Shea, Pete Postlethwaite, George Baker, Peter Vaughan, Cherie Lunghi.
96 min.
An often very funny blend of road movie, buddy-buddy comedy and thriller parody, Johnson's film is short on visual delights (it was made for TV) but full of fine performances, strong throwaway lines (courtesy Stan Hey), and deft off-the-wall touches. Shea and Henry make for a good double act as the AWOL US air force man and the soul-crazy Liverpudlian DJ who find themselves pursued by cops and murderous mobsters, as they travel from Merseyside, via the Lake District, to the Essex coast. Lively, sharp and fast, it also features a wondrous Tamla selection on the sound-track. GA

Cobb
(Ron Shelton, 1994, US) Tommy Lee Jones, Robert Wuhl, Lolita Davidovich, Ned Bellamy, Lou Myers, Stephen Mendillo, William Utay.
128 min.
In the years surrounding WWI, Ty Cobb was baseball's most successful player, but this dark, probing portrait isn't really a sports movie. It focuses on 1960, when the Georgia Peach had gone sour: a bitter, lonely old man intent on fostering his legend even as he knows that death is upon him. Summoning successful sports writer Al Stump (Wuhl) to write his biography, the ego-maniacal, cantankerous Cobb proceeds to dictate a hagiography. The reality is that Cobb's a bully, bigot and woman-beater. Shelton's film is about the nature of truth and popular myth, about the single-minded pursuit of glory, and the horrors

within. It's also very funny. Jones gives a grand-stand performance – this is his Patton, or even perhaps his Macbeth – as the pistol-packin', pill-poppin' Cobb, a monster who daren't look himself in the face, and refuses to apologise. TCh

Cobra, The
(Joseph Henabery, 1925, US) Rudolph Valentino, Nita Naldi.
6,895 ft. b/w.
A film which understandably disappeared after being laughed off the screen on its release. As an impoverished Italian count who comes to America to pursue his career as an 'indoor sheik', Valentino initially parodies his image with a nice sense of comic timing. But the script then saddles him with pure love, a best friend to hold camp hands with, and noble self-sacrifice. Thereafter the main amusement in a turgid melodrama is watching Valentino and Naldi (Queen of the Vampires) slipping into embarrassingly regulation poses as she plays cobra to his mesmerised lion. TM

Cobra (Le Saut de l'Ange)
(Yves Boisset, 1971, Fr/It) Jean Yanne, Senta Berger, Sterling Hayden, Giancarlo Sbragia, Gordon Mitchell, Raymond Pellegrin.
95 min.
Boisset is a usually reliable second-line French director best known for his conspiracy thrillers Plot and Le Sheriff. This early policier is pretty rudimentary revenge stuff revolving around electoral gang war in Marseilles, perked up by a few neat incidentals. Yanne returns from Laotian retirement when his family is wiped out by Sbragia, accompanied by his comic-reading 'commandos', while American friend Hayden plays piggy in the middle. PT

Cobra
(George Pan Cosmatos, 1986, US) Sylvester Stallone, Brigitte Nielsen, Reni Santoni, Andrew Robinson, Brian Thompson.
87 min.
With Stallone as a Dirty Harry-style cop, suffice it to say that there is not nearly enough violence. No one is eviscerated. The villains, all mumblers to a man, are not punished by having their tongues cut out. The body count is only somewhere in the high eighties – and most of these are simply gunned down with a deplorable lack of invention. Very little is done by way of eye-gouging, limb-crushing or tooth-extraction. There are only two points of interest. First, the wimpy liberal cop who wants to do everything by the book is played by Robinson, the man who was once the nastiest killer of the '70s, Scorpio in Dirty Harry. Second, Sly has good taste in cars: a chopped '49 Mercury lead-sled with Nitrous Oxide injection. CPea

Cobra Verde
(Werner Herzog, 1988, WGer) Klaus Kinski, King Ampaw, José Lewgoy, Salvatore Basile.
111 min.
Based on Bruce Chatwin's The Viceroy of Ouidah, this features another of Herzog's doomed outcasts in an alien environment. A farmer-turned bandit in early 19th century Brazil, Cobra Verde (Kinski) is exiled to West Africa to gather slaves while fending off the murderous cohorts of the mad king of Dahomey. Here Herzog's taste for spectacular exotica comes to the fore with extended scenes of mass activity: the restoration of a slave-fortress, tribal processions, a 1,000-strong Amazon army in training, mile after mile of a human telegraph line. Though less apocalyptical than usual, the imagery is as lavish as ever, but the film is wrecked by an underwritten narrative. Certainly, Herzog fulfills his aim of portraying Africa as a cruel, highly civilised continent – the clichés are his own rather than those of conventional movie iconography – but the picture of colonialism is woefully one-dimensional. Finally, however, the film's greatest shortcoming is its inability to stir the emotions. GA

Cobweb, The
(Vincente Minnelli, 1955, US) Richard Widmark, Lauren Bacall, Gloria Grahame, Charles Boyer, Lillian Gish, John Kerr, Oscar Levant, Susan Strasberg.
124 min.
One of the best of Minnelli's 50s dramas, set in an up-market psychiatric clinic with Widmark as the head man, Grahame as the unusually sexual wife and mother, Bacall as the unusually mater-

nal 'other woman'. It is this inversion which disrupts the paternal law and order of the clinic and the home: a worried Widmark appears to be losing his place in both, and only when the two women are back in conventional place can sanity be restored. Don't be put off by the crude surface Freudianism: it's fascinating, with fine performances. JCl

Coca Cola Kid, The
(Dusan Makavejev, 1985, Aust) Eric Roberts, Greta Scacchi, Bill Kerr, Max Gillies, Kris McQuade, Chris Haywood.
98 min.
One-time proud sex warrior and anarchist liberator of the libido, Makavejev has lost his bottle on The Coca Cola Kid. A Coke missionary arrives in Australia with the intention of ousting the local soft drinks king. Aside from the old man's shotgun methods of dissuasion, there are also the distractions of a rapacious Scacchi, a hotel waiter who thinks he's from the CIA, and the Oz fauna. As usual there are some incidental pleasures (among them a 'roo with its arm in a sling, and Scacchi continuing in her mission to spontaneously combust the male population of the planet). Against these, however, is a plot that goes AWOL in the interests of true love, and Roberts, as the kid from Coke, who is well on his way to becoming the world's worst actor. CPea

Cocaine (Mixed Blood)
(Paul Morrissey, 1984, Fr) Marilla Pera, Richard Ulacia, Angel David, Geraldine Smith, Ulrich Berr, Marcelino Rivera, Linda Kerridge.
99 min.
A Lower East Side Story of everyday drug dealers (filmed in English though a 'French' film). Down in Alphabet City, the queues stretch round the block, the cops turn a blind eye, and matriarch Rita La Punta, coming on like Carmen Miranda, surrounds herself with 14-year-old boys because they're too young to get sent down when they kill people. But Rita's Maceteros are being picked off by a rival gang, and her dumb son is being seduced from under her thumb by a floozie from uptown. Morrissey takes this world apart in typically deadpan style, and relies on character and dialogue to provide laughs (although viewers of a certain mentality might also chuckle at the sight of people being shot in the head or having ciggies stubbed out on their chests). For lovers of low-life and would-be sultans of sleaze. AB

Cocaine Fiends, The
(William A O'Connor, 1936, US) Lois January, Noel Madison, Sheila Manners, Dean Benton, Lois Lindsay, Eddie Phillips.
68 min. b/w.
A blatant piece of muck-raking made in obscure conditions in the '30s which delivers its nominal anti-drugs theme with comical relish. A rake's progress of drug-induced degeneracy starts promisingly, but then gets rather bogged down in the banalities of the film's outlook, with the cocaine itself increasingly a side issue.

Cockfighter
(Monte Hellman, 1974, US) Warren Oates, Richard B Shull, Harry Dean Stanton, Ed Begley Jr, Laurie Bird, Troy Donahue, Warren Finnerty, Millie Perkins, Charles Willeford.
83 min.
Charles Willeford's adaptation of his own novel, shot on authentic locations, with Oates as the obsessive trainer of prize fighting cocks who undertakes a vow of silence after the defeat of his best bird. Even bleaker than Two Lane Blacktop, what emerges is what Phil Hardy has called 'one of the most explicit studies of repression that the American cinema has produced' (competitiveness as a substitute for sex). Its commercial failure in the States was hardly surprising. Hellman's films, always terminal in their implications, have been edging closer and closer to self-destruction. Cockfighter in many ways carries the stamp of a 'last' movie. Indeed, Hellman has directed only one since. CPe

Cockleshell Heroes
(José Ferrer, 1955, GB) José Ferrer, Trevor Howard, Victor Maddern, Anthony Newley, David Lodge, Peter Arne, Dora Bryan.
97 min.
As the Empire blew away on the winds of change, a spate of films celebrating Britain's heroic

achievements in WWII attracted huge box-office success. Bond producer Cubby Broccoli proved adept at finding the right formula: pipe-smoking humanitarian Ferrer battles it out with embittered disciplinarian Howard while tough sergeant-major Maddern licks the bunch of good-for-nothing 'volunteers' into a crack fighting force for a glorious Technicolor finale (breaking the blockade of Bordeaux by limpet-mining German battleships). Fortunately there's more. Ferrer directs with a freshness of vision which cuts through the usual coy clichés, and Howard's magnificently bad-tempered performance lifts the film a degree beyond jingoistic flag-waving. RMy

Cockroach, The (Böcek)

(Ümit Elçi, 1995, Tur) Halil Ergün, Nurseli Idiz, Füsun Demirel, Meltem Cumbal.
91 min.
A cod-Freudian drama (from a novel by Erhan Bener) about an Istanbul police chief who dreams back over his life while dying in an ambulance bound for hospital. His pathological hatred of cockroaches seems to be a metaphor for the fascistic imbalance of his mind. His harsh treatment as a young man and the blame that accrued to him for the fiery death of his sister are presented as the motors for his own brutality. (We see him abusing prisoners, but what is the sequence in which he hunts down Leninist revolutionaries meant to be about?) Less clear are his reasons for marrying a slatternly asthmatic young woman who refuses him sex, love and respect. From the evidence here Istanbul seems in a severe state of run-down, unless that's meant to be another expressionistic device. A far from rosy picture of Turkey. Shame about the grating repetitive piano score. WH

Cocktail

(Roger Donaldson, 1988, US) Tom Cruise, Bryan Brown, Elisabeth Shue, Lisa Banes, Laurence Luckinbill, Kelly Lynch, Gina Gershon.
103 min.
If a visitor from Mars needed a crash course in sexism, this would serve. Freshly demobbed, Brian Flanagan (Cruise) takes a Greyhound to NYC, hell-bent on self-improvement. He enlists in business school, but soon concludes that 'notta goddam thing those professors say makes any difference on the streets'. Brian opts instead to imbibe wisdom (and vast quantities of alcohol) at the feet of grizzled bartender Doug (Brown), a would-be guru of the *in vino veritas* school. Soon Bri is the most dazzling barman on the Upper East Side, and finds that women fall for his bottle-juggling technique and 'killer' smile (permanent rictus is nearer the mark). When he finds his true love (Shue) – no make-up, a 'good' girl – she immediately becomes dependent, cries a lot, and becomes pregnant. Conveniently she's also massively rich. The inevitable occurs, and a long happy future of monogamy, money-making and self-righteousness is in the offing. A tale of cock, signifying nothing. RS

Cocoanuts, The

(Joseph Santley/Robert Florey, 1929, US) The Marx Brothers, Kay Francis, Oscar Shaw, Mary Eaton, Margaret Dumont.
96 min. b/w.
The Brothers' first feature, for Paramount, adapted from their 1925 Broadway hit and set in a Florida hotel running wild with jewel thieves, romantic leads, dancing bellhops, a stately matron (Dumont), a conniving manager (Groucho) and assorted riff-raff (Harpo and Chico). It shows its age, what with indistinct sound, fluffed lines, quaint choreography, quainter songs, a stilted supporting cast and positively arthritic direction. But the Brothers' energy and madness is never in question: when the laughs come, they come loud and long. GB

Cocoon

(Ron Howard, 1985, US) Don Ameche, Wilford Brimley, Hume Cronyn, Brian Dennehy, Jack Gilford, Maureen Stapleton, Jessica Tandy, Gwen Verdon.
117 min.
A trio of old folks are in the habit of sneaking out from their wrinkly refuge for dips in the pool next door. But there are amiable aliens about (in human skinsuits) turning the pool into a veritable fountain of youth. Soon the oldsters are shrug-

ging off their creeping senility. All this might have been unseemly and embarrassing were it not for no-nonsense performances from spunky old veterans like Ameche and Brimley. But even they cannot prevent the film from lapsing into cringe territory towards the end. AB

Cocoon: The Return

(Daniel Petrie, 1988, US) Don Ameche, Wilford Brimley, Courtney Cox, Hume Cronyn, Jack Gilford, Steve Guttenberg, Maureen Stapleton, Elaine Stritch, Jessica Tandy, Gwen Verdon, Linda Harrison, Brian Dennehy.
116 min.
Not a patch on *Cocoon*; what merit this sequel has comes entirely from the superb cast of veterans, with very little help from a script which seems to have been ghosted by Justice Shallow. The story is so badly recapitulated that anyone not familiar with the situation will wonder why some of the cast seem fitter than others. The rejuvenated leavers return to Earth for a visit, find Bernie (Gilford) suicidal in an old folks' home, and fix him up with a merry widow (Stritch). Ben and Mary (Brimley, Stapleton) start to regret their grandson growing up. Art and Bess (Ameche, Verdon) miraculously conceive a child. Joe and Alma (Cronyn, Tandy) straddle what tension there is, since he will die if he stays. Ameche and Cronyn wring the heartstrings during all the emergency ward scenes. BC

Codename: The Soldier

see Soldier, The

Code of Silence

(Andrew Davis, 1985, US) Chuck Norris, Henry Silva, Bert Remsen, Mike Genovese, Nathan Davis, Molly Hagan.
101 min.
Chuck is very much the strong, silent type. People turn to him for advice when the chips are down: 'What do you do if you don't have someone?' sobs a woman-in-peril. 'You find someone' says Chuck. To be fair, a Chicago cop doesn't have to wax lyrical. What he does do is organise drug busts, rid the force of a trigger-happy old boozer, get beaten up, and prevent two gangs from wiping each other out by wiping out both gangs himself. It is all very moral. AB

Coeur qui bat, Un (Your Beating Heart)

(François Dupeyron, 1991, Fr) Dominique Faysse, Thierry Fortineau, Jean-Marie Winling, Steve Kalfa, Daniel Laloux, Christophe Pichon, Dominique Abel, Roland Amstutz.
99 min.
Eyes meet across a crowded Paris metro carriage. She gets out. Percussion builds. He follows her into a bar. 'Do you know a hotel around here?' They leave together. At least this starts with a teasing come-on, but it shares the problem faced by its central couple, Mado (Faysse) and Yves (Fortineau): how to recapture the thrill of that run-up to hot sex with a nameless stranger? Though she's not particularly interested after the deed is done, he gives her his phone number. She's married with a teenage son; husband Jean keeps a little antiques business ticking over, while she earns her crust acting in rather-too-pretentious radio plays. Perhaps that lightning strike of excitement is missing from her life, after all. It's a classic set-up. However, writer/director Dupeyron's flabby, uninspired treatment lets it go for almost nothing. As the couple trawl the Pigalle hotels and agonise over their uncertain future, one hopes for a shard of insight, another angle on the old eternal threesome that would lift the film from its torpor. In vain. TJ

Coeur en hiver, Un (A Heart in Winter) (100)

(Claude Sautet, 1991, Fr) Daniel Auteuil, Emmanuelle Béart, André Dussollier, Elisabeth Bourgine, Brigitte Catillon, Maurice Garrel, Myriam Boyer, Jean-Luc Bideau.
104 min.
On the surface, an unassuming, low-key study of a *ménage à trois* that never really takes off physically; dig deeper, however, and it's filled with dark, disturbing emotions and unsettling power-games. Stéphane (Auteuil) and Maxime (Dussollier) are old friends and partners in a violin-making business; Camille (Béart) is a concert

violinist and Maxime's lover, who comes increasingly to dominate the taciturn Stéphane's thoughts. As time passes, while she seems to respond to his apparent interest in her, he remains reticent: out of shyness, loyalty to Maxime, or something more perverse? What distinguishes the film is that Sautet and his excellent trio of leads manage to convey complex emotional nuances without resorting to explicit dialogue, plot contrivance, or hackneyed visual metaphor. Everything is underplayed, made manifest through subtle glances, brief but pregnant silences, the rhythms of the editing, the moody qualities of the lighting, and the occasional bursts of Ravel played by Camille. There's not an ounce of fat on this deceptively quiet movie, which at times achieves a real sense of pain and confusion. GA

Coffy

(Jack Hill, 1973, US) Pam Grier, Booker Bradshaw, Robert DoQui, William Elliott, Allan Arbus.
91 min.
Superficially just another black exploitation film (one of the first to feature a woman in a strong central role), *Coffy* is distinguished by its unremitting moral blackness. With a yellow press feel to the script and a welcome sexual frankness, the world Coffy inhabits is revealed as one where social, sexual and political exploitation are simply the norms. What makes the film is essentially the character of Coffy as played by Pam Grier with increasing alienation: a nurse out to get the men who are responsible for her little sister's addiction, she makes a conscious decision to manipulate the sexual situations which the men around her force her to engage in. It is a performance that defies and subverts the genre. VG

Cohen and Tate

(Eric Red, 1988, US) Roy Scheider, Adam Baldwin, Harley Cross, Cooper Huckabee, Suzanne Savoy.
86 min.
Eric Red, scriptwriter of *The Hitcher*, turns his hand to writing and directing for this suspenseful low-budget thriller. Both films revolve around the theme of innocent captured by raving sadist. Travis (Cross) is a nine-year-old boy who has witnessed an underworld killing. Cohen (Scheider) and Tate (Baldwin) are professional killers who must kidnap the boy and transport him from Oklahoma to their bosses in Houston. The nightmarish journey takes place at night, with the jaded taciturn Cohen increasingly angered by the lunatic ramblings of his violent sidekick. Added to this is their young hostage, who sets the men up against each other, and concocts various escape plans. Red does wonders with a simple budget and scenario; the sparsity of props and dialogue enhances the often brutal tension, while balance is struck with hefty doses of black humour. Cohen wears a hearing aid and dreams of retirement, while Tate chews matchsticks and 'has shit for brains': unlikely villains made credible by the context and Scheider's low-key performance. CM

Coilin & Platonida

(James Scott, 1976, GB) Marion Joyce, Seán Bán Breatnach, Katrina Joyce, Bairbre Bolustrom, Bairbre Mac Donncha.
86 min.
A transposition of Nikolai Leskov's folk-tale to an Irish setting (refilmed on 16 mm from the original on Super-8), broken up into elusive, ambiguous fragments and using silent movie-type intertitles to convey the dialogue. The result draws a parallel between the act of making a film and the act of picking up and passing on an existing story. Its conceptual challenges are augmented by a harsh, gloomy poetry, crystallised in the Gaelic lament that recurs on the soundtrack. TR

Cold Comfort

(Vic Sarin, 1989, Can) Maury Chaykin, Margaret Langrick, Paul Gross.
88 min.
A disturbed father rescues a businessman (Gross) from a blizzard, then takes him home as a birthday present for his nubile daughter. Apparently based on a cult fringe theatre piece, it's a disquietingly strange offering, powered along by big Maury Chaykin's gradually unravelling performance as the wacko paterfamilias. Former cinematographer Sarin sustains the oddball tension; but of interest chiefly to connoisseurs of the bizarre. TJ

Cold Comfort Farm

(John Schlesinger, 1995, GB) Kate Beckinsale, Eileen Atkins, Ian McKellen, Sheila Burrell, Rufus Sewell, Joanna Lumley, Freddie Jones, Stephen Fry, Miriam Margolyes.
103 min.

England in the '20s. Orphaned at the age of 19, middle-class Flora Poste determines to live off her relatives, rather than do anything so uncivilised as work. The only kin that remotely fit the bill are her distant cousins, the Starkadders, who work a decaying farm in Howling, Sussex, amid sundry yokels seemingly inhabiting another, Hardy-esque era. Made for the BBC, this woeful adaptation of Stella Gibbons' pastoral parody had success with American cinema audiences, who took it, perhaps, as just another British costume drama, rather than a comedy. Mind you, given Malcolm Bradbury's script and John Schlesinger's direction, which between them coarsen, soften and simply lose much of Gibbons' extraordinarily sophisticated, wonderfully funny humour, that's not surprising. The perfromances don't help much either, though that's less the fault of the very broad acting, than of the all-round starry miscasting (Lumley as Mrs Smiling, Fry as Mybug) – Kate Beckinsale in particular is far too sensible as the determined heroine. GA

Cold Dog Soup

(Alan Metter, 1989, US) Randy Quaid, Frank Whaley, Christine Harnos, Sheree North, Nancy Kwan, Pierre Epstein.
88 min.

A lusty young girl (Harnos) promises a wimpy boy (Whaley) that she will be his 'pressure cooker' if he agrees to bury her mother's recently deceased dog in the middle of the night. But his efforts are thwarted by a psychotic cabbie (Quaid), who insists that they sell the dog, and drags the couple on a tour of local nightspots in search of customers. What follows is the cinematic equivalent of water torture, a throbbing migraine of a movie in which our heroes encounter a catalogue of racial stereotypes, all wanting to know 'What's in the bag?' Chinese restaurateur, Jewish furrier, gang of trigger-happy brothers, voodoo coven of frenzied black zombies.. no stone is left unturned by Thomas Pope's horribly repetitive script, or by Alan Metter in his drivelling attempt to create a surreal comic nightmare. Kill yourself rather than endure it. MK

Cold Eye, The

(Babette Mangolte, 1980, US) Kim Ginsberg, Patricia Caire, Paula Court, Ghislaine Caire, George Deem.
90 min. b/w.

The New York art world as seen through the 'cold eye' of another of Mangolte's knowing heroines, a thoroughly modern *Manhattan Maisie* whose vision and experiences we're again invited to share. But the distance implied by the choice of this fictional protagonist, the strangeness of having her friends and acquaintances converse direct-to-camera, the opening titles ironically appraising each in turn, all promise a critical perspective that somehow isn't achieved. James Barth's flaccid script has a lot to answer for. One's heart sinks as the voice-over mournfully intones, 'Why am I so alienated?', and after a long ninety minutes of narrative devoted to assorted bores minutely scrutinising their own sensibilities, one feels that it wasn't nearly ironic enough, and wonders whether this is where so-called *avant-garde* cinema really ought to be. SJo

Cold Feet

(Robert Dornhelm, 1989, US) Keith Carradine, Sally Kirkland, Tom Waits, Bill Pullman, Rip Torn, Kathleen York, Macon McCalman, Vincent Schiavelli.
94 min.

Thomas McGuane fans are in for a treat with this typically off-the-wall tale of obsessives, oddballs and psychos, set in the New West. Reluctant to marry voracious Maureen (Kirkland) and keen to settle down with his folks in Dead Rock, Montana, Monte (Carradine) suddenly abandons partner-in-crime Kenny (Waits), a mass-murderer and would-be executive with whom he has smuggled a stallion, its gut full of emeralds, over the Mexican border. The first half, with Maureen and Kenny joining up to hunt down Monte, plays deliciously anarchic variations on road movie clichés; while the second (Sheriff Rip Torn gets suspicious of the three strangers in town) effectively parodies the small town Western. As written by McGuane and Jim Harrison, characters, situations and dialogue are colourfully eccentric *and* strangely plausible: the madness and mayhem are mere matters of detail, while the overview of contemporary outlaw life is surprisingly cogent. That the film is less messy than earlier McGuane adaptations is due partly to the uniformly engaging OTT acting, partly to Dornhelm's firm but light control of the proceedings. Utterly crazed, utterly charming. GA

Cold Fever

(Fridrik Thór Fridriksson, 1994, Ice/Ger/Switz/US) Masatoshi Nagase, Gisli Halldórsson, Fisher Stevens, Lili Taylor, Seijun Suzuki.
107 min.

This Icelandic odyssey reveals Japanese star Nagase (who first came to notice in the West in Jim Jarmusch's *Mystery Train*) to be a screen actor of deceptive skill and enterprise. Here he's stoicism itself, and the core of the picture, as a Tokyo fish-company salaryman who follows the advice of his grandfather (Suzuki) and travels to Iceland to perform authentic funeral rites for his geologist parents, who died there more than a decade ago. He meets all sorts en route – including a kindly local (Halldórsson, most sympathetic) and a bickering American couple (Stevens and Taylor). But in the end, this is a quirky, touching road movie that actually goes somewhere; its culmination is a striking spiritual affirmation and personal epiphany at journey's end. A one-off that lodges in the memory. TJ

Cold Heaven

(Nicolas Roeg, 1990, US) Theresa Russell, Mark Harmon, James Russo, Talia Shire, Will Patton, Richard Bradford.
105 min.

Roeg's adaptation of Brian Moore's novel fuses deeply felt emotions and religious ideas into a gripping metaphysical thriller that is both moving and intellectually challenging. On holiday in South America, Russell tries to tell her husband (Harmon) about her infidelity with Russo; but before she can do so, he is hit by a boat while swimming and declared dead. When Harmon's body subsequently disappears, avowed atheist Russell is plunged into a maelstrom of guilt, self-doubt and confusion. Sadly, for all its technical brilliance and narrative assurance, the film's climactic scenes require an act of faith that no film-maker – Christian, agnostic or atheist – has any right to ask. NF

Colditz Story, The

(Guy Hamilton, 1954, GB) John Mills, Eric Portman, Christopher Rhodes, Lionel Jeffries, Bryan Forbes, Ian Carmichael, Richard Wattis, Frederick Valk.
97 min. b/w.

The temptation to label this escapist entertainment is just too great. Actually, it's a prosaically inspirational docu-drama on PoW heroism in the notorious World War II fortress, which unambitiously substitutes an obliquely nationalist self-portrait for the critical resonances of an ostensibly similar film like *La Grande Illusion*. PT

Cold Light of Day, The

(Fhiona Louise, 1989, GB) Bob Flag, Martin Byrne Quinn, Geoffrey Greenhill, Lol Coxhill.
81 min.

A very lightly disguised drama-doc on Cranley Gardens serial killer Denis Nielsen (here named Jordan March), who disposed of at least 13 young loners and losers, presumably based on Brian Masters' fine account in his book *Killing for Company*. March (Flag) looks like Roy Orbison wearing a Black-and-White Minstrels wig; the film has the lighting and look of an Andy Warhol home movie – heads cut off, lots of static shots of men on sofas – and a soundtrack composed of deep breathing, the pounding of a demolition ball, and church bells. Little light is thrown by March in the police interrogations on the reasons for his actions ('I didn't mean to. It just happened') or by the film itself. We see March as a boy, presumably traumatised by witnessing the death of his grandfather. Mostly we see strangulations, heads being boiled, viscera being scooped, hands being hacked. Risibility vies with banality; result, objectionability. WH

Cold Nights
(Soguk Geceler)

(Kadir Sözen, 1995, Tur) Menderes Samancilar, Rahim Çakmak, Volkan Pinardag, Levent Elmas, Ferdi Çetinkaya, Engin Inal.
88 min.

This gritty tale of child labour in contemporary Turkey, slight but reasonably engaging, follows three junior folk musicians from gig to gig, sleeping indoors or out according to the disposition of their manager Mahmud, who treats them with a combination of concern, cruelty and chicanery. The future looks promising when they incorporate an older blind boy with an ear-catching voice: they tour, and the boys develop plans of their own, but the boss has his own livelihood in mind. If the film has little time for Mahmud, the director shows an unsensational feel for the plight of children forced into employment and adulthood. More perplexing are occasional bizarre nightmare interludes: not only opaque, in visibility and meaning, but also (interrupting the low-key realism) lapsing into hot-blooded melodrama. NB

Cold Sweat
(De la Part des Copains)

(Terence Young, 1970, Fr/It) Charles Bronson, Liv Ullmann, James Mason, Michel Constantin, Jill Ireland, Jean Topart.
94 min.

Uneasy English language version of a turgid continental thriller. Nominally based on Richard Matheson's very competent early novel *Ride the Nightmare*, which is butchered to yield the usual drearily violent routine about vengeance between crooks. TM

Cold Turkey

(Norman Lear, 1970, US) Dick Van Dyke, Pippa Scott, Tom Poston, Edward Everett Horton, Bob Newhart, Vincent Gardenia.
102 min.

Misbegotten satire of middle American attitudes in which an entire town, coerced by its reverend minister (Van Dyke), gives up smoking to win a $25 million bonanza. Irritation mounts as tiresome running gags run the symptoms of nicotine withdrawal into the ground . TM

Cold Water

see Eau Froide, L'

Collectionneuse, La
(The Collector)

(Eric Rohmer, 1966, Fr) Haydée Politoff, Patrick Bauchau, Eugène Archer, Seymour Hertzberg ie. Eugene Archer, Mijanou Bardot, Donald Cammell.
90 min.

The third of Rohmer's six moral tales, and the first of his films to achieve wide recognition. The collector of the title is a delectable nymphet, footloose in St Tropez, who makes a principle of sleeping with a different man every night until two friends, declining to become specimens, decide to take her moral well-being in hand. In the 18th century game which Rohmer transposes to a contemporary setting, this pair can be seen as intellect trying to dominate instinct, but only succeeding in rousing unwanted passions. Wryly and delightfully witty. TM

Collector, The

(William Wyler, 1965, US/GB) Terence Stamp, Samantha Eggar, Mona Washbourne, Maurice Dallimore.
120 min.

Wyler's adaptation of John Fowles' excruciatingly cunning first novel maintains a velvet-gloved grip throughout. A psychopathically repressed lepidopterist uses his football pool winnings to abduct a vibrant young art student and pin her down at all costs. Fowles extended the desperate captive-captor relationship into a multi-faceted metaphor, probing into everything from primal sexual politics and the class war to the responsibility of the artist and the dead soul of '60s England.

Collector, The

see Collectionneuse, La

College

(James W Horne, 1927, US) Buster Keaton, Ann Cornwall, Harold Goodwin, Snitz Edwards, Florence Turner, Grant Withers.
6 reels. b/w.

Minor Keaton but major almost any other comedian, and notably better than Harold Lloyd's *The Freshman*, whose plot it borrows, with bookworm Buster trying to prove himself a jock to win the girl. There is a marvellous sequence in which he apes – perfectly but disastrously – the tricks of a veteran soda-jerk; an even better one in which he attempts a decathlon of sporting events, but knocks down every single hurdle with metronomic precision, is thrown by the hammer instead of the other way round, etc. Rarely was Keaton's grace and athletic skill demonstrated so clearly, even if he (understandably) had to get a double to perform the great pole vault through a window to rescue the heroine from assault by her jock admirer. TM

Colonel Chabert, Le

(René Le Hénaff, 1943, Fr) Raimu, Marie Bell, Aimé Clairond, Jacques Baumer.
102 min. b/w.

Resurfacing in the wake of the Depardieu rendering, this turns out to be a prime example of how the same story can be construed differently, according to time and circumstance. In 1994, Balzac's tale seemed ideologically unexceptionable, with a faded representative of France's military glory denouncing the violence exercised in the name of *la patrie*, and finally withdrawing from a world that has defeated him, to live out a life of quiet resignation. Fifty years before, however, this must have seemed tailor-made for the occupying Nazis; even the flashbacks to the battle of Eylau would have found favour, since that showed a victory over the Russians. Only the film's status as a faithful adaptation of a literary classic mitigates the collaborationist charge. Less urgently, it's fascinating to compare the two Chaberts – Depardieu crashing around like a baffled bull, Raimu all icy disdain and calculated glimpses of pathos. BBa

Colonel Chabert, Le

(Yves Angelo, 1994, Fr) Gérard Depardieu, Fanny Ardant, Fabrice Luchini, André Dussollier, Daniel Prevost, Olivier Saladin, Maxime Leroux.
111 min.

Cinematographer Yves Angelo marks an auspicious directorial debut with this thoughtful, strongly cast adaptation of a tall tale by Balzac. Depardieu plays a man who's lost everything and left to wonder what life still has to offer: a dishevelled wreck, he wanders into the offices of lawyer Derville (Luchini) to unfold the incredible story of how he was left for dead in the Napoleonic campaigns; how he wandered across Europe for ten years before returning home; how his 'widow' (Ardant) is now a countess after her remarriage to Count Ferraud (Dussollier) – leaving Chabert no option but to reclaim his name and property through the processes of the law. Crackpot or victim of capricious fate? Conniving charlatan or visionary man of principle? It's to Depardieu's immense credit that his grandiloquent Chabert may be all, or any, of these things. Well worth investigating. TJ

Colonel Redl (Redl Ezredes)

(István Szabó, 1984, Hun/WGer/Aus) Klaus Maria Brandauer, Hans-Christian Blech, Armin Müller-Stahl, Gudrun Landgrebe, Jan Niklas.
149 min.

Redl is a man in an iron mask. At the expense of his poverty-stricken family, his Jewishness, homosexuality and friends, he makes a dramatic rise through the ranks of the feuding army of the crumbling Hapsburg Empire, only to discover, under the dyspeptic tutelage of the Archduke, that he will always be a suspicious, disposable intruder into the upper classes. Brandauer's towering performance minutely marks the gradual disintegration of Redl's mask and his final exposure at the point of death. Szabó's film is visually magnificent, shot with a crisp clarity which never succumbs to romantic nostalgia. The suicide of the real-life Redl was the subject of John Osborne's notorious *A Patriot for Me*. But where Osborne revelled in the decadence and debauchery, Szabó gives an extraordinary, chilling, complex account of a man's betrayal of himself. JE

Colorado Territory

(Raoul Walsh, 1949, US) Joel McCrea, Virginia Mayo, Dorothy Malone, Henry Hull, John Archer, Frank Puglia.
94 min. b/w.

A classic Western, this bleak remake of Walsh's own *High Sierra* substitutes McCrea's weary desperation for Bogart's laconic interpretation of the bandit who wants to go straight but signs up for 'just one more job'. Cinematographer Sid Hickox piles on the black to give it the look of a *film noir*, and writer John Twist creates a fitting atmosphere of doom around McCrea and Mayo, but it is Walsh's direction which brings this darkly romantic Western to life. The *bravura* treatment of landscape is particularly impressive, especially in the final sequence where his ant-sized humans meet their malevolent destiny amid barren mountains. PH

Color Me Blood Red

(Herschell Gordon Lewis, 1964, US) Don Joseph, Candi Conder, Scott H Hall, Elyn Warner, Patricia Lee.
74 min.

The first film to reach Britain made by the notorious Lewis, who shocked the US drive-in audiences of the '60s with some of the goriest films ever made, notably *Blood Feast* and *2000 Maniacs*. If this one is anything to go by, Lewis' films make *Friday the 13th* et al look like they were directed by Orson Welles. The narrative – about an artist who paints with human blood – is so token that it verges on abstraction, the acting is unspeakable, even the sound-track sometimes disappears. Set as it is in no kind of context, the mindless, sadistic gore seems all the more depressing, and the film itself becomes unwatchable. DP

Color of Honor, The

(Loni Ding, 1987, US)
101 min. b/w & col.

After Pearl Harbor, several hundred thousand Japanese-Americans were incarcerated in concentration camps. Later, young men drafted from these same camps played a key role in US military intelligence and in battle, while their families continued to be imprisoned back home and anti-Jap propaganda raged. Through extensive interviews with victims of the internment policy and war veterans, this thorough and compelling film highlights a previously undocumented injustice. EP

Color of Money, The

(Martin Scorsese, 1986, US) Paul Newman, Tom Cruise, Mary Elizabeth Mastrantonio, Helen Shaver, John Turturro, Bill Cobbs.
119 min.

25 years on, Fast Eddie Felson (Newman, repeating his role in *The Hustler*) is a part-time liquor salesman who keeps his interest in pool and hustling alive by staking players of promise. Enter Vince (Cruise), whose talents Eddie persuasively harnesses to his own experience *en route* to a nine-ball tournament in Atlantic City. Vince is likeable but arrogant, skilful but naïve, and what's more he's accompanied by a precocious girl-friend (Mastrantonio) who spreads her time between flirting with Eddie and massaging young Vince's cue (*Babushka* or otherwise). Anyone looking for a repeat of the immortal *The Hustler* will not only be disappointed but downright stupid: *The Color of Money* is a film for the '80s with many of that decade's strongest preoccupations. The mixture of mutual need and mistrust in the relationship between Vince and Eddie is only one of the motors in a film that sees Scorsese's direction at its most downmarket and upbeat – never have pool tables, balls and cues looked so rich and strange – and has one of the most protean and compelling music sound-tracks (Clapton, Charlie Parker, Warren Zevon, Bo Diddley, etc) in ages. As Eddie tells Vince, 'Pool excellence is not about excellent pool'; and in a scene in which Newman recoils from the thought that he is a Frankenstein, trying to recreate his own youth in the person of another, the whole meaning of the hustle, the game of life, becomes spectacularly clear. SGr

Color of Night

(Richard Rush, 1994, US) Bruce Willis, Jane March, Ruben Blades, Lesley Ann Warren, Scott Bakula, Lance Henriksen, Brad Dourif, Kevin J O'Connor, Jeff Corey.
123 min.

This – another of Willis's crimes against celluloid – is a special kind of bad. Connoisseurs of crud, however, will treasure its particular brand of klutzy chemistry. It would be unkind to give away too much of the delirious sequence of events that pass for a plot. Suffice to say that it involves hangdog Willis as a shrink understandably troubled by his patients' habit of jumping out the window during sessions; March as a so-called 'struggling actress' with whom Bruce becomes entangled; sundry scenes of murder, nymphomania, schizophrenia, etc; and, most enjoyably, the likes of Henriksen, Dourif and Warren as game members at a group therapy session, presumably intended for those unfortunates who can't spot a duff script to save their lives. TJ

Color Purple, The

(Steven Spielberg, 1985, US) Danny Glover, Whoopi Goldberg, Margaret Avery, Oprah Winfrey, Willard Pugh, Akosua Busia, Rae Dawn Chong.
154 min.

The adaptation of Alice Walker's Pulitzer Prize-winning novel, about growing up 'poor, female, ugly and black' in the Deep South, by a Middle American movie brat not hitherto noted for his interest in any of the above, could be cynically seen as a blatant (and botched) bid for Oscars. And it's easy – but unfair – to stamp on the Spielberg version of Celie's triumphant pursuit of happiness and self-respect. Example: Walker's clear, lyrical patois has been filmed with, well, purple pomposity, a battering ram of flashy editing and tearful emotion (the brutish husband played by Glover, whom Walker finally allows his own small epiphany, gets especially short shrift as yet another of the big, bad authority figures who stalk Spielberg's world). Nor is it altogether surprising that Spielberg treads delicately round the story's more radical elements, like Celie's Lesbian love for free-spirited blues singer Shug (Avery) or the political insights of her sister's African experience. And yet ... due in no small measure to a superb cast spearheaded by Whoopi Goldberg, this is a powerful and honourable attempt to wrest an unusual book into the populist Hollywood mainstream. SJo

Colors

(Dennis Hopper, 1988, US) Sean Penn, Robert Duvall, Maria Conchita Alonso, Randy Brooks, Grand Bush, Don Cheadle, Gerardo Mejia, Glenn Plummer, Sy Richardson, Trinidad Silva.
121 min.

Never as eccentric as *The Last Movie* or *Out of the Blue*, *Colors* nevertheless makes most other cop movies look formulary by comparison. Neither its plot – two mismatched cops take on LA's murderous gangs – nor its violence offer anything out of the ordinary. It wins out, rather, with a raw authenticity: gritty location shooting, plausibly inarticulate dialogue, a chaotic episodic narrative, and excellent performances. To a rather predictable master-pupil relationship, Duvall and Penn bring a refreshing lack of buddy-buddy sentimentality, while Hopper avoids sensationalism, rarely condemning or condoning, but providing a stark, even subtle investigation of misplaced loyalties and a moronic sense of honour. He also copes with car chases, stand-offs, and shootouts as efficiently as any director currently working in Hollywood. Finally, however, it's a film with heart; a moving, beautifully acted death scene at the end effortlessly evokes the sense of waste inevitable in a world of such random, unthinkingly violent macho pride. GA

Colossus of New York, The

(Eugène Lourié, 1958, US) John Baragrey, Mala Powers, Otto Kruger, Robert Hutton, Ed Wolff, Ross Martin.
70 min. b/w.

With the world doomed by over-population, a scientist decides that it's his duty to reanimate the brilliant brain of his dead son in a vast metallic structure. The plot gives out halfway through, but Lourié's visualisation of the monster's metallic agonies – much of them subjective – is cruel and potent. DP

Colossus of Rhodes, The (Il Colosso di Rodi)

(Sergio Leone, 1960, It/Sp/Fr) Rory Calhoun, Lea Massari, Georges Marchal, Mabel Karr, Conrado San Martin.
127 min.

By the time Leone was thirty, he'd worked on well over 50 muscle-and-sweat sagas, including *Helen of Troy*, *Quo Vadis?* and the chariot scene in *Ben Hur*. *The Colossus of Rhodes* was his first attempt at direction, and it was a film remarkable enough, at a time when the peplums had just about reached the end of their particular line, to warrant good notices for its crowd and spectacle scenes. (The Colossus itself is a sophisticated torture chamber hidden behind a persuasively artsy exterior.) After the film's success, Leone turned down attempts to channel him into the manufacture of superman heroics in the Maciste mode, and went back to 2nd Unit work on Aldrich's *Sodom and Gomorrah*.

Colossus of the Stone Age
see Maciste Contro i Mostri

Colossus – The Forbin Project
see Forbin Project, The

Colour of Pomegranates, The (Nran Gouyne) 100
(Sergo Paradjanov, 1969, USSR) Sofico Chiaureli, M Aleksanian, V Galstian, G Gegechkori.
80 min.
Originally refused an export licence, Paradjanov's extraordinary film traces the life of 18th century Armenian poet Sayat Nova ('The King of Song'), but with a series of painterly images strung together to form tableaux corresponding to moments of his life rather than any conventional biographic techniques. Pomegranates bleed their juice into the shape of a map of the old region of Armenia, the poet changes sex at least once in the course of his career, angels descend: the result is a stream of religious, poetic and local iconography which has an arcane and astonishing beauty. Much of its meaning must remain essentially specific to the culture from which the film springs, and no one could pretend that it's all readily accessible, but audiences accustomed to the work of Tarkovsky should have little problem. CPea

Colour of Pomegranates: Director's Cut, The (Nran Gouyne)
(Sergo Paradjanov, 1992, USSR) Sofico Chiaureli, M Aleksanian, V Galstian, G Gegechkori.
73 min.
Paradjanov's most famous film was always a headache for the old Soviet authorities: a queer and obviously dissident paean to the cultures of Armenia and Georgia framed as a spiritual biography of the mysterious 18th century poet Sayat Nova. Paradjanov shot it in 1969. The Kremlin was aghast; it had the film shortened and drastically restructured and didn't allow it out of the country until 1983. Here at last is the director's original *film maudit*, and it's every second the classic of camp/hieratic cinema it promised to be. The film flows uninterrupted from the poet's childhood to his physical death and spiritual resurrection. The 'story' is still told in gorgeously stylised tableaux crammed with Christian and pagan symbols, but the voluptuous psychedelic imagery has a much more organic coherence. It's now much clearer that the poet's ubiquitous muse also represents his female alter ego, and that his inner torments are as much those of the gay icon St Sebastian as those of the Armenian patriotic martyr. And the explicit visual references to Buñuel and Pasolini underline Paradjanov's own ambivalence about the embrace of the church. The film is more profane than sacred, in fact, and all the more magical for it. TR

Colpire al Cuore
see Blow to the Heart

Colt .45 (aka Thundercloud)
(Edwin L Marin, 1950, US) Randolph Scott, Zachary Scott, Ruth Roman, Lloyd Bridges, Chief Thundercloud.
74 min.
Fast-paced Technicolor Western, later the basis for a fondly remembered US TV series. R Scott's a gun salesman whose latest consignment of snazzy new pistols falls into the hands of Z Scott

and his band of desperados. Unpretentious hokum, and one of the last films of Edwin Marin, a prolific second-feature man, who turned out several Randolph Scott Westerns. TJ

Coma
(Michael Crichton, 1977, US) Genevieve Bujold, Michael Douglas, Elizabeth Ashley, Rip Torn, Richard Widmark, Lois Chiles.
113 min.
Crichton's excellent adaptation of Robin Cook's novel is one of the most intelligent sci-fi thrillers in years. Bujold is the doctor who, after a series of mysterious and fatal mishaps with patients going into coma for no clear reason, begins to suspect that something evil is being covered up at the hospital. A simple enough story, but one told in such chilling fashion that visitors to hospitals will never feel the same again. Careful to establish an authentic atmosphere, Crichton only slowly lets events spiral off into nightmarish Hitchcockian fantasy, while the fact that nobody will believe Bujold, attributing her suspicions to female hysteria, only serves to point up the patriarchal nature of the medical profession. See it and worry. GA

Comanche Station
(Budd Boetticher, 1960, US) Randolph Scott, Claude Akins, Skip Homeier, Richard Rust, Nancy Gates, Rand Brooks.
74 min.
The last of the marvellous Westerns partnering Boetticher and Scott, beautifully scripted by Burt Kennedy and performed by a solid cast. Scott's the obsessive man, hunting these last ten years for a wife kidnapped by Comanches, who rescues instead another woman, only to find himself up against Akins and his reward-hungry sidekicks as he ferries her back to civilisation. With characters doomed from the start, it's a bleakly pessimistic film that gains warmth from gently ironic humour and a discreetly elegiac tone.

Come and Get It
(Howard Hawks/William Wyler, 1936, US) Edward Arnold, Joel McCrea, Frances Farmer, Walter Brennan, Andrea Leeds.
99 min. b/w.
Minor Hawks (the last ten minutes were directed by Wyler) in which a 19th century Wisconsin lumber magnate and his son fight for the love of Frances Farmer – daughter of a woman the father once knew. The emphasis on professionalism and definition of character through action (work) is typical Hawks. Good performances all round, especially from Farmer in a dual role. Sadly, the location photography (Gregg Toland, Rudolph Maté) is poorly integrated with the jarringly setbound dramatic scenes. NF

Come and See (Idi i Smotri)
(Elem Klimov, 1985, USSR) Alexei Kravchenko, Olga Mironova, Liubomiras Laucevicius, Vladas Bagdonas.
142 min. b/w & col.
Soviet Belorussia, near the Polish border, 1943. Florya, a young partisan, left behind as his unit moves to prepare for a renewed German advance, returns to his village to find only a mass of bodies, including those of his family, and later witnesses the entire population of a nearby town being machine-gunned and burnt to death. This epic, allegorical and traumatising enactment of the hellish experience of war (especially its effect upon a generation of the Soviet people) is rendered by Klimov – albeit unintentionally – as a disorienting and undifferentiated amalgam of almost lyrical poeticism and expressionist nightmare. WH

Comeback, The
(Pete Walker, 1977, GB) Jack Jones, Pamela Stephenson, David Doyle, Bill Owen, Sheila Keith, Holly Palance, Richard Johnson.
100 min.
It's sad, 17 years on, to see the British horror film still seeking inspiration from *Psycho*...and still getting it all wrong. But that's not difficult when you confuse horror with the horrible. People don't just die in this film, they decay, slowly and unconvincingly. Unconvincing is the best word for a plot that has a perfectly respectable mid-

dle-aged couple driven to heights of murderous passion and lunacy by the filthy songs and lewd gyrations of a singer played by Jack Jones. Not even its brace of transvestite red herrings can help the story stand on its own feet. SM

Come Back Africa
(Lionel Rogosin, 1959, US) Zachariah Mgabi, Vinah Bendile.
85 min. b/w.
Recently unbanned in Johannesburg, Rogosin's docudrama was an early exposé of the evils of apartheid, filmed clandestinely and using a non-professional cast who portray a typical township family, separated by law and drifting through a series of menial jobs until a single infringement (ie. man and wife share a night together) leads to a singularly bleak denouement. Although the film has considerable weaknesses – principally on the narrative level of performance, and the need to spell everything out in the manner of a social science course (this last, an entirely understandable decision for 1959) – its power comes from the location filming of the township, which might have been shot today. This township – Sophiatown – was once the only place in South Africa where blacks could own freehold properties. The area was demolished and is now a white suburb called Triumph. ATu

Come Back Charleston Blue
(Mark Warren, 1972, US) Godfrey Cambridge, Raymond St Jacques, Peter De Anda, Jonelle Allen, Maxwell Glanville, Minnie Gentry.
100 min.
Second of two underrated thrillers (the first was *Cotton Comes to Harlem*) inspired by Chester Himes and his ace Harlem detectives, Grave Digger Jones and Coffin Ed Johnson. Black Bogarts with a natty line in upstaged Chandlerisms, the pair tangle here with murders by cut-throat razor, the resurrection of a gangster who died forty years earlier, a regally crazy old lady (wonderful performance by Gentry), and the hijacking of all the heroin in Harlem. No masterpiece, but very funny and full of bizarre touches. TM

Come Back, Little Sheba
(Daniel Mann, 1952, US) Burt Lancaster, Shirley Booth, Terry Moore, Richard Jaeckel.
99 min. b/w.
Little Sheba is a dog that's gone AWOL, and its owner, Shirley Booth, has also lost her looks and her love. She's married to a reformed alcoholic (Lancaster), and has a lodger (Moore) whose incessant bonking with Richard Jaeckel drives Burt back to the bottle and Booth into self-pity. Dated now, it's still a classic slice of '50s Americana, based on a play by William Inge and treading gracefully between tragedy and comedy. But unlike *Picnic*, it doesn't score heavily as a movie. Daniel Mann refuses to get off his tripod, and the camera seems transfixed by Booth's screen debut (she had played the part on Broadway), which won her an Oscar and the Cannes prize. ATu

Come Back to the 5 & Dime Jimmy Dean, Jimmy Dean
(Robert Altman, 1982, US) Sandy Dennis, Cher, Karen Black, Sudie Bond, Kathy Bates, Marta Heflin, Mark Patton.
110 min.
Startlingly successful translation from one medium to another, with Altman turning the first of his theatrical adaptations into a cinematic tour de force. A group of women, members of a James Dean fan club, reunite in '75 to pay tribute to the death, 20 years earlier, of their hero while shooting *Giant* in the Texan desert nearby. Ed Graczyk's play itself is a humdrum if highly enjoyable affair, gradually proceeding from its comic observations about the way the women aren't quite friends any more to a more serious consideration of shattered dreams and saddened lives, all exposed in a gripping if familiar series of intimate revelations. But beyond the excellent performances and Altman's evident sympathy for his garrulous gathering of beautiful losers, what marks the film is the way he uses both the camera and a wall mirror (which periodically reflects us back to '55) to explore and open up his single dime-store set and the cracks in the masks of his deluded/deluding characters. Stunning stuff. GA

Come Blow Your Horn

(Bud Yorkin, 1962, US) Frank Sinatra, Tony Bill, Lee J Cobb, Molly Picon, Barbara Rush, Jill St John.
113 min.

Routine comedy fodder – domestic squabbles in a New York Jewish family, with playboy sophisticate Sinatra introducing kid brother Bill to the delights of the high life – from the pen of Neil Simon (his first major success), ploddingly transferred to the screen. A few nice lines and an intriguing cast don't compensate for the over-familiarity of the basic idea. GA

Come, Come, Come Upward (Aje Aje Bara-Aje)

(Im Kwon-Taek, 1989, SKor) Kang Soo-Yeon, Jin Yong-Mi, Yu In-Chon, Jon Moo-Song.
123 min.

A female companion-piece to Im's classic *Mandala*, this too rests on a contrast between sacred and profane approaches to Buddhist enlightenment. Sun-Nyo (Kang, superb) runs away from her broken home and her crush on a teacher to become a nun, expecting to pray and meditate. But the convent sends her out into the world, where she mixes with the poor and desperate and forms one sexual attachment after another with rough working-class men. Im compares her self-abasement with the more orthodox asceticism of another young nun, whose retreat from worldly things results in a brutal rape. The drama is rooted in a clear sense of social and psychological realities but lifted above mere social realism by Gu Joong-Mu's sensationally beautiful cinematography, mostly in shades of blue and grey. TR

Comedians, The

(Peter Glenville, 1967, US/Bermuda/Fr) Richard Burton, Alec Guinness, Elizabeth Taylor, Peter Ustinov, Paul Ford, Lillian Gish, Raymond St Jacques.
156 min.

A sadly inept adaptation of Graham Greene's novel (script by Greene himself) about turmoil in Haiti under Papa Doc, with a group of English-speaking stereotypes going through the usual intrigues, despair and romance. The main problem is that Glenville's lumbering direction concentrates so much on Dick, Liz and trivia. Only the performances of Gish, Ford and Guinness give any relief from the endless battery of clichés. GA

Comedy of Terrors, The

(Jacques Tourneur, 1963, US) Vincent Price, Peter Lorre, Boris Karloff, Basil Rathbone, Joe E Brown, Joyce Jameson, Buddy Mason, Beverley Hills, Linda Rogers.
88 min.

Price and Lorre are somewhat over-enthusiastic undertakers in Richard Matheson's disappointingly scripted, self-conscious horror spoof set in New England in the 1890s. With credentials of this calibre, the movie could hardly fail, but it comes perilously close. On the other hand, you've never seen so many scene-stealers together in their natural environment (notably Karloff as Price's senile sleeping partner, and Rathbone as his landlord, a would-be Shakespearean actor with cataleptic tendencies). And Price, of course, deserves a knighthood: Sir Vincent, knight of the long knives. TCh

Come Fill the Cup

(Gordon Douglas, 1951, US) James Cagney, Phyllis Thaxter, Raymond Massey, James Gleason, Gig Young.
113 min. b/w.

Despite a not altogether convincing script, a solid piece of entertainment with Cagney as the journalist whose life is almost ruined by alcoholism, until he sees the light and sets about helping to cure others. Gangsters are brought in to contrived effect towards the end, but the whole thing, despite a tub-thumping message, is lent style by a strong cast and Robert Burks' steely photography. GA

Come Next Spring

(RG Springsteen, 1955, US) Ann Sheridan, Steve Cochran, Walter Brennan, Sherry Jackson, Richard Eyer, Edgar Buchanan, Sonny Tufts, Mae Clarke.
92 min.

Slight but charming slice of rural Americana set in Arkansas and detailing the difficulties facing Cochran (reformed drunkard determined to prove himself) and his wife Sheridan as they try to make a go of their farm. A bit contrived in its incident, and never as tough or as moving as Renoir's superficially similar *The Southerner*; but Sheridan gives her all and breathes life into the proceedings, while Brennan is as reliable as ever. GA

Come on George

(Anthony Kimmins, 1939, GB) George Formby, Pat Kirkwood, Joss Ambler, Meriel Forbes, Cyril Raymond.
88 min. b/w.

Once upon a time in a distant land, Formby – the goofy, gormless, ukelele-playing comedian (?) – was a sure-fire box-office success up North. Here he's an ice-cream seller at a racetrack with ambitions to become a jockey, opportunistically employing his natural empathy with a horse, and tangling with a psychiatrist and hordes of performing fleas before he rides to victory. OK if you like that sort of thing. GA

Come Play with Me

(George Harrison Marks, 1977, GB) Irene Handl, Alfie Bass, George Harrison Marks, Ronald Fraser, Ken Parry, Cardew Robinson.
94 min.

Truly atrocious sex comedy involving forgers on the run and out-of-work strippers staffing a health farm. Accept an invitation to go swimming in a piranha-infested river rather than play with this lot. SM

Comes a Horseman

(Alan J Pakula, 1978, US) James Caan, Jane Fonda, Jason Robards, George Grizzard, Richard Farnsworth, Jim Davis.
118 min.

From the first, with its graveyard claustrophobically hemmed in by mountains, *Comes a Horseman* is a mistit Western, with Pakula using Jane Fonda's uncanny resemblance to her father to set up a curious tangential relationship, respectful and rebellious, with classic Western mythology. Fonda is the rather uneasy 'banshee woman boss' of a Montana ranch in 1945, fighting off cattle baron (and former incestuous cousin) Robards, assisted only by a Walter Brennan-style old-timer and a reluctant recruit: Anzio veteran Caan. The sparring of veteran and banshee sits uneasily between conviction and irony, the set pieces – stampede, saloon fight – seem token; even the ranchers' conflicts of interest are handled too precisely, too 'politically' for genre material. Only in the later stages, with some appropriate acknowledgments – that the ranches are both mortgaged, that the film is more interested in murder than battle – does conflict come alive. Visually superb, though: a doomed attempt to make Fordian metaphors speak a language of corrupting, intimate anxiety. CA

Come See the Paradise

(Alan Parker, 1990, US) Dennis Quaid, Tamlyn Tomita, Sab Shimono, Shizuko Hoshi, Stan Egi, Ronald Yamamoto.
133 min.

Parker's movie about the experience of Japanese-Americans immediately after Pearl Harbor characteristically undermines its socio-political problems by focusing single-mindedly on the lives of a handful of individuals and resorting to simplistic bombast. The opening sequences bode ill: examining the cultural and racial barriers that divide his would-be lovers – ex-union activist Jack McGurn (Quaid) and Lily (Tomita), the Nisei daughter of Jack's employer – Parker even indulges Quaid with a silly, redundant song-and-dance number. Once Jack is drafted, and Lily and her family are interned in a desert camp with thousands of other victims of US xenophobia, the film plunges headlong into turgid melodrama. Dust, death and disintegrating values are the Kawamuras' lot, as the narrative staggers through an endless series of farewells and reunions, fallings-out and reconciliations; tears flow, the music swells, and Jack, affirming his love for Lily, discovers a poetic articulacy that is quite implausible for this working class hero. Except for the historical data inserted here and there into the dialogue, everything on view derives not from reality but from manipulative movie cliché. GA

Comfort and Joy

(Bill Forsyth, 1984, GB) Bill Paterson, Eleanor David, CP Grogan, Alex Norton, Patrick Malahide, Rikki Fulton.
106 min.

When his girl-friend walks out on him, Alan 'Dicky' Bird (Paterson) grits his teeth and plugs away at his sugar-coated job as a DJ on a Glasgow local radio station. Then by a highly unlikely quirk of fate he finds himself mediating in an ice-cream war between Mr McCool and Mr Bunny, both of them branches of the Scotia Nostra. But while Paterson regains his self-esteem through the injection of seriousness into his life, the film is damaged for the same reason: Forsyth stamps too firmly on the comedy which was his forte, while being apparently too nice to believe that the mafia are anything other than high-spirited boys. The result doesn't go far enough in either direction. Other people make comedy thrillers; this is a whimsical mild-surpriser. CPea

Comfort of Strangers, The (Cortesie per gli ospiti)

(Paul Schrader, 1990, It/GB) Christopher Walken, Rupert Everett, Natasha Richardson, Helen Mirren, Manfredi Aliquo.
104 min.

Its lush visuals concealing a core of fetid malevolence, Schrader's film of Ian McEwan's novel inhabits a strange, unsettling territory somewhere between art movie and thriller. Colin (Everett) and Mary (Richardson) are second-honeymooning in Venice, warily striving to repair the fissures in their stale relationship. A seemingly fortuitous encounter with the aristocratic Robert (Walken) bemuses them, his evident hospitality sitting uneasily with his unusually frank questions and confessions. But the suave tale-spinner also catalyses what remains of the couple's sexual feelings for each other, and as if mesmerised, they return to the palazzo he shares with his submissive wife (Mirren), only half oblivious to the dangers awaiting them...Adopting an oblique perspective on motivation, Harold Pinter's script sometimes suffers from awkward, even implausible dialogue; but careful pacing and casting make for a film that, while directed with cool discretion, is sensual and shocking in its casual evocation of erotic violence, emotional manipulation and moral torpor. If much of the credit must go to cameraman Dante Spinotti's use of dense, exotic colours and to Gianni Quaranta's elegant sets, it's finally Schrader who deserves praise for the septic, stifling mood. GA

Comic Book Confidential

(Ron Mann, 1988, Can) Lynda Barry, Charles Burns, Sue Coe, Robert Crumb, Will Eisner, Al Feldstein, Shary Flenniken, William M Gaines, Bill Griffith, Jaime Hernández, Jack Kirby, Harvey Kurtzman, Stan Lee, Paul Mavrides, Frank Miller, Victor Morosco, Françoise Mouly, Dan O'Neill, Harvey Pekar, Spain Rodriguez, Gilbert Shelton, Art Spiegelman.
90 min.

With the comic book industry now enjoying unprecedented respect, Mann's documentary is a timely if unsatisfying look at four decades of comic history, and interviews 22 leading American creators. It opens promisingly with the patriotic '40s and McCarthyite '50s, when comics were burnt and Senate sub-committees investigated questions of depravity and corruption. It's strong, too, on the underground comix of the '60s, but the scope of the film is too broad, and the little time allotted to each writer and artist is further reduced by the fatuous device of having them read out loud their own texts while panels from their comics are shown on the screen. The filming is for the most part an unimaginative and endless succession of talking heads, with narrative links provided by '*Meanwhile*...' – precisely the kind of crass storytelling method modern comics try to avoid. Buffs will no doubt enjoy seeing their heroes, but anyone else will be bored rigid. DW

Comic Magazine (Komikku zasshi nanka iranai)

(Yojiro Takita, 1985, Jap) Yuya Uchida, Yumi Asou, Beat Takeshi, Yoshio Harada.
120 min.

The spirit of Paddy Chayefsky unfortunately lives on in this leaden satire of the dubious ethics of the Japanese media. An increasingly ragged TV journalist endures one humiliating setback after another in an unending quest for exclusive celebrity interviews; he tramples on the private feelings of others until his conscience finally asserts itself and he steps in to stop (rather than report) a murder. Hideously protracted, lumberingly obvious, and completely lacking in real bite. TR

Coming Home

(Hal Ashby, 1978, US) Jane Fonda, Jon Voight, Bruce Dern, Robert Carradine, Penelope Milford.
128 min.
Hal *Shampoo* Ashby takes on (and makes disposable) America's post-Vietnam guilt, with a supremely sentimental tale of war hero's wife (a nurse!) falling for paraplegic war veteran. Cliché piles on cliché to the strains of a garbled '60s sound-track, but the movie's ending goes some way to recognising its failure. Fonda is magnificent. CA

Coming Out

(Heiner Carow, 1990, Ger) Matthias Freihof, Dagmar Manzel, Dirk Kummer, Alex Wandtke, Michael Gwisdek, Werner Dissell.
113 min.
Hailed as the first East German film to deal with homosexuality, this mixes the romantic yearning, melodrama and self-disgust typical of ground-breaking gay work. The plot is reminiscent of *Nighthawks* and *Taxi zum Klo*: respected schoolteacher leads double life, butch by day, cruising the clubs by night. Philipp (Freihof) makes an enthusiastic stab at heterosexuality with a female colleague (Manzel), only to find himself accidentally wandering into a louche bar full of drag queens that looks like an out-take from *Cabaret*. One night of happiness in the arms of another young man (Kummer) ensues, before fate conspires to separate them and leave Philipp facing loneliness, persecution and alcoholism. So far, so miserable. But the redeeming feature, along with a wonderfully open performance from Freihof, is that, given the social climate of East Germany, this is anything but an exercise in self-pity: when the characters speak of loneliness and persecution, they are *not* posturing. RS

Coming to America

(John Landis, 1988, US) Eddie Murphy, James Earl Jones, Arsenio Hall, Shari Headley, Madge Sinclair, Calvin Lockhart.
117 min.
Murphy plays HRH Akeem, Crown Prince of Zamunda, whose pampered existence extends to molly-coddled privates. But when presented by his father (Jones) with the *fait accompli* of a decreed marriage, Akeem rebels and sets off for New York with his loyal manservant (Hall), where he decides that Queens is the most likely whereabouts of the woman who will love him for himself. Lodging in a run-down tenement, the pair find work as cleaners in a hamburger joint, where Akeem soon encounters elegant, sophisticated Lisa (Headley). Much of the credit for this slick, at times very funny movie must go to Landis, since Murphy's previously wasted talent is here harnessed to reveal a considerable finesse; superb comic timing, a satirical edge, and Murphy's extraordinary gift for mimicry lift it right out of the trough of mediocrity to which it is all but consigned by its utterly predictable storyline. SCu

Coming Up Roses

(Stephen Bayly, 1986, GB) Dafydd Hywel, Iola Gregory, Olive Michael, Mari Emlyn, WJ Phillips.
93 min.
In a small Welsh town stands the Rex, an old dog of a cinema showing black-and-white horror pics to an audience of empty seats. Inevitably, the cinema is closed, and the manager Eli, projectionist Trevor, and ice-cream lady Mona are thrown onto the slag-heap of unemployment (this, by the way, is the time of the miners' strike). When Trev's ex-wife needs £700, he borrows the ailing Eli's funeral money, and he and his new love Mona are then faced with the problems of how to pay it back and save the cinema and their jobs. Updating *The Smallest Show on Earth*, this is the second-ever Welsh language movie released in the UK (the

first being *Boy Soldier*). Subtitled in English, it's a chuckling good comedy with an edge. 'Take the cinema away from us and what other means of escape is there?' pleads old Eli; none from the grim realities of Thatcher's Britain. CB

Command, The

(David Butler, 1954, US) Guy Madison, Joan Weldon, James Whitmore, Carl Benton Reid, Ray Teal, Harvey Lembeck.
88 min.
Both the first film in CinemaScope from Warner Bros and the first Western in the widescreen process from any studio. This yarn of a cavalry medical officer inheriting command of a wagon train, and fighting both Indians and smallpox, has its moments; most of them thanks to the script rather than the ponderous direction, although Sam Fuller, credited with the adaptation from a James Warner Bellah novel, disowned the film after screenwriter Russell Hughes' revisions ended up on screen. PT

Command Decision

(Sam Wood, 1948, US) Clark Gable, Walter Pidgeon, Van Johnson, Brian Donlevy, Charles Bickford, Edward Arnold, John Hodiak.
112 min. b/w.
Talkative but soberly gripping World War II drama about the conflict between Gable, commander of a bomber unit determined to rush through the destruction of German factories producing a new breed of jet fighter, and Pidgeon as his politic superior, well aware that the inevitable heavy losses will reflect badly on his plans for daylight precision bombing. Adapted from a stage play and barely opened out, it isn't as good as *Twelve O'Clock High*, made the following year, but a strong cast pulls it through. TM

Commando

(Mark L Lester, 1985, US) Arnold Schwarzenegger, Rae Dawn Chong, Dan Hedaya, Vernon Wells, James Olson.
90 min.
Colonel John Matrix (Schwarzenegger) pits his pecs against a team of ruthless renegades who have kidnapped his daughter in their drive to restore a right-wing dictator to the presidency of a Central American state. It is all rather more light-hearted than Rambo, and consequently much more entertaining, but plot and action are still lodged firmly in Boy's Own territory, and even Rae Dawn Chong can't detract from the all-round gatta-gatta and the steady stream of extras being trampolined out of big explosions. There is some fairly outrageous homo-erotic badinage between Matrix and his chief adversary, but otherwise it's straight-up comic-strip stuff, and never comes near to *The Terminator*. AB

Commare Secca, La (The Grim Reaper)

(Bernardo Bertolucci, 1962, It) Francesco Ruiu, Giancarlo De Rosa, Alvaro D'Hercole, Romano Labate, Lorenza Benedetti.
100 min. b/w.
Bertolucci's first feature, a whodunit about a whore's murder, offers more than filmographic interest. The joint passages of time and adolescence are realised in its combination of febrile sexual alertness and the elaborate reconstruction of each defendant's day, always returning to the doomed woman dressing while the same rainstorm rages. Also intriguing are the portraits of the gormless young soldier on leave, accosting literally every female he meets; the ageing prostitute; and the gay witness to the crime. MM

Comment je me suis disputé... ('ma vie sexuelle')

see Ma vie sexuelle (Paul Dedalus' Journey)

Comme un Boomerang

see Boomerang

Commissar, The (Komissar)

(Alexander Askoldov, 1967, USSR) Nonna Mordyukova, Rolan Bykov, Raisa Niedashkovskaya, Vasily Shukshin, Ludmila Volinskaya.
108 min. b/w.
Askoldov's movie was sat on after initial

screenings in 1967 because it dealt with such unpalatable subjects as anti-Semitism and women's rights. The film, although it enters wholeheartedly into its story and is shot with a certain austere flair, has a hard time engaging the audience. The story, set in 1920, is resolutely stern: Clavdia, a Red Army officer, becomes pregnant by a comrade later executed by the Whites. She is billeted with a poor Jewish family until the birth, by which time her intial racial hostility, and their resentment of her haughty attitude, have worn off, and each side recognises the other's common humanity. Askoldov clearly felt passionately about his subject, but *The Commissar* is a work of promise rather than polish; sadly he was prevented from working again. RS

Commitments, The

(Alan Parker, 1991, US) Robert Arkins, Michael Aherne, Angeline Ball, Maria Doyle, Dave Finnegan, Bronagh Gallagher, Félim Gormley, Glen Hansard, Dick Massey, Johnny Murphy, Kenneth McCluskey, Andrew Strong.
118 min.
Foul-mouthed, fast-talking and *very* funny, this is Parker's best to date. It's an intentionally 'small' movie that treats a familiar subject (kids forming a rock band) with a deft intimacy. But as the young hopefuls from Dublin's working-class Northside go through the round of auditions, rehearsals and gigs, it becomes clear that the film is big in heart. For Parker and his excellent, mostly non-professional cast are indeed committed to characters, milieu *and* music: classics from Otis, Wilson Pickett, Aretha *et al*. For one thing, the script precisely captures both the witty banter and the modest dreams of the streetwise kids. For another, Parker never over-emphasises the unemployment and poverty, nor does he glamorise the band. The result is a gritty, naturalistic comedy blessed with a wry, affectionate eye for the absurdities of the band's various rivalries and ambitions; and the songs are matchless. GA

Committed

(Sheila McLaughlin/Lynne Tillman, 1983, US) Sheila McLaughlin, Victoria Boothby, Lee Breuer, John Erdman, Heinz Emigholz.
79 min. b/w.
A low-budget independent alternative to the Jessica Lange *Frances* made a couple of years earlier, this sees McLaughlin as Hollywood actress Frances Farmer, reliving her memories while incarcerated in the mental institution to which she has been committed, and employs her as a litmus with which to measure American attitudes to political commitment, mental health, and strong women. It's become fashionable to regard Farmer as something of a martyr, and although she was certainly a talented actress treated abysmally by Hollywood, family and friends, it is hard now to ascertain the truth behind her downfall. That apart, this is an original and stylish movie, austere and bitter. GA

Common Threads: Stories from the Quilt

(Robert Epstein/Jeffrey Friedman, 1989, US) Sara Lewinstein, Suzi Mandell, David Mandell, Sallie Perryman, Suzi Mandell, Tracy Torrey.
75 min.
Since 1985, the Names Project has based its work around the assembling of a now massive memorial quilt composed of individually-produced squares, each commemorating an AIDS death. In this Oscar-winning documentary, maintaining the high standards of Epstein's earlier *The Times of Harvey Milk*, he and his co-director Friedman have chosen, from the widest possible spectrum, six people who have suffered loss: the wives of an Olympic athlete and a drug addict, the parents of a haemophiliac boy who died at twelve, and a naval commander and a writer, who have both lost lovers and themselves contracted AIDS. Through their moving testimonies, with the aid of photographs and home videos, faces and histories are put to the names on five of the squares. It's a gentle, sensitive film, the fierce anger felt by its makers evident only in the use of statistics and media snippets which build up to a damning indictment of the social and political response to the AIDS crisis. WH

Communicants, The

see Nattvardsgästerna

Communion

(Philippe Mora, 1989, US) Christopher Walken, Lindsay Crouse, Joel Carlson, Frances Sternhagen, Andreas Katsulas, Terri Hanauer, Basil Hoffman.
101 min.
Novelist Whitley Strieber (Walken), taking friends, wife and young son to his country cabin, wakes up to the first of many meetings with 'non-human' creatures. They whisk him off inside their strange craft and subject him to rigorous, painful examination, yet he subsequently remembers nothing. As the encounters become more frequent, his behaviour becomes more erratic, and he agrees to undergo hypnosis sessions, which reveal the ordeals suppressed by his conscious mind. This misjudged adaptation of Strieber's 'true life' experiences (described in his best-seller) eschews his philosophical and scientific theories about the events, offering instead Strieber wielding rifles against the intruders and, in mellower mood, boogying with them. In aiming for the widest popular appeal, the film ends up in no man's land. CM

Communion (aka Holy Terror)

(Alfred Sole, 1976, US) Linda Miller, Mildred Clinton, Paula Sheppard, Niles McMaster, Rudolph Willrich, Jane Lowry.
108 min.
Did 12-year-old Alice strangle and set fire to her younger sister during her first communion service? As Robin Wood has noted, the American family film has shifted from the comedy genre to the horror film; in this instance a lot of the humour transfers as well. *Communion* delights in confounding expectations as it conducts three separate enquiries. The plot investigates the murder; the film examines the family's self-destruction; and the film-makers construct a running commentary on the themes of Alfred Hitchcock: against a carefully evoked background of Catholicism emerge twin themes of repression and guilt. Numerous parallels and cross-references neatly bind it all together. The result is far more than a sterile exercise in suspense: *Communion* constantly keeps the audience on its toes with a wealth of incidental detail, excellent set pieces and technical versatility. CPe

Como Agua para Chocolate

see Like Water for Chocolate

Como ser mujer y no morir en el intento

see How to Be a Woman and Not Die in the Attempt

Companeros (Vamos a Matar, Companeros!)

(Sergio Corbucci, 1970, It/Sp/WGer) Franco Nero, Tomas Milian, Jack Palance, Fernando Rey, Iris Berben, Francisco Bodalo, Karin Schubert.
118 min.
A spaghetti Western, and a pretty absurd one. Nero, sporting more costumes than expressions, is a Swedish gunrunner in a straw boater who gets mixed up with hidden treasure and communist revolutionaries down Mexico way. Palance, startlingly like Robert Shaw on a bad day, is a slant-eyed mercenary with a pet hawk and an artificial hand who's pissed at Nero for leaving him nailed to a tree in Cuba. Rey, minus his own voice, is a bespectacled commie professor who advocates Gandhi-esque non-violence but graduates to some serious slaughter by the end. Twangy Morricone score. AO

Company Business

(Nicholas Meyer, 1991, US) Gene Hackman, Mikhail Baryshnikov, Kurtwood Smith, Terry O'Quinn, Daniel Von Bargen, Oleg Rudnick, Geraldine Danon.
98 min.
The Cold War is over – or is it? Retired from active duty, CIA agent Sam Boyd (Hackman) is recalled to do one last job: he must travel to Berlin with a former State Department mole (Baryshnikov), plus a briefcase containing $2 million to exchange for a captured American pilot. But Sam discovers that he has been betrayed by his own people, and our unlikely duo go on the run with CIA and KGB in hot pursuit. This offers familiar spy movie clichés, and although Meyer's direction creates a moderately menacing atmosphere, his script is at best undemanding, at worst simplistic. Hackman rises above the material, which is more than can be said for Baryshnikov. CM

Company Limited (Seemabaddha)

(Satyajit Ray, 1971, Ind) Barun Chanda, Sharmila Tagore, Parumita Chowdhary, Harindranath Chattopadhyaya.
112 min. b/w.
Against a background of neo-imperialist India, and set in Calcutta, a city of severe unemployment and unrest, Ray creates a finely judged satire about the gradual compromise that is the price of ambition. His complacent, but not unlikeable, central character works as a sales manager and possesses sufficient ambition to override any doubts about accepting the privileges remaining from colonial days and the rewards of Westernised industry. But two things undermine his smugness: his provincial but astute sister-in-law pays a visit; and a crisis in the export department forces him to resort to political manipulation in order to further his career. Both events leave him a wiser but lesser man. It's basically an old-fashioned film, but none the worse for that. CPe

Company of Strangers, The

(Cynthia Scott, 1990, Can) Alice Diabo, Constance Garneau, Winifred Holden, Cissy Meddings.
100 min.
Deftly skirting the dangers of improvisation, this touching and gently humorous film maroons a group of septuagenarian women (and their younger black minder) in an isolated farmhouse, where they while away the time talking about their families, working lives and past loves, and their hopes and fears for an uncertain future. Simple scenes, like one in which a prissy woman is cajoled into removing her wig, or the realisation that one of the women (now deaf) will never again hear birdsong, are suffused with residual strength and intimations of mortality. The only false note is the carefully selected nature of the group (a Navajo woman, a nun, a lesbian, a wacky stroke-survivor), which undercuts the otherwise free-form structure. NF

Company of Wolves, The

(Neil Jordan, 1984, GB) Angela Lansbury, David Warner, Graham Crowden, Brian Glover, Kathryn Pogson, Stephen Rea, Sarah Patterson.
95 min.
Once upon a time, young Rosaleen was dreaming of an Arcadian past when Granny would tell grim tales of once upon a time when little girls should beware of men whose eyebrows meet in the middle and who are hairy on the inside... And in those dark days, fear accompanied desire and beauty was wed with the beast ... The characters in Jordan's film of Angela Carter's stories inhabit a magical, mysterious world of cruelty and wonder, rarely seen in cinema. In tales within tales within tales, dream is reality, wolves are human, and vice-versa. Rarely has this Gothic landscape of the imagination been so perfectly conveyed by film; there is simply a precise, resonant portrayal of a young girl's immersion in fantasies where sexuality is both fearful and seductive. Like all the best fairy-tales, the film is purely sensual, irrational, fuelled by an immense joy in story-telling, and totally lucid. It's also a true original, with the most beautiful visual effects to emerge from Britain in years. GA

Company She Keeps, The

(John Cromwell, 1950, US) Lizabeth Scott, Jane Greer, Dennis O'Keefe, Fay Baker, John Hoyt.
83 min. b/w.
Dreadful script by Ketti Frings which ties itself up in novelettish knots as a female ex-con (Greer) does battle with her female parole officer (Scott) over the latter's boy-friend. Cromwell does his best in the circumstances, and Greer does wonders. TM

Compartment Tueurs

see Sleeping Car Murder, The

Competition, The

(Joel Oliansky, 1980, US) Richard Dreyfuss, Amy Irving, Lee Remick, Sam Wanamaker, Joseph Cali.
129 min.
Romance in a major key: competitive classical pianists Dreyfuss and Irving spar the sentimental sex war as an inevitable prelude to a four-handed future. The plot's old hat and not half as interesting as any of Michael Ritchie's 'competition' films (*Downhill Racer*, *Smile*, etc), but you have to admire writer/director Oliansky's confidence in playing it again so straight and so strong to the gallery. The ivories are nicely tinkled, and the vets – Remick and Wanamaker – get most of the saving lines. PT

Completely Pogued

(Billy Magra, 1989, Ire) The Pogues, Kirsty McColl, Joe Strummer, Steve Earle, Lynval Golding.
55 min.
'What we did, right, was we broke open the pop market, right? To trad music, right? Irish trad music, yeah? *Now* what happened after that I don't know...' So confesses toothy, hard-drinkin' Shane McGowan, lead man with punk-folk megastars the Pogues, the band that has taken traditional Irish folk and ramshackle rock to the bright pop lights of Wembley. In this rather haphazard but proud spirit, the documentary, like the Pogues' career itself, continues: the band and the various famous rockers they've jammed with offering opinions and anecdotes in a surprisingly entertaining and often revealing manner. Even if you have absolutely no interest in the music, the vast array of pasty-faced uglies is really quite stunning. LD

Compromising Positions

(Frank Perry, 1985, US) Susan Sarandon, Raul Julia, Edward Herrmann, Judith Ivey, Mary Beth Hurt, Joe Mantegna, Josh Mostel.
98 min.
A witty, unbuttoned script by Susan Isaacs, taken from her novel of the same name, puts ex-reporter Sarandon into the middle of a murder scandal that is rocking the well-manicured lawns of commuter-belt New York suburbia. A sleazy dentist, who has been putting more than just his water pick into his female patients' cavities, ends up with one of his own scalpels in the neck. With the help of a *macho simpatico* cop (Julia), Sarandon uncovers a pornography ring, along with some risqué polaroid shots of most of the local female population in various degrees of bondage. What gives her the edge in the investigation is her sympathy with the ladies, and her own wide-eyed innocence. It's all very humorous and engaging, if only for proving that American whodunits don't have to have car chases and brutality; and it has a wicked eye for the vacuity of middle-class good life and what it may conceal. Lots of feelthy girl talk, too. CPea

Compulsion

(Richard Fleischer, 1959, US) Dean Stockwell, Bradford Dillman, Orson Welles, Diane Varsi, EG Marshall, Martin Milner.
103 min. b/w.
Emasculated version of Meyer Levin's novel based on the Leopold-Loeb case, in which two homosexual law students murdered a boy to demonstrate their intellectual superiority. Fine so long as it sticks to the thriller format, but shaky in its period sense (Chicago, 1924) and developing mushy pretensions culminating when Welles is trundled on to deliver an impassioned but hokey boil-down of Clarence Darrow's two-day summation pleading mercy for reasons of insanity. Best performance is Stockwell's, though Dillman and Welles are good value. TM

Comrades

(Bill Douglas, 1986, GB) Robin Soans, Alex Norton, William Gaminara, Philip Davis, Robert Stephens, Freddie Jones, Vanessa Redgrave, Michael Hordern, James Fox.
183 min.
Douglas' epic and very British film about the Tolpuddle Martyrs – 1830s Dorset farm labourers who formed a union to protest against subsistence wages, only to be deported to Australia – employs a minimum of fussy historical detail to offer a didactic but never dogmatic film of wide-ranging relevance. Politically, it foreshadows modern labour disputes; aesthetically, as 'a lanternist's account', the film is an investigation of different, pre-cinematic modes of story-telling. Fuelling the whole is a deeply humane concern for suffering, coupled with a righteous anger directed against hypocrisy and inequality. Equally importantly, however, it works as

often humorous, always intelligently moving spectacle, immaculately performed, structured and shot. GA

Comrades, Almost a Love Story (Tian Mimi)

(Peter Chan, 1996, HK) Leon Lai, Maggie Cheung, Eric Tsang, Irene Tsu, Chris Doyle.
118 min.
A nine-times winner at the 1997 Hong Kong Film Awards, Chan's film charts the lives of two immigrants to Hong Kong from Mainland China across ten years. Li Xiaojun (Lai) is a naive and gullible northerner with a fiancée back home in Tianjin; Li Chiao (Cheung) is a street-smart southerner from Guangzhou who wants no emotional attachments in her life until she hooks up with a triad boss (Tsang). Both of them receive extended sentimental educations, sometimes together, more often apart. Very well played, the central near-romance serves as a barometer of the social and economic changes in Hong Kong since the mid-1980s. The supporting characters and subplots are far less interesting and credible; a dotty old brothel madam with a thing for William Holden (!) is especially wearisome. TR

Comrade X

(King Vidor, 1940, US) Clark Gable, Hedy Lamarr, Felix Bressart, Oscar Homolka, Eve Arden, Sig Rumann.
90 min. b/w.
By no means classic Vidor: its characters – Gable as an American journalist in Soviet Russia, Lamarr as the source of his scoop stories – are simply too bland to animate the film. Only in the last sequence, where Gable and Lamarr escape from Russia in a tank, closely pursued by virtually the whole of the Russian army, does Vidor successfully visualise (albeit comically: the script is by Ben Hecht and Charles Lederer) the tensions that the characters set in motion. A superb piece of entertainment, none the less. PH

Con Air

(Simon West, 1997, US) Nicolas Cage, John Cusack, John Malkovich, Steve Buscemi, Ving Rhames, Danny Trejo, Colm Meaney, Mykelti Williamson, Rachel Ticotin.
115 min.
Led by Cyrus 'The Virus' Grissom (Malkovich), a dozen jailbirds hijack a transport plane. Only parolee Cameron Poe (Cage) – caught up in the middle – stands between the worst of the worst and their freedom. Scott Rosenberg's ingeniously tooled script recalls such vintage entertainments as The Dirty Dozen and The Great Escape. Dialogue is pared to bullet points, punctuation between spectacular set-pieces, but Rosenberg makes every word count. If it needs strong actors to flesh out the characterisation, so be it: Rhames, Buscemi, Trejo – faces you don't forget in a hurry. Sometimes skin deep is close enough. Commercials director West gives us the hard sell non-stop for 115 ear-splitting minutes. There are misjudgments. He gets off on male flesh rippling against slow motion fireballs, and has no time for women, but throws in a transvestite for cheap jibes. The climax looks like an afterthought, and in trying to top itself, the movie finally goes OTT. Very cool, but also very cold. TCh

Conan the Barbarian

(John Milius, 1981, US) Arnold Schwarzenegger, James Earl Jones, Max von Sydow, Sandahl Bergman, Ben Davidson, Cassandra Gaviola.
129 min.
Big blokes, each seized by some grand costume fetish, hack divots out of each other with big broadswords. Deaths take for ever, years pass in a flash as our muscle-bound hero pursues his Quest for the Father (a villain who, delightfully, transmogrifies into a snake). Conan the Barbarian revives the old epics of Steve Reeves, adds some visual sophistication from the Italian Western, and raises a small cheer as a movie for European rather than American illiterates. Milius brags unnecessarily with egghead movie references, manages to lampoon Californian death cults, indulges in some questionable Triumph of the Will stuff, adds an appalling commentary that cries out for O Welles to sell it, and laces the whole thing with intentionally heavy humour

that seems to have been misunderstood. Match verdict: no goals, slow build-up, but much absorbing action off the ball. CPe

Conan the Destroyer

(Richard Fleischer, 1984, US) Arnold Schwarzenegger, Grace Jones, Wilt Chamberlain, Mako, Tracey Walter, Sarah Douglas.
103 min.
Shorn of the intellectual pretensions of its predecessor Conan the Barbarian (ditto the gratuitous sex), this new adventure is far closer to creator Robert E Howard's preference for small minds in big bodies – a requirement Schwarzenegger fills wonderfully. A predictable quest plot is unwound with tremendous verve, and the only real disappointments are some ropey special effects. But Fleischer's zest for action carries it all along splendidly. GD

Concert for Bangladesh, The

(Saul Swimmer, 1972, US) Eric Clapton, Bob Dylan, George Harrison, Billy Preston, Leon Russell, Ravi Shankar, Ringo Starr.
99 min.
The film of the album, distinguished from other roxploitation movies by the fact that it's entirely shot from fixed camera positions, and therefore appears entirely insensitive to both the music and the event as a whole. TR

Concerto of Life

(Xia Gang, 1997, China) Wang Luoyong.
103 min.
A risible melodrama, told in flashback, about a Shanghai piano teacher and his friends who remain devoted to their art (Western classical music) from the '60s to '93. Since the period includes the Cultural Revolution, when foreign music was banned, much secrecy and suffering is involved, but the film often seems perversely apolitical, so that the Revolution registers as a brief, erroneous blip and, as such, part of life's rich tapestry. The tunes, perhaps inevitably, are all popular favourites, the ludicrous, lachrymose finale is overlong and disingenuous ('No regrets' indeed!), and the characterisation facile. Xia Gang should watch some movies by Sirk, who revelled in this kind of tosh, and learn to go with the melodrama, not against it. GA

Concierge, The

see For Love or Money

Concorde – Airport '79, The

see Airport '80 The Concorde

Concrete Jungle, The

see Criminal, The

Condamné à mort s'est échappé, Un (A Man Escaped)

(Robert Bresson, 1956, Fr) François Leterrier, Charles LeClainche, Maurice Beerblock, Roland Monod, Jacques Ertaud.
102 min. b/w.
The true story of a French Resistance worker's escape from imprisonment by the Gestapo in the Montluc fortress at Lyon was the inspiration for A Man Escaped: 'The story is true. I give it as it is, without embellishment,' claimed Bresson. However, by pushing through the authentic details into a more transcendental realm, Bresson in fact subtly transforms the simple story into a metaphysical meditation. This he does by introducing an unseen, transcendental force which helps the young man in simple but crucial ways: 'I would like to show this miracle: an invisible hand over the prison, directing what happens and causing such a thing to succeed for one and not another...the film is a mystery...The Spirit breathes where it will.' The kind of film which inspires awe, even in an atheist. NF

Condorman

(Charles Jarrott, 1981, US) Michael Crawford, Oliver Reed, Barbara Carrera, James Hampton, Jean-Pierre Kalfon, Dana Elcar.
90 min.
Latest ideological intervention from the Disney machine: the Cold War re-heated for the kiddies.

Lamebrain comic artist Crawford gets to play an American-accented Bond and trash the nasty Reds at their own spy games in approved superhero style. A pathetic shadow of the Frank Tashlin/Jerry Lewis Artists and Models; almost as bad as the latest Bond itself. Send the kids to sleep with How to Read Donald Duck instead. PT

Conductor

see Maestro, Il

Conductor, The (Dyrygent)

(Andrzej Wajda, 1979, Pol) John Gielgud, Krystyna Janda, Andrzej Seweryn, Marysia Seweryn.
102 min.
Culture shocks: Wajda's credit appears over New York; Gielgud's lips move and a disembodied Pole speaks his lines. Such incongruities are never quite integrated within this parable about a prodigal elder's attempted return to the fold. Gielgud is the eponymous international maestro whose encounter with a young violinist stirs memories of a provincial Polish début – and an old debt – prompting him to celebrate his jubilee with his long-abandoned ain folk. His reception incorporates simmering jealousies and personality clashes (and Wajda's sly digs at the star system of socialist culture), but the film only really lives in fits and starts. PT

Conduct Unbecoming

(Michael Anderson, 1975, GB) Michael York, Richard Attenborough, Trevor Howard, Stacy Keach, Christopher Plummer, Susannah York, James Faulkner.
107 min.
An alarmingly creaky adaptation of Barry England's play about a regimental outpost in India in Victorian times, and the flutterings about honour occasioned when the bounder in the mess attacks a lady. His secret trial by subalterns' court martial reveals unsuspected murky depths in which rigor theatricalis is warded off only by a valiant starry cast giving their all in the big scenes with which each is thoughtfully provided. TM

Confession, The

see Aveu, L'

Confessional, The (Le Confessionnal)

(Robert LePage, 1995, Can/GB/Fr) Lothaire Bluteau, Patrick Goyette, Jean-Louis Millette, Kristin Scott Thomas, Ron Burrage, Richard Fréchette.
101 min.
Renowned stage director Robert LePage's debut film is dramatically assured and visually inspired. Returning to Quebec for his father's funeral, Pierre Lamontagne (Bluteau) becomes enmeshed in his adopted brother Marc's obsessive search for roots. The quest takes them back to 1952, when Hitchcock was filming I Confess in the city; at that time, Marc's unmarried 16-year-old mother Rachel revealed the father's identity, under the protection of the confessional. Questions of faith and identity are skilfully woven into an entertaining mystery plot. NF

Confessions from a Holiday Camp

(Norman Cohen, 1977, GB) Robin Askwith, Anthony Booth, Doris Hare, Bill Maynard, Sheila White, Liz Fraser, Linda Hayden, John Junkin, Lance Percival.
88 min.
Cherie's dad Tony (playing one Sid Noggett) buddies the dread Askwith through this excruciating parade of mid-'70s British smut (premise: a holiday camp is taken over by a former prison officer). The title establishment languishes under such grey skies that you feel a twinge of sympathy for the female extras called on to disrobe at regular five-minute intervals. TJ

Confessions of a Bigamist (Warum hab' ich bloss 2 x ja gesagt)

(François Legrand, ie.Franz Antel, 1969, WGer/It) Lando Buzzanca, Terry Torday, Raffaella Carrà, Peter Weck.
89 min.

The lucky hero is a wagon-lit attendant on the Rome-Munich train, with a wife at each end of the line – boy, does he have fun? Also on hand to raise a snigger in this Teutonic sex-comedy are some blustering bigwigs and a crazy doctor whose speciality is treating impotence. GB

Confessions of a Driving Instructor

(Norman Cohen, 1976, GB) Robin Askwith, Anthony Booth, Sheila White, Doris Hare, Bill Maynard, Windsor Davies.
90 min.
This third in the *Confessions* series must be a new low for British comedy, displaying a complete indifference to wit, pacing, timing or observation. Nominally based around the rivalry between two driving instruction schools, it soon bankrupts itself on a series of soft-core gropings, manufactured with awesome clumsiness as women fall for the spectacularly lack-lustre hero.

Confessions of a Nazi Spy

(Anatole Litvak, 1939, US) Edward G Robinson, Francis Lederer, George Sanders, Paul Lukas, Lya Lys, Henry O'Neill, James Stephenson.
102 min. b/w.
Anti-Nazi propaganda film from Warners, with Robinson (like Cagney, doing an about-face from gangster roles to more respectable characters) as the G-Man ferreting out Nazi fifth columnists working in America. Topically following hard on the heels of several anti-Nazi trials in 1938, the film achieved great popular and critical success in America (though banned in many Latin American and European countries); now, for all its admirable anti-Fascist relevance, it seems weakened by its patriotic flag-waving and the pseudo-documentary approach (sacrificing suspense) taken by Litvak. But the quietly determined Robinson, the sinister Sanders (as a Nazi villain, a role he would later develop in Lang's *Man Hunt*), and Lederer (the man duped into becoming a spy by his vain egocentricity) lend a power to the film that makes it still worth watching. GA

Confessions of a Pop Performer

(Norman Cohen, 1975, GB) Robin Askwith, Anthony Booth, Bill Maynard, Doris Hare, Sheila White, Bob Todd.
91 min.
No.2 in the *Confessions* series. Although seemingly directed at the lowest common denominator, with nudes sighted every few minutes to revive flagging concentration and plot, glimpses of a time-honoured British comic tradition can occasionally be discerned: good old smut by way of end-of-pier summer shows, What-the-Butlers-Saw and *Carry On* films. It's a world of relentless double entendres, verbal misunderstandings, randy wives and cuckolded husbands, groping couples, snapping braces and perpetual coitus interruptus. All remarkably innocent: no one swears and the family is regarded as sacrosanct (the film, after all, is primarily family entertainment).

Confessions of a Sixth Form Girl (Schulmädchen-Report – Was Eltern nicht für moglich halten)

(Ernst Hofbauer, 1970, WGer) Friedrich von Thun, Günter Kieslich, Rolf Harnish, Helga Kruck.
90 min.
The rag-bag of confessions (in fact, 'true' case histories) in this poorly graded assembly-line exploiter (the first of a series) are related to the parent-teacher association, with suitable Teutonic authority, by a sixth-former's portly father who (surprise, surprise) turns out to be a child psychologist. This dismal barrel-scraper induces bottomless gloom and an indefinite loss of sexual appetite. JPy

Confessions of a Suburban Girl

(Susan Seidelman, 1992, GB)
50 min.
In this slight documentary (commissioned by BBC Scotland) which explores changing sexual attitudes, Seidelman returns to her home town of Huntingdon Valley, just outside Philadelphia, to search out childhood friends. Interspersing interviews with clips from her films, she traces the interest in 'bad girls' which runs through her work to a youth spent in suburbia, when toughnut Italians wore the coolest clothes and looked like being the hottest dates. Bitter-sweet passages contrast youthful expectations with adult reality, but such hopeless Seidelman efforts as *Cookie* and *She-Devil* don't bear up under the weight of this analysis. CM

Confessions of a Window Cleaner

(Val Guest, 1974, GB) Robin Askwith, Anthony Booth, Sheila White, Dandy Nichols, Bill Maynard.
90 min.
As dismal as its successors in the brief *Confessions* series, this was covered widely in the trade press at the time. Something to do with the bravery of the producers actually going ahead and making what they all but acknowledged was a whole lot of garbage, on the principle that garbage is better for the British film industry than not making anything at all. VG

Confessions of Winifred Wagner, The (Winifred Wagner und die Geschichte des Hauses Wahnfried 1914-1975)

(Hans-Jürgen Syberberg, 1975, WGer) Winifred Wagner.
104 min. b/w.
'He had that perfect Austrian warmth and understanding.' Winifred Wagner (78-year-old widow of Richard Wagner's son Siegfried) on the human face and personal charm of Adolf Hitler. Hitler's passion for Wagner inevitably led him to Winifred, organiser of the Bayreuth Festival. During their 22-year friendship, to whose memory she is stubbornly faithful, Hitler doted on her family and mentioned nothing of politics: 'I would say he was too easily influenced and gave in to radical demands,' is her only criticism, made apparently without irony. This film features Winifred Wagner's first interview (shot almost entirely in medium close-up) about Hitler as a patron of the arts. It's an extraordinary document – about the role of art in a society, about its relation to politics, and about degrees of unawareness. CPe

Confidence (Bizalom)

(István Szabó, 1979, Hun) Ildikó Bánsági,, Péter Andorai, O Gombik, Károly Csáki.
117 min.
Confidence may not possess the surface sheen or panache of Szabó's later blockbuster *Mephisto*, but it's a film of near-equivalent substance within its more intimate scope. Acting a role during wartime is again the focus, but here the false identities (as man and wife) of a harmless refugee couple living through the Nazi occupation of Hungary are assumed out of strict necessity. He is a resistance fugitive, she the wife of another underground member, hustled to safety as a net closes on her husband. At first they share only suspicion and insecurity, but they are hemmed by circumstance into an alliance, then an accommodation, then a relationship. Trust is the crucial variable between them; and the more claustrophobic the film becomes, the more it opens out to address the crux of any relationship, sexual or social. Notions of betrayal and commitment resonate far beyond the couple's tenuous haven. This reductionist description may sound dry, but the film isn't: its political-thriller edginess and emotional poignancy intersect absorbingly, and the central performances are flawless. PT

Confidential Agent

(Herman Shumlin, 1945, US) Charles Boyer, Lauren Bacall, Peter Lorre, Katina Paxinou, Victor Francen, Wanda Hendrix.
118 min. b/w.
Striking, literate adaptation of Graham Greene's novel which takes its tone from Boyer's tired, ageing secret agent (in reality a musician) sent to England in 1937 by the Spanish Loyalists to sabotage a Fascist business deal. Shumlin's direction is inclined to be lethargic (a distinguished stage producer, he made only two movies), but is more than made up for by Wong

Howe's moody lighting, which perfectly captures the twilit world of people living constantly in fear. A marvellous cast makes it a must anyway. TM

Confidential Report
see Mr Arkadin

Confirm or Deny

(Archie Mayo, 1941, US) Don Ameche, Joan Bennett, Roddy McDowall, John Loder, Eric Blore, Arthur Shields, Raymond Walburn.
73 min. b/w.
Fast-moving if fairly ordinary tribute to the heroism of American war correspondents covering World War II. Much of the film gets bogged down in the growing romance between agency man Ameche and Ministry of Information switchboard girl Bennett, but it's entertaining enough when the bombs drop; and collector-cultists may derive pleasure from a script by former journalist and future genius Sam Fuller. GA

Conflict

(Curtis Bernhardt, 1945, US) Humphrey Bogart, Alexis Smith, Sydney Greenstreet, Rose Hobart, Charles Drake, Grant Mitchell.
86 min. b/w.
Routine *film noir* with Bogart as a murderer disoriented by the mounting evidence that his victim is still alive. Greenstreet, exuding detached benignity, hovers over Bogart's dilemma and has the line which ought to pin down the theme – 'Sometimes a thought can be like a malignant disease and eat away the will power' – but somehow Bernhardt never realises that promise. The dominant irony of the first reel, in which Bogart and wife Hobart are publicly 'the happiest of couples' and privately tearing each other apart (a dichotomy bridged by their theme tune, 'Jealousy'), is dispelled by the patchy development later. Alexis Smith's role remains unfocused, while Bogart suffers defiantly and spits out the odd characteristic line. Robert Siodmak had a hand in the story. SG

Conflict of Wings (aka Fuss Over Feathers)

(John Eldridge, 1954, GB) John Gregson, Muriel Pavlow, Kieron Moore, Niall MacGinnis, Guy Middleton, Harry Fowler, Sheila Sweet.
84 min.
Produced by Group Three as part of the government's intervention in the British film industry in the '50s. The conflict in question is between birds wings and RAF wings. The Norfolk villagers want to keep their bird sanctuary, and the RAF want a training ground. Needless to say there is a third way: the Great British Compromise. One minor point of interest is that the script is by Don Sharp from his own novel. PH

Conformist, The (Il Conformista) `100`

(Bernardo Bertolucci, 1969, It/Fr/WGer) Jean-Louis Trintignant, Stefania Sandrelli, Gastone Moschin, Enzo Taroscio, Pierre Clémenti, Dominique Sanda.
115 min.
Like *The Spider's Stratagem*, a subtle anatomy of Italy's fascist past, but here the playful Borgesian time-travelling is replaced by a more personal drive which heralds the Oedipal preoccupations that haunt Bertolucci's later work. Stripping Moravia's novel of all its psychological annotations except one – as a child, the hero suffered trauma at the hands of a homosexual – Bertolucci presents him simultaneously as a suitably murky protagonist for a *film noir* about political assassination, and as a conformist so anxious to live a normal life that he willingly becomes an anonymous tool of the state. Juggling past and present with the same *bravura* flourish as Welles in *Citizen Kane*, Bertolucci conjures a dazzling historical and personal perspective (the marbled insane asylum where his father is incarcerated; the classical vistas of Mussolini's corridors of power; the dance hall where two women tease in an ambiguous tango; the forest road where the assassination runs horribly counter to expectation), demonstrating how the search for normality ends in the inevitable discovery that there is no such thing. TM

Confrontation, The
(Fényes Szelek)

(Miklós Jancsó, 1968, Hun) Lajos Balázsovits, Andrea Drahota, András Bálint, Kati Kovács.
86 min.
'What is the role of the individual in history?' asks one of the characters in Jancsó's film, set in the Hungary of 1947 and concerned with the problems of revolutionary tactics, this time posed for a group of students. *The Confrontation* has more talk than is usual in Jancsó's films, precisely because its form is that of a debate on revolutionary tactics, though of course there is the usual recourse to the specifically Hungarian marching, dancing and folk-song rituals which make his movies continually seductive. RM

Confucian Confusion, A
(Duli Shidai)

(Edward Yang, 1994, Tai) Xianggi Chen, Shujun Ni, Weiming Wang, Bosen Wang.
125 min.
Yang's brilliantly achieved comedy follows a selection of modern urban types through two fraught days and nights rife with misunderstandings and cross-purposes. The specific focus is on Taipei now, a city torn between me-generation aspirations and age-old Chinese ideas of social conformity, but almost everything here could equally well take place in neo-conservative London: Yang's semi-affectionate caricatures of civil servants, business and PR people and the arts crowd are all too recognisable. The new streamlined version of the film is tighter and more provocative than that which baffled most of the comatose British press corps (TO excepted) at Cannes '94; the creative energies that fired *A Brighter Summer Day* are sparkier than ever. TR

Congo

(Frank Marshall, 1995, US) Dylan Walsh, Laura Linney, Joe Don Baker, Tim Curry, Ernie Hudson, Grant Heslov, Mary Ellen Trainor.
108 min.
Congo isn't so much a movie as a gigantic theme park, with the name of Michael Crichton (who wrote the original not-half-bad novel) as a flashing attraction. The storylines take in: the return of a talking mountain gorilla to the wilds of central Africa; the discovery of a perfect diamond that can fuel the megalomaniac dreams of Baker's electronics mogul; lots of special effects gadgetry care of explorer-babe Karen Ross (Linney); a grotesquely OTT performance from Curry as a Translyvanian con-man seeking a lost city; an imminently exploding volcano; jungle disasters and mutant animals; Third World governments in turmoil and nice scenery. Dreadfully muddled, but mildly diverting. SGr

Congo Crossing

(Joseph Pevney, 1956, US) George Nader, Peter Lorre, Virginia Mayo, Michael Pate, Rex Ingram.
87 min.
Dull and derivative Casablanca-type tale of fugitives from the law gathering together in Congotanga, where extradition laws are not practised. The routine goings-on are lit up only by the presence of Lorre and by Russell Metty's elegant Technicolor camerawork. GA

Congo Maisie

(HC Potter, 1940, US) Ann Sothern, John Carroll, Shepperd Strudwick, EE Clive, Rita Johnson, JK Kerrigan.
70 min. b/w.
Sothern takes the title role for this second entry in the MGM series about big-hearted showgirl Maisie Ravier. In this one she stows away and is shipped off to a strife-torn rubber plantation. Cut-price filler slung together on a quiet corner of the studio backlot. TJ

Congress Dances
(Der Kongress tanzt)

(Erik Charell, 1931, Ger) Lilian Harvey, Willy Fritsch, Conrad Veidt, Lil Dagover, Adele Sandrock.
92 min. b/w.
Fluffy Viennese super-operetta: among the most celebrated and sumptuous of the musicals that waltzed all over German screens from the coming of sound to the advent of the 'new' film-makers in the '60s. Attractions include Karl Hoffmann, one

of Germany's great cinematographers; matinée idol Fritsch and his lady-love Harvey; lots of lieder, light comedy, pageantry, dance and romance. Ostrich-like escapism from ominous contemporary events, or dazzling entertainment of the first water to vie with Hollywood's best? SJo

Conman and the Kung Fu Kid
(Langbei wei Jian/aka Wits to Wits)

(Wu Ma, 1974, HK) Henry Yue Young, Wu Ma, Suzy Mang, Shih Kien.
107 min.
For fun and profit, this rips off Leone's *Fistful of Dynamite* by translating Coburn's ex-IRA bomber into a compulsive gambling swindler, and Steiger's greedy Mexican thug into a scrofulous oaf on the run from his fiancée. Most Hong Kong action movies are Western-influenced as this wind up as mixtures of lobotomised Chinese popular culture and crass Hollywood plagiarism. This is the happy exception: since it skips all of Leone's more provocative overtones and uses the rambling plot merely to showcase the two lead actors, it retains most of its Chinese identity, and emerges as one of the most genial of its kind. Henry Yue Young and Wu Ma bounce from farce to cynicism and back in the title roles; details are often abrasive or amusing (the swindler severing his 'offending' hand when he's caught cheating in a casino); and the film's anarchic politics keep the physical extravagances on an upswing. TR

Connecticut Yankee
in King Arthur's Court, A
(aka A Yankee in
King Arthur's Court)

(Tay Garnett, 1949, US) Bing Crosby, Rhonda Fleming, William Bendix, Cedric Hardwicke, Henry Wilcoxon.
107 min.
A decidedly muted musical version of Mark Twain's story about a 20th century blacksmith transported back into the world of Camelot. It's a highly amiable affair, enlivened by lush Technicolor photography, mindlessly amusing humour, and a marvellous performance by Bendix (at his best singing 'Busy Doin' Nothin'' with Hardwicke and Crosby). GA

Connecting Rooms

(Franklin Gollings, 1969, GB) Bette Davis, Michael Redgrave, Alexis Kanner, Kay Walsh, Gabrielle Drake, Olga Georges-Picot, Leo Genn.
103 min.
Adapted from a stage play, but still riddled with act and scene pauses. A seedy boarding-house tale, with the inmates' self-constructed illusions protecting their battered souls from bravely borne truths, it's a fairly classic condensation of several fetishistic concerns endemic to British cinema: Redgrave's ex-schoolmaster winces over the painful memory of a sexy little boy with whom he was innocently (of course) involved in a scandal. Davis soldiers through as the musician who turns out to be merely a busker (albeit a remarkably prosperous one), but sadly succumbs.

Connection, The

(Shirley Clarke, 1961, US) William Redfield, Warren Finnerty, Garry Goodrow, Jerome Raphael, James Anderson, Roscoe Lee Browne, Carl Lee.
110 min. b/w.
The gimmicky premise of Jack Gelber's play – that those were real junkies up on the stage waiting for their fix, killing time by improvising jazz and making with street-jive monologues – probably makes more sense as a movie than it ever did in the theatre. Clarke films it as if it were documentary (so that when the cameraman himself takes a fix, the camera-work goes to pieces), and the Living Theatre actors are convincing enough to sustain this close a scrutiny. Some creaky business with a Salvation Army sister recalls the piece's stage origins, but the music and the sense of 'dead time' retain a 'beat' authenticity. TR

Conqueror, The

(Dick Powell, 1956, US) John Wayne, Susan Hayward, Pedro Armendariz, Agnes Moorehead, Thomas Gomez, William Conrad, John Hoyt, Ted de Corsia, Lee Van Cleef.
111 min.

Over-long, very dull epic produced by Howard Hughes, about the territorial and amorous conquests of Genghis Khan. Wayne, who saw the film as an oriental Western, is horribly miscast as the barbaric warrior, drawling lines like 'You're beautiful in your wrath' to the reluctant Hayward, and looking decidedly un-Oriental. GA

Conquest

(Lucio Fulci, 1983, It/Sp/Mex) George Rivero, Andrea Occhipinti, Sabrina Sellers, Corrado San Martin, Violeta Cela.
92 min.
Best known for his gruesome zombie pics, Fulci here turns his hand to an arrow-and-tomato-sorcery epic involving a couple of lightly-clad he-men who roam o'er the smoky plain, make eyes at women with mudstalked tresses, and do battle 'gainst the legions of evil loosed by a naked, snaked sorceress in a mask (I want him and his weapon,' she seethes, playing suggestively with her pythons). Our heroes encounter husky wolf-men, cobwebb'd screechers and (surprise) zombies; and there is an inordinate amount of spurting wounds, severed heads and oozing poison pustules, which jiffs up the action whenever the dumb dialogue and orange-filtered skies threaten to get tiresome. AB

Conquest of Space

(Byron Haskin, 1955, US) Walter Brooke, Eric Fleming, Mickey Shaughnessy, William Hopper, Ross Martin, Joan Shawlee.
81 min.
Totally bizarre sci-fi epic, mounting a 'realistic' attempt at an expedition to Mars, which has some animated segments as pretty as *2001*. This George Pal project tries elaborately (and presumably expensively) for authenticity, and naturally gets it all wrong. But there's something pleasantly loony about the whole thing, from the chicken-pie capsules down to the anti-gravity zip-up boots. At one point the script even has its chief astronaut denouncing the entire mission as a 'cursed abomination' when he gets a touch of religion. A fascinating relic. DP

Conquest of the Earth

(Sidney Hayers/Sigmund Neufeld Jr/Barry Crane, 1980, US) Kent McCord, Barry Van Dyke, Robyn Douglass, Lorne Greene, John Colicos, Robert Reed, Wolfman Jack.
99 min.
The third movie instalment of TV's *Battlestar Galactica*, continuing its sluggish slog in the wake of *Star Wars*. Three directors are credited (presumably three episodes were cobbled), but their efforts are uniformly faceless as the Cylon invaders laboriously make it to Earth. Even Wolfman Jack, making a guest appearance as a disc jockey whose radio transmitter is a prime target for attack, seems under the weather. TM

Conquest of the
Planet of the Apes

(J Lee Thompson, 1972, US) Roddy McDowall, Don Murray, Natalie Trundy, Ricardo Montalban, Hari Rhodes, Severn Darden.
85 min.
Fourth in the series derived from Pierre Boulle's novel, with the pet apes who have evolved into slaves rebelling against their human masters. Dismally lurid stuff, ham-fistedly directed and low on credibility. TM

Conquest of the South Pole

(Gillies MacKinnon, 1988, GB) Stevan Rimkus, Laura Girling, Leonard O'Malley, Gordon Cameron, Ewen Bremner, Alastair Galbraith, John Michie, Julie-Kate Olivier.
91 min. b/w & col.
From the opening credits, featuring archive footage of Amundsen's historic expedition, it's clear that MacKinnon's first feature – a low budget adaptation of Manfred Karge's play – is going to be quite special. Led by the seductive and sinister Sloopianek (Rimkus), a group of unemployed Scottish youngsters decide to fill their time – and fend off fears of failure – by recreating the first successful trip to the Antarctic in their home town. Almost inevitably, the task takes on epic proportions – glaciers, equipment, huskies and penguins must be found – and the group steadily splinters over strategy and purpose. Shot among the ice-houses, docksides and tenement blocks of Leith, the film is at once faithful to Karge and a visually stim-

ulating piece of cinema. Though endowed with a bleak conclusion, it never lacks wit or tenderness, since MacKinnon celebrates the crucial role played by imagination in the youth's fantastic voyage of self-discovery. With strong performances from a young, largely unknown cast, he explores a broad emotional landscape, never slipping into facile pathos or liberal tub-thumping, so that one is finally left invigorated by what might otherwise have seemed a futile, ludicrous odyssey. GA

Conrack
(Martin Ritt, 1974, US) Jon Voight, Paul Winfield, Hume Cronyn, Madge Sinclair, Tina Andrews, Antonio Fargas.
106 min.
Ritt's taste for significant subjects and some heavy underlining of his themes is confirmed by this tale of a white, hip, long-haired, anti-Vietnam war teacher who takes a backwoods assignment which lands him in a one-room black school where he confronts ignorance and deprivation of a depth he had never dreamed existed. Mercifully, the potentially dubious aspects of the subject are mostly exorcised, in part by a strong script (adapted from the book by real-life teacher Pat Conroy), but largely by the engaging and persuasive performance Ritt draws from Voight (equally convincingly backed by the mainly juvenile cast). *Conrack* treads a line perilously close to Sounder, but avoids that film's mawkish contrivance. VG

Consenting Adults
(Alan J Pakula, 1992, US) Kevin Kline, Mary Elizabeth Mastrantonio, Kevin Spacey, Rebecca Miller, Forest Whitaker, EG Marshall.
99 min.
This faltering addition to Hollywood's yuppies in peril cycle starts better than it finishes. Jinglewriter Richard (Kline, wooden) and his supportive wife Priscilla (Mastrantonio) have every reason to be content with their lifestyle until 'financial adviser' Eddy (Spacey) and his improbably blonde partner Kay (Miller) arrive to upset the balance. Friendly relations are soon established, but 'neath the surface simmer sexual tensions which insurance scam-meister Eddy is all too keen to exploit, suggesting that he and Richard do the not-done thing by sleeping with each other's wives. The following day, police discover semen traces on Kay's battered body, and Richard is suddenly prime suspect in a murder case. His life disintegrates before his very eyes, and the movie follows suit. Twenty years after the taut *Klute*, Pakula's touch has deserted him; the glossy, literalist approach he favours here works firmly against the arrant contrivances in Matthew Chapman's screenplay, rendering already convoluted events even more ridiculous. TJ

Consequence, The (Die Konsequenz)
(Wolfgang Petersen, 1977, WGer) Jürgen Prochnow, Ernst Hannawald, Walo Lüönd, Edith Volkmann, Erwin Kohlund.
100 min. b/w.
This charts the fraught course of a gay male romance between an actor (who serves time for seducing a minor) and the cherubic son of a prison warden. A contrived story-line erects every obstacle possible along the way, but the overall sincerity and the genuinely sobering ending help make up for the way the dice are loaded. TR

Conspiracy of Hearts
(Ralph Thomas, 1960, GB) Lilli Palmer, Sylvia Syms, Yvonne Mitchell, Ronald Lewis, Albert Lieven, Peter Arne, Nora Swinburne.
116 min. b/w.
If you want to know what the ultimately synthetic box-office film would look like, then try this weepie. It contains calculated doses of the three magic ingredients guaranteed to gladden all nice old ladies: nuns, animals and children. In fact, it's got Catholic nuns saving Jewish children from naughty Germans. The film conforms to Lawrence's definition of sentimentality as 'working out on yourself feelings you haven't really got'. DP

Conspiracy Theory
(Richard Donner, 1997, US) Mel Gibson, Julia Roberts, Patrick Stewart, Cylk Cozart, Stephen Kahan, Terry Alexander, Alex Mcarthur.
135 min.
Jabbering Mel Gibson is clearly a Manhattan cab-

bie with a troubled past, and his pursuit of upper-bracket love interest Julia Roberts, a Justice Department attorney investigating the murder of her judge father, gets the plot rolling on an expansive, glossy thriller that delivers much less than it at first promises. Donner and cameraman John Schwartzman pull out their best stuff early on when unknown assailants tie Mel to a wheelchair and pump him full of truth drugs. Weird colours. Fast-cuts. All very disorienting, until we realise terminally dull Patrick Stewart is the interrogator with the steel-rimmed glasses. Gibson deserves a nod for taking on a character so obviously fractured by military experiments, but despite having the ultimate paranoiac's pad, he too often settles for playing the lovable wacko, and his memory returns at the convenience of screenwriter Brian Helgeland. A series of increasingly desperate chases, and catchy use of the karaoke classic 'Can't Take My Eyes Off You', masks a lack of confidence in a narrative with too few suspects and the same old CIA bad guys behind it. TJ

Conspirators, The
(Jean Negulesco, 1944, US) Paul Henried, Hedy Lamarr, Sydney Greenstreet, Peter Lorre, Joseph Calleia, Victor Francen, Eduardo Ciannelli, George Macready.
101 min. b/w.
In his days at Warners, Negulesco was as polished a perpetrator of pacy, romantic hokum as Michael Curtiz, and he manages to make this *Casablanca*-type tale entertaining and stylish, despite the contrivances and derivativeness of the plot. Henried is again a resistance fighter, turning up in neutral Lisbon to have an affair with Lamarr (who wouldn't?) and to deal with Nazi spies. With such a cast, and wonderfully dark, contrasty camera-work from Arthur Edeson, enjoyment is assured. GA

Conspirators of Pleasure (Spiklenci slasti)
(Jan Svankmajer, 1996, Czech/Switz/GB) Petr Meissel, Gabriela Wilhelmová, Barbora Hrzánová, Anna Weltlinská.
75 min.
Svankmajer, the Czech genius of surrealism, explores the bizarre erotic impulses of various individuals in modern Prague. One man collects porn magazines, chickens and umbrellas to fashion himself a weird creature. His neighbour does similar things with straw. Their newsagent tinkers with anatomical additions to his hi-tech TV set. The newscaster keeps carp in a bowl in her bedroom, while her neglectful husband hears operatic climaxes in his head whenever he encounters saucepan lids, fur, nails and latex fingers. Finally, there's the postwoman, who rolls bread into doughballs for very odd purposes, after delivering to the first man an ominous note simply saying 'Sunday'. Even though there's an inexorable logic to the meticulous preparation of the 'perversions' finally perpetrated by these loners, Svankmajer's humour is as black, sly and subversive as ever. While there's far less animated material here than in his earlier work (and, indeed, no dialogue), there's a marvellously morbid, grotesque sense of absurd sado-masochistic ritual at play. GA

Constance
(Bruce Morrison, 1984, NZ) Donogh Rees, Shane Bryant, Judie Douglass, Martin Vaughan, Donald McDonald.
103 min.
Imagine that it's 1984 and you go to the cinema dreaming that you're Rita Hayworth, then wake up next morning and find that you are in suburban Auckland, New Zealand – all cheery, scrubbed faces and neat aspirations. A daunting movie subject, which could easily have turned into whimsy and nostalgia; but thanks to a magnificently realised performance by Rees, the film's stab at the tone of the great post-war melodrama is an almost total success. From minor social peccadilloes via debauchery to complete self-abasement, Constance clings to her dream until it destroys her. Combining a real sense of style with some genuine emotion, the film is lush and exhilarating. NR

Constant Factor, The (Constans)
(Krzysztof Zanussi, 1980, Pol) Tadeusz Bradecki, Zofia Mrozowska, Malgorzata Zajaczkowska, Cezary Morawski.
98 min.

Putting a youthful idealist under the microscope, Zanussi demonstrates that in a Communist bureaucracy the constant factor is the network of corruption which ensures that some people are more equal than others. Obviously this notion rang out more boldly in its Polish context. Obviously, too, some of the symbolism is pretty basic, with the hero frustrated in his dream of climbing the Himalayas and having to settle for a window-cleaner's cradle. But Zanussi's quasi-scientific approach, building a mosaic of tangential facts and perceptions out of his findings, often manages to turn ordinary life into something extraordinary. Moments of tenderness and surprise abound, especially in a love affair which illuminates the film with shy, sidelong grace. If boredom nevertheless lurks not too far away, it is because the images are too conventionally framed. TM

Consul, The (Konsul)
(Miroslav Bork, 1989, Pol) Piotr Fronczewski, Maria Pakulnis, Krzysztof Zaleski, Henryk Bista.
104 min.
A frustratingly dry black comedy which satirises bureaucracy, hypocrisy and greed (what else?) as it follows an ingenious and daring con-man around modern Poland. Fronczewski's performance as the eponymous hero is subtly modulated and appropriately charismatic, while the slow-to-start story, which eventually sees him pose as a nonexistent Austrian diplomat, is fascinating enough in a *House of Games* kind of way. But the whole could have benefited from more ebullient direction; as it is, the 'moral' (the swindler couldn't operate successfully if it weren't for the complicity of both his victims and the State) tends to overwhelm any humour or narrative drive. GA

Consuming Passions
(Giles Foster, 1988, GB/US) Vanessa Redgrave, Jonathan Pryce, Tyler Butterworth, Freddie Jones, Prunella Scales, Sammi Davis, Thora Hird, Timothy West, William Rushton, Andrew Sachs, Mary Healey, Bryan Pringle.
98 min.
Recipe for Chocolate Fudge. Take a half-hour TV play about a traditional family-owned confectionery company, the fortunes of which are miraculously revived when three men fall into the chocolate vats one day, creating an overnight tastebud sensation. Flatten it out until it is about three times the length, being careful to remove all but the most cursory references to the original authors, Michael Palin and Terry Jones. Add an inept Norman Wisdom-style hero (Butterworth), and a salacious subplot about a nymphomaniac Malteser (Redgrave) who blackmails him into having esoteric sex. Add a few drops of Essence of Ealing – small family firm threatened by giant conglomerate whose ruthless axemen (Pryce) puts efficiency and image before quality of product. Stir in some soppy love interest. The consistency should be lumpy and the taste insipid. In America these are known as Soylent Brownies. NF

Contact
(Robert Zemeckis, 1997, US) Jodie Foster, Matthew McConaughey, Tom Skerritt, Angela Bassett, John Hurt, David Morse, Rob Lowe, William Fichtner, James Woods.
150 min.
Ellie Arroway (Foster) has devoted her scientific career to scanning the cosmos for signs of life. One day she's rewarded with a radio transmission from a distant galaxy, and the world is transfixed. It's clear that the aliens have plans for us, but whether for good or ill defies human understanding. An intergalactic ambassador is called for, and Ellie wants the job. Zemeckis aims for spiritual reverence reminiscent of *Close Encounters*: the scope and scale of his picture are established by the first shot with a brilliantly sustained zoom through space and time. There are two more virtuoso sequences: a climactic space trip and a breathtakingly outrageous piece of post-modern appropriation with the first images broadcast from outer space. Regrettably, these visual coups only point up the inadequacy of a screenplay (from Carl Sagan's novel) which marries profound philosophical questions with hokey melodramatics, shallow characters and infantile conclusions. It's not just that it resorts to an albino Adventist to inject spurious suspense, nor that it foists McConaughey on us as a randy Luddite priest who is, coincidentally, the love interest (the pillow talk is physics vs meta-

physics). It also features heavy-handed exposition, repetitive, maudlin flashbacks, uneven performances and endless sermonising. TCh

Contact, The (Cheob Sok)

(Chang Yoon-Hyun, 1997, SKor) Han Suk-Kyu, Chun Doo-Yeon, Chu Sang-Mi, Bak Yong Soo.
105 min.
A melancholy radio producer has an on-off affair with a colleague. One of his listeners, however, is so entranced by his playing of the Velvet Underground's 'Pale Blue Eyes' that she starts communicating with him by e-mail – while still carrying a torch for a friend's boyfriend. The pair eventually meet, although cuteness is mostly held at bay by a fragmented narrative which never quite opts for the obvious. Rather too westernised for its own good, but with perceptive insights into what it takes to fuel desire between people who've never met, and nicely acted and shot. GA

Contact Man, The
see Alias Nick Beal

Conte des trois diamants
see Tale of the Three Jewels

Conte d'été
(A Summer's Tale)

(Eric Rohmer, 1996, Fr) Melvil Poupaud, Aurélia Nolin, Amanda Langlet, Gwenaëlle Simon, Aimé Lefèvre, Alain Guellaff, Evelyne Lahana.
113 min.
Rohmer's delicious follow-up to *A Tale of Springtime* and *A Winter's Tale* takes the simplest of stories – a young man torn between three women – and conjures up a cornucopia of emotional, philosophical and comic riches. Gaspard (Poupaud), a moody, introspective and seemingly shy student, is lent an apartment in Brittany for the summer; he hopes to be joined by Léna (Nolin), with whom he thinks he's in love. Whiling away the time, he meets Margot (Langlet), an anthropology student and part-time waitress, whose talent as a confidante introduces him to the idea of platonic friendship with a girl; besides, she already has a boyfriend. Gaspard, however, does get involved with her friend Solène (Simon), since Léna still hasn't contacted him. Then, of course, she turns up out of the blue. So who will he end up taking to the isle of Ouessant for a romantic weekend? Funny, perceptive and, in the end, surprisingly suspenseful, Rohmer's characteristically casual but precise exploration of human desire and delusion proceeds with great subtlety from an initial series of what seem to be dramatically inconsequential scenes to a final act so tightly structured it might almost be farce. As the plotting becomes more complex, so does our understanding of the characters' motives. As ever, Rohmer's fecund insights into love, friendship, manipulation, coincidence and chance are backed up by his typically vivid evocation of time and place, and by superb naturalistic performances. GA

Conte d'hiver
see Winter's Tale, A

Conte de Printemps
see Tale of Springtime, A

Contempt
see Mépris, Le

Contes Immoraux
see Immoral Tales

Contraband (aka Blackout)

(Michael Powell, 1940, GB) Conrad Veidt, Valerie Hobson, Hay Petrie, Raymond Lovell, Esmond Knight, Charles Victor, Peter Bull.
92 min. b/w.
Less stylish than *The Spy in Black*, this espionage thriller is more fun, with its tongue-in-cheek plot revelling in Hitchcockian eccentricities. Making atmospheric use of London under the blackout (including a tout hawking electric torches and gas mask cases at Victoria Station), it has its German agents operating from a warehouse packed with patriotic busts of Neville Chamberlain, while hero and heroine tour a series of bizarre nightclubs before rounding up the villains with enthusiastic help

from a posse of Danish waiters and carousing rugby players picked up en route. Minor by Powell & Pressburger standards, but most enjoyable. TM

Contract, The (Kontrakt)

(Krzysztof Zanussi, 1980, Pol) Maja Komorowska, Tadeusz Lomnicki, Leslie Caron, Magda Jaroszówna, Krzysztof Kolberger.
111 min.
Written and directed by Zanussi for Polish TV, though with production values hardly inferior to those prevalent in the country's cinema output, *The Contract* has a premise just this side of absurdism: a bride has second thoughts at the altar and dashes from the church, leaving the assembled guests to celebrate as if the wedding had taken place. The resulting party, which occupies most of the film's running time, has more than its share of drunken and embarrassing moments, sexual indiscretions and revelations culminating in the discovery that one of the guests has been pilfering from the others' purses and handbags, all of which Zanussi orchestrates with considerable skill to tragi-comic effect. An illumination of the kind of telling details about contemporary Poland, in fact, that one can hardly hope to glean from newspaper and television reports. RM

Contre-allée, La
see Both Sides of the Street

Convent, The (O Convento)

(Manoel de Oliveira, 1994, Port/Fr) Catherine Deneuve, John Malkovich, Luis Miguel Cintra, Leonor Silveria.
90 min.
In which eccentric veteran Oliveira transcends wackiness and achieves utter tosh. US professor Malkovich and wife Deneuve visit a remote Portuguese monastery to research his thesis that Shakespeare was in fact a Spanish Jew, and become embroiled in vaguely sinister sexual shenanigans apparently engineered by the guardian of the place. What might have been an effective horror thriller or psychodrama is turned, by the director's endless erudite allusions to myth, literature and so on, into what looks like a mere blueprint for a more coherent, less tedious meditation on good and evil. GA

Conversa Acabada
see Other One, The

Conversation, The

(Francis Coppola, 1974, US) Gene Hackman, John Cazale, Cindy Williams, Allen Garfield, Frederic Forrest, Teri Garr, Robert Duvall.
113 min.
An inner rather than outer-directed film about the threat of electronic surveillance, conceived well before the Watergate affair broke. Acknowledged as the king of the buggers, Hackman's surveillance expert is an intensely private man. Living alone in a scrupulously anonymous flat, paying functional visits to a mistress who plays no other part in his life, he is himself a machine; and the point Coppola makes is that this very private man only acquires something to be private about through the exercise of his skill as a voyeur. Projecting his own lonely isolation on to a conversation he painstakingly pieces together (mesmerising stuff as he obsessively plays the tapes over and over, adjusting sound levels until words begin to emerge from the crowd noises), he begins to imagine a story of terror and impending tragedy, and feels impelled to try to circumvent it. In a splendidly Hitchcockian denouement, a tragedy duly takes place, but not the one he foresaw; and he is left shattered not only by the realisation that his soul has been exposed, but by the conviction that someone must have planted a bug on him which he simply cannot find. A bleak and devastatingly brilliant film. TM

Conversation Piece (Gruppo di Famiglia in un Interno)

(Luchino Visconti, 1974, It/Fr) Burt Lancaster, Helmut Berger, Claudia Marsani, Silvana Mangano, Elvira Cortese, Stefano Patrizi.
121 min.

A parable about the approach of death, this centres around a slightly Prospero-like professor (Lancaster incarnating a role similar to the one he played in *The Leopard*) who finds his carefully nurtured, opulent solitude upset by the eruption into his life of a wealthy woman (Mangano) and her chaotic jet-set entourage. Berger, for whom the film on one level seems a valedictory love-song, plays an angel of death figure, to whom a certain mystery attaches. If the *dolce vita*-style intrusion is given distinctly Jacqueline Susann-like overtones by the rather dissociated dialogue in the English language version, *Conversation Piece* nevertheless comes across as a visually rich and resonant mystery, far more fluid and sympathetic than *Death in Venice*. VG

Conversations with Willard Van Dyke

(Amalie R Rothschild, 1981, US) Willard Van Dyke, Cole Weston, Ralph Steiner, Joris Ivens, Donald Richie.
58 min.
In the '20s, Willard Van Dyke was a still photographer who apprenticed himself to Edward Weston; in the '30s he moved into socially aware film-making; and during World War II he became an army propagandist. The '50s found him doing personally unsatisfying commercial and documentary work, but the next decade gave him the chance to take over the film department of the Museum of Modern Art, where he introduced the contemporary work of 'downtown' film-makers into the moribund repertory. Now a spry and chipper 76, he has returned to technically pure and richly beautiful still photography; and Rothschild's film allows him to present himself and his career very sympathetically. He is so successful at this, in fact, that subsequent viewing of his famous 1939 documentary, *The City*, is a mite disappointing. The montage is splendid, but the message – that we should abandon squalid cities to live in healthy industrial parks – is embarrassingly naïve, in retrospect at least. MH

Converted, The (Zawrócony)

(Kazimierz Kutz, 1994, Pol) Zbigniew Zamachowski, Anna Waszczyk, Zofia Rysiowna, Marek Kondrat.
79 min.
Lugubrious political satire set in a Polish industrial town in 1981. Tomasz is a Party animal who readily agrees to spy on a Solidarity rally for his bosses in return for a promised holiday in Bulgaria. He later finds himself arrested for his subversive activities. Very Eastern European, this. Zamachowski (*Three Colours: White*) plays Tomasz as a benign, bandly-legged buffoon, a kind of post-revolutionary Norman Wisdom. But as for his conversion, and the logic of his superiors, most mystifying. TCh

Convoy

(Sam Peckinpah, 1978, US) Kris Kristofferson, Ali MacGraw, Ernest Borgnine, Burt Young, Madge Sinclair, Franklyn Ajaye, Seymour Cassel.
110 min.
Taking CW McCall's hit single as starting-point, script-writer Bill Norton (director of *Cisco Pike*) makes Rubber Duck (Kristofferson) a populist hero of the classic Hollywood kind, leading a group of heavy truckers in their war of independence waged on the highways of America; and Peckinpah's direction places the film in the tongue-in-cheek comic vein of his own earlier *Ballad of Cable Hogue*. Its blatant and impossible artifice is also completely in keeping with Peckinpah's pessimistic streak. Police cars, trucks and bars are destroyed in balletic slow-motion, but none of the characters appears to get hurt (and no one dies – even when you think they do). The narrative goes a bit over the top in the second half, but it's after a large dose of the best kind of escapist good humour. RM

Coogan's Bluff

(Don Siegel, 1968, US) Clint Eastwood, Lee J Cobb, Susan Clark, Tisha Sterling, Don Stroud, Betty Field, Tom Tully.
100 min.
The second film in Siegel's rogue cop cycle, this falls between *Madigan* and *Dirty Harry*. It's about an Arizona deputy sent to New York, stetson, boots and all, to escort a prisoner home; the pris-

oner escapes, and Coogan (Eastwood) roams New York, cowboy in the big city, until he eventually recaptures the hippy prisoner and returns home. Siegel's handling of this conflict between the self-reliant Westerner and the big-city rule book is predictably very funny, and he is aided by a very tight script as well as a mercilessly sarcastic performance from Cobb as Coogan's New York superior. Even Siegel's somehow off-centre treatment of New York hippiedom is intriguingly wry. RM

Cookie

(Susan Seidelman, 1989, US) Peter Falk, Dianne Wiest, Emily Lloyd, Michael V Gazzo, Brenda Vaccaro, Adrian Pasdar, Lionel Stander, Jerry Lewis, Bob Gunton, Ben Rayson, Ricki Lake, Joe Mantello.
93 min.
If this light-hearted account of Mafia mayhem fails to deliver, it's through no fault of the performances. Dino Capisco (Falk) is a labour racketeer on parole after 13 years behind bars; Cookie (Lloyd) is his free-spirited daughter. Despite close surveillance from the law, Dino manages to wrest some prestige and power from old 'business' associates, while his biggest headache concerns his troubled relationship with Cookie. There are moments to savour, notably when Wiest (as Cookie's mother/Dino's mistress), Vacarro (Dino's wife) or Falk are on screen. Lloyd affects a convincing Brooklyn accent, and she does her utmost with limited dialogue. Crucially, the central rift which supposedly exists between father and daughter fails to materialise with any sense of conviction; instead, the film falls back on stereotyping. Seidelman brings visual flair, but given the poorly conceived script, *Cookie* fails to touch female sensibilities in the same way as *Desperately Seeking Susan* and the under-rated *Making Mr Right*. CM

Cook, the Thief, His Wife (100) & Her Lover, The

(Peter Greenaway, 1989, GB/Fr) Richard Bohringer, Michael Gambon, Helen Mirren, Alan Howard, Tim Roth, Ciaran Hinds, Gary Olsen, Ewan Stewart, Roger Ashton Griffiths, Ron Cook, Liz Smith, Ian Dury, Diane Langton.
124 min.
Greenaway's film begins with a man stripped naked, force-fed shit and pissed on, and it ends in cannibalism. Between, there lies a simple tale of adultery, jealousy and revenge. Wealthy London hoodlum Gambon nightly visits the ritzy restaurant he has bought, humiliating his wife (Mirren), chef (Bohringer) and thugs with his *nouveau riche* vulgarity and threats of violence. Understandably tired of him, his wife embarks on an affair (in the loos, naturally) with another regular customer, the quiet, bookish Howard. It's the details – as in all Greenaway movies, far from incidental – that provide most interest: odd connections made between sex, eating, love and death. Since the characters are here less educated than usual, the witty wordplay of Greenaway's finest work is missing; and though it looks sumptuous enough – with Sacha Vierny's 'Scope camera relishing the reds, golds and greens of the set and Jean-Paul Gaultier's gaudily stylised costumes – shooting in a studio seems to have cramped the director's taste for elegantly surreal symmetries. For a Jacobean-style drama about deadly emotions, the film lacks passion; only in the final half-hour, with Michael Nyman's funereal music supplying a welcome gravity, does it at last exert a stately power. GA

Cool Breeze

(Barry Pollack, 1972, US) Thalmus Rasulala, Judy Pace, Jim Watkins, Raymond St Jacques, Lincoln Kilpatrick, Sam Laws.
102 min.
An updated black remake of *The Asphalt Jungle* becomes formula cops 'n robbers, with all the ethnocentricity needed to turn on those amused by it (usually whites) and those in need of heroes/self images (generally blacks). Having only a few nice touches (like the robbery in which three of the gang wear grotesque masks of Nixon, Agnew and Johnson), the film is most notable for its array of black asses – perhaps the most exploited outfront on the commercial cinema screen. JPi

Cooley High

(Michael Schultz, 1975, US) Glynn Turman, Lawrence Hilton-Jacobs, Garrett Morris, Cynthia Davis, Corin Rogers.
107 min.

An enormous box-office hit in the States, *Cooley High* – a kind of black *American Graffiti* or *Lords of Flatbush* about a group of high school kids in the '60s (hence Motown sound-track) – is streets ahead of the average blaxploitation effort, yet is still something of a disappointment. Partly the fault lies with the script, and partly with a certain commercial gloss; one or two of the characters nevertheless do come over with some distinctiveness, thanks to OK performances. VG

Cool Hand Luke

(Stuart Rosenberg, 1967, US) Paul Newman, George Kennedy, JD Cannon, Lou Antonio, Robert Drivas, Strother Martin, Jo Van Fleet, Clifton James, Dennis Hopper, Harry Dean Stanton.
127 min.
A caustically witty look at the American South and its still-surviving chain gangs, with Newman in fine sardonic form as the boss-baiter who refuses to submit and becomes a hero to his fellow-prisoners. Underlying the hard-bitten surface is a slightly uncomfortable allegory which identifies Newman as a Christ figure (and reminds one that Rosenberg once directed the awful, Moral Rearmament-ish *Question 7*). But this scarcely detracts from the brilliantly idiosyncratic script (by Donn Pearce from his own novel) or from Conrad Hall's glittering camera-work (which survives Rosenberg's penchant for the zoom lens and shots reflected in sun-glasses). TM

Cool Runnings

(Jon Turteltaub, 1993, US) Leon, Doug E Doug, Rawle D Lewis, Malik Yoba, John Candy, Raymond J Barry.
98 min.
Perhaps the only thing less likely than a Jamaican bobsled team is a Hollywood film inspired by the true story of the crew that competed in the 1988 US Olympics. Not that this sticks closely to the facts; instead, it's another *Rocky*-style sports movie about the underdogs who achieve public recognition and self-respect. Travelogue shots of happy Jamaicans dancing in the sun give way to patronising comedy as slobbish ex-coach Candy is cajoled into teaching four novices. The missing ingredients are snow and ice, but there's plenty of this when the scene shifts to Canada. In his prime, co-writer Michael Ritchie might have turned this into a caustic *Downhill Racer* or *Bad News Bears*-style critique of professional sporting values. Director Turteltaub, on the other hand, patronises both characters and audience with daft knockabout humour, tear-jerking sentiment and racial stereotyping which skates on very thin ice. NF

Cool World

(Ralph Bakshi, 1992, US) Gabriel Byrne, Brad Pitt, (voice of) Kim Basinger.
102 min.
Animator Bakshi promises a hipper version of *Who Framed Roger Rabbit*, but delivers a pale imitation. The action shifts between our world and the Cool World, an anarchic cartoon universe where Detective Frank Harris (Pitt) has to stop the only other human (Byrne) from being seduced by voluptuous Holli Would (voiced by Basinger), or for some reason the end of both worlds would be nigh. Bakshi has triumphed before without much plot, happiest when given free rein to be weird, but here you get the impression that the studio got cold feet. Apart from a thumping acid house soundtrack, and one extraordinary shot which takes the 'camera' into a character's mouth, through the guts and out the anus, the chaos is strangely muted. Even the eventual universe-shaking shag is an anti-climax, and by the time all hell rips loose just before the abysmally contrived happy ending, you're well past caring. DW

Cool World, The

(Shirley Clarke, 1963, US) Hampton Clanton, Yolanda Rodriguez, Carl Lee, Gloria Foster, Bostic Felton, Jerome Raphael.
106 min. b/w.
The Cool World was Frederick Wiseman's first involvement with cinema (he produced it) and Shirley Clarke's second feature as director/writer (after *The Connection*). At heart, it's a not-very-interesting melodrama about a black kid in Harlem learning the hard way that crime is no answer to social problems. But on the surface it's a very much more interesting view of day-to-day

life in the ghetto, patterned as a flow of 'insignificant' incidents, variously angry, frightened and defeated characters, and all too credible pressures. Often crudely photographed, but with a brilliantly multi-layered sound-track which integrates some fine jazz. TR

Cop

(James B Harris, 1987, US) James Woods, Lesley Ann Warren, Charles Durning, Charles Haid, Raymond J Barry, Randi Brooks, Steven Lambert.
110 min.
This mean, moody, and muddled *Dirty Harry*-style thriller, adapted from James Ellroy's crime novel *Blood on the Moon*, brutally manhandles its feminist theme and debases Woods' rare talent for portraying sympathetic psychotics. Other than that it's slickly made, violent, and (intentionally and unintentionally) funny. Woods plays a LAPD detective whose idea of communicating with his seven-year-old daughter is sharing sordid tales of his busts. His wife takes exception, the child, and a one-way ticket to San Francisco. Is he sick or merely work obsessed? A call has him fast on the trail of a serial killer. The first mutilated female victim has books on the shelf with titles like *The Womb Has Teeth*. Another call has him rendezvous with a purveyor of sex parties; she's later found trussed up, blood-spattered and dead. Finally, a diary note leads to a feminist bookshop run by a soured romantic Warren, once gang-raped at the very school Woods attended. Could that be the clue? WH

Cop & ½ (aka Cop and a Half)

(Henry Winkler, 1993, US) Burt Reynolds, Norman D Golden II, Ruby Dee, Holland Taylor, Ray Sharkey.
97 min.
Eight-year-old Devon (Golden) dreams of being a cop: he watches the TV shows, knows the procedures and has learned the lingo – all he needs is a badge and some cuffs. So when he conveniently witnesses a crime in progress, Devon negotiates a little quid pro quo. He'll spill the beans on the bad guys if the good guys will let him play cop for a day. Cynical, battle-weary plainclothes detective Reynolds, who thinks the only cuffs kids should be given are ones round the ears, gets the assignment. Reynolds' lazy performance combines elements of his tough guy persona and his light comic manner, but is a poor photocopy of his best work. As for the cute, grinning Golden, let's just say Macaulay Culkin can rest easy in his bed. NF

Cop au Vin (Poulet au Vinaigre)

(Claude Chabrol, 1984, Fr) Jean Poiret, Stéphane Audran, Michel Bouquet, Jean Topart, Lucas Belvaux, Pauline Lafont.
110 min.
Grotesque murders in a small provincial town; huge meals; a scourging of the bourgeoisie. Where could this be but Chabrol country? The young postboy is investigating the local cartel's murderous business schemes, with the help of his crippled mother (an increasingly aggrieved Audran) and his girl-friend. But he is no match for the out-of-town cop (*poulet*) wonderfully played by Poiret as an omniscient, genial fellow who transforms into a roughhouse two-fister when occasion demands. And it is all done with the skittishness which Chabrol brings to this kind of policier, but given edge by his very mocking eye. CPea

CopLand

(James Mangold, 1997, US) Sylvester Stallone, Harvey Keitel, Ray Liotta, Robert De Niro, Peter Berg, Janeane Garofolo, Annabella Sciorra, Noah Emmerich, Cathy Moriarty, Deborah Harry.
105 min.
When all your citizens are big city cops, NYPD seeking rest in the New Jersey commuter belt, who will police the police? Out of a mixture of complaisance, natural deference and an inferiority complex as big as his middle-age spread, local sheriff Freddy Heflin (Stallone) has let things slide, turning a blind eye to the dubious activities of detective Ray Donlan (Keitel) and his cohorts. Freddy's jerked out of his lethargy when Internal Affairs send Moe Tilden (De Niro) to investigate the apparent suicide of another cop, Donlan's cousin. Writer/director Mangold's lat-

ter-day Western is overloaded with good actors, though the bulk of the drama falls on Stallone's broad shoulders. It's effective casting. Stallone's slow, stunted speech patterns mesh well with Freddy's dim realisation that sometimes integrity isn't enough, that you have to put yourself on the line for what you want. His clumsy, unconsummated relationship with Liz (Sciorra) is especially touching – accompanied by scratchy Springsteen records. The mystery suspense elements, however, grind from implausibility (the set-up), to cliché (the climax), with too much back story in between TCh

Cops and Robbers
(Aram Avakian, 1973, US) Cliff Gorman, Joseph Bologna, Dick Ward, Shepperd Strudwick, Ellen Holly, John P Ryan.
89 min.
Racy script by Donald Westlake about two of New York's finest who decide that their uniforms and badges give them an ideal camouflage for pursuing extra-legal activities. They proceed to perpetrate one of the most spectacular securities heists Wall Street has ever seen. There's an added twist as the cops also try to rip off the Mafia men to whom they're supposed to fence the proceeds of their crime. An insubstantial film, rather clumsily edited, but pleasant enough, especially for those who dislike violence and love happy endings. MHo

Cop's Honour (Parole de Flic)
(José Pinheiro, 1985, Fr) Alain Delon, Jacques Perrin, Fiona Gélin, Vincent Landon, Stéphane Ferrara, Jean-François Stévenin.
98 min.
Alain Delon is a man with a mission. An ex-cop ('the best'), his wife and daughter murdered, he returns from playing great white god among the cheery savages of the Congo to avenge his family and rid Lyons of a vigilante group who, dressed like Ninjas, go round town killing petty criminals under orders from a mysterious Mr Big. Not so mysterious, actually, since everything in this atrocious movie is predictable. The women are disposable love objects, the dialogue risible, and the acting wooden in the extreme. Most notable is the appalling sound-track: disco for the sweaty workout, heavy metal for the action, a totally irrelevant use of Tristan and Isolde for a car stunt, and Delon himself crooning the end-credits pap. Delon has no excuse; after all, besides 'acting' and 'singing', he also produced and co-scripted. GA

Copycat
(Jon Amiel, 1995, US) Sigourney Weaver, Holly Hunter, Harry Connick Jr, Dermot Mulroney, William McNamara, JE Freeman, Will Patton, John Rothman, Shannon O'Hurley.
123 min.
Midway through this gimmicky, derivative serial killer thriller, the murderer sends a message to his pursuers, a line from a song by The Police, promising he'll 'turn a murder into Art'. 'Very witty, this guy,' mutters agoraphobic psychologist Sigourney Weaver. 'He wants to dazzle us.' That goes for the film-makers too, of course, who've come up with this peculiarly tasteless, opportunistic conceit: a serial killer who reproduces the murders of notorious serial killers (Bundy, Dahmer, et al). With even less scruple, the screenwriters proceed to replicate the 'feminist' structure from Silence of the Lambs, with Weaver and cop Holly Hunter splintering the Clarice Starling role, consulting convicted psycho Harry Connick Jr for the inside dope, and finally coming face to face with their fears in a scary/silly climax. There are flashes of interest between the intriguingly matched stars, and Amiel keeps the tension high, but the film's imagination is circumscribed by the clichés of the genre, so that the name of that Police tune seems relevant: it's 'Murder by Numbers'. It leaves a nasty taste in the mouth. TCh

Coquille et le Clergyman, La
see Seashell and the Clergyman, the

Coraje del Pueblo, El
(The Courage of the People/
The Night of San Juan)
(Jorge Sanjinés, 1971, Bol/It) Domitila Chungara, Federico Vallejo, Felicidad Vda. de Garcia, Eusebio Gironda.
94 min.

When a talented political film-maker like Sanjines aims a film at a very specific audience (to elucidate that audience's past and present oppression and, hopefully, radicalise its future), then the film may lose much of its impact when transposed to a different culture. So it is with Courage of the People, a bleak representation of a 1967 massacre of Bolivian tin miners by the army, reconstructed with the participation of survivors. Introduced by the depiction of a similar event in 1942, the film progresses to the '67 massacre, depicting the workers' growing resistance without analysing the move towards more radical action. SM

Corbeau, Le (The Raven)
(Henri-Georges Clouzot, 1943, Fr) Pierre Fresnay, Pierre Larquey, Micheline Francey, Ginette Leclerc, Louis Seigner, Noël Roquevert, Sylvie, Roger Blin.
93 min. b/w.
David Thomson calls Clouzot's a 'cinema of total disenchantment'. This exposé of a malicious small town in France must be one of the most depressed films to emerge from the period of the German Occupation: everyone speaks badly of everyone else, rumours of abortion and drug addiction are rife, and a flood of poison-pen letters raises the spiteful hysteria to epidemic level. Clouzot's misanthropy concludes in total defeat; his naggingly over-insistent style occasionally achieves a great blackness. CPe

Cornered
(Edward Dmytryk, 1945, US) Dick Powell, Walter Slezak, Micheline Cheirel, Luther Adler, Morris Carnovsky, Nina Vale, Edgar Barrier, Steven Geray.
102 min. b/w.
Powell's second and definitive attempt to shed his crooner image, as an ex-PoW tracking down the collaborationist responsible for his young French wife's death, is even better than Murder, My Sweet. Dispensing with the expressionistic flurries, it concentrates on bleak ambiguity (abetted by a fine cast) as the hunt goes up in Buenos Aires for a villain whom no one – not even his own wife – has ever seen (a telling metaphor for the hidden face of Fascism). As one might expect of a film whose credits carry at least four blacklist victims (Dmytryk, producer Adrian Scott, actors Adler and Carnovsky), the hard-boiled dialogue is studded with political warnings and forebodings in a manner that now looms as pleasantly period, but is in any case effortlessly carried by Harry Wild's superb noir camerawork. TM

Correction, Please
or how we got into pictures
(Noël Burch, 1979, GB) Sue Lloyd, Jeff Rawle, Lea Brodie, Jimmy Gardner.
52 min.
Using very early archive material and studio-shot footage, Burch – author of Theory of Film Practice – contrives a witty re-staging of the tropes of very early silent American cinema: the uses of space, dialogue, design and the camera are seen evolving (degenerating?) into the recognisable form of narrative cinema. CA

Corridors of Blood
(Robert Day, 1958, GB) Boris Karloff, Betta St John, Finlay Currie, Francis Matthews, Adrienne Corri, Christopher Lee, Francis de Wolff.
86 min. b/w.
Despite the presence of Karloff – as a humanitarian doctor of the 1840s whose experiments with anaesthetics lead to drug addiction and involvement with body-snatchers – this often seems to be little more than an excuse for detailed coverage of some utterly gruesome operations and the systematic mutilation of patients on the operating table. There are some compensations, however, notably a cunningly atmospheric recreation of Victorian London from Day (who made the infinitely superior Grip of the Strangler), and a brief but superbly stylish appearance by Christopher Lee as a soft-spoken villain. DP

Corrina, Corrina
(Jessie Nelson, 1994, US) Whoopi Goldberg, Ray Liotta, Tina Majorino, Don Ameche, Wendy Crewson, Joan Cusack, Jennifer Lewis.
116 min.
Jessie Nelson's movie is loosely based on his own childhood, and no better for it. The story – little

Molly (Majorino) withdraws into a world of silence after her mother's death, causing more grief for her dad (Liotta), until he discovers the perfect nanny (Goldberg), who teaches her to trust her tongue and him his heart again – is stuff you'd stash in a locket. It's a Whoopi vehicle, and the only interest is in Hollywood's tailoring of the race issue to fit the star. Her Corrina is doing the Mary Poppins gig because she can't get a break in the white world. She dreams of writing the sleeve notes to jazz albums and, to illustrate how the system permits blacks to play but not write about jazz, spins Bill Evans' 'Peace Piece' – which is confusing, since Evans was white. Liotta plays Jewish. That's about the level of the debate, but a nearly transparent Don Ameche turns in his last performance, and cinematographer Bruce Surtees gives Rolls-Royce lensing. BC

Corrupt
see Order of Death

Corsa dell'innocente, La
see Flight of the Innocent

Cortazar
(Tristan Bauer, 1994, Arg) Julio Cortazar, Hugo Carrizo, Agustín Goldschmidt.
80 min.
A profile of the Argentine writer Julio Cortazar, encompassing his boxing career, literary work, political radicalism, and personal (and cultural) exile in Europe, interspersed with self-penned tangos and various grandiloquent musings on subjects to hand. The film is a montage (Cortazar's own tape recordings, readings from his writings, archive television interviews, filmed reconstructions) shorn of any outside narration. It's a disjointed technique, but one which, given patience, achieves a rare meditative quality that helps to temper some of the film's more drily intellectual aspects. As do the tangos. Even so, its appeal is likely to be confined to those with a prior interest in the man and his work. NB

Corvette K-225
(aka The Nelson Touch)
(Richard Rosson, 1943, US) Randolph Scott, James Brown, Ella Raines, Barry Fitzgerald, Andy Devine, Walter Sande.
99 min. b/w.
Standard, though unusually muted, World War II yarn about the sterling work done by a Canadian commander and his corvette crew on convoy patrol in the Atlantic. As one might expect with Howard Hawks as producer, the accent is on the way things are done, but the result – complete with obligatory romantic interest – is not particularly exhilarating. TM

Corvette Summer
(aka The Hot One)
(Matthew Robbins, 1978, US) Mark Hamill, Annie Potts, Eugene Roche, Kim Milford, Dick Miller, Richard McKenzie.
105 min.
One of Hollywood's better 'growing up' movies, this steers well clear of tear-jerker material by tracking the on-off juvenile romance of car-mad (post Star Wars) Hamill and apprentice hooker Annie Potts through the neon glare of Las Vegas. He's lost his cherished customised Stingray and is gradually losing his illusions too, while she's lost her inhibitions a little too early for safety. 'Life's lessons' are pretty easy to take, though, when delivered in such a stylishly shaggy-dog fashion. PT

Cosh Boy (aka The Slasher)
(Lewis Gilbert, 1953, GB) James Kenney, Joan Collins, Hermione Baddeley, Hermione Gingold, Sean Lynch, Laurence Naismith, Sidney James.
75 min. b/w.
The first British-made picture to be awarded an 'X' certificate, and much reviled at the time for its sensationalism, Lewis Gilbert's homegrown crime picture looks pretty tame more than 40 years on. Youthful Kenney, who played the role in Bruce Walker's play Master Crook, from which the film was adapted, is the kind of hoodlum who steals granny's savings and bashes old ladies over the head, while Collins is the girl he gets pregnant then callously rejects. In fact, it's a rea-

sonably worthy social-conscience effort in the British manner. The resemblance to the Craig/Bentley case (see *Let Him Have It*) didn't go unnoticed, and the BBFC softened some scenes where Kenney wields cosh and razor before letting it pass. TJ

Cosi

(Mark Joffe, 1995, Aust) Ben Mendelsohn, Barry Otto, Toni Collette, Rachel Griffiths, Colin Friels, Pamela Raide, Jacki Weaver, Aden Young, Greta Scacchi.
100 min.
Ben Mendelsohn is employed as drama therapist at a mental hospital; completely inexperienced, he finds it tough when Otto, ring leader of the patients, insists they stage a production of Mozart's *Cosi fan tutte*...with predictably chaotic results. Though the film is too broadly 'comic' and, in the end, sentimental to live up to director Joffe's earlier *Spotswood*, and while its treatment of mental illness is at the very least dodgy, it does have a quirky vitality, some good lines and likeable performances by many Australian stalwarts (even Greta Scacchi has a nice, uncredited cameo). GA

Costa Brava (Family Album)

(Marta Balletbò-Coll, 1994, Sp) Desi del Valle, Marta Balletbò-Coll, Montserrat Gausachs, Josep Maria Brugués.
92 min.
Shot in English over 14 days, split between Barcelona and the Spanish coast, this witty and gradually affecting study of a lesbian love affair blossoming against the odds is necessarily constrained, the action taking place chiefly in phone booths, an apartment and on a roof. That's not to say though, that the director hasn't made the most of scant resources. Anna (Balletbò-Coll) is forced to make ends meet as a tourist guide; her free time is spent getting her one-woman show, 'Love Thy Neighbour', off the ground. Until, that is, she falls in love with an exasperating Israeli engineer (del Valle) who turns Anna's world (and underwear draw) upside down. Slight, but endearing. FM

Cottage to Let
(aka Bombsight Stolen)

(Anthony Asquith, 1941, GB) Leslie Banks, Alastair Sim, John Mills, George Cole, Jeanne de Casalis, Carla Lehmann, Michael Wilding, Catherine Lacey, Wally Patch.
90 min. b/w.
Jaunty wartime fare with Cole as a crafty Cockney lad (he'd created the role in Geoffrey Kerr's play) evacuated to rural Scotland in time to stop a Glasgow-based spy ring getting their hands on inventor Banks' revolutionary new bombsight. Mills drops by as a passing parachutist, and Sim makes the most of his role as an *éminence grise*. TJ

Cotton Club, The

(Francis Coppola, 1984, US) Richard Gere, Gregory Hines, Diane Lane, Lonette McKee, Bob Hoskins, James Remar, Nicolas Cage, Allen Garfield, Fred Gwynne, Gwen Verdon.
128 min.
The misconception that sinks this often handsome confection is that revivalism will spread evenly over separate cultures, turning the Prohibition gangsters and backstage romances and old jazz into a winning hand of iconographic flash-cards for the camera. What neck! Neither Ellington's music nor the black dancers will hold still, of course, and fatally detain the emotions while the lovers do not. Gere, with masher's taz and major hair-oil, phones in his performance from the wardrobe department. Hines, his black opposite number, does better with less. Of the hoods, only Hoskins and Fred Gwynne rise above the mundane mayhem, spinning headlines and general dis-dat-doze. The narrative is a mess despite the simplistic twinning of tales, and – worse yet – keeps interrupting the heart-stopping hoofing. BC

Couch

(Andy Warhol, 1964, US) Gerard Malanga, Baby Jane Holzer, Ondine, Allen Ginzberg, Jack Kerouac.
40 min.
Pre-*Chelsea Girls* Warhol, which means silent, black-and-white, fixed-angle stares at nothing

very much. Actually, *Couch* is action-packed by the standards of most early Warhol: it comprises a series of takes of the couch itself, upon which persons in varying stages of undress enjoy carnal relations with each other in varying permutations. Much of it is gay. The print seen here, a dupe of a dupe, almost totally lacks visual definition: less orgasmic than protoplasmic. TR

Couch Trip, The

(Michael Ritchie, 1987, US) Dan Aykroyd, Walter Matthau, Charles Grodin, Donna Dixon, Richard Romanus, Mary Gross, David Clennon.
98 min.
When LA celebrity sex therapist George Maitlin (Grodin) succumbs to a nervous breakdown, a London sabbatical is advised. The call to suitably uncharismatic locum Dr Baird is intercepted by lunatic John Burns Jr (Aykroyd). Assuming Baird's identity, Burns duly shows up in Therapy City, where his dotty advice worries the sponsors of Maitlin's popular radio phone-in show but wows the clients. A fellow con-artist (Matthau) rumbles the scam, and wants a piece of the proceeds. Ritchie's irreverent farce won't tip the balance of Hollywood's love/hate relationship with psychiatry, but it does have fun with the mythology. Aykroyd revels in a role tailor-made for his shoot-from-the-lip talent, his exuberant performance illuminating the film's sometimes flabby sentimentality and slack structure. Intermittently hilarious, if rickety, fun. SCu

Counsellor, The
(Il Consigliori)

(Alberto De Martino, It/Sp, 1973) Martin Balsam, Tomas Milian, Francisco Rabal, Dagmar Lassander, Carlo Tamberlani.
102 min.
Lame Mafia movie made in San Francisco, but with a predominantly Italian cast dubbed into English. Weighty debts are owed to *Bullitt* (locations and car chases) and *The Godfather* (subject and theme). Balsam excepted, the gangsters are all reduced to wide-screen smiles and hostile eyes, which gives most of the cast the appearance of ventriloquists' dummies; and apart from some amusingly heavy-handed symbolism, there's little of consequence to note.

Count a Lonely Cadence
(aka Stockade)

(Martin Sheen, 1990, US) Charlie Sheen, Martin Sheen, F Murray Abraham, Larry Fishburne, Blu Mankuma, Michael Beach, Harry Stewart, John Toles-Bey, James Marshall, Ramon Estevez.
97 min.
'He's an intelligent enough kid, just lacks discipline'. With these words still ringing in his ears, Charlie Sheen is summarily despatched to the US Army, and before you can say AWOL has taken up a 90-day lease in the stockade. The camp commander, a strict disciplinarian, is Martin Sheen, but this displaced father-son conflict turns out to be only one aspect of the story. The bulk of the screen time is devoted to Charlie and the other five prisoners, all of whom are black. The progression from mutual suspicion to friendship may not be revelatory, but the performances (Fishburne, Stewart, Beach) are lively and Sheen's direction assured. If there's something a mite patronising about the 'colourful' sub-patrol antics, the movie comes as near as dammit to acknowledging, at the close, the gulf that still divides the races, and that's a surprise in this eminently liberal work. On the down side, there's no real feel for period (the mid-'60s), and that dull Sheen psychodrama doesn't go away. TCh

Countdown

(Robert Altman, 1967, US) James Caan, Robert Duvall, Joanna Moore, Barbara Baxley, Michael Murphy, Steve Ihnat.
101 min.
Made before *M*A*S*H* (and subjected to re-editing by the studio), Altman's drama about American astronauts being rushed to the moon in an attempt to beat the Russians is a surprisingly human affair, concentrating less on sci-fi hardware than on the emotional crises affecting the men and their families. Slightly soapy in parts, but overall it's an intelligent and taut little film, interesting for the way it foreshadows not only the actual look of the Apollo capsules but

also Altman's later style: the lack of interest in 'plot', the overlapping dialogue, and the imaginative use of the 'scope frame are all there, if in embryonic form. GA

Count Dracula
(El Conde Dracula)

(Jesús Franco, 1970, Sp/It/WGer) Christopher Lee, Herbert Lom, Klaus Kinski, Frederick Williams, Maria Rohm, Soledad Miranda.
98 min.
With Kinski gibbering away in the padded cell as the puppet-like Renfield, and Lee re-running his seductive Hammer suavity as the Count, this near-forgotten low-budget version seems to have laid much groundwork for later forays into cinematic vampire lore. The script's ambitions (early marked by a not over-extravagant title claim to be illustrating Stoker's novel 'as written') are high and distinctly dead-pan, though perhaps not best served by direction that veers with some consistency to the endearingly inept (or, more charitably, to rigorous anti-illusionism?). Yet the movie emerges as a soberly intelligent reappraisal of a potent and oft-misrepresented mythology. PT

Count Dracula and
His Vampire Bride

see Satanic Rites of Dracula, The

Counterfeiters

(Peter Stewart ie Sam Newfield, 1948, US) John Sutton, Doris Merrick, Hugh Beaumont, Lon Chaney, George O'Hanlon.
73 min. b/w.
Scotland Yard man Sutton heads for Los Angeles to help the local force bring in a counterfeiting ring. Posing as a confidence trickster, he infiltrates Beaumont's gang, but romance with the alluring Merrick may prove not to be such a good idea after all. Passable support-slot thriller with horror star Chaney as one of the heavies. TJ

Countess Dracula

(Peter Sasdy, 1970, GB) Ingrid Pitt, Nigel Green, Sandor Elès, Maurice Denham, Patience Collier, Lesley-Anne Down, Peter Jeffrey.
93 min.
Stiff performances and shoddy sets apart, this late Hammer depiction of the activities of Countess Elisabeth Bathory – who used to bathe in the blood of slain virgins in an attempt to regain her youth – is still intriguing for its emphasis on corruption and decay rather than vampirism. Pitt is excellent as the baleful Countess. GA

Countess from Hong Kong, A

(Charles Chaplin, 1966, GB) Marlon Brando, Sophia Loren, Sydney Chaplin, Tippi Hedren, Patrick Cargill, Michael Medwin, Margaret Rutherford, Charles Chaplin.
120 min.
Everybody wanted to like Chaplin's first film in ten years (and his last, as it turned out), but it just wasn't funny. His direction is antiquated and almost anonymous, and there is a strange stagy atmosphere, almost as if the cast were continually waiting for prompts. Apparently Chaplin worked hard with his actors, but the fact remains that even if Brando weren't hopelessly miscast as a diplomat who finds a Russian émigré countess (Loren) stowed away in his cabin, it would still have been difficult for anyone to speak Chaplin's stilted lines with conviction. Margaret Rutherford comes off better than most as one of the ship's passengers. DP

Count of Monte-Cristo, The

(David Greene, 1974, GB) Richard Chamberlain, Tony Curtis, Trevor Howard, Louis Jourdan, Donald Pleasence, Kate Nelligan.
104 min.
Shot in Italy and very obviously designed as a TV special (plenty of small gaps for ads, plus a big gap halfway through), this is an above-average piece of junk. The familiar Dumas material is put over with a touch of style (Greene indulges his usual fondness for fancy compositions and loony camera angles), and the equally familiar cast provide good value as they don fancy outfits and parade their clashing mannerisms (Curtis is especially ludicrous, and ends up with a dashing skunk hairdo). The script comes up with the occa-

c

sional gem as well: 'I didn't know – we'd moved away,' the heroine explains after learning that Chamberlain's dad starved to death. Not very good, in other words, but there are worse ways of wasting time. GB

Country

(Richard Pearce, 1984, US) Jessica Lange, Sam Shepard, Wilford Brimley, Matt Clark, Therese Graham, Levi L Knebel.
109 min.
A gritty examination of the way that Reaganite economics is squeezing the life out of the small farmer. Shepard is very fine as the farmer, who, with Lange as his land-owning wife, faces foreclosure by the loan company. The scenes of the hard life are becoming familiar from the down-home type of film, but what sets this one apart is the emphasis placed upon Lange, who becomes the mainstay of family and farm. It's not a comfortable film, nor even a very optimistic one, but its power lies in a very truthful depiction of the men and women that the movies tend to forget. CPea

Country Dance
(aka Brotherly Love)

(J Lee Thompson, 1969, GB) Peter O'Toole, Susannah York, Michael Craig, Harry Andrews, Cyril Cusack, Brian Blessed, Robert Urquhart.
112 min.
The US release title, *Brotherly Love*, better signalled the incestuous relationship at the core of this quirkily comic melodrama of emotional Highland flings (scripted by James Kennaway from his own novel). O'Toole's Scots aristocrat, comes across as an outline first draft for his later role in *The Ruling Class*. The use of Irish landscapes as a stand-in for all the pastoral bits doesn't help much. PT

Country Girls, The

(Desmond Davis, 1983, GB) Sam Neill, Maeve Germaine, Jill Doyle, John Olohan, Britta Smith, Patricia Martin.
108 min.
Clever Kate and naughty Baba are ingenuous heroines typical of novelist Edna O'Brien's shamrock imaginings. Growing together in leaps and bounds, the girls progress honourably from village to convent school, propelled from there by the boot of notoriety to Dublin. Maeve Germaine and Jill Doyle are splendid, cutting an irreverent swathe through this lyrical romance, transforming guilty pleasures into innocent delights. And Sam Neill deserves a mention for recreating yet again a character of urbane charm and simian morals with no discernible sign of boredom. But it is finally director Davis' verdant vision of southern Ireland that opens out O'Brien's novel of '50s mores and manners to something that, although essentially a TV film, plays gracefully on the cinema screen. FD

Country Life

(Michael Blakemore, 1995, Aust) Kerry Fox, Greta Scacchi, Sam Neill, Michael Blakemore, John Hargreaves, Googie Withers, Patricia Kennedy.
117 min.
Blakemore's 'quality' riff on *Uncle Vanya* is set down under in 1919. Deborah (Scacchi) is the object of desire, the frustrated younger wife of a pompous theatre critic (Blakemore). Returning from London to his stepfamily's ornate ancestral pile in New South Wales, the pair, respectively, spark ardour and resentment in the Anglophile household: Dr Askey (Neill), drinker, pacificist and conservationist, is smitten with Deborah, as is his rival, the nervous, artistic and saturnine master of the house, Uncle Jack (Hargreaves). Meanwhile, fresh and self-effacing as the critic's abandoned daughter, Fox steals the acting honours. Blakemore introduces some intriguing reflections on colonial coming-of-age, but they are sketched in such bald, symbolic strokes, it feels easy to be ahead of the game. For the rest, there's a lot of the camera gazing on impressive Hunter Valley locations, and a working over of small snobberies, racism and manners in candle-lit dinner scenes. Neill takes Scacchi for a walk in the bush among the rutting 'roos, where he gets – 'Hadn't we better get back!' – to unbuckle her shoe. Well-dressed, entirely respectable drama, but with little cinematic frisson. WH

Countryman

(Dickie Jobson, 1982, GB) Countryman, Hiram Keller, Carl Bradshaw, Basil Keane, Freshey Richardson, Kristina St Clair.
100 min.
First production from Island Pictures, whose parent record company did so much to introduce reggae to a white audience, but *The Harder They Come* it ain't. An underworked script by writer/director Jobson has Countryman, a Jamaican village fisherman, rescuing two Americans whose small plane has crashed, then sheltering them as they become the quarry of a national man-hunt conducted to disgrace the opposition party during a national election. Unfortunately, the film never works out its political confusions. But even more problematic are the supernatural powers with which its innocent protagonist is endowed, probably the sticking point for wide audience acceptance. An excellent sampler-style sound-track – Marley, Toots, Scratch Perry, Aswad, etc – isn't enough to paper over the deficiencies. Nor is the film's superbly lush landscape cinematography. RM

Count Yorga, Vampire

(Bob Kelljan, 1970, US) Robert Quarry, Roger Perry, Michael Murphy, Michael Macready, Donna Anders, Judith Lang, Edward Walsh.
90 min.
This low-budget modern-day vampire movie is primitive but not unimaginative. Robert Quarry is the Count, a new arrival in California who knows a superstitious state when he sees it. He soon enlists a series of genuinely disgusting vampire brides (one of them tucks into her pet cat), despite the efforts of their mortal husbands. The flip humour and gruesome effects have lost the novelty value that appealed to cult audiences in 1970, but Yorga remains an intriguing off-shoot to the vampire family tree. TCh

Coup de Foudre
(At First Sight/Entre Nous)

(Diane Kurys, 1983, Fr) Miou-Miou, Isabelle Huppert, Guy Marchand, Jean-Pierre Bacri, Robin Renucci, Patrick Bauchau.
111 min.
After dealing with the growing pangs of being a teenager during the '60s in *Diabolo Menthe*, Diane Kurys here turns to the problems of her parents' generation. In 1942, Huppert buys her way out of a camp for Jews in occupied France by marrying an ex-Legionnaire who proposes in a *coup de foudre*. Ten years later, a prosperous bourgeoise in Lyon, she meets an artist (Miou-Miou) who is equally disaffected with her marriage to a good-natured no-hoper. Their developing relationship, 'a little more than friendship and a little less than passion', is the core of the film, enabling them to kick against the pricks. It's all very much in line with the sort of 'Women's Picture' at which Dorothy Arzner was once adept in Hollywood: hardly likely to stretch or threaten the system, but showing – without resorting to melodrama – the desire and heartbreak of everyday life. CPea

Coup de Grâce
(Der Fangschuss)

(Volker Schlöndorff, 1976, WGer/Fr) Margarethe von Trotta, Matthias Habich, Rüdiger Kirschstein, Mathieu Carrière, Valeska Gert.
95 min. b/w.
Of all Schlöndorff's many literary adaptations, this sombre movie from Marguerite Yourcenar's novel is probably the best. It's set in a Baltic country house in 1919, surrounded by echoes and traces of the war, and the meat of it is a gay/straight triangle: Communist sympathiser Sophie (von Trotta) loves German officer Erich (Habich), who seems to be repressing a passion for her brother (Kirschstein). But it's drained of (melo)drama: Schlöndorff films it with eerie detachment, like a *noir Effi Briest*, the better to underline the politics. One memorable indulgence is a squawking performance from Valeska Gert as a crazed aunt. TR

Coup de Menhir, Le

see Asterix and the Big Fight

Coup de Torchon

see Clean Slate

Coupe de Ville

(Joe Roth, 1990, US) Patrick Dempsey, Arye Gross, Daniel Stern, Annabeth Gish, Rita Taggart, Joseph Bologna, Alan Arkin, James Gammon.
99 min.
Roth's low-budget comedy bottles sibling rivalry inside a vintage Cadillac on a cross-country journey, shakes it up, fuels on '60s rock, quarrels and caring, and proves to be a sweetheart of a film. Three dissimilar brothers – a bully in uniform (Stern), a dreamer (Gross) and a teenage rebel (Dempsey) – are directed by their father (Arkin) to deliver the car intact and without a scratch for their mother's birthday. The assignment proves tricky, but along the way the boys learn about co-existence and family loyalty, which was dad's idea in the first place. Nothing spectacularly original about the plot, but the playing throughout is so juicy and the writing so idiosyncratic that it feels like hot news. Fans of major chromium and the white-wall tyre will go through hell with the title vehicle. BC

Coup pour Coup
(Blow for Blow)

(Marin Karmitz, 1972, Fr/WGer) Anne-Marie Bacquier, Danielle Chinsky, Eva Damien, Jean Hébert, Annick Fougéry.
90 min.
For anyone who has suffered a boring, meaningless job and wasted hours planning exquisite revenge on domineering officials, *Coup pour Coup* – a fictional reconstruction of the successful occupation by women of a French textile factory – is the stuff that dreams are made of. At one stage, a group of seamstresses do in fact subject their boss to some of the treatment normally accorded them. More important, the film is a study of the general conditions of many working class women in France, and the suppression they endure both at work and at home. An often exhilarating film, based on actual events, it was made as a collective effort: all the workers in the cast are genuine, but actors were called on to play the management 'heavies'. Its momentum should be enough to dispel any doubts you might have about its naïveté.

Courage Fuyons
(Courage – Let's Run)

(Yves Robert, 1979, Fr) Jean Rochefort, Catherine Deneuve, Philippe Leroy-Beaulieu, Robert Webber, Michel Aumont.
98 min.
One would have thought that the subversive ironies of *Préparez vos Mouchoirs* might have trashed the current run of lightweight French comedies of adultery, but *Courage Fuyons* proves to be yet another bastard offspring of *Pardon Mon Affaire*. In its favour it does have the lugubrious Rochefort, a congenital coward given to such acts as stoning his own car rather than irritate some like-minded students (May 1968), and the ever-watchable Deneuve as the *chanteuse* for whom he forsakes all. But the main theme of cowardice and its toxic effects soon loses its impetus: incidental humour shrinks to a brittle misanthropy, and the underlying suggestion that true love is best contained in the realms of deceit is no more than boulevard comedy has been proclaiming for centuries. CPea

Courage Mountain

(Christopher Leitch, 1989, US) Juliette Caton, Charlie Sheen, Leslie Caron, Yorgo Voyagis, Laura Betti, Jan Rubes, Joanna Clarke, Jade Magri, Nicola Stapleton, Kathryn Ludlow.
98 min.
Since Shirley Temple's *Heidi* of 1937, numerous rehashes have ensued. In this innocuous sequel, set in October 1915, 14-year-old Heidi (Caton) is despatched to school in Italy by her loveable grandfather (Rubes), leaving behind her 'best friend' and prospective lover (Sheen). When the school is commandeered by the Italian army, Heidi and three chums are separated from their guardian (Caron) and fall into the clutches of a fiendish, child-exploiting workhouse owner (Voyagis). Will the girls escape and make it back across the Alps for Christmas? Will Heidi's rustic charm sustain the city-bred cissies through their ordeal? Will Sheen's astonishingly square jaw save the day? Cynical exploitation aside, this is actually an amiable rites-of-passage movie for pre-pubescent audiences. MK

Courage of the People, The

see Coraje del Pueblo, El

Courage Under Fire

(Edward Zwick, 1996, US) Denzel Washington, Meg Ryan, Lou Diamond Phillips, Michael Moriarty, Scott Glenn, Matt Damon, Bronson Pinchot.
116 min.
The Gulf War. In a night engagement, Lt Col Nathaniel Serling (Washington) gives the order to fire on one of his own tanks and kills his best friend. Later, having taken a desk job under Gen Hershberg (Moriarty), he's detailed to investigate helicopter pilot Karen Walden (Ryan), who's been recommended for the Medal of Honor. He discovers conflicting testimonies in Walden's case, and also that his own guilt can no longer be hidden. Will the combination of absence from his family, drink, the promptings of journalist Tony Gartner (Glenn), and the conflicting pulls of 'truth' and 'honour' take away his moral courage to deliver the right report? Zwick's second movie with Washington, following his Civil War epic Glory, is a rolling campaign. It starts well, with an opening 'fog-of-war' sequence of old-fashioned panache. And as the detective-story flashback structure gets under way, what initially seemed adherence to dramatic and moral cliché becomes more complex and interesting. But having set up the pins and knocked 'em down, Zwick disappointingly starts standing them up again – to demonstrate the compromising nature of his 'liberal' values. WH

Courier, The

(Joe Lee/ Frank Deasy, 1987, Eire) Gabriel Byrne, Ian Bannen, Cait O'Riordan, Kevin Doyle, Mary Ryan, Michelle Houlden, Padraig O'Loingsigh.
85 min.
This independent Irish thriller has Mark (O'Loingsigh), a young dispatch rider, becoming embroiled in the nefarious network of horse-trading controlled by Val, a vicious video-dealer played with great malignancy by Byrne. When druggy Danny, an old buddy, is set up by the police and snuffs it sniffing strychnine, Mark determines to get the whole lot of them, and in so doing win the heart of Colette (ex-Pogue O'Riordan). The film's lovey-dovey scenes degenerate into a photo-romance, but the frequent violence is handled with an often distressing realism, and the suspense is generally kept taut. Gabriel Beristain photographs the Dublin locations with a seedy stylishness, and it is clear that Deasy and Lee will one day be directors of flair. Never mind if the flaws provide the odd giggle, this is a work of imagination and ambition. MS

Courtesans of Bombay, The

(Ismail Merchant, 1982, GB) Saeed Jaffrey, Zohra Segal, Kareem Samar.
75 min.
Docu-drama set in the huge Bombay tenement of Pavanpul, where scores of dancing girls go through their paces in a warren of tiny, squalid rooms for the benefit of rapt, occasionally lecherous, male audiences. A fascinating insight, ill-served by Merchant's strangely coy approach, and his device of interspersing reportage with the fictional reminiscences of imaginary habituées. The effect is confusing as well as extremely irritating, and casts a pall of artifice over the whole proceedings. Devotees of Indian dancing will no doubt find much of interest, but those who attempt to follow the recipe for lime pickle are likely to end up scratching their heads, as instructions have been severely truncated in the cutting-room. JP

Court Jester, The

(Norman Panama/Melvin Frank, 1956, US) Danny Kaye, Glynis Johns, Basil Rathbone, Angela Lansbury, Cecil Parker, Mildred Natwick, John Carradine, Robert Middleton.
101 min.
Spasmodically effective spoof of Robin Hood-style adventures, with Kaye as the former circus clown joining up with a band of outlaws to overcome a tyrannical usurper king. Whether it's really watchable depends on what you feel about the charmless Kaye, whose vehicle this is from start to finish. GA

Court Martial

see Carrington VC

Court-Martial of Billy Mitchell, The (aka One Man Mutiny)

(Otto Preminger, 1955, US) Gary Cooper, Charles Bickford, Ralph Bellamy, Rod Steiger, Elizabeth Montgomery, Darren McGavin.
100 min.
Based on fact, Preminger's impressively low-key film is about an American general who, in 1925, accused the military of incompetence and criminal negligence for their lack of interest in building up an air force, and was court-martialled for his views. With Cooper as the crusading officer, one is never in any doubt as to the correctness and sincerity of his views (Mitchell was posthumously rehabilitated in 1947), while Steiger puts in one of his inimitably flashy performances as the prosecuting attorney. GA

Courtneys of Curzon Street, The (aka The Courtney Affair)

(Herbert Wilcox, 1947, GB) Anna Neagle, Michael Wilding, Gladys Young, Coral Browne, Michael Medwin, Daphne Slater, Jack Watling.
120 min. b/w.
Tedious family soaper stretching over three generations, starting with romance between a parlourmaid and a baronet's son, and gradually moving on to the working classes. With the once popular but whimsy pairing of Neagle and Wilding, it's emotionally restrained in that typically frustrating British cinema fashion. GA

Cousin Bobby

(Jonathan Demme, 1992, US)
69 min.
It's perhaps characteristic of Demme's quirky integrity that he should follow The Silence of the Lambs with a low-key, 16mm documentary about a long-lost relative. Typical, too, that the film, for all its seeming amateurishness, ends up being far more than a home movie. For the Reverend Robert Castle, the cousin Demme hasn't seen for over 30 years, is not only a colourful figure – a politically radical Episcopalian minister battling against the poverty, racism and drugs that blight Harlem – but a welcome reminder that even in Bush's America the Left has just about managed to survive. If the film's loose structure means it occasionally lacks focus, Demme's relaxed, open narrative style allows him to paint a wide-ranging portrait of America. GA

Cousin Cousine

(Jean-Charles Tacchella, 1975, Fr) Marie-Christine Barrault, Victor Lanoux, Marie-France Pisier, Guy Marchand, Ginette Garcin.
95 min.
Two families become united by marriage, and a slightly bored wife finds herself falling for one of her new relatives. A sardonic look at family life in France, with winning performances, well handled peripheral details and characters, all as tasty and insubstantial as a marshmallow. GB

Cousins

(Joel Schumacher, 1989, US) Ted Danson, Isabella Rossellini, Sean Young, William Petersen, Lloyd Bridges, Norma Aleandro, Keith Coogan, Gina De Angelis, George Coe.
113 min.
In this uninspired remake of the 1975 French film Cousin Cousine, dance instructor Larry (Danson) and flirtatious wife Tish (Young) become, through complications attendant upon a marriage, distant relatives of some sort to aggressive car rep Tom (Petersen) and his dithering spouse Maria (Rossellini). Celebrations hardly begin before Tish is openly attaching herself to Tom. Confiding their mutual sense of an impending collapse of family ties, Larry and Maria find themselves platonically drawn to one another. Tom, being aware of his wife's growing relationship, does what any butch hypocritical chauvinist would do, and thumps Larry. Will Tom and Tish and Larry and Maria find total happiness, or just go back to being odd couples? The answer's sadly obvious. The film's failure lies in its characterisation: far too many folk have been flung in from all directions, allowing little chance for the central figures to emerge, let alone gell. A ragged, unfunny affair. DA

Cousins, Les (The Cousins)

(Claude Chabrol, 1958, Fr) Gérard Blain, Jean-Claude Brialy, Juliette Mayniel, Claude Cerval, Guy Decomble, Corrado Guarducci, Stéphane Audran.
103 min. b/w.
The town mouse and his country cousin. Or, the story of two students, one who was very, very good, and one who was very, very bad; but the bad one passed his exams, got the girl (when he wanted her), and survived to live profitably ever after. A fine, richly detailed tableau of student life in Paris, and Chabrol's first statement (in his second film) of his sardonic view of life as a matter of the survival of the fittest. The centrepiece, as so often in the early days of the nouvelle vague, is an orgiastic party climaxed, as the guest sleeps it off next morning, by a sublimely cruel and characteristic 'joke' by the bad cousin (Brialy) when he performs an eerie Wagnerian charade with candelabra and Gestapo cap to wake a Jewish student into nightmare. TM

Cousins in Love (Tendres Cousines)

(David Hamilton, 1980, Fr/WGer) Thierry Tevini, Jean Rougerie, Catherine Rouvel, Anja Shute, Valerie Dumas, Laure Dechasnel.
91 min.
Feeble sexploiter set in the French countryside at the start of World War II. A male lead with the build of a nine-year-old (and a dubbed voice like Dustin Hoffman circa The Graduate) beds an almost endless queue of palpitating teenage girls. The oily-lensed soft-focus of 'respectable' erotica merchant Hamilton more often looks like a badly processed Super-8 home movie, with playing and dialogue to match, and all the sexuality of a stale meringue. GD

Cover Girl

(Charles Vidor, 1944, US) Rita Hayworth, Gene Kelly, Phil Silvers, Lee Bowman, Eve Arden, Jinx Falkenburg, Otto Kruger.
107 min.
Cliché-ridden as it follows Hayworth's rise to fame as a magazine model, this musical nevertheless offers plenty of style: Kelly dances up a dream, Hayworth is elegance incarnate, the Jerome Kern-Ira Gershwin score – including the marvellous 'Long Ago and Far Away' – is tuneful throughout, and the whole thing, especially the comic stuff from Silvers and Arden, is executed with considerable brio. And Rudolph Maté's Technicolor photography is faultless.

Cover Girl Killer

(Terry Bishop, 1959, GB) Harry H Corbett, Felicity Young, Spencer Teakle, Victor Brooks, Tony Doonan, Bernadette Milnes, Dermot Kelly, Charles Lloyd Pack.
61 min. b/w.
Compact British filler set against the background of pin-up publishing which pits have-a-go Spencer Teakle, a young Canadian who inherits 'Wow' magazine, against the crazed slayer of a string of glamour models, Harry H Corbett no less. TJ

Cow, The (Gav)

(Daryush Mehrjui, 1968, Iran) Ezat Entezami, Ali Nasirian, Jamshid Mashayekhi.
101 min. b/w.
Beguilingly bizarre tale of a peasant who so adores his cow, the only one in the village, that he is driven insane by suspicion when it dies and he is told (in an attempt to lessen the blow) it has disappeared. Basically the film is designed as a naturalistic portrait of village life, with its sense of community, its petty intrigues and rivalries, its primitive ways and means. But over it, quite literally, hangs the dark of the moon as the bereaved hero sits on the roof of his stable, staring out into the night before descending to take the cow's place, terrified of being stolen in his turn. The man's delusion (or is it a self-protecting magic?) boils up into a dark, demonic possession which suddenly bursts like a star-shell in an ending which speaks volumes about the failure to understand which turns some men into beasts. Truly fascinating, even if Mehrjui occasionally loses his way. TM

Cowboy

(Delmer Daves, 1957, US) Glenn Ford, Jack Lemmon, Anna Kashfi, Brian Donlevy, Dick York, Richard Jaeckel.
92 min.

Likeable attempt to show what life was really like in the old West (ironically based on reminiscences by the notoriously mendacious Frank Harris), with Lemmon as the hotel clerk who joins a 2,000 mile cattle drive from Chicago to the Rio Grande in the 1870s. The episodic narrative, taking in an Indian attack, a Mexican fiesta and a cattle stampede, is more romantic than realistic; but it remains consistently atmospheric and enjoyable, with the striking use of landscape characteristic of Daves. TM

Cowboys, The

(Mark Rydell, 1971, US) John Wayne, Roscoe Lee Browne, Bruce Dern, Slim Pickens, Colleen Dewhurst.
127 min.
Offbeat and intriguing Western, with Wayne as a cattle driver who, deserted when his cowhands head off to a gold-rush, gathers together eleven schoolboys to help him get his herd to market. En route they are easy prey for villains; meanwhile, Wayne introduces them to the joys of shooting, drinking, whoring and killing. Although the film is well performed and beautifully shot by Robert Surtees, its ideology is highly objectionable, celebrating as it does the turning of the boys into hardened killers. Interesting to compare to *The Shootist*, in which young Ron Howard's desire to emulate the skills of his hero, an ageing gunfighter (Wayne again) is criticised at every turn. GA

Cows

see Vacas

Crackers

(Louis Malle, 1983, US) Donald Sutherland, Jack Warden, Sean Penn, Wallace Shawn, Larry Riley, Trinidad Silva.
91 min.
Whatever your opinions of the art-house gloss that used to varnish Malle's films from *Lacombe Lucien* to *Atlantic City*, they did at least suggest a beating heart at work. This thin concoction, based on a 1958 Roman comedy, *I Soliti Ignoti*, has a gang of villains gathering around Warden's rickety pawnshop, mostly to avoid the mean backstreets of San Francisco. Spurred on by poverty and frustration, they decide to crack his safe, only to botch the whole caper in a welter of escalating cack-handedness. There's a nice cameo from Shawn, doing nothing but eat dinner without André, but Sutherland is uncharacteristically null. Cardiac arrest finally seizes the film, after a long case of terminal whimsy. CPea

Crack in the Mirror

(Robby Benson, 1988, US) Robby Benson, Tawny Kitaen, Danny Aiello, Kevin Gray, Cliff Bemis, Tony Levine, Paul Herman.
94 min.
Yes, this is about drug-taking in New York. The movie wants to do two things: to attract a lucrative young audience, and to deliver a heavy anti-drugs message. The two, unfortunately, are mutually exclusive in this case. Scott (Benson) and Vanessa (Kitaen) are young, beautiful, and upwardly mobile. To look at their Park Avenue apartment and trendy attire, you'd never believe they were short of dosh, but they are; so short that preppy, clean-living Scott goes AWOL to take over a drugs empire for a villain he hardly knows. Unlikely? Well, get this. While the dealer is hiding from the mob, Scott settles into his employer's high-tech penthouse, and within days has taken to coke-dealing and crack manufacturing like a duck to water. The downward spiral of self-debasement begins as Vanessa gets into crack in a big way, and Scott discovers that, when high, he'll sleep with any old beautiful girl, but will come too quickly. It ends in tragedy. Score by Nile Rodgers (funky); fashion by Rosemary Ponzo (tacky); moral (missed opportunities); drugs (uncredited). Gross movie. EP

Crack in the World

(Andrew Marton, 1965, US) Dana Andrews, Janette Scott, Kieron Moore, Alexander Knox, Peter Damon.
96 min.
Infinitely better than the appalling *Day the Earth Caught Fire*, which developed along similar lines. A team of scientists are attempting to harness the energy at the earth's core, and explode some nuclear bombs underground in order to speed up their probe. The result is a nightmarish rupture in the earth's crust, which begins to have apoca-

lyptic consequences in terms of climate, earthquakes and human devastation. The theme often seems awesomely credible and the special effects are excellent, although the usual character conflicts in the scientific team become trying at times. The images of chaos at the end are particularly disturbing. DP

Cracksman, The

(Peter Graham Scott, 1963, GB) Charlie Drake, George Sanders, Dennis Price, Nyree Dawn Porter, Eddie Byrne, Finlay Currie.
112 min.
Charlie Drake, like many British comedians, was never able to transfer his style of humour to the screen. All his films were much of a muchness, and this one – in which he's a locksmith shanghaied into big-time crime – is merely funny in parts. Co-star Sanders looks embarrassed. DP

Crack-Up

(Malcolm St Clair, 1936, US) Peter Lorre, Brian Donlevy, Helen Wood, Ralph Morgan, Thomas Beck.
70 min. b/w.
Basically B movie espionage hokum, but with ideas behind both script (Charles Kenyon and Sam Mintz) and direction as Donlevy, an arrogant test pilot disgruntled because he feels (justifiably) he has been cheated over a new patent, decides to recoup his losses by selling the plans to a foreign power. When things seem on the verge of falling into routine, Lorre emerges from his disguise as an amiable half-wit, tolerated around the airport as a harmless mascot, to reveal himself – inimitably – as the ruthless spymaster. The final sequence, in which their escape plane crash-lands in the sea and the prospect of imminent death prompts both Lorre and Donlevy to a wry re-examination of the masks they have assumed, is contrived but bizarrely effective. TM

Crack-Up

(Irving Reis, 1946, US) Pat O'Brien, Claire Trevor, Herbert Marshall, Ray Collins, Wallace Ford, Dean Harens, Erskine Sanford.
93 min. b/w.
A modest but gripping little thriller set in and around a big New York art gallery, with O'Brien as the expert on forgeries who is dismissed when his erratic conduct – due, he claims, to having been in a train crash of which there proves to be no record – is put down to drunkenness. Setting out to clear his name through a fog of amnesia (in fact the train wreck was an illusion produced by way of an injection of sodium pentothal), he uncovers a vast, ramifying plot to substitute forgeries for masterpieces on loan to the museum. Marginally intriguing for its view of art (pro populist, anti élitist stuff like surrealism), it's made as a thriller by the excellent supporting cast and fine, *noir*-ish camera-work from Robert de Grasse. TM

Craft, The

(Andrew Fleming, 1996, US) Fairuza Balk, Neve Campbell, Rachel True, Robin Tunney, Christine Taylor, Skeet Ulrich, Cliff De Young, Helen Shaver.
101 min.
A tale of supernatural LA high-school high jinks featuring the three members of a teenage 'coven' – 'The Bitches of Eastwick'. Outsiders all – Nancy (Balk), the punk with an alcoholic single parent; Bonnie (Campbell) with facial scars from a childhood car crash; and Rochelle (True) who's, well, black – they're in need of a fourth to complete their empowered circle. When new girl Sarah (Tunney) arrives, her brooding demeanour and telekinetic powers announce her as the natural candidate. The school's a hothouse of resentment, conflict and hurt, and the girls' experiments in spellcraft are regarded as deliciously dangerous excursions into adolescent self-discovery. There are some fine set-pieces, including a magical release of butterflies and a disturbing dream sequence, but the end opts disappointingly for standard horror-house effects. WH

Craig's Wife

(Dorothy Arzner, 1936, US) Rosalind Russell, John Boles, Billie Burke, Jane Darwell, Dorothy Wilson, Alma Kruger, Thomas Mitchell.
75 min. b/w.
A '30s rarity: a Hollywood picture written and directed by women. Russell is a strong-willed but glacial spouse determined to rule both husband

Boles and their home. She comes to regret her intransigence, however, when she becomes meshed in a murder case and finds there are few friends around to help out. Arzner gives Mary C McCall Jr's adaptation of a play by George Kelly a remarkably austere tone. TJ

Crash

(David Cronenberg, 1996, Can) James Spader, Holly Hunter, Elias Koteas, Deborah Kara Unger, Rosanna Arquette.
100 min.
Arguably the closest commercial Western cinema has come to Oshima's *Ai No Corrida* – what 'story' there is consists chiefly of a series of obsessive, claustrophobic, transgressive sex-scenes – Cronenberg's film of JG Ballard's novel is both imaginative and, notwithstanding its 'scandalous' content, strangely 'respectable' (in terms of fidelity and finding appropriate solutions to problems of adaptation). Basically, it's about a couple (Spader and Unger), already so disenchanted by notions of conventional sex that they tell each other in detail about their various other liaisons, who are further aroused when they encounter Hunter (widowed victim of a car collision with Spader) and Koteas, a near-crazy car-crash freak who introduces them to the perverse erotica of scars, wrecked debris and the threat of violent death itself. It's a dark, disturbing, languorous movie, as ludicrous, hermetic and repetitive, perhaps, as Ballard's original, but admirably assured and true to itself. GA

Crash

(Alan Gibson, 1976, US) Joe Don Baker, Susan Sarandon, Larry Hagman, Alan Vint, Parnelli Jones.
78 min.
Gibson, a former employee of BBC TV, attempts to enter his low-budget rally movie in the mini-disaster stakes. Motorists and motor-cyclists roar round Manila, while sweaty promoter (Hagman) strives to drum up excitement at base, dealing with a string of implausible catastrophes. Documentary footage of floods and car crashes constitute the film's most spectacular moments. A hilarious song ('Checkered flag or crash/Going for the heavy green/There ain't no in between/So do me right, you damned machine') momentarily enlivens an otherwise thoroughly moribund venture. JPy

Crash of Silence

see Mandy

Craze

(Freddie Francis, 1973, GB) Jack Palance, Diana Dors, Julie Ege, Edith Evans, Hugh Griffith, Trevor Howard, Michael Jayston, Suzy Kendall.
95 min.
London antique shop owner Palance becomes enslaved to an African idol which demands female sacrifices in return for worldly goods. But with such a poor and perfunctory script which quickly establishes Palance as nutty as they come and reduces him to uttering every line as though it had been dragged out of him only after half-an-hour's torture, there's little joy in the numerous cameo roles. At least Evans, Howard, Griffith and Dors ensure that the film is in safe hands, but ultimately their brief appearances can't compensate for the yawning gaps elsewhere. Francis does little to make it atmospheric, so it's soon down to the staple diet of sex'n'murder. CPe

Crazies, The

(George A Romero, 1973, US) Lane Carroll, WG McMillan, Harold Wayne Jones, Lloyd Hollar, Richard Liberty, Lynn Lowry.
103 min.
Night of the Living Dead suggested that Romero was an unusual if none too clearly defined talent; two non-horror movies later, *The Crazies* proved it. The main plot premise echoes *The Andromeda Strain*: an accident with a virus creates a terrifying civil emergency, and incidentally reveals that the US government is working towards germ warfare. Romero, however, is more interested in effect than cause. First, he brilliantly updates the riddle Don Siegel posed in *Invasion of the Body Snatchers*: how can one tell who is infected and who isn't? The virus drives its victims mad before killing them, but what is the line between 'nor-

mal' hysteria and actual insanity? Second, and equally brilliantly, he demonstrates the difficulty in imposing martial law on a community of gun-owners, thereby creating a highly feasible vision of social collapse. Good dialogue and performances, too. Altogether, enough plusses to excuse weak plotting and occasional lapses into cliché. TR

Crazy Family (Gyakufunsha Kazoku)

(Sogo Ishii, 1984, Jap) Katsuya Kobayashi, Mitsuko Baisho, Yoshiki Arizono, Yuki Kudo, Hitoshi Ueki.
107 min.
On the surface, Ishii's 'crazy family' is as normal as you or me: husband, wife and two pretty, healthy teenage kids, living in the suburban house of their dreams. But Ishii rips aside this bourgeois façade to show the horror festering beneath. Dad's mind is a seething can of paranoid worms, convinced that his 'love' is the only cure for the 'sickness' he detects in the others, and well before the end he's trying to trick them into a painless group suicide with a stout dose of insecticide in the coffee. The problems come to a head when his senile father (disgusting as only the elderly know how to be) visits and outstays his welcome, forcing Dad to take a chainsaw to the living-room floor with the perfectly reasonable intention of digging a cellar-cum-fallout shelter to accommodate the old misery. But that's when he strikes the nest of white ants... Seeing Ishii's film is a bit like rediscovering the thrill of your first encounter with Monty Python all those years ago: black humour at its most vicious (ie. funniest), paced like a commuter express and spiked with a dash of science fiction to keep even the most micro-chipped viewer unsure where he, she or it is going. TR

Crazy for Love

see Trou Normand, Le

Crazy for You

see Vision Quest

Crazy Horse of Paris, The (Crazy Horse de Paris)

(Alain Bernardin, 1977, Fr) John Lennox, Dickie Henderson, Alain Bernardin, George Carl, Senor Wences.
95 min.
A sort of concert film of the naughty show at the Crazy Horse Saloon in Paris, with a backstage 'story' concocted around the arrival of a repulsive hack who claims to come from the Dundee Chronicle to do a story on 'the girls'. The acts are wholesome and lifeless – on-the-spot dancing and strips which take one from next-to-nothing to absolutely nothing. The guy who runs the joint seems on the level, but a dirty-old-man note creeps into his voice when asked to describe the qualities he looks for in a prospective chorine. Out comes stuff about poitrines agressives and thighs being the pillars of temples. It's just a clean, old-fashioned peep-show, really, tedious beyond belief. JS

Crazy Joe

(Carlo Lizzani, 1973, US/It) Peter Boyle, Paula Prentiss, Fred Williamson, Charles Cioffi, Rip Torn, Luther Adler, Fausto Tozzi, Eli Wallach, Henry Winkler.
99 min.
Crazy Joe sprawls, but for the most part it sprawls with a certain style. The film opens with four hoods singing opera while driving to make a killing, and goes on to a 10-year retrospective on the history of the New York Mafia. Not content with that, Lizzani throws in a good 20 minutes' worth of prison movie (including a riot), a bit about the gangster as existentialist and his relationships to the media. And that's topped off by Peter Boyle doing imitations of Bogart and Widmark for his mates. The film is at its best when examining the Mafia power structure. It encompasses the farce of the Italian-American Federation (no more than a PR whitewash by the Mafia, which succeeded only in drawing attention to itself); deals with Mafia-Negro relations; and generally boasts an awareness that few recent Mafia movies have had. It does, in fact, emerge as something of a B picture epic. CPe

Crazy Love

(Dominique Deruddere, 1987, Bel) Josse De Pauw, Geert Hunaerts, Michaël Pas, Gène Bervoets, Amid Chakir.
87 min.
It's easy to see why Charles Bukowski loves this interpretation of his work. The linking of three Bukowski short stories shows one boy/youth/man's progression from one carefree, fairytale prepubescence, through a sexual education which starts conventionally (and wittily) enough but which is derailed in the second episode by the development of the most heart-rendingly grotesque case of acne. De Pauw, as the older Harry Voss, proves a startlingly good actor, leading us gently and sadly from the standpoint of the youth's growing alienation from love and women, down a strange path to an awful place typically reeking of Bukowskian angst, spunk, death, booze, and loneliness. Norra lorra laffs? Untrue. The film is mordantly funny, stunningly designed, exquisitely photographed, quirkily directed, and all too brief. This director, in his debut, knows how to tell a story. Bizarre and beautiful. TC

Crazy Mama

(Jonathan Demme, 1975, US) Cloris Leachman, Stuart Whitman, Jim Backus, Ann Sothern, Donny Most, Linda Purl, Bryan Englund, Merie Earle, Dick Miller.
82 min.
Not so much a sequel to Corman's Bloody Mama, more a good-natured parody of the Bonnie and Clyde family gangster genre, scripted by Robert Thom. Demme took on this riotous Corman production at very short notice, and played up the laughs rather than the violence. Set in the '50s, the story centres on Depression child Melba Stokes (Leachman) and her journey from West to East coast along with mom (Sothern) and daughter (Purl), gathering together en route a motley band united in their sufferance at the hands of the law. Demme brings to the sly social commentary his usual deft choice of rock'n'roll standards, and draws enthusiastic performances from his wacky cast. DT

Crazy People

(Tony Bill, 1990, US) Dudley Moore, Daryl Hannah, Paul Reiser, JT Walsh, Bill Smitrovich, Alan North, David Paymer, Mercedes Ruehl.
92 min.
Dudley Moore plays a jaded copywriter who ends up in a sanatorium after he decides to produce ads devoid of hype. His fellow patients suffer from a variety of stereotypes, the worst case being Daryl Hannah, who harbours a dangerous penchant for loose dresses and baggy cardigans. Everyone feels much better once spurred into writing ads; and the agency snaps up their copy when consumers become hungry for truth. This is a lazy, obvious film, functionally directed and crudely characterised, which testifies to, rather than criticises, the power and influence of advertising. John Malkovich, originally cast, walked out on the project. Now there's an actor who knows when to make an exit. CM

Crazy Ray, The

see Paris qui Dort

Crazy Stranger, The

see Gadjo Dilo

Creator

(Ivan Passer, 1985, US) Peter O'Toole, Mariel Hemingway, Vincent Spano, Virginia Madsen, David Ogden Stiers, John Dehner, Jeff Corey.
107 min.
A not unlikeable dog's dinner of a campus comedy, centring on Nobel prize-winning professor O'Toole's attempts to recreate his dead darling wife in his garden shed. Despite workaday direction, a slightly forced optimism, and the centrifugal force of Jeremy Leven's untogether script (adapted from his own novel), the cheeriness and enthusiasm of the playing carries it through. The film comes on like a dumb 1970s version of a Shaw play, with O'Toole running his University Research Department like a happy Captain Shotover, appropriating funds and equipment with carefree abandon and forever inviting his assistants to search for the 'Big Picture'. Hemingway plays the 'Life Force', a free spirit

with a permanent orgasm who agrees to provide an egg for O'Toole's experiment. Spano's gadget-obsessed assistant gives outline to O'Toole's paternal qualities, and David Ogden Stiers' small-minded colleague provides the foil for O'Toole's flamboyant irresistability. It's a Peter O'Toole show, and it's worth it for his craggy-stoned face alone. WH

Creature

see Titan Find, The

Creature from the Black Lagoon

(Jack Arnold, 1954, US) Richard Carlson, Julia Adams, Richard Denning, Antonio Moreno, Whit Bissell, Nestor Paiva, Ricou Browning.
79 min. b/w.
The routine story – members of a scientific expedition exploring the Amazon discover and are menaced by an amphibious gill man – is mightily improved by Arnold's sure sense of atmospheric locations and by the often sympathetic portrait of the monster. Interestingly, the threat is perceived as partly sexual (notably in the scene where the creature swims mesmerised beneath the tightly swimsuited Adams), and thus the film can be seen as a precursor of Jaws. GA

Creatures the World Forgot

(Don Chaffey, 1970, GB) Julie Ege, Brian O'Shaugnessy, Tony Bonner, Robert John, Marcia Fox, Rosalie Crutchley.
95 min.
Actually, it was Hammer who forgot the creatures, for this sequel to the money-spinning One Million Years B.C. is a resolutely dinosaur-free zone. Instead, there's unconscionable amounts of grunting, a daft plot involving a tribe of cave-dwellers on a trek across the desert to a new home, and enough of trash icon Julie Ege in (and out of) a fur bikini to earn the thing an 'X' certificate . Despite so much cult potential, however, one abiding problem remains: it's unbelievably tedious. TJ

Creature Walks Among Us, The

(John Sherwood, 1956, US) Jeff Morrow, Rex Reason, Leigh Snowden, Gregg Palmer, Ricou Browning, Don Megowan.
78 min. b/w.
Third outing for the creature from the black lagoon, a dim affair in which the amphibious man is subjected to laboratory experiment (and is naturally cross). Jack Arnold's guiding hand is sorely missed. TM

Creepers (Phenomena)

(Dario Argento, 1984, It) Jennifer Connelly, Daria Nicolodi, Dalila Di Lazzaro, Patrick Bauchau, Donald Pleasence, Fiore Argento.
110 min.
You know where you are with a Dario Argento film. You're in the Swiss Transylvania, at a girls' school, with a crazed killer on the loose. Another characteristic of an Argento movie is that the plot is every bit as mad as the murderer: an excuse for a lot of stalk'n'slash with panache, maggots a-go-go, and some outrageous overacting from Donald Pleasence and Daria Nicolodi. At the centre is an excellent performance by Connelly, who fondles bees, communicates with ladybirds and develops a meaningful relationship with a Great Sarcophagus Fly, which results in her classmates, the headmistress and the murderer all wanting her put away. Not nearly as stylishly bonkers as Suspiria or Inferno, but it'll do. AB

Creeping Flesh, The

(Freddie Francis, 1972, GB) Christopher Lee, Peter Cushing, Lorna Heilbron, George Benson, Kenneth J Warren, Duncan Lamont.
91 min.
Above-average horror, positively crammed with Gothic themes and put together with some care, with Freddie Francis' camera recapturing that crystal-sharp quality which he understandably abandoned for Tales from the Crypt. The sheer multiplication of ideas sometimes becomes contrived, but Cushing is right back on form as a Wilhelm Reich-like scientist who

is convinced that he has detected 'the principle of evil' under the microscope. This intrinsically fascinating theme (which implies a liaison between the rational and the mystical) is never properly developed, but does give rise to good moments, especially when Cushing injects the 'evil' into his prim little daughter (Heilbron) and she is transformed into a wildly sensual image of female libido. DP

Creepshow

(George A Romero, 1982, US) Hal Holbrook, Leslie Nielsen, Adrienne Barbeau, Fritz Weaver, Viveca Lindfors, Carrie Nye, Stephen King, EG Marshall.
120 min.
'I waanntt myy caaakkkeee!' gurgles the decaying birthday revenant of the first segment of this well-dressed and frequently beautifully framed tribute to the graveyard hoots of Bill Gaines's EC horror comics, complete with links in the original cartoon style. Sadly, the combined talents of King and Romero fail to sustain the opener's deft mesh of blood-letting and black humour. King himself is excellent as a bumpkin with fungus-from-space problems, but the other stories – a watery re-run of Cask of Amontillado, EG Marshall as a Howard Hughes type overrun by cockroaches during a power failure, etc. – are simply too long for anybody's comfort. The old Amicus movies used EC originals to better effect and with more brevity, for all their cardboard sets. GD

Creepshow 2

(Michael Gornick, 1987, US) George Kennedy, Dorothy Lamour, Lois Chiles, Tom Wright, Stephen King, Tom Savini.
90 min.
Just as you can't judge a '50s comic book by its lurid cover, so you can't judge a cheapo, three-part film by its sources: in this case, original stories by Stephen King and a screenplay by George Romero. The linking animation sequences featuring a young comic reader are reasonably effective, but first-timer Gornick's direction is so painfully inept that not one of the episodes is even slightly scary, let alone horrifying. See a wooden cigar-store Indian come to life and bump off even more wooden teenage delinquents in Old Chief Wood'nhead! See dope-smoking teenage swimmers terrorised by a floating bin-liner in The Raft! See a sexually-active married woman, who has just enjoyed six orgasms ('count 'em') with a paid stud, terrorised by the indestructible Hitch-hiker! Marvel at the film's hypocritical moralising! The only terrifying thing about Creepshow 2 is the thought of Creepshow 3. NF

Cremaster 5

(Matthew Barney, 1997, US) Matthew Barney, Ursula Andress, Joanne Rha, Susan Rha.
55 min.
Fifth in the series of weird films by Californian artist Barney, this consists of stunning visuals that are like animated paintings – Greenaway without the narrative flow. Andress plays the Queen of Chains. Overlooking the empty stage, she sings mournful arias to her dead lover – the black knight (Barney). Flashbacks recall his bizarre end. Throwing off his cloak, he reveals his nakedness. He perches on the balustrade of the bridge, peering down into the dark waters of the Danube. He topples down to a watery grave and comes to rest among white lilies. In a sequence shot in Budapest's famous Gellért baths, Barney also appears as an exotic satyr with a glass headdress, fungoid ear and beard extensions, hooves and frilled red waders. The water nymphs who inhabit the pool are blessed with decorative genital growths and marbled skin resembling porcelain. In a catalogue accompanying the film you can study these exotica, but on screen many of the gorgeous details are lost, especially as your attention is occupied in trying to unravel the symbolism of these strange and beautiful sights. SK

Cremator, The (Spalovac Mrtvol)

(Juraj Herz, 1968, Czech) Rudolf Hrušinský, Vlasta Chramostová, Jana Stehnová, Milos Vognic, Jiri Menzel.
102 min. b/w.
A promising idea for a black comedy about a mild-mannered family man who runs a crematorium, this works well enough for a while as he fusses simultaneously over the details of his

trade and matters of personal hygiene, gradually becoming obsessed with the notion that his ovens are a last defence against earthly torments. The trouble is that the time is the late 1930s, and Herz makes such heavy allegorical weather of his tale that one is giving absolutely nothing away by revealing that the hero and his ovens eventually find fulfilment under the Nazis. TM

Crescendo

(Alan Gibson, 1969, GB) Stephanie Powers, James Olson, Margaretta Scott, Jane Lapotaire, Joss Ackland.
95 min.
This lazy variation on script-writer Jimmy Sangster's Taste of Fear (1961) is further crippled by the lack of Seth Holt's assured direction. At a villa in southern France, American heroine Powers gets mixed up with a strange widow (Scott), her invalid, heroin-addicted son (Olson), and their attentive maid (Lapotaire). When the maid is murdered, Powers is drawn into a conspiracy by the scheming widow, while the son drives himself crazy with nightmares about being murdered himself. Some cursory soft-core sex scenes fail to enliven the mechanical plot, and the contrived ending never rises to the promised crescendo. NF

Cría Cuervos (Raise Ravens)

(Carlos Saura, 1975, Sp) Geraldine Chaplin, Ana Torrent, Conchi Perez, Maite Sanchez, Héctor Alterio.
110 min.
A mesmerising film which conflates the drive to wish-fulfilment – a young girl, after watching the death of her father, comes to believe she holds the key to life and death – with a partial account of the last days of Fascism in Spain. At the root of both strands of Saura's elliptical script lies the idea of repression as the motor force behind the strange goings-on in the isolated (yet in the middle of Madrid) house of the Anselmo family. Intriguingly, the film suggests that the spirit of the dusty surrealism of Buñuel lives on in his native Spain. PH

Cri du Coeur, Le

(Idrissa Ouedraogo, 1994, Fr) Richard Bohringer, Saïd Diarra, Félicité Wouassi, Alex Descas.
80 min.
Writer/director Ouedraogo, maker of the acclaimed Yaaba, travelled to Paris from his native Burkina Faso to shoot this intriguing tale of an African boy adjusting to life in France, where he's troubled by memories and visions of his homeland. Although the overall feel isn't as idiomatic as the film-maker's previous work, Bohringer is on mercurial form as the former truckdriver who befriends the child, and the blend of the experiences of two worlds and cultures is arresting, if not fully achieved. TJ

Cries and Whispers (Viskingar och Rop)

(Ingmar Bergman, 1972, Swe) Harriet Andersson, Kari Sylwan, Ingrid Thulin, Liv Ullmann, Erland Josephson, Henning Moritzen.
91 min.
You can interpret Cries and Whispers through a whole religious metaphysic, and no doubt Bergman himself would; but latterly this has been something of a red herring for a director whose talent lies more in straight psychodrama. None of the films immediately preceding have been more visually seductive than Cries, so much so that form, repeatedly, gets the better of content. Mostly Bergman is able to regain control, which is where the scenes that make the film come in: for instance, the short sequence where Thulin, in period costume, is undressed by her maid, which says all there is to say about clothes, disguise, repression. Cries is about bodies, female bodies, in extremity of pain, isolation or neglect (the cards are heavily stacked). Karin (Thulin) mutilates her cunt with a piece of broken glass and, stretched out on her marital bed, smiles through the blood she's smeared across her mouth at her husband in celebration of a marriage that's a 'tissue of lies'. Maria (Ullman) finds herself lacking a thread that would tie her irreversibly to life. Bergman's hour remains resolutely that of the wolf. VG

Crime and Punishment

(Josef von Sternberg, 1935, US) Edward Arnold, Peter Lorre, Marian Marsh, Tala Birell, Elisabeth Risdon, Mrs Patrick Campbell.
88 min. b/w.
Far from Sternberg's best, but still a fairly impressive, if overly condensed, adaptation of Dostoevsky's novel. Lorre is highly effective as the arrogant Raskolnikov, committing a murder and then battling it out both with his conscience and with police inspector Arnold. The strongest scenes, in fact, are those dealing with the cat-and-mouse games between the two men, although the whole thing benefits from Lucien Ballard's characteristically fine photography. Of course it falls a long way short of the book in terms of philosophical import and characterisation, but it's pretty compelling nevertheless. GA

Crime and Punishment (Rikos ja Rangaistus)

(Aki Kaurismäki, 1983, Fin) Markku Toikka, Aino Seppo, Esko Nikkari, Olli Tuominen, Hannu Lauri.
93 min.
Kaurismäki does Dostoevsky, and though it's not exactly a straight adaptation, the gloom and foreboding are authentic. Here Raskolnikov is Rahikainen, a Helsinki slaughterhouse worker who shoots the man responsible for killing his wife in a hit-and-run incident three years earlier. At the victim's house, however, he meets a young woman with whom he gets into a relationship, and she, for the moment, withholds his name from the police. TJ

Crime Busters (Due Superpiedi quasi Piatti)

(EB Clucher, ie. Enzo Barboni, 1976, It) Terence Hill, Bud Spencer, David Huddleston, Luciano Catenacci, Laura Gemser.
115 min.
Laurel and Hardy become first Starsky and Hutch, then Robin Hood and Little John, as lovable layabouts Hill and Spencer fetch up in Miami, try to rob a supermarket, and stumble by accident into a police recruiting parade. This is Italian hybrid at its most tiresome, covering up a threadbare second-hand plot with thick slapstick and sentiment. AN

Crime de Monsieur Lange, Le (The Crime of Monsieur Lange)

(Jean Renoir, 1935, Fr) René Lefèvre, Jules Berry, Odette Florelle, Nadia Sibirskaïa, Sylvia Bataille, Marcel Levesque.
90 min. b/w.
One of Renoir's most completely delightful movies (scripted by Jacques Prévert in the euphoria of the Popular Front days), a comedy-thriller-romance about employees of a publishing firm setting up a glorious collective when their lecherous and oppressive boss suddenly goes missing. Chaos sets in when he unexpectedly reappears to reap the fruit of their success, built on the imaginative efforts of a writer of Westerns who also finds a way out of the predicament by using a gun. Fantasy, politics and gentle naturalism combine to perfection, while Renoir's sympathies for his domestic revolutionaries are so infectious as to make the film genuinely uplifting. GA

Crime in the Streets

(Don Siegel, 1956, US) James Whitmore, John Cassavetes, Sal Mineo, Mark Rydell, Virginia Gregg, Peter Votrian.
91 min. b/w.
A rain-slicked wharf, a foghorn sounds, and the rumble starts. With just a single back-alley set and a five-and-ten cent script, Siegel's B gang picture can make 'the street' more real than all the stylisations of later efforts like The Wanderers. There's a street-corner girl who dances with her mouth, and there's Cassavetes as Frankie, the leader who can't bear to be touched, dripping all the bug-eyed surliness of his grown-up movies and hiding all the dirty little secrets that each family contains. Coil-spring tension is supplied by the long run-in to the first test of manhood – the big kill. If it's a shade heavy on the psychodrama at the expense of the action, at least the confrontations have spine; and if the ending is neces-

sarily happy, at least it's due to a kid brother rather than the earnest social worker. Like a zip-gun, cheap and effective. CPea

Crime of Monsieur Lange, The
see Crime de Monsieur Lange, Le

Crime of Passion
(Gerd Oswald, 1956, US) Barbara Stanwyck, Sterling Hayden, Raymond Burr, Fay Wray, Royal Dano, Virginia Grey.
86 min. b/w.
'Behind every successful man...': the old cliché gets full-bloodedly melodramatic illustration as Stanwyck takes detective husband Hayden's prospects for LAPD promotion into her own hands (soon bloodied). Oswald, son of German director Richard and responsible for one of the most visually arresting and thematically over-the-top episodes of *The Outer Limits* (*Shape of Things Unknown*), could usually be relied on to turn budgetary constraints to energetic advantage. PT

Crime of the Century
(Mark Rydell, 1996, US) Stephen Rea, Isabella Rossellini, JT Walsh, Michael Moriarty, David Paymer, John Harkins, Allen Garfield, Barry Primus.
111 min
An impressive cast weigh in for this HBO period drama, a re-creation of the Lindbergh kidnap case based on Ludovic Kennedy's *The Airman and the Carpenter*. Richard Hauptmann (Rea) was picked up with marked ransom notes and charged with the murder of the famous aviator's baby. America was baying for blood, and Hauptmann, a German immigrant, fitted the bill. The limited budget makes for so-so production work and competent, but severely constrained direction by old pro Mark Rydell. The upside is an eloquent, thoughtful screenplay by William Nicholson and some juicy character acting by the likes of Harkins (as an alcoholic defence lawyer), Moriarty (the concerned local Governor), Paymer (the prosecuting attorney) and Walsh (the police chief). It takes a while to get used to Rea talking with an aksent lak dis, but he comes through with a couple of burning speeches. TCh

Crimes and Misdemeanors
(Woody Allen, 1989, US) Caroline Aaron, Alan Alda, Woody Allen, Claire Bloom, Mia Farrow, Joanna Gleason, Anjelica Huston, Martin Landau, Jenny Nichols, Jerry Orbach, Stephanie Roth, Sam Waterston.
104 min.
In the first of two loosely interwoven stories, rich, philanthropic ophthalmologist Judah Rosenthal (Landau), afraid his lover (Huston) will reveal all to his wife (Bloom), decides to dispose of the former with the help of a hit-man friend of his brother. In the second, more comic story, earnest, impoverished documentarist Clifford Stern (Allen), falls for the producer (Farrow) of a TV tribute he has reluctantly agreed to make about the brother-in-law he hates (Alda), a conceited, successful maker of sitcoms. Judah and Clifford meet only in the final scene: what links them throughout is guilt, stemming from an obsessive interest in matters of faith and ethics. It's an extremely ambitious film, most akin perhaps to *Hannah and her Sisters*, the narrative and tonal coherence of which it sadly lacks, though the assured direction and typically fine ensemble acting manage partly to conceal the seams. Dramatically, the film seldom fulfils its promise, and its pessimistic 'moral' – that good and evil do not always meet with their just deserts – looks contrived and hollow. Intriguing and patchily effective, nevertheless. GA

Crimes at the Dark House
(George King/David MacDonald, 1940, GB) Tod Slaughter, Sylvia Marriott, Hilary Eaves, Hay Petrie, Geoffrey Wardwell, David Horne.
69 min. b/w.
Cheap, cheerful and none too faithful adaptation of Wilkie Collins' *The Woman in White*, with the barnstorming Slaughter purveying prime ham as the murderous opportunist wreaking havoc at the mansion of an impoverished aristocratic family. Juicy stuff, entertaining enough if not taken at all seriously. GA

Crimes of Passion
(Ken Russell, 1984, US) Kathleen Turner, Anthony Perkins, John Laughlin, Annie Potts, Bruce Davison.
107 min.
First and foremost, an extremely uninhibited satire on American sexual dreams and nightmares. Turner, a career woman who doubles by night as the ultra-hooker China Blue, acts out every male fantasy in the book until she picks up a cop, sees him turn into a piece of meat beneath her, and gets carried away with her stiletto heels and his nightstick. She meets her Baudelairean match in Perkins, a deranged fundamentalist consumed by lust and slowly mustering the energy to act out his own dark fantasies. In between, the film lays into an 'average' suburban couple, living a sexual fantasy of their own – of marital fulfilment. It relies on sheer pace and stylistic bravura, and talks dirty more wittily than anything since Bogart and Bacall. There are lapses, but this is in the main a comedy so black that it recaptures some of the cinema's long-lost power to shock. TR

Crimes of the Future
(David Cronenberg, 1970, Can) Ronald Mlodzik, Jon Lidolt, Tania Zolty, Jack Messinger, Paul Mulholland.
65 min. b/w
Crimes of the Future explores a world of genetic mutations, in which all adult women have died from the use of cosmetics and the surviving men keep finding themselves reverting to more primitive forms. The mainspring of Cronenberg's humour is the discrepancy between theory and actual experience; as with the earlier *Stereo*, the movie is dominated by an 'absent' theorist (in this case the mad dermatologist Antoine Rouge), whose hapless disciple struggles to uphold his master's teachings in situations of escalating absurdity and anarchy. The humour couldn't be blacker, and the quality of invention is outrageously high. TR

Crimes of the Heart
(Bruce Beresford, 1986, US) Diane Keaton, Jessica Lange, Sissy Spacek, Sam Shepard, Tess Harper, Hurd Hatfield, David Carpenter.
105 min.
When Meg (Lange) steps off the Greyhound bus, trailing behind her a blown-out singing career and a series of failed relationships, Babe (Spacek) has just emptied a gunful of lead into her noxious senator husband, and buttoned-up, neurotic Lenny (Keaton) is singing herself 'Happy Birthday' all alone in the kitchen. The stage is set for an escalating black farce on the theme of broken dreams; but all we get, sadly, is a meandering display of half-hearted Mississippi drawl as these three dizzy sisters wander from room to room trading reminiscence and recrimination. Symptomatically, it is only when Meg and her old flame (Shepard) take off to the bayou that the movie starts to sing. Elsewhere, Beresford fails to generate sufficient chemistry to bind the performances. Occasional bursts of delicious tragic humour nevertheless make this a not unlikeable 'feminist' mood piece. WH

Crime Story (Zhong'an Zu)
(Kirk Wong, 1993, HK) Jackie Chan, Kent Cheng, Law Kar-Ying, Ko Shou-Liang, Ng Wing-Mei.
106 min.
Kirk Wong's determination to play this straight (there's no space for any of Jackie Chan's comedy schticks, and not much for set-piece stunts either) makes this the best pure thriller Chan has ever starred in. He plays a cop assigned to rescue a wealthy but morally dubious property developer (Law) from the gang which is holding him to ransom. But even his most ingenious efforts to trick the kidnappers go awry – because his corrupt superior Inspector Hung (Cheng) is secretly behind the whole thing. Moody visuals, expertly paced montages and climactic sequences aboard a rusting sea-tanker and in a burning slum tenement all deliver above and beyond genre norms. TR

Crimetime
(George Sluizer, 1996, GB/US/Ger) Stephen Baldwin, Pete Postlethwaite, Sadie Frost, Geraldine Chaplin, Karen Black, James Faulkner, Philip Davis, Marianne Faithfull.
118 min.
A struggling actor (Baldwin) gets a job on

'Crimetime', a TV show reconstructing hideous recent killings. But when the murderer (Postlethwaite) arrives at a hiatus in his activities, it's a decisive moment for his small-screen counterpart: lose a nice little earner, or kill to continue the mayhem. A worthless London-set shocker purporting to comment on the values of the media. TJ

Crimewave
(Sam Raimi, 1985, US) Louise Lasser, Paul Smith, Brion James, Sheree J Wilson, Edward R Pressman, Reed Birney.
86 min.
It isn't surprising to find that Sam *Evil Dead* Raimi has here plundered the conventions of comic strip capers. What is surprising is that a screenplay co-written by Raimi with the Coen brothers (*Blood Simple*) should bleed all over the block without ever congealing into a properly nasty tale of zany doings in '40s-ish-going-on-present-day Detroit. Superschmuck Vic Ajax, about to fry for the murder of his employers, generates the film as one long flashback protesting his innocence. The real murderers are professional exterminators Crush and Coddish, who zoom around with a giant stuffed rat on their van roof, wreaking havoc with the multi-settinged Megahorts machine. There is much visual pow-zap-zowie, and excruciatingly extended bouts of gormless goofing by Vic at the girl of his dreams. Only in a couple of wacky chase set pieces does Raimi show himself capable of dementedly one-dimensional cartoony discipline. AB

Criminal
(David Jacobson, 1994, Ger) Ralph Feliciello, Liz Sherman, Sheila York, Eric Reid.
80 min. b/w.
Shot in English, and in grainy high-contrast b/w in the US, this reflective, stylish but heavy-handed blend of muted realism, melodrama and *film noir* focuses on a gentle businessman who embezzles a fortune to buy his nagging wife her dream house, only to find that she's been cheating on him. As he takes to the road, meeting up with a disenchanted damsel in distress, the film begins to exert a strange, poetic power not unlike that of, say, *Detour* – but far more tender. Bleak, crude even, but decked out with fine performances and a good use of music ('50s kitsch and John Adams' *Shaker Loops*). GA

Criminal, The (aka The Concrete Jungle)
(Joseph Losey, 1960, GB) Stanley Baker, Sam Wanamaker, Margit Saad, Patrick Magee, Grégoire Aslan, Jill Bennett, Rupert Davies, Laurence Naismith.
97 min. b/w.
Terrific performance from Baker as the criminal, an existential loner whose violence is essentially self-destructive as, literally trapped within the bars of a prison, he finds himself metaphorically caught between two complementary systems: one represented by the sadistic chief warder (Magee), who feeds his sense of power by fomenting a dog-eat-dog code in the cells, the other by the underworld kingpin (Wanamaker) waiting outside to kill Baker and hijack his stashed loot. Losey's American eye and expertise make it jaggedly explosive and visually brilliant, a million miles beyond other British crime movies. TM

Criminal Code, The
(Howard Hawks, 1931, US) Walter Huston, Phillips Holmes, Constance Cummings, Mary Doran, Boris Karloff, De Witt Jennings, John Sheehan.
97 min. b/w.
Detailing the conflict between a cynical prosecuting attorney turned warden (Huston) and a green young killer (Holmes), whose stretch in the slammer threatens to destroy not only his faith in life but also his sanity, the taut, unsentimental plot about betrayal and revenge proposes that the convicts' sense of honour and justice is not so very different from that of the authorities: 'Someone's gotta pay' lies all too easily on the lips of both vengeful hard-asses like Karloff and self-righteous perpetrators of the law such as Huston. But there's no facile moralising here; rather, the fast pacing, grimly realistic atmosphere, and superb performances summon up a tragic battle of wits and power in which both sides are equally right and wrong, forced to do what their posi-

tion in life requires them to, and from which the only way out is death. Hawks' later concerns are in full bloom here – pride in professionalism, loyalty and betrayal within the group, the difficulties facing men forced to live without women, responsibility and respect – and his totally assured style is reflected in the quick, naturalistic dialogue, quirky black humour, and the ability to turn potentially risible set pieces – like Huston's first confrontation with a yard full of riotous cons – into electrifying suspense. GA

Criminal Face
see Ho!

Criminal Law
(Martin Campbell, 1989, US) Gary Oldman, Kevin Bacon, Karen Young, Joe Don Baker, Tess Harper, Ron Lea, Karen Woolridge, Elizabeth Sheppard.
118 min.
After winning an acquittal for wealthy client Martin Thiel (Bacon), defence attorney Ben Chase (Oldman) discovers that he is in fact guilty of rape and murder. Will the attorney follow the advice of his fellow professional – 'Justice is for God' – or use privileged knowledge to expose Thiel? Given the basic plot, behind-camera talent and cast, the film should be better than it is. Martin Campbell (who directed the superb *Edge of Darkness* for television) uses tight frames and a sense of restlessness to convey tension, but this makes for uneasy viewing when combined with Mark Kasdan's overwrought script. A crude, confused psychology operates here: Thiel blames everything on Mother, and a conscience-stricken Chase turns homicidal while his old mentor offers quiet advice from the death-bed. CM

Criminal Life of Archibaldo de la Cruz, The (Ensayo de un Crimen/La Vida Criminal de Archibaldo de la Cruz)
(Luis Buñuel, 1955, Mex) Ernesto Alonso, Miroslava Stern, Ariadna Welter, Rita Macedo, José Maria Linares Rivas.
91 min. b/w.
Buñuel marshals all of his characteristic amoral wit in this tale of a would-be murderer frustrated at every turn in his efforts to get his kicks from a successful sex killing. As usual, the master eschews the visual fussiness of 'style', opting for the straightforward camera set-up at all times. The use of props like the toy music box from his childhood which triggers off Archibaldo's lust, and the wax dummy burned after one of his attempts is thwarted, is all the more stunning (and hilarious) as a result. RM

Crimson Blade, The
see Scarlet Blade, The

Crimson Cult, The
see Curse of the Crimson Altar

Crimson Kimono, The
(Samuel Fuller, 1959, US) Victoria Shaw, Glenn Corbett, James Shigeta, Anna Lee, Paul Dubov, Jaclynne Greene.
82 min. b/w.
Fuller developing his theme of urban alienation: landscape, culture and sexual confusion are all juxtaposed, forcing the Japanese-born detective (who, along with his buddy, is on the hunt for a burlesque queen murderer) into a nightmare of isolation and jealousy. Some fine set pieces – like the disciplined Kendo fight that degenerates into sadistic anarchy – and thoughtful camera-work serve to illustrate Fuller's gift for weaving a poetic nihilism out of his journalistic vision of urban crime. GSa

Crimson Pirate, The
(Robert Siodmak, 1952, GB) Burt Lancaster, Nick Cravat, Eva Bartok, Torin Thatcher, James Hayter, Noel Purcell, Margot Grahame.
104 min.
Marvellous semi-serious swashbuckler, with Lancaster and Cravat – his diminutive acrobat colleague – taking on a tyrant in the 18th century Mediterranean. Racily but elegantly directed by Siodmak, it effortlessly merges thrills and spoofery to produce entertainment that really is, for once, suitable for 'kids of all ages'. But the

film's strongest point is the opportunity it offers to watch its stars' relaxed, energetic stunt-work: never has Burt looked so graceful. GA

Crimson Tide
(Tony Scott, 1995, US) Gene Hackman, Denzel Washington, George Dzundza, Viggo Mortensen, Matt Craven, James Gandolfini, Rocky Carroll, Jaime P Gomez.
116 min.
The crisis in the former Soviet Union has intensified. With a nuclear base in the hands of nationalist rebels, the world is waking up to another Cuban missile crisis, and the USS 'Alabama' is dispatched to deep waters within striking distance of Moscow. Only executive officer Hunter (Washington) stands between hawkish Captain Ramsey (Hackman) and a pre-emptive strike. Conceived as a post-Cold War update on *Fail Safe*, this tense, lucid brinksmanship drama also incorporates elements from *The Caine Mutiny*, *A Few Good Men*, and every submarine movie you've ever seen. There's no disguising the braggadocio with which director Scott plays cat-and-mouse with nuclear holocaust, cranking up the excitement with crazy angles, hot reds and greens, and Dariusz Wolski's hyper, heat-seeking camera. The screenplay may be credited to Michael Schiffer, but the punchy dialogue has Quentin Tarantino written all over it. The cast has a ball. Hackman, especially, brings immense reserves of humour, dignity and conviction to his meatiest role since *Unforgiven*. TCh

Crise, La
(Coline Serreau, 1992, Fr) Vincent Lindon, Patrick Timsit, Annik Alane, Valérie Alane, Gilles Privat, Zabou.
95 min.
Serreau, who made *Romuald et Juliette* and *Trois Hommes et un Couffin*, is determined to bring her troubled male protagonist around to a more feminine, even feminist, understanding of the world. Like *Romuald*, this begins with a harassed but apparently successful businessman losing both job and wife. As one might expect, however, *La Crise* has a less romantic, more coruscating edge: Romuald had his Juliette after all. But when Victor (Lindon) turns loser, he's stuck with Michou (Timsit), a kind, if slow-witted social outcast. This is a black comedy which takes itself very seriously. There's a pervasive sense of bankruptcy and malaise as Victor rebounds from one rejection to the next. Every couple is breaking up, racism is rife, politicians are hypocrites. The shrill opening is probably intentionally aggravating, but it ebbs into affecting, melancholy moments of transcendence and a more gently droll, if still spiky, sentimental education. There are problems: Michou's 'holy fool' takes some swallowing, and Serreau would do better to refrain from sermonising. Nevertheless, this is urgent, scalding satire, with a terrific performance from Lindon. TCh

Crisis
(Richard Brooks, 1950, US) Cary Grant, José Ferrer, Signe Hasso, Paula Raymond, Ramon Novarro, Gilbert Roland.
96 min. b/w.
Screenwriter Richard Brooks kicked off a largely distinguished directorial career with this highly charged political melodrama. Grant plays an American doctor forced to perform a brain tumour operation on South American dictator Ferrer (based, it seems, on Peron). The success of the endeavour places the medic and his wife Raymond in even greater danger themselves. Although the storyline bears a strong resemblance to the British thriller *State Secret*, also made in 1950, Brooks is adept at maintaining the tension. Grant looks as though he'd rather be holding a dry martini than a scalpel. TJ

Criss Cross
(Robert Siodmak, 1948, US) Burt Lancaster, Yvonne De Carlo, Dan Duryea, Stephen McNally, Richard Long.
88 min. b/w.
Wonderfully seedy tale of betrayal and obsession from superb *noir*-thriller stylist Siodmak. Beautifully shot (Franz Planer) and scripted (Daniel Fuchs), it bears more than a slight resemblance to the same director's *The Killers*. Again Lancaster is the fall guy, an armoured-car payroll guard still brooding over his ex-wife (De

Carlo), who has taken up with gangster Slim Dundee (Duryea) but leads Lancaster to believe that they can make a new start with booty gained from a daring heist if he will go through with it. As always with Siodmak, the suspense is maintained throughout by taut pacing, visual precision, and excellent characterisation. GA

Critters
(Stephen Herek, 1986, US) Dee Wallace Stone, M Emmet Walsh, Billy Green Bush, Scott Grimes, Nadine Van Der Velde, Don Opper.
86 min.
The Critters in question, aliens escaping from a space prison, are rolling amok in the small town of Grovers Bend, Kansas, where they've penned up Farmer Brown's family. They've cut the phone lines, killed the electricity, and eaten his goldfish. Now they want him. Judging from the title, Spielberg's *Gremlins* would be the immediate target, and indeed *Critters* does share a sardonic similarity. In fact, *Critters* looks like several dozen films without looking like any one of them, the action and characters lifted whole from a dissimilar plethora of cinematic sources and underscored with a sizzling sarcasm which elevates it from its source material. As a local puts it when he encounters the outer-space bounty hunters who've come to save humanity dressed in what look like worn-out Flash Gordon pyjamas (the locals wear bowling shirts with a *Ghostbusters* logo), 'They must be from Los Angeles.' No they don't make 'em like they used to, they make 'em exactly like they used to, only with a bit more bite. SGo

Critters 2: The Main Course
(Mick Garris, 1988, US) Scott Grimes, Liane Curtis, Don Opper, Barry Corbin, Terrence Mann.
87 min.
Critters, you may remember, concerned a group of oversized mothballs from space who landed on Earth and ate everybody, until some intergalactic bounty hunters turned up and fried them. The 'Krites', however, had the good business sense to lay some eggs before getting splattered, so now Grover's Bend is up to its neck in the little buggers again, and the space-borne pest control are back on the job. Garris plays it for laughs, and despite dull moments (and the obvious plagiarisation of *Gremlins*), does a pretty good job. Massive guns go KABOOM! everywhere as one gribbly after another gets stiffed, each exploding in a fountain of what looks strangely like the green gunk Linda Blair spewed over von Sydow in *The Exorcist*. The superimposure (particularly at the end when the hero meets his double) is diabolical, and the Chiodo brothers' creations are, as before, both spectacularly silly and disconcertingly vicious as they munch people's vital organs. The effect is perhaps not unlike watching Sooty in a video nasty. MK

Crocodile Dundee
(Peter Faiman, 1986, Aust) Paul Hogan, Linda Kozlowski, John Meillon, David Gulpilil, Mark Blum, Ritchie Singer.
98 min.
Dundee is a sort of living legend in his own outback, a man who once narrowly escaped being croc-fodder and who's got the scars to prove it. He's at home among the aboes and the poisonous snakes, but his robust, unpretentious outlook ensures that he can also thrive in the urban jungle of New York when American journalist Sue transports him there for publicity purposes. He deals efficiently with all the muggers, druggers and drag artists, and class distinctions fade before his exotic appeal. Hogan and his collaborators have managed to invest the original lager ad Ozzie stereotype with a good deal of rugged charm and native wit. AB

Crocodile Dundee II
(John Cornell, 1988, Aust) Paul Hogan, Linda Kozlowski, Charles Dutton, Mark Blum, John Meillon, Hechter Ubarry.
112 min.
In the mega-hit series league, the trick is to keep the bits that went down well. Thus writer/producer/star Hogan has retained instances of the naive Natural Man in the metropolis: he falls off a ledge on learning that a would-be suicide is driven by unrequited gay love, and fishes with dynamite off New York's Battery. Back home in the outback,

he repeats the sophisticated Aborigines stuff – 'It needs garlic', comments one, crouching over some unspeakable tucker. But there's little time for character in this standard issue plot about a rascally coke baron (Ubarry) trying to recover incriminating evidence from Dundee's sheila (Kozlowski). The violence is still pleasantly paddling-pool stuff, but the disarming G'day factor has been pasteurised away. BC

Croix de Bois, Les (Wooden Crosses)
(Raymond Bernard, 1931, Fr) Pierre Blanchar, Charles Vanel, Antonin Artaud, Aimos, Raymond Cordy, Paul Azaïs.
107 min. b/w.
An adaptation of Roland Dorgelès' celebrated (back then) WWI novel, this differs from its near contemporaries All Quiet and Westfront 1918 by having no explicit pacifist message. The intended audience were probably the veterans themselves, the movie being a necessarily circumspect but reasonably honest-seeming account of their collective experience. It's set throughout at the front, eschewing the customary 'home on leave' episode and concentrating remorselessly on the process of attrition, culminating in Blanchar's lonely calvary, as he slowly dies of a stomach wound in no man's land. The combat scenes, which go on and on, are filmed conventionally but sensibly with the camera, static or tracking, at ground level except when – unusually for the time – it seems to be hand-held. The sequence where the poilus listen nervously in their dugout to the sound of the Germans mining below them has the excitement of the newly feasible, characteristic of such early talkies. BBa

Cromwell
(Ken Hughes, 1970, GB) Richard Harris, Alec Guinness, Robert Morley, Dorothy Tutin, Frank Finlay, Timothy Dalton, Patrick Magee.
141 min.
Turgid history lesson which never quite makes up its mind whether it means to be subtle or spectacular, and eventually compromises on both counts. Fact is considerably fictionalised in order to present Cromwell (loudly played by Harris) as a blameless champion of the underprivileged. The battle scenes are staged vigorously enough, but also play havoc with history. TM

Cronaca di un Amore (Chronicle of a Love Affair)
(Michelangelo Antonioni, 1950, It) Lucia Bosè, Massimo Girotti, Ferdinando Sarmi.
96 min.
Antonioni's early work has been overshadowed by the international acclaim which greeted L'Avventura and L'Eclisse (though David Thomson for one celebrates the 'triumphant' vitality and 'tender rigour' which characterise the director's first films). It's difficult to watch his feature debut, Cronaca di un Amore, without looking ahead to the elliptical masterpieces which grew out of it. The film might as well be called Identification of a Woman: a detective is hired to investigate the past of an industrialist's wife, but the assignment only precipitates further loss and disappointment. If the form is more conventional than what was to follow, the mood of decadent ennui, alienation and anguish is instantly recognisable. TCh

Cronos
(Guillermo Del Toro, 1993, Mex) Federico Luppi, Ron Perlman, Claudio Brook, Margarita Isabel.
92 min.
Luppi, an elderly antiques dealer, discovers a gold gizmo which a mysterious alchemist had hidden inside a statue centuries before. The old man becomes immortal, his body undergoes a bizarre transformation, and he develops a thirst for blood. Resisting the efforts of dying businessman Brook and his henchman Perlman to get hold of the so-called Cronos device (it has strange body-piercing abilities), Luppi struggles to hold on to his humanity even beyond the grave. Del Toro gives an intriguing spin to the time-honoured vampire pic. Out goes gratuitous blood letting, in comes dry wit, a sombre pace and a substantial emotional kick, as Luppi seeks to maintain the powerful bond with his wife and young granddaughter, even though he looks,

well, like something from a horror movie. A most startling genre piece: tender, imaginative and wholly its own. TJ

Crooklyn
(Spike Lee, 1994, US) Alfre Woodard, Delroy Lindo, David Patrick Kelly, Zelda Harris, Carlton Williams, Sharif Rashed, Tse-Mach Washington.
114 min.
This semi-comic look at middle-class family life in Brooklyn, New York, in the mid-'70s was written by Spike Lee and his siblings Joie and Cinqué. As well as hanging out on the stoop and battling with four idle brothers, ten-year-old Troy (Harris) – from whose point of view the story is told – witnesses the tensions between her mother (Woodard) and father (Lindo). While Lee's customary visual style and sense of street vitality are much in evidence, it's easy to see why this fond, semi-autobiographical evocation of a largely vanished lifestyle bombed in the US. It's not just the misjudgment of depicting Troy's lengthy visit to an aunt in Virginia through the squeezed perspective of an anamorphic lens, nor even the final scenes in which the story lurches from comedy to half-hearted melodrama: the key problem is that the film is simply a ragged series of anecdotal sketches. GA

Crooks' Tour
(John Baxter, 1940, GB) Basil Radford, Naunton Wayne, Greta Gynt, Abraham Sofaer, Charles Oliver, Gordon McLeod.
84 min. b/w.
A relic from the days of radio spin-offs, this genially rickety comedy features Caldicott and Charters, the two amiable asses from the old boy network – impersonated by Radford and Wayne – who enlivened The Lady Vanishes and Night Train to Munich, then graduated to a radio series. The stock plot has them stranded in an Arabian desert while on a package tour, being mistakenly entrusted with secret information in a Baghdad nightclub, and then pursued all over the place by Nazi agents. Uninspiring stuff, but the patter remains endearingly funny. Rescued from a nasty fate in the desert by a sheik who also proves to be a member of the old boy network and invites them to dinner (sheep's eyes, of course), Wayne remains distraught: 'But we haven't got dinner jackets,' he protests. TM

Cross, The (La Cruz)
(Alejandro Agresti, 1997, Arg) Norman Briski, Mirta Busnelli, Carlos Roffe, Laura Melillo.
90 min.
After the delightful Buenos Aires Vice Versa, this is a disappointment. It starts well, with Briski's drunkard film critic arguing vehemently with the editors who find his reviews too negative. But as the film goes on to chart his mid-life crisis born of his drinking and his wife's departure for another man, it turns into an indulgent rant, enlivened only by the critic's ludicrous attempts to impersonate his wife's lover in order to discredit the man's sexual past. Strong performances, but the drama ends up going nowhere. GA

Cross and Passion
(Claire Pollak/Kim Longinotto, 1981, GB)
60 min.
A film documenting how the Troubles affect the Catholic women living on and around a cheerless, battle-scarred Belfast estate. A schoolgirl, a housewife, a nun speak fluently (though in accents often elusive to an English ear) of the forces shaping their daily lives. British soldiers are shown only as distant figures in khaki squatting by house corners, rifles cocked, next to kids who imperviously continue their games. The film's title (the name of a Catholic girls' school) proposes as more immediate, more powerful a source of oppression the papist catechism of chastity and sexual guilt passed on through generations of Irish women. The nuns also preach meekness and resignation in the face of the God-sent Troubles, but the implied connections between Church and occupying forces are never fully explored. SJo

Cross and the Switchblade, The
(Don Murray, 1970, US) Pat Boone, Erik Estrada, Jackie Giroux, Jo-Ann Robinson, Dino DeFilippi.
105 min.

Trash has a certain attractiveness, especially when it's the sort that claims to be based on fact and at the same time pits Pat Boone against a ghetto full of black and Puerto Rican kids. A preacher from Pennsylvania launching into reform work in New York, Boone comes out with phrases like 'God'll get you high, but he won't let you down', and there's layings-on of sweaty palms, a lady on heroin reclaimed, bible handouts, gang fights out of West Side Story, betrayals, young love, even light forming an unmistakable cross on the screen at a crucial moment. The best thing about it, this being one of those movies that seem unconscious of what they're really about, is that Boone's motivations are never less than equivocal, so that the switchblade wins hands down over God-is-loveism.

Cross Creek
(Martin Ritt, 1983, US) Mary Steenburgen, Rip Torn, Peter Coyote, Dana Hill, Alfre Woodard, Joanna Miles.
122 min.
Sporting a fancy line in hats and a dangerously overripe sensibility, writer Marjorie Kinnan Rawlings (Steenburgen) abandons her husband and journeys south to grapple with The Great American Gothic Novel. Stuck in a renovated backwoods shack, the local colour soon proves far more vivid than anything her imagination can conjure up. There's the suave hotelier who gets her jalopy back on the road, the doting black maid with an errant lover, and punting through the swampwand cackling balefully here's Torn as the resident rustic loon. Never one to stint herself when it comes to romantic overkill, Ritt piles on the slush with even more gusto than usual. Broadly – and self-consciously – signposted as The Stirring Story of a Woman's Struggle to Find Herself, the result suffers from a bad case of the cutes and a quite intolerable smugness. JP

Crossfire
(Edward Dmytryk, 1947, US) Robert Ryan, Robert Young, Robert Mitchum, Gloria Grahame, Sam Levene, Paul Kelly, Jacqueline White, Steve Brodie.
85 min. b/w.
This ultra-low-budget thriller did what all great B movies do: it broached a subject that 'respectable' movies wouldn't touch. In this case, the racist murder of a Jew (although it was a homosexual in Richard Brooks' source novel, The Brick Foxhole), and the exposure of the murderer's fanatical anti-Semitism. Dmytryk exploits the poverty-row sets for their claustrophobic quality, and introduces 'expressionist' lighting and distorted angles to dramatise the tensions that simmer and finally explode between the characters, GIs back from the war in Europe but not yet discharged. This was the kind of movie that provoked the McCarthy witch-hunt in Hollywood. TR

Crossing Delancey
(Joan Micklin Silver, 1988, US) Amy Irving, Peter Riegert, Reizl Bozyk, Jeroen Krabbé, Sylvia Miles, George Martin, John Bedford Lloyd.
97 min.
Izzy Grossman (Irving) is a NY Upper West Sider, managing a bookstore, arranging readings and literary soirées, whose grandmother Bubbie Kantor (Bozyk) decides that, at 33, she should be married to a nice Jewish man. So she employs the matchmaking services of the overbearing Mrs Mandelbaum (Miles), who introduces Izzy to Sam Posner (Riegert), the pickle man. Meanwhile, Izzy is flirting with egocentric novelist Anton Maes (Krabbé). Her dilemma begins: should she opt for Posner's peck of pickles – dull, reliable, and resistable – or for Maes' seductive sophistication? Some poignant and charming moments undercut the Munchkin aspect of the ethnic elderly portrayed here, but on the whole Silver's direction spoon-feeds chicken soup covered in a slightly unpalatable patina of schmaltz. JGI

Crossing Guard, The
(Sean Penn, 1995, US) Jack Nicholson, David Morse, Robin Wright, Anjelica Huston, Piper Laurie, Richard Bradford.
114 min.
After six years of desperate, unrelieved mourning, Freddy Gale (Nicholson) feels his life has just one terminus: the murder of John Booth (Morse) who killed his daughter in a drunk-driving acci-

188 Time Out Film Guide

dent. Writer/director Penn cuts between Gale's impotent, pent-up rage, aimed also at his ex-wife (Huston), and Booth's equally consuming remorse after his release from prison. Only a hesitant affair with a painter (Wright) proffers hope. This is a naive film. Very evidently the work of an actor, it follows the performances with a dogged faith which lands you in all sorts of nooks and crannies, some no more than dead ends. Yet Nicholson delivers his most committed, penetrating work in years. Penn is at his best simply pointing a camera at lonely men in anonymous rooms, choking for air in emotional vacuums of their own devising. TCh

Crossing the Bridge
(Mike Binder, 1992, US) Josh Charles, Jason Gedrick, Stephen Baldwin, Cheryl Pollak, Jeffrey Tambor, Rita Taggart.
103 min.
Mike Binder's directorial debut (he previously scripted the superior teen comedy Coupe de Ville) is a self-consciously wrought portrait of the artist as a young man; a series of comic and melancholy vignettes in the vein of Stand by Me and Diner. It's a likeable, engagingly woolly affair, the story of three friends dragging their feet after high school, pondering whether they should grow up and go to college or run drugs over the bridge from Canada and make some money – or both. This is one of those movies where a rough-and-ready game of football is endowed with near-metaphysical significance. But that's how middle-aged lads like to remember their youth, and there's usually a well-turned gag to undercut the nostalgia. Charles is good as the aspiring writer, but Threesome co-star Baldwin steals the movie from him all over again. TCh

Cross My Heart
see Fracture du myocarde, La

Cross My Heart and Hope to Die (Ti Kniver I Hjertet)
(Marius Holst, 1994, Nor) Martin Dahl Garfalk, Jan 'Devo' Kornstad, Kjersti Holmen, Reidar Sørensen.
96 min.
An intriguing but not wholly successful coming-of-age saga which blends mystery, comedy and Oedipal drama as Otto, a teenager abandoned by his friends for the summer holidays, strikes up a love-hate relationship with an enigmatic older kid who seems to exert a strange, malign influence (largely sexual) over the local women, including Otto's mother. The quiet small-town '60s setting is well conveyed, but the mystery is finally a somewhat annoying red herring. GA

Cross of Iron
(Sam Peckinpah, 1977, GB/WGer) James Coburn, Maximilian Schell, James Mason, David Warner, Klaus Löwitsch, Senta Berger.
133 min.
Peckinpah's only war film, based on a novel by Willi Heinrich, displays his familiar preoccupation with the individual confronted by events beyond his control. Dealing with a German platoon involved in the 1943 retreat on the Russian front, the film reveals a special feeling for the universalities of war: lives in the balance, the single-mindedness of daily survival, and the suppression of emotion. Sombre and claustrophobic photography, an intelligent script, and Peckinpah's clear understanding of a working platoon of men, are all far removed from the monotonous simplicity of most big-budget war films. CPe

Crossover Dreams
(Leon Ichaso, 1985, US) Rubén Blades, Shawn Elliot, Elizabeth Peña, Tom Signorelli, Virgilio Marti.
86 min.
Despite the boil-in-the-bag plot – struggling musician (salsa superstar Blades) hits big time and goes off the rails – this has lots going for it. It's the story of countless jazz and rock musicals, and the song remains the same, that rich whites in their 5th Avenue eyries still run and ruin people's lives. But this deals with the new leisure marginals: the salsa musicians of America's massive barrio populations. Barring one set piece, the music is subordinate to the narrative, sometimes annoyingly so. That said, the sound-track

remains a powerful cultural, er, signifier, and Blades and cast turn in strong, unsentimental performances. Apart from some choc-boxy scenes, Ichaso films New York with a hard-edged realism, presenting the mixed Latin communities cusping on their own social crossover. JG

Crossroads
(Jack Conway, 1942, US) William Powell, Hedy Lamarr, Basil Rathbone, Claire Trevor, Margaret Wycherly, Felix Bressart.
84 min. b/w.
Hollywood's cannibalisation of the 1939 French psychological thriller Carrefour, here developed along lighter lines to match Powell's Thin Man image. He plays a happily married diplomat who, on the eve of an ambassadorial appointment, finds himself being blackmailed as a supposed former crook (amnesia has conveniently left a hole in his memory), and confronted by proof in the form of a confederate, a mistress and a mother. It emerges as a typical MGM confection, but the cast remains very watchable. TM

Crossroads
(Walter Hill, 1986, US) Ralph Macchio, Joe Seneca, Jami Gertz, Joe Morton, Robert Judd, Harry Carey Jr.
96 min.
While it begins as a variation of sorts on The Karate Kid, with young Macchio learning life lessons and string-picking from an old bluesman (Seneca) he rescues from a New York nursing-home, when their odyssey on the road reaches the Mississippi Delta this atypical Walter Hill movie develops into a strange fantasy mingling the legends of Faust and Robert Johnson. The latter element works better than the Devil business, and the script, by John (Young Guns) Fusco, might have had more resonance than the finished film, which is too slick for its own good. But Seneca is worth watching, Ry Cooder's score is among his best work, and this certainly isn't sequel fodder. TCh

Crossup
see Tiger by the Tail

Crossways (Jujiro)
(Teinosuke Kinugasa, 1928, Jap) Junosuke Bando, Akiko Chihaya, Yukiko Ogawa, J Soma.
5,841 ft. b/w.
Kinugasa's second film with his experimental theatre company, made two years after the better-known Page of Madness. At root, it's a simple melodrama about a young man's infatuation with a geisha, and his sister's frantic attempts to save him from himself. As such, it may seem too slow and over-emphatic for some tastes. But its imagery, lighting and montage effects are at least as daring as those in the earlier film, and fully the equal of anything done in the West at the time. Kinugasa's fidelity to physical realities (like breath misting in the freezing air and steam rising from sodden clothing) is often chilling, but his vision of the Yoshiwara pleasure district as a 'hell' of lights, shadows and frenetic movement also brings out his remarkable gifts as an expressionist. Certainly much more than an archive curiosity. TR

Crow, The
(Alex Proyas, 1994, US) Brandon Lee, Michael Wincott, Rochelle Davis, Ernie Hudson, David Patrick Kelly, Angel David.
101 min.
Lee died making this supernatural rock-star revenge movie, and, after the lawsuits, recriminations and distribution problems, it has mopped up at the US box office. Lee had almost completed filming, so the thrust of the story (from James O'Barr's graphic novel) is intact. The footage has been bumped up with flashbacks, stand-in shots, and hi-tech tweaking whereby Lee was extracted from spare scenes and installed in new ones. It's unobtrusively done, but makes the action a touch repetitive. More radically, the sicko storyline has been softened, becoming an elegiac, not to say maudlin, portrait of lost love. This has, sadly, worked to the advantage of the film: what was once slick, vacuous and trashy is now shot through with a terrible post-production irony. This is a most morbid film, a twisted Gothic romance with shards of the original black wise-cracking splintering through the portentousness. Visually, it's a treat; characterisation is sharp,

particularly the nicely defined villains; and the action scenes, though soft-pedalled, still pack a satisfying crunch. SFe

Crow: City of Angels, The
(Tim Pope, 1996, US/GB) Richard Brooks, Vincent Perez, Mia Kirshner, Vincent Castellanos, Ian Dury, Iggy Pop.
86 min.
Following Brandon Lee's death in an on-set accident, the producers of the first Crow movie completed it using computer graphics, thus proving that there's no limit to Hollywood's cynical exploitation of a star's box-office appeal. This necrophiliac sequel, the first feature of a British pop promo-maker, tries to sidestep the Lee issue by resurrecting the cathartic purity of James O'Barr's original comic book. Sadly, like its unfortunate protagonist, it's very soon dead in the water. Although the setting has moved from Detroit to LA, the stylised urban wasteland, morbid atmosphere and basic plot remain the same: gunned down by Judah (Brooks) and his gang of low-lifes, Ashe (Perez) returns from the dead, inheriting the dark mantle of the first film's Eric Draven. On the plus side, legendary rock survivor Iggy Pop exudes raw power as Judah's search-and-destroy sidekick. NF

Crowd, The
(King Vidor, 1927, US) James Murray, Eleanor Boardman, Bert Roach, Estelle Clark, Daniel G Tomlinson, Dell Henderson.
90 min. b/w.
Certainly one of Vidor's best films, a silent masterpiece which turns a realistically caustic eye on the illusionist of the American dream. A young man ('born on America's 124th birthday') arrives in the big city convinced that he is going to set the world on fire, only to find that life isn't quite like that. A humble but steady job leads to love, marriage, kids and a happiness arbitrarily cut short by an accident (one of the children is run over and killed) which leads to the loss of his job, despairing unemployment, and impossible tensions starting to erode the marriage. The performances are absolutely flawless, and astonishing location work in the busy New York streets (including a giddy tour of Coney Island on a blind date) lends a gritty ring of truth to his intensely human odyssey, bounded by his eager arrival among the skyscrapers (the camera slowly panning up the side of a vast office block to discover him at work, lost in a sea of identical desks), and the last shot that has him merging as just another face in the crowd. Simple but superb. TM

Crows (Wrony)
(Dorota Kedzierzawska, 1994, Pol) Karolina Ostrozona, Kasia Szczepanik, Anna Prucnal.
66 min.
A charming if sad film about a ten-year-old girl – mischievous, brave, isolated at school, and hungry for the love denied by her mother – who decides to run away 'to the end of the world', abducting a four-year-old with whom she recreates a kind of mother-daughter relationship. Beautifully shot, the film might seem a little too studiously poetic were it not for young Karolina Ostrozona's performance: vibrant, touching, natural, and totally free of sentimentality. GA

Crucible, The
(Nicholas Hytner, 1996, US) Daniel Day-Lewis, Winona Ryder, Paul Scofield, Joan Allen, Bruce Davison, Rob Campbell, Jeffrey Jones, Peter Vaughan, Charlayne Woodard.
123 min.
Salem, Massachusetts, 1692. The town tears itself apart during the investigations testing the claims of a group of young girls that their nocturnal forest gatherings were the result of satanic possession. At the root of the hysteria is the sexual and emotional turmoil of Abigail Williams (Ryder), bent on vengeance against Elizabeth Proctor (Allen) who put a stop to Abigail's affair with her husband John (Day-Lewis); but that particular power struggle, with its deceit, suspicion and resentment, is as nothing to the deadly vortex that consumes Salem when Judge Danforth (Scofield) arrives to take control with trials and hangings. The ironies of the piece, adapted by Arthur Miller from his own 1953 play on the perils of McCarthyism, are savage and well served by a top-notch cast perfectly attuned to the poetry of the dialogue and the parable's fiery passions. Hytner

holds the action together with solid, unflashy, well-paced direction, ensuring that this is no mere period piece but a compelling, pertinent account of human fear, frailty and cold ambition. GA

Crucible of Terror
(Ted Hooker, 1971, GB) Mike Raven, Mary Maude, James Bolam, Ronald Lacey, Betty Alberge, Melissa Stribling.
91 min.
A modest but quite enjoyable variation on the *House of Wax* theme, which has some well-used location footage of Cornwall and a couple of good scenes to make up for the trite script, obviously low budget, and total miscasting of Mike Raven as the psychotic sculptor. DP

Crucified Lovers, The
see Chikamatsu Monogatari

Cruel Passion
(Chris Boger, 1977, GB) Koo Stark, Lydia Lisle, Martin Potter, Hope Jackman, Katherine Kath, Maggie Petersen.
97 min.
The improbabilities of this awkward period sex-ploiter (which pathetically attempts to emulate the look of *Barry Lyndon*) are compounded by a strain of casual nastiness which would be thoroughly offensive were it not so carelessly handled. Two sisters are expelled from a nunnery; one takes to harlotry, the other hangs on to her virginity, only to be raped in the last reel prior to being torn to pieces by Doberman Pinschers. Drawn from Sade, the film is veneered with a spurious morality which supposedly made its catchpenny cruelty somehow acceptable to the censor. JPy

Cruel Sea, The
(Charles Frend, 1952, GB) Jack Hawkins, Donald Sinden, Stanley Baker, John Stratton, Denholm Elliott, Virginia McKenna, Moira Lister, Liam Redmond, Alec McCowen.
126 min. b/w.
A sterling, old-fashioned war film of the type too readily devalued these days. Jack Hawkins gives perhaps his most notable performance as the captain of a Royal Navy corvette, suggesting as much life above as below that stiff upper lip, while Eric Ambler's adaptation of Nicholas Monsarrat's book gives the minnows their due as the enlisted men face storms and German U-boats with more courage than experience. Best of all, Frend's documentary style puts us smack in the middle of the Atlantic – the cruel sea indeed. TCh

Cruising
(William Friedkin, 1980, US) Al Pacino, Paul Sorvino, Karen Allen, Richard Cox, Don Scardino, Joe Spinell.
106 min.
Starting from a classic undercover premise (Pacino descends into Manhattan's SM gay underworld to track a psychopathic killer), and opening with some powerful moments, Cruising soon drifts into bloody Village People-type caricature, with Pacino overplaying his nameless angst as the script patently refuses to tackle the central issue – its hero's sexual ambivalence. The structure continues to loosen, and although Friedkin – like Coppola – has always had difficulty with endings, this one is so arbitrary it's as if he just gave up. DP

Crumb
(Terry Zwigoff, 1995, US) Robert Crumb, Aline Kominsky, Charles Crumb, Maxon Crumb, Robert Hughes, Martin Muller, Don Donaghue, Dana Crumb, Trina Robbins, Spain Rodriguez.
120 min.
At four, Robert Crumb would hump his mother's cowboy boots while singing 'Jesus Loves Me'. At six, he developed a sexual attraction to Bugs Bunny. At 17, he became driven by an obsession: to take his revenge on the alpha-males of his school by going down in history as a great artist. Crumb was an unlikely hero of the '60s counter-culture, but strips like *Fritz the Cat*, *Mr Natural* and *Keep on Truckin'* made him the toast of Haight-Ashbury. More interesting still is his later, confessional work, analysed and berated in the film by a series of female comic pundits and ex-girlfriends. So far, so good, but when focusing on Crumb's relationship with his two

brothers the documentary occasionally goes off the rails to become a prurient, though undeniably fascinating, freakshow. Still, it remains an outstandingly interesting portrait of obsession and genius. DW

Crush
see Kung Fu Fighting

Crush
(Alison Maclean, 1992, NZ) Marcia Gay Harden, Donogh Rees, Caitlin Bossley, William Zappa, Pete Smith.
97 min.
An intriguing and often impressive debut feature in which, following a car crash, the driver (Harden) – a predatory young American – takes the place of her injured literary critic friend (Rees), then insinuates herself into the home and hearts of a famous writer (Zappa) and his teenage daughter (Bossley). A study in deceit, manipulation, obsession and awakening awareness, Maclean's film starts unsteadily – the narrative a mite too elliptical and enigmatic for its own good – but slowly resolves itself into a powerful if faintly overheated melodrama. Beautifully performed, however, and shot with a great deal of dramatic resonance in a bleak, dank New Zealand countryside full of glooping geysers and precarious footholds. GA

Crush, The
(Alan Shapiro, 1993, US) Cary Elwes, Alicia Silverstone, Jennifer Rubin, Amber Benson, Kurtwood Smith.
89 min.
A harmless sex-teaser, from a first-time writer/director, which develops into a confused, cynical and third-rate exploitationer. Upcoming journalist Nick Eliot (Elwes) cruises into Seattle in his bashed-up jalopy to take up a job at *Pique* magazine. Fortune finds him accommodation with a wealthy family whose 14-year-old daughter Darian (Silverstone), a would-be Lolita, soon despatches her mate to check him out. Leaves much to be desired. WH

Crusoe
(Caleb Deschanel, 1988, US) Aidan Quinn, Ade Sapara, Warren Clarke, Hepburn Graham, Shane Rimmer, Elvis Payne, Jimmy Nail, Tim Spall.
94 min.
Deschanel's intriguing variation on Defoe's novel employs a clever if contrived anti-colonial twist. After a storm, ruthless slave-trader Crusoe (Quinn) is washed up on a desert island, where he develops survival skills and a capacity for solitude. The footprints in the sand and the obsequious Friday, however, are nowhere to be found; instead, he saves a black slave (Graham) intended for human sacrifice by fearsome cannibals, arrogantly christening him Lucky ('I have no one to sell you to'). But the next day he wakes to find himself sharing the island with Lucky's headless corpse and a physically and intellectually superior warrior (Sapara) who is clearly unimpressed by Crusoe's efforts to impose the white man's language, table manners and 'civilised' lifestyle on his own sophisticated culture. On the back foot from the outset, Crusoe is forced to endure various indignities and re-examine his own racist elitism. The film works best when dialogue is kept to a minimum, partly because much of it is embarrassingly bad, partly because the island's exotic beauty and the dynamics of the pair's relationship are best conveyed through Deschanel's meticulous attention to telling visual minutiae. NF

Cruz, La
see Cross, The

Cry-Baby
(John Waters, 1990, US) Johnny Depp, Amy Locane, Susan Tyrell, Iggy Pop, Traci Lords, Patty Hearst, Polly Bergen, Troy Donahue, Mink Stole, Joe Dallesandro, Joey Heatherton, Willem Dafoe.
85 min.
An energetic and hyperactively hormonal romp through '50s kitsch from trash-master Waters. In Baltimore, 1954, the town's youth are divided into Squares and Drapes, the latter presided over by gang-leader Wade 'Cry Baby' Walker (Depp), orphaned son of the electrocuted Alphabet bomber. When Cry Baby ('That's *Mister* Baby to

you!') falls for lithesome daughter-of-wealth Allison Vernon-Williams (Locane), she is sucked into a world of 'coloured' music, skin-tight slacks and reckless driving, from which her erstwhile companions seek to extract her forthwith. Replete with a thumpingly good soundtrack mixing old standards with modern pastiches, this is Waters' finest film to date, a worthy successor to *Hairspray* which exudes teen angst and young lust from every pore. Cameos from notable degenerates Iggy Pop and Traci Lords beautifully complement Depp's spunkily hollow-cheeked performance, while Patty Hearst plays the American middle class nightmare to a tee. Seriously sexy stuff. MK

Cry Danger
(Robert Parrish, 1951, US) Dick Powell, Rhonda Fleming, Richard Erdman, William Conrad, Jean Porter, Regis Toomey, Jay Adler.
79 min. b/w.
A former child actor (*City Lights*) and celebrated editor (for Ford; an Oscar-winner for *Body and Soul*), Parrish directed one masterpiece (*The Wonderful Country*), one almost-masterpiece (*The Purple Plain*) and a gallery of engaging, civilised movies before getting tangled in the shoals of the swinging British '60s. His major theme is of a man seeking not so much an identity as a place to belong, and here, in his directorial début, the theme lurks behind a low-budget thriller framework as ex-bookie Powell exits the slammer to get revenge on the bad guys who put him there. Shot in 22 days (Parrish rewrote the script with William Bowers), it's the kind of movie in which, told to expect someone extra for dinner, delicious Fleming smiles 'OK, I'll put more water in the soup'. With excellent support players like a young, thin (for him) William Conrad and Jay Adler, this is a fast, crisp and laconic delight. CW

Cry Freedom
(Richard Attenborough, 1987, GB) Kevin Kline, Penelope Wilton, Denzel Washington, John Hargreaves, Alec McCowen, Kevin McNally, Zakes Moke, Ian Richardson.
158 min.
Donald Woods (Kline), editor of the *Daily Dispatch*, following the publication of a critical article on black activist Steve Biko (Washington), is challenged to meet him, and is won over. After Biko's brutal murder by the South African police, Woods refuses to accept the official cause of death (hunger strike) and campaigns for a full public enquiry. Viciously persecuted along with his wife and family, he finds that flight is the only answer. The initial stages of this epic movie are somewhat stodgy, but once Attenborough achieves his momentum there's no holding him. The performances are excellent, the crowd scenes astonishing, and the climax truly nerve-racking. An implacable work of authority and compassion, *Cry Freedom* is political cinema at its best. MS

Cry from the Mountain
(James F Collier, 1986, US) James Cavan, Wes Parker, Rita Walter, Chris Kidd, Coleen Gray.
90 min.
When Parker takes his ten-year-old son on a canoeing trip in the Alaskan wilderness to break the news of his impending divorce, he bashes his head when their kayak collapses. An old mountain dweller (Cavan) comes to the rescue, and – he's an ardent evangelist – accompanies the pair home, where he convinces the wife (Walter) to go to a Billy Graham crusade. The sermon convinces her, like her hospitalised husband, that there is a way to solve their problems. She and her son are born again, the old man is born again, and the viewer is invited by Graham's voice to follow suit. It's a well-worn weepie formula, but there's little in the simplistic working out of the plot or the idea of salvation as an all-round happy ending to move sceptics very far. EP

Crying Freeman
(Christophe Gans, 1995, Fr/Can/US/Jap) Mark Dacascos, Julie Condra, Rae Dawn Chong, Byron Man, Tcheky Karyo.
102 min.
Based on an epic Japanese comic book of rare intelligence and detail, this is almost too reverential towards its source material: several sequences inspire déjà vu, having literally been story-boarded in the original manga; and both

Dacascos, as the eponymous Chinese assassin who cries when he makes a hit, and Condra, as the virgin who falls for the soft-hearted hard man, look the part uncannily. Director Gans tries honourably to put the Art into martial arts, but comes fatally unstuck. Though slo-mo fight sequences distance the action from your traditional Jackie Chan beat-'em-ups, you find yourself longing for some good, old-fashioned shit-kicking. When we finally get it, and discover that Dacascos not only looks like Johnny Depp on steroids, but that he could whup Jean-Claude Van Damme's sorry ass as Hollywood's next action hero, you just wonder what took him so long. DW

Crying Game, The

(Neil Jordan, 1992, GB) Forest Whitaker, Miranda Richardson, Stephen Rea, Adrian Dunbar, Jaye Davidson, Breffini McKenna, Joe Savino, Birdie Sweeney, Jim Broadbent, Tony Slattery.
112 min.
Drunk at a South Armagh fairground, black British soldier Jody (Whitaker) is abducted by the IRA and held hostage on a farm. His jailer Fergus (Rea) comes to respect and understand his prisoner, and after an army raid, heads for London to seek out Jody's lover, hairdresser and chanteuse Dil (Davidson)... It's perhaps surprising that Jordan's thriller hangs together at all. After the opening carnival scene, it virtually turns into a statically theatrical two-hander; then, when Fergus reaches London, both locations and focus become more diffuse as the narrative steadily winds itself up for a bloody finale. There's a problem not only in the clumsy structure, but in Jordan's determination to keep surprising us with twists. Even though the whole is never more than the sum of its parts, the film does work, raises a plethora of questions concerning loyalty, violence and the nature of desire, and is in some respects a summation of the various themes that have emerged from Jordan's work. GA

Cry in the Dark, A

(Fred Schepisi, 1988, Aust) Meryl Streep, Sam Neill, Charles Tingwell, Kevin Miles, Jim Holt, Nick Tate.
121 min.
On a family camping trip, Lindy Chamberlain (Streep) sees a dingo emerge from the tent and finds her baby gone. A torchlight search ensues, and a bloody baby suit is discovered. Lindy and her husband Michael (Neill) go on TV, and seize the opportunity to plug their Seventh Day Adventist faith, which does not go down well. They don't seem to be grieving. Australia takes against this unnervingly self-contained victim of disaster. The press go for the jugular, the Australian public ridicule the dingo story, and the couple go on trial for murder. Schepisi's matter-of-fact direction and the rather undernourished screenplay don't mine much beyond the lousiness of the press and the unknowableness of the victims, but Streep (the best thing she has done in ages) carries it along. BC.

Cry of the Banshee

(Gordon Hessler, 1970, GB) Vincent Price, Elisabeth Bergner, Essy Persson, Hugh Griffith, Sally Geeson, Patrick Mower, Hilary Dwyer.
87 min.
Screenwriter Chris Wicking's third collaboration with director Hessler is set in 16th century England, where evil spirit Mower exacts revenge on witch-hunting magistrate Price. Despite authentic location work and rather opportunistic flashes of graphic mayhem, this has none of the narrative concision, thematic richness or overall conviction of Michael Reeves' *Witchfinder General*, in which Price and Dwyer also appeared, two years earlier. TJ

Cry of the City

(Robert Siodmak, 1948, US) Victor Mature, Richard Conte, Shelley Winters, Fred Clark, Debra Paget, Hope Emerson, Betty Garde.
96 min. b/w.
Riveting example of Siodmak's skill not only in transforming indifferent material, but in giving the feel of studio *noir* to location shooting. The familiar '30s theme (cop and criminal sharing the same deprived background in New York's Little Italy) acquires an almost metaphysical ring in being displaced by what turns into a literal cry of the city as the wounded gangster (Conte, ter-

rific) goes on the run for the last few hours of his life, leaving behind him a dark trail of murder, pain and betrayal. Rarely has the cruel, lived-in squalor of the city been presented in such telling detail, both in the vivid portrayal of ghetto life and in the astonishing parade of corruption uncovered in the night (a slug-like shyster; a monstrous, sadistic masseuse; a sleazy refugee abortionist, etc.). TM

Cry of the Hunted

(Joseph H Lewis, 1953, US) Vittorio Gassman, Barry Sullivan, Polly Bergen, William Conrad.
95 min. b/w.
Far from Lewis' best, this chase thriller is nevertheless an engagingly taut affair, its various visual flourishes climaxing in a characteristically atmospheric swamp shoot-out (one of several in his work). Gassman is the escaped con who, for none too clear reasons, heads back home to his beloved Louisiana bayous, Sullivan the pursuing lawman with whom he shares a strange bond. Hardly original, but highly enjoyable. GA

Cry of the Penguins

see Mr Forbush and the Penguins

Cry Onion (Cipolla Colt)

(Enzo Castellari, 1975, It/Sp/WGer) Franco Nero, Martin Balsam, Sterling Hayden. Emma Cohen, Duilio Cruciani.
91 min.
Attempting to spice up this lamentable slapstick Western, those responsible for the dubbing have foisted an inappropriate James Stewart drawl on freckle-faced Franco Nero (a gormless, onion-eating fanatic who refuses to sell a patch of land to Balsam, an oil baron with a dart-firing mechanical hand), while his juvenile sidesick spouts Al Pacino Brooklynese. Nero spends most of the movie throwing onions at the baddies, or rendering them unconscious with his malodorous breath. JPy

Crystal Gazing

(Laura Mulvey/Peter Wollen, 1982, GB) Gavin Richards, Lora Logic, Mary Maddox, Jeff Rawle, Alan Porter, Patrick Bauchau.
92 min.
Wollen and Mulvey's most narrative feature to date marks time in London during the Thatcher recession as it follows (and digresses from) the paths of two men who have less of a future than the two women who make up the centre of the film. The main object of its makers is to make connections, placed somewhere between Brecht and Breton, in a city where the wires are either crossed or the lines down and things are falling apart under Thatcher, leaving only isolated pockets of activity. If the subject matter is dour, tragic even according to Wollen and Mulvey, they take pains to disrupt the sombreness with deliberate levities, and their playfulness in establishing connections recalls early Godard. Its achievements are to show how life proceeds at different rhythms, not often caught in fiction, and to make everything in the film more clearly recognisable – for once the title says it all. CPe

Crystal Voyager

(George Greenough, 1974, US)
78 min.
Boring surfing film saved by the last twenty minutes, the only segment with music by Pink Floyd and actually shot from a surfboard.

Cry Uncle (aka Super Dick)

(John G Avildsen, 1971, US) Allen Garfield, Madeleine Le Roux, David Kirk, Devin Goldenberg, Deborah Morgan, Nancy Salmon.
87 min.
Perhaps the least likely candidate ever for the 'extended version' trend is Avildsen's early cheapo feature: a contemporary of *Joe*, but made before the respectability of *Save the Tiger*, the bankability of *Rocky*, or the honour of removal from *Saturday Night Fever*. First released here as *Super Dick*, in deference to Garfield's private eye/cocksman role, it re-emerged with its original US title and ten minutes of footage restored to its choppy continuity. A bizarre soft-core comedy-thriller, its frantically parodic sexual anarchism is of a pretty reactionary species, and even the guilty guffaws sometimes obstinately refuse to come; though Garfield's gargoyle slob is definitely one for the Divine crowd to savour. PT

Cry Wolf

(Peter Godfrey, 1947, US) Barbara Stanwyck, Errol Flynn, Geraldine Brooks, Richard Basehart, John Ridgely, Jerome Cowan.
83 min. b/w.
Stanwyck makes a brave attempt as the woman in peril in this old dark house thriller with its creaky plot about her coming to claim the inheritance of her recently deceased husband and suspecting that his uncle (Flynn) may have murdered him. The twists in the plot don't really improve matters much, but the cast is generally watchable, if wasted. GA

CS Blues

(Robert Frank, 1972, US). The Rolling Stones, Dick Cavett, Lee Radziwill, Truman Capote.
90 min.
It's *Cocksucker Blues* of course, a film made of the Rolling Stones on tour in North America, 1972 (at the time of their excellent *Exile On Main Street* LP). It has acquired considerable cult status, largely on account of the group's reluctance to have it shown – whether because they are portrayed as Satanic Majesties, or just an above-average rock group, is not altogether clear. There is some intravenous use of heroin, not by the principal characters, natch, and some mucking about with groupies. There are also some well composed and shot concert sequences, but what the film does best is present a picture of the mini-society that attached itself to the group at its peak. A pretty dismal society it is, too. For fans this is practically unmissable, but less partisan voyeurs are likely to concur with guitarist Mick Taylor's observation on one of the many dreary drug-taking scenes: 'I've never seen a hotel room filled with such Olympian ecstasy.' He's joking. MC

Cuba

(Richard Lester, 1979, US) Sean Connery, Brooke Adams, Jack Weston, Hector Elizondo, Denholm Elliott, Martin Balsam, Chris Sarandon, Lonette McKee.
122 min.
'Havana, Cuba, 1959'. Lucky they print this on the screen, as it's the first and last coherent piece of information you can glean from Lester's political love story, which mentions neither politics nor love but plays out its actions against a background of both. Confused? So, it would seem, was Lester, for his indecision over making either element dominant produces a central love affair which is hollow, and a revolution which is just so much local colour. Ultimately, it's about corruption, apathy and crumbling values, in all their seedy splendour. Everyone is on the lam: Connery, a mercenary for Batista; Adams, a female cuckold with her eyes wide open, but wedded to wealth and power; Elliott, a crop-sprayer turned gunrunner. Not so much 'Cuba Si' as Cuba...what? FF

Cuba Libre

(David Riondino, 1996, It/Cuba) David Riondino.
88 min.
This putative update of *Bicycle Thieves* is full of rambling but seductive incident. It focuses on the arrival in Havana of a plane load of Italians: a venal promo director seeking revolutionary posters and poverty as a backdrop to shoe commercials; a bossy 'capitalist' setting up a restaurant; a self-obsessed 50-year-old poet forever declaiming his verse from the rooftops; a student come to research Zavattini's Cuban period, who fails to notice a real-life version of the De Sica tale re-run before his eyes. Writer/director Riondino, who also stars, may not turn tourist clichés about Cuba on their heads, but he leads them a merry, salsa seasoned dance. WH

Cuerpo en el Bosque

see Body in the Forest, A

Cugini Carnali

see Visitor, The

Cugino Americano, Il

see Blood Ties

Cujo

(Lewis Teague, 1983, US) Dee Wallace, Daniel Hugh-Kelly, Danny Pintauro, Christopher Stone, Ed Lauter, Kaiulani Lee.
91 min.

This adaptation on a modest budget from Stephen King's bestseller about a rabid St Bernard is a pleasing illustration of the filmic simplicity at the heart of King's better writing. Any old pulp writer can trap heroine and child in a broken-down car menaced by a vicious dog, but it takes a King to spot the enormous advantage of keeping them there for two-thirds of the book. Fortunately Teague follows his lead, making considerable visual and narrative mileage out of the struggle between dog and car, as his actors scream and cry their way through the movie with commendably little shame. But for all its ingenuity, *Cujo* does lose an awful lot of ground from the fact that rabid St Bernards tend to evoke pity rather than terror. Perhaps that explains why the film's US earnings would buy few dog biscuits. DP

Cul-de-Sac

(Roman Polanski, 1966, GB) Donald Pleasence, Françoise Dorléac, Lionel Stander, Jack MacGowran, Robert Dorning, Iain Quarrier, Jacqueline Bisset.
111 min. b/w.
Shot through with the same surreal, absurdist wit as Polanski's shorts, this bizarre variation on a classic theme – a couple who have withdrawn from the world (Pleasence and Dorléac) to live on an isolated island are visited by gangsters on the run (Stander and MacGowran) – centres around the director's abiding concerns: sexual perversity, insecurity and humiliation, the eruption of nightmarish chaos into a seemingly ordered world, human betrayal, corruptibility and self-destruction. If the subject matter is bleak and bitterly serious, the tone throughout is darkly comic, while the precise imagery effortlessly conveys the tension, the claustrophobia, and the madness of the situation. GA

Culloden

(Peter Watkins, 1964, GB) George McBean, Alan Pope, the people of Inverness.
71 min. b/w.
Watkins' films are compulsively interesting almost in spite of themselves. His *oeuvre* may be characterised as a progression from polemical hysteria towards formal paranoia, yet it is impossible to deny his films their emotive, affective power, derived from an innovatory manipulation of technique. *Culloden* (made for TV) exhibits Watkins' virtues and vices in about equal proportions, and takes on a critical centrality as an initiator of the 'drama-doc' strain of British TV. These quasi-newsreels of the past and future, feeding off the documentary tradition to bolster the 'realism' of their speculative fictions, and usurping the medium's primary resources for capturing 'actuality' to present reconstructions, effectively efface their artifice by playing on the 'integrity' of certain strategies of representation. Yet Watkins must still here rely on an omniscient/propagandist commentary to convey the contextual discourses around his 'horror movies': a problem superseded in his later, similar, but increasingly worrying work. PT

Culpepper Cattle Co., The

(Dick Richards, 1972, US) Gary Grimes, Billy Green Bush, Luke Askew, Bo Hopkins, Geoffrey Lewis, Wayne Sutherlin, Matt Clark.
92 min.
Engaging 'demythologising' Western, with Grimes as the naive young Texan who joins a cattle drive with romantic dreams of the cowboy life, only to have them dashed as he encounters death, crime and compromise. Deliberately downbeat, aided no end in its aims at authenticity by the excellent photography (Laurence Edward Williams and Ralph Woolsey). GA

Culture Club –
A Kiss Across the Ocean

(Keith MacMillan, 1984, GB) Culture Club: Boy George, Jon Moss, Ron Hay, Mikey Craig.
64 min.
Filmed in December 1983 at the band's Hammersmith Odeon gig (and first released on video), this features all their singles and material from both albums. The picture quality is superb, due no doubt to the special equipment used in the filming, but that's more than can be said for the digital-sound mix. The drums dominate most of the time (probably because drummer Jon Moss mixed it), with George and Helen Terry's vocals often lost in the sea of scream from adoring fans. Other than that, a tight, well-paced show. DA

Cumbres borrascosas
see Abismos de pasión

Cup Final

(Eran Riklis, 1991, Isr) Moshe Ivgi, Muhamad Bacri, Salim Dau, Basam Zuamut.
107 min.
June, 1982. Israel invades Lebanon. When his squad is ambushed, Sergeant Cohen (Ivgi) is captured by a retreating PLO foot patrol. As the patrol pick their way through the unmarked minefield their country has become, back towards the dubious safety of Beirut, Cohen tries to reach out to his captors. English provides the means, but the real common language proves to be a shared passion for football: Palestinian and Israeli alike are stunned to learn of West Germany's defeat by Algeria in the World Cup finals in Spain, while Cohen's passionate support for Italy commends him to the patrol-leader Ziad (Bacri). Although his gripping, fundamentally humanist movie doesn't break any new ground, Riklis doesn't shirk from the complexity of the Arab-Israeli conflict, maintaining an admirably even-handed political stance as Cohen and Ziad gravitate from mutual incomprehension to grudging respect, with the tension between them never far away. After a slightly stilted opening, Riklis steers confidently between irony, menace and warmth, helped by a uniformly excellent cast. NF

Curdled

(Reb Braddock, 1992, US) Angela Jones, William Baldwin.
88 min.
In 1992, while doing the rounds with *Reservoir Dogs*, Tarantino saw a short which he later encouraged director Reb Braddock to expand to a feature. The result is this smart, over-stretched black comedy about a young Latino woman, Gabriela (Jones), who gratifies her morbid obsession with murder by working for a cleaning company that specialises in mopping up its gruesome aftermath. The childlike quality of Gabriela's macabre fascination is deftly sketched, as she pores over her collection of newspaper cuttings or tries to recreate the choreography of death suggested by the chalk marks, bullet holes and blood stains. Fantasy and reality finally merge when she comes face to face with the Blue Blood Killer, a smooth sociopath (played with icy charm by Baldwin) who preys on wealthy women. In a confrontation filmed as a single four-and-a-half-minute shot, the killer forces her to re-enact the dance of death implied by the murder scene, from both the victim's and the assailant's point of view. This bravura sequence virtually justifies the price of admission, but elsewhere the congealed blood is spread a little too thinly, a deficiency only partly made up for by a catchy, Spanish-influenced soundtrack. NF

Cure, The

(Peter Horton, 1995, US) Brad Renfro, Diana Scarwid, Joseph Mazzello, Bruce Davison, Aeryk Egan.
97 min.
Stillwater, Minnesota: Erik (Renfro) lives alone with his sourpuss mom Gail (Scarwid). He's bored. Next door is Dexter (Mazzello), who has AIDS. The two 11-year-olds have never met – Gail's too bigoted – but that doesn't stop the lads at school from dubbing Erik 'homo' and generally cramping his social options. So he figures, what the hell, may as well jump over the fence and strike up a friendship; next thing, the pair are inseparable. Gail finds out, threatens to take Erik away, and so the boys board a raft for a wholly irresponsible escapade, heading downriver to New Orleans where, claims a *National Examiner* headline, a Dr Fishburne has found a miracle cure for AIDS. A first feature from a 'thirty-something' actor: well played, lots of jaunty episodes, unobtrusively squidgy emotions, a good cry at the end. The real weakness arises from the weepie format itself. There's never any ambition here to delve into those more interesting facets of the story littered around its edges. Avoids the worst excesses of mawkishness, but essentially just the usual mix of life-affirming, flabby humanist hogwash. NB

Cure in Orange, The

(Tim Pope, 1987, GB) The Cure: Robert Smith, Laurence Tolhurst, Simon Gallup, Porl Thompson, Boris Williams.
114 min.

An astonishingly lavish production number for one of the world's less dynamic live bands, rendered noteworthy by its setting against the magnificent backdrop of an ancient amphitheatre (the Théâtre Antique d'Orange in France). Smith, in a non-stop run through their best-known numbers, proves that he is not one of the world's great frontmen, but for Cure fans this is as perfect and cinematographically compelling a record of a gig as could be asked for. For the rest of us, it's a bit of a yawn. DPe

Cure Show, The

(Aubrey Powell/Leroy Bennett, 1993, GB) The Cure.
96 min. b/w & col.
The Cure have spent 15 years championing the ultimate shoe-shuffling indie music for staying in to, so it's perhaps strange that this is their *second* live film. Mumbling into the microphone from behind a guitar and tumbleweed haircut, leadman Robert Smith carries these huge concerts surprisingly well, and this is an attractive, well-shot movie of a colourful (if not imaginatively) staged concert (Palace Stadium, Detroit, July 1992). The songs range from 'Let's Go to Bed' to 'Never Enough'. Even fans of trendy bands, it seems, get their lighters out for the slowies. LD

Curly Sue

(John Hughes, 1991, US) James Belushi, Kelly Lynch, Alisan Porter, John Getz, Fred Dalton Thompson, Cameron Thor.
102 min.
Tousle-haired urchin Curly Sue (Porter) and her down-and-out guardian Bill (Belushi), are carrying out a tried-and-tested scam which involves deliberately colliding with an expensive car to elicit favours from the remorseful driver. As luck would have it, their latest victim is a posh, high-powered lawyer (Lynch). The first collision brings free grub, and a second, unintentional encounter also brings accommodation in her apartment, new wardrobes for both, and – bingo! – romance. From the opening montage of childhood moments through to the contrived resolution, this is utterly formulaic. Hughes' leaden direction and script give no hint of the skill that distinguishes his best work. CM

Curse of Frankenstein, The

(Terence Fisher, 1957, GB) Peter Cushing, Christopher Lee, Hazel Court, Robert Urquhart, Valerie Gaunt.
82 min.
The first of the Hammer Frankensteins, bringing blood and amputated limbs to the story but cursed with an inept make-up for Lee's monster (Jack Pierce's Karloff creation was copyright). The whole thing in fact looks surprisingly tacky for a film which sparked a box-office bonanza. Fisher's voluptuous use of colour was much more assured in the following year's *Dracula*. TM

Curse of Greed, The
see Twin Pawns

Curse of the Cat People, The

(Robert Wise/Gunther von Fritsch, 1944, US) Simone Simon, Ann Carter, Kent Smith, Elizabeth Russell, Julia Dean, Jane Randolph, Sir Lancelot.
70 min. b/w.
Though very different in purpose and tone to *Cat People*, Val Lewton's 'sequel' is far more closely tied to its predecessor than is commonly believed. For one thing, all the main characters remain very much the same as they were in the earlier film, to which there are many specific references; for another, both films concern the way that guilt, fear and fantasy can arise from isolation and misunderstanding. In this case, it's a small girl, lonely and repeatedly scolded by her parents and shunned by her friends for indulging in day-dreaming; when she populates her solitary world with the ghost of her father's dead first wife (Simon, heroine of *Cat People*), her imagination (or is it?) gets her into serious trouble. Far from being a horror film, it's a touching, perceptive and lyrical film about childhood, psychologically astute and occasionally disturbing as it focuses entirely on the child's-eye view of a sad, cruel world. GA

Curse of the Crimson Altar (aka The Crimson Cult)

(Vernon Sewell, 1968, GB) Boris Karloff, Christopher Lee, Mark Eden, Virginia Wetherell, Barbara Steele, Rupert Davies, Michael Gough.
89 min.
A shoddy horror pic, notable only as the 81-year-old Karloff's last completed feature. Robert Manning (Eden) traces his vanished brother to Craxted Lodge in the village of Greymarsh, but the owner (Lee) – in fact taking revenge against the Manning family on behalf of a witch ancestor, Lavinia (Steele), burned in the 17th century – denies all knowledge of him. Robert has strange dreams featuring Steele, her face painted green, her lips blood-red, and wearing a ram's horn headpiece; but he and his girlfriend (Wetherell) are ultimately saved by a wheelchair-bound witchcraft expert (Karloff). The story has (uncredited) similarities to HP Lovecraft's *Dream in the Witch House*, but director Sewell never gets to grips with the muddled script. NF

Curse of the Demon

see Night of the Demon

Curse of the Mummy's Tomb, The

(Michael Carreras, 1964, GB) Ronald Howard, Terence Morgan, Fred Clark, Jeanne Roland, George Pastell, Jack Gwillim, Dickie Owen.
80 min.
Limp Hammer sequel to *The Mummy*, with the bandaged one (Owen) escaping from his Pharaoh's sarcophagus when it is excavated and exhibited on tour, going on the rampage in London and ending up in the sewers. Resolutely unimaginative. GA

Curse of the Pink Panther

(Blake Edwards, 1983, GB) David Niven, Robert Wagner, Herbert Lom, Joanna Lumley, Capucine, Robert Loggia, Harvey Korman, Burt Kwouk, Ted Wass, Leslie Ash.
110 min.
'What has happened to France's greatest detective?' There's no Peter Sellers in this PP film, not even an out-take (just a puny Clouseau impersonation from a guesting Roger Moore). *Les flics* are about to set the World's Greatest Detective on Clouseau's trail; but Inspector Dreyfus tics up the computer, and they get Officer Clifton Sleigh (Wass from *Soap*), resident drongo of NYC's not-so-finest. You can guess the rest. Sleigh sniped at from all angles. Everybody misses. Dreyfus in fishpond. Dreyfus in traction. Burt Kwouk hai-karate. Stolen diamond. Professor Balls. Inflatable dog. Côte d'Azur. Wacky car chase. Inflatable woman. Blow-up. Boom boom. Valenthia. Leslie Ash. Kiss kiss bang bang. Joanna Lumley. Hang-gliding. Mud bath. Capucine's cheekbones. What has happened to France's greatest detective? He's dead dead dead and necrophilia is dead boring. AB

Curse of the Werewolf, The

(Terence Fisher, 1960, GB) Oliver Reed, Yvonne Romain, Catherine Feller, Clifford Evans, Anthony Dawson, Richard Wordsworth, Warren Mitchell.
91 min.
The life and times of a lycanthrope down in sunny but sinister Spain, developing the story from the mutant's conception (when a beggar rapes a deaf-mute servant girl), through his early years when he causes church fonts to bubble, to his final death at the hands of a lynch mob incensed by his murders. Sex, naturally, is the catalyst that sets Reed off on his homicidal binges. More ambitious and complex than most Hammer films in its investigation of the opposing forces that rule the life of the monster (though still a drastic simplification of Guy Endore's marvellous source novel, *The Werewolf of Paris*), but badly lacking in dramatic tension. GA

Curse of the Wraydons, The

(Victor M Gover, 1946, GB) Tod Slaughter, Bruce Seton, Gabriel Toyne, Andrew Lawrence, Lorraine Clewes, Pearl Cameron.
94 min. b/w.
Adapted by director Gover from the play *Springheeled Jack, the Terror of London*, this is a ridiculously overcooked period melodrama. Slaughter (b. 1885), not as young or nimble as in his Sweeney Todd days, looks a little out of breath as the villain of the piece, a murderous Napoleonic spy with a hatred of all things British. Watching him wobble and roar his way through the film, you can only regret he was never given the chance to work with Ed Wood Jr, the one director who would surely have cherished his pantomime style. GM

Curtain Up

(Ralph Smart, 1952, GB) Robert Morley, Margaret Rutherford, Olive Sloane, Kay Kendall, Michael Medwin, Liam Gaffney, Joan Rice.
82 min. b/w.
Intriguing potboiler set in the world of seaside rep (adapted from Philip King's play *On Monday Next*): Morley and Rutherford, two of the dottiest character actors in the British movie firmament, are given rare leading roles. He's a hectoring director, she's the equally stubborn playwright whose latest, quite atrocious work the company's mounting for purely mercenary reasons. GM

Curtis's Charm

(John L'Ecuyer, 1995, Can) Maurice Dean Wint, Callum Keith Rennie, Rachael Crawford, Barbara Barnes-Hopkins, Hugh Dillon.
75 min.
Small but beguiling movie, based on a story by Jim Carroll. A recovering heroin addict runs into an old comrade-in-arms in the park, but Curtis is crawling the bench with fright: he thinks he's being followed by a squirrel. His voodoo juju mother-in-law has put a spell on him, he explains. The man needs a talisman to protect him. Even at 75 minutes this feels over-extended, and the budget evidently didn't stretch to New York locations, but it's a cool, off-the-wall conversation piece, snappily put together with a darkly humorous sense of the metaphysical. TCh

Custard Boys, The

(Colin Finbow, 1979, GB) Tony Collins, Chris Chescoe, Les Scott, Glenn Dunderdale, Eric Milliet, Peter Setram.
82 min.
An Indian summer, 1942: 'When I was thirteen, all I wanted to be was a hero.' A young evacuee's response to the surrounding war-obsessed adult world seems the only one available to him, until he forms 'a particular friendship' with another boy, a Jewish refugee. This threatens the stability of his gang (who also mirror the racist/jingoist attitudes of adulthood), and he is caught in Forster's great liberal crux: your country or your friend? A celebration of all that is lost and found in the process of growth, all the more remarkable for the performances of the boys involved, who act the adults into the ground. CPea

Custer of the West

(Robert Siodmak, 1966, US/Sp) Robert Shaw, Mary Ure, Jeffrey Hunter, Ty Hardin, Robert Ryan, Lawrence Tierney, Kieron Moore, Marc Lawrence.
146 min.
Siodmak's penultimate movie which, as an epic Cinerama Western lumbered with the need for irrelevant spectacle, manages to be far less affecting than his less expensive *noir* thrillers of the '40s. Nevertheless, it's an ambitious and occasionally stylish work, expertly crafted but let down by a script which doesn't quite decide what angle to take on its controversial protagonist. Shaw's erratic American accent doesn't help either, though some of the supporting performances (Ryan especially) are very watchable. GA

Custodian, The

(John Dingwall, 1993, Aust) Barry Otto, Anthony LaPaglia, Hugo Weaving, Kelly Dingwall.
109 min.
Quinlan (LaPaglia) is a cop on the verge of a nervous breakdown. He is separating from his drunken wife, who hates that he's honest but poor, and suspicious of his best mate Church (Weaving), who's dishonest but rich. After a bout on the bottle, which gets him passed over for promotion and suspended, Quinlan goes in with Church, but simultaneously dishes the dirt to crusading journalist Reynolds (Kelly Dingwall) who passes on the info to nice guy Ferguson (Otto) of Internal Affairs. A somewhat involving but on the whole rather heavy-handed thriller on the theme, 'Who will watch over our protectors?' AO

Cut Above, A

see Gross Anatomy

Cutter and Bone

see Cutter's Way

Cutter's Way (aka Cutter and Bone)

(Ivan Passer, 1981, US) Jeff Bridges, John Heard, Lisa Eichhorn, Ann Dusenberry, Stephen Elliott, Nina Van Pallandt, Arthur Rosenberg, Patricia Donahue.
109 min.
A dazzling *film noir* out of the same paranoiac mould as *Klute*. It begins with classic murder as a girl's body is stuffed into a trash-can one stormy night. When the killer is tentatively identified as a fat-cat oil tycoon, stern retribution against the powers who never pay for their sins is demanded by Cutter (Heard), a horribly mutilated Vietnam veteran who hounds the tycoon to his doom, guilty or not. But the quixotic Cutter is gradually transformed into an Ahab pursuing his Moby Dick, and the hallucinatory quality of the film comes from its view of California as a paradise turned into a hunting-ground for the leviathans of speculation. As three minnows threshing desperately to avoid being engulfed, Cutter, his drunken wife (Eichhorn), and his beach-bum best friend (Bridges) are caught in a nightmarish personal triangle of extraordinary, constantly shifting complexity, rippling with secrecies and ambivalent emotions that escape easy definition. Amazing performances from Heard, Bridges and Eichhorn in one of the key films of the decade. TM

CutThroat Island

(Renny Harlin, 1995, US) Geena Davis, Matthew Modine, Patrick Malahide, Frank Langella, Maury Chaykin, Stan Shaw, Rex Linn, Harris Yulin.
125 min.
The pirate movie requires a dashing male star and a dose of lightly self-deprecating humour. In this $90m revisionist swashbuckler, we get Geena Davis doing the all-action honours, and a hotch-potch script that seems to think pirate movies are so funny in themselves the need for more humour is superfluous. The plot's well worn: a treasure map is sought by the star, her ill-matched cohort Modine, dully rhubarbing villain Langella, and others. On screen the money has bought yards of 17th century Jamaican fixtures and fittings, a couple of attractive galleons, and a warehouse of Semtex. Harlin is never a man to shy away from the lure of Very Big Explosions, and, on a technical level, the spectacle's impressive. The only actor to make much of an impact is Malahide's colonial officer, who extracts tart irony from the merest crumbs. TJ

Cutting Edge, The

(Paul Michael Glaser, 1992, US) DB Sweeney, Moira Kelly, Roy Dotrice, Terry O'Quinn, Dwier Brown, Chris Benson.
102 min.
When a collision on the ice robs Olympic ice hockey player Doug Dorsey (Sweeney) of his peripheral vision, his life falls apart. Kate Moseley (Kelly) is one of the most talented and temperamental figure-skaters in the world, her sights fixed firmly on winning gold at the 1992 Winter Olympics. Her only problem is that she can't get a regular partner. In desperation her trainer turns to Dorsey, but can the former sportsman forget his old ways, acquire a new skating style, overcome his natural loathing for his new partner, *and* win gold at the Olympics? What do you think? A lobotomised ice-skating obsessive (since many of the skating sequences are choreographed by former Olympic gold medallist Robin Cousins) *might* find something praiseworthy in all this predictable, ham-fisted, romantic tosh. NKe

Cutting It Short (Postrizini)

(Jiri Menzel, 1980, Czech) Jiri Schmitzer, Magda Vasáryová, Jaromir Hanzlik, Rudolf Hrusinsky.
98 min.
Caution was obviously still the watchword for Menzel after his political troubles. Charming but desperately thin, like *Those Wonderful Movie Cranks* this is a period comedy, set in a provin-

cial brewery and working very hard to extract some fun out of the local dignitaries who serve on the board. A gorgeous performance from Vasáryová, as a local beauty delighting in her bounteous sensuality, lends a welcome touch of Maupassant to the rustic frolics. TM

Cycle, The (Dayereh Mina)

(Daryush Mehrjui, 1974, Iran) Ezat Entezami, Ali Nassiriane, Frouzan, Said Kangarani.
102 min.
A surprisingly eloquent piece of poetic neo-realism. A young man accompanies his dour old father to hospital in Tehran; while waiting there, both become enmeshed in the corrupt business cycle which surrounds it. It's arty but articulate, a social allegory in which the hospital's contaminated blood supply poisons exactly those people (the urban poor) who are also its desperate donors. This cyclical logic of exploitation unfortunately yields moral rather than political conclusions, and produces some heavy-handed thematic oppositions – honesty versus corruption, country versus city. But with its overwhelming intuitions of visual truth (the luminous hospital, the dusty waste of an industrial hinterland), the central drama of lost hope and tyrannical poverty in the Shah's 'free' market state retains considerable force; you can see why it was banned for three years. CA

Cyclo (Xich Lo)

(Tran Anh Hung, 1995, Fr/Vietnam) Le Van Loc, Tran Nu Yen Khe, Tony Leung Chiu-Wai, Nguyen Nhu Quynh.
129 min.
The story's set in motion by the theft of a pedal cab essential to the economic survival of an 18-year-old Vietnamese. But forget *Bicycle Thieves*, and forget, too, writer/director Tran Anh Hung's debut feature, *The Scent of Green Papaya*. When the 'cyclo' (Le Van Loc) tells his boss that his vehicle's been stolen by professional rivals, he finds himself at the mercy of the Poet (Tony Leung Chiu-Wai), a taciturn gangster who diverts the boy from self-improvement (as advised by his late father) and into a life of crime. What the boy doesn't know, however, is that the Poet has also lured his sister (Tran Nu Yen Khe) into prostitution: in the desperate, hustling world of Ho Chi Minh City, it seems, innocence is unprotected. With its dazzling camerawork, feverish energy and dark, visceral power, this admirably unsentimental film paints a compelling portrait of moral derailment and salvation in a city in social and spiritual turmoil. The plot's packed with absent, uncaring or malign father figures; the tone is alternately tender or brutally violent; and the use of water and fire as symbols of purification and destruction gives rise to vivid dreamlike imagery. It'll have you reeling. GA

Cyclone, The (Il Ciclone)

(Leonardo Pieraccioni, 1996, It) Leonardo Pieraccioni, Lorena Forteza, Barbara Enrichi, Massimo Ceccherini, Mario Monicelli.
94 min.
A huge hit in Italy (indeed, the biggest local box office smash ever), this simply doesn't travel. The 'cyclone' is a touring flamenco dance company whose bus breaks down in an insular Tuscan town. Our accountant hero, a flustered romantic, puts them up in the family barn. He has an idiot brother who sleeps in a coffin, a butch lesbian sister, and a sex mad friend – he doesn't seem to know anyone who isn't a stereotype. The endless stream of avuncular ribaldry occasionally hits paydirt, but only if you have the patience for it. TCh

Cyrano de Bergerac

(Jean-Paul Rappeneau, 1990, Fr) Gérard Depardieu, Jacques Weber, Anne Brochet, Vincent Perez, Roland Bertin, Philippe Morier-Genoud, Philippe Volter.
138 min.
Rappeneau's version of Rostand's theatrical warhorse never puts a foot wrong. Much of the credit goes to Depardieu, perfect as the 17th century Gascon swordsman and braggart whose unsightly nose prevents him from confessing his love for his cousin Roxane. The text, cut, reworked and still in alexandrine verse, exudes all the grace and pace of a deftly orchestrated *rondo* (admirably served by Anthony Burgess' English subtitling), and this almost musical sense of meaning reinforced by rhythm extends throughout: the camera swoops at moments of ebullience, the performers' gestures, movements and delivery of lines seem almost choreographed. Everything has been fleshed out to its full potential; the entire scale of the piece, too, is augmented, so that landscapes, sets, battles and countless extras reflect the enormity of the poet Cyrano's unspoken torment. Rappeneau's movie-making demonstrates an unshowy confidence in itself and its subject that is wholly justifiable. GA

d

The Deer Hunter

Da

(Matt Clark, 1988, US) Barnard Hughes, Martin Sheen, William Hickey, Doreen Hepburn, Karl Hayden.
102 min.
Hugh Leonard's stage play translates dully to the screen in this valentine to a dead Dublin father. Da (Hughes) is dead and buried but comes back to exasperate his son Charlie (Sheen), now a successful playwright in New York. The ghost device releases a flood of flashbacks from Charlie's boyhood and young manhood, in all of which ineffectual Da plays the spoiler's part. His prospect of certain sex, for instance, is banjaxed when Da approaches the park bench and, by dint of garrulity, unearths the girl's family history and queers the lad's pitch. Any hope of presenting an emotional exorcism, as Charlie wins through to the realisation that his Da loves him, is shafted by the sheer obviousness of the old man's affection from the start. Mildly entertaining. BC

Dad

(Gary David Goldberg, 1989, US) Jack Lemmon, Ted Danson, Olympia Dukakis, Kathy Baker, Kevin Spacey, Ethan Hawke, Zakes Mokae, JT Walsh.
118 min.
Sharp, successful businessman John (Danson), out of step with his folks, grudgingly comes home to help care for his confused and helpless father Jake (Lemmon) while his indomitable mom Bette (Dukakis) is in hospital. Roles are reversed as son coaxes father from his childlike state, and John's success leads him to reassess his failed relationship with his own teen son (Hawke). Lemmon wrings genuine pathos from his role, as does Dukakis as shrewish, sardonic Bette. It's Danson in sincere mode who makes the film difficult to endure, especially in the later learning, caring and sharing scenes. Eventually, Jake falls foul of the Big C. He's sick! He gets better! He has a relapse! He rallies! This is called milking it. The film does assert there are some things positive thinking won't conquer, like sickness, senility and death. But it smothers any serious intent in cheap homily, modern mythology and sickly sentimentality. SFe

Dadetown

(Russ Hexter, 1995, US) Bill Garrison, David Phelps, Pete Nagler, Tom Nickenback, Ed Hubble.
93 min.
The film's crew sets out to make a documentary about an archetypal small town, and realises it's on the brink of breakdown. The antagonism between the town's older inhabitants (mostly employed at a factory going out of business) and newcomers who've moved on to smart new estates in order to work at an obscure but powerful communications company looks set to turn horribly violent. Hexter's involving analysis of the social, economic, political and technological factors undermining a once happy community is absolutely persuasive – and entirely false, for this is a dazzlingly authentic bogus documentary, whose status as a forgery is admitted only in a few hilarious, faintly absurdist gags. A brilliant debut, perfectly shot, scripted and performed; the tragedy is that Hexter died, still in his mid-30s, soon after it was made. GA

Daddy

(Peter Whitehead, 1973, GB/Switz) Niki de St Phalle, Gwynne Rivers, Mia Martin, Clarisse Rivers, Rainer von Dietz.
What began as a documentary on sculptress Niki de St Phalle finished up as a fantasy about a woman's attempts to exorcise the influence of her sexually domineering father. It provides an excuse for a whole ragbag of Freudian neuroses, six-foot phalluses in coffins, nubile girls in nun's habits stripping in front of altars, masturbation, some obvious jokes, pretty photography, abysmal acting, and a commentary that reads and sounds like a Home Service children's story for adults. Still, with father looking like a hangover from vaudeville and mother coming on like Jean Harlow, along with a laughably insistent piano score thumping away in the background, any girl would have her problems. CPe

Daddy Long Legs

(Jean Negulesco, 1955, US) Fred Astaire, Leslie Caron, Thelma Ritter, Fred Clark, Terry Moore, Larry Keating.
126 min.
This third film version (fourth if you count Shirley Temple and Curly Top) of Jean Webster's novel/play, about an orphaned waif who falls for a playboy sophisticate who has become her anonymous benefactor, is for the most part an unusually flaccid Astaire musical, despite sterling efforts from the two leads plus Clark and Ritter (as, respectively, Fred's manager and secretary). The chief problem is the story's utter predictability, although the score and choreography (with the single exception of 'Something's Got to Give') are also uninspired. Shot to no apparent advantage in 'Scope, this is Hollywood escapism at its most mediocre. GA

Daddy Nostalgie

see These Foolish Things

Daddy's Dyin' – Who's Got the Will?

(Jack Fisk, 1990, US) Beau Bridges, Beverly D'Angelo, Tess Harper, Judge Reinhold, Amy Wright, Patrika Darbo, Bert Remsen, Molly McClure, Keith Carradine.
95 min.
A flaccid adaptation by Del Shores of his own play in which the title tells all: while Texan patriarch Bert Remsen lies on his death-bed, his offspring assemble for a binge of bickering greed. Beer-swilling Beau Bridges and six-times divorced C&W singer Beverly D'Angelo are only concerned with who gets what; older sister (Wright) is into that old-time religion, while the other (Harper) is worried fiancé Keith Carradine will fall prey to the promiscuous charms of D'Angelo, whose neglected hippy lover (Reinhold) seems to be mighty fond of Bridges' dumpy wife (Darbo). Meanwhile grandmomma (McClure) strives to invest Remsen's last days with a modicum of peace and dignity. Dull, dated and displaying its stage origins at every turn, this clichéd account of sibling strife convinces neither as black comedy nor in its dim final hymn to family unity. Worse, a largely superior cast is let down by Fisk's stolid direction. GA

Dad's Army

(Norman Cohen, 1971, GB) Arthur Lowe, John Le Mesurier, Clive Dunn, John Laurie, James Beck, Ian Lavender, Arnold Ridley, Liz Fraser.
95 min.
Since the original was one of the few TV series which successfully resisted the temptation to broaden its effects as time went by, one might have expected this spinoff to translate painlessly to the big screen. Lowe (sublimely unaware as he barks 'I must ask you to keep you hands off my privates') and the rest of the regulars are as irresistible as ever. But the script digs several pits for itself by needlessly recapitulating the history of the platoon, by foregrounding details best left to the imagination (like Sgt Wilson's relationship to Pike's mother), and worst of all by offering a climax involving real Germans. Surely only an invisible enemy, never materialising but ineffably menacing, can exist in the same world as this moonshine Home Guard crew. TM

Dad Savage

(Betsan Morris Evans, 1997, GB) Patrick Stewart, Kevin McKidd, Helen McCrory, Joe McFadden, Marc Warren, Jake Wood.
104 min.
This first feature – a Fen country heist drama knee-deep in illicit banknotes, callous youths, betrayal, confusion and general bellicosity – evidently takes Shallow Grave as its inspiration. But it's a hash job, a blank, tiresome muddle of vapid characters and threadbare plotting. The one distinction is the show-role provided for senior actor Patrick Stewart as tulip farmer Dad Savage, known just as 'D' to his boys: son Sav (Wood) and his buddies H (McKidd), Vic (Warren) and Bob (McFadden), D's recently hired hands. This being (supposedly) an East Anglian Western, Dad wears a stetson and cowboy boots, enjoys Country and Western line dancing, and has scant regard for the law and a stash of loot buried in the woods. Likewise, the boys get off on guns, killing and blood – as a brief introductory montage informs us – and evince just enough wherewithal to hatch a half-baked scheme which instantly unravels for the duration of the film. NB

Daemon

(Colin Finbow, 1986, GB) Arnaud Morell, Susannah York, Bert Parnaby, Sadie Herlighy, Donna Glaser, Orlando Swayne.
71 min.
This Children's Film Unit production is bound to grip young audiences: a horror story told from a child's point of view, the new kid in town who's convinced he's possessed by the devil. In all, a remarkable achievement from a production crew whose average age is twelve, highlighted by a warm performance from Susannah York, who neither steals the show from the featured young performers nor from the young audiences it will undoubtedly entertain. SGo

Daens

(Stijn Coninx, 1993, Bel/Fr/Neth) Jan Decleir, Gérard Desarthe, Antje De Boeck, Michael Pas, Johan Leysen, Idwig Stéphane.
138 min.
A Belgian chronicle of a notorious 'red' priest and the formative years of his country's democratic process. During the closing decades of the 19th century, Aalst has become a thriving provincial mill town, a boon for the wealthy owners of the textile factories, less happy for the workers toiling for subsistence pay. The poor find a champion in Father Adolf Daens (Decleir), who is elected against opposition to represent the Christian People's Party in Belgium's new assembly. It's not long, however, before the establishment closes ranks to protect its interests. Without Decleir's gruff authority, the film would probably go for very little. As it is, the combination of stirring music, rippling indignation and plenty of idealistic speechifying marks it down as earnest, decent, middlebrow viewing. TJ

Daisies (Sedmikrásky)

(Vera Chytilová, 1966, Czech) Jitka Cerhová, Ivana Karbanová, Julius Albert, Jan Klusák.
76 min. b/w & col.
Visually hideous, tiresomely gimmicky satire on materialism, with two bored girls, both named Marie, who spend the entire movie causing havoc in restaurants and nightclubs, ripping off unsuspecting men and generally eating and behaving like pigs. As an allegory it lacks any resonance, as a movie it stinks. ATu

Daisy Kenyon

(Otto Preminger, 1947, US) Joan Crawford, Dana Andrews, Henry Fonda, Ruth Warrick, Martha Stewart, Peggy Ann Garner, Connie Marshall.
99 min. b/w.
Fascinating melodrama (from the novel by Elizabeth Janeway) which has anguished Crawford torn between the two men in her life, army sergeant Fonda and married lawyer Andrews. She's a fashion designer (cue costume changes); as always with Crawford, though, it's her gaunt, angular face that dominates the screen. She may only have agreed to do the film on condition that Andrews and Fonda were her co-stars, but fine actors though they are, they can't match her pitch of intensity. GM

Daisy Miller

(Peter Bogdanovich, 1974, US) Cybill Shepherd, Barry Brown, Cloris Leachman, Mildred Natwick, Eileen Brennan, Duilio Del Prete.
92 min.
Bogdanovich's nervous essay in the troubled waters of Henry James, where American innocence and naiveté are in perpetual conflict with European decadence and charm, reveals him to be less an interpreter of James than a translator of him into the brusquer world of Howard Hawks. The violence done James in this is forgiveable – indeed, Cybill Shepherd's transformation of Daisy into a Hawks heroine is strangely successful – but as a result there is no real social conflict in the film, and it becomes just a period variant on The Last Picture Show, without the vigour of that film or the irony of the original James novel. PH

Dakota Incident

(Lewis R Foster, 1956, US) Linda Darnell, Dale Robertson, Ward Bond, John Lund, Regis Toomey, Skip Homeier.
88 min.

The stagecoach breaks down in the desert, the Indians attack, but bad girl Darnell and bad boy Robertson survive (in best *Stagecoach* tradition) to walk into the sunset. Usually slagged off as routine, it is in fact beautifully shot (by Ernest Haller), vividly characterised, and surprisingly well written. Frederic Louis Fox's script functions as a sort of parable, with Robertson's bank robber, dogged on the one hand by a bank clerk blamed for one of his exploits and hoping somehow to win his good name back, and on the other by a senator preaching peace with the red man, cynically maintaining his belief in the power of the gun. Both these good people are killed, and the 'miracle' of Robertson's redemption is a complex mix arising out of their deaths, his own unexpected inability to kill the last surviving Indian with his bare hands, and the arrival of a storm out of a clear sky just as death from thirst seems imminent. Superbly embroidered in and around the characters, the 'message' is much less naive than it sounds when spelled out. TM

Dakota Road

(Nick Ward, 1991, GB) Charlotte Chatton, Amelda Brown, Alan Howard, Jason Carter, Rachel Scott, Matthew Scurfield, David Warrilow.
88 min.
Ward, an experienced writer/director of stage, radio and TV, displays a talent for intimate cinema in his first film. Bored by her existence in rural Norfolk, 15-year-old Jen Cross (Chatton), daughter of a farm labourer, dreams of reaching the heights of passion with a pilot from the local American air base. Brought down to earth by fumbling sex with orphaned signalman Raif (Carter), Jen is later caught in the act by the Reverend Stonea (Warrilow). Her father Bernard (Scurfield), already angry at being sacked by landowner Alan Brandon (Howard) – a frustrated widower who adds to the indignity by employing Bernard's wife (Brown) as a cleaning woman – now sinks into a smouldering, jealous rage which hints at some darker family secret... Framing both the wide vistas and the claustrophobic interiors with a painterly eye, Ward coaxes sympathetic performances from a good cast. Occasionally, the inertia that afflicts the characters also arrests the flow of the narrative; but for the most part, Ward's direction and Ian Wilson's sublime photography capture the feel of a bleak fen country with just a glimmer of hope on the distant horizon. NF

Dak van de Walvis, Het

see On Top of the Whale

Daleks – Invasion Earth 2150 A.D.

(Gordon Flemyng, 1966, GB) Peter Cushing, Bernard Cribbins, Ray Brooks, Andrew Keir, Roberta Tovey, Jill Curzon, Godfrey Quigley.
84 min.
Second and last to date of the big screen *Dr Who* spinoffs. Very tame but marginally better than the first, with the Daleks unsurprisingly coming to grief after invading a ruined London of the future and robotising the inhabitants. Very variable special effects and often excruciatingly cheapo sets. TM

Dallas

(Stuart Heisler, 1950, US) Gary Cooper, Ruth Roman, Raymond Massey, Steve Cochran, Antonio Moreno.
94 min.
Civil War renegade Cooper fakes death in a shootout with Wyatt Earp and heads for Texas to revenge himself on the brothers who massacred his family. A routine plot, but plenty of diversions on the trail – Coop pretending to be a danified US marshall in frock coat and top hat, horseback chases, furtive romance. The star sleepwalks, though since he's supposed to be the laconic outsider-type, this doesn't matter at all. Impressive production values and blazing Technicolor camerawork by Ernest Haller. Basically a B-Western though. GR

Dallas Doll

(Ann Turner, 1994, US) Sandra Bernhard, Victoria Longley, Frank Gallagher, Jake Blundell, Rose Byrne.
104 min.

US golf pro Bernhard is invited to enliven an Australian club in suburban Sydney and ends up staying with a nice, normal family. Only the young daughter and the dog are suspicious of her seductive, go-getting character; nevertheless, the family is duly transformed. Bernhard is boringly herself, and Longley's born-again housewife steals the film from her. Occasionally coming on like a satirical update of Theorem, it's neither funny nor frightening; indeed, it's hard to fathom what it's really meant to be about, though its attitude to both America and Japan lay it open to charges of xenophobia (which might, of course, be part of the satire). Oddly unsatisfying. GA

Dal Polo all'Equatore

see From Pole to Equator

Dama do cine Shanghai, A

see Lady from the Shanghai Cinema, The

Damage

(Louis Malle, 1992, GB/Fr) Jeremy Irons, Juliette Binoche, Miranda Richardson, Rupert Graves, Leslie Caron, Ian Bannen, Gemma Clarke.
111 min.
This good-looking version of Josephine Hart's bestseller – a cautionary tale of *amour fou*, risqué sex and power play 'twixt a married Tory minister and an enigmatic young French-born auctioneer – is a dull affair. We follow Irons' MP to a crowded cocktail party, where he falls in lust at first glance with his son's girlfriend (Binoche), and soon we're motoring through one ritzy London postal district after another, along a predictable road to disaster – but for whom? The acting strays in different directions. Binoche is reduced to an elegant-chic clothes-horse; Irons, to point up the explosive, mysterious nature of erotic attraction, has to stress ordinariness, which strangely makes his motivation seem mysterious and the erotic attraction ordinary. Richardson, as the wife, gives a shuddering, raging howl of a breakdown, which stuns the movie into silence. The sex scenes make you consider the acting. Boredom is maybe the clue: Malle has been charting this territory since the late '50s, and co-scriptwriter David Hare said it all before in *Paris by Night*. WH

Dam Busters, The

(Michael Anderson, 1954, GB) Michael Redgrave, Richard Todd, Ursula Jeans, Derek Farr, Patrick Barr, John Fraser, George Baker, Brewster Mason, Basil Sydney.
124 min. b/w.
At one time seemingly up as a candidate for culting by those who found the surrounding footage of *Pink Floyd: The Wall* to taste (this was the movie playing incessantly on Pink's TV). Anderson and RC Sherriff's tribute to Barnes Wallis (inventor of World War II's bouncing bomb) and Wingco Guy Gibson (who spearheaded their use in destroying strategically-important Ruhr dams) slips some thoughtful reservations and some gross sentimentality into its bouncing bombast. With its final cost-counting, it contorts the stiff upper lip into something like a deathly grimace. PT

Dame aux Camélias, La

(Mauro Bolognini, 1981, Fr/It) Isabelle Huppert, Gian Maria Volonté, Fabrizio Bentivoglio, Fernando Rey, Jann Babilée, Bruno Ganz.
121 min.
Not based on the play or novel, but on the real-life romance that inspired the tearful tale of Marguerite Gautier. But the unhappy love of Dumas *fils* for Marie Duplessis is turned into hoary melodrama, as lavishly tatty as any rep performance of the play. Matters are not improved by a very choppy narrative, adapted from a longer TV version. TM

Dame dans l'auto avec des lunettes et un fusil, La

see Lady in the Car with Glasses and a Gun, The

Dames

(Ray Enright, 1934, US) Joan Blondell, Dick Powell, Ruby Keeler, ZaSu Pitts, Hugh Herbert, Guy Kibbee.
90 min. b/w.
A predictable puttin'-on-a-show plot is basically

a superfluous framework for some bright comic acting from the likes of Blondell and Pitts, and for typically ornamental musical scenes staged by Berkeley, with dozens of girls waving their legs around while lying on their backs (and they call that dancing?). GA

Dames du Bois de Boulogne, Les

(Robert Bresson, 1945, Fr) Maria Casarès, Elina Labourdette, Paul Bernard, Lucienne Bogaërt.
90 min. b/w.
Like *Les Anges du Péché*, Bresson's second feature, based on a self-contained anecdote in Diderot's novel *Jacques le Fataliste*, is in many ways atypical of his oeuvre. He uses, quite brilliantly, professional actors. The visual texture is not muted grey, but sharp and contrasty. The camera is constantly prowling and tracking. The dialogue (by Cocteau) is brilliantly jewelled, literary to the point of preciousness, the very antithesis of the later monosyllabics. Yet as one watches the elegant socialite (played by Casarès with superbly steely venom) spin a cold-blooded plot to destroy her rival after being humiliatingly spurned in a liaison in the interests of true love, one could hardly be anywhere but in Bresson's world. Sexuality takes precedence over salvation, but there is the same interiority, the same intensity, the same rigorous exclusion of all inessentials. TM

Damien – Omen II

(Don Taylor, 1978, US) William Holden, Lee Grant, Jonathan Scott-Taylor, Robert Foxworth, Nicholas Pryor, Lew Ayres, Sylvia Sidney.
109 min.
This sequel lacks the bravura pacing of the original, and though it tries to maintain the biblical tone in following the adolescence of its antichrist anti-hero, immense problems emerge. Murderous adolescents are much more routine movie material than murderous five-year-olds, and making Damien vaguely unhappy about his identity only serves to make him more irritating. The number of surrogate demons is also vastly inflated, thereby stacking the decks against the angels from the beginning and undermining any real tension. DP

Damnation Alley

(Jack Smight, 1977, US) Jan-Michael Vincent, George Peppard, Dominique Sanda, Paul Winfield, Jackie Earle Haley, Kip Niven.
91 min.
Insanely jettisoning the Hell's Angel protagonist of Roger Zelazny's cult novel of a post-holocaust odyssey, this dire slice of uninspired sci-fi tracks an amphibious armoured truck from a California missile base cross-country towards the source of taped signs of life in Albany, NY. Military redneck Peppard and rebel Vincent gather a model post-nuclear family (one black, one woman, one kid) like tokens en route, hampered by appalling process work and by derivative confrontations with mutant mountain men and man-eating cockroaches. A real mess. PT

Damned, The (aka These Are the Damned)

(Joseph Losey, 1961, GB) Macdonald Carey, Shirley Ann Field, Alexander Knox, Viveca Lindfors, Oliver Reed, James Villiers.
87 min. b/w.
Certainly the strangest Hammer film ever made, this combines apocalyptic sci-fi, teen rebellion, and portentous philosophising to awkward but riveting effect. Set, strangely but successfully, in Weymouth, it begins as a rather mundane romance, with Carey and Field threatened by local Teddy Boys, before spiralling into a dour mystery about a scientist's experiments with radioactive kids. The performances are universally weak, and Losey's clearly ambivalent attitude towards the demands of the genre ensures that the film is never exciting. But as an ambitious oddity, it exerts not a little fascination. GA

Damned, The (La Caduta degli Dei/Götterdämmerung)

(Luchino Visconti, 1969, It/WGer) Dirk Bogarde, Ingrid Thulin, Helmut Griem, Helmut Berger, Renaud Verley, Umberto Orsini, Charlotte Rampling, Florinda Bolkan.
164 min.

Visconti on the rise of Nazism as reflected within in a German industrialist family in the '30s is as operatic and overblown as you'd expect, often to extremely impressive effect. But the overall languorousness finally swamps even the carefully elaborated decadence, making heavy going of otherwise interesting performances from Bogarde and Rampling. And the indulgence of Helmut Berger (who debuts in drag, impersonating Dietrich) is already unmistakeable. TR

Damn the Defiant
see HMS Defiant

Damn Yankees (aka What Lola Wants)
(George Abbott/Stanley Donen, 1958, US) Tab Hunter, Gwen Verdon, Ray Walston, Russ Brown, Shannon Bolin, Rae Allen, Bob Fosse.
110 min.
A musical lumbered with too much plot and tiresome Walston as the Devil who tempts an ageing baseball fan into rejuvenation for a year (in the person of Tab Hunter). But it also has scintillating choreography by Bob Fosse (his duet with Verdon, 'Who's Got the Pain?' is an eye-opener), and an equally brilliant score by Richard Adler and Jerry Ross (a songwriting team also responsible for the marvellous The Pajama Game, and only prevented from becoming the best on Broadway by the latter's untimely death). TM

Damsel in Distress, A
(George Stevens, 1937, US) Fred Astaire, Joan Fontaine, George Burns, Gracie Allen, Reginald Gardiner, Constance Collier, Montagu Love.
101 min. b/w.
Temporary parting of the ways for Fred and Ginger, with Astaire (in hopes of avoiding comparisons) saddled with a non-dancing partner plus Burns & Allen for comic relief. Nicely directed but a bit on the twee side with its Wodehouse plot and mock Englishness, the result would be questionable but for a rich Gershwin score. Though shackled to Fontaine for 'Things Are Looking Up', Astaire has some sparkling solos, notably the beautiful 'A Foggy Day' and his intermezzo with percussion instruments to 'Nice Work if You Can Get It'. TM

Dan Candy's Law
see Alien Thunder

Dance Craze
(Joe Massot, 1981, GB) Bad Manners, The Beat, The Bodysnatchers, Madness, The Selecter, The Specials.
91 min.
As a blueprint for an investigation of rock's 2-Tone phenomenon, Dance Craze works well. Not only does Joe Dunton's photography make the movie look sumptuous, but the music catches the genre's brittle beat and loose-limbed spontaneity. However, if you're over 14 and have seen any of the bands, the experience soon becomes relentlessly dull. Despite scattered wakey-wakey devices (like Pathé News footage from the '50s and '60s), the catalogue of live footage is devoid of any context that might explain the origins, development and effects of the movement. Pity. IB

Dance, Girl, Dance
(Dorothy Arzner, 1940, US) Maureen O'Hara, Lucille Ball, Louis Hayward, Ralph Bellamy, Virginia Field, Maria Ouspenskaya.
90 min. b/w.
Arzner's internal critique of Hollywood ideology (woman as silent object of male scrutiny) works within the confines of a stock vaudevillian golddiggers comedy-drama, tagging along with the old vamp/virgin dichotomy between dancers Ball and O'Hara until the latter upsets the spectacular equation by turning on her (the) audience of leering males with her observations. PT

Dance Hall
(Charles Crichton, 1950, GB) Natasha Parry, Diana Dors, Petula Clark, Jane Hylton, Donald Houston, Sydney Tafler, Kay Kendall, Bonar Colleano, Geraldo, Ted Heath.
80 min. b/w.
Perhaps the closest the British cinema of its period came to a neo-realist fresco: a matrix of low-key melodramatic narratives converging on the communal (rather than institutional) core of the local palais, and on an upcoming dance contest. The diffuse focus on working-class women marks it as a welcome rarity (presumably to the credit of unsung Ealing screenwriter Diana Morgan), and even the domestic cliché situations communicate a lively sense of resistance to dominant social and economic austerity. Director Crichton moved on to some of the cosier Ealing comedies, but working on Dance Hall, as co-writer and editor respectively, were more abrasive talents Alexander Mackendrick and Seth Holt. PT

Dance Little Lady
(Val Guest, 1954, GB) Terence Morgan, Mai Zetterling, Guy Rolfe, Mandy Miller, Eunice Gayson, Reginald Beckwith.
87 min.
Tepid British melodrama which reunites Terence Morgan and child actress Mandy Miller (they first appeared together in Mandy – Ealing's outstanding 'serious' picture – in 1952). Morgan's again a tyrannical bullying father, this time determined to make Mandy into a Hollywood star. Estranged wife Mai Zetterling, a former ballerina, is set against the idea. GM

Dance Me to My Song
(Rolf de Heer, 1998, Aust) Heather Rose, Joey Kennedy, John Brumpton, Rena Owen.
102 min.
Julia (Rose, persuasive) is bound to a wheelchair and her carer Madeleine (Kennedy) is a man chasing bitch pushed by frustration and jealousy towards violence against her vulnerable charge; Eddie (Brumpton) is the faintly mysterious but ultimately angelic local guy who, much to Mad's jealous annoyance, takes a shine to Julia. The third film in de Heer's loose trilogy dealing with the fraught relationship of the marginalised with the world is his bravest yet (it was scripted by Rose, who is herself confined to a wheelchair); often, however, it resorts to fairytale coincidence and contrivance, while the characterisation is cartoon thin and the message heavy handed. GA

Dance of Love (Reigen)
(Otto Schenk, 1973, WGer) Senta Berger, Maria Schneider, Helmuth Lohner, Sydney Rome, Peter Weck, Helmut Berger.
122 min.
Described as 'delightfully mischievous' by its distributors, Schenk's film – not so much a remake of Max Ophüls' classic La Ronde as a return to Arthur Schnitzler's more sardonic play – takes full advantage of relaxing censorship attitudes. Predictably, all the visual richness and stylish elegance of the Ophüls version has given way to bumbling sexual romps. Censorship at least had the positive value of forcing directors to be imaginative in the way they presented Eros on the screen. GSa

Dance of the Vampires (aka The Fearless Vampire Killers)
(Roman Polanski) Jack MacGowran, Roman Polanski, Alfie Bass, Jessie Robbins, Sharon Tate, Ferdy Mayne, Iain Quarrier, Terry Downes.
107 min.
Messy vampire spoof-cum-homage to Hammer, which doesn't really come off on either count. On the other hand, no film can be all bad which has a screen credit reading 'Fangs by Dr Ludwig von Krankheit'; and Polanski does pull out some gems, like the very Jewish monster menaced with a crucifix who cheerfully gloats, 'You got the wrong vampire, girl!' Other pluses include very attractive sets and Douglas Slocombe's camerawork, Krzysztof Komeda's bat-winged musical score, and the marvellous sequence of the great vampire ball, in which the guests rise from their graves to embark on a stately minuet that ends in front of a vast mirror reflecting only the three human interlopers. With all its faults, an engaging oddity. TM

Dance of the Wind (Wara Mandel)
(Rajan Khosa, 1997, GB/Fr/Ger/Neth) Kitu Gidwani, Bhaveen Gosain, Roshan Bano, BC Sanyal.
85 min.
Though visually arresting and making beautiful use of classical Indian music, this film by British-based Rajan Khosa never opts for a picture postcard view of life in contemporary Delhi. It centres on an acclaimed singer who finds herself unable to perfom after the death of her mother and mentor. The loss affects her career, and her relationship with her students and her husband. Lyrical and meditative it may be, but the film shows us things seldom depicted in Indian cinema (the heroine vomiting in the lavatory) and firmly contextualises the singer's life, steeped in art, tradition and taste, within a world that also includes poverty, violence, injustice and bhangra. Simple, elegant and as resonant as the lovely sounds heard throughout. GA

Dancers
(Herbert Ross, 1987, US) Mikhail Baryshnikov, Alessandra Ferri, Leslie Browne, Thomas Rall, Lynn Seymour, Victor Barbee, Julie Kent.
99 min.
A lot of ballet nonsense with Baryshnikov as a celebrated dancer who likes to play hide the salami with his leading ladies, but has for the moment lost contact with his creative muse. Naive American teenager Lisa (Kent) arrives in Southern Italy to join his production of Giselle. Their brief liaison fans Baryshnikov's creative spark, allowing him to dance with new passion while Lisa weeps in the wings. Predictably, the off-screen entanglements are echoed by the on-stage action, in which the rake is haunted by the ghosts of his wronged lovers. Ross stages the extended dance sequences with considerable flair, and it's a treat to see the graceful Alessandra Ferri stealing the show. However, in a terpsichorean turkey stuffed with silliness, the pliés and pirouettes are a long time coming. NF

Dances with Wolves
(Kevin Costner, 1990, US) Kevin Costner, Mary McDonnell, Graham Greene, Rodney A Grant, Floyd Red Crow Westerman, Tantoo Cardinal, Robert Pastorelli, Maury Chaykin.
180 min.
Disenchanted after being wounded in the American Civil War, Lt Dunbar (Costner) is assigned to a frontier outpost. Finding nothing but a deserted fort and left to his own devices, Dunbar gradually gains the friendship and trust of both a wolf and the Sioux Indians. Won over by the native Americans' love of the land, the honourable soldier joins in their buffalo hunt, courts a white woman the tribe adopted in childhood, transfers allegiance from predatory white man to peaceful Indian, and discovers en route his true self. At three hours long, and with a largely Indian cast delivering (subtitled) Lakota dialogue, Costner's debut as a director is a genuinely, impressively epic Western. It may lack complexity and political sophistication – the Sioux are a mite sentimentalised, the US Cavalry too obviously ignorant bigots, and Costner's two-dimensional hero too prone to cute pratfalls – but its sentiments are conspicuously sincere and its dramatic sweep hugely confident. Historical and cultural authenticity is virtually an end in itself, and although the last half-hour founders in repeated farewells, it looks great. Once you're sucked into the leisurely narrative, it's hard to resist. GA

Dances with Wolves – Special Edition
(Kevin Costner, 1990-91, US) Kevin Costner, Mary McDonnell, Graham Greene, Rodney A Grant, Floyd Red Crow Westerman, Tantoo Cardinal, Robert Pastorelli, Maury Chaykin.
236 min.
The additional footage in this extended version of Costner's Western epic is basically more of the same, fleshing out relationships and making no radical difference to the film. Splendid panoramas abound, but a couple of extra sequences do serve to enhance understanding and motivation: notably, the battered state of Fort Sedgwick (with its caves and wreckage), and a scene in which an unsettled Lt Dunbar watches Sioux celebrate their slaughter of white settlers. CM

Dance With a Stranger
(Mike Newell, 1984, GB) Miranda Richardson, Rupert Everett, Ian Holm, Matthew Carroll, Tom Chadbon, Jane Bertish.
102 min.
Newcomer Richardson is Ruth Ellis, peroxided

'hostess' in a Soho drinking club and the last woman to be hanged in Britain for the murder of her upper middle class lover. Not so much star-crossed as class-crossed, the affair has all the charm of fingernails on a blackboard, and it's filmed with a merciless eye for the sort of bad behaviour that Fassbinder made his own. But what the movie captures perfectly is the seedy mood of repression, so characteristic of austerity Britain in the '50s. Richardson gives full rein to the two things that British cinema has hardly ever had the guts to face: sexual obsession and bad manners. And, since this is England, it's the latter that finally sends her to the scaffold. It's shot, designed and acted with an imaginative grasp that puts it straight into the international class. CPea

Dancing Bull (Wuniu)
(Allen Fong, 1990, HK) Cora Miao, Lindzay Chan, Anthony Wong, Fung Kin-Chung.
116 min.
The strains of running a modern-dance company in the Thatcherite cultural climate of Hong Kong cause a marriage to break up: the choreographer husband lapses into inertia with a new girlfriend, while the dancer wife becomes a cultural mover. Not much of a storyline to support a movie that aims to take the temperature of present-day Hong Kong (in the aftermath of the Beijing massacre), and it must be said that the film is neither as impassioned nor as incisive as it thinks it is. But it does sustain interest at several levels, and Cora Miao (the first bona fide star to appear in an Allen Fong movie) copes with the director's improvisational methods as if born to them. TR

Dancing in the Dark
(Leon Marr, 1985, Can) Martha Henry, Neil Munro, Rosemary Dunsmore, Richard Monette, Elena Kudaba.
99 min.
Marr's first feature offers a tunneled vision of the 20-year marriage of Edna and Harry in their small suburban home (not just the centre of Edna's world, but her entire universe), where the camera catches the woman like a grub burrowing its way in the soil. Edna's story is told in flashback: sitting in her white dressing-gown in a psychiatric hospital, she examines her notebook (the diary of a mad housewife?) and proceeds to reveal the details of a 20-year career of cleaning, screwing and cooking for her mate before one day deciding to sharpen a kitchen knife against the bones of his ribcage. This murderous act of 'liberation' becomes, in a sense, Edna's birth, where the grub finally asserts its identity after a life led solely to complement that of her boorish husband. Unfortunately it is difficult to base a feature-length film on a character who has no character. Inevitably it makes for a rather tedious and highly non-moving use of exposed silver nitrate on plastic. SGo

Dancin' Thru the Dark
(Mike Ockrent, 1989, GB) Claire Hackett, Con O'Neill, Angela Clarke, Julia Deakin, Louise Duprey, Sandy Hendrickse, Andrew Naylor, Conrad Nelson, Simon O'Brien, Peter Watts, Mark Womack, Colin Welland.
95 min.
'It's raised more misery than all the wars and revolutions put together', mutters a jaded soul on the subject of marriage. Certainly Willy Russell's adaptation of his own play Stags and Hens is unequivocal about tying the knot too soon. The action takes place the night before Linda and Dave's wedding: Linda (Hackett) is out with the girls for a hen night, Dave (Nelson) is carousing with the boys. Both parties unwittingly converge on the same nightclub, where Linda has gone to see her almost-famous ex-boyfriend (O'Neill) perform with his group. Emotions run high when Linda is overwhelmed by second thoughts... It's a straightforward tale about a well-worn theme – it has no pretensions to be otherwise – but the frequent moralising about marriage tends towards excess. The more obvious jokes (I'm gregarious' –'Pleased to meet you, Greg') hold far less humour than the trenchant observations of disco politics: from early-evening boogies around handbags to booze-fuelled advances. Overall, with a solid cast, Ockrent makes an assured and lively film debut. CM

Dancing With Crime
(John Paddy Carstairs, 1947, GB) Richard Attenborough, Sheila Sim, Barry K Barnes, Barry Jones, Garry Marsh, Bill Owen.
83 min. b/w.
Attenborough as an earnest young taxi-driver, recently demobbed, who, though headed for marriage on a shoestring, stoutly refuses the temptation to come in on a mysterious black market deal with an ex-army pal (Owen). Setting out to investigate when he finds the dead pal dumped in his taxi, he tracks the villains to a local dance hall they use as a front, and – with his girl (Sim) intrepidly going undercover on his behalf – brings them to justice. Strictly conventional all the way, but not unlikeable, despite some clumsily staged fisticuffs for the climax. TM

Dandy in Aspic, A
(Anthony Mann, 1968, GB) Laurence Harvey, Tom Courtenay, Mia Farrow, Lionel Stander, Harry Andrews, Peter Cook, Per Oscarsson, Barbara Murray, John Bird.
107 min.
Scripted by Derek Marlowe from his own novel, Anthony Mann's last film (he died during shooting and was replaced as director by Laurence Harvey) is the story of a Russian double agent, Krasnevin (Harvey), given a difficult mission by the British secret service: to hunt down and eliminate himself. Driven by a byzantine plot that would turn out to be characteristic of the writer (compare Stuart Cooper's The Disappearance, adapted from Marlowe's Echoes of Celandine), the film is strong on Cold War atmospherics and notable for its superior cast. NRo

Dandy, the All-American Girl (aka Sweet Revenge)
(Jerry Schatzberg, 1976, US) Stockard Channing, Sam Waterston, Franklyn Ajaye, Richard Doughty, Norman Matlock.
90 min.
Determinedly offbeat comedy, with Channing as a slightly crazy car-thief, stealing and selling a variety of autos as she attempts to gain enough cash to buy herself a Ferrari. Meanwhile, she plays a complex romantic game with three very different male admirers. Schatzberg, forsaking the serious and muddled statements of films like Scarecrow and Puzzle of a Downfall Child, here comes up with a relaxed and meandering study of eccentric characters on the fringes of society, as messy and occasionally likeable as Henry Jaglom's far more garrulous efforts. Indulgent, directionless, but well-performed and often witty. GA

Dang Bireley's and the Young Gangsters (2499 Antapan Krong Muang)
(Nonzee Nimibutr, 1997, Thai) Jesdaporn Pholdee, Noppachai Muttaweevong, Attaporn Teemakorn, Suppakorn Kitsuwan.
110 min.
Ths stylish and assured first feature is based on the true story of a '50s gangster, who modelled himself on Dean and Elvis, and became famous in Bangkok after killing two men by the age of 18. The film charts his rise to power, his exile in the countryside after a martial law clampdown, and his battles with two friends turned hothead thugs. Told in flashback, from the day he's ordained a monk (to please his mum), the film seldom moralises, but never glamorises the violence either. Clearly influenced by the early work of John Woo, it's best seen as a tale of honour, loyalty and love among hoodlums. GA

Danger by My Side
(Charles Saunders, 1962, GB) Maureen Connell, Anthony Oliver, Alan Tilvern, Bill Nagy.
63 min. b/w.
Plucky Connell gets a job in a shady nightclub to follow up her hunch that the sleazy proprietor was involved in her detective brother's murder. An unexceptional British B-thriller with an anonymous cast and a risible striptease which even in 1962 can't have set many hearts aflutter. TJ

Danger: Diabolik (Diabolik)
(Mario Bava, 1967, It/Fr) John Phillip Law, Marisa Mell, Michel Piccoli, Adolfo Celi, Terry-Thomas, Claudio Gora.
105 min.

A delightfully outlandish comic strip directed by the master of the Italian B movie, a former cameraman who could always be relied on to ravish the eye with wonderfully bizarre imagery. Part James Bond parody, part Feuillade serial, it sends itself up as cheerfully as anything else as its hero dallies with his beloved under a snowfall of banknotes or prowls about his nefarious (but always chivalrous) purposes in black leotards, armed with suction pads that turn him into a human fly. But from time to time it also hits a high note of fantasy worthy of Cocteau, notably in a scene where Diabolik, encased in plumes of molten gold, is transformed into a living statue by his arch-enemy. TM

Dangerous
(Alfred E Green, 1935, US) Bette Davis, Franchot Tone, Margaret Lindsay, Alison Skipworth, John Eldredge.
78 min. b/w.
Davis, as a former star actress now wallowing in the gutter and self-pity, is rehabilitated by Tone's handsome young architect. Even Davis says she found the script maudlin and mawkish, though she won an Oscar for her performance.

Dangerous Female
see Maltese Falcon, The

Dangerous Game
see Snake Eyes

Dangerous Ground
(Darrell James Roodt, 1996, SAf/US) Ice Cube, Elizabeth Hurley, Sechaba Morojele, Eric 'Waku' Miyeni, Ving Rhames.
95 min.
Feisty South African academic Vusi (Ice Cube) was thrown into America's 'fugee-loving arms at 14, but now, with the death of his father, it's time to pop home. Thanks to an inability to stick big knives into squirming goats, he finds himself at odds with his family. Nevertheless, as first-born, he's the one sent to find an errant brother in Johannesburg, where he teams up with his brother's girlfriend Karen (Hurley), a crack-addled stripper. Directed by Darrell Roodt, a white South African, this set-up promises some interesting conflicts: 'sophisticated' America vs 'authentic' Africa; the old apartheid South Africa vs the new. But you get the feeling there was a kerfuffle about who the film was aimed at, and that someone plumped for adolescent boys weaned on Beverly Hills Cop. The doom and gloom surrounding South Africa's future merely serves as an excuse for America's finest to take matters in hand. Why, you might ask, can't the South Africans do it for themselves? Because, according to this film, they're ineffectual kaftan-wearers or effete junkies. CO'Su

Dangerous Liaisons
(Stephen Frears, 1988, US) Glenn Close, John Malkovich, Michelle Pfeiffer, Swoosie Kurtz, Keanu Reeves, Mildred Natwick, Uma Thurman, Peter Capaldi.
120 min.
Choderlos de Laclos' 18th century novel is a monument to lust, guilt and duplicity, written in letter form. One of the film's enormous strengths is scriptwriter Christopher Hampton's decision to go back to the novel, and save only the best from his play. Frears, under commercial pressure but also determined to start afresh, has chosen American actors for the main roles: Malkovich as the professional philanderer Valmont; Close as the sadistic aristocrat with whom he plots to ruin both a social union and a virtuous woman (Pfeiffer, splendid). The result is a sombre, manipulative affair in which the décor is never allowed to usurp our interest. Broader, nastier even than the play, it uses recurring epistolary motifs, shadow and close-up to convey the themes of the piece: the relationships between pleasure and pain, our inability to control others, our endless desire to do so. Malkovich's final demise, run through, wasted and resigned, recalls the misty-eyed days of Fairbanks and Flynn; while Close, all eye-contact, front, and self-possession, ends the film unforgettably as a sacrificial lamb on the altar of decency. SGr

Dangerously They Live
(Robert Florey, 1942, US) John Garfield, Nancy Coleman, Raymond Massey, Moroni Olsen, Lee Patrick, Esther Dale, Christian Rub.
77 min. b/w.

Creaky spy melodrama in which Coleman, working for British intelligence, is abducted in New York by Nazi sympathisers intent on gaining access to a message she has memorised concerning the route to be taken by a big convoy. When the car crashes, she lands in hospital, and confides in a young intern (Garfield) after recovering from temporary amnesia. Garfield's doubts about her story are confirmed when the man she insists *isn't* her father (Olsen) summons a distinguished psychiatrist (Massey) under whom Garfield had once studied. Florey can't do much about the lumbering script or about Coleman's inept performance. But once the girl has been taken 'home' – a large, lonely mansion where she and Garfield (brought along to lull lingering suspicions) find themselves held prisoner while Massey and his Nazi cohorts do their dirty work – Florey seems more interested, bringing off some nice semi-Gothic atmospherics. The ending, alas, reverts to routine histrionics and heroics. TM

Dangerous Minds

(John N Smith, 1994, US) Michelle Pfeiffer, George Dzundza, Courtney B Vance.
99 min.
A surprise hit at the US box office, this is a standard 'inspirational' foray into the blackboard jungle, a place where over-age ethnic actors vye for the attention of the camera and pay no heed to their English teacher until she gets relevant by quoting Bob Dylan. Actually it's quite a respectable piece of work, with an impressive tough-love performance from Pfeiffer, but Ronald Bass's hackneyed screenplay is all carrot and no stick. TCh

Dangerous Mission

(Louis King, 1954, US) Victor Mature, Piper Laurie, Vincent Price, William Bendix, Betta St John, Dennis Weaver.
75 min.
A thriller which opens resonantly with a man being gunned down as he sits at the piano in a dark, deserted nightclub. But despite good performances, the presence of Horace McCoy, WR Burnett and Charles Bennett among the credited writers, and a potentially workable story – detective Mature sets out in pursuit of a girl who witnessed the murder, ostensibly to protect her from the Mob – this never really takes off. Mature is so nudgingly pointed up as the killer that it's painfully obvious he isn't, and the supposedly nail-biting climax among the treacherous mountain crevasses (shot in the Glacier National Park, Montana, with excessive attention to scenic grandeur) is absurdly hamfisted. TM

Dangerous Moonlight

(Brian Desmond Hurst, 1941, GB) Anton Walbrook, Sally Gray, Derrick de Marney, Cecil Parker, Keneth Kent, Guy Middleton.
98 min. b/w.
Splendidly slushy World War II melodrama, with Walbrook an angst-ridden Polish pianist torn between success in America and death in the skies above beleaguered Britain. Hurst, the wild Irishman of British cinema, proves surprisingly proficient at investing his slight, improbable story with power and resonance. The issues may be trittly resolved – only a miracle allows us a final encore of the Warsaw Concerto – but in taking the myth of the great artist and subordinating it to the more immediately relevant one of the do-or-die fighter-pilot hero, Hurst conjures up a satisfying concoction of fantasy and propaganda. RMy

Dangerous Moves (La Diagonale du Fou)

(Richard Dembo, 1983, Switz) Michel Piccoli, Alexandre Arbatt, Liv Ullmann, Leslie Caron, Daniel Olbrychski, Michel Aumont.
110 min.
Set during the World Chess Championship, and focusing on the intense rivalry between ageing, ailing Soviet champion Liebskind (Piccoli) and his former pupil, the unorthodox young rebel Fromm (Arbatt) – himself a Russian defector whom the Soviet authorities wish to humiliate – the film's fascination lies partly in the bizarre, underhanded tactics employed to distract keyed-up competitors, partly in the vivid characterisations. Also of interest, however, is the wider context which reveals the rivals as reluctant pawns in political power struggles. Expertly performed (particular-

ly by Piccoli), and shot through with moments of memorably absurd humour, Dembo's miniature thriller is an unusual delight. GA

Dangerous Summer, A

(Quentin Masters, 1981, Aust) Tom Skerritt, Ian Gilmour, Wendy Hughes, Ray Barrett, James Mason, Guy Doleman.
100 min.
Ludicrous conspiracy thriller set in the Blue Mountains during the bush fire season, with the plot huffing and puffing round attempts to sabotage a multi-million dollar resort project. Made the same year as Phillip Noyce's skilful but slightly tub-thumping *Heatwave*, which looks like a masterpiece of subtlety and discretion by comparison. TM

Dangerous When Wet

(Charles Walters, 1953, US) Esther Williams, Charlotte Greenwood, William Demarest, Fernando Lamas, Jack Carson.
95 min.
A ludicrous plot, designed to cash in on Williams' rather specialised talent, sees her and her Arkansas family preparing for a cross-channel swim. Arthur Schwartz and Johnny Mercer's songs are pleasant enough, as are the performances; but the highlight of the humdrum proceedings is the sequence in which Esther swims with Tom and Jerry. GA

Dangerous Woman, A

(Stephen Gyllenhaal, 1993, US) Debra Winger, Barbara Hershey, Gabriel Byrne, Chloe Webb, David Strathairn, Laurie Metcalf.
102 min.
Gyllenhaal's third feature (from a script by his wife Naomi Foner) is happily less hackneyed than one might anticipate. The cast are a great help: Debra Winger as Martha, a gauche social and emotional misfit whose naive insistence on telling the truth gets her into trouble with those around her; Barbara Hershey as her attractive aunt Frances, who finds that looking after Martha is taking its toll on her affair with a married politician; Chloe Webb as Martha's friend Birdy, and the ever-excellent David Strathairn as Birdy's lover Getso; and Gabriel Byrne as Mackey, the drunken handyman who's taken on to repair Frances and Martha's home, only to upset the already precarious applecart. Much here may be routine, in the lyrical small-town genre, but now and then a welcome sense of pain, confusion and frustrated desire erupts from the well-honed narrative. GA

Danger Route

(Seth Holt, 1967, GB) Richard Johnson, Carol Lynley, Barbara Bouchet, Sylvia Syms, Gordon Jackson, Diana Dors, Sam Wanamaker.
92 min.
The late British director Seth Holt has something of a cult reputation, although even his supporters would probably admit that his was a frustrated and frustrating career, being full of films that are half-impressive, half-banal. This espionage thriller, with Johnson as a hired assassin caught in a complex web of betrayal and violence when he's commissioned to murder a Czech scientist, is typical; the narrative is confused and fragmented, but the tension is taut, especially when Johnson is called upon to kill his own girlfriend. GA

Daniel

(Sidney Lumet, 1983, US) Timothy Hutton, Mandy Patinkin, Lindsay Crouse, Edward Asner, Ellen Barkin, Julie Bovasso, Tovah Feldshuh, Joseph Leon, Amanda Plummer.
129 min.
Adapted by EL Doctorow from his own novel, *The Book of Daniel*, this fictional telling of the story of the Rosenbergs (executed in the 1950s in Chicago for Soviet espionage concerning the atom bomb) jerks every tear, rehearses every cliché, and obscures every insight that the perspective of thirty years might grant us. Hutton plays the son of the Rosenbergs (called here the Isaacsons), who becomes a hippy in the '60s and is convinced that if he can find the truth about his parents' guilt or innocence he will be able to free his schizophrenic sister from her madness. Unfortunately, Doctorow and Lumet mix this story up with a polemic about capital punishment. They also destroy their focus by never

coming clean about what they think the Rosenbergs actually did. This leaves *Daniel* as just a psycho-political melodrama. MH

Daniel and the Devil

see All That Money Can Buy

Daniel Takes a Train (Szerencsés Dániel)

(Pál Sándor, 1983, Hun) Péter Rudolf, Sándor Zsótér, Kati Szerb, Mari Törőcsik, Dezsö Garas.
92 min.
In 1956 two teenage boys, one an army deserter whose unit turned against the government when the Russians rolled in, the other an apolitical youth called Daniel who aims to follow his girlfriend and her family to the West, take one of the last, overcrowded trains from Budapest to Vienna during the brief period when emigration was allowed. The atmosphere of panic and moral dilemma (whether to stay loyal to Hungary or escape to 'freedom') is keenly sustained, and the period reconstruction well bolstered by Elemér Ragályi's clever camerawork. But apart from the buddy relationship of the two fugitives, characterisation is thin, and there's almost too much plot incident to keep it on the rails. Still, it rattles along and is by turns amusing and heartstopping. (The conflict between the generations is more than touched on, but the implications – of the ending in particular – might have emerged more clearly had censorship not eliminated the information that Daniel has in fact killed his father). MA

Danny Jones

(Jules Bricken, 1971, GB) Frank Finlay, Jane Carr, Len Jones, Jenny Hanley, Nigel Humphreys.
91 min.
Some nice shots of the Welsh countryside, but mostly a cliché story about a Welsh carpenter, his apprentice son, and a posh bint who comes between them. The father learns that the boy must have his independence; the boy figures out that women who see themselves as sex objects can be used as such; and the posh bint ends up happy to have someone whom she thinks loves her in spite of her weight problem. Visit Wales instead. JK

Danny the Champion of the World

(Gavin Millar, 1989, GB) Jeremy Irons, Robbie Coltrane, Samuel Irons, Cyril Cusack, Michael Hordern, Lionel Jeffries, Ronald Pickup, Jean Marsh, Jimmy Nail, William Armstrong, John Woodvine, Jonathan Davis.
99 min.
Roald Dahl takes on green politics in this adaptation of his children's book: screenwriter John Goldsmith introduces the theme of rural conservation and injects topicality into a tale of post-war village life. But the basic conflict is more personal: between loveable poacher William (Irons) and crass, *nouveau riche* lord of the manor Hazell (Coltrane). Widower William runs a garage and lives in a caravan with his nine-year old son Danny (Samuel Irons). One day their peace is shattered when Hazell decides that all he surveys should become a housing estate, but his plans are thwarted by the fact that William's patch of land is smack in the middle of the estate. In the ensuing battle of wills, we can thrill to the dangers of poaching, and hiss at Hazell's dastardly schemes. Millar directs with authority and loving attention to period detail. There's also a pleasing ring of truth about the relationship built up between real-life father and son Jeremy and Samuel Irons. Family entertainment: cosy, intimate, a touch cloying. CM

Dans le Ventre du dragon

see In the Belly of the Dragon

Dante's Inferno

(Harry Lachman, 1935, US) Spencer Tracy, Claire Trevor, Henry B Walthall, Alan Dinehart, Scotty Beckett, Rita Hayworth.
88 min. b/w.
Despite the rather over-the-top moralising of the finale, which posits a dramatic comeuppance for Tracy, the ambitious and cynical showman who has built himself into a wealthy carnival- and

ship-owner by exploiting and manipulating people, this is still a very enjoyable film. Partly for its bizarre, pre-*Nightmare Alley* Gothic vision of circus life, partly for Tracy's admirably tough performance, and partly for the spectacular insertion of the famous 'hell' sequence (later re-used in Ken Russell's *Altered States*). The allegory may be banal, the vision pure kitsch, but it's hard to deny the sheer fun of seeing so many scantily-clad extras cavorting wildly amid such architecturally extravagant sets. GA

Dante's Peak

(Roger Donaldson, 1997, US) Pierce Brosnan, Linda Hamilton, Jamie Renée Smith, Jeremy Foley, Elizabeth Hoffman, Charles Hallahan.
108 min.
The first of 1997's two volcano movies acquits itself well in the spectacle department, but its colourless characters, dwarfed from the outset by a computer-generated peak, finally get lost among the deadly emissions. There's a familiar feel to the film's *Jaws*-like set-up, with Brosnan's intuitive volcanologist predicting imminent catastrophe while local councillors insist there's no need for panic. As an exercise in disaster-movie logistics, this is on a par with *Twister*, although the jaw-dropping SFX are far more varied and genuinely terrifying. NF

Danton

(Andrzej Wajda, 1982, Fr/Pol) Gérard Depardieu, Wojciech Pszoniak, Anne Alvaro, Patrice Chéreau, Roger Planchon, Alain Mace.
136 min.
Despite Wajda's denials, it's hard to resist the superficial comparison between Robespierre and Danton, and Jaruzelski and Lech Walesa. Granted there are huge distinctions in ideology, but on the level of political personalities, Robespierre's ruthless dedication to the Revolution and Danton's man-of-the-people charisma carry potent contemporary resonance. Maybe history does repeat itself, and to some extent Wajda does too, here fleshing-out a costume drama with the kind of historical details that work in favour of the film's meaning rather than just prettifying it. OK, it's a message movie with a predictable punchline, but as Depardieu cries on the scaffold: 'Show them my head. It will be worth it'. It is. MA

Danzón

(Maria Novaro, 1991, Mex) Maria Rojo, Carmen Salinas, Blanca Guerra, Tito Vasconcelos, Victor Carpinteiro, Margarita Isabel.
96 min.
Danzón is the name of a dance and its music: a style particularly attractive to Julia (Rojo) a 40-year-old single mother, telephonist and star of the local *salon de baile* in Mexico City. When her white-suited Danzón partner of 20 years standing – a real *caballero* – disappears one day, Julia is thrown into crisis and embarks on a trip to the coastal port of Vera Cruz in search not only of him but of herself too. Described as 'hot and spicy' in the programme for London's 1992 Latin American Film Festival, it is anything but. Instead, it is a gentle, affirmative and honest depiction of a particular culture (what the Danzón expresses about the emotional and sexual longings of its adherents) from the woman's point of view, which uses song to structure the narrative. It is directed by Novaro with non-obtrusive sensitivity. WH

Darby O'Gill and the Little People

(Robert Stevenson, 1959, US) Albert Sharpe, Jimmy O'Dea, Sean Connery, Janet Munro, Kieron Moore, Walter Fitzgerald, Jack MacGowran.
90 min.
Walt Disney had wanted to make this Oirish fantasy (suggested by HT Kavanagh's stories) for more than 20 years and even visited Ireland to do the research, acknowledging the co-operation of 'King Brian of Knocknasheega', lord of the little people, on the final credits. Forty years on, with M'Lord Fitzpatrick's caretaker Darby O'Gill (Sharpe) falling down a well and landing in the realm of the leprechauns where he's given three wishes, it registers as a pretty hokey entertainment. But Peter Ellenshaw and Eustace Wallace's effects are put together with the studio's customary care – and there's even a banshee sequence with flame throwers to put the wind up the kids,

begorrah begob. For those of a sentimental turn, there is the delight of watching young Connery romancing the ineffably wholesome Janet Munro, a couple of years before things turned nasty for Commander Bond at Crab Key with the somewhat more knowing Ursula Andress.

Dark Angel

(Craig R Baxley, 1989, US) Dolph Lundgren, Brian Benben, Betsy Brantley, Matthias Hues, David Ackroyd, Michael J Pollard, Jesse Vint, Jay Bilas, Sherman Howard.
91 min.
An unpretentious sci-fi action pic in which Lundgren does battle with extra-terrestrial drug-dealers armed with lethal space-age flying CDs. Caine (Lundgren) is a conventionally 'unconventional' Houston vice cop, who works on instinct and would rather die than break his word. When his buddy is blown away infiltrating a local drug ring, Caine finds himself forced into partnership with strait-laced, by-the-book Laurence Smith (Benben, nicely irritating). Relations between the two are strained to breaking point as Caine announces his belief that a spate of peculiarly vampiric killings are being carried out by drug-fiends from outer space. But Smith's incredulity naturally turns to awed acceptance as the corpse-count rises. With an upbeat script and a healthy sense of humour, this is an unashamedly ridiculous affair with moderate ambitions and matching success. MK

Dark Angel, The

(Sidney Franklin, 1935, US) Fredric March, Merle Oberon, Herbert Marshall, Janet Beecher, John Halliday.
110 min. b/w.
Lush Goldwyn weepie, based on a Guy Bolton play previously filmed by George Fitzmaurice in 1925, with Ronald Colman and Vilma Banky. Man loves woman who turns to his equally smitten cousin when he's reported killed in the war, but finds (gulp) that he's only blinded and living in self-sacrificial hiding. Irredeemable tosh (with a distinctly tepid performance from Oberon), despite Lillian Hellman script and sleek Gregg Toland camerawork. TM

Dark at the Top of the Stairs, The

(Delbert Mann, 1960, US) Robert Preston, Dorothy McGuire, Eve Arden, Angela Lansbury, Shirley Knight, Lee Kinsolving.
123 min.
A Pulitzer Prize winner in its Broadway version, William Inge's play based on memories of his Oklahoman youth in the '20s suffers here from undue reverence from both Mann and screenwriters Irving Ravetch and Harriet Frank – usually much sharper with oddball Westerns or liberal dramas for Martin Ritt – and undue hamming from a wildly disparate cast. Small-town domestic intrigues push one way, sub-plots about adolescent fears and anti-Semitism pull another. PT

Dark Avenger, The (aka The Warriors)

(Henry Levin, 1955, GB) Errol Flynn, Joanne Dru, Peter Finch, Yvonne Furneaux, Patrick Holt, Michael Hordern, Moultrie Kelsall, Robert Urquhart.
85 min.
The sets left at Borehamwood after MGM's *Ivanhoe* provided the excuse for this rather more modest production to nip in and show that even a 46-year-old Flynn still had a modicum of swash and buckle left in him – and if he didn't, there was always the stunt double. The Black Prince (Flynn) must subdue the restless nobles in English-held Aquitaine and defeat the machinations of duplicitous count Finch. Unpretentious hokum, and any movie that casts Michael Hordern as Errol Flynn's dad has to raise a smile, especially since he was two years the star's junior. TJ

Dark Circle

(Chris Beaver/Judy Irving/Ruth Landy, 1982, US)
81 min.
A well done, preaching-to-the-converted anti-nuclear documentary. An intense, low-key production which shows up the flashy decontextualising of *Atomic Café*, it ranges from Nagasaki survivors, through neighbours of a plu-

tonium plant near Denver, to the fiasco of Diablo, the Californian nuclear power plant described as 'the most analysed building in the world' which, at the last minute, turned out to have been built back to front. JCo

Dark City

(William Dieterle, 1950, US) Charlton Heston, Lizabeth Scott, Viveca Lindfors, Dean Jagger, Jack Webb, Don Defore, Ed Begley, Henry Morgan, Mike Mazurki.
88 min. b/w.
Given that Heston spent most of his career playing monumental heroes, it's a surprise to find him cast as a petty hood in this, his Hollywood debut. He's a war hero fallen on tough times who makes a living hustling at poker. There's a homicidal maniac on his heels, out to avenge the death of his brother who committed suicide after losing a fortune to Heston at the table. As the title makes clear, we're in the realm of *film noir*. A plaintive score from Franz Waxman and moody camerawork from Victor Milner ensure the picture scores on atmosphere, but veteran director Dieterle hasn't been dealt much of a hand by his scriptwriters. GM

Dark City

(Alex Proyas, 1997, US/Aust) Rufus Sewell, Kiefer Sutherland, Jennifer Connelly, Richard O'Brien, Ian Richardson, Colin Friels, William Hurt.
100 min.
At midnight the city stops. Citizens black out, transfixed in whatever activity they're engaged in, while all around them 'The Strangers' modify the urban environment, transforming streets and buildings, the fabric of people's lives. When the clock starts again, collective amnesia shrouds the general unease. John Murdoch (Sewell) wakes up to face a murder rap he knows makes no sense. Tipped off by the mysterious Dr Schreber (Sutherland), he evades captures and sets about unearthing his apparently metaphysical pursuers. Proyas' overwrought MTV camera jitters tend to highlight characterisation that's two dimensional even by comic book standards, and the film can't stand the inevitable comparisons with *Blade Runner* or *Brazil*. Nevertheless, Murdoch's quandary proves surprisingly engrossing, the art direction is always striking, and unlike most contemporary sci-fi, the movie does risk a cerebral approach, tapping a vein of postmodern paranoia. TCh

Dark Corner, The

(Henry Hathaway, 1946, US) Mark Stevens, Lucille Ball, Clifton Webb, William Bendix, Constance Collier, Kurt Kreuger, Cathy Downs, Reed Hadley.
99 min. b/w.
Fine *noir* thriller, superbly paced by Hathaway, equally superbly shot by Joe MacDonald, and benefiting from the Fox trademark (at this time) of location shooting. Stevens is the private eye just released from jail after being framed for murder, only to find a sinister thug tailing him and gradually driving him into a nightmare which ends with him wanted for murder all over again. Although Webb's suave villain is carried over virtually intact from *Laura* (complete with the manic possessiveness about beautiful women), *The Dark Corner* manages its own note of individuality by casting the vulnerable Stevens as a tough Sam Spade whose façade is systematically cracked ('I'm backed up in a dark corner and I don't know who's hitting me') until his devoted, wisecracking secretary (Ball) has to mother him through. Terrific performances, not least from Bendix as the thug in a white suit, Downs as the dark angel of the piece, and Kreuger as a Teutonic snake. TM

Dark Crystal, The

(Jim Henson/Frank Oz, 1982, GB) character performers: Jim Henson, Kathryn Mullen, Frank Oz, Dave Goelz, Brian Muehll.
93 min.
Every attempt to film in the epic fantasy style of *The Lord of the Rings* has foundered on the technical difficulties involved, particularly Equity's failure to produce trolls, orks and hobbits in sufficient quantities. Henson, creator of the Muppets, has put all his energies into creating a spectacular range of live-action creatures who prance and gobble their way across the screen with an unprecedented conviction. Given this enormous

advantage, it is therefore disappointing that this $26 million film should restrict itself to a very basic pulp fantasy plot – the hero's quest to free his world from the ravages of an evil race – when there are superior models available in any bookshop. Monstrous characterisations, and the relish with which the strange rituals of evil creatures are portrayed, make up for this deficiency. Desiccated, clawing villains feasting on rotting food in a castle as unprepossessing as the crashed spaceship in *Alien* have a splendour that is almost operatic. DP

Dark Enemy

(Colin Finbow, 1984, GB) David Haig, Douglas Storm, Rory MacFarquhar, Martin Laing, Chris Chescoe.
97 min.

Finbow set up the Children's Film Unit in 1981 in order to encourage youngsters to participate in all aspects of film-making, and it looks to be paying off. This, the unit's third film, is centered around a group of children who are living in a post-nuclear world, unaware of the civilisation before them. Only two Most Elders remain, the rest were either too young or not yet born at the time of the holocaust. And now the time has come for a new leader to be elected. Apart from a rather slow start, the film encompasses some excellent acting, a great music score, and a haunting underlying moral. DA

Darker Than Amber

(Robert Clouse, 1970, US) Rod Taylor, Suzy Kendall, Theodore Bikel, Jane Russell, James Booth, Janet McLachlan, William Smith.
96 min.

An attempt to crash the then popular *Tony Rome* market with John D Macdonald's seedy eye Travis McGee – Kendall's first appearance is as a 'lady in cement' – that flounders around confusedly in the Florida underground. Russell here made her final appearance, while Kendall gets two roles, one hideously dubbed. PT

Dark Eyes (Oci Ciornie)

(Nikita Mikhalkov, 1987, It) Marcello Mastroianni, Silvana Mangano, Marthe Keller, Elena Sofonova, Pina Cei, Innokenti Smoktunovski.
118 min.

Mikhalkov's adaptation of several of Chekhov's short stories makes for bland viewing indeed. Mastroianni is in fine form as the fickle, philandering and finally irritatingly spineless Romano, a wealthy Italian whose dismay at the imminent bankruptcy of his wife's bank takes him away from family and mistress to the distracting lassitudes of a health spa, where he encounters and seduces the shy, reluctant Anna (Sofonova). When Anna returns to Russia and husband, Romano follows, but will he do the honourable thing and tell his wife (Mangano) the truth? Mikhalkov manages, remarkably, to render the harrowing dilemmas thrown up by problems of adultery, commitment, disillusionment and solitude woefully shallow. Mastroianni apart, the film is a glossy, unprepossessing example of the mainstream art movie. GA

Dark Eyes of London
(aka The Human Monster)

(Walter Summers, 1939, GB) Bela Lugosi, Hugh Williams, Greta Gynt, Wilfred Walter, Arthur Owen, May Hallatt.
76 min. b/w.

Engaging chiller based on an Edgar Wallace novel, with Lugosi giving one of his better performances as the director of an insurance company and (incognito) of a home for the blind where the newly-insured are drowned in a tank and disposed of in the Thames. Let down by extremely conventional characterisation of the intrepid hero and heroine (Williams and Gynt), but weirdly atmospheric, with good use made of the Thames mudflats and a splendidly macabre denouement involving two blind henchmen, one of them a hulking Frankenstein monster (Walter). TM

Dark Habits (Entre Tinieblas)

(Pedro Almodóvar, 1983, Sp) Cristina S Pascual, Marisa Paredes, Mari Carrillo, Lina Canalejas, Manuel Zarzo, Carmen Maura, Chus Lampreave.
116 min.

Almodóvar's third feature is slapdash, occa-

sionally slow-moving, haphazardly plotted. That it's also wildly funny, bitchy, affecting and surreal is a tribute to his perennial warmth and wit. Nightclub singer Yolanda (Pascual) is impelled, via a bit of drug trouble, into the arms of the Mother Superior of the Convent of Humble Redeemers. Lying low in a spacious cell, decked with the trappings of Catholic kitsch, she finds the demands of the religious life needn't cramp her style too much: Sister Rat (the wonderful Lampreave) pens bodice-rippers, the Mother Superior jacks off in the privacy of her office, Sister Manure has LSD-fuelled religious ecstasies, and Sister Sin (Maura, radiant) is spotted from a bedroom window wrestling with a tiger. The whole thing winds up with the inevitable scandal and is almost completely silly; but as ever, Almodóvar's adoration of his female stars is heart-warming, and his visual style a delight. SFe

Dark Half, The

(George A Romero, 1991, US) Timothy Hutton, Amy Madigan, Michael Rooker, Julie Harris, Roger Joy, Kent Broadhurst, Rutanya Alda.
121 min.

Proof that not all films derived from Stephen King's books need be intellectually banal and cinematically dull. Romero's movie centres on Thad Beaumont (Hutton), a small-town author and creative-writing tutor, who, threatened with exposure, decides to kill off his literary doppelgänger, crime novelist George Stark. Soon afterwards, Thad's friends and colleagues start meeting violent deaths, apparently at the hands of the late Stark. Thad's wife Liz (Madigan) is frightened for the children, but although the local lawman (Rooker) is sympathetic, he refuses to believe that Thad's fictional alter ego is the razor wielding culprit. It's a strong conceit, but precisely how it's linked to a feather-brained subplot about the black-outs and aural hallucinations Thad suffered as a child remains obscure. This one-paced psychological horror movie delivers its share of visual shocks, but relies mainly on a controlled build-up of tension. NF

Dark Journey

(Victor Saville, 1937, GB) Vivien Leigh, Conrad Veidt, Joan Gardner, Anthony Bushell, Ursula Jeans, Austin Trevor.
82 min. b/w.

An amiable melodrama in which two World War I spies (witty Leigh, icy Veidt) fall for each other in high society Stockholm (treated by the movie as some Nordic Casablanca!). The film ultimately bears the stamp of its director less than of its producer (Korda) and studio, and a certain blandness pervades. Fascinating, though, for the date it was made and its appropriately confused sympathies (pacifist? militarist? continental? British? – hard to say). CA

Darklands

(Julian Richards, 1996, GB) Craig Fairbrass, Rowena King, Jon Finch, David Duffy, Roger Nott, Richard Lynch, Nicola Branson.
91 min.

This £500k first feature has been called the Welsh *Wicker Man*. Writer/director Richards readily acknowledges his debt to the 1973 horror classic – partly out of fanboy respect, partly, one suspects, to defuse accusations of plagiarism. In his least action-oriented role to date, Fairbrass plays Frazer Truick, a Welsh-born, London-raised journo whose investigations into the death of a young steelworker suggest links between the industrial 'accident', fervent nationalist politician David Keller (Finch), and an uppity group of Celtic neo-pagans. Truick's nose for a story and lust for the dead youth's beautiful sister, cub reporter Rachel (King), soon have him knee-deep in desecrated churches, slaughtered pigs, crazy priests and a revivalist political conspiracy. The confident direction and Zoran Djordevic's atmospheric visuals are complemented by a score that effectively blends Test Department's percussive industrial noise with gentler Welsh folk songs. NF

Darkman

(Sam Raimi, 1990, US) Liam Neeson, Frances McDormand, Colin Friels, Larry Drake, Nelson Mashita, Jesse Lawrence Ferguson.
91 min.

Dr Westlake (Neeson) is on the verge of perfect-

ing a synthetic skin which conceals disfigurements; the problem is, the skin dissolves in sunlight after 99 minutes. When his laboratory is ransacked and blown up by gangster Durant (Drake), Westlake is left for dead, face down in a vat of caustic chemicals. But he survives (*sans visage*) as Darkman, an avenging angel who uses temporary masks to impersonate and destroy his enemies, while simultaneously attempting to win back his estranged love (McDormand). Drawing self-consciously on the 'misunderstood monster' tradition of Universal's golden age, Raimi's major studio debut abounds with conflicting ambitions, juggling pathos, horror and incongruous slapstick as it attempts to meld (with variable success) an archaic narrative structure with a kinetic, modern visual style. Neeson's performance encapsulates these contradictions, mixing camp histrionics with moments of touching precision. But the breathtaking action sequences find Raimi in his element: wild, woolly and occasionally wondrous, *Darkman* has the chaotic charm of untrammelled, undisciplined talent. MK

Dark Mirror, The

(Robert Siodmak, 1946, US) Olivia de Havilland, Lew Ayres, Thomas Mitchell, Richard Long, Charles Evans.
85 min. b/w.

Impressively unusual thriller with typically simplistic Freudian elements as psychiatrist Ayres is called in by the police to help investigate a murder committed by one of two identical twins...but which one? Intriguing cat-and-mouse games and perverse power struggles as both he and we try to fathom which of the sisters is the warped psycho, with de Havilland (in the dual role) and Siodmak managing admirably to counteract the contrived plot. What really makes it work, though, is Siodmak's firm grasp of mood and suspense; the opening scene, in which the camera prowls a darkened room until it finds a corpse, sets the tone perfectly for the sense of uncertainty and chaos that follows. GA

Darkness in Tallinn
(Tallinn pimeduses/
Tallinnan pimeys)

(Ilkka Järvilaturi, 1993, Fin/US/Swe/Estonia) Ivo Uukkivi, Milena Gulbe, Monika Mäger, Enn Klooren, Vainö Laes.
99 min. b/w & col.

This ultra-black comedy by Finnish film-maker Järvilaturi is an unexpected joy. It begins, almost disconcertingly, with Estonia's newly re-established independence being marked by a secret gathering of criminals, who plan to nab the country's massive bullion reserves when they're brought from Paris back to Tallinn. Thus is Toivo (Uukkivi), a small-time caviar smuggler and electrician, advised by his very pregnant wife Maria (Gulbe) to abandon ideals for the promise of money, brought in on a daring night hold-up. True to form, the scheme hits the skids with in-fighting among the ill-matched hoods. Ingeniously written (by Paul Kolsby), tautly paced with b/w photography that never fails to surprise, this is *noir* at its blackest. The characters, too, are pleasingly quirky, but never contrived. A funny, suspenseful heist movie with a properly sharp moral/political edge. GA

Dark of the Sun

see Mercenaries, The

Dark Passage

(Delmer Daves, 1947, US) Humphrey Bogart, Lauren Bacall, Bruce Bennett, Agnes Moorehead, Tom D'Andrea, Clifton Young, Douglas Kennedy.
106 min. b/w.

Classic thriller based on the David Goodis novel about a man wrongly convicted of murder who escapes, has his face changed by plastic surgery, and clears his name with the aid of a girl whose father was similarly framed. Brilliantly atmospheric San Francisco settings, memorably bizarre supporting performances, a superb use of subjective camera (much more effective than in *Lady in the Lake*) throughout the entire first third of the film. The only flaw is the momentary absurdity when the bandages are finally unwrapped to reveal the 'new' face as dear old Bogart's (although prepared for by the use of his distinctive voice from the start). TM

Dark Past, The

(Rudolph Maté, 1949, US) Lee J Cobb, William Holden, Nina Foch, Adele Jergens, Stephen Dunne.
75 min. b/w.
Cast against type, Holden's the ringleader of a gang which takes over shrink Cobb's lakeside retreat while they await their getaway in this competent remake of the 1939 Chester Morris picture *Blind Alley*. The twist, and it's not altogether convincing, is that Cobb uses his professional insights into his captor's personality profile to turn the tables, with much pop pyschology along the way. One's not absolutely flabbergasted to learn that it all started life as a stage play. TJ

Dark Star

(John Carpenter, 1974, US) Brian Narelle, Dre Pahich, Cal Kuniholm, Dan O'Bannon, Joe Saunders, Miles Watkins.
83 min.
Carpenter's fondly remembered first feature, which the director himself described as 'One big optical – *Waiting for Godot* in space'. Four bombed-out astronauts journey endlessly through the galaxy, whiling away the time with jokes, sunlamp treatment, personal diaries on videotape, and games with their own pet alien. Arguably the last great hippy movie with its jokey references to drugs, the Absurd and California surfing (one crew member makes it back to earth on an improvised board), it also anticipates the sci-fi vogue of the '70s (*Alien* and Carpenter's own gem *The Fog*) as well as taking a healthy sideswipe at the pretensions of *2001*. Sheer delight. MA

Dark Summer

(Charles Teton, 1994, GB) Joeline Garner Joel, Steve Ako, Chris Darwin, Bernie Deasy.
85 min.
The skanking reggae heard over shots of a decaying Liverpool seems promising. Abe and Jess exchange glances over the rubble when Jess starts working for her Dad on site. They're young and in love (we must assume it's that old 'chemistry', since there's little dialogue or emotional build-up), but her Dad is appalled, though whether it's because Abe's black or an employee isn't clear. Jess moves out to be with Abe, which is fine until the heartbreak begins. The five years writer/director Teton spent in advertising do not seem to have given him a grip on the basics of dramatic film-making. A self-financed first feature which fails to take flight. EPe

Dark Victory

(Edmund Goulding, 1939, US) Bette Davis, George Brent, Humphrey Bogart, Geraldine Fitzgerald, Ronald Reagan, Cora Witherspoon.
106 min. b/w.
Davis has a field day as the petulant Long Island heiress who wields her riding-crop to humble the Irish chauffeur (Bogart, no less, badly miscast), then learns she has only months to live and spends the rest of her time discovering resignation and romantically dying (partnered, alas, by the soggy Brent). She and Goulding almost transform the soap into style; a Rolls-Royce of the weepie world. TM

Dark Waters

(André De Toth, 1944, US) Merle Oberon, Franchot Tone, Thomas Mitchell, Fay Bainter, John Qualen, Elisha Cook Jr, Rex Ingram.
90 min. b/w.
Woman-in-peril thriller with Oberon, orphaned and left a nervous wreck by a World War II torpedoing, recuperating with relatives living in Louisiana (in an old dark house, naturally) who conspire to have her declared insane so that they can claim her fortune. Oberon is tiresomely tremulous, and the script almost as shaky; but the sterling efforts of De Toth and cameraman John Mescall (whose lighting invests the bayou swamplands surrounding the house with a magically eerie mystery) combine to turn dross into a wonderfully mean and moody slice of Southern Gothic. TM

Dark Wind, The

(Errol Morris, 1991, US) Lou Diamond Phillips, Gary Farmer, Fred Ward, Guy Boyd, John Karlen, Jane Loranger, Gary Basaraba.
111 min.
Produced by Robert Redford, this was the first in a proposed series of films based on Tony Hillerman's contemporary Navajo thrillers. Phillips stars as Tribal Policeman Jim Chee, embroiled in four complicated cases ranging from vandalism to drugs and murder – or are they all the same case? It seems appropriate that Errol Morris, the film-maker/detective whose documentary *The Thin Blue Line* freed a convicted murderer, should make his first fiction feature about a shaman/cop. Evidently, he shares Hillerman's respect for Native American culture, but this is a less distinctive film than might have been anticipated (Redford might almost have directed it). What we get is an engrossing, thoughtful and unusual mystery which arguably tips us the wink too early. It's very faithful to the novel – perhaps that's the problem. TCh

Darling

(John Schlesinger, 1965, GB) Dirk Bogarde, Laurence Harvey, Julie Christie, Roland Curram, Alex Scott, Basil Henson.
127 min. b/w.
No one need look further than *Darling* for a succinct guide to the reasons for the rapid decline of the British 'New Wave' in the '60s: the film supports the argument that the movement was stillborn. Frederic Raphael's script tramples its own studied issues (Third World poverty, corrupt Western values, jet-set alienation) under its equally studied Sophisticated Characterisation. Schlesinger's direction is a leaden rehash of ideas from Godard, Antonioni and Bergman, which nonetheless contrives to remain firmly rooted in British theatre of the Royal Court school. Excruciatingly embarrassing at the time, it now looks grotesquely pretentious and pathetically out of touch with the realities of the life-styles that it purports to represent. TR

Darling Lili

(Blake Edwards, 1969, US) Julie Andrews, Rock Hudson, Jeremy Kemp, Lance Percival, Michael Witney.
136 min.
A commercial failure that was savaged and ridiculed at the time, *Darling Lili* is a glorious film. Edwards' wedding present to Julie Andrews, it is yet another instalment of his ongoing celebration of innocence as the great virtue of life. To understand the film, a simple enough love/spy story set in World War I, one simply has to accept that love (and jealousy) is more important than winning wars. That done, the seemingly bizarre emotional switches of the film stand revealed as the perfect pivots around which Edwards has carefully constructed one of the most satisfying lyrical films in years. PH

D'Artagnan's Daughter

see Fille de D'Artagnan, La

Darwin Adventure, The

(Jack Couffer, 1971, GB) Nicholas Clay, Susan Macready, Ian Richardson, Christopher Martin, Robert Flemyng.
91 min.
About Darwin's journey to the Galapagos Islands, and the evidence he found there for evolution rather than individual creation of each species. The film refuses to go into the implications in the realm of ideas of Darwin's discovery, and suffers through the innate ambiguity of Hollywood-type movie-making towards its thinking characters. A good subject spoilt through unimaginative handling of both animal and human sequences.

D.A.R.Y.L.

(Simon Wincer, 1985, GB) Mary Beth Hurt, Michael McKean, Kathryn Walker, Colleen Camp, Josef Sommer, Ron Frazier, Barret Oliver.
100 min.
He's smart, nice, liked by all, so why make a film about this boring little jerk? The first half is somewhat short on drama as the new boy in town (Oliver) establishes himself as a wiz at advanced calculus, brill at baseball, and insufferably cute. Eventually, however, the heavies arrive: this microchip marvel (Data Analysing Robot Youth Lifeform) is the Pentagon's most powerful secret weapon since Cruise, and now the army wants it back, please. Oz director Wincer has produced a bland slice of ersatz Americana that's about as folksy as MacDonalds apple pie; a filming-by-numbers mix of small-town nostalgia, soapy family drama and high-tech sfx, this Dreary Android Runaway Yarn Lags way behind the Spielberg thoroughbreds it tries so hard to ape. SJo

Daughter of Rosie O'Grady, The

(David Butler, 1950, US) June Haver, Gordon MacRae, Debbie Reynolds, Gene Nelson, James Barton, SZ Sakall, Jane Darwell.
104 min.
Nowhere near as satisfying as *Stage Door* as a backstage epic, this period musical attempts to evoke the good old days of vaudeville, an era for which Hollywood had an extravagant, irrational affection. June Haver plays an ingenue who hits the boards against her father's wishes; the ensuing drama tends towards wide-eyed sentimentalism. Still, it's worth watching if only to witness the struggle to get into the next big musical number, and for a sterling performance from SZ 'Cuddles' Sakall, the rotund, white-haired comedian who duplicated this bumbling, fatherly role in dozens of films, including *Casablanca*. ATu

Daughter of the Nile (Niluohe Nüer)

(Hou Xiaoxian, 1987, Tai) Yang Lin, Gao Jie, Yang Fan, Xin Shufen, Li Tianlu.
91 min.
At first sight, you wouldn't clock this as a film from the director of *A Summer at Grandpa's* and *The Time to Live and the Time to Die*. But despite the shift from his usual rural settings to the extremely mean streets of present-day Taipei, this is another of Hou's haunting accounts of the joys and terrors of adolescence. The central character is a young woman struggling to keep her father and elder brother (cop and thief respectively) from each other's throats, while nursing a distant crush on one of her brother's friends, a too-pretty gigolo who gets into trouble when he starts dating a gangster's moll. The tangled relationships resolve themselves into a mesh of disappointments and frustrations, but despite the downbeat mood there are charming eruptions of humour, and the sheer eloquence of Hou's mellow visual style makes the film a lot more life-enhancing than most. TR

Daughter of the Puma, The

(Ulf Hultberg, 1994, Guatemala/Den/Swe) Angela Cruz, Gerardo Taracena, Alfonso Lopez, Dolores Heredia, Elpdia Carillo.
86 min.
Deceptively simple, moving tale, set in the aftermath of the 1982 San Francisco massacre, of a Mexico-exiled Amero-Indian girl's search across 'the border of death' for her 'disappeared' brother (partly financed by the Danish and Swedish Save the Children fund and supported by the Nobel Peace Prize-winner Rigoberta Menchu). At its heart is the fine, almost wordless performance of Angela Cruz as the girl, the horrific re-enactment of the massacre of her village, and the finely crafted scenes of personal intimacy, as the family members attempt to live their lives torn between the irreconcilable demands of the murderous military and the guerrillas, whom the girl's brother joins. WH

Daughters of Darkness (Le Rouge aux Lèvres)

(Harry Kümel, 1970, Bel/Fr/WGer/It) Delphine Seyrig, Danièle Ouimet, John Karlen, Andréa Rau, Paul Esser, Georges Jamin, Fons Rademakers.
96 min.
Like so many vampire films, this one begins with a couple of newlyweds. But Stefan looks a bit...dissipated. And why is he so reluctant to tell his mother about the marriage? They check into a deserted hotel on the Ostend seafront ('It's rather dead around here this time of year', says the porter). Kümel's is no ordinary vampire film, but then Seyrig, as the Countess Bathory, is no ordinary vampire. You'll never catch her flashing her fangs at people, probably because it would smudge her perfect scarlet lipstick. Instead, draped in fur and silver lamé, she vamps it up like crazy, accompanied by her charming young 'secretary' Ilona. Meanwhile, young girls are found with their throats cut, and not a trace of blood...Kümel wrings a new twist out of traditional vampire banes like running water, but also brings the myth's kinkier

aspects to the fore in their full glory. The screen oozes deathless style, and enough cod dialogue to stop the whole thing degenerating into Great Art. Gorgeous, absolutely bloody gorgeous. AB

Daughters of Satan
(Hollingsworth Morse, 1972, US) Tom Selleck, Barra Grant, Tani Phelps Guthrie, Paraluman, Vic Diaz.
96 min.
Made in the Philippines back-to-back with *Superbeast*, only it doesn't look like there was very much money left. Selleck buys an old painting of witches being burned at the stake, fascinated because one of them closely resembles his wife. The witches are out for revenge, the wife starts going into murderous trances, and it's a fiendishly boring plod all the way. TM

Daughters of the Dust
(Julie Dash, 1991, US) Cora Lee Day, Alva Rogers, Barbara-O, Trula Hoosier, Umar Abdurrahamn.
112 min.
Set in 1902, on a barrier island off Georgia, this first feature is an impressionistic portrait of the ritual last supper of the Peazant family before migrating to the mainland. The younger generations are leaving the matriarch Nana (Day) and the insulated traditional life she symbolises. Tensions are raised by the return of family members Viola, a Baptist missionary, and Yellow Mary (Barbara-O), a proud whore, and by Eli's apprehension that his wife Eula (Rogers) is carrying the child of a rapist. Nana fears these rifts will destroy her family when they leave the home of their African ancestors and calls on the spirit of Eula's unborn child to heal them. Steeped in symbolism, superstition and myth, this disconcertingly original film is structured in tableaux which jump through time. The characters speak in the islanders' Gullah dialect and little is explained; however, Dash's universal message about holding on to tradition in face of change rings clear. CO'S

Dave
(Ivan Reitman, 1993, US) Kevin Kline, Sigourney Weaver, Frank Langella, Kevin Dunn, Ben Kingsley, Charles Grodin.
110 min.
This warm-hearted film casts the copiously talented but still underrated Kline in the double role of Dave Kovic, nice, unassuming, uncoordinated but helpful Mr Nobody, and Bill Mitchell, unpleasant, cynical and adulterous incumbent of the White House. Kline is magnificent as the man who moves in when the President goes down with a sex-induced stroke, and the supporting cast are first rate, with Weaver as Mitchell's estranged, increasingly baffled consort, and Kingsley as the idealistic Vice President. Politicians such as Tip O'Neill supply celebrity cameos. A buoyant comedy in the Capra tradition. SGr

David Copperfield
(George Cukor, 1935, US) Freddie Bartholomew, Frank Lawton, WC Fields, Roland Young, Edna May Oliver, Basil Rathbone, Maureen O'Sullivan, Lionel Barrymore, Lewis Stone, Lennox Pawle, Elsa Lanchester.
132 min. b/w.
As one might expect from Cukor, an exemplary adaptation of Dickens' classic, condensing the novel's sprawl with careful clarity, and yielding up a host of terrific performances from its superb cast. Pride of place, of course, goes to Fields as Micawber, refusing to conceal his American accent, relishing the verbal gems, and for once allowing us to inspect the heart of tarnished gold that lay beneath his crusty exterior. One of those rare things: a blend of Art and Hollywood that actually works. GA

David Copperfield
see Charles Dickens' David Copperfield

David Holzman's Diary
(Jim McBride, 1967, US) LM Kit Carson, Penny Wohl, Louise Levine, Fern McBride.
73 min. b/w.
An enduring delight from the Underground era, cleverly sowing arrant lies at the then-sacred 24 fps. McBride's good-humoured gag on 'personal cine-

ma' and the diary genre casts a wry sidelight on a generation's self-obsession and cinephilia. *David Holzman* commits his life (film-making) to film – directing and starring in the film we're watching, his home-movie autobiography. So far, so faddish. But 'David' is actor Kit Carson, behind the camera he's apparently twiddling is Michael Wadleigh, and the auto-vérité amounts to as much of McBride's script as could be filmed before his $2,500 ran out. Retrospective ironies pile up with interim career leaps: Carson shot a documentary on Dennis Hopper, married Karen Black, and is now a Hollywood screenwriter; Wadleigh tripped through *Woodstock* to *Wolfen*; and McBride has limped through sci fi and softcore satire to the added narration credit for *The Big Red One* and the remake of *Breathless*. The illusion is complete. PT

Dawn!
(Ken Hannam, 1979, Aust) Bronwyn Mackay-Payne, Tom Richards, John Diedrich, Bunney Brooke.
120 min.
One might have expected Ken Hannam, who made one of Australia's breakthrough movies in *Sunday Too Far Away*, to have brought a bit more bite to this bland biopic of swimming ace Dawn Fraser, the Olympic gold medallist whose clashes with authority culminated in a flag-stealing incident at the 1964 Tokyo games that saw her banned from competition for ten years. Mackay-Payne, a swimmer herself, looks more confident in the pool than out of it. TJ

Dawn, The (To Harama)
(Alexis Bistiskas, 1994, Greece) Katerina Kouka, Stavros Zalmas, Smaragda Karydi.
110 min.
A conventional tale of a rake's downward progress and his ingenue's rise from rags to riches. An Athens clothes shop assistant Vasso (Kouka, fine) befriends (it turns out) a selfish, drunken night-club singer (Zalmas) and ends up taking the limelight herself. Of interest mainly for its mild feminism and the extended sequences of Greek ballad singing. WH

Dawning, The
(Robert Knights, 1988, GB) Rebecca Pidgeon, Anthony Hopkins, Jean Simmons, Trevor Howard, Tara MacGowran, Hugh Grant.
97 min.
This modest period drama, set in the south of Ireland before partition in 1921, successfully avoids most of the pratfalls and preciousness inherent in the genre. Based on Jennifer Johnston's elegant and expressive novel *The Old Jest*, it mirrors the events of the mounting IRA terrorist campaign in the maturing mind and eyes of an 18-year-old girl. The setting is the world of fading grandeur of the old Anglo-Irish ascendancy. Independent-minded Nancy (Pidgeon) lives in a great house presided over by her aunt (Simmons) and wheelchair-ridden ex-General grandfather (Howard, visibly his last role). Wilful and arty, she thinks herself enamoured of a straitlaced ex-army stockbroker (Grant), but with the arrival of a mysterious stranger (Hopkins), events take a tragic turn; a crisis is triggered, and Nancy is forced to examine her loyalties. Knights' film is solidly crafted, but its main strength lies in the performances. Rebecca Pidgeon makes a remarkable debut, exhibiting a rare ability to externalise thought and feeling. WH

Dawn of the Dead (aka Zombies)
(George A Romero, 1979, US) David Emge, Ken Foree, Scott H Reininger, Gaylen Ross, David Crawford, David Early.
126 min.
Undoubtedly the zombie movie to end 'em all, *Dawn of the Dead* starts roughly where *Night of the Living Dead* ended, and then proceeds to build mercilessly on its vision of a USA engulfed and decimated by murderous flesh-eating corpses. The horror/suspense content is brilliant enough to satisfy the most demanding fan, and the film uses superb locations like a huge shopping mall to further its Bosch-like vision of a society consumed by its own appetites. But take no munchies. DP

Dawn Patrol, The
(Howard Hawks, 1930, US) Richard Barthelmess, Douglas Fairbanks Jr, Neil

Hamilton, William Janney, Gardner James, Clyde Cook, James Finlayson, Frank McHugh.
90 min. b/w.
A group of men doing what men have to do during World War One, with a characteristically Hawksian emphasis on professionalism, self-respect and loyalty: Brit pilots Barthelmess and Fairbanks respond to German taunts about their flying prowess by massacring a squadron, thus incurring the displeasure of commander Hamilton, who points out the need to act more responsibly. If the early recording techniques in Hawks' first talkie entail a stiltedness in dialogue and performance, he compensates by contrasting the claustrophobic psychological tension of the interior scenes with the liberating, expertly shot action of the aerial footage (so good that it was used again in Goulding's 1938 remake). GA

Dawn Patrol, The
(Edmund Goulding, 1938, US) Errol Flynn, Basil Rathbone, David Niven, Donald Crisp, Melville Cooper, Barry Fitzgerald.
103 min. b/w.
Remake of the 1930 Howard Hawks film, from which it borrows its fine aerial footage (mostly shot by Elmer Dyer). Neither version (pace Hawks fans) is exactly a masterpiece, since the dialogue scenes in the first version are stiff and stodgily directed, while Goulding gets smoother performances (Flynn in particular is excellent), but has doctored dialogue more suited to bellicose times: not altering the thematic concern with the psychological stresses of combat leadership, but discreetly stressing the heroism of the young World War I flyers rather than the terrible waste of their deaths. TM

Day After Trinity, The
(Jon Else, 1980, US) Frank Oppenheimer, II Rabi, Robert Wilson, Jane Wilson, Dorothy McKibbin, Stirling Colgate.
89 min. b/w & col.
Los Alamos, 1941. A boom town (literally) where some of the best and brightest minds of the age, summoned by J Robert Oppenheimer, fabricated America's first atomic bomb. In this documentary they recall how the initial win-the-war fervour, and euphoria that their contraption actually worked, faded fast when they realised they'd replaced one Final Solution with another. Awe-inspiring footage of the Bomb in action, though the film's tiresome obsession with moral anguish and reliance on anecdote, sometimes revealing but often rambling, makes the film less than explosive. SJo

Day a Pig Fell into the Well, The (Daijiga Umule Pajinnal)
(Hong Sang-Soo, 1996, SKor) Kim Eui-Sung, Park Jin-Sung, Jo Eun-Sook, Lee Eun-Kyung.
115 min.
No pigs or wells in sight in Hong's justly acclaimed first feature, which looks at the lives of five very recognisable urban types as if all of them were witnesses at the scene of some freak accident. These men and women make mistakes and suffer frustrations in the ways we all do: a failed novelist blames everyone but himself for his inability to keep a relationship going; a woman dreams of divorcing her husband and pins her hopes on a lover who has already moved on; a generally faithful husband impulsively rents a hooker while on a business trip and catches an STD. Part of the pleasure here comes from the skill with which Hong interweaves these seemingly unconnected lives; the rest comes from the excellence of the images, sounds and performances and from Hong's warm but unsentimental engagement with his characters. TR

Day at the Races, A
(Sam Wood, 1937, US) The Marx Brothers, Allan Jones, Maureen O'Sullivan, Margaret Dumont, Douglass Dumbrille, Sig Ruman.
111 min. b/w.
The Brothers' second film for MGM should be retitled 'A Week at the Races' at least: it's overlong, overweight, overplotted. Even the comedy scenes are often played to excess, with too much raucous slapstick (like Harpo's destruction of Chico's piano). The plot formula established in *Opera* is repeated, but the script and characterisations are shallow: who'd have thought to find the Brothers fighting to save a sanatorium when there's a nice racetrack alongside? Still, worth seeing for its good stretches; you can always stock up with refreshments when anyone starts singing. GB

Daybreak

see Jour se lève, Le

Daydream Believer

(Kathy Mueller, 1991, Aust) Miranda Otto,
Martin Kemp, Anne Looby, Alister Smart, Gia
Carides, Bruce Venables, Howard Vernon.
86 min.
Australian schoolgirl Nell (Otto) thinks she is a
horse, whinnying her way through conflict until
a shrink tells her that 'deep down in all of us, there
lurks an animal'. Flash forward. Now an adult,
she trades hay for acting and self-help, still communing with horses but reverting to their lingo
only during moments of acute stress. There's
plenty of *that* about after she drives into the flash
sports-car belonging to Digby (Kemp), one-time
London orphan turned wealthy theatrical pro-
ducer/horse-breeder, who juggles attempts to
raise backing for a musical with efforts to find a
stallion to impregnate his prize mare. This is
where Nell comes in handy: can she get the name
of the mare's mate during a session of horse-talk?
An involving premise, which sees parental abuse
giving rise to Nell's escapism, is wasted on a ludicrous romantic comedy full of signposted jokes
and pratfalls. CM

Day for Night
(La Nuit Américaine)

(François Truffaut, 1973, Fr/It) Jacqueline
Bisset, Valentina Cortese, Jean-Pierre Aumont,
Jean-Pierre Léaud, Dani, Alexandra Stewart,
Jean Champion, François Truffaut.
116 min.
One of Truffaut's most captivating sentimental
comedies, built around his obvious love for cinematic illusionism. What story there is concerns the
various emotional upsets, logistical difficulties,
and moments of sheer elation during the shooting
of a rather silly-looking feature called *Meet
Pamela*. Basically it's all just an excuse for a marvellous series of delicately observed gags about
how things are really done behind the scenes on a
film set: grande dame Cortese infuriates everyone
by forgetting her lines, a cat awkwardly refuses to
drink its milk, Léaud throws adolescent fits every
few hours. Coupled with Georges Delerue's uplifting score and some superb performances (none
more so than the director himself), it's a must for
anyone besotten with the glamorous trivialities of
the cinematic medium. GA

Daylight

(Rob Cohen, 1996, US) Sylvester Stallone, Amy
Brenneman, Jay O Sanders, Viggo Mortensen,
Dan Hedaya, Karen Young, Claire Bloom.
114 min.
The disaster movie returns. Manhattan: a motley
group – including a lonesome gal (Brenneman)
and a dog – is trapped in a tunnel beneath the
Hudson. After a garbled mishap involving joyriders and trucks carrying nitroglycerine, they face
further explosions, flood water and panic-induced
bickering. Their survival depends on the heroic
efforts of Stallone; they're lucky to have him,
since he trod this line of work before, until taking
the rap for an earlier fatal incident. Director
Cohen keeps the vehicle cruising in fourth gear,
hoping the audience won't get too impatient with
the familiar scenery. Big, efficient, mindless entertainment. NB

Day of the Animals

(William Girdler, 1976, US) Christopher
George, Leslie Nielsen, Lynda Day George,
Richard Jaeckel, Michael Ansara, Ruth Roman.
98 min.
Twelve ill-assorted people (and twelve low-volt-
age performers) on a survival trek in the High
Sierras are attacked by bears, wolves, birds,
snakes, dogs – all of whom aren't feeling quite
themselves. The cause of their unease is ultra-vio-
let rays, seeping through an atmosphere polluted with aerosol sprays. The result is the most
routine kind of thrills, packed with all the lack of
imagination Girdler lavished on *Grizzly*. GB

Day of the Beast, The
(El día de la bestia)

(Alex de la Iglesia, 1995, Sp/It) Alex Angulo,
Armando De Razza, Santiago Segura, Terele
Pávez, Nathalie Seseña, Jaime Blanch.
104 min.
Alex de la Iglesia's clever, more assured follow-

up to *Acción Mutante* is a devilishly funny horror-comedy in which Angulo's priest becomes
convinced that the Antichrist will be born in
Madrid on Christmas Day. Immersing himself in
evil, he searches for clues among the city's human
detritus and in the lyrics of 'death metal' songs,
before kidnapping, with the help of a gonzoid
record-shop assistant (Segura), a famous TV
para-psychologist (De Razza). Meanwhile, somewhere out there, El Diablo is waiting to be born.
This is essentially a black comedy about two hapless individuals caught up in an impending cataclysm way beyond their understanding.
Responding to the robust humour and underlying seriousness of the script, Angulo brings an
engaging subtlety to his theologically inspired
madman, Segura's HM fan is likewise bonkers
yet oddly loveable. NF

Day of the Dead

(George A Romero, 1985, US) Lori Cardille,
Terry Alexander, Joseph Pilato, Jarlath
Conroy, Antone DiLeo, Gary Howard Klar,
Ralph Marrero, John Amplas, Richard Liberty.
102 min.
The odds are now 400,000 to one. Romero's zombies may be flesh-eaters, but they're far more
sympathetic than most of his living protagonists,
an unsavoury bunch who are holed up in an
underground bunker, dragging sundry walking
stiffs into the lab of 'Dr Frankenstein' to fund his
messy experiments into the domestication of
dead things – this means giving them Sony
Walkmans and Stephen King books. Between
shocks, he delves beyond the normal reach of the
Film Nasty to evoke the intolerable isolation of
ordinary beings in a situation which they cannot
fully comprehend. There are allegories there, if
you want them, and plenty of innard exposure.
There is also evidence of a master horror film-
maker at work. This, a fitting end to the trilogy
that kicked off with *Night of the Living Dead*, is
an awesome monument to the eternal zombie that
lurks within us all. AB

Day of the Dolphin, The

(Mike Nichols, 1973, US) George C Scott, Trish
Van Devere, Paul Sorvino, Fritz Weaver, Jon
Korkes, Edward Herrmann.
104 min.
Having taught his beloved marine playmate to
speak (ie. to say 'Fa, Ma, Pa' and other fascinating
gems), scientist Scott discovers that the creature's
intelligence is being exploited by horrible humans
in a plot to kill the president. A bizarre and often
ridiculous attempt to merge documentary, suspense and comedy that is marginally less silly than
Nichols' best-loved film, *The Graduate*. GA

Day of the Evil Gun

(Jerry Thorpe, 1968, US) Glenn Ford, Arthur
Kennedy, Dean Jagger, John Anderson, Paul
Fix, Harry Dean Stanton, Parley Baer, Royal
Dano, Ross Elliott.
93 min.
A Western directed with lazy assurance, and
scripted by Charles Marquis Warren as something like a cross between *The Searchers* and
Peckinpah's *The Deadly Companions*. Glenn Ford
is an ageing gunfighter, tired of the macho kick,
who returns home after three years only to learn
from a neighbouring farmer (Kennedy) that his
wife and two small daughters have been carried
off by Apaches. Kennedy claims that the wife
intended to marry him, presuming her husband
dead; and in uneasy alliance the two men set out
on the trail. Their odyssey, with the two men subtly changing places as the farmer begins to revel
in the hunt and the gunfighter leaves him to get
on with the killing, is studded with pleasingly
bizarre encounters: a minister's wife brooding in
a darkened room over her experiences as an
Apache captive; Indians who disarm them with
lassoes and stake them out to die from buzzard's
beak; a cluster of burning shacks that turns out
to be a town in the death-throes of cholera; a
Mormon ghost town that harbours a sinister
band of Confederate deserters. No masterpiece,
but distinctly effective. TM

Day of the Jackal, The

(Fred Zinnemann, 1973, GB/Fr) Edward Fox,
Michel Lonsdale, Alan Badel, Eric Porter,
Jean Martin, Cyril Cusack, Delphine Seyrig,
Donald Sinden.
142 min.

Inherently suspenseless (history would give us
several more years of assassination-target De
Gaulle), this adaptation of Frederick Forsyth's
bestseller yet provides an occasionally satisfying
core of tension that owes less to Zinnemann's penchant for *High Noon*-ish clock-watching than to
his schematic opposition of a cold, chameleonic
lone killer (Fox, the OAS's hired pro) with a
messy, though equally ruthless, bureaucracy of
'democratic' defence. Low on documentary conviction and political context, but an intriguing
exercise in concealing the obvious. PT

Day of the Locust, The

(John Schlesinger, 1974, US) Donald
Sutherland, Karen Black, Burgess Meredith,
William Atherton, Geraldine Page, Richard A
Dysart, Bo Hopkins, Jackie Earle Haley.
143 min.
Schlesinger's misguided version of Nathanael
West's cynical classic about a tormented
Tinseltown, peopled by no-hopers trying in vain
to work their way into the glamorous, starry life
of the Hollywood studios. Admittedly the book,
an elusive, mesmeric work of associated images
and ideas, surreal and analytical, would present
problems for the most talented of film-makers.
But Schlesinger really blows it. West's thin plot
is stretched out to excessive length, with little
sense of pace or the significance of events; the
characters are cut down, stranded without pasts
and motivations; images are emphasised with no
sense of context; the narrative is often confused
and confusing. Only the hysterical holocaust at
the end of the film gives any idea of West's conception, and even then the power of the scene is
betrayed by a pathetic, superfluous coda. GA

Day of the Outlaw

(André De Toth, 1959) Robert Ryan, Burl Ives,
Tina Louise, Nehemiah Persoff, Jack Lambert,
Alan Marshal.
96 min. b/w.
Day of the Outlaw carries further (and further
inward) the viciousness of *The Indian Fighter*,
with its claustrophobic tensions coiled tight in a
snowbound township when the arrival of a murderous renegade cavalry unit interrupts Ryan's
attempt to reclaim his woman and his land. The
incisive bleakness of Philip Yordan's script finds
its perfect complement in the absurdist violence
of De Toth's direction.

Day of the Premiere
of 'Close Up'

see Giorno della prima di 'Close Up', Il

Day of the Triffids, The

(Steve Sekely, 1962, GB) Howard Keel, Nicole
Maurey, Janette Scott, Kieron Moore,
Mervyn Johns.
94 min.
Not a particularly faithful adaptation of John
Wyndham's novel, though it sticks to the basic
theme about a world epidemic of blindness followed by the attack of strange plant-like creatures
called 'triffids'. The film shows signs of having
been put together rather patchily, with several
uncertain performances and some rather dodgy
process work. But quite a few of Wyndham's ideas
do translate to the screen most effectively, like the
airliner whose crew and passengers are suddenly
struck blind, and the electric fortress surrounded
for miles and miles around by invading triffids.
Sometimes unintentionally funny, and it could
have done without the customary moralising. DP

Day of Wrath (Vredens Dag)

(Carl Dreyer, 1943, Den) Thorkild Roose,
Lisbeth Movin, Sigrid Neiiendam, Preben
Lerdorff Rye, Anna Svierkier, Albert Hoberg.
105 min. b/w.
Often seen as an allegory on the Nazi occupation
of Denmark, this austere and very sombre
account of the persecution of witches in 17th century Denmark is arguably Dreyer's most pessimistic film. When a pious elderly parson sends
an old woman to the stake, she curses him. His
young wife (the daughter of a woman suspected
of witchcraft) falls in love with her stepson: the
affair induces the parson's death. Is the wife, then,
herself a witch? Dreyer remains wisely ambivalent, preferring instead to focus on the powerful,
earthly emotions of fear and love: the grim, grey
confession chambers – location of perhaps the

most discreet yet horrific torture scenes in cinema – embody the former, rippling streams and sun-dappled meadows the latter. Almost paradoxically, Dreyer evokes the soul through the physical world; the result is a masterpiece, its slow, measured pace and stark visuals achieving an almost unbearable emotional intensity. GA

Days, The
(Dong-Chun de Rizi)
(Wang Xiaoshuai, 1993, China) Yu Hong, Liu Xiaodong, Lou Ye.
75 min. b/w.
To those whose experience of Chinese cinema has been limited to the visually exotic films of Chen Kaige and Zhang Yimou, this rather wonderful movie by young independent Wang Xiaoshuai may come as a surprise. Shot in lyrical, melancholy b/w, it begins with a sensual, languorous scene of a couple making love in a Beijing bedsit, before proceeding to chart the slow, inexorable break-up of their relationship. Dong and Chun are both unsuccessful artists-turned-tutors, but shared interests and sexual passion haven't managed to stave off boredom and petty domestic tensions, with the result that she now wants to go to America, and he hasn't the fire left in his soul to tell her he'd rather she didn't. The days pass, and Chun's proposed departure gets even closer. What makes the movie so compelling is Wang's subtle control of mood: the stark, elegant visuals, the music, the elliptical approach to narrative, the long takes, the taciturn but telling performances – all work together to produce a hauntingly poetic elegy to the transience of love. GA

Days and Nights in the Forest
(Aranyer din Ratri)
(Satyajit Ray, 1969, Ind) Soumitra Chatterjee, Sharmila Tagore, Subhendu Chatterjee, Samit Bhanja, Robi Ghose, Pahari Sanyal, Kaberi Bose.
115 min. b/w.
Ray's most overtly Renoir-ish film, this might almost be a remake of Une Partie de Campagne, transposed to another time and place and through another sensibility. Instead of the French bourgeois family setting off for a picnic, four young men leave Calcutta for a few days in the country, trailing their westernised careerist attitudes, a middle class indifference to the lower orders, a self-satisfaction that leaves them closed to experience. Out of a series of delightfully funny mishaps as the visitors eagerly try to pursue acquaintance with their two promisingly attractive neighbours, Ray gradually distils a magical world of absolute stasis: a shimmering summer's day, a tranquil forest clearing, the two women strolling in a shady avenue, wistful yearnings as love and the need for love echo plangently. Elsewhere jobs have to be won or lost, problems faced and solved, but not here; an illusion of course, revealed as time lifts its suspension but leaves one of the quartet a changed man, the other three assailed by tiny waves of self-doubt. Beautifully shot and acted, it's probably Ray's masterpiece. TM

Days in London
(Ayam fi London)
(Samir Al Ghosaini, 1977, Leb) Samira Tawfeek, Yossif Shaaban, Rafeek Al Soubeiy, Khaled Taja.
97 min. b/w.
On this evidence, Arab musical escapism is directly comparable with the Bombay variety, but it is to be hoped that the film industries of the Middle East can boast some writers and directors better capable of stringing images and characters together than those responsible for this pathetic comedy-thriller. The leading lady, as a gaudily dressed shepherdess stranded in tourist London, is required to register confusion and mime three songs; reputed to be a big star in her home market, she is not, by any European definition of the word, an actress. TR

Days of Being Wild
(A-Fei Zhengchuan)
(Wong Kar-Wai, 1990, HK) Leslie Cheung, Andy Lau, Maggie Cheung, Carina Lau, Tony Leung, Jacky Cheung.
94 min.
Wong Kar-Wai's second feature is a brilliant dream of Hong Kong life in 1960. A young man of Shanghainese descent drifts through a series of

casual friendships and uncommitted affairs, unconsciously pining for a relationship with his mother, who has started a new life in Manila. He finally takes off for the Philippines, where he sets himself up for the ultimate fall... The terrific, all-star cast enacts this as a series of emotionally unresolved encounters; the swooningly beautiful camera and design work takes its hallucinatory tone from the protagonist's own uncertainties. The mysterious appearance of Tony Leung only in the closing scene heralds a sequel that will sadly never be made. But this is already some kind of masterpiece. TR

Days of Glory
(Jacques Tourneur, 1944, US) Gregory Peck, Alan Reed, Maria Palmer, Lowell Gilmore, Tamara Toumanova, Hugo Haas.
86 min. b/w.
Peck making his debut as a Russian guerrilla in one of those World War II tributes to our gallant Soviet allies which caused so much embarrassment later on. Actually, while making no bones about the fact that the protagonists are Communists, Casey Robinson's script is much more concerned with their doggedly gallant resistance under siege than with any political or propagandist purpose. No one had much to say for the film at the time, but it's sober and surprisingly convincing, even making the romantic interludes with Toumanova (a Catholic ballerina who joins the godless guerillas in their fight) unforced and natural. Quite beautifully directed by Tourneur. TM

Days of Heaven
(Terrence Malick, 1978, US) Richard Gere, Brooke Adams, Sam Shepard, Linda Manz, Robert Wilke, Jackie Shultis, Stuart Margolin.
94 min.
Wide-eyed, streetwise Abby (Adams) and her lover come (amidst thousands of other croppers from the industrial north) to the startlingly fertile harvest landscape of World War I Texas. Once there, they are caught up in a diffident, ultimately fatal triangle with their ailing young landowner-boss (Shepard): these are the surreal, idyllic, numbered Days of Heaven. This strange fusion of love story, social portrait and allegorical epic, by the director of Badlands, is rooted like that film in recent history, and held together only by its voice-over commentary and staggering visual sense. Where it goes further is in a profound chilling of romantic style, which treats lovers and insects alike as they flit through the vast wheat fields at dusk. Eventually (with a plague-of-locusts climax and the lovers' flight) the narrative collapses, leaving its audience breathlessly suspended between a 90-minute proof that all the bustling activity in the world means nothing, and the perfection of Malick's own perverse desire to catalogue it nonetheless. Compulsive. CA

Days of Hope
see Espoir

Days of Thunder
(Tony Scott, 1990, US) Tom Cruise, Robert Duvall, Nicole Kidman, Randy Quaid, Cary Elwes, Michael Rooker, Fred Dalton Thompson, JC Quinn.
107 min.
A flashy, pre-packaged racing picture featuring stock cars and stock situations. Veteran crew chief Duvall's efforts to get the naturally gifted Cruise to drive within the mechanical limits of the car provide the character-building father/son conflict. Kidman meanwhile provides the obligatory love interest as an improbably young doctor who offers TLC and a little more besides after Cruise is involved in a near-fatal crash. The plot's driving momentum is lost when Cruise's arch-rival (played with quiet intensity by Rooker) is badly injured in the same crash, to be replaced by insipid Val Kilmer-lookalike Cary Elwes. The resulting tedium is relieved only by Kidman's spirited berating of Cruise for his infantile macho desire to control his unruly emotions, and by yet another sterling performance from the ever-excellent Duvall. NF

Days of Water, The
(Los Dias del Agua)
(Manuel Octavio Gómez, 1971, Cuba) Idalia Anreus, Raúl Pomares, Adolfo Llaurado, Mario Balmaseda, Omar Valdés.
110 min.

Based round the true case of a woman who became a saint and 'miracle' worker in 1936 Cuba, The Days of Water, with its restless camerawork, offers broad and sweeping intimations of the popular revolution to come: the exploited and pent-up energies of an oppressed peasantry will eventually transform themselves into revolutionary forces (symbolised towards the end by the firing of the first shot of defiance). Appropriately, the atmosphere is near hysteria, culminating with the wish fulfilment of the final carnage. Huge crowds harangued by a commercial conman wait to be blessed or healed; the Church rails impotently while a fantasy sequence reveals that its Virgin Mary has a malevolent face; decadent and opportunist politicians exploit the 'saint's' popularity with typically gangster-ish methods. Voodoo and Catholicism combine to produce what can only be described as primitive baroque – an array of startling images, often as crude as they are effective. CPe

Days of Wine and Roses
(Blake Edwards, 1962, US) Jack Lemmon, Lee Remick, Charles Bickford, Jack Klugman, Alan Hewitt, Tom Palmer, Debbie Megowan, Jack Albertson.
116 min. b/w.
A heartrending saga of alcoholic dependency, adapted by JP Miller from his own teleplay. Cast heavily against type, Lemmon plays a San Francisco PR man uneasy about his job (which involves procuring women for business parties) and covering it by convivial drinking. When he marries Remick, they drink to celebrate. They drink to everything else, too. And then they start drinking simply to drink. The couple's battle to get off the bottle is harrowingly chronicled, so much so that you almost forget it's a Blake Edwards picture – his best by some margin, with a touching score by Henry Mancini. TJ

Day the Earth Caught Fire, The
(Val Guest, 1961, GB) Edward Judd, Janet Munro, Leo McKern, Michael Goodliffe, Bernard Braden, Reginald Beckwith, Arthur Christiansen.
99 min. b/w.
Thoroughly old-fashioned disaster film about a Daily Express reporter who learns that the earth has been tilted off its axis by the impact of two simultaneous H-bomb tests. Its 'authentic' newspaper setting looks quaint now, but there's some effective atmospheric build-up to the big one as London swelters in fog and heat. Perhaps inevitably, given the period and the film's medium budget, the ending is a cop-out. DP

Day the Earth Stood Still, The
(Robert Wise, 1951, US) Michael Rennie, Patricia Neal, Hugh Marlowe, Sam Jaffe, Billy Gray.
92 min. b/w.
A classic science fiction fable, its ambitious storyline conveying a surprising pacifist message. A flying saucer lands in Washington DC, and the humanoid alien which emerges is immediately shot and wounded by nervous state troopers. A ten-foot tall robot, Gort, emerges and disintegrates guns and tanks, before being deactivated by the wounded alien (Rennie). Rennie later delivers an ultimatum to the world's leaders: stop these senseless wars or face the awesome consequences – demonstrated by a period of one hour in which all the world's power is stopped. The scenes in which the fugitive Rennie learns about life on Earth by living incognito in a boarding-house with a young widow (Neal) and her son (Gray) are particularly effective, and it is telling that it is the boy who prevents Gort from destroying the world by uttering the immortal line, 'Gort! Klaatu barada nikto'. Edmund H North's intelligent script and Wise's smooth direction are serious without being solemn, while Bernard Herrmann's effectively alien-sounding score reinforces the atmosphere of strangeness and potential menace. NF

Day the Fish Came Out, The
(Michael Cacoyannis, 1967, Greece/GB) Tom Courtenay, Colin Blakely, Sam Wanamaker, Candice Bergen, Ian Ogilvy, Patricia Burke.
109 min.
In 1972, a military aircraft crashes near a tiny

Greek island after jettisoning its nuclear load, and a team of experts is sent to conduct a discreet search for the missing bombs. Their presence, supposedly as representatives of a hotel development company, turns the island into a thriving tourist resort, and the beaches are packed with holiday-makers by the time the fish start mysteriously dying. Directing with an eye to *Dr Strangelove*, Cacoyannis turns it all into hideously lumbering farce, so unconvincing that one is heartily glad when the unprepossessing characters at last seem likely to be overwhelmed by radiation. TM

Day the Sun Turned Cold, The (Tianguo Niezi)

(Yim Ho, 1994, HK) Siqin Gaowa, Tao Chung-Hua, Ma Jingwu, Wei Zhi.
100 min.
Yim Ho's sober, engrossing and finely observed film is based on actual events in China, but it's not an exercise in docu-drama. A young man goes to the police in Changchun to confide his fear that his mother murdered his father in their village home ten years earlier; the cops don't take him too seriously, but his persistence forces them to launch an investigation. The core issue, though, is not whether or not murder was done, but the love/hate relationship between a mother and son, and casting of the extraordinary Mongolian actress Siqin Gaowa as the mother gives full play to the Oedipal implications. The mix of realist detail and psychological insight takes the film way beyond the limitations of traditional Chinese melodrama. TR

Day the World Ended, The

(Roger Corman, 1955, US) Richard Denning, Adele Jergens, Lori Nelson, Mike Connors, Paul Birch, Raymond Hatton, Paul Dubov.
81 min. b/w.
An early Corman sci-fi movie (his first, in fact, as a director) which has survivors of the holocaust fending off an unfriendly mutant, and is engaging (almost convincing, even) in its pervasive seediness. The use of locations and the interplay between the desperate characters is surprisingly ambitious. TR

Day Time Ended, The

(John 'Bud' Cardos, 1979, US) Jim Davis, Chris Mitchum, Dorothy Malone, Marcey Lafferty, Natasha Ryan.
80 min.
Targeted at a family audience in the wake of Spielberg and *Close Encounters*, but the narrative won't hold any child's attention as it wanders incoherently around the cosmic chaos caused by – wait for it! – a trinary supernova. And the crucial special effects are zilch, although a pixie-sized alien scores simply because of its cow-eyed charm. IB

Daytrippers, The

(Gregg Mottola, 1995, US) Hope Davis, Parker Posey, Anne Meara, Stanley Tucci, Liev Schreiber, Pat McNamara, Campbell Scott, Marcia Gay Harden.
88 min.
Loving wife Davis finds a love letter in husband Tucci's pocket. He's a publisher, so it may be more innocent than it seems, but then, mysteriously, he's not at the office. The wife, her parents, her sister and the sister's boyfriend cram into the car and drive into the city to confront him. Mottola's dysfunctional family comedy is a bit arch, but sometimes sharp. Indie cinema and Neil Simon intersect on the corner of pathos and farce. TCh

Dazed and Confused

(Richard Linklater, 1993, US) Jason London, Joey Lauren Adams, Milla Jovovich, Shawn Andrews, Rory Cochrane, Adam Goldberg.
102 min.
School's breaking up for the summer of '76. The seniors debate party politics while next term's freshmen run the gauntlet of brutal initiation rites, barely comforted by the knowledge that they'll wield the stick one day. No one's looking much farther ahead than that. This has a free-wheeling, 'day-in-the-life-of' structure which allows writer/director Linklater, in his second feature, to eavesdrop on an ensemble cast without much in the way of dramatic contrivance. There's a quirky counter-cultural intelligence at work: sympathy for those on the sidelines, and a dead-pan pop irony which places this among the

hippest teenage movies. While the camera flits between some two dozen youngsters (played by uniformly excellent unknowns), Linklater allows himself to develop a handful of stories. Seriously funny, and shorn of any hint of nostalgia or wish-fulfilment, this is pretty much where it's at. TCh

D.C. Cab (aka Street Fleet)

(Joel Schumacher, 1983, US) Max Gail, Adam Baldwin, Mr T, Charlie Barnett, Gary Busey, DeWayne Jessie, Gloria Gifford.
99 min.
Fast-rappin' hi-jinks with the staff of the lowliest cab company in Washington DC. Basically a cross between TV's *Taxi* and the Schumacher-scripted *Car Wash*. Unfortunately, the sharp one-liners and quickie situation-jokes stop about halfway through, when an attempt at a plot is introduced. Ironically, despite a Keystone chase sequence, all this does is slow things down. Still, most of the jokes are a hoot (even Mr T parodies himself), and the soundtrack really frizzles. If this screen debut is anything to go by, Charlie Barnett should give Eddie Murphy a run for his money in the New Richard Pryor race – a Black Power Harpo, no less. GD

Dead, The

(John Huston, 1987, US/GB) Anjelica Huston, Donal McCann, Helena Carroll, Cathleen Delany, Ingrid Craigie, Rachel Dowling, Dan O'Herlihy, Donal Donnelly, Marie Kean.
83 min.
John Huston's last film is a small masterpiece on the order of Welles' *The Immortal Story*, perfectly achieved and unapologetic towards its literary antecedents. Joyce's novella is extraordinary for – among other virtues – the seamless flow from the mosaic approach to a dinner party into an anguished examination of the varieties of love, and the director delicately captures this musical movement. 'Is love worse living?' Joyce joked elsewhere, but at this stage allows the deceived husband (McCann) to make his peace with a shattered dream. His wife (Anjelica Huston) is moved by a song to remember a long-ago suitor who died for love – an impossible card for her decent, conventional husband to trump, and in turn leading him to reflect upon the transience of human lives. The closing shots of falling snow carry a complex emotional charge and a sort of resolution. The married couple get the lion's share of the drama and are wonderfully moving, while the rest of the cast – Donnelly, in particular, as Freddy the loveable drunk – are perfect. Tony Huston's script adds only the masterly stroke of the reading of a poem, and leaves the import of hope-achieved-at-a-cost intact. BC

Dead Again

(Kenneth Branagh, 1991, US) Kenneth Branagh, Andy Garcia, Emma Thompson, Derek Jacobi, Wayne Knight, Hanna Schygulla, Robin Williams, Campbell Scott, Richard Easton.
108 min.
Branagh's lame stab at a romantic psychological thriller makes no sense. Sloppily constructed and cut, riddled with clichés and cant, it tells the old tale of a tough, wisecrackin' LA private eye (Branagh) hired to discover the identity of a mute, amnesiac woman (inevitably Thompson). Her nightmares derive from a violent past, from which, it seems, only an eccentric hypnotist (Jacobi) can free her. The none-too-plausible and unexplained twist is that Em's flashbacks are to a previous life (1949) when she was a famous pianist and Ken was her famous composer hubby, who was executed for her murder. The leads are dreadful, and Garcia as a news-hack who fires the muso's jealousy, Schygulla as the muso's loyal German housekeeper, and Williams as the dick's defrocked shrink pal are all awfully misused. Could it be that nothing – not the over-bearingly 'Hitchcockian' score, nor the OTT art direction – must distract our attention from the subtext: that Ken and Em are destined to dance through eternity together? GA

Dead and Buried

(Gary A Sherman, 1981, US) James Farentino, Melody Anderson, Jack Albertson, Dennis Redfield, Nancy Locke Hauser, Lisa Blount.
95 min.
Establishing shots of a bleak, colourless Atlantic seaboard fishing town, and the presence of *Alien*

scriptwriter Dan O'Bannon on the credits, combine to make one expect a more adult-aimed variation on Carpenter's *The Fog*. Unfortunately a series of progressively grisly murders intervenes, suggesting a mere overtime-earner for the chaps at SFX; but after some irritating meanderings, the film picks up momentum and, via a splendidly staged confrontation in a Mabuse-style lab, progresses to a 'surprise' climax which, even if anticipated, must still rank a close second to the false ending of *Carrie*. Gruesome almost to a fault, but not quite, it emerges as an efficient shocker. GD

Dead Bang

(John Frankenheimer, 1989, US) Don Johnson, Penelope Ann Miller, William Forsythe, Bob Balaban, Frank Military, Tate Donovan.
102 min.
Based on the career of a real-life homicide cop, this is a vehicle for the still-pending big screen launch of Johnson, the casual fashion-plate from *Miami Vice*. To show his range, this time he looks like shit, with specs held together by tape, and Hoke Moseley-style personal problems. He vomits on a suspect, too, but don't think the camera doesn't love him, right down to the freeze-frame finish. Popeye Doyle he ain't. Having Johnson aboard entails a certain amount of tailored scenario that doesn't drive the story. The brief affair with cop's widow Miller is unconvincing, and the scene with the psychiatrist seems to be there to show the star getting the giggles. The plot begins with race murders, leads to a cross-country pursuit, and ends daftly with neo-Nazis in underground caverns. Routine stuff. BC

Dead Beat

(Adam Dubov, 1994, US) Bruce Ramsay, Natasha Wagner, Balthazar Getty, Meredith Salenger, Alex Cox, Deborah Harry.
93 min.
Produced by Christopher Lambert, this is a quirky US indie about a rock'n'roll rebel stuck in a Midwestern hole in the early '60s. He wears cowboy boots, make-up, and models himself on Elvis. He's a real ladykiller. Literally. Dubov's debut has plenty of zip, but it doesn't entirely come off, perhaps because it shows its hand too soon, perhaps because the hip amoral tone just doesn't gel with the bozo narrator young Balthazar Getty provides. Intriguing all the same, with cameos from Alex Cox and Deborah Harry, and a ticklish, narcissistic turn from Ramsay. TCh

Dead Calm

(Phillip Noyce, 1988, Aust) Nichole Kidman, Sam Neill, Billy Zane, Rod Mulliner, Joshua Tilden, George Shevtsov, Michael Long.
96 min.
Recuperating from a family tragedy, a seasoned seaman (Neill) and his young wife (Kidman) sail their yacht, the Saracen, off the coast of Australia. Spotting a stricken boat, the Orpheus, they are amazed when a terrified young man (Zane) rows towards them, climbs aboard, and tells a horrifying story about an attack of food poisoning which he alone survived. But when Neill rows to the Orpheus to investigate, he is astonished to see his yacht, complete with wife and dog, sail off in the opposite direction with Zane at the wheel. Aboard the sinking Orpheus, Neill finds evidence of the marine hitchiker's lunacy; meanwhile, on the Saracen, Kidman is learning the hard way. A classic piece of pared-down genre film-making is lent extra depth by an emotional subtext stressing Kidman's transition from dependent wife to resourceful individual. Director Noyce's bravura camerawork conspires with Terry Hayes' spare script (adapted from the novel by Charles Williams) and some edgy cutting to exploit every ounce of tension, right down to a killer ending. NF

Dead Can't Lie, The

(Lloyd Fonvielle, 1988, US) Tommy Lee Jones, Virginia Madsen, Colin Bruce, Kevin Jarre, Denise Stephenson, Frederic Forrest, Michael Chapman.
98 min.
Eddie Mallard (Jones) is a piss-poor PI hired by Charlie, a very rich man, to find his wife Rachel (Madsen), whom he buried 10 years ago. She asked to be entombed naked except for her priceless jewels, and her husband obliged, but later had second thoughts, dug her up, and retrieved the rocks. Now she has returned to the land of the living to get them back. Soon Rachel and Eddie

are power-showering away, Eddie convinced that Rachel is real, which she ain't. She's a succubus using him for her own evil ends, which entails quite a bit of nudity: Mr Jones is too old for this kind of thing. There's one good joke, albeit an old and sexist one. It might have been possible to view this catalogue of clichés as a tongue-in-cheek tribute to cornball cinema if irony hadn't been wholly absent. Mallard's movie is just a dead duck. MS

Dead Cert.

(Tony Richardson, 1974, GB) Scott Antony, Judi Dench, Michael Williams, Nina Thomas, Mark Dignam, Julian Glover.
99 min.
A film about racing from Richardson, who made *The Charge of the Light Brigade* so he must know all about horses. An amateur jockey (well, none of them professionals can speak proper) tries to discover who is nobbling the favourite for the National (well, they do say that racing attracts the worst of every class). Seems he's having an affair with the wife of a racehorse owner and getting a bit on the side with a masseuse. But it's OK. They both help him to go and win the Grand National. Despite a few concessions to our times, and a potentially promising subject, the film manages nothing in the way of suspense, insight or entertainment. There ought to be a steward's enquiry. CPe

Dead End

(William Wyler, 1937, US) Sylvia Sidney, Joel McCrea, Humphrey Bogart, Wendy Barrie, Claire Trevor, Marjorie Main, Allen Jenkins, the Dead End Kids.
93 min. b/w.
A muscle-bound Goldwyn production with an inflated reputation, interesting now chiefly in that, transposed virtually intact from the stage, it lets you see what the original Broadway production of Sidney Kingsley's play must have been like; particularly fascinating is the composite set which makes a metaphor of the rich man's terraces overhanging the slums. The social thesis (deprived backgrounds may make criminals, but they can make good guys and padres too) is familiar from countless problem pictures of the period, and the Dead End Kids are about as menacingly streetwise as Shirley Temple in her naughtier moods. Cruising along like a well-oiled machine tended by an excellent cast, it remains highly watchable, even if the basic mawkishness – in evidence everywhere from the rhyming of Sidney's dewy-eyed good girl with Trevor's ravaged bad one, down to the fact that Bogart's gangster is risking his neck to see mom one more time (she slaps him and sends him packing, true, but that just adds to the pity of it all) – keeps sticking in the craw. TM

Deadfall

(Bryan Forbes, 1968, GB) Michael Caine, Giovanna Ralli, Eric Portman, Nanette Newman, David Buck, Carlos Pierre, Leonard Rossiter, Vladek Sheybal.
120 min.
Question: When is a thriller not a thriller? Answer: When it's a Forbes. A jewel thief (Caine) falls in love with the wife (Ralli) of his homosexual accomplice (Portman). She has been mentally scarred by her father's membership of the Gestapo, and her husband, a former French resistance fighter, is buggering a gigolo. And then, bugger *moi*, it transpires that the wife is also her husband's daughter, and they all commit suicide happily ever after. Replete with a Shirley Bassey theme tune and a 20-minute John Barry guitar concerto to accompany the robbery, this isn't a Freudian *Rififi*. It's rubbish. ATu

Dead Funny

(John Feldman, 1994, US) Elizabeth Peña, Andrew McCarthy, Paige Turco.
118 min.
It's hard to fathom what Feldman intended with this smug, excessively 'smart' tale, related largely in flashback, of the rise and fall of a passionate but shallow New York love affair between Peña and the resistible McCarthy. She returns home from work one day to find him in the kitchen stabbed with a samurai sword. (They are practical jokers.) How did it happen? Who did it? Who cares? Probably not Feldman who seems more interested in shooting his actresses' naked thighs. GA

Dead Heart

(Nick Parsons, 1996, Aust) Bryan Brown, Angie Milliken, Ernie Dingo, Aaron Pedersen.
105 min.
When a young Aborigine is found dead in a police cell, the local cop (Brown, who also produced) finds that his rule-bending ways of keeping the peace in a remote Aboriginal settlement are no longer sufficient to prevent racial conflict and violence. Not without appeal as a culture-clash thriller, this suffers from an occasional lack of narrative clarity, perhaps inevitably given the magical beliefs held by the older Aborigines whose notions of justice fuel the plot. That said, there are nice touches here (notably some scenes featuring white liberal documentarists), and strong performances from Brown and Milliken. GA

Deadline at Dawn

(Harold Clurman, 1946, US) Susan Hayward, Bill Williams, Paul Lukas, Joseph Calleia, Osa Massen, Lola Lane, Jerome Cowan, Marvin Miller, Roman Bohnen, Steve Geray.
83 min. b/w.
'Golly, the misery that walks around in this pretty, quiet night!' murmurs Hayward's vibrant dance-hall dame, chasing round Manhattan trying to get her sailor pal off a murder rap. Golly, indeed, for the script by playwright Clifford Odets never lets up for a moment. Terse and flowery by turns, it elaborates the plot of Cornell Woolrich's novel almost to the point of incomprehension, yet movingly enhances the notion of New York as a fatal presence, teeming with the homeless and unhappy. Clurman, moonlighting in Hollywood after the collapse of his Group Theatre in New York, later dismissed it as just 'a run-of-the-mill RKO movie', but take no notice: it's made with cockeyed artistry from beginning to end, and shouldn't be missed. GB

Deadline – USA
(aka Deadline)

(Richard Brooks, 1952, US) Humphrey Bogart, Ethel Barrymore, Kim Hunter, Martin Gabel, Ed Begley, Paul Stewart, Jim Backus.
87 min. b/w.
Former newspaperman Brooks made a good fist of this media drama. He has Bogey in his favour as the crusading editor of a New York daily, battling to expose crime kingpin Gabel, while at the same time persuading owner Barrymore from selling the whole operation. Tautly scripted and put over with a feeling for authenticity (it was shot in the offices of the *New York Daily News*), it's one of those films where Brooks' liberal sympathies and no-nonsense storytelling is squarely on target. TJ

Dead Liqueur

(Georges Karypides, 1992, Greece) Yiannis Karabellas, Costas Karabellas, Vaso Youlielmaki, Spyros Fokas.
91 min.
A remembrance of a '50s bourgeois childhood in a major Greek city, with something of the 'forbidden games' mystery tale about it, Karypides' film follows the life of two younger boys (one the narrator) who undergo a secret double marriage rite to their adolescent sister in the memory-laden cellar of their house. The basement is a place of mysteries – including a strange story that their father may have murdered a girl in a vat in the liqueur still – that need to be exorcised. Much of the tale is obscure, full of intimations of a class and society struggling to survive past its time, and doing so in the absence of a strong male presence. The pace is slow, and the film is shot with a restrained cinematic style. Odd, moody but intriguing. WH

Deadly

(Esben Storm, 1991, Aust) Jerome Ehlers, Frank Gallagher, John Moore.
101 min.
This competent, moderately nail-biting feature belongs to that uneasy genre, the investigative thriller with a political point to make. As often happens, the point (here, the brutal treatment meted out to Australia's aboriginal community) is driven home with hammerhead subtlety and at the same time obscured by hard-guy shenanigans. Ehlers is a Sydney cop sent to the outback to investigate the apparent suicide of an Aboriginal in police custody. Predictably, he's required to rubber-stamp a

cover-up, but his maverick tendencies get the better of the situation... Director-writer Storm is good at setting the scene, and the sense of the outback town as a bastion of apartheid and entrenched hatred is the film's strongest point. But the jaw-clenched heroics are pedestrian and the mystery too transparent to hold interest. JRo

Deadly Advice

(Mandie Fletcher, 1993, GB) Jane Horrocks, Brenda Fricker, Imelda Staunton, Jonathan Pryce, Edward Woodward, Ian Abbey, Billie Whitelaw, Hywel Bennett, John Mills, Eleanor Bron.
91 min.
Set in Hay-on-Wye, infamous locally as the home of 1920s poisoner Major Herbert Armstrong, this competent, intermittently funny film casts Horrocks as Jodie, a mother-dominated shrew for whom life is anything but sweet. While her sister Beth (Staunton) is out and about with male stripper Bunny (Abbey), Jodie is stuck at home with her lazy, oppressive mother (Fricker). Inspired by a book about Armstrong's exploits, Jodie decides to bump her off, receiving unexpected help when the Major (Woodward) slides into reality from the pages of the book. Soon Jodie's bedroom is crammed with veteran British character actors playing real-life killers with conflicting advice on how best to dispose of the troublesome mother. Horrocks easily holds her own in this distinguished company, while Fricker is far more terrifying than any of the genteel killers. Mandie Fletcher's handling of Glenn Chandler's script is, however, sketchy and hurried, a legacy perhaps of her background in formula TV (*Blackadder*, *Only Fools and Horses*). NKe

Deadly Affair, The

(Sidney Lumet, 1966, GB) James Mason, Simone Signoret, Maximilian Schell, Harriet Andersson, Harry Andrews, Kenneth Haigh, Roy Kinnear, Max Adrian, Lynn Redgrave.
107 min.
The usual John Le Carré net of intrigue, betrayal and death (based on his *Call for the Dead*) as Mason's Foreign Office security inspector investigates a colleague's suicide and finds himself under threat from an espionage ring. Lumet handles the atmosphere and performances with solid professionalism, and manages to tease out emotional strands from the knotty plotting; but there's no denying it's all been done before and since, even if rarely so efficiently. GA

Deadly Blessing

(Wes Craven, 1981, US) Maren Jensen, Susan Buckner, Sharon Stone, Jeff East, Lisa Hartman, Lois Nettleton, Ernest Borgnine.
102 min.
An excellent example of a mundane project elevated into quite a palatable genre movie by its director. Craven (who previously made *The Hills Have Eyes*) faced a script with one laborious idea in which a woman is terrorised by a rural religious sect. Realising the limitations, Craven has to keep audience interest alive with some desperate but occasionally inspired strategies: several unpredictable plot twists have been added, as well as an atmospheric sub-theme involving the heroine's nightmares. The shock sequences are punchy and varied, including one disturbingly Freudian horror of a snake in a bathtub, while the visual style is a deliberate attempt to make Texas look as lonely and lost as an Andrew Wyeth painting. Best of all, the impudent ending seeks to imply that all the sect's demonic imaginings are literally true. *Deadly Blessing* isn't a very good movie, but it holds out distinct promise that Craven will soon be in the front rank of horror film-makers. DP

Deadly Companions, The

(Sam Peckinpah, 1961, US) Brian Keith, Maureen O'Sullivan, Chill Wills, Steve Cochran, Strother Martin.
90 min.
Peckinpah's first film, a not altogether characteristic but nevertheless quirky Western which sees Keith's ex-army sergeant making amends for killing a boy by ferrying his corpse and his mother on a funeral procession through Apache territory. Routine in places, but enlivened by the sardonic characterisation (reminiscent in some ways of Faulkner's superficially similar *As I Lay Dying*) and by odd moments of visual bravura. GA

Deadly Eyes

see Rats, The

Deadly Females, The

(Donovan Winter, 1976, GB) Tracy Reed, Bernard Holley, Scott Fredericks, Heather Chasen, Brian Jackson.
105 min.
'Tart I may be, thanks to you, but cheap I am not!' someone bawls at her boorish hubby before summoning one of Tracy Reed's gang of Kensington hit-women to dispose of him. Writer/producer/director/editor Winter strives to make exactly the same distinction in this sex-and-crime potboiler with classy notions ('you' in his case would be the impecunious, short-sighted British film industry). The film's nasty goings-on are supposedly a comment on the 'Savage Seventies'; but it takes more than close-ups of newspaper headlines screaming about IRA attacks and Bunny Girl murders to establish a fruitful connection, and the film's inept pretensions make it even more pernicious than your straightforward sexploiter. Reed's Godmother figure is cool enough to win the respect of any praying mantis, but the only glimmer of style Winter shows is to shoot one set-up through the back of a wicker chair. GB

Deadly Friend

(Wes Craven, 1986, US) Matthew Laborteaux, Kristy Swanson, Michael Sharrett, Anne Twomey, Anne Ramsey, Richard Marcus.
90 min.
Teenage boffin Paul has developed a robot, BB, that can think for itself but it still has a silly voice. It suddenly starts seeing red, but no matter – Elvira, a paranoid neighbour, blows it away. Samantha, though, is a nice neighbour, and Paul is off his rocker when her kooky father kills her. But love will find a way: Paul implants BB's brain into Samantha's. She jerks into action. She is set on revenge...Although the prevailing tone is comic, there is plenty of grue and gore; the heart stops several times. This may be Craven at his crummiest, but the resulting sick still ranks higher than anything his imitators can come up with. MS

Deadly Maria

see Tödliche Maria, Die

Deadly Pursuit

see Shoot to Kill

Deadly Run
(Mortelle Randonnée)

(Claude Miller, 1982, Fr) Michel Serrault, Isabelle Adjani, Guy Marchand, Stéphane Audran, Macha Méril, Genevieve Page, Sami Frey.
120 min.
Miller in Chabrol territory with an intriguing thriller, based on Marc Behm's novel *The Eye of the Beholder*, in which Serrault's somewhat eccentric private eye is given a case following a young runaway couple. When the woman (Adjani) murders the man, Serrault simply follows her through a series of further killings, suspecting (or wishing) she might be his long-lost daughter. A colourful if not altogether successful study in obsession and guilt transference, it features excellent performances all round (Serrault is magnificent, as always) and a surprisingly appropriate score by Carla Bley. GA

Deadly Strangers

(Sidney Hayers, 1974, GB) Hayley Mills, Simon Ward, Sterling Hayden, Ken Hutchison, Peter Jeffrey.
93 min.
Old-fashioned psychopathic goings-on in the West Country. Ward, a travelling salesman, shoe fetishist and voyeur, gives a lift to nice Hayley Mills while we're left to guess which one's the nutter escaped from the local funny farm. The script disastrously lumbers itself with this cumbersome suspense mechanism at the expense of developing more profitable themes, and the camerawork stresses the obvious with its movements. Sole redeeming feature is Hayley Mills, who suggests an actress capable of much better things than she has been offered recently. Hayers, to his credit, does exploit her best quality – an insolent, slightly offhand sex appeal. CPe

Deadly Trackers, The

(Barry Shear, 1973, US) Richard Harris, Rod Taylor, Al Lettieri, Neville Brand, William Smith, Paul Benjamin, Pedro Armendariz Jr.
110 min.
Primarily a vehicle for Richard man-called-horse-lost-in-the-wilderness Harris. It's a formula pursuit Western, Harris starting out as reason-loving, gun-hating sheriff, ending up seeking revenge for his wife and son killed in a bank hold-up. Once south of the border, the excuses are all set for what the film's really about: a comedy of cruelty for us, seemingly a masochistic indulgence for Harris. He's beaten by a mob, almost lynched, and temporarily blinded before he exacts his revenge. The perfunctory questioning of the morality of revenge lacks any real conviction; Taylor as the villainous bandit leads an uninspired wild bunch; and the film never more than plods along under the weight of Harris' long-suffering performance. RM

Deadly Trap, The
(La Maison sous les Arbres)

(René Clément, 1971, Fr/It) Faye Dunaway, Frank Langella, Barbara Parkins, Michèle Lourié, Patrick Vincent, Karen Blanguernon, Maurice Ronet.
100 min.
A leisurely but cunningly paced story which starts off looking like a *Woman's Own* romance, and by the time it's finished has somehow involved you in domestic drama, murder, kidnapping and espionage intrigue. The ending has an impact similar to the punchline of a shaggy dog story, but the lead-up is always interesting thanks to Clément's nice Hitchcockian-flavoured style and deft use of menacingly 'ordinary' locations. VG

Deadly Weapons

(Doris Wishman, 1974, US) Zsa Zsa, Harry Reems, Greg Reynolds, Saul Meth.
73 min.
Wishman directs a lady boasting a 73-inch bust, and variously known as Zsa Zsa or Chesty Morgan, in a bizarre softcore sex movie in which she ultimately takes to suffocating mobsters between her mammaries. The whole thing is put together with such amateurishness that it almost seems as though the director is consciously rebelling against every convention of narrative cinema: close-ups of carpets, tracking shots of the sky, technicians weaving in and out of vision. But (just in case you're wondering) it hasn't enough unintentional humour or erotic content to make a visit worthwhile.

Dead Man

(Jim Jarmusch, 1995, US/Ger) Johnny Depp, Gary Farmer, Robert Mitchum, Lance Henriksen, Gabriel Byrne, John Hurt, Alfred Molina, Crispin Glover.
120 min. b/w.
A bizarre, funny, almost mystical take on the Western, Jarmusch's film charts the sentimental education of a clerk, William Blake (Depp), when he travels out West and finds himself, after an unexpected violent incident, pursued by vicious bounty hunters and taken up by a decidedly eccentric Indian (Farmer) who believes his new friend is the English visionary poet. Looser in structure than the director's earlier work, but pervaded with the same deadpan humour and superb imagery (cameraman,Robby Müller), this is an original and very weird account of the American wilderness. Haunting electric guitar score by Neil YoungGA

Deadman, The

(Peggy Ahwesh/Keith Sanborn, 1989, US) Jennifer Montgomery, Ramon Quanta la Gusta, Dianne Torr.
40 min. b/w.
A woman leaves her dead lover and staggers through torrential rain to a dingy bar where she fucks, sucks and pisses on the assembled staff and clientèle. Based on a story by Georges Bataille, high-priest of Erotico-Necro Theory, *The Deadman* is a joyless exercise in the transgressive imagination that gets its kicks defiling the mouldering body of silent cinema. Shot through monochrome drizzle with an exaggeratedly raw soundtrack that makes every cough a thunderous eruption, every urinary trickle a sonic deluge, the story is framed as a fragment from some apocryphal silent era, the libertine visuals intercut with funereally solemn, wryly redundant intertitles. As a dour exercise in 'anti-porn', liberating excess from the titillating rhetoric of 'erotic' cinema, you can see where it's aiming, but it never really engages the viewer in any interrogation of the viewing process, largely because it's dull. JRo

Dead Man Walking

(Tim Robbins, 1995, US) Sean Penn, Susan Sarandon, Robert Prosky, Scott Wilson, R Lee Ermey, Raymond J Barry, Celia Weston, Lois Smith, Roberta Maxwell, Margo Martindale.
122 min.
Sister Helen Prejean (Sarandon) is a nun who works with the mainly black poor. When she first visits the Louisiana State Penitentiary, however, she's unprepared for the ethical, emotional and spiritual turmoil which follows. Inmate Matthew Poncelet has requested her help in his appeal against execution. With politicians and radio fundamentalists advocating tougher measures, the chances of a stay of execution are slim for an unrepentant white-trash racist who insists he only watched, rather than participated in, the rape and murder of a teenage couple. If his appeal fails, will Helen have the strength not merely to continue as his spiritual adviser, but to guide her arrogant, hate-filled charge towards some sort of redemption? Though it finally takes a firm stand against institutionalised murder, director Robbins' tough, balanced script (from an autobiographical book) never succumbs to special pleading. Poncelet is a very nasty piece of work (superbly played by Penn with bouffant hair and goatee), while the vengeful grief of the victims' families is depicted with sympathy and respect. Though the message is underlined by the questions raised (whose pain, exactly, is the 'humane' method of lethal injection finally intended to diminish?), this brave, intelligent and very moving film is no dry thesis – thanks principally to the vivid excellence of the performances. GA

Dead Men Don't Die

(Malcolm Marmorstein, 1991, US) Elliott Gould, Melissa Anderson, Mark Moses, Mabel King, Jack Betts, Philip Bruns.
91 min.
A TV newsman who stumbles on a major scoop is wiped out by the Mob, resurrected by a voodoo priestess and, in zombified state, sets out to track down his killers. Not good. TJ

Dead Men Don't Wear Plaid

(Carl Reiner, 1981, US) Steve Martin, Rachel Ward, Carl Reiner, Reni Santoni, George Gaynes.
88 min. b/w.
Not the first movie to be built around cameo performances, but these are somewhat less novel. Forties stars (Bergman, Bogart, Cagney, etc.) are exhumed from the Hollywood vaults to live again in a new mystery comedy whose convolutions stem not least from forcing various clips from old thrillers to look as though they belong together. Some amusement is derived from watching a film that so obviously had to be worked out backwards. The bits in between feature likeable Martin as a bone but clumsy detective – with all the good lines, which is no bad thing because he's the best part of this fairly amusing, clever exercise in editing. CPe

Dead of Night

(Robert Hamer/Basil Dearden/Charles Crichton/Alberto Cavalcanti, 1945, GB) Mervyn Johns, Michael Redgrave, Frederick Valk, Googie Withers,, Sally Ann Howes, Basil Radford, Naunton Wayne, Roland Culver.
102 min. b/w.
Still spooky after all these years, this superb Ealing chiller is still the most effective example of the portmanteau style: five separate ghost stories embedded in a framework of a country house party, where an architect is experiencing sinister sensations of *déjà vu*. The ghost stories are related in turn by the other guests, and events gradually move into total nightmare territory. The best episode is Hamer's 'Haunted Mirror', run a close second by Redgrave's definitive ventriloquist turn in 'The Ventriloquist's Dummy', directed by Cavalcanti. See it with a friend. AB

Dead of Night (aka Deathdream)

(Bob Clark, 1972, Can) John Marley, Lynn Carlin, Henderson Forsythe, Richard Backus, Anya Ormsby.
90 min.
Modest and reasonably intriguing horror film. Andy (Backus) is reported killed in action, but returns from the grave to seek retribution from the family and small-town society that drove him to enlist in the first place. The film's novelty lies in its observation of Andy's home life; notably the tensions between Mom (impressively played by Carlin) and Dad which degenerate from minor squalls to major sores. Andy emerges as the hapless problem child forced into a vampiric blood habit through the sins of his parents. The film plunges in the final chase sequence, however, where Clark's artless direction strains against almost comic strip events. IB

Dead of Winter

(Arthur Penn, 1987, US) Mary Steenburgen, Roddy McDowall, Jan Rubes, William Russ, Ken Pogue, Wayne Robson.
100 min.
Struggling actress Katie (Steenburgen) auditions for a part that entails travelling upstate to a rambling country house inhabited by crippled Dr Lewis (Rubes) and his amanuensis (McDowall). She should, however, be less concerned about her acting prospects than about the missing actress she is to replace, Julie Rose. Were she a thriller fan, she'd realise that her life is in danger; after all, she's the pawn in a game reminiscent of Joseph H Lewis' *My Name Is Julia Ross*. While beautifully shot, admirably old-fashioned (sexual violence and explicit gore are absent), and endowed with pleasing plot twists, the film is too formulaic and offers little opportunity for Penn to display his prodigious talents. GA

Dead Pigeon on Beethovenstrasse (Kressin und die tote Taube in der Beethovenstrasse)

(Samuel Fuller, 1972, WGer) Glenn Corbett, Christa Lang, Anton Diffring, Eric P Caspar, Sieghart Rupp, Anthony Chin, Alex D'Arcy.
103 min.
Those misguided individuals who didn't like *White Dog* had better stay clear of this, Fuller's most bizarre film. Made for German TV, it's a complex crime thriller about an American agent visiting Bonn to find the killer of his partner, and getting involved in a treacherous world of blackmail, drugs, nude photography and murder. In conventional terms it's ruined by wooden acting (notably Fuller's wife Lang as femme fatale) and a wayward plot. But its great attraction lies not only in the typically vigorous direction (pacy action scenes accompanied by the music of Can), but in the madcap humour which turns the entire film into a parody of thuggish thrillers. Add to that the wicked movie references (*Alphaville* is presented as a skinflick, *Rio Bravo* is shown with a German Dean Martin ordering schnapps), and the startling, even surreal use of locations, not to mention a weird credits sequence, and you have what is virtually a professional home movie that delights by its sheer sense of fun and absurdity. GA

Dead Poets Society

(Peter Weir, 1989, US) Robin Williams, Robert Sean Leonard, Ethan Hawke, Josh Charles, Gale Hansen, Dylan Kussman, Allelon Ruggiero, James Waterston, Norman Lloyd, Kurtwood Smith, Alexandra Powers.
129 min.
With Tom Schulman's script scrutinising educational conformity, the casting of Robin Williams as English teacher John Keating is inspired. Keating's eccentric teaching methods, exhorting his students with cries of 'Carpe Diem', promote spontaneity and idealism. But in the prestigious Welton Academy circa 1959, these male offspring are put on the same career path as their fathers, and face stern opposition from the educational establishment when they choose to indulge their imaginations. Keating's gospel breeds hope for some, frustration and despair for others. To a large degree, Schulman avoids cliché by focusing almost exclusively on entrenched paternal prejudice against artistic pursuits. Weir infuses the film with his customary mysticism, but more impor-

tantly, draws sensitive performances from his largely inexperienced cast (Leonard is particularly impressive). Williams does wonders with a role that tends to be reduced to one of catalyst. CM

Dead Pool, The

(Buddy Van Horn, 1988, US) Clint Eastwood, Patricia Clarkson, Liam Neeson, Evan C Kim, David Hunt, Michael Currie, Michael Goodwin.
91 min.
Dirty Harry part five ain't much cop. True, the morgues and breakers' yards are filled to brimming, but the sight of Lt Callahan (Eastwood) and new partner Lt Quan (Kim) trying to look scared as they are chased through San Francisco by a 6-inch remote-controlled model car quickly un-suspends disbelief. Down in Chinatown there are murderous thugs flying through windows into his lap; worse, now that he's hit the headlines and has go-getter newscaster Samantha Walker (Clarkson) on his back, Harry fears he may become a victim in a series of psychopathic murders of local celebrities. So many ethical debates later, a prolonged burst of Uzi machine-gun fire forces Walker into his arms and his way of thinking; and the anonymously sent hit-list – the eponymous dead pool – is traced to sicko horror film director Peter Swan (Neeson). Eastwood still manages to run about almost energetically, and there are occasional flashes of the old laconic wit; but the direction is woefully loose, and can't marry the parody with the thrills. WH

Dead Presidents

(Allen Hughes/Albert Hughes, 1995, US) Larenz Tate, Rose Jackson, Freddy Rodriguez, Chris Tucker, N'Brushe Wright, Bookeem Woodbine.
121 min.
The twins' follow-up to *Menace II Society* is essentially a classic gangster movie (*The Roaring Twenties*, say) revamped and remoulded for a new context: black experience in the late '60s and early '70s. The war this time is Vietnam, but Anthony Curtis (Tate) comes back to face the age-old problems: unemployment and a woman he hasn't seen for too long. There are intriguing aspects to this yarn, and the brothers can choreograph a scene, but you get the impression that they learned all they know from other movies, the blood and guts is gratuitous, and the episodic narrative takes an awful long time to get nowhere very rewarding. Great heist sequence though. TCh

Dead Reckoning

(John Cromwell, 1947, US) Humphrey Bogart, Lizabeth Scott, Morris Carnovsky, Charles Cane, William Prince, Marvin Miller, Wallace Ford.
100 min. b/w.
Faced with the synthetic Scott instead of genuine Bacall, Bogart reacts with a hint of self-parody. Or maybe it's just that the film, cast in flashback form with a guilt-ridden narration by Bogart, tries too hard to maintain its note of doomed *noir* romance. Excellent hardboiled shenanigans as Bogart's ex-paratrooper sets out with a 'Geronimo!' on his lips to investigate the disappearance of his buddy, uncovering a web of duplicities at the centre of which is the alluringly equivocal Scott. But the relationship never quite convinces, leading to a faintly embarrassing emotional climax as death conjures one last 'Geronimo!' Highly enjoyable all the same. TM

Dead Ringers

(David Cronenberg, 1988, Can) Jeremy Irons, Genevieve Bujold, Heidi von Palleske, Jonathan Haley, Nicholas Haley.
115 min.
Cronenberg's emotionally devastating study of the perverse relationship between identical twin gynaecologists, Beverly and Elliot Mantle, is an intense psychological drama which confronts his familiar preoccupations – fear of physical and mental disintegration, mortality, the power struggle between the sexes – without the paradoxical protection of visceral disgust. Instead, the abstract, expressionist imagery synthesises the physical and the mental. Courtesy of clever, unobtrusive trick camerawork, Irons gives a superlative performance as both twins. The delicate symbiotic balance between the brothers is suddenly upset by the eruption into their lives of hedonistic actress Claire (Bujold). As always, they share everything, including Claire, until Beverly

realises that he has at last found something he does not want to share, and he is plunged into a whirlpool of emotional confusion; when Elliot tries to help, he too is sucked into the vortex of pain and despair. Likewise, Cronenberg pulls us deeper and deeper into his harrowing tale of separation and loss, the disturbing, cathartic power of which leaves one drained but exhilarated. NF

Dead Zone, The

(David Cronenberg, 1983, US) Christopher Walken, Brooke Adams, Tom Skerritt, Herbert Lom, Anthony Zerbe, Colleen Dewhurst, Martin Sheen.
103 min.
This numbs those nerve-ends all the other films failed to reach, but can't quite flesh out the original skeletal story (one of Stephen King's least memorable), despite Walken's haunted performance as a schoolteacher who crashes into a milk-truck and, five years later, wakes from a coma to find himself cursed with second sight. Cronenberg indulges his fondness for nightmares in a damaged brain, but forgoes his usual flesh-flinging in favour of some subtler flesh-tingling. The visceral shockerama of *Videodrome* has given way to a brooding atmosphere of bleak unease in snow-covered landscapes. Apart from some brief bleeaggh with a pair of scissors, there's nothing here to send you home retching. AB

Deaf and Mute Heroine, The (Longya Jian)

(Wu Ma, 1971, HK) Helen Ma, Tang Dic, Shirley Wong, Tang Ching, Lee Ying.
102 min.
A superbly rendered fantasy, dominated by brilliantly handled tussles of sheer wit and ingenuity (rather than muscle power) as the heroine of the title disorientates and confounds assailant after assailant. Wu Ma sustains his idealised world with almost as many visual sleights-of-hand as his heroine, having his camera actively recoil from the entrance of a giant knight (whose face remains unseen for a whole sequence, and who has attained the state of weightlessness) to perch somewhere near the ceiling, or filling the screen with a diffuse flood of red which, for a moment, the eye is unable to interpret: is it a pool of blood or merely a floating scarf? The climactic conflict, too, is fought out in a genuinely dreamlike atmosphere. VG

Deaf Smith & Johnny Ears (Los Amigos)

(Paolo Cavara, 1972, It) Anthony Quinn, Franco Nero, Pamela Tiffin, Ira Furstenberg, Franco Graziosi.
92 min.
An unmemorable Italian Western spoilt by an over-complicated, over 'historical' plot (about the Republic of Texas in 1834 and its entry into the Union); not to mention some some very unfunny business between Quinn, in his nature man guise as a deaf mute, and Nero as his would-be engaging 'ears'.

Dealers

(Colin Bucksey, 1989, GB) Paul McGann, Rebecca De Mornay, Derrick O'Connor, John Castle, Paul Guilfoyle, Rosalind Bennett, Adrian Dunbar, Nicholas Hewetson, Sara Sugarman.
91 min.
This strangely dated City drama is set, they suggest, in the near future, even though it notches up all those mid-'80s obsessions: need, greed, gratification. Daniel Pascoe (McGann), bad boy of the dealer room, takes insane risks but does nicely, ta very much: lord of the manor lifestyle, seaplane, portable phone, vintage sportscar. We get a glimpse of other values as a sexy girlfriend (Bennett) gives him the shove for being money-driven, though she's soon shown to be as pretentious and self-indulgent as every other character. The top trader has offed himself, and the job's been given to stuck-up, by-the-book Anna (De Mornay, surprisingly convincing). Anna just ain't got that flair, so bad boy and good girl have to cooperate to win back the lost millions. You know the scenario: it's loathe at first sight, but soon they're allies, and she hangs back admiringly while he pulls off the big one. The climax comes in the dealer room as the cast all stare mesmerised at flashing green numbers. The most likeable performance is O'Connor's

Robby Barrell, a dire warning of what happens when you stay in the mythic City over the age of 35: coke-snuffing, booze-sloshing, graven with lines, emotionally undisciplined. Poetic, really. SFe

Dealers Among Dealers

(Gaylen Ross, 1995, US)
77 min.
An engrossing fly-on-the-wall study of New York's Jewish jewellery trade. As Orthodox cutters sing Yiddish songs, and their bosses buy and sell stones for millions, we become privy to a profoundly conservative society devoted equally to craftsmanship and capitalism, and determined to perpetuate social and economic transactions built on notions of honour, hierarchy and tradition endlessly passed from father to son. Throughout the film runs a keen sense of history – whether of the pogroms, when owning a diamond could make the difference between life and death, or of the early '90s recession, when hitherto successful dealers might be reduced to working as chauffeurs. GA

Dear America: Letters Home from Vietnam

(Bill Couturie, 1987, US) David Brinkley, Fred DeBrine, Edwin Newman, Fred McGee, Jack Perkins, Howard Tuckner, Sander Vanocur.
87 min.
This beautifully crafted documentary brings home the tragedy of the Vietnam war in ways well out of the reach of feature films. Nothing is re-enacted, and the interweaving of newsreel and amateur footage puts you right there next to the bloody stumps and the booby-traps in the elephant grass. The letters home – read by Robert De Niro, Martin Sheen, Sean Penn, Tom Berenger, Robin Williams among others – range from family ordinary to the staring horror of Joseph Conrad's Kurtz. Tears and fear are a constant refrain. An intensely moving and disturbing experience. BC

Dear Boys
(Lieve Jongens)

(Paul de Lussanet, 1980, Neth) Hugo Metsers, Hans Dagelet, Bill van Dijk, Albert Mol.
88 min.
Writer Wolf lures Tiger and Beaver to his country home, ditching Beaver's wrinkled old sugar daddy so that the Pinteresque games can start. Wolf's only currency in the bargain is the fantasies he weaves for Beaver: sweet boys, fast cars, romance. His own fantasy, it seems, is of marrying both boys in church, but he's faced with the same problem as the banished old lover – no one loves an ageing queen. The trio, with the axe-wielding ex- in tow, pass through a series of bizarre tableaux, erotic, humorous, surreal, pathetic, occasionally firing off intellectual squibs. But ultimately Dear Boys hovers unsatisfactorily between contrived wank literature and the inspired narrative conceits of Roeg, Resnais et al. A gay Providence it is not. JG

Dear Diary
(Caro Diario)

(Nanni Moretti, 1994, It/Fr) Nanni Moretti, Renato Carpentieri, Antonio Neiwiller, Jennifer Beals.
100 min.
Moretti's three-part movie-essay is structured as a wry, affectionate and very funny odyssey through the Roman suburbs, the Aeolian Isles, and the Italian health system. Relaxed and leisurely, it's an effortless blend of documentary and fiction, part road movie, part sociological satire, part polemical reminiscence. As Moretti travels around, investigating and commenting, he manages to provoke not only laughter, but the sense that we are seeing Italy anew. Accordingly, just as he includes offbeat gags about, say, movie critics being fed a taste of their own medicine, so when he drives to the site of Pasolini's murder, he forces us simply to look and listen, to take in light, space, shape, movement and music; in other words, to recognise the essence of cinema shorn of story and superfluous stylistic tropes. That's no mean achievement in these days of narrative and technological overkill, though the movie is too modest to insist even on its own quirkiness, let alone its more serious subtextual concerns. GA

Dearest Love

see Souffle au Coeur, Le

Dear Inspector
(Tendre Poulet)

(Philippe de Broca, 1977, Fr) Annie Girardot, Philippe Noiret, Catherine Alric, Hubert Deschamps, Paulette Dubost, Roger Dumas.
105 min.
De Broca hit gold regularly with entertainments like That Man from Rio and King of Hearts, but for the witty panache of the former and the cultish whimsy of the latter Dear Inspector substitutes a tired, slapdash soufflé of middle-aged romance and comedy-thriller. Ex-Sorbonne classmates, bearded Greek professor Noiret and female cop Girardot meet cute. She keeps quiet about her job, until the strains of hunting the murderer of a lengthening list of Deputies prove too much. They part, she resigns, turns to spring-cleaning. They reunite in scenic Honfleur; she solves the case, he gets involved; they limp off towards bliss. Routine froth. PT

Dear Mother, I'm All Right
(Liebe Mutter, mir geht es gut)

(Christian Ziewer, 1972, WGer) Claus Eberth, Nikolaus Dutsch, Heinz Herrmann, Ernest Lenart, Kurt Michler.
87 min.
If Tout va Bien was a movie about industrial relations for a middle class audience, then this is the equivalent movie for workers themselves. Shot with guileless simplicity, it analyses the situation of workers at a West Berlin factory where cutbacks are proposed; a strike is called, but it proves difficult to maintain solidarity. It's seen mainly from the point of view of one 'average' employee, but there are also glimpses of management machinations. The links between general economic policies and such facts of life as workers' problems with accommodation are made absolutely explicit. The approach has the immediacy of a good comic strip, naive in the best, non-patronising sense. It looks exemplary. TR

Dear Summer Sister
(Natsu no Imoto)

(Nagisa Oshima, 1972, Jap) Hosei Komatsu, Hiromi Kurita, Lily, Akiko Koyama, Shoji Ishibashi, Rokko Toura.
95 min.
A film in which Oshima tackles Japan's 'Okinawa problem'. The Japanese today treat Okinawa as a holiday resort, and so this begins as a light, summery dream of sun, sand and teenage flirtation. But the underlying thread (a girl's search for her long-missing brother) conjures up darker spectres, and before long the entire idyll has been effectively undercut by guilt-ridden memories of the past – and especially the atrocities perpetrated on the island during the war. TR

Death and the Maiden

(Roman Polanski, 1994, GB/US/Fr) Sigourney Weaver, Ben Kingsley, Stuart Wilson, Krystia Mova.
103 min.
In a newly democratised South American country, Escobar (Wilson) heads a commission investigating the abuse of political prisoners. One such prisoner was his wife Paulina (Weaver). When one night Escobar comes home late, having been given a lift by seemingly liberal Dr Miranda (Kingsley), Paulina is convinced that their guest is the tormentor who 15 year ago subjected her to sexual humiliation and violence. Escobar feels duty-bound to defend the stranger from the woman he loves, but who may be lying, even insane. In filming Ariel Dorfman's adaptation of his own stage hit, Polanski wisely never opens out the action from the remote clifftop house. In keeping things claustrophobic, close-up and ambivalent, he heightens the suspense (not to mention the sexual tension) and allows for a fluent, lucid exploration of notions of justice, responsibility, forgiveness, and corruption by power. At the same time, the three powerful, sensitively nuanced performances ensure that the characters never become mere mouthpieces for an ethical enquiry. GA

Death at Broadcasting House

(Reginald Denham, 1934, GB) Ian Hunter, Donald Wolfit, Henry Kendall, Austin Trevor, Mary Newland, Jack Hawkins, Val Gielgud, Betty Ann Davies.
74 min. b/w.
'Thirty-five million people hear actor strangled on the air', scream the headlines. Radio producer Val Gielgud had the intriguing idea of making one of those quaintly melodramatic BBC murder mysteries the fulcrum for an archetypically English whodunit, with everyone apart from Sir Herbert Farquharson (homage to Sir John Reith!) likely suspects. This may be a low-budget quickie, but with efficient direction and a very knowledgeable script, the film becomes an evocative reminder of the seminal influence the BBC – with its Blattnerphones and sound-FX men and toffee-nosed producers – must have exercised on the cultural life of the 30s. You'll never guess whodunit, either. RMy

Death Becomes Her

(Robert Zemeckis, 1992, US) Meryl Streep, Bruce Willis, Goldie Hawn, Isabella Rossellini, Ian Ogilvy, Adam Storke, Nancy Fish, Alaina Reed Hall, Michelle Johnson.
104 min.
Zemeckis' black comedy seems oddly old-fashioned, reminiscent less of Roger Rabbit and Back to the Future than of '40s screwball and horror spoofs. When fading star Madeline (Streep) finds that Ernest (Willis), the plastic surgeon fiancé of her friend Helen (Hawn), is besotted by her tarnished glamour, her vanity demands that she marry this wimp who can restore her looks. Years later, 'Hell' plots revenge, and all is set for a bitching battle of Baby Jane proportions; but what finally drags the murderous trio into a maelstrom is the Faustian pact Madeline makes with Lisle Van Rhuman (Rossellini) in return for an elixir of eternal youth. Sporadically very funny indeed, the script features some nicely wicked one-liners, which are well complemented by Zemeckis' sight gags and by performances of great gusto. Far from sophisticated in its satire of narcissism, but enormous fun. GA

Death by Hanging (Koshikei)

(Nagisa Oshima, 1968, Jap) Yun-Do Yun, Kei Sato, Fumio Watanabe, Toshiro Ishido, Masao Adachi.
117 min. b/w.
All of Oshima's films deal in a challenging and committed way with specifically Japanese questions and problems. Death by Hanging is an 'absurd' comedy about the situation of Korean immigrants in Japan, centering on a state execution that goes wrong, mounted as a sort of witty Brechtian argument. TR

Death Collector

(Ralph De Vito, 1975, US) Joseph Cortese, Lou Criscuola, Joe Pesci, Bobby Alto, Frank Vincent.
85 min.
A tarted-up Mafia morality tale, redeemed by Joseph Cortese's striking central performance as a bad-tempered small-town hoodlum down on his luck (yet icy in his resolution). Routinely 'picturesque' butchery is punctuated by memorable details, incidental observations of character, underworld jargon, oafish bravado. Effective, but flawed. AC

Deathdream

see Dead of Night

Death in a French Garden
(Péril en la Demeure)

(Michel Deville, 1985, Fr) Michel Piccoli, Nicole Garcia, Anemone, Christophe Malavoy, Richard Bohringer, Anaïs Jeanneret.
101 min.
A handsome young man arrives at a suburban mansion to give guitar lessons to an attractive teenage girl, and before you can say plectrum her mother launches into a grand seduction. But does her formidable husband know? Is their curious neighbour sane? Who is video-taping their affair? And who is the man following the guitarist? An elegant, teasing narrative unfolds, complete with elliptical dialogue, sleight-of-hand editing, and poised performances all round. A sophisticated entertainment from French stylist Deville, whose films have been little seen here since the '60s period romp Benjamin. DT

d

Death in Brunswick

(John Ruane, 1990, Aust) Zoe Carides, Sam
Neill, John Clarke, Yvonne Lawley, Nico
Lathouris, Nicholas Papademetriou.
109 min.
Drinking heavily, stuck as the cook for a trendy
rock club, and nagged by his visiting mother,
Sam Neill desperately hopes that a romance with
Sophie (Carides), a Greek-Cypriot barmaid, will
alter his luck. Instead, the death of his drug-dealing Turkish washer-up embroils him in a black
comic nightmare involving an inconvenient body,
a sadistic bouncer, and Sophie's club-owner
fiancé. This being a comedy, though, Neill eventually 'sees the light' and resolves to change his
life. A likeably offbeat and often surprisingly
dark comedy thriller, set amid a seldom acknowledged working class ethnic community. NF

Death in the Seine

(Peter Greenaway, 1989, GB/Fr)
44 min.
Made for TV and the French Bicentennial celebrations, this is an extreme case of Peter
Greenaway's obsession with cataloguing and
classification. Comprising 23 case histories of
corpses fished out of the Seine between 1795 and
1801, it forms a kind of micro-reprise of his monumental The Falls, piling up its narratives,
Holmesian speculations and slow, clinical tracking shots over corpses, in a rigidly uniform structure. But within this forbidding system,
Greenaway breaks up the frame, much as in
Prospero's Books, using Paintbox graphics to
play on the comparative textures of television and
paper. Death in the Seine is a pedantic film,
because it's about pedantry and the systematic
collecting of facts which might or might not constitute evidence. It wasn't taken up by British TV,
which considering the film's sign-off comments
about the transience of memory and recorded
knowledge, is a rather sour irony. JRo

Death in the Sun
(Der Flüsternde Tod)

(Jürgen Goslar, 1975, WGer) Christopher Lee,
James Faulkner, Trevor Howard, Sibyle
Danning, Erik Schumann, Sam Williams.
96 min.
Rape and revenge in the African veldt. What
matters more than the plot are the assumptions
that the movie (made in Rhodesia) parades up
front: Lee's police chief is eminently humane
(under crusty exterior), Howard's white settler
eminently soft-hearted (under crusty exterior),
the blacks sorely in need of the white man's
guiding hand, and the terrorist leader an albino
sexual pervert. CPe

Death in Venice
(Morte a Venezia)

(Luchino Visconti, 1971, It) Dirk Bogarde,
Björn Andresen, Silvana Mangano, Marisa
Berensen, Mark Burns, Romolo Valli.
128 min.
Dire adaptation of Thomas Mann's novella,
which turns the writer of the original into a composer, simply so that Visconti can flood his luscious, soft-focus images of Venice with the
sombre sounds of Mahler, thus attempting to give
a heartfelt emotional core to the hollow, camped-
up goings-on. Bogarde is more than a little mannered as the ageing pederast whose obsession
with a beautiful young boy staying at the same
hotel (Andresen in sailor-suit and blond locks)
leads him to outstay his welcome in the plague-
ridden city. Everything is slowed down to a funereal (some might claim magisterial) pace, Mann's
metaphysical musings on art and beauty are jettisoned in favour of pathetic scenes of runny mascara, and the whole thing is so overblown as to
become entirely risible. GA

Death Is Child's Play

see Quién Puede Matar a un Niño?

Death Is My Trade (Aus
einem deutschen Leben)

(Theodor Kotulla, 1977, WGer) Götz George,
Elisabeth Schwarz, Kurt Hübner,
Kai Taschner.
145 min.
Though the fundamental sincerity of Death Is My
Trade is unchallengeable, one gags on it never-

theless. With explicative chapter headings and a
visual texture so grainily sepia as to make the
film look as if it's being projected on sandpaper,
Kotulla traces the gradual transformation of an
earnest young World War I hero into the commandant at Auschwitz, mulling over plans to
step up the 'output' in the crematoria and finally
confessing to his baffled American captor that he
is 'physically incapable' of disobeying an order.
But that arresting admission only exposes the
film's inadequacy: the intimate contingency of the
holocaust on an individual (or national) psyche is
cited rather than dramatised, and we are confronted yet again with the obscene aping of concentration camp victims by bony old extras in
striped pyjamas. GAd

Death Japanese Style

see Ososhiki

Death Kick (Huang Feihong/
aka The Master of Kung Fu)

(Ho Menghua, 1973, HK) Chen Ping, Gu Feng,
Wang Xie, Lin Weidu, Xu Shaoxiong.
100 min.
Set in '20s China and based around the life of the
famous Cantonese boxer/martial arts master
Huang Fei-hong, Death Kick doesn't really manage to surmount the drawback of its over-complicated plot to convey much of the feeling of the
period, or much of its latent theme either. Perhaps
surprisingly, its strong points are its humour,
some engaging if broad characterisations, and its
sly view of the activities of the opium- and jade-
dealing Europeans who ran China's concessions
at the time. Amiable enough, but its fight
sequences lack the style to make them more than
competent. VG

Death Line (aka Raw Meat)

(Gary Sherman, 1972, GB) Donald Pleasence,
Norman Rossington, David Ladd, Sharon
Gurney, Christopher Lee, Hugh Armstrong.
87 min.
One of the great British horror films, Death Line
is a classic example of what Hellraiser director
Clive Barker calls 'embracing the monstrous'. The
film's basic premise is a gruesome one: following
a cave-in during the construction of an underground tunnel in 1892, successive generations of
plague-ridden cannibals have survived and developed their own subterranean culture. Forced out
of hiding by the death of his wife, the sole surviving cannibal begins abducting passengers
from Russell Square tube station. The disgust provoked by the corpse-filled underground world
inhabited by the cannibal is offset by the tenderness with which he treats his dying wife, and by
the unutterable sadness of his lonely plight. The
film's great achievement is in eliciting sympathy
for a creature whose residual capacity for human
feeling amid such terrible degradation is ultimately more moving than horrifying. NF

Death of a Bureaucrat
(Muerte de un Burocrata)

(Tomás Gutiérrez Alea, 1966, Cuba) Salvador
Wood, Silvia Planas, Manuel Estanillo.
85 min.
This arresting early work by one of Cuba's foremost film-makers is a black comedy about institutionalised bureaucracy at its most pedantic.
After a model factory worker is killed in an accident at work, he's buried with his union card as
a mark of eternal solidarity; trouble is, when his
wife applies for a pension, she's told she must present the card before she can get any money – and
there's a law forbidding exhumation within the
first two years of burial. It's a surprising piece to
have been made in the Cuba of the mid-'60s, but
the laughs come as much from a Buñuelian sense
of absurdity as they do from any outright criticism of Castro's regime. TJ

Death of a Cameraman
(Morte di un Operatore)

(Faliero Rosati, 1978, It) Daniele Griggio,
Remo Remotti.
65 min.
Attempting dubious homage to his former mentor Antonioni, Rosati merely succeeds in evoking
tinny echoes of The Passenger with this debut
feature. His journalist in the desert is retracing
with the aid of video equipment and a surviving
tape the final journey through Sinai of a 10-years-

dead cameraman colleague – whose surname just
happens to be an anagram of his own. Such glibly
suggestive 'profundity' props up a boringly arty
succession of arid compositions and 'enigmatic'
silences, betraying little more than a director with
nothing to say. PT

Death of a Gunfighter

(Allen Smithee, ie. Robert Totten/Don Siegel,
1969, US) Richard Widmark, Lena Horne, John
Saxon, Michael McGreevey, Darleen Carr,
Carroll O'Connor, Kent Smith.
100 min.
A fringe Siegel Western (he spent two weeks finishing it off). The theme of a law and order marshal who has tamed a frontier town, only to
become an embarrassment to the 'civilised' community, is sufficiently interesting for one to wonder what it would have been like if Siegel had
done the whole thing.

Death of a Salesman

(Volker Schlöndorff, 1985, US) Dustin
Hoffman, Kate Reid, John Malkovich, Stephen
Lang, Charles Durning, Louis Zorich.
136 min.
The setting is awful: sludgy indoors and sunsets
on painted backdrops in the yard. That apart, all
that's wrong with this version of the 1984
Broadway revival of Arthur Miller's play is the
salesman himself. Dustin Hoffman's Willy Loman
is a hard-working actor playing old; it's a technical performance, starting at such a pitch of sound
and fury that it has nowhere to go when the humiliations really clock in. Loman is a complex character, pompous, self-deluding, bullying, laughable,
pitiable, and ultimately tragic – this last never
tapped by the actor. It isn't until the salesman's
wife (Reid) lays into her sons (Malkovich and
Lang) that you feel the dynamic of this family, the
power of the play, and what acting can do to the
emotions. This trio is terrific, trapped in the hell of
the unattainable American Dream, and tearing
into each other. Hoffman hadn't been on the stage
for 17 years, and it shows. BC

Death of a Soldier

(Philippe Mora, 1985, Aust) James Coburn, Reb
Brown, Bill Hunter, Maurie Fields, Belinda
Davey, Max Fairchild.
96 min.
Edward Leonski (Brown) was the first American
soldier to be sentenced to death by a US military
tribunal in World War II, convicted for the murder of three women while stationed in Australia.
His motive, as he told his defence counsellor Major
Dannenberg (Coburn) was a need to possess the
women's 'voices'. The American military, seeking
to defend their reputation, responded to public outcry by prosecuting Leonski themselves, while
Dannenberg pushed to save the soldier's life with
an insanity plea. Mora uses the trial in an attempt
to examine the fragile relationship that existed
between Americans and Australians during the
war, and to demonstrate the need for due process
of law. But sadly for any intelligent treatment of
these issues, the film concentrates on the depiction
of the murders and the manhunt which ensued,
with Melbourne presented as an outrageous Frat
party for the GIs, while Coburn struggles with stilted dialogue and what would seem to be an inordinate amount of starch in his jockeys. SGo

Death of Maria Malibran, The
(Der Tod der Maria Malibran)

(Werner Schroeter, 1972, WGer) Magdalena
Montezuma, Christine Kaufmann,
Candy Darling.
104 min.
A series of tableaux illustrating the life and death
of a celebrated 19th century German opera singer.
Each tableau has a different motif, and each
comes across with a decadent romanticism that
lies somewhere between the Pre-Raphaelites and
a quick flick through the pages of a '40s copy of
Vogue. Schroeter's film is a delight to the eye –
rich, strange and perverse.

Death of Mario Ricci, The
(La Mort de Mario Ricci)

(Claude Goretta, 1983, Switz/Fr/WGer) Gian
Maria Volonté, Magali Noël, Heinz Bennent,
Mimsy Farmer, Jean-Michel Dupuis,
Michel Robin.
101 min.

A country road glimpsed through a dirty windscreen...a mangled car wreck on a garage forecourt... Volonté blowing up an inflatable coat hanger and reminding his assistant that 'it's the details that count'. And so they clearly do in Goretta's film, although quite what they add up to is never sharply defined. A crippled TV journalist (Volonté) arrives in a Swiss village to interview a specialist in world food shortages disillusioned by the non-application of his theories. But he soon becomes embroiled in a web of local intrigue resulting from the death of a young immigrant worker. Goretta counterpoints his two stories with deft assurance, letting them strike subdued ironies off one another; there are thematic strands galore here, clearly signposted but seemingly left deliberately smudged. Yet there is no shortage of delights either: fine atmospherics, immaculately fluid camerawork, and a towering performance from Volonté, sympathy and disdain flickering back and forth across those marvellously expressive features. JP

Death of the Flea Circus Director, The (Der Tod des Flohzirkusdirektors)

(Thomas Koerfer, 1972, Switz) François Simon, Paul Gogel, Norbert Schwientek, Janine Weill.
111 min. b/w.
Fleas, like the Swiss, operate a risky balancing act of neutrality: in part this political comedy of the absurd revolves around the problems of radical action in that stolid, prosperous, complacent country. After losing his flea circus in a pesticide accident, Ottocaro Weiss (Simon) tries to seek compensation from the authorities, undergoes a ritual death during an anniversary ceremony for the plague, and rises again, with two assistants and a mysterious financial backer, to unleash his theatre of the plague upon the public. Starkly comic and distanced, the film explores the symbolic significances of this theatre from various perspectives, wryly noting the paradoxes thrown up and how polar arguments often in fact overlap: ideas are as infectious as diseases. And until the final scene, Weiss' dreams of a new political liberty are part of a terrifying grand design of which he knows nothing. In that sense, the film seems to offer little hope, the humour of the first half a reflex action against what is to come. CPe

Death on the Nile

(John Guillermin, 1978, GB) Peter Ustinov, Bette Davis, Mia Farrow, Jane Birkin, David Niven, Jack Warden, Angela Lansbury, Maggie Smith, George Kennedy, Lois Chiles.
140 min.
Over-extended and sloppily characterised Agatha Christie whodunit, with Ustinov's Poirot investigating the murder of an heiress aboard a steamer in the 30s. Nostalgic period recreation is everything, with the cast reduced to a gallery of stylish eccentrics and the whole film slavishly modelled on the earlier *Murder on the Orient Express*. GA

Death Race 2000

(Paul Bartel, 1975, US) David Carradine, Simone Griffeth, Sylvester Stallone, Mary Woronov, Roberta Collins, Joyce Jameson.
79 min.
The perfect example of a 'corporation' movie; dreamed up as a quickie rival to *Rollerball*, it follows its big brother in playing for bust on its basic concept – here, a coast-to-coast road race in which drivers score points by mowing down pedestrians. It could have been made by anybody; the fact that it was actually produced by Corman and directed by Bartel is so much icing on the cake. Corman's involvement doubtless accounts for the general vigour and the careful attention to exploitation values; Bartel was probably behind most of the quirky incidental humour and the unexpected casting (including Warhol's Chelsea girl Mary Woronov as the driver Calamity Jane). Overall the movie isn't as synchromeshed as it might be; the rivalry between champions Carradine and Stallone isn't very interesting, and some of the gags aren't sick or funny enough. But it's a great audience film. TR

Death Sentence (Mrityudand)

(Prakash Jha, 1997, Ind) Shabana Azmi, Madhuri Dixit, Om Puri, Ayub Khan, Shipla Shirodkar.
115 min.
This conspiracy thriller kicks like a frenzied mule.

After an introduction in the style of a news report, on the sponsored village murder of a 22-year-old widow, it turns abruptly into a convoluted *faux* political documentary, detailing the networks of business, religious and familial ties that form the dense mass of upper caste politics in Bilaspur. It's a world rife with corruption, avarice, sabotage – and misogyny. New recruit Vinay tries to play the game, using his bride Ketki's dowry to sign a quarry contract with local government businessmen, despite Ketki's pleas that they won't play fair. So the bride (Dixit) and her sister-in-law Chandravati (Azmi, commanding) take a stand, whereupon all the weight of entrenched male power mobilises against them. NB

Death Ship

(Alvin Rakoff, 1980, Can/GB) George Kennedy, Richard Crenna, Nick Mancuso, Sally Ann Howes, Kate Reid.
91 min.
A crewless Nazi torture-ship malevolently hunts down and sinks Caribbean pleasure cruisers. Good enough. But a *Ten Little Indians* plot soon takes over which is as rusty as the evil vessel. Kennedy gradually, but without much conviction, becomes the demented embodiment of the Third Reich as the corpses pile up; the *Psycho* shower murder is 'borrowed' again; the direction never moves beyond endless zooms to mirror pumping engines. SJ

Deaths in Tokimeki (Tokimeki ni Shisu)

(Yoshimitsu Morita, 1984, Jap) Kenji Sawada, Kanaka Higuchi, Naoki Sugiura.
105 min.
The man who fell to earth this time is an unnamed hit-man cloistered in a seaside villa, awaiting the arrival of his victim, the leader of a new religious cult. Morita (young director of *Family Game*) structures the movie like a computer game, in which unexpected new information is required to move on to the next phase; he exerts vice-like control over the images and moods, juggling moments of eroticism, inner violence, misogyny and black humour. It all works like a pacemaker with induced hiccoughs. TR

Deathsport

(Henry Suso/Allan Arkush, 1978, US) David Carradine, Claudia Jennings, Richard Lynch, William Smithers, Will Walker, Jesse Vint.
83 min.
Mutant offspring of the *Death Race 2000* line of cheapo sci-fi. The inhabitants of its post-holocaust society are familiar enough: cannibal freaks, sadist overlords of the fascist city-states, and the samurai-like 'Range Guides' gladiatorially pitched against the death-machines (dressed-up trail bikes). The plot, however, soon escalates into a frenzied biker chase pic, embracing both Kung-fu mysticism and the heavy pyrotechnics which push it to its most effective level. If it never quite rises to the kind of parable one half expects from the Corman factory, it's still OK. CPea

Deathtrap

(Sidney Lumet, 1982, US) Michael Caine, Christopher Reeve, Dyan Cannon, Irene Worth, Henry Jones.
116 min.
Undeterred by the resistance to translation from the stage of *Sleuth* and its parlour murder game, Michael Caine tries again, this time as a harassed Broadway playwright, a one-time master of the mystery thriller now driven to plot murder as a way of getting round his writer's block. Beautifully played (especially by Cannon, listening with increasing unease as her husband expounds his death trap), this adaptation of Ira Levin's play is witty, edgy and teasingly compelling until about the end of act one. Then, with the ingenious groundwork laid, all reality is tossed overboard as the multiplication of Chinese boxes begins, revealing murder within murder, play within play. Turned into puppets arbitrarily shunted round at the service of a plot much too clever for its own good, the characters are soon creaking as loudly as the stage machinery. TM

Death Trap (aka Eaten Alive)

(Tobe Hooper, 1976, US) Neville Brand, Mel Ferrer, Carolyn Jones, Marilyn Burns, William Finley, Stuart Whitman, Roberta Collins.
96 min.

Hooper's follow-up to *The Texas Chainsaw Massacre* is a further exploration of American rural degeneracy, about a senile swamp dweller (Brand) with a hook arm who likes to feed tourists and their children to his alligator. At its best, the film's lurid tone matches the evocative gloom of the EC horror comics of the '50s, in particular the amazing swamp stories drawn by 'Ghastly' Graham Inglis. Otherwise, it's trite and unconvincing. DP

Death Valley

(Dick Richards, 1981, US) Paul Le Mat, Catherine Hicks, Stephen McHattie, Wilford Brimley, Peter Billingsley, Edward Herrmann.
88 min.
An achingly average low-rent slasher. Noisome kid (Billingsley), on vacation in Arizona with his mom and her new boyfriend to establish the seeds of familial love, stumbles across a clue to what appears to be a novel way of (literally) cutting down the tourist trade, and spends the rest of the movie getting the adults into tight corners. A touch of the Spielbergs in that the action is seen from the kid's viewpoint, but the plot's predictability is well-matched by short measures in both acting and direction. The obnoxious kid becomes the slasher's target, and one feels rather cut up when he isn't. FL

Death Vengeance

see Fighting Back

Death Watch (La Mort en Direct)

(Bertrand Tavernier, 1979, Fr/WGer) Romy Schneider, Harvey Keitel, Harry Dean Stanton, Max von Sydow, Thérèse Liotard, Caroline Langrishe.
130 min.
As so often with Tavernier, a film that promises more than it delivers. Science fiction set in a near future, it starts from the intriguing premise that, in a society from which death has been effectively banished or at least tucked out of sight, a TV network plans to transmit a real-life soap opera for the benefit of curious viewers. A network employee (Keitel) has a miniature camera planted in his brain to record everything he sees, and the subject of his death watch (Schneider) is told she has an incurable disease. But as rebellious emotions begin to rage in both parties, the humanist in Tavernier gets the better of his fantasy, leading to some windy preachment and loss of credibility. A film to be seen, nevertheless, strikingly cast and with Glasgow lending its persuasive presence as a city of the future. TM

Death Weekend (aka The House by the Lake)

(William Fruet, 1976, Can) Brenda Vaccaro, Don Stroud, Chuck Shamata, Richard Ayres, Kyle Edwards, Don Granberry.
94 min.
Inordinately wealthy dentist takes incredulous date for dirty weekend at his secluded mock-Tudor mansion. Fun (which doesn't look like materialising anyway) is spoiled by the arrival of four irate middle-aged greasers (led by Stroud in best bovine form). They take their time smashing the place up, killing the dentist and raping the girl. Spunky Vaccaro fights back (slitting the throat of smallest psycho at moment of orgasm), and at this point matters begin to pick up. Moderately exciting manhunt wraps up this excessively violent exploiter. Uneasy performances all round, however, don't help the tediously unbelievable premise of Fruet's dog-eared script. JPy

Death Wish

(Michael Winner, 1974, US) Charles Bronson, Hope Lange, Vincent Gardenia, Stuart Margolin, Steven Keats, William Redfield.
94 min.
Objectionable vigilante trash from the objectionable Winner, with the stony Bronson taking the law into his own vengeful hands when his wife is killed and his daughter turned into a traumatic vegetable after an attack by muggers. The sense of location is strong, emphasising a hostile, nightmarish terrain; but Winner's recourse to caricature when dealing with police and thugs, and his virtually overt sympathies with the confused, violent Bronson, make for uncritical, simplistic viewing. GA

Death Wish II

(Michael Winner, 1981, US) Charles Bronson, Jill Ireland, Vincent Gardenia, JD Cannon, Anthony Franciosa, Ben Frank.
95 min.

It's difficult to decide here which appeals to the nastier of audience instincts, the rape or the retribution. But what is clear about this sequel is that its attitude to its death-dealing urban vigilante is now much less ambivalent. Where *Death Wish* 'persuaded' its audience that its protagonist might be justified in his crusade, this takes popular support for granted, and even allows the stoic Bronson a certain relish in blowing away the LA street gang responsible for the rape and death of his teenage daughter (still recovering from the trauma of the 1974 story). Overall, it's as unstylish as anything Winner has put his name to. RM

Death Wish 3

(Michael Winner, 1985, US) Charles Bronson, Deborah Raffin, Ed Lauter, Martin Balsam, Gavan O'Herlihy, Kirk Taylor.
90 min.

An ageing Bronson is released from gaol to clear the local territory of human trash. The muggerslugger shows Brooklyn how to fight back, and provides much ammunition for anti-liberals: warfare not welfare. Initial excitement at the welter of violence soon palls into boredom, only intermittently relieved by the preposterousness of the action. With the strong element of fantasy, the frenetic attempts to create an end-product, and the squandering of resources, this is nothing more than cinematic masturbation. MS

Death Wish 4: The Crackdown

(J Lee Thompson, 1987, US) Charles Bronson, Kay Lenz, John P Ryan, Perry Lopez, George Dickerson, Soon-Teck Oh.
99 min.

When his girlfriend's daughter dies of a coke overdose, semi-retired vigilante Bronson deals out some summary justice to the pusher who sold the stuff. Shortly afterwards, he is summoned by businessman Ryan, who encourages Old Stone Face to take on the gang controlling 90 percent of the LA drugs trade. Director Thompson ignores the thick-ear dialogue and wooden acting, and blows up every car and building in sight. Gail Morgan Hickman's complicated script manages a couple of nice twists, but it's too formulary to pursue the ambiguities it reveals. Most enjoyable is the clear thread of self-parody, which keeps the laughs and bullets coming thick and fast. NF

Decadence

(Steven Berkoff, 1993, GB) Joan Collins, Steven Berkoff, Christopher Biggins, Michael Winner.
108 min.

Berkoff is the sneering adulterer, Collins the snooty aristo – and the parallel characters, scuzzbag private dick and arriviste housewife. The fringe play (from which this is drawn) usually delivers a short, sharp shock, but here Berkoff's stagy direction dissipates most of the scathing wit and pleasing vulgarity. The film resembles a video shot from the front row of the audience. She romps on silk sheets; he writhes at the crack of a riding crop. Dreadful. ACh

Décade Prodigieuse, La

see Ten Days' Wonder

Decameron, The (Il Decamerone)

(Pier Paolo Pasolini, 1970, It/Fr/WGer) Franco Citti, Ninetto Davoli, Angela Luce, Patrizia Capparelli, Pier Paolo Pasolini.
111 min.

Pasolini manages in his uninhibited fashion to capture the anarchic comic spirit of Boccaccio's bawdy tales in this episodic romp; but the sight of the endless assembly of seemingly toothless proles Pasolini picked up as extras can be a bit intimidating.

Deceived

(Damian Harris, 1991, US) Goldie Hawn, John Heard, Ashley Peldon, Robin Bartlett, Tom Irwin, Amy Wright, Jan Rubes, Kate Reid, Beatrice Straight.
108 min.

After the comedy fiasco of *Bird on a Wire*, Hawn gets serious for this psychological thriller, only to find herself immured in an equally preposterous plot. She plays Adrienne, whose seemingly blissful life with museum curator Jack (Heard) conceals all manner of horrors. After six happy years of marriage, Jack's apparent death in a car crash leaves his grieving wife to unravel the mystery of why he assumed a false identity sixteen years earlier. With increasingly macabre/laughable developments in the story, poor Goldie is left stomping around, convincingly distraught as she vacillates between threats and toe-curling terror. Too bad, because slick direction and rich textures created by longtime Eastwood cinematographer Jack Green prove enticing, as does a strong performance from Heard. CM

Deceivers, The

(Nicholas Meyer, 1988, GB) Pierce Brosnan, Saeed Jaffrey, Shashi Kapoor, Helen Mitchell, Keith Michell, David Robb, Tariq Yunus.
103 min.

Insecure young Englishman Savage (Brosnan) breaks colonial taboos by dyeing his skin to infiltrate the 'thuggees', a band of murderers dedicated to the goddess Kali. John Masters' novel is a great story, but the movie misses much of it. The opening set of clichés – a tiger hunt, a *Gone With the Wind* dance, a regimental wedding – give way to better film-making as the bizarre thuggery gets under way, but it's a case of too little too late for this shock-horror costume caper. Actors as powerful as Kapoor, Jaffrey and Keith Michell are reduced to hackneyed cameos, India looks like something out of a travel brochure, and blasting Hollywood-Viennese music ensures that we know it's a major motion picture. PHo

December Bride

(Thaddeus O'Sullivan, 1990, GB) Donal McCann, Saskia Reeves, Ciaran Hinds, Patrick Malahide, Brenda Bruce, Michael McKnight, Dervla Kirwan, Peter Capaldi, Geoffrey Golden.
88 min.

In turn-of-the-century Ireland, Sarah (Reeves) and her mother (Bruce) are servants in the Echlin household; but after the old master's death, the remote Presbyterian community is shocked when Sarah starts having sexual relations with both Echlin brothers (McCann and Hinds), all three resisting overtures from the minister (Malahide) to join his flock. Sarah becomes pregnant: unsure which man is the father, reluctant to marry and embrace the hypocrisies of the church, she chooses to let both share in the child's upbringing. David Rudkin's intelligent adaptation of Sam Hanna Bell's novel explores national conflicts within the context of the community's intense divisions. 'The three curses of Ireland: England, religion and the drink' muses the elder brother as he strives to maintain equilibrium between the enraged locals and his defiant family. O'Sullivan's careful compositions and Bruno de Keyzer's exquisite cinematography lend the film a stark, simple grandeur, which in turn emphasises the harsh, physical nature of the characters' lives. The measured pace – beautifully sustained by the performances – ensures a film of sharp insight and striking clarity. CM

Deception

(Irving Rapper, 1946, US) Bette Davis, Claude Rains, Paul Henreid, John Abbott, Benson Fong.
112 min. b/w.

Four years after *Now Voyager*, *Deception* resurrects the same team for another grand emotional wallow – the 'woman's picture' at its historical zenith. Here, though, the passions are even more overblown, with Rains, excellent as a mad, bad composer, exerting a Svengali-like influence over Davis, his duplicitous pupil, and Henreid, as the master cellist who needs Rains' new composition to make his reputation but needs Davis even more. As she lies her way out of Rains' clutches and into marriage with Henreid, so the effects of her 'deceptions' become more corrosive. Blazing histrionics in the concert hall, *crime passionel* in the salon, and outside on the streets of Manhattan it's always raining. CPea

Decline and Fall...of a Birdwatcher!

(John Krish, 1968, GB) Robin Phillips, Genevieve Page, Donald Wolfit, Colin Blakely, Robert Harris, Leo McKern, Patience Collier, Felix Aylmer, Griffith Jones.
113 min.

Rather softened adaptation of Evelyn Waugh's first novel satirising the mores of decadent wealthy Britain, with Phillips as the innocent undergraduate being sent down from Oxford and suffering a sentimental education (while teaching in a seedy Welsh boarding-school) at the hands of various darkly comic characters. Faithful to the letter if not quite the spirit of Waugh (it lacks the novel's bite, and is also unwisely updated), it's nevertheless endowed with strong performances all round and civilised, if literary, direction by Krish. GA

Decline of the American Empire, The (Le Déclin de l'Empire Américain)

(Denys Arcand, 1986, Can) Dominique Michel, Dorothée Berryman, Louise Portal, Geneviève Rioux, Pierre Curzi, Rémy Girard, Yves Jacques, Daniel Brière.
101 min.

Four university history professors, three married and one gay, gather at a country retreat and prepare a large meal for the evening. They talk about their sex lives. Meanwhile their wives are at a health club. They too trade dirty secrets. Finally they all converge for the big dinner and the knives come out...Arcand has assembled a band of middle class professionals, sinking onto that middle-age plateau of resignation, and with little to occupy their minds but the pursuit of personal pleasure. His achievement is to make the subject appear by turns black and satiric, without ever falling out of love with his characters. A penetrating, discomforting study; recommended for all those who worry about feeling too smug about their private lives. CPea

Decline of Western Civilization, The

(Penelope Spheeris, 1980, US) Black Flag, Germs, Catholic Discipline, X, Circle Jerks, Alice Bag Band, Fear.
100 min.

By far the most noteworthy aspect of Penelope Spheeris's LA punk movie is its timing, late on two counts. To her credit, she is keen neither to bury nor to champion the movement; and if that means throwing the appalling bands in with the talented, and the dodo interviewees in with the perceptive, then so be it. Hence, of the seven bands featured heavily, one can be grateful for the lasting hardcore beatings of John Doe's X, the grim all-or-nothing mania of the Germs' singer Darby Crash, and the hugely insulting spewings of John Belushi's faves Fear. Memories to squeal at, on the other hand, are the Alice Bag Band and critic Claude Bessy's Catholic Discipline – both wholly disastrous shots of pea-brains with amps meet social realism. The interviews are mostly very funny, probably not always intentionally so. It's far from unmissable, but it's valuable rock history with some great noise. SGa

Decline of Western Civilization Part II: The Metal Years, The

(Penelope Spheeris, 1988, US) Aerosmith, Alice Cooper, Kiss, Motorhead, Ozzy Osbourne, Chris Holmes, Poison, Lizzy Borden, Faster Pussycat, Seduce, Odin, London, Megadeth.
93 min.

Spheeris's second look at what the sweet young things of the City of Angels get up to when they're not free-basing and setting fire to classrooms or their hair. She puts a camera in front of a number of kids and Heavy Metal 'stars', and lets them talk about their music and their lives – both ultimately worthless. There are musical interludes from the likes of Faster Pussycat, London, and other almost indistinguishable crap acts, all wanting and waiting to be as big and bigoted as Guns'n'Roses, who wanted too much money to appear. Osbourne is the greatest walking example of just how stupid the HM creed of drugs, booze and macho sexism really is: fat and funny at first, sickening after a while. Holmes is pathetic, Alice Cooper is sad, Paul Stanley displays amazing penis envy, and Aerosmith are simply stupid. The regular HM girlfriends are tough and strangely feminist, the groupies singularly ugly and dumb. The boys all brag about sex but look like Mother Fist is their main mistress. The values stink, the music stinks, and Lemmy from Motorhead is a dickhead, but the movie is totally compelling. Rather like watching a car wreck on the opposite side of a motorway. MPe

Deconstructing Harry

(Woody Allen, 1997, US) Woody Allen, Kirstie Alley, Bob Balaban, Richard Benjamin, Billy Crystal, Judy Davis, Hazelle Goodman, Mariel Hemingway, Amy Irving, Julie Kavner, Elisabeth Shue, Stanley Tucci, Robin Williams.
96 min.
Harry Block (Allen) is a priapic foul-mouthed author whose ex-wives and lovers, family and friends object to his philandering and unreliability, and his habit of using them, thinly disguised, as fodder for his work. He goes to receive a fellowship at his alma mater with his nine-year-old son, his best friend and a black hooker in tow, and you'd think – this being Woody's *Wild Strawberries* – that Harry will learn something. But will he? Thankfully, despite many similarities to Bergman's film, this is not one of Allen's arty efforts (though the jump cuts are tiresome). As it alternates events from Harry's life with their fictionalised versions, proceeding towards a meeting of art and reality, the film is mainly very funny – most memorably in a vignette with Robin Williams as an actor who literally lacks focus. The sour take on artistic endeavour makes a welcome change from Allen's earlier work (as, indeed, does the inclusion of a significant black character – albeit a whore). But whether the idea of a man able to live and love only through his art is original or deep is another matter entirely. GA

Décroches les étoiles
see Unhook the Stars

Deep, The

(Peter Yates, 1977, US/GB) Jacqueline Bisset, Nick Nolte, Robert Shaw, Dick Anthony Williams, Earl Maynard, Louis Gossett, Eli Wallach.
124 min.
If *Star Wars* is basically a movie for people who like to play amusement arcades, then *The Deep* (adapted by Peter Benchley from his own novel) is the ultimate disco experience. It unerringly evokes all those misspent hours: it has sex objects for all tastes, instant fun, danger and boredom in unequal proportions, strobe-light climaxes, and Donna Summer in stereo. Furthermore, it does away with a storyline and dances on the spot for two hours, taking voodoo, buried treasure, violence and sea monsters in its stride. The Bermuda locations conjure up adverts for rum, but nothing much else has anything to do with the cinema. TR

Deep Cover

(Bill Duke, 1992, US) Larry Fishburne, Jeff Goldblum, Victoria Dillard, Charles Martin Smith, Sydney Lassick, Clarence Williams III, Gregory Sierra, Roger Guenveur Smith.
106 min.
Fishburne, sensational in his first starring role, is a mid-West undercover cop brought in to infiltrate a West coast drugs ring whose members stretch up to the Latin American diplomatic corps. In a stunning opening sequence, we see a ten-year-old boy (who grows up to be Fishburne's John Q Hull) cradling his junkie father as the latter dies on a doomed Christmas attempt to rob a liquor store for dope money. Twenty years later, Hull is a cop with an attitude problem, a man who obeyed his father's order never to touch drugs but still has all the animal instincts of the dark side of the street. In the course of his work, Hull has to feign indifference to scenes of hideous violence, and gradually becomes embroiled with Goldblum's on-the-edge lawyer/user/dealer. Eventually, biting on a little more than it can chew, the film reverts to type. But in addition to Fishburne, it gives us a first-rate soundtrack, a clutch of splendid cameos, fine, grainy direction from Duke, and much pointed stuff about the hypocrisy behind the USA's so-called war against drugs. SGr

Deep Crimson (Profundo carmesí/Carmin profond)

(Arturo Ripstein, 1996, Mex) Regina Orozco, Daniel Giménez Cacho, Marisa Paredes, Verónica Merchant, Julieta Egurrola, Patricia Reyes Spíndola.
115 min.
This version of the true story that inspired Leonard Kastle's *The Honeymoon Killers* (1969) is set in Mexico in 1949. Black comedy informs both films, but where Kastle's was notable for its grim austerity, Ripstein opts for a sumptuous yet strangely detached variation on the traditional Mexican melodrama. For all their protestations of undying love, Coral (Orozco) and Nicolás (Giménez Cacho) are hardly the most sympathetic of protagonists. Besides murdering a series of widows, Coral, an obese, slatternly, Charles Boyer-obsessed nurse, dumps her kids at the first opportunity, while her beloved Nicolás is a deceitful gigolo con-man. The sickly, overheated emotions are reflected in the ornate, even gaudy decor and lighting, while Ripstein's grasp of the couple's cowardice and cruelty and of the social, sexual and psychological circumstances which render their victims gullible and vulnerable is evident both in his matter-of-fact depiction of the killings, and in the subtly ironic tone of the dialogue and performances. Imagine late Fassbinder filtered through a Latin sensibility and you're only halfway there. GA

Deep End

(Jerzy Skolimowski, 1970, WGer/US) Jane Asher, John Moulder-Brown, Diana Dors, Karl Michael Vogler, Christopher Sandford.
88 min.
Set in a decidedly unglamorous and unswinging London, Skolimowski's sex comedy posits a beautifully bizarre and totally unsentimental education for his adolescent hero, employed at a rundown swimming baths and obsessively pining for colleague Asher. Often very funny, tainted perhaps by a whiff of misogyny, and blessed with a thudding soundtrack from early Can, it's a brief and highly original delight. GA

Deep Impact

(Mimi Leder, 1998, US) Robert Duvall, Téa Leoni, Elijah Wood, Vanessa Redgrave, Maximillliam Schell, Morgan Freeman, James Cromwell.
121 min.
A meteor is heading for Earth. The first 40 minutes are the least bad. Astronomers are caught napping when schoolboy Wood spots something strange coming this way. Washington keeps a lid on it, until TV reporter Leoni stumbles across 'the biggest story in history'. A year hence, we will be destroyed, unless the US-Soviet space mission Messiah can deflect the asteroid's course by detonating nuclear explosions deep in its core. It's at this point – when the President (Freeman) places the fate of the world into the hands of astronaut Duvall and his crew – that the movie really goes into under-drive. They learn the value of self-sacrifice and togetherness. If director Leder fails to make the personal stories come to life, she's even sketchier on the big picture – her idea of social breakdown begins and ends with a traffic jam. TCh

Deep in the Heart
see Handgun

DeepStar Six

(Sean S Cunningham, 1988, US) Taurean Blacque, Nancy Everhard, Greg Evigan, Miguel Ferrer, Nia Peeples, Matt McCoy, Cindy Pickett, Marius Weyers, Elya Baskin, Thom Bray, Ronn Carroll.
99 min.
The 11-strong crew of the DeepStar Six are wrapping up their six month research project on the ocean floor when a mysterious blip appears on their radar screens: an unidentified swimming object! What follows is a particularly messy game of sardines, the only rule being that no one attemps anything remotely unpredictable. The actors put up a good fight, but the cod technobabble is so unremitting ('Stabilise stabilisers' – 'Stabilisers stabilised') that it is tempting to cheer when they are finally shut up. The only inventive aspects of the movie are the variously contrived

fatalities, and a sea monster so ugly it makes Jaws look like a tadpole. Cunningham apes Ridley Scott and James Cameron competently enough, and there are scary moments, but he has not got the 'vision thing'. This simply rehashes the phony trappings of countless TV shows, to baldly go where we have been before. TCh

Deer Hunter, The (100)

(Michael Cimino, 1978, US) Robert De Niro, John Cazale, John Savage, Christopher Walken, Meryl Streep, George Dzundza, Chuck Aspegren.
182 min.
This is probably one of the few great films of the decade. It's the tale of three Pennsylvanian steelworkers, their life at work, at play (deer-hunting), at war (as volunteers in Vietnam). Running against the grain of liberal guilt and substituting Fordian patriotism, it proposes De Niro as a Ulyssean hero tested to the limit by war. Moral imperatives replace historical analysis, social rituals become religious sacraments, and the sado-masochism of the central (male) love affair is icing on a Nietzschean cake. Ideally, though, it should prove as gruelling a test of its audience's moral and political conscience as it seems to have been for its makers. CA

De eso no se habla
see We Don't Want to Talk About It

DEF by Temptation

(James Bond III, 1990, US) James Bond III, Kadeem Hardison, Bill Nunn, Samuel L Jackson, Cynthia Bond.
95 min.
Mixing singles bar seduction with bestial bloodsucking, this all-black horror movie offers a vampiric variation on Spike Lee's *She's Gotta Have It*. Drawn to New York by strange dreams, religious country boy Joel (Bond) competes with his streetwise brother K (Hardison) for a *bad* vamp temptress who prefers Blood Marys to screwdrivers. The sexist overtones of Cynthia Bond's predatory vampire leave a nasty taste in the mouth, the special effects are poor, and the plot sags badly in the middle. Nevertheless, the stylish visuals, sharp dialogue and incidental humour make this an unusually classy Troma release. The production values are B negative, but actor/producer/director Bond's debut feature rates a B plus. NF

Defence Counsel Sedov

(Yevgeny Tsymbal, 1988, USSR) Vladimir Ilyin, Tamara Chernova, Tatiana Rogozina, Natalia Schukina.
45 min. b/w & col.
Just when you thought *glasnost* had allowed Soviet film-makers to say all there was to say about the horrors of the Stalin years, along comes this astonishing short feature (based on fact) to peel away more layers of the onion. Harassed, middle-aged Sedov is the only lawyer in Moscow willing to take on the defence of four farmers accused of sabotaging their commune and tortured into making false confessions. His dogged persistence against the state's legal and political bureaucracy gets the men off, but results in his own canonisation as a Stalinist zealot – and in the execution of dozens of other men. A genuinely shocking parable of the biter bit, it incorporates some staggering newsreel footage from the '30s, never seen before. TR

Defence of the Realm

(David Drury, 1985, GB) Gabriel Byrne, Greta Scacchi, Denholm Elliott, Ian Bannen, Fulton Mackay, Bill Paterson.
96 min.
A conspiracy yarn which looks to the tradition of Buchan as well as the more recent one of *Three Days of the Condor*. A far from crusading hack uncovers a mystery behind a political scandal and feels impelled to investigate. What's going on? Something not very nice at all involving nuclear weapons, that's what. Drury coaxes an excellent performance from newcomer Byrne, and directs with a style and sense of location rarely present in homegrown cinema. The Fenland scenes and those in London by night are notably atmospheric, and while the ending isn't entirely satisfactory, there is no questioning the quality and pedigree of the film. RR

Defending Your Life

(Albert Brooks, 1991, US) Albert Brooks, Meryl Streep, Rip Torn, Lee Grant, Buck Henry, Michael Durrell, James Eckhouse, Gary Beach.
111 min.

Although gentle and sentimental, Brooks' satire is better by far than most Hollywood movies about the afterlife. As LA advertising man Daniel, killed in a car crash, Brooks brings his familiar neuroses to bear on a pristine purgatory where self-acceptance, as opposed to goodness, determines one's progress through infinity. Nervy and self-centred, Daniel is clearly ill-qualified for promotion to a higher plane, but with help from brave, becalmed Julia (Streep) and his celestial advocate (Torn), he might just make it through the official review of his sojourn on earth to emerge as something more than a lowly amphibian. Much of the comedy centres around life in Judgement City, where American obsessions are indulged to a utopian degree; if there's something a tad New Age about the emphasis on feeling good, at least that ol' time religion is mercifully absent, while the satire hits target more often than not. The film is finally too soft, but the performances are uniformly strong, the humour intelligently adult, and Brooks once again proves a pleasing alternative to Woody Allen. GA

Defiance

(John Flynn, 1979, US) Jan-Michael Vincent, Theresa Saldana, Fernando Lopez, Danny Aiello, Santos Morales, Rudy Ramos, Art Carney.
102 min.

A nasty and simplistic urban-Western parable for Reagan's America. Stranger-in-town Vincent takes it from a marauding Puerto Rican street gang 'til he can't take no more, then comes on like a righteous Cruise missile to trash the bad guys on a wave of populist reaction. Objectionable. PT

Defiant Ones, The

(Stanley Kramer, 1958, US) Tony Curtis, Sidney Poitier, Theodore Bikel, Charles McGraw, Lon Chaney, King Donovan, Cara Williams.
96 min. b/w.

Typical piece of liberal pleading from Kramer in which two escaped cons (Curtis and Poitier) go on the run manacled together in an oh-so-obvious metaphor for racial hatred. The suspense of the manhunt in the swamps never really overcomes the dead weight of Kramer's 'message', but pleasures are to be found in the supporting roles of McGraw and Chaney. MA

Def Jam's How to Be a Player

(Lionel C Martin, 1997, US) Bill Bellamy, Natalie Desselle, Lark Voorhies, Mari Morrow, Max Julien.
94 min.

A ponderous, compromised essay in misogyny. Dray Jackson (insipid MTV comic Bellamy) has a loyal if jealous girlfriend Lisa (Voorhies) but remains an incorrigible Don Juan. Sister Jenny (Desselle) and sexy Katrina (Morrow) decide to teach him a lesson. Dray's visits to his well-heeled women, for all the attempted glamour, seem essentially the rounds of a high-class male prostitute. CO'Su

De Grands Evénements et des Gens Ordinaires

see Of Great Events and Ordinary People

Degree of Murder, A (Mord und Totschlag)

(Volker Schlöndorff,1966, WGer) Anita Pallenberg, Hans P Hallwachs, Manfred Fischbeck, Werner Enke.
87 min.

Schlöndorff's second film. Pallenberg plays a Munich waitress who shoots her ex-boyfriend in a quarrel, and then ropes in two strangers to help her dispose of the body. She sleeps with both of them, but nothing much else happens on the way to the open ending. Schlöndorff presents it all as a detached observer, and accompanies it with a score by the soon-to-be-late Brian Jones.

Déjeuner sur l'Herbe, Le (Lunch on the Grass/Picnic on the Grass)

(Jean Renoir, 1959, Fr) Paul Meurisse, Catherine Rouvel, Jacqueline Morane, Fernand Sardou, Jean-Pierre Granval.
92 min.

Often seen as a paean to Nature (and Renoir père – it was shot at Auguste Renoir's house at Les Collettes). With its odd tale of a future bureaucrat liberated from glacial rationalism through enforced submission to Nature's whims, Le Déjeuner sur l'Herbe is one of Renoir's most ravishing, and simultaneously most irritating films. Again and again, sumptuous photography collapses into cold argument. PH

Dekalog 1: 'I am the Lord thy God, Thou shalt have no other God but me'

(Krzysztof Kieslowski, 1988, Pol) Henryk Baranowski, Wojciech Klata, Maja Komorowska.
53 min.

It's a freezing early winter morning on the Warsaw estate where Pavel (Klata), an intelligent boy approaching teenage, and his lecturer father (Baranowski) are playing with computers. Using a scientific formula, they input the recent ground temperatures, which confirms the safety of the ice on the nearby ponds; and thus reassured, father allows Pavel to have his Christmas present (a pair of ice skates) early. That day, Pavel's pleasure in his intellectual accomplishments is tempered by the sadness he feels about a dead dog; and prompted by the Catholic talk of his beloved aunt (Komorowska), he is moved to question his father on the nature of the soul. 'Why' he asks, 'do people have to die at all?'. Kieslowski's moving drama unfolds with all the force of a metaphysical ghost story as the father, having heard that three children are feared dead on the ponds, begins a frenetic search to locate his son. The performances and direction are calibrated to perfection; the result is a film of shattering insight, laced with black humour and savage irony. WH

Dekalog 2: 'Thou shalt not take the name of the Lord thy God in vain'

(Krzysztof Kieslowski, 1988, Pol) Krystyna Janda, Aleksander Bardini, Olgierd Lukaszwicz.
57 min.

Bardini plays a consultant at the local hospital, a lonely, diffident man in his sixties, who has just begun to relate, in weekly instalments, the sad story of his life (his wife and children were killed during the war). A neighbour (Janda), a chain-smoker, knocks insistently on his door, much to his annoyance, demanding news of her husband, a patient of his who may be dying of cancer. Her problem, it transpires, is that she is pregnant (by another), and the decision whether she has an abortion or not is dependent on the survival or otherwise of her husband. The consultant refuses to play God by saying whether the husband will live or die. As he says, 'I have a God, but it's only enough for me'. As in Dekalog 1, the film's power comes from the precise, economic delineation of character and circumstance. WH

Dekalog 3: 'Honour the Sabbath Day'

(Krzysztof Kieslowski, 1988, Pol) Daniel Olbrychski, Maria Pakulnis, Joanna Szczepkowska.
56 min.

Taxi-driver Janusz, his mother, wife and two kids leave a chair free, in the traditional manner, at their Christmas Eve dinner-table. At midnight mass, Janusz spots a familiar-looking woman looking at him, and later, back at his flat, receives a call from her and meets her in the street. Her husband is missing; he must help find him. He reluctantly agrees, and having lied to his wife about his taxi being stolen, embarks with the woman – with whom it becomes clear he has had an affair – on a search through the lonely city and its hospitals, dry-out clinics and railway terminuses. A film of enormous compassion, this long night's journey into day says more in under an hour about the suffering con-sequent on exclusion (the film is full of closing doors), infidelity and the absence of charity than a life-time of sermons. WH

Dekalog 4: 'Honour thy father and thy mother'

(Krzysztof Kieslowski, 1988, Pol) Adrianna Biedrzynska, Janusz Gajos, Artur Barcis.
55 min.

Easter. Young acting student Anka (Biedrzynska) lives with her architect father, as she has since her mother's death in childbirth. They have a close relationship, and josh each other with the easy intimacy of lovers. Her relationship with her boyfriend, on the other hand, she finds far more difficult. Her father leaves for a trip abroad, and asks her to attend to some unpaid bills. Looking in a drawer for them, she finds an old envelope marked in her father's hand, 'To be opened in the event of my death', and inside it another envelope addressed, presumably in her mother's writing, to 'My darling Anka'. What truth can it contain? When her father returns, they drink vodka and she challenges him to a game of Truth or Dare... Kieslowski's masterly film addresses the question of incest – more properly, incestuous impulses and their roots – and has all the discomforting compulsion of watching open-heart surgery. The performances by Biedrzynska and Gajos as the father are astounding. WH

Dekalog 5: 'Thou shalt not kill'

(Krzysztof Kieslowski, 1988, Pol) Miroslaw Baka, Krzysztof Globisz, Jan Tesarz.
57 min.

Kieslowski's extraordinary film depicts two acts of slaughter. Pimply country kid Yatzek (Baka) unexplainedly kills a taxi-driver. The State then kills him. Both are deaths by hanging, of different kinds, both shown in graphic detail and in real time, shocking in itself. The effect is deeply unsettling. Kieslowski shoots in a calm, heightened-realist style, using multiple filters to bleed and darken the colours of the dour locations, and gets to the heart of our inability to obey the edict 'Thou shalt not kill', thus suggesting the mystery of our deepest motives, without preaching or simplification. A raw, edgy, challenging work originally made, like the rest of the Dekalog, for TV; Kieslowski himself expanded it into an 85-minute theatrical version entitled A Short Film About Killing. WH

Dekalog 6: 'Thou shalt not commit adultery'

(Krzysztof Kieslowski, 1988, Pol) Grazyna Szapolowska, Olaf Lubaszenko, Stefania Iwinska, Piotr Machalica.
58 min.

Hints of a Rear Window-style thriller give way to an unorthodox love story when teenage postal clerk Tomek (Lubaszenko) confesses to spying on artist Magda (Szapolowska). The older woman's interest is piqued, and though initially angry, she draws him into a tremulous, ultimately humiliating love affair. Kieslowski maintains a dispassionate objectivity, and presents the simplest gestures, expressions and words with calculated restraint, allowing the audience to bring their own compassion to bear on the ill-fated relationship. Mature and profoundly moving. Expanded to 87 minutes, the theatrical version was called A Short Film About Love. NF

Dekalog 7: 'Thou shalt not steal'

(Krzysztof Kieslowski, 1988, Pol) Anna Polony, Maja Barelkowska, Wladyslaw Kowalski, Boguslaw Linda.
55 min.

Kieslowski's camera roves past the windows of a Warsaw housing estate and looks in on a family of four. Majka (Barelkowska), a sad-faced woman in her early twenties, is having trouble comforting four-year-old Anka – screaming from nightmares about wolves – when she is roughly pushed aside by a 50-year-old woman. Majka herself takes comfort from her father, a gentle organ-pipe maker. What are the relationships between these four? And what is the cause of the awful tension in the air? Dekalog 7 is only nominally about stealing (Majka kidnaps Anka and takes the child to her teddy-bear-making ex-boyfriend's cabin in the Josefow woods). It is really a questioning – and insightful – examination of the difficulty of growing up (for all generations), and the true meaning and implications of fathering and mothering. WH

Dekalog 8: 'Thou shalt not bear false witness'

(Krzysztof Kieslowski, 1988, Pol) Maria Koscialkowska, Teresa Marczewska, Artur Barcis, Tadeusz Lomnicki.
55 min.
One of the more schematic – though no less fascinating, nor less acute – of the series, this concerns the question of choice 'in a moral hell'. An elderly female university professor of ethics is introduced to an American academic who is researching the fate of Jews after WW2. Sitting in on the professor's lectures, the American offers a story – which has personal significance both for her and the professor – for the students to analyse. A Jewish child, during the Nazi occupation of Warsaw, is offered sanctuary on condition that she obtain a certificate of baptism. The Catholic couple who have promised to help refuse on the grounds that they will not bear false witness, thus condemning the child to almost certain death. But, of course, that is not the whole story... WH

Dekalog 9: 'Thou shalt not covet thy neighbour's wife'

(Krzysztof Kieslowski, 1988, Pol) Ewa Blaszczyk, Piotr Machalica.
58 min.
Promiscuous surgeon Roman (Machalica) is told by his doctor that he can no longer have children, nor sex. He tells his airport-receptionist wife Hanka, who replies that there are more things in a relationship than five minutes of panting in bed once a week. The unspoken things count – but what are they? They cuddle. Soon, however, his curiosity and nascent jealousy aroused by mysterious phone calls, Roman begins to suspect her of having a lover. He takes to spying on her, a process that threatens to destroy his spirit... A complex, unsettling movie (Roman's diagnosis could be AIDS) that digs deep to find the 'irreducible' in people, but offers no simplistic answers (save that of Love, the subject and object of all ten of the Dekalog series). WH

Dekalog 10: 'Thou shalt not covet thy neighbour's goods'

(Krzysztof Kieslowski, 1988, Pol) Jerzy Stuhr, Zbigniew Zamachowski, Henryk Bista.
57 min.
Kieslowski lightens up somewhat in the last of the series, a black comedy on the potentially destructive effect of material wealth. Two brothers, one a singer in punk band 'City Death', the other older and married, discover a stamp collection in their dead athlete father's flat. As the collection's significance (and value) dawns on them, they are forced to turn the flat into a mini Fort Knox, replete with security systems, Rottweilers and window bars. But are they guards or prisoners? Zamachowski and Stuhr are perfect as the brothers, moving and comic at the same time. The film plays like a version of Bresson's L'Argent directed by Bertrand Blier. WH

Delicate Balance, A

(Tony Richardson, 1974, US/GB) Katharine Hepburn, Paul Scofield, Lee Remick, Kate Reid, Joseph Cotten, Betsy Blair.
134 min.
Albee's powerful, coruscatingly brilliant study of tribal rites among the New England jet set. It is also first and foremost a stage play, utterly dependent on direct confrontation between actors and audience, verbal in origins, drawing-room in setting and, on the surface, eminently static. Richardson (as is the norm in this American Film Theatre series) settles for 'filming' the proceedings, and only succeeds in evaporating the tension and the clarity of the original. That said, the cast on show is unbeatable. They make the whole grinding affair bearable, but you'll still get a stiff neck. SGr

Delicate Delinquent, The

(Don McGuire, 1956, US) Jerry Lewis, Martha Hyer, Darren McGavin, Horace McMahon, Milton Frome.
100 min. b/w.
Jerry's first solo pic after his split-up with Dino sends up the '50s 'problem' teenflick something rotten. Lewis is the odd kid out in a gang of urban ruffians, so kindly cop McGavin takes him under his wing – and before long he wants to join the force too. Excessive physical slapstick, gooey sentiment, plain dumbness. TJ

Delicatessen (100)

(Jean-Pierre Jeunet/Marc Caro, 1990, Fr) Dominique Pinon, Marie-Laure Dougnac, Jean-Claude Dreyfus, Karin Viard, Ticky Holgado, Anne-Marie Pisani, Jacques Mathou, Rufus, Howard Vernon.
99 min.
The near future: taking a job and a bedsit at a shabby rooming-house above a butcher's shop, ex-clown Louison (Pinon) falls for the butcher's daughter. But her father, unhappy about the blossoming romance, deals in human flesh: will Louison fall victim, or will the Troglodistes, an underground group of vegetarian fanatics, come to his rescue? On to this slim story, writer-directors Jeunet and Caro pile a wealth of delicious comic detail. Each grotesquely larger-than-life inhabitant of the scrofulous tenement has his own little story; visually, the film evokes Gilliam, Lynch, the Coens and Carné, but the allusions never get in the way of the nightmarish humour. The sets, special effects, photography, pace and performances all contribute to the brash comic-strip vivacity, and even the fairy-tale romance avoids sentimentality. Increasingly inventive as it progresses, Jeunet and Caro's fast, funny feature debut entertains from sinister start to frantic finish. GA

Delinquents, The

(Chris Thomson, 1989, Aust) Kylie Minogue, Charlie Schlatter, Angela Punch McGregor, Bruno Lawrence, Todd Boyce, Desiree Smith, Melissa Jaffer, Lynette Curran, Jonathon Hardy.
105 min.
Lola (Minogue, winsome and wimpy) and American Brownie (Schlatter, presumably cast because he looks like a young Mel Gibson) share so very, very much: they both love books, rock-'n'roll and lolling around in their underwear, and are both entirely lacking in charisma or acting ability. Small wonder, then, that the adults, who are all bastards, just don't understand; small wonder, too, that when this small-town Australian Romeo and Juliet decide to make a go of it alone in the big city, they find it bloody hard. After all, Lola and Brownie are not very bright, even allowing that it is 1957. For one thing, despite forever professing their romantic spirit of adventure, all they really want to do is chuck away their lives by producing a brat at the age of 15; for another, they shack up with a couple of squatters, one of whom is a brainless, Pythonish parody of a DH Lawrence Yorkshireman. Retards flock together, apparently. The acting is universally atrocious, the direction flat and tedious, and the script, which cuts a dash through every cliché in the book, risible. GA

Delinquent School Girls (aka Sizzlers)

(Gergory Corarito, 1975, US) Michael Pataki, Bob Minor, Stephen Stucker, Sharon Kelly, Brenda Miller, Ralph Campbell.
83 min.
An insipid dilution of the women's prison movie. Three male convicts (a black rapist, a gay dress designer, and a relentless mimic whom Opportunity Knocks would have had difficulty in presenting) escape from a State Asylum for the Criminally Insane. They accidentally hit upon a Corrective Institute for girls, and the results are obvious. A snail's pace, lumbering direction, lame script, and performances that keep caricature one-dimensional and top-heavy, make this well worth avoiding. IB

Delirious

(Tom Mankiewicz, 1991, US) John Candy, Mariel Hemingway, Emma Samms, David Rasche, Charles Rocket, Raymond Burr, Dylan Baker, Jerry Orbach.
96 min.
The idea of a writer finding himself within the fictional world he creates (after a bang on the head) is here developed with jokes so obvious they don't need to be made. Candy plays the scriptwriter of an American daytime soap. A fat fool, in reality he's a failure, abused by the soulless producers of Beyond Our Dreams, used by the leading bitch (Samms, who acts as if Dynasty had never been axed), and blind to the only woman worth caring for (Hemingway). In Ashford Falls, the world of his creation, he is transformed into a hero. After an hour of high farce, he finally sees Samms and Hemingway for what they are. His still being able to sit down at the typewriter and play God is used to drive home the moral – which Capra conveyed with far more charm in It's a Wonderful Life – that if you stop trying so hard happiness will find you. Old jokes are piled on top of incomprehensible plot development until you feel truly delirious. CO'S

Delitto in pieno sole

see Plein Soleil

Deliverance

(John Boorman, 1972, US) Jon Voight, Burt Reynolds, Ned Beatty, Ronny Cox, Billy McKinney, James Dickey.
109 min.
Four Atlanta businessmen decide to prove that the frontier spirit is not dead by spending a canoeing weekend shooting the rapids of a river high in the Appalachians. Terrific boy's own adventure stuff with adult ingredients of graphic mutilation and buggery, but Boorman is never content either to leave it at that or to subscribe to the ecological concerns of James Dickey's novel (where man's return to nature becomes vital because 'the machines are going to fail, and then – survival'). Instead, he adds a dark twist of his own by suggesting that concern is too late. From the quartet's first strange encounter with the deformed albino child in a mountain community almost Dickensian in its squalor, down to the last scene where Voight watches coffins being unearthed and removed to safety before the new dam floods the valley, their trip down the river becomes an odyssey through a land that is already dead, killed by civilisation and peopled by alien creatures rather than human beings. Signposted by the extraordinary shot of a corpse, surfaced from the water with one arm grotesquely wrapped round its neck and the other pointing nowhere, it's a haunting, nightmarish vision. TM

Delta, The

(Ira Sachs, 1996, US) Shayne Gray, Thang Chan, Rachel Zan Huss, Colonious Davis.
85 min.
No less striking than Gus Van Sant's debut Mala Noche, this low-budget first feature by the assistant director of Longtime Companion offers a completely fresh perspective on life in Memphis, Tennessee. Lincoln (Gray) is a cute, 17-year-old kid from a good Jewish family with a nice girlfriend and plenty of straight buddies. But something draws him to the city's gay subculture – and into a dangerous relationship with the disturbed and unreliable Minh (Chan), child of a Vietnamese mother and a black GI, victim of every prejudice going. Sachs allowed his actors to develop situations and dialogue through improvisation, giving the film a meandering, naturalistic feel. When plot does assert itself, in the abrupt closing scenes, the effect is truly disconcerting. TR

Delta Force, The

(Menahem Golan, 1986, US) Chuck Norris, Lee Marvin, Martin Balsam, Joey Bishop, Robert Forster, Lainie Kazan, George Kennedy, Hanna Schygulla, Susan Strasberg, Bo Svenson, Robert Vaughn, Shelley Winters.
129 min.
Once more the dream machine rewrites US foreign policy; after Rambo, we now get their Delta Force. Amid all the pyrotechnics of airport hijackings, blown over stunt men, rackety chases through bazaars, all of it quite competently handled, there are a few asides of interest. Students of minimal acting techniques can compare Marvin and Norris: impassivity versus vacancy. Students of the disaster film should write a short thesis on why George Kennedy is ubiquitous. Everyone else might wonder why the film is so virulently anti-Arab. CPea

Deluge, The (Potop)

(Jerzy Hoffman, 1974, Pol) Daniel Olbrychski, Malgorzata Braunek, Tadeusz Lomnicki, Wladyslaw Hancza.
183 mins

A bum-shifting 17th century war epic drawn from a highly popular Henryk Sienkiewicz novel. Formations march through impressive countryside, finally battling it out with a flurry of horses, cannon fire, wounded bodies and spurting blood – none of which comes over visually with the force one might expect, despite nice colour photography in shades of brown. Worming his way through it all, miraculously unscathed, is the courageous adventurer (Olbrychski) who also finds time for a little routine romancing. A long trek at three hours, though it does pick up its heels towards the end, but in Poland, presented in two parts, it ran for 312 minutes. GB

Delusion

(Carl Colpaert, 1990, US) Jim Metzler, Jennifer Rubin, Kyle Secor, Jerry Orbach, Robert Costanzo, Tracey Walter.
100 min.
When computer exec Metzler embezzles half a million dollars or so and heads off for Reno, he thinks he's got it made, but that's before he picks up showgirl Rubin and boyfriend Secor. Obviously, he hasn't watched many *films noirs*, because we're talking Big Mistake here in an unsung little picture that's got pace and a handful of diverting twists, but not quite the requisite star power. TJ

Dementia

(John Parker, 1953, US) Adrienne Barrett, Bruno VeSota, Richard Barron, Ben Roseman, Ed Hinkle, Debbie VeSota.
60 min. b/w.
This genuinely bizarre oddity seems to have been masterminded by Bruno VeSota (later a Corman associate), who produced and plays the Orson Welles part as the villain; the director, Parker, is obscure to the point that his name is missing from the print under review. The movie spends an hour exploring a lonely woman's sexual paranoia through a torrent of expressionist distortions which would look avant-garde if the vulgar Freudian 'message' weren't so reminiscent of '50s B features. Still, parts of it anticipate Welles' *Touch of Evil*. TR

Dementia 13 (aka The Haunted and the Hunted)

(Francis Ford Coppola, 1963, US/Eire) William Campbell, Luana Anders, Bart Patton, Mary Mitchell, Patrick Magee, Eithne Dunn.
81 min. b/w.
Produced by Roger Corman, and evidently made under his presiding spirit, this runs briskly through one of those family reunion plots in which the challenge is to guess which seemingly benign member of the family is the mad axe-murderer who's steadily picking off the rest. The location (an Irish castle) is used imaginatively, the Gothic atmosphere is suitably potent, and there's a wonderfully sharp cameo from Patrick Magee as the family doctor. TR

Demetrius and the Gladiators

(Delmer Daves, 1954, US) Victor Mature, Susan Hayward, Michael Rennie, Debra Paget, Anne Bancroft, Ernest Borgnine, Richard Egan.
101 min.
Sequel to *The Robe* and just as absurd, with Christ's garment now the object of a quest by Caligula. But the pieties have gone, to be replaced by the tortuous court machinations of Caligula, Messalina and Claudius; there are some spiffing gladiatorial combats; and with Daves showing much more ease in the CinemaScope format than Henry Koster, it's a lot of fun. TM

Demi-Paradise, The (aka Adventure for Two)

(Anthony Asquith, 1943, GB) Laurence Olivier, Penelope Dudley Ward, Marjorie Fielding, Margaret Rutherford, Miles Malleson, George Cole.
115 min. b/w.
Russian engineer Olivier invents a special propeller for ice-breakers and comes to England to supervise the building of a new ship in this pro-Soviet propaganda piece. A stranger in a strange land comes to understand our funny ways. Says a lot about how homefront film-makers thought Britain should be represented in 1943 – very cosy it all is, too. TJ

Demoiselles de Rochefort, Les (The Young Girls of Rochefort)

(Jacques Demy, 1967, Fr) Catherine Deneuve, Françoise Dorléac, George Chakiris, Grover Dale, Danielle Darrieux, Michel Piccoli, Gene Kelly, Jacques Perrin, Henri Crémieux.
126 min.
Jolliest of the Demy-Michel Legrand operettas, sometimes wholly entrancing (especially the ecstatic Darrieux-Piccoli celebration of long lost love), but also foolishly inviting comparison with the Hollywood musical by borrowing Gene Kelly (painfully awkward in toupee and dubbed voice) and a couple of alumni from *West Side Story* (accompanied by a good deal of pastiche Jerome Robbins choreography). The result lacks the delicate purity of *The Umbrellas of Cherbourg*, but makes up for it with boundless vitality and the ravishing spectacle of Rochefort itself, with the town square freshly repainted as a pastel-coloured dreamscape. TM

Demolition Man

(Marco Brambilla, 1993, US) Sylvester Stallone, Wesley Snipes, Sandra Bullock, Nigel Hawthorne, André Gregory.
115 min.
This state-of-the-art action comedy is a cruel satire on a PC society where sex, smoking, swearing and salt are banned, and violence has been eradicated. Cryogenically frozen in 1996, psychotic criminal Phoenix (Snipes) and LA cop Spartan (Stallone) are defrosted in 2036: the former to sort out sewer-dwelling eco-terrorists, the latter to clear up the mess left by his old arch-enemy. In sprawling 21st century San Angeles, under benevolent dictator Dr Cocteau (Hawthorne), the only weapons are in a museum. Phoenix escapes and heads straight for them, and the duplicitous Cocteau admits that Spartan's ultra violent methods may be necessary to restore boring normality. First-time director Brambilla stages the senseless violence with skill and relish, aided by producer Joel Silver's trademark mega-explosions. Forget your preconceptions, but not your brain cells and sense of irony. NF

Demon

see God Told Me To

Demon Lover Diary

(Joel DeMott, 1980, US) Joel DeMott, Don Jackson, Jerry Youngkins, Jeff Kreines, Carol Lasowsky.
90 min.
A documentary about the filming of *The Demon Lover* (1976), a movie/dream realised by two factory workers who sacrificed security (mortgaged home) and a finger (industrial 'accident') to raise the funds. But amateurs and professionals don't mix, and the non-communication between producers and crew leads to disturbing outbursts of frustration, filmed – and in part caused by – this film-within-a-film. FF

Demons (Demoni)

(Lamberto Bava, 1985, It) Urbano Barberini, Natasha Hovey, Karl Zinny, Fiore Argento, Paolo Cozzo.
93 min.
Produced by Dario Argento and directed by Mario Bava's son, a horror movie set in a red plush fleapit where an assortment of juveniles and degenerates have been assembled to watch some hokum about Nostradamus' tomb. While the film-within-the-film turns splattery, members of the audience are transformed, one by one, into flesh-eating demons. And the exits have been bricked up. It's a terrific idea which gets bogged down in stalk 'n slash stereotyping: the guys hunker down, the girls get hysterical and people are picked off. But it's all jolly gory. *Evil Dead*-ish fun, with a particularly squeamy bit which will put you off spot-squeezing for life, and some outrageous business with a helicopter. AB

Demons 2 (Demoni 2)

(Lamberto Bava, 1986, It) David Knight, Nancy Brilli, Coralina Cataldi Tassoni, Bobby Rhodes, Asia Argento.
91 min.
Accidentally reanimated, the Demons killed off in the original invade a tower block through the TV screens. Cue the obligatory party full of

bright young things who bop till they drop dead, then, transformed, rampage about the building like Hooray Henries with a dental hygiene problem. The cliché meter keeps pace with the body count as Argento and Bava throw in the old claustrophobic-trapped-in-lift chestnut, the cute kid all alone with toy ray gun, and the pregnant woman terrorised by same when a plastic Gremlin bursts from his stomach. Only a gym full of demon-bashing body-builders provides any real spark, and even the gore isn't in sufficient abundance to satisfy the diehards. DW.

Demon Seed

(Donald Cammell, 1977, US) Julie Christie, Fritz Weaver, Gerrit Graham, Berry Kroeger, Lisa Lu.
95 min.
Back from the post-*Performance* wilderness, Cammell was offered the thankless task of spinning a cripplingly restrictive premise – Christie trapped, menaced and impregnated by a super-computer desperate to produce a 'brainchild' offspring before its plugs are pulled – to feature length. A few of his labyrinthine concerns and much advanced animation work (plus optical assistance from once-celebrated avant-gardist Jordan Belson) spice the thin conceit, but it's a doomed project. PT

Demons of the Mind

(Peter Sykes, 1971, GB) Paul Jones, Gillian Hills, Robert Hardy, Michael Hordern, Patrick Magee, Shane Briant, Yvonne Mitchell.
89 min.
Sykes' first feature, an exotic Wildean horror story, visually as extravagant and tantalising as a decadent painting: rose petals drop lightly over corpses, an emaciated and incestuous brother and sister communicate through a keyhole dividing their sickrooms, a father hunts and shoots his children in the woods. These are some of the surreal fragments around which the plot revolves, and the script by Christopher Wicking is a striking attempt to introduce new themes and ideas to British horror. Badly let down, though, by some grotesque overacting, notably from Hardy, who sabotages a key role by playing it as ced Shakespeare. DP

Denise Calls Up

(Hal Salwen, 1995, US) Alanna Ubach, Tim Daly, Caroleen Feeney, Dan Gunther, Dana Wheeler Nicholson, Liev Schreiber, Aida Turturro, Sylvia Miles.
80 min.
It's the morning after the night before, and Linda's clearing up. Lots of food's still on the table because nobody turned up. Gail calls up to check how things went and apologise for being too busy to come. Afterwards she calls Frank who calls Jerry. None of them made it either. We're talking to New York's home office set here, laptops à go-go, busy busy busy. Still there's something which might drag them away from their keyboards. Gail wants to set up Jerry with her friend Barbara, but she needs Frank to call Jerry to get them together. Oh yes, and Denise calls up Martin, because she found out he made a donation to the sperm bank, and she's having his child. Maybe they could meet up, if he can get out the door, or even get off the phone. And so it goes on and on. Seventy minutes of phone conversations, cordless and mobile, call-waiting and 'Call you right back.' After about three minutes, though, the joke runs dry, the gimmickry (death on the phone, a birth on the phone) grates, the irony flattens out, and the constant yabbering of a bunch of thespian also-rans is enough to set you screaming. TJ

Dennis the Menace (aka Dennis)

(Nick Castle, 1993, US) Walter Matthau, Mason Gamble, Joan Plowright, Christopher Lloyd, Paul Winfield.
96 min.
John (*Home Alone*) Hughes is a dab hand at reconstituted family comedies. The script for this one he based on characters from Hank Ketcham's comic strip. Cherubic blond moppet Dennis (Gamble) – not to be confused with the *Beano*'s tousle-haired anarchist – is about as naughty as a choirboy on a Sunday school outing, and in terms of mischief only half as imaginative. Abandoned by his parents to the care of grouchy Mr Wilson (Matthau) and his childless wife

(Plowright), Dennis runs amok. Wilson rashly prepares to exhibit his ultra-rare Moon Plant at the local horticultural society's annual beanfeast…A smooth blend of sentiment and slapstick. NF

Dentellière, La
(The Lacemaker)
(Claude Goretta, 1977, Fr/Switz/WGer) Isabelle Huppert, Yves Beneyton, Florence Giorgetti, Anne Marie Düringer, Renata Schroeter, Michel de Ré.
107 min.
As much as anything, it's probably the intriguing ambivalence of a narrative in which connections are never overtly made that turned this into an unexpected box-office hit. Where *A Girl from Lorraine* treads a clearcut feminist path, *The Lacemaker* lurks in more shady byways. Its heroine (beautifully played by Huppert as a passive object) seems less a candidate for women's lib than a helpless prisoner of the incommunicability Goretta had in mind when he defined the film as being about the problem between two people 'who are unable to love each other because they do not express themselves in the same way'. The refreshing quality of the film, as one listens to the expressive eloquence of its silences, is that it cannot be reduced to ideological terms. The heroine may be a victim of both social convention and a suave though sympathetic seducer, but with a mysterious inner radiance glowing behind her patient suffering, she is also much, much more. TM

Dentist in the Chair
(Val Guest, 1960, GB) Bob Monkhouse, Peggy Cummins, Kenneth Connor, Eric Barker, Ronnie Stevens, Eleanor Summerfield, Reginald Beckwith.
88 min. b/w.
Stock up on the laughing gas, you'll need it to get through this farce involving student driller killer Monkhouse, dodgy petty crook Connor and a vanload of 'hot' dental instruments. The storyline may be full of cavities, but at least it's funnier than *Marathon Man*. TJ

Départ, Le
(Jerzy Skolimowski, 1966, Bel) Jean-Pierre Léaud, Catherine Duport, Jacqueline Bir, Paul Roland, Léon Dony.
91 min. b/w.
Skolimowski's first film made outside Poland, this perhaps laid the seeds for the later troubles and misunderstandings of his years in the wilderness with its sharp contrast between surface visual excitements and the shallow substance underneath. The hero (Léaud, hot from Godard's *Masculin Féminin*, along with Catherine Duport) is as much of a firecracker as the director, playing a Brussels hairdresser who gets up to crazy, startling tricks in order to secure a Porsche for a weekend racing rally. His obsessive quest allows Skolimowski to score some points about Capitalist excess and isolation, but not enough to keep the film properly balanced. Still, if you feel in the mood for frenzied hijinks, you'll get your money's worth. GB

Deranged
(Jeff Gillen/Alan Ormsby, 1974, US) Roberts Blossom, Cosette Lee, Robert Warner, Marcia Diamond, Brian Sneagle.
82 min.
This dark, stark account of the murderous activities of Wisconsin necrophile Ed Gein (the real-life character who inspired *Psycho* and *The Texas Chain Saw Massacre*) impresses not only through its occasional flashes of black humour (Gein, distressed by his beloved mother's death, exhumes her, and when she proves a little taciturn at the dinner-table, kills various women to keep her company), but by the sheer austerity of the direction. The more sensationalist aspects of the story are admirably underplayed, and Blossom's nicely gauged performance lends the film surprising conviction. GA

Derby (aka Roller Derby)
(Robert Kaylor, 1970, US) Mike Snell, Charlie O'Connell, Butch Snell, Christina Snell, Eddie Krebs.
96 min.
A documentary which follows one Mike Snell through his decision to leave his job and become a derby skater, incorporating interviews with his family, friends, and team members. The derby

itself is a natural for film: violent, colourful, full of great sweeping movements. In practice it seems all but devoid of rules. Everyone very definitely stomps hard on everyone else. Kaylor, formerly a still photographer, makes full use of the sport's spectacular aspects (filming from high up over Madison Square Gardens, for instance, so that the skaters become a blur of colour in a small ring of light), and delights in tracing the rituals that separate the game from the mainstream of life. He also allows people and events to explain themselves; the result is a remarkably lucid exposition of the roller derby at all points (not least its appeal to violent and masochistic instincts). VG

Derby Day
(aka Four Against Fate)
(Herbert Wilcox, 1952, GB) Anna Neagle, Michael Wilding, Googie Withers, John McCallum, Nigel Stock, Ralph Reader, Alfie Bass.
84 min. b/w.
Deeply unchallenging portmanteau of stories, from the Wilcox-Neagle stable, following the comic and dramatic adventures that befall visitors to Epsom's biggest race day, these include a taxi driver, a French maid and a murderer. Retitled for its US release, just in case it caused confusion in Kentucky. TJ

Dernier Combat, Le
see Last Battle, The

Dernières Vacances, Les
(Roger Leenhardt, 1947, Fr) Odile Versois, Michel François, Berthe Bovy, Pierre Dux, Renée Devillers, Jean d'Yd.
95 min. b/w.
Modest, unassuming and tremblingly fresh, this is the kind of miracle that will always pass unnoticed. If its theme (the end of adolescence), period (the '20s) and mood (elegiac) have all become clichés of contemporary cinema, it only confirms how much the dilettante Leenhardt, a critic, documentarist and *éminence grise* of the New Wave, was ahead of his time. Not to be missed – honestly. GAd

Dernier Mélodrame, Le
see Last Melodrama, The

Dernier Métro, Le
see Last Metro, The

Dernier Milliardaire, Le
(René Clair, 1934, Fr) Max Dearly, Renée Saint-Cyr, Marthe Mellot, Raymond Cordy, José Nogueiro, Aimos.
100 min. b/w.
Turning his patrician gaze for a moment on the real world (in the squalid aftermath of the Stavisky affair), Clair characteristically set this comedy on political chicanery in a Mediterranean Ruritania of Monte Carlo dimensions. Feeble as satire, and only occasionally amusing, it can best be described as a cross between *The Merry Widow* (without Lehar) and *Duck Soup* (without the Marx Brothers). GAd

Dernier Tournant, Le
(Pierre Chenal, 1939, Fr) Fernand Gravey, Michel Simon, Corinne Luchaire, Robert Le Vigan, Florence Marly, Marcel Vallée.
90 min. b/w.
When it comes to *noir*, we Anglos may have appropriated the word, but the *thing* was the result of the most delicate Franco-American reciprocity, well illustrated here. Preceding Visconti (*Ossessione*), Garnett and Rafelson, this is the first adaptation of James M Cain's 1934 novel *The Postman Always Rings Twice*, with its triangle of slobbish husband/bored wife/tough drifter. Apart from an accommodation with Michel Simon's star status, which required the husband to live longer, it's a faithful transposition of the novel's tone and content. But it's the style of the actors – Gravey's soulful eyes and mournful presence, Luchaire's other worldly beauty and air of resignation – which makes the difference, nudging the distinctively French world of 'poetic realism' and that of American pulp finally and irrevocably into alignment. (Luchaire's career stopped in 1940; she was the daughter of pro-Nazi writer Jean Luchaire, shot after the Liberation, and she herself was dead at 29.) BBa

Dérobade, La (The Life)
(Daniel Duval, 1979, Fr) Miou-Miou, Maria Schneider, Daniel Duval, Niels Arestrup, Brigitte Ariel.
113 min.
Based on a book by a French ex-prostitute, this is the extremely unpleasant story of a woman (Miou-Miou) dominated, despised and frequently beaten up by her pimp (played by the director). Perhaps seen in a French social context there might be an excuse to make for the film: it is in part set up to attack their very vicious system of pimps. However, it remains fetishistic, voyeuristic and racist, with its arty camera lingering over bodies, kinky outfits, and scenes of stomach-turning brutality perpetrated for the most part by swarthy men. HM

Dersu Uzala
(Akira Kurosawa, 1975, USSR/Jap) Maksim Munzuk, Yuri Solomin, M. Bichkov, V. Khrulev.
141 min.
Kurosawa went to Russia because he'd found it impossible to get work in Japan, but sadly he succumbed almost completely to the Mosfilm line in crude spectacle and simplistic, lumbering drama. Drawn from the autobiographical novels of a military explorer who encounters an elderly Goldi forest-dweller at the turn of the century, what emerges is a transparently sincere but entirely predictable account of the friendship between 'civilised' urban Russian and 'primitive' Oriental man of nature. TR

Der var engang en Krig
see Once There Was a War

Des Enfants Gâtés
(Spoiled Children)
(Bertrand Tavernier, 1977, Fr) Michel Piccoli, Christine Pascal, Michel Aumont, Gérard Jugnot, Arlette Bonnard.
113 min.
Only partly autobiographical, this account of a film director's brief affair with a young neighbour, and his involvement in the social and political ramifications of a tenancy dispute in an apartment block, still carries the weight of Tavernier's convictions about the injustices everyone (including film-makers) is forced to contest, domestically and at work. A striking performance from Pascal and the familiar leonine one from Piccoli. More 'parochial' than most Tavernier, but worth catching up with. MA

Desert Bloom
(Eugene Corr, 1985, US) Annabeth Gish, Jon Voight, Jobeth Williams, Ellen Barkin, Jay D Underwood, Allen Garfield.
106 min.
A near flawless mood piece. It is the '50s and nuclear testing is about to begin in the Nevadan wastes, but back in Las Vegas 13-year-old Rose (Gish) finds family life quite volatile enough. Her alcoholic stepfather (Voight), a traumatised World War II military-freak, seems to hate her but love her glam-puss aunt (Barkin). Written and directed by Corr, the film's main strength is its humorous understatement: it may take a little time to exert its considerable power, but once achieved its control never slips. The performances all round are excellent, avoiding histrionics and conveying with total authenticity the terrifying naivety of the mushrooming atomic age: 'Rise and shine, it's A-bomb time!' MS

Désert des Tartares, Le
(Valerio Zurlini, 1976, Fr/It/WGer) Jacques Perrin, Max von Sydow, Philippe Noiret, Vittorio Gassman, Laurent Terzieff, Jean-Louis Trintignant, Fernando Rey, Francisco Rabal.
148 min.
Something nasty is lurking on the steppes outside the fort, while inside the years pass and the occupying garrison sits around brooding. Is it the dread Tartars, the vengeance of God, or simply a figment of the uneasy military imagination? Difficult to care much, since portentousness hangs heavy over this handsome but hamfisted adaption of Dino Buzzati's Kafkaesque novel, abstracted in time, place and almost everything else way beyond the reach of a fine cast. TM

Deserter and the Nomads, The (Zbehovia a Poutnici)

(Juro Jakubisko, 1968, Czech/It) Stefan Ladizinsky, August Kubán, Gejza Ferenc, Jana Stehnová.
102 min.

Three tales of war, the first being by far the best. A young WWI soldier flees from the battlefield carnage and returns to the native village he has dreamed of as a haven of peace. But his return sparks off violent dissensions; he is betrayed to the Hussars as a deserter; and soon the whole village is a welter of brutal killings. With colour and images guided by folk art and a tang of surrealism, Jakubisko shapes his material into a sort of medieval death's jest-book, with Death himself – a grinning, skull-like refugee from a Bergman film – eagerly waiting to reap his harvest. Technique unfortunately begins to run rather wild in the rest of the film, all zooms, filters, distortions and wild arabesques. But the main problem is that the two remaining stories (WWII and a future nuclear holocaust) tend to ram home the message about the continuing horrors of war with a dull thud. An extraordinary, offbeat movie all the same. TM

Desert Fox, The (aka Rommel – Desert Fox)

(Henry Hathaway, 1951, US) James Mason, Cedric Hardwicke, Jessica Tandy, Luther Adler, Everett Sloane, Leo G Carroll, George Macready, Richard Boone.
88 min. b/w.

Considered daring at the time for its sympathetic view of a World War II enemy general as tragic hero. A whitewashed Rommel, returning to Germany disillusioned after the African defeat, becomes involved in the abortive Operation Valkyrie plot to assassinate Hitler, and opts for suicide rather than stand trial. Not really persuasive, despite careful performances and the journalistic flair of Hathaway's direction. TM

Desert Hearts

(Donna Deitch, 1985, US) Helen Shaver, Patricia Charbonneau, Audra Lindley, Andra Akers, Dean Butler, Gwen Welles.
93 min.

To Reno (in 1959) comes a mid-thirtyish New York teacher, her hair in a bun and her nerves in shreds, in search of a divorce from a stultified marriage. She puts up at a local ranch, and it's not long before she is succumbing to the advances of a much younger woman, though not without resistance. Suspicions that the film will simply be a period piece, viewed through the modern lens of post-feminist wishful thinking, are soon allayed however. Redneck Reno might still adhere to the old frontier notions of anything-goes morality, but it still harbours enough of the puritan spirit to make life uncomfortable for lesbians. Moreover, the ranch is more of an emotional snake-pit than first appears. Deitch is well served by Shaver as the teacher and Charbonneau as the young seducer. Best of all, however, is the way the movie dignifies all its characters. There is also an incendiary consummation of the affair, and Patsy Cline on the soundtrack; two features which had this paleneck by the throat. CPea

Desert Mice

(Michael Relph, 1959, GB) Alred Marks, Sidney James, Dick Bentley, Patricia Bredin, Dora Bryan, Irene Handl, Kenneth Fortescue, Reginald Beckwith, Joan Benham, Marius Goring, Liz Fraser.
83 min. b/w.

Groundbreaking melodrama about the love that dare not squeak its name…No, no, just taking the mickey. Africa, 1941: a third-rate ENSA concert party captures German officer (Goring) masquerading as one of ours. Strong odour of mouldy cheese. GM

Deserto Rosso

see Red Desert, The

Desert Song, The

(H Bruce Humberstone, 1953, US) Gordon MacRae, Kathryn Grayson, Steve Cochran, Raymond Massey, William Conrad, Ray Collins.
110 min.

The third movie of Sigmund Romberg's operetta in three decades – and if the result (adapted by Max Steiner) is utter tosh, at least it's utter tosh done dead straight. Full-throated Kathryn Grayson is the general's daughter who takes her time in realising gentleman anthropologist Gordon MacRae, the object of her affections, is also moonlighting as El Khobar, daring leader of North Africa's rebel contingent. TJ

Desert Trail, The

(Cullen Lewis ie Lewis D Collins, 1935, US) John Wayne, Mary Kornman, Paul Fix, Eddy Chandler, Carmen LaRoux, Lafe McKee, Al Ferguson, Henry Hall.
54 min. b/w.

Larky, no-account Western: rodeo rider John Scott (Wayne, unusually talkative), and his gambling buddy Kansas Charlie (Fix) are framed for murder, but John's girl, orphan Anne (Kornman), saves the day, after many a double-cross, when her mortally wounded brother admits to the crime. The stock rodeo footage suggests the two-horse town of Rattlesnake Gulch has a population of fifty thousand. The title's a mystery. JPy

Desert Victory

(Roy Boulting, 1943, GB)
60 min. b/w.

The full story of Montgomery's World War II campaign in North Africa as recorded by 26 combat cameramen attached to the 8th Army. Boulting's role as director and supervising editor kept him in London, cutting the footage as it was rushed from the front. The result is a classic wartime propaganda job, refreshingly soft in the commentary and unflinching in its visuals. GA

Designated Mourner, The

(David Hare, 1996, GB) Miranda Richardson, Mike Nichols, David de Keyser.
94 min.

Three people sit behind a desk: an old man (de Keyser), his daughter (Richardson), and his son-in-law (Nichols). They talk, not to each other, but to us, the audience. They reminisce about Judy's relationship with her father, a poet and dissident, and her husband Jack, who wilts under his own sense of intellectual inferiority. Gradually Jack takes centre stage to trace the contours of a narrative, the story of his failed marriage, his political and moral cowardice, his increasing alienation from the world of words and ideas. Hare's subtle, artful film of Wallace Shawn's play exists purely in that abstract, literary world – it is, defiantly, a piece of theatre, pared and minimalist. The film has something of the intimate quality of an actors' read through: what you lose in action, you gain in concentration and insight. Hare says the play is about 'the death of culture, the danger of culture becoming a minority pursuit', which obviously reflects his conviction that 'Keats is better than Dylan', highbrow better than lowbrow; certainly the film fulfils his own elitist criteria. Me? I could barely keep my eyes open. TCh

Design for Living

(Ernst Lubitsch, 1933, US) Gary Cooper, Fredric March, Miriam Hopkins, Edward Everett Horton, Franklin Pangborn.
90 min. b/w.

Noël Coward's teacup wit and elegance hardly suits the beer glass temperament of his screen adaptor Ben Hecht, who later complained of the author's 'vaudeville patter with an English accent', not to mention a 'superiority complex that went over big with sofa-cushion menders'. The script galumphs when it should glide, and neither the director nor the stellar cast can bring this would-be soufflé about a bohemian ménage-à-trois (Cooper paints, March writers, Hopkins flits between them) to the right fluffy consistency. GB

Designing Woman

(Vincente Minnelli, 1957, US) Gregory Peck, Lauren Bacall, Dolores Gray, Sam Levene, Chuck Connors, Mickey Shaughnessy, Ed Platt.
118 min.

A bubbly comedy in the best plush MGM style, following a fashion designer's amiable clash of interests with her sports journo husband. Peck however, is not an actor with the featherweight comic touch, and Bacall, herself a late replacement for the Monaco-bound Grace Kelly, had to get through the death of partner Bogart during production. A misfire. TJ

Desire

(Frank Borzage, 1936, US) Marlene Dietrich, Gary Cooper, John Halliday, Akim Tamiroff, William Frawley, Alan Mowbray.
96 min. b/w.

Elegant romantic comedy in the style of Lubitsch (who produced), but lacking his nudging innuendo thanks to Borzage's less cynical romanticism. Dietrich is the sprightly, sophisticated jewel thief who uses naive young Cooper to smuggle a necklace from France into Spain, only for love to bloom despite the difference in their moral outlooks. Marlene's best movie away from Sternberg, it's relaxed, funny and charming. GA

Desire Under the Elms

(Delbert Mann, 1958, US) Sophia Loren, Anthony Perkins, Burl Ives, Frank Overton, Pernell Roberts.
114 min. b/w.

Surprisingly faithful to the play, but still a leaden travesty. Director and cast (Loren especially) are hopelessly at sea with Eugene O'Neill's tragedy of familial lust (for land as much as for the body), which is a loose transposition to 19th century New England of Euripides' Hippolytus. TM

Desk Set (aka His Other Woman)

(Walter Lang, 1957, US) Spencer Tracy, Katharine Hepburn, Joan Blondell, Gig Young, Dina Merrill, Neva Patterson.
103 min.

Most reviewers agreed at the time that Hepburn got far more out of this mere bauble of a sex comedy than the 1955 Broadway play deserved. In it she plays the leader of an all-female TV network research team fearful of being rendered redundant by the arrival of an electronics expert's computer, with Tracy wooing her into acceptance. If Tracy was never quite as interesting as Hepburn's best comic foil, Cary Grant, he always allowed his offscreen lover ample scope. The results are some splendidly crisp exchanges between the pair, and the inevitable scene of embarrassment where he is literally 'caught with his pants down'. RM

Des Nouvelles du Bon Dieu (News from the Good Lord)

(Didier Le Pêcheur, 1996, Fr) Marie Trintignant, Maria de Medeiros, Christian Charmetant, Isabelle Candelier, Michel Vuillermoz, Jean Yann, Mathieu Kassovitz.
110 min.

A superbly inventive and witty first feature charting the effects of a trendy philosopher's suicide on his widow, a priest with shaky faith, and a near incestuous brother and sister who are the writer's greatest fans. The plot is driven by the siblings' belief that they're living out a novel written by God, and since the story's lousy they want to line up a chat with Him. If it all sounds weird, it is – but also rather wonderful. The Pope gets his, cops and mediums join in the search, the increasingly outrageous black comedy is seamlessly mixed with proper (if parodied) metaphysical ideas, and the plotline has enough surprises for several features. Subversive, sexy, thought-provoking. GA

Despair

(Rainer Werner Fassbinder, 1978, WGer/Fr) Dirk Bogarde, Andrea Ferreol, Volker Spengler, Klaus Löwitsch, Alexander Allerson, Bernhard Wicki.
119 min.

This generally ill-received assault (in both senses) on the art house market, filmed in English, toys perversely with its signifiers of 'class' (Nabokov novel, Stoppard script, Bogarde performance) to both plainly outrageous and oddly hermetic effect. The novel's surprises are merrily given away half way through (when distressed chocolate manufacturer Hermann Hermann decides to opt out of proto-Nazi Germany by murdering a 'double' who in fact looks nothing like him), and Fassbinder increasingly aligns the material with his more personal studies in schizophrenia like Satan's Brew or World on a Wire, while matching his own concerns with illusionism to Nabokov's with delusion. Bold, garish and obsessive, but more than a little irritating. PT

Desperado

(Robert Rodriguez, 1995, US) Antonio
Banderas, Salma Hayek, Joaquim De Almeida,
Steve Buscemi, Cheech Marin, Quentin
Tarantino.
105 min.
Less a sequel than a loose, bigger-budget remake
of *El Mariachi*, Rodriguez's second feature may
be a rambling, derivative exercise in gratuitous
violence, but its determination to proceed as if the
word 'restraint' never existed makes for gleeful
entertainment. The story takes off from and
rehashes the first film. Out to avenge his girlfriend's death, the mariachi (Banderas) turns up
in a lawless border town, determined, against the
advice of his buddy Buscemi (Steve, that is), to kill
drug-lord Bucho (De Almeida). There's a hitch:
Bucho knows he's targeted, and orders his myriad henchmen to waste anybody new in town.
Happily, after a run-in with one such thug, the
mariachi falls in with bookstore proprietor
Carolina (Hayek), who offers him shelter from the
storm of bullets. Humour comes mainly via
Buscemi, De Almeida and, in a pleasingly curtailed cameo, a mugging Tarantino. If the irony
and invention lacks the light touch of *El Mariachi*,
there's more than enough preposterous pleasure
to be had from Rodriguez's expertise with the
action set-pieces and absurdist approach to the
story's mythical aspirations. Bloody good fun. GA

Desperate

(Anthony Mann, 1947, US) Steve Brodie,
Audrey Long, Raymond Burr, Douglas
Fowley, William Challee, Jason Robards Sr,
Freddie Steele.
73 min. b/w.
Mann's B thrillers are as tough and harshly
stylised as they come. Here Steve Brodie and wife
flee both the mob fingering him for murder and
the law. Burr is a superb gangleader, and one
scene – a beating-up in a dark basement lit by a
single swinging light – is essence of *noir*. SJ

Desperate

(Rico Martinez, 1991, US) Kimberli Ghee,
Elvis Christ.
90 min. b/w.
So hip it hurts, the first film from Martinez, 'a
Chinese-Filipino/Mexican-American', chronicles
the desperate lives and times of Troy and Tan-
Yah: fame-fetishists, losers hooked on bogus
dreams, desperate for success. When we first meet
them, Tan-Yah (Ghee) is Tina Toilet, a would-be
punk singer with pseudo-English accent and attitude to match, while Troy (Christ) is desperately
over-extended in an investment pyramid that's
about to crash. It's 1979, a desperate year. Cut to
1984 – a desperate year – and Tan-Yah Tempter's
Heavy Metal thing doesn't happen. The 'Big New
Hair' is a washout, the record deal a bust. Troy's
acting career climaxes at the bottom: porno,
steroids, liposuction, collagen injections. Both
know that making it is murder. It's 1989, a desperate year... at 90 minutes, this is exactly 75 minutes too long (we all deserve 15 minutes, okay?).
For a film about 'now', it is laboured, repetitive,
derivative. In a word, desperate. TCh

Desperate Hours

(Michael Cimino, 1990, US) Mickey Rourke,
Anthony Hopkins, Mimi Rogers, Lindsay
Crouse, Kelly Lynch, Elias Koteas, David
Morse, Shawnee Smith.
105 min.
From its two opening scenes – scenic and sen-
sational(ist) respectively – it's pretty clear that
Cimino's remake of Joseph Hayes' thriller (a virtual
remake of William Wyler's 1955 version) will be
strong on visuals, weak on continuity and characterisation. Three hoodlums (Rourke, Koteas,
Morse) randomly choose the Cornell home as a
hideaway, and hold the family (Hopkins, the
estranged husband Hopkins, and two kids)
hostage. But where Wyler was content to wind
up the claustrophobic tension, and focus on getting the best out of Bogart and Fredric March,
Cimino appears distinctly frustrated by the scale
of his materials. He does, however, manage to
keep Rourke's escaped con – a volatile mix of
charm and menace – under control, while
Hopkins is dependably solid, if miscast as a
Vietvet. Mostly, however, the impression is of
Cimino trying to prove he can behave himself,
and deserting his cast in the process. Not desperate, but disappointingly ordinary. GA

Desperate Hours, The

(William Wyler, 1955, US) Humphrey Bogart,
Fredric March, Arthur Kennedy, Martha Scott,
Dewey Martin, Gig Young, Mary Murphy,
Robert Middleton.
112 min. b/w.
From a Broadway play, with Bogart giving his
penultimate performance as the desperate fugitive, a role played on stage by Paul Newman. A
trio of convicts on the run terrorise an average
American suburban family headed by March. One
of a number of '50s films which revealed the paranoia lurking under the facade of the American
dream, this time the respectability and security of
the family being disrupted with a vengeance.
Bogart clearly enjoys himself as a man with no
redeeming features, and he's well supported by
the other two (Martin, Middleton). Wyler directs
efficiently, if somewhat mechanically. CPe

Desperate Journey

(Raoul Walsh, 1942, US) Errol Flynn,
Raymond Massey, Ronald Reagan, Nancy
Coleman, Arthur Kennedy, Alan Hale.
107 min. b/w.
Boy's Own adventure as Flynn and his World
War II bomber crew (RAF courtesy of
Hollywood) escape from Nazis sneeringly led by
Massey after being shot down over the Black
Forest. Aside from some expendable propagan-
da heroics, rousingly handled by Walsh. TM

Desperate Living

(John Waters, 1977, US) Liz Renay, Mink Stole,
Susan Lowe, Edith Massey, Mary Vivian
Pearce, Jean Hill.
91 min.
Revelling in the travesty of carnal excess,
Desperate Living transforms the standard
elements of fairytale into a pastiche of dominant
sexual mores. The wicked queen is an omnivo-
rous barracuda-mother with a predilection for
leather boys, who devours her empire's
sub-lumpen populace with an appetite that is
tempered only by perverse sadism. Her princess
daughter, trapped in the heterosexual pursuit of
a Love Story, is finally saved by a rebellious
uprising of lesbian transsexual heroines who
bring about the collapse of the maternal dictatorship. Single-mindedly tracing the limits where
hedonism becomes revulsion, this is a celebration
of the flesh, a revindication of marginalised sex-
ualities, of desire as artifice, which is a lot less
misogynist than the tasteful aestheticism of 'natural' sexuality in softcore porn. CPa

Desperately Seeking Susan

(Susan Seidelman, 1985, US) Rosanna
Arquette, Madonna, Aidan Quinn, Mark Blum,
Robert Joy.
103 min.
Bored suburban housewife Roberta becomes
obsessed with mysterious messages placed in
The Times and starts looking all round New York
for 'Susan'(who has meanwhile arrived in town
from Atlantic City with a killer on her tail), until
eventually a bump on the head propels her into
Susan's persona and sets the hitman on her tail.
Susan is a sublimely self-sufficient slut with a
wacky wardrobe and a string of boyfriends, and
she is played by the Queen of Belly Buttons;
Arquette, as Roberta, outdoes her in sexy posing,
sultry pouting and kooky comic timing as she
swaps her humdrum canapé-ridden existence for
a magic act and a pink tutu. The female characters are neither merely love interest, nor man-fix-
ated mealy-mouthers, nor 'in peril'. They are
offbeat, off-the-wall, out-to-lunch and thoroughly engaging: Céline and Julie let loose in a Big
Apple subculture. AB

Desperate Measures

(Barbet Schroeder, 1998, US) Michael Keaton,
Andy Garcia, Brian Cox, Marcia Gay Harden,
Erik King, Efrain Figueroa.
100 min.
Frank Connor, a lone parent cop, competes with
the police force on a manhunt for escaped con
McCabe, and finds himself in a no man's land
between hunter and prey. The cops want the fugitive dead, and Frank wants his bone marrow to
save his little boy. The title describes the film's
strategy of victimising the child, a leukaemia
patient whose pre-op vulnerability is exploited
first to enable McCabe's escape, and then later as
he becomes a hostage to the latter's fortunes.

Keaton plays the con like Hannibal Lecter: a multiple murderer who can outwit his captors,
unblinking, droll and occasionally vicious. Garcia
is a rather dull embodiment of earnest persistence, and Harden flits in and out in an under-
explored role as the boy's surgeon. NB

Desperate Remedies

(Stewart Main/Peter Wells, 1993, NZ) Jennifer
Ward-Lealand, Kevin Smith, Lisa Chappell,
Cliff Curtis, Michael Hurst.
93 min.
This preposterous 19th century bodice-ripper is
set Down Under in a raunchy harbour town periodically injected with fresh blood in the form of
grimy transportees. One such is Hayes (Smith)
who is enlisted by an opulent but penniless dressmaker (Ward-Lealand) to save her opium-addict-
ed sister from a callous fop (Curtis). Stagy,
set-bound, and dazzling enough to trigger a
migraine. A film that dares to be bad, and succeeds quite splendidly. SFe

Desperate Search

(Joseph H Lewis, 1952, US) Howard Keel, Jane
Greer, Patricia Medina, Keenan Wynn, Robert
Burton, Lee Aaker.
73 min. b/w.
Not much dramatic fat on Lewis's involving open-
air suspense picture about the search for a couple
of children who have survived an air crash somewhere in the mountains of British Columbia. A
familiar set-up brings professional and personal
rivalries between Keel's reformed alcoholic father,
his iron-willed ex-wife, pilot Patricia Medina, and
latest (non-airborne) flame Jane Greer, but there's
little sentiment in the handling of the children's
plight and good-egg support from moustachioed
Keenan Wynn. A minor thing perhaps, but they
did a sound job with what they had. TJ

Desperate Siege

see Rawhide

Destination Gobi

(Robert Wise, 1953, US) Richard Widmark,
Don Taylor, Casey Adams, Murvyn Vye,
Darryl Hickman.
89 min.
A WWII action movie with a difference, this
somewhat implausible adventure has US Navy
officer Widmark seconded to the Gobi desert to
take charge of a group of American meteorolo-
gists at a remote weather station. Ambitiously,
he tries to engage local Mongol tribesmen to
attack the Japanese, who respond by bombing the
station, leaving Widmark and company alone in
the wilderness to fend for themselves. TJ

Destination Moon

(Irving Pichel, 1950, US) John Archer, Warner
Anderson, Tom Powers, Dick Wesson, Erin
O'Brien Moore.
91 min.
One of the George Pal-produced series of sci-fi
movies from the '50s, this is characteristically thin
on plot and characterisation, high on patriotism,
and impressive in its colour photography and special effects; a true precursor to *Star Wars*, in fact.
A group of scientists defy the familiar bunch of
superstitious and unadventurous philistines
(politicians, businessmen) and take off in their
new rocket to beat the Russians to the moon. GA

Destiny (Al Massir)

(Youssef Chahine, 1997, Egypt/Fr) Nour El
Cherif, Laila Eloui, Mahmoud Hémeida, Safia
El Amary, Mohamed Mounir.
135 min.
Its occasional dramatic longueurs notwithstanding, Chahine's film about the 12th century
Moorish philosopher Averroës is a brave,
engrossing attack on Islamic fundamentalist
dogma and oppression. Averroës and his followers are shown as free-thinking liberals, the
Caliph (who ordered his work burnt) a mere political pawn, but secondary to the narrative itself
is the glorious, stirring (and generically traditional) use of song and dance – frowned on by
the philosopher's enemies – as an energising, liberating force which embodies Chahine's notion
that 'thought has wings'. Common sense and sensuality merge in the intelligent script and
vibrant, colourful *mise-en-scène* to often exhilarating effect. GA

Destiny (Der müde Tod)

(Fritz Lang, 1921, Ger) Bernhard Goetzke, Lil Dagover, Walter Janssen, Rudolph Klein-Rogge, Georg John.
7,566 ft. b/w.
Lang's first major success was inspired by the *Intolerance* device of mixing parallel settings and cultures. Death gives a young girl three chances to save her lover's life, in old Baghdad, in 17th century Venice, and in mythical China. The tone ranges from baroque melodrama to eccentric whimsy, and the plotting is full of digressions and asides, but Lang's design sense and use of architectural space gives the film a basic consistency. And the plentiful special effects still look amazingly inventive. TR

Destiny Turns on the Radio

(Jack Baran, 1995, US) Dylan McDermott, Nancy Travis, James Belushi, Quentin Tarantino, James LeGros, Allen Garfield.
102 min.
This naff comedy-romance has McDermott's escaped con pitch up in Vegas looking for his heist loot and his beloved (Travis). The news is poor. Torch singer Travis is shacked up with Belushi's casino boss, and partner-in-crime LeGros explains his empty pockets with an incredible yarn. Cue a flashback to Tarantino's Johnny Destiny rising like Neptune from the hotel swimming pool, naked amidst thunderbolts and flashing neon light. No wonder he lost consciousness! And there's more. The guy who stole the booty was the same guy who gave McDermott a lift into Vegas. It's sad when deliberately self-mocking films backfire. This whimsical morass is a genuine trip to Palookaville. McDermott is no romantic hero, and the script is a woeful hash of *Bus Stop*, *Repo Man* and the musical sequences of *The Fabulous Baker Boys*. WH

Destroy All Monsters (Kaiju Soshingeki)

(Inoshiro Honda, 1968, Jap) Akira Kubo, Jun Tazaki, Yoshio Tsuchiya, Kyoko Ai.
89 min.
A romping Japanese monster rally, the 20th production in this vein from Toho studios, who have energetically devastated Japan on film virtually every year since 1954. Their output is frequently graphic and witty, with a weird gladiatorial style which has emerged under the guidance of Honda since his first *Godzilla*. In some ways these features are more like sporting events than fantasies, with a radio commentary ('It's Godzilla leading the attack') as the monsters of this world rally to protect it from extraterrestrial invasion.

Destry Rides Again

(George Marshall, 1939, US) James Stewart, Marlene Dietrich, Charles Winninger, Brian Donlevy, Una Merkel, Mischa Auer, Samuel S Hinds, Jack Carson, Billy Gilbert.
94 min. b/w.
Marvellous comedy Western, with Stewart's pacifist, reputedly wimpy marshal taming the lawless town of Bottleneck by means of words and jokes rather than the gun Donlevy's villain repeatedly provokes him to use. What is remarkable about the film is the way it combines humour, romance, suspense and action so seamlessly (with individual scenes – Dietrich singing 'See What the Boys in the Back Room Will Have', Stewart's delicious parable about a homicidal orphan, Mischa Auer losing his pants – indelibly printed in the memory). Flawless performances, pacy direction and a snappy script place it head and shoulders above virtually any other spoof oater. GA

Desvio al Paraiso (Shortcut to Paradise)

(Gerardo Herrero, 1994, Sp) Charles Dance, Assumpta Serna, Morgan Weisser, Katrina Gibson.
97 min.
To a backwoods Puerto Rican apartment complex comes Dance's Quinn, who lies his way into a job as janitor, befriends a tenant's ten-year-old daughter, and becomes murderously heavy with anyone who gets in his way. Much of this is nonsense of the OTT sort, but Herrero certainly gives it a patina of style, and here and there it almost works. Indeed, as a schlocky psycho-thriller, it's

not unwatchable, helped out by some decent performances and a nice sense of milieu. Trashy but, for the most part, fun. GA

Détective

(Jean-Luc Godard, 1985, Fr) Nathalie Baye, Claude Brasseur, Johnny Hallyday, Jean-Pierre Léaud, Alain Cuny, Laurent Terzieff.
98 min.
The trouble with Godard films is the weight of expectation brought to them: sometimes they're strained and serious (*Passion*), sometimes they're megabores (*Hail Mary*), and sometimes mini-masterpieces like *Détective*. This is a cross between a *Grand Hotel* for the 1980s and *film noir*: a crumbling Paris hotel houses four groups of people whose paths occasionally cross. One is the group around house-detective Terzieff, still trying to solve a murder of years ago; another is the entourage of boxer Tiger Jones, in training under the eye of his manager (Hallyday); another is a couple on the verge of breaking up; and the last is the Mafia. Much of it, especially Léaud (Terzieff's nephew-aide) and Cuny as a Godfather who judges men by their toilet habits, is riotously funny. Built on the charisma of its stars and on memories of the great thrillers of the 40s, tenuously held together by Godard's romantic pessimism, curiosity and sense of humour, it's co-dedicated, sensibly, to Clint Eastwood. TR

Detective, The

(Gordon Douglas, 1968, US) Frank Sinatra, Lee Remick, Jacqueline Bisset, Ralph Meeker, Jack Klugman, Horace McMahon, Lloyd Bochner, Robert Duvall.
114 min.
Fairly strong follow-up to the Sinatra/Douglas private eye caper *Tony Rome*, with the former now a New York cop fighting crime and corruption in a determinedly sleazy environment. Well acted and directed, though Abby Mann's script is an uneasy mixture of toughness and preachiness, while the succession of gays and man-hungry women looks badly dated. GA

Detective Story

(William Wyler, 1951, US) Kirk Douglas, Eleanor Parker, William Bendix, Horace McMahon, Cathy O'Donnell, George Macready, Joseph Wiseman, Lee Grant.
103 min. b/w.
Twenty-four hours in the life of a precinct station, just another day during which Douglas' jutting-jawed cop uses sadistic strong-arm tactics on a variety of suspects, discovers that his wife has had dealings with a slimy abortionist, throws a hysterical tantrum or two, and runs accidentally on purpose into a hoodlum's bullet. Underlying it all is a morality about the good man driven over the edge by the evil all around him, not made any less stagy by the way several characters come on as though auditioning for a Method class. It has a certain compulsiveness, but as with *Dead End* (also based on a play by Sidney Kingsley), the main interest lies in the admirable set. TM

Detenuto in Attesa di Giudizio

see Why?

Detour

(Edgar G Ulmer, 1945, US) Tom Neal, Ann Savage, Claudia Drake, Edmund MacDonald, Tim Ryan.
68 min. b/w.
The kind of film (made in six days, almost entirely in a Poverty Row studio, its extensive road scenes shot with back projection) that would be impossible to make today, even as a TV movie. Now it would require 100% locations (the 'art' of studio shooting having been discredited and thus lost), and the minimal narrative would never justify a go-ahead (pianist Neal is bumming from New York to rejoin his girl in California until tripped by hostile fate and the literally amazing femme fatale Savage). Neither pure thriller nor pure melodrama (though it has its true complement of doomed lovers, dead bodies, and a cruel sexual undertow), on an emotional level it most resembles the wonderful purple-pulp fiction of David Goodis. Passion joins with folly to produce termite art *par excellence*. CW

Deus, Patria e Autoridade (God, Fatherland and Authority)

(Rui Simoes, 1976, Port)
120 min.
For this documentary about Portugal's political explosion, Simoes had access to the archives of Portuguese TV, but he has cut the material together in a very different way from its original presentation (most of the archive footage predates the April 1974 coup). In addition, he includes filmed interviews with workers about their conditions, and with others about their own and the Portuguese colonies' part in the downfall of the Caetano regime. The film is less a history than a statement about class realities, and how political power in Lisbon never left the hands of the bourgeoisie.

Deutsche Kettensagenmassaker, Das

see German Chainsaw Massacre, The

Deux Anglaises et le Continent, Les (Anne and Muriel/Two English Girls)

(François Truffaut, 1971, Fr) Jean-Pierre Léaud, Kika Markham, Stacy Tendeter, Sylvia Marriott, Philippe Léotard.
132 min.
One of Truffaut's most tantalising romances, a discreet *ménage à trois* involving a French writer of the *belle époque* and two sisters living on the romantic Welsh coast. It's a tale of art born from emotional sacrifice as – all in love with one another and reluctant to cause hurt – the three withdraw from any final conflict or consummation of their feelings. As such, it's as much about what doesn't happen as about what does, and the form employed by Truffaut and Henri Pierre Roché's source novel (he also wrote *Jules et Jim*) – a literary narration – is thus entirely appropriate to the film's detached, gently nostalgic mood. Concerned not so much with feelings as with feelings about feelings, the film is simultaneously introspective and passionate, a perfect complement to the artistic era it portrays. Originally released in both Britain and America in a cut version. GA

Deux Hommes dans Manhattan

(Jean-Pierre Melville, 1958, Fr) Pierre Grasset, Jean-Pierre Melville, Christiane Eudès, Ginger Hall, Monique Hennessy, Jean Darcante, Jerry Mengo.
84 min. b/w.
If *Bob le Flambeur* was Melville's love letter to Paris, *Deux Hommes* is his billet-doux to New York. The chief pleasure from this fast, laconic movie is in the appearance of Melville himself, playing one of two journalists who are sent to Manhattan to trace the French UN delegate, only to discover that he died in his mistress' arms, thus creating possible scandal. The New York scenes were shot on the run, and mainly consist of Melville racing from a cab and into the entrances of famous buildings, which are then matched with suspiciously Parisian-looking interiors. A well-sustained, cheeky joke, full of life and a love for all things American, indispensable for an overview of the man. CPea

Deuxième Souffle, Le (Second Breath)

(Jean-Pierre Melville, 1966, Fr) Lino Ventura, Paul Meurisse, Raymond Pellegrin, Christina Fabrega, Pierre Zimmer, Michel Constantin, Denis Manuel.
150 min. b/w.
Made after three years 'in the wilderness' for Melville, this is his most elaborate and intricately plotted *film noir*, a labyrinthine exploration of loyalties and betrayals in the French underworld. It centres on an ageing gangster (Ventura at his most gnarled), in hiding after escaping from jail, who involves himself in a daring highway robbery while waiting to be smuggled out of the country. The steely location photography gives the action a veneer of realism, but the film's real energies are subterranean, and suffused with Melville's typical poetry: the bizarre interdependence of cop and criminal here is seen with the same eyes as the passionate love/hate of the brother and sister in *Les Enfants Terribles*. TR

Deux ou Trois Choses que Je Sais d'Elle (Two or Three Things I Know About Her)

(Jean-Luc Godard, 1966, Fr) Marina Vlady, Anny Duperey, Roger Montsoret, Jean Narboni, Christophe Bourseiller, Marie Bourseiller, Raoul Lévy.
95 min.
Despite some time-bound concerns and irritating conceits, the sheer energy of Godard's dazzling sociological fable is enough to commend it. Paris and prostitution, seen through 24 hours in the life of a housewife-prostitute (Vlady), tell a story of selling yourself to buy happiness, but getting paid in bad dreams. A fictional documentary of *Alphaville*'s nightmare, its virtuoso display of confession and analysis, the sublime and ridiculous, show Godard's deft grasp of the subversive nature of laughter and passions. Too good to miss. DMacp

Devi (The Goddess)

(Satyajit Ray, 1960, India) Chabi Biswas, Sharmila Tagore, Soumitra Chatterjee, Karuna Bannejee.
93 min. b/w.
Less obviously a work of humanist realism than the Apu trilogy, Ray's film is nevertheless a carefully nuanced study in religious obsession, with Biswas convinced that his young daughter-in-law (Tagore) is in fact the goddess Kali reincarnated. Comparitively baroque and melodramatic both in terms of its images and story, it still manages to mount a lucid, finally very moving argument against the destructive nature of fanaticism and superstition, with Tagore gradually losing all sense of her own individuality. Without a doubt, it is impressive film making; but whether its very Indian concerns are of widespread interest remains a moot point. GA.

Devil and Daniel Webster, The

see All That Money Can Buy

Devil and Max Devlin, The

(Steven Hilliard Stern, 1981, US) Elliott Gould, Bill Cosby, Susan Anspach, Adam Rich, Julie Budd, David Knell.
95 min.
This inspiring story of how an out-and-out slob makes a pact with the Devil but is finally converted to the Disney organisation would make better entertainment if the studio hadn't thrown so many disparate elements together in an attempt to grab their audience. We get one played out anti-hero, one winsome child actor, one Streisand clone who keeps belting out the same song, one wry black comic; the wonder is that there's no cute dolphin chortling in the swimming-pool. The script has its moments, especially when Cosby is around as the Devil's aide, but the film finally subsides in a welter of structural flaws and heartwarming sentiment. GB

Devil and Miss Jones, The

(Sam Wood, 1941, US) Jean Arthur, Robert Cummings, Charles Coburn, Edmund Gwenn, Spring Byington, SZ Sakall, William Demarest.
92 min. b/w.
A pleasant enough script by Norman Krasna lends sparkle to a Capra-corn style comedy about a cantankerous department store tycoon seeing the light when, in an attempt to put down a labour dispute, he disguises himself as a worker. Coburn is fine as the converted boss, Arthur is her usual professional self as the committed shopgirl with a heart of gold, but Cummings' wooden performance and Wood's stolid direction are something of a let-down. GA

Devil at 4 O'Clock, The

(Mervyn LeRoy, 1961, US) Spencer Tracy, Frank Sinatra, Jean-Pierre Aumont, Kerwin Mathews, Barbara Luna, Grégoire Aslan, Alexander Scourby.
126 min.
Spencer Tracy plays Ingrid Bergman in this hideous Polynesian variation on *The Inn of the Sixth Happiness*. He is a drunken and soul-searching missionary on an island about to be fire and brimstoned by a volcano, and can't save the leper children on his own. Enter three escaped convicts whose souls need saving. Everyone goes to heaven. ATu

Devil Commands, The

(Edward Dmytryk, 1941, US) Boris Karloff, Richard Fiske, Anne Revere, Amanda Duff, Ralph Penney.
65 min. b/w.
Karloff, at the time in the middle of a mad scientist rut that threatened to bog him down completely, is here attempting to contact his dead wife with weird machinery (involving Frankensteinian electricity, metallic space suits and hijacked bodies) and predictably disastrous results. Basically, it's a thick-ear version of a fine novel by William Sloane (*The Edge of Running Water*), but Karloff's performance is as reliable as ever, and Dmytryk injects what style he can on the budget, notably an atmospheric opening sequence more than reminiscent of the beginning of *Rebecca*. TM

Devil-Doll, The

(Tod Browning, 1936, US) Lionel Barrymore, Maureen O'Sullivan, Frank Lawton, Robert Greig, Lucy Beaumont, Henry B Walthall, Rafaela Ottiano.
79 min. b/w.
Anticipating both *Dr Cyclops* and *The Incredible Shrinking Man* in its miniaturisation effects, this was co-scripted by Erich von Stroheim from an excellent novel, *Burn Witch Burn!*, by A Merritt. Barrymore is an escaped convict who masquerades as the proprietress of a toy shop. The dolls he sells are actually real people reduced in size; and much of the film shows them – charmingly and only occasionally disturbingly – coping with giant furniture, evading their schoolgirl owners, and carrying out Barrymore's murderous revenge on those who sent him to Devil's Island. Browning had made *Freaks* at MGM, much to Mayer's disgust, and in working out his contract he had to lighten his uniquely dark vision, though the scene of a doll climbing out of a Christmas tree is effectively chilling. ATu

Devil in a Blue Dress

(Carl Franklin, 1995, US) Denzel Washington, Tom Sizemore, Jennifer Beals, Don Cheadle, Maury Chaykin, Lisa Nicole Carson, Terry Kinney, Mel Winkler.
101 min.
Recently fired and desperate to keep up the payments on his beloved home, WWII veteran Easy Rawlins (Washington) is offered a job by the shady Dewitt Albright (Sizemore): to discover the whereabouts of one Daphne Monet (Beals), a politician's fiancée scandalously rumoured to hang out in black bars. Assured that there's nothing illegal involved, Easy accepts. Pretty soon, however, he finds himself suspected of murdering a friend's girl (Carson) and under threat from both the cops and Albright's thuggish henchmen. Reluctantly, he puts in a call to Mouse (Cheadle), an old friend from his native Texas – reluctantly, because while Mouse has guts and loyalty to spare, he's also a volatile psychopath. Franklin's follow-up to *One False Move* is an impressively complex, polished and intelligent adaptation of Walter Mosley's thriller. It not only shows us an immaculately recreated world hitherto ignored by the movies (the black neighbourhoods of late '40s LA), but locates race, alongside more familiar elements like money and power, as a central motivating force for the various characters' actions. Mercifully, however, Franklin never preaches but allows the racial theme to emerge naturally from story and situation. Everything – the performances, Tak Fujimoto's angled camerawork, the jazz and blues soundtrack, the snappy script – slots neatly into his overall design. Sheer pleasure. GA

Devil in Miss Jones, The

(Gerard Damiano, 1972, US) Georgina Spelvin, Harry Reems, John Clemens, Marc Stevens, Rick Livermore.
68 min.
A milestone in hardcore history. Damiano (of *Deep Throat*) produced what was, for the genre, a film both technically proficient and dramatically coherent. He also introduced the marvellous Georgina Spelvin, a mature and attractive sex star who can really act, in the role of the frustrated spinster who commits suicide, relives her life as a wanton hussy, and ends up stranded for eternity in an existential Hell where orgasm is always just out of reach. AB

Devil in Miss Jones Part II, The

(Henri Pachard, 1982, US) Georgina Spelvin, Jack Wrangler, Jacqueline Lorians, Joanna Storm, Anna Ventura.
84 min.
An altogether jollier affair than the original. The first 15 minutes depict a delirious vision of Hell as a bad night at the Camden Palace, art direction courtesy of a Derek Jarman Fan Club, populated with luminaries such as Cyrano de Bergerac (specialist in 'nose jobs'), Marie-Antoinette ('the last time I gave head was in 1793') and, um, the Duke of Windsor. Getting the (literal) hots for Miss Jones, who has other ideas about his no orgasms regime, he grants her wish of eternal erotic existence in New York City. Alas, this is where the film itself gets shot to hell, because the stupendous Spelvin is transmuted into a series of bland bosomy starlets while Lucifer, getting hornier by the minute, searches for a suitable receptacle for her sex-hungry soul. Still, with some nice notions and witty one-liners, it's a cut above the average softcore feature. AB

Devil in the Flesh

see Diable au corps, Le

Devil Is a Woman, The

(Josef von Sternberg, 1935, US) Marlene Dietrich, Lionel Atwill, Cesar Romero, Edward Everett Horton, Alison Skipworth.
83 min. b/w.
Sternberg's final film with Dietrich, as precisely aimed as a whiplash to the coccyx. Marlene is Concha Perez, cigarette factory girl, sailing serenely through a comic-opera Spain in a steely, deeply-felt analysis of male masochism. Sternberg adapts the same Pierre Louys novel as Buñuel did for *That Obscure Object of Desire*, but he does it from the inside, centreing on the experience of two men (a young revolutionary and an older military man) who love Marlene and compulsively submit to the agonies of being rejected by her. Even those who go only for the Dietrich glamour can't miss these underlying tensions, since the stoic acceptance of emotional pain undermines all the surface frivolity. Some will find the glittering cruelty sublime. Unique now, as it was then. TR

Devil Never Sleeps, The

see Satan Never Sleeps

Devil, Probably, The

see Diable Probablement, Le

Devil Rides Out, The

(Terence Fisher, 1967, GB) Christopher Lee, Charles Gray, Nike Arrighi, Leon Greene, Patrick Mower, Gwen Ffrangcon-Davies, Sarah Lawson, Paul Eddington.
95 min.
Over the years, this film's reputation has grown enormously, and its cult status must be as high as any horror movie. Richard Matheson, who scripted it, was able to improve immeasurably on Dennis Wheatley's ponderous novel, and it is consequently the best film that Fisher and Hammer ever made, an almost perfect example of the kind of thing that can happen when melodrama is achieved so completely and so imaginatively that it ceases to be melodrama at all and becomes a full-scale allegorical vision. Christopher Lee has never been better than as the grim opponent of Satanism, and the night in the pentacle during which the forces of evil mobilise an epic series of cinematic temptations rediscovers aspects of mythology which the cinema had completely overlooked. DP

Devils, The

(Ken Russell, 1971, GB) Oliver Reed, Vanessa Redgrave, Dudley Sutton, Max Adrian, Gemma Jones, Murray Melvin, Georgina Hale.
111 min.
Russell's overwrought adaptation of John Whiting's play and Aldous Huxley's book *The Devils of Loudun*, full of much spiritual and physical writhing, is best approached as a diabolical

d

comedy. No matter how thickly Russell piles on the masturbating nuns, tortured priests and dissolute dauphins, there's no getting round the fact that it's all more redolent of a camp revue than a cathartic vision. Derek Jarman's sets, however, still look terrific. TR

Devil's Advocate, The (Des Teufels Advokat)

(Guy Green, 1977, WGer) John Mills, Stéphane Audran, Jason Miller, Paola Pitagora, Daniel Massey, Leigh Lawson, Timothy West, Patrick Mower.
109 min.
Spiritual torment is written all over this excruciating adaptation of Morris West's bestselling tale of betrayal and redemption, with Mills as the monsignor investigating a dubious case for canonisation, and having a torrid time (quite apart from dying of cancer) as he uncovers evidence of a murky story. Filmed in English, peopled entirely by caricatures, risibly righteous in its attitude to homosexuality, the film rivals *The Hiding Place* as an example of misplaced religiosity. JPy

Devil's Advocate, The

(Taylor Hackford, 1997, US) Keanu Reeves, Al Pacino, Charlize Theron, Jeffrey Jones, Judith Ivey, Craig T Nelson, Connie Nielsen, Tamara Tunie, Delroy Lindo.
144 min.
In this enjoyably daft legal thriller, from a novel by Andrew Neiderman, Reeves is a small time Florida defense attorney corrupted by ambition, greed and vanity. At one point, Al Pacino, impressive head of the multinational law firm that's lured him to New York with promises of fame and fortune, takes Reeves to the top of a high building, and promises to make him lord of all he surveys. But what does it profit a man to gain the whole world, if he loses his sexy girlfriend (Theron) and quaint, church-going mother? As the epitome of charismatic evil, Pacino is perversely attractive, his seductive performance making Reeves' temptation all the more believable. For his part, Keanu never quite convinces that he has the brain power necessary for exacting legal work. Tongue planted gently in his cheek, director Hackford makes his anti-materialist points without ever taking things too seriously. Regrettably, an overblown finale and redundant trick ending undercut the mild subversiveness of what's gone before. NF

Devil's Brigade, The

(Andrew V McLaglen, 1968, US) William Holden, Cliff Robertson, Vince Edwards, Andrew Prine, Claude Akins, Carroll O'Connor, Richard Jaeckel, Jack Watson, Harry Carey, Dana Andrews, Michael Rennie, Patric Knowles.
130 min.
Apparently based on fact, this emerges as a pretty slavish reprise of Aldrich's *The Dirty Dozen*. This time round, Holden is the unconventional officer assigned the task of knocking a bunch of thugs and misfits into shape for a special do-or-die mission. Appealing to their pride by pitting them against a crack Canadian regiment, he naturally succeeds. Thereafter, while not behaving impeccably on the battlefield, they sing 'For He's a Jolly Good Fellow' and hold birthday celebrations for the man who showed them the path to glory. The characterisations are strictly cardboard and the direction sluggish. TM

Devils, Devils (Diably, Diably)

(Dorota Kedzierzawska, 1991, Pol) Justyna Ciemny, Pawel Chwedoruk, Grzegorz Karabin.
86 min.
This is rather like everyone's idea of the Polish art film – slow-moving, shadow-laden, practically silent, and packed with significant close-ups and baleful looks. There's not much narrative either: gypsies come to a gloom-laden small town and small-minded souls rail at their alien ways, while a young girl finds the presence of the Other curiously in synch with her (you guessed it) burgeoning sexuality. At times soporific in its drowsy pace, it's nevertheless strangely seductive, not least for its tendency to dissolve into formalism. The occasional gypsies' knees-ups seem to have wandered in from another film entirely, but overall this is a curious, extremely atmospheric exercise. JRo

¡Devils Don't Dream! Research on Jacobo Arbenz Guzmán (¡Devils don't dream! Nachforschungen über Jacobo Arbenz Guzmán)

(Andreas Hoessli, 1995, Switz) Maria Vilanova de Arbenz, Howard E Hunt, Pio Quinto Hernandez, Richard Nixon, Winston Churchill.
80 min.
Documentary on the '40 years of war' that have troubled and haunted Guatemala since the US-executed coup against the liberal regime of Jacobo Arbenz Guzmán – a young army officer who himself led a coup against the prevailing right-wing dictatorship and, on being elected president, instituted a programme of progressive reforms. The absence of witnesses willing to talk (with the exception of Arbenz's widow) betokens the climate of fear that still obtains in Guatemala, and also limits the scope of the documentary. On the other hand, writer/director Hoessli has located much footage long thought lost in the private archives of a contemporary news cameraman. CIA-man Howard Hunt, chief of propaganda and political action in 1954, gives first-hand testimony of the arrogance of the US towards this one-time 'banana republic'. WH

Devil's Doorway

(Anthony Mann, 1950, US) Robert Taylor, Louis Calhern, Paula Raymond, Marshall Thompson, Edgar Buchanan.
84 min. b/w.
Actually made before *Broken Arrow*, but held up by a nervous MGM so that the Delmer Daves film reaped all the kudos for spearheading the pro-Indian cycle of Westerns. Taylor is the Indian who, having fought for the North in the war between the states, returns to his homelands only to find that the war against racism has still not been won. Mann's first Western, which he shoots as if it were a *film noir* and makes into a tough, bleak and cynical tragedy. CW

Devil's Envoys, The

see Visiteurs du Soir, Les

Devil's Eye, The (Djävulens Öga)

(Ingmar Bergman, 1960, Swe) Jarl Kulle, Bibi Andersson, Nils Poppe, Sture Lagerwall, Stig Järrel, Gunnar Björnstrand.
90 min. b/w.
Bergman's first earnest attempt to grapple with the question of theatricality in cinema. It retells the key incidents in the life of Don Juan, but its account of the seducer's shallow bravado and inner angst and his final despatch to hell is like Fellini's *Casanova* to the power of ten: a 'comedy' from which the laughs have all been drained. It's mounted as an overtly theatrical performance throughout: the episodes are introduced by Bergman veteran Björnstrand, who lectures the audience on what they're seeing and instructs them to view it as comedy. The episodes themselves are highly stylised, with (non-musical) hints of *Don Giovanni* foreshadowing Bergman's declared passion for Mozart opera. The dominant impression, though, as in so many early Bergman movies, is of a deep pessimism that is imposed rather than felt as necessary or productive. TR

Devil's Island

(William Clemens, 1939, US) Boris Karloff, Nedda Harrigan, James Stephenson, Adia Kuznetzoff, Will Stanton, Robert Warwick.
62 min. b/w.
B movie variation on *The Prisoner of Shark Island*, with Karloff as a French doctor sentenced to ten years on Devil's Island after tending an escaped prisoner convicted of treason. The predictable exposé of barbaric conditions is leavened by some nice touches (a mini-guillotine used for clipping cigars by Stephenson's corrupt governor), but falls apart latterly in a flurry of sentimental contrivance: Karloff performs delicate brain operation on governor's injured child; grateful mother helps him escape with evidence of governor's evildoings; he's recaptured, but saved from guillotine by arrival of *deus-ex-machina*. Karloff's sobering presence (he's excellent throughout) keeps it watchable. TM

Devil's Island (Djöflaeyjan)

(Fridrik Thór Fridriksson, 1996, Ice/Nor/Ger/Den) Baltasar Kormákur, Gisli Halldórsson, Sigurveig Jónsdóttir, Halldóra Geirhardsdóttir.
103 min.
A decade after WWII, the Americans abandon Camp Thule, Iceland – bestowing makeshift homes on the slum dwellers of Reykjavik. Gógó departs with them, but leaves behind her three grown kids – Baddi, Danni and Dolli, who live with their grandparents, Tommi (Halldórsson) and Karolina (Jónsdóttir). At first glance, Fridriksson's charmer looks studiedly eccentric. There's something cartoonish about the motley bunch of ne'er-do-wells. They may be out of it, but they're not immune to the world, in fact they're peculiarly vulnerable to change. Baddi (a stellar performance from Kormákur) visits his mother in the States, and comes back a rock'n'roll hound dog who rules the roost with his Cadillac, hep talk and cocksure moves. It's soon obvious there's nothing for him in Iceland any more. This is a bright, tangy, highly engaging account of the old world trying to get to grips with the new. The incidental structure gives the extended cast plenty of room to make their mark, and despite the sometimes harrowing circumstances, Fridriksson always keeps the energy up. TCh

Devil's Own, The

(Alan J Pakula, 1997, US) Harrison Ford, Brad Pitt, Margaret Colin, Rubén Blades, Treat Williams, George Hearn, Mitchell Ryan, Natascha McElhone.
111 min.
A Hollywood blockbuster in which Northern Ireland comes over as the usual assemblage of gentle natives, scheming Brits, down-home knitwear, and gunfire stilling the plaintive sound of the uileann pipes. His fisherman dad a victim of the 'security forces', IRA man Pitt takes the battle to the sanctuary of the US, where he plots a missile shipment from a safe house set up by republican sympathisers. His unwitting host, decent Irish-American cop Ford, is kind enough to offer shelter to the young man from a troubled homeland, but as the visitor settles in, an ominous shadow is already looming over his Transatlantic sojourn. The tension between the dedicated terrorist and the family nest that might yet redeem him proves the piece's strongest dramatic suit, buoyed by Ford's believable performance as the hard-pressed NYPD man trying to do the decent thing against the odds. Otherwise, lacking the adrenalin of an out-and-out action movie, and without the intelligence to be much of anything else, the film has nowhere to go. Pitt's accent, most convincing when he says 'aye', is somewhat tested by whole sentences. TJ

Devil's Playground, The

(Fred Schepisi, 1976, Aust) Arthur Dignam, Nick Tate, Simon Burke, Charles McCallum, John Frawley, Jonathan Hardy.
107 min.
Stirrings of style in this semi-autobiographical first feature (Schepisi matured markedly in *The Chant of Jimmie Blacksmith* and *Barbarosa*). But its tale of troubles in a Catholic boys' school follows the familiar catechism of crises of faith and puberty, told in the impressionistic manner that was the quality hallmark of the 'new' Australian cinema. TM

Devil's Rain, The

(Robert Fuest, 1975, US) Ernest Borgnine, Eddie Albert, Ida Lupino, William Shatner, Keenan Wynn, Tom Skerritt, Joan Prather, John Travolta, Claudio Brook.
86 min.
After a luxuriant Bosch credit sequence, we plunge into thirty minutes of bewildering but entertaining events that revolve around a dissolving dad, a satanic register, a protective amulet, a Mansonesque coven of dead-eyed converts led by a reincarnated witch, plus an expert in the fields of ESP and demonology. When the explanations begin (mainly a flashback to 17th century ancestors), things become heavy-handed, revealing the ragged direction, a dire script, and performances which range from the bemused (Albert) to the awful (Borgnine). Fuest butters on the special effects, which culminate in a tediously extended final splurge when almost the whole cast dissolves into a puddle of green slime. IB

Devil's Wheel, The (Chyortovo Koleso)

(Grigori Kozintsev/Leonid Trauberg, 1926, USSR) Ludmila Semyonova, N Foregger, Pyotr Sobolevsky, Sergei Gerasimov, Emil Gal.
8,695 ft. b/w.
Typically of the heady days of early Soviet cinema, this is constructed according to the fast, sharp editing principles advocated by Eisenstein, complete with symbolic inserts; but in terms of subject matter, it's much less explicitly political than most movies emerging from Russia in the '20s. Chronicling a young sailor's descent into a murky, treacherous underworld of pimps and thieves, after having encountered a Louise Brooks lookalike at a fairground and missed his departing boat, it's a lively moral fable that delights in vivid visual effects and quirky characterisations. If the plot occasionally reveals gaping holes, and the tacked-on ending urging the clearance of the Leningrad slums seems to be rather gratuitous, there's enough going on to keep one attentive and amused. GA

Devil Within Her
see Chi Sei?

Devil Within Her
see I Don't Want to be Born

Devotion

(Curtis Bernhardt, 1943, US) Ida Lupino, Olivia de Havilland, Nancy Coleman, Paul Henreid, Sydney Greenstreet, Arthur Kennedy, Montagu Love.
107 min. b/w.
Pure hokum. In a studio-recreated Haworth parsonage, Charlotte (bitchy de Havilland) and Emily (dreamy Lupino) indulge in various highly romantic intrigues and passions, overshadowing the quieter Anne (Coleman) even before they set to writing and become the famous Brontë sisters. Silly even to the point of having the beloved curate inexplicably played by Austrian Henried, but endowed with a charm and conviction all its own, helped enormously by Bernhardt's swooning direction and Ernest Haller's photography. Enjoyably absurd. GA

Diable au corps, Le (Devil in the Flesh)

(Claude Autant-Lara, 1947, Fr) Gérard Philipe, Micheline Presle, Jean Debucourt, Germaine Ledoyen, Denise Grey, Jacques Tati.
112 min. b/w.
One of the cornerstones of the *cinéma de papa* so opportunistically maligned by Truffaut, this solid adaptation (by Aurenche and Bost) of the Raymond Radiguet novel hasn't lost its power to move. While all around celebrate the end of the war in 1918, a schoolboy (Philipe) remembers his impossible affair with an older married woman (Presle), from whose funeral he is barred. Autant-Lara unfortunately overplays some of his stylistic devices (such as the slowed-down sound that announces each flashback), but for the main part he elicits sensitive performances from his leads, and the smoky photography and sets evoke a unique period atmosphere. DT

Diable Probablement, Le (The Devil, Probably)

(Robert Bresson, 1977, Fr) Antoine Monnier, Tina Irissari, Henri de Maublanc, Laetitia Carcano, Régis Hanrion, Nicolas Deguy.
95 min.
Bresson observes his Parisian student protagonist in numb recoil from a culture, almost a species, compromised beyond recall. As so often in Bresson, the process of detachment ends in deliberately sought death. Here Charles' proxy suicide stands, as Jan Dawson has perceptively noted, both as an affirmation of a purity no longer possible within society, and 'as a portent of the millions of deaths, not self-willed, which must inevitably follow', given the ruthless course of society's crimes. Charles and the two women in his life are offered less as convincing portrayals of life on the student fringe than as indices of a particular state of consciousness. Beside the toughness of *Pickpocket*, the depth of feeling of *Une Femme Douce*, the rigour of *Lancelot du Lac, The Devil, Probably* has a certain opaque quality. Its case is presented rather than argued: one buys its cosmic bleakness or one doesn't, but there is no doubt about the conviction with which it is put. VG

Diabolik
see Danger Diabolik

Diabolique
see Diaboliques, Les

Diabolique

(Jeremiah Chechik, 1996, US) Sharon Stone, Isabelle Adjani, Chazz Palminteri, Kathy Bates, Spalding Gray, Shirley Knight, Allen Garfield.
107 min.
Remake of Clouzot's 1954 chiller with an arty veneer. Stone's the hard-bitten mistress and Adjani the fearful, ailing wife of Palminteri, sadistic head of a Philadelphia boarding school. Bates is the sassy private eye who smells something fishy after Palminteri's reported missing. We, of course, have already seen the ladies drown him in the bath, so how come it seems he may still be alive or, at the very least, haunting his killers? Working from a rickety script, Chechik coughs up a string of Grand Guignol clichés and attempts to give a 'modern' twist to a plot over-familiar from inferior imitations. The cast is wasted: Adjani, suitably vulnerable in the Véra Clouzot role, has little scope to deliver the raw emotions she's so good at; Stone is two-dimensionally terse and tough; Bates is lumbered with some dubious gags about mastectomy; and Palminteri mugs as the sneering ogre. Not scary. DA

Diaboliques, Les (Diabolique/The Fiends)

(Henri-Georges Clouzot, 1954, Fr) Simone Signoret, Véra Clouzot, Paul Meurisse, Charles Vanel, Pierre Larquey, Michel Serrault, Jean Brochard.
117 min. b/w.
Headstrong mistress (Signoret) and retiring wife (Clouzot) conspire to murder the man they share, a tyrannical headmaster of a seedy boarding-school whose curriculum offers nothing but stagnation and decay. But in this black world (where, ironically, only the dead comes to life) everyone is in the end a victim, and their actions operate like snares setting traps that leave them grasping for survival. The camera watches these clammy proceedings with a cold precision that relishes its neutrality. At least one source claims that all Clouzot's films were shot in an atmosphere of bitterness and recrimination. It shows. But in this case it makes for a great piece of Guignol misanthropy. CPe

Diabolo Menthe (Peppermint Soda)

(Diane Kurys, 1977, Fr) Éléonore Klarwein, Odile Michel, Anouk Ferjac, Michel Puterflam, Yves Rénier, Robert Rimbaud.
101 min.
Kurys' impressive feature debut, based on autobiography, is a sensitive account of a year in the lives of two sisters – 13-year-old, introverted Anne, and outgoing 15-year-old Frédérique – in the early '60s. Without ever lapsing into melodrama, the film adopts a decidedly un-nostalgic tone, lucidly charting the everyday oppressions of school life and the girls' difficult relationships with their parents – a separated Jewish couple – their friends and each other. Indeed, it's a harsh, unsentimental look at adolescence, with the '60s setting serving primarily to define the social and political context of the girls' rites of passage; at the same time, however, the film is invested with great warmth through Kurys' assured, sympathetic handling of her cast. GA

Día de la bestia, El
see Day of the Beast, The

Diagnosis: Murder

(Sidney Hayers, 1974, GB) Jon Finch, Judy Geeson, Christopher Lee, Tony Beckley, Dilys Hamlett, Jane Merrow, Colin Jeavons.
90 min.
A lumbering, shakily scripted essay in the kind of emotional area (actions stemming from hatred, greed and possessiveness) that Chabrol effortlessly activates into his fraught and loving critiques of the bourgeoisie. Consultant psychiatrist Lee's wife disappears; notes appear blaming him for her murder. Enter Finch's police inspector, dragging with him an ambitous but awkward subplot involving his girlfriend and her crippled husband (not only is the poor guy confined to a wheelchair, he is also given the most unspeakable lines in the script). Hayers' pedantic, explanatory style, and failure to sustain any very revealing mood or to probe his characters with the necessary relentlessness, makes the going grim. VG

Diagonale du Fou, La
see Dangerous Moves

Dial M for Murder

(Alfred Hitchcock, 1953, US) Ray Milland, Grace Kelly, Robert Cummings, Anthony Dawson, John Williams.
105 min.
Shot in 3-D – which resulted in some rather strained and awkward compositions – this nevertheless remains one of Hitchcock's very stagiest films. Milland is the has-been tennis star who decides to have his wife killed in order to lay his hands on her fortune; Kelly is the potential victim who cannot, at first, work out why a stranger should enter her house and try to murder her. It all moves along in a rather efficient if lifeless fashion, with only John Williams shining as a canny police detective, and only the murder scene itself breaking the tedium induced by Hitchcock's decision to shoot on a single apartment set. GA

Dialogue des Carmélites, Le

(RL Bruckberger/Philippe Agostini, 1959, Fr/It) Jeanne Moreau, Alida Valli, Pascale Audret, Madeleine Renaud, Pierre Brasseur, Georges Wilson.
113 min. b/w.
Only Bresson, perhaps, could have done justice to Gertrud von le Fort's novel of Carmelite martyrdom during the French Revolution (already adapted for the stage by Bernanos and opera house by Poulenc). What it got instead was the ultra-static co-direction of Bresson's cinematographer (Agostini) and a fashionable 'literary' priest (Bruckberger). Though a potentially moving study of grace (in the most literal, theological sense) under pressure, neither of these qualities is very conspicuous in this pallid Sunday school picnic of a film. GAd

Dialogues With Madwomen

(Allie Light, 1993, US)
90 min.
Seven articulate women speak about manic depression, schizophrenia and multiple-personality disorders. Director Allie Light, who adds her own experience of depression, offsets the interviews with experimental montage sequences. Archive footage and reconstructed images illuminate the darkest corners of the psyche: a keyhole drips blood; a silhouette dances in front of the moon; an interviewee walks into the sea with a suitcase; horrific photographs of self-mutilation. The material draws heavily on early childhood, the reasons for insanity being attributed to life-experience rather than biochemistry; and abuse at the hands of fathers and stepfathers features strongly. JBa

Dial Rat for Terror
see Bone

Diamond Mercenaries, The

(Val Guest, 1975, Switz) Telly Savalas, Peter Fonda, OJ Simpson, Maude Adams, Hugh O'Brian, Christopher Lee.
101 min.
'Is that Miss or Ms?' Savalas asks of Adams. 'That depends on the man,' she replies. In other words, we have here an old-fashioned adventure given the veneer of modernity. The crooks planning the desert heist are Vietnam veterans rather than league of gentlemen; but in other respects we're back in the world of Val Guest hokum (Savalas wanders about showing off his wardrobe, you don't quite get to see anything in the bed scene, all the interiors are in medium-shot). Still, the robbery is a smart piece of editing, the desert looks handsome, and Christopher Lee staggers around in it wearing khaki – a rare delight. AN

d

Diamonds

(Menahem Golan, 1975, US) Robert Shaw,
Richard Roundtree, Barbara Hershey, Shelley
Winters, Shai K Ophir.
108 min.

All jokes apart from a boy's best friend aside, this is
an irredeemable disaster of a caper movie. Shot
in Israel, it has Shaw in an embarrassing double
role as both security head of the Tel Aviv
Diamond Exchange and his playboy brother, out
to outwit him with a pair of love-bird thieves. PT

Diamonds Are Forever

(Guy Hamilton, 1971, GB) Sean Connery, Jill St
John, Charles Gray, Lana Wood, Jimmy Dean,
Bruce Cabot, Joseph Furst.
120 min.

Apart from a clumsy climax, a wry and exhilarating bit of entertainment. The film's virtues stem
mainly from a sense of self-parody, an intelligent
script, the deft handling of the Las Vegas locations,
and the presence of Jill St John instead of the usual
array of pneumatic androids that super-bureaucrat
Bond preys upon. Although the Bond films have
succeeded in referring only to themselves,
Diamonds achieves somewhat of a breakthrough
by being set in a kind of socio-political reality: the
Howard Hughes-type recluse in his Vegas empire;
the implications of the nuclear blackmail game; the
peculiarly Californian obsession with mortuaries;
right down to the fey but villainous homosexuals
and the pair of beautiful killer-karate female bodyguards who initiate 007 into contemporary femininity. On the debit side, the plot is about as
watertight as a sieve, and the unwillingness of
Bond's enemies to fill him with lead – instead opting for elaborate and ludicrous devices from which
he escapes far too easily – has become tiresome. PG

Diamond Skulls

(Nick Broomfield, 1989, GB) Gabriel Byrne,
Amanda Donohoe, Michael Hordern, Judy
Parfitt, Ian Carmichael.
87 min.

'It begins as if it's going to be a film about class,
which is obviously what people expect from the
British cinema'. Nick Broomfield goes on to
protest that his film deals with the murkier subject of obsession, but in fact it dabbles with both
themes – and neither satisfactorily. Lord Hugo
Buckton (Byrne, the exceptionally jealous husband of ex-model Ginny (Donohoe), thinks she's
having an affair with her publishing colleague.
After a heavy night wining and dining, Buckton
gets behind the wheel of a car, while fellow officers from his former regiment pile into the back.
A woman is run down. After momentary dithering, they decide to close ranks, and so leave her
fatally injured. One of the group, noting the victim's strong resemblance to Buckton's wife, suffers from a pricked conscience. But will he run
squealing to the police? In documentarist
Broomfield's transition to fiction, the camera
lingers over Byrne's sculptured features and captures each careful gesture from Donohoe. The
controlled technique echoes the theme of domination, but combined with the largely unsympathetic characters, results in a film that affects
emotion and remains curiously hollow. CM

Diane

(David Miller, 1955, US) Lana Turner, Pedro
Armendariz, Roger Moore, Marisa Pavan,
Cedric Hardwicke, Henry Daniell.
110 min.

A 16th century romp: young Roger Moore is the
king's son, Lana Turner the French countess who
falls for him – but he can't reciprocate since Dad
wants him to marry Catherine de Medici. Despite
a script from Christopher Isherwood and one of
Miklos Rozsa's ludicrously overblown scores, this
is stodgy, soporific stuff. Turner's ridiculously
miscast while Moore hadn't yet mastered the let's-
raise-my-eyebrows style of acting he later used
to show off to Miss Moneypenny. GM

Diaries

(Ed Pincus, 1981, US) Jane, Sami, Ben and Ed
Pincus, David Neuman, David Hancock.
200 min.

If you set out to make a film diary of your family and friends over five years – births, deaths,
break-ups, etc. – would you wish it on the public? Ed Pincus does. Hailed by some as a remarkable piece of cinéma-vérité validated by the
film-maker's disarming honesty, Diaries comes

across to anyone not living among the artistic
elite of Cambridge Mass. as a self-indulgent suf-
fering-Seventies bore. MA

Diary for My Children (Napló Gyermekeimnek)

(Mártá Mészáros, 1982, Hun) Zsuzsa Czinkóczi,
Anna Polony, Jan Nowicki, Tamás Tóth,
Mari Szemes.
107 min. b/w.

After the war, teenage Juli and her grandparents
return from exile in Russia to Budapest. But Juli's
hopes of happiness in her homeland are gradually
eroded by the strictures of a disciplinarian society;
her guardian offers love but no freedom; a free-
thinking older man who befriends Juli is incarcerated. The fact that the film is based on Mészáros'
own experiences makes for a certain veracity about
life in Hungary during the Stalinist era, and certainly one is struck by its sincerity, intelligence and
strong performances. But the film is so coldly
directed, and the portrait of period and place so resolutely joyless that it is hard to care in any real way
about the grim fates of its characters. GA

Diary for My Loves (Napló Szerelmeimnek)

(Mártá Mészáros, 1987, Hun) Zsuzsa Czinkóczi,
Anna Polony, Jan Nowicki, Irina Kouberskaya,
Mari Szemes.
130 min. b/w & col.

Mészáros' second semi-autobiographical film
diary picks up where Diary for My Children left
off in the Hungary of 1953. Alter-ego Juli, still
played by the frosty but winningly resolute
Czinkóczi, is now 18, has lost her lover in the
Stalinist purges, and is placed in the care of her
party-puppet foster mother. Juli's dream of becoming a film director comes true in Moscow, but her
adherence to documentary truths troubles the
comrades back in Budapest, even after the death
of Bad Father Joe. Taking us up to the '56
Uprising, Mészáros creates a superbly confident
portrait of her country's traumatic past, painted
through individual passions and more than a
touch of psychoanalysis. Sometimes her points
may miss their mark without a crash course in
East European history, official and more especially unofficial; but her integrity binds the mixture of psychodrama and newsreel, monochrome
and colour, novelette and history lesson. DT

Diary of a Chambermaid, The

(Jean Renoir, 1946, US) Paulette Goddard,
Hurd Hatfield, Francis Lederer, Burgess
Meredith, Judith Anderson, Reginald Owen,
Florence Bates, Irene Ryan.
86 min. b/w.

In its own strange way, even more genuinely surreal than Buñuel's later version of Mirbeau's
novel about a keyhole-peeking chambermaid
whose arrival in the household of a decadent and
eccentric aristocratic family wreaks havoc.
What's so bizarre about Renoir's adaptation
(scripted and produced by Meredith, then husband of Goddard) is the sheer artificiality of both
setting and performances, emphasising the
power struggles that develop as a theatre of
deceit and delusion. Less bitterly savage than
Buñuel, but equally sharp in its satire, it stands
on an otherwise uncharted point between La
Règle du Jeu and, say, The Golden Coach. GA

Diary of a Chambermaid, The (Le Journal d'une Femme de Chambre)

(Luis Buñuel, 1964, Fr/It) Jeanne Moreau,
Georges Géret, Michel Piccoli, Françoise
Lugagne, Daniel Ivernel, Jean Ozenne,
Gilberte Géniat.
98 min. b/w.

Moreau as the beautiful, ambitious Célestine makes
it from Downstairs to Upstairs by manipulating her
right-wing boss (Piccoli), his leftish neighbour
(Ivernel) and his fascist gamekeeper (Géret). Octave
Mirbeau's muckraking 1900 novel has abiding
insight into the deep structures of French political
instability. Buñuel shifts the story to the rise of
Fascism in the '30s: the dogs right down to that spiritual gunge which links political, sexual and social
positions (and impositions) as equal perversions of
human desires (in turn perversions of animal
desires). Like most Buñuel heroines, Célestine is
intuitively a feminist, but before her time, and
blows it by her egoism and ambivalence before

male ruthlessness. Moreau's baleful charisma complements Buñuel's sardonic sadness. It's his greyest
film since Nazarin, and all the more troubling for
its impassive flow, which successive explosions of
strange desire can never quite disturb. RD

Diary of a Country Priest (Journal d'un Curé de Campagne)

(Robert Bresson, 1950, Fr) Claude Laydu,
Marie-Monique Arkell, André Guibert, Jean
Riveyre, Nicole Ladmiral, Nicole Maurey.
120 min. b/w.

Alone and dying of cancer, a young curate faces
the mortal torment of failure in his task of saving
souls. What he finds in the ultimate victory over
self is that mysterious touch of grace which
remains one of the immutable signs of a Bresson
film. Watching this spiritual odyssey is almost a
religious experience in itself, but one which has
nothing to do with faith or dogma, everything to
do with Bresson's unique ability to exteriorise an
interior world. TM

Diary of a Lost Girl (Das Tagebuch einer Verlorenen)

(Georg Wilhelm Pabst, 1929, Ger) Louise
Brooks, Edith Meinhardt, Vera Pawlowa, Josef
Rovensky, Fritz Rasp, André Roanne,
Arnold Korff.
9,393 ft. b/w.

An elegant narrative of moral musical chairs,
Pabst's last silent film not only plays on who holds
what kind of legitimate place in society, but is also
a starkly direct view of inter-war Germany.
Feasting the camera on Brooks' radiant beauty,
Pabst follows the adventures of innocence led
astray in the shape of Thymian, a pharmacist's
daughter. Her progress from apple of her father's
eye, through sexual lapse and approved school, to
darling of an expensive brothel and finally to
dowager countess, gives Pabst the opportunity to
measure the Germany of the Weimar republic
against Brooks' embodiment of a vitality so exuberant that it equals innocence. However damning, though, Pabst's indictment of the bourgeoisie
as torn between powerless compassion, greed and
scandal-lust, his alternatives – the brothel as the
one place of true friendship, or the aristocratic
father-figure who puts everything right in the end
– smack very much of a cop-out, allowing him to
both revel in decadence and enjoy the moral superiority of denouncing it. RB

Diary of a Mad Housewife

(Frank Perry, 1970, US) Richard Benjamin,
Frank Langella, Carrie Snodgress, Lorraine
Cullen, Frannie Michel, Peter Boyle.
95 min.

Perry and his scriptwriter-wife Eleanor have consistently made provocative, offbeat films about
mental and spiritual reawakening (until the disastrous Mommie Dearest, that is). Some of them,
like the allegorical The Swimmer, have been
intriguing catastrophes; this is one of the more
successful. Bored New York housewife Snodgress
tires of smug, over-ambitious husband Benjamin
and his persistent nagging, and decides to gamble on an affair with narcissistic writer Langella,
only to find that relationship equally dissatisfying. Often very funny in its acerbic swipes at
American success-orientated society (as revealed
at a camp art preview and an unsuccessful party),
imaginatively scripted and acted (Benjamin is
superbly repellent), it's an entertaining satire that
disappoints only in the stereotypically limited
choices it offers to the woman. GA

Diary of Anne Frank, The

(George Stevens, 1959, US) Millie Perkins,
Joseph Schildkraut, Shelley Winters, Richard
Beymer, Lou Jacobi, Diane Baker.
170 min. b/w.

One of those extremely long and well-meaning
adaptations of plays, this doesn't really amount
to very much, despite its intrinsically moving
subject matter. The story of a Jewish family, who
had to hide in a concealed attic for two years
before they were captured by the Nazis, is
poignantly true, but remains a little too theatrical in this production. Millie Perkins looks good
as Anne (though her personality seems wrong),
while Shelley Winters' hysterical performance as
Mrs Van Daan won her an Oscar as best supporting actress. DP

Diary of a Shinjuku Thief (Shinjuku Dorobo Nikki)

(Nagisa Oshima, 1968, Jap) Tadanori Yokoo, Rie Yokoyama, Moichi Tanabe, Tetsu Takahashi, Kei Sato, Fumio Watanabe.
94 min. b/w & col.
One of Oshima's most teasing and provocative collages, inspired by the student riots of '68 and contemporary 'youth culture' generally. The main thread running through it is the relationship between a passive and vaguely effeminate young man and an aggressive and vaguely masculine young woman. They meet when he steals books and she poses as a shop assistant who catches him in the act; they spend the rest of the movie trying to reach satisfactory orgasms with each other. Their route takes them through a dizzying mixture of fact and fiction, from an encounter with a real-life sexologist to involvement in a 'fringe' performance of a neo-primitive kabuki show. The logical connections are there, but they're deliberately submerged in a welter of contrasting moods, styles and lines of thought. TR

Diary of Lady M, The
see Journal de Lady M, Le

Dias Contados (Running Out of Time)

(Imanol Uribe, 1994, Sp) Carmelo Gomez, Ruth Gabriel, Javier Bardem, Candela Peña.
93 min.
A slick contemporary thriller loosely inspired by Carmen (really very loosely: Gomez is an ETA terrorist and part-time photographer, Gabriel a junkie prostitute). Uribe keeps threatening to take it somewhere interesting, but never really gets there – the terrorist background feels opportunistic and the characters don't have lives of their own. What's more, the director's penchant for photographing women naked from the waist down is unalloyed voyeurism. TCh

Dick Barton – Special Agent

(Alfred Goulding, 1948, GB) Don Stannard, Jack Shaw, George Ford, Gillian Maude, Colin Douglas, Geoffrey Wincott.
70 min. b/w.
The ace radio 'tec and his faithful sidekicks Jock and Snowy made their film debut in this cheap programmer (the first of three) which pitted them against dastardly foreign saboteurs tampering with the water system. Elementary stuff – the nostalgist's equivalent of steam cinema. PT

Dick Deadeye, or Duty Done

(Bill Melendez, 1975, GB) voices: Victor Spinetti, Peter Reeves, George A Cooper, Miriam Karlin.
81 min.
An animated feature designed by Ronald Searle and based on the plots, characters and songs of Gilbert and Sullivan. Those in love with G & S may find the narrative line stupid, the new lyrics silly, and the reggae accompaniment sedate (compared, that is, with the rollicking Black Mikado). Animation fans will no doubt moan that Melendez' movie is hardly animated at all – just a series of grandly designed backgrounds and characters who are jerked about like puppets. But those with a taste for Searle's ornately grotesque style will find much pleasure, both in the elaborate settings and in the hideous array of barmaids, whores, pirates, policemen, rear admirals, sisters, cousins and aunts (with not a well-formed human body among them). GB

Dick Down Under
see True Story of Eskimo Nell, The

Dick Tracy

(Warren Beatty, 1990, US) Warren Beatty, Al Pacino, Madonna, Glenne Headly, Charlie Korsmo, Charles Durning, Paul Sorvino, Dustin Hoffman, James Caan, Mandy Patinkin, Dick Van Dyke, Michael J Pollard, Estelle Parsons, William Forsythe, Henry Silva, Allen Garfield, John Schuck, Seymour Cassel, Ed O'Ross, RG Armstrong, Bert Remsen, Mike Mazurki.
105 min.
Set in the '30s, Beatty's film culls its villains – a gallery of grotesques with names like Pruneface,

Flattop and The Brow – from the later '40s strips. As Tracy (Beatty) sets about foiling the plans of Big Boy and The Blank to take over the city, Breathless Mahoney (Madonna) introduces emotional conflict for the careerist detective, whose long-standing relationship with Tess Trueheart (Headly) is going nowhere fast. Beatty has rejected 'psychology and behaviour' (read complexity) in characterisation; this is old-fashioned, clearly defined morality, with literally no shades of grey (the use of colour is wonderfully imaginative and carefully modulated). Pleasing restraint is evident in the way Beatty allows his character to be outshone by his adversaries. As mobster Big Boy, a brash thug fond of misquoting Lincoln, Nietzsche and Plato, Pacino is virtually unrecognisable and hugely enjoyable; and Madonna gives confident renditions of the Stephen Sondheim numbers. A spectacular movie whose technical achievements – notably the sharp editing – will surely provide a gauge by which subsequent comic strip films are judged. CM

Didn't You Kill My Brother?

(Bob Spiers, 1987, GB) Alexei Sayle, Beryl Reid, Graham Crowden, Pauline Melville, Peter Richardson, David Stafford.
52 min.
Comic Strip's radical remake of Bicycle Thieves has Alexei Sayle as twins: Sterling Moss is bad and ignorant, Carl Moss is good and prison-educated. Carl makes bikes with the help of a gang of dole-ites; Sterling, with their help, nicks them. Their murder-mad mum (Beryl Reid, as wonderful as ever: 'You should always put a dead badger on a head wound...') encourages the sibling rivalry with lethal results. Sayle's 'satirical' script takes social awareness to new shallows: the charges of a horribly realistic social worker are called Laura and Ashley. You'll laugh. MS

Die! Die! My Darling
see Fanatic

Die Hard

(John McTiernan, 1988, US) Bruce Willis, Alan Rickman, Alexander Godunov, Bonnie Bedelia, Reginald Veljohnson, William Atherton, Paul Gleason, James Shigeta.
132 min.
A hi-tech thriller with a human heart, offering slam-bang entertainment on a par with Lethal Weapon or Aliens. On Christmas Eve, visiting New York cop McClane (Willis) enters the highrise LA office block where his estranged wife works, not realising that it has already being taken over by sadistic smoothie Hans Gruber (Rickman) and his ruthless terrorists. Inside the building, having taken wife (Bedelia) and celebrating colleagues hostage, the gang tries to crack open the Nakotomi corporation's computerised vault; outside, LA cops and FBI agents squabble over jurisdiction, while opportunistic TV reporters gather like jackals; it's up to McClane, having established a chance radio link with a passing patrolman (Veljohnson), to use the building's 39 empty floors, lift shafts, and heating ducts to improvise diversionary tactics. McTiernan excels in the adrenalin-inducing action scenes, staging the murderous mayhem and state-of-the-art violence as if he were born with a camera in one hand and a rocket launcher in the other. NF

Die Hard 2

(Renny Harlin, 1990, US) Bruce Willis, Bonnie Bedelia, William Atherton, Franco Nero, William Sadler, John Amos, Dennis Franz, Sheila McCarthy.
123 min.
Yet again, humble detective John McClane (Willis) stumbles into a terrorist plot, this time to hijack a whole airport. Yet again, the authorities dismiss him as a jerk, and he must save the day single-handedly. 'Man, I can't believe this' he moans, 'How can shit like this happen to the same guy twice?' This kind of self-referential irony, stopping just short of full-blown parody, saves the film; no one carries a one-liner better than Willis. He's also unusual among Hollywood's Action Men in seeming vulnerable at the same time as being invincible. Harlin fails to bring out the claustrophobic tension that made the original a masterpiece among blockbusters, but more than compensates in timing, speed and sheer volume. So

what if there are reservations? We're talking action not art, and on that level Die Hard 2 succeeds magnificently. DW

Die Hard with a Vengeance

(John McTiernan, 1995, US) Bruce Willis, Samuel L Jackson, Jeremy Irons, Graham Greene, Colleen Camp, Nick Wyman, Sam Phillips, Larry Bryggman.
128 min.
The first (entertaining) Die Hard film put an ordinary Joe in an extraordinary situation – namely, saving an office block from terrorists. The second just squeaked by on the same formula – saving an airport from terrorists – with the ironic line, 'How can shit like this happen to the same guy twice?' But you can only suspend disbelief so far, and by the third in the series – saving a city from terrorists (led by Irons) – the joke wears thin. With Willis's John McClane transformed by his previous experiences into a more traditional action superman, it's left to sidekick Jackson to play vulnerable. As the racist, Caucasian-hating Harlem store-owner Zeus, he provides some of the best moments with his inversion of 48 HRS, as well as the incidental pleasure of seeing two disparate characters from Pulp Fiction united at last: 'What have you been doing all this time?' the drunken ex-cop McClane is asked at the outset. 'Smoking cigarettes and watching Captain Kangaroo,' he replies cryptically – a line recognisable to Taranteenies as coming from the song which played while Marcellus was being buggered. Apart from that, there's little wit or originality on offer, just the familiar escalation of car chases and big bangs. DW

Die, Monster, Die!
see Monster of Terror

Different for Girls

(Richard Spence, 1996, GB) Steven MacKintosh, Rupert Graves, Miriam Margoyles, Saskia Reeves, Charlotte Coleman.
97 min.
When a traffic accident brings together laddish biker Paul and greetings card versifier Kim, it takes a while for them to realise they're acquainted. True, it's nearly two decades since they left school, but Kim has changed – after all, before her operation, she used to be Paul's best mate Karl. As they try tentatively to revive their friendship, Kim (MacKintosh) finds herself attracted to Paul (Graves), whose own emotions are a confused blend of protectiveness, curiosity and ill-repressed desire. But wary of attracting unwanted attention, Kim prefers a life of tidy tranquil conformity, which Paul's hot headedness threatens to disrupt. While Tony Marchant's script and Spence's direction suffer from a certain stolid inevitability, the movie never degenerates into mere worthiness, and in narrative terms, special pleading about the plight of transsexuals is kept low. Crucial to the slim story is MacKintosh's extraordinarily subtle performance: every expression, gesture, glance and vocal nuance rings true. It's a performance, in fact, as frank, sensitive and brave as the troubled character he plays, and affecting enough even to triumph over the film's final predictability. GA

Different Story, A

(Paul Aaron, 1978, US) Perry King, Meg Foster, Valerie Curtin, Peter Donat, Richard Bull.
108 min.
Actually, the same old schlock, except that the first thirty minutes are in drag: a sort of Touch of Class screwball comedy which has been uneasily welded to a homosexual subject. Albert (King) wears aprons, designs frocks, and shacks up with Stella (likeable Meg Foster, playing a happily adjusted lesbian). But when Albert starts staying out nights, it looks like he's backsliding...A glossily persuasive film which presents its 'real' gays as neurotics or gangsters, and offers us so many clichés about role reversal, marriage and pregnancy that it makes An Unmarried Woman look like an intelligent study of divorce. SHi

Digby – the Biggest Dog in the World

(Joseph McGrath, 1973, GB) Jim Dale, Spike Milligan, Angela Douglas, John Bluthal, Norman Rossington, Milo O'Shea.
88 min.

Surprisingly, this attraction for all the family isn't at all bad. McGrath has taken a rather thin and unimaginative children's fantasy (dog drinks Project X and grows thirty feet high) and developed it into a cross between a spoof horror film and a gag show for his mates. A pity the special effects are so shoddy. DMcG

Diggstown
(aka Midnight Sting)
(Michael Ritchie, 1992, US) James Woods, Louis Gossett Jr, Bruce Dern, Oliver Platt, Heather Graham, Randall 'Tex' Cobb, Thomas Wilson Brown, Duane Davis.
98 min.
Ritchie's scam movie, based on a Leonard Wise novel, is about a backwoods community famous as the 'rural capital of cash fighting'. The town is named after a fallen hero called Charles Macum Diggs, who was set up so nastily by the town's current boss, Gillon (Dern), that Diggs now sits in a wheelchair. So what better than to con the con-man? Enter Caine (supercool Woods), just out of jail, and his sidekick Fitz (the brilliant Platt), who aim to take Gillon to the cleaners by setting up a huge bet that Caine's ageing protégé, 'Honey' Roy Palmer (Gossett) can beat ten consecutive opponents in 24 hours. Of course, there's more to it than this: old-fashioned racism, Mafia involvement, killings, copious side-bets, and all the chicanery that goes on when big bucks are at stake. Though the blood flows copiously, the film is mainly a mass of punchy one-liners, sight gags, sporting and heroic fantasies, and champion performances. Naturally the film bears no relation to the physical laws of bodily damage, but in the end, who cares? SGr

Dillinger
(Max Nosseck, 1945, US) Lawrence Tierney, Edmund Lowe, Anne Jeffreys, Eduardo Ciannelli, Elisha Cook Jr, Marc Lawrence.
70 min. b/w.
Dubbed 'the first conceptual gangster epic', this unmoralistic, detached portrayal of Public Enemy Number One is a fine example of a sensational story, cheaply produced with stock footage, that gets away with artistic murder. Tierney is the glum psychopath, a skilled professional hitting the headlines with his dubious talent. Unemotional and rough at the edges, it's a sobering inventory of a fabulous myth. DMacp

Dillinger
(John Milius, 1973, US) Warren Oates, Ben Johnson, Michelle Phillips, Cloris Leachman, Harry Dean Stanton, Steve Kanaly, Richard Dreyfuss, Geoffrey Lewis, John Ryan.
107 min.
Against a background of Depression America, where legendary status is bestowed on anyone who can beat the System, Dillinger and his gang rob banks with one eye already on posterity. Milius rightly makes no apology for endorsing the mythic qualities of his characters and setting his film firmly in the roots of American folklore. Bonnie and Clyde are dismissed as two-bit hoodlums, while the film's style condemns the knowing chic of Penn's film. Rather, it's closer in spirit to standard Western myths, or as if Corman had got his hands on Peckinpah's 'Pat Garrett and Billy the Kid'. Milius filters his story through countless B movies and detective stories, indirectly paying homage to all the different media that have contributed to the Dillinger legend, but keeps things the right side of nostalgia. Good to see AIP delivering the goods and producing movies like this. CPe

Dimanche à la Campagne, Un
see Sunday in the Country

Dimenticare Venezia (Forget Venice/To Forget Venice)
(Franco Brusati, 1979, It/Fr) Erland Josephson, Mariangela Melato, Eleonora Giorgi, David Pontremoli, Hella Petri, Fred Personne.
110 min.
Bergman's icy world of guilts and repression transposed wholesale to sunnier Italian climes in Brusati's curiously allusive Art Movie (a surprise Oscar contender). An extended family reunion becomes (inevitably) an exorcism of childhood for its reticent participants, two discreetly gay couples spellbound by an operatic matriarch; while

the eternal abstracts – sex, death, religion and art – provide a hermetic seal of 'class', only pierced by a few sharp edges of pain and a single shaft of optimism. PT

Dimples
(William A Seiter, 1936, US) Shirley Temple, Frank Morgan, Helen Westley, Robert Kent, Stepin Fetchit.
78 min. b/w.
Dimples you want, Shirley Temple you get, in this unstoppably cute vehicle for 1936's top attraction at the US box office. Even sceptics have to admit that Shirley's instinctive abilities acted most of her co-stars off the screen, but here loveable Morgan gives as good as he gets as the kindly grandfather who battles to keep custody of the dear little brat when rich socialite Helen Westley tries to adopt her. The tug-of-love plot is followed by the moppet's success on Broadway. TJ

Dim Sum – A Little Bit of Heart
(Wayne Wang, 1985, US) Laureen Chew, Kim Chew, Victor Wong, Ida FO Chung, Cora Miao.
87 min.
A wonderful film about a more-or-less westernised Chinese family in San Francisco. Geraldine is perfectly happy going steady with her long-standing boyfriend, and she doesn't want to leave her widowed mother alone. But Mrs Tam is convinced that she will die soon, and she's determined to see Geraldine married. It's hard to say what makes this modest, undramatic story so extremely appealing. Maybe it's because Wang uses one family's experience as a key to a larger picture of the Chinese immigrant experience. Maybe because he's learned from Ozu and Allen Fong how to structure scenes that faithfully record the chaotic sprawl of everyday life. Or maybe it's just because of the great sense of humour. A real treat. TR

Diner
(Barry Levinson, 1982, US) Steve Guttenberg, Daniel Stern, Mickey Rourke, Kevin Bacon, Timothy Daly, Ellen Barkin, Paul Reiser, Kathryn Dowling.
110 min.
Directing from his own script, Levinson revels in detailed observation in this rites-of-passage movie about a college student returning home to Baltimore for the Christmas holidays in 1959, and picking up with the old gang as they try to fend off adulthood and marriage by hanging out at the local diner and talking about football, women, cars and rock'n'roll (Stern is particularly fine as the R&B buff, memorising record label serial numbers with religious awe). Not a lot to it, but the sense of period is acute, the script witty without falling into the crude pitfalls that beset other adolescent comedies, and the performances are spot-on. GA

Dinner at Eight
(George Cukor, 1933, US) Marie Dressler, John Barrymore, Wallace Beery, Jean Harlow, Lionel Barrymore, Billie Burke, Lee Tracy, Edmund Lowe, Jean Hersholt.
113 min. b/w.
Edna Ferber-George Kaufman play about sophisticated New York society, adapted for the screen by Frances Marion and Herman J Mankiewicz and perfect material for Cukor's satirical touch, despite his forebodings that Marie Dressler, starring as a haughtily impoverished Broadway star, 'looked like a cook and had never played this kind of part'. The laughs are mainly at the expense of the *nouveau riche* couple, a comedy of manners in which Harlow reveals her natural gift for humour and Beery confirms his status as the definitive boor. But the film also reflects the vagaries of the 1930s social scene, and John Barrymore virtually plays himself as the all-time lush. Perfect viewing for a wet Saturday afternoon. MA

Dinosaurus!
(Irvin S Yeaworth Jr, 1960, US) Ward Ramsey, Paul Lukayher, Kristina Hanson, Gregg Martell, Fred Engelberg, Alan Roberts.
85 min.
A tropical island that time has half forgotten. Thanks to some very contrived plotting (freak flashes of lightning and the like), various animals of Jurassic vintage are brought back to life. There's a bizarre sub-plot about the friendship between all-American teenager Alan Roberts and

caveman Gregg Martell, and a surprising vein of sentimentality. Ludicrous but mildly more engaging than the customary Killer-B. GM

Diplomatic Courier
(Henry Hathaway, 1952, US) Tyrone Power, Patricia Neal, Stephen McNally, Hildegard Knef, Karl Malden.
97 min. b/w.
Neat, taut espionage thriller, with Power out to avenge a friend's death and finding himself on the trail of a secret document which will alert America to Soviet plans for the invasion of Yugoslavia. Cold War simplistics rule, as always in the early '50s. But the plot, adapted from a Peter Cheyney novel (*Sinister Errand*) runs mainly to fast-moving action, and with Trieste as the principal location, it's beautifully shot by Lucien Ballard in a globe-trotting equivalent to the semi-documentary style Hathaway evolved in *The House on 92nd Street, 13 Rue Madeleine* and *Call Northside 777*. TM

Diplomatic Immunity
(Sturla Gunnarsson, 1991, Can) Wendel Meldrum, Michael Hogan, Michael Riley, Ofelia Medina.
94 min.
An Ottawa diplomat arrives in El Salvador after a coup to find that the Canadian housing project for the homeless has been taken over by soldiers and prostitutes. Though it doesn't shrink from the brutalities of civil war, this is not an action movie, but an intelligent investigation of the nature of Western aid, the hidden political agendas that control its distribution, and the desire of these 'victims' to determine their own future rather than just gratefully accept hand-outs. DW

Directed by Andrei Tarkovsky (Regi – Andrej Tarkovskij)
(Michal Leszczylowski, 1988, Swe) Larisa Tarkovsky.
101 min.
As documentaries on film-makers go, this is exemplary. The late Russian director's style and creative methods are illustrated, respectively, by clips from *The Sacrifice* and by shots of him on location in Sweden for that film; rehearsing his actors, functioning as his own camera operator during practice shots, discussing points of design and lighting with ace lensman Sven Nykvist, and perhaps most endearingly, revealing himself to be possessed of an easy sense of humour. But Tarkovsky is most widely revered for his spirituality and his ideas, which are manifested here in readings from his own book *Sculpting in Time*, and in excerpts from a lecture delivered to adoring students and fans. Indeed, where Leszczylowski comes up trumps is in the way he shows Tarkovsky turning theory into practice. Inevitably, given the man, the accent is on Art and Poetry, and it's arguable that there are too many shots of him in characteristic 'great director' pose, framing a scene with his hands and looking suitably intense. But overall, the film is to be commended for its objectivity. GA

Directed by William Wyler
(Aviva Slesin, 1986, US) Narrator: A Scott Berg.
58 min. b/w & col.
Any biographical documentary that wheels on La Streisand as the first witness to genius is hardly likely to be profoundly critical or analytical, and this film rarely rises above the factual and sycophantic. That said, it's a watchable enough account of the career of one of Hollywood's most craftsmanlike directors, and with testimonies from Bette Davis, Billy Wilder, Lillian Hellman et al, does occasionally come up with unfamiliar information. Wyler's own contributions (recorded three days before his death) reveal a likeable, intelligent man. And the clips – from his debut A feature *Counsellor-at-Law*, through Goldwyn classics like *Wuthering Heights, The Letter* and *The Best Years of Our Lives*, to the final mess of *Funny Girl*, are well chosen. GA

Dirigible
(Frank Capra, 1931, US) Jack Holt, Ralph Graves, Fay Wray, Hobart Bosworth, Clarence Muse, Roscoe Karns.
102 min. b/w.
Two Navy pilots testing dirigibles for use in antarctic regions; one crashes, and the other, off to the rescue, covets his wife. Actually, it isn't

quite so sappy as it sounds, thanks to good performances and careful pacing, but the triangle still creaks a little in a strangled, peculiarly British way: Wray tires of hubby Graves never being home, since he's always swashbuckling off to risk his neck and keep his name in the news; Holt loves her in quiet, strong-jawed self-abnegation; but he knows where her true love lies, even when he proposes to divorce Graves to marry him, and so bows out gracefully. There's compensation in some fine special effects involving the irresistibly photogenic dirigibles. TM

Dirty Dancing
(Emile Ardolino, 1987, US) Jennifer Grey, Patrick Swayze, Jerry Orbach, Cynthia Rhodes, Jack Weston.
100 min.
In many ways, a routine teen-flick with its '60s setting, sex, rock'n'roll and interfering stereotypical adults; but after so many movies trading on the oats-sowing traumas of male adolescence, here's one that looks at a young girl's sexual adventures in a serious and self-effacing manner. College-bound Baby (Grey), on holiday with her parents at a Borscht-Belt hotel, finds her way to a party where the resort's resident dance partners (Swayze and Rhodes) are feeling each other up and rubbing crotches in time to the music. Baby is shocked and thrilled, and when Rhodes is put out of action by an abortion, jumps at the chance to partner Swayze. This involves being coached to professional standard in just a few days, which stretches credibility but allows for some movingly coy scenes as the two fall in love and into bed, with none of the incumbent fretting about loss of respect, integrity or virginity on Baby's part. A safe combination of laughs, tears and an improbably happy ending, but sensitive performances, a burning rock'n'soul soundtrack and sleazy choreography carry the day. EP

Dirty Dozen, The
(Robert Aldrich, 1967, US/GB) Lee Marvin, Ernest Borgnine, Charles Bronson, John Cassavetes, Richard Jaeckel, Robert Ryan, Telly Savalas, Donald Sutherland, George Kennedy, Jim Brown.
150 min.
Over the years, The Dirty Dozen has taken its place alongside that other commercial classic, The Magnificent Seven. The violence which liberal critics found so offensive has survived intact. Aldrich sets up dispensable characters with no past and no future, as Marvin reprieves a bunch of death row prisoners, forges them into a tough fighting unit, and leads them on a suicide mission into Nazi France. Apart from the values of team spirit, cudgeled by Marvin into his dropout group, Aldrich appears to be against everything: anti-military, anti-Establishment, anti-women, anti-religion, anti-culture, anti-life ('We got enough here to blow up the whole world'). Overriding such nihilism is the super-crudity of Aldrich's energy and his humour, sufficiently cynical to suggest that the whole thing is a game anyway, a spectacle that demands an audience. (The Mean Machine offers the reverse: American football as total war). The then-unknown Donald Sutherland's moronic performance is a treat. CPe

Dirty Harry
(Don Siegel, 1971, US) Clint Eastwood, Harry Guardino, Reni Santoni, John Vernon, Andy Robinson, John Larch, John Mitchum.
101 min.
Uncredited writer John Milius was thinking of Kurosawa's detective movies, and of outrageous antagonists differentiated only by the badge one wears; director Siegel was thinking of bigotry and, as ever, in terms of questions rather than answers. Critics were immediately thinking of effects ('Every frame votes Nixon'). Siegel's ambiguity wins out, as it had done with Invasion of the Body Snatchers (anti-Red? anti-McCarthy?). Seminal law-and-order cinema, and the site of revival for the oldest cine-political argument of all: does an articulated theme necessarily constitute an ideological position, especially when it's so transparent (cop Callahan's fascism) that it's noticed by everyone who's ever written about the film? It's more than a little embarrassing when critics trust audiences less than film-makers do. PT

Dirty Ho (Lantou He)
(Lau Kar-Leung aka Liu Jialiang, 1979, HK) Gordon Liu, Wong Yu, Lo Lieh, Hui Yinghong, Wang Longwei.
99 min.
Marking the very highest point ever reached by the kung fu genre, Lau's masterpiece concerns an imperial prince (Liu) travelling incognito in South China who 'enslaves' the petty thief Ho (Wong) by wounding him with a poison to which he alone possesses the antidote. When the prince is summoned back to Beijing for an urgent meeting about the imperial succession, the thief has no choice but to tag along; there are daily traps and ambushes on the road because a rival wants the prince out of the way. The film lovingly exploits the ambiguity of the central relationship: does the prince pick up the thief because he lusts after his body, because he wants to improve him morally or simply because he needs a bodyguard? Working with two of his own most brilliant pupils, Lau constructs several of the genre's most intricately choreographed set-pieces: the 'disguised' fight conducted while examining priceless antiques is in the Gene Kelly class. The UK video release of this 'Scope film is correctly letterboxed but poorly dubbed – because Shaw Brothers refused to supply a Chinese-language master. TR

Dirty Knight's Work
see Trial by Combat

Dirty Laundry
(Michael Normand/Robert Sherwin, 1996, US) Jay Thomas, Tess Harper, Tresa Hughes, Michael Marcus, Stanley Earl Harrison.
92 min.
Worried about his dry-cleaning business and unduly concerned about hair loss, Thomas finds himself unable to respond sexually to his wife Tess Harper. A shrink's advice that infidelity might buck him up backfires, and soon Harper's gone off with her chiropractor. This black marital comedy is in many ways a conventional, even predictable affair, though it's enlivened by neat one-liners and occasionally transmits a genuine sense of pain, confusion and absurdity. Minor but watchable. GA

Dirty Little Billy
(Stan Dragoti, 1972, US) Michael J Pollard, Lee Purcell, Richard Evans, Charles Aidman, Dran Hamilton, Willard Sage, Gary Busey.
100 min.
A surreally realistic account of the pre-fame days of Billy the Kid (characterised by Pollard as the mental retard of history) that culminates in the first of his many killings. A film full of contradictions: Dragoti's vision of the West is truly unromantic, Coffeyville, Kansas, being seen as a mudbath with the saloon as a womb no one wants to leave, yet at the same time the visuals are breathtakingly beautiful. Well worth a look. PH

Dirty Mary
see Fiancée du Pirate, La

Dirty Mary, Crazy Larry
(John Hough, 1974, US) Peter Fonda, Susan George, Adam Roarke, Vic Morrow, Kenneth Tobey, Eugene Daniels, Roddy McDowall.
92 min.
B road-movie that serves only to underline how much Monte Hellman transformed the genre with Two-Lane Blacktop. This outing offers little more than plastic, would-be superstars playing at being kooky people as Fonda holds up a supermarket and drives around furiously, the police in pursuit, with his mechanic and girl-along-for-the-ride in tow (yes, another fashionable three-way relationship). The script, about small-timers who wished they were bigger, is soon totally undermined by Fonda's most complacent performance to date and Susan George's sub-Goldie Hawn antics. By way of compensation, the locations are quite pretty and the car stunts are handled with a certain verve. CPe

Dirty Money
see Flic, Un

Dirty Rotten Scoundrels
(Frank Oz, 1988, US) Steve Martin, Michael Caine, Glenne Headly, Anton Rodgers, Barbara Harris, Ian McDiarmid.
110 min.

Two con men working the Riviera town of Beaumont-sur-mer set a wager to decide which of them should have the rights to the patch. In standard 'odd couple' style, our heroes' credentials are diametrically opposed: Caine is all text-book sophistication, posing as a prince in exile; Martin is a two-bit hustler whose party-piece involves a bedridden granny about to pop her clogs. The wager involves screwing the first available woman for $50,000, although the money becomes secondary as the boys' hearts are set aflame by Headly's physical charms. Since the film's publicity tells you that there's a 'delightful final twist', you'd have to be a bit dippy not to figure out that the lads are themselves being soft-soaped. There's little enough to keep you occupied as Caine and Martin go through their comic set pieces in workaday fashion while the film moves mechanically from one contrived situation to the next. MK

Dirty Weekend
(Michael Winner, 1992, GB) Lia Williams, Rufus Sewell, Michael Cule, David McCallum, Sean Pertwee, Ian Richardson.
103 min.
Is it too easy to say that Winner's version of Helen Zahavi's brutal feminist best-seller resembles the shoddier end of the Death Wish series? Could the director, perhaps, be playing a deeper game? Winner has cunningly shot whole tracts to resemble out-takes from local cinema advertising, which distances the audience from the material and indeed from wakefulness itself. The story is pie simple. Bella (Williams), sick of gropers and peeping toms, visits an Iranian clairvoyant (Richardson in cocoa butter) who advises her to join the predators – and donates his flick knife. Over a weekend in Brighton, she dispatches chaps with a hammer, a polythene bag, a car, a gun and the knife. Fans of the gross will savour the bondage freak and the forced blow-job with vomiting. Pretty rotten. BC

Disappearance, The
(Stuart Cooper, 1977, GB/Can) Donald Sutherland, Francine Racette, David Hemmings, John Hurt, David Warner, Peter Bowles, Virginia McKenna, Christopher Plummer.
102 min.
Impressive and glossy thriller, scripted by Paul Mayersberg from Derek Marlowe's novel Echoes of Celandine, about a hired killer forced to take on an assignment in England even though his wife has mysteriously disappeared. Although the direction is occasionally a little precious – with studiedly stylish tableaux accompanied by Ravel – Sutherland is suitably haunted and cold as the confused assassin, and John Alcott's superb camerawork, on location in an icy Canada and a leafy Suffolk, is a definite bonus. And there are some fine supporting performances, particularly from Warner, Hurt and, most memorably, McKenna. GA

Disappearance of Kevin Johnson, The
(Francis Megahy, 1995, US) Pierce Brosnan, James Coburn, Dudley Moore, Alexander Folk, Bridget Baiss, Ian Ogilvy, Richard Beymer.
106 min.
A British documentary crew, making a feature about Hollywood Brits, wants to interview prospective mogul Kevin Johnson. Then Johnson's announced missing. No one's perturbed, so the film-makers start to investigate, interviewing studio execs and estate agents, screenwriters and gardeners, girlfriends, starlets, models and waitresses. This 'mockumentary' (from a former BBC documentarist) is structured like Spinal Tap, looks like Heidi Fleiss – Hollywood Madam, and appears to have broadly scandalous (if light hearted) ambitions in the vein of The Player. With its enigmatic central figure set against the hermetic, shallow and guileful ways of LA's movie-making class, the movie recalls diverse examples of great American art: Gatsby, Kane, Sunset Boulevard, The Long Goodbye. Deliberate or not, this multiplicity of reference points fails the film, since essentially it's never anything more than slight, diverting entertainment. NB

Disciple of Death
(Tom Parkinson, 1972, GB) Mike Raven, Ronald Lacey, Stephen Bradley, Marguerite Hardiman, Virginia Weatherell, Rusty Goff.
84 min.

Words cannot convey the awfulness of this Grand Guignol about a revivified corpse vampirising maidens in 18th century Cornwall. It might well have been made over a weekend. The watchword was obviously one take of everything: people fluff lines and mess up entrances (particularly on the horses, which nobody can ride), and close-ups reveal the gauze holding wigs, beards and eyebrows together. The acting is preposterous, and towards the end, the appearance of a Jewish magician ('Trinity schminity') heralds an irrationally jokey (but quite unfunny) climax which is either an indication that the whole thing is a leg-pull or a last-ditch attempt to pump some life into the proceedings (it's difficult to tell).

Disclosure
(Barry Levinson, 1994, US) Michael Douglas, Demi Moore, Donald Sutherland, Caroline Goodall, Dennis Miller, Roma Maffia, Dylan Baker.
128 min.
DigiCom executive Tom Sanders (Douglas) expects a promotion. Instead he gets shafted: first, an old flame, Meredith Johnson (Moore), gets the job, then she attempts to seduce him in the office. He resists her advances, and next day finds himself accused of sexual harassment. When he counter-sues, DigiCom close ranks against him. This slick Michael Crichton adaptation certainly knows its business. It's glossy, suspenseful, and features what – for a mainstream movie – must be the most explicit unconsummated sex scene in years. Screenwriter Paul Attanasio has effectively neutralised Crichton's meretricious sexism with a string of impressive, independent female roles, and a surprisingly sophisticated take on gender discrimination, even if the casting of Douglas and Moore suggests a more reductive reading. Hokey and classy in equal measure, this is better than it ought to be. TCh

Discreet Charm of the Bourgeoisie, The (Le Charme Discret de la Bourgeoisie)
(Luis Buñuel,1972, Fr) Fernando Rey, Delphine Seyrig, Stéphane Audran, Bulle Ogier, Jean-Pierre Cassel, Paul Frankeur, Julien Bertheau.
105 min.
Delightful if overrated comedy from Buñuel, flitting about from frustrating situation to frustrating situation as six characters in search of a meal never manage actually to eat it. Are they prevented by their own fantasies? by their lack of purpose? by their discreet charm? Buñuel never really lets us know, while managing to skip through some very funny scenes en route. But it does lack the savage bite and genuinely nightmarish feel of his earlier work (comparison with *The Exterminating Angel* shows up the later film's complacency), while the chic stylishness of the characters comes over as overbearing rather than satirically revealing. GA

Discrète, La
(Christian Vincent, 1990, Fr) Fabrice Luchini, Judith Henry, Maurice Garrel.
95 min.
In this very Rohmer-esque film, Rohmer alumnus Fabrice Luchini is wonderfully cringesome as a literary dilettante who revenges himself on womankind by writing a seduction diary at the expense of a randomly chosen victim. The interest lies not so much in the predictable intrigue – it almost reads like a commonplace seduction comedy – as in the treatment of a particularly unpalatable strain of French amorous discourse. Seen from the perspective of Old World *libertinage* – the film drops its eighteenth century references liberally enough to tip you off – it takes issue with a tradition of socially-sanctioned nastiness. It is also perilously balanced on the quality of its performances: idiosyncratic new name Judith Henry, and Luchini displaying a fabulous repertoire of prissy tics and moues. If nothing else, see it for the way he answers the telephone. JRo

Dishonored
(Josef von Sternberg, 1931, US) Marlene Dietrich, Victor McLaglen, Lew Cody, Warner Oland, Gustav von Seyffertitz.
91 min. b/w.
'1915...Strange figures emerge from the rubble of the Austrian Empire': among them X-27 (Dietrich) and H-14 (McLaglen), military spies and the best-loving enemies. Sternberg's absurd espionage melodrama is just one more peg on which to hang

his familiar, outrageous pictorial stylistics and to extend his fetishisation of Marlene – yet the result is amazing. Beyond improbability lies another of Sternberg's systematic examinations of the feminine mystique, and the tragedy of a woman sacrificed on the altar of her own sexuality. And right on the surface lies the inevitable patina of telling innuendo; in one deliciously transparent scene, Marlene is betrayed by her own pussy(cat), which eventually lands up safe in the arms of the church as Marlene is shot for her sins. PT

Disorderly Orderly, The
(Frank Tashlin, 1964, US) Jerry Lewis, Glenda Farrell, Everett Sloane, Karen Sharpe, Kathleen Freeman, Susan Oliver, Alice Pearce.
89 min.
Some longueurs, but also wonderful gags in Tashlin's best cartoon style (ranging from Lewis helping an astonished patient to brush the teeth he isn't wearing yet, or furtively sweeping dust away under a corner of artificial lawn, to the mathematically precise demolition of a supermarket by runaway stretcher). How much you enjoy the film probably depends on the extent to which you can stomach the Lewis sentimentality, here given fulsome rein since he is not only forlornly in love but practically canonised in his desire to help suffering humanity. There is also, alas, plenty of opportunity for characteristic Lewis mugging each time his would-be doctor, afflicted with a severe case of squeamishness, meets his nemesis in the shape of a patient (the inimitable Pearce) with an inexhaustible supply of ghastly symptoms on tap. TM

Disparen a Matar (Shoot to Kill)
(Carlos Azpurúa, 1992, Ven) Amalia Pérez Díaz, Jeancarlo Simancas, Daniel Alvarado.
90 min.
A minister's son is killed passing a troubled working-class estate on the outskirts of the Venezuelan capital, Caracas. A woman from the estate (whose husband was killed by dictatorship forces 30 years before) witnesses her son being beaten up by the police in a reprisal attack. He later dies, and she approaches journalist Santiago, insisting that he expose the injustice, a course of action which brings him into conflict with his editor, the corrupt police and security forces, and his own political conscience. This first fiction film by veteran documentarist Azpurúa is a hard-hitting, deeply felt attack on the mechanics of political corruption, injustice and repression, made into a stylish thriller in the Costa-Gavras mould. WH

Disparus de Saint-Agil, Les
(Christian-Jaque, 1938, Fr) Michel Simon, Erich von Stroheim, Aimé Clariond, Serge Grave, Armand Bernard, Robert le Vigan, Marcel Mouloudji.
102 min. b/w.
Odd that a charming, facile and wholly unmemorable journeyman like Christian-Jaque (the Vadim of Martine Carol) should have excelled in that most problematic of genres: the children's film. An almost surrealistically creepy thriller set in a boys' school (with faint echoes of *Zéro de Conduite*) and boasting a cast that would have done credit to a more heavyweight movie, *Les Disparus* can be recommended to all grown-ups from eight to eighty. GAd

Distant Drums
(Raoul Walsh, 1951, US) Gary Cooper, Mari Aldon, Richard Webb, Arthur Hunnicutt, Ray Teal.
101 min.
A reworking of *Objective Burma* in Western terms, with Seminoles replacing the Japanese as Cooper's veteran scout leads a motley group through jungle swamplands during an Indian uprising. The characters are fairly basic, but marvellous use is made of the Florida Everglades, and the set pieces (the nocturnal attack on the fort garrisoned by Indians and their renegade gun-runners, Coop's underwater duel with the Seminole chief) are terrific. TM

Distant Thunder
(Rick Rosenthal, 1988, US/Can) John Lithgow, Ralph Macchio, Kerrie Keane, Reb Brown, Janet Margolin, Dennis Arndt.
114 min.
The dependable Lithgow is a Vietnam vet who's taken to the wilderness to be alone with his psy-

chological wounds, while Macchio tries his best as the son he hasn't seen in more than 15 years. A putative reunion is the motor for this drearily uninvolving offering: a very well-trodden trail. Not for Satyajit Ray fans. TJ

Distant Thunder (Ashani Sanket)
(Satyajit Ray, 1973, Ind) Soumitra Chatterjee, Babita, Romesh Mukerji, Chitra Bannerji, Gobinda Chakravarty.
101 min.
Middle period Ray in that its political theme is powerfully evident, yet remains filtered through a prime concern with the characters. The setting is Bengal in 1942, with millions threatened by man-made famine (food is diverted for military use; prices rise; profiteers profit). Against this background, Ray delicately sketches the coming of age of a young Brahmin (an endearingly funny and tender performance from Soumitra Chatterjee); from a caste traditionally acting as priest, teacher and doctor, supported by his village as a mark of respect, the Brahmin first has to learn – mainly through the agency of his strong-minded and sensitive wife (Babita) – not only just what it is he is supposed to be preaching, teaching and prescribing, but how to earn the respect he is accorded. The crux for these two good people comes when, faced by their own hunger as well as the starving beggars by now omnipresent, an untouchable dies outside their house. The Brahmin's decision (tacitly approved by his wife) to break taboo by touching the body (to bury it, safe from the jackals) rings out in Indian terms as a call to revolution. Distant thunder, indeed; a superb film. TM

Distant Trumpet, A
(Raoul Walsh, 1964, US) Troy Donahue, Suzanne Pleshette, James Gregory, Diane McBain, William Reynolds, Claude Akins.
116 min.
Walsh's last film, saddled with an average script and a colourless lead performance from Donahue, but nevertheless emerging as a majestically simple, sweeping cavalry Western, a little reminiscent of Ford in mood and manner. Brilliantly shot by William Clothier, it tends to have its cake and eat it by indulging in a spectacular massacre before introducing the liberal message, but still goes further than most in according respect to the Indian by letting him speak his own language (with subtitles). The laconic mastery here belies the accusations of decline levelled at Walsh, even if many of his later films were disappointing. TM

Distant Voices, Still Lives
(Terence Davies, 1988, GB) Freda Dowie, Pete Postlethwaite, Angela Walsh, Dean Williams, Lorraine Ashbourne.
84 min.
Through a fragmented series of almost ritualistic gatherings drawn from his own family's memories of the '40s and '50s, Davies paints a vivid picture of the painfully restrictive knots bound around a working class family by a stern, unforgiving patriarch who lords it over wife, son and daughters with mute menace and brute force. These stark, impressionistic vignettes are explained, deepened, counterpointed and savagely undercut by the popular songs of the period that fuel the narrative: never have 'Taking a Chance on Love', 'O Mein Papa' and 'Up a Lazy River' been heard to such ironic and emotionally devastating effect. Music is crucial to Davies' decidedly neo-realist method, partly as a self-protective strategy adopted by his downtrodden creatures. If all this sounds either unbearably cerebral or excruciatingly melancholy, fear not. It all looks superb, the largely unknown cast performs to perfection, and the entire movie works beautifully, both as an unprecedentedly honest, unpatronising account of British working class life, and as a tribute to the human spirit's capacity to survive immense setbacks with dignity. Ambitious, intelligent, profoundly moving, it thrills with a passion, integrity and imagination unseen in British cinema since Powell and Pressburger. GA

Distinguished Gentleman, The
(Jonathan Lynn, 1992, US) Eddie Murphy, Lane Smith, Sheryl Lee Ralph, Joe Don Baker, Victoria Rowell, Grant Shaud, Kevin McCarthy, Charles S Dutton, James Garner.
112 min.

Murphy makes a partial return to form as a con-artist in this *Trading Places*-style comedy. After Senator Jeff Johnson (Garner) dies while giving job satisfaction to his attractive female researcher, Thomas Jefferson Johnson (Murphy) shortens his name, lengthens his CV, and breezes into Congress on the strength of mis-placed 'name recognition'. Once elected, abetted by a political wheeler-dealer (Smith) and a power lobbyist (Baker), he wastes no time in greasing the right palms, making the best social connections, and getting on to financially advan-tageous committees. The film's credibility takes a sudden dive, though, when Murphy, con-fronted by a young female constituent whose cancer *may* have been caused by her school's proximity to high-voltage power lines, instant-ly abandons avarice and cynicism. Lynn han-dles the set-ups and verbal fencing deftly, but there is only so much he can do with former political speech-writer Marty Kaplan's crass script, which aims at easy targets, lacks momen-tum, and ultimately fails to pay off. NF

Disturbed
(Charles Winkler, 1990, US) Malcolm McDowell, Geoffrey Lewis, Priscilla Pointer, Pamela Gidley, Irwin Keyes, Deep Roy, Clint Howard, Kim McGuire.
96 min.
A black comic tale of medical madness, Winkler's debut feature stars McDowell as Dr Russell, a perverted psychiatrist whose past misdemeanours come back to haunt him. Ten years ago, Russell drove a patient to suicide with his forced sexual attentions. But when he tries it again with Sandy Ramirez (Gidley), it all goes wrong. Drugged into submission like the last victim, Sandy is seized by spasms and appar-ently dies; but the following day her body has vanished. Soon Russell starts getting night-mares, hallucinations, and pertinent singing telegrams from beyond the grave. McDowell gives a gloriously deranged performance, while the beautiful Gidley gets strong support from Lewis (as a sympathetic fellow-patient) and Pointer (a professionally compromised nurse). Who could resist a film which contains this pithy exchange: Nurse Francine to the wigged-out Dr Russell, 'You need professional help'; Russell, 'I *am* professional help!' NF

Dites-lui que Je l'aime
see This Sweet Sickness

Diva
(Jean-Jacques Beineix, 1981, Fr) Frédéric Andrei, Richard Bohringer, Wilhelmenia Wiggins Fernandez, Thuy An Luu, Chantal Deruaz, Jacques Fabbri, Gérard Darmon.
123 min.
Marvellous amalgam of sadistic thriller and fairy-tale romance, drawing on a wild diversity of gen-res from *film noir* to Feuillade serial. The deliriously offhand plot, cheekily parodying Watergates and French Connections, has switched tapes setting a pair of psychopathic hoods on the trail of a young postal messenger, turning his obsessive dream – of romance with a beautiful black opera singer whose performance on stage he has secretly recorded – into a night-mare from which he is rescued by a timely *deus-ex-machina* (clearly a descendant of the great Judex). The most exciting debut in years, it is uni-fied by the extraordinary decor – colour supple-ment chic meets pop art surrealism – which creates a world of totally fantastic reality situat-ed four-square in contemporary Paris. TM

Dive Bomber
(Michael Curtiz, 1941, US) Errol Flynn, Fred MacMurray, Ralph Bellamy, Alexis Smith, Robert Armstrong, Regis Toomey.
133 min.
Released just months before the Japanese attack on Pearl Harbor, this isn't the wartime propa-ganda effort you'd expect from the title and star, but a tautly handled study of flying-relat-ed medical problems in which doc Flynn puts a few hours in the cockpit so he can discover exactly what it is that makes his fellow pilots blackout when they go into a dive. A surefire bet for plane nuts, only moderately engrossing for the rest of us. Rich camerawork courtesy of Technicolor specialists Bert Glennon and Winton C Hoch. TJ

Divided Heart, The
(Charles Crichton, 1954, GB) Cornell Borchers, Yvonne Mitchell, Armin Dahlen, Michel Ray, Alexander Knox, Geoffrey Keen, Theodore Bikel, Alec McCowen.
89 min. b/w.
A change of tack for comedy specialist Crichton in Ealing's true-life tug-of-love saga (written by Jack Whittingham and Richard Hughes) about a Bavarian couple, Borchers and Dahlen, who raise war orphan Ray as their own, then have to face the difficult consequences when the boy's real mother, a survivor of Auschwitz, is traced back in Yugoslavia. Mitchell is impressive as the dis-traught genuine mum trying to win back her child's affection through the language barrier that's grown up between them, and producer Michael Balcon rated this stolid, earnest drama one of the best films made at Ealing. TJ

Dividing Line, The
see Lawless, The

Divine Body
(Divine Carcasse)
(Dominique Loreau, 1998, Bel/Benin) Szymon Zaleski, Alphonse Atacolodjou, Simonet Blakou.
88 min.
This debut feature by a Belgian woman director traces the trajectory of a battered old Peugeot exported from Belgium to Benin (West Africa), where its white owner, an economic development adviser, hands it on to his black houseboy. Frequently in for repairs, the car is run into the ground as a makeshift taxi and eventually left to be scavenged for its parts by the roadside – whereupon its remains are recycled by an artist who has been asked to fashion a sculpture of the god of nightwatchmen. The vague air of porten-tousness that hangs over a mainly lightweight film is offset by the modest charm of its glimpses of village life and people. But the overriding sense of 'us' and 'them' leaves it uncomfortably close to Jamie Uys territory. TR

Divine Emma, The
(Bozká Ema)
(Jiri Krejcik, 1979, Czech) Bozidara Turzonovová, Juraj Kukura, Milos Kopecky, Jiri Adamira.
111 min.
An old-fashioned, slow-moving biopic, redeemed by some luscious photography and the gorgeous singing of Gabriela Benacková as the off-screen voice of Emma Destinn, opera singer and Czech nationalist at a time when Bohemia was sub-merged in the Austro-Hungarian Empire. Turning her back on fortune and fans in America at the start of WWI, Destinn rashly returned home carrying a cape with a concealed decoding device, to be arrested at the border and interned in her own stately home. Spurned by the opera houses, with only a deteriorating relationship with her estate manager and lover to sustain her, she rejected opportunities to escape and held hugely popular open-air concerts, to the severe embarrassment of her imprisoners. The film glo-ries in her courage and talent, and she emerges as a sad, passionate woman. JE

Divine Madness
(Michael Ritchie, 1980, US) Bette Midler, 'The Harlettes' (Jocelyn Brown, Ula Hedwig, Diva Gray).
93 min.
Wearing what looks like an old dressing-gown, hair shoved up any old how, pouring sweat and mascara, Bette Midler closes her stage show a heaving wreck, and the audience love it. As 'The Divine Miss M', 'Sophie Tucker' and 'Dolores DeLago, the Toast of Chicago', she has cracked the dirtiest jokes, sung the raunchiest songs, derided the audience ('You'll laugh at any old thing'), belittled the Royals, the French, the Germans, herself, strutted, gone through her bump and grind routine, and yet at the end of it all manages to convince you with that tremulous smile that she is as insecure as any little girl from the Bronx just starting out in showbiz. It is the precise dash of self-mockery that she adds to even her crudest stories and gestures that takes the sting from the tail, that makes the wonder-fully slaggy Greek chorus ('The Harlettes') her partners and not just a titillating sideshow, and

that raises the 'smutty joke' from the gutter to the flyover. Unsullied, despite her efforts, Bette triumphs. FF

Divorce American Style
(Bud Yorkin, 1967, US) Dick Van Dyke, Debbie Reynolds, Jason Robards, Jean Simmons, Van Johnson, Shelley Berman, Joe Flynn, Martin Gabel, Tom Bosley, Lee Grant, Eileen Brennan.
108 min.
'When was the last time you had relations, Mr Harmon?' With this question, put by a marriage counsellor to Dick Van Dyke – who is of course excused from answering – Norman Lear's script toys uneasily with the realities of marital life but carefully preserves the conventions. Despite the trappings of hard-boiled satire – a couple break-ing up in a welter of money-grubbing ill-temper, children facing up to broken homes, other divorcees hovering in hopes of snaring a remar-riage that will get them off the alimony hook – this is in fact divorce Hollywood style. Li'l ol' love wins out, with Dick and Debbie coming together again like the beautiful people they are. Two or three very funny scenes, all the same, and a first-rate batch of supporting performances. TM

Divorce of Lady X, The
(Tim Whelan, 1938, GB) Merle Oberon, Laurence Olivier, Binnie Barnes, Ralph Richardson, Morton Selten, JH Roberts.
91 min.
Korda lavished an expensive Technicolor pro-duction job on this wafer-thin comedy, a remake of the 1933 quota quickie *Counsel's Opinion*. Unable to find a room at a top London hotel, Oberon spends an innocent night in stranger Olivier's bed under the pretence that they're a married couple. Next day the latter is visited by Lord Richardson, ready to divorce his wife on the ground that she'd been in another gentleman's room the night before. Major-league thesps in their fresh-faced youth. TJ

Dixie
(A Edward Sutherland, 1943, US) Bing Crosby, Dorothy Lamour, Billy De Wolfe, Marjorie Reynolds, Lynne Overman, Raymond Walburn, Eddie Foy Jr.
89 min.
Routinely whitewashed biopic of blackface min-strel Daniel Decatur Emmett, finding fame, for-tune and love in 19th century New Orleans, and managing to turn the title song into the Confederate battle hymn en route. A surprising-ly attractive film, nevertheless, with the impres-sive period reconstructions – shot in glowing colours – helping to flesh out a desperately man-ufactured plot. Above all, it's directed by Sutherland with a care and affection that shows, relying on nostalgic, old-fashioned groupings that cunningly echo the quaintly formalised stage groupings of the resurrected minstrel show acts. Excellent cast, too. TM

Dixie Dynamite
(Lee Frost, 1976, US) Warren Oates, Jane Anne Johnstone, Kathy McHaley, Christopher George, Wes Bishop, Stanley Adams, RG Armstrong.
88 min.
After the ramshackle delights of *Race with the Devil* and *The Thing with Two Heads*, this is a dis-appointing addition to the Lee Frost/Wes Bishop collection. Though the story – sisters Patsy and Dixie enlist the help of motor-cycling drunk Warren Oates in a campaign of explosive revenge after the death of their pa in a moonshine war – is told with its authors' usual exuberance in both action and dialogue, there's no disguising how humdrum the basic material is. It's time Lee and Wes graduated to more ambitious budgets. AN

Django
(Sergio Corbucci, 1966, It/Sp) Franco Nero, Eduardo Fajardo, Loredana Nusciak, José Bodalo, Angel Alvarez, Rafael Vaquero.
95 min.
Originally banned in Britain for its comic-strip iconoclasm and graphic violence, this rates along-side Leone's *Dollars* trilogy as one of the dad-dies of the spaghetti/paella Western. It's a clean-up-and-paint-the-town-blood-red revenge drama with a difference. Nero's mud-spattered ex-Yankee soldier, first seen squelching towards

a US-Mexican border ghost town, a coffin forever in tow, has every Western hero's quality *in extremis*. His speed-of-light gunslinger outlaw has a romantic heart – his wife was killed by one of Major Jackson's KKK-like henchmen – and an enigmatic morality. He solves the war between Jackson's men and General Rodríguez' bandidos by dispensing death to all, but his sympathies are shown when he later teams up with Rodríguez for a gold heist. Corbucci's style is a mix of social realism, highly decorative visuals, and finely mounted action sequences. For the rest, there are enough mud-wrestling prostitutes, whippings, ear-loppings, explosions and scenes of wholesale slaughter to keep any *muchacho* happy. Funny, visceral, bloody, no-nonsense entertainment with a touch of class. WH

Django Kill (Se Sei Vivo, Spara)

(Giulio Questi, 1967, It/Sp) Tomas Milian, Piero Lulli, Milo Quesada, Paco Sanz, Roberto Camardiel.
120 min.
Giulio Questi (a former associate of Fellini) and Franco Arcalli (later Bertolucci's regular writing partner) devised this dour, notoriously excessive spaghetti Western, which pushes the brutality of the genre to almost surreal ends. Milian's the double-crossed Mexican gang leader out for revenge on his former partner (Lulli). The film begins promisingly but then loses its way in a succession of melodramatic grotesqueries, including suffocation by molten gold, roastings on a spit, and the killing of children. The Italian version runs two hours – 19 minutes longer than the original international release print. Not for the squeamish. TJ

D.O.A.

(Rudolph Maté, 1950, US) Edmond O'Brien, Pamela Britton, Luther Adler, Beverly Campbell, Lynn Baggett, Willing Ching, Neville Brand.
83 min. b/w.
Delirious descent into the maelstrom of '40s *film noir* as a small town businessman trades dull days and a loyal lover for a fling in the jazz nights of San Francisco. How he becomes enmeshed in the crueller, deadlier corruption of LA, solving the case of his own murder, involves a succession of ingenious twists too good to give away. Maté shoots fast and always to the point as he drives his protagonist through endless doorways and rooms which are like trapdoors and boxes in an accelerating nightmare. Maté, whose credits as cameraman include *Vampyr*, *Foreign Correspondent* and *Gilda*, holds it all together with no trouble, and without the slightest appeal to art gives the images the intensity of a dying man's last story. Breathless, indeed. CPe

D.O.A.

(Rocky Morton/Annabel Jankel, 1988, US) Dennis Quaid, Meg Ryan, Charlotte Rampling, Daniel Stern, Jane Kaczmarek, Christopher Neame, Robin Johnson, Rob Knepper.
97 min. b/w & col.
A remake of the 1950 *film noir*, presumably attracted by the lure of that implacable opening in which the hero staggers into the precinct house to report a murder: his own. Morton and Jankel's version likes that enough to re-stage it in black and white, and to issue the pert, boozy, disillusioned Eng Lit prof Dexter Cornell (Quaid), with a bellyful of slow-acting poison which gives him a day or so to find his murderer. Aided by adoring student Sydney (Ryan), to whom he attaches himself (literally) with superglue, Cornell batters against an impenetrable nighttown of red herrings. After a welter of murders, suicides, adulteries, buried birthrights, and a struggle with a tar-pit, Cornell learns the real meaning of publish or die on the campus. Borrowings apart, the plot is a muddle, and further confused by the Max Headroom team's mania for angle shots and distortions. Quaid is miles better than his material. BC

Doc

(Frank Perry, 1971, US) Stacy Keach, Faye Dunaway, Harris Yulin, Mike Witney, Denver John Collins, Dan Greenberg.
96 min.
A stab at the Doc Holliday/Wyatt Earp/OK Corral story which has pretensions towards 'stripping away the myth', but there are still the narrowed eyes, the staccato demands for whisky,

and lines like 'One hand of five-card stud; my horse against your woman'. In return we have constant reminders of Doc's TB, and pregnant pauses which, in eschewing the tongue-in-cheek intensity of the Italian Westerns, are simply empty. The result is very downbeat, and ultimately fails to replace the excitement of total involvement in the myth with any deeper understanding of the real West. JC

Doc Hollywood

(Michael Caton-Jones, 1991, US) Michael J Fox, Julie Warner, Barnard Hughes, Woody Harrelson, David Ogden Stiers, Frances Sternhagen, George Hamilton, Bridget Fonda, Mel Winkler, Helen Martin, Roberts Blossom.
103 min.
Washington intern Ben Stone (Fox at his frenetic best) nurses hopes of fun, sun, bimbos and bucks from cosmetic surgery in California. Setting off for an interview in Beverly Hills, he loses his way in the Bible Belt and crashes his car in Grady, 'Squash Capital of the South'. The town seems stuck in the '50s. The natives initially resent the squirt from the city; also unwelcome are the manipulatory moves by man-hungry Nancy Lee (Fonda), and by the town elders who want a replacement for old Dr Hogue. But from the moment Stone sees ambulance-woman Lou (Warner) emerge from a lake naked, love raises its head. Will the charms of Grady and the independent Lou erode his determination before the car is rebuilt? Caton-Jones views all the characters with undisguised affection; the whole thing bubbles along nicely in a fresh, witty, unselfconscious manner, making you forget the dated Capra-corn message. WH

Doc Savage – The Man of Bronze

(Michael Anderson, 1975, US) Ron Ely, Paul Gleason, Bill Lucking, Michael Miller, Eldon Quick, Darrell Zwerling, Paul Wexler.
100 min.
George Pal's last effort is a gargantuanly awful visualisation of the first in Kenneth Robeson's popular '30s pulp series, with Ron Ely (TV's Tarzan) as the superhuman leader of 'The Amazing Five' world experts as they track down the murderer of his father in South America. The special effects are pretty grim (unusual for a Pal production), but Anderson's direction is even grimmer, adopting the now obligatory (in the wake of Batman and Flash Gordon) camp attitude towards its pre-war fantasy subject. It's almost as though America is taunting itself for ever having taken its superheroes seriously. PM

Doc's Kingdom

(Robert Kramer, 1987, Port/Fr/GB) Paul McIsaac, Vincent Gallo, Ruy Furtado, Cesar Monteiro, Roslyn Payne.
90 min.
James 'Doc' Matter (McIsaac) might be a character from *Milestones*, Kramer's *cinéma-vérité* documentary-fiction about '60s activism in the US. Doc finds himself in a shack on the Lisbon waterfront. He's put his time in the political underground behind him, and he's survived (so we're told) a stint in a 'permanent war zone' in Africa and a disease which was never diagnosed. The writer/director, who credits himself simply 'Kramer', as though, like his anti-hero, he's mislaid his personal identity, takes a very long time reaching his point. Jimmy, the son Doc's never seen (he was conceived in the office of a prison chaplain while Doc was doing time), comes from America bringing news of his mother's death. Their meeting settles only that they need never meet again. JPy

Docteur Jekyll et les Femmes (The Blood of Doctor Jekyll/ Doctor Jekyll and Miss Osbourne)

(Walerian Borowczyk, 1981, Fr) Udo Kier, Marina Pierro, Patrick Magee, Howard Vernon, Clément Harari.
92 min.
Borowczyk brings to this the same bizarre, poetic sensibility which made *Goto, Island of Love* and *Blanche* such outlandish wonders, but which forced him into working in the margins of the sex-film industry. He takes the traditional elements

of the Stevenson story and turns them to his own surreal ends: the good doctor is transformed into a ravening beast and then stalks the corridors of a rambling Victorian house; the inhabitants find themselves under siege from within, and the threat is largely sexual. As usual Borowczyk exercises his immaculate, painterly eye for unusual objects and settings, and a fetishist's delight in costume (especially shoes). God knows what the raincoat trade makes of it: a film of strange and outrageous beauty which seems to emanate from that place where our fears are also desires. CPea

Docteur Petiot

(Christian de Chalonge, 1990, Fr) Michel Serrault, Pierre Romans, Zbigniew Horoks, Berangère Bonvoisin, Aurore Prieto, André Chaumeau, Axel Bogousslavski.
102 min. b/w & col.
De Chalonge's true story of mass murder in Occupied Paris has Dr Petiot stalking the city like a Nosferatu reborn, surrounding his murders with an obsessive theatrical ritual to a scratchy tango accompaniment. Self-conscious cinematic trickery – all expressionist *chiaroscuro* and silent-era iris shots – makes an unsettling frame for Petiot's career. The factual part is that Petiot ran a roaring trade persuading Jews that he could ship them safely to Argentina; after handing over their possessions, they ended up in his oven rather than Hitler's. Grisly as the tale is, de Chalonge gives it an almost comic air of Grand Guignol. A hideously flamboyant Serrault plays the killer as a Demon King with kohled eyes and flapping coat-tails. Yet there's a real sense of history, of the emergence from the night of Occupation into the tainted daylight of Liberation. This is a powerfully idiosyncratic shadow-show, an inventively cold-blooded inquiry into the way war breeds monsters – and an unqualified marrow-chiller to boot. JRo

Docteur Popaul (High Heels/Scoundrel in White)

(Claude Chabrol, 1972, Fr/It) Jean-Paul Belmondo, Mia Farrow, Laura Antonelli, Daniel Ivernel, Daniel Lecourtois, Dominique Zardi, Henri Attal.
101 min.
The project on which Chabrol first gave his cynicism full rein and took his mordant playfulness to outrageous lengths. This coarse farce, hardly worth the vitriol poured on its apparent misogyny, always looked more like the director's revenge on the French mass audience, who had consistently ignored his good movies, but would accept anything with Belmondo, and in this case did. Ironic inversions of the star's image, charming ugly women for their 'moral beauty', or 'unmanned' as his schemes rebound, ring pretty hollow. PT

Doctor, The

(Randa Haines, 1991, US) William Hurt, Christine Lahti, Elizabeth Perkins, Mandy Patinkin, Adam Arkin, Charlie Korsmo, Wendy Crewson, Bill Macy.
123 min.
Reunited five years after *Children of a Lesser God*, Haines and Hurt are trapped here by a trite, predictable script. Jack McKee is a brilliant, happily married surgeon who lacks compassion for his patients. Only when he himself develops cancer does he start to appreciate the trials and terrors of being under the knife. McKee's search for inner goodness is guided by June (Perkins), a terminally ill fellow-patient. Can he right the wrongs of his thoughtless past and become a kinder, gentler man? Of course he can. This is American sitcom morality writ large: a lesson to be learned the hard way, but everyone comes out smiling at the end. Both Hurt and Lahti as his wife struggle valiantly with the material, but you can't help but wonder why they took it on in the first place. NKe

Doctor and the Devils, The

(Freddie Francis, 1985, GB) Timothy Dalton, Jonathan Pryce, Twiggy, Julian Sands, Stephen Rea, Phyllis Logan, Lewis Fiander, Beryl Reid, TP McKenna.
92 min.
Based on a screenplay by Dylan Thomas, this thinly disguised story of the notorious 'resurrectionists' Burke and Hare, supplying freshly killed bodies to a Victorian surgeon, comes across as watered-down Hammer Gothic, com-

plete with trite metaphysical meditations. The depiction of the huddled Victorian whores, hags, beggars, drunks, idiots and street-pedlars forever rhubarbing in the grimy gloom is risible. The cast is as wooden as the three admittedly elegant studio sets. Twiggy's Cockney prostitute takes the Golden Stiff Award for sheer ineptitude, but surely even she didn't deserve the random, irrelevant inclusion of her tuneless tavern song spot? GA

Doctor Blood's Coffin

(Sidney J Furie, 1960, GB) Kieron Moore, Ian Hunter, Hazel Court, Gerald C Lawson, Kenneth J Warren, Fred Johnson, Paul Hardtmuth, Paul Stockman.
91 min.
Surprisingly grisly low-budget British exploitation effort in which surgeon Hunter and son Moore attempt to cheer up their widowed receptionist by exhuming her late husband and performing a primitive heart transplant. TJ

Dr Cyclops

(Ernest B Schoedsack, 1940, US) Albert Dekker, Thomas Coley, Janice Logan, Victor Kilian, Charles Halton.
75 min.
Marvellous performance by Dekker as the villainous Dr Cyclops – as bald as Lorre's Dr Gogol and going blind behind his pebble glasses, hence the echo of Homer's Polyphemus in his name and his ultimate fate – who lurks in the Amazonian jungle conducting experiments in which he shrinks people to manikin size. An engaging fantasy with brilliantly executed (though mostly rather unimaginative) special effects which look back to *The Devil Doll* and forward to *The Incredible Shrinking Man*. Let down by a dull supporting cast, but retrieved by the attractively pale, tremulous Technicolor. Based on a fine story by Henry Kuttner, writing under the pseudonym of Will Garth; beware the novelisation, also published as by 'Garth' but unmistakably the work of a hack. TM

Doctor Death: Seeker of Souls

(Eddie Saeta, 1973, US) John Considine, Barry Coe, Cheryl Miller, Stewart Moss, Leon Askin, Jo Morrow, Moe Howard.
89 min.
Ludicrous hokum apparently completely recut at one stage in its history, about one Doctor Death who transplants souls. It all turns completely hilarious when the good doctor repeatedly fails to implant another soul in our hero's recently dead wife. The amateurishness of the proceedings give the whole thing the appearance of a pantomime, or maybe a stray episode from the TV *Batman* series. VG

Dr Ehrlich's Magic Bullet

(William Dieterle, 1940, US) Edward G Robinson, Ruth Gordon, Otto Kruger, Donald Crisp, Maria Ouspenskaya, Sig Ruman.
103 min. b/w.
Misleadingly titled biopic of a doctor (Robinson) whose dedication to research brings him into conflict with the staid late-19th century German hospital in which he works. His subsequent discovery of a cure for syphilis vindicates his methods and earns him a wealthy patron. The screenplay – by John Huston (shortly to begin directing), Heinz Harald and Norman Burnside – earned a deserved Oscar nomination. NF

Doctor in the House

(Ralph Thomas, 1954, GB) Dirk Bogarde, Kenneth More, Donald Sinden, Donald Houston, Kay Kendall, Muriel Pavlow, James Robertson Justice.
91 min.
First in the *Doctor* series spawned by Richard Gordon's novels, a steady slog through the medical student joke-and-jape book, made bearable by the amiable (if somewhat over-age) cast. The sequel, *Doctor at Sea*, took Dr Simon Sparrow (Bogarde) on his first job as medical officer on a cargo steamer, starting the steady degeneration into mechanical farce that accelerated as the series progressed. Basically a slightly more sophisticated variation on the *Carry On* films, subtler in innuendo but even more predictable in situations, the series produced five more films up

to 1970 (*Doctor at Large, Doctor in Love, Doctor in Distress, Doctor in Clover, Doctor in Trouble*), but found a more welcome refuge as a TV sitcom.

Doctor in the Nude, The

see Traitement de Choc

Doctor Jekyll and Miss Osbourne

see Docteur Jekyll et les Femmes

Dr Jekyll and Mr Hyde

(John S Robertson, 1920, US) John Barrymore, Brandon Hurst, Martha Mansfield, Charles Lane, Nita Naldi, Louis Wolheim.
5,670 ft. b/w.
Dominated by Barrymore's stagy bravura, and especially by the celebrated transformation scenes, this early adaptation of Stevenson's story elsewhere rarely rises above the routine, despite the efforts of cinematographer Roy Overbough to shadow the squalid streets of London expressionistically. PT

Dr Jekyll and Mr Hyde

(Rouben Mamoulian, 1932, US) Fredric March, Miriam Hopkins, Rose Hobart, Holmes Herbert, Halliwell Hobbes, Edgar Norton.
98 min. b/w.
Still the best version of Stevenson's novella, shot in pre-Hayes Code days and therefore able to trace Jekyll's troubles to their source in sexual repression. Jekyll's frustration over the enforced delay in his marriage becomes a reiterated motif in the dialogue, and just in case anyone misses the point, it is underlined by diagonal wipes linking him to his fiancée at moments of stress preceding transformation. Cunningly, Mamoulian opens the film with a lengthy subjective sequence, so that our first real view of Jekyll (an admirable performance from March) is when he embarks on his lecture on the possibility of separating the two natures of man: a ploy which simultaneously arouses curiosity about this man, indicates his soaring intellectual arrogance, and divorces him from society as represented by his distinguished, disapproving audience. The rest, stunningly shot by Karl Strauss as a visual tour de force, is both superb and slyly subversive. TM

Dr Jekyll and Mr Hyde

(Victor Fleming, 1941, US) Spencer Tracy, Ingrid Bergman, Lana Turner, Donald Crisp, Ian Hunter, Barton MacLane, C Aubrey Smith.
127 min. b/w.
Glossy MGM version of Stevenson's horror classic about the good and ambitious doctor whose experiments on himself turn him into a raving homicidal beast. Not a patch on Mamoulian's 1932 version, since it jettisons the overt sexuality (which saw repression as the reason for Jekyll's experiments), and never really allows us to identify with the demonic protagonist, thus forfeiting the opportunity to make the audience complicitous in his guilt. Furthermore, though Bergman (admittedly a little too fresh-faced for a prostitute, even if MGM had allowed such a thing) makes a reasonable barmaid, Turner is badly miscast as the upmarket fiancée. Well shot by Joseph Ruttenberg, and the transformations are effectively handled, but it's generally shallow and anaemic. GA

Dr Jekyll and Ms Hyde

(David F Price, 1995, US) Sean Young, Tim Daly, Lysette Anthony, Stephen Tobolowsky, Harvey Fierstein, Polly Bergen.
90 min.
The old yarn gets a gender-bending twist in this crass comedy (not to be confused with the enjoyably imaginative *Dr Jekyll and Sister Hyde*). Using Victorian journals belonging to his grandfather, perfume developer Richard Jacks (Daly) discovers a formula which transforms him into his female alter ego, Helen Hyde (Young). Suddenly sprouting breasts in public can be a little embarrassing, but there are predictable side effects: instead of an ineffectual male dork, he/she is now a self-confident, go-getting woman. In a lead role intended for the frenetic Jim Carrey, the anonymous Daly seems trapped in a state of suspended animation. As the ballsy Helen, Young looks a million dollars, but acts like she's being paid loose change. Yves DuBois, a token gay (Fierstein), gets one of the few mildly amusing pieces of comic dia-

logue: mightily perplexed by his desire for Helen, he exclaims, 'Twenty years in therapy and I start liking girls! That's malpractice.' NF

Dr Jekyll and Sister Hyde

(Roy Ward Baker, 1971, GB) Ralph Bates, Martine Beswick, Gerald Sim, Lewis Fiander, Dorothy Alison.
97 min.
Admirably successful attempt to ring new changes on an old theme, with the good doctor turning himself into a beautiful femme fatale who lures prostitutes to their death in an East End in panic at the Jack the Ripper killings. The transgression thus being sexual as well as moral, the already rich story takes on a wealth of new meanings, while Brian *Avengers* Clemens' script is both witty and imaginative. Enormous fun. GA

Dr M

(Claude Chabrol, 1989, Ger/It/Fr) Alan Bates, Jennifer Beals, Jan Niklas, Hanns Zischler, Benoît Régent, William Berger.
116 min.
Chabrol's futuristic thriller, set in a still divided Berlin, turns out to be something of a *folie de grandeur*, flawed but fascinating. Dr Marsfeldt (Bates, playing like a Bond villain) is head of the omnipotent Mater Media corporation, and has his headquarters in a technology-filled back room of the 'Death' nightclub, where youngsters dance while mushroom clouds blossom on screens. Screens also fill the streets, the thousand faces of Sonja Vogler (Beals) inviting an increasingly suicidal populace to get away from it all at Theratos holiday camp. Detective Hartmann (Niklas) pads the mean polluted streets to fathom the rash of self-destruction. Chabrol's film, intended as a loose homage/reworking of Fritz Lang's proto-fascist master criminal Dr Mabuse, is at heart a sombre, timely meditation on our millenial, self-destructive instincts. Retained from Lang is the use of overawing architectural compositions, and his mix of silent serial, comic strip melodrama and expressionism. Less rewarding are a hopelessly difficult exposition, and the dial-a-country casting exigencies of the new Euro-productions. WH

Dr Mabuse, the Gambler (Dr Mabuse, der Spieler)

(Fritz Lang, 1922, Ger) Rudolf Klein-Rogge, Alfred Abel, Aud Egede Nissen, Gertrude Welcker, Bernhard Goetzke, Paul Richter.
Part I, 11,470 ft; Part II ('Inferno'), 8,399 ft. b/w.
Lang's introduction to Mabuse is typical of his early work in being disorganised and erratically paced as a narrative, but shot through with flashes of inspiration. The master criminal (taken from a pulp novel by Norbert Jacques) is presented as an overlord of the contemporary social chaos in Berlin: he profits from the ills of the time, and adopts countless disguises to instigate new varieties of exploitation. Lang has said that he intended the film as a kind of social criticism, and his sprawling plot does take glimpses of night-life decadence and themes like economic inflation in its stride. But overall the grasp of social reality is as shaky as the plotting, and the film's interest – certainly by comparison with the later *Testament of Dr Mabuse* – remains basically historical. TR

Dr No

(Terence Young, 1962, GB) Sean Connery, Ursula Andress, Joseph Wiseman, Jack Lord, Anthony Dawson, John Kitzmiller, Zena Marshall.
105 min.
The first Bond film, made comparatively cheaply but effectively establishing a formula for the series – basically a high-tech gloss repackaging of the old serials – and setting up a box-office bonanza with its gleeful blend of sex, violence and wit. As memorable as anything in the series (the arteries hadn't hardened yet) are modest highlights like Bond's encounter with a tarantula, Honeychile's first appearance as a nymph from the sea, the perils of Dr No's assault course of pain. Looking back with hindsight, one realises the extent to which the later films got bigger but not better, relying on expertise rather than creativity, and reducing film-making to committee decisions. One Bond film can be tighter, wittier, better cast, more outrageous than the next, but basically soulless, they remain as individually unmemorable as computer printouts.

Dr Phibes Rises Again

(Robert Fuest, 1972, GB) Vincent Price, Robert Quarry, Valli Kemp, Fiona Lewis, Peter Cushing, Beryl Reid, Terry-Thomas, Hugh Griffith.
89 min.
Dull, witless rehash of *The Abominable Dr Phibes*, with Price murderously buckling down to the task of securing the ancient Egyptian elixir which will resurrect his wife. The same wasted opportunities with art deco sets, a scattering of pointless guest appearances, and only one death scene with balls (murder by scorpion). Pity it wasn't given to a director who could exploit the real possibilities. TR

Dr Rhythm

(Frank Tuttle, 1938, US) Bing Crosby, Mary Carlisle, Beatrice Lillie, Andy Devine, Laura Hope Crews, Sterling Holloway, Franklin Pangborn.
80 min. b/w
Lamebrained musical which makes a hash of O Henry's story *The Badge of Policeman O'Roon*, about a hungover doctor who takes over bodyguard duties (falling for the heiress, naturally) from a policeman friend unable to work because he was bitten by a recalcitrant seal. Enlivened (although even she seems under the weather) by the marvellous Bea Lillie, who unleashes a wild gypsy dance, and entraps a bemused Franklin Pangborn as recipient of her famous 'Two dozen double damask dinner napkins' routine. TM

Dr Strangelove: or, How I Learned to Stop Worrying and Love the Bomb ▮100▮ (100)

(Stanley Kubrick, 1963, GB) Peter Sellers, George C Scott, Sterling Hayden, Keenan Wynn, Slim Pickens, Peter Bull, Tracy Reed, James Earl Jones.
94 min. b/w.
Perhaps Kubrick's most perfectly realised film, simply because his cynical vision of the progress of technology and human stupidity is wedded with comedy, in this case Terry Southern's sparkling script in which the world comes to an end thanks to a mad US general's paranoia about women and commies. Sellers' three roles are something of an indulgent showcase, though as the tight-lipped RAF officer and the US president he gives excellent performances. Better, however, are Scott as the gung-ho military man frustrated by political soft-pedalling, and – especially – Hayden as the beleaguered lunatic who presses the button. Kubrick wanted to have the antics end up with a custard-pie finale, but thank heavens he didn't; the result is scary, hilarious, and nightmarishly beautiful, far more effective in its portrait of insanity and call for disarmament than any number of worthy anti-nuke documentaries. GA

Dr Syn, Alias the Scarecrow

(James Neilson, 1963, GB) Patrick McGoohan, George Cole, Tony Britton, Michael Hordern, Geoffrey Keen, Kay Walsh, Eric Pohlmann.
98 min.
Conventional adventure yarn with a mysterious smuggler (actually the Vicar of Dymchurch) performing deeds of derring-do up and down the Kent coast during the reign of George III. It's a Disney production, so naturally the piratical vicar (previously incarnated by George Arliss in 1937) takes on tiresomely po-faced Robin Hood traits. The cast is exceedingly British, so many minutes can be whiled away spotting familiar figures in side-whiskers and breeches. GB

Dr Terror's House of Horrors

(Freddie Francis, 1964, GB) Peter Cushing, Christopher Lee, Donald Sutherland, Max Adrian, Roy Castle, Neil McCallum, Michael Gough, Ursula Howells, Alan Freeman.
98 min.
The first Amicus portmanteau film, which combines five stories comprising a vampire, a severed hand, a man-eating plant, a voodoo curse and a werewolf. The production suffers from some weak moments (notably the feeble voodoo story with even feebler comedy relief from Roy Castle), but two of the episodes are good; and who can resist the spectacle of Alan Freeman being engulfed by a man-eating plant?

Dr Who and the Daleks

(Gordon Flemyng, 1965, GB) Peter Cushing, Roy Castle, Jennie Linden, Roberta Tovey, Barrie Ingham, Michael Coles, Geoffrey Toone.
83 min.
The first big-screen spinoff from the TV series, plodding through a shopworn plot in which the good Doctor helps an outcast tribe (a singularly camp crew they are too) against their Dalek oppressors. The settings are moderately imaginative in a tacky sort of way; even tackier comedy on the side from Castle; OK for undemanding kids. TM

Doctor X

(Michael Curtiz, 1932, US) Lionel Atwill, Lee Tracy, Fay Wray, Preston Foster, Mae Busch, John Wray.
80 min.
Despite its high reputation, a disappointing movie that dithers somewhere between horror and whodunit, never quite coming good on either and further crippling itself with some horrendous comic relief. The mystery concerns a moon murderer who cannibalises his victims and a one-armed scientist (Foster) working on a synthetic flesh substitute (and if you don't guess the killer's identity way ahead of time, your head needs examining). Stylish sets, though, and Curtiz adds some nice expressionistic flourishes, plus a bizarrely stilted but effective re-enactment of the crimes. It looks better if you're lucky enough to catch one of the rare two-colour Technicolor prints. TM

Doctor Zhivago

(David Lean, 1965, US) Omar Sharif, Julie Christie, Geraldine Chaplin, Rod Steiger, Alec Guinness, Tom Courtenay, Ralph Richardson, Siobhan McKenna, Rita Tushingham.
193 min.
Visually impressive in a picture postcard sort of way. Otherwise an interminable emasculation of Pasternak's novel, seemingly trying to emulate *Gone With the Wind* in romantic vacuity as Russia is torn by revolution and Sharif's Zhivago moons on about the elusive love of his life. Steiger and Courtenay excepted, all the performances are very uncomfortable. TM

Dodes'ka-den

(Akira Kurosawa, 1970, Jap) Zuchi Yoshitaka, Kin Sugai, Kazou Kato, Junzaburo Ban, Kiyoko Tange.
140 min.
A highly ambitious social panorama, with the shanty dwellers of a contemporary Tokyo rubbish dump serving as a microcosm for Kurosawa's Gorki-style celebration of the human condition through the triumph of loyalty and the imagination. Many of the threatened shortcomings of earlier Kurosawa films here reach fruition: extremely crude psychological characterisation of the gallery of down-and-outs, lushly melodramatic score, explicit statement of themes by several of the characters for anyone who's missed the point, grossly stylised acting and design (particularly the use of colour symbolism, this being Kurosawa's first film in colour). Nevertheless, there's a laudable fluidity in the way the characters are knitted together into a cyclical narrative, and some of them have moments of quiet poignancy. RM

Dodge City

(Michael Curtiz, 1939, US) Errol Flynn, Olivia de Havilland, Ann Sheridan, Bruce Cabot, Alan Hale, Victor Jory, John Litel, Frank McHugh, Guinn Williams.
105 min.
A leisurely 'epic' Western, hugely enjoyable in its skilful marshalling of stock ingredients as Flynn, wagonmaster turned sheriff, tames the rumbustious cattle town at the end of the railroad line with the aid of the crusading newspaper editor's daughter (de Havilland). Nothing here you haven't seen before (in fact the marathon saloon brawl turns up all over the place as stock footage), but it's put together with great freshness and skill. Ann Sheridan, though given little enough screen time as the saloon girl, is as usual a standout. TM

Dog Day Afternoon

(Sidney Lumet, 1975, US) Al Pacino, John Cazale, Sully Boyar, Penelope Allen, Beulah Garrick, Carol Kane, Charles Durning, James Broderick, Chris Sarandon.
130 min.
At first sight, a film with large, self-conscious ambitions where a bank siege (the film is based on a real incident that occurred in the summer of '72) seems a metaphor for Attica and other scenes of American overkill and victimisation. But it turns into something smaller and less pretentious: a richly detailed, meandering portrait of an incompetent, anxiety-ridden, homosexual bank robber (played with ferocious and self-destructive energy by Pacino) who wants money to finance a sex-change operation for his lover. The film's strength lies in its depiction of surfaces, lacking the visual or intellectual imagination to go beyond its shrewd social and psychological observations and its moments of absurdist humour. LQ

Dog of Flanders, A

(James B Clark, 1959, US) David Ladd, Donald Crisp, Theodore Bikel, Max Croiset, Monique Ahrens.
96 min.
Less about a dog than a boy of (19th century) Flanders: Nelo, who lives in poverty with his grandfather and wants to become an artist. His progress towards this ambition is helped by a painter who befriends him and, in the happy ending, takes him as an apprentice. But the film is really about the kind of life led by Nelo and his grandfather, blending attractive images of the Flemish countryside with a story of personal and social values (Nelo is forbidden by the well-off miller to play with his daughter; the priest won't let him see the Rubens in the cathedral because he can't pay). An old-fashioned tearjerker for kids (the grandfather dies), it's pretty, but not pretty-pretty. JWi

Dogpound Shuffle (aka Spot)

(Jeffery Bloom, 1974, Can) Ron Moody, David Soul, Pamela McMyler, Ray Stricklyn, Raymond Sutton.
97 min.
In Vancouver, rasping Irish bum (Moody) loses his little old terrier Spot, and can't fork up the thirty dollars to get the mutt out of the dogpound, but eventually raises the money in a rather enchanting way. Despite this gooey storyline, the movie has a good bit of guts, and the director/producer/writer shows a nice talent for wittily depicting life's seamier side: there's a brief moment in a rock-bottom café where Moody digs into a cesspit masquerading as a bowl of soup, and a hearty off-screen cougher turns out to be the cook; scenes in the dog-pound bristle with well-modulated violence and general unpleasantness. Moody's acting is agreeably restrained, as is the dog's. GB

Dogs

(Burt Brinckerhoff, 1976, US) David McCallum, George Wyner, Eric Server, Sandra McCabe, Sterling Swanson.
90 min.
Bearded, be-jeaned and sporting a Beatle cut, McCallum's biology professor stumbles through the movie – usually accompanied by beercan – mumbling his disgust over the idiocy of his students and cynicism about his dilettante colleagues at a small, isolated college campus. The local dogs seem to share his view that the planet could do without this particular bunch of morons, and proceed to dispose of them with much slavering and gnashing of teeth. McCallum suspects that olfactory stimuli can cause mass behaviour in animals, and he just manages to survive; perhaps it was his resemblance to an Old English Sheepdog that fooled 'em. FF

Dogs, The

see Chiens, Les

Dogs in Space

(Richard Lowenstein, 1986, Aust) Michael Hutchence, Saskia Post, Nique Needles, Deanna Bond, Tony Helou, Chris Haywood, Peter Walsh.
109 min.
A squat in Melbourne, 1978: discernible among the roaches, mouldering cans of beans, Eno albums and the odd sheep, are the truly terrible punk band Dogs in Space, a gaggle of hippies, students and nurses, and sundry visitors including a chainsaw fanatic and two strangely amiable cops. Into this seething heap drifts the Girl,

a taciturn waif whose perceptions of the house's giggling, garrulous grotesques form the narrative springboard for Lowenstein's admirably adventurous film. No mere rock movie, it is a remarkably rich portrait both of a much-maligned subculture and of the end of an era: story, for the most part, is held at bay, with the vividly realised fragments as apparently chaotic yet as tautly structured as *Nashville*. Lowenstein generously but unsentimentally allows his initially irritating, immature characters to become interesting and sympathetic. A funny, elegiac, uplifting, and deliciously different movie. GA

Dogs of War, The
(John Irvin, 1980, GB) Christopher Walken, Tom Berenger, Colin Blakely, Hugh Millais, Paul Freeman, Jean-François Stévenin, JoBeth Williams, Roberet Urquhart.
118 min.
If you thought *The Deer Hunter* was racist, then get your eyes round this: Frederick Forsyth's novel about a mercenary coup in a small African dictatorship adapted with all the lost-empire sentimentality that the book avoided. And, given Irvin's reputation after directing *Tinker, Tailor, Soldier, Spy* for the BBC, it's odd to find a film which muffs locations (New York, London, 'the tropics') and themes (solitude, the joy of action) with such indifference. Ten out of ten to Colin Blakely for his cameo (as an itinerant o'booze), but otherwise this is just another weary hack job from a rootless British film industry in decline. CA

Dog Soldiers
see Who'll Stop the Rain?

Dog Star Man
(Stan Brakhage, 1961/4, US) Stan Brakhage.
83 min. b/w.
Brakhage revitalises the Romantic concept of the artist as heroic protagonist, struggling with Nature, the seasons, life, death, and above all with his own developing consciousness. This work introduced to the '60s avant-garde a new use of visual analogy and metaphor, in a language based on wild camera movement, hand painting, superimposition, and the reconstruction and recapitulation of series of images and whole sequences. DC

Doing Time for Patsy Cline
(Chris Kennedy, 1996, Aust) Richard Roxburgh, Miranda Otto, Matt Day.
95 min.
Ralph (Day), a teenager, dreams of leaving the Australian outback and seeking fame in Nashville. Hitching to Sydney, with his guitar under his arm, he's picked up by the flamboyant Boyd (Roxburgh) and his girl Patsy (Otto), and yep, you guessed, an adventure of an entirely different nature begins. Ralph falls in love with the pallid, breathy Patsy, while being dragged into Boyd's tangle of lies and crime. It's a slight affair, retreading familiar territory, albeit against the photogenic Australian skyline, with the help of a handful of country tunes. Otto and Roxburgh do their own singing, which in Otto's case is fine. FM

Dolce Vita, La (The Sweet Life) 100 (100)
(Federico Fellini,1960, It/Fr) Marcello Mastroianni, Yvonne Furneaux, Anouk Aimée, Anita Ekberg, Alain Cuny, Annibale Ninchi, Magali Noël, Lex Barker.
176 min. b/w.
The opening shot shows a helicopter lifting a statue of Christ into the skies and out of Rome. God departs and paves the way for Fellini's extraordinarily prophetic vision of a generation's spiritual and moral decay. The depravity is gauged against the exploits of Marcello (Mastroianni), a playboy hack who seeks out sensationalist stories by bedding socialites and going to parties. Marcello is both repelled by and drawn to the lifestyles he records: he becomes besotted with a fleshy, dimwit starlet (Ekberg), he joins in the media hysteria surrounding a child's alleged sighting of the Virgin Mary, yet he longs for the bohemian life of his intellectual friend Steiner (Cuny). There are perhaps a couple of party scenes too many, and the peripheral characters can be unconvincing, but the stylish cinematography and Fellini's bizarre, extravagant visuals are absolutely riveting. EP

Doll, The (Gudia)
(Goutam Ghose, 1997, Ind) Pran Sikand, Mithun Chakraborty, Nandana Dev Sen, Avtaar Gill.
107 min.
This quietly subversive Indian drama in Bollywood garb, adapted from a novel by the Bengali writer Mahashweta Devi, does well by its central metaphor. Johnny Mendes (Chakraborty) is a young musician under an ageing master ventriloquist who passes on his prize lifesize female dummy. To the dismay of his would-be girlfriend, Johnny's new act blends pop music with sharp social comment from the doll's lips, swiftly gaining mass popularity that local politicos seek to exploit. Images of Indian femininity, the lack of genuine political debate and the corruption of the system come in for searching examination, though the frequent stops for musical numbers may inhibit the involvement of a Western audience. TJ

Doll, The (Lalka)
(Wojciech Has, 1968, Pol) Beata Tyszkiewicz, Mariusz Dmochowski, Jan Kreczmar, Tadeusz Fijewski, Janina Romanówna.
159 min.
A handsomely mounted Polish marathon based on a celebrated 19th century novel set in Warsaw about a merchant who falls in love with a beautiful aristocrat. For the first half-hour or so the going is pretty heavy, but after that, although the numerous characters remain confusing, it begins to mesmerise. The acting is persuasive, and the scope of the production is quite vast, with Has' camera sweeping through 19th century Warsaw, setting up a satirical portrait of social decadence as the obsessional love of the wealthy merchant, scorned by the aristocracy behind his back, is meticulously probed. DP

$ (aka The Heist)
(Richard Brooks, 1971, US) Warren Beatty, Goldie Hawn, Gert Fröbe, Robert Webber, Scott Brady, Arthur Brauss.
121 min.
Detailing in meticulous fashion a perfect bank robbery, committed by Beatty and Hawn after he, as a security expert, has installed an apparently impenetrable safe in a Hamburg bank. The comedy sits uneasily with the admittedly efficient action scenes, although at least here we have none of the usual Brooks sermonising to dilute the brew. It's all a bit flashy – lots of emphasis on technology, and shot in a mosaic of short, snappy scenes that seem to converge only after a while – but entertaining if you can stand the pace. GA

Dollar Mambo
(Paul Leduc, 1993, Mex) Dolores Pedro, Roberto Sosa, Raul Medina, Litico Rodriguez, Olga de la Caridad Diaz, Gabino Diego.
80 min.
The third part of Leduc's loose trilogy (after *Barocco* and *Latino Bar*) is a kind of Mambo-ballet, a more or less wordless series of dance cabaret sequences, intercut with short narrative sections, centred around the 'Panama Saloon' in a small town on the Canal Zone in the period leading up to the American invasion. One of the group of entertainers, a mime artist, warns about the penalty of silence over this sad episode of Panamanian history; and certainly the last part of the movie (as soldiers descend on the club and then have sex and snort cocaine with their masks still on) enacts events that are nasty in the extreme. A weird entertainment. WH

Dollmaker, The
(Daniel Petrie, 1983, US) Jane Fonda, Levon Helm, Amanda Plummer, Geraldine Page.
104 min.
A film which failed to go out on release, and it doesn't take long to discover why. Fonda (and she's one of the producers) is grossly miscast as a hillbilly farmer's wife, fighting the world on behalf of her children and her land, and disastrously uprooted into wartime Kentucky where to her horror the women wear flashy underwear and the men go on strike. Sophisticated Fonda is hardly the sacrificial earth mother type, given to whittling in her spare time surrounded by angelic children. She would have had the farmers' wives doing aerobics to improve their figures. Sentimental nonsense. JE

Doll's Eye
(Jan Worth, 1982, GB) Sandy Ratcliff, Bernice Stegers, Lynne Worth, Paul Copley, Nick Ellsworth, Richard Tolan.
75 min.
This examines contradictory male attitudes to women as they affect a researcher, a prostitute and a switchboard operator. Documentary evidence and fictionalised scenes are interwoven to produce a daunting picture of incomprehension and abuse. But in its apparent determination to be non-didactic, the film ends up a victim of its own honesty, constantly undercutting its arguments. Nevertheless, if it ultimately bites off rather more than it can chew, there are plenty of incidental pleasures along the way; not least Worth's sharp eye for absurdity, and her resolve to forge a style of British political cinema that is daring and informative as well as entertaining. JP

Doll's House, A
(Patrick Garland, 1973, GB) Claire Bloom, Anthony Hopkins, Ralph Richardson, Denholm Elliott, Anna Massey, Edith Evans, Helen Blatch.
95 min.
Ibsen's discussion of marriage is so strong, so contemporary, so close to the bone that it can survive even being submitted to the uncomfortable stylistic hybrid of filmed theatre. If the production wanders a little and suffers through the declamatory acting style, then the acuteness of the play itself is there to compensate. Money and the attendant charade of security confront the unexpected miracle of change. It is absurd how little progress we have made, how little of the play sounds redundant, and how tenacious the situation of Ibsen's heroine (for that's what she turns out to be) is. The crippling love of the patriarchal society rides on, strong as ever. Richardson makes a completely credible Dr. Rank, Hopkins is solid as Torvald, and when Bloom forgets about performing she manages to speak with something like conviction.

Doll's House, A
(Joseph Losey, 1973, GB/Fr) Jane Fonda, David Warner, Trevor Howard, Delphine Seyrig, Edward Fox, Anna Wing.
106 min.
Here we are no longer in the realm of a play brought to the screen with marginal concessions, as was the case with Patrick Garland's version, but in that of film. Losey has deliberately cooled the 'dramatic' confrontations of the play, and drawn them out so that they form a complex emotional tapestry against which his superb floating camera movements, his ominous shots of skating figures and his long vistas through ornate rooms, serve to diffuse the spotlight from Nora herself to those around her. Her husband, as played by Warner, is no longer the dry pedant of Garland's version; he ends up less dismissable, and therefore more dangerous. In a sense, playing devil's advocate to Fonda's Nora, Losey has assured her feminist metamorphosis a strength (helped by echoes of the actress' own evolution) not found in a simple interpretation. Both versions are worth seeing, but this one shades it. VG

Dolores Claiborne
(Taylor Hackford, 1995, US) Kathy Bates, Jennifer Jason Leigh, David Strathairn, Judy Parfitt, Christopher Plummer, Vernon Bogosian.
131 min.
Reporter Selena (Leigh) returns home to a remote island off the Maine coast for the first time in 15 years. Her mother Dolores (Bates) has been charged with the murder of her wealthy employer (Parfitt). She's shocked at the dilapidated state of their lonely old house, but her mother is even more shocked at how much Selena has blanked out from the past, about Dolores's husband Joe (Strathairn), and about his death. A melodrama with Grand Guignol trappings, adapted from a first-person novel by Stephen King, Hackford's film invites comparison not only with *Misery*, but a whole sub-genre of movies, including *What Ever Happened to Baby Jane?* and *Marnie*, which cast a beady eye over the 'Monstrous Feminine'. In terms of suspense, it becomes wrapped up in itself in a series of long and overwrought flashbacks, but there's a strong, pervasive sense of barely contained dementia, and it's a rare movie which presents three formidable female roles. No classic, but a real kettle of fish. TCh

Domicile Conjugal (Bed and Board)

(François Truffaut, 1970, Fr/It) Jean-Pierre Léaud, Claude Jade, Hiroko Berghauer, Daniel Ceccaldi, Claire Duhamel, Barbara Laage.
97 min.
For those who found Truffaut's later work becoming flaccid, this fourth instalment in the continuing saga of Antoine Doinel provides plenty of critical ammunition. The early years of marriage for Truffaut's quasi-autobiographical character involve estrangement from his wife, an affair with a Japanese mistress (ending in long silences and cramp in the legs for Doinel), reunion with his wife, fatherhood, and acceptance of his lot. Truffaut takes immense pains to keep his characters interesting, scenes being built around elaborate (and often very funny) sight gags and running jokes, but ultimately they only serve to remind us what a pompous and self-regarding bore Doinel has become. Funny enough, if that's all you want. RM

Dominick and Eugene (aka Nicky and Gino)

(Robert M Young, 1988, US) Tom Hulce, Ray Liotta, Jamie Lee Curtis, Todd Graff, Bill Cobbs, David Strathairn, Mimi Cecchini.
109 min.
Pittsburgh trash collector Nicky Luciano (Hulce), dropped on his head as a boy (the truth about that event is held over for a last-reel revelation), is all misguided good intentions, easily led (he runs drugs unknowningly for neighbourhood hoods), and clearly a considerable burden to his brother Gino (Liotta). Constantly having to fend off Nicky's fears of abandonment, Gino also has guilt of his own: Nicky's wages pay for his medical schooling (and his internship will call him to Stanford for two years), while his efforts to have a life and a girlfriend (Curtis) of his own cause irreconcilable jealousy. Coming in the wake of Rain Man, Young's socially-concerned drama is unafraid of tackling complex emotional issues, but what few patronising and hackneyed insights it offers are waved like red flags. Unsophisticated. WH

Dominique

(Michael Anderson, 1978, GB) Cliff Robertson, Jean Simmons, Jenny Agutter, Simon Ward, Ron Moody, Judy Geeson, Michael Jayston, Flora Robson.
100 min.
Convoluted and comatose psychological horror film. Tap your toes and twiddle your thumbs while the weary cast fumble around trying to hide from you who is trying to drive who mad and for which implausible reason. All is explained in one Niagara Falls-velocity speech, but only after the zomboid stars have made at least eleven snail-paced trips through the mansion down to the conservatory to discover who's hanging down from the creaking beam again. Definitely for the Will-the-Real-Criminal-Please-Sit-Down category. CR

Domino Killings, The

see Domino Principle, The

Domino Principle, The (aka The Domino Killings)

(Stanley Kramer, 1977, US) Gene Hackman, Candice Bergen, Richard Widmark, Mickey Rooney, Edward Albert, Eli Wallach.
100 min.
Paranoid conspiracy thriller with Hackman as a crackshot Viet vet sprung from prison by unidentified government agencies for a sniping mission. With a lame script and the leaden hand of Kramer's direction, it blows most of its chances: dreadful clichés in the reunion scenes between Hackman and loyal waiting wife (Bergen); waste of interesting guest stars like Widmark and Rooney; dull use of establishing long shots for atmosphere; pretentious exchanges like 'Did you ever hear of Franz Kafka?' – 'Who's he?' – 'Nobody. Just a guy'. Worst of all – and unforgiveable in an action thriller – is that it simply fails to thrill. RM

Doña Flor and Her Two Husbands (Doña Flor e Seus Dois Maridos)

(Bruno Barreto, 1976, Braz) Sonia Braga, José Wilker, Mauro Mendonça, Dinorah Brillanti.
110 min.

An occasionally engaging Brazilian comedy, taken from a novel by Jorge Amado, about a woman whose irresponsible husband Vadinho drops dead dancing in a carnival. She subsequently remarries the respectable but, alas, not-so-sexy pharmacist Teodoro. The comedy format allows a neat reconciliation of her conflicting urges for sex and security: she simply calls up Vadinho as a ghost, and lives happily with both husbands. Unfortunately, the film tries to get it both ways too, by marrying arty satire with Carry On innuendo. JM

Doña Herlinda and Her Son (Doña Herlinda y su Hijo)

(Jaime Humberto Hermosillo, 1986, Mex) Arturo Meza, Marco Antonio Treviño, Leticia Lupercio, Guadalupe del Toro, Angelica Guerrero.
91 min.
Doña Herlinda, despite her indulgent front, is a woman of implacable will. She wants her son to marry, produce children, and be happy, but Rodolfo is gay. She proceeds to take charge of his love life. Ramón, Rodolfo's lover, is moved into the family house, and drops his taco in shock when she suggests adjoining beds. 'What if you need something in the middle of the night?' she says, without innuendo. The film has some of the subversive charm of Agnès Varda's 'Le Bonheur', and adds a new dimension to the concept of extended family. Serenaders appear with small guitars at the drop of a sombrero, camping key moments with their sentimental songs – just one amusing detail in this nicely judged satire. BC

Donald Cammell: The Ultimate Performance

(Chris Rodley/Kevin Macdonald, 1998, GB) James Fox, Mick Jagger, Nicolas Roeg, Kenneth Anger, Cathy Moriarty, Barbara Steele, Johnny Shannon.
75 min.
For Cammell, the ultimate performance, of course, was to shoot himself (only to remain lucid for some while as he spoke to his wife China before dying): a shocking but strangely appropriate end for the writer/co-director of Performance. He had led a dramatic life – a precocious painter, a charismatic sexual adventurer and a member of fashionable/arty sets in Paris and London during the Swinging '60s, a reclusive exile in LA occasionally hanging out with the likes of Kenneth Anger and (less happily) Brando – but was he, finally, an underachiever? Post-Performance, his career was littered with uneven or unmade films, and perhaps one can't blame others for being wary of his artistic risk-taking, his abiding interest in sexuality, violence and death, Crowley and Borges, and some of his near mystical ideas. He may have had a dissociative personality, someone says here. This excellent documentary is enthusiastic but never hagiographic. At its core lies the fascinating history of Performance – a movie that looks even more insanely uncompromising now than when it first appeared. GA

Donato and Daughter

(Rod Holcomb, 1993, US) Charles Bronson, Dana Delaney, Xander Berkeley.
90 min.
After its Death Wish heyday, Bronson's career has slowly faded. He still has one of the most gloom-ridden faces in contemporary US cinema, but given most of his recent material, it's not surprising he looks so miserable. He's in typically saturnine form in this routine police thriller about a father and daughter in the LAPD. They're on the trail of a serial killer. The killer's also preying on them. Not much cop. GM

Don Giovanni

(Joseph Losey, 1979, It/Fr/WGer) Ruggero Raimondi, John Macurdy, Edda Moser, Kiri Te Kanawa, Kenneth Riegel, José van Dam.
176 min.
Losey's Don Giovanni is a social study out of Brecht, who once argued: 'We find the glamour of this parasite less interesting than the parasitic aspects of his glamour'. As the orchestra strikes up the Overture, the Don is touring his glass factory, suspended on a single plank above the fires which will finally consume him. Here labour vies with leisure, license with liberty, in a production mindful of Mozart's (and Sade's) era: the opera antedated the French Revolution by a mere two years. Filmed largely in formal long shot against

Palladian Vicenza, Losey's cinematic version is a conscious attempt to 'make the unreal tangible'. Mostly – despite the odd Zeffirelli-ism and occasional 'motivation' – it succeeds. Appropriately histrionic performances from an excellent opera cast (notably Raimondi's vampiric Don and Kiri Te Kanawa's hysterical harlequin Elvira) and a very vocal mix which displeases record reviewers, but clarifies the libretto, combine with autumnal colours out of Masaccio and Giorgione to map the declining empire of the ancien regime. MM

Don Is Dead, The

(Richard Fleischer, 1973, US) Anthony Quinn, Frederic Forrest, Robert Forster, Al Lettieri, Charles Cioffi, Angel Tompkins.
117 min.
All too obviously trying to cash in on the success of The Godfather, this tale of Mafiosi dividing up Las Vegas between themselves, and then resorting to doublecross to get more than their fair share, still manages to hold the interest. Quinn is surprisingly subdued and effective as the big boss, Forrest turns in a nice performance as a young member of the family wanting out, and Fleischer handles the material in pleasantly forthright fashion. GA

Don Juan DeMarco

(Jeremy Leven, 1995, US) Marlon Brando, Johnny Depp, Faye Dunaway, Rachel Ticotin, Bob Dishy, Geraldine Pailhas, Richard Sarafian.
97 min.
Depp is Don Juan. Or is he? He claims to be the world's greatest lover – at 21, to have seduced more than a thousand women – but in his cape and mask, he looks more like the world's greatest loony tune. Retiring psychiatrist Jack Mickler (Brando) has ten days to figure the kid out, to commit him or recommend his release. Juan is a charmer, but how do his picaresque tales of love in Mexico and the East square with the few known facts: the father who died in an auto accident, the mother who turned to religion in her grief? Mickler isn't sure, but his patient's romantic vision of the world proves highly infectious. Written and directed by novelist and former psychiatrist Leven, this is a slight, likeable comedy (despite inelegant camerawork and a somewhat slack pace) trading heavily on the emotional pull of its stars. It's a joy to see Brando throwing himself into the spirit of the thing, ardently courting his perplexed wife of 30 years, a ravished Dunaway (they share a lovely five-minute bed scene – in one, uninterrupted take). And not many young actors would (or could) have played the purity and innocence of Don Juan with Depp's sensitivity (especially as such obvious centrefold-types are cast as his conquests). His soft, Castillian lilt and natural elegance are well-nigh irresistible. TCh

Don Juan or If Don Juan Were a Woman (Don Juan 1973 ou si Don Juan était une Femme)

(Roger Vadim, 1973, Fr/It) Brigitte Bardot, Jane Birkin, Maurice Ronet, Mathieu Carrière, Robert Hossein, Michèle Sand, Robert Walker Jr.
94 min.
Nearly forty, and Bardot's facade is still intact, but the films don't get any better. She makes a good enough feminine incarnation of Don Juan, but the three stories of her lethal prowess look as though they were designed as some form of tortuous revenge by her ex-husband, director Vadim. VG

Donnie Brasco

(Mike Newell, 1997, US) Al Pacino, Johnny Depp, Michael Madsen, Bruno Kirby, James Russo, Anne Heche, Zeljko Ivanek, Gerry Becker.
126 min.
A small-time operator specialising in stolen jewellery, Donnie Brasco knows a 'fugazi' – a fake – when he sees one. So he should, because he's fugazi himself, an FBI undercover agent working his way into the good graces of the Mob by way of Lefty Ruggiero, a wiseguy who takes him under his wing. Brasco's so successful, the operation becomes open-ended: for months, even years, he amasses evidence reaching throughout the Mafia – but his wife and kids never see him, and his friendship with Lefty goes beyond the

parameters of the job. When push comes to shove, which way will he jump? A tense, sharp and compelling character study, Newell's film is a worthy addition to the Mob-movie canon. Comparison with *GoodFellas* is inevitable, though these wiseguys are no high-rollers, and the tone is much more measured; low-key, even. While Depp is admirably controlled in the necessarily passive, contained title role, Donnie is rather overshadowed by his more sympathetic mentor. Even when he's scrupulously underplaying, Pacino's Lefty dominates every scene he's in: relishing the comic foibles supplied by Paul Attanasio's witty script, the gruff, coded vocabulary and a strong element of pathos. TCh

Do Not Disturb

(Ralph Levy, 1965, US) Doris Day, Rod Taylor, Sergio Fantoni, Hermione Baddeley, Reginald Gardiner, Maura McGiveney, Leon Askin.
102 min.
An American woollen executive (Taylor) is transferred to England: at home in the big country house, spouse Day wring her hands over her husband's imagined infidelity with his London secretary, then gets back at him by dallying with sultry antique dealer Fantoni. An inane comedy of marital complications, from a play by William Fairchild, with the usual off-beam Hollywood views of London and Paris. TJ

Donovan's Brain

(Felix Feist, 1953, US) Lew Ayres, Gene Evans, Nancy Davis(Reagan), Steve Brodie, Lisa K Howard.
83 min. b/w.
Curt Siodmak's neat horror/sci-fi novel, about a human brain which is brought back to life after an air crash, was first filmed by George Sherman in 1944 as *The Lady and the Monster*, and remade by Freddie Francis as *Vengeance* in 1962. This version (sticking closest to the novel), scripted and directed by a rather obscure film-maker who subsequently went into television, is modest but effective, distinguished by an excellent performance from Ayres as the well-meaning scientist taken over by the vengeful brain.

Donovan's Reef

(John Ford, 1963, US) John Wayne, Lee Marvin, Jack Warden, Elizabeth Allen, Cesar Romero, Dorothy Lamour, Jacqueline Mazurki, Mike Mazurki, Marcel Dalio.
108 min.
Most critics agree that *Donovan's Reef* is a fun film – 'A couple of Navy men who have retired to a South Sea island now spend most of their time raising hell', runs one brief description of the film – but beneath the fun lies one of Ford's most desperate films. Set on an idyllic island, the film seemingly depicts a 'natural' (semi-feudal) society in which Ford's wandering elders (Wayne, Marvin and Warden) can at last settle down and find peace. However, the arrival of Warden's Boston-reared daughter (Allen) reveals that, like the town in *The Sun Shines Bright*, the island of Ailakaowa is a paradise built on ritual and racial division. In short, a very bleak – but very funny – comedy. PH

Don Quichotte

(Georg-Wilhelm Pabst, 1932, Fr) Fedor Chaliapin, Dorville, Renée Vallier, Mireille Balin, Mady Berry, Jean de Limur, Vladimir Sokoloff.
63 min (originally 85 min approx). b/w.
Along with an English-language doppelgänger, shot concurrently, this has long been a hard film to find, so we should be grateful for even an abridged, disjointed version (all that remains?). The film's commercial wash-out is easy to understand. This is a bleak, comfortless adaptation, emphasising madness (Chaliapin is grotesque, though not inappositely so), failure and death. But as an evocation of period (sets by Andrejew) and of sun-baked Iberian languor, it shows how stylish a film-maker Pabst could be. The ending is pure despair: Quixote dead, the police burning his books, and long, long slow-motion shots (reprised by Truffaut in *Fahrenheit 451*) of pages curling up in agony, accompanied by Ibert's vigorous score. (Students of the composer's work will be best placed to identify such songs as have been excised in this copy.) BBa

Don Quixote

(Grigori Kozintsev, 1957, USSR) Nikolai Cherkassov, Yuri Tolubeyev, Serafima Birman, T Agamirova, V Friendlich, L Vertinskaya.
105 min.
Like Kozintsev's *Hamlet* and *King Lear*, this is a marvellously sensitive adaptation of a notoriously difficult classic text. Of course, Cervantes' epic has been curtailed and condensed so that it focuses on the picaresque odyssey of Quixote and Sancho Panza, rather than on the countless tales with which the author parodied chivalric literature. But it's absolutely faithful in spirit: not only are the arid Spanish plains admirably evoked by the Crimean locations (with Moskvin's masterly 'Scope camerawork weaving its own magic spell), but Cherkassov (Eisenstein's Nevsky and Ivan) and Tolubeyev are magnificent, respectively, as the gangly, naive and idealistic knight errant and his loyal friend and servant. Witty, elegant and touching. GA

Don Quixote

(Rudolf Nureyev/Robert Helpmann, 1973, Aust) Robert Helpmann, Ray Powell, Rudolf Nureyev, Francis Croese, Lucette Aldous, Colin Peasley.
111 min.
A film of Petipa's 19th century Russian ballet, publicised as being produced with 'full film techniques' rather than as a straightforward record of a stage performance. It nevertheless falls into the trap of theatre conventions (heavy make-up, even heavier hamming, unvarying lighting for each separate scene, crude blackouts to indicate changes of locale, identical dress for the populace) without taking advantage of the fluidity and mystery possible in film. The one sequence that works is a moonlit pas de deux for Nureyev as the jolly Barber of Barcelona (a more suitable title, as the ballet bears no resemblance to Cervantes' masterpiece) and coquettish Lucette Aldous of the steely feet and spiky eyelashes. Otherwise it's unremitting dancing, enthusiastically performed by members of the Australian Ballet. For Rudi-watchers and balletomanes only. JMu

Don's Party

(Bruce Beresford, 1976, Aust) Ray Barrett, John Hargreaves, Jeanie Drynan, Graham Kennedy, Graeme Blundell, Clare Binney.
90 min.
An adaptation of leading Aussie playwright David Williamson's stage hit about a suburban 1969 Sydney election telly party predominantly attended by about-to-be-disappointed-yet-again Labour supporters. The play crackled with a nice line in witty, scatological abuse as characters tore strips off each other's psyches, marital infidelities were unmasked, and sexual vanities (particularly masculine ones) were deflated. Beresford's clumsy direction blows much of the carefully orchestrated gag timing in the text, leaving it mostly up to the (good) actors. Otherwise, it's a moderately successful statement about the marginality of politics in the lives of the philistines, who profess socialism but are completely preoccupied with booze and birds. RM

Don't Answer the Phone!

(Robert Hammer, 1979, US) James Westmoreland, Flo Gerrish, Ben Frank, Nicholas Worth, Pamela Bryant.
95 min.
This routinely mindless sickie – identikit psycho on the loose; women in peril; macho cop to the rescue – crept out shamefacedly over Christmas without the dubious benefit of either press screening or poster campaign. An encouraging sign that Wardour Street might be getting just a wee bit perturbed by the feminist backlash? PT

Don't Bother to Knock

(Roy Baker, 1952, US) Richard Widmark, Marilyn Monroe, Anne Bancroft, Jeanne Cagney, Elisha Cook Jr, Jim Backus.
76 min. b/w.
This psychodrama takes place in a hotel, and the feel of the film is dominated by the sense of both distance and closeness between things happening in different parts of it. Bancroft is the singer in the hotel bar, who breaks up with Widmark's airline pilot because he doesn't have 'an understanding heart'. Encountering the mentally disturbed Monroe babysitting in a guest's bedroom, Widmark goes through rapid (!) personal growth (he *cares*); which makes him ultimately worthy of his girlfriend. The plot is so simple that psychological interest is needed to sustain it, and this would require stronger performances than those Widmark and Monroe give. The film's most powerful effect is the play-off between sound and image in hotel geography (Monroe and Widmark speak on the phone across a courtyard; Bancroft's singing is switched on via internal radio, in counterpoint with visual cuts to the bar), which provides a coherence lacking in the emotional drama. JWi

Don't Bother to Knock (aka Why Bother to Knock)

(Cyril Frankel, 1961, GB) Richard Todd, Elke Sommer, June Thorburn, Nicole Maurey, Eleanor Summerfield, Judith Anderson.
89 min.
Surprisingly, Frederic Raphael had a hand in this limp attempt at a sophisticated sex farce, about a philandering Edinburgh travel agent who hands out numerous keys to his flat to different girls. Of course they all turn up just when he gets together again with an old flame (Thorburn) he seriously wants. The sort of thing that a few years later Leslie Phillips would make his own dire speciality. GA

Don't Call Me Frankie

(Thomas A Fucci, 1992, US) Peter van Norden, Elizabeth Ann Bowen, Martin Beck, Nan Moog.
70 min.
Frank Connally is holed up in a truly sleazy California hotel with a gun in his hand. A week ago his wife walked out with the kids, pausing only to empty the bank account and sell Frank's beloved record collection. Now he just wants to end it all. Trouble is, his eccentric neighbour-tenants keep getting in the way. Fucci (producer of *Purple Haze* and *Nightsongs*) tells on the West Coast clichés and stereotypes in his debut feature, which looks and plays like off-Hollywood fringe theatre. Good soundtrack, though. TR

Don't Cry for Me Little Mother (aka Little Mother)

(Radley Metzger, 1972, WGer/Yugo) Christiane Kruger, Siegfried Rauch, Ivan Desny, Mark Damon, Anton Diffring.
100 min.
Metzger's commercially disastrous attempt to get away from the framework of orthodox sex-ploitation. Filmed in English, it's a direct rehash of the Eva Peron story, using an exceedingly tricksy flashback structure to follow its 'heroine' from her illegitimate birth in the slums, through a lifetime of whoring, torturing and backstabbing, to a planned martyrdom by public assassination. There are only two scenes that aim to titillate; the rest is played for 'drama', complete with theatrical repartee and a generous quota of recrimination scenes. But the flash shooting and cutting cannot disguise the sheer dinginess of the Yugoslav locations, any more than they can compensate for a script and performances of hopeless banality. TR

Don't Forget You're Going to Die

see N'oublie pas que tu vas mourir

Don't Get Me Started (aka Psychotherapy)

(Arthur Ellis, 1994, GB/Ger) Trevor Eve, Steve Waddington, Marion Bailey, Ralph Brown.
76 min.
First shown at Cannes under the title *Psychotherapy*, this British Film Institute fiasco has been trimmed (mainly at the beginning and end), recut and retitled. Sure, the awkward mix of black comedy and psychological thriller – it's about a quiet insurance salesman whose taste for murder is awakened by the tensions of his giving up smoking – never quite plumbs the absurd depths of the earlier version, but the stilted dialogue, wooden performances, ugly visuals, and overall wrong-headedness, still make it a clinker. A shame, since the director's short films have been a joy. GA

Don't Just Lie There, Say Something!

(Bob Kellett, 1973, GB) Leslie Phillips, Brian Rix, Joan Sims, Joanna Lumley, Derek Royle, Peter Bland, Katy Manning.
91 min

Sir William Mainwaring-Brown (Phillips) is the spokesman for a Government anti-porn Bill; Under Secretary Ovis (Rix) is kidnapped, on his way to to be married, by hippies opposed to the legislation; Sir William gets in a muddle with his mistress and his secretary (Lumley, then in bimbo mode); the leader of the Opposition (Royle) turns out to be the grandfather of the leader of the hippies (Katy Manning). Based on a play by Michael Pertwee: farcical political 'sleaze' from the era of Edward Heath – dire and very stagebound.

Don't Knock the Rock

(Fred F Sears, 1956, US) Alan Dale, Bill Haley and His Comets, Alan Freed, Little Richard, The Treniers.
84 min. b/w.

A swift follow-up to *Rock Around the Clock* from producer Sam Katzman resulted in this rudimentary teenflick, in which singing sensation Alan Dale returns to his hometown to convince the fuddy-duddy mayor that rock'n'roll is no threat to civilisation, merely the Charleston of its day. Witnesses for the defence: Bill Haley, who does 'Hook, Line and Sinker', and Little Richard, who clinches the argument with 'Tutti Frutti' and 'Long Tall Sally'. TJ

Don't Look Back

(DA Pennebaker, 1967, US) Bob Dylan, Joan Baez, Donovan, Alan Price, Allen Ginsberg.
96 min. b/w.

1965. Bob Dylan's Yankee caravan moves through a dreary, unswinging Britain. The attendant press and entourage look to the beautiful Mr D for answers ('Do you read the Bible?') which he doesn't provide, being too busy with his metamorphosis from nice folkie to withdrawn rockstar. His mask slips, fascinatingly, as he struggles between affection and disaffection. Only the wardrobe is definitely set: shades, leather jacket, tight pants and raked back hair (a rocker, no less) set him aside from the denim and fringes, dating him less than his surroundings. While Dylan plays a part and apart, nearly all the others, drawn like moths to his flame, appear in the grip of some great masochism. The abiding memories of *Don't Look Back* are lack of privacy, dull cliques, stumble-drunkenness, very insecure British artists (Price, Donovan), and Dylan's bored, amused sparring with anyone trying to point him in the direction of Damascus. The restless hand-held camera is the main disadvantage of a fascinating document: a sore sight for the eyes, with enough whip-pans to defeat the most determined self-flagellant. CPe

Don't Look Now 100 (100)

(Nicolas Roeg, 1973, GB/It) Donald Sutherland, Julie Christie, Hilary Mason, Clelia Matania, Massimo Serrato.
110 min.

A superbly chilling essay in the supernatural, adapted from Daphne du Maurier's short story about a couple, shattered by the death of their small daughter, who go to Venice to forget. There, amid the hostile silences of an off-season resort, they are approached by a blind woman with a message of warning from the dead child; and half-hoping, half-resisting, they are sucked into a terrifying vortex of time where disaster may be foretold but not forestalled. Conceived in Roeg's usual imagistic style and predicated upon a series of ominous associations (water, darkness, red, shattering glass), it's hypnotically brilliant as it works remorselessly toward a sense of dislocation in time; an undermining of all the senses, in fact, perfectly exemplified by Sutherland's marvellous Hitchcockian walk through a dark alley where a banging shutter, a hoarse cry, a light extinguished at a window, all recur as in a dream, escalating into terror the second time round because a hint of something seen, a mere shadow, may have been the dead child. TM

Don't Make Waves

(Alexander Mackendrick, 1967, US) Tony Curtis, Claudia Cardinale, Robert Webber, Joanna Barnes, Sharon Tate, David Draper, Mort Sahl, Edgar Bergen, Jim Backus, Dub Taylor.
97 min.

Mackendrick's last film is a determinedly hip and wacky '60s comedy drawn from Ira Wallach's novel *Muscle Beach*. Curtis plays Carlo, a little like the Sidney Falco of *Sweet Smell of Success* gone West, whose accident-strewn introduction to California leads him to sell swimming pools to the rich and famous. A range of women cross his path – including a rather one-note Cardinale and, in her first role, Sharon Tate – in a fitful satire on spaced-out beach folk and greedy businessmen. Mackendrick's customary visual elegance and sense of timing lead to occasional highlights, and he at least delivers a good finale with a house sliding into the sea, reminiscent of *The Gold Rush*. But the tasteless hand of producer Marty Ransohoff results in much awkward cutting and dodgy script turns, making the film barely eligible for cult status. DT

Don't Move, Die and Rise Again! (Zamri, Umri, Voskresni!)

(Vitaly Kanevsky, 1989, USSR) Dinara Drukarova, Pavel Nazarov, Elena Epova, Valery Ivchenko, Vyacheslav Bambushek.
103 min. b/w.

This unrelentingly severe autobiographical nightmare is probably the dourest memoir of childhood ever made. Twelve-year-old Valerka (Nazarov) lives in a far-flung corner of Soviet Asia in 1946, in a mining town partly inhabited by Japanese PoWs. His tense hustle of an existence is relieved only by Galia (Drukarova), a rival tea-vendor in the market. Rarely was a film so single-mindedly devoted to the proposition that life is hell, but Kanevsky's philosophy is rather less compelling than his way of conveying it. Jerky camera movements and monochrome photography so grainy it's better described as grubby – these trademarks of high *vérité* pall quickly. It's the often baffling cuts and jumps that let the story breathe. Kanevsky ends his thorough dramatic drubbing by pulling out a Brechtian 'only-a-movie' twist that whiffs somewhat of bad faith. This apart, the film has an undeniable authority, though with the best will in the world you couldn't call it life-enhancing. JRo

Don't Play With Fire (Diyi Leixing Weixian/ aka Dangerous Encounter – First Kind)

(Tsui Hark, 1980, HK) Lo Lieh, Lin Chen-Chi, Albert Au, Paul Che.
95 min.

An extraordinary thriller in which Tsui Hark matches the graphic horror-comic violence of his narrative – involving arms-dealing Vietnam vets, Triad gangsters, and a dash of anarchic urban terrorism – with an equally 'violent' sense of character and mise en scène. As genre limits are stretched in an atmosphere of seemingly constant hysteria, the security of even the most cynical viewer must crumble. SJ

Don't Take It To Heart

(Jeffrey Dell, 1944, GB) Richard Greene, Patricia Medina, Alfred Drayton, Edward Rigby, Richard Bird, Wylie Watson, Moore Marriott, Brefni O'Rorke.
91 min. b/w.

Dell, a novelist/screenwriter here making his writer-director debut, reveals a pleasing lightness of touch in this whimsical comedy in the manner of *The Ghost Goes West* (restless spirit, stirred up by bomb, helps to settle ruffled village politics). Stuffed to the brim with quaint characters, it is occasionally guilty of milking its jokes (Rigby's delightfully crumbling butler does his arthritic patter through the castle corridors, with accompanying theme, just once too often). On the other hand there are nicely offhand jokes like the village high street with shopfronts all indicating ownership by members of the Bucket family except for one interloping Pail; and the resolution, with the squire (O'Rorke) happily looking forward to life as a poacher when it turns out that he owes his position to an ancestral usurpation, is perfectly in keeping with the spirit of gently anarchic satire. TM

Don't Tell Her It's Me

(Malcolm Mowbray, 1990, US) Shelley Long, Steve Guttenberg, Jami Gertz, Kyle MacLachlan, Madchen Amick, Kevin Scannell, Perry Anziolotti.
102 min.

Guttenberg is cartoonist Gus, bald, bloated and bitter after a course of chemotherapy; Long is busybody sister Lizzie, aka romantic novelist Vivica Lamoureaux. Lizzie determines to fix Gus up with Ms Right in the shape of rag journo Emily (Gertz); and by the miracle of modern workout techniques, Gus is transformed into Lobo, a lone-wolf macho bike boy. It would take a virulently mean-minded director to make anything of this gruesome plot, but Mowbray turns in a very mawkish piece of work. He's not helped by Gertz, and especially not by Long. Guttenberg just about musters interest as a dryly charming nebbish; but as a variant on the ever popular wimp-into-love-god scam (pay-off: she prefers the wimp), it's a poor second to *The Nutty Professor*. JRo

Don't Tell Mom the Babysitter's Dead

(Stephen Herek, 1991, US) Christina Applegate, Joanna Cassidy, John Getz, Josh Charles, Keith Coogan, Concetta Tomei, Kimmy Robertson, Eda Reiss Merin.
105 min.

This isn't just another teen movie. Mom is notable only for her absence, packed off for two months to Australia. That leaves 17-year-old Sue 'Swell' Ellen, her brothers Kenny, Zach and Walter, 6-year-old Melissa, and a little old lady who is clearly some sort of serial babysitter. 'TV rots your brain' she wheezes menacingly, before Kenny's satanic bedroom brings on a coronary. Once the 'sitter' has snuffed it, the kids opt to fend for themselves, and elect Swell as their breadwinner. So far, so predictable. But this is a sassy little comedy of wit and intelligence from the director of *Bill and Ted's Excellent Adventure*. As Swell, Applegate is appealing and resourceful, while Coogan's dope-head Kenny contributes to a wonderfully dry, on-going marital spoof. Getz is the unctuous boardroom chauvinist to a tee, and Cassidy rounds off the picture's relaxed *Cosmo*-feminism as Swell's scatty boss. TCh

Doomed Cargo

see Seven Sinners

Doom Generation, The

(Gregg Araki, 1995, Fr/US) James Duval, Rose McGowan, Johnathon Schaech, Heidi Fleiss.
85 min.

'Welcome to Hell': this 'heterosexual movie' by Gregg Araki is not for the faint-hearted. A couple-on-the-road movie, with a sexually voracious third party along for the ride, this is a highly stylised, luridly coloured provocation, aimed squarely at the moral majority (not that they'd be seen dead at a flick like this). Firing on all cylinders for the first time, Araki throws in decapitation, spunk munching, outrageous visual and structural puns, Hollywood madam Heidi Fleiss, and a running 666 gag, all in the service of American sexual liberation. Imagine *Natural Born Killers* with a sense of humour. TCh

Doomwatch

(Peter Sasdy, 1972, GB) Ian Bannen, Judy Geeson, John Paul, Simon Oates, George Sanders, Percy Herbert.
92 min.

Spinoff from the muddled ecological teleseries, with the gang of scientists here investigating the effects of a sunken oil tanker on the inhabitants of a remote island off the Cornish coast. Predictably, the serious intentions of the original series have been forsaken on the big screen for a half-baked horror thriller. GA

Doors, The

(Oliver Stone, 1991, US) Val Kilmer, Frank Whaley, Kevin Dillon, Meg Ryan, Kyle MacLachlan, Kathleen Quinlan, Billy Idol, Dennis Burkley.
140 mins.

It's one of several compensatory surprises in this foray into the '60s that, as Jim Morrison, erstwhile paperweight Val Kilmer almost does for screwed-up rock stars what De Niro did for hapless middleweights; and less so that Stone all but manages to save his biopic of the hazy, crazy days of yore from becoming just another well-worn variation on the theme of self-destructive cock-rock and self-styled shamanism. This swirling dervish of a film charts the Doors' rise from avant-gardists to pop sensations to notoriety symbols, with Morrison rapidly alienating his less visionary and far less pretentious colleagues, led by MacLachlan's pragmatic Ray Manzarek. Stone sometimes loads the narrative with too much sub-Freudian baggage about Morrison's childhood, but the music, the excess and the excitement come across well; there are splendid cameos of the likes of Warhol and the Velvet Underground's Nico (giving Jim good head in a New York elevator); and Meg Ryan (as Jim's 'lady') shows commendable patience in the role of band ornament. SGr

Doppelganger: The Evil Within

(Avi Nesher, 1992, US) Drew Barrymore, George Newbern, Dennis Christopher, Leslie Hope, Sally Kellerman, Luana Anders.
104 min.
Barrymore proves she's grown into a mature, talented actress in this psychological horror movie about a young woman haunted by a lethal, ghostly double. Following the brutal murder of her mother in New York, Holly Gooding (Barrymore) leaves Los Angeles, moving into a shared apartment with aspiring screenwriter Patrick Highsmith (Newbern), who can't believe his luck. But Holly's confusing mood swings leave him wondering whether he's dealing with a volatile nymphomaniac or a vulnerable child-woman. The answer, of course, is both. Nesher's direction never does justice to his own script, which moves forward smoothly without neglecting emotional texture: the spiky exchanges between Patrick and his jealous old flame/writing partner Elizabeth (Hope) are especially good. NF

Dossier 51, Le

(Michel Deville, 1978, Fr/WGer) François Marthouret, Claude Mercault, Roger Planchon, Nathalie Juvet, Philippe Rouleau, Françoise Lugagne.
108 min.
An effectively sinister paranoid thriller, an exercise in voyeuristic point-of-view which consists almost entirely of the detailed surveillance file constructed by a foreign intelligence agency in an attempt to 'turn' a totally unwitting minor French diplomat. A sleek technocratic nightmare of the impossibility of maintaining privacy, it plays fearfully ambiguous games with its audience, inviting complicity in piecing together manipulatable 'evidence', while advising the wisdom of an over-the-shoulder glance, and reveals even such ostensibly healing techniques as psychoanalysis to be easily amenable to annexation to the impersonal mechanics of espionage. Compelling ammunition for the 'information is power' anti-databank lobby. PT

Do the Right Thing

(Spike Lee, 1989, US) Danny Aiello, Ossie Davis, Ruby Dee, Richard Edson, Giancarlo Esposito, Spike Lee, Bill Nunn, John Turturro, Paul Benjamin, John Savage.
120 min.
After the dismally miscalculated School Daze, Spike Lee returns to splendid form with a pacy, punchy ensemble piece set in Brooklyn during one stiflingly hot 24 hours. Lee himself plays Mookie, pizza delivery-man for Sal (Aiello) and his two sons; though selfishly neglectful of his Hispanic lover and child, Mookie is mostly Mr Nice Guy, ever ready to lend his calming influence to the storm of insults that fly between the local blacks, Italians, Koreans and white cops. Eventually, however, the heat takes its toll, and petty disagreements escalate into a full-scale riot. Effortlessly moving from comedy to serious social comment, eliciting excellent performances from a large and perfectly selected cast, and making superb use of music both to create mood and comment on the action, Lee contrives to see both sides of each conflict without falling prey to simplistic sentimentality. Best of all, the film — at once stylised and realistic — buzzes throughout with the sheer, edgy bravado that comes from living one's life on the streets. It looks, sounds, and feels right: sure proof that Lee's virtuoso technique and righteous anger are tempered by real humanity. GA

Double Agent 73

(Doris Wishman, 1974, US) Chesty Morgan, Frank Silvano, Saul Meth, Jill Harris, Louis Burdi.
72 min.

Another cheapo epic from the director and star of Deadly Weapons, with 'Chesty' this time playing a Bond-style secret agent chosen to root out a heroin gang because her 73-inch physical attributes enable her to have a camera embedded in her left breast – an excuse to let it all hang out. With the plot to all intents and purposes out of commission, we are left with a series of grotesquely filmed, weird, almost symbolic acts. A kind of cryptic, distorted meditation on femaleness develops, given the obvious alienation 'Chesty' experiences from her body, with breasts as objects of fear to be operated on and deployed in the context of various phallic objects. Despite maternal connotations, she is associated totally with death and loneliness, and the film becomes a monument to pathological male fantasies. VG

Double Game

see Maestro, Il

Double Headed Eagle, The

(Lutz Becker, 1973, GB)
93 min. b/w.
A documentary in which Becker uses contemporary footage, some of it extremely rare, to trace the rise of the Nazis up to Hitler's first speech as Chancellor in 1933. As a study it's anthropological rather than historical, discarding the tortuous intrigues of the scrabble for power in favour of a broader survey that shows the tacit acquiescence of a people. The film is best on gradual development: the transformation of the ill-kempt party gatherings, watched by a few amused villagers, into the half-baked symbolism and phrase-mongering of the mass rallies. It also implies that against such a background, moral stands were not as easy as we might assume. Einstein and Thomas Mann slip away, supposedly for their holidays, leaving the club-foot dwarf Goebbels to tell the nation that one day patience towards the Jew will come to an end. A chilling moment. CPe

Double Impact

(Sheldon Lettich, 1991, US) Jean-Claude Van Damme, Geoffrey Lewis, Alan Scarfe, Alonna Shaw, Cory Everson, Philip Chan Yan Kin, Bolo Young.
118 min.
Hong Kong: two babes-in-arms, present when Mater and Pater are shot to noodles by Triad hitmen, are so traumatised they both grow up to be Van Damme. Chad is a kickboxing LA aerobics instructor and something of a fop; twin brother Alex is a strong, mean, silent headbutt merchant with a cigar grafted to his lower lip. Chad's Vietvet Uncle Frank (Lewis) reunites the boys, who swiftly set about the sibling snarling, but soon team up to kick the baddies. Lettich directs with the limpness you associate with the vegetable he's very nearly named after. The idea of two Van Dammes must have seemed workable on paper, but both exude the charisma of a packet of Cup-a-Soup, and not even Van Damme seems able to tell himselves apart. JRo

Double Indemnity 100 (100)

(Billy Wilder, 1944, US) Barbara Stanwyck, Fred MacMurray, Edward G Robinson, Porter Hall, Jean Heather, Tom Powers, Fortunio Bonanova.
106 min. b/w.
Before he settled down to being an ultra-cynical connoisseur of vulgarity, Wilder helped (as much as any of his fellow Austro-German emigrés in Hollywood) to define the mood of brooding pessimism that laced so many American movies in the '40s. Adapted from James M Cain's novel, Double Indemnity is certainly one of the darkest thrillers of its time: Wilder presents Stanwyck and MacMurray's attempt at an elaborate insurance fraud as a labyrinth of sexual dominance, guilt, suspicion and sweaty duplicity. Chandler gave the dialogue a sprinkling of characteristic wit, without mitigating any of the overall sense of oppression. TR

Double Life, A

(George Cukor, 1947, US) Ronald Colman, Signe Hasso, Edmond O'Brien, Shelley Winters, Ray Collins, Millard Mitchell.
104 min. b/w.
The first of Cukor's string of fruitful collaborations with screenwriters Garson Kanin and Ruth Gordon, a curious melodrama about a Broadway matinée idol who so loses himself in his role as

Othello that he carries it over, murderously, into a backstreet affair with a waitress. The theatre scenes are so brilliantly observed, so rich in the sort of affectionate detail that made The Actress a small masterpiece, that the film seems to grind gears uncomfortably when venturing into the grey and shabby B movie world of the murder. All the more so in that it then returns to its happier idiom for a grand finale of on-stage retribution. Flawed, undoubtedly, but fascinating. TM

Double Life of Véronique, The

see Double Vie de Véronique, La

Double Man, The

(Franklin J Schaffner, 1967, GB) Yul Brynner, Britt Ekland, Clive Revill, Anton Diffring, Moira Lister, Lloyd Nolan.
105 min.
Barely passable spy thriller in which Brynner's CIA agent is lured to Europe in search of his son (reported dead) and finds himself abducted by the Commies, who replace him with his double (Brynner again). The cast do their best (Brynner, Revill and Lister especially) to enliven the routine spy larks, while Denys Coop's camerawork makes an elegant picture postcard spread of the Tyrolean Alps. GA

Double Suicide (Shinju Ten no Amijima)

(Masahiro Shinoda,1969, Jap) Kichiemon Nakamura, Shima Iwashita, Hosei Komatsu, Yusuke Takita.
106 min. b/w.
Shinoda's interesting film is a generally faithful adaptation of a play by Chikamatsu, preserving all the theatrical conventions of the puppet theatre original, and even trumping that level of artifice with bizarre devices of his own: eccentric framing, ultra-formal compositions, and a very stylised use of black-and-white. The trouble is that the very simple plot (a married man's fateful love for a courtesan) sometimes gets lost amid all the stylistic bustle: the formal beauty comes dangerously close to sheer formalism, and the 'fantastic' elements risk degenerating into Fellini-esque excess. TR

Double Team

(Tsui Hark, 1997, US) Jean-Claude Van Damme, Dennis Rodman, Paul Freeman, Mickey Rourke, Natacha Lindinger, Valeria Cavalli.
93 min.
More than just another action director, Tsui Hark is one of world cinema's great fantasists, with The Butterfly Murders and Once Upon a Time in China among his many credits. But this is rubbish: an incoherent James Bond-ish yarn distinguished only by its formal decadence and the presence of basketball's Dennis Rodman. He looks like a punk, but has a disarmingly fey, debonair manner which gives his scenes a fillip. In contrast, Van Damme is puny and square as a CIA operative pressganged into The Colony, a secret think-tank for 'retired' international agents. After that, the filmmakers can't think of anything more interesting for him to do than the rescue of wife and new-born child from the clutches of villain Stavros (Rourke). Directing on autopilot-gone-haywire, Tsui rips off that old HK gag of the shoot-out in a baby ward, throws in a tiger for the gladiatorial climax, and blows up the Coliseum as an afterthought. TCh

Double Trouble

(Norman Taurog, 1966, US) Elvis Presley, Annette Day, John Williams, Yvonne Romain, Chips Rafferty, Norman Rossington, The Wiere Brothers.
92 min.
Presley, well into his descent towards celluloid oblivion, tours a Europe which a mere gust of wind would have dislodged, pursued by comical policemen, oafish villains, and girls, girls, girls. AC

Double Vie de Véronique, La (The Double Life of Véronique) (100)

(Krzysztof Kieslowski, 1991, Pol) Irène Jacob, Halina Gryglaszewska, Kalina Jedrusik, Aleksander Bardini, Wladyslaw Kowalski, Jerzy Gudejko.
98 min.

Two physically identical girls, living in Poland and France, are mysteriously linked in numerous respects. Each has a talent for music, each entertains doubts about her current lover, and each has a weak heart. And although they have never met, when Veronika collapses on stage during a recital, Véronique immediately feels that her life has changed in a profound way. Kieslowski may not proffer the lucid moral insights of his earlier *Dekalog* series, but it's hard to imagine anyone else making a more mesmerising study of spiritual disquiet. If the story is simplicity itself, this is certainly not an easy film, but coherence is assured by Irène Jacob's luminous double performance, by Kieslowski's effortless control of mood, and by his subtle use of repeated motifs. Whether you swallow what seems to be Kieslowski's thesis (if we can recognise our affinities with some obscure soul-twin, we may learn from their suffering) comes down to a matter of faith; but there's no denying his compassion or ability to invest places, objects and passing moments with an almost numinous power. GA

Double X

(Shani S Grewal, 1991, GB) Simon Ward, William Katt, Norman Wisdom, Bernard Hill, Gemma Craven, Leon Herbert, Chloe Annett, Derren Nesbitt, Vladek Sheybal.
97 min.
The brainchild of its director, this is an unspeakably dreadful, amateurish affair which shows, if nothing else, the desperate straits the British film industry has come to. What possessed actors of the calibre of Ward, Hill and Craven to consider this clueless cheapo about British organised (or rather, unorganised) crime is a matter only for speculation; Wisdom was presumably resurrecting his ambitions to be a serious actor in the part of a bank robber who tries to protect himself and his young daughter from a band of vicious crooks. There is absolutely no level – not even in the realms of self-parody – on which the film works. Inauspiciously, it's the first product of the Business Enterprise scheme. SGr

Douce

(Claude Autant-Lara, 1943, Fr) Odette Joyeux, Roger Pigaut, Marguerite Moréno, Jean Debucourt, Madeleine Robinson.
111 min. b/w.
If Harold Robbins had been alive and well in Paris under the German Occupation, he might have produced something like *Douce*: a story which follows the conflicting passions of a young girl and her governess in a stately Parisian home in 1887. What he would have missed is the delicately detailed charm, the burning class antagonisms, and a handsome young spectre who appears out of nowhere to wreak destruction upon all. In short, it wouldn't be what it is: enchanting. Melancholic melodrama at its best, knocking the soapbox out from under the legs of upperclass landlords, the ambitious bourgeoisie who seek to usurp their position, even Cupid himself. SGo

Dougal and the Blue Cat (Pollux et le Chat Bleu)

(Serge Danot, 1970, Fr) voices: Eric Thompson, Fenella Fielding.
82 min.
When blue-furred Buxton turns up in the Magic Garden, Dougal suspects that all is not well. The new feline friend's habit of hanging around in the nearby deserted glue factory and talking to the disembodied 'Blue Voice' (Fenella Fielding) doesn't increase his confidence one jot. And indeed in no time at all our hero's worst fears are realised: Zebedee's moustache is hijacked, the chums are chucked in a dungeon, and Dougal himself gets sent to the moon by Madame Blue. It's a tribute to Eric Thompson's superb voice-overs that this remains a quite inspiring animation movie, by turns witty, satirical, and occasionally downright weird. Kids will love it, adults go bananas over it, and spaced-out acid casualties think they've astrally projected onto another planet. MK

Doulos, Le (The Finger Man)

(Jean-Pierre Melville, 1962, Fr/It) Jean-Paul Belmondo, Serge Reggiani, Jean Desailly, René Lefèvre, Fabienne Dali, Michel Piccoli, Marcel Cuvelier, Monique Hennessy, Daniel Crohem.
108 min. b/w.
Darker than *Bob le Flambeur*, Melville's second foray into the Parisian underworld borrows its epigraph from Céline: 'One must choose: die... or lie?' Appropriately, in a film devoted to the principle of duplicity, Melville teases the spectator by reproducing the police station from Mamoulian's *City Streets*, while his Paris features American lampposts, call-boxes, subway entrances. At the heart of this ambiguous world is Silien (Belmondo), by repute a professional informer, who juggles twin friendships with a police inspector (Crohem) and a burglar (Reggiani). Just out of jail, afraid he can't cut it in the underworld any more, involved in an act of revenge that leaves him with a nasty taste in his mouth, Reggiani finds Crohem lurking in ambush when he undertakes his next job. The images point unequivocally to Belmondo as the informer, until Melville skims through them again to reveal a different story; but either way, the doubt conjures disaster. Terrific performances, and equally terrific camerawork from Nicolas Hayer – more *gris* than *noir* – conjure a rivetingly treacherous, twilit world. TM

Dove, The

(Charles Jarrott, 1974, US) Joseph Bottoms, Deborah Raffin, John McLiam, Dabney Coleman, John Meillon.
104 min.
The five-year, round-the-world voyage of teenage Californian yachtsman ('I just had to get out and see what else was going on') Robin Lee Graham, produced by Gregory Peck as a chaste romance in picturesque locations for the family film market. Boring as hell, with even cinematographer Sven Nykvist's invention sorely taxed by the tedious succession of seascapes. PT

Down Among the Z Men

(Maclean Rogers, 1952, GB) Michael Bentine, Spike Milligan, Peter Sellers, Harry Secombe, Carole Carr, Robert Cawdron.
71 min. b/w.
The sole feature film with all four original Goons, going their own sweet way through an absurd plot about foiling crooks who are after an obscure atomic formula. Rickety and pretty juvenile, though Sellers' Major Bloodnok, played more or less straight, is nice. Bentine, as the mad professor, does his stage act with the all-purpose chairback as part of a show at the army camp. Milligan does his gormless Eccles as a private. Secombe is straight man. GA

Down and Dirty

see Brutti, sporchi e cattivi

Down and Out in Beverly Hills

(Paul Mazursky, 1986, US) Nick Nolte, Bette Midler, Richard Dreyfuss, Little Richard, Tracy Nelson, Elizabeth Peña, Evan Richards.
103 min.
When Nolte's gentleman of the road tries to drown himself in a Beverly Hills swimming-pool, coathanger baron Dreyfuss welcomes him into a family riddled with the whole gamut of late 20th century neuroses. Another of Mazursky's looks at the pursuit of happiness, this update of Renoir's *Boudu Saved from Drowning* starts life as a satire on the tribal rites of the new and filthy rich, but goes badly wrong somewhere down the line. Renoir's anarchic hobo romantically ditched bourgeois bliss for the open road; Mazursky presents his bag people as pathetic basket cases, with Nolte's upwardly mobile tramp only too happy to take up permanent residence in Lotusland. And it betokens some kind of desperation (or perhaps the fact that this was produced by Disney's adult offshoot) that the comedy rests increasingly on the cute antics of the family dog. As one of David Mamet's characters would say, money talks and bullshit walks. SJo

Down by Law

(Jim Jarmusch, 1986, US) Tom Waits, John Lurie, Roberto Benigni, Nicoletta Braschi, Ellen Barkin, Billie Neal.
107 min. b/w.
Jack (Lurie) and Zack (Waits), super-cool no-hopers, meet up in a New Orleans jail. Initially at odds with one another, they are soon distracted by the arrival of Roberto (Benigni), whose pidgin English, memories of old movies, and quotations from Robert Frost in his native Italian keep them both irritated and amused. Finally, however, it is this garrulous and eternally optimistic little man who leads the two self-appointed tough guys to freedom. Jarmusch's fairytale amalgam of prison movie, *noir* thriller and offbeat comedy bears some resemblance to his earlier *Stranger than Paradise*: both are in three parts; both concern jaded Americans transformed by contact with a foreign innocent; both are shot in stunning, sharp black-and-white. And again music (by Waits and Lurie) and mood are essential components to Jarmusch's poetry. But what makes this more accessible (and perhaps less ambitious) is the emphasis on humour; after the initial establishment of character and atmosphere, the laughs come thick and fast, most notably from the marvellous Benigni. For all the wit and style, however, the film's most delightful triumph is to demonstrate that 'Ees a sad an' beautiful world'. GA

Downhill Racer

(Michael Ritchie, 1969, US) Robert Redford, Gene Hackman, Camilla Sparv, Joe Jay Jalbert, Timothy Kirk, Dabney Coleman, Karl Michael Vogler.
101 min.
Fine first feature from the once wonderful Ritchie, concentrating – as in so much of his work (*The Candidate, Smile, Semi-Tough*) – on the cost and rewards of winning. Redford is the ambitious skier, out to break all records, and contemptuous of the teamwork advocated by the coach (Hackman) when he goes to Europe for the Olympics. The understated performances and reluctance to emphasise plot result in convincing characterisations, to such an extent that the often narcissistic Redford actually allows himself to come across as a dislikeably selfish, arrogant and icy man. And the location skiing sequences, revealing Ritchie's background and interest in documentary styles, are simply astounding, even for those with little interest in the sport. GA

Down Memory Lane

(Phil Karlson, 1949, US) Steve Allen, Franklin Pangborn, Mack Sennett, Frank Nelson.
72 min. b/w.
A Steve Allen TV show provides a pretty dumb frame for re-runs of some cherishable Sennett material: silent clips and longer extracts from WC Fields' *The Dentist* and Bing Crosby's *Blue of the Night*. An oddball credit for tough-guy director Karlson, who knocked it out, with his radio discovery Allen, in a mere two days at Eagle-Lion. PT

Down Periscope

(David S Ward, 1996, US) Kelsey Grammer, Lauren Holly, Bruce Dern, Rob Schneider, Harry Dean Stanton, William H Macy, Ken Hudson Campbell, Rip Torn.
93 min.
The Navy doesn't know what to do with Tom Dodge – he's due his own command, but he's such an impulsive maverick, he has more enemies among the top brass than most officers face in wartime. That's how he finds himself at the helm of a rusty diesel-powered submarine that should have been junked decades ago, with a crew of no-hopers to match. His mission impossible: a war game pitting the technology of yesteryear against the nuclear powered might of today's US Navy. Grammer's first major feature after his TV success with *Frasier* finds him embracing a new persona. Out goes the intellectual cold fish, in comes the intuitive, warm, fun-loving leader of men. The role looks good on him, but it's a shame that he's also jettisoned the sophisticated dry wit which has been his hallmark in favour of a much broader, wetter humour. But what would you expect of a movie directed by Ward and co-written by Hugh (*Police Academy*) Wilson? The funniest bit plumbs the depths for a silent-running gag which could seriously damage any future submarine picture. The construction is so ramshackle (or the mood so PC) that the film-makers put a woman (Holly) on board, then can't find a thing to do with her. TCh

Down the Ancient Stairs (Per le Antiche Scala)

(Mauro Bolognini, 1975, It/Fr) Marcello Mastroianni, Françoise Fabian, Marthe Keller, Barbara Bouchet, Pierre Blaise, Lucia Bosè.
102 min.
A film that hardly deserves the outright dismissal it has generally received; it at least shows evidence of an intelligent awareness of the issues it broaches, and a loving attention to period detail (Italy in the '30s). Its biggest handicap is probably its central metaphor, ultimately too facile,

which has the mental asylum in which most of the action takes place, dominated by an all-powerful and supposedly much-loved Professor, standing as a microcosm of the fascist state. But Françoise Fabian's rational and sensitive performance, as the young doctor come to investigate the professor's methods, is a major plus; and Mastroianni is totally credible as the self-deluding professor who finds the veiled tyranny he has practised within the walls reproducing itself frighteningly outside. VG

Down Three Dark Streets
(Arnold Laven, 1954, US) Broderick Crawford, Ruth Roman, Martha Hyer, Marisa Pavan, Kenneth Tobey.
85 min. b/w.
Watchable enough, thanks to the performances, despite an overblown finale. But with its commentary and backstage glimpses of new detection techniques as Crawford's FBI agent unravels three cases on which his buddy was working when killed, it looks like a slightly sheepish echo of *Dragnet* (whose first movie spinoff also appeared in 1954). TM

Downtime
(Bharat Nalluri, 1997, GB/Fr) Paul McGann, Susan Lynch, Tom Georgeson, David Roper, Denise Bryson, Adam Johnston, David Horsefield.
91 min.
Imagine Ken Loach remaking *Die Hard*. Police shrink McGann talks single mum Lynch out of jumping off the tower block that's home to her and her small son, but the place also has a vandalism problem and a creaking old lift – where the three end up, dangling and fighting for their lives. Director Nalluri makes the best of this, but can do little about the script's tin ear for would-be hard boiled dialogue, and Georgeson's overheated performance as the unemployed dad who's not going to take it any more. Credibility doesn't really come into it. TJ

Down to Earth
(Alexander Hall, 1947, US) Rita Hayworth, Larry Parks, Marc Platt, Roland Culver, James Gleason, Edward Everett Horton.
101 min.
Terpsichore, Muse of the Dance (Hayworth), is sent to terra firma to help Broadway producer Parks with his latest musical extravaganza. The result, however, never quite gleams as bright as Rudolph Maté's Technicolor photography, despite the return of Culver and Horton as the helpful angelic types from the earlier and superior *Here Comes Mr Jordan*. TJ

Drachenfutter
see Spicy Rice

Dracula
(Tod Browning, 1931, US) Bela Lugosi, Helen Chandler, David Manners, Dwight Frye, Edward Van Sloan.
85 min. b/w.
Not by any means the masterpiece of fond memory or reputation, although the first twenty minutes are astonishingly fluid and brilliantly shot by Karl Freund, despite the intrusive painted backdrops. Innumerable imaginative touches here: the sinister emphasis of Lugosi's first words ('I...am...Dracula') and the sonorous poetry of his invocation to the children of the night; the moment when Dracula leads the way up his castle stairway behind a vast cobweb through which Renfield has to struggle as he follows; the vampire women, driven off by Dracula, reluctantly backing away from the camera while it continues hungrily tracking in to Renfield's fallen body. Thereafter the pace falters, and with the London scenes growing in verbosity and staginess, the hammy limitations of Lugosi's performance are cruelly exposed. But the brilliant moments continue (Renfield's frenzy in his cell, for instance), and Freund's camerawork rarely falters. TM

Dracula
(aka Horror of Dracula)
(Terence Fisher, 1958, GB) Peter Cushing, Christopher Lee, Michael Gough, Melissa Stribling, Carol Marsh, Valerie Gaunt.
82 min.

This was the first Hammer remake of *Dracula*, and it is by now more or less established as a classic. The film is perhaps typified by its beautiful opening sequence in which Christopher Lee appears, a menacing shadow between pillars at the top of a staircase, then glides down the stairs in a prolonged take to reveal not the grotesque figure that Lugosi portrayed but, on the contrary, a crisply charming aristocrat 'with pale face and unforgettable eyes'. Other parts, however, have worn less well. DP

Dracula
(Dan Curtis, 1973, GB) Jack Palance, Simon Ward, Nigel Davenport, Pamela Brown, Fiona Lewis, Penelope Horner, Murray Brown.
98 min.
A TV movie theatrically released in Britain. Despite traditionally atmospheric touches in the direction, a disappointing adaptation which boasted of going back to source in Bram Stoker's novel but lets Richard Matheson's script stray into silly infidelities and inventions. Radically miscast, Palance does have his moments as a Dracula mourning his lost love, but misses out on the chance to be romantically Byronic since, with his love reincarnated as Lucy Westenra (Lewis), he is mostly required to rage because she is killed again. TM

Dracula
(John Badham, 1979, US) Frank Langella, Laurence Olivier, Donald Pleasence, Kate Nelligan, Trevor Eve, Jan Francis, Tony Haygarth.
112 min.
Langella offers the best interpretation of Stoker's villain since Christopher Lee and, Badham's film, shot in England, gives him a classy environment to devastate. But the decision to create such a sympathetic vampire (especially alongside Olivier's hammy Van Helsing) leaves the film short of suspense, and so romance has to take most of the weight. As a result, it begins to drift badly at the climax. TM

Dracula (aka Bram Stoker's Dracula)
(Francis Ford Coppola, 1992, US) Gary Oldman, Winona Ryder, Anthony Hopkins, Keanu Reeves, Richard E Grant, Cary Elwes, Bill Campbell, Sadie Frost, Tom Waits, Jay Robinson.
127 min.
From the moment Dracula (Oldman) trails a bloodied razor across his tongue with a look of ecstasy, you know that this version, going back to source in Stoker's novel, isn't going to offer a silver-tongued bloodsucker hovering over swooning damsels. In the opening sequences, Dracula's soul-mate Elisabeta (Ryder) commits suicide in the mistaken belief that he had died in battle. Forsaking God, he seems doomed to an endless existence of guilt and loneliness, until lawyer Jonathan Harker (Reeves) shows up a picture of his fiancée, who just happens to be the spitting image of Elisabeta. A gorgeous, stylised adaptation, full of visual tricks and dazzling camerawork, this places the emphasis firmly on perverse, rampant eroticism. Equally forceful is Oldman's extraordinary performance, especially in his older guise, complete with buffant hairdo and elongated fingers. In contrast to Hopkins' aggressive performance as vampire-hunter Van Helsing, a stupefied Reeves puts in a hopeless show of defiance. This lack of a convincing central dynamic leads to the occasional sense that the film is little more than a spectacular edifice, but you'll be too spellbound to resist seduction. CM

Dracula A.D. 1972
(Alan Gibson, 1972, GB) Christopher Lee, Peter Cushing, Stephanie Beacham, Michael Coles, Christopher Neame.
98 min.
Feeblest of the early 1970s cycle of Dracula revivals, set in contemporary London and decorated with scantily-clad female victims. Plot revolves around a trendy party-goer, Johnny Alucard (geddit?), who suggests livening up a party with a spot of devil worship. Guess who materialises, ludicrously rigged out in traditional period garb? Crass Hammer trash. MA

Dracula: Dead and Loving It
(Mel Brooks, 1995, US) Leslie Nielsen, Peter MacNicol, Steven Weber, Amy Yasbeck, Lysette Anthony, Harvey Korman, Mel Brooks, Clive Revill, Anne Bancroft.
90 min.
Brooks has always grounded his humour on high production values, a practice admirers claim achieves satirical effect and fond *hommage*. Certainly, this is as lavish as ever, and the narrative likewise takes care to keep up with both Stoker's original and the Coppola facsimile. There are some slight shortcuts. Renfield (MacNicol), not Jonathan Harker, travels to Transylvania, where Dracula (Nielsen) entrances and enslaves him, thus securing food (the crew of the *Demeter*) and shelter (Carfax Abbey). The Count provides the clothing himself – a Gary Oldman-esque buffant wig, for instance, which he takes off indoors (one of the surviving jokes). Coppola had trouble stuffing the book into two hours, and this hasty hour-and-a-half feels perfunctory in the extreme. Brooks, as Van Helsing, is one of the more successful aspects, but he hasn't imbued in his stock company a similar ability to rise above their underwritten roles. NB

Dracula Has Risen from the Grave
(Freddie Francis, 1968, GB) Christopher Lee, Rupert Davies, Veronica Carlson, Barbara Ewing, Barry Andrews.
92 min.
With the exception of Peter Sasdy, none of the Hammer directors who followed Terence Fisher into the Dracula series have been able to relate the atmosphere and poetry of vampirism to the rest of the plot. Here, Freddie Francis creates some admirable atmosphere and tension in the first half-hour, but ultimately reduces the film to an inconsequential splurge of arbitrary religious and sexual motifs. DP

Dracula, Prince of Darkness
(Terence Fisher, 1965, GB) Christopher Lee, Andrew Keir, Barbara Shelley, Francis Matthews, Suzan Farmer, Thorley Walters.
90 min.
Full of the sensual mysteriousness which Hammer used to achieve so effortlessly during their long occupation of Bray studios. Starting with a re-run of the Count's dusty demise at the hands of Van Helsing, this was the official sequel to *Dracula*, and – though it tails off – the first hour has real grandeur as Dracula's servant uses a prudish Victorian couple to effect his master's restoration. DP

Dracula's Daughter
(Lambert Hillyer, 1936, US) Gloria Holden, Otto Kruger, Marguerite Churchill, Irving Pichel, Edward Van Sloan, Nan Grey.
72 min. b/w.
A genuine sequel to Tod Browning's *Dracula* (based on Bram Stoker's story *Dracula's Guest*), Universal's low-budget shocker finds Van Helsing placed under arrest for the murder of the Count, only for a mysterious woman (Holden) to turn up and take away Dracula's body for ritual consignment to a funeral pyre. Though she has inherited the vampic urge from her father, this princess of darkness desperately seeks release from her condition through an understanding psycologist (Kruger). Apart from its haunting, low-key mood, the film is also notable for its subtle suggestion (hardly expected from a former director of B Westerns) of the lesbian nature of the female vampire. DT

Dragnet
(Tom Mankiewicz, 1987, US) Dan Aykroyd, Tom Hanks, Christopher Plummer, Harry Morgan, Alexandra Paul, Jack O'Halloran, Elizabeth Ashley, Dabney Coleman.
106 min.
The contemporary perspective is even less kind to '50s TV's sententious Sergeant Joe Friday than to Elliot Ness. Aykroyd really has the character down, too – the stolidly purposeful walk, the endless uninflected speeches about decency and proper procedure, punctuated with time checks – but where Jack Webb was little more than the Mount Rushmore of public service, Aykroyd's big soft nellie features and prissy mien trawl for laughs. All of which is wonderful, but little else is. Friday's new partner, Hanks, is not so much a character as

an unnecessary intermediary between us and the joke. He is here to point up the risibility of the procedural rule book, so he's been issued with instinct and major dishevellment. Porn king Coleman and evangelist Plummer plan to rig the struggle of good against evil for profit, which somehow involves sacrificing an Orange County virgin on the altar. Entertaining enough, but a pity they didn't draft in more of the Eisenhower context. BC

Dragon Dies Hard, The (aka The Bruce Lee Story)
(Shih Ti, 1974, US) Li Hsiao-Lung, Tang Pei, Yamada, Na Yin-Hsiu.
90 min.
Produced by Chinese businessmen in the States and withdrawn there as libellous, this fictionalised biography of Bruce Lee has its heart firmly in the dirt-digging world of Hong Kong movie gossip. Very rough and perfunctory, it's nonetheless diverting as a curiosity. VG

DragonHeart
(Rob Cohen, 1996, US) Dennis Quaid, David Thewlis, Dina Meyer, Julie Christie, Peter Postlethwaite, Jason Isaacs.
103 min.
Brave knight-turned-bounty-hunter Bowen (Quaid) teams up with Draco, an 18 by 43 ft last-surviving dragon (voice by Sean Connery). They go from village to village, faking the dragon's capture and pocketing the reward. Thus Bowen is kept in turnips, while Draco escapes extinction. Being a medieval Hollywood romp for the '90s (notable computer-generated effects), the film has a villainous king played by an English actor – here, the wonderful Thewlis, who distracts attention from Quaid's obvious inability to match the technology. When he finds out his mother the Queen (Christie) has tried to have him killed, he pauses before muttering, 'How unmotherly of you.' Engaging fare: part Dungeons and Dragons, part buddy movie – in the style of 'The Good, the Bad and the Very Ugly' – and, finally, a tale of redemption. Connery's dragon doesn't baulk at chatting up the leading lady. SGr

Dragonslayer
(Matthew Robbins, 1981, US) Peter MacNicol, Caitlin Clarke, Ralph Richardson, John Hallam, Peter Eyre, Albert Salmi, Sydney Bromley.
110 min.
The saga is simple enough in this hybrid sword-and-sorcery fantasy: Dark Ages necromancer, summoned to conquer tyrannical dragon, inconveniently dies testing his powers; Sorcerer's Apprentice takes over, falls foul of virgin-sacrificing king; eventually takes on the impressively monstrous 'Vermithrax Pejorative' with a little help from the beyond. But it's the universal resonance of myth and legend that works against the film despite its creditable packaging: Richardson's 'last sorcerer' is inevitably close kin to the Merlin of Excalibur, while the callow youth with an ambitious half-grasp of his mentor's magic comes to us ready-filtered through the likes of Luke Skywalker. Verges on the nasty for the nippers; sails close to déjà vu for fantasy fans; fated, probably, to damnation by faint praise. PT

Dragon: The Bruce Lee Story
(Rob Cohen, 1993, US) Jason Scott Lee, Lauren Holly, Robert Wagner, Nancy Kwan, Michael Learned.
120 min.
In this lively if inevitably compromised biopic of the charismatic Hong Kong martial arts star, Jason Scott Lee (no relation) looks good and moves well as the Chinese street kid who came to America, set up his own martial arts school, landed a supporting role in the Green Hornet TV series, then returned to Hong Kong to find he had become a national celebrity. Unlike most film star biopics, this is especially strong on the films themselves, with skilful re-creations from Fists of Fury and Enter the Dragon. Less successful is the subplot in which Lee faces up to his inner demons, depicted as a fantastical giant samurai figure. NF

Dragonwyck
(Joseph L Mankiewicz, 1946, US) Gene Tierney, Vincent Price, Glenn Langan, Walter Huston, Anne Revere, Henry Morgan, Jessica Tandy.
103 min. b/w.
Mankiewicz's directing debut is a far cry from the acerbically scripted satires – A Letter to Three Wives, All About Eve – for which he is best known; indeed, though it inhabits basically the same Gothic territory as his later The Ghost and Mrs Muir, it lacks that film's charm, easy wit and ambivalent psychological insights. Still, it's an efficient enough drama in the tradition of Rebecca, with innocent young Tierney leaving her rural home to stay with wealthy and sophisticated cousin Price. Needless to say, she marries him only to discover that he's a cruel, brooding tyrant who maltreats his workers and has a sinister skeleton in his closet. Few surprises, but the performances are vivid and the recreation of the 1840s setting is subtly plausible. GA

Dragoon Wells Massacre
(Harold Schuster, 1957, US) Barry Sullivan, Dennis O'Keefe, Mona Freeman, Katy Jurado, Sebastian Cabot, Jack Elam.
88 min.
A motley group – it includes a cavalry officer, a sheriff, two convicts, two women (one haughtily respectable, one not), a renegade gun-and-whisky runner – fight a desperate rearguard battle as they trek across the Arizona desert with marauding Apaches on their tail. It's a stock Western situation but a highly enjoyable film, magnificently shot by William Clothier and with a surprisingly tight, inventive script by Warren Douglas (the Apaches need the renegade alive for future use, for example, so they merely pick off the horses as the first stage in a war of attrition) which is particularly strong on characterisation (with the good/bad balances subtly shifting under pressure). Excellent performances, too, with Elam especially memorable as a man so accustomed to being pigeonholed as an ugly desperado that he is doggily abashed by an orphaned child's unhesitating acceptance of him as a trustworthy protector. TM

Drama of the Rich (Fatti di Gente Perbene)
(Mauro Bolognini, 1974, It/Fr) Giancarlo Giannini, Catherine Deneuve, Fernando Rey, Marcel Bozzuffi, Corrado Pani.
115 min.
In late 19th century Italy, the Murri family caused a scandal. Bolognini's reconstruction of their story looks like nothing so much as a Visconti sub-text: a slowly unfurled melodrama full of weighty but unexplored themes (political power, incest, science, religion) whose passion is almost entirely spent on the aristocratic stylishness of its looks. At least Morricone's resonant score lends emotional life. HM

Dramma della Gelosia (Jealousy, Italian Style/ The Pizza Triangle)
(Ettore Scola, 1970, It/Sp) Marcello Mastroianni, Monica Vitti, Giancarlo Giannini, Manolo Zarzo, Marisa Merlini, Hercules Cortez.
106 min.
Scola's satire on screaming, gesticulating, Italian romantic dramas inevitably and unfortunately falls into the trap of indulging in the same overheated histrionics that it attacks. But, as it tells its melodramatic story of a beautiful florist torn between her two jealous lovers – a pizza-cook and a bricklayer – it still manages to be intelligently entertaining, with its eclectic humour (parody, social satire, and a nice line in cool, throwaway dialogue counterbalancing the boiling emotions) and polished performances. GA

Draughtsman's Contract, The
(Peter Greenaway, 1982, GB) Anthony Higgins, Janet Suzman, Anne Louise Lambert, Neil Cunningham, Hugh Fraser.
108 min.
Although set in an English country house in 1694, this is essentially science fiction of the most dazzling kind, being a far more vivid exploration of an alien world than 99 per cent of big budget Hollywood films. The story about a painter who undertakes to draw an estate is as intriguing as the culture it displays. Greenaway's 17th century is a place of ribald honesty as well as unfathomable mystery, and it revels in the spoken word. Of course this is non-genre, low-budget cinema, and some people will be irritated by its singlemindedness; but for others it's proof that wit can sometimes carry a film to places special effects just don't reach. DP

Draws
see American Tickler or The Winner of 10 Academy Awards

Dreamchild
(Gavin Millar, 1985, GB) Coral Browne, Ian Holm, Peter Gallagher, Caris Corfman, Nicola Cowper, Jane Asher.
94 min.
At eighty, Alice Liddell is met in New York in 1932 by intrusive hacks who thrust a pink nylon bunny in her arms and demand a message for the children of America. Confronted with these alien surroundings, the hoity-toity and terribly British Alice is forced to unbend a little and piece together the fragments of her life. Dennis Potter's screenplay contrasts sassy New York with Alice's recollections, both of an idyllic youth in Oxford with the stammering Dodgson (Holm), and of Carroll's classic dominated by Jim Henson's ferocious puppets. An imaginative tour de force which is more than matched by Millar's direction of his first feature film. JE

Dream Demon
(Harley Cokliss, 1988, GB) Jemma Redgrave, Kathleen Wilhoite, Timothy Spall, Jimmy Nail, Mark Greenstreet, Susan Fleetwood.
89 min.
A fantasy thriller with an intricate dream-within-a-dream structure, low on budget but high on ambition, this offers a breathless run down the corridors of the unconscious mind. As her wedding to a Falklands hero approaches, virgin Diana (Redgrave) suffers disturbing nightmares. When wacky Jenny (Wilhoite) turns up claiming to have lived in Diana's house during a childhood since blotted from her mind, their fates become intertwined. Catalysed by her memories, Jenny's repressed past also surfaces as a recurring nightmare. Blurring the line between reality and dream, the film keeps the audience off-balance, while the effects are employed sparingly but to good effect. With more time and money, Cokliss might have sorted out the shaky plot and made more of some intriguing ideas. Still, stylish photography, excellent sets, and Bill Nelson's jagged soundtrack ensure scariness. NF

Dreamer
(Noel Nosseck, 1979, US) Tim Matheson, Susan Blakely, Richard B Shull, Jack Warden, Barbara Stuart, Pedro Gonzalez-Gonzalez.
86 min.
Matheson's the dewy-eyed idealist of the title, a handsome lad who hopes to make it big on the professional bowling circuit. Craggy old-timer Warden (who seems to be doing an impersonation of Burgess Meredith in Rocky) offers to coach him. Tim's girlfriend, Blakely, is dead set against his choice of career, but if he knocks down enough skittles, he's sure to win her round. Not much polish on this particular ball. GM

Dream Flights (Polioty Vo Sne Naiavou)
(Roman Balayan, 1983, USSR) Oleg Yankovsky, Liudmila Gurchenko, Oleg Tabakov, Liudmila Ivanovna.
90 min.
Clowning his way through life, 40-year-old Seryozha feels infinitely superior to his far more staid and steady colleagues and friends; he's ambitious, attractive and, it seems, free. But beneath the wayward liveliness lies a sad reality of loneliness, insecurity and despair; when his wife and mistress meet each other, they both leave him; when he accuses his fellow workers of moral hypocrisy, he loses his job. Balayan's film, a subtle, sensitive tragicomedy, traces its charismatic but dislikeable hero's picaresque odyssey from complacency to confusion with an admirable ambivalence of attitude. On the one hand, a petulant, selfish prankster who's never grown up; on the other, someone who refuses to play by the rules of conformist society. Central to the film's ability not only to hold interest but also to convince is Tarkovsky's leading man Yankovsky's remarkable performance, as edgy, exciting, charming and suggestive of vulnerability as De Niro at his best. GA

Time Out Film Guide 243

Dreaming of Rita (Drömmen om Rita)

(Jon Lindström, 1993, Swe) Per Oscarsson, Marika Lagercrantz, Philip Zandén, Yaba Holst.
108 min.

Having recently buried his wife, Oscarsson goes in search of an old flame who reminds him of his beloved Rita Hayworth; trouble is, he's far from young and healthy himself, so his daughter sets off in pursuit, leaving her workaholic husband behind, and meeting a more appreciative hitcher en route. Cue for a romantic farce-cum-road movie endowed with engaging twists, but not exactly startling or original – indeed, the end is a disappointing cop-out. The landscape is a bonus, as is the charismatically beautiful Lagercrantz. GA

Dream Life (La Vie Rêvée)

(Mireille Dansereau, 1972, Can) Liliane Lemaître-Auger, Véronique Le Flaguais, Jean-François Guité, Guy Foucault.
90 min.

A film about sexism and women's liberation which is ideologically clear and cohesive, uncompromising, and well made. Two young girls, one working class, the other middle class, meet at work and become friends. Finding it hard to live in the present, and that their fantasies bear no relation to the way they experience men's attitudes to them, they lure one of their dream lovers to act out 'his' reality; he fails, and the grip is broken; they have proved that the real men they know are peripheral to their lives, and thus are no longer dependent on their own fantasies. Filmed as a punctuated story – with narrative, fantasy, flashback and slow-motion – it's a superbly rounded and sensual presentation of ideas. MV

Dream Life of Angels, The

see Vie Revée des Anges, La

Dream Lover

(Alan J Pakula, 1986, US) Kristy McNichol, Ben Masters, Paul Shenar, Justin Deas, John McMartin, Gayle Hunnicutt.
104 min.

McNichol plays a tyro musician plagued by nightmares after fatally stabbing an assailant in her apartment; but the 'dream therapy' she undertakes to shake off the shock brings with it new traumas. Pakula treats all this as a Bergmanesque case study, but the male figures besieging the heroine's mind aren't drawn with sufficient firmness. Intriguing idea; ramshackle plotting. TJ

Dream Lover

(Nicholas Kazan, 1993, US) James Spader, Mädchen Amick, Fredric Lehne, Bess Armstrong, Larry Miller, Kathleen York.
103 min.

Spader is high-earning yuppie-type Ray Reardon who thinks, having gone through one divorce, that he's found the ideal mate in alluring Lena (Amick). But after several years of apparent happiness, her increasingly erratic behaviour strikes doubt in his heart. Here's the person he should know best – but is she the woman he thought she was? Promising material, disappointingly frittered away. TJ

Dream of Kings, A

(Daniel Mann, 1969, US) Anthony Quinn, Irene Papas, Inger Stevens, Sam Levene, Val Avery.
110 min.

Quinn doing his Zorba act as a cheerful Chicago loafer who despises money and spends his days brightening the neighbourhood (not to mention a sex-starved widow) with his life-giving presence. Insisting ad nauseam that as a Greek he belongs to a race of kings, he is brought down to earth only when he discovers that his small son is dying. Dripping with ludicrously overblown dialogue to match the performance. TM

Dream of Passion, A

(Jules Dassin, 1978, Switz/Greece) Melina Mercouri, Ellen Burstyn, Andreas Voutsinas, Despo Diamantidou.
110 min.

This disastrous blend of Euripides, Bergman (credited inspiration) and sub-Cassavetes role-confusion glibly juxtaposes the theatrical angst of Mercouri, grappling with her interpretation of

Medea for a new production of the play, alongside the cold religious fanaticism of Burstyn, jailed for a triple infanticide in response to her husband's infidelity, and fails miserably in attempting to invoke 'Persona-I' correspondences between them. A hammer-blow insistence on the 'relevance' of Greek tragedy, a modish 'distancing' of the creative process, and a token exploration of feminist implications conspire to produce a nightmare of pretension. Filmed (basically) in English. PT

Dream On

(Amber Production Team, 1991, GB) Amber Styles, Maureen Harold, Anna-Marie Gascoigne.
115 min.

There's something remarkable about the low-budget work of North Shields' Amber Collective. *Seacoal* was politically sharp Loachian realism; *In Fading Light* saw a growth in confident technique and a flair for the epic; here, they move still further from the documentary naturalism of their beginnings, with an engaging, coherent, continually surprising blend of realism and fantasy, witty comedy and serious social comment. It depicts the problems faced by three women (alcoholism, anorexia, abuse and battering) with honesty, depth of feeling and an unexpected touch of magic. As ever, the performances are highly convincing (even the men – however stupid or nasty – are never reduced to stereotypes), the politics are spot-on, and the finale, firmly rooted in the gritty reality of a celebration dance after the women's darts-night, is wholly moving. GA

Dreams

see Kvinnodröm

Dreams

see Akira Kurosawa's Dreams

Dreamscape

(Joseph Ruben, 1983, US) Dennis Quaid, Max von Sydow, Christopher Plummer, Eddie Albert, Kate Capshaw, David Patrick Kelly, George Wendt.
99 min.

Quaid is a gambler with psychic powers. To pay off debts, he is persuaded to take part in an experiment where he links up with sleepers and tours through their dreams, solving a neurosis here, dealing with a demon there. Some of the dreams are funny (one middle-aged man's fidelity nightmare is hysterical); most are pretty nasty, though, especially a trip through an 8-year-old's primal fears. In the end, things get a bit silly: Quaid has to save the USA by fighting off the forces of evil in the President's nightmares. But as a night out this is as good a piece of solid, down-the-line schlock as anything to come along since *Halloween III*. NR

Dreams That Money Can Buy

(Hans Richter/Max Ernst/Fernand Léger/Man Ray/Marcel Duchamp/Alexander Calder, 1946, US)
90 min.

The movie's artistic credentials couldn't be more imposing (in addition to the various expatriate Surrealists/Dadaists who contributed episodes, there is music by John Cage and Darius Milhaud, among others), but that makes its manifest failure all the more striking. Richter has created a feeble pastiche of the contemporary *film noir* as the framing story, centering on a man with the power to generate dreams; other contributions are therefore integrated as dream sequences. The movie quickly degenerates into a series of party pieces: Duchamp rehashes his 'roto-reliefs' of 1927, Léger animates dolls, Calder animates his mobiles, and so on. Only Ernst, who recreates an image-sequence from his collage-novel *La Semaine de la Bonté* in live action terms, emerges with much credit. TR

Dream Team, The

(Howard Zieff, 1989, US) Michael Keaton, Christopher Lloyd, Peter Boyle, Stephen Furst, Dennis Boutsikaris, Lorraine Bracco, Milo O'Shea, Philip Bosco, James Remar, Jack Giplin.
113 min.

The Dream Team is a collection of fruitcakes, locked away because they're just too *annoying* for polite society. Only Billy (Keaton), with his violent temper, poses any threat, but even this is a symptom of his being too in tune with his emotions. Of

the others, Albert (Furst), after 12 years of institutionalised TV viewing, can communicate only in telespeak; Jack (Boyle) thinks he's Christ; and Henry (Lloyd) thinks he's a doctor. These openhearted innocents are misunderstood but not mistreated: *One Flew Over the Cuckoo's Nest* is acknowledged and dismissed in an inspired opening scene. Caring psychiatrist Dr. Weitzman (Boutsikaris) escorts the Team on a day out to the Yankee Stadium, and is separated from his charges in the heart of Manhattan. Abandoned in the madness of the urban jungle, they are forced to overcome their mental handicaps in order to trace the missing doctor and foil a murder plot. Halfway through, the plot settles into an obvious stride, but by then we're hooked into each character's personal voyage of self-discovery. Despite the barrage of one-liners and almost farcical plot twists, Zieff's light touch and some unselfish ensemble acting make this team genuinely endearing. EP

Dreigroschenoper, Die (The Threepenny Opera)

(GW Pabst, 1931, Ger) Rudolf Forster, Carola Neher, Reinhold Schunzel, Fritz Rasp, Lotte Lenya, Valeska Gert.
111 min. b/w.

Brecht and Weill may have sued Pabst over what they considered his manhandling of their musical (the director rewrote Brecht's script and dropped several songs), but the social satire remains thankfully intact. The story itself is preserved: in Victorian London, womanising gentleman thief Mack the Knife joins, through marriage, both the king of the beggars and the chief of police in setting up a bank. If Brecht's anti-capitalist sentiments are muted by Pabst's heavily stylised lyricism, there is no denying either the sheer visual eloquence of the sets and photography or the charismatic power of the performances, most notably, perhaps, Lenya as the whore Jenny. GA

Dressed to Kill

(Brian De Palma, 1980, US) Michael Caine, Angie Dickinson, Nancy Allen, Keith Gordon, Dennis Franz, David Margulies.
104 min.

Beginning and ending with a pair of shower frissons, this brazen reworking of *Psycho* is most striking for its sheer audacity, and actually lifts that film's most shattering device. But having achieved this coup, the film degenerates into near-farce, punctuated by a number of hollow audience-grabbing moments which hang together not at all. Ultimately, the film amounts to little more than a consummate study of suspense technique, all dressed up with nowhere to go. DP

Dresser, The

(Peter Yates, 1983, GB) Albert Finney, Tom Courtenay, Edward Fox, Zena Walker, Eileen Atkins, Michael Gough.
118 min.

An accomplished film of Ronald Harwood's theatrical two-hander, animated by two gigantic performances. Finney, grossly Shakespearean as Sir, the imperious, declamatory actor-manager with a Moses-like command of his company and inanimate objects ('St-o-o-p th-a-a-a-t tr-ai-ai-n!' he bawls, bringing British Rail to its knees), is fully matched by Courtenay's pantomime poof Norman, Sir's devoted dresser: mincing, nagging, but the only one able to reach to the furthest depths of Sir's hair-tearing madness and coax him into the costumes and roles that have by wicked irony destroyed him. Especially pleasing, then, that in the final act it is the quiet craft of an actress – Atkins as the long-suffering, love-lorn stage manageress – that rises above constrictions of plot and thankless part to upstage them. FD

Dressmaker, The

(Jim O'Brien, 1988, GB) Joan Plowright, Billie Whitelaw, Jane Horrocks, Tim Ransom, Peter Postlethwaite, Pippa Hinchley, Tony Haygarth.
91 min.

Liverpool, 1944. Nellie (Plowright), elderly dressmaker to her upper-working-class neighbourhood, has a scatty, sexually-active younger sister Margo (Whitelaw), and rules with a Victorian rod of iron over their repressed niece Rita (Horrocks). Nellie is not amused to disocer that Margo and Rita attended a raucous bonking bash with GIs stationed locally; still less, that Rita had fallen in love with boring Southern GI Wesley (Ransom). But

d

Rita fails to meet the horny GI half-way, thereby ensuring an early end to the romance....and subsequently plunging the family into unexpected tragedy. In his first feature O'Brien admirably conveys an atmosphere of arsenic and old lace through realistic period sets, claustrophobic camerawork, and dim lighting, while John McGrath's wittily scripted adaptation of Beryl Bainbridge's novel is played with stylish gusto by all concerned. Horrocks plays the innocent so well that you feel like strangling her; Plowright and Whitelaw are a joy throughout. DA

Drifting Clouds (Kauas Pilvet Karkaavat/Au loin s'en vont les nuages)

(Aki Kaurismäki, 1996, Fin/Ger/Fr) Kati Outinen, Kari Väänänen, Elina Salo, Sakari Kuosmanen, Markku Peltola.
97 min.
When the Helsinki restaurant where Ilona (Outinen) works is taken over, the new owners decide not to retain the existing staff. To make matters worse, Ilona's tram-driver husband Lauri (Väänänen) is made redundant. There are a few jobs around and the couple are no longer in the bloom of youth. Will their marriage survive the belt-tightening and the blows to dignity that unemployment brings? The potentially depressing subject matter is superbly offset by Kaurismäki's customary deadpan brand of gently absurdist comedy, by the use of primary colours in the set designs, and by the quiet yet real sense of supportiveness that imbues Ilona and Lauri's relationship not only with each other but with their friends and colleagues. As ever, the performances from Kaurismäki regulars are understated to the point of minimalism, but the writer/director treats the lives, aspirations and anxieties of his less-than-beautiful losers with such unsentimental affection that we care about every one of them (Ilona and Lauri's magnificently solemn mutt Pietari included). As ever, too, the semi-ironic use of music (Tchaikovsky, old-fashioned tango), Timo Salminen's subdued, precise camerawork, and Kaurismäki's miniaturist's eye for the telling detail yield rewards aplenty. GA

Drifting Life, A (Chunhua Menglu)

(Lin Cheng-Sheng, 1996, Tai) Lee Kang-Sheng, Vicky Wei, Grace Chen, Chen Shi-Huang, Wang Yu-Wen, Lang Jing.
123 min.
An intensely moving directorial debut from Lin, hitherto best known as a comic actor in movies like Buddha Bless America. A family in rural Taiwan starts to break up when the son's young wife dies giving birth to her second child. The son Kun-Cheng (Lee) leaves home and drifts into another sexual relationship, but tries to be a good father to his kids and a tolerant, filial son to his parents, both of whom irritate the hell out of him. The storyline is minimal, but Lin builds up a commanding picture of the ways parents influence children and children resist parents. It's a film about cutting ties and mending ties, acted with total conviction and directed with light-handed control. TR

Driftwood

(Allan Dwan, 1947, US) Natalie Wood, Dean Jagger, Walter Brennan, Ruth Warrick, Charlotte Greenwood, Jerome Cowan.
90 min. b/w.
Fascinating and unusual movie about a young, orphaned girl found wandering in the wilderness by an idealistic doctor, and taken back to be cared for at his village, a hothouse of political intrigue where the authorities refuse him full medical facilities, and where the girl herself provokes outrage among the locals with her outspoken honesty and strange, biblical morality. At times the religious allegory is pushed a bit too far, and there's a certain amount of sentimentality about a dog the girl finds. But generally, it's an admirably dreamlike and often dark conjuring up of the way the adult world is viewed by children, in its own way almost as effective as Curse of the Cat People, made three years earlier. GA

Driftwood

(Ronan O'Leary, 1996, Ire/GB) James Spader, Anne Brochet, Barry McGovern, Anna Massey, Aiden Grenell.
100 min.

Man washes up, wounded and without memory, on windswept Irish shore. Woman takes Man back to remote cottage, tending his crippled leg, and telling him she's the island's sole inhabitant and he can't leave till the boat brings supplies in three months' time. Weeks pass. Man, attracted and grateful, sleeps with Woman, but still plans to leave; Woman, between sculpting naked Men and having intense conversations with her dead mum, plans otherwise. This determinedly arty, allegorical and anaemic look at the emotional and psychological power plays that constitute male-female interaction comes across as a lame rip-off of such female-fruitcake fare as Misery, Images and Repulsion. At best it's gynophobic, at worst misogynistic – though Spader's amnesiac no-name seems incapable of committing, that's peanuts compared to the neurotic disorders displayed by Anne Brochet's Sarah, whose smothering, possessive obsession pushes her from simple repeated deceits to deadly violence. GA

Driller Killer, The

(Abel Ferrara, 1979, US) Jimmy Laine (ie. Abel Ferrara), Carolyn Marz, Harry Schultz, Baybi Day, Richard Howorth.
85 min.
When your attempts at expressing yourself artistically are being sabotaged by an accumulation of unpaid bills, when your peace is ruptured by the punk band practising next door, when your loved one is packing her bags – oh God, don't you feel like grabbing an electric drill (with Porto-Pak) and boring through the nearest cranium? No, perhaps not, and anyway it's still no excuse to go round piercing stray down-and-outs from NYC's drifting poor population. But this film has fallen victim to its catchy title and publicity bluurrgh, and is now firmly, unfairly established in the vanguard of video nastiness. Only one murder is shown in lingering technogore – a bit of drill driven through the brain of an unfortunate bum. The rest of the victims are despatched via fast-action wobblicam or submerged in shadow, and it makes a refreshing change that none of the female characters are even threatened, let alone drilled. The psychopathic painter (played by the director) has more in common with the Deneuve schizo from Repulsion (with skinned rabbit thrown in as reference) than with the bloodcrazed slashers of other gore movies. Gloomy, doomy and disturbing; as depressing a picture of urban decay as you're likely to see, with its earsplitting collage of noisome nightmare depicting a reality that is probably a million miles from the sheltered suburbia of the video nasty nixers. AB

Dritte Generation, Die

see Third Generation, The

Drive, The (Saigo no Drive)

(Shunichi Nagasaki, 1992, Jap) Koji Tamaki, Shigeru Muroi, Yoko Nogiwa, Takeshi Naito, Kaori Mizushima, Tatsuo Yamada, Tomoko Otahara.
93 min.
This is more restrained and less spectacular than Nagasaki's subversive thriller The Enchantment, but ultimately just as chilling . A divorced single mother (Muroi) is desperate to keep her married lover and business partner (Tamaki). With loan sharks circling, she picks up a schoolgirl, murders her, and tries to extract a ransom from the child's senile grandfather, while enticing her 'innocent' partner into a weekend on the lam. An anguished, misplaced love story, with a wrenching performance from Muroi, and no cop-outs. TCh

Drive, He Said

(Jack Nicholson, 1970, US) William Tepper, Karen Black, Michael Margotta, Bruce Dern, Robert Towne, Henry Jaglom.
90 min.
It's strange that while Easy Rider has often been credited with opening up Hollywood, its prime movers should subsequently have had such a hard time. But Hopper, Fonda and Nicholson all overreached next time out, and the fascinating Last Movie, Hired Hand and Drive, He Said each got pigeonholed – or shelved – as 'failures'. Nicholson's movie was nothing less than his own variant on W.R. – Mysteries of the Organism: a boldly-shot campus yarn of basketball and revolution turning on notions of Reichian sex-pol. No way can it be said to work, despite the cast's cultish distinction,

but it still knocks most of its quasi-radical contemporaries sideways as an index of doomed '60s/'70s causes and confusions. PT

Drive-In

(Rod Amateau, 1976, US) Lisa Lemole, Glenn Morshower, Gary Cavagnaro, Billy Milliken, Lee Newsom.
96 min.
Frantic goings-on during a performance of Disaster '76, a movie showing at a Texas drive-in theatre (The Alamo), are the promising ingredients of this cod catastrophe movie. That they constitute no more than an unsatisfying hodge-podge is less the fault of Bob Peete's indulgent, idiosyncratic story (two engaging amateur crooks bungle hold-up in theatre concession stand), than the frenetic pace of its execution and Amateau's overriding concern with busy narrative mechanics. A successful directorial debut demands more than incidental charms and a string of formulary sight gags in a by now thoroughly overworked parodic style. JPy

Driver, The

(Walter Hill, 1978, US) Ryan O'Neal, Bruce Dern, Isabelle Adjani, Ronee Blakley, Matt Clark, Felice Orlandi.
91 min.
Scriptwriter-turned-director Walter Hill's Hard Times (retitled The Streetfighter in Britain) received deservedly excellent reviews when it opened a few years back. His second feature is even better, a combination of brilliantly edited car chases and existential thriller which recalls the sombreness of Melville and the spareness of Leone in a context which is the 'classical' economy of directors like Hawks and Walsh. A brilliant plot of cross and double-cross, with cop Dern out to nail ace getaway driver O'Neal, unravels with a tautness to put it on a par with the same year's action hit, Assault on Precinct 13. RM

Driving Licence, The

see Permis de Conduire, Le

Driving Me Crazy

(Nick Broomfield, 1988, GB) André Heller, Andrew Braunsberg, Nick Broomfield, Joe Hindy, Edek Bartz, Roy Lichtenstein.
81 min.
A hilarious cautionary tale tracing documentarist Broomfield's efforts to film the genesis of a glitzy stage show, to be produced in Munich by singer/impresario André Heller, reflecting the diversity of black musical experience. The budget for the associated documentary film is slashed from $1.4 million to $300,000, and a fictional subplot is introduced against Broomfield's will. Efforts to salvage the Fame-style feature founder, and fearing the collapse of the whole project, Broomfield continues on the understanding that he is allowed to film everything. The New York auditions give a first hint of the show's likely quality, a synthetic showbiz extravaganza incorporating a mish-mash of calypso, gospel, rap, tap, ballet and breakdance. More captivating by far are the off-stage machinations, including surreal conversations with neurotic scriptwriter Joe Hindy, a clandestine meeting between Broomfield and his producer in a broom cupboard, and crisis discussions conducted in financial double-speak. Several memorable characters emerge as Broomfield struggles to keep things in focus, his intrusive camera revealing artistic compromise, fragile egos, and a great deal of unintentional humour. NF

Driving Me Crazy

see Dutch

Driving Miss Daisy

(Bruce Beresford, 1989, US) Morgan Freeman, Jessica Tandy, Dan Aykroyd, Patti Lupone, Esther Rolle, Joann Havrilla, William Hall Jr, Alvin M Sugarman.
99 min.
Beresford and writer Alfred Uhry have produced a polished adaptation of the latter's play, but it's the sharp performances from Freeman and Tandy which save it from being overwhelmed by hazy filters and a surfeit of gleaming low-angle shots of period cars. Tandy plays a spirited Jewish matron who takes on black chauffeur Freeman; and the story, set in Atlanta

against the social changes of the American South, charts their relationship over 25 years as they progress from caution to affection. Real events in the city's history are pinpointed (the bombing of the synagogue in 1958, the 1965 hotel reception in honour of Martin Luther King), with Tandy refusing to acknowledge prejudice, Freeman all too painfully aware of its consequences. Far too cosy to serve as an effective social or political metaphor; better to regard it as a solid ensemble piece. CM

Drôle de Drame (Bizarre, Bizarre)

(Marcel Carné, 1937, Fr) Louis Jouvet, Michel Simon, Françoise Rosay, Jean-Louis Barrault, Jean-Pierre Aumont, Nadine Vogel, Alcover.
97 min. b/w.
At the centre of a farcical plot, scripted by Jacques Prévert from a novel by J Storer Clouston and supposedly set in London, is a mild, bumbling botanist (Simon), secretly the author of murder stories and accused of murdering his wife by the Bishop of Beckford (Jouvet), who disappears, reappears in disguise as a detective, and turns a table or two. Meanwhile a real killer goes happily about his business (Barrault, who murders butchers because he loves animals). Carné isn't renowned for his wacky temperament, and he fails to extract all the fun possible from such rich material. But there are plenty of piquant absurdities, from the proliferating milk bottles delivered by Aumont's lovelorn Express Dairy milkman, to the gents in Limehouse robbed of the flowers in their buttonholes (a typical Prévert touch). And Simon is marvellous. GB

Drôle d'Endroit pour une rencontre

see Strange Place to Meet, A

Drop Dead Fred

(Ate De Jong, 1991, US) Phoebe Cates, Rik Mayall, Marsha Mason, Tim Matheson, Bridget Fonda, Carrie Fisher, Keith Charles, Ashley Peldon.
99 min.
This boisterous comedy allows Mayall to be completely naughty, to shock, to offend... and to exasperate beyond belief. Elizabeth (Cates) reverts to youthful fantasies in a bid to escape the trauma of losing both her husband and her job. Tucked up in her own bed back home with Mom, she revives her imaginary childhood friend Fred (Mayall), and together they make sweet music. Too bad for adult viewers that this entails smearing dog shit on the living-room carpet, concocting mud pie for dinner, destroying a houseboat, etc; while Elizabeth's desperate attempts to get back together with her husband and to exorcise childhood demons aren't likely to appeal to younger viewers. Mason (as Elizabeth's domineering mother) and Fisher (as her best friend) lend strong support. But Cates appears strangely resigned to each life-shattering episode; even the goggle-eyed, frantic Mayall fails to galvanise her. CM

Drop Zone

(John Badham, 1994, US) Wesley Snipes, Gary Busey, Yancy Butler, Michael Jeter, Corin Nemec, Kyle Secor, Luca Bercovici.
102 min.
After Demolition Man and Sugar Hill, action hero Snipes plummets to earth in this sky-diving picture. Busey is characteristically out of order as the leader of an aerial team that swoops into Drug Enforcement Agency offices and downloads information about their undercover agents. The crooks then sells the information to drug barons, who in turn arrange for the exposed DEA agents to disappear. So US Marshal Snipes and his fearless partner (Butler) take to the skies in pursuit of the bad guys. Some spectacular sky-diving sequences, but a very unpersuasive story. NF

Drowning by Numbers

(Peter Greenaway, 1988, GB) Bernard Hill, Joan Plowright, Juliet Stevenson, Joely Richardson, Jason Edwards, Bryan Pringle, Trevor Cooper.
119 min.
Obsessed with obscure English folk games and father to corpse-collecting Smut, coroner Madgett becomes involved with three generations of women all named Cissie Colpitts. Unsurprisingly, his amorously optimistic agreement to keep mum about the aquatic deaths of their husbands lands him in deep water. Greenaway returns to the playful punning, ludicrous lists, and quizzical conundrums of his earlier work: opening with a girl counting a hundred stars, the 'plot' then proceeds with those same numbers appearing either in the dialogue or in suitably bizarre images. Equally teasing is the film's complex web of absurdly interlocking allusions to games, sex and mortality: famous last words, Samson and Delilah, Breughel, circumcision, etc. Elegantly scored and luminously shot, it's a modernist black comedy filled with arcane, archaic and apocryphal lore, and hugely enjoyable. GA

Drowning Pool, The

(Stuart Rosenberg, 1975, US) Paul Newman, Joanne Woodward, Tony Franciosa, Murray Hamilton, Gail Strickland, Melanie Griffith, Coral Browne, Richard Jaeckel.
108 min.
Newman, playing Ross Macdonald's private eye for the second time (the first was in Harper), embarks on a Deep South excursion through broads, nymphet daughters, twitchy cops, hookers, hoods, and gangsters of a more refined but dangerous sort. As so often with Macdonald, it's the corruption of rich families that is exposed: dominated by a grotesque mother figure (Browne) who is at least morally responsible for their sins, both weak and strong are warped by perversions. What matters in this type of film is not so much the plot as the way in which an atmosphere is created. Unfortunately, Rosenberg directs flatly, hopping from one set piece to the next, disjointedly throwing characters of varying interest across Newman's path, while the latter – in his coarsest performance yet – remains content to wisecrack and ham outrageously. Murray Hamilton scores as the villain, however, and the title sequence offers some sort of compensation. CPe

Drugstore Cowboy

(Gus Van Sant, 1989, US) Matt Dillon, Kelly Lynch, James Le Gros, Heather Graham, Beah Richards, Grace Zabriskie, Max Perlich, William S Burroughs, James Remar.
101 min.
Bob (Dillon), his wife Dianne (Lynch), Rich (Le Gros) and Nadine (Graham) are junkies who survive by robbing pharmacies in Portland, Oregon, in 1971. The natural leader of the gang, Bob decides they had better leave town after one too many scrapes with the law. It's Bob, too, who finally elects to straighten out after one of their number ODs. Though hardly earth-shakingly original, Van Sant's low-budget movie takes a cool, contemplative and sometimes comic look at American drug-culture, manages for the most part to dispense with easy moralising, and comes close to grasping why the addiction to chemicals of every kind ('A dope fiend always knows how he's gonna feel'). Despite some Coppola-esque touches with speeding clouds, the stark simplicity of Bob's fantasies suitably complements the overall gritty realism. But it's the acting that carries the day: Dillon's wildly obsessive and sporadically articulate Bob avoids the usual bratpack mannerisms, Remar makes a plausibly boorish cop, and William Burroughs brings a raddled, fragile integrity to the role of a junkie ex-priest Bob meets at a detox hostel. GA

Drum

(Steve Carver, 1976, US) Warren Oates, Isela Vega, Ken Norton, Pamela Grier, Yaphet Kotto, John Colicos, Fiona Lewis, Paula Kelly.
110 min.
'Niggers fornicating's what Falconhurst's all about', growls Warren Oates in this dire sequel to Richard Fleischer's magnificent Mandingo. Likewise the movie itself, except that even this aspect remains unfocused. Much of the blame rests with the chaotic and clumsy script fashioned from Kyle Onstott's potboiling bestseller: an incoherent introductory sequence takes the Onstott crudeties, which Fleischer was scrupulous in making a function of the characters themselves, and gives them the status of a voice-over, thereby fatally altering the audience's relationship to what is on the screen. VG

Drum, The (aka Drums)

(Zoltan Korda, 1938, GB) Sabu, Raymond Massey, Roger Livesey, Valerie Hobson, Desmond Tester, Francis L Sullivan.
104 min.
Korda's lively slice of imperialist adventure set on the Northwest Frontier during the days of the Raj, with true blue Brit officer Livesey helping out young prince Sabu against the machinations of his evil uncle, the snarling Massey. Good fun, brimful of action and Boy's Own heroics, given a touch of class by Georges Périnal's Technicolor camerawork. GA

Drums

see Drum, The

Drums Along the Mohawk

(John Ford, 1939, US) Claudette Colbert, Henry Fonda, Edna May Oliver, John Carradine, Arthur Shields, Robert Lowery, Ward Bond.
103 min.
A typical Ford hymn to the pioneer spirit, his first film in colour and absolutely stunning to look at. Set on the eve of the Revolutionary War, it's a stirring account of the trials of a young couple setting up home in an isolated farming community, particularly memorable for the sequence in which Fonda outdoes Rod Steiger's 'run of the arrow', racing two Mohawks in a fantastic cross-country marathon to bring help to the beleaguered fort. Very funny too, on occasion, as witness the redoubtable Edna May Oliver's confrontation with a band of marauding Indians. TM

Dry Rot

(Maurice Elvey, 1956, GB) Ronald Shiner, Brian Rix, Peggy Mount, Lee Patterson, Sidney James, Joan Sims, Heather Sears, Miles Malleson.
87 min. b/w.
John Chapman's stage farce opened in London in the summer of 1954 and was still running to full houses when this film version came out. Here, however, it all begins to creak. Bent bookies Shiner, Rix and James plan a killing at the races by switching their decrepit nag for a so-called French wonder horse but, unsurprisingly, things don't exactly go to plan. TJ

Dry White Season, A

(Euzhan Palcy, 1989, US) Donald Sutherland, Janet Suzman, Zakes Mokae, Jürgen Prochnow, Susan Sarandon, Marlon Brando, Winston Ntshona, Thoko Ntshinga, Leonard Maguire.
107 min.
Behind the credits, two boys play happily together. Within minutes, the black boy is caught up in the Soweto uprising, the murderous violence of which is cross-cut with the white boy's family sitting on a manicured lawn to the strains of classical music. That, unfortunately, is the end of the film. Oh, there's business to clear up over the next 100 minutes, as Afrikaaner Ben du Toit (Sutherland) sees that Something Is Wrong in South Africa and that Something Should Be Done. There's Brando's star turn as a lawyer jaded by the realisation that justice cannot exist in matters of race, puffing, pausing, snorting, looking like he's wandered in from another movie. There's Prochnow's nicely understated Special Branch officer, and Suzman playing the bitch again; horrific tortures in police custody; and a sub-plot, not in André Brink's novel, designed to include a few black faces (South African exile Zakes Mokae is particularly good). But like Cry Freedom, it's still whites debating racial injustice: fine for a book published in Afrikaans a decade ago, but a poor premise for a message movie. DW

D2: The Mighty Ducks

(Sam Weisman, 1994, US) Emilio Estevez, Kathryn Erbe, Michael Tucker, Jan Rubes, Carsten Norgaard, Maria Ellingsen, Wayne Gretzky, Kareem Abdul Jabbar.
107 min.
Weisman's sequel to The Mighty Ducks is the formula again, and probably mandatory for fans of juvenile ice hockey. Gordon Bombay (Estevez) is grounded from the minor leagues and returns to coaching the Mighty Ducks. This time, however, they are entered in the Junior Goodwill Games as Team USA and sponsored to the hilt. Weakling

that he is, Bombay prefers a penthouse over-looking the sea to the team barracks, gets his hair swept back like the evil coach of the opposing Icelandic team, Wolf (Norgaard), and stops using the beloved duck whistle. Iceland wipes the ice with the tiny multi-ethnic Yanks until...but one's lips must remain sealed. There's a spark of interest when Estevez renders the Michael Moriarty speech from *The Deadliest Season*, invoking duckpond memories of the lost touchstone of integrity. Sports moralists will faint at the ease with which the introduction of a goon element into a children's team is accepted by all, not to mention the business with the lasso. Puck off. BC

DuBarry Was a Lady
(Roy Del Ruth, 1943, US) Red Skelton, Lucille Ball, Gene Kelly, Virginia O'Brien, Zero Mostel, Rags Ragland, Douglas Dumbrille, Donald Meek, Tommy Dorsey and his Orchestra.
101 min.
Produced by Arthur Freed, who should have known better, this adaptation of the Cole Porter musical ditches most of the songs – and the lusty bawdiness that went with them – to fashion a vehicle for Skelton and Ball, in the process interpolating more 'suitable' numbers (including a dismal girlie calendar item). It begins well with Ball (dubbed by Martha Mears) singing the title song with suitably costumed chorus, exquisitely shot by Karl Freund in delicate pastels. The colour then glossies up, and acres of unfunny comic business are expended on Skelton, a nightclub cloakroom attendant loved by the cigarette girl (O'Brien) but smitten by singer Ball. Ball loves an aspiring songwriter (Kelly), but has set her sights on a millionaire, and settles for Skelton when he wins a sweepstake. Hit with a Mickey Finn, Skelton imagines the situation transposed to 18th century France: 30 minutes of witless parody which supposedly sorts out the romantic tangle. Kelly has a good song-and-dance solo (staged by Charles Walters) to one of the surviving Porter songs, 'Do I Love You'; another, 'Friendship' is perfunctorily sung by the cast to bring the curtain down. TM

Duchess and the Dirtwater Fox, The
(Melvin Frank, 1976, US) George Segal, Goldie Hawn, Conrad Janis, Thayer David, Roy Jenson.
104 min.
Segal and Hawn, card sharp and happy hooker respectively, form an uneasy alliance for this amiable if calculated comedy Western. Some sharp Jewish humour displays an eye for the bawdy and profane, but finally the rest of the film falls behind the one-liner jokes as the comedy becomes increasingly contrived. CPe

Duck Soup
(Leo McCarey, 1933, US) The Marx Brothers, Margaret Dumont, Louis Calhern, Edgar Kennedy.
70 min. b/w.
The greatest of the surreally anarchic threesome's films (foursome here), this is a breathtakingly funny and imaginative spoof of war movie heroics, with a couple of Ruritanian states going to war because someone calls President Groucho an upstart (anyway, he's paid a month's advance rent on the battlefield). Totally irreverent towards patriotism, religion (a song proclaims 'We Got Guns, They Got Guns, All God's Chillun Got Guns'), diplomacy, courtroom justice, and anything even vaguely respectable, it also includes what is perhaps the Brothers' funniest scene ever: an immaculately timed and performed sequence with a broken mirror in which Groucho, Chico and Harpo look absolutely identical. A masterpiece. GA

Duck, You Sucker
see Giù la Testa

Dudes
(Penelope Spheeris, 1987, US) Jon Cryer, Catherine Mary Stewart, Daniel Roebuck, Lee Ving, Flea, Pete Willcox, Read Morgan.
97 min.
Continuing her preoccupation with terminal punks, Spheeris mines unexpected humour by relocating the sub-culture Way Out West, neatly combining random savagery and whimsy. 'Looking for exit signs', the despairing Grant

(Cryer) leads his spiky band out of New York, but doesn't discover a 'reason to live' until one of them is murdered in the desert by bad guy Missoula (Ving). Ghost riders in the sky in the shape of the Marlboro Cowboy and a tribe of Indians appear to the surviving punks during a night of bootleg whisky, but more practical help is offered by a gunslinging girl gas-station owner (Stewart) and an Elvis impersonator (Willcox). It's all pretty daft, but there are felicities – Elvis transfixing a bull at a rodeo with a golden oldie, 'punk Biscuit (Roebuck) requesting 'Holidays in Cambodia' by the Dead Kennedys from the drunk in the sheriff's lockup, and a genuine shoot-up in a cinema showing *Jesse James*. Visually it's a good deal more inventive and accomplished than the sketchy material. BC

Duel
(Steven Spielberg, 1972, US) Dennis Weaver, Jacqueline Scott, Eddie Firestone, Lou Frizzell.
90 min.
Spielberg's first film, superbly scripted by Richard Matheson, made for TV but booking its own place on the big screen: an absolute cracker about a salesman driving along the highway who gradually realises that the huge petrol tanker playfully snapping at his heels – apparently driverless – has more sinister designs. There are no explanations and no motivations, except perhaps for a hint of allegory in the script (the motorist's name is Mann) and an intriguing visual suggestion that this is the old, old battle between the shining, prancing, vulnerable knight and the impervious, lumbering dragon. Simply a rivetingly murderous game of cat and mouse that keeps you on the edge of your seat. TM

Duel at Diablo
(Ralph Nelson, 1965, US) James Garner, Sidney Poitier, Bibi Andersson, Bill Travers, Dennis Weaver, William Redfield, John Hoyt, John Crawford.
102 min.
Not as suggestive as Nelson's subsequent Vietnam Western, *Soldier Blue*, this is an action-packed oater with racial overtones. Garner hankers after revenge as his Indian wife has been murdered and scalped by Bibi Andersson's soldier boy husband (Weaver); for her part, Andersson has been kidnapped and held captive by Indians. Poitier is the only one without a racial hang-up. The story unravels itself with bouts of vicious bloodletting, Garner is his usual excellent self, and Neal Hefti contributes an especially good score. ATu

Duel at Silver Creek, The
(Don Siegel, 1952, US) Audie Murphy, Stephen McNally, Faith Domergue, Susan Cabot, Gerald Mohr, Lee Marvin.
77 min.
Siegel's first Western and his first film in colour (very nicely shot by Irving Glassberg). Statutory stuff about wicked claim-jumpers and the quick-draw artiste who sees justice done. But it's handled with great verve and more than a suspicion of tongue-in-cheek by Siegel, who rewrote as much as he could, giving the characters outrageous names (Silver Kid, Lightning Tyrone, Opal Lacy, Tinhorn Burgess), stretching the amorous complications and the villainies into near-absurdity, and building up a special explosive bit for Marvin in one of his earliest roles. TM

Duel in the Sun
(King Vidor, 1946, US) Jennifer Jones, Gregory Peck, Joseph Cotten, Lionel Barrymore, Lillian Gish, Walter Huston, Charles Bickford, Herbert Marshall, Harry Carey.
138 min.
If ever a Western deserved the title of horse opera, this is it: a soaring extravaganza variously described as 'Lust in the Dust' and 'Liebestod Among the Cactus' as two brothers play Cain and Abel in rivalry for a steamy halfbreed sexpot while their father broods over his crumbling empire. Luridly beautiful, with stunning passages jostling near-bathos in a patchiness not surprising since Selznick went through three cameramen and half-a-dozen directors in his vaulting ambition to outdo *Gone With the Wind*, it has rare power and a great supporting cast. The climax, which has Peck and Jones consummating their tempestuous passion by orgasmically shooting each other to bits has an absurdist magnificence that defies criticism. TM

Duellists, The
(Ridley Scott, 1977, GB) Keith Carradine, Harvey Keitel, Albert Finney, Edward Fox, Cristina Raines, Robert Stephens, Tom Conti, John McEnery, Diana Quick.
101 min.
A curious mixture. This British film, based on a Conrad story, received heavy US financial backing and stars two Americans conspicuously at odds with their British supporting cast. The filmmakers dubiously opt for a kind of Napoleonic Western: a tale of honour and obsession with one French officer pursued down the years by another. Keitel struggles gamely against a wooden Carradine, but the American influences further dislocate a script that delivers little observation, psychological or social, on their running feud. Instead, the film concentrates on the look of things, backed up by heavy research into contemporary French fashions. Scott, a name in TV commercials making his first feature, brings little overall thrust, working instead in short bursts. CPe

Duet for One
(Andrei Konchalovsky, 1986, US) Julie Andrews, Alan Bates, Max von Sydow, Rupert Everett, Margaret Courtenay, Cathryn Harrison.
107 min.
In this sensitive adaptation of Tom Kempinski's play, Andrews, as the internationally acclaimed concert violinist whose career, marriage and life are shattered by the onset of multiple sclerosis, is as professional as ever; the supporting cast – Bates as the surly, selfish composer husband, Everett as a rebellious protégé, von Sydow as the psychotherapist whose seemingly callous attitude conceals his own fear of dying – is equally solid. And, with the exception of a couple of scenes concerning sexual jealousy, Konchalovsky's direction is reliable and unsentimental. But the use of the sugary slow movement from Bruch's Violin Concerto – a real family favourite – to accompany the crucial moments of Andrews' dark night of the soul is symbolic of the film's limited achievement: to confront anxiety, illness and the realisation of life's meaninglessness without ever exuding a real sense of pain. GA

Due to an Act of God
(Im Zeichen des Kreuzes)
(Rainer Boldt, 1983, WGer) Renate Schroeter, Wigand Witting, Johanna Rudolph, Mathias Nitschke, Antje Hagen.
106 min.
Detailing the effects that a collision between juggernauts transporting liquid nitrogen and radioactive waste has on the area surrounding a quiet and tidy German village, Boldt paints a grim and unsentimental picture. The nightmare lies not merely in the atrocious physical aftermath (though there are no *Day After* Nosferatu lookalikes here), but in the way the faceless and culpable authorities deal with the situation: to prevent panic, a massive cover-up is implemented, contagious victims are incarcerated like criminals, martial law is imposed, and the most seriously contaminated are left to die without any real aid. Tense without being melodramatic, tough but fuelled by a passionate concern for human life, it's a fine, intelligent film that offers little hope and plenty of cause for worry. And as a thriller, it takes an honourable place in the tradition best represented by Romero's *The Crazies*. GA

Duffer
(Joseph Despins/William Dumaresq, 1971, GB) Kit Gleave, Erna May, James Roberts (ie.William Dumaresq), Lisa Doran, Marcelle McHardy.
75 min. b/w.
A first feature by two expatriate Canadians, this tells the mock-ingenuous tale of a passably attractive lad who spends most of his life submitting to a homosexual sadist but occasionally scurries to a golden-hearted whore for relief. Duffer's account of himself in a voice-over narration starts out ultra-subversive ('I didn't much enjoy the things that Louis-Jack did to me, but they seemed to give him pleasure, and there really isn't much of that around') and gets more and more Joycean. The plot gets rather lost in musings on fantasy versus reality, but the imagery

remains funny and, when needed, tough; the mood is predominantly wistful, well caught by Galt MacDermot's simple piano score. TR

Duffy
(Robert Parrish, 1968, GB) James Coburn, James Mason, James Fox, Susannah York, John Alderton, Guy Deghy.
101 min.
Parrish, it has been observed, was a director happiest when dealing with outsider figures, but above all in need of a good scriptwriter. Donald Cammell, who co-directed *Performance*, looked to be just the person to provide him with his best opportunity since *Wonderful Country*, made ten years earlier. The script promisingly featured a dropout ex-criminal, enlisted to aid two English boys in robbing their own millionaire father; and an excellent cast was assembled. The results were woeful: the last word in modishness, and the final nail in the coffin of '60s pop. CPe

Dulces Horas
see Tender Hours

Dulcima
(Frank Nesbitt, 1971, GB) Carol White, John Mills, Stuart Wilson, Bernard Lee, Sheila Raynor, Dudley Foster.
98 min.
Product of Bryan Forbes' uneasy reign at EMI Film Productions. An adaptation of an HE Bates story about a randy, miserly old farmer and the golddigging girl who comes to work for him. Nothing more than a *Woman's Own* story, with one point of interest: it deals with a sort of society rarely thought interesting enough for movies, and therefore the Gloucestershire locations and bits of 'country lore' are refreshing. It's neat, but nothing.

Dulcimer Street
see London Belongs to Me

Dumb & Dumber
(Peter Farrelly, 1994, US) Jim Carrey, Jeff Daniels, Lauren Holly, Teri Garr, Karen Duffy, Charles Rocket.
107 min.
Notes on a motion picture recollected in tranquillity. Story: the two dumbest guys in the world drive across America to return a lady's briefcase. Inside the case is a $1m ransom. Complications ensue. Character: Carrey and Daniels. The lady is blonde (Holly). Un film de: Farrelly, who previously worked on rewrites for *Wagons East!* Both *Wagons East!* and *Dumb & Dumber* feature sequences where a minor character unwittingly drinks piss. Carrey: he's trying too hard to please (no one has mugged this much since Steve Martin's *The Jerk*), but the force is with him. He's like Jerry Lewis, but less recherché. Less sentimental, too. Context: given American cinema's current obsession with innocence and ignorance (*Forrest Gump, Nell, I.Q.*), at least this never romanticises its protagonists. They are genuinely, irredeemably, 100 per cent no-hopers. They are not kind to strangers (except wealthy blondes), they are lousy conversationalists, they have no social graces – no grace at all in fact – and terrible haircuts. Economics: they paid Carrey $7 million. The entire budget totalled $15m. In the US to date [1995], the film has grossed $117m. TCh

Dumbo
(Ben Sharpsteen, 1941, US) voices: Edward Brophy, Herman Bing, Sterling Holloway, Cliff Edwards, Verna Felton.
64 min.
One of the best of Disney's animated features. An ugly duckling variation, lifted by those unforgettable characters: the ancient, haywire stork who delivers Dumbo late, the circus train reminiscent of the Tin Man, the irrepressible mouse who befriends the rejected hero, the bitchy old elephant troupe ('Hey girls, have I got a trunkful of dirt..!'), and the beautifully characterised crows – stolen by Bakshi for *Fritz the Cat* – who sing the classic 'When I See A' Elephant Fly'. The artwork, of course, is magisterial: aerial views of the States, the erecting of the big top in a storm, and the brilliant drunken vision of pink elephants. Magic. SG

Dumb Die Fast, the Smart Die Slow, The (Galok Bang Tai Cha, Galok Na Tai Gon)
(Manop Udomdej, 1991, Thai) Sorasak Wongthai, Khachonsak Ratana-nidsai, Aungkana Timdee, Manop Aswathep.
123 min.
The hard-boiled thriller, Thai-style – obviously indebted to *The Postman Always Rings Twice* and other models, but irreducibly Thai in its plotting and characterisations. The kindly owner of a gas station with a no-good wife takes on a hitch-hiker as a handyman, unaware that he's on the run. The wife learns the newcomer's secret, and tries to blackmail him into robbing her husband. Manop started out as an 'underground' political film-maker, which doubtless explains the hints of social comment here. Mostly, though, he has fun in the plot's moral quicksand. Very entertaining, and very novel to see these conventions through Thai eyes. TR

Dune
(David Lynch, 1984, US) Kyle MacLachlan, Francesca Annis, Sting, Jürgen Prochnow, Brad Dourif, José Ferrer, Kenneth McMillan, Linda Hunt, Max von Sydow, Silvana Mangano, Freddie Jones, Dean Stockwell.
140 min.
Trying desperately to stay faithful to Frank Herbert's fat novel, this opens with a lengthy voice-over concerning the cosmos circa 10,991 and the tactical importance of the planet Dune, where a life-enhancing spice is mined. A first half of bewildering exposition follows: a mish-mash of characters and feudal, feuding empires, which is only ironed out for a second half of Flash Gordon-type action. Buried deep in the welter of not-so-special effects are globs of pure Lynch, notably some of the most impressive sci-fi set design since *Blade Runner* (all Victorian Gothic pipes, hissing steam and heavy-duty brass). The star-studded cast does its best with dialogue dripping in silly names, and Kenneth McMillan is enjoyably outrageous as a bloated, floating boil-covered baddy. The anticlimactic ending leaves so many loose ends that *Dune II* was no doubt in the offing. AB

Dunkirk
(Leslie Norman, 1958, GB) John Mills, Richard Attenborough, Bernard Lee, Robert Urquhart, Patricia Plunkett, Maxine Audley.
134 min. b/w.
Overlong, stolid account of the famous World War II rescue operation from the Normandy beaches in 1940, reconstructed by Ealing with exactly the sort of cast you would expect, doing their plucky Brit acts as they portray a small group separated from the main force. The usual quiet heroics, dressed up with a semi-documentary atmosphere. GA

Dunston Checks In
(Ken Kwapis, 1995, Can) Jason Alexander, Faye Dunaway, Eric Lloyd, Rupert Everett, Graham Sack, Glenn Shadix, Nathan Davis.
88 min.
An unruly orang-utan plus an opulent hotel setting equals a natural disaster, or in this case a kids' movie. Robert (Alexander) manages the Majestic Hotel, New York, owned by avaricious Mrs Dubrow (Dunaway). She's convinced that the so-called Lord Rutledge (Everett) is really a hotel critic, and insists that everything runs extra smoothly. But Robert's sons discover that the lord's a jewel thief with an anthropoid accomplice. When the gangly one, Dunston, finally escapes Rutledge's clutches, the kids spend the rest of the film trying to conceal him. The children we took adored the cheerful scenario and sad-cum-happy signposted climax. Adults, on the other hand, will probably be stupefied by Everett's unrecognisable twit, complete with lip-distorting gum guard, and Dunaway's raging Ivana Trump turn. Alexander, though, is a likeable comic player in the Charles Grodin manner, and younger sibling Lloyd makes for a more loveable character than Macaulay Culkin. The film's admirably bereft of realistic violence, but then the makers blow it by slipping in a scene featuring Dunston innocently puffing on a cigarette. DA

Durante l'Estate
see During the Summer

Du Rififi à Paname (Rififi in Paris/The Upper Hand)
(Denys de la Patellière, 1965, Fr/It/WGer) Jean Gabin, Claudio Brook, Gert Fröbe, Nadja Tiller, George Raft, Claude Brasseur, Mireille Darc, Daniel Ceccaldi.
98 min.
One of those latter-day vehicles in which, portly and white-haired, Gabin brushes importunate girls aside to lavish attentions on his pet Boxer, meanwhile masterminding a series of unenterprising crimes which win him the usual admiring accolade: 'He's a real man!' Thoroughly routine stuff, it mixes some passable action sequences with statutory travelogue footage (London, Munich, Tokyo), allows Gabin to coast through without exerting himself, and finds time for George Raft to do his coin-flipping act. But Claudio Brook, taking time off from Buñuel (he was the major-domo in *The Exterminating Angel* and the nutty saint in *Simon of the Desert*) makes a refreshingly unstereotyped hero, and Gert Fröbe steals his scenes as a crook with leftist leanings. TM

Du Rififi chez les Hommes (Rififi)
(Jules Dassin, 1955, Fr) Jean Servais, Carl Möhner, Robert Manuel, Perlo Vita(i.e.Jules Dassin), Magali Noël, Pierre Grasset, Robert Hossein.
117 min. b/w.
Archetypal heist thriller, with a group of thieves banding together for a daring jewel robbery and falling out afterwards. Highly acclaimed for the 35-minute robbery sequence, conducted without a word being spoken, and for the generally downbeat atmosphere, it's actually rather overrated, lacking the tension, profundity, and vivid characterisation of similar films by, say, Becker and Melville. Like even the best of Dassin's work, in fact, it never penetrates beneath its fashionable, self-conscious surface. GA

During the Summer (Durante l'Estate)
(Ermanno Olmi, 1971, It) Renato Parracchi, Rosanna Callegari.
105 min.
The marvellously quaint and funny tale of a timid, unprepossessing little man – self-styled as The Professor – who busies himself with designing coats-of-arms, and presenting them to anyone who matches up to his private assessment of nobility. Recipients include an old man patiently waiting on a railway station for the son who doesn't turn up, a hall porter who brings a cup of coffee when he hurts his leg, a girl with whom he embarks on a sidelong little romance, and who proves that she deserves his accolade of 'Princess' when the law finally catches up and he is jailed for his 'malpractices'. Stunningly shot in colour, with a non-professional cast and very much the same wryly observant sense of humour as *Il Posto*, it has a touch of real Olmi magic to it. TM

Dust
(Marion Hänsel, 1985, Bel/Fr) Jane Birkin, Trevor Howard, John Matshikiza, Nadine Uwampa.
88 min.
Cape Province, South Africa. In a remote farmhouse, spinsterly Magda tends to her stern, imperious father. Life might continue this way forever, were it not for an intrusion into the household by a new maid that arouses a maelstrom (or Magda's dreams) of seduction, jealousy, murder and rape. Hänsel's stark adaptation (shot in English) of JM Coetzee's *In the Heart of the Country* is a strangely interior film, viewed through the lonely eyes of the repressed Magda (Birkin). As the film somewhat uneasily blends reality and fantasy, family bonds are twisted, master-servant roles are reversed, and 'the work of generations falls to ruins'. But for all its admirable evocation of Magda's mounting hatred and hysteria, Hänsel's approach is finally flawed by its careful adherence to introspective, literary qualities. GA

Dust Devil
(Richard Stanley, 1993, GB) Robert Burke, Chelsea Field, Zakes Mokae, Marianne Sägebrecht.
105 min.
More personal and ambitious than Stanley's killer-android debut *Hardware*, this boldly juxtaposes

murder, magic and South African politics. A near-wordless opening reel leads us into a nightmarish world of mysticism and ritual slaughter. Drawn to the drought-ridden town of Bethany by the smell of death, shape-shifting 'Hitcher with No Name' (Burke) kills and dismembers a lonely young woman who picks him up. While the hitcher feeds off the despair of others, including fugitive wife Field, local policeman Mokae enlists the help of a half-mad, half-blind cinema projectionist in his search for a suspected serial killer. The non-linear storyline relies more on atmosphere than forward momentum, and the tone veers wildly between dream-like mysteriousness and indulgent incomprehensibility. A sidewinder snaking across a dune, hazy desertscapes, and an extraordinary scene in a sand-filled cinema are evidence of a visionary talent. But Field's vacant performance, some poorly realised dream sequences, the leaden dialogue, and a mortuary scene with Sägebrecht are grim. NF

Dust in the Wind
(Lian Lian Feng Chen)
(Hou Xiaoxien, 1987, Tai) Wang Ching-wen, Hsing Shu-fen, Ch'en Shu-fang, Li Tien-lu.
100 min.
Faintly disappointing by Hou's own very high standards, this story of teenage love and betrayal (framed by a move from village to city) is notable for its sociological precision and its oblique criticism of Taiwanese militarism. As often in Hou's movies, mainland China is a huge off-screen presence, here briefly stumbling on-screen in the person of a terrified fisherman whose boat has sailed off-course. Performances and technical standards are both superb, but there's a nagging sense that the director is marking time rather than moving forward. TR

Dutch (aka Driving Me Crazy)
(Peter Faiman, 1991, US) Ed O'Neill, Ethan Randall, JoBeth Williams, Christopher McDonald, Ari Meyers, EG Daily, L Scott Caldwell, Kathleen Freeman.
107 min.
Little positive to report on this John Hughes production (he also scripted, and must therefore carry the can for the below-par dialogue). The rite-of-passage here is a car ride, from school in Atlanta to Thanksgiving dinner in Chicago, undertaken under protest by adolescent rich kid Doyle (Randall) in the company of Dutch (O'Neill), his separated mother's working-class boyfriend. Doyle is superior sonofabitch personified, his only rival in loathsomeness Doyle's absentee father (McDonald). O'Neill displays lazy charm, a Matthau-like rambling bear of a man-child with a grin set somewhere between gormless and amiable. The set pieces, involving fireworks, a walk in the cold, a car crash and a pair of prostitutes who turn Doyle's cheeks cherry red, are the milestones on the path to friendship and respect. It's all assembly-line stuff. WH

Dutchman
(Anthony Harvey, 1966, GB) Shirley Knight, Al Freeman Jr.
56 min. b/w.
Harvey's transition from editor to director is a brilliantly spare, edgy adaptation of LeRoi Jones' play, basically a two-hander set on a New York subway train: a grim duel between cat and mouse as a rangily sexy white woman circles a young black sitting alone, deliberately teasing, taunting, flaunting herself in a perverse attempt to break his control. Resentment and attraction crackle through the dialogue (and the superb performances) in an almost orgiastic expression of provocation and desire, until she wins and the black is goaded into retaliation. It ends, of course, in violence: a devastating acknowledgment that this is just about the only ground on which black and white can meet. The film's one minor flaw is when the camera eventually pulls back from the duo to reveal that the carriage has filled with commuters studiously minding their own business; true to life, perhaps, but it comes over as a facile trick. TM

Dybbuk, The
(Michael Waszynski, 1938, Pol) Abram Morewski, Lilli Liliana, Dina Halpern, Leon Liebgold.
125 min. b/w.
In this Yiddish language version of Ansky's play, the immersion in the traditional culture of the Eastern European 'shtetl' (Jewish village) is complete, and even heightened by the expressionistic style of acting and filming amid fairly realistic sets and costuming. From the initial shots in the synagogue to the marvellous singing and dancing at peak moments of the plot, this supernatural tale of the tragic possession of a bride by the soul of her true loved one is as weird and wonderful as an Isaac Bashevis Singer story. The Jewish absorption in the inexplicable suffering of humanity is made almost unbearably poignant by the knowledge that not only the traditional culture of the Polish Jews, but even the lives of the makers and actors of this film, were to be utterly destroyed over the next few years by an evil beyond even the imagination of a society that could produce irrational, tragic tales as remorseless as The Dybbuk. MH

Dying Swan, The
(Umirajuseij lebed)
(Evgenij Bauer, 1917, Rus) Vera Karalli, V Polanskij, A Gromov, I Perestiani.
1,078 metres. b/w.
Bauer was one of the two leading figures in pre-Soviet Russian cinema; he trained in fine arts and made films prolifically for only five years before dying in an accident. This lugubrious melodrama, evidently quite representative of his output, suggests that he was a big fan of Dorian Gray, Salome and other Wilde perversities. The mute Gizella Raccio, raised in the countryside, longs to dance in Moscow. Her father (a dead ringer for Boris Yeltsin) persuades an impresario to give her a break, and she becomes a star as the Dying Swan. This attracts the attention of painter Valerian Gliiniski, a talentless psychotic who believes that perfect beauty is found only in death. Gizella innocently poses for him. She later has recurrent nightmares, but a reunion with her first love Viktor helps her to shake them. Valerian, however, is enraged by the new light in her eyes. He lures her back to his studio. Within the limiting conventions of the period, Bauer's staging and the performances remain valid and in some ways surprisingly fresh. Vera Karalli, an Imperial Theatre ballerina, is even quite touching as Gizella. But it's the necrophilia motif – developed in the skull-strewn design of Valerian's studio and the starkly Freudian dream scene, not to mention the no-concessions ending – which gives the film its lasting interest. TR

Dying Young
(Joel Schumacher, 1991, US) Julia Roberts, Campbell Scott, Vincent D'Onofrio, Colleen Dewhurst, David Selby, Ellen Burstyn, Dion Anderson, George Martin.
111 min.
Shamateurishly directed, this Roberts vehicle traversing the clichéd class-clash/love story territory of Pretty Woman is a dog. Working-class, Catholic, unemployed and single, Hilary (Roberts) applies for a job as live-in carer for Victor Geddes (Scott), a millionaire's son suffering from leukemia, but is given the thumbs-down by Geddes père. Soon, however, she is summoned to the basement flat where Victor lives in splendid social isolation, surrounded by the morbid works of Klimt and Rossetti. Sadly, down at the disco where Hilary gets her kicks, nobody told her about art history... The surprising thing is the film's coyness. As their relationship grows and we finally get to sex – after all the business of her helping him through frightening post-chemotherapy attacks – the camera pulls away ashamedly to view their contact through mirrors. Judy Holliday and Jean Hagen would have sent the script back. WH

Dynamite Chicken
(Ernest Pintoff, 1971, US) Richard Pryor, Paul Krassner.
76 min. b/w & col.
Pryor's gags and monologues, mostly delivered while toying with a basketball on the site of a derelict building, link a series of archive clips of marginal hippies being really free, man, and politically didactic. 'Stars' such as Warhol and Lennon and Yoko appear fleetingly and to no great effect. Sketches by the Ace Trucking Co are mildly amusing. Are there better ways to spend 76 minutes? Only about 26,958. Yep, Dynamite Chicken lays egg. GB

Dynamite Women
see Great Texas Dynamite Chase, The

Dyn Amo
(Stephen Dwoskin, 1972, GB) Jenny Runacre, Pat Ford, Catherine Kessler, Linda Marlowe, John Grillo.
120 min.
From (a long way apparently) Chris Wilkinson's play of the same name. The film is set in a strip club. The girls go through their routines to shreds of Zippety-doo-dah and Sweet Dream Baby on the pocket-sized stage amid the usual cheap tinsel and glitter tat, acting out sour fantasies that point to a painful divorce from self – woman as servant, as little girl, as programmed seductress – each more grotesque than the last. It's typical Dwoskin, examining faces, gestures, half-movements. Rewarding unless you're after a good story.

Dynasty
(Qian Dao Wan Li Zhui)
(Zhang Meijun, 1977, Tai/HK) Bobby Ming, Pai Ying, Tang Wei, Jin Gang.
95 min.
A very average swordplay/martial arts movie, enlivened by proficient 3-D photography in the Polaroid process. The plot (vengeful young monk has seven days to kill wicked Imperial Court eunuch) is rehashed from a 1966 King Hu film called Dragon Gate Inn, and Pai Ying – one of the heroes in A Touch of Zen – reprises his role as the eunuch from that film. The rest is typical '70s kung-fu stunts. Reasonably engaging exposition, very flat climax, feeble gestures towards the Ming Dynasty historiography. Best 3-D effect: arrows fired directly into the audience. TR

e

Easy Rider

Each Dawn I Die

(William Keighley, 1939, US) James Cagney, George Raft, George Bancroft, Jane Bryan, Stanley Ridges, Maxie Rosenbloom, Alan Baxter.
92 min. b/w.
Somewhat routine Warner Brothers social-conscience movie, with Cagney as the crusading reporter fighting political corruption and getting framed for murder; in prison he meets up with gangster Raft, becomes a hardened victim of the tough system, and eventually becomes involved in a riot. Theoretically interestingly bleak, in that Cagney, already disillusioned about justice, also loses his faith in friendship (thinking himself betrayed by Raft) and goes round the bend in solitary. But the muddled script ties itself up in knots, and the broody direction is unremarkable. Cagney's fiery presence gives the whole thing a much-needed lift. GA

Eadweard Muybridge, Zoopraxographer

(Thom Andersen, 1974, US) narrator: Dean Stockwell.
59 min. b/w & col.
There are many pleasures in this film about the 19th century photographic pioneer, not least that of seeing a complicated subject laid out with crystal clarity. With the aid of multiple cameras, Muybridge made tiny strips of film containing consecutive shots of humans and animals in motion – embryonic moving pictures, in fact. Andersen dwells on all angles of interest, from the technical through to the philosophical and the sociological. Muybridge himself had many personal quirks, too: he shot his wife's lover (but was acquitted of murder), and he documents his animal models with more care than the humans (excepting some of the women). Andersen, previously a sly parodist of underground styles, brings to the material the ironist's penchant for brevity and suggestive implication; his film is a delight. GB

Eagle, The

(Clarence Brown, 1925, US) Rudolph Valentino, Vilma Banky, Louise Dresser, Albert Conti, James Marcus.
7 reels. b/w.
Clarence Brown was better than most of his contemporaries at handling the kernel of human interest at the heart of large-scale action dramas; his direction here serves Valentino unusually well, bringing equal intensity to the romantic intrigue and the set-piece thrills. This was Valentino's penultimate film (made a year before his death), and is probably the best surviving key to an understanding of the death-cult that swept the world in 1926. Bonus: William Cameron Menzies' sets are astounding. TR

Eagle Has Landed, The

(John Sturges, 1976, GB) Michael Caine, Donald Sutherland, Robert Duvall, Jenny Agutter, Donald Pleasence, Anthony Quayle, Jean Marsh, Judy Geeson, Treat Williams.
135 min.
Plodding time-passer about a Nazi plot to kidnap Churchill from his Norfolk retreat in 1943. Tom Mankiewicz, adapting Jack Higgins' bet-hedging bestseller ('at least half documented historical fact'), goes for an examination of good/bad German motivations that cuts across the sub-*Jackal* suspense; Sturges turns in a tired study of Cherman and Oirish accents, and little else. There's not one iota of the two-way menace of a partly similar Germans-in-Britain picture like *Went the Day Well?* PT

Eagle Has Two Heads, The

see Aigle à Deux Têtes, L'

Eagle With Two Heads

see Aigle à Deux Têtes, L'

Eagle's Wing

(Anthony Harvey, 1978, GB) Martin Sheen, Sam Waterston, Harvey Keitel, Stéphane Audran, Caroline Langrishe, John Castle, Jorge Luke.
111 min.
Set in the as yet untamed American wilderness 'long before the myths', this is unusual not only as a first-class Western made by a British director, but in being virtually a silent movie as an Indian and a white man (Waterston and Sheen), each a failure in his own world and determined to prove otherwise, pursue a strange, obsessive duel for possession of the glorious white stallion that gives the film its title. Quirkishly funny as the duel evolves into a sort of medieval quest attended by its own rituals and chivalries, the film gradually weaves its concentric subplots (various other parties tag along behind, driven by their own passions) into a plaintively spiralling lament for lost illusions. Marvellously shot by Billy Williams, it's weird, hypnotic and magical. TM

Ear, The (Ucho)

(Karel Kachyna, 1969, Czech) Jirina Bohdalová, Radoslav Brzobohaty, Gustav Opocensky, Miloslav Holub.
93 min. b/w.
By far the best of the Czech movies banned when Dubcek was toppled in 1969, this uses a flashback structure to explore a crucial night in the lives of Ludvik, a high-ranking bureaucrat, and his semi-estranged wife Anna. They come home from a reception (at which Ludvik learns that his boss and other government officials have just been arrested in a political purge) to find that their home has been comprehensively bugged. During the long and sleepless night, they tear each other apart with Albee-like ferocity while imagining the worst that the future may hold for them. The dawn brings a twist ending that makes Kachyna's film the bitterest and most scathing account of what it takes to get ahead in a Communist bureaucracy. TR

Early Bird, The

(Robert Asher, 1965, GB) Norman Wisdom, Edward Chapman, Jerry Desmonde, Paddie O'Neil, Bryan Pringle, Richard Vernon.
98 min.
Norman Wisdom, like much of Jerry Lewis, should perhaps be reserved exclusively for kids. The continual emphasis on slapstick, the sentimental celebration of the downtrodden but happy moron, and the total inability to rise above the invariably banal plots, tend to induce teeth-gritting agony for the adult viewer. This 'comedy' sees the staggering cretin as a milkman for a small firm whose inept antics save his unappreciative employers from a takeover. GA

Early Spring (Soshun)

(Yasujiro Ozu, 1956, Jap) Ryo Ikebe, Chikage Awashima, Keiko Kishi, Chishu Ryu, Daisuke Kato.
149 min. b/w.
A typically low-key domestic drama in Ozu's mournful, defeatist vein: it deals with the breakup between an office-worker and his wife when the husband embarks on a tentative affair, and surrounds both partners with extensive webs of friends, relatives, acquaintances and colleagues. It's shot and edited in Ozu's characteristic 'minimalist' style, with hardly any camera movement, a carefully circumscribed syntax, and an editing method that's as unconventional by Japanese standards as it is remote from the Western norm. Ozu's pessimism is deeply reactionary, and the idiosyncrasy of his methods is more interesting for its exoticism than anything else; but anyone who finds the socio-psychological problems of post-war Japan engaging will find the movie both fascinating and rather moving, simply as evidence. TR

Earrings of Madame de..., The

see Madame de...

Earth

see Tierra

Earth (Zemlya)

(Alexander Dovzhenko, 1930, USSR) Semyon Svashenko, Stepan Shkurat, Mikola Nademsky, Yelena Maximova.
5,591 ft. b/w.
One of the last of the silents, and though increasingly an absentee from Ten Best lists, a very great film indeed. The director's trademarks – a field of sunflowers all waving goodbye, a lowering sky filling three-quarters of the frame – remained well nigh constant throughout his career, but he seldom recaptured the pantheistic phosphorescence of this hymn both to nature and to the gleaming new tractors and ploughs which aimed to transform it. Such is the authenticity of its pictorialism, in fact, that one has to remind oneself that it was actually shot like other films. GAd

Earth Girls Are Easy

(Julien Temple, 1988, US) Geena Davis, Jeff Goldblum, Jim Carrey, Damon Wayans, Julie Brown, Michael McKean, Charles Rocket, Larry Linville, Rick Overton, Diane Stillwell.
100 min.
Crass, silly, tacky: it's not easy to depict the complexities of being a Valley Girl, but in this zany musical, Temple and co-writer/star Julie Brown have a go. The plot is about a day in the lives of three aliens (led by Goldblum) who, after crash-landing in LA, set off to explore the hot-spots in the company of a lovelorn manicurist (Davis). But first they're introduced to beauty-salon owner Candy (Brown), who transforms the furry freaks into human-looking specimens capable of partying and falling in love. The plot ain't much, nor is it supposed to be. This is deliberately, gleefully vacuous entertainment, and any satirical edge is blunted by the film's obvious affection for its subject. But there are excesses, as when Brown, in a beach-movie parody, kicks up sand and warbles about the virtues of being blonde. It's one of several redundant moments, aimed at patently dated, soft targets. But by the time the aliens are shaved and shimmying in the beauty parlour, you'll either be shamelessly hooked or hopelessly bored. CM

Earth Is a Sinful Song (Maa on Syntinen Laulau)

(Rauni Mollberg, 1973, Fin) Maritta Viitamäki, Pauli Jauhojärvi, Aimo Säukko, Milja Hiltunen.
102 min.
Set in a remote rural Lapp community, economically deprived, culturally backward and repressed. A spirited young girl is broken by her family and friends as they discourage her relationship with a nomadic herdsman whose loose reputation they despise and envy. For the villagers, escape comes from drink, bouts of joyless sex, or through the hysteria of the occasional church meeting. Mollberg infuses his film with a gloomy sensuality, sodden colours, virtually no music and little relief. In between the feverish action, he groups his characters in painterly tableaux in which they look more than usually stunned. The film works best at placing its figures in landscapes, less so with characterisation and momentum. The melodramatic ending lacks impact for all its cyclical neatness. CPe

Earthquake

(Mark Robson, 1974, US) Charlton Heston, Ava Gardner, George Kennedy, Lorne Greene, Genevieve Bujold, Richard Roundtree, Marjoe Gortner, Barry Sullivan, Lloyd Nolan, Walter Matthau.
123 min.
Lovers of bizarre cinematic gimmickry will find much to enjoy thanks to an ingenious aural device known as Sensurround which induces a minor tremor in the cinema during climactic sequences. The special effects are of a high order as Los Angeles is razed, so it is unfortunate that the same intelligent attention is not extended to either script or direction. Both settle for flat, generally laughable hokum, and the film ends up nowhere near as interesting a comment on the psychological aspects of disaster as *Juggernaut*. DP

Earth vs the Flying Saucers (aka Invasion of the Flying Saucers)

(Fred F Sears, 1956, US) Joan Taylor, Hugh Marlowe, Harry Lauter, Morris Ankrum, Donald Curtis.
81 min. b/w.
Androids in flying saucers give the Earth sixty days in which to surrender. Scientist Hugh Marlowe sets about devising a sonic gun which will show 'em who's boss. Despite a mundane script, this works quite effectively by adopting a dry, documentary tone and splurging the budget on Ray Harryhausen's spectacular special effects. Check out the wholesale destruction of Washington DC's most famous landmarks. TCh

Earth vs the Spider (aka The Spider)

(Bert I Gordon, 1958, US) Ed Kemmer, June Kenney, Gene Persson, Gene Roth, Hal Torey, June Jocelyn, Mickey Finn.
73 min. b/w.
Routine creature feature in which a small town teenage couple, looking for the girl's missing father, stumble on a giant spider lurking in a network of caves and narrowly escape its trampoline-style web (dad, of course, is already a victim). A sheriff's posse manages to knock the creature out with DDT; and supposedly dead, it is parked in the school gym to await shipment for scientific study. Cue for teenagers to break in for some rock'n'roll larks, while the monster revives and goes on the rampage before being finally electrocuted. The special effects are nothing to write home about, with the spider fitting comfortably into the gym, but once outside, towering over two- and three-storey buildings. The Carlsbad Caverns in New Mexico provide a spectacular setting, used to remarkably little effect. Altogether inferior to its obvious model, Jack Arnold's *Tarantula*. TM

Easter Parade

(Charles Walters, 1948, US) Fred Astaire, Judy Garland, Peter Lawford, Ann Miller, Jules Munshin.
103 min.
The only time the two greatest Hollywood musical stars teamed up was an accident – Gene Kelly had broken his ankle and suggested the initially reluctant Fred as his replacement. In the event, it's not an ideal coupling, a stylistic unease between them – save in the legendary novelty song 'A Couple of Swells' – being often apparent. Nevertheless, *Easter Parade* is the sort of musical to put your feet up for, lifted by three bursts of dynamism: Fred's show number 'Steppin' Out with My Baby', his brilliantly inventive 'Drum Crazy', and Ann Miller's knock-down broadside 'Shakin' the Blues Away'. The story is Pygmalionesque, the songs vintage Irving Berlin. And if you think they can't sing in 'At Long Last Love', bend an ear to Peter Lawford wrestling with 'A Fella with an Umbrella'. SG

East LA

see My Family

East of Eden

(Elia Kazan, 1955, US) James Dean, Raymond Massey, Julie Harris, Richard Davalos, Jo Van Fleet, Burl Ives, Albert Dekker.
115 min.
Notable mainly for the electrically emotional scenes between Massey as the stiff, stern patriarch, and Dean as the rejected 'bad' son, Kazan's adaptation of Steinbeck's novel, about the rivalry between two teenage boys for the love of their father, is as long-winded and bloated with biblical allegory as the original. That said, it's a film of great performances, atmospheric photography, and a sure sense of period and place (the California farmlands at the time of World War I). A pity, however, about Leonard Rosenman's dreary score, which goes way over the top in attempting to underline the intensity of the various familial conflicts. GA

East of Elephant Rock

(Don Boyd, 1976, GB) John Hurt, Jeremy Kemp, Judi Bowker, Christopher Cazenove, Anton Rodgers, Tariq Yunus, Vajira.
92 min.
Old Hollywood traditions hang heavy and ridiculous over this depressingly redundant sample of British independent cinema. It's a colonial romantic tragedy, set somewhere in South East Asia during 1948. In place of people like Gable, Harlow or Bette Davis, a cast of British stalwarts gamely beat their breasts over sexual and racial problems brought to the boil by the philandering of Embassy secretary Hurt, whose mistresses include a native girl and the far from native wife of a plantation owner. Boyd's direction revives antique clichés like newspaper headlines spinning into close-up to pull the plot forward, but nothing seems likely to pull the audience out of its slumbers. Peter Skellern's score provides a parallel musical pastiche, and the photography recalls ads for Bacardi and Coke. GB

East of Sumatra

(Budd Boetticher, 1953, US) Jeff Chandler, Marilyn Maxwell, Anthony Quinn, Suzan Ball, Peter Graves, John Sutton.
82 min.
A striking opening sequence has Chandler, a ruthlessly efficient mining engineer, summarily shoot a member of his crew for turning up drunk and endangering lives on the site by playing silly games with dynamite. When the crew is packed off to prospect on a remote Pacific island, budget limitations begin to show in the terrible backdrop of rocks and jungle as their plane lands; and before too long, box-office considerations loom large in the curvaceous shape of a jungle princess disporting herself in a rock pool. The Hawksian theme nevertheless survives, sporadically taking fire in the mutually respectful relationship between Chandler and the island's king (Quinn), a man of honour and some civilisation, who has ceded the mineral rights against a promise of medical supplies for his people. When the penny-pinching head office decides to palm off some tacky trade goods instead, the jungle drums naturally begin to throb and poisoned darts to fly. It's a typical concoction, in other words, not without its moments thanks to Boetticher, with excellent performances from Chandler and Quinn. TM

East of the Rising Sun

see Malaya

East Palace, West Palace (Dong Gong Xi Gong)

(Zhang Yuan, 1996, China) Hu Jun, Si Han, Liu Yuxiao, Lu Rong, Ma Wen.
94 min.
The most daring and achieved of all the 'illegal' independent films made in China in the '90s – and quite probably the last, since it prompted the Film Bureau to formally outlaw unauthorised production and confiscate Zhang Yuan's passport. A-Lan, a young gay man, is arrested in a Beijing cruising park and held for overnight interrogation by Shi, a macho but latently ambivalent cop. As he describes his life since childhood and his sexual history, it becomes clear that his stories are actually expressions of his desire for the cop. This realisation makes Shi more aggressive. The film is an intense chamber drama with large resonances: its ultimate implication is that the bond between the people and the authorities in China is essentially a sado-masochist one. This is the closest cinema has ever come to the spirit of Jean Genet, closer even than Genet's own *Chant d'amour*. TR

Easy Living

(Mitchell Leisen, 1937, US) Jean Arthur, Edward Arnold, Ray Milland, Franklin Pangborn, William Demarest, Luis Alberni.
91 min. b/w.
Unmistakably scripted by Preston Sturges (stout tycoon falls down stairs; 'I see you're down early today, sir' remarks the imperturbable butler), this irresistible screwball comedy with a dash of Wall Street satire has the penniless Arthur and pompous Arnold meet cute when his wife's fur coat (thrown out of the window in a marital spat) falls on her head. Subsequently assumed to be the tycoon's mistress and encouraged to live on credit in an extravagance beyond anyone's wildest dreams, she is brought down from her cloud by falling for the poor boy met in an automat diner (Milland), who ironically turns out in best fairytale tradition to be the tycoon's son. Directed by Leisen with his airy elegance, his infallible eye for decor (the outrageous splendours of the hotel suite in which Arthur is installed have to be seen to be believed), and injections of slapstick which must have given Sturges ideas when he came to direct his own movies (in particular the custard-pie food riot in the automat), it is a delight. TM

Easy Living

(Jacques Tourneur, 1949, US) Victor Mature, Lucille Ball, Lizabeth Scott, Sonny Tufts, Lloyd Nolan, Paul Stewart, Jeff Donnell.
77 min. b/w.
Scripted by Charles Schnee (*The Bad and the Beautiful, Two Weeks in Another Town*) from an Irwin Shaw story, this might have been another *Sweet Smell of Success* with a lowdown angle on professional sport. Tourneur does his best (always concisely, sometimes brilliantly) as Mature's ageing football star gambles his life to ensure security while his wife (Scott) turns the screw on his troubles by ruthlessly pursuing fame as a designer. But studio interference and script compromises (notably in begging the question of whether the wife screws her way to success, and in treating her ambitions with routine bias) sugar the sourness. TM

Easy Money

(Jim Signorelli, 1983, US) Rodney Dangerfield, Joe Pesci, Geraldine Fitzgerald, Candy Azzara, Tom Ewell.
95 min.
The tale of an all-American slobbo (Dangerfield) who spends his days photographing overweight babies and nights swilling beer, guzzling pizza, gambling, doping and generally whooping it up with his 'regular guy' buddies. When his mother-in-law (cue 1001 mother-in-law jokes) leaves him a fortune, it's with the proviso that he gives up these little pleasures for a whole year. If one fails to give a toss for his ensuing sufferings, it's largely because he is a character so repellent he makes Alf Garnett look like a Salvatian Army sergeant. The fact that it took four writers (among them National Lampoon's PJ O'Rourke) to concoct this pile of doggy-doo riddled with sexism and racism doesn't make it any funnier than woodworm in a cripple's crutch. FL

Easy Rider

(Dennis Hopper, 1969, US) Peter Fonda, Dennis Hopper, Antonio Mendoza, Phil Spector, Jack Nicholson, Warren Finnerty.
95 min.
'Some day I'd like to see some of this country we're travelling through' says one of the fugitive couple in *They Live By Night*. Two decades later, their spiritual children had gone 'underground', discovered dope, rock and road...and a preference for male friendships. In this simplistic amalgam of travelogue and the zoom lens, a beatific Fonda and his mumbling St John go looking for America, financed courtesy of a coke deal with Phil Spector. The film was right about one thing at least: the advent of cocaine as the drug. CPe

Easy Virtue

(Alfred Hitchcock, 1927, GB) Isabel Jeans, Franklin Dyall, Eric Bransby Williams, Ian Hunter, Robin Irvine, Violet Farebrother.
7,300 ft. b/w.
Based on a Noël Coward play about the effects of scandal and gossip on a young woman after a much-publicised divorce by her brutal and jealous husband. Though occasional acerbic touches remain, the sections that are drawn directly from the original remain hampered by the loss of Coward's dialogue. But the first half of the film, an addition detailing events only described in the play, is pure Hitchcock, its combination of conciseness and idiosyncrasy demonstrating his mastery of silent narration. A typically bold example is the scene where a proposal of marriage is both made and accepted by telephone without either speaker being shown: Hitchcock traces the conversation via the reactions of the switchboard operator who's eavesdropping on the call. But he's almost certainly right about the final title, which he describes as being the worst he ever wrote. AS

Eat a Bowl of Tea

(Wayne Wang, 1989, US) Victor Wong, Russell Wong, Cora Miao, Eric Tsang Chi Wai, Lau Siu Ming, Wu Ming Yu, Hui Fun.
103 min.
New York, in the late '40s: Ben Loy (Russell Wong) is a loyal Chinese-American son, and when he visits his mother in China after the war, he takes advantage of the recently changed US immigration laws and returns to New York with a wife, Mei Oi (Miao), to live in a closed Chinese community almost entirely made up of men (until the end of the war, America forbade male Asian immigrants to bring wives and daughters with them). Their fathers want the couple to be both prosperous and parents, but Ben Loy works so hard he becomes impotent; meanwhile, understandably bored, Mei Oi encounters temptation in the form of a smooth womaniser. Wang's semi-comic romance is a light-hearted account of the problems faced by young lovers in a displaced and oppressively watchful society. It's a charming rather than probing film, with Wang successfully focusing attention on performances and period atmosphere rather than on

moral nuance. Although rather more emotional pain would not have gone amiss, the result is enjoyable, assured and stylish. GA

Eat Drink Man Woman (Yinshi Nan Nu)

(Ang Lee, 1994, Tai) Sihung Lung, Kuei-Mei Tang, Yu-Wen Wang, Chien-Lien Wu, Winston Chao, Sylvia Chang, Ah-Leh Gua.
124 min.
Comedy drama about a widower and his three unmarried daughters. Mr Chu, a retired Taipei chef, would like his girls to leave home, but is too repressed and stubborn to communicate frankly with them, relying instead on the ritual Sunday dinners he serves up to preserve a sense of family. They, however, feel guilty about their own needs: Jia-Jen, a Christian teacher, nursing a broken heart and covert desire for the sports coach; Jia-Chien, a career woman into casual sex with her ex; and the youngest, Jia-Ning who works in a burger-joint and gets on uncomfortably well with a friend's boyfriend. Which daughter, if any, will stay with Dad? Or will he succumb to predatory widow Mrs Liang – if his health holds out? Tasty ingredients (Sihung Lung's Mr Chu and Chien-Lien Wu's Jia-Chien are especially good), but the food metaphor never carries weight, and the characterisations are too shallow to lend the film emotional punch. GA

Eaten Alive
see Death Trap

Eating Raoul

(Paul Bartel, 1982, US) Paul Bartel, Mary Woronov, Robert Beltran, Susan Saiger, Ed Begley Jr, Buck Henry.
83 min.
The most delicious blackly comic collision of sex, food and murder, Bartel's film arrives as a delightful surprise from the former court jester of Roger Corman's exploitation stable. Featuring Bartel himself and his frequent B-queen, Woronov, as the Blands, innocently stranded amid the hedonist detritus of LA, dreaming (like their Hollywood forebears, the Blandings) of rural retreat, Paul and Mary's Country Kitchen. And dreaming vainly, until 'accidental' homicide propels them into a scheme to exploit carnal as well as culinary appetites, luring disposable perverts to a deadpan doom with the haphazard help and hindrance of such figures as Doris the Dominatrix and Hispanic hustler Raoul. The style stays straight-faced, the more to crease ours with the disparity between sick joke frenetics and a gentle, unruffled sitcom sensibility. A genuine treat for civilised cannibals. PT

Eat My Dust!

(Charles B Griffith, 1976, US) Ron Howard, Christopher Norris, Warren Kemmerling, Dave Madden, Robert Broyles.
89 min.
With the camera on the bumper and David Grisman's country swing on the soundtrack, the opening sequence of this movie raises false hopes that it will offer some sort of distillation of the 'hot-car' cycle put out by exploitation studio New World. Griffith's directorial debut – after 20 years of scripting for Corman – does deliver the expected race/chase/demolition derby mayhem, but every time the focus switches to Ron Howard's adolescent romantic worries, it stalls. Strange that a writer's movie should rely so heavily on stunting and second unit work; sad that it does so little new with its regulation good ol' boys and dumb cops. PT

Eat the Peach

(Peter Ormrod, 1986, Eire) Stephen Brennan, Eamon Morrissey, Catherine Byrne, Niall Toibin, Joe Lynch, Tony Doyle.
95 min.
When their Japanese employers decide to up sticks and take their jobs with them, are brothers-in-law Arthur (Morrissey) and Vinnie (Brennan) the type to sit back and mope? Nope! It takes only a viewing of Elvis risking life and limb motorcycling around the Wall of Death in Roustabout for them to decide to employ their idle hours erecting their very own Wall (on Arthur's wife's vegetable plot). Money's the problem (not to mention Arthur's wife, who ups sticks and legs it too), so there's nothing to it but a stint of bootlegging

across the nearby border to raise the readies, finish the job, and wait for the crowds we know will never come. Within the modest dimensions of his small budget, Ormrod succeeds remarkably well, with a deft touch, a light heart, and not a trace of patronising, to give a true human measure to the dreams and ambitions, failures and disappointments of this collection of likeable loonies. Eat the peach and hear the mermaids sing. WH

Eat the Rich

(Peter Richardson, 1987, GB) Ronald Allen, Sandra Dorne, Jimmy Fagg, Lemmy, Lanah Pellay, Nosher Powell, Fiona Richmond, Ron Tarr, Robbie Coltrane.
98 min.
In this second feature from the Comic Strip team (following The Supergrass), genderless black waiter Pellay takes to the road to lead a People's Revolution, while arch-adversary Powell, a fascistic East End tough turned Home Secretary, bids for top office through headlines in The Sun. True to Comic Strip form, the film lampoons the lunacy of every social group it touches (political extremists, civil servants, the press, the royals, the rich, the poor); make what you will of the politics, as a series of sketches it delivers the laughs. Powell turns in one of the funniest performances of the year, and Pellay's transformation of a swank London restaurant into an eatery on the lines of a pie shop is not to be missed. SGo

Eau Froide, L' (Cold Water)

(Olivier Assayas, 1994, Fr) Virginie Ledoyen, Cyprien Fouquet.
92 min.
Commissioned as part of a series in which directors went back to their adolescence, this is a brave, moving film, set in the outskirts of Paris in 1972. It's a portrait of two delinquents, both from broken homes, and both about to be packed off to institutional care. Christine is on the verge of a mental breakdown, and Gilles, who buys dynamite for kicks, is headed for boarding school. Assayas shoots with a hand-held camera and favours cold, blue lighting and diagetic sound. He's rewarded with two resolutely natural, unshowy performances by Ledoyen and Fouquet, and a tremendous emotional pull. The centrepiece is a marvellously sustained midnight party sequence (a requirement of the series), where a horde of teens group, groove and get off to the sounds of Janis Joplin, Creedence Clearwater Revival, Leonard Cohen and Alice Cooper. Recommended. TCh

Ebirah – Terror of the Deep (Nankai no Daiketto)

(Jun Fukuda, 1966, Jap) Akira Takarada, Toru Watanabe, Hideo Sunazuka, Kumi Mizuno.
86 min.
The film's title notwithstanding, the real star of this Toho production is Godzilla, who – with the aid of another friendly monster, Mothra – puts paid to Ebirah ('an enormous crab' that looks very much like a boiled lobster) and the hordes of The Red Bamboo, a SMERSH-like organisation intent on world domination, and rescues various humans in distress. PH

Echo Park

(Robert Dornhelm, 1985, Aus) Susan Dey, Tom Hulce, Michael Bowen, Christopher Walker, Shirley Jo Finney, Heinrich Schweiger.
89 min.
An aspirant actress turned stripagrammer, her songwriting pizza-delivery-boy lodger, and the Austrian body-builder neighbour (not a hundred umlauts from one Arnold S) bid fair to become the Jules et Jim of the seedy clapboard milieu of suburban LA. Romanian-born, Vienna-trained Dornhelm has the quirky mitteleuropäisch eye (cf. Milos Forman) for the freaks and oddities of American life. Tom Hulce, a long way from Amadeus, reveals a splendidly individual comic presence; and the hopes, shocks, sulks and loyalties of this free-wheeling trio are a small but real delight. MHoy

Eclipse

(Jeremy Podeswa, 1994, Can) Von Flores, John Gilbert, Pascale Monpetit, Manuel Aranguiz, Maria Del Mar, Greg Ellwand, Matthew Ferguson.
95 min. col & b/w.

This debut feature updates the La Ronde idea of a chain of lovers, but with a multi-cultural mix of straight, bi and gay characters and without the focus on the etiquettes of romance and seduction. From the opening financial transaction between a middle-aged businessman and an Asian rent boy, it's clear that the characters will all be more or less up-front about their sex drives. What's difficult for them is not the quick squelch of the sex act itself, but the feelings that follow: the fears, the insecurities, the expectations that the encounter will be either forgotten or parlayed into something more substantial and durable. The same anxieties that haunt La Ronde, in fact. Each of the ten sexual encounters is credible and superbly acted, but the film really takes off around halfway with the episode involving a nervous immigration lawyer and an angelic boy student. This and subsequent scenes combine novelistic depth with short-story concision: entire lifetimes of unspoken longings and unthought assumptions are laid bare with remarkable skill. The acute wit of the sex scenes isn't, however, always present in the linking material, which tries to conjure an impending solar eclipse into a grand metaphor, but doesn't really make it stick. TR

Eclipse

(Simon Perry, 1976, GB) Tom Conti, Gay Hamilton, Gavin Wallace, Paul Kermack, David Steuart.
85 min.
Twin brothers take a small boat out into the Atlantic to watch a lunar eclipse. The body of one is subsequently found on the beach. Showing a fine eye for domestic detail (the main action occurs over Christmas in an isolated cliffside house occupied by the dead brother's widow, where the surviving brother broods over his twin and their relationship), Simon Perry's palpably well-crafted first feature leaves the viewer to decide whether the death was murder or an accident. Despite occasional over-strong symbols, the result is an intelligent attempt to breach the philistine bastions of British commercial cinema. JPy

Eclipse, The (L'Eclisse)

(Michelangelo Antonioni, 1962, It/Fr) Monica Vitti, Alain Delon, Francisco Rabal, Lilla Brignone, Rossana Rory, Louis Seigner.
125 min. b/w.
With L'Avventura and La Notte, L'Eclisse completes an Antonioni trilogy on doomed relationships in a fractured world. This time, Vitti has a traumatic bust-up with the bookish Rabal, and apathetically lets herself get involved with brash young stockbroker Delon. At first glance it's a more formally innovative movie than its predecessors (witness the ending: a long montage that doesn't show the principal characters), but it's underpinned by the same hackneyed symbolism: dawn and nightfall, construction sites, the Bomb, 'ethnic' spontaneity and the rest. Anyone disenchanted with the vacuity of later Antonioni will find the seeds of their dissatisfaction well-rooted in the mannerism and facile anguish evident here. TR

Ecoute Voir... (See Here My Love)

(Hugo Santiago, 1978, Fr) Catherine Deneuve, Sami Frey, Florence Delay, Anne Parillaud, Didier Haudepin, Antoine Vitez.
110 min.
A weird political thriller, this features Deneuve as a private eye (part Emma Peel, part Bogart), investigating a group practising thought control via doctored radio waves, shuffling trench-coated through a country house mystery. Not entirely free of the metaphysical riddles that swamped the earlier work of Argentinian exile and Borges enthusiast Santiago, this hit-and-miss effort is at least shot with flair and works the senses (particularly by way of its complex stereo soundtrack) without ever quite making sense itself. PT

Eddie

(Steve Rash, 1996, US) Whoopi Goldberg, Frank Langella, Dennis Farina, Richard Jenkins, Lisa Ann Walter, John Benjamin Hickey, Malik Sealy.
101 min.
Trying to add bounce to her well worn flounce, Whoopi's the eponymous, mouthy basketball fan who's caught up in the machinations of rhine-

stone cowboy Wild Bill (Langella). Bill has been brought in to save New York's ailing basketball team, the Knicks, and plucks Eddie from the crowd to act as a rinky-dink mascot coach. But she's the real thing – grabs a'hold of those NBA boys, shakes 'em up and you can guess the rest. They're all present and correct, the elements of a Goldberg vehicle we've come to know and dread. What saves the film from abomination is the basketball. It may not look good (TV values reign), but the floor pounding games are edited to create real rushes of glee. The NBA stars, too, are superb, particularly real-life hoop-dreamer Sealy as arrogant golden boy Stacy Patton. CO'Su

Eddie and the Cruisers
(Martin Davidson, 1983, US) Tom Berenger, Michael Paré, Joe Pantoliano, Matthew Laurance, Helen Schneider, Ellen Barkin.
95 min.
1964. The band are poised for national success when singer Eddie drives his car off a bridge. His body is never found...cue, 20 years later, the inevitable Cruisers revival, and a rock'n'roll mystery ensues with renewed speculation over the singer's fate. Overlong live sequences of the band threaten to take over from the fairly reasonable storyline, and relationships don't have the chance to develop. Add to this the fact that the band sound more like Springsteen than Del Shannon, and it all seems a little unrealistic. Clothes and settings, too, seem strangely anonymous. Where it works is in the present, and a sharper look at how various band members had made out 20 years on would have made it still more interesting. Low key and, despite the music, rather likeable. GO

Eddie Murphy Raw
(Robert Townsend, 1987, US) Eddie Murphy.
90 min.
In an immaculate record of his one-man show, the self-appointed superstud levels his sights against anyone who isn't black, male or Murphy. Women come in for more than their fair share of the offensive, as castrating bitches whose duty is to fuck husbands and cook burgers for hungry sons; the predatory infidelities of men, however, would seem excusable through Nature, Destiny, or simply because it's Okay with Eddie. Lisping gays, Rocky-obsessed Italians, whites in general, and Murphy's rivals are also subject to the foulmouthed brew of complaint and contempt. It's impossible to deny the virtuosity of his non-stop delivery, but the relentless macho onslaught sadly lacks the saving grace of Richard Pryor's self-irony. Even if Murphy doesn't mean what he says (and he probably does), laughs are forestalled by the feeling that it's all too mechanically manipulative. GA

Eden Valley
(Amber Production Team, 1994, GB) Brian Hogg, Darren Bell, Mike Elliott, Jimmy Killeen, Mo Harold, Amber Styles.
95 min.
When Billy (Bell), a listless, disaffected teenager from a neglected housing estate, is put on probation for stealing drugs from a chemist's, his mother sends him to the country to stay with his dad Hoggy (Brian Hogg), who left the family some ten years earlier to live in a caravan and raise horses for harness-racing. Interested only in raves, drugs and music, Billy remains resolutely unimpressed by his dad's home, his passion for racing, and the working-class sense of honour that impels him to work on, however cold the wind that blows over the snowy hills of Co Durham. But is this harsh new life better than serving time? Once again, the Amber Production Team has produced a film notable for its authenticity, its muscular, naturalistic performances, and its lack of sentimentality. The film is marked by a droll humour, a celebratory sense of community, and a responsiveness to nature and landscape. A British film made with limited resources standing foursquare on its own ground. GA

Edge, The
(Lee Tamahori, 1997, US) Anthony Hopkins, Alec Baldwin, Elle Macpherson, Harold Perrineau, LQ Jones, Kathlee Wilhoite.
117 min.
Getting back to nature in the Alaskan hinterland, billionaire Charles Morse (Hopkins) peruses a tattered book, Lost in the Wild. Soon a plane crash allows him to show off his encyclopedic memo-

ry, coping with shame, fear, hunger and the elements, plus a smarmy photographer (Baldwin) and his wounded assistant (Perrineau, who should have 'Dead Meat' tattooed on his forehead). Moreover, there's a Kodiak bear on their trail. This boasts an original screenplay by David Mamet and enough outdoor pursuit to fill a men's monthly for a year. They've even worked in a cameo by Elle Macpherson as the wife who may or may not be fooling around behind Morse's back. This last plot wrinkle gives the boys something to thrash out. The movie's on stronger ground with the rudiments of survivalism, in particular the long central battle with the bear, so exciting it makes everything afterwards seem anti-climactic. Hopkins keeps his hamminess in check, and Baldwin finds layers of insidious charm, frailty and menace. TCh

Edge of Darkness
(Lewis Milestone, 1943, US) Errol Flynn, Ann Sheridan, Walter Huston, Nancy Coleman, Helmut Dantine, Judith Anderson.
120 min. b/w.
WWII propaganda piece, scripted by Robert Rossen, paying tribute to the Norwegian resistance movement, which now appears too worthy for even the most die-hard action fancier. Flynn was then getting over the scandal surrounding his trial for statutory rape, so it's not surprising, perhaps, that he looks as though he'd rather be elsewhere.

Edge of Doom
(aka Stronger Than Fear)
(Mark Robson, 1950, US) Farley Granger, Dana Andrews, Joan Evans, Robert Keith, Paul Stewart, Mala Powers, Adele Jergens, Mabel Paige.
99 min. b/w.
Goldwyn-produced chunk of religious trumpery, with Granger indulging heavily sulky histrionics as a young man driven to murder a priest when, with dad already refused consecrated burial as a suicide, he can't raise the money (or persuade the church) to bury mom with suitably ostentatious solemnity. Beautifully shot in noir terms by Harry Stradling as Granger wanders the seamy side of the city on his dark night of the soul, it might have been more effective had Goldwyn not hired Ben Hecht to expand Andrews' role (as the priest who realises that Granger did the killing, and tries to persuade him to relieve his torment by confessing) after the New York opening. Now saddled with prologue and epilogue in which Andrews tells the story in flashback to a young priest with 'doubts' (by way of restoring his faith, as it did his own, though why remains a mystery), the whole thing is impossibly sententious. TM

Edge of Sanity
(Gerard Kikoine, 1988, US) Anthony Perkins, Glynis Barber, Sarah Maur-Thorp, David Lodge.
90 min.
Although allegedly based on Stevenson's classic horror tale, The Strange Case of Dr Jekyll and Mr Hyde, this tawdry slasher pic seems more like an attempt to cash in on 1988's Jack the Ripper centenary. After inhaling the fumes from a substance he has been using on a laboratory monkey, Dr Jekyll is transformed into his baser alter ego, though he looks more a seasick Dr Caligari than a bestial Mr Hyde. Perkins doesn't so much chew up the cardboard scenery as swallow it whole, as his debauched Hyde stalks the dark streets and lurid brothels in search of sensual pleasures and potential victims. The tarts all wear fetishistic underwear, and there is some blasphemous stuff involving a crucified client and a writhing nun, but Stevenson's underlying allegory is itself tortured to death by the atrocious dialogue, wooden acting, and inept direction. NF

Edge of Terror, The
see Wind, The

Edge of the City
(aka A Man Is Ten Feet Tall)
(Martin Ritt, 1957, US) John Cassavetes, Sidney Poitier, Jack Warden, Kathleen Maguire, Ruby Dee, Ruth White, Robert Simon.
85 min. b/w.
Ritt's first feature, scripted by Robert Alan

Aurthur from his own teleplay A Man is Ten Feet Tall. Cassavetes and Poitier become friends down on the waterfront. Cassavetes is the mixed-up, insecure white boy picked on by the brutal, bigoted foreman/union racketeer (Warden); Poitier the wiser, maturer black who defends him (at the cost of his life) in an attempt to teach him to stand up for the right thing. A worthy enough piece, well acted and making excellent use of locations on the New York docks; but when you get down to it, no less dramatically artificial than On the Town, and this boy Poitier is whiter than white. TCh

Edge of the World, The
(Michael Powell, 1937, GB) Niall MacGinnis, John Laurie, Belle Chrystall, Finlay Currie, Eric Berry, Grant Sutherland.
81 min. b/w.
Powell's first major movie, shot on location and as much an account of the harshness of life on the isolated Shetland Isles as the story of two friends torn apart by the elements they struggle against for sustenance. In an interesting move in 1978, Powell was commissioned by BBC TV to return to the island of Foula and film a new introduction and epilogue to his original film. The resulting 'bookends', in colour, give Edge of the World (retitled Return to the Edge of the World) even greater strength, pushing the story further back and emphasising the mysterious and frightening poetry that Powell captures in his search for images that define the waywardness of nature. PH

Edie & Pen
(Matthew Irmas, 1996, US) Stockard Channing, Jennifer Tilly, Scott Glenn, Stuart Wilson, Chris Sarandon, Randy Travis, Michael McKean, Beverly D'Angelo, Louise Fletcher, Martin Mull.
97 min.
Edie (Tilly) and Pen (Channing) meet in Reno. They're both getting divorced, but Edie's marriage lasted only a fortnight, and she's planning to remarry the very same day, while Pen's still in love with her husband of ten years. Together, they embark on an ill-advised nocturnal adventure with Harry, a womanising cowboy (Glenn). This post-romantic comedy has a lot of charm. The direction leaves something to be desired, but Victoria Tennant's script is witty and well structured without seeming mechanical, and cameos from the likes of McKean, D'Angelo, Mull and Travis keep things ticking over nicely. Channing and Glenn work up an easy rapport, and it's another notch in Tilly's promising career. TCh

Edipo Re
see Oedipus Rex

Edison the Man
(Clarence Brown, 1940, US) Spencer Tracy, Rita Johnson, Lynne Overman, Charles Coburn, Gene Lockhart, Henry Travers.
107 min. b/w.
Glossily polished biopic made as a sequel to Young Tom Edison, with Tracy in suitably earnest form, struggling through the trials and tribulations of poverty and neglect en route to inventing the light bulb. Something of a whitewash job, it never begins to suggest the stubborn and sometimes shortsighted side to the inventor's character that led him, for example, first to fail to recognise the potential of his invention of the movie camera and projector, and secondly, to hang so firmly on to his patent that the movie medium was in thrall to him for many years. GA

Edith and Marcel (Edith et Marcel)
(Claude Lelouch, 1983, Fr) Evelyne Bouix, Jacques Villeret, Francis Huster, Jean-Claude Brialy, Jean Bouise, Marcel Cerdan Jr, Charles Aznavour.
140 min.
Voilà the passionate affair between Edith Piaf and Marcel Cerdan, welterweight champion of Europe (played by his son). Cue for lots of heartfelt warbling intercut with the biff-bam of the boxing-ring, circumscribed by dizzying camerawork and strung along to the strains of Francis Lai. All this is spliced with a barely relevant subplot about a mismatched romance between two 'ordinary' fictional folk: a bookloving young dreamer and a slobbish PoW who has never even heard of Proust. Bouix is compellingly sparrow-

like and doesn't once sing 'Je ne regrette rien'. Aznavour, as himself, croaks croonfully down the blower whenever he thinks up a new tune for Edith to sing. 'Avec toi, avec toi, avec toi,' she trills, meaning every word. Marcel's plane crashes, toute la France goes into mourning, and the film critic, between snuffles, declares the whole thing to be a load of raging bull. AB

Educating Rita
(Lewis Gilbert, 1983, GB) Michael Caine, Julie Walters, Michael Williams, Maureen Lipman, Jeananne Crowley, Malcolm Douglas.
110 min.
Willy Russell's adaptation of his own slick theatrical two-hander pits Liverpudlian housewife Walters, in pursuit of true learning via the Open University, against alcoholic academic hack Caine. Apart from the odd cinematic in-joke (Caine's booze concealed behind a copy of *The Lost Weekend*), Gilbert's direction remains serviceable but stolid: the film's faults – and merits – are mostly those of the play. A few flashes of wit and insight lie embedded in a morass of prejudice, cliché and evasion. Only Walters' ebullient movie debut as the chirpy working class sparrow wanting to 'sing a different song' (the role she created on stage) almost succeeds in infusing the exercise with infectious life. SJo

Edvard Munch
(Peter Watkins, 1976, Nor/Swe) Geir Westby, Gro Fraas, Iselin von Hanno Bart.
167 min.
Watkins' biography of the formative years of the pioneer Expressionist easily vindicates its running time. As Munch moves through his youth, quiet and alienated, we realise that he too was eluded by any lasting intimacy: a long, abortive affair with an older woman joins the ubiquitous ghosts of a childhood scarred by sickness and death. In the end it's the paintings which do Munch's talking for him, both directly and through the prefigurations and echoes in the film's set pieces, a fuzzed, mutely anguished procession of half-profiles and silently helpless groups with numb, naked eyes. A remarkable film. GD

Edward II
(Derek Jarman, 1991, GB) Steven Waddington, Kevin Collins, Andrew Tiernan, John Lynch, Dudley Sutton, Tilda Swinton, Jerome Flynn, Nigel Terry, Roger Hammond, Annie Lennox.
90 min.
This modern dress adaptation of Marlowe's play excites through its sheer guts and combativeness. Despite the visual lyricism, the mood is raw and angry. Jarman re-uses his sub-Brechtian clothes-as-class characterisation: scheming Mortimer (Terry) in army officer kit; nobles in business suits; Isabella (Swinton) in a *Vogue*'s gallery of designer dresses; Edward's supporters as gay *Outrage* activists. Jarman rips from Marlowe what is relevant to our times, to comment on the repressive nature of the British state; but this is problematic. The tragic, idealistic love of Edward (Waddington) for lowly-born, upstart Gaveston (Tiernan) speaks volumes about gay relationships in repressive, class-conscious societies, but Isabella's relationship with Mortimer is shown in images redolent of horror movies. This ambivalence, however, does not deny the film's power. Central to its pleasures are the performances; it isn't Jarman 's best film, but it's his most accessible. WH

Edward Scissorhands
(Tim Burton, 1990, US) Johnny Depp, Winona Ryder, Dianne Wiest, Anthony Michael Hall, Kathy Baker, Vincent Price, Alan Arkin, Robert Oliveri, Conchata Ferrell.
105 min.
With his electric-shock hairdo and kinky black gear, Edward (Depp) is a model of trendy respectability – except for one thing. This manmade creature has got shears instead of hands, because his creator (Price) died mid-project. He sits lonely and lethal in his gloomy mansion, until the Avon Lady (Wiest) comes to call. She invites him home, and he proceeds to dazzle her family and neighbours with his flair for topiary and surreal hair-styling. With its skewed vision of suburbia, Burton's film bears comparison with his earlier *Pee-Wee's Big Adventure*. It's a visual treat, complete with pastel bungalows, surreal shrubbery and grotesque outfits, but it remains curiously hollow. CM

Ed Wood
(Tim Burton, 1994, US) Johnny Depp, Martin Landau, Sarah Jessica Parker, Patricia Arquette, Jeffrey Jones, Vincent D'Onofrio, GD Spradlin, Lisa Marie, Juliet Landau, Bill Murray, George 'The Animal' Steele, Mike Starr, Max Casella, Brent Hinkley.
127 min. b/w.
Burton's biopic of the man often described as the world's worst film-maker (*Glen or Glenda*, *Plan Nine from Outer Space*, etc) may offer a somewhat favourably distorted account of the man and his films – it ends before his slide into porn, penury and alcoholism and, while recreating certain scenes from Wood's work with astonishing accuracy, manages to avoid showing his most tiresomely nonsensical sequences – but it certainly succeeds as a funny, touching tribute to tenacity, energy, ambition and friendship. Affection shines through warm and bright, aided no end by Stefan Czapsky's evocative b/w camerawork, and by a host of spot-on lookalike performances. Landau, especially, is superb, bringing fire, acid, pathos, wit and real dignity to the role of the pitiful, occasionally deranged former horror hero Bela Lugosi; and, in the film's most conspicuous, outrageous but surprisingly appropriate bit of fictionalisation, Vincent D'Onofrio makes a notably beleaguered Welles. Depp himself, all innocence, bright-eyed zeal and itchy obsession, never really lets us get beneath Wood's skin, but gives such a good-natured performance that it's hard not to end up rooting for someone who was talentless, naive and misguided in virtually everything he did. GA

Eel, The (Unagi)
(Shohei Imamura, 1997, Jap) Koji Yakusho, Misa Shimizu, Fujio Tsuneta, Mitsuko Baisho.
117 min.
After a deceptively dark, brutal beginning in which Yakusho murders his adulterous wife, Imamura's *Palme d'Or* winner lightens up quite considerably to present an offbeat, occasionally even comic account of his reintegration into the world after eight years in prison. Unusually, it's the protagonist's own hesitancy and introversion that makes rehabilitation difficult, rather than society; indeed, the eccentric folk who frequent his remote barber's shop, and especially a young woman he saves from suicide, are mostly very supportive and helpful. Still, the past catches up with him, leading to a climax as violent, farcical and ultimately affecting as Imamura's cool, clear direction is subtle and assured. GA

Efecto Mariposa, El
see Butterfly Effect, The

Effect of Gamma Rays on Man-in-the-Moon Marigolds, The
(Paul Newman, 1972, US) Joanne Woodward, Nell Potts, Roberta Wallach, Judith Lowry, Richard Venture.
101 min.
An engaging adaptation of Paul Zindel's Pulitzer Prize-winning play, which sees Newman's cool, lucid direction transforming what could have been a pretentious domestic drama into a touching account of small joys in sad and stunted lives. Woodward is excellent as the slatternly mother of two daughters, one introverted and hiding a tenacious interest in science (the title refers to her school project), the other a boy-chasing cheerleader destined to follow in her mother's unsuccessful footsteps. Newman and Woodward's daughter Potts steals the movie, but what makes it so watchable is Newman's reluctance to sentimentalise. GA

Effi Briest
(Rainer Werner Fassbinder, 1974, WGer) Hanna Schygulla, Wolfgang Schenck, Ulli Lommel, Karl-Heinz Böhm, Ursula Strätz.
140 min. b/w.
Late 19th century Germany. A wholly inexperienced teenage girl is pushed into a marriage with a minor aristocrat many years her senior. She bears him a child, but her first knowledge of emotional warmth is gained when a neighbour makes moves to seduce her. Fassbinder's *Effi Briest* is quite literally a film of Theodor Fontane's novel: everything about the way it's conceived and structured draws attention back to the literary source. As a result, Effi is not just another

Fassbinder victim-figure, but (true to Fontane) an index of her society's morality; she is exploited in various ways by everyone around her, but she suffers only because she hasn't the strength to challenge the social codes that bind her. Schygulla plays her with absolute conviction. Filmed in black and white, with extraordinary delicacy and reserve, this is one of Fassbinder's best films. TR

Effrontée, L'
see Impudent Girl, An

Egyptian Story, An (Hadduta Misriya)
(Youssef Chahine, 1982, Egypt) Mohiel Dine, Ussama Nadir, Magda-El-Khatib, Leila Hamada.
130 min.
Boldly blending personal and political histories, intercutting its fast-moving fictional scenes with documentary footage, this sort of sequel to *Alexandria – Why?* follows the fortunes of Chahine's charismatic film-maker hero and alter ego, forced to review his past and learn to love himself by a critical open-heart operation. The occasionally clumsy central conceit – Yehia/Chahine standing trial for his life during surgery – is amply offset by the energy and style of this indulgent, exuberant, and immensely likeable self-portrait. SJo

Ehe der Maria Braun, Die
see Marriage of Maria Braun, The

Eiger Sanction, The
(Clint Eastwood, 1975, US) Clint Eastwood, George Kennedy, Vonetta McGee, Jack Cassidy, Heidi Bruhl, Thayer David.
125 min.
The most puzzling of Eastwood's self-directed films, lacking the ironic detachment that characterised his long journey from the Man with No Name to *Bronco Billy*. Shot in a straightforward adventure style, with Eastwood as the art lecturer cum cold-blooded assassin hired to kill his victim while climbing the North face of the Eiger, the movie is little but a series of nice panoramas and clichéd action sequences. PH

8½ (Otto e Mezzo) [100]
(Federico Fellini, 1963, It) Marcello Mastroianni, Claudia Cardinale, Anouk Aimée, Sandra Milo, Rossella Falk, Barbara Steele, Guido Alberti.
138 min. b/w.
The passage of time has not been kind to what many view as Fellini's masterpiece. Certainly Di Venanzo's high-key images and the director's flash-card approach place 8½ firmly in its early '60s context. As a self-referential work it lacks the layering and the profundity of, for example, *Tristram Shandy*, and the central character, the stalled director (Mastroianni), seems less in torment than doodling. And yet...The bathing of Guido sequence is a study extract for film-makers, and La Saraghina's rumba for the seminary is a gift to pop video. Amiably spiking all criticism through a gloomy scriptwriter mouthpiece, Fellini pulls a multitude of rabbits out of the showman's hat. BC

8-Diagram Pole Fighter, The (Wulang Bagua Gun/aka The Invincible Pole Fighters)
(Lau Kar-Leung aka Liu Jialiang, 1983, HK) Fu Sheng, Gordon Liu, Lily Li, Hui Yinghong, Lau Kar-Leung, Ke Ming, Gao Fei.
99 min.
Turned upside down during production by the death of Fu Sheng in a car crash, this is by far Lau's most sombre and serious minded film. It set out to retell the famous Song Dynasty legend of the Yang family, massacred by Mongol invaders with the connivance of a Chinese traitor. In the film, Yang's 5th and 6th sons (Liu and Fu respectively) survive the massacre: 6 returns home deranged to be nursed by his mother and sisters (but, due to Fu's death, never to fight again), while 5 eventually finds his way to a temple where he learns to use his now bladeless spear as a weapon, mastering the art of 8-Diagram pole fighting. The many scenes of combat, choreographed to Lau's usual high standard, are relent-

e

lessly grim and bloody; the monks who back up 5 in his climactic revenge respect their Buddhist principles by disabling rather than killing their enemies – by knocking out all their teeth. The dubbed UK video release is a horrible pan-and-scan job. TR

18 Again!

(Paul Flaherty, 1988, US) George Burns, Charlie Schlatter, Tony Roberts, Anita Morris, Miriam Flynn, Jennifer Runyon, Red Buttons.
100 min.
This production-line vehicle for nonagenarian comic Burns is notable in that he plays a younger man: 81-year-old company director Jack Watson, a dictatorial and lecherous pain-in-the-ass, who makes a birthday wish to be 18 again which – no really? – comes true. Shy grandson David (Schlatter), bullied by the frat jocks, has a near-fatal car accident at the very moment Jack has a heart-attack, and bodies and souls swop partners. For two weeks, David wanders around in Jazz Age gear, fisting a cigar and cocktail, cracks vaudeville jokes, and stuns the girl of his dreams (Runyon, the usual blonde with piano-keyboard teeth) by his prowess on track and field, skills courtesy of grandpa. Meanwhile, newly humanised, Jack boots out parasitic playmate Madelyn (Morris struggling womanfully with an ugly role) and recognises the neglected talents of son Arnold (Roberts). A ramshackle, uninspiring enterprise, full of vaguely objectionable humor and gags of pensionable age. WH

Eighth Day, The (Le Huitième Jour)

(Jaco Van Dormael, 1996, Fr/Bel/GB) Daniel Auteuil, Pascal Duquenne, Miou-Miou, Henri Garcin, Isabelle Sadoyan.
118 min.
For sales executive Harry (Auteuil), life has gone terribly wrong: he's so caught up in the system, his wife (Miou-Miou) and kids have left, and happiness eludes him. One starry night, he closes his eyes, takes his hands off the steering wheel – and runs over a dog belonging to Georges (Duquenne), a Down's syndrome fugitive from an institution who's searching for his (dead) mother. As Harry searches for somewhere suitable to dump the chaotically unpredictable Georges, his initial grumpiness and prejudice turns to understanding and affection, revived by his charge's spontaneity, innocence and warmth. After a visually gorgeous, brilliantly executed opening, which evokes through a bizarre creation myth Georges' skewed but beautiful perceptions of the world, Van Dormael's follow-up to Toto the Hero slowly but surely turns into something altogether more conventional, simplistic and, regrettably, sentimental. The contrast between the emotional riches of Georges' life and the dessicated orderliness of Harry's world is often trite, and the plotting frequently implausible. Clearly Van Dormael has a huge heart and a fertile imagination, but here he seems too close to his subject for the film's good. GA

8 Heads in a Duffel Bag

(Tom Schulman, 1997, US/GB) Joe Pesci, Andy Comeau, Kristy Swanson, Todd Louise, George Hamilton, Dyan Cannon.
95 min.
Two identical duffel bags: one belongs to cocky mobster Tommy Spinelli (Pesci), the other to meek medical student Charlie (Comeau). Charlie's bound for a holiday in Mexico with girlfriend Laurie (Swanson) and her parents, smarmy Dick and neurotic Annette (Hamilton and Cannon). Spinelli's bag contains eight human heads, grisly 'proof' of a Mob hit. If Spinelli fails to deliver all the evidence to his boss, his head will roll too. But then the bags get mixed up at the airport, and, worse, some of the heads go missing. The black humour's shovelled on in the first ten minutes, giving the impression that we're in for a swell bit of dark bad-taste comedy. But when Cannon lunges into frame, having discovered the contents of Charlie's bag, all becomes clear: the film's actually several shades lighter than Hamilton's tan and better suited to TV. DA

Eight Men Out

(John Sayles, 1988, US) John Cusack, Clifton James, Michael Lerner, Christopher Lloyd,

Charlie Sheen, David Strathairn, DB Sweeney, John Mahoney, Michael Rooker, Perry Lang, Don Harvey, Kevin Tighe, Maggie Renzi, Studs Terkel, John Sayles.
120 min.
Sayles tells the story of the 1919 World Series baseball scandal as an allegory of the way the uneducated poor can be manipulated, corrupted and destroyed by the rich and powerful. The Chicago White Sox were tempted, thanks to the paltry salaries paid by their penny-pinching boss, to take bribes from a group of gambling hoodlums (Arnold Rothstein included) in return for throwing the World Series to the Cincinnati Reds. The affair rocked America; and Sayles' movie, sticking close to the known facts, reflects the disillusionment that came with the realisation that these heroic figures were merely weak, corruptible humans. At the same time, however, his use of a near-legendary story to comment on the economic and social factors which made such corruption possible pushes him into a black-and-white polarisation of the characters which is only partly redeemed by the overall excellence of the acting. Given the inevitably knotty plotting, the message is oddly unrevealing, although the film features more than enough intelligently, wittily scripted moments to remain a fascinating insight into a crucial episode in the souring of that old American Dream. GA

8 Million Ways to Die

(Hal Ashby, 1986, US) Jeff Bridges, Rosanna Arquette, Alexandra Paul, Randy Brooks, Andy Garcia.
115 min.
What happened? With Ashby, Bridges, Arquette and a script co-written by Oliver Stone, you expect the result to be better than a long drawn-out episode of The Equalizer. Bridges plays a dipso cop who gets dropped from the force for blowing away a man going berserk with a baseball bat. When an unhappy hooker comes to him for protection, she ends up in a storm drain, and our decrepit hero determines to get even with her killer, a pigtailed drug-dealer. People say 'shit' and 'fuck' a lot; the spurts of action are too few and far between to hold the interest. However, there are a couple of things that make you sit up. Firstly, a fanny-flaunting floozie says 'Streetlight makes my pussy-hair glow in the dark'. And second, Arquette pukes over Bridges' groin. No wonder. MS

Eight O'Clock Walk

(Lance Comfort, 1953, GB) Richard Attenborough, Cathy O'Donnell, Derek Farr, Maurice Denham, Lily Kann.
87 min. b/w.
Taxi driver Attenborough's the chief suspect in the killing of an eight-year-old girl, and though spouse O'Donnell never doubts his innocence, circumstantial evidence seems damning. Led by an effectively squirming Attenborough, the performers are more credible than the creaking screenplay. TJ

8 Seconds

(John G Avildsen, 1994, US) Luke Perry, Cynthia Geary, Stephen Baldwin, James Rebhorn, Red Mitchell, Ronnie Claire Edwards, Carrie Snodgress, George Michael.
105 min.
Perry stars as a demon rodeo rider Lane Frost. From the moment tiny tot Frost is hoisted on to a baby bull, charges 20 feet and falls off on his head, his path to fame is assured. It's a true story, so the plot is perfunctory – is Frost too common for cute rodeo gal Kellie (Geary)? Next thing you know he's married and buckling on the World Championship belt. But soon he's canoodling with the 'buckle bunnies', neglecting doe-eyed Kellie and proving his inability to tame too unridden monsters, the wild bull Red Rock and his marriage. Perry is too petulant to convince us of Frost's dark side; while Avildsen remains a proponent of the point-and-shoot school of direction. The film redeems itself somewhat by its downbeat ending. SFe

Eight Taels of Gold (Ba Liang Jin)

(Mabel Yeun-Ting Cheung, 1989, HK) Sammo Hung, Sylvia Chang.
119 min.
Mabel Cheung's previous movie was a bittersweet romance set in New York: stuffy middle class Chinese girl meets working class Chinese layabout. This one reverses the formula: work-

ing class achiever from New York's Chinatown visits China and falls for a glamorous peasant girl who is already engaged to someone else. Conspicuously lacking in depth, and all too ready to go for easy laughs and pathos, this is partially redeemed by the strength of its two lead performances. Sylvia Chang and Sammo Hung, both cast somewhat against type, relish the chance to play off each other, and both are highly watchable. Hard to forgive the endlessly dragged-out unhappy ending, though. TR

1871

(Ken McMullen, 1989, GB) Roshan Seth, John Lynch, Timothy Spall, Alexandre de Sousa, Maria de Medeiros, Ian McNeice, Ana Padrao, Jack Klaff, Dominique Pinon, Med Hondo, Lutz Becker.
100 min.
McMullen's film about the Paris Commune offers a stirring rendition of the 'Internationale' sung, at a moment of seeming defeat, by the actors in Ramborde's Theatre in Paris, as reactionary government forces close in to remove, as it were, the masses from the stage of history. McMullen depicts the events of those heady days – from the assassination of Emperor Maximilian of Mexico in 1867, through the crazy Franco-Prussian war, to the crushing of the communards – as a farcical theatrical event, taking his cue, no doubt, from Marx's famous remarks about how history repeats itself (his words themselves repeated imperiously by a black Marx played by director Med Hondo). In and out of Ramborde's Theatre or the nearby Café Anglais, a gallery of historical cutouts impersonates the various mighty forces at work in society. It's a grand, ambitious, three-act, sub-Brechtian affair, which exhibits the McMullen trademarks: a painterly eye, an unashamed taste for Big Ideas and allusive puns, and a tendency to lapse into obscurity and pretentiousness. WH

80th Step, The (80. Adim)

(Tomris Giritlioglu, 1996, Tur) Zuhal Olcay, Levent Ulgen, Haluk Bilginer.
105 min.
Korkut Laçin lies in hospital, arguably in a coma, certainly with three bullets inside him. Who put them there, and why? And just who is this man? With an idiosyncratic flashback structure involving both the reminiscences of state investigators' interviewees and Korkut's own memories, we painstakingly unravel a history involving childhood at an orphanage, a 1975 burnt-down chemistry lab, flight abroad, 1978 capture in Bangkok, protracted torture by the Turkish military authorities, and various unexplained phenomena. The net result is unexpectedly wacky: partly because of the impenetrability of the drama, partly because of the strange fascination of its enigmatic central figure, a man 'just more ordinary than others', says his ex-lover, but also hard and lonely, a man who alienates his old friends with his deadpan fearlessness, but who seems to have picked up an inscrutable chip on his shoulder somewhere along the way. NB

Eight-Tray Gangster: The Making of a Crip

(Thomas Lee Wright, 1993, US) Kershaun Scott.
65 min.
This documentary gives the camera over to LA gang members – of whom there are an estimated 80,000 – and a community activist, Kershaun 'Lil Monster' Scott, a member of the CRIPs (Common Resources for an Independent People). His is not a savoury tale. We follow Scott through the neighbourhoods and up into the hills for gun practice, as he explains what he sees as the inevitable process of initiation into gang membership: the need for self-defence and survival. The other interviewees are his brother 'Kody Monster', jailed aged 14 for first-degree murder, filmed in prison, and their mother. Director Wright offers no analysis, little distance, and regrettably, in the end, little genuine insight. The most moving scene is in the casualty department of the Daniel Freeman Hospital, which resembles a WWI first-aid post: mothers sit with heads bowed and nurses are left, literally, to pick up the pieces. WH

8-Wheel Beast, The (Il Bestione)

(Sergio Corbucci, 1974, It/Fr) Giancarlo Giannini, Michel Constantin, Giuseppe Maffioli, Giuliana Calandra, Dalila Di Lazzaro.
102 min.

A truck-driving movie with pretensions towards social realism. Events start unpromisingly with an utterly predictable conflict between the cool old hand and the hothead novice. Things turn lukewarm with some background detail. Then the last third raises questions about going independent, and the ensuing problems with the unions and the Mafia. It ends up with more than a nod in the direction of *The Wages of Fear*. That the film improves on its atrocious beginnings is more a matter for relief than any indication of quality.

80 Blocks from Tiffany's
(Gary Weis, 1980, US)
60 min.
Bring 'em back alive documentary for which the crew ventured into the wilds of the South Bronx street-gang territory to talk to members of the Savage Skulls and Savage Nomads. Picturesque shots of the natives posing with steel helmets and swastikas, muttering darkly about dastardly deeds and codes of honour. Muddled and messy, the film is as inarticulate as its heroes. TM

84 Charing Cross Road
(David Jones, 1986, US) Anne Bancroft, Anthony Hopkins, Judi Dench, Jean De Baer, Maurice Denham.
99 min.
David Jones' film of Helene Hanff's book, recording the bizarre transatlantic relationship between a New York bibilophile and a London bookseller, comes as a pleasant surprise. Though inevitably literary in tone – the letters between Hanff and the Marks employees structure the narrative – it is never less than intelligent, touching, humorous. Central to this success is the subtle contrast between the austerity of postwar London and the comparatively bright affluence of Hanff's New York; also rewarding is the way images wittily counterpoint and comment on the lovingly intoned letters. And the film somehow manages to convey Hanff's almost sensual passion for pages bound in leather and still resounding with the pleasurable reactions of previous readers. None of which qualities would be evident were it not for the performances: Hopkins as the staid, shy family man Frank P Doel, and the marvellous Bancroft, relishing the vagaries of English pronunciation, as the headstrong Ms Hanff. Thankfully, the film has nothing to do with easy nostalgia; it's about real, credible people, and as such finally becomes very moving. GA

84 Charlie Mopic
(Patrick Duncan, 1988, US) Jonathan Emerson, Nicholas Cascone, Jason Tomlins, Christopher Burgard, Glenn Morshower, Richard Brooks, Byron Thomas.
95min.
This independently produced Vietnam film presents an unusual perspective on the familiar platoon movie scenario. '84 Charlie Mopic' is a two-man army documentary film crew assigned to accompany an average platoon and 'record procedures peculiar to this combat situation'. Black leader OD and his mixed-bag platoon – joker Easy, tough guy Cracker, hillbilly Cracker etc – are therefore filmed and interviewed, on the job and at rest, as they hump the boonies in search of 'Charlie'. The dense slang, attention to detail and ensemble acting lend an air of immediacy and authenticity, although the use of hand-held camera throughout is hard on the eyes. One short scene gives an intimation of what's in store: cameraman Mopic talks about developing reels of film that have come back from the front line, minus their cameraman – 'You never knew what you were gonna see', he says ominously. A shade too worthy, perhaps, but quietly effective. NF

Eijanaika
(Shohei Imamura, 1981, Jap) Kaori Momoi, Shigeru Izumiya, Ken Ogata, Shigeru Tsuyuguchi, Masao Kusakari.
151 min.
Picking his way through the anarchy and absurdity of a society in violent transition like some oriental Makavejev, Imamura breathes bawdy life into the bones of Japanese history with this mosaic portrait of the political chaos preceding the Imperial Meiji Restoration. A confusing welter of factions and mercenary figures flit through a complex of allegiances and relationships, but

as the title translates – echoing the rioters' cries – 'What the hell'. The canvas is vivid enough to impress the most Eurocentric of spectators. PT

Eika Katappa
(Werner Schroeter, 1969, WGer) Magdalena Montezuma, Gisela Trowe, Rosa von Praunheim
144 min.
Any adjectives that you might (with reasonable objectivity) apply to grand opera, apply just as much to Schroeter's hysterical celebration of the form. *Eika Katappa* is interminably long, highly repetitive, commitedly clichéd, and very camp indeed. It is also, at times, extremely funny. It begins with a preview of coming attractions (a skinny Siegfried, a battleaxe Brunhilde) and ends with a survey of past highlights; in between lies a vast melting pot of scenes, situations and characters from your best and least loved operas, shifting restlessly in and out of narratives like an addict on overdrive. Just when it appears to be drawing its threads together, it launches into a tragic gay love story likely to cause a massive increase in Kleenex sales. Those hardy souls who stay the course are lavishly rewarded. TR

Einmal Ku'damm und Zurück
see Girl in a Boot

Ek Baar Phir (Once Again)
(Pande, 1979, GB) Deepti Naval, Suresh Oberoi, Pradeep Varma, Saeed Jaffrey.
125 min.
The first Hindi film to be shot in London (with English subtitles), *Ek Baar Phir* should provide students of the genre with enough material to keep them distracted (unusual locations, heroine demanding a divorce from husband over the phone). Non-Hindi filmgoers might find other elements of interest – Saeed Jaffrey playing himself, an intriguing account of rupee black market finance – but are more likely to be deterred by the inordinate length, eccentric use of song, and heavy emotional underlining. Something like reading 2,000 pages of Mills & Boon romance. CPea

El
(Luis Buñuel, 1952, Mex) Arturo de Córdova, Delia Garcés, Luis Beristáin, José Pidal, Aurora Walker, Carlos Martinez Baena.
100 min. b/w.
Why would a fanatically jealous husband creep up on his sleeping wife clutching a bottle of anaesthetic and a needle and thread? In the gospel according to Buñuel, it's because he's a typical bourgeois male, terrified of female sexuality, projecting his own heavily repressed lusts on to every other male in sight. Buñuel examines him dispassionately, as a victim of himself and of the society that formed him; his story is neither a tragedy nor a comedy, but a necessary working out of certain moral and psychological tensions that are intrinsic in his class. The tone couldn't be further from the self-congratulation of an exercise like *The Discreet Charm of the Bourgeoisie*. TR

E la Nave Va
see And the Ship Sails On

El Cid
(Anthony Mann, 1961, US/Sp) Charlton Heston, Sophia Loren, Raf Vallone, Geraldine Page, John Fraser, Hurd Hatfield, Herbert Lom, Michael Hordern, Douglas Wilmer, Frank Thring.
184 min.
One of the very finest epics produced by Samuel Bronston, equally impressive in terms of script (by Philip Yordan, who mercifully steers clear of florid archaisms) and spectacle. Heston is aptly heroic as the 11th-century patriot destined to die in the fight for a Moor-less Spain, Mann's direction is stately and thrilling, and Miklos Rozsa's superb score perfectly complements the crisp and simple widescreen images. Sobriety and restraint, in fact, are perhaps the keynotes of the film's success, with the result that a potentially risible finale (in which Cid's corpse is borne into the realm of legend, strapped to his horse as it leads his men to battle) becomes genuinely stirring. GA

El Condor
(John Guillermin, 1970, US) Jim Brown, Lee Van Cleef, Patrick O'Neal, Mariana Hill, Iron Eyes Cody, Imogen Hassall, Elisha Cook Jr.
102 min.

A real hotch-potch, this: an American spaghetti Western, shot in Spain, set in Mexico, directed by British expatriate Guillermin, produced by the Hungarian Andre De Toth (who would probably have made a better job of directing it), and written by Steven Carabatsos and Larry (*It's Alive, Demon*) Cohen. Plus, its story features a black chaingang fugitive, a Yankee conman and an Apache, hunting down buried gold in a desert fortress. Unfortunately, too many cooks spoil the unappetising broth; the film is emptily flashy, fashionably violent, and totally lacking in subtlety or real tension. GA

El Dorado
(Howard Hawks, 1966, US) John Wayne, Robert Mitchum, James Caan, Charlene Holt, Michele Carey, Arthur Hunnicutt, RG Armstrong, Edward Asner.
127 min.
Hawks' effortless Western gathers together a gunfighter, a drunken sheriff, a young hopeful, a couple of tough women, and sets them up in a jail, fighting for their lives against a cattle baron and his hired killers. Sounds familiar? In many ways the plot resembles Hawks' earlier *Rio Bravo*, and several of the themes are again present: the importance of group solidarity, self-respect, professionalism, and acceptance of others' faults. But the tone here is transformed by the emphasis on his two central heroes' infirmity: not only is Mitchum a drunk, but Wayne suffers badly from age and a gun wound. Seemingly a lazy, leisurely coast towards the final shootout, it is in fact an elegy on lost youth assuaged by friendship, moving from lush pastures to dusty township, from light to darkness. This is an old man's movie only in the sense that it deals with the problems of approaching the valley of death. In other words, it's a witty, exciting and deeply moving masterpiece. GA

El Dorado
(Carlos Saura, 1988, Sp/Fr) Omero Antonutti, Eusebio Poncela, Lambert Wilson, Gabriela Roel, José Sancho, Feodor Atkine, Inés Sastre.
123 min.
Saura's account of Spain's quest for Peruvian gold differs from Herzog's *Aguirre, Wrath of God* in intention and budget. Loopy Lope de Aguirre and his conquistadors sail themselves up a creek without gold or paddle, decimated by unseen assailants, hostile environs, exhausted provisions, and mad, merciless self-slaughter. Aguirre (the excellent Antonutti) is a tired 50-year-old way down the military pecking order; if voice-overs suggest he sees himself as God's instrument, Saura portrays his murderous deeds as a product of the clashing forces of Spanish society. His attempt to demythologise this *folie de grandeur* within the conventions of the big budget epic (at $9 million, Spain's most expensive film to date) excels in evoking the destructive effects of sexual jealousy, envy, greed and the Spanish obsession with death. But despite lush 'Scope photography and the meticulous display of authentic armour and finery, the film is often oppressive, and too dependent on faces to communicate meaning, adding obscurity to something already complex and ambiguous. Not Saura's best, perhaps, but a fascinating attempt to get to the heart of myths, men and history. WH

Elective Affinities (Le Affinità Elettive)
(Paolo Taviani/Vittorio Taviani, 1996, It/Fr) Isabelle Huppert, Fabrizio Bentivoglio, Jean-Hugues Anglade, Marie Gillain.
98 min.
The Tavianis' adaptation of Goethe's novel may seem strangely restrained compared to their other fables, but it's still a work of exquisite elegance and precision. Set in Tuscany during the Napoleonic era, it charts the forces of attraction and repulsion that shape the complex relationships between a happily married baron and his wife (Anglade, Huppert), the baron's architect friend (Bentivoglio) and the wife's goddaughter (Gillain). If the story itself (engrossing enough) never seems very much more than an unusually formal period romance, the immaculate performances and the Tavianis' masterly control of colour, composition and music (a poignant but unexpectedly modernist score from Carlo Crivelli) make for absorbing viewing. GA

Electra Glide in Blue

(James William Guercio, 1973, US) Robert Blake, Billy Green Bush, Mitchell Ryan, Jeannine Riley, Elisha Cook, Royal Dano.
113 min.

Striking one-off by a former record producer. A weirdly funny black comedy about an undersized cop, barely five feet tall but nursing a dream of becoming a Clint Eastwood hero. He makes the grade (after a fashion, since the dream turns sour) by way of an alarmingly funny echo of *Dr Strangelove* (his mentor in detection has no use for evidence, preferring instead to stand in the moonlight listening to his inner voices) and some spiky mockery of police methods. The message may be a little naïve when he finally opts for humanity rather than authoritarianism, but the film has an extraordinary texture, peeling away layer after layer to reveal dark depths of loneliness and despair as this cop Candide learns that he isn't living in the best of all possible worlds. And Conrad Hall's photography, especially of the Monument Valley landscapes, is a joy. TM

Electric Dreams

(Steve Barron, 1984, GB/US) Lenny Von Dohlen, Virginia Madsen, Maxwell Caulfield, Don Fellows, voice of Bud Cort.
112 min.

A gauche West Coast architect called Miles has a pash on the concert cellist who lives upstairs, and guess who's competing for her supple hand? It's Miles' computer, name of Edgar, programmed to compose spoony tunes for the lady's delectation. It's mildly amusing to watch Miles plug his new machine into household appliances, but anthropomorphism soon rears its ugly head, and Edgar turns out to be a fractious bore with a peevish desire to grasp the essence of true love. The climax is pure coca-cola and likely to rot the teeth of human viewers. Come back HAL, all is forgiven. AB

Electric Horseman, The

(Sydney Pollack, 1979, US) Robert Redford, Jane Fonda, Valerie Perrine, Willie Nelson, John Saxon, Nicolas Coster, Allan Arbus, Wilford Brimley.
120 min.

Simple-minded tract disguised as a romantic comedy in which Redford's has-been rodeo cowboy, condemned to star in breakfast food commercials, takes off for the wide open spaces to stage a protest when he finds that his horse is being kept drugged. Beguilingly sharp at first, but the later stages, with Fonda's toughie reporter tagging along for a story but going all mushy inside, wallow in sentimentality about integrity, ecology and all that jazz. TM

Electric Man, The

see Man-Made Monster

Electric Moon

(Pradip Krishen, 1991, GB) Roshan Seth, Naseeruddin Shah, Leela Naidu, Gerson Da Cunha, Raghubir Yadav, Alice Spivak, Frances Holm, James Fleet, Barbara Lott.
103 min.

A former Maharajah (Da Cunha), known as Bubbles to his friends, spends his advancing years running the Machan holiday lodge in the forests of central India. And while his sister (Naidu) shares his weary resignation at the disruption caused by tourists, their go-getting brother (the wonderful Seth) is keen to package his culture for Western consumption. But the mean-minded bureaucrat who oversees the national park seems determined to hinder the enterprise. Writer Arundhati Roy relies far too heavily on comic stereotype, from the women who lust after Bubbles to the patronising Brit harbouring memories of Empire; while director Krishen fails to control the rambling narrative. As a comedy, the film lacks pace; as a serious look at cultural and social exploitation, it lacks edge. CM

Elektreia (Szerelmem, Elektra)

(Miklós Jancsó, 1975, Hun) Mari Törőcsik, Jozsef Madaras, György Cserhalmi, Mária Bajcsay, Lajos Balázsovits.
74 min.

There are two main levels in Jancsó's enthralling reinvention of the Elektra myth as a fable of permanent revolution. One is the troubling analysis of people's capacity for submission to tyranny; the other is the triumphant celebration of the 'firebird' of revolution, reborn daily with the rising sun. Grounding the political fable in the story of Elektra and Orestes' revenge on their father's murderer, Aegisthus, gives it an implicit psychoanalytical dimension of a kind new in Jancsó's work. The film's balletic and musical elements are even more central than they are in *Red Psalm*: the rhapsody of song and dance replaces conventional dramatic exposition, leaving Jancsó free to explore the dialectical cross-currents of his subject. It's mesmerising. TR

Element of Crime, The (Forbrydelsens Element)

(Lars von Trier, 1984, Den) Michael Elphick, Esmond Knight, Me Me Lai, Jerold Wells, Ahmed El Shenawi, Astrid Henning-Jensen.
104 min.

Von Trier's first feature, and it shows: all the stops are pulled out in this operatic horror-thriller, filmed in English and set in the blitzed-out, rain-lashed hinterlands of Northern Europe, steeped in a sulphurous yellow light. Bogart meets Borges as battered detective Elphick agonises over the mad mathematical computations behind the diabolical 'lotto murders' under the baleful gaze of his mentor (mesmerisingly played by Knight), whose method involves entering the criminal mind. A cinephile's film, stuffed with influences and allusions which, together with the precocious brilliance of every single image, can become numbing at times rather than stunning; but the absolute assurance and ingenuity make this a debut as startling as *Eraserhead* and every bit as spectacular. SJo

Eléna et les Hommes (Paris Does Strange Things)

(Jean Renoir, 1956, Fr/It) Ingrid Bergman, Jean Marais, Mel Ferrer, Pierre Bertin, Jean Richard, Juliette Greco, Magali Noël, Gaston Modot.
95 min.

With Renoir at the height of his later artifice, this completes what was effectively a trilogy begun by *The Golden Coach* and *French Cancan*, exploring both the glorious innocence of the past and the power of theatrical illusion. A prancing ballet of love's surprises, set amid the military manoeuvres and Quatorze Juillet carnivals of France in the 1880s, it is sheer delight as Bergman's entrancing Polish princess (or goddess from Olympus) weaves her spell over destiny to inspire men to fame and fortune until – in a magnificent *coup de théâtre* – she is herself finally trapped and rendered human by love. Fantasy, yes, but hardly escapist in the astonishing pertinence with which it reduces the hawkish military and political ambitions of the day to derisory farce while demonstrating the infallibility with which love goes on making the world go round. TM

Eleni

(Peter Yates, 1985, US) Kate Nelligan, John Malkovich, Linda Hunt, Ronald Pickup, Oliver Cotton, Rosalie Crutchley.
117 min.

After the considerable delights of *Breaking Away* and *The Janitor*, Yates and writer Steve Tesich are clearly floundering with this adaptation of Nicholas Gage's book. A *New York Times* reporter (Malkovich) gets himself transferred to the Athens office on the pretext of investigating atrocities committed during the Greek Civil War of the '40s. There, he traces the events that led to his mother Eleni's execution at the hands of the Commie 'liberators'. Bent on revenge, he tracks down the main culprit...As an obsessive vengeance thriller, this is strangely flat, flawed by a cool performance from the usually reliable Malkovich. Worse, however, are the flashbacks to the peasant village of Lia, an arena of endless betrayal and self-sacrifice among the black-clad womenfolk. Nelligan's eponymous martyr is both a paragon of maternal virtue and a caricature of Hellenic emotionalism, while life in Lia is portrayed in shallow fashion as picturesquely primitive and poverty-stricken. Worst of all is Cotton's villain, an unmotivated sadistic oppressor with all the subtle characteristics of a '40s Hollywood Nazi. GA

Elenya

(Steve Gough, 1992, GB) Pascale Delafouge Jones, Klaus Behrendt, Margaret John, Seiriol Tomes, Sue Jones Davies, Iago Wynn Jones.
82 min.

An all-too-familiar tale of a lonely young Welsh girl who, ostracised during WW2 because her mother was Italian, cares for a wounded German pilot who has crashed in the local woods, keeping him a secret from both the aunt she lives with and the cruelly jingoistic villagers. Rather like a cross between *Whistle Down the Wind* and *Another Time, Another Place*, the film is elegantly shot, nicely acted, worthy in its liberal sentiments, and almost entirely predictable. GA

Elephant Boy

(Robert Flaherty/Zoltan Korda, 1937, GB) Sabu, Walter Hudd, Allan Jeayes, WE Holloway, Bruce Gordon, Wilfrid Hyde-White.
80 min. b/w.

Amiable but dated version of Kipling's tale about a boy who has a way with elephants helping out government hunters in their transportation of a herd through the jungle. Fiction and documentary footage rub shoulders uneasily, but the latter (shot by Flaherty in India) is vividly watchable. GA

Elephant Man, The

(David Lynch, 1980, US) John Hurt, Anthony Hopkins, Anne Bancroft, John Gielgud, Wendy Hiller, Freddie Jones, Michael Elphick, Hannah Gordon.
124 min. b/w.

More accessible than Lynch's enigmatically disturbing *Eraserhead*, *The Elephant Man* has much the same limpidly moving humanism as Truffaut's *L'Enfant Sauvage* in describing how the unfortunate John Merrick, brutalised by a childhood in which he was hideously abused as an inhuman freak, was gradually coaxed into revealing a soul of such delicacy and refinement that he became a lion of Victorian society. But that is only half the story the film tells. The darker side, underpinned by an evocation of the steamy, smoky hell that still underlies a London facelifted by the Industrial Revolution, is crystallised by the wonderful sequence in which Merrick is persuaded by a celebrated actress to read Romeo to her Juliet. A tender, touching scene ('Oh, Mr Merrick, you're not an elephant man at all. No, you're Romeo'), it nevertheless begs the question of what passions, inevitably doomed to frustration, have been roused in this presumably normally-sexed Elephant Man. Appearances are all, and, like the proverbial Victorian piano, he can make the social grade only if his ruder appendages are hidden from sensitive eyes; hence what is effectively, at his time of greatest happiness, his suicide. A marvellous movie, shot in stunning black-and-white by Freddie Francis. TM

Elephant Song

(Go Riju, 1994, Jap) Miyuki Matsuda, Seiichiro Shimotsuki, Susumu Terajima, Yuki Takamura.
60 min.

A small, perfectly formed gem. Coffee-shop waitress Kanako, divorced with a young son, finds herself obliged to honour a rash promise she made to a long-time customer. She always wanted to be buried in the land rather than a cemetery, so that his body would be 'useful' – and now he's dead. Kanako and her boy enlist the help of a friendly florist with a small truck (Terajima, a regular in Takeshi Kitano's films), steal the corpse, and head for the mountains. All three learn a lot on the trip: about death, about friendship, about self-esteem and about keeping promises. Funny and touching, and probably more than a little profound. TR

11 Harrowhouse

(Aram Avakian, 1974, GB) Charles Grodin, Candice Bergen, John Gielgud, Trevor Howard, James Mason, Peter Vaughan, Helen Cherry.
108 min.

Engaging caper movie which manages to breathe some new life into the old formula: American outsider (Grodin) grappling with a bland wall of English bowlers, brollies and phlegm as he becomes involved in an elaborate plan to rob a London diamond house. Some pleasingly fantastical notions (painted cockroaches used to blaze a trail to the target vault), and witty use made of Grodin's offscreen commentary to spoof the usual genre heroics. But the last quarter of the film, already undercut by the fact that the amateur thieves suddenly and inexplicably develop professional skills, degenerates into direly facetious knockabout. TM

Elisa

(Jean Becker, 1994, Fr) Vanessa Paradis, Gérard Depardieu, Clothilde Courau, Sekkou Sall, Florence Thomassin, Michel Bouquet, Philippe Léotard, Catherine Rouvel.
114 min.
This vehicle for the gamine pop-star/actress Vanessa Paradis is by Jean Becker, a director who has done, and should know, better. Here, she prances her hot-panted way as an ex-children's home rebel who leaves her surrogate 'family' (Courau's fellow home-girl Solange, Sall's Arab sidekick Ahmed) to wreak emotional revenge for her mother's suicide on both her suburban grandparents and her 'real' father. The first half is a series of loosely linked scenes of posturing 'rebellion'. Older men figure strongly. She twists a late-middle-aged bookseller around her little finger, seduces an older man in the (mistaken) belief he may have been her mother's lover, and (at last!) tracks down her father, who turns out to be Depardieu. Thrown in, for good measure, is a bemusing scene with Léotard doing a Serge Gainsbourg impression at the piano as 'the Gitanes Smoker'. The final sequence is more diverting. She finds Depardieu brawling and boozing among the matelots in a port-side bistro, and strips for him on the sands before slowly realising that redemption is a game two must play. WH

Elles n'oublient pas
see Love in the Strangest Way

El Mariachi
(Robert Rodriguez, 1992, US) Carlos Gallardo, Consuelo Gomez, Peter Marquardt, Jaime de Hoyos, Reinol Martinez.
80 min.
In terms of plot, there's little remarkable about Rodriguez's debut feature: the tale of a loner mistaken for a killer and hounded by all manner of vengeful furies has blessed countless movies. But it's not the story, or the low budget, which makes this polished foray into mythic conflict so deliciously fresh; it's the sheer joy taken in the medium of film. As the hobo musician of the title (Gallardo) drifts into a small, dusty Mexican township – only to find himself the target of armed gangs in search of a kindred – Rodriguez goes for broke with a breakneck pace, swarms of bullets, cinematic tricks, and a tone as playful as it is knowing of genre conventions. The director's light touch is all his own; and this unpretentious offering delivers in all departments. GA

Elmer Gantry
(Richard Brooks, 1960, US) Burt Lancaster, Jean Simmons, Arthur Kennedy, Shirley Jones, Dean Jagger, Edward Andrews, Hugh Marlowe, Rex Ingram.
145 min.
A 'controversial' look at revivalist religion which, with the passing of the years, is unlikely to raise many eyebrows. That said, it's still an entertaining, intelligent movie, thanks largely to the magnetic presence of Lancaster. As the charming charlatan with the powerfully persuasive tongue who joins up with Sister Simmons' touring grass-roots evangelist circus during the depressed '20s, he has only to flash that silvery smile for us to believe that it's not the good will of the Good Lord he's after, but a rather more carnal acquaintance with the Bible-spouting glamour girl who employs him. Brooks' script and direction never really delve beneath the surface, leaving the relationship between faith, corruption, sex and money largely unexplored (one would have loved to see this filmed by Sirk or Minnelli); but with a host of fine performances, and a strong sense of period and place conveyed by John Alton's lush camerawork, there's still plenty to enjoy. GA

Elmore Leonard's Gold Coast
see Gold Coast

El Norte
(Gregory Nava, 1983, US) Ernesto Gomez Cruz, David Villalpando, Zaide Silvia Gutierrez, Alicia Del Lago, Miguel Gomez Giron.
140 min.
After a military massacre of labourers in Guatemala, which leaves his father's head dangling from a tree, Enrique takes his sister Rosa and heads off for the fabled land of opportunity, El Norte or North America, where every house has running water, every man a job. Unfortunately Mexico, with its border guards and illegal operators who smuggle wetback labour, stands in the way; but after crawling several miles through a sewage pipe full of rats, Los Angeles is within sight. Life there without a permit, however, proves harder than down among the rats. Traditional immigrant films from Hollywood (The Godfather?) end in fame, money and beautiful women for the inheritors of the new found land's promise; but El Norte gives us a vision of the downside of the American dream. The film's concentration on the plight of its young hopefuls, however, is done with much humour and compassion, so that the tragedy of its message is very bracing. CPea

El Salvador: Another Vietnam
(Glenn Silber/Tete Vasconcellos, 1981, US)
50 min.
Next wobbly domino in Central America after Nicaragua was El Salvador, whose progress from banana republic to flashpoint for Cold War paranoia is traced in this documentary. American military support for the Duarte dictatorship and the suppression of popular dissent are recorded in footage from diverse sources; US public protest and consternation in Congress swell; and the Vietnam parallels become ever more apparent. A companion piece (and ominous sequel) to Silber's record of the anti-Nam movement, The War at Home, it's more urgent and cogent than that neat historical package. SJo

El Salvador – Decision to Win (El Salvador – La Decision de Vencer)
('Ceró a la Izquierda' Film Collective, 1981, ElS)
67 min.
This documentary catalogues largely non-violent images of the continuing internecine guerilla war, in which everyday tasks become part of the revolution and politically precocious children cry 'the last one's a fascist' as they race. It's all in accordance with FMLN hero Farabundo Marti's 1932 scheme for 'mass organisation in cities and countryside to establish an effective rearguard'. Sadly, the film is as valid but uninspiring as these words, and does little to revive deflected world interest in El Salvador. FD

El Salvador – Portrait of a Liberated Zone
(Michael Chanan/Peter Chappell, 1981, GB)
61 min.
In January 1981, the Farabundo Marti Liberation Front launched a General Offensive represented as a failure by the US and international press. However, this film, shot after the offensive in the liberated zone east of the capital, presents a highly organised guerilla army with high morale and the overwhelming support of the peasant population. The interview format allows time for peasant fighters to speak not only of the current situation, but of the years of poverty and daily oppression motivating the war. JWi

El Salvador – The People Will Win (El Salvador – El Pueblo Vencerà)
(Diego de la Texera, 1980, El S)
80 min.
In a forest clearing, a freedom fighter carrying a movie camera approaches a peasant woman with a large basket. She produces a rifle from her basket, he gives her the camera to hide. Guerilla war means guerrilla cinema. Both weapons are equally vital in the struggle against a barbarous US-backed junta and a pernicious US-mediated TV account of the two-year-old civil war. This documentary collates material from European TV and clandestine film crews to update the account of the war already lost in Vietnam being re-fought by America's new warlords. MA

Elstree Calling
(Adrian Brunel/Alfred Hitchcock/André Charlot/Jack Hulbert/Paul Murray, 1930, GB) Will Fyffe, Cicely Courtneidge, Jack Hulbert, Tommy Handley, Lily Morris, Gordon Harker, Anna May Wong, Donald Calthrop.
86 min. b/w & col.
Brunel's 'revolutionary plans for camera and editing treatment' for Britain's first musical were thwarted by the Elstree establishment, but the film's display of revue artists and music hall stars of another age has a hypnotic quality hardly affected by its primitive technique. Worth seeing, if only as a belated guide to 'What's On in London, 1930'. In the print under review, the stencil-coloured dancing girls have been restored. Brunel served as supervising director; Hitchcock directed the sketches; Charlot, Hulbert and Murray the ensemble numbers. RMy

El Topo
see Topo, El

Elusive Corporal, The
see Caporal Epinglé, Le

Elusive Pimpernel, The
(Michael Powell/Emeric Pressburger, 1950, GB) David Niven, Margaret Leighton, Jack Hawkins, Cyril Cusack, Robert Coote, Edmond Audran, Charles Victor, Danielle Godet.
109 min.
A reasonably faithful adaptation of Baroness Orczy's tale of the French Revolution and the debonair Englishman who spirited aristos out of reach of the Terror. Somewhat over-elaborated, especially in the lavish court sequences, it contrives to get bogged down in a marshy area somewhere between straightforward boy's adventure and classic P & P territory. Powell's original intention was to make it a musical, but Korda and Goldwyn objected; with relics of this conception surviving in the return to Orczy's adventure yarn, the result was that, as Powell commented, 'it really was a terrible mess'. Not terrible, since it is characteristically vivid and colourful, and sparked by bright flashes of sardonic humour. TM

Elvira Madigan
(Bo Widerberg, 1967, Swe) Pia Degermark, Thommy Berggren, Lennart Malmer, Nina Widerberg, Cleo Jensen.
95 min.
Candidate for the prettiest pic ever award. A lyrical elegy about a circus tightrope walker and a soldier who elope in 19th century Sweden, and eventually commit suicide. Photographed and set to a Mozart piano concerto; you may be enchanted by it if you don't laugh yourself sick.

Elvira, Mistress of the Dark
(James Signorelli, 1988, US) Cassandra Peterson, W Morgan Sheppard, Daniel Greene, Susan Kellerman, Jeff Conway, Edie McClurg.
96 min.
Elvira (Peterson), a camp vamp modelled on Morticia Addams and all other screen vampires, is fired from her job with an LA TV station. A telegram arrives telling her a great aunt has died and she is named in the will, which could mean the $50,000 she needs to appear in Vegas. Hot-pedalling it to Massachusetts to collect her loot in her vampmobile, she upsets puritan locals with her appearance and outgoing charms, gains a house, a recipe book, and a familiar in the shape of a poodle called Algonquin, and falls foul of her great uncle, the warlock (Sheppard). Elvira realises that she, like her mother, has Powers, nearly ends up being burned at the stake, inherits more money, and opens in Vegas. A predictable plot and cheapskate effects deaden Elvira's occasional witty lines, while references to the horror genre make the film busy without going anywhere. Vamp high camp, where Elvira is more mistress of the dork. JGl

Elvis (aka Elvis – The Movie)
(John Carpenter, 1979, US) Kurt Russell, Shelley Winters, Pat Hingle, Season Hubley, Bing Russell.
150 min.
The TV movie trimmed by half-an-hour and with a hyphenated The Movie added when released theatrically in Britain in 1979. A biopic ending in

1969 (and framed by Elvis' triumphant return to Las Vegas in July of that year), it alternates periods of brash psychologising with creditable re-enactments of some legendary performances. Carpenter copes best with the minutiae of a star at tenuous leisure, but wasn't around for the post-production overseen by Dick Clark. The result is inevitably compromised, but compulsive. PT

Elvis! Elvis!
(Kay Pollak, 1977, Swe) Lele Dorazio, Lena-Pia Bernhardsson, Fed Gunnarsson, Elisaveta, Allan Adwall.
100 min.
A smart, slightly lonely 7-year-old finds that growing up in Sweden isn't made any easier when mother has named you after Swivel-Hips. Occasionally diverting, mostly over-familiar rites-of-passage story, from a novel by Maria Gripe. TJ

Elvis on Tour
(Pierre Adidge/Robert Abel, 1972, US) Elvis Presley, Vernon Presley, Jackie Kahane, James Burton, Charlie Hodge.
93 min.
An unrevealing portrait of the Presley army on tour – Colonel Parker forever hovers around, just offscreen as it were – Elvis on Tour is nonetheless eminently watchable, if only for the sight and sound of James Burton's incredible guitar-playing and the re-run of an early Presley performance on the Ed Sullivan show. The'history of Elvis' montage at the end – the film is basically directionless and veers from subject to subject – was 'supervised' by Martin Scorsese. PH

Elvis – That's the Way It Is
(Denis Sanders, 1970, US) Elvis Presley.
108 min.
A documentary chronicling Presley's second Las Vegas season following his welcome return to the stage in 1969. Its concern with underlining the obsessive zeal of his followers leads to too many irritating interviews; but the off-stage material is curiously revealing, and the performance itself enjoyable if only occasionally exciting. AC

Emanuelle and the Last Cannibals (Emanuelle e gli Ultimi Cannibali)
(Joe D'Amato, ie. Aristide Massaccesi, 1977, It) Laura Gemser, Gabriele Tinti, Susan Scott, Donald O'Brien.
87 min.
Deeply involved in her journalist career, and glowing with the earnest nobility of a sixth form prefect, black Emanuelle (descended from the French softcore heroine but with only one 'm' to her name) finds little time for sex in this hilariously gruesome tale set in the Amazon jungles.

Emerald Forest, The
(John Boorman, 1985, GB) Powers Boothe, Meg Foster, William Rodriquez, Yara Vaneau, Estee Chandler, Charley Boorman.
114 min.
An American engineer working on a dam project in Brazil loses his seven-year-old son in the rain forest to an isolated Indian tribe, and spends the next ten years in a tireless search. The film's ultimate message – that we continue to destroy this hot house at our peril – is the uncomfortable truth to which he returns in a final caption. What lies between is a half-fantasised view of Indian tribal culture, with its peculiar codes of existence and bewildering intimacy with nature. For despite some flamboyant violence, this is less the despairing Boorman of Deliverance than the unabashed visionary who twisted The Exorcist into its over-ambitious sequel. The forest scenery is ravishingly photographed, and the sheer visual sweep more than compensates for some occasionally shaky acting. Full marks, too, for giving us sub-titles for the Indian language; as an ethnographic adventure, there is more to these decorated natives than Mad Max Factor. A rare delight. DT

Emergency
(Francis Searle, 1962, GB) Glyn Houston, Zena Walker, Dermot Walsh, Colin Tapley, Anthony Dawes.
63 min. b/w.
Dim little drama about an injured child awaiting a blood transfusion (rare blood group, naturally)

and the police round-up of donors – including, would you believe it, a convicted killer and an atomic scientist in jeopardy – who save her life. Meanwhile, of course, the anguished parents patch up their marital problems. Any resemblance to Emergency Call of 1952 is hardly coincidental, since both films were produced by British B movie specialists Butcher's. TM

Emergency Call
(Lewis Gilbert, 1952, GB) Jack Warner, Anthony Steel, Joy Shelton, Sidney James, Earl Cameron, Freddie Mills, Sydney Tafler.
90 min. b/w.
Three pints from a rare blood group are desperately sought to save a child's life. Slick enough as a thriller, but the script – with the potential donors a black with a chip on his shoulder, a boxer about to throw a fight, and a murderer on the run – is pure novelettish crap. TM

Emigrants, The (Utvandrarna)
(Jan Troell, 1970, Swe) Max von Sydow, Liv Ullmann, Eddie Axberg, Svenolof Bern, Aina Alfredsson, Allan Edwall.
191 min.
First half of a two-film adaptation of a quartet of novels by Vilhelm Moberg: an austere, long, and picturesque recreation of the hardships which led Swedish farmers in the 1850s to leave home and travel in search of a better life in America. It's very slow, subtly acted, and if you can last the course, quite moving. Troell not only directed, but also photographed, co-scripted and edited the film, which becomes something of an assertion of human courage, determination and dignity. The second part, The New Land, deals with the pioneers' arrival and settlement in America. GA

Emily – Third Party Speculation
(Malcolm Le Grice, 1979, GB) Malcolm Le Grice, Judith Le Grice, Margaret Murray.
60 min.
Le Grice's Blackbird Descending the previous year signalled such witty potential for exploring narrative and perpetual time and space that this retread disappoints by its ponderousness and unrelieved seriousness. Constructed around a repeating 'neutral' domestic scene, the film examines its material elements in relation to point-of-view, first in the conventional sense of the film-maker's objectivity and subjectivity, then by an assumption of the spectator's perception. But the visual/verbal punning is so strained, and the focused narrative fragment so barren, that the opening image, of the film-maker-cum-spectator sitting blankly in front of a screen, transfers all too easily to the 'real' – and bored – viewer. PT

Emitaï
(Ousmane Sembene, 1972, Sen) Robert Fontaine, Michel Remaudeau, Pierre Blanchard, Ibou Camara.
103 min.
A strong statement from Sembene about the forms of oppression practised by the French in West Africa. Set during World War II, it deals with the staggered annihilation of a small tribe that attempts to resist the exploitation of its labour and resources. The initial part of the film presents the theft of their labour, conscripted into the White Man's War. The French quash resistance by separating the village into groups that can be held hostage against the others. Allowing the separation, the village elders bemuse themselves with their unhelpful gods, losing the last chance to organise themselves into militant resistance. Sembene makes his point with a humour all the more powerful for the anger it induces at the genocidal antics of the whites. A conventional film, but it succeeds in its aim, clarifying the logic of the colonial struggle through a specific example. JDuC

Emma
(Douglas McGrath, 1996, GB/US) Gwyneth Paltrow, Toni Collette, Juliet Stevenson, Alan Cumming, Ewan McGregor, Jeremy Northam, Sophie Thompson, Greta Scacchi, Polly Walker, Phyllida Law.
120 min.
Paltrow looks the part as pretty, wealthy, would-be social engineer Emma Woodhouse, doesn't alienate our sympathies in her patronising attempt to find a match for orphan Harriet Smith (Collette),

and pulls off an affecting arc into chastened self-knowledge when circumstances turn her machinations back on herself. Throughout, the acting's the thing, with Cumming's oleaginous cleric vying to outdo Stevenson's screeching harridan, McGregor's modern charmer, and the smooth voice of reason from the agreeably understated Northam – though they all give way to Sophie Thompson as bespectacled Miss Bates. Indeed if the performers catch the eye, it's largely because McGrath (an American screenwriter here directing his first feature) has given them substantial chunks of Austen's dialogue and more or less left them to it, since the background's generic period-England adds little but the usual breeches, bonnets and gauzy soft-focus. Sadly, when the going gets tougher the film doesn't have many answers, and the odd unsettling surge of over-emphasis betrays an eye on the American market. TJ

Emmanuelle
(Just Jaeckin, 1974, Fr) Sylvia Kristel, Marika Green, Daniel Sarky, Alain Cuny, Jeanne Colletin.
94 min.
Very glossy, very French voyage into sexual discovery that mingles cliché and elegant posturing with an attempt to broaden the horizons of the sex film. As such, it looks like a softcore version of The Story of O commissioned by Vogue magazine. CPe

Emmanuelle 2 (Emmanuelle II, L'Anti-Vierge)
(Francis Giacobetti, 1975, Fr) Sylvia Kristel, Umberto Orsini, Catherine Rivet, Frédéric Lagache.
92 min.
Unashamedly endorses all the clichés of Emmanuelle, particularly the lure of the Orient. The camera moves smugly through spacious colonial rooms, occasionally padding things out with ethnic travelogue footage. Plotting is marginal and characterisation zero, lacking even its predecessor's pretence of a voyage into sexual discovery. CPe

Emmanuelle in Tokyo (Tokyo Emmanuelle Fujin)
(Akira Kato, 1975, Jap) Kumi Taguchi, Mitsuyasu Maeno, Katsunori Hirose, Midori Otani.
91 min.
The first example of the genre known as Nikkatsu roman-porno (romantic porn) to have reached British distribution. Since Japanese censorship is much stricter in sexual matters than our own, it didn't get far here. It is, of course, both sexist and idiotic, but genre specialists might find comparisons between the underlying attitudes and those of European sexploitation instructive. TR

Emma's War
(Clytie Jessop, 1985, Aust) Lee Remick, Miranda Otto, Mark Lee, Terence Donovan, Donal Gibson, Bridey Lee.
96 min.
Yet another Australian period drama in which an independent woman suffers from Life and a surfeit of syrupy sentiment. With husband away at the war, Anne Grange (Remick) has taken to drinking and dancing with cushions. Meanwhile, daughters Emma and Laurel thrive under the eccentric tuition of stout Miss Arnott, until their panicky mother packs them off to the country to avoid the threatened Japanese bombing raids. Striking a distinctly autobiographical note, and prey therefore to the unwieldy nature of personal recollection, Jessop's film has a disjointed, episodic quality. It also contorts itself to include the pacifist sentiments and puberty blues of 14-year-old Emma's friendship with a young, poetry-reading conscientious objector. As the dipso, Remick reprises her most famous role, but in more ways than one these are not The Days of Wine and Roses. NF

Emmène-moi (Last Chance Hotel)
(Michel Spinosa, 1994, Fr) Karin Viard, Antoine Basler.
86 min.
Authentically painful study (with a Peter Hammill string score) of an ill-matched couple's forlorn attempts to revive their relationship after a two-year break. Sophie is headstrong, domi-

nant, irresponsible, and incapable of finishing what she starts; Vincent, her deserted hotel-receptionist lover, is resentful, cautious and a mite dull. Though the film sometimes seems a little too self-consciously sordid, it's generally a fine effort, beautifully acted, shot through with real sexual passion and torment, and astute on the psychology of self-destruction. GA

Emmerdeur, L' (A Pain in the A**)

(Edouard Molinaro, 1973, Fr/It) Lino Ventura, Jacques Brel, Caroline Cellier, Nino Castelnuovo, Jean-Pierre Darras.
84 min.
Good crazy comedies are few and far between these days. This one (disappointingly remade by Billy Wilder as *Buddy Buddy* in 1981) takes off nicely after about twenty minutes thanks to the solid presence of Ventura, an unwordy script, and a deceptively deadpan beginning. Ventura, a hired killer with one shooting already under his belt, takes a hotel room from which he plans a political assassination. Meanwhile, in the next room, the pain in the arse of the title attempts to hang himself. Ventura's calm exterior slowly shatters as the incompetent idiot slowly latches onto him; he ends up driving pregnant women to hospital, falling off ledges, getting drugged in a case of mistaken identity, looking for a garage distributing free plastic saints, and finally sharing a cell with the amiable idiot, the possessor of a mammoth persecution complex. Ventura's slow disintegration is a delight to watch, and Brel manages well at being extremely irritating. CPe

Emperor of the North Pole, The (aka Emperor of the North)

(Robert Aldrich, 1973, US) Lee Marvin, Ernest Borgnine, Keith Carradine, Charles Tyner, Simon Oakland, Matt Clark, Elisha Cook.
119 min.
Set during the Depression, Aldrich's film starts out from a lovely gamesmanship premise derived from the legendary enmity between railwaymen and the hoboes who rode the rails. It's a duel to the death, developed with dark humour and nail-biting excitement, between Borgnine's sadistic guard – up to all the tricks and armed with a fearsome array of sledgehammers and steel chains – and Marvin's laconically contrary hobo, who cannot resist the challenge of making a lie of Borgnine's boast that no one has ever jumped his train and lived to tell the tale. A pity, perhaps, that the script pursues a vague political allegory instead of exploring its characters more deeply, but the vivid background detail (including a Baptist river-dunking which is the occasion for a cheeky theft of clothes) is brilliantly realised. TM

Emperor's Naked Army Marches On, The (Yuki Yukite Shingun)

(Kazuo Hara, 1987, Jap) Kenzo Okuzaki, Shizumi Okuzaki, Kichitaro Yamada, Iseko Shimamoto.
123 min.
A documentary portrait of Kenzo Okuzaki, a 62-year-old WWII veteran who acquired a prison record (for killing a man and for firing *pachinko* balls at the Emperor) in the course of his fanatical campaign to lay the blame for Japan's conduct of the war on the Emperor. Here the self-proclaimed messenger of God seeks to uncover what truly happened in New Guinea in 1945, 23 days after the war ended, when two Japanese soldiers were killed by their colleagues in *very* mysterious circumstances. The outcome of his investigations is gruesomely weird (cannibalism figures heavily), but stranger still is his style of interrogation, a volatile mix of apologetic politeness, deceit (his wife and anarchist friend pose as victims' relatives), and sudden violence, so relentless that one of his many ageing interviewees, fresh from hospital, ends up in an ambulance. Kazuo Hara's fly-on-the-wall documentary fascinates both for its bizarre protagonist, and for its brutally frank portrait of a society constrained by notions of shame rather than guilt. Jigsaw-like in construction, alleviated by mad wit, the film is unlike any other: rough, raw and sometimes surprisingly moving, it's absolutely compelling. GA

Emperor's Shadow, The (Qin Song)

(Zhou Xiaowen, 1996, HK/China) Jiang Wen, Ge You, Xu Qing.
127 min.
Although designed and staged on a fairly spectacular scale, this Qin Dynasty epic is at heart a chamber tragedy centred on the love-hate bond between Ying Zheng, China's first emperor, and his one-time blood brother, a musician named Gao Jianli. The unapologetic modernity of Jiang Wen's great performance as the emperor suggests that Zhou Xiaowen is less concerned with history than with present-day relations between the artist and the Chinese state. But the film feels more like an aesthetic adventure than a political commentary, and Zhou (director of *Ermo*) makes it all the more extraordinary by stressing the homo-erotic feelings which run just beneath the surface of the central relationship. TR

Emperor Waltz, The

(Billy Wilder, 1947, US) Bing Crosby, Joan Fontaine, Richard Haydn, Roland Culver, Lucile Watson, Sig Ruman.
106 min.
Generally reckoned to be Wilder's worst movie, as thick a slice of *sachertorte* as ever served – even Lubitsch would have thrown up. One of Wilder's favourite themes – the confrontation between New and Old World values – is given an early airing with Crosby's phonograph salesman washing up in a mythical mittel-European kingdom, where he sets about usurping Strauss with a clambake. Fontaine is a countess and there's a dodgy romance as well. There are acres of wasted space, yet occasionally this movie bursts into life, and the whole thing is tinged with a postwar nostalgia for a Europe that has been snuffed out. Oh yes, Wilder prefigured Antonioni by having the hills dyed a nicer shade of green. ATu

Empire des Sens, L'

see Ai No Corrida

Empire of Passion (L'Empire de la Passion/Ai no Borei)

(Nagisa Oshima, 1978, Fr/Jap) Kazuko Yoshiyuki, Tatsuya Fuji, Takahiro Tamura, Takuzo Kawatani, Akiko Koyama.
105 min.
At once a companion film to *Ai no Corrida* and a compulsive reaction against it: the dominant themes here are guilt, repression and censorship. It's set in rural Japan, around the turn of the century, and it centres on a *crime passionel*: the murder of an elderly rickshaw-man by his wife and her lover, a soldier recently discharged from the army. But the couple are literally haunted by their crime (in the person of the old man's ghost), cannot separate themselves from their own society, and finally pay for their crime at the hands of a grotesquely cruel policeman. It now seems obvious that the film expressed Oshima's reaction to the worldwide 'scandal' generated by *Ai no Corrida*, but it's worth remembering that while he made it, Oshima was undergoing a prosecution in Japan for publishing the script of his previous film. His hatred of the 'authority' figure here reaches heights unseen since *Death by Hanging*. TR

Empire of the Ants

(Bert I Gordon, 1977, US) Joan Collins, Robert Lansing, John David Carson, Albert Salmi, Jacqueline Scott.
89 min.
'Have you ever taken a close look at what the ant is all about?' a voice harangues us in the opening minutes of this flat-footed piece of stupidity, supposedly derived (like the same director's *Food of the Gods*) from HG Wells. Thanks to Gordon's special effects, a close look reveals that the ant is really an incredibly hairy octopus and about as frightening as a muppet. The plot hardly grabs one either: the giant ants (fed on spilled atomic waste) attack a motley bunch of dithering idiots being taken round an isolated spot of Florida swamp by fraudulent land developer Joan Collins. The sleekly mature Joan acts as though she's always about to say 'Look at me, I'm still sexy!' What she does say, however, is things like 'Oh my God', as does everybody else. It's all drastically boring. GB

Empire of the Sun

(Steven Spielberg, 1987, US) Christian Bale, John Malkovich, Miranda Richardson, Nigel Havers, Joe Pantoliano, Leslie Phillips, Masato Ibu, Emily Richard, Rupert Frazer.
152 min.
JG Ballard's autobiographical novel, about his experiences in the WWII Japanese concentration camps in China, is a mild version of the events he witnessed; Spielberg's is milder still. young Jim Graham (Bale) is Ballard, an obnoxious expat brat separated from his parents as the war overwhelms Shanghai. His world of balsa-wood models and servants is blown apart and replaced by prison camp brutality. Stripped of its sci-fi trappings, Ballard's text is about what shits we may become in order to survive. Spielberg includes a strand of populist heroism, yet even this fails to dent the awful message. And the budget makes itself seen, as does Bale's superlative Jim. JG

Empire Records

(Allan Moyle, 1995, US) Anthony LaPaglia, Liv Tyler, Rory Cochrane, Maxwell Caulfield, Robin Tunney, Debi Mazar.
89 min.
Twenty-four incident-packed hours in a groovy New Jersey record store. This Hollywood attempt to plug into 'Generation X' mixes together all those things twenty-somethings are meant to care about: top sounds past and present, the uncertainties of the future, the problems of self-esteem, and how to get off with other twenty-somethings. Pile in lots of bright young talent plus a jukebox soundtrack, and you'd think hipster status was guaranteed, were it not for that Carol Heikkinen's screenplay resolves all its dilemmas with cornball tidiness. Remember those old movies where the kids put the show on in a barn and save the day? Well, the Oldest Living Plot Device shakes an elderly hoof in the big finale here, too, scuppering the film's nose-diving cred for good. Still, even if it's not as cool as the execs would like to hope, Moyle's movie is not unenjoyable in a synthetic kind of way. Tyler confirms her star status as the ill-advised lass who decides to lose her virginity with has-been teen idol Caulfield (admirably self-satirising), while the rest of the junior cast hold their own. Overall, fatally ersatz but good natured at heart. TJ

Empire State

(Ron Peck, 1987, GB) Ray McAnally, Cathryn Harrison, Martin Landau, Emily Bolton, Lee Drysdale, Elizabeth Hickling, Ian Sears.
102 min.
Outside the futuristic Empire State nightclub in London's docklands, yuppie housing developments and fly-by-night warehousing projects are rapidly replacing the old working class communities. Wide boy Paul (Sears) tries to set up a deal with American businessman Chuck (Landau), but his plans to cut former boss Frank (McAnally) out of the game seriously underestimate the strength of old East End money. The fates of a chorus of minor characters criss-cross one another before finally converging on the club, where the rivalry between Paul and Frank explodes into primitive bare knuckles pugilism. For all its stylised images and electro muzak, the film's two-dimensional characters are simply static figures in what wants to be a hard-edged Hollywood-style thriller, but is in fact a cold hi-tech design. A brave but flawed attempt to escape the straitjacket of British realism. NF

Empire Strikes Back, The

(Irvin Kershner, 1980, US) Mark Hamill, Harrison Ford, Carrie Fisher, Billy Dee Williams, Anthony Daniels, David Prowse, Kenny Baker, Alec Guinness.
124 min.
Familiarity breeds content; from the corny 'droids to the tired and emotional Wookie, the events, recognitions and revelations of the sequel have the rhythm of *Soap* in 70 mm – and we love it, it makes us better people. As it appears that the plot is now infinitely extendable, a li'l oedipal confidence works in; there's more passion, more pain and more riddles in this family plot. With a goddam muppet as its spiritual guide, '*Star Wars*: Episode V' is an impressive indulgence in Hollywood style for the TV generation. RP

Empire Strikes Back: Special Edition, The

(Irvin Kershner, 1980, US) Mark Hamill, Harrison Ford, Carrie Fisher.
124 min.

This second instalment of the 'Star Wars' series, directed not by George Lucas but by his former USC tutor Irvin Kershner, is the tautest – an extended ricochet from one incendiary set-piece battle to another which still finds time to attend to plot, pace and character. After the destruction of the Rebel base on icy Hoth, Han (Ford), Leia (Fisher), et al, escape in the Millennium Falcon, eventually finding dubious sanctuary in the city of Bespin. Meanwhile, Luke (Hamill) heads for the Degobah system to be schooled in Jedi lore by Yoda. These two plot strands dovetail in the final quarter, when Luke rushes to Bespin to save his friends and confront Darth Vader, ignoring Yoda's pleas that he finish his training and risking his own helpless conversion to the Dark Side. The 'special edition' restoration work is impressive, though there's barely a minute's worth of extra footage this time round. In fact, the film's reliance on stop-frame animation means that, visually at least, it hasn't dated quite as well as *Star Wars*. The dialogue, too, will have you chewing your fist in places. Fisher and Hamill are clearly relishing the challenge to Be More Feisty and the robot comedy, driven by an outrageously camp Threepio, is almost funny. JO'C

Empress Yang Kwei Fei, The (Yokihi)

(Kenji Mizoguchi, 1955, Jap/HK) Machiko Kyo, Masayuki Mori, So Yamamura, Eitaro Shindo, Sakae Ozawa.
98 min.

Mizoguchi's first film in colour is set in 8th century China during the latter years of the T'ang dynasty, and contrasts the 'pure' love story of Emperor Huan Tsung and his mistress Yang Kwei Fei with the corruption and opportunism rife in the imperial court. Those who find Mizoguchi's later films guilty of arid formulism will find fuel for their arguments here. The director's lifelong preoccupation with the position of women in feudal society is undoubtedly diminished by the idealised treatment of his heroine, while the depiction of members of her family seeking preferment and promotion within the court often borders on caricature. On the other hand, there are sequences of stunning beauty, notably Yang Kwei Fei's execution scene (accompanied by some terrific music). RM

Empty Table, The (Shokutaku no Nai ie)

(Masaki Kobayashi, 1985, Jap) Tatsuya Nakadai, Mayumi Ogawa, Kie Nakai, Kiichi Nakai, Takeyuki Takemoto.
142 min.

When a student is arrested for his part in a terrorist siege, his apparently cool, callous father resists the customary Japanese social pressures to resign from his job (or even kill himself), and instead stands firm in his refusal to take the blame for his son's criminal acts. Result: virtually total breakdown of the family's stability. Glossily stylish, with impeccably composed visuals, the film focuses throughout on the dilemmas facing the unbending, outwardly unfeeling father (played with stoic taciturnity by Nakadai), charting the conflict between individual needs and emotions and the demands of society at large. Overlong and overschematic, it would benefit from a more total immersion in the hysterical conventions of melodrama to bring it to life, but admirers of vaguely politicised psychodramas may find much to enjoy. GA

Enamorada (Woman in Love)

(Emilio Fernández, 1946, Mex) María Félix, Pedro Armendáriz, Fernando Fernández, José Morcillo.
99 min. b/w.

A deliriously romantic reworking of *The Taming of the Shrew*, set during the Juarez Revolution. When general Armendáriz seizes the town of Cholula, he immediately falls for the beautiful but volatile Félix, daughter of a wealthy landowner; unsympathetic to the revolutionary cause, she treats his attempts at courtship with fiery contempt. Acted and directed with wit, verve and passion, the film also benefits from Gabriel Figueroa's stunning b/w photography; see it, too, for the overwhelmingly lovely scene when Armendáriz finally begins to win over the stubborn Félix with a heart-rending serenade. GA

En avoir (ou pas)

(Laetitia Masson, 1995, Fr) Sandrine Kiderlain, Arnaud Giovaninetti.
90 min.

Despite a certain predictability in the ending, Masson's film is an unusually bleak 'meeting of misfits' drama, in which Kiderlain's sacked Boulogne fish-packer – she dreams, vaguely, of becoming a singer – moves virtually at random to Lyon, and meets Giovaninetti's terminally depressive labourer, just dumped by his girl because he's scared of women. Determinedly downbeat in its raw realism (the soundtrack includes Marianne Faithfull and Nick Drake!), and packed with strong performances from various young stalwarts of the New French Cinema, it's well observed, intelligently written, and finally quite moving. GA

En Cas de Malheur (La Ragazza del Peccato/ Love Is My Profession)

(Claude Autant-Lara, 1958, Fr/It) Brigitte Bardot, Jean Gabin, Edwige Feuillère, Franco Interlenghi, Nicole Berger.
122 min. b/w

Considering she was operating at a time of such constraint, when 24 frames of exposed nipple constituted at least a month's ration of cinematic erotica, it's surprising how potent a sexual presence the vintage Bardot remains 40 years on. She's offset here by Gabin at his most world-weary and Autant-Lara at his most sardonic: when the director finally permits the audience to ogle BB's bare breasts, they're soaked in blood, after she's been butchered by a deranged ex-lover (a shot widely censored at the time). Essentially this is bourgeois nightmare – successful lawyer seduced away from marriage and career by proletarian pussy – but presented non-judgementally and with icy control. BBa

Enchanted April

(Mike Newell, 1991, GB) Josie Lawrence, Miranda Richardson, Alfred Molina, Jim Broadbent, Michael Kitchen, Joan Plowright, Polly Walker.
99 min.

London, 1922. Lottie (Lawrence) is fed up: her fuddy-duddy husband (Molina) is the sort who says cut flowers are 'extravagant', and the weather is miserable. She decides to rent a small Italian castle for a month-long holiday, minus spouse. Joining her plans for temporary escape are a writer's disgruntled wife (Richardson), a snobbish widow (Plowright), and an aloof aristocrat (Walker). Period is tastefully evoked, and loving care has gone into the visuals; but crucially, a weak script (based on Elizabeth von Arnim's novel) lets down any spirit of adventure. Personalities clash but are cheerfully reconciled, and marital tensions are swiftly resolved. Newell does manage to draw out fine performances (although Lawrence struggles with an impossibly simplistic role), but this is a sentimental journey you'd be wise to avoid. CM

Enchanted Cottage, The

(John Cromwell, 1945, US) Dorothy McGuire, Robert Young, Herbert Marshall, Mildred Natwick, Spring Byington, Hillary Brooke.
91 min. b/w

Icky romantic whimsy adapted from Pinero's play about a honeymoon cottage which waves the magic wand of love to transform a pair of uglies into an ideal couple. Full of sanctimonious guff, and not made any more palatable by the glamour convention whereby Young's war wounds give him Frankensteinian facial scars (nobody thinks of plastic surgery) while McGuire's blemishes just need a touch of the hairdos to set right. Ted Tetzlaff's clean camerawork comes out of it with distinction, but Herbert Marshall (as the blind pianist who composes a tone poem to the lovers) wins the yuk of the year award. TM

Enchantment, The (Yuwakusha)

(Shunichi Nagasaki, 1989, Jap) Kumiko Akiyoshi, Masao Kusakari, Kiwako Harada, Takeshi Naito, Tsutomu Isobe.
109 min.

Nagasaki's assured teaser produces several surprises. As it begins, with Tokyo shrink Dr Sotomura being visited by Miyako, a beautiful young woman claiming to suffer beatings from her flatmate (who may be a lesbian lover), the film looks set to be an intelligent if faintly formulary psychodrama on the theme of sexual jealousy. Within minutes, however, another patient is discovered dead with a knife in his back, and as the good doctor becomes increasingly besotted with Miyako, the film shifts into moody *femme fatale* territory. So far, so intriguing, but by the film's end Nagasaki has repeatedly pulled the rug from under our feet, so that our assumptions, like Sotomura's, are shaken by a truly subversive conclusion. This seductively cunning movie, whose preposterous twists contain a provocative questioning of traditional ideas on sex, sanity and masculine authority, should appeal not only to feminists of every hue, but to anyone looking for crisp visuals, subtle suspense and inventive direction. GA

Encino Man (aka California Man)

(Les Mayfield, 1992, US) Sean Astin, Brendan Fraser, Pauly Shore, Megan Ward, Robin Tunney, Mariette Hartley, Richard Masur, Michael DeLuise.
88 min.

This depressingly witless teen comedy continues the revenge-of-the-nerds theme popularised by Bill, Ted, Wayne and Garth. 'It's not enough to be a geek from Encino,' Harold (Astin) tells spaced-out friend Dave (Shore), 'I'm gonna be Prom King'. The message of these films is not just that the last shall be first, but that it's cool to be a dweeb. What's striking is that the underdogs are not transformed by their experiences – the ugly ducklings don't become swans – but their values are completely vindicated, and the world (Wayne's world) remade in their image. Here, Dave and Harold dig up a frozen caveman in their back yard, defrost and groom him, and in no time 'Link' (Fraser) is all but indistinguishable from the other high school neanderthals. That Link's make-over proves so painless – so devoid of comic or dramatic situations – suggests that this high-concept movie forgot what it was about. TCh

En Compagnie d'Antonin Artaud (My Life and Times with Antonin Artaud)

(Gérard Mordillat, 1993, Fr) Sami Frey, Marc Barbé, Julie Jézéquel, Valérie Jeannet.
90 min. b/w.

A fascinating re-creation of post-war bohemian Paris and the relationship between the dying and paranoid theatre polemicist Antonin Artaud and the young poet Jacques Prevel who kept the cultural titan in drugs. Superb performances by Frey as Artaud, whose Theatre of Cruelty was a great influence on Brook, Berkoff, Marowitz and Grotowski, and by Barbé as Prevel looking like a young Chet Baker. SGr

Encore

(Harold French/Pat Jackson/Anthony Pélissier, 1951, GB) Nigel Patrick, Roland Culver, Alison Leggatt; Kay Walsh, Noel Purcell, John Laurie; Glynis Johns, Terence Morgan, Ferdy Mayne.
86 min. b/w.

After the success of *Dead of Night* in the mid-1940s, portmanteau pictures enjoyed a vogue in British cinema. This is the third film adapted from Somerset Maugham's short stories. It starts brightly enough with 'The Ant and the Grasshopper' (script, TEB Clarke). A typically English variation on *The Rake's Progress*, this follows an upper-class ne'er-do-well who sponges mercilessly off his brother. 'Winter Cruise' (Arthur Macrae), set on an ocean liner, and 'Gigolo and Gigolette' (Eric Ambler), about a circus performer who loses her nerve, are less convincing, if only because their endings seem so contrived. Maugham introduces the stories himself. GM

Encounter at Raven's Gate

(Rolf de Heer, 1988, Aust) Steven Vidler, Celine Griffin, Ritchie Singer, Max Cullen, Vince Gil, Saturday Rosenberg, Terry Camilleri.
89 min.

Arriving to investigate the smouldering wreck-age of an outback property, Special Branch agent Hemmings (Camilleri) seems disconcerted to find local police sergeant Taylor (Cullen) already at the scene. Taylor senses that he has stumbled on Something Big, and as the two men piece togeth-er the events leading up to the disappearance of the house's three inhabitants, he begins to sus-pect a government cover-up. In flasback, we observe the fraught triangular relationship between paroled car-thief Eddie (Vidler), his responsible older brother Richard (Singer), and Richard's frustrated artist wife Rachel (Griffin). Meanwhile, cars grind to a halt, wells dry up, dead sheep and birds litter the sun-parched earth. De Heer's disconcerting images suggest not only an intangible link between the seething emotions and the unexplained physical events, but also an invisible, all-seeing alien presence. The original screenplay apparently explained the strange occurences; the film itself is more enigmatic and open-ended, using an elliptical narrative and bizarre camera angles to reinforce the prevailing mood of mystery and unease. NF

End, The

(Burt Reynolds, 1978, US) Burt Reynolds, Dom DeLuise, Sally Field, Strother Martin, David Steinberg, Joanne Woodward, Norman Fell, Myrna Loy, Kristy McNichol, Pat O'Brien, Carl Reiner.
100 min.
Reynolds' second film as director, casting him-self as a man learning that he is terminally ill, is an engaging attempt to take the piss out of the crocodile tears that have been gleefully exploited since Love Story. The early sequences are by far the best, teasing a wry black comedy out of the revelations of inadequacy and failure of communication as the condemned man sets out to seek comfort and take leave of his loved ones. Strain shows later on as his frenzied attempts to achieve suicide, both aided and hin-dered by a genial lunatic (the direly mugging DeLuise), veer into Mel Brooks slapstick. Pretty funny, all the same. TM

Endangered Species

(Alan Rudolph, 1982, US) Robert Urich, JoBeth Williams, Paul Dooley, Hoyt Axton, Peter Coyote, Marin Kanter, Dan Hedaya, Harry Carey Jr.
92 min.
A strange, stylish, bizarrely eclectic conspiracy thriller. Out in the rural American Midwest, cows are found slaughtered and mutilated, the crimes having been perpetrated by UFO-like flashing lights in the sky. Purportedly based on facts connected with regular illegal tests con-ducted into the effectiveness of germ and chem-ical warfare, Rudolph's film fascinates partly by its oddball characterisation – the investigators include a juvenile delinquent, her drunken detec-tive father, and a raunchy woman sheriff – and partly by the enigmatic, almost impressionistic structure of the narrative, which throws up weird, thought-provoking connections and cor-respondences. For all its occasional pretensions, a film that offers many rewards, thanks largely to its firm alliance with the sci-fi genre: a strat-egy that entails rather more intelligence and emotional power than a superficially similar exercise like Silkwood. GA

End as a Man

see Strange One, The

Endless Love

(Franco Zeffirelli, 1981, US) Brooke Shields, Martin Hewitt, Shirley Knight, Don Murray, Richard Kiley, Beatrice Straight.
115 min.
Almost fifteen years after Romeo and Juliet, Zeffirelli delivered yet another film about star-crossed young lovers. Endless? It's interminable – a tale of consummated puppy love between two high school kids, at first sanctioned by parents and then frustrated by them, whereupon the male partner burns down their house, is com-mitted for psychiatric care, and from then on pur-sues his obsession of sexual reunion. Pitched at an audience of teenagers, it's of no interest to anyone else, except for a peculiar undertow of incest, inter-generational sex and giant death wishes. As excruciating as the Diana Ross/Lionel Richie title tune. RM

Endless Night

(Sidney Gilliat, 1971, GB) Hayley Mills, Hywel Bennett, Britt Ekland, George Sanders, Per Oscarsson, Peter Bowles, Lois Maxwell.
99 min.
Based on the novel by Agatha Christie. An Olde English mystery developing (eventually) from Bennett's marriage to the sixth richest girl in the world (Mills). An example of the sort of thing Christie was writing in her later years: moody psychological studies very different from, and not so much fun as, her early thrillers.

End of an Era (Telos Epochis)

(Antonis Kokkinos, 1994, Greece) Demosthenes Papadopoulos, Costas Kazanas, Giorgis Pyrpassopoulos, Peggy Trikalioti, Despina Kourti.
98 min.
This rites-of-passage movie set in late-'60s Athens (the musical references are somewhat misdated) is not exactly gripping, but gets by on fair performances, as Christos, shy, intelligent son of a Patras workman determined that his boy study medicine, begins to make friends at his new school. Not much happens – they discuss music, date girls, stage Rhinoceros, and the father of one of them is arrested (this is the era of the Colonels) – but at least it avoids the usual macho adoles-cent pitfalls. GA

End of August, The

(Bob Graham, 1981, US) Sally Sharp, Lilia Skala, David Marshall Grant, Kathleen Widdoes, Paul Roebling, Paul Shenar.
107 min.
Another earnest attempt by film-makers gripped by that proselytising zeal which affects those who read good novels (in this case, Kate Chopin's The Awakening). After some years of married restraint in turn-of-the-century New Orleans Creole society, Edna (Sharp) abandons propriety and exchanges her life of comfort, dependence and 2.4 kids for the Bohemian Way. More vital-ly (and shockingly), she rejects the duty of the conjugal bed in order to find sensual and sexual fulfilment between the sheets with the charis-matic Arobin (Shenar), and on a more cerebral plane with the callow Robert (Grant). Regrettably, the film finds no satisfactory substitute for reflec-tive insights into the female mind, condemning the well-acted characters to a two-dimensional existence and inadvertently relegating Chopin's work to the genre of 'local colourist' from which she endeavoured to escape. A potboiler. FD

End of St Petersburg, The (Konyets Sankt-Peterburga)

(Vsevolod Pudovkin, 1927, USSR) AP Chistyakov, Vera Baranovskaya, Ivan Chuvelyov, V Chuvelyov, V Obolensky.
8,202 ft. b/w.
Pudovkin's account of the 1917 Revolution is less celebrated than Eisenstein's October, and will be (for a while at least) than Warren Beatty's Reds. Not entirely without justification, for this is text-book cinema (the film was mapped out in advance, not with a storyboard, but with a kind of 'montage-board') which, unlike October, relies on a prototypical worker hero to embody the soul of the masses. Ironically, it's the power of the images themselves rather than the way they are edited that has kept it alive. GAd

End of the Day, The

see Fin du Jour, La

End of the Golden Weather, The

(Ian Mune, 1992, NZ) Stephen Fulford, Stephen Papps, Paul Gittins, Gabrielle Hammond, David Taylor, Alexandra Marshall.
103 min.
Co-writer/director Mune's adaptation of Bruce Mason's one-man show is full of the sort of frantic hamming which makes for bad theatre and bad cin-ema. Set against the unspoilt beaches of Auckland, the cluttered plot revolves around the imaginings of 12-year-old Geoff Crome (Fulford): the gallery of eccentrics on offer include an athlete who carries boulders while he trains, an overweight matron, and a lonely loony with a parasol. But Geoff reserves his affection and support for crazy Firpo (Papps), whose oft-repeated mantra of 'made-man' alludes to his ambition to run in the Olympics. The

domestic tension between the budding Walter Mitty and his father is clichéd and laboured; but most maddening of all is Firpo, whose wide-eyed tantrums evoke memories of nails scraped against blackboards. Pee-wee kiwi. CM

End of the Road

(Aram Avakian, 1969, US) Stacy Keach, Harris Yulin, Dorothy Tristan, James Earl Jones, Grayson Hall, Ray Brock, James Coco.
110 min.
First feature as director from Avakian, a former editor, this adaptation of John Barth's black com-edy deals somewhat incoherently with the prob-lems of operating 'normally' amid the aberrations and monstrosities of middle class America. Tracing the progress of college graduate Jake Horner (Keach) from mental hospital (ie. 'normal' society as nightmare) to life outside – spent undermining the marriage of a teacher colleague – the film holds the attention despite its mess of styles: a mixture of incisive black comedy (Terry Southern had a hand in the script), inarticulate rage and self-indulgence. The main problem is a lack of perspective: the implications of issues, like the roles of psychiatry and women, for example, are virtually ignored. Muddled but interesting, the strengths and weaknesses of its nihilism are summarised by the pointed quote from Shakespeare: 'A tale told by an idiot, full of sound and fury, signifying nothing'. CPe

End of Violence, The (Am Ende der Gewalt)

(Wim Wenders, 1997, US/Fr/Ger) Bill Pullman, Andie MacDowell, Gabriel Byrne, Loren Dean, Traci Lind, Daniel Benzali, Marisol Padilla Sanchez, K Todd Freeman, Pruitt Taylor-Vince, Udo Kier, Frederic Forrest, Sam Fuller.
122 min.
At once infuriatingly solemn and the best thing from Wenders in a decade, this visually resplen-dent LA 'thriller' concerns Mike Max (Pullman), a wealthy producer of violent movies who goes to ground with a group of Mexican gardeners after escaping an attempt on his life, and the movie-obsessed cop Doc Block (Dean) and the surveillance expert Ray (Byrne) who search, sep-arately, for a solution to the crime. It's a compli-cated affair, involving – or does it? – Max's wife (MacDowell); stuntwoman Cat (Lind); a refugee from El Salvador (Sanchez) hired by Ray's boss (Benzali); rap poet Six (Freeman); and expat European film-maker Zoltan (Kier). As the film explores links between life and the movies, poli-tics and power, venality and violence, crime and new technology, it occasionally slips into mediocre comedy and smug self-reflexiveness, but for the most part it's stylish and intelligent. As a love-hate letter to the movie-making capital, it's superbly designed and shot; as a contempo-rary film noir expressing a European unease at the future of the world as presaged by this blessed/damned city on the Western edge, it's strangely compelling. GA

End Play

(Tim Burstall, 1975, Aust) John Waters, George Mallaby, Ken Goodlet, Robert Hewett, Delvene Delaney, Charles Tingwell.
110 min.
Absolutely appalling dross. Two brothers – one on shore leave, one paraplegic – play theatrical cat and mouse with each other and the witless police over who's been knocking off hot-panted hitchhikers and dramatically dumping their bod-ies. It could all take place on amateur dramatics night at the local village hall, and would proba-bly come across with more conviction. PT

Endstation Freiheit

see Slow Attack

Enemies, a Love Story

(Paul Mazursky, 1989, US) Anjelica Huston, Ron Silver, Lena Olin, Margaret Sophie Stein, Judith Malina, Alan King, Rita Karin, Paul Mazursky.
120 min.
The war is over, but for Herman (Silver) conflict continues. It's New York, 1949; Herman is an edu-cated Jew married to the gentile peasant girl (Stein) who saved him from the Nazis. Life gets complicated. He's carrying on a turbulent affair with Masha (Olin), a deeply troubled survivor of

the camps. Enter his first wife Tamara (Huston), long presumed dead. 'Ten enemies can't harm a man as much as he can harm himself': in its reference to the Yiddish saying, Isaac Bashevis Singer's novel sums up Herman's predicament. A 'fatalistic hedonist' makes for a seemingly unsympathetic lead character, but in this intelligent adaptation, Mazursky (co-scripting with Roger L Simon) conveys emotion without manipulation, sensitively distilling despair and self-hatred, but lifting the mood with dark humour. Philosophical issues are brought into focus rather than generated by the Holocaust, and are examined within the realm of relationships rather than intellectual debate. The performances (from Lena Olin in particular) are perfectly suited to the mood, while period is beautifully evoked in subdued tones and subtly lit interiors. CM

Enemy, The (Düsman)

(Zeki Ökten, 1980, Tur) Aytaç Arman, Güngör Bayrak, Güven Sengil, Kâmil Sönmez.
160 min.
Written from jail by Yilmaz Güney, as was *The Herd*, this is a gritty, atmospheric story of the struggle for survival in Third World urban poverty, and its impact on a marriage. Overlaid with symbolism, some of which is inevitably lost in the culture gap (the dog poisoning, one gathers, is specially meaningful to Turks), its style is at once compelling and disturbing. Regrettably, in the interests of low Western attention spans, some 20 minutes have been cut, and the loss of one arguably crucial scene reduces the ending to a deus-ex-machina resolution rather than the narrative progression of the original. JCo

Enemy Below, The

(Dick Powell, 1957, US) Robert Mitchum, Curt Jurgens, David Hedison, Theodore Bikel, Doug McClure.
98 min.
Powell's subaquatic suspense picture follows war-weary US destroyer captain Mitchum as he tracks Jurgens' U-boat across the Atlantic, hoping to stop the vessel before she joins up with other German subs. The psychology of personal confrontation and the mechanics of marine combat are the focus here, rather than flagwaving, so we're allowed some sympathy for Jurgens, an old hand from the Great War who loves his country but despises the Nazis. Mitchum holds up the American end with his customary stoic reserve. Shot in CinemaScope. TJ

Enemy Mine

(Wolfgang Petersen, 1985, US) Dennis Quaid, Louis Gossett Jr, Brion James, Richard Marcus, Carolyn McCormick.
108 min.
Little more than a buddy movie set in space which, sadly, relies like Petersen's earlier *Neverending Story* more upon special effects than storyline. Earth warrior Quaid shoots it out with 'Drac' warrior Gossett, then both man and creature crash-land on the deserted Fyrine IV. The gloomy planet, with its meteor storms and bug-eyed monsters, soon draws the combatants together as they realise that the greatest threat to their survival is not each other, but the planet itself. *Enemy Mine* then mutates into a story of friendship, understanding and eventual love between the two Robinson Crusoes in space. Both Quaid and Gossett, the latter doing a passable imitation of a fish, perform like troopers, and one special effect in particular, where Gossett gives birth to a Drac-brat, is impressively moving. What the film lacks, however, is the epic vision to match its epic pretensions, something to bind together the action and the ideas. CB

Enemy of the People, An

(George Schaefer, 1977, US) Steve McQueen, Bibi Andersson, Charles Durning, Richard A Dysart, Michael Cristofer.
107 min.
The casting of Steve McQueen as the hero of Ibsen's play (a scientist determined to expose the pollution of a prosperous small town's water supply) threatens the worst. But his performance, together with Durning's as his brother the mayor (equally determined to put the lid on any scandal) make it fairly creditable. Sure, it's stagebound. But decent production values, and direction which preserves the suspense of Ibsen's

exposition, ensure that it remains watchable until the play's own unsatisfactory last act. The only really offensive aspects are the denunciation scene, and the degeneration of the hero into an increasingly sentimentalised Christ-like martyrdom, as much the fault of the text as of McQueen's interpretation. RM

Enemy of the People, An (Ganashatru)

(Satyajit Ray, 1989, Ind) Soumitra Chatterjee, Ruma Guhathakurta, Dhritiman Chatterjee, Mamata Shankar, Dipankar Dey, Subhendu Chatterjee, Vischwa Guhthakurta, Manoj Mitra.
100 min.
This transplant of Ibsen's play to present-day Bengal, with Soumitra Chatterjee as the doctor foiled by vested interests in his fight to secure a costly overhaul of the town's polluted water supply, has to get everyone's sympathy vote: it was Ray's first movie since his heart attack, and doctor's orders limited him to a studio shoot. Sadly, the film needs all the sympathy it can get. Ray's own script remains locked in a 19th century sense of 'dramatics', reducing the characters to mouthpieces for positions, and the plot to a thin and unconvincing set of political manoeuvres. The actors struggle gamely to breathe life into it, but their efforts are hopeless. And the ludicrously optimistic ending is blatantly imposed from above; nothing in the preceeding 95 minutes earns or justifies it. TR

Enfance nue, L' (Naked Childhood/Me)

(Maurice Pialat, 1968, Fr) Michel Terrazon, Marie-Louise Thierry, René Thierry, Marie Marc, Pierrette Deplanque.
80 min.
Pialat's first feature is a wonderfully delicate study of a ten-year-old boy and his decline into delinquency when boarded out with foster parents after being abandoned by his mother. With Truffaut as co-producer, comparisons with *Les Quatre Cents Coups* are inevitable, but there is really little resemblance between the two films except in theme and refusal to sentimentalise. Instead of focusing on the child, Pialat concentrates on the adults: the foster parents puzzled by the boy's delinquency since he so clearly responds to their affection; the ancient grandmother with whom he breaks through to a special relationship (very warm and funny); the welfare and adoption officers, carrying out their jobs with weary patience, but tending to treat the children as pets rather than as human beings. It's a film in which nuance is everything; amazingly, given that Pialat was working exclusively with non-professionals, the performances are stunning. TM

Enfant Sauvage, L' (The Wild Child)

(François Truffaut, 1969, Fr) Jean-Pierre Cargol, François Truffaut, Jean Dasté, Françoise Seigner, Paul Villé.
84 min. b/w.
The story, based on fact, of a late 18th century behavioural scientist's attempts to condition a wild boy found in the woods in the ways of 'civilisation'. The confrontation of Rousseau's noble savage with Western scientific rationalism makes for a film with enormous philosophical implications: emotional subjectivity versus scientific objectivity, nature versus nurture, society versus the individual. Given the semi-documentary treatment and the subject itself, the film could have been excruciatingly dull in lesser hands. In fact it's as lucid and wryly witty a film as you could wish for, uncluttered by superfluous period detail. A beautiful use of simple techniques – black-and-white photography, Vivaldi music, even devices as outmoded as the iris – give it a very refreshing quality. The use of much voice-over from Dr Itard's original journals, set against images patently contradicting the scientist's detached assumptions, make for some pretty ironies, and fundamentally question the morality of much scientific investigation, as well as attempting to evaluate the worth of many of our social constructs (such as education). A deeply moving film, dedicated to Jean-Pierre Léaud, the actor who plays Truffaut's semi-autobiographical hero, Antoine Doinel. RM

Enfants de Lumière, Les (The Children of Lumière)

(André Asseo/Pierre Billard/Pierre Philippe/Alain Corneau/Claude Miller/Claude Sautet, 1995, Fr)
102 min. b/w & col.
A delicious sprint leading us through about 300 sensitively chosen and juxtaposed clips from 100 years of French cinema, from the Lumières' *Workers Leaving the Factory* to the latest version of *Les Misérables* starring an aged Belmondo. Loosely structured around various topics (history, fantasy, crime, war, love, travel, food) and featuring a mercifully unwordy narration from Jacques Perrin, it's a joyous, uplifting tribute to a national industry whose major achievements are countless – impossible, indeed, to imagine a British equivalent. GA

Enfants du Paradis, Les (Children of Paradise) 100 (100)

(Marcel Carné, 1945, Fr) Pierre Brasseur, Arletty, Jean-Louis Barrault, Marcel Herrand, Maria Casarès, Louis Salou, Pierre Renoir, Fabien Loris, Jane Marken.
187 min. b/w.
A marvellously witty, ineffably graceful rondo of passions and perversities animating the Boulevard du Crime, home of Parisian popular theatre in the early 19th century, and an astonishing anthill of activity in which mimes and mountebanks rub shoulders with aristocrats and assassins. Animating Jacques Prévert's script is a multi-layered meditation on the nature of performance, ranging from a vivid illustration of contrasting dramatic modes (Barrault's mime needing only gestures, Brasseur's Shakespearean actor relishing the music of words) and a consideration of the interchangeability of theatre and life (as Herrand's frustrated playwright Lacenaire elects to channel his genius into crime), to a wry acknowledgment of the social relevance of performance (all three men are captivated by Arletty's insouciant whore, who acts herself out of their depth to achieve the protection of a Count, establishing a social barrier which Lacenaire promptly breaches in his elaborate stage management of the Count's murder). Flawlessly executed and with a peerless cast, this is one of the great French movies, so perfectly at home in its period that it never seems like a costume picture, and at over three hours not a moment too long. Amazing to recall that it was produced in difficult circumstances towards the end of the German Occupation during World War II. TM

Enfants Terribles, Les (The Strange Ones)

(Jean-Pierre Melville, 1949, Fr) Nicole Stéphane, Edouard Dhermitte, Jacques Bernard, Renée Cosima, Roger Gaillard, Mel Martin.
107 min. b/w.
One of Cocteau's most satisfying contributions to the cinema, largely because of Melville's lucid interpretation of the writer's poetic vision. Essence and myth lie at the centre of Cocteau's story of a young sister (a startling performance from Nicole Stéphane) and brother who retreat into their private world to play out their erotically charged games. It is easy to see why the film was so influential with subsequent French film-makers, especially in the way it anticipates the self-obsessiveness of an adolescent culture that grew up in the '50s. How Melville achieved its lightness of touch – a quality much admired by Cocteau – remains a small mystery, given Cocteau's constant interference and a wooden male lead (Cocteau's protégé, not Melville's choice). CPe

Enfer, L' (Torment)

(Claude Chabrol, 1993, Fr) Emmanuelle Béart, François Cluzet, Nathalie Cardone, André Wilms, Marc Lavoine, Dora Doll, Jean-Pierre Cassel.
103 min.
Paul (Cluzet) is charming, attractive, hard-working; Nelly (Béart) is beautiful and carefree, devoted to her husband and more than happy to help him make a success of his Edenic lakeside hotel. They're madly in love. Nelly has a baby. Paul has trouble sleeping; he can't shake off a nagging inner voice which needs to know what Nelly's up to every minute of the day. Little by little his suspicions take shape, and jealousy plunges him into

an unfathomable purgatory of doubt and dementia. Chabrol's film is a relentlessly bleak, gripping study of pathological jealousy which finds the director more thoroughly engaged than he's been for some while. Based on a rediscovered screenplay by Henri-Georges Clouzot (whose 1964 production was abandoned after six days' shooting), this is a black comedy which evolves into a long dark night of the soul. The nihilistic vision may be Clouzot's, but the economy, concentration and oppressive atmosphere are pure Chabrol, as is the eruption of the suppressed into the public arena. A work of enthralling virtuosity. TCh

Enforcer, The
(aka Murder, Inc.)

(Bretaigne Windust/Raoul Walsh, 1951, US) Humphrey Bogart, Everett Sloane, Zero Mostel, Ted de Corsia, Roy Roberts, Bob Steele, King Donovan.
88 min. b/w.
Based on the 1940 revelations of Abe Reles as to the existence of an organisation called Murder Inc, but prompted by the Kefauver Committee investigations of 1950, this is very much a transitional film between the *noir* Forties and the syndicate Fifties. Unveiling the argot of the murder business for the first time (eg. 'contract', 'hit', 'finger'), it scored another notable first by using its intricate web of flashbacks, conjured by the interrogations of Bogart's crusading assistant DA, to explore the mysterious structures of organised crime. In a typically *noir* aura of fear, shot by Robert Burks in a semi-documentary style, and with a laconically witty script by Martin Rackin, it only occasionally reveals the cracks one might expect given that part of the footage had to be restaged by Walsh (who contributed, most notably, the climactic shootout with the killer finally nailed in a doorway). TM

Enforcer, The

(James Fargo, 1976, US) Clint Eastwood, Tyne Daly, Harry Guardino, Bradford Dillman, John Mitchum.
96 min.
Dirty Harry part three doggedly revives the formula of its predecessors, with Eastwood again the tough San Francisco cop, at odds with his liberal superiors, stalking psychopaths, this time a supposedly revolutionary group of kill-crazy kids. Whereas the earlier films went some way to exploring the political and personal tensions of operating as a modern lawman, this simplifies to the point of crudity – 'It's a war, isn't it?' – and misuses Eastwood's monolithic presence, primarily as a butt for gags like lumbering him with a female partner. This last could have worked, especially with Eastwood tiring of his image (cf. *The Outlaw Josey Wales*), but the scriptwriters fail dismally to develop the relationship, opting instead for a predictable one-note comedy of encumbrance. Yet despite inferior contributions from most departments, Eastwood carries the picture, and Tyne Daly does well as the female cop against very stacked odds. CPe

Engelchen

see Little Angel

England Made Me

(Peter Duffell, 1972, GB) Peter Finch, Michael York, Hildegard Neil, Michael Hordern, Joss Ackland, Tessa Wyatt.
100 min.
Duffell's adaptation of Graham Greene's novel retreads the path of both *Cabaret* and *The Damned*, but comes far closer to the spirit of Isherwood's *Goodbye to Berlin*. The film never allows its characters to be dwarfed by set pieces, and instead concentrates on conveying the ingenuous and ineffectual charm of a young Englishman (York) caught between the decadence and encroaching violence of Nazi Germany and a potentially incestuous twin sister (Neil). It's a pity that the film was unfairly neglected at the time, thereby throwing a hitch into Duffell's promising career. DP

Englishman Who Went Up a Hill, But Came Down a Mountain, The

(Christopher Monger, 1995, GB) Hugh Grant, Ian McNeice, Colm Meaney, Tara Fitzgerald, Ian Hart, Tudor Vaughn, Kenneth Griffith.
95 min.

English cartographer Reginald Anson (Grant, blinking and stammering) and his colleague George (McNeice) arrive at a quiet Welsh village in 1917 to measure Ffynnon Garw – the 'first mountain in Wales', the locals boast. The Englishmen's findings dismay them. At 984 ft the summit is 15 ft short of a mountain. Led by the landlord, Morgan the Goat (Meaney), and his arch-rival, the Rev Jones (Griffith), the villagers determine that the surveyors will not leave until the hill has become a mountain. Monger (*Just Like a Woman, Waiting for the Light*) heard this yarn from his father and his father's father, but the film owes as much to the parochial charm of the Ealing comedies of the 1940s, and that obsession with size which runs through much British film humour (*The Mouse That Roared, The Smallest Show on Earth*, etc). It's a gentle, indulgent celebration of community values, heart and home, with a sprinkling of Welsh nationalist propaganda. Well crafted as it is, and hard to dislike, it's harder still to shake the suspicion that Monger is making a mountain out of a molehill. TCh

English Patient, The ⑩⓪

(Anthony Minghella, 1996, US) Ralph Fiennes, Juliette Binoche, Willem Dafoe, Kristin Scott Thomas, Naveen Andrews, Colin Firth, Julian Wadham, Jürgen Prochnow, Kevin Whately, Clive Merison.
162 min.
Tuscany, as the Allies pursue the Germans north at the end of WWII: traumatised by loss and carnage, Canadian nurse Hana (Binoche) decides to stay behind in an abandoned, bombed monastery and care for her dying patient (Fiennes). He seems to recall little of his life, but when Caravaggio (Dafoe), a vengeful, morphine-addicted thief, turns up and quizzes him over past dark secrets, and as Hana reads from his beloved Herodotos, memories return of the pre-war years when, as an archaeologist/cartographer in the Sahara, he had a passionate affair with Katharine (Scott Thomas), wife of a British colleague. Though Anthony Minghella's adaptation of Michael Ondaatje's novel simplifies, jettisons and changes certain elements of the original story, it remains a rich, complex, entrancing piece of work. Part poignant romance, part suspenseful adventure, part enigmatic mystery, it's essentially a study in different responses to love and war, honour and betrayal, nationality and identity, falsehood and forgiveness, which sounds subtle echoes as the narrative flashes to and fro between two main time frames. Needless to say, the performances are flawless; more surprising is the fluency, poetry and scale of Minghella's direction (John Seale's sensuous desert photography is superb), equally eloquent whether depicting boudoir intimacies, bomb-disposal skills, drunken dementia or a deadly sandstorm. GA

Enid Is Sleeping
(aka Over Her Dead Body)

(Maurice Phillips, 1989, US) Elizabeth Perkins, Judge Reinhold, Jeffrey Jones, Maureen Mueller, Rhea Perlman, Brion James, Charles Tyner, Henry Jones, Michael J Pollard.
102 min.
Enid (Mueller) catches her cop husband (Reinhold) in bed with her sister (Perkins), and in the ensuing fracas is killed. What to do with the body? Everything goes wildly wrong...The troublesome corpse as a comic theme is usually a bit of a flounder. Even Hitchcock couldn't do much with it in *The Trouble with Harry*, and Phillips does even less, though he's noisier about it. In fact, the cast shout a lot to make things funnier, or stand about mugging to give the gag a chance to go down. Pity, since Reinhold and Perkins are accomplished comic players when they get the material. BC

Enigma

(Jeannot Szwarc, 1982, GB/Fr) Martin Sheen, Sam Neill, Brigitte Fossey, Michel Lonsdale, Derek Jacobi, Frank Finlay.
122 min.
In this disastrous mid-Atlantic spy thriller, Sheen plays an expatriate American who grew up behind the Iron Curtain and now makes propaganda broadcasts for Free World Radio in Paris. Learning that the KGB has a plan to assassinate five leading Soviet dissidents now living in Europe, the CIA recruit Sheen to obtain a cru-

cial scrambling device fitted to a Communist word processor in East Berlin. Sheen changes his appearance almost as often as John Briley's script changes its mind (about every five minutes), and both of them are forever rushing down blind alleys in search of an excitement which continually eludes them. NF

Enigma of Kaspar Hauser, The

see Jeder für sich und Gott gegen alle

Enigma Rosso

see Red Rings of Fear

Ensayo de un Crimen

see Criminal Life of Archibaldo de la Cruz, The

Ensign Pulver

(Joshua Logan, 1964, US) Robert Walker Jr, Burl Ives, Walter Matthau, Tommy Sands, Millie Perkins, Kay Medford.
104 min.
Sequel to Thomas Heggen's long-running play *Mister Roberts* which, in the film version at least, coasted along largely on the strength of fine performances from Cagney, Lemmon and William Powell. The substitute cast taking over here is competent enough, but the script has nothing whatsoever to add, and soon runs out of invention in trying to prolong the feud between the ship's crew and its martinet captain. TM

Entertainer, The

(Tony Richardson, 1960, GB) Laurence Olivier, Brenda de Banzie, Albert Finney, Joan Plowright, Roger Livesey, Alan Bates, Shirley Anne Field, Thora Hird, Daniel Massey.
96 min. b/w.
John Osborne's quirky indictment of '50s stagnation still looks stagebound, despite extensive location shooting and the cool, inventive photography of Oswald Morris. Too many words, too many tantrums, too much kitchen-sink sentimentality; yet there are moments when this looks like a good film. The performances are remarkable: Plowright and de Banzie beating desperately against the bars of the mad male family; Livesey, a resurrected Colonel Blimp, inspiring the OAPs with 'Don't Let Them Scrap the British Navy'; and Olivier, throwing Shakespearean dignity to the winds to play Archie Rice, the epitome of '50s tattiness with his gratifyingly awful theme song, 'Thank God We're Normal'. RMy

Entertaining Angels: The Dorothy Day Story

(Michael Ray Rhodes, 1996, US) Moira Kelly, Heather Graham, Melinda Dillon, Lenny Von Dohlen, Martin Sheen, Brian Keith.
111 min.
An evangelical biography of the firebrand reporter, feminist and philanthropist Dorothy Day (Kelly, persuasive): in 1933, following her conversion, she co-founded *The Catholic Worker* with Peter Maurin (Sheen), an eccentric philosopher. The film opens in Greenwich Village, 1917, where Dorothy boozes with anarchists, communists and Eugene O'Neill, and argues journalistic priorities at *The Call*. But as the opening credit ('A Paulist Picture') and the end-list of 'thank yous' (including the Conrad Hilton Foundation) testify, the makers are more interested in her later mission to bring Christ into the lives of the poorest and most dejected of New York's Lower East Side. The first hour, 1917-33, rushes through too much placard-waving social history, rendered in nicely composed but familiar umbra washes. The second deals at tedious length with Day's conflicting commitment to the poor, her daughter and the paper. WH

Entertaining Mr Sloane

(Douglas Hickox, 1969, GB) Beryl Reid, Harry Andrews, Peter McEnery, Alan Webb.
94 min.
Joe Orton's four-hander about a sister and brother (nympho and queer respectively) vying for the favours of a desirable stud (under the eyes of their ancient dadda) loses much of its savoury charm in this movie version. Clive Exton's script opens out the play conventionally, to little effect, and Hickox's direction shows little flair for farce in general or Orton in particular. The cast are good enough for the original, though. RG

Enter the Dragon

(Robert Clouse, 1973, US/HK) Bruce Lee, John Saxon, Shih Kien, Jim Kelly, Bob Wall, Yang Sze, Ahna Capri.
98 min.

The first of a burgeoning series of American film industry attempts to colonise the kung-fu market, this manages to be inferior to even the weakest of Bruce Lee's *echt*-Chinese movies. A sorry mixture of James Bond and Fu Manchu, it tacks together the exploits of a multi-national crew of martial artists converging on Hong Kong for a tournament, infiltrated by Lee – fresh from his Shaolin temple – on an assignment to bust an opium racket. Worth seeing for Lee, but still unforgivably wasteful of his talents.

Enter the Ninja

(Menahem Golan, 1981, US) Franco Nero, Susan George, Sho Kosugi, Alex Courtney, Will Hare, Zachi Noy, Christopher George.
99 min.

A Z-grade international cast fumbles its way through a tiresome series of action movie clichés (impotent wealthy farmer and his frustrated wife ask their Ninja friend to defend them from ruthless oil baron and his incompetent hoods), with the characters mouthing appallingly clumsy lines in a startling variety of post-dubbed accents ('Why is Hasegawa so frustrated?' – 'Because it's the twentieth century'). With monotonous regularity the story pauses for graceless and unexciting fight scenes, complete with incessant death gurgles and bone-creaking, or for banal cod-Zen philosophising and rituals. Even on the level of unintentional humour this fails to entertain: the mark of a truly dreadful movie. GA

Enter the 7 Virgins (aka Virgins of the Seven Seas)

(Kuei Chih-Hung/Ernst Hofbauer, 1974, HK/WGer) Yueh Hua, Tamara Elliot, Gillian Bray, Sonja Jeanine, Diana Drube, Deborah Rulls, Wang Hsieh, Liu Hui-Ling.
92 min.

Kuei Chih-Hung's magnificently atmospheric direction (making consummate use of the Shaw sets), and supremely dignified playing by Yueh Hua and Liu Hui-Ling, go for nothing in this co-production. Some idiot has seen fit to burden the film with intensely degrading, not to say racist dubbing into joke Chinese full of 'vellys' and 'walkee plankees' (the story starts on board ship). There is also a liberal sprinkling of hip Americanisms of the 'Man, I'm really into kung-fu' variety. The appalling Hofbauer, veteran of innumberable leaden sex farces, presumably contributed the derisory sex scenes. VG

Entity, The

(Sidney J Furie, 1981, US) Barbara Hershey, Ron Silver, David Labiosa, George Coe, Margeret Blye, Jacqueline Brooks.
125 min.

Perhaps any movie with such a wretched central idea (woman sexually assaulted by an invisible demon), supposedly based on fact or not, deserved the feminist picket-line which attended its West End screening. But for reasons that may be fortuitous, *The Entity* doesn't emerge quite as one-dimensionally nasty as its synopsis suggests. The film's men are so uniformly creepy, and its heroine so strong and sympathetic, that apart from a couple of unpleasant moments the story often seems less like horror than feminist parable, especially when Hershey (giving a fine performance) is reduced to a laboratory object with her home recreated in the psychology department. None of this may be intended, of course, but it goes to show that commercial movies sometimes hit spots that more intentionally didactic efforts can't reach. DP

Entre Nous

see Coup de Foudre

Entre Tinieblas

see Dark Habits

Equilibristes, Les (Walking a Tightrope)

(Nico Papatakis, 1991, Fr) Michel Piccoli, Lilah Dadi, Polly Walker.
128 min.

Based on an episode in the life of Jean Genet – but possessing none of the depth of play with sex and power in his writing – this features Piccoli as a supposedly great poet, playwright and all-round manipulator who falls for a young German-Algerian sweeper-up at the circus (Dadi), and resolves to make him a great tightrope-walker. Needless to say, the young man is soon tossed aside for a sexy would-be racing driver, and retreats for histrionic hair-tearing sessions with his beer-sodden mother. Ludicrously overwrought, and with a positively 19th century notion of gay sex – all ageing Svengalis and gamy young Ganymedes – this wears its symbolism heavily, to say the least; and worst of all, it's stultifyingly dull, right up to the daft apocalyptic climax. Polly Walker, as Piccoli's confidante and 'cock-catcher', is mysteriously got up as a dead ringer for Grace Kelly. JRo

Equinox

(Alan Rudolph, 1992, US) Matthew Modine, Lara Flynn Boyle, Tyra Ferrel, M Emmet Walsh, Fred Ward, Marisa Tomei, Lori Singer.
103 min.

After a dip into the mainstream with *Mortal Thoughts*, the wildest card in American cinema is back on his own bizarre terrain. This modern urban fairytale is a beautifully ambivalent re-telling of *The Prince and the Pauper*. Modine is the separated-at-birth twins (both of them), one a hood whose dream life – moppet children, a cooing fashion-plate wife (Singer) – is coupled with violent megalomania, the other a cringing wimp who can't bring himself to date his best friend's anguished, poetry-reading sister (Boyle). The whole is held together with a plot about an aspiring writer (Ferrel) on the track of her first real-life drama, and by an atmospheric soundtrack (Terje Rydal, Ali Farka Toure) that accompanies the characters' hypnotically crazed manoeuvres. M Emmet Walsh steals the show as a garage boss in a drolly choreographed homage to Jacques Demy. Delirious stuff. JRo

Equus

(Sidney Lumet, 1977, GB) Richard Burton, Peter Firth, Colin Blakely, Joan Plowright, Harry Andrews, Eileen Atkins, Jenny Agutter, Kate Reid.
137 min.

Lumet's reverential adaptation of Peter Shaffer's play all but defies sane comment: the sub-Lawrentian pretensions that theatre audiences took so seriously stand revealed in all their Pythonesque absurdity when transposed to the screen. The problem is very basic: theatrical symbolism just isn't the same as filmic realism. Add to this that Burton lacks even a shred of credibility as the psychiatrist, and that Firth's performance – technically faultless – is periodically interrupted by scenes in which the awe-struck camera simply observes him undressed, and you begin to comprehend the film's true wretchedness. TR

Era Notte a Roma

(Roberto Rossellini, 1960, It/Fr) Leo Genn, Giovanna Ralli, Sergei Bondarchuk, Hannes Messemer, Peter Baldwin, Sergio Fantoni, Enrico Maria Salerno, Paolo Stoppa, Renato Salvatori, Laura Betti, Rosalba Neri.
120 min. b/w.

Stylistically an intriguing (and not wholly successful) mixture of Rossellini's early 'realism', Bergman-period melodrama, and the contemplative didacticism of his later films, this return to the milieu of Nazi-occupied Rome may not have the raw power of *Rome, Open City*, but is immensely affecting all the same. Three escaped Allied PoWs – a Brit, an American and a Russian – take refuge in the home of Roman black marketeer Ralli, whose Communist lover (Salvatori) is executed when they are betrayed by a corrupt, Nazi-collaborator priest. On one level, it's a fairly straightforward suspense movie, detailing the countless threats to the safety of the fugitives and the woman who provides sanctuary; on another, it's an unsentimental, *Paisà*-like celebration of the shared humanity that allows the various characters to communicate with one another despite linguistic differences and the wariness born of perilous circumstance. An uneven, flawed, but very intelligent work of enormous humanity. GA

Eraser

(Charles Russell, 1996, US) Arnold Schwarzenegger, James Caan, Vanessa Williams, James Coburn.
114 min.

A cumbersome, resolutely formula thriller of the kind that Arnie made before he *was* Arnie (think of *Commando* or *Raw Deal*). Still, it intermittently takes off into the realms of comic fantasy hyper-drive, with our hero leaping from burning jets at 11,000 feet, grappling with alligators in the New York Zoo ('You're luggage!'), and trading lead with the latest hi-tech X-ray weaponry – the influence of John Woo, perhaps, or simply the result of the current fetish for digital effects. Schwarzenegger is Kruger, the government's best agent in the federal witness protection programme. When a mole in the organisation seeks to wipe out his latest charge (Williams), Kruger only has his old clients to turn to. It's a movie constructed around three or four self-consciously 'cool' episodes, and passably entertaining as such, but there's also an awful lot of uncool contrivance, coincidence and contempt for the audience. TCh

Eraserhead

(David Lynch, 1976, US) John Nance, Charlotte Stewart, Allen Joseph, Jeanne Bates, Judith Anna Roberts, Laurel Near.
89 min. b/w.

Lynch's remarkable first feature is a true original. There's little in the way of a coherent story: nervy Henry, living in a sordid industrial city of smoke, steam and shadows, is forced to marry his girlfriend when she pronounces herself pregnant, and finds himself the father of an all-devouring, inhuman monster. But, almost like a surrealist movie, it has its own weird logic, mixing black comedy (concerning nuclear families and urban life), horror and sci-conventions, and pure fantasy. Best seen as a dark nightmare about sexuality, parenthood and commitment in relationships, it astounds through its expressionist sets and photography, the startling, sinister soundtrack, and relentlessly imaginative fluency. Only the sequence that gives the film its name – a dream within the dream about Henry's head being lopped off and turned into a pencil-eraser – fails to work, and that's a small reservation for a film with so many cinematic coups. GA

Ercole alla conquista di Atlantide (Hercules and the Captive Women/Hercules Conquers Atlantis)

(Vittorio Cottafavi, 1961, It/Fr) Reg Park, Fay Spain, Ettore Manni, Luciano Marin, Laura Altan, Enrico Maria Salerno, Ivo Garrani, Gian Maria Volonté.
101 min.

Some extreme claims have been made for Cottafavi's sword and sandal epics, but essentially this example impresses by its simplicity and excellent pictorial values. Reluctant hero Hercules (Park) is hoodwinked into serving the Greek cause by quashing the scheme of the Queen of Atlantis (Spain) who, under the influence of the god Uranus, is producing a race of supermen. The knockabout comedy is unexceptional and most of the cast only adequate, though Spain delivers a high camp performance as the arrogant queen, letting off coloured puffs of smoke for her pleasure. Best of all is the dynamic design: deep and mysterious hallways, a team of white horses flying through subterranean tunnels, and a wholly identical superrace revealed from beneath their equally identical armoured visors. DT

Eredità Ferramonti, L'

see Inheritance, The

Erendira

(Ruy Guerra, 1982, Fr/Mex/WGer) Irene Papas, Claudia Ohana, Michel Lonsdale, Oliver Wehe, Rufus, Blanca Guerra, Pierre Vaneck.
105 min.

Once upon a time there was a comely maiden who lived with a tame baby ostrich and her wicked granny in a windswept hacienda dripping with alabaster and gilt and paper flowers. But the foolish girl forgot to snuff out the candles one night, and the magnificent palace blazed into ashes. 'My poor darling,' murmured the grandmother gently, 'your life will not be long enough to repay me', and she set the virgin to work as a courtesan. And admirers came from far and wide to follow their exotic progress through the Mexican desert and to lie with Erendira...This febrile fairytale, adapted by Gabriel García Márquez from his own novella, is handsome to behold and laden with symbols, though of what it's difficult to say. Only Irene Papas, as the imperious, peacock-plumed beldame, brings a touch of mad comic grandeur to brighten the portentous solemnity. SJo

Eric Clapton and His Rolling Hotel

(Rex Pyke, 1980, GB) Eric Clapton, Muddy Waters, George Harrison, Elton John.
70 min.
The Rolling Hotel, which carried the Clapton entourage on their 1979 European tour, is a luxury train originally built by Goering and usually reserved for the German chancellor. On board, and on various European stages, Pyke shot what, surprisingly, was the first documentary footage about this veteran rock guitarist. The film gives space to the man as well as his music, and treats his talents with the seriousness they deserve. SWo

Erik the Viking

(Terry Jones, 1989, GB) Tim Robbins, Mickey Rooney, Eartha Kitt, Terry Jones, Imogen Stubbs, John Cleese, Tsutomu Sekine, Antony Sher, Gary Cady, Charles McKeown, Tim McInnerny, John Gordon Sinclair, Freddie Jones.
108 min.
Terry Jones' post-Python frolic, inspired by his own Norse saga children's book, is not a funny film, and neither well-directed nor exciting. Robbins plays a kind of lovelorn gentle giant, dismayed by the daily drudgery of conquest, pillage and rape, who seeks enlightenment from a cave-dwelling seer/hag (Kitt). This is the Dark Age of Ragnarok, she tells him, which will end in an orgy of fighting and destructiveness. He thus sets out with a long-ship full of squabbling warriors with names like Sven the Berserk and Thorfinn Skullsplitter, to awaken the gods with the Horn Resounding so that they may usher in the new era of peace and light. In pursuit are snivelling Loki (Sher), maker of weapons, and the very-evil-indeed Halfdan the Black (Cleese). There's a certain precocious schoolboy mentality at work in the film: an indulgent delight in making fantasies come to life. Its disarming mix of blood-and-muck realism, researched detail, and soaring wish-fulfillment, wonder and irreverence, does provide lots of small incidental pleasures. WH

Erl King, The

see Roi des Aulnes, Le

Ermo

(Zhou Xiaowen, 1994, China) Alia, Liu Pieqi.
98 min.
This highly entertaining tragi-comedy is the best film yet about the ups and downs of 'modernisation' in the Chinese countryside. The heroine Ermo is a doughty noodle-maker bent on regaining her social status in the village; she sets her heart on earning and saving enough to buy the largest TV set in the country, even if it kills her – which it begins to look like doing. Wry, sexy and very wittily observed, the film sees China now as a tangle of materialism, amorality and left-overs from both feudalism and communism. Buñuel himself couldn't have come up with a more devastating account of stone-ground passions or preservative-free desires. TR

Ernest Saves Christmas

(John Cherry, 1988, US) Jim Varney, Douglas Seale, Oliver Clark, Noëlle Parker, Gailard Sartain, Billie Bird, Robert Lesser.
91 min.
What can you expect from a cheap seasonal movie directed by an advertising executive and starring a character devised as a vehicle for selling American couch-potatoes anything from milk to financial services? Santa Claus (Seale) arrives in America (by plane) in search of Joe Carruthers (Clark), unemployed children's entertainer and heir apparent to Father Christmas' throne. Not surpisingly, everyone thinks Mr Claus is a fruitcake, but with the help of a 'wacky' cab-driver and a 'streetwise' runaway girl, rampant festivity triumphs. At the centre of the film is the said taxi-driver, Ernest P Worrell (Varney), a twisted, cheap imitation of the young Jerry Lewis, whose comic turns make Paul Hogan's repertoire seem

a galaxy of creativity. This, combined with Cherry's staggeringly inept direction, is not unlike watching 91 solid minutes of commercials, with Varney's resolutely unfunny zaniness interspersed with tooth-rottingly saccharine messages from the sponsor (Christmas is nice, children are nice, etc). MK

Erotic Quartet

(Radley Metzger, 1970, US/WGer/It) Sylvana Venturelli, Frank Wolff, Erika Remberg.
90 min.
The brash, all-American certainties of Russ Meyer's sexploiters find their exact opposites in the work of Metzger, whose stylishly shot and designed movies are riddled with 'European' ambiguities of mood, theme and sexual identity. *Erotic Quartet* is his most ambitious and 'personal' film: a study of an Italian bourgeois family's involvement with a girl who might or might not be a star in one of the 8mm blue movies they like to run at home. The films-within-the-film generate some almost Pirandellian games with appearance and reality, but the movie's real claims to distinction in its field are its balanced sensitivity to male and female sexuality, and its bravura set pieces (notably the library set, decorated with blown-up dictionary definitions of erotic terms). TR

Erotique

(Lizzie Borden/Monika Treut/Clara Law, 1993, US/Ger/HK) Kamala Lopez-Dawson, Bryan Cranston, Priscilla Barnes, Camilla Soeberg, Ron Orbach, Marianne Sägebrecht.
84 min.
Three feminist stories confront and subvert the standard porn movie (up to a point). Borden and Treut are comfortable with the brief, allowing their central characters fantasy, force and passion, but Law's cinematic concerns lie in cultural rather than gender differences, and she opts (out) for humour. 'Let's Talk About Sex', Borden's tale of phone sex worker Rosie (Lopez-Dawson), reworks themes from *Working Girls*. It's a sometimes steamy little affair, though Borden does well to question Rosie's own fantasy which slips easily into stereotype. Treut's deadly lesbian vignette, 'Taboo Parlour', plays hard ball. Her dildo-wearing heroine works out a variation of the Black Widow scenario – an uncompromising gender power game likely to alienate any man hoping for titillation. Law's meditation on the future of Hong Kong, 'Wonton Soup', ends the film with a a soft-core wimper as a couple explore a version of the Kama Sutra. FM

Escalier C

(Jean-Charles Tacchella, 1985, Fr) Robin Renucci, Jean-Pierre Bacri, Catherine Leprince, Jacques Bonnaffé, Jacques Weber, Claude Rich, Michel Aumont.
101 min.
Tacchella's film centres on the inhabitants of one staircase in a 14th arrondissement apartment block. A dipso, a widow and a novelist *manqué* all take second place to a lugubriously handsome art critic (Renucci), who is cynical, obnoxious and very rude to women. It takes the death of a neighbour to effect his moral reawakening, whereupon he declares his intention to move in with a caring gay and makes a pilgrimage to Jerusalem. Even if the fact that the film treats indulgence in all its manifestations doesn't quite excuse its total implausibility,it's superbly acted and contrives to be both amusing and affecting. MS

Escape

(Basil Dean, 1930, GB) Gerald du Maurier, Edna Best, Gordon Harker, Madeleine Carroll, Austin Trevor, Lewis Casson, Ian Hunter, Nigel Bruce.
70 min. b/w.
'Do you know how I spend most of my time in prison? Holding imaginary conversations with the Respectable'. Dean's early talkie is interesting not only for its innovatory location shooting, but for its charmingly archaic concern for the upper class outcast. Killing a policeman in defence of a lady of the streets, our officer and gentleman hero finds himself breaking rocks on Dartmoor and 'treated like a dog'. With a 'By gosh I'll do it!' he's away, and before being caught by a gaggle of policemen, warders, bellringers and peasants, encounters genuine class solidari-

ty among the local gentry. 'I can't bear to see a man like that chased by a lot of yokels', exclaims one of his genteel admirers. Quite so. RMy

Escape

(Mervyn LeRoy, 1940, US) Norma Shearer, Robert Taylor, Conrad Veidt, Alla Nazimova, Felix Bressart, Albert Basserman, Elsa Basserman.
104 min. b/w.
Glossy wartime sentiment from MGM, as American widow Shearer turns against her German lover (Veidt in his Hollywood debut) to help a young compatriot artist (Taylor) rescue his mother from a pre-war Nazi concentration camp. Adapting from a bestselling novel by Ethel Vance, LeRoy forsakes the hard-nosed 'realism' learned during his days with Warners, and goes all out for a well-crafted, controlled, but finally rather bland weepie. Supporting roles are performed by the usual group of stock European actors – Bressart, the Bassermans, all highly watchable – and there's an added bonus in Taylor's incarcerated mother being played by Nazimova, exotic temptress of silent movies, here returning to the screen after an absence of 15 years. But lacking the romantic conviction of Borzage, LeRoy all too often seems stranded in a smooth, unruffled sea of MGM banality. GA

Escape (Szökés)

(Livia Gyarmathy, 1997, Hun) Daniel Olbrychski, Artur Zmijewski, Krzysztof Kolberger, Adám Schnell, Zsolt László.
92 min.
Hungary, just a few years on from the country's liberation from fascism, and the new Communist regime is settling in nicely, filling the prisons with political dissenters. This is the true story of one such innocent, as he spends two years in a secret labour camp before effecting a daring escape. He has memorised the names of his fellow internees in the hope of bringing the story to the outside world, but half the Hungarian army seems to be on his trail. Not unexpectedly, a fairly dour piece of film-making, but it does tell its story with a certain gritty urgency, and there's a fine performance from Olbrychski as the steely camp commandant. TJ

Escape from Alcatraz

(Don Siegel, 1979, US) Clint Eastwood, Patrick McGoohan, Roberts Blossom, Jack Thibeau, Fred Ward, Paul Benjamin, Larry Hankin.
112 min.
Siegel's finest film since *The Shootist*, this tells the story of the one successful escape ever believed to have been made from the island penitentiary of Alcatraz. It's not an action film: there's little in the way of exciting set pieces, and Eastwood's restrained performance is low-key almost to the point of minimalism. Rather, as he slowly tries to tunnel out with a pair of nail-clippers, it's an austere depiction of the tedious routines of prison life, and of the courage and strength of spirit needed in coping with unpleasant warders, tough fellow-inmates, and a life sentence. As such, it's closer to Bresson's *A Man Escaped* (although obviously without the Catholic theme of redemption) than to the Hollywood prison escape movie. GA

Escape from Fort Bravo

(John Sturges, 1953, US) William Holden, Eleanor Parker, John Forsythe, Polly Bergen, William Demarest.
98 min.
Western set in Arizona during the Civil War, neatly sustained from a familiar set of ingredients. Femme fatale Parker helps some Confederate soldiers escape their Union captors, whose efforts to recapture them are hindered by hostile Indians. Holden's suitably steel-jawed as the cavalry captain leading the boys in blue. Photographed by Robert Surtees. TJ

Escape from L.A.

see John Carpenter's Escape from L.A.

Escape from New York

(John Carpenter, 1981, US) Kurt Russell, Lee Van Cleef, Ernest Borgnine, Donald Pleasence, Isaac Hayes, Season Hubley, Tom Atkins, Harry Dean Stanton, Adrienne Barbeau.
99 min.

Sporting a black eye-patch and a mutinous sneer, anti-hero Snake Plissken (Russell) prepares to invade the Manhattan of 1997, sealed off as a self-regulating maximum security prison following a 400% rise in the crime rate, and ruled over by a black drug-dealing Prospero (Hayes) attended by his punk Ariel. Victim of a Catch-22 situation and primed to self-destruct if he fails, Snake's task is to rescue the hijacked US President (Pleasence) from this ominous underworld; and for about half the film, Carpenter's narrative economy and explosive visual style (incorporating some marvellous model work of the new Manhattan skyline) promise wonders. The trouble is that his characters neither develop nor interact dynamically, so the plot gradually winds down into predictable though highly enoyable histrionics. TM

Escape from the Dark (aka The Littlest Horse Thieves)

(Charles Jarrott, 1975, US) Alastair Sim, Peter Barkworth, Maurice Colbourne, Susan Tebbs, Geraldine McEwan, Prunella Scales, Leslie Sands, Joe Gladwin.
104 min.
A loathsome Disney attempt to foist the standards of *Upstairs Downstairs* on a turn-of-the-century Yorkshire colliery: anyone taking children to see it will have to put up with 'Can I go down a mine, too?' for the rest of the week. In a daringly flagrant disregard for the Industrial Revolution, our story shows how humble pit-ponies can beat new-fangled mechanisation every time, and how honest colliers only want to get on with their job without interference from The Bosses. 'Them ponies belong in the pit, same as us' is the line of the film: it's as if Lawrence and Orwell, let alone *Kes*, had never existed. England's class-ridden society of acting talent (Sim as crusty earl, beaming Joe Gladwin down t'pit) does its duty, but all are on a hiding to nothing. AN

Escape from the 'Liberty' Cinema (Ucieczka z Kina 'Wolnosc')

(Wojciech Marczewski, 1990, Pol) Janusz Gajos, Zbigniew Zamachowski, Teresa Marczewska.
92 min.
A complex, allusive and deeply-felt examination of the nature and effects of censorship, directed by one of Poland's leading intellectual – and much censored – film-makers. It employs a rich mixture of dark political satire and poetic allegory as it details the life of the head of an unnamed town's District Censorship Office, a divorced ex-poet, journalist and literary critic suffering from psychosomatic headaches and heart palpitations. There are ructions outside his local cinema, the Liberty: the actors on screen stage a strike (shades of *The Purple Rose of Cairo*), refuse their allotted lines and roles, and begin to assert their freedom to make demands on the audience. The pressure on the head censor becomes unbearable, so when the local political bosses get involved and his vodka bottle runs out, he decides on extraordinary action... WH

Escape from the Planet of the Apes

(Don Taylor, 1971, US) Roddy McDowall, Kim Hunter, Bradford Dillman, Ricardo Montalban, Natalie Trundy, Sal Mineo, Albert Salmi, M Emmet Walsh.
97 min.
The third in the series. Quite a cheat, really, as Cornelius, Zira and Milo slip through a bend of time and avoid the holocaust. They find themselves back on human-dominated earth. Which is good for the budget as there is hardly a space device in sight. Instead, all we get is hysterical reactions from the local US Gov. fascist, Zira lecturing to the Women's Institute, a friendly circus owner...But the pessimism of the earlier two films remains, as well as another loophole, for the follow-up. It's a long way down from even the second in the series.

Escape from Zahrain

(Ronald Neame, 1961, US) Yul Brynner, Sal Mineo, Jack Warden, Madlyn Rhue, Tony Caruso, James Mason, Jay Novello.
93 min.
Turgid desert-trek drama, featuring Brynner and various bottle-tanned cohorts as escapee political

prisoners in an Arab oil state. A predictable combination of the woeful exotic urges of both director Neame (*Mister Moses*) and screenwriter Robin Estridge (the dire Frankie Avalon-starring *Drums of Africa*). PT

Escape of The Amethyst

see Yangtse Incident

Escape Route to Marseilles (Fluchtweg nach Marseilles)

(Ingemo Engström/Gerhard Theuring, 1977, WGer) Katharina Thalbach, Rüdiger Vogler.
210 min.
Studies of Germany's recent fascist past – especially from film-makers on the left – are notorious for their length (eg. *Confessions of Winifred Wagner*), but this would put even Hans-Jürgen Syberberg to the test. Basically, it's an analysis of how people escaped from Occupied France through the so-called Free Zone to Marseilles and, with a lot of luck, abroad by sea. But the film also aims to point the significance of these events for all those involved in resistance activities today. Mixing documentary, interview and newsreel footage, but deliberately avoiding the 'dramatic' aspects of the mass exodus, this quasi-documentary is comprehensive to the point of pedantry and sober to the point of solemnity, lacking the essential irony that made Kluge's *The Patriot* such an entertaining yet progressive treatise on 20th century German history. Overburdened by a sense of expiation, and unrelieved by any feeling for accessible film-making. MA

Escape to Athena

(George P Cosmatos, 1979, GB) Roger Moore, Telly Savalas, David Niven, Claudia Cardinale, Stefanie Powers, Richard Roundtree, Sonny Bono, Elliott Gould, Anthony Valentine.
117 min.
Planning a summer holiday? *Escape to Athena* suffers from that tourist brochure look, with bouzouki music throbbing as we skim across the Aegean back to the sun-soaked days of 1944 and a PoW Camp *Méditerranée* on an idyllic isle, frequented by film stars like Moore, Niven and Gould. Take a drop of ouzo with colourful local characters like Savalas (as the island's big, sensitive Resistance leader) and Cardinale (the island's patriotic madame). The plot is like something knocked together by Alistair MacLean in his sleep, but was actually devised by the director. Awful. JS

Escape to Burma

(Allan Dwan, 1955, US) Barbara Stanwyck, Robert Ryan, David Farrar, Robert Warwick, Murvyn Vye, Lisa Montell, Reginald Denny, Peter Coe.
88 min.
Pure hokum in which Ryan goes on the run through the Burmese jungle after supposedly murdering the local ruler's son, pursued by a British police officer (Farrar) intent on bringing him back for trial, and by the ruler's underlings, bent on summary justice. He finds succour and romance in the unlikely person of Stanwyck, who runs her late father's teak plantation, rules the natives with matriarchal benevolence (they call her Gwen Ma), and has a special soft spot for her labour force of elephants. Dwan does his best with a script which doesn't miss a potboiling ingredient: a ravening tiger for Ryan to save Stanwyck from, a baby elephant that performs cute tricks, a bagful of rubies to incite a roving gang of bandits to thoughts of robbery and murder. The three leads give good performances, but the film's sole distinction is John Alton's brilliantly lucid Technicolor/Superscope camerawork. TM

Escape to Happiness

see Intermezzo

Escape to Victory

see Victory

Escape to Witch Mountain

(John Hough, 1974, US) Eddie Albert, Ray Milland, Donald Pleasence, Kim Richards, Ike Eisenmann, Walter Barnes.
97 min.
A Disney adventure with quite a lot going for it, even if it does end up spreading itself too wide

for the sakes of the entire family. Two orphans, gifted with extra-terrestrial powers, get sidetracked in their search for their origins by an unscrupulous Milland, who hopes to use their clairvoyance to increase his own wealth. What emerges is a chase film – with the kids aided by a gruff but friendly Eddie Albert – which employs fast cars and a helicopter in much the same manner as Hough's earlier *Dirty Mary, Crazy Larry*. Most of the credit must rest with the adult actors, who refuse to patronise their material; interestingly, the film's underlying themes ('Our planet was dying. The only industry left was the manufacture of spaceships') are both topical and quite serious. CPe

Escort, The

see Scorta, La

Eskiya

see Bandit, The

Esperanza & Sardinas

(Roberto Romeo, 1996, Sp) Manuel de Blas, Paulina Gálvez, Luis Beviá, Juan Antonio Blasco.
92 min. b/w.
Shot quite stylishly in b/w on a very low budget, this example of the new Spanish cinema is formless, meandering and inconsequential. Set in an Alicante village, it simply observes the not particularly arresting relationships between sundry unsavoury characters – the men are mostly braggarts and brawlers into drink, drugs and sex talk, the women objects of their desire. GA

Espion Lève-toi

(Yves Boisset, 1982, Fr) Lino Ventura, Michel Piccoli, Krystyna Janda, Bruno Crémer, Heinz Bennent, Bernard Fresson.
98 min.
Here's a belated digest of mid-'60s espionage clichés, from the bandstand rendezvous at the start (*The Ipcress File*) to the perforated hero and heroine at the end (*The Spy Who Came In From the Cold*). Once again government agencies and their creatures are characterised as ruthless, cynical and devious beyond comprehension, crushing the innocent in the interests of some great obscure McGuffin. The setting (Zurich, with all its Franco-German confusions) might have stimulated some originality, but no: this is all cold-eyed hitmen, spot the traitor and shoot-outs on the funicular. Ventura, Piccoli and the composer Morricone in their different ways keep their heads below the parapet, but Janda unwisely charges forth, acting away as though all this might mean something. From George Markstein's novel *Chance Awakening*. BBa

Espions, Les

(Henri-Georges Clouzot, 1957, Fr) Curd Jurgens, Peter Ustinov, Gérard Séty, Sam Jaffe, Paul Carpenter, Martita Hunt.
125 min. b/w.
A lunatic asylum in remote countryside, a top secret patient smuggled on to the premises at dead of night, the arrival in the village of a flock of sinister strangers. Turns out the Secret Service has invented a pretend spy to fox the foe and this is all in aid of spinning out the deception. The fiction-about-a-fiction idea aside, this bears no resemblance to Hitchcock's similar set up *North by Northwest*, and it's hard to know whether the wildly fluctuating tone was a matter of accident or design. The multi-national casting doesn't help, with the humourless Jurgens apparently suffering the agonies of the damned, and Ustinov's very presence shifting all his scenes into waggishness. Beginning as gothic horror, ending as cynical shaggy dog story, this is one of the more peculiar contributions to the '50s Cold War cycle. BBa

Espoir (Days of Hope/Man's Hope)

(André Malraux, 1939, Fr/Sp) José Sempere, Andres Mejuto, Nicolas Rodriguez, Pedro Codina, José Lado.
90 min. b/w.
Begun in 1938 in Barcelona, but interrupted by the arrival of Franco's troops, Malraux's crudely made but historically fascinating film only drew on one episode from his novel of the same title. Basically an assemblage of memories of the anti-Fascist fighting during the Civil War, the dialogue scenes

now look very inadequate. What are extraordinary, however, are the sequences of combat, a bombing raid filmed from the air, and the film's climactic set piece, a procession of over 2,000 carrying dead and wounded pilots down the mountain of the Sierra de Teruel to the music of Darius Milhaud. DT

Esther Waters

(Ian Dalrymple/Peter Proud, 1948, GB)
Kathleen Ryan, Dirk Bogarde, Cyril Cusack, Fay Compton, Ivor Barnard, Mary Clare, Julian d'Albie, Morland Graham, Shelagh Fraser.
109 min. b/w.
Having made her mark in Reed's *Odd Man Out*, Irish actress Ryan got herself a real showcase in this period melodrama, from the novel by George Moore (1894), suffering nobly and at length as the honest serving wench in a country house who gets herself pregnant by rapscallion groom Bogarde (in his second screen appearance). He, on the other hand, is more interested in horse racing, and there'll be a fortune won and lost before the day is done. The actors win our sympathy despite the hoary subject matter, though the well-staged racecourse sequences almost convince you the movie's a lot better than it actually is. TJ

Estratagia del Caracol, La

see Strategy of the Snail, The

Etat de Siège

see State of Siege

Et Dieu Créa la Femme (And God Created Woman/ And Woman...Was Created)

(Roger Vadim, 1956, Fr) Curd Jürgens, Brigitte Bardot, Christian Marquand, Jean-Louis Trintignant, Georges Poujouly.
91 min.
Cautiously titled *And Woman...Was Created* for its British release, this was the film that started the Bardot thing. Basically a clever piece of pre-New Wave programming with its St Tropez locations, 'daring' sex and amoral youth, it adds up to little more than a series of semi-nude posturings as the sex kitten flits nymphomaniacally from man to man and back again. But the lively characterisations and wry wit make the first half a good deal more watchable than most of Vadim's abject later creations.

Eté à La Goulette, Un

see Summer in La Goulette, A

Eté inoubliable, Un

see Unforgettable Summer, An

Eté Meurtrier, L'

see One Deadly Summer

Eternal Love

see Eternel Retour, L'

Eternel Retour, L' (Eternal Love/Love Eternal)

(Jean Delannoy, 1943, Fr) Madeleine Sologne, Jean Marais, Jean Murat, Yvonne de Bray, Pierre Pieral, Jane Marken.
111 min. b/w.
Made during the German Occupation in World War II, Cocteau's updating of the Tristan and Isolde legend remains a sadly neglected film, largely because postwar critics jumped on the Aryan blondness of the two leads to tag it as collaborationist. Actually the pair look more like a tribute to camp chic, drifting photogenically but sexlessly through the grand passion that unites the lovers in death. But the film itself, broodingly set in an ancient castle overhanging the sea, has a rare, dreamlike beauty that captures the quality of legend almost as successfully as *La Belle et la Bête*. Some stunning performances, too, not least from Pieral as the malevolent dwarf and de Bray as his horribly complacent mother. TM

Eternity and a Day (Mia Eoniotita Ke Mia Mera)

(Theo Angelopoulos, 1998, Greece/Fr/Ger) Bruno Ganz, Isabelle Renauld, Achileas Skevis, Despina Bebedeli.
130 min.

A dying author (Ganz) prepares to leave his beloved family home by the sea, and settle things with his daughter; his feelings of despair are interrupted, complicated and finally, to some extent, banished by memories of happier times with his wife (Renauld) and by an encounter with a young Albanian orphan. Angelopoulos' film, a deserving winner of the Palme d'Or at Cannes '98, is a characteristically elegant, eloquent and idiosyncratic meditation on the relationships between personal and political histories, and between life and art. More intimate than, say, *The Travelling Players* or *Ulysses' Gaze*, the film nevertheless reaches out, as its long, fluid takes escort us through space and time, to universal themes and broader topicalities, effortlessly fending off charges of hermetic aestheticism. GA

Ethan Frome

(John Madden, 1992, US) Liam Neeson, Patricia Arquette, Joan Allen, Tate Donovan, Katharine Houghton, Stephen Mendillo.
107 min.
The landscapes of winter mirror the emotions in this adaptation of Edith Wharton's 1911 novel. Ethan Frome (Neeson), the New England farmer struggling to make ends meet, is one side of an eternal triangle, the others are his sickly cousin Zeena (Allen) and his fragile relative Mattie (Arquette). Their story is related by Mrs Hale (Houghton), the sexton's wife, to Rev Smith (Donovan), the new minister, who wants to help the Fromes. Although the dutiful husband, the bed-ridden wife and the poor relation are staples of melodrama, audiences should be able to identify with characters who see their hopes crushed, revivified and crushed again. Plainly filmed this tale may be – it is an 'American Playhouse' theatrical release – but it is honestly played and deeply felt. Bobby Bukowski's bleak cinematography and Rachel Portman's mournful score make the pain palpable. AO

Etoile du Nord, L' (The Northern Star)

(Pierre Granier-Deferre, 1982, Fr) Simone Signoret, Philippe Noiret, Fanny Cottençon, Julie Jezequel, Liliana Gérace, Gamil Ratib.
124 min.
Clearly borrowing both inspiration and key personnel from the Bertrand Tavernier school of eccentric thrillers, Granier-Deferre teases this Simenon adaptation towards irresistible absurdity. The brilliant Noiret is a forgetful killer on the lam, spinning exotic yarns to fend off compound disappointments and derangements (prompting the film to incongruous cross-fades between the Belgian boarding-house where he's staying and his previous home in Egypt), stirring in his ageing landlady (Signoret) the memory of her own long-abandoned dreams of 'escape', and cueing several nice black ironies about travel broadening the mind. There's a flighty femme fatale, a murder on a train, dirty money burnt – but all the conventions of the genre make scant impression on Noiret's fantastic fakir act. Which, however you look at it, is the only conceivable abiding impression of this incoherent, oddball joy. PT

Etrange Monsieur Victor, L'

(Jean Grémillon, 1938, Fr) Raimu, Madeleine Renaud, Pierre Blanchar, Viviane Romance.
102 min. b/w.
Or the strange Monsieur Grémillon...Though unquestionably a major film-maker, Grémillon – also an accomplished musician, painter and documentarist – has remained a marginal figure even in his native land, a French Humphrey Jennings, perhaps. In this bleak study of malevolence, an example of his painterly rather than poetic realism, Raimu plays (magnificently) a modest clerk whose mousy respectability conceals the psychology of a monster. GAd

E.T. The Extra-Terrestrial

(Steven Spielberg, 1982, US) Dee Wallace, Henry Thomas, Peter Coyote, Robert MacNaughton, Drew Barrymore.
115 min.
Returning to the rich pastures of American suburbia, Spielberg takes the utterly commonplace story of a lonely kid befriending an alien from outer space, and invests it with exactly the same kind of fierce and naive magic that pushed Disney's major masterpieces like *Pinocchio* into

a central place in 20th century popular culture. Moreover, with its Nativity-like opening and its final revelation, the plot of *E.T.* has parallels in religious mythology that help to explain its electric effect on audiences. But although conclusively demonstrating Spielberg's preeminence as the popular artist of his time, *E.T.* finally seems a less impressive film than *Close Encounters*. This is partly because its first half contains a couple of comedy sequences as vulgar as a Brooke Bond TV chimps commercial, but more because in reducing the unknowable to the easily loveable, the film sacrifices a little too much truth in favour of its huge emotional punch. DP

Eureka

(Nicolas Roeg, 1982, GB/US) Gene Hackman, Theresa Russell, Rutger Hauer, Jane Lapotaire, Mickey Rourke, Ed Lauter, Helena Kallianiotes, Joe Pesci.
129 min.
The usual nervy Roeg cross-cutting has almost vanished in favour of a cleaner but just as distanced narrative, in two plain parts: a prospector (Hackman) in Canada in the '20s finally strikes it lucky, engulfed in a river of gold; and then the rest of his life, immured in his house ('Eureka') in the Bahamas and wondering what on earth there is left. While the weight of Roeg's success is usually stylistic, this is more of a harkback to the cosmic scale of *The Man Who Fell to Earth*, with enormous themes streaming through a strange tale. Alongside the bass-line of a man who 'once had it all, and now just owns everything', there are games of knowledge and power (voodoo, cabbalahs, magick), a devouring relationship with his daughter (Russell), and a nebulous running battle with business competitors who want their own share of the planet. The man who raped the earth and lost his demon is finally the victim of 'business interests' in the same way that Jagger was in *Performance*. It's a great, *Kane*-like notion – the price we pay for gaining what we want – and overflowing with awkward ideas and strange emotion. CPea

Europa

(Lars von Trier, 1991, Den) Jean-Marc Barr, Barbara Sukowa, Udo Kier, Ernst-Hugo Järegård, Erik Mark, Jergen Reenberg, Henning Jensen, Eddie Constantine.
114 min. b/w & col.
Von Trier's *Element of Crime* was one of the great love-it-or-hate-it films, and this divided opinions even more furiously. Portentous but hypnotic, it's a mannered delve into postwar history: an American German (Barr) returns to work on the German railways after WW2, only to get entangled in underground politics and the dark machinations of a railway dynasty. The grandiose scale and visual pyrotechnics paradoxically combine to claustrophobic effect (imagine something between Fassbinder and Lynch's *Dune)*; and like the constantly shuttling sleeping car in which much of the film is set, where it's going is hard to say. Max von Sydow's ominously mesmeric opening voice-over makes for a wind-up from the outset, but if you can stay awake through that, you're in for a highly idiosyncratic mystery tour. JRo

Europa, Europa

(Agnieska Holland, 1991, Fr/Ger) Marco Hofschneider, Julie Delpy, Hanns Zischler, André Wilms, Andrzej Mastalerz, Delphine Forest.
112 min.
Although both look and subject matter are familiar – from *Mephisto* and *The Tin Drum* – Agnieska Holland's war story is all the more unsettling for being true. Salomon Perel (Hofschneider) is a young German Jew who flees eastwards as the Nazis move in. Fate ensures his survival by landing him first in a Soviet Komsomol school, where he learns to be a fervent young Stalinist, then in a German front-line detachment where he passes as the flower of pure Aryan youth. Enrolled in an élite Hitler Youth academy, he falls for lovely Jew-hating Leni (Delpy); but by this point the effort of hiding behind so many masks, not to mention hiding the most physical evidence of his Jewishness, is beginning to take its toll... The story is so absurd that it could have made a grotesque historical burlesque of the Günter Grass variety. Holland takes a more prosaic approach, but the ironies bite hard, and occasional farcical moments add

an unsettling edge to Perel's fortunes. Holland plays on the paradox of role-playing with moderation, but the moral uncertainties of Perel's survival are no less dizzying for all that. JRo

Europe After the Rain
(Mick Gold, 1978, GB) Marcel Duchamp, Max Ernst.
88 min. b/w & col.
As an idiosyncratic anthology of Dadaist and Surrealist artifacts and attitudes, Gold's film for the Arts Council is fine. A chock-full collage of texts, reproduced artworks, actual footage and dramatised reconstructions, it constantly unearths delights, both visual and aural (some strictly tangential, such as Joan Bakewell interviewing Marcel Duchamp). But as an analysis of the movements' aesthetic ideas, aims and achievements, it flounders: by reducing the 20th century historical and cultural context to two world wars, plus the thought of Freud and Trotsky; and by crucially failing to make adequate distinction between 'authentic' surrealism and its latter-day manifestations in, for instance, cigarette advertising and TV comedy. PT

Europeans, The
(James Ivory, 1979, GB) Lee Remick, Robin Ellis, Tim Woodward, Wesley Addy, Lisa Eichhorn, Nancy New, Tim Choate, Kristin Griffith.
92 min.
A wonderfully elegant adaptation of Henry James' early novel about the impact of a sophisticated but impecunious European countess and her brother on their wealthy country cousins in America. Staged with affection, insight, a whole fistful of superb performances and exquisite settings. Odd, though, that Ruth Prawer Jhabvala's otherwise excellent script fails to note James' distinction between the Countess, who is a fortune-hunter, and her brother who is not; without it, the subtlest irony of this comedy of manners goes by the board. TM

Eve
(Joseph Losey, 1962, Fr/It) Jeanne Moreau, Stanley Baker, Virna Lisi, Giorgio Albertazzi, James Villiers, Riccardo Garrone, Lisa Gastoni.
118 min. b/w.
The film is set in Venice, in the season that most suits that city (winter), shot in Losey's characteristic baroque style of the period, and features Baker as the upstart Welsh novelist, engaged to an empty marriage but gradually ensnared into an *amour fou* by the ferocious, loose temptress Eve. Love hardly enters into it; it is corruption by power, money and bad faith that are Losey's obsessions, and they are dwelt upon insistently with more sheerly scathing disaste than he allowed himself subsequently. The film undoubtedly belongs to Moreau who, in one of her finest performances, gives a portrait of terrifying honesty – the heartless self-possession of a woman who does nothing unless for money or whim. The figures of alienation wandering through an elegant landscape may be familiar from the Antonioni trilogy of the period, but the pessimism, energetic misanthropy and disenchantment with the world are all Losey's own. CPea

Evel Knievel
(Marvin Chomsky, 1971, US) George Hamilton, Sue Lyon, Bert Freed, Rod Cameron, Dub Taylor, Ron Masak.
90 min.
A fascinating and enjoyable film about the daredevil motorcyclist-stuntman (played ebulliently by Hamilton, although the spectacular stunt scenes are documentary footage of Knievel himself). Piecing together events in his life – his early delinquent driving, an attempted safe-cracking career, and the increasing audacity of his legendary rides – it portrays something of an egomaniac, basking in the light of his own fame while privately racked by neuroses. Chomsky's seemingly nonchalant direction, from a script by John Milius and Alan Caillou, sensibly refuses neat psychological explanations, and instead opens out to provide a finely detailed portrait of middle America. GA

Even Cowgirls Get the Blues
(Gus Van Sant, 1993, US) Uma Thurman, John Hurt, Rain Phoenix, Keanu Reeves, Lorraine Bracco, Angie Dickinson, Carol Kane, Roseanne Arnold, Ken Kesey, Buck Henry, William Burroughs.
96 min.

This adaptation of Tom Robbins' cult novel finally emerges as an embarrassing miscalculation. Thurman is Sissy Hankshaw, a model by profession and hitch-hiker by vocation. On a photo-shoot at a Dakota beauty ranch, Sissy is caught in the middle of a cowgirl sexual revolution against the feminine hygiene regimen of the Countess (Hurt). The film is a sour comedy and a curiously inert road movie. Mostly, though, it's a wacky allegory of the kind in vogue in the '70s, which is roughly when this sort of material might have had some sort of relevance. It's actually more like a time capsule: anyone nostalgic for woolly women's lib metaphors, feckless counter-culturalism, hippy-dippy rhetoric and bird symbolism, this is the trip you've been waiting for. TCh

Even Dwarfs Started Small (Auch Zwerge haben klein angefangen)
(Werner Herzog, 1970, WGer) Helmut Döring, Gerd Gickel, Paul Glauer, Erna Gschwnedtner, Gisela Hartwig.
96 min. b/w.
A film about man's relation to the world of objects he surrounds himself with. Dwarfs are used to emphasise the extent to which objects dominate our personal relations: their alienation from the institution and its products is ours too. The anarchist uprising is a beautiful negation of bourgeois values, sometimes savage, but usually compassionate and amusing. The dwarfs are great, and the tribal music superb.

Evénement le plus Important depuis que l'Homme a Marché sur la Lune, L'
see Slighty Pregnant Man, The

Evening Dress
see Tenue de Soirée

Evening Performance (Función de Noche)
(Josefina Molina, 1981, Sp) Lola Herrera, Daniel Dicenta, Natalia Dicenta Herrera, Luis Rodriguez Olivares.
90 min.
Intensely private, largely improvised, this portrait of a middle-aged actress struggling with a role that propels her into personal crisis (echoes of Cassavetes' *Opening Night*) consists mainly of an emotional confrontation between Lola Herrera and her ex-husband Dicenta. But the brief moments showing her with friends, children and doctor aren't enough to open up a painfully introverted central scene into the promised analysis of 'machismo'; and although it's impossible not to admire Herrera's honesty, as the endless hysterics/histrionics mount, so unfortunately does the spectator's tedium. SJo

Evening Star, The
(Robert Harling, 1996, US) Shirley MacLaine, Miranda Richardson, Bill Paxton, Juliette Lewis, Ben Johnson, Scott Wolf, Jack Nicholson.
129 min.
Fifteen years after the death of her daughter (and 14 years after *Terms of Endearment*), the sun's setting on Aurora Greenway (MacLaine). She's fighting with her grandchildren, feuding with her neighbour Patsy (Richardson) and succumbing to a shrink with a mother complex (Paxton). While Lewis is convincingly cast as Debra Winger's daughter, and you can always look to Richardson for poised bitchery, writer/director Harling ensures that everyone is but further grist to Aurora's already monstrous ego: even the ubiquitous Jack Nicholson pops in to pay tribute. This isn't so much a movie as a memorial service. MacLaine, though, is still very much alive and kicking, more than able to take a scene by the scruff of the neck. If there's no edge, at least there's a centre. Harling is best known for his play *Steel Magnolias*, and he also had a hand in the scripts for *Soapdish* and *First Wives Club*, so it's no surprise that the film's female characters have more going on than their feckless partners, but this adaptation of Larry McMurtry's novel irons out depth without tightening up a baggy shapeless narrative. TCh

E Venne un Uomo
see Man Named John, A

Evensong
(Victor Saville, 1934, GB) Evelyn Laye, Fritz Kortner, Conchita Supervia, Emlyn Williams, Alice Delysia, Carl Esmond.
84 min. b/w.
Irish diva (Laye) is moulded by Viennese impresario (Kortner) into a top opera star and romancer of the Austrian nobility, but refusal to acknowledge the approach of her twilight years leads to an inevitable fall from grace. A touch more sophisticated than the usual run of homegrown '30s musicals, genre specialist Saville's film benefits no end from the commanding and courageous central performance. TJ

Event Horizon
(Paul Anderson, 1997, US/GB) Laurence Fishburne, Sam Neill, Kathleen Quinlan, Joely Richardson, Jack Noseworthy, Richard T Jones, Jason Isaacs, Sean Pertwee.
96 min.
After 35 years lost in the cosmos, the spaceship 'Event Horizon' re-establishes contact. A team of crack astronauts, led by Fishburne and accompanied by scientist Neill, is sent from Earth to salvage the vessel and pick up survivors. When they arrive, they get more than they bargained for. For all its big budget effects and scenery, Brit director Anderson's third feature – after *Shopping* and *Mortal Kombat* – is less sci-fi spectacular than old fashioned ghost-cum-horror yarn, set 56 days away from Earth. Walls drip blood and shapeless evil hovers. Horror piles on horror without much intervening suspense. Even the fine supporting cast (Pertwee, Richardson and Quinlan) fails to raise the ghost of a smile to ease the tension. But, despite its shortcomings, this is never dull. The movie avoids *Alien* space monster clichés brilliantly and the soundtrack contains more of the 'Boo!' effects than I've heard since *Halloween*. NKe

Eve of Destruction
(Duncan Gibbins, 1991, US) Renee Soutendijk, Gregory Hines, Michael Greene, Kurt Fuller, John M Jackson, Loren Haynes, Ross Malinger.
98 min.
In her American debut, Soutendijk plays Dr Eve Simmons, a beautiful research scientist who creates a cyborg in her own image. A military robot endowed with her body, brains and emotional hang-ups, it turns into a super-destructive, castrating, father-hating RoboSlut. Sadly, too little is made of the premise that Soutendijk's damaged doppelgänger is giving vent to her own repressed urges. Also, the bursts of explosive action are punctuated by turgid, talky scenes in which angry cop Hines harangues Soutendijk about the ethics of military science. In short, an attention-catching idea in search of a movie. NF

Eve of St Mark, The
(John M Stahl, 1944, US) Anne Baxter, William Eythe, Michael O'Shea, Vincent Price, Dickie Moore.
96 min. b/w.
Maxwell Anderson's blank verse play, a Broadway hit, comes over on screen as a slightly artsy WWII flag-waver, as GI Eythe survives conditions in the Pacific campaign with the help of Midwestern sweetheart Baxter. The treatment of familiar material is more sensitive than usual, but some of the ambitious dialogue sticks in the craw. TJ

Everest
(David Breashears, 1997, US)
43 min.
The Himalayan vistas viewed from the world's tallest mountain on an IMAX screen 'seven storeys' high is breathtaking. Cameraman Rob Schauer and the rest of the team clearly went through hell: the crew (including the son of Sherpa Tenzing who accompanied Hillary on the first ascent) was required to cart more than 100lb of IMAX stock across crevasses and over unpredictably icy boulders. They witnessed the misfortune of eight climbers from another expedition perishing on the same slopes. And then there was the frost bite and altitude sickness. George Harrison provides the swirling soundtrack, Liam Neeson the sincere commentary. DA

Evergreen

(Victor Saville, 1934, GB) Jessie Matthews, Barry Mackay, Sonnie Hale, Betty Balfour, Ivor McLaren.
91 min. b/w.

Matthews, the stallholder's daughter from Berwick Street, paid heavily for the acclaim she won as Britain's leading musical star. Despite Saville's sympathetic direction, she suffered horrifying nervous rashes and temporary mental breakdown during the making of this, her most famous film. She nevertheless gives a dazzling performance in the dual role of a famous music hall star and the daughter, an unemployed chorus-girl, who impersonates her in a desperate bid for fame and fortune. If Saville fails to explore the sexual undertones of the story, the exciting post-*Metropolis* sets designed by Alfred Junge provide an impressive showcase for Jessie's elfin beauty and superb dancing (to a Rodgers and Hart score). RMy

Everlasting Secret Family, The

(Michael Thornhill, 1987, Aust) Arthur Dignam, Mark Lee, Heather Mitchell, Dennis Miller, Paul Goddard, Beth Child, John Clayton.
93 min.

Sports day at an exclusive Australian boys' school. One of the gorgeous youths, watched by a sinister black-clad figure, is whisked off to a hotel room, divested of clothes and ravished. As he doesn't object, he is taken to a party and seduced by a Japanese gent who insists on doing things to him with a large live crab. Next, he undergoes an initiation ceremony à la Knights Templar and joins 'the family', an ancient sex-ring which wreaks terrible punishment on those who blab. From then on, it's a confused tale of the boy's attempts to flee, his search for eternal youth, and his burgeoning relationship with his master's son, with lots of male nudity and some fairly explicit sex. All the gay characters are 'elderly pervert' stereotypes, cruel, calculating and vampirish; yet, for a film that takes so rigidly homophobic a stance, an awful lot of time is spent dwelling on youthful tanned muscles, taut buttocks, and the like. Revolting, ludicrous, infuriating, and (blush) often very erotic, it is about nothing but self-hatred. RS

Everybody Does It

(Edmund Goulding, 1949, US) Paul Douglas, Linda Darnell, Celeste Holm, Charles Coburn, Millard Mitchell, Lucille Watson.
98 min. b/w.

A typically Hollywoodised version of James M Cain's fine novella (*Career in C Major*, previously filmed in 1939 as *Wife, Husband, and Friend*) about a rough-diamond building contractor whose life is made a misery by the socialite wife he adores. Intent, like Charles Foster Kane's beloved, on parlaying a tiny talent into a career as a concert singer, she loses no opportunity to walk over her husband's supposed cultural inferiority. Her comeuppance is neatly contrived when a celebrated diva, sought for an opinion of her voice, discovers not only that the despised husband has the sensational voice in the family, but that his body is desirably hunky. Shorn of most of Cain's acid social and sexual overtones, the script turns into a routine romantic comedy. Given elegantly sharpish direction, plus fine performances by the leads (Douglas as the husband, Holm as the wife, Darnell as the diva), it makes for pleasantly civilised viewing all the same. TM

Everybody's All-American (aka When I Fall in Love)

(Taylor Hackford, 1988, US) Jessica Lange, Dennis Quaid, Timothy Hutton, John Goodman, Carl Lumbly, Ray Baker, Savannah Smith Boucher, Patricia Clarkson.
127 min.

Based on the novel by Frank Deford, this spans 25 years in the lives of three characters: Gavin Grey (Quaid), Babs (Lange), and Gavin's nephew Donnie (Hutton). Everybody loves Gavin. Revered as a footballer, he leaves college to go professional and marries Babs, while peripheral Donnie – juggling his naive regard for Gavin alongside a latent passion for Babs – heads for an academic career. Typically of such scenarios, the story charts the trials which beset the golden couple, and the self-realisation which comes with hardship and maturity. The idolatry which surrounds Gavin verges on the absurd, making it nearly impossible to establish sympathy for him or those who adore him. Given the material, the performances are competent enough; but Hackford and cinematographer Stephen Goldblatt are too indulgent in creating a near-religion out of the characters' self-absorption. CM

Everybody's Cheering

see Take Me Out to the Ball Game

Everybody's Fine (Stanno tutti bene)

(Giuseppe Tornatore, 1990, It/Fr) Marcello Mastroianni, Michèle Morgan, Salvatore Cascio, Valeria Cavalli, Marino Cenna, Roberto Nobile.
126 min.

Tornatore's follow-up to *Cinema Paradiso* isn't quite so dewy-eyed, but will still have cynics retching into their popcorn. Amiable old buffer Matteo (Mastroianni) lives a lonely life in Sicily. On a whim, he ups sticks and travels to the mainland; his aim, to reunite his family round a dinner table. But his children seem strangely embarrassed by him. Contrasted with the highly unsatisfactory behaviour of his adult offspring are his vivid memories of them as kids. His son Alvaro remains absent, and as the old man camps miserably on the doorstep, young Alvaro (the terminally cute Cascio) shimmers into view. There is a melodramatic plot lurch, a haunting dream sequence, a well-handled autumnal love affair, and a neat twist at the end. Like *Cinema Paradiso*, it's expertly manipulative and good-looking, though a tad darker. Mastroianni gambols through it. SFe

Everybody Wins

(Karel Reisz, 1990, GB) Debra Winger, Nick Nolte, Will Patton, Judith Ivey, Jack Warden, Kathleen Wilhoite, Frank Converse, Frank Military.
97 min.

Arthur Miller's play, *Some Kind of Love Story*, was a black comedy on the themes of fantasy and corruption played out over a *film noir* framework, exciting speculation as to how far marriage to Marilyn Monroe had been source material. Expanded into film, it's a tantalising, brave failure. Here, the central relationship between private investigator Tom O'Toole (Nolte), variously encouraged by *femme fatale* Angela Crispini (Winger) to dig into the false conviction of a lad for murder, is significantly altered. On stage, their relationship has been going on for years; but film being film and stasis meaning stalled, they've been issued with a beginning and an end. This weakens a symmetry of compromised interdependence between the lovers, and between cops, judges and crooks in society at large. Everywhere is Chinatown; the town could be Hammett's Poisonville, USA. The film also introduces a biker cult of a weirdness that at times touches *Twin Peaks*. With infinitely changeable Angela on the strength, and viewed by her amazingly credulous gumshoe, human behaviour is unfathomable enough already. He looks Amish and plays patsy for his Cleopatra, who turns in an outstanding performance despite a difficult script, while Karel Reisz negotiates most of the shoals like a master. BC

Every Little Crook and Nanny

(Cy Howard, 1972, US) Lynn Redgrave, Victor Mature, Paul Sand, Maggie Blye, Austin Pendleton, John Astin, Dom DeLuise.
92 min.

It had to come – the Mafia family comedy. Plus the English nanny gag. Plus a hamfisted script routine around a kidnapped son. Gee whizz...Victor Mature points his profile and doesa-da-dago accent.

Every Little Thing (La Moindre des Choses)

(Nicolas Philibert, 1996, Fr)
104 min.

The La Borde clinic, a stately chateau surrounded by forest, takes an unorthodox approach to psychiatric care. The clinic's regime resembles that of a laidback boarding school for eccentrics, with pills – although there's no introduction to or analysis of such matters. Rather, we're straight in to an intimate documentary record of the several months the patients and staff take to prepare their summer theatrical production. Sometimes the patients talk – to each other or the camera; other times they just watch, or whistle, or walk slowly across the gravel...or we see trees blowing in the wind. The play (briefly excerpted) looks interesting, but the film as a whole doesn't repay one's patience. NB

Every Man for Himself

see Sauve Qui Peut – la Vie

Every Man for Himself and God Against All

see Jeder für sich und Gott gegen alle

Everyone Says I Love You

(Woody Allen, 1996, US) Alan Alda, Woody Allen, Drew Barrymore, Lukas Haas, Goldie Hawn, Gaby Hoffmann, Natasha Lyonne, Edward Norton, Natalie Portman, Julia Roberts, Tim Roth, David Ogden Stiers, Billy Crudup.
101 min.

Springtime in New York. Norton and Barrymore stroll hand in hand around a fountain, then burst into a deliciously sloppy rendition of 'Just You, Just Me', and immediately we're right into it, and you can't imagine why it's taken Woody Allen so long to get round to reviving the musical. Romantic, nostalgic and decadent as Fred Astaire, this might as well be an old movie, for all its relevance to the '90s or Allen's on-going problems. In some ways, it's not like a Woody Allen film at all. The plot – a frippery about the affairs of an extended upper-class family – transports us from Manhattan to Venice and Paris; there are black faces about the edges, a female, teenage narrator; even some fancy special effects work. Yet it never feels cynical or self-serving; indeed, it feels like the work of a younger, more open-hearted man. Unlike *Mighty Aphrodite*, in which Allen's on-screen character is apparently irresistible to Mira Sorvino, here his courtship of Roberts is accomplished only through underhand means, and the joke's ultimately on him. The musical standards are beautifully orchestrated, staged with wit and invention, and enthusiastically performed, particularly by Norton, Tim Roth and Hawn, three stand-outs in a charming, sweet-natured *divertissement*. Enjoy yourself (it's later than you think). TCh

Every Picture Tells a Story

(James Scott, 1984, GB) Phyllis Logan, Alex Norton, Leonard O'Malley, Mark Airlie, John Docherty.
83 min.

Scott reaches back into his family history to describe the adolescence of his father, painter William Scott. The film traces William Scott's life from his childhood in an Irish Catholic family in Scotland to his teenage years in Enniskillen and Belfast. The fundamental theme is the emergence of the boy's talent as an artist, part rooted in his harsh childhood experiences and part born of his need to break away from those roots. Handsomely stylised images and performances of unassailable authority make it very beautiful, and sometimes very moving. TR

Everything for Sale (Wszystko na Sprzedaz)

(Andrzej Wajda, 1968, Pol) Andrzej Lapicki, Beata Tyszkiewicz, Elzbieta Czyzewska, Daniel Olbrychski, Witold Holtz.
105 min.

Here they are again, our old friends illusion and reality, battling it out to unsettling effect in a film with more layers than an onion and umpteen references to Wajda's own career. A film director called Andrzej tries to continue shooting after his lead (clearly modelled on Zbigniew Cybulski, the actor who became the personification of postwar Polish cinema through his work with Wajda, and who had recently died in tragic circumstances) has disappeared. The result is stylistically and emotionally overwrought, but Wajda's technical assurance helps enormously in maintaining tension. GB

Everything You Always Wanted to Know About Sex, But Were Afraid to Ask

(Woody Allen, 1972, US) Woody Allen, Lynn Redgrave, John Carradine, Burt Reynolds, Anthony Quayle, Gene Wilder, Lou Jacobi, Tony Randall, Louise Lasser.
87 min.

Seven sketches parodying a sex manual, in which Allen – before trying to change his name to Fellini-Bergman – strung together 'every funny idea I've ever had about sex, including several that led to my own divorce'. Some dross, but the parodies of Antonioni (all angst and alienation of a wife who can achieve orgasm only in public places) and of TV panel games ('What's My Perversion?') are brilliantly accurate and very funny. Best of all is the sci-fi parody entitled 'What Happens During Ejaculation?', which has the miniaturised scientists of *Fantastic Voyage* inside a life-sized male robot, busily checking data and providing the necessary bodily reactions by hand-turned winch as the robot wines, dines and seduces a real-life woman. Allen achieves his finest hour here, dressed as one of the sperm, poised anxiously with parachute by the escape hatch and crying 'Gung ho!' as he jumps, 'We're gonna make babies!' TM

Every Time We Say Goodbye
(Moshe Mizrahi, 1986, US) Tom Hanks, Cristina Marsillach, Benedict Taylor, Anat Atzmon, Gila Almagor.
98 min.
Hanks' aptitude for romantic comedy can do nothing for this corny World War II love story, which has a script so sugary it goes for your fillings. A heavily American-accented RAF officer, he meets a beautiful young Jewish girl (Marsillach) in Jerusalem. While she is as fresh and pure as her little white underslips, with smouldering eyes and a 180 degree wiggle that he finds irresistible, she is also a Sephardim, a branch of Jewry which permits marriage only within the faith. True love is in for a rocky ride. She fights her feelings for him, saying no a lot when she means yes. 'I'll wait a hundred years for you' she wails as her dashing flight lieutenant departs to do his bit for the desert campaign. Strictly for addicts of Mills & Boon. EP

Every Which Way But Loose
(James Fargo, 1978, US) Clint Eastwood, Sondra Locke, Ruth Gordon, Geoffrey Lewis, Beverly D'Angelo, Walter Barnes.
114 min.
A huge disappointment after *The Outlaw Josey Wales* and *The Gauntlet*, this rambling comedy forsakes the subtle, self-deprecating humour of those films and opts for a far rowdier and broader comedy that never really goes anywhere or says anything. Clint is the somewhat dumb prizefighter who wins an orang-outan and sets off with his new buddy in pursuit of hard-to-get C&W singer Locke. The attempt to counter his apparent superiority over other men with his gauche reactions to the woman makes no interesting points, and the whole thing seems like an indulgent, expensive home movie created by and for Eastwood's customary stock company of actors. GA

Evictors, The
(Charles B Pierce, 1979, US) Vic Morrow, Michael Parks, Jessica Harper, Sue Ane Langdon, Dennis Fimple, Bill Thurman.
92 min.
'Let 'em have it!' yells a G-Man behind the credits, initiating a chain of mayhem that will continue unabated for 90 minutes. Pierce toiled unspectacularly in the low-budget mills for several years, but scored a bullseye with this energetically ghoulish exploiter which relocates the Old Dark House on Bonnie and Clyde terrain. The plot (city couple buy a lonely farm whose massacred former owners refuse to stay dead) may be perfunctory, but there are likeable performances, nice period details, and terrific set pieces, as well as a final twist incredible enough to be mildly surprising. TP

Evil Dead, The
(Sam Raimi, 1982, US) Bruce Campbell, Ellen Sandweiss, Betsy Baker, Hal Delrich, Sarah York.
86 min.
Raimi's first feature, a sensationally bad-taste effort which narrates the rapid decline into demonic mental and physical possession of a clean-cut, all-American holiday party holed up in a mountain Tennessee retreat. The woods come alive, devils possess the living, and Tom Sullivan's amazing make-up effects climax with a final fiery exorcism which makes George Romero look like *Playschool*. Short on characterisation and plot but strong on

atmospheric horror and visual churns, this movie blends comic fantasy (EC Tales) with recent genre gems like *Carrie* and *Texas Chainsaw Massacre* to impressive effect. SGr

Evil Dead II
(Sam Raimi, 1987, US) Bruce Campbell, Sarah Berry, Dan Hicks, Kassie Wesley, Theodore Raimi, Denise Bixler.
84 min.
Not so much a sequel, more a self-parodic reprise, like some black comic nightmare in the damaged brain of sole survivor Ash (Campbell). This time though, tired of cowering in the corner, Ash gets tooled up with a shotgun and a chainsaw, and lets the monsters suck on some abuse. Meanwhile, four other victims – none of whom has ever seen a horror movie – arrive at the shack and start settling in, unaware that they'll be dead by dawn. The dialogue has been pared to the bone, the on-screen gore toned down, and the maniacal laughter cranked up to full volume. Using the same breathless pacing, rushing camera movements and nerve-jangling sound effects as before, Raimi drags us screaming into his cinematic funhouse. Delirious, demented and diabolically funny. NF

Evil Eden
see Mort en ce Jardin, La

Evil That Men Do, The
(J Lee Thompson, 1983, US) Charles Bronson, Theresa Saldana, Joseph Maher, José Ferrer, René Enriquez, John Glover, Raymond St Jacques.
90 min.
Bronson as a hit man persuaded out of retirement to terminate a sadistic professional torturer in the pay of an oppressive South American government. Right from the opening sequence the film is a clumsy catalogue of pain and death, from the mutilated victims of the torturer to the trail of wasted baddies who were foolish enough to incur Bronson's wrath. The title openly declares a moral stance, but with the film quite happy to accept the assassin as a meter of justice, its ethics are as muddled and erratic as the editing and camerawork. There's only one lesson that comes through loud and clear: don't mess with Charles Bronson. DPe

Evil Trap, The
see Folle à Tuer

Evil Under the Sun
(Guy Hamilton, 1981, GB) Peter Ustinov, Jane Birkin, Colin Blakely, Nicholas Clay, Maggie Smith, Roddy McDowall, James Mason, Sylvia Miles, Denis Quilley, Diana Rigg.
117 min.
With Ustinov's energetic impersonation of Poirot and Anthony Shaffer's traditionally structured script, *Death on the Nile* offered a fair recreation of Agatha Christie's world, but this time Christie herself would rightly have disowned the film. It's not just that her novel's English coastal setting has been switched to an Adriatic island; for some reason, Shaffer and Hamilton have swopped the elegant English-style menace for a splurge of theatrical camp. The emphasis on gaudy costumes and bitchy back-biting is hideously amplified by a composite Cole Porter score, and it is only in the last section that Shaffer finally drops the *double entendres* and allows the golden-age-of-detection feel to reassert itself. DP

Evita
(Alan Parker, 1996, US) Madonna, Antonio Banderas, Jonathan Pryce, Jimmy Nail, Victoria Sus, Julian Littman, Peter Polycarpou.
134 min.
The most significant Hollywood musical in 15 years (virtually the only Hollywood musical in 15 years) turns on the dubious political integrity of one Eva Duarte, 1930s actress, working-class heroine, and consort of Argentina's fascist leader Col Juan Perón. Born into poverty, Eva worked her way up a ladder of men, then hitched her star to the military dictator to become the self-appointed 'spiritual leader of the nation'. Her political rhetoric may have been at odds with her glamorous lifestyle, but her death in 1952 caused an outpouring of grief. Is the musical still a credible genre in these cynical times? On the basis of this

film, the answer's a qualified yes. Parker has no embarrassment when it comes to putting over a song, and he's assembled a strong cast in Madonna, Pryce (Perón) and a fiercely brow-beating Banderas as the ubiquitous narrator. Unfortunately, for all its popularity on stage, the Andrew Lloyd Webber/Tim Rice show makes an unlikely movie. Parker does his best to disguise the fact with extensive cross-cutting and plentiful crowd scenes, but there's no real dynamic to the story, no sense of movement. The film cries out for the liberation of choreography to supplement the thin, repetitive score. An unholy cocktail of Emiliano Zapata, Eva Braun, and Princess Di, Evita's politics are intriguing; presumably that's what attracted Parker and co-screenwriter Oliver Stone to the material, but the movie's so seriously weighty, the bombast rather tips the balance against Evita charisma. Despite Madonna's impressive performance, we're never remotely tempted to cry for her – and, in the end, that must make the film a failure. TCh

Ewok Adventure, The (aka Caravan of Courage)
(John Korty, 1984, US) Eric Walker, Warwick Davis, Fionnula Flanagan, Guy Boyd, Aubree Miller.
100 min.
Ewoks (first seen in *Return of the Jedi*) have lifeless eyes, nuclear families, short fuses, clean bums, hang-gliders, priestesses, wise men and rhythm. They look like short, furry Colin Wellands, and sound like David Rappaport clearing his throat in a subway. They live on Endor, which is like California with rocky bits painted in front of the lens. The caravan is a vehicle for a kiddy-quest for lost parents – young, curly-top cutie and big, bolshie brother coming to terms with his inner obnoxiousness via confrontation with alien culture. Short on action by Lucasfilm standards, stuffed with toothy teddies which lack the charm of Phase One Gremlins, or the wit of any muppet...I blame Thatcher. RP

Excalibur
(John Boorman, 1981, US) Nigel Terry, Helen Mirren, Nicholas Clay, Cherie Lunghi, Paul Geoffrey, Nicol Williamson, Robert Addie, Gabriel Byrne.
140 min.
Visually impressive but generally muddled and uneven adaptation of Malory's *Morte d'Arthur*, both overlong and incoherent as it follows the quest for the Holy Grail and the climactic battle between Arthur and Mordred. Almost determinedly bizarre (or stupid?) in some of its characterisation – most notably Williamson's eccentric Merlin – it also adds a dash of gore and a touch of sex for good modernist measure. Nothing, however, can counter the film's inability to sway the emotions. For all its audacity, a misguided folly. GA

Excess Baggage
see Bulto, El

Excess Baggage
(Marco Brambilla, 1997, US) Alicia Silverstone, Benicio Del Toro, Christopher Walken, Jack Thompson, Nicholas Turturro, Michael Bowen, Sally Kirkland, Harry Connick Jr.
101 min.
Rich girl Emily (Silverstone, irritating) kidnaps herself and demands a ransom from neglectful father. But then car thief Del Toro unwittingly steals the vehicle in which she's locked herself. Emily takes charge of the abduction. Pursued by the cops, two incompetent hoods, and a cool ex-CIA agent (Walken), the couple flee across country and fall in love. Del Toro, so brilliant as the vowel-gargling felon in *The Usual Suspects*, is just too weird to convince as a romantic lead. The action covers 72 hours and, despite some classy visuals, it sometimes feels like it. NF

Executioner, The
see Verdugo, El

Executioners from Shaolin (Hong Xiguan)
(Lau Kar-Leung aka Liu Jialiang, 1977, HK) Chen Guantai, Wong Yu, Lo Lieh, Lily Li, Gordon Liu.
103 min.

Not as finely crafted as Lau's later Shaw Brothers films, but this reframing of one of the key Shaolin legends in explicitly sexual terms is an amazing achievement. After the sack of the Shaolin Temple, monk Hong Xiguan (Chen) goes into hiding and marries; but he neglects his wife and son because he's set on fighting the eunuch Bai Mei (Lo), who destroyed Shaolin. His macho 'Tiger Stance' cannot equal the eunuch's quasi-mystical power, and he dies in the duel. His widow (Li) trains their son Wending (Wong) in the feminine 'Crane' style, which is all she knows, and the boy is ridiculed as a sissy by his schoolmates. Wending eventually picks up scraps of his father's techniques from a worm-eaten training manual and confronts his father's killer as a 'bisexual' fighter: half male, half female. The eunuch, conversely, is a sexual 'black hole' who can suck opponents into his body through the void where his genitals once were. If only Freud could have seen it. The UK video release of this 'Scope film is panned-and-scanned and wretchedly dubbed. TR

Executioner's Song, The

(Lawrence Schiller, 1982, US) Tommy Lee Jones, Christine Lahti, Rosanna Arquette, Steven Keats, Jordan Clarke, Richard Venture, Eli Wallach.
135 min.
Schiller and Norman Mailer's docu-drama – about double-killer Gary Gilmore, who demanded to be executed – exists in a curiously harsh netherworld beyond traditional genre, skirting the realm of the clinical dossier. Sensation (crimes and punishment: two murders and a firing squad) and incongruity (Gilmore as media event) produce a troubled, quizzical analysis of background and context, but seem as displaced from being the movie's elusive subject as does Gilmore himself. Jones (playing Gilmore) goes his own fascinating route to the loser's nirvana without recourse to psycho-style tics, while strong character performances from Arquette and Lahti constantly shift the focus back towards the scurvy straitjacket of Utah underdogs. In all, easier to recommend than to define. This is an edited version of the 2-part TV movie, running 200 minutes. PT

Execution in Autumn
(Qiu Jue)

(Li Xing, 1971, Tai) Ou Wei, Tang Pao-Yun, Ko Hsiang-Ting, Fu Pi-Hui
99 min.
It's hard to pinpoint why a film apparently as simple as this should be so extraordinarily moving. The story couldn't be more direct: in Han Dynasty China, executions are confined to the autumn, and the selfish, brutal Pei finds himself in prison for eleven months, waiting for his sentence to be carried out. During that period he is inveigled into marrying, so that his wife can bear him an heir, and his character gradually begins to mellow. The film's real richness seems to lie in its web of undercurrents; the tangle of hopes, dreams, memories and desires that enmeshes the characters, sometimes almost tangible, sometimes elusive.

Execution Protocol, The

(Stephen Trombley, 1992, GB)
90 min.
The Potosi Correctional Center is the showcase maximum security prison for Missouri's 'most dangerous criminals'; every inmate has been convicted of capital murder, and sentenced either to 50 years or life without parole, or to death by lethal injection. Trombley's exemplary film focuses not only on the ethics of capital punishment, with officials and prisoners alike allowed to give their opinions on the issue, but on the minutiae of who does what and how whenever an execution takes place. The prisoners (including one whose execution was stayed with just three hours to go) are especially articulate in their condemnation of the centre's 'humane' methods; and Trombley's cool tone, sharp images, and use of a superb modern jazz score, make for powerful viewing. One complaint only: we never learn what the prisoners actually did, which – while it doesn't alter the fact that the State is committing institutionalised murder – rather weakens the force of the film's argument. GA

Executive Action

(David Miller, 1973, US) Burt Lancaster, Robert Ryan, Will Geer, Gilbert Green, John Anderson, Ed Lauter.
91 min.

A compelling dramatic hypothesis constructed by Dalton Trumbo from the conspiracy theories advanced by persistent Kennedy assassination investigator Mark Lane, in turn based on evidence the Warren Commission refused to hear. Fudged slightly towards tidy fictional coherence by an unwillingness to acknowledge the very discrepancies that Lane had earlier illustrated with Emile de Antonio in the documentary Rush to Judgement, but a plausible enough attempt to weld the 'political thriller' style of Costa-Gavras onto Hollywood. Producer Edward Lewis, nine years later, was responsible for setting up Costa-Gavras' Hollywood debut with Missing. PT

Executive Decision

(Stuart Baird, 1995, US) Steven Seagal, David Suchet, Kurt Russell, Oliver Platt, John Leguizano, Halle Berry, Joe Morton, JT Walsh, Marla Maples Trump.
132 min.
This 'bomb on a plane' action-thriller takes off smoothly, hits some terrorist turbulence at cruising altitude, and doesn't come down until the palm-sweating finale. Koran-quoting Arab Nagi Hassan (Suchet) and his team take over a 747 bound for Washington, DC, and threaten to kill all on board if their imprisoned leader isn't freed. But intelligence analyst David Grant (Russell) senses that Hassan has a more heinous plan: to land the plane, release its (supposed) payload of lethal nerve toxin, and wipe out the Eastern seaboard. So, while on the ground the military men and politicians decide whether to down the plane and cut their losses, an anti-terrorist unit led by Lt Col Austin Travis (Seagal) uses a prototype 'sleeve' to board the aircraft in midair. Providing high-altitude intelligence back-up are pencil-pusher Grant and the sleeve's designer Cahill (Platt), both way out of their depth. As befits an editor-turned-director, Baird has a strong sense of pace and suspense, but even his cross-cutting skills are no match for a plot that fragments the action and blurs the narrative focus. Even so, the escalating tension largely compensates for the lack of character involvement, and the climax will have you reaching for your safety belt. NF

Executive Suite

(Robert Wise, 1954, US) William Holden, June Allyson, Barbara Stanwyck, Fredric March, Walter Pidgeon, Louis Calhern, Shelley Winters, Paul Douglas, Nina Foch, Dean Jagger.
104 min. b/w.
Slick MGM account of intrigues that take place among five viciously opportunistic company executives, jostling for position when their president dies. Taut and gripping, its chief strengths are a finely structured script by Ernest Lehman, and top-notch acting by the starry ensemble. March is particularly memorable, cast against the grain as a devious, maliciously selfish company controller. For all its sheerly entertaining wallowing in spiritual corruption, however, it never approaches the acerbic pungency of Lehman's collaboration with Clifford Odets on Sweet Smell of Success. GA

Exile, The

(Max Ophüls, 1947, US) Douglas Fairbanks Jr, Maria Montez, Paule Croset (ie.Rita Corday), Henry Daniell, Nigel Bruce, Robert Coote).
95 min. b/w.
Fairbanks Jr may have written and produced The Exile, but thankfully Ophüls' camera performs more gymnastics than he does as Charles II, the escapee king tiptoeing through the tulip fields of Holland. The obligatory swashbuckling is held well in check in Ophüls' first American movie, and an essentially lightweight, star-oriented period piece is transformed into a pertinent series of reflections on love and duty, on identity and role, and on destiny. PT

Exit to Eden

(Garry Marshall, 1994, US) Dana Delany, Paul Mercurio, Rosie O'Donnell, Dan Aykroyd, Hector Elizondo, Stuart Wilson, Iman.
114 min.
Garry (Pretty Woman) Marshall's sexploiter makes Zalman King's 'women's fantasy' movies seem sophisticated and daring. His film begs the question – how humiliatingly it begs! – 'What do women really want?' On this issue, dominatrix Delany, unbending mistress of the SM sex

ranch island 'Eden', takes a while to accept the missionary position: lots of foreplay and a straight 'kindness and cute butt' pay-off in the form of Paul (Strictly Ballroom) Mercurio's photographer, here mostly naked and canine-collared. Given the film is such a foolish exercise (you have to accept O'Donnell in bondage attire and Aykroyd's dumb-klutz maintenance man as a pair of LA cops investigating a jewel heist in deep cover), you'd expect excess or a camp romp à la Russ Meyer at least. But no such luck. There's certainly plenty of tits'n'ass, male and female, scantily adorned in Fellini-Satyricon-style gold lamé Roman chic, but it's not an erotic show. There are a few in-jokes and droll moments, but otherwise you wouldn't know it was a Garry Marshall movie. Neither bad enough for cult status, nor good enough for vicarious thrills. WH

Exodus

(Otto Preminger, 1960, US) Paul Newman, Eva Marie Saint, Ralph Richardson, Peter Lawford, Lee J Cobb, Sal Mineo, John Derek, Hugh Griffith, Felix Aylmer, Jill Hayworth.
220 min.
Touted as a masterpiece by stout Premingerites; but with one eye on the box-office, the other on avoiding giving offence, this adaptation of Leon Uris' blockbusting novel about the founding of modern Israel could hardly be anything but a compromise. Moral issues are raised, only to be forgotten in urgent deluges of action or romance; characters are all fashioned strictly to stereotype; and for all its caution, it finally comes across (especially in view of subsequent history) as a pretty objectionably blinkered slice of Zionist propaganda. Watchable mainly for the sheer skill and drive of Preminger's direction, although at 220 minutes even that long outstays its welcome. TM

Exodus – Bob Marley Live

(Keith Macmillan, 1978, GB) Bob Marley and the Wailers.
74 min.
An excellent low-key high fidelity record of a stage set (at the Rainbow Theatre, North London, in June 1977) miraculously welds musical restraint to wild exuberance. It catches all Marley's moments and moods – angry, jiving, teasing, wasted – a great antidote to the rock-machine calculations and reverence of The Last Waltz. Only the exclusion of the audience disappoints. The climactic high is irresistible: Marley in the spotlight, a chalk-blue bird hovering in the dark, reaching out to the howling crowd – 'Don't give up your rights...' CA

Exorcist, The

(William Friedkin, 1973, US) Ellen Burstyn, Max von Sydow, Lee J Cobb, Kitty Winn, Jack MacGowran, Jason Miller, Linda Blair.
122 min.
Friedkin's film about the possession of a 12-year-old girl works as an essay in suspension of disbelief and on the level of titillatory exploitation. Although harrowing, its effects depend entirely on technical manipulation, and with Friedkin's pedestrian handling of background story and supporting characters, we're left more or less willing the film towards its climax. Sure enough, during the act of exorcism the girl obliges with a spectacular levitation. It would all be forgiveable, somehow, if the film was at all likely to alter anyone's perceptions one jot. But all The Exorcist does is take its audience for a ride, spewing it out the other end, shaken up but none the wiser. CPe

Exorcist II: The Heretic

(John Boorman, 1977, US) Linda Blair, Richard Burton, Louise Fletcher, Max von Sydow, Kitty Winn, Paul Henried, James Earl Jones, Ned Beatty.
117 min.
Substantially recut by Boorman after his original version was derided in America, but it's still easy to see why New Yorkers jeered. Boorman completely avoids gore and obscenity, treating the original as a kind of sacred good-versus-evil text, and weaving its sets and characters into a highly traditional confrontation of occult forces. The theme is attacked with engaging intensity, and Boorman brings off more than one visual coup (notably the ingenious locust photography in the African sequences). Dennis Wheatley fans, at least, will love it. DP

Exorcist III, The

(William Peter Blatty, 1990, US) George C
Scott, Ed Flanders, Brad Dourif, Jason Miller,
Nicol Williamson, Scott Wilson, Nancy Fish,
Viveca Lindfors, Zohra Lampert, Barbara
Baxley.
110 min.
Fifteen years after the execution of the Gemini
killer, Georgetown falls prey to grisly serial slayings bearing the Gemini's trademark mutilations.
Meanwhile, deep in the bowels of the town's psychiatric institution, a patient emerges from catatonia, claiming to be the Gemini and demanding
recognition. Investigating the case is Lt
Kinderman (Scott), whose world-weary scepticism is challenged not only by the patient's exact
knowledge of the crimes, but by his uncanny
resemblance to Father Damien Karras, who fell
to his death fifteen years earlier while performing an exorcism. Blatty's sequel eschews the visceral effects of its predecessor (it ignores
Boorman's *The Heretic*) to rely instead on the
chilling power of suggestion. The excessively
wordy dialogue is interrupted by intervals of
brooding malevolence, and by a couple of contrived but startlingly effective shocks. The real
terror, however, comes from Dourif's straight-to-
camera serial killer monologues, which breathe
eerie life into the script. With the exception of an
unnecessary spectacular climax, this is a
restrained, haunting chiller which stimulates the
adrenalin and intellect alike. MK

Exotica

(Atom Egoyan, 1994, Can) Don McKellar, Mia
Kirshner, Arsinée Khanjian, Elias Koteas,
Bruce Greenwood.
103 min.
Characteristically stylish, intriguing film from
Atom Egoyan, heavy on the eroticism and mystification as it delves into the lives of a number
of characters connected by their relationship to
the strip joint of the title: the owner and MC; a
table-dancer; a taxman obsessed with the dancer;
and a pet-shop proprietor, whose business the
taxman is auditing. It's another excursion into
projected fantasies, anxiety, exploitation and
secret needs; the elegant camerawork and intense
performances sustain interest, although the fragmentation of the plot sometimes seems unnecessarily obscurantist – finally, the mystery is not
so very startling or significant. Fascinating,
though, and without the pretensions that have
marred some of Egoyan's earlier work. GA

Experience Preferred
But Not Essential

(Peter Duffell, 1982, GB) Elizabeth Edmonds,
Sue Wallace, Geraldine Griffiths, Karen
Meagher, Maggie Wilkinson, Ron Bain.
75 min.
Small, basically honest, very English film, made
for 'Film on Four' by David Puttnam's Goldcrest,
about a girl from Cleveland filling in the summer
before college with a job as a maid at a Welsh seaside hotel. The chef, an ex-seaman from Paisley,
lays siege to the girl's virginity. This is the
Campaign for Nuclear Disarmament '60s.
Nothing particularly surprising here (Ivan the
wine waiter sleepwalks naked; backstairs life is
uncarpeted, cheerful and over-emotional), but the
sentiment is notably unforced. Found particular
favour in America. JPy

Experiment in Terror
(aka The Grip of Fear)

(Blake Edwards, 1962, US) Glenn Ford, Lee
Remick, Stefanie Powers, Roy Poole, Ned
Glass, Ross Martin, Clifton James.
122 min. b/w.
After seven lightish comedies and dramas,
and directly following *Breakfast at Tiffany's*,
Edwards launched himself in a new direction
with this thriller: an experiment for him (although
he had trodden thick-ear territory with his TV
series, such as the legendary *Peter Gunn*) and also
for the genre. Years before John Carpenter and
other movie brats began to play with audience
expectations and memories, Edwards constructed his film – about an asthmatic psycho pursuing Lee Remick – around precisely similar
attitudes. Gone was the whodunit mystery formula; gone the need for psychological explanations; in their place, an exercise in steely style,
with the audience split between its concern for
the victim and its fascination with the psycho's

activities. After Carpenter and De Palma, it may
seem a little dated; yet Edwards' classical feel for
pure cinema remains unalloyed. CW

Experiment Perilous

(Jacques Tourneur, 1944, US) Hedy Lamarr,
George Brent, Paul Lukas, Albert Dekker,
Margaret Wycherly, Julia Dean.
91 min. b/w.
A comparatively minor but characteristically elegant Tourneur costume melodrama-cum-psy-
chological thriller in the vein of *Rebecca* and
Gaslight, this features Lamarr as the wife of a
wealthy philanthropist; inevitably, she comes to
fear not only for her own sanity, but also for that
of her genuinely dangerous husband, a manic
authoritarian patriarch whose violence is the
product of a troubled, traumatic childhood.
Equally inevitably, doctor/detective Brent is there
to save her and supply romantic interest, but
Tourneur manages to overcome the formulaic
plotting and cod-Freudian characterisations
through carefully controlled performances and
Tony Gaudio's fine camerawork. GA

Experts, The

(Dave Thomas, 1989, US) John Travolta, Arye
Gross, Charles Martin Smith, Kelly Preston,
Deborah Foreman, James Keach, Jan Rubes,
Brian Doyle Murray.
83 min.
A lame-brain Cold War comedy. New York trendies
Travolta and Gross are hired to open a disco in a
small Midwestern town – or so they think. In fact,
they have been flown in to a top-secret KGB installation modelled on a supposedly average American
burgh. The Russkies hope these innocents abroad
will authenticate and update their project. In terms
of the Super Powers, this is very thin stuff.
Fractionally more interesting is the implicit contrast between the pure '50s Americana the Soviets
have reproduced, and the '80s values (Japanese
hardware, *et al*) Travolta brings to it. TCh

Explorers

(Joe Dante, 1985, US) Ethan Hawke, River
Phoenix, Jason Presson, Amanda Peterson,
Dick Miller, Robert Picardo.
109 min.
Three kids are inspired by strange nightmares
and a stroke of scientific luck to build their own
spaceship, but suddenly find themselves out of
control, yanked towards an encounter with some
extremely oddball aliens. What really lifts this
into the stratosphere of heady entertainment is
its dizzy wit and intelligence. The dialogue is
deliriously deadpan, the story surreal but surprisingly convincing, and the wealth of references
to movie and TV classics hilarious rather than
mere smartass posing. Dante's wacky comedy-
thriller never degenerates into Spielbergian sentimentality, but mixes its inventive originality
with a winning self-deprecating irony. It looks
terrific, moves along at a gallop, and is marvellously good-natured. GA

Exposé

(James Kenelm Clarke, 1975, GB) Udo Kier,
Linda Hayden, Fiona Richmond, Patsy Smart,
Vic Armstrong, Karl Howman.
82 min.
This follow-up to Clarke's *Man Alive* TV report
on sexploitation movies ran into censorship troubles with its explicit links between sex and violence. A paranoid author (Kier) living in an
isolated country house hires a secretary (Hayden)
to help him complete an overblown but potentially successful sex novel. The secretary turns out
to be a psychopath who, before exposing the
author as bogus, blasts two rapists with a shotgun, cuts the throat of an elderly woman, and then
kills the author's girlfriend (Richmond) in the bath
with the same knife. Clarke directs this derivative
screenplay (a diluted solution of *Psycho* and *Straw
Dogs*) with more economy than one expects from
the genre. But Richmond demonstrates little of her
renowned sexual athleticism, and the decorous,
carefully placed sexual encounters are as predictable and passionless as ever. JPy

Exposed

(James Toback, 1983, US) Nastassja Kinski,
Rudolf Nureyev, Harvey Keitel, Ian McShane,
Bibi Andersson, Ron Randell, Pierre Clémenti,
James Toback.
99 min.

An eccentric thriller meandering an uneasy route
between jet-set melodrama – Kinski quits small
town college to become top model – and terrorist
activities, with Keitel not really at his most convincing as terrorism's Paris kingpin. Toback's
earlier *Fingers* won some critical support, and his
script here is not without philosophical moments
concerning the ambiguities of the 'look' and the
'self'; but *Exposed* does not entirely have the
courage of its frequently heady high art absurdities, despite moments like the one in which
Nureyev (cast as a renowned violinist) literally
attempts to play Kinski's body like a violin. For
this kind of material the temperature must not be
allowed to drop, but it frequently does. VG

Exposure

(Kieran Hickey, 1978, Eire) Catherine Schell,
TP McKenna, Bosco Hogan, Niall O'Brien,
Mairin O'Sullivan, Leslie Lalor.
48 min.
Alongside his excellent and chilling short *A
Child's Voice*, *Exposure* demonstrates that Hickey
is an Irish director of considerable power and
assurance who seems intent on making the most
of the tradition in Celtic fiction for quiet and subtle terror. Set on the desolate west coast of Ireland,
the film explores a Polanski-like plot in which
three surveyors find themselves stuck in a remote
hotel with a French girl photographer. There are
a few unsuccessful moments (notably a jarring
beach-montage sequence), but in general the tone
is deft and sharp, and the use of the tiny hotel bar
to convey accumulating tension is masterly. DP

Expresso Bongo

(Val Guest, 1959, GB) Laurence Harvey, Cliff
Richard, Sylvia Syms, Yolande Donlan,
Kenneth Griffith, Meier Tzelniker, Hermione
Baddeley, Wilfrid Lawson.
111 min. b/w.
An adaptation of Wolf Mankowitz's 1958 showbiz musical, bristling with period flavour, from
the cast's brylcreemed coiffures and snazzy ties
to the presence of Gilbert Harding playing himself. More surprisingly, it also bristles with energy and wit, and even survives the presence of the
19-year-old Cliff Richard as the bongo-thumping
boy pushed up to stardom by Harvey's impeccably smarmy agent. The result is probably
Britain's most abrasive and entertaining film
musical. GB

Exquisite Tenderness

(Carl Schenkel, 1995, US/Ger) Isabel Glasser,
James Remar, Malcolm McDowell, Peter Boyle,
Charles Dance, Sean Haberle.
100 min.
Schenkel handles this medical chiller with the
sledge-hammer subtlety he brought to *Knight
Moves*. Ironically, although he expressed reservations about the gore quotient, the set-piece
nastiness is the one element that works. A giant
syringe being shoved up someone's nostril is
guaranteed to provoke a response. By contrast,
attempts at suspense fail dismally, due to lack
of narrative control and a surfeit of flashy camerawork. A monochrome pre-credits sequence
in which a boy witnesses the blood-spattered
demise of his sick brother explains the killer's
psychological trauma. We then flash forward
to the present, where Dr McCann (Glasser), desperate to clear her name after the gruesome
death of a dialysis patient, enlists the help of an
ambitious toxicologist (Remar). As the mystery
unfolds, it becomes clear that someone with a
grudge is bumping off the hospital's patients,
in order to disgrace the medical staff and further his own Frankensteinian research into tissue and bone regeneration. The presence of
McDowell as the fanatical Dr Stein offers a
glimmer of hope, but when he dies, the film dies
with him. Schenkel's reputation rests on his
tense, lift-bound suspenser *Out of Order*, but
on this evidence he's never going to get past the
first floor. NF

Extasis

(Mariano Barroso, 1996, Sp) Javier Bardem,
Federico Luppi, Silvia Munt, Daniel Guzmán,
Leire Berrocal, Alfonso Lusson, Guillermo
Rodriguez.
87 min.
Disaffected rebels who dream of opening their
own bar, Bardem, Guzmán and Berrocal are firm
friends who even rob their own families to get the

cash together. But when Bardem impersonates Guzmán in order to trick the latter's wealthy, long-estranged theatre-director father (Luppi), the trio's plans start to fall apart: seduced by Luppi's affections and fortune, not to mention the fame he offers in trying to turn the boy into a star, Bardem begins to enjoy bourgeois society. Though a little too chic and overwrought (all that symbolism and metaphor!), this succeeds thanks to a nicely ambiguous take on Bardem and Luppi's motives and an assured control of mood and pace. GA

Exterminating Angel, The (El Angel Exterminador)

(Luis Buñuel, 1962, Mex) Silvia Pinal, Enrique Rambal, Lucy Gallardo, Claudio Brook, Tito Junco, Bertha Moss.
95 min. b/w.
In the best surrealist tradition, Buñuel claimed that his brilliant, disconcertingly funny joke – after an upper class dinner party, the guests find some mysterious compulsion making it impossible for them to leave the premises – has no rational explanation. True enough, but there are meanings aplenty in his powerful central image of decay as the vast, magnificently appointed bourgeois salon is gradually reduced to a sordid rubbish-heap where the once elegant guests squat and gnaw at bones. Significantly, the whole thing takes place under the sign of the church, but what still delights about the film is the way it refuses to be pigeonholed. Devastatingly funny, illuminated by unexpected shafts of generosity and tenderness, it remains one of Buñuel's very best. TM

Exterminator 2

(Mark Buntzman, 1984, US) Robert Ginty, Deborah Geffner, Mario Van Peebles, Frankie Faison, Scott Randolph.
90 min.
As an upholder of justice and fairness, both Ginty and his vigilante alter-ego, the Exterminator, are sadly deficient. Despite tuning in to police airwaves, he never quite makes it in time to rescue the little old liquor-store owner, or the armoured vehicle guard, or even his own girlfriend. They all end up as salami, with Ginty left to turn the offenders into blazing balls of heavily padded stuntmen. One can't help pondering the practical aspects of humping ten tons of flamethrowing equipment around midtown Manhattan; and whether it makes the city safer for honest citizens is debatable. It sure rubs up X (Van Peebles) the wrong way: he's a vicious gangleader with a Grace Jones haircut and a tendency to sound off at his attendant junkies, punkies and breakdancers with psychobabble like 'I am the Street'. One can be forgiven for losing interest, and instead musing on the Significance of the Garbage Truck in Contemporary Film Culture. AB

Extraordinary Adventures of Mister West in the Land of the Bolsheviks, The (Neobychainiye Priklucheniya Mistera Vesta v Stranye Bolshevikov)

(Lev Kuleshov, 1924, USSR) Porfiri Podobed, Vsevolod Pudovkin.
80 min. b/w.
Satirical look at Western versus Soviet manners, politics and realities with a high-fur-coated American tourist first casting a superficial eye over the new Moscow, only to be taken off by a bunch of abductors and then escaping their clutches and glimpsing the 'real essence' of the Soviet Union.

Extreme Close-Up

(Jeannot Szwarc, 1972, US) James McMullan, James A Watson Jr, Kate Woodville, Bara Byrnes, Al Checco, Anthony Carbone.
82 min.
The idle fantasies provoked by watching a pretty girl become rather more concrete for a young TV reporter (McMullan), conducting a series on invasion of privacy ('Privacy is not clearly a legal right'), when he gets his hands on the latest bugging devices. From lazily scanning the block opposite, through some more dedicated spying, his voyeurism culminates with self-appraisal in the mirror while his wife reaches orgasm beneath him. Because the central character is given little

motivation (he's ordinary, personable, reasonably married), the audience is forced into an examination of its own condoning of the voyeur's actions. Unfortunately, with the sex scenes so routinely softcore, this investigation doesn't necessarily go very deep. As scripted by Michael Crichton, however, the pitfalls of peeping are well accounted for: the fear of being found out, the mixture of guilt and elation, and above all, the lengths to which people are prepared to go. As our reporter says on TV, 'If someone wants to spy badly enough, he'll find a way to do it'. Even if it means squatting behind a tree in the pitch black with an infra-red scanner. CPe

Extreme Measures

(Michael Apted, 1996, US/GB) Hugh Grant, Gene Hackman, Sarah Jessica Parker, David Morse, Bill Nunn, John Toles-Bey, Paul Guilfoyle, Debra Monk.
118 min.
A promising start for Hugh Grant and Liz Hurley's Simian Films. Grant's a junior doctor in the A&E department of a NY teaching hospital who's intrigued by the perplexing symptoms of a fatally disturbed mystery patient. The disappearance of the body spurs him to dig deeper into the case. With nurse Parker on hand to lend support and romantic involvement, Grant doesn't realise he's getting into dark conspiratorial waters, which will threaten his life and livelihood, implicate revered neurologist Hackman, and take him to parts of the city he didn't even know existed. Grant has just the right amount of offhand decency to sustain the film's moralising impetus and bring an emotional relevance to its spiralling plot reversals. Perhaps screenwriter Tony Gilroy's adaptation of Michael Palmer's novel slightly labours the discussion of medical ethics, but Hackman's involving performance, as the researcher bending the rules in the treatment of spinal injuries, never leaves the arguments cut and dried. An effective crowd-pleaser which never goes dumb on you. TJ

Extreme Prejudice

(Walter Hill, 1987, US) Nick Nolte, Powers Boothe, Michael Ironside, Maria Conchita Alonso, Rip Torn, Clancy Brown, William Forsythe.
104 min.
A thinly disguised remake of Sam Peckinpah's The Wild Bunch, set on the US/Mexico border, updated to include a CIA team of Vietnam veterans trained in the use of sophisticated hi-tech weaponry. The central conflict between Texas Ranger Nolte and his former buddy turned drug baron (Boothe) is textbook Western stuff, complete with the standard rivalry over the love interest (Alonso). Covert CIA team leader Ironside asks Nolte for help in recovering secret government documents allegedly in Boothe's possession, thus forcing the ranger to choose between old loyalties and the demands of duty. The action is lean and tough, the body count huge, and the final shootout an obvious reprise of Peckinpah's finale. But where the latter's vision transformed The Wild Bunch into a savage elegy for the passing of the Old West, Hill can only duplicate its choreographed violence. NF

Extremities

(Robert M Young, 1986, US) Farrah Fawcett, James Russo, Diana Scarwid, Alfre Woodard, Sandy Martin.
89 min.
Attacked by a masked would-be rapist (Russo), Fawcett manages to escape but leaves her ID behind. The police ('Ever been picked up for prostitution before?') are less than sympathetic, and her two flatmates are kind enough to take her car with them when they leave her alone to face, as she and we know, her assailant's inevitable return. What follows is an hour of violent and voyeuristically relished confrontation as Fawcett, initially stripped, humiliated and terrorised, manages to turn the tables to blind and cage her 'animal' aggressor. This offensive adaptation of William Mastrosimone's controversial play suggests that there was never much question of making any serious attempt to deal with the important subjects raised. The use of subjective camera and meaningless circling shots cannot disguise either the essential abuse of cinematic technique or the crippling lack of psychological insight and detail. Under the restrictive hand of Young's direction, Russo's

moronic 'Method' maniac and Fawcett's grimy avenger are equated as mere beasts in this one-room zoo. WH

Eye for an Eye

(John Schlesinger, 1995, US) Sally Field, Kiefer Sutherland, Ed Harris, Olivia Burnette, Alexandra Kyle, Joe Mantegna, Beverly D'Angelo.
101 min.
A virulent throwback to the vigilante movies of the '70s. Field is a respectable middle-class wife and mother who turns into a gun toting suburban Rambette after her daughter's raped and murdered before her very ears (she's on the phone). The police have an airtight case, but a technicality allows the killer to walk free, and Sally takes to following him. What she sees confirms her already low opinion: not only is he bearded, tattooed and Sutherland, he's also rude and unrepentant, tortures animals, and pisses on the sidewalk. For this, he must die. Vigilante thrillers are by nature contrived and manipulative, but Schlesinger's reactionary film knows no bounds when it comes to emotional blackmail. Does it make the crime more terrible that it's committed on the victim's birthday? Are such judicial miscarriages so prevalent that a victim support group could shield a summary execution agency? While assorted authority figures pay lip service to law and order, compassion and forgiveness, their words ring hollow: the film operates as propaganda for capital punishment. Mercifully, it's not very effective propaganda. The characterisation is so thin, and the plotting so crude, it's only the violence which sets this apart from the banalities of TV fare – that and the novelty of seeing Sally Field come on like Travis Bickle. TCh

Eye for an Eye, An

(Steve Carver, 1981, US) Chuck Norris, Christopher Lee, Richard Roundtree, Matt Clark, Mako, Maggie Cooper, Rosalind Chao.
104 min.
Norris, the Great White Hope of the Hollywood martial arts movie, beefcakes his way through an Oriental Connection drug ring with a bullet-proof spiritual aura and a dated fantasy line in abode, wardrobe and transportation. An undercover narc who quits the San Francisco force when his buddy is set up and blown away, his lone-wolf biblical revenge gets further prompts from the ravages of a mammoth Mongolian henchman and such minor irritants as a machine-gun helicopter raid by boiler-suited Triad lackeys. His facial muscles twitch for love or laughter; otherwise it's a frozen-frown, feet first routine all the way to the signposted Bad Guy. PT

Eye of the Cat

(David Lowell Rich, 1969, US) Michael Sarrazin, Gayle Hunnicutt, Eleanor Parker, Tim Henry, Laurence Naismith, Jennifer Leak.
102 min.
A nicely extravagant tale of horror in which an army of cats protect a rich invalid (Parker) from her two-faced hairdresser-confidante (Hunnicutt), who has set a nephew with a phobia about cats (Sarrazin) to scheming for her money. Its success can be largely attributed to two of Hitchcock's collaborators: writer Joseph Stefano, who turned in the script for Psycho, and Ray Berwick, who trained the birds for The Birds. CPe

Eye of the Needle

(Richard Marquand, 1981, GB) Donald Sutherland, Kate Nelligan, Christopher Cazenove, Ian Bannen, Alex McCrindle, Stephen MacKenna.
113 min.
Sutherland, a Canadian, plays a German who is pretending to be an Englishman, and makes a convincing job of it. At the outset seeming to be an old-fashioned World War II spy thriller, with its steam trains, fog, lacquered advertisements and Bulldog Spirit, this keeps up with the times by also offering a string of sudden 'necessary' murders, a half-severed hand, a ration of naked top-half bed-thrashing, and a hopeless, vicious triangle relationship. The war is ultimately reduced to three people, stranded on a rain-soaked Scottish island. But the drama remains strangely unengaging: we soon realise that the legless (in both senses) ex-Spitfire pilot is going to have to go, and though the hysterical, bullet-

ridden climax is impressive, we know that there can be only one survivor. On an afternoon as wet as those on the island, the film would pass the time agreeably, nothing more. JC

Eyes in the Night

(Fred Zinnemann, 1942, US) Edward Arnold, Ann Harding, Donna Reed, John Emery, Allen Jenkins, Stephen McNally, Reginald Denny, Mantan Moreland.
80 min. b/w.
Zinnemann's second film, from Baynard Kendrick's novel *Odor of Violets*, is a minor but jolly slice of ingenious sleuthery with Arnold as a blind detective whose dog Friday helps him clear up the mystery that may connect the death of Harding's old flame Emery, a Nazi spy ring and the involvement of her scientist husband. The result's a spruce little MGM second feature, neatly worked out within its limits. TJ

Eyes of a Stranger

(Ken Wiederhorn, 1980, US) Lauren Tewes, Jennifer Jason Leigh, John DiSanti, Peter DuPré, Gwen Lewis, Kitty Lunn.
85 min.
A muddled piece of misogynistic violence, which tries to offset its all too common tale of a murderous rapist by having a Fonda-style newscaster (Tewes) bravely investigate while confronted by apathy and accusations of hysteria from boyfriend, police and male colleagues at work. This promising (?) aspect, however, is betrayed both by the repeatedly voyeuristic assaults, and by the objectionable climax in which the newscaster's younger sister (Leigh), made deaf, dumb and blind by a childhood rape, is 'cured' by the killer's attack. GA

Eyes of Hell, The

see Mask, The

Eyes of Laura Mars

(Irvin Kershner, 1978, US) Faye Dunaway, Tommy Lee Jones, Brad Dourif, Rene Auberjonois, Raúl Julia, Frank Adonis.
103 min.
John Carpenter's intriguing original script, about a woman telepathically keyed-in to the sight of a murderer, underwent a cautionary transformation before its final emergence on screen as a glossily gimmicky murder mystery, featuring Dunaway as a female Helmut Newton. Carpenter baled out after nine months' work for producer Jon Peters, trying to soften his conception into a possible Streisand vehicle; and co-credited David Zelag Goodman was but the last of eight or nine scriptwriters subsequently employed to turn it into a shallow, chic confusion of eyes, camera lenses, and saleable images of violence of the sort it now purports to question as an 'issue'. Almost incidentally, it no longer works as a thriller, with a final revelation that one would have thought *Psycho* rendered impossible to re-use. PT

Eyes Without a Face

see Yeux sans Visage, Les

Eyewitness

(John Hough, 1970, GB) Mark Lester, Lionel Jeffries, Susan George, Tony Bonner, Jeremy Kemp, Peter Vaughn, Peter Bowles, Betty Marsden.
91 min.
Scripted by Ronald Harwood from the novel by Mark Hebden, this runs a lame variation on *The Window*. Lester is the eleven-year-old who witnesses a murder (in fact of the wrong man), isn't believed because he's always spinning yarns, and can't go to the cops because the killers are two policemen (Vaughn and Bowles). The Maltese locations are unusual and attractive, but the plot blows up into an absurd mayhem of chases and corpses. With credibility low, watchability gets even lower thanks to Hough's hideously mannered efforts at style (zooms, distortions, weird angles, images reflected in spectacle lenses, etc). TM

Eyewitness (aka The Janitor)

(Peter Yates, 1981, US) William Hurt, Sigourney Weaver, Christopher Plummer, James Woods, Irene Worth, Kenneth McMillan, Pamela Reed, Albert Paulsen.
108 min.
It's easy to say that this is much less than the sum of its parts – part fairytale love story, in which a poor boy loves and wins rich TV reporter, part soufflé of New York paranoia, which involves a murder (with a Vietnamese background) in the building where the poor boy works as a janitor. However, it is rare to find an American film these days that manipulates its plot to accommodate the relationships (and there are lots of them – friends, families, dogs), and whose characters are at least interesting. Steve Tesich's script sometimes smacks of screenwriting classes, but Yates (who worked with Tesich on *Breaking Away*) easily accommodates these lapses with his unfussy, medium-fast direction. Indeed, he guides his cast around the furniture better than most. The result is an enjoyable entertainment whose box-office failure was thoroughly undeserved. CPe

f

Fabulous Baker Boys, The

(Steve Kloves, 1989, US) Jeff Bridges, Michelle Pfeiffer, Beau Bridges, Wendy Girard, Ellie Raab, Jennifer Tilly, Xander Berkeley, Dakin Matthews.
113 min.
Piano duo Jack and Frank Baker (Jeff and Beau Bridges) have been gigging so long that their act has become a stale routine of schmaltzy intros and cocktail favourites. Auditioning for a singer to spice up the brew, they land themselves with Susie Diamond (Pfeiffer), a tough cookie if ever there was one. The new act is a success, but Susie's intrusion into the brothers' settled ways causes complications: family-man Frank, half-preferring things the way they were, is worried that womaniser Jack will seduce and drop Susie, while she wants a say in shaping the musical repertoire. If Steve Kloves' directing debut, from his own script, is hardly original, it does play fresh variations on an old theme. Much of the credit must go to the actors, with the Bridges brothers making a superb double act. Jeff, especially, manages with very sparse dialogue to convey a wealth of information about a less than sympathetic character; indeed, understatement is crucial to the script's success, keeping us puzzled about characters and situation for longer than one might hope. Sadly, Susie doesn't fully escape stereotyping (though Pfeiffer proves she can belt out a song). Otherwise, with more than enough witty, well-observed details, it's a little charmer. GA

Face

(Antonia Bird, 1997, GB) Robert Carlyle, Ray Winstone, Steven Waddington, Phil Davis, Damon Albarn, Lena Headey, Peter Vaughn, Gerry Conlon, Arthur Whybrow.
105 min.
Ray (Carlyle), a lapsed East End communist, has long since given up the common good for private gain. Still, even he's shocked when his brothers-in-arms turn their guns on each other after persons unknown steal the stash from their latest raid. The suspects are limited: there are five in the gang, and Ray knows at least he's staunch. After Antonia Bird's unhappy Hollywood venture, Mad Love, this heist-gone-wrong picture reclaims lost ground on home turf, and shares with Bird's BBC films Safe and Priest a determination to get in where the action is. It's muscular, raw, and aggressive. These un-English qualities make for rough edges, but also for vividly authentic popular cinema and plenty to argue about in the pub afterwards. Ronan Bennett's hard-boiled script keeps the tension simmering, the excellent Carlyle and a knockout cast somehow make you care, and there's a palpable sense of London in the dark days of winter, dog eat dog, and time running out. TCh

Face, The

see Ansikte t

Face at the Window, The

(George King, 1939, GB) Tod Slaughter, Marjorie Taylor, John Warwick, Leonard Henry, Aubrey Mallalieu, Robert Adair.
65 min. b/w.
The last of the great theatrical barnstormers, particularly famed for his lusty impersonation of the Demon Barber of Fleet Street, Slaughter generally disappoints on film, not only because the movies themselves tend to be creaky reproductions of stage performances, but because his speciality – the hissable villains of Victorian melodrama – really requires live audience participation to complete its larger-than-life mockery. The Face at the Window, closer to Grand Guignol in its tale of a mysterious killer who terrorises Paris in the 1880s, stabbing his victims while their attention is claimed by a bestial face at the window, is probably the best of them. The plot, statically but effectively staged as a series of tableaux, and filled out by a mad scientist who revives corpses by electricity (and proposes to assist the police by reviving a victim to finger the killer), is agreeably dotty. But Slaughter's performance, stylised in movement and gesture to an almost Brechtian degree, as self-parodic as a pantomime demon yet oddly chilling in its assumption of a sadism gleefully shared with the audience, is extraordinary. TM

Face Behind the Mask, The

(Robert Florey, 1941, US) Peter Lorre, Evelyn Keyes, Don Beddoe, George E Stone, John Tyrell
69 min. b/w.

Lorre is superlative as an immigrant watchmaker who arrives in America full of beaming enthusiasm for the promised land (his scenes with Beddoe, as the neighbourhood cop totally disarmed by his naive friendliness, are a joy), but whose reward is horrible disfigurement in a tenement fire. Forced to turn to crime to pay for the expensive facial mask without which he is unemployable, suicidally distressed by the betrayal of his own ideals, he is redeemed by the love of a blind girl (Keyes)...a tender, totally unsentimental idyll ended when her death by violence leaves him to plot a cold-blooded, self-immolating revenge. With Lorre's own sensitive features serving miraculously as the expressionless 'mask', while Florey's direction and Franz Planer's camerawork put scarcely a foot wrong, the film effortlessly transcends its B horror status to become a bleak, plangently poetic little tragedy. TM

Face in the Crowd, A

(Elia Kazan, 1957, US) Andy Griffith, Patricia Neal, Anthony Franciosa, Lee Remick, Walter Matthau, Kay Medford, Burl Ives, Rip Torn.
126 min. b/w.
When radio producer Neal discovers the homespun philosophy and musical talents of Griffith's Lonesome Rhodes in an Arkansas jail, she little knows that the hobo she's about to launch on a massively successful television career is going to turn into a monstrous national demagogue, not only cherished by his public but listened to by politicians. In the opening scenes of Kazan and writer Budd Schulberg's satire on the dangers of television and advertising, Griffith's virtuoso, likeably irreverent performance makes for genuinely amusing viewing; but once he's mixing with the bigwigs, the film-makers' political messages start flying thick and fast, and the drama soon becomes overheated and unconvincing. Nor is it politically sophisticated: as in late-'30s Capracorn, the ordinary 'little people' are presented as being so gullible that what starts out as a seemingly liberal tract rapidly becomes a smug, cynical exercise in misanthropy. GA

Face of Darkness, The

(Ian FH Lloyd, 1976, GB) Lennard Pearce, John Bennett, David Allister, Gwyneth Powell, Roger Bizley.
58 min.
After an uncertain start (through over-use of close-up), this feature debut settles into an interesting occult thriller that treats its subject with some intelligence. Concentrating on an MP's extremist ambitions, it deals with his recruitment of (and, unwittingly, by) the powers of evil, and his raising of one of the undead to further his totalitarian plans. Although inexperience sometimes shows in both plotting and direction, Lloyd manages his set pieces with conviction and a talent for bringing out the uneasy sexual undertones of necromancy. CPe

Face/Off

(John Woo, 1997, US) John Travolta, Nicolas Cage, Joan Allen, Alessandro Nivola, Gina Gershon, Dominique Swain, Nick Cassavetes, Harve Presnell, CCH Pounder.
139 min.
Pay attention, none of this makes much sense. Five years after the murder of his son, FBI agent Sean Archer (Travolta) finally has the drop on terrorist Castor Troy (Cage) – but with Castor comatose and a bomb ticking somewhere in LA, Archer's persuaded to undergo facial surgery, swapping Castor's features for his own. In this way, Archer-as-Troy (Cage) hopes to trick the location out of Castor's brother Pollux (Nivola). Unfortunately, Castor wakes up, and makes off with Archer's face, killing everyone who's in on the secret, and moving into his enemy's office. Woo's poetic-kinetic style has evolved, if not to the point of desperation, then to delirium: he makes a virtue of incredulity. With two of Hollywood's most flamboyant actors playing each other, the movie becomes a kind of pop Heat, an elaborate self-parody and quasi-serious examination of the art of film acting. Yet there's an authentic subversive frisson as Travolta (as-Troy-as-Archer) sizes up his rebellious teenage daughter, puts the sizzle back into a stale marriage, and generally carries on with the air of a sociopath getting the most out of life. 'Are we having any fun yet?' he demands. Twice over. TCh

Face of Fu Manchu, The

(Don Sharp, 1965, GB) Christopher Lee, Nigel Green, Joachim Fuchsberger, Karin Dor, Tsai Chin, Howard Marion Crawford, Walter Rilla.
94 min.
Sax Rohmer's fiendish Yellow Peril revived and played straight in a beautifully designed, perfectly paced and genuinely exciting thriller, with terrific performances from Lee (Fu Manchu) and Green (a magnificently imperturbable Nayland Smith). The Chinoiserie sets are gorgeous; even better are the locations, so carefully chosen for their period possibilities that the spirit of Feuillade hovers benignly over sequences like the great chase with rattletrap cars speeding along cobbled alleys while the pilot of a pursuing aeroplane leans, entrancingly, over the side to drop his squat, fin-tailed bombs by hand. Stylish, witty and a treat to watch. TM

Faces

(John Cassavetes, 1968, US) John Marley, Gena Rowlands, Lynn Carlin, Fred Draper, Seymour Cassel, Val Avery.
130 min. b/w.
Cassavetes' first independent film since Shadows – made after the severely compromised, if fascinating, studio movies Too Late Blues and A Child Is Waiting – is a compelling, sometimes harrowing account of the seemingly random and inconsequential events leading to marital breakdown. As always, the excellent, nervy performances are the thing, and the result – a classic of modern realism – is a convincingly bleak precursor to Husbands and A Woman Under the Influence. GA

Faces of Women (Visages de Femmes)

(Désiré Ecaré, 1985, Ivory C) Eugénie Cissé Roland, Albertine Guéssan, Véronique Mahile, Alexis Leatche, Désiré Bamba.
105 min.
A wonderfully unpredictable and lively triptych on the financial, sexual and emotional emancipation of African women, pieced together over twelve years by a film-maker who hasn't a single dull thought in his head. Traditional choruses and dances link the episodes and comment on the action, lending the film a structure that owes no debts to colonial models. The middle episode, about a woman who tires of her possessive husband and goes out to get herself a lover, is a real eye-opener: an extremely naked scene of seduction in and around a river lays a hundred puritan ghosts. TR

Face to Face (Ansikte mot Ansikte)

(Ingmar Bergman, 1975, Swe) Liv Ullmann, Erland Josephson, Gunnar Björnstrand, Aino Taube-Henrikson, Kari Sylwan, Sif Ruud, Sven Lindberg.
136 min.
Try to catch the original four-part TV series rather than this truncation for cinema release (especially the hideously dubbed English version); it emerges as Bergman's most potent psychodrama from the cycle that began with Cries and Whispers and ended with Autumn Sonata. The story concerns the gradual and agonising breakdown of a successful psychiatrist (Ullmann, married to another shrink played by Lindberg), who returns to her family home and becomes overwhelmed by memories of the past. The acting is intense, as you would expect from Ullmann and Josephson, working under a director who was coming to terms with his own breakdown in this film; and the nightmare imagery (washed-out backgrounds clashing vividly with stark colours) delivers a strong jolt to the subconscious. Laugh if you like, but check your dreams over the next few weeks after seeing it and you'll find fragments of this film corroding your conscience. MA

Fade to Black

(Vernon Zimmerman, 1980, US) Dennis Christopher, Tim Thomerson, Gwynne Gilford, Normann Burton, Linda Kerridge, Morgan Paull.
102 min.
Christopher's teenage angst-ridden movie addict with the nervous pre-murder giggle is a darker cousin of Billy Liar. But what promises to be sublime turns gradually to ridiculous as the young antihero's banes – wheelchaired ma, teasing

workmates, boss – are obliterated in a mess of gore and nostalgia as he turns Dracula (marvellous), Mummy, Hopalong Cassidy etc. The film aspires to hommage, it's true, but its references are altogether too obvious. That said, there's a *Psycho* bathroom pastiche that's almost worth the price of a ticket all by itself; and no collector of movie mush will want to miss it for its good bits, which are more than a few. GD

Fahrenheit 451

(François Truffaut, 1966, GB) Oskar Werner, Julie Christie, Cyril Cusack, Anton Diffring, Bee Duffell, Jeremy Spenser.
112 min.
An underrated film, perhaps because it is less science fiction than a tale of 'once upon a time'. Where Ray Bradbury's novel posited a strange, terrifyingly mechanised society which has banned books in the interests of material well-being, Truffaut presents a cosy world not so very different from our own, with television a universal father-figure pouring out reassuring messages, and the only element of menace a fire-engine tearing down the road. A bright, gleaming childhood red, the engine is like a reminder of toyhood days; and as Werner's fireman hero goes about his task of destroying literature, his growing awareness of the almost human way in which books curl up and die in the flames gradually assumes the dimensions of a quest for a legendary lost treasure – movingly glimpsed as he slowly and painfully deciphers the title-page of *David Copperfield*. Here the rich, nostalgic pull of the past wins out over technocracy, and the film ends, as it began, with a scene lifted right out of time: a wonderful shot of the rebels – each dedicated to the preservation of a literary masterpiece by committing it to memory – wandering in contented, idyllic exile by the edge of a glitteringly icy lake. TM

Fail Safe

(Sidney Lumet, 1964, US) Henry Fonda, Dan O'Herlihy, Walter Matthau, Frank Overton, Edward Binns, Fritz Weaver, Larry Hagman.
112 min. b/w.
Eclipsed by its contemporary, *Dr Strangelove*, *Fail Safe* eschews the former's black humour and opts for a deadly serious mix of cold-war melodrama and rampant psychosis. Creeping unease builds up to terminal paranoia as the machines run away from their masters, the 'fail safe' fails, and the unstoppable 'Vindicator' bomber homes in on Moscow – all by accident. Lumet sensibly avoids pyrotechnics in favour of tightening the psychological screws, as Larry Hagman (the president's translator – nice looking kid) does nervy trade-offs on the hot-line, and everyone, from President Fonda down, starts drowning in a sea of cold sweat. CPea

Fair Game (Mamba)

(Mario Orfini, 1988, It) Trudie Styler, Gregg Henry, Bill Mosley.
81 min.
I'm slithering around on my belly in a chic warehouse flat with no windows and a jammed front door, *Psycho* shower scene sound effects shrieking in my ears, injected with a fatal overdose of sex hormone that only gives me 30 minutes to sink my teeth into 150 pounds of thirty something-ish designer flesh while squinting through an 8am fish-eye lens. What am I? Right. I'm a bemused black mamba with a schizophrenic libido (a randy poisonous snake to you) chasing Trudie Styler around because her rich ex-husband can't deal with the business parties on his own, nor with the fact that she hates his designer gadgets and executive toys. Welcome to the flip side of *Fatal Attraction*: 7,287 feet of 'serious' camera work with a plot worthy of a third-rate acid trip. The heavy mythological pointers (Styler plays Eva) are completely subverted by Orfini's insistence on fondling Styler's bum from as many obscure angles as possible. JCh

Fair Game

(Andrew Sipes, 1995, US) William Baldwin, Cindy Crawford, Steven Berkoff, Christopher McDonald, Miguel Sandoval, Johann Carlo, Salma Hayek, John Bedford Lloyd.
90 min.
Miami lawyer Crawford, whose life is threatened by Berkoff and his team of over-armed baddies (she knows not why), finds detective Baldwin her

only salvation. Cue shoot-out, car chase, explosions, repeated ad nauseam. One of her alimony cases is (somehow) connected to ex-KGB agents looking to transfer savings from Cold War-era Swiss bank accounts. But who cares, since no one lets either her or us in on the secret. Dire in all departments. NB

FairyTale – A True Story

(Charles Sturridge, 1997, US) Florence Hoath, Elizabeth Earl, Paul McGann, Phoebe Nicholls, Bob Peck, Harvey Keitel, Peter O'Toole, Anton Lesser, Mel Gibson.
98 min.
One of two 1997 films inspired by Elsie Wright and Frances Griffiths' photographs of the fairies resident at the bottom of their Cottingley garden. While Nick Willing's *Photographing Fairies* used the hullabaloo surrounding the pics to spin a distinctly ambivalent, adult story about bereavement, imagined realities and the post-WWI national psyche, Sturridge's film takes up the same issues in the children's film format, proclaims a whole hearted, affirmative response to the Fairy Question, and induces a more ambiguous reaction. Despite the high production values, however, the glitzy cast and several tried-and-tested storytellers, I never truly believed that the film-makers believed. Children, on the other hand, may not be so cynical. It's a respectable tale, but there's too much baggage for the fancy fully to take flight. NB

Faithful Narrative of the Capture, Sufferings and Miraculous Escape of Eliza Fraser, A

see Rollicking Adventures of Eliza Fraser, The

Fakebook

see American Blue Note

Falcon and the Co-eds, The

(William Clemens, 1943) Tom Conway, Jean Brooks, Rita Corday, Amelita Ward, Isabel Jewell, George Givot, Cliff Clark.
68 min. b/w.
Despite the off-putting title, an attractive little thriller in which the Falcon investigates murder in a girl's school, where an atmosphere of fear and loathing centres on a girl with second sight, while she herself is driven to suicidal despair by her predictions of murder. Scripted by Ardel Wray, who worked regularly with Val Lewton (*I Walked with a Zombie, Leopard Man, Isle of the Dead*), it is beautifully characterised and has some vividly eerie touches (better exploited in Roy Hunt's camerawork than by Clemens' direction). It's one of the best in a series which took over from *The Saint* after RKO tired of paying Leslie Charteris for rights, and turned instead to a Michael Arlen story (*The Gay Falcon*, retained as the title of the first film in 1941). George Sanders, with five appearances as the Saint behind him, was clearly bored playing virtually the same character (less ruthless, more honest); and after three appearances, he was killed off by Nazi assassins in *The Falcon's Brother* (1942), leaving his real-life brother Conway to succeed him. Of the four Sanders films, *The Falcon Takes Over* (1942) is distinguished as the first adaptation of a Raymond Chandler novel: a breathless scurry through the plot of *Farewell My Lovely* with an excellent performance from Ward Bond as the moronically lovelorn Moose Malloy, it finds the suave Sanders distinctly anomalous in Chandler territory. Conway, bringing a lighter touch to the series (which managed its comic relief better than most), starred in nine films after *The Falcon's Brother*, most of them deft and surprisingly enjoyable. *The Falcon Strikes Back* (1943), for instance, though saddled with a dull plot about missing war bonds, is directed by Edward Dmytryk with strikingly elliptical economy, and has the bonus of Edgar Kennedy as a mad puppeteer villain. *The Falcon in Hollywood* (1944) is a lively studio murder mystery directed by Gordon Douglas, with RKO itself serving as the set. *The Falcon in San Francisco*, vividly directed by Joseph H Lewis (particularly the opening sequence with the little girl on the train), makes excellent use of locations. *The Falcon in Mexico* enlivens a stock plot with some elaborate location footage clearly not shot on a B movie budget: could it possibly be errant footage from Welles' abortive *It's All True*? TM

Falcon and the Snowman, The

(John Schlesinger, 1985, US) Timothy Hutton, Sean Penn, Pat Hingle, Joyce Van Patten, David Suchet, Lori Singer, Richard Dysart.
131 min.
Seminary drop-out Hutton fetches up in a job deep in the heart of the CIA telex circuit; sick with his country, he persuades his ex-altar boy buddy and current dope dealer, Penn, to peddle secrets to the Russians in Mexico City. Much is made of the mechanics of the business, and in this area the movie belongs to Penn, his eyebrow-pencil moustache dissolving in cocaine as he keeps up a front of jittery bravado. Hutton succumbs firstly to a thin role, and secondly to the film's lack of any strong viewpoint about its leading men. As usual Schlesinger is more than half in love with what he might be satirising. CPea

Fallen

(Gregory Hoblit, 1998, US) Denzel Washington, John Goodman, Donald Sutherland, Embeth Davidtz, James Gandolfini, Elias Koteas, Robert Joy.
127 min.
Super-clean cop John Hobbes (Washington) unleashes evil spirit 'Azazel' when he sends a serial killer (Koteas) to the chair. Unlike Morgan Freeman's learned sleuth in *Seven*, the parochial Hobbes is convinced that cops are 'the chosen people'. Having captured the killer, he appears on TV smug and smiling. Things turn intriguing, however, when later his attention is drawn to the biblical injunction 'Hide your good works.' His consequent fear that the whole city is against him is straddled between paranoia and intuition. Azazel's spirit is passed along by touch: in a crowded, aggressive city (Philadelphia), anyone can turn nasty. On a metaphorical level, this makes sense – AIDS and a fear of the city are central to the '90s. But God (or the Devil) is in the detail: every time a fluid is taken into the body, the fidgety camera zooms in, fascinated, suspicious. Excellent support from Davidtz, Goodman, and Joy, as Hobbes' brother, though as the plot twists take precedence over character, much of the film's nuance trickles away and, along with it, the tension. CO'Su

Fallen Angel

(Otto Preminger, 1945, US) Alice Faye, Dana Andrews, Linda Darnell, Charles Bickford, Anne Revere, Bruce Cabot, John Carradine.
97 min. b/w.
Dana Andrews marries sweet little Alice Faye for her money in order to keep his waitress mistress (Darnell) in the style to which she would like to be accustomed. But things go wrong when the waitress is murdered. A sharp, small town melodrama, with the contrasts between the two ends of town well observed: the suburban houses and the seedy roadhouse with its run-down rooms. CPe

Fallen Angels (Duoluo Tianshi)

(Wong Kar-Wai, 1995, HK) Leon Lai, Michele Reis, Takeshi Kaneshiro, Karen Mong, Charlie Young.
96 min.
Tired of the wounds incurred at work, Hong Kong hitman Wong Chi-Ming (Lai) decides to break his partnership with the agent (Reis) who hires and secretly loves him; when he meets the punkish Baby (Mong), there's a small chance his loneliness will come to an end, but the agent's still keen to revive their relationship. Meanwhile, mute ex-con He Zhiwu (Kaneshiro), who makes a living by re-opening shops closed for the night, meets up with Charlie (Young). Helping her hunt down her ex-boyfriend's new lover, He Zhiwu falls for Charlie himself, but after she disappears, he fills his time shooting videos of his flophouse-proprietor father. As stylish and audacious as *Days of Being Wild* and *Chungking Express*, Wong Kar-Wai's film is another poignant but occasionally playful study of forlorn romance and melancholy solitude. Good-looking twenty-somethings struggle to make it through the night in the neon-lit streets, bars and diners of a Hong Kong rendered magically moody by the extreme wide-angle lens of Chris Doyle's fluid camera. Exhilarating and, in the end, unexpectedly touching. GA

f

Fallen Idol, The

(Carol Reed, 1948, GB) Ralph Richardson, Michèle Morgan, Bobby Henrey, Sonia Dresdel, Denis O'Dea, Jack Hawkins, Dora Bryan.
95 min. b/w.
A perfect example of the respectable quality film which achieved its apotheosis in late '40s Britain: tasteful, restrained, carefully crafted, but in the long run a little anaemic. Reed, once considered the great British director, had his clay feet mercilessly exposed by the *auteur*ist critics of the '60s. Now stripped of his inflated reputation, it is possible to appreciate his virtues: an ability to elicit remarkable performances from his actors – here an engaging Anglo-French child and an admirably controlled Richardson – and a fine skill for exploring psychological depths without sacrificing narrative coherence. Taking Graham Greene's story of the relationship between an (upper class) boy and his (working class) hero, he expands it into a sophisticated analysis of the intersections between the separate realities of children and adults. RMy

Falling Down

(Joel Schumacher, 1992, US) Michael Douglas, Robert Duvall, Barbara Hershey, Frederic Forrest, Tuesday Weld, Lois Smith.
115 min.
Schumacher's film goes beyond the confines of vigilante films like *Death Wish* whose concerns stop at the criminal justice system. 'D-Fens' (Douglas), named after his own car number plate and his now redundant job as a bastion of America's nuclear defence industry, is a one-man terrorist in the Los Angeles jungle. Forced by a traffic jam to make his way 'home' on foot, Douglas strikes at various targets: rude car drivers, obstructive fast-food workers, violent gangs, overcharging Korean shopkeepers, snobby golf-course wrinklies. However, the only person he directly murders is a disgusting, homophobic neo-Nazi. The scumbag is played by the invariably excellent Forrest who, along with Duvall as a speak-softly cop and Hershey as Douglas's estranged wife, gives the cast an air of huge respectability. There are reservations: too many plot and moral loose-ends, while the film veers giddily between Douglas the psycho-menace and Douglas the sad sympathy-object. Sometimes funny, sometimes touching, and certainly unnerving. SGr

Falling For You

(Robert Stevenson/Jack Hulbert, 1933, GB) Jack Hulbert, Cicely Courtneidge, Tamara Desni, Garry Marsh, Alfred Drayton, OB Clarence.
88 min. b/w.
Patchy vehicle for West End revue darlings Courtneidge and Hulbert. As rival journalists on the trail of Ruritanian heiress Desni, they tangle with haunted castles, irate editors, runaway sleighs, a ghost called Stephen and a villain called Sausage. Hulbert's snow and ice slapstick is embarrassingly unfunny, but the film is saved by the bit-part players and the exuberantly inventive Courtneidge. Disguised as a twitching rabbit-toothed hypochondriac, as 'onest, affable and 'elpful ladies 'elp Hettie Bartholomew, and finally as a kangaroo leading her bemused adversaries in a chorus of 'Why Has a Cow Got Four Legs?', she is absurdly magnificent. RMy

Falling in Love

(Ulu Grosbard, 1984, US) Robert De Niro, Meryl Streep, Harvey Keitel, Jane Kaczmarek, George Martin, David Clennon.
106 min.
De Niro and Streep play two Manhattan commuters who fall in love, *Brief Encounter* style; but to invoke Coward and Lean's film is to realise just how thin and unsatisfying this one is. Coincidences are difficult to get right in any romantic movie, yet here they are piled on without regard for sense or subtlety, while the script is so concerned to give its big names equal screen time that it fails to establish an innocuous but hardly compelling love story of the old school. De Niro merely coasts, while Streep's woman-at-the-emotional-crossroads now seems as familiar as a stale variety turn. DP

Fall of the House of Usher, The

see House of Usher, The

Fall of the Roman Empire, The

(Anthony Mann, 1964, US) Sophia Loren, Stephen Boyd, James Mason, Christopher Plummer, Alec Guinness, Anthony Quayle, John Ireland, Mel Ferrer, Omar Sharif, Eric Porter.
187 min.
Though lacking the mythic clarity of *El Cid* – Mann's other epic for Samuel Bronston – this is a superior example of the genre. Deserting the usual conflict of Christians and Romans, the story moves to a later era and charts the intrigues surrounding the Imperial throne, held by Marcus Aurelius and coveted by the corrupt Commodus, that led to the Romans' downfall at the hands of the Barbarians. Largely accurate in historical terms, thanks to a wordy but intelligent script by Philip Yordan (a master of the epic style), it is surprisingly restrained, both in terms of action and acting. But the atmosphere is consistently convincing: darkness holds sway on the fringes of the Empire, where the armies are struggling to repel the invading hordes, while Rome is presented as a magnificent but decadent monument to the unimaginative pragmatism of the Roman mind. Terrific sets, a stirring score by Dimitri Tiomkin and the overall quality of the production values manage to counteract the film's excessive length. GA

Fall of the Romanov Dynasty, The

(Esther Shub, 1927, USSR)
5,578 ft. b/w
In 1927, when Eisenstein was making *October*, Esther Shub was working on neglected newsreel footage from the Moscow archives to create a dramatic 'montage of film document' spanning 1913-1917. In 1967, Mosfilm re-produced the film, adding an introduction and a soundtrack of classical piano music to counterpoint and underline her juxtaposition of images and terse intertitles. The result is a highly entertaining and visually interesting history lesson, which charts in succinct and often amusing terms the decline of the Tsars (the Romanov dynasty) and the rise of the masses. HM

Falls, The

(Peter Greenaway, 1980, GB) Peter Westley, Aad Wirtz, Michael Murray, Lorna Poulter, Patricia Carr.
185 min.
Greenaway's fantasy expands enormously the same obsessions as his earlier *A Walk Through H* and *Vertical Features Remake*: a cross between Alice after the Holocaust and the ramblings of a deranged film librarian. Set in a strangely serene future – after a Violent Unexplained Event which has irrevocably changed Life as We Know It – *The Falls* sets out to document the biographies of 92 victims of the event, all selected on the basis that their names begin with the letters 'Fall'. The strategy is ingenious, substituting an amazing excess of 'content' for the formalism that has (usually) defined the avant-garde. Not recommended to people who like one story, two characters, and a happy ending. But for those who like riddles, acrostics, sudden excursions, romantic insights, and the eerie music of Michael Nyman (plus bits of Brian Eno)...come to Xanadu. CA

Fall Time

(Paul Warner, 1994, US)
Stephen Baldwin, Mickey Rourke, Jason London, David Arquette, Jonah Blechman, Sheryl Lee, J Michael Hunter.
88 min.
High-school grads London, Arquette and Blechman plan a play-acted 'murder' in front of the bank which major sleazo Rourke and psychotic accomplice Baldwin just happen to be holding up. The dear young chaps find themselves sucked into a miasma of paranoia, violence, muddled scripting and drearily mannered turns from the two hoods. The plot delivers up a ludicrous roadside sex scene involving harassed female hostage Lee, before crumbling to a grandiose and deeply bathetic conclusion. A singularly unpromising first feature. TJ

Falsche Bewegung

see Wrong Movement

Fälschung, Die

see Circle of Deceit

Fame

(Alan Parker, 1980, US) Irene Cara, Lee Curreri, Laura Dean, Antonia Franceschi, Paul McCrane, Barry Miller, Gene Anthony Ray, Maureen Teefy.
133 min.
A British-directed, New-York based musical which follows the heartbreak-and-success story of a group of youngsters as they're put through their paces at the High School of Performing Arts. The main characters, all lightly sketched in, offer a brief showcase for just about every kind of performing talent from classical ballet to stand-up comedy; the song'n'dance numbers are edited to an unstoppable disco beat; and the brazen jokes (Jews, blacks, women, gays, etc.) keep coming to show that we're all part of the same pie in the sky. It's a crack at the American Dream which carries all the exhilaration and depth of a 133-minute commercial break. HM

Family Album

see Costa Brava

Family Business

(Tom Cohen, 1982, US) Howard Snider, Judy Snider, the Snider children.
87 min.
A fly-on-the-wall documentary examining the dodgy finances of a pizza parlour in Muncie, Indiana, and the strain on the family who run it. Howard Snyder is Mr Shakey, the pizza man who hasn't made it to Hamburger Row. He embraces the American way of life with zest as he serves his mouthwateringly massive pizzas, sings to the customers, records his own radio ads, and works enormously long hours; but beneath the 'have a nice day' exterior, he is struggling to retain his franchise and to balance his books. Wrong orders, bickering and dating take place against a background of mounting anxiety which culminates in an emotional family meeting. They are all extraordinarily unselfconscious in front of the camera, but in the end one longs for a little less vérité and rather more creativity. JE

Family Business

(Sidney Lumet, 1989, US) Sean Connery, Dustin Hoffman, Matthew Broderick, Rosana DeSoto, Janet Carroll, Victoria Jackson, Bill McCutcheon, Deborah Rush, BD Wong.
113 min.
The credits imply class; but while everyone is proficient, this uneasy mix of comedy, thriller and melodrama fumbles its way through a forest of clichés and contrivances. Vito (Hoffman) is a respectable New York meat-trader who has renounced the criminal ways of his roguish dad Jesse (Connery). But in giving son Adam (Broderick) the best education money can buy, Vito has alienated himself from both, driving them into conspiratorial buddydom. When Adam plans a million-dollar scam involving the theft of plasma from a low-security lab, Jesse wants in, but Vito is co-opted only when he realises that the only way to protect his son is to be there. The heist goes awry, and a vaguely light-hearted romp enters the register Emotional. This being Lumet, issues are broached – genes and generational conflict, the relationship between morality and law, the purpose of life – but meaningful dialogues do not a good movie make: the battle lines, clear from the start, proceed with the inevitability of a computer game towards weepy reconciliation. Worse, it's hard to like or care for the characters; and since writer Vincent Patrick (adapting his own novel) stacks the odds to favour Jesse's selfish anarchy, the end result is at best morally confused, at worst devious. GA

Family Game (Kazoku Game)

(Yoshimitsu Morita, 1983, Jap) Yusaku Matsuda, Ichirota Miyagawa, Junichi Tsujita, Juzo Itami, Saori Yuki.
107 min.
A subtly cruel satire on the Japanese obsession with corporate and academic success which blends striking visual compositions, pithy dialogue and absurdist humour. Matsuda plays a young private tutor hired by ambitious parents to cram their youngest son into the 'right' school. The father

works all the hours God sends, while the wife busies herself with obsessive cleaning. Both are alienated from their sons, for whose benefit they are supposedly making these sacrifices, and the presence of the tutor opens up the cracks which the formalities of parental love and filial duty are meant to paper over. The juxtaposition of meticulously framed images with terse, ironic dialogue and explosions of slapstick violence exposes the frustrations generated by an unhealthy preoccupation with material aspiration and social status. Sogo Ishii ripped into similar issues with a chainsaw in *Crazy Family*, but Morita dissects equally tellingly with a scalpel. NF

Family Jewels, The

(Jerry Lewis, 1965, US) Jerry Lewis, Sebastian Cabot, Donna Butterworth, Gene Baylos, Robert Strauss, Anne Baxter.
100 min.
Lewis could never be a father, but here he plays seven uncles from whom a rich industrialist's orphaned daughter must pick a daddy. Parodying a gangster film, it's a tour de force of Lewisian disguise, slowly unfolding gags, and monstrous sentimentality. A morose clown, a Terry-Thomas style pilot, a gaga photographer, and an incomprehensible old sea captain all figure; but nothing so funny as when the gangster uncle sheds his 'funny mask' disguise to reveal a worse real face beneath. Ups and downs on the laughter scale, perhaps, but there's more than meets the eye. DMacp

Family Life

(Ken Loach, 1971, GB) Sandy Ratcliff, Bill Dean, Grace Cave, Malcolm Tierney, Hilary Martyn, Michael Riddall, Alan Macnaughtan.
108 min.
A fictional documentary (scripted by David Mercer) that charts the influence of family relations on a young girl's deteriorating ability to handle her environment. It presents a highly biased attack against the techniques of drug and electro-convulsive therapy, in favour of a more personal approach that takes into account the complexities of the individual's social context. As propaganda, the film tends to distort and oversimplify the issues, with a method disturbingly similar to that which it is attacking. *Family Life* continues Loach's examination of class exploitation, and because its purpose and function are clearer than *Poor Cow* or even *Kes*, it's arguably a better film, even if remaining limited by its TV-derived visual puritanism. JDuC

Family Life (Zycie Rodzinne)

(Krzysztof Zanussi, 1970, Pol) Daniel Olbrychski, Maja Komorowska, Jan Nowicki, Jan Kreczmar, Halina Mikolajska.
93 min.
Tricked into returning home for the first time in six years, a successful young Polish engineer is forced to decide whether or not to take responsibility for the destructive lifestyle of his estranged, alcoholic father, bitter that the family's wealth has gone, his furniture is being sold, and his grandfather's glass factory is now state-owned. Despite the laconic passivity of Olbrychski's performance as the engineer, *Family Life* compels attention by its richly detailed evocation of the family's crumbling mansion, its overgrown garden under siege from modern apartment buildings, and the precision with which Zanussi develops the engineer's struggle to accept, and finally to free himself from, the tentacles of his father's capitalist past. A neatly dismissive coda wraps up this taut, supremely well-made example of formal Polish film-making. JPy

Family Plot

(Alfred Hitchcock, 1976, US) Karen Black, Bruce Dern, Barbara Harris, William Devane, Ed Lauter, Cathleen Nesbitt, Katherine Helmond.
120 min.
With his last film, Hitchcock made a triumphant return to form in the comic thriller. His most relaxed, witty and urbane movie since *North by Northwest* (also scripted by Ernest Lehman), it's a dense but extremely entertaining collection of symmetric patterns, doubles and rhymes. One couple (Dern/Harris) are amiable fakes, dealing in bogus spiritualism; another (Black/ Devane) are sinister fakes, trading in the physical merchandise of kidnapped diplomats and ransomed

jewels. Linking these two pairs is an illegitimate child, an empty grave, and a mountain of misunderstandings. Hitchcock ties together the complex strands in a delightful way, with a series of symbols and set pieces which demonstrate that the Old Master had lost his touch not one jot. Beneath all the fun, there's a vision of humans as essentially greedy and dishonest, presented with a gorgeously amoral wink from Hitchcock, and performed to perfection by an excellent cast. GA

Family Portrait (Sishi Buhuo)

(Li Shaohong, 1992, China) Li Xuejian, Song Dandan, Ye Jing.
90 min.
After laying bare backward village mentalities in *Bloody Morning*, Li Shaohong turns her attention to China's urban middle class. Cao is a photographer, married to an opera singer and with an infant son, caught in the usual professional morass of political compromise. His life starts to fall apart when he learns that his ex-wife also bore him a son some months after their divorce – and when the boy turns up looking for his father. Nothing wildly dramatic, just believable people in believable situations. If the ending seems a touch forced, this is nevertheless a sign that 'Fifth Generation' cinema is changing and coming to terms with up-to-date realities. TR

Family Viewing

(Atom Egoyan, 1987, Can) David Hemblem, Aidan Tierney, Gabrielle Rose, Arsinée Khanjian, Selma Keklikian.
86 min.
Dad seems like a regular, middle class guy, but his penchants for mild sado-masochism and phone sex have driven his wife to leave him. He packes his senile mother-in-law off to a low-rent old people's home, and instals a charming, sitcom-style bimbo to meet his domestic and sexual needs. His son, meanwhile, spends all his free time visiting Granny in the home, where he strikes up a friendship with a young woman who happens to work for the phone-sex business patronised by his father.... Egoyan's movie offers a rare – in 1988, unique – blend of black comedy, parody, formal fun-and-games, and emotive drama, and finally proves to have a remarkable range and maturity, giving equal weight to everything from the implications of video surveillance to the plight of elderly ethnic immigrants. You laugh one minute, gasp the next, and grope for the Kleenex moments later. TR

Fan, The

(Edward Bianchi, 1981, US) Lauren Bacall, James Garner, Maureen Stapleton, Hector Elizondo, Michael Biehn, Anna Maria Horsford, Griffin Dunne.
95 min.
Tacky adaptation of Bob Randall's novel in which (prefiguring the Jodie Foster case) a Broadway star's youthful fan (Biehn) graduates from epistolary devotion to homicidal mania when his overtures receive increasingly curt responses. Since impending shocks are loudly telegraphed in advance, and mainly comprise a series of virtually identical slasher attacks with open razor, the result is crude, nasty and predictable. Sole reason for watching the film is the wonderful Bacall as the toast of Broadway, currently celebrating yet another forty-ninth birthday, curling her basso purr round lines to make their banality sound like wit, and rehearsing a musical (songs by Marvin Hamlisch) that gives her the chance to strut her stuff as a song-and-dancer. TM

Fan, The

(Tony Scott, 1996, US) Robert De Niro, Wesley Snipes, Benicio del Toro, Ellen Barkin, John Leguizamo, Patti D'Arbanville-Quinn, Chris Mulkey.
115 min.
It's hard to imagine what De Niro saw in this crass 'study' of a delusional stalker, which merely requires him to reprise, in cruder form, two of his best-known roles, Rupert Pupkin and Travis Bickle. Alienated from his job as a hunting-knife salesman, and separated from a wife who resents any time he spends with their young son, Gil Renard (De Niro) hones his obsession with the San Francisco Giants baseball team and their classy new signing Bobby Rayburn (Snipes). When Rayburn hits a slump, Renard focuses his

resentment on usurper Juan Primo (del Toro), whose winning streak he brings to a sudden, brutal end. Facile pop psychology, hysterical performances, frenetic editing and a deafening, aggressive soundtrack. NF

Fanatic
(aka Die! Die! My Darling!)

(Silvio Narizzano, 1965, GB) Tallulah Bankhead, Stefanie Powers, Peter Vaughan, Maurice Kaufman, Yootha Joyce, Donald Sutherland, Robert Dorning.
96 min.
One of the best of Hammer's psychological thrillers, mainly thanks to Richard Matheson's ingenious and terrifying script (adapted from a novel by Anne Blaisdell) about a religious crank who gradually becomes homicidal. There are plenty of *Psycho* rip-offs – notably at the climax – but Tallulah Bankhead is great in the title role, and for once the basis of the plot seems disturbingly credible. Admittedly Narizzano (who made the awful *Georgy Girl*) has little to offer in the way of direction, but then Matheson's scripts tend to be able to look after themselves. DP

Fandango

(Kevin Reynolds, 1985, US) Kevin Costner, Judd Nelson, Sam Robards, Chuck Bush, Brian Cesak, Marvin J McIntyre, Suzy Amis.
91 min.
Five college friends strike out on one last fling – and the buddy buddy coming of age road movie is born. Despite patronage from Steven Spielberg, *Fandango* made no box-office impact. There is a sense of *déjà vu* all right, but this is an extremely attractive valediction to youth, with farcical underpinnings ably handled by Reynolds. His potential as a film-maker has since been confirmed (check out *The Beast*), and his pal Costner (surely the most important star to emerge from the '80s: Howard Hawks would have loved him) holds this one together. As a consequence, the picture's jumpy tone is safely grounded in character. BC

Fanny

(Marc Allégret, 1932, Fr) Raimu, Pierre Fresnay, Orane Demazis, Alida Rouffe, Fernand Charpin, Robert Vattier, Milly Mathis.
126 min. b/w.
Part two of Marcel Pagnol's Marseilles trilogy, which began with *Marius*. The story so far: Marius, eager-beaver son of choleric but loveable César, has deserted Fanny, the love of his life, for the other love of his life, the sea – leaving Fanny bearing his child. Panisse, a middle-aged old fool, offers to solve all problems by marrying the girl himself, thus securing the son he longs for. However, when Marius returns...But plots are the last thing to worry about in the trilogy; one's best bet is to savour instead the finely drawn character studies, the triumphant acting, the warmth, humanity, and tightly-reined sentimentality of Pagnol's whole outlook. Allégret's direction is notably neater than Korda's in the first part or Pagnol's own for *César*. GB

Fanny

(Joshua Logan, 1960, US) Leslie Caron, Maurice Chevalier, Charles Boyer, Horst Buchholz, Salvatore Baccaloni, Lionel Jeffries.
133 min.
Curious adaptation of the 1954 Broadway musical (book by SN Behrman and Logan) which cavalierly cut out the excellent Harold Rome score, leaving only the title song for background orchestrations. What's left, clumsily compressed from Pagnol's Marseilles trilogy so as to play up the romantic complications, is both dire and dull. Jack Cardiff's pretty Technicolor photography is some compensation. TM

Fanny and Alexander
(Fanny och Alexander) [100]

(Ingmar Bergman, 1982, Swe) Gunn Wållgren, Jarl Kulle, Erland Josephson, Jan Malmsjö, Harriet Andersson, Bertil Guve, Allan Edwall, Mats Bergman, Gunnar Björnstrand.
189 min.
Bergman's magisterial turn-of-the-century family saga, largely seen through the eyes of a small boy and carrying tantalising overtones of autobiography. Perhaps more accurately described as

an anthology of personal reference points, designed as an auto-critique analysing his repertoire of artistic tricks. Years ago, in *The Face*, Bergman was agonising over the humiliations of the artist caught out in his deceptions and manipulations; but *Fanny and Alexander* cheerfully acknowledges his role as a charlatan conjuring his own life into dreams and nightmares for the edification or jollification of humanity. Here again are the smiles of a summer night (transferred to a dazzling evocation of traditional Christmas celebrations), the terror of the small boy harried by a sternly puritanical father, the crisis of religious doubt, the apocalyptic materialisation of God through a glass darkly (but seen this time to be only a marionette). Pulling his own creations apart to show how they tick, Bergman demonstrates the role of art and artifice, ocassionally slipping in a stunning new trick to show that the old magic still works. Certainly the most illuminating and most entertaining slice of Bergman criticism around, even better in the uncut TV version which clocks in at 300 minutes. TM

Fanny Hill

(Gerry O'Hara, 1983, GB) Lisa Raines, Oliver Reed, Wilfrid Hyde-White, Shelley Winters, Alfred Marks, Jonathan York, Paddie O'Neil.
92 min.
A pale blue production, like its bestselling 1749 smut-opus source, this smooths over the sordid face of 18th-century peccadillo in favour of wholesome rosy-tinted coitus. Young Fanny progresses from penniless provincial freshy adrift in olde London, to wealthy Woman of Pleasure via brothels which throw terrific-looking parties, and where the other whores make great bosom pals. Apart from a few tastefully arranged bums and brief glimpses of torpid tool, the onus of creative expression is on the nipple and all the interesting things it can do in big close-ups. Firmly grasping the fundamental part of Fanny, Lisa squeezes out a well-rounded performance, and holds her own against Reed's lawyer and Winters' madam, before coming into money and rutting off into the credits with her true lurve. The optimistic ending merely validates a specious subtextual interpretation of the plot as Cinderella with Knobs On. AB

Fantasia

(Ben Sharpsteen, 1940, US) Animation feature; music performed by the Philadelphia Orchestra, conductor Leopold Stokowski.
135 min.
Renowned abstract film-maker Oskar Fischinger, employed in a distant capacity on the Bach sequence, called this Disney effort a 'conglomeration of tastelessness'. He wasn't kidding. Only the Dukas *Sorcerer's Apprentice* sequence, with Mickey Mouse, where the storyboard is effectively provided by the composer, achieves a respectable kind of success. For the rest, Disney's attempts at the visual illustration of Beethoven and Co – a dubious exercise anyway – produce Klassical Kitsch of the highest degree. Awesomely embarrassing; but some great sequences for all that, and certainly not to be missed. GB

Fantasist, The

(Robin Hardy, 1986, Eire) Moira Harris, Christopher Cazenove, Timothy Bottoms, John Kavanagh, Mick Lally, Bairbre Ni Chaoimh.
98 min.
Down Dublin's mean streets stalks a psychopath who, before pouncing for the kill, mesmerises his victims-to-be with lengthy telephone monologues that blend blarney, threats and pure poetry. Armed only with a strange mixture of canny courage and coy innocence, Patricia – a young Southern Irish farmgirl leaving home to try her luck teaching in the city – is simultaneously attracted to and terrified by three admiring males, each of whom might turn out to be her saviour or her slayer. Hardy's thriller is often as offbeat as his earlier *The Wicker Man*, embellishing its suspense with oddball characters, intimations of magic and the polarities of innocence and experience, country and city, dream and reality. Attempting to investigate different aspects of sexual/romantic fantasy (all four central characters might lay claim to the film's title), Hardy nevertheless remains constricted by both the narrative formulas and the moral conventions of the woman-in-peril film: too often, Patricia, as played by Moira Harris, seems not just foolhardy

but actually compliant in her dangerous predicament. That said, however, Hardy deserves praise for his very evident ambitions. GA

Fantastic Disappearing Man, The

see Return of Dracula, The

Fantastic Night, The

see Nuit fantastique, La

Fantastic Planet (La Planète Sauvage)

(René Laloux, 1973, Fr/Czech) Graphic designs by Roland Topor.
71 min.
Are you ready for the struggle of the Oms against their oppressive masters, the 40-foot Draags? Something of a revelation to anyone who thinks animation extends only as far as *Fritz the Cat*, Roland Topor's graphics create a world reminiscent of two of the greatest artists of the fantastic, Bosch and Odilon Redon. He sketches a menacing landscape full of womb-like passages, intestinal plants, strange phallic and vaginal shapes, and extraordinary posthistoric monsters. CPe

Fantastic Voyage

(Richard Fleischer, 1966, US) Stephen Boyd, Raquel Welch, Donald Pleasence, Edmond O'Brien, Arthur Kennedy, Arthur O'Connell.
100 min.
Very nearly a corking sci-fi lark, kicking off from the premise that when a top scientist defecting to the West suffers brain damage in an assassination attempt, the only answer is to inject a miniaturised submarine and medical team through his bloodstream to deal with the clot on his brain. The voyage through the fantastic landscapes of the body is brilliantly imagined, with the heart a cavernous vault, tidal waves menacing the canals of the inner ear (caused when a nurse drops an instrument in the operating theatre), cyclonic winds tossing the sub helplessly about as the lungs are reached. The script, alas, is pretty basic, expending half its energies on delivering a gee-whiz medical lecture, the other on whipping up suspense around the mysterious saboteur who lurks aboard (and is so sweatily shifty-eyed that there isn't much mystery). An opportunity missed, therefore – especially as the imaginative sets are slightly tackily realised – but fun all the same. TM

Fantômas contre Fantômas

(Robert Vernay, 1948, Fr) Yves Furet, Alexandre Rignault, Maurice Teynac, Marcelle Chantal, Odile Versois.
91 min. b/w.
Here's another example of an obscure work by a disregarded director turning out to have worn better than many of the official key movies of the day. Blithely transcending all concepts of period and genre, this deploys the hooded master criminal from the Belle Epoque alongside a berserk brain surgeon intent on creating an army of killer zombies (in the backlog of Universal horrors must just have hit France), a gang of comic black marketeers, and an abandoned Gestapo torture centre with handy pool of sulphuric acid. It's hectic and ruthless, shot in self-conscious deep-focus (the Greg Toland backlog…) and incorporates so much location filming to render the director an accidental documentarist of Paris, summer of '48. It may not be Feuillade, it may not add up to anything very coherent, but it would certainly have been a waste had this uninhibited fever dream been left in the vaults. BBa

Fantôme de la Liberté, Le (The Phantom of Liberty)

(Luis Buñuel, 1974, Fr) Bernard Verley, Jean-Claude Brialy, Monica Vitti, Milena Vukotic, Michel Lonsdale, Jean Rochefort, Claude Piéplu, Julien Bertheau, Michel Piccoli, Adriana Asti.
104 min.
As a good Surrealist who aimed to disturb rather than to please, Buñuel must have felt that the Oscar which crowned the worldwide success of *The Discreet Charm of the Bourgeoisie* was the last straw. At any rate, he made sure that this isn't such an easy pill to digest, though its delightful humour goes down just as easily. The Chinese

box structure, with a series of bizarre episodes never quite reaching the point of resolution, is exactly the same as in the earlier film. But where *The Discreet Charm* used the interrupted dinner-party as a comfortably recognisable motif, *The Phantom of Liberty* works more disconcertingly by stringing its episodes on an invisible thread woven by the prologue (where Spanish patriots welcome the firing-squad with cries of 'Long live chains!', and a Captain of Dragoons falls in love with a statue of a saint). Thereafter, beneath the surface, the film busily explores the process whereby the human mind, burying itself ostrich-like in convention, invariably fails to recognise the true nature of freedom and sexuality. TM

Fantôme du Moulin Rouge, Le

(René Clair, 1925, Fr) Albert Préjean, Sandra Milovanoff, Georges Vaultier, José Davert, Maurice Schutz, Paul Olivier.
6,900 ft. b/w.
Made immediately after the experimental short *Entr'acte*, this uses many of the same devices – superimposition, trick effects, comic occurrences caused by 'magic' – but harnesses them to a much more conventional narrative. A young man, unsuccessful in love, manages to leave his body and tours Paris, disembodied and invisible, playing practical jokes: a row of coats walks off from a hotel cloakroom; an unattended taxi drives itself away; a row of top hats appears on the pavement. This reconciliation of romantic comedy and surrealist gags, using fantasy to present avant-garde motifs, is typical of Clair, as is the largely irrelevant but utterly inspired 'Eccentrics' Bar' sequence. AS

Far and Away

(Ron Howard, 1992, US) Tom Cruise, Nicole Kidman, Thomas Gibson, Robert Prosky, Barbara Babcock, Cyril Cusack, Eileen Pollock, Colm Meaney, Michelle Johnson.
140 min.
A change of pace for Cruise and Kidman, after the dismal *Days of Thunder*, with this old-fashioned period romance. In 19th century Ireland, tenant farmer Joseph Donelly (Cruise) sets his handsome face against injustice, planning to avenge his father's death at the hands of unscrupulous landowners. Instead, he falls in with Shannon (Kidman), his intended victim's daughter, who persuades him to travel to America as her servant-companion. Once in Boston, Joseph makes good with bouts of bare-knuckle fighting, Shannon sweats and fumes in a chicken-plucking factory, and the pair feud and tease. Howard's lifelong ambition to make a film about his Irish ancestry results in a light confection, full of sweeping overhead shots and predictable pulp-fiction intrigue. CM

Faraway, So Close (In weiter Ferne, so nah!)

(Wim Wenders, 1993, Ger) Otto Sander, Peter Falk, Horst Buchholz, Nastassja Kinski, Heinz Rühmann, Bruno Ganz, Solveig Dommartin, Lou Reed, Willem Dafoe, Mikhail Gorbachev.
144 min. b/w & col.
Wenders' follow-up to *Wings of Desire* is a considerable disappointment, a sprawling metaphysical caper movie which has much in common with his previous picture, *Until the End of the World*. Beginning a few years after Damiel (Ganz) hung up his wings to settle down with Marion (Dommartin), the film follows the angel Cassiel (Sander) as he too becomes mortal. Life doesn't throw him any great romance, however – instead, he finds himself in an extraordinary convoluted (and extremely tedious) mystery thriller. We get jokes, whimsy, hijinks and escapades; we get Lou Reed strumming a new song; we even get bungee-jumping at the climax. What's lacking is any sense of form. The movie meanders for two and a half hours, has glaring continuity gaps, and repeatedly confuses self-consciousness with irony, sincerity with significance. There are grace notes here, but Wenders' ambitions seem far, far away. TCh

Far Country, The

(Anthony Mann, 1954, US) James Stewart, Walter Brennan, Ruth Roman, Corinne Calvet, John McIntire, Jay C Flippen, Harry Morgan.
97 min.
A strange, almost self-conscious Western writ-

ten, like *Where the River Bends*, by Borden Chase.
Stewart travels north to the Oregon territory with
old-timer Brennan and a herd of cattle, only to be
cheated out of the steers by corrupt judge
McIntire. Signing up with saloon owner Roman's
wagon-train to the gold-mining camps, ostensibly to earn some money, Stewart in fact plans to
steal back his cattle and take his revenge. Stewart
again plays the driven, vengeful loner, and the
emphasis is again on his eventual acceptance of
a social rather than an individual sense of justice.
What distinguishes this from *Where the River
Bends*, though, is Mann's use of painted backdrops, rear-projections and other artificial devices
which tend – like the odd, cryptic dialogue – to
undermine any sense of realism. NF

Farewell (Proshchanie)

(Elem Klimov, 1981, USSR) Stefaniya Stayuta,
Lev Durov, Alexei Petrenko, Leonid Kryuk,
Vadim Yakovenko.
126 min.
This monitors the dying gasps of a remote
Siberian village, its vibrant peasant culture
threatened by a government hydro-electric
scheme, and examines the conflict – desire for
individual happiness versus pragmatic plans for
the greater good of society – in balanced, fruitful
terms. What really distinguishes the movie, however, and offers allegories for the asking, is the
resonant, mystical nature of Klimov's images:
Mother Earth, symbolised most notably by a
gigantic, seemingly indestructible tree, is imbued
with a primitive, pantheistic power, while the
engineers sent to raze the island first appear as
hazy angels of death emerging from the mists of
the lake. As guilt and recrimination, fear and confusion take grip of the villagers, who prepare for
evacuation with a mixture of melancholia and
bawdy celebration, Klimov paints a haunting picture of the onset of death that culminates in a
stunning sequence located in a fearful limbo. All
of which suggests Russian ruminations of an
impenetrably joyless kind; nevertheless, despite
the stately pace and excessive length, the film's
assured, elegiac evocation of a virtually pagan
world, both defined and doomed by its traditions,
exerts considerable fascination. GA

Farewell Again
(aka Troopship)

(Tim Whelan, 1937, GB) Leslie Banks, Flora
Robson, Patricia Hilliard, Sebastian Shaw,
René Ray, Anthony Bushell, Robert Newton,
Edward Lexy, Wally Patch.
85 min. b/w.
Carrying the same call to preparedness as *Fire
Over England* (both were produced by Erich
Pommer and scripted by Clemence Dane), this is
a prototype *In Which We Serve* about a troopship
bringing men home on leave after five years army
service in India. Trouble stirs when orders
require an immediate return to duty, but – after
six hours in port during which all the carefully
planted domestic problems and heartbreaks get
a cursory airing – everybody nobly buckles to.
Quite warmly praised at the time, but the class
attitudes accepted as perfectly normal – the officers, suffering stoically, soothe other-rank grumbles with a patronising pat on the head; the
gentry cavort over cocktails and dancing in the
saloon while the lower orders huddle like squalid
sardines below decks – are positively cringe-making. No wonder Churchill and the Conservatives
were elected out after World War II. TM

Farewell My Concubine
(Ba Wang Bie Ji)

(Chen Kaige, 1993, HK/China) Leslie Cheung,
Zhang Fengyi, Gong Li, Lu Qi, Ying Da, Ge
You, Li Chun, Lei Han.
156 min.
Hitherto, Chen Kaige's films have specialised in
poetic, allusive allegory: in *King of the Children*
and *Life on a String*, especially, socio-political
content was conveyed by elliptical narratives and
vivid but often enigmatic images. Here, however, Chen adopts a direct and less personal
approach to his country's troubled history as he
charts the similarly troubled relationship, from
1925 to 1977, of two Peking Opera actors. Their
boyhood friendship arises in protective reaction
to the disciplines of the Academy; but by the time
they've become stars, Dieyi (Cheung) has fallen
for his friend Xiaolou (Zhang Fengyi), mirroring
the on-stage devotion of the concubine he plays

for Xiaolou's King of Chu. Inevitably, he is distraught when Xiaolou marries a prostitute, Juxian
(Gong Li), who is more than a match for Dieyi's
jealous hysteria; but the trio are also caught up
in bigger events so that over the decades their
mutual suspicion, deceits, divided loyalties,
betrayals and acts of desperate support for one
another chime with the mood of China itself.
Appropriately operatic, Chen's visually spectacular epic is sumptuous in every respect.
Intelligent, enthralling, rhapsodic. GA

Farewell My Darling
(Haksaeng Bukunshinwi)

(Park Chul-Soo, 1996, SKor) Park Chul-Soo,
Choi Sung, Kwon Sung-Duk, Moon Jung-Sook,
Jung Ha-Hyun, Bang Eun-Jin.
124 min.
A very old man dies in his home village and the
members of his family – now scattered far and
wide – converge for the three-day funeral. The
eldest son happens to be a Seoul-based film director (guess who plays him), who neglects his
duties as chief mourner and stands to one side to
watch – as film directors do – the tensions build
and elements of grotesquerie multiply. Before
long skeletons are tumbling out of family closets.
Park marshals a huge cast and episodic narrative
with assurance and delivers a very filmic tragi-
comedy. TR

Farewell, My Lovely

(Dick Richards, 1975, US) Robert Mitchum,
Charlotte Rampling, John Ireland, Sylvia
Miles, Anthony Zerbe, Harry Dean Stanton,
Jack O'Halloran, Sylvester Stallone, Jim
Thompson.
95 min.
After Altman's intensive analysis of Philip
Marlowe in *The Long Goodbye*, it's hard to imagine another straightforward adaptation. Yet
Farewell, My Lovely deliberately courts nostalgia
with lovingly recreated '40s settings and film tech-
niques recalling the thrillers of the time, besides
the casting of Mitchum, who made his name in
just such films. As such, it lies alongside the successful 1944 adaptation rather than the current
Californian detective pictures, whose troubled
introspections it lacks. The film's triumph is
Mitchum's definitive Marlowe, which captures
perfectly the character's down-at-heel integrity
and erratic emotional involvement with his cases.
Purists may find the script's tinkering with
Marlowe's character irritating. But there are plenty of compensations: strong supporting performances, moody renderings of the underbelly of
Los Angeles nightlife, and a jigsaw plot with
Marlowe's chase through seven homicides to find
an ex-nightclub singer, six years disappeared. CPe

Farewell, My Lovely
(aka Murder My Sweet)

(Edward Dmytryk, 1944, US) Dick Powell,
Claire Trevor, Anne Shirley, Otto Kruger,
Mike Mazurki, Miles Mander, Esther Howard.
95 min. b/w.
Fine adaptation of Chandler's novel (which had
served as plot fodder for *The Falcon Takes Over*
only two years earlier), evocatively creating a
seedy, sordid world of shifting loyalties and
unseen evil as Marlowe goes in search of the
young and missing Velma at the urgent behest
of Moose Malloy (Mazurki in fine form), a brutish
ex-con unaware that the girl he left behind when
he went to jail has metamorphosed into the dangerously duplicitous Claire Trevor (another marvellous performance). Powell is surprisingly good
as Marlowe, certainly more faithful to the writer's
conception than Bogart was in *The Big Sleep*,
while the supporting cast make the most of John
Paxton's superb dialogue. And Harry Wild's
chiaroscuro camerawork is the true stuff of *noir*.
Although released in America as *Murder My
Sweet*, the film was in fact originally screened
there as *Farewell, My Lovely*. GA

Farewell, Stranger
(Lebewohl Fremde)

(Tevfik Baser, 1991, Ger) Grazyna Szapoloska,
Musfik Kenter.
98 min.
Sensitive if familiar romantic drama, from a
Turkish director, set on a remote German island
(Langeness), with a 40-year-old woman forming
a relationship with an exiled Turkish writer and

poet in the absence of her husband and daughter.
The closed community's response is deftly handled, and the couple's courting watched with tenderness. The cinematography is fine too – lovely
night-time vistas against cold blue light. It's a
film that stresses common humanity rather than
political outrage, but it's none the less for that.
Tevfik Baser relies on rather obvious symbolism
(storms, floods, fires), but otherwise directs with
confidence and emotional restraint. WH

Farewell to Arms, A

(Frank Borzage, 1932, US) Gary Cooper, Helen
Hayes, Adolphe Menjou, Mary Philips, Jack
LaRue, Blanche Frederici, Henry Armetta.
78 min. b/w.
Not only the best film version of a Hemingway
novel, but also one of the most thrilling visions
of the power of sexual love that even Borzage
ever made. An American ambulanceman, serving in Italy in World War I, falls in love with an
English nurse; he finally goes AWOL to rejoin
her, only to find her carrying his child and dying
of hunger and loneliness. No other director got
performances like these: Cooper at his youngest
and sexiest, moving from drunkenness to intox-
ication; moon-faced Hayes, at once a mother-fig-
ure and a lover; and Menjou as Cooper's repressed
homosexual friend, jealously coming between the
lovers. And no other director created images like
these, using light and movement like brush-
strokes, integrating naturalism and a daring
expressionism in the same shot. This is romantic
melodrama raised to its highest degree, fittingly
set to the music of Wagner's 'Liebestod'. TR

Farewell to Arms, A

(Charles Vidor, 1957, US) Rock Hudson,
Jennifer Jones, Vittorio De Sica, Alberto Sordi,
Mercedes McCambridge, Elaine Stritch, Oscar
Homolka, Victor Francen.
152 min.
Inflated remake of Frank Borzage's classic 1932
adaptation of the Hemingway novel (almost literally twice the length), with Hudson as the US
ambulance driver and Jones the British nurse
finding their World War I romance crushed
beneath surplus production values and spectacle.
A padded Ben Hecht script and Selznick's invari-
able tendency to overkill are equally to blame. PT

Farewell to False Paradise
(Abschied vom Falschen
Paradies/Yalanci Cennete
Elveda)

(Tevfik Baser, 1989, WGer/Tur) Zuhal Olcay,
Brigite Janner, Ruth Olafsdottir, Barbara
Morawiecz, Ayse Altan, Serpil Inanc.
92 min.
Baser's film describes the emotional journey of a
woman who, sentenced to six years in a German
prison for murdering her cruel husband, finds
that the friendship of her fellow female cellmates
serves to renew her spirit, until she hears that on
release she will be deported to Turkey and retrial... WH

Farewell to the King

(John Milius, 1988, US) Nick Nolte, Nigel
Havers, Frank McRae, James Fox, Marilyn
Tokudo, Marius Weyers.
117 mins.
Dr *Apocalypse Now* revisited. When, in a World
War II mission to mobilise resistance against the
Japs, plucky Brit officer (Havers) and his black
radioman (McRae) parachute into Borneo, they
find the tribes united in peace under US Army
deserter-turned-king Nolte. This Great White
God proves reluctant to fall in with the fork-
tongued Allied forces until a surprise Jap attack
on his village. Persuaded that he 'can't avoid
History', Nolte leads his men into war against the
brutal, oddly honourable enemy, and thus enters
the dominion of Myth. Havers and Nolte proceed
from initial suspicion, through wary respect, to
the kind of unspoken love between men that
remains a matter of adoring glances; and Havers
braves the top brass in an effort to guarantee
post-war freedom for Nolte's Noble Savages.
Despite the craftsmanlike visual bravura, entire
scenes verge on incoherence, and the portentous
script serves only to expose how vague and misplaced is Milius' faith in anarchism. Where once
he seemed an original, now he merely regurgitates his own woolly, vacuous clichés. GA

f

Far from Home: The Adventures of Yellow Dog

(Phillip Borsos, 1994, US) Bruce Davison, Mimi Rogers, Jesse Bradford, Tom Bower, Josh Wannamaker, Margot Finley, Dakotah.
81 min.

This movie about a lad and his dog surviving in the British Columbian wilderness is better than the formula might suggest. Playing the parents is normally a thankless gig, but Davison and Rogers bring a believability to the frantic pair: their 14-year-old son, Angus (Bradford), hasn't emerged from the tall timbers after three weeks. Parted from his father when their boat sinks in a storm, the boy and the dog survive on fish, grubs, berries and confection, and traverse the Book of Genesis terrain despite attacks by wolves. As usual, Angus is stuck in ravines every time the air-rescue helicopter goes over. As usual, the dog supplies resolution in the darkest hour. Yellow Dog (Dakotah) is a splendidly trained labrador who brings off a brilliant leap into a lineful of washing that had at least one junior audience cheering. Simple, effective stuff. BC

Far from the Barbarians

see Loin des Barbares

Far from the Madding Crowd

(John Schlesinger, 1967, GB) Julie Christie, Terence Stamp, Peter Finch, Alan Bates, Fiona Walker, Prunella Ransome, Alison Leggatt, Freddie Jones.
168 min.

Another classic bites the dust. Thomas Hardy's Bathsheba, a country girl who attempts to better her station and find true love, miscast Julie Christie just as effectively as did Dr Zhivago; for some mysterious reason, the notion that she should play classic roles was one that persisted for several years. Nicolas Roeg's evocative photography of the West Country dominates the film, and shows up the characters as just going through the motions. PH

Far from Vietnam (Loin du Viêt-nam)

(Alain Resnais/William Klein/Joris Ivens/Agnès Varda/Claude Lelouch/Jean-Luc Godard, 1967, US)
115 min. b/w & col.

Necessarily dated but still a fascinating document, this collective protest against the Vietnam war begins with a graceful ballet of bomb-loading and take-off preparations aboard an American carrier, contrasted with shots of civilians in Hanoi hurrying to pathetically inadequate improvised shelters. Suspected Vietcong sympathisers are beaten up; peace marchers in America are confronted by counter-demonstrators shouting 'Bomb Hanoi!'; General West-moreland appears reassuringly on TV to state that 'Civilian casualties do not result from our firepower; they result from mechanical errors'. All good, stirring stuff, edited into a remarkably coherent whole by Chris Marker. But the film goes on to probe the ambiguity behind the protest. Inherent throughout (but explicitly explored in fictional interludes directed by Renais and Godard) is the dilemma that, although this was 'the first war everyone can watch' and all of us were involved, the very remoteness (in every sense) of the conflict carried inevitable obfuscations. There is a certain amount of navel-gazing here, but at least the film acknowledges the sense of impotent frustration shared by many in trying to decide what to *do*. TM

Fargo (100)

(Joel Coen, 1995, US) Frances McDormand, Steve Buscemi, Peter Stormare, William H Macy, Harve Presnell, Kristin Rudrüd.
98 min.

Car salesman Jerry Lundegaard (Macy) hires low-lifes Carl and Gaear (Buscemi and Stormare) to kidnap his wife, hoping that her wealthy father will pay a ransom from which Jerry can cream a share. The abduction goes according to plan, but the kidnappers commit three murders as they drive by night through the snowy Minnesota wastes. Police chief Marge Gunderson (McDormand), a slow-talkin', smart-thinkin', pregnant housewife, investigates. Joel and Ethan Coen's beguiling film is both very funny and, finally, very moving. Performed to perfection by an imaginatively assembled cast, it displays the

customary Coen virtues, at the same time providing a robust emotional core unaffected by the taint of mere technical virtuosity. The talk is more leisurely than usual, the camera largely static, the focus firmly on relationships, character, ethics. However banal the lives and aspirations of the leading figures, there's nothing condescending about the humour. Marge and her husband are genuinely good, ordinary people caught up in extraordinary events of, to them, unfathomable evil. Suspense, satire, mystery, horror, comedy and keen (if faintly surreal) social observation combine to prove yet again that (bar very few) the Coens remain effortlessly ahead of the American field. GA

Farinelli Il Castrato

(Gérard Corbiau, 1994, It/Bel) Stéfano Dionisi, Enrico Lo Verso, Elsa Zylberstein, Caroline Cellier, Marianne Basler, Jacques Boudet, Omero Antonutti, Jeroen Krabbe.
111 min.

Today the average opera isn't over till the diva trills her high notes, but in the 18th century the major stars were the male castrati. The film is soon ripping bodices and bunging three in a bed, allowing the angel-voiced Farinelli (Dionisi) and his composer sibling Riccardo (Lo Verso) to display their perfected love-making routine. Physiological queries thus answered, we can get on with the musical meat of a substantially true story. The castrato voice powered baroque opera through exquisite ornamentation and long-breathed melody, and here the dramatic conflict sparks between the brothers' loyalty to each other and the demanding presence of composer Handel (Krabbe) who wants to write for Farinelli, but ditch Riccardo. Corbiau's film gives convincing attention to the process of musical creation, but complicates itself with a tricksy narrative framework and an underwritten romantic subplot (Zylberstein wasted as the woman who flits between the brothers). Lavish sets and costumes make a colourful impression, the unusual material compels attention in its own way, but it's the vocal and authentic instrumental performances that raise the film momentarily towards the sublime. (The castrato voice was created by the IRCAM synthesis of soprano and countertenor voices.) TJ

Farmer's Wife, The

(Alfred Hitchcock, 1928, GB) Jameson Thomas, Lillian Hall-Davies, Maud Gill, Gordon Harker, Louise Pounds.
67 min. b/w.

Charming comedy of rural manners, about a morose middle-aged farmer, having recently lost his wife, making inept and irascible attempts to find himself a new spouse. His final humble discovery of true love is signalled far too early in the film, but that doesn't destroy the effects of a great deal of subtle slapstick and witty caricature, especially in a marvellously sustained sequence at a tea-party.

Far North

(Sam Shepard, 1988, US) Jessica Lange, Charles Durning, Tess Harper, Donald Moffat, Ann Wedgeworth, Patricia Arquette, Nina Draxten.
89 min.

Save us from Renaissance men. Shepard writes plays, directs them, acts in plays and movies, and now wants to direct movies. Think again, Sam. This opens promisingly, with wonderfully gritty acoustic music from the Red Clay Ramblers on the soundtrack, and Durning slowly losing control of his horse and coming to grief. Cut to a big close-up of the offending beast's dark, mysterious eye. Later, the music turns synthetic and so do the emotions. Citified daughter Lange gets the job of shooting the nag ('While it still knows why' rumbles the hospitalised Durning) and returns to the homestead, somewhere near the Great Lakes. Will she do it? Or will she be prevented by her older sister (Harper) and the sister's fun-loving daughter (Arquette)? What does barmy mother (Wedgeworth) think? Will Sam lose interest in all this women's stuff and concentrate on the boring, boorish double act of Durning and his brother Moffat as they drink their way out of hospital and into the wild woods? The characters wander around emoting and shouting at one another, but saying nothing; and Shepard's cod-Eisensteinian montage effects (jump cuts between women and owls, most notably) belong in a film museum. JMo

Far Off Place, A

(Mikael Salomon, 1993, US) Reese Witherspoon, Ethan Randall, Jack Thompson, Sarel Bok, Maximilian Schell.
116 min.

An updated but old-fashioned eco-adventure (from Laurens van der Post's A Story Like the Wind and A Far Off Place), with the accent on the adventure. Teens Witherspoon and Randall, don't get on at the start but end up in love. The elements include ruthless poachers; a craggy game warden (Schell), irate at the villains for slaughtering not only elephants but the teens' parents; a wise African guide (Bok); and a trek across the Kalahari. A cameraman's directorial debut; handsome and quite sincere. AO

Farrebique

(Georges Rouquier, 1947, Fr)
85 min. b/w.

Shot between 1944 and '46 in the Aveyrand area of the rugged Massif Central, this documentary milestone called on three generations of a peasant family to act out their lives for the camera. It charts cycles of birth, death and work, and records the coming of electrification. The protagonists sometimes appear slightly stiff (to modern eyes), but there's compact storytelling in the way Rouquier binds our sympathies to their on-going grind, and an exquisite moment of lyricism (despite the superfluous voice-over) when stop-motion photography catches the turn of the seasons. TJ

Fast Charlie, the Moonbeam Rider

(Steve Carver, 1978, US) David Carradine, Brenda Vaccaro, LQ Jones, RG Armstrong, Terry Kiser, Jesse Vint, Noble Willingham.
99 min.

Corman and Carradine teamed up again for yet another version of the coast-to-coast race with no holds barred. This time it's 1919 and motorcycles, not cars as in Death Race 2000. Not just a straightforward win-or-bust movie, it often goes for laughs with its miraculously injury-free carnage, and demonstrates how the scorn of a good woman can make an honest man out of free-wheelin' Charlie, ex-army dispatch rider and conman extraordinaire. FF

Fast Company

(David Cronenberg, 1979, Can) William Smith, Claudia Jennings, John Saxon, Nicholas Campbell, Cedric Smith, Judy Foster.
91 min.

Drag racing may seem an aberrant subject for the Carl Dreyer of Splatter, but the sport is the man's secret passion, and it shows. The hokey plot is strictly off the peg: when soft-hearted hairy-arse drag racers are shit-sandwiched between corrupt team manager (Saxon at his most reptilian) and the mean-minded neanderthal opposition, they come up smelling like roses. But Cronenberg's obsessive attention to the detail of preparing the machines, mixing the fuel, armour-plating the drivers and the tactical skills of winning, makes the track sequences enthralling. The weakness (in line with every other racetrack saga) is that once off the track, the picture hits the skids. Instead of following through the ruthless drive of the drag strip, it indulges in ill-advised sidetracks into soft-core sex, gags and rock'n'roll, a brand of exploitation the late Claudia Jennings (here in her last screen role) made her own in the likes of Truck Stop Women. But at the beginning, middle and end, there are still the races, staged amid the racket and the razzmatazz with Cronenberg's customary skill. AT

Faster, Pussycat! Kill! Kill!

(Russ Meyer, 1965, US) Tura Satana, Haji, Lori Williams, Susan Bernard, Stuart Lancaster, Paul Trinka.
83 min. b/w.

This shows Meyer to be a fine action director as well as America's best-known tit man. Though decorated with the usual array of top-heavy starlets – a trio of homicidal disco dancers on rest-and-recreation in the Californian desert (which means fast cars and whatever kinky thrills come their way) – it was in fact made as an exploiter for the Southern states' undemanding drive-in market. A cheap and efficient comic horror movie, it's funniest when its dialogue and characters' behaviour are at their most non sequitur.

The twaddlesome plot about the cover-up of a man's murder by the (lesbian) leader of this girlie gang is helped enormously by a brooding music score which sounds as if it had walked in from a paranoid Cold War sci-fi film; and the weirdo desert farmhouse family the trio happen upon pre-dates *The Texas Chain Saw Massacre* by almost a decade. RM

Fastest Gun Alive, The

(Russell Rouse, 1956, US) Glenn Ford, Jeanne Crain, Broderick Crawford, Russ Tamblyn, Allyn Joslyn, Leif Erickson, John Dehner, Noah Beery Jr, JM Kerrigan, Rhys Williams.
92 min. b/w.
Similar in theme to Henry King's *The Gunfighter*, this begins impressively, with Crawford riding into town to challenge a complete stranger ('They say you're faster than me') and triumphantly out-drawing him ('Get him a headstone to say he was killed by the fastest gun alive'), only to be faced by a blind man's prophetic warning ('No matter how fast you are, there's always someone faster'). Meanwhile, mild storekeeper Ford wrestles with his promise to his wife (Crain) to forget about his prowess with a gun. Unfortunately, having set up the inevitability of confrontation, the script loses its ballad-like directness, meandering through a bank robbery, taking in a dance number for Tamblyn, and providing yards of psychological explanation (Ford, afraid of guns, is obsessed with his failure to avenge his father's death; Crawford, whose wife left him for another man, is out to prove he is mucho macho). That said, the reactions of the townsfolk are detailed with some complexity, the key scenes are extremely well staged, and the performances are excellent. TM

Fast, Fast (Deprisa, Deprisa)

(Carlos Saura, 1980, Sp) Berta Socuéllamos, José Antonio Valdelomar.
98 min.
Meandering through the suburbs of Madrid and its empty hinterlands, an episodic plot follows the sex, drugs and crime life-style of four felonious but likeable punks (played by real-life delinquents, two of whom were later apprehended for robbing banks). A teen-gang movie, and in many ways an unassuming genre piece, but mercifully free of moralising. Distinguished by an inventive soundtrack and stirring flamenco music score, and a mobile, intimate camera that follows its characters like a shadow, closely capturing not only action but reaction, ephemeral moments of camaraderie, friction and a perfidious 'freedom': fast living, leisurely observed. SJo

Fast Forward

(Sidney Poitier, 1984, US) John Scott Clough, Don Franklin, Tamara Mark, Tracy Silver, Cindy McGee, Constance Towers, Irene Worth.
110 min.
Wish fulfilment on a grandiose scale with the cotton candy saga of eight alarmingly attractive teenagers from Ohio. Convinced of their own dance talents, they storm the Big Apple, and in a mere three weeks have the rock world knocked for a loop. Poitier's direction is earnest, and the four-square camerawork comes from someone who never heard of Bob Fosse. Still, there is some high energy performing going on – notably from Franklin, a proud and sexy black who could go far. It's all too sanitised, and has nothing to do with rock reality, but it's always fun to see the underdog triumph over the moguls. AR

Fast Lady, The

(Ken Annakin, 1962, GB) James Robertson Justice, Stanley Baxter, Leslie Phillips, Kathleen Harrison, Julie Christie, Dick Emery, Frankie Howerd, Monsewer Eddie Gray.
95 min.
Mercurial Scots TV comedian Baxter plays a cycling enthusiast determined to win the heart of roadhog Robertson Justice's daughter (Julie Christie, in her second movie, again with Baxter) by impressing her with a vintage Bentley acquired expressly for the purpose. Amiable but faddish, with Phillips in splendidly slimy form as a used car salesman. TJ

Fast Talking

(Ken Cameron, 1983, Aust) Rod Zuanic, Toni Allaylis, Chris Truswell, Gail Sweeny, Steve Bisley, Tracy Mann.
95 min.

Comedy about a delinquent dope-dealing 15-year-old with a quick-thinking scam for every possible occasion. Of course he's got problems, with an alcoholic father and teachers out to get him, but he always has the last laugh, until one day...The acting is superb, and Cameron makes his characters even more believable through some swift, sure touches: a teacher obsessed with gardening, a classmate with a bad line in Frank Spencer impersonations. A sharp, entertaining portrait of teenage life based around the admirable idea that there's far more to happiness and dignity than simply doing what you're told. CS

Fast Times at Ridgemont High (aka Fast Times)

(Amy Heckerling, 1982, US) Sean Penn, Jennifer Jason Leigh, Judge Reinhold, Phoebe Cates, Brian Backer, Ray Walston.
92 min.
Although nominally based on journalist Cameron Crowe's investigative study of high school kids, this is essentially a straight sex'n'fun exploitation movie. There's the usual array of school stereotypes (the lecher, the stoned surfer, the hustler), a rock score, and endless attention to the rituals of dating and mating. Taken purely on this level, it's a relatively witty example of its kind, with an enjoyable performance from Penn as the stoned surfer, and some good lines. But it lacks the frenzied energy which allowed *Porky's* to beat all competitors in its field. DP

Fast Trip, Long Drop

(Gregg Bordowitz, 1993, US) Gregg Bordowitz, Bob Huff.
54 min.
In 1988, Gregg Bordowitz, a New York videomaker, tested HIV positive, and set about making an autobiographical documentary. It's a freewheeling, funny, irate, provocative look at attitudes – his, ours, the media's – towards AIDS; at how one might 'live' with such an immediate, persistent awareness of imminent mortality. On one level, the film's 'documentary' aspects are conventional: Bordowitz speaks confessionally and straight-to-camera about his sex life and Jewish heritage, discusses his illness and his assumption of gay identity with his mother and stepfather, and mulls over the impossibility of hope with his support group. All this, however, is intercut not only with archive footage of various risky activities (car stunts, a man juggling a baby atop a skyscraper) and with sour satirical sketches featuring Borodwitz's surly Alter Allesman and various broadcasters, doctors and activists played by one Bob Huff. The resulting *mélange*, faintly reminiscent of early Makavejev, is troubled and troubling, occasionally exhilarating, and admirably honest; more surprisingly, against the odds, Bordowitz finally steers us towards some sort of gentle hope. GA

Fast-Walking

(James B Harris, 1982, US) James Woods, Tim McIntire, Kay Lenz, Robert Hooks, M Emmet Walsh, Timothy Carey, Susan Tyrrell.
115 min.
A characteristic, off-beam offering from James B Harris, a former Kubrick collaborator, this starts out as a straightforward prison movie but soon splinters into a wayward character study of morally irredeemable individuals. Woods' prison warden, 'Fast-Walking' Miniver, is up to every scam in the book, but his trade in pimping and the like is disrupted by the rumpus over the arrival of black political activist Hooks and the growing megalomania of trustee inmate McIntire. Downbeat, greasy and with a genuinely eccentric sense of humour. TJ

Fatal Attraction

see Head On

Fatal Attraction

(Adrian Lyne, 1987, US) Michael Douglas, Glenn Close, Anne Archer, Ellen Hamilton Latzen, Stuart Pankin, Ellen Foley, Fred Gwynne.
120 min.
A glossy, Hitchcock-by-numbers thriller, with Douglas as a happily married New York attorney whose clandestine weekend of passion with business associate Close provokes the wrath of a woman scorned when he tries to give her the brush-off. Angered by his insensitive chauvinism,

Close becomes increasingly unhinged, progressing from insistent phone calls to acid attacks on Douglas' car, and finally to physical attacks on his family. Lyne employs the same flashy imagery as in *92 Weeks*, but his overheated visual style seems curiously inappropriate to James Dearden's tepid script. The film finally comes to the boil in the brilliantly staged, crowd-pleasing finale – a nail-biting showdown between a knife-wielding Close, a frightened wife and an enraged Douglas. A predictable dog's dinner of Pavlovian thriller clichés, this will appeal strongly to those who think women should be kept on a short lead. NF

Fatal Beauty

(Tom Holland, 1987, US) Whoopi Goldberg, Sam Elliott, Rubén Blades, Harris Yulin, John P Ryan, Jennifer Warren, Brad Dourif, Mike Jolly, Charles Hallahan, David Harris, Cheech Marin.
104 min.
A designed-by-committee vehicle for Whoopi Goldberg, allowing her to keep her comedy act and extend her range into territory staked out by Eddie Murphy, with risible – therefore enjoyable – results. Unorthodox undercover cops Rita Rizzoli – a Dirty Harriet with an MA in wisecracks – is a mean fatherfucker dedicated to keeping 'snow' off the streets of LA. Down in Chinatown, nude coolies are adulterating cocaine with lethal proportions of Ventonol; she figures one Conrad Kroll (Yulin) for the villain of the piece, but it takes days and nights of padding the streets in disguise – hobbling heels, leopard-skin, and Tina Turner rup – before the breaks come. Meanwhile, a trio of giggling psychopaths muscle in (Brad Douril's staring-eyed Leo Nova is a gem), and all is set for a 15-minute showdown in a shopping mall. Sam Elliott's love interest takes too long warming up, but a confused plot and plenty of poor taste leave Whoopi relatively unscathed. WH

Fatal Bond

(Vincent Morton, 1991, Aust) Linda Blair, Jerome Ehlers, Stephen Leeder, Donal Gibson, Caz Lederman, Joe Bugner.
90 min.
Blair heads down under in search of a decent part and winds up in this so-so thriller playing an American-born hairdresser who drifts across Australia with boyfriend Ehlers, and discovers too late that a trail of murders seems to follow them wherever they go. No prizes for guessing who's the next victim. TJ

Fatal Reaction: Singapore

(Marijke Jongbloed, 1996, Neth)
78 min.
Documentaries about dating agencies are scarcely original, but this foray into the genre (the second part of a series about the problems single women face finding suitable partners) has a novel twist: the dating agency in question is a government organisation. As we hear the ex-leader Lee Kuan Yew proclaim, Singapore needs to boost its population to compete in the world market. The director follows a handful of Singaporeans as they attend various 'dating' events, including a love cruise. Men and women have very different expectations. The grimmest, most poignant moment comes as a die-hard chauvinist, used to bullying his mother, tells the young woman he hopes to marry what he expects in terms of obedience and housework. As he gorges himself on a pizza, she breaks down in tears. GM

Fata Morgana

(Werner Herzog, 1971, WGer).
78 min.
Herzog's completely non-narrative movie is cast in the mock-heroic form of an epic poem, each of its chapter headings ('Creation', 'Paradise', 'The Golden Age') being more ironic than the one before. Shot in and around the Sahara, its images evoke the idea of the desert as a terminal beach, littered with colonial debris, spanning extremes of poverty and misery, peopled with the dispossessed and the eccentric, haunted by mirages. It's the nearest thing yet to a genuine political science-fiction movie. Brilliantly original, utterly haunting. TR

Fat City

(John Huston, 1972, US) Stacy Keach, Jeff Bridges, Susan Tyrrell, Candy Clark, Nicholas Colasanto, Art Aragon.
96 min.

Marvellous, grimly downbeat study of desperate lives and the escape routes people construct for themselves, stunningly shot by Conrad Hall. The setting is Stockton, California, a dreary wasteland of smoky bars and sunbleached streets where the lives of two boxers briefly meet, one on the way up, one on the way down. Neither, you sense instantly, for all their tally of past successes and future glories, will ever know any other world than the back-street gymnasiums and cheap boxing-rings where battered trainers and managers exchange confidences about their ailments, disappointments and dreams, and where in a sad and sobering climax two sick men beat each other half to death for a few dollars and a pint of glory. Huston directs with the same puritanical rigour he brought to *Wise Blood*. Beautifully summed up by Paul Taylor as a 'masterpiece of skid row poetry'. TM

Fate of Lee Khan, The (Ying-chun-ge zhi Fengbo)

(King Hu, 1973, HK) Li Li Hua, Angela Mao, Hsu Feng, Hu Chin, Tien Feng.
105 min.
The Fate of Lee Khan is to the Chinese martial arts movie what *Once Upon a Time in the West* in to the Italian Western: a brilliant anthology of its genre's theme and styles, yielding an exhilaratingly original vision. It's set in the Yuan Dynasty, when China was under Mongol rule, and centres on the efforts of a band of Chinese patriots (mostly women) to retrieve a map that has fallen into the hands of Mongol baron Lee Khan. A lighthearted exposition (especially witty in its handling of the sexual politics) leads up to a tense stalemate, with the patriots posing as manager and staff of an inn where their enemy is lodging, but unable to follow through their original plan. King Hu's mastery of pace, humour, colour and design makes most other movies around look tatty. TR

Father

(John Power, 1990, Aust) Max Von Sydow, Carole Drinkwater, Julia Blake, Steve Jacobs.
100 min.
Drinkwater's world is upended when her elderly father, Von Sydow, is identified as a concentration camp functionary by Holocaust survivor Blake. The difficult material needed firmer handling than it gets here, however, for the film fudges the central issue of Von Sydow's culpability and turns the victim of injustice into a batty neurotic scheming for revenge. (See also Costa-Gavras' *Music Box*, 1989.) TJ

Father, The (Fadern)

(Alf Sjöberg, 1969, Swe) Georg Rydeberg, Gunnel Lindblom, Lena Nyman, Jan-Olof Strandberg, Tord Stål, Sif Ruud, Axel Düberg.
100 min.
A battle between a retired army captain and his wife for dominance and possession of their only daughter ends in madness and death. The dice are probably loaded from the start in Strindberg's play, but a rather too engaging Rydeberg, as the father, isolates the much stronger performance of the wife to a point where the conflict does not mesh, and at the end emerges as more melodramatic than tragic. Matters aren't helped by some curious technical effects altogether more appropriate to Disney (writing appears as if by magic on a page), along with obtrusive and often unnecessary use of flashback. Too often the attempts to find a visual metaphor for Strindberg's imagery are so literal (hallucinatory sequences to illustrate the captain's madness) that they must detract from the original. A pity that Sjöberg didn't extend his treatment of the background to the central drama. There he successfully portrays a twilight world of sombre colours, full of eavesdroppers, a world where the central drama is played out in front of, and constantly interrupted and inhibited by, servants who say nothing but know everything. Straight theatre, in other words. CPe

Father, The (Pedar)

(Majid Majidi, 1996, Iran) Mohammad Kasebi, Parivash Nazarieh, Hassan Sadeghi, Hossein Abedini.
96 min.
'I know of no other world than a child's world,' director Majid Majidi has said. 'A small and simple world, yet vast and magnificent. Blue like the sky, clear like the river, and upright like the mountains.' This statement captures Majidi's style: its child-like directness sidesteps naivety to achieve singular emotional clarity. Following the death of his father, a 14-year-old Iranian boy, Mehrollah (Sadeghi), travels south to find work, returning later to find that the local policeman is now a domineering presence in his mother's house. Fleeing from his occupied home, he's pursued and caught by his new father, but the journey back is longer and harder than either of them could have imagined. NF

Father and Son (Fuzi Qing)

(Allen Fong, 1981, HK) Shek Lui, Lee Yu-Tin, Cheng Yu-Or, Chan Sun.
96 min.
A boy from a poor family struggles to survive in a shanty town suburb of Hong Kong, clashing with his father and with a society that denies him almost every opportunity to realise his dream of making movies. The boy is an autobiographical portrait by Fong, who finally broke into film, making martial arts adventures for Hong Kong Television. Even then, when he went independent, he had to hassle with producers to get the freedom to make this personal film, which satirises the traditional Chinese notion of self-improvement through education. Warmly understated in its central performances, it's replete with humour and sympathy for the father as much as for the son. MA

Father Brown

(Robert Hamer, 1954, GB) Alec Guinness, Peter Finch, Joan Greenwood, Cecil Parker, Bernard Lee, Sidney James, Ernest Thesiger.
91 min. b/w.
Far from Hamer at his best, but still a stylishly civilised comedy thriller, with an engagingly sly (if occasionally too ingratiating) performance from Guinness as GK Chesterton's sleuthing priest, here calmly countering the suave criminal mastermind Flambeau (played by Finch with a fine touch of sardonic melancholy) in his attempt to purloin the priceless Cross of St Augustine. One of the most attractive things about the film is the way Hamer manages to update the story to a contemporary setting without losing any of its quintessential period flavour. Basically the performances are the thing, although there are two outstanding sequences: the Hitchcockian auction set up as a trap for Flambeau, and the delightfully eccentric encounter between Father Brown and the ancient Vicomte de Verdigris (Thesiger), a veritable ballet of misadventures which ends in two sets of broken spectacles. TM

Father Goose

(Ralph Nelson, 1964, US) Cary Grant, Leslie Caron, Trevor Howard, Jack Good, Stephanie Berrington, Jennifer Berrington.
116 min.
It's a shame that Grant, one of the finest actors ever to grace a cinema screen, should have logged this sentimental claptrap as his penultimate film. He plays an irascible South Pacific beachcomber who becomes a military observer for the island during World War II, and finds his independence softened by a French schoolmarm and her seven cloyingly sweet girl pupils. Admittedly, Grant frequently looks as if he really didn't want to be there, wading lost in a sludge of turgid drama and pallid comedy. GA

Fatherland

(Kenneth Loach, 1986, GB/WGer/Fr) Gerulf Pannach, Fabienne Babe, Cristine Rose, Sigfrit Steiner, Robert Dietl, Heike Schrotter.
111 min.
An intriguing departure for Loach, scripted by Trevor Griffiths, this concerns the voluntary exile of an East German Liedermacher (a kind of radical singer/songwriter) to West Berlin, where his worst fears are confirmed: he has swopped intimidation and censorship for the kind of 'repressive tolerance' that only American record executives and progressive GDR capitalists can convey in all its seductive horror. So far, so good. Superbly composed and cleverly paced, this story of one man's unillusioned exile gives way to a second half in which a thriller-style subplot concerning the singer's vanished father (tracked down to England) takes over, but fails to match the tension and interest of what has gone before. A flawed but always stimulating and intelligent film, with fine performances from Pannach (debuting as the exile) and Steiner (as his father). SGr

Father of the Bride

(Vincente Minnelli, 1950, US) Spencer Tracy, Joan Bennett, Elizabeth Taylor, Don Taylor, Billie Burke, Leo G Carroll.
93 min. b/w.
Thoroughly enchanting comedy about the trials and tribulations a middle-aged family man faces when the daughter he dotes on decides to get married. As one might expect, Tracy is superb, and while the film is never as impressive as Minnelli's all-out melodramas (*Some Came Running, Two Weeks in Another Town*), it's still fascinating for the rather bleak undercurrents coursing beneath the many laughs: the father's problems are engendered by his own jealousy, insecurity and fears about getting old. A less effective sequel, *Father's Little Dividend* (1951), had Tracy facing the trial of becoming a grandfather. GA

Father of the Bride

(Charles Shyer, 1991, US) Steve Martin, Diane Keaton, Kimberley Williams, Kieran Culkin, George Newborn, Martin Short, BD Wong, Peter Michael Goetz.
105 min.
Minnelli's 1950 comedy about wedding-day horrors is updated for the '90s, but is tamer stuff than the original. Co-writer/co-producer Nancy Meyers and co-writer/director Shyer go for broad laughs; the closest they come to recreating Minnelli's dark, disturbing nightmare sequence is a scene in which the bride's father fantasises about a cut-price reception. Martin is the harassed dad, wrestling with ever-escalating costs and rapidly diminishing pride; mom (Keaton) is the voice of moderation. Some sequences and dialogue are lifted directly from the original, but in the wider context, this merely serves to underline the remake's comparative lack of tenderness and subtlety. CM

Father of the Bride Part II

(Charles Shyer, 1995, US) Steve Martin, Diane Keaton, Kimberly Williams, Martin Short, George Newborn, Kieran Culkin.
107 min.
Having scored an unexpected hit with their bland update of the Minnelli classic *Father of the Bride* (1950), the production team of Charles Shyer and Nancy Meyers knew where to go for inspiration for the sequel: *Father's Little Dividend* (1951), wherein pa becomes a granddaddy. The result's a collection of feelgood clichés advertising the benefits of a massive house, children and grandchildren, beige furnishings and a racing green sportster. The narrative has to conjure up obstacles to Martin's happiness (a nastily caricatured Arab buys the family nest, then spouse Keaton and daughter Williams fall pregnant at the same time) before resolving them all in a multiple-childbirth finale. Martin has nothing to work with, and mugs away thoughtlessly; Keaton strains credibility in the cushion-up-the-jumper role; while the ill-used Short is the family's design adviser, an egregious camp stereotype, vowel-strangler and master of Viennese frippery. Very unexciting. TJ

Fathers' Day

(Ivan Reitman, 1997, US) Robin Williams, Billy Crystal, Julia Louis-Dreyfus, Nastassja Kinski, Charlie Hofheimer, Patti D'Arbanville, Jared Harris, Mel Gibson.
99 min.
Kinski's teenage son runs away from home in LA, after yet another row with dad. She calls old boyfriend Crystal, informs him he has a son, and suggests he go find the kid. Then she calls old boyfriend Williams, and informs him that he has a son, etc. Crystal's the relatively straight guy, a self-centred lawyer with a taste for time-saving social shortcuts, Williams – somewhat restrained – his goofier accomplice, a wimpy failed writer who flaps and emotes. Writers Ganz and Mandell (*Parenthood, City Slickers*) go pleasingly light on the syrup and sentimentality. NB

Father-to-Be

see Jag Är Med Barn

Fathom

(Leslie Martinson, 1967, GB) Tony Franciosa, Raquel Welch, Ronald Fraser, Greta Chi, Richard Briers, Clive Revill, Tom Adams.
99 min.
Raquel Welch as an amateur sky-diver who turns

Modesty Blaise to recover a missing nuclear device which isn't what it seems. The mind boggles, but she is really sweet and funny in an 007 parody which maintains a remarkably light touch, and also offers the admirable Revill as a sinister, fish-blooded villain. Low on surprises, but strong on sunny good humour. TM

Fat Man and Little Boy (aka Shadow Makers)

(Roland Joffé, 1989, US) Paul Newman, Dwight Schultz, Bonnie Bedelia, John Cusack, Laura Dern, Ron Frazier, John McGinley, Natasha Richardson, Ron Vawter.
127 min.
Co-scripted by Bruce Robinson, Joffé's film explores the wartime race between America and Germany to develop the atom bomb. Even when it transpires that the enemy is not seriously beavering away on such a project, the American military, under the guidance of General Groves (Newman) continue with development. J Robert Oppenheimer (Schultz) is the tortured genius heading the project, his public litany about scientific objectivity at odds with private agony over ethics. Groves and Oppenheimer strike an uneasy pact of sorts; their conflict makes the moral issues manifest and is well played. Other characters, however, remain half-realised and functional: Oppenheimer's neglected wife (Bedelia) and mistress (Richardson); an idealistic young physicist (Cusack) and his nurse girlfriend (Dern). On one level, the film compels through force of intellect, but ultimately it lacks the cohesive emotional force, the ferocity, to consistently nurture its conviction over two hours. CM

Faust

(FW Murnau, 1926, Ger) Emil Jannings, Gosta Ekman, Camilla Horn, Wilhelm Dieterle, Yvette Guilbert, Frieda Ricard.
7,875 ft. b/w.
Murnau's version of the story of the man who sold his soul to the Devil (Jannings) in return for youth is visually extraordinary but dismally uneven in terms of its dramatic effect. Certainly, its opening scenes (the prologue between an Angel and Satan, and the temptation of Faust, after which Mephistopheles takes him on an astonishing, beautiful journey through the skies) easily hold the attention, but a long, tedious central section, portraying in farcical detail Faust's courtship of Marguerite, sits awkwardly with what has preceded it. The finale finds Murnau returning to form, but too late: one is left merely marvelling at the way he and cameraman Carl Hoffman have imitated the old Dutch, German and Italian masters, and the German romanticists. GA

Faust (Lekce Faust)

(Jan Svankmajer, 1994, Czech Republic/Fr) Peter Cepek; voices: Andrew Sachs, Jan Kraus, Vladimir Kudla.
95 min.
Opening in a determinedly familiar contemporary milieu – a man emerging from a crowded Prague subway is handed a map – this film by the Czech surrealist Jan Svankmajer soon moves into stranger, darker territory. The man visits the spot on the map marked 'X' – a courtyard and a theatre dressing-room complete with costumes, make-up and a copy of Goethe's Faust. Reading the book, he becomes embroiled in a world of obscure spells, alchemy and deals with the Devil. On to this the director grafts a wealth of themes, motifs, allusions and gags, his method an expertly executed, profoundly imaginative combination of live action, claymation, puppet theatre, stop-motion animation and special effects. There are a couple of dramatically flat moments, when one feels Svankmajer hasn't quite got the measure of the feature-length narrative, but for the most part this is a film which galvanises the mind and astonishes the eye. In a word, magic. GA

Fausto

(Rémy Duchemin, 1992, Fr) Jean Yanne, Ken Higelin, Florence Darel, François Hauteserre, Maurice Bénichou, Bruce Myers.
82 min.
Teenage orphan Fausto Barbarico (Higelin) gets a gig as an apprentice tailor with old-school tradesman Mietek (Yanne). Under his mentor's guidance and support, Fausto lets his imagination run free on a series of fantastical couture designs that bring him fame and fortune, cement his relationship with flatulent pal Raymond (Hauteserre), and win the heart of winsome lass Tonie (Darel). And that's pretty much it. Just when you're ready for some conflict to rear its head and give the narrative some ballast, up come the credits and you're out in the street again pondering the undeniable but slight charm of a movie that dares to be so cheerily wistful. Fausto's creations are fun at the time, and Yanne does a really warm turn as the hunchback bespoke tailor learning to change his ways. But there's just so little to it; only the most desperate fantasist could be borne away on the gossamer wings of this fixed smile fairy-tale. TJ

Faustrecht der Freiheit (Fox/Fox and His Friends)

(Rainer Werner Fassbinder, 1975, WGer) Rainer Werner Fassbinder, Peter Chatel, Karl-Heinz Böhm, Harry Bär, Adrian Hoven, Ulla Jacobsen, Kurt Raab.
123 min.
One of Fassbinder's excellent melodramas focusing on the manipulation and destruction of a working-class victim-figure, in this case a surly fairground worker who is taken up by effete bourgeois gays when he wins a small fortune on a lottery. It's the usual vision of exploitation and complicity hidden under the deceiving mantle of love, but Fassbinder's precision, assured sense of milieu, and cool but human compassion for his characters, make it a work of brilliant intelligence. And the director himself is superb as the none-too-intelligent hero. GA

Faute de l'Abbé Mouret, La (The Sin of Father Mouret)

(Georges Franju, 1970, Fr/It) Francis Huster, Gillian Hills, Tino Carrero, André Lacombe, Margo Lion, Lucien Barjon.
93 min.
An adaptation of Zola's novel by one of the world's most idiosyncratic and fascinating directors. As always, Franju finds fantasy and surreal images in the everyday world, and taking a 'naturalistic' anti-clerical novel – in which a young priest, obsessed with the Madonna, is led to a far more openly physical passion for a young girl – he creates an amoral, poetic vision of a world where religious dogma and fanaticism are imbued with a sense of Gothic expressionism. Faithful to Zola, the film is nevertheless recognisably a creation of Franju: beautiful, bizarre and lucid. GA

Faute de Soleil (For Want of Sun)

(Christophe Blanc, 1995, Fr) Jean-Jacques Benhamou, Sarah Hazaire.
57 min.
When lonely Lucie makes her debut dancing at a strip joint, she meets and falls for Jean, brother of the show's compere. Trouble is, he's blind from an accident, and given to drunken binges, bitter self-pity and fits of rage. A bleak variation on the meeting-cute theme, with an accent on the roles played by need and acceptance in the development of love. Downbeat, but the performances punch home. GA

Favourites of the Moon (Les Favoris de la Lune)

(Otar Iosseliani, 1984, Fr) Katia Rupe, Hans Peter Cloos, Alix De Montaigu, Maïté Nahyr, François Michel.
102 min.
The lunatic dance which constitutes the action need trouble no one who remembers the pool-table ploy of Nashville by which an endless supply of characters are cannoned off each other. More difficult is the remoteness and enigma which mark many of the episodes; the moods are fragile and often shifting. The tale woven by the crossing paths of these thieves and lovers may be about the way that, as the price of a work of art increases, so art itself is devalued, but this is pursued tenuously, allowing many crazed asides. What unifies the episodes is a patient moral scourging of our greed and futile desires; but where the British would use satire, this opts for the French form of Tatiesque anarchy and fun. And fun it certainly is. CPea

Favour, the Watch and the Very Big Fish, The (Rue Saint-Sulpice)

(Ben Lewin, 1991, Fr/GB) Bob Hoskins, Jeff Goldblum, Natasha Richardson, Michel Blanc, Jacques Villeret, Angela Pleasence, Jean-Pierre Cassel.
89 min.
Louis (Hoskins) earns his crust photographing devotional pictures in Paris, but his tyrannical boss (Blanc) has threatened the sack unless he can find the perfect model for Christ. All appears lost until he meets actress Sybil (Richardson), who sweeps him off his feet and straight into her muddled life: she's traumatised by an abortive affair with a grumpy pianist (Goldblum), who attempted to set fire to the last rival for her affections. Now released from prison, he's a changed man – morose, vengeful, and a dead ringer for Christ. Based on a Marcel Aymé short story, this 'surreal romantic comedy' stretches its ideas too far. Writer-director Lewin heightens language and gesture until the central relationship is rendered absurd; Goldblum broods menacingly and deludes himself that he really is Christ. The effect is dislocating. CM

Fear

(Rockne S O'Bannon, 1989, US) Ally Sheedy, Pruitt Taylor Vince, Lauren Hutton, Michael O'Keefe, Stan Shaw, Dina Merrill, Keone Young, John Agar.
95 min.
Despite its attention-grabbing opening and intriguing central conceit – a psychic 'detective' capable of entering the minds of serial killers – this erratic thriller never lives up to its initial promise. Egged on by her manager (Hutton), successful author and media celebrity Cayce Bridges (Sheedy) teams up with a pair of sceptical LA detectives to track down a ruthless murderer. She soon realises, however, that the Shadow Man (Vince) has tuned into her psychic wavelength and is drawing her into his sick scenario, not only by forcing her to see through his eyes but by sending her telepathic messages. One or two scenes do achieve a genuine frisson. But a poorly integrated romance with a hunky neighbour (O'Keefe) serves only to introduce tedious red herrings, and eventually the unsettling switchback logic of the early scenes gives way to the cheap thrills of a fairground finale. NF

Fear

(James Foley, 1996, US) Mark Wahlberg, Reese Witherspoon, William Petersen, Amy Brenneman, Alyssa Milano.
97 min.
A replay of Cape Fear for a teenage audience. Wahlberg takes the De Niro role seducing both the virginal 16-year-old Nicole (Witherspoon), and, at least metaphorically, her stepmother (Brenneman). He's a charmer on the surface, but big trouble underneath, as Nicole's father (Petersen) quickly recognises. Trying to keep them apart, he only makes things much, much worse. The film, set in Seattle, begins very gloomily and ends well off the rails in Straw Dogs territory. There's just enough play on the idea of paternal jealousy to merit the term 'subtext', but the text itself is hackneyed, and the invitation to take this macho pissing contest seriously is all too resistible. TCh

Fear (La Paura)

(Roberto Rossellini, 1954, It/WGer) Ingrid Bergman, Mathias Wiedman, Renate Manhardt, Kurt Kreuger, Elise Aulinger.
81 min. b/w.
Pretty much passed over at the time, Rossellini's Bergman films are now being touted, not always too convincingly, as supremely personal masterpieces. This one, the last in the series, has a fine central idea: a woman, driven to infidelity and then suicidal angst by her husband's hostility, is viewed as yet another victim of his vivisectional experiments. But the sense of moral preachment that so often marred Rossellini's work remains inescapable. TM

Fear and Loathing in Las Vegas

(Terry Gilliam, 1998, US) Johnny Depp, Benicio Del Toro, Christina Ricci, Ellen Barkin.
118 min.

Everyone tries so hard at getting this adaptation of Hunter S Thompson's gonzo classic just right that one would love to like it more. Certainly, Gilliam pulls out the stops with the hallucinatory madness – the film does at least look good – and Depp and Del Toro, as the drug deranged heroes exploring the darkest excesses of the American Dream in 1971 Vegas, give their energetic all. The trouble is, they end up mugging like mad, and it's all too relentlessly weird, wacky and tacky: it takes an hour before the pace calms down sufficiently to let in a few laughs, and only Barkin, in a brief (and superior) scene towards the end anchors the manic antics in some sort of human reality. A film of brilliant moments, but sadly less coherent – and, one senses, rather less personal – than most of Gilliam's work. GA

Fear Eats the Soul (Angst essen Seele auf)

(Rainer Werner Fassbinder, 1973, WGer) Brigitte Mira, El Hedi Ben Salem, Barbara Valentin, Irm Hermann, Rainer Werner Fassbinder, Karl Scheydt.
92 min.
A deceptively simple tale of the doomed love affair between an ageing cleaner (Mira) and a young Moroccan gastarbeiter (immigrant worker) which exposes the racial prejudice and moral hypocrisy at the heart of modern West German society. Drawing upon the conventions of Hollywood melodrama (the film has many similarities to Douglas Sirk's *All That Heaven Allows*), Fassbinder uses dramatic and visual excess to push everyday events to extremes, achieving a degree of political and psychological truth not accessible through mere social realism. Watch for Fassbinder himself as the reptilian son-in-law, and relish the scene in which Mira's son kicks in the television to demonstrate his disgust at the idea of her marrying an Arab. NF

Fear In the Night

(Maxwell Shane, 1947, US) DeForest Kelley, Paul Kelly, Ann Doran, Kay Scott, Robert Emmett Keane.
72 min. b/w.
A remarkable thriller about a young man's torture by nightmare when he dreams he committed a murder, and then finds himself in possession of tangible evidence proving that somehow, somewhere, he actually did kill. An adaptation of Cornell Woolrich's story *Nightmare*, it's a real poverty row quickie produced by the Pine-Thomas team. Admirably acted in a raw-boned way, tricked out with a barrage of cheap but surprisingly effective expressionistic tricks, above all using a subjective narration which orchestrates the hero's terrors with Bressonian intensity, it creates (almost by accident, it would seem) a hauntingly exact visualisation of the dark, seedy world of Woolrich's imagination that made him the patron saint of *film noir*. Shane remade the film in 1956 as *Nightmare*, with twice the budget and half the effect. TM

Fear in the Night

(Jimmy Sangster, 1972, GB) Judy Geeson, Joan Collins, Ralph Bates, Peter Cushing, Gillian Lind, James Cossins.
85 min.
One of those neatly constructed but slightly mechanical psycho-thrillers which make you feel as if someone is pushing buttons connected to electrodes in your brain. Geeson plays a young woman recovering from a nervous breakdown who is terrorised into wanting to kill the aged, deranged headmaster of the prep school where her husband (Bates) teaches. What she doesn't know is that Bates is in league with the headmaster's wife (Collins). There is a sporadically effective use of prowling camera movements and atmospheric sounds, but Hammer fans will soon recognise the plot as a thinly disguised reworking of *A Taste of Fear*, which Sangster scripted for Seth Holt back in 1961. GA

Fear Is the Key

(Michael Tuchner, 1972, GB) Barry Newman, Suzy Kendall, John Vernon, Dolph Sweet, Ben Kingsley, Ray McAnally.
108 min.
Slightly obscure plot from Alistair MacLean's novel about a gang of thugs out to hijack a planeload of gold and jewels. The hero's wife, brother and kid are on the plane, which is shot down into the sea. So he (Newman) vengefully sets out to infiltrate his way into the organisation, as salvage expert to retrieve the loot, by means of spectacular car chases and assorted killings. A sexless, insubstantial movie, but it's fast and clean, with a reasonable line in suspense.

Fearless

(Peter Weir, 1993, US) Jeff Bridges, Isabella Rossellini, Rosie Perez, Tom Hulce, John Turturro, Benicio Del Toro.
122 min.
By the time Max Klein (Bridges) has grabbed Carla (Perez) for a quick liberating fandango in downtown Oakland, Weir's ambitious movie has already hit the skids. Having survived a terrible air crash, Max goes AWOL before returning to his devoted wife (Rossellini) and their son – reborn, as it were, afraid of nothing. Is he in shock, or has his near-death experience given him special insight, power even, as Max feels? After an intriguing, laconic first half hour, the film sinks into portentous solemnity. One problem is that Weir and writer Rafael Yglesias can't make up their minds about Max's status and state of mind; moreover, the director's much-advertised 'mysticism' often results in spasms of incoherence, not to mention tedium. As often with Weir, there's considerably less here than meets the eye. GA

Fearless Vampire Killers, The

see Dance of the Vampires

Fear of a Black Hat

(Rusty Cundieff, 1992, US) Mark Christopher Lawrence, Larry B Scott, Rusty Cundieff, Kasi Lemmons, Howie Gold.
88 min.
A derivative, sporadically funny comedy that chronicles a year in the life of rap band Niggaz with Hats, and tries to do for rap what *This Is Spinal Tap* did for heavy metal. Given the lyrical and sartorial excesses of rap luminaries such as Ice T, Public Enemy and Niggaz with Attitude, the idea has potential. But while individual interviews, pop-video parodies and album titles hit the mark, the film as a whole is insufficiently clearcut in its satire of the bands' dubious antics and attitudes. NF

Feast at Midnight, A

(Justin Hardy, 1994, GB) Freddie Findlay, Christopher Lee, Robert Hardy, Edward Fox, Lisa Faulkner, Samuel West, Aled Roberts, Andrew Lusher.
106 min.
A throwback to the days of the Children's Film Foundation: well-spoken kids teach a few bumbling adults a thing or two and sort everything out in time for a happy ending. Arriving at bleak Dryden Park prep school, new boy Magnus (Findlay) starts a secret food club to win over his classmates, tangles with a variety of public school types (Lee, Hardy, West), and falls in puppy love with a master's daughter (Faulkner). All the while, he writes to his sick father (Fox), honorary chairman of the Scoffers, and upperclass dispenser of culinary and life-related wisdom. There's the germ of a good family movie here but neither the script nor the production values are of a very high order. AO

Feast of July

(Christopher Menaul, 1995, GB) Greg Wise, Embeth Davidtz, Ben Chaplin, Tom Bell, James Purefoy, Kenneth Anderson, Jemma Jones.
118 min.
Dismissed from her job when she's found to be pregnant, and subsequently miscarrying, young Bella Ford (Davidtz) is in a parlous way when she arrives, cold and alone, in an unfamiliar late-Victorian town in search of Arch Wilson (Wise), the cad who promised to marry her. She's taken in for the night by Pa Wainwright (Bell) and next day Ma Wainwright (Jones) offers her food and board alongside their three sons – Jed (Purefoy), a brash, cocksure soldier home on leave, Matty (Anderson), a more retiring shoemaker, and dark horse Con (Chaplin), slow of mind, hot of temper. Inevitably, Bella's presence stirs up rivalry between the three. Moreover, her past may yet return. This is another landscape- and costume-driven piece, a lavishly designed, earnestly acted period drama which risks smothering its charac-

ters' emotions under their bonnets and livery. Closer examination reveals the problem to be less the props than Christopher Neame's screenplay, which troubles neither to develop the characters nor to allow the drama respite from a raft of narrative clichés. It's no disaster, but grand and ultimately tragic goings-on like these ought to inspire more than a raised eyebrow. NB

Fedora

(Billy Wilder, 1978, WGer) Marthe Keller, William Holden, Hildegard Knef, Jose Ferrer, Mario Adorf, Frances Sternhagen, Michael York, Henry Fonda.
113 min.
A shamefully underrated film, *Fedora* is Wilder's testament and one of the most sublime achievements of the '70s. Only superficially does it resemble *Sunset Boulevard*, since time has moved on; appropriately, *Fedora* is about a star's disastrous attempt to make time stop, and a washed-up producer's efforts to cope with Hollywood's inexorable new generation. Atmospherically set on Corfu, it explores the basics of cinema: realism, illusion, romance and tragedy – in a word, emotion. It's not a flashy film, let alone a cynical one, and it has a narrative assurance beyond the grasp of most directors nowadays: finely acted, mysterious, witty, moving and magnificent. ATu

Feds

(Dan Goldberg, 1988, US) Rebecca De Mornay, Mary Gross, Fred Dalton Thompson, Ken Marshall, Larry Cedar, Raymond Singer.
82 min.
Two young women try to make the grade at the FBI Training Academy. They're given a predictably hard time by their male colleagues, a leering, chauvinist bunch of halfwits and bullies who seem to have strayed out of a National Lampoon movie, but the feisty lasses prove their mettle by the final reel. Director Goldberg seems uncertain whether he should be aiming for slapstick or an earnest docu-drama about sexism in the FBI. Despite an engaging Goldie Hawn-style performance from De Mornay, the end result is bland, toothless satire with neither the gusto of *Police Academy*, nor the charm of *Private Benjamin*. GM

Feedback

(Bill Doukas, 1978, US) Bill Doukas, Myriam Gibril, Denise Gordon, Taylor Mead.
90 mins.
Shades of Kafka and the '60s cinema of narcissism haunt this rambling film in which the actor-*auteur* wanders blankly through both comic-strip New York street life and the intricacies of plea-bargaining after receiving a summons on a mysterious conspiracy charge. Though fitfully encouraging speculation on the relativity of guilt, it's essentially a movie of moments. Some, such as Taylor Mead's characteristically quirky cameo as a judge, are definitely worth waiting for; but finally there aren't quite enough to sustain the feature length. PT

Feeling Minnesota

(Steven Baigelman, 1996, US) Keanu Reeves, Cameron Diaz, Vincent D'Onofrio, Delroy Lindo, Courtney Love, Tuesday Weld, Dan Aykroyd, Levon Helm.
99 min.
The title comes from a Soundgarden song: 'I'm looking California and feeling Minnesota.' Unfortunately, the movie pretty much looks Minnesota too: drab, flat, and overcast (in both senses). There are germs of interest in director Baigelman's screenplay: a shotgun wedding in which Diaz is forcibly married off to accountant D'Onofrio by the local mob bigwig (Lindo) as a kind of incentive payment – she ends up humping her husband's tearaway brother (Reeves) during the reception. They take to the road, but foolishly come back for the money. The movie strains for cool, but the result's something of a mess. TCh

Feelings

(Lawrence Britten, 1975, GB) Kate O'Mara, Paul Freeman, Edward Judd, David Markham, Bob Sherman, Frances Kearney.
92 min.
Learning of his sterility, a prosperous record producer (Freeman) reluctantly agrees that his wife (O'Mara) should be artificially inseminated.

Nothing happens. A distinguished sexologist (Markham) suggests her chances of conception will improve if she submits to normal sexual intercourse. A physiotherapy student obliges. A child is born which in due course inherits a fortune from a great uncle. The student attempts blackmail to get his hands on the cash. Ludicrous yarn based on clinical balderdash about AI, with an unsavoury attitude to miscegenation and lesbian mothers. JPy

Feet First

(Clyde Bruckman, 1930, US) Harold Lloyd, Barbara Kent, Robert McWade, Lillian Leighton, Henry Hall, Noah Young, Sleep 'n' Eat, Willie Best.
70 min. b/w.
Harold Horne (Lloyd), a not very practised Honolulu shoe salesman, falls for the boss's 'daughter' (in reality his far more accessible secretary) and having pursued his loved one on to an oceangoing liner finds himself tied up in a mail sack with an important business bid in his pocket. All of which tedious business takes up the first two-thirds of the picture. However, once the mail sack lands on a rising builder's hoist outside a skyscraper, the acrobatic fun begins in earnest. A familiar reprise, to be sure, of Safety Last, but none the worse for that. The high spot has Lloyd flailing halfway down the building at the end of a gushing high-pressure fire hose. Be warned, there's a lot of prehistoric business in the skyscraper with a slow, barely verbal Negro servant (Best), played to the n-th degree of dumbness and then some. JPy

Felix the Cat: The Movie

(Tibor Hernádi, 1989, US) voices: Chris Phillips, Maureen O'Connell, Peter Neuman, Alice Playton, Susan Montanaro.
82 min.
Felix made his screen debut as an animated short in 1919, passing through newspaper strips to become a major TV star in the '50s and '60s. Unfortunately, updating him for today's kids seems to mean ripping off Star Wars. A beautiful princess sends off a hologrammatic plea for help when she is captured and relieved of her kingdom by an evil duke. There follows a Quest through an alternative dimension inhabited by all manner of hybrid creatures (beasts with detachable heads, carnivorous marsh gas, rampaging robots), in which Felix fills in for Luke Skywalker (with the same combination of wide-eyed innocence and happy-go-lucky optimism that set him apart from more scurrilous cartoon cats like Sylvester, Top Cat and Fritz). Felix always had a surrealist slant, but this inane fantasy lacks the motor of good plot or dialogue. True, the animation is consistently inventive and the voicing good, but the end result is a TV cartoon padded out to feature length. DW

Fellini's Casanova (Il Casanova di Federico Fellini)

(Federico Fellini, 1976, It) Donald Sutherland, Tina Aumont, Cicely Browne, Carmen Scarpitta, Clara Algranti.
163 min.
Imbued with an air of funereal solemnity and elegance, this forsakes realism in favour of a stylised romantic pessimism which confronts impotence, failure, sexuality and exploitation as fully as Pasolini's Salò. Although teetering at times dangerously close to Ken Russell, the visual daring and pure imagination of every image leave it as an elegiac farewell to an era of Italian cinema; and Sutherland's performance is the most astonishing piece of screen acting since Brando's in Last Tango in Paris. SM

Fellini's Roma (Roma)

(Federico Fellini, 1972, It/Fr) Peter Gonzales, Fiona Florence, Marne Maitland, Britta Barnes, Anna Magnani, Federico Fellini, Gore Vidal.
128 min.
Fellini in the self-indulgent mood that mars so much of his later work, taking us on an extravagantly sentimental and grotesque tour of 'his' Rome. The lack of any structural organisation of his 'insights' and 'memories' – though flaccid fantasies would be a better description – and the familiar gallery of obese, noisome stereotypes quickly become tiresome. But there is no denying that the man still has the capacity to pull off startling visual coups. GA

Fellini-Satyricon

(Federico Fellini, 1969, It/Fr) Martin Potter, Hiram Keller, Salvo Randone, Max Born, Fanfulla, Capucine, Alain Cuny, Lucia Bosè.
129 min.
Sprawling and conspicuously undisciplined, this is less an adaptation of Petronius than a free-form fantasia on his themes. Fellini's characteristic delirium is in fact anchored in a precise, psychological schema: under the matrix of bisexuality, he explores the complexes of castration, impotence, paranoia and libidinal release. And he pays homage to Pasolini's ethnographic readings of myths. It's among his most considerable achievements. TR

Fellow Traveller

(Philip Saville, 1989, GB/US) Ron Silver, Imogen Stubbs, Hart Bochner, Daniel J Travanti, Katherine Borowitz, Julian Fellowes, Richard Wilson, Doreen Mantle.
97 min.
1954: blacklisted Hollywood screenwriter Asa Kaufman (Silver) arrives in London to work anonymously on scripts for the new independent television series 'Robin Hood'. Shattered by the news of the Hollywood suicide of his actor friend Cliff Byrne (Bochner) but unable to return home (he faces a HUAC subpoena), Asa enlists the reluctant help of Cliff's ex-lover Sarah (Stubbs), and dredges through his dreams and memories in search of clues to Cliff's death. As scripted by Michael Eaton, this McCarthy-period thriller interweaves numerous themes: guilt, confession and repression; privacy, paranoia and betrayal; the difference between America and Britain in the '50s; the role played by obsession in artistic creativity; the conflict between Marxist and freudian concepts of socio-political change. But it's also a moody, gripping suspense drama, reminiscent of classic film noir, its tortuous narrative full of mysterious flashbacks and dream sequences. Saville elicits some very fine performances, notably from Silver, and Travanti as a 'pink shrink' who treats Hollywood's Left; but finally it's the sheer wealth of detail and the uncommonly intelligent ambitions of the script that carry the day. GA

Feluettes, ou La Répétition d'un drama romantique

see Lilies

Female Jungle, The

(Bruno Ve Sota, 1956, US) Lawrence Tierney, John Carradine, Jayne Mansfield, Kathleen Crowley, Rex Thorsen, Bruno Ve Sota.
56 min. b/w.
When a Hollywood actress is found dead, drunken cop Tierney (the heist organiser in Reservoir Dogs some decades later) has an obvious murder suspect in Carradine's gossip columnist, but a further killing gives him second thoughts. Murky B melodrama with a cult value cast. After her screen debut as a passing good-time girl, Mansfield went back to selling popcorn at a cinema, but not for long. TJ

Female Perversions

(Susan Streitfeld, 1996, US/Ger) Tilda Swinton, Amy Madigan, Karen Sillas, Frances Fisher, Clancy Brown.
113 min.
Adapted from an academic tome by US feminist Louise J Kaplan, this first feature centres on the crimes and misdemeanours of two thirty-something sisters. It's a fiery polemic/sex romp/watery Mamet soap. Tilda Swinton is a successful attorney, Eve, a brittle beast forever candying over her 'masculine' ambition with lipstick, lingerie and high heels. Politically correct Madelyn (Madigan) is attempting to hide 'femaleness' (she steals frilly underwear). Events focus on Eve's interview for the post of judge and Madelyn's arrest for theft. As family secrets unravel, the question becomes which side of the law should women want to be on? The film totters under the weight of its earnest symbolism (an ageing, overweight woman, for instance, struggling on a tightrope). Moreover, for all director/co-writer Streitfeld's desire to explode our culture's fascination with beauty, she herself seems besotted with Swinton, fixating on her perfect, scrubbed-with-nails aesthetic; the more homely Madigan, wonderfully restrained in her dead-eyed lunacy, just doesn't

attract the same attention. Among the po-faced dross, however, there's much that's stunning. Interminable and flawed though the film is, the images that work grip like ivy. CO'Su

Female Trouble

(John Waters, 1974, US) Divine, David Lochary, Mary Vivian Pearce, Mink Stole, Edith Massey.
95 min.
Waters scrapes the bottom of the flash/trash barrel as artlessly as he did in Pink Flamingos. Again starring the wonder wobble Divine, Female Trouble documents the winsome life of one Dawn Davenport, from the moment she mashes Mum under the Christmas tree (having failed to receive her coveted cha-cha heels from Santa) to her shocking end in the electric chair. In between, accepted notions of beauty get flipped over on their bum as the sublime Divine sails through her various guises (loving mother, mugger, model and mass murderer), taking time out to double as her own deflowerer. Hilarious moments pockmark the movie like a bad case of acne, but like the person with only one joke to tell, it soon loses its appeal and laughter is replaced by lethargy. FL

Female Vampires

(Jess Franco, 1973, Fr) Lina Romay, Alice Arno, Jack Taylor.
94 min.
A wretched soft-porn piece which substitutes oral sex for blood-sucking. For Lina Romay vampirism manifests itself mainly as a lack of make-up and a surly expression. Even the genre's sartorial elegance has passed her by as she mooches round the woods in nothing but a pair of boots, cape and belt. Plenty of below-the-belt sex. SFe

Femme d'à côté, La

see Woman Next Door, The

Femme Défendue, La (The Forbidden Woman)

(Philippe Harel, 1997, Fr) Isabelle Carré, Philippe Harel, Nathalie Conio, Sophie Niedergang, Julien Niedergang.
100 min.
An intriguing if flawed experiment in cinematic storytelling. A 22-year-old woman (Carré) hesitantly enters into an affair with a 39-year-old man (Harel), who's married with a kid. The film's a shrewd analysis of an adulterous relationship, but what lifts it out of the ordinary is that it's shot with a subjective camera from the man's PoV (Harel appears only briefly in reflection). The narrative is limited to the man's conversations with his lover, so that what we see is almost entirely Carré (who carries the film impressively). More than a gimmick, this device puts the viewer in a complex position – somewhere between contempt and complicity – with regard to the weak-willed, manipulative seducer. Regrettably, the story sometimes lacks the dramatic drive to match this potentially interesting conceit. GA

Femme de l'Aviateur, La

see Aviator's Wife, The

Femme de Mon Pote, La

see My Best Friend's Girl

Femme Douce, Une (A Gentle Creature)

(Robert Bresson, 1969, Fr) Dominique Sanda, Guy Frangin, Jane Lobre.
88 min.
Bresson's first film in colour, a wonderfully lucid adaptation of Dostoievsky's enigmatic short story about a young woman who kills herself for no apparent reason. An elliptical intimation of the suicide; a shot of the husband staring at his dead wife's face in an attempt to understand; then in a flat, even monotone, his voice embarks on its voyage of exploration – part confession, part accusation – and a series of heart-rendingly non-committal flashbacks fill in the details of their story. By the end, in a sense, one is no wiser than before. Was it because he loved her too much or too little, because he gave her too little money or too much, because he felt she was too good for him or not good enough? The extraordinary thing about the film is that any or all of these interpretations can be read into it, still leaving, undis-

turbed at the bottom of the pool, an indefinable sense of despair. Time was when Bresson's characters could look forward to salvation as a reward for their tribulations; but around this time the grace notes disappeared, his world grew darker, and the people in it – like this haplessly unhappy husband and wife – seemed doomed to a pilgrim's progress in quest of the secret which would allow the human race to belong again. TM

Femme du Boulanger, La (The Baker's Wife)

(Marcel Pagnol, 1938, Fr) Raimu, Ginette Leclerc, Charles Moulin, Fernand Charpin, Robert Vattier, Robert Bassac, Charles Blavette.
116 min. b/w.
'Lucky people who will be seeing La Femme du Boulanger for the first time', said the 'New Statesman's William Whitebait when Pagnol's movie was on one of its periodic reissues in 1944. One only hopes that today's audiences will feel equally lucky: if they've no objections to seeing something flagrantly unfashionable, but bursting with bucolic vigour and sly satirical wit, they ought to be happy enough. Raimu, a French clown sans pareil, plays a baker in Provence who refuses to bake another loaf until his flighty wife (currently in the arms of a local shepherd) is returned to him. Pagnol's direction has been described as 'elaborately unobtrusive', whatever that means. GB

Femme entre Chien et Loup, Une (Woman In a Twilight Garden)

(André Delvaux, 1978, Bel/Fr) Marie-Christine Barrault, Roger Van Hool, Rutger Hauer, Bert André, Raf Reyman, Senne Rouffaer, Mathieu Carrière.
111 min.
Elliptical tale of a World War II triangle (and its aftermath) in which a Belgian woman falls for a French-speaking Resistance leader while her husband, an idealistic Flemish-speaking nationalist, is serving on the eastern front as a volunteer with the German SS. Delicately shaded and much less schematic than it sounds, it still emerges as little more than a specifically Belgian/ Flemish rehash of the usual traumas. Exquisitely shot, but a disappointment from the usually evocative and subtle Delvaux. TM

Femme est une Femme, Une (A Woman Is a Woman)

(Jean-Luc Godard, 1961, Fr) Anna Karina, Jean-Paul Belmondo, Jean-Claude Brialy, Marie Dubois, Nicole Paquin, Marion Sarraut, Jeanne Moreau, Catherine Demongeot.
84 min.
Most of Godard's early movies are so much of their particular time that they'll need explanatory footnotes before long. This was the first of his colour/cinemascope tributes to the changing moods of Karina (his then wife); the film's own soundtrack notes that it might equally be a comedy or a tragedy because it's certainly a masterpiece. It has a thin thread of plot about Karina's desire to get pregnant, it flanks her with the pragmatic Brialy on one side and the romantic Belmondo on the other, then stands all of them in the shadow of MGM musical stars of the '40s and '50s, and it collages these elements together with sundry gags, worries, contradictions and asides into a kind of movie that nobody had seen before. The result is brash, defiant, gaudy and infinitely fragile. TR

Femme Fatale

(André Guttfreund, 1991, US) Colin Firth, Lisa Zane, Billy Zane, Scott Wilson, Lisa Blount, Carmine Caridi.
90 min.
Joseph (Firth) meets enigmatic Cynthia (Lisa Zane) at his nature centre. A brief courtship and marriage follow, but when Cynthia walks out on the eve of their honeymoon, the distraught groom embarks on a search of her old Los Angeles neighbourhood, and discovers that she is not who he thought she was. The path to discovery is difficult – not so much for Joseph as for the weary viewer. The camera roves around a landscape scattered with affected sycophants and wide-eyed drug dealers before jolting on, periodically, into flashbacks of life in the countryside. With each bizarre revelation, the film descends further into hysterical nonsense. CM

Femme française, Une (Eine Französische Frau)

(Régis Wargnier, 1994, Fr/GB/Ger) Emmanuelle Béart, Daniel Auteuil, Gabriel Barylli, Jean-Claude Brialy, Geneviève Casile, Michel Etcheverry, Heinz Bennent.
98 min.
After bathing Deneuve in exotic colonial finery for the dull Indochine, writer/director Wargnier reserves a worse fate for Béart in this bathetic, absurdly misjudged trawl through the emotional wreckage of an army marriage. Summer 1939 brings the union of Jeanne (Béart) and youthful lieutenant Louis (Auteuil) and fleeting bliss before he spends the next five years in a German PoW camp. Release finds him returning home to a wife who's scandalised the family by having an affair, and the couple are only just reconciled before the next set of orders sends them to Berlin, where Louis joins the Allied occupation force. Jeanne finds herself irresistibly drawn to her German landlord's son Mathias (Barylli), a passion that causes intolerable tensions. Pushed hither and thither, Auteuil is right to look ill at ease, but Béart is sadly reduced to an empty repertoire of stamping mini-mélo, swaths of décolletage and sheer pouty desperation. The star chemistry (the leads split off-screen during production) is pure corrosion, while Patrick Doyle's overblown score merely expands the agony. TJ

Femme Infidèle, La (Unfaithful Wife)

(Claude Chabrol, 1968, Fr/It) Stéphane Audran, Michel Bouquet, Maurice Ronet, Serge Bento, Michel Duchaussoy, Guy Marly.
98 min.
One of Chabrol's mid-period masterpieces, a brilliantly ambivalent scrutiny of bourgeois marriage and murder that juggles compassion and cynicism in a way that makes Hitchcock look obvious. The obligatory cross-references are still there (blood in the sink; the exactly duplicate final use of simultaneous backtrack and forward zoom adapted from Vertigo), but they're no longer there to legitimise a vision now mature. Audran and Bouquet, as the first of Chabrol's recurring Charles/Hélène couples, are superb in discovering 'secret' parts of each other denied as much by complacency as convention. PT

Femme Mariée, Une (A Married Woman)

(Jean-Luc Godard, 1964, Fr) Macha Méril, Bernard Noël, Philippe Leroy, Roger Leenhardt, Rita Maiden.
98 min. b/w.
Relatively minor Godard which, characteristically, plays off fictional form (a day in the life of an adulterous wife) against documentary moments (face-on interviews in which characters lecture on abstracts like 'Memory' and 'Childhood'). Another of his socio-sexual fables, in fact, curious for the way it was censored. Outraged by its mockery of Marriage and Family, the authorities insisted that the title be changed – from La Femme Mariée (Married Woman, a collectivity, a condition) to Une Femme Mariée (A Married Woman, an individual, unrepresentative case). CA

Femme ou Deux, Une

see Woman or Two, A

Fencing Master, The (El Maestro de Esgrima)

(Pedro Olea, 1992, Sp) Omero Antonutti, Assumpta Serna, Joaquin de Almeida, José Luis Lopez Vazquez.
88 min.
Madrid, 1868: Queen Isabel's regime is crumbling, and Don Jaime de Astarloa (Antonutti) lives only for fencing. When the beautiful Adela de Otero (Serna) asks him to teach her, he refuses to instruct a lady. A demonstration of her skill, however, has him curling his moustache. Soon he's infatuated, but Adela has a more prominent partner in mind. Olea's adaptation of Arturo Pérez Reverte's novel begins in a solemn register, but just as you're about to write it off as a museum piece, it abruptly changes tack and develops into a lively old-fashioned melodrama: Don Jaime is duped in love, a friend is murdered, a woman's corpse is fished out of the river. This intrigue has enough cut and thrust to tickle all but the most

jaded palate, while Serna makes a fine foil for Antonutti's crafty performance. Only Olea's wider socio-historical pretensions seem a mite sketchy. TCh

Fengriffen

see And Now the Screaming Starts!

FernGully: The Last Rainforest

(Bill Kroyer, 1992, Aust) voices: Tim Curry, Samantha Mathis, Christian Slater, Jonathan Ward, Robin Williams, Grace Zabriskie, Cheech Marin, Tommy Chong.
76 min.
The FernGully of this animation feature is a pretty, pastel-coloured glade in the middle of a rainforest where animals and plants live in harmony, tended by Magi Lune and her gentle nature-spirits. 'Everything in Creation is connected by the delicate web of life,' says the aptly named Ms Lune. As if to put this theory to the test, Crysta flies out to the smoke at the edge of the rainforest. It is her first encounter with Man. Impetuously, she saves the life of Zak, a particularly cute specimen, and shrinks him to her size. Alas, Zak's colleagues at the logging operation are possessed by the evil spirit Hexxus, and the whole forest is imperilled. FernGully is black and white and Green all over. Aimed squarely at the under-12s, it won't displease most parents, if only for the welcome absence of marketable accessories. TCh

Ferris Bueller's Day Off

(John Hughes, 1986, US) Matthew Broderick, Alan Ruck, Mia Sara, Jeffrey Jones, Jennifer Grey, Cindy Pickett.
103 min.
Ferris (Broderick) is a boy who gets anything he wants, screws over anyone who gets in his way, and gets patted on the back for doing so. Gathering his best friend (Ruck) and his best girlfriend (Sara), he skips school for the day out in Chicago. Hughes revels in Ferris' ingenuity, then neatly adds dimension after a ninety-minute parade of hubris and material wealth by telling us that people count more than their possessions. Ferris is an admittedly entertaining, at times delightful fellow. How unfortunate that no one got to wring the little bastard's neck. SGo

Ferry Cross the Mersey

(Jeremy Summers, 1964, GB) Gerry Marsden, Fred Marsden, Les Chadwick, Les Maguire, Julie Samuel, Eric Barker, Deryck Guyler.
85 min. b/w.
Grotesquely inept and dated pop musical featuring Gerry and the Pacemakers which is so bad that it doesn't even make it as nostalgia. Shot in a very short space of time to cash in on the Liverpool sound; the other pop personalities involved are Cilla Black, Jimmy Savile and the Fourmost. Ken Tynan, whose film reviewing was not always so succinct and penetrating, gave it the most accurate five-word review ever in The Observer when he called it 'a little glimpse into hell'. DP

Ferry to Hong Kong

(Lewis Gilbert, 1958, GB) Curd Jürgens, Sylvia Syms, Orson Welles, Jeremy Spenser, Noel Purcell.
113 min.
The first of Rank's clueless strikes at the international market is a moronic male melodrama-cum-adventure movie with Curd Jürgens as a shiftless Austrian drifter who's in his element when Orson Welles' ferry is threatened by a typhoon off Macao. All at sea away from his favoured British subject matter, Lewis Gilbert tries to navigate by the stars, but he's duly scuppered by his own rocky script. Filmed in CinemaScope. TCh

Festen

see Celebration, The

Festival (Chukje)

(Im Kwon-Taek, 1996, SKor) Ahn Song-Gi, Oh Jung-Hae, Han Eun-Jin, Chung Kyung-Soon, Park Seung-Tae, Lee Kem-Joo.
108 min.
Odd there should be two major Korean films

centred on funerals in the same year, but this one is very different in form, tone and style from *Farewell My Darling*, even if it also shows a family at risk of tearing itself apart. Im directs with his usual classical restraint and places great weight on the many rituals that form part of the ceremonies; the beauty and serenity of these customs ultimately see the mourners through the parade of bad behaviour, drunken outbursts and hitherto unvoiced resentments. One element marks it as Im's most experimental film in some time: the story is filtered through glimpses of a child's picture-book vision of the death of her grandma – arresting, stylised sequences whose meaning falls into place only at the very end. TR

Festival

(Pupi Avati, 1996, It) Massimo Boldi, Isabelle Pasco, Gianni Cavina, Margaret Mazzantini.
95 min.
An over-the-hill comic, scrambling for bookings on the provincial club circuit, Franco (Boldi) cuts a sad figure. His only prospect is the release of a low-budget film by a first-time director – a hateful experience for a star of Franco's former stature. Then, a miracle! The film's invited to the Venice festival, in competition. The critics start buzzing, and suddenly Franco is tipped for the Golden Lion. Avati's melancholy answer to *The King of Comedy* is sour and unfunny. Chiefly shot at the Venice fest in 1995, and screened there in '96, the film holds up a mirror to the vanity of the event, but echoes with empty laughter. TCh

Fetishes

(Nick Broomfield, 1996, US) Mistresses Raven, Catherine, Beatrice and Delilah, Goddess Natasha.
84 min.
Pandora's Box, downtown Manhattan, caters to a niche market. They do sadism, the clientele provide the masochism. If you're into bondage, rubber, female wrestling or toilet-licking, this is your place. Of course there are two fetishes being explored here: SM and voyeurism. Perhaps that's why Broomfield plays a less aggressively upfront role than usual – though we do see him flirting with the mistresses and sticking his microphone in some unexpected places. TCh

Feu Follet, Le (A Time to Live and a Time to Die/ The Fire Within/Fox Fire/ Will o'the Wisp)

(Louis Malle, 1963, Fr) Maurice Ronet, Lena Skerla, Yvonne Clech, Hubert Deschamps, Jeanne Moreau, Alexandra Stewart.
121 min. b/w.
Arguably the finest of Malle's early films, this is a calmly objective but profoundly compassionate account of the last 24 hours in the life of a suicide. Ronet gives a remarkable, quietly assured performance as the alcoholic who, upon leaving a clinic, visits old friends in the hope that they will provide him with a reason to live. They don't, and Malle's achievement lies not only in his subtle but clear delineation of his protagonist's emotions but in his grasp of life's compromises; his portrait of Parisian society is astringent, never facile. A small gem, polished to perfection by an unassuming professional. GA

Feverhouse

(Howard Walmesley, 1984, GB) Joanne Hill, Graham Massey, Patrick Nyland.
46 min. b/w.
Scripted by Ken Hollings, this short feature might better be considered as a poem: something out of Baudelaire's *Fleurs du Mal* via the French Surrealist cinema and Throbbing Gristle's brutalist chic. Shot in expressionist monochrome, it roams the rooms and corridors of what might be the titular hospital, a grim Victorian edifice where bodies lie untended on trolleys, nurses murder inmates, a nurse-patient love affair flutters in the shadows, the sick and blind stumble in Beckettian repetition, and the oblique, disturbing narrative only hints at larger horrors. Given all that, it hovers dangerously close to pretension, sometimes teetering over the edge, but still remains a darkly individual visual essay, despite its precedents. It's also blessed with an exciting score, a brew of metal gamelan and junkyard bebop from Biting Tongues. JG

Fever Pitch

(Richard Brooks, 1985, US) Ryan O'Neal, Catherine Hicks, Giancarlo Giannini, Bridgette Andersen, Chad Everett, John Saxon.
96 min.
Hollywood old-stager Brooks' last completed feature to date (1996) is an old-fashioned and numbingly predicable problem pic of the kind that he used to do rather better (*The Blackboard Jungle*, for instance). Here the horror of gambling comes under the microscope as ace reporter O'Neal sets out to write an exposé of Las Vegas, but (surprise, surprise) ends up a slave to the gaming table. TJ

Fever Pitch

(David Evans, 1996, GB) Colin Firth, Ruth Gemmell, Neil Pearson, Lorraine Ashbourne, Mark Strong, Holly Aird, Ken Stott, Stephen Rea.
102 min.
Nick Hornby's done a clever thing. While a Hollywood studio has bought the rights to his best-seller *High Fidelity*, and are trying to work out how to Americanise it, he's transposed the battle of the sexes scenario on to this most parochial of romantic comedies – only he's passing it off as *Fever Pitch*, an adaptation of his first, strictly unfilmable book. Firth is Paul, an English teacher with an unhealthy obsession for Arsenal Football Club. Gemmell is Sarah, a starchy colleague who despises the game and the hooligans who follow it – Paul, especially. You don't need a crystal ball to predict the result. Mercifully dispensing with the best part of 25 seasons of Highbury inaction, the film concentrates on the championship hopes of 1988-9, with brief, explanatory flashbacks to Paul's childhood. The focus is a kind of reverse angle on conventional soccer coverage, with the camera trained on the fans, not the players. Director Evans doesn't catch the psychological acuity of Hornby's prose, but he brings the push and pull of that fateful season to life even for non-Arsenal fans, and scores early on with a very funny seduction scene. Gradually, though, the energy sags. It's so much more in love with football than heterosexual relationships. The mismatched couple is a staple of screwball comedy, but these characters are fundamentally dislikeable – he's an arrested adolescent with a one-track mind, she's got nothing going for her at all. TCh

Few Good Men, A

(Rob Reiner, 1992, US) Tom Cruise, Jack Nicholson, Demi Moore, Kevin Bacon, Kiefer Sutherland, Kevin Pollak, James Marshall, JT Walsh, Wolfgang Bodison.
138 min.
Scripted by Aaron Sorkin from his own play, considerably less interesting than *A Soldier's Story*, this centres on a fatal case of bullying in the US Marines and the ensuing trial. The intellectual cut-and-thrust of the courtroom is largely absent here, and the denouement seems slick, arbitrary, and derived from the Captain Queeg catalogue. Even worse, Cruise is cast as the dilettante Navy lawyer with a brilliant legal brain, and jives about in much the same manner as he did in *Top Gun*. Lieutenant Commander Demi Moore wants him to get serious, praises his brain repeatedly in case we missed it, and finally gets him shouting idealistically in court. The pair of them are useless in uniform, and shown up by the highly professional Bacon, who gives a layered performance as the opposing counsel. Unfortunately, the most interesting character is little more than a cameo for Nicholson, but he does give an alarming sketch of the élitist military mind. BC

F for Fake (Vérités et Mensonges)

(Orson Welles, 1973, Fr/Iran/WGer) Orson Welles, Oja Kodar, Elmyr de Hory, Clifford Irving, Edith Irving, François Reichenbach, Joseph Cotten, Laurence Harvey, Richard Wilson.
85 min.
A triumphantly self-amused, self-aware reflection on the verities of art and creativity and the lies that sustain them, Welles' quizzical homage to forgery and illusionism is both a self-portrait and a wry refutation of the *auteur* principle, a labyrinthine play of paradoxes and ironies that comes off as the cinematic equivalent of an Escher painting. Starting with some 'found' footage of art forger Elmyr de Hory shot by doc-

umentarist François Reichenbach, Welles manipulates it into a mock inquisition on the mysteries of authorship, autonomy, attribution and associative editing, arriving back at *Kane* and the *War of the Worlds* broadcast via Howard Hughes and his hoax biographer Clifford Irving. Alongside the films of Jacques Rivette, the epitome of cinema-as-play. PT

Fiancée du Pirate, La (Dirty Mary/A Very Curious Girl)

(Nelly Kaplan, 1969, Fr) Bernadette Lafont, Georges Géret, Michel Constantin, Julien Guiomar, Jean Parédès, Francis Lax, Claire Maurier.
106 min.
Kaplan's first feature is a cruel inversion of the Cinderella fable: the story of a 'pirate' woman, social outcast of a backbiting, bigoted provincial village, who takes her revenge by turning prostitute in order to seduce and blackmail her clients and oppressors into ruin. The mockery is harsh, despite the bright colours and playful tone: greed, malice and bigotry are satirised with merciless, atheistic scorn, and the final blow for sexual and social revenge is struck in the hamlet's church. Piggy eyes, once popping out of their sockets with lust, burn with hatred, while the heroine (the marvellous Lafont) dances off down the open road, leaving behind only a strange abstract sculpture of fridges, showers and bric-a-brac, as though thumbing her nose at the very possibility of marriage and homely virtue. CA

Fiddler on the Roof

(Norman Jewison, 1971, US) Chaim Topol, Norma Crane, Leonard Frey, Molly Picon, Paul Mann, Rosalind Harris, Michael Glaser.
180 min.
Jewison fairly wallows in ethnic roots in this adaptation of the Sheldon Harnick/Jerry Bock musical, set in a Jewish village community in the pre-Revolutionary Ukraine: three hours of pure schmalz, buried up to its neck in noisy national traditions as the hero marries off three daughters in turn, pausing each time to unload buckets of song, sentiment and homespun philosophy. Very hard to take with the film sitting up and practically slobbering in its eagerness to prove how loveable it is. A pity, because the score isn't half bad (the show-stopping 'If I Were a Rich Man' almost gets lost), the choreography has possibilities, and Topol is distinctly personable. TM

Fiddlers Three

(Harry Watt, 1944, GB) Tommy Trinder, Frances Day, Sonnie Hale, Francis L Sullivan, Diana Decker, Elisabeth Welch, James Robertson Justice.
88 min. b/w.
Sailors Trinder and Hale plus plucky Wren Frances Day are struck by lightning on Salisbury Plain and transported back to Ancient Rome, where they're acclaimed as powerful seers and outwit Sullivan's cheerily debauched Nero. Cheeky wartime British comedy with odd imaginative touch (associate producer Robert Hamer reshot a good deal of it). James Robertson Justice appears as a young centurion. TJ

Field, The

(Jim Sheridan, 1990, GB) Richard Harris, John Hurt, Tom Berenger, Sean Bean, Frances Tomelty, Brenda Fricker, John Cowley, Ruth McCabe, Sean McGinley.
110 min.
John B Keane's play takes on some of the resonances of an Irish *Lear* in Jim Sheridan's adaptation. West Coast tenant farmer Bull McCabe (Harris) has lavished all his love upon a rented field which he hopes to leave to his weak son (Bean), in the belief that a man is nothing without land. His dream is shattered when the widowed owner puts it up for auction, and he is outbid by an outsider, an American (Berenger) with plans to modernise the area. Following the American's murder, Bull cracks apart, driving wilfully ever deeper into tragedy. Some of the ingredients are given – Bull's wife (Fricker) hasn't spoken to him in a decade, his second son killed himself – but most of the burden of developing a tragic character is down to Harris, and he layers it richly without too much thespian tilting of the beard into the elements. His Bull is a spectrum of patience, violence, parsimony and ceilidh, intimidating to his son and awesome to

his fawning creature Bird O'Donnell (Hurt, also at his peak). Sense of place, time and custom are faultless, and despite a few narrative lurches, it's a moving experience. BC

Field Of Dreams

(Phil Alden Robinson, 1989, US) Kevin Costner, Amy Madigan, James Earl Jones, Timothy Busfield, Ray Liotta, Burt Lancaster, Gaby Hoffmann, Frank Whaley, Dwier Brown.
106 min.
Despite a happy family life, Iowa farmer Ray Kinsella (Costner) is left musing over lost idealism and a squandered relationship with his father, a former baseball player now dead. Hearing a disembodied voice urging 'If you build it, he will come', he is propelled on a quest which initially involves putting a baseball pitch in the middle of his crop. This in turn heralds the arrival of ghostly baseball players – including the infamous Shoeless Joe Jackson, implicated in the fixing of the 1919 World Series. Taken in bare outline, the plot may appear faintly ridiculous; but this often beautiful film (John Lindley's cinematography is breathtaking) – using baseball as a metaphor for other issues, namely the bonding or lack of it between father and son – embraces qualities which are skilfully amplified and *not* sentimentalised. Writer/ director Robinson has embellished WP Kinsella's novel to examine the ideological conflict between the '60s and the '80s; together with moments of dry humour and fine performances, the political element lends the film gravity sufficient to counterbalance any sense of whimsy. Pure magic. CM

Fiendish Plot of Dr Fu Manchu, The

(Piers Haggard, 1980, US) Peter Sellers, Helen Mirren, David Tomlinson, Sid Caesar, Simon Williams, Steve Franken, Stratford Johns, John Le Mesurier, Burt Kwouk.
108 min.
Sadly, this final movie from Sellers is also one of his worst. Most of the jokes one anticipates seconds before they occur; many are of the ethnic stereotype sort; the visual running gag palls at its second appearance. Co-star Helen Mirren continues her determined bid to give up acting for the role of ripest screen-tease sex object of the '80s. RM

Fiends, The

see Diaboliques, Les

Fiend Without a Face

(Arthur Crabtree, 1958, GB) Marshall Thompson, Kim Parker, Terence Kilburn, Kynaston Reeves, Stanley Maxted.
74 min. b/w.
Close by a US Army base in a remote corner of Canada, a trail of corpses leads Thompson to uncover a hideous experiment gone wrong. A familiar plot right down to the atomic mutation premise, but the special effects – killer brains that propel themselves through the air with a whip of the spinal cord and latch onto the backs of their victims' necks – are among the most memorable in the eco-horror genre. Crabtree (a former cinematographer who graduated to Gainsborough melodramas and also made the bizarre *Horrors of the Black Museum*) is one of the unsung *auteurs* of the pre-*Outer Limits* era. This may be his finest hour and a bit. MA

Fierce Creatures

(Robert Young/Fred Schepisi, 1996, US/GB) John Cleese, Kevin Kline, Jamie Lee Curtis, Michael Palin, Ronnie Corbett, Carey Lowell, Robert Lindsay, Maria Aitken.
93 min.
Not a sequel, but a belated reunion for Cleese and his co-stars from *A Fish Called Wanda*, and as strained as such occasions tend to be. The set-up's silly. Rollo Lee (Cleese) runs a small British zoo, a surprisingly prominent blip on Aussie tycoon Rod McCain's plans for global conglomeration. Obsessed with profit margins, Rollo decides only dangerous animals pay – the rest will have to go. The staff are appalled, but things get even worse when McCain (Kline) drafts in corporate hotshot Willa (Curtis) and his no-good son Vince (Kline again), who embark on a crass sponsorship scheme. There's some funny business with the zoo-keepers pretending that meerkats

are the most vicious beasts on four legs, and Cleese briefly reminds us of Python's cutting edge when he dispatches a handful of the cutest creatures with a shotgun, but the movie soon settles for dismally obvious running gags about bestiality, Curtis's body, and Cleese's sexual charisma. Just about musters enough laughs to cover up the cracks. TCh

Fièvre Monte à El Pao, La (Republic of Sin)

(Luis Buñuel, 1959, Fr/Mex) Gérard Philipe, Maria Félix, Jean Servais, Miguel Angel Ferriz, Raúl Dantés, Domingo Soler.
97 min. b/w.
Philippe's last role before his death from cancer, playing a small-time government administrator – the setting is a South American dictator-state – whose time comes when the governor is assassinated and he temporarily takes over until a successor is appointed. The film is a study in the futility of liberal sentimentality when it refuses to acknowledge the fascist mechanism for what it is: Philippe's few attempts to improve the lot of political prisoners prove useless in face of a stronger rival and his own desire for security and power. It's hardly major Buñuel – he himself blamed its shortcomings on the inevitable compromises of a co-production – but his view of greed, hypocrisy and cruelty is as lucidly sardonic as ever, and the portrait of the dangers of trying to improve a totalitarian regime from the inside remains as relevant today as when the film was made. GA

Fifth Avenue Girl

(Gregory LaCava, 1939, US) Ginger Rogers, Walter Connolly, Verree Teasdale, James Ellison, Tim Holt, Franklin Pangborn, Kathryn Adams.
83 min. b/w.
LaCava seems to have lost his touch, usually good for some sharpish social satire, in this comedy about a jobless and homeless girl taken into his stately mansion by a despondent millionaire, mainly with a view to shaking up his money-grubbing family by having her come on as a gold-digger. The family duly fulminate while the millionaire happily plays with his pet pigeons instead of attending to business, and true love predictably looms to provide a happy resolution for his protégée. Even Rogers seems curiously listless. TM

Fifth Element, The (Le Cinquième Elément)

(Luc Besson, 1997, Fr) Bruce Willis, Gary Oldman, Milla Jovovich, Ian Holm, Chris Tucker, Luke Perry, John Neville, Mathieu Kassovitz, Julie T Wallace.
126 min.
The 23rd century: Earth's being threatened by a fireball – Absolute Evil – and our only hope lies with the Fifth Element, sent by friendly aliens and given human form as the waifish Leeloo (Jovovich), who's rescued from a suspicious militia by Korben Dallas, spacefighter turned Brooklyn air-cabbie (Willis). Until he takes her to the priest Cornelius (Holm), who alone understands the ancient mysteries, Dallas has no idea of his charge's role in the scheme of things – though her exceptional powers and the unwelcome attentions of Zorg (Oldman), a power-maniac aligned with Evil, soon convince him she's something special. While there's enjoyment to be had from Willis's amiably tongue-in-cheek performance, Dan Weil's production design, Jean-Paul Gaultier's outlandish costumes and Digital Domain's special effects, Besson's futuristic fable is flawed by a messy narrative which strains to incorporate far too many grotesque and eccentric characters. Leeloo's sorrowing horror at humanity's propensity for violence and war is a bit rich in a movie that delights in, and depends for effect on, firepower, explosions and loudly destructive mayhem. GA

Fifth Monkey, The

(Eric Rochat, 1990, US) Ben Kingsley, Mika Lins, Vera Fischer, Silvia De Carvalho.
93 min.
A poor Brazilian trapper sees the lucrative sale of four rare chimpanzees as his pathway to marital happiness with high maintenance widow De Carvalho, but after a perilous journey to the city to find a buyer he realises he's formed a stronger rela-

tionship with his primate pals than he's ever had with his would-be bride. Modest but not unpleasing tropical adventure with a strong eco-friendly message and eye-catching location work. TJ

55 Days at Peking

(Nicholas Ray, 1962, US) Charlton Heston, David Niven, Ava Gardner, Robert Helpmann, Flora Robson, Leo Genn, John Ireland, Kurt Kasznar, Paul Lukas, Harry Andrews.
154 min. U
From its marvellous opening – in the Legation compound at Peking, the troops of eight foreign powers raise their national flags to the accompaniment of a cacophony of national anthems – to the final relief of the diplomats to whom the Boxers have laid siege in the compound, Ray almost transcends the spectacular world of international co-production film deals. He carefully orchestrates the big action sequences (the sine qua non of the Epic) so that they form a mere background to the unfolding drama of the awkward love affair between Heston and Gardner. The result, Ray's farewell to Hollywood, is admittedly a broken-backed movie – producer Samuel Bronston re-cut it – but one full of delicious moments as Ray's camera cranes and swoops around his protagonists, almost taking us back to the nervous grandeur of *Johnny Guitar* on occasion. A magnificent failure. PH

52 Pick-up

(John Frankenheimer, 1986, US) Roy Scheider, Ann-Margret, Vanity, John Glover, Robert Trebor, Clarence Williams III, Lonny Chapman.
110 min.
This is the one Elmore Leonard fans were waiting for, the one that lost least on the swings and roundabouts of translation to the screen. It has, damagingly, exchanged the precise economic placing of Detroit for impersonal LA, fiddled a bit with the plot, but courageously sticks by the unheroic tone of the book. Married Harry's passing fling with a young 'model' places him in the hands of a trio of extortionists. They show him the evidence on video, and when he refuses to pay up, execute his mistress with his gun, and play him the subsequent snuff movie. Harry's survival depends upon his ability to play the unstable trio off against each other. Excellent performances. Best of all is the casting of Williams as Bobby Shy – as shamblingly conspicuous as the brother from another planet, golliwog hair and a too-tight raincoat that clings like a hobo's fart, this is a guy who wants a good leaving alone. BC

Fighting Back

(Michael Caulfield, 1982, Aust) Lewis Fitzgerald, Kris McQuade, Caroline Gillmer, Paul Smith, Robyn Nevin, Wyn Roberts, Ben Gabriel.
100 min.
After much frustrated head-banging, a troublesome boy (Smith) finds a friend (brother, mentor, father figure, etc.) in a well-meaning teacher (Fitz-Gerald) whose revolutionary methods stretch to playing AC/DC in class. Caught between developing the individual relationship of pupil to teacher and exposing the injustices of the educational system, the film opts for an unhelpful sentimentality. The teacher's lack of sexual definition, and the film's refusal to raise the question of sex in general – strange, as its real subject is puberty – makes the subtext of the relationship decidedly odd. Analysts will have a field day, others needn't bother. CPe

Fighting Back (aka Death Vengeance)

(Lewis Teague, 1982, US) Tom Skerritt, Patti LuPone, Michael Sarrazin, Yaphet Kotto, David Rasche.
98 min.
'We gotta go out and scare some respect into these punks.' It's urban vigilante time again, though here more of a clean-streets variant on the current craze for survivalism. Skerritt plays an Italian-American deli owner who organises his People's Neighbourhood Patrol along textbook paramilitary lines, and mounts a violent campaign to stomp all 'deviants' and restore the local park to his kids. There's political conscience somewhere in the script which places its hero as a blood-lust racist and an opportunist politico, but it's all too easily drowned by the crowd-pleaser set pieces of 'righteous' revenge. PT

Fighting Elegy (Kenka Elegy)

(Seijun Suzuki, 1966, Jap) Hideki Takahashi.
86 min. b/w.

Suzuki made more than his share of genre classics, but this (his penultimate film for Nikkatsu) is something else: a completely original anatomy of young male hormones that shows how repressed violence can be channelled into fascism. Being the director he is, Suzuki films it as comedy. It's set in the militarist 1930s, and the 'hero' is a high-school student who finds that a good rumble beats a cold shower. The film has none of Suzuki's usual florid visuals, and doesn't need them. It catches the tone of adolescent fumblings precisely, and its cool 'Scope images give it the contours of a masterpiece. TR

Fighting Justice

see True Believer

Fighting Mad

(Jonathan Demme, 1976, US) Peter Fonda, Lynn Lowry, John Doucette, Philip Carey, Scott Glen, Kathleen Miller.
90 min.

Engaging piece of exploitation that manages to both paint in broad colours and pay attention to detail at the same time. It's rednecks vs yellow hardhats as Arkansas farmers find themselves bulldozed off their property by the unscrupulous mining corporation. Into this conflict comes Fonda, who has got scruples, and a bow-and-arrow. Once his brother and sister-in-law and father have been murdered, he wreaks his own vengeance, blowing up, and maiming, and adjusting his liberal spectacles after every killing. Where writer/director Demme scores is in extracting maximum story value from his cast and location, so that every scrap of sex and violence is highly realistic, and advances the plot. Altogether, another winner from the House of Corman. AN

Fighting Seabees, The

(Edward Ludwig, 1944, US) John Wayne, Susan Hayward, Dennis O'Keefe, William Frawley, Grant Withers, Duncan Renaldo.
100 min. b/w.

Standard World War II flagwaver in which Wayne, having fought for the principle that a non-combatant pioneer corps should nevertheless be armed, spends his time wiping out loads of brutish Japs in between bouts of romancing the pretty (and pretty unbelievable) war correspondent who happens to be on hand in the person of Susan Hayward. TM

Fighting 69th, The

(William Keighley, 1940, US) James Cagney, Pat O'Brien, George Brent, Jeffrey Lynn, Alan Hale, Dennis Morgan, Frank McHugh.
90 min. b/w.

Sentimental propagandist claptrap recounting the heroic adventures of New York's famous Irish regiment during World War I. With distinct echoes of Angels With Dirty Faces – Cagney's the brash punk knocking the company's traditions until he discovers patriotism, O'Brien's the pious priest giving him guidance – the film is one of its star's most sugary, and therefore most disappointing efforts. Still, he does make the film come alive during a couple of hysterical screaming scenes. GA

Figures in a Landscape

(Joseph Losey, 1970, GB) Robert Shaw, Malcolm McDowell, Henry Woolf, Christopher Malcolm.
110 min.

A misguided adaptation of Barry England's excellent novel about two Englishmen on the run from an unspecified prison camp in the Far East (Burma, Korea, Vietnam, take your pick). Re-located in Europe, with Robert Shaw's script still harping insistently on their nationality, one is left wondering bemusedly what military authority two evidently apolitical Englishmen can be running from in fear of instant annihilation. A Kafka nightmare of totalitarianism seems to be the answer, alas. But if you can forget the pretensions and the clumsy characterisations, Losey's direction is a dazzling example of pure mise en scène, with every shot perfectly calculated to frame the theme of two figures caged in a landscape. The sequences in which

they are stalked by a helicopter playing cat-and-mouse are good enough to suspend disbelief in the game. TM

File of the Golden Goose, The

(Sam Wanamaker, 1968, GB) Yul Brynner, Edward Woodward, Charles Gray, John Barrie, Bernard Archard, Adrienne Corri.
109 min.

Lots of red London buses and telephone boxes in this touristy-looking thriller from the scrag end of the Swinging London scene. Brynner's the American agent who hits Blighty in search of the gang of murderous counterfeiters who killed his girl, while Woodward is the decent British copper Scotland Yard insist on having in on the case. The movie's a bit of a plod too, though Gray enjoys himself as the chief villain. TJ

File on Thelma Jordon, The

(Robert Siodmak, 1950, US) Barbara Stanwyck, Wendell Corey, Paul Kelly, Joan Tetzel, Stanley Ridges, Richard Rober, Barry Kelley.
100 min. b/w.

A fine film noir which works an ingenious, intricate variation on the situation in Double Indemnity, but which takes its tone, unlike Wilder's film, not from Stanwyck's glittering siren who courts her own comeuppance ('Judgement day, Jordon!'), but from the nondescript assistant DA she drives to the brink of destruction. The part is played (remarkably well) by Corey, whose haunted, hangdog persona as a perennial loser is echoed so perfectly by the deliberately slow, inexorable tempo of Siodmak's direction (not to mention George Barnes' superbly bleak lighting) that the film emerges with a quality akin to Lang's dark, romantic despair. TM

Fille de D'Artagnan, La (D'Artagnan's Daughter)

(Bertrand Tavernier, 1994, Fr) Sophie Marceau, Philippe Noiret, Claude Rich, Charlotte Kady, Sami Frey, Jean-Luc Bideau, Raoul Billerey, Nils Tavernier.
130 min.

1654, the South of France. When horsemen follow a runaway black slave into the convent where he's taken sanctuary and kill both the fugitive and the Mother Superior, they little realise that one of the novices is Eloïse (Marceau), spirited sprog of retired musketeer D'Artagnan (Noiret). Suspecting that the murders are somehow linked to a plot against Louis XIV, the girl dons buckskins and sword and rides off, accompanied by an adoring poet (Tavernier) acquired en route, to ask her dad to protect the boy king. Only when the headstrong Eloïse seems set to fall into the hands of the villainous Duc de Crassac (Rich) and his scarlet mistress (Kady) does D'Artagnan return to the fray. Tavernier's swashbuckler never quite turns into parody and never quite plays it straight. Sadly, it never quite takes off, either. Yes, it's as good-natured and elegant to look at as one might expect, but the leisurely pace sags at times, and the two main conceits – centring the film on a feisty female and stressing the way age has affected the musketeers' skills and ideals – are hardly original. Good swordplay, but a bit too much breezy banter. GA

Fille de l'Air, La

(Maroun Bagdadi, 1992, Fr) Béatrice Dalle, Thierry Fortineau, Hippolyte Girardot, Roland Bertin, Liliane Rovère.
106 min.

This big-screen treatment of a notorious 1986 French prison breakout plays rather like an extended TV 'reconstruction'. It's based on the autobiography of Nadine Vaujour (Dalle), a secretary who fell for fugitive armed robber Michel (Fortineau), when her petty-crook brother asked her to shelter him. After a doomed attempt to go straight, Michel was recaptured and given a heavy sentence, while Nadine served several months on a complicity charge – during which time the couple married and she gave birth to a son. On release, distressed by Michel's mental deterioration, this determined woman learned to fly a helicopter and successfully freed her husband from prison. Lebanese director Bagdadi handles the physical details with visceral aplomb (a raid on the Vaujour household is, for example, absolutely terrifying), but neglects the contextualising niceties of characterisation. It's

one thing to allow the audience room to consider their own moral perspective, another, surely, to leave the motivations of these real-life people so frustratingly opaque. A stellar cast can do little but look scruffy and hope the narrative's factual interest gets them through. It does (just), but the psychological grit of the story is clearly elsewhere. TJ

Fillmore

(Richard T Heffron, 1972, US) The Grateful Dead, Jefferson Airplane, Hot Tuna, NRPS, Quicksilver Messenger Service, Santana, Cold Blood and Lamb, Bill Graham.
105 min.

A clumsy, cluttered, grainy tribute to San Francisco's former music Vatican, shot during the venue's final week. The views of promoter Bill Graham (a manic, chest-thumping telephone thug) quickly cease to amuse as he's allowed to thunder one-dimensionally onwards, volume constantly on the up. In between times, a motley selection of performers deliver predominantly lacklustre material to an unimaginative film crew. A still splendidly gritty Box Scaggs is the easy victor, while only the most fervent Jefferson Airplane fans are advised to wade through the surrounding swamp for the measly minute or so of 'Up Against the Wall' offered here. Cinephiles may be able to squeeze an odd laugh from the cretinous use of split screen, but that's pitiful compensation for one of the worst music films of the past decade. GD

Film

(Alan Schneider, 1965, US) Buster Keaton.
22 min. b/w.

A man scrambles through a silent grey landscape to his sparsely decorated room, where he systematically rids himself of every possible witness to his existence: pets, mirror, a picture of a staring ancient god, photos of his own past. But also watching him is someone else, embodied by the gaze of the camera, which remains behind the man virtually throughout the film. There is a profound philosophical theme in Beckett's sole foray into cinema, based on the idea to be/exist is to be perceived. But perhaps more intriguing than Beckett's largely successful attempt to examine an abstract epistemological concept through the materialist medium of film, is the wholly appropriate casting of Keaton who, in the classic comedies of the '20s, envisaged a universe notable for its cruel, arbitrary absurdity, and who, perhaps, anticipated Beckett's thesis on perception (and cinema) in Sherlock Junior. Dark, witty and fascinating.

Film About a Woman Who...

(Yvonne Rainer, 1974, US) Dempster Leech, Shirley Soffer, John Erdman, Renfreu Neff, James Barth.
105 min. b/w & col.

Rainer's second feature takes 'performing' as a central theme and metaphor. The protagonists are at once dancers, actors and lovers – for others, for an audience. The context they are set in constitutes a remarkable juxtaposition of visual and verbal descriptive methods: inter-titles, written texts, voices off, dance, slides and acted sequences. Insight, irony and wit are marvellously combined, reaching a height in the appropriately labelled central section, 'An Emotional Accretion in 48 Steps'. SF

Film from the Clyde

(Cinema Action, 1977, GB)
83 min.

Halfway through this documentary study of the work-in at Upper Clyde Shipbuilders in 1971, one of the workers says, 'This is a group of workers who are not going to grovel, tugging their forelocks, to the labour exchange'. Such clarity of expression and considered determination to participate in the political process powerfully highlights the platitudinous gobbledegook of declared official policy: 'to keep what is in the long term keepable'. The film serves as an enlightening view of exactly how workers can help determine their own future by refusing to be sacrificed to the forces of capitalism (albeit in the name of economic expediency). SM

Filofax

see Taking Care of Business

Fils du Requin, Le
see Shark's Son

Final Analysis
(Phil Joanou, 1992, US) Richard Gere, Kim Basinger, Uma Thurman, Eric Roberts, Paul Guilfoyle, Keith David, Robert Harper, Harris Yulin.
124 min.
It's not clear whether this film's genesis is Hitchcock homage or an attempt to build on the success of *Prime Suspect* and *Jagged Edge*. The result is an overlong, hardly believable psychological thriller in which Gere plays a San Francisco shrink involved with the older sister of one of his more disturbed patients. Gere (who spends much of his time testifying in court for the defence) becomes embroiled with Basinger in no time at all. After a heady trip to a very obviously phallic lighthouse, the 'double jeopardy' plot spins off into the blue yonder when she bumps off her fashionable but sadistic American-Greek gangster husband (Roberts, acting with his muscles). While Basinger has the projection, it's Thurman as her younger sister who has most of the real allure, though much of the film's latter half is taken up with a rather tedious game to decide which sis is the psycho. It's hard to care in the end. SGr

Final Combination
(Nigel Dick, 1993, US) Michael Madsen, Lisa Bonet, Gary Stretch, Tim Russ, Damian Chapa, Carmen Argenziano.
93 min.
Detective Madsen teams up with reporter Bonet to track down serial killer Stretch. Cop falls for scribe, scribe knows something about the nutcase, nutcase has things in common with cop, etc. Very ordinary. AO

Final Conflict, The
(Graham Baker, 1981, US) Sam Neill, Rossano Brazzi, Don Gordon, Lisa Harrow, Barnaby Holm, Mason Adams, Robert Arden,
108 min.
The third part of *The Omen* trilogy is contrived as a series of set pieces whose point is the grisliest possible end for the Antichrist's victims. Damien is now head of the world's largest multinational corporation, a powerful and charismatic man in his early thirties, and the eventual corpses are a band of seven Italian monks armed with sacred daggers, out to stop Damien from preventing the Second Coming (by slaughtering all first-born males). If these elements make it a suitable entrant in the cinema's long blood sports lists, it must be said that the non-delivery of Satan's promised reign is something of a letdown. Still, it does mark a return of sorts to the stylishness of *The Omen* after the tackiness of *Damien – Omen II*. RM

Final Countdown, The
(Don Taylor, 1980, US) Kirk Douglas, Martin Sheen, Katharine Ross, James Farentino, Ron O'Neal, Charles Durning.
105 min.
What happens when the mighty US aircraft carrier 'Nimitz' is carried through a timewarp to find itself off Pearl Harbor minutes before the Japs attack in 1941? An idea worthy of Harlan Ellison, but disappointingly fumbled. Taylor handles most of the aircraft carrier material like a recruiting film, and though the script manages a few deft twists and turns, and even a neat final frisson, it ultimately works more on the tease level of a TV episode than as a movie. Sheen's performance, as always, is engagingly low-key. DP

Finally Sunday!
see Vivement Dimanche!

Final Programme, The
(aka The Last Days of Man on Earth)
(Robert Fuest, 1973, GB) Jon Finch, Jenny Runacre, Sterling Hayden, Harry Andrews, Hugh Griffith, Julie Ege, Patrick Magee, Graham Crowden, George Coulouris.
89 min.
Read Michael Moorcock's novel first and you might make sense of this garbled sci-fi fantasy about scientists trying to breed a self-reproducing

hermaphrodite as the end of the world approaches. Concentrating as always on giving his work a chic gloss, Fuest (acting as his own set designer) simply lets things drift from muddle to muddle while a few moments of black comedy surface. TM

Final Terror, The
(aka Campsite Massacre)
(Andrew Davis, 1981, US) John Friedrich, Adrian Zmed, Daryl Hannah, Rachel Ward, Ernest Harden Jr.
84 min.
The carnage count turns out to be remarkably low for this sort of crud. Also low is the originality quotient, but the borrowings (*Psycho* meets *Texas Chainsaw* via *Southern Comfort* and *Deliverance*) are cobbled together with a surprising amount of flair. A group of young persons go out into the woods and immediately break all the Rules for Characters in Horror Movies; they split up, turn their backs to the camera, and commit sylvan fornication (for which sin, as we all know, the penalty is aaagghh). It only confirms everything you have always feared about camping holidays; but at least one of the party is as loony as the maniac, and the fledgling forest-rovers prove to be a mite more resourceful than the usual teens in peril, most notably when Rachel Ward patches up someone's slashed throat with needle and thread. AB

Finders Keepers
(Richard Lester, 1984, US) Michael O'Keefe, Beverly D'Angelo, Louis Gossett Jr, Pamela Stephenson, Ed Lauter, David Wayne, Brian Dennehy, John Schuck.
96 min.
While Lester's variable output has been a lot more variable than most, nothing in his assorted canon quite prepares one for the full ghastliness here. Apparently starting from the assumption that *Honky Tonk Freeway* was one of the major movies of our time, this sets off in hot emulation, by rail this time rather than road. The plot has the luckless O'Keefe teaming up with D'Angelo (doing her by now depressingly familiar screwball kookie routine) on the trail of the usual cache of stolen goodies. Lester, whose soft spot for particularly witless capers has been well documented, tries to shore things up with as much trickery as he can muster, but it's a doomed exercise. JP

Fin du Jour, La
(The End of the Day)
(Julien Duvivier, 1939, Fr) Louis Jouvet, Michel Simon, Victor Francen, Madeleine Ozeray, Gabrielle Dorziat, François Périer, Sylvie.
108 min. b/w.
Set in an abbey that serves as a retirement home for actors, rife with squabbles, jealousies and remembrances of past glory, to which a threat of closure adds waves of despairing self-pity, *La Fin du Jour* once rated highly as a biting depictment (like *La Règle du Jeu* though in a different key) of the decadence of France just before World War II. Despite its dark edges, it hasn't worn nearly so well as Renoir's masterpiece, with a complacently whimsical sentimentality constantly threatening to break through. The performances, though, are terrific: Jouvet as the suave ladykiller determined to maintain his image at all costs; Simon as the hopeless man who lived out a marginal career as the eternal understudy; Francen as the classical artist too proud to court popular success and still regretting it. TM

Fine Madness, A
(Irvin Kershner, 1966, US) Sean Connery, Joanne Woodward, Jean Seberg, Patrick O'Neal, Clive Revill, Jackie Coogan.
104 min.
An engaging, sharply scripted comedy (Elliott Baker, from his own novel), with Connery oddly but not inaptly cast as a poet driven berserk by the frustrations of wage-earning in New York. Perceptive, persuasive and often very funny, especially in a sequence where Connery, forced to address a staid group of female culture-vultures because he needs the fee, gets drunk and proceeds to relieve his feelings ('Open your corsets and bloom…let the metaphors creep above your knees'). Silly farce takes over latterly as a doctor he has cuckolded vengefully prescribes a pre-frontal lobotomy (which has no effect). Ted McCord's location camerawork, and Woodward's performance as the poet's harassed, embarrassed wife, are outstanding. TM

Fine Mess, A
(Blake Edwards, 1986, US) Ted Danson, Howie Mandel, Richard Mulligan, Stuart Margolin, Maria Conchita Alonso, Jennifer Edwards, Paul Sorvino.
90 min.
Clever of Blake Edwards to review his frenetic comedy in the title, but after that it's downhill all the way to the tune of screeching tires, the jabber of gibberish, and a hysteria count likely to leave audiences gasping like goldfish. What plot there is has movie extra Danson blundering into a racehorse-nobbling racket, and attempting to stay one car chase ahead of the cops, the mob and a string of irate old flames long enough to collect his ill-gotten winnings. This involves more crashes than the M1 on a Bank Holiday, a host of throwaway jokes which should all have been thrown away, and wild overacting all round. The biggest disappointment is Danson, who created an exquisite satire on the American superstud in TV's *Cheers*; his extension of the role here, as Sex Machine Spence, is a downright embarrassment. DAt

Finger Man, The
see Doulos, Le

Finger of Guilt
see Intimate Stranger, The

Fingers
(James Toback, 1978, US) Harvey Keitel, Jim Brown, Tisa Farrow, Michael V Gazzo, Tanya Roberts.
91 min.
Bearing not a little resemblance to Scorsese's *Mean Streets*, not to mention Toback's earlier script for Karel Reisz's *The Gambler*, this is a raw thriller-cum-psychodrama about a split personality: Keitel plays an aspiring concert pianist strangely fascinated by the violence he encounters while enforcing the payment of 'debts' owed to his criminal father. The idea is none too original, and the film can certainly be faulted for its macho posturing and unquestioning misogyny. Nonetheless, Toback, making his directing debut, is clearly exorcising – or indulging – a few personal demons, and the perverse conviction of Keitel's tormented performance, reinforced by restless, sometimes volatile visuals, prevents the overheated plot from becoming entirely risible. It's not exactly pleasant, but it is compelling. GA

Finian's Rainbow
(Francis Ford Coppola, 1968, US) Fred Astaire, Petula Clark, Tommy Steele, Don Francks, Barbara Hancock, Keenan Wynn, Al Freeman Jr.
144 min.
An underrated musical, admittedly a little dated in the social comment (on labour exploitation and race relations) which probably seemed quite daring on the original's Broadway debut in 1947. But Burton Lane's score – intact save for the curious omission of the marvellous 'Necessity' – is still first rate, and Coppola steers his motley cast through it with an instinct for rhythm and movement which shows that the choreographic preoccupation which surfaced in his work starting with 'One From The Heart' was nothing new. Certainly the best of the latter-day musicals in the tradition of Minnelli and MGM. TM

Finnegans Wake
(aka Passages from James Joyce's Finnegans Wake)
(Mary Ellen Bute, 1965, US) Martin J Kelly, Jane Reilly, Peter Haskell, Page Johnson, John V Kelleher, Ray Flanagan.
97 min. b/w.
A surprisingly successful attempt to bring Joyce's gargantuan novel to the screen – especially surprising considering Mary Ellen Bute's previous work for the cinema (some very footling animation à la McLaren). The reason probably lies in her use of the play adaptation by Mary Manning, which transforms much of the original's humour and verbal fireworks into stunning theatre. The film isn't stunning cinema, but it's consistently entertaining and far more Joycean than Joseph Strick's pedantic efforts. GB

Finyé (The Wind)

(Souleymane Cissé, 1982, Mali) Fousseyni Sissoko, Goundo Guisse, Balla Moussa Keita, Ismaila Sarr, Oumou Diarra.
105 min.

A campus protest movie, complete with drugs, generation gaps, fascistic policing and boy-girl problems. Cissé's students actually are living under a military dictatorship and trying to come to terms with a patriarchal society still weighed down with hundreds of superstitions. No one is caricatured, and the film develops its conflicts with splendid directness, shifting easily between realism and fantasy. It boils down to a fairly simple argument for liberal democracy, but the specifics of the setting give it an immediacy that an equivalent western film could never approach. TR

Fiore delle Mille e una Notte, Il

see Arabian Nights

Fiorile

(Paolo Taviani/Vittorio Taviani, 1993, It/Fr/Ger) Claudio Bigagli, Galatea Ranzi, Michael Vartan, Lino Capolicchio, Constanza Engelbrecht.
118 min.

The Tavianis' film recounts the changing fortunes of a Tuscan family – the Benedetti ('blessed'), later known as the Maledetti ('cursed') – from the time of the Napoleonic Wars, when a young girl's love for a French soldier is thwarted by her brother's theft of gold from the invading army's coffers, to the present day, when one of the girl's descendants returns from France with his children to introduce them to their disillusioned, reclusive grandfather. In the intervening years, even when the family was at its wealthiest at the start of the 20th century, ambition, guilt, power and desire for vengeance dominated the Benedettis' lives – but what of the future? Will the children at last be able to shake off the 200-year-old 'curse'? A film of immense elegance, the Tuscan landscape ravishingly photographed by Giuseppe Lanci, the poignant emotions subtly underscored by Nicola Piovani's characteristically lovely music. GA

Fire

(Earl Bellamy, 1977, US) Ernest Borgnine, Vera Miles, Patty Duke Astin, Alex Cord, Donna Mills, Lloyd Nolan, Neville Brand, Ty Hardin, Gene Evans.
100 min.

Spectacularly ham-fisted disaster movie (made for TV). The disaster this time is a forest fire, ignited by convict Neville Brand as part of an elaborate escape plan. Bellamy's sluggish direction dampens every opportunity for suspense as he brings together groups of gruff rangers, public-spirited prisoners, an anguished teacher and her cosmetic schoolchildren, an incredibly silly couple of doctors whose marriage is on the rocks, and two ageing sweethearts. Curdled sentiment predominates, the performances are uniformly awful, and the script ('Any psychiatrist would tell us that our real problem is your father') is stilted in the extreme. IB

Fire

(Deepa Mehta, 1996, Can) Shabana Azmi, Nandita Das, Kulbushan Kharbanda, Jaaved Jaaferi, Ranjit Chowdhury.
104 min.

Adultery, masturbation and lesbianism...this taboo-breaking Indian film from the producer of Bandit Queen has 'em all. Significantly, perhaps, it's in English, but otherwise the portrait of a New Delhi household caught between the contradictory impulses of duty and desire rings reasonably true (though the emancipated new bride Sita may be a somewhat idealised figure). It's a courageous picture that never gets too pompous – writer/director Mehta isn't above interjecting a parodic fantasy sequence or a song – very attractively photographed by Giles Nuttgens, with radiant performances from Azmi and Das. TCh

Fire and Ice

(Ralph Bakshi, 1982, US) voices: Randy Norton, Cynthia Leake, Steve Sandor, Sean Hannon, Leo Gordon.
82 min.

More cut-ups from Bakshi's animated cut-outs.

Here his collaborator is Frank Frazetta, dean of Sword'n'Sorcery illustration – and with predictable results. It's all Chas Atlas heroes slicing one another to bits in order to win ladies with more curves than a bunch of grapes. Complete with sub-Wagnerian score and just a hint of subliminal racism – the disposable 'subhumans' are dusky chaps, the hero an Aryan blond – it may well satisfy a low IQ, pubescent (probably) male Iron Maiden fan, but the rest of us are poorly served. GD

Firebirds (aka Wings of the Apache)

(David Green, 1990, US) Nicolas Cage, Tommy Lee Jones, Sean Young, Bryan Kestner, Dale Dye, Mary Ellen Trainor, JA Preston, Peter Onorati.
86 min.

When the American military decides to wade in against Latin American drug cartel terrorism, young pilot Jake Preston (Cage) joins the task force, and undergoes training by Brad Little (Jones) on the wonder attack-helicopter known as the Apache. Brad can spot a soul-mate: 'I joined the army to kick ass' he tells Jake, 'and so did you'. Problems with his sight and ex-girlfriend/fellow pilot Billie Lee (Young) ruffle Jake's plans. Inevitable comparisons with Top Gun leave this action adventure wanting. With a gung ho script, sometimes rudimentary editing and uninvolving relationships, the whole effect is rather flat. None of the aerial sequences boast the visual thrills of Top Gun, while even the attempt to inject controversy in the shape of Hollywood's first female combatant is half-realised. In mid-battle, a pursued Billie Lee pleads, 'Oh Jake, save my ass'. She should have heard his reason for enlisting. CM

Fire Festival (Himatsuri)

(Mitsuo Yanagimachi, 1984, Jap) Kinya Kitaoji, Kiwako Taichi, Ryota Nakamoto, Norihei Miki, Rikiya Yasuoka.
120 min.

This deals with Grand Themes – mankind versus nature, the immanence of the divine – without seeming either stupid or pretentious. Yanagimachi starts from a brilliant location (a small coastal town ringed by mountains), and then tells an extraordinary tale. An ultra-macho lumberjack identifies completely with the forests he pillages. He is sexually unfulfilled by his marriage, by an old flame, and by the vaguely gay thing he has going with the teenage boy on his team; his sexual energies, nurtured by the pantheist tradition of shinto, are focused on the goddesses of the place. His mind finally snaps during the town's annual fire festival, leading to a truly shattering climax. Ecological and social issues resonate in the background, and the haunting sounds and images will leave most audiences shaken, stirred and awed. TR

Firefox

(Clint Eastwood, 1982, US) Clint Eastwood, Freddie Jones, David Huffman, Warren Clarke, Ronald Lacey, Kenneth Colley.
136 min.

Ex-Vietnam flier with poor nerves (and bad case of flashbacks) is ordered to steal deadly Russian jet from behind 'enemy' lines. The simple storyline is quickly grounded by flying chunks of exposition that director/actor Eastwood tries to ignore. Eastwood the director disregards many Cold War possibilities, preferring to dawdle over a first hour that mooches along while Eastwood the actor enjoyably dons various disguises, playing a man who can't act (or so everyone tells him) and is happiest left alone with his gippy nerves. Only in the airborne climax – a prolonged chase of modest ability – does he achieve solitary ecstasy, while, with a touch so perverse as to be admirable, the wordy finale is left to a foreign actor whose English is actually incomprehensible. CPe

Fire in the Sky

(Robert Lieberman, 1993, US) DB Sweeney, Robert Patrick, James Garner, Craig Sheffer, Peter Berg, Henry Thomas.
109 min.

This modest sci-fi movie treads the same ground as Communion, but more purposefully. The small community of Snowflake, Arizona, is thrown into confusion when loggers return from the forest claiming one of their number has been taken away in a spacecraft. A sceptical special investi-

gator (Garner) shares the locals' doubts, believing the story is a cover for murder...until the missing man (Sweeney) turns up with his own incredible story. The imagery is familiar: scientific experiments in which orifices are penetrated, and womblike interiors representing primal fears about the integrity of the body. Surely this is inner, not outer space. Even so, the handling of the small-town social dynamics, the media circus and the scary special effects provide an engrossing build-up and satisfying pay-off. NF

Firemen's Ball, The (Horí, má Panenko)

(Milos Forman, 1967, Czech/It) Jan Vostrcil, Josef Kolb, Josef Svet, Frantisek Debelka, Josef Sebánek.
73 min.

The scene is the annual firemen's ball in a small Czech town. The action, characteristically tenuous but packed with detail, concerns the committee's efforts to round up girls for a beauty contest, the winner to make the presentation of a golden hatchet to their 86-year-old retiring president. As the ball proceeds, a patchwork of comic incident unfolds: the committee, finding girls too shy and mothers too ferocious, are busily trying to hijack any girl, pretty or not; an anxious official watches as the lottery prizes mysteriously vanish one by one; and the ancient president, desperate to slip away for a pee, is kept forcibly waiting and waiting. Quietly, irresistibly funny in the early Forman manner (this was his first film in colour); but the belated switch to allegorical satire (in the closing sequences, an elderly peasant's house burns down while the firemen revel; a sympathetic whip-round nets the now worthless lottery tickets for him) seems altogether too sour in the context. TM

Fire Monsters Against the Son of Hercules

see Maciste contro i Mostri

Fire Over England

(William K Howard, 1936, GB) Flora Robson, Laurence Olivier, Leslie Banks, Raymond Massey, Vivien Leigh, Tamara Desni, James Mason.
92 min. b/w.

Lavish Korda production designed partly as a coronation year spectacular, partly as a call to arms against the Nazi threat. The script is the usual historico-romantico bunk, tricked out with some literary frills and providing some mild swashbuckling for Olivier, playing a young man seeking revenge for his father's death at the hands of the Spanish Inquisition, and simultaneously serving Queen and Country by obtaining advance news of the Armada. Directed stylishly enough, but it gets by mainly on the handsome sets, superb camerawork (Wong Howe), and some sterling performances (notably Robson's pawky Queen Elizabeth and Massey as the villainous Philip of Spain). Pity the climactic burning of the Armada is so obviously tank-bound. TM

Firepower

(Michael Winner, 1979, GB) Sophia Loren, James Coburn, OJ Simpson, Eli Wallach, Anthony Franciosa, George Grizzard, Vincent Gardenia.
104 min.

Typically brash and lurid thriller from Winner, which starts off with Loren's chemist husband being blown up as he's on the point of exposing a racket in contaminated drugs. As Loren and an ex-lover (Coburn) try to track down the killers, the film turns into an endless series of noisy, colourful explosions and crashes in glossily picturesque locations. Tiresome. GA

Firestarter

(Mark L Lester, 1984, US) David Keith, Drew Barrymore, Freddie Jones, Heather Locklear, Martin Sheen, George C Scott, Art Carney, Louise Fletcher, Moses Gunn, Antonio Fargas.
114 min.

Stephen King's novel not only concerns that most awkward of all combinations, the CIA and paranormal psychology, it has the episodic quality that is a hallmark of King's less filmable fiction. Barrymore (the sister in E.T.) plays a girl with telekinetic powers who is eventually captured and shoved into a government laboratory. Lester manages to maintain a fair level of suspense, and he is greatly helped by Scott, giving his best performance in years as the demonic CIA man sporting a sneer and a pony tail, but King's supernatural ideas need a human focus or they seem nearly idiotic. And, unlike the central figures in *Carrie* or *The Shining*, the heroine of *Firestarter* is just a rather wet little girl who happens to throw fireballs. DP

Fires Were Started (aka I Was a Fireman)
(Humphrey Jennings, 1943, GB) George Gravett, Philip Dickson, Fred Griffiths, Loris Rey, Johnny Houghton.
80 min. b/w.
Jennings' one venture into feature-length drama-documentary narrowly escaped being brutally chopped down by the publicity men at the Ministry of Information. Certainly it lacks the tight narrative structure common in good commercial films, but Jennings is a strong enough film-maker to ignore formulae and conventions to build his own unique structures. Here he used real firemen and real fires – kindled among the blitzed warehouses of London's dockland – but with the aim of creating something more than documentary realism. It is the epic quality of the firemen's struggle that excites Jennings, and his celebration of the courage and dignity of ordinary people working together in the shadow of disaster makes the film extraordinarily impressive. RMy

Fire with Fire
(Duncan Gibbins, 1986, US) Virginia Madsen, Craig Sheffer, Jon Polito, Jeffrey Jay Cohen, DB Sweeney, Kate Reid, Jean Smart, Ann Savage.
103 min.
It's romance across the tracks time as reform school kid Sheffer goes on the run with Catholic schoolgirl Madsen in this time-passer which went straight-to-video in Britain. Trivia fans will tick the presence of *Detour*'s Ann Savage in a small role as one of the nuns. The title conceals a tragic irony: Duncan Gibbins, the British-born writer/director, perished when a forest inferno swallowed up his Los Angeles home in 1994. TJ

Fire Within, The
see Feu Follet, Le

Fire Within, The (Onibi)
(Rokuro Mochizuki, 1997, Jap) Yoshio Harada, Reiko Kataoka, Sho Aikawa, Yashushi Kitamura, Noriko Hayami, Eiji Okuda.
101 min.
There's nothing startlingly original about this tale of a gangster trying to go straight on his release from prison (no, he doesn't succeed for long), but Mochizuki finds a fresh, sidelong slant on even the most hackneyed situations. Yoshio Harada – a laconic tough guy in the Takeshi Kitano mould – makes Kuni a decent, if impatient man. His actions carry real weight, allowing the director to develop an unexpectedly romantic tone. TCh

Fireworks
see Anger Magick Lantern Cycle, The

Firm, The
(Sydney Pollack, 1993, US) Tom Cruise, Gene Hackman, Gary Busey, Holly Hunter, Jeanne Tripplehorn, Hal Holbrook, Ed Harris, Toibin Bell.
154 min.
Pollack's conventional race-against-time version of John Grisham's best-seller soft pedals on the novel's conspiracy-paranoia atmosphere, makes goons of the Mob, and shows signs of having been rewritten. But it does have Cruise as the go-for-it law graduate, whose now rather faded physical charm takes nothing from his dumb-but-earnest ingénu appeal. The plot has Cruise scorn the advances of the big Eastern law firms for a small 'family'-oriented outfit in Memphis, only to find rottenness at the heart and hearth of the New South. Adorning the film, in supporting roles, are its saving graces: Hackman's moving and dissolute *consigliere*/father-figure; madcap investigator Busey and floozy helpmeet Hunter; and Bell's eerily engaging white-haired psychopath. WH

First a Girl
(Victor Saville, 1935, GB) Jessie Matthews, Sonnie Hale, Griffith Jones, Anna Lee, Alfred Drayton, Martita Hunt.
94 min. b/w.
The last in a series of German musicals transposed into English (and later remade with Julie Andrews as *Victor/Victoria*). Matthews is, as usual, an aspiring seamstress whose singing and dancing ambitions are fulfilled only after a sequence of sexual shenanigans. In *Evergreen* she won fame and fortune by impersonating her granny. Here, doing a *Tootsie* in reverse, she resorts to playing a female impersonator – with understandably convincing results. Saville doesn't quite get his Busby Berkeley act together, and an aura of inane innocence keeps at bay the interesting undertones of the plot. But for an English musical, this is tight, professional and unpretentious, and Matthews has a winsome vitality which is irresistible. RMy

First Blood
(Ted Kotcheff, 1982, US) Sylvester Stallone, Richard Crenna, Brian Dennehy, David Caruso, Jack Starrett, Michael Talbott.
97 min.
A long-haired undesirable, run off-limits by a small town sheriff, turns right around and comes back. Taken to the police station for a spot of persuasion, he suffers flash recalls of torture in Vietnam. Going momentarily berserk, and hounded like a mad dog, he leads his pursuers a frightening dance through the woods before returning to give the town its comeuppance. As a Stallone vehicle this is sleek, slick and not unexciting, but crassly castrates the David Morrell novel on which it is based. Read the book: tough, provocative, savagely ironical and infinitely more complex, it's much better value. TM

First Deadly Sin, The
(Brian G Hutton, 1980, US) Frank Sinatra, Faye Dunaway, David Dukes, George Coe, Brenda Vaccaro, Martin Gabel, Anthony Zerbe, James Whitmore.
112 min.
Dull, confused thriller, with cop Sinatra tracking down an apparently motiveless murderer, meanwhile worrying about his wife becoming increasingly unhealthy after a kidney operation. Totally superfluous religious imagery haunts the plot, the relationship between Sinatra and Dunaway seems to have been inserted entirely for sentimental reasons, and the whole thing fails to convince throughout. GA

First Effort (Opera Prima)
(Fernando Trueba, 1979, Sp) Oscar Ladoire, Paula Molina, Antonio Resines, Kitty Manver, Marisa Paredes.
Romantic comedy of manners manqué, set in the post-Franco Swinging '70s and centred on a super-conventional Antoine Doinel clone and his encounters: with a sweet young thing and her swain; his waspish ex-spouse; one Belch, nihilist author of *Dried Shit* (subtle humour this isn't); Zoila, blue movie-maker who gets off on bestiality and ball-breaking fornication; and a bizarrely incongruous Ingmar Bergman, who luckily never appears. Well-liked in New York ('a new Woody Allen') and France ('neo-Truffaut'), this peevish and impatient portrait of Spain's late-blossoming flower generation has the generosity and incisiveness of neither. SJo

First Great Train Robbery, The (aka The Great Train Robbery)
(Michael Crichton, 1978, GB) Sean Connery, Donald Sutherland, Lesley-Anne Down, Alan Webb, Malcolm Terris, Robert Lang, Michael Elphick.
111 min.
Connery and Sutherland as a pair of freewheeling Victorian criminals in the Butch and Sundance mould who attempt to rob a bullion train. Crichton's adaptation of his own novel falls badly between genres, never quite making up its mind whether it's aiming for comedy or suspense, and not succeeding very conclusively at either. The characters stay largely undeveloped, while – despite superficially peculiar features – the robbery is stripped of the ingenious exposition of the novel to become just another heist. There are

some excellent sequences, notably those built around the search for the bullion keys; but in general this odd hybrid cuts through the crap of much period melodrama without finding anything very substantial to put in its place. DP

First Knight
(Jerry Zucker, 1994, US) Richard Gere, Sean Connery, Julia Ormond, Ben Cross, Liam Cunningham, Christopher Villiers, Valentine Pelka, Colin McCormack, John Gielgud.
134 min.
This expensive, star-heavy retake on the Arthurian legend works well enough as Hollywood Gothic hokum: Connery is his usual reliable self as the renowned first among equals; Ormond is quite excellent as a thoroughly modern maiden torn between love and duty; and Gere's fearless Lancelot may be about as medieval as a roller disco but still has charm and athleticism (less Lancelot du Lac than Lancelot du Lacquer). William Nicholson's script produces a few dud lines, but the big scenes are spaciously put together and the final sequence in which Arthur is launched towards Avalon on a raft ignited by a lone arrow is genuinely touching. There's even a cameo by Gielgud and the semblance of a happy ending to a story that is usually shrouded in mist and tears. No Merlin, no Holy Grail, and no Lady of the Lake. Lots of lovely torches though and some really neat crossbows. SGr

First Legion, The
(Douglas Sirk, 1950, US) Charles Boyer, William Demarest, Lyle Bettger, Barbara Rush, Leo G Carroll, HB Warner, George Zucco.
86 min. b/w.
Something of an oddity in the Sirk canon, in that it was shot on location and is unusually static and talky. It concerns various crises of religious faith suffered by a number of priests in a Jesuit seminary; Sirk admitted that he wanted to push it towards comedy, since the subject as he saw it related religion to the absurd, namely a bogus 'miracle', performed by an atheist doctor on a crippled priest, which revives belief among the brotherhood. The film, it must be said, is not one of the director's best; his interest in his material seems academic rather than inspired, and there's scant evidence of the irony that informs his finest work. Even so, the performances are generally very impressive (perhaps most notably Demarest, cast against type) and the film is for the most part free of the winsome pieties commonly found in Hollywood films dealing with devotion and divine mystery. GA

First Love
(Joan Darling, 1977, US) William Katt, Susan Dey, John Heard, Beverly D'Angelo, Robert Loggia, Tom Lacy, Swoosie Kurtz.
92 min. 15.
College romance set in an unspecified American institution. Katt, alternately called 'sweet' or 'a very special person', takes love seriously and loses his marbles over Dey. He describes her as 'fragile', but she seems surprisingly resilient, having been involved with a charmless older man (Loggia) for three years, no doubt a surrogate for the father who shot himself. Through this ogre the relationship sours, but they adapt and life goes on. Not a bad story, but a pity that director Darling spends so much time setting up such a condescending approximation of contemporary college life, full of merry japes, poignant incoherence, and all those clichés about sex for the under 21s. Don't rate Cat Stevens' mood music much either. JS

First Love (Chut Sarang)
(Lee Myung-Se, 1992, SKor) Kim Hae-Soo, Song Young-Chang, Cho Min-Gi, Choi Jong-Won.
108 min.
Shot almost entirely on the studio lot, Lee's extraordinary vision of a shy 19-year-old student's unrequited love for her drama teacher unfolds in the run-up to a college production of Thornton Wilder's *Our Town*. The film's own tonal emphasis balances the touching romantic innocence of the girl with the knowing by-play of florid fantasy and down-home reality surrounding her. There's humour and deft observation here; but it's rare to find a movie deep-hearted enough to

give touching consideration to the purity of a love untainted by bitter experience, or indeed to view the loss of these illusions with such warm compassion. Unexpectedly impressive. TJ

First Man into Tokyo

see First Yank into Tokyo

First Monday in October

(Ronald Neame, 1981, US) Walter Matthau, Jill Clayburgh, Barnard Hughes, Jan Sterling, James Stephens, Joshua Bryant, Wiley Harker.
99 min.
In which the rule is disproved that any film starring Walter Matthau can't be all bad. The date of the title marks the opening session of the US Supreme Court, when liberal Justice Snow (Matthau) discovers to his disgust that the first woman Justice is to be the dread conservative, Judge Loomis (Clayburgh). A half-heartedly serious script about integrity in high places is further degraded by Neame to a lifeless comedy about professional antagonism conquered by grudging affection. The pair confront each other in a series of private debates about matters judicial/ethical, which are about as intellectually bracing as Snow-White-meets-Grumpy. The scene where Matthau rises from the coronary unit to Right a Wrong, and marches into the Supreme Court hand-in-hand with the Widow Loomis, simply confirms that we're in fairyland Washington. JS

First Name: Carmen (Prénom Carmen)

(Jean-Luc Godard, 1983, Fr/Switz) Maruschka Detmers, Jacques Bonnaffé, Myriem Roussel, Jean-Luc Godard, Hyppolite Girardot, Christophe Odent.
84 min.
Something like a remake of *Pierrot le Fou* in its cosmic despair, doom-laden romanticism, and stinging, insolent wit. Replacing Bizet with Beethoven and recasting the operatic cigarette girl as a cheapo terrorist, this is really an intimate journal musing about three movies in one. As in *Passion*, there is a bleak acknowledgement of the difficulty of making films (with the string quartet's Beethoven rehearsals indicating how the film-maker is going astray in the tone and tempo of his attempts to communicate). Then there is the story of Carmen and Don José, which obstinately refuses to get off the ground, grinding into a grim stasis where *l'amour fou* dies miserably as the naked lovers take sexual stock. And finally there is Godard himself, drawing all the threads together in a confessional performance as a burnt-out film-maker languishing in a lunatic asylum, out of which he is tempted only to suffer both professional and personal betrayal by Carmen (last name Karina?). Not for nothing does the film carry a nostalgic dedication 'in memoriam small movies'. This, throwaway jokes and all, is Godard back at his most nouvelle vague in years. TM

First of the Few, The (aka Spitfire)

(Leslie Howard, 1942, GB) Leslie Howard, David Niven, Rosamund John, Roland Culver, Anne Firth, Cyril Raymond, Bernard Miles, Miles Malleson.
117 min. b/w.
Detailed and assured chronicle of RJ Mitchell's trials and triumphs in designing and building the Spitfire, the fighter plane whose aerial superiority won the Battle of Britain. Director/star Howard – who died on an RAF mission in 1943 – brings appropriate dedication to his final screen role, while Niven is suitably chummy as his test-pilot pal. Stirring score by William Walton. TJ

First Power, The

(Robert Resnikoff, 1990, US) Lou Diamond Phillips, Tracy Griffith, Jeff Kober, Mykel T Williamson, Elizabeth Arlen, Dennis Lipscomb.
98 min.
Before Gary Gilmore was executed, he announced his belief in reincarnation and his intention of coming back. Inspired by this, writer-director Resnikoff's silly thriller has LA detective Logan (Phillips), who headed the successful investigation, up against the evil soul of an executed serial killer, Channing (Kober). Logan's nightmares begin as he is terrorised by a disembodied voice, lurid graffiti, and a resumption of the killings. He

recruits the services of a psychic (Griffith) and the local convent, where a nun recognises Satan's handiwork. Resnikoff fails to sustain the tension established in the opening sequences, and the plot quickly degenerates into a repetitive pattern of possession and exorcism for the victims requisitioned by Channing's soul to do its bidding. With the exception of Phillips, the performances are remarkably unconvincing. CM

First Strike (Jingcha Gushi 4 zhi Jiandan Renwu)

(Stanley Tong, 1996, HK) Jackie Chan, Jackson Lau, Annie Wu, Bill Tung, Jerzi Petrov.
107 min.
A lot more fun than the Bond movies it gets into bed with, this sprawling action-adventure (nominally No 4 in Jackie Chan's *Police Story* series) shuttles from Hong Kong to the Ukraine and on to Australia for a climactic fight under water amid real live sharks. The McGuffin is the usual stolen nuclear warhead, but the stunts are the movie's raison d'être: a chase/shoot-out up a snowy mountain, immersion in an icy lake, a tussle on the outside of a tall building, a fight with improvised weapons including an aluminium step-ladder. The highpoint is Chan singing 'I Will Follow Him' while stripping at gunpoint. Watch out for substantial differences between the original Chinese version and the re-edited, dubbed US version. TR

First Time with Feeling (Vous Intéressez-vous à la Chose?)

(Jacques Baratier, 1973, Fr/WGer) Nathalie Delon, Muriel Catala, Didier Haudepin, Bernard Jeantet, Renée Saint-Cyr.
82 min.
If Eric Rohmer ever went crackers and plunged into porno, the results could be something like this. The hero – suffering, need one say, from awful inhibitions – spends one of those idyllic French summers where everyone talks, drinks, writes journals, drinks, and gives their personal codes a good shake. By the end of it all he is able to treat his heart's desire – a lovely cousin – in the style she deserves. Baratier has seen better days: time was when he wowed the critics with a New Wave/cinéma-vérité send-up called 'Dragées au Poivre'. GB

First Wives Club, The

(Hugh Wilson, 1996, US) Goldie Hawn, Bette Midler, Diane Keaton, Stockard Channing, Maggie Smith, Dan Hedaya, Eileen Heckhart, Philip Bosco.
103 min.
It's 1969 and four young women, full of peace, love and ambition, are about to graduate. Cut to present-day New York, and the bleary spectacle of Cynthia (Channing), the gang's leading light, thrown over by her husband for pert-breasted wife number two. Lonely as hell, she takes a short walk off a tall building. At her funeral, superstar Elise (Hawn), mouthy frump Brenda (Midler) and doormat Annie (Keaton) realise they too are dizzyingly close to the edge; now saggy and a bit loose at the seams, they've been turned in for younger models. What to do? You've got it – revenge: they're going to kick those badfellas where it hurts – in the pocket. This comedy finds all three stars in wryly cartoonish form, with Keaton particularly charming/irritating. One-liners aside, however, there's no disguising the film's social smugness or predictability. CO'Su

First Yank into Tokyo (aka First Man into Tokyo/ Mask of Fury)

(Gordon Douglas, 1945, US) Tom Neal, Barbara Hale, Marc Cramer, Richard Loo, Keye Luke, Benson Fong, Leonard Strong.
83 min. b/w.
A wartime potboiler in which a Japanese-speaking US pilot (Neal), his features orientalised by plastic surgery, is smuggled into Japan to retrieve vital data from a scientist (Cramer) captured while testing a component for the A-Bomb. Desperate plotting ensures that the commandant (Loo) of the PoW camp was once Neal's college room-mate, while a US nurse (Hale) playing Florence Nightingale to the prisoners is his long-lost sweetheart. Will either penetrate his inscrutable disguise when he worms his way in

as a guard? The mission is accomplished with the aid of more plot contrivances, and Neal – his plastic surgery irreversible – elects to die while killing innumerable Japs rather than force his new features on his beloved. Skilful direction and camerawork (Harry Wild) just about keep things going. The A-Bomb theme and a gloating commentary ('Hiroshima destroyed! Nagasaki devastated!') were added when the war's abrupt end caught up with the film's release. TM

Fish Called Wanda, A

(Charles Crichton, 1988, GB) John Cleese, Jamie Lee Curtis, Kevin Kline, Michael Palin, Maria Aitken, Tom Georgeson, Patricia Hayes, Geoffrey Palmer.
108 min.
A perfectly old-fashioned romantic comedy, big on caper, generous on Ealing, and heavy on the twisted stereotypes. Cleese scripts and stars as London barrister Archie Leach, hired to defend a gem thief, and earning a much-vaunted 'sex symbol' tag with the affections of gangster's moll Wanda Gershwitz (Curtis). It's a plot too jagged to document in full – Where are the gems? Who has the safe-deposit key? Who's betraying whom? Is the London Underground really a political movement? – but the interest lies less in outcome than in character: Palin as a madly stuttering, animal-loving dog-murderer, Kline as a maybe-CIA cruel paranoid pseud who's intermittently Wanda's lover/gay brother, and Cleese and Curtis as the most unlikely rug-tearers since Miller and Monroe. There's nothing deep, nothing groundbreaking, but it's a never-dull, tightly scripted yarn with some very funny gags. SGa

Fisher King, The

(Terry Gilliam, 1991, US) Robin Williams, Jeff Bridges, Amanda Plummer, Mercedes Ruehl, Michael Jeter, Harry Shearer.
137 min.
When New York radio DJ Jack Lucas (Bridges) inadvertently drives a listener to commit mass murder, his confidence and career crumble. Three years on, he's rescued from suicide and muggers by Parry (Williams), a deranged hobo whose wife died in the massacre. A former professor of medieval history, Parry has two dreams: to retrieve the Holy Grail, and to win the heart of the fair Lydia (Plummer). Consumed by guilt, doubtful about his future with his lover Anne (Ruehl), Lucas concludes he can redeem himself if only he can bring Parry and Lydia together. The plot may be wayward, but Gilliam's film is mostly funny and exhilarating: at once nightmarish and deeply romantic, a partly fantastic study in loneliness, lunacy, despair and violence, it's also spectacularly visual (despite the atypical dearth of special effects). Moreover, Gilliam allows his actors unprecedented space, and they respond admirably (Bridges and Plummer especially). Scary, touching, often hilarious, this modern fairytale is surprisingly enchanting. GA

F.I.S.T.

(Norman Jewison, 1978, US) Sylvester Stallone, Rod Steiger, Peter Boyle, Melinda Dillon, David Huffman, Tony Lo Bianco.
145 min.
Despite its Watergate scars, *F.I.S.T.*, with its marches on Washington and its attacks on conspiracy and monopoly, is a striking reaffirmation of traditional populism. Stallone, the all-American *auteur*/contender of *Rocky* (and how much of this film too?), plays an industrial worker in Depression Ohio who makes good as the boss of the (thinly disguised) Teamsters Union. With few exceptions, Hollywood has proved consistently unwilling to treat questions of labour, and the political drama here remains substantially conventional, anchoring the issues in violence, romance and righteous individualism. Stallone's performance is a superb blend of stubborn-jawed gravity and ironic hamming as he heads, Godfather-like, for a confrontation with the Senate. It, and a curious historical leap in the narrative from 1930 to 1960, together push the film beyond the point where it can supply a traditional conclusion or a hero. The climactic murder of the Union boss by his Mafia backers is a puzzled attempt to resolve the contradiction between individualist demands (Law & Order, enterprise: Capital) and social needs (subsistence, justice: Labour). CA

Fistful of Dollars, A
(Per un Pugno di Dollari)
(Sergio Leone, 1964, It/WGer/Sp) Clint
Eastwood, Gian Maria Volonté, Marianne
Koch, Pepe Calvo, Wolfgang Lukschy.
100 min.
Though far less operatic and satisfying than
Leone's late work, his first spaghetti Western
with Eastwood still looks stylish, if a little rough
at the edges. Based on Kurosawa's *Yojimbo*, it set
a fashion in surly, laconic, supercool heroes with
Eastwood's amoral gunslinger, who plays off two
gangs against one another in a deadly feud. All
the classic Leone ingredients were there – the
atonal score, the graphic violence, the horrendous
dubbing – and the film's Stateside success
changed the face of a genre. GA

Fistful of Dynamite, A
see Giù la Testa

Fistful of Fingers, A
(Edgar Wright, 1995, GB) Graham Low, Oliver
Evans, Martin Curtis, Quentin Green,
William Cornes.
81 min.
This is a homemade spaghetti Western (budget
£10,000, cardboard horses and a handful of sixth-
formers) which parodies itself along with the
genre archetypes. The moving story of a bounty
hunter's love for his murdered horse is a ragbag
of the surreal, the satiric and the plain lame in the
tradition of *Hot Shots! Part Deux*, with one
Graham Low, a tour guide at Wookey Hole Caves,
doing an uncanny impersonation of Eastwood's
'No Name'. Wright may not be in the class of
Robert (*El Mariachi*) Rodriguez, but he has talent. Best seen after a couple of beers. TCh

Fistful of Flies
(Monica Pellizzari, 1996, Aust) Dina Panozzo,
Tasma Walton, John Lucantonio, Anna
Volska, Maria Venuti, Rachael Maza, Giordano
Gangl.
85 min.
Here's the angle, in the words of the heroine's
mother: 'Men are all like toilets: all engaged, all
pissed-off or all full of shit!' Sixteen-year-old
refusenik Mars (Walton) finds growing up is hard
to do in the repressive, racist, hypocritical, male-
dominated Italian-Australian Catholic community she has the privilege to live in. This is
daughter-of-Jane-Campion stuff, an off-kilter, suburban surrealist drama, shot in primary colours,
with its broad satirical swipes accompanied by
droll social observation, brutal episodes of
domestic cruelty and an ending of male-van-
quishing wish-fulfilment. The performances are
in the farce-meets-realist tradition of *Sweetie*,
with Walton giving an especially brave one as
the Girl on the Road to Empowerment. Great fun,
and all power to the sisters. WH

Fist of Fury (Jingwu Men/
aka The Chinese Connection)
(Lo Wei, 1972, HK) Bruce Lee, Nora Miao,
James Tien, Robert Baker, Maria Yi,
Tien Feng.
106 min.
One of the best of the Chinese chop sock dramas.
It has a basically serious story: the inmates of one
kung-fu school have poisoned the teacher of a
rival school, and our devoted hero sets out on a
course of revenge. But a potential revenge
tragedy turns into a film of comic strip outrageousness as Bruce Lee tries, but fails, to reconcile his natural thirst for revenge with his desire
to keep the name of his school clean. The result
is a patently absurd and funny movie, involving
a series of spectacular fight routines, often filmed
in slow motion, which are highly acrobatic and
exciting.

Fist of Fury Part II
(Jingwu Men Xuji)
(Li Zuonan, 1976, Tai) Bruce Li, Lo Lieh, Tien
Feng, Lee Quinn, Shikamura Yasuyoshi.
104 min.
One of a flood of Bruce Lee spin-offs, this purports to be a sequel to the Lee vehicle *Fist of Fury*
(but is in fact an ultra-low-budget rehash of its
script), and it stars Lee lookalike Ho Tsung-Tao
(whom it bills as 'Bruce Li'). It's not the worst of
its kind, but it is unremittingly feeble, both as a

drama and as a kung-fu exploiter. Only the final
duel is given set piece status; the rest is so much
scrappy action and emoting. TR

Fist of the North Star
(Toyoo Ashida, 1990, Jap)
112 min.
If you thought *Akira* was strange, violent and
hard to understand, get a load of this animated
feature, based on the comic available in translation from specialist shops. Like many Japanese
manga, it's set in a barren, post-apocalyptic world
where only men's muscles can grow. The plot is
the usual fantasy rubbish about fraternal betrayal and maiden-rescuing; but what distinguishes
it is the stylised visuals, the existentialist landscapes, and the quite exceptional levels of violence perpetrated by the martial arts supermen.
Heads bulge and explode, arms fall to the ground,
blood gushes skywards, torsos are severed, bodies are crushed to pulp. If Sam Peckinpah had
murdered Walt Disney and disembowelled
Bambi, the result would have been tame in comparison. DW

Fists in the Pocket
(I Pugni in Tasca)
(Marco Bellocchio, 1965, It) Lou Castel, Paola
Pitagora, Marino Masè, Liliana Gerace, Pier
Luigi Troglio.
113 min. b/w.
A synopsis of Bellocchio's amazing first film
might suggest an Italian version of US TV's
Soap, with its story of a family variously plagued
by epilepsy, blindness, low IQs and raging frustration. But Bellocchio orders his material and
directs his actors with such verve and passion
that audiences have little time and less
inclination to giggle. In particular, Lou Castel's
performance as Alessandro, a teenage epileptic
ultimately driven to frenzied acts of violence,
seethes with a hateful energy rarely seen on the
screen. Both Castel and Bellocchio have been simmering down quietly ever since. A stunning film,
literally. GB

Fists of Fury
see Big Boss, The

Fit to Be Untied
(Matti da Slegare)
(Marco Bellocchio/Silvano Agosti/Sandro
Petreglia/Stefano Rulli, 1975, It)
For a tale of misery, woe and black despair, a surprisingly optimistic film. Focusing on Parma, this
documentary (really two, put together by a collective) claims insanity as a social disease, the
predictable result of compounding poverty with
ignorance, and banishing the halt and lame to
secretive (often church-run) institutions where
they are beaten and tormented. The film's unspoken question is who is really insane, the inmates
or their cruel keepers. Certainly Paolo, the
youngest of the cases studied, does not seem mad.
Although oblivious to the discipline of parents or
school, and forever tugging at jumper, hat or hair,
Paolo's discussion of his problem shows a reasoning unclouded by naivety or insanity. He's not
looking for a miracle, but he knows what would
help – a job. And as Part Two shows, the effects
of just this upon the truly mentally handicapped
can be miraculous when the job comes complete
with fellow-workers who offer friendship as well
as instruction. FD

Fitzcarraldo
(Werner Herzog, 1982, WGer) Klaus Kinski,
Claudia Cardinale, José Lewgoy, Miguel Angel
Fuentes, Paul Hittscher.
158 min.
Though there was a distinct possibility that the
much-publicised and characteristically fraught
production saga of Herzog's movie would overshadow the completed film itself, it turned out to
be some kind of appropriately eccentric and monumental marvel. Operatic excess is both the subject and the keynote, as Kinski's visionary Irish
adventurer obsessively hatches grandiose
schemes to finance a dream of bringing Caruso
and the strains of Verdi to an Amazon trading-
post. Staked by loving Molly, a madam
(Cardinale), he pilots the resurrected tub 'Molly-
Aida' down an uncharted tributary in search of
untapped rubber, wooing the fierce natives with
gramophone arias before securing their inexplic-

able collaboration in the ludicrous task of hauling the ship manually over a hill towards a parallel waterway. Overcoming his own disparaged
image as an inspired madman, Herzog charts an
ironically circular course around an indulged,
benevolent Aguirre; perversely illuminates colonialism with surrealism; and demonstrates once
again in his always suspect yet somehow irresistible way that 'only dreamers move mountains'. PT

Five
(Arch Oboler, 1951, US) William Phipps, Susan
Douglas, James Anderson, Charles Lampkin,
Earl Lee.
93 min. b/w.
A quintet of survivors – idealist, pregnant
woman, black doorman, hunk and wimp – debate
mankind's future in this naive post-apocalyptic
drama, set mainly in the writer/director's Frank
Lloyd Wright-designed apartment. Earnest and
not very pacy. TJ

Five and the Skin
(Cinq et la Peau)
(Pierre Rissient, 1982, Fr/Phil) Feodor Atkine,
Eiko Matsuda, Gloria Diaz, Rafael Roco,
Phillip Salvador, Louie Pascua, Roberto
Padua.
97 min.
A completely unclassifiable feature from
Frenchman-about-cinema Rissient, but clearly
autobiographical at heart. The images show a
Frenchman in Manila, and explore his move-
ments, his meetings, his enthusiasms, and his
sexual fantasies. There is synch-sound, but no
dialogue; instead, his thoughts and reflections are
heard in an exquisitely literary voice-over. The
blend of specifics and abstracts is mesmerising.
RG

Five Came Back
(John Farrow, 1939, US) Chester Morris, Lucille
Ball, Wendy Barrie, John Carradine, Joseph
Calleia, C Aubrey Smith, Patric Knowles, Allen
Jenkins, Elizabeth Risdon, Kent Taylor.
75 min. b/w.
If the plot sounds familiar, that's partly because
Farrow himself remade this film in 1956 as *Back
from Eternity* (also for RKO), partly because it's
the old warhorse about air passengers crash-landed in a hostile wilderness that has left its mark on
everything from Buñuel's *La Mort en ce jardin* and
Aldrich's *The Flight of the Phoenix* to the *Airport*
sagas and *Alive*. But despite what now seem
clichés – the headhunters, the cowardly braggart,
the tart with a heart, the noble revolutionary – this
one still comes up fresh, thanks to a taut, economic script (by Jerry Cady, Dalton Trumbo and
Nathanael West!) full of twists and vivid characters, and to Farrow's eminently civilised handling
of his material. (A devout Catholic, he even manages to make the scenes of redemption and sacrifice both plausible and remarkably unsentimental.)
And Nick Musuraca's photography is as atmospheric as in his later *films noirs*. GA

5 Card Stud
(Henry Hathaway, 1968, US) Dean Martin,
Robert Mitchum, Roddy McDowall, Inger
Stevens, Katherine Justice, John Anderson,
Yaphet Kotto, Denver Pyle.
103 min.
A card-sharp caught palming an ace is lynched
by six of the seven men he was playing poker
with (Martin protests in vain); and panic spreads
through the small Colorado town as the lynchers
begin to die one by one, killed in gruesome parodies of the hanging. Hathaway directs this
Western *Ten Little Indians* with a sort of weary
authority, alternating patches of boredom with
fresh, striking detail. What chiefly keeps it afloat
is the excellent cast, headed by Martin as the
gambler who turns Sherlock Holmes to solve the
mystery, and Mitchum – in a variation on his performance in *Night of the Hunter* – as the mysterious hellfire preacher who rides into town with
a secret and a faster draw than anyone else. TM

Five Corners
(Tony Bill, 1987, US) Jodie Foster, Tim
Robbins, Todd Graff, John Turturro, Elizabeth
Berridge, Rose Gregorio, Gregory Rozakis,
John Seitz, Cathryn de Prume.
94 min.

The teenage Bronx in '64 was divided into the concerned and the heads. Harry (Robbins) is on the brink of joining civil rights Down South. Melanie (Berridge) and Brita (de Prume) sniff from bags and play yo-yo on top of elevators. Linda (Foster) works in a pet store and is preoccupied with stopping psychotic Heinz (Turturro) from attempting rape again now that he's out of the slammer. The latter's courtship is unconventional. Unbidden, he steals a pair of penguins for her from the zoo, and when she demurs, clubs one to death. Like *American Graffiti*, all these teenie tales take place against a specific historical time, with TV and electioneering vans everywhere on the go to remind us. Some tales work better than others, with the mysterious killings by bow-and-arrow convenient but low on credibility. The investigating cop duo (Rozakis and Seitz) could have strayed in from Chabrol at his daftest; Linda's crippled boyfriend (Graff) is a curdler; Turturro's Heinz, however, is rivetingly over the top. Lots of good ideas and memorable scenes, but it's a bit of a mess. BC

Five Days One Summer

(Fred Zinnemann, 1982, US) Sean Connery, Betsy Brantley, Lambert Wilson, Jennifer Hilary, Isabel Dean, Gerard Buhr, Anna Massey.
108 min.
A film which creates drama more out of gesture and nuance than dialogue, and employs a lush setting which overwhelms instead of pointing up the characters' emotions. Older, married doctor takes his young niece for a dirty week in the Swiss Alps in the 1930s. The mountain climbing footage is remarkable, but the plot gathers so little pace that when the girl runs to find out whether the doctor she loves or the handsome young guide she fancies has been killed in an avalanche, our interest in her dilemma is academic. MB

Five Easy Pieces

(Bob Rafelson, 1970, US) Jack Nicholson, Karen Black, Lois Smith, Susan Anspach, Billy Green Bush, Helena Kallianiotes, William Challee.
98 min.
Rafelson's second film – in which Jack Nicholson, seemingly a redneck oil-rigger, turns out to be a fugitive from a musical career inherited from a family of classical musicians – is a considered examination of the middle-class patrician American way of family life. Centreing on Nicholson's drifter, the film unswervingly brings him into confrontations with his past as he equally unswervingly attempts to evade everything, preferring to make gestures rather than act consistently. The result is less a story and more a collection of incidents and character studies, all of which inform each other and extend our understanding of Nicholson's mode of survival: flight. PH

Five Evenings
(Pyat Vecherov)

(Nikita Mikhalkov, 1978, USSR) Liudmila Gurchenko, Stanislav Liubshin, Valentina Telichkina, Larisa Kuznetsova, Igor Nefedov.
101 min. b/w & col.
Taken from a theatrical text, filmed in grimy, tinted black-and-white, the minimal narrative tracks the prosaic interaction of four characters, young/old, male/female, through the interiors of urban Russia a generation or so ago. Mikhalkov transforms these unpromising ingredients with consummate skill into a film quite unlike the heroic or prestigious bombast prevalent in Russian cinema. At worst, a delightful, meticulous tour de force, and at least, a resonant and revealing miniature. SH

5 Fingers

(Joseph L Mankiewicz, 1952, US) James Mason, Danielle Darrieux, Michael Rennie, Walter Hampden, Oscar Karlweis, Herbert Berghof.
108 min. b/w.
An elegantly witty espionage movie, founded on fact but no slave to the facts as recounted by German military attaché LZ Moyzisch in his account (*Operation Cicero*) of an Albanian-born valet to the British ambassador in Turkey in 1944 who hawked top secret allied documents to the Germans. In Mankiewicz's hands, characteristically elaborated into a teasing rondo of political

and sexual intrigue where each new double-crossing move is mated by a totally unexpected irony of fate, the tale becomes an irresistibly dry, cynical comedy of manners in which the crafty gentleman's gentleman (a marvellous performance from Mason), scheming to secure the means to promote himself as a member of the leisured classes, falls victim to his own pretensions when a beautiful but unprincipled refugee Countess (the equally marvellous Darrieux) trails a heady promise of romance across his path. An irresistible treat. TM

Five Fingers of Death

see King Boxer

5:48, The

(James Ivory, 1979, US) Mary Beth Hurt, Laurence Luckinbill, Laurinda Barrett, John DeVries, Robert Hitt, Ann McDonough.
58 min.
Ivory's only feature film to date (1996) not produced by his business partner Ismail Merchant, this short suspense picture was adapted by the playwright Terrence McNally from a story by John Cheever and commissioned by New York's Channel 13 TV. Hypocrites abound in Merchant Ivory's work, but the unvarnished cruelty which runs through the character of John Blake (Luckinbill), the ad-man held at gunpoint on his train journey home to Shady Hill, Westchester County, by his wronged secretary (Hurt), may come as a shock to those who've grown accustomed to the elegant subtleties of Ruth Jhabvala's MIP scripts. Made back-to-back with *The Europeans*. JPy

Five Graves to Cairo

(Billy Wilder, 1943, US) Franchot Tone, Anne Baxter, Akim Tamiroff, Erich von Stroheim, Peter Van Eyck, Fortunio Bonanova, Konstantin Shayne.
96 min. b/w.
An impressive wartime espionage thriller, with Tone as a British corporal holed up in a Nazi-controlled hotel in the North African desert, and posing as a German in an attempt to discover the whereabouts of Rommel's secret fuel dumps. The script by Wilder and his long-term associate Charles Brackett is taut and intelligent, but the film's real strengths are John Seitz's superb photography of the desert and hotel, and von Stroheim's resumption of his 'man you love to hate' persona as Rommel. Lajos Biro's source play had been filmed twice before as *Hotel Imperial* (1927 and 1939), and in 1951 resurfaced in an engaging parody version as *Hotel Sahara*. GA

Five Heartbeats, The

(Robert Townsend, 1991, US) Robert Townsend, Michael Wright, Leon, Harry J Lennix, Tice Wells, Diahann Carroll, Harold Nicholas, Chuck Patterson.
121 min.
The year is 1965, and five young guys aim for fame with a sloppy but impassioned vocal group. They're a bit Four Tops, a bit Temptations, and a lot Smokey Robinson and the Miracles, since starstruck songwriter 'Duck' (Townsend) seems conceived as an adoring homage to the acknowledged laureate of soul. The film stands mainly on its characterisations, and the band itself is fairly flawlessly cast: not so much the rather listless Townsend, but certainly Duck's Casanova brother JT (Leon), the virtuous Choirboy (Wells), and lead singer Eddie (Wright), whose fate is blatantly a Dire Warning. For all the specificity of the soul background, Townsend gives us a retread illustration of the familiar pitfalls of fame; while some of the broader music biz gags seem left over from his earlier *Hollywood Shuffle*, as do the strictly 2D female characterisations. By the time it ends in a heartwarming nuclear family hoedown, we've learned nothing new. JRo

Five Star Final

(Mervyn LeRoy, 1931, US) Edward G Robinson, Marian Marsh, HB Warner, Anthony Bushell, Boris Karloff, George E Stone, Ona Munson, Aline MacMahon.
89 min. b/w.
Much praised in its day as a biting attack on gutter journalism (one of dozens trotted out during the first years of sound), this early entry in the Warner 'social protest' cycle hasn't worn nearly

so well as Hecht-Milestone's much less solemn and self-righteous *The Front Page*. Robinson is more than adequate as the editor persuaded to boost circulation by reviving an old scandal, with tragic results ending in a double suicide. But with the victims coming on like characters in a Victorian melodrama, and LeRoy's direction accentuating the plot's stage origins with its graceless gestures towards 'cinema' (including a clumsy attempt at split screen), the film hovers more than once on the brink of risibility. Worth seeing mainly for Karloff's wonderfully Uriah Heep-ish performance as a reporter ('the most blasphemous thing I've ever seen,' his editor drily observes) formerly expelled from divinity school for some evident but unspecified sexual misdemeanour. TM

5000 Fingers of Dr T, The

(Roy Rowland, 1953, US) Tommy Rettig, Hans Conried, Peter Lind Hayes, Mary Healy.
88 min.
The 5000 Fingers of Dr T can barely contain its multiple fascinations within the 'kids' movie' format, attempting as it does to make explicit the connections between dreams, surrealism and psychoanalysis. Using the child's fantasy structure of *The Wizard of Oz*, it's the tale of nine-year-old Bart (Rettig), who resents his piano lessons and projects teacher Terwilliker (Conried) as an authoritarian madman bent on mesmerising his mother, killing the friendly plumber, imprisoning all other musicians, and enslaving 500 little boys at a giant keyboard to rehearse his own masterpiece for eternity. There's enough colourful whimsy here to divert a young audience; but also enough pop Freud and political allegory to keep even the most compulsively note-taking adults happy. And with a couple of musical routines that come close to defining camp, this awesome entertainment really does have something for everyone. PT

Five Women Around Utamaro
(Utamaro o Meguru Go-nin no Onna)

(Kenji Mizoguchi, 1946, Jap) Minosuke Bando, Kotaro Bando, Tanaka Kinuyo, Kowasaki Hiroko, Izuka Toshiko.
94 min. b/w.
Made immediately after the war, despite continuous opposition from the Occupation Forces, this remarkable film about the late 18th century artist marks the beginning of Mizoguchi's commitment to the theme of female emancipation: Utamaro himself is seen as the 'neutral' centre of a series of emotional intrigues which illustrate the corruption of Edo period morals and highlight the particular vulnerability of women. The film is also something of a meditation on the status of the artist; scriptwriter Yoshikata Yoda is on record as saying that he intended it as a reflection on Mizoguchi himself. In style it's much like Mizoguchi's later work, but less emotional, more formalised, more mysterious, and a great deal more daring aesthetically. TR

Fixed Bayonets

(Samuel Fuller, 1951, US) Richard Basehart, Gene Evans, Michael O'Shea, Richard Hylton, Craig Hill, Skip Homeier, Henry Kulky, James Dean.
92 min. b/w.
'His films are like scenarios made from communities of rats, the camera itself a king rat,' David Thomson wrote of Fuller. The rat trap is the Korean war, in a studio set of fake rock and fake snow, literally a theatre of war. The constantly moving camera isolates the tensions within an American platoon fighting a rearguard action. As the leaders are picked off by the 'alien' reds, one sensitive corporal's struggle with the responsibilities of leadership drags the plot in a slow dance of death; only to be blasted apart by a typical cigar-chewing affirmation of good old Yankee guts. RP

Fixer, The

(John Frankenheimer, 1968, US) Alan Bates, Dirk Bogarde, Georgia Brown, Jack Gilford, Hugh Griffith, Elizabeth Hartman, Ian Holm, David Warner, Murray Melvin, Peter Jeffrey.
130 min.
Blacklisted screenwriter Dalton Trumbo adapted Bernard Malamud's heavyweight novel, a tale of injustice set in pre-revolutionary Russia, but despite obvious effort all round this remains one

of those worthy responsible movies trading on its self-proclaimed prestige. Bates suffers his way to an Oscar nomination as Yakov Bok, the Jew who refuses to confess to a crime (the ritual murder of a child) of which he's innocent and is imprisoned without trial. Bogarde, on the other hand, as the melancholy lawyer, who's murdered for attempting to help Bok, has a touch more charisma. Not a patch on the director's earlier *Bird Man of Alcatraz*. GM

Flambierte Frau, Die
see Woman in Flames, A

Flame (aka Slade in Flame)
(Richard Loncraine, 1974, GB) The Slade, Tom Conti, Johnny Shannon, Kenneth Colley, Alan Lake.
91 min.
A straightforward account of the rise and ultimate disillusionment of a typical teenage rave band, tightly scripted and directed. The seediness of the behind-the-scenes machinations runs through the story: they are seedy whether perpetrated by a third-rate Midlands agent or by the suave director of a London management and investment company. The film (which isn't a moment too long, a welcome rarity) doesn't say much that you don't know already; good performances, though, from Shannon, Conti, and Lake as the all-time loser vocalist. JC

Flame
(Ingrid Sinclair, 1995, Zim/Fr/Namibia) Marian Kunonga, Ulla Mahaka, Norman Madawo, Moise Matura.
90 min.
The war that transformed Rhodesia into Zimbabwe is shown through the experiences of two young women freedom fighters, one dedicated to improvement through study, the other a more robust type with a tendency to fall for the wrong man. An intelligent, sympathetic first feature, but a tad predictable and so rushed in places that it slides into less than persuasive melodrama. 'Flame' (Kunonga) finds she's pregnant, gives birth in a truck and loses the baby in an air raid, all in about five minutes. GA

Flame and the Arrow, The
(Jacques Tourneur, 1950, US) Burt Lancaster, Virginia Mayo, Robert Douglas, Aline MacMahon, Nick Cravat.
88 min.
The first of Burt Lancaster's attempts to revive the swashbuckling spirit of Douglas Fairbanks Senior. Perhaps not quite so irresistibly ebullient as *The Crimson Pirate*, but also less arch in its use of verbal anachronisms. Great fun, at any rate, beautifully paced by Tourneur, as Lancaster and Cravat romp through their incredible gymnastic stunts while rescuing medieval Lombardy from wicked oppressors. TM

Flame in My Heart, A (Une Flamme dans Mon Coeur)
(Alain Tanner, 1987, Fr/Switz) Myriam Mézières, Aziz Kabouche, Benoît Régent, Biana, Jean-Yves Berthelot, André Marcon.
110 min.
A folly from Tanner, scripted by its heavily emoting star Mézières, this tells the ludicrous tale of a woman who can never get what she wants, whether she's rehearsing Racine on stage or stripping in an immigrants' bar in Paris. She spends the first half of the movie trying to shake off an exceptionally persistent Arab lover, then picks up a journalist on the Métro and launches into an affair that takes her to Egypt. Ms Mézières' overheated performance would not be out of place in a Rosa von Praunheim movie; the embarrassment quotient is off the scale. TR

Flame in the Streets
(Roy Baker, 1961, GB) John Mills, Brenda de Banzie, Sylvia Syms, Earl Cameron, Johnny Sekka, Ann Lynn, Wilfrid Brambell.
93 min.
A relatively early attempt to come to terms – in melodramatic form – with racism and the aspirations of black immigrants in Britain. Mills owns a furniture factory and is proud of his tolerance, endorsing a Jamaican's candidacy as shop steward. However, enlightened shop floor attitudes are one thing; his daughter marrying a black is

quite another. It's a bit like a social thesis – Discuss – but its background of poor housing and gangs of teddy boys roving the streets like the Ku Klux Klan is convincing enough. ATu

Flame of New Orleans, The
(René Clair, 1941, US) Marlene Dietrich, Bruce Cabot, Roland Young, Mischa Auer, Andy Devine, Laura Hope Crews, Franklin Pangborn.
78 min. b/w.
After the end of her partnership with Josef von Sternberg, Dietrich didn't regain her professional stride until 1939, when she was cast as a roistering bar hostess in the spoof Western, *Destry Rides Again*. Here, two films later, she's playing a variation on the role: an émigré adventuress with a dubious past in St Petersburg, trying to pose as a countess in New Orleans, torn between a 'sensible' marriage and her wild passion for the butch young captain of a Mississippi steamer. This was the first of the four films that Clair directed in Hollywood during his wartime exile from France, and he was clearly content to swim with the tide: he simply films the formulary but entertaining script, with a minimum of directorial touches. It is, of course, Dietrich who carries it. TR

Flame Over India
see North West Frontier

Flame Top (Tulipää)
(Pirjo Honkasalo/Pekka Lehto, 1980, Fin) Asko Sarkola, Rea Mauranen, Kari Franck, Esko Salminen.
135 min.
Finnish epic about a celebrated national hero, Maiju Lassila: novelist, revolutionary and wealthy businessman. From his poor, rural childhood, through his arrival in St Petersburg in 1900, his success as a writer, his exile in the Finnish forests, and his eventual imprisonment and death, the film charts Lassila's political development – his terrorist activities against the Russians, and his part in the 1918 Finnish Civil War. Shot on location not only in Finland but also in Leningrad, the film is well-crafted and authentic, but the slow pace and broodingly melancholic atmosphere make it generally heavy-going. GA

Flaming Creatures
(Jack Smith, 1962, US) Mario Montez.
43 min. b/w.
One of the legendary *maudit* films, Smith's extravaganza of underground pleasure(ing)s doesn't quite stand up to its chequered fame. Shot in murky black-and-white, it visibly belongs to the early '60s, but nevertheless appears to originate from some arcane time pocket of the '20s, populated by vampy drag queens and draggy vampires, guests at a boisterous but strangely innocent orgy orchestrated with pulpy pop ditties and flapper anthems. Admittedly, it now comes across as an archive piece, and proves that boredom has always been a factor in the avant-garde's articulation of perverse desire. But as a missing link between prehistoric ciné-camp and the dazed excesses of Warhol and the infinitely more trenchant George Kuchar, it is of academic interest at the very least. JRo

Flaming Ears
(Angela Hans Schierl/Dietmar Schipek/Ursula Pürrer, 1991, Aus) Susanna Heilmayr, Angela Hans Schierl, Ursula Pürrer, Margarethe Neumann.
89 min.
It's safe to say that this apocalyptic lesbian fantasy is one of a kind, but that's as far as it goes. Set in 2700 in the mouldering city of Asche, it chronicles the star-crossed amours of a group of women: Volley (Pürrer), a roller-skating pyromaniac; her plastic-suited, possibly extraterrestrial lover Nun (Schierl); and Spy (Heilmayr), a comics artist who vows revenge on Volley for burning down her printing press. There's little coherent narrative; the directors are more concerned with elaborating a wild and woolly style, comprising daft decor, lurid colours and free-floating camerawork. They merrily cut corners with the futurism, knocking up a passable *Alphaville* world from table-top Meccano and leaving the rest to creaky stop-motion animation. Despite oddball gags seemingly beamed in from another dimension, the feel is leadenly Teutonic. JRo

Flamingo Kid, The
(Garry Marshall, 1984, US) Matt Dillon, Hector Elizondo, Molly McCarthy, Martha Gehman, Richard Crenna, Jessica Walter, Fisher Stevens.
100 min.
In 1963, Brooklyn-born Jeffrey (Dillon) takes a summer job at the El Flamingo beach club on Long Island, and receives an education in the art of making money; his family, however, is dismayed by the boy's dreams of speedy upward mobility. Hardly original stuff, and morally the film wants to have its cake and eat it, celebrating working-class simplicity while revelling in the luxuriance of beach club life. But the performances compensate, with Dillon turning in a light and touching portrait of confused ambitions. GA

Flaming Star
(Don Siegel, 1960, US) Elvis Presley, Barbara Eden, Steve Forrest, Dolores Del Rio, John McIntire, Rodolfo Acosta.
101 min.
By far and away Presley's best film, in which he sings only one song (apart from the title number), and is used emblematically rather than required to act as the half-breed son in a mixed race family which is gradually torn apart as the Kiowas go on the rampage against white settlers and both sides draw up their racist lines. Despite the stolid liberal intentions behind the script, Siegel keeps the tensions finely balanced on a knife edge, with the inevitable violence threatening to explode at every moment and the tortured emotions cutting surprisingly deep. A fine Western. TM

Flap (aka The Last Warrior)
(Carol Reed, 1970, US) Anthony Quinn, Claude Akins, Tony Bill, Victor Jory, Don Collier, Shelley Winters, Rodolfo Acosta.
106 min.
A feeble comedy. Quinn reprises his primitive savage-with-savvy bit as the drunken Indian who inaugurates a public relations war for Indian rights, Red Power. Reed's leaden direction and the script's poetry-as-prose language trivialise every issue the film touches upon. Even the wonderful idea of lassooing a helicopter is thrown away. PH

Flashback
(Franco Amurri, 1990, US) Kiefer Sutherland, Dennis Hopper, Carol Kane, Cliff De Young, Paul Dooley, Michael McKean, Richard Masur.
108 min.
Hopper gives a strong performance as a '60s radical who came near to murdering Vice-President Spiro Agnew back in 1969. After emerging from two decades in hiding, he finds himself being escorted to face trial in Washington state by reactionary FBI man Sutherland. He manages to change clothes with his minder and both land in trouble with a local sheriff. The main pleasure here is the repartee between the stars. Lots of appeal for ageing hippies, too. TJ

Flashdance
(Adrian Lyne, 1983, US) Jennifer Beals, Michael Nouri, Lilia Skala, Sunny Johnson, Kyle T Heffner, Belinda Bauer.
98 min.
The term *Flashdance* conveys the concept of incorporating everyday ephemera into a self-taught dance routine. This is what Alex (Beals) does, in between her day job as a welder and her night work dancing in a working-men's club. Abetted by trusty stereotypes such as warm-hearted boss, ex-Ziegfeld mentor, and tart with a heart, she pursues her dream of entering the Big Ballet School. She's unusually fortunate in appearing at a club whose ambience owes more to Hot Gossip than to Minsky's, but this flash-dancing stuff appears strikingly unoriginal (even if she can do 38 pirouettes on her bum); and tricksy filming prevents the routines from ever properly letting rip. Not a film for dance lovers, but rather for the starry-eyed who fancy themselves as budding Terpsichores amid romantic trappings of loin-revealing leotards, live-in lofts large enough for a family of 14, and icky kissy interludes. It's worth noting as symptomatic that most of the dance sequences were performed not by Beals, but by uncredited French dancer Marine Jahan. AB

Flash Gordon

(Michael Hodges, 1980, GB) Sam J Jones, Melody Anderson, Chaim Topol, Max von Sydow, Ornella Muti, Timothy Dalton, Brian Blessed, Peter Wyngarde, Mariangela Melato, John Osborne.
115 min.

Forget the hi-tech droidery of the current strain of sci-fi, *Flash Gordon* time warps us thirty years back into the baroque world of wedding-cake sky castles, crystal swords, hawk-men, and chaps who have just twelve hours to save the world, armed only with a lantern jaw and a clean pair of tights. The narrative is a little plodding, but adult punters will soon slip back into a reverie for the lost visions of Saturday morning cinema, and their kids can get off on the extraordinary undercurrent of febrile sexuality. Acting honours go to von Sydow as Ming the Merciless and Mariangela Melato as his dark-eyed henchperson. Flash himself is as thick as a brick, but will no doubt appeal to gentlemen who prefer blonds. CPea

Flatliners

(Joel Schumacher, 1990, US) Kiefer Sutherland, Julia Roberts, Kevin Bacon, William Baldwin, Oliver Platt, Kimberly Scott.
114 min.

Med school student Nelson Wright (Sutherland) is so obsessed with research into the near-death experience that he recruits four friends, and they take turns at stopping their hearts until the monitors reading their vital signs indicate nothing but flat lines. Once revived by other members of the team, armed with their new-found knowledge they set about rectifying past misdeeds. Schumacher's aggressive direction sweeps across weird panoramas and dives headlong into terrifying memories. We're in mystical territory here, hence the flamboyant visuals; but that's no excuse for Peter Filardi's affected script, which culminates in Bacon railing against the heavens, fists and feet flying. There's also a sorry lack of restraint from production designer Eugenio Zanetti, whose other-worldly atmosphere reaches its apotheosis in Sutherland's all-white apartment, which contains only one piece of furniture (a bed, of course). CM

Flavia la Monaca Musulmana

see Rebel Nun, The

Flavour of Green Tea Over Rice, The (Ochazuke no aji)

(Yasujiro Ozu, 1952, Jap) Shin Saburi, Michiyo Kogure, Koji Tsuruta, Chishu Ryu, Chikage Awajima, Keiko Ksujima.
116 min. b/w.

Beginning in light-hearted mood with four women deceiving their husbands to go drinking at a spa, this exquisite Ozu film gradually turns dark as it charts the marital crisis of one of the women and her taciturn husband. At once a study of the shortcomings and strengths of the arranged marriage, and an exploration of what constitutes deceit, and an understated celebration of love tentatively rekindled (one might almost call it Ozu's *Viaggio in Italia*), this is also one of the director's most 'active' films; the camera frequently moves, there are car rides, train journeys and planes taking off, as well as scenes at baseball games and cycle races. Very funny and very moving. GA

Fled

(Kevin Hooks, 1996, US) Stephen Baldwin, Laurence Fishburne, Will Patton, Robert John Burke, Victor Rivers, David Dukes, Ken Jenkins, Salma Hayek.
98 min.

A disgraced cop (Fishburne) and a hacker-with-a-heart (Baldwin) go on the lam in Georgia – first from jail-house nasties, then from cops and crims alike – while trading (witless) insults and punches. There's an intrepid local sheriff (Patton) who won't accept the official line; sinister expat Cubans with slicked hair and shades; a double-dealing superior (Burke) in the witness protection programme; and an accommodating driver (Hayek) whose car the boys co-opt, and who has to stop falling for cops. Add in elusive computer disks with vital info, regular soft-core violence, a baddy who won't stay dead, chases on foot, by car, truck, motorbike, and a cable-car finale. Lots of physical energy, but little else. NB

Flesh

(Paul Morrissey, 1968, US) Joe Dallesandro, Geraldine Smith, Maurice Bradell, Louis Waldon, Geri Miller, Candy Darling, Jackie Curtis, Patti Darbanville.
105 min.

About a hustler who goes to work to earn money for his wife's girlfriend's abortion. Self-consciously analytical, self-consciously beautiful. Visually always fine, persuasive, flattering, curious, and occasionally blatantly sociological. A product of the Warhol factory, it keeps the non-edited appearance of Warhol's own films. VG

Flesh & Blood

(Paul Verhoeven, 1985, US/Neth) Rutger Hauer, Jennifer Jason Leigh, Tom Burlinson, Jack Thompson, Fernando Hillbeck, Susan Tyrrell, Ronald Lacey.
127 min.

Verhoeven's first American feature gets landed with the handle to sum up his entire oeuvre: lashings of flesh and bags of blood, slopping around in a triumph of tastelessness. We be back in ye Middle Ages, when peasants are revolting and so are their table manners. Hauer plays Martin, leader of a raggle-taggle band of renegades who nab Agnes, virgin bride-to-be of Steven, a limp wimp and would-be Leonardo. After much rollicking rape'n'looting, Martin and his chums murder the inhabitants of a castle and settle in for a sort of Massacre of the Red Death, with bits of plague-ridden dog being lobbed at them over the battlements. With an English script crafted by Dutchmen, it's a bit Carry On Up the Codpiece, but one gets the feeling that Verhoeven hasn't quite got to grips with female psychology: Agnes may be a manipulative little bint who knows how to butter up a bumpkin's libido, but would she really have developed such a soft spot for her rapist, less a loveable rogue as played by Hauer than a steel-eyed psycho? AB

Flesh and Bone

(Steve Kloves, 1993, US) Dennis Quaid, James Caan, Meg Ryan, Gwyneth Paltrow, Scott Wilson, Christopher Rydell.
126 min.

When Arlis Sweeney (Quaid) was a kid, he saw his dad Roy (Caan) kill an entire farmstead family, except the screaming baby. Thirty years on, Arlis is content to drift around Texas fixing candy and condom machines; at least until he meets Kay Davies (Ryan), a volatile young woman keen to escape an unhappy marriage. Their hesitant relationship blooms – then, one night, the past catches up with Arlis in the shape of his father, for whom blood ties override all other considerations. Writer/director Kloves seems preoccupied with character and milieu. The performances are sound, but for much of the time the film seems undecided whether it's a mystery, a romance, a social document or an art movie. And that indecision is fatal, stifling the life out of what might have been an effective little thriller. GA

Flesh and Fantasy

(Julien Duvivier, 1943, US) Charles Boyer, Edward G Robinson, Barbara Stanwyck, Betty Field, Robert Cummings, Thomas Mitchell, Robert Benchley.
93 min. b/w.

Three tales of the supernatural, rather tiresomely linked by reflections on superstition from Benchley and his clubmen friends. A wonderfully atmospheric shot, with Mardi Gras revellers huddling on the riverbank, suddenly hushed as the body of a drowned girl is retrieved from the water, introduces the charming but slightly icky tale of a plain and embittered Cinderella (Field) who is given a mask of beauty to wear at the ball by a mysterious old man in a novelty shop, thereby precariously ensnaring the heart of the student prince (Cummings) who has hitherto ignored her. The second and best episode adapts Wilde's *Lord Arthur Savile's Crime*, with Robinson as the distraught man told by a fortune-teller (Mitchell) that he's going to commit murder, deciding to get it over with, and finding that fate is not so easily cheated. Superb throughout, the camerawork (Paul Ivano and Stanley Cortez) excels itself here. The third tale (Boyer as a tightrope walker haunted by visions of Stanwyck) is negligible, despite excellent performances. TM

Flesh and the Devil

(Clarence Brown, 1927, US) John Gilbert, Greta Garbo, Lars Hanson, Barbara Kent, William Orlamond, Marc MacDermott.
9 reels. b/w.

Renowned for its electric love scenes between Garbo and Gilbert (though these days they don't seem that torrid), this is an elegant bit of melodramatic fluff, with Garbo in swooning form as the adulterous Countess coming between her soldier lover (Gilbert) and his best buddy (Hanson), who marries her after the count (MacDermott) is killed in a duel. Much ado about nothing, really, but Garbo is as luminous as ever, thanks to William Daniels' camerawork. GA

Flesh and the Fiends, The (aka Mania/Psycho Killers/The Fiendish Ghouls)

(John Gilling, 1959, GB) Peter Cushing, Donald Pleasence, George Rose, Billie Whitelaw, June Laverick, Renee Houston, Dermot Walsh, Melvyn Hayes.
97 min. b/w.

A somewhat rickety old chiller (to the backdoor of Dr Knox's Edinburgh medical academy come the 'Resurrectionists') not helped by the stiff second leads, Laverick and Walsh, but much enlivened by the black-comic caperings of Pleasence (Ulster accent and rolling eyes) and Rose (a very simple-minded killer) as the body-snatchers Hare and Burke. The film, written by John Gilling and Leon Griffiths, is notably cold-hearted when it comes to the off-hand murders, young 'Daft' Jamie (Hayes), for instance, being strangled in a pig pen, amid the squealing of the porkers. Incidental pleasures include Billie Whitelaw, as a noisy trollop, and Renee Houston, as Mrs Burke, a most businesslike murderess. JPy

Flesh for Frankenstein (Carne per Frankenstein)

(Paul Morrissey, 1973, It/Fr) Joe Dallesandro, Monique Van Vooren, Udo Kier, Carla Mancini, Srdjan Zelenovic.
95 min.

Here Morrissey stops pretending that he's making Warhol movies and sets his sights on the US drive-in market, which takes its sex softcore but its violence unbridled. The plot boils down to Baroness Frankenstein entertaining the local stud in her boudoir, while hubby Victor chops up the rest of the peasant population in the lab downstairs. Trouble is, Morrissey just doesn't cut it as a 'real' director: there's no way that he can conjure even a sickie horror comedy from one overplayed concept (yards of bursting entrails), a three-page script, a bunch of game but mostly talentless players, and a few decorative sets. Well aware of his problems, he stakes everything on a gimmick and films in a 3-D process. Somehow, it's not enough. TR

Flesh Gordon

(Michael Benveniste/Howard Ziehm, 1974, US) Jason Williams, Suzanne Fields, Joseph Hudgins, William Hunt, John Hoyt, Candy Samples.
90 min.

Flesh Gordon, to save the world from a Sex-Ray attack, takes on the evil Wang, ruler of the planet Porno. Unsatisfying as a sex film, not much cop as anything else, this sci-fi ski-fli manages to be visually compulsive and dully unimaginative at the same time. AN

Fletch

(Michael Ritchie, 1985, US) Chevy Chase, Joe Don Baker, Dana Wheeler-Nicholson, Richard Libertini, Tim Matheson, M Emmet Walsh, George Wendt, Kenneth Mars.
98 min.

Based on the lightweight but likeable thriller by Gregory Mcdonald, *Fletch* kicks off with its eponymous investigative reporter bumming on the beach in pursuit of a drugs story. He is approached by a wealthy executive (Matheson) who declares himself to have terminal cancer, and offers our hero big bucks to break into his mansion and bump him off. Fletch, unfortunately, is played by the goofy but charmless Chevy Chase. His efforts to uncover the executive's real aims are little more than an excuse for him to ramble around in assorted disguises – but merely looking like Chevy Chase in disguise giving out silly in-joke pseudonyms – and uttering flippant unwisecracks. AB

Fletch Lives

(Michael Ritchie, 1989, US) Chevy Chase, Hal Holbrook, Julianne Phillips, R Lee Ermey, Richard Libertini, Randall 'Tex' Cobb, Cleavon Little, Patricia Kalember.
95 mins.
Bequeathed an 80-acre plantation in the Deep South, Fletch jets off to his new-found ancestral home. Surprise, surprise, the mansion turns out to be a ruin, but Fletch decided to hang around just long enough to get his end away with a 'lovely local lawyer' (Kalember), who promptly drops dead. Chase makes *fnar fnar* jokes about her death being a result of his sexual prowess, but a more likely explanation would be that Ms Kalember had read the script and decided it was a good time to get out. The ensuing plot, in which Chase gets tangled up in murder, mystery, intrigue, and derring-do, isn't worth describing since it serves only as a vehicle for Fletch to don various disguises and deliver his own 'inimitable' comic patter. The humour throughout is alternately mindless, sexist, racist, and homophobic, and would probably offend if you managed to stay awake. MK

Flic, Un (Dirty Money)

(Jean-Pierre Melville, 1972, Fr/It) Alain Delon, Catherine Deneuve, Richard Crenna, Ricardo Cucciolla, Michael Conrad, Simone Valère, Jean Desailly.
98 min.
The great Melville's thirteenth and last film – another French gangster thriller filtered through American hard-nosed conventions – is stylistically his most pared-down. Aside from the two set-piece heists, as ingeniously planned and meticulously shot as ever, the connecting story-line of an increasingly inept 'flic' (Delon) pursuing his alter ego across a darkening urban landscape has a near psychotic disregard for place, time or even plot, but total coherence in terms of mood – more blue than *noir*. A bitter meditation on disenchantment and defeat, as glacial and hermetic as Deneuve's face. CPea

Flickering Roads (Asphaltflimmern)

(Johannes Hebendanz, 1994, Ger) Fäti Sengul, Thorsten Schatz, Oda Pretschner.
80 min.
An unpretentious road movie through the underside of contemporary Germany. Swaggering delinquent teenager Micka and abandoned Rumanian immigrant Gena try to steal the same car. When they subsequently swindle café waitress Phillipa out of their bill and her job, all three find themselves on the lam, estranged from society and hounded by the police. Despite losing his way in places, director Hebendanz treats his several subjects in a light and determinedly balanced fashion, forgoing both judgment and cliché. The open ending leaves one rather more optimistic about the prospects for this makeshift family than for the society they finally abandon. NB

Flight from Ashiya

(Michael Anderson, 1963, US/Jap) Yul Brynner, Richard Widmark, George Chakiris, Suzy Parker, Shirley Knight, Danièle Gaubert, Eiko Taki.
102 min.
Tepid adventure movie, with an American Air-Sea Rescue Service team flying to save the crew of a ship sunk off the Japanese coast in a typhoon. The lumbering action scenes are further deflated by flashbacks to previous disasters the heroes have experienced; and Anderson, master of the overblown twaddle-movie (*Around the World in 80 Days, Logan's Run*), miraculously even manages to waste the photographic talents of Burnett Guffey and Joe MacDonald. GA

Flight of the Doves

(Ralph Nelson, 1971, GB) Ron Moody, Jack Wild, Dorothy McGuire, Stanley Holloway, Helen Raye, William Rushton.
101 min.
Having perpetrated a repellent mixture of bloody violence, pacifist plea and spoony romance in *Soldier Blue*, Nelson followed up with this equally odious whimsy about two Liverpudlian moppets who take flight from a cruel stepfather and head for Ireland, where a loving granny (McGuire) waits with open arms in a little

thatched cottage. Various grotesques met along the way, plus Moody as a wicked uncle with an eye to their inheritance (and adopting a series of wild disguises as he gives chase), provide some laborious relief from the maudlin sentiment. Nelson produced and co-scripted as well as directing, so the sorry mess is all his. TM

Flight of the Innocent (La Corsa dell'innocente)

(Carlo Carlei, 1993, It) Manuel Colao, Francesca Neri, Jacques Perrin, Federico Pacifici, Sal Borgese, Lucio Zagaria.
105 min.
Deep in the Calabrian countryside, young Vito (Colao) stumbles across a shooting, the bleeding victim fleeing before an unknown assailant. When Vito returns home, his father is marked as the killer by a red blot on his shoes – and further shocks are to come. Later that evening, gunmen break into the farmhouse and slaughter the family. Pitched into the stuff of nightmares, Vito barely escapes with his life. Writer/director Carlei constructs a bravura, killer opening, but later – as angelic Colao imagines himself a surrogate son to the wealthy parents (Neri and Perrin) of an abducted boy – the plot becomes mired in sentimentality and wish-fulfilment. TJ

Flight of the Intruder

(John Milius, 1991, US) Danny Glover, Willem Dafoe, Brad Johnson, Rosanna Arquette, Tom Sizemore, J Kenneth Campbell, Dann Florek, Madison Mason, Ving Rhames.
113 min.
'My politics are strange,' John Milius has said, 'I'm so far to the right, I'm almost an anarchist'. *Almost?* Judging by this gung-ho tale of a pair of frustrated Navy fliers – vengeful, disillusioned pilot Brad Johnson, and jaded, cynical bombardier Willem Dafoe – flying an unauthorised two-man mission to knock out a Vietcong missile dump in Hanoi, he's gone beyond good and evil. Sadly, his direction is as muddled as his ideology, stodgy exchanges of dialogue punctuating the disappointingly dull action sequences, which are long on military hardware but short on adrenalin. Even a diehard Milius fan would be hard-pressed to find anything of merit in this leaden, macho nonsense. NF

Flight of the Navigator

(Randal Kleiser, 1986, US) Joey Cramer, Veronica Cartwright, Cliff De Young, Sarah Jessica Parker, Matt Adler, Howard Hesseman.
89 min.
One dark night, 12-year-old David goes looking for his younger brother Jeff. Falling into a ditch, he knocks himself out. Moments later he awakens and walks home, only to find that his family have moved. Not only that, for the past eight years he's been missing, presumed dead. It's a pity the film can't quite live up to the promise of this opening: the boy's confusion is nicely handled, and the reaction on his face when he discovers that the revolting Jeff is now four years older than he and twice his size is one of the high spots of the movie. But as the answer to this strange little riddle unfolds, with NASA scientists discovering that his head is full of space charts and that he can communicate with computers, we're back on familiar Hollywood hi-tech territory. One for the none too discerning youngster. CB

Flight of the Phoenix, The

(Robert Aldrich, 1965, US) James Stewart, Richard Attenborough, Peter Finch, Hardy Kruger, Ernest Borgnine, Ian Bannen, Ronald Fraser, Christian Marquand, Dan Duryea, George Kennedy.
149 min.
Basically a disaster movie about survival problems when a cargo-passenger plane crashes miles from anywhere in the Arabian desert. The pilot (Stewart), conscious of his responsibility for the lives of all concerned, suffers doubts; his navigator (Attenborough), a man accustomed to relying on the bottle for his courage, starts shaping up; a regular army officer (Finch) courts suicide because he blindly insists on playing by regulations...So far, so conventional, although beautifully characterised and directed by Aldrich with a grip that keeps tension high and heroics low. What takes the film right out of the rut is the gradual emergence of the group's saviour: a

youthful German designer of model aircraft (Kruger), who develops a strain of pure Nazi fanaticism in his determination to prove that he can build a plane which will fly from bits of the wreck. He does it, too, although his only previous experience has been in toy-making; and in doing so, he raises spiky questions about leadership (democratic/dictatorial) and the survival of the fittest. A fadeout handshake of mutual congratulation finally shoves those questions aside – this is a Hollywood movie, after all – but not before they've achieved their abrasive task. TM

Flight to Berlin (Fluchtpunkt Berlin)

(Christopher Petit, 1983, WGer) Tusse Silberg, Paul Freeman, Lisa Kreuzer, Jean-François Stévenin, Ewan Stewart, Eddie Constantine, Tatjana Blacher.
90 min.
A mysterious death, a dissatisfied loner who may or may not be somehow guilty, a journey, introspection all round...where else but in Petit territory? As the film throws up plentiful questions regarding Tusse Silberg's relation to a dead woman, her sister, and the strange city of the title, Petit films in a terse, thought-provoking but oddly classical style, sounding echoes not merely of Godard, Rivette and Wenders, but also of older masters like Lang. Whether it works or not depends on your attitude towards the script's hesitantly elliptical way with narrative, but there's no denying that Petit is one of Britain's most ambitious film-makers. Infuriating or inspired, either way it's still worth a look. GA

Flim-Flam Man, The (aka One Born Every Minute)

(Irvin Kershner, 1967, US) George C Scott, Michael Sarrazin, Sue Lyon, Harry Morgan, Jack Albertson, Alice Ghostley, Albert Salmi, Slim Pickens, Strother Martin.
115 min.
Aside from a long and outrageously destructive car chase, this is mainly a matter of mild charm and much cracker-barrel philosophy as an ageing confidence trickster (Scott) sardonically undertakes to instruct a youthful army deserter (Sarrazin) in the ways of the world. Good performances all round, but it's a long haul before the boy, having proven himself an apt pupil but deciding to do the right thing, teaches his mentor that there is at least one honest person in the world. TM

Flintstones, The

(Brian Levant, 1994, US) John Goodman, Elizabeth Perkins, Rick Moranis, Rosie O'Donnell, Kyle MacLachlan, Halle Berry, Elizabeth Taylor.
91 min.
This 'Spielrock' production is faithful to the original in everything but scale. The trick was not to stray too far from the cartoon simplicity of the Hanna-Barbera TV series, so the movie is a spectacular celebration of the superficial and the reassuring. The town of Bedrock is a genuine foam-design wonder: the bustling quarry, the monumental high street with its stone-roller cars. The exploited Jurassic-era fauna, from Dino the pet dinosaur to the lobster lawnmowers, all courtesy of Henson puppet technology and enhanced computer animatronics are as sympathetic as you wish they'd organise a 'toon union. The actors, on the other hand – Goodman's Fred, Moranis's Barney, Perkins' Wilma – replicate the voices, manners, tics and tropes of the originals so accurately, they seem like programmed automatons. WH

Flipper

(James B Clark, 1963, US) Chuck Connors, Luke Halpin, Kathleen Maguire, Connie Scott.
90 min.
Straightforward tale of a boy and a dolphin which proved popular enough to merit a movie sequel and launch a fondly remembered '60s TV series. You know the score by now: young Halpin nurses the dolphin back from injury, then has to persuade a grouchy old pop to let him keep his new-found pal as a pet. Will pacify small children. TJ

Flipper

(Alan Shapiro, 1996, US) Paul Hogan, Elijah Wood, Chelsea Field, Jessica Wesson, Isaac Hayes, Jonathan Banks, Jason Fuchs.
96 min.

Amiable yarn based on the mid-'60s TV series about a growing youngster and an 'orphan' dolphin. Wood is the diffident single-parent child, Sandy, who vacations in a Caribbean backwater with his uncle Porter (Hogan), an ex-Beach Boys roadie turned salty sea dog (plus Hemingway cap and parrot). It's something of a muted comeback for Hogan, waltzing through his role as the eccentric but straight-arrow father-substitute with a pared version of his real man 'Dundee' persona. Writer/director Shapiro blends the elements of romance, adventure and comedy with easy if anonymous competence. Sandy trysts with bright-eyed Kim (Wesson), Porter romances marine biologist Cathy (Field); no wonder the dolphin keep springing into the air as if to protest he's been forgotten. Excellent technical credits, notably Bill Butler's camerawork, but the best stuff is the kid's lingo – 'Gotta jet, here comes the hippy.' WH

Flirt

(Hal Hartley, 1995, US/GB/Jap) Bill Sage, Parker Posey, Martin Donovan, Robert Burke, Karen Sillas, Dwight Ewell, Dominik Bender, Geno Lechner, Elina Lowensöhn, Miho Nikaido, Toshio Fujiwara, Chikako Hara, Hal Hartley, Masatoshi Nagase.
84 min.
Hartley's jeu d'esprit starts from an intriguing premise: the same script is delivered three times, by three different casts, thus allowing local cultural differences and the viewer's cumulative knowledge to influence various shifts in tone and treatment. Shot first as a stand alone short, 'New York, February 1993' brings the tart romantic confusions familiar from the director's earlier work, as Bill Sage gives himself 90 minutes to decide if his future lies with partner Posey, and has his decision shaped by barfly Donovan's suicidal response to rejection by Sage's other lover. In 'Berlin, October 1994' black American Dwight Ewell hesitates over his affair with art dealer Bender, and a chorus of refreshingly straightforward workmen explain the film's self-reflexive strategies. 'Tokyo, March 1995' sets down with *butoh* performer Nikaido (Hartley's off-screen wife) and visiting American film-maker 'Hal', played with quizzical self-consciousness by the writer/director himself. Although the aphoristic dialogue and sly wit are by now a given, the structure allows Hartley to jettison more and more of the narrative exposition as he goes along, creating a Godardian sense of playfulness and also renewing the director's interest in purely choreographic nuance. TJ

Flirting

(John Duigan, 1989, Aust) Noah Taylor, Thandie Newton, Nicole Kidman, Bartholomew Rose, Felix Nobis, Josh Picker, Kiri Paramore.
99 min.
The second part of a trilogy which began with *The Year My Voice Broke*. Teenage student Danny (Taylor) divides his time between being bullied for his stutter and being bewitched by Thandiwe (Newton), a Ugandan pupil from a nearby girls' school. Both misfits, the two find solace in each other's affection, crossing the lake in search of adulthood. Beautifully written and directed by Duigan, the film maintains a delicate balance between wry satire, childish laughter, and dark, brooding malevolence. Not since Bill Forsyth's *Gregory's Girl* has a movie so precisely captured the goose-bumps, grunts, giggles and gorgeous rapture of teenage love. Taylor is a jowly delight, while 16-year-old newcomer Newton throws savage glances and sensuous smiles with the assured air of a seasoned professional. Electrifying and heartbreaking; cherish it. MK

Flirting with Disaster

(David O Russell, 1996, US) Ben Stiller, Patricia Arquette, Téa Leoni, Mary Tyler Moore, George Segal, Alan Alda, Lily Tomlin.
92 min.
Mel (Stiller) has a wife, Nancy (Arquette), an as yet unnamed baby, and a 'psychic need' to track down his biological parents. An adoption agency provides him with information so efficiently that he readily agrees to let research psychologist Tina (Leoni) witness the reunion. Besides, she's an attractive ex-dancer and he and Nancy aren't exactly back up to speed in the bedroom. Unfortunately, there's been a mix-up in the records, and the next 'father' he checks out isn't legitimate either; so the threesome – plus baby –

work their way across the country, picking up a couple of gay federal agents en route. Writer/director Russell's follow-up to the incest comedy *Spanking the Monkey* confirms his gift for acute mischief-making.The neurotic frenzy threatens to annoy, but Russell's edgy, abbreviated style generates farcical comic friction without sacrificing character. When, early on, that icon of wholesomeness Mary Tyler Moore flashes her support bra, it's clear that, henceforth, nothing's sacred. It must be excruciatingly embarrassing to be related to this film-maker, but he's fast becoming a favourite son to the rest of us. TCh

Floating Life

(Clara Law, 1996, Aust) Annette Shun Wah, Annie Yip, Anthony Wong, Edwin Pang, Cecilia Fong Sing Lee, Toby Wong.
95 min.
A fascinating if flawed tale of a Hong Kong family who emigrate to Australia, where the bossy, largely Westernised second daughter's warnings about pit-bulls, killer wasps and skin cancer only add to the difficulties of adjustment; meanwhile, the eldest sister tries to persuade her husband that they should leave Germany, and the womanising eldest son wonders whether he too should see in 1997 or join his family. Shifting steadily from gentle comedy to something more poignant, the film never quite adds up to anything very compelling or cohesive. Watchable, none the less. GA

Flor di me Secreto, La

see Flower of My Secret, The

Florentine Dagger, The

(Robert Florey, 1935, US) Donald Woods, Margaret Lindsay, C Aubrey Smith, Robert Barrat, Henry O'Neill, Eily Malyon.
69 min. b/w.
Genuinely bizarre thriller about a young man, tormented by his heritage as 'the last of the Borgias', who tries to commit suicide to put an end to his impulse to kill. Advised by a psychiatrist to sublimate his fears, he writes a successful play about the Borgias, only to come to fear that his leading lady, who has problems of her own – a mother horribly burned in a theatrical fire, an amorous stepfather who is found stabbed with a Florentine dagger – may be being taken over by the personality of Lucretia. Over-compressed from Ben Hecht's novel, the script emerges as a bit of a ragbag, meandering from a classically stylish horror movie opening into conventional whodunit and back again to Grand Guignol. It is held together a trifle uncertainly by some Freudian analysis (the setting is Vienna), and rather more securely by Florey's consistently inventive, moodily evocative direction. Acting honours go to Barrat for his marvellously witty performance as the susceptibly gallant police chief. TM

Flower of My Secret, The (La Flor di me Secreto/La Fleur de mon secret)

(Pedro Almodóvar, 1995, Sp/Fr) Marisa Paredes, Chus Lampreave, Rossy de Palma, Juan Echanove, Imanol Aria, Carmen Elias.
107 min.
Here we have Almodóvar's most open, unadorned, emotive and maybe even courageous film to date, an intimate portrait of pain and regeneration that strikes the heart without trickery. Gone are the chic excesses of *Kika* and the uneasy balance between superficial sensationalism and pocket melodrama that's marked the director's work since *Women on the Verge*. Paredes is immensely sympathetic as Leo, a forty-something writer of romantic fiction who hits crisis point when she's rejected by her absentee husband and finds she's trapped by her reputation when she tries to expand her literary horizons. Although she's supported by Angel (Echanove), cultural editor of *El Pais*, the constant bickering between her mother and sister doesn't help matters (Lampreave and de Palma, in a double-act to treasure); a trip home to her native village in La Mancha proves, however, an unlikely source of solace. Rarely has Almodóvar focused so closely on a single character, and the challenge of developing an individual portrait has reconnected him with the emotional realities of an everyday damaged life, where loneliness, professional frustration and the irritation and commitment that permeate family relationships are observed with perceptiveness, honesty and the usual incisive humour. TJ

Flowers in the Attic

(Jeffrey Bloom, 1987, US) Louise Fletcher, Victoria Tennant, Kristy Swanson, Jeb Stuart Adams, Ben Ganger, Lindsay Parker.
92 min.
Tennant is the perfect little mother whose husband dies in a car crash, and who puts herself and her four children at the mercy of her dying father and sadistic mother. Daddy never approved of her marriage and wrote her out of his will, and her unforgiving mother (Fletcher) insists that the children be kept locked in the attic to prevent him ever discovering their existence. Months pass, and the children, suffering from exhaustion and poisoned cookies, realise that their loving mother is just as deranged as their granny, and plot their escape. Incestuous desires run rampant in the original novel by VC Andrews, but all the movie has to offer is soft-focus innuendo. As fantasy stripped of all its metaphorical trimmings, the sublimely ridiculous plot is more likely to reduce an audience to laughter than to tears. TRi

Flowers of Shanghai (Hai Shang Hua)

(Hou Xiaoxian, 1998, Tai) Tony Leung Chiu-Wai, Michelle Reis, Jack Gao, Carina Lau.
125 min.
Entirely studio shot, Hou's most formally daring film to date is less an adaptation of a century old novel by Han Ziyun than a distillation of the lost world it describes. The 'flower houses' of old Shanghai were technically brothels, but not primarily places for sex; at a time when arranged marriages were the norm, China's male elite patronised them to get an *éducation sentimentale*. Hou organises the film around two strands of narrative. In one, Cantonese civil servant Wang (Leung) turns his back on his favourite 'flower girl' after catching her with another lover. In the other, a 'gentleman caller' and a cynical 'flower girl' conspire to profit from arranging to cover up the scandal of an attempted suicide. Each scene is a continuous take, bracketed by fades up from and back to black; the one (crucial) exception is the insert of Wang's point-of-view as he witnesses Ms Crimson's unfaithfulness. Hauntingly sad, the film elegantly deranges the viewer's sense of time: this seemingly unchanging world is in fact riven by off-screen incidents – which change everything. TR

Flubber

(Les Mayfield, 1997, US) Robin Williams, Marcia Gay Harden, Christopher McDonald, Raymond J Barry, Clancy Brown.
94 min.
'Flubber' – Prof Brainard (Williams) informs us, pseudo-scientifically – is an elastomer, ductile and elastic. All we really really need to know, however, is that the Professor's flying rubber superballs cause spectacular destruction. Top honours in this Disney remake of *The Absent-Minded Professor* go to cameraman Dean Cundey and the effects and design teams: to the whizzing balls, flying cars, aerial simulations, the 'Time Machine' laboratories and the Heath Robinson-style domestic aids. Williams produces another of his strangely sympathetic cartoons, an arrested adult so forgetful he's three times missed his own wedding (to Harden). He wears the same bow ties as Fred MacMurray, but dispenses with any residual traces of maturity. The script (by John Hughes and Bill Walsh) has Brainard selling the flubber to save the college. He's frustrated by fiancée-stealing McDonald, and the henchmen of entrepreneur Barry, who, naturally enough, want to exploit the green goo. WH

Fluchtweg nach Marseilles

see Escape Route to Marseilles

Fly, The

(Kurt Neumann, 1958, US) David Hedison, Patricia Owens, Vincent Price, Herbert Marshall, Kathleen Freeman, Charles Herbert.
94 min.
Differing greatly from David Cronenberg's very loose remake, this sci-fi classic is equally entertaining in its love of the grotesque. When scientist Hedison's matter-transference experiment goes wrong, he ends up with a fly's head and wing, while the insect in question is lumbered with his head and arm. His attempts to reverse the process inevitably fail, and he gradually goes insane, lead-

ing to a pleasingly bleak finale in which his wife crushes his head in a steam press and the fly gets trapped in a spider's web. Ludicrous stuff, of course, but Price lends his own inimitable and delightful brand of bravura to the role of Hedison's concerned brother, while James (*Shogun*) Clavell's script successfully treads a fine line between black comedy and po-faced seriousness. GA

Fly, The

(David Cronenberg, 1986, US) Jeff Goldblum, Geena Davis, John Getz, Joy Boushel, Les Carlson, George Chuvalo, David Cronenberg.
100 min.
The year's blockbuster romance, but they'll probably do a fair amount of retching as well as sobbing in the aisles, since it's directed by Cronenberg, the man who gave you the original exploding head. The story pupates much like its 1958 predecessor, with scientist Seth Brundle (Goldblum) failing to notice the fly that sneaks a lift when he teleports himself between the 'designer phone booths' in his warehouse laboratory. But instead of ending up with a gigantic insect head, Brundle is fused with the little fucker at a molecular-genetic level, triggering an insidious process whereby his character is changed along with his body. What makes the story more than just a gore-fest of corroded limbs and inside-out baboons is the touching relationship between Brundle and journalist Veronica Quaife (Davis), and their respective attitudes to the 'disease', which is representative of any modern scourge of the flesh, from cancer and AIDS to plain old age. Frail stomachs may heave at the film's high yuck-factor and Grand Guignol climax, but the poignancy is that of a *Love Story* for the '80s, with real raw meat on it. AB

Fly II, The

(Chris Walas, 1989, US) Eric Stoltz, Daphne Zuniga, Lee Richardson, John Getz, Frank Turner, Anne Marie Lee, Gary Chalk, Saffron Henderson.
104 min.
With the original director and leads having nothing to do with this sequel, we suffer a nasty opening scene in which an unconvincing Geena Davis lookalike gives birth to a crusty chrysalis, whence emerges Seth Brundle's son, Martin (Stoltz). He looks normal on the outside, but inside his genetic wiring is seriously crossed. Growing up under the clinical eyes of the sinister Bartok industries, Martin zips from boyhood to manhood in a ridiculously short period, and in no time at all is getting it together with Beth Logan (Zuniga), who doesn't know about his dad being a creepy-crawly. But when Martin's skin starts falling off, she begins to suspect that it's more than just a case for Clearasil, and resolves to help her loved one sort out his confused chromosomes – too late to avoid the onslaught of latex and squishy special effects for which we've all been waiting, and which is indeed the movie's only interesting commodity. Other than that, it's standard directionless fare. MK

Fly a Flag for Poplar

(Roger Buck/Caroline Goldie/Ron Orders/Geoff Richman/Marie Richman/Tony Wickert, 1974, GB)
81 min. b/w & col.
Those convinced that the proper translation of cinéma-vérité is cinema boredom will have their belief confirmed by this documentary tribute to Poplar's community spirit. Large, inert slabs of it are devoted to the day-to-day doings of its people, particularly those organising a neighbourhood festival: mums prepare meals, a clergyman greets passers-by, a Ford worker drives to Dagenham, someone performs on the spoons. The fragmentary reconstruction of Poplar's past, using newsreels and photographs, is far more interesting; and the print quality is often better, too. GB

Fly Away Home

(Carroll Ballard, 1996, US) Jeff Daniels, Anna Paquin, Dana Delany, Terry Kinney, Holter Graham, Jeremy Ratchford.
107 min.
An inspirational movie from the director of *The Black Stallion*. The shock opening, however, sets a tone of emotional realism unusual for a children's film. (A car crash leaves 13-year-old Amy traumatised and her mother dead.) The ostensible (true-life) adventure – Amy is shipped to backwoods Canada to live with her eccentric sculptor/

inventor father (Daniels), learns to fly a microlight aircraft in order to reach the breeding grounds of the orphaned geese she's raised – is made a metaphor for the girl's empowerment thanks to the enabling support of her parent. It's a common enough image, but it's realised here without strain. Caleb Deschanel's cinematography is as arresting as Mark Isham's score is discreet. But the performances are key: as Amy, Anna Paquin proves again what an expressive, soulful actress she is, and Daniels' madcap dad is a winning study in hippy ingenuity and indefatigability. WH

Flying Camel, The

(Rami Na'Aman, 1994, Isr) Gidon Singer, Salim Dau, Laurence Bonard, Gilat Ankori.
92 min.
Slight Israeli comedy in which an ageing Jewish professor (determined to stop the city council's demolition of Bauhaus buildings) and an Arab garbage collector (whose father owned an orange grove on the site of the Jew's shack) first lock horns and then, predictably, join forces. Focused on questions of land, tradition and cultural difference, the film is easy to read, but too broad to provoke more than the odd chortle. GA

Flying Down to Rio

(Thornton Freeland, 1933, US) Dolores Del Rio, Gene Raymond, Raul Roulien, Ginger Rogers, Fred Astaire.
89 min. b/w.
Fred and Ginger teamed for the first time as featured artists in the big production number, 'The Carioca': 'I'd like to try this thing just once' says Fred, launching the movies' greatest partnership. Otherwise notable mainly for the non-stop opticals which turn the film into a series of animated postcards. The nominal star, the wooden Raymond, is swept off his feet by the exotic Del Rio (one of those actresses who age only ten years in forty-odd), of whom a Yankee girl cries, 'What have these South Americans got below the equator that we haven't?'. The Berkeleyesque aerial ballet is a gas. SG

Flying Fool, The

(Walter Summers, 1931, GB) Henry Kendall, Benita Hume, Wallace Geoffrey, Ursula Jeans, Martin Walker.
76 min. b/w.
One of those 'thick-ear' melodramas which made up the bulk of British B movies, with Kendall as a pilot assigned by the Secret Service to unmask a killer. Not quite up to *Dark Eyes of London* or *Traitor Spy*, but old maestro Summers, structuring his cardboard story around low-life Paris and Croydon airport, manages some marvellous moments. An airsick passenger swearing never again to cross the Channel, a villain rising Dracula-like from his coffin, some superbly seedy can-can dancers, even an Antonioni-ish car/plane duel. Maybe not great cinema, but for those with happy memories of Saturday morning pictures, an essential part of life. RMy

Flying Leathernecks

(Nicholas Ray, 1951, US) John Wayne, Robert Ryan, Don Taylor, Janis Carter, Jay C Flippen, William Harrigan, James Bell, Barry Kelley.
102 min.
Made between the marvellous *In a Lonely Place* and *On Dangerous Ground*, this is arguably Ray's least distinguished film, a relatively conventional, anonymous WWII drama made for RKO mogul Howard Hughes – hence the authentic, Technicolor aerial footage of fighters in combat, as a Marine Corps squadron fight the Japs at Guadalcanal. Rather more interesting, perhaps, is the private conflict between Wayne's sternly nonnesense disciplinarian CO and Ryan's more openly compassionate executive officer, who is afflicted with several of the neuroses commonly found in Ray's protagonists. Finally, however, it's all very predictable, even culminating in a flag-waving endorsement of traditional heroism. Thanks to the solid performances and fine camerawork, the film is not bad, merely professional. GA

FM

(John A Alonzo, 1978, US) Michael Brandon, Eileen Brennan, Alex Karras, Cleavon Little, Martin Mull, Cassie Yates, Norman Lloyd, James Keach.
104 min.

Set in a slick little LA music station, QSKY (7.11 on your FM dial), *FM* barely concerns itself with the daily business of radio. Really it's the story of a group of hip (but nice) dedicated broadcasters, led by sexy, buddy-hugging Jeff Dugan (Brandon), out to combat the interfering idiocy of the indentured slaves of the network corporation. Dugan, who's heavily into the music biz, is against commercials on commercial radio (but since QSKY pumps out an endless stream of Ronstadt, the Eagles and Queen, wouldn't a few mindless jingles go unnoticed?) The crunch comes when Dugan is forced to resign after refusing to broadcast a recruiting ad from the army. His crew of husky-voiced neurotics pull themselves together and start a sit-in. Much solidarity and hugs. Deus-ex-machina, the head of the corporation flies into LA, and as you might guess, he admires guts...A lot of Pie in the QSKY. JS

[Focus]

(Satoshi Isaka, 1996, Jap) Tadanobu Asano, Keiko Unno, Akira Shirai, Tetsuro Sano.
73 min.
Despite an escalation into melodrama as it heads towards its climax, this is an almost completely believable fake documentary. A TV current affairs crew is interviewing a shy, repressed nerd about his addiction to listening in on short-wave radio and mobile phone conversations. But the director is a scuzzy opportunist whose sole ambition is to land a sensational scoop; an overheard call about a gun in a coin-locker starts them on a descent into hysteria and disaster. The casting of the film's actual cameraman as the TV crew's off-screen cameraman gives the overall credibility a huge boost. It's also extremely well acted (Asano, who plays the nerd, is currently Japan's hottest young star) and executed with considerable skill and welcome shafts of humour. In sum, it's as good as 'social-conscience' movies ever get. TR

Fog, The

(John Carpenter, 1979, US) Adrienne Barbeau, Hal Holbrook, Janet Leigh, Jamie Lee Curtis, John Houseman, Tom Atkins, Nancy Loomis.
91 min.
The Fog will disappoint those expecting a re-run of the creepy scares from *Halloween*. Instead, expanding enormously on the fantasy elements of his earlier films, Carpenter has turned in a full-scale thriller of the supernatural, as a sinister fog bank comes rolling in off the sea to take revenge on the smug little town of Antonio Bay, N.Calif. No shotguns running; no prowling of dark corners; no tricksy dry-ice chills. Instead you'll find a masterful simplicity of style, a lonely and determined group of characters under siege, and a childlike sense of brooding fear that almost disappeared in the '70s. Carpenter's confidence is outrageous; the range of his models even more so (from Poe to RKO); and the achievement is all his own, despite ragged moments and occasional hesitations. CA

Fog Over Frisco

(William Dieterle, 1934, US) Bette Davis, Lyle Talbot, Margaret Lindsay, Donald Woods, Henry O'Neill, Hugh Herbert, Robert Barrat.
68 min. b/w.
No masterpiece, but a fascinatingly brisk thriller about a journalist (Woods, living up to his name) and a young heiress (Lindsay) searching for the kidnappers of her wayward, irresponsible sister (Davis). The plot is complex enough to hold the attention, the performances by and large passable (Davis unfortunately disappears after about twenty minutes), though the injections of comedy with Hugh Herbert's inept photographer are excruciating. But Dieterle directs for all he's worth, moving the plot along at a furious pace and making excellent use of Tony Gaudio's chiaroscuro camerawork. GA

Folies Bergère

(Roy Del Ruth, 1935, US) Maurice Chevalier, Ann Sothern, Merle Oberon, Eric Blore, Walter Byron, Ferdinand Munier.
84 min. b/w.
A real Chevalier show as he demonstrates his saucy Gallic charm in two roles: as a wealthy Baron in financial straits, and as a Folies comedian the Baron employs to impersonate him to help him out of an awkward scrape. The comedy that arises from mistaken identities and complications with wife and girlfriend is brisk enough,

though the musical numbers – even the one starring Chevalier's trademark straw hat – hardly match the Warners Busby Berkeley style that Fox's Zanuck was so keen to emulate. GA

Folks!

(Ted Kotcheff, 1992, US) Tom Selleck, Don Ameche, Anne Jackson, Christine Ebersole, Wendy Crewson, Robert Pastorelli, Michael Murphy.
109 min.
Jon Aldrich (Selleck) has a solid job on the Chicago Stock Exchange, a spacious home, lovely wife (Crewson), two kids and a dog. Then, one day, his perfect life is thrown into chaos: while he's visiting his sick mother (Jackson) in Florida, the FBI invades his office to investigate insider trading, freezing his private account in the process. No money means no nursing care for Mom, but worse is to come when Jon visits his senile father (Ameche), who burns down his own home in a fit of forgetfulness. All Mom and Dad want is a swift journey to that trailer park in the sky, and when Jon is enlisted to help their (abortive) suicide attempts, a series of signposted accidents leaves him *sans* sight, toe and testicle. Masquerading as a commentary on the greedy '80s, this is clearly the sort of moronic comedy beloved of the *Weekend at Bernie's* team of Kotcheff and writer Robert Klane. CM

Folle à Tuer
(The Evil Trap)

(Yves Boisset, 1975, Fr/It) Marlène Jobert, Tomas Milian, Victor Lanoux, Michel Lonsdale, Jean Bouix.
95 min.
A fair thriller that begins with one of WC Fields' anti-kid quotes, and promisingly looks like despatching one averagely noxious brat quite early on, but settles instead for making his survival a condition of its heroine's redemption. Having just been released from a mental clinic and hired as a governess, Jobert finds herself at the centre of a kidnap-and-murder conspiracy hatched by her apparent benefactor, and involving a studiedly vicious Milian as its agent. On the run from both killer and media-fanned frame-up, she's perhaps just a little too much the bastion of resourceful sanity in a mad world, but Boisset conjures a pleasing momentum for her flight, and allows some of the absurd humour of her plight to seep blackly out. Based on the gloriously titled *série noire* novel *O Dingos, O Châteaux* by Jean-Patrick Manchette (*Aggression, Nada*), it leans surprisingly little on modish paranoia, and pleases most for its essential modesty. PT

Follow a Star

(Robert Asher, 1959, GB) Norman Wisdom, June Laverick, Jerry Desmonde, Hattie Jacques, Eddie Leslie, Richard Wattis, John Le Mesurier, Fenella Fielding, Ron Moody, Sydney Tafler, Joe Melia.
104 min. b/w.
His old producer, Hugh Stewart, used to reckon Wisdom was as close British cinema had come to a comedian in the mould of Harold Lloyd or Buster Keaton. It's certainly true that Wisdom was in his heyday a consummate acrobat with a knack for slapstick. But little Norman had a fatal flaw: he always sugared his comedy with spoonfuls of outrageous, cloying sentiment. This picture (which he co-scripted) is a case in point. He's a tailor's assistant with a beautiful singing voice. Unflappable straightman Desmonde is the faltering crooner who gets Wisdom to stand off-stage and sing while he mimes. There are plenty of laughs, but the script again relies on making us feel sorry for our poor mistreated hero. GM

Following

(Christopher Nolan, 1998, GB) Jeremy Theobald, Alex Haw, Lucy Russell, John Nolan.
70 min. b/w.
Shot at weekends on a shoestring, Nolan's 16mm b/w feature is more *Shallow Grave* than Shane Meadows. Blocked writer Bill (Theobald) takes to following strangers through the streets of Soho, ostensibly to kickstart his fiction. One day, one of his 'targets' bites back: Cobb (Haw) introduces himself as a burglar skilled at 'reading' people's identities from rifling through their possessions, and he insists that Bill should tag along to experience the thrill for himself. A complicated time structure (the film flashes backwards and for-wards) signals that more is going on here than meets the eye. Sure enough, the denouement involves two double crosses, a femme fatale, a murder and a crowning triple cross. The generic pay off is a little disappointing after the edgy, character based scenes of exposition, but the film is acted and directed confidently enough to work well as a wry mystery thriller. TR

Follow That Dream

(Gordon Douglas, 1962, US) Elvis Presley, Arthur O'Connell, Anne Helm, Joanna Moore, Jack Kruschen, Simon Oakland.
110 min.
Presley made 33 films, and at least 30 were considered duds by the critics. However, they all made money, and they're still a fixture on TV. Here, he's a homeless army veteran who heads south to Florida with his father and four orphans (songs include 'Home Is Where the Heart Is'). Opportunities for sneering and hip-swivelling are limited. One of Hollywood's most celebrated (and cynical) screenwriters, Charles Lederer, provided the script (from the novel *Pioneer Go Home* by Richard Powell), but it's such a feeble, mawkish affair that you half suspect he wrote it tongue-in-cheek. Or perhaps he thought Perry Como was the star. GM

Follow the Fleet

(Mark Sandrich, 1936, US) Fred Astaire, Ginger Rogers, Randolph Scott, Harriet Hilliard, Astrid Allwyn, Lucille Ball, Betty Grable.
110 min. b/w.
Fred plays an ex-exponent of 'genteel dancing' who became a gob when Ginger wouldn't marry him. They meet up again at the Paradise Club and, in this revamp of *Hit the Deck*, put on a show and save a floundering romance between four-square Scott and awful-pain Hilliard. The numbers, being by Irving Berlin, are top-hole. 'I'm Putting All My Eggs in One Basket' gets a hilarious sparring dance routine, 'Let Yourself Go' is a marvellous piece of showing off, and 'Let's Face the Music and Dance' the most beautifully integrated of any of their evening dress jobs. Fred's piano-playing and typing turn out just like his dancing – no surprise: his hands always danced as much as his feet. SG

Folly To Be Wise

(Frank Launder, 1952, GB) Alastair Sim, Roland Culver, Elizabeth Allan, Martita Hunt, Colin Gordon, Janet Brown, Miles Malleson.
91 min. b/w.
National Service and Launder & Gilliat comedies are such clearly marked symptoms of the '50s that one might expect their combination to distil the very essence of that dreary decade. Indeed, Launder brings James Bridie's play to the screen with a minimum of flair and ingenuity, but the themes the film deals with are intriguing. Bumbling entertainments officer Sim attempts to come to terms with youth and modernism by dispensing with the services of the local lady violinists and giving the masses what they want. That it should be a 'brains trust' of local celebrities that draws the crowds in is highly implausible, but the resulting display of middle class moral bankruptcy and celebration of working class common sense is extraordinary. RMy

Fong Sai-Yuk
(aka Fang Shiyu)

(Yuan Kwai, 1993, HK) Jet Li, Josephine Siao, Adam Cheng, Chen Songyonh.
100 min.
Fast action comedy in period costume. The cobbled script uses real characters and organisations, but whips up an entirely fictitious froth of martial arts tournaments, undeclared passions and underground resistance movements. It centres less on the nominal star Jet Li than on the sublime Josephine Siao, in and out of drag as the hero's protective mother, her performance a show-stopping culmination of three decades of fine work in the Hong Kong cinema. TR

Food of the Gods, The

(Bert I Gordon, 1976, US) Marjoe Gortner, Pamela Franklin, Ralph Meeker, Ida Lupino, Jon Cypher, Tom Stovall.
88 min.
Gordon's reworking of his *Village of the Giants* (1965), replacing the giant teenagers with amazing colossal chickens, wasps and (especially) rats, all of whom have gorged themselves on a vile fluid found bubbling on the ground near Lupino's farm and put into bottles helpfully labelled FOTG. It's a piece of low-budget rubbish (based on a portion of HG Wells' 1904 fantasy) featuring all the genre's well-loved ingredients: a frightful script, variable special effects, and a weird bunch of actors who manage to look just a little less ludicrous than the giant rats. Unfortunately, the film's attractions pall about half way through: Gordon can't muster the lunatic verve necessary to bind things together, and one marauding rodent soon begins to look like any other, no matter what its size. GB

Fool, The

(Christine Edzard, 1990, GB) Derek Jacobi, Cyril Cusack, Ruth Mitchell, Maria Aitken, Irina Brook, Paul Brooke, Jim Carter, Rosalie Crutchley, Patricia Hayes, Don Henderson, Michael Hordern, Stratford Johns, Miriam Margolyes, John McEnery, Michael Medwin, Murray Melvin, Miranda Richardson, Joan Sims.
140 min.
Edzard's *Little Dorrit* was rightly acclaimed for its impeccable attention to detail; the same care, if not the literary pedigree, has gone into this successor, co-written by Edzard with her editor Olivier Stockman, but owing its inspiration to the more prosaic if equally socially-conscious work of Henry Mayhew. She has again produced an authentic period feel, but what the film lacks is a strong narrative. The confusing premise lies in the fact that Jacobi is leading a double life: first as Mr Frederick, a lowly theatrical booking clerk of humble means and charisma; then as Sir John, the effortless darling of polite Victorian society, able almost to create money out of the air, and accepted not because of who he is but how he behaves. Much has been made of the parallels between the ebullience of 1857 and the stock market scandals of today, but more intriguing is a fine theatrical climax in which Jacobi turns on the representatives of True-Brit greed, tearing their selfishness to bits – much to their seeming incomprehension. Jacobi is as usual superb, well supported by a galaxy of British actors. SGr

Fool for Love

(Robert Altman, 1985, US) Sam Shepard, Kim Basinger, Harry Dean Stanton, Randy Quaid, Martha Crawford.
108 min.
Sam Shepard's play was a short, Strindbergian chamber piece, in which a semi-incestuous affair between half-brother and sister was enacted largely by them hurling each other off the walls of their small motel room. While maintaining the claustrophobia, Altman's adaptation is much more leisurely in approach, allowing a good half-hour for the arrival of Eddie (Shepard himself) at the motel in the Mojave desert, before getting down to the hurting match between the two obsessive would-be lovers. The play had a ghostly figure, the Old Man, who hovered in the wings, breaking into occasional monologue to comment on the affair, in which it was revealed that he was in fact their father. The film successfully weaves him into the action, still standing slightly apart as a Greek chorus, but nonetheless integrated: Stanton is his usual excellent self as the man who may be a spirit from the past. Shepard is perfect as the dumb hick in cowboy gear who likes lassoing the bedpost; and Basinger, as the faded girl in a red dress, brings a curious, tatty dignity to the role, and proves at last that she can act when not required to pout in her underwear. It's the best of Altman's series of theatre adaptations, capturing the original's dreamlike musings on the nature of inherited guilt; what one misses is the sexual ferocity. CPea

Foolish Wives

(Erich von Stroheim, 1921, US) Erich von Stroheim, Maude George, Mae Busch, George Christians, Cesare Gravina, Malvine Polo, Dale Fuller.
13,800 ft. b/w.
The first full-scale working-out of Stroheim's explorations of the ground between high society manners and terminal squalor and depravity. The plot centres on the sexual and criminal activities of Count Karamzin (Stroheim). The sumptuous visual style continually invites the viewer

to indulge Karamzin's fantasies, only to undercut them with 'real life' details designed to shake the whole edifice. TR

Fools of Fortune

(Pat O'Connor, 1990, GB) Julie Christie, Iain Glen, Mary Elizabeth Mastrantonio, Michael Kitchen, Niamh Cusack, Tom Hickey, Neil Dudgeon.
109 min.
An adaptation of the novel by William Trevor (whose *Ballroom of Romance* O'Connor adapted for TV a few years back), following the fortunes of a wealthy middle class Irish family during the violent period of revolutionary Republicanism and British military repression in the 1920s and '30s, this is made with such loving care that one can easily forgive its minor weaknesses. The tranquil life of the Quinton family is shattered when an attack on their rural home by the notorious 'Black and Tans' leaves young Willie's father and two sisters dead. Five years later, his mother (Christie) is a drunken wreck, and not even a tender love affair with his childhood friend Marianne (Mastrantonio) can free Willie (Glen) from his morbid obsession with the man (Dudgeon) who destroyed his family. O'Connor's assured direction effortlessly evokes the historical period without detracting from the emotional core of the unfolding drama; only some puzzling flashes forward and Iain Glen's over-pitched grimacing seem out of key. There are times too, when Hans Zimmer's musical score seems to be straining for a dramatic impact that the quietly engrossing emotional drama can't always match. Special praise, though, for Julie Christie, who is equally convincing as the vivacious young wife and as the dipsomaniac widow. NF

Fools Rush In

(Andy Tennant, 1997, US) Matthew Perry, Salma Hayek, Jon Tenney, Carlos Gomez, Tomas Milian, John Bennett Perry, Jill Clayburgh.
109 min.
A nervy NY exec (Perry) has a fling in Las Vegas with a Mexican photographer (Hayek). Result, pregnancy. His stern New England poetry, however, is at odds with her vibrant magic realism (literally, a battle of the books). Playing a smart alec terrified by his own lack of substance, Perry seems genuinely in need, as helpless in his own way as old stars like Grant or Stewart. Hayek is also impressive, endowing the photographer with an unaffected moral strength. The scenes with Alex's WASPish parents are amusingly jagged: reactionary in-laws are usually 'brought round', but these two (Perry and Clayburgh) remain politely vile throughout. Scriptwriter Katherine Reback rather takes her time answering all the old questions. CO'Su

Footlight Parade

(Lloyd Bacon, 1933, US) James Cagney, Joan Blondell, Ruby Keeler, Dick Powell, Frank McHugh, Guy Kibbee, Ruth Donnelly, Hugh Herbert.
104 min. b/w.
The third of Warners' major backstage musicals to appear in 1933, unlike *42nd Street* and *Gold Diggers of 1933* in that it deals not so much with putting on a Broadway show as with combating the threat of talking pictures; unlike them, too, in that it pins its atmospheric faith less on the Depression than on Roosevelt optimism as personified by Cagney's irrepressibly bouncy choreographer. It ends with a string of three grandiose numbers by Busby Berkeley, that kitschy darling of current fashion, two of which (*Honeymoon Hotel* and *By a Waterfall*) are well suited to the wimpish personalities of Powell and Keeler; but the third, *Shanghai Lil*, is given a terrific boost by Cagney and by a camera raptly tracking through smoky Chinese bars, nightclubs and opium dens. But by far the best part of the film is its first hour, fast, furious and funny as Cagney sets out to convince his nervous backers that his idea for live prologues to accompany talkies can be made to work. TM

Footloose

(Herbert Ross, 1984, US) Kevin Bacon, Lori Singer, John Lithgow, Dianne Wiest, Christopher Penn, Sarah Jessica Parker.
107 min.
The opening credits of *Footloose* are irresistible: sneakered, socked, stilettoed Big Feet bopping out the signature tune. What follows doesn't quite

make the groove, but it has a jolly good swing at it. Storyline involves bible-bashing, book-burning smalltownship versus thrill-seeking teens straining against the total local nix on rock'n'roll dancing. Their spokesman is Ren, played by Bacon as a beefy-biceped hipster with a ziggy haircut. The dancing is snappy and zappy, mostly of the pent-up frustration variety which emphasises music and movement as a sociable alternative to bloodying noses. It leaves *Flashdance* standing in the Bopsical stakes, and there's not a loin-revealing leotard in sight. AB

Footman, The (Il Portaborse)

(Daniele Luchetti, 1991, It) Silvio Orlando, Nanni Moretti, Giulio Brogi.
95 min.
A dry satire on corruption and compromise in contemporary Italian politics. A schoolteacher obsessed with poetry and experienced in ghost-writing is hired by an ambitious young minister to write his speeches and tend to the credibility of his image. Occasionally contrived, even obvious, and never quite as funny as it would like to be, it's nevertheless an agreeably adult film, far more telling than what generally passes for political satire in British and American movies. GA

Footsteps in the Fog

(Arthur Lubin, 1955, GB) Stewart Granger, Jean Simmons, Bill Travers, Ronald Squire, Finlay Currie, Belinda Lee, William Hartnell, Peter Bull, Victor Maddern.
90 min.
Granger and Simmons, husband-and-wife team of the time, are well matched in this florid Edwardian thriller (from WW Jacobs' *The Interruption*), in which he's the master of the house and she's the maid hoping to blackmail her way up the pecking order by threatening to reveal that he's just done away with his wife. The twisty plot stretches credibility here and there, but the film's gusto is infectious and Granger's limited range is much suited to period caddishness. TJ

For a Few Dollars More (Per Qualche Dollari in più)

(Sergio Leone, 1965, It/Sp/WGer) Clint Eastwood, Lee Van Cleef, Gian Maria Volonté, Klaus Kinski, Mara Krup, Aldo Sambrell, Mario Brega.
130 min.
The one in which Eastwood and Van Cleef, bounty hunters both, reluctantly join forces to take on psychotic bandit Volonté and his gang (which includes Kinski as a hunchback). Not as stylish as *The Good, The Bad and The Ugly*, but a significant step forward from *A Fistful of Dollars*, with the usual terrific compositions, Morricone score, and taciturn performances, not to mention the ubiquitous flashback disease. GA

For All Mankind

(Al Reinert, 1989, US)
90 min. b/w & col.
Between 1968 and 1972, NASA sent 24 astronauts into space as part of its Apollo Space Program. All nine missions (six of which involved lunar landings) were accompanied by a plethora of on-board cameras. It was left to producer-director Reinert to sift through a staggering six million feet of footage and over 90 hours of interviews in order to arrive at this fascinating record. The footage is astonishingly good. It begins with an early launch filmed from every conceivable angle, and in such fine detail that you'd be forgiven for thinking George Lucas and his effects team had a hand in the making. From those fierce images of the launch blast, the tone then shifts to the serenity of space... There is no commentary as such. Instead, Reinert allows the stunning slo-mo images and the many conversations between the astronauts and mission control to speak for themselves. It works a treat, as does the accompanying sound track by atmospheric soundsmiths Brian Eno and Daniel Lanois. DA

For Better, For Worse

see Zandy's Bride

Forbidden

(Frank Capra, 1932, US) Barbara Stanwyck, Adolphe Menjou, Ralph Bellamy, Dorothy Peterson, Henry Armeta.
81 min. b/w.

This early Capra melodrama plays as a tear-jerker. Stanwyck has an illegitimate child by politician Menjou, whose refusal to leave his invalid wife forces the single mother into a marriage of convenience with the unscrupulous Bellamy. He in turn threatens to ruin Menjou by revealing his infidelities, bullish tactics that prove no match for Stanwyck's obsessive love. Unsophisticated and hammy, it's a soap opera that hasn't stood the test of time. TJ

Forbidden

(Anthony Page, 1984, GB/WGer) Jacqueline Bisset, Jürgen Prochnow, Irene Worth, Peter Vaughan, Robert Dietl, Avis Bunnage.
114 min.
Set in Nazi-Occupied Berlin, a ploddingly dull World War II Resistance drama, based on a true story. Bisset plays a German countess as good as she is beautiful, who studies veterinary medicine, joins the underground, saves hundreds of lives, and falls in love with the equally nice Prochnow who, being Jewish, is forced to play Anne Frank in the dark corners of Bisset's cramped apartments. Fassbinder would soon have set the lovers at each other's throats, but here they behave with unimpeachable forbearance and nobility. It shouldn't happen to a vet – or to filmgoers. SJo

Forbidden Games

see Jeux Interdits

Forbidden Planet

(Fred M Wilcox, 1956, US) Walter Pidgeon, Anne Francis, Leslie Nielsen, Warren Stevens, Jack Kelly, Richard Anderson, Earl Holliman, James Drury.
98 min.
Classic '50s sci-fi, surprisingly but effectively based on *The Tempest*, with Nielsen's US spaceship coming across a remote planet, deserted except for Pidgeon's world-wearied Dr Morbius (read Prospero), his daughter (Miranda) and their robot Robby (Ariel). Something, it transpires, has destroyed the planet's other inhabitants, and now, as Bard and Freud merge, a monster mind-thing Caliban begins to pick on the spaceship's crew. An ingenious script, excellent special effects and photography, and superior acting (with the exception of Francis), make it an endearing winner. GA

Forbidden Relations (Visszaesök)

(Zsolt Kézdi-Kovács, 1982, Hun) Lili Monori, Miklós B Székely, Mari Törócsik, József Horváth, József Tóth.
92 min.
It opens with a suicide and ends with a birth – the second child of a brother-sister love affair. So *Forbidden Relations* is a film of illicit passions haunted by fears of insanity and the strictures of state morality. But don't expect high melodrama, or indeed a panting, prettified art house parable: this is spare social realism from Hungary, with a young widow falling for a returning ex-con whom she later learns is her half-brother. Feckless in the eyes of their rural community but obstinately faithful to their *amour fou*, the couple wind up in jail, despite the compassion of police and magistrates required to implement the law. Controversial and courageous in its home country, largely because of the humanist warmth Kézdi-Kovács brings to the subject; but despite the vigorous earthiness of the sexuality on display, this is a rather too muted, meandering attack on the ancient taboo. MA

Forbidden Woman, The

see Femme Défendue, La

Forbidden World (aka Mutant)

(Allan Holzman, 1982, US) Jesse Vint, Dawn Dunlap, June Chadwick, Linden Chiles, Fox Harris, Raymond Oliver, Scott Paulin.
86 min.
Delightful *Alien* rip-off from the Corman fun factory, with a 'genetic wildcat' using its teeth and tentacles to pick protein off the members of an isolated planet outpost. Oodles of gore, gratuitous nudity (a sauna on a sandswept planet station!), and an exhilarating thumb-in-cheek to *Close Encounters*. The Final Solution offers sacs more liquefaction than Ridley Scott's sterile shocker. AB

Forbin Project, The (aka Colossus – The Forbin Project)

(Joseph Sargent, 1969, US) Eric Braeden, Susan Clark, Gordon Pinsent, William Schallert, Leonid Rostoff.
100 min.
Two giant defence plan computers, distrustful of man's eternal stupidity, link terminals across the Iron Curtain to hold an agitated world in thrall. After an excellent beginning, the craven script (based on DF Jones' novel *Colossus*) develops cold feet, injects some tiresome comic relief, and gradually begins to drag the whole thing down to *Dr Who* level. A pity, since the first half is chillingly persuasive. TM

Force: Five

(Robert Clouse, 1981, US) Joe Lewis, Bong Soo Han, Sonny Barnes, Richard Norton, Benny Urquidez, Ron Hayden, Pam Huntington, Mandy Wyss.
96 min.
Potentially interesting martial arts caper of battle against a Rajneesh-like guru, allowed to stagnate in a mire of sickening gore, endless destruction, and simplistic, humourless sermonising. As the stereotypically mixed *Force: Five* – a black, a Chicano, a woman, a psychotic, and a Handsome Leader – sets out to save gullible disciples from the wicked Reverend Rhee's Palace of Celestial Tranquillity (a minotaur's labyrinth of torture and carnage), it becomes increasingly difficult to distinguish morally between the opposing sides. All the breathtaking brutality makes for tiresome viewing. GA

Force of Evil

(Abraham Polonsky, 1948, US) John Garfield, Beatrice Pearson, Thomas Gomez, Howland Chamberlain, Roy Roberts, Marie Windsor.
78 min. b/w.
One of the key films of the '40s. From a novel by Ira Wolfert (*Tucker's People*), it extracts a clinical analysis of the social, moral and physical evils attending on the numbers racket, centering this on a remarkably complex portrayal of the mutual guilt of two brothers caught at opposite ends of the same rat trap: one (Garfield) torn by the realisation that his corruption means the destruction of his brother, the other (Gomez) by his awareness that he was responsible for that corruption in the first place. If their conflict has the authentic ring of tragedy, it is partly because Polonsky uses the iconography of the underworld thriller so skilfully that his touches of allegory and symbolism – like Garfield's last bleak descent down a stairway to discover the reality of his personal hell – are natural outcroppings rather than artificial injections; and partly because the dialogue, terse and unpretentious but given an incantatory quality by its calculated hesitations and repetitions, has an unmistakable tang of gritty urban poetry that floods the entire film. Like no other film of the period, it stands as a testament, its mood – as Polonsky has confessed – being compounded on the one hand by fear of the McCarthy witch-hunts, and on the other by conflict in potential victims doubting the absolute justice of their cause. TM

Force of One, A

(Paul Aaron, 1978, US) Jennifer O'Neill, Chuck Norris, Clu Gulager, Ron O'Neal, Bill Wallace, Eric Laneuville, James Whitmore.
91 min. 15.
With a dope epidemic on the streets and a karate cop-killer on the loose, undercover narc Jennifer O'Neill enlists the martial artistry of (real-life champ) Norris to help stomp the bad guys. A typically plot-heavy script from Ernest Tidyman survives unimaginative direction to deliver that current rarity, an unpretentious action movie. A bit out of its depth at the top of a bill, but vastly superior to the ostensibly similar *Jaguar Lives*. PT

Force 10 from Navarone

(Guy Hamilton, 1978, GB) Robert Shaw, Harrison Ford, Barbara Bach, Edward Fox, Franco Nero, Carl Weathers, Richard Kiel, Alan Badel.
118 min.
Survivors of *The Guns of Navarone* mission return to deal with the spy who betrayed them.

Under Hamilton's moribund direction, this becomes a Bond-in-uniform saga, with a can-they-spike-the-Kraut-guns-in-time plot. All the potentially exciting set pieces (traitor in our midst, whose side are the Gucci-clad partisans on?) are thrown away with a disregard for the basic mechanics of suspense, and the climax is literally cardboard thin. Edward Fox is consistently watchable, but on the whole a damned poor show from the chaps down at EMI HQ. CPea

Fords on Water

(Barry Bliss, 1983, GB) Elvis Payne, Mark Wingett, Kathryn Apanowicz, Jason Rose, Allister Bain, David Ryall.
83 min.
Two London kids, one black, one white, are cast into the outer darkness of the dole. But as this duo leave behind the night-locked city, speeding northwards in a stolen motor, it's soon clear that Bliss' first feature celebrates resistance not resignation; and that with its lustrous, colourful images and laconic screenplay, its jump cuts and jazzy score, it owes less to drab naturalism than to the moody poetry of Neil Jordan's *Angel*, spiked with *Nouvelle Vague* verve and nerve. There is much to enjoy: an irreverent sense of humour, a great saxy soundtrack by 'Angel' composer Keith Donald, and above all an upbeat ending that has Thatcher's flotsam cheekily waving, not drowning. SJo

Foreign Affair, A

(Billy Wilder, 1948, US) Jean Arthur, Marlene Dietrich, John Lund, Millard Mitchell, Bill Murphy, Stanley Prager, Peter von Zerneck.
116 min. b/w.
Shot amid the ruins of Berlin, Wilder's satire on the corruption among GIs fraternising with the locals did not go down too well with the Defence Department. Arthur plays a prim congresswoman investigating an army officer (Lund), and when she realises she really has fallen for her man, she has to win him away from the exotic charms of chanteuse Dietrich. This may not be Wilder at his best – the story develops along fairly predictable lines, with Arthur switching her starchy uniform for a glistening evening gown – but there are some precious set pieces, notably a seduction among a row of filing cabinets and Dietrich's club act, not to mention a crackling script. DT

Foreign Body

(Ronald Neame, 1986, GB) Victor Banerjee, Warren Mitchell, Geraldine McEwan, Denis Quilley, Amanda Donohoe, Eve Ferret, Anna Massey, Stratford Johns, Trevor Howard.
111 min.
The major problem here is determining the most offensive performance. Is it Banerjee as Indian immigrant Ram Das, or Mitchell in blackface as his scheming cousin IQ? The comedy centres on the daydreaming Das, who comes to England in '75 after losing his job as night porter in a Calcutta brothel. He takes a job as bus conductor until IQ – a toilet attendant at Heathrow – persuades him to pose as a Harley Street chiropractor. Das attends to wealthy female patients in need of attention rather than medical advice, bowing and gesticulating his way into the hearts of the English aristocracy. Despite the make-up, Mitchell charms, his comedy based in character rather than the rabbit punchlines. It's Banerjee, the wide-eyed fool, whose antics are not only less than entertaining, but also alarming. SGo

Foreign Correspondent

(Alfred Hitchcock, 1940, US) Joel McCrea, Laraine Day, Herbert Marshall, George Sanders, Albert Basserman, Edmund Gwenn, Eduardo Ciannelli, Robert Benchley.
120 min. b/w.
Despite the now rather embarrassing propagandistic finale, with McCrea urging an increase in the war effort against the Nazis, Hitchcock's espionage thriller is a thoroughly enjoyable affair, complete with some of his most memorable set pieces. McCrea and Day are the lovers searching out Nazi agents in London and Holland after the disappearance of a peace-seeking diplomat, while Sanders, Gwenn amd the normally wooden Marshall lend fine support. Something of a predecessor of the picaresque chase thrillers like *Saboteur* and *North by Northwest*, its main source

of suspense comes from the fact that little is what it seems to be: a camera hides an assassin's gun, sails of a windmill conceal a sinister secret, and the sanctuary of Westminster Cathedral provides an opportunity for murder. Not one of the director's greatest – there's little of his characteristic cruelty or moral pessimism – but still eminently watchable. GA

Foreigners (Jag Heter Stelius)

(Johan Bergenstråhle, 1972, Swe) Konstantinos Papageorgiou, Anastasios Margetis, Savas Tzanetakis, Andreas Bellis.
113 min.
A worthy, sometimes telling film about the experiences of Greek immigrants in egalitarian Sweden, scripted from a novel based on the (Greek) author's own experiences. Sadly, though, the processing from life-to-book-to-film hasn't made for conviction, and the film's fictionalised aspects tend to be more intrusive than revealing. Oddly memorable, though. VG

Foreign Land

(Walter Salles, 1995, Braz) Fernanda Torres, Fernando Pinto, Laura Cardosa, Luis Mello, Alexandre Borges.
110 min. b/w.
Salles' second feature, fluently shot in b/w, focuses on Brazilian youth torn between the hardships of the newly democratic homeland and exile in the corrupted émigré sub-culture of Lisbon. The story eventually settles on a young man on a bungled smuggling operation to Portugal, who finds himself on the run with a disenchanted Brazilian woman. Their sudden plunge into violence and romance, as well as their struggle for identity, is reminiscent of Antonioni's *The Passenger*. Despite not quite steering clear of road movie clichés, the film's stylistic bravura, occasional moments of real humour and excellent performances are pretty invigorating. DT

Foreign Moon

(Zhang Zeming, 1995, GB/HK) Chen Hsiao Hsuan, Harrison Liu, Chen Daming, David Tse.
90 min.
Deeply unconvincing from the start, this loose assemblage of clichés about émigré Chinese has only its London setting to distinguish it from a dozen predecessors set in New York. The three central characters (impossibly naive girl, sad exradical and muscle-queen wide-boy) plod through a highly predictable teaming-up and falling-out; there's no psychological depth, sociological insight or even credible emotion. Maybe the excellent *Swan Song* was the only real film that Zhang Zeming had in him. TR

Foreman Went to France, The

(Charles Frend, 1941, GB) Tommy Trinder, Constance Cummings, Clifford Evans, Robert Morley, Gordon Jackson, Francis L Sullivan.
87 min. b/w.
Preceding Ealing's marvellous *Went the Day Well?*, this contribution to the war effort is less imaginative but almost as effective in its more conventional way. Based on fact, it has Evans as a factory foreman sent to France in 1940 and, aided by two soldiers (Trinder, Jackson) and an American girl (Cummings), contriving to spirit vital machinery away from the advancing Germans. Beautifully dovetailing comedy and drama, it is remarkably discreet in its patriotics, aside from a final scene where French refugees nobly give up their possessions to make room for the machines on the last boat out. A pity the efforts of some of the cast – notably Morley – to pass as Frenchmen are disastrous. TM

Forest of Bliss

(Robert Gardner, 1986, US)
90 min.
Basically, a documentary day in the life of the Ganges riverbank at Benares. Well shot, but it has all been seen before in countless variations from Ray's *Aparajito* to Malle's *Phantom India*, except that here the stress is on the jostling extremes of sacred and profane: worshippers standing absorbed in their rituals while dogs gnaw hungrily at corpses floating by. Oddly, though made for the Harvard Film Study Center, it is presented as an impressionistic travelogue

without either commentary or subtitles. Several of the rites and customs, and at least one dialogue scene, demand elucidation. TM

Forever Amber

(Otto Preminger, 1947, US) Linda Darnell, Cornel Wilde, Richard Greene, George Sanders, Richard Haydn, Jessica Tandy, Anne Revere, Glenn Langan.
140 min.

A cleaned-up adaptation of Kathleen Winsor's novel about a peasant wench's rise to riches – by means of sexual favours – during the reign of Charles II, this was originally planned as a John Stahl film, with Peggy Cummins in the role of the opportunistic Amber. Stahl, in fact, would probably have been better suited to the lurid emotional melodrama than Preminger, though Darnell – blonde for once but as sultrily sensuous as ever – is fine in the central role, while the supporting cast (notably Sanders as the king) is excellent. It's all lavish enough, beautifully shot in Technicolor by Leon Shamroy, but Preminger's direction lacks the sophisticated lightness of touch that Mitchell Leisen brought to the in some ways similar *Kitty*. GA

Forever England
(aka Born for Glory)

(Walter Forde, 1935, GB) Betty Balfour, John Mills, Jimmy Hanley, Barry McKay, Felix Aylmer.
80 min. b/w.

This Michael Balcon production, a rather creaky adaptation of CS Forester's WWI nautical novel *Brown on Resolution*. Mills is bright-eyed and full of pluck as an ordinary seaman whose bravery in German captivity leads single-handedly to the sinking of an enemy vessel. The rest of the movie only just passes muster, but you can see the young star was clearly destined to move up the ranks. TJ

Forever in Love
see Pride of the Marines

Forever Mary
(Mery per sempre)

(Marco Risi, 1988, It) Michele Placido, Claudio Amendola, Francesco Benigno, Alessandro Di Sanzo, Tony Sperandeo.
106 min.

Teacher Marco Terzi (Placido) deliberately picks the short straw in the Italian educational lottery and chooses a posting to the Rosaspina reform school, home to Palermo's toughest delinquent youth. There he wins these hard nuts' hearts by setting them essays on love, letting them draw on him with felt tip pen, and snogging Mary the class transvestite to prove he's a real man. Before long, the boys are eating out of his hand; the authorities are, naturally, less enamoured. This is a fairly standard exercise in the boys-behind-bars genre, with all the usual ingredients – cruelty, camaraderie, and a surprisingly teasing attitude to the sodomy that never quite takes place. The main appeal lies in the honest, unshowy performances of the non-professional cast of real reform school alumni. JRo

For Ever Mozart

(Jean-Luc Godard, 1996, Fr) Madeleine Assas, Bérangère Allaux, Ghalya Lacroix, Vicky Messica, Frédéric Pierrot, Harry Cleven.
82 min.

Godard (director/writer/editor) casts a quizzical eye on Sarajevo, art and the cinema: in the first half, a group of naive youngsters drive to Bosnia to perform Alfred de Musset's play *On ne badine pas avec l'amour*; in the second, a film-maker strives to get 'Fatal Bolero' in the can. The two parts are linked by Godard's insistence on a cinema of the intellect (dis-chord; absurdism; quotation; provocation), and by his recognition of the futility of the exercise ('Cinema substitutes our gaze with a world in harmony with our desires…something essential is renounced'). TCh

Forever Young

(David Drury, 1983, GB) James Aubrey, Nicholas Gecks, Karen Archer, Alec McCowen, Liam Holt, Jane Forster, Ruth Davies.
84 min.

On stage a trendy curate strums his way through

'Donna', while a long-lost friend looks on in amazement to see his one-time singing partner still reliving his teenage memories 20 years on. It's Ray Connolly parading his '50s fantasies once more, but this time with a more ironic gloss than usual, since his script is about the way both friends are still trapped by unresolved problems. As a series of flashbacks shows, they used to be inseparable – testing each other's pop knowledge in the school showers, chatting up girls, performing their Everly Brothers-style act – until in their different ways they betrayed each other…a treachery which is about to repeat itself 20 years on. Made as a TV movie in Channel 4's *First Love* series, *Forever Young* catches well the psychology of the relationship, but it also has the cosiness and soft nostalgia one has come to expect from executive producer David Puttnam. Basically, a night out for the middle-aged. CS

Forever Young

(Steve Miner, 1992, US) Mel Gibson, Jamie Lee Curtis, Elijah Wood, Isabel Glasser, George Wendt, Joe Morton, Nicolas Surovy.
101 min.

In 1939, test pilot Daniel McCormick (Gibson) finds his courage deserting him whenever it comes to proposing to his childhood sweetheart (Glasser). Overwhelmed by grief when she is hit by a truck and rendered comatose, he agrees to be cryogenically frozen by a scientist pal (Wendt); but when he wakes up, it is 1992. Fortunately, single mother Claire (Curtis) and her young son (Wood) are on hand to help him adjust to modern living and piece together his lost past. Jeffrey Abrams' script gets the tone just right, playing everything straight and never lapsing into knowing irony; while Miner, content to let the storyline unfold, leaves it to the actors to flesh out the sometimes touching, sometimes comic collision between Daniel's old-fashioned gallantry and modern-day cynicism. Looked at with a jaundiced eye, the scenario is slushy and full of holes; surrendered to in a spirit of careless romanticism, it works. NF

Forever Yours
see Forget-Me-Not

For Fun (Zhao Le)

(Ning Ying, 1992, HK/China) Huang Zongluo, Huang Wenjie, Han Shanxu, He Ming.
97 min.

Ning Ying hit the jackpot with this her second feature, financed from Hong Kong but shot entirely in Beijing. The story, about retired old codgers who team up to form an amateur Peking Opera troupe and enter a talent contest, is warm, funny and extremely likeable. It's also quite sharp politically, since it pricks the bubble of pomposity associated with Chinese officialdom – incarnated in the story by a former stage-doorman who sees himself as a natural leader. Wonderful performances from the two queens in the troupe, and from Huang Zongluo as the petty tyrant. TR

Forget-Me-Not
(aka Forever Yours)

(Zoltan Korda/Stanley Irving, 1936, GB) Beniamino Gigli, Joan Gardner, Ivan Brandt, Hugh Wakefield, Jeanne Stuart.
72 min. b/w.

Majestic Italian tenor Gigli was the raison d'être for this soppy sea-going romance, made by the Kordas in simultaneous English and Italian versions. Having lost his wife, Gigli is much taken with fellow passenger Gardner and resolves to marry, though the reappearance of her former fiancé is to test their love. Undistinguished elsewhere, but whenever the big man sings you'll understand why he's reckoned one of the greats. Best approached as an addendum to the records for interested fans. TJ

Forget Paris

(Billy Crystal, 1995, US) Billy Crystal, Debra Winger, Joe Mantegna, Cynthia Stevenson, Richard Masur, Julie Kavner, Cathy Moriarty.
101 min.

Waiting for friends to arrive at their engagement party, Andy (Mantegna) tells Liz (Stevenson) about the bizarre romance between his pal Mickey (Crystal) and Ellen (Winger): how the airline she worked for in Paris mislaid the coffin carrying Mickey's father, and how despite this

inauspicious beginning (and her rich husband) they fell in love, married and lived happily…for a while. Craig (Masur) and Lucy (Kavner) take up the story: Mickey, a basketball referee, was always on the road, and Ellen started climbing the walls of their suburban LA home. She'd given up everything for the marriage; what would Mickey give up? We've been this way before. An alternative title might be 'When Mickey Met Ellen'. Produced, directed and co-written by Crystal, the film has a generous number of acerbic asides and some memorable slapschtick, but as Ellen discovers, laughs aren't enough, and, like the relationship it depicts, everything goes terribly slack in the middle. TCh

Forget Venice
see Dimenticare Venezia

For Keeps (aka Maybe Baby)

(John G Avildsen, 1987, US) Molly Ringwald, Randall Batinkoff, Kenneth Mars, Miriam Flynn, Conchata Ferrell, Sharon Brown, Jack Ong.
98 min.

The main claim to fame of Kenosha, Wisconsin, is that it was the birthplace of Orson Welles; the fact that the town is also now the setting of Avildsen's film is unlikely to increase its reputation. High school kids Darcy (Ringwald) and Stan (Batinkoff) are very much in lerv, but when Darcy becomes pregnant all hell breaks loose: their folks argue over adoption and abortion, the kids get spliced, and the sacrifices demanded by parenthood (Darcy's future in journalism, Stan's in architecture) temporarily threaten to split the pair asunder. Though the film finally opts for ear-bashing histrionics, its prevailingly pedagogic tone is both coy and tricksy. The dialogue is relentless in its banality, the stereotype characters unattractive and poorly motivated, the plot protracted and predictable. GA

For Love or Money

(Megan McMurchy/Jeni Thornley, 1983, Aust) Jane Clifton, Diane Craig, Nick Enright, Vivienne Garrett.
109 min.

Documentaries probably don't come more ambitious than this: co-produced by an Australian women's collective, its subject matter is little less than a feminist analysis of Australian women's fortunes in (and out of) the work force – where Australian includes Aborigine and migrant women – across a 200-year sweep from the arrival of the first women convicts to the present day. To document this huge and diverse subject, the film-makers use a dense montage of footage – archive material, clips from feature films, TV ads, even donated home movies – which is complemented or ironically counterpointed with a medley of narrative voices and incidental music. In more crudely didactic hands, the material could have been unpalatable, but agile editing, some grimly humorous footage, and a prevailing sense of conviction keep it moving along, while the strength of the analysis it develops justifies its exhausting means. HH

For Love or Money
(aka The Concierge)

(Barry Sonnenfeld, 1993, US) Michael J Fox, Gabrielle Anwar, Anthony Higgins, Michael Tucker, Bob Balaban.
96 min.

Michael J Fox was the acceptable face of '80s yuppiedom: the little guy who thinks big, the all-American optimist who believes in profit without loss. Mercenary he may be, but the manners are impeccable. Here, as concierge in New York's elite Bradbury Hotel, he's a one-man service industry who'll do anything for a tip. This supposedly romantic comedy is every bit as hackneyed as it sounds. TCh

For Me and My Gal

(Busby Berkeley, 1942, US) Judy Garland, Gene Kelly, George Murphy, Stephen McNally, Marta Eggerth, Keenan Wynn, Ben Blue, Richard Quine.
104 min. b/w.

Set just before World War I, this corny musical introduced 30-year-old debutant Gene Kelly in the intially unsympathetic role of an ambitious hoofer who joins up with fellow vaudevillians

Garland and Murphy in the, hope of fulfilling his/their dream of playing at the famous Palace Theatre. Their plans are complicated by Kelly's selfish scheming to avoid the draft, and by a romantic triangle in which Murphy loves Garland, Garland loves Kelly, and Kelly loves, besides himself, the idea of being famous. Kelly's contrived transformation from ruthless heel to self-effacing war hero is totally unconvincing, but the excellent numbers – including the title song, 'When You Wore a Tulip' and 'Ballin' the Jack' – may help to numb the pain. NF

Formula, The
(John G Avildsen, 1980, US) George C Scott, Marlon Brando, Marthe Keller, John Gielgud, GD Spradlin, Beatrice Straight, Richard Lynch.
117 min.
Laborious thriller about a formula for synthetic fuel which reaches back to the Nazi past and forward to contemporary terrorism. Avildsen and Steve Shagan (scripting from his own novel) go wildly astray in trying to mine some more of the breast-beating vein they opened up in *Save the Tiger*, with Brando playing some particularly loony tunes as the tycoon who orates in defence of big business and power games. TM

For Pete's Sake
(Peter Yates, 1974, US) Barbra Streisand, Michael Sarrazin, Estelle Parsons, William Redfield, Molly Picon.
90 min.
Yates sure is an erratic talent. *Bullitt* made one think he was only good with action scenes. *The Friends of Eddie Coyle*, *Breaking Away* and *The Janitor* suggested that he could indeed handle strong characterisation and droll humour. Everything else makes him look almost totally talentless. Here he's adrift in a sea of poor performances and bad comic timing, as Streisand gets farcically involved with loan sharks et al in an attempt to supplement the income of herself and her student-cum-cab driver hubbie Sarrazin. GA

For Queen and Country
(Martin Stellman, 1988, GB/US) Denzel Washington, Dorian Healy, Amanda Redman, Sean Chapman, Bruce Payne, George Baker.
106 min.
For his debut as a director, Stellman (scriptwriter on *Quadrophenia*, *Babylon* and *Defence of the Realm*) has produced an ambitious but disappointing piece about class and race in 'Thatcher's Britain'. His storyline concerns Reuben, a Falklands war hero whose return to a dreadfully run-down South London council block is marked by rejection from white cops and the blacks with whom he grew up. When the immigration authorities inform Reuben, who was born in St Lucia, that he's no longer officially a British citizen, something snaps. Stellman's script contains an intelligent appraisal of a country divided more subtly by loyalty and habit than the media often realise. But the choice of Washington doesn't help: he isn't bad in the part, but his accent strays absurdly. More worrying is the often corny plotting, the by now tired-looking exploitation of Broadwater violence, and a preposterous shootout ending. Stellman's direction is often as sluggish as the daily routines of his protagonists. SGr

Forrest Gump
(Robert Zemeckis, 1994, US) Tom Hanks, Robin Wright, Gary Sinise, Mykelti Williamson, Sally Field.
142 min.
Played by Hanks with a sing-song Southern drawl and an evangelical earnestness, Gump is the quintessential simpleton, his only characteristic the inert righteousness instilled in him by his mama (Field). Gump's story is as extraordinary as he is banal. He conducts us on what amounts to a virtual-reality tour of late twentieth century American history. Beneath its babyboomer soundtrack, its restive feel-good aesthetic and conventional liberal veneer, this is a dismayingly reactionary work. Consider Forrest's one true love, Jenny (Wright), a 'nice' girl who takes a wrong turn when she abandons home for showbusiness. Throughout director

Zemeckis contrasts Gump's charmed progress with Jenny's unhappy engagement with the counter culture. It's only when she's dying that Jenny realises she should have stayed with Forrest all along. He's asexual, square and a tedious conversationalist, but God knows he loves his mother – as this mawkish conservative movie ultimately goes to prove: ignorance is bliss. Winner of a raft of Oscars. TCh

For Roseanna
see Roseanna's Grave

Fort Apache
(John Ford, 1948, US) Henry Fonda, John Wayne, Shirley Temple, Pedro Armendariz, John Agar, George O'Brien, Ward Bond, Victor McLaglen, Anna Lee.
127 min. b/w.
The first of Ford's cavalry trilogy (to be followed by *She Wore a Yellow Ribbon* and *Rio Grande*), and an intriguing development of questions of leadership, responsibility, heroism and legend, first raised in the muted officers' conflict of *They Were Expendable*. West Point stiffness (the Custer-like Fonda) meets the more organic Western community of an isolated Arizona outpost, and inflexible notions of 'duty' lead inexorably to disaster, historically rewritten as glory. Not for the last time, Ford gives us telling evidence of tragic ambiguity, but none the less decides to 'print the legend'. PT

Fort Apache, the Bronx
(Daniel Petrie, 1981, US) Paul Newman, Edward Asner, Ken Wahl, Danny Aiello, Rachel Ticotin, Pam Grier, Kathleen Beller.
123 min.
It's not that Newman turns in anything less than his customarily diligent performance as a greying career cop, nor that his affair with a Puerto Rican nurse played by an actress who must be 30 years his junior strains credibility (since that blue-eyed sex appeal remains intact). But the material strung together in a script about urban police work is so familiar from countless cop shows that it's difficult to see who needs this movie. The litany of routine duties includes disarming crazy knifers, saving gays from suicide, delivering babies, chasing muggers, preventing pimps from beating their whores, all depicted in ramblingly episodic fashion and without a shred of street credibility. RM

For the Boys
(Mark Rydell, 1991, US) Bette Midler, James Caan, George Segal, Patrick O'Neal, Christopher Rydell, Arye Gross, Norman Fell, Rosemary Murphy, Bud Yorkin, Jack Sheldon.
145 min.
A drama spanning three wars and professional/emotional skirmishes over two generations. Dixie (Midler) is to be awarded a medal for a career spent entertaining US troops, an honour she shares with her one-time partner Eddie (Caan). A television ceremony is planned, but at the last minute, she won't budge from her house. A long-standing grudge against Eddie is to blame, and it's up to a sweet-talking studio minion to coax an explanation. Cue a flashback to her life story, complete with battle footage and the occasional tune... Rydell charts the decline in American values: good-natured soldiers of WWII give way to druggies in Vietnam, and quick-witted writer Art (Segal) enjoys fame and fortune before falling victim to McCarthyism. Marshall Brickman's script is full of marvellous one-liners, but despite its aspirations, this sentimental Midler road-show is hopelessly unrestrained. CM

For Them That Trespass
(Alberto Cavalcanti, 1948, GB) Richard Todd, Stephen Murray, Patricia Plunkett, Joan Dowling, Michael Laurence, Rosalyn Boulter.
95 min. b/w.
For Them That Trespass, scripted by J Lee Thompson of all people, is notable for the way Cavalcanti transforms his story, of how Richard Todd, wrongly imprisoned for murder, clears his name, into a bleak account of guilt. Shot so as to bring out both the poetry and the squalor of working class life, it was one of the postwar British films that presaged the arrival of *Room at the Top* and *Saturday Night and Sunday Morning* a decade later. PH

Fortini/Cani
(Jean-Marie Straub/Danièle Huillet, 1976, It/Fr/WGer/GB/US) Franco Fortini, Luciana Nissi, Adriano Aprà.
85 min.
The film essay is a fairly recondite genre, but it's safe to say that there has never been an example like this. It's a film of a book: the Italian writer Franco Fortini is seen and heard reading sections from his book *The Dogs of Sinai*, in which he attacks Italian reactions to the war in Palestine in the light of his own part-Jewish upbringing. Although Straub completely respects the integrity of Fortini's words, he 'contexts' the argument in a number of provocative ways. A haunting image of a seashore at night, or a brief extract from Schoenberg's *Moses and Aaron*, are enough to underline the element of melodrama in Fortini's autobiography; a placid study of the hills where Nazis massacred the Italian resistance is enough to generate a meditation on the meaning of Fortini's anti-fascism. The film draws attention to issues of frightening relevance, and yet allows the viewer plenty of space to think and feel. TR

Fortress
(Stuart Gordon, 1992, US/Aust) Christopher Lambert, Kurtwood Smith, Loryn Locklin, Lincoln Kilpatrick, Jeffrey Combs, Tom Towles.
95 min.
Stuart Gordon calls this prison movie 'a sort of science-fiction version of *The Great Escape*'. Regrettably, Lambert, imprisoned because his pregnant wife is about to exceed the government limit of children allowed a married couple, is no Steve McQueen. Built 30 storeys below ground, the state-of-the-art prison features laser bars, robot guards and a nasty device called the Intestinator. While confined to the futuristic prison interiors, the film works reasonably well; but once Lambert springs his wife and escapes, the limitations of budget and narrative imagination start to show. As it moves away from the ensemble feel of the early scenes, this quickly degenerates into a part explosive, part sentimental star vehicle. NF

Fortune, The
(Mike Nichols, 1974, US) Jack Nicholson, Warren Beatty, Stockard Channing, Florence Stanley, Richard B Shull, Tom Newman, Scatman Crothers, Dub Taylor.
88 min.
This starts promisingly as a sardonic comedy about an absurd *ménage-à-trois*, the mechanics of sex in the '20s, and the men's bewilderment about matters female. Beatty and Nicholson, as the sleazy lounge lizard and halfwit accomplice who conspire to run away with an heiress, send up their own images as though indulging a private joke, but still manage a couple of delirious moments. Their flight west (incognito, but with Nicholson constantly drawing attention to them) throws away its gags shamelessly, but once in California lethargy settles in. The film becomes almost static, a series of stagy, glossy tableaux: such lack of momentum may be an adequate assessment of the characters' limited capacity for development, but it has a disastrous effect on the film's pacing. Events degenerate into miscalculated farce and underline Nichols' continuing slick superficiality. Adrien Joyce's much hackedabout script sounds as though it was once excellent: a pity everyone treats it so off-handedly. CPe

Fortune and Men's Eyes
(Harvey Hart, 1971, Can/US) Wendell Burton, Michael Greer, Zooey Hall, Danny Freedman, Larry Perkins, James Barron.
102 min.
Clumsy adaptation of John Herbert's play (he scripted himself) about homosexual brutalisation in men's prisons. If you believe in a prison that tolerates Michael Greer's flamboyant queen, then you'll probably also believe in Wendell Burton's progress from cute/butch innocence to rapist in the showers. TR

Fortune Cookie, The (aka Meet Whiplash Willie)
(Billy Wilder, 1966, US) Jack Lemmon, Walter Matthau, Ron Rich, Cliff Osmond, Judi West, Lurene Tuttle, Harry Holcombe.
124 min. b/w.

Wilder's first match of Matthau and Lemmon pushes the idea of role-playing even further than *Some Like It Hot*: TV cameraman Lemmon gets knocked out accidentally during a football game, and his shyster attorney-cum-brother-in-law Matthau gets him to feign partial paralysis in order to claim huge damages. On the surface it's a complete delight, with Matthau's relentlessly funny lines taking most of the honours, but underneath lies a disenchantment as bleak as *The Apartment*: amoral, misogynist characters (in Lemmon's case, literally spineless) racing through ever more futile efforts to outmanoeuvre each other. The friction between the laughs and the cynicism generates more heat than most Hollywood comedies even aim at, including Wilder's later *The Front Page* with the same stars. TR

48 HRS
(Walter Hill, 1982, US) Nick Nolte, Eddie Murphy, Annette O'Toole, Frank McRae, James Remar, David Patrick Kelly.
97 min.
Having built a creditable reputation by standing slightly to one side of his action material and looking at it from a different angle, Hill finally comes clean and delivers a down-the-line thriller, plain, fast and efficient. After losing his gun to some low-life, cop Nolte springs a black ex-member of the gang (Murphy) from jail to help him, and has just *48 HRS* in which to recover his piece and wrap up the case. Superfly Murphy proves the perfect foil for the gruff, shambling Nolte; together they shoot it out with what looks suspiciously like the remnants of the street gangs from *The Warriors*, while thankfully sidestepping most of the old buddy-buddy pitfalls. For the first time, Hill gives himself enough time to allow a fair amount of fast-talk dialogue through his usually gritted teeth, and enough space to pay his respects to such sources as Peckinpah and Siegel. It takes an honourable place in a line of San Francisco thrillers from *Point Blank* through *Bullitt* and *Dirty Harry* to *Killer Elite*. CPea

40 Graves for 40 Guns (aka The Great Gundown)
(Paul Hunt, 1971, US) Robert Padilla, Richard Rust, Malila St Duval, Steven Oliver, David Eastman, Stanley Adams.
100 min.
Sombre half-breed robs train, is betrayed by gang, returns to deserted wife, loses her, assembles new bunch of misfits, then bloodily offs old gang. Borrowing heavily from Peckinpah for his themes (conflicting allegiances, the lore of machismo, the letting of blood, etc), Hunt never attains the former's understanding, control or grace, with the result that his film degenerates into a series of random slaughters which lack even sufficient cruelty to be interesting. CPea

Forty Guns
(Samuel Fuller, 1957, US) Barbara Stanwyck, Barry Sullivan, Dean Jagger, John Ericson, Gene Barry, Robert Dix.
80 min. b/w.
Possessed of a gun-crazy sting all its own, Fuller's near-legendary B Western still excites dazed amazement and still resists critical shorthand. As an explicitly sexual range-war yarn, you'd automatically dub it a Freudian Western, except that the good doctor's shade could never cope with dreams like Fuller's: vivid, abstract, brutal affairs of naked emotion and violence. So you're left cataloguing the movie's startlingly pleasurable elements – the daring, darting camera style; the keynote performances from Stanwyck as a sensual autocrat and Sullivan as a tired, Earp-like killer; the radical jettisoning of comfortable myth – until you happily concede that essences are irreducible. And this is the essence of American action cinema. Just watch, and be stunned speechless yourself. PT

40 Metre Square Germany (40 Metrekare Almanya)
(Tevfik Baser, 1986, WGer) Özay Fecht, Yaman Okay, Demir Gökgöl, Mustafa Gülpinar.
80 min.
This makes a pair with Baser's *Farewell to False Paradise* (1989). Both are prison films, one literal, the other domestic, and both describe the travails of Turkish women brought to Hamburg by

guest-worker husbands. Here a young 'bride', Turna (first seen trying to light an electric stove), is virtually imprisoned in the dingy apartment she shares with a factory worker. 'Why did you lock me in, I'm not an animal!' she screams, which doesn't stop him having sex with her as if she were one. The flashbacks to the 'old country' aren't, however, vaseline-lensed, as they were in *Farewell to False Paradise*: Turna is going to have to make her own way in Germany. WH

49th Parallel
(Michael Powell, 1941, GB) Eric Portman, Anton Walbrook, Leslie Howard, Raymond Massey, Laurence Olivier, Finlay Currie, Niall MacGinnis, Glynis Johns.
123 min. b/w.
Commissioned by the Ministry of Information in hopes of swaying public opinion in favour of America's entry into the war, this now seems a little dated in patches, with the characterisations all too self-consciously tailored to the propaganda notion of providing a cross-section of ethnic types united in their resistance to Nazism (Leslie Howard's stereotypically laconic Englishman suffers most). But the episodic account of a stranded U-Boat crew's brutal foray into Canada still grips (Emeric Pressburger's script is beautifully structured), and the running debate on democracy versus dictatorship is conducted in terms far from simplistic. What really lifts the film, though, is what David Thomson calls 'a primitive feeling for endangered civilisation': a feeling very much akin to the passionate concern for England's green and pleasant land which flowered in the marvellous *A Canterbury Tale* three years later. TM

42nd Street
(Lloyd Bacon, 1933, US) Warner Baxter, Ruby Keeler, Bebe Daniels, Dick Powell, Guy Kibbee, George Brent, Ginger Rogers, Una Merkel.
89 min. b/w.
Seminal backstage musical in which the leading lady sprains her ankle on the opening night. Waiting in the wings is chorus-girl Keeler, who is ordered to get on out there: 'Sawyer, you're going out a youngster, but you've got to come back a star!' Includes some sensationally naughty Busby Berkeley numbers like 'Shuffle Off to Buffalo' and 'Young and Healthy', but it takes a lot to beat Bebe lolling on a piano as she trills 'You're Getting to Be a Habit with Me'. You too probably know someone who dances like Ruby Keeler: he might not be too flattered if you tell him so. AB

For Valour
(Tom Walls, 1937, GB) Tom Walls, Ralph Lynn, Veronica Rose, Joan Marion, Henry Longhurst.
95 min. b/w.
Aldwych farce from the pen of Ben Travers. Walls is the private who saves his compatriot's life in the Boer War and Lynn the soldier who nominates his rescuer for a VC and unwittingly reveals that he's an escaped con. Later, the plot whips into overdrive with the pair playing their own sons, but it doesn't raise much laughter these days. TJ

For Want of Sun
see Faute de Soleil

For Whom the Bell Tolls
(Sam Wood, 1943, US) Gary Cooper, Ingrid Bergman, Akim Tamiroff, Katina Paxinou, Joseph Calleia, Arturo de Cordova, Vladimir Sokoloff, Mikhail Rasumny, Fortunio Bonanova.
168 min.
One of Paramount's prestige pictures in 1943, when Katina Paxinou won an Oscar for best supporting actress, and the film picked up nominations in virtually every major category – but not in writing and in direction, and that's the *tell*. As an American fighting with the partisans in the Spanish Civil War, Cooper makes a perfect Hemingway hero, robust and romantic in equal measures. Falling in love with Ingrid Bergman's peasant guerrilla makes a lot of sense too, but the film's a mess dramatically. Wood approaches the material with kid gloves, when Hemingway was always a bare-knuckle fighter. Most later prints were tightened dramatically by being reduced to 130 minutes. TCh

For Your Eyes Only
(John Glen, 1981, GB) Roger Moore, Carole Bouquet, Chaim Topol, Lynn-Holly Johnson, Julian Glover, Cassandra Harris, Jill Bennett, Michael Gothard.
127 min.
An inflation-fighter Bond dumps the giant sets and mechanical gizmos of recent years in favour of stunts galore, courtesy of John Glen, who was second unit director on earlier 007s. Worth a try, but without his Art Dept clothes on, Bond is like the naked Emperor. Look, ma, no plot and poor dialogue, and Moore really is old enough to be the uncle of those girls. MB

Foul Play
(Colin Higgins, 1978, US) Goldie Hawn, Chevy Chase, Burgess Meredith, Rachel Roberts, Eugene Roche, Dudley Moore, Brian Dennehy, Marc Lawrence.
116 min.
A big budget, San Francisco-set comedy thriller, with Goldie Hawn playing self-contained kook Gloria Mundy. A significant name, since the deliberately ridiculous plot involves an attempt to murder the pontiff. (Or is it because Hawn's a little too well-worn in this kind of role, sic transit Gloria Mundy?). Unsatisfactory as a whole, the film is hilarious and tense in bits. For while writer/director Higgins uses almost every stock thriller device – sinister dwarf, albino, scarfaced man, moving shower curtain, disappearing corpses, a chase, an escape or two, even the identical twin wheeze – he approaches this semi-parody with more zest and originality than is common, and careers from farce to thrills before you can say 'Spot the hommage'. JS

Fountain, The (Fontan)
(Yuri Mamin, 1988, USSR) Asankul Kuttubaev, Sergei Dontsov, Zhanna Kerimtaeva, Viktor Mikhailov, Anatoli Kalmikov.
101 min.
Mamin's film is already a historical record of a certain phase of *perestroika*. But as an extremely broad social comedy, as well as a swingeing critique of personal and bureaucratic (ir)responsibility, it's little short of irresistible. Kazakhstan herdsman Kerbabaev moves to Moscow to live with his daughter and her husband Peter, the harassed maintenance official of a rancid, crumbling apartment block beset by constant disasters. With its catalogue of accumulating mishaps, *The Fountain* fires off its barbs in ample salvos, some of them perhaps too obviously allegorical of Russia's woes. But as an adeptly choreographed ensemble piece, and for its fairly pullulating sense of place, the film gushes with anarchic pleasures. JRo

Fountainhead, The
(King Vidor, 1949, US) Gary Cooper, Patricia Neal, Raymond Massey, Kent Smith, Robert Douglas, Henry Hull, Ray Collins.
114 min. b/w.
The most bizarre movie in both Vidor's and Cooper's filmographies, this adaptation of Ayn Rand's first novel mutes Ms Rand's neo-Nietzschean philosophy of 'Objectivism' but lays on the expressionist symbolism with a 'free enterprise' trowel. Cooper plays the up-and-coming architect with unorthodox ideas who dynamites a building that doesn't conform with his plans, marries wealthy heiress Neal, and winds up building the world's tallest tombstone as a memorial to a friend who committed suicide. As berserk as it sounds, although handsomely shot by Robert Burks and directed with enthusiasm. TR

4 Adventures of Reinette & Mirabelle (4 Aventures de Reinette & Mirabelle)
(Eric Rohmer, 1986, Fr) Joëlle Miquel, Jessica Forde, Philippe Laudenbach, Yasmine Haury, Marie Rivière, Fabrice Luchini.
99 min.
In Rohmer's slight but delightful low-key account of the up-and-down friendship between two teenage girls, the naturalistic performances are, as ever, supremely credible, with unknowns Miquel and Forde stealing the honours as the eponymous heroines. Reinette is a charming if changeful country girl longing to become a successful painter, Mirabelle the Parisian student

who offers to share her flat in town. The four largely un-dramatic adventures, first in the remote countryside, then in Paris, concentrate on their different reactions to the world: nature, social injustice, money, and in the wonderful final sequence, the familiar Rohmeresque problem of too much talk. It's all inescapably French (in the best sense) and concerned with the joys not only of good conversation but of seeing. Finally, for all its deliciously light humour and anecdotal quality, the film is essentially about people. Which other film-maker loves us, warts and all, so perceptively or so generously? Therein lies Rohmer's abiding genius. GA

Four Against Fate
see Derby Day

Four Days in July
(Mike Leigh, 1985, GB) Des McAleer, Stephen Rea, Shane Connaughton, Brid Brennan, Charles Lawson.
92 min.
Commissioned by producer Kenith Trodd and shown by the BBC in 1985, this is deviser/director Leigh's Northern Ireland film. This is alien territory for Leigh, who had some difficulty getting used to the grubby terrain of working-class Belfast and hanging a storyline on characters taken from both sides of the sectarian divide. Another departure for the now internationally established director is that the film has none of those people whom Leigh just can't portray properly: the English middle or upper classes. The result is a low-key but intriguing film which depicts the relations and friends of two families, Catholic and Protestant, linked by the arrival of babies in the month of the Orange marches. There are no shoot-outs or killings, even if the impact of the Troubles is exemplified by the crippled Eugene (McAleer, superb and understated) and ex-internees Brendan and Dixie, who swap yarns about using the prison lavatory system to distil poteen. Although strongly cast, the film has its longueurs (plus a Catholic bias), but it's sometimes very funny and tinged with sadness, even tragedy, throughout. A miserable man in hospital whose wife is expecting their first child asks: 'Three hours she's been in there. What does she think she's playing at?' SGr

Four Days in September (O Que é Isso, Companheiro?)
(Bruno Barreto, 1997, Braz) Alan Arkin, Pedro Cardoso, Fernanda Torres, Luiz Fernando Guimaraes, Claudi Abreu, Nelson Dantas.
113 min.
1969: a little known revolutionary group kidnaps US ambassador Charles Burke Elbrick in order to spotlight Brazil's military dictatorship. The kidnappers demand the release of political prisoners and, more importantly, air time. The authorities track them down – but dare they endanger the ambassador? The film (from a book by Fernando Gabeira, a journalist who'd participated in the abduction) is somewhat reminiscent of Costa-Gavras, but without the ideological programme. Indeed, Bruno Barreto goes out of his way both to round out the ambassador (Arkin, excellent as usual), and to humanise one of the official torturers. Nor are the radicals romanticised: they're young, naive, and in over their heads. A tense, absorbing, character piece – and a clear, balanced, historical study. TCh

Four Days of Snow and Blood (226)
(Hideo Gosha, 1989, Jap) Kenichi Hagiwara, Tomokazu Miura, Masahiro Motoki, Naoto, Takenaka, Daisuke Ryu.
114 min.
Based on Kazuo Kasahara's book 226, Gosha's turgid and hopelessly undramatic movie reconstructs the failed military coup of 26 February 1936, when a group of emperor-worshipping army officers tried to overthrow the civilian government. Dozens of earlier Japanese movies have dealt with these events, but few have been so wrong-footed: Gosha devotes most of two hours to the political and ethical debates that followed the assassinations, pausing only to weep along with the officers' long-suffering wives. A wretched dog of a movie. TR

4 Faces of Eve (4 [Si] Mian Xiawa)
(Jan Lamb/Eric Kot/Kam Kwok-Leung, 1996, HK) Sandra Ng, Eric Kot, Jan Lamb, Karen Mok, Wyman Wong.
91 min.
Four-episode vehicle for comedienne Sandra Ng, designed both to show off her versatility and to give some of the orthodoxies of Hong Kong film production a kick in the arse. Sadly, despite Ng's obvious talent, most of it is neither fresh nor funny. The second episode, played in a guttural invented language, is almost unwatchable (she's a Mainland Chinese wife ministering to her husband's every cruel need) and the final episode, in which she's a housewife winning prizes on a TV game show for exposing the full misery of her marriage, pales beside such realities as The Jerry Springer Show. But the first and third episodes have their moments, and Chris Doyle's anarchic cinematography is, to say the least, unpredictable. TR

Four Faces West
see They Passed This Way

Four Feathers, The
(Zoltan Korda, 1939, GB) John Clements, June Duprez, Ralph Richardson, C Aubrey Smith, Allan Jeayes, Jack Allen, Donald Gray.
130 min.
Classic British imperialist adventure, about a man accused of cowardice and redeeming himself through lofty heroics during the Sudan campaign of the 1890s. Produced by Alexander Korda, and directed by his brother Zoltan with flair and imagination, it's a typically polished vehicle for saluting a certain British mythology, with a rousing score by Miklos Rosza, superb Technicolor camerawork by a crew that included Périnal and Jack Cardiff, and solid performances all round. The fourth (and best) version of AEW Mason's ripping yarn, previously filmed in 1915, 1921 and 1929. GA

Four Feathers, The
(Don Sharp, 1978, GB) Beau Bridges, Robert Powell, Simon Ward, Jane Seymour, Harry Andrews, Richard Johnson.
105 min.
Redundant sixth version of the Mason yarn aimed squarely at the US TV audience who lapped it up shortly after its royal premiere here, complete with episodic structure (climaxes before commercials) and insistence on close-ups. Hardly worth a giggle, even over Bridges' 'English' accent, Ward's Monty Python beard, or Johnson in blackface. Harry Andrews gets to articulate the Boy's Own ethos: 'I doubt if a woman could understand'. PT

Four Flies on Grey Velvet (Quattro Mosche di Velluto Grigio)
(Dario Argento, 1971, It/Fr) Michael Brandon, Mimsy Farmer, Jean-Pierre Marielle, Francine Racette, Calisto Calisti.
105 min.
Rock drummer Brandon finds himself at the centre of a blackmail murder mystery in Rome. The script remains a distinct handicap, but Argento's handling of set pieces (mainly a series of elaborate murders) shows flair. A pity that he doesn't spend more time concentrating on heightening the atmosphere of hysteria and menace. DP

Four Friends (aka Georgia's Friends)
(Arthur Penn, 1981, US) Craig Wasson, Jodi Thelen, Michael Huddleston, Jim Metzler, Reed Birney, Julia Murray, James Leo Herlihy.
115 min.
To some extent drawing on the experiences of its scriptwriter Steve Tesich, this traces key moments in the life of Yugoslav immigrant Danny (Wasson), from his arrival in the States as a boy to the time when, thirty years later, his parents return to the old country. Although its episodic narrative entails a certain lack of unity, it's nevertheless an ambitious and impressive work that deals intelligently with a number of themes: the way time and distance play havoc with relationships, particularly with Danny's beloved Georgia, a lively, infuriating and gener-

ous girl whom he shyly rejects with saddening results; the way personal lives often rhyme with wider history; and most of all, the difficulties romantic Danny faces in trying to come to terms with the many contradictions and polarities – poverty and wealth, rural simplicity and urban sophistication – inherent in his adopted homeland. A dense but never pretentious film that manages to convey the atmosphere of the '50s and '60s succinctly, it offers delights galore, not least a light, perceptive wit and an unsentimental ability to touch the emotions. GA

400 Blows, The
see Quatre Cents Coups, Les

Four Just Men, The
(Walter Forde, 1939, GB) Hugh Sinclair, Griffith Jones, Francis L Sullivan, Frank Lawton, Anna Lee, Basil Sydney.
85 min. b/w.
Edgar Wallace's vigilante quartet save the Empire from foreign agents plotting to block the Suez Canal. Ludicrously jingoistic (even remembering 1956), and further blemished by a bland romance between an intrepid girl reporter (Lee) and the most handsomely boyish of the four (Jones). But still quite fun thanks to Forde's Hitchcockian flair for everyday menace (murder by poisoned suitcase at Victoria Station, by electrocution in a bathroom, by empty lift-shaft). TM

Four Men and a Prayer
(John Ford, 1938, US) Loretta Young, Richard Greene, George Sanders, David Niven, Sir C Aubrey Smith, J Edward Bromberg, William Henry, Alan Hale, John Carradine, Reginald Denny, Barry Fitzgerald, Berton Churchill.
85 min. b/w.
A ripping yarn in which Colonel Sir C Aubrey Smith is cashiered on the Northwest Frontier for conduct unbecoming that resulted in a massacre. His four sons (Sanders, Greene, Niven and Henry) rally round in London, and have time to learn that the old boy was framed by a munitions syndicate before he is murdered. Determined to clear the family name, the sons disperse to India, South America and Egypt. Once the preliminaries are over, their adventures are more enjoyable than they have any right to be, given that Ford directs with pace, wit, and tongue firmly in cheek. Clichés are exaggerated to the point of absurdity; Niven is given a good deal of subversively funny business as the flightiest brother; and pomposities (like the royal vindication at the end) are deflated by the malice with which they are staged. Loretta Young is particularly cleverly used: a wealthy socialite in love with Greene, she keeps popping up wherever the action is, downgrading it into a romantic comedy, and making the point that heroics solve nothing (her father is the armaments king the sons unmask, but he isn't the villain). TM

Four Musketeers: The Revenge of Milady, The
(Richard Lester, 1974, Pan/Sp) Oliver Reed, Raquel Welch, Richard Chamberlain, Michael York, Frank Finlay, Simon Ward, Christopher Lee, Faye Dunaway, Charlton Heston, Geraldine Chaplin, Jean-Pierre Cassel.
106 min.
The second half of Lester's brilliant The Three Musketeers is a reasonably beguiling, if noticeably padded coda, with the best bits containing in abundance that quality of penetrating period wit which made its predecessor such a delight. The tone is darker and more oppressive; there are sequences that lapse into boredom; but the scenes involving Dunaway – whether she's lobbing poisoned darts at her lovers or busily seducing her English warder – have a lushly ironic fairytale quality that the movies capture all too rarely. DP

Four Nights of a Dreamer (Quatre Nuits d'un Rêveur)
(Robert Bresson, 1971, Fr/It) Isabelle Weingarten, Guillaume des Forêts, Jean-Maurice Monnoyer, Jérôme Massart.
82 min.
Adapted from Dostoevsky's story of a couple's chance encounter and the advance of their parallel obsessions over four successive nights. The hallucinatory light and colour of Paris at night act as both mirror and landscape for their fragile relationship. Shot through with a mystical, almost frosty compassion, the film is rescued

from occasional moments of pretension by the gentle eroticism and absolute conviction with which it is made. The Dostoevsky story, *White Nights*, was filmed under that title by Luchino Visconti in 1957. CA

Four Rooms

(Allison Anders/Alexandre Rockwell/Robert Rodriguez/Quentin Tarantino, 1995, US) Tim Roth, Marisa Tomei, Sammi Davis, Valeria Golino, Madonna, Jennifer Beals, David Proval, Antonio Banderas, Lana McKissack, Quentin Tarantino.
97 min.
It's New Year's Eve in a Hollywood hotel; Ted the bellboy (Roth) is on his own. In Anders' episode, a witches' coven is after his semen; in Rockwell's he stumbles into a SM marital nightmare; Rodriguez has him looking after two mischievous children; and Tarantino reruns an 'Alfred Hitchcock Presents...' yarn involving a machete, a drunken wager, and a pinkie. Ted is the lynch-pin, but Roth's is a gibbering, fidgeting, nervous breakdown of a performance. Only Rodriguez paces and shapes the material; his virtuoso story has the authentic black comic lunacy of a Tom and Jerry cartoon brought to life. And Tarantino? Unwisely holding court as a Hollywood star, he offers further proof of his own acting limitations, with dialogue so patently Tarantino-esque it might be intentional self-parody. Most worryingly, his self-conscious, meandering takes raise doubts about his hitherto infallible cinematic intuition. They should have called this 'One Room' and released it as a Rodriguez short. TCh

Four Seasons, The

(Alan Alda, 1981, US) Alan Alda, Carol Burnett, Len Cariou, Sandy Dennis, Rita Moreno, Jack Weston, Bess Armstrong.
108 min.
The dialogue written by Alda for his directorial debut has the cut and thrust, but not the edge, of his script for *The Seduction of Joe Tynan*. Three married couples, friends of long standing, have their complacency challenged when one of their number replaces his wife with a younger woman. The camerawork is unadventurous (the only variation on static observation of the characters being the nature footage signalling the seasonal changes), but the performances Alda elicits from his co-actors almost justifies this. Within the characterisations, most of the fears and foibles of middle class, middle-aged America may be found. Amusing and worth a look. FD

Four Sons

(Archie Mayo, 1940, US) Don Ameche, Eugenie Leontovich, Mary Beth Hughes, Alan Curtis, George Ernest, Robert Lowery.
89 min. b/w.
Solid propaganda effort demonstrating the effects of the German invasion of Czechoslovakia on an ordinary family, with Ameche standing firm to fight the good fight and brother Curtis embracing the Nazi cause. Schematic but not ineffective melodrama responding to the crisis in Europe. A remake of a 1928 John Ford silent about a German family surviving the horrors of WWI. TJ

Fourteen Hours

(Henry Hathaway, 1951, US) Richard Basehart, Paul Douglas, Barbara Bel Geddes, Debra Paget, Agnes Moorehead, Robert Keith, Howard da Silva, Jeffrey Hunter, Grace Kelly, Jeff Corey.
92 min. b/w.
Back in 1938, John Warde perched on a ledge 17 floors up a skyscraper, and, for 14 hours, threatened to jump. This vertiginous melodrama recounts the event in professional low-key journalistic fashion. As in *Ace in the Hole*, the emphasis is as much on the reaction of bystanders as on the plight of the would-be suicide. Cab-drivers take bets, while cops and psychiatrists try to talk him down. Grace Kelly, in her debut, appears among the onlookers. GM

1492: Conquest of Paradise

(Ridley Scott, 1992, US) Gérard Depardieu, Armand Assante, Sigourney Weaver, Loren Dean, Angela Molina, Fernando Rey, Michael Wincott, Tchéky Karyo, Kevin Dunn, Frank Langella, Mark Margolis.
155 min.

Christopher Columbus: hero, or villain paving the way for genocide? Scott straddles the quincentenary controversy, painting him as a rebellious sort who finds reality at variance with his dreams. The film covers 20 years, from his early efforts to raise backing to his ensuing triumphs and, ultimately, the disillusionment of seeing Eden turning into Hell. It was a shrewd move to cast Depardieu in the role: few actors could so skilfully reconcile the necessary qualities of enthusiasm, vulnerability and arrogance. As Queen Isabel, Weaver proves a good foil, while spectacular visuals convey the brutality and grandeur of the age. But in attempting to explore the man, Roselyne Bosch's script also embraces the myth, most obviously in some initial exchanges laden with significance. Vangelis' thunderous, intrusive score doesn't help; even more tedious is foppish villain Wincott, fashion victim and confirmed sadist.

Fourth Man, The
(De Vierde Man)

(Paul Verhoeven, 1983, Neth) Jeroen Krabbé, Renée Soutendijk, Thom Hoffman, Dolf De Vries, Geert De Jong.
102 min.
Gerard is a writer; he is also Catholic, alcoholic and homosexual. And en route to give a lecture in the Dutch seaside town of Flushing, he has visions of oozing eyeballs and the Virgin Mary, dreams of castration, and is later hit on the head by a dead seagull. Although he shacks up with Christine (owner of the Sphinx Beauty Parlour, who lathers his hair with Delilah shampoo before cutting it), Gerard is true to his proclivities and hankers after her man Herman. But what became of Christine's three ex-husbands, eh? And who will be fourth? All this might be risible, but in Verhoeven's hands it's also an elegant Gothic entertainment, decorated with layers of deliciously over-the-top detail, explicit fleshy pursuits, artistic sickness and double-Dutch delirium tremens. Never a dull moment. AB

Fourth Protocol, The

(John MacKenzie, 1987, GB) Michael Caine, Pierce Brosnan, Ned Beatty, Joanna Cassidy, Julian Glover, Michael Gough, Ray McAnally, Ian Richardson.
119 min.
This adaptation of Frederick Forsyth's espionage thriller is neither fish nor fowl. Brosnan, who plays the ice-cool and ruthless Soviet undercover agent sent to an East Anglian American airbase to execute a 'devastating' plan to destabilise Anglo-American nuclear cooperation, poses and pouts so much that there are hopes of the film developing into a Bond-like spoof. No such luck. Still, Caine – a kind of middle-aged Harry Palmer – is at his shambling best as the no-nonsense spycatcher overcoming the deviousness or incompetence of his Intelligence bosses; and MacKenzie gives this home-grown blockbuster the requisite glossy, if predictable finish. What is missing is any real tension or psychological detail that might lend plausibility to all the hocus-pocus about East-West political and military intrigue. WH

Fourth War, The

(John Frankenheimer, 1990, US) Roy Scheider, Harry Dean Stanton, Jürgen Prochnow, Tim Reid, Lara Harris.
90 min.
When asked what kind of weapons would be used in the third world war, Einstein replied that he didn't know, but that the fourth war would be fought with stones. Nothing in this rather old-fashioned thriller has the bite of this remark. Scheider plays the clichéd military hardass, a veteran of Vietnam, divorced, disenchanted. 'A warrior', says his old comrade General Harry Dean Stanton, who intuitively installs him as a base commander on the German-Czech border. Soon Scheider is mounting one-man nocturnal sorties behind the Iron Curtain, partying with Soviet patrols and incurring the wrath of his Russian counterpart (Prochnow). The latter is Scheider's kind of guy; he was in Afghanistan. As Stanton puts it, in a rare animated moment, these are two 'disillusioned, pissed-off malcontents', and when the inevitable macho stand-off develops, it's to hell with the consequences. *The Fourth War* may have been conceived as the thinking person's *Rambo*, but in the event it isn't a patch on *First*

Blood; for a simple story, it's quite a mess, the very dubious voice-over hardly clarifying a clumsy sense of chronology. With the twists in the intrigue all too blatant, the climactic fight is a relief when it comes. TCh

Four Weddings and a Funeral

(Mike Newell, 1994, GB) Hugh Grant, Andie MacDowell, Kristin Scott Thomas, James Fleet, Simon Callow, John Hannah, David Bower, Corin Redgrave, Rowan Atkinson, Sophie Thompson.
117 min.
A British comedy that's classy and commercial – and, most important, very, very funny. Admittedly, as it charts the social, sexual and romantic fortunes of thirty-something Charles (Grant), a self-confessed serial monogamist, and the friends, old flames and potential lovers (notably MacDowell's rather enigmatic American beauty), who are his fellow guests at one wedding after another, the film's focus on well-heeled jovial oafs and its conventional attitude to modern relationships hardly make for 'radical romantic comedy'. But that's quibbling. Newell's direction switches smoothly between affecting intimacy and sequences of rowdy chaos; perhaps the film's trump card, however, is its emotional honesty, particularly in the poignant and sobering funeral scene. Genuine feel-good entertainment. GA

Fox
see Faustrecht der Freiheit

Fox, The

(Mark Rydell, 1967, US) Sandy Dennis, Anne Heywood, Keir Dullea, Glen Morris.
110 min.
Overdone adaptation of DH Lawrence's novella, making explicit everything that was implicit in his study of two women living together on an isolated poultry farm (menaced by a marauding fox), and the opposition of one to the marriage of the other. Dullea and Dennis, two of the worst overactors in the business, don't help any; but most of the blame must go to Rydell for his heavily emphatic direction. CPe

Fox and His Friends
see Faustrecht der Freiheit

Fox and the Hound, The

(Art Stevens/Ted Berman/Richard Rich, 1981, US) voices: Mickey Rooney, Kurt Russell, Pearl Bailey, Jack Albertson, Jeanette Nolan.
83 min.
One of the more homely Disney animated features, neither hip like *The Jungle Book* nor (pardon the expression) trippy like *Fantasia*. We're back in that serene Disney woodland where bright flowers dot heavily shaded glades and snow plops off branches like ice-cream. Here female creatures bat long eyelashes and kindly old Widow Tweed lives in a cosy cabin. She domesticates Tod, an orphaned fox cub who plays happily with a puppy hound until they grow up (and Tod acquires Mickey Rooney's voice). 'Two friends who didn't know they were supposed to be enemies', runs the catch-line. But the moral aimed at the children is a very conservative one: duty to your kind must come before personal friendship, that's nature's way. JS

Foxes

(Adrian Lyne, 1979, US) Jodie Foster, Cherie Currie, Marilyn Kagan, Kandice Stroh, Scott Baio, Sally Kellerman, Randy Quaid, Adam Faith.
105 min.
Almost like an inverted *Saturday Night Fever*, *Foxes* follows four LA teenage girls who seduce, humiliate, adore and befriend various men, but whose primary loyalties are always to each other. The first half, unfortunately, is poor: the producers (Casablanca Record) have lumbered it with undigested lumps from the company rock catalogue; there is some pretty variable comedy, dreary travelogue footage, and a very ugly use of filters and soft focus. But gradually a much more interesting film takes over. The tone becomes darker and more moralistic, concentrating on the relationship between Foster (looking uncannily old) and her impossible, dope-happy friend (a fine performance from ex-Runaway Cherie Currie),

both contemplating with real hurt the certainty of separation. The ending takes this feeling to its logical conclusion, and works a hell of a lot better as post-'60s tragedy than *The Rose*. DP

Fox Fire
see Feu Follet, le

Foxy Brown
(Jack Hill, 1974, US) Pam Grier, Antonio Fargas, Kathryn Loder, Peter Brown, Terry Carter, Sid Haig.
94 min.
Grier's follow-up to *Coffy*, also scripted and directed by Hill, lacks all the fine, subversive qualities she lent that film. She continues the avenger role, but in much diluted form, simply exacting retribution for the murder of her narcotics officer boyfriend (gone is *Coffy's* environment of all-pervasive and over-weening corruption); and in any case this is subsumed in a general racial tone, with every white within spitting distance made a bigot, for the sole purpose of milking audience reactions in the most blatant way possible. Grier is an actress able to convey an amazing and unflinching strength, and she reveals the film for the dross it is. VG

F.P.1 antwortet nicht
see No Answer from F.P.1

Fracture du myocarde, La (Cross My Heart)
(Jacques Fansten, 1990, Fr) Sylvain Copans, Nicolas Parodi, Cécilia Rouaud, Delphine Gouttman, Olivier Montiège, Lucie Blossier.
105 min.
Snapped up by Hollywood for a remake by Spielberg, this is the best story about kids since *Stand by Me*. 12-year-old Martin (Copans), terrified that he will be sent to an orphanage, conceals the fact that his mother has died. His classmates band together to keep the secret and outwit the authorities. The burial of the corpse in baking foil with a grandfather clock as a coffin is funny, touching, and memorably surreal. Martin's friends steal food from home for him, learn to forge his mother's signature, and devise scams at school to derail parent meetings. The adult world – and the usual sexual rites of passage – are seen as largely irrelevant. Social workers are useless, teachers have forgotten what it was like to be a child, and there are no villains. Neither sentimental nor melodramatic, the film earns its tragic ending. Collective playing by the large cast of kids is excellent. BC

Fragments of Isabella
(Ronan O'Leary, 1989, Ire) Gabrielle Reidy.
79 min.
O'Leary's film is a transposition of a stage play based on a book written by Holocaust survivor Isabella Leitner. As a teenager, Leitner was taken from the Hungarian Jewish ghetto of Kisvarda to Auschwitz, thence to Birnbaumel. On the death march to Bergen-Belsen, she escaped with two of her sisters. The horrors and atrocities she witnessed on that darkest of journeys – including the deaths of her mother and two young sisters – are related here in the form of a long monologue by Reidy. Her performance is hard to fault, not least because of its restraint. The monologue is interspersed with newsreel footage, but no shots of horror. If the film's power derives essentially from the word, it is a compliment to the unobtrusive sensitivity of O'Leary's direction – the film is staged on simple sets, carefully lit by Walter Lassally, and incorporates a very subtle use of music (by Carl Davis) and sound – that nothing gets in the way of our hearing it. WH

Framed
(Phil Karlson, 1974, US) Joe Don Baker, Conny Van Dyke, Gabriel Dell, John Marley, Brock Peters, John Larch, Warren Kemmerling, Paul Mantee.
106 min.
Everything about this film is ugly and elephantine. A barely audible Joe Don Baker becomes the victim of a baffling frame-up involving people in 'high places', does a spell in jail, then sets out full of vengeful bitterness to unravel the whys and wherefores. The fragmented direction, which persists in spotlighting the irrelevant, is not even within shouting distance of creating any sus-

pense or intrigue; one violent act merely mindlessly succeeds another. The performances are tediously one-dimensional: Joe snarls, Conny breaks down, while the various legal guardians bully. The final twist loses any power it might have had when the one vaguely sympathetic cop, leafing through evidence of top-level corruption, passionately declares, 'Oh no, not him!' IB

Franc, Le
(Djibril Diop Mambéty, 1995, Switz/Fr/Senegal) Dieye Ma Dieye, Aminta Fall, Demba Bâ.
45 min.
Mambéty's short final part of the trilogy he began way back when with the acclaimed *Touki Bouki* is a winning cautionary tale about a poor Senegalese congoma player who wins the lottery. Shot (in beautiful colour) in a lively composite style that brings to mind the experimental freshness of '20s Soviet cinema, it veers easily and joyfully between realist, surrealist and almost-documentary modes, with jangling camera angles and a foot-tapping soundtrack featuring music in French, English and Arabic (including a delightful Tom Waits-like, deep-toned vocalist). It's a satire, of course, on Senegal's economic and social contradictions (the S. Franc has recently devalued, the lottery's an irrelevant fantasy), delivered as the sweetest of pills. WH

Frances
(Graeme Clifford, 1982, US) Jessica Lange, Sam Shepard, Kim Stanley, Bart Burns, Christopher Pennock, James Karen.
140 min.
The sad life of '30s and '40s actress Frances Farmer is surely the stuff of melodrama: the story of an intelligent, uncompromising young actress with strong radical political opinions, who fell or was pushed from grace in Hollywood and ended up undergoing a lobotomy in an asylum. But in this version the vein becomes increasingly American Gothic; the potential romantic exploration of the American Left is abandoned in favour of a concentration on the star's incarceration in a series of increasingly Hogarthian asylums. Indeed, Farmer, as scripted here and played by Lange, unsurprisingly remains something of a cypher. VG

Francesco, giullare di Dio (Francis, God's Jester)
(Roberto Rossellini, 1950, It) Aldo Fabrizi, Brother Nazario, Arabelle Lemaître, and the monks of Nocere Inferiore Monastery.
75 min. b/w.
Like *Rome, Open City* and *Paisà*, this was co-written by Federico Fellini. Inspired by the *Little Flowers of St Francis*, it's the story of Francis of Assisi and his acolytes, the first Franciscans. They're a motley crew – simple, humble, joyful – quite prepared to give away anything they have (even their cassocks!) if it is required. Rossellini's film shares their qualities. How you react to it probably depends on your own state of grace... or your sense of humour. TCh

Franchesca Page
(Kelley Sane, 1997, US) Varla Jean Merman, Rossy de Palma, Tara Leon, Mark Dendy, Linda Smith, Leigh Rose, Marc Cunningham.
92 min.
The *faux* Almodóvar opening credits are pretty fab, but from then on this cross-dressing NY frolic entertains only fitfully. The problem isn't in Jeff Robertson's central turn as fun-sized drag queen Varla Jean Merman, who makes the late Divine look like a wilting flower. It's in the plot line spun around her (romance, ambition and murder behind the scenes of an off-off-off-Broadway disco extravaganza, 'The Lady Does It All'), the director's timing of the sundry catty one-liners, and the enthusiastic, but distinctly amateur-hour supporting cast. For indulgent connoisseurs of high camp. TJ

Franchise Affair, The
(Lawrence Huntington, 1950, GB) Michael Denison, Dulcie Gray, Anthony Nicholls, Marjorie Fielding, Athene Seyler, Peter Jones, John Bailey, Ann Stephens, Hy Hazell, Kenneth More.
88 min. b/w.
A strangled adaptation of Josephine Tey's mys-

tery (itself based on the 18th century Elizabeth Canning case). Denison is the country solicitor retained by two women new to the area (Gray as the distressed daughter, Fielding as her battleaxe mother) accused of sequestering, starving and beating a local girl (Stephens) in an attempt to make her their servant. In the novel, the solicitor is shaken out of his complacency by what transpires, but you would never guess as much from Denison's wooden performance in a context – the direction consists largely of posing the actors in static groupings – which looks very much like a repertory company matinée, with risible 'opening out' attempts to portray the town's mounting harassment of the interlopers. All tension is soon dissipated, with Gray so palpitatingly innocent, and her accuser so clearly a lying minx, that the lengthy trial sequence becomes tiresomely redundant (except to explain the plot). TM

Francis
(Arthur Lubin, 1949, US) Donald O'Connor, Patricia Medina, ZaSu Pitts, Ray Collins, John McIntire, Tony Curtis.
91 min. b/w.
First of Lubin's sextet of Universal comedies 'starring' Francis the Talking Mule alongside Donald O'Connor. With information culled (as near as dammit) from the horse's mouth, raw second lieutenant O'Connor becomes a hero of the Burma campaign and, not unnaturally, a candidate for the funny farm. The series pegged out when Charles Lamont and Mickey Rooney replaced Lubin and O'Connor in 1955. Chill Wills provided Francis' voice. PT

Francis, God's Jester
see Francesco, giullare di Dio

François Truffaut, Portraits Volés (François Truffaut, Stolen Portraits)
(Serge Toubiana/Michel Pascal, 1992, Fr) Eric Rohmer, Claude Chabrol, Bertrand Tavernier, Olivier Assayas, Fanny Ardant.
93 min.
It's not hard to guess why people like Jean-Pierre Léaud and Jean-Luc Godard wouldn't participate in this autopsy of Truffaut's reputation as a man and as a film-maker, but it's harder to understand why the directors pass over their absence in silence. In essence, this is a clips-and-talking-heads documentary, notably mainly for prying into some of the darker corners of Truffaut's psyche, including the ruthlessness with which he craved attention during his days as a young critic. Both fans and non-fans will come away with their prejudices confirmed. TR

Frank Capra's American Dream
(Kenneth Bowser, 1997, US) Robert Altman, André De Toth, John Milius, Martin Scorsese, Richard Schickel, Fay Wray, Edward Zwick.
109 min. b/w & col.
An expansive, sympathetic and well-illustrated survey of Capra's career, this bio-doc by-passes archive interviews with the garrulous and self-centred director, but then sometimes dwells too long on celebrity gush. Concentrating on the golden '30s and '40s, and skipping over Capra's decline in the '50s, the film gives due weight to such significant collaborators as screenwriter Robert Riskin. Especially piquant is the loyal sound man (sole survivor of the team) declaring his exasperation over Capra's indulgences on *Lost Horizon*. DT

Frankenhooker
(Frank Henenlotter, 1990, US) James Lorinz, Patty Mullen, Charlotte Helmkamp.
90 min.
'Jesus Christ, this could get ugly', says Jeffrey, nerdy would-be Frankenstein, as a laboratory guinea pig explodes after inhaling fumes from his patented Super-Crack. And it does. When his bride-to-be is turned into a tossed salad by a runaway lawnmower, Jeffrey salvages her head and reconstructs her with limbs, breasts and torsos gleaned from hookers he has tricked into 'cracking up' in similar fashion. Revived by the obligatory bolt of lightning, Elizabeth is not quite her old self; even her clients find her too hot to han-

dle. Henenlotter indulges his penchant for sleaze to the max, throwing in a few bad-taste puns and a little therapeutic head-drilling for laughs. The resulting fragmented mess will no doubt keep some in stitches, but it is definitely less than the sum of its body parts. NF

Frankenstein

(James Whale, 1931, US) Boris Karloff, Colin Clive, Mae Clarke, John Boles, Edward Van Sloan, Dwight Frye, Frederick Kerr.
71 min. b/w.

A stark, solid, impressively stylish film, overshadowed (a little unfairly) by the later explosion of Whale's wit in the delirious *Bride of Frankenstein*. Karloff gives one of the great performances of all time as the monster whose mutation from candour to chill savagery is mirrored only through his limpid eyes. The film's great imaginative coup is to show the monster 'growing up' in all too human terms. First he is the innocent baby, reaching up to grasp the sunlight that filters through the skylight. Then the joyous child, playing at throwing flowers into the lake with a little girl whom he delightedly imagines to be another flower. And finally, as he finds himself progressively misjudged by the society that created him, the savage killer as whom he has been typecast. The film is unique in Whale's work in that the horror is played absolutely straight, and it has a weird fairytale beauty not matched until Cocteau made *La Belle et la Bête*. TM

Frankenstein

see Mary Shelley's Frankenstein

Frankenstein: The True Story

(Jack Smight, 1973, GB) James Mason, Leonard Whiting, David McCallum, Jane Seymour, Nicola Paget, Michael Sarrazin, Michael Wilding, Agnes Moorehead, Margaret Leighton, Ralph Richardson, John Gielgud.
123 min.

Scripted by Christopher Isherwood and Don Bachardy, this is not exactly a faithful rendering of Mary Shelley's novel, although it deserves full marks for using the magnificent Arctic ending so long ignored by the cinema. Difficult to assess properly, since the feature is a boil-down from the 200-minute version shown on American TV, although a misogynistic reading is clearly intended (with the two brides, Frankenstein's and the monster's, emerging as more treacherously villainous than either of their mates). For a while it comes on like bad Hammer, until the arrival of the monster – a handsome lad, but the process is reverting – perks things up considerably. Particularly memorable is a scene where the monster's demurely virginal Bride sings 'I Love Little Pussy, Her Coat Is So Warm', before gleefully attempting to strangle a sleepy persian and lasciviously licking a drop of mauve blood from her scratched arm; and a glorious moment of delirium when the monster disrupts a society ball to collect his bride, ripping off her pearl choker to reveal the stitched neck, then annexing her head as his property. Whiting is a weak Frankenstein, but more than made up for by Sarrazin (the monster), Seymour (his bride), Richardson (the hermit) and Mason (first cousin to Fu Manchu as Polidori). TM

Frankenstein and the Monster from Hell

(Terence Fisher, 1973, GB) Peter Cushing, Shane Briant, Madeline Smith, John Stratton, Bernard Lee, Dave Prowse, Patrick Troughton.
99 min.

Fisher's last film is a disappointment. Using the already well-proven formula, it offers the Baron this time as a doctor in a criminal asylum for the insane, secretly working with his assistant towards creating yet another life. Things begin well, with Fisher adding some atmospheric touches and Cushing suggesting a man undermined by his excessive rationality. Unfortunately the script, which treads a wavering line between jerky comedy and seriousness, soon dissipates anyone else's better intentions. Things are further weakened by a listless assistant, a monster that looks as if it has strayed from some never-realised 'Apes' project, and a gratuitously unpleasant brain transplant. CPe

Frankenstein Created Woman

(Terence Fisher, 1966, GB) Peter Cushing, Susan Denberg, Thorley Walters, Robert Morris, Duncan Lamont, Alan Macnaughtan.
86 min.

Fisher's third film in the Hammer *Frankenstein* series is a subtly decadent reworking of the *Bride of Frankenstein* theme (although it bears absolutely no relation to the Universal picture), about a Lamia-like seductress who returns from the grave to seduce and slaughter her former tormentors. It's full of cloying Keatsian imagery, which somehow transcends the more idiotic aspects of the plot. DP

Frankenstein Meets the Wolf Man

(Roy William Neill, 1943, US) Lon Chaney Jr, Bela Lugosi, Lionel Atwill, Ilona Massey, Patrick Knowles, Maria Ouspenskaya, Dwight Frye.
74 min. b/w.

The first of Universal's frantic attempts to halt falling box-office receipts by doubling up on its monsters, with Chaney's despairing Wolf Man coming to consult Dr Frankenstein in the hope of finding cure or release. The good doctor is dead, but another overweening scientist (Knowles) is on hand to be tempted to revive the monster, found frozen in ice, for a last-reel showdown with the Wolf Man in which both are swept away when the villagers blow up a dam. Fast-paced and quite atmospheric in its tacky way, but definitively sabotaged by Lugosi as the monster; at last getting to play the role he missed out on in 1931, he gives a performance of excruciatingly embarrassing inadequacy. TM

Frankenstein Must Be Destroyed

(Terence Fisher, 1969, GB) Peter Cushing, Veronica Carlson, Simon Ward, Freddie Jones, Thorley Walters, Maxine Audley, George Pravda.
97 min.

Hammer's fifth Frankenstein film shifts the horror from the Monster, now a sad and pathetic victim, to the Baron (Cushing), now an embittered and ruthless tyrant. Abducting his former assistant Dr Brandt (Pravda) from a lunatic asylum, the Baron transplants his brain into the body of Dr Richter (Jones). Restored to sanity but with his brain trapped within an alien body, the newly bandaged Brandt/Richter monster is able to talk to his grief-stricken wife (Audley) but unable to understand or explain the transformation that has 'cured' him. Fisher taps a rich vein of Romanticism here, making this the high point of a series that afterwards degenerated into the sloppy self-parody of Jimmy Sangster's *The Horror of Frankenstein*. NF

Frankie & Johnny

(Garry Marshall, 1991, US) Al Pacino, Michelle Pfeiffer, Hector Elizondo, Nathan Lane, Jane Morris, Kate Nelligan, Greg Lewis, Al Fann, Glenn Plummer.
118 min.

Adapted by Terrence McNally from his own play *Frankie and Johnny in the Clair de Lune*, this shares the squashiness of Neil Simon. Against a klaxon background of New York, Frankie (Pfeiffer), a waitress at the Apollo Café, has problems responding to the courting of Johnny (Pacino), the short-order cook. She's withdrawn, wants a VCR, and seems content to observe her neighbours' relationships through the window. But Johnny, after a mousy one-night stand with another waitress (Nelligan), won't take no for an answer. He gatecrashes her bowling night, they go to bed, she supplies the condom, and this time he lets rip with an orgasmic cry. Quaint cameos from Morris as a species of Dandy Nichols waitress, and Elizondo as the loveable cheap Greek cafe-owner. Pacino wears a vest and bandanna and moons through the part. Pfeiffer plays dowdy. Marshall directs as if *Marty* had never happened. BC

Frankie Starlight

(Michael Lindsay-Hogg, 1995, US/Ire) Anne Parillaud, Matt Dillon, Gabriel Byrne, Rudi Davies, Georgina Cates, Alan Pentony, Corban Walker.
101 min.

This tale of a physically impaired Irishman (a dwarf) and the literary success of his family reminiscences does itself no favours by courting comparison with producer Noel Pearson's *My Left Foot*. Frankie's mam Bernadette (Parillaud) lands in Ireland by accident after WWII (she's discovered stowing away on a ship from France with homebound GIs). In Cork, naval officer Jack Kelly (Byrne) sees her alone and pregnant and becomes a father figure to young François (Pentony). Later, Frankie takes a shine to one of Jack's daughters, Emma, until the Kellys are transferred elsewhere. Next, from Texas, comes biker Terry Klout (Dillon), who whisks Bernsie and Frank to the States. Meanwhile, the adult Frank (Walker) is selling his life story to a publisher, reading the reviews, attending book-signings, crossing paths once more with Emma. Alas, the effect of these episodes is feeble. Whereas *My Left Foot* built up around the formidable figure of Christy Brown, here there's a void. The diffuseness is central to the star-gazing metaphor, but more than a tight plot is needed to entrance the audience, and director Lindsay-Hogg's picture postcard naturalism isn't it. The film does, however, have some charm, and the performances help it amble along pleasantly. NB

Frantic

see Ascenseur pour l'Echafaud

Frantic

(Roman Polanski, 1988, US) Harrison Ford, Betty Buckley, Emmanuelle Seigner, Alexandra Stewart, David Huddleston, Robert Barr, Boll Boyer.
120 min.

Polanski's thriller boasts several superb set pieces, even if it doesn't quite snap shut on the mind the way *Chinatown* did. Dr Walker (Ford) checks into a Paris hotel with his wife (Buckley) to attend a conference. She has collected the wrong suitcase at the airport, their problems escalate, and to watch how Polanski calibrates the build-up of disquiet in a standard hotel suite until the wife disappears is deeply satisfying. Walker is suddenly alone with the unimaginable in alien territory, asking for help. Officialdom won't take him seriously and he resorts to clues lit by match flares. We are in *film noir* territory. The wrong suitcase leads him to a corpse, and then to Michelle (Seigner), a swinging chick who attaches herself to his quest. Polanski's penchant for the surreal goes adrift on one dislocation involving the Statue of Liberty through a porthole, but scores heavily with Ford's increasingly disreputable returns to base, a discreet, tiptoe hotel into which he creeps shoeless, and with a bubblegum punkette in tow. Funny and unsettling. BC

Frantz Fanon: Black Skin, White Mask

(Isaac Julien, 1996, GB/Fr) Colin Salmon, Al Nedjari, John Wilson, Ana Ramalho, Noirín Ni Dubhgaill; Homi Bhabha, Stuart Hall, Françoise Vergès.
70 min.

A fine introduction to the life and work of the Frantz Fanon (1925-61), the Martinican-born, Paris-educated author, intellectual and activist. Isaac Julien and co-writer Mark Nash's study shows the influence of Derek Jarman's similar work on Wittgenstein. Mixing the talking heads (notably Stuart Hall), interviews with relatives, co-workers and friends, and archive footage, clips and reconstructions, they have produced a clear résumé of Fanon's ideas, but also something rarer, a strong, affecting sense of the man's complex personality. With his interest in violence, black identity and psychiatry (it was Fanon's professional work with war-damaged 'natives' and French soldiers in early '50s Algeria that was to revolutionise his politics, leading him later to join the FLN), Fanon is in many ways a perfect subject for Julien, enabling him to pursue themes that have figured in his work since *Territories* in the early '80s. In many ways this is the director's most mature film and not without the lyricism of his earlier discursive documentaries. Fanon died young (of leukaemia), just before the publication of *The Wretched of the Earth*, the analytical manifesto which became the freedom fighter's bible. WH

Französische Frau, Eine

see Femme française, Une

Fraternally Yours

see Sons of the Desert

Frauds

(Stephan Elliott, 1992, Aust) Phil Collins, Hugo
Weaving, Josephine Byrnes, Peter Mochrie,
Helen O'Connor.
94 min.
Phil Collins as an insurance investigator?
Unctuous, supercilious, insidious, Roland
Copping is surely the part he was born to play.
A pair of dice always in hand, he allows Lady
Luck to rule his destiny – which is bad news for
ill-fated middle-class couple Jonathan and Beth
Wheats (Weaving and Byrnes), vulnerable to
blackmail after their opportunistic insurance
claim. Copping tempts the couple into a spiral
of defiance and defeat, his brinkmanship taking
them ever closer to disaster; and as the stakes
get higher, the movie gets wilder, mutating into
a surreal black comedy with a brash carniva-
lesque tone. Copping's apartment looks like a
spare set from *Toys*, while acute camera angles
ensure that any semblance of reality is purely
coincidental. But while this movie may be different, it's not *that* different; actually, it resembles an extended episode of *The Avengers*.
Elliott's thesis is that all men are children at
heart – and that children are malicious, vindictive beasts. It's hardly an edifying conceit, and
the movie has an over-insistent, meretricious
feel about it. TCh

Frau im Mond

see Woman in the Moon

Freaked

(Tom Stern/Alex Winter, 1993, US) Alex
Winter, Randy Quaid, Megan Ward, Michael
Stoyanov, Brooke Shields, Keanu Reeves, Mr
T, Bobcat Goldthwait.
81 min.
Clearly a labour of love for co-writer, co-director
and star Alex Winter (the other one in the *Bill and
Ted* movies), this freewheeling, anarchic, gross-
out comedy should satisfy the six-pack post-pub
crowd, but it can't really stand up to sober viewing. It's the vaguely satirical story of a spoiled
young movie star (Winter) whose South
American product endorsement tour turns sour
when he's waylaid in Quaid's bizarre jungle-freak
circus and given a dose of the truly evil medicine
he's been pushing. The wit is all in the casting:
Mr T as the bearded lady (you got a problem with
that?), Bobcat Goldthwait as 'Sockhead', Brooke
Shields as a TV presenter, and Keanu Reeves
behind layers of hair as 'Ortiz the Dog Boy'. Brian
(*Society*) Yuzna's surreal make-up effects are also
worth a look – check out those gun-toting Rasta
eyeballs! – but the sum is less than its (very ugly)
parts. TCh

Freaks

(Tod Browning, 1932, US) Harry Earles, Olga
Baclanova, Wallace Ford, Lelia Hyams, Henry
Victor, Daisy Earles.
64 min. b/w.
A superb and unique film from that master of the
morbid, masochistic and macabre, Tod Browning.
Set in a travelling circus – a milieu Browning
knew and loved from his own experience – it
shows the revenge taken by a group of circus
freaks on a beautiful trapeze artist and her strong-
man lover after they have tried to kill a midget
(the marvellous Harry Earles, one of the stars of
Browning's *The Unholy Three*) for his fortune.
The basic themes of the film are the strength in
solidarity of the individually weak freaks, and the
inner beauty of the physically malformed as compared to the greed and deceit of the physically
resplendent. Although using real freaks,
Browning's treatment is never voyeuristic or condescending, but sympathetic in such a way that
after a few minutes we almost cease to perceive
them as in any way abnormal. There is a strong,
black humour that, remarkably, lacks cruelty, and
a real sense of terror in the awful revenge the
wronged freaks exact. MGM never knew what hit
them with this film; they virtually disowned it,
and it remained unseen in Britain until the '60s.
It has now achieved deserved recognition as a
masterpiece. GA

Freaky Friday

(Gary Nelson, 1976, US) Barbara Harris, Jodie
Foster, John Astin, Patsy Kelly, Dick Van
Patten, Vicki Schreck, Sorrell Booke, Ruth
Buzzi, Marie Windsor.
100 min.
'I wish I could swop places with her for just one
day', is the mutual cry of suburban mom and
teenage daughter. And sure enough, Jodie Foster
duly informs the audience, 'Mom's body has got
my mind in it!' But in 'some ways nothing
changes: Barbara Harris merely becomes her
usual scatty self, while Foster adds another display of unbridled precocity to her credits. This
being a Disney comedy, nothing too drastic happens; and attendant adults can rest assured that,
because Dad is so dithering and ineffectual, awkward questions about potentially incestuous relations, sadly, do not arise. Good performances
struggle gamely to overcome the increasingly
predictable plot. CPe

Freddie as F.R.0.7.

(Jon Acevski, 1992, GB) voices: Ben Kingsley,
Jenny Agutter, Brian Blessed, Nigel
Hawthorne, Michael Hordern, Jonathan Pryce,
Prunella Scales, Billie Whitelaw, John
Sessions.
91 min.
Prince Frederic is transformed into a magical frog
by his wicked aunt in a fairytale preamble to this
animation feature. Bizarrely, we cut to the modern day, where he is the pride of the French secret
service. Meanwhile, Blighty is losing its heritage
at an alarming rate. Nelson's Column has vanished. The Tower of London disappears
overnight. With 007 in Hollywood, MI6 turn in
desperation to F.R.0.7. Billed as 'An Amazing
Fantasy of a New Kind', the movie is a hotch-
potch of half-baked ideas ransacked from Disney,
Bond and, at a guess, cult shows like *The
Avengers* and *Dr Who*. The most intriguing
notion is that by stealing historic monuments, the
Snake Queen hopes to extract the country's life
force and plunge the population into inertia. The
rest is lame jokes and outmoded stereotypes. TCh

Freddy's Dead:
The Final Nightmare

(Rachel Talalay, 1991, US) Robert Englund,
Lisa Zane, Shon Greenblatt, Lezlie Deane,
Ricky Dean Logan, Breckin Meyer, Yaphet
Kotto.
89 min.
Once again, a spurious piece of Freddy mythology – involving an adopted daughter – provides
the excuse for some not-so-special effects
sequences and flip one-liners in this terminally
boring conclusion to the *Nightmare on Elm Street*
series. An amnesiac teenager, christened 'John
Doe' (Greenblatt), lands up at the centre for disturbed adolescents run by child psychologist
Maggie Burroughs (Zane). Apparently providing
the link Freddy needs to get at rich runaway
Spencer (Meyer), bellicose martial arts expert
Tracy (Deane) and aurally impaired Carlos
(Logan), 'John' is also drawn into Freddy's nightmare world. All that remains, therefore, is for
Freddy to bump off each of the disposable teens
in turn, by exploiting their psychological weaknesses. Plus, of course, the long overdue demise
of Freddy himself. Even the much-heralded 3-D
finale is murky and unimaginative. NF

Freebie and the Bean

(Richard Rush, 1974, US) Alan Arkin, James
Caan, Loretta Swit, Jack Kruschen, Mike
Kellin, Paul Koslo, Valerie Harper.
113 min.
Not the latest Disney, as the title implies, but yet
another cop movie, a strangely callous exercise
that divides its time between comic destruction
of *It's a Mad World* proportions, and a super-vio-
lence that makes no distinction between the people and the machinery that it destroys. Caan and
Arkin manage just enough to justify the presence
of yet another wisecracking male duo, but the
general feeling is of an attempt at audience
manipulation, assembled by computer, apart
from the truly bizarre final confrontation that
looks like something strayed from another movie.
On the whole, a film one can live without. CPe

Freedom for Us

see À Nous la Liberté

Freedom Is Paradise (SER)

(Sergei Bodrov, 1989, USSR) Volodya Kozyrev,
Alexander Bureyev, Svetlana Gaitan, Vitautas
Tomkus.
75 min.
Bodrov's excellent movie has no more flab than
its young hero, a tough but doe-eyed teenager in
a black-leather jacket who escapes from reform
school and traverses the USSR in search of his
father, also in prison. The title really ought to be
FIP since, like the other kids in the reform school,
13-year-old Sasha has the acronym *SER* ('svobo-
da eto rai') tattooed on his arm as a kind of badge
of hope. His quest takes him from Alma Ata (the
city where Bodrov got his own first break) all the
way to Archangel (site of Lenin's first gulag): an
ideal itinerary for a road movie, full of regional
and ethnic variety and rich in political associations. Bodrov, a one-time satirical journalist,
starts from the assumption that almost everyone
in the USSR is conditioned to think and behave
like a prisoner. But his focus is squarely on
Sasha's resilience, imagination and emotional
needs. As a picture of childhood's end, it's strong
enough to stand alongside genre classics like *My
Life as a Dog* and *A Summer at Grandpa's*; and
the fluency and simplicity of Bodrov's film language makes it a pleasure to watch. TR

Freedom Road

(Ján Kadár, 1979, US) Muhammad Ali, Kris
Kristofferson, Ron O'Neal, Edward Herrmann,
Barbara-O Jones, Sonny Jim Gaines.
100 min.
Originally a four-hour tele-drama in the States,
but mercifully trimmed to feature length here,
Freedom Road marks a sad close to the career of
the late expatriate Czech director, Kadár. Howard
Fast's bulky novel is transposed with all the
numbing insistence and impeccable stacked-deck
liberalism of an old Stanley Kramer message-
movie, with Muhammad Ali struggling to
portray a quiet black Spartacus in the midst
of the fight for post-Civil War emancipation.
Flashbacks span 13 years' shallow history of
'the story so far', while former slave niggers and
poor white trash together prepare for martyrdom
in battle with the baby-burning Klan. The
sentiments are fine; the sermonising's not. PT

Freejack

(Geoff Murphy, 1992, US) Emilio Estevez,
Mick Jagger, Rene Russo, Anthony Hopkins,
Jonathan Banks, David Johansen, Amanda
Plummer.
109 min.
Catapulted into the future a split second before a
motor-racing accident, Alex Furlong (Estevez)
wakes up in 2009, just in time to avoid a lobotomy. Dazed and confused, he flees across a polluted New York divided between the rich, powerful
executives of the McCandless Corporation and the
poor who live on the streets. Monosyllabic
'Bonejacker' Vacendak (Jagger) is despatched to
capture Alex, a 'Freejack' intended for a mind-
transplant that will allow an ailing client to transfer to his youthful body. The central idea is never
explored, despite the obvious potential of a scenario in which Alex is confronted with old flame
Julie (Russo), now a high-flying executive with the
Corporation owned by her love-struck but unrequited boss (Hopkins). Whenever things get boring, which is often, the double-crossing factor is
increased, which complicates the plot without
adding substance to the two-dimensional characters or to the mechanical suspense. NF

Freelance

(Francis Megahy, 1970, GB) Ian McShane,
Gayle Hunnicutt, Keith Barron, Alan Lake,
Peter Gilmore, Charles Hyatt.
81 min.
Kept on the shelf for five years, this surfaced for
one week in London as a supporting feature, then
disappeared. In fact, it's a very straightforward,
serviceable thriller about a small-time con man
who is trapped into graduating to bigger crime.
Filmed essentially as a chase, the film boasts a
couple of good action sequences and some nicely
low-key location shooting. CPe

Freeway

(Matthew Bright, 1996, US) Reece
Witherspoon, Kiefer Sutherland, Dan Hedaya,
Amanda Plummer, Brooke Shields.
98 min.

The directorial debut for *Guncrazy* screenwriter Matthew Bright, this enthusiastically grotesque exploitation flick turns out to be Little Red Riding Hood transposed to '90s California. In her most engaging performance to date, Witherspoon is a polite, affectionate, shit-kicking teen stuck with a fuck-up mom, an abusive stepdad, and all the bad luck in the world. Fleeing welfare officers for Grandma's house, she breaks down on the freeway, and gets a lift from a concerned psychologist – Sutherland – who isn't all he appears to be. There's not much edification in store, and Bright cruises over some bumpy plot holes, but the teen's perspective does put a black comic spotlight on wider social hypocrisies. Danny Elfman contributes a rusty, rollicking carnival-esque theme tune. TCh

Free Willy

(Simon Wincer, 1993, US) Jason James Richter, Lori Petty, Jayne Atkinson, August Schellenberg, Michael Madsen.
112 min.
Sweeping strings accompany the opening sequence of balletic whales cavorting in brilliant blue sea, changing abruptly to a cacophony as the bad guys with nets chug up in their tugs. Willy is trapped and his family swims mournfully away. Cut to an angelic street-kid, Jesse (Richter), caught graffiti-ing Willy's tank; the only way to escape 'baby jail' he discovers is to go to well-meaning but stiffo foster parents and clean up the tank under the tutelage of Haida Indian whale-trainer Randolph (Schellenberg). Willy, meanwhile, has turned ornery. Soon, however, Jesse's mouth organ is echoing Willy's whalesong and the message is spelt out: boy and whale get on because they're both looking for a family. This well-acted film has a straight-faced tone which is hard to resist. SFe

Free Willy 2

(Dwight Little, 1995, US) Jason James Richter, Jon Tenny, Michael Madsen, Jayne Atkinson, Elizabeth Peña, August Schellenberg.
97 min.
Maybe it takes three to mix the formula, but this is tons better entertainment than the original. Dwight Little has understood the visual appeal of these black-and-white killer whales in open, chromium sea and cinematographer Laszlo Kovacs has done them proud. Last time, the threat to Willy was continued imprisonment in the aquarium, but here, more excitingly, it's an oil slick down the blowhole, plus an oil explosion at sea, and another threat of imprisonment in the aquarium to make up the weight. Disturbed teenager Jesse (Richter) is issued with an even more disturbed younger half-brother Elvis, who lies all the time, but they make common cause on the plight of the whale. Their foster father (Madsen) has reconciled himself to the role, and Randolph the Native American (Schellenberg) gets to mix some magic herbs and chant healingly over the waters. BC

Free Willy 3: The Rescue

(Sam Pillsbury, 1997, US) Jason James Richter, August Schellenberg, Annie Corley, Vincent Berry, Patrick Kilpatrick.
86 min.
Jesse, now 17, and Max, aged ten, team up to gather evidence needed by the authorities to clamp down on the illegal trade in whale meat. The film tactfully brings home the cruelty of the whaling industry (a U certificate notwithstanding), and declines to treat Max's dad (himself a whaling captain) as a black-hearted monster. A satisfying family movie, with plenty of aquatic frolicking, and not too preachy. TJ

French Cancan

(Jean Renoir, 1955, Fr) Jean Gabin, Françoise Arnoul, Maria Félix, Gianni Esposito, Philippe Clay, Michel Piccoli, Edith Piaf, Dora Doll, Patachou.
102 min.
Renoir's return to film-making in France after an absence of fifteen years is a nostalgic studio reconstruction of the Paris of his painter father. Despite its artificiality and meandering plot construction – with Renoir falling in love with some of his minor characters – it brilliantly evokes the world of the French Impressionists, building into a comic riot of colour and movement. The story is a backstage musical on the founding of the Moulin Rouge and the training of the famous cancan dancers. The climactic cancan scene is one of the finest dance sequences ever filmed, and worth the price of a ticket on its own. RM

French Connection, The

(William Friedkin, 1971, US) Gene Hackman, Fernando Rey, Roy Scheider, Tony Lo Bianco, Marcel Bozzuffi, Frédéric de Pasquale.
104 min.
An urban crime thriller which won undeserved acclaim for its efficient but unremarkable elevated-railway chase and its clumsy, showy emphasis on grainy, sordid realism. The performances are strong, although Hackman has done far better than this portrayal of a hard-nosed cop obsessively tracking down a narcotics ring in New York, using methods disapproved of by his superiors. The real problems, however, are that Friedkin's nervy, noisy, undisciplined pseudo-realism sits uneasily with his suspense-motivated shock editing; and that compared to (say) Siegel's *Dirty Harry*, the film maintains no critical distance from (indeed, rather relishes) its 'loveable' hero's brutal vigilante psychology. GA

French Connection II

(John Frankenheimer, 1975, US) Gene Hackman, Fernando Rey, Bernard Fresson, Jean-Pierre Castaldi, Charles Millot, Cathleen Nesbitt, Ed Lauter.
119 min.
Far superior to Friedkin's original, simply because Robert Dillon's script is much more critical in its probing of the Popeye Doyle character. As Doyle visits Marseilles to track the drugs ring to its source, his natural, bigoted arrogance and sense of superiority are undermined, not merely by being a stranger in a strange land, but also by being shot full of heroin and forced to suffer the terrors of cold turkey. Hackman takes the enlarged role by the scruff of the neck and delivers yet another fine performance of doubt and the dawning awareness of his own weakness. Frankenheimer directs in taut, pacy fashion to keep the suspense high. GA.

French Kiss

(Lawrence Kasdan, 1995, US) Meg Ryan, Kevin Kline, Timothy Hutton, Jean Reno, François Cluzet, Susan Anbeh, Renee Humphrey.
111 min.
This is a tissue-thin affair tarted up with phoney continental charm. Kate, a skittish control freak (Ryan), follows her fiancé to Paris when he tells her he's fallen in love with another woman. En route, she meets Gallic con-man Luc (Kline), who stows his contraband in her valise for customs, and reluctantly stands by when it's promptly stolen. Directed by Kasdan, this plays like a lighter version of *The Accidental Tourist* – there's the same cautious exhortation to open yourself to life's risks. Like the wine Luc treasures, the film wants to be sophisticated but not pretentious, cynical yet sincere. In other words, it wants it both ways. There's farce, slapstick, Kline's Clouseau accent, gibes at American puritanism and French driving, and then there's the desultory pacing, the plaintive life-enhancing sentiments and the travelogue cinematography. TCh

French Lieutenant's Woman, The

(Karel Reisz, 1981, GB) Meryl Streep, Jeremy Irons, Hilton McRae, Emily Morgan, Charlotte Mitchell, Lynsey Baxter, Leo McKern.
123 min.
John Fowles' novel is a full-blooded 19th century romance, but written in 1969 and addressed to the intellectual vanity of the modern reader by means of confidential asides, footnotes which titillate while purporting to add documentary authority (all that absurdly solemn stuff about sausage skins and condoms), and frequent recourse to passwords (like Darwin, Marx and (just once) Freud. As a result it places that easy target – repressed Victorian sexuality – well within our drooling sights. Harold Pinter's screenplay gives flesh to this 20th century perspective with a parallel story: not only do Streep and Irons play the 19th century lovers, they are also cast as a pair of adulterous sophisticates, swotting up on Victorian social history between takes during filming of *The French Lieutenant's Woman*. As a solution to the almost impossible problem of adapting the book, this film-within-a-film idea is an honourable failure, providing a modest, nearly redundant framework since the Victorian sequences stand on their own merits, with performances (the pre-Raphaelite Streep is outstanding), exquisite photography (Freddie Francis) and Reisz's direction combining to deliver a powerful and persuasive anatomy of passion. JS

French Line, The

(Lloyd Bacon, 1953, US) Jane Russell, Gilbert Roland, Arthur Hunnicutt, Mary McCarty, Craig Stevens, Steven Geray.
102 min.
Jane Russell shown 'flat' is perhaps an anatomical impossibility, but the film was originally made in 3-D, and most screenings nowadays will unfortunately prevent you from testing the accuracy of RKO's publicity slogan: 'It'll knock both your eyes out!' The woman who once gave Howard Hughes his greatest technical challenge plays a Texan tycoon who disguises herself as a model and goes to Paris to find a man unaware of her vast fortune. Enter Gilbert Roland as a French musical comedy star and the excuse for some song-and-dance routines that look like outtakes from *Gentlemen Prefer Blondes* and *How to Marry a Millionaire*. ATu

Frenchman's Creek

(Mitchell Leisen, 1944, US) Joan Fontaine, Arturo de Cordova, Basil Rathbone, Nigel Bruce, Cecil Kellaway, Ralph Forbes.
113 min.
Captivatingly extravagant piece of escapism from the much underrated Leisen: an adaptation of a Daphne du Maurier story about a 17th century aristocratic woman who leaves London for Cornwall with her children – mainly to escape pressingly unwelcome attentions from her complaisant husband's best friend (Rathbone) – and there falls in love with a swashbuckling French pirate. Fontaine is a little too prissy to enter fully into the spirit of things (although this brings dividends when she is faced with the heartbreaking problem of her children), but the combination of exquisite colour, sets and location photography with Leisen's light touch is a winning formula. GA

French Mistress, A

(Roy Boulting, 1960, GB) James Robertson Justice, Cecil Parker, Raymond Huntley, Ian Bannen, Agnès Laurent, Irene Handl, Kenneth Griffith, Thorley Walters.
98 min. b/w.
One of the great disappointments in post-war British film history is the decline of the Boulting Brothers. It's a mystery how film-makers capable of turning out thrillers as accomplished as *Brighton Rock* and *Seven Days to Noon* spent the latter half of their career churning out flaccid satirical comedies. This effort, set in an English public school, is typical late Boulting nonsense, a prurient yarn about how excited teachers and students alike become when a glamorous new female teacher arrives on their doorstep. There's a certain pleasure in seeing warhorses like Justice and Parker try to out-ham one another, but no hiding the feebleness of the material (from a play by Robert Munro) or the Boultings' approach to it. GM

French Mustard (La Moutarde Me Monte au Nez)

(Claude Zidi, 1974, Fr) Pierre Richard, Jane Birkin, Claude Piéplu, Jean Martin, Danou Minazzoli.
98 min.
Generally insufferable farce which steers an unhappy course between odd moments of style, heavy Gallic charm, and tasteless bursts of visceral slapstick. Harmless enough to have been seen on BBC TV, it shows not very much of Birkin as scandalous starlet Jackie Logan, who gets repeatedly embroiled with the mayor's son. Here and there among all the falling about there are swipes at spaghetti Westerns, anti-pornographers, and Henry Kissinger. Sometimes the chapter of accidents befalling the mayor's son snowballs to good nutty effect; mostly not though. AN

French Twist

see Gazon maudit

French Without Tears

(Anthony Asquith, 1939, GB) Ray Milland, Roland Culver, Guy Middleton, Ellen Drew, David Tree, Janine Darcy, Jim Gérald.
85 min. b/w.

In an idyllic little French language school, trainee diplomats and a sex-starved naval commander lose their hearts and minds to a winsome, gooey adventuress. Terence Rattigan's 'well made play' – a mixture of sophisticated badinage and schoolboy misogyny – now looks utterly inconsequential, redolent only of the anaemic '30s complacency which led to Munich. PM's son 'Puffin' Asquith struggles valiantly but in vain to turn it into something cinematic, and even Culver's nicely judged performance as the stoically lovesick sailor fails to life the film beyond being simply a historical curiosity. Needless to say the critics at the time thought it was wonderful. RMy

Frenzy

(Alfred Hitchcock, 1972, GB) Jon Finch, Alec McCowen, Barry Foster, Barbara Leigh-Hunt, Anna Massey, Vivien Merchant, Billie Whitelaw.
116 min.

Hitchcock's return to Covent Garden, 'wrong man' plotting, the neuroses of sexual immaturity, and black-humoured slapstick ironies, tied up neatly in Anthony Shaffer's screenplay about the panic wrought by the 'necktie murderer', and glossed with the usual quota of stand-out sequences: the camera's descending recoil from a murderer's first-floor flat; a grisly wrestling match with a corpse in a lorry-load of potatoes; the inspector's mealtimes (almost a reverse homage to Chabrol); the one extended, disturbing seduction/rape/murder scene. A series of variations on themes of excess, surplus and waste from the most fastidious of directors. PT

Frenzy

see Hets

Fresa y Chocolate

see Strawberry and Chocolate

Fresh

(Boaz Yakin, 1994, US/Fr) Sean Nelson, Giancarlo Esposito, Samuel L Jackson, N'Bushe Wright, Ron Brice, Jean LaMarre, Luis Lantigua.
115 min.

A stylish, affecting, ingeniously plotted first feature in which a 12-year-old black kid, beset by drug-dealers, a junkie sister, and his clean-living aunt, struggles to put his life in order by means of lessons he's learned from his chess-playing dad. Yakin never settles for the easy, last-minute moralising and macho posturing that has afflicted much of the otherwise intriguing new black cinema; here, story and character take priority, helped no end by Nelson's quiet, riveting central performance. GA

Fresh Horses

(David Anspaugh, 1988, US) Molly Ringwald, Andrew McCarthy, Patti D'Arbanville, Ben Stiller, Leon Russom, Molly Hagan, Viggo Mortensen, Chiara Peacock.
105 min.

We know things aren't right between lovebirds Matt (McCarthy) and Alice (Peacock) when he turns up late for his engagement party. A conventional guy, training for a conventional career, Matt is having a crisis of faith, and only bourbon-drinking, dishevelled Jewel (Ringwald) can help him. While Alice talks about wedding china, Matt enjoys secret assignations with Jewel in a trackside shack. She's lower class, been abused, a high school dropout. Matt is appalled, attracted, confused, and has an uncontrollable urge to correct her syntax. Wordily scripted by Larry Ketron from his own play, this tortured attempt to sustain the bratpack formula fails dismally. Ringwald's performance is fine, but McCarthy suffers unconvincingly, with exaggerated looks and pauses to convey inner torment; the contrast between urban and rustic values is forced; and there's no real emotional depth in the lead character's tedious, muddled excesses. CM

Freshman, The

(Andrew Bergman, 1990, US) Marlon Brando, Matthew Broderick, Bruno Kirby, Penelope Ann Miller, Frank Whaley, Jon Polito, Paul Benedict, Richard Gant, Maximilian Schell.
103 min.

Film student Clark Kellogg (Broderick) arrives in New York ready to start his first term, but within minutes smooth-talking hustler Victor Ray (Kirby) has relieved him of money and luggage. When Kellogg later chances across Ray, the latter makes amends by offering the distraught teen a part-time job with his uncle Carmine Sabatini (Brando) who, seen sprawled behind his desk at an Italian 'social club', looks every inch the Godfather. Kellogg's first assignment seems fraught with hazards...Writer-director Bergman's good-natured comedy makes light of gangster genre conventions, and humorously undercuts some of the more portentous aspects of film academia: Kellogg's plight is rendered farcical when, at a seminar on Coppola's The Godfather, he begins to find disturbing similarities between his life and the movie. The casting, needless to say, is perfect, and Bergman keeps the various escalating intrigues clipping along at a brisk pace. CM

Freud

(John Huston, 1962, US) Montgomery Clift, Susannah York, Larry Parks, Susan Kohner, Eileen Herlie, Fernand Ledoux, David McCallum, Rosalie Crutchley, Eric Portman.
140 min. b/w.

Huston concentrates on the young Freud, driven by a pathological desire to 'know', discovering the existence of the unconscious. The narrative suggests similarities between Freud and other Huston heroes who are inexorably compelled to acknowledge the unacceptable faces of the self. But the banal misconceptions about psycho-analysis repeated in the film are contradicted by the force of the mise en scène, with its narrative dislocations and the excessive pictorialism of the image track making 'Freud' an extraordinary, uncanny film noir. As if the telling of this particular tale could not but re-inscribe into the text what the trivialisation of psychoanalysis seeks to repress. Together with The Asphalt Jungle, Freud is Huston's most remarkable film.

Freudlose Gasse, Die

see Joyless Street, The

Friday

(F Gary Gray, 1995, US) Ice Cube, Chris Tucker, John Witherspoon, Anna Maria Horsford, Tiny 'Zeus' Lister Jr, Nia Long.
92 min.

'It's Friday – let's get high!' pretty much sums up this so-so 'hood comedy. Craig (Ice Cube, motionless) is a soft-natured teen who still resides with his parents. His best buddy is quick-talking Smokey (Tucker, OTT), a drug-dealing dope-fiend with a cash-loan problem. What action there is rarely shifts beyond the parents' porch. Director Gray tries (unsuccessfully) to create a '90s Cheech and Chong with inane lavatory humour, manic facial expressions, and plenty of close-ups of a tokin' Smokey. Passé the spliff. DA

Friday the 13th

(Sean S Cunningham, 1980, US) Betsy Palmer, Adrienne King, Jeannine Taylor, Robbi Morgan, Kevin Bacon, Harry Crosby.
95 min.

A motley crew of teenagers whose idea of relaxation is a game of strip Monopoly take jobs at a run-down summer camp, but get gorily hacked and sliced to death by a local nutter almost before they've had time to unpack. A tame, poorly plotted serving of schlock, less horrific for its ketchup-smeared murders than for the bare-faced fashion in which it tries and fails to rip off Carpenter's Halloween in matters of style and construction. TP

Friday the 13th Part 2

(Steve Miner, 1981, US) Amy Steel, John Furey, Adrienne King, Kirsten Baker, Stu Charno, Warrington Gillette.
87 min.

This first sequel to Friday the 13th opens with mild panache when a summary recapitulation of the story so far ends with the sole survivor of the previous massacre being unexpectedly despatched by a new killer (the grief-crazed woman's supposedly dead son). The script then jumps five years, assembles a new set of victims at the summer camp, and repeats the gory carnage as before. The formula reached Part VIII by 1989. Cynically manipulative, stultifying in their sameness, they require no comment except that

Part III was shot in 3-D, Part V (A New Beginning) toyed with being tongue in cheek, and Part VI (Jason Lives) took the rather desperate step of resurrecting its psycho like Frankenstein's monster.

Friday the 13th Part VIII: Jason Takes Manhattan

(Rob Hedden, 1989, US) Jensen Daggett, Kane Hodder, Scott Reeves, Peter Mark Richman, Barbara Bingham.
100 min.

For what it's worth (very little), probably the best in the series. Human threshing-machine Jason is scraped up from the bottom of Crystal Lake by the anchor of a passing pleasure boat and soon finds himself on a cruise to New York with a bunch of eminently scythable high school students. With more flair and less gore than the other eight, Jason Goes to Hell: The Final Friday brought matters to a grim conclusion four years later. TJ

Frieda

(Basil Dearden, 1947, GB) Mai Zetterling, David Farrar, Glynis Johns, Flora Robson, Albert Lieven, Barbara Everest, Gladys Henson.
98 min. b/w.

With World War II hostilities just over, RAF officer Farrar brings home a German bride (Zetterling), having married her in gratitude for her part in helping him to escape from a PoW camp (unaware that Johns, whom he loved but who married his brother, is now a widow). 'It's a pleasant, peaceful spot...like any town in England', he tells her as he looks out of the train taking them home. Cue for one of those comfortable slices of social criticism in which rabid prejudice is gradually broken down by sweet reasonableness. But with Farrar and Zetterling doing their respective glowering and cowering acts, he treating her with increasing callousness as she becomes increasingly unnerved by her hostile reception, the whole thing begins to shape up as a melodramatic thriller. Highly watchable, perhaps for the wrong reasons. TM

Fried Green Tomatoes at the Whistle Stop Café

(Jon Avnet, 1991, US) Kathy Bates, Jessica Tandy, Mary Stuart Masterson, Mary Louise Parker, Gailard Sartain, Stan Shaw, Cicely Tyson, Gary Basaraba, Lois Smith, Grace Zabriskie.
130 min.

Southern housewife Evelyn (Bates) has had enough of her couch-potato husband (Sartain). Their sex life is dying, and even wrapping her naked body in cling-wrap merely provokes further apathy. Then, at a nursing-home, she meets old-timer Ninny (Tandy), who launches into a rambling recollection of long-gone friends and family: tales of feisty Idgie (Masterson) and Ruth (Parker) who once ran a café in Ninny's small Alabama home town. Gradually, Evelyn finds strength in the bravery of these two, and solace in Ninny's evocation of simpler times. With director Avnet, Fannie Flagg co-scripted this adaptation of her novel; but while the book deftly juggles separate narratives, the device proves clumsy on screen. More dizzying than the jumps between past and present is the speed with which consciousness-raised Evelyn swaps caricatures, evolving from Frump to Fighter. Essentially, the film is about fine performances – with Tandy securing an Oscar nomination – but it wins no prizes for subtlety. CM

Friendly Persuasion

(William Wyler, 1956, US) Gary Cooper, Dorothy McGuire, Marjorie Main, Anthony Perkins, Richard Eyer, Robert Middleton, Walter Catlett.
140 min.

Wyler in characteristically earnest form with a Western-style story of a family of Quakers whose faith in a non-violent way of life is sorely tried by the outbreak of the Civil War. Solid performances, particularly from Perkins as the anguished son, and odd touches of humour (which might, ironically, offend Quakers, since their way of life is presented as eccentrically old-fashioned); but the basic dilemma – whether to take up arms or not – is presented in simplistic and predictable fashion. GA

Friends

(Lewis Gilbert, 1971, GB) Sean Bury, Anicée
Alvina, Ronald Lewis, Toby Robins, Joan
Hickson, Pascale Roberts.
102 min.
Hideous schmaltz, all lyrical slow motion and soft
focus, in which a fourteen-year-old French girl
(Alvina) and a fifteen-year-old English boy (Bury)
run away from their respective unhappy homes
to the Camargue (complete with wild horses).
There, in a cosy cottage, they play at marriage,
have a baby, and *almost* manage to live happily
ever after in their Garden of Eden. Complete with
Elton John on the soundtrack. Yuck. TM

Friends

(Elaine Proctor, 1993, GB/Fr) Kerry Fox,
Dambisa Kente, Michele Burgers, Marius
Weyers, Tertius Meintjes.
109 min.
Set in South Africa just before the release of
Nelson Mandela, this film focuses on three representative women who meet at university: Sophie
(Fox) comes from an affluent white Johannesburg
suburb; Thoko (Kente) is a Zulu teacher; Aninka
(Burgers) a working-class Afrikaner. They live
together, defiantly, but their friendship is tested
when Sophie, an anti-apartheid activist, plants a
bomb, with bloody consequences, This fiction
film, by a South African-born documentary-
maker, rather labours its points. Powerful prison
scenes, though, and convincing snapshots of
Johannesburg social life. JBa

Friends and Husbands
(Heller Wahn)

(Margarethe von Trotta, 1982, WGer/Fr)
Hanna Schygulla, Angela Winkler, Peter
Striebeck, Christine Fersen, Franz Buchrieser.
106 min.
Something of a disappointment after *The German
Sisters*. Von Trotta's theme – the obsessive interdependence of two women, one (Schygulla)
assured and outgoing, the other (Winkler) timid
and reclusive – resembles her earlier chamber
piece, *Sisters, or the Balance of Happiness*. But here
her more ambitious scope opens up glaring weaknesses in the minor roles, particularly the husbands, and the story rambles furiously, with little
added by location shooting in Cairo and Provence.
And a heavy pall of Teutonic neuroticism sits over
the whole thing, stemming not from Hitler's legacy as in *The German Sisters*, but more diffusely
from the German Romantics, whose suicides and
madmen and women exercise a highly ambivalent
fascination. But von Trotta does extract excellent
performances from her two leads, making this a
delicate and penetrating study of (platonic) love
between women. SJo

Friendship's Death

(Peter Wollen, 1987, GB) Bill Paterson, Tilda
Swinton, Patrick Bauchau, Ruby Baker,
Joumana Gill.
78 min.
In September 1970, a British war correspondent
(Paterson) is distracted from his coverage of the
bloody conflict between Palestinians and
Jordanians when he rescues a young lady
(Swinton) from a PLO patrol. Simply named
Friendship, she claims to be an extraterrestrial
robot sent to Earth on a peace mission and accidentally diverted from her original destination,
the Massachusetts Institute of Technology. Is she
insane, a spy, or telling the truth? Wollen's film
comes across as a two-set *Dr Who* for adults,
complete with political, philosophical and more
pettily personal problems; the use of the alien outsider's way of seeing the world is perceptive and
provocative, the plentiful ideas counterbalance
the lack of extravagant spectacle. Best of all, the
film displays a droll wit (Friendship viewing a
typewriter as a distant cousin, or concocting a
surreal thesis on the big toe's importance in the
oppression of women) and a surprising ability to
touch the heart. With two impressive central performances, Wollen at last proves himself able to
direct actors, and has made by far his most
rewarding movie to date. GA

Friends of Eddie Coyle, The

(Peter Yates, 1973, US) Robert Mitchum, Peter
Boyle, Richard Jordan, Steven Keats, Alex
Rocco, Joe Santos, Mitchell Ryan.
102 min.

Yates' downbeat dissection of Boston's underworld, based on the novel by George V Higgins,
revolves around the dilemma of Mitchum's weary
small-time mobster and all-time loser Eddie
'Fingers' Coyle (somebody shut a drawer on his
hand), under pressure to turn stoolie in the wake
of a couple of murderous bank heists. The cast lend
the film an authority that Yates' curiously pedestrian approach fails to provide, and Mitchum's
agonies over codes of underworld honour segue
perfectly into his subsequent explorations of loyalty and obligation in *The Yakuza*. PT

Frightened City, The

(John Lemont, 1961, GB) Herbert Lom, John
Gregson, Sean Connery, Alfred Marks, Ruth
Romain, David Davies, Olive McFarland,
Kenneth Griffith, Bruce Seton.
97 min. b/w.
When dodgy accountant Waldo Zhernikov (Lom)
convenes a meeting of London's top racketeers,
the craggy, grandfatherly characters who turn up
seem more like grocers than gangsters. At least
Connery, pre-Bond, brings a little muscle to the
proceedings; but Gregson, as Insp Sayers, is simply too wholesome a cop for the protection-bust-
ing job in hand. GM

Frighteners, The

(Peter Jackson, 1996, NZ/US) Michael J Fox,
Trini Alvarado, Peter Dobson, John Astin,
Jeffrey Combs, Chi McBride, Jim Fyfe, Jake
Busey, Dee Wallace Stone, R Lee Ermey.
110 min.
Jackson's follow-up to *Heavenly Creatures* is an
sfx-heavy scarefest that looks at first like a return
to the slapstick horror-comedy of *Braindead*.
Later, however, it flips into a grim, disturbing
horror movie about the malevolent spirit of a serial killer back from the grave to increase his body
count. Fake para-psychologist Frank Bannister
(Fox) is in cahoots with a trio of tortured souls –
hip dude Cyrus (McBride), creaky-boned old-
timer The Judge (Astin), and nerdy bookworm
Stuart (Fyfe): they scare the shit out of
Fairwater's inhabitants while Frank cleans up the
mess. A series of unexplained deaths heralds the
arrival of a Grim Reaper-like spirit that Frank
alone can see. This may be connected to a thrill-
kill case in which Patricia Bradley (Stone), now a
middle-aged, mother-dominated recluse, and her
hospital orderly boyfriend Johnny Bartlett
(Busey) massacred a dozen patients and hospital
staff. Though funded by Hollywood, this New
Zealand-shot movie was creatively controlled by
Jackson and co-writer Fran Walsh. So while the
on-screen violence is toned down, there's no soft-
pedalling the ugliness of mass murder or the
obscenity of ill-deserved media celebrity. At
times the relentless special effects and tangled
plotting veer towards visual and narrative
overkill, but the final tonal swerve is shocking
and effective. NF

Frightmare

(Pete Walker, 1974, GB) Rupert Davies, Sheila
Keith, Deborah Fairfax, Paul Greenwood, Kim
Butcher, Fiona Curzon.
86 min.
With *Frightmare* following on *House of
Whipcord*, David McGillivray's scriptwriting is
undoubtedly having a marked effect on Walker's
exploitation pictures. Where he used to settle for
routine plots, his films now teem with demonic
life, plus vicious and genuinely disturbing shock
effects. *Frightmare* is about a psychopathic mum
(Keith) who has the nasty habit of going at her
victims with an electric drill before devouring
them raw. It is far better written and acted than
you might expect, and Walker's direction is on
another level altogether from *Cool It Carol!* or *The
Flesh and Blood Show*. The problem is that there
is absolutely no exposition or analysis, no flexi-
bility about the theme; still contained within a
basic formula, it tends to leave a highly unpleasant aftertaste. DP

Fright Night

(Tom Holland, 1985, US) Chris Sarandon,
William Ragsdale, Amanda Bearse, Roddy
McDowall, Stephen Geoffreys, Jonathan Stark.
106 min.
Nobody believes in vampires any more:
scriptwriter Holland (*Psycho II*) makes his directorial debut with a reworking of the boy who
cried wolf. Teenager Charley (Ragsdale) cries

vampire when he sees what his next door neighbour is up to, and tries to enlist the fearless vam-
pire-killing skills of TV's *Fright Night* host
(McDowall), who turns out to be a cynical has-
been. All-round scepticism is further fuelled by
the neighbour: no creepy Lugosi lookalike, but
handsome, urbane Sarandon, who has a way (and
has away) with the girls, and is furthermore adept
at sexy disco-dancing. The likeable juve leads are
more than mere fang-fodder, the MORish soundtrack is actually quite toothsome, and the vampy-
rotechnic effects are special enough to satisfy the
most jaded SFX aficionado. AB

Fright Night Part 2

(Tommy Lee Wallace, 1988, US) Roddy
McDowall, William Ragsdale, Traci Lin, Julie
Carmen, Jonathan Gries, Russell Clark.
104 min.
Another stop-me-if-you've-heard-this sequel, with
young Ragsdale emerging from three years of
psychotherapy to find that the vampires he's
been persuaded are imaginary really do exist.
Having convinced TV horror-show host
McDowall that the fanged ones are back in business, Ragsdale confronts the deliciously dangerous Carmen, sister of suave bloodsucker Chris
Sarandon whom they stalked in Part 1. With
Carmen's fatal allure substituted for Sarandon's
sexually ambiguous charm, the intriguing homo-
erotic overtones of the original give way to a more
blatant equation of hunger and desire. What few
innovations there are – notably Carmen's spectacular usurpation of McDowall's show – go for
nothing. Wallace's direction lackes the clear and
intelligence that Tom Holland brought to *Fright
Night*. NF

Fringe Dwellers, The

(Bruce Beresford, 1986, Aust) Kristina Nehm,
Justine Saunders, Bob Maza, Kylie Belling,
Denis Walker, Ernie Dingo.
98 min.
This adaptation of Nene Gar's novel about contemporary life among the Aborigines of Australia
shows them as outcasts in their own country,
despised by the whites, disinclined to work at
what menial jobs they can get, and with a big par-
tiality for hitting the booze. The Comeaway family is persuaded by their 15-year-old daughter
Trilby (Nehm) to move from the shantytown
where they live to a new estate. She is determined
not to fall into the same overbreeding, under-
achieving trap as the women around her, but
finds that events seem constantly to be conspiring against her. Beresford evidently feels considerable sympathy with the Aborigines, but this
is tinged with despair at their apparent penchant
for self-destruction. The film never really jells,
but is notable for an engaging performance from
Nehm. JP

Frisk

(Todd Verow, 1995, US) Michael Gunter, Craig
Chester, Parker Posey, James Lyons, Alexis
Arquette, Raoul O'Connell.
83 min.
Dennis (Gunter) begins to explore his violent
homosexual fantasies when he meets Henry
(Chester), a masochist who's also a necrophiliac
pin-up. His friends are alarmed, but sceptical,
when Dennis begins to write confessional letters
describing acts of murder. The dubious equation
of homosexuality, perversity and murder made
in mainstream Hollywood thrillers like *Basic
Instinct* or *Cruising* has outraged the gay community. Is it a sign of decadence or maturity that
gays can now exploit gay-on-gay violence? And
is it for edification or entertainment? Neither,
probably. Verow made his mark as cameraman
on Gregg Araki's *Totally F***ed Up* and MTV's
Real World series. His first film as director (from
a cult novel by Dennis Cooper) boasts occasional bursts of flashy editing, lousy performances
(exception: Parker Posey in a ten-minute cameo
as a fag hag only too happy to participate in a
spot of orgiastic murder), and a sour sensibility
quite in keeping with the characters. TCh

Frisson des Vampires, Le
(Sex and the Vampire/
Vampire Thrills)

(Jean Rollin, 1970, Fr) Sandra Julien,
Dominique, Nicole Nancel, Michel Delahaye,
Jacques Robiolles.
90 min.

An involved vampire story, badly acted and with an idiotic plot, but visually a feast. It features a fantastic gaunt lady vampire in vermilion make-up who materialises at one stage out of a grandfather clock, and at another comes down the chimney. Also two gentlemen in Carnaby Street evening gear. Quite sexy. Great curiosity value.

Fritz the Cat
(Ralph Bakshi, 1971, US) voices: Skip Hinnant, Rosetta Le Noire, John McCurry, Judy Engles.
78 min.
Animated feature based on Robert Crumb's comic strip, detailing a young hipster cat's exploits with dope, Harlem, the police, the Angels, etc. Despite some ingenious effects, a generally trivial exercise that never matches the punch of the original.

Frog Dreaming
(Brian Trenchard-Smith, 1985, Aust) Henry Thomas, Tony Barry, Rachel Friend, Tamsin West, Dempsey Knight, John Ewart.
93 min.
Something's alive at the bottom of an uncharted pond, and 10-year-old adventurer Cody (Henry Thomas of ET) is determined to find it. Director Trenchard-Smith sets the action of this children's movie (involving aboriginal magic) in a remote town in southern Australia, constructing the parallel worlds of doting adults and their irrepressible children as a foundation for his adventure in minutiae. The real adventure, however, is Trenchard-Smith's rediscovery of boyhood, with all its inventiveness, innocence and independent, fearless strength. SGo

Frog Prince, The
(Brian Gilbert, 1984, GB) Jane Snowden, Alexandre Sterling, Jacqueline Doyen, Raoul Delfosse, Jeanne Herviale, Françoise Brion.
90 min.
Paris, 1960: a wicked city where English ingénue Snowden, sent to polish her French, acquires a sentimental education, fending off lecherous frogs with varying degrees of Gallic smarm. The film, with David Puttnam as executive producer, has a nostalgic Film on Four blandness about it, although Posy Simmonds' semi-autobiographical screenplay adds a little spice with its sharp ear for dialogue and its broadly farcical slant, indulging much humour at the expense of those funny French. SJo

Frogs
(George McCowan, 1972, US) Ray Milland, Sam Elliott, Joan Van Ark, Adam Roarke, Judy Pace, Lynn Borden.
90 min.
A 'nature strikes back' eco-drama built on sturdy, if predictable, Ten Little Nigger lines. Elliott plays an ecological photographer snapping wildlife and garbage around the private island home of a millionaire family with nasty habits like spraying insecticide, collecting hunting trophies, catching butterflies. They gather annually for birthday celebrations under the iron fist of patriarch Milland; multiplying and mutating into giant (but not unbelievable) species as a result of the pollution, the reptiles become malevolent, causing the deaths of one after another of the family. Two good points: no revenge-on-frog scenes after they climactically overwhelm Milland in the abandoned house; and apart from some manipulation by cross-cutting, all the reptiles behave fairly normally. Filmed in the usual crisp AIP style, with dazzling sunlight and ominous shadows.

From Beyond
(Stuart Gordon, 1986, US) Jeffrey Combs, Barbara Crampton, Ken Foree, Ted Sorel, Carolyn Purdy-Gordon.
85 min.
A horror movie from beyond the pale. While experimenting with a sound resonator, mad scientist Dr Edward Pretorius (Sorel) has his head bitten off by an eel which swims in the air. Arrested and charged with his boss' murder, Crawford Tillinghurst (Combs), released into the care of a psychiatrist, later repeats the experiment to prove his innocence. This opens up another can of worms, to improbable results. NF

From Beyond the Grave
(Kevin Connor, 1973, GB) Peter Cushing, David Warner, Donald Pleasence, Ian Bannen, Diana Dors, Angela Pleasence, Margaret Leighton, Nyree Dawn Porter, Ian Carmichael, Ian Ogilvy, Lesley-Anne Down.
98 min.
Although a vast improvement on the derisory Vault of Horror, this seventh Amicus horror omnibus, using stories by R Chetwynd-Hayes, suffers from much the same faults as its immediate predecessors. As usual there's one really good episode (a remarkable sub-Pinter piece on witchcraft with a stunning performance from Angela Pleasence), but the others are at best average. And the linking story, with Cushing manning an antique shop, is feeble even by Vault of Horror standards. The script's concentration on suspense and visual effects, with a minimum of dialogue, should be a virtue; but the Amicus budgets are so low (with name casts a priority) that the technique frequently results in sequences of cramping boredom. DP

From Dusk till Dawn
(Robert Rodriguez, 1995, US) Harvey Keitel, George Clooney, Quentin Tarantino, Juliette Lewis, Cheech Marin, Fred Williamson, Salma Hayek, John Saxon.
107 min.
It might be more interesting to watch this Tarantino/Rodriguez film without knowing what's in store, in which case, skip this review and take your chances. But don't come running back to me if double-barrelled schizophrenic gun-crazy gut-shot evangelical sleaze, incendiary, popcorn-blowing macho mayhem, slinky, soul-searching zombie strippers, and vampiric cult-infested cinemania don't light your pipe. Tarantino and Clooney are the Gecko brothers, sick and ruthless killers, respectively. They commandeer the motor home of the Rev Fuller (Keitel) to evade the cops en route to a midnight rendezvous at the Titty Twister, hottest whorehouse in all Mexico. Along for the ride are Fuller's teen kids, and the Reverend himself, who has most definitely picked the wrong day to lose his faith. Written by Tarantino in 1990 on a commission from a special effects company, the film is aimed squarely at (male) horror movie fans who appreciate the nuances of impalement by pool cue, pencil and table leg. Rodriguez has a lot of fun dreaming up cool ways to kill people (he's making this his life's work), but he also gets something resembling a performance from Tarantino and transforms Clooney into a full-fledged movie star. Bikers, head-bangers and film geeks will rave to the grave. TCh

From Hell It Came
(Dan Milner, 1957, US) Tod Andrews, Tina Carver, Linda Watkins, John McNamara, Gregg Palmer, Robert Swan.
71 min. b/w.
'And to hell it can go!' A South Sea island prince is put to death by the tribal elders for fraternising with scientists. He returns as Tabanga...the people-eating tree.

From Hell to Texas (aka Manhunt)
(Henry Hathaway, 1958, US) Don Murray, Diane Varsi, Chill Wills, Dennis Hopper, RG Armstrong, Jay C Flippen.
100 min.
When cowboy Murray accidentally murders one of the sons of powerful rancher Armstrong, the old man despatches his other boy Hopper at the head of a posse to hunt down the killer. Meanwhile, Murray finds refuge with kindly farmer Wills and falls for his daughter, but trouble won't remain far away for long. Capably handled (in 'Scope) by Hathaway, with Murray and young Hopper particularly striking, and the script achieving a timeless resonance by focusing on the morality of vengeance and the power of forgiveness. TJ

From Hell to Victory (De l'Enfer à la Victoire)
(Hank Milestone, ie. Umberto Lenzi, 1979, Fr/It/Sp) George Peppard, George Hamilton, Horst Buchholz, Jean-Pierre Cassel, Capucine, Sam Wanamaker, Anny Duperey.
102 min.

As the title suggests, a large slice of epic schlock, which criss-crosses the cosmopolitan cast of second-string heavies through the fortunes of war and the woman they love. Some make it, some don't. In spite of Euro-computer dialogue and a general makeshift air, it's still hard to dislike the awesome nerve of a movie which has incidentals like a shootout on the Eiffel Tower and George Hamilton wasting a Panzer Brigade single-handed. Merde! CPea

From Here to Eternity
(Fred Zinnemann, 1953, US) Burt Lancaster, Deborah Kerr, Frank Sinatra, Montgomery Clift, Donna Reed, Ernest Borgnine, Philip Ober, Jack Warden.
118 min. b/w.
Bowdlerised version of James Jones' novel about physical passion, jealousy and anti-semitism in a Honolulu barracks immediately prior to Pearl Harbor. Best known for Lancaster and Kerr's adulterous romp in the surf, but besides Burnett Guffey's crisp monochrome camerawork and Daniel Taradash's taut screenplay, it's the performances that stay in the memory, particularly those of Clift and Sinatra. Zinnemann's flat direction does produce its dull moments, though; one can only dream of what Minnelli, say, might have made of the steamy melodrama. GA

From Mao to Mozart: Isaac Stern in China
(Murray Lerner, 1980, US) Isaac Stern, David Golub, Tan Shuzhen.
83 min.
Far more than a tribute to the man and his music; as well as virtuoso violinist Stern on his 1979 tour of China, we also see a China eager to hear and learn about Western music. Chinese conservatory students' technically superb renditions of Sibelius and Brahms understandably lack the nuances of emotion customary in the West, but playing their own music, or in action at the Peking Opera and the gymnasium, they display dazzling talents. The enthusiastic, amiable Stern occasionally offers paternalistic judgments on Chinese musical abilities, and is thoroughly confused when asked to consider Mozart in a sociopolitical context. But he's a musician, and his violin sings passionately. Most remarkable, however, are a Shanghai professor's account of his incarceration during the Cultural Revolution, and some truly amazing child prodigies. An uplifting film, made with intelligence and love. GA

From Noon Till Three
(Frank D Gilroy, 1975, US) Charles Bronson, Jill Ireland, Douglas V Fowley, Stan Haze, Damon Douglas, Hector Morales.
99 min.
A Western, adapted by Gilroy from his own novel, whose ideas are executed with an uncertainty that makes whole chunks of the film virtually unwatchable. After a premonition, Bronson sends his gang to their deaths while he passes the afternoon conning a rich widow (Ireland) into bed. Later, thinking he has died a heroic death, she turns the memorabilia of their relationship into a flourishing tourist industry; and when he finally turns up again (after an ignoble spell in jail), she safeguards the legend by ensuring that no one will heed his attempts to reclaim his identity. In its unfolding, the story becomes distinctly uncomfortable, an unhappy mixture of light romantic comedy and something altogether darker (after all, it begins with a nightmare and ends in madness). On top of this, there's the added torture of watching Bronson trying to struggle out of the acting straitjacket that he has worn for some years.

From Pole to Equator (Dal Polo all'Equatore)
(Yervant Gianikian/Angela Ricci Lucchi, 1986, It/WGer)
96 min. tinted.
Archivalism was never like this. The film-makers have explored a mass of 'travelogue' footage shot by the Italian explorer-cameraman Luca Comerio in the early years of this century, and turned it into a magical, terrifying journey through inner space. The original images have been stretch-printed and colour-tinted, giving them a fragile surface beauty, but also creating a crucial distance from the original content: the slaughter of big game, the taming of colonised

peoples in Africa and Asia, the glorification of imperial conquest. There's no moralising commentary to point up the contradictions; each viewer is left to dream his/her way through a phantasmagoria that extends the definition of Empire-building to the act of photography itself. *Sauve qui peut.* TR

From Russia With Love

(Terence Young, 1963, GB) Sean Connery, Daniela Bianchi, Pedro Armendariz, Lotte Lenya, Robert Shaw, Bernard Lee, Eunice Gayson.
116 min.
Bond number two and probably the best of the lot, with a remarkably gritty, wittily exciting plot in which the international crime organisation SPECTRE implements a diabolically complex scheme, hatched by a chess grand master, designed to cause terminal deterioration in Cold War relations. Memorable for the brilliant precredits stalk, Lenya's lesbo sadist, Shaw's psycho assassin, the cat-and-mouse game on the Orient Express, and – by no means least – the enchanting Daniela Bianchi, so vividly alive by comparison with the plastic dollies later Bonds toyed with. To see the film again now is to see all too vividly the abject depths of mechanical mindlessness into which the series has been sinking. TM

From Russia with Rock (Sirppi ja Kitara)

(Mafjaana Mykkanen, 1988, Fin) Alliance Aquarium, Avia, Bravo, Brigada K Cruise, Mister Twister, Nuance, Televizor, Nautilius Pompilius, Va Bank, Uriah Heep.
108 min.
In December 1987, a seven-day rock festival was staged in Moscow, the first ever such event in the Soviet Union. Mykkanen and her crew were there to cover the festival, a mixture of state-sanctioned pop and 'underground' Soviet bands, many of whom belong to a Moscow-based collection, Rock Laboratory. One band, Nautilius Pompilius from Siberia, shot into the charts as a result of their festival appearance, and the last third of the film records their reactions to fame and final retreat to Siberia. Throughout, there is a sense of the importance of rock music to young Russians, their enthusiastic embrace of perestroika, and, sadly, a sense that the medium is totally played out in the West. RS

From the Cloud to the Resistance (Nube alla Resistenza)

(Jean-Marie Straub/Danièle Huillet, 1979, It/Fr/WGer/GB) Olimpia Carlisi, Walter Pardini, Mauro Monni, Carmelo Lacorte, Luigi Giordanello.
103 min.
Straub and Huillet expand their concerns with dazzling scope and beauty: the struggle between gods and men, the eruption of the past into the present. From the first shots of a goddess seated in a tree, through a long debate between mythological characters, to the exploration of a village's fascist past, the film constantly startles by its imaginative and historical leaps. Operatic and documentary in approach, the film carefully juxtaposes two texts by Cesare Pavese, one a series of dialogues on fate and destiny, the other an elliptical narrative about the search for memories in an Italian village after the Liberation. A work of provocation which strips ornament and leaves essences, and whose integrity gives it a distinct sense of the sublime. DMacp

From the Hip

(Bob Clark, 1987, US) Judd Nelson, Elizabeth Perkins, John Hurt, Darren McGavin, Ray Walston, Dan Monahan, David Alan Grier, Allan Arbus.
112 min.
Judd Nelson – the 'rebel' in *The Breakfast Club* – perfects his impersonation of a wild bronco in this flashy drama from the director of *Porky's*. The only trouble is, he's supposed to be playing ambitious yuppie lawyer Robin Weathers (nickname: 'Stormy'). Assigned to defend John Hurt on a murder rap, he loses his cool when he figures out his client may in fact be guilty of some greater evil. Cue self-righteous moralising and a contrived courtroom denouement. A trial, for sure. TCh

From the Journals of Jean Seberg

(Mark Rappaport, 1995, US) Mary Beth Hurt.
97 min.
Rappaport's remarkable documentary works through Seberg's life, from her Midwest school days, through her much-publicised debut in Preminger's *Saint Joan* and her success in *A Bout de Souffle*, to her nightmarish marriage to Romain Gary, her involvement with the Black Panthers, and her eventual suicide in 1979. But it also uses the actress's experiences as a starting point for the exploration of an array of subjects. Hurt's Seberg is impressive as she reminisces straight to camera from beyond the grave, but what makes the film so extraordinary is the way Rappaport weaves illuminating connections between the threads of his densely informative thesis. This is intertextuality at its most accessible, provocative and surprising: a scene in *Saint Joan*, for example, leads to observations on Jane Fonda that take in *Klute*, Vadim, Vietnam, Josh Logan, workout tapes, Ted Turner, Lev Kuleshov and the opportunities afforded ageing actresses – even as Fonda is rhymed with Falconetti, Vanessa Redgrave and Seberg herself. Entertaining, moving, intellectually sharp and imaginatively brilliant. GA

From the Life of the Marionettes (Aus dem Leben der Marionetten)

(Ingmar Bergman, 1980, WGer) Robert Atzorn, Christine Buchegger, Martin Benrath, Rita Russek, Lola Müthel.
104 min. b/w & col.
Bergman's not exactly successful examination of the events and warped psychology leading up to a bourgeois businessman's murder of a prostitute. Laden with sexual traumas, fading marriages and nightmare death wishes, it's a trip through Bergman territory that we've all taken before. But Sven Nykvist's camerawork is as usual impeccable, and a certain curiosity value is afforded by the spectacle of Swedish angst filtered, as through a glass darkly, by way of an entirely German cast. TM

From the Terrace

(Mark Robson, 1960, US) Paul Newman, Joanne Woodward, Myrna Loy, Ina Balin, Leon Ames, Felix Aylmer, George Grizzard, Patrick O'Neal , Elizabeth Allen, Barbara Eden, Mae Marsh.
144 min.
An adaptation of John O'Hara's bestseller which settles for soapy melodrama instead of the novel's more sardonic perspective on a young ex-serviceman's rise to success among the idle rich of Pennsylvania. Robson's film is still highly watchable, with Paul and Joanne pretending their marriage is on the rocks, and all sorts of machinations in the boardroom and the bedroom. It's an American cousin to *Room at the Top*, shot in CinemaScope and DeLuxe colour, with an Elmer Bernstein score and plenty of histrionics. TCh

Front, The

(Martin Ritt, 1976, US) Woody Allen, Zero Mostel, Herschel Bernardi, Michael Murphy, Andrea Marcovicci, Remak Ramsay, Lloyd Gough.
95 min.
Woody Allen, miscast in his first straight role (as a schnook who lends his name to blacklisted writers for ten percent of the take, eventually coming under scrutiny himself), struggles through a reenactment of the communist witch-hunting of the '50s. Although made by those who suffered blacklisting at first hand, the film pulls all its political punches, settling instead for sentimental narrative. Its suggestion that each individual can buck the brutality of political oppression by standing up against the bullies lies squarely in the great reactionary tradition: 'a man's gotta do what a man's gotta do' replaces political analysis, and turns the film into an empty monument to the senility of American liberalism. SM

Frontera, La

(Ricardo Larrain, 1991, Chile/Sp) Patricio Contreras, Gloria Laso, Aldo Bernales, Hector Noguera, Alonso Venegas, Grisela Nuñez 'La Batacuna'.
115 min.
This absorbing first feature explores one man's internal exile in a country whose recent history has known the worst of political repression. Ramiro (Contreras), a Santiago teacher, is banished to a remote coastal community for putting his name to a public denunciation of the military authorities' abduction of one of his colleagues. His enforced sojourn takes him under the restrictive care of the local police; yet the unexpected resonance of his encounters with the locals – Maite (Laso), a fugitive from Franco's Spain with her own troubled past, and Buzo (Bernales), a half-crazed diver – prompts him to rethink his life and his political commitment. With its wry treatment of the prisoner's bumbling captors and an uplifting climactic coup to savour, we witness a journey of discovery from a national cinema where the term 'political film' still means something. TJ

Front Page (Xin Ban Jin Ba Liang)

(Philip Chan, 1990, HK) Michael Hui, Samuel Hui, Ricky Hui, Catherine Hung.
92 min.
Although it does feature a sub-text criticising tabloid journalism in Hong Kong, this is first and foremost a Michael Hui comedy – the first in many years to reunite him with his brothers Sam and Ricky, young hero and eternal fall guy respectively. It's not as funny as Hui's *Chicken and Duck Talk*, but the patchwork script has a satisfying integrity of structure, the performances are terrific, and there are plenty of droll situations and sight gags. Michael Hui himself shines in his usual role as the would-be tyrant unable to sustain his tyranny; this time the character is a news magazine editor trying to stave off the official receiver. TR

Front Page, The

(Lewis Milestone, 1931, US) Adolphe Menjou, Pat O'Brien, Mary Brian, Walter Catlett, Edward Everett Horton, Mae Clarke, George E Stone.
101 min. b/w.
The first screen version of Hecht and MacArthur's fast-talking play set in a cynical newspaper world is, not surprisingly, rather less hilarious than Hawks' definitive *His Girl Friday* or Wilder's '70s vulgarisation. The main problem is that O'Brien, as Hildy Johnson, torn between his obsession for journalism's glamour and his desire to marry, never actually looks very interested in committing himself to either life; thus the dilemma at the heart of the drama barely seems to matter, and it's left to Menjou, suave, hard and mendacious, to bring the film alive during his regrettably brief appearances as Walter Burns, the editor lacking all human qualities except ambition. Milestone's direction, veering between stagey two-shots and extravagant but purposeless camera movements, doesn't help either. But it's still worth seeing, if only to hear the jokes which the Hays Code later put an end to. GA

Front Page, The

(Billy Wilder, 1974, US) Jack Lemmon, Walter Matthau, Carol Burnett, Allen Garfield, David Wayne, Vincent Gardenia, Herbert Edelman, Charles Durning, Susan Sarandon, Austin Pendleton, Martin Gabel.
105 min.
Third and least of the movie versions of Hecht and MacArthur's classic stage comedy about a manic editor's attempts to win back his star reporter – on the eve of the latter's marriage – by means of working up a hysterical storm about the forthcoming execution of an insane killer. Quite simply vulgar in comparison to its predecessors (especially Hawks' brilliant *His Girl Friday*), it relies too much on foul language, inappropriate slapstick, and superficial cynicism. That said, the cast – particularly the Gentlemen of the Press, acting as a profane Greek chorus to the battle between Walter Burns and Hildy Johnson (Matthau and Lemmon in usual form) – is impressive. GA

Front Page Woman

(Michael Curtiz, 1935, US) Bette Davis, George Brent, June Martel, Joseph Crehan, Roscoe Karns, Winifred Shaw.
82 min. b/w.
Not exactly a proto-feminist text (despite being based on a story called *Women Are Born Newspapermen*), nor for that matter an at all accu-

rate picture of journalism, but still a vivid comedy-drama with Davis and Brent in fine form as the wisecracking couple working for rival papers and trying to better each other in following up a murder story. Absurd at times, with the two papers at one point printing absolutely identical stories, but directed and acted with sparkle and speed. GA

Frozen (Jidu Hanleng)

('Wu Ming', 1997, China) Jia Hongshen, Ma Xiaoqing.
90 min.
Shot in 1994 and reflecting the dark mood in Beijing's 'underground' art circles at that time, this was an independent production – hence illegal in the eyes of the Film Bureau. The subsequent outlawing of unauthorised film-making in China forced the director to hide behind the pseudonym 'Wu Ming' (No Name). A young performance artist decides to trump the nihilism and self-destructive theatrics prevailing among the avant-garde crowd by staging a series of four symbolic deaths for himself, each coinciding with an equinox. He appears to die during the last, frozen to death on midsummer's day. But this 'death' was as much a fake as the others. A wry, semi-detached narration expresses a precise ambivalence about the protagonist and his friends, mocking their pretensions but respecting their helpless feelings of impotence in the China of the 1990s. TR

Fruit Machine, The

(Philip Saville, 1988, GB) Emile Charles, Tony Forsyth, Robert Stephens, Clare Higgins, Bruce Payne, Robbie Coltrane, Carsten Norgaard.
108 min.
Eddie (Charles) is a chubby 17-year old dreamer who loves scoffing chocs and watching old movies with his blowsy mum. Dad thinks he's a nancy boy, so when his mate Michael (Forsyth) calls for help the two scousers take off in search of adventure, and find it in a nightclub called 'The Fruit Machine', presided over by Annabelle (Coltrane, marvellous), an outsize drag queen whom they witness receiving too close a shave from a sicko called Echo (Payne). Running for their lives, the pair fall in with an opera singer (Stevens) and his agent (Higgins), who takes them to Brighton. Michael pays for their fares by horizontally dancing with both of them. Eddie remains oblivious to all this – he's too involved with a dripping dolphin man (Norgaard) who keeps appearing in front of him...Saville films Frank Clarke's script in a mishmash of styles, and the pace sometimes flags. But what the hell, it's as camp as Christmas, and if it rarely hits the jackpot, playing along with it is wildly enjoyable. MS

Fruits of Passion, The (Les Fruits de la Passion)

(Shuji Terayama, 1981, Fr/Jap) Klaus Kinski, Isabelle Illiers, Arielle Dombasle, Peter, Kenichi Nakamura, Takeshi Wakamatsu.
83 min.
Terayama supposedly knocked off this piece of arse-with-class to finance his theatre work. Certainly it's a highly dispiriting plunge into latter-day Borowczyk territory: softcore gropings dished up with arty trappings and fetishistic gloss to guarantee French box-office action. The narrative (based on the sequel to The Story of O) has Kinski testing his young love's affection in an Oriental brothel. Lashings of surrealist 'touches', so male culture-hunters needn't feel guilty when aroused. SJ

F.T.A.

(Francine Parker, 1972, US) Jane Fonda, Donald Sutherland, Len Chandler, Holly Near, Pamela Donegan.
94 min.
A documentary inevitably dated by the very success of the cause of which it was part. The title's an acronym for the Free Theatre of America revue's slogan 'Free the Army/Fuck the Army', and the film records performances by the group at US military bases on the Pacific Rim – Hawaii, Okinawa, the Philippines – in an openly subversive attempt to motivate sentiment within the rank-and-file of the US forces against the war in Vietnam. It's pretty conventional stuff, comprising footage of the revue in performance (campus-style anti-war sketches, protest songs) and interviews with soldiers. Even more so than when

it was made, it will be of interest mostly to fans intrigued by the prospect of Fonda and Sutherland hoofing their way through song'n'-dance routines. RM

F.T.W.

(Michael Karbelnikoff, 1994, US) Mickey Rourke, Lori Singer, Brion James, Rodney Grant, Peter Berg.
97 min.
Either 'Fuck the War', which is tattooed across Lori Singer's knuckles, or Frank T Wells – being the name of Mickey Rourke's ex-con rodeo rider. She's on the run from the law after the death of her psychotic brother (Berg), and he's the gentle loser who tries to straighten her out. Rourke's face has become fascinating. He's aged quickly, and that dimple is now surrounded by the craggy features of a real cowboy. He gives a strong performance in a very capable little movie: a melancholy love story with bloody bookends. TCh

Fugitive, The

(John Ford, 1947, US) Henry Fonda, Dolores Del Rio, J Carrol Naish, Pedro Armendariz, Ward Bond, Leo Carrillo, Robert Armstrong, John Qualen.
104 min. b/w.
Graham Greene's The Power and the Glory given typically Fordian treatment, in that the moral complexities of the novel have been replaced by simplicity, picturesque poetry, and emotional power. Fonda plays the priest pursued by police and informers in an anti-clerical Latin American country, wandering the countryside in search of sanctuary and someone to understand him. It's generally one of Ford's most turgid efforts, slow, overstated, and with an annoying tendency towards obvious religious symbolism. But one cannot deny the beauty of Gabriel Figueroa's glowing photography. GA

Fugitive, The

(Andrew Davis, 1993, US) Harrison Ford, Tommy Lee Jones, Sela Ward, Julianne Moore, Jeroen Krabbé, Andreas Katsulas.
130 min.
A glossy, formula chase movie with the requisite number of extravagant action sequences (most notably a massive train crash). Brilliant doctor Richard Kimble (Ford) flees death row after wrongful conviction for his wife's murder. He vaguely recalls what the culprit looked like, but can he evade the authorities long enough to track him down? More or less as soon as you see him you know who the villain is. Ford is up to par for the strenuous stuff, but falls short on the grief, anxiety and compassion, allowing Tommy Lee Jones to walk away with the show as the wise-cracking marshal on Kimble's trail. GA

Fugitive Kind, The

(Sidney Lumet, 1959, US) Marlon Brando, Anna Magnani, Joanne Woodward, Maureen Stapleton, Victor Jory, RG Armstrong.
135 min. b/w.
Despite its stellar credentials, just about everything is wrong with this adaptation of Tennessee Williams' play Orpheus Descending. Brando plays a mysterious drifter who ignores a local tramp (Woodward doing her well-practised degenerate shtick) in favour of a lady of maturer years with a cancer-ridden husband. Magnani, with her unintelligible English, is not much worse than Brando, who undergoes the ultimate indignity of having to sing through another man's voice (for this role he became the first actor to be offered a million dollars, which he needed badly to cover his debts on One-Eyed Jacks). Lumet's direction is either ponderous or pretentious, and he failed to crack the problem of the florid stage dialogue and a dangerously weak role for Brando. DT

Full Circle (aka The Haunting of Julia)

(Richard Loncraine, 1976, GB/Can) Mia Farrow, Keir Dullea, Tom Conti, Jill Bennett, Robin Gammell, Cathleen Nesbitt, Mary Morris.
97 min.
Mia Farrow's fragile air of neurotic self-possession equips her well for the central role as a woman slowly destroyed by the ghost of an evil child. The narrative, from a story by Peter Straub, juggles ambiguously – if not carelessly – with themes

thrown up and better developed in The Turn of the Screw, Don't Look Now and Rosemary's Baby: corrupted innocence, dead children, obsession with the past, introversion, possession, guilt, the haunted house, etc. But there is much to commend in Farrow's performance, complemented by Colin Towns' softly chilling score, which is more than can be said for Conti and Dullea. JS

Full Confession

(John Farrow, 1939, US) Victor McLaglen, Joseph Calleia, Sally Eilers, Barry Fitzgerald, Elisabeth Risdon.
73 min. b/w.
McLaglen as a dumb-ox killer, Calleia the priest forced to respect the sanctity of the confessional. Heavy echoes of The Informer as McLaglen is hounded by the voice of conscience. Much capering Irishry, too, from Barry Fitzgerald as the wrong man awaiting execution. Calleia is remarkably good, while Farrow does his best, steering a smoothly moody course between the twin reefs of McLaglen and Fitzgerald. TM

Full Contact (Xia Dao Gao Fei)

(Ringo Lam, 1992, HK) Chow Yun-Fat, Simon Yam, Bonnie Fu, Ann Bridgewater, Anthony Wong.
97 min.
Jeff (Chow Yun-Fat), a tough guy with a sense of honour, saves his debt-ridden friend Sam from loan sharks. Hooking up with gay gangster Judge (Simon Yam) and his dubious henchmen, the friends are double-crossed in a violent heist. Sam saves his own skin, while Jeff is left for dead. Big mistake. When Jeff comes back, he's mad. Ringo Lam is like John Woo, but lapsed – there are none of those spiritual affectations to clog up the works; he'll pay lip service to macho codes, but that's as far as it goes. Super-slick, making opportune use of Bangkok locations, and relishing every violent episode, the film's unquestionably good of its type, but also sleazy and soulless. TCh

Full House

see O. Henry's Full House

Full Metal Jacket

(Stanley Kubrick, 1987, GB) Matthew Modine, Adam Baldwin, Vincent D'Onofrio, Lee Ermey, Dorian Harewood, Arliss Howard.
116 min.
The first half of Kubrick's movie steers clear of South East Asia altogether, focusing on the dehumanising training programme undergone by a group of novice US Marines. Then, after a suitably melodramatic bloodbath, the action switches to 'Nam, where star recruit Pvt Joker (Modine) soon tires of his behind-the-lines job as military journalist and provokes his CO into sending him forth into the shit. Black but obvious irony abounds, madness and racist bigotry are rampant, and a muddled moral message arises from the mire of a sprawling second half when the cynical, nominally heroic Joker finally learns to kill. None of which is to suggest that the film is bad; despite a certain stereotyping and predictability there are moments of gripping interest. Finally, however, Kubrick's direction is as steely cold and manipulative as the régime it depicts, and we never really get to know, let alone care about, the hapless recruits on view. GA

Full Moon in Blue Water

(Peter Masterson, 1988, US) Gene Hackman, Teri Garr, Burgess Meredith, Elias Koteas, Kevin Cooney, David Doty.
95 min.
A low-budget comedy-drama, slow to start, in which Masterson's uncinematic direction, and first-time screenwriter Bill Bozzone's reliance on characterisation, reveal their shared theatrical backgrounds. Hackman helps no end with a strong performance as the self-pitying, cynical owner of a poky bar on the Texas Gulf Coast. Mounting debts, combined with the disappearance of his wife, lead him to the verge of selling out to unscrupulous land-grabbers. But that same day he also has to contend with the muddled kidnapping of his wheelchair-bound father-in-law (Meredith), a hold-up, and a bust-up with his casual girlfriend (Garr). Low-key stuff with an assortment of eccentric rednecks, probably better suited to the small screen.

Full Moon in New York (Ren zai Niu-Yue)

(Stanley Kwan, 1989, HK) Maggie Cheung, Sylvia Chang, Siqin Gaowa, Josephine Koo, Richard Hsiung.
89 min.

Kwan's New York feature overcomes a spurious 'political' subtext (women from Hong Kong, Taiwan and Mainland China must figure out how to get along) thanks to some fairly trenchant observations about the émigré Chinese experience. Chang is the would-be Shakespearean actress from Taiwan, stuck playing horses in off-off-Broadway clinkers; Cheung is the Hong Kong restaurateur/property magnate coming to the end of a lesbian affair; and Siqin Gaowa is the bride from China, barely coping with strange Western ways. Richer and more imaginative than most Chinatown movies, persuasive enough as a sketch of female bonding, and superbly shot by Bill Wong. TR

Full Moon in Paris (Les Nuits de la Pleine Lune)

(Eric Rohmer, 1984, Fr) Pascale Ogier, Tchéky Karyo, Fabrice Luchini, Virginie Thévenet, Christian Vadim, Laszlo Szabo.
101 min.

Ogier and Karyo are an ill-matched couple; she longs for freedom, love and excitement, and moves out into her own Parisian pied-à-terre in order to see him only at weekends. But rumours, misunderstandings and flirtations hold sway with such vengeance that Ogier's double life backfires. It's as elegant and incisive a comedy of manners as ever from Rohmer, deriving much wit and subtlety from the simplest of plots, merely by concentrating on conversations and the mixed-up motives that fuel them. But accusations that the film is too literary or verbal miss the point entirely: performance, decor and composition – not to mention narrative structure – are all at the service of the film's meaning, perhaps most notably in a marvellous party scene where the body language of dancing and glances speaks volumes. GA

Full Monty, The (100)

(Peter Cattaneo, 1997, US/GB) Robert Carlyle, Tom Wilkinson, Mark Addy, Lesley Sharp, Emily Woof, Steve Huison, Paul Barber, Hugo Speer, Deirdre Costello, Bruce Jones.
91 min.

Sheffield. Unemployment. Men battling for their self-respect in a post-industrial waste land. Like *Brassed Off*, this turns feel-bad clichés on their head. The men here don't make a sentimental stand by blowing their own trumpets: their shot at self-respect involves stripping to the bare essentials – out-raunching the Chippendales before a horde of noisy local lasses. Carlyle's assured with the self-deprecating humour of the unlikely bump 'n' grind, and the understated, but still palpable desperation underlining the men's plight – and his able cohorts have enough problems of their own to stop matters developing into out-and-out farce. With the women virtual bystanders, there's some attempt at addressing manhood-in-crisis – squaring loss-of-breadwinner status with the finale's cheering reassertion of sexual identity. Along the way, screenwriter Simon Beaufoy slips in an affectionate gay subplot, makes things awkward for himself by exposing Carlyle's pubescent son to the chaps' developing routines, and never quite manages to convince the head as much as the heart. Still, director Cattaneo thrives on the sheer incongruity of it all. TJ

Full of Life

(Richard Quine, 1956, US) Judy Holliday, Richard Conte, Salvatore Baccaloni, Esther Minciotti.
91 min. b/w.

Breezy comedy, with gargantuan Baccaloni (a popular New York opera singer of the '50s) pissing off Italian-American couple Holliday and Conte by interfering in the birth of their child. Holliday has no special religious convictions but her boozy father-in-law-to-be insists she confirm her faith before the sprog is born. Holliday is vivacity itself; Baccaloni is a roly-poly firecracker; and the script by cult author John Fante (from his own novel) strikes just the right note. NF

Full Speed

see A Toute Vitesse

Fun

(Rafal Zielinski, 1994, US) Renee Humphrey, Alicia Witt, Leslie Hope, William R Moses.
105 min.

Two teenage girlfriends murder an old lady – for fun. The film unfolds in flashbacks as a court psychiatrist and a reporter probe the girls' motives (past in colour, present in grainy blue and white). The girls keep talking about the TV movie they'll inspire ('Is that how you expect to see yourself: Drew Barrymore?'), and that's exactly what this feels like: a TV movie. There's even a *Pretty Woman*-type pop promo in the middle. There is one big plus though – two arresting, naturalistic performances from Humphreys and Witt. TCh

Fun Bar Karaoke

(Pen-ek Ratanaruang, 1997, Thai)
100 min.

With its racked up soundtrack, fancy dissolves, slo-mo camera and moments of Tarantino-like casual violence, this dreamy tale of a young commercials film-assistant (or is she a check-out girl?) seems more an exercise in style than an exploration of modern Bangkok. Young Pu lives with her dad, who forgets her birthday, more concerned, it seems, with the femme fatale down at the karaoke bar. He's beaten up by a gang of bouncers including a cool young hitman whom Pu fancies. Pu goes to the swimming pool a lot and visits a fortune teller who predicts her father's death. The director, whose debut this is, comes from commercials, so maybe he's fed up with unmistakable meanings. WH

Fun Down There

(Roger Stigliano, 1989, US) Michael Waite, Nickolas B Nagourney, Martin Goldin, Jeanne Smith.
85 min.

Stigliano takes the grainy docu-drama angle in following the fortunes of Buddy (Waite) a young gay man from upstate New York who leaves home for the Big Apple. He soon finds himself involved with a group of typical urban bohemians, with whose help he loses his virginity, makes friends, and gets a job. It's all shot with dispassionate detachment, by means of fixed camera angles that record party small talk and sexual acts without comment or sensationalism. Occasionally the home movie mood is annoying: one feels the cast are allowed to do their party pieces a little too much (they're just not interesting enough to hold attention). But in general it's an engaging piece, with a central performance by Waite that radiates a convincing innocence and an electric sexuality. RS

Funeral, The

(Abel Ferrara, 1996, US) Christopher Walken, Isabella Rossellini, Vincent Gallo, Annabella Sciorra, Chris Penn, Benicio del Toro, Gretchen Mol.
99 min.

Walken, Penn and Gallo are brothers in 1930s New York. When one is killed, the lives of the other two quickly unravel. This stylishly shot mobster comedy-thriller has a flashback structure of such complexity – it starts with the funeral and works backwards – that the makers themselves seem confused by it. There are some distracting plot strands (for instance, Gallo's sudden embrace of workers' rights) and a few too many nods to *The Godfather*, but this is still a brilliant, very visceral piece of film-making with an infectious strain of morbid humour. GM

Funeral in Berlin

(Guy Hamilton, 1966, GB) Michael Caine, Eva Renzi, Paul Hubschmid, Oscar Homolka, Guy Doleman, Rachel Gurney, Hugh Burden.
97 min.

Second outing for Caine and Len Deighton (after *The Ipcress File*). This time the plot thickens almost to the point of congealing, with everybody seemingly tailing everybody else (you soon give up caring why) as Harry Palmer is despatched to Berlin to get the real story when a Russian intelligence colonel, chief of security on the Wall, is reported to be anxious to defect. Left to twiddle your thumbs while the plot gradually strangles, you can relish some nice location photography, two straightfor-

ward action sequences, and a lovely performance from Homolka as the bluffly sinister defector. TM

Funeral Rites

see Ososhiki

Funhouse, The

(Tobe Hooper, 1981, US) Elizabeth Berridge, Cooper Huckabee, Miles Chapin, Largo Woodruff, Shawn Carson, Sylvia Miles, Wayne Doba, William Finley.
96 min.

Which is socially acceptable – to love Tobe Hooper movies for their perverse but stubborn puritanism, or to love them for the incredible way they decoy your attention with stylish homages to other horror classics, then spring on you new and inventive means of scaring you out of your seat? *The Funhouse*, a story of two amorous young couples who arbitrarily enter the sleazoid world of a sinister travelling carnival (despite warnings) and Find They Are Not Alone, is a little too long, but what the hell? It's not every day the fright genre produces a film capable of commenting on epic subjects like the ties that bind and the disintegration of the modern family, the foolishness of dabbling voyeuristically in others' pain, and the possible detrimental effect of the Polaroid Instamatic on American moral fibre (a theme touched upon also in *The Texas Chainsaw Massacre*, Hooper's extreme pro-vegetarianism tract), while doing its proper job providing plenty of cheap thrills. Not that taste is nesessarily involved here, but it's rare that any film follows through its chosen themes with such attention to detail, much less leavening the package with a truly anarchic blend of black humour. CR

Funny About Love

(Leonard Nimoy, 1990, US) Gene Wilder, Christine Lahti, Mary Stuart Masterson, Robert Prosky, Stephen Tobolowsky, Anne Jackson, Susan Ruttan, David Margulies.
101 min.

As interminably cute as its title suggests, Nimoy's film strains for a sophisticated view of adult relationships, while in reality taking the director's obsession with babies to new depths. Wilder plays Duffy, a satirical cartoonist – so we're told, though on the evidence presented he seems no more than a rather pathetic chauvinist in mid-life crisis. Be that as it may, he can boast good taste in women. First, he woos the wonderful Christine Lahti in double quick time; then, when she has failed to reproduce and been put aside, he turns to the young, spunky Masterson. A stronger actor than Wilder – a cabbage patch doll of a man – might have persuaded us that he is more than a sentimental sexist. As it is, the movie drowns in a maudlin sea of sickly sentiment. TCh

Funny Bones

(Peter Chelsom, 1994, US/GB) Oliver Platt, Jerry Lewis, Lee Evans, Leslie Caron, Richard Griffiths, Oliver Reed, Ian McNeice, Gavin Millar, Terence Rigby.
128 min.

Writer/director Chelsom's follow-up to *Hear My Song* throws plenty of comic ideas around, but only one or two stick. Platt stars as Tommy Fawkes, a stand-up comic overshadowed by his father (Lewis), whose Las Vegas show falls so flat he takes off to relearn his trade – in Blackpool. There he comes across Jack Parker (Evans), a natural-born comedian with a talent so pure it's positively dangerous. This paternalistic yarn inhabits a curiously nostalgic neverland where sentimental whimsy and showbiz escapism ultimately drown out acute psychological trauma. Evans is okay in his cinema debut, but his role seems to have been emasculated in large-scale cuts which play havoc with what was evidently an undeveloped script (it still runs over two hours). What any of this has to do with Oliver Reed, French smugglers and an ancient immortality drug we may never know. TCh

Funny Dirty Little War, A (No Habrá más Penas ni Olvido)

(Héctor Olivera, 1983, Arg) Federico Luppi, Héctor Bidonde, Victor Laplace, Rodolfo Ranni, Miguel.
79 min.

A profound, aptly titled insight into the madness of recent Argentinian political history. Set in a fictional town near Buenos Aires, the year is 1974: an aged Peron has been returned to power and is encouraging a purge of the leftist forces (his original supporters in the '40s) by the same right wing opportunists who brought about his exile in 1955. Mayor, Secretary General and Police Chief each pass down the responsibility of removing a 'Peronist' administrator and his 'subversive' assistant from the town hall. Verbal banter and threats escalate into a full-scale bloody siege when the building itself becomes a refuge to those who cling to a position variously labelled Marxist or even apolitical. Olivera's skill is to proceed from a farcical opening to a dramatic and black conclusion without losing sight of the appalling reality behind the jokes: torture here is casually enacted in a schoolroom where physical agony is juxtaposed with portraits of national heroes and the naive drawings of children. Wittily scripted, furiously paced, deftly performed, this is explosive political comedy that demonstrates the absurd division of groups who believed in some sort of salvation through Peron. Don't die for me, Argentina – but they did. DT

Funny Face
(Stanley Donen, 1956, US) Fred Astaire, Audrey Hepburn, Kay Thompson, Michel Auclair, Suzy Parker, Robert Flemyng.
103 min.
The musical that dares to rhyme Sartre with Montmartre, *Funny Face* – surprisingly from Paramount rather than MGM – knocks most other musicals off the screen for its visual beauty, its witty panache, and its totally uncalculating charm. The beauty is most irresistible in the sylvan scene, shimmering through gauze, when Astaire and Hepburn find they 'empathise', to use the film's joke. The panache is most sustained in the 'Clap Yo' Hands' number, in which Astaire and Thompson shuffle on as a couple of beats and develop a dazzlingly inventive send-up. The charm is everywhere. Love triumphs over capitalist exploitation, joyless intellectualisation, and all things phony; and the thesis persuades because of the commitment and skill of the team and the lightness of the underrated Donen's touch. SG

Funny Games
(Michael Haneke, 1997, Aus) Susanne Lothar, Ulrich Mühe, Frank Giering, Arno Frisch, Stefan Clapczynski.
103 min.
Continuing the fascination with violence and its representation evident in his earlier films, Haneke's movie may be shocking, but it's also entirely serious. A couple and their young son arrive at their lakeside holiday home, only to have it invaded by two strange, ultra-polite young men who turn out to be sadistic, homicidal psychopaths. No facile explanations are offered for the killers' behaviour; rather, through their regular asides to the camera, and by occasionally disrupting the otherwise 'realist' narrative, Haneke explores both the emotional and physical effects of violence, and interrogates our own motives in consuming violent stories. Amazingly, very little violence is actually seen; we hear its perpetration and witness its aftermath, which (though no less disturbing) is absolutely crucial to the responsible treatment of such a horrific subject. Brilliant, radical, provocative, it's a masterpiece that is at times barely watchable. GA

Funny Girl
(William Wyler, 1968, US) Barbra Streisand, Omar Sharif, Kay Medford, Anne Francis, Walter Pidgeon, Lee Allen, Gerald Mohr.
147 min.
Wyler's only musical, *Funny Girl* is the fictionalised biography of Fanny Brice (Streisand), the ugly duckling who became a glamorous Ziegfeld star and achieved fame as a comic, so puncturing the mythic public eroticism of the *Ziegfeld Follies*. The film's central irony is not the usual one of public success at the expense of private pain, but the complex one of success at the expense of personal knowledge. Streisand never looks into the mirrors that Wyler surrounds her with. Well worth watching, even if most later Streisand movies aren't. PH

Funny Lady
(Herbert Ross, 1975, US) Barbra Streisand, James Caan, Omar Sharif, Roddy McDowall, Ben Vereen, Carole Wells.
138 min.
Funny Girl becomes Funny Lady as Streisand completes the tragi-comic tale of Fanny Brice in a curate's egg of a musical blockbuster. The opening is good, with Streisand taking off Brice again with astounding ease and the plausible Billy Rose soon established by Caan. But the inexorable slide into stodge begins early with merely efficient numbers, and the unspeakable flash-forward at the end brings it flatulently to earth. Ben Vereen goes some in 'Clap Hands, Here Comes Charley'; while Streisand and the dancers doing 'Great Day' is one for the anthologies. The lady can still turn a one-liner with sweet malevolence – 'when you're a star, everything you do is magic' as she falls over in the wardrobe – but she can't save a galumpher any more than she could save the (far worse) *Hello Dolly*. Neither can the glowing cinematography of James Wong Howe. SG

Funny Man
(Simon Sprackling, 1994, GB) Tim James, Christopher Lee, Benny Young, Matthew Devitt, Pauline Black, Ingrid Lacey.
93 min.
Christopher Lee appears at the start of this farrago as a suave aristo who on the turn of a card loses his beloved ancestral home to a sleazy record producer, but neglects to warn the new owner that his des res comes complete with an evil jester who slaughters unwelcome visitors. Lee subsequently pops up chuckling from the madhouse, as the sick and sad jester disposes of the cast in various repellent ways. There's the threat of a sequel. AO

Funny Money
(James Kenelm Clarke, 1982, GB) Gregg Henry, Elizabeth Daily, Gareth Hunt, Derren Nesbitt, Annie Ross, Joe Praml.
97 min.
A love-on-the-lam movie about credit card fraud, with guest zombies and second-rate leads playing out a totally charmless fiction in one and a half locations. The money is plastic but the love, eventually, is true: he (Henry) is a balding cocktail pianist with deeply hidden talent, she (Daily) is an irrepressible (ha!), elfin American, fresh in town with a tote-bag full of stolen cards. In the seamless sleaze of a Park Lane hotel, the couple turn their tricks and discover the piles of pathos on the jet set bum. If it had in any critical way been about this grubby little criminal sub-culture it just might have been watchable. RP

Funny Thing Happened on the Way to the Forum, A
(Richard Lester, 1966, US) Zero Mostel, Phil Silvers, Jack Gilford, Buster Keaton, Michael Crawford, Annette Andre, Patricia Jessel, Michael Hordern.
98 min.
Mix a bawdy story in the style of the Roman satirist Plautus with modern New York humour and the flashy direction of Lester, and what have you got? Not surprisingly, a spasmodically successful farce taken along at breakneck pace so that half of the good gags don't have time to sink in, and half of the bad ones fortunately disappear in the mêlée. All in all, a middling affair, with the overrated Mostel playing the slave on the lookout for freedom, and many of Stephen Sondheim's songs from the original Broadway musical thrown out in the rush. GA

Fun With Dick and Jane
(Ted Kotcheff, 1976, US) George Segal, Jane Fonda, Ed McMahon, Dick Gautier, Allan Miller, John Dehner, Hank Garcia.
100 min.
Aerospace engineer Segal's redundancy puts his and acquisitive wife Fonda's one-up materialism on the line for some incongruous satire; but the easy option lure of crazy comedy soon has them turning ineptly to crime, and the attack on the values they incarnate leads so desperately cling to peters out into fuzzy independent/corporate criminal contrasts. Compromised intentions mean that the cynical premise leaks all its acid as we're

actually asked to sympathise with the artificial 'poverty' of the executive class. It's the sort of thing that would undoubtedly amuse Norman Tebbitt. PT

Für Elise
(Paulo Thiago, 1993, Braz) Norma Bengell, Maria Zilda Bethlem.
95 min.
Focused on the relationship between three very different women who share an apartment, this meandering, allegorical movie may be intended as some sort of statement on the female condition, but with the trio (wary, promiscuous and neurotic respectively) all defined exclusively by their attitudes to men, it's certainly not feminist. GA

Furies, The
(Anthony Mann, 1950, US) Barbara Stanwyck, Walter Huston, Wendell Corey, Gilbert Roland, Judith Anderson, Beulah Bondi, Thomas Gomez, Albert Dekker, Wallace Ford, Blanche Yurka.
109 min. b/w.
A fraught, violent Freudianism stampedes through Charles Schnee's script (adapted from Niven Busch's novel) for Anthony Mann's intense Western – only his second stab at the genre which would bring out his very best qualities: his gritty treatment of physical and mental conflict, his classical intelligence and expressive use of landscape. In comparison, *The Furies* smacks of primitivism, its central feud between Stanwyck and her cattle baron father Walter Huston being both overwritten and underdeveloped. That said, these two performers are so compelling in their own right that Mann could get away with murder with them on the screen together. TCh

Further and Particular
(Steve Dwoskin, 1988, GB) Richard Butler, Bruce Cooper, Jean Fennell, Irene Marot, Julie Righton, Nicola Warren, Carola Regnier.
110 min.
This film dovetails two obsessions: a man's with woman's sexuality, and a film director's with the nature of the camera's gaze. Needless to say, there is a lot of repetition. The camera approximates Memory, firstly that of a young boy, and of the sexual encounters arranged for him by his mother, and eventually that of an old man, with corresponding fragmentation. Many of the images of sexual stereotypes, and the games they play, are arresting if over-long, but too much of the film is taken up with commonplace profundities ('Truth is change') and doubtful maxims ('Love is reality transformed into a sport') spoken directly into the camera. References to Hitchcock's *Rope* and Welles' *The Lady from Shanghai* serve mainly to highlight the discrepancy between what the film demands of the viewer and what it gives back in the way of ideas and entertainment. MC

Further Gesture, A (aka The Break)
(Robert Dornhelm, 1997, GB/Ger/Jap/Ire) Stephen Rea, Alfred Molina, Rosana Pastor, Brendan Gleeson, Pruitt Taylor Vince, Maria Doyle Kennedy.
101 min.
Dowd (Rea), an IRA prisoner in the H-blocks, is gloomily facing his sentence, until he spontaneously joins a comrade (Gleeson) in a risky escape. Dowd begins a new life in New York, but he might as well be in prison again – until he strikes up a friendship with co-worker Tulio (Molina) and gets to know his close group of Guatemalan exiles. A bond with Monica (Rosana Pastor) seals his acceptance among the exiles, and Dowd learns the dark truth behind their presence in the US. Ronan Bennett's screenplay, based on an idea by Rea, is free from special pleading: there's no turning back, for instance, once you've used violence in the service of ideology. Director Dornhelm peaks in the opening burst of action, but keeps control of a narrative that asks spectators to assess their own sympathies. In trying to combine action thriller, love story and political think piece, the film bites off more than it can chew, but Rea and Gleeson are absolutely credible, and there's black Ulster humour in abundance. TJ

Furtivos
see Poachers

Fury

(Fritz Lang, 1936, US) Spencer Tracy, Sylvia Sidney, Walter Abel, Bruce Cabot, Edward Ellis, Walter Brennan.
94 min. b/w.

Lang's first American film, with Tracy as the man wrongly accused of a kidnapping who escapes summary justice by lynch mob as the jail burns down, then goes into hiding, plants evidence to suggest he died, and sits back gloatingly as his 'killers' are brought to trial. Softened along pious lines at the end (what else from MGM, who tinkered cravenly with the script all down the line?), so not quite the masterpiece of reputation: Lang later made much better, much less touted films. Still impressive, all the same, especially in the build-up to the lynching sequence. TM

Fury (Il Giorno del Furore)

(Antonio Calenda, 1973, It/GB) Oliver Reed, John McEnery, Raymond Lovelock, Carol André, Claudia Cardinale.
118 min.

An adaptation of Lermontov's novel *Vadim* which must rate as one of the crassest ventures in years, so God knows how Edward Bond, respected playwright, got himself muddled up with it. Presumably the director, who also has a hand in the script, must shoulder most of the blame; if his writing is anything like his direction, then it must have represented the kiss of death to Bond's contribution. As for the film, it has Reed as an 18th century Russian landowner, given to telling his dog that he's the only one he can trust, and to fondling girls' nighties while one of his peasants is flogged half to death outside. Meanwhile, Vadim (McEnery), a strange new servant bent on avenging the death of his parents at the hands of the tyrannical Reed, incites the masses to agitate. Agitation is likely to be already rife in the audience. CPe

Fury, The

(Brian De Palma, 1978, US) Kirk Douglas, John Cassavetes, Carrie Snodgrass, Charles Durning, Amy Irving, Fiona Lewis, Andrew Stevens.
118 min.

Here De Palma poses the burning question: is there still commercial mileage in demonic possession? But this attempted follow-up to *Carrie* almost entirely lacks its predecessor's narrative thrust and suspense. At centre it's another common-or-garden story of children screwed up by their own telekinetic powers, but there are several distracting subplots: one about secret US government research into psychic phenomena (masterminded by Evil Incarnate in the person of Cassavetes), more on the hero's paternal angsts as he approaches the male menopause. Stylistic pretensions further defuse whatever punch the original script might have had. In so far as the film lives at all, it's in its shock effects, which are adequately cruel if too thin on the ground – although the heartwarming sight of Cassavetes getting his just deserts compensates for a lot. TR

Fuss Over Feathers

see Conflict of Wings

Future Cop

see Trancers

Future Is Woman, The (Il Futuro è Donna)

(Marco Ferreri, 1984, It/Fr/WGer) Ornella Muti, Hanna Schygulla, Niels Arestrup, Maurizio Donadoni, Michèle Bovenzi.
100 min.

Once upon a time Ferreri made sprightly little sexual fables with a tasty black humour. Then the shock factor took over, culminating in Ferreri's beloved phallocracy capitulating to feminism with Depardieu chopping off his dong in *The Last Woman* Now Ferreri seems to have gone soft in this uninspiring tale of an attempted New Deal in relationships, in which a bored bourgeois couple take in a wistful *femme maudite* and squabble over her body and baby. Terrific design and loud disco music are no compensation for the spectacle of this tiresome trio, who weep, pout and beat each other up, giving little hope for the result of Ornella Muti's (real-life) pregnancy. DT

Future of Emily, The (L'Avenir d'Emilie)

(Helma Sanders-Brahms, 1984, Fr/WGer) Brigitte Fossey, Hildegard Knef, Ivan Desny, Herman Treusch, Camille Raymond.
116 min.

Sanders-Brahms' films are not for the faint-hearted. Compared to *No Mercy, No Future*, her coruscating study of schizophrenia, this is almost a joyride, a long day's journey into O'Neill territory with three generations of mothers and daughters at each other's throats. Fossey, successful actress and single mother, returns home to Normandy to visit daughter and parents. Recriminations multiply, with Fossey and Knef (her mother) living through a dark night of the soul, each balancing the family/career equation and baring her passionate obsession with the other. Strong meat, but the actresses sink their teeth into it with consummate relish. SJo

Futureworld

(Richard T Heffron, 1976, US) Peter Fonda, Blythe Danner, Arthur Hill, Yul Brynner, John Ryan, Stuart Margolin.
107 min.

Set in 1985, this sequel to the pithy *Westworld* is all gloss and no substance. *Westworld's* vast pleasure centre, where any and every fantasy could be fulfilled by means of highly sophisticated humanoid robots, is rebuilt on an even more lavish and supposedly fail-safe scale. Leading diplomats plus the press are invited to sample the goods, and only one intrepid newshound (Fonda) suspects that all is not well. Instead of expanding the possibilities, the film opts for a guided tour of the various simulated marvels, from a Cape Kennedy blast-off and a chess game with holograms as the pieces to a ski-race down a Martian hillside. At one point there is an asinine dream sequence whose only relevance seems to be as a reminder that Yul Brynner played the lead resurgent robot in the parent film. The script, which labours under polysyllabic mumbo-jumbo at times, is infantile, while the performances, apart from a sprightly Danner as Fonda's TV cohort, are spineless. IB

F/X (aka F/X – Murder by Illusion)

(Robert Mandel, 1985, US) Bryan Brown, Brian Dennehy, Diane Venora, Cliff De Young, Mason Adams, Jerry Orbach.
108 min.

'Nobody cares about making movies about people any more; all they care about is special effects' says an actress who has just been riddled with bullets. Yes, and it must have seemed like a beezer idea to make a film about an FX wizard, veteran of masterpieces such as 'Vermin from Venus' and 'Rock-a-Die Baby', who is forced to use his skills in order to survive when bad men from the Justice Department start gunning for him. Their motive: Tyler (Brown) helped them set up a fake assassination, and must now be eliminated to maintain watertight security. This sort of plot has to be watertight as well, if it is to probe the space between reality and illusion; but here the leaks start with a whopping credibility gap when Tyler takes on such a fishy-smelling job in the first place. The contrast between faked death and real bodies spilling real blood is never properly exploited, and the FX themselves rarely rise above the level of 'Get me the smoke pods, like the ones we used in Hell Raisers'. Vaguely amusing, but *The Stunt Man* did it all so much better. AB

F/X2 (aka F/X2 – The Deadly Art of Illusion)

(Richard Franklin, 1991, US) Bryan Brown, Brian Dennehy, Rachel Ticotin, Joanna Gleason, Philip Bosco, Kevin J O'Connor, Tom Mason, Dominic Zamprogna, Josie DeGuzman, John Walsh.
108 min.

Six years after part one, special effects ain't what they used to be. While *F/X – Murder by Illusion* relied heavily on explosions and smoke for excitement, here we're offered a 'telemetry' suit (enabling the wearer to control a robot's movements via remote control) and advanced video technology. But certain things remain constant: Rollie (Brown) and Leo (Dennehy) are still at odds with a corrupt system. After the traumatic events which left his girlfriend dead, special effects wizard Rollie has settled for a peaceful life as a toymaker. But when he is recruited to help the police on a case, he becomes embroiled in an intrigue involving the Vatican, the Mafia and precious gold medallions. Although this sequel spends more time developing the friendship between the crime-busting buddies, it remains rather flat and uninvolving. CM

g

MORON ASSHOLE
PUTZ BONEHEAD

Grumpy Old Men

Gabbeh

(Mohsen Makhmalbaf, 1995, Iran/Fr)
Shaghayegh Djodat, Hossein Moharami,
Abbas Sayahi.
74 min.
In Iran, a *gabbeh* is a colourful woollen carpet
woven by the women of sheep-herding nomadic
tribes. In this visually gorgeous film, Gabbeh
(Djodat) is also a young woman prevented from
marrying her horseman suitor by her father, who
keeps coming up with lame excuses about her
uncle needing to find a bride first, or his own wife
having to give birth to their latest child. On one
level, the film functions as fascinating ethnographic semi-documentary; on another, as a
study in storytelling, both traditional and mod-
ern(-ist). Gabbeh, herself a figure depicted in a
carpet, relates her tale of love and frustration to
an ancient, bickering couple who may just be her
future self and her lover. The tone is at once lyrical and epic, charming and whimsical. GA

Gable and Lombard

(Sidney J Furie, 1976, US) James Brolin, Jill
Clayburgh, Allen Garfield, Red Buttons,
Joanne Linville, Melanie Mayron.
131 min.
A disastrous example of a short-lived mid-'70s
cycle of Lives of the Stars (see also *WC Fields and
Me*), *Gable and Lombard* gets neither the history
nor the glamour right. The film seems as insulated and remote from the 'real' Hollywood as
Hollywood vehicles of the time were from the
'real' world. Allen Garfield does a reasonable turn
as Louis Mayer, but Brolin is a wax dummy and
Clayburgh produces a very modern version of the
Lombard larkishness. Furie completes the pretence by presenting the Gable and Lombard story
as if it were one of the crazy comedies they
appeared in. MA

Gabriela

(Bruno Barreto, 1983, Braz) Sonia Braga,
Marcello Mastroianni, Antonio Cantáfora,
Paulo Goulart.
99 min.
Brazilians go gaga over Sonia Braga, for she it
was who put the Bra in Brazil. It is therefore ironic that she is barely to be seen wearing one in this
film. Ironic also that it is a costume drama set in
1925, for Sonia has little need of a costume to
emote effectively, and even when clothed is usually busting out all over. Mastroianni, as the
wealthy bar-owner who tries to make a
respectable woman of her, looks understandably
bemused as Sonia steals his thespian limelight by
taking showers, cooking, doing the laundry, playing leapfrog and going to bed (while the soundtrack is forever crooning 'Gabriela, Gabriela' to a
background of sultry guitar strings). After being
socked in the eye by Sonia, there can be little hope
that the viewer will bother to untangle the convoluted cross-tracery of subplots, even though
some of these also feature big-bosomed Brazilians.
It would be unfair to call *Gabriela* smut, since it
consists of so much wishy-washy soap. AB

Gabriel Over the White House

(Gregory La Cava, 1933, US) Walter Huston,
Karen Morley, Franchot Tone, Arthur Byron,
C Henry Gordon, Samuel S Hinds, Jean Parker.
87 min. b/w.
A party stooge in the pockets of 'special interests',
the newly elected US President, Hammond
(Huston), has no intention of squaring up to the
Great Depression... until he wakes up from a car
accident a changed man: a visionary leader. What
distinguishes La Cava's political fable from ostensibly similar populist fantasies by Frank Capra is
not so much ideology as urgency. Where John Doe
preached neighbourliness and Mr Smith talked
boys' camps, Hammond sidesteps Congress to
declare a state of emergency, establishes an 'Army
of Construction' (a prototype for Workfare), pits
the military against the mob, and instigates World
Disarmament. His 'divine madness' smacks of fascism, though La Cava might have enlisted Plato
in his support as well as Lincoln; and in any case,
American movies are as paradoxical as American
politics: Louis B Mayer – a staunch Republican –
held up the film's release because he saw it as an
insult to ex-President Hoover and a boost for
Franklin Roosevelt's New Deal. Any similarities
with Messrs Bush and Clinton are *entirely* coincidental. TCh

Gadael Lenin

see Leaving Lenin

Gadjo Dilo (The Crazy Stranger)

(Tony Gatlif, 1997, Fr) Romain Duris, Rona
Hartner, Izidor Serban, Florin Moldovan,
Ovidiu Balan, Dan Astileanu.
100 min.
Tony Gatlif, a Rom himself, continues his exploration of gypsy culture with this tale of a young
Parisian (Duris) who travels to Romania in search
of a gypsy singer. Slowly accepted by a clan suspicious of the outside world, he witnesses the joys
and heartbreaks of Romany experience. This
funny, bawdy, moving blend of gritty drama, glorious music and dance, and ethnographic semi-
documentary never romanticises the characters:
while they're lively, lusty, talented and passionate, they also have a tendency towards drunkenness, theft, xenophobia and foul-mouthed
aggression – the result, probably, of being treated as unwanted outsiders by the world around
them. Simultaneously stirring and illuminating,
and as well worth catching as Gatlif's earlier *Les
Princes* and *Lacho Drom*. GA

Gai Savoir, Le

(Jean-Luc Godard, 1968, Fr/WGer) Juliet Berto,
Jean-Pierre Léaud.
91 min.
Commissioned (in a moment of exceptional naiveté)
by French TV, *Le Gai Savoir* was Godard's first
'radical' break with established methods of exhibition and distribution; the film was never televised,
and has been seen only by political groups and film
societies. Two militants meet in a darkened film
studio to educate themselves in the ideological
meanings of specific sounds and images: their work
is essentially 'de-constructive', and it represents an
important step in Godard's own return to a 'degree
zero' of cinema. In Godard's own terms, the film is
not at all revolutionary: it's a confused, idiosyncratic attempt at an analysis of the way things are,
not yet a committed attempt to construct the way
they should be. TR

Galahad of Everest

(John-Paul Davidson, 1991, GB) Brian Blessed,
Chris Bonnington.
90 min.
This spectacular but extremely bizarre BBC documentary recounts the madcap efforts of actor
Brian Blessed to exorcise an obsession that has
dogged him since childhood: to follow the footsteps of mountaineers George Leigh Mallory and
Andrew Irving's fated 1924 attempt on Everest.
It charts his preparation in England, the trip to
India, a blessing by the Dalai Lama, to a final
assault on the summit, kitted out *à la* Mallory in
'20s plus-fours and umbrella. Davidson intercuts
archive footage of Mallory's original expedition
with a snow-blasted Blessed reading Mallory's
last letters from five miles high. If this sounds like
your average 'climbing movie', it isn't. It adds up
to a hilarious study in English eccentricity. WH

Galaxy of Terror

(Bruce Clark, 1981, US) Edward Albert, Erin
Moran, Ray Walston, Bernard Behrens,
Zalman King, Sig Haig.
80 min.
A Roger Corman tummy-ripper on the *Alien*
theme, involving a rescue mission's dash into
deep space to discover the whereabouts of one of
their craft. However, they soon end up
wishing they hadn't, as one crew member after
another is exterminated by those nasty slimy
things that usually inhabit such desolate places.
Forget the story, 'cause there isn't one, but see it
for the gory bits and marvellous gutsy make-up.
Yech! DA

Galileo

(Liliana Cavani, 1968, It/Bulg) Cyril Cusack,
Gheorghi Kolaiancev, Irene Kokonova, Lou
Castel, Gigi Ballista.
108 min.
Cavani's second feature, a film that makes an
impassioned plea for the primacy of the
evidence of the senses as against a seemingly
undentable wall of dogma and passively
accepted consensus opinion. And the plea is articulated in the early part of the film with real
urgency, fervour and individuality. The

impenetrable, monolithic quality of state-authen-
ticated truth is wittily rendered in the rigid
curlicues and ostentatious grandeur of Papal
architecture, and the argument is convincingly
developed around the person of Giordano Bruno
(Kolaiancev), Galileo's fellow scientist and martyr. The film, however, becomes a lot more conventional and less passionate on Bruno's death,
and Cavani is unable to solve the perennial
Galileo problem: he (played here by Cusack) turns
by degrees into an unastonishing symbol. VG

Galileo

(Joseph Losey, 1974, GB/Can) Chaim Topol,
Edward Fox, Michel Lonsdale, Richard
O'Callaghan, Tom Conti, Mary Larkin, Judy
Parfitt, John McEnery, Patrick Magee.
145 min.
Maybe Losey simply lived too long with a
project he had been trying to get off the ground
ever since he first directed Laughton in Brecht's
play in 1947, and which emerges here as a curiously academic exercise. For one thing, giving a
likeable but lightweight performance, Topol is
allowed to get away with presenting Galileo as a
hero, which makes nonsense of Brecht's condemnation of him as a coward for his betrayal of
science (the crucial carnival scene now becomes
just a jolly romp). For another, Losey hedges
uncertainly between theatre and cinema, so that
Brecht's linking songs and captions are retained,
but rendered in 'cinematic' ways that make them
both clumsy and tautological. By far the most
striking sequence is also the most purely theatrical (Galileo's daughter and disciples waiting anxiously to hear whether he has recanted, shot on a
bare stage with stark, theatrical groupings and
spotlights projecting a shadow-play of their emotions on the cyclorama behind). Elsewhere,
smooth theatrical continuity tends to blunt the
raw edges of Brecht's distancing effects. TM

Gallery Murders, The

see Uccello dalle Piume di Cristallo, L'

Gallipoli

(Peter Weir, 1981, Aust) Mark Lee, Mel
Gibson, Bill Hunter, Robert Grubb, Tim
McKenzie, David Argue, Bill Kerr, Ron
Graham.
111 min.
Australia's answer to *Chariots of Fire*, similarly
buoyed up by a fulsome nationalistic fervour, and
coincidentally also featuring two sprinters whose
friendly rivalry leads not to the Olympic track
but to the World War I battlefront of Gallipoli.
Expensively and handsomely shot, the Gallipoli
reconstructions (complete with conventional message about the waste of war) are impressively
done. Much less appealing, the central section
devoted to training in Egypt sags badly through
its crass buddy antics and its crude caricatures
of wogs and pommies. TM

Gallivant

(Andrew Kötting, 1996, GB) Andrew Kötting,
Gladys Morris, Eden Kötting.
100 min.
A delightfully offbeat road movie in which the
oddball director Andrew Kötting, his grandmother Gladys, and his daughter Eden, who has
learning difficulties and communicates by sign
language, travel around the coast of Britain. If the
camerawork occasionally veers towards the
tricksy, this first feature is still a warm, enlightening and often very funny look at Britain and
what it means to be British. GA

Gal Young 'Un

(Victor Nuñez, 1979, US) Dana Preu, David
Peck, J Smith, Gene Densmore, Jennie
Stringfellow.
105 min.
Very much a personal film, with Nuñez not only
directing but also scripting (from a story by
Marjorie Kinnan Rawlings), producing, editing
and photographing, this likeable independent feature tells of a quiet, ageing widow being duped by
a caddish young man, who first uses her money
to build a still (the setting is Prohibition Florida)
and then adds insult to injury by bringing home
a young mistress. A little soft-centred, it never
really manages to convince when the widow finally takes her revenge, but the period reconstruction, careful pacing, and compassion towards its
characters make it well worth a look. AB

Gambit

(Ronald Neame, 1966, US) Shirley MacLaine, Michael Caine, Herbert Lom, Roger C Carmel, John Abbott, Arnold Moss.
108 min.

Likeable performances from Caine and MacLaine as the Cockney con-man and the Eurasian show-girl in Hong Kong who conspire to steal a price-less statue from Lom. But it's all pretty thin as the conventionally unconventional caper, involv-ing cross and double-cross, veers erratically from comedy to thriller and back again to romance. GA

Gambler, The

(Karel Reisz, 1974, US) James Caan, Paul Sorvino, Lauren Hutton, Morris Carnovsky, Jacqueline Brookes, Burt Young, Vic Tayback, M Emmet Walsh, James Woods.
111 min.

Caan's gambler (a fine performance) is a universi-ty lecturer who gets into hot water with the mob-sters over his debts, and uses Dostoievsky to intellectualise his weakness into tragic compul-sion. Predictably, his increasingly desperate mea-sures are at the expense of those closest to him, and are accompanied by a deepening masochistic streak. In keeping with this definition of classic impulses, Reisz's direction is panoramic, with aspi-rations towards the epic, when it should have been closer in and faster. The result is a highly melo-dramatic and romantic film, for all the veneer of disillusion, whose weighty statement too often swamps the potentially strong suspense. *The Gambler* looks all the more old-fashioned for com-ing in the wake of Altman's systematic demythol-ogy of the subject in *California Split*; and James Toback showed how his script might perhaps have been tackled when he came to make his own directing debut with *Fingers*. CPe

Gambler, The

(Károly Makk, 1997, GB/Neth/Hun) Michael Gambon, Jodhi May, Polly Walker, Dominic West, John Wood, Johan Leysen, Angeline Bell, Luise Rainer.
97 min.

St Petersburg, 1866: debt-ridden Dostoevsky (Gambon) has struck a deal with his publisher – in exchange for an advance, he must meet the dead-line for his next book, or forfeit the rights to all his published work. With a month to go, doom looks inevitable, unless stenographer Anna Snitkina (May) can channel the author's violent mood swings into sustained creativity. Yet, as he unfolds an autobiographical story of obsessive desire and self-destruction around the roulette wheel, this prim naive girl begins to experience unexpected feelings for the much troubled artist. Gambon has the dis-solute look down pat, but earns our compassion as a man shaped for good and ill by the contours of his own weakness. In a less obviously showy role, May deftly suggests a woman coming to terms with desires she never knew she had, and her underplaying blends nicely with the larger-than-life contributions from Walker's voluptuous femme fatale and Rainer's marvellously vibrant grand-mother. Makk balances dramatic interest across the twin-track narrative and delivers an absorbing ven-ture into the psychology of addiction. TJ

Game, The

(David Fincher, 1997, US) Michael Douglas, Sean Penn, James Rebhorn, Deborah Kara Unger, Peter Donat, Carroll Baker, Armin Mueller-Stahl.
128 min.

San Francisco. Ruthless financier Nicholas Van Orton (Douglas) is a control freak who no longer knows the meaning of fun or friendship. When his estranged, addictive brother Conrad (Penn) enrolls him with Consumer Recreation Services for his birthday, his curiosity's aroused by the offer of a mysterious 'game' tailored to the needs of each participant. At first his application is rejected, but when, on TV, a newscaster starts talking directly to him, Nicholas realises the game's already begun and that his actions are being monitored and manipulated. As his priva-cy is progressively invaded and the situations in which he finds himself become ever more life-threatening, Van Orton tries to pull out of the game, but too late. Though the film's 'message' about complacency transformed by chaos and uncertainty is hackneyed, the alarming twists of the witty, ingenious script (by John Brancato and Michael Ferris) hold the attention throughout. GA

Game for Vultures

(James Fargo, 1979, GB) Richard Harris, Richard Roundtree, Joan Collins, Ray Milland, Sven-Bertil Taube, Denholm Elliott.
106 min.

Rhodesia...1979...guerilla warfare in the bush...arms smuggling in the Hilton...torrid pas-sion (Collins + Harris) between the bed-sheets. If this attempt to cash in on international news (made in South Africa, incidentally) were a little more reactionary and a little less 'responsible', it might have made a decent action film and turned its images of men at war (platoons skirmishing hope-lessly in the bush) to some use. As it is, the plot meanders in desperation, and the increasing arch-ness of Joan Collins in her usual role becomes just another dead-weight irrelevance. If white Rhodesia feels as dispirited as this movie looks, the war of black liberation has already been won. CA

Gamekeeper, The

(Kenneth Loach, 1978, GB) Phil Askham, Rita May, Andrew Grubb, Peter Steels, Michael Hinchcliffe, Philip Firth.
80 min.

Loach's adaptation for TV of a script by Barry (*Kes*) Hines is a superb study of a year in the life of a gamekeeper working on an aristocrat's Northern estate, subtly examining his relation-ships with his family, his employer, his dog, and the land itself. Avoiding didactic simplifications, beautifully shot by Chris Menges, and superbly acted, it's the type of totally honest social docu-ment that shows up a film like *Begging the Ring* for the half-baked idea it is. GA

Game of Danger

see Bang! You're Dead

Gandhi

(Richard Attenborough, 1982, GB) Ben Kingsley, Candice Bergen, Edward Fox, John Gielgud, Trevor Howard, John Mills, Martin Sheen, Ian Charleson, Athol Fugard.
188 min.

By virtue of its subject matter, and of the prodi-gious effort that has gone into its production, *Gandhi* has to be considered one of the major British films of the year. Its subject is an Indian spiritual leader almost unknown to today's Western youth, who not only preached a more sophisticated and forceful version of the pacifist ethic than ever flowered in the '60s, but succeed-ed in using it to help liberate his country and change its political history. Of course the film raises more questions than it comes near to answering, but its faults rather pale beside the epic nature of its theme, and Kingsley's perfor-mance in the central role is outstanding. FD

Gang, Le

(Jacques Deray, 1976, Fr/It) Alain Delon, Maurice Barrier, Roland Bertin, Adalberto Maria Merli, Xavier Depraz, Raymond Bussières, Nicole Calfan, Laura Betti.
103 min.

Old-fashioned, simple-minded stuff, with a bewigged Delon leading the notorious but effort-lessly elusive 'front-wheel-drive gang' in a not too serious succession of hold-ups in postwar France. Deray periodically clobbers the audience with second-hand chunks of morality, but for the most part is content to move the action along with a minimum of violence and the occasional pastoral interlude evocative of a simpler age when crooks – however psychopathic – all had hearts of gold and faithful molls. The gendarmes, we are told, are busy purging their ranks of collaborators; it falls, therefore, to a jeweller's comely wife to despatch our hero (his demise coming as no sur-prise, since the movie is one long flashback). JPy

Gang's All Here, The (aka The Girls He Left Behind)

(Busby Berkeley, 1943, US) Alice Faye, Carmen Miranda, Phil Baker, James Ellison, Charlotte Greenwood, Eugene Pallette, Edward Everett Horton, Sheila Ryan.
103 min.

Busby Berkeley's first in colour, reaching some sort of apotheosis in vulgarity with Carmen Miranda's 'Lady in the Tutti-Frutti Hat' accom-panied by a parade of chorines manipulating out-size bananas. Basically terrible, although Berkeley fans get some bizarre eyefuls and Benny

Goodman provides some bland Big Band swing. But Alice Faye does get to sing two terrific Harry Warren numbers, 'No Love, No Nothing' and 'A Journey to a Star'. TM

Garde à Vue (The Inquisitor)

(Claude Miller, 1981, Fr) Lino Ventura, Michel Serrault, Guy Marchand, Romy Schneider, Didier Agostini, Patrick Depeyrat.
88 min.

A fine psychological thriller, adapted from an English mystery novel (John Wainwright's *Brainwash*) already accented by a *Série Noire* translation. The potential staginess of the mate-rial – a New Year's Eve interrogation in a provin-cial police station – is admirably shaken by inspired adaptation, *mise en scène* and editing as cop Ventura turns 'witness' Serrault (an attorney obsessed with his own mediocrity) into a sus-pected rapist and murderer. No descent to glib cat-and-mouse cleverness, and no recourse to actorly fireworks: Miller's confidence in dialogue and an ever more tightly twisting plot is simply a gripping joy. PT

Garden, The

(Derek Jarman, 1990, GB) Tilda Swinton, Johnny Mills, Kevin Collins, Pete Lee-Wilson, Spencer Leigh, Jody Graber, Roger Cook.
92 min.

At first this looks like *The Last of England 2*, but there's a crucial difference: this time, there's no pretension to objectivity. Jarman's own presence is central, and everything else on the screen is pre-sented as his subjective dreams. Hence Jarman looks at his own garden near the sea in Dungeness, and imagines that it's the Garden of Eden or Garden of Gethsemane; Jarman reads about the government passing Section 28 and about the Synod witch-hunting gay priests, and imagines that Christ died for downcast gays; Jarman contemplates his own mortality (he is HIV-positive), and imagines that the end of the world is nigh. Touching, intense, sometimes unexpectedly amusing, sometimes agonising, and always achingly sincere. TR

Garden, The (Záhrada)

(Martin Sulik, 1995, Slovakia) Roman Luknar, Marian Labuda, Zuzana Sulajova.
99 min.

There are a few amusing moments (notably the drunken reunion between the teacher hero and his generally hostile father) in this offbeat tale of spiritual renewal, but most of the time it's too oblique, allegorical and, perhaps, tinged with misogyny for its own good. Jakub, asked to leave his tailor dad's flat, goes to live in and tidy up his late grandfather's rundown rural cottage and gar-den; while there, he meets saintly and philosoph-ical types, not to mention a teenage girl ('The Virgin Miraculous') whose mother beats her. Sadly, the film never lives up to its 14 intriguing chapter headings. GA

Garden of Allah, The

(Richard Boleslawski, 1936, US) Marlene Dietrich, Charles Boyer, Basil Rathbone, Tilly Losch, C Aubrey Smith, Joseph Schildkraut, John Carradine.
80 min.

Selznick's first colour production, a load of lush tosh about the complicated romance in the Algerian desert between disillusioned socialite Dietrich (grieving after her father's death) and Boyer's deserting Trappist monk. Based on a hideously dated Robert Hichens novel, complete with absurdly portentous dialogue, it's all pretty dull as well as silly, despite the rich Technicolor camerawork and sturdy attempts by Dietrich and Boyer to breathe life into the turgid story. GA

Garden of Eden, The

see Jardin del Eden, El

Garden of the Finzi-Continis, The (Il Giardino dei Finzi-Contini)

(Vittorio De Sica, 1970, It/WGer) Dominique Sanda, Lino Capolicchio, Helmut Berger, Romolo Valli, Fabio Testi, Camillo Cesarei, Inna Alexeief.
95 min.

De Sica's most watchable film in years of crude farces and coarse melodramas. Based on the novel by Giorgio Bassani and set in Ferrera in 1938, it deals with the net of persecution that gradually closes in on Italian Jews as Mussolini models his state ever more closely on Hitler's Germany. External events hold the film in a vice-like grip, while its dreamy evocation of a doomed way of life ambivalently records the placidity with which the aristocratically wealthy Finzi-Continis – retreating within their walled estate when they are no longer welcome outside – simply wait for fate to overtake them. Formally beautiful, sometimes moving, it's ultimately rather hollow. TM

Gardens of Stone

(Francis Coppola, 1987, US) James Caan, Anjelica Huston, James Earl Jones, DB Sweeney, Dean Stockwell, Mary Stuart Masterson, Dick Anthony Williams, Lonette McKee, Sam Bottoms.
112 min.
Coppola's oblique, muted and curiously revisionist drama of life on the home front during the Vietnam war. Sgt Hazard (Caan), a battle-seasoned veteran frustrated by his present role in the 'toy soldier' regiment guarding the Arlington military cemetery, is shaken out of his self-pitying cynicism by his love affair with an anti-war journalist (Huston) and a spiky father/son relationship with a gung-ho rookie (Sweeney). Caan is against the war – 'It's not even a war. There's nothing to win, and no way to win it' – but for the military; he won't go back to Vietnam, but desperately wants a transfer to Fort Benning, where he can train young recruits to die valiantly. Meanwhile, the bodies arrive daily, to be boxed up and buried with full military honours. While Ronald Bass' subtly understated dialogue, Coppola's meticulous direction, and some exceptional acting (especially from Caan) never fail to rivet the attention, there's a pervasive and worrying sense of the central issues being gently but undeniably fudged. NF

Garlic Is as Good as Ten Mothers

(Les Blank, 1980, US)
54 min.
Better than any dry martini as an aperitif, even in the non-Smellaround version, this documentary eulogy to garlic sure gets the juices going. Featuring such eccentrics as the Chief Garlic Head, and tabling the many and varied delights of the 'stinking rose', this is a real breath of fresh air. Will repeat and repeat. FF

Garment Jungle, The

(Vincent Sherman/Robert Aldrich, 1957, US) Lee J Cobb, Kerwin Mathews, Gia Scala, Richard Boone, Valerie French, Robert Loggia, Joseph Wiseman, Wesley Addy.
88 min. b/w.
Cut from familiar *noir* cloth – all eerie ceiling fans and empty elevator shafts expressionistically shot and lit – *The Garment Jungle*'s off-the-peg plot concerns a coming-home Korean war veteran's discovery of foul play in the family firm and political gangsterism on either side. It's a sort of 'pro-labour' (Aldrich's term) retort to *On the Waterfront*'s anti-union allegory three years earlier (both films were Columbia releases, both were set in New York, and both cast Cobb as a proto-capitalist patriarch). Uncredited director Robert Aldrich was replaced by Sherman only one week before shooting ended for his refusal to tone down a tough screenplay. In spite of Sherman's efforts, though, *The Garment Jungle* makes latter-day labour films like *F.I.S.T.*, *Norma Rae* and *Blue Collar* look comparatively unstarched. PK

Gasbags

(Marcel Varnel, 1941, GB) The Crazy Gang, Moore Marriott, Wally Patch, Peter Gawthorne, Carl Jaffe, Irene Handl, Billy Russell.
77 min. b/w.
Moore Marriott, grizzled, knobbly-kneed, and looking old enough to be Wilfrid Brambell's great-grandfather, steals the picture from under the very noses of the Crazy Gang – no small feat, considering this is probably the Gang's finest comedy. He plays a venerable PoW who just happens to have the plans of a secret weapon drawn on his back. The plot is set in motion by a flying fish-and-chip stall, no less, and barminess prevails throughout. Ranks with *The Goose Steps Out* as one of Britain's funniest wartime films. GM

Gas Food Lodging

(Allison Anders, 1991, US) Brooke Adams, Ione Skye, Fairuza Balk, James Brolin, Robert Knepper, David Landsbury, Jacob Vargas, Donovan Leitch.
101 min.
Nora (Adams) waits tables and scrapes by, single-handedly raising two teenage daughters in a clapped-out trailer. Romance seems as scarce as rain in her New Mexico backwater: Nora and elder daughter Trudi (Skye) know what it means to be left high and dry, and even young Shade (Balk) suffers rejection at the hands of dreamy Darius (Leitch). But hopes of love die hard, and there's escapism to be found at the local Spanish fleapit. Shade decides to go father-hunting, but an attempt at match-making and the hunt for her long-absent dad (Brolin) yield decidedly mixed results. Far from gloomy fare, this debut from an American independent offers humour, wry observation and sympathetic characterisation. Without patronising her characters, writer-director Anders captures the frustrations of both generations, and the concluding optimistic note isn't forced. Delightfully oddball and strangely sane. CM

Gaslight

(Thorold Dickinson, 1939, GB) Anton Walbrook, Diana Wynyard, Frank Pettingell, Robert Newton, Jimmy Hanley, Cathleen Cordell.
88 min. b/w.
The first film version of Patrick Hamilton's stage play about a Victorian criminal who tries to drive his wife mad in order to prevent her from discovering his guilty secret while he searches their house for a stash of precious rubies. Nothing like as lavish as the later MGM version with Charles Boyer and Ingrid Bergman, but in its own small-scale way a superior film by far. Lurking menace hangs in the air like a fog, the atmosphere is electric, and Wynyard suffers exquisitely as she struggles to keep dementia at bay. It's hardly surprising that MGM tried to destroy the negative of this version when they made their own five years later. NF

Gaslight (aka The Murder in Thornton Square)

(George Cukor, 1944, US) Ingrid Bergman, Charles Boyer, Joseph Cotten, Angela Lansbury, Dame May Whitty, Terry Moore, Barbara Everest.
114 min. b/w.
Lusher and less resonant than the 1939 British version of Patrick Hamilton's moody period melodrama, which had a much surer sense of background (in particular the English class thing, trailing an inbred distrust of the smarmy foreigner), and mined a chilling vein of psychosis in Walbrook's performance. Directed with consummate skill, all the same, as Cukor plants an indefinable sense of unease during the sunnily romantic Italian honeymoon (a lengthy addition in this version), then gradually orchestrates it into a genuinely harrowing crescendo of terror in the claustrophobically cluttered house in fogbound London where the husband is methodically driving his wife insane. One of Bergman's best performances, with Boyer not too far behind, and Lansbury unforgettable as the sulkily insolent parlourmaid whom the husband cunningly uses to add insult to his wife's injury. TM

Gas-s-s-s, or it became necessary to destroy the world in order to save it

(Roger Corman, 1970, US) Robert Corff, Elaine Giftos, Pat Patterson, George Armitage, Alex Wilson, Alan Braunstein, Ben Vereen, Bud Cort.
79 min.
This started life as a serious science fiction movie, but relatively late in the day Corman decided to transform it into a wacky comedy. He dispenses with his usual tight construction, and the almost non-existent plot chronicles the activities of America's youth after the adult population has been wiped out, with many of the themes and characters from his earlier movies turning up in a caricatured form. It may sound promising, but thanks to Country Joe's tedious score and an endless succession of feeble jokes, it is likely to be of more interest to Cormanologists than anyone else. DP

Gate, The

(Tibor Takacs, 1986, Can) Stephen Dorff, Christa Denton, Louis Tripp, Kelly Rowan, Jennifer Irwin.
86 min.
Glenn (Dorff), a Canadian in his early teens, has a thing about rockets, a 16-year-old sister who cares, an HM-loving demonologist buddy, and parents who make untimely decisions to go away for the weekend. As such, this spunky, diminutive Everyman is clearly well equipped to deal with the Forces of Darkness when, for no apparent reason, they come steaming out of a hole in his back garden. After an eventful but soporific first half, the plot, as full of holes as the Albert Hall, takes off into surreal nonsense that is almost delightful: inappropriately cute and beautifully animated SFX monsters thrown up from Hell; a hand stigmatised with a functionless eye; and a dead workman who never existed in the first place arriving zombie-like to wreak revenge for nothing in particular. The lunacy on view is strangely dreamlike, and no bad thing. It's only a pity the film actually tries to make sense. More abandon all round, and the result could have been a Z-grade cult classic. GA

Gate of Flesh (Nikutai No Mon)

(Seijun Suzuki, 1965, Jap) Jo Shishido.
90 min.
A deliciously torrid melo in which the solidarity of a group of prostitutes – based on mutual anarchy, and the threat of torture and humiliation for anyone who offers a freebie – disintegrates when they shelter a criminal whom they all fall for. Fascinating for its lurid colour-coding, theatrical lighting, quirky editing, and the overall artifice of design, which revels in both the dog-eat-dog decrepitude of post-war Tokyo and the bitter, sweaty mood of sado-masochistic cruelty. GA

Gate of Lilacs

see Porte des Lilas

Gates of Heaven

(Errol Morris, 1978, US) Floyd McClure, Joe Allen, Martin Hall, Mike Koewler.
85 min.
Is the canine after-life a concept sufficiently dear to the heart of California to form an exploitable basis for corporate capitalist credibility? Well, it may seem a dumb question, but at least two family concerns profiled in this winningly absurdist documentary think the answer is yes. For it's the unpredictable market economy of pet cemeteries over which Morris' subjects wax both lyrical and hymnal, as they affirm in endearingly ludicrous detail their earnest commitment to dead doggies and the dollar, and insistently hard-sell alternative routes through the eponymous portals. Morris respects the manic integrity of his interviewees, and handles his Great American Metaphors with the lightest of touches; incidentally winning a bet that saw Werner Herzog eat his shoe (having wagered that the film would never get made), he ultimately achieves a real treat of everyday surrealism. PT

Gates of Hell

see Paura nella Città dei Morti Viventi

Gates of Paris

see Porte des Lilas

Gates of the Night

see Portes de la Nuit, Les

Gathering of Eagles, A

(Delbert Mann, 1962, US) Rock Hudson, Mary Peach, Rod Taylor, Barry Sullivan, Kevin McCarthy, Henry Silva, Leora Dana.
115 min.
This loose remake, transposed to a peacetime setting, of producer Sy Bartlett's script for the much superior *Twelve O'Clock High* sees Rock Hudson struggling vainly to imitate the former version's Gregory Peck, as a colonel determined to improve the alertness and efficiency of a Strategic Air Command base. The conflict that arises from his ruthlessness – and the rumours surrounding his relationship with another officer's wife – are a pale shadow of the desperate strain evoked by Peck's wartime predicament. The flying footage, how-

ever, with its impressive if disturbingly hawkish shots of B-52 bombers, gives the film a sense of life; hardly surprising, since Bartlett and his director were both former fliers themselves. GA

Gathering of Old Men, A
(Volker Schlöndorff, 1987, US/GB/WGer) Louis Gossett Jr, Richard Widmark, Holly Hunter, Joe Seneca, Julius Harris, Will Patton, Woody Strode, Tiger Haynes.
91 min.
A murderous white Louisiana farmer chases a black man and is killed for his trouble by an anonymous shotgun blast. Plantation owner Hunter rounds up all her retired hands (Gossett, Seneca, Harris, Strode), each bringing with him a discharged shotgun. All confess to the shooting. Sheriff Widmark parks his car and awaits developments. A hot day with nothing to do but go fishing, and a stand-off in front of a shack where a white man of no great consequence lies spread-eagled on his back, slowly unfolds. Taken from a novel by Ernest J Gaines, an affecting moralist, the film has a dry tone and an appropriate lack of display, but the old stars, for all their impassivity, rather overwhelm the proceedings. JPy

Gatica
(Leonardo Favio, 1993, Arg) Edgardo Nievas, Juan Costa, Cristina Child, Horacio Taicher.
136 min.
A wearisome boxing picture about the rise and fall of lightweight boxing champ Gatica set in Argentina during the Peronist period of the 1940s and '50s: very, very derivative of Raging Bull. TJ

Gator
(Burt Reynolds, 1976, US) Burt Reynolds, Jack Weston, Lauren Hutton, Jerry Reed, Alice Ghostley, Dub Taylor, Mike Douglas.
116 min.
A sequel to the thick-eared White Lightning, this offers marginal interest as Burt Reynolds' directorial debut. The plot is formula pulp – Reynolds is blackmailed into exposing a former buddy, now a big-shot Southern crook – but it takes far too long to tell. Much of the two hours rather quaintly concerns Reynolds' star image. After a tongue-in-cheek he-man opening, and between further bouts of action, things dawdle to a standstill while Reynolds projects his sensitivity, lazy singalong good nature, and old-fashioned romanticism; he even expresses doubts about his 'style' and inability to cope with independent women. Too much of this is tedious, rather like off-cuts from his recent movies, but the reasonable photography and good action material help. Country singer Jerry Reed makes a good heavy, and when Reynolds keeps it simple, his direction suggests the makings of a modest craftsman. CPe

'Gator Bait (aka Swamp Bait)
(Ferd Sebastian/Beverly Sebastian, 1974, US) Claudia Jennings, Sam Gilman, Doug Dirkson, Don Baldwin, Ben Sebastian, Bill Thurman, Clyde Ventura.
93 min.
Despite the tantalising title, this exploiter is a woefully sodden, Z-grade fusion of Deliverance and Gator. In the Louisiana swamplands, the local sheriff's boy (Ventura) frees swamp Valkyrie (Jennings) for what was an accidental killing. The film is devoted to the lumbering efforts of the demented family of the deceased, together with the lapsed forces of law and order, to track down the 'wildcat'. The directors manage to blow every opportunity of the pulp genre. The location is totally wasted (were alligators out of season?), the script and performances devoid of any real energy or brash humour. Sadly, even Claudia Jennings, heroine of the excellent Truck Stop Women, doesn't deliver as she catches snakes with her bare hands and leads her male pursuers a merry dance. IB

Gattaca
(Andrew Niccol, 1997, US) Ethan Hawke, Uma Thurman, Alan Arkin, Jude Law, Loren Dean, Gore Vidal, Ernest Borgnine, Blair Underwood, Tony Shalhoub, Elias Koteas.
106 min.
In the future, geneticists will design test-tube babies to be disease-free. Physical perfection will become the norm, and those flawed specimens born the old-fashioned way will form the new underclass – the 'in-valids'. Vincent Freeman (Hawke), an in-valid

with a heart defect, is only taken seriously in the powerful Gattaca space programme when he assumes the identity of Jerome (Law), a 'valid' who supplies blood, tissue and urine samples in return for shelter (he himself having been crippled in a car accident). The subterfuge is successful – until a murder draws unwelcome scrutiny from the authorities. Self-consciously at a remove from the trashy B-movie sensibilities which have dominated science-fantasy movies in recent times, this harks back to the vacuum-packed, classically alienated dystopia of Brave New World and Fahrenheit 451. Chilly, elegant, and a little bloodless. TCh

Gattopardo, Il
see Leopard, The

Gauntlet, The
(Clint Eastwood, 1977, US) Clint Eastwood, Sondra Locke, Pat Hingle, William Prince, Bill McKinney, Michael Cavanaugh, Carole Cook, Mara Corday.
109 min.
'Big .45 calibre fruit! Macho mentality!' – Eastwood under siege as Sondra Locke leads the assault on his monolithic image. As much comedy as action picture, The Gauntlet mines the vein of humour discovered in The Outlaw Josey Wales: again most of the laughs are at Eastwood's expense. In his most mellow cop role yet, he plays a long-suffering, rather dumb officer who extradites a smart, fast-talking hooker, but ends up hiking her cross country, pursued by mob and cops alike (more identical than alike). The well paced script is an effective mixture of worldliness and naïveté: despite the couple's graphic sparring scenes, in which Eastwood more than meets his match, their relationship remains curiously innocent; a kind of fugitive romanticism pervades. A major source of amusement is watching Eastwood the director leaving Eastwood the actor barely in control throughout. Eastwood's Annie Hall? CPe

Gaunt Stranger, The (aka The Phantom Strikes)
(Walter Forde, 1938, GB) Wilfrid Lawson, John Longden, Alexander Knox, Sonnie Hale, Louise Henry, Patrick Barr, Patricia Roc.
73 min. b/w.
Michael Balcon's experiment in independent production, an adaptation of Edgar Wallace's The Ringer, still looks good despite its low budget. An intelligent script by Sidney Gilliat effectively tightens up the typical Wallace tale of a master of disguise who outwits the police to carry out his errand of righteous vengeance. From nervy opening to unexpectedly upbeat ending, Forde copes in bold, workmanlike fashion with the convoluted plot, and Ronald Neame's moody photography is adequate compensation for the limited studio setting. Splendidly slimy Lawson gives a virtuoso performance as the degenerate miscreant who doggedly refuses to face his doom, Patricia Roc – the darling of the '40s – makes her debut as a snootily wrong-headed secretary, and Hale proves surprisingly proficient at providing comic relief. All in all, a classic British thriller. RMy

Gawain and the Green Knight
(Stephen Weeks, 1973, GB) Murray Head, Ciaran Madden, Nigel Green, Anthony Sharp, Robert Hardy, David Leland, Murray Melvin, Ronald Lacey.
93 min.
Ye olde Englishe poem, filtered through Mallory, Weeks, and United Artists (who tampered with the director's original cut). It's an only just watchable tale of the Arthurian gallant having a go at the grass-coloured magical being, which never makes it as a serious attempt to film the original text, nor as an out-and-out fantasy. Weeks had another try ten years later, remaking it as Sword of the Valiant, with very little more success.

Gawin
(Arnaud Selignac, 1991, Fr) Jean-Hugues Anglade, Wojtek Pszoniak, Catherine Samie, Bruno.
91 min.
Making ET look like a right hard bastard, Gawin is the winsome space-hopping chum of little Felix, sci-fi crazy and suffering from leukaemia. When Felix's doctor starts to mutter balefully that medicine can do no more, stricken widowed Papa (Anglade) decides it's time for extra-terrestrial

forces to take a hand... They seem to have taken a hand in the script as well, since Gawin proceeds with a blithe disregard for plausibility. Clearly conceived as a three Kleenex-box movie, it's guaranteed to leave you dry-eyed, not to say slack-jawed with disbelief. Give or take a couple of flash Beineixian gliding shots in the first minute, it's unmitigated astro-piffle. JRo

Gay Divorcee, The
(Mark Sandrich, 1934, US) Fred Astaire, Ginger Rogers, Alice Brady, Edward Everett Horton, Eric Blore, Erik Rhodes, Betty Grable.
107 min. b/w.
Having insured Fred's legs for the equivalent of £200,000, RKO producer Pandro S Berman launched the Astaire-Rogers musicals with this extensive revamp of Cole Porter's famous stage show. Only the classic 'Night and Day' was retained in the score, with an archetypal dance duet set to it; new songs included 'Let's K-nock K-neez' for the divine Horton and a starlet called Betty Grable. A big, brash production number, 'The Continental', tries to cap the similar item from Flying Down to Rio ('The Carioca'). SG

Gazebo, The
(George Marshall, 1959, US) Glenn Ford, Debbie Reynolds, Carl Reiner, John McGiver, Mabel Albertson, Doro Merande, Bert Freed, Martin Landau.
102 min. b/w.
An amiable black comedy, adapted from Alec Coppel's play, in which Ford plays a TV writer-director, on the verge of the big time (a script commission from Hitchcock), who decides in desperation to murder the blackmailer who is bleeding him white over an amorous indiscretion, afterwards disposing of the body under the gazebo being erected in the garden. It's much too long and leisurely, needlessly incorporating a routine song-and-dance number for Reynolds (as Ford's showbiz wife), and belabouring the plot to show that Ford didn't actually kill anyone. But the central sequence in which Ford (excellent throughout) nervously executes his perfect murder, only to find everything going wrong except the murder itself, is hilarious, and perfectly capped by a call from Hitchcock to ask how his script is coming on, whereupon the despairing Ford asks the Maestro how he would solve the dilemma of a killer with a body to bury and no shovel to do it with. Nice supporting cast, too. TM

Gaze of Ulysses, The
see Ulysses' Gaze

Gazon maudit (French Twist)
(Josiane Balasko, 1995, Fr) Victoria Abril, Josiane Balasko, Alain Chabat, Ticky Holgado, Miguel Bosé, Catherine Hiegel, Catherine Samie, Telsche Boorman, Katrine Boorman.
107 min.
Serial adulterer Laurent (Chabat) has all the women he wants, and in Loli (Abril), a beautiful, blissfully ignorant wife. At first the intrusion of butch, cigar-smoking Marijo (Balasko) seems no more than a minor irritation (her van breaks down outside their home, and Loli immediately takes a shine to her), but when she puts the moves on his wife, Laurent cannot contain his shock and revulsion. His reaction sends the women into each other's arms, and soon he's negotiating for equal conjugal rights. An astute, modern spin on the ménage-à-trois farce, this begins like one of Bertrand Blier's tongue-in-cheek intellectual provocations, with Balasko reprising her unlikely seductress role from Trop belle pour toi! Unlike Blier, however, Balasko (who also wrote and directed) actually seems to like her characters, even as she accentuates their foibles: Laurent's chauvinist hypocrisy, Loli's naïve pride and jealousy, and Marijo's domineering self-confidence. These stereotypes are endowed with rather more dignity than their circumstances allow, and most of the playing is marvellously sympathetic. A very funny and expertly timed farce. TCh

Gebroken Spiegels
see Broken Mirrors

Geburt der Nation, Die
see Birth of a Nation, The

Geheimnisse einer Seele
see Secrets of a Soul

Geisha Boy, The

(Frank Tashlin, 1958, US) Jerry Lewis, Marie McDonald, Sessue Hayakawa, Nobu McCarthy, Barton MacLane, Suzanne Pleshette.
98 min.
One of Jerry Lewis' first comedies away from former partner Dean Martin, this rather flaccid vehicle reveals the mawkish side that would arise more often in his solo efforts. Lewis plays an unsuccessful magician who takes a job entertaining the troops in the Far East. In Japan, a young orphan (as he's euphemistically labelled) becomes attached to this goofy surrogate father. Fortunately, Tashlin's direction supplies some great visual jokes, principally with a live rabbit that is made to seem more of an animated human character. DT

General, The 100

(Buster Keaton/Clyde Bruckman, 1926, US) Buster Keaton, Marian Mack, Glen Cavender, Jim Farley, Frederick Vroom, Joe Keaton.
7,500 ft. b/w.
Keaton's best, and arguably the greatest screen comedy ever made. Against a meticulously evoked Civil War background, Buster risks life, limb and love as he pursues his beloved railway engine, hijacked by Northern spies up to no good for the Southern cause. The result is everything one could wish for: witty, dramatic, visually stunning, full of subtle, delightful human insights, and constantly hilarious. GA

General, The (100)

(John Boorman, 1998, Ire/GB) Brendan Gleeson, Adrian Dunbar, Sean McGinley, Maria Doyle Kennedy, Angelina Ball, Jon Voight, Joe Melia.
124 min.
Dublin, the 1980s and '90s. Martin Cahill (Gleeson) is forever a few steps ahead of the police, cocking a snook at all the authority figures he's detested since a childhood in the slums, defined by poverty, petty crime and priestly abuse. Determined to get his man, Inspector Ned Kenny (Voight) nevertheless views him with grudging respect, but it's only when he arranges full time surveillance that Cahill's loyal gang begin to buckle under pressure; even then, the self-styled Godfather can probably count on the support of his wife (Kennedy), her sister (Ball), his right-hand man Noel (Dunbar), and an amused, hero-hungry public, so that his pranks and perversions of justice go unpunished. But how long can he get away with refusing to hand over a portion of his spoils to the IRA? Boorman's energetic account of Cahill's real-life escapades is notable for its deft characterisations and authenticity: while Cahill's sentiments and actions are appreciated as the exploits of a canny born rebel, we're never allowed to forget that he's also volatile, violent and, whatever his feelings for his family, ultimately self-obsessed. All the performances are impressive, but Gleeson and Voight are especially memorable, lending an almost tragic air of inexorability to Cahill and Kenny's cat-and-mouse games. GA

General Amin (Général Idi Amin Dada)

(Barbet Schroeder, 1974, Fr)
90 min.
The only moment of real insight in a rambling and overlong documentary comes at its climax: 'After a century of colonialism' the commentary asks, 'isn't it in fact a deformed image of ourselves that Amin reflects?' It's a highly pertinent question, and one that a film-maker like Godard could have used to shattering effect. Here, however, it arrives as a postscript to a patchy assemblage of footage. The facts presented are disturbing, but Amin himself emerges as a dumber, more naïve, and more boring version of countless Western politicians. Occasionally, and surprisingly, the man seems prepared to laugh at himself: one of the few unexpected features in an otherwise profoundly depressing and exploitative film. DP

General Line, The (Staroye i Novoye; aka Old and New)

(Sergei Eisenstein, 1929, USSR) Marfa Lapkina, Vasya Buzenkov, Kostya Vasiliev, I Yudin.
8,102 ft. b/w.
The General Line was the project Eisenstein interrupted to make *October*, the epic commissioned to mark the tenth anniversary of the USSR. Neither of these two celebrations of his theory of 'associative montage' (which remain among his most powerful and innovative movies) met with official approval or popular success; Eisenstein was condemned as a 'formalist'; and began the world travels that eventually led him to Mexico. *The General Line* is a comprehensive account of Soviet agricultural policies, showing the struggle for collectivisation of the farms, distinguished (like *October*) by Eduard Tisse's phenomenal photography, by Eisenstein's muscular homo-erotic poetry, and by extraordinary sado-masochistic undercurrents. Fans of Kenneth Anger's *Eaux d'Artifice* should not miss the daringly erethistic cream-separator sequence in *The General Line* on which it is based. TR

General Sahib

see Burra Sahib

Generation, A (Pokolenie)

(Andrzej Wajda, 1954, Pol) Tadeusz Lomnicki, Urszula Modrzynska, Tadeusz Janczar, Roman Polanski, Zbigniew Cybulski.
91 min. b/w.
First part of Wajda's trilogy, completed by *Kanal* and *Ashes and Diamonds*. Those were exciting times for Polish cinema: 'In Poland art fulfils a special function...it carries a certain burden of tradition through the fact that for a hundred years the state did not exist, or it existed only in literature, in art, to which everyone could refer'. Cinema, sometimes laboriously, had to carry the Polish identity. In the '50s, Wajda processed great public events (later too, perforce through analogy), and the trilogy covers the Resistance in Warsaw. *A Generation*, set in occupied Warsaw in 1942 and revolving around the setting up of a youth resistance group, was his first feature, and hews to the Socialist Realist line. Courage, honour and self-sacrifice inform the actions of his hero, who discovers a sense of purpose in unity, the collective and the Party. Hope opens the trilogy, disillusionment closes it, and the final part centres on an individual crisis and a great star performance fit to rank beside James Dean from Zbigniew Cybulski, here featured in a supporting part. One from the heart. BC

Genesis (Génesis)

(Mrinal Sen, 1986, Fr/Ind/Bel/Switz) Shabana Azmi, Naseeruddin Shah, Om Puri, MK Raina.
109 min.
In the past, Mrinal Sen's leftist films have eschewed mystical visions of an India outside history; here he focuses on the collapse of just such an escapist dream. Two men, the Farmer and the Weaver (Shah and Puri) have abandoned the poverty of contemporary India to start life anew in the sprawling ruins of a long lost village. Their only tie with the outside world is the Merchant (Raina), who provides the raw materials and markets for their product; their only connection with the 20th century is the roar of the odd plane jetting across the desert. Alone in their world, the pair build a new society, and their land begins to bloom...until harmony is shattered with the arrival of the Woman (Azmi), a refugee from recent floods. Though Sen's sexual politics may strike western eyes as dubious, the simplistic power of the film is unquestionable. The fifth character is the landscape which comes to bloom, beautifully complemented by a score from Ravi Shankar. GA

Genevieve

(Henry Cornelius, 1953, GB) Dinah Sheridan, John Gregson, Kay Kendall, Kenneth More, Geoffrey Keen, Joyce Grenfell.
86 min.
Everyone seems to remember this gentle comedy – about two couples entering the London to Brighton veteran car race, and indulging in friendly rivalry – with great affection. But with the exception of the delectable Kay Kendall, gorgeously belting out jazz on the trumpet, it just isn't very funny any more; and Larry Adler's whining harmonica score only makes things worse. GA

Genghis Cohn

(Elijah Moshinsky, 1993, GB) Anthony Sher, Robert Lindsay, Diana Rigg, John Wells.
80 min.
Twelve years on, Jewish stand-up comic Cohn (Sher) returns to haunt the SS officer (Lindsay) – now a successful Bavarian police commissioner – who commanded the firing squad which executed him. At the same time, the town is beset by a series of bizarre murders of lovers caught in flagrante, and rumour, intrigue and ambition tip the community into self-destructive chaos. Not a bad idea (from a novel by Romain Gary), and not exactly a bad film – but the black comedy would be far blacker and funnier if the direction and acting weren't so awfully, awfully theatrical. GA

Genou de Claire, Le

see Claire's Knee

Gens de la rizière, Les (Rice People)

(Rithy Panh, 1994, Cambodia/Fr) Peng Phan, Mom Soth, Chhim Naline, Va Simorn, Sophy Sodany.
130 min.
Paris-resident Rithy Panh's first feature (he was previously a documentarist) is an elegaic, unsentimental tribute to his native Cambodia (in 1979, he escaped, aged 16, from a Khmer Rouge camp), and its peasant people, the farmers of the paddy fields. Impressive as it is – the cast of professionals and non-professionals show extraordinary commitment; the landscape, interiors and actors are finely photographed; and the tone is ably sustained – the film is somehow neither as moving nor as satisfying as it promises to be. Focused on a hard-pressed rice-growing family with its Russian-doll-pack of seven daughters, the film, based on a novel by Shannon Ahmad, follows their travails as the seasons turn and the wife takes over the burden of responsibilty after her husband succumbs to a deadly thorn. Rithy Panh elegantly evokes in ethnographic detail the centuries-old agrarian pattern of their lives, the Buddhist icons, the portentous owls. A mysterious dream of the Khmer Rouge entering the village and an end quote from Rilke suggest that narrative is a metaphor for the people's suffering as a whole under Pol Pot. This is not, however, fully developed. Heartbreaking depictions of pestilence, though, and some memorably expressive scenes with children. WH

Gentle Creature, A

see Femme Douce, Une

Gentle Gunman, The

(Basil Dearden, 1952, GB) John Mills, Dirk Bogarde, Elizabeth Sellars, Robert Beatty, James Kenney, Joseph Tomelty, Barbara Mullen, Jack MacGowran.
86 min. b/w.
An Ealing production, this stiff, overplotted tale of IRA internal feuding, shot in spurious *noir* style, nevertheless betrays interesting attitudes. The fact that some emphasis is given to the IRA and its claims is defused by abandoning the political issue in favour of a generalised, wet humanism – Mills and Bogarde, as reconciled Irish brothers (!), slouching into the sunset – and by a typically English focus on Irish character. Beatty, the hard man, can say 'You English came into Ireland as if you stormed into a Cathedral and settled into the nave', and the sense of desecration is nevertheless lost because he is 'Irish', ie. poetic, daft or sinister. If Ealing once mirrored English attitudes, then clearly film-making has progressed but the attitudes haven't. CPea

Gentleman Jim

(Raoul Walsh, 1942, US) Errol Flynn, Alexis Smith, Jack Carson, Alan Hale, Ward Bond, John Loder, Minor Watson, Arthur Shields.
104 min. b/w.
Walsh's reputation is as an action director, but he was equally good as a period illustrator (witness the lazily loving *The Strawberry Blonde*). Here he has the best of both worlds, matching a rich evocation of San Francisco in the 1880s (perhaps a bit heavy on the Irish family brawls) with a vivid account of the pre-Queensberry fight scene, and capping a rumbustious sequence of bouts with a superbly shot version of the gruelling heavyweight championship match between Gentleman Jim Corbett and John L Sullivan in 1892. Lavish, lustrous and none too accurate historically, it's Hollywood at its cavalier best, with a perfectly judged performance from Flynn, brash yet engaging, as the social-climbing Corbett. TM

Gentleman's Agreement

(Elia Kazan, 1947, US) Gregory Peck, Dorothy McGuire, John Garfield, Celeste Holm, Anne Revere, June Havoc, Albert Dekker, Jane Wyatt, Dean Stockwell.
118 min. b/w.
Academy Award-winning but sentimental and muddled account of a journalist (Peck) who passes himself off as a Jew in order to research a series of articles on anti-Semitism, only to find the masquerade entailing a backlash of grief and pressure for his own family. Archetypal Hollywood social comment in that it wears its heart on its sleeve rather than offers any analysis of the problem; and the Fox studio's fondness for 'realism' looks remarkably dated in places. Good performances, however, particularly from Garfield and Holm. GA

Gentlemen Prefer Blondes

(Howard Hawks, 1953, US) Jane Russell, Marilyn Monroe, Charles Coburn, Tommy Noonan, Elliot Reid, George Winslow.
91 min.
A classic musical/social satire, featuring tight script, Hawks' usual humanity of style, and a line-up of sardonic song'n'dance numbers ('Diamonds Are a Girl's Best Friend', etc). A cynical plotline (golddigging cabaret artistes on transatlantic liner crossing) is wonderfully belied by generous sentiment, and the Monroe/Russell sexual stereotypes are used ironically to generate a whole range of erotic gambits: innocence, brashness, temptation, seduction. Interesting, too, that the male parts remain mere foils to the sympathetic sparring relationship of the female leads. Smashing. CA

Gentle Sex, The

(Leslie Howard/Maurice Elvey, 1943, GB) Rosamund John, Joan Greenwood, Lilli Palmer, Joan Gates, Jean Gillie, Joyce Howard, Barbara Waring, Leslie Howard.
93 min. b/w.
Howard's silly framework for this account of the initiation of seven women into the army is annoying and patronising; but beneath the sugary surface there is a frank acknowledgment of the changes wrought by the war. Under the inspired leadership of a wily, sweet-sucking Glaswegian (John), the group grasp their opportunities to become gunners and lorry-drivers with both hands, and unlike the women in the more widely lauded Millions Like Us, without the approval and support of men. The documentary realism necessary to fulfil the film's propagandist function is extended by Howard into a welcoming, if rather bemused celebration of the new equality between the sexes. A fascinating barometer of the changing moral climate of the '40s. RMy

Genuine

(Robert Wiene, 1920, Ger) Fern Andra, Harald Paulsen, Ernst Gronau, John Gottoht, Hans von Twardowsky.
b/w.
Same director, same writer, same cameraman, but...Rushed out six months after The Cabinet of Dr Caligari, Genuine merely goes to prove how dependent the earlier film was on its cast and designers: painted cinema animated by the extraordinary acting skills of Veidt and Krauss. Here, with rotten actors mugging away in César Klein sets which look like recycled leftovers from a Christmas pantomime, Caligari-ism is reduced to grisly travesty. The Pygmalion plot concerns a painter whose creation comes alive, turns nasty after being sold in a slave market, and gloatingly drives her admirers to murder and suicide. Playing this supervamp in unfortunate costumes which at one point lend her a passing resemblance to the Tinman of Oz, Fern Andra leers and squirms like a demented Theda Bara. TM

Geordie (aka Wee Geordie)

(Frank Launder, 1955, GB) Bill Travers, Alastair Sim, Norah Gorsen, Raymond Huntley, Miles Malleson, Duncan Macrae, Stanley Baxter.
99 min.
Worried he's going to lose out on the girl he's after, confirmed weakling Travers builds himself up and enters the Melbourne Olympics as a hammer thrower. An affectionate triumph-of-the-

underdog fable from Launder and Gilliat, chock full of Scots clichés, with Sim stealing every scene as the local laird and lots of familiar faces right down the cast list. From a novel by David Walker. TJ

George and Mildred

(Peter Frazer Jones, 1980, GB) Yootha Joyce, Brian Murphy, Stratford Johns, Norman Eshley, Sheila Fearn, Kenneth Cope.
93 min.
Spun off from a spin-off of a TV sitcom that began in the '60s, this threadbare farce provides lamentable evidence of Wardour Street's profitless dependency on the British TV ratings chart. Murphy's runtish Roper, traditionally played as one of the gambling, grumbling unemployed, has been given a job (setting a Thatcherite example) as a traffic warden. Otherwise it's the same ageist, sexist class structure you know and loathe. Feeble humour even in its half-hour slot, and desperately unfunny at three times the length. MA

George Balanchine's The Nutcracker

see Nutcracker, The

Georg Elser

see Seven Minutes

George of the Jungle

(Sam Weisman, 1997, US) Brendan Fraser, Leslie Mann, Thomas Haden Church, Richard Roundtree, Greg Crutwell, Abraham Benrubi.
92 min.
Based on the characters of Jay Ward's TV cartoon series, this live action feature pitches itself on the level of exotic, anything-goes pantomime, with Tarzan-like George, a talking ape, a pelican, a pet elephant, a pith-helmeted eco-villain (Church), and a willowy but plucky love interest (Mann). Fraser is a natural for the hero, brought up in Bukuvu National Park, Africa, by Ape, his snobbish bookworm butler – incompetently, though, since George can't swing on a vine without crashing his tackle. His mix of bare-faced cheek, infantilism and physical exuberance sets the tone, while the plot's absurdities are acknowledged with disarming candidness. The story is incidental – the villain wants to abduct the talking ape for financial gain – and thankfully the animatronics and computer effects aren't allowed to overwhelm the proceedings. WH

Georgette Meunier

(Tania Stöcklin/Cyrille Rey-Coquais, 1989, WGer) Tiziana Jelmini, Dina Leipzig, Thomas Schunke, Manfred Hulverschiedt.
82 min.
This independent feature, indulgently described as 'black comedy', tells of Georgette's frustrated love affair with brother Emile and her career as a 'black widow' – seducing and poisoning the male citizens of a small German town circa 1900. The necessarily minimalist treatment and a paternal voice-over which prompts the action suggest an adult fairy tale of sorts, though the combination of Inexorable Destiny and inexplicable behaviour tends to obscure any quasi-feminist intent, the incest theme actually debasing the radical thrust of the femme fatale. Likewise, a potentially absorbing fantasy element (she kills with kisses) is thrown away. The writer-directors optimistically equate pretension with wit, and only Jelmini's alarmingly potent Georgette carries much conviction. A mainstream production might have demanded tighter logic, an exploitation movie could have pushed the subversive stuff, but this drab effort comes from no man's land. TCh

Georgia's Friends

see Four Friends

Georgy Girl

(Silvio Narizzano, 1966, GB) Lynn Redgrave, Alan Bates, James Mason, Charlotte Rampling, Bill Owen, Clare Kelly, Rachel Kempson.
99 min. b/w.
Though tame by modern standards, this candid comedy of sexual manners in 'Swinging London' was considered bold for its day. Redgrave is a

frumpy, unattractive dance teacher who is offered an escape from her loneliness by her ageing, married but amorous employer (Mason). Inevitably dated, yet often funny and sometimes surprisingly bleak. A nice cameo by Rampling, too, as Georgy's bitchy, sniping flatmate. NF

German Chainsaw Massacre, The (Das deutsche Kettensagenmassaker)

(Christoph Schlingensief, 1990, Ger) Udo Kier, Karina Fallenstein.
63 min.
A bloody and demented blend of Brechtian political satire and Texas Chainsaw Massacre-style horror, this shrieking gore-fest is set during the first hours after German reunification. Fleeing from the East, hapless victims fall prey to a crazed family of human butchers, who introduce them to the pleasures of the Free Market by noisily hacking, bludgeoning and chainsawing them to death. Abrasive, relentless, cruelly funny and enjoyably deranged. NF

German Sisters, The (Die Bleierne Zeit)

(Margarethe von Trotta, 1981, WGer) Jutta Lampe, Barbara Sukowa, Rüdiger Vogler, Doris Schade, Verenice Rudolph, Luc Bondy.
107 min.
Inspired by the cases of Gudrun Ensslin – the Baader-Meinhof terrorist and Stammheim 'suicide' – and her journalist sister, von Trotta once again takes up questions of the roots and potential paths of women's resistance and revolt, creating a disturbing mosaic of personal and state histories around a sisterly relationship of intriguingly contradictory complexity. As in The Lost Honour of Katharina Blum, terrorism itself is an offscreen phenomenon; its ramifications at the personal level, and its unlabelled reactionary equivalents, marking the film's painful subject across at least a generation: from two schoolgirls watching film of the concentration camps to a young son almost burned alive in the '80s because of his now notorious parentage. A bold assertion of the continuity of history from the culture most willing to deny it, and fine, accessible political film-making. PT

Germany in Autumn (Deutschland im Herbst)

(Heinrich Böll/Alf Brustellin/Bernhard Sinkel/Hans Peter Cloos/Katja Rupé/Rainer Werner Fassbinder/Alexander Kluge/Beate Mainka-Jellinghaus/Maximiliane Mainka/Peter Schubert/Edgar Reitz/Volker Schlöndorff, 1978, WGer) Hannelore Hoger, Katja Rupé, Hans Peter Cloos, Angela Winkler, Helmut Griem.
134 min. b/w & col.
A genuinely collaborative movie, aiming to deal with the state of the West German nation in the months between the Schleyer kidnapping and the Baader-Meinhof deaths in Stammheim Prison. The result centres on paranoia rather than on terrorism as such. Fassbinder brings the issues squarely back home, showing himself arguing with his mother and taking out his aggressions on his late boyfriend Armin. At its best, the film argues that it's impossible to have a 'coherent' left wing position on terrorism. TR

Germany, Pale Mother (Deutschland bleiche Mutter)

(Helma Sanders-Brahms, 1979, WGer) Eva Mattes, Ernst Jacobi, Elisabeth Stepanek, Angelika Thomas.
150 min.
This highly personal account of Sanders-Brahms' own childhood was made for her daughter. Broken into three parts, it simultaneously traces the history of Germany before, during and after World War II, and her own history. In the first part she's the as yet unborn child who comments ironically on her parents; during the war the angle shifts as we watch the mother gather strength and their relationship develop; after the war the husband/father returns, unwittingly bringing emotional destruction with him. The film is overloaded with visual symbolism and runs too long, but the concept and performances more than compensate for the flaws. HM

Germany, Year Zero
(Germain, Anno Zero)
(Roberto Rossellini, 1947, It/WGer) Edmund
Moeschke, Werner Pittschau, Barbara Hintz,
Franz Krüger, Erich Gühne.
74 min. b/w.
A long opening tracking shot through Berlin's
ruins under the Occupation in 1945 is both documentary and a hallucinatory voyage through a
stone age city, the perfect illustration that realist
film can also forge fantasy. It sparks against the
story of a thirteen-year-old boy who works the
black market, sells Hitler souvenirs for chewing-
gum, and who will kill his sick father out of naïve
mercy and regard for the whisperings of his old
Nazi teacher. A horror movie that declines to
tease. DMacp

Germinal
(Claude Berri, 1993, Fr/Bel/It) Gérard
Depardieu, Judith Henry, Renaud, Miou-Miou,
Jean Carmet, Jean-Roger Milo, Laurent
Terzieff.
158 min.
This adaptation of Zola's novel looks superb, as
befits the most expensive French film to date.
From the opening with the coal mine, belching
orange flame, looming out of the dark, to the
strike and riot, all 160 million francs is on screen.
In the novel the miners' unionisation and strike
are matched by the frustrated love story of
Etienne (folk singer Renaud, making an impressive debut) and Catherine (Henry), in the film,
however, the miners are much to the fore – with
the result that the pace slows. The film, from the
director of Manon des Sources, is at its best
exploring man's uneasy relationship with the
earth; the coal dust these people extract from the
ground is killing them as surely as it's keeping a
roof over their heads. Depardieu, as Maheu, is
solid if unspectacular; but Miou-Miou, as his long-
suffering wife, is astonishing, her performance
gaining strength as she loses her beloved family,
one by one, to the pit. NKe

Geronimo:
An American Legend
(Walter Hill, 1994, US) Jason Patric, Gene
Hackman, Robert Duvall, Wes Studi, Matt
Damon, Rodney A Grant, Kevin Tighe,
Steve Reevis.
115 min.
This is the authentically bloody chronicle of the
last Apache leader, as recorded in the memoirs
of one of the cavalrymen who hunted him down.
It's a film about the land and who owns it, the
clash between incompatible cultures, and the
telescoping of history with the apparently inexorable progress of 'civilisation'. Although Wes
Studi (Geronimo) is only fourth billed in the
title role, he has roughly equal screen time with
the other three principals: Southern cavalry officer Gatewood (Patric), General Crook
(Hackman) and chief scout Al Sieber (Duvall).
This being a John Milius story, you'd expect to
find some unspoken bond between enemies, and
there is, but it's a surprise how uncompromisingly the film conveys the ruthlessness of both
sides, the racism and hypocrisy of the white
men, and the ferocity with which the Apache
respond. Walter Hill proves unexpectedly reluctant to force the story, but he makes the red
earth of the Moab desert burn with blood and
shame. TCh

Gert and Daisy's Weekend
(Maclean Rogers, 1941, GB) Elsie Waters,
Doris Waters, Iris Vandeleur, John Slater,
Elizabeth Hunt, Wally Patch, Annie Esmond,
Aubrey Mallalieu.
79 min. b/w.
Music hall's favourite Cockneys, Gert and
Daisy (Elsie and Doris Waters) do their patriotic bit for British cinema in this ramshackle
but lively wartime comedy when they help
evacuate a gang of East End kids to a smart
country house. Needless to say, neither the toffs
nor their butlers and maids much care for the
visitors, who are soon accused of stealing jewellery. Social historians will doubtless be fascinated by the ease with which the sisters turn
the class system upside down. It's hard to
believe that in real life, their brother was that
nice Jack Warner, who used to play PC Dixon
of Dock Green. GM

Gertrud
(Carl Theodor Dreyer, 1964, Den) Nina Pens
Rode, Bendt Rothe, Ebbe Rode, Baard Owe,
Axel Strøbye, Anna Malberg.
116 min. b/w.
Dreyer's last film was adapted from a 1919 play
by Hjalmar Söderberg, but it remains one of the
most purely cinematic discourses of the 1960s. Its
forty-ish protagonist rejects the compromise of
her marriage, but suffers disappointment in her
younger lover and retreats into a serene isolation.
Dreyer directs his actors into performances that
are understated to the point of stillness, and composes shots with a daring economy of decor and
design; he also slows the overall pace to a contemplative minimum. At the same time, though,
he explodes the film's syntax (consecutive shots
that don't quite match; camera movements that
are never quite resolved), so that the placid surface is undermined by a quarry of tiny fissures.
Similarly, the spiritual serenity of the subject is
built upon an aching sense of emotional pain –
and the fact that it's only half-articulated makes
it all the more shattering. TR

Geschichtsunterricht
see History Lessons

Geschriebene Gesicht, Das
see Written Face, The

Getaway, The
(Sam Peckinpah, 1972, US) Steve McQueen, Ali
MacGraw, Ben Johnson, Sally Struthers, Al
Lettieri, Slim Pickens, Richard Bright, Dub
Taylor, Bo Hopkins.
122 min.
An evident precursor to The Driver (Walter Hill
scripted both, this one from Jim Thompson's
novel). The major strength of The Getaway rests
solidly on McQueen's central role, a cold tense
core of pragmatic violence. Hounded by furies (2
mobs, police, a hostile landscape), he responds
with a lethal control, blasting his way through
shootouts that teeter on madness to the loot, the
girl, and Peckinpah's mythic land of Mexico.
Survival, purification, and the attainment of
grace are achieved only by an extreme commitment to the Peckinpah existential ideal of action
– a man is what he does. Peckinpah's own control of the escalating frenzy is masterly; this is
one of his coldest films, but a great thriller. CPea

Getaway, The
(Roger Donaldson, 1994, US) Alex Baldwin,
Kim Basinger, Michael Madsen, James Woods,
David Morse, Jennifer Tilly, Richard
Farnsworth.
115 min.
An efficient if somewhat echoing remake of Sam
Peckinpah's 1972 thriller. Basinger is loving wife
Carol, who sleeps with crooked politico (Woods) to
spring ungrateful husband Doc (Baldwin) from
jail. A big heist turns bloody, and the couple head
for the Mexican border with the Mob, the cops and
double-crosser Madsen on their tail. Peckinpah's
take on Jim Thompson's novel was scripted by
young Walter Hill, and the remake is based on the
same screenplay updated by Amy (Indecent
Proposal) Jones. Director Donaldson keeps the
atmosphere hot and sweaty, with salty dialogue
('The plan is: Shut Up'), exciting shoot-outs at regular intervals and plenty of suspense in between.
It's a treat to see the double-barrelled menace of
Woods and Madsen together at last. TCh

Get Back
(Richard Lester, 1991, GB)
89 min.
This documentary chronicles, in sometimes dated
intercut fashion, the spate of gigging from Paul
McCartney that culminated in his 1990 Get Back
world tour. Despite the fussiness of Lester's
approach, which bungs in lots of '60s footage,
wacky imagery, vegetarian propaganda and
home movies, the best thing here is the music
itself, from McCartney and a (mostly) very good
band. On vintage Beatles rockers like 'Back in the
USSR', 'I Saw Her Standing There' and 'Can't Buy
Me Love', McCartney's voice sounds as good as
the editing room can make it. There are lots of
shots of adoring fans, and Lester even tries to
make them the stars by showing them 'off-duty':
one in a nurse's uniform, another doing bodybuilding exercises. Generally, the style hits that
level of coy futility throughout, split-screens and
all, but at least there are some great songs to
remember from Macca, shamelessly nostalgic in
a way that most pop always has been. SGr

Get Carter
(Mike Hodges, 1971, GB) Michael Caine, Britt
Ekland, John Osborne, Ian Hendry, Bryan
Mosley, Geraldine Moffatt, Dorothy White.
112 min.
Caine plays a London wide-boy who moves up to
Newcastle to sort out a spot of bother, only to discover that his niece is up to her neck in a blue
movie racket. It's slick and cynical, but interesting for the Newcastle locations and its study of a
provincial crime syndicate. In fact it's one of the
relatively few British films of the period, along
with Gumshoe, to exploit its setting to advantage.
CPe

Get Charlie Tully
see Ooh…You Are Awful

Get on the Bus
(Spike Lee, 1996. US) Richard Belzer,
DeAundre Bonds, Andre Braugher, Thomas
Jefferson Byrd, Gabriel Casseus, Albert Hall,
Harry Lennix, Isaiah Washington, Ossie
Davis.
122 min.
Lee assembles a crew of African-Americans travelling from South Central LA to attend Louis
Farrakhan's Million Man March in Washington,
DC, not only to celebrate an historic event, but to
depict a microcosm of black (male) America – and
to highlight the experiences and attitudes that
divide, define and unite men bent on achieving a
sense of brotherhood. Despite evident good intentions and the sterling performances, this ambitious road movie, set over three days in October
1995, never gets very far. Ironically (given some
of Lee's earlier efforts), that's partly down to the
director's determination to create a sense of balance: as scripted by Reggie Rock Bythewood, the
passengers are more ciphers than fully rounded
characters, while the conflict-driven narrative,
which embraces issues of colour, class, criminality, age, religion and sexual politics, is schematic. Whether Farrakhan himself is simply
pro-black, or sexist, anti-white and anti-Semitic
is never really confronted, but the problem is less
one of ideology than drama: though Lee's deft
expertise keeps things pacy and (mostly) plausible, the material can't avoid a certain predictability and, in the end, a preachy
sentimentality. GA

Get Out Your Handkerchiefs
see Préparez vos Mouchoirs

Get Shorty
(Barry Sonnenfeld, 1995, US) John Travolta,
Gene Hackman, Rene Russo, Danny DeVito,
Dennis Farian, Delroy Lindo, James
Gandolfini, John Gries, David Paymer, Linda
Hart, Barry Sonnenfeld.
105 min.
Miami loan shark Chili Palmer (Travolta) follows
a bad debt from one coast to the other, but he
feels right at home when he touches down in LA.
Instead of putting the squeeze on schlock movie-
maker Harry Zimm (Hackman), Chili pitches his
own story concept, agrees to back-off Harry's
most impatient investor, ruthless drugs kingpin
Bo Catlett (Lindo), and casually breaks into
showbiz. Retired scream queen Karen Flores
(Russo) provides an intro to her ex, diminutive
Hollywood superstar Martin Weir (DeVito), and
soon the deal is taking shape: money, murder
and mayhem in Lalaland. By sticking closely to
Elmore Leonard's novel (often word for word),
director Sonnenfeld and screenwriter Scott
Frank have plugged straight into the king of
crime's most underrated attribute: the comedy of
manners. Leonard's flashy characters are always
trying on personalities for size, feeling each other
out with flip remarks and attitude – everybody's
looking for a piece of the action, and the movie
fair fizzes with memorable double-talk and
backchat. As satire, it's pretty broad, and so
throwaway it almost cancels itself out, but the
film-makers never overplay their hand: it's a
breezy, smoothly sophisticated affair, capitalising on Travolta's low-key charisma. Snappily
scored and edited – everything clicks. TCh

Getting Any? (Minna Yatteruka)

(Takeshi Kitano, 1994, Jap) Minoru Iikuza, Shouji Kabyashi, Testuya Yuuki.
108 min. ['export cut' 76 min.]
Kitano may have recut this film since I saw it a few weeks ago [in October 1994], when it was half hilarious, half surprisingly leaden. It begins as an absurd comedy about a young dope bent on losing his virginity: because he believes a fast car or a first-class air ticket will make him irresistible, he gets up to a series of crazy antics in pursuit of sex. The repetitive gags about obsession and incompetence, not unlike those in a *Roadrunner* cartoon, are marvellous; then, when he gets a job acting in a samurai film, the humour drifts off into ever more tired parody (yakuza and monster movies follow). GA

Getting Even With Dad

(Howard Deutch, 1994, US) Macaulay Culkin, Ted Danson, Glenne Headly, Saul Rubinek, Gailard Sartain, Hector Elizondo.
109 min.
Widower Ray Gleason (Danson) is an ex-con who wants to go straight. Timmy (Culkin) is his estranged son who wants to have a father again. When the boy's aunt dumps him on Ray's doorstep, Timmy finds that dad is less interested in looking after him than in carrying out the final heist that will pay for his bakery business, so he videos the crime, hides the loot, and threatens to blow the whistle if father and son don't spend some time together. Hence, the way is paved for an ending visible from a distance of some miles. The script is formula and so is the direction, which leaves the acting. According to the credits, Danson had an acting coach, but he's a warm enough presence to be able to carry a film as slight as this without needing one; instead the coach should have worked with Culkin, who can't even eat a sandwich convincingly. AO

Getting It Right

(Randal Kleiser, 1989, US) Jesse Birdsall, Helena Bonham Carter, Peter Cook, John Gielgud, Jane Horrocks, Lynn Redgrave, Shirley Anne Field, Pat Heywood, Bryan Pringle, Judy Parfitt.
102 min.
Poor Gavin (Birdsall), shy, sensitive, still living at home, and at 31 the oldest virgin in Christendom. But fear not: Gav is about to discover *gurls* in a big way, in all their stereotypical glory. There's Minerva (Carter), anorexic daughter of wealth-seeking Mr Buy-Rite; Joan (Redgrave), a flame-haired 40-year-old who has had material splendour heaped upon her but has 'never been loved'; and Jenny (Horrocks), heart-of-gold hairdresser's assistant. All have the hots for nice boy Gavin. Adapted by Elizabeth Jane Howard from her own novel, the film flits between light comedy and raging pathos, a male fantasy (despite the female author) drenched in a kind of Hampstead world-view. Cameos come and go: Cook adjusts his toupée, and Gielgud camps it up as Minerva's *arriviste* father. half-hearted attempts are made to evoke the style of '60s films like *Georgy Girl*, but it just never clicks. Birdsall is fine, but top marks to Pat Heywood as his mother, who fair steals the whole movie. MK

Getting of Wisdom, The

(Bruce Beresford, 1977, Aust) Susannah Fowle, Sheila Helpmann, Patricia Kennedy, John Waters, Barry Humphries, Kerry Armstrong.
101 min.
Drenched in lushly tasteful Victorian production values, this evocation of a warmly sentimental education, set in a Melbourne girls' boarding school, achieves little by way of justifying an adaptation of Ethel Richardson's autobiographical novel of 1910. A perky feminine independence may have proved controversial at the time of its writing, but here emerges as a mere cliché-ridden prelude to an unseen but inevitable brilliant career. Barry Humphries plays straight as a cleric, when a little of his invigorating vulgarity might have pepped the proceedings up considerably, while Beresford's display of versatility only points up his comparative strengths in the almost all-male worlds of *The Club* and *The Money Movers*. PT

Getting Straight

(Richard Rush, 1970, US) Elliott Gould, Candice Bergen, Robert F Lyons, Jeff Corey, Max Julien, Cecil Kellaway.
125 min.
Muddled (and now dated) campus revolt comedy, distinguished by Elliott Gould's marvellously grizzly performance as an ageing dropout who decides to drop back in again, and resolutely keeps his nose glued to his books in self-defence. Robert Kaufman's script casts a wryly caustic eye not only on the juvenility of the student demands, but also on the hopeless desiccation of academia. Instead of following up, he opts for the easy way out, offering a kitschy metaphor – make love not protest – in a ridiculous scene where Gould strips off to do just that amid the flying fists of a campus riot. Rush's mannered direction is no help, but there are some very funny scenes, not least an oral in which Gould is driven into a corner like a caged lion by an examiner determined to make him admit, through a reinterpretation of *The Great Gatsby*, that Scott Fitzgerald was a closet homosexual. TM

Gettysburg

(Ronald F Maxwell, 1993, US) Tom Berenger, Martin Sheen, Stephen Lang, Jeff Daniels, Sam Elliott, C Thomas Howell, Brian Mallon, Ken Burns.
136 min (Part 1). 118 min (Part 2).
This epic account (made for Turner Television) of the events of the American Civil War preceding, during and after the great battle of 1863 is, finally, a film about men with whiskers – the prodigious facial hair being a signifier of manly courage, moral resolve, undying honour and sensitivity to deathly resolve. It's a movie that parades authenticity, but never settles on its own point of view. Clearly, even now, film-makers are wary of stirring up or offending old allegiances, and here, regrettably, writer/director Maxwell wishes to have his cake and eat it. That said, as officers like Lee (Sheen), Longstreet (Berenger), Chamberlain (Daniels) and Buford (Elliott) struggle to cope with the heavy mantle of history, gazing off to the horizon or tearfully exhorting their men to sacrifice themselves for the greater good, Maxwell does make with the massed troops to spasmodically impressive effect (notably in the Little Round Top fiasco). Of interest chiefly to Civil War buffs and make-up artists. GA

Ghetto

(Mladen Maticevic/Ivan Markov, 1996, Serbia) Goran Cavajda, Partibrejkers, DLM, Svarog, Direktori, Dead Ideas, Darkwood Dub, Plejboj, Supernaut.
72 min.
A drummer wanders though Belgrade in slo-mo, musing on how dreadful life in the city has become over the last few years, and visits rock bands, poets, alternative artists and other rebels and posers. If you know the city, its buildings and rock'n'roll traditions, this all may mean something; others are likely to find it dull, cynical and pretentious. GA

Ghost

(Jerry Zucker, 1990, US) Patrick Swayze, Demi Moore, Tony Goldwyn, Whoopi Goldberg, Vincent Schiavelli, Rick Aviles.
127 min.
The premise is a staple of teen romance: separate hero and heroine so that there's plenty of yearning but no danger of any squelchy business. The difference here is that the young couple are allowed a brief but memorable moment of on-screen passion; and the thing that comes between them is death. Swayze, he of the acting ability of a corpse, is ideal as the murdered yuppie who learns how to use his ghostly powers to foil a dastardly plot; Moore, as the grieving girlfriend, displays the animation of a dishcloth. Luckily, Whoopi Goldberg is on hand to ham it up gloriously in abetting the lovers with her newly discovered psychic powers. But the real credit for turning a minor mystic romance into one of the most enjoyable movies of the year rests on an excellent script by Bruce Joel Rubin, and on the surprisingly sure direction of Jerry Zucker. He borrows a roving camera from Sam Raimi, a penchant for shooting into and through solid matter from David Lynch; and the dissolves between scenes cleverly echo Swayze's ability to walk through walls. DW

Ghost and Mrs Muir, The

(Joseph L Mankiewicz, 1947, US) Gene Tierney, Rex Harrison, George Sanders, Edna Best, Vanessa Brown, Anna Lee, Robert Coote, Natalie Wood.
104 min. b/w.
Apprentice work, comparatively speaking, not scripted by Mankiewicz himself (although he contributed), but still astonishingly characteristic in its airy philosophical speculations about the imagination and its role as a refuge when the salty ghost of a sea captain (Harrison) befriends a beautiful widow (Tierney) and intervenes to save her from the cad she is thinking of marrying. Leaning too heavily towards light comedy, Mankiewicz doesn't get the balance quite right, so that the tale of a romance tenuously bridging two worlds isn't quite as moving as it should be when reality ultimately reasserts its claims. A hugely charming film, nevertheless, beautifully shot (by Charles Lang), superbly acted, and with a haunting score by Bernard Herrmann. TM

Ghost and the Darkness, The

(Stephen Hopkins, 1996, US) Michael Douglas, Val Kilmer, Tom Wilkinson, Bernard Hill, John Kani, Om Puri, Emily Mortimer.
110 min.
The British Empire's steaming progress across East Africa is stalled by two lions that wreak such terror on the natives pressed into building a railway bridge that the project falls dangerously behind schedule. As the bodies mount, Irish engineer John Patterson (Kilmer) is joined by the famous game hunter Remington (Douglas) to tackle 'The Ghost' and 'The Darkness'. Teddy Roosevelt called Col Patterson's *The Man-Eaters of Tsavo* 'the most thrilling book of true stories ever written', and William Goldman's script begins with the boast: 'Even the most improbable parts of the story really happened.' Too bad director Hopkins (*Predator 2*) wouldn't know the truth if it bit him. He renders this mildly promising material so crassly, we might be watching a belated *Jaws* rip-off. All the elements are here: the prowling POV shots as the lions size up their next victim; the merciless capitalist who's the real villain of the piece (Wilkinson – 'I don't care about you; I don't care about 30 dead; I only care about my knighthood!'); and Douglas doing his Robert Shaw impression as the swaggering, whisky-swigging hunter. The film looks expensive and is, occasionally, tense. It's also risibly staged and edited, with incongruous cutaways to flora and fauna, and downright sheepish when it comes to explaining away colonialism. TCh

Ghost Breakers, The

(George Marshall, 1940, US) Bob Hope, Paulette Goddard, Richard Carlson, Paul Lukas, Willie Best, Anthony Quinn, Noble Johnson.
82 min. b/w.
One of Hope's finest comedies, a sequel from Paramount to the success of the previous year's *The Cat and the Canary*, this sees him accompanying the gorgeous Ms Goddard to the West Indies, where she has inherited a haunted Gothic castle. Meetings with ghosts, zombies, and all manner of spooky phenomena occur, allowing Hope ample space to demonstrate his customary capacity for cowardice and alarm. But although the general situation is much the same as in *The Cat and the Canary*, it works better here because the film provides thrills as well as laughs, thanks to Marshall's deft and delicate direction, Charles Lang's shadowy camerawork, and Hans Dreier's authentically Gothic art direction. GA

Ghostbusters

Ivan Reitman, 1984, US) Bill Murray, Dan Aykroyd, Sigourney Weaver, Harold Ramis, Rick Moranis, Annie Potts, William Atherton.
105 min.
Ghostbusters combines two of the most popular Hollywood products in recent years: *National Lampoon/Saturday Night Live*-style comedy and state-of-the-art special effects. But the story of a trio of incompetent 'experts' in the paranormal (Murray, Aykroyd and Ramis), who set up as ghostbusters after they are canned from their college sinecures, is less cynical a construction than it sounds. Reitman shows greater flair at controlling the anarchic comic rhythms of the *Lampoon/SNL* crowd than most of the directors who have attempted that hopeless task, and the

effects are truly astonishing. *Close Encounters* meets *Animal House*, incidentally giving Murray's sleazily self-confident persona his best leading part to date. MB

Ghostbusters II

(Ivan Reitman, 1989, US) Bill Murray, Dan Aykroyd, Sigourney Weaver, Harold Ramis, Rick Moranis, Ernie Hudson, Annie Potts, Peter MacNichol, Harris Yulin, David Margulies, Kurt Fuller, Janet Margolin, Wilhelm von Homburg.
108 min.
A river of gunk flows beneath the sidewalks of New York, growing ever bigger in response to people's nasty thoughts. The Ghostbusters confront the sticky philosophical issues with characteristic finesse, but overall this much-hyped sequel fails to recapture the energy of the original. Even the demonic stature of the chief villain (von Homburg), who wants to possess Weaver's baby, fails to inject consistent tension. The film is largely an excuse for a cast get-together, with the Ghostbusters, under judicial restraining order after the havoc wreaked in part one, suffering lives of semi-obscurity. Murray fronts a cable TV show, Aykroyd and Hudson are entertainers to the 'ungrateful yuppie larva' at children's parties, Ramis continues his research. Weaver is a single parent divorcee (and ex-lover of Murray), and her imperilled sprog brings the team back into action. This attempt to inject novelty into the plot by way of an endangered infant is little more than a convenience, while the rest is all too familiar. CM

Ghost Camera, The

(Bernhard Vorhaus, 1933, GB) Henry Kendall, Ida Lupino, S Victor Stanley, George Merritt, Felix Aylmer, Fred Groves, John Mills, Davina Craig.
64 min. b/w.
A rough and ready little comic mystery, from a story by J Jefferson Farjeon, about a chemist who finds a camera in the backseat of his car, develops the film and smells a murder, with John Mills as the ultra innocent suspect of shifty detective Merritt. This 'quota quickie' was made by Vorhaus at Twickenham for Julius Hagen and, aside from the David Lean editing credit, is chiefly of interest for the upper-class innocence and what now seems the utterly extraordinary accent and delivery of Henry Kendall, as the chemist. JPy

Ghost Catchers

(Edward F Cline, 1944, US) Ole Olsen, Chic Johnson, Gloria Jean, Martha O'Driscoll, Leo Carrillo, Andy Devine, Lon Chaney Jr, Walter Catlett.
67 min. b/w.
Third of the four zany comedies with which Olsen and Johnson revived a flagging career during the '40s. Best remembered for *Hellzapoppin*, they were even better in *Crazy House*. This one, with the pair as nightclub entertainers exorcising a haunted house, is patchier, not least because it is saddled with far too much plot. Funny, though, with the same riot of non-sequiturs and vaudeville gags. TM

Ghost Chase

(Roland Emmerich, 1987, WGer) Jason Lively, Jill Whitlow, Tim McDaniel, Paul Gleason, Chuck Mitchell, Leonard Lansink.
89 min.
With its silly script, lame acting, naff special effects, and laughable model work, this unfunny supernatural comedy looks like the sort of film its leading characters – a pair of teenage home moviemakers (Lively and McDaniel) – might have made themselves. Lively is hoping his grandfather's bequest will save their latest production and lure back his much put-upon leading lady, Whitlow. His inheritance, however, turns out to be a suitcase of junk, including an old clock. But piranha-loving studio boss Gleason is very interested in the suitcase, and hires a bumbling Kraut stereotype (Lansink) to steal it. The clock's chimes at midnight fail to turn McDaniel into Orson Welles, but they do help him to dream up some ideas for a new movie. Wisps of fog then bring to life an animatronic model of grandfather's old butler, and a predictable tale of stolen inheritance unfolds. The most inventive thing here is footage from *Night of the Living Dead* shown on a projector without the spools going round. NF

Ghost Dance

(Ken McMullen, 1983, GB) Leonie Mellinger, Pascale Ogier, Robbie Coltrane, Jacques Derrida, Dominique Pinon.
100 min. b/w & col.
A film to watch rather than to analyse or write about (though it stubbornly encourages both activities). Its pleasures – which are not consistent over 100 minutes – are intensely visual: a beachscape, blighted urban landscape, a city by night, evocatively photographed by Peter Harvey. Evocation is the film's key theme. A 'calling up' of images, myths and memories from a past which, according to philosopher Jacques Derrida (who is 'interviewed' in one sequence), was never present. Ghosts, then, but in the Freudian sense of 'internalised figures from the past' who collectively make their presence known to us. These myths, the film argues, seek to make historical sense out of historical chaos, and in the present electronic age they are omnipresent – in data banks, and even at the end of a telephone line. Quite how the thesis connects with the narrative – Ogier and Mellinger drifting around Paris and London and running into the bulky frame of Coltrane – remains a mythtery. MA

Ghost Goes West, The

(René Clair, 1936, GB) Robert Donat, Jean Parker, Eugene Pallette, Elsa Lanchester, Everley Gregg, Hay Petrie.
90 min. b/w.
Only the obsessively cosmopolitan Korda could have put together this British film, with its French director, its American writer (Robert Sherwood) and its story from *Punch* about a Scottish castle transported to Florida along with its ghost. The result of this geographical potpourri is so silly that it's almost disarming – especially with the gracefully romantic Donat wandering about with his honey voice, kilt and bagpipes. But total delight is kept at bay by the obviousness of the satire on US habits, the obviousness of the sets, and the comparative waste of Clair's talents. GB

Ghost in the Shell (Kokaku Kidotai)

(Mamoru Oshii, 1994, Jap/GB) voices: Richard George, Mimi Woods, William Frederick.
83 min.
Set in 2029 and using inspired computer animation, Oshii's sci-fi *anime* conjures up a dazzling, futuristic cityscape that, sadly, is not matched by the human landscapes at the heart of the story. The *Blade Runner* theme of identity as a function of memory is raised but not explored. Cybercop Kusanagi has a synthetic personality, silicon breasts and an identity crisis. Ordered to track down the Puppetmaster, who can hack into human brains, she and her bland sidekick Bateau become embroiled in a conspiracy involving a secret government project, inter-departmental rivalries and a computer virus that's mutated into a being with a sense of its own destiny. All credit to Britain's Manga Entertainment for co-funding this ambitious project with the Japanese producers of *Akira*, but much more attention should have been paid to the script and disastrous dubbed dialogue. NF

Ghost of Frankenstein, The

(Erle C Kenton, 1942, US) Cedric Hardwicke, Lon Chaney Jr, Lionel Atwill, Bela Lugosi, Ralph Bellamy, Evelyn Ankers, Dwight Frye.
68 min. b/w.
No masterpiece but better than its reputation, this picks up where *Son of Frankenstein* left off, with Lugosi's Igor retrieving the monster (now played by Chaney, alas) from the sulphur pit. Relishable performances from Hardwicke and Attwill as scientists at cross-purposes, the former determined to endow the monster with a sane brain, the latter slyly playing along with Lugosi's mad plan to have his transplanted so that he can dominate the world in the monster's body. The pair make it great fun. TM

Ghost of St Michael's, The

(Marcel Varnel, 1941, GB) Will Hay, Claude Hulbert, Charles Hawtrey, Derek Blomfield, Felix Aylmer, Raymond Huntley, John Laurie.
82 min. b/w.
Hay's first picture with Ealing stuck to a tried routine, with his seedy schoolmaster and bois-

terous pupils evacuated from the Blitz to a spooky castle on Skye where rebellious Hawtrey whisks up further mischief among his fellow students. Meanwhile, the rest of the plot (by Angus Macphail and John Dighton) works in a mystery bagpiper and the by now customary unmasking of a Nazi spy ring. TJ

Ghosts from the Past

see Ghosts of Mississippi

Ghost Ship, The

(Mark Robson, 1943, US) Richard Dix, Russell Wade, Edith Barrett, Ben Bard, Edmund Glover, Skelton Knaggs, Lawrence Tierney, Sir Lancelot.
69 min. b/w.
This Val Lewton production may not scale the heights of *Cat People* or *I Walked with a Zombie*, but it has its impressive moments. A brooding tale of mysterious deaths on board a ship captained by the haunted, moody Dix, it's perhaps most notable for its scene of a sailor crushed to death by an enormous chain in the hold, and for its remarkable narration by a seemingly omniscient deaf-mute. The first, sea-girt half is best, darkly atmospheric and full of pulp poetry; when the story moves ashore, things come down to earth a little, but by then the spell is cast.

Ghosts of Mississippi (aka Ghosts from the Past)

(Rob Reiner, 1996, US) Alec Baldwin, Whoopi Goldberg, James Woods, Craig T Nelson, Susanna Thompson, Lucas Black, William H Macy.
130 min.
Thirty years after the event, Assistant DA Bobby DeLaughter (Baldwin) is out to secure a conviction for the murder of Medgar Evers, one-time chief civil rights worker in the frontline state of Mississippi. True, DeLaughter, in association with several hard-working colleagues and with the key involvement of Evers' widow Myrlie, tracked down new witnesses and a lost murder weapon to help bring a case against Byron De La Beckwith (Woods, Oscar nominated), originally acquitted after two hung juries. Certainly the DA, who'd been 11 at the time of the killing in 1963, had marital problems because of the pressure and unpopularity of the case, but no amount of emotional ballast in the film can make up for the tedium and repetition inevitable when a murder is shown and then dissected in two separate court hearings. Indeed, the only pluses are the ever-watchable Woods and Whoopi Goldberg's excellent, understated showing as Evers' widow. SGr

Ghosts...of the Civil Dead

(John Hillcoat, 1988, Aust) Dave Field, Mike Bishop, Chris De Rose, Nick Cave, Freddo Dierck, Vincent Gil.
93 min.
Hillcoat makes a remarkable debut with this brutal depiction of prison life. The technology appears futuristic, but the New Generation prison under scrutiny is very much a contemporary phenomenon based on the production team's research. The film unfolds in flashback, detailing the violent incidents which necessitated a 'lockdown' at Central Industrial prison. Despite the protection offered to guards by hi-tech supervision rooms, the inmates – after months of administrative provocation and manipulation – exact bloody revenge on what they perceive to be their oppressors. Hillcoat makes few concessions to commercial conventions, such as establishing a sympathetic protagonist. The result is unrelenting and harrowing as the focus rapidly shifts between all the aggrieved. Pornography, murder, rape, theft, and drugs are all dealt with in raw fashion, and although the cumulative effect is exceptionally disturbing, the film ultimately manages to elicit passionate concern over the future of our prison service. CM

Ghost Story

(John Irvin, 1981, US) Fred Astaire, Melvyn Douglas, Douglas Fairbanks Jr, John Houseman, Craig Wasson, Patricia Neal, Alice Krige, Jacqueline Brookes.
110 min.
Disastrous distillation of Peter Straub's overrated but at least tolerably coherent novel. The action is now almost as arthritic as the perfor-

mances of the quartet of golden oldies who sit around regaling each other with ghost stories while the demonic spirit of a girl they wronged in their youth rampages around wreaking vengeance. The horror, weakly and predictably managed by Irvin, is mainly confined to tiresomely repetitive shots of the rotting flesh that lurks beyond the demon's pretty face. TM

Ghoul, The

(T Hayes Hunter, 1933, GB) Boris Karloff, Ernest Thesiger, Cedric Hardwicke, Dorothy Hyson, Anthony Bushell, Ralph Richardson, Kathleen Harrison.
79 min. b/w.
Slow-burning and extremely uneven chiller with Karloff as a professor who believes that a ring stolen from an Egyptian tomb will grant him immortality. However, when Karloff lays down to die, his servant steals the gem, and the professor comes back to life to wreak a terrible revenge. The build-up is too slow, and the later scenes degenerate into ill-judged humour and Old Dark House clichés. Keep an eye out for Richardson, making his screen debut as a phony vicar. NF

Ghoul, The

(Freddie Francis, 1975, GB) Peter Cushing, John Hurt, Alexandra Bastedo, Gwen Watford, Veronica Carlson, Don Henderson.
87 min.
We're back in the world of Hammer production values (now subtly calling themselves Tyburn), where no moorland scene is complete without a smoke-bomb billowing away just out of camera range, and well up to the usual mediocre level of British horror. Violin-playing ex-missionary Cushing arrives back from India with A Horrible Secret and a mystical servant (Watford). Bright young things crash their motor outside the front gate, and are whisked away in by poor mad Tom (Hurt, sadly wasted). You should be able to fill in the other details. The familiar brisk script ('These marshes were used by the army as a training area, but they lost too many men') is by John Elder. AN

Ghoulies

(Luca Bercovici, 1984, US) Peter Liapis, Lisa Pelikan, Michael Des Barres, Jack Nance, Peter Risch, Tamara De Treaux.
84 min.
Like Trancers, an amiable low-budget confection from the fun factory of Charles Band, who seems to be following in Corman's footsteps as the eminence grise of the rip-roaring rip-off exploiter. Jonathan (Liapis) moves with his girlfriend into a dilapidated mansion he has inherited, and soon develops an unhealthy interest in black magic rites. His eyes glow dayglo green as he literally assumes the mantle of his father and conjures up the toothy little familiars of the title, a duo of dwarves and a temptress with a lethally long tongue. Dad's putrefying corpse gets tired of pushing up daisies and instead pushes up grave dirt to make a spectacular comeback. Most of the supporting cast wind up wound in sheets, but the stalk'n'slaughter is of a distinctly lighthearted hue, and the ghoulies themselves (sort of down-market gremlins) are given to hiding their eyes when anything remotely gruesome occurs. More zesty black comedy than horror. AB

Ghouls, The

see Flesh and the Fiends, The

Giant

(George Stevens, 1956, US) Elizabeth Taylor, Rock Hudson, James Dean, Mercedes McCambridge, Carroll Baker, Dennis Hopper, Chill Wills, Jane Withers, Sal Mineo, Rod Taylor.
201 min.
Stevens' sprawling epic of Texan life, taken from Edna Ferber's novel, strives so hard for Serious Statements that it ends up as a long yawn. Dealing with the two men who love Taylor – strait-laced cattle baron Hudson, and the less respectable rancher who strikes it rich with oil (Dean, a strange spectacle in himself as he turns grey) – the film attempts to conduct some sort of attack on rampant materialism, as well as offering an elegy for the times that have a-changed. But the pace is so plodding, and the general effect so stultifyingly unsubtle, that one is left impressed only by the fine landscape photogra-

phy and Dean's surprisingly convincing portrayal of a middle-aged man. To see the overblown, soft-centred nature of the film, one need only compare it with Sirk's vitriolic account of Texan family life in Written on the Wind. GA

Giant of Marathon, The (La Battaglia di Maratona)

(Jacques Tourneur, 1959, It/Fr) Steve Reeves, Mylène Demongeot, Daniela Rocca, Daniele Varga, Sergio Fantoni, Alberto Lupo, Gianni Loti, Ivo Garrani, Philippe Hersent.
87 min.
Philippides (Reeves), victor of the 490 BC Olympics, is proclaimed leader of the Athenian Sacred Guard and in due course defeats Darius the Persian at the Battle of Marathon. A well-plotted (in a bare-bones sort of way) and quite sprightly tale of double dealing, photographed by Mario Bava (who a year later launched his career as a cult horror director), with Fantoni as the heartless woman-killer Theocritus, and Rocca as the matronly sacrificial love interest. Pretty ordinary (not to say ludicrous), but some inventive and brutal underwater sequences. JPy

Giant Spider Invasion, The

(Bill Rebane, 1975, US) Barbara Hale, Steve Brodie, Leslie Parrish, Alan Hale, Robert Easton, Kevin Brodie, Bill Williams.
82 min.
Something of a hotch-potch as Rebane jumbles comic strip with genuinely unsettling horror. Real spiders are used to reasonably good effect, whereas the one giant specimen, despite a spirited first appearance, is patently mechanical and sadly undemonstrative. Still, the film starts with gusto: gamma rays crash into a Wisconsin farm, opening up a sort of grisly parallel universe, and scattering alien rocks that in addition to housing the spiders are lined with diamonds. Thereafter it becomes a tangle of technological mumbo-jumbo, an elderly courtship between Hale and Brodie, Old Testament fire and brimstone from a revivalist preacher, a painfully jolly sheriff, an asinine cub reporter, and a drunken wife who constantly berates her slobbish husband. Apart from the monumentally stilted script which provides many a chuckle, one of the highlights must be when Leslie Parrish (the drunken wife) sips a Bloody Mary which, unknown to her, contains a pulverised arachnid enemy. IB

G.I. Blues

(Norman Taurog, 1960, US) Elvis Presley, Juliet Prowse, Robert Ivers, Leticia Roman, James Douglas, Arch Johnson.
104 min.
First in a series of nine bland Presley vehicles directed by Taurog, and the film which engendered a career formula of tepid, routine comedy-musicals. Just out of the army himself, a subdued Elvis plays a guitar-strumming GI in West Germany, romances the forbidding Prowse, serenades unpardonably cute children, has the occasional fist fight, and sleepwalks to the set of his next film. AC

Gidget

(Paul Wendkos, 1959, US) Sandra Dee, Cliff Robertson, James Darren, Arthur O'Connell, Joby Baker, Yvonne Craig, Doug McClure.
95 min.
Dee hangs out for the summer with clean-living college surfers on Malibu Beach. She falls for Darren, but he's in love with his surfboard. Sandra soon puts matters right by making the big chump jealous. This winsome comedy – a sort of Baywatch of its day – spawned several sequels and a TV series (with Sally Field) and made a mint for Columbia. GM

Gift, The

(Marc Evans/ Red Saunders, 1990, GB) Tat Whalley, Jodhi May, Emma-Louise Harrington, Cynthia Greville, Jeff Rawle, Jacqueline Tong.
102 Min.
Loosely based on the TV Series, this is a fairly gripping supernatural drama for older children. On a visit to his grandparents' Welsh cottage, 14-year-old Davy (Whalley) learns that he has inherited the family gift for clairvoyance. returning home with his young sister (Harrington), he is assailed by a stream of disturbing premoni-

tions involving armed men in grotesque masks and Western-style coats – the very men with whom Davy's father has been overheard in clandestine converstation. Younger kids may get restive because of the lack of action with the situation only becoming clear towards the end. That said, there are a number of nail-biting moments, extremely inventive camera angles, and marvellously understated performances from Whalley, Jodhi May (as the only classmate to understand Davy's predicament), and Cynthia Greville as the kindly but somewhat sinister grandmother. Pity about the cotton-wool soundtrack. DA

Gigi

(Vincente Minnelli, 1958, US) Leslie Caron, Maurice Chevalier, Louis Jourdan, Hermione Gingold, Jacques Bergerac, Eva Gabor, Isabel Jeans.
116 min.
Not a Broadway-based musical but a screen original, derived from Colette's short novel set in turn-of-the-century Paris, with famous if vapid songs by Lerner and Loewe ('I Remember It Well', 'Thank Heaven for Little Girls'). But the dominating creative contribution comes from Minnelli and Cecil Beaton (responsible for production design and costumes). The combination of these two visual elitists is really too much – it's like a meal consisting of cheesecake, and one quickly longs for something solid and vulgar to weigh things down. No doubt inspired by the finicky, claustrophobic sets and bric-à-brac, the cast tries (with unfortunate success) to be more French than the French, especially Chevalier. The exception is Gingold, who inhabits, as always, a world of her own. GB

G.I. Jane

(Ridley Scott, 1997, US/GB) Demi Moore, Viggo Mortensen, Anne Bancroft, Jason Beghe, Scott Wilson, Lucinda Jenney.
125 min.
This humourless variant on Private Benjamin puts Moore through her paces as an intelligence officer selected as the first woman to undergo combat training with the US Navy SEALs. Everyone expects her to fail. Mortensen – the sadistic/benevolent master chief – abuses his recruits, but Demi takes it like a man. She shaves her head – a moment covered with half a dozen cameras, as if it were the helicopter attack in Apocalypse Now! All the movie lacks is real combat, so the script cooks up an excuse for a raid on Libya, where the star can celebrate the ultimate emancipation: she can kill for her country. It's a toss up what's most depressing about all this. Moore's grim self-determinism is self-defeating. She's fit all right – but an exercise video might have been more entertaining. The hardline feminism is such a reductionist position, and the basic training genre affords so little room for manoeuvre, that the picture's an irrelevance before it's even begun. TCh

Gilda

(Charles Vidor, 1946, US) Rita Hayworth, Glenn Ford, George Macready, Joseph Calleia, Steve Geray, Gerald Mohr.
110 min. b/w.
Ford plays a drifting gambler who gets adopted by a German casino owner (Macready) in Buenos Aires, only to become embroiled in a misogynistic ménage-à-trois with the German and his wife (Hayworth). The script is laced with innuendoes and euphemisms; and Ford finds himself as a character whose sexual attributes are not only ambiguous, but bordering on the perverse as his misogyny gradually gains the upper hand. Never has the fear of the female been quite so intense; and the themes that took wing in this extraordinary piece of cinema finally came to roost in such sexual noirs as Carnal Knowledge and Last Tango in Paris. GSa

Gilsodom

(Im Kwon-taek, 1985, SKor) Kim Ji-mi, Sin Song-il, Han Ji-il, Kim Ji-yong.
102 min.
In the summer of 1983, South Korea's national obsession was a TV programme designed to reunite families separated in the Korean War thirty-three years earlier. Im Kwon-taek's movie takes the broadcasts as a documentary starting point, then spins off into a Fassbinderesque

fiction about a dispersed family that comes back together, only to find that the pieces no longer fit. The issues are adult, and so is the treatment: no melodrama, no tub-thumping, but a piercing analysis of social and psychological blocks. TR

Gimme Shelter
(David Maysles/Albert Maysles/Charlotte Zwerin, 1970, US) The Rolling Stones, Ike and Tina Turner, Jefferson Airplane.
90 min.
The Altamont movie, and something of a bummer: if you love the Stones, you're likely to be irritated by the fact that the camera stays on Mick Jagger for virtually every frame; if you're keen to understand why the notorious murder took place and what responsibility the musicians should admit to, you're left with a vacuous look of shock and confusion on the singer's face; and if you get off on violence accompanied by music played loud and raw, you'll love it. Still, it is a reminder that the '60s were not entirely about love, peace and limp liberalism. GA

Ginger & Fred (Ginger e Fred)
(Federico Fellini, 1986, It/Fr/WGer) Giulietta Masina, Marcello Mastroianni, Franco Fabrizi, Frederick von Ledenburg, Augusto Poderosi, Martin Maria Blau.
127 min.
The absence of Fellini's name before the title seems a just indication of a return to something warmer, quieter and more intimate than his grandiose freak shows. Confirming this is his reunion with his wife Masina after a gap of some 23 years, and with Mastroianni, so often his alter ego in the past. They play a couple of old hoofers, who used to tour the boards doing a respectful homage to Astaire and Rogers; they are being brought together after all these years by a TV show in Rome. A long first half, chronicling Ginger's return to the city, shows the place to be in the grip of much general urban decay, and allows Fellini his usual wallowing in all the quirky sideshows (a dead pig, lit up with fairy lights, dangles from the railway station roof). But once the couple finally get together, a warmth which Fellini has not displayed for years gradually seeps all over the screen. She is still trim, a courageous old fighter; he is seedy, but with an ironic detachment. Not even Fellini's deadly sarcasm about TV's horrible degradation of all human values can quite dim the magic that they restore with their little dance. As usual, Fellini doesn't have a lot to say; but it amounts to considerably more than his usual marginal doodlings, and it is irresistibly charming. CPea

Giornata Particolare, Una
see Special Day, A

Girasoli, I
see Sunflower

Girl Can't Help It, The
(Frank Tashlin, 1956, US) Jayne Mansfield, Tom Ewell, Edmond O'Brien, Julie London, Henry Jones.
99 min.
The quintessential '50s rock film, containing legendary appearances from Fats Domino, the Platters, Little Richard and Gene Vincent among its seventeen numbers, though the greatest musical moment is perhaps Eddie Cochran belting out '20 Flight Rock'. The story is a fairly biting satire on the PR worlds of rock and advertising, with Ewell as a press agent and Mansfield as a dumb blonde who rockets to stardom after imitating a prison siren on a rock record. This is the film in which Tashlin made Mansfield hold two milk bottles next to her boobs for a momentary visual gag; and he was capable of even crueller humour, as the sequel *Will Success Spoil Rock Hunter?* proved. DP

Girlfriends
(Claudia Weill, 1978, US) Melanie Mayron, Anita Skinner, Eli Wallach, Christopher Guest, Amy Wright, Viveca Lindfors, Bob Balaban, Mike Kellin.
88 min.
The heroine of Weill's chronicle of a woman in New York today – not pretty, not gamine, not even *jolie laide* – is an apprentice 'art' photogra-

pher, an uneasy heterosexual in a world of obsessively potato-mashing males, who is bereft when her poetry-writing flatmate marries and moves out. The slightly spaced gay dance freak who replaces her gets chucked (nice touch) when she borrows our heroine's blouse. But not before she catalyses the film's sidelong appraisal of lesbianism – treated, unusually, as a fair option. The net effect is a warm (if not entirely cosy) liberal feminism. MM

Girlfriends, The
see Amiche, Le

Girlfriend, The (La Amiga)
(Jeanine Meerapfel, 1988, WGer/Arg) Liv Ullmann, Cipe Lincovsky, Federico Luppi, Victor Laplace, Harry Baer, Lito Cruz.
108 min.
This fragmented history of a relationship between two women explores elasticity of friendship, loyalty and strength, and attempts to parallel the women's differing experiences of oppression. Raquel, a Jewish child refugee from Berlin, and Maria grow up in Buenos Aires in the '40s and '50s. Raquel (Lincovsky) realises her desire to become a well-known actress; Maria (Ullmann) marries a local boy and has three children. The two meet again in 1978, shortly after Maria's eldest has been abducted by 'security forces'. Anti-Semitic attacks scare Raquel into fleeing to Berlin, to return to an uneasy democracy of sorts when Argentina's military government falls. Maria has devoted herself to an uncompromising struggle to locate her missing son, one of many. Raquel has exorcised herself in Berlin (but it's a shady part of the narrative) and returns somehow more reflective; Maria has been transformed from passive onlooker to vociferous leader of 'The Mothers'. The story rattles on movingly and competently, but might have been more fulfilling had the themes been better balanced: the dialectic only hints at similarities between the opression faced in Europe in the thirties and Argentina in the seventies, at the anti-Semitism that surfaced during both traumatic periods. JGl

Girl from Lorraine, A (La Provinciale)
(Claude Goretta, 1980, Fr/Switz) Nathalie Baye, Angela Winkler, Bruno Ganz, Dominique Paturel, Roland Monod, Jean Obé, Henri Poirier.
112 min.
Single, stifled and 31, Baye's 'provinciale' uproots for a Paris peopled largely with fellow exiles (Swiss pill salesman Ganz, struggling German actress Winkler) in search of work and...well, she's not quite sure what else. What she doesn't want, but all she finds, is a succession of relationships set in parentheses, circumscribed as much by economics as emotions. Ganz's promotion ends their affair; friend Winkler sells herself to keep kids and career together. Baye is an only slightly tougher cousin of Goretta's tragic 'lacemaker', but every bit as 'innocent', and her director really has nothing new to say in this insubstantially vague portrait of sensitivity and metropolitan moral recession. A romanticist's tut-tutting just doesn't cut deep enough: it's no more than a wistful sigh of a movie. PT

Girl from Maxim's, The
(Alexander Korda, 1933, GB) Frances Day, Leslie Henson, George Grossmith, Stanley Holloway, Lady Tree, Evan Thomas, Eric Portman.
82 min. b/w.
Made before Korda hit the big time with *The Private Life of Henry VIII* and the lavish Denham epics, this adaptation of a Feydeau farce impresses despite the budgetary constraints. With brother Vincent's meticulous art direction and Périnal's photography, Korda convincingly creates the ambience of hypocritical decadence that epitomises the 'gay nineties'. Maxim's, presided over by Day's cunningly quixotic coquette, becomes a palace of boisterous female exhibitionism where men pay for their pleasure by exposing themselves as fatuous ninnies. The brilliant farce-playing from snorting old buffer Grossmith, spluttering pompous Henson, and the gnarled and knotty Lady Tree, completes the ingredients for a bold, elegant, visually exciting film. RMy

Girl from Trieste, The (La Ragazza di Trieste)
(Pasquale Festa Campanile, 1983, It) Ben Gazzara, Ornella Muti, Mimsy Farmer, Andrea Ferreol, Jean-Claude Brialy, William Berger.
103 min.
Muti is saved from a watery grave, artificially respirated, and then confronted on the beach by expatriate cartoonist Gazzara, who in no time is brazenly squinting down her bodice. When she confesses to doing such suicidal things for kicks, it's plain he should duck for cover, but as her eccentricity runs on down to barking lunacy, so he becomes more and more obsessive, the fool. By the time she has shaved her head bald, it's clear that it's going to end badly, and her desperate yearning for punishment is going to allow Campanile full rein in showing all its festering detail. Gazzara coasts through it, rumbling away in his best Hemingway manner; and Muti seems to be cornering the market in doe-eyed doxies with a serious Catholic problem; the rest is just a gaudy treadmill. CPea

Girl in a Boot (Einmal Ku'damm und Zurück)
(Herbert Ballmann, 1983, WGer) Ursela Monn, Christian Kohlund, Evelyn Meyka, Peter Schiff, Peter Seum, Bettina Martell, Brigitte Mira.
96 min.
The girl is Ulla, a spunky East Berlin fräulein, a little bored with her job at the Engineering Works and her long-standing boyfriend; given a lift one day by Thomas, a suave chef at the Swiss Embassy, she finds herself more than ready to indulge in a little nocturnal East-West relations. Thomas has taken to nipping across Checkpoint Charlie for pizzas at his favourite restaurant, so Ulla suggests he take her for a quick 'Ausflug' to the West, secreted in the boot of his Merc...But, oh yes, things go wrong. Shot with all the panache of a McDonalds advertisement with music to match, the movie adds up to little more than an unimaginative love story that reduces the traumas of life in the 'divided city' to casuistic cliché. Symptomatically, the only enlivening diversion is provided by two minor performances: Peter Schiff as Ulla's concerned Communist father, and Fassbinder regular Brigitte Mira as a toilet attendant. WH

Girl in Every Port, A
(Howard Hawks, 1928, US) Victor McLaglen, Robert Armstrong, Louise Brooks, Marcia Casajuana, Myrna Loy, William Demarest, Sally Rand.
6 reels. b/w.
'That big ox means more to me than any woman!' says Armstrong's sailor (via an intertitle) in Hawks' engagingly naive fourth film, thus paving the way for decades of buddy love. A strange choice, you might think, when the ox is McLaglen and the woman is the almost divine Louise Brooks, glowing with beauty in a cloche hat and beguiling fringe. But the film's allegiances remain so much with the triangle's male sides – two sailors who stumble over each other befriending the same girls in the same ports – that the result is dramatically lopsided. Technically, however, it's perfectly adroit, swiftly paced, clearly detailed, with only a modicum of overacting from the lads when they're tanked up and spoiling for trouble ('Let's pick another fight and go fifty-fifty on the fun'). No Hawksperson should miss it. GB

Girl in the Picture, The
(Cary Parker, 1985, GB) John Gordon Sinclair, Irina Brook, David McKay, Gregor Fisher, Paul Young, Rikki Fulton.
91 min.
Sinclair plays a photographer's assistant who doesn't know when he's well off. Having decided to give his live-in girlfriend (Brook) the boot – some nice comic moments as he tries to pluck up the courage to tell her – he's soon mooning about wondering why he can never get a slice of the action; a feeling shared by his workmate Kenny (McKay), who is pining for a mystery 'girl in the picture' he has just developed. But of course there's always someone worse off, and into the shop to order some wedding photos comes Bill (Fisher), harbouring catastrophic doubts about his forthcoming marriage. The comic confusions and misunderstandings as these three incompe-

tents try to help each other out look a little like pastiche Bill Forsyth. But it's still an engaging debut from writer/director Parker, a classy light comedy with a firmer hold on reality than most of its American teenage counterparts. CS

Girl Most Likely, The

(Mitchell Leisen, 1957, US) Jane Powell, Cliff Robertson, Keith Andes, Tommy Noonan, Kaye Ballard, Una Merkel.
98 min.
Leisen's last theatrical feature – a musical remake of *Tom, Dick and Harry*, with Powell agonising prettily over which of three beaux (mechanic Robertson, wealthy Andes, real estate salesman Noonan) to wed – is admittedly far from his best, but not without interest. True, the cast don't have the necessary talent or fizz to do justice to either Gower Champion's choreography or the often splendidly gaudy art direction (shot in Technicolor, of course). But Leisen's handling of his hand-me-down material is civilised and vibrant, and while it's nowhere near as memorable as his *Lady in the Dark*, the film provides further evidence that he was one of Hollywood's most underrated directors. GA

Girl of Good Family, A (Liangjia funü)

(Huang Jianzhong, 1985, China) Cong Shan, Zhang Weixin, Wang Jiayi, Liang Yan, Zhang Jian.
110 min.
Much influenced by *Yellow Earth* (whose director, Chen Kaige, worked as Huang Jianzhong's assistant on two previous movies), this tale of an arranged marriage between an 18-year-old girl and an infant boy confirms that Chinese cinema has acquired a new candour and readiness to broach 'difficult' material. The girl naturally get the hots for a strapping lad of her own age, pushing the film to a climax that comes straight from traditional melodrama. But most of it is freshly observed, understated, and lushly imagistic. TR

Girl on a Motorcycle (La Motocyclette/Naked Under Leather)

(Jack Cardiff, 1968, GB/Fr) Marianne Faithfull, Alain Delon, Roger Mutton, Marius Goring, Catherine Jourdan.
91 min.
Thrill as adulterous Faithfull zips off into the arms of former lover Delon for a bout of leather-clad, tank-straddling, high-octane how's-your-father, shot by director/cameraman Cardiff as if it were high art indeed. Proof that the Swinging '60s could be toweringly soporific. TJ

Girl Rosemarie, The

see *Mädchen Rosemarie, Das*

Girls! Girls! Girls!

(Norman Taurog, 1962, US) Elvis Presley, Stella Stevens, Laurel Goodwin, Jeremy Slate, Guy Lee, Nestor Paiva.
106 min.
Elvis as a nightclub singer, pursued by girls but more concerned about his beloved fishing-boat. Co-scripted by Edward Anhalt, who won an Oscar for the 'Becket' screenplay two years later, this is not exactly a feast of wit and erudition; but it is one of Presley's better lightweight vehicles, thanks largely to the presence of Stella Stevens, one of the few leading ladies who gave him any competition. AC

Girls He Left Behind, The

see *Gang's All Here, The*

Girls in Uniform

see *Mädchen in Uniform*

Girl Shy

(Fred Newmeyer/Sam Taylor, 1924, US) Harold Lloyd, Jobyna Ralston, Richard Daniels, Carlton Griffin.
88 min. b/w.
Lloyd is a timid tailor's apprentice who after hours has been writing a fantasy book, 'The Secret of Making Love' (later retitled 'A Boob's Diary'), two episodes of which are exactly illustrated: 'My Vampire', in which Harold professes

'indifference', and 'My Flapper' in which he adopts the caveman approach. There are in addition three classic sequences: one in which Harold becomes glued to the girl he's wooing; another when he visits the LA publishers to whom he's submitted his book and is mobbed by the hysterical typing pool; and finally the climactic rescue chase, to prevent the marriage of the girl to a mustachioed bigamist, with its glorious string of knife-edge stunts. JPy

Girl 6

(Spike Lee, 1996, US) Theresa Randle, Isaiah Washington, Spike Lee, Jennifer Lewis, Quentin Tarantino, Debi Mazar, Naomi Campbell, Larry Pine, Madonna, John Turturro, Ron Silver.
108 min.
Lee's follow-up to *She's Gotta Have It* has been a long time coming, but this freewheeling comic celebration of an independent New York City gal fits the bill: it even starts with Judy (Randle) auditioning with a monologue from the earlier film. When the director (Tarantino) insists she strip, she quits, and her acting career appears to be over until she lands a job as a phone-sex operator. Although her friend Jimmy (Lee) is appalled, in many ways 'Girl 6' is a liberating, therapeutic role: sexually she's always in control, she's well paid, and there's no colour barrier. But is Judy hung-up on Girl 6? If this synopsis suggests a plot, Lee must have had other things on his mind. Instead, the film's eclectic, New Wave-ish pick'n'mix of fantasy, parody and pastiche sets the stage for star cameos à go-go. Randle changes her look with every scene, throws in faultless impersonations of Dorothy Dandridge and Pam Grier, and almost holds it all together. After this role, she should never have to audition again. There's something refreshing about the film's reckless proximity to anarchy, the stylishly imaginative cinematography and lusciously exorbitant Prince soundtrack, even if it does ring hollow when Lee tries to get serious on us. TCh

Girls Just Want to Have Fun

(Alan Metter, 1985, US) Sarah Jessica Parker, Lee Montgomery, Helen Hunt, Morgan Woodward, Jonathan Silverman, Ed Lauter, Holly Gagnier.
89 min.
This sticks to the old bopsical formula: Terpsichorean teen hits town, gets boyfriend, battles misguided parents, and wins big dance contest. The protagonist here is white, middle class, Catholic schoolgirl Janey (Parker), whose aim is to hoof her way into a regular slot on the local Dance TV. With dumb jock Jeff (Montgomery) as her dancing partner, she evades the protective custody of her father and gets the better of rich bitch Natalie (Gagnier), in one of those stupendously uninspired dance routines which look like Olga Korbut crossed with *Come Dancing*. AB

Girls to be Married, The (Chujia Nü)

(Wang Jin, 1991, China) Shen Rong, Tao Huimin, Ju Xue.
99 min.
Five young girls, faced with the prospect of marriage (four of them arranged), make a suicide pact: it's to be hanging *en masse*, bedecked in festive red corduroy. As they wait, their family travails give them every reason to wish for a rapid getaway. From the shocking, perverse tableau at the beginning – a bride hangs herself during a wedding procession – the film draws links between love and death, underscoring the grim lot reserved for women in the rural community in which it is set. Admirers of *Ju Dou* will recognise some of the settings, and even some of the visual style; but in typical Hong Kong fashion, the more sober themes are tempered by splashes of spectacle and heart-tugging rhetoric (it's heavy on the soft-focus). Moving, beautiful, and not a little unsettling. JRo

Girl with Brains in Her Feet, The

(Roberto Bangura, 1997, GB) Joanna Ward, Amanda Mealing, John Thompson, Jamie McIntosh, Joshua Henderson, Jodie Smith.
98 min.
This directorial debut may explore familiar territory (a girl's coming of age), but it opens up Joanna Hodges' screenplay with a light touch, and elicits engaging performances from its prin-

cipals, notably Joanna Ward as 13-year-old 'Jack'. Secret smoker, T-Rex fan and nascent track runner, this energetic Leicester schoolgirl shows a nifty ability to sidestep the challenges and irritations life throws up, be it domestic interference (her mum's a nag), scarcely veiled racism, the perils of adolescent sex – or the lack of training shoes. It's not in the league of *Kes*, on which it leans for inspiration, but it gives notice of sensitive new talent. WH

Girl with Green Eyes

(Desmond Davis, 1963, GB) Rita Tushingham, Peter Finch, Lynn Redgrave, Marie Kean, Arthur O'Sullivan, Julian Glover, TP McKenna.
91 min. b/w.
Co Clare colleen Tushingham heads up to Dublin, where she shares digs with her best pal Redgrave, works in a grocer's, and falls for middle-aged writer Finch, whose wife and kids have long since left him. Unlike other British films of the time, cameraman Davis's assured debut, scripted by Edna O'Brien from her own novel, doesn't pile on the kitchen sink realism. It concentrates on the characters' fumbling emotional insecurities and the keenly observed background of emotional repression. Has worn well. TJ

Girl with the Red Hair, The (Het Meisje met het Rode Haar)

(Ben Verbong, 1981, Neth) Renée Soutendijk, Peter Tuinman, Ada Bouwman, Robert Delhez, Johan Leysen.
114 min.
A remarkably assured first feature, charting the real-life resistance activities of the (for the Dutch) almost legendary World War II heroine Hannie Schaft. It paints a detailed, lucid portrait of a respectable woman abandoning her legal studies and overcoming qualms to become an efficient killer, hunted by the occupant Nazis and increasingly at odds with the acquiescent Dutch authorities. Avoiding 'aren't Nazis slimy' clichés, Verbong constructs a resonant context in which his courageous heroine discovers the personally tragic consequences of her militant choice. If the film is finally too restrained to achieve the emotional power of its acknowledged models (Melville's *L'Armée des Ombres*, Bertolucci's *The Conformist*), the precise, exquisite images – in desaturated sepia colours – and strong performances nevertheless convey both honesty and intelligence: it's engrossing, sensitive, and despite the period setting, totally relevant. GA

Giorno della prima di 'Close Up', Il (Day of the Premiere of 'Close Up')

(Nanni Moretti, 1995, It) Nanni Moretti.
7 min.
Pointed, poignant and marvellously droll Moretti short in which he worries about the opening, at his Nuovo Sacher cinema in Rome, of a Kiarostami masterpiece against stiff competition from the likes of *The Lion King*. One of the best and most honest movies ever made about the headaches of running an indie art cinema. GA

Giro City

(Karl Francis, 1982, GB) Glenda Jackson, Jon Finch, Kenneth Colley, James Donnelly, Emrys James, Karen Archer.
102 min.
Exercising something of the fascination of a crossword puzzle, this angry parable about media censorship is cast as an investigative report about two investigative reports, often assuming thriller form as reporters lurk and cameras whirr, the stories are worried over and painstakingly reworked, until the exhilarating moment when the pieces finally fall into place. One story is about a Welsh farmer stubbornly resisting eviction, the other about the political situation in Ireland. Both prove to involve 'higher interests'; both end on the cutting-room floor; and the reporters are left to bite on the bullet: 'You never learn, do you? You have to compromise'. Guilty itself of a little (understandable) compromise in casting star names for what comes on like a documentary, the film nevertheless still bites, and is honest enough to query (without really exploring) the honesty of reporters who rage against, but accept, the status quo of compromise. TM

Giselle

(Victor Di Mello, 1981, Braz) Alba Valéria, Carlo Mossy, Maria Lucia Dahl, Nildo Parente, Ricardo Faria, Monique Lafond.
95 min.
Pretty Giselle returns from her studies in Europe to Brazil where, on the ranch that is home to her father and stepmother, she rolls head, shoulders and eyes in the orgasmic embrace of all and sundry to the accompaniment of an international MOR soundtrack. The distinguishing feature of this not unenjoyable softcore is the sheer variety of sexual permutation (homo and heterosexual two, three and foursomes, paedophilia), while elements of politics and violence which threaten to introduce a new dimension to the film are quickly manipulated to eliminate any hindrance to the family's lovemaking. All finally go their separate ways, with Giselle returning to Europe – for more of the same. FD

Gito, the Ungrateful (Gito, l'Ingrat)

(Léonce Ngabo, 1992, Burundi/Switz/Fr) Joseph Kumbela, Marie Bunel, Aoua Sangare, Louis Kamatari.
90 min.
In outline, Ngabo's (and Burundi's) first feature sounds like an Eric Rohmer comedy of manners. Back home with a Parisian diploma in his pocket and expecting to walk into a civil service job, Gito finds himself both unemployed and caught between two women: his current French girlfriend Christine and his local old flame Flora. If it plays more like sit-com than Rohmer, then that reflects Ngabo's need to appeal to audiences at home *and* abroad and his well-developed sense of humour: the film runs rings round both male pride and the emerging African bourgeoisie. Minor, but highly watchable. TR

Giù la Testa (Duck, You Sucker/A Fistful of Dynamite/Once Upon a Time – the Revolution)

(Sergio Leone, 1971, It) James Coburn, Rod Steiger, Romolo Valli, Maria Monti, Rik Battaglia.
150 min.
Having already, in *Once Upon a Time in the West*, taken energetic liberties with the typical (John) Fordian Western, it's not surprising that Leone should have taken a sideswipe at another of the director's stereotypes, the revolutionary Irishman, in the second part of his trilogy of political fables. But the specific IRA background of Coburn's Sean is as ultimately unimportant as the specific Mexican setting: with characteristic flamboyance, Leone is more concerned to build a composite of the all-purpose, all-causes revolutionary 'John Doe' from Sean's informed commitment and the naïve brute force of Steiger's Juan. The most wry of the political spaghettis, and wholly wonderful. PT

Giulietta degli Spiriti

see Juliet of the Spirits

Give My Regards to Broad Street

(Peter Webb, 1984, GB) Paul McCartney, Bryan Brown, Ringo Starr, Barbara Bach, Linda McCartney, Tracey Ullman, Ralph Richardson.
108 min.
Pop star Paul zooms around in his own Herbie car, records at the Beeb, attends board meetings, smiles kindly at aged autograph hunters, takes champers, and performs an awful lot of music. The documentary stuff is propped up by a plot about some missing master tapes (which has the distinction of being both uneventful and baffling), some embarrassingly old-fashioned visual set pieces, and cameo roles in which Ullman manages to be unfunny and Richardson looks understandably tired. Token attempt at street cred: if Paul doesn't get the tapes back, he'll be taken over by a sunglasses-wearing business shark. SGr

Give Us Tomorrow

(Donovan Winter, 1978, GB) Sylvia Syms, Derren Nesbitt, James Kerry, Donna Evans, Matthew Haslett, Alan Guy.
94 min.

Good old True Brit cinema does it again with this half-hearted headline exploitation, in a sub-TV thriller vein, that leaves you in no doubt that it was 'entirely shot on location in Orpington, Kent'. It's unlikely that it even disturbed the residents with its tale of a bank robbery gone wrong and a suburban siege in which heavyweight lumpen yob (Nesbitt) and dole-queue kid (Guy) hold 'respectable' bank manager's family hostage. If tempted to lay down money for this rubbish, you should get a few compensatory chuckles from a captor-captive slanging match on the economics of the class system, and from the instant love affair between virgin daughter and afore-mentioned kid; but you'll still want your cash back by the time the script's stabs at Social Comment are exhausted. PT

Gladiator

(Rowdy Herrington, 1992, US) James Marshall, Cuba Gooding Jr, Brian Dennehy, Robert Loggia, Ossie Davis, John Heard, Jon Seda, Cara Buono, Lance Slaughter.
102 min.
Herrington follows up the state-of-the-art violence of *Road House* with a leaner, more controlled tale of back-street boxing in Chicago. Blackmailed by corrupt promoter Horn (Dennehy), white schoolboy boxer Tommy Riley (Marshall) is forced into a fight scene where cheating is normal. Horn bills Tommy as 'The Great White Hope', but Tommy's motivation – paying off his father's gambling debts – hardly sets him alongside 'hungry' white champions of the past. For his black opponents, on the other hand, their fists are their only passport out of the ghetto. It's this desperation, and the racial undercurrent of black versus white, that Horn is keen to exploit. Marshall makes a promising feature debut; and Herrington, pushing beyond the expected triumph-of-the-underdog clichés, underpins the crowd-pleasing Rocky-style fight action with some unobtrusive social comment and confident visual storytelling. NF

Glass Key, The

(Stuart Heisler, 1942, US) Brian Donlevy, Alan Ladd, Veronica Lake, Joseph Calleia, William Bendix, Bonita Granville, Richard Denning.
85 min. b/w.
Not quite so resonant an early example of *noir* as *The Maltese Falcon*, partly because the novel's ending has been clumsily softened, but still a remarkably successful Hammett adaptation. Best sequence by far is the marathon beating-up sustained by Ladd in a bout of grating sado-masochism as Bendix ('He's a tough baby, he likes this') coyly begs his 'little rubber ball' to bounce back for more. Shot and played with deceptive casualness, the sequence is central to the film, flaunting an erotic undertow that sows continuing doubts throughout. Playing with his usual deadpan as he weaves warily through a maze of political machinations and underworld snares in the service of his boss, Ladd remains equally frozen whether expressing his love for Lake or his loyalty to Donlevy. The result is a teasing sexual ambiguity, considerably enhanced (at least until the copout ending) by the fact that Hammett's hero – here callous enough to admit a willingness to let Lake hang if necessary in furtherance of his aims – has been toughened up by being reduced to a *noir* cipher for the film. TM

Glass Menagerie, The

(Paul Newman, 1987, US) Joanne Woodward, John Malkovich, Karen Allen, James Naughton.
135 min.
Newman's movie of the Tennessee Williams play, about a family disintegrating in a gloomy, claustrophobic St Louis apartment during the depression, is uncompromising and at times unbearably poignant. The mother (Woodward) is a stifling combination of emotional blackmail and self-glorifying reverie; her crippled daughter Laura (Allen, a revelation here), is a timid, gentle creature, as fragile as the world of glass animals into which she retreats. When the long-awaited gentleman caller accidentally breaks both her favourite unicorn and her heart, she finally drifts away for good into her fantasies. Her brother Tom (Malkovich) is weak and aware of it, and his self-loathing testimony brackets the confined action. The acting is bruisingly true; the deep

guilts of family are present throughout; everybody feels martyred. Newman trusts the words to conjure up the old crushed magnolia. BC

Glass Mountain, The

(Henry Cass, 1949, GB) Michael Denison, Dulcie Gray, Valentina Cortese, Tito Gobi, Sebastian Shaw.
94 min. b/w.
Shot down over Italy in WWII, composer Denison is inspired by the glacial beauty of the Alps and his illicit desire for the young Cortese to write an opera based on the legend of the Glass Mountain. When he returns to Blighty, his wife Dulcie Gray waits stoically for his indifference to thaw. This solidly directed, lavishly mounted romantic tosh was a huge hit in its day. NF

Glass Shield, The

(Charles Burnett, 1995, US) Michael Boatman, Lori Petty, Bernie Casey, Ice Cube, Michael Ironside, Elliott Gould, Richard Anderson, Don Harvey.
108 min.
Burnett's first film since the provocative *To Sleep with Anger* in 1990 is a Lumet-style *policier* inspired by an everyday tale of LAPD-sponsored murder, racism and corruption. Boatman is the first black cop to serve in Anderson's precinct. He's proud to pull on his uniform, and readily bends the truth to put away a bad guy, but he can't just stand by and watch when he realises his colleagues are framing an innocent man, and they'll kill to keep it quiet. It's a familiar story, but Burnett draws strong character work from the cast (Petty is outstanding as a rookie who latches on to Boatman as a fellow outsider). Ultimately, however, the movie feels sketchy, as if Burnett chopped the flesh off his screenplay and left us only the bare bones.

Glastonbury: The Movie

(Robin Mahoney, 1995, GB) The Verve, Lemonheads, Omar, Airto Moreira.
96 min.
A marvellously honest, beautifully shot documentary celebrating 25 years of rock 'n' rolling around in the mud somewhere in a field in Somerset. Filmed over several years, this widescreen Dolby digital excursion dispenses with voice-overs, interviews and scrolling subtitles and just lets the music – from crusty rockers The Verve, Evan Dando's Lemonheads, spaced-cadets Spiritualised, groove-meister Omar, percussion genius Airto Moreira, et al – do the talking. DA

Gleaming the Cube

(Graeme Clifford, 1988, US) Christian Slater, Steven Bauer, Richard Herd, Le Tuan, Minh Luong, Art Chudabala, Ed Lauter, Charles Cyphers.
105 min.
'Gleaming the cube' is the term applied for that moment when pirouetting skateboarders momentarily leave the ground to carve their way through the air. It's the type of thing rebel without a high school diploma Brian (Slater) loves to do, much to his parents' despair. But he's first to rally to their cause when tragedy strikes, getting his act together to take the law into his own hands. According to the hackneyed conventions of this so-so thriller, this involves ridding himself of tatty clothes and stubble. He delves into the Orange County underworld, which is racier than you might think. The Vietnamese community is up to no good, with corruption infiltrating a seemingly respectable medical supply business. Slater and Le Tuan (as a Vietnamese ex-colonel) put in decent performances, but the best moments come from the action sequences in which Brian and his buddies perform their sporty feats. But with the screenplay dabbling with too many issues and stereotypes, the characters are largely one-dimensional and the relationships unconvincing. CM

Glengarry Glen Ross

(James Foley, 1992, US) Al Pacino, Jack Lemmon, Alec Baldwin, Alan Arkin, Ed Harris, Kevin Spacey, Jonathan Pryce, Bruce Altman, Jude Ciccolella.
100 min.
David Mamet's play about the wheelings and dealings of real-estate salesmen gets dedicated playing from a splendid cast, but gains nothing by the transfer from stage to screen. Foley takes us outside the office a bit, but essentially it's a

claustrophobic story of men under pressure revealing cracks in character. 'Always be closing,' is the motto of these high-pressure hustlers, but after a brutal pep talk from bossman Blake (Baldwin), many of the team are faced with personal closure if they don't perform at peak. In this competitive climate, one of them steals the 'leads' (names of prospective clients). Mamet's aphasic dialogue and profanities fit perfectly with the accents, and it's possible to imagine how hotshot Ricky Roma (Pacino) will end up like pitiful, pleading Levene (Lemmon). Both turn in superb performances, but it's an ensemble piece, and Harris, Arkin and Spacey are just as good. BC

Glenn Miller Story, The

(Anthony Mann, 1954, US) James Stewart, June Allyson, Harry Morgan, George Tobias, Frances Langford, Louis Armstrong, Gene Krupa, Charles Drake.
116 min.
This ends where Scorsese's *New York, New York* begins, at the height of the big band era in the '40s; and some striking similarities end with the remorseless good nature of the Glenn Miller movie. Allyson beams and twinkles as Miller's practical wife; Stewart, looking remarkably like Miller, is disarmingly eccentric. They make an exemplary American couple, finding the road to success lined with nice friends, swirling *Variety* headlines, and key moments like Glenn saying to wife (long-distance), 'My number's Pennsylvania 6-5000'. But it works beautifully, especially if you like the music. Musical direction is by Henry Mancini, who abandons his own particular 'sound' for a credible homage to Miller's. Watch for Louis Armstrong leading a jam session on 'Basin Street Blues' in a speakeasy in Harlem, and Frances Langford doing 'Chattanooga Choo-Choo' in a well-boned strapless. JS

Glen or Glenda? (aka I Led Two Lives/ I Changed My Sex)

(Edward D Wood Jr, 1952, US) Bela Lugosi, Lyle Talbot, Daniel Davis (ie. Edward Wood Jr), Dolores Fuller, Tommy Haynes.
61 min. b/w.
This well-meaning disaster, rescued from the obscurity it surely craves, is without doubt a candidate for one of the worst films ever made. The main story – a documentary-style look at the problems of transvestites – is a masquerade of good intentions shot with all the panache of an Indian restaurant commercial. Glen (pseudonymously played by the director himself) eyes ladies' underwear in clothing stores, covets his fiancée's angora; and when dressed to kill s/he looks like a straggler from the Monty Python lumberjack song. Snicker, snicker. Presiding over proceedings – goodness knows why – is a senile Lugosi looking as though he had strayed in from another movie. His advice as an 'expert' takes the form of endless taunts...but see for yourself, it's a film that defies description. CPe

Glimmer Man, The

(John Gray, 1996, US) Steven Seagal, Keenen Ivory Wayans, Bob Gunton, Brian Cox, Michelle Johnson, John M Jackson, Stephen Tobolowsky.
91 min.
Although this slick Seagal action pic won't convert die-hard detractors, aficionados will note that he's both gained weight and lightened up. Ever since playing the ship's cook in *Under Siege*, the slab-faced one has been leavening his straight man image with a pinch of humour. The magic ingredient here is Wayans who, as his fast-talking, street-wise partner, allows Seagal to introduce something new into the mix, self-mockery. While Seagal cleanses his mind with Tibetan prayer beads, Wayans worships Saint Jack – Daniels, that is. The mismatched buddies are hunting a California serial killer called 'The Family Man', who slaughters and crucifies entire Catholic families; but Seagal suspects the latest killing was the work of a pro. Anonymously scripted and directed, this at least suggests that if Seagal can ever learn to deliver a kiss-off line, he might get within shouting distance of being likeable. As his old Special Ops boss, an overripe Cox confirms his status as the Rod Steiger of the '90s. NF

Glissements Progressifs du Plaisir

(Alain Robbe-Grillet, 1974, Fr) Olga Georges-Picot, Jean-Louis Trintignant, Anicée Alvina, Michel Lonsdale.
105 min.
Trintignant, in trenchcoat and trilby, investigates a bondage slaying, grilling the heroine in the victim's bedroom which somehow contrives to be also a monastery cell, with trussed-up nuns languishing compliantly in the adjacent sanctum sanctorum. This is Robbe-Grillet amusing himself by scrambling together images and situations out of the overlapping conventions of the murder mystery and the S/M fantasy, taking care never to join the dots to form a coherent narrative and indeed ensuring that no such joining-up can possibly be achieved. This being Robbe-Grillet, none of the characters is permitted anything so crass as everyday sexual congress, though the numerous erotic tableaux should stir even the jaded or disinclined, thanks to the presence of Olga Georges-Picot, playing (but of course!) both victim and defence counsel. Amid all the sleight of hand, the most impressive feat is Trintignant's performance which manages to be simultaneously poker-faced and extravagantly comic. BBa

Glitterball, The

(Harley Cokliss, 1977, GB) Ben Buckton, Keith Jayne, Ron Pember, Marjorie Yates, Barry Jackson.
56 min.
Enterprising little feature from the Children's Film Foundation which told – but five years earlier – precisely the same story as Spielberg's *E.T.* The extraterrestrial (a metal sphere) is insufficiently characterised and the adults are a drag, but it's neat and pacy with (on a limited budget) some excellent special effects. TM

Glitter Dome, The

(Stuart Margolin, 1984, US) James Garner, Margot Kidder, John Lithgow, John Marley, Stuart Margolin, Paul Koslo, Colleen Dewhurst.
94 min.
As a one-time member of the LAPD, Joseph Wambaugh presumably has the merit of authenticity in his very personal treatment of police procedure; all the more worrying, then, that he chooses to cast his scenarios in the form of black farce. Cases get solved more by accident and coincidence than by detection, the police chiefs are all rattled idiots, and the detectives are divided between the 'survivors' – hard-drinking wearies, given to carnal jags of mind-bending proportion – and the 'sensitives', who can't find the release of outrageous behaviour and tend to crack up. Margolin's direction of this Tinsel-town thriller about kiddy porn and murder (designed for cable TV) is too diffuse to be faithful to the particularities of Wambaugh's vision. But Garner contributes a very watchable wrinkly 'tec with lines like 'In Hollywood, Halloween is redundant'; and as his partner, Lithgow acquits himself perfectly in the role of the 'sensitive' with nightmares of an especially nasty case of child abuse. CPea

Global Affair, A

(Jack Arnold, 1963, US) Bob Hope, Lilo Pulver, Michèle Mercier, Elga Andersen, Yvonne De Carlo, Robert Sterling, John McGiver, Nehemiah Persoff, Mickey Shaughnessy.
84 min. b/w.
What did poor Jack Arnold do to deserve this? Bob Hope plays a bachelor United Nations official, saddled with a foundling baby and flatulent wisecracks, who spurs furious competition between the 117 member nations – hitherto uninterested in welcoming the orphan – by announcing that it will be awarded to the best and most deserving country. All patch up their differences to applaud his eventual decision to adopt the little charmer himself (surprise, surprise) after marrying Michèle Mercier. Nobody is likely to applaud anything else, except perhaps a brief flare from Lilo Pulver as a Russian gynaecologist. TM

Gloire de mon père, La (My Father's Glory)

(Yves Robert, 1990, Fr) Philippe Caubère, Nathalie Roussel, Didier Pain, Thérèse Liotard, Julien Ciamaca, Joris Molinas, Paul Crauchet, Victor Garrivier.
111 min.

The first part of Marcel Pagnol's four-volume autobiography represents an unclouded homage to a childhood of apparently unchanging sunshine. In comparison to *Jean de Florette* and its sequel, this is a film of small pleasures. Robert eschews the top rank of French actors in favour of those with a genuine Provençal background, a decision Pagnol would surely have admired. But other decisions seem less successful. The book's charm comes from the sly contrast between the grown-up Pagnol's narration and his young self's naivety. Robert does use a narrator, but much of the verbal humour is lost on audiences reliant on subtitling or struggling to decipher the vernacular. The child actors have charm in good measure, but charm cannot be built into a film: you have to let it arise. Although the landscape is as impressive as ever, the film always looks too pretty, and Robert can't resist the temptation to swamp key scenes with Vladimir Cosma's heavy Mantovani strings. JMo

Gloria

(John Cassavetes, 1980, US) Gena Rowlands, John Adames, Buck Henry, Julie Carmen, Lupe Guarnica, Basilio Franchina.
121 min.
A near stunner: half art movie, half chase thriller, with a breathless, commanding performance from Gena Rowlands as the ex-chorus girl of the title. Hard as nails and twice as brassy, she takes unwilling charge of a neighbour's doe-eyed kid after his family has been slaughtered by the Mafia; the mismatched pair find themselves on the run with a bookful of Mafia accounts. Cassavetes' movies are a kind of frenzied gulp, quivering with emotion, under-motivated, over-long, and this is no exception: sublime, but infuriating. CA

Glory

(Edward Zwick, 1989, US) Matthew Broderick, Denzel Washington, Cary Elwes, Morgan Freeman, Jihmi Kennedy, André Braugher, Raymond St Jacques, Cliff DeYoung.
133 min.
Glory heralds the bravery of the American Civil War's first black fighting unit. Most of the emphasis has gone into evoking a firm sense of period: screenwriter Kevin Jarre reveals less talent for full-blooded characterisation and dialogue. Led by white officers headed by Colonel Robert Gould Shaw (Broderick), the men set off from the North for confrontation, which culminates in the bloody storming of a Confederate fort. Among the soldiers (and giving the best performances) are a calm gravedigger (Freeman) and a belligerent runaway slave (Washington). Voice-over narration makes effective use of the real-life Shaw's correspondence, but in terms of authenticity the battle sequences are truly impressive. Marching across open fields amid cannon-shot, or plunging into hand-to-hand combat, the stark clarity of Freddie Francis' cinematography combined with Zwick's intimate style evokes immediacy and fear. It's an ambitious and purposeful film, but complexities have been pared to meet the demands of the all-important '15' certification. CM

Glory Alley

(Raoul Walsh, 1952, US) Ralph Meeker, Leslie Caron, Kurt Kasznar, Gilbert Roland, Louis Armstrong, John McIntire, Dan Seymour, Jack Teagarden.
79 min. b/w.
Set among the 'pugs and mugs' of Bourbon Street, New Orleans, this is long on atmosphere but short on credibility. Meeker plays (very well) a boxer who literally runs out on the bout that might have made him a contender. Hounded as a coward, especially by the blind father (Kasznar) of the girl he loves (Caron), he is too proud to explain that, as a child, he suffered a fractured skull at the hands of his drunken father; under the bright lights of the ring, the trauma recurred of schoolmates jeering at his shaven, stitched skull. After a bout with alcohol, he enlists, returning from the war a much-publicised hero. Only Kasznar refuses to relent, until an eye specialist (secretly summoned by Meeker) suggests an operation that might restore his sight. It doesn't, but ('there are various kinds of blindness') does effect a change of heart. Meeker, now a welcome son-in-law, goes on to become champ. Disgorged in clumsy chunks by Art Cohn's script, this farrago becomes much easier to take when leavened by Walsh's ebullient response to the low-life fellow-

ship of the milieu. The jazz score, with Armstrong in good voice and Caron contributing some charmingly quaint honky tonk/ballet routines, is a bonus, too. TM

Glory Guys, The

(Arnold Laven, 1965, US) Tom Tryon, Harve Presnell, Andrew Duggan, Senta Berger, James Caan, Michael Anderson Jr, Slim Pickens, Wayne Rogers.
112 min.
Screenwriter Sam Peckinpah might have made more of this fatalistic Western adventure, from the novel The Dice of God by Hoffman Birney, than journeyman Laven, but it's a diverting picture all the same. Tryon's the cavalry captain sent to join general Duggan's frontier regiment, only to find the latter obsessed with defeating the combined local Indian forces. If anything, the film should be called 'The Glory Guy' because it's Duggan's drive to personal fulfilment, even at the cost of his men's lives, which is the central strand of this examination of control-gone-mad. The result's hardly a masterpiece, but it builds to a nicely mounted battle that pushes the point home. TJ

Glory Stompers, The

(Anthony M Lanza, 1967, US) Dennis Hopper, Jody McCrea, Chris Noel, Jock Mahoney, Saundra Gale, Jim Reader, Robert Tessier.
85 min.
AIP biker movie in which plastic Chris Noel ('I just want something more than being a Stomper's girl') gets herself kidnapped by a rival gang and sparks off a series of fantasies of varying violence among Dennis Hopper's boys. Hopper ogles Noel's reincarnation of high school days, while his younger brother (Reader) dreams of meaningful love (and gets run over by a primitive hulk for his pains). While its framework is that of a Western, the film sticks relentlessly to its B picture format, successfully exuding an atmospheric haze. There's the sad sight, though, of Jock Mahoney (erstwhile Tarzan and Range Rider, famous for vaulting on to his horse back in the '50s) so aged he can scarcely straddle his machine. CPe

G-Men

(William Keighley, 1935, US) James Cagney, Ann Dvorak, Margaret Lindsay, Robert Armstrong, Lloyd Nolan, Barton MacLane.
85 min. b/w.
The film that put Cagney on the right side of the law after pressure groups (and Hoover's FBI) had castigated Hollywood's glorification of the gangster hero. In fact, it's hard to distinguish Cagney's Brick Davis – a punk from the wrong side of the tracks who becomes a lawyer, turning federal agent to take on the mob who killed his buddy – from his earlier incarnations, since he's still violent, trigger-happy, and motivated by personal impulses rather than a sense of legal justice. That said, however, it's a typical Warners thriller: fast, gutsy, as simplistic and powerful as a tabloid headline. GA

Gnome Named Gnorm, A (aka Upworld/Adventures of a Gnome Named Gnorm)

(Stan Winston, 1988, US) Anthony Michael Hall, Jerry Orbach, Eli Danker, Claudia Christian, Mark Harelik, Robert Z'Dar.
88 min.
A particularly desperate addition to the cycle of buddy-cop pics, in which LAPD workhorse Hall (who's filled out somewhat from his geeky John Hughes days) finds himself teamed with one of the little people (a creature who's burrowed up from beneath the earth in search of a life-giving crystal) to track down some diamond thieves. Director Stan Winston made his name as the effects wizard behind Aliens. TJ

Goalkeeper's Fear of the Penalty, The (Die Angst des Tormanns beim Elfmeter)

(Wim Wenders, 1971, WGer/Aus) Arthur Brauss, Kai Fischer, Erika Pluhar, Libgart Schwarz, Marie Bardischewski.
101 min.
The Goalkeeper's Fear of the Penalty outdoes even Wenders' subsequent Alice in the Cities in its sense that everything shown is at once subjective and objective. German goalie Bloch

(Brauss) walks out of a game in Vienna, hangs around, commits an arbitrary murder, and then takes a coach to the Austrian border to look up an old flame. It's the journey of a man who's getting too old for his job, living off his nerves, sustained by his taste for Americana, movies and rock (everything from Hitchcock to 'Wimaway'). Brauss' engagingly hangdog face anchors it all in recognisable human feelings, while avoiding the least hint of 'psychological' explanation. More than in his later movies, Wenders' style here has a remarkably charged quality: every frame haunts you for goddam weeks. TR

Goat Horn, The (Koziyat Rog)

(Metodi Andonov, 1972, Bulg) Katia Paskaleva, Anton Gortchev, Milene Penev, Kliment Dentchev.
97 min. b/w.
A straightforward 17th century tale of revenge which comes to the screen with the well-worn air of a film made at least a decade earlier. A Bulgarian farmer raises his daughter as a boy, training her to kill the men who raped and murdered her mother, a role against which she eventually revolts. The film fails because it refuses to explore the girl's growing awareness beyond the basic requirements of the plot, except once in a scene where she watches one of her mother's killers make love to a woman. In this instance her realisation of the inadequacies of her own concepts, founded as they are on revenge, is well handled. Elsewhere, as in her subsequent relationship with a young shepherd, cliché predominates. Altogether something of an anachronism. CPe

Go-Between, The

(Joseph Losey, 1970, GB) Julie Christie, Alan Bates, Dominic Guard, Margaret Leighton, Michael Redgrave, Michael Gough, Edward Fox.
116 min.
Losey's adaptation of LP Hartley's novel is one of his more impressive later works. Together with screenwriter Harold Pinter, he creates another of his depictions of the destructive side of the English class system, as a love affair between the daughter of an affluent country family and a local farmer is tragically thwarted by prejudice and convention. Seen through the eyes of a young boy who acts as the instrument for the couple's assignations, the affair becomes the nexus for all the repression and unspoken manipulations brewing under the fragile facade of an apparently civilised society; battle becomes personal on the cricket field, and the chink of teacups hides vicious whispers and plotting. It occasionally becomes a bit too precious, especially with the inserts of the grown-up go-between visiting his past haunts, but it's strong on atmosphere (the Norfolk locations are beautifully shot by Gerry Fisher), performance and moral nuance. GA

GoBots: Battle of the Rocklords

(Ray Patterson/Don Lusk/Alan Zaslove, 1986, US) voices: Margot Kidder, Roddy McDowall, Michael Nouri, Telly Savalas.
74 min.
Whatever evil lurks in the dark corners of the galaxy, have no fear: the GoBots are there – a new line of toys from the Tonka corporation, now starring in their first feature-length animated advertisement by Hanna-Barbera. Leader One and the GoBots are faced with a dangerous mission. Cy-Kill, the renegade GoBot, has travelled through the dimensions of hyperspace to the planet Quartex to join forces with the evil Magmar (voice by Savalas). There, where inanimate rocks have the ability to transform themselves into living, breathing anthropomorphic forms, Magmar seeks to take the planet by force, and the GoBots aim to stop him. Save your pennies and watch the GoBots on TV instead. SGo

Goda Viljan, Den

see Best Intentions, The

Goddess, The

see Devi

Goddess, The

(John Cromwell, 1958, US) Kim Stanley, Lloyd Bridges, Betty Lou Holland, Steven Hill, Patty Duke, Joan Copeland.
105 min. b/w.

Just as he later ridiculed the inanities of American TV in Network, writer Paddy Chayevsky took the Hollywood star system to task in this equally savage satire. He cribbed the story directly from Ava Gardner's life: a small town girl of the Depression marries her way out of her background, abandons her husband, changes her name and sleeps her way to stardom. Once at the top, she can't cope with her fame and becomes increasing suicidal. Although brilliantly played in best Method style by Kim Stanley, this would-be screen goddess is more a caricature than a character. Given what happened to Monroe a few years later, the script seems both cruel and strangely prophetic. GM

Goddess, The (Shennü)

(Wu Yonggang, 1934, China) Ruan Lingyu, Li Keng, Zhang Zhizhi, Li Junpan.
78 min. b/w.
Written, directed and designed by the 27-year-old Wu Yonggang, this is the kind of film that demands a rewriting of the film history books. The Garbo-esque Ruan Lingyu plays a single mother driven into prostitution (the title is a euphemism) to pay for her young son's schooling. Her best efforts to maintain some personal dignity run aground on social hypocrisy and male misogyny, the latter personified by the brutal pimp who co-opts her services. Free of moralism and melodrama, expressively composed and lit and very naturalistically acted, this is a film of startling modernity. TR

Godfather, The [100] (100)

(Francis Ford Coppola, 1971, US) Marlon Brando, Al Pacino, James Caan, Richard Castellano, Robert Duvall, Sterling Hayden, John Marley, Richard Conte, Diane Keaton, John Cazale, Talia Shire.
175 min.
An everyday story of Mafia folk, incorporating severed horses' heads in the bed and a number of heartwarming family occasions, as well as pointers on how not to behave in your local trattoria (ie. blasting the brains of your co-diners out all over their fettuccini). Mario Puzo's novel was brought to the screen in bravura style by Coppola, who was here trying out for the first time that piano/fortissimo style of crosscutting between religious ritual and bloody machine-gun massacre that was later to resurface in a watered-down version in The Cotton Club. See Brando with a mouthful of orange peel. Watch Pacino's cheek muscles twitch in incipiently psychotic fashion. Trace his rise from white sheep of the family to budding don and fully-fledged bad guy. Singalong to Nino Rota's irritatingly catchy theme tune. Its soap operatics should never have been presented separately from Part II. GA

Godfather Part II, The

(Francis Ford Coppola, 1974, US) Al Pacino, Robert Duvall, Diane Keaton, Robert De Niro, John Cazale, Talia Shire, Lee Strasberg, Michael V Gazzo.
200 min.
Far superior to The Godfather, this ambitiously flashes both backwards to Vito's arrival from Sicily at the turn of the century, when his struggles to make a living turn him towards a life of small-time crime; and forwards to Michael's involvement in Vegas, Cuba and a Senate hearing on organised crime. The basic thesis here seems to be that what started out as Vito's defence of his family's pride and safety becomes, by the time of Michael's absolute control over a nationwide criminal empire, an aggressive obsession with power for power's sake, so warped and ruthless that the Don is reduced to killing family and friends. All well and good, except that Coppola, so impressed by the rituals of the Corleone clan, still fails to actually show the Mafia's pernicious effect on society at large: all the violence is directed against characters directly involved with the Mob. It was, in fact, this dishonest slant (combined with the evident ambition and style of Coppola's conception) that allowed the films to become so popular. In 1977, acknowledging the awkwardnesses resulting from the split into two films, Coppola re-edited them into a chronological whole for TV, adding almost an hour of previously unseen footage. AB

Godfather Part III, The

(Francis Ford Coppola, 1990, US) Al Pacino, Diane Keaton, Talia Shire, Andy Garcia, Eli Wallach, Joe Mantagna, George Hamilton, Bridget Fonda, Sofia Coppola, Raf Vallone, Donal Donnelly, Helmut Berger, John Savage.
162 min.

The chief impression is of *déjà vu*: extravagant ceremonies, parties, shady meetings behind closed doors. The implausible story doesn't help: Michael Corleone (Pacino), grey and bowed in 1979, misses his ex-wife (Keaton) and kids so much that he decides to abandon crime and make the family business legitimate. If it's nicely ironic that bastard nephew Vincent (Garcia), Michael's right-hand man, is almost psycopathically violent, this strand is weakened when Michael objects to daughter Mary's falling for Vincent. And the unwise insertion of elements from real life – the laundering of money through the Vatican – founders because so many details are skated over that the exact implications of Michael's brush with Old World power-brokers are often obscured. Plot apart – much of which concerns Michael's struggles to defend both his empire and his intergrity against Mafia peers – it often looks like Coppola is going through the motions. The acting is merely passable, several characters are given nothing to do, and Michael's paranoid self-pity lends the film an absurd morality: Coppola expects us to sympathise with the *semblance* of virtue. GA

God, Fatherland and Authority

see Deus, Patria e Autoridade

Godfather of Harlem, The

see Black Caesar

God's Alcatraz

(Boris Stout, 1993, GB) Dr Johnny Ray.
36 min.

Sketchy but intriguing documentary about one man's struggle to instil black pride into the impoverished 'village' of St Paul in East Brooklyn. Radical Christian preacher Dr Johnny Ray has a mission, and self-acknowledged charisma. But as we follow him from sermons and men's consciousness-raising sessions to his Mississippi home, the precise import of his ideas (including voluntary segregation for the black community) are never fully examined – a pity, since his influence on his parishioners is evidently substantial. GA

God's Army (aka The Prophecy)

(Gregory Widen, 1994, US) Elias Koteas, Christopher Walken, Eric Stoltz, Virginia Madsen, Amanda Plummer.
94 min.

A novice priest-turned-cop (he lost his faith after a string of searing apocalyptic visions), Koteas finds himself caught between heaven and hell in a battle of the angels, as predicted in the 23rd chapter of Revelations (there's no 23rd chapter, Bible fans). For the God squad, we have Stoltz sucking face with a little girl to lodge the evil soul of a war criminal where fallen angel Gabriel (Walken) will not find it, he hopes. This weird metaphysical thriller comes on like a cross between *Wings of Desire* and an exploitation rip-off. Widen (who wrote *Highlander*) hasn't quite got the budget to stage Armageddon, but he would if he could. As it is, the movie never quite delivers on the Big Idea, but at least Walken comes through in spades: he's out of this world. Acting doesn't get more brazen than this. TCh

God's Country

(Louis Malle, 1985, US)
90 min.

A truly lovely little film from the sadly underrated Malle. As ever, in this documentary about the inhabitants of the small farming town of Glencoe, Minnesota, the director reveals an extraordinary compassion for his subjects, viewed as well-meaning, dignified, but flawed. The gently comic tone of the beginning – happy, united families mowing the lawns, cow inseminators enjoying their literally shitty work, farmboys driving enormous tractors – gradually deepens to a darker hue as the legacies of Vietnam and Reagan are examined, and the tightly-knit community is shown as a breeding-ground of ignorance and intolerance (blacks are absent, gays invisible). Then, for the final 20 minutes, Malle shows us Glencoe six years on: dreams severely damaged, prosperity threatened, newlyweds become prematurely middle-aged. Malle never mocks, merely understands, in this extremely personal document of one European's love-hate for middle America. GA

Godsend, The

(Gabrielle Beaumont, 1980, GB) Malcolm Stoddard, Cyd Hayman, Angela Pleasence, Patrick Barr, Wilhelmina Green, Joanne Boorman.
90 min.

There's more than a hint of *The Omen* in this horror movie about a family that is slowly destroyed by a little girl they adopt after her mother has mysteriously vanished. Despite some moments of artfully sustained menace, and the fact that both little girls playing the cuckoo-child look superbly malevolent, the script by Olaf Pooley rapidly becomes stilted, and the narrative development makes little sense. DMcG

God's Little Acre

(Anthony Mann, 1958, US) Robert Ryan, Tina Louise, Aldo Ray, Buddy Hackett, Jack Lord, Fay Spain, Michael Landon.
110 min. b/w.

God's Little Acre completely bypasses its exotic origins in Erskine Caldwell's sensational novel. Instead, Mann and scriptwriter Philip Yordan transform their subject matter to create out of it a study of two 'over-reachers' struggling for control over the destiny of their family. Accordingly, the film is best seen in the light of the treatment of the family in *Man of the West* and *The Fall of the Roman Empire*. Ryan, the family's monomaniacal patriarch, has successfully harnessed the energy of his constantly squabbling flock for 15 years into an impossible search for his grandfather's mythic hidden gold. Similarly, Ray's son-in-law is driven by the dream of reinvigorating the homestead (and the valley) by turning the mill-power back on. While the film's resolution – peace and harmony – is impossible to take, the previous 100-odd minutes offer the most concise account of Mann's conception of the power and tensions that lie at the root of family life. PH

Gods Must Be Crazy, The

(Jamie Uys, 1980, SAf) Xao, Marius Weyers, Sandra Prinsloo, Nic de Jager, Louw Verwey.
109 min.

Savour the profound imperialist symbolism of a Coke bottle dropping out of the sky like an apple of discord into a Botswana bush tribe of beatific innocents; delight in gags of such stunning originality as banana-skin pratfalls and speeded-up car chase scenes; gladden in positive, new images of the developing countries (bumbling black bureaucrats; evil but incompetent terrorists, of course routed mainly by the white 'stars'; and the simple, primitive tribe, with a plummy, patronising voice-over constantly reminding us how quaint and comical they are). Offensively racist and too gormless even for the kids at whom it is evidently aimed: Third World cinema of a quite...uncommon kind. SJo

Gods Must Be Crazy II, The

(Jamie Uys, 1988, SAf) N!Xau, Lena Farugia, Hans Strydom, Eiros.
98 min.

Mindless, immature, slapstick twaddle. Clearly aimed at under-fives, it follows the plight of several unconnected folk, all running about the vast Kalahari veldt like headless chickens: Bushman Xixo (N!Xau) has lost his two offspring on the back of a poacher's lorry; New York City lawyer Ann Taylor (Farugia), in Africa to front a conference, crashes on an airborne sightseeing trip and meets up with Tom Selleck-lookalike Dr Marshall (Strydom), who does his darndest to impress the city waif with his bushwhacking skills; and a couple of armed guerillas with nothing better to do than spend most of their time arresting each other. As with its predecessor, the Pathé-style 'gee, aren't these natives cute' narrative mingles speeded-up Keystone capers, a never-ending supply of mechanically-operated wildlife, and some of the naffest aerial SFX you're ever likely to see. DA

Gods of the Plague (Götter der Pest)

(Rainer Werner Fassbinder, 1969, WGer) Harry Baer, Hanna Schygulla, Margarethe von Trotta, Günther Kaufmann, Ingrid Caven.
91 min. b/w.

Remade (in more impressive form) as *The American Soldier* later the same year, Fassbinder's early gangster movie is slow, absurd, and quite mesmerising. Baer's the pretty criminal 'hero' who gradually sinks back into his underworld ways by hanging around with the wrong types: card-playing crooks and layabouts with trenchcoats and ever-present cigarettes, fickle molls hanging languorously on the sidelines. Any social comment is implicit rather than explicit, the world depicted is related more closely to classic American *noir* than any contemporary reality, and there is very little plot indeed. But it's a witty, stylish meditation on the genre, filtered through the decidedly dark and morbid sensibility of its director. GA

God Told Me To (aka Demon)

(Larry Cohen, 1976, US) Tony Lo Bianco, Sandy Dennis, Sylvia Sidney, Deborah Raffin, Sam Levene, Richard Lynch, Mike Kellin, Andy Kaufman.
95 min.

A delirious mix of sci-fi, pseudo-religious fantasy and horror detective thriller, with Lo Bianco as the perfect existential anti-hero – a New York cop and closet Catholic, guiltily trapped between wife and mistress. His investigations into a bizarre spate of mass murders lead right to the top: Jesus Christ, no less, is provoking innocent citizens to go on a murderous rampage. The wonderfully insane plot – involving spaceships, genetics and police corruption – builds to an ambiguous climax: a 'gay' confrontation which suggests an outrageous alternative to anal intercourse. *God Told Me To* overflows with such perverse and subversive notions that no amount of shoddy editing and substandard camerawork can conceal the film's unusual qualities. Digging deep into the psyche of American manhood, it lays bare the guilt-ridden oppressions of a soulless society. SW

Godzilla

(Roland Emmerich, 1998, US) Matthew Broderick, Jean Reno, Hank Azaria, Maria Pitillo, Michael Lerner, Harry Shearer.
138 min.

Toho's nuclear nightmare comes to America, like a very big chicken coming home to roost. This self-appointed box office behemoth from the makers of *Independence Day* is a plodding non-event. After a promising start, the movie falls apart almost as soon as Godzilla arrives in Manhattan – we'll buy a mutant lizard the size of a church, but it's a stretch to accept that the authorities keep losing track of the creature (then again, it does appear to change size according to the demands of the art director). Emmerich's sub-Spielbergian awe is constantly undercut by his own squeamishness – it's just not scary – and by the irritatingly drippy leads. You can't help praying for Broderick to get the chop, while Pitillo seems to think she's auditioning for a sitcom; only Reno comes out with head held high. Populist cataclysm requires a lighter touch than this. TCh

Godzilla 1985 (Gojira)

(Kohji Hashimoto/RJ Kizer, 1985, Jap) Raymond Burr, Keiju Kobayashi, Ken Tanaka, Yasuko Sawaguchi, Shin Takuma.
87 min.

Godzilla! exclaims a harassed Japanese PM, 'I was hoping I'd never hear that name again'. So, probably, was Raymond Burr, who featured in additional American footage for the 1954 original and here reprises his role as a reporter, summoned out of retirement to advise the wet-eared oiks in the Oval Office. In these times of megabuck SFX, it is refreshing to be presented with a man in a monster suit stomping on Dinky toys and punching holes through cardboard skyscrapers. Yet Godzilla is more than a mere monster, he is a 'product of our civilisation' and a dire warning to a weapon-wielding world. He is also an ambassador for peace: Americans (speaking American) find themselves ranged alongside Soviets (speaking subtitles) and Japanese (speaking dubbed). With the advent of ecological awareness, Godzilla has assumed heroic, even tragic status – Nature bites back with flashing fins and bad breath. Radioactive fallout cannot faze him, cadmium bombs merely stun him, and it is to the call of nature (in the form of birdsong) that this mighty behemoth finally succumbs. 'He's looking for something', observes one of the characters, 'Searching...' Yes! There is something of the Godzilla in us all. AB

Godzilla vs the Bionic Monster (Gojira tai Mekagojira)

(Jun Fukuda, 1974, Jap) Masaki Daimon, Kazuya Aoyama, Akihiko Hirata, Hiroshi Koizumi.
80 min.
A patchy romp in which villainous spacemen (apes at heart) plan to devastate Earth using Mechagodzilla, a fearsome bionic ogre disguised to look like the real champ. After a breathless intro during which a royal geisha has visions of the impending disaster, a spooky cave is unearthed, pieces of 'space titanium' are found, and Mechagodzilla makes mincemeat of one of our hero's mates (a sort of inflated, leaping hedgehog), the film becomes bogged down in a clutter of subplots, characters and technicalities. Things begin to pick up in the final epic confrontation between the two Godzillas and war god Ghinrah, who is woken up from his million year kip to lend a hand. Death rays zigzag and mouths belch fire with cartoon gusto, through overall the special effects are disappointing. IB

Godzilla vs the Smog Monster (Gojira tai Hedora)

(Yoshimitsu Banno, 1971, Jap) Akira Yamaguchi, Hiroyuki Kawase, Toshie Kimura, Toshio Shibaki, Keiko Mari.
85 min.
The tenth sequel to the original Godzilla. Your favourite oriental monster's sparring partner here is a king-sized lump of sludge (supposedly evolved from the industrial waste of a coastal town) that poses under the name of Hedora (Hopper? tails? sexual?) and looks like a cross between an owl and a festering turd. While the special effects aren't exactly Harryhausen (in fact two Jap midgets in costumes stomping around shoe-boxes painted to look like factories), and it's certainly no great shakes as sci-fi, there are a few laughs and an unintentionally funny 'Save the Earth' theme tune. PM

Go Fish

(Rose Troche, 1994, US) VS Brodie, Guinevere Turner, T Wendy McMillan, Migdalia Melendez, Anastasia Sharp.
83 min. b/w.
A lively romantic comedy set in Chicago which blows fresh air on the fusty conventions applied to the representation of lesbian and gay lives. Five women – aspirant writer Max, college lecturer Kia, reserved vet's assistant Ely, sharpminded Daria, divorced nurse Evy – do the thing twenty- and thirty-somethings do. They hang out, cook, drink, talk and then talk some more. Here for a change are people who seem to come from somewhere. Troche makes sure that detail is minutely, tellingly observed, and quite naturally adds a moral political dimension. What's also welcome is that the characters' sexual identity is given – they're lesbians. If you can accept that, now we're talking. WH

Go for a Take

(Harry Booth, 1972, GB) Reg Varney, Norman Rossington, Sue Lloyd, Dennis Price, Julie Ege, Patrick Newell, David Lodge.
90 min.
Varney and Rossington as two characters who find themselves pursued by a gang and seek refuge in a film studio, where Varney turns his hand to stunting and Rossington to hustling. They end up stealing a necklace and avoiding the gang in an extended chase sequence. A very weak comedy, equally uninspired whether hammering away at its twin themes of money and girls or putting Varney through yet another painful routine. DP

Goin' Down the Road

(Donald Shebib, 1970, Can) Doug McGrath, Paul Bradley, Jayne Eastwood, Cayle Chernin, Nicole Morin.
88 min.
Joey and Pete are running from a poverty-stricken region of the Maritimes in a fated attempt to escape a sequence of drab inevitabilities. Of course Toronto can only offer the same sort of job; of course one of them's going to hit a girl on an unlucky night; of course he'll marry her and set up house on hire purchase; he's going to get laid off from work because that's the nature of the work; they're going to huddle in depressing rooms, and argue more and more as the money hits zero; they're going to try robbing a supermarket; something's going to go wrong. The whole inescapable spiral is charted without ever putting an emotional foot wrong. We've all had bad times, but there's usually been something to get us on to the next plateau: luck, background, education. These two have none of this, and Shebib's first feature awakens anger at a society that invites dreams it cannot fulfil, teaching us a bit more about what's wrong. JC

Going in Style

(Martin Brest, 1979, US) George Burns, Art Carney, Lee Strasberg, Charles Hallahan, Pamela Payton-Wright.
96 min.
The director of Beverly Hills Cop and Scent of a Woman made an auspicious start to a Hollywood career as a purveyor of neatly crafted commercial undertakings with this warm and entertaining story of old codgers Burns, Carney and Strasberg hitting back at the society that's abandoned them by successfully robbing a Manhattan bank. A trio of contrasting personalities, the veterans bring both a mischievous wit and a sense of subdued anger to a familiar comic plotline, and the film achieves a rare balance of laughter and compassion. TJ

Going My Way

(Leo McCarey, 1944, US) Bing Crosby, Barry Fitzgerald, Rise Stevens, Gene Lockhart, Frank McHugh, Jean Heather, Stanley Clements.
126 min. b/w.
Godawful Oscar-winning schmaltz, with Crosby as a crooning, imbibing and golf-playing priest who saves the souls in his New York parish and wins over the man who holds the mortgage on the church as well. All this and Barry Fitzgerald doing his crotchety leprechaun act too. Go anywhere to avoid it. ATu

Going Places

see Valseuses, Les

Going Steady (Yotz' im Kavua)

(Boaz Davidson, 1979, Isr) Yiftach Katzur, Yvonne Michaels, Zacki Noy, Rachel Steiner, Jonathan Segal, Daphna Armoni.
88 min.
Brought to you by the makers of the disastrous Lemon Popsicle, this is equally dire and unremittingly sexist. 'Never pass up a potential piece' is the philosophy of one of its puerile heroes, and the film indulges his every whim. It's supposed to be an Israeli version of American Graffiti, but all it manages is an obscene level of childishness, and the ruination of 22 classic '50s hits (from The Platters to Brenda Lee). HM

Goin' South

(Jack Nicholson, 1978, US) Jack Nicholson, Mary Steenburgen, Christopher Lloyd, John Belushi, Veronica Cartwright, Richard Bradford, Danny De Vito.
108 min.
Nicholson's second film as director, a wonderfully beguiling Western in which he plays a sad sack outlaw (ex-cook to Quantrill's Raiders) snatched from the gallows by Steenburgen's prim spinster (taking advantage of a special ordinance occasioned by man shortage after the Civil War), who weds him and puts him to work mining for gold. Tender, bawdy and funny in its shaggy dog ramifications, their evolving relationship – she hankering for prosperous propriety in Philadelphia, he for lazy lustfulness in a Mexican cantina – is irresistible, and comes complete with a hilarious variation on the genre's inescapable shootout with the law. TM

Go, Johnny, Go!

(Paul Landres, 1958, US) Alan Freed, Jimmy Clanton, Sandy Stewart, Chuck Berry, Jo-Ann Campbell, Richie Valens, Eddie Cochran.
75 min. b/w.
As if the hilarious cynicism of The Girl Can't Help It had never happened, the almost-charming naïveté of Alan Freed's movies continued, ignoring racialism and presenting a painfully low-budget, cleaned-up version of rock'n'roll to calm parental fears. Hero Clanton (later to perpetrate 'Venus in Blue Jeans', but coming from the raunchy New Orleans school) grins his way stoically from rags to riches via a demo disc played on Freed's radio show. Everyone is so damned decent that the occasional sour comments from Freed and a studio bandleader sound like blasphemy. Laugh if you like, but as well as the crude fictionalising and dreadful miming, the film offers the only moving evidence of Ritchie Valens (even if Freed does rush out half-way through the song), a rare fragment of Eddie Cochran, the great Cadillacs camping through two Coasters-like numbers, and Chuck Berry struggling to be a nice guy in a 'major acting role'. JC

Gold

(Peter Hunt, 1974, GB) Roger Moore, Susannah York, Ray Milland, Bradford Dillman, John Gielgud, Tony Beckley, Simon Sabela.
124 min.
Moore fights a conspiracy to flood a gold mine and thus increase the world price of gold, allowing the villains to profit by prior investment. Apart from neat performances by Milland and Gielgud, the only point of note is that Gold was made in South Africa against union wishes. Predictably, black miners are depicted as a loyal army of cheery coons, a notion that concludes with a black overseer sacrificing his life to save Moore's. Ah, well, at least the film's idea of justice extends as far as having the villain (Dillman) run over by his own Rolls Royce. CPe

Gold Coast (aka Elmore Leonard's Gold Coast)

(Peter Weller, US, 1997) David Caruso, Marg Helgenberger, Jeff Kober, Barry Primus, Richard Bradford.
105 min.
Strange thing about Elmore Leonard adaptations, you can stick closely to the book, and it all comes right (Get Shorty, Jackie Brown), or you can stick closely to the book, and everything goes horribly wrong (as here). This has a plot set-up which takes some swallowing: Karen, a widowed Miami millionairess, appears to have it all – what she doesn't have is sex, because her husband decreed it in his will (the executor hires a heavy to enforce it, too). Ex-con/dolphin ringmaster Maguire (Caruso) comes into her life, and decides to help her out. Jeff Kober steals the show as Roland, the strong arm, but the leads are distinctly lacklustre, and Weller botches the behind-the-camera stuff – he seems to have discovered a new toy, 'shaki-cam'. TCh

Gold Diggers, The

(Sally Potter, 1983, GB) Julie Christie, Colette Laffont, Hilary Westlake, David Gale, Tom Osborn.
89 min. b/w.
It's all happening in this feminist experiment: frantic chases, gold rushes, horseback escapes, ballroom dances. But this is no action movie, for its heart is in its mouth, and the value of each character and scene is measured in metaphors. Sadly, Potter's cyclical, stylised, surreal film about a quest for knowledge, power and much more, illustrates nothing better than the difficulties inherent in this kind of undertaking. Hers is a cryptic world of shadows and ciphers, with meanings that are too elusive (or didactic) to command attention or encourage interest; and it is ironic that the best made point is achieved off-camera (by the assembly of an all-women crew to make the film). FD

Gold Diggers of 1933

(Mervyn LeRoy, 1933, US) Warren William, Joan Blondell, Aline MacMahon, Ruby Keeler, Dick Powell, Ginger Rogers, Ned Sparks, Guy Kibbee.
96 min. b/w.
Second of the archetypal backstage musicals

from Warners (it followed hard on the success of *42nd Street*) which established the idiosyncratic geometrics of Busby Berkeley. Some semblance of a plot (songwriter Powell turns against his wealthy parents in wishing to marry chorus girl Keeler), and enough Depression wisecracking from Blondell, MacMahon and Rogers; but most notable is the vulgar, absurd and wonderfully surreal Berkeley choreography. Great numbers: Ginger Rogers adorned in dollars singing 'We're in the Money'; young lovers interrupted by rain while 'Pettin' in the Park'; and on a strangely bleak note, the files of unemployed ex-servicemen during 'Remember My Forgotten Man'. Delirious and delightful. GA

Gold Diggers of 1935

(Busby Berkeley, 1934, US) Dick Powell, Adolphe Menjou, Gloria Stuart, Alice Brady, Hugh Herbert, Gloria Farrell, Frank McHugh, Winifred Shaw.
95 min. b/w.
Not a patch on *Gold Diggers of 1933*, this is set in a hotel where Powell, a medical student doubling as hotel clerk, falls for the daughter (Stuart) of a stingy multi-millionairess (Brady). The annual charity show is naturally being put on, and the plot revolves around the efforts of a mad Russian director (Menjou) and assorted associates to take the millionairess for as much as they can. Since Berkeley (his first solo as director) seems to have no idea how to handle actors, the result is acres of atrocious mugging (Menjou being the worst offender) and a couple of Powell ballads. Survive the first 70 minutes, however, and there are two big production numbers. The first ('The Words Are in My Heart') is standard Berkeley fare, involving chorines and waltzing white pianos. But 'The Lullaby of Broadway' is one of his most inventive choreographies: a mini-chronicle of a day in the life of the Great White Way, ending with the night bringing on an exhilarating horde of tap dancers. TM

Gold Diggers of 1937

(Lloyd Bacon, 1936, US) Dick Powell, Joan Blondell, Glenda Farrell, Victor Moore, Lee Dixon, Osgood Perkins.
100 min. b/w.
Dick Powell as a singing insurance salesman who interests ageing, hypochondriac producer Victor Moore in a million dollar policy, and puts on a show with the proceeds... Nuggets include two memorable Busby Berkeley set pieces. Fifty couples canoodling on fifty giant rocking-chairs in 'Let's Put Our Heads Together', and spunky Joan Blondell leading seventy chorus girls in a military-style tattoo called 'All's Fair in Love and War'. TCh

Golden Ball, The

see Ballon d'Or, Le

Golden Balls (Huevos de Oro)

(Bigas Luna, 1993, Sp) Javier Bardem, Maria De Medeiros, Maribel Verdu, Elisa Touati, Raquel Bianca, Alessandro Gassmann.
95 min.
Bardem plays Benito Gonzalez, a hustler who dreams of building the biggest skyscraper in Benidorm. After plump, two-timing Rita (Touati) breaks his heart, he determines not to let any woman past his defences; model Claudia (Verdu) is strictly a trophy broad. He marries Marta (De Medeiros) for her money and juggles his sharp, intelligent wife and compliant mistress while doing dodgy deals and wailing along to Julio Iglesias on his home karaoke machine, showing off his Rollex and jingling his bollocks like so much small change. Director Luna mixes admiration for this full-blooded fool with a rueful warning about the dangers of machismo. Reinforcing the central image of a vaunting skyscraper – can he get it up? – are phallic symbols galore, with eggs and lobsters the key foodstuffs. SFe

Golden Boy

(Rouben Mamoulian, 1939, US) Barbara Stanwyck, William Holden, Adolphe Menjou, Lee J Cobb, Joseph Calleia, Sam Levene, Edward Brophy.
99 min. b/w.
If Clifford Odets' play seems impossibly shop-worn today – boy from poverty row is tempted to abandon Art and his violin for the quick but brutalising rewards of the boxing-ring – at least this adaptation prunes away the worst, pseudo-poetical excesses of the original dialogue. Gone, too, is the character of the labour organiser, mouthpiece for Odets' flabby plea that the hero's choice is a matter for concern in terms of the ongoing struggle between Capital and Labour. What's left is melodrama, with the dilemma couched largely in moral and personal terms, and it stands up pretty well under Mamoulian's stylish direction, with its chiaroscuro lighting effects, savage final fight (shot with subjective camera), and gallery of excellent performances. Holden (in his film debut) is good in the title role; but the real treats are Menjou's mournfully cynical fight manager, Stanwyck's melting moll, and Calleia's wonderfully serio-comic, trigger-itchy gangster. TM

Golden Braid

(Paul Cox, 1990 Aust) Chris Haywood, Gosia Dobrowolska, Paul Chubb, Norman Kaye, Marion Heathfield, Monica Maughan.
91 min.
Inspired by Guy de Maupassant's short story *La Chevelure*, this is slighter than usual for Cox, but as witty as ever. Bernard (Haywood) is a fastidious clock-repairer with a history of collecting as many women as he does clocks. But his home is his true repository of pleasure, full of antiques and works of art, and chiming to the music of time. Into it he brings his newest conquest, the married Terese (Dobrowolska), but it's a perfect lock of golden hair, found secreted in a dresser, that unlocks his erotic passions and threatens to tip him into insanity. Though essentially a melancholy chamber piece, sustained by Haywood's quietly expressive performance, it is not without bursts of deliciously dark humour. Nino Martinetti's cinematography ensures a rich painterly surface, and the film is edited to produce a slow metronomic rhythm which lulls one rewardingly. WH

Golden Child, The

(Michael Ritchie, 1986, US) Eddie Murphy, Charles Dance, Charlotte Lewis, Randall 'Tex' Cobb, James Hong, Shakti, JL Reate.
94 min.
Hot on the heels of *Big Trouble in Little China*, this similarly attempts to weld the thrills of oriental martial arts movies on to the Hollywood comic thriller, and similarly swan dives between the two stools to fall flat on its fanny. Murphy is a freelance LA social worker who specialises in finding lost children. Spotted by various wise oriental persons as The Chosen One, he embarks on his mission to retrieve The Golden Child, an appealing little waif who will convert the world to goodness, but has been captured for the forces of darkness by Dance. As in *Big Trouble*, there is much playing around with oriental mythic nonsense: underground caverns, magic daggers, even a trip to Tibet. But where the movie really misses a trick is its inability to reproduce the balletic splendours of martial arts. There is a comely Tibetan wench who can sink the odd villain, but her leaping wouldn't get her past an audition for the Peking Opera. Dance, sporting an orange goatee, is a splendid villain, looking like a Victorian actor-manager. The surprise is Murphy, who relies more on his undoubted charm than on the stream of wisecracks he usually delivers. CPea

Golden Coach, The (La Carrozza d'Oro/ Le Carrosse d'Or)

(Jean Renoir, 1953, It/Fr) Anna Magnani, Duncan Lamont, Odoardo Spadaro, Riccardo Rioli, Paul Campbell, Nada Fiorelli, Jean Debucourt.
100 min.
The first film in what came to be seen as a trilogy (completed by *French Cancan* and *Eléna et les Hommes*) celebrating Renoir's continuing love affair with the theatre. Magnani plays the lead actress in a troupe of commedia dell'arte players in 18th century Peru. The story (derived from Prosper Mérimée) revolves around her pursuit by three different lovers. Both story and characterisations are remarkably silly, in fact, but Renoir makes gold of the interaction between theatre and life, the distinction between them continually shifting with the plot. Exquisitely shot by Claude Renoir, this is one of the great colour films. RM

Golden Eighties

(Chantal Akerman, 1986, Fr/Bel/Switz) Delphine Seyrig, Myriam Boyer, Fanny Cottençon, Lio, Pascale Salkin, Charles Denner, Jean-François Balmer, John Berry.
96 min.
A zippy, brightly coloured musical – rather like Jacques Demy on speed – which is a far cry from Akerman's earlier slow, serious examinations of women and their place. The setting is the enclosed world of a shopping mall: on one side Lili's hair salon, busy with excitable young shampoo girls; on the other a clothes boutique run by Monsieur Schwartz and wife Jeanne (played with a nervous false smile by Seyrig). Their son Robert lusts after Madonna-lookalike Lili, who shamelessly shifts between him and a lovelorn gangster. One of her girls, Mado, is hopelessly in love with Robert. Then Jeanne's old American lover turns up...Akerman breathlessly switches from one group to another, merging bustling set pieces with wistful solos, until somehow the threads come together in a celebration of tears for fears and rampant amour. Dangerously flirting with kitsch – some sections do resemble a wacky French pop special – Akerman once again gets away with the impossible by virtue of her energy, insight and enveloping sensuality. DT

GoldenEye

(Martin Campbell, 1995, GB/US) Pierce Brosnan, Sean Bean, Izabella Scorupco, Famke Janssen, Desmond Llewelyn, Joe Don Baker, Judi Dench, Robbie Coltrane, Tchéky Karyo, Alan Cumming, Minnie Driver, Samantha Bond.
120 min.
Six years after Timothy Dalton's last po-faced outing as 007, Brosnan takes over the role which Sean Connery once said was 'as difficult as Hamlet'. There's also a new Miss Moneypenny (Bond), a new M (Dench) and a new post-Communist world order. This Bond has been ruthlessly updated for '90s Russia: one scene takes place in a breaker's yard full of redundant Soviet statues. There's also an attempt to add depth to his character by introducing moral dilemmas – should he surrender, or let agent 006 (Bean) die? – and a hint of inner struggle. Thankfully, some things stay the same: Llewelyn makes his 15th appearance as Q, and there's another baddy who wants to inflict damage on the world, by stealing and controlling the 'GoldenEye' satellite activator, which disables everything electronic from outer space. Brosnan is most comfortable fighting, escaping or making the odd quip; in the more pensive scenes, particularly with impressive love interest Natalya (Scorupco), he seems lost. Director Campbell keeps matters bowling along and even manages to recapture something of the look of the earlier films. NKe

Golden Lady, The

(José Larraz, 1979, GB/HK) Christina World, June Chadwick, Suzanne Danielle, Anika Pavel, Stephen Chase, Edward de Souza, Patrick Newell.
94 min.
Bizarrely unimaginative mix of ingredients from *Charlie's Angels* and the Bond series: cute women agents whose greatest victories are scored in the sack. The location is London, the plot too complicated to believe (KGB, CIA, Israelis and Arabs in one ridiculous espionage arena), and the tone depressingly reminiscent of *The Bitch*. Forget it.

Golden Marie

see Casque d'Or

Golden Needles

(Robert Clouse, 1974, US) Joe Don Baker, Elizabeth Ashley, Jim Kelly, Burgess Meredith, Ann Sothern, Roy Chiao, Frances Fong.
92 min.
Another of the Weintraub/Heller rip-offs of the Chinese cinema, and certainly the most dull, cynical and reactionary yet, lacking the slim saving graces of either *Enter the Dragon* or *Black Belt Jones*. Its plot ties itself in dreary knots around the attempts of a couple of hired freelancers (Ashley and Baker) to obtain possession of an ancient Chinese statue which indicates the seven forbidden acupuncture points. The martial arts are peripheral, and anyway no match for Western muscle. Clouse once again proves himself one of the least competent directors around. VG

g

Golden Rendezvous

(Ashley Lazarus, 1977, US) Richard Harris, Ann Turkel, David Janssen, Burgess Meredith, John Vernon, Gordon Jackson, Keith Baxter, Dorothy Malone, John Carradine.
103 min.

Dud ship-board drama based on one of Alistair MacLean's more preposterous yarns (a cargo ship catering to wealthy gamblers is taken over by terrorists as prelude to a dastardly caper). Attention is briefly held as mercenaries machine-gun the casino. Unfortunately they miss Burgess Meredith, wearing a silly hat, big Ann Turkel as the bitch with a heart of gold bullion, and dear old Dorothy Malone with her secret sorrow. JS

Golden Salamander

(Ronald Neame, 1949, GB) Trevor Howard, Anouk Aimée, Herbert Lom, Miles Malleson, Walter Rilla, Jacques Sernas.
87 min. b/w.

Lame thriller about an English art expert on the trail of some priceless antiques in North Africa (including the jewel-studded allegorical creature of the title), but crossing the path of a gang of gun-runners. At least there's Anouk to look at, along with some photogenic locations, and Howard gives a sturdier performance than the material warrants. TM

Golden Seal, The

(Frank Zuniga, 1983, US) Steve Railsback, Michael Beck, Penelope Milford, Torquil Campbell, Seth Sakai, Richard Narita.
94 min.

Set on one of the bleak Aleutian islands off the coast of Alaska, this is not in fact a Disney film but it has the formula down pat. Boy loves seal. Dad hunts seal. Boy hates dad. Dad sees light. Stir in some postcard scenery, plus some guff about the golden seal's magical ecological properties, and that's about it. TM

Golden Swallow (Jin Yanzi)

(Chang Cheh, 1968, HK) Wang Yu, Cheng Pei-Pei, Lo Lieh, Wu Ma, Gu Feng.
104 min.

Shaw Brothers produced this sequel to King Hu's Come Drink with Me to 'punish' Hu for ending his contract with them (and for cleaning up with his first Taiwanese film, Dragon Gate Inn). Cheng Pei-Pei returns as the righteous swordswoman Golden Swallow, lured out of hiding by news that her trademark pin has been found near the bodies of assorted dead villains. The man responsible is Silver Roc (Wang Yu at his most impassive), who has loved her since childhood and kills bad guys by the score to prove it. Trouble is, her friend Han (Lo Lieh) also secretly loves her – and so emotional complications underpin the plot's martial mayhem. Better written, shot and edited than Shaw movies of the '70s (Bao Xueli's 'Scope cinematography includes some daring hand-held work), this carries rhetorical excesses to sublime heights. High points include Roc, in spotless white, despatching an entire army singlehanded and the climax, in which Roc fights on with four daggers embedded in his chest. Yes, it was a seminal influence on John Woo, soon to be Chang's assistant. TR

Goldfinger

(Guy Hamilton, 1964, GB) Sean Connery, Honor Blackman, Gert Froebe, Shirley Eaton, Harold Sakata, Bernard Lee.
112 min.

Vintage Bond from the moment our hero pops up out of the sea under a bobbing seagull attached to his frogman's suit which, having duly accomplished his explosive mission, he strips off to reveal an impeccable white dinner-jacket underneath. Ken Adam's sets, capped by the marvellous Fort Knox fantasy, are superb; and although Blackman's Pussy Galore is less than might be desired, there is suitably outsized villainy from Froebe and Sakata. Paul Dehn had a hand in the script, doubtless accounting for the unusually high incidence of wit in a script pleasantly laced with diabolic fantasy (from Eaton's demise by gold paint to Connery's near-emasculation by laser beam). TM

Goldfish (Huangjin Yu)

(Wu Di, 1995, China) Ma Xiaoyong, Zheng Tianwei, Yang Lu.
70 min.

This comic-edged first feature by Wu Di (cinematographer of The Days and Postman) has the same feel for street-level realities found in other Beijing indies, but a jauntier tone than most of them. Ma is the only guy his age in urban China who is scared to emigrate. One girlfriend has already left him over this issue; another gets him as far as the airport before he chickens out of flying to San Francisco. Trouble is, they've said their goodbyes to family and friends – and so they find themselves hiding in a rented farmhouse outside the city, pretending to be abroad. Retour d'Afrique had a similar premise, but this turns into a much sharper meditation on mental and other prisons when Ma starts breeding and selling goldfish, envying them their 'freedom'… TR

Gold Rush, The [100]

(Charles Chaplin, 1925, US) Charlie Chaplin, Mack Swain, Georgia Hale, Tom Murray, Henry Bergman, Betty Morrissey.
8,555 ft. b/w.

The Little Tramp is here the Lone Prospector, poverty stricken, infatuated with Hale, and menaced by thugs and blizzards during the Klondike gold rush of 1898. Famous for various imaginative sequences – Charlie eating a Thanksgiving meal of an old boot and laces, Charlie imagined as a chicken by a starving and delirious Swain, a log-cabin teetering on the brink of an abyss – the film is nevertheless flawed by its mawkish sentimentality and by its star's endsome winsome attempts to ingratiate himself into the sympathies of his audience. Mercifully, it lacks the pretentious moralising of his later work, and is far more professionally put together. But for all its relative dramatic coherence, it's still hard to see how it was ever taken as a masterpiece. GA

G'Olé!

(Tom Clegg, 1982, GB)
101 min.

Settling for redundantly regurgitating the spectacle of the final stages of the 1982 World Cup, this documentary compilation (narrated by Sean Connery, with commentary by Stan Hey) emerges as blandly unimaginative as its 'official film' status might imply. Where its 1966 precursor 'Goal' sustained itself on the potent novelty values of an England victory and flexible colour camerawork, this lags helplessly in the wake of high-quality blanket TV coverage, relying on a futile recreation of excitement over results and their immediate reverberations, while the penchant for low-angle close-ups on play ill serves a level of the game that's predominantly about finding and exploiting space. PT

Golem, The (Der Golem, Wie er in die Welt Kam)

(Paul Wegener, 1920, Ger) Paul Wegener, Albert Steinrueck, Ernst Deutsch, Lyda Salmonova.
69 min. b/w.

Spirited Ufa re-telling of the famous Jewish myth. When new anti-semitic laws are passed in 16th century Prague, an old rabbi, who's foreseen misfortune in the stars, brings the Golem to life. This ungainly hulking monster, made from clay with a pudding bowl haircut, terrorises the court into rescinding its laws against the Jews, but then goes on a wrecking spree of its own. Notable for its imaginative use of armies of extras and Karl Freund's expansive camerawork, Wegener's horror pic anticipates the many monster movies later made in Hollywood. The director was obsessed by the story of the Golem (he made two other films on the subject), quite an irony considering his later association with the Nazis. GM

Goliath and the Barbarians (Il Terrore dei Barbari)

(Carlo Campogalliani, 1959, It/US) Steve Reeves, Chelo Alonso, Giulia Rubini, Livio Lorenzon, Andrea Checchi, Bruce Cabot.
95 min.

AD 568: The Longobards sack Verona, in the process killing the father of young Emiliano, aka Goliath (Reeves, aka Mr Universe). Goliath organises a guerilla band, counterattacks, and is taken prisoner. He falls in love with the daughter of his captor, a barbarian duke. Everything works out, thanks to Goliath returning the sacred crown of the Longobard king. After much bloodshed Emiliano marries the girl (Alonso). Kitsch fare from that fondly remembered, but in fact irredeemably tacky age of TotalScope Italian epics. JPy

Go Naked in the World

(Ranald MacDougall, 1960, US) Gina Lollobrigida, Anthony Franciosa, Ernest Borgnine, Luana Patten.
103 min.

Don't get excited, the title is only a lurid fly. Franciosa brings home his new girlfriend, La Lollo, but dad Borgnine and the Italian siren go way back already. The players do not seem to have their hearts in this lumpen melodrama. TJ

Gone in 60 Seconds

(HB Halicki, 1974, US) HB Halicki, Marion Busia, Jerry Daugirda, James McIntyre, George Cole, Ronald Halicki.
103 min.

A rousing exercise in auto-snuff: how many cars can you demolish inside 103 minutes and still maintain interest in a plot? Almost half that time is taken up by another chase to end them all as 'Eleanor', the stolen Ford Mustang needed to complete a gigantic consignment (the title means how long it takes to steal a car, not to destroy it), creates a trail of havoc through LA and environs. 'Eleanor' is quite rightly credited at the start, since she has at least as much character as the human wrecking crew, who adopt a take-it-or-leave-it attitude about letting you know what's going on. If you take it, the wealth of sketched-in technical detail is fairly engrossing, and the energy of this Halicki production (he also wrote, directed, stars and supplied the vehicles) is arresting. It's a pity that it had to descend into such routine carnage. AN

Gone To Earth

(Michael Powell/Emeric Pressburger, 1950, GB) Jennifer Jones, David Farrar, Cyril Cusack, Esmond Knight, Sybil Thorndike, Edward Chapman, Hugh Griffith, George Cole, Beatrice Varley.
111 min.

A film much maligned in its time, not least by producer David O Selznick, who issued an American version retitled The Wild Heart, incorporating additional footage directed by Rouben Mamoulian and running only 82 minutes. Mary Webb's 1917 novel was the archetypal bodice-ripper – wicked squire, pious yokels, adultery and redemption –out of which Powell and Pressburger made a visually spellbinding romance. Christopher Challis' photography evokes Shropshire and the Welsh borders so that you can smell the earth. Menace, the bloodlust of the chase (of the fox or the outcast sinner), is omnipresent as trees bend and wild creatures panic before an unseen primal force. Cruelty besides beauty sweeps these pastoral vistas. Forget Jones' rustic English (Kentucky? Australian?) and the melodramatic clichés (boots trampling posies): the haunting, dreamlike consistency recalls that other fairy story of innocence and menace, The Night of the Hunter. MHoy

Gone With the Wind [100] (100)

(Victor Fleming, 1939, US) Clark Gable, Vivien Leigh, Leslie Howard, Olivia de Havilland, Thomas Mitchell, Hattie McDaniel, Ona Munson, Ann Rutherford, Evelyn Keyes.
222 min.

What more can one say about this much-loved, much discussed blockbuster? It epitomises Hollywood at its most ambitious (not so much in terms of art, but of middlebrow, respectable entertainment served up on a polished platter); it's inevitably racist, alarmingly sexist (Scarlett's submissive smile after marital rape), nostalgically reactionary (wistful for a vanished, supposedly more elegant and honourable past), and often supremely entertaining. It never really confronts the political or historical context of the Civil War, relegating it to a backdrop for the emotional upheavals of Leigh's conversion from bitchy Southern belle to loving wife. It's also the perfect example of Hollywood as an essentially collaborative artistic production centre. Cukor, Sam Wood and Fleming directed from a script by numerous writers (including Scott Fitzgerald and Ben Hecht); William Cameron Menzies provided the art designs; there's a top-notch cast; and producer David O Selznick oversaw the whole project obsessively from start to finish. Yet, although anonymous, it's still remarkably coherent. GA

Time Out Film Guide **349**

Gong Show Movie, The

(Chuck Barris, 1980, US) Chuck Barris, Robin Altman, Brian O'Mullin, Mable King, Murray Langston, Jaye P Morgan, Jamie Farr.
89 min.

A hit on US TV in the latter part of the '70s, *The Gong Show* was a forum for the talentless – the dentist who played tunes on his drill, the man who blew his trumpet through his navel – who got laughed at by a celebrity panel, or, worse, suffered the ignominy of the gong which terminated their plucky efforts. Unfortunately, Barris, the show's creator/presenter, seemed to be succumbing to megalomania by the time this cringingly diabolical spin-off appeared, detailing his own crises of confidence and mounting personal problems as he tries to keep his beloved show on the road. TJ

Gonin

(Takashi Ishii, 1995, Jap) Koichi Sato, Masahiro Motoki, Jinpachi Nezu, Naoto Takenaka, Toshiyuki Nagashima, 'Beat' Takeshi Kitano.
109 min.

Five rank social outsiders (bankrupt businessman, unemployed salaryman, dismissed cop, pimp and male prostitute) team up to rob a huge amount of money from the outwardly respectable Ogoshi yakuza gang; an implacably gay hitman ('Beat' Takeshi in an eyepatch) is sent to hunt them down. Both the visuals and the all-star cast are knockout, but it's the mix of genre renewal, social allegory and dirty (mostly gay) sexuality which makes the film extraordinary. The climaxes are so exciting they should come with a health warning. TR

Gonin 2

(Takashi Ishii, 1996, Jap) Ken Ogata, Shinobu Otake, Kimiko Yo, Yui Natsukawa, Yumi Nishiyama, Mai Kitajima, Yumi Takigawa, Toshiyuki Nagashima.
107 min.

Not quite the equal of the first film, but it was a typically smart idea to make the five outsiders women this time. Each has a deftly sketched reason to hate society in general and men in particular. They are about to rob an ultra-chic jewellery story when the Ogoshi gang beats them to it, so they set about relieving the yakuza of their haul. The wild card in play is Toyama (Ogata), the owner of a metalworks, who has his own major grudge against the gang and is bent on violent revenge. For sheer graphic flair and visual attack, Ishii's film-making is head-and-shoulders above what passes for comics-influenced cinema in the West. TR

Gonza the Spearman
(Yari no Gonza)

(Masahiro Shinoda, 1986, Jap) Hiromi Go, Shima Iwashita, Shohei Hino, Misako Tanaka, Haruko Kato, Takashi Tsumura, Kaori Mizushima.
126 min.

Osai's husband, shogun leader of the clan of Izumo, is called away on business. In his absence, she asks his favoured retainer, Gonza, to marry her young daughter. But Gonza is caught up within the intra-clan power struggle, as others seek to usurp his prominent position. Beneath structured ritual, beneath the unstructured dichotomy of masculine and feminine culture, Shinoda uncovers the motivating passions which slowly simmer before boiling to the surface. Based on the 18th century play by Monzaemon Chikamatsu, the film's triumph comes with its final samurai confrontation, two dishonoured men left with no choice but to fulfil their prescribed roles. SGo

Goodbye, Boys
(Do Svidanija, Maltsjiki)

(Mikhail Kalik, 1966, USSR) Yevgeni Steblov, Mikhail Kononov, Nikolai Dostal.
97 min.

Directed by a great lost name of '60s Soviet cinema, this was shelved and forbidden for export, emerging only 25 years later. It shouldn't be seen purely as a historical curio, though. Very much of its time, but still extremely fresh, it's an alternately lyrical and cynical evocation of youth in a Black Sea resort before World War II. Three adolescent boys enjoy their last summer together

before being packed off reluctantly to military school. The use of newsreel footage – which was partly what got the film into trouble – is somewhat jarring, but otherwise it is light on polemic. The boys' quirks and follies are sympathetically observed, and the sense of place is flawless. JRo

Goodbye, Columbus

(Larry Peerce, 1969, US) Richard Benjamin, Ali MacGraw, Jack Klugman, Nan Martin, Michael Meyers, Lori Shelle, Royce Wallace.
105 min.

A wonderfully beady-eyed adaptation of Philip Roth's novella satirising the Jewish *nouveau riche* and/or the American Dream, with Benjamin as the impoverished graduate courting a Radcliffe girl (MacGraw), and discovering what he's got into only when she invites him (to the exasperation of her socially ambitious mother) to stay as a house guest. Self-effacingly directed by Peerce, the film stakes everything on minute observation of detail: the ghastly gusto of mealtimes in the *parvenu* dining-room; the loose-limbed insolence in every movement made by the scion of the family; the worship of appearances rather than accomplishments in everything that is said or done. With Philip Roth's barbed dialogue retained intact, and faultlessly delivered by an admirable cast, the film is funnier than *The Graduate* (made a couple of years earlier) and much less pretentious. TM

Goodbye Emmanuelle

(François Leterrier, 1977, Fr) Sylvia Kristel, Umberto Orsini, Jean-Pierre Bouvier, Charlotte Alexandra, Jacques Doniol-Valcroze, Olga Georges-Picot, Alexandra Stewart.
98 min.

This awful episode in the *Emmanuelle* saga takes a curious moral turn. When one of her passing fancies calls her a whore, her only recourse is to fall in love with him. The double standard evident in previous adventures – where Kristel portrays a woman apparently choosing to practice sexual freedom, while in fact being savagely exploited – is dropped. Suddenly it's all jealousy, privacy and tears around bedtime. Much agony, low on ecstasy. JS

Goodbye Girl, The

(Herbert Ross, 1977, US) Richard Dreyfuss, Marsha Mason, Quinn Cummings, Paul Benedict, Barbara Rhoades.
110 min.

Written by Neil Simon, it's no surprise that this is a classy piece of Broadway sitcom. Mason and Dreyfuss play with comic panache and vitality as the couple reluctantly obliged to cohabit, even if occasionally their physical energy adds to the impression that this is simply theatre on celluloid. Equally, interest flags after they get to bed, endorsing the line that 'It's amazing how flabby you get when you're happy'. But overall Simon's ego-splitting wisecracks make for many good laughs, even though, in contrast to Woody Allen's nervous New York humour, which has the discomforting ring of truth, Simon opts for a playwright's ring of confidence. JS

Goodbye, Mr Chips

(Sam Wood, 1939, GB) Robert Donat, Greer Garson, Terry Kilburn, John Mills, Paul Henreid, Judith Furse, Lyn Harding, Milton Rosmer, Guy Middleton, Nigel Stock.
113 min. b/w.

With his cane, scarf, mortar-board and perpetual hangdog expression, Robert Donat seemed to embody Neville Chamberlain – 'I have a piece of paper and it's spelt incorrectly. One hundred lines, Master Hitler, or you'll be slippered'. Actually, the movie always was a museum piece, and– if you are in the right mood – a deeply affecting one. Donat's schoolmaster looks back upon his life – his surrogate fatherhood to scores of boys, his marriage to Mrs Miniver, who dies during childbirth – and Olde England passes before our very eyes. ATu

Goodbye, Mr Chips

(Herbert Ross, 1968, GB) Peter O'Toole, Petula Clark, Michael Redgrave, George Baker, Michael Bryant, Jack Hedley, Sian Phillips.
147 min.

Incredibly bloated remake, with Mrs Chips an ex-showgirl (allowing for some vacuous songs), a continental holiday (allowing for a travelogue wallow),

and Herbert Ross (his first film as director), trying to match Wyler's choreographed camera movements on *Funny Girl* but failing to make them serve any meaningful purpose. The pity of it is that Peter O'Toole sketches an excellent performance amid the debris – angular and desiccated as a stick insect, but endowing the character with both an inside and an outside, so that his metamorphosis from passionless pedant into loveable eccentric is perfectly credible. Good support too, from Redgrave and Bryant in particular, but they're trapped like flies in the sticky confection. TM

Goodbye New York

(Amos Kollek, 1984, Isr) Julie Hagerty, Amos Kollek, Shmuel Shiloh, Aviva Ger, David Topaz.
90 min.

Garrulous insurance saleswoman Hagerty, betrayed by her unfaithful hubby, sets out for Paris in seach of peace of mind, only to end up penniless and stranded in Israel. Kollek offers us a predictable plot and dismal propaganda about the values of kibbutz culture. A fatal flaw in the film is that both Hagerty and Kollek himself, playing an Israeli army reserve who becomes her chief suitor, are so unsympathetic. Another is that Hagerty's sub-Judy Holliday kook is simply not strong enough to carry such thin and clichéd material. GA

Goodbye, Norma Jean

(Larry Buchanan, 1975, US/Aust) Misty Rowe, Terrence Locke, Patch Mackenzie, Preston Hanson, Marty Zagon.
95 min.

Managing the feat of holding its nose and leering at the same time, this 'biopic' mixes scurrility and a token feminism with rock-bottom production values. 'Not legend, nor the way she told it, this is how it was' promises the introduction, thereby allowing for a highly speculative hour-and-a-half about Marilyn Monroe's early career on the casting couch. Even the sustained loathing of men ('That's the last cock I'll ever have to suck' are the film's final words) is diluted by the presence of an unlikely father-figure producer who takes Marilyn's career in hand. Misty Rowe fails spectacularly as a reincarnation of Monroe.

Goodbye Pork Pie

(Geoff Murphy, 1980, NZ) Tony Barry, Kelly Johnson, Claire Oberman, Shirley Gruar, Jackie Lowitt.
105 min.

Using the well-established caper-chase road movie format, this follows two 'irrepressible' buddies on a 1,000 mile 'let's get smashed' odyssey in a stolen car, in pursuit of love and pursued by cops. But for all its admittedly speedy pace, the film pays mere lip service to the idea of characterisation and to 'earthy' humour with its lame, often objectionable jokes: 'irrepressible' means sexist antics such as betting on a girl's virginity, cursing 'stupid bloody bitches' ad nauseam, indulging in drink, dope and drearily juvenile zaniness. Only towards the end does the film pick up in its predictably darkening mood. But even then too many elements are plagiarised; *Sugarland Express*, especially, told a similar tale with far more thrills, wit and humanity. GA

Goodbye South, Goodbye
(Nanguo Zai Jian, Nanguo)

(Hou Xiaoxian, 1996, Tai) Jack Kao, Hsu Kuei-ying, Lim Giong, Anne Shizuka Inoh.
110 min.

Though Hou has said that he wanted this to have a different rhythm from the slow, even static pace of his previous work, it remains immediately recognisable as a Hou movie, not only because of the very lengthy takes (here, admittedly, often of moving trains, cars, motorbikes, etc), but because of his determinedly oblique approach to narrative and the way it provides information. This time round, the 'story' of a group of small-time punks on the fringes of the underworld is designed to offer insights into the moral, political and economic climate of '90s Taiwan; it does, and the movie looks as marvellous as ever. But for all the expertise on view, one can't help feeling a sense of déjà vu. The film echoes much of Hou's own previous work, and the plot's central strand – an ambitious guy and his younger, more volatile buddy finally get their comeuppance in a car crash – is oddly reminiscent of *Mean Streets*. GA

Good Burger

(Brian Robbins, 1997, US) Kenan Thompson, Kel Mitchell, Abe Vigoda, Sinbad, Shar Jackson.
95 min.
This TV spinoff asks us to root for the trash food joint of the title, and specifically its hero, Ed (Mitchell), an exceptionally annoying imbecile. The staff of Good Burger are more adept at driving out would-be customers with execrable puns than serving their orders, so the bad boys across the road at Mondo Burger need no help in driving their small fry rivals out of business. Enter Dexter (Thompson), a more conventionally wayward adolescent than Ed, who needs to work through the school vacation to pay off the insurance on two sportscars he's wrecked. Dexter notes that Ed makes very nice homemade burger sauce, and suddenly Good Burger is back in business. Few people can be so big-hearted as to tolerate Ed's agonising brand of pedantic humour. NB

Good Companions, The

(Victor Saville, 1933, GB) Edmund Gwenn, Mary Glynne, John Gielgud, Jessie Matthews, Percy Parsons, AW Baskcomb, Max Miller.
113 min. b/w.
JB Priestley's fantasy, in which a demure spinster, an elderly mill-worker and an effete schoolteacher throw security to the winds to seek fortune and adventure with a broken-down band of travelling players, is so engaging that one easily forgives its sentimentality. Saville's direction is adequate rather than inspired, but he elicits marvellous performances from his disparate cast. Matthews' portrayal of a bubblingly neurotic soubrette is wonderful, and not surprisingly shot her to stardom. The film does feed on rather than explore the twee camaraderie of the provincial touring company, but an English backstage musical as witty and well-handled as this is something to be thankful for indeed. RMy

Good Companions, The

(J Lee Thompson, 1956, GB) Celia Johnson, Eric Portman, John Fraser, Janette Scott, Hugh Griffith, Joyce Grenfell, Rachel Roberts, Thora Hird, Mona Washbourne, Alec McCowen, John Le Mesurier, Anthony Newley.
104 min.
Priestley's novel is given a Technicolor and CinemaScope update making it far plusher than the tightly budgeted 1933 version. This time Johnson, Portman and Fraser are the spinster, the bluff Northerner and the teacher who bring new life to the Dinky Doos pierrot troupe, and put youngster Scott's name up in lights. It doesn't have quite the same charm as the earlier adaptation, but is solidly done all the same, with a regiment of familiar faces in the minor roles. TJ

Good Die Young, The

(Lewis Gilbert, 1954, GB) Laurence Harvey, Gloria Grahame, Richard Basehart, Joan Collins, John Ireland, Stanley Baker, Margaret Leighton, Robert Morley.
98 min. b/w.
Producer Jack Clayton and director Lewis Gilbert (the most hard-working of all British post-war film-makers) assembled a top Anglo-American cast for this predictable but not unentertaining thriller (from a novel by Richard Macauley). Psychotic playboy Harvey finds himself short of the readies so he persuades ex-GI Basehart, AWOL Air Force sergeant Ireland and no-hope boxer Baker to join him in holding up a mail van. This being a British picture from the '50s, you don't expect them to get away with it – but neither do you quite anticipate Joan Collins and Gloria Grahame popping up in such low-key supporting roles as they do here. GM

Good Earth, The

(Sidney Franklin, 1937, US) Paul Muni, Luise Rainer, Walter Connolly, Charley Grapewin, Jessie Ralph, Tilly Losch, Keye Luke.
138 min. b/w.
'Who wants to see a picture about Chinese farmers?' asked LB Mayer of his production chief Irving Thalberg. Thalberg had asked the same question about a Civil War picture called Gone With the Wind. The answer in both cases was millions, but in the case of The Good Earth the reasons are quite bewildering. A kind of Lychees of Wrath, it's a typically lumbering, cautious,

overblown Thalberg project, saved by Rainer's genuinely moving, Oscar-winning portrayal of Chinese peasantry, and by an immensely spectacular storm of locusts. Thalberg died during the production, and Mayer accorded him a special tribute on the credits, the only time that the name of the last tycoon appeared on a film. ATu

Good Father, The

(Mike Newell, 1986, GB) Anthony Hopkins, Jim Broadbent, Harriet Walter, Frances Viner, Simon Callow, Miriam Margolyes, Joanne Whalley.
90 min.
Hopkins is a middle-aged, middle-class, middle-minded man, impaled on the post-feminist hook. Having once been a subscriber to the cause, he has since been thrown out of his home, and pays alimony for the privilege of having his child turned against him. The worm turns and he embarks on a none-too-fair legal battle, in order to 'jerk her lead'. The early stages of this battle of the sexes are by turns hilarious and squirm-making, but Christopher Hampton's script finally opts for an uneasy truce, perhaps a soft option after the initial viciousness. But it's a very brave foray across the minefield; its detonations will have you ducking for cover, whatever your sex or persuasion. CPea

GoodFellas (100)

(Martin Scorsese, 1990, US) Robert De Niro, Ray Liotta, Joe Pesci, Lorraine Bracco, Paul Sorvino, Frank Sivero, Gina Mastrogiacomo, Frank Vincent, Chuck Low.
145 min.
Scorsese's fast, violent, stylish mobster movie is a return to form, De Niro, and the Italian-American underworld. But in following, from '55 to the late '70s, the true-life descent into big-time crime of Henry Hill (Liotta), he and co-writer Nick Pileggi seem less concerned with telling a lucid, linear story than with providing sociological evidence of an ethically (ethnically?) marginalised society united by the desire to make a fast buck. Because Hill and the older 'good fellas' he first falls in with as an awestruck kid – De Niro, Pesci, Sorvino – exist almost totally on the surface, we watch shocked and beguiled but never come to care. The camera and cutting style is as forcefully persuasive as a gun in the gut, so that we are not enlightened but excited by the cocky camaraderie, bloody murder, and expansive sense of 'family' on view. Still, the movie excites the senses in a way few film-makers even dream of, and its epic sweep and brilliantly energetic film language rest on a cluster of effortlessly expert performances. GA

Good Fight, The

(Noel Buckner/Mary Dore/Sam Sills, 1983, US) Bill Bailey, Ed Balchowsky, Ruth Davidow, Evelyn Hutchins.
98 min. b/w & col.
Just about the most stirring documentary you'll ever see. Through newsclips, old photographs and interviews with survivors, it tells the story of the 3,200 men and women who fought with the American Lincoln Brigade during the Spanish Civil War: men like Bill Bailey, the longshoreman who laughs as he describes how, during an anti-Nazi demonstration in New York in 1935, he and a friend boarded a German ship and tore down its swastika; women like Evelyn Hutchins, who had to fight to persuade her colleagues into letting her serve as the only female ambulance driver. What seems to have motivated them was America's deliberate non-intervention. 'That was my brother out there', says one volunteer; 'You had to put up or shut up' says another; and they all describe 'an enormous feeling of wanting to come to grips' with what they saw as the tide of Fascism about to engulf Europe. What comes over most strongly is the resolute idealism of those who fought, and did so in a way that seems impossibly heroic in these unheroic times. They were young, 'just chickenshit kids', untrained, and with no idea of what they were letting themselves in for. Yet they went and suffered terrible casualties. Now, although in their seventies, their enthusiasm for the cause remains undimmed, and a bunch of them are seen marching proudly as Lincoln Brigade veterans in a huge demo against US involvement in El Salvador. They may have lost the battle, but as one of them concludes, but the war against Fascism was won, and the good fight continues. CB

Good Guys and the Bad Guys, The

(Burt Kennedy, 1969, US) Robert Mitchum, George Kennedy, David Carradine, Tina Louise, John Davis Chandler, John Carradine, Marie Windsor.
90 min.
Burt Kennedy's characteristically affectionate Western comedy sees ageing sheriff Mitchum join forces with his old bandit enemy George Kennedy to outwit Carradine and his gang of younger, rather less honorable robbers, and in so doing, cock a snook at Balsam, the opportunist and self-inflated mayor who has demanded Mitchum's retirement. In noting the passing of the Old West, and upholding honour and age over expediency and youth, Kennedy comes closer to the Peckinpah of Ride the High Country than of The Wild Bunch; even so, the humour here is broad and cheery rather than elegiac and violent. The performances are delightful throughout, and Kennedy, quite rightly, gives them free rein. GA

Good Guys Wear Black

(Ted Post, 1977, US) Chuck Norris, Anne Archer, James Franciscus, Lloyd Haynes, Dana Andrews, Jim Backus.
95 min.
Whether taken as a cynical companion to prestigious Hollywood Vietnam movies, a twisting political conspiracy, or a starring vehicle for world karate champion Chuck Norris, this complicated action caper hovers between OK and mediocre. A mysterious spate of assassinations follow a top secret US raid into North Vietnam, with veteran Norris suspecting that they were set up by corrupt politicians as part of an expedient deal with the reds to end the war. Norris ties it all up and biffs sense into those too yellow to own up in a post-Watergate world where expediency is all, and honour is a dirty word. A successor to Go Tell the Spartans from the studiously unsentimental Post. DMacp

Good Life, The (La Buena Vida)

(David Trueba, 1996, Sp) Fernando Ramallo, Lucia Jiménez, Luis Cuenca, Isabel Oetero, Joel Joan, Victoria Peña, Jordi Bosch.
105 min.
This uneven, but not uninteresting first feature starts alarmingly (in sub-Toto the Hero vein) with the 14-year-old protagonist, a would-be writer, recalling his life from pre-natal days – before picking up a little when he learns that his parents have died in a car crash, while he's planning to lose his cherry to a whore. Thereafter the film concerns the boy's efforts to overcome loneliness and guilt, to sort out his own problems and those of his relatives, and generally to get through growing up without too much pain. Weakest when most whimsical, the film is nevertheless sporadically perceptive about adolescent experience. Lively, amiable, and eminently forgettable. GA

Good Man in Africa, A

(Bruce Beresford, 1993, US) Colin Friels, Sean Connery, John Lithgow, Diana Rigg, Louis Gossett Jr, Joanne Whalley-Kilmer.
94 min.
Just as casting can be the making of a film, so it can be its ruination. A case in point is this adaptation of William Boyd's comic novel about the political, diplomatic and sexual machinations surrounding an impending election in the emerging oil-rich state of Kinjana. As frustrated mid-level British diplomat Morgan Leafy, a role tailor-made for Timothy Spall, we have the more bankably handsome Australian actor Colin Friels; as his boorish boss, High Commissioner Fanshawe, we have American John Lithgow, whose 'English' accent has improved not a jot since Cliffhanger; and as Professor Adekunle, wily would-be president of the corrupt African state, Louis Gossett Jr, who appears to be more basketball player than politician. Screenwriter Boyd has turned his laugh-out-loud novel into a groan-out-loud movie. NF

Good Marriage, A

see Beau Mariage, Le

Good Men, Good Women
(Haonan, Haonü)

(Hou Hsiao-hsien, 1995, Jap/Tai) Annie
Shizuka Inoh, Lim Giong, Jack Kao.
108 min.
Hou again looks at recent Taiwanese history.
The story centres on an actress mourning her
lover who's convinced she's receiving silent
phone calls from the person who stole her diary.
She begins to identify with the character she's
playing in a movie about a couple involved in the
Resistance during the '40s and '50s. With its narrative switching between past and present, 'reality' and the film-within-a-film, Hou's movie is
complex and challenging, but never inaccessible.
Blending the personal with the political to typically resonant effect, it's a multi-layered exploration of changing cultural ideals, haunted
memories, and the joys and pains of love. With
patience, it soon becomes clear this is some sort
of masterpiece. GA

Good Morning

see Ohayo

Good Morning, Miss Dove

(Henry Koster, 1955, US) Jennifer Jones, Robert
Stack, Kipp Hamilton, Robert Douglas, Peggy
Knudsen, Chuck Connors, Jerry Paris.
107 min.
Sentimental but professionally assembled classroom chronicle follows much-loved spinster
schoolma'm Jennifer Jones through generations
of diverse pupils at a small town high school,
before a spine tumour sends her to hospital where
surgeon Stack, a former student, must undertake
a risky operation to save her. Few sharp edges,
but just the thing for a homespun Sunday afternoon wallow. TJ

Good Morning...and Goodbye
(aka The Lust Seekers)

(Russ Meyer, 1967, US) Alaina Capri, Stuart
Lancaster, Pat Wright, Haji, Karen Ciral, Don
Johnson, Tom Howland.
78 min.
Connoisseurs of camp who revere Russ Meyer's
majestic *Beyond the Valley of the Dolls* will be
disappointed by this low-budget earlier effort.
Although loins quiver, studs flex their pectorals, and cantilevered breasts career across
the screen, the film is distinctly skimpy and
down-market. Despite the sonorous moralising
in prologue and epilogue about 'humble sex,
that three-letter word whose power cannot be
demeaned by the foulness of four-letter words',
such splendid silliness is not maintained
throughout the story of Burt, impotent middle-
aged businessman, and his randy, taunting wife
Angel, for whose legs anytime is opening time.
DJe

Good Morning Babylon
(Good Morning Babilonia)

(Paolo Taviani/Vittorio Taviani, 1986,
It/Fr/US) Vincent Spano, Joaquim De Almeida,
Greta Scacchi, Désirée Becker, Omero
Antonutti, Charles Dance, Bérangère
Bonvoisin.
117 min.
The Taviani brothers' first (mainly) English language film, set just before and during World War
I, concerns two inseparable Tuscan brothers,
stonemasons who – like their forefathers –
restore Romanesque cathedrals. Suddenly finding themselves without work, they travel to
America in search of the fortune that will allow
them to return to revive their father's business;
after endless setbacks, they finally win acclaim
for their work on the Babylonian elephants for
DW Griffith's *Intolerance*. As in their previous
films, the Tavianis take an oblique and deeply
personal look at history to create a fable of enormous resonance. Realism merges with the surreal, fact with fiction, and a *faux-naïf* surface (not
unlike that of the films from the period depicted)
conceals a complex interweaving of familiar
Taviani themes: the continuing strengths and
shortcomings of tradition and patriarchy, the
importance of imagination, memory and collective endeavour. Typically, sentimentality is held
at bay by the cool, formalised direction. The performances throughout are splendid, the symbolism never intrusive, the entire achievement witty
and elegant. GA

Good Morning, Boys!
(aka Where There's a Will)

(Marcel Varnel, 1937, GB) Will Hay, Graham
Moffatt, Lilli Palmer, Martita Hunt, Mark
Daly, Charles Hawtrey.
79 min. b/w.
This brisk vehicle for Hay's idiosyncratic talents
has him in the tailor-made role of a roguish
schoolmaster, whose wayward teaching methods
win him a trip to Paris with his French class.
There's a stowaway in the party and they become
involved in the theft of the Mona Lisa. Hay's persona is a much more cynical and devious than the
gauche type George Formby played for director
Varnel, which goes some way to explaining why
this, his finest hour, hasn't dated too badly. TJ

Good Morning Vietnam

(Barry Levinson, 1987, US) Robin Williams,
Forest Whitaker, Tung Thanh Tran, Chintara
Sukapatana, Bruno Kirby, Robert Wuhl, JT
Walsh, Noble Willingham.
108 min.
As US Armed Forces Radio DJ Adrian Cronauer,
dumped in Saigon, in '65, Williams reveals how
easy it is to hang a slim, bathetic idea on a virtuoso performance. Cronauer is your archetypal all-
American anti-hero, an achingly funny, irreverent
motormouth with a taste for hot soul and a subversive vision of the Vietnam conflict as a mad
Wizard of Oz scenario which enrages the top brass
as inevitably as it boosts the morale of the grunts.
Williams' rendition of the broadcasting sequences
is terrific, as speedily inventive as the comic's
finest stand-up moments, even though Levinson
has an irritating habit of cutting away to
Cronauer's colleagues and audience cracking up,
simply to show that the guy's funny. But the story
itself is bunk. Besides the DJ's heroic set-to with
petty-minded superiors, there's a crass romance
with a shy young Vietnamese, and a friendship
with her brother, which allows our fine liberal protagonist to play great white god to the gooks.
Offering only hackneyed insights into the war, the
film makes for stodgy drama. But Williams' manic
monologues behind the mike are worth anybody's
money. GA

Good Mother, The

(Leonard Nimoy, 1988, US) Diane Keaton,
Liam Neeson, Jason Robards, Ralph Bellamy,
Teresa Wright, James Naughton, Asia Vieira.
103 min.
Heartbreak time in this rigged tug-of-love drama.
Divorced Anna (Keaton) brings up six-year-old
daughter Molly (Vieira) on her own, and is making
out nicely until she discovers the realm of the senses in the bed of sculptor Leo (Neeson). It's a shock
when Molly reports to her father (Naughton) that
Leo let her touch his penis, and he sues for custody.
That was in fact all very innocent, but their taking
the sleeping child into their bed during sex was
questionable, and Anna's lawyer (Robards) advises her to throw Leo to the wolves if she wants to
keep her kid. Is it possible to combine sexual ecstasy with motherhood, asks the blurb, but that's hardly made into a universal brain-teaser, nor into a
comment on society's transition from permissive
'60s to staid '80s, by this special case. Performances
are good, though Keaton's snorting laughs and distracted manner are a bit of an obstacle course.
Three hankie job. BC

Goodnight Vienna
(aka Magic Night)

(Herbert Wilcox, 1932, GB) Jack Buchanan,
Anna Neagle, Clive Currie, Gina Malo, William
Kendall, Joyce Bland.
76 min. b/w.
'Vienna in the summer of 1914 – gayest, hand-
somest city in Europe, famous alike for the lilt of
its waltzes and the beauty of its women...Vienna,
capital of love, where days are made for love and
nights for kisses.' As the gushing introduction
suggests, this romantic musical, adapted from a
radio play, is sheer syrup from beginning to end.
Buchanan plays a dashing Austrian cavalry officer (with his lopsided grin and braying diction,
he looks and sounds as if he's just slipped out of
a PG Wodehouse novel). Neagle, making her
screen debut, is the Eliza Doolittle-like flower seller he falls in love with. War comes between them.
He ends up a penniless shoe salesman, while she
rises to become a great singer. The two are no
longer on talking terms, but not even Neagle can
resist Buchanan in full song. GM

Good Old Daze

see Péril Jeune, Le

Good People of Portugal, The
(Bom Povo Português)

(Rui Simoes, 1980, Port)
130 min. b/w.
An exemplary piece of agit-documentary which,
in its own context, is as experimental and revolutionary as Vertov's *Man with a Movie Camera*.
The events of Portugal's 'Carnation' Revolution
and the subsequent eighteen months are complex,
but this combination of heady lyricism and sharp
political analysis transmits the popular energy
that gave western Europe its most uplifting mass
movement of recent years. Newsreel, satire, re-
enactments and popular music come together
dynamically in a film that is both about the people and for the people. MA

Good Son, The

(Joseph Ruben, 1993, US) Macaulay Culkin,
Elijah Wood, David Morse, Wendy Crewson,
Daniel Hugh Kelly, Jacqueline Brookes,
Quinn Culkin.
87 min.
Now, here's a thing: two years after its US
release, this bad seed thriller reaches Britain,
by-passing cinemas despite healthy US box-
office takings. The reason has nothing to do
with the film's shortcomings and everything to
do with the murder of the Liverpool toddler
James Bulger by two small boys and the media
uproar which followed. Based on an original
screenplay by Ian McEwan (who disowned the
film), the story concerns young Mark (Wood),
who comes to stay with his aunt and uncle and
gradually discovers that his cousin Henry
(Macaulay Culkin) is psychotic. Despite a few
crude philosophical stabs at the nature of evil,
the film is basically a straight-ahead melodrama, driven home with force if not finesse by the
director of *The Stepfather*. Kit Culkin apparently held Fox to ransom over *Home Alone 2* to
extend his son's range with this role – in the
event, young Mac is decisively upstaged by
Wood, but the film's strongest selling point has
to be a cliff-top finale in which the tyke's own
mother has to choose whether he'll live or die.
A summer camp classic. TCh

Good, the Bad and the ⑩⑩
Ugly, The
(Il Buono, il Brutto, il Cattivo)

(Sergio Leone, 1966, It) Clint Eastwood, Eli
Wallach, Lee Van Cleef, Aldo Giuffrè,
Mario Brega.
180 min.
Hard to tell who's good, bad or ugly in this bitterly cynical portrait of America during the Civil
War, with the three leads indulging in ruthless
violence and self-help as they search for a buried
fortune. Nevertheless, for all its shortcomings as
a study in relative morality, Leone's final *Dollars*
Western delights through its subversive, operatic parody of genre conventions, undercutting
heroism by means of black comedy and over-the-
top compositions, all deep focus and zooms. And
Morricone's score is as powerful as always. It's
enormous fun. GA

Good to Go

(Blaine Novak, 1986, US) Art Garfunkel,
Robert Doqui, Harris Yulin, Reginald
Daughtry, Richard Brooks, Paula Davis.
90 min.
A vindictive cop (nastily well-played by Yulin)
pursues a young black gang who've perpetrated rape and murder while low on Angel Dust
and after they had been prevented from attending a Washington Go-Go gig. The music is culpable by association. Reporter/lush Garfunkel
(limp) is duped into abetting the racist cop, until
indignant blacks force Art's pink eyes open.
The real star, of course, is the music of Trouble
Funk, Chuck Brown & The Soul Searchers, and
Redds & The Boys. Go-Go is Washington's
form of superhard funk. It's heavy duty but
clean and proud, and makes you dance like you
always knew you could. GBr

Good Wife, The

see Umbrella Woman, The

Good Wife of Tokyo, The

(Kim Longinotto/Claire Hunt, 1992, GB)
52 min.

This thoroughly captivating, amusing documentary records singer Kazuko Hohki's visit to her home town of Tokyo where, in between performances with her group the Frank Chickens, she gets married and canvasses women's views on their changing role in Japanese society. The most fascinating revelations come from Hohki's wonderful mother who, as a priest in the religious group House of Development, preaches the benefits of laughter within a doctrine for positive living. Her Zen demonstration on the art of a long and happy marriage is a sequence to be cherished. CM

Good Will Hunting

(Gus Van Sant, 1997, US) Robin Williams, Matt Damon, Ben Affleck, Stellan Skarsgård, Minnie Driver, Casey Affleck, Cole Hauser.
126 min.

Good Will Hunting's sincerity comes capitalised, which is not to deny the film is honest and moving in its way. Damon (who co-scripted, with Ben Affleck) plays Will, a janitor at the Massachusetts Institute of Technology. He's a closet genius, a volatile orphan who'd rather hang out with his beer buddies than parlay his brains into the lucrative career that would seem to be his destiny. Appalled that such a talent should be lost to science, maths professor Lambeau (Skarsgård) takes the boy under his wing, arranges for him to get psychiatric help, and watches Will make monkeys of the shrinks. Sean (Williams) is the last resort: another South Boston guy who never really made it, maybe he can break through where his distinguished peers failed. There are tensions here. To an extent, the film challenges America's ingrained anti-intellectualism, yet its anti-elitist instincts lead it close to equating academia with a dubious effeminacy. In the end it even falls back on that old cinematic panacea: get in touch with your inner Robin Williams. It's acted and directed with care, and Damon is outstanding, his scenes with Driver being especially sparky. TCh

Good Woman of Bangkok, The

(Dennis O'Rourke, 1991, Aust)
Yaowalak Chonchanakun
82 min.

The economics of prostitution out East haven't changed since Suzie Wong's day, and O'Rourke's documentary doesn't break new ground either, apart from his declaration of *mea culpa*. Aoi, from a village, becomes a bar girl to support her family. 'Good or bad, I don't think. I get money. OK'. Direct-to-camera interviews with Aoi and her mother are spuriously ennobled with opera, and there are plenty of shock cuts to the roaring life of the bar, bulging with lager louts demanding 'pussy shoot balloon'. BC

Goofy Movie, A

(Kevin Lima, 1996, US) voices: Bill Farmer, Jason Marsden, Jim Cummings, Kellie Martin, Rob Paulsen, Wallace Shawn.
77 min.

The first full-length movie starring Disney's toothy 63-year-old hound. For much of his career Goofy remained in the shadow of Mickey and Donald until the studio resurrected him for a series of 'Goof Troop' TV shorts, in which he played alongside his slightly more intelligent son Max. Here Max shows signs of adolescent rebellion. Realising he's gotta do something if he's to bridge the generation gap, Pa takes reluctant son on a mind-expanding fishing trip. Max would much rather be impressing his girl Roxanne with his Michael Jackson routine. Insipid songs and not much story. DA

Goonies, The

(Richard Donner, 1985, US) Sean Astin, Josh Brolin, Jeff Cohen, Corey Feldman, Kerri Green, Martha Plimpton, Ke Huy Quan.
114 min.

Dreamed up in a story by Steven Spielberg, the goonies are seven restless kids in a coastal town who, deserted by parents fighting a local real estate takeover bid, discover an old treasure map pointing to famed pirate One-Eyed Willie's galleon. Unfortunately, a family of incompetent thieves are also after the loot, and are not above shoving the hand of one of the little mites into a liquidiser to extort information. And while the pre-pubescents continually scream, their doting parents prove equally odious in a finale of astounding sentimentality. DT

Goopy Gyne Bagha Byne

see Adventures of Goopy and Bagha, The

Gordon's War

(Ossie Davis, 1973, US) Paul Winfield, Carl Lee, David Downing, Tony King, Gilbert Lewis, Carl Gordon.
90 min.

Once director Davis settles down and leaves gimmickry well alone, this unfolds nicely enough. The idea is the old one of a group of professionals dedicated to wiping out crime and evil, this time in modern Harlem. Ex-Green Beret Winfield reassembles the old black platoon from 'Nam and declares war on the pusher after his wife is found dead from an overdose (cue for red-filtered flashbacks). Wartime expertise hits the concrete jungle, and from then on it's mindless action all the way, with the platoon having unlimited access to material – 'Hey, man, this infra-red is outta sight!' – to help wage their war. Raised out of the ordinary by an ingenious safe raid, an above-average car chase, and some nice location work.

Gorgeous Bird Like Me, A

see Belle Fille comme moi, Une

Gorgeous Hussy, The

(Clarence Brown, 1936, US) Joan Crawford, Lionel Barrymore, Robert Taylor, Melvyn Douglas, Franchot Tone, James Stewart, Beulah Bondi.
102 min. b/w.

A lavishly appointed nineteenth century costumer in which Joan Crawford, as glamorous as she ever was, inveigles her way into a position of high influence in the White House of childhood friend Andrew Jackson (Barrymore, who steals the picture) – so much so that the President sacks his entire cabinet when rumours start to circulate. Crawford's role was based on the real Peggy Eaton, but it was Beulah Bondi, playing Jackson's bona fide wife, who came out of the film with an Oscar nomination. TJ

Gorgo

(Eugène Lourié, 1961, GB) Bill Travers, William Sylvester, Vincent Winter, Christopher Rhodes, Joseph O'Conor, Bruce Seton.
79 min.

An irresistibly tacky cross between *King Kong* and *The Beast from 20,000 Fathoms*. Midsize monster Gorgo is awoken from millennia of slumber and shipped off for exhibit in Battersea Funfair. This prompts its mammoth mummy to come and stomp a number of model-work London monuments in a display of maternal kinship. The final film, more's the pity, to be directed by Lourié, an art director who also perpetrated *The Beast from 20,000 Fathoms*, *The Colossus of New York* and *Behemoth the Sea Monster*. PT

Gorgon, The

(Terence Fisher, 1964, GB) Peter Cushing, Richard Pasco, Barbara Shelley, Christopher Lee, Michael Goodliffe, Patrick Troughton, Prudence Hyman.
83 min.

One of the few Hammer films with a female monster, this very English slice of Grand Guignol is undermined by failings in the make-up department. The Gorgon, a harridan with a snake-encrusted wig, would be hard pressed to frighten the proverbial mouse, let alone turn anyone to stone. Barbara Shelley's the young woman who acts ghoulish whenever there's a full moon. (The actual monster was played by Prudence Hyman.) Given that so many thrillers are predicated on the idea of the murderous male gaze, it's a novelty to have the woman staring back. Fisher directs in his usual brisk style, as if he's making a public information documentary, not a baroque horror pic. The settings are disconcerting (in Vandorf, an imaginary country somewhere between Transylvania and suburban Surrey) and Christopher Lee's scientist always looks uncomfortable in his tweed suit. GM

Gorilla Bathes at Noon

(Dusan Makavejev, 1993, Ger) Svetozar Cvetkovic, Anita Mancic, Alexandra Rohmig, Petar Bozovic, Andreas Lucius.
83 min.

For Makavejev, it's as if nothing has changed in 20-odd years. This collage-comedy may be set in the no-man's-land at the heart of the unified Berlin, but the images, the ideas and the bathetic juxtapositions could all be out-takes from *Innocence Unprotected* or *W.R. – Mysteries of the Organism*. The protagonist is a Russian soldier left behind in Berlin when his platoon goes home, haunted by scenes from the 1949 Stalinist epic *The Fall of Berlin* and nonplussed by the demolition of a gigantic statue of Lenin. So: socialism dies, socialist illusions crumble, and we're back to the same old socialist punch-ups and social contradictions. Not riveting. TR

Gorillas in the Mist

(Michael Apted, 1988, US) Sigourney Weaver, Bryan Brown, Julie Harris, John Omirah Miluwi, Iain Cutherbertson, Constantin Alexandrov.
129 min.

Apted's biopic about the late Diane Fossey's mission to save the endangered mountain gorilla has, to some extent, been pre-empted by wildlife programmes on TV. This is not to denigrate Sigourney Weaver's committed performance, but to question the dramatic rigging around the humans. One of those spiky crusaders with tunnel vision, Fossey pitched herself on a wet, cold mountain in Rwanda, and set about her life's work. Her research cleared away a mass of misinformation about gorilla behaviour, and the scenes in which she gradually establishes a communication with the reclusive species are the real interest of the film. Her relationship with the photographer (Brown) who puts her cause on the map, initial hostility turning into love affair, feels like a box-office consideration; over the years, her battles with poachers and government officials distort her into a dangerous Messianic crank, but the transition here seems abrupt. Script problems apart, the film is too long, but the footage with the gorillas is always extraordinary. BC

Gorky Park

(Michael Apted, 1983, US) William Hurt, Lee Marvin, Brian Dennehy, Ian Bannen, Joanna Pacula, Michael Elphick, Richard Griffiths, Rikki Fulton, Alexander Knox, Alexei Sayle.
128 min.

Neither Dennis Potter's screenplay nor the heavyweight cast can raise this adaptation of Martin Cruz Smith's best-selling spy novel above the ordinary. The discovery of three faceless bodies in Moscow's Gorky Park sets Soviet policeman Hurt's investigation in motion, but while subsequent interference by KGB man Dennehy hints at espionage, the involvement of fur-coated businessman Marvin suggests more mercenary motives. Hurt and Dennehy are excellent, as ever, but Marvin is badly miscast as a ruthless smoothie; and the film as a whole, while never less than involving, seldom generates any real suspense as it moves towards a curiously muffled showdown. NF

Gospel According to St Matthew, The (Il Vangelo Secondo Matteo)

(Pier Paolo Pasolini, 1964, It/Fr) Enrique Irazoqui, Margherita Caruso, Susanna Pasolini, Marcello Morante, Mario Socrate.
142 min. b/w.

Certainly Pasolini's most satisfying movie, devoid both of the frequent lapses into pretentiousness that mar (for example) *Theorem* and *Medea*, and the sloppy editing and awkward acting of movies like *The Decameron*. The director's Catholicism and Marxism serve him well here as the Messiah is presented as a determinedly political animal fuelled by anger at social injustice, while the miracles are allowed to remain unexplained (but also never presented in terms of flashy special effects). The film's beauty, in fact, derives from its simplicity, with the Italian landscape (and non-professional actors) turned into a convincing milieu for the all-too-familiar goings-on by marvellous monochrome camerawork. And Pasolini's use of music, from Bach to Billie Holiday, is astounding. GA

Go Tell the Spartans

(Ted Post, 1977, US) Burt Lancaster, Craig
Wasson, Jonathan Goldsmith, Marc Singer,
Evan Kim, Joe Unger, Dennis Howard.
114 min.
Moving from the home front – and tentative or
oblique treatments of Vietnam – towards confrontation with the action, American cinema was
gradually extricating itself from a position of
silent complicity and stuttering out the sort of
moralistic mush that permeates *Go Tell the
Spartans*, one of the first 'platoon movies' of
Vietnam. Post's film is fundamentally that old
post-World War II standby, the anti-war-movie,
a second generation offspring of the conscience-
stricken cavalry movie. It's brought up to date to
the extent that our human/wise/rebellious hero
(Lancaster – count his speeches) can die with a
final exclamation of 'Oh, shit!' – an apt summation of a film that parades characters and quotes
expressly included to be dismissed with a self-
satisfied cynical shrug. Message-mongering for
morons. PT

Gothic

(Ken Russell, 1986, GB) Gabriel Byrne, Julian
Sands, Natasha Richardson, Myriam Cyr,
Timothy Spall, Alec Mango.
87 min.
June 16, 1816. The Villa Diodati on the shores of
Lake Geneva. An illustrious gathering: Lord
Byron and his biographer-physician Polidori play
host to Shelley, his lover Mary Godwin, and her
half-sister Claire. They're an unruly, incestuously entangled lot, as artistic types in Russell's films
tend to be, given to imbibing laudanum, making
each other, and tossing off gratuitous insults. Not
surprisingly, matters get out of hand. As a storm
gathers, the flamboyant fops and fantasists hold
a séance, to test their propensity for wickedness
by conjuring into life their innermost demons.
With this fictionalised recreation of the events
leading to the writing of *Frankenstein*, Russell is
in his element, revelling in the seething psychodramas, the fetid atmosphere of sexual abandon, the gloops of slime and decaying flesh.
Unfortunately, Stephen Volk's script is so banal
that the final eruption of absolute evil comes not
as a nightmarish climax but as a nonsensical
mish-mash of all we've seen before. Pretensions
aside, it's an entertaining enough roller-coaster
ride, but it's sad to see the darker, more fertile
labyrinths of this particular literary funhouse
ignored in favour of scatological silliness. GA

Goto, l'île d'amour
(Goto, Island of Love)

(Walerian Borowczyk, 1968, Fr) Pierre
Brasseur, Ligia Branice, Ginette Leclerc, René
Dary, Jean-Pierre Andréani, Guy Saint-Jean.
93 min. b/w & col.
Borowczyk's first live-action feature was simultaneously a brilliant debut and a seamless transition from his earlier animation-based work. The
story is a simple fable of the destructive force of
passion: on a mythical island, the beautiful wife
(Branice) of the weak ruler Goto III (Brasseur) is
shown to be unfaithful by his chief fly-catcher,
Grozo (Saint-Jean). But Grozo's own infatuation
for her leads to tragedy. Borowczyk's highly
stylised direction, with consciously flattened
images, and objects rendered as animate and as
significant as human beings, is well complemented by the imperious Brasseur and the extraordinary beauty of Branice. The sudden flashes
of colour in a very monochrome context, and the
soaring use of a Handel organ concerto, further
consolidate a true 'art' film, in the sense that
everything is composed and designed to create a
wholly imagined – yet tangible – world. DT

Gotti

(Robert Harmon, 1997, US) Armand Assante,
Anthony Quinn, William Forsythe.
117 min.
No-holds-barred four-letter words, strong acting
from a name American-Italian cast and good
writing from Steve Shagan add up to the life and
crimes of the 'Teflon Don', John Gotti, who murdered his way to the top of the Gambino crime
family of New York. There are some strange sani-
tisations: Gotti is known to have personally dismembered the neighbour who accidentally ran
over his beloved son. Here the neighbour is simply shot by Gotti's close associate and betrayer
Sam Gravano, who is now part of the witness pro-

tection program and presumably can't complain.
A touch of cynical humour perhaps? Assante
excels as Gotti, a man of undoubted complexity,
while Quinn as his mentor Neil DeLaCroce
absolutely peels away the years. Highly recommended. SGr

Goupi-Mains-Rouges
(It Happened at the Inn)

(Jacques Becker, 1943, Fr) Fernand Ledoux,
Georges Rollin, Blanchette Brunoy, Line Noro,
Robert le Vigan, Maurice Schutz.
95 min. b/w.
The French peasantry sometimes affects that traditionally 'Welsh' habit of distinguishing each
owner of a widely shared name by affixing some
characteristic trait to it. Thus 'Goupi the Red-
Handed', a poacher and the blackest sheep of a
rural family in the throes of treasure-hunting.
Black, not red, is in fact the dominant tonality of
this bracingly mean-spirited melodrama, whose
sombre, underlit visuals give the impression that
the whole film was shot during a curfew. GAd

Go West

(Buster Keaton, 1925, US) Buster Keaton,
Howard Truesdale, Kathleen Myers,
Ray Thompson.
6,293 ft. b/w.
The only Keaton feature in which he discreetly
tapped a vein of Chaplin pathos (his character is
'Friendless' and his leading lady a mournful cow),
this is not one of his masterpieces, but is almost
as enchanting in its quiet way. Some wonderful
touches mark the progress of Buster's romance
with the cow as he sits patiently waiting for her
to milk herself after placing a pail in the appropriate position, ties antlers to her head so that she
can defend herself against the herd, and – on realising that his liking is reciprocated – essays a gingerly pat while politely raising his hat. The
spirited climax has Buster, dressed in a red
Mephistopheles costume with demented cops
clinging to his tail, trying to head off a stampeding herd as it rampages through town: a chase
which never really escalates properly in the manner of *Cops* or *Seven Chances*, largely (as Keaton
later explained) because of problems experienced
in controlling the cattle. TM

Go West

(Edward Buzzell, 1940, US) The Marx
Brothers, John Carroll, Diana Lewis, Tully
Marshall, Robert Barrat.
80 min. b/w.
Relatively late, and therefore far from great,
Marxian mania, in which Groucho, Chico and
Harpo find themselves victims both to a West
they can barely hoodwink or subvert, and to a
script which is only spasmodically funny. That
said, it starts well enough, with Harpo and Chico
gleefully outwitting Groucho's attempts to fleece
them of ten dollars; and the final, frantic train
chase climax – while falling dismally short of
Keaton's *The General* – has its (admittedly slap-
sticky) moments. GA

Grace of My Heart

(Allison Anders, 1996, US) Illeana Douglas,
Matt Dillon, John Turturro, Eric Stoltz, Bruce
Davison, Patsy Kensit, Jennifer Lee Warren,
Bridget Fonda.
115 min.
There's a lovely sequence about a third of the way
into Anders' delightful movie which follows a
song from conception – the street scene that
inspires it – through the writing, to the recording
session. This seamlessly edited passage swings
like the snappy '60s girl pop it emulates. Like the
film as a whole, it works as a musical in its own
right, and as history and critique of the pop
process. Anders charts the progress of Denise
Waverly (the excellent Illeana Douglas), an aspiring singer signed up to write songs at the Brill
Building by impresario Joel Millner (outrageously wigged-out Turturro). Denise is tough and
smart, but often ill-served by a series of amorous
and professional partners: beatnik radical Eric
Stoltz, married DJ Bruce Davison, and finally surf
sensation Matt Dillon, none of whom allows her
to develop her own voice, though they all provide
plenty of song material. Loosely inspired by the
life of Carole King, this is a light, feminist take on
15 years of pop: hits and Ms, if you will. It begins
with a bright, peppy tone, pastiching the nascent
rock'n'roll scene with an affectionate smile and

perfect pitch – the Larry Klein-produced soundtrack is spot on. But it's not all kitsch nostalgia:
the period coincides with great social changes,
particularly regarding the role of women, a recurrent Anders theme. Sharp cameos include Patsy
Kensit's rival songwriter and Bridget Fonda's teen
songbird with a secret love. TCh

Grace Quigley

(Anthony Harvey, 1984, US) Katharine
Hepburn, Nick Nolte, Kit Le Fever, Chip Zien,
William Duell, Elizabeth Wilson, Walter Abel.
87 min.
Professional hit man Nolte lacks self-confidence.
But when he fetches up against Hepburn, who
hires him first to help ease her out of this life, and
then to oblige all her old friends, he gains self-
esteem from these philanthropic acts of euthanasia, and a mother figure to comfort him. Good
black comedies about death are rare, and this certainly proves spry and knowing. But its tough
line on sentimentality goes squashy at the three-
quarter point, and there is evidence of re-editing
to provide a soft-option ending. Originally
screened as *The Ultimate Solution of Grace
Quigley*, running 102 minutes, it was then re-edited, partly re-shot, and re-titled. CPea

Graduate, The

(Mike Nichols, 1967, US) Anne Bancroft,
Dustin Hoffman, Katharine Ross, William
Daniels, Murray Hamilton, Elizabeth Wilson,
Norman Fell, Buck Henry.
108 min.
Modish, calculated, but hugely popular film
which, with the help of an irrelevant but diverting Simon and Garfunkel soundtrack, proved one
of the biggest hits of the '60s. Hoffman, looking
for the most part like a startled rabbit, got caught
between the rapacious Mrs Robinson and her
daughter, and suggested a vulnerability that was
sufficiently novel to turn him into as big a movie
star as all the he-men like McQueen and Newman.
The film itself is very broken-backed, partly
because Anne Bancroft's performance as the
mother carries so much more weight than
Katharine Ross' as the daughter, partly because
Nichols couldn't decide whether he was making
a social satire or a farce. As a comment on sex in
the West Coast stockbroker belt, the film falls a
long way short of Clint Eastwood's later *Breezy*,
which makes much more of a lot less promising
material. CPe

Grand Amour, Le

(Pierre Etaix, 1968, Fr) Pierre Etaix, Annie
Fratellini, Nicole Calfan, Ketty France,
Louis Mais.
86 min.
The diminishing returns apparent in Etaix's
films, derived from Tati but without the touch of
genius (unmistakable even if you find Tati unfunny), came to a head with this tiresome whimsy
which chose the unfortunate year of 1968 in
which to satirise French bourgeois morality with
a gentle affection that turns into approbation.
About a respectable married man who escapes
into fantasies about his nineteen-year-old secretary, only to return to the status quo a contentedly wiser man, it is witless, self-indulgent and
cloyingly sentimental. TM

Grand Canyon

(Lawrence Kasdan, 1991, US) Danny Glover,
Kevin Kline, Steve Martin, Mary McDonnell,
Mary-Louise Parker, Alfre Woodard, Jeremy
Sisto, Tina Lifford, Patrick Malone.
134 min.
The things that can happen in LA! If you're an
immigration lawyer, like Kline, you can break
down in a poor black area and get saved from the
homeboys by a black road-rescue driver (Glover).
Or if you're the wife (McDonnell) of that lawyer,
and he's had a fling with his secretary and your
teenage son is turning to thoughts of love, you
can go gooey-eyed over a baby you find abandoned in the bushes. Or if, like Glover, you've got
a deaf daughter, and a poor but hard-workin' sister with a son who's tempted by the neighbourhood gangs, you can befriend the rich lawyer and
wax philosophical about one of your country's
loveliest natural landmarks. Or if you produce
slasher movies, like Martin, and then get shot,
you can reconsider your whole life and career.
Then again, like Kasdan, you could make an
ambitious, entertaining and seriously indulgent

film about the modern malaise afflicting your home town. If this disaster-packed parable often smacks of melodramatic contrivance, it does at least benefit from solid performances and direction, and a leavening line in sardonic humour. GA

Grand Central Murder

(S Sylvan Simon, 1942, US) Van Heflin, Sam Levene, Patricia Dane, Cecilia Parker, Virginia Grey, Tom Conway, Samuel S Hinds, Connie Gilchrist, Mark Daniels, Millard Mitchell.
73 min. b/w.

A traditional whodunit, scripted at a breathless pace by Peter Ruric from Sue MacVeigh's novel, with private eye Van Heflin solving the murder of a golddigging actress (Dane) under the nose of a biliously dim cop (Levene). After a couple of scenes edgily and excitingly staged amid the rolling stock at Grand Central Station, the suspects are assembled at police HQ. Fortunately, they're a lively bunch, and their stories keep the action jumping in unexpected directions by way of a series of intriguing flashbacks. The resolution stemming from a reconstruction of the murder is a little flat, but the rest makes for an enjoyable B movie: good performances, tolerably witty dialogue, excellent camerawork (George Folsey), and a pleasant leavening of both comedy and hard-boiled thriller. TM

Grand Chemin, Le

(Jean-Loup Hubert, 1987, Fr) Anemone, Richard Bohringer, Antoine Hubert, Vanessa Guedj, Christine Pascal, Raoul Billerey.
107 min.

Hubert's story of a 9-year-old Parisian boy's billeting in a Breton village has the universal appeal of a beloved genre. Birth, death, sex, kids' games, and adult secrets are seen through the eyes of sensitive little Louis (Antoine Hubert). Dumped on Marcelle (Anemone) and Pelo (Bohringer) while his mother goes into hospital to have a baby, Louis finds himself in a desperately troubled and sometimes violent household. Pelo booze, and has to be brought home in a wheelbarrow, because Marcelle has become unresponsive after the death of their child. Both clutch for the boy's love, and bicker over him. A little village tomboy (Guedj) teases and instructs him in the ways of grown-ups, but Louis has to go through his familial insecurity on his own. The squabbling couple won French Oscars and richly deserve them – Anemone for her sassy walk and prissy ways, Bohringer for his rough, bawdy tenderness. The sense of a childhood summer remembered is sensitively conveyed, the barleysugar sweetness of days in the trees, the nocturnal alarms with the pillow over the ears. BC

Grande Bouffe, La

see Blow-Out

Grande Illusion, La 100

(Jean Renoir, 1937, Fr) Jean Gabin, Pierre Fresnay, Erich von Stroheim, Marcel Dalio, Julien Carette, Gaston Modot, Jean Dasté, Dita Parlo, Jacques Becker.
117 min. b/w.

Renoir films have a way of talking about one thing while being about another. La Grande Illusion was the only one of his '30s movies to be received with unqualified admiration at the time, lauded as a warmly humane indictment of war, a pacifist statement as nobly moving as All Quiet on the Western Front. Practically nobody noted the irony with which this archetypal prison camp escape story also outlined a barbed social analysis, demonstrating how shared aristocratic backgrounds (and military professionalism) forge a bond of sympathy between the German commandant (von Stroheim) and the senior French officer (Fresnay); how the exigencies of a wartime situation impel Fresnay to sacrifice himself (and Stroheim to shoot him) so that two of his men may make good their escape; and how those two escapees (Gabin and Dalio), once their roles as hero-warriors are over, will return home reduced being working class and dirty Jew once more. The Grand Illusion, often cited as an enigmatic title, is surely not that peace can ever be permanent, but that liberty, equality and fraternity is ever likely to become a social reality rather than a token ideal. TM

Grandeur et Décadence d'un Petit Commerce de Cinéma

see Rise and Fall of a Little Film Company

Grand Hotel

(Edmund Goulding, 1932, US) Greta Garbo, John Barrymore, Wallace Beery, Joan Crawford, Lionel Barrymore, Lewis Stone, Jean Hersholt.
115 min. b/w.

The 'Nashville' of its day, Grand Hotel's reputation has outgrown its actual quality, and it is now interesting only as an example of the portmanteau style: an interwoven group of contrasting stories allowing a bunch of stars to do their most familiar bit. Cigarette cards here include lonely Garbo, mercurial John Barrymore, crusty Lionel, business-like Joan Crawford, bent Beery. Supervising and commenting on the operation are ageing Lewis Stone and twittering émigré Jean Hersholt. Throw in Cedric Gibbons as art director and cameraman William Daniels, and you have the perfect MGM vehicle – dead boring. Made a year later with a similar cast, Dinner at Eight is of more note in that it provides acidic insight into the star system that Grand Hotel represents. AN

Grand Isle

(Mary Lambert, 1991, US) Kelly McGillis, Adrian Pasdar, Glenne Headly, Julian Sands.
95 min.

A soporific adaptation of The Awakening, Kate Chopin's proto-feminist, turn-of-the-century novel about a Kentucky-born wife and mother of two (McGillis) whose summer season on Grand Isle with her husband's easy-going Creole friends frees her from inhibitions. Courted by the young Pasdar, she finds herself through swimming, unrequited love, painting and other unconventional behaviour. Produced by McGillis herself, this is primarily a celebration of her extraordinary beauty, with endless loving close-ups of her flattering costumes, veiled face and naked body. Thanks to Siesta director Lambert's inept direction, there's no erotic charge, and the liberating ideas that are so strong in the book are lost amid the frocks and period detail. NF

Grand Jeu, Le (Card of Fate)

(Jacques Feyder, 1934, Fr) Françoise Rosay, Pierre-Richard Willm, Marie Bell, Charles Vanel, Georges Pitoeff, Pierre Larquey.
115 min. b/w.

Once famed for its supposedly Pirandellian casting of Bell as a honky tonk temptress whose chiselled features remind hero Willm of the Parisian beauty (also played by Bell) he had joined the Foreign Legion precisely 'to forget'. Le Grand Jeu is short on directorial presence, but long on atmosphere: heat, sand, flies, cheap absinthe, and Rosay poring over greasy Tarot cards behind a rustling bead curtain. GAd

Grand Meaulnes, Le

see Wanderer, The

Grand Prix

(John Frankenheimer, 1966, US) James Garner, Eva Marie Saint, Yves Montand, Brian Bedford, Toshiro Mifune, Jessica Walter, Antonio Sabato, Françoise Hardy, Jack Watson, Adolfo Celi, Claude Dauphin, Genevieve Page.
175 min.

Probably the best of the formula motor racing films, though that isn't saying much. Frankenheimer was a keen fan of the sport, and took great pains to convey the experience cinematically. There are no process shots; a 70mm camera was fixed to Garner's car, and the suspension jacked up on the other side to balance it. Long lenses were used for a slow-motion effect, and split screen boosts the racing footage. But in following an entire season, the movie was always too long, and the bits in-between are the usual soapy off-track drama. The Brian Bedford character, incidentally, was inspired by Stirling Moss. TCh

Grand Theft Auto

(Ron Howard, 1977, US) Ron Howard, Nancy Morgan, Marion Ross, Peter Isackson, Barry Cahill.
85 min.

Looking like something that Peckinpah might have made as a boy, this can best be described as an automotive snuff movie. Howard's debut as a director (he also scripts and stars), it leaves not a vehicle untotalled. There are some feeble attempts

to make statements about young love, political ambition, money and the media, but wrecking cars is what it's all about. As stunts go, they don't go very far, but watching a Roller get wiped out in a demolition derby has its appeal. JCo

Grandview U.S.A.

(Randal Kleiser, 1984, US) Jamie Lee Curtis, C Thomas Howell, Patrick Swayze, Jennifer Jason Leigh, Troy Donahue, Ramon Bieri, John Cusack, Joan Cusack.
97 min.

The assembled cast would've cost a great deal more ten years on. Howell does the rites-of-passage stuff, and Curtis looks after pa's demolition derby business while number one driver Swayze pines vigorously for her. It's pleasant enough, as a view of small-town Americana, but played very straight. No theatrical release in Britain. TJ

Grapes of Wrath, The

(John Ford, 1940, US) Henry Fonda, Jane Darwell, John Carradine, Russell Simpson, Charley Grapewin, Dorris Bowden, John Qualen.
129 min. b/w.

This classic Ford film eclipses much of the action of John Steinbeck's well-known novel of the Oklahoma farmers' migration from the dustbowl to the California Eden during the Depression years. The Okies were unwelcome in California, of course; they threatened the jobs of the locals. The brutal police hassled and harassed them unmercifully. The migrants formed unions in self-defence and struck for decent fruit-picking wages. This inevitably multiplied the official violence. Ford's film, shot by Gregg Toland with magnificent, lyrical simplicity, captures the stark plainness of the migrants, stripped to a few possessions, left with innumerable relations and little hope. MH

Grass

(Merian C Cooper/Ernest B Schoedsack, 1925, US)
5,220 ft. b/w.

A fascinating, visually splendid film about the massive annual migration undertaken by Persia's Bakhtiari tribes in search of fresh pastures for their cattle. Due partly to some pretty awful intertitles ('Brrr. The water's cold!') as the nomads make their journey through fast-flowing rivers, across snowy glaciers and so forth, partly to the suspicion (encouraged by statements from the Persians themselves) that the odyssey was made more difficult at the insistence of the film-makers to render it more dramatic and picturesque, the film doesn't exactly fit the notion of a modern documentary. None the less, if viewed as a Herzog-like tribute to man's courage, determination, and ability to tame nature without destroying it, the film has an impressive scale and poetry. GA

Grass Arena, The

(Gillies MacKinnon, 1991, GB) Mark Rylance, Lynsey Baxter, Pete Postlethwaite, Billy Boyle, Gerard Horan, Bunny May, Harry Landis.
90 min.

Having already impressed with Conquest of the South Pole and Needles, MacKinnon here offers a tough, intelligent version of John Healy's autobiography. Brutalised by his father during a sickly childhood, Healy later ditched a promising boxing career to indulge his obsession for booze among the dossers in London's parks. Repeated stints in prison didn't help, and only when a cellmate taught him the game of chess did salvation seem a prospect. While MacKinnon makes great use of a highly mobile camera – though made for TV, this is real film-making – he and scriptwriter Frank Deasy respect the inherent drama of Healy's painful, often drily funny story, aided by an astonishing performance from Rylance as the shy, innocent and none-too-articulate Healy. GA

Grass Harp, The

(Charles Matthau, 1995, US) Piper Laurie, Sissy Spacek, Walter Matthau, Edward Furlong, Nell Carter, Jack Lemmon, Mary Steenburgen, Sean Patrick Flannery, Joe Don Baker, Charles Durning, Roddy McDowall.
107 min.

The American South, a town full of eccentrics, the late '30s – and Furlong is the chap with the growing up to do when his mother dies and he's left in the company of his aunts (Spacek is the sensible one, Laurie the nature loving, touchy-feely sister she doesn't get on with). The plot (adapted from a Truman Capote novel by Stirling Silliphant and Kirk Ellis) rouses itself when Laurie's home-brew herbal dropsy cure attracts the attention of Lemmon's 'chemical engineer', a shyster with his eye on Spacek's fortune. His arrival causes such division in the household that Laurie retires to a tree house, a crisis requiring the intervention of kindly retired judge Matthau. Town barber McDowall, Durning's blustery reverend and Steenburgen's travelling evangelist also make their contributions to Furlong's life lessons, in a movie so old fashioned it makes *Fried Green Tomatoes* looks like a Gregg Araki picture. Old fashioned but not much cop, unfortunately, since director Charles Matthau (son of Walter) indulges his crusty old hams to the *n*th degree. Capote's prose glitters on the page, but this moves like treacle through its own wrong-headed sense of self-importance. TJ

Grass Is Always Greener, The (Uberall ist es besser, wo wir nicht sind)

(Michael Klier, 1989, WGer) Miroslaw Baka, Marta Klubowicz, Michael Krause, Josef Zebrowski, Anna Pastewka, Anja Klein.
79 min. b/w.
Klier's dour black-and-white feature stars Baka (from Kieslowski's *Short Film About Killing*) as the gentle but alienated youth who tires of the futility of his eked-out existence in depressed Poland – changing money, fencing cheap stolen goods – and hotfoots it to Berlin while he prepares his emigration plans for the US. The film scores in its documentary-style comparative tour around the low dives and low-lives of the marginals and petty criminals found in the dead-end parts of Warsaw and West Berlin, but suffers overly from miserabilism, muted performances, and the lack of an overall organising perspective. WH

Grass Is Greener, The

(Stanley Donen, 1960, US) Cary Grant, Deborah Kerr, Robert Mitchum, Jean Simmons, Moray Watson.
105 min.
Everyone in this movie – adapted from a flummery stage comedy by Hugh and Margaret Williams – stands around like mannequins in Bond Street stores. Dior and Hardy Amies are the real stars. On the plot front, Mitchum is an oil millionaire on holiday in England when he falls for Miss Kerr, a Countess who invites him for tea in her stately home. There follow some indiscretions in London and a duel with Mr Grant, as the cuckolded aristo. ATu

Grass Is Singing, The

(Michael Raeburn, 1981, Zam/Swe) Karen Black, John Thaw, John Kani, Patrick Mynhardt, John Moulder-Brown, Margaret Heale.
109 min.
Two of Doris Lessing's recurring themes come together here: the descent into madness, and the debilitating effect of the environment (in this case, the oppressively permanent swelter of Southern Africa). In a courageously abandoned performance, Karen Black, overdressed and anxious about spinsterhood, leaves the relative social and physical comforts of the town for marriage with a none-too-successful bush farmer (Thaw). Installed in the ramshackle homestead, her automatic and unconsidered racism (it's only 1960) towards the African workers, and the film's violent, quasi-mystical resolution. A dramatically potent adaptation which, while seriously polemical, is also shot through with the hallucinatory and the poetic. JS

Gravesend

(Salvatore Stabile, 1996, US) Tony Tucci, Michael Parducci, Tom Malloy, Thomas Brandise.
85 min.
Given that this first feature was written and directed by a 19-year-old, with a cast of unknowns and an initial budget of $5,000, it's hard not to be impressed by its raw, dark tale of four young, white Brooklyn friends who find

themselves swept up in a spiralling nightmare after one of their number accidentally kills another's brother in one of his many moments of volatile, psychotically macho aggression. Cue the night-long search for a way, with help from Jojo the junkie, to dispose of the body… or, as it turns out, bodies. There's nothing especially new here, and the narrative is perhaps over-eventful, but Stabile clearly has talent; this is compulsively watchable, blessed by muscular performances, occasional incursions of grisly black humour, and a real sense of pace and place. GA

Graveyard of Dreams (Ochnebebis Sasaplao)

(Georgi Khaindrava, 1997, Georgia)
95 min. b/w.
Every culture, it seems, needs to discover for itself that war is hell. Khaindrava's version of this *aperçu* is in every sense a front line bulletin: it's b/w docu-drama about Georgia's attempts to subdue the rebellion in Abkhazia, made with real young soldiers and partly shot in the thick of battle. It starts from the eagerness of students and intellectuals to volunteer for the Georgian army and ends (with rather facile irony) with the deaths of many. Khaindrava, several times imprisoned for dissidence in USSR days, knows all about the conflict: he helped launch it when he was made Minister for Abkhazian Affairs – a post he soon quit. He should have watched *Hell Is for Heroes* before he took the job. TR

Graveyard Shift

(Ralph S Singleton, 1990, US) David Andrews, Kelly Wolf, Stephen Macht, Andrew Divoff, Vic Polizos, Brad Dourif, Robert Alan Beuth.
86 min.
Where *Misery* restored one's faith in Stephen King adaptations, this travesty buries his reputation alive. Bland hunk John Hall (Andrews) drifts into a small Maine town and lands a job at a dilapidated mill. Working the graveyard shift in a basement, he is on hand when a crew of disposable extras discover the subterranean lair of a giant rat-like monster. Introduced to up the love interest, spunky co-worker Jane (Wolf, making what she can of a poorly written role) sweats a lot and holds her own among the all-male crew. The most engaging character, Dourif's crazed Vietvet vermin exterminator, adds some much-needed humour and class before suffering a premature burial. Neither Singleton nor scriptwriter John Esposito has grasped the anti-capitalist undercurrents of King's story, relying instead on cheap shocks and dodgy creature effects. NF

Grayeagle

(Charles B Pierce, 1977, US) Ben Johnson, Iron Eyes Cody, Lana Wood, Jack Elam, Paul Fix, Alex Cord, Jacob Daniels.
104 min.
Right from the opening of this simple Cheyenne legend – an ageing chief intoning in his ancestors' graveyard – the mood evoked by the widescreen Montana landscape is fractured by nonsensical jumps. With 40 minutes removed, the film has been not so much cut as butchered for distribution here. What's left is a disjointed narrative, marvellous performances from Johnson and Elam (whose moments of quiet dignity are ludicrously curtailed), and a picture of Indian life that carries sufficient authenticity only to be undercut by some un-folkloric music and slow-motion. A mess, but one which carries intimations of something better: a would-be mood piece celebrating Indian cycles of death and rebirth. CPea

Gray Lady Down

(David Greene, 1977, US) Charlton Heston, David Carradine, Stacy Keach, Ned Beatty, Stephen McHattie, Ronny Cox, Rosemary Forsyth.
111 min.
A tedious disaster movie that amounts to no more than a straightforward salvage operation (the film is plastered with dedications to the US Navy). Heston, strong and silent commander of the jeopardised nuclear sub that sinks after a collision, is given lines which strain credulity even more than his hairpiece: 'Stow that crap, sailor, now!' Character makes little impression in this almost entirely pointless military exercise. David Carradine at least makes some impact as the

strong, silent, nonconformist captain who mounts the rescue operation, but everyone else is more mechanical than the hardware. CPe

Grazie Zia (Thank You, Aunt)

(Salvatore Samperi, 1968, It) Lou Castel, Lisa Gastoni, Gabriele Ferzetti, Luisa De Santis.
96 min. b/w.
For his first feature, a black comedy modelled on Bellocchio's *Fists in the Pocket*, Samperi even borrowed Lou Castel to embody his anti-hero, the son of a business tycoon, who initially expresses his rebellion by pretending to be unable to walk, and snarling insults at all and sundry from his wheelchair. Sent to recuperate in the care of an aunt (Gastoni) – a doctor but also a beautiful woman – he snares her into a kind of sexual complicity, forcing her to humour him in a series of bizarre rites which rise in crescendo to his final invention, a game of euthanasia. Uneven, more black than comic, but capturing much the same sense of rapt perversity as Bellocchio's film: an undeniably striking debut. TM

Grease

(Randal Kleiser, 1978, US) John Travolta, Olivia Newton-John, Stockard Channing, Jeff Conaway, Barry Pearl, Didi Conn, Eve Arden, Joan Blondell, Sid Caesar.
110 min.
The real progenitor of this musical celebrating the rock'n'roll '50s, had it not fudged some of the less adequate dance numbers by shooting above the knees, would be *West Side Story*. Otherwise, the film aspires to some of the pretensions of *Rebel Without a Cause*, from which it borrows liberally while saddled with the liabilities of its dumb stage musical script. Its flashy opportunism (nostalgia pitched squarely at an audience too young to even recall the era) quickly becomes very irritating. Allusions to french letters and high school pregnancies, and double entendres allowed by the hindsight of this more 'permissive' society, scarcely conceal the fact that *Grease* is even more simplistic (and finally reactionary) than the beach blanket movies of the era. Lots of colour, movement, surface glitter, only one decent song (the title track sung by Frankie Valli). RM

Grease 2

(Patricia Birch, 1982, US) Maxwell Caulfield, Michelle Pfeiffer, Adrian Zmed, Lorna Luft, Didi Conn, Eve Arden, Sid Caesar, Tab Hunter.
114 min.
As gaudily tempting as a soft-centre as ever graced a Woolworth counter. Liberally picking'n'mixing assorted elements of American popular culture, Birch picks up the story of Rydell High a few years on from where Randal Kleiser left it. Travolta and Newton-John have moved on, Conn is back from beauty school, and straight skirts have replaced full ones; these changes apart, we're on familiar ground. Pink Lady Pfeiffer steals the heart of Caulfield, a straight A, strait-laced student from England who is excruciatingly dull (rating 8 on a chuckability scale of 10). However, he gets himself a pair of wheels and wins his girl. Such niceties as a plausible plot and three-dimensional characters are trampled under Weejun-shod foot, but sheer energy, a handful of good tunes (including a great theme song from the Four Tops), and some very funny one-liners save the day. FD

Greased Lightning

(Michael Schultz, 1977, US) Richard Pryor, Beau Bridges, Pam Grier, Cleavon Little, Vincent Gardenia, Richie Havens.
96 min.
Anyone who enjoyed *Car Wash* should be warned that Schultz admits only to having done a wrap-up 'fireman's job' on this woeful biopic featuring a smiling Pryor as Wendell Scott, the first black US stock car driver. Although Melvin Van Peebles evidently directed most of it, a doubt still remains as to who should be held finally responsible for the finished cornball mish-mash, since Schultz's subsequent film (*Which Way Is Up?*) bears an ominous resemblance to the style and tone of this relentlessly indulgent comedy-romance. JPy

Great Armored Car Swindle, The

see Breaking Point, The

Great Balls of Fire!

(Jim McBride, 1989, US) Dennis Quaid, Winona Ryder, John Doe, Joe Bob Briggs, Stephen Tobolowsky, Trey Wilson, Alec Baldwin, Steve Allen, Lisa Blount, Peter Cook.
107 min.

The trouble with this biopic is that it attempts to convey too many aspects of the Jerry Lee Lewis legend. His marriage (to his 13-year-old second cousin)and the ensuing scandal are the focus and deserve serious treatment, but instead the pace is disrupted by the kind of spontaneous musical routine that is more at home in a light-hearted romantic comedy. When the film switches to London, the playful approach is utterly out of keeping with the unfolding drama. And what is Peter Cook doing as a newspaper hack? Stranger yet is the miscasting of Quaid, whose attempts to affect Lewis' boundless energy and Southern naiveté are alternately amusing and perplexing. Taken in isolation. Quaid's keyboard scenes are splendidly carried by the strength of the music, but alas, such moments are short-lived. Other performances are better, notably from Alec Baldwin as Lewis' Bible-thumping, disapproving cousin, and Ryder as his winsome bride. CM

Great Day in Harlem, A

(Jean Bach, 1994, US) Art Kane, Dizzy Gillespie, Marian McPartland, Art Farmer, Milt Hinton, Sonny Rollins, Johnny Griffin.
60 min. b/w & col.

Bach's documentary avoids all the clichés of jazz retrospective by concentrating on a single event on an August morning back in 1958. *Esquire* magazine's then art director, Robert Benton (yes, he of *Bonnie and Clyde* and *Nobody's Fool*), commissioned a photo from Art Kane containing as many jazz musicians as possible standing outside a brownstone in Harlem (57, plus one club-owner, in the event), and, unofficially, bassist Milt Hinton brought along his home-movie camera. There are so many stories here. The musicians had hardly seen each other in daylight before – 'They never knew there were two 11 o'clocks in one day,' said one. They were so pleased to talk to each other it was difficult to get them to stand still, and even then Dizzy Gillespie pulled a face which cracked up Roy Eldridge, and street urchins stole Count Basie's hat. Thelonious Monk was late. He'd been deciding on an outfit to eclipse the competition. Johnny Griffin today remembered Monk with awe, and Sonny Rollins remembered Lester Young as someone briefly visiting from another planet. All the contemporary interviews are fascinating and touching, too: Blakey and Diz are gone now. The musical clips aren't over-familiar and are killingly good. A wonderful, warm little movie. BC

Great Day in the Morning

(Jacques Tourneur, 1956, US) Robert Stack, Virginia Mayo, Ruth Roman, Alex Nicol, Raymond Burr, Leo Gordon.
92 min.

A fine Western, set on the eve of the Civil War, with Stack as a Southern gambler/gunslinger who agrees, for a price, to help ferry a shipment of gold desperately needed to buy guns for the Rebel cause. Adapted from a bestseller and set in the booming Colorado Territory, it starts with the advantage of a remarkably literate script by Lesser Samuels which beats a lucid path through the tangle of conflicting interests: not only between North and South, but between public need and private lust for gold, between the realities of love and the illusions of desire. Focal point of the various subsidiary battles between self-interest and selfless commitment is Stack's anti-hero, who is finally cornered not only into offering his services to the South free of charge, but to acknowledge that he loves Roman's shop-soiled saloon girl rather than Mayo's pristine lady. But he does so – the script never quite abandons its abrasive edge of cynicism – only when it is too late for his gold (otherwise all of it would fall into Northern hands) and for his girl (although he doesn't know it, he left her behind to be murdered). Tourneur stages it all impeccably, with outstanding performances from Stack and Roman. TM

Great Dictator, The

(Charles Chaplin, 1940, US) Charles Chaplin, Paulette Goddard, Jack Oakie, Reginald Gardiner, Maurice Moscovich, Billy Gilbert, Henry Daniell.
128 min. b/w.

Chaplin acts the roles of Hitler (alias Adenoid Hynkel) and a Jewish barber who returns as an amnesiac, decades after an accident in World War I, totally unaware of the rise of Nazism and the persecution of his people. The representation of Hitler is vaudeville goonery all the way, but minus the acid wit and inventive energy that Groucho Marx managed in his impersonation of authoritarianism gone berserk in *Duck Soup*. Mr Nobody is eventually carted away to a concentration camp, which leads to a reversal of roles when the barber escapes and is mistaken for Hynkel on the eve of the invasion of Austria. Cue for an impassioned speech about freedom and democracy calculated to jerk tears out of the surliest fascist, in a manner startlingly similar to Hitler's very own delivery. VG

Great Ecstasy of Woodcarver Steiner, The (Die Grosse Ekstase des Bildschnitzers Steiner)

(Werner Herzog, 1975, WGer) Walter Steiner.
47 min.

A film about flying in the face of death. In Steiner's case, the flying is literal: he is a champion ski-jumper, in Herzog's view the best in the world because the most profoundly fearless. Convention would call this a 'documentary reportage', but convention would be wrong: the angle of approach is wholly unexpected, and Herzog's own participation as commentator/interviewer/hero-worshipper/myth-maker guarantees a really extraordinary level of engagement with the subject. Watch especially how he coaxes a truly revealing story about a pet raven out of a highly embarrassed Steiner in the closing moments. Herzog, a surrealist to the core, knows that the real world offers more fantastic phenomena than anything he can imagine. TR

Great Escape, The

(John Sturges, 1962, US/WGer) Steve McQueen, James Garner, Richard Attenborough, James Donald, Charles Bronson, Donald Pleasence, James Coburn, Gordon Jackson, David McCallum.
173 min.

Uneven but entertaining World War II escape drama, which even when it first appeared seemed very old-fashioned. Based on Paul Brickhill's factual account of the efforts of Allied prisoners to break out of Stalag Luft North, it contains memorable sequences and a sea of well-known faces. McQueen comes off best as 'The Cooler King'; Bronson and Garner (perhaps surprisingly) give good support; Coburn is totally miscast as an Australian, yet turns in an amusing performance. Worth seeing the last half hour, if nothing else, for one of the best stunt sequences in years: McQueen's motor-cycle bid for freedom. CPe

Greatest, The

(Tom Gries, 1977, US/GB) Muhammad Ali, Ernest Borgnine, Roger E Mosley, Lloyd Haynes, Malachi Throne, John Marley, Robert Duvall, David Huddleston, Ben Johnson, James Earl Jones.
101 min.

It's hard to define exactly where this highly selective biography, with Muhammad Ali playing himself, goes so wrong, but it's like one of his later fights: heavy in unrealised potential, poor value considering the stars involved, yet with Ali himself emerging unscathed at the end. The script – credited to Ring Lardner Jr – veers between some felicitous use of the young Clay's poetry which grows into the fluent speeches given to Ali himself, and hamfisted bridging passages that gloss over any details out of tune with the *Rocky* image (eg. the death of his mentor Malcolm X, Zaire). Likewise the direction, which evokes some early nigger-baiting tensions, then as soon as Ali takes over the role and dodges the draft, settles for straight hero-worship. AN

Greatest Show on Earth, The

(Cecil B DeMille, 1952, US) James Stewart, Betty Hutton, Charlton Heston, Cornel Wilde, Dorothy Lamour, Gloria Grahame, Lawrence Tierney, Henry Wilcoxon.
153 min.

Characteristically elephantine Big Top epic from DeMille, thumped across with a winning brashness and garnering the veteran showman his first Best Picture Oscar. Heston crosses his Moses-to-be with Noah as he leads his 'children' and menagerie cross-country, while Stewart's killer-on-the-lam does a wonderfully affecting 'tears of a clown' number in the true, tacky circus tradition of sawdust, spectacle and sentiment. PT

Greatest Story Ever Told, The

(George Stevens,1965, US) Max von Sydow, Carroll Baker, Pat Boone, Victor Buono, Richard Conte, Jose Ferrer, Van Heflin, Charlton Heston, Angela Lansbury, David McCallum, Roddy McDowall, Dorothy McGuire, Sal Mineo, Donald Pleasence, Sidney Poitier, Claude Rains, Telly Savalas, John Wayne, Shelley Winters, Ed Wynn.
260 min.

Interminable and intolerably reverential rendering of the Life of Christ, originally made in Ultra Panavision 70mm, and soon cut for general release to 225 minutes (with subsequent versions even further shorn, the most ruthless being 127 minutes). Max von Sydow's remarkable performance is consistently undermined by dozens of ill-chosen cameos, such as John Wayne's 'Truly, this man was the Son of Gaaard' Centurion, and Shelley Winters yelling 'I'm cured!' as the Woman of No Name. Sydow resists the temptation to engage the Devil (Pleasence) in a game of chess. ATu

Great Expectations (100)

(David Lean, 1946, GB) John Mills, Valerie Hobson, Martita Hunt, Bernard Miles, Francis L Sullivan, Finlay Currie, Jean Simmons, Anthony Wager, Alec Guinness, Freda Jackson.
118 min. b/w.

Still Lean's best film, and probably – along with Cukor's *David Copperfield* – the best of all the cinema's many stabs at Dickens. It begins on a high note with young Pip's nervous scurry home along the bleak seashore as darkness falls, past lowering gibbets and blasted trees leading him straight into his hair-raising encounter with Magwitch the convict in the graveyard. A hard act to follow, but Lean tops it effortlessly with his eerie evocation of the Gothic yet strangely gentle fantasy world inhabited by poor, mad Miss Havisham, nesting her broken heart amid the cobwebby remains of her wedding finery. For once the transition from childhood (with Mills and Hobson taking over from Wager and Simmons) is managed with total credibility, and the fine performances keep on coming (Mills and Hobson have never been better; Hunt is fantastic; Currie, Guinness, Simmons and Sullivan all memorable). Visually flawless, perfectly paced, it's a small masterpiece. TM

Great Expectations

(Joseph Hardy, 1975, GB) Michael York, Sarah Miles, James Mason, Margaret Leighton, Robert Morley, Anthony Quayle, Joss Ackland, Rachel Roberts, Heather Sears, Andrew Ray.
124 min.

Many distinguished names who should have known better lend themselves to what looks like a TV musical version of Dickens' tale, minus the songs. This plodding, charmless adaptation is long on coincidences which become increasingly preposterous. Most notable, however, are the wigs: over a hundred, the press handout revealed. And you can spot every one of 'em. Poor old Joss Ackland's ruins an otherwise good performance (as Joe Gargery). And the same bowl of fruit rests on the sideboard...twenty years later. CPe

Great Expectations

(Alfonso Cuarón, 1997, US) Ethan Hawke, Gwyneth Paltrow, Hank Azaria, Chris Cooper, Anne Bancroft, Robert De Niro, Josh Mostel, Kim Dickens.
111 min.

While remaining largely faithful to the narrative thrust of Dickens' novel, Cuarón's version is hugely different from the David Lean classic, displaying all the wit, vitality and unpretentious assurance the Mexican brought to his delightful *A Little Princess*. It kicks off with orphan Finn (Hawke) fatefully making the acquaintance of an escaped con (De Niro), crazy old Nora Dinsmoor (Bancroft), and her beautiful niece Estella (Paltrow) in '70s Florida; before fast-forwarding to '80s New York where, as a promising artist, Finn continues to pursue his childhood beloved, now engaged to rich, snobby Walter (Azaria). The transposition to modern America works very well. Since we're advised from the start that we're about to see the story not as it happened, but as it's remembered by the older, wiser Finn, both the magical, natural paradise of the Everglades and the success-oriented New York art world beautifully evoke the twin poles of hopeful innocence and harsh experience. Cuarón plays up this fabulous romance, never departing from Finn's obsessive view of the bewilderingly changeable Estella, and underlining the cruel ironies of a life transformed yet tainted by love. Stylish, sexy, involving, and great fun. GA

Great Garrick, The
(James Whale, 1937, US) Brian Aherne, Olivia de Havilland, Edward Everett Horton, Melville Cooper, Lionel Atwill, Luis Alberni, Etienne Girardot, Lana Turner, Marie Wilson, Albert Dekker.
91 min. b/w.
Not the 'ponderous biography' of Steven Scheuer's *Movies on TV*, but an unusual, comical divertissement in which the legendary 18th century English actor accepts an invitation to the Comédie Française in Paris, announcing that he'll teach them a thing or two about their craft. When they catch wind of his remark, the entire French company stages an elaborate hoax at a country inn in an attempt to humiliate their guest (who has a trick or two in hand). A swish, witty production with a droll performance from the underrated Aherne as David Garrick. TCh

Great Gatsby, The
(Elliott Nugent, 1949, US) Alan Ladd, Betty Field, Macdonald Carey, Barry Sullivan, Ruth Hussey, Shelley Winters, Howard da Silva.
92 min. b/w.
The first sound adaptation of Scott Fitzgerald's classic. Although some of the detail of the novel has been changed (and Betty Field gives an unusually weak performance, miscast as Daisy Buchanan), this scores over Jack Clayton's lavish and longer 1974 version by the casting of Alan Ladd as Gatsby, so much more convincing as a man with a dark and mysterious past than one-dimensional glamour-puss Robert Redford. At the same time, the picture is less a '20s costume drama than a '40s *film noir*, shot in moody monochrome by the maestro John F Seitz. ATu

Great Gatsby, The
(Jack Clayton, 1974, US) Robert Redford, Mia Farrow, Bruce Dern, Karen Black, Scott Wilson, Sam Waterston, Lois Chiles, Howard da Silva.
146 min.
A literary adaptation that continually begs detrimental comparison with the novel, this relies too much on appearance, making little attempt to explore behind the beguiling '20s façade. Given little support, the characters are left scratching the surface, their feverishness expressed in an unfortunately literal manner, as though they're running high temperatures most of the time. Redford occasionally conveys Gatsby's private obsession and his unease, but too often he's merely decorative, certainly no enigmatic figure of gossip. Farrow's Daisy is disastrously lightweight, a cross between squeaky child and flapper hard to imagine as the object of anyone's infatuation. It's sadly logical that their love is celebrated as the ultimate Babycham experience. Although no catastrophe, uneven pacing and length make *The Great Gatsby* over-schematic and overt, at its best when dealing with the lesser characters, and safely middle-of-the-road.

Great Gilbert and Sullivan, The
see Story of Gilbert and Sullivan, The

Great Gundown, The
see 40 Graves for 40 Guns

Great K & A Train Robbery, The
(Lewis Seiler, 1926, US) Tom Mix, Dorothy Dwan, William Walling, Harry Grippe, Carl Miller, Edward Piel.
53 min. b/w.
Typically energetic escapist Western from one of

the earliest stars to set the generic formula. Officially listed as an army deserter in 1902, Mix became national rodeo champion in 1909, and entered films with the Selig company a year later. With the accent on pace, stuntwork and a modicum of comic relief, his films achieved massive success, and a Fox contract followed from 1917 to 1928, until the coming of sound and the lure of the circus conspired to slow his prolific output. Here, as a railroad detective going undercover to foil a persistent gang, he crossed paths with versatile B director Seiler, a former Fox gagman who was still churning 'em out in 1958. PT

Great Lie, The
(Edmund Goulding, 1941, US) Bette Davis, Mary Astor, George Brent, Lucile Watson, Hattie McDaniel, Grant Mitchell, Jerome Cowan.
107 min. b/w.
Sudsy melo as George Brent divorces concert pianist Astor, marries Davis, and then leaves a metaphorical Amazon jungle for the real one, where he apparently dies in a plane crash. Meanwhile, back in the big smoke, Astor discovers that she's pregnant and Davis wants to adopt the baby as a souvenir of her darling hubby. The leading ladies blast away at each other like pocket battleships, while Max Steiner and Tchaikovsky provide a sumptuous musical background. ATu

Great Manhunt, The
see State Secret

Great Man Votes, The
(Garson Kanin, 1939, US) John Barrymore, Peter Holden, Virginia Weidler, Donald MacBride, William Demarest.
72 min. b/w.
Virtually a B movie, but featuring a wittily outsize performance from Barrymore as a Harvard professor, turned nightwatchman and souse since his wife's death, who demands the right to educate his own children and finds himself arguing from a position of strength because of a quaint electoral anomaly. In Capra vein but rather too whimsical, the film is constantly dragged down by a pedestrian script which offers Barrymore no help at all (and indeed, often makes him appear to be guilty of cute overplaying). TM

Great McGinty, The
(Preston Sturges, 1940, US) Brian Donlevy, Muriel Angelus, Akim Tamiroff, Allyn Joslyn, William Demarest, Louis Jean Heydt.
81 min. b/w.
Sturges' first film as writer/director, a wonderfully dry satire which takes the American political system apart through the tale of a bum (Donlevy) who rides on a tide of corruption to become state governor. A totally dishonest man, he gets his comeuppance only because – through the influence of his wife, a sweet prig whose liberal conscience comes in for some rude knocks – he is for one fatal moment tempted to be honest. Cast in flashback from the sleazy banana republic cantina where the disgraced Donlevy has found refuge as a barman – and tells his story to a bank cashier (Heydt) suicidally regretting a momentary temptation to embezzlement – the script is underpinned by some slyly subversive thoughts about the success ethic and living up to expectations. Although the Sturges stock company was not yet fully formed, a number of familiar faces keep popping up to give the whole thing a delightfully quirky vitality. TM

Great McGonagall, The
(Joseph McGrath, 1974, GB) Spike Milligan, Peter Sellers, Julia Foster, Julian Chagrin, John Bluthal, Valentine Dyall.
89 min.
Revue-type sketches inspired by the life of William McGonagall, the 19th century Scot and self-styled poet who wrote verse not unlike Milligan. Potentially amusing material comes to grief as the film fails to find an appropriate visual style for Milligan's predominantly verbal humour. The Goonery between Sellers (as Queen Victoria) and Milligan (as McGonagall) comes off, but elsewhere the humour is forced and the social/political comment embarrassingly exposed. With its musical hall setting, it looks like some tiresome theatrical junket brought out

in the wake of the departing Lord Chamberlain, crammed full of previously vetoed references to the Royal Family.

Great Moment, The
(Preston Sturges, 1944, US) Joel McCrea, Betty Field, Harry Carey, William Demarest, Louis Jean Heydt, Franklin Pangborn, Grady Sutton, Jimmy Conlin.
83 min. b/w.
The odd Sturges film out, a more or less serious biopic of WTG Morton, the Boston dentist who accidentally discovered the use of ether as an anaesthetic in 1846, receiving neither fame nor fortune as a reward for this great service to humanity. But Sturges couldn't be solemn for long, and though telling a basically tragic story (like the hero of *The Great McGinty*, Morton ruined himself through one 'great moment' of charitable impulse), he injects some delightful doses of slapstick and verbal fancy, while using members of his stock company in very unexpected ways. Recut by the studio and generally considered to be a failure, it's nevertheless an oddly moving film that sticks obstinately and agreeably in the mind. TM

Great Mouse Detective, The (aka Basil the Great Mouse Detective)
(John Musker/Ron Clements/Dave Michener/Burny Mattinson, 1986, US) voices: Vincent Price, Barrie Ingham, Basil Rathbone.
80 min.
Animated feature from Disney in which the one true rival to the old coke-fiend lives down in the basement of 221b Baker Street. Basil, like his alter ego, plays the violin; he also has his Moriarty, in the shape of the magnificent Professor Ratigan, a Napoleon of crime with the wardrobe and neurotic wit of a Nineties dandy, and the absolute conviction that his rat-like form is one of nature's mistakes. Donning his best mousestalker, Basil takes to the mean streets once more, in aid of an eight-year-old Scots mouse whose toymaker father has been abducted. As usual with *film noir*, however, it is the villain who steals the heart and one is rooting for in the breathtaking showdown high up in the cogs and ratchets of Big Ben. CPea

Great Muppet Caper, The
(Jim Henson, 1981, GB) Diana Rigg, Charles Grodin, John Cleese, Robert Morley, Peter Ustinov, Jack Warden, Joan Sanderson.
97 min.
Second big screen outing for TV's favourite inanimates, with Kermit, Fozzie and Gonzo as reporters intrepidly investigating the theft of jewels belonging to Rigg, an international couturière soon being besieged by Miss Piggy as an aspiring model. The songs are routine, but the inconsequential plot leaves plenty of space for engaging asides like the blandly silly dinner-table dialogue between a well-bred couple (Cleese and Sanderson) determined not to notice that their home has been invaded by little furry creatures. Or a charming moment when Kermit and friends tangle with a fold-up bed which shuts them away into the wall. Pause, then a contentedly muffled, 'Hey, this is nice!' TM

Great Northfield Minnesota Raid, The
(Philip Kaufman, 1971, US) Cliff Robertson, Robert Duvall, Luke Askew, RG Armstrong, Dana Elcar, Donald Moffat, John Pearce, Matt Clark.
90 min.
This Western concerning the Younger and James brothers' gang covers familiar ground, borrowing freely from *Bonnie and Clyde, McCabe and Mrs Miller*, etc. Interesting for its demonstration of how exploitative capitalism leads simple-minded farmers' boys into outlawry, though somewhat marred by Duvall's manic interpretation of the role of Jesse James.

Great Rock'n'Roll Swindle, The
(Julian Temple, 1979, GB) Malcolm McLaren, Sid Vicious, Johnny Rotten, Steve Jones, Paul Cook, Ronnie Biggs.
104 min.

A brilliant, infuriating final chapter in the Sex Pistols saga, exposing the corruption of a lethargic roll generation and the morbid tastes of the English. Smartly mixing early Pistols fragments with virtuoso set pieces (including Sid in 'My Way'), it adds up to the most innovative comic strip fantasy since Tashlin. DMacp

Great Santini, The

(Lewis John Carlino, 1979, US) Robert Duvall, Blythe Danner, Michael O'Keefe, Stan Shaw, Lisa Jane Persky, Julie Anne Haddock.
115 min.
Duvall is Colonel 'Bull' Meechum – ace Marine fighter pilot, obsessive disciplinarian and family man who drives his wife and kids perilously close to the edge. His performance, and that of O'Keefe as his confused, loyal elder son, hold together the shoddy script by force of Method acting alone. But Carlino's direction doesn't help: he was responsible for the atrocious *Sailor Who Fell from Grace with the Sea*, and *The Great Santini* suffers from the same triteness, with its Deep South setting and a 'progressive' racial subplot that plunges deep into tear-jerk territory. See it for the acting; wallow in the sentiment. CA

Great Scout & Cathouse Thursday, The

(Don Taylor, 1976, US) Lee Marvin, Oliver Reed, Robert Culp, Elizabeth Ashley, Strother Martin, Sylvia Miles, Kay Lenz.
102 min.
Marvin revives an old feud with a politically ambitious railroad man and teams up with Reed, who plays an improbable half-breed fired with an ambition to give all white women the clap. This dreary and eminently forgettable Western has Marvin's increasingly tedious hamming matched, and even topped, by Reed's hapless mugging; not a pretty sight. CPe

Great Sinner, The

(Robert Siodmak, 1949, US) Gregory Peck, Ava Gardner, Melvyn Douglas, Walter Huston, Agnes Moorehead, Ethel Barrymore, Frank Morgan.
110 min. b/w.
The year is 1860, the great sin is gambling, and the sinner (Peck) is a young novelist, 'Fyodor', if you will. Christopher Isherwood had a hand in the script, which unceremoniously culls episodes and characters from Dostoievsky's youth, *Crime and Punishment*, and *The Gambler*. Unfortunately, this prestigious MGM production is heavy-going and overdone. Moorehead plays a bleary pawnbroker; Barrymore, Morgan and Huston are roulette fiends; Gardner is the love interest. They're all out of luck. TCh

Great Smokey Roadblock, The

see Last of the Cowboys, The

Great Texas Dynamite Chase, The (aka Dynamite Women)

(Michael Pressman, 1976, US) Claudia Jennings, Jocelyn Jones, Johnny Crawford, Chris Pennock, Tara Strohmeier, Miles Watkins.
90 min.
Traditionally raunchy New World fare, a gimmicky outlaw yarn that stands genre roles on their heads, with Jennings and Jones as dynamite-totin' best-buddy bankrobbers. It gleefully exhibits all the essential radicalism of the exploitation format, and brims with anarchic energy. PT

Great Train Robbery, The

see First Great Train Robbery, The

Great Waldo Pepper, The

(George Roy Hill, 1975, US) Robert Redford, Bo Svenson, Bo Brundin, Susan Sarandon, Geoffrey Lewis, Edward Herrmann, Margot Kidder.
108 min.
A surprising box-office flop next to its precursors, *Butch Cassidy and the Sundance Kid* and *The Sting*, this by and large refuses cute nostalgic manipulation (an easy option for a vivid yarn on the declining days and shrinking frontiers of aerial barnstorming) to place some coherent emphasis on a critique of the unquestioned 'hero-

ic' hooks of the earlier films: adventurism, conmanship and male bonding. Redford's World War I flier has by 1926 tailored his sustaining lies about his daredevil rivalry with former German opponent Brundin (now extended into stuntsmanship) to the point where he almost believes them himself, and is certainly convincing enough to employ them with a dangerous seductiveness. His deeds and his deceptions (and his irresponsibility) are, however, rhymed with those of cinema itself, presented as the only scheme within which they really make any sense. An underrated attempt to scrutinise the immature American screen hero, which simultaneously works as a fine belated addition to Hollywood's recurrent romantic fascination with flying. PT

Great Wall, A

see Great Wall Is a Great Wall, The

Great Wall Is a Great Wall, The (aka A Great Wall)

(Peter Wang, 1985, US/China) Wang Xiao, Li Qinqin, Xiu Jian, Sharon Iwai, Shen Guanglan, Kelvin Han Yee, Peter Wang.
102 min.
The first American feature film shot in China amounts to rather more than an album of holiday snaps, thanks to the unfamiliarity of the resort and the universality of the situation. A Chinese-American computer executive (Peter Wang) takes his family to visit relatives in Peking. Both branches of the family are enormously curious about each other, so there is plenty of experimenting with language, lipstick, electric blankets, music and squat toilets. Ideological differences are kept at arm's length, and the concept of privacy which is debated would have been as incomprehensible in Imperial China as it is to the Red Chinese. There's no Chinese word for it. Comparative economics don't get much of a look in either, beyond the statistic that a bottle of Coke costs half a day's wages. West confronts East only at the ping-pong table, and the star of the film is Peking itself, still an elegant city of shady courtyards, tree-lined avenues and ancient pagodas, despite *Godzilla*-type redevelopers. BC

Great Waltz, The

(Julien Duvivier, 1938, US) Luise Rainer, Fernand Gravey, Miliza Korjus, Hugh Herbert, Lionel Atwill, Minna Gombell, Sig Ruman.
102 min. b/w.
Sumptuous MGM kitsch, shot with great panache by Joseph Ruttenberg but treating Johann Strauss and his music to most of the clichés known to the biopic book (the snivelling romantic complications are very hard to take). Victor Fleming took over direction latterly from Duvivier, but the final sequence (Strauss' instant composition of 'The Blue Danube' and tearful farewell to his illicit love) was conceived and directed by Josef von Sternberg. TM

Great Waltz, The

(Andrew L Stone, 1972, US) Horst Buchholz, Mary Costa, Rossano Brazzi, Nigel Patrick, Yvonne Mitchell, James Faulkner.
134 min.
For perhaps half-an-hour, with every door opening to reveal couples whirling gaily in the Viennese waltz and Nigel Patrick cheerfully sending up the character of Johann Senior, this Strauss biopic is lively if exhausting. Then Senior dies, Junior gets amorous, and love's platitudes are given the freedom of the screen. There is even a moment when Strauss, struck by instant inspiration while dallying in the Vienna Woods, scribbles an immortal melody on his cuff. It makes the Duvivier film look like a masterpiece by comparison. TM

Great White Hype, The

(Reginald Hudlin, 1996, US) Samuel L Jackson, Peter Berg, Jeff Goldblum, Jon Lovitz, Damon Wayans, Corbin Bernsen, Cheech Marin, Salli Richardson.
91 min.
When it comes to heavyweight boxing: never bet on the white guy. But what if America got bored with blacks beating each other up? A flamboyant promoter, the Reverend Fred Sultan (Jackson), decides the sport needs a Great White Hope to bring back the big bucks. In the absence of any qualified contenders, he settles on retired

amateur pugilist Terry Conklin (Berg), the peace-loving lead singer of Massive Head Wound, and the only man ever to floor the champ. Despite some promising credentials – notably a script by Ron Shelton (*Bull Durham*) and Tony Hendra (*Spinal Tap*) – this lackadaisical comedy stings like a butterfly and floats like a bee. Still, Jackson supplies an engaging gloss on Don King, and the script takes a refreshingly irreverent approach to media pieties ('Do you covet racism?' demands the politically correct Conklin of his bemused new manager). Indeed, the film's clued-in on most fronts. It doesn't insult the intelligence, lands a sucker punch or two, but fails to deliver a knockout combination. A contender, then, but only a flyweight. TCh

Greed [100]

(Erich von Stroheim, 1923, US) Gibson Gowland, ZaSu Pitts, Jean Hersholt, Tempe Pigott, Frank Hayes, Dale Fuller.
7,900 ft. b/w.
Originally planned to run around ten hours but hacked to just over two by Thalberg's MGM, von Stroheim's greatest film still survives as a true masterpiece of cinema. Even now its relentlessly cynical portrait of physical and moral squalor retains the ability to shock, while the Von's obsessive attention to realist detail – both in terms of the San Francisco and Death Valley locations, and the minutely observed characters – is never prosaic: as the two men and a woman fall out over filthy lucre (a surprise lottery win), their motivations are explored with a remarkably powerful visual poetry, and Frank Norris' novel is translated into the cinematic equivalent of, say, Zola at the peak of his powers. Never has a wedding been so bitterly depicted, never a moral denouement been delivered with such vicious irony. GA

Greek Tycoon, The

(J Lee Thompson, 1978, US) Anthony Quinn, Jacqueline Bisset, Raf Vallone, Edward Albert, James Franciscus, Camilla Sparv, Charles Durning, Roland Culver.
106 min.
Set somewhere in a timeless Martini-land, *The Greek Tycoon* is an everyday love story of a shipping magnate and an assassinated president's widow – a sort of Harold Robbins out of *TitBits* tabloid biopic. Quinn's ageing Zorba is certainly no Citizen Kane, and Bisset's contribution rarely veers beyond the soulful pose, but it matters hardly a jot to a publicly rehearsed, pre-sold jet-set jamboree. Upmarket exploitation pics tend to make it (ie. profit) on the merest smell of money, sex and scandal, and this effort just reeks. Trashy it may be (though classily trashy, on a $6 million budget); vulgar it ain't – the Tomasis and the Cassidys are at bottom really ordinary, unhappy folks who just happen to have untold wealth and power. Your sympathy is earnestly solicited; it would be better spent on anyone tempted to sit through this glossy travesty. PT

Green Berets, The

(John Wayne/Ray Kellogg, 1968, US) John Wayne, David Janssen, Jim Hutton, Aldo Ray, Raymond St Jacques, Jack Soo, Bruce Cabot, Patrick Wayne, Luke Askew.
141 min.
The Duke tells it like it was in Vietnam from a hawk's eye view, with the Vietcong spending their time setting fiendish booby-traps, while he and his gallant men defend the peace-loving, victimised peasantry. A war correspondent (Janssen) starts by expressing mild doubts about the situation, but grabs a rifle when he sees how it is. What offends about the film, even more than its flag-waving one-sidedness, is that it is such a ponderously silly, tear-jerking melodrama. Every cliché is given a whirl, even the Vietnamese orphan lurking about the camp as a cute mascot. At the end, when his favourite Yank is killed in action, Wayne leads the kid comfortingly off into the sunset (honest he does) saying 'You're what this is all about'. TM

Green Card

(Peter Weir, 1990, US) Gérard Depardieu, Andie MacDowell, Bebe Neuwirth, Gregg Edelman, Robert Prosky, Jessie Keosian, Ethan Phillips, Mary Louise Wilson.
107 min.
French musician George Faure (Depardieu)

needs a green card to work in America; New York horticulturist Brontë Parrish (MacDowell) is after an apartment with greenhouse available only to a married couple. So they undergo a marriage of convenience, which turns out to be anything but when the authorities decide to investigate. After months apart, flamboyant George and uptight Brontë must reunite in order to memorise a fictionalised life together... Rarely did New York look so exotic and entrancing; Weir's signature is evident in the driving beat of the opening musical sequence and in the lush splendours of Brontë's greenhouse. Weir's first romantic comedy boasts a central relationship which is tentative and hopeful, a mood beautifully realised by Depardieu (venturing into new territory with a major English-speaking role). Complemented by the refined MacDowell, his gracious, generous performance is never dominating, and their exchanges offer unexpected pleasures. In terms of the genre's conventions, Weir likens this film to 'a light meal'. It's one to savour. CM

Green Fire
(Andrew Marton, 1954, US) Grace Kelly, Stewart Granger, Paul Douglas, John Ericson, Murvyn Vye.
100 min.
Expansive but routine romantic adventure, with Kelly coming between expat emerald miners amid the local (Eastman) colour of South America. A profusion of natural disasters give Marton the chance to show his paces, usually better appreciated when confined to action sequences and second unit inserts on the films of others (as in the chariot races of *Ben Hur*). An early script from the writing team of Ivan Goff and Ben Roberts who, despite signing proficient stuff for directors like Walsh and Mann, will probably be best remembered for creating *Charley's Angels* over 20 years later. PT

Green for Danger
(Sidney Gilliat, 1946, GB) Alastair Sim, Sally Gray, Rosamund John, Trevor Howard, Leo Genn, Megs Jenkins, Judy Campbell, Moore Marriott.
91 min. b/w.
Two murders in a cottage hospital leave the surgeon, the anaesthetist and three attendant nurses as major suspects. But this is no ordinary country house whodunit; Launder and Gilliat's long experience as scriptwriters enables them to undermine the conventions to macabrely humorous effect. Amid the unpredictable explosions of World War II 'doodlebugs', Sim's eccentrically fallible detective rakes over the dirty secrets of his guilt-ridden suspects and leads us carefully up the garden path. 'Not one of my most successful cases', he is driven to confess; but one of Launder and Gilliat's most likeable films. RMy

Greengage Summer, The (aka Loss of Innocence)
(Lewis Gilbert, 1961, GB) Kenneth More, Danielle Darrieux, Susannah York, Jane Asher, Maurice Denham.
99 min.
Before Gilbert descended to mush like *Friends* and *Paul and Michelle*, he made a number of interesting failures, of which this is probably one of the best. Susannah York, in one of her best performances, plays a young schoolgirl holidaying in France, where she falls in love with an Englishman, a mysterious older man (More). The main problem is that the plot degenerates into silly dramatics at the expense of character development, with More turning out to be – of all things – a jewel thief. DP

Green Grow the Rushes (aka Brandy Ashore)
(Derek Twist, 1951, GB) Richard Burton, Honor Blackman, Roger Livesey, Frederick Leister, Geoffrey Keen, Bryan Forbes.
79 min. b/w.
The film technicians' union ACTT (as it then was) set up its own production company to break the grip which the British majors then had on the industry and thus provide extra work for its members. Their first offering, from the novel by Howard Clewes, was this diluted combination of *Whisky Galore!* and *Passport to Pimlico* in which a bunch of Kent brandy smugglers call on

ancient rights to prevent the men from the ministry shutting down their operations. The film had distribution problems at the time, and these days is chiefly of archival interest. TJ

Green Ice
(Ernest Day, 1981, GB) Ryan O'Neal, Anne Archer, Omar Sharif, Domingo Ambriz, John Larroquette, Philip Stone.
116 min.
Clodhopping attempt to make a jolly romantic comedy set against a background of torture, murder and rebel guerillas being fed to the hogs in the prisons of Colombia. O'Neal and Archer play a couple of Americans meeting cute in Mexico, then heading for Colombia, where she takes over from a sister shot while working for the rebel cause, and he (at first with itchy fingers for the loot) helps her replenish the rebel coffers through a daring heist of emeralds from a government stronghold right out of a James Bond movie (with Sharif a villain to match). Painfully miscalculated from the word go, it's a load of offensive old cobblers coated in picture postcard scenery. TM

Greenkeeping
(David Caesar, 1992, Aust) Mark Little, Lisa Hensley, Max Cullen.
90 min.
A meandering, *very* low-key comedy in which Little, greenkeeper at the local bowls club, finds it hard to cope with a dope-dependent wife and her unpaid dealers, with a born-again moneylender brother, with racists and temptresses in the club, and with his own complete ignorance on matters horticultural. The script is often droll in its observation of the mind-numbing banalities of mate-culture, though there are times when it seems unfocused and all too ready to rest on sub-Jane Campion eccentricity. Slim, then, but finally rather likeable. GA

Green Light
(Frank Borzage, 1937, US) Errol Flynn, Anita Louise, Margaret Lindsay, Cedric Hardwicke, Walter Abel, Henry O'Neill, Spring Byington.
85 min. b/w.
Adapted from a novel by Lloyd C Douglas, this is a typically heady brew of medico-religious claptrap. Flynn is a young surgeon, left to take the blame when a patient dies during an operation, who refuses to exculpate himself on realising that the senior colleague responsible (O'Neill) is an old man terrified of total ruin. It's love at first sight when Flynn meets the dead woman's daughter (Louise); but she blames him for her mother's death; so he departs for the wilds of Montana, places his life on the line as a human guinea pig, and comes up with a vaccine against the deadly spotted fever. The jello binding the characters together in a welter of forgiveness and redemption is a wise old crippled cleric (Hardwicke), who assures them that God's red light means man must pause to learn through suffering before getting the green light to go on into eternity. Given that the script comes on like a volubly po-faced sermon, Borzage directs with admirable cool, and gets excellent performances from the entire cast. TM

Green Man, The
(Robert Day/(uncredited) Basil Dearden, 1956, GB) Alastair Sim, George Cole, Terry-Thomas, Jill Adams, Raymond Huntley, Eileen Moore, Avril Angers, Dora Bryan, John Chandos, Colin Gordon, Peter Bull, Arthur Lowe.
80 min. b/w.
A splendid black comedy, adapted by Frank Launder and Sidney Gilliat from their own play *Meet a Body*. Sim is up to his old tricks as a timid watchmaker who is a professional assassin in his spare time. All the right people get bumped off (headmasters, businessmen, and other assorted dictators), and the movie is quite vulgar enough to be funny. It is fascinating to compare Sim's hilarious schizophrenia with Alec Guinness in *The Ladykillers*. Inside every Englishman there lurks a ruthless criminal, impatient to steal scenes. TCh

Green Pastures, The
(William Keighley/Marc Connelly, 1936, US) Rex Ingram, Oscar Polk, Eddie Anderson, Frank Wilson, George Reed, Myrtle Anderson.
93 min. b/w.
There is nothing intrinsically offensive about this all-white use of all-black stereotypes to illustrate

the artless simplicities of the gospel religion of Deep South slavery. Constructed as a series of Sunday School Bible stories linked by spirituals, it has enormous charm in its folklorish fancies (Heaven as a cushy cotton plantation, Babylon as a dingy backstreet dive), and a performance of great gentleness and good humour from Ingram ('Ain't no bed of roses bein' De Lawd') which is never tainted by the mawkish religiosity that creeps in towards the end. What is offensive is the way in which the depths of plangent suffering that inspired the spirituals are totally ignored. Instead we get white society's wish-fulfilment image of happy Uncle Toms who will be content with their due reward of a ten-cent cigar and a fish-fry in heaven. TM

Green Ray, The (Le Rayon Vert)
(Eric Rohmer, 1986, Fr) Marie Rivière, Vincent Gauthier, Carita, Basile Gervaise, Béatrice Romand, Lisa Hérédia.
99 min.
It's July, and Delphine (Rivière), a young Parisian secretary, is suddenly at a loss regarding her holiday; a friend has just backed out of a trip to Greece, her other companions have boyfriends, and Delphine can't bear spending August in Paris. She also hopes to find a dream lover, but receives only the unwelcome attentions of pushy predators, until...There's a whiff of fairytale to this particular slice of realism à la Rohmer, but what's perhaps most remarkable is that the film was almost completely improvised; though not so as you'd know it. It's as flawlessly constructed, shot and performed as ever, with France's greatest living director effortlessly evoking the morose moods of holidaying alone among crowds, and revelling in the particulars of place, weather and time of day. Deceptively simple, the film oozes honesty and spontaneity; the word, quite bluntly, is masterpiece. GA

Green Room, The
see Chambre Verte, La

Greenwich Village
(Walter Lang, 1944, US) Carmen Miranda, Don Ameche, William Bendix, Vivian Blaine, Felix Bressart, Tony and Sally DeMarco, Adolph Green, Betty Comden, Judy Holliday, Alvin Hammer.
82 min.
The Village in the Roaring '20s and the new boy in town is dapper Don Ameche, a talented composer hoping to get his latest concerto performed at Carnegie Hall. What happens, though, is that he falls in with Carmen Miranda, exotic hostess at William Bendix's swingin' speakeasy, who persuades him to let her boss turn it into a Broadway revue – and just the vehicle for singing sensation Vivian Blaine, with whom young Ameche is already besotted. The fluff factor is high in this easygoing Fox frolic, but trainspotters will note the fleeting presence of cabaret artistes The Revuers, who included future star Billy Holliday and *Singin' in the Rain* writers Betty Comden and Adolph Green. TJ

Greetings
(Brian De Palma, 1968, US) Jonathan Warden, Robert De Niro, Gerritt Graham, Megan McCormick, Ashley Oliver, Allen Garfield.
88 min.
De Palma's third feature freewheels and jumpcuts its three weirdo leads through a late '60s obstacle course of draft-dodging, sex and assassination politics, picking up more than its share of unforced laughs on the way. A quintessential Movie Brat apprentice piece. Godardian disruptions, documentary coups, peeping-tom Hitchcock incisions: the film school textbooks and movie house memories assimilated, evaluated, turned inside-out and spring-cleaned, with only the budget to keep it all streetbound. Silly *and* substantial.

Gregorio Cortez
see Ballad of Gregorio Cortez, The

Gregory's Girl
(Bill Forsyth, 1980, GB) John Gordon Sinclair, Dee Hepburn, Jake D'Arcy, Claire Grogan, Robert Buchanan, William Greenlees, Allison Forster.
91 min.

g

Slight but highly entertaining comedy about a Scottish schoolgirl who becomes a wizard on the football team (arousing male resentment, naturally), and the lanky Gregory who fancies her from afar. Strong performances and a naturalistic script, which zooms in on adolescent delusions and embarrassments, keep things going at a leisurely pace. Quirky and utterly endearing, it nevertheless reveals the director's definite lack of interest in the visual textures of his films. GA

Gremlins

(Joe Dante, 1984, US) Zach Galligan, Phoebe Cates, Hoyt Axton, Polly Holliday, Frances Lee McCain, Dick Miller, Keye Luke, Scott Brady.
111 min.
Eccentric inventor Axton gives a cute little Christmas present to his 20-year-old son Billy (Galligan): it's a mogwai, latest in the long line of coy, furry creatures to send the blockbuster audience into paroxysms of communal cooing. When accidentally splashed with water, it spawns nasty offspring which, when fed after midnight, transmute into brawling, boozing, murderous gremlins, who proceed to trash the Spielbergian, Disneyish, Capraesque small town setting. Though sloppily plotted and stickily whimsical in parts, *Gremlins* is kept afloat by its splendid special effects and set pieces, which culminate with its nasty wee beasties whooping it up at a screening of *Snow White*, much in the manner of the mewling, puking blockbuster movie audience which will no doubt be lapping up all this tomfoolery. AB

Gremlins 2: The New Batch

(Joe Dante, 1990, US) Zach Galligan, Phoebe Cates, John Glover, Robert Prosky, Robert Picardo, Christopher Lee, Haviland Morris, Dick Miller, Jackie Joseph, Keye Luke, Kathleen Freeman, Paul Bartel, John Astin.
106 min.
A chaotic affair which eschews narrative coherence for rapid-fire sight gags and self-referential silliness. The risibly slender plot finds Billy (Galligan) and prissy girlfriend Kate (Cates) in the employ of the Clamp Organisation, into whose money-grubbing hands falls the newly-orphaned *mogwai* ('Gizmo' to his friends). Narrowly evading dissection by ever-so-slightly fiendish Dr Catheter (Lee), Gizmo is reunited with Billy, who hardly has time to say 'don't get them wet or feed them after midnight' before his moistened pet gives birth to a skyscraper full of late-night feasting beasties. Thereafter, film-inspired pandemonium reigns. Gizmo, his head full of Rambo, 'becomes war', gribblies wave dentists' drills about their ears and chatter 'Is it safe?', and the whole diminutive cast dons spangled dresses and top hats for a Busby Berkeley-style chorus of 'New York, New York'. There's almost enough in-joke ingenuity to justify the total absence of plot. MK

Grey Fox, The

(Phillip Borsos, 1982, Can) Richard Farnsworth, Jackie Burroughs, Ken Pogue, Wayne Robson, Timothy Webber, Gary Reineke, David Petersen.
91 min.
Oldster stagecoach-robber Bill Miner (impeccably played by Farnsworth) emerges from the San Quentin rest home at the turn of the century, after a stay of some 30 years. Journeying through America into Canada, he discovers a country in transition: cars, cameras, rampaging Pinkerton men, etc. Still in love with the romance of the old West, Miner both disinters his career in crime and embarks on an oddball love affair, before committing himself to the inevitable one blag too many. The pacing is gentle, the style conditioned by documentary. Borsos infuses this story with wry observation, an appropriately elegiac feel, and a brooding sense of landscape. It's hard not to be charmed. RR

Grey Gardens

(David Maysles/Albert Maysles/Ellen Hovde/Muffie Meyer, 1975, US) Edith Bouvier Beale, Edith B Beale Jr.
95 min.
America's obsession with Jackie Kennedy-Onassis-who-next is overwhelming, and presumably the reason for the success there of this documentary about two of her family who live in isolated squalor on Long Island; a film that is voyeuristic in the extreme, extending no warmth to the bizarre mother and daughter as they battle out their lives together, but choosing instead to film them in the most offensive of ways. Like the shots of 'Little' Edith Bouvier Beale, a large 56-year-old, taken from below as she climbs upstairs in a miniskirt, rambling to herself; or 'Big' Edith, the demanding 79-year-old mother, with her towel falling off her withered, naked body. As Big Edie sings and Little Edie dances, both adoring the transient attentions of the film crew, you can only wonder what happened once the party was over. HM

Greystoke – The Legend of Tarzan Lord of the Apes

(Hugh Hudson, 1984, GB) Christopher Lambert, Ralph Richardson, Ian Holm, James Fox, Andie MacDowell, Cheryl Campbell, John Wells, Nigel Davenport.
130 min.
What would it be like for a lost child of the British aristocracy to be reared by apes in the African jungle? Cue for some skilfully handled action and a vivid realisation of the ape community in which a man eventually becomes boss-cat. The film changes gear when our hero returns to Edwardian Britain and his ancestral home, Greystoke. Torn between two cultures, confused by his love for Jane, desolated by the loss of his grandfather (man) and his father (ape), he undergoes...culture schlock. It is here that *Greystoke* pops its valves, pushing a simple yarn to the point of philosophical overload. Rhetoric apart, the film offers some stirring entertainment, and a memorable ham sandwich from Richardson, allowed to steal the show as the grandfather in what proved to be his last film. RR

Gridlock'd

(Vondie Curtis-Hall, 1996, US/GB) Tim Roth, Tupac Shakur, Thandie Newton, Charles Fleischer, Howard Hessman, John Sayles, Vondie Curtis-Hall.
91 min.
When fellow musician Cookie (Newton) overdoses on New Year's Eve, Stretch and Spoon resolve to get into rehab asap. They reckon, however, without the federal welfare system, a bureaucratic spaghetti junction which isn't about to help anyone in a hurry, least of all a couple of itchy smack addicts with attitude. Trekking from office to office, queue to queue, the pair take another hit to help them through the day, only to get mixed up with a brutal gangster and a murder investigation. A hip take on heroin addicts kicking against the pricks (*Trainspotting in New York*, you might say), the film has a fairly uninteresting narrative motor in its thriller subplot, but hits on an edgy black comic tone for Stretch and Spoon's increasingly pained dealings with the unsympathetic representatives of authority. Roth (Stretch) and the late Tupac Shakur (Spoon) work up a delicious, deadpan rapport, in which Stretch is the wild card and Spoon the long-suffering straightman, and which climaxes with a hilariously sick scene in which the former repeatedly stabs his compliant pal in the chest, in a last desperate bid for medical attention. TCh

Grief

(Richard Glatzer, 1993, US) Craig Chester, Jackie Beat, Illeana Douglas, Alexis Arquette, Carlton Wilborn, Lucy Gutteridge, Paul Bartel, Mary Woronov.
87 min.
'There are many ways to tell a story, realism is just the most dull.' That, at any rate, is the ethos of the writers of 'The Love Judge', a TV show set in a California divorce court. Here circus lesbians vie with schizophrenic opera divas and stripper nuns for truth, justice and alimony. The writers' lot seems mundane in comparison, though these maladjusted under-achievers are a colourful group: Mark (Chester) is still grieving for his lover who died a year ago of AIDS, but he's in with a chance for a production job and is besotted with Bill (Arquette). Jeremy (Wilborn) says Bill's a lost cause, and Leslie (Douglas) agrees with him; she prefers Ben, the photocopy repairman. Meanwhile, the boss, Jo (Beat), is incensed to find her new sofa despoiled with sperm stains every morning. While Glatzer's debut boasts a good number of campy, enjoyable scenes (notably 'extracts' from 'The Love Judge' featuring the likes of Paul Bartel and Mary Woronov) and a stand-out performance from Jackie Beat, it's a surprisingly well structured, carefully nuanced affair (taking place over a working week, and, except in the extracts, never leaving the office). A genuinely moving comedy. TCh

Grieta, La

see Rift, The

Grievous Bodily Harm

(Mark Joffe, 1988, Aust) Colin Friels, John Waters, Bruno Lawrence, Shane Briant.
90 min.
Flat Australian thriller which follows the uneasy partnership between crime journalist Friels and opportunistic cop Lawrence as they combine expertise to stop serial killer Waters from continuing a trail of mayhem. The film's habit of undercutting audience expectation is so overused it becomes tiresome, so Joffe throws in an odd snippet of sexual perversity in a bid to restore interest. TJ

Grifters, The

(Stephen Frears, 1990, US) Anjelica Huston, John Cusack, Annette Bening, Pat Hingle, Henry Jones, Michael Laskin, Eddie Jones, JT Walsh.
110 min.
The title refers to con artists like Roy Dillon (Cusack), who makes a living palming dollar bills in bars, or Myra (Bening), the feisty drifter who tries to steer him to the big time after a petty scam lands him in hospital. But the most ruthlessly survivalist is Roy's mother Lily (Huston), employed by the Mob to work a 'playback' scam at racetracks, and liable to be beaten up or have a cigar stubbed out on her hand just to teach her a lesson. Lily is perceived as a woman of great tragedy, still possessed of the maternal instincts she needs to try to save her long-neglected son, imbued with a toughness that helps her overcome constant terror and loneliness, and sufficiently tainted by life to both desire and finally destroy her offspring. Donald Westlake's excellent screenplay does some justice to the starkness of Jim Thompson's novel; and Frears' direction never fails to grab the attention, even given the weaknesses of Cusack and Bening as the existentialist young love interest. Anjelica Huston is quite astonishing; as Thompson is a kind of dimestore Dostoievsky, so Huston's Myra seems straight from the pages of Euripides and Sophocles. SGr

Grim Prairie Tales

(Wayne Coe, 1990, US) James Earl Jones, Brad Dourif, William Atherton, Lisa Eichhorn, Will Hare, Marc McClure, Michelle Joyner, Scott Paulin.
94 min.
This first feature by Coe (who designed the posters for *Back to the Future* and *Out of Africa*, among others) is a stand-out US independent. A prim New Englander (Dourif) finds his campsite invaded by a grizzled, smelly mountain man (Jones), who turns up with a fresh corpse slung over his saddle. Mutual mistrust spurs them to scare each other with horror stories through the night. The four tales are ingeniously varied (and intelligently keyed to the character of the teller and the situation around the camp-fire); but it's the writing of the framing story and the two lead performances that make the film so special. As the T-shirt has it, it sucks you in. TR

Grind

(Chris Kentis, 1996, US) Adrienne Shelly, Billy Crudup, Paul Schulze, Frank Vincent, Saul Stein.
96 min.
The filmic equivalent of a Springsteen song: Eddie (Crudup) returns to his industrial home town and moves in with his brother and his bored, brow-beaten wife, Janey. Eddie goes to work as a machinist, but switches to night shifts so he can work on his hotrod by day. It sounds grindingly predictable (and it doesn't disappoint), but this is a subtler, more emotionally honest film than most American indies are concerned to come up with. It doesn't look like much, but the cutting's sharp, and the three principals turn in carefully nuanced performances. It's easy to see why everyone's getting excited about Crudup – but don't write off Kentis either. In its own quiet, cumulative way this is an impressive, authoritative debut. TCh

Gringo in Mañanaland, A

(Dee Dee Halleck, 1995, US)
61 min. b/w & col.

This documentary constructs an argument about the representation of South America by its northern neighbours without recourse to commentary or interviews: the film is entirely made up of archive footage from Hollywood features, cartoons, ads and newsreels. At first it seems shapeless and neutral, but gradually the insidious political nature of the material becomes explicit, not least when the unmistakable Ronald Reagan turns up in a long-forgotton melodrama, *Tropic Zone*, and Charlton Heston takes to battling the armies of invading Red Ants in *The Naked Jungle*. TCh

Grip of Fear, The

see Experiment in Terror

Grip of the Strangler
(aka The Haunted Strangler)

(Robert Day, 1958, GB) Boris Karloff, Elizabeth Allan, Jean Kent, Vera Day, Anthony Dawson, Tim Turner, Diane Aubrey.
79 min. b/w.

A Jekyll and Hyde tale set in London in the 1880s, with an immaculate performance from Karloff as a distinguished novelist and social reformer who investigates the case of 'The Haymarket Strangler' – suspecting that a sailor found guilty and executed was in fact innocent – and finds the trail leading in alarmingly compromising directions. Opening grimly with a public hanging (with callous crowd hungry for a spot of entertainment eagerly in attendance), and making evocative use of 'The Judas Hole' (a sleazy music hall whose scantily-clad girls become the target for murder), the whole film is powerfully underpinned by the repressive nature of Victorian society. Uncommonly gripping, wonderfully atmospheric, it has a real touch of the Val Lewtons. TM

Grisbi

see Touchez pas au Grisbi

Grissom Gang, The

(Robert Aldrich, 1971, US) Kim Darby, Scott Wilson, Tony Musante, Robert Lansing, Connie Stevens, Irene Dailey.
128 min.

One of Aldrich's finest and most complex films, this adaptation of James Hadley Chase's notorious *No Orchids for Miss Blandish* is far more than just another contribution to the nostalgic rural gangster cycle initiated by *Bonnie and Clyde*. For one thing, the eponymous family, who kidnap '30s heiress Miss Blandish, are never glamorised but portrayed as a pathetic, ignorant bunch of grotesques; for another, as the petulant and spoilt heroine turns the sadistic and murderous Slim Grissom's love for her to her own cruelly humiliating purposes, the film becomes an unsentimental exploration of perverse power-games played between two characters whose very different family backgrounds cannot conceal the latent vulnerability they both share. As such it is simultaneously witty and surprisingly touching, its disturbing emotional undercurrents lent depth by the assured playing of both Darby and Wilson. GA

Grizzly

(William Girdler, 1976, US) Christopher George, Andrew Prine, Richard Jaeckel, Joan McCall, Joe Dorsey.
91 min.

'No way!' twice in the first five lines of dialogue let you know what to expect from this attempt to ape *Jaws*, so to speak. The strictly B feature cast plays a team of Forest Rangers (including boozy maverick and fey conservationist, as in *Jaws*) chasing an alleged twenty-footer who eats girl campers. Alleged, because whenever the bear is seen from a normal angle, he is quite obviously of medium build; much of the other marauding is done from his own point of view (as in *King Kong*), which equally fails to convince. The heavy-breathing soundtrack accompanying these attacks is at least preferable to lines like 'While you've been sitting on your fat ass, I've made this forest part of me'. AN

Groove on a Stanley Knife

(Tinge Krishnan/Beth Kotler, 1997, GB) Alison Burrows, Samantha Hoyle.
42 min.

Two lasses hole up in a gross public lavatory, after a violent confrontation with three drug dealers. They gab about drugs and sex (one is a lesbian) until a dramatic revelation tears everything apart. At least one of the co-directors here has talent: there's a real intensity when the film pushes beyond its grimy realism. It's let down by some over-written dialogue and uneven acting, but on the whole it's an impressive calling card from Sheffield's Disruptive Element Films – let's hope MTV doesn't swallow them up. TCh

Groove Tube, The

(Ken Shapiro, 1974, US) Ken Shapiro, Richard Belzer, Chevy Chase, Buzzy Linhart, Richmond Baier.
75 min.

A series of one-dimensional parodies on aspects of American life that lampoons all the expected targets – corporations, TV, commercials, politics – but in a way that makes few dents. Jokes extend little beyond their not-so-original ideas: a news broadcast about Suk Muc Dik and Phuc Hu; some ads that make explicit the implicit sex of most advertising; a TV pundits' tea party; 'Fanny Hill' being read out on a tots' programme. The only permutations the film seems happy with are two sex sketches: one dealing with a heavy petting session in a cinema, the other a sporting commentary on the German performance in the International Sex Games. Throughout a fairly healthy vulgarity prevails over insight. CPe

Gross Anatomy
(aka A Cut Above)

(Thom Eberhardt, 1989, US) Matthew Modine, Daphne Zuniga, Christine Lahti, Todd Field, John Scott Clough, Alice Carter, Zakes Mokae.
109 min.

The trials and tribulations of a first year med 'gross anatomy' class. Modine is a charismatic lead as Joe Slovak, the cocky young lad who bounces in with his basket-ball to find that not everyone views dissecting cadavers in the same carefree manner. The group's reaction to this maverick is sensitively – if not adventurously – scripted as they resist his influence and put him in his place. Mild and humorous, the film dodges the melodrama traps it sets for itself, making pleasant if forgettable viewing. RK

Grosse Fatigue

(Micheal Blanc, 1994, Fr) Micheal Blanc, Carole Bouquet, Philippe Noiret, Giles Jacob.
92 min.

Actor Blanc's ambitious blend of doppelgänger fable and movie-movie comedy isn't, unfortunately, as funny as it'd like to be. It begins intriguingly, with Blanc up to mysteriously awful antics in Cannes and, later, Paris; then, as the puzzle moves towards its ingenious if excessively belated solution, matters get bogged down in in-jokes and bad timing. Noiret, especially, contributes an engaging cameo, but the film as a whole is much too clever for its own good. And really, Michel, gags about rape are a bit off. GA

Grosse Pointe Blank

(George Armitage, 1997, US) John Cusack, Minnie Driver, Alan Arkin, Dan Aykroyd, Joan Cusack, Jeremy Piven, Hank Azaria, Barbara Harris.
107 min.

Contract killer Martin Blank (John Cusack) finds himself going home to Grosse Pointe, Detroit, for his high school reunion weekend. His shrink (Arkin) thinks it might help with his spiritual crisis. So does his secretary (Joan Cusack). And besides, there's a job in town. More to the point, maybe Debi (Driver) is ready to forgive him, ten years after he stood her up on prom night. Coming on the heels of *Swingers* and *Palookaville*, this hip black comedy is another droll study in the neuroses of the modern American male. As his name suggests, Blank is a void – his life has no meaning – but he thinks he's smart enough to get back on track, to buck those twin truisms: you can't go home again, and there are no second acts in American lives. Cusack is an engaging, lively actor with a keen sense of irony, and those qualities are much in evidence here. Director Armitage doesn't quite get the edge he brought to *Miami Blues*, but for what is essentially a one-joke movie, this has an awful lot going for it; not least the persuasive

notion that psychiatrists all over America are being terrorised by angst-ridden hitmen intent on liberating their inner selves. TCh

Grotesque, The

(John-Paul Davidson, 1995, GB) Alan Bates, Theresa Russell, Sting, Lena Headey, Steven Mackintosh, Jim Carter, Anna Massey, Trudie Styler, Maria Aitken, James Fleet, John Mills, Annette Badland.
98 min.

Having scripted this moribund adaptation of his own meticulously wrought, black comic novel, Patrick McGrath must take some blame, but Davidson's stultifying direction and listless performances from Sting and Bates deal the death blow. In the novel, McGrath evokes an atmosphere of Gothic gloom, moral decay and insidious malice; here his elegant weirdness and sly humour sink into a bog of boredom. The new obsequious butler Fledge (Sting) insinuates himself into the postwar household of Sir Hugo Coal (Bates), an eccentric aristo who hopes to stun the Royal Society with his crackpot theories of dinosaur genealogy. Seduced by Fledge's charm, Sir Hugo's wife Harriet (Russell) becomes embroiled in a subtle conspiracy that undermines her husband's authority, compromises her daughter Cleo's marriage plans, and culminates in the death of Cleo's would-be suitor Sidney Giblet (Mackintosh). Sting fails to capture the class hatred and sly ambition that inform Fledge's actions, and it's a crime to have wasted such character actors as Carter, Massey and Mills on such a dramatically dull, visually impaired treatment. NF

Groundhog Day

(Harold Ramis, 1993, US) Bill Murray, Andie MacDowell, Chris Elliott, Stephen Tobolowsky, Brian Doyle-Murray, Marita Geraghty.
101 min.

How would it feel to wake up to the same day *every* day? Would you crack up at the sheer tedium of it all? Cynically exploit others (*they* don't know they're trapped in a time warp) with what you learned about them the day before? Or use the situation to better yourself? That's the dilemma facing misanthropic TV weatherman Phil Connors (Murray) when he once more visits the small town of Punxsutawney, Pennsylvania – 'weather capital of the world' – to report on its annual Groundhog Day ceremony. What's so satisfying about Danny Rubin and Harold Ramis' script – besides the sheer plethora of gags – is the way it rigorously covers every last nuance of Connors' nightmarish predicament: he can drink himself legless without fear of the morning after, endlessly refine his chat-up lines, become an expert in 19th century French verse, but whatever he does he ends up back where he was on the dot of six. Ramis directs this surreal suburban fantasy with an admirably light touch, revelling in its absurd repetitions, surprising us with narrative ellipses, and allowing Murray ample space to indulge his special mix of sarcasm and smarm. But this is first and foremost a comedy of *ideas*, on which score it never falters. GA

Groundstar Conspiracy, The

(Lamont Johnson, 1972, US) George Peppard, Michael Sarrazin, Christine Belford, Cliff Potts, James Olson.
95 min.

Johnson fashions a neatly edgy film out of an investigation into sabotage at a space research plant, where the blank mind of an amnesiac (Sarrazin) lies at the centre of the mystery. With an excess of surveillance hardware on display, the film carefully sows the seeds of paranoia, and expresses grave doubts about the morality of security control as Peppard's security agent goes about his enquiry answerable to no one. Apart from one lapse into the field of human emotions, the script deals intelligently with the programmed responses of its automaton-like characters.

Group, The

(Sidney Lumet, 1966, US) Candice Bergen, Joan Hackett, Elizabeth Hartman, Shirley Knight, Joanna Pettet, Mary-Robin Redd, Jessica Walter, Kathleen Widdoes, James Broderick, Larry Hagman, Richard Mulligan.
150 min.

Basically soap opera, but a beautifully crafted and brilliantly acted adaptation of Mary McCarthy's novel chronicling the fortunes of eight Vassar graduates, class of '33, up to the beginning of World War II. Sidney Buchman's script does a remarkable tailoring job on the book, pruning away all the fat and cutting the rest into hundreds of sharp little scenes which are pieced together as an attractively witty mosaic of the decade. Particularly clever is the way in which the girls, each one neatly and distinctively characterised, are seen to evolve personality-wise: looking, for instance, at the Dottie (Hackett) of the last scenes – proud wife of an Arizona oil-man, growing slightly hatchet-faced and probably a pillar of the local ladies' league – and remembering her first, despairingly daring affair with a Greenwich Village painter, one thinks with astonishment that's exactly how she would turn out. Should the lengthy array of amorous hopes and disillusionments threaten boredom, there's always Boris Kaufman's wonderfully handsome camerawork to admire. TM

Grumpy Old Men
(Donald Petrie, 1993, US) Jack Lemmon, Walter Matthau, Ann-Margret, Burgess Meredith, Daryl Hannah, Kevin Pollak, Ossie Davis, Buck Henry.
103 min.
The Odd Couple are reunited to curious effect, since Lemmon has long since moved convincingly into dramatic parts, while Matthau has stayed pretty much where he was. They play elderly, feuding neighbours in small-town Wabasha, Minnesota. They've been insulting each other about their fish catch for five decades, when on to the scene arrives wacko teacher Ariel (Ann-Margret) to intensify their rivalry. Who gets the newcomer is as predictable as the outcome of a subplot romance between their respective children (Hannah and Pollak). It's a dawdling affair – apart from the outtakes at the end, which are funnier than anything in the picture itself – memorable chiefly for the Hanna-Barbera appearance of Matthau in a trapper's cap uttering lines like, 'The guy's straight as a grizzly's dick.' Also on hand is Burgess Meredith as an L-Dopa grandpa – 'Didya mount her?' – and Buck Henry as the flinty repo man. Mediocre, regrettably. BC

Guadalcanal Diary
(Lewis Seiler, 1943, US) Preston Foster, Lloyd Nolan, William Bendix, Richard Conte, Anthony Quinn, Richard Jaeckel, Roy Roberts, Minor Watson, Lionel Stander.
93 min. b/w.
Twentieth Century-Fox lost no time in bringing the US Marines' successful Solomon Islands campaign to the screen (it was the first important victory of the Pacific war). Respected at the time for its authenticity, Seiler's film no longer seems particularly remarkable, featuring the usual cross-section of acceptable American types (with a heroic chaplain at their head) as they go about their business. The cast is better than most, and it is impressively staged, given that location filming actually took place in Camp Pendleton, California. TCh

Guantanamera
(Tomás Gutiérrez Alea/Juan Carlos Tabio, 1994, Cuba) Carlos Cruz, Mirtha Ibbara, Raúl Eguren, Jorge Perugorria.
105 min.
A familiar retread of the Cuban political satires of the '60s and '70s, this road movie deals with the aftermath of the now settling Cuban financial crisis of the early '90s. An ageing opera singer, 'Yoyita', the 'Guantanameran' of the song and title, who has been abroad to earn her fortune, returns to Cuba where she dies in the arms of her old flame. As a result, the intransigent bureaucrat husband of her unhappily married daughter, who has organised a crazy petrol-saving relay scheme for Havana burials, finds Yoyita is his first road test. There are jibes at shortages, the black market and sexual politics, but, as the daughter has a fling with a truckdriver, the film subsides into another celebration of the Cuban adage: 'Love is the Salt of Life'. WH

Guard, The (Karaul)
(Alexander Rogozhkin, 1989, USSR) Alexander Smirnov, Alexei Buldakov, Sergei Kupriyanov, Alexei Poluyan.
96 min. b/w & col.

Less stunning than bludgeoning, Rogozhkin's grisly movie is like the old Living Theater play The Brig, but on wheels. It is set almost entirely on a prison train transporting jailbirds across the USSR. It focuses on a rookie guard, Chlustov, and the endlessly humiliating hazing he undergoes at the hands of his older colleagues; finally, the atmosphere of extreme violence and brutality causes him to crack. Prison metaphors aside, the movie is notable for pushing certain images of Russian masculinity as far as they will go; it strips men naked morally, spiritually and, ultimately, physically too. TR

Guardian, The
(William Friedkin, 1990, US) Jenny Seagrove, Dwier Brown, Carey Lowell, Brad Hall, Miguel Ferrer, Natalia Nogulich.
93 min.
Deep in the lush canyons of upmarket LA, the tranquillity of an all-American family (Brown, Lowell and infant son) is threatened by the arrival of Camilla (Seagrove). Posing as a nanny sent by the Guardian Angel agency, she turns out to be a blood-thirsty, baby-sacrificing tree-worshipper. Based on Dan Greenburg's novel The Nanny, Friedkin's first foray into horror since The Exorcist contains many of the trademarks which characterised that epochal work: prying cameras track constantly through the shadowy corridors, sneaking up on occupants, while blinded scientists (police and doctors) impotently explain away supernatural disturbances. This time, though, Friedkin opts for up-front hokum, interspersed with impressively ridiculous special effects, including man-eating trees, flying nannies and coniferous chainsaw carnage. A severely flawed but not unamusing venture from a director who should know better. MK

Guarding Tess
(Hugh Wilson, 1994, US) Shirley MacLaine, Nicolas Cage, Richard Griffiths, Austin Pendleton, Edward Albert, James Rebhorn.
95 min.
Doug Chesnic (Cage) has the worst assignment in the secret service: he's bodyguard to former First Lady Tess Carlisle (MacLaine). Doug wants to be where the action is; Tess wants to go golfing every three or four years (usually in the dead of winter), with perhaps an annual trip to the opera for variety. Worse, she treats her bodyguards like butlers; she expects breakfast in bed, and no guns in the house. Hugh Wilson, creator of the Police Academy series, was once responsible for some modestly engaging TV sitcoms – and that's essentially what this is. He gets some amiable, low-key play out of the slippery ground between protocol and authority, the battle of wills between the determined, by-the-book agent and stubborn, independent Tess, but it's going nowhere slow until an implausible kidnap plot is hatched much too late in the day. Cage is on best behaviour here, but he's not an especially sympathetic performer. MacLaine more than keeps her end up (picking an outfit for an official affair, she opts for 'elegant disdain, yet sincere concern'); and her tetchy hauteur just about keeps the movie alive. TCh

Guerre d'un Seul Homme, La
see One Man's War

Guerre des Boutons, La (The War of the Buttons)
(Yves Robert, 1962, Fr) André Treton, Michel Isella, Martin Lartigue, Jean Richard, Yvette Etiévant, Jacques Dufilho.
95 min. b/w.
The buttons in question belong to the trousers of two rival gangs of urchins and are snipped off, along with braces and shoelaces, in a crescendo of running battles. If that notion doesn't, as they say, grab you, then how about an atrociously mugging and coyly foul-mouthed little hero with a twinkle in his eye as big as the Ritz, who proposes to drive the enemy from their lair by farting them out? A huge commercial success, like all films with naked children. GAd

Guerre est finie, La (The War is Over)
(Alain Resnais, 1966, Fr/Swe) Yves Montand, Ingrid Thulin, Genevieve Bujold, Dominique Rozan, Françoise Bertin, Michel Piccoli, Jean Bouise, Jean Dasté.
122 min. b/w.

Stylistically, La Guerre est finie is probably Resnais' most orthodox film, covering three days in the life of a Spanish exile in Paris involved in a plot to overthrow Franco. Working from a script by Jorge Semprun, Resnais explores his hero's doubts and insecurities through his relationships with two very different women: a mistress (Thulin) who represents potential stability, and a vivacious young student (Bujold) who offers him a new life. Perhaps it is the film's directness and obviously dated aspects (middle-age male angst faced with effervescent feminine adoration having become such a staple 'art movie' subject) that have made it seem a minor item in an often challenging director's career. DT

Guerre sans nom, La (The Undeclared War)
(Bertrand Tavernier, 1992, Fr)
246 min.
The 1954-1962 Algerian War was undoubtedly one of the most bitter and destructive of modern conflicts. Nearly three million French combatants were involved, 25,000 lost their lives, and the French political establishment was shaken to its foundations. Officially, of course, there was no war, only 'a police action'. In the 30 years since, precious little has been written or filmed on the subject, and it was in a sense to break the taboo, to give voice to the repressed past, that producer Jean-Pierre Guérin and Tavernier undertook this documentary, hacked down from 50 hours of footage shot in Grenoble, the venue of one of the two largest anti-war riots in the '50s. They made the decision to focus exclusively on the testimonies of 28 veterans and a few of their wives; Tavernier uses a few of their own snapshots, a few shots of the Algerian desert, some footage of the site of the riots and of a veterans' rally; there is no stock footage, of carnage or otherwise. The film's remarkable power and universality lies in the human scale of these testimonies. The veterans – all of them conscripts, and of every shade of political conviction – are clearly talking about their experiences for the first time, and describe the events of 30-odd years ago with exceptional vividness and honesty. With anguished memory captured so tangibly, it is sometimes difficult to watch as so many of them break down in tears. The film, however, is shot with full allowance for their integrity. WH

Guess Who's Coming To Dinner
(Stanley Kramer, 1967, US) Spencer Tracy, Katharine Hepburn, Sidney Poitier, Katharine Houghton, Cecil Kellaway, Beah Richards, Roy E Glenn Sr.
108 min.
One can hardly complain about the performances when Tracy and Hepburn combine as the leads, but Kramer's well-meaning comedy-drama about racism – a liberal couple suffer a few doubts when their daughter brings home the black she intends to marry – is a leaden and stilted affair, wrecked by the cautious move of making the groom-to-be singularly good-looking, respectable (he's a doctor) and well-to-do. A wishy-washy, sanctimonious plea for tolerance, directed with Kramer's customary verbosity and stodginess. GA

Guest, The
see Caretaker, The

Gueule d'Amour
(Jean Grémillon, 1937, Fr) Jean Gabin, Mireille Balin, René Lefèvre, Marguerite Deval, Jeanne Marken, Jean Aymé.
102 min. b/w.
When Gabin chances to return – older, sadder and in unbecoming civvies – to the shady bar where, as a legionnaire, he once held sway, a taxi-girl remarks incredulously (and callously) on his former reputation as the garrison's Don Juan. The intense poignancy of this 'privileged moment' is symptomatic of the way in which both actor and director have revitalised what is basically a trite, off-the-peg melodrama about a man destroyed by his passion for a woman. GAd

Gueule Ouverte, La
see Mouth Agape, The

Guide for the Married Man, A

(Gene Kelly, 1967, US) Walter Matthau, Robert Morse, Inger Stevens, Sue Ane Langdon, Claire Kelly, Elaine Devry, Lucille Ball, Jack Benny, Sid Caesar, Art Carney, Jeffrey Hunter, Jayne Mansfield, Carl Reiner, Phil Silvers, Terry-Thomas.
91 min.
Walter Matthau, who was passed over for the film version of *The Seven Year Itch* at the beginning of his Hollywood career after playing it on Broadway, comes down with the 12-year itch in this garbled bourgeois satire. Robert Morse is the adulterous neighbour who gives his friend the lowdown on the dos and don'ts of doing it, with star-studded illustrations featuring Lucille Ball, Phil Silvers, Jayne Mansfield and the like (among a host of guest cameos). These occasionally inventive situations score intermittently, but it's an unappealing effort on the whole. TCh

Guiltrip

(Gerard Stembridge, 1995, Ire) Andrew Connolly, Jasmine Russell, Peter Hanly, Michelle Houlden.
89 min.
Brutal, bleak, full of the bitterness of life, this isn't much fun. But it's an impressive, disturbing glimpse of fear and loathing in a provincial Irish town. Late at night, Tina (Russell) waits for her army corporal husband Liam (Connolly) to return from work. When he finally makes it, a long argument erupts. Each is suspicious of what the other's been up to. They never find out, but we do. Liam's a calculating skirt-chaser; Tina fancies the wares at a hi-fi shop and also an absurdly enthusiastic salesman (Hanly). Juggling flashbacks, writer/director Stembridge masters a difficult structure: unfolding past and present, building up character, counterpoising word and deed, and finally suggesting a ruinously unbalanced relationship that obscures and distorts issues of blame and guilt. More than just a domestic drama, the film's an unflinching picture of communal discord and alienation amid the banalities of small-town life. It's also an indictment of the place of violence in society: the abuse of personal power and the hopelessness of keeping military-bred qualities confined to barracks. An auspicious debut. NB

Guilty as Sin

(Sidney Lumet, 1993, US) Rebecca De Mornay, Don Johnson, Stephen Lang, Jack Warden, Dana Ivey.
107 min.
Though the title suggests a *Jagged Edge*-style thriller, Lumet has a taste for weightier courtroom dramas. Audiences expecting a legal thriller will get something deeper and darker, but if they stay long enough, they'll also get what they came for. Jennifer Haines (De Mornay), an ambitious lawyer with a killer instinct, meets her match in David Greenhill (Johnson), a 'ladies man' and alleged wife killer. Locked in a dangerous game with her seductive, manipulative client, yet bound by the rules of confidentiality, she slowly realises she was chosen for a reason: Greenhill knew he could push her buttons. Lumet and scriptwriter Larry Cohen emphasise the erotic tension and psychological cross-currents sparking between the couple. Regrettably, De Mornay resorts to quivering histrionics for Haines' slide from confident professional to hysterical victim, while the potentially fascinating battle, gives way to crass women-in-peril clichés, before finally tipping over the edge into melodrama. NF

Guilty by Suspicion

(Irwin Winkler, 1990, US) Robert De Niro, Annette Bening, George Wendt, Patricia Wettig, Sam Wanamaker, Luke Edwards, Ben Piazza, Martin Scorsese, Barry Primus, Gailard Sartain, Stuart Margolin.
105 min.
Film director David Merrill (De Niro) refuses to name names to the House Un-American Activities Committee in 1951, despite the recommendations of studio boss Darryl F Zanuck (Piazza) that he resort to a slippery lawyer (Wanamaker). Everybody assumes he'll give in since his work means everything to him – it cost him his marriage – but will he? The only fringe benefit of blacklisting, since friends split for Europe, kill themselves or denounce each other, is the support of his ex-wife (Bening) and his developing relationship with his son. The resolute ban on heroics in Winkler's

directorial debut spreads something of a monochrome mood. What happens to friendship, marriage and work when the blacklist descends is schematically displayed without mining much that's memorable. Still, it's an interesting film, convincingly played and mature in its conception. BC

Guinea Pig, The
(aka The Outsider)

(Roy Boulting, 1948, GB) Richard Attenborough, Cecil Trouncer, Robert Flemyng, Sheila Sim, Bernard Miles, Peter Reynolds, Timothy Bateson.
97 min. b/w.
Thanks to the first cinematic sounding of the word 'arse', a vaguely controversial examination of what would happen if you let working class yobs into the country's public schools. Attenborough is the tobacconist's son whose uncouth manners give him a hard time as he shocks the snobbish teachers and pupils of an old-established institution. Solid entertainment, even if barely convincing, distinctly soft on the political side (he eventually wins respect and friendship, of course, having been moulded to the public school image), and riddled with special pleading. GA

Gulag

(Roger Young, 1984, US) David Keith, Malcolm McDowell, David Suchet, Warren Clarke, John McEnery, Nancy Paul.
119 min.
A film thoroughly mediocre in every aspect – acting, writing, the very idea. An American journalist (Keith), victim of a KGB plot, is arrested while covering a sports tournament in Moscow. This honest and innocent hero is beaten and humiliated by various black-hearted flunkies of the Russian legal system before being carted off to a Siberian prison camp for ten years. There he eventually persuades a stiff-lipped Englishman (McDowell) – very democratic, this film, when it comes to handing out national stereotypes – to join him in an outrageous escape attempt across more than 1,000 miles of snowdriven Siberian wastes. At which point one roots for a pack of wolves to come and put an end to everyone's misery. A moving performance from Suchet (as a Jewish academic imprisoned for requesting an exit visa to Israel) simply points up what an insulting load of old cobblers the rest is. CS

Gulliver's Travels

(Peter Hunt, 1976, GB) Richard Harris, Catherine Schell, Norman Shelley, Meredith Edwards.
81 min.
Singing Richard Harris is shipwrecked in pasteboard Lilliput, and junior patrons will find that the ensuing, distinctly un-Swiftian fun leaves almost everything to be desired. Immense trouble, so we're informed, went into the film's animation (though Harris, the only human being seen for most of the running time, gives the impression of having been uneasily shoe-horned into the frantic, scampering action). The enterprise as a whole, featuring a tubby king and a lacklustre court conspiracy, is bogged down in treacly sentiment. JPy

Gumball Rally, The

(Chuck Bail, 1976, US) Michael Sarrazin, Normann Burton, Raúl Julia, Gary Busey, Tim McIntire, Susan Flannery.
106 min.
The first, and some say best, of the cross-country car race cycle that spawned the likes of *The Cannonball Run*. As the customised cars burn rubber from New York to Long Beach, Florida, we are treated to the usual squealing tyres, clouds of dust and metal-crunching crashes. Pitched at cartoon level, with a bizarre collection of speed enthusiasts crudely taking care of the comedy, it relies almost exclusively on the exceptional stunt work, the plot only occasionally dropping into first gear for some boring and irrelevant dramatic stuff. NF

Gummo

(Harmony Korine, 1997, US) Jacob Sewell, Nick Sutton, Lara Tosh, Jacob Reynolds, Darby Dougherty, Chloe Sevigny, Carisa Glucksman, Max Perlich, Linda Manz.
89 min.

This impressionistic portrait of a half-imaginary Midwestern suburb confirms Harmony (*Kids*) Korine as a creative force to be reckoned with. Be warned, however, it is often an unpleasant experience. When the two teenage boys at its centre aren't killing stray cats, they're sniffing glue, paying for sex or messing with life support machines. But for all the immature fixation on depravity, Korine's refusal to condemn or condescend to his characters saves the film from freak show voyeurism. Twisting from *cinéma vérité* to improvisation to pre-scripted lines, often within the same scene, he's audaciously upfront about his stratagems (his command of rhythm and pace is also quite brilliant). Problematic, troubling, dangerous even, but breathtakingly original, and absolutely true to the times. The cutting edge doesn't get any sharper than this. TCh

Gumshoe

(Stephen Frears, 1971, GB) Albert Finney, Billie Whitelaw, Frank Finlay, Janice Rule, Fulton Mackay, Carolyn Seymour, George Silver.
84 min.
A beautifully observed and hilariously funny film about a bingo-caller in a Liverpool working-men's club (Finney) who dreams of writing (and starring in) *The Maltese Falcon* and recording 'Blue Suede Shoes', only to be plunged into a real murder mystery when he tries to bring his dream world to life. *Gumshoe*, unlike most pastiches, doesn't get bogged down in references beyond itself. The credit for this is due to Finney, who is careful to make it clear that Eddie is a self-conscious dreamer, and to Stephen Frears who, in his first feature, is similarly careful to anchor the film in the gritty world of petty Liverpool crime before animating Eddie's all-encompassing dreams. PH

Guncrazy

(Tamra Davis, 1992, US) Drew Barrymore, James LeGros, Joe Dallesandro, Billy Drago, Michael Ironside, Rodney Harvey.
97 min.
Straight to video in Britain, but audience support in the US eventually won it a theatrical release. Inspired by *They Live by Night* and the original *Gun Crazy*, this is a love-on-the-run yarn, with the incendiary Barrymore immensely sympathetic as the promiscuous, sexually mistreated teen who goes on the lam with former prison pen-pal LeGross. They leave behind an unwitting trail of death and destruction, begun by her shooting of abusive guardian Dallesandro. Although it doesn't seek to excuse their wrongdoing, the film stands out for its convincing depiction of the up-against-it white-trash mentality and the overriding demands of youthful desire. TJ

Gun Crazy
(aka Deadly Is the Female)

(Joseph H Lewis, 1949, US) Peggy Cummins, John Dall, Berry Kroeger, Morris Carnovsky, Annabel Shaw, Harry Lewis, Nedrick Young.
87 min. b/w.
Basically a love-on-the-run saga, this concerns a misfit couple, drawn to each other by their mutual love for guns, who turn to robbing banks when married life gets tough. Much praised as an amoral, gripping study in the fraught relationship between sex, violence and money, it sees Lewis – one of the very finest B movie directors – firing on all cylinders, prompt ing his leads to a very real evocation of *amour fou*, and turning his budgetary limitations to advantage, notably in the lengthy uncut take (shot from inside a car) of a small-town heist, and in the finale, shot in a misty swamp to avoid the need for extras. Far more energetic than *Bonnie and Clyde* – the most famous of its many progeny – its intensity borders on the subversive and surreal. GA

Gunfight, A

(Lamont Johnson, 1970, US) Kirk Douglas, Johnny Cash, Jane Alexander, Raf Vallone, Karen Black, Keith Carradine.
89 min.
A self-conscious Western which conflates the showdown with showmanship, as ageing gunmen Douglas and Cash prepare to charge admission to townsfolk eager to view the eponymous event, to be held (in parodic homage to the 'corrida' finales of Leone's *Dollar* films) in the local bullring. Director Johnson's heavyweight tele-movie reputation was then still to be established;

while writer Harold Jack Bloom, who here cheats badly with an inconclusive double ending, was also later to taste small-screen fame as a Jack Webb associate and creator of the series *The DA* and *Hec Ramsey*. PT

Gunfight at the O.K.Corral

(John Sturges, 1957, US) Burt Lancaster, Kirk Douglas, Rhonda Fleming, Jo Van Fleet, John Ireland, Lee Van Cleef, Frank Faylen, Kenneth Tobey, DeForest Kelley, Earl Holliman.
122 min.
This peculiar film resembles Sturges' more famous *The Magnificent Seven*: not unlikeable, not uninteresting, but as many times as you see it, it gets neither better nor worse. Passion, certainly, is lacking, and being a 'town' Western, it's all very conventionally domestic. The Earp/Clanton family shootout is a Western legend, and was treated by Ford with romantic righteousness in *My Darling Clementine* a decade earlier. For Sturges, the shootout remains a kind of grudging necessity, and has no more relationship with any real historical truths than Ford's did. Curiously, Sturges returned to the Earp saga with *Hour of the Gun* (1967), which picked up where this one leaves off; but by then he was caught between a dying traditionalism and the growing audience need for the genre to criticise itself. CW

Gunfighter, The

(Henry King, 1950, US) Gregory Peck, Helen Westcott, Millard Mitchell, Jean Parker, Karl Malden, Skip Homeier, Richard Jaeckel, Mae Marsh.
84 min. b/w.
A superb Western, almost classical in its observance of the unities (clock-watching as obsessively as *High Noon*, it's an altogether tougher, bleaker film), and a ground-breaker in its day with its characterisation of Peck's notorious gunfighter Jimmy Ringo as a man just about over the hill, haunted by the dead weight of his reputation, the fear of loneliness, the certainty of dying at the hands of some fast-draw punk sneering 'He don't look so tough to me'. Riding into the small town where the wife and child he abandoned are living incognito, he insists on waiting in the saloon in the hope that she will agree to see him. The kids play hookey from school to gape open-mouthed; the bartender gleefully rubs his hands at the thought of the profits; indignant rustling from the good ladies of the town serve notice that an outlaw is unwelcome; and with assorted grudge-bearers already assembling, along with the aforesaid fast-draw punk, there is clearly no future for Johnny Ringo. Magnificently directed and shot (by Arthur Miller), flawlessly acted by Peck and a superb cast, governed by an almost Langian sense of fate, it's a film that has the true dimensions of tragedy. TM

Gun Fury

(Raoul Walsh, 1953, US) Rock Hudson, Donna Reed, Phil Carey, Lee Marvin, Neville Brand.
83 min.
Straightforward Western from a generally straightforward film-maker. Hudson and new bride Reed are on their way West when she's kidnapped by bad 'un Carey and his gang (including youthful varmint Marvin), leaving her man no choice but to lay down his pacifist ideals and give chase. 'A man's gotta do,' in other words, though in this instance Rock's flamboyant performance rather overdoes it. TJ

Gunga Din

(George Stevens, 1939, US) Cary Grant, Victor McLaglen, Douglas Fairbanks Jr, Joan Fontaine, Sam Jaffe, Eduardo Ciannelli, Montagu Love.
117 min. b/w.
Of course one winces a little at the smug colonialist attitudes, and at the patronising 'You're a better man than I am, Gunga Din' which commemorates the humble native water-bearer's sacrifice after he dies blowing a bugle to save the Raj from falling into an ambush. All the same this is a pretty spiffing adventure yarn, with some classically staged fights, terrific performances, and not too much stiff upper lip as Kipling's soldiers three go about their rowdy, non-commissioned, and sometimes disreputable capers. What, one wonders, did William Faulkner contribute, uncredited, to the bulldozing Hecht/MacArthur script? TM

Gung Ho

(Ron Howard, 1986, US) Michael Keaton, Gedde Watanabe, George Wendt, Mimi Rogers, John Turturro, Soh Yamamura.
112 min.
In a Pennsylvanian town, works foreman Keaton persuades a Japanese car company to reopen a local factory. But his problems have just begun, because as employee liaison officer, he has to smooth over the introduction of streamlined practices and zero-defect efficiency. Soon he is unable to contain the workers' resentment: a walkout threatens the future of the partnership. Keaton, with bizarre facial expressions and smart-aleck wisecracks, makes much of the comic situations, but Howard fails to keep the line moving. Further, the hero, though funny, is ultimately unsympathetic, securing through his cosy pacts nobody's position but his own, while the upbeat ending justifies strike-breaking. With comrades like this, who needs class enemies? NF

Gunhed

(Masato Harada, 1989, Jap) Landy Leyes, Masahiro Takashima, Brenda Bakke, James B Thompson, Aya Enjyoji.
100 min.
It's the 21st century, and on the Pacific island 8J0, the super-computer Chiron 5 lies in the 400-storey Mother Tower, dormant since it defeated the World Union Government back in 2026. Arriving on 8J0, bounty hunter Brooklyn and Texas Ranger Nim team up after the Mother Tower's reactivated defence system has massacred their various comrades. With the help of two children who survived the robot war, they discover and repair the last 'Gunhed', an unmanned combat robot, and use it to save the world as they know it. Impenetrable tosh (at least in this English version). AO

Gunmen

(Deran Sarafian, 1993, US) Kadeem Hardison, Christopher Lambert, Mario Van Peebles, Brenda Bakke, Sally Kirkland, Denis Leary, Patrick Stewart, Richard Sarafian.
90 min.
This buddy-buddy action movie begins promisingly with a South American drug baron Patrick Stewart attending his wife's funeral. 'Do you think I'm over-reacting?' he asks coolly, as the gravediggers shovel on the dirt, slowly muffling the poor woman's screams. He sends right-hand man Leary to find a cache of stolen loot, putting him on collision course with charming adventurer Lambert and US special agent Van Peebles, unlikely allies, each of whom knows half of the treasure's location. Sarafian is an unpretentious, easy-to-please director, with an eye for quirky character detail and a dab hand at the macho stuff. Leary makes a good fist of the heavy, but the movie's real subject is the elaborate bonding rituals of the hunks. TCh

Gunpoint

see At Gunpoint

Gun Runner, The

see Santiago

Guns Across the Veldt

see Spoor

Guns and the Fury, The

(Tony Zarindast, 1981, US) Peter Graves, Albert Salmi, Cameron Mitchell, Michael Ansara, Shaun Curry, Barry Stokes.
99 min.
An abysmal desert adventure which totally wastes the inherent promise of being set in Persia in 1908, amid early international conflict over Arab land and Gulf oil. What happens is that mercenary Yanks cluster manfully round a single drilling rig, getting furious as swarthy locals, gung-ho Bengal Lancers and dastardly Russians try to give them and each other some pragmatic lessons in gun-power ideology. The history's as risibly re-written as the dialogue; the only woman in sight is inevitably raped by marauding Cossacks; the local hero seems to have graduated from Oxford in guerilla tactics; and two charging horsemen fall dead for every shot fired. PT

Guns for San Sebastian (La Bataille de San Sebastian)

(Henri Verneuil, 1967, Fr/Mex/It) Anthony Quinn, Anjanette Comer, Charles Bronson, Sam Jaffe, Silvia Pinal, Jaime Fernández, Ivan Desny, Fernand Gravey.
111 min.
Anthony Quinn plays a lusty rogue with a heart of gold (what else?) who allows himself to be mistaken for a priest, and goes on to inspire some craven villagers to defend themselves against assorted un-Christian marauders (including Bronson as a nasty half-breed who has taken up with the Indians). The setting is nominally 18th century Mexico. It's a one-man Seven Samurai by any other name, competently enough directed and with a Morricone score, but strictly routine stuff. TM

Guns in the Afternoon

see Ride the High Country

Guns of Darkness

(Anthony Asquith, 1962, GB) Leslie Caron, David Niven, James Robertson Justice, David Opatoshu, Derek Godfrey, Richard Pearson, Eleanor Summerfield, Ian Hunter.
102 min. b/w.
Set in South America, and at first glance a hangover from the Empire films of the '50s, with their familiar paraphernalia of rebellions, plantations and exotic locales. There is, in fact, rather more to it. The story, taken from a Francis Clifford novel, moves through similar territory to Graham Greene's 'entertainments'. Both writers deal with questions of conduct faced by the Englishman abroad, although Clifford's heroes show more practical application and less imagination in the face of moral crises, thereby skirting the spiritual malaise that besets Greene's characters. Here Niven's Britisher finds himself unwillingly dragged off the fence when his own and his wife's safety is threatened. John Mortimer manages an intelligent script. CPe

Guns of Navarone, The

(J Lee Thompson, 1961, GB) Gregory Peck, David Niven, Anthony Quinn, Stanley Baker, Anthony Quayle, James Darren, Irene Papas, James Robertson Justice, Richard Harris.
157 min.
Producer Carl Foreman specialised in downbeat movies questioning the nature of wartime heroism. But the on-going debates about the morality of warfare that are scattered through this Alistair MacLean adaptation only serve to drag out the action climaxes, in which our WWII heroes take out two big gun-posts on a Turkish cliff. Lots of studio rock-climbing, and everybody gets very wet. TR

Guru, The

(James Ivory, 1968, US/Ind) Utpal Dutt, Michael York, Rita Tushingham, Aparna Sen, Madhur Jaffrey, Barry Foster, Saeed Jaffrey.
112 min.
Fox budget meets slender subject, and East uncomfortably meets West. With York as a '60s pop idol (he even sings) tripping to India for sitar lessons, and Tushingham on an unidentified spiritual quest, not even Utpal Dutt's splendid performance as their Western-susceptible guru can prevent Ivory's mockery from nose-diving into caricature, or his favourite theme – of incongruous cultural collisions – from being awkwardly reinforced by his own hybrid style. JD

Guy

(Michael Lindsay-Hogg, 1997, GB/Ger) Vincent D'Onofrio, Hope Davis, Kimber Riddle, Diane Salinger, Richard Portnow.
94 min.
This intriguing oddity attempts to blend the experimental with the mainstream. Shot with 'subjective camera', it begins with the unseen, anonymous film-maker (Davis) selecting Guy Dade (D'Onofrio) as the subject for her latest 'documentary'. Initially uncertain about her motives and understandably reluctant to let her invade his privacy, he eventually agrees to let her follow him around LA, shooting his dodgy car deals, dates with girlfriend Veronica (Riddle), and his endless vain attempts to get to know his chronicler/interrogator better. She, however, remains an aloof observer – or does she? This is an intelligent if rather unfocused

examination of the way people may be both nervous about, and aroused by, the prospect of exposing themselves to the prying but sometimes liberating gaze of a voyeuristic camera. D'Onofrio is adept at suggesting Guy's increasingly evident, faintly desperate need to feel attractive or desired; though aware he's playing with fire, he's clearly turned on by – what? – the chance of fame, a woman's attention, self-revelation? Though entertaining and thought provoking, it's not a patch, say, on *Spinal Tap*, let alone *Close-Up*. GA

Guyana: Crime of the Century (Guyana: El Crimen del Siglo)

(René Cardona Jr, 1979, Mex/Sp/Pan) Stuart Whitman, Gene Barry, John Ireland, Joseph Cotten, Bradford Dillman, Jennifer Ashley, Yvonne De Carlo.
108 min.
Guyana, 1978: 912 members of James Jones' People's Temple cult commit mass suicide – an act of 'revolutionary death' – as their dream of a promised land shatters. Hounded by press, congressmen, and his own paranoid imagination, the Bible-thumping socialist visionary Jones (played by Whitman) emerges as no more than a cardboard cut-out in this penny-dreadful hash which is somehow both uninformative and tedious. The strictly token emphasis on lurid sex/torture, and its ageing rent-a-star cast, shows up producer/director Cardona's past reputation for factory-line quickies for South American markets. DMacp

Guys and Dolls

(Joseph L Mankiewicz, 1955, US) Marlon Brando, Jean Simmons, Frank Sinatra, Vivian Blaine, Stubby Kaye, Robert Keith.
150 min.
A musical fairly glittering with intelligence and invention. Too much talk, its critics said (not for the first time with Mankiewicz). But quite apart from the fact that much of this talk is delectable Runyonese, some defence is necessary against the frenzied brilliance of Michael Kidd's choreography, which threatens to deluge the screen in energy and eccentricity right from the pyrotechnic opening number that establishes the teeming underworld of Times Square. Relaxed and caressing, the dialogue sequences serve as a kind of foreplay, enhancing not merely the exquisite eruptions of pleasure aroused by the musical numbers, but the genuine lyricism of the romance between gambler Sky Masterson and his Salvation Army doll. Inspired casting here, with Brando and Simmons – a Method counterbalance to the more traditional showbiz coupling of Sinatra and Blaine – lending an emotional depth rare in musicals. TM

Gycklarnas Afton (The Naked Night/Sawdust and Tinsel)

(Ingmar Bergman, 1953, Swe) Harriet Andersson, Åke Grönberg, Hasse Ekman, Anders Ek, Gudrun Brost, Annika Tretow, Gunnar Björnstrand.
96 min. b/w.
Acknowledging the influence of Dupont's *Variety* – one of the keystones of German expressionism, in which marriage was seen as a perilous highwire act – Bergman here employs the circus as a metaphor for the humiliating hoops through which men and women are put by their sexual dreams and desires. Heavily masochistic in its anguished account of the futile attempts of an ageing circus owner (Grönberg) and his steely young mistress (Andersson) to escape the dreary limitations of their mutually destructive involvement, it isn't exactly prepossessing in theme. But visually it is a treat, with Bergman's richly baroque compositions and persistent use of deep focus brilliantly exploiting the circus and theatre settings. And the performances are first-rate. TM

Gymkata

(Robert Clouse, 1985, US) Kurt Thomas, Tetchie Agbayani, Richard Norton, Edward Bell.
90 min.
High-kicking balderdash featuring Thomas as a former US Olympic gymnast who enters an endurance test in the small Himalayan country of Gymkata just so he can biff his opponents and, if he wins, persuade the authorities to instal an American 'Star Wars' defence post on their soil. Mediocre action pulp. TJ

Gypsy

(Mervyn LeRoy, 1962, US) Rosalind Russell, Natalie Wood, Karl Malden, Paul Wallace, Betty Bruce, Parley Baer, Ann Jilliann.
149 min.
Blowsy, miscast Technirama musical, with Rosalind Russell as the horrendous stage mother Mama Rose. Ethel Merman had a Broadway triumph with the role, but Russell is horrendous. As her unfortunate offspring, Ann Jillian isn't really there as June Havoc, and Wood doesn't have what it takes as stripper Gypsy Rose Lee. On the plus side: songs by Jule Styne and Stephen Sondheim. TCh

Gypsy

(Emile Ardolino, 1994, US) Bette Midler, Peter Riegert, Cynthia Gibb, Jennifer Beck, Ed Asner, Lacey Chabert, Elisabeth Moss, Keene Curtis.
142 min.
This second screen adaptation of the musical on the life of stripper Gypsy Rose Lee is a traditional genre piece in '40s mode. Midler's hellish showbiz mom steals the picture against not much opposition. JBa

Gypsy and the Gentleman, The

(Joseph Losey, 1957, GB) Melina Mercouri, Keith Michell, Patrick McGoohan, Lyndon Brook, June Laverick, Flora Robson, Mervyn Johns.
107min.
In an uneven Regency-period melodrama, neither Mercouri as a flashy-eyed gypsy girl nor Michell as the arrogant minor aristocrat she pursues to raise her standing could be said to give subtle performances. Neither are they aided by by a story that echoes the worst aspects of the costume romp in its mechanical contrivance. But seen as a typical Losey film in which class and sexual passion lead to death and destruction, it's not without interest, particularly in view of the director's bold attempt to match prints by Rowlandson and avoid Technicolor prettiness. DT

Gypsy Moths, The

(John Frankenheimer, 1969, US) Burt Lancaster, Deborah Kerr, Gene Hackman, Scott Wilson, William Windom, Bonnie Bedelia, Sheree North.
106 min.
In many ways a flawed film – the attempt at mixing the action of a *Grand Prix* and the small town disillusionments of an *All Fall Down* doesn't entirely come off – *The Gypsy Moths* is nonetheless one of Frankenheimer's most satisfying works. Dealing with a trio of sky-divers who for a variety of reasons are growing ambivalent about their 'careers', and the inhabitants of a small town who feel both threatened and attracted to the parachutists, the film manages to catch equally well the quiet desperation of small town life and the growing disillusionment of incessant travellers in search of glamour. The performances by Lancaster, Kerr and Hackman are superb. PH

Gypsy Soul (Alma Gitana)

(Chus Gutiérrez, 1995, Sp) Amara Carmona, Pedro Alonso, Peret, Loles León, Rafael Alvárez 'El Brujo', Julieta Serrano.
92 min.
Taking inspiration from *Romeo and Juliet*, and also probably *Strictly Ballroom*, this flamenco romance is a fairy tale set in Madrid. Handsome, womanising Antonio wants to become a flamenco star, but hasn't enough gypsy in his soul to pass muster – that's also the problem when he meets and falls for Lucia, a serious student whose patriarchal family don't want her hanging out with non-gypsies. Stylishly shot but with no new spin on macho mores. GA

The Hunchback of Notre Dame (1939)

h

Hackers

(Iain Softley, 1995, US) Jonny Lee Miller, Angelina Jolie, Jesse Bradford, Matthew Lillard, Laurence Mason, Fisher Stevens, Renoly Santiago.
105 min.

Blurring the line between heightened reality and hi-tech fantasy, this presents the virtual world that hackers imagine, rather than the one they inhabit. Busted seven years earlier for causing computer chaos on Wall Street, the legendary 'Zero Cool' (Miller) is now 18 and hooked up with a wacky, multi-ethnic gang of hackers and phone phreaks. While Zero and spiky femme 'Acid Burn' (Jolie) channel their sexual attraction into competing for the top hacker slot, 'Cereal Killer', 'Phantom Freak' and 'Crash Override' define their place in the rebel tribe by pulling harmless on-line stunts. But things get serious when the Secret Service cracks down and 'The Plague' (Stevens), hacker turned security expert, sets them up to take the fall for his internal scam, siphoning millions of dollars from the mega-corporation that employs him to keep them out. Directed with verve, and driven forward by a wrap-around electronic score, this brilliantly captures the energy and insolence of virtual teen rebellion. The sappy ending's hard to take, but the on-line showdown between The Plague, the Secret Service and the united worldwide community of hackers is nail-biting. NF

Hail! Hail! Rock'n'Roll

(Taylor Hackford, 1987, US) Chuck Berry, Eric Clapton, Robert Cray, Johnnie Johnson, Etta James.
121 min.

Early on in Hackford's well-researched documentary and concert film about the legendary Chuck Berry, we see Berry outside the Fox Theatre in St Louis, from which he was excluded as a boy because of his colour, and now to be the scene of his 60th birthday concert. Interviews with Berry's contemporaries – pianist and former partner Johnnie Johnson, wild man Little Richard and Bo Diddley – stress his originality, while family members fill in the personal background. Unusually, the emphasis is on the development of his unique guitar sound, with keen insights into his diverse influences. Berry's voice is shot, and several songs – 'School Days', 'Sweet Little Sixteen', 'Memphis' – fall hopelessly flat, but his guest stars do him proud: Richard's clanging riffs on 'Little Queenie', Clapton's bluesy licks on 'Wee Wee Hours', and R & B queen Etta James' gutsy, soulful singing on 'Rock'n'Roll Music'. The sound recording is excellent, and the fluid camerawork and sharp editing capture the live concert atmosphere. NF

Hail, Mary
(Je Vous Salue, Marie)

(Jean-Luc Godard, 1984, Fr/Switz) Myriem Roussel, Thierry Rode, Philippe Lacoste, Manon Andersen, Juliette Binoche.
107 min.

Wily Godard has located the Biblical story of the Virgin Birth among the present-day Swiss. Godard's Mary (beautifully incarnated by Roussel, his Karina-like discovery) has to cope with an unconvinced and irritable Joseph, eventually almost beaten into submission by an oafish Gabriel, who performs the Annunciation at a petrol station. While Joseph learns the hardest of ways that love is not all fleshly desire, a parallel story tells of a young girl called Eva receiving a painful lesson in male inconstancy. Composed like a brilliant mosaic, Godard's film gives fresh meaning to everyday images; makes us listen to Dvorak with renewed appreciation; and shows the female nude as though never filmed before. DT

Hail the Conquering Hero

(Preston Sturges, 1944, US) Eddie Bracken, Ella Raines, Raymond Walburn, William Demarest, Elizabeth Patterson, Jimmy Conlin, Franklin Pangborn.
101 min. b/w.

Wonderful satire on small-town jingoism, all the more remarkable in that it was made during World War II. Bracken is the scrawny marine, son of a World War I hero, instantly invalided out because of hay fever. Terrified at this mortal blow to family pride, he hides out as a shipyard worker while pretending to be overseas, until forcibly escorted home by six sympathetic marines who learn his story. But a quirk of the telephone wires has trans-

lated 'hay' into 'jungle' fever, and to his horror he finds a civic welcome awaiting him as a Pacific war hero, with worse to come when he is adopted by acclaim as candidate for mayor. The ending has been taxed with sentimentality, although it is in fact deeply ironic. Otherwise no Middle American sacred cow (from mom and apple pie to heroic fathers) is spared in this hilarious blend of satire, slapstick and comedy of manners, with marvellous dialogue full of dizzy non-sequiturs and an amazing gallery of grotesque characters. TM

Haine, La (Hate)

(Mathieu Kassovitz, 1995, Fr) Vincent Cassel, Hubert Kounde, Saïd Taghmaoui, Karim Belkhadra, Edouard Montoute, François Levantal.
98 min. b/w.

Twenty-four hours in the Paris projects: an Arab boy is critically wounded in hospital, gut-shot, and a police revolver has found its way into the hands of a young Jewish skinhead, Vinz (Cassel), who vows to even the score if his pal dies. Vinz hangs out with Hubert (Kounde) and Saïd (Taghmaoui). They razz each other about films, cartoons, nothing in particular, but always the gun hovers over them like a death sentence, the black-and-white focal point for all the hatred they meet with, and all they can give back. Kassovitz has made only one film before (the droll race-comedy Métisse), but La Haine puts him right at the front of the field: this is virtuoso, on-the-edge stuff, as exciting as anything we've seen from the States in ages, and more thoroughly engaged with the reality it describes. He combats the inertia and boredom of his frustrated antagonists with a thrusting, jiving camera style which harries and punctuates their rambling, often very funny dialogue. The politics of the piece are confrontational, to say the least, but there is a maturity and depth to the characterisation which goes beyond mere agitprop: society may be on the point of self-combustion, but this film betrays no appetite for the explosion. A vital, scalding piece of work. TCh

Hair

(Milos Forman, 1979, US) John Savage, Treat Williams, Beverly D'Angelo, Annie Golden, Dorsey Wright, Don Dacus.
121 min.

Other than providing the full stop to his would-be '60s trilogy (previous episodes: Taking Off and One Flew Over the Cuckoo's Nest), it's difficult to determine what could have attracted Forman to a musical as hopelessly leaden as Hair and its uneasy amalgam of draft-card burning, cosmic consciousness, ill-judged comedy and dopey sentimentality. Sounding, and for the most part looking, like a National Lampoon parody of some ghastly Swinging Sixties compendium, it lacks even the vitality of the stage show, which was at least persuasively ingenuous. The problem with Hair is that it's neither old enough to have acquired the picturesque dignity of a period piece, nor young enough to have the slightest contemporary relevance. The result is a smug, banal fairytale-with-a-message, redeemed only by the intermittently imaginative staging of the songs. AC

Hairdresser's Husband, The
(Le Mari de la coiffeuse)

(Patrice Leconte, 1990, Fr) Jean Rochefort, Anna Galiena, Roland Bertin, Maurice Chevit, Philippe Clevenot, Jacques Mathou.
80 min.

Aged 12, Antoine has two passions: dancing to Arabic music, and having his hair cut by an ample Alsacienne who unwittingly introduces him to the world of sex. In middle age, Antoine (Rochefort) has lost none of his ardour: when he glimpses shy coiffeuse Mathilde (Galiena), he is so struck that he immediately proposes marriage. Amazingly she accepts, and he moves into her salon, where their blissful romance remains barely touched by the outside world... While Leconte's study in erotic obsession is, like Monsieur Hire, hardly sophisticated in its sexual politics, that's not to deny its eccentric charm. Lighter in tone than its predecessor, it benefits from a genuinely scatty performance by Rochefort, and from a fine line in off-the-wall humour. Less successful is the shift to a darker mood: this bitter-sweet comedy barely justifies its downbeat outcome. That said, Eduardo Serra's elegant photography and Michael Nyman's score perfectly complement the blend of wit and melancholia. GA

Hair Opera, The
(Mohatsu Kageki)

(Yuri Obitani, 1992, Jap) Yuri Obitani, Yosefu Kosuzu, Tomoko Kamisaki.
61 min.

Obitani is a trainee opera singer and aspiring film-maker casting about for ways to entertain his audience when he learns of an exhibition by woman artist Yosefu Kosuzu; it comprises neatly mounted and dated specimens of pubic hair from all the men she has slept with. Obitani excitedly interviews her and then invites her to exchange film 'letters' with him. The film is mostly a compilation of those letters, chronicling a conceptual relationship which begins to break down when it emerges that what Obitani wants most is a place in Kosuzu's next exhibition. Already a classic of Japanese independent cinema, this is the most startling first-person film-making since David Holzman's famous Diary. The climactic shaving scene left me almost on the floor. TR

Hairspray

(John Waters, 1988, US) Divine, Debbie Harry, Sonny Bono, Ricki Lake, Colleen Fitzpatrick, Ruth Brown, Pia Zadora, Ric Ocasek.
92 min.

Waters' most hygienically commercial film is a Retro schlock-fancier's delight. Remember backcombing and the beehive, pale-pink lipstick, acid yellows, that first kiss? Tracy Turnblad (Lake), fat teenie offspring of fatter Edna (Divine), dreams of winning the dance crown on The Corny Collins Show on TV, but falls foul of bitchy queen-of-the-hop Amber von Tussle (Fitzpatrick) and her grotesquely unscrupulous parents (Harry and Bono). Also on the strength are Ruth Brown as Motormouth Maybelle, Pia Zadora as a beatnik, and plenty of vigorous hoofing to the unlamented Madison. BC

Halbe Welt (Half the World)

(Florian Flicker, 1993, Aus) Rainer Egger, Dani Levy, Maria Schrader, Mercedes Egheiler.
83 min.

This ultimately exasperating slice of Austrian sci-fi conjures up a metropolitan society where the sun's rays have become fatal and life continues at night or behind shades. Controlling all images of the sunlit world now off-limits is the all powerful Luna organisation, but a disparate band of rebels stands determined to free themselves from the dark and re-embrace the light. Unfortunately, this is only half the movie. There's the germ of an idea, excellent use of Vienna and Hamburg locations, and impressive high-contrast photography, yet the plotting and characterisation are dispiritingly minimal and one's interest soon flags. A missed opportunity. TJ

Half a Sixpence

(George Sidney, 1967, GB/US) Tommy Steele, Julia Foster, Cyril Ritchard, Penelope Horner, Elaine Taylor, Hilton Edwards, Pamela Brown, James Villiers.
146 min.

Tommy Steele originated the role of the draper's assistant who comes into money and moves up the social scale without automatically finding the happiness he desires in Beverley Cross's musical play adapted from HG Wells' novel Kipps. Made in the days when American studios were throwing money at anything British that could move under its own power, the film lays on the period charm rather exhaustingly, and the songs ('Flash! Bang! Wallop! What a Picture!' being the highlight) don't exactly sweep you along. The star smiles and smiles – and smiles. TJ

Half-Breed, The

(Stuart Gilmore, 1952, US) Robert Young, Janis Carter, Jack Buetel, Reed Hadley, Barton MacLane, Porter Hall.
81 min.

Well-meaning but rather dull Western, clearly derivative of the earlier Broken Arrow as it ladles out a message about how the Indians were only mean because some white men had been mean to them first. Buetel (Billy the Kid in The Outlaw) is ineffectual as the title character, trying to forge the bonds of friendship between whites and Indians in the face of gold-greedy shit-stirring from Hadley, although Young adds a touch of class as the good liberal gambler who saves the day. GA

Half Life

(Dennis O'Rourke, 1985, Aust)
84 min. b/w & col.
After World War II, the Marshall Islands were entrusted by the United Nations to the care of Uncle Sam, who generously staged some 66 nuclear tests in this Pacific paradise. This documentary focuses on Operation Bravo, an explosion over 1,000 times bigger than Hiroshima, detonated in (the film claims) full knowledge that winds would carry radiation straight to two of the atolls. Navy officials stood by in specially insulated ships as kids played in the nuclear 'snow'; US propaganda films crowed over the 'stupendous blast' and the (quote) 'happy, amenable savages' providing 'valuable data' on the bomb's hideous long-term effects. Drawing on recently declassified US Defense footage, O'Rourke presents his case with textbook clarity and intelligence. The fallout from this blast from the past lingers on, and the breathtaking cynicism of the Americans in the whole affair should, at the very least, give pause to ponder the speed at which our own sceptred isle is turning into Airstrip One. SJo

Half Moon Street

(Bob Swaim, 1986, US) Sigourney Weaver, Michael Caine, Patrick Kavanagh, Faith Kent, Ram John Holder, Keith Buckley, Annie Hanson.
89 min.
An American linguist and economist working in London, Dr Slaughter (Weaver) supplements her meagre income by prostitution. The relationship she strikes up with a regular client, troubleshooting diplomat Lord Bulbeck (Caine), not only follows the customary course of clandestine trysts and growing jealousy, but also entangles her in a web of violent political intrigue. Adapted from Paul Theroux's novel *Dr Slaughter*, Swaim's follow-up to *La Balance* is a dud. Without decent direction, Weaver's portrayal of a woman intent on exercising full control over her life, but unwittingly manipulated by all around her, seems merely embarrassed, while – with the exception of the dependable Caine – the supporting characterisations are woefully thin. London becomes a familiar topographical mish-mash, the narrative is ramshackle, and even the action set pieces – the most memorable aspect of the earlier film – are clumsily executed. GA

Half the World

see Halbe Welt

Hallelujah, I'm a Bum

(Lewis Milestone, 1933, US) Al Jolson, Madge Evans, Harry Langdon, Frank Morgan, Chester Conklin, Bert Roach.
82 min. b/w.
An intriguing but curiously botched follow-up to the enchanting *Love Me Tonight*, again using a Rodgers & Hart score structured by rhyming recitative. Jolson, hardly the ideal R & H interpreter anyway, is horribly miscast as the leader of a band of Depression down-and-outs who haunt Central Park: he just hasn't the persona to play a Byronic hero of social protest who accepts a job because he falls in love, and drops out again when love fails him. The script, mixing cynicism with sentimentality in a manner typical of Ben Hecht (who co-authored with SN Behrman), also veers uncertainly between pursuing its Depression themes and elaborating its singularly turgid romantic complications (where the heroine, conveniently amnesiac, shuttles between two equally unlikely suitors). Some of the infelicities were probably due to production problems, since the film was started by Harry D'Abbadie D'Arrast, continued by Milestone (who brought in R & H), and completed (apparently at Jolson's insistence) by Chester Erskine. The songs make pleasant but not great listening. TM

Hallelujah the Hills

(Adolfas Mekas, 1962, US) Peter H Beard, Sheila Finn, Martin Greenbaum, Peggy Steffans, Jerome Raphael, Taylor Mead.
86 min. b/w.
A highpoint from the 'innocent' years of American underground cinema, and something of an enduring delight for real film buffs. Mekas' comedy starts from an enthusiastic parody of French 'new wave' concepts like using two actresses to play one character, and manages to

go on to incorporate references (part satire, part homage) to what seems like every other branch of cinema extant. It ranges from samurai movies to Chaplinesque slapstick, and it hits the intended tone between love and scepticism far more often than you'd have thought possible. The main thing is that it's recklessly enthusiastic about itself and about cinema in general – and the enthusiasm is infectious. TR

Halliday Brand, The

(Joseph H Lewis, 1956, US) Joseph Cotten, Viveca Lindfors, Betsy Blair, Ward Bond, Bill Williams, Jay C Flippen.
78 min. b/w.
If ever a movie justified the once-modish tag of 'psychological Western', it's this one. Lewis' film has been unforgiveably neglected, for it matches his unique visual intelligence to a remarkably explicit critique of patriarchal law. Ward Bond's tyrannical authority, exerted over both family and community (of which he is 'founding father' and sheriff) is classically grounded in an obsessive fear of otherness. His brutal defence of race purity (against the Indians whose fathers he 'tamed' and dispossessed) sparks off the conflict with his own son (Cotten) which gives the film its headlong impetus and its characteristic violence. The psychological – and political – resonances are specified in the clarity of Lewis' visual metaphors (the gun in the foreground; dead wood littering the frame), which gloriously transcend the minor irritants of miscasting and underbudgeting. Impressive. PT

Halloween (100)

(John Carpenter, 1978, US) Donald Pleasence, Jamie Lee Curtis, PJ Soles, Charles Cyphers, Kyle Richards.
91 min.
A superb essay in Hitchcockian suspense which puts all its sleazy *Friday the 13th* imitators to shame with its dazzling skills and mocking wit. Rarely have the remoter corners of the screen been used to such good effect as shifting volumes of darkness and light reveal the presence of a sinister something. We know, and Carpenter knows we know, that it's all a game as his psycho starts decimating teenagers observed in the sexual act; and he delights in being one step ahead of expectation, revealing nothing when there should be something, and something – as in the subtle reframing of the girl sobbing in the doorway after she finally manages to kill the killer, showing the corpse suddenly sitting up again behind her – long after there should be nothing. Perhaps not quite so resonant as *Psycho* to which it pays due homage, but it breathes the same air. TM

Halloween II

(Rick Rosenthal, 1981, US) Jamie Lee Curtis, Donald Pleasence, Charles Cyphers, Jeffrey Kramer, Lance Guest, Pamela Susan Shoop.
92 min.
The first *Halloween* had such an ancient maniac-on-the-loose theme that it was easy to miss just how original the film was in its use of the new gliding Steadicam to prolong audience identification with the villain. Rosenthal is no Carpenter, but he makes a fair job of emulating the latter's visual style in this sequel (co-scripted by Carpenter) which takes up where the earlier film left off. The action is now largely set in a terrorised local hospital, while the villain has so palpably become an agent of Absolute Evil that any associations with contemporary sexual violence are fortunately diminished. The result won't make any converts, but Jamie Lee Curtis is as good as ever. DP

Halloween III: Season of the Witch

(Tommy Lee Wallace, 1983, US) Tom Atkins, Stacey Nelkin, Dan O'Herlihy, Ralph Strait, Michael Currie, Jadeen Barbor.
98 min.
The title is a bit of a cheat, since the indestructible psycho of the first two films plays no part here. With the possibilities of the character well and truly exhausted, *Season of the Witch* turns more profitably to a marvellously ingenious Nigel Kneale tale of a toymaker and his fiendish plan to restore Halloween to its witch cult origins (involving a TV commercial for toy masks that are in fact diabolical engines). Kneale had his name removed from the credits after tampering

with his script had reduced O'Herlihy's toymaker – originally bathed in Celtic mists of myth and magic – to the conventional mad doctor. The end result is a bit of a mess but hugely enjoyable, and often (thanks to Dean Cundey's camerawork and John Carpenter's close supervision as producer) as striking visually as its predecessors. TM

Halloween 4: The Return of Michael Myers

(Dwight H Little, 1988, US) Donald Pleasence, Ellie Cornell, Danielle Harris, Michael Pataki, Beau Starr, Kathleen Kinmont, Sasha Jenson, George R Wilbur.
88 min.
Ten years after his incarceration in a maximum security prison, catatonic ex-knife-wielder Michael Myers (Wilbur) finds himself transferred to a 'normal' hospital. In no time at all our boy snaps out of his decade-long coma, stiffs a few ambulance men, and trudges off to his old haunting ground of Haddonfield, intent upon introducing his cutesy-pop little niece (Harris) to the cutting edge of his eccentric behaviour. 'Evil...on two legs!' exclaims deranged, disfigured Dr Loomis (Pleasence), before steaming off in search of his favourite patient. Then it's the usual town-under-siege-by-indestructible-psycho nonsense: the Halloween celebrations are curtailed by Michael's festive antics; police officers are massacred (off-screen, naturally); kiddies are terrorised; promiscuous teenagers discover that id f you make out behind your parents' backs the bogeyman will slice you up. *Halloween III* ditched Myers, realising that as an archetypal harbinger of doom he was a dead duck. It's a shame that the lure of the cash registers resurrected the beleagured bore. The shocks are infinitesimal, the script diabolical. MK

Halloween: The Curse of Michael Myers

(Joe Chappelle, 1995, US) Donald Pleasence, Paul Rudd, Marianne Hagan, Leo Geter.
92 min.
You know you're in trouble when they stop numbering the sequels; this is the sixth, if anyone's counting. The unkillable chappie remains unkilled after offing a host of unknown faces on Halloween, only this time he's egged on by evil doctors and black magic. A series of competently engineered shock moments jollied along by a jazzed-up version of John Carpenter's original electronic score: slicker than crude oil and just as unattractive. AO

Halls of Montezuma

(Lewis Milestone, 1951, US) Richard Widmark, Walter [Jack] Palance, Robert Wagner, Jack Webb, Karl Malden.
113 min.
Rough tough US Marines hunt down a Japanese rocket base in the Pacific Basin in this standard guts-or-glory WWII flagwaver. Capably put together by Milestone, who cut in real combat footage with the mock-up set-pieces shot in the US at Camp Pendleton, but it's hard to believe this is the same man who 21 years earlier made the landmark anti-war movie *All Quiet on the Western Front*. TJ

Hambone and Hillie (aka The Adventures of Hambone and Hillie)

(Roy Watts, 1983, US) Lillian Gish, Timothy Bottoms, Candy Clark, OJ Simpson, Robert Walker, Alan Hale.
90 min.
After visiting her family in NYC, Grandma Hillie embarks for her LA home; left behind, her beloved dog Hambone decides to do the distance by paw. So begins this transcontinental trot past the trouser-leg of democracy as the canine Kerouac doggedly woofs his way west. He wags tails with other picaresque pooches, cocks a kindly ear at a trucker's life story, rolls liquid eyes at a lonely paraplegic, and saves a pregnant woman from an escaped convict. As Hambone hits the Grand Canyon, he passes against a craggy backdrop and ghostly voices strike up a patriotic chorus in honour of this humble yet stouthearted hound, a four-legged embodiment of the Great American virtues, and an example to all of us who want the dog licence fee bumped up to at least £500. AB

h

Hamburger Hill
(John Irvin, 1987, US) Dylan McDermott, Steven Weber, Tim Quill, Don Cheadle, Michael Patrick Boatman, Anthony Barrile.
110 min.
Highly conventional in form, this traces the brutally brief odyssey of a group of infantrymen from training to bodybags in Vietnam. Hamburger Hill, for which most of the attacking grunts die, proves as pointless as the objective in *Paths of Glory*, but Irvin and screenwriter James Carabatsos reserve their indignation for the unappreciative citizenry back home. It isn't quite the old ours-is-not-to-question-why encomium, however, since the troops are poor whites and uneducated blacks who bitch continually about protesting hippies, each other, and do-or-die largely unreconciled. Applied sociology is all over the dialogue, though the obscenity quota mercifully drops as battle begins. There are a couple of rocky moments, but the large cast of unknowns go through hell convincingly, and illustrate the randomness of mortality. In its juggernaut functionalism, *Hamburger Hill* may be the McDonald's of the war movie. BC

Hamlet
(Hay Plumb, 1913, GB) Johnston Forbes-Robertson, Gertrude Elliott, Walter Ringham, Adeleine Bourne, JH Barnes, SA Cookson, Alex Scott-Gatty, JH Ryley.
5,800 ft. b/w.
Forbes-Robertson was known by London's theatre critics as 'the supreme Hamlet of his time'. This film, made on location at a specially built castle on the Dorset coast under the auspices of producer Cecil Hepworth, attempts to preserve his stage performance, as in aspic. Featured alongside the actor-knight are his American wife Gertrude Elliott (Ophelia) and the rest of the cast from a famous Drury Lane production. It's fascinating to see Forbes-Robertson's mannered, gestural performance, but at 60, he was 35 years too old for the part. Shakespeare without sound: a typically quixotic endeavour from Britain's pioneer film-makers. GM

Hamlet
(Laurence Olivier, 1948, GB) Laurence Olivier, Eileen Herlie, Basil Sydney, Jean Simmons, Felix Aylmer, Stanley Holloway, Terence Morgan.
155 min. b/w.
Despite winning several Oscars, Olivier's (condensed) version of Shakespeare's masterpiece makes for frustrating viewing: for all its 'cinematic' ambitions (the camera prowling pointlessly along the gloomy corridors of Elsinore), it's basically a stagy showcase for the mannered performance of the director in the lead role (though he's ably supported by a number of British theatrical stalwarts). Not half as powerful as Kozintsev's marvellous Russian version. GA

Hamlet
(Grigori Kozintsev, 1964, USSR) Innokenti Smoktunovsky, Mikhail Nazwanov, Elza Radzin-Szolkonis, Yuri Tolubeyev, Anastasia Vertinskaya.
150 min. b/w.
Featuring a positive hero (predictably, the 'Now might I do it pat' soliloquy of prevarication has been cut), the action unfolds between shots of lowering rocks and turbulent seas, with Hamlet pattering through a very tangible Elsinore of massive portcullises, stone walls, endless corridors and chunky oaken furniture. A little monolithic in theory, but it works magnificently because Kozintsev has thought his interpretation right through to the end with complete consistency, and gives the film a genuinely exciting epic sweep. What one remembers, though, is the superb marginal detail: the appearance of the Ghost on the battlements, vast black cloak billowing in the wind, like a Titan striding across the sea; the dying Polonius pulling down the arras to reveal row upon row of tailor's dummies in Gertrude's wardrobe; above all, the wonderfully moving conception of Ophelia as a frail blonde marionette, first seen jerked into motion by the tinkling music of a cembalo at her dancing lesson, and gradually becoming the helpless plaything of court politics. There's a genuine cinematic imagination at work here. TM

Hamlet
(Tony Richardson, 1969, GB) Nicol Williamson, Anthony Hopkins, Judy Parfitt, Mark Dignam, Marianne Faithfull, Gordon Jackson.
117 min.
The perennial problem in filming Shakespeare is what to do with all those stagy settings and backdrops; or alternatively, what to do with all those words, which tend to sound impossibly literary when set off against natural surroundings. Filming entirely in the Round House, where he had previously staged the play, Richardson solves the dilemma by concentrating almost exclusively on faces. Flurries of dark stone, vague impressions of courtiers and rich hangings; but mostly faces lower obsessively from the screen, surrounded by mysterious pools of darkness in which figures stealthily appear and disappear. The reason may be economy, but the result is an extraordinarily naked emphasis on the words and their meaning. Nicol Williamson's Hamlet, not exactly mellifluous but intelligent, mocking and volcanically explosive, is neatly disciplined by this approach; and apart from some roughnesses in the casting (and some curious textual omissions), it's interesting, imaginative, and certainly Richardson's best film. TM

Hamlet
(Celestino Coronado, 1976, GB) Anthony Meyer, David Meyer, Helen Mirren, Quentin Crisp, Barry Stanton, Vladek Sheybal.
67 min.
Made impossibly cheaply (shot and mixed on video, then transferred to film) this obviously took great effort and dedication. But was it worth it? As a compression of the play, it's initially inventive but all too soon predictable: the device of having twin brothers play Hamlet wears very thin indeed. As an interpretation, it is most notable for taking the misogyny of the 'get thee to a nunnery' scene and applying it liberally to the rest of the play: having Helen Mirren play both lead women helps Coronado to sustain this reading. The misogynist bias puts the film's over-all gay-camp sensibility in a very questionable light, and preening performances from Crisp and Sheybal don't help. At worst, offensive; at best, joyless. TR

Hamlet
(Franco Zeffirelli, 1990, US) Mel Gibson, Glenn Close, Alan Bates, Paul Scofield, Ian Holm, Helena Bonham-Carter, Stephen Dillane, Nathaniel Parker, Pete Postlethwaite.
134 min.
There are very few actors who could carry the risks of another cinematic reworking of *Hamlet* in an age when many younger film fans think the name refers to a small cigar. Mel Gibson and Glenn Close are two such stars, and, though the name of Franco Zeffirelli is unlikely to mean much to anyone under the age of 30, it must have been the Italian director's cultish *Romeo and Juliet*, rather than his recent string of cinematic no-nos such as *Endless Love* and *The Champ*, that soothed the backers. It's a surprisingly successful venture, decked out in Anglo-Saxon styles and with a brooding, robust castle setting which oozes horse muck. Gibson never gets much beyond the antic disposition and sports some bizarre curls, but Close gambols lustily as Gertrude, Helena Bonham-Carter makes a splendidly under-age Ophelia and, in other supporting roles, both a boozy-looking Bates and a pompous-sounding Ian Holm add great worth to the parts of Claudius and Polonius. Zeffirelli's darting, aerial, I-spy perspective more often adds to, rather than repeats, the effect of the verse, and all the cuts (including the opening battlements sequence) are eminently justified in the cause of narrative thrust. SGr

Hamlet
(Kenneth Branagh, 1996, US) Kenneth Branagh, Julie Christie, Billy Crystal, Gérard Depardieu, Charlton Heston, Richard Briers, Derek Jacobi, Jack Lemmon, Robin Williams, Rufus Sewell, Richard Attenborough, Brian Blessed, Michael Bryant, Judi Dench, Reece Dinsdale, Ken Dodd, John Gielgud, Rosemary Harris, Michael Maloney, John Mills, Timothy Spall, Kate Winslet.
242 min.
If Branagh's ambitious film needs any kind of compliment, it is that at around four hours it carries itself perfectly well. The star/director has assembled one of the finest casts ever seen on the big screen: so the Player King is played by Heston, who at least gets to speak, unlike Gielgud, Dench, John Mills and Ken Dodd in a succession of parts which underline the text through imagined interludes. Sometimes the casting is regrettable (Jack Lemmon looking ill-at-ease as a superannuated sentry); at others tongue-in-cheek (Attenborough as the English ambassador) or wasteful (Depardieu as a one-scene monosyllabic spy). The role-playing scores most in the world of work and politics, warfare and diplomacy, as imagined by Briers' superb Polonius and Jacobi's Claudius. Branagh's prince is admirable: popular, versatile, frank, kind, ruthless, athletic, straight-backed, with a little-boy-lost voice to go with the martial one. Tim Harvey's production design makes Elsinore a highlight, creating a snow-swept Ruritania of chessboard floors, mirrored corridors, freezing courtyards. Drawbacks: an intrusive score; spurious sex scenes between Kate Winslet's Ophelia and Branagh's pre-antic Hamlet; and a full-scale Norwegian invasion during the final duel. But all in all, as near to Branagh's masterwork as dammit, and far better fun than a jig, or even a tale of bawdry. SGr

Hamlet Goes Business
(Hamlet Liikemaailmassa)
(Aki Kaurismäki, 1987, Fin) Pirkka-Pekka Petelius, Esko Salminen, Kati Outinen, Elina Salo, Esko Nikkari, Pentti Auer.
86 min. b/w.
Kaurismäki's idiosyncratic reworking of Shakespeare is concerned with money rather than melancholia. Transposed to modern Finland, it begins with the poisoning of the head of a family firm, leaving shiftless son Hamlet with a controlling 51% interest. Learning that unprofitable mills and factories are to be sold off to buy a world monopoly in rubber-duck manufacture, Hamlet vetoes the move and starts a boardroom battle. Kaurismäki keeps this wacky idea afloat with farcical plotting, deadpan humour and cryptic dialogue. The overall tone is pure B-movie, the exaggerated emotions and Timo Salminen's glistening *noir* photography recalling Warners' crime melodramas of the '40s. The characters are ciphers, too: reduced to pawns in the board games, they have no life outside their assigned roles. Viewed in isolation, this might have seemed merely promising; seen in combination with *Ariel* and *Leningrad Cowboys Go America*, it confirms Kaurismäki's unique and unpredictable talent. NF

Hammers Over the Anvil
(Ann Turner, 1992, Aust) Russell Crowe, Charlotte Rampling, Alexander Outhred.
101 min.
In a rural community in Australia at the turn of the century, handicapped teenager Outhred discovers the mysteries of the adult world when he becomes the unwitting go-between in the affair of lusty horse-trader Crowe and romantically-inclined Englishwoman Rampling, wife of the local landowner. The result – with its voice-over documenting the artistic growth of the teenager, its glimpses of half-understood sexuality, and its trail of conflict between father and son – isn't badly made, just familiar. Ann Turner's *Celia*, an arresting rites-of-passage story about the terrors of childhood, promised better than this literary saga. TJ

Hammett
(Wim Wenders, 1982, US) Frederic Forrest, Peter Boyle, Marilu Henner, Roy Kinnear, Lydia Lei, Elisha Cook, RG Armstrong, Richard Bradford, Sylvia Sidney, Samuel Fuller.
97 min.
Wenders' first American movie is no conventional biopic, but a stunningly achieved fiction about the art and mystique of creating fiction. By 1928, Dashiell Hammett is a retired Pinkerton agent, aridly glossing the exploits of his old sidekick Jimmy Ryan as raw material for his magazine stories. But when the real Ryan turns up in San Francisco to plunge Hammett into a Chinatown conundrum of underage hookers, gunsel punks, stag movies, blackmail and murder, he uncovers at first hand

the characters and canvas for such subsequent triumphs as *The Maltese Falcon*, and discovers within himself the seeds of Sam Spade. Wenders' double-edged examination of what Spade later called 'the stuff that dreams are made of' is rich and audacious, as much a homage to bygone Hollywood as to Hammett and the '*roman noir*' he pioneered: almost entirely studio-shot, bit-cast with iconic veterans, hauntingly scored. Forrest incarnates the writer as a rumpled but uncreased Bogart; Boyle is the archetypal Archer-type loser; the whole cast plays just one beat away from the genre staples their characters would become in print and the movies. One to savour. PT

Hamsin

(Daniel Wachsman, 1982, Isr) Shlomo Tarshish, Hemda Levy, Ruth Geler, Shawaf Yassin, Daou Selim.
88 min.
This shows that art can sometimes do what no amount of political commentary and reporting can accomplish: provide the understanding that comes from knowing people, rather than knowing about them. In a small farming village in Northern Israel in 1982, suspicions arise that the central government intends to expropriate the local Arab lands. The consequent bitterness and hostility destroy old Arab-Jewish friendships and loyalties. The film is particularly good at conveying the texture of Israel: the look and character of a country that combines Third World and Western ways. There are weaknesses – some clumsy exposition and a too obvious Lawrentian sexuality – but they do not seriously diminish the film's pleasures, nor its importance. MH

Hamster Factor and Other Tales of Twelve Monkeys, The

(Keith Fulton/Louis Pepe, 1996, US)
90 min.
A documentary on the making of *12 Monkeys*, giving insights into its director Terry Gilliam (perfectionist but pragmatic, ambitious but amiable), and taking us through virtually the entire production process, from receiving the script and working out the budget, through shooting, editing and other aspects of post-production, to the marketing, previews, promotion and final release of the movie. Entertaining and illuminating. GA

Hana-Bi

(Takeshi Kitano, 1997, Jap) 'Beat' Takeshi, Kayoko Kishimoto, Ren Osugi, Susumu Terajima, Tetsu Watanabe.
103 min.
Kitano's Venice prize-winner mixes tenderness, violence and droll humour. A recently retired cop drifts towards a one-off crime, to help out a suicidal colleague crippled in a disastrous stake-out, and to take his terminally ill wife on one last trip around Japan. It's exceptionally assured, imaginative and idiosyncratic: the violence is sudden, brutal and almost all in the editing; the working of Kitano's own delightful paintings into the story is astonishingly resonant; the *mise-en-scène* as sharp and inventive as in *Sonatine*; and it's all held together by Beat Takeshi's unprecedentedly taciturn, impassive, but expressive performance, which is crucial to the film's emotional punch. Fans of Melville, Keaton, Hawks and Peckinpah should be especially impressed, but anyone with a modicum of patience, an open mind and a little love in their heart will probably recognise it as a masterpiece. GA

Hand, The

(Oliver Stone, 1981, US) Michael Caine, Andrea Marcovicci, Annie McEnroe, Bruce McGill, Viveca Lindfors, Rosemary Murphy.
104 min.
Anyone having seen *Salvador* or *Platoon* who thinks that Oliver Stone is the best thing since sliced bread would do well not only to remember his scripts for *Midnight Express* and *Year of the Dragon*, but to catch this grotesque, unimaginative fiasco – clearly ripped off from *The Beast with Five Fingers* – in which cartoonist Caine has his mitt severed in an accident, and sees it commit a series of murderously vengeful crimes against his enemies. Silly and nasty. GA

Handful of Dust, A

(Charles Sturridge, 1987, GB) James Wilby, Kristin Scott Thomas, Rupert Graves, Anjelica Huston, Judi Dench, Alec Guinness, Graham Crowden.
118 min.
Here we go again, with the inevitable follow-up to *Brideshead Revisited*: heritage, haircuts and hooray Henries. This time the country house is a Gothic pile called Hetton, where the 'madly feudal' Tony Last (Wilby) lives with wife Brenda (Thomas) and young son John Andrew. Brenda, out of boredom, has an affair with John Beaver (Graves), a common golddigger. As these are the '30s, she pays for her infidelity with the death of her son. Evelyn Waugh's novel is a savage, ironic indictment of worthless people, but you wouldn't know it from the film. Sturridge directs the proceedings with all the gob-smacked wonder of a stable-boy at the ball; everything is taken at face value. Only when Brenda thinks John Beaver has copped it, and is relieved to discover that it is John Andrew instead, do we register any moral disgust. Great performances, glorious scenery, a magnificent waste of time. MS

Handgun
(aka Deep in the Heart)

(Tony Garnett, 1982, US) Karen Young, Clayton Day, Suzie Humphreys, Helena Humann, Ben Jones.
101 min.
Garnett's first American movie, set in Dallas, is a curious amalgam of 'concerned' docudrama and *Lipstick*-style exploitation. Kathleen (Young), a nice Irish Catholic girl from Boston, squares up to the cowboy charmer (Day) who dates her and then rapes her at gunpoint. Unfortunately for the film's sexual politics, Kathleen opts for rough justice the Charles Bronson way, arming herself with a new 'masculinised' image (cropped hair, combat gear), a handgun and sharpshooting skills, before luring the baddie out to a midnight face-off and dumping him symbolically outside the County Courthouse. Garnett is clearly as seduced as his heroine by Wild West frontier mythology and life in the Lone Star state. Misfiring as serious social commentary, *Handgun* ends up, beneath its veneer of casual naturalism, as a pseudo-feminist vigilante movie that celebrates the attitudes it affects to deplore. SJo

Handgun

(Whitney Ransick, 1993, US) Treat Williams, Paul Schulze, Seymour Cassel, Anna Thompson.
90 min.
This engaging thriller, set in New York, starts with a bang, as villain Jack (Cassel), father of George (Williams), ends up the sole survivor of a mega-heist firefight. The cops descend on George, catch him *in flagrante delicto*, and locate his handgun. He goes on the run and is finally forced to hole-up with his brother Mike, a sleazebag conman with a Woody Allen-like verbal delivery. Independent writer/director Ransick's debut is another offbeat post-modern character study of thieves without honour. Hand-held, droll and well-observed: maybe some of the dialogue could have been tightened, and some of the scenes rehearsed one more time, but it's still a winner, and Treat's a treat. WH

Händler der vier Jahreszeiten

see Merchant of Four Seasons, The

Handmaid's Tale, The

(Volker Schlöndorff, 1990, US/Ger) Natasha Richardson, Faye Dunaway, Aidan Quinn, Elizabeth McGovern, Victoria Tennant, Robert Duvall, Blanche Baker, Traci Lind.
108 min.
Margaret Atwood's novel is a remarkable tour de force, a kind of feminist *1984* which gradually builds up detail so that the full horror of the world created creeps up like a killer in the night: a vision of an America so obsessed with physical, environmental and moral pollution that it returns to a mix of old Calvinism and newer Fascism. It should have transferred well to the screen, particularly as Schlöndorff is a veteran of literary adaptation. Of the fine cast, both Richardson (as the titular surrogate mother chosen to give birth on behalf of the state) and Duvall (as her unwelcome mate, an ageing military bigwig) are particularly fine. Sadly, the faults in the film lie in

Harold Pinter's uncharacteristically bland script, and often woefully inadequate design and direction: the latter often missing opportunities in key scenes, the former full of rather tacky and silly uniforms, symbols, vehicles, and particularly crass watchtowers. SGr

Hands Across the Table

(Mitchell Leisen, 1935, US) Carole Lombard, Fred MacMurray, Ralph Bellamy, Marie Prevost, William Demarest, Astrid Allwyn.
80 min. b/w.
After telling a friendly paraplegic that she's after money, not love, hotel manicurist Lombard bumps into MacMurray's impecunious man-about-town hopscotching down the corridor, and her personal credo slowly crumbles. But not in the riotous way of some other Paramount comedies from the period: Leisen skilfully moves his players through some occasionally creaky set pieces (a meal full of hiccups, a simulated long-distance telephone call) to arrive, in the last half-hour, at thoughtful scenes of considerable tenderness whose erotic undertow prevails even when MacMurray is bared to the waist under a sun lamp. And Lombard, in the first part tailor-made for her, proves herself as the only Hollywood person ever to be a great beauty, a great comedienne and a great actress all at once. GB

Hands of Orlac, The
(Orlacs Hände)

(Robert Wiene, 1924, Aus) Conrad Veidt, Alexandra Sorina, Carmen Cartellieri, Fritz Kortner, Fritz Strassny.
92 min. b/w.
Wiene spent the early '20s trying to repeat his surprise success with *The Cabinet of Dr Caligari*. This adaptation of Maurice Renard's celebrated novel finds him exploring another 'horrific' theme, but using his repertoire of Expressionist effects more coolly. His version of the story (about a concert pianist who loses his hands in a train crash, and has the hands of an executed murderer grafted on in their place) opts for a 'realistic' denouement rather than a 'fantastic' one, but it still manages to generate some potent shocks from its confrontation between the hero and villain. Its most enduring quality is Veidt's tormented performance as Orlac. TR

Hands of Orlac, The

see Mad Love

Hands of the Ripper

(Peter Sasdy, 1971, GB) Eric Porter, Angharad Rees, Jane Merrow, Keith Bell, Derek Godfrey, Dora Bryan.
85 min.
Late Hammer horror with a hefty dose of cod Freud, as Jack the Ripper's daughter grows up to become a sexually disturbed homicidal maniac after seeing daddy butcher mommy. Rees is particularly effective in the role, while Sasdy keeps the tension reasonably high; nevertheless, one can't help experiencing a certain sense of *déjà vu*, for all the narrative ingenuity. GA

Hands Over the City

see Mani sulla Città, Le

Hands Up! (Rece do Góry)

(Jerzy Skolimowski, 1967/1981, Pol) Jerzy Skolimowski, Bogumil Kobiela, Joanna Szczerbic.
90 min. b/w & col.
Though doubts have been expressed as to the wisdom of re-editing the original footage to make space for a prologue shot in 1981 in London and Beirut, Skolimowski's film, more aptly titled than he realised, proves well worth waiting for since its suppression by the Polish authorities in 1967. Shot in sepia and grey, bursting with '60s energy and invention, funny yet vitriolic, it details in consistently vivid imagery a collective psychodrama staged by four disillusioned students in an abandoned cattle truck. Unforgettable. GAd

Handsworth Songs

(John Akomfrah, 1986, GB) voice-overs: Pervais Khan, Meera Syal, Yvonne Weekes.
61 min.
An invigorating and thoughtful documentary from the London-based Black Audio Film

Collective that examines elements of the Black experience in Britain from the perspective of the tragic events of 1985: the Handsworth riots, the death and funeral of Cynthia Jarrett, and the – seemingly – ever downward path of race relations, brought to a head by the deteriorating economic plight of Britain in the '80s. What is in evidence here is a fertile and imaginative cinematic intelligence which, in waging 'the war of naming the problem', musters a range of archive material, interviews, and filmed records of the disturbances in such a way as to provide an essay that is as full of subtle, rich and allusive argument as it is devoid of empty didacticism and stridency. WH

Hand That Rocks the Cradle, The

(Curtis Hanson, 1992, US) Annabella Sciorra, Rebecca De Mornay, Matt McCoy, Ernie Hudson, Julianne Moore, Madeline Zima, John de Lancie.
110 min.
Claire (Sciorra), happily married and pregnant, is molested during a visit to her gynaecologist. The ensuing investigation results in the doctor's suicide, thus causing his pregnant wife (De Mornay) to miscarry. De Mornay finds solace in an elaborate revenge which involves posing as a nanny and gaining employment with Claire in order to wreak havoc. Screenwriter Amanda Silver gleefully exploits parental fears, and skilfully depicts the shifting loyalties, malevolence and escalating paranoia within Claire's household. But as the film progresses, malicious schemes and loony excesses are combined, with Hanson's self-conscious direction rendering one particularly sensational murder even more implausible. Subtler and more involving are sequences which show the splendidly unnerving De Mornay in coercive, threatening mode. CM

Hang 'em High

(Ted Post, 1967, US) Clint Eastwood, Inger Stevens, Ed Begley, Pat Hingle, Arlene Golonka, James MacArthur, Ben Johnson, Ruth White, Charles McGraw, LQ Jones, Alan Hale Jr, Dennis Hopper, Bruce Dern, Bert Freed, Bob Steele.
114 min.
More interesting as a way station in Eastwood's career than for anything intrinsic to its lawman/vigilante scenario, this was his first American Western after the spaghettis. Made by his own company, Malpaso, with an old 'Rawhide' director on board (Eastwood is said to have shot some of it himself), the film anticipates the obsession with the dichotomy between natural and legal justice. Saved by chance after being summarily strung up as a presumed rustler and left to die, Eastwood sets out to avenge himself on the nine men who constituted the lynch mob and left him with a scar on his neck. TCh

Hanged Man, The

(Don Siegel, 1964, US) Robert Culp, Edmond O'Brien, Vera Miles, Norman Fell, Brenda Scott, Gene Raymond, J Carrol Naish.
87 min.
Nowhere near as effective as Siegel's other telefilm (The Killers), this second version of Dorothy Hughes' Ride the Pink Horse comes over as a thriller with considerable directing flair and little substance. As Culp travels to New Orleans to take revenge on the man he believes responsible for the death of his friend, only to discover that he is the victim of manipulative deception, Siegel makes the most of his colourful locations (notably during the Mardi Gras festivities), but is let down by a hackneyed, incoherent script, which has Culp getting involved with a beautiful young girl of astonishing, implausible innocence. Of interest to Siegel completists only. GA

Hanging Garden, The

(Thom Fitzgerald, 1996, Can/GB) Chris Leavins, Troy Veinotte, Kerry Fox, Sarah Polley, Seana McKenna, Peter MacNeill.
91 min.
Writer/director Fitzgerald's first feature starts conventionally as Sweet William (all the characters are named after plants) returns home to rural Nova Scotia after a long absence for his sister's wedding. Then matters turn spectacularly surreal: he encounters his former self, an unhappy grossly overweight teenager who hanged himself in despair over his homosexuality. A question

mark hangs over which William is the 'true' one, and which the ghost, or the fantasy. Leavins and Fox head a strong cast in this unusual witty twist on the old dysfunctional family plot. SJo

Hanging Gardens

see Jardines Colgantes

Hangin' with the Homeboys

(Joseph B Vasquez, 1991, US) Doug E Doug, Mario Joyner, John Leguizamo, Nestor Serrano, Kimberly Russell, Mary B Ward, Reggie Montgomery.
89 min.
Four Bronx likely lads – two black, two Puerto Rican – start their Saturday night by being booted out of a salsa party, and end up, one battered car and several battered egos later, wiser guys. It's one of those films in which the lessons of a lifetime are learned in one night, but it all works to brisk comic effect. The guys are basically cutouts, each defined by his own tic, but they're done to a fault. There's Tom (Joyner), an aspiring actor, shiftless Willie (Doug), and shy, morose Johnny (Leguizamo). But the star turn is Nestor Serrano's obnoxious hustler, Vinnie. The film is a little too episodic, and being a buddy movie, never quite pulls the rug from under the boys' braggadocio. But Vasquez makes pointed play with some of the current movie clichés of race and sex politics, and the pace never lets up. A lot of fun, with a lot of heart, and pretty hip into the bargain. JRo

Hangmen Also Die!

(Fritz Lang, 1943, US) Brian Donlevy, Anna Lee, Walter Brennan, Gene Lockhart, Dennis O'Keefe, Alexander Granach, Margaret Wycherly.
131 min. b/w.
Marvellous anti-Nazi propaganda film structured as noir thriller, with Donlevy as the man who assassinates Heydrich in Prague in 1942, hiding out with the Resistance when the Gestapo implement a retributory reign of terror in the city. Brecht, who originally worked on the script with Lang, claimed that his ideas were betrayed by the final product; but Lang's insistence that for most of the film he did employ the writer's work seems borne out by many fine sequences, with the taut, typically Langian action often interrupted by speeches that comment both didactically and intelligently on the proceedings. The atmosphere is dark and oppressive, the Nazis are portrayed as ideological gangsters, and the themes of loyalty and betrayal, passive and active resistance, beautifully worked out. Superb performances throughout, while James Wong Howe's photography perfectly captures the spirit of the occupied city, where hiding places are few and far from safe. GA

Hangover Square

(John Brahm, 1944, US) Laird Cregar, Linda Darnell, George Sanders, Glenn Langan, Faye Marlowe, Alan Napier.
77 min. b/w.
Loosely based on Patrick Hamilton's novel, this is a slightly self-conscious attempt to repeat the success of The Lodger, immensely stylish in its evocation of Edwardian London but failing to reproduce quite the same sense of subtle psychological nightmare. Playing a composer driven to murderous blackouts by discordant sounds (a fine cue for Bernard Herrmann's score), Cregar – in his last film – again gives a superbly ambivalent performance; and Darnell is terrific as the scheming chanteuse who seduces him into prostituting his talent to supply her with popular songs. But with the script using histrionics to patch its holes, Brahm is sometimes forced to respond with Grand Guignol excesses like the climax, which provides flaming apotheosis in the concert hall for the composer and his finally-completed concerto; pitched on a far too hysterical and grandiose note, this finale never quite rhymes, as it should, with the superb earlier sequence in which Cregar, anonymous in the crowd of Guy Fawkes celebrants, casually consigns Darnell's body to a bonfire. TM

Hangup

(Henry Hathaway, 1973, US) William Elliott, Marki Bey, Cliff Potts, Michael Lerner, Wally Taylor, George Murdock.
93 min.
A curiously dated and unconvincing tone of

moral outrage envelops this creaking tale of a black policeman (Elliott) who redeems and then falls in love with a young heroin addict (Bey), only to abandon her upon discovering that she lied about having worked as a hooker. Driven back to the toils, she dies and he is left with a 'hangup'. The septuagenarian Hathaway's creative powers were once to be reckoned with intermittently, but this rudimentary, straggling revenge picture – his last – should have been left tactfully on the shelf. JPy

Hanky Panky

(Sidney Poitier, 1982, US) Gene Wilder, Gilda Radner, Kathleen Quinlan, Richard Widmark, Robert Prosky, Josef Sommer, Johnny Sekka.
110 min.
An unashamed attempt to repeat the success of Stir Crazy, again directed by Poitier and taking the high security leak of a weaponry system for its soft centre, this comedy-thriller lets Wilder do his hysterical hero act yet again as he gets unwittingly embroiled with double-crosses, moles and cabbies who are allergic to elephant shit. Unfortunately, Hanky Panky doesn't have Richard Pryor in a chicken suit. Instead, there's TV comedienne Radner, whose efforts to pull a performance out of a poorly drawn female romantic lead are valiant, to say the most. Shored up by the mildly funny situation jokes and a superbly evil performance from the papyrus-faced Widmark as a horrid henchman, this is slick fun at best and cringing nonsense at its worst. FL

Hanna's War

(Menahem Golan, 1988, US) Ellen Burstyn, Maruschka Detmers, Anthony Andrews, Donald Pleasence, David Warner, Vincenzo Ricotta, Christopher Fairbank.
148 min.
1944. When Hanna (Detmers) abandons the rough comforts of her kibbutz to help kilted Andrews chase the Nazis out of the Balkans, nothing goes as it should. They are astonished to discover cattle trucks full of Jews, and even more surprised to learn that the ferryman paid to smuggle them into Hungary is a German spy. Hanna consequently falls into the capable hands of torturer Pleasence, who persuades her to betray her mother, brave, moving Burstyn. But all's well that ends well. Mum is released, and Hanna finds the slick Hollywood martyrdom she seems to be after. Written, produced and directed by Golan, the film's supposed to be a serious piece, refuting the anti-Semitic slur that the Jews were a load of namby-pamby defeatists when, in fact, they fought the Nazis like everybody else. The bad script is based on a stale polemic, which produces an expensive and self-righteous piece of propaganda. Top-notch performances by Detmers and Pleasence do nothing to make it the slightest bit gripping. PHo

Hannah and Her Sisters

(Woody Allen, 1986, US) Woody Allen, Michael Caine, Mia Farrow, Carrie Fisher, Barbara Hershey, Lloyd Nolan, Maureen O'Sullivan, Daniel Stern, Max von Sydow, Dianne Wiest, Sam Waterston.
107 min.
Allen's previous three films (Zelig, Broadway Danny Rose, The Purple Rose of Cairo) were thin, clever sketches fleshed out with characteristic one-liners. Here he returns to the territory he knows best, Manhattan. Of the three sisters (this is very much Chekhov landscape), the youngest (Hershey) lives with a spiritual mentor (Von Sydow), an intellectual recluse who rails against the iniquities of modern culture. The middle one (Wiest) is a frantic urban neurotic, forever borrowing money to pursue her latest career whim. And the eldest (Farrow) is apparently the most stable, a successful actress and mother presiding over a warm family circle. All is not well, however; Farrow's husband (Caine) is pursuing an affair with the youngest sister; sibling rivalry is rife. Wandering in and out of this extended dissection of family love life is Allen himself, playing his familiar nebbish hypochondriac; when a medical crisis brings him uncomfortably close to death, he samples all the different religions, before turning to the Marx Brothers' films as evidence that life is to be enjoyed. It is an articulate, literate film, full of humanity and perception about its sometimes less-than-loveable characters, which nonetheless comes down on the side of the best things in life: the primacy of love and

feeling, qualified hope, and the fragility of it all. It also returns to much of the humour from his 'early, funny' films; Allen seems finally to have found the ability to please not just everyone, but also himself. CPea

Hannibal Brooks

(Michael Winner, 1968, GB) Oliver Reed, Michael J Pollard, Wolfgang Preiss, Helmut Lohner, Karin Baal, Peter Karsten, John Alderton, James Donald.
102 min.
British PoW Brooks (Reed) is assigned to look after an elephant named Lucy, to whom he grows devoted. En route with the elephant from Munich to a safer zoo in Innsbruck, Brooks accidentally kills the Nazi member of the escort (Karsten) and then sets off with Lucy over the mountains to Switzerland. Pollard is tiresomely flaky as one 'Packy', leader of a private army, and Oliver Reed is not much more than Oliver Reed. Pretty good, though, for a Michael Winner film. TJ

Hannie Caulder

(Burt Kennedy, 1971, GB) Raquel Welch, Robert Culp, Ernest Borgnine, Strother Martin, Jack Elam, Christopher Lee, Diana Dors.
85 min.
Gimmicky British-financed Western, terminally indecisive over whether to parody or indulge the then familiar motifs of the spaghetti style, featuring Welch as the poncho-clad avenger of her own gang-rape and her husband's murder by the gnarled triumvirate of Borgnine, Elam and Martin. An opportunistic hiatus in Kennedy's comedy-Western decline. PT

Hanover Street

(Peter Hyams, 1979, GB) Harrison Ford, Lesley-Anne Down, Christopher Plummer, Alec McCowen, Richard Masur, Michael Sacks, Max Wall.
108 min.
Gung-ho American World War II bomber pilot falls for an already married English rose during teatime rendezvous in war-torn Hanover Street. Presumably the fragile 'brief encounters' of war had some immediate poignancy for the audiences of that period; here, though, tricked out with all sorts of 'modern' intrusions (bed scenes, *Catch-22* aircrew) and saddled with dialogue of quite staggering banality, they merely straggle into the wayward irrelevancies of his creeping cowardice and her increasing guilt. The second half ignores the obvious irony of husband and lover circumstantially trapped on the same suicide mission, settling instead for heroics of the 'Tell her I died a brave man' variety. Anaemic and foolish. CPea

Hans Christian Andersen

(Charles Vidor, 1952, US) Danny Kaye, Zizi Jeanmaire, Roland Petit, Farley Granger, John Qualen.
120 min.
Determined that he was going to make a movie about the celebrated storyteller, producer Sam Goldwyn went through every conceivable permutation of directors (William Wyler!), stars (Gary Cooper!) and scripts (16 of 'em) before ending up with this garish epic of musical puerility. You'll remember the songs – from 'Wonderful, Wonderful Copenhagen' to 'The Ugly Duckling' – but does Kaye have to play it as though he has a mental age of ten? A sugary one. TJ

Hanussen

(István Szabó, 1988, Hun/WGer) Klaus Maria Brandauer, Erland Josephson, Ildikó Bánsági, Walter Schmidinger, Károly Eperjes, Grazyna Szapolowska.
117 min.
The third collaboration, after *Mephisto* and *Colonel Redl* between Szabó, Brandauer and cinematographer Lajos Koltai. Klaus Schneider (Brandauer) is an Austrian sergeant whose clairvoyant gifts first attract moderate acclaim during his recuperation from fighting in WWI. In hospital he forms friendships with two people who will help him to shape his future: Jewish psychologist Bettelheim (Josephson) and Nowotny (Eperjes), an ambitious army acquaintance who decides to promote Schneider's talents. On tours of Vienna and Berlin under the stage name of Hanussen, Schneider's phenomenal predictions bring him into contact with the

decadent post-war elite; and despite his apolitical stance, his prophecies of Hitler's rise to power inevitably implicate him with the Nazis, threatening his friendships and precarious sense of stability... Brandauer's dominating screen presence is perfectly suited to the role of the charismatic seducer, whose abilities to transfer his will and to control respondents serve as a not so subtle metaphor for the rise of Fascism. Szabó heightens the mysticism with a pervading sense of menace which, together with Koltai's exquisite visuals, captivates attention throughout. CM

Hap-Ki-Do (aka Heqidao)

(Huang Feng, 1972, HK) Angela Mao, Carter Huang, Pai Ying, Ji Han Jae.
97 min.
A well-mounted action pic with a female lead who practises the martial art of Hap-Ki-Do. There is an undoubted, if limited, kick to be had from seeing a woman in there giving as good as she gets instead of waiting under the cherry blossoms. Set in 1934 Korea, when the country was under the domination of those perennial baddies, the Japanese, the plot concerns the efforts of the Chinese to fight back against constant provocation. The biggest culprits are the denizens of the notorious Black Bear School, and inevitably it is left to Angela Mao to storm the place alone. VG

Happening, The

(Elliot Silverstein, 1966, US) Anthony Quinn, George Maharis, Michael Parks, Faye Dunaway, Robert Walker, Oscar Homolka, Martha Hyer, Milton Berle.
101 min.
Four Miami beach bums find they've kidnapped cleaned up gangster Quinn in this dated excuse for an anti-establishment comedy, which gave Dunaway her first role, as one of the abductors (a few months later she was to play Bonnie Parker), and The Supremes a chart-topping hit. Infuriated that his wife Martha Hyer, partner Berle, Mafia boss Homolka, and his mother won't pay up for his release, the gangster blows his top, takes over his own kidnapping, secures the ransom by a faked death and blackmail, and then, to the horror of the purblind hippies, who he's turned into his soldiers, burns the supposedly marked loot. Co-scripted by Frank R Pierson, with evocative camerawork by Philip Lathrop. TJ

Happiest Days of Your Life, The

(Frank Launder, 1950, GB) Alastair Sim, Margaret Rutherford, Joyce Grenfell, Guy Middleton, Edward Rigby, Richard Wattis, George Cole.
84 min. b/w.
With hindsight, this uproarious farce, adapted from a play by John Dighton, heralds a retreat. Throughout the 1940s, Launder and Gilliat had been making ambitious, heartfelt films about ordinary people (*Millions Like Us*, *Waterloo Bridge*), but with the new decade, they began to rely more and more on stylised English humour and stock characters. Sim plays a headmaster who learns that thanks to Civil Service bungling, he's going to share his premises with a girls' school. Vintage moments include Rutherford, tweedy, formidable headmistress, marching at the head of a column of girls, like Hannibal about to attack the Alps, and Joyce Grenfell's games mistress Miss Gossage ('just call me sausage') banging the school gong with the fervour of a bodybuilder auditioning for Rank. GM

Happiest Millionaire, The

(Norman Tokar, 1967, US) Fred MacMurray, Tommy Steele, Greer Garson, John Davidson, Lesley Ann Warren, Geraldine Page, Gladys Cooper, Hermione Baddeley.
159 min.
Antiseptic, over-long (there have been various cut-down versions) but not unpleasant Disney musical. MacMurray exudes characteristically quizzical charm as the eccentric Philadelphian millionaire with a penchant for fisticuffs and alligators, while Tommy Steele does a winsome Oirish act as the butler who takes care of problems that arise when his master's tomboy daughter (Warren) falls for a youth (Davidson) who initially doesn't quite come up to expectations. What with Greer Garson thrown in

as MacMurray's gracious wife, it's all very bland and cosy. Best moment is when Gladys Cooper and Geraldine Page sing the respective praises of aristocratic and *nouveau riche* social graces in a nicely bitchy song called 'There Are Those'. TM

Happiness

(Todd Solondz, 1998, US) Jane Adams, Dylan Baker, Lara Flynn Boyle, Philip Seymour Hoffman, Ben Gazzara, Louise Lasser, Jared Harris.
134 min.
Centred loosely on a New Jersey family of three grown-up sisters, their parents, partners and children, Solondz's brave and adventurous second feature takes misery, loneliness and cruelty as a given in contemporary life; everyone here is (justifiably or otherwise) unhappy with their lot – or should be, if they could only stop deluding themselves. Right from the painfully funny opening, it's a bible-black comedy of considerable assurance, but gradually the humour subsides to be replaced by a core of despairing human sympathy, most noticeably for the paedophile father whose heart-to-hearts with his teenage son come to form the emotional backbone of the movie. Very often, you're unsure whether you want to accompany Solondz on his journey into a modern purgatory, but you should take the trip; it's worth it, and something you'll never forget. GA

Happiness (Schaste)

(Alexander Medvedkin, 1934, USSR) Piotr Zinoviev, Elena Egorova, L Nenascheva, W Uspenski.
5,840 ft. b/w.
One of the last Soviet silent movies, rediscovered and restored by French cine-chameleon Chris Marker in 1971, *Happiness* proved an easily accessible counterpoint to the exotic obscurities of *The Wishing Tree*. For this rare and often hilarious example of socialist slapstick is likewise grounded in the seeming eccentricities of Russian folk culture; but on the less culturally specific dynamics of those hopes and dreams which forever sustain the exploited, and which may or may not flourish after the revolution. Medvedkin's infectiously happy oddity emerged surprisingly from a slough of social-realist orthodoxy, and prompted none other than Eisenstein to the admiring tribute: 'Today I saw how a Bolshevik laughs'. PT

Happiness

see Bonheur, Le

Happiness in Twenty Years (Le Bonheur dans 20 Ans)

(Albert Knobler, 1971, Fr) narrator: Orson Welles.
93 min. b/w.
A series of astonishing documentary sequences illustrating the Czech experience, everything from the arrival of the Russian liberating tanks after World War II to the 'confessions' of the show trials, from chunks of Stalinist newsreels to the first blossoming of what was to become the cinematic new wave in the café theatre satires of the '60s. Its argument is achieved visually: although it does inevitably relish the tatty absurdity of the whole iconography of the Stalinist period, the film also carefully charts its progress so that we actually see a visual expression of a political idea forming on the screen as crowds harden, literally, into massed ranks. VG

Happy Birthday, Wanda June

(Mark Robson, 1971, US) Rod Steiger, Susannah York, George Grizzard, Don Murray, William Hickey.
105 min.
Kurt Vonnegut's adaptation of his own off-Broadway play about a big game hunter (Steiger) who returns from the jungle after being believed dead for eight years. He finds his dim wife (York) turned intellectual, and undecided whether to marry a pacifist doctor or a vacuum cleaner salesman. Though these ingredients may sound promising, add a precocious child and you have all the ingredients for the tedious satire of American attitudes that it is. Steiger's overacting and the film's obvious theatrical origins don't help either.

Happy Ever After
(aka Tonight's the Night)
(Mario Zampi, 1954, GB) David Niven, Yvonne
De Carlo, Barry Fitzgerald, George Cole,
Robert Urquhart, Michael Shepley, AE
Matthews, Liam Redmond.
78 min.
Passable comedy with Niven as the new squire
of an Irish village, blissfully unaware that the
devious locals are drawing lots to see who gets
the chance to bump him off. It's actually not bad
as these things go, because the money was spent
on the cast, and they did even go to Ireland to
shoot it (in Technicolor). TJ

Happy Family, The
(aka Mr Lord Says No)
(Muriel Box, 1952, GB) Stanley Holloway,
Kathleen Harrison, Naunton Wayne, Dandy
Nichols, George Cole, Miles Malleson,
Margaret Barton.
86 min. b/w.
Another Ealing-style triumph for the 'little people' (adapted by Sydney and Muriel Box from a
play by Michael Clayton Hutton): Holloway and
family barricade themselves in their grocery store
when the authorities inform them it has to be
demolished to make way for an access road to the
Festival of Britain site on London's South Bank.
Nichols is fun as a spiritualist spinster, but otherwise there's not a great deal to celebrate. TJ

Happy Gilmore
(Dennis Dugan, 1996, US) Adam Sandler,
Christopher McDonald, Julie Bowen, Frances
Bay, Carl Weathers, Alan Covert,
Dennis Dugan.
92 min.
Happy Gilmore (Sandler) is a life-long ice hockey
fanatic. Snags: his skating's wretched, and his
temper short and explosive. In fact, his one talent's a thundering slap shot that's as liable to hit
the spectators as the net. While the home of his
beloved grandma is being repossessed by tax
officials he discovers his power shooting lends
itself to a 400-yard golf drive. So, hoping to rescue grandma from a diabolical nursing home,
Happy goes on the Pro Golf Tour, hindered by
his putting, his short fuse and the jealous attentions of smarmy favourite Shooter McGavin
(McDonald). Given that the chief pleasure of
Dugan's film is watching a maniac on golf greens,
a liking for the sport is incidental to the enjoyment of this immensely silly film. And while it
may be dumb, the film-makers refuse to force the
fact as funny in itself, relying instead on well-
drawn characters, goofy slapstick, cartoon violence and occasionally inspired dialogue. The
result falls somewhere between early Steve
Martin, the Marx Brothers and a Looney Tune.
The only real let-down is the handling of the love
interest; otherwise, this is superior disposable
comedy. NB

Happy Hooker, The
(Nicholas Sgarro, 1975, US) Lynn Redgrave,
Jean-Pierre Aumont, Lovelady Powell,
Nicholas Pryor, Elizabeth Wilson, Tom
Poston, Conrad Janis, Richard Lynch.
98 min.
The only spark in this cheapskate version of
Xaviera Hollander's much-touted life story is provided by Lynn Redgrave's believable and consistently interesting incarnation of Xaviera as a
rather practical lady of no great imagination but
a deal of energy. The script and direction are both
doggedly routine. Anything like a sex scene is
promptly elided out of existence, a promising line
of social satire fails to develop, and the sorry light
cast on the male characters, all roundly and condescendingly patronised by the women, is
allowed to develop swiftly into overripe farce. A
distinct aura of missed opportunity hangs about
the proceedings, which make quite a good job of
sidestepping the relevant issues. VG

Happy New Year
see Bonne Année, La

Happy Together
(Mel Damski, 1989, US) Patrick Dempsey,
Helen Slater, Dan Schneider, Marius Weyers,
Brad Pitt, Barbara Babcock.
102 min.
College comedy in which freshman Dempsey dis-

covers that an admin error has given him Slater
as a roommate, a situation that's bound to lead to
embarrassment, amorous complications and a
clunking resolution. If you're really interested a
young Brad Pitt pops up as a fellow student. TJ

Happy Together
(Chunguang Zhaxie)
(Wong Kar-Wai, 1997, HK) Leslie Cheung,
Tony Leung Chiu-Wai, Chang Chen.
97 min.
Under the Chinese title used for Antonioni's Blow-
Up (it connotes the exposure of something indecent), Wong Kar-Wai and cameraman Chris
Doyle have crafted their most lyrical film. The
romance between two gay men from Hong Kong
ends soon after they arrive in Argentina. Lai
(Leung) gets a job as a doorman at a Buenos Aires
tango bar and starts saving for his ticket home.
Ho (Cheung) turns tricks for fun and profit, but
comes running back to Lai for comfort when one
of his clients leaves him bruised and bleeding. Lai
befriends – and somehow draws emotional
strength from – a Taiwanese kid on his way
south to 'the end of the world'. The three main
characters give Wong all he needs for a piercing
meditation on the meaning of partings, reunions,
and attempts to start over. From afar (Buenos
Aires is Hong Kong's antipodes), he crystallises
the anxieties and hopes of Hong Kong people on
the eve of the return to China. TR

Happy We
see Tva Killar och en Tjej

Hardbodies
(Mark Griffiths, 1984, US) Grant Cramer, Teal
Roberts, Gary Wood, Michael Rapport,
Sorrells Pickard.
87 min.
What this needs to make it a great film is a new
script, a completely different cast, a decent director, and a soundtrack void of any dismal disco
muzak. The plot, which revolves around the
efforts of three middle-aged creeps to pick up big-
bazoomed extras, would have been vastly
improved by the addition of a psychopath with
an axe. The hero, a slobby-mannered beach bum,
would have been more sympathetic had he been
run over by a truck before filming. AB

Hard-Boiled
(Lashou Shentan)
(John Woo, 1991, HK) Chow Yun Fat, Tony
Leung, Mo Shun Kwan.
132 min.
In essence, John Woo's characteristic take on
movies like Die Hard: a supercharged thriller in
which a renegade cop and an undercover man
take on Triad gun-runners who store their munitions in a hospital morgue. Anyone who saw The
Killer will have a fair idea what to expect, from
the intense male bonding to the hyper-kinetic
editing style. What's new here is a rich vein of
anarchic humour (will they evacuate the maternity ward before the hospital blows up?) and a
bluesy back-beat of philosophical musings on a
cop's sad lot. No surprise that Woo (who cameos
as a barman) has been courted by Hollywood. TR

Hard Contract
(S Lee Pogostin, 1969, US) James Coburn, Lee
Remick, Lilli Palmer, Burgess Meredith,
Patrick Magee, Sterling Hayden, Claude
Dauphin, Helen Cherry, Karen Black.
106 min.
A sometimes intelligent examination of the mind
of a professional killer (Coburn) sent to Europe to
dispose of three men. Plans start to go awry when
his emotional reserves (he deliberately seeks
transactions with prostitutes) are plumbed by
Remick. Unfortunately there are too many distractions for the film to really work: Coburn
appears too inflexible, the pretty European locations look deliberately chosen for the American
market, and too many well known faces (Magee,
Palmer, Dauphin) are left with too little to do. CPe

Hardcore
(aka The Hardcore Life)
(Paul Schrader, 1978, US) George C Scott, Peter
Boyle, Season Hubley, Dick Sargent, Leonard
Gaines, David Nichols.
108 min.

Schrader tackled Middle American dilemmas
with eloquence in the radical Blue Collar, and he
had touched on incest and child sexuality in
scripts like Obsession and Taxi Driver. Hardcore
stakes out similar ground: the pre-teen daughter
of Midwesterner Scott disappears from a
Calvinist youth camp, then surfaces in a porn
film. And Scott gets things off to a titanic start
as we voyeuristically watch his agony when confronted with a porn movie of his own daughter.
But credibility wavers when he impersonates a
seedy producer with suspicious ease, then forms
a sentimental detective partnership with a whore
(Hubley). The action meanders around to a hackneyed end, and because Hardcore is softcore, it
doesn't convincingly convey that climate of self-
hatred which pervades the sexual ghetto. It's a
reminder, though, that the culturally respected
cinema demands far gorier, more inventive and
more technically accomplished depictions of sexual violence than the flesh flicks. CR

Hard Day's Night, A
(Richard Lester, 1964, GB) The Beatles, Wilfrid
Brambell, Norman Rossington, Victor Spinetti.
85 min. b/w.
A sanitised semi-documentary version of life on
the road with John, Paul, George and Ringo, with
a paper-thin storyline about difficulties with their
manager and Paul's Grandpa (Brambell) serving
as a linking device to connect scenes of the Fab
Four in the studio, in concert, and in flight from
frantic fans. Lester's gimmicky camera-trickery
– jump-cuts, fast and slow motion, etc, etc – is so
much icing on the cake, and has dated badly; but
the mop-tops are likeably relaxed, with Lennon
offering a few welcome moments of his dry, acerbic wit. GA

Hard Eight
(Paul Thomas Anderson, 1996, US) Samuel L
Jackson, Gwyneth Paltrow, John C Reilly,
Philip Baker Hall, F William Parker.
101 min.
Sidney (Baker Hall) – old, well-kept – approaches a roadside café. John (Reilly) – young, down-
and-out – is slumped in front of the joint. Sidney
offers John cigarettes and coffee, $50 and a ride
to Vegas, and advice on playing the money at the
crap tables. Reno, two years later, and the stakes
have doubled. John's making a steady living gambling under Sidney's tutelage; he's also hooked
up with Clementine (Paltrow), a cocktail waitress
who turns tricks on the side. Outside Sidney's
orbit is John's pal Jimmy (Jackson), a small-time
hood with scant respect for Sidney – a catalyst
for trouble. There's a timeless quality to this first
feature (from the director of Boogie Nights): while
owing particular debts to the low-life worlds of
'40s B-movies and '70s neo-noir, it could have
been made almost any time in the last 50 years.
But it's in no way a pastiche. With a smart, savvy,
but unshowy script and quietly confident direction, this is a subtle, understated reworking of
noir conventions. Jackson and Paltrow both
prove their talents as character actors; Reilly
brings a credible, wide-eyed fecklessness to his
part; and Baker Hall is a revelation. NB

Harder They Come, The
(Perry Henzell, 1972, Jam) Jimmy Cliff, Carl
Bradshaw, Basil Keane, Janet Bartley,
Winston Stona, Bobby Charlton.
110 min.
The age-old story of country boy, urban corruption, and a bad end. The guy is Jimmy Cliff, the
city is Kingston, the bad business is the reggae
industry, and the crime is killing a cop who's in
on the 'ganja' trade. The film's tone is righteously angry, but it doesn't go for the easy targets: it
views Cliff's image of himself as a hero as ironically as it denounces police violence and mis-
sionary-style religion. Along the way, it offers a
richly textured picture of Jamaican shanty-town
life, composed with a terrific eye for detail. The
action is as gutsy as the well-integrated score,
which makes the movie's Hollywood-style gloss
a little anomalous, but the basic humour and
toughness emerge unscathed. TR

Harder They Fall, The
(Mark Robson, 1956, US) Humphrey Bogart,
Rod Steiger, Jan Sterling, Mike Lane, Max
Baer, Edward Andrews.
109 min. b/w.
A boxing drama with Bogart (in his last role) type-

cast as the sports publicist who finally does the right thing and sets out to expose the syndicate. The *Harder They Fall* bears the hallmark of its producer/writer Philip Yordan all over it. Robson tries vainly to give the movie the look of a thriller with lots of shadows and bleak lighting, but Yordan consistently returns it to the field of melodrama by setting his drama in the home – as Bogart and his wife Sterling agonise over his job of exposing the fixed fights – rather than in the boxing ring. PH

Hard, Fast and Beautiful

(Ida Lupino, 1951, US) Claire Trevor, Sally Forrest, Carleton Young, Robert Clarke, Kenneth Patterson.
79 min. b/w.
An intriguing little melodrama from the under-rated Lupino, with Trevor as an ambitious, domineering mother who pushes her daughter (Forrest) to become a tennis champion, only to accuse her of ingratitude when she falls for Clarke and tires of the tournament circuit. Rather like a *Mildred Pierce* of the sporting world but with sympathies reversed, it's a mite predictable in its plotting, but Trevor is typically excellent, and Lupino never sentimentalises the mother-daughter relationship. Nowhere near as rewarding as either *The Hitch-hiker* or *The Bigamist*, but a very watchable entertainment all the same from one of Hollywood's few women directors. GA

Hard Men

(JK Amalou, 1996, GB/Fr) Vincent Regan, Ross Boatman, Lee Ross, 'Mad' Frankie Fraser, Ken Campbell, Mirella D'Angelo.
87 min.
A bankrupt effort which begs to be seen as a British *Reservoir Dogs*. It's a callous, sentimental drama about an East End hitman who wants out, now he's a dad. The acting's uniformly terrible (imagine the cast of *Grange Hill* imitating Joe Pesci) and the dialogue's chiefly monotonous obscenity. Dire. TCh

Hard Rain

(Mikael Salomon, 1997, US/GB/Jap/Ger/Den) Morgan Freeman, Christian Slater, Randy Quaid, Minnie Driver, Edward Asner, Richard Dysart.
97 min.
After weeks of rain, the floods are rising around the town of Huntingburg, Indiana. Slater's armoured-car courier is out on his usual money collection run. It's bad enough being stuck in water with $3m in the back – what he doesn't need is a man like Freeman planning a robbery with his gang, nor a damsel in distress like Driver's art restorer, too stubborn to leave her beloved stained glass windows in the local church. Thankfully, good ol' sheriff Quaid is around, but maybe even he can't resist the temptation of an evacuated town there for the taking. Meanwhile, it's still bucketing. *Speed* screenwriter Graham Yost came up with this nifty spin on the high concept thriller, which puts everything under water several feet deep and rising. *Hard Rain* may not be the most inventive of thriller plots, essentially boiling down to an extended chase with all concerned after the moneybags, but it's extremely impressive as a physical production. TJ

Hard Road

(Colin Finbow, 1989, GB) Francesca Camillo, Max Rennie, John Louis Mansi, Andrew Mulquin, David Savile, Amanda Murray, Peter Bayliss.
90 min.
The tenth feature from the Children's Film Unit centres on the adventures of two bored and disillusioned 13-year-olds: working class Kelly (Camillo), an incessant liar whose favourite pastime is winding up the Children's Help Line about her so-called abusing father; and quiet, withdrawn Max (Rennie), a poor rich kid with a fondness for faking suicides. Kelly persuades Max to take the driving seat of a scarlet 1959 Ferrari he is due to inherit when he's 17) for an illegal spin round the countryside, where the joy of new-found freedom eventually has them settling Crusoe-style deep in the Sussex undergrowth. Although some children will find the pace a trifle slow at times, it's still easily the CFU's best work to date: technically proficient (especially bearing in mind that most of the production team are well under 16), and with shining performances from the children. DA

Hard Target

(John Woo, 1993, US) Jean-Claude Van Damme, Lance Henriksen, Yancy Butler, Arnold Vosloo, Wilford Brimley.
97 min.
Sporting hair extensions and a Cajun accent, Van Damme plays Chance Boudreaux, a drifter who comes to the aid of one Natasha Binder (Butler) as she searches for her transient father in New Orleans. He turns up dead, the luckless prey in a deadly bloodsport: a clandestine safari through the urban jungle in which the very rich hunt and kill derelicts. Matters improve considerably once the hunt is on – the movie's firepower would shame the devil. It's what Hollywood wanted Woo for: bigger, brighter explosions. That we can hope for more is evinced by the film's most memorable sequence: a wounded black man stumbles through a busy main street begging for help, ignored by everyone except his hunters. As the man becomes resigned to his fate, Woo homes in on his face in three arresting jump-cut freeze-frames. The scene doesn't just betray an alien viewpoint, it distils an undertow of social alienation more sharply than any American director would have dreamed of. TCh

Hard Times
(aka The Streetfighter)

(Walter Hill, 1975, US) Charles Bronson, James Coburn, Jill Ireland, Strother Martin, Maggie Blye, Michael McGuire, Robert Tessier.
97 min.
Hill's debut as a director: a surprisingly arresting and tight film about illegal bare-knuckle fighting in Depression era New Orleans. Rather than open up the story with the type of pretentious moralising that bedevils the majority of American sporting and gambling films, this utilises Bronson's limited range to produce a laconic, unemotional, almost Oriental celebration of the mythic fighting hero. Strong supporting performances, good locations, and well-staged fights contribute to what is an impressive example of how to assemble this kind of material. CPe

Hard Times (Tempos Difíceis, Este Tempo)

(Joao Botelho, 1988, Port/GB) Luis Estrela, Julia Britton, Isabel de Castro, Ruy Furtado, Inéz Medeiros.
96 min. b/w.
Botelho's third feature is a modern-day adaptation of Dickens' novel, set in a strangely timeless Lisbon. Constructed for the most part from static tableaux shot in stunning black-and-white, performed with a stylised detachment, and littered with intriguing, even startling narrative ellipses, it is serious but never solemn. Indeed, for all the personal tragedy on view, much of the film is very funny with Dickens' purple and eccentric text (often spoken in voice-over) complemented by and contrasted with Elso Roque's starkly poetic images. It's a tale of jealousy, robbery, and disillusionment; of stern, forbidding patriarchs, downtrodden wives and orphans, and orphans making good, in a world both defined and confined by its unflinching commitment to facts as opposed to feelings. The film's manifest intelligence and profound sense of irony knocks spots off most British literary adaptations, while simultaneously constituting a love letter to cinema itself. GA

Hard to Handle

(Mervyn LeRoy, 1933, US) James Cagney, Mary Brian, Ruth Donnelly, Allen Jenkins, Emma Dunn, Claire Dodd, Robert McWade.
78 min. b/w.
This breezy comedy is a real product of the Depression, with Cagney blustering away as the scheming promotions man ducking and diving his way from fronting marathon dance contests, to pushing new wonder diets and making America grapefruit-conscious (an allusion perhaps to the star's notorious fruit-in-the-face scene from *Public Enemy*). He meets his match in determined mom Donnelly, who's set on marrying him off to daughter Brian, and if the whole thing doesn't make a heck of a lot of sense, at least it speeds along. TJ

Hard to Kill

(Bruce Malmuth, 1990, US) Steven Seagal, Kelly Le Brock, Bill Sadler, Frederick Coffin, Bonnie Burroughs.
96 min.

A routine cop thriller with plenty of bodies but no brains. Waking from a lengthy coma, LA cop Mason Storm (Seagal) swears revenge on the corrupt senator, crooked cops and vicious hoodlums who killed his wife and son and put him to sleep for seven years. With a little TLC from nurse Andy Stewart (LeBrock) and some help from a retired Internal Affairs officer, Storm regains gale force and blows away everyone in sight. he also recovers an incriminating videotape which will put the senator, now aspiring Vice President, behind bars for a long time. While Seagal is spraying bullets, breaking bones and throwing interchangeable bad guys through windows, this has a certain mindless appeal. But Malmuth's flaccid direction lacks the vicious muscularity and authentic edge of Seagal's previous feature, *Nico*; while the poorly integrated romantic subplot – not to mention the drippy, Chuck Norris-style flashback scenes involving the dead wife and son – lead to some awkward, choppy scene transitions. Why do these tough guys always insist on showing their sensitive side too? NF

Hardware

(Richard Stanley, 1990, GB/US) Dylan McDermott, Stacey Travis, John Lynch, William Hootkins, Iggy Pop, Carl McCoy, Mark Northover.
94 min.
In the barren wastelands of the future, a zone trooper stumbles upon the remains of an advanced killing machine, the Mark 13 cyborg. Purchased by rugged space trooper Mo (McDermott) as a gift for his sculptress girlfriend Jill (Travis), the dismembered fragments reconstruct themselves from household appliances, turning Jill's apartment into a combat zone as the reborn machinery goes on the rampage. Former pop-promo director Stanley's feature debut is an impressive assault on the senses, a shamelessly plagiaristic robotics nightmare laden with OTT apocalyptic symbolism and brash cinematic homages, from Argento's *Deep Red* to Cameron's *The Terminator*. Stanley's gaudy vision achieves a roller-coaster pace, swept along by an incessant industrial soundtrack, the perfect backdrop for Image Animation's deliciously fetishistic creation, all pumping pistons and sinewy flex. An energetic, low-budget Pandora's Box of delights, tailor-made for the disposable '90s. MK

Hard Way, The

(John Badham, 1991, US) Michael J Fox, James Woods, Stephen Lang, Annabella Sciorra, Delroy Lindo, Luis Guzmán, Mary Mara, Penny Marshall.
111 min.
Action-man actor Nick Lang (Fox), tired of cartoon characters (his latest is 'Smoking Gunn II') wants to land the part of a gritty New York homicide detective, so his agent fixes up some real-life experience with John Moss (Woods). But this reluctant 'Yoda among cops' has no intention of babysitting, and continues his search for a dangerous killer, all the while dragging the movie star through his chaotic and dangerous life. This light, bright comedy counterbalances Hollywood convention with some very funny swipes at the film industry. A breathtaking opening chase sequence gives way to a gloriously playful, carping exchange between Lang and his agent (Marshall) as they review the current state of Hollywood, ranging from the success of *Henry V* ('It won awards for that little Scottish fellow') to the unstoppable career of Mel Gibson. Badham handles the numerous action sequences with confidence, but the real enjoyment comes from the interplay between the two leads, who revel in the opportunity to send up their images. The ever-amazing Woods recalls *Cop* during speeches about his life, and Fox's 'dickless Tracy' tries to debunk nice-guy McFly. CM

Harem

(Arthur Joffé, 1985, Fr) Nastassja Kinski, Ben Kingsley, Dennis Goldson, Michel Robin, Zohra Segal, Juliette Simpson.
114 min.
It is hard not to be impressed by the single-mindedness of Joffé who, with only a few shorts to his credit, garnered $10 million, Kinski and Kingsley, and made his own movie. Kinski plays a single-minded New York demoiselle, working at full stretch on Wall Street and firmly not on the lookout for 9 weeks of passion. But mysterious gifts begin arriving, and before long she appears to be

a prize catch for the white slave market, waking up one day in an isolated Arabian harem. Fortunately, though, her captor is an educated and lonely prince who has desired her from afar. What might have been an intriguing clash of cultures soon dissipates into a listless drama of will they/won't they, until the Tragic Irony of the finale falls completely flat. Fine credentials (attractive decor by Trauner, delicate photography by De Santis) but little inspiration. DT

Harlan County, U.S.A.
(Barbara Kopple, 1976, US) Nimrod Workman, EB Allen, Bessie Lou Cornett, Jim Thomas.
103 min.
With its plundering of Hollywood narrative conventions – notably an action pic crescendo climax, and establishment 'villains' who could have come straight from Central Casting – Kopple's documentary about a Kentucky miner's strike fails in ways typical of many American political films which strike a chord in the liberal conscience and go on to win Oscars. Harlan County inevitably gets very confused/confusing at times, but there's some extraordinary footage by the courageous crew, and to its credit the film eschews any BBC notions of 'impartiality' or 'balance'. The role of women in the strike (as pickets, debaters about tactics, morale-boosters and strengtheners of solidarity) begs comparison with Salt of the Earth. Required viewing, therefore, but there should have been more analysis and less emotive effect. RM

Harlem Nights
(Eddie Murphy, 1989, US) Eddie Murphy, Richard Pryor, Redd Foxx, Michael Lerner, Danny Aiello, Della Reese.
116 min.
New York 1938, and the city's nocturnal revelries are centered upon Club Sugar Ray, where gambling, booze and hookers are available in equal quantities. Presided over by the paternal Sugar Ray (Pryor) and his hot-headed adopted son Quick (Murphy), the illegal venue's profitable future is threatened when rival clubster Bugsy Calhoune (Lerner) demands a slice of the action, aided and abetted by crooked cop Phil Cantone (Aiello). Resolving to head for pastures new, Ray and Quick plot to stitch up Calhoune and Cantone once and for all before exiting swiftly with the loot. Written, produced, directed by and starring Mr Murphy, Harlem Nights is a bloated period piece, brandishing big production values, one or two good performances (notably Pryor and Aiello), the occasional laugh, and a spectacularly duff sub-Sting storyline that doesn't so much climax as go prematurely limp. Murphy's screenplay abounds with the usual doses of misogynistic dialogue, interspersed with a few gags about people who stutter and multiple use of the word 'motherfucker', all of which are tiresome. the imposing Della Reese meanwhile camps it up as a ball-busting Madame, who says 'Kiss my entire ass' endlessly and beats Murphy up, which is a vicarious delight for all. MK

Harlequin
(Simon Wincer, 1980, Aust) Robert Powell, David Hemmings, Carmen Duncan, Broderick Crawford, Gus Mercurio, Alan Cassell, Mark Spain.
93 min.
The multi-headed beast of international packaging got its fangs into the struggling Australian film industry and spat out this lump of drivelling horror. The potentially interesting notion of re-running the Rasputin legend in the context of a modern political campaign is sunk by a dumb script, a lot of telekinetic flummery, and a performance from Robert Powell which desperately lacks the sense of irony that might at least have transformed his studded leather and mascara into high camp instead of the simply ridiculous. With its English leads, its supporting cast dubbed into American, and its carefully non-specific locations, the whole miserable thing flounders somewhere in mid-Pacific. CPea

Harley Davidson and the Marlboro Man
(Simon Wincer, 1991, US) Mickey Rourke, Don Johnson, Chelsea Field, Daniel Baldwin, Giancarlo Esposito, Vanessa Williams, Tom Sizemore, Julius Harris.
98 min.

Set in sunny Burbank, this disastrous modern Western veers between camp pastiche and po-faced machismo as two tough-but-tenderhearted tearaways accidentally steal some drugs. Pursued by mobsters who want their merchandise back, Harley (Rourke) and Marly (Johnson) bike, smoke, flex biceps, jump off tall buildings, and indulge in various limp male-bonding rituals. They make a ludicrously vain double act, Johnson modelling sporty stetson and kinky boots, Rourke opting for a black-and-red leather jump-suit with his name emblazoned on the back. The baddies, meanwhile, are dressed to kill in fetching ankle-to-neck, wet-look overcoats. Utter rubbish, and badly dressed at that. MK

Harold and Maude
(Hal Ashby, 1971, US) Ruth Gordon, Bud Cort, Vivian Pickles, Cyril Cusack, Charles Tyner, Ellen Geer.
92 min.
Like Bob Rafelson, a director similarly obsessed with the trials and tribulations of the children of the rich, Ashby forever treads the thin line between whimsy and absurdity and 'tough' sentimentality and black comedy. Harold and Maude is the story of a rich teenager (Cort) obsessed with death – his favourite pastime is trying out different mock suicides – who is finally liberated by his (intimate) friendship with Ruth Gordon, an 80-year-old funeral freak. It is most successful when it keeps to the tone of an insane fairystory set up at the beginning of the movie. PH

Harper (aka The Moving Target)
(Jack Smight, 1966, US) Paul Newman, Lauren Bacall, Julie Harris, Arthur Hill, Janet Leigh, Pamela Tiffin, Shelley Winters, Robert Wagner, Robert Webber.
121 min.
Newman plays Ross Macdonald's private eye Lew Harper, a role he was to repeat for Stuart Rosenberg in 1975's The Drowning Pool. William Goldman, in his first solo script credit, plays knowing games with the Chandlerish conventions, while director Smight pumps up the pace and tags along with the allusive casting of Bacall. Enjoyable performances throughout. Just the same, a very minor Big Sleep. PT

Harrad Experiment, The
(Ted Post, 1973, US) James Whitmore, Tippi Hedren, Don Johnson, B Kirby Jr, Laurie Walters, Victoria Thompson, Robert Middleton.
97 min.
Or 'Gidget Meets Masters and Johnson'. Set in an American co-ed college where the pupils are taught self-discovery through sex and (discreet) nudity, the film merges teen romance and sexposé so beguilingly that it ends up as one of the most amusing Hollywood romps since Beyond the Valley of the Dolls. The sexual agonies and dilemmas are straight out of True Romances, and frequently crass; but occasionally they have a lurid authenticity, and Post, who employs long, voyeuristic takes, reveals more gusto here than one would ever have thought possible from his previous work. The film, with its incredibly awful theme song and old-fashioned conception of sexological research, well deserves the cult success it had in America. DP

Harriet the Spy
(Bronwen Hughes, 1996, US) Michelle Trachtenberg, Gregory Smith, Vanessa Lee Chester, Rosie O'Donnell, Eartha Kitt, J Smith-Cameron, Robert Joy, Charlotte Sullivan.
101 min.
Adapted from Louise Fitzhugh's 1964 novel about a determined 11-year-old, this primary-coloured piece is a sweet but flawed take on the inspirational children's film. Harriet (Trachtenberg) is indeed a spy – self-employed – roaming the neighbourhood, observing life in all its multi-cultural glory, and taking comprehensive readings in her private notebook. She wants to remember everything, because she's going to be a writer. Meet her world: best friends Janie (Lee Chester), a budding home chemist, and Sport (Smith), a house-kid tending to his starving-writer dad; the rest of her class, including prim Marion, class president; her well-to-do parents; and her guiding light, nanny Golly (O'Donnell).

That's the set-up. Pity it takes most of an hour, without proposing where we might be going. Much of the Nickelodeon-assembled cast and crew share a background in commercials, and it shows: good-looking, insistently hip 'fun' – it's also quite boring. Then Marion steals Harriet's notebook, reads out her rather hurtful character assessments of her friends; they take revenge; Harriet takes her revenge; everyone shuns her; her parents get worried and stop her note-taking; bad emotions take hold…and we have a story. Engaging dilemmas, solutions, experiences – great. And maybe it was worth the wait, but the wait wasn't needed. NB

Harry & Son
(Paul Newman, 1984, US) Paul Newman, Robby Benson, Ellen Barkin, Wilford Brimley, Judith Ivey, Ossie Davis, Joanne Woodward.
117 min.
Taken sequence by sequence, this is a well acted and elegantly photographed social drama, with Newman as a depressed widower who loses his job and quarrels with his kids. The plot is a little thin, but Big Acting Scene follows Big Acting Scene quite pleasantly for a while, until you begin to realise that Newman (who co-scripted as well as directed) has decided to compose his entire film out of them. It is nothing more than a constant succession of the kind of emotional peaks actors love to do on screen. Humbler scenes involving background or narrative, which may be immensely tedious to act but help the plot unfold, have in general been left out altogether. The result is a curiously indigestible phenomenon, like being forced to eat five courses of avocado by an overbearing dinner-party host. DP

Harry and the Hendersons (aka Bigfoot and the Hendersons)
(William Dear, 1987, US) John Lithgow, Melinda Dillon, Margaret Langrick, Joshua Rudoy, Kevin Peter Hall, David Suchet, Don Ameche, M Emmet Walsh.
111 min.
'A William Dear Film'? Come off it, this has Steven Spielberg, whose Amblin company produced, written all over it. While the Hendersons are on a hunting holiday, their car collides with the legendary Bigfoot of the Pacific Northwest. Mistakenly believing the Yeti-like creature dead, they take him to their Seattle home, which he promptly demolishes before proving himself a genial giant of enormous compassion. Nevertheless, nosey neighbours and fame-hungry hunters smell something suspicious, and pretty soon the gun-crazy citizens of Seattle are on the trail of the hapless, hirsute 'Harry'. This cloying mixture of sitcom and fantasy is clearly designed to pluck the heart-strings, tickle the funnybone, and sow seeds of doubt about the moral worth of hunting. GA

Harry and Tonto
(Paul Mazursky, 1974, US) Art Carney, Ellen Burstyn, Chief Dan George, Geraldine Fitzgerald, Larry Hagman, Arthur Hunnicutt, Joshua Mostel.
115 min.
Mazursky's odyssey traces elderly widower Harry's flight/trip across America with cat Tonto after the demolition of his NY apartment. It's Candide again, with Harry not so much an innocent as a sympathetic, who is mugged, seduced, welcomed, depended upon, rejected, ever so gently. Its charm has a calculated feel, though, its individualities an edge of whimsy, its poetry is rhyming couplets. Harry's freedom to mix it with the kids, squeezing out their oppressed parents, is hammered home. Still, Mazursky has escaped Fellini's shadow; when everyone's back from going to 'look for America', he might have something interesting to say. SG

Harry and Walter Go to New York
(Mark Rydell, 1976, US) James Caan, Elliott Gould, Michael Caine, Diane Keaton, Charles Durning, Lesley Ann Warren, Val Avery, Jack Gilford.
123 min.
A caper film set in the 1890s whose weightily established period atmosphere (carefully gaslit interiors, tones of muted brown and gold) creates

a mausoleum-like environment in which all attempts at comedy die the death. The disastrous casting of Caan and Gould as a variety song-and-dance act – unsuccessful, as they demonstrate only too effectively – dooms the project further. There is some fleetingly acute re-creation of the mores of the upper crust of the criminal world, a climax of chaotic mayhem, and a neatly dotty performance from Lesley Ann Warren. The film provides its own epitaph when Caine's underworld star, asked why he keeps on cracking safes, remarks that 'every cell tingles with the possibility of failure'. Failure realised, and with precious little tingle. VG

Harry In Your Pocket
(Bruce Geller, 1973, US) James Coburn, Michael Sarrazin, Trish Van Devere, Walter Pidgeon, Michael C Gwynne, Tony Giorgio.
103 min.
Coburn as a jet-set pickpocket in a film that looks as if it should have been sold straight to the TV networks. Too much time is devoted to the least interesting aspect of the story, a rather silly love triangle involving Coburn, Sarrazin and Devere. Coburn's profession demands that he remain a cipher in the society in which he has chosen to operate, but this implication is never developed; and too little time is devoted to the art of the professional pickpocket at work, something else that would have made for a more interesting time. CPe

Harvest, The
(David Marconi, 1992, US) Miguel Ferrer, Leilani Sarelle, Harvey Fierstein, Henry Silva.
97 min.
One of those moody thrillers where down-on-his-luck gringo (Ferrer's blocked scriptwriter) heads down to Mexico and finds himself involved with a femme fatale, corrupt officialdom and various seedy ex-pats. Nothing very original, then, although there's a nice twist when Ferrer wakes to find himself short of one kidney. The hothouse atmosphere, boozy interludes and fishing-nets on the beach suggest that Marconi has seen the likes of *The Big Steal* and *Out of the Past* once too often. GA

Harvey
(Henry Koster, 1950, US) James Stewart, Josephine Hull, Cecil Kellaway, Peggy Dow, Jesse White, Charles Drake, Wallace Ford.
104 min. b/w.
Stewart in his batty but amiable persona as small-town boozer Elwood P Dowd, who imagines a close friendship with a 'pooka' (a mischievous familiar of Irish folklore), in this case a 6' 4" white rabbit called Harvey. His anxious sister (Hull) tries to get him certified, and the film suggests that the fantasy is quite harmless. Charming, lightweight stuff so long as you can take Stewart's ingenuousness, but it does wear thin. GA

Harvey Girls, The
(George Sidney, 1946, US) Judy Garland, John Hodiak, Ray Bolger, Angela Lansbury, Virginia O'Brien, Preston Foster, Marjorie Main, Kenny Baker.
101 min.
A likeable but aimless musical which doesn't know what to make of its plot (designed to cash in on the pioneer spirit of *Oklahoma!*) about the Harvey House restaurants which followed the railroad into the West, bringing demure waitresses into the domain of rowdy saloon girls. The highly inappropriate Harry Warren/Johnny Mercer songs are mostly romantic numbers or specialties for the deadpan O'Brien, with even the bustling 'On the Atchison, Topeka and the Santa Fe' failing to rouse any real echoes of the Western. It is symptomatic that the film's best and most legitimate number, with Angela Lansbury leading a saloon girl chorus of 'Oh, You Kid', is thrown away in favour of a dialogue exchange between Garland and Hodiak which could well have waited. TM

Harvey Middleman, Fireman
(Ernest Pintoff, 1965, US) Gene Troobnick, Hermione Gingold, Patricia Harty, Arlene Golonka, Will Mackenzie, Charles Durning.
76 min.
In animator Pintoff's first live-action feature, Harvey is a fireman with a nice wife, nice children, nice house. He rescues a girl, falls in love

with her, has attacks of conscience, and cools it; whereupon the girl stages another fire, falls into the arms of another fireman, and Harvey goes happily back to his domestic routine. At first this simple story is used as a peg for very effective humour derived from the contrast between the mundane, frightening 'normalness' of Harvey's daily routine, and the pride in it which he confides to camera in a series of monologues. But the film changes direction, and what started as sharp, subtle satire on a 'normal' American ends up as little more than standard domestic comedy, complete with pat happy ending. JC

Has Anybody Seen My Gal?
(Douglas Sirk, 1952, US) Charles Coburn, Piper Laurie, Rock Hudson, Gigi Perreau, Lynn Bari, Larry Gates, Skip Homeier.
89 min.
One of a projected series of films about small town America, this was Sirk's first in colour. Coburn plays an eccentric millionaire investigating the Blaisdell family, to whom he is thinking of leaving all his money. The $100,000 he gives them as a test goes to the parents' heads, but the children and their commonsensical values save the day. From this perspective the film is an admirable companion piece to *All That Heaven Allows*. In contrast to the devastating view of selfish children and mean-minded respectable citizens of that film, *Has Anybody Seen My Gal?* is one of Sirk's gentler – and lesser – works, making charming use of its '20s setting and songs. James Dean made his brief debut in one of the drugstore scenes. PH

Hasta Morir (Until Death)
(Fernando Sarinana, 1994, Mex) Demian Bichir, Juan Manuel Bernal, Vanessa Bruche, Veronica Merchant.
100 min.
Well-directed, effective contemporary tragidrama of disenchanted Mexico City youth focusing on two friends since childhood. One is a cool criminal dude with a 'Pachucho' tattoo, a pork-pie hat and a belief in knives (a noble weapon) rather than guns; the other a weak vessel with an dog who adopts an empty machismo when the pressure builds following a store robbery. Blending familar staples such as the Cain and Abel story, the doppelgänger and the conventions of the US ghetto movie, writer/director Sarinana nevertheless manages to turns a fresh eye on notions of couth and cool for today's barrio boys. Its enjoyable music track of acoustic guitar rock and Mexican-style funk sets the tone perfectly. No masterpiece, but it keeps you involved. WH

Hasty Heart, The
(Vincent Sherman, 1949, GB) Richard Todd, Patricia Neal, Ronald Reagan, Anthony Nicholls, Howard Marion Crawford, Ralph Michael, Orlando Martins.
107 min. b/w.
Leaden version of John Patrick's tearjerking play, set in a World War II army hospital in Burma, about a dour, chip-on-shoulder Scottish soldier who gradually discovers the meaning of friendship after learning that he has only weeks to live. Todd won some plaudits at the time for his stubborn performance, but subsequent appearances confirmed that the wooden look was habitual. TM

Hatari!
(Howard Hawks, 1962, US) John Wayne, Elsa Martinelli, Hardy Kruger, Red Buttons, Gérard Blain, Michèle Girardon, Bruce Cabot.
159 min.
Marked by the relaxed pace and tone of Hawks' later work, this could easily be seen as *Only Angels Have Wings* transferred from the Andes to the African bush. There's little plot but plenty of typically Hawksian situations as it follows the travails of a group of safari hunters (preservationists, not killers) working a game reserve. All the usual themes emerge as gently and naturally as bubbles from champagne: the need for professionalism and self-respect; the importance of the group and integration; attraction between men and women seen as conflict; and (echoing *Monkey Business* and *Bringing Up Baby*) asides on humans as animals. Light, sunny, and effortlessly switching between action and comedy, it also fascinates through its superb footage of the actual capture of the wildlife, in which the dan-

ger and the excitement of the chase are beautifully, precisely evoked. All in all, one of those rare films that genuinely constitutes a 'late masterpiece'. GA

Hatchet Man, The (aka The Honourable Mr Wong)
(William Wellman, 1932, US) Edward G Robinson, Loretta Young, Dudley Digges, Blanche Frederici, Leslie Fenton, Tully Marshall, J Carrol Naish.
74 min. b/w.
Robinson is the hit man of the title, a Chinaman who has made it as an American businessman, and who is called back to his traditional responsibilities when a Tong War breaks out in San Francisco. To complicate matters, his task is to kill his best friend, and he must then look after the latter's daughter. It's a subject that would surely have excited Sam Fuller. As handled by Wellman, the idea of friendship and responsibility is called into question rather than that of cultural identity. An intriguing film. PH

Hate
see Haine, La

Hatter's Castle
(Lance Comfort, 1941, GB) Robert Newton, Emlyn Williams, James Mason, Deborah Kerr, Beatrice Varley, Henry Oscar, Anthony Bateman.
102 min. b/w.
An entertaining slice of Victorian melodrama adapted from AJ Cronin's novel. Not quite Gothic, but edging that way through Newton's performance (one of his more controlled efforts) as the social-climbing Glasgow hatter who builds himself an opulent mansion, sets about keeping his family in line with a brutal relish that would have made Mr Barrett of Wimpole Street wince, and ends up in madness and conflagration. Damped down by flat direction, but the sets and camera-work are excellent. TM

Haunted
(Lewis Gilbert, 1995, GB) Aidan Quinn, Kate Beckinsale, Anthony Andrews, Simon Lowe, Anna Massey, Liz Smith, John Gielgud.
107 min.
Adapted from James Herbert's novel by veteran Lewis Gilbert, this old-fashioned ghost story benefits from craftsmanship, but lacks atmosphere and imagination. All is present and correct, from the Edwardian pile where things go bump in the night, to the ghostly figures by a moonlit lake. Quinn brings an emotional dimension to the professional sceptic David Ash whose rational beliefs are challenged by a confrontation with the spiritual world. Summoned to Edbrook House by dotty servant Miss Webb (Massey), David's drawn into the intrigues of its other three inhabitants, Christina and the brothers Robert (Andrews) and Simon (Lowe). Unsettled by the weird goings-on, David starts to lose his grip on reality. Massey's twitchy, unhinged old lady sets the tone for what will follow, while Beckinsale's sexy Christina fuses childlike recklessness with adult manipulation. Ironically, as the shocking revelations and sfx kick in with a vengeance, it's Quinn's disintegrating professor who holds things together, his outstanding performance a solid dramatic axis around which things spin wildly out of control. NF

Haunted
(Michael Roemer, 1984, US) Brooke Adams, Jon De Vries, Ari Meyers, Trish Van Devere, Mark Arnott, Scottie Bloch, Roseanna Cox.
118 min.
With Brooke Adams in fine form as the young woman fleeing an unhappy marriage and taking refuge with a family in a more drastic state of disintegration than her own, this out-and-out melodrama sees her confronting as heavy a mix of cruelty, confusion and incipient insanity as Barbara Stanwyck ever had to face in the '50s. Far darker than the likes of *Dallas* and *Dynasty* (since it avoids their drossy gloss and plasticky plotting), it impresses due to a careful script, superb naturalistic performances, and – perhaps most importantly – a profound and rare awareness that upset/unbalanced people sorely in need of help are very often a total pain in the ass. GA

h

Haunted and the Hunted, The
see Dementia 13

Haunted Honeymoon
(Gene Wilder, 1986, US) Gene Wilder, Gilda Radner, Dom DeLuise, Jonathan Pryce, Paul L Smith, Peter Vaughan, Bryan Pringle.
84 min. PG.
In the opening scene of this comedy chiller, a sinister spectre, seen only from his white spats down, kicks a loveable family dog. After which it's familiar formula: stick a group of loonies in a draughty mansion, kill one of them off, and kill the lights, with honeymoon couple Wilder and Radner – 1939 stars of radio's *Manhattan Mystery Theatre* – present because he's set to inherit if he can survive the night. Wilder, of course, is playing with genre here, and while it's familiar (Mel Brooks with *Young Frankenstein*, gets his fingers burnt. It's flat, unfunny, and full of slavish borrowings. SGo

Haunted Palace, The
(Roger Corman, 1963, US) Vincent Price, Debra Paget, Lon Chaney, Frank Maxwell, Leo Gordon, Elisha Cook, John Dierkes.
86 min.
This supposed version of Poe's poem, beautifully scripted by Charles Beaumont with a good deal more than a dash of Lovecraft's *The Case of Charles Dexter Ward*, boasts a superb performance from Price as a New England warlock who is burned alive for his evil practices, though not before putting a curse on his tormentors. In due course he returns, taking over the body of his great-great-grandson to wreak a picturesque revenge, well-flavoured with ground fogs, creaking doors, cobwebs, electrical storms and mutant monsters. If there is a flaw, it is that Daniel Haller's art direction rings too few changes on the style he established in *House of Usher;* but Corman, with his prowling camera omnivorously probing the darker recesses of nightmare, paces his direction to perfection. TM

Haunted Strangler, The
see Grip of the Strangler

Haunted Summer
(Ivan Passer, 1988, US) Philip Anglim, Laura Dern, Alice Krige, Eric Stoltz, Alexander Winter.
106 min.
As in Ken Russell's *Gothic*, it is the summer of 1816. Shelley, his lover Mary Goodwin, and her half-sister Claire Clairmont, gather at the Hôtel d'Angleterre in Secheron, where who should turn up but Lord Byron. We can tell that Shelley (Stoltz) is an untrammelled spirit because he flashes his willy in a waterfall, and that Byron (Anglim) is a free-thinker because he smokes opium provided by his adoring catamite Dr Polidori (Winter). When they have nothing better to do, the queer quintet attempt to scare the hell out of each other in the dungeons of Chillon castle, but all that comes out is yawns. Quivering glances, sensitive silences, pretty photography, and Haydn harmonies do not in themselves make a film serious. Passer, who directed the excellent *Cutter's Way*, has turned coy here, opting for soft lighting, soft focus, and shots through sheets of gauze for the sedate sex scenes. MS

Haunting, The
(Robert Wise, 1963, GB) Julie Harris, Claire Bloom, Richard Johnson, Russ Tamblyn, Fay Compton, Rosalie Crutchley, Lois Maxwell, Valentine Dyall.
112 min. b/w.
Often overwrought in its performances, this adaptation of Shirley Jackson's novel *The Haunting of Hill House* – a group of people gather in a large old house to determine whether or not a poltergeist is the source of rumours that it is haunted – still manages to produce its fair share of frissons. What makes the film so effective is not so much the slightly sinister characterisation of the generally neurotic group, but the fact that Wise makes the house itself the central character, a beautifully designed and highly atmospheric entity which, despite the often annoyingly angled camerawork, becomes genuinely frightening. At its best, the film is a pleasing reminder that Wise served his apprenticeship under Val Lewton at RKO. GA

Haunting of Julia, The
see Full Circle

Hauptdarsteller, Der
see Main Actor, The

Havana
(Sydney Pollack, 1990, US) Robert Redford, Lena Olin, Raúl Julia, Alan Arkin, Tomás Milián, Daniel Davis, Richard Farnsworth, Mark Rydell.
145 min.
Cuba, 1958. Revolution is in the air, American gangsters and corrupt politicians enjoy a last taste of unrestrained capitalism. Slick gambler Jack Weil (Redford) prefers poker to politics, but then he meets glamorous Swedish revolutionary Bobby (Olin) and her rich husband (Julia). Suddenly he's making radical gestures, braving financial loss and life-threatening situations in a bid to save her from dictator Batista's men. Redford's seventh collaboration with Pollack has a romantic, dramatic sweep which glosses over some of the most intense scenes. Crisp, luminous images alternate with dusty filters to help create a sense of heightened reality. Sexual attraction leads to political awareness; the speed at which the central relationship develops provides an indication of social change, with Bobby betraying her class and Jack forced to acknowledge some difficult truths about himself. But the whole thing lacks conviction. CM

Having a Wild Weekend
see Catch Us If You Can

Having It All
(Edward Zwick, 1982, US) Dyan Cannon, Barry Newman, Hart Bochner, Melanie Chartoff, Sylvia Sidney.
100 min.
Glossy comedy featuring high fashion and the jet set life. Guilt-ridden Thera (Cannon), a rich, successful fashion designer, has a cool, sophisticated spouse in New York, and an artistic, passionate one in LA. Her personality changes too, one can tell by the changes in hairstyle from soignée to rampant curls. Bedroom doors are out of date, and it's more a question of popping in and out of airports, and even then you can get caught. Naturally the first husband finally wins out, and the comedy follows its predictable course unto its dreary end. Made for cable TV, it should have stayed there. JE

Hawaii
(George Roy Hill, 1966, US) Max von Sydow, Julie Andrews, Richard Harris, Carroll O'Connor, Torin Thatcher, Gene Hackman, Jocelyn La Garde.
186 min.
A sprawling adaptation of James A Michener's doorstop novel about an 1820s Yale divinity student (Sydow) who becomes a missionary to the underdeveloped Hawaiian islands. The conflict between naïve dogma and naïve innocence is effectively established, but the spectacle is always broader than it is deep. Dashing sea captain Harris' desire for Sydow's friendly, outgoing wife (Andrews) provides the love interest, the storm scene a much-needed dose of riproaring spectacle. NF

Hawk, The
(David Hayman, 1992, GB) Helen Mirren, George Costigan, Rosemary Leach, Owen Teale, Melanie Hill.
86 min.
Annie Marsh (Mirren) fears her husband (Costigan) may be the serial killer whom the media have dubbed 'The Hawk'. But is the father of her children – a roving service engineer – capable of bludgeoning women to death and gouging out their eyes? Hayman's low-key direction of Peter Ransley's script (from his own novel) and Andrew Dunn's moody urban photography work well in developing Mirren's escalating paranoia. But with so much of the detail taken directly from the Yorkshire Ripper case, it seems absurd and disorienting when, in a departure from both real and fictional sources, Annie finally finds the strength to turn the tables on her husband. GA

Hawks
(Robert Ellis Miller, 1988, GB) Timothy Dalton, Anthony Edwards, Janet McTeer, Camille Coduri, Jill Bennett, Robert Lang.
110 min.

It's a worthy idea: a dark comedy about two men, in their prime but terminally ill in hospital, who decide to live their last days to the full. So in surgeon's greens and hijacked ambulance, the handsome lawyer (Dalton) and American football player (Edwards) make for Amsterdam with the intention of bonking their balls off in a brothel. Waylaid, however, by a couple of Sharons (McTeer, Coduri), they discover that nice girls will do it for the dying with a glad heart and kinky négligée. Miller's attempts to set a life-affirming tone hit hysteria, although the script by Roy Clarke (*Last of the Summer Wine*) doesn't help, with its relentless innuendo and offensively stereotyped characters dragging the humour through black to blue. Ultimately, the over-zealous exploitation of anything that might make an unappealing subject more commercial kills the film. EP

Hawks and the Sparrows, The
see Uccellacci e Uccellini

Hawk the Slayer
(Terry Marcel, 1980, GB) Jack Palance, John Terry, Bernard Bresslaw, Ray Charleson, Peter O'Farrell, Patricia Quinn, Morgan Sheppard, Harry Andrews, Roy Kinnear, Patrick Magee.
94 min.
Somewhere in the mists of time (or dry ice to you and me), Hawk the Slayer (Terry) roamed a land of painted backdrops, cardboard castles, and gauze-infested forests, fighting Evil and bringing Peace. His team: a dwarf, an elf, a giant, and a witch who can turn a useful trick or two. His opponents: the rest of the world captained by big brother Palance, a dirty player if ever there was one. The object of the game: kill each other. The wonder of it is that the cast can deliver their lines without cracking up. It is all so unbelievably tacky that it almost works. FF

Häxan
see Witchcraft Through the Ages

Head
(Bob Rafelson, 1968, US) The Monkees (Micky Dolenz, David Jones, Mike Nesmith, Peter Tork), Victor Mature, Annette Funicello, Timothy Carey, Logan Ramsey.
85 min.
Rafelson's first feature, made when Monkee mania had all but died, *Head* proved too experimental for the diminishing weenybop audience which had lapped up the ingenious TV series. It flopped dismally in the US, and only achieved belated release here. Despite obviously dated aspects like clumsy psychedelic effects and some turgid slapstick sequences, the film is still remarkably vital and entertaining. Rafelson (who helped to create the group), together with Jack Nicholson (co-writer and co-producer), increased the TV show's picaresque tempo while also adding more adult, sardonic touches. The calculated manipulation behind the phenomenon is exposed at the start, when the Monkees metaphorically commit suicide. The typical zany humour is intercut with harsher political footage and satire on established genres of American cinema, exploding many a sacred cow into the bargain. IB

Head Above Water
(Jim Wilson, 1997, US/GB) Harvey Keitel, Cameron Diaz, Craig Sheffer, Billy Zane, Shay Duffin.
92 min.
Alone in a remote holiday beach house in Maine, while her judge husband (Keitel) and local childhood friend (Sheffer) go sea-fishing, ex-party girl Diaz is visited by old flame Zane – whose dead body she finds next morning on the living room couch. Keitel's miscast as a pipe-chewing father figure, while Diaz, clad mostly in a one-piece yellow swimsuit, is left floundering in the shallows of a script which relies on ludicrous human behaviour and mechanical plot twists, the latter signposted by an over-emphatic score. (Remake of Nils Gaup's superior black comic thriller *Hodet Over Vannet*, 1993.) NF

Headhunter
(Francis Schaeffer, 1990, US) Kay Lenz, Wayne Crawford, John Fatooh, Steve Kanaly, June Chadwick, Sam Williams.
92 min.
A complete non-starter of a horror movie featur-

ing a quite astonishing dearth of imagination: a pagan beast comes to Boston, kills off a lot of people, and then gets defeated in hand-to-hand combat with two cops. End of story. A subplot about one of the cops (Crawford) discovering that his wife is a lesbian comes and goes, leaving you wondering if somebody switched movies on you. Gratuitous tedium. MK

Head On
(aka Fatal Attraction)
(Michael Grant, 1980, Can) Stephen Lack, Sally Kellerman, John Huston, Lawrence Dane, John Peter Linton.
98 min.
Stephen Lack, star of *Scanners*, and Sally Kellerman, her usual off-beam self, meet after a car crash and begin to act out their sexual fantasies. The process starts by taking inspiration from children's stories, but develops into something more dangerous. Much of this misfires, but there are sparks of interest. (Released in the US in 1985 – would you believe –as *Fatal Attraction*.) TJ

Head Over Heels
(Joan Micklin Silver, 1979, US) John Heard, Mary Beth Hurt, Peter Riegert, Kenneth McMillan, Gloria Grahame, Nora Heflin, Jerry Hardin.
98 min.
Occasionally engaging romantic comedy (based on Ann Beattie's novel *Chilly Scenes of Winter*), with Heard as the Salt Lake City civil servant doing his damnedest to win back the woman with whom he had an affair the year before. The trouble is, she's not too sure about his idolisation of her, nor of whether she wants to leave her husband. Strong naturalistic performances and an unforced script keep the ogre of wackiness at bay, although – as in *Between the Lines* – Silver's attitude all too often becomes rather ingratiatingly indulgent towards the determinedly 'nice' characters, resulting in a soft, mushy centre. GA

Health
(Robert Altman, 1979, US) Lauren Bacall, Glenda Jackson, Carol Burnett, James Garner, Dick Cavett, Paul Dooley, Donald Moffat, Henry Gibson.
102 min.
Never released theatrically in Britain, and widely considered as exemplifying the trap into which Altman's free-wheeling, loosely structured social comedies were sooner or later destined to fall, *Health* nonetheless has its admirers who claim that the movie's incidental jokes justify the thinness of the storyline. It's about a health foods convention in Florida, where leading lights from the yoghurt and museli industries are competing for the presidency of the national organisation. Jackson plays her butch number, complete with cigar; Bacall plays an 83-year-old virgin (!); Garner contributes his engagingly wry *Rockford* persona; Burnett and Gibson are reliably wacky. But Altman's character-based, semi-improvised plotting, so successful in *Nashville*, misses its target more often than it scores. MA

Health Warning (Da Leitai)
(Kirk Wong, 1983, HK) Wong Lung-Wai, Ko Hung, Ray Lui, Venus Nguyen, Monica Lam, Alexandre Lee, Tsui Kam-Kong.
83 min.
Kirk Wong's most daring film: a deeply cynical take on the kung-fu genre crossed with dystopian sci-fi and an attitude towards sexual kinks straight out of an early Lou Reed song. Ray Lui (the nominal hero) is killed off early, allowing the chunky Wong Lung-Wai to move centre stage as the stolid but highly corruptible fighter who takes on transvestites, robotic dykes, newly synthesised hallucinogens and neo-Nazi megalomaniacs. This is what the French mean by *film maudit*. TR

Hear My Song
(Peter Chelsom, 1991, GB) Ned Beatty, Adrian Dunbar, Shirley Anne Field, Tara Fitzgerald, William Hootkins, Harold Berens, David McCallum, John Dair, Stephen Marcus.
105 min.
Loosely inspired by events in the life of Irish tenor Josef Locke, Chelsom's first feature is an 'old-fashioned' comedy whose shameless stabs at cockle-warming charm make for a sludge of ingratiating whimsy. Liverpool club owner Micky O'Neill

(Dunbar, who co-wrote with Chelsom) is in a fix. His inability to say 'I love you' has provoked a walk-out by his girlfriend Nancy (Fitzgerald), and his ambitious plans to revive the club's fortunes by bringing back tax exile Locke (Beatty) go awry: the singer he has booked is an imposter (Hootkins) who takes advantage of Locke's old flame Cathleen (Field), who happens to be Nancy's mum. Micky's dreams can be fulfilled only if he tracks down the real Locke in Ireland and tempts him to Liverpool for one last concert. It's hard to fathom why this film was received so warmly. Despite Beatty's sterling performance, the overall tone is one of maudlin blarney. GA

Hear No Evil
(Robert Greenwald, 1993, US) Marlee Matlin, Martin Sheen, DB Sweeney, John C McGinley, Christina Carlisi, Greg Elam.
97 min.
Journalist McGinley finds a valuable ancient coin, stolen in a daring heist, and hides it in the bleeper of his deaf physical-trainer. When the journalist meets with an explosive 'accident', the physical-trainer, Matlin, doesn't know she's been left carrying the booty. But crooked psycho-cop Sheen does. Only reliable restaurateur Sweeney can save the day. A ludicrous variation on *Wait Until Dark* in which Matlin and Sweeney remain laudable deadpan, while Sheen goes swiftly into rent-a-mental overdrive. MK

Hearse, The
(George Bowers, 1980, US) Trish Van Devere, Joseph Cotten, David Gautreaux, Donald Hotton.
100 min.
Still recovering from a mental collapse, Devere moves to an inherited house in a small town, an antique hearse keeps driving up at night, and, to add to her troubles, a diary suggests that she is related to a witch possessed by the devil. Standard guff.

Heartaches
(Donald Shebib, 1981, Can) Margot Kidder, Annie Potts, Robert Carradine, Winston Rekert, George Touliatos.
93 min.
Winsome (female) buddy movie which offers a roundly satisfying tragi-comic role to Kidder, but substantially less to its audience. The plot hinges on plain-looking Potts running away from her track-racer husband (Carradine) and shacking up with Kidder in downtown Toronto. One-time great hope of Canadian cinema, Shebib contents himself with schematic contrasts between the two women's approach to sex, and a sentimental excursion into an Italian immigrant community. Anyone homesick for Toronto might find compensations in the location photography; but if you ask more of a movie, this one is not answering. MA

Heart Beat
(John Byrum, 1979, US) Nick Nolte, Sissy Spacek, John Heard, Ray Sharkey, Anne Dusenberry, Margaret Fairchild, Tony Bill.
108 min.
A minor (low budget) gem, with Nolte ambling ruefully through twenty years of the American Dream as Neal Cassady, the superman-hero-hobo-lover of Jack Kerouac's *On the Road*. Based on the autobiography of Carolyn Cassady (who is played with calm brilliance by Spacek), the movie centres on her triangular life with two men, warily sidestepping the hype and narcissism of Beat mythology and the parallel temptation to indulge in an essay on Literary Genius. Instead, out of an episodic narrative emerges a quiet contemplation of the vast spaces and suburban dreams of the postwar period, a glowingly designed, occasionally tacky epic of America from the Bomb to the Pill. CA

Heart, Beating in the Dark
(Yamiutsu Shinzo)
(Shunichi Nagasaki, 1982, Jap) Shigeru Muroi, Takeshi Naito, Taro Suwa, Tesuji Onda.
75 min.
A boy and a girl in a room, seemingly on the run from something. Are they in love? They fuck compulsively, and their sex has a disturbing edge of sado-masochism. They enact 'flashbacks' to their pasts, but it's the girl who speaks the boy's

aggressive, 'macho' lines and vice versa. What brought them there is finally revealed in a terrifying monologue. It often plays like a 'wrong side of the tracks' answer to Oshima's *In the Realm of the Senses*: a love story which is brutal, messy, hopeless and finally horrifying, but a love story none the less. (Shot on Super-8, transferred to video.) TR

Heartbreakers
(Bobby Roth, 1984, US) Peter Coyote, Nick Mancuso, Carole Laure, Max Gail, James Laurenson, Carol Wayne, Kathryn Harrold.
99 min.
Blue is an angry young artist, facing up to the departure of his long-time girlfriend. His greatest buddy is Eli, a handsome, reluctant rich boy desperate to be in love. Written and directed with tremendous assurance, Roth's first commercial feature deals with the close friendships splintered by the competitive instincts of dissatisfied souls, and the secret jealousies and impulsive attractions that cause the greatest wounds. There are brilliant lead performances from Coyote and Mancuso; fine too are Laure, and James Laurenson as a campy art dealer. Add a pulsating Tangerine Dream score and Michael Ballhaus' glowing photography, and the result is an emotional cocktail that is provocative, touching and witty as hell. DT

Heartbreakers, The
(Die Heartbreakers)
(Peter F Bringmann, 1983, WGer) Sascha Disselkamp, Mary Ketikidou, Uwe Enkelmann, Michael Klein, Mark Eichenseher, Hartmut Isselhorst.
114 min.
It's 1964, and bitten by the Beatle bug from Berlin to Bavaria, kids are buying guitars, forming groups with English names, and setting out to emulate the Fab Four. One such band is Die Heartbreakers: four pimply individuals, their pint-sized impresario and chanteuse excluded on the grounds that Mick Jagger would never have shared the stage with a girl. Bringmann tells their story with droll humour, drawing unforced performances from his cast of young unknowns, and playing the gigs and gags out against interesting locations. A likeable, unassuming movie whose very passable renditions of '60s classics will bring a glow of nostalgia to anyone who was there, and perhaps a flash of pleasurable surprise to those too young to remember. SJo

Heartbreak Island
(Qunian Dongtian)
(Hsu Hsiao-Ming, 1995, Tai) Vicky Wei, King Jieh-Wen, Chang Ching-Ju, Tsai Chen-Nan.
120 min.
An intelligent but rather studied film about idealism and its betrayal, set against the 'Formosa Incident' (a troubled pro-democracy rally of the '70s) and its aftermath. A woman is released from prison where she was locked up for a decade or so for terrorism; in seeking out friends and colleagues, and the lover who inspired her to become an activist, she comes painfully to realise that not only the world but people's feelings have changed. The movie, beautifully acted and visualised, is a blend of the personal and political, somewhat in the style of Hou Hsiao-hsien, but lacking the resonance and emotional punch that make Hou's films so compelling. GA

Heartbreak Kid, The
(Elaine May, 1972, US) Charles Grodin, Cybill Shepherd, Jeannie Berlin, Eddie Albert, Audra Lindley, William Prince.
106 min.
Marital comedy with its characters distanced just enough to prevent the barbs coming too close to home. Lenny (Grodin) woos and weds Lila (Berlin), only to have his carefully nurtured pre-wedding romantic ideas bite the dust from the moment the ceremony is concluded. His inaccessible goddess becomes the all too accessible Lila, gorging herself on egg salad sandwiches, getting sunburned, and generally behaving like a normal human being. It's too much for Lenny, stuck as he is in a state of pre-wedding hots. He finds another object for his fantasies (Shepherd), and pursues her with a kind of crass desperation all the way to her midwest college, where she is, as expected, every football hero's dream date. Wittily directed by May, and neatly scripted by

Neil Simon (from Bruce Jay Friedman's story *A Change of Plan*), though somewhere the film loses its thread and forgets how to draw things decently to a close. VG

Heartbreak Ridge

(Clint Eastwood, 1986, US) Clint Eastwood, Marsha Mason, Everett McGill, Moses Gunn, Eileen Heckart, Bo Svenson, Boyd Gaines.
130 min.
After three tours in Vietnam, gunnery sergeant Tom Highway (Eastwood) approaches retirement, and is assigned to the Reconnaissance Platoon where he started. Alas, the US Marines are now run by penpushers, theorists and time-servers; so when Grenada looms, there is only Highway between his rookies and a row of body-bags. In format, this is no more than the classic mission movie: first they train, then they do it for real. But the film belongs to Eastwood. Now looking increasingly like an Easter Island statue, he has a voice pickled in bourbon, a tongue like razor wire, and a body so full of shrapnel that he can't walk through airport metal detectors. When he isn't putting his men through hell, he is sobering up in the brig or reading women's magazines to get a clue on how to speak to his ex-wife. CPea

Heartburn

(Mike Nichols, 1986, US) Meryl Streep, Jack Nicholson, Jeff Daniels, Maureen Stapleton, Stockard Channing, Richard Masur, Milos Forman.
109 min.
Heartburn is taken from Nora Ephron's book about her marriage to Watergate champ Carl Bernstein. Streep and Nicholson play the two journalists (under different names), although you will be forgiven if this fact passes you by. For the substance of the film is the kind of *Guardian* Women's Page slop in which the getting and raising of babies is suddenly a unique experience, deemed to be of undying interest to all observers, and the greatest tragedy in a woman's life is the discovery of her husband's adultery. Real life in between is supplied by dinner party gossip and group therapy. A movie of colossal inconsequence. Heartburn? No, just a bad attack of wind. CPea

Heart Condition

(James D Parriott, 1990, US) Bob Hoskins, Denzel Washington, Chloe Webb, Jeffrey Meek, Ray Baker, Roger E Mosley.
95 min.
This mismatched-buddy cop movie with a neat supernatural angle has Hoskins as an LA vice cop with a penchant for fast food, beer, smoking and using the 'N-word' when referring to his black brothers. So when he sees his old flame (Webb) being smuggled away from a crime scene by her new lover, a suave black lawyer (Washington), racist sparks fly. Hoskins' real problems start when he suffers a heart attack and, with Washington meanwhile dying, receives his black heart in a transplant. More problematically, Washington's ghost is along for the ride, complaining that he was murdered and coaxing Hoskins into smartening up his act. So Hoskins starts wearing flash clothes, driving a Merc, and asking awkward questions of a dead senator. Making effective use of its central conceit, this offbeat gem delivers the necessary plot twists and action, but never soft pedals on the racial angle. Chloe Webb contributes a finely balanced performance as a woman whose appreciation of both men's qualities finally finds expression in one composite male. NF

Heart in Winter, A

see Coeur en hiver, Un

Heart Is a Lonely Hunter, The

(Robert Ellis Miller, 1968, US) Alan Arkin, Sondra Locke, Laurinda Barrett, Stacy Keach, Chuck McCann, Percy Rodriguez, Biff McGuire, Cicely Tyson.
123 min.
A deaf mute (Arkin), left alone when his only friend (similarly afflicted) is committed to an asylum, moves to a new town, waiting expectantly. This being the Deep South, assorted misfits soon gather round him: an alcoholic drifter (Keach), a gawkily unhappy teenage girl (Locke), a black doctor with an outsize chip on his shoulder (Rodriguez). All of them pour out their troubles

in his silent, sympathetic presence, feeling that their lives are richer for the shared relationship. Yet suddenly, for reasons they know nothing about, the deaf mute commits suicide (he has learned of the death of his friend), and they are left to reflect bitterly on how much they took, how little they gave. The theme is sentimental, of course, but as directed by Miller in a series of oblique, self-contained scenes – with excellent performances all round and superb camerawork from James Wong Howe – the film has much the same haunting, poetic quality as the Carson McCullers novel (her first) on which it is based. TM

Heartland

(Richard Pearce, 1979, US) Rip Torn, Conchata Ferrell, Barry Primus, Lilia Skala, Megan Folsom, Amy Wright.
96 min.
Directed by a former documentarist, and based on the letters and papers of real-life 'wilderness woman' Elinore Stewart, this looks to be the kind of Western that Ken Loach might make. The Wyoming hills of 1910 may be past the earliest days of the frontier, but Rip Torn's taciturn Scots rancher hasn't changed his attitudes since his forebears disembarked the Mayflower. Torn is the housekeeper he first buys, then later weds, and she provides an admirable testimony to the central role that women must have played in building the new-found land. Rooted firmly in TV-style docudrama, the film charts the appalling rigours of pioneer life (lost herds, lost children) with an oblique respect and an insistence on the gritty (see Torn up to his elbows in a cow's backside). Whether or not you go for it rather depends on whether you like your Westerns mythologised or demythologised: 'circle the wagons' versus the Wyoming hills with a washing-line stretched across them. CPea

Heartland Reggae

(Jim Lewis, 1982, Can) Bob Marley & the Wailers, The I-Threes, Peter Tosh, Jacob Miller Inner Circle Band, Junior Tucker.
87 min.
Using concert footage shot between 1977-78 (climaxing with the 'One Love Peace Concert' where Marley, elevated to prophet status, unites on stage the leaders of the two Jamaican political parties), this falls into exactly the same trap as its predecessors in reggae documentary. For whom was the film made? If Black, the rasta talkover is unnecessary; if White, it is almost incomprehensible. Despite a scissors-and-sellotape approach to editing, and a sound quality never better than variable, the film does have its joyous moments: the gleeful Tosh as he anthemises the 'erb in 'Legalise It'; the sadly missed wobbling antics of Jacob Miller, whose enthusiasm is hard not to respond to and ultimately saves the film from being a ganja-fogged mess. FL

Heart Like a Wheel

(Jonathan Kaplan, 1983, US) Bonnie Bedelia, Beau Bridges, Leo Rossi, Hoyt Axton, Bill McKinney, Dean Paul Martin, Dick Miller.
113 min.
Kaplan's bold film yokes together two unlikely themes, the 'woman's picture' and drag racing, then stands slightly to the side of both and narrows its eyes. For while the roaring glamour of quarter-mile sprint cars would have tempted many action directors into dwelling at length on the spectacle, Kaplan's focus shifts slowly away from the flames and the noise and onto the problems facing the rise of a woman racer, Shirley Muldowney. Even than the movie is far from simple: of course there is unthinking prejudice from race officials and other drivers, but the real problem is Muldowney's struggles with her own affections and loyalties. Race fans won't be disappointed, but the real bonus comes from a perfect performance of tough understatement from Bedelia as the three-time winner. The wheel may be a flash chrome slot-mag, but the heart is gold. CPea

Heart of Glass (Herz aus Glas)

(Werner Herzog, 1976, WGer) Josef Bierbichler, Stefan Guttler, Clemens Scheitz, Volker Prechtel, Sepp Müller.
94 min.
It's hard to imagine that anyone other than

Herzog would have wanted to make a film like *Heart of Glass*. It returns to the formal and conceptual extremism of his work before *Kaspar Hauser*: almost the entire cast are performing under hypnosis throughout, and the plot unfolds in increasingly oblique fragments, making it Herzog's most stylised film to date. It's certainly extremely bizarre, but by no means unapproachable. The tale it tells is plainly allegorical: a glass factory declines into bankruptcy when its owner dies without divulging the formula for its special ruby glass, and the village that depended on the factory for employment goes down with it. But one doesn't have much chance to mull over the implications during the film itself: Herzog directs attention squarely at the performances (which are almost agonisingly intense) and at the imagery (which is very beautiful in a German Gothic way). Any film that dares to hover so close to sheer absurdity needs – and deserves – a sympathetic audience. TR

Heart of Midnight

(Matthew Chapman, 1988, US) Jennifer Jason Leigh, Peter Coyote, Brenda Vaccaro, Denise Dummont, Gale Mayron, Frank Stallone, Nick Love, Tico Wells, James Rebhorn.
105 min.
Chapman's psychological thriller is an interesting failure, which so indulges the psycho viewpoint that it finally prevents his plot from working. Heroine Carol (Leigh) has a history of mental illness, and when she inherits a neglected downtown club, her raucous mum (marvellous Vaccaro) doubts the wisdom of letting her move in and renovate. Swiftly, so do we. Three degenerate builders turn into rapists one night, objects whizz about by telekinesis, taps drip blood, and upstairs is a maze of SM parlours, orgy dorms, and spyholes, besides which Carol has flashbacks, hallucinations, and an ankle in plaster. There is an explanation, but having gone through hell with camera angles and panting corridors, you may not buy it. The Powell of *Peeping Tom*, Polanski, and Lynch are in the mix, and there are disquieting and powerful sequences. BC

Heart of the Matter, The

(George More O'Ferrall, 1953, GB) Trevor Howard, Elizabeth Allan, Denholm Elliott, Maria Schell, Gérard Oury, George Coulouris, Peter Finch, Earl Cameron, Michael Hordern, Cyril Raymond.
105 min. b/w.
Despite its betrayal of Graham Greene's concluding chapters, this is still an atmospheric adaptation; and as the tormented Scobie, Trevor Howard gives what is possibly his finest screen performance. The setting is Sierra Leone in 1942, and Scobie, a Catholic, is the deputy police commissioner whose sympathy for the Africans doesn't go down well with the ex-pats. But Scobie has more serious problems: no longer loving his wife yet consumed by his pity for her, he sends her back to Britain on holiday, having borrowed the money from a local trader. He then falls in love with Maria Schell, a survivor from a torpedoed liner, and when his wife returns, he is blackmailed. Sinking into the depths of despair and religious guilt, he dies fatefully by accident. In the novel he commits suicide, the gravest sin for Catholics, and the heart of the matter was God's capacity for forgiveness. Even so, the intensity of Howard's performance more than compensates, as does the supporting cast (including Finch as a priest, Oury as the blackmailer, and Hordern as Scobie's boss). ATu

Heart-Rending

see Love Hurts

Hearts and Minds

(Peter Davis, 1974, US)
110 min.
An Oscar-winning documentary dissection of the post-Vietnam American conscience. Davis, a controversial documentarist whose previous work included the notorious *The Selling of the Pentagon* for CBS television, described it as 'more psychological than political'; which is precisely where it falls down, using pathos-eliciting footage (interviews with veterans, their parents, a Buddhist monk; footage of a bombed village) instead of the hard political analysis so obviously needed. The result is that, while this has the required emotional effect, the film's characters

polarise all too easily into the heroes and villains of the anti-Commie, anti-gook propaganda movies extensively 'quoted'. Nevertheless, there is much interesting and exclusive interview material from American militarists and policymakers, and most notably a previous French president, to compensate for the overall mood of chest-beating remorse. RM

Hearts of Darkness: A Filmmaker's Apocalypse

(Fax Bahr/George Hickenlooper, 1991, US) 96 min.
Even at the time *Apocalypse Now* was completed, back in 1979, Coppola likened its genesis to the Vietnam war itself: 'It was crazy... we had access to too much money and too much equipment, and little by little we went insane'. This documentary is entirely in agreement with that verdict. Assembled from later interviews and from some 60 hours of footage shot on location in the Philippines (much of it by Coppola's wife Eleanor), the documentary lists a catalogue of disasters: problems with weather and the Filipino government; massive over-expenditure; Martin Sheen's heart attack; actors spaced out on whatever drugs were available; and an elephantine Brando refusing to play a fat character. At once anecdotal and revealing, this excellent film both illuminates the catastrophes that beset one particular project, and shows, by way of comparison, exactly what American film has foregone since the '70s. GA

Hearts of Fire

(Richard Marquand, 1987, US) Fiona Flanagan, Bob Dylan, Rupert Everett, Suzanne Bertish, Julian Glover, Susannah Hoffmann, Larry Lamb.
95 min.
A half-baked rock'n'roll fable. Star-struck teenager Flanagan quits her job and flies to England with retired rock star Dylan. Together, they are whisked off to a country house retreat by hot but jaded pop star Everett, and Flanagan launches herself into the recording of her debut album, while Everett recovers his song-writing ability. Nothing much happens, except that Flanagan is seduced by fame and Everett, while Dylan hovers enigmatically on the sidelines, offering jaundiced comments. Everett parades his affected proletarian accent once more, hilariously typecast as a talentless wanker. The only sympathetic character is the blind girl fan who wants to shoot him. Hampered by a meandering script, Marquand's last film has none of the functional slickness of *Jagged Edge*; the concert scenes in particular are hopelessly unexciting. NF

Hearts of the West (aka Hollywood Cowboy)

(Howard Zieff, 1975, US) Jeff Bridges, Blythe Danner, Andy Griffith, Donald Pleasence, Alan Arkin, Richard B Shull, Herbert Edelman.
103 min.
Few films in recent years have dealt with the Hollywood dream factory so wittily, sympathetically and incisively. In the early '30s, a hick from the sticks (Bridges) signs up with a bogus university to improve his talent at writing Zane Greystyle Western novels; stranded in LA, he takes a job as saddletramp extra for a film being made by the irascible Arkin. Rob Thompson's script gently nudges at the plagiarism, narcissism, corruption and rampant materialism infecting Tinseltown during its heyday, and allows sufficient space for the characters to grow, convince and command sympathy. A delicate balancing act is achieved as reality and fantasy are juxtaposed, and the performances are top-notch throughout (Bridges is particularly fine as the likeable innocent eager to make good). The jokes may not make you guffaw, but are carried out with a subtle, understated sense of timing and characterisation that will surely leave you with a quietly satisfied smile stretching from ear to ear. GA

Heartstrings (Xin Xiang)

(Sun Zhou, 1992, China) Fei Yang, Wang Yumei, Zhu Xu.
97 min.
Jingjing, ten-year-old son of Peking Opera actors, is sent to stay with his grandfather in the Guangdong countryside while his parents get divorced. The boy hates Opera; the old man used

to be an Opera star. Sun Zhou follows their progress from prickly estrangement to rapprochement with unblushing sentimentality, pausing only to dwell on the old man's emotional perplexity in romancing the local grass widow. Mushy stuff with rather too many ideas recycled from Hou Xiaoxian's *A Summer at Grandpa's*. TR

Heat

(Michael Mann, 1995, US) Robert De Niro, Al Pacino, Val Kilmer, Jon Voight, Amy Brenneman, Wes Studi, Dennis Haysbert, Tom Sizemore, Mykelti Williamson.
171 min.
Investigating a bold armed robbery which has left three security guards dead, LA cop Vincent Hanna (Pacino), whose devotion to work is threatening his third marriage, follows a trail that leads him to suspect a gang of thieves headed by Neil McCauley (De Niro). Trouble is, McCauley's cunning is at least equal to Hanna's, and that makes him a hard man to nail. Still, unknown to Hanna, McCauley's gang have their own troubles: one of their number is a volatile psychopath, while the businessman whose bonds they've stolen is not above some rough stuff himself. Such a synopsis barely scratches the surface of Mann's masterly crime epic. Painstakingly detailed, with enough characters, subplots and telling nuances to fill out half a dozen conventional thrillers, this is simply the best American crime movie – and indeed, one of the finest movies, period – in over a decade. The action scenes are better than anything produced by John Woo or Quentin Tarantino; the characterisation has a depth most American filmmakers only dream of; the use of location, decor and music is inspired; Dante Spinotti's camerawork is superb; and the large, imaginatively chosen cast gives terrific support to the two leads, both back on glorious form. GA

Heat

(Paul Morrissey, 1971, US) Joe Dallesandro, Sylvia Miles, Andrea Feldman, Pat Ast, Ray Vestal, Lester Persky, Eric Emerson.
103 min.
A pool, a crummy hotel, a luxury mansion, and the ever-retreating charade of showbiz and stardom. Sylvia Miles plays an ageing actress with her hooks into Little Joe. Little Joe plays an out-of-work ex-child star in a TV Western series, buffeted languidly by circumstance. Andrea Feldman plays an unloved child/mother. *Sunset Boulevard* as it never was, often looking like a softcore foray into poolside sex. Some great lines, some campy sequences, much humour. VG

Heat and Dust

(James Ivory, 1982, GB) Julie Christie, Greta Scacchi, Christopher Cazenove, Shashi Kapoor, Madhur Jaffrey, Charles McCaughan, Barry Foster, Nickolas Grace, Zakir Hussain.
130 min.
Adapted by Ruth Prawer Jhabvala from her own novel, *Heat and Dust* fuses several Merchant Ivory themes: the exoticism of India stirring English blood, the past hanging heavy over the present, dirty dealings flourishing behind a cloak of good manners. Anne (Christie) arrives in India to investigate the story of her great-aunt Olivia (Scacchi), cause of a considerable Raj scandal in the '20s. Ivory cuts back and forth between the newly-married Olivia's discovery of India, crashing colonial boredom relieved only by outings with the local Nawab (Kapoor); and Anne's as she follows obsessively in her great-aunt's footsteps. But whereas Olivia's spirited disregard for convention lands her in disgrace, the same path 60 years later leads Anne towards self-awareness and contentment. Directed with Ivory's customary charm, the film boasts fine performances (Christie and Scacchi in particular), and switches periods with effortless ease, striking up a fine network of ironies along the way. Passion, never one of Ivory's strong points, does get rather submerged beneath a welter of local colour; a delight none the less. JP

Heathers

(Michael Lehmann, 1988, US) Winona Ryder, Christian Slater, Shannen Doherty, Lisanne Falk, Kim Walker, Penelope Milford, Glenn Shadix, Lance Fenton, Patrick Labyorteaux.
103 min.
A wicked black comedy about teenage suicide and pernicious peer-group pressure, this refresh-

ing parody of high-school movies is venomouslt penned by Daniel Waters and sharply directed by Lehmann. The Heathers are three vacuous Westerburg High school beauties who specialise in 'being popular' and making life hell for socially inadequate dweebettes and pillowcases. Having sold out her former friends in these categories, Veronica (Ryder) becomes an honorary member of the select clique – but turns monocled mutineer. Aided by handsome rebellious newcomer JD (Slater), she devises a drastic plan to undermine the teen-queen tyranny, but underestimates JD's ruthlessness: the scheme backfirs dangerously. The compromised ending (forced on the film-makers by New World) is a serious let-down, but there is some exceptional ensemble acting, several stylish set pieces, and more imaginative slang than you could shake a cheerleader's ass at. More crucially, the film uses an intimate knowledge of teen-movie clichés to subvert their debased values from the *inside*. NF

Heatwave

(Phillip Noyce, 1981, Aust) Judy Davis, Richard Moir, Chris Haywood, Bill Hunter, John Gregg, Anna Jemison, John Meillon.
95 min.
Goon squads roughly evict demonstrating squatters: people in the way of 'progress', their homes on the site of a speculative prestige building project. No more than a scenario for worthy sentiments, it seems, until the focus rapidly narrows to the curious common-ground confrontation between an ambitious architect (Moir) and an impulsive local activist (Davis); and amid the heatwave that is Sydney's Christmas climate, the plot unexpectedly sours, thickens, and solidifies into a complex conspiracy thriller. A campaigning community journalist disappears, companies change hands, unions change sides, arson takes care of stubborn residents. Noyce puts the suspense screws on in time, and tight, and the odd allies' spiralling progress towards a nightmarish New Year's Eve shootout stylishly scars the unacceptable face of Lego-brick capitalism, with a memorably disturbing final image confirming this film as a genuine urban horror movie. PT

Heaven

(Diane Keaton, 1986, US)
88 min. b/w & col.
Quirky first film from Diane Keaton which blows a great idea – various inhabitants of America talk about their ideas of death and the after-life – by tarting it up with horrendously pretentious studio sets, unnecessarily silly camera angles, and somewhat over-clever cutting. The use of old film and TV clips, while funny, palls after a while; but most damaging is Keaton's snidely condescending tone towards her manipulated subjects. A cooler, more conventionally objective approach would have produced a far more revealing, humane and witty documentary. GA

Heaven & Earth

(Oliver Stone, 1993, US) Tommy Lee Jones, Joan Chen, Haing S Ngor, Hiep Thi Le, Debbie Reynolds.
140 min.
Admirable though it may be for Stone to have followed *Platoon* and *Born on the Fourth of July* with an account of the Vietnam War as experienced by a Vietnamese woman, good intentions don't necessarily make for good movies. This is awful. When a prologue set in 1953 introduces young Le Ly and her peaceful farming community just before the arrival of French troops, it's clear from an autobiographical voice-over, the gleeful peasant faces and the swelling music that we're not about to see an understated movie. And as Le Ly (Hiep Thi Le) proceeds on her physically dangerous and spiritually devastating odyssey, Stone scuppers what could have been an affecting story with visual, verbal and dramatic bombast. In going again for the big one, the director resorts to damp sentimentality, cod poeticism and facile preachiness – and it seems to last forever. GA

Heaven Can Wait

(Ernst Lubitsch, 1943, US) Don Ameche, Gene Tierney, Charles Coburn, Laird Cregar, Marjorie Main, Spring Byington, Allyn Joslyn, Eugene Pallette, Signe Hasso, Louis Calhern.
112 min.
Classic Lubitsch, disarmingly light in tone but in

fact quite astute in its social and sexual satire. Ameche plays Henry Van Cleeve, a dandy who pitches up in Hell believing his past sex life in the naughty Nineties qualifies him admirably for eternal damnation; but as he recounts his story, he emerges as a kindly and sympathetic man. Tierney plays the faultless wife, and Lubitsch handles the whole delightful business with characteristic delicacy. The bonus is the brilliant Technicolor photography which shows off Basevi and Fuller's marvellous decor for Hell to memorable advantage. MA

Heaven Can Wait
(Warren Beatty/Buck Henry, 1978, US) Warren Beatty, Julie Christie, James Mason, Jack Warden, Charles Grodin, Dyan Cannon, Buck Henry, Vincent Gardenia.
101 min.
Beatty's directing debut is a perverse remake of the 1941 *Here Comes Mr Jordan*, a whimsical tale of a dead boxer returning to earth in another chap's body through a celestial mix-up. What mordant wits like Elaine May (who co-scripted with Beatty) and Buck Henry saw in this is another heavenly mystery: the script provides only the thinnest of lunatic fringes to decorate the soggy comic material. Beatty ambles nicely enough through the hero's part (remodelled as a quarter-back), and Charles Grodin turns up trumps playing another of his chinless, spineless wonders. But Christie's comedy gifts are as minuscule as ever, and the film drags its feet uncertainly from beginning to end. GB

Heaven Help Us
(aka Catholic Boys)
(Michael Dinner, 1984, US) Donald Sutherland, John Heard, Andrew McCarthy, Mary Stuart Masterson, Kevin Dillon, Wallace Shawn, Kate Reid.
104 min.
A sharply observed rites-of-passage comedy set in Brooklyn in 1965. At St Basil's Catholic School for Boys, the pupils find their growing pains made more painful by the ministrations of stern-faced Brethren, who lecture them on the Seventh Deadliest Sin just before a long-awaited junior prom, and patrol the dance floor ready to disentangle any clinches too close for chastity. Sutherland presides in a perm and a cassock over fellow-monks Heard and Shawn, the schoolboy cast give good-natured performances, and Dinner (his first film) brings sensitivity and freshness to a threadbare theme. SJo

Heaven Knows, Mr Allison
(John Huston, 1957, US) Deborah Kerr, Robert Mitchum.
107 min.
On the one hand, Huston's typically wry contribution to Hollywood's long-established, censor-baiting fascination with nuns. On the other, a quirky and superior reworking of his own *The African Queen*. Deborah Kerr, back in the habit ten years after *Black Narcissus*, is stranded on a Jap-held Pacific island with marine corporal Mitchum, whose wonderfully low-key portrait of melting machismo is everything Bogart's respectably Oscar-chasing irascibility wasn't. The favourite film of its veteran screenwriter, John Lee Mahin. PT

Heavenly Creatures
(Peter Jackson, 1994, NZ) Melanie Lynskey, Kate Winslet, Sarah Peirse, Diana Kent, Clive Merrison, Simon O'Conner.
98 min.
Based on a real-life murder case that scandalised New Zealand in the '50s, Peter Jackson's movie marks a welcome change from the splatter of *Bad Taste* and *Braindead*. Rather than focus on the final act of violence, the film explores the over-heated encounter between two teenagers: clever, cocky Juliet (Winslet), from a well-to-do English family, and pudgy, initially more introspective Pauline (Lynskey), a working-class girl. The pair's obsession with books, Mario Lanza, the fearsome Orson Welles and other 'saints' leads them to create their own 'Fourth World', a medieval fantasy involving royal romance and bloody intrigue; but when their parents decide that the friendship is 'wayward' and 'unhealthy', the girls' terror at the prospect of separation impels daydreams to invade reality, with deadly results. Jackson's film is distinguished by the

intensity of the girls' secretive relationship. If the busy camera movements used to convey the heady exhilaration of their early encounters are irritating, the sense of claustrophobic immersion in private mysteries is palpable. Acted with conviction, and directed and written with febrile vibrancy. GA

Heavenly Pursuits
(Charles Gormley, 1986, GB) Tom Conti, Helen Mirren, David Hayman, Brian Pettifer, Jennifer Black, Dave Anderson.
91 min.
An engaging satire on the miracle business, set in a Catholic school in Glasgow whose status-seeking authorities are much taxed by the problem of canonisation for their patron, the Blessed Edith Semple, who died in 1917 with one authenticated miracle to her credit. She needs two more, the Vatican sternly decrees. Meanwhile a sceptical remedial teacher (Conti) is quietly performing miracles of his own with backward kids, and is as startled as anyone when a couple of bizarre circumstances intervening in his life seem to smack of the miraculous. Treated with tongue-in-cheek seriousness, the resulting confusion of cross-purposes as the media jump on the band wagon treads a delicate path through the morass of cynicism, gullibility and wishfulness. Quirkily funny and admirably acted, it works beautifully largely because Gormley (scripting as well as directing) refuses to undersell any of his characters: everybody has his reasons. TM

Heaven, Man, Earth
(Laurens C Postma, 1984, GB)
78 min.
The problem in making a film about the Triad gangs of Hong Kong is that there's very little you can actually show. This deeply dishonest movie used miles of irrelevant travelogue to cover the gap, and has clumsily staged sequences masquerading as 'documentary'. Even the alleged movie clips are actually scenes from TV. All this duplicity produces a very damp squib, despite the dogged sensation-seeking. TR

Heavens Above!
(John Boulting, 1963, GB) Peter Sellers, Cecil Parker, Isabel Jeans, Eric Sykes, Bernard Miles, Brock Peters, Ian Carmichael, Irene Handl, Miriam Karlin.
118 min. b/w.
Playing a clergyman who applies his Christian charity literally, having been translated by error to a posh parish from his prison chaplaincy, Sellers works valiantly to wring a laugh or two out of this cringe-making satire on the church. Based on an idea by Malcolm Muggeridge, no less, the script is peopled exclusively by stereotypes, skitters uneasily into farce, and indulges a penchant for schoolboy sniggers that makes it a not-so-distant relative of the *Carry On* family. TM

Heaven's Burning
(Craig Lahiff, 1997, Aust) Russell Crowe, Youki Kudoh, Kenji Isomura, Ray Barrett, Robert Mammone, Petru Gheorghiu.
99 min.
It takes a while for this road movie thriller to take off, as the director labours through an opening section which lays out how Japanese honey-mooner Midori (Kudoh) happens to find herself on the run (and loving it), chased by bank robbers and her 'disgraced' ex-husband, with only a hot-rodder (Crowe) as reluctant helpmate. In a film of blunt genre strokes, Kudoh's transition to kooky 'liberated' chick is as rudimentarily sketched as the reactions to her foreignness are awkwardly played out. Nevertheless, director Lahiff manages to balance the action and human interest, using transport truck metal and the horizontal swaths of the Australian landscape to emulate the sweep and gleam of the American prototype, and undercutting the machismo through the sympathetic playing of Kudoh and, especially, Crowe. WH

Heaven's Gate
(Michael Cimino, 1980, US) Kris Kristofferson, Christopher Walken, John Hurt, Sam Waterston, Brad Dourif, Isabelle Huppert, Joseph Cotten, Jeff Bridges, Geoffrey Lewis.
219 min.
For all the abuse heaped on it, this is – in its com-

plete version, at least – a majestic and lovingly detailed Western which simultaneously celebrates and undermines the myth of the American frontier. The keynote is touched in the wonderfully choreographed opening evocation of a Harvard graduation in 1870: answering the Dean's ritual address urging graduates to spread culture through contact with the uncultivated, the class valedictorian (Hurt) mockingly replies that they see no need for change in a world 'on the whole well arranged'. Twenty years later, as Hurt and fellow-graduate Kristofferson become involved in the Johnson County Wars, their troubled consciences suggest that some change in the 'arrangements' might well have been in order. Watching uneasily as the rich cattle barons legally exterminate the poor immigrant farmers who have taken to illegal rustling to feed their starving families, they can only attempt to enforce the law that has become a mockery (Kristofferson) or lapse into soothing alcoholism (Hurt). Moral compromise on a national scale is in question here, a theme subtly echoed by the strange romantic triangle that lies at the heart of the film: a three-way struggle between the man who has everything (Kristofferson), the man who has nothing (Walken), and the girl (Huppert) who would settle for either provided no fraudulent compromise is asked of her. The ending, strange and dreamlike, blandly turns a blind eye to shut out the atrocities and casuistries we have witnessed, and on which the American dream was founded; not much wonder the American press went on a mass witch-hunt against the film's un-American activities. TM

Heaven-6-Box
(Hiroyuki Oki, 1995, Jap) Yasuhisa Kiyooka, Gensho Takasaki, Yoshie Takasaki, Jun Osaki, Tei Osaki, Kenji Tsuzuki, Daijiro Hashimoto.
60 min.
Commissioned by the city of Kochi to mark the opening of its Museum of Modern Art, this experimental feature by Japan's foremost gay indie filmmaker almost defies description. The film is divided into six 10-minute chapters (or 'boxes') which, says Oki, add up to an image of 'heaven'. They certainly do add up to a portrait of the city and its people, from the mayor posing outside the railway station to the undressed boys lying around Oki's own apartment, from a strange piece of performance art outside the new museum to the fish market and the youth orchestra playing on the seashore. Ineffably idiosyncratic and mildly sexy, it rewards repeated viewings. TR

Heaven's Prisoners
(Phil Joanou, 1996, US) Alec Baldwin, Kelly Lynch, Mary Stuart Masterson, Eric Roberts, Teri Hatcher, Vondie Curtis-Hall, Badja Djola.
131 min.
This unspeakably tedious adaptation of a book by James Lee Burke is hampered by the fact that the leading man looks and sounds like an LA tourist, rather than a bruised ex-New Orleans cop recovering from violence and alcoholism by running a bait farm. Taking on the role of Dave Robicheaux, Baldwin gets back into his old baddie routine when he rescues a child from a spectacular air wreck. The crash concerns villains involved in dope, women and illegal immigrants, and leads to the killing of Dave's wife, at which point Baldwin gives what is one of the most embarrassingly unconvincing examples of Hollywood emoting by refusing to believe that she's dead. Joanou has a strong affinity for the violent, the religiously symbolic and the musical – one of the best things about this film is a solid blues soundtrack. But he can also be a deeply boring storyteller, and at 131 minutes this piece is way over its natural timespan; by about two thirds in, you pray for the alligators to get you. SGr

Heaven Tonight
(Pino Amenta, 1990, Aust) John Waters, Kim Gungell, Rebecca Gilling, Sean Cully, Guy Pearce.
93 min.
Although most films about the tribulations of rock stars are utterly awful, the occasional oddball which slips through the net keeps the 'pop film' genre alive and interesting. This tiny-budget Antipodean offering centres on an ageing has-been whose son's flourishing singing career provokes much domestic hassling and heartache.

Taking a resolutely downbeat approach, and featuring some convincing footage in which the participants actually appear to be playing their instruments (a miracle!), this avoids all the naff 'let's-do-the-gig-here' clichés, for which praise is due indeed. Not as hard-hitting as *Slade in Flame*, perhaps, but nicely grim none the less. MK

Heavy

(James Mangold, 1995, US) Pruitt Taylor Vince, Shelley Winters, Liv Tyler, Deborah Harry, Joe Grifasi, Evan Dando.
103 min.
The humming undertow of Thurston Moore's electronic score lends this American indie a brooding intensity right from the start. We're in small-town territory: a rundown diner, a new girl behind the counter, and growing romantic attachment from the owner's plump, retiring son. Disaster's rather obviously brewing; Tyler's fresh-faced Callie may be bringing new life to the place, but she's sparked resentment in fellow waitress Delores (Harry), while the occasional presence of her muso boyfriend Jeff (Dando) seems bound to cause the gentle, corpulent Victor (Vince) some ill-defined yet inevitable hurt. As proprietress Dolly (Winters) presides over failing business and a few loyal regulars, the future appears more uncertain than ever. Writer/director Mangold's careful, essentially serious approach puts the characters under the microscope and relies on the performers not to let him down. They don't. Newcomer Tyler is breezy and touching. Vince meanwhile is hugely sympathetic as the shy boy daring to reach out, capturing deep repression and tiny everyday acts of courage with meticulous command. A potent, if slightly precious first feature, that's distinctive enough to remain long in the mind. TJ

Heavy Metal

(Gerald Potterton, 1981, US) voices: Don Francks, John Romanus, John Candy, John Vernon.
90 min.
Among those listed in the credits are a handful of collaborators whose reputations should be rescued from the cosmic junkheap this deserves to rust on – notably writer Dan O'Bannon – but the collective animators of this dopey Disney parody (reportedly 1,000 artists working in five cities simultaneously) still have a lot to answer for. Fantasies that are gratuitously sexist and Fascist (macho whoring and warmongering), and whose roots reach all the way back to post-hippie paranoia, feed the tangled plot-lines of a movie that, given the orchestral overkill and surprisingly low profile of heavy metal music, should disappoint even the teenage wet-dreamers it's aimed at. MA

Heavy Petting

(Obie Benz, 1988, US) David Byrne, Sandra Bernhard, Allen Ginsberg, William Burroughs, Ann Magnuson, Spalding Gray, Josh Mostel, Laurie Anderson, John Oates, Abbie Hoffman.
78 min. b/w & col.
A documentary whose subject matter (sexual initiation and education) tempted assorted celebrities and intellectuals to recount their earliest intimate encounters. Sandra Bernhard let a boy see her bottom in return for a fudgsicle, David Byrne wondered if he would use up all his sperm if he masturbated, Spalding Gray ponders whether the raccoon hats so popular during his adolescence were used to stimulate the wearer's genital area. By incorporating archival footage (educational, television, feature films), Benz and his researchers explore shifts in sexual codes of conduct in America from the '50s. They've unearthed some wonders, from *How to Say No to Physical Aspects of Puberty*, and as newshounds quiz teens about the evils of rock'n'roll, one presenter warns that moral depravity could leave the country vulnerable to Communist conquest. The 'witnesses' lend a structure of sorts; when it works, the material is funny and direct, even though the comparison of the two eras doesn't exactly prove revelatory. CM

Heavy Traffic

(Ralph Bakshi, 1973, US) Joseph Kaufmann, Beverley Hope Atkinson, Franke de Kova, Terri Haven.
75 min.

An animated follow-up to *Fritz the Cat* that must have been worked out on a computer. Take one pinball wizard, plus one godfather, plus one underground comic artist, plus black chickette power, plus anything else that grabbed the boppers ten years ago, and you should have what they all want to see. Despite the occasional stream of animated piss, stretched cock or flashed twat, or the 'innovation' of combined live and animated sequences, the movie falls apart at every seam, a humourless mess, a stale joke. The quality of the animation is cornflake packet standard, the script – one or two minor moments excepted – a disaster. JDuC

Hedda

(Trevor Nunn, 1975, GB) Glenda Jackson, Peter Eyre, Timothy West, Jennie Linden, Patrick Stewart, Constance Chapman.
102 min.
The abbreviated title of this Brut production (transposing Nunn's Royal Shakespeare Company staging of Ibsen's play) is the clue: leaving out the *Gabler* implies a Woman's Picture and the plastic surface of high-class soap opera. So it is for much of the time, with close-ups of Glenda Jackson reacting archly to the out-of-focus figures in the background. Luckily the supporting cast is outstanding; so that once the nods to opening out the play have been made, the film settles into its hypnotic story of manipulation and sexual tensions, with no fancy angles to obscure the power of Hedda's climactic burning of the Lovborg manuscript. AN

Hedd Wyn

(Paul Turner, 1992, GB) Huw Garmon, Sue Roderick, Catrin Fychan, Ceri Cunningham, Lilo Silyn, Grey Evans.
110 min.
Subtitled 'The Armageddon Poet', this Welsh-language feature is the story of WWI poet Ellis Evans, known under the pen name Hedd Wyn. Ellis – who failed on his first attempt to fulfil his ambition of winning the Chair at the National Eisteddfod – left school at 14 and three years later was conscripted (in place of his brother) into the Army. While serving in France, he used every spare moment to work on his poem 'Yr Arwr' (The Hero), which he finally completed and submitted by post. A month later, on the first day of the Battle of Passchendaele, he was mortally wounded, but his poem survived and he was awarded the prize he had always coveted. Little noted in England, *Hedd Wyn* received an Oscar nomination in 1994 for best foreign-language film. NF

He Died with His Eyes Open (On ne Meurt que 2 Fois)

(Jacques Deray, 1985, Fr) Michel Serrault, Charlotte Rampling, Xavier Deluc, Elisabeth Depardieu, Jean Leuvrais, Jean-Paul Roussillon.
106 min.
An adaptation of Robin Cook's first thriller (written under the pseudonym of Derek Raymond). A washed-up concert pianist is found dead beside a railway track, leaving back at his apartment the biggest heap of clues anyone could wish for: a pile of tape recordings in which he rambles on about his obsessive love for one Barbara. When the lady in question turns up (Rampling), she immediately confesses to the bemused cop on the case (Serrault). In true *noir* style, however, this is only the beginning; there is now poor, ugly Serrault's long haul to establish proof, his fatal attraction to the femme fatale, his bizarre identification with the dead man, and of course his sad choice between feelings and duty. Rampling is fine as the sloe-eyed temptress with the murderous level gaze and a certain taste for incest; and Serrault is rapidly establishing himself as the French Walter Matthau, a marvellous melancholic with perfect timing. It's the sort of thriller at which the French excel; lovely stuff. CPea

Heidi Fleiss – Hollywood Madam

(Nick Broomfield, 1995, GB) Heidi Fleiss, Ivan Nagy, Madam Alex, Cookie.
106 min.
Broomfield's characteristically feisty, intrusive documentary about the Tinseltown prostitute/madam is packed with biographical detail, eye-catchingly sleazy characters (but unfortunately no real stars), and lots of unanswered questions. Fleiss is clearly a pretty shrewd mover; Madam Alex, her mentor, now seems merely a sad eccentric; while Fleiss's on-off, love-hate relationship with film-maker, lover and alleged pimp Ivan Nagy, is a wonder to behold: exploitative in the extreme, but who's exploiting who? Fascinating, but then, however sharp or persuasive Broomfield's sleuthing methods, that's almost inevitable. GA

Heidi's Song

(Robert Taylor, 1982, US) voices: Lorne Greene, Sammy Davis Jr, Margery Gray, Michael Bell.
94 min.
The much loved, oft retold story of Heidi gets the Hanna-Barbera treatment: it remains the tale of a cute little blonde who refuses to see catastrophe (grandfather breaks his leg, Klara is still no better, and Heidi herself is almost devoured by rats) other than as an opportunity for a grating cheerfulness, spiced with a Disney-like catalogue of anthropomorphic mutts and vermin and a few tunes. But, interestingly, the film-makers seem to have taken the classic animation of Chuck Jones as their model (where they have not cannibalised their own TV series), introducing a saving strain of acerbity into an otherwise cloying cartoon. FD

Heimat (Homeland)

(Edgar Reitz, 1984, WGer) Marita Breuer, Dieter Schaad, Michael Lesch, Eva Maria Bayerswaltes, Rüdiger Weigang.
924 min. b/w & col.
In this eleven-part film made for TV, Reitz portrays his country's difficult history from 1919 to the present day without recourse to soap operatics. Maria, born in 1900, is the still point around whom others move emotionally, economically, and politically, with the narrative developing through a superbly sustained accumulation of detail. Humane and comic, it's very finely acted, exact in period detail, and immaculately photographed in monochrome with occasional bursts of colour of an epiphanic resonance. A magnificent achievement that will reward every hour it demands of your time. DT

Heiress, The

(William Wyler, 1949, US) Olivia de Havilland, Ralph Richardson, Montgomery Clift, Miriam Hopkins, Vanessa Brown, Ray Collins, Mona Freeman.
115 min. b/w.
Wyler's version of Henry James' *Washington Square* (based on a play adaptation) is typically plush, painstaking and cold. James' heroine, whose young love is thwarted by a grasping fiancé and an equally selfish father, at least turned into a spinster with moral integrity, but Wyler's simply grows into a malevolent old witch. Olivia de Havilland is a millstone round many a film's neck, but she soon leaves off smiling sweetly in this one, clashing swords in deep focus with Richardson (magnificently imperious) and an oily Clift. And Aaron Copland contributes some suitably icy music. It's all highly professional and heartless. GB

Heist, The

see $ [Dollars]

He Knows You're Alone

(Armand Mastroianni, 1980, US) Don Scardino, Caitlin O'Heaney, Elizabeth Kemp, Tom Rolfing, Lewis Arlt.
94 min.
There's a psycho on the loose. Having once been traumatically jilted, Rolfing specialises in brutally despatching brides-to-be, and becomes obsessed with one in particular (O'Heaney). News reaches police chief Arlt, who snorts fire as his erstwhile bride-to-be was an early Rolfing victim. For a more curdled piece of chiller incompetence, this would be hard to beat. Newcomer Mastroianni directs with leaden predictability. A myopic eye for overblown and voyeuristic imagery, he moves from one murder to another, a synthesiser signpost helping to rob every spill of any surprise at all. The final twist is especially dumb and obvious. And characterisation means stereotype; Tupperware dialogue for passive women, racy dialogue for shower-room, protective men. It's almost distastefully bad. IB

Held for Questioning
(Der Aufenthalt)
(Frank Beyer, 1983, EGer) Sylvester Groth, Fred Düren, Klaus Piontek, Matthias Günther, Horst Hiemer.
102 min.
Beyer's film is a study of prison life and of personality. A young German soldier is imprisoned after the end of the war in 1945: is he wittingly or unwittingly a war criminal? Are the other inmates more dangerous than the guards? Never less than interesting, the film is flawed by a central inconsistency of approach: never quite a study of the minutiae and banality of the day-to-day existence of the prisoner, it also never fully explores the possibilities of a potentially Kafkaesque situation. SM

Helen, Queen of
the Nautch Girls
(Anthony Korner, 1973, Ind/GB)
31 min. b/w & col.
A documentary on the Anglo-Indian Helen, best remembered by Western audiences, perhaps, as the Heroine in Gold dancing on the giant typewriter in Merchant Ivory's *Bombay Talkie*. The star of more than 500 Hindi films turns out to be straightforward, unaffected professional, modestly concerned that her film's have a consistent point of view and that, above all, her eyes hold the spectator's attention. Her ambition, when she finally retires? To open a modest boutique in Bombay's still to be completed Sheraton Hotel. JPy

Helicopter Spies, The
(Boris Sagal, 1967, US) Robert Vaughn, David McCallum, Carol Lynley, Bradford Dillman, Lola Albright, John Dehner, Leo G Carroll, John Carradine, Julie London.
93 min.
A *Man from UNCLE* film which sees Solo and Kuryakin on the trail of a notorious safecracker (Dillman) in Greece. Inevitably their quest leads to a plot to dominate the world, this time by a sect of white-haired mystics, and the team fight their way through several continents. It's all pretty static low-budget stuff, with only a few guest appearances to help things along: Carol Lynley, for example, as a mini-skirted all-American girl, bent on revenge. DP

Hell and High Water
(Samuel Fuller, 1954, US) Richard Widmark, Bella Darvi, Victor Francen, Cameron Mitchell, Gene Evans, David Wayne.
103 min.
Known for his uninhibited camera movements, Fuller was the obvious person for Fox to ask to make a CinemaScope movie in an enclosed space in order to prove to doubting executives that the walls of the cinema would not appear to rotate during tracking shots or pans. The result was *Hell and High Water*, which is mostly set aboard a submarine, and tells the story of a group of patriots and mercenaries who stop the Chinese from dropping an atomic bomb from an 'American' plane at the time of the Korean war. A deeply pessimistic film, it questions the roots of loyalty and identity by examining the stated motives of its characters at every stage of the film. Widmark is at his ambiguous best. PH

Hellbound: Hellraiser II
(Tony Randel, 1988, GB) Claire Higgins, Ashley Laurence, Kenneth Cranham, Imogen Boorman, Sean Chapman, William Hope, Doug Bradley.
93 min.
A disappointing sequel to Clive Barker's innovatory 'body horror' pic, which – while making some effort to flesh out the Cenobite mythology – simply performs cosmetic surgery on the original. This time, it's a skinned Julia (Higgins) who writhes up from a blood-caked mattress, while depraved psychiatrist Dr Channard (Cranham) summons Pinhead and his pals with the help of Tiffany (Boorman), a dumb teenager with a penchant for solving puzzles. And when Kirsty (Laurence) receives a message in blood from her Hell-bound father, she plunges into a subterranean labyrinth to save him. Directed with staggering ineptitude, this never approaches the visceral intensity and flesh-crawling terror of the first film. The teenage heroines are too insipid to elicit either interest or sympathy,

Julia's graduation from wicked stepmother to Evil Queen erases a crucial element of moral ambiguity, and the labyrinth looks like a cross between an MC Escher painting and a '70s 'progressive rock' album cover. Only Channard's transformation into a Cenobite, and subsequent celebration of his perverse power, match the intellectual complexity and visual ferocity of *Hellraiser*. NF

Hellcat Mud Wrestlers
(David Sullivan/John M East, 1983, GB) Queen Kong, Shelley Selina Savage, Sadistic Sadie, Helen Hammer, Miss Death Wish.
48 min.
Somewhere between docudrama and *cinéma-vérité*, this features the likes of Selina Savage, Miss Death Wish and Helen Hammer, all grappling with the extremely civilised art of mud wrestling (in front of a grotesquely staggish audience). One wonders why so much effort is lavished in attempting to establish individual personalities since, with the exception of 20-stone Queen Kong, they all become indistinguishable once they hit the muck. Pure smut for people with muddy minds. AB

Hellcats of the Navy
(Nathan Juran, 1957, US) Ronald Reagan, Nancy Davis, Arthur Franz, Henry Lauter, Selmer Jackson.
82 min. b/w.
Ron'n'Nancy's only screen appearance together is the chief reason why anyone still remembers this dull WWII actioner. On a US Navy sub out to attack Japanese merchant shipping, Capt Reagan hits conflict with Chief Officer Franz over command decisions which may have been influenced by feelings for Miss Davis. TJ

Hell Drivers
(Cy Endfield, 1957, GB) Stanley Baker, Patrick McGoohan, Herbert Lom, Peggy Cummins, William Hartnell, Wilfrid Lawson, Jill Ireland, Sidney James, Gordon Jackson, Sean Connery.
108 min. b/w.
Energetic and violent trucking thriller marked by the raw, angry edge of the best of blacklist victim Endfield's Hollywood work, and by his appreciation (shared, oddly enough, by fellow exile Joseph Losey) of the markedly out-of-the-mainstream talent of Stanley Baker. Playing an ex-con hired as one of a team of drivers forced to drive at dangerous speeds in rattletrap lorries over rugged roads to meet the daily quota of loads to be delivered (a touch of *The Wages of Fear* here), Baker further becomes involved in a deadly duel with a sadistic rival (McGoohan) on his way to smashing the haulage company's racket. Baker and Endfield eventually formed their own production company for *Zulu*. PT

Heller in Pink Tights
(George Cukor, 1960, US) Sophia Loren, Anthony Quinn, Margaret O'Brien, Steve Forrest, Edmund Lowe, Eileen Heckart, Ramon Novarro.
100 min.
Cukor's one stab at the Western genre was a typically personal response to the conventions, playing much of the adventure for comedy, and centering the plot around a touring theatrical troupe. As in so many of his films, the relationship between life and theatre is explored as the company, performing to ramshackle communities in an untamed frontier, act out heroic tales of love, passion and honourable death, surrounded by an altogether less romantic reality in which people struggle simply to survive. As in *A Star Is Born* and *Les Girls*, Hoyningen-Huene's colour designs are magnificent, and under the expert eye of Cukor, even Loren and Quinn give superb performances. GA

Heller Wahn
see Friends and Husbands

Hellfire Club, The
(Robert S Baker/Monty Berman, 1960, GB) Keith Michell, Peter Arne, Adrienne Corri, Kai Fischer, Peter Cushing, Bill Owen, Tutte Lemkow, Miles Malleson, Andrew Faulds.
93 min.
Baker and Berman produced, directed and shot this yarn, written by Leon Griffiths and Jimmy

Sangster, and based, peripherally, on the dodgy doings of the 18th century club for sensation-seeking gentlemen. Jason, an orphaned acrobat in a travelling circus (Michell, suitably energetic), is heir to the Netherden estate, which has been usurped by his cousin Thomas, the Hellfire's decadent new president (Arne). To retrieve what's his, Jason becomes a Netherden groom, arouses Thomas's mistress (Corri) and ends in Newgate under sentence of death, until the Prime Minister intervenes to save him. Surprisingly light on debauchery and occasionally perhaps too jocular for its own good, this costume melodrama nevertheless occasionally skips out of the rut. TJ

Hellhounds of Alaska, The
(Die Blutigen Geier von
Alaska)
(Harald Reinl, 1973, WGer) Doug McClure, Harald Leipnitz, Angelika Ott, Roberto Blanco, Kristina Nel, Klaus Löwitsch.
90 min.
West German, or schnitzel Westerns, have never had the crossover appeal of the spaghettis, but there was quite a sub-genre there for a while. This is an obscure, moderate adventure, with McClure as a fur-trapper battling the elements and sundry villains to sled a sick boy cross country for medical treatment. TJ

Hell in Korea
see Hill in Korea, A

Hell in the Pacific
(John Boorman, 1968, US) Lee Marvin, Toshiro Mifune.
103 min.
Intriguing but finally dissatisfying movie in which Marvin and Mifune repeatedly get into macho standoffs as a US Marine pilot and a Japanese naval officer stranded together on a desert island during World War II. Boorman makes the most of a limited situation through strong performances and dramatically employed scope compositions, but it gradually descends into woolly allegory. Obviously on the principle that something was lacking, the British release prints were saddled with an ending in which a bomb from the skies literally blew everything apart. In Boorman's original, rather more acerbic ending, after the two men get happily drunk together, having just discovered civilisation (an abandoned military camp, with stocks of food, cigarettes and drink) they simply walk angrily off in opposite directions, their enmity rewakened by photographs of the war in an old magazine. GA

Hell Is a City
(Val Guest, 1959, GB) Stanley Baker, John Crawford, Donald Pleasence, Maxine Audley, Billie Whitelaw, Joseph Tomelty, George A Cooper.
98 min. b/w.
A persuasively sweaty crime thriller set in Manchester, written and directed by the once reliable Guest (from a novel by Maurice Proctor), this atypical Hammer production benefited from a strong cast and fine use of location photography (in 'Hammerscope'). Square-jawed Baker toughs it out as a harassed police inspector with a volubly frustrated wife (Audley) at home, and the arduous assignment on the streets of tracking down a jailbreaker (Crawford) wanted for murder. The atmosphere is persuasively seedy and downbeat, and there's a striking performance by Billie Whitelaw in a period when she seemed to specialise in 'fallen women'. DT

Hell Is for Heroes
(Don Siegel, 1962, US) Steve McQueen, Bobby Darin, Fess Parker, Nick Adams, Bob Newhart, Harry Guardino, James Coburn.
90 min. b/w.
A war film is a war film is a war film...except that Siegel, brought into the project at the last moment when Steve McQueen refused to work with the scheduled director, toughened the standard war-is-hell screenplay into an extraordinary study of psychopathology. He centres everything squarely on the McQueen character (one of his best performances, a human war machine), and emphasises the tensions within the American platoon rather than the conflict with the offscreen

Germans. The ending, which stresses the enormous human cost of a small tactical gain, is remarkably powerful, precisely because it's the first time that Siegel allows his audience any perspective on what they've been seeing. TR

Hell Night
(Tom De Simone, 1981, US) Linda Blair, Vincent Van Patten, Peter Barton, Kevin Brophy, Jenny Neumann, Suki Goodwin.
102 min.
Producer Irwin Yablans spent the time between *Halloween* and *Halloween II* cooking up more of the same. This time the innocent lambs set up for slaughter are a quartet of students (sporting fancy dress for more picturesque effect) who are locked overnight into a haunted house as a fraternity initiation test. To nobody's surprise but their own, jokey efforts to stage manage some nocturnal frights turn into the real thing. Amazing, though, what a competent director, cameraman and cast can do to help out a soggy plot. Tolerably watchable by comparison with the average *Halloween* rip-off. TM

Hello Again
(Frank Perry, 1987, US) Shelley Long, Judith Ivey, Gabriel Byrne, Corbin Bernsen, Sela Ward, Austin Pendleton, Carrie Nye.
96 min.
Lucy Chadman (Long) is the ideal suburban housewife, devoted to her medic hubby Jason (Bernsen) and son Danny, who wants to be a chef. Her sister is quite the opposite. In tune with the cosmos, zany Zelda (Ivey) has no problem bringing Lucy back from the dead when she chokes on a South Korean chicken ball. But in the meantime a year has elapsed, and Jason has married Lucy's horizontally-mobile friend Kim (Ward). Lucy doesn't like it. Enlisting the help of a doctor friend (Byrne), she fights off the attentions of the alerted media and sees off her rival in love. Merely the excuse for a parade of expensive clothes and opulent locations, with Shelley Long milking her role for any drop of pathos, this is good for a giggle at best. MS

Hello, Dolly!
(Gene Kelly, 1969, US) Barbra Streisand, Walter Matthau, Michael Crawford, Marianne McAndrew, EJ Peaker, Tommy Tune, Louis Armstrong.
148 min.
Only Streisand's second movie, but already (as co-star Matthau grumbled) she was hogging the screen. The trouble is that there isn't much to hog in this elephant which gave *Star!* a helping hoof in burying the Hollywood musical. The Jerry Herman score is unmemorable, Michael Kidd's choreography is foreshortened to accommodate yards of additional dialogue by Ernest Lehman, and the rest is Streisand grandly doing her thing in a series of plushily colossal sets. PT

Hello, Frisco, Hello
(H Bruce Humberstone, 1943, US) Alice Faye, John Payne, Jack Oakie, Lynn Bari, June Havoc, Laird Cregar.
98 min.
Lush but formulaic Fox musical, set on the Barbary Coast during the Naughty Nineties and charting the constancy of Faye's broken heart as she quietly rises to fame as a singing star while Payne, brashly getting ideas above his station, gets into entrepreneurial messes and tags after a Nob Hill heiress. Notable mainly for the vivid Technicolor and Faye's rendition of the Oscar-winning song 'You'll Never Know' (although it's repeated once too often as she waits for Payne to get the message). GA

Hello, Hemingway
(Fernando Pérez, 1990, Cuba) Laura de la Uz, Raúl Paz, Herminia Sánchez, Caridad Hernández, Enrique Molina.
88 min.
'Why did they make birds so delicate and fine as those sea swallows when the ocean can be so cruel?', a bookseller quotes from Hemingway's *The Old Man and the Sea;* but his young friend Laurita (de la Uz, terrific) dismisses the darker passages of the story. In '50s Cuba, she applies for a scholarship to an American university, thereby attempting the first steps away from her impoverished family. Pérez beautifully interweaves complex moods as his film ranges over

personal and social upheaval. Laurita's decision to try to go to America unleashes increasingly hostile reactions from relatives and her politicised boyfriend, but this is balanced against tender exchanges with her grandmother. Initially, the film parallels Laurita's determination with that of Hemingway's Old Man; but more effectively, it dwells on the function of fantasy as both catalysing and comforting force. Fresh, lively and intelligent. CM

Hellraiser
(Clive Barker, 1987, GB) Andrew Robinson, Clare Higgins, Ashley Laurence, Sean Chapman, Oliver Smith.
93 min.
In the bare bedroom of a London suburban house, bored sensualist Frank Cotton solves the mystery of a Chinese puzzle-box and enters a world of exquisite cruelty presided over by the Cenobites, glamorous sadists with a penchant for ripped flesh, steaming viscera and flayed muscle. Later, restored to life by his brother Larry's blood, Frank rises half-formed from a pool of slime. When Larry's wife (and Frank's ex-lover) Julia agrees to provide the human meat he needs to put flesh on his bones, the three become involved in an infernal triangle...Barker's dazzling debut as a director creates such an atmosphere of dread that the astonishing visual set pieces simply detonate in a chain reaction of cumulative intensity. His use of the traditional 'teenage screamer' heroine (Larry's daughter) tends to undercut the unsettling moral ambiguities of the adult triangle, and the brooding menace of the Cenobites is far more terrifying than the climactic rollercoaster ride. These are small quibbles, however, in a debut of such exceptional promise. A serious, intelligent and disturbing horror film. NF

Hellraiser II
see Hellbound: Hellraiser II

Hellraiser III: Hell on Earth
(Anthony Hickox, 1990, US) Doug Bradley, Terry Farrell, Paula Marshall, Kevin Bernhardt, Ken Carpenter, Peter Boynton.
96 min.
With its bravura camerawork, fetishistic Cenobite designs, nerve-jangling soundtrack, and literate Peter Atkins script, Anthony Hickox's film is a worthy successor to Clive Barker's flesh-ripping original. Freed from the stone prison of the Pillar of Souls, Pinhead (Bradley) quickly dispatches decadent rock club owner JP Monroe (Bernhardt). Hearing of JP's gruesome death, TV reporter Joey Summerskill (Farrell) sniffs a scoop, but what she finds is something more nightmarish: Pinhead and his new purveyors of pain, Camerahead, CD and Barbie. Forget the disastrous *Hellbound: Hellraiser II;* this is adult horror to die for. NF

Hell's Angels
(Howard Hughes, 1930, US) Ben Lyon, James Hall, Jean Harlow, John Darrow, Lucien Prival.
135 min. b/w & col.
The Hughes folly over which he laboured for nearly three years, going through a slew of directors (including Luther Reed, James Whale and Howard Hawks) at various stages in the hope of making the greatest and most impressively realistic flying movie ever. Saddled with an atrocious boy's own paper plot about a good brother and a bad brother, both in the Flying Corps and clashing over a girl, the end result is barely adequate. But it does feature a spectacularly elaborate World War I dogfight, and an equally fine Zeppelin sequence. And of course there's Harlow, unflatteringly lit and making a nonsense of the plot by playing her character as an unmistakable floozie, but undeniably making an impact. TM

Hell's Angels on Wheels
(Richard Rush, 1967, US) Adam Roarke, Jack Nicholson, Sabrina Scharf, Jana Taylor, John Garwood.
95 min.
Rush's film came second after Corman's *Wild Angels* in the late '60s biker-movie cycle, and like the earlier film was banned by the British cen-

sor. It now looks a real weirdie: notorious Angel Sonny Barger is credited as 'adviser'; the Oakland Angels feature; B movie directors Jack Starrett and Bruno VeSota have cameo parts; and Jack Nicholson – as a gas pump attendant called Poet who falls in with the road rats by accident – already possesses, fully-fledged, the cynical charm that made him a star. But nothing prepares you for the simple brutality of the film and its off-the-cuff style (it was shot in two weeks). The camera (Laszlo Kovacs) thunders in and out of the pack on dusty roads; barroom fights boast bottles and chains; and Nicholson's nervousness looks real. The whole project, in fact, with its violence and love interest (Nicholson fighting for the leader's 'momma') is schizophrenic, cutting from psychedelia and group sex to private angst and night-time stompings. Rush said that he found the whole bike phenomenon 'distasteful', and it shows in the uneven treatment. But who can resist a bike movie whose pack-leader, asked for a motive, resorts to Milton: 'It is better to rule in Hell than to serve in Heaven'. Eat your heart out, Hunter Thompson. CA

Hellstrom Chronicle, The
(Walon Green, 1971, US) Lawrence Pressman.
90 min.
A curious mixture of entomological documentary and cheapjack horror movie, with Pressman impersonating a supposed visionary Swedish scientist called Nils Hellstrom, and intoning apocalyptic warnings about mankind's imminent come-uppance. The insects are taking over, is the message: scientifically possible and even probable, no doubt, but dramatised with laughable over-emphasis. The microphotography, on the other hand, is amazing, making the insects (everything from bees and termites to Black Widow spiders and driver ants) look like horrendous monsters, and containing quite enough chills in its own right. TM

Hell Up in Harlem
(Larry Cohen, 1973, US) Fred Williamson, Julius W Harris, Gloria Hendry, Margaret Avery, D'Urville Martin.
96 min.
This sequel to *Black Caesar* sparks from a marked tension between blaxploitation conventions and Cohen's maintenance of an ironic distance from his 'hero', who survives an opening semi-reprise of the earlier film's ending (having Harlem Hospital commandeered at gunpoint) to rise/fall/resurrect himself as underworld overlord of New York. The jerkily episodic narrative loosens its tremendous pace about half-way in, even if Cohen keeps jostling the formula with inventive story loops and staccato bursts of action, but it's the overall evidence of a film shot literally 'on the run' that makes this such a delight. Action constantly erupts to general bewilderment and brilliant effect on unsanctioned New York streets, while tourist trap monuments to American democracy serve as hit-and-run locations for conspiracy or corruption, as if in a dry run for Cohen's *Private Files of J Edgar Hoover*. Black maids force-feeding soul food to Mafiosi, a colour-reverse lynching, and a ludicrous foot-plane-foot chase sequence constitute just a few of the sly energies emitted en route to a characteristically ambivalent ending. PT

Hellzapoppin'
(HC Potter, 1941, US) Ole Olsen, Chic Johnson, Martha Raye, Mischa Auer, Hugh Herbert, Elisha Cook Jr, Jane Frazee, Robert Paige.
84 min. b/w.
A genuinely bizarre oddity, this madcap comedy is fascinating not only for its many very funny moments, but also for the way it includes, amid the material taken directly from the original stage revue, various purely cinematic gags which are surprisingly modern in tone and significance. The fact that Olsen and Johnson's revue-style material dispenses with plot, creating instead an almost Monty Pythonesque series of loosely, lunatically linked vignettes (many of them parodies of Hollywood clichés, such as Elisha Cook invariably getting killed with lead), allows them to ignore realism and play around with the medium itself: at one point the stars have problems with the careless projectionist screening the film out of rack, upside-down, etc. Although lacking the satirical edge of the Marx Brothers,

Hellzapoppin frequently outstrips the works of Groucho and Co in terms of speed, imagination and sheer craziness. GA

Help!

(Richard Lester, 1965, GB) John Lennon, Paul McCartney, Ringo Starr, George Harrison, Leo McKern, Eleanor Bron, Victor Spinetti, Roy Kinnear, Patrick Cargill.
92 min.
The second of Lester's two films with the Beatles is obviously a must on grounds of nostalgia, but it never really lives up to the engaging opening sequence in which the evil Maharajah throws darts at the Beatles performing on film. Many of the gags subsequently fall flat, and the final frenetic chase scarcely makes it as either slapstick or satire. *A Hard Day's Night* may be more primitive, but it also seems more spontaneous. DP

Helter Skelter

(Tom Gries, 1976, US) George DiCenzo, Steve Railsback, Nancy Wolfe, Marilyn Burns, Christina Hart.
92 min.
A dramatised documentary about the wave of brutal killings that swept LA back in 1969, and the investigations and trials that eventually led to the conviction of Charles Manson and several members of his 'family'. Based on the book of the same name by prosecuting DA Vincent Bugliosi, it's hardly surprising that the movie is factually reliable, although having been cut down to half its original length (it was first shown as a two-part telefilm), it inevitably omits many important details, such as the fact that one of the defence lawyers was killed by the 'family' during the trial. More disturbingly, it never really examines the generally confused and shifting moral climate in which the murders took place: the sympathy that Manson won from various far outposts of the counter-culture is totally ignored, while the lackadaisical and incompetent methods of the police investigations are barely mentioned. Still, it's thankfully low on gore, and (for an enormously complicated story) told with sufficient narrative simplicity to remain gripping, even though the premise that Manson and his right-hand woman Susan Atkins were mad is too often signalled by ludicrously widened staring eyes. GA

Hen in the Wind, A
(Kaze no naka no mendori)

(Yasujiro Ozu, 1948, Jap) Shuji Sano, Kinuyo Tanaka, Chieko Murata, Chishu Ryu, Takeshi Sakamoto, Eiko Takamatsu.
84 min. b/w.
Ozu himself considered this a failure, but its tale of a soldier who returns home from the war to find his wife has resorted to prostitution in order to nurse their sick child shames many a lesser director's manifest successes despite its overtly melodramatic elements. The symmetrically structured narrative, concentrating first on the woman's plight, then on the husband's rejection of her and eventual reconciliation, and the outbreak of angry violence extraordinarily heightened against the placid domestic background, leave no doubt where Ozu's sympathies lie and of his concern for the erosion of the traditional family system. RM

Hennessy

(Don Sharp, 1975, GB) Rod Steiger, Lee Remick, Richard Johnson, Trevor Howard, Eric Porter, Peter Egan, Stanley Lebor, Ian Hogg.
104 min.
Only American International Pictures could come up with a rollicking cheapie based on the situation in Northern Ireland, utilising both the royal family and the cabinet as plausible extras. Steiger is better than he's been for ages as Hennessy, an embittered Belfast demolition worker who plans to blow up the Royal Opening of Parliament. The film deftly avoids the sectarian issue by making him a lone maverick, pursued by both Special Branch and the IRA (who are to all intents and purposes indistinguishable), and by moving so fast that the improbabilities simply don't have time to catch up. The casting (Porter, Remick and Howard especially), the locations and the use of newsreel at the climax are all spectacularly good, and Sharp's direction proves that he is more than a match for any of AIP's Hollywood hands. DP

Henri

(Simon Shore, 1993, GB) Kara Bowman, John Hewitt, Joe McPartland, Cheryl O'Dwyer, Michael Gregory.
60 min.
A BBC 'Screenplay' from Northern Ireland which treats local events with a light comic touch, without losing sight of the serious underlying issues. John Forte's script uses the piano accordion as a symbol of the divided communities' mutual distrust, following rural Protestant schoolgirl Henri(etta) as she travels to Belfast to try her luck in a music competition – despite a repertoire limited to old Orange anthems. TJ

Henry & June

(Philip Kaufman, 1990, US) Fred Ward, Uma Thurman, Maria De Medeiros, Richard E Grant, Kevin Spacey, Jean-Philippe Ecoffey, Juan Luis Buñuel.
136 min.
Kaufman's account of the triangular affair between Henry Miller (Ward), his wife June (Thurman) and Anais Nin (Medeiros) in '30s Paris is certainly good to look at, edited like a dream, and about an hour too long. Intelligently scripted, particularly good on the pain in relationships, it doesn't shed much light on the literary commerce between the writers. Bohemian society here sometimes resembles the setting for a Gene Kelly number, and the much-vaunted explicitness seems to have strayed in from a Zalman King production. Both Miller and Nin choose June as their Muse, draining away at her until she flees to preserve her sanity, but the actual disclosure that provokes the break – in bed with Nin, she learns that Nin and Miller have been a number – seems uncharacteristically illiberal. Neither Thurman nor Medeiros do much with their roles, but Ward has a fine old time screwing with his hat on and hammering at the Remington. BC

Henry Fool

(Hal Hartley, 1997, US) Thomas Jay Ryan, James Urbaniak, Parker Posey, Maria Porter, Kevin Corrigan.
137 min.
Looser, more expansive and certainly more scatological than Hartley's earlier work, this very funny, finally touching fable focuses on the way Henry Fool (Ryan) – a bawdy, rebellious, intellectually gifted drifter, and quite possibly a charlatan – transforms the lives of the inhabitants of a small town: notably, shy, put-upon Simon Grim (Urbaniak), who under Fool's auspices becomes both celebrated as a writer and demonised as a pornographer; his promiscuous sister (Posey) and depressive mother (Porter). For all its outrageous black humour, however, it remains a Hartley movie, with its wittily stylised dialogue, droll performances, crisp camerawork and its profoundly ironic musings on the nature of art and its status in society – musings which surely reflect on Hartley's own status as an ambitious but marginalised film-maker. GA

Henry: Portrait
of a Serial Killer

(John McNaughton, 1986, US) Michael Rooker, Tracy Arnold, Tom Towles.
90 min.
McNaughton's compelling study of a blithe sociopath makes the flesh crawl and the mind reel. Turning up at the Chicago apartment shared by old prison buddy Otis and his timid sister Becky, Henry (Rooker) slowly draws Otis into his dark, obsessive world of casual murder. The violence is at first oblique, with Henry's past murders presented as a series of grotesque tableaux accompanied by the (recorded) sounds of the victims death struggles. Later, the violence becomes more graphic, but what makes it so disturbing, and sometimes almost unwatchable, is the cool matter-of-fact tone McNaughton sustains throughout. Whether presenting a halting conversation or bloody carnage, he observes events with the unblinking eye of a surveillance camera. It is this air of detachment that makes the blood run cold. Rooker achieves frightening intensity as an ice-killer for whom murder and taking a beer out of the fridge are much the same thing. The remote possibility of moral redemption seems to be held out by Henry's tentative relationship with Becky, but even that faint glimmer of hope is extinguished by a devastatingly downbeat ending. A film of ferocious, haunting power, and a highly impressive directing debut. NF

Henry V

(Laurence Olivier, 1944, GB) Laurence Olivier, Renée Asherson, Robert Newton, Leslie Banks, George Robey, Esmond Knight, Leo Genn, Felix Aylmer, Max Adrian.
137 min.
In Olivier's first attempt at direction there's a certain, limited delight in the possibilities of a new-found medium. The transitions from the stage-bound settings of the Globe to the ringing plains of Agincourt (as stirring as any sequence from *Triumph of the Will*) suggest a flexing of cinematic muscle that, sadly, he later allowed to atrophy by returning to acting his head off and simply recording it by camera. CPea

Henry V

(Kenneth Branagh, 1989, GB) Kenneth Branagh, Brian Blessed, Richard Briers, Robbie Coltrane, Judi Dench, Ian Holm, Derek Jacobi, Alec McCowen, Geraldine McEwan, Michael Maloney, Paul Scofield, John Sessions, Robert Stephens, Emma Thompson, Michael Williams.
137 min.
Branagh adapted and directed this opus as well as starring, and he's found jobs for all his pals. Look, there's John Sessions mugging frantically at the back! Scurvy knave Bardolph is a be-latexed Briers; Mistress Quickly is a dusty Judi Dench; plus there's the grim spectacle of Emma Thompson bounding around in a red wig, gabbling Franglais. Coltrane is Falstaff: great idea, but as the fat man doesn't appear in the play, he's wedged in by way of fumbling flashbacks. Most of the scenes, including exteriors, could have been filmed on the stage of the National, and devices like Jacobi's Chorus, in anachronistic black greatcoat and woolly scarf, serve to accentuate the theatricality of the enterprise, as does the fact that Hal appears to be attacking France with 25 men. The fog of war is convincingly portrayed, though other scenes have an unmistakable whiff of the BBC production: the clip-clop-whinny sound effects, the sudden downpours, the swirling dry ice. Quibbles apart, Branagh succeeds in his blunt, robust portrayl of the Soldier-King, hauling the film along in the wake of his own gung-ho performance. SFe

Henry VIII and His Six Wives

(Waris Hussein, 1972, GB) Keith Michell, Frances Cuka, Charlotte Rampling, Jane Asher, Jenny Bos, Lynne Frederick, Barbara Leigh-Hunt, Donald Pleasence, Michael Gough.
125 min.
The BBC series *The Six Wives of Henry VIII* was a typically well-costumed and researched affair, if rather predictable in its desire to show that underneath the infamous king's bluff and headstrong exterior there lay a lonely and reasonable man. This big-screen spin-off retains that predictability, while losing a lot of historical detail in its compression of the nine-hour original. Most annoying, however, is Michell's mannered and determinedly larger-than-life performance. GA

Her Alibi

(Bruce Beresford, 1989, US) Tom Selleck, Paulina Porizkova, William Daniels, James Farentino, Hurd Hatfield, Ronald Guttman, Victor Argo, Patrick Wayne, Tess Harper.
94 min.
One of those predictable comedies about reclusive writers living vicariously through the adventures created in their work. Selleck is a mystery novelist, suffering from writer's block, who attends court one day in the hope that inspiration will strike, and encounters beautiful Romanian Nina (Porizkova). His powers of perception are such that he can tell straight away she's incapable of stabbing a man as charged, and it transpires that she's being coerced by nasty KGB agents. Suitably intrigued, he offers refuge at his palatial country hideout, in the knowledge that the unfolding adventures will offer him plenty of material. The plot is ludicrous, which in itself would be perfectly acceptable given sharper handling, but both script and direction devote so much time to romantic undercurrents that the central intrigue is further divested of credibility. CM

Herbie Goes Bananas

(Vincent McEveety, 1980, US) Cloris Leachman, Charles Martin Smith, John Vernon, Steven W Burns, Elyssa Davalos, Harvey Korman, Richard Jaeckel.
100 min.

In the ten years since the Disney Organisation made *The Love Bug* and an off-white VW Beetle called Herbie shot to stardom, he's grown with the part and become more assertive, while his supporting actors become more and more like car components. This is Herbiefilm IV (last in the series), in which 26 versions of the star car got trashed; with that kind of turnover in stand-ins, it's not surprising that they haven't got around to changing the plot formula, only the scenery. This year's model chases around some of the less political clichés of Central America in pursuit of villains and pre-Colombian artefacts. If you can stomach the lovey bits, the film has a lot of good car stunts, some innuendo for the adults, and the ultimate accolade for the Chaplinesque Herbie – a chance to play opposite a cute Mexican orphan. RP

Herbie Goes to Monte Carlo
(Vincent McEveety, 1977, US) Dean Jones, Don Knotts, Julie Sommars, Jacques Marin, Roy Kinnear, Bernard Fox.
105 min.
Herbie the thinking VW is all tuned up for the Paris to Monte Carlo road race, but falls for a pert little Lancia (who must be considerably under-age), to the dismay of his handsome driver (Jones) and eye-rolling mechanic (Knotts). Successfully combining excitement, romance and simple comedy, this stock Disney (third in the series) follows an entirely predictable course with masterful precision. And there's sunny weather all the way. JS

Herbie Rides Again
(Robert Stevenson, 1974, US) Helen Hayes, Ken Berry, Stefanie Powers, John McIntire, Keenan Wynn, Huntz Hall.
88 min.
Sequel to Disney's *The Love Bug*, about a Volkswagen with a mind of its own. Despite some insipid characterisation and one or two lapses, things move along at a fair pace and there's a surprising plot all about property speculation in San Francisco. Can Grandma Steinmetz save her home from the grasping magnate Alonzo Hawk? The comedy is on the whole inventive, occasionally aspiring to almost surrealist heights. CPe

Hercules
(John Musker/Ron Clements, 1997, US) voices: Tate Donovan, Danny DeVito, James Woods, Rip Torn, Samantha Eggar, Hal Holbrook.
93 min.
Ancient myth the Disney way, with all the incest, virgin-ravishing and animal cruelty merrily replaced by sound family values and a whole urnful of peppy 1990s pop references. It could easily seem crass, but it's hard to get all serious about a film that so revels in its own infectious humour, distributes gags to all ages, and displays great craft in art director Gerald Scarfe's angular integrated visual design. In short another benchmark achievement for the *Aladdin* team of Musker and Clements. As in *The Hunchback of Notre Dame*, the makers are clued-in enough to take a rise out of their conventional hero, and the grown-up Herc here is a likeable big lug, though not too smart – game enough to slay the Hydra, but not so savvy he can spot the machinations of honey-voiced siren Megara, who's secretly in league with Hades, the megalomaniac ruler of the Underworld. As voiced by Woods, this cigar-chomping super-bad guy remains the chief attraction for grown-ups, who'll also relish the gospelling diva of the none-too-Greek chorus, and the cheeky send-up of ancient Thebes' own merchandising industry. Littl'uns will go for DeVito's knockabout hero-training satyr. TJ

Hercules and the Captive Women
see Ercole alla conquista di Atlantide

Hercules Conquers Atlantis
see Ercole alla conquista di Atlantide

Hercules Returns
(David Parker, 1993, Aust) David Argue, Michael Carman, Mary Coustas, Bruce Spence, Brendon Suhr, Nick Polites.
80 min.
Brad (Argue) is booted out of the Kent Cinema Corporation, a heartless multiplex monolith, and fights back by reopening an old-fashioned picture palace with the help of projectionist Sprocket (Spence). But evil boss Sir Michael Kent tries to scupper them by ensuring that their trash-fest opener, *Hercules*, is supplied in the original Italian without subtitles. What to do? Why, dub it themselves of course, live from the projection box. Actually, this pretence doesn't hold up. But the merciless caricature of these baby-oil poseurs is pretty irresistible. SFe

Herd, The (Sürü)
(Zeki Ökten, 1978, Tur) Tarik Akan, Melike Demirag, Tuncel Kurtiz, Levent Inanir.
118 min.
Shot by Ökten under instruction from its writer Yilmaz Güney, at the time imprisoned for murdering a judge, this slice of social realism is never simplistic, always powerful as it follows the disintegration of a nomadic family of shepherds as they herd their sheep from the Anatolian pastures to the markets of modern Ankara. Problems abound: the traditional ways of the nomads – superstition, feuding, ignorance – are no better than the corrupt and exploitative officialdom of modern industrialised Turkey, although being poor and barely recognised as real human beings, the family are continually at the mercy of their more 'sophisticated' compatriots. Though never quite as telling or brilliant as the later *Yol*, it's a fine film that achieves its effect through its total sincerity and conviction. GA

Here Beneath the North Star
see Täällä Pohjantähden alla

Here Comes Mr Jordan
(Alexander Hall, 1941, US) Robert Montgomery, Evelyn Keyes, Claude Rains, Rita Johnson, Edward Everett Horton, James Gleason.
93 min. b/w.
Mildly engaging fantasy, remade as *Heaven Can Wait* in 1978, with Montgomery as the boxer despatched to his eternal rest by clerical error and returned to earth with Rains as his avuncular guardian angel. Lovely supporting performances from Rains, Horton (the anxiously over-zealous heavenly messenger who made the mistake in the first place) and Gleason (a hopelessly bemused fight manager); but the comedy of errors as Montgomery casts around for a new body in which to pursue his championship ambitions is rather uncomfortably tinged with the fey archness which so often came over Hollywood when envisaging an afterlife. TM

Here Comes the Groom
(Frank Capra, 1951, US) Bing Crosby, Jane Wyman, Franchot Tone, Alexis Smith, James Barton, Anna Maria Alberghetti.
113 min. b/w.
Typically whimsical Capra comedy (with lots of sentiment) in which Crosby adopts a couple of war orphans who will be exiled from the land of democracy unless he can win his fiancée Wyman back from an infatuation with a handsome millionaire (Tone). Tedious romantic shufflings slightly enlivened by some songs and a brief guest spot for Louis Armstrong (playing and singing 'Misto Christofo Columbo'). TM

Here Come the Waves
(Mark Sandrich, 1944, US) Bing Crosby, Betty Hutton, Sonny Tufts, Ann Doran, Catherine Craig.
99 min. b/w.
Fairly dull musical stacked full of patriotic propaganda as it pays tribute to the seafaring warriors – both men and women – of the US Navy. Bing croons and spoons as he joins up and falls in love with identical twin sisters, both played by Hutton. The variable score by Harold Arlen and Johnny Mercer includes 'That Old Black Magic' and 'Accentuate the Positive'. GA

Here We Go Round the Mulberry Bush
(Clive Donner, 1967, GB) Barry Evans, Judy Geeson, Angela Scoular, Sheila White, Adrienne Posta, Vanessa Howard, Diane Keen, Moyra Fraser, Denholm Elliott, Michael Bates, Maxine Audley.
96 min.
Swinging London days, so poor Hunter Davies' pleasant sub-Salinger novel, about the sexual tribulations of a grammar school sixth-former (he longs for something a bit more up-market than the snotty-nosed local bints), gets the full gloss treatment. Jamie MacGregor (Evans) worked part-time for a small local Co-op, but here he's much more smartly located in a supermarket; the Stevenage council estate where he lives looks like King's Road-cum-Carnaby Street, fairly dripping with dolly birds; his dream fantasies are Dick Lester lookalikes, using speeded-up motion for good measure; and when he finally gets invited to a party, the scene looks as fashionably clichéd as the photographer's studio antics in Antonioni's *Blow-Up*. Donner's eagerness to pour 'swinging style' and pop songs over everything makes nonsense of the socially critical attitudes that filter weakly through from the script (by Hunter Davies himself). So charmless as to be almost unwatchable. TM

Heritage, The
(Amnon Rubinstein, 1993, Isr) Avi Toledano, Yael Abecassis, Alon Aboutboul.
86 min.
An old-fashioned costume drama, which cuts between present-day Jerusalem and Toledo, Spain, at the time of the Inquisition and the suppression of the seders. Its parallel love stories – in the modern story an Israeli Jew befriends an air hostess on his trip to locate a house described on an ancient family document brought to him by a lawyer; in the past, a Gentile falls for the imprisoned Jewish woman he's assigned to spy on – function poorly as a means of bringing history 'alive'; and as a 'reconciliation' love story, the film leaves much to be desired, as do its awkward transitions and plot contrivances. It's strangely compulsive, none the less, in a sandal-saga kind of way. WH

Her Majesty, Love
(William Dieterle, 1931, US) Marilyn Miller, WC Fields, Ben Lyon, Leon Errol, Ford Sterling, Chester Conklin.
76 min. b/w.
Fields plays second fiddle to bright-eyed Marilyn Miller (a fellow Ziegfeld star) and the all-smiling, all-leaping Ben Lyon in his first sound feature, an adaptation of a German film with few belly laughs but much charm. He plays the unpresentable father of a barmaid engaged to a dashing young toff, and enjoys himself scandalising dinner guests with a few juggling routines perilously performed with food and kitchenware. Aside from such set pieces, he's still good value, for Fields is one of the few screen comics who could take on the part of a doting father and retain credibility. GB

Hero
(Barney Platts-Mills, 1982, GB) Derek McGuire, Caroline Kenneil, Alastair Kenneil, Stewart Grant, Harpo Hamilton.
92 min.
Brave venture for the fiercely independent Platts-Mills (who had been silent since making *Bronco Bullfrog* and *Private Road* over ten years previously): a Gaelic-speaking epic set in the fifth century, shot on some beautiful locations along the south-west coast of Scotland, and telling the tale of a young knight-errant who joins the band of 'heroes' led by Finn MacCool and sung by the bard Ossian. The non-professional cast, alas, are distressingly amateurish, and since the script seems half-strangled in what it is trying to say, the result looks not unlike a clumping village pageant. TM

Hero
(Tony Maylam, 1986, GB) narrator: Michael Caine.
86 min.
For those who take on the task of making the official documentary of the FIFA World Cup, there is one crucial question: with an impossible number of games to cover, how do you make sure that the most important moments are committed to celluloid? This team thought they had all bases covered by concentrating on the progress of ten key players from various countries; and although, by and large, it's a fairly sensible way of approaching the problem, there is still too much left out for this film to be entirely satisfactory. The commentary, by an awestruck Caine, is embarrassingly over the top, but the film's real weakness is that two of the tournament's most significant games – Russia's 6-0

drubbing of Hungary, and then their defeat by Belgium in the best game of the whole series – barely get a mention. As a celebration of the talent of Diego Maradona, it's spellbinding, but as a record of the 1986 World Cup, it stinks. DPe

Hero, The
see Bloomfield

Hero at Large
(Martin Davidson, 1979, US) John Ritter, Anne Archer, Bert Convy, Kevin McCarthy, Harry Bellaver, Anita Dangler.
98 min.
Very obvious comedy with uncharismatic Ritter as an unemployed actor who gets a job running around in a costume to promote the Captain Avenger comic strip, then after bravely stopping a grocery store robbery decides he'd quite like to go into the superhero business himself. Archer's the wholly disinterested girl-next-door, Convy the scheming PR exec who sees a way of exploiting the Captain's derring-do to his own ends. TJ

Heroes
(Jeremy Paul Kagan, 1977, US) Henry Winkler, Sally Field, Harrison Ford, Val Avery, Olivia Cole, Hector Elias.
113 min.
Henry 'The Fonz' Winkler's first starring feature purports to deal with the 'forgotten' subject of Vietnam veterans. But well-meaning references to a lost generation are quickly dropped in favour of routine odyssey as Winkler travels from NY to Eureka, California (yes, afraid so), teams up with Sally Field (casualty of a non-military engagement), and comes on like the only sane man in a crazy world (of course he's certified and on the run). 'The only one who is chasing you is you', she tells him, and he finally exorcises his ghosts of Vietnam with his gal by his side. One brief interlude of interest features Harrison Ford as a speedy but kinda slow vet who'd make Clint Walker look smart. CPe

Heroes, The (Gli Eroi)
(Duccio Tessari, 1972, It/Fr/Sp) Rod Steiger, Rosanna Schiaffino, Rod Taylor, Claude Brasseur, Terry-Thomas, Gianni Garko.
110 min.
Badly dubbed and inferior successor to *Kelly's Heroes* and other such wartime caper movies. A motley assortment of Germans and Allies call an uneasy truce and opt out of the desert conflict in pursuit of £2 million. Steiger does his German accent (which is beginning to pall a bit), Schiaffino shows a lot of leg, and everyone hams outrageously. A few happy coincidences and a lot of doublecrossing keeps a creaky plot going, and the photography helps some, but the relentless jokiness, plus the inevitable problems of co-production, ensure that it ends up being tedious.

Heroes of Telemark, The
(Anthony Mann, 1965, GB) Kirk Douglas, Richard Harris, Ulla Jacobsson, Michael Redgrave, David Weston, Anton Diffring, Eric Porter.
131 min.
Panavision vistas of Norwegian snowscapes dwarf the characters of Mann's spectacular World War II mission movie, in appropriate correlation to the atomic threat posed by the Nazi heavy water plant Douglas and his resistance allies must destroy. If the landscape no longer mirrors psychology as it did in Mann's classic Westerns, at least it still dominates the narrative with impressive ironic force. PT

Heroic Trio, The (Dongfang San Xia)
(Johnny To, 1992, HK) Maggie Cheung, Michelle Yeoh, Anita Mui, Anthony Wong, Damian Lau.
82 min.
The gimmick is all three are women. Superheroines of the near future battle ancestral evils in labyrinthine caverns beneath city streets. This is quintessential Hong Kong pulp fiction, conflating elements of sci-fi, horror, *noir*, thriller, the supernatural, action-adventure and instant pathos. The plot involves kidnapped boys, one of whom will be chosen as puppet monarch of some imaginary China, the rest turned into zombie cannibals. Good support from Anthony Wong as a meathead sentinel who eats his own severed fingers. TR

Herostratus
(Don Levy, 1967, GB) Michael Gothard, Gabriella Licudi, Peter Stephens, Antony Paul, Mona Chin, Helen Mirren.
142 min.
This 'triumph' for the British avant-garde – an inverted Mephistopheles story in which a poet sells his suicide to an ad agency – now looks charmingly naive. It's Antonioni crossed with Lester's Beatles generation: polite, irreverent, inarticulate, with an irredeemably narrative construction (love story), and much proudly-presented but embarrassed improvisation. While the film's choice of models (tragic grandiloquence versus minimalism, capitalism versus existential angst) remains confused, it's still clever and pretty. Leather fetish fantasy turns wittily into rubber glove ad, striptease is intercut with abattoir – and juxtaposition nearly reduces both to advertising slickness. Intriguing to see how even the avant-garde was mesmerised by the 'beautiful life' of the '60s. CA

Héros très discret, Un (A Self-Made Hero)
(Jacques Audiard, 1995, Fr) Mathieu Kassovitz, Anouk Grinberg, Sandrine Kiberlain, Albert Dupontel, Nadia Barentin, Jean-Louis Trintignant.
106 min.
Audiard's marvellous follow-up to his impressive *Regarde les hommes tomber* is a deliciously inventive comedy about a shy, cowardly, none-too-bright nobody (Kassovitz, director of *La Haine*) who through a mixture of luck, determination and downright lies manages to pass himself off as a WWII Resistance hero. It may be seen as a sly satire on France's illusions about its own wartime record, but more importantly it's a dazzlingly written, consistently funny, and finally very moving tale about identity, fame, storytelling and the way heroic acts often occur on the most intimate plane. GA

Herz aus Glas
see Heart of Glass

He Said, She Said
(Ken Kwapis/Marisa Silver, 1991, US) Kevin Bacon, Elizabeth Perkins, Sharon Stone, Nathan Lane, Anthony LaPaglia, Charlaine Woodard.
115 min.
A pair of yuppie Baltimore hacks use their romance as material for their rival newspaper columns. Later they become TV stars. The story's told from two perspectives, with Kwapis directing his and Silver hers. It may seem a novel conceit, but like the lifestyle journalism it celebrates, the film is grating, narcissistic and shallow. GM

He's a Woman, She's a Man (Jinzhi Yuye)
(Peter Chan Ho-sun, 1994, HK) Leslie Cheung, Anita Yuen, Carina Lau.
106 min.
The United Film-makers Organisation (UFO) has made a splash in the tough Hong Kong market with a series of comedy-dramas about the problems facing yuppies. This one purports to deal with gender issues and has a smattering of gay supporting characters. A young woman (Yuen) tries to break into showbiz by posing as a male singer; a straight talent manager (Cheung) is disturbed to find himself fancying her, unaware of her actual gender. Almost unwatchably shallow and insincere, the film tries to give its affirmative hetero ending a gay-friendly spin. TR

Hester Street
(Joan Micklin Silver, 1974, US) Steven Keats, Carol Kane, Mel Howard, Dorrie Kavanaugh, Doris Roberts.
92 min. b/w.
Tackling a potentially fascinating and neglected area – Jewish immigrants in end-of-last-century New York – this limits itself to an affectionate and predictable chronicle of the Americanisation of Jake and Gitl. Clarity of emotion at the expense of subtlety, larger than life performances (with the exception of Carol Kane, whose greenhorn wife ends up learning the fastest), confine the film to warmheartedness and gentle, ironic observation at the expense of any real insight. Only towards the end, as the couple split up and remar-

ry, does the film satisfactorily come to terms with a society in a state of flux and its relation to the American Dream: the passing of old customs, self-improvement, ghetto mentality and matriarchy are all touched upon. But an unimaginative camera and misty monochromes do little beyond conveying some self-conscious period recreation. CPe

Hets (Frenzy/Torment)
(Alf Sjöberg, 1944, Swe), Stig Järrel, Mai Zetterling, Alf Kjellin, Olof Winnerstrand, Stig Olin, Gunnar Björnstrand.
101 min. b/w.
A vaguely rebellious teenager (Kjellin), bullied by his sadistic Latin master (Järrel), falls for a young prostitute (Zetterling) who tells him she is being persecuted by a sinister man; when the boy finds her dead, he also discovers the teacher hiding in the room... As scripted by Ingmar Bergman (it was his first filmed scenario), Sjöberg's film is a relentlessly cruel study in sadomasochistic relationships, structured as a bleak, sordid thriller. Full of superb expressionist shots which serve to highlight the intensity of the film's highly emotional subject matter, it also benefits from the excellent performances of Järrel and the young Mai Zetterling. Interestingly, Järrel was made up to resemble Himmler, prompting interpretations of the film as an allegory on Fascism; more crucially, however, its harsh pessimism anticipates the spiritually tormented universe of Bergman's own work. GA

He Walked By Night
(Alfred Werker, 1949, US) Richard Basehart, Scott Brady, Roy Roberts, Whit Bissell, Jack Webb.
79 min. b/w.
Minor but taut thriller in the semi-documentary vein so popular in the second half of the '40s, about detectives tracking down thief-turned-cop killer Basehart (and making much play with the new Identikit methods). The fact that Anthony Mann had an uncredited hand in the direction may have something to do with the successful creation of a tense atmosphere, although most notable is the superb *noir* photography by John Alton, who really comes into his own during the final chase through the LA sewers. Basehart is excellent as the strange, lone wolf electronics expert/killer, an enigmatic threat haunting the paranoid dreams of the witch-hunting era. GA

He Walks Like a Tiger
see King of Kung Fu

He Who Gets Slapped
(Victor Sjöström, 1924, US) Lon Chaney, Norma Shearer, John Gilbert, Tully Marshall, Marc MacDermott, Ford Sterling.
6,953 ft. b/w.
Based on Leonid Andreyev's 1914 play, which prefigures Beckett and the Absurd in expressing the angst of pre-Revolutionary Russia, *He Who Gets Slapped* is about a scientist shattered to discover that his patron has appropriated not only his researches but his wife. Frozen into the fixation that he must become a clown in body as well as in spirit, he joins a circus. There, literally wearing his heart on his sleeve, he willingly suffers agonies of humiliation while the crowd roars. Chaney's performance is extraordinary, but the real amazement of the film is Sjöström's direction, incorporating incredibly subtle lighting effects (which are his, not the cameraman's), and perfectly blending its daring Expressionist devices with the horror movie ethos which takes over when the clown finally seeks revenge. This, undoubtedly, is the source Bergman drew on for *Sawdust and Tinsel*. TM

Hex
(Leo Garen, 1973, US) Tina Herazo [Cristina Raines], Hilarie Thompson, Keith Carradine, Mike Combs, Scott Glenn, Gary Busey, Robert Walker, John Carradine.
93 min.
Largely a mess, but an engaging one. A horror film/Western/World War I biker movie, it exudes an improbable degree of charm precisely because of a freewheeling script that refuses to be tied to any one genre. Very obviously made in the shadow of Corman's *Gas-s-s-s*, it traces the consequences of the accidental meeting between two Lawrentian sisters – living

alone on the Nebraskan farm left to them by their Indian father – and a gang of oddly innocent bikers in the early years of the century. While the expected thuggery and rape almost come about, mayhem of another kind is introduced when one of the sisters begins to conjure her dead father's familiars to do their worst, resulting in a string of psychedelic sequences. Although the girls' motivations remain consistently traditional (well, almost), on the whole the film exudes the feeling of being, almost subliminally, a nostalgic valediction to the counter-culture. VG

Hey Cousin!
see Salut Cousin!

Hi, Are You Alone? (Hola, estás sola?)
(Icíar Bollaín, 1995, Sp) Silke, Candela Peña, Alex Angulo, Elena Irureta, Arcadi Levin.
90 min.
Like her performance as the red-haired Maite in Ken Loach's Land and Freedom, actress-turned-writer/director Icíar Bollaín's first feature is simple, direct and infused with feeling. Part road movie and part domestic drama, it follows two 20-year-olds, moody Niña (Silke) and vivacious Trini (Peña), as they wander about Spain in search of money, love and a sense of belonging. Alternating between spells on the road and brief experiments with various forms of domesticity, the ill-matched pair share rooms, a boyfriend (the Russian-speaking 'Olaf') and, more problematically, Niña's estranged mother Mariló (Irureta). The uncontrived situations, flawed characters and unforced humour are revealing yet never judgmental. NF

Hibiscus Town (Furong Zhen)
(Xie Jin, 1986, China) Liu Xiaoqing, Jiang Wen, Zheng Zaishi, Zhu Shibin, Xu Songzi.
136 min.
Cut for international distribution from the 165 minute, two-part original, this – like Xie Jin's Two Stage Sisters – is a potent blend of the political and personal. It begins in 1963, in the remote rural backwater of the title: through determination and hard work, beancurd-seller Hu Yuyin makes enough money to build a new house for herself and her timid husband. But Maoist plans are afoot to clean up the country, and Hu Yuyin is accused of self-enrichment at the expense of the state. Betrayal, denunciation and humiliation abound as her life steadily falls apart; with the advent of the 1966 'Cultural Revolution', intrigue and paranoia are epidemic. Xie's portrait of China's traumatic, turbulent history ranges from '63 to the post-'Gang of Four' years, his palette the changing fortunes of an entangled group of individuals. It's impressive both for the elegant precision with which the director fills his scope frame with small, significant details, and for the discreet understatement that controls his own special brand of epic melodrama. In some ways similar to the classic romances of Frank Borzage, Hibiscus Town is a moving account of survival in the face of widespread social and political madness, told with clarity, compassion and insight. GA

Hickey & Boggs
(Robert Culp, 1972, US) Bill Cosby, Robert Culp, Rosalind Cash, Louis Moreno, Ron Henrique, Robert Mandan, Vincent Gardenia, James Woods.
111 min.
The first film from a Walter Hill script turns out to be as interesting for the assurance of Culp's direction as for Hill's contribution. Hickey & Boggs pairs television's I Spy team of Cosby and Culp as two down-at-heel private eyes caught in the crossfire of a very messy attempt to fence a suitcase full of banknotes. The laconic and cynical pair inhabit a familiar '70s noir thriller world where if you blink you miss a crucial plot point, and Cosby's relationship with his estranged wife and kid more than once threatens to turn sentimental. But the film scores with set pieces like the complicated shootout in a baseball park (where neither of them manage to hit anything), and many moments of fine throwaway humour. Peckinpah or Siegel couldn't have done it any more crisply. RM

Hidden, The
(Jack Sholder, 1988, US) Kyle MacLachlan, Michael Nouri, Claudia Christian, Clarence Felder, Clu Gulager, Ed O'Ross, William Boyett.
97 min.
A fast-paced, blackly comic sci-fi thriller about a power-hungry alien organism which invades the bodies of law-abiding citizens and transforms them into deranged criminals with a penchant for fast cars, blasting rock music, and violent anti-social behaviour. When a respectable businessman robs a bank, guns down the security guards, and crashes into a road block, LA cop Nouri thinks it's all over. But at the hospital, the inciting organism slips into a neighbouring patient, who then continues the previous host's crime spree. Forced to team up with FBI cop MacLachlan, Nouri's frustration is exacerbated by his new partner's quirky behaviour and air of debauched stillness. Created by ace SFX man Kevin Yagher, the organism is a classic (mostly kept hidden); the developing relationship between the two cops is nicely handled; and there's a neat twist concerning the origins of MacLachlan's vendetta against the organism. Powered by a driving rock score, this is by turns sleek, reckless, and smoothly effective, like a Ferrari with a psycho killer at the wheel. NF

Hidden Agenda
(Ken Loach, 1990, GB) Frances McDormand, Brian Cox, Brad Dourif, Mai Zetterling, Maurice Roëves, Bernard Bloch, Brian McCann, Michelle Fairley.
108 min.
Loach's film has the feel of a Costa-Gavras political thriller and a script by controversial Marxist Jim Allen. Despite its sometimes flailing conspiracy-theory narrative, and its upstaging by TV projects like Stalker, Death on the Rock and Who Bombed Birmingham?, this deserves to be seen simply because it takes the debate on Ireland further than most such docudramas, asking questions about the nature of the British presence and its effect on the mainland's justice system. The plot, based on both the Stalker and Colin Wallace affairs, concerns the murder of an American civil liberties campaigner by security forces, and the subsequent enquiry by Brian Cox's Stalker-style police officer which leads to the heart of the military and political establishment. Whatever one thinks of the political line on offer, there's plenty of evidence of Loach's undiminished power as a film-maker, and equally ample evidence that something is very rotten in the state of Northern Ireland. SGr

Hidden City
(Stephen Poliakoff, 1987, GB) Charles Dance, Cassie Stuart, Bill Paterson, Richard E Grant, Alex Norton, Tusse Silberg.
108 min. b/w & col.
Poliakoff's first film as writer-director, at least partly inspired by an article in Time Out on Secret London, in particular a building in Wandsworth which was used for the interrogation of prisoners during the war. The film bristles with deceptively mundane settings – tunnels, shafts, tearooms, workmen's huts – all throwing up secrets of the surveillance trade. Not merely the Le Carré kind either, but the sort which affects all of us in the end. The thriller plot in which Charles Dance and Cassie Stuart track down one of these secrets is chilling enough, but far less powerful than the superb use of real locations and the mazy, hazy recreation of a modern city of computers, chicanery and dark secrets. The sort of movie that ensures you never feel secure walking down the street again. SGr

Hidden Fortress, The (Kakushi Toride no San-Akunin)
(Akira Kurosawa, 1958, Jap) Toshiro Mifune, Misa Uehara, Takashi Shimura, Susumu Fujita, Eiko Miyoshi.
139 min. b/w.
The movie that confirmed Kurosawa's greatest strength, his innovative handling of genre. Set amid the civil wars of 16th century Japan, and concerns samurai Mifune escorting a princess and two oafish peasants through enemy territory. Kurosawa's treatment is part traditional (the plotting, the concept, the use of Noh theatre music), part eclectic (there are reminiscences of

John Ford Westerns), and part truly idiosyncratic (the Shakespearean contracts between clowns and heroes). It was clearly only a small step from this to the delights of Yojimbo and Sanjuro. TR

Hidden Room, The
see Obsession

Hide in Plain Sight
(James Caan, 1980, US) James Caan, Jill Eikenberry, Robert Viharo, Joe Grifasi, Barbra Rae, Kenneth McMillan.
98 min.
A promising subject for James Caan's directorial debut: the true story of a divorced Buffalo factory-worker who finds that his two children have disappeared because their stepfather has been given a new, secret identity by the government after testifying against underworld associates. But as a director, Caan's sense of mood and construction proves desperately uncertain, with the result that the film uneasily mixes suspense thriller elements in with its more realistic study of a blue collar worker up against civil authority; and his own mannered portrayal of the inarticulate, fiery hero with a heart of gold is frequently hard to take. DP

Hider in the House
(Matthew Patrick, 1989, US) Gary Busey, Mimi Rogers, Michael McKean, Kurt Christopher Kinder, Candy Hutson, Elizabeth Ruscio, Chuck Lafont.
108 min.
When Tom Sykes (Busey) is released from an institution some 20 years after murdering his sadistic parents, all he wants is a family and a home. Obsessively pragmatic, he installs himself into a newly refurbished house, building a secret room behind a false wall in the loft. By the time the Dryers take up residence, all the rooms are bugged and Sykes has his own entry. Adopting this 'perfect' family, he finds himself increasingly involved in family affairs: cowering like the kids when the parents argue, and then taking an overtly Oedipal role, manoeuvering the father (McKean) out of the picture and introducing himself to the mother (Rogers) as a friendly neighbour. Accept the unlikely premise (director Patrick puts economy over plot exposition), and you'll find a tense psychological suspense film which cannily explores family politics with sour wit and distinctly macabre conclusions. It's a very promising debut from Patrick, resisting the overt violence of the horror movie in favour of uneasy intimacy and intelligent characterisation. Rogers and McKean are first-rate, but Busey in particular has seldom been better employed, his hulking physique a reminder of the tragic monsters of movie yore, immensely threatening but intrinsically vunerable. TCh

Hiding Out
(Bob Giraldi, 1987, US) Jon Cryer, Keith Coogan, Annabeth Gish, Gretchen Cryer, Oliver Cotton, Tim Quill, Anne Pitoniak.
98 min.
A twenty-something stockbroker (Jon Cryer), about to give evidence against a mobster, learns there's a contract out on his life. He flees town, dyes his hair, and enrolls in a suburban high school alongside his cousin. Predictable, slackly plotted nonsense, marginally redeemed by a genial young cast. GM

Hiding Place, The
(James F Collier, 1974, US) Julie Harris, Eileen Heckart, Arthur O'Connell, Jeannette Clift, Robert Rietty.
147 min.
At the centre of this story of Corrie and Betsie ten Boom, Dutch sisters who, with their family, helped smuggle countless Jews out of Holland during World War II and were incarcerated in a German concentration camp, lies a would-be celebration of Christian faith. The good intentions of all concerned notwithstanding, the film falls flat. Collier's ersatz heroic style is inadequate as suggesting either the torments of concentration camp life or the consolations of true faith; so much so that the real Corrie ten Boom appears personally in a prologue to testify how faith kept her and her sister alive. In short, the film – produced for Billy Graham's Evangelistic Association – lacks the commitment of its protagonist, preferring instead religious clichés and production values. PH

High and Dry

see Maggie, The

High and Low (Tengoku to Jigoku)

(Akira Kurosawa, 1963, Jap) Toshiro Mifune, Kyoko Kagawa, Tatsuya Mihashi, Yutaka Sada, Tatsuya Nakadai, Takashi Shimura.
143 min. b/w.
Adapted, unexpectedly, from one of Ed McBain's 87th Precinct novels (King's Ransom), this emerges as part thriller and part morality play in the manner characteristic of Kurosawa. After bringing off a big financial coup, a tycoon finds that his son has been kidnapped. Prepared to ruin himself to pay the ransom, he realises that his chauffeur's son was abducted by mistake. The first half, set in a single room, echoes Hitchcock's Rope in exploring his moral dilemma while the action takes place off-screen. The second is disconcertingly different in that it focuses excitingly on the police procedures deployed in the hunt for the kidnapper. But the connections, though sometimes overly obvious in appealing to the liberal conscience, span fascinating Dostoievskian depths. TM

High Anxiety

(Mel Brooks, 1977, US) Mel Brooks, Madeline Kahn, Cloris Leachman, Harvey Korman, Dick Van Patten.
94 min.
Generally juvenile and crass spoof of Hitchcock thrillers, filching themes and scenes from Vertigo, Psycho, The Birds, Spellbound etc., in its story of a psychologist going to work at a very strange and sinister Institute for the Very Very Nervous. Most of the gags are either incredibly obvious or depressingly scatological, or both. But there are a couple of nice touches, one satirising Hitchcock's use of orchestral scores, and the other his relentlessly prowling, voyeuristic camera. GA

High Boot Benny

(Joe Comerford, 1993, Ire) Frances Tomelty, Alan Devlin, Marc O'Shea, Fiona Nicholas.
82 min.
The occasional playfulness of Reefer and the Model (1987) is replaced here – another response by director Comerford to the political impasse in present-day Ireland – by a more sombre mood. This is a more straightforward allegorical tale than its predecessor, set around a 'neutral' school run by 'The Matron' (Tomelty) and Manley (Devlin), a maverick ex-priest, on the windswept border between North and South. Teenage delinquent Benny, who sports a mohican and steel-shinned boots, is a metaphorical and literal outsider, who wanders the rugged landscape that surrounds the former fort, looking after animals, and taking refuge (and physical comfort) at the school. When the school 'caretaker' is found dead, Benny is drawn into the conflict between the police, the British Army, the Loyalist paramilitaries, and the IRA. Into the arms of which group will he be drawn? This is a potent blend of didactic history lessons, flourishes of elegant dark beauty, brooding psycho-drama and cold-blooded analysis. Strong performances. WH

High Bright Sun, The (aka McGuire Go Home!)

(Ralph Thomas, 1965, GB) Dirk Bogarde, George Chakiris, Susan Strasberg, Denholm Elliott, Grégoire Aslan, Colin Campbell, Joseph Fuerst, Nigel Stock.
114 min.
A misguided Ralph Thomas/Betty Box production for the Rank Organisation which tries to create a romantic drama out of the British military presence in Cyprus in the late '50s. Bogarde's British intelligence man whose efforts to stem Eoka guerilla activity are compromised when he falls for American-Cypriot gal Strasberg, an archeology student lodging at a villa where the chief guerilla (Aslan) is in hiding. Sadly the script by Ian Stuart Black (from his own novel) doesn't make it through the political minefield created by a very messy independence conflict. Chakiris lays it on as a fanatical student patriot. TJ

High Commissioner, The

see Nobody Runs Forever

High Encounters of the Ultimate Kind

see Cheech & Chong's Next Movie

Higher Learning

(John Singleton, 1995, US) Ice Cube, Laurence Fishburne, Kristy Swanson, Jennifer Connelly, Michael Rapaport, Omar Epps, Jason Wiles, Tyra Banks.
128 min.
The setting is 'Columbus' University, where freshmen arrive believing that they're there in pursuit of higher learning, wilder parties or whatever – whereas what they're really after is some individual sense of sexual, racial or political identity: hard to achieve when they also want to belong, and when various teachers, cliques and loudmouths are out to influence them. Among the newcomers are Malik (Epps), a black athlete who soon has to work and run harder than expected, and finds himself caught between the conflicting attitudes to racial struggle of Fudge (Ice Cube) and Professor Phipps (Fishburne); Kristen (Swanson), a gullible WASP who after being date-raped falls under the spell of feminist Taryn (Connelly); and Remy (Rapaport), a gauche misfit whose loneliness renders him prey to the camaraderie of local neo-Nazis. A stylish, intelligent film-maker, Singleton interweaves the threads of his demographic tapestry with assurance, passion and a welcome awareness of the complexities of the college community's contradictory impulses towards integration and separatism. Minus points: some schematic stereotyping and a rather sniffy attituted towards lesbianism. GA

Highest Honor – A True Story, The

see Southern Cross

High Heels

see Docteur Popaul

High Heels (Tacones lejanos)

(Pedro Almodóvar, 1991, Sp) Victoria Abril, Marisa Paredes, Miguel Bosé, Pedro Diez del Corral, Féodor Atkine, Ana Lizarán.
114 min.
Almodóvar ditches gender-bending, drug-abusing anarchy for a more sober meditation on the importance of family. Newsreader Rebecca (Abril) is obsessed by her glamorous pop singer mother (Paredes), who left her as a child. The reunion after 15 years is difficult, not least because Rebecca has married her mother's old boyfriend; and when he is murdered, suspicion alights on them both. The performances are superb, with a raw emotion that is uncomfortably voyeuristic to watch; and the central scene, around which the rest of the film was constructed, is an astonishing tragic-comic tour de force: Rebecca broadcasts the latest news on the murder of her own husband, then almost breaks down as she shows snapshots of ordinary household objects. It's sad and funny, but like the rest of the film, mostly sad. And therein lies the problem: the overwrought, almost physical love/hate relationship between the two women never quite rings true, and Almodóvar has crossed the thin comedic line that separated Law of Desire and Matador from cloying melodrama. You come out bruised, thoughtful, but unredeemed. DW

High Hopes

(Mike Leigh, 1988, GB) Philip Davis, Ruth Sheen, Edna Doré, Philip Jackson, Heather Tobias, Lesley Manville, David Bamber.
112 min.
Mike Leigh describes this film (his first for the big screen since his debut in 1971 with Bleak Moments) as his most optimistic work to date; and in the splendidly unfashionable figures of Cyril and Shirley (Davis and Sheen), two downmarket residents of old King's Cross, comes an enormous upsurge of warmth, despite Cyril's continuing confusion on the subject of procreation in a divided world. Less successful are the nastier creations of Leigh's blend of improvisation and script: the monstrous car salesman Martin and his consumerist spouse (Jackson and Tobias); two yuppie neighbours played by Bamber and Manville with a permanent sneer on their minds. But in the figure which draws all these strands together for a very amusing birthday party, Cyril's ageing and indomitable mum (Doré), he

offers a superbly crafted and unsentimentalised study of age and survival. Very long, prone to the longueur, but finally triumphant in its sombre, raw meditation on how we live. SGr

Highlander

(Russell Mulcahy, 1986, GB) Christopher Lambert, Roxanne Hart, Clancy Brown, Sean Connery, Beatie Edney, Alan North.
116 min.
Narrative coherence is not a quality which director Mulcahy brings to this mondial of machismo, about a bizarre (and shrinking) band of immortals engaged in mortal combat down the ages. Highlander hops to and fro, from the Scottish highlands in the middle ages to contemporary America, allowing Lambert to don a variety of kits to match the perpetually pained expression in his eyes, and Connery, as his mentor, to make tosh dialogue sound like it was written by Noël Coward. It has lots of energy, a frenzied pace, and a villain who sings Tom Waits while mowing down innocent pedestrians. It's a lot of utterly preposterous fun, even if it doesn't quite hang together. Scotch missed. RR

Highlander II – The Quickening

(Russell Mulcahy, 1990, US) Christopher Lambert, Sean Connery, Virginia Madsen, Michael Ironside.
100 min.
The time travellers with a flair for decapitation and swordplay are back, though this time Mulcahy's slick visuals merely serve to emphasise how vacuous the concept has become. It's the 21st century, and the ozone layer has been replaced by a protective shield built by what rapidly becomes the world's most powerful, corrupt corporation. The shield's original creator is Connor MacLeod (Lambert), now an old man who has opted to end his days in peaceful oblivion on Earth. But back home on the planet Zeist, evil dictator Katana (Ironside) has other plans for him... The film-makers opt this time for plenty of comic-strip gore, with the irredeemably wicked Katana leering his way through a series of spine-shattering escapades. "This is going to be fun" he mutters before a particularly tedious sequence in which subway train passengers endure a bloody ride to hell. Leaden, laden with effects, short on imagination.

Highlander III – The Sorcerer

(Andy Morahan, 1995, Can/Fr/GB) Christopher Lambert, Mario Van Peebles, Deborah Unger, Mako, Raoul Trujillo, Jean-Pierre Pérusse.
98 min.
Evil magician Kane (Van Peebles), one of three immortals buried in a Japanese magician's cave for 400 years, returns to confront his nemesis, the Highlander (Lambert). Using brute strength and the power of illusion, he wrests the Prize from his adversary's grasp. Observing from the sidelines is research scientist Alex Johnson (Unger), whose archaeological dig first unearthed them. Lambert is as uncharismatic as ever, while Van Peebles is as frightening as a wrestler in mock angry mood, and just as ridiculous. The choicest moment is when Connor MacLeod's flashback romp in the hay with Sarah (Unger, again) is interrupted by a flunky who insists he's needed in Paris immediately, 'because the Revolution's started'. With dialogue and storylines like these, director Morahan is on a hiding to nothing. To his credit, however, he smoothly continues the series' tradition of flashy images, showy sfx, aerial landscape shots and driving rock tunes. Polished photography from Steven Chivers. NF

Highly Dangerous

(Roy Baker, 1950, GB) Margaret Lockwood, Dane Clark, Marius Goring, Naunton Wayne, Wilfrid Hyde-White, Michael Hordern, Anthony Newley.
88 min. b/w.
Eric Ambler must have enjoyed himself cooking up this daffy blend of espionage spoof and straightforward thriller. Lockwood's the rather prim entomologist who heads for the Balkans, is arrested as a spy, then escapes and teams up with crusading Yank journo Clark while under the influence of a truth serum that makes her believe she's the heroine in a radio serial. It doesn't really come off, but larky moments raise a smile – like casting Naunton Wayne as the Chief of the Imperial General Staff. TJ

High Noon (100)

(Fred Zinnemann, 1952, US) Gary Cooper, Grace Kelly, Lloyd Bridges, Katy Jurado, Thomas Mitchell, Otto Kruger, Lon Chaney, Henry Morgan.
85 min. b/w.
A Western of stark, classical lineaments: Cooper, still mysteriously beautiful in ravaged middle-age, plays a small town marshal who lays life and wife on the line to confront a killer set free by liberal abolitionists from the North. Waiting for the murderer's arrival on the mid-day train, he enters a long and desolate night of the soul as the heat gathers, his fellow-citizens scatter, and it grows dark, dark, dark amid the blaze of noon. Writer Carl Foreman, who fetched up on the HUAC blacklist, leaves it open whether the marshal is making a gesture of sub-lime, arrogant futility – as his bride (Kelly), a Quaker opposed to violence, believes – or sim-ply doing what a man must. *High Noon* won a fistful of Oscars, but in these days of pasteboard screen machismo, it's worth seeing simply as the anatomy of what it took to make a man before the myth turned sour. SJo

High Plains Drifter

(Clint Eastwood, 1972, US) Clint Eastwood, Verna Bloom, Mariana Hill, Mitchell Ryan, Jack Ging, Stefan Gierasch, Billy Curtis, Geoffrey Lewis.
105 min.
As gravestone inscriptions in the town of Lago (painted red and renamed Hell by the phantom drifter) make clear, this was supposed to be Eastwood's fond adieu to the worlds of Sergio Leone and Don Siegel; and indeed he cuts the operatic excess of the former with the punchy economy of the latter. Yet the way Ernest Tidyman's script is submitted to distortion and distension, and fitted with Bruce Surtees' almost surreal images (and several twists of the ghostly revenge plot itself), suggest nothing so much as Eastwood returning for reference to the popular Japanese cinema from which Leone himself first borrowed for the *Dollars* films. Whatever, there's a boldness, confident stylisation, and genuine weirdness to the movie that totally escaped other post-spaghetti American Westerns, with a real sense of exorcism running both through and beyond it. PT

High Risk

(Stewart Raffill, 1981, US/GB) James Brolin, Lindsay Wagner, Anthony Quinn, Cleavon Little, Bruce Davison, Chick Vennera, James Coburn, Ernest Borgnine.
94 min.
To the accompaniment of news bulletins dis-pensing gloom about inflation and unemploy-ment, an out-of-work cameraman (Brolin) collects three similarly situated buddies for an improba-ble raid on the Colombian hacienda of dope-deal-er Coburn. Veering between comic caper and homily on the danger of living out depression fan-tasies, *High Risk* has something of an identity problem. For all his bull-slaying bravado, the suavely sinister Coburn proves to be just a paper tiger, while Quinn and a band of corrupted revo-lutionaries provide little more than light relief. There are nicely observed moments – the trepi-dation with which these 'ordinary Americans' confront the necessity for violence, their right-eous indignation at being taken for CIA agents ('Christ, we're on Welfare!') – but they do tend to get lost in a finale of dago-bashing heroics. RMy

High Road to China

(Brian G Hutton, 1983, US) Tom Selleck, Bess Armstrong, Jack Weston, Wilford Brimley, Robert Morley, Brian Blessed, Cassandra Gava.
120 min.
No better or worse than other film-making-by-numbers imitations of *Raiders of the Lost Ark*. Armstrong plays a headstrong '20s heiress searching for her father, an inventor; Selleck plays the grizzled alcoholic flying ace who owns the only available planes. There is absolutely no feeling for the period, and the actors make no attempt to rise above the script's feeble idea of verbal sparring. But the Yugoslav locations are scenic, the aerial stunts are efficient, and there's an explosion every time interest starts to flag. Assuming, of course, that the interest was there in the first place. TR

High School

(Frederick Wiseman, 1968, US)
75 min. b/w.
Wiseman's second film, one of the documentaries marked by a certain compulsive austerity – they reject the traditional crutches of commentary, background music, gloss colour or fancy camer-awork – in which he explored aspects of American institutional life. In *High School*, as might be expected, the American Dream is watched in the making. It is in the oppression of the adult/child relations that the full squalor of the bourgeois ideal is squeezed out. JDuC

High School High

(Hart Bochner, 1996, US) Jon Lovitz, Tia Carrere, Mekhi Phifer, Guillermo Díaz, John Neville, Malinda Williams, Louise Fletcher.
85 min.
Gag-wise, this spoof from the Zucker Bros – actu-ally just David plus major production help and lightweight scriptwriting assistance from Robert LoCash and Pat Proft – is an under-achiever. Lovitz plays the naive teacher son of a WASP headmaster who escapes the paternal shadow by accepting a post in the internecine groves of Marion Barry High. His beliefs set him at odds with rival Latino/Afro gangs and headmistress Louise Fletcher, who wields a baseball bat, but soon gets him 'skin-slapping' with 'educational assistant' Victoria (Carrere). Strangely, the direc-tor plays too much of the movie straight, slow and slushily romantic. This grants us dangerous leisure time to notice the script's dependence on racism, sexism and homophobia, ensuring that the moments of unrestrained, non-PC excess (a hilarious travesty of Chinatown clichés, for instance) prove the most rewarding. WH

High Season

(Clare Peploe, 1987, GB) Jacqueline Bisset, James Fox, Irene Papas, Sebastian Shaw, Kenneth Branagh, Lesley Manville, Robert Stephens.
101 min.
This messy moussaka of a film purports to iden-tify the changes effected by tourism on a colour-brochure Greek village, but it is in fact symptomatic rather than diagnostic. A pack of foreigners, their cameras whirring, have descend-ed upon an unspoilt location, made hoo-ha, ridiculed the natives, and gone home with their skin peeling but their preconceptions intact. Characteristically for such a Carry On, the feeble plot wanders all over the place and involves a Grecian urn, a statue of the unknown tourist and a Russian spy. Bisset is a photographer, and her estranged hubby (Fox) a sculptor. Their cultural pretensions are on a level with those of the script by Mark and Clare Peploe. MS

High Sierra

(Raoul Walsh, 1941, US) Humphrey Bogart, Ida Lupino, Alan Curtis, Arthur Kennedy, Joan Leslie, Henry Hull, Henry Travers, Cornel Wilde, Barton MacLane.
100 min. b/w.
A momentous gangster movie which took the genre out of its urban surroundings into the bleak sierras, and in so doing marked its transition into *film noir*. It isn't just that Bogart's Mad Dog Earle is a man 'rushing towards death', infallibly doomed and knowing it, from the moment he is paroled and through the half-hearted hold-up to his last stand on the mountainside. He also in a sense wills his own destruction, his dark despair fuelled by the betrayal of an innocent, clubfoot-ed country girl whose operation he pays for, and who casually abandons him as soon as she can 'have fun'. Terrific performances, terrific camera-work (Tony Gaudio), terrific dialogue (John Huston and WR Burnett from the latter's novel), with Walsh – who in fact reworked the material as *Colorado Territory* eight years later – giving it something of the memorable melancholy of a Peckinpah Western. TM

High Society

(Charles Walters, 1956, US) Bing Crosby, Frank Sinatra, Grace Kelly, Celeste Holm, Louis Armstrong, Louis Calhern, John Lund.
107 min.
Musical remake of *The Philadelphia Story* which scores over the original only in its score. Crosby (especially) and Sinatra are miscast in the Cary Grant/James Stewart roles, and Grace Kelly only really catches the icy class of Tracy Lord, where-as Katharine Hepburn made her a complex comic creation. But despite many commentators' thumbs-down to one of Cole Porter's best late scores, the numbers are good, particularly the lesser-known ballads (like Bing's archetypal note-bending 'Samantha'). And there's not much gain-saying 'Well Did You Evah' (the only song not written for the movie, and it looks an intrusion) or 'Who Wants to Be a Millionaire?' (with the undervalued Celeste Holm). A slightly misbegot-ten musical, but with many pleasures and Louis Armstrong, growing into sweet avuncularity. SG

High Spirits

(Neil Jordan, 1988, US) Peter O'Toole, Daryl Hannah, Steve Guttenberg, Beverly D'Angelo, Jennifer Tilly, Martin Ferrero, Liam Neeson, Ray McAnally.
96 min.
Written and directed by the man who gave you *Angel*, *Company of Wolves* and *Mona Lisa*, this dreadful movie carries on the love affair between Ireland and Hollywood with a vengeance, begin-ning as a tribute to '50s flea-bag theatre, contin-uing as a banal commercial for the joys of Celtic rural life, and ending as a cross between *Beetlejuice*, *Cymbeline* and *The Quiet Man*. O'Toole is the decrepit owner of decrepit Plunkett Castle, which he hopes to preserve from the hands of a rich American developer by renting it out to gullible, ghost-hunting rich Americans. Lo and behold, real ghosts emerge, time zones are crossed, silly buggers played, Hannah rattles her bones, and Guttenberg plays Guttenberg. The script seems a collection of loose ends and rewrites; the direction is deeply dispirited; and with the exception of O'Toole and a couple of engaging vignettes, it's a complete turkey. SGr

High Tide

(Gillian Armstrong, 1987, Aust) Judy Davis, Jan Adele, Claudia Karvan, Colin Friels, John Clayton, Frankie J Holden.
104 min.
Lilli (Davis) is one of a trio of mophead backing singers for an Elvis lookalike. Bet (Adele) works in a fish factory, drives an ice-cream van in the summer, and sings at the local nightspot at week-ends. Ally (Karvan), her granddaughter, wants to be as great a surfer as her late father. When Lilli gets the sack, she is stranded in the Australian backwater where Bet and Ally live in a caravan park. Ally is her abandoned daughter. Gillian Armstrong's terrific film centres on the after-shocks of this discovery. Without a trace of schlock or schmaltz, she depicts the viewpoints of these three women with great skill, aided in no small way by Laura Jones' admirable script. A distinctive sense of place, a generous sense of humour, and three remarkable performances comine to produce a movie with an undertow of astonishing emotional power. MS

High Time

(Blake Edwards, 1960, US) Bing Crosby, Fabian, Tuesday Weld, Nicole Maurey, Richard Beymer.
103 min.
Bing does a Rodney Dangerfield and goes back to school in this early Edwards offering, before *Breakfast at Tiffany's* made his name or the *Pink Panther* films lodged him in a creative rut. Had you been a bona fide teenager at the time, one sus-pects you'd probably have hated it, but from a '90s vantage point, it's an inoffensive caper, gamely played by the old groaner and prodded along by an easygoing Henry Mancini score and some Cahn/Van Heusen songs ('The Second Time Around' picking up an Oscar). TJ

Highway Patrolman (El Patrullero)

(Alex Cox, 1991, US/Mex) Roberto Sosa, Bruno Bichir, Vanessa Bauche, Zaide Silvia Gutierrez, Pedro Armendariz Jr, Malena Doria.
105 min.
When he graduates from the National Highway Patrol Academy to the dusty desert roads around Durango, young Pedro (Sosa) is determined to serve with honour. He's even against bribes, though the woman he marries soon puts paid to that with her repeated demands for a more com-fortable life. Gradually the poverty, crime, mari-tal tension and growing self-hatred get to Pedro, and when he stumbles across a drugs operation,

he must decide which path to take…back to his old lofty ideals, or on to ill-gained wealth, a new pragmatism, or death. Graced with an aura of authenticity, the movie succeeds as a low-key blend of cautionary tale and downbeat actioner, despite the sometimes glaring budgetary restraints. In short, not as ambitious, let alone as quirky, as most of Cox's earlier work, but it delivers. GA

Highways by Night

(Peter Godfrey, 1942, US) Richard Carlson, Jane Randolph, Jane Darwell, Barton MacLane, Ray Collins, Gordon Jones.
62 min. b/w.
Based on a story by Clarence Buddington Kelland but with one eye seemingly on Howard Hughes, this RKO B movie features Carlson as a millionaire whiz-kid content to enjoy a sheltered existence at home while contributing revolutionary designs to the family engineering plant. Since he is shortly to become a leader of men in the navy, his uncle (Collins) suggests he go and find out how those men live. Obediently visiting a sleazy nightclub, he witnesses a murder, is framed for the killing by a racketeer (MacLane), and finds shelter with a working girl (Randolph), whose brother (Jones) runs a one-man trucking firm the racketeer is trying to put out of business. Adding his brains to the brother's brawn, Carlson saves the day and wins the girl. It's all efficiently done, but not very interesting: *Sullivan's Travels* reworked by Capra, with the wit replaced by bromides about the sterling worth of ordinary folk, the benefits of manual labour, and the joys of ham sandwiches. TM

Highway to Hell

see Running Hot

High Wind in Jamaica, A

(Alexander Mackendrick, 1965, GB) Anthony Quinn, James Coburn, Ben Carruthers, Lila Kedrova, Kenneth J Warren, Gert Fröbe, Nigel Davenport, Isabel Dean.
103 min.
Mackendrick paved the way towards the risky triumph of *A High Wind in Jamaica* with an equally unsentimental scrutiny of the innocent savageries of childhood in the underrated *Sammy Going South*. But his adaptation of Richard Hughes' novel was still received uncomfortably on its release, for widescreen buccaneering adventures were hardly expected to incorporate emotional and psychological resonances of the sort only recently locked up in the art-house visions of *Lord of the Flies*. Yet the colourful gusto Mackendrick brings to his yarn of pirate-captured children adrift between primitivism and Victorianism is pure cinema and pure entertainment, with comedy and tragedy ironically balanced in the combination of childhood dreams and adult dread. PT

High Window, The

see Brasher Doubloon, The

Hilda Was a Goodlooker

(Anna Thew, 1986, GB) Mary Thew, Hermine Demoriane, Jacky Davy, Kevin Allen, George Saxon.
59 min.
Broken fragments of narration accompany broken fragments of 'Hilda's' physique. A woman recalls the early aspects of her family's life, centering on her older sister's rejection and subsequent acceptance of her suitor (who, in a lighter moment, wins the girl over by banging his head against the wall). Thew's intention is unclear; we are able to get an idea of what Hilda's life might have been like, but to what end? The mystical images with their repetitious depictions of the parts of the whole, the passionate silhouettes, the fragments of thought and footwear, amount to little more than mystical images of parts of the whole, passionate silhouettes, and fragments of thought and footwear. SGo

Hill, The

(Sidney Lumet, 1965, GB) Sean Connery, Harry Andrews, Ian Bannen, Alfred Lynch, Ossie Davis, Roy Kinnear, Jack Watson, Ian Hendry, Michael Redgrave.
123 min. b/w.
Sean Connery took a break from Bond to give a sterling performance in this awesomely intense drama set in a North African British army camp, where the favourite punishment for prisoners is to send them clambering up and down a man-made hill in the full heat of the day. A lot of screaming and barking issues from the British thesps, and every bead of sweat is visible in Oswald Morris' brilliant monochrome photography. Lumet's strengths (the moral universe as an all-male enclave) and weaknesses (set the volume high, then turn it up higher) are all here. Not for the faint-hearted. DT

Hill in Korea, A
(aka Hell in Korea)

(Julian Amyes, 1956, GB) George Baker, Stanley Baker, Harry Andrews, Michael Medwin, Ronald Lewis, Stephen Boyd, Victor Maddern, Percy Herbert, Robert Shaw, Michael Caine.
81 min. b/w.
'Old enough to fight, too young to vote' – the cry of National Service conscripts in Korea who resented being placed in the firing line of someone else's civil war. The conflict wasn't popular with British film-makers either – too many sensitive areas. This patrol movie, shot in Spain three years after the armistice, touches lightly on most of them, though it deflects the National Service issue by making the most hysterical malcontent (Lewis) equally indignant that a lad of his calibre is having to muck in with all these rough proles. Tension with army regulars and death from 'friendly fire' are also addressed. Otherwise, it all seems slightly pointless, though inventively shot by Freddie Francis (his first). BBa

Hill's Angels

see North Avenue Irregulars, The

Hills Have Eyes, The

(Wes Craven, 1977, US) John Steadman, Janus Blythe, Arthur King, Russ Grieve, Virginia Vincent, Susan Lanier, Dee Wallace, Robert Houston.
90 min.
A baby cries, granddaddy is crucified, cannibals with CB radios stalk a land where even the hills have eyes. Somewhere in the desert a clean WASP family of six are stranded; there are murmurs of atomic tests, and at the local gas station, an old man talks of a monster mutant son he abandoned in the wilds. To little avail: the Carters are besieged in their trailer and the nightmare begins. The baby is kidnapped (for supper), half the family die. From there, it's a question of the 'civilised' family acquiring the same cunning as their cannibal counterparts in a fight to the death. Parallel families, Lassie-style pet dogs who turn hunter-killers, savage Nature: exploitation themes are used to maximum effect, and despite occasional errors (the cannibal girl who protects the 'human' baby), the sense of pace never errs. A heady mix of ironic allegory and seat-edge tension. CA

Himmel über Berlin, Der

see Wings of Desire

Hi, Mom!

(Brian De Palma, 1969, US) Robert De Niro, Jennifer Salt, Lara Parker, Gerrit Graham, Nelson Peltz, Allen Garfield, Charles Durning.
86 min. b/w & col.
A blast from the past which recalls De Palma's beginnings as a really eclectic independent. Made for $95,000 after the unexpected success of his anarchic *Greetings*, this is the sequel to end all sequels. De Niro plays variations on a Vietnam vet returning to NY as, variously, a 'peep art' porno movie-maker, an urban guerilla, and an insurance salesman. At least that's the framing excuse for an increasingly lunatic series of set piece gags. 'Be Black Baby' is a skit on off-Broadway 'encounter theatre', in which a middle class white audience is terrorised by black actors in whiteface. Shot by De Palma in visceral *vérité*, it actually is terrifying. Structurally, the film never recovers – but then its main merit is a refusal to 'hang together'. Anarchic and very appealing. IC

Hindenburg, The

(Robert Wise, 1975, US) George C Scott, Anne Bancroft, William Atherton, Roy Thinnes, Gig Young, Burgess Meredith, Charles Durning.
125 min. b/w & col.
The disaster movie whose big bang is based on the assumption that the Hindenburg airship, the pride of Nazi Germany, was in fact sabotaged when it burst into flames while landing at New York in 1937. The formula is much as one would expect – lots of switching from the dirigible to plot developments on land in the USA and Germany which are accompanied by day/time/place checks, all part of the big countdown to disaster. Special effects are reasonable, and the final holocaust is shot in black-and-white to enable the incorporation of newsreel footage. The cast, most of them under suspicion as potential saboteurs, are both more imaginatively selected and kept in better check than usual; but the picture of Nazi Germany scratches scarcely deeper than *Cabaret*.

Hindered (Behindert)

(Steve Dwoskin, 1974, GB/WGer) Stephen Dwoskin, Carola Regnier.
96 min.
Certainly one of Dwoskin's most immediately accessible movies, *Hindered* is also one of his most rigorous examinations of the 'look' of the spectator, of the camera, and of his actors. Made in cooperation with German TV, the film traces the ebbing and flowing relationship between Dwoskin – a polio victim who can only move, and then with great difficulty, with the use of crutches – and Carola Regnier. In contrast to most of Dwoskin's works, the content of *Hindered* is not overtly erotic. Nonetheless, like films such as *Dyn Amo* and *Girl*, it works by denying the spectator full satisfaction of the voyeuristic interests raised by the film's images. Dwoskin forces the spectator to take sides with the trapped actors – including Dwoskin himself, of course – whom his camera mercilessly probes. PH

Hindle Wakes

(Victor Saville, 1931, GB) Belle Chrystall, John Stuart, Sybil Thorndike, Norman McKinnel, Edmund Gwenn, Mary Clare, Muriel Angelus.
79 min. b/w.
This glitteringly effective celebration of the financial and sexual independence of Lancashire mill-girls, based on Stanley Houghton's celebrated play from 1912, must have aroused mixed feelings among working class audiences in the '30s, when unemployment was driving women into prostitution. While Sally Hardcastle of *Love on the Dole* sells her body and soul to the bookmaker, fierce, fiery Jenny Hawthorne (Chrystall) snubs her nose at marriage to the boss' son and gaily assures her parents that, 'I'm a Lancashire lass, and so long as there's weaving sheds in Lancashire I shall earn enough to keep me going'. Ironic that the economic basis of her independence had been eroded by the time the film appeared; but Jenny, storming out into the night in clogs and shawl, makes a splendidly indomitable icon of feminist independence. RMy

Hi, Nellie!

(Mervyn LeRoy, 1934, US) Paul Muni, Glenda Farrell, Ned Sparks, Robert Barrat, Kathryn Sergava, Hobart Cavanaugh, Douglass Drumbrille, Donald Meek.
75 min. b/w.
Paul Muni, the Hollywood '30s favourite in heavyweight social-conscience roles, reteamed with his *I Am a Fugitive from a Chain Gang* director for a rare crack at a comedy in this Warners newspaper frolic, rather uncertainly pepped up with a gangster angle. Refusing to condemn an apparently embezzling banker, Brad (Muni) is demoted from managing editor of the *Times-Star* to the latest incumbent of the 'Nellie Nelson' agony column, a task he resents at first, before falling on a clue that might help clear his reputation. The title's a reference to the sardonic teasing he repeatedly receives from fellow journos. The studio had conveyed newspaper life with more veracity and punch three years earlier in *Five Star Final*. TJ

Hired Hand, The

(Peter Fonda, 1971, US) Peter Fonda, Warren Oates, Verna Bloom, Robert Pratt, Severn Darden, Ted Markland.
90 min.
Peter Fonda's follow-up to *Easy Rider* is a strange hybrid of a movie which starts off as a ghastly Western parody of Dennis Hopper's film, and then develops into something much more interesting:

the last half is primarily concerned with the problems of a woman in a male-oriented Western culture, and Bloom captures the part magnificently, adding another dimension to the film by her performance. Oates, too, is as good as ever, and there are a few scenes between them of real subtlety and intelligence before the uninteresting mechanics of the plot reassert themselves. DP

Hireling, The
(Alan Bridges, 1973, GB) Robert Shaw, Sarah Miles, Peter Egan, Elizabeth Sellars, Caroline Mortimer.
108 min.
Not uninteresting adaptation of LP Hartley's novel, consciously styled in echo of Losey's *The Go-Between*, with excellent performances from Miles as the upper class widow recuperating from a nervous breakdown, and Shaw as the chauffeur of the car she hires daily to escape her empty world of tinkling teacups and social chitchat. Talking to the chauffeur's back, reassured by the monosyllabic pragmatism of an ex-RSM who views life's problems in terms of black and white, she gradually realises the emptiness of her self-torment, becomes gay, flirtatious, ready to resume her place in society; he, meanwhile, is gradually caught in the toils of an inarticulate, almost mystic adoration. The social barrier is subtly evoked in terms which have nothing to do with *Lady Chatterley* snobbery and sexual challenge; the point Hartley makes is that because neither ever really sees the other as a human being, neither of them can consciously admit the other as a possible partner, and frustration is inevitable. At which point, alas, the film falls apart. Electing to sound a blast of contemporary social protest totally at odds with the '20s setting, it has the chauffeur going berserk and using his Rolls as a battering-ram to the accompaniment of ironical snatches of 'Rule Britannia' and 'God Save the Queen'. Crass is hardly the word for it. TM

Hiroshima, Mon Amour
(Alain Resnais, 1959, Fr/Jap) Emmanuelle Riva, Eiji Okada, Bernard Fresson, Stella Dassas, Pierre Barbaud.
91 min. b/w.
Hiroshima's mushroom cloud has probably inspired more glib statements and images than any other 20th century phenomenon. So it's particularly refreshing to find that it still has some meaning in Resnais' first feature, now almost thirty years old. Marguerite Duras' script – part *nouveau roman*, part Mills & Boon – centres on a Japanese man and a French woman coming together in Hiroshima, exploring each other and their past lives, both of which have been far from rosy. The woman was punished as a wartime collaborator after an affair with a German soldier; the man's whole life was shattered by the bomb. Duras and Riva revel masochistically in the woman's sad story (she had her head shaved in prison), but Resnais does his best to soft-pedal the novelettish touches, and presents a melancholy disquisition on the complex relationships between world calamities and personal histories, between the past, present and future. GB

His Affair
see This Is My Affair

His Girl Friday (100)
(Howard Hawks, 1940, US) Cary Grant, Rosalind Russell, Ralph Bellamy, Gene Lockhart, Porter Hall, Helen Mack, Roscoe Karns, John Qualen, Ernest Truex, Billy Gilbert.
92 min. b/w.
Perhaps the funniest, certainly the fastest talkie comedy ever made, this inspired adaptation of Hecht and MacArthur's *The Front Page* adds an extra dimension of exploitation by turning Hildy Johnson into Walter Burns' ex-wife. Grant's Burns performs astonishing feats of super-quick timing as he garrulously manipulates a gallows case – Qualen, a simpleton mercilessly jailed for killing a black policeman – to further his own ends: first, to win back his wife from staid insurance salesman Bellamy (wonderfully slow in gumboots and bovine smile); second, to win back his star reporter (Hildy again); and third, to beat the rival rags to the full story of the political corruption that casts a shadow over the judicial system demanding Qualen's death. But Grant is not

alone in his masterly expertise: Charles Lederer's frantic script needs to be heard at least a dozen times for all the gags to be caught; Russell's Hildy more than equals Burns in cunning and speed; and Hawks transcends the piece's stage origins effortlessly, framing with brilliance, conducting numerous conversations simultaneously, and even allowing the film's political and emotional thrust to remain upfront alongside the laughs. Quite simply a masterpiece. GA

His Kind of Woman
(John Farrow, 1951, US) Robert Mitchum, Jane Russell, Vincent Price, Tim Holt, Charles McGraw, Marjorie Reynolds, Raymond Burr, Jim Backus.
120 min. b/w.
A supreme oddity from Howard Hughes' RKO, which starts off with a relatively straightforward *noir* thriller plot – gambler Mitchum is pressurised under threat of violence to help exiled hoodlum Burr return to the States – and about halfway through turns into surreal parody. Mitchum has said that much of it was made up as the production went along, and certainly scenes such as his ironing of dollar bills, and the frequent innuendo-laden backchat with Russell, have an air of spontaneity. Funniest, however, is Price as a mad and conceited actor, given to spouting cod Shakespeare even at the most dangerous of moments. The thing, not unlike a taut, sadistic thriller peppered with incursions from the Monty Python crew, hardly hangs together; but it is excellently performed and directed, and remains an unforgettable delight. GA

His Other Woman
see Desk Set

Histoire d'Adèle H., L'
see Story of Adèle H., The

Histoire inventée, Une (An Imaginary Tale)
(André Forcier, 1990, Can) Jean Lapointe, Louise Marleau, Charlotte Laurier, Marc Messier, Jean-François Pichette, France Castel, Tony Nardi, Marc Gélinas.
100 min.
This bizarre farrago of Québecois humour raises a few laughs and just about makes sense, but rarely at the same time. It revolves around an arty production of *Othello*, staged by a manic director (Nardi) whose ex-mobster uncle has roped in the Palermo old folks club to attend every performance. Or around a boozy cop (Messier), first seen having a mild altercation with a rambunctious parrot; or a jazz trumpeter (Lapointe) whose on-the-skids trio is being rent asunder by sorrows romantic and religious; or a love goddess (Marleau) whose 40 ex-swains follow her around in a moonstruck cortège; or even her daughter (Laurier), agonising over a two-timing Othello. There's some of the flavour of an Alan Rudolph movie – the characters keep bouncing off each other in the same desultory way – but there's too much reliance on running gags that don't really run anywhere. The cast's great, though, and Forcier has a way of making bleak old Montreal look charmingly baroque. JRo

Histoires d'Amérique: Food, Family and Philosophy
see American Stories

Histoires Extraordinaires (Spirits of the Dead/ Tales of Mystery)
(Roger Vadim/Louis Malle/Frederico Fellini, 1967, Fr/It) Jane Fonda, Peter Fonda, Françoise Prévost, Alain Delon, Brigitte Bardot, Terence Stamp.
121 min.
A compendium of three Poe stories. Vadim's (*Metzengerstein*) carries with it an aura of perversity, due not so much to the fetishistic clothes and decor as to the casting of Jane Fonda and brother Peter as the lovers. With his death, she resorts to a totem black stallion as a substitute, and the film itself falls apart. Malle's piece (*William Wilson*), a not particularly riveting variation on the Doppelgänger theme, has Alain Delon 1 (looking slightly bewildered) being chased by Alain Delon 2 (looking even more

bewildered). Bardot puts in an appearance, looking odd in a black wig. Meticulously done, but not much to do about Poe; only Fellini (*Toby Dammit*) really manages to make much of his source. Stamp comes to Rome as the actor chosen to play Christ in the first Catholic Western (a cross between Dreyer and Pasolini, with a touch of Ford). He plays a man at the end of his tether, and as his obsessions take over, so do Fellini's. In many ways the sequence foreshadows *Roma*. It's overdone and strained, but worthwhile for Stamp's curious performance. CPe

Historia Oficial, La
see Official Version, The

Historias del Kronen
see Stories of the Kronen

History Is Made at Night
(Frank Borzage, 1937, US) Charles Boyer, Jean Arthur, Leo Carrillo, Colin Clive, Ivan Lebedeff, George Meeker.
97 min. b/w.
A bizarre movie from Borzage, who invades the sophisticated territory of Lubitsch and Leisen – Paris hotels, cruise liners, impersonations, two-timing wives, jealous husbands – and turns it all into a romantic thriller, complete with an ending that recalls *A Night to Remember*. Jean Arthur's marriage to Colin Clive is on the rocks, and suave Boyer – a waiter who poses as a thief, later turning up as patron of a Manhattan restaurant – comes to her rescue. Emotions run high, implausibilities pile up, but Borzage keeps the motor running, and the stars – especially the rather neglected Arthur, who is now a Carmelite recluse – are immensely watchable. ATu

History Lessons (Geschichtsunterricht)
(Jean-Marie Straub/Danièle Huillet, 1972, It) Gottfried Bold, Johann Unterpertinger, Henri Ludwigg, Carl Vaillant.
85 min.
History Lessons derives from sections of Brecht's incomplete novel *The Business Affairs of Mr Julius Caesar*. It comprises four interviews with contemporaries of Caesar's (every word on the soundtrack is Brecht's): a banker, a former soldier, a lawyer and a writer, all of whom place Caesar's exploits in direct political perspectives. Typically, though, the film-makers insist on doing more than merely re-examining historical fact. They inscribe the dissection of Rome's imperialist past within three detailed studies of Rome today, establishing links that work both ways. And they leave the city altogether for the scenes in which their actors quote Brecht's dialogue; these scenes make a radical (Brechtian) break with the 'rules' of narrative film grammar. Illusions of all kinds are, in fact, ruthlessly pared away, leaving a series of concrete facts and statements in the forms of sounds and images that the viewer is free to use to construct meanings. This is arguably political cinema at its most advanced and provocative. TR

History of Mr Polly, The
(Anthony Pelissier, 1949, GB) John Mills, Sally Ann Howes, Finlay Currie, Megs Jenkins, Diana Churchill, Dandy Nichols, Juliet Mills.
95 min. b/w.
Timid draper Mills, tired of his dull life and nagging wife, torches his shop and takes to the open road, landing up at the Potwell Inn, where he battles with fearsome Currie before settling down with the pub's jolly plump landlady, Megs Jenkins. A pleasant, rosy-cheeked adaptation of HG Wells's rural fantasy novel. NF

History of Post-War Japan as Told by a Bar Hostess (Nippon Sengo Shi: Madamu Omboro no Seikatsu)
(Shohei Imamura, 1970, Jap) Etsuko Akaza.
105 min. b/w.
The links between the two halves of the title are generally left to work themselves out in terms of American influence, which we see both in the newsreels of political events and, on its most basic level, in the hostess' bar. They are sufficiently tenuous for our interest to rest mainly with the hostess herself. Fortunately she's an amazing lady, talkative and humorous, posses-

sor of enormous charm. Shot in an appropriately rough-edged style, partly to distance itself from its own claim that film is a manipulative medium. Imamura's film ironically has an ending like something out of Hollywood fantasy. Our hostess, rumoured to be about fifty by then, leaves for the States with her 23-year-old Marine husband in tow and her sights set on US citizenship.

History of the World Part I

(Mel Brooks, 1981, US) Mel Brooks, Dom DeLuise, Madeline Kahn, Harvey Korman, Cloris Leachman, Gregory Hines, Sid Caesar, Spike Milligan.
92 min.
It's difficult to dislike Brooks' parody of the historical epic, as old-fashioned as it is anarchic: a series of comic sketches playing through scenes from Kubrick's *2001*, DeMille's *Ten Commandments*, Roman sandal epics, and Louis XIV's court immediately prior to the French Revolution. Brooks piles on the scatological humour thick and fast, including many of the world's worst jokes, and as usual there's a high number of misses for every gag that hits the target. Centrepiece is a lavish Busby Berkeley-style production number, 'The Inquisition', a bad taste attempt to recapture the kitsch glories of 'Springtime for Hitler' (in *The Producers*). And, like the Monty Python team, Brooks knows full well that one of his best jokes is production values at least as impressive as what he's lampooning. RM

Hit, The

(Stephen Frears, 1984, GB) John Hurt, Tim Roth, Laura Del Sol, Terence Stamp, Bill Hunter, Fernando Rey.
98 min.
After ten years meditating on his new life down in Spain, supergrass Willie Parker (Stamp) is rudely awakened by some visitors – two hit men come to take him back to Paris to settle a few scores. But Willie is a changed man, completely unfazed by the imminence of death, and it is the killers whose nerves are stretched on the long road back to 'the hit'. Frears returned here to the big screen thirteen years after *Gumshoe* and a retreat to the stunting effect of TV; the wide, sunlit plains of Spain seem to have broadened his horizons, allowed a flexing of cinematic muscle, and inspired him to something both exciting and lofty. Hurt is in good vicious form as the shaded hit man; Stamp once more wears a smile like a halo; and the prospect of approaching death is handled without too much metaphysical puffing and blowing. All in all, a very palpable hit. CPea

Hit!

(Sidney J Furie, 1973, US) Billy Dee Williams, Richard Pryor, Paul Hampton, Gwen Welles, Warren Kemmerling, Janet Brandt, Todd Martin.
134 min.
Furie continued his association with Williams, Pryor and Hampton from *Lady Sings the Blues* into this over-stretched vendetta action movie, which also overdoes the improvised jive-talk comedy relief in its yarn about a renegade federal agent (Williams) forming his own ad hoc revenge squad to take out nine Marseilles heroin dealers after his daughter ODs. Furie's penchant for silly camera angles and meaninglessly arresting images is here muted, but not replaced by much of distinction. PT

Hitcher, The

(Robert Harmon, 1986, US) Rutger Hauer, C Thomas Howell, Jennifer Jason Leigh, Jeffrey DeMunn, John Jackson, Billy Green Bush.
97 min.
There's a killer on the road (everyone's favourite Dutch psycho, Hauer) with a Nietzschean gleam in his eye and an ugly knife in his pocket. When Howell picks him up at dawn on a deserted Texan highway, he immediately makes his intentions plain by scaring the boy witless. When the boy fights back, however, then the hitcher has found what he needs – a decent adversary – and the game begins. By an apparent near-magical ability to be in several places at once, Hauer embarks on his round of gory slaughters, while sucking Howell into appearing at the scene, only to be nabbed by the cops. If you can swallow the unlikely nature of the killer's powers (like dismembering an entire police station while the boy is asleep in a cell), then you are in for a good

rough ride down a murky road. There's a little toying with the old *doppelgänger* idea of the hero and villain coming to resemble one another, and the ending is rather straightforward; but it's a highly competent sick-fright version of the evergreen chase formula. And you'll never eat french fries again without looking at them closely. CPea

Hitch-hiker, The

(Ida Lupino, 1953, US) Edmond O'Brien, Frank Lovejoy, William Talman, José Torvay, Sam Hayes, Jean Del Val.
71 min. b/w.
Although made in the same year as Lupino's impressive weepie *The Bigamist*, this inhabits a totally different universe. Two men on a fishing trip pick up a mass-murdering hitcher (Talman), and are forced at gunpoint to drive him through Mexico until the fatal moment when he no longer needs them. Absolutely assured in her creation of the bleak, *noir* atmosphere – whether in the claustrophobic confines of the car, or lost in the arid expanses of the desert – Lupino never relaxes the tension for one moment. Yet her emotional sensitivity is also upfront: charting the changes in the menaced men's relationship as they bicker about how to deal with their captor, stressing that only through friendship can they survive. Taut, tough, and entirely without macho-glorification, it's a gem, with first-class performances from its three protagonists, deftly characterised without resort to cliché. GA

Hitler – a Career (Hitler eine Karriere)

(Joachim C Fest/Christian Herrendoerfer, 1977, WGer) narrator: Stephen Murray.
157 min. b/w & col.
The first big hit of the Hitler revival in West Germany: it came as a book-plus-film package, just like *Jaws*. The movie is a long compilation of documentary footage, tracing Hitler's political trajectory from its early setbacks in the '20s to its end, with just enough contexting material to support its simple linear-history argument; this English version is garnished with a grave, moralising commentary. There's a strong bias towards footage from the '20s and '30s, presumably because images of the blitzkrieg and the concentration camps would be less saleable to a modern German audience. British audiences, of course, haven't been protected from Hitler, and much of the material is familiar here from TV compilations and movies like *The Double-Headed Eagle* and *Swastika*. But whether one finds the material intrinsically interesting or not, there's no mistaking the nature of the packaging: this is 'history' conceived, edited and scored like fiction, self-sufficient and comfortably remote. TR

Hitler, a Film from Germany

(Hans-Jürgen Syberberg, 1977, WGer/GB/Fr) Heinz Schubert, André Heller, Harry Baer, Peter Kern, Hellmuth Lange.
360 min.
The third and longest part of Syberberg's extraordinary trilogy on German culture, history and nationalism (the two earlier films were *Ludwig – Requiem for a Virgin King* and *Karl May*), best described as a high camp, heavy-duty analysis of both history and historical analysis itself. The chosen method is to single out, act out, alter, and finally comment on the lives of a handful of 'awkward' German historical figures, from Ludwig of Bavaria through fantasy author Karl May to Hitler, the 'madman'. Behind aesthetic complexity lies a simple purpose: to show up the sort of historical contradictions solved by Marxists with bare economic models, and by others with suspect reference to the 'greatness' or 'madness' of the figures involved. Visually lyrical, the style is eclectic to the point of hysteria; and the tone oscillates between the operatic (Wagner figures large) and the colloquial (Hitler in conversation with his projectionist) without ever quite coming unstuck. Humour mixes with mythology and analysis in the attempt to reunite art, history and ideology. It's a quite remarkable film, with a sense of metaphor equal to its intellectual courage. CA

Hitler Gang, The

(John Farrow, 1944, US) Robert Watson, Roman Bohnen, Martin Kosleck, Reinhold Schunzel, Fritz Kortner, Alexander Granach, Alexander Pope, Ludwig Donath.
101 min. b/w.

Although sometimes tempted to caricature and inclined to simplify by suggesting that Hitler was no more than an addle-pated psychotic, this stands head-and-shoulders above most of Hollywood's attempts to deal with the Nazi peril. Semi-documentary in approach, it traces the rise of the Nazi party from 1918 to 1934 with the aid of some brilliant impersonations of Hitler, Goebbels, Goering, Himmler, Hess, Ludendorff, Streicher, Strasser et al, mainly by refugee actors. Its set pieces, in particular the Munich putsch and the Night of the Long Knives, are staged with real flair. But the fascination of the film, as its title suggests and as Parker Tyler noted, is its view of Hitler as a gangster (and therefore likely to get his comeuppance from betrayal by his own generals), where gangsterism is defined as 'the interest of minorities hallucinated as the interest of majorities and prosecuted in an extra-legal or anti-legal way...so that the nation became a gang'. The lucidly intelligent script, surprisingly enough, is by Frances Goodrich and Albert Hackett, a partnership otherwise notable mainly for a clutch of distinguished musicals. TM

Hitler's Madman

(Douglas Sirk, 1942, US) John Carradine, Patricia Morrison, Alan Curtis, Ralph Morgan, Howard Freeman, Edgar Kennedy, Ava Gardner.
85 min. b/w.
Sirk's first American film may, like Lang's *Hangmen Also Die!*, centre on the true story of the Nazi commander Heydrich, whose assassination by the Czechs brought about horrendous reprisals by the German forces, but it is less *noir*-thriller than a committed, moving tribute to the spirit of resistance amongst the occupied Czech people. Its low budget is all too evident in the back-lot sets and the none-too-inspiring cast (though Carradine is superb as the sadistic Heydrich, and Ava Gardner has a brief cameo as a peasant girl tormented by brutal Nazis), but the overall effect is surprisingly powerful; from the opening shots of a statue of St Sebastian pinned with arrows, the film's emphasis on physical suffering and martyrdom is kept well to the fore. GA

Hitler: the Last Ten Days

(Ennio De Concini, 1973, GB/It) Alec Guinness, Doris Kunstmann, Simon Ward, Adolfo Celi, Diane Cilento, Gabriele Ferzetti, Eric Porter, Joss Ackland.
104 min.
For all its specious moralising – the Simon Ward character is clearly intended to be the 'conscience of Germany', and Alistair Cooke's scene-setting narration is similarly intended as the 'voice of authority' – this account of life in the bunker quickly topples over into uneasy farce, with Alec Guinness' Hitler seeming more like a character from *Kind Hearts and Coronets* than the frightening political figure he was. Juxtaposing newsreel footage with dramatised reconstructions doesn't help either. PH

Hit List

(William Lustig, 1989, US) Jan-Michael Vincent, Lance Henriksen, Rip Torn, Leo Rossi, Jere Burns, Charles Napier.
87 min.
For people who like seeing heads being shut in doors, stuck inside ovens, or being cut to french fry size by a steel grid. Henriksen does a great job playing the psycho hitman working for Mafia boss Torn, but – all because of a floppy house number 9 – gets the wrong address for a hit, shoots the wrong man, gives the wrong wife a miscarriage, and even kidnaps the wrong child. Sadly for the Mob, the child belongs to civilian hero Vincent. Cue vengeance, thrills, gore, and even a touching finale. WSG

Hit Man

see Scoumoune, La

HMS Defiant (aka Damn the Defiant)

(Lewis Gilbert, 1962, GB) Alec Guinness, Dirk Bogarde, Anthony Quayle, Tom Bell, Nigel Stock, Murray Melvin, Victor Maddern, Maurice Denham, Bryan Pringle.
101 min.
This late 19th century seafaring saga has some impressive credentials: a strong cast, a script by

Nigel Kneale and Edmund H North (the latter did the adaptation for Ray's *In a Lonely Place* and co-wrote *Patton*), beautiful CinemaScope photography by Christopher Challis, crisp editing by Peter Hunt (later to become a Bond stalwart), and superb design by Arthur Lawson. It was nothing special in 1962, but today seems rather cherishable, and to make it now would cost rather more than $40 million. As an evocation of class conflicts among the officers and bitter resentments among the pressganged crew, the movie is tense and convincingly acted, with the traditional *Mutiny on the Bounty* roles reversed: Captain Guinness is the humanitarian, and First Lieutenant Bogarde is the unrepentant cat-lover. ATu

Ho! (aka Criminal Face)

(Robert Enrico, 1968, Fr/It) Jean-Paul Belmondo, Joanna Shimkus, Sydney Chaplin, Paul Crauchet, Stéphane Fey, Tony Taffin, Alain Mottet.
168 min.
Indulgent Belmondo fans only for this turgid, badly dubbed effort from the time when the star could churn out any old rubbish and still clean up at the French box office. In this one, he's a disgraced former racing driver reduced to chauffeuring for a bunch of thieves who simply call him 'Ho!' Meanwhile, his other interests in life are society girl Shimkus and (ahem) his collection of smart ties. TJ

Hobson's Choice

(David Lean, 1953, GB) Charles Laughton, Brenda de Banzie, John Mills, Daphne Anderson, Prunella Scales, Richard Wattis.
107 min. b/w.
Set in the 1890s, this adaptation of Harold Brighouse's working class comedy, a favourite rep company standby since it was first performed in 1916, sees Laughton's tyrannical Lancashire bootmaker brought to heel when his plain-speaking daughter (de Banzie) marries his downtrodden, simple-minded employee (Mills) and sets up a competitive business. It could so easily have been a load of old cobblers; but Lean's sharp direction and impeccable performances all round transform a slight comedy into a timeless delight. NF

Hocus Pocus

(Kenny Ortega, 1993, US) Bette Midler, Sarah Jessica Parker, Kathy Najimy, Omri Katz, Thora Birch, Amanda Shepherd.
96 min.
This comedy ghoulfest – about three hanged 17th century Salem witches revivified on Halloween 1993 – toes a wobbly line between genuinely scaring the tinies and diverting the seen-it-all teens. New-kid-in-town Katz believes witches and stuff to be all hocus pocus until heart-throb Shepherd takes him to her family's disused museum – the old witches' house – where he foolishly lights a black-flamed candle and brings back the blood-seeking daughters of darkness. The ugly trio – Midler, Najimy and Parker – perform a show-stopping version of 'I Put a Spell on You' at a Halloween party, but otherwise it's slim pickings. WH

Hoffa

(Danny DeVito, 1992, US) Jack Nicholson, Danny DeVito, Armand Assante, JT Walsh, John C Reilly, Robert Prosky, Natalija Nogulich, Kevin Anderson, John P Ryan, Paul Guilfoyle.
140 min.
Written by David Mamet, and starring Nicholson as the legendary union boss who disappeared one summer's evening in 1975, DeVito's film disappoints, though there are always compensations. Nicholson's Hoffa and his all-purpose sidekick/co-conspirator Bobby Ciaro (De Vito) move all the way from hard-nosed pre-war trucking, through union organisation, struggle and arson, into the full-scale corruption and racketeering that were to lead Hoffa into the arms of attorney general Robert Kennedy (Anderson), to jail, and finally to an anonymous grave – courtesy, in all probability, of his erstwhile Mafia cohorts. DeVito's scale is grand, but the language is foul and the sets sometimes look tacky, while the score is unspeakable. Nicholson's performance dominates, but fails finally to hold the film together. Still, in the courtroom confrontations with

Anderson's boyish Bobby, and in the flashforward scenes with an aged DeVito, waiting for that last, late rendezvous in a freeway cafeteria, there is much to admire. Ambiguous, but probably not sufficiently so: yooze catch ma drift? SGr

Hog Wild

(Les Rose, 1980, Can) Patti D'Arbanville, Michael Biehn, Tony Rosato, Angelo Rizacos, Martin Doyle, Claude Phillipe.
95 min.
A mite pleasanter and funnier than the awful title suggests, this is a good-natured, dumb movie about a high school feud between Waspy wimps and leathered bike heavies. Quick to anger, easily moved to violence (of the custard pie sort), the bikers are led by Rosato, who has perfected an incomprehensible mumble (sounding like early Brando on a bad line) and is as menacing as anyone with doggy eyes and an owlish blink can be. Although the bikers are blessed with a Morricone-esque theme tune, the film lacks the sort of musical thread which might make it a viable teen movie (it's obvious that all the 'kids' should have graduated at least a decade earlier). JS

Hola, estás sola?

see Hello, Are You Alone?

Holcroft Covenant, The

(John Frankenheimer, 1985, GB) Michael Caine, Anthony Andrews, Victoria Tennant, Lilli Palmer, Mario Adorf, Michel Lonsdale, Bernard Hepton.
112 min.
From the blood-soaked ashes that is Berlin in 1945, rises a mighty plan hatched by the doomed *Übermensch*, involving some $4 billion and a vault in Geneva. Caine, as the unwitting son of the ringleader, is elected to administer the fund; a job which entails spending most of the movie jetting to international tourist locations so that he can be filled in on the next plot twist by an obliging minor character. From the blood-soaked ashes of a dog's dinner like this it is yet possible to glean moments of derisive pleasure. And Caine, once again, strides through the rubble with the air of a man who has read the script but is still hoping for a miracle. CPea

Hold Back the Dawn

(Mitchell Leisen, 1941, US) Charles Boyer, Olivia de Havilland, Paulette Goddard, Victor Francen, Walter Abel, Rosemary de Camp, Mitchell Leisen.
115 min. b/w.
As scripted by Brackett and Wilder and directed by the underrated Leisen (who appears, as himself, in a brief cameo as the Hollywood director to whom Boyer tries to sell his story), this romantic weepie is both moving and effectively stylish. Boyer's vaguely sinister charm is well deployed as the stateless Latin gigolo who tricks a plain-jane schoolmarm (de Havilland) into marriage purely in order to gain entry to the US from Mexico, while the depiction of their faltering relationship is achieved with a welcome degree of dark, ironic wit. But it's Leisen's assured, polished handling of a potentially soapy story that lends surprising conviction to the whole affair; so fluent is the narrative that disbelief at de Havilland's naïveté is suspended throughout. GA

Hold Me, Thrill Me, Kiss Me

(Joel Hershman, 1992, US) Adrienne Shelly, Max Parrish, Sean Young, Diane Ladd, Timothy Leary.
93 min.
It's probably inevitable that a thrusting young director on the make should come up with much the same 'outrageous' ideas as his predecessors of the last generation did, but it's kinda sad that Hershman's debut feature should turn out to be such a flabby rehash of *Pink Flamingos*. A burglar (Parrish) on the run from a shotgun marriage in which the gun went off hides out in a California trailer park peopled with would-be droll eccentrics, and finds true lurv with the virginal sister (Shelly) of a vicious go-go dancer. The casting is right – Young and Ladd parody their established screen images, Timothy Leary does a cameo – but the sense of going through the motions is overwhelming. This is more like an American *Carry On Columbus* than a brave new voice in alternative comedy. TR

Hold You Tight
(Yue Kuai Le, Yue Duoluo)

(Stanley Kwan, 1998, HK) Chingmy Yau, Sunny Chan, Ke Yulun, Eric Tsang, Sandra Ng, Tony Rayns.
93 min.
Kwan's '1997 movie' avoids politics and melodrama, focusing instead on characters who oscillate between Hong Kong and Taiwan, between marriage and divorce, between commitment and adultery. Chingmy Yau plays two Hong Kong career women (or is that one woman at two phases of her life?), one of them stuck in a not very fulfilling marriage with a computer obsessed husband, the other a divorcee who has emigrated to Taipei and opened a boutique. The story turns on the sudden death of the first woman in an air crash; her husband (Chan), more numbed than grief stricken, is helped through the aftermath by a gay friend (Tsang), only to be devastated afresh by discovering that he's long been an object of desire for a teenager confused about his sexuality (Ke). Sexually frank and emotionally intense, the film's stature is enhanced by strong performances and Kwan Poon-Leung's virtuoso cinematography. RG

Hole, The

see Trou, Le

Hole, The

see Onibaba

Hole, The

(Tsai Ming-Liang, 1998, Tai) Yang Kuei-Mei, Lee Kang-Sheng, Miao Tien, Tong Hsiang-Chu.
95 min.
The last week before the 21st century: a mysterious epidemic has resulted in mass evacuation from Taipei, with only a few residents refusing to leave their homes, two of whom – a man and the woman who lives in the flat below – become involved in a mysterious, unspoken relationship when the latter's ceiling collapses, due to the non-stop rain, and they suddenly become aware of one another. The premise is weird enough, but interrupting the metaphorical story with delightfully amateurish song and dance sequences (by way of homage to '50s star Grace Chang, though they also reflect on the woman's fantasies) takes it still further into uncharted territory. Somehow, it all comes off: the characters are depicted with insight and wit, the mood is kept controlled, and the ending is genuinely moving. Idiosyncratic, of course, but immensely impressive. GA

Hole in the Head, A

(Frank Capra, 1959, US) Frank Sinatra, Edward G Robinson, Eleanor Parker, Carolyn Jones, Thelma Ritter, Keenan Wynn.
120 min.
Capra's penultimate movie lacks the resonance of his '30s work, and is a fairly wilful attempt to make our hearts heave. Sinatra plays the widowed (with small son) owner of a peeling Miami Beach hotel which is about to be foreclosed by the banks. Robinson is his elder brother, and Parker is a lonely widow who might have the money to save the hotel, but Sinatra isn't that much of a heel. Frank sings 'High Hopes', and despite some good moments, one wishes the whole thing was a musical. ATu

Holiday

(George Cukor, 1938, US) Cary Grant, Katharine Hepburn, Lew Ayres, Doris Nolan, Edward Everett Horton, Henry Kolker, Binnie Barnes, Henry Daniell.
93 min. b/w.
Marvellous 'sophisticated comedy' about a prototype dropout (Grant in one of his best performances) who takes a rich upper class family by storm: arriving engaged to the conventionally snobbish younger daughter (Nolan), stirring up latent doubts and resentments through his carefree disregard for material proprieties and properties, he ends up by showing the yearningly dissatisfied elder sister (Hepburn) the way to a declaration of independence. Despite some very funny barbed dialogue, mostly centering on two clashing couples among the engagement party guests (one liberal, the other proto-Fascist), the film is less a satire on the rich than an acknowledgment that privilege has its drawbacks; its key

scene, accordingly, takes place in the nursery playroom, a place redolent of childhood hopes and dreams, which Hepburn and her unhappily alcoholic brother (Ayres) unconsciously use as a retreat from their unwelcome social obligations. Often underrated by comparison with *The Philadelphia Story* (both are based on plays by Philip Barry), but even better because its glitteringly polished surface is undermined by veins of real feeling, it is one of Cukor's best films. TM

Holiday Camp
(Ken Annakin, 1947, GB) Flora Robson, Dennis Price, Jack Warner, Kathleen Harrison, Hazel Court, Jimmy Hanley, Esmond Knight, Emrys Jones, Peter Hammond.
97 min. b/w.
Surprisingly unpatronising in its portrayal of the working classes triumphing over organised leisure, Annakin's kaleidoscope of life in a Butlin's concentration camp reflects something of the populist feeling which swept the Labour Party to victory in 1945. Time has mellowed the documentary quality of the film, and location shooting and authentic detail now seem less important than the presence of the whole range of British acting talent, from Dame Flora Robson to Cheerful Charlie Chester, among the cast of thousands. Annakin is able to build up a microcosm of British society, with Price's killer airman embodying post-war anxiety, and acting as a sinister antidote to Warner and his Huggett family. The only thing missing is the presence of voluptuous Jean Kent, struck down by flu on the inhospitable East Coast location. RMy

Holiday in Mexico
(George Sidney, 1946, US) Walter Pidgeon, Jane Powell, Jose Iturbi, Ilona Massey, Roddy McDowall.
127 min.
Absurdly over-extended musical confection in which Pidgeon as the US Ambassador to Mexico looks on in disdain as daughter Powell falls for local classical pianist Iturbi. That's the cue for a string of musical interludes bringing in everything from Xavier Cugat and his Latin combo doing the 'Walter Winchell Rumba', an arrangement of 'Three Blind Mice' by the then 17-year-old André Previn, and, to top it all, Schubert's 'Ave Maria'. MGM threw everything they had at this one, but it still just lies there and dies there. TJ

Holiday Inn
(Mark Sandrich, 1942, US) Fred Astaire, Bing Crosby, Marjorie Reynolds, Virginia Dale, Walter Abel.
101 min. b/w.
Despite opportunities for some fine dancing from Astaire at his most energetic, he's lumbered not only with Crosby, crooning 'White Christmas' for the first time, but also with Marjorie Reynolds, clearly no replacement for Ginger Rogers. But the Irving Berlin score, including 'Easter Parade' and 'Let's Say It with Firecrackers' (which gives Fred his best moment) makes up for the thin story about a love triangle at the eponymous vacation resort. GA

Hollow Reed
(Angela Pope, 1995, GB/Ger) Sam Bould, Martin Donovan, Ian Hart, Joely Richardson, Jason Flemyng, Shaheen Khan, Roger Lloyd Pack, Annette Badland.
104 min.
Martyn (Donovan) is a gay doctor estranged from his wife Hannah (Richardson). Visited by their 9-year-old son Oliver, who lives with his mother, Martyn suspects that the blood on the boy's face is not the result of school bullying but something more sinister. Is Oliver being abused by Hannah's lover Frank (Flemyng)? Hannah, however, rejects the notion out of hand, impelling Martyn to sue for custody. Trouble is, Oliver's so frightened, and reluctant to upset his mum, that he won't speak out against Frank. Besides, there's also the fact that Martyn lives with Tom (Hart) – and a gay man, in the eyes of the law, is unlikely to be deemed a better parent than a heterosexual woman. Sensitive, intelligent and affecting, Pope's film derives much of its emotional punch from its cast: Donovan gives an especially fine, focused performance, Richardson scrapes together some sympathy for a character whose blinkered gullibility is frequently infuriating, and young Sam Bould is admirable as Oliver. GA

Hollow Triumph
(aka The Scar)
(Steve Sekely, 1948, US) Joan Bennett, Paul Henreid, Eduard Franz, Leslie Brooks, John Qualen, Mabel Paige.
82 min. b/w.
Not half bad, despite a loopy plot about a con-man/thief hiding from pursuit who kills a look-alike psychiatrist and assumes his identity (conveniently skilled in surgery through interrupted studies, he is even able to reproduce a facial scar). The tension is kept ticking nicely by a flaw in the impersonation (working by mirror, he scars the wrong cheek), even more so by the fact that he unexpectedly inherits dire troubles from the dead man's past. Good supporting performances, a satisfyingly bleak ending, and absolutely stunning lighting and LA location shooting from John Alton. TM

Hollywood Boulevard
(Joe Dante/Allan Arkush, 1976, US) Candice Rialson, Mary Woronov, Rita George, Jeffrey Kramer, Dick Miller, Paul Bartel, Jonathan Kaplan.
83 min.
Prentice work from the carefree young persons who went on to give you *Piranha* and *Rock'n'Roll High School*. Reputedly cobbled together in ten days, most of which must have been spent collating the outtakes from *Death Race 2000*, this is probably the ultimate movie in-joke: a parody of Roger Corman's outfit (New World Pictures), made by the people who work for it. The plot includes several murders, an unscrupulous star (Woronov), a director (Bartel, of course) who can't decide whether to pay homage to Von Sternberg or Godzilla, and a great many clips from actual New World product. The relentless obviousness is ultimately rather wearying, but the finale manages to be suitably outrageous, and it's undoubtedly a treasure trove for Corman buffs. TR

Hollywood Cavalcade
(Irving Cummings, 1939, US) Don Ameche, Alice Faye, J Edward Bromberg, Buster Keaton, Al Jolson, Mack Sennett, Chester Conklin, The Keystone Kops.
96 min.
Agent Ameche brings Faye to silent-era Hollywood in this loving re-creation of the movies' pioneer days. The first half is the best, with Mack Sennett on hand to supervise the slapstick and Buster Keaton to chuck a custard pie or two. Personal problems and unconvincing melodrama take over, but the sight of the genuine Rin-Tin-Tin Jr will send viewers off into the sunset well satisfied. TJ

Hollywood Cowboy
see Hearts of the West

Hollywood on Trial
(David Helpern Jr, 1976, US)
narrator: John Huston.
102 min. b/w & col.
It's hardly surprising that *Hollywood on Trial* ends up being interesting mostly for the footage of individual testimonies at the 1947 House Un-American Activities Committee hearings on Hollywood. Helpern's documentary begins with a short potted newsreel history of America from the early '30s until the end of World War II. From there it gradually zeroes in on the persecution of the group of (mainly) screenwriters who were to become known as the Hollywood Ten for their defiance of the burning question, 'Are you now, or have you ever been a member of the Communist Party?' The film sometimes succumbs to the simplistic in its attempts to adequately contextualise the HUAC hearings. And the interviews with the jailed and blacklisted thirty years on – Dalton Trumbo, Edward Dmytryk, Zero Mostel and many others – add little to our comprehension of the paranoia rampant in the McCarthy era. Worth seeing for the film of the hearings themselves, though. RM

Hollywood or Bust
(Frank Tashlin, 1956, US) Dean Martin, Jerry Lewis, Pat Crowley, Maxie Rosenbloom, Anita Ekberg.
95 min.
Last (and one of the best) of the Martin and Lewis comedies, in which Lewis is a mentally retarded movie freak enamoured with La Ekberg, and Martin a gambler on a losing streak. They team up and drive a Cadillac convertible, which they have both won as a prize, to Hollywood. For protection, Lewis takes along his Great Dane. A particular favourite of Truffaut, who pointed out that the title refers to financial insolvency as much as to Ekberg's chest, its gags have real momentum, and the parody of *War and Peace*, which Paramount were making at the time with Ekberg, is delightful. ATu

Hollywood Shuffle
(Robert Townsend, 1987, US) Robert Townsend, Anne-Marie Johnson, Starletta Dupois, Helen Martin, Craigus R Johnson, Ludie Washington.
81 min.
Bobby is a struggling black actor. The few roles offered by white movie writers and producers reek of artifice: punks, pimps, sassy soul brothers and Eddie Murphy clones. What's a man to do? Townsend's satire may be gentle, but more often than not it's spot on. As Bobby (Townsend) escapes the sad reality of racial stereotyping through daydreams that expose the absurdity of whites telling blacks how to be Black, we're treated to visions of a Black Acting School (learn how to play a yodelling butler Stepin Fetchit-style), a truly *noir* TV-*noir* (Sam Ace in *Death of a Breakdancer*), and best of all, a Bros' version of a Bazza Norman-type movie round-up. Despite the film's conspicuously minuscule budget and shaky narrative structure, it *is* funny. If you value enthusiasm and imagination more than glossy sophistication, you'll laugh. GA

Holocaust 2000
(aka The Chosen)
(Alberto De Martino, 1977, It/GB) Kirk Douglas, Simon Ward, Agostina Belli, Anthony Quayle, Virginia McKenna, Alexander Knox, Adolfo Celi.
102 min.
A straight rip-off from *The Omen*. This time it's an American industrialist, not an American ambassador, who sires the Anti-Christ, but in other respects the familiar rush-towards-apocalypse is all here, right down to the various decapitations. If only the film-makers had paid less attention to plot detail in *The Omen* and more to its acute construction and direction, they might have pulled it off; but *Holocaust 2000* bears most of the worst traces of international co-production, notably a sense of disunity between cast and direction, some poor dubbing, and lines of dialogue that sound just like subtitles ('Your mother used to blame you subconsciously for being the only one to survive'). Everyone's pulling hard, only it's all too obvious they're not pulling in the same direction. DP

Holy Innocents, The
(Los Santos Inocentes)
(Mario Camus, 1984, Sp) Alfredo Landa, Terele Pávez, Francisco Rabal, Augustín González, Juan Diego.
105 min.
In the '60s, a young soldier on leave returns to the humble rural croft of his youth to visit his prematurely ageing parents, and recalls, in a series of flashbacks, the lives and quotidian grind of his family. This is Franco's Spain; and for the poorest workers on the estates, life is feudal and brutal. The scenes speak for themselves: the soldier's father crawling like a dog to sniff out fallen game, too proud of his prowess to notice his debasement; his simpleton uncle gently cradling the family's retarded child, only to infect her with lice; his ever-suffering mother, sadly and stoically accepting the loss of her child's chance of an education. If Camus places his sympathy firmly with these innocent victims rather than their morally impoverished employers, his mood is nevertheless one of restraint, shot through with moments of symbolism and dark spirituality. Save only finally, when the cruelty and claustrophobia are punctured by a moment of cold catharsis. A moving and mournful valediction to an unforgotten and unforgiven past. WH

Holy Matrimony
(Leonard Nimoy, 1994, US) Patricia Arquette, Joseph Gordon-Levitt, Armin Mueller-Stahl, Tate Donovan, John Schuck, Lois Smith.
93 min.

Time Out Film Guide 397

This comedy thriller has Arquette, the 'Marilyn Monroe' of her local Midwestern State Fair, hotfooting it with amour Donovan to a Hutterite colony on the Alberta plains, there to hide from the FBI following a cash robbery. Donovan is only cautiously welcomed back from the land of temptation by elder Mueller-Stahl; but when he's seen off in a car accident, Hutterite law demands that Arquette must marry his 12-year-old brother. The elders hope the law will provoke her swift egress. Instead, she accepts. Matching the culture clash of *Witness* with a rock'n'roll movie would be daunting for even the most inventive director. Leonard Nimoy plays it straight. Arquette is a vital, kooky presence, but here she looks merely embarrassed. WH

Holy Terror
see Communion

Hombre
(Martin Ritt, 1966, US) Paul Newman, Fredric March, Richard Boone, Diane Cilento, Martin Balsam, Barbara Rush, Cameron Mitchell, Frank Silvera.
111 min.
Based on a novel by Elmore Leonard which works a neat variation on the *Stagecoach* theme, this has Newman first outcast by the passengers who think he is an Apache, then elected as their guardian angel when they are menaced by bandits. White, but brought up by Apaches to believe that civilisation is hell, Newman very sensibly – but to humanitarian protests from his flock – starts coldly and calculatedly picking off the bandits one by one before they are ready for him. Developing its own liberal conscience, the film has Newman finally see the light – 'People must help each other' – so that he perishes (nobly rather than ironically) in making a doomed bid to rescue Rush, staked out by the bandits to die in the sun. Even so this is one of Ritt's best films, with fine performances all round, impressive Death Valley locations, and superlative camerawork from James Wong Howe. TM

Hombre Mirando al Sudeste
(Eliseo Subiela, 1986, Arg) Lorenzo Quinteros, Hugh Soto, Ines Verengo.
110 min.
Faced with a patient who insists he's from another planet, a doctor reacts with incredulity, yet the better he gets to know his subject, the more inclined he is to believe him, even if this means challenging his most basic assumptions. A straight-faced Argentinian drama which Hollywood would doubtless have played as farce. TJ

Home Alone
(Chris Columbus, 1990, US) Macaulay Culkin, Joe Pesci, Daniel Stern, John Heard, Roberts Blossom, Catherine O'Hara, John Candy.
103 min.
After *Planes, Trains and Automobiles*, writer-producer John Hughes turns once more to the nightmare of travel, this time from a child's perspective. Set to spend Christmas in Paris with parents and assorted relatives, young Kevin (Culkin) wishes everyone would just disappear, a desire granted when he is accidentally left behind by his preoccupied parents (Heard and O'Hara). But the novelty starts to wear off when a couple of burglars (Stern and Pesci, excellent) target the house. Hughes confidently mixes elements of precocious self-awareness with childlike wonderment: the boy truly believes his dream has become manifest, so he gorges on junk food and television until the reality of the situation brings loneliness and fear. Broader in humour, however, with an inconsistency of mood not helped by abrupt editing and Columbus' sometimes self-conscious direction, Home Alone lacks the sustained tension of the earlier film. CM

Home Alone 2:
Lost in New York
(Chris Columbus, 1992, US) Macaulay Culkin, Joe Pesci, Daniel Stern, Catherine O'Hara, John Heard, Devin Ratray, Brenda Fricker, Eddie Bracken, Tim Curry.
120 min.
This routine sequel has a trio of nice cameos, but no surprises. Through mix-ups, Kevin (Culkin)

gets detached from the family again, and while they fly on holiday to Florida, he fetches up alone in New York. Bad burglars Harry (Pesci) and Marv (Stern) turn up again to rob a toyshop of its Christmas takings, which owner Mr Duncan (Bracken) has earmarked for a children's hospital. Wandering about Central Park, Kevin encounters a sinister-seeming but actually lonely pigeon lady (Fricker), and advises her about love and life (much as he did the sinister-seeming but lonely snow-shoveller in the earlier film). His sojourn at the Plaza Hotel is fraught with suspicious staff (Curry), but his battle with the burglars – surely the point of these flicks – mistakes the pain threshold for hilarity. BC

Home Alone 3
(Raja Gosnell, 1997, US) Alex D Linz, Olek Krupa, Rya Kihlstedt, Lenny Von Dohlen, David Thornton, Haviland Morris.
102 min.
In place of Macaulay Culkin, comes mop-top newcomer Linz, and in place of Pesci and Stern, a quartet of similarly stupid espionage thieves. What remains the same is yet another chain of 'ouch that hurt' cartoon set-pieces. The first two films saw Kevin inadvertently left alone because of mistakes made by his preoccupied parents. Here writer/producer John Hughes has manufactured a situation whereby Alex, suffering from chicken pox, is intentionally left at home by his working parents. This low-IQ nonsense is becoming very tiresome. DA

Home and the World, The
(Ghare-Baire)
(Satyajit Ray, 1984, Ind) Soumitra Chatterjee, Victor Banerjee, Swatilekha Chatterjee, Gopa Aich, Jennifer Kapoor.
140 min.
Based on a novel by Rabindranath Tagore and set in 1908 Bengal, this tells of a woman who, after being persuaded by her wealthy but liberal husband to break with the tradition of female seclusion, falls not only for his old friend but also for the latter's revolutionary ideals, intended to unite Bengalis against the British colonial policy of 'divide and rule' regarding Hindus and Moslems. Although it becomes clear where Ray's political sympathies lie, his customary sense of balance and generosity towards his characters prevents him from tipping the scales in facile fashion, while motivations and issues are presented with great clarity. One could accuse the film of being talky and static, but the formal elegance, sure sense of pace, and uniformly excellent performances guarantee a moving experience. GA

Home at Seven
(aka Murder on Monday)
(Ralph Richardson, 1952, GB) Ralph Richardson, Margaret Leighton, Jack Hawkins, Meriel Forbes, Campbell Singer, Michael Shepley.
85 min. b/w.
Bank clerk Richardson returns home from work to quiet suburbia at his usual time, only to be told by his wife (Leighton) that he's been missing for 24 hours. Suffering from apparent amnesia, he gets another shock when evidence incriminates him in theft and murder committed during the time he can't account for. Richardson had starred on stage in RC Sherriff's source play. His air of concerned bewilderment is just right for this modest suspenser; and in his only time behind the camera, he makes a decent fist of maintaining tension, although the proscenium arch never seems far away. TJ

Home Before Midnight
(Pete Walker, 1978, GB) James Aubrey, Alison Elliot, Mark Burns, Juliet Harmer, Richard Todd, David Hamilton.
111 min. b/w.
A confused but salacious piece of exploitation which takes the tale of a London Lolita and places it in an unconvincing world of '70s rock'n'roll. Its only possible appeal is to the sexist who might be able to identify with David Hamilton's line about the girl at his side: 'I've got to handle this little hot shot here'. The script rarely rises above the asinine until the end, where it becomes truly offensive, making a case for believing that little girls who cry 'rape' are probably lying. HM

Homebodies
(Larry Yust, 1973, US) Paula Trueman, Frances Fuller, William Hansen, Ruth McDevitt, Peter Brocco, Ian Wolfe, Douglas Fowley.
96 min.
Low budget black comedy about six senior citizens who, refusing to vacate their condemned brownstone haven for a gaunt, antiseptic block of flats, begin a murderous guerilla war against their opponents. The subsequent mayhem is depicted with much humour, nicely controlled tension, and – somehow – with dignity. Towards the end, the group's leader (76-year-old Paula Trueman, a saner version of Ruth Gordon) gets carried away into excess, and the film goes off the rails with her. But on balance it's remarkably convincing. GB

Homeboy
(Michael Seresin, 1988, US) Mickey Rourke, Christopher Walken, Debra Feuer, Thomas Quinn, Kevin Conway, Antony Alda, Jon Polito.
116 min.
Rourke has usually played knock-nutty, but this time, as an ageing boxer from Arkansas, at least he has an alibi. Johnny Walker winds up at a run-down seaside resort, is befriended by small-time entertainer and petty thief Wesley (Walken), and falls for The Nice Girl (Feuer) who runs the carousel and pony rides. Resisting Wesley's plan to rob some orthodox Jews of diamonds, Johnny fights for the big purse, although he knows that with his cranium one blow can kill him (he needs the money to repair the carousel, see). Rourke is credited with the story, and it's a compendium of his screen characteristics – the inner tenderness postulate that can only be reached by cracking the kernel against the wall for reel upon reel, the preposterous walk, gobbing in two kinds (blood and saliva), lots of up-ended bottles, and very sparse dialogue. Sentimental and self-indulgent, with snot added. BC

Homecoming
(Si Shui Liu Nian)
(Yim Ho, 1984, HK) Siqin Gaowa, Josephine Koo, Xie Weixiong, Zhou Yun.
97 min.
After ten years in Hong Kong, a girl returns for a visit to her native village on the mainland. Cue for a familiar clash between nostalgia and necessity, busy fleshpots and rustic backwaters, the 'free' and the Communist worlds. But effortlessly confounding expectations, Yim Ho's film sidesteps all the pitfalls with grace, wit and even touches of quaint fantasy. A real charmer. TM

Homecoming, The
(Peter Hall, 1973, US/GB) Cyril Cusack, Ian Holm, Michael Jayston, Vivien Merchant, Terence Rigby, Paul Rogers.
114 min.
The Homecoming was first performed in 1965 after Pinter had taken a five-year pause over full-length stage work. Significantly, it concerns the return of academic son Teddy (Jayston) to his North London familial nest, a smouldering pyre of hatred and resentment presided over by Max (Rogers). This demonic Alf Garnett, when not spitting contempt for his poovy bachelor brother (Cusack), waxes hateful, rapturous and disgusted about his dead wife, best friend, and homebound sons, loquacious pimp Lenny (Holm) and dumbbell pugilist Joey (Rigby). In this battle of wills, Teddy's enigmatic wife (Merchant) finally triumphs, while hubby returns to his US campus unsure of his ability to operate 'on' situations rather than 'in' them. Hall has produced his best work for the cinema with this sensitive adaptation: a riveting, often hilarious piece (with outstanding performances from Holm, Cusack and Rogers) which makes one quite melancholy about Pinter's self-willed decline into a Bakerloo Line imitation of Samuel Beckett. SGr

Home for the Holidays
(Jodie Foster, 1995, US) Holly Hunter, Anne Bancroft, Robert Downey Jr, Charles Durning, Dylan McDermott, Steve Guttenberg, Cynthia Stevenson, Claire Danes, Geraldine Chaplin, David Strathairn.
103 min.
'Wait till you see your father's organ – he can't keep his hands off it!' No, not a line from some forgotten British farce, but Bancroft to Hunter in

Jodie Foster's family-relationships comedy that stoops to fart jokes and dotty maiden aunts before divesting itself of a none-too-pressing homily: 'We don't have to like each other – we're family.' Hunter is Claudia, who makes the pilgrimage home for Thanksgiving with a bad cold and a worse temper: her life's a mess. Her parents (Bancroft and Durning) bicker constantly, her brother (Downey) shows up with a mysterious male friend (McDermott), and her sister (Stevenson) can't contain her resentment towards all and sundry. It's shaping up to be a hell of a weekend. A modest film (in every sense) which pushes the gags too hard. TCh

Home from the Hill
(Vincente Minnelli, 1959, US) Robert Mitchum, Eleanor Parker, George Peppard, George Hamilton, Luana Patten, Everett Sloane, Constance Ford.
150 min.
In this small-town America melodrama, Mitchum plays the coolly licentious head of a Texan family, Parker his frigid wife. Both vie for the allegiance of their son (Hamilton), coming to terms with his patriarchal inheritance until he discovers the existence of an illegitimate half-brother (Peppard). Then all hell breaks loose as the sins of the father are visited on the son. Minnelli's intelligent use of scope, colour and all the technical resources Metro could offer would make it watchable enough. His ability to present the network of relationships between his quartet of characters so that all four are presented in a sympathetic light, and particularly his portrayal of the central oedipal psychodrama (Hamilton is excellent), make it explosive viewing. RM

Home in Indiana
(Henry Hathaway, 1944, US) Walter Brennan, Jeanne Crain, June Haver, Charlotte Greenwood, Lon McCallister, Ward Bond.
103 min.
Homespun Americana to the max as orphan McCallister is packed off to uncle Walter's farm, teams with local lasses Crain and Haver, then finds his métier as a champion horse breeder. Brightly coloured and impossibly optimistic, it's a missive from another era, and not recommended to those of a curmudgeonly disposition. Later remade as the Pat Boone vehicle April Love. TJ

Home-Made Melodrama
(Jacqui Duckworth, 1982, GB) Lyndey Stanley, Joy Chamberlain, Cass Bream, Madelaine McNamara, Joy Watkins.
51 min.
This frankly autobiographical account of the director's painful experiences developing a lesbian ménage à trois remains caught in a cloistered domestic world that, despite a real concern to open up a wider perspective, masks the political dimension and external pressures enclosing intimate emotions. Its address is to a committed, if limited audience, which will doubtless disregard the mostly unimaginative visuals and 'home-made' technical quality dictated by lack of money, equipment and expertise. SJo

Home of Our Own, A
(Tony Bill, 1993, US) Kathy Bates, Edward Furlong, Clarissa Lassig, Sarah Schaub, Miles Feulner, Soon-Teck Oh.
104 min.
Frances Lacey (Bates) has no money, no husband, six kids and a broken-down '48 Plymouth. Undeterred, she settles on an abandoned farm shack in a middle-American pothole and convinces its owner, Mr Moon (Soon-Teck Oh), to let the Lacey clan set up house there in return for chores and odd jobs. With bits and pieces from the local scrap merchant, and a great deal of determination, the family begins to fix up the place. Hardship takes its toll, however, and the eldest son, Shayne (Furlong), becomes increasingly embittered towards his indomitable mom. It's hard to imagine much of an audience for this gritty, poignant movie. Tony Bill presents a vision of working-class American experience that is, perhaps, a shade sentimental, but still largely authentic and unpatronising. With notably tough and tender performances from Bates and Furlong, and good work from cinematographer Jean Lepine, this is a solid, small-scale film with its heart in the right place. TCh

Home of the Brave
(Laurie Anderson, 1986, US) Paula Mazur, Laurie Anderson, William S Burroughs.
91 min.
Written and directed by Anderson, this is far removed from the monochrome epics of her earlier shows, relying on colour imagery, dance, and fair helpings of Anderson's spooky humour. All the hits and album faves are here, although the adoption of the rock format contradicts the initial, idiosyncratic charm of her work. Fans should flock, while others are guaranteed 91 minutes of the strangest pop entertainment ever. If there is a flaw, it's in Anderson's work itself, which pretends to comment on weapon culture and information technology, when in fact all that Anderson is doing is playing around with signs. JG

Hometown
(Furusato)
(Kenji Mizoguchi, 1930, Jap) Yoshie Fujiwara, Shizue Natsukawa, Fujiko Hamaguchi, Kunio Tamura, Heitaro Doi.
86 min. b/w.
Mizoguchi's first sound film (some of it's talkie, some with music and intertitles) may feature a fairly crude Star Is Born-style melodramatic story, broad humour and some distinctly unsubtle cutting, but it still impresses for its fluid camerawork and its sympathy for the woman whose singer husband, attracted by fame, fortune and a femme fatale, gradually grows more distant and uncaring. Very much of its time, but memorable for a dazzling party scene with jazzed-up Dvorak. (Original running time 107 minutes, but all extant copies 86 minutes.) GA

Homeward Bound:
The Incredible Journey
(Duwayne Durham, 1993, US) Rattler (Michael J Fox), Tiki (Sally Field), Ben (Don Ameche), Don Adler.
85 min.
Disney's live-action hit The Incredible Journey (1963) saw two dogs and a cat trek across Canada on their way home. This is the remake. Verities are passed from age to youth; races and creeds bonded by adversity. The creatures are voiced – Fox is the tearaway pup, Ameche the venerable hound, Field the Himalayan cat. Totally uncorrupting. WH

Homework
(La Tarea)
(Jaime Humberto Hermosillo, 1990, Mex) María Rojo, José Alonso, Xanic Zepeda, Christopher.
85 min.
Virginia (Rojo) sets up a hidden video camera, discards jeans for figure-hugging dress, and awaits a knock on the door. Enter Marcelo (Alonso), an old paramour of the preening variety... Hermosillo's inventive and deceptive sex comedy comes on like a minimalist sex, lies and videotape revisited a la Mexicana, though the spin here is placing a woman in control of the camera. This is a less cool relative of the serious 'filming and fucking' movies from the likes of Soderbergh and Atom Egoyan, but here the meditations on power, pornography, voyeurism, the camera as weapon of control, fantasy and the like, have a more formal, old-fashioned feel. It's shot in ten-minute takes to fake real time, and being forced to view the proceedings from the static camera position is like participating in an experiment, with the viewer as object. Still, it's good to be implicated now and again. WH

Homicidal
(William Castle, 1961, US) Glenn Corbett, Patricia Breslin, Jean Arless, Eugenie Leontovich, Richard Rust.
87 min. b/w.
One from cult shock-meister William Castle, of The Tingler fame. Castle himself introduces this passably creepy tale about an Old Dark House, a murderous blonde, a paralysed old Swedish woman, and a mysterious young man. Not quite his loopiest film, it cribs brazenly from Psycho, to good effect. This time, the gimmick-fixated maestro didn't go as far as wiring up cinema seats or dangling creepy crawlies from the ceiling; instead, the faint-hearted were offered a 'fright break' in which to make their excuses and leave. JRo

Homicide
(David Mamet, 1991, US) Joe Mantegna, William H Macy, Natalija Nogulich, Ving Rhames, Vincent Guastaferro, Rebecca Pidgeon, Lionel Mark Smith.
102 min.
Mamet's third film comes from a disturbing thriller, Suspects, by William Caunitz. Honest cop Bobby Gold (Mantegna) is taken off a hot case to babysit a Jewish family. An old pawnbroker has been murdered, and the family, fearing an anti-semitic conspiracy, believe that they're next. Gold starts out resenting the assignment, but gradually begins to accept their take on events. His long-suppressed Jewishness surfaces. The twist at the end is devastating, forcing you to view the film as a character study rather than a thriller, which places it in the Detective Story and The Offence bag. Unfortunately, the transitions are sometimes abrupt and unconvincing, despite Mantegna's intensity. We can see how bigotry drives him away from his adoptive police family toward his own people, but not how his new militancy escalates so steeply. Gripping, though. BC

Homme Amoureux, Un
see Man in Love, A

Homme de Désir, L'
(Dominique Delouche, 1970, Fr) François Timmerman, Eric Laborey, Emmanuelle Riva, André Falcon.
100 min. b/w.
Delouche's film is reverentially shot in the style of Bresson: the pious, anguished hero inhabiting a world in which everyday objects are infused with mystical significance, and where natural sounds serve to emphasise the individual's essential isolation in a universe where man's only possible relationship is directly with God. Uneasily grafted on to this act of homage is the ménage à trois tale of a man's infatuation for a hitchhiking youth he has picked up, a relationship which develops with all due encouragement from his wife. The story is reminiscent of Chabrol's Les Biches, in fact, and is best enjoyed as a thriller. The contrast between the urbane, relaxed world of the man, and the underworld night existence of the youth, is handled with a remarkable sureness until the working-out of the respective fates of the two characters, when our sympathy is shifted from the corrupt impotence of the man to the unworthy pocket-picking boy unwillingly drawn into the man's cruel and ultimately masochistic pursuit.

Homme de Marrakesh, L'
(Our Man in Marrakesh/
That Man George)
(Jacques Deray, 1966, Fr/It/Sp) George Hamilton, Claudine Auger, Alberto De Mendoza, Daniel Ivernel, Tiberio Murgia.
90 min.
Dubbed '60s international hotchpotch with Hamilton and cohorts planning a gold bullion heist in the Moroccan desert. It's the sort of would-be-hip fluff that Belmondo had made popular in France and overseas (L'Homme de Rio, etc), but Hamilton's glazed presence doesn't do the business. TJ

Homme de ma vie, L'
(The Man in My Life)
(Jean-Charles Tacchella, 1995, Fr/Can) Maria de Medeiros, Thierry Fortineau, Jean-Pierre Bacri, Anne Letourneau, Ginette Garcin, Ginette Mathieu.
103 min.
A very moderate comedy of manners, à la Woody Allen: Fortineau's impecunious bookseller Maurice affects an air of misanthropic mystery but needs de Medeiros' coquettish Aimée to put him at ease with the world. She, however, has determined to marry money, donning slinky red dress and cheesy grin to snare bastard restaurant-critic Malcolm (Bacri). The resolution is not unexpected, but along the way writer/director Tacchella toys with the audience to exasperating, if not terribly interesting effect. TJ

Homme de Rio, L'
(That Man from Rio)
(Philippe de Broca, 1964, Fr/It) Jean-Paul Belmondo, Françoise Dorléac, Jean Servais, Simone Renant, Milton Ribeiro, Adolfo Celi.
120 min.

A delightfully preposterous thriller (the McGuffin is some stolen Amazonian treasure), wittier than any of the Bond spoofs that subsequently flooded the market and a good deal racier than *Raiders of the Lost Ark*. Handsomely shot on location in Brazil, with Belmondo as the cheerfully indestructible hero who cliffhangs, climbs buildings, imitates Tarzan, parachutes almost into the jaws of a crocodile, and does his best to cope with the enchantingly unpredictable Dorléac (late lamented sister of Catherine Deneuve). The dubbing in the transatlantic version isn't too disastrous. TM

Homme est Mort, Un
see Outside Man, The

Homme et une Femme, Un (A Man and a Woman)
(Claude Lelouch, 1966, Fr) Anouk Aimée, Jean-Louis Trintignant, Pierre Barouh, Valérie Lagrange, Simone Paris, Paul le Person.
102 min.
The notoriously schmaltzy but still undeniably eye-catching film in which Aimée and Trintignant conduct an intense and often unhappy affair against an elegant, colourful background. Lelouch tricks it out with every elaborate cinematic effect he can beg, borrow or steal, ransacking both Welles and Godard for titillating devices which look good but never even begin to mesh with the subject matter (note in particular the 360 degree tracking shot at the end). In some ways the film's sheer zest and the talented cast might have won the day, were it not for Francis Lai's dreadfully corny and monotonous theme music. DP

Homme qui Aimait les Femmes, L'
see Man Who Loved Women, The

Homme qui Dort, Un (A Man in a Dream)
(Bernard Queysanne/Georges Perec, 1974, Fr/Tun) Jacques Spiesser.
90 min. b/w.
A hypnotic solo by its mute hero, a young man who decides to withdraw from the world and whose mental journal of his experience is confided to us by a girl's voice offscreen, *Un Homme qui Dort* is an astonishing tour de force. What distinguishes it from all those ventures in spiritual navel-gazing is that his decision to not-be is purely practical, and the parabola he traces from boredom to terror – as he gradually detaches himself to float free within an indefinable menace – is brilliantly conveyed by the other leading character in the film: the city of Paris. The influence of Franju is unmistakable, and wholly beneficial. TM

Hommes femmes Mode d'emploi
see Men, Women: User's Manual

Homme sur les Quais, Les
see Man by the Shore, The

Hondo
(John Farrow, 1953, US) John Wayne, Geraldine Page, Ward Bond, Michael Pate, James Arness, Rodolfo Acosta, Leo Gordon, Lassie.
93 min.
John Wayne's favourite John Wayne movie. Louis L'Amour's source novel is a variation on *Shane*, with Wayne as the eponymous stranger, a cavalry scout, whose manly ways recommend him to a homesteader (Page) and her boy, though here her husband's a ne'er-do-well the Duke kills in self-defence. The film extends liberal respect to the Indians, and even implicitly endorses a romance between a white woman and the half-breed Hondo. Page won an Oscar nomination for this, her first film role, but Wayne's guileless performance is even better: gently self-mocking, while still every inch the embodiment of the conviction that 'a man ought to do what he thinks is best'. Robert Burks' cinematography is a major plus (the film was originally released in 3-D, but there's precious little gimmickry). A rarity until restored by the John Wayne Society for re-release in 1995. TCh

Honey and Venom
(Jun Mori, 1990, GB) Georgia Byng, Tom Knight, Emma Croft.
41 min.
An intriguing but faintly over-aesthetic short feature, made in London by a young Japanese director. A woman painter, in a lifeless apartment that she must have designed herself, finds her privacy invaded by a drunken man from the noisy party upstairs. The incident seems trivial, but the reverberations are massive: the woman's house of cards begins to collapse. Mori films without comment or explanation, trusting his emphasis on details to tease out the unspoken implications. Hard to imagine the method working in a full-length feature, but he just about gets away with it at this length. TR

Honey, I Shrunk the Kids
(Joe Johnston, 1989, US) Rick Moranis, Matt Frewer, Marcia Strassman, Kristine Sutherland, Thomas Brown, Jared Rushton, Amy O'Neill, Robert Oliveri.
93 min.
While batty inventor Szalinski (Moranis) boffins away in the attic, his kids Amy and Nick (O'Neill, Oliveri) are left to shift for themselves. Russ Thompson (Frewer), his sports-jock neighbour, looks on in scorn, but is comically insensitive to the needs of his own two sons (Brown, Rushton). The Thompson boys whack a baseball through the attic window, the as yet imperfect shrinking machine is activated, and the warring youngsters wind up tiny, swept into a bin-bag and dumped at the bottom of the garden. During their trek back, there are wonderful moments like a flight *on* the bumble bee, a fall into a giant flower, and the adoption of a discarded lego brick as a night shelter. Perhaps unavoidably, there sre inconsistencies of scale, and though the characterisation is generally warm and believable, there's still the 'Your sister's all right – for a *gurl*!' syndrome. Sterling entertainment, though. SFe

Honey, I Blew Up the Kid
(Randal Kleiser, 1992, US) Rick Moranis, Marcia Strassman, Robert Oliveri, Lloyd Bridges, John Shea, Keri Russell, Ron Canada, Amy O'Neill.
89 min.
Kleiser's follow-up to *Honey, I Shrunk the Kids* is a disappointment. Much of the problem is that it's impossible to place a 112-foot high baby in peril, or excite the sort of concern that was generated by the miniaturised children. This big baby gurgles happily as he picks up cars with adults in them and toddles about grabbing neon signs in Las Vegas, threatened only – and briefly – by a man with a tranquilliser dart in a helicopter. The rest of the problem is lousy back-projection, with ill-matched scenes in which the proper-sized people seem to be responding several yards to the left and right of the stimulus. Very boring. BC

Honeymoon (Luna de Miel)
(Michael Powell, 1959, Sp/GB) Anthony Steel, Ludmila Tcherina, Antonio, Leonide Massine, Rosita Segovia.
109 min.
The last of Powell's ballet films, unfortunately not a patch on *The Red Shoes*, or even *The Tales of Hoffman*. A slim story – prima ballerina Tcherina travelling on honeymoon with Steel in Spain, and being drawn into performing again by Antonio – is thankfully enlivened by a couple of beautifully shot ballet sequences (music by Theodorakis and de Falla) choreographed by Antonio and Massine. Many of Powell's customary themes are there, including that of the ambivalence of artistic creation, but delivered in fairly lifeless fashion compared to his best work. That said, Georges Périnal's Technicolor camerawork is as stunning as ever. GA

Honeymoon in Vegas
(Andrew Bergman, 1992, US) Nicolas Cage, Sarah Jessica Parker, James Caan, Pat Morita, Anne Bancroft, Peter Boyle, Seymour Cassel.
105 min.
A long awaited wedding between the maternally fixated Jack Singer (Cage) and his boisterous bride Betsy (Parker) seems finally on the cards when the couple take a break in Vegas. But the decks are stacked against Jack, who loses big in a poker game to arch knave Tommy Korman

(Caan, sublimely slimy). In lieu of payment, Tommy demands a weekend with Betsy, who reminds him of his long-lost wife. Will Tommy steal Jack's ace from under his nose? Beautifully written and directed by Bergman, this paradoxically modern slice of nostalgia energetically revives the long mourned 'oddball' comedy. For once, Cage is pleasantly understated, playing the straight guy beset by nine shades of madness: lunatic mothers, deranged mobsters, singing Chieftains, and sky-diving Elvis impersonators by the dozen, they're all here in this joyous, uplifting romp. MK

Honeymoon Killers, The
(Leonard Kastle, 1969, US) Shirley Stoler, Tony Lo Bianco, Mary Jane Higby, Doris Roberts, Kip McArdle.
108 min. b/w.
This tells, bleakly, unsentimentally, in shady black-and-white tricked out with a scratchy Mahler soundtrack, the true tale of Martha Beck and Ray Fernandez: she a grotesquely overweight nursing sister from Mobile, Alabama; he a Latin gigolo living off aged spinsters and widows, tricking them of their money and, after a torrid team-up with Martha, bumping them off in a manner no way sanitised in Kastle's hands. The couple were electrocuted in 1951, but the film shows them not so much as monsters as a weird, passionate appendage to the love and marriage stakes glibly represented by the collection of down-home mommas, randy would-be wives and patriotic widows on whom the couple prey (with Martha posing as Ray's sister, though so overcome with jealousy that attempted suicide, murder, and eventually betrayal to the police ensue). An eerie, negected classic of its kind. SGr

Honey Pot, The
(Joseph L Mankiewicz, 1966, US/It) Rex Harrison, Susan Hayward, Cliff Robertson, Capucine, Edie Adams, Maggie Smith, Adolfo Celi, Herschel Bernardi.
150 min.
Adapted from a play out of a novel based on Ben Jonson's *Volpone*, Mankiewicz's screenplay finds a contemporary millionaire (Harrison in fine waspish form) inspired after a performance of Jonson's play to re-enact the same plot device on his three former mistresses (Hayward, Capucine and Adams) – posing as a dying man to test their reactions. The structure continually threatens to cave in under the weight of over-fussy dialogue and confusing plot twists, but the high-grade cast (with a pleasingly restrained Maggie Smith as the hypochondriac Hayward's nurse), and some sumptuous photography by Gianni Di Venanzo, make it highly watchable. If cinema and stage farce have to get in bed together, this is one of the more fruitful unions around. DT

Honeysuckle Rose
(Jerry Schatzberg, 1980, US) Willie Nelson, Dyan Cannon, Amy Irving, Slim Pickens, Joey Floyd.
119 min.
Schatzberg might be a very urban cowboy (*Panic in Needle Park, Puzzle of a Downfall Child, Sweet Revenge*, et al), but there's no evidence here of slick, Altman-style condescension to country 'n' western culture. Instead there's an unforced equation of the upfront emotional currency of c & w lyrics with a simple triangular plotline pared down from *Intermezzo* (singer Nelson and wife Cannon almost come apart over the lure of the road and one more infidelity). Nothing new under the sun – but the easy-going fringe benefits are well worth the ticket: Nelson's a natural, and the duets with Cannon are pure gold. PT

Honkers, The
(Steve Ihnat, 1971, US) James Coburn, Slim Pickens, Lois Nettleton, Anne Archer, Richard Anderson, Ted Eccles, Jim Davis.
103 min.
Ageing rodeo rider Lew Lathrop (Coburn) may not still be at his competitive best, but the cameraderie and womanising of the touring circuit continue to exert a strong pull when he makes a rare visit home to New Mexico to his estranged spouse Nettleton. Melancholy, slow, closely detailed post-Western drama which lets rip with the moralising at the close as Lew's partner Clete (Pickens) is trampled to death by a bucking bull.

Coburn has a watchable charm, though *Junior Bonner* and *J.W. Coop* (both also from the early '70s) rode the same range with greater distinction. TJ

Honky Tonk Freeway

(John Schlesinger, 1981, US) William Devane, Beau Bridges, Teri Garr, Beverly D'Angelo, Hume Cronyn, Jessica Tandy, Geraldine Page.
107 min.
Ealing in its heyday might have coaxed some mild satire out of the idea of a small town prepared to go to any lengths to ensure that it is not bypassed by a new freeway. Officials swallow bribes but fail to deliver, the townsfolk resort to terrorist tactics, hordes of grotesques converge on the town bringing the tourist money all the ghoulish greed is about. The material is there, but in Schlesinger's hands the whole thing is battered into a shapeless, witless mess as a barrage of slapstick gags, each more crudely conceived and badly timed than the last, leaves one numb with disbelief. Even Abbott and Costello were funnier. TM

Honkytonk Man

(Clint Eastwood, 1982, US) Clint Eastwood, Kyle Eastwood, John McIntire, Alexa Kenin, Verna Bloom, Matt Clark.
123 min.
One of the most oddball and heroically unfashionable superstar vehicles ever contrived. Only Eastwood, with the rest of Hollywood obsessed with taking us up where we belong, could have the audacity to play a comparatively odious and untalented country singer dying of consumption during the Depression. Much of the film is concerned with his picaresque pilgrimage to a Nashville audition along with nephew (played by Eastwood's son) and grandpappy (the excellent McIntire), and it culminates in a last-chance recording session during which the singer nearly coughs himself to death. The whole thing veers wildly in quality, and no Eastwood-hater should go within a mile of it; but few lovers of American cinema could fail to be moved by a venture conceived so recklessly against the spirit of its times. DP

Honno

see Lost Sex

Honorary Consul, The (aka Beyond the Limit)

(John MacKenzie, 1983, GB) Michael Caine, Richard Gere, Bob Hoskins, Elpidia Carrillo, Joaquim de Almeida.
104 min.
Deep in torpid, guerilla-riddled, brothel-centric South America (a currently popular destination for film-makers and a land Graham Greene's fiction has visited many times, always carrying two battered suitcases labelled 'Betrayal' and 'Errant Catholicism'), honorary British consul Charlie Fortnum (Caine) is mistakenly kidnapped. And no one really wants him back. MacKenzie directs with a literal flourish, brandishing Hoskins, charm-like, as an unlikely Argentinian policeman. But even a rabbit's foot as solid as Hoskins cannot ward off the evil charm of Gere reworking his unloving *American Gigolo* persona that is all wrong for Dr Eduardo Plarr, a character to whom machismo is totally alien. One wonders what Greene, whose thoughts on the cinema and charlatans are always worth hearing, would have to say. Yet even he could hardly find fault with Caine who, as the anti-heroic middle-aged lush (a character he first began to sketch in *Educating Rita*) gives the performance of his life. FD

Honor Thy Father

(Paul Wendkos, 1973, US) Joseph Bologna, Raf Vallone, Brenda Vaccaro, Richard S Castellano, Joe De Santis, Marc Lawrence.
100 min.
Based on Gay Talese's account of the '60s Mafia war between the Organisation and recalcitrant member Joe 'Bananas' Bonanno, Wendkos' film (actually made for TV) compares favourably with the more ambitious but superficial *The Godfather*. Against the familiar settings of anonymous rooms, city backlots, and streets at night, a feeling of futility erodes the Mafia assumptions of honour. An archetypal slob of a gunman giggles his way through old gangster movies, yet reads Sartre's *Being and Nothingness*. For all the shootings, the two most graphic deaths are natural: heart attack and cancer. Above all, there's

the bewilderment of Bonanno's daughter-in-law (Vaccaro). Already a nervous wreck, her patience snaps when two more gangsters turn up expecting to eat. Apart from a weak ending and a plot that both needs and uses a narrator, an altogether intelligent film. CPe

Honourable Mr Wong, The

see Hatchet Man, The

Honour Among Thieves

see Touchez pas au Grisbi

Hoodlum Empire

(Joseph Kane, 1952, US) Brian Donlevy, Claire Trevor, Luther Adler, John Russell, Forrest Tucker, Vera Ralston, Gene Lockhart, Grant Withers, Taylor Holmes.
98 min. b/w.
Designed to cash in on the televised Kefauver hearings, this was originally intended as a Frank Costello biopic. When George Raft refused to play his old buddy, the project metamorphosed into the story of Joe Gray (Russell), brought up in the rackets by his mobster uncle (Adler) until combat service in WWII teaches him the all-American values his army buddies are ready to die for. In feeble imitation of the vastly superior *The Enforcer*, a string of flashbacks from the Senate Committee hearings reveal how Gray tries to go straight in a rural community; how the Mob's expanding gambling activities encroach; and how he is deliberately inculpated so that, should threats fail and he decide to testify, his evidence will be compromised. Absurdly melodramatic when it isn't being pompous, sermonising or hopelessly simplistic about syndicate activities, the film is kept afloat solely by the fine cast (Adler, Russell and Trevor, in particular). TM

Hook

(Steven Spielberg, 1991, US) Dustin Hoffman, Robin Williams, Julia Roberts, Bob Hoskins, Maggie Smith, Caroline Goodall, Charlie Korsmo, Amber Scott, Laurel Cronin, Phil Collins.
144 min.
Spielberg's *Hook* looks like a theme park. The *Peter Pan* plot has been rejigged to suit Hollywood's dreary preoccupation with redemption; not that it matters much, since the story is largely becalmed so that we can wallow in the production values. The sets are variable but often unpleasant on the eye. To say that the best thing about the film is the miniaturised Roberts as Tinkerbell, wearing motorised Arthur Rackham wings, gives some idea how duff it is. The $60 million-plus enterprise first nosedives in the sprawling sequence where the Lost Boys train the paunchy grown-up Peter Pan (Williams) for combat against arch-enemy Hook (Hoffman), who has kidnapped his children. Hoffman's Old Etonian accent slips a bit; Hoskins as Hook's sidekick has nothing to do, and does it raucously. By the end, Peter has ditched his Wall Street cell phone and rediscovered the child in himself, so that's all right. BC

Hoop Dreams

(Steve James, 1994, US) William Gates, Arthur Agee.
170 min.
Steve James' essential inner-city epic chronicles the lives of two young blacks growing up in a Chicago housing project. At 14, basketball prodigies Arthur Agee and William Gates win scholarships to a suburban high school, St Joseph's. Then their fortunes diverge. William looks set to follow in the footsteps of St Joe's favourite son, all-star Isiah Thomas. Arthur doesn't make the cut. Skinny and immature, he finds himself back in the inner city with his parents fall behind on the fees. Over the next four years, however, the boys' lives are to intersect more than once, and in unexpected ways. A three-hour documentary about basketball is probably not most people's idea of a night out, but this one rewards the effort. James and his collaborators shot more than 250 hours of footage, and the cumulative emotional power is simply devastating. Sport is the only dream Arthur and William are allowed, their only ticket out of the ghetto, but they also have to carry the weight of their parents' aspirations – and if they make it, they will become role models for thousands of kids just like them. Unforgettable. TCh

Hooper

(Hal Needham, 1978, US) Burt Reynolds, Jan-Michael Vincent, Sally Field, Brian Keith, John Marley, Robert Klein, James Best, Adam West.
99 min.
The rich vein of 'innocent' anarchy running through Burt Reynolds comedy showcases around this time is mined again to good effect as his *Smokey and the Bandit* persona transmutes seamlessly into the ace Hollywood stuntman of the title, and director Needham (an ex-stuntman himself) slips effortlessly into a lightweight satire of the movie biz and an almost Hawksian action-comedy of male-group professionalism. Formula stuff as Reynolds' over-the-hill stuntman faces the toll of his injuries, and battles against the multiple hazards of low budget, high risk production, irate girlfriend and challenge from younger rival. Plus, naturally, The Big Stunt. But it's all surmounted by the irrepressible and irresistible Reynolds ego, which accommodates both the hagiography of a Tammy Wynette soundtrack dirge and the self-mockery of a screening of stunt footage from *Deliverance* to a sleeping audience. PT

Hoosiers (aka Best Shot)

(David Anspaugh, 1986, US) Gene Hackman, Barbara Hershey, Dennis Hopper, Sheb Wooley, Fern Persons, Chelcie Ross.
115 min.
Back in 1951, a hick high school basketball team could achieve self-respect just by getting into the State Finals. Or so this cloyingly nostalgic sports movie would have us believe. Hackman plays the belligerent coach who, in knocking the underdogs into shape, is absolved of his past sins. Actually, the film starts promisingly, with his entry into the tight-knit rural community complicated by suspicion and by his prickly relationship with fellow-teacher Hershey. There's also a brilliant cameo by Hopper as the sometime player turned town drunk whom Hackman redeems by taking him on as his assistant. However, once Hackman's uncompromising integrity lures the team's recalcitrant star player out of self-imposed retirement and the team hits a winning streak, it's just a case of going through the hoops. NF

Hoots Mon!

(Roy William Neill, 1939, GB) Max Miller, Florence Desmond, Hal Walters, Davina Craig, Garry Marsh, Gordon McLeod.
77 min. b/w.
Ramshackle vehicle for the Cheeky Chappie, who used to appear on stage through a trapdoor, 'up from the sewers, like the jokes you're going to get': his act is carefully deodorised here, though he still makes a pretence of keeping a wary eye on the wings in expectation of being hauled offstage. The excuse for a plot has him get rather more than he bargained for when he accepts a challenge from a rival Scots comedienne (Desmond) to try his Cockney comedy on her native folk. Fast-moving, cheerful and a mite tiresome, it is enlivened by Desmond's impersonations of Miller himself, Syd Walker, Bette Davis and – best of all – a hideously simpering Elisabeth Bergner. TM

Hope and Glory

(John Boorman, 1987, GB) Sebastian Rice-Edwards, Geraldine Muir, Sarah Miles, David Hayman, Sammi Davis, Derrick O'Connor, Ian Bannen.
112 min.
Boorman's autobiographical film about family life during the Blitz is subversively light on the blood, sweat, tears and sacrifice, and a joy throughout. Seen through the eyes of nine-year-old Bill Rohan (Rice-Edwards), the war was a wonderland of superior fireworks displays every night, and adventure playgrounds of rubble and ruined houses. Dad joins up and Mum starts to see a lot of Dad's best friend Mac, while teenage sister Dawn runs wild with GIs. 'They know we're mad on jam' warns Mum, regarding a captured tin of German jam with deep suspicion; a barrage balloon breaks free of its moorings, bumps about the rooftops, and has to be shot down by a Home Guard firing squad. Tragedy is touched upon only in the episode of an orphan who refuses to leave her bombed home, and is offered a shrapnel collection by a sympathetic child. When the Rohan family are burned out, they take refuge with eccentric Granddad (Bannen, astonishingly good) at Shepperton on

the river. The wind in the willows and the willow on the cricket ball – Boorman's long-lost England communicates its affectionate poetry. BC

Hopscotch
(Ronald Neame, 1980, US) Walter Matthau, Glenda Jackson, Herbert Lom, Sam Waterston, Ned Beatty, George Baker, David Matthau, Ivor Roberts.
107 min.
Despite the equal star billing, this is not another comic two-hander following up *House Calls* in pitting the misanthropic slobbishness of Matthau against the elegant bitchery of Jackson. Really it's a solo vehicle for Matthau as a CIA operative who, disciplined by demotion to a desk job, takes his revenge through an elaborate practical joke: mysteriously disappearing, he starts mailing – with the order soon out that he has got to be stopped – chapter by chapter instalments of his memoirs (with the promise of revelations to come) to intelligence agencies in the world's capitals. Less weakly scripted and directed, less reliant on globetrotting locations and technological hardware, it could have become a worthy successor to *Charley Varrick*, as it is, Matthau just about carries it. But only just. RM

Horizon (Horizont)
(Pál Gábor, 1971, Hun) Péter Fried, Lujza Orosz, Szilvia Marossy, Zoltán Vadász, József Madaras.
87 min. b/w.
This study of the contemporary Hungarian generation gap is unfortunately reminiscent of the British social dramas of the early '60s (a sequence from Anderson's *If...* is included by way of indirect tribute), with the jazz and pop music used reinforcing the period feel: a dance-hall sequence looks like something from early Beatle days. A teenage boy, representative of many his age, rejects all that his parents have fought and been imprisoned for. He drops out of school, quits his job, dreams of nihilism, and ends up working in a factory, the despair of his elders. The film is best at gauging the fundamental confusion that lies behind the boy's facade of toughness (illustrated when he carefully copies an acquaintance's man of the world mannerisms, much to the scorn of his schoolfriends). Coming down on the side of youth, it does invest them with a mobility that contrasts pointedly with the often sedentary older generation. But it is in its assertion that the old has to make way for the new that *Horizon* flounders. Given his hero's lack of stance, Gábor is left making detailed observations and little else.

Horizons West
(Budd Boetticher, 1952, US) Robert Ryan, Julie Adams, Rock Hudson, John McIntire, Raymond Burr, James Arness, Dennis Weaver.
81 min.
Still apprentice work, so don't expect anything quite so stylishly spare as the Boetticher-Randolph Scott cycle from this Western about two brothers returning to Texas after the Civil War, one to get rich quick by cattle rustling and terrorisation, the other to become his nemesis as town marshal. Burt Kennedy's superb scripting was probably the decisive factor in those later movies; here, despite impressive patches, the script by Louis Stevens too often settles for crude routine, while Hudson makes a slightly laborious meal of the good brother. But Ryan's performance as the gangster-tycoon reverberates in a manner that sometimes anticipates Boetticher's classic *The Rise and Fall of Legs Diamond*. TM

Horloger de St Paul, L' (The Clockmaker/The Watchmaker of Saint-Paul)
(Bertrand Tavernier, 1973, Fr) Philippe Noiret, Jean Rochefort, Jacques Denis, Yves Alfonso, Sylvain Rougerie, Christine Pascal.
105 min.
For his film-making debut, ex-critic Tavernier took a novel by Simenon, made the lightly polemical choice to collaborate on the screenplay with veterans Aurenche and Bost (victims of Truffaut's early New Wave ire), set the result in Lyon, and emerged with a work of old-fashioned precision that the craftsman of the title would doubtless have been proud of. Noiret is superb as the eponymous 'horloger', realigning his self-willed solitude into credible relationships with his son, on the run with girlfriend after killing a swinish

security guard, and the sympathetic police inspector (Rochefort) in charge of the case; while the physical and political ambience is rendered with a classically 'invisible' aura of authenticity. PT

Horror Chamber of Dr Faustus, The
see Yeux sans Visage Les

Horror Express (Pánico en el Transiberiano)
(Eugenio Martin, 1972, Sp/GB) Christopher Lee, Peter Cushing, Telly Savalas, Silvia Tortosa, Jorge Rigaud, Alberto de Mendoza.
90 min.
An inferior reworking of *The Thing from Another World*, which still manages to keep interest alive despite some poor special effects, a flat jokiness and stereotype characters. The idea itself is intriguing enough: anthropologist Lee's ancient fossil found in China, believed to be the missing link, comes back to life on the Trans-Siberian railway, adding the knowledge of its victims to its own. From their first greeting of 'Well, well, look who's here!', Lee and his arch-rival Cushing, at their most urbane, ensure that it remains watchable, while the express train setting keeps it all moving at a better speed than it perhaps deserves. CPe

Horror Hospital
(Antony Balch, 1973, GB) Michael Gough, Robin Askwith, Vanessa Shaw, Ellen Pollock, Skip Martin, Dennis Price, Kurt Christian.
91 min.
Anticipating the day of the video nasty, Balch – who had collaborated with William Burroughs on *Towers Open Fire* and *The Cut-Ups* – here twisted the conventional elements of the horror movie to a new level of grotesquerie. The plot concerns a mad Pavlovian doctor, whose body is a hulk of third-degree burnt tissue, boring holes in young persons' brains in an attempt to master their minds. The object is somehow to persuade beautiful ladies to fuck him, appearances notwithstanding; but despite turning into mindless zombies, they are still resistant to his charms. Hence much frustration vented by scything heads off with a Boadicea chariot of a Rolls Royce, Cocteau-like biker henchmen given to beating people up, and mutant dwarves chopping skulls with hatchets or burning flesh with cigarettes. All of which takes place in a charming castle masquerading as a health farm. Cliché after cliché is ruthlessly hammered into a telling stomach-gripper: one for sophisticates of undergrowth horror of the Chas Addams variety. JDuC

Horror of Death
see Asphyx, The

Horror of Dracula
see Dracula

Horrors of the Black Museum
(Arthur Crabtree, 1959, GB) Michael Gough, Graham Curnow, June Cunningham, Shirley Ann Field, Geoffrey Keen, Gerald Anderson, Beatrice Varley.
95 min.
The first of Anglo-Amalgamated's loose trilogy of Sadian horror movies – the others being *Circus of Horrors* and Michael Powell's infinitely superior *Peeping Tom* – anticipates Powell's interest in voyeurism with its opening scene of a woman's eyes being gouged out by a pair of viciously spiked binoculars. Thereafter, as Gough's novelist devises a series of horrible crimes in order to make his work more appealing to a sensation-hungry readership, the film continues as a tacky catalogue of gratuitously nasty tortures and murders. Indeed, it's as lascivious and leering in its approach as the great British public it purports to condemn. Lurid and innuendo-laden, it's an intriguing oddity. GA

Horse Feathers
(Norman Z McLeod, 1932, US) The Marx Brothers, Thelma Todd, David Landau, Robert Greig, Nat Pendleton.
70 min. b/w.
The title means bunk or baloney – a fitting epithet for the Brothers' second screen original for Paramount, where the lads and their writers

threw sanity to the winds with a wildly disorganised parody of academic life. Groucho is president of Huxley College, where none of the students appear to be under thirty-five. Chief subjects on the curriculum seem to be football, sex, the delivery of heinous puns (haddock/headache) and the refurbishing of old vaudeville routines (the biology lecture). The Brothers have never been so chaotic or so aggressively funny. GB

Horseman on the Roof, The
see Hussard sur le toit, Le

Horsemen, The
(John Frankenheimer, 1970, US) Omar Sharif, Jack Palance, Leigh Taylor-Young, David De, Peter Jeffrey, Mohammad Shamsi, George Murcell, Eric Pohlmann, Saeed Jaffrey.
109 min.
The story, adapted by Dalton Trumbo from Joseph Kessel's novel, is a good and suitably emblematic one about a champion Afghan horseman and the famous last-of-the-line stallion who undertake a perilous journey to regain the honour the man feels he has lost after his defeat in the ceremonial game of Buzkashi. On the journey he loses a leg, is confronted by his groom and an untouchable woman who want to kill him, meets a blind scribe who tells him the tale of his blindness, and a nomad who fights his scraggy one-horned sheep against a champion ram. Each encounter contains within it the seeds of his own predicament, from which a moral can be drawn. Sadly, the whole thing comes grindingly to grief on compromise (not least the absurdities of Hollywood stars speaking pidgin and rubbing shoulders with genuine Afghan extras). Some good things survive: the Afghan landscape, the horse-riders (including Sharif's double), and Palance (the only actor who seems to know what it's all about). VG

Horse's Mouth, The
(Ronald Neame, 1958, GB) Alec Guinness, Kay Walsh, Renée Houston, Mike Morgan, Robert Coote, Arthur Macrae, Michael Gough, Ernest Thesiger.
95 min.
Uneasy adaptation of Joyce Cary's marvellous novel (itself an integral part of a trilogy) about the anti-social nature of genius. Guinness builds a clever, painstakingly detailed character study as the scruffily disreputable Gulley Jimson, an ageing artist prepared to go to any lengths to ensure that he can go on setting down his vision in paint. But despite using John Bratby paintings to represent that vision, the film itself is more concerned with the artist's eccentricities than with his creativity. Flatly directed, loosely scripted, it emerges as little more than a lightweight slice of Ealing-style whimsy. TM

Horse Soldiers, The
(John Ford, 1959, US) John Wayne, William Holden, Constance Towers, Althea Gibson, Hoot Gibson, Anna Lee, Russell Simpson.
119 min.
Underrated Civil War Western, leisurely and sometimes simplistic, but mostly quintessential Ford as Wayne's pragmatic colonel and Holden's humanitarian doctor debate (and embody) aspects of war while leading a Union cavalry patrol deep behind Confederate lines, with their conflict extended by the presence of a fiery Southern belle (a lovely performance from Towers) taken along for the ride because she's overheard their plans and bursting to undermine their mission. There's a magnificent payoff in the sequence where children from the military academy cheerfully march off to the tune of fife and drum to mount a last-ditch defence of the Confederacy, flimsy toy soldiers so ripe for the slaughter that the baffled enemy simply turn tail and flee. TM

Horse Thief (Daoma Zei)
(Tian Zhuangzhuang, 1986, China) Tseshang Rigzin, Dan Jiji, Jayang Jamco, Gaoba, Daiba.
88 min.
This is Zhuangzhuang's dream project: a film about the real Tibet, from the hardship and cruelty of life on the plains to the splendour and mystery of Buddhist ceremonial, a film about life and death in the Buddhist scheme of things. The story is told in pictures, not words. Norbu is a horse thief, expelled from his clan, forced to become a

nomad, pitching his tent wherever he can find casual work. He and his wife are devout Buddhists, regularly visiting the temples to turn the prayer-wheels, but their son falls sick and dies. Norbu reaches his lowest ebb when a tribe hires him to carry the death-totem in a ritual exorcism of a plague of anthrax. In desperation, he returns to his clan to beg to be taken back. Filmed on locations in Tibet, Gansu and Qinghai and acted by local people, it offers the most awesomely plausible account of Tibetan life and culture ever seen in the west. It's one of the few films whose images show you things you've never seen before. TR

Hors la vie (Out of Life)
(Maroun Bagdadi, 1991, Fr/It/Bel) Hippolyte Girardot, Rafic Ali Ahmad, Hussein Sbeity, Habib Hammoud, Magdi Machmouchi, Hassan Farhat.
97 min.
When Patrick Perrault (Girardot), a French photographer covering the war in Beirut, is taken hostage, his life turns into a waking nightmare. Kept blindfold in an airless, initially darkened room, prey to injury, illness and sheer terror, Perrault alternates between simply struggling to survive and trying to persuade the more communicative of his continually changing captors to help him escape. Lebanese director Bagdadi's gripping thriller is exemplary of its kind. Neither flinching from nor sensationalising the violence, humiliation and sordid circumstances of Perrault's ordeal (inspired by the real-life experiences of Roger Auque), the film comes across as frighteningly authentic. The captors are never just faceless villains, but rounded, often sympathetic characters evoking the variety of causes at work in the war. Bagdadi never takes sides or offers easy answers, and Girardot's powerhouse performance renders Perrault's fear remarkably palpable. GA

Hospital
(Frederick Wiseman, 1970, US)
84 min. b/w.
Wiseman's fourth film, one of his celebrated vérité projects on American institutions: a series of despairing (or blackly comic) vignettes from the low priority end of the health/wealth equation, shot with comprehensive austerity at Metropolitan Hospital in New York City. As with most of Wiseman's films of this period, a marshalling of evidence that's angrily illustrative of symptoms of the 'system's' malaise, but mute with regard to analysis of their cause or their cure. PT

Hospital, The
(Arthur Hiller, 1971, US) George C Scott, Diana Rigg, Barnard Hughes, Nancy Marchand, Stephen Elliott, Donald Harron, Roberts Blossom.
102 min.
Paddy Chayefsky's black comedy about the head of a hospital facing disasters all round him while he undergoes a bout of personal depression. It starts off with some marvellously cruel moments, and Scott's performance towers over the proceedings throughout. But Hiller's direction is pretty shoddy, while the script eventually loses its way and begins to look increasingly hysterical, at the same time shamelessly trivialising Scott's crisis (sex cures all ills). GA

Hostile Hostages
see Ref, The

Hot Blood
(Nicholas Ray, 1956, US) Jane Russell, Cornel Wilde, Luther Adler, Joseph Calleia, Mikhail Rasumny.
95 min.
While admittedly far from being one of Ray's best films, his tale of the stormy courtship of Wilde and Russell – gypsies from rival tribes introduced to one another by their parents for an arranged marriage which obeys the laws not only of tradition but financial enterprise – is fascinating both for its *mise-en-scène* and as an example of the director's interest in ethnology. Indeed, the two elements combine to create a boldly flamboyant celebration of ritual, the gypsies' love of music, dance and colourful costumes allowing Ray to transform a potentially clichéd romantic sparring session into lurid, restless images often strangely

reminiscent of the musical. An oddity, then, but one distinguished by Ray's characteristic refusal to patronise or glamorise his characters. GA

Hot Box, The
(Joe Viola, 1972, US) Andrea Cagan, Margaret Markov, Rickey Richardson, Laurie Rose, Carmen Argenziano, Charles Dierkop.
89 min.
Though co-scripted and produced by Jonathan Demme, a film so hampered by basic lack of skill that an interesting storyline becomes buried under a whole load of destructive ambiguities. Four American Peace Corps nurses are kidnapped by the Revolutionary Army of a Latin American republic to teach medical aid. Having tasted ill-treatment by Government forces, they become sufficiently convinced of the rightness of the cause to fight a bloody battle on the revolutionaries' side. Their 'enlightenment', though, remains a perfunctory foible of the plot. VG

Hot Dog...The Movie
(Peter Markle, 1983, US) David Naughton, Patrick Houser, Tracy N Smith, John Patrick Reger, Frank Koppola.
98 min.
The callow hero from hicksville hopefully lugs his sticks across the States for the World Free-Style Ski Championships. He has a tendency toward John Denver guitar interludes, mostly brought on by a spunky blonde hitchhiker. There's a lot of swish slomo ski-strutting of the Winter Fun in Wunderberg (it's a piece of piste) variety. And there's the Chinese Downhill, when the madcap Rat Pack (loveable lads with a liking for lager and big tits) pit their poles, lemming-like, against the arrogant scheisskopf ski-champ Rudi. If you're fond of snow and it's après-math, you'll get your money's worth, but basically it's Porky Park, on sticks. AB

Hôtel de la Plage, L'
(Michel Lang, 1977, Fr) Daniel Ceccaldi, Myriam Boyer, Francis Lemaire, Guy Marchand, Jean-Paul Muel, Anne Parillaud, Michel Robin.
111 min.
Michel Lang's dated (arrested?) preoccupation with the supposed comic dimensions of adolescent skirt-chasing – already displayed in *A Nous les Petites Anglaises!* – re-emerges intact in this omnibus version of every dire French holiday-romance movie you've ever seen. Ticking off the predictable, prudishly 'permissive' permutations of a dozen or so stereotyped holidaymakers lends the film about as much narrative tension as filling in last week's football coupon. Lang alternately indulges and exploits the intended objects of his satire, and for the genuine toughness of a generically related film like *The Lace-maker*, merely substitutes a cloying sentimentality. PT

Hotel de Love
(Craig Rosenberg, 1996, Aust) Aden Young, Craig Rosenberg, Saffron Burrows, Simon Bossell, Pippa Grandison, Ray Barrett, Julia Blake.
97 min.
A gaudy, kitsch, neo-romantic Australian comedy, in which, by some oversight, there are no ABBA tunes, but 10CC serve almost as well. Twins Rick (Young) and Stephen (Bossell) both carry a ten-year torch for Melissa (Burrows), an old flame from their teens. Rick is cynical and assertive, Simon shy and romantic. Melissa re-enters their lives at the titular honeymoon hotel, arm in arm with her fiancé, the very week that the twins' bickering parents are to renew their wedding vows. With its dapper cocktail piano player, theme suites, and 'Niagara Smalls' water feature, the de Love is quite tacky enough to complement a handful of enjoyably broad performances, but writer/director Rosenberg doesn't allow the dressing to swamp the salad – yes, it's occasionally crass, but it's also sometimes laugh-out-loud funny. TCh

Hôtel du Nord
(Marcel Carné, 1938, Fr) Annabella, Arletty, Louis Jouvet, Jean-Pierre Aumont, André Brunot, Jane Marken, Paulette Dubost, Bernard Blier, François Périer.
90 min. b/w.
A very likeable film, but for once denied a Jacques Prévert script, Carné's 'poetic realism' seems a tri-

fle thin and hesitant in this populist yarn about a sleazy Parisian hotel and its inhabitants. While the sad young lovers (Annabella, Aumont) defy their jobless future in a suicide pact, Arletty and Jouvet run cynically away with the film as a pair of hardbitten rogues. But the real star is Trauner, whose studio sets – the mournful canal bank, the little iron bridge, the shabby rooms – are as amazingly evocative as Maurice Jaubert's score. TM

Hôtel du Paradis
(Jana Bokova, 1986, GB/Fr) Fernando Rey, Fabrice Luchini, Berangère Bonvoisin, Hugues Quester, Marika Rivera, Carola Regnier, Michael Medwin, Juliet Berto, Lou Castel.
113 min.
Joseph (Rey) is an ageing actor whose movie career has been dogged by a succession of villainous cameos in Bond movies. Spending a working vacation in Paris, he enters in vain to stage Camus' *The Fall*, his path crossing with the hotel's other variously estranged residents: Frédérique (Bonvoisin), a photographer on the run from her ex-boyfriend; Arthur (Luchini), a would-be film-maker; and Maurice (Quester), a theatre owner in the grip of severly diminishing returns. Bokova's feature debut is a melancholy portrait of exile which threatens to fall into sentimentality. Yet her conviction that apparent non-events frequently embody the most important episodes of human communication, and her resolute refusal to compromise atmosphere by forcing the narrative forward, constantly elevates her work above such mundanity. Casting Rey was a stroke of genius; the almost painful parallel between his own career and that of the beleaguered Joseph is turned into caustic humour by his fatally grim, understated delivery. MK

Hotel New Hampshire, The
(Tony Richardson, 1984, US) Rob Lowe, Jodie Foster, Beau Bridges, Nastassja Kinski, Paul McCrane, Lisa Banes, Jennie Dundas, Wallace Shawn, Wilford Brimley.
108 min.
Why is this so dreary? Could it be the fault of John Garp Irving, author of the original book? So many potentially interesting things happen to Win Berry (Bridges) and his family as he attempts to create the hotel of his dreams. Daughter Jodie Foster gets gang-banged. The farting dog gets stuffed. The family move to Vienna and a new hotel. Mrs Berry (Banes) and youngest son are killed. Jodie has sex with Nastassja. Mr Berry is blinded. Jodie has sex with...But knocking off your characters, or giving them sexual hang-ups, doesn't make them anything more than pawns in some trite yet ponderous scheme which hammers home its every banal comment on Life and flogs its every slim joke to Death. AB

Hotel Sahara
(Ken Annakin, 1951, GB) Yvonne De Carlo, Peter Ustinov, David Tomlinson, Roland Culver, Albert Lieven, Bill Owen, Ferdy Mayne, Sydney Tafler, Anton Diffring.
96 min. b/w.
Ustinov plays it very broad as the accommodating North African hotel owner, caught in WWII, who switches allegiances whenever a new army comes to town. There are fitful hints that satire may be intended, but the end result is basically jingoistic farce. One plus is a fine comic turn from Yvonne De Carlo (soon to be Mrs Munster) as Ustinov's fiancée.

Hotel Sorrento
(Richard Franklin, 1994, Aust) Caroline Goodall, Caroline Gillmer, Tara Morice, Ray Barrett, Joan Plowright, John Hargreaves.
112 min.
Meg Moynihan (Goodall), an Australian based in London, is the author of a feminist memoir nominated for the Booker Prize. The book's caused waves back in her small hometown. Here Meg's sister Hilary (Gillmer) has been joined by their youngest sibling Pippa (Strictly Ballroom's Morice), who's flown in briefly from business in the US. By the time Meg's anxiety has sent her back to the family nest, a death has upped the stakes in sisterly recrimination. At which point, Marge Morrisey (Plowright), a literary local, turns the domestic turmoil into a debate on the changing face of Australian cultural identity. An earnest trawl through the personal and artistic legacy of Ocker patriarchy, based on a play by Hannie Rayson. TJ

Hotel Terminus: The Life and Times of Klaus Barbie

(Marcel Ophuls, 1987, US)
267 min.

Ophuls' documentary about the infamous Nazi war criminal, expelled from Bolivia and returned to France for trial, is a mass of interview and newsreel spliced and juxtaposed to produce a narrative *which* is also a moral and historical record *which* is also a set of questions *which* can be reduced here to two crunchers: who are you to judge? what would you have done? The film rarely flags, despite copious location shifts and languages and subtitles which run the gamut and the gauntlet. From wartime France to fascist Bolivia, from boyhood admirers to aggrieved business partners and victims of the Nazis' butchery turning almost as much upon each other as their persecutor, the film is as much about selective memory and the vagaries of moral responsibility as a story of one man who affected so many, and who managed to work for not only the SS but also the Allies, the Bolivian arms runners and the romantically conceived Bolivian navy, and return to Lyons at the age of 71 more sprightly and confident than most of the people whose lives he wrecked. Superb. SGr

Hot Enough for June

(Ralph Thomas, 1963, GB) Dirk Bogarde, Sylva Koscina, Robert Morley, Leo McKern, Roger Delgado, John Le Mesurier, Richard Vernon, Derek Nimmo, Richard Pasco.
98 min.

A plodding spy spoof, with Czech-speaking writer Dirk Bogarde unwittingly hired by the British Secret Service for a mission in Prague. The early scenes are fun, as the late James Bond's effects are filed away, and as Robert Morley's spy chief shows his knowledge of geography. But the movie rapidly goes downhill until the ending, when the number one sightseeing spot in Britain for a Czech refugee turns out to be Aldermaston. ATu

Hot Money

(Selig Usher, 1979, Can) Orson Welles, Michael Murphy, Michelle Finney.
80 min.

Presumably this Canadian offering kept Welles in cigar money for a couple of weeks, but it's sad to see him reduced to such dreck. Murphy's the ex-con, now working as a small-town deputy, who pulls off a $1m theft from a local widow, then worries that his boss, sheriff Welles, will lose his job because of it. TJ

Hot One, The

see Corvette Summer

Hot Rock, The (aka How to Steal a Diamond in Four Uneasy Lessons)

(Peter Yates, 1972, US) Robert Redford, George Segal, Zero Mostel, Ron Leibman, Paul Sand, Moses Gunn, William Redfield.
105 min.

Donald E Westlake, who also writes under the name of Richard Stark, has quietly been providing material for some of the better American thrillers for some years. *Point Blank, The Split* and *The Outfit*, all with similar plots and themes, were adaptations from Stark novels. Like *Cops and Robbers, The Hot Rock* is by Westlake. Both of them touch on the themes of teamwork and capitalism, crime being just another form of free enterprise. Redford and Segal are both good, parodying their normal images, as the thieves who steal the Sahara Stone from the Brooklyn Museum and spend the rest of the film chasing after it. Like *Cops and Robbers* it's a lightweight film, but enjoyable nonetheless. CPea

Hot Roof, A (Gyaegotun Nalui Ohu)

(Lee Min-Yong, 1996, SKor) Sook Son, Ha Yoomi, Jung Sun-Kyoung, Lee Jean-Son.
108 min.

The subtitles are kind of dodgy and there's the odd lapse in the script, but Lee Min-Yong's debut feature is basically a gas. Already the most widely-sold Korean film ever made (but it doesn't have distribution in Britain), it's a daydream about a major skirmish in the sex-war: women, who come to the rescue of a battered wife and accidentally kill her husband, barricade themselves on the roof of their apartment block, resist arrest, and win national support. The women's struggle for solidarity (most tested when they find out that one of them is actually a drag queen) is wittily contrasted with the quasi-gay bonding of two burglars trapped in an apartment below by the police siege. Funny, raunchy and unashamedly pulpy, this knockout entertainment could only have come from a society and culture in the throes of rapid change. TR

Hot Shots!

(Jim Abrahams, 1991, US) Charlie Sheen, Cary Elwes, Valeria Golino, Lloyd Bridges, Kevin Dunn, Jon Cryer, William O'Leary, Kristy Swanson, Efrem Zimbalist Jr.
85 min.

Enlisted in a top secret bombing mission alongside the élite of the Navy's air corps, hot-headed flyboy Topper Harley (Sheen) must first convince the beautiful base psychiatrist (Golino) that his mental quirks won't endanger the operation. In the event, he earns her love, his comrades' respect, and a one-way ticket to Disneyland. This Kentucky Fried movie dogs *Top Gun* like canned laughter dogging a feeble joke. There's nothing as subtle as parody here. Instead, Abrahams and co-writer Pat Proft keep the narrative framework out of harm's way while taking pot shots at whatever takes their fancy, from *9½ Weeks* to *Dances with Wolves*. These spoofs are funny up to a point, but Abrahams can't summon much conviction for the job; too often, a mere allusion does all the work, while wackier gags are stretched beyond breaking point. It might be funnier. TCh

Hot Shots! Part Deux

(Jim Abrahams, 1993, US) Charlie Sheen, Lloyd Bridges, Richard Crenna, Valeria Golino, Rowan Atkinson.
89 min.

Part Deux turns to the Rambo saga, reinventing Sheen's lunkhead 'Topper' Harley as a pseudo-Stallone, while drafting in the real Richard Crenna to reprise his sturdy colonel schtick. With President 'Tug' Benson (Bridges again) ensconced in the mother of all hostage crises – his country's finest captive in the Middle East – Charlie dons upper-body definition, bullet-belt and bandana to rescue 'the men who went in to get the men who went in to get the men'. Unlike its grim predecessor, there are at least two chuckles this time round, a slapstick routine at a Buddhist monastery and a witty *Apocalypse Now* gag. TJ

Hot Spot

see I Wake Up Screaming

Hot Spot, The

(Dennis Hopper, 1990, US) Don Johnson, Virginia Madsen, Jennifer Connelly, Charles Martin Smith, William Sadler, Jerry Hardin, Barry Corbin, Jack Nance.
130 min.

After an impressively laconic, enigmatic opening – Harry Madox (Johnson) drifts into a dusty Texan town and successfully makes a sale at a used-car lot owned by a complete stranger – Hopper's film sinks steadily into *film noir* cliché. Taken from Charles Williams' 1953 novel *Hell Hath No Fury*, it's a determinedly sleazy account of small-town corruption. When canny con-man Madox finds his affections torn between a troubled, virginal waif (Connelly) and his new employer's dangerously seductive wife (Madsen), you soon get the gist: he's headed for a fall. Robbery, adultery, blackmail and murder are on the agenda, but the pacing is so sluggish, the plotting so repetitive, and the characters so formulary that everything is imbued with an unilluminating inevitability. Ueli Steiger's camerawork conveys the overheated torpor of small-town Texas, and odd brief scenes bring a touch of fire; but for the most part the impression is of a talented man going rather lazily through the motions. GA

Hot Stuff

(Dom DeLuise, 1979, US) Dom DeLuise, Suzanne Pleshette, Jerry Reed, Ossie Davis, Luis Avalos, Marc Lawrence, Dick Davalos.
91 min.

The raucous comedy of *Hot Stuff* is even broad-er than its sizeable director/star. The plot, co-scripted by Donald Westlake, concerns four Miami cops who pose as fences in order to entrap a ridiculously bizarre gaggle of thieves (not as bizarre, though, as the perfect social mix back at the cop shop, which includes a black chief, a volatile Cuban, and Pleshette as the perfectly groomed policewoman who always has a fresh magnolia in her hair). But despite the right wing premise (the story is based on a real police entrapment operation) and tedious funny-chases, nice characterisations and witty dialogue make it almost winning. CR

Hot Times

(Jim McBride, 1974, US) Henry Cory, Gail Lorber, Amy Farber, Steve Curry, Bob Lesser.
84 min.

A kind of Jewish comic reply to *The Lords of Flatbush*, in which a number of misogynist, Portnoy-esque sex hang-ups are laid bare in a High School USA setting. However, if one peels away the phony zaniness lent by the bleeping out of 'offensive language' (defensive tampering by the producers) and the supposedly zappy voice-over narration, one is left with a film surprisingly true to McBride's underground origins, notable for some persuasively bizarre touches and a superlatively fluid visual style. Best scenes are those involving the shooting of a sex film in which a series of male performers struggle to come-or-not-to-come on cue, and a sequence involving a Times Square pick-up with a 'liberated' mother. Superb performances. VG

Hot Winds (Garm Hava)

(MS Sathyu, 1973, Ind) Balraj Sahni, Vikas Anand, Rajendra Raghuvanshi, Raj Verma, Gita.
136 min.

A highly ambitious first feature which examines the Indian situation just after the liberation, and the aftermath of the partition of the subcontinent. What is remarkable about the film is the degree to which it refuses to follow well-trodden 'epic' paths in its story of a Muslim family coming to terms with the political realities of an increasingly hostile Hindu Agra (where to remain is to be hounded as outcasts). Despite something of an undertow of conventional melodrama, particularly in the ill-fated romance and eventual suicide of the daughter of the house, Sathyu directs with grace and perceptiveness, and reveals a noteworthy political awareness. VG

Hound Dog Man

(Don Siegel, 1959, US) Fabian, Stuart Whitman, Carol Lynley, Arthur O'Connell, Betty Field, Royal Dano, Jane Darwell, Edgar Buchanan, Claude Akins.
87 min.

Fred Gipson's bucolic novel of Southern country folk was the main attraction for Siegel here (Peckinpah thought of filming it too), but he reckoned without producer Jerry Wald's insistence that Fabian get the lead as the young chap learning about life and love on a hunting jaunt with older, wiser Whitman. This meant eight songs from a star who admitted his own frailty in the vocal department, but Siegel integrates them into the action, has the rest of the cast join in on occasion, and swiftly moves on with the action. The music certainly doesn't detract from an amiable outdoor adventure with a pleasing line in deflating macho bullshit. And nothing whatsoever to do with Elvis. TJ

Hounded

see Johnny Allegro

Hound of the Baskervilles, The

(Sidney Lanfield, 1939, US) Richard Greene, Basil Rathbone, Nigel Bruce, Lionel Atwill, Wendy Barrie, John Carradine, Morton Lowry.
80 min. b/w.

First in the Rathbone-Bruce Sherlock Holmes series, making disappointingly little of the baleful hound (Roy William Neill later provided much more imaginative direction). Highly enjoyable as a period thriller, nevertheless, with lovely support from Carradine and Atwill as a pair of richly sinister red herrings, and one scene enchantingly played by Bruce in which, unable to resist claiming to be Holmes in questioning a tramp, Watson has to pretend he knew all the time when the tramp reveals himself to be Holmes in disguise. This is the only film in the series to allude to Holmes' addiction, through his weary curtain-line aside: 'The needle, Watson!' TM

Hound of the Baskervilles, The

(Terence Fisher, 1958, GB) Peter Cushing, Christopher Lee, André Morell, Marla Landi, David Oxley, Miles Malleson, Francis de Wolff.
86 min.
The best Sherlock Holmes film ever made, and one of Hammer's finest movies. Fisher, at the peak of his career, used Conan Doyle's plot to establish a stylish dialectic between Holmes' nominally rational Victorian milieu and the dark, fabulous cruelty behind the Baskerville legend. This opposition is expressed within the first ten minutes, when he moves from the 'legend' with its strong connotations of the Hellfire Club (the nobleman tormenting a young girl with demonic satisfaction) to the rational eccentricities of Baker Street. Holmes is indeed the perfect Fisher hero, the Renaissance scholar with strong mystical undertones, and Cushing gives one of his very best performances, ably supported by Morell (who does not make the usual mistake of overplaying Watson). Lee is in equally good form as the Baskerville heir, and Jack Asher's muted Technicolor photography is superb. DP

Hound of the Baskervilles, The

(Paul Morrissey, 1977, GB) Peter Cook, Dudley Moore, Denholm Elliott, Joan Greenwood, Terry-Thomas, Max Wall, Irene Handl, Kenneth Williams, Hugh Griffith, Roy Kinnear, Spike Milligan.
85 min.
A 'homage' to the spirit of English film comedy that is truly one of the crummiest movies ever made. In case the idea of a Conan Doyle send-up doesn't itself have you in stitches, Morrissey and his stars/co-scripters Cook and Moore try to slay you with every other kind of joke their clapped-out minds can remember. There's even a pathetic lampoon of *The Exorcist*, a mere four years too late. Every single gag and every single comedy role is mistimed, misplayed or simply misconceived. It also looks worse than any film from a 'name' director in years: a first-year film student would be ashamed of the flat, stilted compositions and the dingy little sets. TR

Hounds of Notre Dame, The

(Zale Dalen, 1981, Can) Thomas Peacocke, Frances Hyland, Barry Morse, David Ferry, Lawrence Reece.
95 min.
Not, in fact, Quasimodo's pets, but the ice-hockey team of Notre Dame, a boys' school in the frozen Canadian outback, run by nuns and a priest, which dispenses the usual vile mixture of learning by rote, inedible food and patriotic speeches for World War II. Hero of the piece is the 'larger than life' headmaster/priest who runs the place like a Hitler Youth Camp and is duly loved by all the boys. Miss Jean Brodie on ice? CPea

Hounds of Zaroff, The

see Most Dangerous Game, The

Hour of Liberation – the Struggle in Oman, The (Saat el Tahrir Dakkat Barra Ya Isti'Mar)

(Heiny Srour, 1974, Leb) narrator: Youssef Salman Youssef.
62 min. b/w & col.
An urgent and fast-moving documentary/propaganda film on the struggles of the People's Liberation Army in Oman, in the Persian Gulf. The resistance of the PLA in the early '60s is placed in the context of British/US economic and political interests, in which a sophisticated oil-extractive technology in the north has produced a deliberate political maintenance of poverty and underdevelopment elsewhere. Establishing their base in Dhofar, in the south, the PLA's task is both military and ideological. As they seek to gain ground, since 1970 they have started a school, trained a people's militia, helped stop inter-tribal feuding among the nomads by helping them to build secure water-holes and learn farming. It's technically compelling, using stills, slogans, songs, documentary material, aimed as much at the Arab-speaking world as at all national liberation movements. MV

Hour of the Gun

(John Sturges, 1967, US) James Garner, Jason Robards, Robert Ryan, Steve Ihnat, Frank Converse, Albert Salmi, Jon Voight.
101 min.
Sturges' sequel to his own *Gunfight at the O.K. Corral*, written by Edward Anhalt and shot in Panavision by Lucien Ballard, is a notable addition to the run of Wyatt Earp movies chiefly for its unexpected bitterness of tone. Garner's lawman leaves the moral high ground to seek hot-blooded revenge for the murder of his brothers by henchmen working for Ryan's Ike Clanton. Classic opening gunfight and first-rate performances from Garner, and from Robards as the tubercular, laconically resigned Doc Holliday. A determinedly old-style Western, made two years before Peckinpah shook things up with *The Wild Bunch*. TJ

Hour of the Pig, The

(Leslie Megahey, 1993, GB/Fr) Colin Firth, Donald Pleasence, Ian Holm, Nicol Williamson, Michael Gough, Harriet Walter, Elizabeth Spriggs.
117 min.
In darkest medieval France, legislation languishes beneath the pendulum sway of ecclesiastical caprice and peasant superstition. Against this backdrop, Renaissance man and Parisian lawyer Richard Courtois (Firth) makes his grand entrance, only to find that his first case in an isolated rural community is to defend a pig charged with the murder of a young boy. As the drama uncoils into folds of seigneurial corruption and forbidden sexuality, ethnic tension and church indifference, the slightly ramshackle narrative proves both educational and highly entertaining. Although revelling in the bawdy absurdities of lovingly textured authenticity, writer/director Megahey's film remains thoroughly modern in outlook, refreshingly irreverent in tone and remarkably accomplished in execution. TJ

Hour of the Star (A Hora da Estrela)

(Suzana Amaral, 1985, Braz) Marcélia Cartaxo, José Dumont, Tamara Taxman, Umberto Magnani, Denoy De Oliveira.
95 min.
19-year-old Macabéa works as a typist in Brasilia. With little money, less grace or beauty, and almost no education, she leads a wretched life: her roommates say she smells, her only pal calls her ugly, and her boyfriend Olimpico – no great shakes himself – tells her she's an idiot. Unusually, the director places this plain Jane nonentity centre-screen to present a beguilingly unsentimental portrait of ignorance, cultural poverty, and stunted emotions. Nothing much happens: the girl avoids being sacked, eats like a pig, rides the Metro, and takes aimless walks with her not exactly beloved Olimpico. But Amaral's precise and never condescending direction ensures that we follow this most unsympathetic of heroines to the end of the line, forestalling bathos by means of a stark, robust humour. Only Bresson's *Mouchette* suggests a precedent for this film's determination to reveal, rather than dignify, a life of utter banality; but what the comparison fails to evoke is Amaral's ability to uplift without Catholic contrivance. GA

Hour of the Wolf (Vargtimmen)

(Ingmar Bergman, 1967, Swe) Max von Sydow, Liv Ullmann, Erland Josephson, Gertrud Fridh, Gudrun Brost, Ingrid Thulin.
89 min. b/w.
A brilliant Gothic fantasy about an artist who has disappeared, leaving only a diary; and through that diary we move into flashback to observe a classic case history of the Bergman hero haunted by darkness, demons and the creatures of his imagination until he is destroyed by them. The tentacular growth of this obsession is handled with typical virtuosity in a dazzling flow of surrealism, expressionism and full-blooded Gothic horror. First the hour of the wolf, the sleepless nights of watching and waiting, when the artist (von Sydow) describes – but we do not see – the horde of man-eating birdmen and insects who have invaded his sketch-book. Then the daylight encounters when a car crawling over the horizon, a girl picking her way through the rocks on a sun-bleached beach, look momentarily like weird, threatening insects. Finally, the full nightmare of the *soirée* at a château gradually transformed into Dracula's castle as its aristocratic inhabitants become werewolves and vampires, and the artist flees into a forest of blackened, clutching trees, pursued by monstrous birds of prey. In its exploration of the nature of creativity, haunted by the problem of whether the artist possesses or is possessed by his demons, *Hour of the Wolf* serves as a remarkable companion-piece to *Persona*. TM

Hours and Times, The

(Christopher Münch, 1991, US) David Angus, Ian Hart, Stephanie Pack, Robin McDonald, Sergio Moreno, Unity Grimwood.
60 min. b/w.
In the spring of 1963, John Lennon allowed Brian Epstein to take him away for four days in Barcelona. It was a chance for John to recharge his batteries. Also, Epstein was gay. Münch's film is a speculative fiction, based on these facts but with no pretence at Albert Goldman-style *faction*. Instead, he presents a lively, subtle conversation piece, an intimate dialogue between two very different men. Epstein is urbane, cosmopolitan and deeply insecure; Lennon working-class, intellectually curious and absolutely sure of himself. They discuss art, check out a Bergman film, discuss the ins-and-outs of buggery. Epstein is in love; Lennon pulls back from the brink. Both turn elsewhere to make half-hearted pick-ups. Whatever really happened, this poignant, fragmentary, assured and beautifully paced film rings true. Validation enough, surely? TCh

House

(Steve Miner, 1986, US) William Katt, George Wendt, Richard Moll, Kay Lenz, Mary Stavin, Michael Ensign.
93 min.
This starts promisingly with a malevolent mansion casting its malign influence over horror writer Katt, who is suffering from the Dreaded Nam Flashback disease and trying to exorcise his traumas in memoir form while puzzling over the mysterious disappearance of his young son. It rapidly degenerates into disconnected episodes of spooky sitcom farce. Katt is menaced by a stuffed swordfish, the animated contents of a tool-shed, and a number of monsters which are about as bloodcurdling as the Care Bears. The next door neighbour turns out to be the fat chap from *Cheers*, and the house itself gets forgotten as the script bungs in a bit of conservatory foliage to represent Vietnam and Katt's war experiences come back to haunt him, not very hauntingly, by way of the bathroom cabinet. Mildly amusing in a Fairy Liquid, fun-for-all-the-family sort of way, but the occasional guffaw cannot compensate for the total lack of guts. AB

House II: The Second Story

(Ethan Wiley, 1987, US) Arye Gross, Jonathan Stark, Royal Dano, Bill Maher, John Ratzenberger.
88 min.
Jesse McLaughlin (Gross) inherits a house with a secret: his great-great grandpappy, a notorious outlaw from the Old West, was buried in the back garden with a valuable crystal skull imbued with magic powers. So Jesse digs him up. But once the skull is installed on its altar, it creates a series of magic portals by which various baddies travel through time to try to steal it. This sequel to *House* offers another blend of humour and horror, but the gags aren't particularly sweet, the chills aren't particularly spicy. On the whole an indigestible affair, which fortunately passes quickly through the system. SGo

House

(Laurie Lynd, 1995, Can) Daniel MacIvor, Patricia Collins, Stephen Ouimette, Ben Cardinal.
86 min.
Basically a one-man show, with MacIvor venting his spleen before an audience of small town curiosity-seekers. His Carver-esque, neurotic/psychotic autobiographical anecdotes touch on the

lives of one or more of those in attendance. Sort of alternative group therapy. MacIvor is not happy: his mother's possessed by the devil, his father's the saddest man alive, his sister's in love with a dog, the one he loves does not love him, and he has no place to live. TCh

Houseboat

(Melville Shavelson, 1958, US) Cary Grant, Sophia Loren, Martha Hyer, Harry Guardino, Eduardo Ciannelli, Murray Hamilton.
110 min.
Widower Grant takes his kids in tow and shacks up in a new floating domicile to find romance with maid Loren, who (surprise!) just happens to be a wealthy socialite doing a bit of slumming. Tame VistaVision family frolic. TJ

House by the Cemetery, The (Quella Villa accanto al Cimitero)

(Lucio Fulci, 1981, It) Katherine MacColl, Giovanni De Nari, Paolo Malco, Giovanni Frezza, Silvia Collatina.
86 min.
Cut-price spaghetti gore cooked up from the not exactly brand-new narrative premise of a nice middle class family moving to a house in New England with a sinister sitting tenant, the nefarious Dr Freudstein. Bits of *Amityville* and *The Shining*, plus every other imaginable mad-scientist, screaming-in-the-cellar, haunted-house horror cliché, shamelessly ripped off, cut and stuck together into (literally) a hack-work of almost awesome incoherence. Even Henry James, irreverently quoted in the closing epitaph, fails to confer any respectability upon the proceedings. Strictly for pulp cultists. SJo

House by the Lake, The

see Death Weekend

House by the River

(Fritz Lang, 1950, US) Louis Hayward, Jane Wyatt, Lee Bowman, Dorothy Patrick, Ann Shoemaker, Kathleen Freeman, Peter Brocco, Jody Gilbert.
88 min. b/w.
One of Fritz Lang's deathly constructs: a patently artificial period melodrama about an author (Hayward) who strangles his wife's maid and implicates his brother (Bowman) in the crime. It's a bleak, gloomy film, one in which the psychological undercurrents seem to be flooding over the banks, drowning any fleeting vestige of rationality in a perverse Teutonic romanticism. TCh

House Calls

(Howard Zieff, 1978, US) Walter Matthau, Glenda Jackson, Art Carney, Richard Benjamin, Candice Azzara, Dick O'Neill, Thayer David.
98 min.
Concocted by an unhealthy quartet of writers, this suggests a slightly wacky, liberated variant on Universal's comedies of eighteen years earlier, when Rock Hudson flashed his pearly teeth at Doris Day. Once again it's love between two pros: Matthau is a shambling, philandering doctor at a mediocre hospital, while Jackson leads one of those nebulous American business lives, making and selling cheesecake. He doesn't put a foot wrong, but the garrulous, charmless Jackson character comes over as the original pain in the neck. Background details of hospital life are handled much more astutely than the main plot. It's a big mystery how Zieff (of *Slither* and *Hearts of the West*) allowed it to go off at half-cock. GB

Householder, The

(James Ivory, 1963, Ind) Shashi Kapoor, Leela Naidu, Durga Khote, Achla Sachdev, Hariendernath Chattopadayaya.
101 min. b/w.
James Ivory's first feature was adapted by Ruth Jhabvala from her fourth novel and shot, on a shoestring, in Delhi, using a house belonging to a friend of the producer. A young teacher Prem (Kapoor) finds himself married to an exquisite but trying girl (the part-French Leela Naidu). He's not yet ready, however, to assume the responsibilities of a 'householder'. He feels, like many later Merchant Ivory protagonists – Olivia in *Heat and Dust*, Leonard Bast in *Howards End* – that there

must be something more to life, something spiritual, something better and higher. Prem searches (comically), but in the end settles for domesticity. The predicaments of Olivia and Leonard were resolved with greater dramatic conviction, but there's much that's authentic and touching in this small, sharply observed drama about the necessity of a man turning a deaf ear to the sighs of his mother. Ivory showed an early version of the film to Satyajit Ray who offered to reshape it. The task took three days, and Ivory recalls the explosive force of the Master's repeated command, *Cut!* JPy

House in Nightmare Park, The

(Peter Sykes, 1973, GB) Frankie Howerd, Ray Milland, Hugh Burden, Kenneth Griffith, John Bennett, Rosalie Crutchley, Ruth Dunning.
95 min.
Howerd plays a Victorian ham actor invited to an eerie stately home, supposedly to entertain. In reality it's a question of inheritance (he's the long-lost heir, and this is *The Cat and the Canary* all over again). Sykes directs in his best high romantic style (the opening is brilliant) and Howerd restrains himself sufficiently; but though some gags work, towards half time the strain begins to tell and it all falls apart.

Housekeeping

(Bill Forsyth, 1987, US) Christine Lahti, Sara Walker, Andrea Burchill, Anne Pitoniak, Barbara Reese, Margot Pinvidic.
116 min.
Adolescent sisters Ruthie (Walker) and Lucille (Burchill) live by a threatening black lake; their mother lies at its bottom, and Aunt Sylvie (Lahti) flaunts death by rowing on it late at night. Sylvie rocks the boat in other ways too. Arriving out of the blue to care for her nieces, she has habits that challenge the small town's conventions and eventually come between the girls: she collects tins, sleeps on park benches, hoards newspapers, condones the girls' truancy, almost sets the house on fire while cooking. Gentle humour stems from such idiosyncrasies, but Sylvie is irresponsible, dangerously so. When Lucille's schoolgirl desire to be 'normal' forces her out of the house, we sense an ominous flipside to the kookie, childish adventures Sylvie dreams up to entertain Ruthie. Weather, period (the '50s) and place (Idaho) are so emphatically detailed they're oppressive; while Sylvie and the girls come to life with greater depth and wholeness than Forsyth's characters have hitherto enjoyed. Here the director's characteristic other-worldly charm is overshadowed by a dark intensity; with its backdrop of death, isolation and portent, the movie is sombre, very strange, but wonderful. EP

Housemaid, The (Hanyo)

(Kim Ki-Young, 1960, SKor) Lee Un-shim, Chu Jung-nyo, Kim Chin-kyu.
90 min
An extraordinary film anywhere, not least in Korea, this heightened melodrama is often cited as the uneven maverick Kim Ki-Young's masterpiece. It's a deliberately overblown, if deadpan and Hitchcockian tale of a music teacher's demise through the twin agencies of his wife's greed (she wants a two-storey house) and his maidservant's supposed sexual predatoriness (she comes on like Kathleen Byron in *Black Narcissus*). Kim's is a bleak, Nietzschean view of human motivation, and the whole, with its jazz-score, location shooting, hot-house Sirkian drama and Clouseau-like horror suspense makes for a notably delirious experience. WH

House of America

(Marc Evans, 1996, GB/Neth) Siân Phillips, Matthew Rhys, Steven Mackintosh, Lisa Palfrey, Richard Harrington.
96 min.
In an isolated prairie-style house built from corrugated iron, the Lewis family – mad mam (Phillips), teenage dreamers Sid and Gwenny (Mackintosh and Palfrey), and their down-to-earth young brother Boyo (Rhys, sympathetic) – struggle to cope with the void left by their absent husband/father who 15 years before traded the green green grass of South Wales for the wide open spaces of America. More like an overwrought Sam Shepard psycho-drama than a downbeat study of doleful teenagers, this adapt-

ed play (by Edward Thomas) eschews miserabilism in favour of a poetic celebration of naive teen dreams about burning bright and dying young. With no local heroes to call their own, the Harley-riding Sid and Gwenny lose themselves in a drink and drug-fuelled fantasy of the American Dream derived from Kerouac's *On the Road*. The bleached photography and Welsh-dominated soundtrack adds notable texture to an ambitious debut. NF

House of Angels (Änglagård)

(Colin Nutley, 1992, Swe) Helena Bergström, Rikard Wolff, Sven Wollter, Reine Brynolfsson, Ernst Gunter.
119 min.
After a rural community's elderly patriarch snuffs it, anticipation runs high that his neighbour, wealthy farmer Axel (Wollter), will buy up his property, but his granddaughter Fanny (Bergström) turns up on a Harley Davidson with leather-clad companion Zac (Wolff) and decides to move into the house. The locals are suspicious that the pair will bring Big City ways to this sleepy corner of the country, and though harmony is eventually restored, Nutley by no means makes this a sure thing. The film's slow to start, but the measured pacing clearly delineates the two parties' separate agendas, as tension builds between them and the ostensibly decent villagers start haranguing the newcomers out of narrow-mindedness, anxiety and mistrust. While the portrayal of open-hearted oldster Gottfried (Gunter) sugars the pill, there's an unexpectedly trenchant analysis of simmering everyday prejudice: a movie that smiles at you with gritted teeth. TJ

House of Bamboo

(Samuel Fuller, 1955, US) Robert Ryan, Robert Stack, Shirley Yamaguchi, Cameron Mitchell, Sessue Hayakawa, Brad Dexter.
102 min.
1954. American-led gang pulls raids in Tokyo, Yokohama. Ex-GI involvement suspected. Lone American infiltrates gang. Identity, motives unclear. *House of Bamboo* offers all Fuller's key themes and motifs in a characteristic thriller form: dual identities, divided loyalties, racial tensions, life (and cinema) as war. Part of it is Fuller the war correspondent, reporting from the front, leaving the viewer to fight out meanings alongside the characters. Part of it is Fuller the American tourist, shamelessly reducing Japan to stereotypes, twisting local colour to his own ends. Godard used to think it was Fuller's best movie. TR

House of Bernarda Alba, The (La Casa de Bernarda Alba)

(Mario Camus, 1987, Sp) Irene Gutiérrez, Ana Belén, Florinda Chico, Enriqueta Carballeira, Vicky Peña, Aurora Pastor, Mercedes Lezcano.
103 min.
In this adaptation of Lorca's last play, the matriarchal edict proclaimed by Bernarda on her husband's death condemns her five unmarried daughters to an aeon in black behind the locked doors of an all-female household. The one male to get a look in is glimpsed in shadows, keeping minight trysts through barred windows; planned for the eldest daughter, he loves the youngest, stoking the flames of jealous rivalry until the whole pressurised can of blocked emotions blows apart. Camus' forte lies in his precise delineation of period detail and buttoned-up behaviour, and he makes palpable the savage destructiveness of Franco's dictatorship – here in its birth throes but rooted, as Lorca tried to show, in the restricted social and sexual codes of Spanish society. The performances play on one unrelenting note – fever-pitched misery – though the whole cast admirably sustains the intensity throughout. Camus rarely opens the drama out, but neither does he achieve the cathartic rush demanded by Lorca's denouement. The result is cold, and a little tiresome. WH

House of Cards

(Michael Lessac, 1993, US) Kathleen Turner, Tommy Lee Jones, Asha Menina, Park Overall, Shiloh Strong, Esther Rolle.
109 min.
When the death of their archeologist father causes a family to return to the US after years on the site of a Mayan dig in Mexico, mom Turner grows concerned by daughter Menina's increas-

ingly withdrawn behaviour. Jones is the kindly psychiatrist with whom she clashes when his diagnosis doesn't match her own theories. A mediocre family saga in which a striking turn from young Menina eclipses the two stars. TJ

House of Doom
see Black Cat, The

House of Dracula
(Erle C Kenton, 1945, US) Lon Chaney Jr, John Carradine, Martha O'Driscoll, Lionel Atwill, Glenn Strange, Onslow Stevens.
67 min. b/w.
A follow-up to Universal's *House of Frankenstein* monster omnibus, this time adding a girl hunchback to the usual fauna. Stevens plays a benevolent doctor who cures the Wolf Man, fails with Dracula, and while running amok himself with an inadvertently acquired bloodlust, gleefully revives the Frankenstein monster. It all ends in a grand holocaust borrowed from *The Ghost of Frankenstein*. Nicely shot by George Robinson, it's agreeably loony fun if you don't expect too much. TM

House of Evil
see House on Sorority Row, The

House of Exorcism, The
(La Casa dell'Exorcismo)
(Mickey Lion, 1975, It) Telly Savalas, Elke Sommer, Sylva Koscina, Alida Valli, Robert Alda, Gabriele Tinti.
93 min.
A wildly incoherent *Exorcist* spin-off directed, in part at least, by the talented Mario Bava. The film alternates pointlessly between stops-out hocus pocus and some devilish comedy from a lollipop-sucking Telly Savalas. The pseudonymous director credit conceals the fact that this is Bava's *Lisa and the Devil* (1972), much hacked about and tricked out with clatteringly crude new footage involving Alda as an exorcising priest. RC

House of Fear, The
(Roy William Neill, 1945, US) Basil Rathbone, Nigel Bruce, Aubrey Mather, Paul Cavanagh, Dennis Hoey, Holmes Herbert, Gavin Muir.
69 min. b/w.
A cursed mansion named Drearcliff provides the setting for this passably atmospheric adaptation of Conan Doyle's *Adventure of the Five Orange Pips*, with Holmes and Watson joining the heavily insured old buffers of 'The Good Comrades' club for a weekend of cryptic warnings and mutilated corpses. Watson, for once, makes the elementary deduction. PT

House of Frankenstein
(Erle C Kenton, 1944, US) Boris Karloff, Lon Chaney Jr, John Carradine, Glenn Strange, Lionel Atwill , George Zucco, J Carrol Naish.
74 min. b/w.
Universal's second horror stew, which tried to go one better than *Frankenstein Meets the Wolf Man* by featuring, in addition to those two luminaries, Dracula, a mad doctor, a psycho hunchback and a Chamber of Horrors. It's absurdly indigestible but surprisingly watchable, thanks to classy camera-work from George Robinson, with Carradine making – all too briefly – a superb Dracula. Mad doctor Karloff and the Frankenstein monster (Strange) meet their end in quicksands. TM

House of Fright
see Two Faces of Dr Jekyll, The

House of Games
(David Mamet, 1987, US) Lindsay Crouse, Joe Mantegna, Mike Nussbaum, Lilia Skala, JT Walsh, Steve Goldstein.
102 min.
In playwright David Mamet's directorial debut, best-selling psychiatrist Margaret Ford (Crouse) decides to confront the gambler who has driven one of her patients to the verge of suicide, and leaves her orderly, antiseptic life for a visit to the downtown lowlife House of Games. Mike (Mantegna) turns out to be swift and shifty, promising to cancel the patient's debts if Margaret sits in with him on a big money card game in the back room. Fascinated by the similarities between her trade and Mike's – both

study human nature and trade on trust – Margaret hangs out with Mike and learns, to her cost, the intricacies of the sting. Mamet's glee in tracking the rackets and his ear for the great American aphasia – 'I'm from the United States of Kiss My Ass' –more than compensate for the sometimes flat direction, and the performances are splendid. BC

House of Madness
(La Mansión de la Locura)
(Juan López Moctezuma, 1972, Mex) Claudio Brook, Arthur Hansel, Ellen Sherman, Martin Lasalle, David Silva.
88 min.
A curiosity based on an obscure Poe story, *The System of Doctor Tarr and Professor Fether*, which is well worth a look. Definite echoes of Jodorowsky and Arrabal, but in general Moctezuma, who has a fetching visual style, steers clear of the obvious pitfalls of absurdist horror. His film is about a kind of 'kingdom' of madness which is established when the inmates of a vast and surreal insane asylum lock up their wardens and establish their own bizarre hierarchy of activities and ideas. Many of the images and sequences have a weird beauty, though the pace flags towards the end. DP

House of Mortal Sin
(Pete Walker, 1975, GB) Anthony Sharp, Susan Penhaligon, Stephanie Beacham, Norman Eshley, Sheila Keith, Hilda Barry.
104 min.
House of Whipcord and *Frightmare*, the first two films David McGillivray scripted for Walker, suggested that the two of them might possibly invigorate low-budget British exploitation. *Mortal Sin*, however, is a disappointment, although it has its moments. Crazed old Catholic priest terrorises young girl after her confession, while her sister is getting the other curate, a liberal young priest, all hot under the collar. The script relies too much on mild sacrilege for its effects, instead of concentrating on more interesting aspects of religious repression. CPe

House of Pleasure
see Plaisir, Le

House of Rothschild, The
(Alfred Werker, 1933, US) George Arliss, Boris Karloff, Loretta Young, Robert Young, C Aubrey Smith, Arthur Byron, Helen Westley, Reginald Owen, Alan Mowbray.
88 min. b/w & col.
A lavish Selznick biopic in which Arliss first plays Mayer, founder of the House of Rothschild, then his son Nathan, the financial wizard who made London his HQ. A lengthy prologue, set in Prussia in 1780, argues that money was the only way out of the ghetto for a Jew. Thereafter, infused with the spirit of the New Deal, Nunnally Johnson's script waxes lyrical over the great social good that Nathan achieved by putting his resources behind the fight to save Europe from Napoleon's empire-building (no comment is made on the fact that this also made him the richest man in Europe). Rather more interesting are details concerning the expansion of Mayer's humble money-changing business, and about the tricky insider deals which brought Nathan to a position of power. Commenting on the legacy of anti-semitism (with Karloff's sinister Prussian baron pointedly coming on like a Nazi), the film hedges its bets by casting non-Jews in the leading roles, and by bursting into Technicolor for a tendentious finale in which Nathan finally achieves social acceptance along with a knighthood from the Prince Regent. TM

House of Smiles
(La Casa del sorriso)
(Marco Ferreri, 1990, It) Ingrid Thulin, Dado Ruspoli, Vincenzo Cannavale.
98 min.
Ferreri's film concerns old age (the old provocateur is in his sixties himself), and centres around the relationship between two 'inmates' of a home for the elderly: lively, eccentric Adelina (Thulin) and dapper charmer Andrea (Ruspoli). All Ferreri's films have elements of surreal black farce, and here the farce resides in the outrageous institutional repressiveness of the home and its staff. Ferreri turns everything on its head.

Transgressors (and those unable any longer to perform basic functions for themselves) are threatened with dispatch to 'Africa', an outbuilding staffed by immigrant Maghrebi workers. It is there that the celebrant couple go for privacy and sex (in the Watermelon caravan belonging to their African friends). A film of sharp insight, filled with humanity and mischievous subversiveness. WH

House of Spirits, The
(Bille August, 1993, Ger/Den/Port) Jeremy Irons, Meryl Streep, Glenn Close, Winona Ryder, Antonio Banderas, Vanessa Redgrave, Armin Mueller-Stahl.
138 min.
Isabel Allende's dynastic fable begins in the 1920s, when fate throws together the driven, macho Esteban Trueba (Irons) and the mysterious, magical Clara Del Valle (Streep). A self-made man, Esteban whisks Clara off to his sprawling estate, where they live in discord with his spinster sister Ferula (Close as a butch, black-eyed Catholic martyr). Time passes. The Truebas' felicitously named daughter Blanca grows up to be Winona Ryder: an independent-minded young woman who gets pregnant by peasant agitator Banderas. And so it goes on for two hours and five decades, until a dramatic political coup jerks these characters from the magical realist soap that is their life into a traumatic melodrama in which Blanca is brutally tortured by Esteban's bastard son. This final passage belatedly musters some conviction; elsewhere, director August plods through his own unwieldy, literal script without betraying any sensitivity to the material. Irons gives an excruciating performance – what Streep's genuinely warm, wonderful Clara sees in him you'd need ESP to fathom. TCh

House of Strangers
(Joseph L Mankiewicz, 1949, US) Edward G Robinson, Richard Conte, Susan Hayward, Luther Adler, Paul Valentine, Efrem Zimbalist Jr, Debra Paget.
101 min. b/w.
The story of a patriarchal Italian-American banker and the internecine strife created by his attempts to dominate his four sons (remade as the Western *Broken Lance*). Much darker than most Mankiewicz movies, almost *noir* in fact, though cast in his favourite flashback form so that it becomes a sort of confessional memoir probing ambiguities of motive (and allowing Robinson to make a stunning first appearance, conjured in Conte's memory by a portrait, a Rossini aria, and the camera prowling endlessly up a grand staircase in the family mansion). Terrific performances (Conte, Robinson, Adler) and even better camerawork by Milton Krasner which uses lighting and composition to stake out the screen, the house and the family groupings into sharply defined areas of conflict. TM

House of the Long Shadows, The
(Pete Walker, 1982, GB) Vincent Price, Christopher Lee, Peter Cushing, Desi Arnaz, John Carradine, Sheila Keith, Richard Todd.
101 min.
A jumble of dark house clichés (loosely based on that old standby, *Seven Keys to Baldpate*) which stacks up the *zzzzz* for a good hour before even admitting it's a spoof. Thereafter, two gags for Price, the unavoidable sad ghoulishness of Carradine's mere presence, and a Christopher Lee so wooden that it's hard to tell if he's in a coffin or not. Only Cushing retains any dignity, even coming up with a fresh characterisation – a lisping, drunken rendition of the Upper Class Twit at 70 – that might turn Michael Palin green. The rest is vacuum: bus-ticket script, the usual faceless juvenile support, and bathchair direction. GD

House of Usher, The (aka The Fall of the House of Usher)
(Roger Corman, 1960, US) Vincent Price, Myrna Fahey, Mark Damon, Harry Ellerbe.
80 min.
The first of Corman's eight-film Poe cycle, and one of his most faithful adaptations. Price is his usual impressive self as the almost certainly incestuously inclined Roderick Usher who, having buried his sister alive when she falls into a cataleptic trance, becomes the victim of her ghostly revenge; but it is Corman's overall direction that lends the

film its intelligence and power. The sickly decadence and claustrophobia of the Usher household – which is both disturbed and temporarily cleansed by the fresh air that accompanies Damon's arrival as suitor to Madeline Usher – is admirably evoked by Floyd Crosby's 'Scope photography and Daniel Haller's art direction, the latter's sets dominated by a putrid, bloody crimson. But Richard Matheson's script is also exemplary: lucid, imaginatively detailed and subtle. GA

House of Wax

(André De Toth, 1953, US) Vincent Price, Phyllis Kirk, Frank Lovejoy, Carolyn Jones, Paul Cavanagh, Charles Bronson.
88 min.
One of the better 3-D epics (Warners' first, pioneering effort). Handsomely mounted and directed with great care, it nevertheless remains oddly lacklustre by comparison with the 1933 *Mystery of the Wax Museum*, despite being an often word-for-word remake. One reason is that where the original acquired an additional charge of bizarrerie by locating its Grand Guignol monster within a private enclave of bustling, contemporary New York, this remake is much more conventionally set in the fantasy world of gaslight, ground fogs and opera cloaks. Still, Price is fun (this was the film that typed him as a horror star), the fire in the waxworks is good for a gruesome thrill, and De Toth brings off one classic sequence with Kirk fleeing through the gaslit streets pursued by a shadowy figure in a billowing cloak. TM

House of Whipcord

(Pete Walker, 1974, GB) Barbara Markham, Patrick Barr, Ray Brooks, Anne Michelle, Penny Irving, Sheila Keith.
101 min.
An above average sexploitation/horror that has been put together with some polish and care from a fairly original script. The film is dedicated ironically to all those who wish to see the return of capital punishment in Britain, and it's about a senile old judge and his wife who are so appalled by current permissiveness that they set up a gruesome house of correction for young girls. The only trouble is that the film undercuts its potentially interesting Gothic theme by some leering emphases, and the final result is likely to be seen and appreciated only by the people who will take the dedication at its face value. DP

House of Yes, The

(Mark Waters, 1997, US) Parker Posey, Josh Hamilton, Tori Spelling, Freddie Prinze Jr, Genevieve Bujold, Rachael Leigh Cook.
85 min.
There's something quite lethal about Parker Posey in pearls, and for that inspiration director Mark Waters deserves our gratitude. The film plays like *Rocky Horror* rewritten by Strindberg and Oliver Stone: Hamilton brings his fiancée Spelling home to meet the family, arriving on a dark and stormy night to be greeted by the daintily bonkers Bujold (his mom), a deeply nervy Prinze (brother), and the glamorous Jackie-O, as Posey styles herself (his incestuous twin). Soon, Spelling is witness to a strange, erotic ritual of humiliation, role playing, sex and death – because blood doesn't just run in this family, it positively flows. Quite insane, very arch, and viciously funny (from a play by Wendy MacLeod). TCh

House on Carroll Street, The

(Peter Yates, 1987, US) Kelly McGillis, Jeff Daniels, Mandy Patinkin, Jessica Tandy, Jonathan Hogan, Remak Ramsay, Ken Welsh, Christopher Rhode.
101 min.
Idealistic Emily (McGillis) comes up before a senate committee in 1951 and refuses to name names, loses her job on *Life* magazine, and is subjected to surveillance. By chance, she stumbles upon a plot to smuggle Nazis into the country, and FBI agent Cochran (Daniels) believes her story but is repeatedly warned off. Yates isn't Hitchcock, however, and the cruel cat-and-mouse structure of *Notorious* crumbles to allow for *The Janitor* to make another pass. Walter Bernstein's script unfortunately can't quite make up its mind to finger the American government for giving useful Nazi war criminals sanctuary in the early '50s, and hedges its bets. On the entertainment level, though, it's an efficient, good-looking movie, thanks to Michael Ballhaus' photography of peri-

od New York. The tension relies a bit too much on footfalls on gloomy stairwells, and the villain's silkinesss lacks menace. But there are plenty of nice touches: straight-arrow Cochran making love to Emily between surveillance duties at a stake-out; Tandy's imperious old lady with the binoculars. BC

House on Garibaldi Street, The

(Peter Collinson, 1979, US) Topol, Nick Mancuso, Janet Suzman, Martin Balsam, Leo McKern, Charles Gray, Derren Nesbitt, Alfred Burke.
101 min.
Topol as an Israeli secret agent kidnapping Nazi Eichmann from Buenos Aires? The mind boggles. In fact the problems of this humourless piece of faction (made for TV) are elementary: since the real raid (in the '60s) was a perfect success (ending in Eichmann's trial and execution in Israel), the possibilities for action and suspense are severely limited; the acting is often comic; the plot remains juvenile. What survives surprisingly well is a lack of pretension and a workmanlike sense of limitations which, at times – the nighttime kidnapping scene, for example – even generates a mood of gritty low-budget energy. CA

House on 92nd Street, The

(Henry Hathaway, 1945, US) William Eythe, Lloyd Nolan, Signe Hasso, Gene Lockhart, Leo G Carroll, Lydia St Clair, Harry Bellaver.
88 min. b/w.
Much touted at the time as the first of Louis (*The March of Time*) De Rochemont's documentary thrillers, made with the full cooperation of the FBI. It still works well enough, even though the breathless revelation of the hardware of counterespionage (hidden cameras, two-way mirrors, microfilm, etc) has become slightly old hat. More fascinating, given J Edgar Hoover's personal interest in the project – he even appears on screen to introduce it – is the way the Nazi spy ring, foiled before they can get away with the secrets of the atom bomb, could be read as dirty Commies. The low-key performances contribute effectively to the sense of actuality, despite clumsy mistakes like having Signe Hasso masquerade none too convincingly in drag as the mysterious spymaster. TM

House on Sorority Row, The (aka House of Evil)

(Mark Rosman, 1982, US) Kathryn McNeil, Eileen Davidson, Lois Kelso Hunt, Christopher Lawrence, Janis Zido.
92 min.
As soon as an anguished mother starts yelling 'Where's my baby?' right after delivery in the pre-credits sequence, anyone with half a brain will surmise that, twenty years later and in the same house, Baby is going to make his presence felt. Especially as the house is now part of a college campus. With few surprises to be gleaned from the well-worn format, the main pleasure lies in ticking off 'references' – about a hundred of them from *Halloween* and its lesser offshoots, plus a hefty nod towards Clouzot and his *Diabolique* swimming-pool. Of course, shot with the screen-slash-with-panache one might expect of an ex-assistant to De Palma, there is some unsettling imagery; but seeing yet another dead maniac coming back to life after the ostensible *coup de grace* is enough to make one scream. AB

House on Trubnaya, The (Dom na Trubnoi)

(Boris Barnet, 1928, USSR) Vera Maretskaya, Vladimir Fogel, Anna Sudakevich, Yelena Tyapkina, Sergei Komarov.
5,765 ft. b/w.
This is the greatest movie by Barnet, an ex-actor and boxer who made several of the freshest and most entertaining Soviet films of the 1920s. The plot hinges on a petit bourgeois hairdresser (hilariously caricatured by Fogel) who tries to hire a non-union housemaid; but the film's pleasures are less in the writing than in the try-anything-once attitude to film form, and the agile camerawork, which cranes up and down a crowded tenement and roams the streets of Moscow. It has much the same spontaneity that the early Godard films had, only it's a whole lot funnier. A *bona fide* classic. TR

House Party

(Reginald Hudlin, 1990, US) Kid'n'Play (Christopher Reid/Christopher Martin), Robin Harris, Martin Lawrence, Tisha Campbell, AJ Johnson, Paul Anthony.
104 min.
Wanna party? Kid's grounded, but he's gotta itch to scratch, and tonite could be his night. Par-Tee! After *School Daze*, what else but school nights? The Hudlin brothers' rap comedy (Reggie wrote and directed, Warrington produced) doesn't aspire to Spike Lee's political attitude, but Spike set a precedent for the commercial black-youth pic, his influence evident here in bright day-glo colours, disparate characters, and righteous role models (no alcohol, no drugs, safe sex). Clearly this is no masterpiece, but as its US reception indicated, it is a product overdue in the market, and it compares well with its anaemic counterparts: it's loud, hip and vibrantly styled. Salt'n'Pepa labelmates Kid'n'Play take lead roles, and as someone says, 'they've got a cute thing happening'. Campbell and Johnson from *School Daze* impress again, Full Force and George Clinton crop up in cameos, and Marcus Miller contributes a funky score. TCh

Housesitter

(Frank Oz, 1992, US) Steve Martin, Goldie Hawn, Dana Delany, Julie Harris, Donald Moffat, Peter MacNicol, Richard B Shull, Laurel Cronin.
102 min.
It's back to wacky mode for Hawn after her dismal adventures in *Deceived*. She plays waitress Gwen, whose modest means fail to support her grand ambitions. But that's before she meets stuffy architect Newton Davis (Martin): during their one-night stand, she learns of the custom-made dream house rejected by his long-term love (Delany). Gwen secretly traces his empty property to a New England town. She moves in, and proceeds to regale the locals with stories of her marriage to a dashing, professionally successful Newton. For a romantic comedy, there's little in the way of romance, but the film's strength lies in the escalating lies concocted by Gwen as she struggles to maintain a toehold on her new life. Although it doesn't add up to a whole, and screenwriter Mark Stein fudges the issue of Gwen's motivation, he does provide some very funny, cheerfully contrived scams. CM

House That Dripped Blood, The

(Peter Duffell, 1970, GB) Denholm Elliott, Peter Cushing, Christopher Lee, Jon Pertwee, Joanna Dunham, Joss Ackland, Chloë Franks, Nyree Dawn Porter, Ingrid Pitt, John Bennett.
102 min.
Third in the Amicus portmanteau horror series, incorporating four stories by Robert Bloch and marking Duffell's highly promising debut as a director. Three of the episodes are rough-and-ready but vigorous Grand Guignol fun, involving Elliott as a novelist confronted by the mad strangler created for his latest yarn; Cushing as a retired stockbroker whose head lands up in the hands of a waxworks Salome, image of his long-lost love; and Pertwee (it should have been Vincent Price) as a veteran star of horror movies who finds himself inexplicably in the grip of a vampiric urge. The fourth is something else again, a marvellous mood piece of chilling intensity about a lonely, angelic child (the remarkable Chloë Franks) who compensates rather nastily – with wax image and pins – for the neglect to which she has been condemned, not without cause, by her widowed father (Lee). TM

Howards End

(James Ivory, 1991, GB) Anthony Hopkins, Vanessa Redgrave, Helena Bonham Carter, Emma Thompson, James Wilby, Samuel West, Prunella Scales, Jemma Redgrave, Joseph Bennett, Simon Callow.
142 min.
Margaret, Helen and Tibby Schlegel are bright, beautiful and, compared with most Edwardians, open-minded. The Wilcoxes, with the sole exception of Mrs Wilcox, are not. When Helen (Bonham Carter) carries a torch for Paul Wilcox (Bennett), she gets her fingers burned, but Margaret (Thompson) strikes up a friendship with Mrs Wilcox (Vanessa Redgrave), who then goes and spoils it all by dying. Her last wish is for Margaret to have her house in the country, Howards End,

but the wicked Wilcoxes destroy the will and deny Margaret her inheritance. Then, would you believe it, Mr Wilcox (Hopkins) falls for her... Thus the stage is set for a saga of marriage, idealism, despair, pregnancy, exile and manslaughter conducted to the sound of skeletons rattling in the closet. This is as close as EM Forster ever came to a revenger's tragedy, and the only way Ruth Prawer Jhabvala's overlong screenplay can incorporate all the incident is by having more blackouts than a convention of epileptics. The performances are impeccable, but honours go to Thompson, who manages to make Margaret's saintliness actually seem seductive. MS

Howard the Duck (aka Howard...a new breed of hero)

(Willard Huyck, 1986, US) Lea Thompson, Jeffrey Jones, Tim Robbins, Paul Guilfoyle, Liz Sagal, Dominique Davalos.
111 min.
Howard T Duck, of Marvel Comics, might well have a beef against Lucasfilm for transforming his magnetic comic strip personality into a zipperless polyester duck-suit (filled interchangeably by eight different actors, each apparently under four feet in height) in this aimless movie. As it begins, its hero is zapped out of his tranquil life in Duck World and mysteriously transported to Cleveland, Ohio, where he meets the lead singer (Thompson) of an all-girl punk band. Moved by the violent, anarchic lyrics which sink to depths of depravity only previously reached by the kids from *Fame*, Howard takes an interest in the girl. But the consummation of their love must wait, as the same forces which brought him to earth now threaten the planet itself. Eventually, some wonderful special effects mercifully take over as Jeffrey Jones is transformed into the evil 'Dark Overlord' and slugs it out with one of the duck-suited thespians. SGo

How Does It Feel

(Mick Csaky, 1976, GB) RD Laing, RL Gregory, Elkie Brooks, Michael Tippett, David Hockney.
60 min.
This pretentious documentary, financed by the Arts Council, allegedly examines 'many ideas and activities developed to heighten our sensory awareness and feelings', but is in fact little more than an excuse for a stream of blather. Neuro-psychologist RL Gregory lectures on human sensory mechanisms while watching a movie of two people apparently making love; RD Laing pontificates ('We either want to live or we want to die, and while we're alive we surely want to live more abundantly...'), and later abstractedly watches the birth of his own son; David Hockney chatters engagingly about his art, and answers questions on the level of 'Can you see without your glasses?'; Annie Ross delivers a stentorian commentary, and Elkie Brooks interminably belts out Bob Dylan's 'Like a Rolling Stone'. Only Michael Tippett, passionately discussing the genesis of his Third Symphony, addresses himself to the subject with conviction. These matters were dealt with more energetically and with less solemnity in *WR – Mysteries of the Organism*. JPy

How Green Was My Valley

(John Ford, 1941, US) Walter Pidgeon, Maureen O'Hara, Roddy McDowall, Donald Crisp, John Loder, Anna Lee, Barry Fitzgerald, Patric Knowles.
118 min. b/w.
The backlot mining village (impressive as it is) and the babel of accents hardly aid suspension of disbelief in this nostalgic recollection of a Welsh childhood, based on Richard Llewellyn's novel. An elegant and eloquent film, nevertheless, even if the characteristically laconic Fordian poetry seems more contrived here (not least in the uncharacteristic use of an offscreen narration). Its tale of the calamitous break-up of a traditional way of life – with immigration to America offering a despairing hope of salvation – looms larger in the mind if you think of it (as Ford obviously did) as dealing with Ireland rather than Wales. TM

How I Won the War

(Richard Lester, 1967, GB) Michael Crawford, John Lennon, Roy Kinnear, Lee Montague, Jack MacGowran, Michael Hordern, Jack Hedley, Karl Michael Vogler, Ronald Lacey.
110 min.

Dated, maybe, but Lester's gruesomely black anti-war comedy still looks inventive, and manages occasionally to hit home with its blend of surreal lunacy and barbed satire. Concerning the futile mission of a troop of British soldiers in Egypt during World War II, sent behind enemy lines to set up a cricket pitch to impress a visiting VIP, Charles Wood's script, which attacks war movie conventions as much as war itself, is not always well served by Lester's determinedly zany direction; but the performances are well attuned to the single-minded mood of brash bitterness. GA

Howling, The

(Joe Dante, 1980, US) Dee Wallace, Patrick Macnee, Dennis Dugan, Christopher Stone, Belinda Balaski, John Carradine, Slim Pickens.
90 min.
An absolutely spiffing werewolf movie from the man who later gave you *Gremlins*. John Sayles co-wrote the script, which manages to pack in a whole bundle of lycanthropic buffery while still delivering the grue. Dee Wallace plays a TV reporter who has a nasty experience in a peepshow, and convalesces with a weirdo consciousness-raising group which turns out to be hairy on the inside. Aficionados will have fun spotting such faces as Sayles, Roger Corman, Kevin *Bodysnatchers* McCarthy and Dick Miller, while sicko types will appreciate the warped humour. 'I'm gonna give you a piece of my mind', growls a wolfman, proffering a bit of his brain. AB

How Old Is the River? (Fuyu no Kappa)

(Shiori Kazama, 1994, Jap) Akiko Ito, Cho Bang-Ho, Seiichi Tanabe, Rijin Wakuta, Makiko Kuno.
114 min.
Three half-brothers (their father was a serial husband) share an old-style house by a river outside Tokyo; but the house is on the market, and they have a week to vacate it. The youngest boy has a very secret crush on the eldest, and the other two are rivals for their female cousin; it doesn't take much to shatter their precarious emotional equilibrium. Making her first feature, Kazama sets out to pinpoint the exact moment when young adults surrender their adolescent sense of independence and begin to face a future in society. The film is sometimes so low-key that it threatens to float off down-river itself, but it sketches its characters with unassertive skill. TR

How Sweet Is Her Valley (Unterm Dirndl wird gejodelt)

(Alois Brummer, 1974, WGer) Gisela Schwartz, Annemarie Wiese, Edgar Anliker, Bertram Edelmann.
90 min.
Unimaginably heavy-handed and ill-assembled German so-called sex comedy, populated by a brace of village idiots in lederhosen (one with a chicken in his shorts, the other fishing with a cow-bell), several others who spend large amounts of time rubbing their privates in anticipation, and a couple of leading ladies got up to fulfil the more uninteresting fantasies of the pigtail, miniskirt and knicker brigade. VG

How Sweet It Is!

(Jerry Paris, 1968, US) James Garner, Debbie Reynolds, Maurice Ronet, Paul Lynde, Terry-Thomas, Marcel Dalio, Penny Marshall.
98 min.
Garry Marshall and partner Jerry Belson wrote and produced this fairly ordinary comic travelogue, which follows concerned parents Garner and Reynolds to Europe so they can keep an eye on their son and his girlfriend on their continental vacation. Reynolds finds romance with dallying Ronet, best remembered for his searing portrayal of the suicidal playboy in Louis Malle's *Le Feu Follet*. Started life as a novel by Muriel Resnick titled *The Girl in the Turquoise Bikini*. TJ

How the West Was Won

(Henry Hathaway/John Ford/George Marshall, 1962, US) John Wayne, James Stewart, Henry Fonda, Gregory Peck, Carroll Baker, Debbie Reynolds, Richard Widmark, Walter Brennan, Raymond Massey, Agnes Moorehead, Karl Malden, Robert Preston, George Peppard, Eli Wallach.
155 min.

A vast, sprawling Western, shot in the short-lived three-strip Cinerama process, which chronicles the development of the American West through the adventures of one family over three generations. Hathaway's sequence, 'The Rivers, The Plains, The Outlaws', comes off best, while Ford's section on the Civil War looks as much a survey of his own career as of the war. The main problem remains the impossibility of subjecting a film that is fundamentally about landscape and history to the demands of such a coarse dramatic form. CPe

How to Be a Player

see Def Jam's How to Be a Player

How to Be a Woman and Not Die in the Attempt (Como ser mujer y no morir en el intento)

(Ana Belén, 1991, Sp) Carmen Maura, Antonio Resines, Carmen Conesa, Tina Sainz, Juan Diego Botto, Paca Casares, Victor García, Juanjo Puigcorbé.
89 min.
This sweet film probably meant so much more in its native Spain, where director Belén is a film star and singer, and writer Carmen Rico-Godoy is a well-known novelist and journo. It's presumably autobiographical: the heroine (Maura) is also a journalist called Carmen, and the film has an episodic structure similar to a series of gently humorous newspaper columns. Carmen's husband (Resines) is a genial-slob record producer. It's up to Carmen to clean up, deal with the kids and the maid, and work. The point is hammered home quite relentlessly, but it's a mid-life crisis without the crisis. Maura is as watchable as ever, even when the material is as desultory as this. SFe

How to Be Very, Very Popular

(Nunnally Johnson, 1955, US) Betty Grable, Robert Cummings, Charles Coburn, Sheree North, Fred Clark.
89 min.
Originally, Marilyn Monroe was pencilled in to partner Forces pin-up Betty Grable in this frantic comedy about two chorus girls who hide out in a boys' college to escape a murderer. When Monroe turned down the role, Fox's platinum blonde in reserve, Sheree North, was brought in as replacement. Johnson tries too hard to be as zany as possible, but North's outrageous dance routines make this well worth a look. GM

How to Commit Marriage

(Norman Panama, 1969, US) Bob Hope, Jackie Gleason, Jane Wyman, Leslie Nielsen, Maureen Arthur, Joanna Cameron, Tim Matheson, Tina Louise, Irwin Corey, Paul Stewart.
98 min.
One of the dire sitcoms in which Bob Hope latterly got bogged down. Hope and wife Wyman initiate divorce proceedings. Daughter (Cameron) learns this on the way to the altar, and decides to cohabit instead of marrying. Much ado, especially when she becomes pregnant, with Hope and Wyman adopting silly disguises and contriving to commit the young couple (and themselves, of course) to marriage. Hope also gets to masquerade as a hippy and an oriental guru, to play golf with a chimpanzee (he loses), and to see Jackie Gleason (as the prospective groom's cynical father) steal the few laughs on offer. TM

How to Destroy the Reputation of the Greatest Secret Agent (Le Magnifique)

(Philippe de Broca, 1973, Fr/It) Jean-Paul Belmondo, Jacqueline Bisset, Vittorio Caprioli, Monique Tarbès, Raymond Gérôme.
94 min.
Nine years earlier, with *L'Homme de Rio*, de Broca and Belmondo came up with a delightful parody of James Bondery. They try again here, much less successfully, with Belmondo as a writer of pulp spy thrillers, pressured by deadline fever, who slips out of his seedy garret into the fantasy world of his novels. Imagining himself as his secret agent hero Bob Saint-Clair, he gets involved in the usual sub-Bond spy-jinks, and lures the girl across the courtyard,

Christina/Tatiana (Bisset), between the covers. Routine shoot 'em up stuff is laced with casual sexism and marred by atrocious dubbing. GA

How to Get Ahead in Advertising

(Bruce Robinson, 1989, GB) Richard E Grant, Rachel Ward, Richard Wilson, Jacqueline Tong, John Shrapnel, Susan Wooldridge, Mick Ford. Jacqueline Pearce, Roddy Maude-Roxby.
94 min.
The very model of a successful '80s man, with a lifestyle to match, advertising executive Dennis Bagley (Grant) has a severe zit problem: he can't work up a pitch for a new pimple cream campaign. Things come to a head when he has a very real commercial break, realises that what's wrong with the world is advertising's fault, and proceeds to rid his home of anything that is contaminated with the deadly virus of the promoters. Pustules are forgotten, until a check in the mirror reveals a talking boil on his neck. As Bagley's disgust at his profession grows, so does the carbuncle, a wretched alter ego taking over his life. Grant, as the charmingly meglomaniac Bagley, turns in a high-energy, bravura performance. The opening half-hour is outrageously brilliant, but descends into a pot-boiler of repetitive, if animated, soap-box preaching about the manipulation of punters by the denziens of Madison Avenue and their international brotherhood. That said, writer/director Robinson's dark comedy is bursting with inspired scenes taking the pus out of this powerful industry, and is spot on. JGl

How to Make an American Quilt

(Jocelyn Moorhouse, 1995, US) Winona Ryder, Anne Bancroft, Dermot Mulroney, Ellen Burstyn, Kate Nelligan, Alfre Woodard, Kate Capshaw, Lois Smith, Jean Simmons, Rip Torn, Maya Angelou, Melinda Dillon, Gail Strickland.
117 min.
Struggling to finish a thesis on women's handiwork in tribal cultures and to come to terms with her imminent marriage, Berkeley student Finn Dodd (Ryder) returns to spend the summer with her grandmother (Burstyn) and great aunt (Bancroft). Their idyllic retreat is also the work place of the Grasse Quilting Bee, and as its members make her wedding quilt, Finn becomes privy to their tales of love and betrayal. Unlike the glib accounts of bonding in Waiting to Exhale and Now and Then, this adaptation of Whitney Otto's best-seller is a lyrical, intelligent attempt to create a specifically 'female' cinema. Moorhouse keeps the narrative, which spans 130 years, on a tight rein, never allowing it to wander aimlessly from one anecdote to the next. Admittedly, the metaphor (life's rich tapestry) is facile, but the direction, Janusz Kaminski's pastoral photography and Jane Anderson's finely tuned dialogue combine to produce a subtle, surprisingly witty film. Nevertheless, it's the remarkable performances which really enhance the mixture of nostalgia and world-weary realism: Ryder, as gamine as ever, delivers her most credible performance to date, while the luminous Simmons and imposing Angelou infuse the film with grace and understated charm. KM

How to Marry a Millionaire

(Jean Negulesco, 1953, US) Marilyn Monroe, Betty Grable, Lauren Bacall, William Powell, Rory Calhoun, David Wayne, Alex D'Arcy, Cameron Mitchell, Fred Clark.
95 min.
The first film to be shot in CinemaScope (although it was the second to be released) opens with a pre-credit sequence called Street Scene, which was designed to show off the new anamorphic and stereophonic system. Then follows this feeble little comedy, which hardly needed a wide screen and which just about gets by on star power. Filmed immediately after Gentlemen Prefer Blondes, it's basically the same story, with divorcee Bacall and her chums Monroe and Grable turning a New York apartment into a man-trap. It was made solely to boost Monroe's celebrity, and her short-sighted bimbo is the best thing in it. The men – including Calhoun's fur trapper, Powell's oil tycoon, and Wayne's tax evader – are a wan lot and meant to be. ATu

How to Steal a Diamond in Four Uneasy Lessons

see Hot Rock, The

How to Steal the World

(Sutton Roley, 1968, US) Robert Vaughan, David McCallum, Barry Sullivan, Eleanor Parker, Leslie Nielsen, Daniel O'Herlihy, Leo G Carroll.
89 min.
Kitsch '60s thrills as the Men from UNCLE, Napoleon Solo and Illya Kuryakin, battle yet another evil genius, who's been kidnapping their fellow spies and plotting world domination from his hideaway high in the Himalayas. From the days when Leslie Nielsen was a serious actor. Well, sort of. TJ

How to Succeed in Business Without Really Trying

(David Swift, 1966, US) Robert Morse, Michele Lee, Rudy Vallee, Anthony Teague, Maureen Arthur.
121 min.
A blandly outrageous and occasionally sharp-toothed musical satirising big business, with a likeable score by Frank Loesser, which takes pot-shots at everything from coffee breaks to advertising campaigns. Morse, somehow contriving to be horrendous and endearing at one and the same time, repeats his stage role to brilliant effect as the all-American boy who employs scientific knowhow to rise like a meteor, licking asses and trampling heads every step of the way. Swift's direction is a little stiff and stagy, and there are dull patches; but with handsome camerawork from Burnett Guffey, witty Bob Fosse choreography, and the ineffable Vallee playing the compulsive-knitting, fussbudget boss, this was one of the liveliest musicals of the '60s. TM

H.P. Lovecraft's Necronomico

see Necronomicon

Huckleberry Finn (aka The Adventures of Huckleberry Finn)

(Richard Thorpe, 1939, US) Mickey Rooney, Walter Connolly, William Frawley, Rex Ingram, Minor Watson.
90 min. b/w.
Disappointingly routine follow up to The Adventures of Tom Sawyer, prosaically shot (in black-and-white) with none of the care lavished on the earlier film, despite extensive use of locations. With the characters stuck in cliché (Connolly and Frawley labouring for comic effect as the riverboat conmen, Ingram in the Uncle Tom bit as the runaway slave), the leisurely adventures – though entertaining enough, thanks largely to a subdued and admirable Rooney – seem to roll by as sluggishly as ol' man river. TM

Huckleberry Finn

(J Lee Thompson, 1974, US) Jeff East, Paul Winfield, Harvey Korman, David Wayne, Arthur O'Connell, Gary Merrill, Natalie Trundy.
118 min.
With the facsimile B & W minstrels crooning 'Huckle-berry, Huckle-berry, where you bin?' and Roberta Flack 'performing' (so the credits say) the title song, you get the tenor of this Reader's Digest musical adaptation. The lying and deception that run through Twain's original become incidental rather than thematic, and much of the sense of sheer adventure gets lost. Instead, Huck's adventures with runaway slave Jim remain amiable and episodic rather than memorable and integrated. Everyone 'performs' larger than life, singing their forgettable songs rather badly. Laszlo Kovacs' camerawork, consistently several notches above the rest of the production, remains its only distinctive feature. CPe

Hud

(Martin Ritt, 1962, US) Paul Newman, Melvyn Douglas, Patricia Neal, Brandon de Wilde, John Ashley, Whit Bissell, Crahan Denton, Val Avery.
111 min. b/w.
Along with Hombre, one of Ritt's best films, less abrasive than it thinks but still a remarkably clear-eyed account of growing up in Texas to mourn the old free-ranging ways of the frontier days. Its focus is the antagonism between a sternly moralising, patriarchal ranch-owner (Douglas) and his free-drinking, free-whoring 'no account' son (Newman); the conflict between them, ambivalently observed by the two other members of the household, both emotionally involved with Newman – the ranch housekeeper (Neal) and a hero-worshipping nephew (de Wilde) – boils to a head over a government order to slaughter the ranch's entire herd as a precaution against foot-and-mouth, with Newman urging outlaw defiance and Douglas siding with the law. The film sometimes seems to be busting its britches to attain the status of Greek tragedy in delineating the disintegration of a heritage, with dialogue haunted by images of death and decay. But pretensions are kept nicely damped down by the performances (all four principals are great) and by Wong Howe's magnificent camerawork. TM

Hudson Hawk

(Michael Lehmann, 1991, US) Bruce Willis, Danny Aiello, Andie MacDowell, James Coburn, Richard E Grant, Sandra Bernhard, Donald Burton, Frank Stallone.
100 min.
This quirkily amusing piece of vanity film-making is essentially a ludicrously expensive cult movie. Fresh from prison, reformed thief Hawk (Willis) is coerced by filthy rich megalomaniacs Darwin and Minerva Mayflower (Grant and Bernhard) into a plot to steal three Leonardo masterpieces that provide the key to an alchemical machine for turning lead into gold. Hovering in the backgroud are CIA man Coburn and beautiful Vatican spy MacDowell. Shades of TV's Moonlighting remain, with a cavalier disregard for plot logic and henchmen named after candy bars. Unfortunately, neither Lehmann's direction nor the in-jokey script achieve a consistent tone, veering from knockabout fun to vicious, throat-slashing gore. Willis smirks and smarms his way through some neatly staged set pieces, but funnier by far are MacDowell's drug-induced display of dolphin-speak and the deliciously demented antics of Grant and Bernhard. NF

Hudsucker Proxy, The

(Joel Coen, 1994, US) Tim Robbins, Paul Newman, Jennifer Jason Leigh, Charles Durning, Jim True, John Mahoney, William Cobbs, Steve Buscemi.
111 min.
New Year's Eve, 1958, Norville Barnes (Robbins) climbs on to a window-ledge of the Hudsucker Industries skyscraper in snowy Manhattan. We flash back a month: company chairman Waring Hudsucker (Durning) shocks board members by plunging 45 floors to the sidewalk below – at the moment young Norville, a hayseed business graduate from Indiana, first enters the building to take a post in the mail room. Norville didn't, however, expect immediate promotion to company boss, a move plotted by vice-chairman Sidney Mussburger (Newman); with an idiot pawn in charge, stock will plummet and Sid can take over. Or he could, if only hard-bitten hack Amy Archer (Leigh) hadn't smelt a rat and gone undercover as Norville's secretary. Directed by Joel Coen, produced by Ethan Coen, and scripted by both brothers (plus Sam Raimi), this is a notably well-executed, very funny and very well-acted movie: a quirky, sardonic take on '50s faddishness, fame, power, friendship, character and ethics. A minor work, but confirmation of the Coens' position among America's most ambitious, able and exciting film-makers. GA

Hu-Du-Men (aka Stage Door)

(Shu Kei, 1996, HK) Josephine Siao, Anita Yuen, Daniel Chan, Chung King-fai, Lee Chi-hung.
87 min.
Tailored to fit the impossibly wonderful Josephine Siao, Shu Kei's comedy drama centres on a woman who makes her living playing men on stage and has trouble fulfilling the roles of wife and mother off stage. The film sensibly makes no attempt to disguise the story's own stage origins, but concentrates instead on weaving together the several strands of plot, the emotional complications and the rapid shifts from humour to pathos and back again. The slightly surprising appearance of a lesbian subplot confirms that sexual politics are somewhere on the agenda, but the stance is closer to farce than Freud. Charmingly old-fashioned. TR

Hue and Cry

(Charles Crichton, 1947, GB) Alastair Sim, Jack Warner, Harry Fowler, Valerie White, Douglas Barr, Jack Lambert.
82 min. b/w.
Reminiscent of *Emil and the Detectives* as a gang of East End kids excitedly realise that their favourite blood-and-thunder comic is being used as a means of communication by crooks, and (since the police turn a deaf ear) set out in hot pursuit. One of Ealing's first postwar successes, it is given an enormous boost by locations around the bomb sites of London's East End and by Sim's sinister eccentricities as the author of the serial in question. Its charm, in these days of headlines about kids and video nasties, is of another world: capturing a blonde moll (White) and requiring information, the gang subject her to the most vicious tortures they can think of – tickling by feather (which doesn't work) and menace by white mouse (which does). TM

Huevos de Oro

see Golden Balls

Hugo the Hippo

(William Feigenbaum, 1975, US) voices: Robert Morley, Paul Lynde, Ronny Cox, Percy Rodriguez.
90 min.
An animation feature with terrible songs from Burl Ives and Osmonds Marie and Jimmy. But at least there's an attempt at a liberal theme in its story about the friendship between a village boy (a black kid in Africa) and the sole survivor of a hippo slaughter, and how the local kids come to Hugo's aid against the mindless cruelty of the adults. VG

Huitième Jour, Le

see Eighth Day, The

Hullabaloo over Georgie and Bonnie's Pictures

(James Ivory, 1978, Ind/GB) Peggy Ashcroft, Larry Pine, Saeed Jaffrey, Victor Banerjee, Aparna Sen, Jane Booker.
83 min.
Originally made for LWT's *The South Bank Show*, this is probably one of the most successful of all Merchant/Ivory collaborations. Ruth Prawer Jhabvala's script sets two collectors (Ashcroft and Pine) and two adventurers (Jaffrey and Sen) after a group of Indian miniatures, hidden away in a crumbling palace. The owner, the Maharajah of Jodhpur (Banerjee), watches dispassionately as the four scrabble decorously but desperately after his family's fortune. As delicate and as beautiful as the miniatures at its centre, the film poses, in the most acceptable and accessible way, central questions about the function and value of art. JW

Human Beast, The

see Bête Humaine, La

Human Desire

(Fritz Lang, 1954, US) Glenn Ford, Gloria Grahame, Broderick Crawford, Edgar Buchanan, Kathleen Case, Grandon Rhodes, Dan Seymour.
90 min. b/w.
Lang's version of Zola's *La Bête Humaine* is, like all his best '50s work, as cold, hard and steely grey as the railway tracks which here mark out the action. Glenn Ford, the perfect embodiment of these qualities, returns from Korea, only to be pulled into the murderously destructive marriage between Grahame and Crawford (both superb). The bleak, dark marshalling yards are the perfect backdrop for the playing out of adulterous relationships where 'desire' signifies only fear, jealousy and hatred. SJ

Human Experiments

(Gregory Goodell, 1979, US) Linda Haynes, Geoffrey Lewis, Ellen Travolta, Lurene Tuttle, Aldo Ray, Jackie Coogan, Mercedes Shirley.
86 min.
Solo country singer Linda Haynes runs foul of the law (Ray and Coogan cameos) and takes the rap for a mass killing that sees her committed to the state penitentiary, where a crazed regime zombifies its women inmates. Trailing well behind

Jackson County Jail, but firing off a cruder mixture of backwoods misogyny and nightmarish incarceration, it's a severe case of Southern discomfort. MA

Human Factor, The

(Edward Dmytryk, 1975, GB) George Kennedy, John Mills, Raf Vallone, Arthur Franz, Rita Tushingham, Haydée Politoff, Barry Sullivan.
96 min.
Despite some heavily loaded exploitation of middle class fears of irrational terrorist violence, this movie achieves a certain bulky conviction of its own. After the pointless slaughter of his family in Naples, the cerebral war-games of a NATO electronics expert (Kennedy) are undermined by baser instincts of revenge. Thrashing around like a stunned ox, Kennedy takes on the extremists single-handed, finally wiping them out after they take over a crowded supermarket. His disintegration into a brute force gives the film its momentum, and more or less everyone stands back in disbelief to let him get on with it. The computer hardware is diverting, and treated with greater respect than the terrorists, who are given no credibility whatsoever, ideological or otherwise. CPe

Human Factor, The

(Otto Preminger, 1979, GB/US) Nicol Williamson, Richard Attenborough, Joop Doderer, John Gielgud, Derek Jacobi, Robert Morley, Ann Todd, Richard Vernon, Iman.
114 min.
As directed by the erratic Preminger and scripted by Tom Stoppard, this is pretty faithful to Graham Greene's novel about loyalty and betrayal in the espionage world, at least in terms of plot. Dealing with a couple of British agents suspected of leaking information to the Russians, it comes across well enough in its portrait of loneliness and conscience, and – despite being worthy and almost totally bereft of any real action – the plot mechanics are unusually clear for a spy movie. But the whole thing badly lacks any sort of central thematic focus, and the strangely obsessive Englishness of Greene's world is altogether missing. Craftsmanlike rather than inspired, it's watchable thanks largely to its solid performances. GA

Human Monster, The

see Dark Eyes of London

Humanoid, The (L'Umanoide)

(George B Lewis, 1979, It) Richard Kiel, Corinne Clery, Leonard Mann, Barbara Bach, Arthur Kennedy, Ivan Rassimov.
100 min.
Star Wars may have been puerile, but at least it was fun, which is more than can be said for this space cowboys and Indians movie: a tedious compound of everything from *Frankenstein* (the irradiated mutant monster) to Zen Buddhism (the boy Dalai Lama floats in from Tibet on a glass ashtray), with Darth Vader baddies and a robodog thrown in for good measure. The sets resemble Brent Cross and the spaceships could have come out of a cornflakes packet. 'Nuff said? FF

Humanoids from the Deep (aka Monster)

(Barbara Peeters, 1980, US) Doug McClure, Ann Turkel, Vic Morrow, Cindy Weintraub, Anthony Penya.
81 min.
Despite the sex of the director, a more blatant endorsement of exploitation cinema's current anti-women slant would be hard to find: the strain of humanoid ecological mutants featured here don't stick simply to killing everyone in sight, but carry the sexual premise of the Black Lagoon a stage further into a compulsion to rape. Peeters also lays on the gore pretty thick amid the usual visceral drive-in hooks and rip-offs from genre hits; and with the humour of an offering like *Piranha* entirely absent, this turns out a nasty piece of work all round. PT

Hummingbird Tree, The

(Noella Smith, 1992, GB) Tom Beasley, Desha Penco, Sunil Y Ramjitsingh.
84 min.
A BBC 'Screen One' production, set in Trinidad at the time of the 1946 elections, when the vote was being extended to black Caribbeans and Indians and the call for independence was grow-

ing louder. A far from unpredictable take on the tensions wrought by racial, religious and class divisions, it focuses on a young white boy whose friendship with two local Hindustani kids is constantly being discouraged by his supposedly liberal parents. Performances, script and direction are adequate rather than inspired, though the flaws will probably be less apparent on the small screen. GA

Humoresque

(Jean Negulesco, 1946, US) Joan Crawford, John Garfield, Oscar Levant, J Carrol Naish, Craig Stevens, Tom D'Andrea, Paul Cavanagh, Robert Blake.
125 min. b/w.
Full-tilt Warner Brothers melodrama: slum kid Garfield rises to concert pitch as a classical violinist (dubbed by Isaac Stern) under the far-from-disinterested patronage of wealthy/lonely/bottle-happy/yearning socialite Crawford, and amid ludicrously intense shoulder-chip, tear-jerk sparrings, has to choose between his bow and her heartstrings. Levant plays resident cynic/voice of conscience from the piano stool; Clifford Odets, no less, contributes to the adaptation of Fannie Hurst's madcap tushery. PT

Hunchback of Notre Dame, The

(Wallace Worsley, 1923, US) Lon Chaney, Patsy Ruth Miller, Norman Kerry, Ernest Torrence, Brandon Hurst.
12 reels. b/w.
Chaney's first big-budget film, and the one which made his reputation. Laden down with massive sets and milling extras, bowdlerised even by comparison with the Laughton version of 1939, it emerges more as a historical spectacle than as a horror movie – and a rather tedious one at that, thanks to Worsley's often painfully ponderous direction. Worth seeing mainly for Chaney's remarkable performance: even bowed and constricted by the heavy weights he used to help simulate Quasimodo's crippled gait, his body remains extraordinarily expressive. TM

Hunchback of Notre Dame, The

(William Dieterle, 1939, US) Charles Laughton, Maureen O'Hara, Cedric Hardwicke, Thomas Mitchell, Edmond O'Brien, Harry Davenport, George Zucco.
117 min. b/w.
Although Laughton doesn't attempt the acrobatics that Lon Chaney performed in the silent version, his hunchback comes across as one of the cinema's most impressive 'grotesque' characterisations. Dieterle directs in a way that reminds you of his background as actor/director in the German expressionist cinema: the visuals here impressively recall earlier movies from *Metropolis* (the crowds) to *The Last Laugh* (tracking shots through the shadows). Richly entertaining. TR

Hunchback of Notre Dame, The (Notre Dame de Paris)

(Jean Delannoy, 1956, Fr/It) Anthony Quinn, Gina Lollobrigida, Jean Danet, Alain Cuny, Robert Hirsch.
107 min.
Embarrassingly awful, with Quinn labouring under a slapdash make-up and not rendering the crude dubbed dialogue (it's difficult to imagine that Jacques Prévert had a hand in the original script) any more palatable by indulging in some weird vocal mannerisms. A totally misbegotten venture. TM

Hunchback of Notre Dame, The

(Gary Trousdale/Kirk Wise, 1996, US) voices: Tom Hulce, Demi Moore, Kevin Kline, Tony Jay.
91 min.
While Victor Hugo might not entirely recognise his novel, this Disney animated blockbuster more or less remakes the formidable 1939 Charles Laughton version, marking another milestone for the studio with its dazzling technique and surprisingly mature content. As voiced by Hulce, Quasimodo is, despite the misshapen form that restricts him to the company of three bantering

gargoyles in the cathedral bell tower, a fairly cuddly chap. But *Beauty and the Beast* directors Trousdale and Wise marshal their energies to different ends, lining up this King of Fools alongside the Parisian gypsies and beggars, united in the harsh treatment they receive from the chilling Judge Frollo – an index of society's attitude to the outsider which even the youngest minds should grasp. Elsewhere, while Kevin Kline injects a dash of irony into the conventionally heroic Phoebus, the modelling of free spirited Esmeralda on voice artist Demi Moore (vital statistics and all) confirms the underlying sexual tension – in a Disney cartoon! – of Frollo's confrontation with his own inner demons. Though Alan Menken's music misses the big tune that would cap Stephen Schwartz's nimble lyrics, it's the thematic sophistication that brings the movie to life, making older children and adults its best audience. Sure, the pacy slapstick is up to par, but the 'mobile' camera and extraordinary vistas really come into their own in the dramatic set-pieces, breakneck chases and the climactic assault on Notre Dame itself. TJ

Hungarian Fairy Tale, A (Hol Volt, Hol nem Volt)

(Gyula Gazdag, 1987, Hun) Arpád Vermes, Mária Varga, Frantisek Husák, Eszter Czákányi, Szilvia Tóth.
97 min. b/w.
The fairytale in question is the legend of a giant bird that flies down to save Hungary, but Gazdag's film is less a reinvention of national myth than an attempt to get to the bottom of a typically communist paradox: the way that human impulses turn into inhuman pratices under the dead hand of bureaucracy. The bird turns up at the start in a TV cartoon; and reappears at the end to carry a little boy and his surrogate parents away from their troubles. In between, the film uses Mozart's *Magic Flute* to waft its way through the story of a young orphan searching for a father who was only ever a fictitious name on a birth certificate. Gazdag's approach has something in common with the 'magic realism' of Latin American novelists; he shoots in silvery black-and-white, and feels free to jump from social observation into areas of fantasy and absurdist humour. The result is undeniably distinctive, and the shifts in tone sometimes have a genuinely disconcerting punch; but basically, Gazdag is looking back nostalgically to earlier social fables like De Sica's *Miracle in Milan* than forward to the Hungary of the '90s. TR

Hunger, The

(Tony Scott, 1983, US) Catherine Deneuve, David Bowie, Susan Sarandon, Cliff De Young, Beth Ehlers, Dan Hedaya.
99 min.
Deneuve is the ageless, possibly final survivor of an ancient immortal race dependent on humans for both sustenance and companionship. Her superior blood allows her lovers a triple lifetime until they ultimately succumb to instant decline. Not all of this is apparent in the film, where style rules at the expense of coherence. But that style is often glorious, from a bloody sun sinking over a gothic hi-tech Manhattan skyline to living quarters that are sumptuous. Neat touches of grim humour also: Deneuve and Bowie manhunt in a disco as Bauhaus sing 'Bela Lugosi's Dead'; and Bowie rots away in a hospital waiting room where the 20 minutes wait becomes a subjective century of ageing. Visual sensualities will have a feast, but you'll have to read Whitley Strieber's novel if you don't want to emerge with a badly scratched head. GD

Hungry Hill

(Brian Desmond Hurst, 1946, GB) Margaret Lockwood, Cecil Parker, Michael Denison, Dermot Walsh, Dennis Price, Jean Simmons, Siobhan McKenna, Dan O'Herlihy.
109 min. b/w.
Lockwood isn't her usual Wicked Lady self in this overcooked piece of blarney about 19th century Irish copper-mining folk. She plays a high-spirited colleen who toys with the affections of two brothers, Denison and Price. The storyline, adapted by Daphne du Maurier (and Terence Young) from her own novel, ladles on fire, flood and disease in its grim moments, and throws in Irish jigs, horse riding and waltzing whenever

a little levity is needed. There's the usual bad feeling between the villagers and the big businessman (Parker) who's taken over their land to open his mine. Lockwood is the one who suffers, losing her husband and ending up (somewhat improbably) as a sad old woman with a drug and gambling problem. The dialogue's often laughable, the attempts at Irish accents grate, but this is still enjoyable, full-blooded entertainment. GM

Hungry Wives

see Jack's Wife

Hunt, The

see Caza, La

Hunter, The

(Buzz Kulik, 1980, US) Steve McQueen, Eli Wallach, Kathryn Harrold, LeVar Burton, Ben Johnson, Richard Venture, Tracey Walter.
117 min.
McQueen's last movie has him cast as a latter-day bounty hunter making a living bringing in bail absconders. Routinely scripted and directed, but McQueen gives a likeable enough performance as the anachronistic born-out-of-his-time man. Best running joke is his beaten-up auto which he seems unable to move without crunching metal. RM

Hunters, The

(Dick Powell, 1958, US) Robert Mitchum, Robert Wagner, Lee Phillips, Peter Egan, Mai Britt.
108 min.
Mitchum snoozes his way through this Korean War drama as an Air Force major so cool in the face of combat he's called 'the Iceman'. Not much flying, instead there's a soapy subplot involving the nerve-wracked Phillips and his two-timing spouse Mai Britt – more than enough going on though for those who'd happily watch the star recite the phone book. Filmed in 'Scope. TJ

Hunter's Blood

(Robert C Hughes, 1986, US) Sam Bottoms, Clu Gulager, Ken Swofford, Mayf Nutter, Joey Travolta, Kim Delaney, Lee DeBroux.
102 min.
'When a man gits old enough, he needs to go a-huntin' says one of the five bozos in this film. These men are not cine-literate, and they cheerfully infiltrate remote parts of Arkansas which are littered with telltale signs like 'Tobe's Gas Stop' and 'Razorback Meat Co'. They spot some locals. 'These guys look like something out of National Geographic' they observe. Wrong, bozos; these guys look like rejects from the cast of *The Hills Have Eyes*. After lots of driving along redneck routes, lots of bozo campfire chat ('A man's gotta feel his balls!'), and lots of loony locals chanting 'We're gonna get you', the bozos finally realise they are trapped in a slice of substandard exploitation and decide to git the hell out. Things liven up a little bit when people start gitting half their heads blown away. But not much. AB

Hunt for Red October, The

(John McTiernan, 1990, US) Sean Connery, Alec Baldwin, Scott Glenn, Sam Neill, James Earl Jones, Joss Ackland, Richard Jordan, Peter Firth, Tim Curry.
135 min.
The 'Red October' is a silent submarine. Virtually undetectable on sonar, it constitutes a deadly first strike weapon, more than enough to tip the nuclear balance in the Soviets' favour. No sooner has it left port on its maiden voyage than Captain Raimus (Connery, terrific) breaks from the official course and heads for the US. Will he start a war, or defect? Despite the Cold War implications (the action is set disingenuously before Gorbachev), there's enough nuclear frisson and multi-lateral cynicism here to evoke *Fail Safe*, if not *Dr Strangelove*. McTiernan guides us surely through the convolutions of an admittedly over-complicated plot, and adeptly links hi-tech with character. At its best, with Soviets, Americans and Raimus all at cross-purposes, the movie is an engrossing and exciting battle of wits. But when it attemptsto suggest an interior life in the characters beyond the job at hand, the results are at best perfunctory, more often corny, despite the high-calibre cast. TCh

Hunting Scenes from Bavaria (Jagdszenen aus Niederbayern)

(Peter Fleischmann, 1969, W Ger) Martin Sperr, Angela Winkler, Else Quecke, Michel Strixner, Maria Stradler.
85 min. b/w.
Between the seemingly idyllic opening and closing scenes depicting a rural community, first at church, then at the village festival, Fleischmann attacks that community's prejudices and ignorance without remorse. His very precisely observed portrait of Bavarian life begins with little more than a display of the villagers' constant ribbing, bawdy humour, continuous gossip, and more than a hint of their slow-wittedness. With the return of a young man, their idle malice and childish clowning, always on the edge of unpleasantness, receive some focus: quite without foundation, the lad is victimised as a homosexual. The crippling conformity of their ingrained conservatism leads the villagers to reject anything 'different': a young widow is ostracised, more for her crippled lover and idiot son than her morals; a teacher is frozen out because she's educated; the casual destruction of the young 'homosexual' is given no more thought than the cutting up of a pig. Not Germany in the '30s but the '70s; nevertheless the political parallels are clear. An impressive film. CPe

Hurricane

(Jan Troell, 1979, US) Jason Robards, Mia Farrow, Max von Sydow, Trevor Howard, Dayton Ka'ne, Timothy Bottoms, James Keach.
120 min.
This melodrama of murder and miscegenation was to have been directed by Polanski, who might perhaps have introduced some sexual curiosity. Troell's version is more polynesian pap than polymorphous perversity. American naval commander's virginal daughter (Farrow) is seduced by the pulsating beat of native loins in Pago Pago. The enviable loins belong to Dayton Ka'ne, a bronzed cross between Arnold Schwarzenegger and Robby Benson, but their love augurs badly – the entire cast overacts at the mention of it, and Mia's dad (Robards) can't decide whether he's Captain Queeg or Captain Ahab. As it becomes clear that lots of scenes didn't make it into the final cut, the hurricane does to the landscape what everyone else has done to the script. And even the effects don't cut it. SM

Hurricane, The

(John Ford, 1937, US) Dorothy Lamour, Jon Hall, Mary Astor, C Aubrey Smith, Raymond Massey, Thomas Mitchell, John Carradine, Jerome Cowan.
102 min. b/w.
A breezy South Seas melo, with Dorothy Lamour, having no need to apologise for slinking around in a sarong, canoodling with Hall and giving starchy Governor Raymond Massey the sweats. Ford knocks off the hour or so of filler efficiently enough before the special effects team (headed by James Basevi) take over for the biggest blow-job in Hollywood history. Infinitely more enjoyable than the 1979 remake. ATu

Hurricane Streets

(Morgan J Freeman, 1997, US) Brendon Sexton III, Shawn Elliott, José Zuñiga, David Roland Frank, Carlo Alban, Edie Falco, LM Kit Carson, Isidra Vega.
89 min.
This slice of wrong-side-of-the-tracks New York teenage life has a sympathetic heart, but lacks the passion and originality to convince. It centres on crew member Marcus (Sexton), a spotty, asthmatic, vulnerable 15-year-old being raised by his grandmother in the absence of his father, and with his mother in jail (for helping Mexicans hop the border). It's a story of breaking away, with Marcus making his first (sweetly outlined) romantic forays with pretty young Latino Melena (Vega), running in with her dad and being hauled up by the cops for thieving. Writer/director Freeman is initially at pains to restrain the usual hyperrealist clichés, patching out the boy's existence in desultory, almost inconsequential scenes of street life, hanging out in the 'club house', fencing stolen goods by the school gates. Here the movie seems most at ease, but as it gears up with gunplay episodes and an all too familiar heist, the

uncertainties – inappropriateness, rather – of tone, and the shortcomings of the acting and directing become more evident. WH

Hurry Sundown

(Otto Preminger, 1966, US) Michael Caine, Jane Fonda, John Phillip Law, Robert Hooks, Diahann Carroll, Burgess Meredith, Faye Dunaway, George Kennedy, Rex Ingram.
146 min.
Set in Georgia in 1946 and dealing with the attempts of land-grabbers to dispossess a Negro smallholder, this is the sort of film in which the good guys are very, very good, the bad ones just plain horrid, and you recognise the hero because he gazes at his son, pauses for a count of three, and solemnly intones, 'A man's gotta do what his conscience says is right'. When Preminger makes a problem movie, he really piles on the agony: not just black-baiters and black-lovers, but a judge prejudiced to the point of imbecility, a conscienceful white minister serving his black brethren, a child traumatised after being tied up in his cot, and rampant sex all over the place. The Preminger flair which made The Cardinal so enjoyable, despite its hackneyed script, seems to have deserted him in this lumbering melodrama, put together with the sort of crudely opportunistic 'style' which alternates scenes of the rich folks parading in a stately mansion with shots of the poor sitting down to their humble fare while thumping mood music makes sure you get the point. TM

Husbands

(John Cassavetes, 1970, US) Ben Gazzara, Peter Falk, John Cassavetes, Jenny Runacre, Jenny Lee Wright, Noelle Kao.
154 min.
One of the Cassavetes improvisations made before he began profitably subjecting the technique to genre limitations in The Killing of a Chinese Bookie, Opening Night and Gloria, this is a maddening mixture. Cliché is never too far away as three New York commuters, middle-aged, married and disturbed by the death of a friend, embark on a despairing odyssey (partly on a flying visit to London) of drink, sex and self-discovery. Yet for all the rambling repetitions and noisy generalisations, the film does add up to a devastatingly bleak view of the emptiness of suburban life. TM

Husbands and Wives

(Woody Allen, 1992, US) Woody Allen, Blythe Danner, Judy Davis, Mia Farrow, Juliette Lewis, Liam Neeson, Sydney Pollack, Lysette Anthony, Cristi Conaway, Ron Rifkin, Bruce Jay Friedman.
108 min.
When Sally (Davis) and Jack (Pollack) announce their amicable break-up, their friends Gabe and Judy (Allen and Farrow) start looking at their own marriage more critically. Do they keep secrets from each other? Why have they never had kids? Would Lit lecturer Gabe follow Jack's example and fall for a woman half his age – student Rain (Lewis), for example? Why is Judy so keen to get the highly-strung Sally together with her eligible colleague, the very romantic Michael (Neeson)? To put it another way, what is this thing called love? So vividly drawn are all the characters that one becomes wholly caught up in their tangled whirl of emotional/psychological confusion: though not consistently hilarious, the film is engrossing from start to finish. If the use of hand-held camera is occasionally overdone, Allen's decision to shoot and structure his study of mid-life crisis in the style of fly-on-the-wall documentary pays dividends. With excellent performances (Davis and Pollack in particular), it's his finest film since Hannah and Her Sisters. GA

Hush-a-Bye Baby

(Margo Harkin, 1989, Ire) Emer McCourt, Michael Liebmann, Cathy Casey, Julie Marie Reynolds, Sinead O'Connor.
72 min.
A delightful film from the Derry film and Video Collective, about the lives of four working class convent school chums, one of whom (played by the excellent McCourt) forms a romantic affair – consolidated during an evening Irish class – with a boy who is later detained by the British Army. Something of an exemplar of low-budget, locality-based film-making, the film homestraight in on the realities of its protagonists' lives, engaging such issues as adolescence, the British prescence, isolation and abortion through finely observed and finely played details in their daily lives. Its vigour, clarity and compassion make the sad predicament of McCourt's heroine all the more moving. Sinead O'Connor has a cameo and provides an excellent music soundtrack. WH

Hush...Hush, Sweet Charlotte

(Robert Aldrich, 1964, US) Bette Davis, Olivia de Havilland, Joseph Cotten, Agnes Moorehead, Cecil Kellaway, Victor Buono, Mary Astor, William Campbell, Wesley Addy, Bruce Dern, George Kennedy.
134 min. b/w.
Loony Grand Guignol, with Aldrich and Davis retreading the territory charted in What Ever Happened to Baby Jane? a couple of years earlier. This time round, Davis is the victim, a woman suspected of murdering her fiancé and driven to the point of insanity by the dead man's repeated hauntings of her in her lonely Gothic mansion. Over the top, of course, and not a lot to it, but it's efficiently directed, beautifully shot (Joseph Biroc), and contains enough scary sequences amid the brooding, tense atmosphere. Splendid performances from Davis and Moorehead, too. GA

Hussard sur le toit, Le
(The Horseman on the Roof)

(Jean-Paul Rappeneau, 1995, Fr) Oliver Martinez, Juliette Binoche, Claudio Amendola, Pierre Arditi, Isabelle Carré, François Cluzet, Jean Yanne, Gérard Depardieu.
136 min.
1832. Provence is gripped by cholera. Angelo (Martinez), a hussar, flees Austrian assassins determined to stamp out exiled Italian revolutionaries. Although he attempts to help victims with know-how garnered from a doctor, he's almost lynched as a suspected water-poisoner. To cap it all, he meets mysterious Pauline de Théus (Binoche), a woman so brave and loyal that she's prepared to travel the ravaged land alone in search of her husband. The entranced Angelo insists on delaying his return to Italy to accompany her on the quest. But is there hope? Rappeneau's follow-up to Cyrano de Bergerac is a sumptuous costumer adapted from another literary favourite (one of Jean Giono's 'Hussar' novels). He avoids the static pictorialism that afflicts most heritage movies by focusing on dynamic action and using a speedy, kinetic camera and cutting style. Sadly, however, this runs the risk of turning what is clearly intended to be a serious romance into a lusty romp. Binoche's customary gravitas lends the proceedings some emotional depth, while Martinez makes for a handsome, energetic hero. The Provençal villages and landscapes look good (as usual), but in the end there's not enough development, thematic or otherwise, to sustain interest. GA

Hussy

(Matthew Chapman, 1979, GB) Helen Mirren, John Shea, Daniel Chasin, Murray Salem, Paul Angelis, Jenny Runacre, Patti Boulaye.
94 min.
A love story requiring wads of Kleenex – if not for dabbing at the eyes, then for stuffing in the mouth to stifle frequent yawns – Hussy follows the path of true love as it never runs smooth for a whore with a heart of mould (Mirren) and the lighting man at the nightclub she operates. Set against the sex, drugs and chicken-in-the-basket ambience of London's niteries, their attempts to find happiness (like the scriptwriter's efforts to avoid clichés) get bogged down in a welter of increasingly banal plot devices. A violence-crazed ex-lover, a coke-crazed ex-friend, and a football-crazed 10-year-old son do all they can to mess things up, but like Mirren's virulent essays at acting, it's never quite enough. FL

Hustle

(Robert Aldrich, 1975, US) Burt Reynolds, Catherine Deneuve, Ben Johnson, Paul Winfield, Eileen Brennan, Eddie Albert, Ernest Borgnine, Catherine Bach, Jack Carter.
118 min.
Remarkable contemporary film noir that cuts the dirt and corruption of Los Angeles with a strain of allusions to (and, in the case of Reynolds' cop, illusions of) European romance. A perverse network of lies, guilts and evasions encompasses even Reynolds' love for hooker Deneuve, despite his misguided sense that he can exorcise one world to gain access to another by pursuing a spiralling investigation into the death of a call-girl on behalf of her dangerously distraught father. The toughly ironic parallels Aldrich imposes on Steve Shagan's customarily bitter script draw out a sense that everyone is hustling masochistically for impossible dreams; most audaciously, if the love story is seen as central, Aldrich provides Reynolds and Deneuve with the ultimate tinsel role model of Lelouch's A Man and a Woman. PT

Hustler, The

(Robert Rossen, 1961, US) Paul Newman, Jackie Gleason, George C Scott, Piper Laurie, Myron McCormick, Murray Hamilton, Michael Constantine.
135 min. b/w.
Newman is Fast Eddie, doing his best to convince the world that he can take on Minnesota Fats (Gleason) at pool and walk away with the world title. As always with Walter Tevis (the author of the original book), it takes defeat, and a longish dark night of the soul with Laurie, a drunken, lame waif of a woman, before he can summon the self-respect to return to battle. Rossen allows much space to the essentially concentrated, enclosed scenes of the film, and so it rests solidly on its performances. A wonderful hymn to the last true era when men of substance played pool with a vengeance. CPea

Hustler White

(Bruce LaBruce/Rick Castro, 1996, US) Tony Ward, Bruce LaBruce, Alex Austin, Kevin Kramer, Ron Athey, Glen Meadmore, Ivar Johnson.
79 min.
Bruce LaBruce surfaces somewhere closer to the mainstream with this picaresque LA story. There are no women and, no drugs (and no AIDS-consciousness) in this sideways spin on the rituals of meeting cute. But there is LaBruce himself as visiting writer Jürgen Anger (no relation to Kenneth, as he says repeatedly), who falls for the beatific presence of fugitive hustler Ward, as the two negotiate Santa Monica Boulevard's parade of perversities. It's on the level of mid-'70s John Waters, delighting more in shock value than technical accomplishment (grungy 16mm). TJ

Hwa-om-kyong
(Hwa-eom-gyung)

(Jang Sun-Woo, 1993, SKor) Oh Tae-Kyung, Lee Hye-Young, Kim Eun-Mi, Kim Hye-Sun, Chung Soo-Young.
110 min.
Hwa-om-kyong is the Korean name of the Avatamsaka Sutra, used by Ko Eun as the title for his novel about a young man's tortuous path to Buddhist enlightenment in the India of the Fifth Century BC. Jang proves that he's not only the bad-boy provocateur of Korea's 'new cinema' but a world-class talent by reinventing Ko's novel as a commentary on present day Korea. In Jang's version a boy orphan who never ages physically journeys through the country in search of the mother he never knew; he goes from city streets and polluted dumps to the remotest areas of the country, meeting a prostitute blinded by her pimp, a political prisoner, a professor of astronomy, a Goddess of Mercy. Less a Buddhist film than a way of seeing the chaos of the present from an unexpected perspective, this is a devastating achievement. TR

Hyenas (Hyènes)

(Djibril Diop Mambety, 1992, Sen) Mansour Diouf, Ami Diakhate, Mahouredia Gueye.
110 min.
Partly based on Friedrich Dürrenmatt's play The Visit, Hyenas could be read as a simple parable about political corruption, but it's far too strange to be reduced to that. Stylistically and visually, it's reminiscent of the García Márquez-inspired film Erendira – there's the same sense of heightened unreality and (dare one say it?) magic realism. Set in a small village which mysteriously blossoms into a metropolis (ie. it's set nowhere), it's the story of a local notary shunted into the moral front line when the town is visited by one of its daughters made good – the now omnipotent grand dame Linguere. Director Mambety displays a slightly cruel comic touch as he manipulates his cast of fools and avenging deities in what seems like Africa's equivalent of a Krazy Kat landscape. Not quite fascinating, but more than intriguing. JRo

Hyenas' Sun
(Soleil des Hyènes)

(Rihda Behi, 1977, Tun/Neth) Larbi Doghmi,
Mahmoud Morsi, Habachi, Ahmed Snoussi,
Helene Catzaras.
100 min.

Tunisia turns up trumps with this rough but
quite striking study in the awful consequences of
capitalist madness and tourism in a small fishing
village. The quick-witted jump on the bandwagon with the development's German financiers, the
others tag behind as employees, deserting their
boats to sell tinned sardines and hawk postcards
to the overweight foreign funsters who crowd the
beaches. Behi, making his first full-length feature,
uses a strident visual style, with a little too much
distorted camerawork for comfort; but the film's
sense of commitment (and acidly ironic sense of
humour) helps to steady the course. GB

Hypothesis of the Stolen
Painting, The (L'Hypothèse
du Tableau Volé)

(Râul Ruiz, 1978, Fr) Jean Rougeul, Gabriel
Gascon, Chantal Paley, Jean Raynaud,
Daniel Grimm.
66 min. b/w.

For anyone sceptical about the big claims made
for Ruiz, this is the film to see. It's the equivalent
of a vintage Ken Russell arts psycho-doc, commissioned by French TV as a study of the
philosopher, novelist (and high-class pornographer) Pierre Klossowski. The result is more like
a haunted-house occult whodunit in suspended
animation. A bumbling collector of pictures takes
us on a guided tour of his *Tonnerre* collection –
not the canvases, but their weird compositions re-
enacted as tableaux vivants in a mansion and its
gardens. Between his far-fetched interpretations
of these pictures (mythological subjects with relevance to the society of the day), an enigma takes
shape that can only be explained through 'the
hypothesis...etc'. A tale of mystery and imagination that gives new meaning to the phrase 'intellectual thriller'. This is the real thing. IC

i

The Ipcress FIle

I Accuse!

(José Ferrer, 1957, GB/US) José Ferrer, Anton Walbrook, Emlyn Williams, Viveca Lindfors, Herbert Lom, Leo Genn, Donald Wolfit, David Farrar, Felix Aylmer, Harry Andrews, George Coulouris, Michael Horden, Laurence Naismith.
99 min. b/w.
MGM's version of Alfred Dreyfus' trial, imprisonment on Devil's Island, retrial, pardon and exoneration runs through the facts, and only once or twice touches on the ambiguities of the 'Dreyfus Affair' which made the infamous case, for France at the end of the 19th century, a compelling national tragedy. Ferrer, the star/director, plays Capt Dreyfus, of French military intelligence, with a contained dignity, highlighted by the histrionics of his indignant enemies (notably Lom and Wolfit). The film purrs along, helped by Freddie Young's b/w 'Scope photography and a competent all-star cast, and rises satisfyingly to its big moments, the public humiliation of Dreyfus and Emlyn Williams' impassioned rendition of Zola's noble call to arms ('J'accuse'). Scripted by Gore Vidal from a book by Nicholas Halasz, this is the sort of confident historical picture which from time to time Hollywood used to feel called upon to make, tackling big issues head on, while taking good care not to become mired in human and political paradoxes. JPy

I Am a Camera

(Henry Cornelius, 1955, GB) Julie Harris, Laurence Harvey, Shelley Winters, Anton Diffring, Lea Seidl, Tutte Lemkow.
99 min. b/w.
Julie Harris is Sally Bowles in this version of Christopher Isherwood's '30s Berlin saga (via John Van Druten's stage adaptation), later filmed as the far superior *Cabaret*. You'd hardly expect an adult drama from the director of *Genevieve*, and sure enough the end result is sadly bowdlerised and lacking any sense of the divinely decadent. (The movie which inspired the famous critical quip: 'Me no Leica.') TJ

I Am a Dancer (Un Danseur: Rudolph Nureyev)

(Pierre Jourdain, 1970, Fr) Rudolph Nureyev, Margot Fonteyn, Lynn Seymour, Deanne Bergsma, Carla Fracci.
93 min.
With a seemingly ideal subject to hand, one might have expected a film that would convey something of the excitement of disciplined movement, give some insight into the grinding commitment of a professional dancer's life. Instead, Jourdain has produced a badly lit, boringly photographed, *Vogue*-style portrait of a man with good cheek bones and a leap that regularly carries him out of the frame. Developing into a record of performances, it is useful to the archivist, but captures little of the Nureyev magic. Much the most impressive sequence is a rehearsal of Glen Tetley's 'Field Figures', watched by the choreographer and performed by Nureyev and Deanne Bergsma. Here the proximity of the camera is of real benefit, allowing exploration of this contemporary work in a way never possible over the gulf of an orchestra pit. But once again Jourdain neglects a valuable opportunity: instead of Tetley discussing his piece, which has baffled and intrigued many, we are simply offered Bryan Forbes' voice reading a narration written by John Percival. JMu

I Am a Fugitive from a Chain Gang

(Mervyn LeRoy, 1932, US) Paul Muni, Glenda Farrell, Helen Vinson, Preston Foster, Edward Ellis, Allen Jenkins.
90 min. b/w.
Muni gives a brilliant performance as a regular guy wrongly convicted of murder and subjected to the hardships and beatings of a dehumanising chain gang regime. Later, Muni escapes and makes a successful career as a civil engineer, only to be dragged back to jail some years after when his real identity is discovered. Some of the social commentary now seems a little heavy-handed, but the film still packs a hefty punch. The details of chain gang life are tough and harrowing; the scene in which the governor cites Muni's outstanding contribution to society as evidence of the character-building benefits of the chain gang system defies belief; and the downbeat ending is a killer. NF

I Am Anna Magnani (Io Sono Anna Magnani)

(Chris Vermorcken, 1979, Bel) Anna Magnani, Vittorio De Sica, Pier Paolo Pasolini, Roberto Rossellini, Luchino Visconti, Claude Autant-Lara, Marco Bellocchio, Susi Cecchi D'Amico.
100 min. b/w & col.
This conventional scrapbook biography of legendary actress Anna Magnani features clips from her performances in vaudeville, neo-realist movies and Hollywood, alongside interviews with such directors as her former husband Rossellini, and De Sica and Visconti. Apart from trotting out showbiz paeans to her human warmth, dignified resistance to '50s sex-typing and so forth, it manages glimpses of a complex life scarcely touched upon before. DMacp

I Am a Sex Addict

(Vikram Jean/John Powers, 1993, GB/US) Hubert Selby Jr.
98 min.
In America, it's said, 300,000 people are trying to break the habit of sex addiction. An off-shoot of the vogue sex-talk TV show, this documentary was deemed too explicit for the BBC. In fact, it's unsensational, but on occasion unapologetically voyeuristic. Most of the eight interviewees are sad and lonely – not so much dependent, perhaps, as just plain desperate. Hubert Selby Jr provides whimsical intellectual annotations. TCh

I Am Frigid...Why? (Je Suis Frigide...Pourquoi?)

(Max Pécas, 1972, Fr) Sandra Jullien, Marie-George Pascal, Jean-Luc Terrade, Anne Kerylen, Thierry Murzeau.
92 min.
If there's anything worse than a French underground movie, it's a French sex movie, especially those of Pécas: a less sensual director is hard to imagine, and he has a most calculated and unpleasant way of mixing instant trend into his banal little stories. Our heroine in this effort – last seen suffering from a contrary malady under the same director in *I Am a Nymphomaniac* – is frigid due to some sexual game-playing on the part of the son and daughter of her father's employer (she's just a gardener's daughter). One finishing school, accommodation agency, brothel and theatrical assistantship later, she's realised that her only hope lies with her first true love, he realises he always loved her too, and that's that. Hardly enlightening.

I Am My Own Woman (Ich bin meine eigene Frau)

(Rosa von Praunheim, 1992, Ger)
90 min.
The best yet film from the generally dodgy Rosa von Praunheim: a German equivalent to *The Naked Civil Servant*, centred on the indomitable 'Charlotte von Mahlsdorf', who has braved familial rejection, social ostracism, Nazi persecution, East German Communist persecution, and latterly skinhead persecution with a frock and a smile. Skilfully scripted and paced, the film wisely allows Charlotte herself to shine; she even wanders into reconstructed scenes from her past to correct details. Magnus Hirschfeld should be alive to see it. TR

I Am the Law

(Alexander Hall, 1938, US) Edward G Robinson, Otto Kruger, Barbara O'Neil, John Beal, Louis Jean Heydt.
83 min. b/w.
It may not be terribly good, but this feisty vehicle for Edward G plays to the star's strengths. He's a never-say-die law professor who takes on the city's racketeers, and even carries on the good fight by himself after he's removed from the post, finally putting together the evidence that mayor's son Beal is actually the local crime kingpin. TJ

I Bought a Vampire Motorcycle

(Dirk Campbell, 1989, GB) Neil Morrissey, Amanda Noar, Michael Elphick, Anthony Daniels, Andrew Powell, George Rossi, Daniel Peacock, Burt Kwouk.
105 min.
Falling somewhere between *The Evil Dead* and *Carry On Screaming*, this refreshingly effective horror spoof throws caution to the wind and entrails to the floor when hirsute biker Noddy (Morrissey) buys a Norton which turns out to be a spawn of Hades. Garagebound by day, at night the satanic cycle fuels up on the blood of Hell's Angels, traffic wardens and streetwalkers. When Noddy turns to a priest for assistance, he is met first with scepticism, then with steely resolve as the eccentric cleric (Daniels, neatly twitchy) tools up for an exorcism, God on his side and sacred Ninja weaponry in reserve. Filmed on a minute budget around Birmingham's back streets, Campbell's debut maintains a base level of quick-witted humour while ladling on grungy gore, courtesy of the Image Animation team. The uniformly respectable performances are rather overshadowed by Elphick's deadpan Inspector Cleaver (all sour-faced garlic-breathiness). Schoolboy toilet humour with teeth. MK

Ice

(Robert Kramer, 1969, US) Robert Kramer, Tom Griffin.
132 min. b/w.
A film that has gained hugely with the passage of time. It may not 'explode in people's faces like a grenade' or 'open minds like a can-opener' as Kramer has stated he wished it to, but there's no doubt that it stands alone as a sympathetic, frequently brilliant ideological thriller. Dealing with urban insurrection and armed revolt by the youth of America, Kramer's film occupies intriguingly shifting territory between documentary and science fiction. The result is a unique testament to the political consciousness of a decade. Kramer constantly astonishes with his ability to draw performances and find images that fix this particular consciousness with unnerving precision. It is beautifully shot in black-and-white. VG

Ice Castles

(Donald Wrye, 1978, US) Robby Benson, Lynn-Holly Johnson, Colleen Dewhurst, Tom Skerritt, Jennifer Warren, David Huffman.
109 min.
The pirouetting free-skater heroine, blonde nymphette Lexie Winston (Johnson), leaves backwoods Iowa for the rigorous discipline of Olympic coaching. Escaping the claustrophobia of home (where her father sees her as a substitute for her dead mother), she attains a degree of independence comparable to that of her dilettante ice hockey-playing boyfriend Nick (Benson). Aided by worldly people (the coach, a TV sportscaster), she gains success and fame – at a price: the loss of her native innocence (competition is a cutthroat business), the estrangement of Nick, and finally the tragic loss of her eyesight through a fall. What this three-hanky weepie really says is 'Don't get ideas above your station', for Lexie can only come to terms with her handicap by re-accepting the dominance of her father and Nick, and rejecting her ambitions and herself. You'd have to be blind to miss the moral. FF

Ice Cold in Alex

(J Lee Thompson, 1958, GB) John Mills, Harry Andrews, Anthony Quayle, Sylvia Syms, Diane Clare.
129 min. b/w.
It may not be a very good film, but as Raymond Durgnat demonstrates in *A Mirror for England*, it's an interesting account of 'Britain's sense of inferiority in the post war world'. After the fall of Tobruk in World War II, a battle-fatigued army captain (Mills), a sergeant-major (Andrews) and two nurses drive an ambulance back to Alexandria. On the way they pick up a Dutch South African officer (Quayle) who does everything brilliantly. He's pointedly tougher and more sensible than the suicidally, and manslaughterously, hysteric captain. He's pointedly stronger than the strong sergeant-major, and he's also, it seems, a brilliant diplomat (twice persuading ugly-looking panzers who've captured them to release them). Even when they've found out that he's a German spy, they reckon he's a decent chap as well, having saved their lives several times over. So they save his, by pretending he wasn't in Allied uniform when they caught him. The capability ranking is unmistakeable: Germans or colonial, top; loyal NCO, next; English officer last. PH

Iceland (aka Katina)

(H Bruce Humberstone, 1942, US) Sonja Henie, John Payne, Jack Oakie, Felix Bressart, Osa Massen.
79 min. b/w.

A sluggish comedy-romance with Payne as a marine stationed in Iceland and Henie working her tiresome pixie charm overtime as the local miss who determinedly snares him. Even the skating routines, loaded with fulsome tributes to the good old USA, are tough going. TM

Iceman Cometh, The (Jidong Qixia)

(Clarence Fok Yiu-Leung, 1989, HK) Yuen Biao, Maggie Cheung, Yuen Wah, Wong Jing, Yuan Kui.
114 min.
For reasons too complicated to explain, ancient antagonists Ah Ching (Yuen Biao, the good guy) and Fung San (Yuen Wah, the bad guy) are frozen alive in a glacier. The modern scientists who discover their entwined bodies take them as proof that homosexuality existed in imperial China, but no love is lost between them when they are defrosted and reanimated in present day Hong Kong. This is the cue for a barrage of serio-comic fight scenes, Buddhist mythology and special visual effects, much enhanced by Maggie Cheung's way with the stock character of a brassy hooker. TR

Ice Palace

(Vincent Sherman, 1960, US) Richard Burton, Robert Ryan, Carolyn Jones, Martha Hyer, Jim Backus, Ray Danton, Shirley Knight.
143 min.
Edna Ferber's sprawling novels and populous plays were naturals for never-mind-the-quality-feel-the-width Hollywood (and occasionally produced such happy results as *Giant*, *Dinner at Eight* or the numerous versions of *Cimarron* and *Showboat*). This monster about the founding of Alaska, however, was well and truly betrayed, freezing into a series of icy confrontations between man of progress Burton and simple rival Ryan amid the Warners studio snow. Soap specialist Sherman had already logged the entry of Texas into the Union in 1951's *Lone Star*. PT

Ice Palace, The (Is-slottet)

(Per Blom, 1987, Nor) Line Storesund, Hilde Nyeggen Martinsen, Merete Moen, Sigrid Huun.
78 min.
In the depths of a deep-frozen Norwegian winter, two just-adolescent girls, Siss and Unn, sneak off to Unn's attic bedroom and undress for each other. Although nothing concrete happens, the following day Unn is so overwhelmed by guilt that she runs off to a nearby frozen waterfall, and wandering through caves of ice, finally lays down and dies. The rest of the film focuses on Siss' almost wordless grieving, unable to tell the town elders why her friend disappeared, becoming progressively numbed herself by her inability to understand what has happened. With little dialogue and minimal action, Blom uses the landscape of winter to express strong longing and stronger repression. A cross between *Picnic at Hanging Rock* and the poetic melancholia of an Ibsen play, *The Ice Palace* is a bitter-sweet dream of snow and shadow, beautiful to watch. RS

Ice Station Zebra

(John Sturges, 1968, US) Rock Hudson, Ernest Borgnine, Patrick McGoohan, Jim Brown, Tony Bill, Gerald S O'Loughlin, Lloyd Nolan.
152 min.
A passable yarn about a race for a Russian satellite that comes down near the North Pole, blighted by some heavy-handed irony. Borgnine hams outrageously, Hudson manages better than you'd expect, and McGoohan turns in a good performance. It's not saying much, but Sturges has been responsible for two of the more successful Alistair MacLean adventures, this and *The Satan Bug*. CPe

Ice Storm, The

(Ang Lee, 1997, US) Kevin Kline, Sigourney Weaver, Joan Allen, Jamey Sheridan, Christina Ricci, Elijah Wood.
113 min.
With its meticulous script by James Schamus, strong performances and elegant direction, this tragi-comic look at the lives of a couple of comfortably-off small town Connecticut families in the winter of 1973 is a gem of witty, perceptive observation. Unbeknown to Allen his wife, Kline is car-

rying on with neighbour Weaver, an affair discovered when he comes across his teenage daughter Ricci playing her own sexually explorative games with Weaver's sons. Cue marital discord, adolescent disenchantment and family crises in a thoroughly enjoyable blend of comedy and melodrama which is spot-on both in its evocative recreation of the habits, fads and attitudes of the early '70s, and in its sense of an America at a particular point in its socio-political history. GA

I Changed My Sex

see Glen or Glenda?

Icicle Thief (Ladri di Saponette)

(Maurizio Nichetti, 1989, It) Maurizio Nichetti, Caterina Sylos Labini, Heidi Komarek, Federico Rizzo, Renato Scarpa.
98 min. b/w & col.
The director of a monochrome *hommage* to *Bicycle Thieves* is invited on to a TV programme to discuss his film before a screening. But during the transmission, his movie is interrupted by colour commercials, the characters slip from one world into another, and eventually the director himself intervenes to sort out the mess. Nichetti's wacky satire on the big screen/small screen war is technically very effective, but his own manic performance as the mustachioed director is a major irritant. Some good in-jokes (like a housewife complaining about boring introductions to films on TV) help to pass the time. DT

I Confess

(Alfred Hitchcock, 1953, US) Montgomery Clift, Anne Baxter, Karl Malden, Brian Aherne, OE Hasse, Dolly Haas.
95 min. b/w.
One of Hitchcock's most overtly 'serious' and portentous murder plots, about a Catholic priest who faces the death penalty because of his refusal to break the secrecy of the confessional. Its theological theme and exploration of personal guilt once made it a cardinal point in the pro-Hitchcock arguments of the French critics, notably Chabrol and Rohmer. But now that most critics accept Hitchcock as more than just entertainment, the more strained and serious movies look a lot less formidable than the so-called roller-coaster rides like *Psycho*. Clift (as the priest) and Malden (as the cop) make this worth watching, but it's heavy going at times and the more literary aspects of the script, adapted from Paul Anthelme's play (written in 1902), are uncinematic to say the least. DP

I Could Go On Singing

(Ronald Neame, 1963, GB) Judy Garland, Dirk Bogarde, Jack Klugman, Aline MacMahon, Gregory Phillips, Pauline Jameson.
100 min.
Well-built people have been known to keel over under the intense glare of Garland's emotions in this old-fashioned tug-of-love melodrama (her last film). And the narrative provides very little shelter, as she plays a famous singer topping the bill at the London Palladium, struggling to wrest her illegitimate son away from his surgeon father (Bogarde). Naturally, this is required viewing for Garland devotees, but with Neame's glacial, humourless manner of directing it's hardly the film if you just want fun. GB

i.d.

(Philip Davis, 1994, GB/Ger) Reece Dinsdale, Warren Clarke, Claire Skinner, Richard Graham, Perry Fenwick, Philip Glenister, Saskia Reeves, Sean Pertwee, Charles De'Ath, Philip Davis.
107 min.
An impressive first feature following a group of undercover policemen who attach themselves to the louts who follow a fictional second-division London football club. John (Dinsdale) is your average ambitious cop, early twenties, eye on promotion, a charmer with a nice wife at home, but still with some mileage in the pulling and rucking stakes. The film takes him through the stages of brutalisation, from learning how to drink, smoke and fight dirty, through the addiction of fandom, to eventual disintegration as he loses family, dignity and much more in a descent into the kind of violence he's been sent to prevent. The film has weaknesses: sometimes the low budget shows, and there are irritating lapses (the fans'

scarves are all brand new and the same design), while the script's notes on aggression are far more convincing than its attempt to tackle racism – almost a politically correct afterthought. But Dinsdale's riveting, and the supports, notably Clarke's tattoo-encrusted, skinhead pub landlord and Skinner's housewife, more than make up the numbers. Intriguing stuff, and as English as a cold bacon butty. SGr

Ideal Husband, An

(Alexander Korda, 1947, GB) Paulette Goddard, Michael Wilding, Diana Wynyard, Hugh Williams, C Aubrey Smith, Glynis Johns, Constance Collier, Michael Medwin.
96 min.
Producer/director Korda had fellow Hungarian Lajos Biro adapt Wilde's play for this rather turgid screen version, which has imported American star Goddard as a reasonable Mrs Cheveley, the Victorian adventuress whose blackmail attempt on politico Williams is stymied by nobleman Wilding's decisive counter-attack. Lots of technical gloss on display, including costumes by Cecil Beaton and Georges Périnal's elegant camerawork, but the film is so reverent towards its source material it's almost embalmed. TJ

Identification of a Woman (Identificazione di una Donna)

(Michelangelo Antonioni, 1982, It/Fr) Tomas Milian, Daniela Silverio, Christine Boisson, Sandra Monteleoni, Giampaolo Saccarola.
131 min.
Very much the film of an elder statesman arrogantly conscious of being the most 'modern' director of his generation. It is a contemporary love story – based upon a film-maker's chance encounters with two women – designed to bury the controversies of his courageous video manifesto (*The Oberwald Mystery*) and to regain access to Hollywood. Visually this is perhaps Antonioni's most beautiful film to date, effortlessly fleshing out familiar themes around the difficulties of establishing relationships in our times. But there is much more. Most notably, a refreshing irony prevents the hardened art house pundit from wallowing in nostalgia and the metaphysics of 'portentous messages'. Emphasis is very much on the 'investigation' suggested by the title rather than possible meanings to be derived from it. Everything in the film comes in twos: two women from different social and sexual backgrounds, two films about to be made, two extraordinary key sequences – the first enshrouded in thick fog, the other in the desolation of the Venetian lagoon. In the end the central character chooses not to make his film about the 'ideal woman' but to lose himself in a space oddity with skull-like spacecrafts journeying towards the sun. Probably not a sign of Spielbergian things to come from Antonioni – more a subdued admission from the 'apostle of incommunicability' that the best place for alienation these days is in megabuck fantasies. DR

I Died a Thousand Times

(Stuart Heisler, 1955, US) Jack Palance, Shelley Winters, Lori Nelson, Lee Marvin, Gonzales Gonzales, Lon Chaney, Earl Holliman.
109 min.
While not a patch upon Walsh's version of WR Burnett's *High Sierra*, of which this is a remake, there are still entertaining moments in this tale of a con out to pull one last bank job before retiring. It's often too talky and lethargically paced, but Heisler has an enthusiastic eye for spectacle (notably in the climax up in the mountains), while Palance and Winters, though no real replacement for Bogart and Ida Lupino, demonstrate their own rough charm. GA

Idiot, The (Hakuchi)

(Akira Kurosawa, 1951, Jap) Masayuki Mori, Toshiro Mifune, Setsuko Hara, Takashi Shimura, Yoshiko Kuga, Chieko Higashiyama.
165 min. b/w.
Kurosawa's adaptation from his favourite novelist Dostoievsky has an undeserved reputation as a failure. True, it has a plot which is at first extremely difficult to follow if you don't know the novel, but its literal faithfulness (transferred from St Petersburg to modern Hokkaido) hardly deserves rebuke. The acting has an eerie, trance-like quality; and the perpetually snowbound sets

and locations, warmed by scarcely adequate fires and bulky clothing, together with a continually turbulent music soundtrack, make up the perfect expressionist metaphor for the emotional lives of Dostoievsky's characters. Tom Milne has noted similarities to Dreyer's *Gertrud*; like that film, it repays the initial effort required to get into it. RM

Idiots, The (Idioterne)
(Lars von Trier, 1998, Den) Bodil Jørgensen, Jens Albinus, Louise Hassing, Troels Lyby, Nikolaj Lie Kaas.
117 min.
Often looking rather like a filmed acting workshop, von Trier's first movie made according to the back-to-basics 'Dogma 95' manifesto centres on the emotional and social dynamics of a group of people who, for various reasons, go around pretending to be mentally and/or physically handicapped. What little plot there is charts the tensions that lead some of them to consider leaving the cult, but the film's real interest lies in its exploration of different kinds of 'performance', and in its often very funny satirical look at the way 'normal' society treats 'abnormal' people. Emotionally and intellectually, the movie never quite delivers on its promise, and the frequent views of the boom, the shadow of the camera crew and so forth are irritating distractions (manifesto or not, this is *not* 'pure' cinema), but it is consistently intriguing, involving, and finally quite unlike anything else. GA

Idiot's Delight
(Clarence Brown, 1939, US) Clark Gable, Norma Shearer, Edward Arnold, Charles Coburn, Joseph Schildkraut, Burgess Meredith, Virginia Grey.
105 min. b/w.
Crass adaptation of Robert Sherwood's pacifist play, which not only reduces Sherwood's political arguments to a few whimpers about futility (they weren't any too hot in the first place), but adds a prologue revealing how the broken-down hoofer (Gable) and the mysterious Russian mistress of an armaments king (Shearer) had met and fallen in love when she too was just an all-American showbiz hopeful. What we are then faced with is simply the cloyingly predictable romance when they meet again – she now shorn of all dramatic mystery and all too obviously ripe for comeuppance because she put ambition before love. To make matters worse, the fateful romance takes place in a hotel somewhere in Europe with war hammering ominously at the doors: a hollow Ship of Fools peopled by the usual token selection of rats about to desert (armaments king, German scientist, fervent Communist, etc). Although Clarence Brown works hard to cast his usual elegant spell, the film remains as dead as a doornail, with the exception of one scene in which Gable does a delightfully shoddy top hat and white tie Astaire routine, raising morale in the audience if not the hotel guests. TM

Idle on Parade
(John Gilling, 1959, US) Anthony Newley, William Bendix, Anne Aubrey, Lionel Jeffries, David Lodge, Sidney James.
92 min. b/w.
An interesting curiosity, this is a kind of folksy British parody of Elvis Presley's controversial drafting into the US Army: Newley plays a prototype rock singer who is called up, with all the ensuing complications. In retrospect it all seems very quaint, but it was the film that launched Newley (up to that point a straight actor) on a singing career; and the rock songs that Newley sings ('Idle Rock-a-boogie', 'I've Waited So Long', etc) were great hits in their time. DP

I Don't Kiss
see J'embrasse pas

I Don't Want to Be Born (aka The Devil Within Her)
(Peter Sasdy, 1975, GB) Joan Collins, Eileen Atkins, Donald Pleasence, Ralph Bates, Caroline Munro, Hilary Mason.
94 min.
Sasdy, once thought by many to be the great black hope for British horror films, here turned in – aptly enough – an abortion. Comparing unfavourably with *It's Alive* (made the previous year), it is both derivative and disastrous in every respect: a poor idea (Joan Collins gives birth to a

big baby possessed by a devil whose medium is a dwarf she once spurned), an abominable screenplay by Stanley Price ('I keep getting these awful premonitions'), ludicrous acting (poor Eileen Atkins as an Italian nun), and worst of all, Sasdy's direction. The market for this film must have been planned as the Continent or the States, because almost every foot of film not concerned with the baby is travelogue at its most banal – extraneous shots of Westminster and Oxford Street, plugs for Fortnum & Mason and Holiday Inns. Completing this sorry tale of rip-off is borrowing from *The Exorcist*, Hilary Mason from *Don't Look Now*, and any number of details from Amicus, Hammer and Swinging London horrors. Give it a wide berth. AN

I Escaped from Devil's Island
(William Witney, 1973, US) Jim Brown, Christopher George, Richard Rust, James Luisi, Bob Harris, Paul Richards.
89 min.
Despite an air of unrelieved cruddiness, relentless machismo, bad acting and over-insistent animal imagery of a dog-eats-dog nature, this Corman-produced epic, unlike *Papillon*, at least adopts the right approach. As the title suggests, the film is very much on the level of those old 'True Adventure' stories. Jim Brown has no apparent motive for escaping, but then prison life is painted in sufficiently graphic terms for that not to matter. Favouritism and brutality are rife, prisoners are prepared to rat on each other, and the film admits (albeit crudely) an aura of homosexuality and political agitation that was never properly allowed to infiltrate *Papillon*. Life after the escape looks like a rejected draft of the other film, and includes an encounter with lepers, a tumble with a native girl, and an equally perfunctory ending. Not exactly recommended, unless you misspent your youth reading stories like 'How I Wrestled with a Python and Won'. CA

If...
(Lindsay Anderson, 1968, GB) Malcolm McDowell, David Wood, Richard Warwick, Robert Swann, Christine Noonan.
111 min. b/w & col.
A modern classic in which Anderson minutely captures both the particular ethos of a public school and the general flavour of any structured community, thus achieving a clear allegorical force without sacrificing a whit of his exploration of an essentially British institution. The impeccable logic of the conclusion is in no way diminished by having been lifted from Vigo's *Zéro de Conduite*, made thirty-five years earlier. *If...* was also a timely film – shooting began two months before the events of May 1968 in Paris. Along with *The White Bus*, it put Anderson into a pretty high league; the major disappointment of *O Lucky Man!*, followed by the disastrous *Britannia Hospital*, took him back out of it again. SG

If All the Guys in the World...
see Si tous les gars du monde...

If I Had a Million
(Ernst Lubitsch/Norman Taurog/Stephen Roberts/Norman Z McLeod/James Cruze/William A Seiter/H Bruce Humberstone, 1932, US) Gary Cooper, George Raft, WC Fields, Charles Laughton, Jack Oakie, Charlie Ruggles, Mary Boland, Wynne Gibson, Gene Raymond, May Robson.
88 min. b/w.
The title tells all in this episodic entertainment (variations on the theme of what happens to assorted characters each left a million dollars by a wealthy eccentric), written by eighteen pairs of hands and directed by seven, from cool geniuses like Lubitsch to jolly hacks like Humberstone. The famous Lubitsch episode in which Laughton's mild-mannered clerk gives his boss the raspberry now warrants nothing stronger than a wet smile, but the WC Fields episode is still fun (he goes on a joyride in various old cars, bashing them vengefully against every passing road-hog). The non-comic sequences, however, are all very painful; this is one of those curate's eggs with far more curate than egg. GB

I.F. Stone's Weekly
(Jerry Bruck Jr, 1973, US) I F Stone; narrator: Tom Wicker.
62 min. b/w.

A fascinating portrait of the maverick Washington journalist who, blacklisted during the McCarthy era, started his own paper (running it for some seventeen years) and became a master political gadfly. Stone himself is a delight: witty, irreverent, forever puncturing the lies he claims it is in the nature of all politicians to tell. Brilliantly edited throughout, the real triumph of the film is the way it intercuts Stone's comments with newsreel footage to demonstrate how much of a point he has. TM

If These Walls Could Talk
(Nancy Savoca/Cher, 1996, US) Demi Moore, Shirley Knight; Sissy Spacek, Xander Berkeley; Cher, Anne Heche.
94 min.
A triptych of half-hour films, set in the same house, in 1952, 1974 and 1996, with new occupants reflecting rather obviously the changing times. (Cher makes her directing debut in the third film.) The theme is abortion and the sometimes life-threatening responsibility faced by pregnant women: nurse Demi Moore widowed in the war and pregnant after a fling; harassed housewife/mature student Spacek; and student Anne Heche, who has no home and little income. The films suffer from dramatic compression (there's enough social context to service a soap opera series) and a didactic liberal tone, but they're fleshed out with strong performances and a keen sense of the women's dilemmas. Cher casts herself as a clinic doctor (in bulletproof vest) who literally takes her life in her hands in the fight against hysterical pro-life Christians. WH

If You Feel Like Singing
see Summer Stock

I Hired a Contract Killer
(Aki Kaurismäki, 1990, Fin/Swe) Jean-Pierre Léaud, Margi Clarke, Kenneth Colley, Trevor Bowen, Nicky Tesco, Charles Cork, Serge Reggiani, Peter Graves.
79 min.
This droll thriller displays the same melancholy vision as Kaurismäki's brilliant *Ariel*. After 15 years as a London waterworks clerk, French émigré Henri (Léaud) is made redundant. Lonely and friendless, he hires a hit-man to put him out of his misery; but after meeting flower-seller Margaret (Clarke) in a pub, he tries to cancel the contract. Shot in English on barely recognisable London locations, the film's oblique camera angles, moody colours and short, sharp scenes create a stylised world which still has the feel of everyday life. Kaurismäki's plots and dialogue often give the impression of having been improvised at the last moment, but his framing and narrative concision are extremely rigorous. He also allows lots of space for some sympathetic performances, in particular the laconic Léaud, Colley as the hangdog assassin, Tesco and Cork as a pair of small-time villains. Meanwhile, Timo Salminen's atmospheric images once again catch the seedy ambience of a B movie world where talk is cheap but love is precious. In short, it plays like an Ealing comedy on downers. NF

I Huvet på en Gammal Gubbe
see Out of an Old Man's Head

Iki Kadin
see Two Women

Ikiru (Living/To Live)
(Akira Kurosawa, 1952, Jap) Takashi Shimura, Nobuo Kaneko, Kyoko Seki, Makoto Kobori, Kumeko Urabe.
143 min. b/w.
Easy to patronise as a classic of humanism; a celebration of the intrinsic nobility of human nature as a humble civil servant, following a drunken bout of panic, aimless wandering, and odd encounters on learning that he is dying of cancer, finally discovers a meaning to his empty life by patiently pushing through a project to turn a city dump into a children's playground. An intensely moving film all the same, elegiac and sometimes quirkishly funny in the manner of Kurosawa's elective model, John Ford. Shimura is superb in the central role, and not the least of Kurosawa's achievements is his triumphant avoidance of happy ending uplift; in the crucial (and beautiful) shot of the old man sitting huddled alone in the

park on a child's swing, as the snow falls and he croons happily to himself as he waits for death, the sense of desolation remains complete. TM

I Know What You Did Last Summer

(Jim Gillespie, 1997, US) Jennifer Love Hewitt, Sarah Michelle Geller, Freddie Prince Jr, Anne Heche.
101 min.
This crude slasher movie from *Scream* scriptwriter Kevin Williamson fails to spice up the old recipe and is far too sparing with the basic ingredient – the gruesome slaughter of nauseating American teenagers by a terrifying killer. Here a hook-handed fisherman (a sort of transmogrified Cap'n Birds Eye) terrorises four teenagers involved in a hushed-up hit-and-run accident. There are shoals of red herrings, lots of dumb 'Behind you!'-type scares, and not a scrap of imagination. Heche adds a dash of class as a weird country hick haunted by her brother's suicide, but otherwise the bland teenage cast simply go through the motions. NF

I Know Where I'm Going!

(Michael Powell/Emeric Pressburger, 1945, GB) Wendy Hiller, Roger Livesey, Finlay Currie, Pamela Brown, John Laurie, Norman Shelley, Nancy Price, Catherine Lacey, George Carney.
92 min. b/w.
Alongside *A Canterbury Tale*, Powell's most eloquent tribute to the mysteries of the British landscape. Hiller is the headstrong young girl who travels to Scotland to marry a wealthy but elderly man, only to be confused and distracted by the presence of dashing young laird Livesey. Full of well-integrated symbols (islands, hawks, a whirlpool) and lyrically shot in monochrome by Erwin Hillier, it's all quite beautiful, combining romance, comedy, suspense and a sense of the supernatural to winning effect. GA

Ile au trésor, L' (Treasure Island)

(Raúl Ruiz, 1991, Fr/US) Melvil Poupaud, Martin Landau, Vic Tayback, Lou Castel, Jeffrey Kime, Anna Karina, Jean-François Stévenin, Charles Schmidt, Jean-Pierre Léaud, Pedro Armendariz Jr.
115 min.
Not so much an adaptation as an extended riff on a Robert Louis Stevenson standard. It begins with young Jim Hawkins – who's really called Jonathan, played in excruciating dubbed American by the angelic Poupaud in the English language version – watching his favourite TV serial, and then making the rest up from life when a power failure cuts him off in mid-episode. The hotel where he lives with his ill-matched parents (Castel and Karina) is visited by a motley crew of salt-encrusted sea-wrecks, and by Léaud as Jim's mentor in narrative, or as his alter ego. Midway, the film turns into something like a traditional seafaring yarn, and takes a decided downturn from the wildly artificed first half. But through the morass of entangled story, false clues, and literary references to Borges, Melville and quite possibly Thomas Pynchon, it weaves a dense web of allusions that carry it away from straight narrative into a strange terrain that's part dream, part psychoanalysis, part film theory, and several parts piss-take. Delayed for five years by litigation, cut down from the original four-hour conception, it's extraordinary, if patchy. JRo

I Led Two Lives

see Glen or Glenda?

I Like It Like That

(Darnell Martin, 1994, US) Lauren Vélez, Jon Seda, Griffin Dunne, Rita Moreno, Tomas Melly, Desiree Casado, Jesse Borrego.
106 min.
Chino (Seda), a monstrous husband, is outraged to discover that his wife Lisette (Vélez) wants to work in order to pay for a new stereo. When their Puerto Rican neighbourhood in the South Bronx is hit by a blackout, he goes looting to procure the hi-fi himself, but is caught and jailed – leaving Lisette to raise their three children alone. Helped by her transsexual brother Alexis (who lends her his false breasts), she heads uptown to try to make it as a model. A series of chance encounters

gets her a job in a record company working for Stephen Price (Dunne), who falls in lust with her, and drives her home in his red Lamborghini, much to the displeasure of Chino's mother (Moreno). An impressive fast-paced first feature. Director Darnell Martin emerges as an unusually perceptive chronicler of fragile sexual relationships and complex family ties, and draws strong performances from an inspired cast. A singular, hard-edged romantic comedy. ACh

I Like You, I Like You Very Much (Anata-ga suki desu, dai suki des')

(Hiroyuki,Oki 1994, Jap) Shibuya Kazunori, Kitakaze Hisanori, Nishimoto Kazufumi, Hiroyuki Oki.
58 min.
Made by the most high-profile of Japan's avant-garde film-makers, this is in the same freewheeling style as Hiroyuki's Oki personal short films: hand-held camerawork, refocusing, reframing and adjustment to the camera aperture. These informal methods are used to tell the committedly everyday story of a relationship between two boys which threatens to break apart when one impulsively cruises a straight guy on the street. Shot in the port city of Kochi, the film offers a panorama of small-town gay lives from quasi-monogamous partnerships to night-groping in the park. Highly credible as an account of a glitch in a relationship, it strikes me as one of the most candid films ever made about the vagaries of male desire, albeit with a deliciously romantic ending. TR

I Live in Fear (Ikimono no Kiroku)

(Akira Kurosawa, 1955, Jap) Toshiro Mifune, Eiko Miyoshi, Takashi Shimura, Yutaka Sada, Minoru Chiaki, Haruko Togo.
113 min. b/w.
Made between *Seven Samurai* and *Throne of Blood*, this contemporary social problem movie is Kurosawa's least commercially successful work. Mifune is the ageing, patriarchal head of a Tokyo family who, terrified at the prospect of a nuclear war, decides to sell up the family business and emigrate to a farm in Brazil. With Mifune uncomfortable playing a character twice his real age, and the character himself rendered incoherent by a script which seems uncertain whether it's him or society which is insane, a volunteer court official (Shimura) – required to adjudicate in the ensuing family squabble – a little awkwardly assumes the role of moral centre. It's a problematic film, wearing its uncertainties on its sleeve; but whether shooting in long takes or cutting the footage from multiple camera shooting, Kurosawa remains the cinema's supremely humanist emotional manipulator. See it and worry. RM

I'll Be Seeing You

(William Dieterle, 1944, US) Ginger Rogers, Joseph Cotten, Shirley Temple, Spring Byington, Tom Tully, John Derek.
85 min. b/w.
Interestingly cast mainstream melodrama with Rogers a late replacement for Joan Fontaine as the woman shell-shocked soldier Cotten falls in love with before her 17-year-old daughter (Shirley Temple in her first adult role) blurts out a well-kept secret that threatens to destroy their romance. The contrivance is handled with a good deal of dignity by the ever-refined Dieterle, but producer Selznick wasn't satisfied with Temple's key monologue and hired in George Cukor to reshoot the crucial scene. Spot the joins? TJ

Ill Fares the Land

(Bill Bryden, 1982, GB) Fulton Mackay, David Hayman, Robert Stephens, Morag Hood, JG Devlin.
102 min.
From Michael Powell to Bills Forsyth and Douglas, Scotland endures as the resonant repository for British cinematic mythology. An impressive addition to that tradition, this is a moving, factually-based investigation of the last gasps of life on remote St Kilda. Besieged by hunger, inbreeding, and a remarkable lack of contact with the outside world, the five families remaining in 1929 finally wrench themselves from their wild, beautiful island in a semi-voluntary act of evacuation to the mainland. The film both celebrates

the close-knit community's daily life and examines why, in its reluctance to adapt, it could not but disappear. Neither pastoral idyll nor a 'we had it tough' catalogue of survival strategies, it's more a laconic account of the strengths and strictures of family and ritual – the Sabbath, funerals, a wedding, work and coming-of-age. Here, indeed, lie the connections with Bryden's script for Walter Hill's *The Long Riders*, and with his stylistic idol John Ford. GA

Illicit Interlude

see Sommarlek

Ill Met by Moonlight (aka Night Ambush)

(Michael Powell, 1957, GB) Dirk Bogarde, Marius Goring, David Oxley, Cyril Cusack, Laurence Payne, Wolfe Morris, Michael Gough.
104 min. b/w.
It's sad that Powell and his long-standing collaborator Emeric Pressburger were forced into the grind of British war movies so soon after they had managed to transcend the limitations of most local cinema in movies like *The Red Shoes* and *A Matter of Life and Death*. Like their *The Battle of the River Plate*, this is superior of its kind, but that isn't enough to lift it into the areas that Powell and Pressburger mastered a few years earlier. It's based on an actual incident in World War II: British officer Bogarde is working with partisans in occupied Crete, and decides to kidnap the German commander-in-chief to boost the war effort. General Kreipe (Goring) is duly hijacked and trekked across country by night into custody on a British vessel. The scrupulous reconstruction is all pluck, stiff upper lips and mutual respect for one's foe. It's distinguished by Powell's sense of landscape (as in *49th Parallel*), and by a vigorous Theodorakis score. TR

Illumination (Illuminacja)

(Krzysztof Zanussi, 1972, Pol) Stanislaw Latallo, Monika Denisiewicz-Olbrychska, Malgorzata Pritulak, Edward Zebrowski, Jan Skotnicki.
91 min.
Zanussi's film follows its questing hero, a physics student, through his twenties. A meditation on the human condition, its title is taken from medieval philosophy. The hero's development is episodic and familiar: student days, first sexual encounter, the death of a friend, a marriage that falters and recovers, economic security – a development marked by the gradual abandoning of his search for absolutes. With maturity comes a limiting of horizons and the beginning of decline. The film's depth and individual perception stem from its background of physics, mathematics and medicine, which transforms it into an objective look at the human species. The rapid editing and self-conscious technique is sometimes irritating, but more often proves sufficiently provocative to hold attention. CPe

Illusions

(Julie Dash, 1984, US) Lonette McKee, Ned Bellamy, Rosanne Katon.
34 min.
In which McKee repeats her black-seen-as-a-white role from *The Cotton Club*, this time as a '40s Hollywood producer's assistant determined to fight the way the movies rewrite history (particularly war propaganda) without reference to blacks. Some nice lines, performances and music, although the narrative could be much tighter, and – as in so many low-budget independents – the quality of the sound recording is abysmal. In general, what tends to be described as 'worthy'. GA

Illustrated Man, The

(Jack Smight, 1968, US) Rod Steiger, Claire Bloom, Robert Drivas, Don Dubbins.
103 min.
A much maligned film, loosely derived from Ray Bradbury's collection of short stories and spinning out a fascinating triangle relationship which ranges disconcertingly through past, present and future, and in which the three participants never meet on the same time plane. A young hitchhiker (Drivas) encounters a stranger on the road (Steiger) whose skin is covered with fantastic tattoos which foretell the future. They were done, he says, by a witch-

woman (Bloom) who disappeared 'back into the future', leaving him to roam the earth like the Wandering Jew in quest of vengeance against the woman who made him an outcast. Fascinated, already falling in love, the young man begins to conjure an image of the witch; and through the Illustrated Man's tattoos, sees three stories from the distant future in which he, the witch and the Illustrated Man play the leading roles, all hingeing obliquely on the betrayal of love, with sometimes one character, sometimes another, becoming the victim. Time suddenly ceases to exist, and the characters are caught in a reenactment of the story of the Garden of Eden (or of Cain and Abel) over a campfire where the Illustrated Man and the young hitchhiker fight a mental/physical battle over their enigmatic, absent Eve. Hesitantly directed by Smight, the script is nevertheless genuinely imaginative, and both settings and performances are admirable. TM

Illustrious Corpses (Cadaveri Eccellenti)

(Francesco Rosi, 1975, It/Fr) Lino Ventura, Alain Cuny, Paolo Bonacelli, Marcel Bozzuffi, Tina Aumont, Max von Sydow, Fernando Rey, Charles Vanel, Renato Salvatori.
120 min.
While not as immediately tough as Rosi's political case histories, Illustrious Corpses burns on a slow fuse. A lone policeman (Ventura) investigates the murders of prominent legal figures. But as he stumbles on a conspiracy of national dimensions, the mystery thriller expands into an exploration of the mysteries of political power. The machinations of both Right and Left are set against the constant fact of human mortality (as referred to in the film's title). And a sense of the past is ever present: huge public monuments sit in judgment on the grey men who move through their corridors of power. What impresses most are scenes displaying Rosi's bravura: an obsessive judge shot in his tomb-like mansion; a party calculatedly shocking in its lavishness; Ventura alone in his flat when the horror of his discovery hits him. The photography serves perfectly the growing sense of unease, and Ventura is as quietly excellent as ever. CPe

I Love a Man in Uniform

(David Wellington, 1993, Can) Tom McCamus, Brigitte Bako, Kevin Tighe, David Hemblen, Alex Karzis, Graham McPherson.
97 min.
Henry Adler realises his acting ambitions when he lands the part of a tough-guy sergeant in a TV cop show. Sporting the full black-leather regalia, he acquires a sense of self-importance he can't wait to test out by walking the streets and passing himself off as a real police officer. At first, Wellington's debut plays Henry's misadventures as dark comedy; but when shooting begins of the authentically cheesy Crimewave and Henry's off-screen relationship with his co-star fails to develop satisfactorily, the writer/director's wider scheme falls into place. McCamus's compelling lead performance delineates the increasingly violent results when one anguished individual starts blurring the distinctions; and the film as a whole is provocative and disturbing in the way it leaves viewers to decide how much their sympathies are implicated in the power trip from alienation to psychosis. TJ

I Love Melvin

(Don Weis, 1953, US) Donald O'Connor, Debbie Reynolds, Una Merkel, Allyn Joslyn, Jim Backus, Richard Anderson.
76 min.
Really attractive little musical, with O'Connor as a magazine photographer's gofer pretending to make a cover girl of a chorine (Reynolds) in order to impress her, then heading for disaster as he tries to make good his empty promises. The family scenes have a touch of Meet Me in St Louis, and the numbers choreographed by Robert Alton – including a football ballet (with Reynolds as the football) and a roller-skating dance for O'Connor – are bright and breezily inventive. TM

I Love Trouble

(Charles Shyer, 1994, US) Julia Roberts, Nick Nolte, James Rebhorn, James Loggia, Saul Rubinek, Olympia Dukakis, Marsha Mason.
123 min.

Ace columnist Peter Brackett (Nolte), a Pulitzer hack, is scooped out of complacency by cub reporter Sabrina Peterson (Roberts). They clash on the story of a train wreck, and spur each other on until they've got to the bottom of a not very interesting corporate conspiracy – and each other. Charles Shyer and producer Nancy Meyers usually purvey old-fashioned comedies with a topical twist, but this is just old fashioned: a '90s star vehicle transposed from the '30s. You can't replicate charm, however, and the Shmeyers' movie isn't witty or glamorous; it's smug and glossy, sparkling as tap water, and – when it finally decides it's a suspense picture – tense as an arthritic earthworm. TCh

I Love You Again

(WS Van Dyke, 1940, US) William Powell, Myrna Loy, Frank McHugh, Edmund Lowe, Nella Walker, Donald Douglas, Pierre Watkin.
99 min. b/w.
Powell, Loy and 'one-shot Woody' Van Dyke (the latter didn't dawdle) put The Thin Man series on hold to film this equally zestful screw-ball comedy. The gambit's a corker: when he's clocked with an oar, fusty small-town businessman Powell suddenly remembers he's a con-man, not the model citizen he's been playing for eight years. He forgets everything else about his life while he's an amnesiac and falls in love anew with his beautiful but bored wife. Loy, however, wants a divorce. The pace flags after the first reel, but cracking dialogue and the stars' perfect rapport ensure plenty of giddy fun. GM

I Love You, Alice B Toklas

(Hy Averback, 1968, US) Peter Sellers, Jo Van Fleet, Joyce Van Patten, Leigh Taylor-Young, David Arkin, Herbert Edelman, Grady Sutton.
93 min.
Dispiritingly trendy comedy, co-scripted by Paul Mazursky, in which Sellers briefly sketches a brilliant performance as a middle-aged lawyer tormented by asthma, by a mistress intent on being a wife, and by a car with parking problems. When everyone begins romping around under the influence of marijuana cookies, Sellers becomes a long-haired dropout, and one can only cringe in embarrassment. TM

I Love You, I Don't (Je t'aime, moi non plus)

(Serge Gainsbourg, 1975, Fr) Jane Birkin, Joe Dallesandro, Hugues Quester, René Kolldehoff, Gérard Depardieu.
88 min.
'Some days I just feel I could flush myself down the bowl', bemoans Dallesandro, summing up the excremental flavour of this riotously bleak and brutalised love story. Writer/director Gainsbourg employs a ludicrously grotesque approach – monosyllabic script, overblown symbolism, high-pitched performances, refuse-tip landscape, and small town aggressive boredom. A romance for our times. IB

I Love You, I'll Kill You (Ich liebe Dich, Ich töte Dich)

(Uwe Brandner, 1971, WGer) Rolf Becker, Hannes Fuchs, Helmut Brasch.
94 min.
A young, vaguely effete schoolteacher takes a post in a remote village community, which turns out to be an 'ideal' society: the all-but unemployed macho cops administer downers to keep public deviations in check, but anything from whips to sheep-fucking goes in private. Teach meets his butch 'opposite', the hunter of wolves; the two recognise their hidden kinship, and become lovers. But the experience leads our hero off the rails. He starts poaching (the game is reserved for the 'masters' who descend on the village by helicopter once a year), and so his lover has to track him down...Brandner presents all this in short, seemingly oblique fragments (his own metaphor is a kaleidoscope), a method that takes a while to adjust to: it really takes a second viewing to realise how funny the film is, for example. Brandner seems to have aimed at a L'Age d'or for the valium generation, but the result is very close indeed to a rural version of Performance (right down to a similarly unsatisfactory ending). TR

I Love You to Death

(Lawrence Kasdan, 1990, US) Kevin Kline, Tracey Ullman, Joan Plowright, River Phoenix, William Hurt, Keanu Reeves, James Gammon, Jack Kehler, Miriam Margolyes.
97 min.
Based on a real-life story – jealous wife Fran Toto made or contracted for five attempts on her unfaithful husband's life, landed in prison, and was eventually reconciled with her forgiving spouse – this sketchy comedy sinks beneath the weight of predictability. While Joey (Kline) spins pizzas and compliments female customers, his wife Rosalie (Ullman) puts his flirtation down to Italian blood. When she learns that the dalliances involve sex, however, her murderous rage knows no bounds. But assorted ploys to end his life are all futile; not even bullets fired at point blank range can kill him. A starry cast assists Ullman in her plans – Hurt, Plowright and Phoenix all have a go at Joey – but their presence is just one more symptom of the film's extraordinary lack of restraint. In straining towards humour, John Kostmayer's script falls back on crude exaggeration, and the result is woefully unfunny. CM

Images

(Robert Altman, 1972, Eire) Susannah York, Rene Auberjonois, Marcel Bozzuffi, Hugh Millais, Cathryn Harrison, John Morley.
101 min.
Underrated film about a lonely woman cracking up and suffering disturbing hallucinations about sex and death. Unlike most of Altman's movies, which parody and reinvent genres, Images stands rather in a loose trilogy with That Cold Day in the Park and 3 Women, in its investigation of madness and its concentration upon a female character. The fragmented style of the film, in which York's mental life is portrayed as substantially as her 'real' life, might have become pretentious; but the director controls things beautifully, proffering credible biographical reasons for her inner disturbances, and borrowing shock effects from the thriller genre to underline the terrifying nature of her predicament. It's brilliantly shot by Vilmos Zsigmond (without a hint of psychedelic trickery in sight), superbly acted, and lent extra menace by the sounds and music of, respectively, Stomu Yamashta and John Williams. GA

Imaginary Crimes

(Anthony Drazan, 1994, US) Harvey Keitel, Fairuza Balk, Kelly Lynch, Vincent D'Onofrio, Diane Baker, Chris Penn, Elisabeth Moss, Seymour Cassel, Annette O'Toole.
105 min.
Keitel is good but not stretched as Ray, a small man with big dreams, doomed both as a barely legit businessman and as a husband and father. His eldest daughter (Balk, good) is a bright high school kid and budding author, who uses the emotions he provokes as raw material for her stories about one girl's experience growing up in '60s Colorado. It's a rites-of-passage story in which the daughter's loss of innocence is compared and contrasted with the father's almost childlike destructiveness and delusion; his crimes, real or imaginary, provide the panic which she will use to shape her success. Drazan's careful direction certainly suits the heartfelt script (from a book by Sheila Ballantyne), but more than lashings of honest emotion is required. AO

Imaginary Tale, An

see Histoire inventée, Une

Imagine (aka Imagine: John Lennon)

(Andrew Solt, 1988, US) Narrator: John Lennon.
106 min. b/w & col.
When a poor boy who can do nothing else but play in a rock and roll band dies, we the public get treated to more golden tributes than all the barbiturates he ever took. This documentary uses acres of footage shot on Lennon's orders, and documents the one time in the '70s when he was not continually nodding out. The 1971 recording session in the Lennon's country mansion which produced 'Imagine' is the core; the whole of the narration is taken from Lennon interviews, tracing his life in his own words. The result is a mythological media history that paints the man to be more than a saint:

he is a *human* saint. He made mistakes, and he admits to them. No one, not even his ex-wife, has a bad word to say about him. It's a lesson in how to use celluloid to create your own personal version of reality. But then, when did Lennon ever truly deal with reality? MPe

Imago – Meret Oppenheim
(Pamela Robertson-Pierce/Anselm Spoerri, 1989, Switz) narrator: Glenda Jackson.
90 min.
Her fur-lined tea cup is one of the most famous surrealist objects ever made, but its creator, Oppenheim, is practically unknown. Ironically, the success of the sculpture eclipsed other achievements, and contributed to a depression that sent her back to Switzerland. Her self-doubt lifted in 1954, when she began the extraordinary paintings and sculptures shown at the ICA in 1989. This film was begun in collaboration with the artist, but sadly she died before shooting got under way. Glenda Jackson reads letters and diaries with a dull matter-of-factness to an irritating soundtrack. The edifice creaks, and Oppenheim is made to seem ordinary. The woman who said 'Imagination is the landscape in which the artist goes for a walk' deserves more imaginitive treatment. SK

I'm All Right, Jack
(John Boulting, 1959, GB) Ian Carmichael, Peter Sellers, Irene Handl, Richard Attenborough, Terry-Thomas, Dennis Price, Liz Fraser, Margaret Rutherford, Miles Malleson.
105 min. b/w.
The best of the Boultings' warm, vulgar, affectionate satires. The travails of silly-ass hero Carmichael are only mildly amusing, but the film blazes into life with the arrival of Sellers' Stalinist Don Quixote, tilting with alarming predictability at the windmills constructed by his class enemies. The Red Robbos of this world may be an unfairly easy target, but Sellers' caricature is affectionate, not malicious. Accusations of union-bashing are misplaced. The workers may all be dumb clods who sleep with their vests on, but there's a grudging appreciation of their truculent cynicism, and Attenborough's horrid little entrepreneur discovers that in making them the dupes of his capitalist crookery he brings about his own downfall. RMy

I Married a Communist (aka The Woman on Pier 13)
(Robert Stevenson, 1949, US) Laraine Day, Robert Ryan, John Agar, Thomas Gomez, Janis Carter, Richard Rober, William Talman, Paul Guilfoyle.
73 min. b/w.
This was the notorious project with which eager beaver Howard Hughes did his bit for Uncle Sam during the witch hunt days, assigning it to a string of RKO directors (turn it down, and you labelled yourself pinko or worse). Day is the lady who marries Ryan after a whirlwind courtship, knowing only that he is a top executive with a San Francisco shipping company who used to be a stevedore. The Commies, though, know that he was briefly a Party member during the Depression, and begin blackmailing him (Carter just wanting revenge because he ditched her along with the Party, but Gomez intent on forcing him to help foment labour disputes at the shipyard). Ryan plays ball until the game gets rough and corpses start piling up, when he does the right thing (conveniently dying in the process, after explaining that he only joined because he was a disgruntled kid out of a job: 'I thought I'd quit, but you can't quit. They won't let you'). The sterling cast can make no headway against cartoon characters, a fatuous script that defies belief, and an enveloping sense of hysteria. Nick Musuraca's *noir*-ish camerawork, mercifully, is stunning. TM

I Married a Monster from Outer Space
(Gene Fowler Jr, 1958, US) Tom Tryon, Gloria Talbott, Peter Baldwin, Robert Ivers, Ken Lynch, John Eldredge.
78 min. b/w.
Though trailing in the wake of *Invasion of the Body Snatchers* and saddled with a singularly schlocky title, this is a remarkably effective cheapie about an alien takeover, which even manages an undertow of sexual angst as the tentac-

ular creature inhabiting Tryon, inadvertently giving itself away to Talbott on the sentimental occasion of their wedding anniversary, struggles to come to terms with a mysterious humanisation of its instincts. Good performances, strikingly moody camerawork, a genuinely exciting climax (with a particularly nice touch in that the posse of bona fide humans which finally routs the aliens is recruited from expectant fathers at the maternity ward of the local hospital). TM

I Married a Nazi
see Man I Married, The

I Married a Witch
(René Clair, 1942, US) Veronica Lake, Fredric March, Cecil Kellaway, Robert Benchley, Susan Hayward, Elizabeth Patterson.
76 min. b/w.
Heresy here: Clair's '30s musical comedies have always been acclaimed as enormously original, innovative classics, far superior to his American films. But where those French films now seem dated and Chaplinesque in their twee sentimentality and naïve desire to make a serious point, the American films remain delightful: unpretentious, pacy and genuinely witty. *I Married a Witch* sees Clair at his peak, with an ambitious, puritanical politician (March) being plagued by the mischievous Lake, a witch reincarnated and bent on revenge after being burned at the stake by his ancestors. Lake is delightfully effective as the malicious woman, whose ideas of punishment are often beautifully absurd, and March provides an excellent foil. GA

I Married a Woman
(Hal Kanter, 1956, US) George Gobel, Diana Dors, Adolphe Menjou, Jessie Royce Landis, Nita Talbot, Angie Dickinson.
84 min. b/w & col.
One of two disastrous movies British siren Dors made in Hollywood for RKO, this has her opposite timid US TV comic Gobel as a neglected wife of an ad-man who sets out to make her husband jealous. Dors later sued the studio, charging that they'd made her 'an object of disgrace, ill-will and ridicule,' which gives some idea of the movie's quality. TJ

Imitation Game, The
(Richard Eyre, 1980, GB) Harriet Walter, Lorna Charles, Bernard Gallagher, Gillian Martell, Simon Chandler.
95 min.
Ian McEwan's brilliant script, perfectly realised on film by Eyre, was the television drama of 1980. During World War II, an ATS wireless operator (Walter) casually penetrates, and is eventually destroyed by, the circles of secrecy surrounding the code-breaking operation Ultra. Power, patriarchy, and the moral basis of war are threaded together in a drama concerned with history yet charged with contemporary resonance. JW

Imitation of Life
(John M Stahl, 1934, US) Claudette Colbert, Warren William, Louise Beavers, Rochelle Hudson, Fredi Washington, Ned Sparks, Alan Hale, Henry Armetta.
109 min. b/w.
More character study than polemic, wonderfully warm and witty in its observation of two women (one black, one white) who not only crash the race barriers in their friendship but successfully go it alone in a man's world, Stahl's version of Fannie Hurst's novel makes fascinating comparison with Sirk's remake. Where Sirk pushes the final melodramatics into social confrontation, Stahl withdraws in discretion, almost reducing them to naturalistic credibility. But one shot, of a staircase mathematically dividing the house into upstairs and downstairs as the guests arrive for a party which white Colbert hostesses and black Beavers serves from the kitchen, acknowledges Stahl's awareness of the hypocrisy that underlies the script's apparently 'liberal' treatment of blacks. TM

Imitation of Life
(Douglas Sirk, 1959, US) Lana Turner, John Gavin, Sandra Dee, Juanita Moore, Susan Kohner, Dan O'Herlihy, Robert Alda, Mahalia Jackson.
124 min.

There is a marvellous moment towards the end of Sirk's film which encapsulates the cruel cynicism that permeates his best work. As successful actress Turner, leaning over her dying black maid and long-term friend, lifts her head in tears, we see in the background a photograph of the dead woman's half-caste daughter, smiling. The romantic sentimentality of the moment is totally undercut by the knowledge that the girl, who has rejected her mother out of a desire to pass for white, has found a tragic release with her kindly parent's death. Sirk's last movie in Hollywood is a coldly brilliant weepie, a rags-to-riches tale of two intertwined families, in which the materialist optimism is continually counterpointed by an emphasis upon racist tension and the degeneration of family bonds. Despite the happy ending, what one remembers from the film is the steadily increasing hopelessness, given its most glorious visual expression in the scene of the maid's extravagant funeral, the only time in the film when her subordinate status and unhappy distance from her daughter are abolished. Forget those who decry the '50s Hollywood melodrama; it is through the conventions of that hyper-emotional genre that Sirk is able to make such a devastatingly embittered and pessimistic movie. GA

I'm Expecting
see Jag Är Med Barn

I'm Gonna Git You Sucka
(Keenen Ivory Wayans, 1988, US) Keenen Ivory Wayans, Bernie Casey, Antonio Fargas, Steve James, Isaac Hayes, Jim Brown, Janet DuBois, Dawnn Lewis, John Vernon, Clu Gulager, Kadeem Hardison, Damon Wayans.
89 min.
In this spoof of the mean-ass blaxploitation actioners of the '70s, a crisis has struck New York's black neighbourhoods: the brothers are 'OG'-ing (overdosing on gold medallions etc)in their thousands. Into the fray comes army sergeant Jack Spade (Wayans); returning from years of brave desk and latrine duty to find his younger rother has fallen victim, he decides to hunt down evil Mr Big (Vernon). Wayans tosses out black stereotypes in arresting profusion, adopting the *Airplane!* approach: broad rather than subtle visual gags and parodic encounters. The greatest pleasure comes from seeing '70s veterans send themselves up: an overweight Hayes 'tooling up' with enough weaponry to bomb Libya; fargas' Flyguy, winner of the 'Pimp of the Year' competition, in ludicrous flamboyant threads. The music ranges from Hayes through Curtis Mayfield to rap. The film was co-scripted by Robert Townsend, which may account for a faint smell of complacent yuppie bad faith in the air, but that is blown away by the enthusiasm and innocence of the playing. WH

I'm Jumping Over Puddles Again (Uz zase Skácu pres Kaluze)
(Karel Kachyna, 1970, Czech) Vladimir Dlouhy, Karel Hlusicka, Zdena Hadrbolcová, Vladimir Smeral.
92 min.
About a young boy's passion for horses, his paralysis from polio, and subsequent triumph over his handicap by learning to ride. Village life of the period (just before World War I) is well evoked, and the boy's relationship to his wastrel father, anxious mother, and the somewhat scornful village kids is treated with some feeling. It's a whimsical, rather drowsy film, overlaid with an unfortunate technical tricksiness and an insistent music score. Unexpectedly, it improves enormously with the boy's illness and his feverish hallucinations in hospital. Later, treated with a nicely quirky sense of humour, neither his crippled state nor his determination to overcome it are trivialised. Altogether a bit of an oddity, pleasant and irritating in equal proportions as it avoids the obvious pitfalls and then falls flat where least expected.

Im Lauf der Zeit
see Kings of the Road

Immaculate Conception
(Jamil Dehlavi, 1991, GB) James Wilby, Melissa Leo, Shabana Azmi, Zia Mohyeddin, James Cossins, Ronny Jhutti, Tim Choate.
120 min.

Eccentric at first sight, this ends up delivering pretty much what you'd expect from a 'Film on Four' movie: thoughtful scripting, solid acting, questions of cultural and sexual identity. Wilby and Leo play a well-heeled white couple in Karachi – she's Jewish-American with free-spirit mystic tendencies, he's a no-nonsense Brit conservationist. Unable to conceive, they have recourse to a holy shrine attended by a bevy of eunuchs in full drag. After a three-day fertility work-out, their dream seems likely to come true; but there, of course, the trouble begins. This is plentiful premise to be getting on with, but writer-director Dehlavi chooses to stitch in more subplot than his two hours can reasonably accommodate: Wilby's relationship with journalist Samira (Azmi) and her dying uncle; Cossins as a camp old colonial who steps out of line with Islam; and Leo's pushy diplomat brother (Choate), who turns up to nudge matters into the international incident bracket. Dehlavi goes out of his way to skirt the risk of sensationalism, but his diffuse, overcautious approach dilutes matters to the point of tedium. JRo

Immoral Tales (Contes Immoraux)

(Walerian Borowczyk, 1974, Fr) Lise Danvers, Fabrice Luchini, Charlotte Alexandra, Paloma Picasso, Florence Bellamy, Jacopo Berinizi.
103 min.
Made between *Blanche* and *Story of Sin*, *Immoral Tales* takes Borowczyk's celebrated eye for erotic representation about as far as it can go. The result, which is Borowczyk's slightest and most commercial offering to date, has provoked wildly differing responses: great pagan art or ultimate softcore? In one sense it hardly matters: although cool and stylised in approach, the film displays the most sustained erotic content yet seen publicly in this country. Four episodes – three stories of women from history, plus a contemporary Surrealist text – explore manifestations of feminine eroticism in relation to various taboos: a cosmic initiation, a religious ecstasy, incest and a bloodlust. There is nothing to censor as such, because everything is controlled through atmosphere and suggestion. Objects, even decor, are invested with an erotic tactile quality. The story of Countess Bathory, for example, who bathed in the blood of murdered girls, is predominantly a visual catalogue of liquids on flesh. CPe

Immortal Beloved

(Bernard Rose, 1994, GB/US) Gary Oldman, Jeroen Krabbé, Johanna Ter Steege, Valeria Golino, Isabella Rossellini, Miriam Margolyes.
120 min.
This passionately committed Beethoven biopic proves there's life in the old music yet. Held together by Oldman's harrumphing portrayal of the bad-tempered genius, it structures itself around the enduring enigma of the great man's last will (his entire estate went to an unidentified 'Immortal Beloved'), offering a potted personal history, a judicious selection of greatest hits, and an awe-struck contemplation of the creative process. Regrettably, the film-makers' defining question – is the Immortal Beloved youthful heart-throb Golino, world-weary countess Rossellini, or even his brother's wife, Ter Steege? – makes for only limited dramatic interest; and Oldman's performance consists chiefly of a wig, a scowl and a tantrum. The film's strength is writer/director Rose's determination to let the music carry as much of the emotional weight as possible. He builds exhilarating set-pieces from the Violin Concerto and the *Eroica* and proves a persuasive evangelist for the classical repertoire. The film may plod and pulse in equal measure, but the ecstatic visualisation of the climactic *Ode to Joy* is a triumph. TJ

Immortal Sergeant, The

(John M Stahl, 1943, US) Henry Fonda, Thomas Mitchell, Maureen O'Hara, Allyn Joslyn, Reginald Gardiner, Melville Cooper, Bramwell Fletcher, Morton Lowry.
90 min. b/w.
Standard WWII issue lost-in-the-desert exercise set during the North African campaign, with Fonda as the diffident Canadian corporal who has to shape up and assume command of a depleted British Eighth Army patrol on the death of Thomas Mitchell's stalwart veteran sergeant.

Flashbacks fill us in on Fonda's background. He's pleasant but gauche, a would-be writer and a timorous lover who still considers himself 'a civilian with a couple of chevrons on my sleeve'. Rations are low, the Eyeties are everywhere, and an impressive sandstorm is brewing... fortunately, at moments of crisis Fonda is prompted by the voice of experience (that is to say, the voice of Thomas Mitchell), and he returns a hero with a valuable lesson under his belt: 'If I want anything worthwhile in this life, I have to fight for it. That's not a bad thing for a man to learn, is it... or a nation? To fight!' TCh

Immortal Story, The (Histoire Immortelle)

(Orson Welles, 1968, Fr) Orson Welles, Jeanne Moreau, Norman Eshley, Roger Coggio.
60 min.
Though shot for television on a low budget, this is a sumptuous experience, a fairytale-like story, taken from Isak Dinesen, of a wealthy Macao merchant (Welles) who hires a young sailor to sleep with his wife (actually also hired, since he is unmarried) to make an old legend come true. Basically, it's about the conflict between the cold-blooded realism of the merchant and a romanticism he refuses to accept; and inevitably, the myth turns upon him. Welles is his usual megalomaniacal self, and the use of deep focus, deep shadow and colour is superb. The material itself is fascinating, and Erik Satie's music is perfectly chosen. RM

Immortelle, L'

(Alain Robbe-Grillet, 1962, Fr/It/Tur) Françoise Brion, Jacques Doniol-Valcroze, Guido Celano, Catherine Carayon, Catherine Blisson.
100 min. b/w.
The first feature directed by *nouveau roman* writer and film-maker Robbe-Grillet (who had scripted Resnais' *Last Year in Marienbad*), this is a characteristically fragmented mystery-romance set in Istanbul. The arty narrative is occasionally irritating, and one could easily argue that the images of the elusive femme fatale in underwear and bondage are misogynist; but there is no denying the film's extraordinary creation of that strange, unsettling atmosphere one encounters in a foreign and labyrinthine city. GA

I'm No Angel

(Wesley Ruggles, 1933, US) Mae West, Cary Grant, Edward Arnold, Gertrude Michael, Kent Taylor, Gregory Ratoff.
87 min. b/w.
Single-handed, Mae saved Paramount from bankruptcy and provoked the birth of the League of Decency. *I'm No Angel* contains an extraordinary scene in which she's tended by a bevy of black maids ('Hey, Beulah! Peel me a grape'). Sexism coupled with racism. You can't beat it. Grant, Mae's protégé, once said 'I learned everything from her. Well, almost everything'. The films are pretty awful, but no one ever notices. Mae still lays them in the aisles. SG

I, Mobster (aka The Mobster)

(Roger Corman, 1958, US) Steve Cochran, Lita Milan, Robert Strauss, Celia Lovsky, Lili St Cyr, John Brinkley, Grant Withers.
80 min. b/w.
Corman's second gangster movie, contemporary in setting and made on a bigger budget than he was accustomed to after Fox picked up on the success of *Machine Gun Kelly*. Characteristically taut and vivid in chronicling Cochran's rise from bookie's runner to crime czar and candidate for the attentions of Murder Inc, it basically repeats the gangster movie's age-old story. What lifts it right out of the rut, aside from the excellent performances and Floyd Crosby's beautifully crisp camerawork, is the perfectly judged ambivalence that attends Cochran's ruthless drive for the top. A slum kid ready and willing to kill to avoid remaining on the receiving end of life's kicks, he nevertheless retains a streak of puritan conscience; and having seen himself disowned by his adoring mother, seen the innocent girl who loves him deliberately sacrifice her integrity in order to be with him, seen the shallowness of the loyalties he has chosen to live by, he finally comes to understand the inevitability of his own death. In its modest way, a fascinating film. TM

I, Monster

(Stephen Weeks, 1970, GB) Christopher Lee, Peter Cushing, Mike Raven, Richard Hurndall, George Merritt, Kenneth J Warren, Susan Jameson.
75 min.
Directed with a remarkably mature visual sense by Weeks at the age of twenty-two (his first feature), this Amicus adaptation of Stevenson's *Dr Jekyll and Mr Hyde* – with Lee giving a low-key performance in the lead – suffers from its prosaic fidelity to its source, as well as from a rather forced 'moral' parallel between Victorian and contemporary drug cultures. Clearly made on a shoestring, it was apparently started in an abortive 3-D process that eventually had to be abandoned. PT

Impasse

(Richard Benedict, 1968, US) Burt Reynolds, Anne Francis, Lyle Bettger, Rodolfo Acosta, Jeff Corey, Miko Mayama.
100 min.
The sort of film that now probably sorely embarrasses Burt Reynolds, a tedious action-man adventure that has him searching for a cache of gold in the Philippines, stashed away by five soldiers (using a complicated system of safeguards) during World War II. Screenwriter John C Higgins was once under contract to MGM's B unit, bringing him assignments like Zinnemann's *Kid Glove Killer* and Anthony Mann's *Border Incident*; but by this time he'd gone through *Untamed Youth* towards the ultimate dross of *Daughters of Satan*, also made on the cheap in the Philippines. PT

Importance of Being Earnest, The

(Anthony Asquith, 1952, GB) Michael Redgrave, Joan Greenwood, Edith Evans, Dorothy Tutin, Michael Denison, Margaret Rutherford, Miles Malleson.
95 min.
It is typical of Asquith – Grand Master of the Filmed English Classic – that he never attempts any cinematic wit to complement the verbal ping-pong of Wilde's play: his cameras do little more than reverently record a great patriotic theatrical event. But the settings are the epitome of Victorian plushness, the colour is Technicolor at its fruitiest, and most of the playing is disarming, particularly Edith Evans and her handbag. GB

Impostors

(Mark Rappaport, 1979, WGer/US) Peter Evans, Ellen McElduff, Charles Ludlam, Michael Burg, Lina Todd, Randy Danson.
110 min.
Five chameleon New York characters (twin magicians/assassins, two enigmatic women, a rich wimp), their passions masked by aggressive cool, wend their absurdly entertaining way through Rappaport's customary comic-opera catalogue of melodramatic disparities: a series of tableau visuals bursting with allusive emotional movement, sense of skeletal slapstick, a superabundance of inconsequential plot trails. There's enough for anyone half-familiar with out-of-the-rut New York independent film-making to latch onto; and in terms of the wide audience Rappaport deserves, reservations about this film based on higher enthusiasm for the earlier, underexposed *Local Color* and *The Scenic Route* begin to seem pretty irrelevant. PT

Impromptu

(James Lapine, 1989, GB) Judy Davis, Hugh Grant, Mandy Patinkin, Bernadette Peters, Julian Sands, Ralph Brown, Anton Rodgers, Emma Thompson, Anna Massey.
107 min.
Directed by Sondheim collaborator Lapine, this tells the romantic story of Bohemian cross-dressing novelist George Sand's protracted pursuit of Chopin through salon and château, variously foiled and abetted by Liszt (Sands) and mistress (Peters), Alfred de Musset (Patinkin) and Delacroix (Brown). Driven by a quest for perfect love, Sand (Davis), though knee-deep in an operetta of rejected lovers, hears Chopin pelting at the piano through a door and is a goner. Given that the sick stick of a Pole is played by Hugh Grant, her passion seems inexplicable, and the only scene that convinces has the novelist lying aswoon under the piano as the soundtrack pours it on. The acting

comes in different sizes: in contrast to the naturalism of Davis – heiress to the Jeanne Moreau Estate – stands the high camp of Emma Thompson as the Art-struck Duchess, and the swashbuckling of Patinkin. A longish haul. BC

Improper Conduct
(Mauvaise Conduite)
(Nestor Almendros/Orlando Jimenez Leal, 1983, Fr) Lorenzo Monreal, Jorge Lago, Julio Medina, César Bermudez, José Mario, Rafael De Palet.
114 min.
A quietly terrifying documentary on the (mis)treatment of gays in Cuba which opened up a hornet's nest of controversy and political schizophrenia. While Fidel smiles for the cameras, thousands of homosexuals are being rounded up, sent to concentration camps, imprisoned in medieval castles and tortured. The system of family and neighbour denunciation (for as little as a flowery shirt or long hair) echoes Nazi Germany; the work camp banner of 'Work Will Make You Men' echoes Belsen's 'Arbeit macht Frei'. While the likes of Sartre and Sontag recant their support on camera, others still insist on the wider goal of a socialist state. Bullshit. One innocent person oppressed is one too many. JG

Improperly Dressed
(Herkulesfürdöi emlék)
(Pál Sándor, 1976, Hun) Endre Holman, Margit Dayka, Irma Patkós, Carla Romanelli, Dezsö Garas.
85 min.
An oddly elliptical, mournfully elegiac tale of a young Communist, hounded for political reasons, who seeks haven in a remote sanatorium where, disguised as a woman among women, he becomes increasingly seized by the inertia of his time out of war. The year is 1919, the oppressors are White Russians, and the sanatorium stands nicely as a symbol for what is wrong with Hungary, then as now. The trouble is that Sándor seems uncertain what to make of the parable, and the bizarre situation, left pretty much to its own devices, simply fritters itself away in a haze of half-hinted sexual ambiguities and dreamy atmospherics (the camerawork is exquisite). TM

Impudent Girl, An
(L'Effrontée)
(Claude Miller, 1985, Fr) Charlotte Gainsbourg, Bernadette Lafont, Jean-Claude Brialy, Raoul Billerey, Clothilde Baudon, Jean-Philippe Ecoffey, Julie Glenn.
97 min.
The wayward Miller has always pursued his own fancy; from the adolescent problems of The Best Way to Walk, through the detections of This Sweet Sickness and The Inquisitor, up to the scatty Mortelle Randonnée, there has been no obvious thread running through his work. An Impudent Girl, however – an uncredited adaptation of Carson McCullers' The Member of the Wedding – returns to what was his surest ground in his first film: the pangs of adolescence. Sweet Charlotte (Gainsbourg) is a 13-year-old problem looking for somewhere to happen. She is the despair of her widowed father, drives her brother mad, knows she wants something better, but doesn't know what it is. Until Clara (Baudon) walks into her life. Clara too is 13, but she is also a successful concert pianist, wears pretty white dresses, lives in a lakeside mansion, and is generally just too good to be true. All Charlotte's mad hopes and fears, her desires and heel-stamping jealousies, come pouring out with the appearance of this young catalyst; but the experience is therapeutic, and the outcome one of adult optimism. The film exhibits all of Miller's strengths, in particular his canny way with actors; but best of all is its emotional truth. Adolescence is never comfortable; to face its memories honestly is part of being adult. CPea

Impulse
(Graham Baker, 1984, US) Tim Matheson, Meg Tilly, Hume Cronyn, John Karlen, Bill Paxton, Amy Stryker.
99 min.
Smalltown USA. After a minor earth tremor, a farmer's wife tries to blow her brains out in the middle of an irrationally abusive phone call to her daughter. Armed with her doctor boyfriend, the girl returns home to see what drove momma mad, and finds people acting totally on impulse: elderly folk rob banks, barroom brawlers break their own fingers, and mischievous brats attempt to roast her alive. All too reminiscent, most notably of Invasion of the Body Snatchers, the film wastes its predictable but promising premise and quickly degenerates into virtual absurdity. With the exception of its heroine (Tilly), the entire cast is transformed into an almost comic collection of screaming harridans and snarling gunmen, while the 'hints' at what lies behind the epidemic of aggression are delivered with sledgehammer subtlety. Aiming for a realistic ecological allegory, Baker simply stumbles from cliché to cliché. GA

Impulse
(Sondra Locke, 1990, US) Theresa Russell, Jeff Fahey, George Dzundza, Alan Rosenburg, Nicholas Mele, Eli Danker, Charles McCaughan, Lynne Thigpen.
108 min.
Theresa Russell (excellent) plays an undercover cop on the edge, burned out and unable to sustain her relationship with men. Under assessment by the police shrink after shooting a criminal, she is still moonlighting as a decoy hooker, a role that feeds her desire to lose control. Assistant DA Fahey, meanwhile, is looking for a second witness to secure a watertight case against a drug kingpin. Russell is recruited to make a fake drugs buy designed to force a low-life dealer into testifying, but her cover is blown and things get very complicated. Although a subsequent plot twist, linking Russell's dangerous impulsiveness to a loose thread of Fahey's complex case, is a shade too convenient, Sondra Locke directs with great assurance. The action is tough, the low-life atmosphere authentic, and the relationship between Russell and Fahey charged with tremulous eroticism. Stylish, exciting, and emotionally satisfying. NF

Im Zeichen des Kreuzes
see Due To an Act of God

Inadmissible Evidence
(Anthony Page, 1968, GB) Nicol Williamson, Eleanor Fazan, Jill Bennett, Peter Sallis, David Valla, Eileen Atkins, Ingrid Brett, Gillian Hills.
96 min. b/w.
Misfiring adaptation of John Osborne's play about a middle-aged solicitor oppressed by his sense of failure and his feeling that the whole world is conspiring to exclude him, with Williamson repeating his brilliant stage performance to lesser effect. The main problem is the intrusive camera/editing style which reduces the original lengthy diatribes to tetchy little snippets, simultaneously cutting Osborne's magnificently theatrical anti-hero down to size: instead of being effectively inside a man's mind, we are now left outside, wondering why we should be expected to sympathise with such an unprepossessing, self-centred bore. TM

In a Lonely Place
(Nicholas Ray, 1950, US) Humphrey Bogart, Gloria Grahame, Frank Lovejoy, Robert Warwick, Jeff Donnell, Martha Stewart, Carl Benton Reid.
94 min. b/w.
The place is Hollywood, lonely for scriptwriter Dixon Steele (Bogart), who is suspected of murdering a young woman, until girl-next-door Laurel Gray (Grahame) supplies him with a false alibi. But is he the killer? Under pressure of police interrogation, their tentative relationship threatens to crack – and Dix's sudden, violent temper becomes increasingly evident. Ray's classic thriller remains as fresh and resonant as the day it was released. Nothing is as it seems: the noir atmosphere of deathly paranoia frames one of the screen's most adult and touching love affairs; Bogart's tough-guy insolence is probed to expose a vulnerable, almost psychotic insecurity; while Grahame abandons femme fatale conventions to reveal a character of enormous, subtle complexity. As ever, Ray composes with symbolic precision, confounds audience expectations, and deploys the heightened lyricism of melodrama to produce an achingly poetic meditation on pain, distrust and loss of faith, not to mention an admirably unglamorous portrait of Tinseltown. Never were despair and solitude so romantically alluring. GA

In & Out
(Frank Oz, 1997, US) Kevin Kline, Joan Cusack, Matt Dillon, Debbie Reynolds, Wilford Brimley, Bob Newhart, Tom Selleck, Dan Hedaya.
91 min.
Howard Brackett (Kline), an English teacher in a Midwestern town, gets the shock of his life when a protégé turned movie star (Dillon) unthinkingly 'outs' him before the whole world during the Oscar ceremony. Howard isn't even out to himself – in fact he's supposed to be marrying Emily (Cusack) at the weekend. So what if he's a virgin who loves to dance and adores Barbra Streisand movies? A mainstream comedy with a twist, this is surprisingly waspish about gay manners and sexual hypocrisy, especially as practised by Brackett himself. As long as the script by Paul Rudnick (inspired by Tom Hanks' announcement when he won an Academy Award for Philadelphia) is taking itself flippantly, the movie works well enough. Oz wants it both ways, though, and can't resist hammering home the message with a prolonged Spartacus-style climax quite as ludicrous as the Oscar winning film-within-the-film. TCh

Inauguration of the
Pleasure Dome, The
see Anger Magick Lantern Cycle, The

In a Wild Moment
see Moment d'Egarement, Un

In a Year with 13 Moons (In
einem Jahr mit 13 Monden)
(Rainer Werner Fassbinder, 1978, WGer) Volker Spengler, Ingrid Caven, Gottfried John, Elisabeth Trissenaar, Eva Mattes, Günther Kaufmann.
129 min.
Elvira (Spengler) was Erwin until s/he went to Casablanca for a discreet operation. She now lives in Frankfurt, abandoned by her lover, befriended by a hooker who's not much better off than herself, and ripped to shreds by cruelties and social inequalities. In a Year with 13 Moons is not only Fassbinder's last word on victimised innocence, it's also a subjective response to the suicide of his own lover Armin Meier, and a sincere admission that life is messier than his earlier films acknowledged. A movie riven with contradictions and fuelled by vehemence and passion. TR

In Bed with Madonna
see Truth or Dare

In Caliente
(Lloyd Bacon, 1935, US) Dolores Del Rio, Pat O'Brien, Glenda Farrell, Edward Everett Horton, Leo Carrillo, Judy Canova, Wini Shaw.
84 min. b/w.
Magazine editor O'Brien gives Mexican firebrand Del Rio a bad review for her dance extravaganza, but when best pal Horton whisks him south of the border to evade ruthless gold-digger Farrell, there are no prizes for guessing who's back in her home town of Agua Caliente to meet and greet him. Sadly slack Warners extravaganza, but it does warm up a bit for the Busby Berkeley numbers, including the ultra-kitsch 'Muchacha'. TJ

In Celebration
(Lindsay Anderson, 1974, GB/Can) Alan Bates, James Bolam, Brian Cox, Constance Chapman, Gabrielle Drake, Bill Owen.
131 min.
Stage to screen transfer of the David Storey play directed at the Royal Court by Anderson in 1969, with the cast remaining the same. Not strictly autobiographical, but rooted in the playwright's Nottinghamshire mining background, In Celebration is set in the family home on the night three grown-up sons return somewhat reluctantly to celebrate their parents' 40th wedding anniversary. Anderson has said, 'The stage gives the audience a broader aspect of a scene than film, and therefore the rehearsals were perhaps more valid for me than for the actors.' The play was re-rehearsed for three weeks before shooting, and location scenes were filmed in the colliery town, but it still emerges as an awkward compromise between the two forms, though Bates is splendid as Andrew, the failed painter. MA

Incense for the Damned
(Michael Burrowes, ie. Robert Hartford-Davis, 1970, GB) Patrick Macnee, Peter Cushing, Alex Davion, Johnny Sekka, Madeline Hinde, Patrick Mower, Imogen Hassall, Edward Woodward.
87 min.
An adaptation of Simon Raven's novel *Doctors Wear Scarlet* which bears a fictional director credit: Hartford-Davis took his name off the picture after unexplained difficulties, and it must be the first time in screen history that a film-maker has disowned the only remotely good thing he's done. The film bears some marks of its production difficulties, but in general it sticks closely to Raven's novel, in which the act of vampirism becomes for the hero (Mower) a therapeutic acting-out of the stifling, parasitic mental processes of Oxford that surround him. Probably the theme really needs a Polanski or a Franju to do it justice, but here it is at least put together neatly and coherently, with some elegant location camerawork from Desmond Dickinson. DP

In Cold Blood
(Richard Brooks, 1967, US) Robert Blake, Scott Wilson, John Forsythe, Paul Stewart, Gerald S O'Loughlin, Jeff Corey, Charles McGraw.
134 min. b/w.
A low-key adaptation of Truman Capote's 'novel of fact' about the murder of a whole family by two disturbed petty criminals, *In Cold Blood* forever shies away from trying to understand the killers (played by Blake and Wilson). Accordingly, in contrast to Capote, whose obsessive documentation of the pair's every act betrays his fear than he (and his readers) could well do something similar, Brooks explains and sympathises away their act as being unique to them. PH

Incognito
(John Badham, 1997, US) Jason Patric, Irène Jacob, Thomas Lockyer, Ian Richardson, Rod Steiger, Dudley Sutton.
107 min.
Three art dealers employ a tormented forger (Patric) to paint a 'lost' Rembrandt. Director Badham opts to play it straight, as if this will somehow render the whole exercise less preposterous. Choice moments include Patric daubing furiously in an Amsterdam garret, his sweaty torso decoratively splashed with paint, and the jaw-dropping revelation that a gauche Parisian art student (Jacob) is in fact the world authority on the Dutch master. A plot to frame the forger for murdering one of the dealers culminates with a ludicrous scene at the Old Bailey in which Donovan attempts to prove his innocence by reproducing 'live' his fake masterpiece. NF

In Country
(Norman Jewison, 1989, US) Bruce Willis, Emily Lloyd, Joan Alley, Kevin Anderson, Richard Hamilton, Judith Ivey, Peggy Rea, John Terry.
115 min.
Jewison's post-Vietnam movie concentrates on bereavement, with the consequence that it's decent but dull. Kentucky teenager Samantha (Lloyd) never knew her father who died in the war, but discovers his letters and photos. 'Gee, you missed *ET* and the Bruce Springsteen concerts', she says. Her role throughout is to reconcile the community with its unacknowledged tragedy, whether coddling her withdrawn Vietvet Uncle Emmett (Willis) or encouraging an impotent mechanic. Her generation not only knows naught of Country Joe & the Fish, but double-naught about GIs collecting VC ears and burning hooches, an ignorance which recalls post-war Germany. The emotional climax arrives at the Vietnam memorial tablets in Washington, with the family finally achieving closeness as they find their lad's nme among the thousands. The mass grave, little more than a hole in the ground as a relative says, is a good visual equivalent for America's attitude towards the shameful defeat. Vietnam had a closed casket funeral. BC

Incredible Hulk, The
(Kenneth Johnson/Sigmund Neufeld Jr, 1978, US) Bill Bixby, Susan Sullivan, Jack Colvin, Lou Ferrigno, Susan Batson.
104 min.
This fills you in on what's happened to American TV veteran Bixby since the days

when he hosted *My Favourite Martian*. In a nutshell: his marriage (soft-focus flashback) ended when he couldn't pry a two-ton heap of flaming metal off his wife after an accident, and the trauma sent him on a 'scientific' crusade for the secret of superhuman strength. He checks out the possibilities: adrenalin? dextrose? no, you guessed it, another cinematic dose of radiation. Unfortunately, someone was souping up the radiation equipment as well as the 'magnification' tools. So Bixby by accident becomes The Hulk, re-enacts a monster-and-little-girl scene reminiscent of James Whale's *Frankenstein*, and spends aeons of airtime saving a 747 jet. The moral is: two TV shows (which is what this is) do not one coherent movie make. CR

Incredible Journey, The
(Fletcher Markle, 1963, US) Emile Genest, John Drainie, Tommy Tweed, Sandra Scott, Syme Jago.
80 min.
Triumphantly painful Disney adventure; guaranteed to sear the memory, in spite of the 'Derek the Lonely Dingo'-style narration that has always stood for 'nature' in Walt's wonderful world. Across the changing seasons, three anthropomorphised pets find, incredibly, their way home through 250 miles of Canadian tundra to make some back-handed point about the nuclear family.

Incredible Melting Man, The
(William Sachs, 1977, US) Alex Rebar, Burr DeBenning, Myron Healey, Michael Aldredge, Ann Sweeney.
86 min.
What to do with the incredible melting man except have him melt some more? The film-makers never really resolve this sticky problem once their burned-up astronaut busts out of hospital and, at a snail's pace, starts eating the local population. This Z-grade effort, lacking any low-budget energy, takes its cue from the central character: it's tacky and bumbling and sinks into its own morass long before its subject finally dribbles apart, slurp, glub. CPe

Incredible Sarah, The
(Richard Fleischer, 1976, US) Glenda Jackson, Daniel Massey, Yvonne Mitchell, Douglas Wilmer, David Langton, Simon Williams, John Castle, Edward Judd.
106 min.
An obvious chore for Fleischer (as well as for the audience), this is a pretty traditional attempt at the biopic which threads together scenes-from-the-life of Sarah Bernhardt, from tyro rejection to triumph via social ostracism. The script makes an attempt or two to link Bernhardt's tendency to turn her daily life into constant theatricals with the magnetism of her on-stage appearances, but they remain very token. This *Reader's Digest* film carries the bland signature of its sponsors writ large over every set-up. Glenda Jackson emotes effectively enough through a series of cameo pieces from the classics, but is floored by the bits in between. VG

Incredible Shrinking Man, The
(Jack Arnold, 1957, US) Grant Williams, Randy Stuart, April Kent, Paul Langton, William Schallert, Billy Curtis.
81 min. b/w.
Not merely the best of Arnold's classic sci-fi movies of the '50s, but one of the finest films ever made in that genre. It's a simple enough story: after being contaminated by what may or may not be nuclear waste, Williams finds himself slowly but steadily shedding the pounds and inches until he reaches truly minuscule proportions. But it is what Richard Matheson's script (adapted from his own novel) does with this basic material that makes the film so gripping and intelligent. At first, Williams is merely worried about his mysterious illness, but soon, towered over by his wife, he begins to feel humiliated, expressing his shame and impotence through cruel anger. And then his entire relationship with the universe changes, with cats, spiders and drops of water representing lethal threats in the surreal and endless landscape that is, in fact, his house's cellar. And finally, to the strains of Joseph Gershenson's impressive score, we arrive at the

film's philosophical core: a moving, strangely pantheist assertion of what it really means to be alive. A pulp masterpiece. GA

Incredible Shrinking Woman, The
(Joel Schumacher, 1981, US) Lily Tomlin, Charles Grodin, Ned Beatty, Henry Gibson, Elizabeth Wilson, Mark Blankfield.
88 min.
One more high-promise comedy down the drainpipe: *The Incredible Shrinking Woman* still sounds better on paper after you've seen it. The theme should be watertight in the *Nine to Five*, would-be progressive mould: Woman suffering (literal) diminution under the weight of patriarchal, consumerist culture; while the advance prospect of seeing Lily Tomlin biting ankles is tasty enough to quell doubts about the wisdom of tampering with Richard Matheson's original sci-fi premise. But good intentions and one's own goodwill are soon diminished as script and direction conspire to render a sitcom satire that's indistinguishable from its target. A cloying cuteness soon pervades as Tomlin, shrinking after being sprayed with a new perfume marketed by her advertising executive husband, becomes a media celebrity; and the conclusion – curse becomes cure – is recuperative in more ways than one. PT

Incredibly Strange Creatures Who Stopped Living and Became Mixed-Up Zombies, The
(Ray Dennis Steckler, 1964, US) Cash Flagg ie.Ray Dennis Steckler, Brett O'Hara, Carolyn Brandt, Atlas King, Sharon Walsh.
82 min.
An incredibly mixed-up film which can't make up its mind whether it's a monster movie, a delinquent teen pic, or a showcase for a series of incompetent variety acts. When his beehived girlfriend walks out on him at the fairground, budding young rebel Jerry (played by the director) is exposed to a terrifying 'hypnovision' device by a wicked gypsy with a wart, and runs amok with a knife. The gypsy, for some reason, keeps a collection of acid-scarred zombies locked in the back of her fortune-teller's booth. The monsters break out and go on a strangling rampage in the nightclub next door, where a troupe of staggeringly inept dancers are in the middle of a number called 'The Zombie Stomp'. Truly amazing photography, which alternates static, arty set-ups with dizzying bouts of pseudo-expressionistic camera movement. Unmissable kitsch for turkey collectors, the film was originally shown in 'Hallucinogenic Hypnovision'. Which meant that the cinema ushers would don luminous masks and run up the aisles brandishing cardboard axes. AB

Incredibly True Adventure of Two Girls in Love, The
(Maria Maggenti, 1995, US) Laurel Hollomon, Nicole Parker, Dale Dickey, Stephanie Berry, Maggie Moore, Kate Stafford, Sabrina Artel.
94 min.
Punky 17-year-old Randy Dean (Hollomon) is having a desultory affair with a married woman, lives with her aunt in a 'regular lesbo household', and daydreams to the strains of Zeppelin and Hendrix. Evie Roy (Parker) is a glamorous, well-to-do African-American who lives with her mum, prefers Mozart and Walt Whitman, and is getting tired of her insensitive, immature boyfriend. Though they're both in their senior year at the same high school they don't meet until Evie's car starts giving her trouble and she calls in at the garage where Randy works. Still, it's an encounter that will change their lives. This feature debut offers a perky look at the trials of first love as experienced by two very different girls from two very different backgrounds. If there's nothing hugely original about the story, there's a lot of charm here, thanks largely to the easy naturalism of the performances. This is such a conventional telling of a modern-day fairy story that its (vaguely) subversive content should offend virtually no one. There's tenderness, humour, lyricism and a heartfelt plea for universal tolerance; and if the farcical finale seems obvious and contrived, it's

hard to resist a movie so gentle that its most shocking transgression is the unwitting wasting of a bottle of Château Latour. GA

Incubus

(John Hough, 1981, Can) John Cassavetes, Kerrie Keane, Helen Hughes, Erin Flannery, Duncan McIntosh, John Ireland.
92 min.
A demon-rape flick of unusually high technical ineptitude, even for this egregious genre, which features Canada doubling as California and Cassavetes as the doctor trying to solve the problem of just what is doing all those shower-curtain murders and inflicting such massive internal injuries on the female victims. We are indebted to *The Monthly Film Bulletin* for their scholarly note pointing out that the movie chickens out of the central image of Ray Russell's novel – the huge size of the incubus' phallus – and it's a castration that reaches out into the whole film. Cassavetes' presence inevitably raises echoes from *Rosemary's Baby*, but his baleful looks are miscast on the side of the angels. On a visit the only decent hope is that this nonsense made him enough money for one of his own independent films. CPea

In Custody (Hifazaat)

(Ismail Merchant, 1993, GB/Ind) Shashi Kapoor, Om Puri, Shabana Azmi, Sushma Seth, Neena Gupta, Tinnu Anand, Prayag Raj.
126 min.
As the long-time producer of the Merchant Ivory partnership, Ismail Merchant should have understood the problems of adapting literary texts to the cinema. All credit to him, then, for having the sang froid to choose for his first feature as director, Anita Desai's spare, uneventful novel about a once-revered elderly Urdu poet. The film follows the efforts of a pedantic college tutor, Deven (Puri), to record his hero, the poet Nur (Kapoor), reciting his own work. On a visit to the city of Bhopal, Deven finds Nur living in seclusion, drinking and over-eating, or bickering with his two wives, tired of casting pearls before swine. Deven is no master of technology: the taperecorder is a mystery to him, and much low comedy is extracted from his incompetence; and the arch, awkward quality of these scenes typify the film. Shashi Kapoor as the embittered, decayed poet is, regrettably, made to carry more weight than any man can bear – to symbolise a whole tradition: the neglect of the Urdu language and the oral tradition with its attendant philosophies of authority and respect. WH

Indecent Obsession, An

(Lex Marinos, 1985, Aust) Wendy Hughes, Gary Sweet, Richard Moir, Jonathan Hyde, Bruno Lawrence, Mark Little, Tony Sheldon, Bill Hunter.
106 min.
A hospital drama with a difference: it's World War II, the Far East, and the Japs have just surrendered. The inmates of Ward X, a wing for psychiatric and problem patients, have their routines shattered by the arrival of a new, mysterious patient. Lust, homophobia, violent death, cowardice and an exotic location should make for the sort of soap you can get your teeth into; but apart from a few reasonable impressions of mild insanity, the performances are never good enough to make you believe what's happening on screen. The confrontations fizzle out, the flashbacks are incredibly heavy-handed, and the sexual intrigue is...well, limp. Colleen McCullough's source novel provides a decent enough formula, but the filmmakers manage to reduce it to housewives' afternoon TV-slot tedium. DPe

Indecent Proposal

(Adrian Lyne, 1993, US) Robert Redford, Demi Moore, Woody Harrelson, Oliver Platt, Seymour Cassel.
117 min.
Great hook, crap movie. Here's the zinger: Redford offers a seven-figure sum for a night of hormonal judo with Moore, but she loves some other schmuck. This is so high-concept it practically needs breathing apparatus, but Lyne's flash-trash panache reduces it to mere hi-gloss. To call the characters cardboard would ennoble them. David (Harrelson) and Diana (Moore) are happily married, successful architect and real estate salesperson respectively, until the recession all but wipes them out. They head for Las

Vegas, hoping to win an instant fortune, but ill luck polishes them off, and only the million dollar proposition from Redford's enigmatic magnate stands between the couple and financial ignominy. Can their relationship survive this sternest of all tests? The eventual triumph of love over money is so moving, you'd need a heart of stone not to laugh. At last, a movie for people who cry at pop videos. TJ

Inde Fantôme, L'

see Phantom India

Independence Day

(Roland Emmerich, 1996, US) Bill Pullman, Will Smith, Jeff Goldblum, Robert Loggia, Margaret Colin, Mary McDonnell, Vivica A Fox, Judd Hirsch, James Rebhorn, Harvey Fierstein, Harry Connick Jr.
145 min.
Act I is an Anarchists' Ball. Massive metal spaceships loom over the cities of the world. The destruction of the White House is just for starters. Annihilation of the human race is on the agenda. US President Pullman, a wimp ex-fighter jock, listens to communications expert Goldblum (only in a Rupert Murdoch film could a TV exec save the world!). Act II, the survivors regroup at a secret military base in New Mexico to organise Act III, the fightback. Emmerich's globe-buster is an index of American populist fantasy. Forget subtext. This scrappy, spectacular, juvenile remake of *War of the Worlds* and 101 other sci-fi movies can be taken at face value. It's not about *Them*, it's about *US*: At least this America is strongly pluralist; it's black (Smith as the heroic top gun); it's Jewish (Goldblum and Hirsch as comic relief); it's even a little bit feminine – though Fierstein, Margaret Colin, et al, are really just emotional punctuation marks. The politics cut both ways, balancing pro- and anti-government impulses with Pullman as a vaguely Clinton-esque figure in the middle, pacifist by inclination, warrior by experience. Everything feels anti-climactic after the fireworks, but the moral is clear: it's the end of the world as we know it. And we feel fine. TCh

Indiana Jones and the Last Crusade

(Steven Spielberg, 1989, US) Harrison Ford, Sean Connery, Denholm Elliot, Alison Doody, John Rhys-Davies, Julian Glover, River Phoenix, Michael Byrne, Robert Eddison, Alexei Sayle.
127 min.
A film which smacks of *Raiders of the Lost Ark* in both mood and effects, even down to a tank chase which drags Jones' well-worn heels along the desert floor. Saving us from a sense of complete déjà vu is the introduction of Connery, Medievalist professor and Indiana's father. His screen image provides the perfect fatherly foil to the larger-than-life hero. Pursuing a life-long obsession with the Holy Grail brings the prof into the grip of dastardly Nazis, who of course are after the same thing. It's Indiana Jones to the rescue of his father, the Grail, nay democracy itself. Wisely dispersing with attempts to recapture the central romance of *Raiders*, the emotional core is served this time by the sparring relationship between Indiana and his dad. Jeffrey Boam's script dabbles with themes of neglect and reconciliation, but there's nothing ponderous about the duo's near death scrapes and light-hearted tussels over the same blonde Fräulein. CM

Indiana Jones and the Temple of Doom

(Steven Spielberg, 1984, US) Harrison Ford, Kate Capshaw, Ke Huy Quan, Amrish Puri, Roshan Seth, Philip Stone, Dan Aykroyd.
118 min.
Conceived as a prequel to *Raiders of the Lost Ark*, this kids off in old Shanghai and quickly hotfoots it to the Himalayas in pursuit of another magical talisman. While the set pieces are as spectacular as ever (a neat Busby Berkeley pastiche of 'Anything Goes' as an opener, a corker of an underground helter-skelter ride), the intervening filler shows signs of desperation. Part of the trouble is that anything clearly does go, including the slender hold on credibility that *Raiders* managed to maintain. Gone is Karen Allen's tough, no nonsense heroine, and instead we have the off-putting sight of Capshaw wittering on about her broken nails. Foreigners are generally perceived as an

exotic bunch who are essentially savages at heart. The thrills are there all right, and delivered by the hand of a master, but the frantic flash-bang-wallop sounds altogether more hollow than last time around. JP

Indian Fighter, The

(André De Toth, 1955, US) Kirk Douglas, Elsa Martinelli, Walter Matthau, Walter Abel, Diana Douglas, Lon Chaney Jr, Elisha Cook Jr, Alan Hale Jr.
88 min.
A brisk and very polished Western, lacking the intensity of De Toth's later *Day of the Outlaw*, but notable for its sumptuous 'Scope photography and for its interest in the Sioux Indians and their closeness to nature. Douglas is typically robust as the scout hoping to make a peace treaty with the Sioux as he escorts a wagon train through their territory, while Martinelli, as the Indian girl he falls for, achieved some notoriety with a fairly explicit bathing sequence. The storyline is hardly original, but the solid cast and De Toth's effortless, elegant direction lend it a certain flair. GA

Indian in the Cupboard, The

(Frank Oz, 1995, US) Hal Scardino, Litefoot, Lindsay Crouse, Richard Jenkins, David Keith, Steve Coogan, Sakina Jaffrey.
96 min.
A delightful adaptation of Lynne Reid Banks' children's classic: Omri (Scardino), whose parents (Crouse and Jenkins) are sufficiently well off to afford kids' bedrooms large enough to be film sets, receives an old lock-up cupboard for his ninth birthday, and does swapsy for a plastic model of an 'Indian' with his pal Patrick. After a night in the cupboard, the model becomes Little Bear, an 18th century Onondaga-Iroquois brave (Litefoot). Once Little Bear realises Omri is no 'Great Spirit', they swiftly make friends and explain each other's worlds, until, that is, sole confidant Patrick 'brings to life' a 19th century cowboy (Keith), and their game becomes a matter of life and death. The film's conceit ('you should not do magic you do not understand') is prompted by the heart attack from fear of an old Native American chief, which is typical of the neatly (and lightly) concealed moral thrust of Melissa Mathison's screenplay, which teaches respect for people, knowledge and technology. Fine enlarged production design and effects, and appealing acting from the little and the large. WH

Indian Runner, The

(Sean Penn, 1991, US) David Morse, Viggo Mortensen, Valeria Golino, Patricia Arquette, Charles Bronson, Sandy Dennis, Dennis Hopper, Jordan Rhodes.
126 min.
Plattsmouth, Nebraska, 1968. Tattooed tearaway Frank Roberts (Mortensen) returns from Vietnam to be uncomfortably reunited with his brother Joe (Morse), a law-abiding family man. 'Some of the boys are coming back confused,' muses Bronson, excellently cast against type as the helpless father who needs constant reminding that 'Frank *left* confused'. As Joe strives in vain to rekindle the bond which once joined him to his brother, Frank descends into alcohol-addled oblivion. Inspired by Bruce Springsteen's 'Highway Patrolman', Penn's first project as writer-director is a film out of time, drenched in an overbearing '60s worldview which veers between the dated and the dopey. As a brother, Joe is heartbroken; as casual onlookers, we soon tire both of Frank's drunken philosophising and of Penn's reverence for his suffering. Potentially potent and not without naive charm, but ultimately a masturbatory ejaculation of all too personal juices. MK

Indians Are Still Far Away, The (Les Indiens Sont Encore Loin)

(Patricia Moraz, 1977, Switz/Fr) Isabelle Huppert, Christine Pascal, Mathieu Carrière, Nicole Garcia, Anton Diffring.
95 min.
One of the problems facing Swiss cinema is finding interesting and engaging ways of discussing the country's provincialism. The problem is emphasised in this film about the last week in the life of a schoolgirl because it opts for accumulating banalities. Isabelle Huppert, of *The Lacemaker*, registers another flawless recording of passive teenage despair. CPe

Indian Story, An

(Tapan K Bose, 1981, Ind) narrator:
Naseeruddin Shah.
59 min. b/w.
In 1980, thirty-three people were blinded by police
in the Bhagalpur district of India's eastern state
of Bihar. The police claimed they were criminals
and that the measures were necessary to curb the
soaring crime rate in that area. In fact most of
them had no criminal record, had not been convicted, or even charged with any specific crime,
but were picked almost at random from the
streets and villages around Bhagalpur and subjected to this quite horrendous justice. The Bihar
government and its henchmen managed to cover
up the whole thing so well that the only man punished was the police officer who leaked the affair.
This documentary recounts the story with a simple, chilling clarity. It also makes the necessary
connection between the Bhagalpur blindings and
the repressive machinery inherited from the
British and still maintained. MBo

Indian Summer

see Alive and Kicking

Indian Tomb, The

see Tiger of Eschnapur, The

India Song

(Marguerite Duras, 1974, Fr) Delphine Seyrig,
Michel Lonsdale, Mathieu Carrière, Claude
Mann, Vernon Dobtcheff, Didier Flamand.
120 min.
Duras' main protagonist is Anne-Marie Stretter
(Seyrig), a bored consular wife in '30s India, and the
film details the languorous desperation that drives
her to suicide. But the formal approach to this subject is like nothing before in film history: the 'drama'
is entirely aural (a play of off-screen voices blending with Carlos d'Alessio's utterly compulsive
score), and the elegant visuals counterpoint it by
creating an atmosphere of sumptuous enervation.
Many will find it fascinating, not least because its
sense of stifled anguish emerges without the least
hint of aggression in the style. TR

Indiscreet

(Stanley Donen, 1958, GB) Cary Grant, Ingrid
Bergman, Phyllis Calvert, Cecil Parker, David
Kossoff, Megs Jenkins.
99 min.
Despite the casting, far from a re-run of
Notorious. In fact the Norman Krasna script for
this romantic comedy fluff (about diplomat
Grant's insistence that he's already married in the
face of actress Bergman's attentions) originated
in a play of his that flopped on Broadway some
five years previously, Kind Sir. Here the New
York setting gave way to Mayfair, and Donen
piled on the civilised charm. PT

Indiscretion of an
American Wife

see Terminal Station

Indochine

(Régis Wargnier, 1991, Fr) Catherine Deneuve,
Vincent Pérez, Linh Dan Pham, Jean Yanne,
Dominique Blanc, Henri Marteau,
Carlo Brandt.
154 min.
Before Vietnam, there was Indochina; before the
Americans, the French. The languorous first half
of Wargnier's epic historical romance is pretty
much as you'd expect: plantation-owner Deneuve
in impeccably starched jodhpurs, coolies in their
place, civilisation transplanted to a hothouse. She
begins a passionate affair with a young naval
officer (Pérez), but he falls in love with her adopted Vietnamese daughter (Linh Dan Pham). When
he is sent to a remote outpost on the Gulf of
Tonkin, the girl takes after him. And Wargnier
follows. Midway through, having involved us so
deeply in colonial enterprise, he abruptly cuts our
cultural ties and plunges into sweeping revolutionary myth: the lovers go on the run, the girl
discovers her people, their struggle, what her role
must be. If Bertolucci tried his hand at a mini-
series, it would probably look something like this.
The allegorical intimations may not be entirely
credible, given the piece's lush romanticism; it's
rather enervatingly composed; and the pacing
could certainly be tighter. But such grand old-
fashioned melodrama is almost as exotic as the
stunning Vietnamese landscape; it's easy to be
seduced by it. TCh

I Never Promised You a
Rose Garden

(Anthony Page, 1977, US) Bibi Andersson,
Kathleen Quinlan, Sylvia Sidney, Ben Piazza,
Lorraine Gary, Darlene Craviotto, Reni
Santoni, Susan Tyrrell, Signe Hasso,
Diane Varsi.
96 min.
This Roger Corman production, faithful in detail
to Hannah Green's book (generally regarded as
one of the best lay descriptions of schizophrenia),
has 16-year-old Deborah Blake (Quinlan) struggling with her fantasy-world-turned-remorseless-
possessor and gradually being rehabilitated with
the help of her hospital doctor. Unlike the book,
though, the film fairly hurtles along, missing any
real analysis of mental disturbance while going
all out for Emotion. The inevitably beautiful victim suffers heavily sexual demons; the tragi-
comic antics of her fellow inmates are exploited
to the full; and the end is imbued with the peachy
tints of a full-blown rose. But it's enjoyable and
the performances are excellent, in particular Bibi
Andersson's doctor and Kathleen Quinlan's staggering portrayal of Deborah. Nutsploitation of a
superior kind. HM

I Never Sang for My Father

(Gilbert Cates, 1969, US) Melvyn Douglas,
Gene Hackman, Dorothy Stickney, Estelle
Parsons, Elizabeth Hubbard.
92 min.
Summer Wishes, Winter Dreams, and indeed The
Affair, showed how fine a director of actors Cates
is, and this earlier movie provides even more convincing evidence. Based on Robert (Tea and
Sympathy) Anderson's play, I Never Sang for My
Father is a close and fraught piece about that
curious, inarticulate love that turns blood relationships tacky and sour. Hackman makes something remarkable of the wrestling with himself
as well as with his father – Melvyn Douglas in
full flight – and Cates keeps the saccharine, if not
always the over-emphasis, at bay. If you're not
too laid back to stomach a film about emotions,
this is more than just a worthy affair. SG

Inevitable, The (Parinati)

(Prakash Jha, 1988, Ind) Basant Josalkar,
Surekha Sikri, Sudhir Kulkarni, Sharda ·
D'Soares, BD Singh.
125 min.
Set in an indeterminate period, this flawlessly
tells a folk tale that has all the elemental power
of myth. A humble but respected potter, his wife,
and young boy are encouraged by the local chief
to leave town to manage a remote desert well and
inn for travellers. Slowly, ineluctably, the seductive power of potential riches causes their downfall. First they allow their beloved son to be taken
away to be trained as a Seth (merchant). Later,
they abuse their reputation of service to prey on
their trusting guests. Jha, primarily a documentary film-maker, here serving as his own cinematographer, never puts a foot wrong. he
suffuses the screen with colour (gold, ochre, yellows), mines extraordinary performances from
his players, and uses faces and spaces to perfection, controlling and sustaining a mood of tragic
intensity. WH

In Expectation

see Rainclouds Over Wushan

In Fading Light

(Murray Martin/Amber Films, 1989, GB) Joe
Caffrey, Maureen Harold, Dave Hill, Brian
Hogg, Sammy Johnson, Joanna Ripley,
Amber Styles.
107 min.
The admirable Amber Films collective comes up
trumps again, after Seacoal, with another Loachian account of the disillusioned and dispossessed
up North. A teenage girl (Ripley) visits her
estranged father (Hill) in North Shields, and in
joining him aboard his fishing boat, comes up
against male chauvinism, female jealousy, and
the despair of running a traditional small business in the face of Thatcherite corporate investment. If it's sometimes hard to follow the
authentic dialect, there is no denying the convic-

tion of the naturalistic performances or the intelligence of the script, while a suspenseful gale
sequence effortlessly belies the lowly budget. GA

Infernal Street

see Return of the Dragon

Infernal Trio, The
(Le Trio Infernal)

(Francis Girod, 1974, Fr/It/WGer) Michel
Piccoli, Romy Schneider, Mascha Gomska,
Andrea Ferreol, Monica Fiorentini,
Philippe Brizard.
100 min.
An elegant and outrageous black opera, handled
with a panache that deliberately flouts notions of
good taste. Piccoli enjoys himself hugely as the
civic eminent (a distinguished lawyer newly
invested with the Legion of Honour) who swindles and murders unscrupulously with the help
of his lovers, two sisters (Schneider and Gomska).
The result is a finely balanced fairytale (complete
with 'happy' ending), full of a subversive mockery of pathetic respectabilities, unkind but not
callous. Avoid the English-dubbed version,
which coarsens the film to such an extent that it's
scarcely recognisable: the exuberant excesses of
Piccoli's performance are made to look merely
hammy. CPe

Inferno

(Roy Baker, 1953, US) Robert Ryan, Rhonda
Fleming, William Lundigan, Henry Hull, Carl
Betz, Larry Keating.
83 min.
A tight and involving essay in suspense which
works on the ingenious idea of leaving the audience alone in the desert with an unsympathetic
and selfish character (all the more so considering
that he's a millionaire), left to die with a broken
leg by his wife and her lover. Baker then forces us
to change our attitude of contempt to one of sympathy and admiration for his sheer will to survive.
The suspense is well handled, especially a descent
into a canyon with just one rope and a fall of hundreds of feet. The excellent Ryan plays the millionaire, Fleming his wife. Inferno was one of the
best and last movies to be made in 3-D during the
boom in the early '50s. Certainly its use of space
emphasised the dramatic possibilities of 3-D and
reveals, as more than one person has observed,
that the device had largely been squandered in
other films made at the time. CPe

Inferno

(Dario Argento, 1980, It) Leigh McCloskey,
Irene Miracle, Eleonora Giorgi, Daria Nicolodi,
Sacha Pitoeff, Alida Valli, Veronica Lazar.
107 min.
Argento's career has largely centred on a series
of outlandish thrillers, notable for their bizarre
set pieces, elaborate editing and camerawork.
These bravura displays of technique remained at
odds with his banal handling of actors and narrative, but his best known film, Suspiria, seemed
to indicate that Argento had begun to devise a
style of commercial film-making which was moving away from the limitations of conventional
narrative (or certainly treating it in the most perfunctory fashion), and thrilling the audience only
through sound, image and movement. Sadly,
Inferno – murder and the occult in a New York
apartment house – is a much more conventional
and unexciting piece of work. Argento's own
over-the-top score has been replaced by religioso
thunderings from the keyboards of Keith
Emerson, and the meandering narrative confusions are amplified by weak performances. Even
the set pieces fail to set the screen alight, and the
film's remaining virtue is a series of remarkable
individual shots illuminated like masterworks of
comic book art. SM

Informer, The

(John Ford, 1935, US) Victor McLaglen,
Heather Angel, Preston Foster, Margot
Grahame, Wallace Ford, Una O'Connor, JM
Kerrigan, Donald Meek.
91 min. b/w.
What do critics dream about? John Ford got the
best reviews of his career for this heavy-handed,
humourless and patronising art film ('Many consider it the greatest talking picture ever made in
America', wrote Theodore Huff a few years later),
roundly, and rightly, debunked by Lindsay

Anderson for having the 'painstaking explicit-ness of a silent film grimly determined to tell its story without the aid of titles'. Liquored up by Ford, McLaglen won an Oscar for his lumbering portrait of a brainless, boozy Dubliner, Gypo Nolan, who betrays his buddy to the Black and Tans for a kingly £20, then suffers sweatily under the torments of conscience. There were fur-ther awards for the director, Dudley Nichols' script, and Max Steiner's score – all equally over-emphatic. Today, only Joe August's foggy expressionist camerawork still captures the imag-ination, but even this becomes enervatingly por-tentous before long. TCh

Ingaló
(Asdis Thoroddsen, 1992, Ice) Solveig Arnarsdottir, Haraldur Hallgrimsson, Ingvar Sigurdsson.
98 min.
Bearing an uncanny resemblance to Amber Films' *In Fading Light*, this centres on a 'difficult' (ie. feisty and aggressive) 18-year-old, who leaves her family home on the northern coast of Iceland to join her brother on board a trawler: much gut-ting ensues. A low-key fable that leavens its raw emotional authenticity with an unexpectedly sly wit, it's deftly acted, crisply shot, and eventually about issues of sexual chauvinism, economics, and labour intrigue. If it never gets as sharply political as Amber's movie, it's a fine effort all the same. GA

In Georgia (In Georgien)
(Jürgen Böttcher, 1987, EGer)
100 min.
There's a sense of wonder to Böttcher's graceful film about the republic of Georgia on the Black Sea. With a minimal crew, he travels along the coastline, visiting the main cities and holiday resorts and the most isolated mountain villages, touching on the region's history, culture and sim-plicity of life. Breath-taking panoramic views of misty blue-grey mountains, and long, long takes that allow for uncoaxed responses from the peas-ant subjects, create an impression of a mystical lost land. EP

In Harm's Way
(Otto Preminger, 1965, US) John Wayne, Kirk Douglas, Patricia Neal, Tom Tryon, Paula Prentiss, Brandon de Wilde, Burgess Meredith, Henry Fonda, Dana Andrews.
167 min. b/w.
Preminger, having already revealed a taste for excessive length in films like *Advise and Consent*, *Exodus* and *The Cardinal*, here stretches out a rel-atively conventional WWII drama to the point of tedium. Wayne is the discredited admiral whose reactions to the Japanese attack on Pearl Harbor finally convince both the Navy's top brass and his alienated, contemptuous son of his worth; sub-plots include his romance with nurse Neal, and his executive officer Douglas's trajectory towards self-destruction after he learns of his faithless wife's death. It goes on and on, the slowness exac-erbated by Preminger's customary long takes and by the endless parade of star cameos. So what's it all add up to? War may be hell, but courage and honour will triumph in the end. GA

Inheritance, The
(L'Eredità Ferramonti)
(Mauro Bolognini, 1976, It) Anthony Quinn, Fabio Testi, Dominique Sanda, Luigi Proietti, Adriana Asti.
121 min.
The insipid Sanda seduces her way into the affec-tions and bed of self-made millionaire Quinn, to get her hands on his closely guarded lucre. Passionless characterisations abound, and the periodic spasms of carnality offer little relief as we are swanned around the meticulously realised Rome of the 1880s. Punters dishing out good money in the hopes of seeing a sexually explicit version of TV's *Dynasty* may well be disappoint-ed. WH

Inherit the Wind
(Stanley Kramer, 1960, US) Spencer Tracy, Fredric March, Gene Kelly, Florence Eldridge, Dick York, Donna Anderson, Harry Morgan.
127 min. b/w.
Courtroom drama meets pious liberalism in this stolid adaptation of the Jerome Lawrence-Robert

E Lee play about the Tennessee 'Monkey Trial' of 1925 (when a young schoolmaster – played by York – was indicted for illegally teaching Darwinian theory). Tolerably gripping in its old-fashioned way, thanks chiefly to old pro perfor-mances from Tracy and March as the rival lawyers and ideologists, but rather let down by Kelly's inadequacy as the cynical journalist who is comfortably denounced as the real villain of the piece. TM

Inhibitions
(Paul Price i.e. Paolo Poeti, 1976, It) Claudine Beccarie, Ivan Rassimov, Ilona Staller, Cesare Barro.
120 min.
Veteran porn star Claudine Beccarie shows her years in this lavish sex film, set in North Africa (and heavily cut for British distribution). The more than usually fatuous plot revolves around the inhibited proprietress of a stud ranch who spends her time indulging in casual affairs and snubbing an impecunious upper-class English-man. In the last reel she succumbs to his sinceri-ty, and the proceedings conclude with a bout of passionate, long-delayed grappling. Some dread-ful bits of half-baked philosophising crop up from time to time. JPy

Inhumaine, L'
(Marcel L'Herbier, 1924, Fr) Georgette Leblanc, Jaque Catelain, Philippe Hériat, Marcelle Pradot, Fred Kellerman.
6,120 ft. b/w.
Part-financed by American singer Georgette Leblanc, who also stars, this was designed as a sort of showcase for contemporary French arts. So, decorating a tolerably camp story about a heartless woman (Leblanc) who is poisoned by one disappointed lover (Hériat) and scientifically resuscitated into new humanity by another (Catelain), it boasts extravagant Cubist settings (by Fernand Léger, Robert Mallet-Stevens, Claude Autant-Lara and Alberto Cavalcanti), fea-tures costumes by Paul Poiret, incorporates a Jean Borlin ballet, makes coy reference to radio and TV, and was originally accompanied by a Darius Milhaud score. The result, resolutely chic, brought instant sneers about aesthetic dilettan-tism which L'Herbier was subsequently never quite able to shake off. But despite the wretched acting and daft script (by Pierre Mac Orlan), the last third of the film, in which L'Herbier's attempt to apply a different mood and rhythm to each set-ting begins to pay dividends, is often remarkable in the way it manipulates space as an autonomous element in the drama. TM

In Ismail's Custody
(Derrick Santini, 1994, GB) Anthony Hopkins, Simon Callow, Ruth Prawer Jhabvala, Vanessa Redgrave, Andrew Sarris, Shashi Kapoor.
48 min.
This documentary, by Merchant Ivory stillsman Derrick Santini, courses through the life of Ismail Merchant, from childhood in Bombay, the son of a Muslim textile merchant, to his heights in 1994 as producer of *The Remains of the Day*. Bombay is the Indian Hollywood, but it was on a trip to New York for university studies that Merchant first saw De Sica and Satyajit Ray and he realised the type of film he wished to make. Santini has rounded up the usual suspects: Anthony Hopkins, Emma Thompson, Vanessa Redgrave, Simon Callow ('He's a maverick,' echoing the rest), collaborator/writer Ruth Jhabvala, et al. Shashi Kapoor has been a friend since the first MI film, *The Householder* in 1963, so his com-ments on working on *In Custody*, Merchant's fea-ture debut – 'He's the most fascist director in the world!' – could be humorous. Critic Andrew Sarris and ex-Disney supremo Jeffrey Katzen-berg's testimony shows the Yanks have been wowed too. After 30 years of struggle, the world seems to be his oyster – or perhaps his chicken *tikka*. WH

In-Laws, The
(Arthur Hiller, 1979, US) Peter Falk, Alan Arkin, Richard Libertini, Nancy Dussault, Penny Peyser, Arlene Golonka.
103 min.
Much Arkin and Falkin about enlivens this MOR buddy-comedy, which has a bewildered dentist and a loony CIA man hauling stolen Treasury engravings through a Central American banana-

joke republic just before their kids' wedding. Too silly to be particularly offensive or even particu-larly funny – it's simply outstandingly ordinary stuff.

In Like Flint
(Gordon Douglas, 1967, US) James Coburn, Lee J Cobb, Jean Hale, Andrew Duggan, Anna Lee, Hanna Landy, Totty Ames, Steve Ihnat.
115 min.
Dire sequel to the already desperately flashy *Our Man Flint*, with its nudging innuendo stuck at the level of its punning title. Coburn's super-Bond saves the world from women. Ray Danton took over when TV unwisely revived the 'spoofy' (?) formula in the '70s. PT

In Love
(aka Strangers in Love)
(Chuck Vincent, 1983, US) Kelly Nichols, Jerry Butler, Jack Wrangler, Tish Ambrose, Joanna Storm, Samantha Fox, Michael Knight.
90 min.
While everybody goes ape over *Terms of Endearment*, spare a thought for this softcore soap, which pulls off the 20 Years' Edited Highlights trick on about a billionth of the bud-get. It starts in Florida 1962, where Andy and Jill enjoy a torrid holiday fling before scooting back to their separate existences. New York: he gets the sack, gets divorced. San Francisco: she hangs out with the boho crowd. He sprouts a nifty pair of velcro sideburns and gets his Master Charge revoked. She drops acid and winds up in jail. He becomes a filthy rich restaurateur. She becomes a filthy rich writer. And all the time they pine for each other. Merely dancing with a nymphette in white knickers can take him back twenty years to his one true love. Lelouch in the raw: this could be a contender for the Women's Own selection were it not for the odd bit of tit and bum. AB

In Love and War
(Richard Attenborough, 1996, US) Sandra Bullock, Chris O'Donnell, Mackenzie Astin, Emilio Bonucci, Ingrid Lacey, Margot Steinberg.
114 min.
Singularly uninspiring three-handed dramatisa-tion (of a book by Henry S Villard and James Nagel) of the passionate but ill-fated affair of Ernest Hemingway (O'Donnell) and nurse Agnes von Kurowsky (Bullock). This was during the author's formative spell as a volunteer orderly on the Austro-Italian front in 1918. Bullock simply doesn't have a period face, and looks hopelessly lost. Love, war and grand passion ain't her thing, though you can forgive her for looking uncon-vinced in the clinches with eternal jock O'Donnell, who gives the same faintly irritating performance he always does. Attenborough conjures up hordes of extras for the battle scenes and stun-ning Venetian locations for the subplot involving wealthy Italian suitor Bonucci, yet the film's vision of the horrors of war proves so blandly approximate it never quite fixes the central rela-tionship in sharp focus. Bereft of startling the-matic insight or leavening gallows humour, such old-fashioned selfless heroism and breast-heaving romance doesn't really play any more. The kind of movie the director might have made 30 years ago, and after the very moving *Shadowlands*, a considerable let-down. TJ

In Name Only
(John Cromwell, 1939, US) Carole Lombard, Cary Grant, Kay Francis, Charles Coburn, Helen Vinson, Peggy Ann Garner.
94 min. b/w.
Cary Grant has it all: money, a beautiful wife (Francis) – then he goes and falls in love with artist Carole Lombard, and the Mrs won't give him a divorce. It has all the trappings of a won-derful screwball comedy: in fact it's a mushy tear-jerker, handled with a certain amount of style by John Cromwell.

Inner Circle, The
(Il Proiezionista)
(Andrei Konchalovsky, 1991, It) Tom Hulce, Lolita Davidovich, Bob Hoskins, Aleksandr Zbruev, Feodor Chaliapin Jr, Bess Meyer, Maria Baranova.
137 min.
Glasnost and *perestroika* have a bit to answer for

i

with this true-ish story. Allowed back into Russia to film, Konchalovsky was given access to secret police chief Beria's bullet-proof train compartment and the dreaded KGB building. And that, plus Hoskins' amused performance as Beria, is the upside. Ivan (Hulce), believing that he's under arrest, is whisked off to work the projector for movie-fan Stalin (Zbruev), and is soon boasting to his wife Anastasia (Davidovich) about his importance. She doesn't share his worship of Stalin, and is obsessed with the fate of an orphaned Jewish girl (Baranova). None of this is convincing, and errors of judgment reach surreal proportions (passing cattle urinating into the couple's basement flat, an enormous gilt bust of Stalin bulging out the window). While serving on a train, Anastasia is 'requisitioned' by Beria, though Ivan registers only the honour of it all – until she returns pregnant. Grinning Hulce is unbelievably gormless throughout. BC

Innerspace
(Joe Dante, 1987, US) Dennis Quaid, Martin Short, Meg Ryan, Kevin McCarthy, Fiona Lewis, Vernon Wells, Henry Gibson, Dick Miller, Chuck Jones.
120 min.
After an accident, scientifically miniaturised marine Quaid finds himself floating, complete with miniaturised submersible, around the body of neurotic wimp Short. The pair's attempts to return him to normal size are hampered by evil saboteurs keen in killing Short in order to get hold of the magical miniaturising whatsit. Where Dante transcended the formulaic ingredients of *Gremlins* and *Explorers* by means of dark, droll wit, here for the most part he indulges in frenetic slapstick, broad parody, and juvenile mugging. And while the anatomical special effects are imaginative enough, the manic rather than magical tone fails to achieve the sense of awe that made *Fantastic Voyage* – clearly this film's inspiration – so fascinating. GA

Innocence Unprotected (Nevinost Bez Zastite)
(Dusan Makavejev, 1968, Yugo) Dragoljub Aleksic, Ana Milosavljevic, Vera Jovanovic, Bratoljub Gligorijevic.
78 min. b/w & col.
Makavejev's third film, an entrancing collage using excerpts from the first Serbian talkie, a hilariously naïve melodrama made in occupied Belgrade in 1942 with film stock stolen from the Germans. Bad as the film was, it was apparently a huge success, mainly because audiences delighted in flouting German movies to wallow in its pouting heroine's adventures as she is saved from a wicked stepmother and a leering lecher by a strong man with the heart of a lion (played by a real life Charles Atlas-cum-Houdini type). Innocence, though, is preserved in more ways than one, for Makavejev reassembled the surviving members of cast and crew, older, greyer and sadder. The strong man demonstrates that he can still manage some of his milder tricks (and defends himself against a charge of wartime collaboration); the stepmother wistfully recalls that she once won a competition for the most beautiful legs in Belgrade (and does a song-and-dance to prove it); and as they exchange memories of the old days, Makavejev cuts in newsreel shots of the Occupation so that one begins to see the hoary old melodrama with the eyes of 1942. The film, the people, their youth and their dreams, hover before us as miraculously preserved as flies in amber. TM

Innocent, The
(John MacKenzie, 1984, GB) Andrew Hawley, Kika Markham, Kate Foster, Liam Neeson, Patrick Daley, Paul Askew, Lorraine Peters, Tom Bell, Miranda Richardson.
96 min.
Set in a cotton-mill town in the depths of the '30s depression, this professes to offer a truthful picture of life and love on the dole, but too often settles for quaint nostalgia. A young epileptic roams the Yorkshire dales (spectacularly shot) in search of the rare, wonderful kingfisher when the adult world becomes too bewildering and tough. The film has all the makings of a Sunday afternoon tearjerker, only MacKenzie is too honest to pull too heavily on the heartstrings. He is rewarded by merely revealing the thinness of the characterisation and the meagreness of the script. JE

Innocent, The (L'Innocente)
(Luchino Visconti, 1976, It/Fr) Giancarlo Giannini, Laura Antonelli, Jennifer O'Neill, Rina Morelli, Massimo Girotti, Didier Haudepin, Marie Dubois.
128 min.
After several misguided projects, Visconti's last film returns to the territory he knew best, and forms a worthy finale to a distinguished career. The plot is understated melodrama: a turn-of-the-century gentleman of leisure indulges all his own extra-marital whims, but is mortified when his wife has an affair; his whole philosophy crumbles as he desperately tries to preserve his self-respect. It's based (faithfully) on a novel by Gabriele D'Annunzio, and Visconti's treatment is much more novelistic than melodramatic: the style is uninflected, and the stately camerawork directs attention to the period manners and environments and the notably convincing characterisations. The film resolves itself into an almost painfully sincere meditation on masculine self-delusion. It has a great performance from Laura Antonelli as the wife, and excellent ones from Giannini and Jennifer O'Neill as husband and lover. TR

Innocent, The (...und der Himmel steht still)
(John Schlesinger, 1993, GB/Ger) Anthony Hopkins, Isabella Rossellini, Campbell Scott, Hart Bochner, Ronald Nitschke, James Grant, Jeremy Sinden.
119 min.
Berlin, 1955. A gauche young electronics expert, Leonard Marnham (Scott), arrives in a city drawn and quartered by the Cold War. Already dazed to be enlisted by British Intelligence, he's even more at sea when he finds himself working on a top-secret American project under the command of one Bob Glass (Hopkins), and completely out of his depth when he's seduced by the strange, lovely German Maria (Rossellini). Before they're through, the three will be party to a secret as terrible as any covert international operation. The film didn't have an easy route to the screen. The production lost both director (Mike Newell) and leading lady (Lena Olin) before Schlesinger stepped into the breach. Surprising, then, to discover just how much this absorbing, intelligent picture (from a novel by Ian McEwan) has going for it: a strong sense of time and place, interesting characters, an intriguing scenario. Not that the film works. The pace is altogether too genteel, and, crucially, the casting doesn't stick. TCh

Innocent Blood
(John Landis, 1993, US) Robert Loggia, Anne Parillaud, Anthony LaPaglia, David Proval, Don Rickles.
113 min.
If you've been waiting since 1981 for Landis to reprise the clever blend of horror and humour of *An American Werewolf in London*, this black-comic vampire movie will answer some of your prayers. Parillaud plays Maria, a modern-day vampire with glinting eyes and selective eating habits: she only feeds on bad guys, which puts ambitious Mafia boss Sal Macelli (Loggia) on the menu. Also staking out Macelli is undercover cop Joe Gennaro (LaPaglia) who, despite discovering Maria's secret, teams up with her to prevent Sal turning Pittsburgh into an open-air restaurant for Mafia blood brothers. Going easy on the tomato sauce and fx trimmings, Landis and Parillaud instead emphasise the loneliness of Maria's nocturnal existence. Drawing a parallel with Gennaro's undercover isolation and hinting at a cautious affinity in a bravura sex scene, Landis brilliantly captures a carnal craving laced with blood lust and dangerous eroticism; but, regrettably, all too often the tone lurches from stylish suspense to smart-ass in-jokiness and silly slapstick. NF

Innocent Man, An
(Peter Yates, 1989, US) Tom Selleck, F Murray Abraham, laila Robins, David Rasche, Richard Young, Peter Van Norden, Bruce A Young.
113 min.
When wealthy aircraft engineer Jimmie Rainwood (Selleck) is first shot, then framed by a pair of carelessly corrupt drug (taking) cops, his cosily ordered world is thrown into chaos. Considering himself a 'model citizen' (with only an old marijuana conviction to blot his copybook), Rainwood soon dis-

covers that while the law may be an ass, his own ass is in serious danger. Sentenced to prison, where warring gangs of blacks and whites beat, rape and humiliate each other, the naive idealist is taken under the wing of veteran inmate Virgil Cane (Abraham). Rainwood learns that to survive in this hell-hole he must stand up and fight – knowledge he carries with him on his eventual parole. With the exception of Abraham's world-weary performance, and a couple of nicely nasty cameos from David Rasche and Richard Young as the crooked cops, this is a disposable affair. Yates' ham-fisted direction cranks the film up into melodramatic hyperbole, but Selleck is the real villain, portraying his transformation from wide-eyed innocent to hardened man of the world by changing from clean-shaven mop top to stubbly slicked-back, with reflecting shades to boot. Laughable. MK

Innocent Moves
see Searching for Bobby Fischer.

Innocents, The
(Jack Clayton, 1961, GB) Deborah Kerr, Martin Stephens, Pamela Franklin, Megs Jenkins, Michael Redgrave, Peter Wyngarde, Clytie Jessop, Isla Cameron.
99 min. b/w.
Extremely impressive chiller based on Henry James' *The Turn of the Screw*, with Kerr perfectly cast as the prim, repressed Victorian governess who begins to worry that her young wards may be possessed by the evil spirits of dead servants. No shock tactics here, just the careful creation of sinister atmosphere through decor, Freddie Francis' haunting camerawork, and evocative acting. Kerr, especially, is excellent: rarely was her air of struggling to veil growing hysteria under a civilised facade so appropriately deployed. GA

Innocents in Paris
(Gordon Parry, 1953, GB) Alastair Sim, Ronald Shiner, Margaret Rutherford, Claire Bloom, Laurence Harvey, Jimmy Edwards, Richard Wattis, Louis de Funès, Christopher Lee, Kenneth Williams.
102 min. b/w.
It's national stereotyping well to the fore when assorted Brits launch themselves at Gay Paree for the weekend in this dim spot of '50s portmanteau flummery. Treasury man Sim winds up downing a few with the intransigent Russian delegate; Jimmy Edwards zeroes in on an English pub; and Harvey displays his complete lack of any comic timing as a waiter on the make. It makes TV's *'Allo, 'Allo* look relatively sophisticated, but the likes of Sim and Rutherford perk it up while they're on. TJ

Innocent Sleep, The
(Scott Michell, 1995, GB) Rupert Graves, Annabella Sciorra, Michael Gambon, Graham Crowden, Franco Nero.
99 min.
Down and out in London, Alan (Graves) witnesses the assassination of a businessman, left hanging under Tower Bridge. At the local police station, he's horrified to recognise Insp Stephens (Gambon) from the crime. While Stephens sets about tying up this unexpected loose end, Alan begs reporter Billie Hayman (Sciorra) to check out his story. From the very first sequence, Michell's directorial debut belies its no-budget origins to take us on a journey from the fetid humanity of Cardboard City to the cold, hidden bastions of power. Some of the supporting turns are uneven (Crowden holds nothing back as an alcoholic tramp with useful connections), and Ray Villis's underwritten script runs out of ingenuity on the final lap, but Michell keeps the pacing tight and enlists some lively work from Sciorra and Graves (much more interesting now he's out of those linen suits). It's a classical, rather old-fashioned film, with a symphonic score by Mark Ayres and impressive 'Scope cinematography by Alan Dunlop. TCh

Innocent Sorcerers (Niewinni Czarodzieje)
(Andrzej Wajda, 1960, Pol) Tadeusz Lomnicki, Krystyna Stypulkowska, Zbigniew Cybulski, Wanda Koczeska, Teresa Szmigielowna, Roman Polanski, Krzysztof Komeda, Jerzy Skolimowski.
91 min. b/w.

After his war trilogy, Wajda made this 'new wave' style film about contemporary youth from a script by Skolimowski. The subject is the ritual game-playing of the post-war generation, focusing on a dissolute young man (Lomnicki) who finds himself alone one night with a spikily garrulous young woman (Stypulkowska). They play out a kind of psychological striptease that ends with nothing actually happening, since neither will expose any raw feeling to the other. Wajda himself was unhappy with the result, feeling no particular sympathy for such an 'ineffective' hero. If the film still has value, it lies in the compelling lead performances and the vivid portrait of a newly restless milieu – among them (in a small role), one Roman Polanski, clearly eager to leave this Communist *huis clos*. DT

Innocents with Dirty Hands (Les Innocents aux Mains Sales)
(Claude Chabrol, 1975, Fr/WGer/It) Romy Schneider, Rod Steiger, Paolo Giusti, Jean Rochefort, François Maistre, Pierre Santini, Hans Christian Blech, Dominique Zardi, Henri Attal.
125 min.
A superbly stylish and baroque crime thriller which marks a return for Chabrol to the bravura incorporation of pulp conventions that distinguished some of his earlier work. But here the convoluted plot draws us inexorably through a minefield of kaleidoscopically changing relationships at the kind of measured pace that allows the film to accumulate all sorts of tragic resonances. There are innumerable bold strokes as Chabrol treads from irony to irony, ambiguity to ambiguity. Romy Schneider is fascinating as the icy wife plotting to rid herself of her boorish husband (doubts about Steiger fade as the film progresses), and the minor characters – including a characteristically histrionic lawyer and two policemen given to discussing the case over meals of various dimensions – are drawn with absolute precision. VG

Inn of the Frightened People
see Revenge

Inn of the Sixth Happiness, The
(Mark Robson, 1958, GB) Ingrid Bergman, Curt Jürgens, Robert Donat, Michael David, Athene Seyler, Richard Wattis, Ronald Squire.
158 min.
The renowned story of Gladys Aylward (played by Bergman), an ex-housemaid who became a missionary in China in the '30s. Sketchily scripted and shamelessly glamorised (Aylward bitterly resented being depicted as having had an affair with a Chinese army officer, played by Jürgens), the film is nevertheless a proficiently mounted blend of spectacle and human interest; and the famous climax (Aylward leading the orphaned children over the mountains) is a throat-tightener. The last film of Robert Donat, who looked very ill in his part as the Mandarin. DMcG

In Old Chicago
(Henry King, 1938, US) Tyrone Power, Alice Faye, Don Ameche, Alice Brady, Andy Devine, Brian Donlevy.
95 min. b/w.
MGM famously mounted the West Coast's most notorious earthquake in 1936's *San Francisco*, so rival studio Fox came up with their own equally spectacular disaster flick in this impressive recreation of the 1871 Great Fire of Chicago. With a star-filled cast and a fitful sense of drama, it's pretty much the same old recipe as the equivalent cycle of megabudget '70s exploiters, but the climactic conflagration – shot on the backlot under such dangerous conditions that no women were allowed on set and stuntmen in dresses took all the female parts – is certainly worth the wait.

In Praise of Older Women
(George Kaczender, 1977, Can) Tom Berenger, Karen Black, Susan Strasberg, Helen Shaver, Marilyn Lightstone, Alexandra Stewart.
110 min.
Despite its title, this tediously faithful adaptation of Stephen Vizinczey's book proves to be no more than the picaresque adventures of a highly self-satisfied Hungarian Romeo. Glibly reflecting on

the nature of Women, Love, etc., hero and film skate arm-in-arm across an utterly conventional series of sexual encounters: from adolescent seduced by his neighbour (whatever is Karen Black doing here?), via cabaret artiste and 'revolutionary', to the women he meets as a philosophy lecturer in Canada. The film hits a high when one of his pupils has the temerity to declare her sexual preferences. But as that immediately writes her out of the picture, we are back to the soft-focus, softcore actions of a limp prick; a guy who can rise no further than his own dire simile: love is like a supermarket – you can come out with goods you just didn't need. HM

Inquisitor, The
see Garde à Vue

Ins and the Outs, The
see Uns et les Autres, Les

Insatiable
(Godfrey Daniels, 1980, US) Marilyn Chambers, John C Holmes, Serena, Jesie St James, John Leslie.
80 min.
Stash the old raincoat if you venture out to sample this vehicle for American porno star Chambers which, to judge from the marketing, is being offered in Britain as middle class 'acceptable' skinflick. The original *Insatiable* that set Manhattan dinner parties a-chatter was longer by thirteen minutes, as was stud star Holmes by several inches. The censor has snipped all the hardcore but passed the macho brutality of the foreplay and orgasmic cutaways, leaving a handful of reels that could be projected in any order to the same numbing effect. MA

In Search of Famine (Aakaler Sandhane)
(Mrinal Sen, 1981, Ind) Dhritiman Chatterjee, Smita Patil, Sreela Majumdar, Gita Sen, Dipankar Dey.
125 min.
A polemical feature from India's leading political film-maker, whose strident radicalism constrasts starkly with the liberal humanism of fellow-Bengali Satyajit Ray. In 1980, a film unit arrives in a Bengali village to film a story about the terrible famine of 1943. However, their failure to understand or communicate with the villagers threatens the viability of the project. The filmmakers' intention is to recreate the dire poverty of a disabled peasant's household, yet they seem oblivious to the fact that the lot of the villagers has improved very little in the intervening years. Using this film-within-a-film device, Sen calls into question the insensitive assumptions of the privileged film-makers – an afternoon's shopping for the crew, for example, cleans out the village's vegetable market. NF

Insect Woman, The (Chung Nyo)
(Kim Ki-Young, 1972, SKor) Namgung Won, Yun Yo-jong, Chon Kye-hyon.
110 min.
A delirious, overheated melodrama in which a young woman, forced to support her unappreciative family, slides into a life of prostitution, exploitation and sexual violence, with deadly results. Shot in expressionist style, complete with weird camera effects, this is a movie about madness, inflamed passions, impotence, sadism and, unfortunately, 'Ma Cherie Amour'. GA

Inserts
(John Byrum, 1975, GB) Richard Dreyfuss, Jessica Harper, Veronica Cartwright, Bob Hoskins, Stephen Davies.
117 min.
Very few sex films are actually about sexuality. While this makes a few moves in that direction, it takes an unconscionably long time about it. Set in '30s Hollywood, the stagebound action takes place on a single set where a faded director (Dreyfuss) has been reduced by the talkies to grinding out a porno silent, complete with gay stud and junked-up ex-DeMille actress. Stale repartee and Golden Age gags proliferate; nor does the action pick up with the arrival of other characters and the porno queen's overdose. But when the film finally reaches its erotic confrontation between Dreyfuss and

his backer's girlfriend (beautifully played by Jessica Harper), it does momentarily move into a different league. The censor has spared the scissors here, but someone should have used them on the first hour. DP

Inside Daisy Clover
(Robert Mulligan, 1965, US) Natalie Wood, Christopher Plummer, Robert Redford, Ruth Gordon, Katharine Bard, Roddy McDowall.
128 min.
This story of the rise and fall of a '30s musical starlette left audiences rather cold on its release, and it's not hard to see why. Gavin Lambert's screenplay (from his own novel) lives in the land of the ambiguous and fey, which is probably why the film now seems subtle and attractive. Wood's performance is no Meryl Streep number (and arguably the better for it), while Redford as her possibly gay husband is extraordinarily handsome, which all adds to the air of innocence. The songs by Andre and Dory Previn are nothing to get excited about, though. DT

Inside Job
see Alpha Caper, The

Inside Moves
(Richard Donner, 1980, US) John Savage, David Morse, Diana Scarwid, Amy Wright, Tony Burton, Bert Remsen, Harold Russell.
113 min.
Savage, crippled as a result of a suicide attempt, is reborn in a seedy LA bar where most of the regulars are disabled. As if this weren't difficult enough material in itself, the plot is also determinedly optimistic, mingling its neo-realist surface with dreams of basketball stardom which eventually come true. Sheer eccentricity and ambitiousness place *Inside Moves* above the Kramer class, but ultimately the film only reconfirms that good liberal intentions rarely produce good Hollywood movies.

Inside Out
(Peter Duffell, 1975, GB/WGer) Telly Savalas, Robert Culp, James Mason, Aldo Ray, Günter Meisner, Adrian Hoven, Charles Korvin.
97 min.
After Duffell's impressive *England Made Me*, this vehicle for Telly Savalas' continuing over-exposure comes as a disappointment. Based around the springing from gaol of a top Nazi general who can tell a band of ageing misfits about a cache of gold, what emerges is a rather forlorn middle-aged men's fantasy. After some awkward exposition and flashbacks over 30 years, the film settles into a knowing heist caper whose script desperately papers over the implausibilities with wisecracks. One moment of high farce in which the general is confronted with an apparently resurrected Führer in his bunker suggests that events might be taking a belated turn for the better. Sadly, this is not the case. CPe

Insignificance
(Nicolas Roeg, 1985, GB) Michael Emil, Theresa Russell, Tony Curtis, Gary Busey, Will Sampson.
109 min.
1954. As Monroe, Einstein, DiMaggio and McCarthy, Roeg assembles an excellent cast of non-stars, confines them in anonymous hotel rooms, and lets them rip on all his favourite topics: life, love, fame, hate, jealousy, atomic firestorm and the whole damn thing. As usual with Roeg, the firmament is streaming with large ideas and awkward emotions, which grow larger and larger in significance, and most of which come together in a delightful scene when Marilyn (Russell) explains relativity to Einstein (Emil) with the aid of clockwork trains and balloons. Curtis is Senator McCarthy, still witch-hunting phantoms of his mind; Busey is the washed-up ballplayer, aching for Marilyn's return. It may be a chamber piece, but its circumference is vast. CPea

Inspecteur Lavardin
(Claude Chabrol, 1986, Fr) Jean Poiret, Jean-Claude Brialy, Bernadette Lafont, Jean-Luc Bideau, Jacques Dacqmine, Hermine Clair.
100 min.
Shortly after investigating the banning as blasphemous of a play entitled 'Our Father Which Farts in Heaven', a high-minded paterfamilias is

found dead on the beach, PIG scrawled insultingly on his naked backside. With the widow offering a regal display of indifference, a teenage step-daughter skulking furtively in drug-pushing circles, and a gay uncle gloating madly over his collection of glass eyes, this is Chabrol at odds with the bourgeoisie again. But there is a difference as Poiret's police inspector arrives for his second murder investigation following *Cop au Vin*, this time trailing memories of his former love for the widow, a fallen angel who has innocently sinned in her emotional affairs. Discovering what amounts to a paradise lost, Lavardin elects to play God in order to rout the otherwise unassailable forces of evil. Strangely tender, bizarrely funny, with gorgeous performances from Lafont (the widow) and Brialy (the uncle), this is Chabrol back to the mood of eccentric metaphysical mystery he mined in the marvellous *Ten Days' Wonder*. TM

Inspector Calls, An

(Guy Hamilton, 1954, GB) Alastair Sim, Jane Wrenham, Arthur Young, Olga Lindo, Brian Worth, Bryan Forbes, Pat Neal, George Cole.
79 min. b/w.
JB Priestley's play comes to the screen (adapted by Desmond Davis) with a minimum of cinematic imagination. Alastair Sim is still highly watchable, however, as the Yorkshire policeman who materialises in the midst of a comfortably off Edwardian family to reveal how each one of its complacent members bears some responsibility in the suicide of a pregnant pauper. The play survives, just. TJ

Inspector Clouseau

(Bud Yorkin, 1968, US) Alan Arkin, Delia Boccardo, Frank Finlay, Patrick Cargill, Beryl Reid, Barry Foster.
94 min.
The bumbling French policeman – immortalised by Peter Sellers, but only impersonated here by Alan Arkin – is called to Swinging London to help the Yard track down a gang using the proceeds of the Great Train Robbery to siphon funds from every bank on Swiss soil. Sorely contrived.

Institute Benjamenta

(Brothers Quay, 1995, GB) Mark Rylance, Gottfried John, Alice Krige, Daniel Smith, Joseph Alessi, Jonathan Stone.
105 min. b/w.
Sometime this century, somewhere in Europe: Jakob von Gunten (Rylance) enrols at the Institute Benjamenta, a run-down edifice headed by an eccentric tyrant (John) and dedicated to the training of suitably unambitious, humble servants. Though Jakob readily submits to the repetitive regime of incredibly banal lessons in servility, he begins to wonder whether he might be sufficiently princely to rescue his melancholy tutor, Benjamenta's sister Lisa (Krige), from the suffocating half-life she leads inside the school's sinister, shadowy walls. Inspired by the writings of Swiss novelist Robert Walser, the first feature from the Brothers Quay is as outlandishly beautiful, bizarre, mysterious and inventive as one might expect; more surprising, perhaps, given their history as animators specialising in puppetry and rather abstract metaphor, is the firm grasp of narrative and the intense performances elicited from a strong international cast. Overall, the film can be seen as a (finally subversive) variation on traditional fairytale motifs, as an allegory on our progress through – as an alternative title would have it – 'This Dream People Call Human Life', or as a loving tribute to cinema's fantastic capacity for poetry. Genuinely unsettling. GA

Intelligence Men, The

(Robert Asher, 1965, GB) Eric Morecambe, Ernie Wise, William Franklyn, April Olrich, Gloria Paul, Richard Vernon, Warren Mitchell, Tutte Lemkow, Peter Bull.
104 min.
In the late '50s and early '60s, producer Hugh Stewart had success with Norman Wisdom. He hoped to do even better with Eric and Ernie, whose genius was already evident to millions of British TV viewers. Unfortunately, the pair made only three films, and none had the improvisatory wit or cheek of their best TV work. This is their debut, a feeble spy spoof, culminating in the attempted assassination of a Russian ballerina (Olrich) during a performance of *Swan Lake* at Covent Garden. A long way short of a classic, but it does have its sunshine moments. GM

Interiors

(Woody Allen, 1978, US) Kristin Griffith, Mary Beth Hurt, Richard Jordan, Diane Keaton, EG Marshall, Geraldine Page, Maureen Stapleton, Sam Waterston.
91 min.
Interiors must rank as one of the most spectacular changes of direction for an American artist since Clint Eastwood made *Breezy*. Working as director and writer only, Allen put together a beautifully acted, lyrically written exploration of an intelligent middle class American family whose three grown-up daughters are thunderstruck when their father trades in his elegant depressive wife for a lively, but jarringly vulgar, divorcee. The film has moments of humour, but they are integrated into a totally serious structure which isolates the family's countervailing tensions with a scalpel-like penetration. Only in a single character, the failed husband of one of the daughters, does the tone falter towards soap. Otherwise the approach is rock steady and, if the film's surface invites superficial comparisons with Bergman, its real roots lie in the very finest American art. DP

Interlude

(Douglas Sirk, 1958, US) June Allyson, Rossano Brazzi, Jane Wyatt, Marianne Koch, Françoise Rosay, Keith Andes.
90 min.
A minor but entirely delightful film, based on a James M Cain story previously filmed in 1939 by John M Stahl as *When Tomorrow Comes*: American-girl-in-Europe falls in love with famous classical conductor (Brazzi, oozing charm from every pore). Redolent with guidebook sentiment, and resolutely egalitarian, Sirk's film (as always) subverts the crude dictates of his studio model. The lover comes to rely increasingly on the heroine's 'naïve' strength, and Sirk uses a 'dark secret' subplot (Brazzi's dramatically insane wife) to weave fairytale darkness into a landscape of wide, clear colour. The woman's desire, and her (transient) happiness are allowed to transcend the usually tyrannical alternative: torrid passion or marital affection. CA

Interlude

(Kevin Billington, 1968, GB) Oskar Werner, Barbara Ferris, Virginia Maskell, Donald Sutherland, Nora Swinburne, Alan Webb, Bernard Kay, John Cleese.
113 min.
A remake of Sirk's 1958 film about a young girl who falls in love with a married musician seemed a bizarre choice for Billington's first film. Updated to contemporary London and featuring an *Evening Standard* journalist as the heroine, it is an often successful attempt to relate the clichéd story to people working and living against a precisely drawn (albeit trendy) background. Billington mercifully avoids the excesses of 'Swinging London', and his observant delineation of the discrepancy between the characters' would-be sophistication and their actual stock responses is, on the whole, well supported by the performances. CPe

Intermezzo
(aka Escape to Happiness)

(Gregory Ratoff, 1939, US) Leslie Howard, Ingrid Bergman, Edna Best, Cecil Kellaway, John Halliday.
69 min. b/w.
The ultimate in coffee table weepies, with Howard's unhappily married violinist and Bergman's sympathetic piano teacher making sweet music together during a Riviera idyll, ended when paternal longings drag him reluctantly home and the child has a convenient accident to effect marital reconciliation. Making her radiant Hollywood debut in a part she had played in Sweden, Bergman almost makes you believe the tosh, but Howard (dubbed on violin by Jascha Heifetz) comes on like a smarmy elocution teacher, enunciating atrocious dialogue full of arch emptinesses. TM

Internal Affairs

(Mike Figgis, 1990, US) Richard Gere, Andy Garcia, Nancy Travis, Laurie Metcalf, Richard Bradford, William Baldwin, Michael Beach, Faye Grant, Katherine Borowitz, John Kapelos.
115 min.

Gere (a brilliant return to form) plays an experienced LA street cop who clashes with the tight-assed pen-pushers from Internal Affairs ('the cops of the cops'). But what do these bureaucrats (Garcia and Metcalf) know? Well, for a start, they know that Gere's ex-wives own a fortune in real estate, and that his partner's wife drives a Merc and wears a Rolex. At this point, the morality begins to shift and slide, leaving no clear identification figure. A key element in Gere's *modus operandi* is his ability to identify and exploit the weaknesses of others, something he uses to advantage against Garcia, with taunts about his wife's alleged infidelity. But as the Internal Affairs officers home in on Gere's strung-out partner (Baldwin), they show much the same killer instinct. Also, impressively, the film highlights both the working-class contempt Gere feels for college-boy Garcia, and the fact that Garcia's lesbian partner seems driven by resentment of Gere's macho persona. How much of this was in Henry Bean's excellent script is impossible to tell, but Figgis (in his first American feature) handles the explosive action and the psychological undercurrents with equal assurance. Dark, dangerous and disturbing. NF

International House

(A Edward Sutherland, 1933, US) WC Fields, George Burns, Gracie Allen, Peggy Hopkins Joyce, Stuart Erwin, Franklin Pangborn, Bela Lugosi, Rudy Vallee, Sterling Holloway, Cab Calloway and His Band.
73 min. b/w.
A bizarre, juicy comedy in which dozens of eccentric characters are quarantined in a Shanghai hotel where a crazy local doctor has devised a 'radioscope' – a television set. Over the airwaves we get turns by Rudy Vallee, Baby Rose Marie, and Cab Calloway singing about 'that funny reefer man'. Meanwhile, Burns and Allen perform their shtick, and the incomparable WC Fields cocks a snook at Prohibition by his ostentatious consumption of beer – in flight too! TCh

International Velvet

(Bryan Forbes, 1978, GB) Tatum O'Neal, Christopher Plummer, Anthony Hopkins, Nanette Newman, Peter Barkworth, Dinsdale Landen.
132 min.
A pretty equestrian fairytale, in which an orphaned American teenager (O'Neal) sets her sights on a Gold Medal for Great Britain in the 3-day event at some future South African Olympic Games. This gelatinous story, devised by producer/director Forbes, is so unashamedly sentimental, so resolutely devoid of authentic emotion or motivation, that one can only marvel at its lavish audacity. Do families still go to such tosh? Forbes presumably banked the film's appeal on middle-aged parents recalling Elizabeth Taylor winning the Grand National in *National Velvet* and hauling their children off to see this, its woeful – and very belated – sequel. JPy

Internecine Project, The

(Ken Hughes, 1974, GB) James Coburn, Lee Grant, Harry Andrews, Ian Hendry, Michael Jayston, Keenan Wynn.
89 min.
An American professor of economics (Coburn) gets offered a top level advisory job in Washington, on condition that he eliminates four people in London who operate his European industrial espionage network. Once under way, *The Internecine Project* turns into a straightforward, very enjoyable if somewhat implausible murder story. Rather than despatch his victims himself, Coburn sets them to kill each other by orchestrating their motives and their moves. Despite the plot turning around a succession of calls from conveniently empty public phone boxes (all in working order), and the presence of a stereotype female journalist acting as Coburn's conscience, the film gains in weight thanks to its topical implications. All in all, a neat and unpretentious thriller that offers more food for thought than most such unashamedly commercial movies. CPe

Interno Berlinele

see Berlin Affair, The

Interno di un Convento, L'

see Behind Convent Walls

Interrogation (Przesluchanie)

(Ryszard Bugajski, 1982, Pol) Krystyna Janda, Adama Ferencego, Agnieszka Holland, Janusz Gajos, Anna Romantowska.
116 min.
Bugajski's horrifying film was originally banned under martial law. When cabaret artiste Tonia (Janda) is imprisoned without explanation, she assumes there has been a bureaucratic slip-up. Gradually, however, it becomes clear she is there for a reason: betrayal. Days become months. The monotonous deprivation of the prison cell is varied only by the persuasion, intimidation and torture of interrogation, but Tonia will not break. If, in a sense, this is a period film twice over – made in '82, set in '51 – its impact is as current as it ever was, and its allegorical implications have proved prophetic: the trajectory is very much freedom through fortitude and perseverance. Drained of colour, largely without music, resolutely intimate, it makes for a harrowing couple of hours, but the shifting power-plays between Tonia and her inquisitors are subtly conveyed, while the nuances distinguishing subjective and objective guilt inevitably suggest Kafka and Orwell. TCh

Intersection

(Mark Rydell, 1994, US) Richard Gere, Sharon Stone, Lolita Davidovich, Martin Landau, David Selby, Jenny Morrison.
99 min.
A reworking of Claude Sautet's Les Choses de la Vie (1970), this meticulously directed, flawlessly written, romantic melodrama unfolds in flashback – in the time it takes for a fatal car accident to happen. Successful architect Vincent Eastman (Gere) is experiencing a mid-life crisis: his 16-year marriage to the equally talented Sally (Stone) is empty, held together only by inertia and a mutual responsibility to their daughter Megan (Morrison). Vincent's affair with sensual, spontaneous Olivia (Davidovich) at first seems the perfect way out, yet he continues to hanker for the familiar pleasures his loveless marriage continues to offer. As he vacillates, the failure to choose between wife and mistress causes pain and confusion all round. Less neurotic and sexually charged than usual, Gere digs deep to find the source of his character's chronic indecisiveness. The casting of the vampish Stone as a socially proper, sexually repressed woman is a bold stroke, and Davidovich makes much of her role as the emotionally demanding 'other woman'. NF

Interview With the Vampire

(Neil Jordan, 1994, US) Tom Cruise, Brad Pitt, Antonio Banderas, Stephen Rea, Christian Slater, Kirsten Dunst, Roger Lloyd Pack.
122 min.
Contemporary San Francisco – Louis de Pointe du Lac (Pitt) tells a journalist (Slater) the strange details of his life: how two centuries earlier he was attacked by the degenerate vampire Lestat (Cruise); how he rejected his mentor's advice by feeding on rats and poodles; how the pair 'adopted' a young orphan, Claudia (Dunst), whose thirst for blood outstripped even Lestat's; how their individual inclinations and ethical codes gave rise to lethal tensions between the various members of this bizarre, undead 'family'; and so on. For all its ambitions and visual flair, Jordan's adaptation of Anne Rice's novel is a disappointment. It's not only not scary, it's also dull and conventional. True, the emphasis on Dante Ferretti's lavish production design makes for some heavy dollops of 'atmosphere'; true, too, that the acting is adequate. The major problem lies with Rice's own script which is dramatically repetitive and philosophically banal. Profoundly unremarkable. GA

Intervista

(Federico Fellini, 1987, It) Federico Fellini, Marcello Mastroianni, Anita Ekberg, Sergio Rubini.
105 min.
The wait is over! Here is yet another episode from Fellini's relentlessly colourful past: a free-form reminiscence of his first arrival in the Cinecittà studios, prompted by questions from a Japanese TV crew. The searching period reconstruction includes some dark notes (peasants sing Fascist anthems in the fields), but this is mostly a starry eyed celebration of the time when Movies were still Magic, complete with a bitter-sweet pastiche Nino Rota score. As expected, Mastroianni pops

up, and Fellini sweeps everyone off to Anita Ekberg's villa, where a clip from La Dolce Vita is screened and quiet tears are shed for the Good Old Days. Groundbreaking stuff. TR

In That Land (V toi Stranje)

(Lidia Bobrova, 1997, Rus) Dmitri Clopov, Vladimir Borchaninov, Anna Ovsiannikova, Alexander Stakheev, Svetlana Gaytan.
85 min.
The spectre of allegory haunts every frame of this handsome and intriguing movie, but clear-cut meanings remain elusive. The mayor of a snowbound rural community in the north faces two severe problems: traditional farming skills are dying out because of the exodus of young people to the cities, and too many of the remaining residents are drinking themselves to death on moonshine liquor. Bobrova spreads her dramatic focus evenly between several households, building up a viable microcosm of Russian society in the late 1990s; there are elements of dark, absurdist humour, but in general she's less inclined than her contemporary Muratova to stress regressive and stupid tendencies. Her ending, appropriately enough, leaves us on a knife edge: will the ex-con brought into the village as a mail-order husband turn out to be the community's saviour or its nemesis? TR

In the Belly of the Dragon (Dans le Ventre du Dragon)

(Yves Simoneau, 1989, Can) Rémy Girard, Michel Côté, David La Haye.
102 min.
Simoneau's commendable shot at a sci-fi fantasy with teeth is better than most contemporary Canadian movies, but that isn't saying much. A butch young man drops out of his dead-end job (delivering shop brochures to strife-torn tenements) and sells his body to a mysterious research institute, whose crazed woman diretcor is bent on maximising brain power without regard for the physical cost to her subjects. The movie wants to be a cross between Brazil and Subway, but it's crippled by unimaginitive designs and weak scripting; it comes closest to working in its elements of black comedy, which peter out around the half-way mark. TR

In the Best Interests of the Children

(Elizabeth Stevens/Cathy Zheutlin/Frances Reid, 1977, US) Betty Knickerbocker, Lorraine Norman, Pat Norman, Bernice Augenbraun, Camille Le Grand.
51 min.
A documentary which argues the right of lesbian mothers to custody of their children. Constructed in a series of interviews with several mothers and their staggeringly articulate children, the film eschews any real analysis of the situation, but works instead on an emotive level to convince that lesbians are really OK people. Thus, unfortunately, the visual correlative to the spoken statement is given in the clichéd form of these particular women at their housewifely best (the film's homely, non-alienating stance was designed for TV). HM

In the Bleak Midwinter

(Kenneth Branagh, 1995, GB) Richard Briers, Hetta Charnley, Joan Collins, Nicholas Farrell, Michael Maloney, Julia Sawalha, Celia Imrie, Jennifer Saunders, John Sessions.
98 min. b/w.
After the monstrous hubris of Mary Shelley's Frankenstein, Branagh was wise to get back to basics with this unpretentious backstage comedy, and to cede the limelight to a stand-in. That said, Maloney's actor-director Joe Harper is irresistibly Branagh-esque. A passionate apostle of Shakespeare, Joe's determined to mount his own production of Hamlet, even if it means the last of his meagre savings and a mere week's rehearsal in a rundown country church. With the help of his agent (Collins), he rounds up a group of unlikely thespians desperate enough to work for nothing over Christmas (Briers, Farrell, Sawalha). Shot quickly and cheaply, this is Branagh's most modest film, and his most successful. This is not to say there aren't irritations: too many of the jokes have seen better days, and the sit-com characterisations can't support the director's increasingly sentimental designs on them. Still, Branagh knows his

way round an ensemble, his screenplay combines heartfelt commitment to the theatre with a healthy degree of self-mockery, and the film is crisply photographed in b/w. A palpable hit. TCh

In the Company of Men

(Neil LaBute, 1997, US) Aaron Eckhart, Matt Malloy, Stacy Edwards, Emily Cline, Jason Dixie.
93 min.
Playwright Neil LaBute's film-directing debut is an impressively witty yet unsettling study of male insecurity, misogyny and rivalry. Away on a six-week business trip in a strange town, grouchy, resentful thirty-something execs Eckhart and Malloy decide to take revenge for their recently broken relationships by choosing a vulnerable, lonely woman for both of them (unbeknown to her) to date and dump. The scheme is put into action with deaf typist Edwards (a remarkable performance), but the best laid plans…Poised precariously but skilfully between realism and allegory, black comedy and straight drama, the movie makes the very most of its few locations by opting for a strangely timeless feel, and by focusing attention squarely on the three central performances and LaBute's clever, insightful script. Cruel, cool and pleasingly provocative. GA

In the Deep Woods

(Charles Correll, 1992, US) Anthony Perkins, Rosanna Arquette, Will Patton, DW Moffett.
94 min.
Perkins' last film isn't one you'd care to remember by. He looks haggard and tired as a private investigator on the trail of the 'Deep Woods' killer, who's already murdered one of Arquette's best pals and looks like he's made her his next target. A make-weight filler, from a novel by Nicholas Conde, for completists only. Straight to video in Britain. TJ

In Thee I Trust (Na Tebya Upovayu)

(Elena Tsiplakova, 1993, Rus) Evgeniya Dobrovolskaya, Natasha Sokoreva, Irina Rozanova, Vladimir Ilyin.
81 min.
Alla, a lonely, disfigured woman, takes a priest's advice and volunteers at the local orphanage. It's a grim institution, the staff hardened by corruption and contempt for their charges, the facilities barely adequate. But Alla feels for the children and they respond to her warmth. The authority figures are perhaps too harsh, and the kids too cute, but this is a hard-hitting, moving film about the lost souls of the 'New Russia'. TCh

In the Forest

(Phil Mulloy, 1978, GB) Barrie Houghton, Anthony O'Donnell, Ellen Sheean, Joby Blanchard, Nick Burton.
80 min. b/w.
An English Travelling Players? Three peasant types trek across a forest...and through a polemically structured account of 400 years of British history. Not the 'standard' history of monarchs, battles, disasters and dates (although all of those are there), but an 'alternative' history of political and cultural fragments. What emerges is a militant analysis of the origins of the modern British working class, fashioned by Mulloy with exceptional acuity and a brilliant gift for synthesis. TR

In the French Style

(Robert Parrish, 1962, US/Fr) Jean Seberg, Stanley Baker, Philippe Forquet, Jack Hedley, Addison Powell, James Leo Herlihy, Claudine Auger, Moustache.
105 min. b/w.
An ambitious but ultimately flawed attempt to capture the feelings of an American art student in Paris (Seberg) and her passionate but brief love affairs (with Stanley Baker, among others). For Parisophiles, there's some really nice location photography (by Michel Kelber), but Irwin Shaw's scripts from two of his own short stories doesn't succeed in avoiding the obvious sentimental pitfalls. DP

In the Good Old Summertime

(Robert Z Leonard, 1949, US) Judy Garland, Van Johnson, SZ Sakall, Spring Byington, Buster Keaton, Clinton Sundberg.
102 min.

A musical remake of Lubitsch's *The Shop Around the Corner*, with the period moved back to 1906, the setting shifted to a Chicago music store, and Garland at her most captivating as the shop assistant waging a war of attrition with her bossy superior (Johnson), unaware that he is the lonelyhearts pen pal with whom she has already fallen in love. The fragile charm is rather let down by an indifferent score, although Garland makes the most of her numbers and the rest of the cast give sterling support. Liza Minnelli made her bow as the child at the end. TM

In the Heat of the Night

(Norman Jewison, 1967, US) Sidney Poitier, Rod Steiger, Warren Oates, Quentin Dean, James Patterson, Lee Grant, Scott Wilson, Matt Clark.
109 min.
Jewison's multi-Oscared murder melodrama of racial tension – set in a small Mississippi cotton town where Steiger's bigoted sheriff finds himself forced into collaboration with Poitier's arrogant black homicide expert from Philadelphia – oozes sufficient Southern sweat and features enough admirably crumpled character faces to make up for its over-strident liberal rhetoric. It certainly ranks as superior in every respect to the two Virgil Tibbs vehicles (*They Call Me Mister Tibbs!* and *The Organisation*) with which Poitier subsequently exploited his homicide cop role. Stirling Silliphant's adaptation of the John Ball novel was still deemed controversial enough, in 1967, to require the recreation of a Mississippi small town in the less sensitive environs of Illinois. PT

In the Heat of the Sun
(Yang-guang Canlan de Rizi)

(Jiang Wen, 1994, China) Xia Yu, Ning Jing, Geng Le, Sigin Gaowa.
134 min.
Actor Jiang Wen's first feature is a archetypal rites-of-passage film about a group of boys entering puberty one hot summer in Beijing: fooling around, showing off and bonding, spying on girls, clashing with other gangs, dealing with pesky erections. Two things distinguish it. One is Jiang's own wry voice-over, admitting that these are romanticised and sometimes wished-for episodes from his own childhood. The other is the mid-1970s setting, the dog days of the Cultural Revolution, after all the Maoist frenzy, which it shows as no movie has ever done before. TR

In the King of Prussia

(Emile de Antonio, 1982, US) 'The Plowshares Eight', Martin Sheen, John Randolph Jones, Richard Sisk, George Tynan, John Connelly.
90 min.
Reconstructing the trial that followed a 1980 direct action against a General Electric nuclear weapons facility (the title refers to the name of the plant), this has the 'Plowshares Eight' (Daniel and Philip Berrigan et al) as their eloquent selves, and Martin Sheen in excellent greasy form as the judge. With all the structural advantages of a courtroom drama, it's a wonderful vehicle for the radical Christian anti-nuclear message, and as agitprop it's far superior to even well-done preaching-to-the-converted documentaries such as *Dark Circle*. An intense, low-key production, which itself shows up the flashy decontextualising of *Atomic Cafe*, it ranges from Nagasaki survivors, through neighbours of a plutonium plant, to the fiasco of Diablo, the nuclear plant described as 'the most analysed building in the world', which at the last minute turned out to have been built back to front. JCo

In the Line of Fire

(Wolfgang Petersen, 1993, US) Clint Eastwood, John Malkovich, Rene Russo, Dylan McDermott, Gary Cole.
129 min.
An enjoyably slick if not unfamiliar thriller (by Jeff Maguire) in which the fiendishly brilliant psycho-killer repeatedly taunts the cop to man-to-man confrontation. As Secret Service agent Horrigan, Eastwood is as outspokenly independent as ever: at odds with superiors, caught in a teasing, argumentative romance with colleague Lilly Raines (Russo), and determined to do his job. This time, however, he's haunted by the past (30 years ago he failed to stop the bullet that killed Kennedy) and when he learns that a would-be

assassin (Malkovich) has plans for the current Presidential elections, professional duty provides the opportunity for personal redemption or personal failure. Directing each set-piece for all he's worth, Petersen highlights the plot with vivid details and invests several of the action sequences with moral/psychological dimensions. He's helped no end by Malkovich, and by his lead, whose fine, easy performance extends even to tears. GA

In the Mouth of Madness

(John Carpenter, 1994, US) Sam Neill, Julie Carmen, Jürgen Prochnow, Charlton Heston, Frances Bay, Wilhelm von Homburg.
95 min.
In this lightweight but entertaining horror movie, seasoned genre director Carpenter realises the Lovecraftian weirdness hinted at in the eerie atmospherics of *The Fog* and the monstrous excesses of *The Thing*: in short, the idea of an order of beings that exists in a parallel dimension, expelled from this world but waiting patiently to cross back and take control again. There are shades of both HP Lovecraft and Stephen King in the central character, Sutter Cane (Prochnow), a popular horror writer whose works allegedly influence his more susceptible readers, transforming them into homicidal harbingers of global chaos. When Cane vanishes just before his new book is due for delivery, his publishers panic and hire sceptical insurance investigator John Trent (Neill) to track him down. Trent suspects an elaborate publicity stunt; but having entered the writer's hometown of Hobb's End, he too experiences a blurring of the line between reality and fiction. The script by New Line's head of production, Michael (*Freddy's Dead*) de Luca, does not allow Carpenter free range, nevertheless he manages some neat flourishes of his own, handling the narrative twists and unsettling sfx sequences with customary skill. NF

In the Name of the Father
(Nel Nome del Padre)

(Marco Bellocchio, 1971, It) Yves Beneyton, Renato Scarpa, Lou Castel, Piero Vida, Aldo Sassi, Laura Betti, Marco Romizi.
107 min.
As title and opening make clear, a film about the tyrannies of paternalism: with a great deal of surrealist wit and much venom, Bellocchio lays into the absurdities of authority and its institutions. And by setting his film in a seedy boarding school for rich delinquents, run by Jesuits along military lines, Bellocchio creates a rich target indeed: what monsters are spawned! The result is sheer anarchic fantasy, alternately feverish and despondent, but always superbly realised. On a tougher, allegorical register, it's about the failure of a revolution, about the Italian church's capacity to survive, and about replacing one oppression with another. What lifts the film into that special area inhabited by Buñuel is Bellocchio's capacity for healthy blasphemy and its translation into startling images. Rich, bizarre and original. CPe

In the Name of the Father

(Jim Sheridan, 1993, Ire/GB/US) Daniel Day-Lewis, Pete Postlethwaite, Emma Thompson, Corin Redgrave, John Lynch, Beatie Edney, Britta Smith.
133 min.
Sheridan's movie seeks to engage and enrage. It's not, however, a film with an ideological axe to sharpen, but one which unfolds, with a sense of passionate conviction, a story of injustice – that of the four people wrongly convicted of the IRA's Guildford pub bombings in October 1974. Tracing back to Belfast in the early '70s to uncover the roots of the tragedy, the narrative goes on to chronicle the British judicial system's wilful imprisonment of the Guildford Four – Gerry Conlon (Day-Lewis), fellow tearaway Paul Hill (Lynch), and their London acquaintances Carole Richardson and Paddy Armstrong – plus their alleged accomplices, Conlon's father (Postlethwaite) and relatives in the Maguire family. It then follows events leading to the highly publicised release of the Four in 1989. Sheridan and co-writer Terry George make some minor factual alterations in order to underscore the emotional pain of the long fight for legal reappraisal. TJ

In the Name of the People

(Frank Christopher, 1984, US) narrator: Martin Sheen.
75 min.
A clandestine documentary by American filmmakers following eighteen months in the lives (and deaths) of guerrillas and peasants in the liberated areas of El Salvador. The subdued narration by Martin Sheen details the problems of daily life, food, weapons, recruitment, training, education, health and military actions. JCo

In the Navel of the Sea
(Sa Pusod Ng Dagat)

(Marilou Diaz-Abaya, 1998, Phil) Jomari Yllana, Elizabeth Oropesa.
114 min.
Abaya builds up a convincing portrait of day to day life on a poor Phillipine island, using local non-actors, an observational style and a simple, laidback narrative. There's a stunning moment when one villager is crucified to mark Easter, nails and all, though none of the villagers seems particularly impressed. Ethnographic interest aside, however, there's not an awful lot going on here. To his embarrassment, Pepito grows up to become a male midwife ('Sometimes when I look at a woman's face all I can see is a uterus!'), but his romantic longings touch on wider concerns about the future of this way of life. A bit too soft to hold the attention. TCh

In the Realm of the Senses
see Ai No Corrida

In the Shadow of the Sun

(Derek Jarman, 1972/80, GB) Christopher Hobbs, Gerald Incandela, Andrew Logan, Kevin Whitney, Luciano Martinez, Lucy Su.
51 min.
A collection of Jarman's '72-'74 home footage of friends superimposed around and over 1980 footage of a 'car trip to Avebury'. The 'effects' were all architected at the Super-8 stage, before the artyfact achieved its final 16mm form. It features recurrent themes: a figure at a typewriter who may/may not be composing/dreaming the experience; slow cavortings by would-be mythopoeic figures (ie. naked folks); flames; dunes; a woman swinging her skirt; a couple dancing; lots of robed and masked movers; knockoff plaster heads after the Grecian; and a depiction of angst that could easily be mistaken for an Anadin commercial. Mitigating against that sort of mistake is the soundtrack music by Throbbing Gristle (ie. much electronic doodling with swells of 'meaningful' sound as a persistent shuffler of Tarot cards discovers an antique key and waves it at the viewer). Influences are legion here: Tai Chi movement, Murnau's *Nosferatu*, the wonders of the colour Xerox machine, Windscale-style protective clothing, Alan Alan's Holborn magic shop, and thermography. But, alas, zilch emerges from them; indeed, Jarman's genuine imagination as a designer seems totally in abeyance. Over fifty minutes, it's just not possible to keep your mind from wandering out to make a baloney sandwich. CR

In the Soup

(Alexandre Rockwell, 1992, US) Seymour Cassel, Steve Buscemi, Jennifer Beals, Will Patton, Jim Jarmusch, Carol Kane, Elizabeth Bracco.
95 min. b/w.
New Yorker Adolpho Rollo (Buscemi) is your classic head-movie auteur. In his mind he's creating deathless classics of the screen. Back in the real world, he can't pay the rent on the downtown grothole he calls home. He knows he must be getting really desperate when he puts a script 'Unconditional Surrender' – 500 pages of angst-drenched gobbledygook – up for sale and attracts the attentions of one 'Joe' (Cassel), a warm-hearted minor gangland figure. Director Rockwell's affectionate screenplay pits innocence against experience, artist against philistine, but unexpectedly weighs sympathies towards Cassel's force-of-nature mob mentor, who's soon giving his po-faced protégé a life-lesson masterclass in generosity of spirit, wooing the girl-next-door (Beals), and seat-of-the-pants petty crime. Rockwell's wonderfully unassuming movie throws a big hug around youthful ambition, b/w filmstock, and the glowing screen charisma of Cassel. An unheralded gem. TJ

In the Spirit

(Sandra Seacat, 1990, US) Jeannie Berlin, Olympia Dukakis, Peter Falk, Elaine May, Marlo Thomas, Melanie Griffith, Michael Emil, Christopher Durang.
94 min.

At a time when alternative, holistic medicine is rampaging its ugly way through every town in the world, this satirical swipe at all things new-age comes as a welcome antidote. When a prostitute is killed, a chalk-and-cheese pair of women (one worldly, one fey) set about tracking down her killer, using the notorious 'netherworlds' as their unreliable guide. Deftly scripted by Jeannie Berlin, *In the Spirit* is packed with acerbic gibes which deflate the air-headed arrogance of such leading new-agers as Shirley MacLaine. Berlin and Dukakis are fab in the lead roles, Peter Falk is rip-roaring in a sadly brief cameo, and Melanie Griffith is hardly on screen at all. MK

In the White City (Dans la Ville Blanche)

(Alain Tanner, 1983, Port/Switz) Bruno Ganz, Teresa Madruga, Julia Vonderlinn, José Carvalho, Victor Costa.
108 min.

Ganz, that great loner of modernist cinema, here plays a Swiss seaman who jumps ship in Lisbon, gets involved with a barmaid, and sends reels of home movies back to his wife. Adrift in the exotic *White City*, he is robbed and then stabbed, loses the barmaid after a passionate fling, and finally hitting rock bottom he raises the fare home. The home movies, accompanied by Jean-Luc Barbier's beautiful, hard-edged jazz score, terrifyingly reflect the disintegration of a man in flight from himself. But this is no idling tract on alienation, more an intrigue built around silences, blankness, deceptions of space and time. A teasingly simple film that compels and stimulates. JCo

In This Our Life

(John Huston, 1942, US) Bette Davis, Olivia de Havilland, George Brent, Dennis Morgan, Charles Coburn, Frank Craven, Billie Burke, Hattie McDaniel, Lee Patrick.
97 min. b/w.

Bette Davis steals her sister's husband and ruins her life in this out-of-control family melodrama. 'No one is as good as Bette when she's bad,' claimed the publicity, and she's bad in this all right. John Huston (whose second film this was) wrote that 'there is a demon within Bette which threatens to break out and eat everybody, beginning with their ears. I let the demon go'. In the roadhouse sequence, the sharp-eyed will spot most of the cast from Huston's first picture, *The Maltese Falcon*, including Bogart, Astor, Greenstreet, Lorre, and the director's father, Walter. TCh

Intimate Confessions of a Chinese Courtesan (Ai Nu)

(Chu Yuan, 1972, HK) Lily Ho, Yueh Hua, Betty, Tung Lin, Wan Chung-shan.
91 min.

A good looking production, but a rather embarrassed cross between archetypal kung-fu and the sex film. Set in medieval China, the plot involves the Lesbian head of an exclusive brothel who hires a gang of louts to kidnap likely young girls, who are then broken in and sold off to a series of more or less geriatric local officials with inflated ideas of their own desirability. Our heroine, a young teacher, even undergoes multiple rape, almost entirely in reaction shots and freeze frames; in fact almost everything is filmed in reaction shots, whose over-familiarity just makes this comic strip fable that much more ridiculous. Women with any kind of consciousness, however, will be interested in the superbly acted 'false' ending in which the two women are reconciled – hastily followed, of course, by the hugely predictable 'real' climax.

Intimate Games

(Tudor Gates, 1976, GB) Peter Blake, Suzy Mandell, Anna Bergman, George Baker, Ian Hendry, Joyce Blair, Hugh Lloyd, Mary Millington.
90 min.

A tediously unfunny sex comedy masqueraded (for censorship reasons?) as a spuriously moral exposure movie. 'Abnormal phantasies',

we learn late in the proceedings, cause Professor Gottlieb (Baker) to pounce on one of his female psychology students, after which he is carted off to hospital frothing at the mouth. Earlier, Gottlieb's students have been despatched for the summer vac to write up each other's sexual phantasies. Theory, however, inevitably gives way to softcore practice: slow-motion, dimly-lit, featherweight Lesbian groping; some singularly unerotic tumbling in the back seat of a Rolls; frequent old-fashioned naturist shots of pleasant, well-scrubbed girls in the buff; a notable absence of genitalia. Ian Hendry, Hugh Lloyd and Joyce Blair make brief, decidedly uncomfortable appearances; Anna, Ingmar Bergman's daughter, strips off with good humour. JPy

Intimate Reflections

(Don Boyd, 1975, GB) Anton Rodgers, Lillias Walker, Sally Anne Newton, Jonathan David, Peter Vaughan, Derek Bond.
86 min.

Surely the worst film of the year. It would, of course, be wrong to expect a conventional moviegoing experience from something as specifically non-narrative as this concoction of nuance and gesture; but no amount of special pleading, bonhomie towards experiment, or explanation of motive can hide the fact that the result is like a synthesis of every bad detail of every bad undergraduate film you've ever seen. That Anton Rodgers keeps audience interest going during the film's second half is a tribute to a standard of professionalism eschewed elsewhere. AN

Intimate Relations

(Philip Goodhew, 1996, GB/Can) Julie Walters, Rupert Graves, Matthew Walker, Laura Sadler, Holly Aird, Les Dennis.
99 min.

An English market town, 1954. Harold (Graves) takes a room in the Beasley household. All seems dandy, but then Mrs Beasley (Julie Walters – 'Call me Mum') slips into the sheets with him, and won't take no for an answer. The man of the house remains oblivious, but the 13-year-old daughter begins to get ideas of her own, and Harold finds himself in a pickle. Like *The Young Poisoner's Handbook*, this first feature maliciously satirises the sexual hypocrisy of the time. Walters, needless to add, takes full advantage of the material. TCh

Intimate Stranger, The (aka Finger of Guilt)

(Joseph Walton ie. Joseph Losey, 1956, GB) Richard Basehart, Mary Murphy, Constance Cummings, Roger Livesey, Mervyn Johns, Faith Brook.
95 min. b/w.

Pseudonymously directed by Losey, who had been driven from Hollywood by the McCarthyite purge of the studios, *Intimate Stranger* is a wonderfully slow thriller with a baroque climax in a film studio. Richard Basehart is the studio executive pursued by blackmailing letters from a mysterious girl claiming to be his mistress, his problems complicated by the fact that his wife is the boss's daughter, while the star of his current film is a still-amorous ex-lover. As usual with Losey, both predator and victim take an almost pathological pleasure from their game of mutual destruction. PH

Intimate with a Stranger

(Mel Roberts, 1994, GB) Roderick Mangin-Turner, Daphne Nayer, Amy Tolsky, Lorelei King, Janis Lee, Darcey Ferrer.
94 min.

Los Angeles. After the break-up of his relationship with fellow academic Michelle (Nayer), ex-philosophy professor Jack Hawkins (producer/co-writer Mangin-Turner) walls off his emotions and becomes a gigolo. However, while Hawkins is meant to be an intellectual masquerading as a gigolo, Mangin-Turner looks more like a gigolo masquerading as an intellectual. 'You can be intimate with a stranger, but a stranger to intimacy.' The development and visualisation of this notion leave much to be desired. It doesn't help that the first in a series of women who drift into the jaded gigolo's life is Summer (Lee), a beautiful schoolgirl wanting to lose her virginity to an older man who won't brag about it. Nor that his other clients (frustrated housewife, unfulfilled career-woman)

are chiefly 'types' – each with her own monologue (sometimes straight to camera) explaining why she's after sex and solace in unequal measure. Tediously talky. NF

Intolerance 100

(DW Griffith, 1916, US) Lillian Gish, Mae Marsh, Robert Harron, Constance Talmadge, Miriam Cooper, Alfred Paget, Elmo Lincoln, Walter Long, Bessie Love, Seena Owen.
12,598 ft. b/w.

Griffith's immensely influential silent film intercuts four parallel tales from history (spanning Babylon, Christ's Judaea, Reformation Europe, and turn-of-the-century America) to embroider a moral tapestry on personal, social and political repression through the ages. The thematic approach no longer works (if it ever did); the title cards are stiffly Victorian and sometimes laughably pedantic; but the visual poetry is overwhelming, especially in the massed crowd scenes. And the unbridled eroticism of the Babylon harem scenes demonstrate just what Hollywood lost when it later bowed to the censorship of the Hays Code. CA

Into the Night

(John Landis, 1985, US) Jeff Goldblum, Michele Pfeiffer, Richard Farnsworth, Irene Papas, Dan Aykroyd, David Cronenberg, John Landis, Waldo Salt, Daniel Petrie, Jack Arnold, Paul Mazursky, Jonathan Lynn, Paul Bartel, Don Siegel, David Bowie.
115 min.

Goldblum abandons a safe suburban existence in favour of nocturnal prowlings through Los Angeles, and encounters a mysterious blonde on the run. The plot is minimal, but the film scores partly because of a high sense of fun, and partly because of the way Landis uses his LA locations. As the characters race from the yachts of Marina Del Rey via Rodeo Drive to the Marion Davies mansion in Beverly Hills, he adds a visual running commentary of old film and TV ads, to milk our movie fantasies for all they're worth, and to convey a sense of Los Angeles as a truly mythical city. The casting of innumerable major filmmakers in small roles seems an unnecessary bit of elbow-jogging, but David Bowie makes an excellent contribution as an English hit man, and the two leading players are excellent: Pfeiffer in particular takes the sort of glamorous yet preposterous part that generally defeats even the best actress and somehow contrives to make it credible every inch of the way. DP

Into the West

(Mike Newell, 1992, Ire) Gabriel Byrne, Ellen Barkin, Ciarán Fitzgerald, Ruaidhri Conroy, David Kelly, Johnny Murphy.
102 min.

Screenwriter Jim Sheridan follows *My Left Foot* and *The Field* with a soppy tale of life among the Travellers. In his Dublin tower block, a broken man since the death of his wife, one time Traveller king Papa Riley (Byrne) is swayed from his determination to give his sons (Conroy and Fitzgerald) a conventional home when Grandpa Ward (Kelly) returns from his travels, bringing fanciful tales and a white horse which is lodged in the cramped flat. The authorities take a predictably dim view of this, but in confiscating the horse, provide both father and sons with a new lease of life. But the film lapses into tired whimsy when the boys masquerade as lawless cowboys. It's hard to share their vision of the west of Ireland as America's Western frontier, and impossible to perceive any danger from the uniformed incompetents in pursuit. CM

Intruder, The (aka The Stranger)

(Roger Corman, 1961, US) William Shatner, Frank Maxwell, Beverly Lunsford, Robert Emhardt, Jeanne Cooper, Leo Gordon, Charles Barnes, Charles Beaumont.
80 min. b/w.

Raw-edged and startling, scripted by Charles Beaumont from his own novel based on real-life rabble-rouser John Kasper, Corman's film about Southern desegregation was shot on location in Missouri in a mere three weeks, with threats and obstruction from white locals mirroring the fictional action. Adam Cramer (Shatner, mesmerising) represents an organisation which seeks to stop the process of educational desegregation and

thus frustrate plans of the 'Communist front headed by Jews' to 'mongrelise' society. Cramer is an
insidious outsider whose impassioned speeches
rouse the populace; the result is heightened Klu
Klux Klan activity, attacks on black families and
a liberal white newspaper editor, a near-hanging.
Complex characterisation is sacrificed in the interests of representing the broad socio-political
issues. Emotions intensify in accord with searing
summer temperatures; visuals emphasise the economic disparities, memorably in shots of the black
ghetto and of Cramer in his pristine white suit.
Chilling, and especially at the moment Cramer
delivers his battle-cry, 'This is just the beginning',
painfully prophetic. CM

Intruder in the Dust
(Clarence Brown, 1949, US) Claude Jarman Jr,
David Brian, Juano Hernandez, Elizabeth
Patterson, Porter Hall, Will Geer.
87 min. b/w.
By far the best of the race prejudice cycle of the
'40s, a subtle adaptation (by Ben Maddow) of
William Faulkner's novel which goes out of its
way to avoid the usual special pleading in dealing with Lucas Beauchamp (Hernandez), the
elderly black facing a lynch mob when accused
of shooting a white man in the back. Lucas is
clearly innocent but also 'stubborn and insufferable', so scornful of whitey and his patronage
that he refuses to stoop to defending himself; an
arrogant sonofabitch so hard to like that when
two lone citizens come forward in his defence
(an old woman and a young boy), they do so
against their wills, purely so that they can go on
sleeping easy. An amazingly laid back conception for the period, echoed by Brown's calmly
dispassionate direction and by the unobtrusively persuasive ambience (most of the film
was shot in Faulkner's home town of Oxford,
Mississippi). TM

Inutile Envoyer Photo
(Alain Dhouailly, 1977, Fr) Paul Le Person,
Hélène Dieudonné, Danielle Ajoret, Bernard
Lajarrige, Rémy Carpentier.
95 min.
Gentle, almost soporific rural drama about the
travails of a 55-year-old bachelor farmer when
faced by the imminent prospect of two
unsought partnerships. While the dairy
demands that he modernise his milking equipment and a neighbour offers to pool resources,
his feisty old mother starts placing lonelyheart
ads for him in the photo-romance magazines
that she reads interminably with her two
cronies. A French TV production that's a little
too impressed by its own observation of quirky
custom and character, and ends up as naively
'charming' as its unlikely hero. PT

Invaders from Mars
(William Cameron Menzies, 1953, US) Helena
Carter, Arthur Franz, Jimmy Hunt, Leif
Erickson, Hillary Brooke, Morris Ankrum.
78 min.
A sci-fi cheapie about another invasion of the
body snatchers, which has some chillingly effective moments but doesn't really live up to its reputation, despite the unusual ploy of being told
largely from the point of view of a small boy
(Hunt) who is the first to spot the invaders and
whose parents are the first to go under.
Interesting, though, for the extremeness of its
Cold War aura of military preparedness, which
even throws in actuality shots of tanks and troops
massing as the earthlings prepare to fight back
against the green tentacular midget things that
live in glass globes. Its backyard setting, a nostalgic slice of small town Americana which is the
territory to be defended, inspired the opening
sequence of Scorsese's Alice Doesn't Live Here
Any More. TM

Invaders from Mars
(Tobe Hooper, 1986, US) Karen Black, Hunter
Carson, Timothy Bottoms, Laraine Newman,
James Karen, Bud Cort, Louise Fletcher.
99 min.
An updated version of the '50s paranoia classic
in which a young boy wakes up in the middle of
the night to see a spaceship landing over the hill
behind his house. The rest of the film consists of
his efforts to make the adults around him believe
his story, and his increasing despair as more and
more people are taken over by the Martians. The

effects are magnificent (the tripod drones and the
supreme Martian intelligence are horrific), but
whereas the original worked by building up an
increasingly black mood, this version relies
almost entirely on the special effects; and such
limited brooding tension as it has is gratuitously
undermined by a string of sequences played purely for laughs. Black is good as the near-hysteri-
cal school nurse who becomes the boy's only ally,
and forms a lovely double act with her real son
(Carson), who is commendable as the poor lad.
The lame twist in the original's ending has been
retained. Fun, but very silly. DPe

Invasion
(Alan Bridges, 1966, GB) Edward Judd, Valerie
Gearon, Yoko Tani, Tsai Chin, Lyndon Brook,
Eric Young, Barrie Ingham, Glyn Houston,
Anthony Sharp.
82 min. b/w.
Strikingly imaginative little sci-fi thriller in
which two Oriental women, actually aliens but
peaceful in intent, throw a force field round a
hospital while attempting to retrieve a colleague,
a criminal who escaped from their charge and
has been knocked down by a car. Little happens
as the telephones go dead and panic mounts in
the hospital along with the temperature, but the
sense of threat from the unknown becomes
almost tangible as Bridges weaves his Losey-
influenced camera through shadowy landscapes, or lets it linger broodingly on innocent
objects until they begin to acquire an air of alien
malevolence. TM

Invasion of the Body Snatchers
(Don Siegel, 1956, US) Kevin McCarthy, Dana
Wynter, Larry Gates, Carolyn Jones, King
Donovan, Virginia Christine.
80 min. b/w.
A masterpiece of sci-fi cinema, this adaptation
of Jack Finney's novel is set in the small town
of Santa Mira, where the local shrink is alarmed
by the ballooning number of patients who maintain that their nearest and dearest are not quite
themselves. In fact, the town is gradually being
taken over by 'pod people', alien likenesses of
the inhabitants which lack human emotions.
(The original title was Sleep No More: the aliens
do the swap while the victim is snoozing).
Remade in 1978, this version remains a classic,
stuffed with subtly integrated subtexts (post-
war paranoia etc.) for those who like that sort
of thing, but thrilling and chilling on any level.
The late Sam Peckinpah can be spotted in a
cameo role as a meter reader, and look out for
one of the most sinister kisses ever filmed.
You're next! AB

Invasion of the Body Snatchers
(Philip Kaufman, 1978, US) Donald
Sutherland, Brooke Adams, Leonard Nimoy,
Veronica Cartwright, Jeff Goldblum, Art
Hindle, Lelia Goldoni, Kevin McCarthy, Don
Siegel, Robert Duvall.
115 min.
Though it lacks the awesome allegorical
ambiguousness of the 1956 classic of sci-fi/polit-
ical paranoia (here paid homage in cameo
appearances by Kevin McCarthy and Don
Siegel), Kaufman and screenwriter WD Richter's
update and San Francisco transposition of Jack
Finney's novel is a far from redundant remake.
The extraterrestrial pod people now erupt into
a world where seemingly everyone is already
'into' changing their lives or lifestyles, and into
a cinematic landscape already criss-crossed by
an endless series of conspiracies, while the
movie has as much fun toying with modern
thought systems (psychology, ecology) as with
elaborate variations on its predecessor.
Kaufman here turns in his most Movie Brattish
film, but soft-pedals on both his special effects
and knowing in-jokiness in a way that puts De
Palma to shame; even extra bit appearances by
Robert Duvall (Kaufman's Jesse James in The
Great Northfield Minnesota Raid) and
Hollywood archivist Tom Luddy are given a
nicely take-it-or-leave-it dimension. PT

Invasion of the Body Stealers
see Body Stealers, The

Invasion of the Flying Saucers
see Earth vs the Flying Saucers

Invasion of the Saucermen
(Edward L Cahn, 1957, US) Steve Terrell,
Gloria Castillo, Frank Gorshin, Raymond
Hatton, Ed Nelson.
90 min. b/w.
Low-budget '50s sci-fi which doesn't quite
descend to the level of Ed Wood-style ineptitude,
but isn't too far above it either. 'Little green men'
pop in on Middle America, the town drunk gets
zapped, teenagers show their pluck, the military
get called in. All the usual genre elements are
here, though Cahn hasn't the money or the imagination to do more than the barest minimum with
them. TJ

Invasion U.S.A.
(Joseph Zito, 1985, US) Chuck Norris, Richard
Lynch, Melissa Prophet, Alexander Zale, Alex
Colon, Eddie Jones.
107 min.
We can all sleep easy with Chuck 'Neanderthal'
Norris to protect the free world single-handed
from the commie guerrilla force that attempts
Invasion U.S.A. A machine-pistol hanging at
each hip, Norris blasts his way through an invasion force that blows up innocent family homes
as the occupants prepare for Christmas.
Terrorists disguised as Miami cops, they massacre crowds of Hispanics, place bombs in hyper-
markets, and generally sow the seeds for the
street warfare that will undermine the fabric of
democracy. Norris, who doesn't so much act as
point his beard at the camera, weaves his way
through so many explosions that the money
saved on the cast was obviously blown on
pyrotechnics. Leaden, xenophobic, and utterly
stupid, it's far more offensive than Rambo and
far less well executed. DPe

Inventing the Abbotts
(Pat O'Connor, 1997, US) Joaquin Phoenix,
Billy Crudup, Will Patton, Kathy Baker.
Jennifer Connolly, Michael Sutton, Liv Tyler.
107 min.
Haley, Illinois, 1957: Phoenix and Crudup are the
blue-collar Holt brothers who dare to glance at
the glittering Abbott daughters – smart, gawky
Tyler, typecast 'bad girl' Connelly – whose
father has expressly forbidden such contact.
This rankles with the boys, especially since
rumours persist that the Abbott paterfamilias
(Patton) had an affair with their teacher mother, just after their father died, and is also purported to have snaffled the dead man's design
for a suspension file drawer. The central notion
of the gentry callously exploiting the labour of
those less fortunate brings an element of class
tension to the film which, as the title suggests,
shows how the Abbotts' carefully groomed public image is in fact their strongest suit in perpetuating their social status. While we see
behind the facade, the film eschews real bitterness in favour of the hesitant romance between
Tyler and Phoenix, and a hope that future generations can break the cycle of deception and
resentment. O'Connor's follow-up to Circle of
Friends looks the part and is adeptly played, but
isn't quite distinctive enough to be much more
than a pleasant non-event. TJ

Investigation of Murder, An
see Laughing Policeman, The

Invincible Barbarian (Gunan il Vendicatore)
(Frank Shannon ie.MM Tarantini, 1983, It)
Peter McCoy ie. Pietro Torrisi, Marion Lang,
David Jenkins.
90 min.
In a dark barbaric age gone by, savage tyrant
destroys village and massacres inhabitants.
Surviving child grows up into incredibly
strong/manly/muscular hunk who eventually
murders tyrant and avenges dead family. Sounds
familiar? No, it's not Conan the Barbarian but
Gunan the Invincible, an Italian rip-off which has
neither the style nor the special effects of the real
McCoy. But the bills for designer loincloths, eye
make-up and tomato ketchup must have been
astronomical. MG

Invincible Pole Fighters, The
see 8-Diagram Pole Fighter, The

Invisible Adversaries (Unsichtbare Gegner)
(Valie Export, 1978, Aus) Susanne Widl, Peter Weibel, Dr Josef Plavee, Monika Helfer-Friedrich.
109 min.
Dancing a forlorn quickstep along the interface between dreams and waking, Austrian Anna surfaces to that sinister sound of white noise on the radio informing her that aliens, or at least *Invisible Adversaries*, have invaded human beings. Noticeably blasé about this looming revelation, she seems to regard it as yet more evidence of the way that modern life disfigures its artists, men dump on women, the police hit you on the head, and Kreisky's Austria represses everyone. It's possible that this state of mind is brought on by her boyfriend urinating on her head in the mornings, but whatever the reason, she does seem fairly unhappy, morosely photographing faces and leaving the baby in the fridge. It's either a feverish deconstruction of the bourgeois modes of representation, or more likely what you'd expect to find on *Time Out*'s back page under 'The Way It Was, Dec 1972'. Not unlike *W.R. – Mysteries of the Organism*; it will probably age as badly. CPea

Invisible Man, The
(James Whale, 1933, US) Claude Rains, Gloria Stuart, Una O'Connor, William Harrigan, EE Clive, Dudley Digges, Dwight Frye.
71 min. b/w.
Engrossing adaptation of HG Wells' tale of a scientist made invisible by his experiments with the drug monocaine. The megalomania that ensues upon Rains' ability to go about unseen is played for suspense, pathos and tongue-in-cheek humour (he can't go out in the rain, because it would make him look like a ridiculous bubble). The real strengths of the movie are John P Fulton's remarkable special effects (Rains removing his bandages to reveal nothing, footsteps appearing as if by magic in the snow), lending much-needed conviction to the blatant fantasy; and the fact that we never see the scientist without his bandages until the very end of the film. No wonder Karloff, disdainful of a role in which he would for the most part only be heard, turned down the part; but Rains, with his clear, sensitively inflected voice, was lucky: it made him a star. GA

Invisible Man Returns, The
(Joe May, 1940, US) Vincent Price, Cedric Hardwicke, John Sutton, Nan Grey, Alan Napier, Cecil Kellaway.
81 min. b/w.
Not as stylishly bizarre as Whale's original, but a very enjoyable sequel, with Price as a man wrongly convicted of murder who goes invisible with the help of the original invisible man's brother (Sutton). Riding out the madness that is one of the drug's unfortunate side effects, he proves his innocence by unmasking the real killer. The whodunit element is less gripping than the original's study in soaring megalomania, but Price's urbanely mellifluous voice makes him an admirable successor to Claude Rains, and John P Fulton's special effects are well up to par. TM

Invisible Ray, The
(Lambert Hillyer, 1936, US) Boris Karloff, Bela Lugosi, Frances Drake, Frank Lawton, Walter Kingsford, Beulah Bondi, Violet Kemble Cooper.
81 min. b/w.
Last and least of Universal's three co-starring vehicles for Karloff and Lugosi in the '30s, with the latter overshadowed by Karloff in the first of his many mad scientist roles. After a superb opening in the Carpathian laboratory where Karloff learns the secret of 'capturing light rays from the past', it gets a bit rickety in the African scenes, where a meteorite provides his ray with the necessary 'Radium X' and where a demonstration goes disastrously wrong. But it's briskly staged with some fine camerawork, and Karloff – turned into a radioactive killer and melting down a symbolic statue after each death on his vengeance trail against his wife and the colleagues he feels have betrayed him – is great. TM

Invisible Stripes
(Lloyd Bacon, 1939, US) George Raft, Jane Bryan, William Holden, Humphrey Bogart, Flora Robson, Paul Kelly, Lee Patrick, Henry O'Neill, Marc Lawrence, Leo Gorcey.
82 min. b/w.
A thoroughly predictable tale of the tribulations of an ex-con. Released from jail simultaneously, bad boy Bogart goes back to the rackets, good guy Raft to a careworn mother (Robson), a hopeful younger brother (Holden), a fiancée who snottily ditches him (Patrick), and an ill-paid job from which he is summarily fired as untrustworthy. Unable to make a decent living because of his 'invisible stripes', in despair because he can see his brother edging towards crime in his turn, he emulates Sydney Carton's 'far, far better thing' to team up with Bogart in a series of robberies. The gesture costs him his life, but does stake Holden to a garage and enable him to marry his sweetheart (Bryan). The terminally dreary Raft does little to brighten the soggily soapy proceedings. TM

Invitation, The (L'Invitation)
(Claude Goretta, 1973, Switz/Fr) Michel Robin, Jean-Luc Bideau, Jean Champion, Pierre Collet, Corinne Coderey, Rosine Rochette, François Simon.
100 min.
Truly delightful comedy from Goretta, later better known for *The Lacemaker*. A very simple plot – quiet office clerk inherits a marvellous country house when his beloved mother dies, and invites his 'friends' from work over for a summer garden party. But what distinguishes the film is its acute observation, and the way it gently scrapes away the stereotypes – office lecher, buffoon, nymphet, henpecked husband, etc. – to reveal more complex figures all locked in private worlds of hope, loneliness, and despair. The film has aptly been compared to the work of Renoir, not only for its narrative similarity to *La Règle du Jeu*, but also because Goretta's tender yet unsentimental generosity towards his characters is akin to the French master's dictum that 'everybody has his reasons'. GA

Invitation to Bed (Les Confidences Erotiques d'un Lit Trop Accueillant)
(Michel Lemoine, 1973, Fr) Olga Georges-Picot, Janine Reynaud, Michel Le Royer, Anne Libert, Marie-Gabrielle Pascal.
90 min.
The erotic adventures of a large white fluffy bed, which could almost be a fugitive from a Claes Oldenburg art exhibit. Various characters lie on it and find that their passions increase tenfold. The fadeout joke is when the hero and heroine make love in a square one. GB

Invocation Maya Deren
(Jo Ann Kaplan, 1987, GB) Hella Hammid, Sasha Hammid, Amos Vogel, Marcia Vogel, Stan Brakhage, Jonas Mekas.
53 min.
Maya Deren is one of the most important figures in the history of American experimental cinema. Her '40s films established her as a flamboyant, original film poet whose work not only inspired other avant-garde movie-makers but gave rise to America's Creative Film Foundation and the progressive distribution company Cinema 16. This informative documentary may use a familiar format – clips (including unfinished work), talking heads (Jonas Mekas, Stan Brakhage, et al), footage of Deren herself – but its tone, at once celebratory and objectively distanced, is beguiling. The film paints a portrait of a fascinating woman: extrovert, strong-willed, eccentric, deeply competitive, and immensely energetic. Recommended to anyone interested in dance, alternative cinema, forceful women, and ecstatic imagery. GA

In weiter Ferne, so nah!
see Faraway, So Close

In Which We Serve
(Noël Coward/David Lean, 1942, GB) Noël Coward, John Mills, Bernard Miles, Celia Johnson, Joyce Carey, Kay Walsh, Michael Wilding, James Donald, Richard Attenborough.
114 min. b/w.
The story of a destroyer, its crew, and their flashback memories of the folks back home from a raft after being dive-bombed during the Battle of Crete. Staged with what passed at the time for honest understatement, it now looks impossibly patronising, the epitome of stiff upper lip as Coward's captain graciously condescends to his forelock-touching crew like an indulgent auntie. Interesting chiefly as a reminder of the structures of snobbery and privilege in the services which were largely responsible for Labour's postwar election victory. TM

Io ballo da sola
see Stealing Beauty

Iodo
(Kim Ki-Young, 1977, SKor) Lee Hwa-si, Kim Jong-choi, Choi Yun-sok.
110 min.
More sex and death from iconoclast Kim Ki-Young in this bizarre and beautifully shot 'Scope drama. It takes the form of an investigation by a resort promoter and a newspaper editor of the strange death of an Iodo islander turned ecology reporter, who disappears overboard on a trip back to the island. Unfolding in flashback, it relates in mock mythological terms the fate of the island, populated almost entirely by Amazon-like female deep sea divers and their shamans. Atmospheric, ghostly and oneiric, it's a Freudian mind-boggler, filled with male sexual anxiety, culminating in one of the most shocking copulatory denouements in the movies. WH

I Ought to Be in Pictures
(Herbert Ross, 1982, US) Walter Matthau, Ann-Margret, Dinah Manoff, Lance Guest, Lewis Smith, Martin Ferrero.
107 min.
One of those cases of long-lost family rashly turning up unexpectedly and causing radical (also unlikely) changes in peoples' personalities. This time it's the daughter, the unbearably cute and outspoken Libby (Manoff), who sets off for Hollywood to seek fame and her father (Matthau), last seen when she was in diapers. Matthau is a grumpy, scared bachelor who has given up on work and relationships, and who, until transformed by his daughter, is driving his sensible girlfriend (Ann-Margret) into the arms of another man. Far too few jokes to soak up Neil Simon's soggy material. JE

Ipcress File, The
(Sidney J Furie, 1965, GB) Michael Caine, Nigel Green, Guy Doleman, Sue Lloyd, Gordon Jackson, Aubrey Richards, Frank Gatliff.
109 min.
First and best of Caine's three appearances as Len Deighton's Harry Palmer, despite Furie's penchant for flashy images. There's a suitably complex plot involving a missing scientist, an enigmatic piece of recording tape, electronic brainwashing, and top-level treachery; but the best sequences linger in the mind long after the narrative details have been forgotten. Palmer's perky Cockney personality may be irritating at times, but it's worth putting up with it for scenes like the encounter in the reading-room, the unsuccessful raid on a mysterious warehouse, or the psychedelic torture-chamber. DP

IP5
(Jean-Jacques Beineix, 1992, Fr) Yves Montand, Olivier Martinez, Sekkou Sall.
119 min.
Beineix's film ('5' because it's his fifth, 'IP' for *Isle des Pachydermes*) is another idiosyncratic slice of hard-edged romantic whimsy, which sees a pair of Paris delinquents – a graffiti artist and his very young black pal – head south in search of escape and/or love. Down in Toulouse, they come across Montand's asylum escapee *shaman*, a man who talks to the trees and walks on water, but carries a gun. It looks great – urban reds, moon blues and forest greens – and is replete with the usual chic irony and cinematic pyrotechnics. Well acted, too, especially by the two juve leads, Martinez and Sall. It was Montand's last film, and he is visibly – and movingly – dying. A likeable film, but whether it adds up to much is up to you. WH

I.Q.
(Fred Schepisi, 1994, US) Tim Robbins, Meg Ryan, Walter Matthau, Lou Jacobi, Gene Saks, Joseph Maher, Stephen Fry.
96 min.

To judge from the movies, Albert Einstein was a goofy comedian who dabbled in algebraic abstractions on the side. Matthau plays fairy godmother to his brainy niece Catherine (Ryan) and besotted local mechanic Ed (Robbins). Unable to see beyond the size of a man's Mensa score, Catherine is engaged to a stuffy English psychologist (Fry); she only becomes interested in Ed when uncle Albert and his cronies conspire to recognise his (entirely imaginary) scientific genius. Unfortunately, the media become interested too, and soon President Eisenhower is on the phone. A sappy, old-fashioned romantic comedy in pastel hues, which might have been given some backbone by a Billy Wilder or a Howard Hawks. Robbins is amiable enough as a Gary Cooper type, and Meg Ryan does her own sweet thing, but the equation is overbalanced by Matthau's matey old man. TCh

Ireland: Behind the Wire
(Berwick Street Film Collective, 1974, GB)
110 min.
A bleak alternative to the bland footage of Northern Ireland that we normally get to see. The makers of this documentary offer not so much an analysis of the political situation as a record of the psychological toll. The mesh of sectarianism and nationalism is scarcely touched upon. Rather, the film argues in terms of the legacies of British capitalism and colonialism, and states that a minority is being persecuted just as relentlessly as anywhere else in the world. Through interviews with men who have been tortured, images of barricades and destruction, the sight of a decidedly non-passive army in action, and the strain registered on faces young and old, one can begin to understand what it is like to live in perpetual fear in a country that has become a breeding ground for violence. The film, in revealing the economic discrepancies between England and Northern Ireland, and showing up much of the complacency that dominates our thinking, makes a little more comprehensible the desperate measures taken by extremists.

I Remember Mama
(George Stevens, 1948, US) Irene Dunne, Barbara Bel Geddes, Oskar Homolka, Philip Dorn, Cedric Hardwicke, Rudy Vallee, Edgar Bergen, Ellen Corby, Florence Bates.
134 min. b/w.
A rosily nostalgic valentine to family life in San Francisco circa 1910, rather in the manner of Meet Me in St Louis, though cast (without the music) in the form of memories set down by a budding authoress looking back in gratitude and affection. The homespun philosophy with which these Norwegian immigrants face up to life's hard knocks makes it more sentimental than Minnelli's film. A charmer, nevertheless, directed and acted with real delicacy, not least by Hardwicke as the lodger, a broken-down old actor who pays his way with readings from the classics. Beautifully adapted by DeWitt Bodeen from the John Van Druten play (itself based on Kathryn Forbes' book Mama's Bank Account). TM

Irezumi – Spirit of Tattoo (Sekka Tomurai Zashi)
(Yoichi Takabayashi, 1982, Jap) Tomisaburo Wakayama, Masayo Utsunomiya, Yusuke Takita, Masaki Kyomoto, Taiji Tonoyama.
108 min.
Once more into the mystique of Japanese sex. This one is about a grizzled old master tattooist who will only work on his subjects while they are in the act of screwing. Both the tattooing and the sex are tastefully sanitised: no blood, no unsightly scabs, no erotic complications. There's lashings of picturesque old Japan, and it all turns into jolly melodrama for the finale, with suicides, murders and revelations of hidden identities. RG

Irma la Douce
(Billy Wilder, 1963, US) Jack Lemmon, Shirley MacLaine, Lou Jacobi, Bruce Yarnell, Herschel Bernardi, Hope Holiday, Joan Shawlee.
147 min.
Wilder's two-and-a-half-hour comedy set in the prostitute milieu of Paris (Hollywood-built, courtesy of Alexandre Trauner's designs) looks more than anything like a gaudy musical (which it once was) without the songs (which Wilder removed). It's a chance for Lemmon to go through his paces in various guises – zealous boulevard cop, pimp,

and moonlighting worker in Les Halles foodmarket impersonating an English lord by day. Even for Lemmon, there's too much self-pity in the part of a naïve ex-gendarme who falls heavily for a tart, but Shirley MacLaine redresses the balance as the whore with a heart of gold. Wilder's soft-centred cynicism provides frequent enough laughs without too many longueurs. As in The Seven Year Itch and despite the French setting, they come mainly from the hypocritical vulgarity of contemporary American sexual morality. RM

Irma Vep
(Olivier Assayas, 1996, Fr) Maggie Cheung, Jean-Pierre Léaud, Nathalie Richard, Bulle Ogier, Lou Castel.
98 min.
Named after the slinky heroine of Feuillade's Les Vampires (which neurotic, idealistic director Léaud is here planning to remake), Assayas' partly improvised film charts the experiences of Hong Kong actress Cheung (playing herself) when she turns up in Paris to take the lead in Léaud's doomed movie. Crew members come on to her; journalists lecture her on the future of cinema, Léaud cracks up and is replaced by the gloriously seedy Castel, and Cheung starts having strange dreams. A delightfully nonchalant movie, complete with some nice satirical barbs aimed at contemporary French film culture, and fine performances throughout. GA

Iron & Silk
(Shirley Sun, 1991, US) Mark Salzman, Pan Qingfu, Jeanette Lin Tsui, Vivian Wu.
92 min.
Actor/writer Salzman's autobiography provides the source material for this winning semi-documentary outsider's take on contemporary Chinese society. A youthful fan of kung-fu movies, Salzman travels to China, works as an English teacher and falls for student Vivian Wu, while also training with (real-life) martial arts guru Pan Qingfu. Although the film doesn't probe that deeply into the political arena, cultural differences certainly emerge as the enthusiastic protagonist embraces a way of life far removed from his Western upbringing. TJ

Iron Curtain, The (aka Behind the Iron Curtain)
(William A Wellman, 1948, US) Dana Andrews, Gene Tierney, June Havoc, Leslie Barrie, Edna Best, Berry Kroeger, Noel Cravat.
87 min. b/w.
By the late '40s, anti-communist fervour in Hollywood and throughout the US had reached fever pitch. This brisk, documentary-style thriller, based on the experiences of a code clerk in the Russian embassy in Washington, captures the mood of the times. Andrews is the turncoat who wants asylum in the West so his son can grow up in 'freedom'. Given that he's prepared to share all the latest dope about Soviet espionage techniques, it is not surprising his old colleagues are so keen to assassinate him. GM

Iron Eagle
(Sidney J Furie, 1985, US) Louis Gossett Jr, Jason Gedrick, David Suchet, Tim Thomerson, Larry B Scott, Caroline Lagerfelt.
119 min.
A film which captures the misunderstood rationale behind the Reagan administration's foreign policy, and translates it into dramatic form. Doug Masters (Gedrick), high school graduate, is fighting mad: his dad is being held prisoner in an 'Islamic Fundamentalist State'. In a country where negotiation has become an eleven-letter word no one can pronounce, Doug is left with one option; if he's going to save his old man, he's going to have to blast him out. So he and a retired colonel (Gossett) abscond with two US Airforce fighters and splatter the 'little goochies' across the face of the desert. It is regrettable that the highest of production values have been invested in this, the cheapest of stories. SGo

Iron Eagle II
(Sidney J Furie, 1988, Can) Louis Gossett Jr, Mark Humphrey, Stuart Margolin, Alan Scarfe, Sharon H Brandon, Maury Chaykin.
100 min.
A cheapskate sequel to a Top Gun rip-off, with veteran flyer Colonel 'Chappy' Sinclair (Gossett) head-

ing a top-secret combined US/Soviet mission against a common Arab enemy. The villain this time is Iran, apparently only two weeks away from nuclear capability. Circumventing attempts by hawkish top brass on both sides to sabotage the mission (and thereby Soviet-American military cooperation) by assigning a bunch of rebel, misfit flyers, Chappy and his Soviet counterpart get together, disobey orders, and launch an unofficial attack on the Iranian missile base. While the conciliatory attitude towards the Soviet Union is a welcome development, the drippy romance between macho US pilot Humphrey and glamorous Soviet fly-girl Brandon is entirely dispensable. Long on clichéd characters, ludicrous dialogue, and flying sequences accompanied by nondescript rock music, but short on credibility. NF

Iron Horse, The
(John Ford, 1924, US) George O'Brien, Madge Bellamy, Charles Edward Bull, William Walling, Fred Kohler, Cyril Chadwick.
11,335 ft. b/w.
The epic silent Western, made as Fox's response to The Covered Wagon and effortlessly surpassing it. A paean to Lincoln and the notion of Manifest Destiny, it recounts the building of the first transcontinental railroad. Gangs start from both coasts, rebuffing Indian attacks, thwarting greedy landowners, initiating a sweeping trail drive and moving whole towns along the line. After battles against the rigours of blizzard and desert, the final spike is driven home as the hero avenges his father's murder and wins back his childhood sweetheart. Visual glories (and stirring piano accompaniment) sweep aside objections to the tedious passages, the psychological ineptitude, and the racist portrayal of Indians, Irish and 'coolies'. As in Stagecoach, each scene and each character looks fresh struck at the mint of myth, while every frame asserts that this is the making of America and of the American cinema. JW

Iron Maiden, The
(Gerald Thomas, 1962, GB) Michael Craig, Anne Helm, Jeff Donnell, Alan Hale, Noel Purcell, Cecil Parker, Roland Culver, Joan Sims.
98 min.
A sad film, a kind of traction engine version of Genevieve, with Michael Craig as the man of the future (he's an aircraft designer) getting into trouble because of his love of the past, and finally solving his problems through the realisation that 'Britain is the place of continuity...' etc. Thematically the film makes (reactionary) sense, but cinematically it's a disaster. Scenes at Henley, Ascot and Woburn are supplemented by the Duke of Bedford in person. PH

Iron Maze
(Hiroaki Yoshida, 1991, US/Jap) Jeff Fahey, Bridget Fonda, Hiroaki Murakami, JT Walsh, Gabriel Damon, John Randolph, Peter Allas, Carmen Filpi.
102 min.
Based on the same short story as Kurosawa's Rashomon, this shifts the action to a Pennsylvania 'Rust Belt' town where the son (Murakami) of a billionaire Japanese businessman plans to replace the old steel mill with an amusement park. When he is found at the mill with a potentially fatal head injury, an embittered ex-steelworker (Fahey) confesses that he acted in self-defence, a story backed up by the injured man's American wife (Fonda). The local police chief (Walsh) is suspicious, and his investigation reveals a complex maze of personal and cultural conflicts. Rashomon addressed the subjective nature of perception, but Yoshida's debut feature reduces this idea to a mere plot device, designed to sustain suspense. The attempt to deal with the huge subject of US/Japanese economic and cultural relations is similarly fudged by focusing on the triangular relationship between Murakami, Fahey and Fonda. By the time you reach the centre of this iron maze, you may wish you'd opted for the rollercoaster instead. NF

Iron Triangle, The
(Eric Weston, 1988, US) Beau Bridges, Haing S Ngor, Liem Whatley, Johnny Hallyday, Jim Ishida, Ping Wu, Jack Ong, Sophie Trang.
91 min.
Billed as the first Vietnam film to show both sides of the conflict, this tries to have its cake and eat it. Based on the diary of a young, ideal-

istic Vietcong soldier (here called Ho, played by Whatley), it is narrated by the equally sympathetic US officer who finds it, Captain Keen (Bridges). It therefore dispels the myth of the 'faceless enemy', while retaining a convienient Western identification figure. To be fair, as the opposing forces vie for tactical advantage in the heavily militarised 'Iron Triangle', this strategy does yield some intriguing moments. In the American camp, Keen clashes with his ruthless South Vietnamese and French colleagues over their relentless propagandising and routine use of torture. Likewise, Ho's professional soldiering is compromised by the ideological pointscoring of Communist party official Khoi (Ishida). Naturally, when Keen is later captured by Ho and his men, a professional respect develops between the two. Sadly, the sporadic battle scenes are too messy to be fully effective, so one's over-riding feeling is that writer/director Weston has his heart in the right place, but his liberal politics and cinematic technique all over the place. NF

Ironweed

(Hector Babenco, 1987, US) Jack Nicholson, Meryl Streep, Carroll Baker, Michael O'Keefe, Diane Venora, Fred Gwynne, Margaret Whitton, Tom Waits, Jake Dengel.
143 min.
At last, a real part for Nicholson to sink his teeth into. As Francis Phelan, one-time family man and baseball contender reduced by guilt to Depression-era drifter, the star drives for the marrow, for the spiritual dimension beyond the stubble and staggers that eluded Rourke in *Barfly*. Decades ago, Phelan fatally dropped his baby son; during a trolley strike he threw a rock at a scab, accidentally killing him; a boxcar brawl over shoes resulted in another death: ghosts rise up to rebuke him. 'I don't hold grudges for more than five years,' he tells the apparitions, companionably. 'See ya'. His horizons have shrunk to somewhere to sleep for the night, the price of a bottle, and a new pair of shoelaces, but like the Beckett characters who can't go on, he goes on. Weaker derelicts attach themselves to him – Rudy, cheerfully dying of cancer (Waits, terrific), and Helen, a pathetic, muttering bag-lady down from gentility (Streep, resembling Worzel Gummidge). Down here on the wintry streets of Albany, the characteristic Babenco concern for flotsam gets a sombre and lengthy workout, but it's Nicholson's film. BC

Irreconcilable Differences

(Charles Shyer, 1984, US) Ryan O'Neal, Shelley Long, Drew Barrymore, Sam Wanamaker, Allen Garfield, Sharon Stone.
117 min.
This is essentially about the excesses of the Hollywood lifestyle, the egomania it generates, and how success and failure can change 'normal' people into monsters overnight. O'Neal and Long both turn in sensitive and gently comic performances as a couple consumed by it all, and Drew Barrymore is superb as the neglected daughter caught in the middle. It ruthlessly parodies film industry types, and the superficial Beverly Hills set, by way of one-liners, some truly touching moments, and a great cast. Lovely. DPe

Isadora

(Karel Reisz, 1968, GB) Vanessa Redgrave, James Fox, Jason Robards, Ivan Tchenko, John Fraser, Bessie Love.
138 min.
Many hands dabbled in the script – Clive Exton, Melvyn Bragg, Margaret Drabble – which is perhaps why this lavish biopic is rather impersonal, lacking a consistent viewpoint. Isadora Duncan, like Lawrence of Arabia, is an enigma; and whereas David Lean and Robert Bolt found only an enigma and sought to perpetuate it, Reisz seeks to unravel and explain this bizarre, scandalising appendage to the '20s. In some ways it's like a Ken Russell movie at 33 rpm, discovering the ageing Isadora dictating her memoirs and flashing back to her affairs in Berlin (Fox) and France, where she marries Mr Singer (Robards) of sewing-machine fame, then her second marriage to a Russian poet, her rejection and disillusion, and her final ride in a red Bugatti with scarf flying. The source of the scandal, her uninhibited sexuality and her Classical Greek dancing at the height of the Jazz Age,

gives the film a semblance of unity, something to hang on to, and a visual beauty. And there is also Vanessa Redgrave, giving a quite superb performance in which the mannerisms are Isadora's, not hers. ATu

I Saw What You Did

(William Castle, 1965, US) Joan Crawford, John Ireland, Andi Garrett, Sarah Lane, Sharyl Locke, Leif Erickson, Patricia Breslin.
82 min. b/w.
Typical Castle suspense shocker with a nice premise about a couple of silly teenage girls (Garrett, Lane) who while away the tedium of babysitting by making hoax phone calls ('I saw what you did! I know who you are!'), but unfortunately chance on a psycho (Ireland) who has just done away with his wife. A few chilling moments, but it all depends on your susceptibility. In spite of her star billing, Crawford – given to appearing in this type of film in the later stages of her career – has a supporting role, and makes a violent exit as an overwrought mistress jealously trying to blackmail the psycho into marrying her. DP

I See a Dark Stranger
(aka The Adventuress)

(Frank Launder, 1946, GB) Deborah Kerr, Trevor Howard, Raymond Huntley, Liam Redmond, Michael Howard, Norman Shelley, Brefni O'Rorke.
111 min. b/w.
A briskly entertaining (if ideologically cosy) espionage thriller set during World War II, with Kerr as an Irish colleen brought up on her father's tales of his exploits against the wicked English. Setting out to join the IRA but sidetracked into innocently spying for the Nazis in Dublin, she is run ragged all over the place – including the Isle of Man – before suffering a change of heart when she falls for a British officer (Howard). Rather too whimsical, but littered with engagingly Hitchcockian conceits like the disposal of a corpse by taking it for a stroll in a wheelchair. TM

I Shall Return

see American Guerilla in the Philippines

I Shot Andy Warhol

(Mary Harron, 1996, US/GB) Lili Taylor, Jared Harris, Martha Plimpton, Stephen Dorff, Lothaire Bluteau.
100 min.
Engrossing, informative and beautifully performed account of the psychological turmoil and various other pressures that led Valerie Solanas, founder and sole member of SCUM (the Society for Cutting Up Men), to gun down Andy Warhol. Despite a long, rather too self-conscious party scene, complete with Velvets, various superstars and conversations on couches, the re-creation of the Factory and its population is mostly spot-on: Taylor's paranoid but spikily intelligent Solanas is a triumph, as is Dorff's Candy Darling. And if Harris is perhaps a little too enervated as Andy, the film's sharp take on sexual politics, the allure of fame and the artistic pretensions of a vanished era lends it substance a-plenty. There's a score by John Cale, too. GA

I Shot Jesse James

(Samuel Fuller, 1949, US) Preston Foster, Barbara Britton, John Ireland, Reed Hadley, J Edward Bromberg, Victor Kilian, Tom Tyler, Byron Foulger.
81 min. b/w.
Fuller's first film is a virtual illustration of his dictum that the cinema is like a battleground: 'love, hate, action, violence, death...in one word, Emotion'. Having to choose between loyalty to the past and a love for Jesse James (Hadley), or a desire for a future and the love of a woman, Fuller's outlaw hero Bob Ford (Ireland) makes the wrong choice. He shoots James, only to discover that his whole life has become defined by this deed: doomed to re-enact the murder on stage, and condemned to notoriety in 'The Ballad of Jesse James'. His vision of the future fades into jealousy, economic hardship and, as Phil Hardy has pointed out, 'misplaced love'. As such, more a psychological drama (emphasised by the use of close-up) than a Western, and a highly original film. CPe

Ishtar

(Elaine May, 1987, US) Warren Beatty, Dustin Hoffman, Isabelle Adjani, Charles Grodin, Jack Weston, Tess Harper, Carol Kane, David Margulies.
107 min.
So bad it could almost have been deliberate. The faults are many, but the casting of Hoffman and Beatty as a talentless and tacky cabaret duo is fatal: perverse logic makes Hoffman the smooth-talking womaniser and Beatty the bozo. The complex plot takes far too long to establish that they are to Simon and Garfunkel what McGonagall is to Burns before they are whisked off on a tour of the mythical Sahara republic of Ishtar, where they are lured into spying for opposing sides of a planned revolution, each tailing the other while trying to impress the same beautiful freedom fighter (Adjani). Of course the pair make worse spies than they do songwriters, and soon they're trekking into the desert with only a blind camel and CIA snipers for company. May's script is unfunny, and anything approximating a joke is wrung dry; but accept that you're watching one of the worst films ever made and you may find it hilarious. EP

Island, The

(Michael Ritchie, 1980, US) Michael Caine, David Warner, Angela Punch McGregor, Frank Middlemass, Don Henderson, Dudley Sutton, Colin Jeavons.
114 min.
Peter Benchley's script from his own novel is a mad concoction in which Michael Caine and son stumble on a Caribbean island inhabited by bloodthirsty pirates, inbred over 300 years and now sterile, who survive by plundering consumer goodies from luxury yachts. Caine is designated as stud to the only female capable of child-bearing, the son is happily absorbed into the patriarchal dream world, and a thoroughly Oedipal conflict begins between the pair which looks like ending in patricide. The plot's inversion of *Lord of the Flies* (adults without children running amok on an island paradise), the inanely prattling buccaneers straight out of Disneyland, and the anti-materialist glee of their attack against the rich – smashing videos and taunting sunbathers – all add up to one of the most ludicrous yet entertaining mis-hits since *The Other Side of Midnight*. DP

Island, The
(Hadaka no Shima)

(Kaneto Shindo, 1961, Jap) Nobuko Otowa, Taiji Tonoyama, Shinji Tanaka, Masanori Horimoto.
92 min. b/w.
The film that brought Shindo to international attention is a meditatively-paced study of life on the far side of privation: a small family group struggle for survival on a barren island off the west coast of Japan. The 'poetry' is highly contrived, but the feeling is probably authentic. TR

Island at the Top
of the World, The

(Robert Stevenson, 1973, US) Donald Sinden, David Hartman, Jacques Marin, Mako, David Gwillim, Agneta Eckemyr.
94 min.
Despite the promise of its Jules Verne-ish title, a thoroughly pedestrian effort that doesn't even merit comparison with such earlier Disney adventures as *20,000 Leagues Under the Sea*. Unimaginative plot, interminable dialogue in 'Old Norse', some pointless love interest, and a particularly repulsive poodle. DP

Island in the Sun

(Robert Rossen, 1957, US) James Mason, Harry Belafonte, Joan Fontaine, Dorothy Dandridge, John Williams, Joan Collins, Stephen Boyd, Michael Rennie, Diana Wynyard.
119 min.
Eager yet compromised tilt at a mid-'50s race relations movie, which hasn't quite got the courage of its convictions. Diluted from a novel by Alec Waugh, it's set on a fictional West Indian island, Santa Marta, where wealthy would-be politico Mason stirs up matters by opposing union leader Belafonte in the local election, and the challenger's sister Collins frets at the effect it might have on her impending engagement to Governor's son Boyd. Self-important and rather phoney. TJ

Island of Dr Moreau, The

(Don Taylor, 1977, US) Burt Lancaster,
Michael York, Nigel Davenport, Barbara
Carrera, Richard Basehart, Nick Cravat.
104 min.
HG Wells' novel (about a mad doctor who rules
an island by grafting men and animals together
on his operating table) is ideal material for screen
horror because it's filled with subversive political undertones. The 1933 version with Charles
Laughton (*Island of Lost Souls*) made the most of
these, but here director Don Taylor seems determined to iron out all the interesting emphases in
favour of a visual and narrative style that reduces
everything to the level of schoolboy adventure.
The island becomes an antiseptic paradise, and
Moreau (Lancaster) is no longer a white-suited
colonial sadist but the standard misguided scientist. Only Michael York's metamorphosis into
a beast has any impact, and the film predictably
fails to follow through even on that. DP

Island of Dr Moreau, The

(John Frankenheimer, 1996, US) Marlon
Brando, Val Kilmer, David Thewlis, Fairuza
Balk, Ron Perlman, Marco Hofschneider.
96 min.
Third adaptation of HG Wells' sci-fi novel, begun
by Richard Stanley (*Hardware*) and completed by
John Frankenheimer. Like one of Moreau's creatures, it is a sorry patchwork, its jumbled good
and bad parts in constant conflict. Yet despite the
ludicrous antics of Brando's Moreau, and the lazy,
narcissistic Kilmer as his ex-neuro-surgeon sidekick Montgomery, flashes of inspiration remain,
not least in Brando's idiosyncratic but chilling
delivery of the key speech that begins, 'I have
seen the Devil in my microscope, and I have
chained him.' One feels sorriest for Thewlis and
Balk, who as morally repulsed castaway Douglas
and Moreau's beautiful, feline daughter Aissa,
vainly try to counter the indulgent excesses of
their co-stars. Smeared with sun-block and sporting a range of absurd headgear, Brando is too
whimsical to convince as either the gene-splicing
genius or the benevolent dictator, dispensing justice with the aid of pain-inducing implants that
he activates whenever his half-human subjects
threaten to revert to their animalistic ways. In a
more coherent context, Stan Winston's varied
creature designs might have had more impact;
here they barely serve to distinguish one mutant
creation from another. NF

Island of Lost Souls

(Erle C Kenton, 1932, US) Charles Laughton,
Richard Arlen, Leila Hyams, Kathleen Burke,
Bela Lugosi, Stanley Fields.
72 min. b/w.
Not a great success at the time, probably because
its horror is more intellectual than graphic, this
adaptation of HG Wells' *The Island of Dr Moreau*
(repudiated by the novelist, and originally
banned in Britain) is nevertheless a remarkably
powerful film. Laughton is magnificently repellent as the fiendish doctor whose evolutionary
experiments, involving painful vivisectional
graftings, have resulted in a pitiful island community of hideous man-beasts. Satanically bearded, the epitome of imperialist arrogance in his
immaculate white ducks, the whip-toting Moreau
rules his 'natives' through rituals of fear and pain;
and in a subplot that suffuses the film with a perverse erotic sadism, he indulges his intellectual
curiosity by plotting to mate a human (Arlen)
with the beautiful girl he has created from a panther (Burke), but who is already reverting to her
animal state. In the delirious final sequence,
superbly staged and shot by Karl Struss as the
'natives' rebel and drag the screaming Laughton
away to his own 'House of Pain', the film's subversive spirit surfaces with a real vengeance. TM

Island of Mutations
(L'Isola degli Uomini Pesce)

(Sergio Martino, 1979, It) Barbara Bach,
Claudio Cassinelli, Richard Johnson, Joseph
Cotten, Beryl Cunningham.
99 min.
Irresistibly giggly hokum that gives an uncredited airing to *The Island of Dr Moreau*, boasts a
whole school of amphibious 'Black Lagoon'-
styled creatures, and works up a reasonable head
of cheap thrills in a finale uniting an erupting volcano, voodoo, the treasure of Atlantis, the mad
biologist's secret, and a good old graveyard fist-

fight. Some rather dry verbal humour, stylish
camerawork, and performances above par for the
Saturday afternoon genre easily offset the variable SFX, and overall it makes welcome second
feature material. PT

Island of the Damned

see ¿Quién Puede Matar a un Niño?

Island Rescue

see Appointment with Venus

Islands in the Stream

(Franklin J Schaffner, 1976, US) George C
Scott, David Hemmings, Gilbert Roland, Susan
Tyrrell, Richard Evans, Claire Bloom,
Julius Harris.
105 min.
The strongest thing about this ponderous movie
is the redoubtable George C Scott. Basing the
character on Hemingway himself as much as
upon the Hemingway hero of this late novel, Scott
contrives mostly to play Scott; and what makes
his performance so interesting is the tension
between conscientious craftsmanship and an
intelligence too keen to take seriously the whole
charade of acting. Set in the Caribbean in 1940,
this film about father and sons uncomfortably
mixes reflection and action: ageing artist comes
to terms with life (during sons' school holidays)
and death (heroic self-sacrifice). Scott performs
the Hemingway clichés with vigorous conviction,
whether trying to catch the big fish, idealising the
memory of his first wife, or displaying gruff affection for the obligatory rummy friend. Mostly it's
heavy going, though, especially Schaffner's direction, which languishes in the tropical sun as it did
with *Papillon*. CPe

Isle of Love, The

(Fred J Balshofer, 1922, US) Rudolph
Valentino, Julian Eltinge, Virginia Rappe.
5 reels [?]. b/w.
A drag artist, Valentino in his days before stardom, and the actress who was to die in the
Arbuckle scandal: a list perhaps dreamed up in
desperation for a story about the wilder shores of
early Hollywood? In fact, these three came together for this film in 1918. In 1922, after Virginia
Rappe had died and Valentino had become a star,
writer/director Balshofer recut his footage and
boosted Valentino's part with outtakes. The outcome is pretty loopy: Eltinge in drag, a palace revolution, saucy bathing belles, and huge plugs for
US intervention in foreign affairs. Most of the
film's interest comes from its blatant efforts to
cash in: a silent conversation between Rappe and
Valentino takes on dimensions that Balshofer
could never have dreamed of in 1918. CPe

Isle of the Dead

(Mark Robson, 1945, US) Boris Karloff, Ellen
Drew, Marc Cramer, Katherine Emery, Helene
Thimig, Alan Napier.
71 min. b/w.
Set on a Greek island threatened by the plague at
the end of the Balkan war of 1912, this moody but
slightly muddled RKO horror movie involves the
premature burial of the British consul's wife
(Emery), who rises as a new Britannia, a silent,
emblematic figure killing with a trident and saving Greek womanhood (Drew) from the Greek
general (Karloff) to enable her to fall into the arms
of an American. Producer Val Lewton occasionally manages to evoke the wondrous effects
achieved by Jacques Tourneur (who made
Lewton's name as a producer) in *I Walked with a
Zombie*. The film comes magnificently alive with
the burial sequence, and with the zombie-like,
white-robed woman roaming through shadowy
galleries and shuttered rooms. PW

I Start Counting

(David Greene, 1969, GB) Jenny Agutter,
Bryan Marshall, Clare Sutcliffe, Simon Ward,
Gregory Phillips, Lana Morris, Madge Ryan,
Fay Compton.
105 min.
Misfired psychological thriller revolving around
Agutter's schoolgirl fantasies about her older fos-
ter brother and a series of local murders, and
evoking unproductive associations with such pre-
cursors as *The Fallen Idol*. A disappointment to
admirers of *The Shuttered Room* and *The
Strange Affair*, with which Greene appeared to

be establishing himself in the feature market, and
a prompt to his resumption of prolific TV work
(previously in Britain, Canada and the States,
subsequently with such heavyweights as *Rich
Man, Poor Man* and *Roots*) from which he has
sporadically emerged for such impersonal chores
as *Godspell* or *Gray Lady Down*. PT

Is There Sex After Marriage?

(Richard Robinson, 1973, US) John Dunn, Lori
Brown, Keith Benedict, Candy Samples,
Tony Grillo.
87 min.
This little sex epic tells of a housewife and her
husband getting outside rejuvenations (such tit-
illations as a porno movie or two prostitutes in
lesbian embrace) to overcome their awful inhibitions. The acting is reasonably natural and the
number of couplings reasonably plentiful; everything happens with pace and economy, and a
lady named Candy Samples boasts a fine pair of
breasts. What more can you possibly want? GB

I Take This Woman

(WS Van Dyke, 1939, US) Spencer Tracy, Hedy
Lamarr, Verree Teasdale, Kent Taylor,
Laraine Day, Mona Barrie, Jack Carson,
Marjorie Main.
97 min. b/w.
Tracy as a dedicated doctor who dissuades
Lamarr from committing suicide, marries her,
and then an old flame of his shows up, making
Lamarr go off the rails again. Much more interesting than the soapy histrionics is the film's production history: the supporting cast was
changed in mid-stream, and director Josef von
Sternberg was replaced by Frank Borzage, who
was finally replaced by Van Dyke. Known in
Hollywood as 'I Re-take This Woman', it was
really a project of Louis B Mayer's, which would
have been junked had it not been for the mogul's
insistence that Hedy Lamarr would become a
star in it. ATu

Italianamerican

(Martin Scorsese, 1974, US) Catherine
Scorsese, Charles Scorsese, Martin Scorsese.
49 min.
Scorsese used to wrap up each feature by hustling
through a fast documentary on its tail, a practice
that unfortunately he seems to have discontinued.
Made just after *Mean Streets*, *Italianamerican*
proves just as instructive about life in Little Italy
as Johnny Boy's saga. It's simply Catherine and
Charles Scorsese sitting reminiscing on a plastic
sofa; but their son Marty demonstrates an early
maturity by allowing them a lot of living-space
and little interference, from which a likeable and
affectionate portrait emerges. Charles is a regular,
unpretentious guy; Catherine an engaging, garrulous mama, from whom Scorsese obviously
inherited his furious logorrhea. She also makes
meatballs, whose recipe is included on the
credits. CPea

Italian Job, The

(Peter Collinson, 1969, GB) Michael Caine, Noël
Coward, Benny Hill, Raf Vallone, Tony
Beckley, Rossano Brazzi, Irene Handl,
Fred Emney.
100 min.
The planning and execution of a Turin bullion
heist take, for once, a back seat to the stunt-rid-
dled getaway (subsequently pastiched, after
numerous TV screenings of the film, by at least
one car commercial). As a modest fun movie, it
works, much helped by deep casting contrasts
and a nice sense of absurd proportions from
scriptwriter (and *Z Cars* originator) Troy
Kennedy Martin. PT

It Always Rains on Sunday

(Robert Hamer, 1947, GB) Googie Withers,
John McCallum, Jack Warner, Edward
Chapman, Susan Shaw, Patricia Plunkett,
Alfie Bass, Jimmy Hanley, John Slater,
Sydney Tafler.
92 min. b/w.
A resolutely downbeat – remarkably so for Ealing
Studios – account of a day in the life of Bethnal
Green when an escaped convict (McCallum) seeks
shelter at the home of a former girlfriend (Withers),
now respectably married but bored and waspish-
ly discontented. No attempt is made to elicit easy
sympathy for either of the protagonists as they pur-
sue their selfish ends, and the sense of drab squalor,

Time Out Film Guide **439**

with pursuit ending in the railway yards, is a minor key echo of the poetic realism (also carefully studio-built) of prewar Carné and Renoir. Only slightly compromised by a certain pawkiness in some of the minor Cockney characterisations. TM

Italy: Year One (Anno Uno)
(Roberto Rossellini, 1974, It) Luigi Vannucchi, Dominique Darel, Valeria Sabel, Rota Forzano, Ennio Balbo.
123 min.
Rossellini's return to the cinema after twelve years working for television: a sympathetic, idealised – and almost universally reviled – portrait of Italy's postwar statesman Alcide De Gasperi (played by Vannuuchi), the Christian Democrat leader who successfully kept the Communists out of the government, it is indeed hard to swallow. Its flaw is obvious: from 1945's chaos through anti-Communist coalitions, the historical realities are too close to bear De Gasperi's saint-like depiction. Its major saving irony is that it shows the conditions for historical choices in a much more illuminating light than its reactionary ticket would allow. So, although by no means the best, it's the most provocative of Rossellini's historical biographies, looking suspiciously like a triumph for the devil's advocate. DMacp

It Came from Beneath the Sea
(Robert Gordon, 1955, US) Kenneth Tobey, Faith Domergue, Donald Curtis, Ian Keith, Harry Lauter.
80 min. b/w.
Good to see supporting stalwart Tobey get a lead for once, even if it is in this minor entry in the '50s cycle of radiation-paranoia sci-fi pics (effects by Ray Harryhausen). Our man is a sailor whose submarine is almost sunk by an unidentifed object in the Pacific. Before long San Francisco itself is threatened by the mystery marauder, an octopus mutated to giant dimensions by nuclear tests. (The budget allowed for a creature with only six tentacles.) TJ

It Came from Hollywood
(Malcolm Leo/Andrew Solt, 1982, US) Dan Aykroyd, John Candy, Cheech and Chong, Gilda Radner.
80 min. b/w & col.
A sloppy compilation of the lowlights of schlock. Z-movie monsters and specious effects are wheeled on for a few easy laughs, with unfunny introductions by the likes of Dan *My Stepmother Is an Alien* Aykroyd. Most of the clips didn't come from Hollywood at all; they came from Britain, Japan and garages in the Mid-West. Some of them do, but anyone who laughs at scenes from classics like *War of the Worlds* and *The Incredible Shrinking Man* is off my Christmas card list for good. TCh

It Came from Outer Space
(Jack Arnold, 1953, US) Richard Carlson, Barbara Rush, Charles Drake, Russell Johnson, Joseph Sawyer, Kathleen Hughes.
81 min. b/w.
An early attempt at the theme of an encounter with benign but awe-inspiring aliens. The script (nominally from Ray Bradbury's story *The Meteor*) rattles through all the formulary clichés: an amateur astronomer who 'understands', a belligerent sheriff, a woman used as a pawn. But seen in its original 3-D, it's clear that Arnold's direction gives it more than a passing lift. He isn't much good with his second-rate cast, but his compositions in depth are consistently interesting, and his sparing use of special effects keeps the level of visual interest high. The 3-D process leaves the image somewhat murky, but you can discern sparks of authentic pulp poetry throughout. TR

It Conquered the World
(Roger Corman, 1956, US) Peter Graves, Beverly Garland, Lee Van Cleef, Sally Fraser, Charles B Griffith, Russ Bender.
71 min. b/w.
It Conquered the World makes *Dr Who* look like *2001*. A large, triangular Venusian arrives in a California sandpit and starts belching out little bats to vampirise the locals, much to the consternation of the military. You have to see a movie like this to realise that film-makers who feel they have nothing to lose are rarer than you'd think. TR

It Could Happen to You
(Andrew Bergman, 1994, US) Nicolas Cage, Bridget Fonda, Rosie Perez, Wendell Pierce, Isaac Hayes, Victor Rojas, Seymour Cassel, Stanley Tucci.
101 min.
'Cop Tips Waitress $2 Million': that was the headline in the New York press when Charlie Lang showed up at a coffee shop on his beat and presented Yvonne Biasi with the winnings he'd promised to split with her if his number came up in the lottery. This fairy tale is narrated by a tabloid journalist 'Angel' (Hayes) and comes complete with a wicked witch, Charlie's wife Muriel, who wants all the money for herself. Perez has a field day as Muriel, injecting a welcome note of good old-fashioned greed into what is otherwise a relentlessly edifying story. As Charlie, Cage is on best behaviour, while the wan Fonda is white-bread-with-crusts-off as the waitress worth her heart of gold. TCh

It Couldn't Happen Here
(Jack Bond, 1987, GB) Neil Tennant, Chris Lowe, Joss Ackland, Dominique Barnes, Neil Dickson, Carmen Du Sautoy, Gareth Hunt, Barbara Windsor.
86 min.
At a tawdry English seaside resort, mummy's boy Tennant, winsome and sad-eyed in full evening dress, surveys the scene: a ranting blind priest (Ackland) stumbles across shingle trailed by a troop of schoolboys; nuns in suspenders and kinky boots gambol in the shallows; at a funfair drug addicts, gorging fat ladies and perverts whizz past on the big wheel; and Tennant sings that everything he's ever done is a sin. Meanwhile Tennant's pop group sidekick Lowe breaks free of a garish boarding-house where Barbara Windsor is serving mountainous breakfasts. Director Bond's attempt at a narrative stringing together of the Pet Shop Boys' pop themes is witless, aimless and pretentious. If this sickbag of kitsch communicates anything it's the anguish of a young aesthete on discovering that flying ducks still adorn the walls of his mother's house. EP

It Happened at the Inn
see Goupi-Mains-Rouges

It Happened Here
(Kevin Brownlow/Andrew Mollo, 1963, GB) Pauline Murray, Sebastian Shaw, Fiona Leland, Honor Fehrson, Percy Binns, Frank Bennett.
99 min. b/w.
With an immense reputation as a doggedly meticulous historical fantasy, Brownlow/ Mollo's low-budget film of a Nazi invasion of Britain now seems more than ever like a Borges newsreel: though the event never happened, a film of it perhaps exists from which only these scraps of footage survive. A genuinely eccentric curio which names but cannot express its fears or desires.

It Happened in Brooklyn
(Richard Whorf, 1946, US) Frank Sinatra, Kathryn Grayson, Jimmy Durante, Peter Lawford, Gloria Grahame.
105 min. b/w.
Sinatra was still in the bobby-soxer phase when he made this fluffy musical about a returning GI who moves in with Brooklyn janitor Durante, falls for teacher Grayson, and sets his sights on a career in showbiz. 'Time After Time' (not the Cyndi Lauper hit) stands out among the tunes, though Frank and the Schnozz kick up a storm on 'The Song's Gotta Have Heart'. TJ

It Happened One Night
(Frank Capra, 1934, US) Claudette Colbert, Clark Gable, Walter Connolly, Roscoe Karns, Alan Hale, Ward Bond.
105 min. b/w.
The film which lifted Columbia Studios into the big league by winning five Academy Awards and putting Capra's future output among the biggest box-office successes of the '30s. Gable plays a ruthless reporter who adopts a fugitive heiress making her way across America by bus. She (Colbert) is spoiled and snobbish, he is poor but honest, and his attempts to convert her to home-spun pleasures hit the right emotional chord in Depression-weary audiences. Opinions divide about whether the film's comedy and sententious

notions about the miserable rich and happy poor have dated, but some of the set pieces definitely haven't aged. Capra's sense of humour is a little like that of Preston Sturges, though less caustic; and the film shows its stars at their best, Colbert as one of Hollywood's fresher comediennes, Gable as dumb-but-loveable hunk. RM

It Happened One Summer
see State Fair

It Happened Tomorrow
(René Clair, 1944, US) Dick Powell, Linda Darnell, Jack Oakie, Edgar Kennedy, Edward Brophy, John Philliber.
84 min. b/w.
An engaging fantasy about a cub reporter (1890 period) granted a peek at tomorrow's news by a ghostly old man who presents him with newspapers a day ahead of schedule. The resulting scoops bring him star status and a load of troubles, culminating on the third day with headlines accouncing his own death: a rendezvous which he tries frantically – though with unexpected results – to avoid. Not always as inventive as it might have been, but an elegantly beguiling movie. TM

I, the Jury
(Richard T Heffron, 1981, US) Armand Assante, Barbara Carrera, Laurene Landon, Alan King, Geoffrey Lewis, Paul Sorvino, Judson Scott.
111 min.
Apart from Aldrich's extraordinary *Kiss Me Deadly*, the blood-and-guts thrillers of Mickey Spillane have not translated well to cinema. This adaptation delivers more sex and violence than ever before, and Assante plays Mike Hammer in a shambling Italian style, pleasingly reminiscent of De Niro in *Mean Streets*. But (possibly because Larry Cohen was replaced as director after a week) the film soon becomes repetitious, lacking the overall atmosphere of paranoia that makes Spillane's fictions bearable, and dwelling in a nauseating way (even by the standards of its source material) on sadistic sexual violence. The updated plot concerns sex clinics, post-Watergate cover-ups, and such a multitude of bad guys that even Hammer is only able to despatch about eighty of them. But the modern references just get in the way: as with Ian Fleming, an authentic Spillane adaptation would have to be set in the hysterical atmosphere of the Cold War. DP

I, the Worst of All (Yo, la peor de todas)
(María Luisa Bemberg, 1990, Arg) Assumpta Serna, Dominique Sanda, Hector Alterio, Lautaro Murúa, Alberto Segado, Franklin Caicedo, Graciela Araujo.
105 min.
Bemberg's dramatisation of the life of Sister Juana Inés de la Cruz, the 17th century Mexican writer, moves from an austere series of tableaux to a charged atmosphere of repression and calculating ambition. Flashbacks reveal Sister Juana's fatherless, impoverished and intellectually precocious childhood, and there's a suggestion that her decision to enter the convent was a tactical manoeuvre enabling her to pursue her studies and writing. When the archbishop later conspires to stop her work, she becomes embroiled in a counterplot to undermine his authority, with disastrous results. Serna's intense performance in the lead role is never allowed to dominate a plot built around internecine conflict, shifting loyalties, betrayals and individual acts of courage. The drama is progressively unsettling, particularly as the spiritual malaise becomes manifest in the horrific ravages of the plague. CM

It Hurts Only When I Laugh
see Only When I Laugh

It Lives Again
(Larry Cohen, 1978, US) Frederic Forrest, Kathleen Lloyd, John P Ryan, John Marley, Andrew Duggan, Eddie Constantine, James Dixon.
91 min.
Cohen gives his sequel to *It's Alive* a human angle by placing his monster – a large baby of ferocious tendencies – well inside a normal family context and examining the strain this puts on relationships (Kathleen Lloyd is particularly touching as the wife). But on the whole this is a good film in

theory rather than practice. The script is written in the Albert Memorial style – ungainly in structure, weighed down with extraneous detail. And Cohen remains a director of parts, capable of imaginatively conceived shocks once the monster babies being kept under observation get on the rampage (crawling about under bedclothes, putting feet into birthday cakes), but less capable of providing a cumulative effect. GB

It's a Gift
(Norman Z McLeod, 1934, US) WC Fields, Kathleen Howard, Baby LeRoy, Morgan Wallace, Charles Sellon.
73 min. b/w.
It's a masterpiece, and Fields' definitive study in the horrors of small-town family life. Every person and thing around causes sublime winces of irritation, from the town's horrid disabled citizen Mr Muckle, and a passing insurance salesman looking for 'Karl LaFong', to a squeaking hammock and a rolling coconut. And Fields himself is so curmudgeonly that he almost snatches food from his son's mouth. There's little sentiment (or plot) to provide any relief, either; the film's string of set pieces (three of them taken from the 1925 Ziegfeld Follies) maintains a relentless pace and tone, making this easily the most devastating comedy of the '30s. GB

It's Alive
(Larry Cohen, 1973, US) John P Ryan, Sharon Farrell, Andrew Duggan, Guy Stockwell, James Dixon, Michael Ansara, Robert Emhardt.
91 min.
Although it doesn't finally have the courage of its convictions and raises more questions than its standard horror/sci fi format can cope with, there's still a lot that comes off here. The premise is blackly humorous: every monster has a Mom who loves it. A banal Los Angeles family discover that they have brought a homicidal vampire baby into the world when Junior, straight out of the womb, goes on a murder spree and pits his wits against a mobilised police force. Despite such potentially sidesplitting material, the film often manages to instil a genuinely chilling atmosphere, with its initially kitsch family growing into human beings as they plummet into a world unhinged and apart at the seams. John Ryan's performance as the husband is particularly astute, and Bernard Herrmann's score milks the suspense for all it's worth. CPe

It's All Happening
(Don Sharp, 1963, GB) Tommy Steele, Angela Douglas, Michael Medwin, Bernard Bresslaw, Walter Hudd, Jean Harvey, Richard Goolden.
101 min.
Cheesy British pop musical of the early '60s has Tommy (fresh and chipper) doing his bit for 'charidee' as a hard-working talent scout for a recording company, who puts on a benefit concert to save the orphanage where he was brought up. It's nostalgia parade time as the gig goes ahead with the likes of Shane Fenton and the Fentones, Russ Conway, and The Clyde Valley Stompers. TJ

It's All True
(Richard Wilson/Myron Meisel/Bill Krohn, 1993, Fr/US)
85 min.
Some years back, footage of Orson Welles' 'lost' multi-part film – started in South America in 1942 but never completed (the fiasco basically ruined his career) – surfaced in a short documentary. What little there was (some Rio carnival footage, scenes from the fishing story 'Four Men on a Raft') looked stunning. In this documentary, happily, there's much more to show, including a half-hour sequence, with interviews detailing the film's bedevilled history, and an apparently pretty complete restoration of 'Four Men'. GA

It's a Long Way to the Sea (Hkhagoroloi Bohu Door)
(Jahnu Barua, 1995, Ind) Bishnu Kharghoria, Arun Nath, Kashmiri Saikia Baruah, Sushanta Baruah.
106 min.
A village boatman Puwai (Kharghoria) and his grandson (Barooah) attempt to stay in touch with relatives in the city and to cope with a new bridge across the river that has provided the family with employment for generations. Beneath the surface

of this modest Assamese tale, with its familiar metaphorical Indian river, is a moral lesson on the human cost of 'development'. Bar one slight lurch in the middle, the film unfolds with delightful openness and simplicity. NB

It's Always Fair Weather
(Gene Kelly/Stanley Donen, 1955, US) Gene Kelly, Dan Dailey, Cyd Charisse, Dolores Gray, Michael Kidd, David Burns, Jay C Flippen.
102 min.
Donen and Kelly's last musical together, and an exhilarating – if rather odd – follow-up to the marvellous On the Town. Dealing with three soldier buddies who reunite ten years after the war, only to discover that they now have nothing in common, it features some great dance numbers (Kelly on roller-skates, the trio dancing with dustbin-lids for shoes, Charisse and a chorus of plug-uglies in the gym), and a strangely cynical sense of humour about their incompatibility and about television. GA

It's a Mad, Mad, Mad, Mad World
(Stanley Kramer, 1963, US) Spencer Tracy, Milton Berle, Sid Caesar, Ethel Merman, Mickey Rooney, Buddy Hackett, Dick Shawn, Phil Silvers, Terry-Thomas, Jonathan Winters, Edie Adams, Peter Falk, Eddie 'Rochester' Anderson, William Demarest.
192 min.
Originally filmed in Ultra Panavision for showing in Cinerama (subsequent prints were cut to 154 minutes), Kramer's 'comedy to end all comedy' stretches its material to snapping point but offers happy hours of star-spotting (everyone has a cameo, from Buster Keaton, Jimmy Durante and Jim Backus to Jack Benny, Jerry Lewis and the Three Stooges). There are several great sequences, most of which involve Terry-Thomas, whose image of America as a bosom-and-money-fixated society is spot on. It's an epic allegory about greed, centering on a frantic treasure hunt for buried bank loot. ATu

It's a 2' 6" Above the Ground World (aka The Love Ban)
(Ralph Thomas, 1972, GB) Hywel Bennett, Nanette Newman, Russell Lewis, Simon Henderson, Sally-Ann Ferber, Milo O'Shea, Georgina Hale, John Cleese.
93 min.
Heartwarming (?) comedy about a well-off Catholic family with six kids where the wife exiles husband to the spare bedroom until he feels brave enough to buy himself some contraceptives. It compromises itself right, left and centre in an effort not to offend, and ends up not saying anything at all, but throwing out on the way a couple of nasty lines in doublethink. The wife, for instance, decides to go on the pill – which is OK for her as she's C of E – without telling her husband; and having been celibate for ten months, they both start having sex fantasies. As a comedy it relies on played-down double entendres and the lady driver joke.

It's a Wonderful Life ■ 100 ■ (100)
(Frank Capra, 1946, US) James Stewart, Donna Reed, Lionel Barrymore, Henry Travers, Beulah Bondi, Gloria Grahame, Thomas Mitchell, HB Warner, Ward Bond.
129 min. b/w.
An extraordinary, unabashed testament to the homely small-town moral values and glossy studio production values that shaped Capra's films so successfully in the late '30s and rapidly disappeared thereafter. It's a film designed to grab your cockles and warm them till they smoulder, particularly at the end, with its Christmas card setting, its whimsical angel sent down to save the despairing do-gooder (Stewart) from doing evil by committing suicide. Capra has total command of his cast and technical resources, and a touching determination to believe that it is indeed a wonderful life. GB

It's a Wonderful World
(Val Guest, 1956, GB) Terence Morgan, George Cole, Kathleen Harrison, Mylène Demongeot, James Hayter, Richard Wattis, Ted Heath and His Music.
89 min.
Groan-worthy British musical comedy from the

days before rock'n'roll. Cole (at his spivviest) and Morgan are a couple of hard-pressed songwriters, about to be chucked out of their digs by landlady Harrison, when they get their big break – fellow lodger Demongeot, a young mademoiselle in England for her studies, manages to sell one of their tunes to the Ted Heath orchestra. The ensuing complications are unsurprising, but there are enough familiar faces in the cast to make you feel at home, and a pleasing diversion when our chaps pass off a backwards recording as their new progressive jazz opus 'City of Lost Souls'. TJ

It's Great to Be Young
(Cyril Frankel, 1956, GB) John Mills, Cecil Parker, Dorothy Bromiley, Jeremy Spenser, Brian Smith, Eleanor Summerfield.
93 min.
Tempting to see this as a typically British forerunner of Hollywood's cute campus radical movies, with a bunch of musically-minded grammar school kids rebelling against the dismissal of their piano-playing teacher. Actually, it is just a botched imitation of those Garland/ Rooney putting-on-a-show musicals, tediously tame and producing one absurdity to treasure in the sight of John Mills (the teacher in question) jiving over a hot jazz piano in a pub. The music is dubbed by Humphrey Lyttleton's Band (among others less reputable). TM

It Should Happen to You
(George Cukor, 1954, US) Judy Holliday, Peter Lawford, Jack Lemmon, Connie Gilchrist, Michael O'Shea.
81 min. b/w.
One of Judy Holliday's delicious dumb blonde performances as the nobody despairing of being somebody who makes it by splashing her savings on splashing her name across a billboard in Manhattan. Garson Kanin's script doesn't really bite hard enough in its satire of TV and its eager promotion of the nonentity celebrity, nor – after a wonderful opening – does the comedy have anywhere much to go. Bright moments and irresistible performances, though, with Lemmon (in his debut) making a superb foil for Holliday as the solemn documentary film-maker who observes, loves and is baffled by her. TM

It Shouldn't Happen to a Vet
(Eric Till, 1976, GB) John Alderton, Colin Blakely, Lisa Harrow, Bill Maynard, Richard Pearson, Paul Shelley, John Barrett.
93 min.
A sequel to the fresh-faced, scrubbed and earnest All Creatures Great and Small, based on James Herriot's bestselling tales of the life of a Yorkshire vet in the '30s. What Richard Gordon's Doctor books were to the '50s, Herriot's vet books are to the '70s. Certainly both have won their way into the hearts of the middle classes, presumably because both are so reassuring about the order of things (an impending world war is kept discreetly in the background of this instalment). And in both, our medical hero mixes self-deprecation with an ability to pull it off when it really counts. Alderton plays the part originated by Simon Ward with a greater natural ability; but otherwise the film offers the same round of people chasing animals and vice versa, farmyard gags, and nostalgia for a vanished rural lifestyle. CPe

It's Love I'm After
(Archie Mayo, 1937, US) Bette Davis, Leslie Howard, Olivia de Havilland, Patric Knowles, Eric Blore, Bonita Granville, George Barbier, Spring Byington, Veda Ann Borg.
90 min. b/w.
Howard and Davis, as feuding thespians too busy to have got around to getting married yet, have more fun with this romantic comedy than its overwritten script by Casey Robinson deserves. When matinée idol Howard has to cope with the consequences of a young de Havilland's backstage advances, the plot degenerates into a rather uninspired Comedy of Errors set in a well-to-do WASPish family's country house. For connoisseurs of bad acting, however, there's an execrable but funny performance from Blore (as a manservant, naturally), with whom Howard has most of the fun. RM

It's Magic
see Romance on the High Seas

It's My Life

see Vivre sa Vie

It's My Party

(Randal Kleiser, 1996, US) Eric Roberts, Gregory Harrison, Lee Grant, Marlee Matlin, Bronson Pinchot, Margaret Cho, Olivia Newton-John, Roddy McDowall, Bruce Davison, George Segal, Sally Kellerman, Nina Foch.
110 mins.
Nick (Roberts) is a Los Angeles architect, HIV-positive and now, says his doctor, suffering progressive brain lesions, giving him perhaps another ten days of consciousness. Time to implement Plan B: one final shindig with family and friends, at the end of which Nick will take an overdose, dignity intact. But he won't, or can't, invite Brandon (Harrison), his ex-lover with whom he parted acrimoniously after testing positive. Most of the film consists of Nick's two-day party, at which the ensemble cast mill around, joke and squabble, and gradually slide into a ruminative disconsolateness. Brandon too turns up, is first shunned, and finally makes his peace with Nick. Despite the occasional longueur, all this is quietly engaging. Still, for a weepie, let alone one about AIDS, it's peculiarly upbeat. The real traumas stay in flashbacks, to the death of other infected friends, or in photos arranged in testament on Nick's wall; even moments of frisson, as when Nick's estranged father appears unexpectedly, are kept to the edges of frame. NB

It's Only Money

(Frank Tashlin, 1962, US) Jerry Lewis, Zachary Scott, Joan O'Brien, Mae Questel, Jesse White, Jack Weston.
84 min. b/w.
TV-radio repairman Lewis turns shamus in the search for the inheritor of a millionaire's fortune, and finds he's the missing heir. It's a very funny losing battle against the gadgets and machines, as Lewis turns high energy against cannibal electronic lawn-mowers, TV sets, and living stereo. Up-tempo, satirical, and despite a lame plot, it's a collection of excellent gags. DMacp

It Started in Naples

(Melville Shavelson, 1960, US) Clark Gable, Sophia Loren, Vittorio De Sica, Marietto, Paolo Carlini.
100 min.
One-joke romantic comedy in which Gable (stiff with American honesty and hygiene) and Loren (voluble with Italian guile and grubbiness) squabble over the future of an orphan child fast turning into a delinquent amid the *dolce far niente* temptations of a travelogue Italy. Originally intended as a vehicle for Gracie Fields (it happens on Capri), it is kept afloat chiefly by Loren's engaging ebullience. TM

It Started with Eve

(Henry Koster, 1941, US) Charles Laughton, Deanna Durbin, Robert Cummings, Guy Kibbee, Margaret Tallichet, Walter Catlett.
90 min. b/w.
Far better than most Durbin vehicles, enlivened no end by the presence of Laughton as the cantankerous old millionaire who insists on meeting his grandson's fiancée before he dies. The girl can't be reached and so Durbin, a hatcheck girl, is enlisted to deceive the old man, with predictable complications. Cheerful and charming, although one could well do without the chirpy songs warbled by Durbin. GA

It's the Old Army Game

(Edward Sutherland, 1926, US) WC Fields, Louise Brooks, Blanche Ring, William Gaxton.
77 min. b/w.
In her book *Lulu in Hollywood*, Louise Brooks recalls this as a chaotic, drunken shoot ('Nobody in Ocala seemed to have heard of Prohibition'), and dismisses her own role as 'the love interest'. She's right: it's a hit-and-miss affair, and her appearance is peripheral. Centre stage is Fields, playing the small town drugstore proprietor Prettywillie. He has ghastly relatives (including an obnoxious infant), never gets an uninterrupted nap, gets dragged into a seemingly crooked real estate deal, and makes a disastrous visit to New York. In short, Fields gets to recreate many of his stage routines, and in a much 'purer' form than in most of his later movies. Remade as *It's a Gift*. TR

It's Trad, Dad!

(Dick Lester, 1962, GB) Helen Shapiro, Craig Douglas, Felix Felton, Timothy Bateson, Frank Thornton, Bruce Lacey, Chubby Checker, Temperance Seven, Kenny Ball, Chris Barber, Gene Vincent.
73 min. b/w.
Having cut his teeth on Telegoon shows like *Idiots Weekly* and *A Show Called Fred*, expatriate American Lester proceeded to take the staid British film industry by storm with this firework display of cinematic trickery. Boldly throwing realism out of the window, he uses a wafer-thin plot about a Toy Town mayor determined to stamp out creeping jazzism as a device to explore the '60s music scene (25 numbers in 73 mintes), and to celebrate the coming 'Youth Revolution'. Some of the acts stand up better than others – Gene Vincent singing 'Space Ship to Mars', Gary (US) Bonds, the witty, modish Temperance Seven – but even the more boring trad jazz is filmed with such energy and inventiveness that it entertains. RMy

It Takes Two

(David Beaird, 1988, US) George Newbern, Leslie Hope, Kimberly Foster, Barry Corbin, Anthony Geary.
79 min.
While his new bride is stalling in neutral at the altar, a soon-to-be-ex-bachelor spends his last hours of freedom test driving the car of his dreams with a rather attractive saleswoman for company. Breezy Texas-set caper with a few good jokes. One of the better movies of hit-and-miss director Beaird, best known in Britain for writing the over-heated stage melodrama *0900 Oneanta*, and the squiffy celluloid Southern galumphry *Scorchers*. TJ

It Takes Two

(Andy Tennant, 1995, US) Kirstie Alley, Steve Guttenberg, Mary-Kate Olsen, Ashley Olsen, Jane Sibbett, Philip Bosco.
100 min.
Brooklyn: spinster and orphanage worker Diane (Alley) wants to adopt her favourite charge, spunky nine-year-old Amanda (Mary-Kate Olsen). Trouble is, she's still looking for Mr Right, and the adoption authorities would rather she'd already found him. Upstate New York: widower Roger (Guttenberg), millionaire and part-time parent, would like to find a new mum for his daughter, pristine nine-year-old Alyssa (Ashley Olsen). Trouble is, he's just got engaged to gold-digging Clarice Kensington (Sibbett), and Alyssa would rather she took her claws out of him. Funnily enough, Amanda and Alyssa are identical strangers. Two comedy genres – mistaken identity and true romance – are married in forgettable fashion. And, alas, the Olsen girls are not immediately heart-warming. NB

Ivan's Childhood
(Ivanovo Detstvo)

(Andrei Tarkovsky, 1962, USSR) Kolya Burlaev, V Zubkov, E Zharikov, S Krylov, N Grinko, D Miliutenko.
95 min. b/w.
Tarkovsky's first feature is in many ways an orthodox Russian film of its period. Ivan is a teenage Soviet spy on the German front in World War II who undertakes dangerous missions behind enemy lines, until the inevitable mission from which there is no return. Many of Tarkovsky's later images and themes are already present and correct: Ivan silently wading through still water, eerily immanent forestscapes, the poetry of forbidden zones, and life-and-death struggles played out in slow motion. But the glittering black-and-white camerawork has a florid, bravura quality that Tarkovsky later rejected, as if determined to invest this more or less familiar material with touches of 'visionary' beauty. The irony is that the generic storyline provides a much stronger foundation for his visual ambitions than do the religiose and feebly philosophical abstractions that ostensibly underpin the films from *Solaris* onwards. Tha aura of holiness around Ivan registers neither as religious bombast nor as patriotic myth-making, but rather as an awed respect for childhood mysteries. This is Tarkovsky before his peasant sentimentality and sense of self-importance got the better of him, and it still looks hugely impressive. TR

Ivanhoe

(Richard Thorpe, 1952, GB) Robert Taylor, Elizabeth Taylor, Joan Fontaine, George Sanders, Finlay Currie, Guy Rolfe, Robert Douglas, Emlyn Williams.
107 min.
One of the vintage MGM costume epics from the early '50s when Thorpe was making countless medieval movies 'over at Metro' (this usually meant on location in England). *Ivanhoe* is one of the best, with Robert Taylor in the title role, Elizabeth Taylor as Rebecca, and Fontaine as Rowena. The dialogue and script are fatuously Americanised from Scott's original, but these chivalric sagas of Hollywood's still have a strange poetic quality about them, perhaps partly because of the way they unscrupulously and inaccurately ransacked literature and history for ideas and images. DP

Ivan the Terrible
(Ivan Grozny)

(Sergei Eisenstein, 1944/1946, USSR) Nikolai Cherkassov, Serafima Birman, Ludmila Tselikovskaya, Mikhail Nazvanov, Pavel Kadochnikov.
100 min (Part I) – 87 min (Part II). b/w & col.
Probably the most enjoyable of all Eisenstein's films, his last work, a projected trilogy of which only two parts were completed. The historical subject – Tsar Ivan's struggle to consolidate the Russian empire, freeing it from Eastern domination and (in Part II) the self-serving interests of the Boyars – is sufficiently removed from the crucial problem (for Eisenstein) of reconciling film theory and political practice for it to work as comic melodrama. Often criticised for its lack of historical truth, the film still holds up as a camp essay in authoritarian paranoia. Cherkassov's contorted performance as Ivan, absurdly stylised though it is, beautifully expresses the conscience of the state torn between absolutism and factionalism, while managing a miraculous integration with a superbly operatic visual style. RM

I've Gotta Horse

(Kenneth Hume, 1965, GB) Billy Fury, Amanda Barrie, Michael Medwin, Bill Fraser, Leslie Dwyer, The Gamblers, The Bachelors.
92 min.
At the start of his career, Billy Fury's love of animals proved a constant source of embarrassment to his management, who were trying to mould him into a surly rock'n'roller. By 1965, Fury had broadened into a lukewarm entertainer, and this effort, which desperately plugged his affection for his four-legged friends, was a misguided attempt to (a) widen his appeal to mums, and (b) to regain some of the fans that he and other solo artists had lost since the advent of groupmania in 1963. The film slipped by unnoticed. CPe

I've Heard the
Mermaids Singing

(Patricia Rozema, 1987, Can) Sheila McCarthy, Paule Baillargeon, Ann-Marie MacDonald, John Evans, Brenda Kamino, Richard Monette.
83 min.
When Polly, a gauche, 'organisationally impaired' temp who indulges in absurdly ethereal daydreams and photography, gets a job at a trendy gallery, she develops a crush on her sophisticated, seemingly imperturbable boss, Gabrielle, and unwittingly becomes involved in an art fraud. Unlike her protagonist, Rozema never puts a foot wrong. Polly is granted her own subtle dignity, Gabrielle and her lesbian lover transcend conventional villainy, and an allegorical subtext warning against blind faith in false gods is handled so lightly as to be virtually invisible. For all its social satire, however, this is Polly's film. She is, perhaps, the most memorable, genuinely likeable screen creation in years, and Rozema's debut – touching, hilarious, as fresh as a summer breeze – does her ample justice. GA

Ivory Hunter

see Where No Vultures Fly

Ivy

(Sam Wood, 1947, US) Joan Fontaine, Patric Knowles, Herbert Marshall, Richard Ney, Cedric Hardwicke, Henry Stephenson.
99 min. b/w.

Russell Metty's gorgeous low-key camerawork sets the tone for this Edwardian chiller with a wonderfully moody opening sequence at a fortune-teller's where Fontaine learns that her destiny is to become a murderess. Demurely grasping ambition aiding, she is soon on her way to black widowhood by poisoning her husband, framing her lover, and setting her sights on the next victim. Based on a novel by Mrs Belloc Lowndes (of *The Lodger*) and given an exquisite period gloss by William Cameron Menzies' designs, it's a little bland but a real pleasure on the eye. TM

I Wake Up Screaming (aka Hot Spot)

(H Bruce Humberstone, 1942, US) Victor Mature, Betty Grable, Laird Cregar, Carole Landis, Elisha Cook Jr, Alan Mowbray, Allyn Joslyn, William Gargan.
82 min. b/w.
A fine thriller in which the familiar situation of the man wrongly accused of his girl's murder is given a number of brilliant twists. Visually, adhering to the Fox style, the film is basically naturalistic, but its mood becomes increasingly murky as the hero plumbs the depths of nightmare, culminating in his discovery that the obese, soft-spoken detective relentlessly hounding him (the marvellously sinister Cregar) knows he didn't kill her but, himself hopelessly infatuated with the dead girl, blames him for her death and means to exact a perverse vengeance. Intimations of *noir* proliferate in the fact that the dead girl's sister is irresistibly attracted to the presumed killer, in the sleazy little dream world inhabited by the real killer, and in a scene of nightmarish ambivalence where the hero wakes to find the detective brooding lovingly over him as he sleeps. It's a pity that the script, developing cold feet, prevents the film from developing its full *noir* potential by toning down Steve Fisher's source novel in several respects. Most notably, Fisher's detective (intriguingly, a pen portrait of Cornell Woolrich), was presented as a man dying of TB ('He looked sick. He looked like a corpse. His clothes didn't fit him'); this sickness, creeping like a cancer through the story, made more sense of his obsessive vendetta against a man healthy enough not only to live but to win love. TM

I Walked with a Zombie

(Jacques Tourneur, 1943, US) Frances Dee, Tom Conway, James Ellison, Edith Barrett, Christine Gordon, Sir Lancelot, Darby Jones.
69 min. b/w.
The most elegant of Val Lewton's low budget horrors for RKO, an imaginative updating of *Jane Eyre* which anticipates Jean Rhys' *Wide Sargasso Sea* by transposing the action to the Caribbean, with Rochester's first wife not mad but the victim of a voodoo spell. The script, weaving a delicately intricate web of local superstition around a litany of oblique references to the relativity of good and evil, does wonders in creating an ambiguously unsettling atmosphere. But it is Tourneur's caressingly evocative direction, superbly backed by Roy Hunt's chiaroscuro images, that makes sheer magic of the film's brooding journey into fear by way of voodoo drums, gleaming moonlight, somnambulistic ladies in fluttering white, and dark, silent, undead sentries. TM

I Wanna Hold Your Hand

(Robert Zemeckis, 1978, US) Nancy Allen, Bobby DiCicco, Marc McClure, Susan Kendall Newman, Theresa Saldana, Wendie Jo Sperber, Eddie Deezen, Will Jordan.
104 min.
Spielberg-produced debut for Zemeckis: the zany adventures of four teeny fans from New Jersey determined to crash the Ed Sullivan Show the night the Beatles appeared in 1964 (you never actually see the Fab Four, of course). A personal recollection of the more arcane details of Beatlemania is almost essential, plus familiarity with youth movies like *American Graffiti* and characters like The Fonz. The comedy is far too diverse, ranging from pastiche through farce (old elevator and corridor gags) to plain good humour. In the best scenes, Zemeckis suggests how the Beatles' blend of irreverence, romance and innocence encouraged a kind of youthful rebellion that was almost completely sanctioned. Loved the music. JS

I Wanted to See Angels (Ja Chtela Uwidetj Angelow)

(Sergei Bodrov, 1992, Rus) Alexi Baranov, Natasha Ginko, Lia Ahedjanov, Alex Jarkov.
85 min.
Bodrov (director of *Freedom Is Paradise*) divides his time between Moscow and California, which may explain why this vision of Moscow's chaotic sub-culture has a perspective and elegance lacking in other similar Russian movies about juvenile tearaways. Twenty-year-old Bob rides 1000 km to Moscow on his vintage motorbike to collect a bad debt for his boss; the city chews up and spits out this naive country boy, whose head is full of *Easy Rider* dreams. Less *film noir* than elegy for lost chances, the movie gets inside young Russian heads with an acuity that's almost psychedelic. Sexy, bruising and quite haunting. TR

I Want to Go Home (Je veux rentrer à la maison)

(Alain Resnais, 1989, Fr) Adolph Green, Gérard Depardieu, Linda Lavin, Micheline Presle, Laura Benson, Geraldine Chaplin.
110 min.
To make a movie inspired by comic-strip art has been a long-term ambition for renais; sadly, fulfilment of the dream seems too have come to late. Scripted by Jules Feiffer, this is a predictable tale of a boorishly xenophobic American cartoonist (in Paris for an exhibition of his work) and his estranged daughter (an unforgiving Francophile academic), who belatedly make friends thanks to unwitting intermediary Depardieu, a Sorbonne genius with a characteristically French love of pulp art. If it's meant to be funny, moving *or* an essay on the gulf between American and European mores, it fails; worse, however, the central characters are all so downright egocentric and unpleasant that they virtually drive you screaming from the cinema. GA

I Want to Live!

(Robert Wise, 1958, US) Susan Hayward, Simon Oakland, Virginia Vincent, Theodore Bikel, Wesley Lau, John Marley, Dabbs Greer, Gavin MacLeod.
120 min. b/w.
One of the great anti-capital punishment movies, this is based on the life and death of Barbara Graham. At one time or another, Graham was convicted of prostitution, perjury, forgery, and finally murder. Basing their screenplay on contemporary newspaper files and her own letters, Nelson Gidding and Don Mankiewicz make no bones about Graham's anti-social tendencies, but conclude that she was probably innocent of the last charge. Wise paces the film so that the last half-hour, taking us into the gas chamber, is incredibly powerful, and Hayward won an Oscar for her unforgettable performance. The jazz score is by Johnny Mandel. TCh

I Want What I Want

(John Dexter, 1971, GB) Anne Heywood, Harry Andrews, Jill Bennett, Paul Rogers, Michael Coles, Sheila Reid, Virginia Stride.
105 min.
Anne Heywood as the transsexual son of a Major (Rtd, currently working as a supermarket manager) who decides to fully become a woman (one year later he/she has a 'completely successful' operation). Dexter's *The Virgin Soldiers*, his only previous film, had its points; but this absurd non-exploration has none, aside from one image of sexual frustration powerful only because the rest of the film is so misconceived, misbegotten and coy.

I Want You

(Mark Robson, 1951, US) Dana Andrews, Dorothy McGuire, Farley Granger, Peggy Dow, Robert Keith, Mildred Dunnock, Ray Collins, Jim Backus.
102 min. b/w.
Having achieved tremendous success five years earlier with *The Best Years of Our Lives*, producer Samuel Goldwyn had high hopes for this slightly less distinguished domestic drama, written by Irwin Shaw, exploring the effects of the Korean war on a small-town family construction business. Suggested by the recent experiences of the mogul's own son, future movie-maker Sam Jr, it's a well intentioned, low-key effort, and though

it never quite escapes the feeling that all concerned are walking on eggshells, a valuable record of the times still emerges. TJ

I Was a Fireman

see Fires Were Started

I Was a Male War Bride (aka You Can't Sleep Here)

(Howard Hawks, 1949, US) Cary Grant, Ann Sheridan, Marion Marshall, Randy Stuart, William Neff, Kenneth Tobey.
105 min. b/w.
Neatly reversing the usual comic model, where marriage only ever signals 'The End', this is a classic demonstration of Hawks' unsentimental optimism, and a comedy on frustration and sex-roles that is romantic, subversive and extremely funny, all at the same time. Grant is the priggish, bemused French army officer who hates, loves, and marries smart American army lieutenant Sheridan...then discovers that to follow his bride back to the USA and consummate their interrupted wedding night, he must fill in a million forms, wander disconsolately from barrack to barrack in search of a bed, and, final humiliation, dress up in drag to beat the bureaucracy. CA

I Was a Teenage Werewolf

(Gene Fowler Jr, 1957, US) Michael Landon, Yvonne Lime, Whit Bissell, Tony Marshall, Vladimir Sokoloff, Guy Williams.
70 min. b/w.
All-time zero-budget schlock classic capitalising on the late '50s trend for teen problem pictures, and starring Michael Landon, later Little Joe in *Bonanza* and Dad in *Little House on the Prairie*. As a juvenile delinquent, he's sent to an unscrupulous psychiatrist (Bissell) in the hope he'll get the help he needs to reform; instead, said shrink's experiments turn the hapless youth into a werewolf whenever the school bell sounds. CR

I Was Born, But... (Umarete wa Mita Keredo)

(Yasujiro Ozu, 1932, Jap) Hideo Sugawara, Tokkan-Kozo, Tatsu Saito, Mitsuko Yoshikawa, Takeshi Sakamoto, Chishu Ryu.
100 min. b/w.
This is the original version of the story about rebellious kids who feel betrayed by their father that Ozu remade as *Ohayo* thirty-seven years later. *I Was Born, But...* doesn't have the later film's oscillations between comedy and a tragic sense of defeat; rather, it begins as a particularly riotous comedy, and then abruptly switches to a darker tone when the boys lose their respect for their father. It's silent (Ozu resisted talkies until 1935), but its visual style is so dynamic that you hardly notice; both the gags and the emotional disappointments are anchored in a sure sense of characterisation that remains wholly fresh, and the pace of the whole film is worthy of Buster Keaton at his best. TR

I Was Fifteen (Den Sommeren jeg fylte 15)

(Knut Andersen, 1974, Nor) Steffen Rothschild, Anne Lise Tangstad, Kaare Kroppan, Grethe Ryen, Carina Rude.
98 min.
This Norwegian entry in the adolescent-initiation stakes tastefully refrains from an explicit depiction of its hero's first faltering attempts at sexual congress, and instead diverts us at inordinate length with phallic symbols and boyish customs (boasting, blowing up condoms, chaste kissing in the rain). The plot concerns a youngster sent to his uncle's farm for the summer; the uncle is extremely hardy, and his homely wife makes up for his neglect of her by overfeeding their nephew. Going for a swim, uncle discovers the body of an orphaned girl made pregnant by him (her pasty make-up washes off before our very eyes). Set sometime in the past, judging from the magazines the boy ogles, this sombre film aims, rather uncertainly, at highlighting the hypocrisy of adulthood and the winsomeness of youth. JPy

I Was Happy Here

(Desmond Davis, 1965, GB) Sarah Miles, Cyril Cusack, Julian Glover, Sean Caffrey, Marie Kean, Eve Belton, Cardew Robinson.
91 min. b/w.

A horribly pretentious and sentimental film which still manages to retain a degree of emotional power, with moments of real intensity and conviction. It's about an Irish girl (Miles) who returns to her home in Ireland after an unhappy marriage, and is pursued there by her bullying husband (Glover). The film is certainly much better than Davis' earlier Irish story *The Girl with Green Eyes* (also adapted from Edna O'Brien), but it's dogged by the awful tricks of overemphasis which he seems to have learned from his patron Tony Richardson. DP

I Was, I Am, I Shall Be (Ich war, ich bin, ich werde sein)
(Walter Heynowski/Gerhard Scheumann, 1974, EGer)
71 min. b/w.
Some months after the Chilean coup of September 1973, an East German camera crew managed to obtain permission to visit one of the Pinochet regime's prison camps, a former disused saltpetre mine in the arid desert of northern Chile. But they were able to film only under close surveillance, and the chief interest of *I Was, I Am, I Shall Be* is the material with which this footage is intercut. Shot mainly before the coup, it places Chatabuco in a historical context, both as mine and as prison camp. The factual testimony of former mineworkers, including a witness of the 1925 massacre at Marusia, makes a striking contrast with the blandly explanatory Pinochet. One shot provides a continual refrain: a prisoner holds up the handle of a miner's spade with the words, 'It was found here and I think it speaks for itself. It can be interpreted in many ways' – a statement whose multiple ambiguities become increasingly clear as the film progresses. AS

I Was Monty's Double
(John Guillermin, 1958, GB) John Mills, Cecil Parker, Clifton James, Marius Goring, Michael Hordern, Leslie Phillips, Patrick Allen, Bryan Forbes.
100 min. b/w.
Released in America under the marvellous title of *Heaven, Hell and Hoboken*, *I Was Monty's Double* is a low-budget tour de force. Based on real events – an actor (James, who really was used as a double for General Montgomery during the Allied invasion of Europe in World War II) is hired to impersonate Monty and so confuse the Germans by popping up in odd places – the film neatly uses the elevation of a nobody to honoured hero to question the notions of heroism that so many British war movies unquestioningly supported. Highly enjoyable. PH

I Was on Mars
(Dani Levy, 1991, Ger) Maria Schrader, Dani Levy, Mario Giacalone, Antonia Rey.
86 min.
It's taken a few years for them to gestate, but Jarmusch's *Stranger Than Paradise* has fathered a brood of low-budget Euro-movies about the trials and tribulations of foreigners newly arrived in New York. This is one of them: a relentlessly in-your-face tragi-comedy about a young woman from Warsaw who speaks no English and loses the few greenbacks she has to the first guy she meets, a loud-suited spiv. Levi himself plays the conman as a sleazeball who takes the bit-players in *GoodFellas* as role models; co-writer Maria Schrader plays the Polish girl as dogged perseverance personified. Sometimes raucous, sometimes forlorn, but very rarely convincing. TR

I Went Down
(Paddy Breathnach, 1997, Ire/GB/Sp) Brendan Gleeson, Peter McDonald, Peter Caffrey, Tony Doyle, Antoine Byrne, David Wilmot, Michael McElhatton, Joe Gallagher.
107 min.
Lovely, slow-burning shaggy-dog Irish crime movie built around the uneasy partnership of two small-time Dublin chancers. Thrown together for an errand, the lads are to retrieve a fugitive associate of the local crime boss, and return him to face the music. Git (McDonald) is the quiet type, only doing it to help get a mate out of trouble; Bunny (Gleeson) is a bruiser with ginger sideburns and rockabilly shoes, who likes to think he's on top of the situation when, patently, he isn't. Playwright Conor McPherson's mixes broad humour and dialogue (in the Roddy Doyle vein) into a neat thriller plot. He's well served by an as-yet relatively unknown cast, who never allow the skew-whiff turns of phrase to sound self-conscious, and by the director's guiding sense of equilibrium. It's all beguilingly entertaining as we move through a landscape of rural petrol stations, stand-offs on the peat bog, and deepening intrigue; deceptively rich, too, as it reflects on how its reluctant protagonists stand up to the demands of modern masculinity when they're estranged from their womenfolk, and to consider the whys and wherefores of loyalty and integrity when greed and violent persuasion have blurred the lines of moral probity. TJ

I Will...I Will...For Now
(Norman Panama, 1975, US) Elliott Gould, Diane Keaton, Paul Sorvino, Victoria Principal, Warren Berlinger, Candy Clark, Robert Alda.
108 min.
Harry and Walter Go to New York demonstrated that the talents of Diane Keaton, that beautifully composed comedienne who neatly partnered the cack-handed and physically inconsequential Woody Allen, were not equally suited to those of the exuberant and brawny Elliott Gould. The main problem with this leaden marital farce climaxing in a Californian sex clinic, however, is not so much that the Keaton/Gould partnership again fails to spark, but that Norman Panama's lamentable script, based on a Hollywood approach to sex and marriage decades out of date, is executed with all the lack of subtlety and brightly-lit jollity of a Doris Day heartwarmer. Though hardly surprising in view of Panama's creaky comedy antecedents, it is still wincingly embarrassing to see accomplished performers cavorting in such rubbish. JPy

I...You...He...She
see Je tu il elle

j

Jailhouse Rock

Jabberwocky

(Terry Gilliam, 1977, GB) Michael Palin, Max Wall, Deborah Fallender, John Le Mesurier, Annette Badland, Warren Mitchell, Harry H Corbett, Rodney Bewes, Bernard Bresslaw.
101 min.

Honestly, the things people do to make you laugh in this Python-esque medieval epic. They hire a cast of British notables, ranging from Max Wall to Christopher Logue. They seek out some of Britain's nicest ancient monuments. They create a monster with enough horrible features to stock two series of *Dr Who*. They pile on the atmosphere with mist, candles, crowds, dust and blood. They construct a complicated plot and then only give you glimpses of it, as in the foreign films. Oh yes, they write gags too: some are good (jousting knights with daft things like bananas and fish on their helmets), some are bad, and some ugly. Max Wall's fruity enunciation boosts almost all his lines, and Michael Palin makes a pleasingly gormless hero. But nice bits here and there don't amount to a good movie: like the portmanteau words in Lewis Carroll's poem, there's just far too much packed together for anything to make proper sense. GB

Jabula – A Band in Exile

(Jan Bernard Bussemaker, 1981, GB)
41 min.

No great shakes as a movie, but a sympathetic profile of this black South African group, exiled to the 100 Club in London and discussing the problem of maintaining indigenous roots in music designed to help fight apartheid through popular appeal. The mainstay is a rousing performance of their number 'Wake Up!', intercut with stills of Sharpeville. TM

Jack

(Francis Ford Coppola, 1996, US) Robin Williams, Diane Lane, Brian Kerwin, Jennifer Lopez, Bill Cosby, Fran Drescher, Michael McKean.
113 min.

The Francis Ford Coppola signature, usually reserved for personal projects, doesn't appear to square with what looks like another excuse for Robin Williams to do his infantile routine. The plot conceit has Williams as a lad, Jack, whose over-active metabolism masks a 10-year-old in the hairy body of a 40-year-old man; but in taking the time to explore this scenario in genuine human terms, Coppola delivers an ungainly but undeniably arresting hybrid. While the film's too mature for the kids' audience, its juvenile slapstick trappings – collapsed chairs and the like – may blind grown-ups to the deeply felt emotions at its core. Jack's dispatched to school for the first time, and the way he wins over his alarmed classmates proves refreshingly clear-sighted: he can buy porn mags, light his farts, and dominate the basketball court. It's good to see a movie in touch with such realities – though Bill Cosby's sticky turn as Jack's kindly tutor should have been cut at script stage. Where things switch up a gear, however, is in the confrontation with the adult world, for an ill-fated attempt at wooing teacher introduces Jack to a confusing arena of failed relationships and sexual hang-ups, while a simple 'What I want to be when I grow up' assignment impresses on him the sobering burden of time: when his chums are twenty-something, he'll be approaching his century. The star, kept under firm control, grates less than usual, though you wouldn't come to 'a Robin Williams movie' for what you get here: a divided soul, and just possibly Coppola's most honest movie in years. TJ

Jackal, The

(Michael Caton-Jones, 1997, US) Bruce Willis, Richard Gere, Sidney Poitier, Diane Venora, Mathilda May, JK Simmons, Tess Harper, Leslie Phillips.
124 min.

The Cold War's over, but Russia's gangsters don't like FBI interference on their patch. Angered by the death of his brother, one of the Russians decides to punish the Bureau by hiring a top assassin, the Jackal (Willis), to eliminate a high profile target in full view of the American public. Working with Russian intelligence officer Koslova (Venora), the FBI's Deputy Director (Poitier) reckons the only way to stop the killer is to enlist imprisoned IRA terrorist Mulqueen

(Gere) – who has his own reasons for hating the Jackal. So begins a race against time as the assassin, an anonymous master of disguise, moves in on his as-yet unidentified prey. Structurally, of course, this film echoes *The Day of the Jackal*, but where Fred Zinnemann opted for a meticulous, even dull study in procedural methods, Caton-Jones goes for pacy, well-staged action, colourful characters, and determinedly contemporary atmosphere. If it's sometimes hard to accept Gere's accent and tough guy stuff, Willis plays the lone, heartless killer with menace, flair and evident glee. Excellent performances, too, from Poitier and Venora. GA

Jack & Sarah

(Tim Sullivan, 1995, GB) Richard E Grant, Samantha Mathis, Judi Dench, Eileen Atkins, Ian McKellen, Cherie Lunghi, Imogen Stubbs, Kate Hardie, David Swift.
110 min.

As English as it gets, this romantic comedy about a one-parent family is not without a modest charm. Jack (Grant) loses his wife in childbirth but commits to raising baby Sarah himself. The upside is the sympathetic reaction of young women, and the downside the busybody visits of his mother (Dench) and his wife's mother (Atkins). All is solved when he hires a nanny (Mathis), except that her proximity around the house brings a new cargo of woe. The tale avoids most of the fumbling man-and-baby stuff, but tries to beat the formula elsewhere in overly bizarre fashion. Who would believe a posh alcoholic tramp (McKellen), discovered outside sleeping in a builder's skip, pressed into service as a butler? Yes, the film is thesped to the hilt in the minor roles. Grant is very good at conveying his love for his baby and his impatience with family interference, and possibly only stretched when it comes to being enamoured of the American nanny, an intensely dislikeable bill of goods. Passable. BC

Jackie Brown

(Quentin Tarantino, 1997, US) Pam Grier, Samuel L Jackson, Robert Forster, Bridget Fonda, Michael Keaton, Robert De Niro, Michael Bowen, Lisa Gay Hamilton.
154 min.

A pretty faithful adaptation of Elmore Leonard's *Rum Punch*, Tarantino's finest, most mature movie to date centres on airline steward Jackie (Grier), picked up by the Feds at LAX with cash and drugs destined for gun trader Ordell (Jackson). Reluctant to do time and aware that Ordell tends to murder anyone he suspects might turn informer, she decides to play cops and criminals – not only Ordell, but his former cellmate Louis (De Niro) and pothead girlfriend Melanie (Fonda) – against each other, confiding only in Max (Forster), the world-weary bail bondsman Ordell hired to get her out of jail in the first place. What's immediately rewarding is that Tarantino forgoes flash patter, stand-offs and stylistic flourishes in favour of a closer focus on character (women included), relationships, motives and mood. Also crucial to our actually coming to care about these people is the terrific acting (Grier and Forster make you wonder where they've been all these years). But perhaps most surprising and welcome is that this is a subtle poignant account of middle-aged people trying to come to terms with failing faculties, fading looks, diminishing options and a need to make their lives count somehow. GA

Jack's Wife (aka Hungry Wives/Season of the Witch)

(George A Romero, 1972, US) Jan White, Ray Laine, Anne Muffly, Joedda McClain, Bill Thundhurt.
130 min.

Following his hugely successful debut with *Night of the Living Dead*, Romero flopped with a romantic comedy (*There's Always Vanilla*) as well as this curious hybrid, before returning to successful formula with *The Crazies*. Although there's an occult tinge to its story of a woman who turns to witchcraft for relief from her troubles and ends up shooting her husband in the belief that he is the prowler of her nightmares, it's a strange, experimental film, with an unmistakable (but amateurish) aura of Bergman in its fragmented study of a woman caught up in frustrations very much of the '60s. The drug references and

abstract devices date it badly, but it's intriguing to see Romero torn between genre and art. On the evidence of this film (at least in the 89 minute version generally available), he eventually made the right choice. DP

Jackal of Nahueltoro, The (El Chacal de Nahueltoro)

(Miguel Littin, 1969, Chile) Nelson Villagra, Shenda Román, Luis Melo, Ruben Sotoconil, Armando Fenoglio.
88 min. b/w.

Chile's first feature, like other Third World films, was made specifically for its own people and intended as a critique of the social conditions in that country. Littin chose the true story of an illiterate peasant who had murdered a widow and her five children when drunk, to dramatise his belief that the crime was as much the responsibility of the state as it was the individual's. The killing is reconstructed as a blind emotional reflex against the accumulated despair of a life of abject, uncomprehending poverty. Sentenced to death amid enormous publicity, the 'jackal' is taught to read and write, to make guitars, to be a 'useful' citizen. The society which is responsible for his original illiteracy and poverty gives him his first 'sense of life' with one hand and a firing-squad with the other. The film leaves you enraged not only at the futility of capital punishment, but also at the whole repressive system whose essential inhumanity is never more clearly indicated than in the final, furtive murder of their scapegoat, a shallow exorcism of their own guilt. JDuC

Jack Be Nimble

(Garth Maxwell, 1992, NZ) Alexis Arquette, Sarah Smuts-Kennedy, Bruno Lawrence, Tony Barry, Elizabeth Hawthorne, Brenda Simmons.
95 min.

A heady witches' brew of fairy-tale grimness, melodramatic excess and dark supernatural horror, Maxwell's first feature induces disequilibrium and unease. After their father's affairs precipitate their mother's flight into insanity, Jack (Arquette) and Dora (Smuts-Kennedy) endure a painful childhood separation with very different adoptive families. Jack's sadistic 'father' whips him with barbed wire while his hatchet-faced 'mother' and ghoulish 'sisters' look on. By contrast, Dora's parents are kind, if stiflingly respectable, although at school she is ridiculed and bullied. A long-dreamed-of reunion in their teens, after Jack's escape and Dora's discovery of hidden psychic powers, cannot match the damaged Jack's idealised memories; consumed by desperate, frustrated rage, he lashes out at those closest to him. Meanwhile, his vengeful sisters are on his trail. As the disturbed creator of a steam-driven, hypnosis-inducing light-machine, Alexis Arquette proves that his sisters Rosanna and Patricia have no monopoly on the family talent for flakiness, while Sarah Smuts-Kennedy brings a luminous inner strength to the outwardly frail Dora. NF

Jacknife

(David Jones, 1988, US) Robert De Niro, Ed Harris, Kathy Baker, Charles Dutton, Elizabeth Franz, Tom Isbell, Loudon Wainwright III.
103 min.

As Megs, a clearly unstable Vietvet whose sudden reappearance in the life of his now nearly alcoholic former buddy Dave (Harris) is part theraputic, part traumatic, De Niro is touching, funny and entirely convincing. The moment he arrives out of the blue at the Conneticut home Dave shares with his schoolmarm sister Martha (Baker), we immediately believe in Megs' inarticulacy, slobbishness and sensitivity. Dave's welcome is less than warm; Martha shifts from horror through hesitant acceptance to friendship. Unsurprisingly, as Megs' hidden strengths rise to the surface, he and Martha fall for each other; equally unsurprisingly, Dave – afraid of being alone – opposes their relationsip. The stage origins (Stephen Metcalfe's play *Strange Snow*) of this gently humorous, lyrical study in loneliness and the lasting legacy of 'Nam are all too evident; but Jones focuses attention on his three actors, all of whom serve him well. The obligatory 'Nam flashbacks are clumsy, the resolution a little pat; but De Niro, compelling from start to finish, carries the film. GA

Jackson County Jail

(Michael Miller, 1976, US) Yvette Mimieux, Tommy Lee Jones, Robert Carradine, Frederic Cook, Severn Darden, Howard Hesseman, John Lawlor.
89 min.
As the best of the current batch of rape pictures, *Jackson County Jail* – perhaps not surprisingly – exploits its heroine the least. With her job and domestic life in shreds, a middle class career woman leaves the security of LA to drive across the States. On the road she is subjected to by now familiar humiliations, culminating with life on the run after a jail rape. What lifts the film beyond the offensive indignities of its lesser relations is an insistence on the violence and discrimination in American society, and the assured and straight-forward progression through the country's under-belly. In addition, unlike *Death Weekend*, it is unequivocally sympathetic towards its heroine. Right from the deceptive opening, Miller's direction knows what it's about, and the continual emphasis on the woman's plight and her silent bewilderment lends the film dimensions of reflection and compassion probably not in the original script. The assurance of Yvette Mimieux's performance is a real surprise. CPe

Jack the Bear

(Marshall Herskovitz, 1992, US) Danny DeVito, Robert J Steinmiller, Miko Hughes, Gary Sinise, Julia Louis-Dreyfuss, Bert Remsen.
98 min.
Oklahoma, c. 1972. The house that 12-year-old Jack lives in looks like it was abandoned by the Addams family. Mom's dead, Dad (DeVito), the host of a midnight schlock-horror show, teases the neighbours' kids with his realistic monster impressions. He's got a drink problem and he's close to a breakdown. There's little bro' Dylan, but at three years old, he's more of a responsibility than an ally. The loony next door, forever polishing his car, is rumoured to be a Nazi. This weird – if never quite wonderful – entertainment is a rites-of-passage drama in horror-movie clothing. DeVito gives a blue-collar truth to a hard role, and it's rare to find a Hollywood film which tackles such troubling subjects, however uneasily. WH

Jack the Giant Killer

(Nathan Juran, 1961, US) Kerwin Mathews, Judi Meredith, Torin Thatcher, Walter Burke, Roger Mobley, Barry Kelley, Don Beddoe, Anna Lee.
94 min.
Amiable children's fantasy, looking uncannily like one of the Schneer-Harryhausen series. Hardly surprising, perhaps, since Edward Small turned down the chance to produce *The Seventh Voyage of Sinbad*, then set out to duplicate it when it turned out to be a huge success. Unable to persuade Harryhausen to cooperate along with Juran, Mathews and Thatcher, Small had 'Harryhausen' special effects created by Project Unlimited. Far more persuasive than the jerky demonic creatures (including a griffin and an octopedic sea monster) is Torin Thatcher's sinister, Lugosi-like performance as the wicked Master of Demons. TM

Jacob's Ladder

(Adrian Lyne, 1990, US) Tim Robbins, Elizabeth Peña, Danny Aiello, Matt Craven, Pruitt Taylor Vince, Jason Alexander, Patricia Kalember, Ving Rhames, Macaulay Culkin.
115 min.
Lyne's chilling film bombed in the States, probably because of its origins in the murkier side of the now done-to-death Vietnam War. But, messy and maddening though some of it is, *Jacob's Ladder* is also a truly scary film which is never simply a war or horror vehicle. Jacob Singer (Robbins) is a man whose life totters continually between past, present and future, between reality and terrifying illusion brought on by his experiences in Vietnam, where his unit was dosed with a vicious derivative of LSD to improve its killing power. Where the problem arises is that this scenario is only one alternative in the life of a man variously shown as divorced, studying and co-habiting, married and prosperous with children, or dead on a Vietnam field-hospital table. But Lyne's giddying, unsettling direction conjures up moments of horrifying hallucinogenic power from the bad-trip hell of his protagonist. SGr

Jacqueline Susann's Once Is Not Enough

(Guy Green, 1974, US) Kirk Douglas, Alexis Smith, David Janssen, George Hamilton, Melina Mercouri, Gary Conway, Brenda Vaccaro, Deborah Raffin.
122 min.
A film that has Kirk Douglas exclaim 'You just cut my balls off in front of my daughter', that feels moved to rattle such skeletons in the cupboard as impotence and artificial insemination, that has its central character called January because (in the words of her father) 'she was born on New Year's Day and I swore I'd give her the world', and that bothers to incorporate into the plot a minor-league astronaut with an 'aw shucks' attitude to his job. *Once Is Not Enough* brings the late authoress' characteristically unshadowed world of wealth and deodorised amorality to the screen with all the ringing confidence of a sanitary towel commercial. Green's direction is highly professional, and the overall slickness is fascinatingly allowed to lie like the very thinnest of veneers over absolutely nothing. VG

Jacquot de Nantes

(Agnès Varda, 1991, Fr) Philippe Maron, Edouard Joubeaud, Laurent Monnier, Brigitte de Villepoix, Daniel Dublet, Marie-Sidonie Benoist.
118 min. b/w & col.
Varda's tribute to her husband Jacques Demy, who died in 1990, takes the form of a fictional reconstruction of the boy Jacquot's childhood, deriving its sense of authenticity not only from being shot in the real locations where Demy grew up, but from the fact that he himself collaborated with Varda, sifting through his memories. Home footage of Demy – together with clips from his films – casts an uncomfortably melancholic gaze on the proceedings. Extremely evocative, and vivaciously played by a cast of unknowns, this is a curious hybrid: part essay, part nostalgic reconstruction, at times sitting a little too cosily with the French vogue for faultlessly authentic reminiscence. Varda's valedictory may not bring you any closer to Demy the director, but it's an engrossing, moving tribute. JRo

Jade

(William Friedkin, 1995, US) David Caruso, Linda Fiorentino, Richard Crenna, Chazz Palminteri, Michael Biehn, Donna Murphy.
95 min.
This is Friedkin back to the hackery of *The Guardian*. Indeed, from the prowling camera tour of the baroque oriental San Francisco mansion of a millionaire playboy, to the creepy choral music and jarring soundtrack, this ugly murder thriller pushes close to horror movie territory. It's motored by the same engine common to many of that genre: male fear of the female libido. Predictability, risibility and degeneracy vie in Joe Eszterhas's script: assistant DA Corelli (Caruso), regarding the millionaire's flailed corpse, remarks, 'This is rage!', while a colleague, noting it's election year, laments, 'The media is going to turn this into an X-rated gang bang!' The libido in question belongs to unlikely psychologist of workplace violence Trina Gavin (Fiorentino): married to amoral lawyer Matt (Palminteri), and one-time lover of the still ardent Corelli, she was the last person to see the millionaire alive and is thus prime supect. The role strips Fiorentino of charisma and grace. Caruso, too, has little to do and does it poorly. Thrown in are a few hackneyed Friedkin 'show-stoppers': an extended car chase, and a variation on the car-with-cut-brake-cables number. Cameraman Andrzej Bartkowiak does little more than provide a sheeny gloss on standard ritzy SF locations. Bad. WH

Jade Love (Yu Qing sao)

(Chang Yi, 1984, Tai) Yang Hui-shan, Juang Sheng-t'ien, Ling Ting-feng.
104 min.
An affecting and well-acted period melodrama, based on a Chinese short story but suspiciously similar to *The Go-Between*, right down to a climactic glimpse of coitus. It's about a spoiled young brat who becomes the unwitting messenger between his adored nanny and her mysteriously reclusive 'brother'. The atmosphere is rather cloyingly literary, doubtless because the youngish

director (rallying from two recent flops) was determined to prove his 'cultural' mettle. Still, accomplished in its backward-looking way. TR

Jag Är Med Barn (Father-to-Be/I'm Expecting)

(Lasse Hallström, 1979, Swe) Magnus Harenstam, Anki Lidén, Micha Gabay, Ulf Brunnberg, Lis Nilheim.
107 min.
Moderately diverting social comedy, from the director who went on to make *My Life as a Dog*, in which carefree Harenstam dreams of a career as a famous novelist but is brought right back down to earth by girlfriend Lidén's announcement of a new arrival. TJ

Jagdszenen aus Niederbayern

see Hunting Scenes from Bavaria

Jagged Edge

(Richard Marquand, 1985, US) Jeff Bridges, Glenn Close, Maria Mayenzet, Peter Coyote, Robert Loggia.
109 min.
This shows that a contemporary whodunit can still rivet sophisticated modern audiences without retreating into horror or camp. Marquand and screenwriter Joe Eszterhas achieve this coup by ringing brilliant changes on ancient material: Close plays a woman defence lawyer who becomes involved with client Bridges, fighting to prove he's innocent of murdering his wife. The trial scenes are scripted and played with electrifying skill, as every turn and twist is amplified through Close's emotions. But it is much more than a courtroom picture. These days it is almost unheard of for a movie to keep you guessing until the last frame, but this one does, partly because Marquand plays it so beautifully straight. DP

Jaguar

(Lino Brocka, 1979, Phil) Phillip Salvador, Amy Austria, Anita Linda.
110 min.
Originally banned for export by the Marcos government, and only released after pressure from the Cannes Film Festival, where it was the first Filipino film to be shown in competition. Just as *Manila: In the Claws of Darkness* plundered melodrama, *Jaguar* plunders the American gangster movie (plus possibly blaxploitation pix such as *Shaft*) to express Brocka's rage about poverty and repression. Jaguar is slang for bodyguard, and the hero guards a smart apartment block, supports his family, and stays out of trouble. But when he intervenes in a fight, saving the life of a wealthy playboy and landowner, he gets hired as the man's personal guard and falls for his girlfriend. Gradually, in spite of himself, he is dragged down into crime, becoming a murderer and finally going berserk in jail. Despite budgetary limitations and some wooden acting, the passion of the picture comes across powerfully, as does its portrait of a society in which violence and resentment are endemic. ATu

Jaguar Lives

(Ernest Pintoff, 1979, US) Joe Lewis, Christopher Lee, Donald Pleasence, Barbara Bach, Capucine, Joseph Wiseman, Woody Strode, John Huston.
90 min.
Time-warp film-making from ex-cartoonist and once-touted director Pintoff: a no-interest, multi-location 'action movie' that takes its cues from early James Bond and cheapo kung-fu thrillers. The listless, tedious hokum of the old secret-agent-busts-international-crime-ring plot would have looked tacky (and its martial arts catchpenny) at the turn of the last decade; today it looks hopelessly anachronistic in even the baldest commercial terms. Dead from the neck up; dead from the wallet down. PT

Jailhouse Rock

(Richard Thorpe, 1957, US) Elvis Presley, Judy Tyler, Mickey Shaughnessy, Vaughn Taylor, Dean Jones.
96 min. b/w.
Wrestling with the problem of what to do with a

rock'n'roll star, MGM hit on the addled brainwave of using Richard Thorpe, who had made *The Student Prince* for them three years earlier and had a background in costume musicals and adventures. The story, about a rock star with a prison background, was tougher than some of the other Presley pictures, but the musical numbers especially were shot in the MGM tradition, which was totally wrong for rock. DP

Ja, Ja, Mein General! But Which Way to the Front?
see Which Way to the Front?

Jake Speed
(Andrew Lane, 1986, US) Wayne Crawford, Dennis Christopher, Karen Kopins, John Hurt, Leon Ames, Roy London, Barry Primus, Monte Markham.
105 min.
The remarkable thing is that here is a movie that wants to be bad and still fails. There's nothing wrong with its fecund premise: a fictional comicstrip hero let loose on the screen to lampoon and parody himself through every thrills-and-spills adventure caper that has graced our cash-tills in recent years. But Crawford plays Speed with his foot in his mouth rather than tongue-incheek, and instead of glorying in the experiences of the pulp novel dialogue, dissipates all the comic potential by his evident bewilderment. The feckless and dupable Kopins is the sex interest, romanced down the Zambesi in the quest to rescue her abducted sister from an evil gang of white slave traders, led by almost cynically OTT gay nasty Hurt. In danger of making the targeted teen audience kick the cinema habit altogether. WH

Jalsaghar (The Music Room)
(Satyajit Ray, 1958, Ind) Chabi Biswas, Ganga Pada Basu, Kali Sarkar, Padma Devi, Tulsi Lahari.
100 min. b/w.
Ray's fourth film, a wonderfully evocative anecdote about an elderly aristocrat, slowly dying amid the crumbling splendours of the past, who decides to defy the egalitarian age that is encroaching. For all the rough edges, there is something of Welles here as the ageing aristocrat sits alone in his Xanadu, like Mr Clay in *The Immortal Story*, dreaming amid the remnants of past magnificence while the bulldozers of modern civilisation hum outside the walls. Something, too, of Chekhov's tender irony as he rebels in a gesture of glorious folly, bankrupting himself to hire the best classical musicians around, dust off the vast chandelier, and bring his ancestral music room to glittering life once more for just one last regal extravaganza. Slow, rapt and hypnotic, it is – given some appreciation of Indian music – a remarkable experience. TM

Jamaica Inn
(Alfred Hitchcock, 1939, GB) Charles Laughton, Maureen O'Hara, Leslie Banks, Robert Newton, Emlyn Williams, Wylie Watson.
108 min. b/w.
Acting as co-producer as well as star, Laughton ruled the roost even more than usual in this murky melodrama of 18th century Cornish wrecking, smuggling and thuggery, parading about in the top hat, boots and leering eyebrows of the local JP, and giving poor Maureen O'Hara the fright of her life. Hitchcock, who slipped in this Daphne du Maurier adaptation before leaving for America, clearly found it impossible to secure a strong grip on either Laughton or the material. And while the star himself effortlessly commands attention, the film around him too often collapses in a welter of rhubarbing locals, piffling model work, and the most cardboard sets Elstree could offer. The result is weird, but not wonderful. GB

J.A. Martin, Photographer (J.A. Martin Photographe)
(Jean Beaudin, 1976, Can) Marcel Sabourin, Monique Mercure, Marthe Thierry, Catherine Tremblay, Mariette Duval, Denis Hamel.
101 min.
Leaden venture into the world of the period 'art' movie, not so much meditative as cataleptic. Primarily about Rose-Aimée and her decision

to abandon her household temporarily to accompany her photographer husband on one of his annual tours (in 19th century Quebec), the title seems misplaced; indeed, this sort of erratic emphasis dogs the whole farrago. The structure works by too simple a process of accretion – a succession of 'telling' vignettes at each halt, as the couple photographically encounter capitalism, death, marriage, love, sex, even a miscarriage (he impassively reaches for his shovel). Their final rekindling of passion is only barely justified by the previous pedestrian episodes. And it's all heavily sunk with the usual up-market trappings: ochre tints, half-lit interiors, blank inter-scene pauses, long-held reaction shots; as if Bergman had got hold of *The Archers*. CPea

James and the Giant Peach
(Henry Selick, 1996, US) Paul Terry, Joanna Lumley, Miriam Margolyes, Pete Postlethwaite, Steven Culp.
79 min.
Made by the director of *The Nightmare Before Christmas*, this has an enchanting, at times ghoulish, appeal. An adaptation of Roald Dahl's classic story, Selick's film may not have made any spectacular technical advance on his previous work (the animated central section is sandwiched by stylised live-action sequences), but, despite a lightness of plot, it most beautifully captures the book's free-floating, fantastic sense of adventure and wonder. Forced into a life of drudgery by his evil aunts Sponge and Spiker (Margolyes and Lumley), orphan James dreams of escape to New York. An old man (Postlethwaite) appears and gives the boy a jiggling handful of fluorescent, magical crocodile tongues. A dead peach tree bears a gigantic fruit, and diving Alice-like into its core, James enters a world of strange invertebrates. As his wishes take flight, so does the peach, putting to sea and soaring up in the air, hauled majestically by a flock of tethered sea-gulls. The songs and music have the inimitable signature of Randy Newman. WH

James Baldwin: The Price of the Ticket
(Karen Thorsen, 1989, US) Dr Maya Angelou, Amiri Baraka, David Baldwin, David Leeming, Lucien Happersberger.
87 min.
Born in Harlem in 1924, a preacher's son, Baldwin was himself a boy preacher. In some ways the vocation stuck through his life. Thorsen's non-narrated documentary mixes footage covering his speeches, interviews, lectures; extracts from TV plays; testimony from friends, family, pupils, colleagues; and Maya Angelou reading from his letters and books. A powerful portrait emerges of a fighter, idealist, teacher and liberal-baiter; a man whose anger grew in the face of ignorant interviewers. His long search for self and his education into the politics of race, equality and revolution fascinate: from his flight in '48 from a suffocating America to hyp erventilation in Paris; his support of Algerians ('Paris's niggers'); writing *Go Tell It On the Mountain* in a Swiss village (where, the visual antithesis of all he surveyed, he was a friend to every child); coming out with the publication of *Giovanni's Room*: further flight to Turkey; Eldridge Cleaver's vicious attack on him as a traitor to macho Black politics; and the deaths of King, Malcolm X, JFK. Deeply moving, educational and engaging though the film is, the man's lovers are conspicuously absent. Which of these talking heads were they? *Were* they white? Did that matter to him? At 87 minutes, this is tantalising proof that less is not always more. TC

James Brothers, The
see True Story of Jesse James, The

James Dean Story, The
(Robert Altman/George W George, 1957, US) narrator: Martin Gabel.
82 min. b/w.
Something of a curiosity, this documentary about the life and character of the cultish star who had died a couple of years before is short on analysis, long on (sometimes insufferably pretentious) poetic symbolism, and extremely fine for its sharp black-and-white photogra-

phy, especially effective in the bleak wastelands where Dean grew up. A few nice rare clips are included (notably a stunning outtake from *East of Eden*), but otherwise this is probably of interest only to Dean fanatics or Altman collectors. GA

James Dean – the First American Teenager
(Ray Connolly, 1975, GB) Carroll Baker, Natalie Wood, Sal Mineo, Dennis Hopper, Nicholas Ray, Sammy Davis Jr, Leonard Rosenman, Leslie Caron.
80 min.
Connolly's catch-all compilation follows the trail blazed by Joe Boyd's Hendrix movie: lotsa clips of the Star in action (including obscure TV footage and a 'rare' screen test), lotsa glossy interviews with those who loved or hated him, as much rock music as possible, and fragments of memorabilia like a hilariously stilted road safety commercial. The most lucidly expressive contribution comes from Dean's long time 'mentor' Leonard Rosenman; the most affably stoned from Dennis Hopper. But Connolly makes his reliance on the original movies a real problem: when someone mentions Dean getting into a car, for instance, we're shown a clip from *Giant* of him doing just that...and so the film constantly reinforces the Hollywood 'image' it purports to question. And the dismal coyness about Dean's sex life means the movie scarcely makes it even as gossip. TR

James Gang, The
(Mike Barker, 1997, GB/Can) John Hannah, Helen McCrory, Jason Flemyng, Toni Collette, Darren Brownlie, David Brownlie, Lauren McMurray.
95 min.
With its stylish cinematography, eye catching direction and groovy pop soundtrack, this is a British first feature (Scottish characters, Welsh locations) that desperately wants to be hip. Helen McCrory, who gave her all in Karl Francis' *Streetlife*, is similarly committed here, as the mum trying to hold her family together by launching an impromptu crime spree – though errant husband Hannah and trailing policewoman Collette don't really have the grit required. What's more, Stuart Hepburn's script never begins to carry the weight that would justify the involvement of McCrory's children in the various robberies, or lend conviction to the characterisation. TJ

Jamón, Jamón
(Bigas Luna, 1992, Sp) Penélope Cruz, Anna Galiena, Javier Bardem, Stefania Sandrelli, Juan Diego, Jodi Molla.
94 min.
This is 'Carry On' as scripted by Lorca, a hysterically sombre sex farce pointing up the connections between sex and food. The title is an obscure sexual compliment: machinist Silvia (Cruz) enslaves wealthy stripling José with her ham-flavoured nipples. But as one might expect from a man so fixated, José is in thrall to his mother Conchita, who doesn't want him married to the daughter of the town whore. Conchita enrols a chunky would-be *torero*, Raúl, to distract the nymphet. Before long he's up under Silvia's miniskirt, and it's bound to end in tears. One just wants to slap Silvia, a woman who habitually traipses around wailing in wet, clingy, baby-doll dresses. But there are compensations in Sandrelli's monstrous Conchita and Bardem's hilarious Raúl. The sex scenes are so bizarre as to be parodic and it all looks terribly ugly. But wonderful vignettes of rural life, and a terrific performance from Pablito the piglet. Ham indeed. SFe

Jane
(DA Pennebaker/Richard Leacock/Hope Ryden/Gregory Shuker/Abbott Mills, 1963, US) Jane Fonda, Bradford Dillman, Lee Strasberg, Madeleine Sherwood, Walter Kerr.
51 min. b/w.
One of the early Drew/Leacock efforts, a *cinéma-vérité* portrait of Jane Fonda which tracks her through rehearsals for her Broadway debut in 1960 (a comedy called *The Fun Couple*). Since Vadim and *Barbarella* were still to come, this is Jane the eager *ingénue*, with political protest not rating even a whisper. The tensions of rehearsal and opening night are

well caught, but the rest of the story (Sardi's after the show, unkind reviews, ephemeral heartbreak) is no different from the average showbiz epic. TM

Jane and the Lost City

(Terry Marcel, 1987, GB) Sam Jones, Maud Adams, Jasper Carrott, Kirsten Hughes, Graham Stark, Robin Bailey, Ian Roberts, Elsa O'Toole.
92 min.
This would-be romp based around the saucy exploits of the oft-déshabillée, cami-knickered heroine (Hughes) of the *Daily Mirror*'s wartime 'Jane' strip cartoon is bad beyond the promptings of idle curiosity. Churchill stabs at a map of Africa and dispatches clipped-upper-lip Colonel (Bailey) and secretary Jane in search of much-needed diamonds to save the Empire at its darkest hour. A haphazard journey later, they team up with life-saving Yank Jungle Jack Buck (Jones), and trek through the veldt two comic capers ahead of evil Nazis Lola Pagoda (Adams) and hysterical Herr Heinrich (Carrott, a deep mistake), before reaching the cardboard Lost City presided over by Sheba the Leopard Queen, late of Roedean. Notwithstanding the spasmodic salacious shots of Jane's principal silk-clad joints, the film translates the innocent eroticism and tongue-in-cheek adventurism of the strip into a pile of puerile, enervative folie. WH

Jane Austen in Manhattan

(James Ivory, 1980, GB/US) Anne Baxter, Robert Powell, Michael Wager, Sean Young, Tim Choate, John Guerrasio, Katrina Hodiak, Kurt Johnson.
111 min.
A study in cultural cross-pollination from the Merchant-Ivory-Jhabvala team. Prompted by the recent discovery of a piece of Jane Austen juvenilia – a schoolgirl fantasy playlet about abduction at the hands of a rake – the film again finds them exploring the ways in which the past becomes appropriated and re-processed in the present. Two small New York theatre companies, with widely differing ideas about how the unearthed play ought to be staged (period operetta versus avant-gardist 'performance' event), vie with each other for the patronage of a wealthy cultural foundation which has acquired the rights to the manuscript. The contending claims of tradition, experiment and capital are given narrative thrust, but no real focus or amplification, by the developing feud between the two rival directors: an ageing Anne Baxter and her protégé-turned-Svengali, Robert Powell. Personal differences are allowed to oust artistic differences so comprehensively that the film simply loses its way, disappointingly playing itself out as a series of flashy real-life variations on Austen's original abduction theme. Really, it's all just a little too clever for its own good. MPo

Jane Eyre

(Robert Stevenson, 1943, US) Orson Welles, Joan Fontaine, Margaret O'Brien, Peggy Ann Garner, John Sutton, Henry Daniell, Agnes Moorehead, Hillary Brooke, Elizabeth Taylor.
96 min. b/w.
Charlotte Bronte reduced to straight Gothic romance, but surprisingly effective right from the opening shot of a wavering candle being carried down a long, dark corridor. The early sequences of Jane's schooling are probably the most stylistically consistent and vividly realised (Daniell's chillingly pious sadism as the headmaster, Moorehead sourly petting a piggish little fat boy, young Elizabeth Taylor dying from cruel negligence). After Welles makes his thunderous appearance out of the mist, thrown from his startled horse but still able to swirl a cape with fine braggadocio, the film becomes more erratic, but always looks as though Orson had at least one eye behind the camera. And the cracks (notably the discrepancies in acting styles between pallid Jane and full-blooded Rochester) are neatly papered over by a fine Bernard Herrmann score. TM

Jane Eyre

(Delbert Mann, 1970, GB) George C Scott, Susannah York, Ian Bannen, Jack Hawkins, Nyree Dawn Porter, Rachel Kempson, Kenneth Griffith, Peter Copley, Michele Dotrice.
110 min.
A typical hybrid of 'tasteful' adaptation, shot and (briefly) released in Britain before finding its US TV home. For all the Yorkshire location work and pedantic respect for Charlotte Brontë, it's not a patch on the gloriously artificial 1943 movie; and for all Scott's actorly huff and puff as Rochester, he can't disturb memories of Orson Welles. PT

Jane Eyre

(Franco Zeffirelli, 1996, GB/It/Fr/US) Charlotte Gainsbourg, William Hurt, Joan Plowright, Anna Paquin, Geraldine Chaplin, Billie Whitelaw, Maria Schneider, Fiona Shaw, Elle Macpherson, John Wood, Amanda Root, Samuel West.
113 min.
A faithful adaptation, by Hugh Whitemore and director Franco Zeffirelli, aimed squarely at the middle ground. Its cinematic effects are generally banal – the elegant, slow dissolves that befit a prestige classic, hollow footsteps and an eerie laugh echoing through the Tower – but such restraint is welcome given what Zeffirelli is capable of. Mostly, he seems satisfied to let the actors get on with it, tacitly acknowledging that Charlotte Gainsbourg's Jane is his strongest asset. It's unusual to see a lead actress photographed so harshly. She is sallow with shadows under her eyes, yet has a defiant tilt of the chin and embodies a guilelessness which makes her deeply sympathetic. (She's also a credible match for Anna Paquin's forlorn young Jane.) Gainsbourg's so sparing with her smile, that each one cuts to the quick. William Hurt makes a strong fist of a less intimidating Rochester: he's brusque and morose, but altogether more accessible than the brooding romantics portrayed by Welles and Scott in earlier versions. In a way, that's the problem with this adaptation. It's too tame to stir the blood. We understand Jane's pain but not her passion. For all its melodramatic hyperbole, the 1943 version caught Charlotte Bronte's tenor more honestly than this. Very capable support, though, from Fiona Shaw (Mrs Reed), Amanda Root (Miss Temple), Joan Plowright (Mrs Fairfax), and Billie Whitelaw (Grace Poole).TCh

Janice

(Joseph Strick, 1973, US) Robert Drivas, Regina Baff, Barry Bostwick, David Bauer, Beatrice Colen.
84 min.
Strick's rather belated foray into the world of the road movie and through the dregs of the American dream. Two truck drivers (Drivas, Bostwick), leading a life sufficiently precarious to keep them on the fringes of petty crime, pick up Janice (Baff), a prostitute who alternately helps them and helps to destroy them. Strick looks to expose the myth of the road movie through his characters, whose main form of communication lies in outbursts of destructive violence. But with his over-riding concern to make the film look good – the vergeside shots at hubcap height, the rain swirling up from the wheels of overtaking lorries – he ends up merely glamorising the myth that he's purporting to strip bare. CPe

Janis

(Howard Alk/Seaton Findlay, 1974, Can) Janis Joplin.
97 min.
On film, as on stage, Janis Joplin is like a child in complete isolation: holding dialogues with herself that never end, moving gently over her own pain like someone trying to compose an instant autobiography. It's a tribute to the makers of this documentary that you do come out feeling that there will never be anyone else like her. The film contains no mention of her death, only the merest suggestion in a wistful tracking shot around her empty car, but from the amount of energy that we see released it doesn't seem surprising. Her own words, plus a montage of early pictures, go quite a way towards explaining how the quiet suburban kid from Port Arthur who was never asked to the High School prom could have developed into one of the greatest American rock singers. Alk and Findlay simply allow the story to be told in its own terms, especially by the performances: all of the good ones are here, from the legendary Monterey 'Ball and Chain' to 'Try'. DP

Janitor, The

see Eyewitness

January Man, The

(Pat O'Connor, 1989, US) Kevin Kline, Susan Sarandon, Mary Elizabeth Mastrantonio, Harvey Keitel, Danny Aiello, Rod Steiger, Alan Rickman.
97 min.
In New York, eleven murders have taken place in as many months, and the serial killer is about to strike again. So bellicose mayor Steiger reluctantly reinstates maverick sleuth Nick Starkey (Kline), and despite the reservations of the police commissioner (Keitel), who also happens to be Nick's estranged brother, Nick is put on the case. In idiosyncratic fashion, Nick miraculously identifies the apartment that is the killer's next port of call...at which point plot and dramatic tension plummet. Black humour becomes knockabout comedy. Sarandon, as Keitel's wife and sometime lover of his brother, and Mastrantonio as the mayor's daughter who falls for Nick, give good enigmatic performances, but are mislaid in the ensuing tumult. John Patrick Shanley's screenplay, touching on themes of betrayal and corruption, honesty and trust, promises and teases but suffers from coitus interruptus. JGl

Jardin del Eden, El (The Garden of Eden)

(Maria Novaro, 1994, Mex) Renee Coleman, Bruno Bichir, Gabriela Roer, Rosario Sagrav.
104 min.
From the 'feminist' director of the delightful *Danzón*, this is set in Tijuana and concerns the relationship between three disparate women, all in their way border-dwellers – Jane, an American going south, Liz her Spanish-American friend (who can't speak Spanish and is sister of blocked writer Frank who can), and Mexican Serena, a widow struggling to bring up her children alone. It's a discursive, rambling narrative, which may offer a good few insights into the difficulties of both racial identity and the building of alternate means of communication and support between women, but its message or meaning is a little obscure. Likeable and good-hearted none the less. WH

Jardines Colgantes (Hanging Gardens)

(Pablo Llorca, 1993, Sp) Feodor Atkine, Iciar Bollain, Luis Flete, Rafael Diaz.
116 min.
Joining the long line of cinema's shy, bespectacled voyeurs is Flete's repressed tailor, obsessed by his dream of clothing absolutely without decoration. In search of a perfect piece of leather, he falls into the hands of a ruthless warehouse owner (Atkine), who purloins his precious tailor's knife and compels him to make a dashing suit to win the heart of an unwilling local girl (Bollain). Sexual and professional jealousy entwine to make this a slow-burning tale of desire and perversity, studded with erotic symbols (roses, blood, tattoos, knives, tight corsetry). Atkine is stunning as the vain, garrulous, frightening mobster. SFe

Jason and the Argonauts

(Don Chaffey, 1963, GB) Todd Armstrong, Nancy Kovack, Gary Raymond, Laurence Naismith, Niall MacGinnis, Michael Gwynn, Douglas Wilmer, Honor Blackman, Patrick Troughton, Nigel Green.
103 min.
Jolly juvenile adventure in which Jason (the rather stolid Armstrong) is aided – or hindered – by assorted whimsical gods on Olympus as he quests for the Golden Fleece, and the film itself is given an enormous boost by Ray Harryhausen's special effects. The bronze Titan is an arthritic disappointment, but most of the other inventions are pleasingly imaginative, not least the army of waspishly pugnacious, sword-wielding skeletons which pop out of the ground when the Hydra's teeth are sown. Great fun, as these things go, with a Bernard Herrmann score to boot. TM

Jason's Lyric

(Doug McHenry, 1994, US) Allen Payne, Jada Pinkett, Forest Whitaker, Bokeem Woodbine, Suzzanne Douglas, Anthony 'Treach' Criss, Lisa Carson.
119 min.
This begins in lyrical Deep South mood with Jason (Payne) sitting on a Greyhound bus and recalling his traumatic Houston childhood, when

his estranged Viet-vet father Maddog (Whitaker) would go on binges brutally proclaiming his love for Jason's mom (Douglas); the gunshot that put an end to his attacks resulted in Jason's younger brother Josh (Woodbine) turning to a life of drugs and imprisonment. Years later, Jason's still trying to keep the volatile Josh in check, but when he takes up with gang leader Alonzo, elder brother of Lyric (Pinkett), whose romantic sensitivity has allowed Jason's nightmares to turn into dreams of a better life, it's clear that Jason will have to choose between his family and his lover. Bobby Smith Jr's script is an all-black blend of themes from *Romeo and Juliet* and the Cain and Abel story – a risky conceit, but one that in general works surprisingly well, thanks to muscular performances, and an atmospheric portrayal of life in and around the Houston suburbs that rarely descends into stereotype. The movie's a touch too long, and its romantic interludes are sometimes too highly coloured, but McHenry's control of the nicely unsentimental tone is pretty assured, while there's a bonus in the soundtrack which mixes bluesy electric guitar and soul standards. GA

Jassy

(Bernard Knowles, 1947, GB) Margaret Lockwood, Patricia Roc, Dennis Price, Basil Sydney, Dermot Walsh, Nora Swinburne.
102 min.
Splendid tosh from Gainsborough, home of the postwar British movie melodrama, with Lockwood as a 19th century gypsy girl who has the gift of second sight and is saved from the forfeit for witchcraft (a ducking in the village pond) by Dermot Walsh, rightful owner of the local manor house. Later involved in tortuous romantic complications culminating in an accusation of murder, she nevertheless contrives to find true love and see justice done all round. Stock 'period' characters in full-blooded performances; not to everyone's taste, but a testament to the vigour of Gainsborough's style in a period of otherwise dour British cinema. MA

Jaws

(Steven Spielberg, 1975, US) Roy Scheider, Robert Shaw, Richard Dreyfuss, Lorraine Gary, Murray Hamilton, Carl Gottlieb, Jeffrey Kramer.
125 min.
A reminder that, once upon a time, Spielberg used to make films for adults rather than infants and critical regressives. Maybe it is just a monster movie reminiscent of all those '50s sci-fi films, but it's at least endowed with intelligent characterisation, a lack of sentimentality (in contrast to, say, *E.T.*), and it really is frightening. And, added to the Ahab/Moby Dick echoes in the grizzled sailor Shaw's obsession with the Great White Shark, there are moments of true darkness, expressed most eloquently in the John Milius-scripted speech about the wreck of the 'Indianapolis'. GA

Jaws 2

(Jeannot Szwarc, 1978, US) Roy Scheider, Lorraine Gary, Murray Hamilton, Joseph Mascolo, Jeffrey Kramer, Collin Wilcox, Ann Dusenberry
116 min.
'Children of Jaws' might have been a better title for this teen version of the big fish story. The switch in emphasis – away from an adult world in which expert and monster play out their duel, to one where healthy, wealthy but dumb kids are merely terrorised prawns – can't disguise the sense of *déjà vu*. The townsfolk of Amity appear to be suffering from amnesia as far as sharks are concerned; the mayor is still corrupt and moneyhungry; the disappearance of tourists is shrugged off; and as usual, nobody believes Scheider. Suspension of disbelief might have been possible had this been a ripping good yarn; but the kids are just plain silly, and it's a toss-up to decide which is more unconvincing, the shark or Scheider. FF

Jaws 3-D

(Joe Alves, 1983, US) Dennis Quaid, Bess Armstrong, Simon MacCorkindale, Louis Gossett Jr, John Putch, Lea Thompson, PH Moriarty, Dan Blasko.
99 min.
Just when you thought it was safe (yet again) to go back into the cinema, a new *Jaws* hits the screen, this time in 3-D (you need some form of

gimmick to sell a film with little or no storyline). A new 'Undersea Kingdom', fashioned out of a lagoon at Sea World, Florida, is about to be opened to the public. Everything goes according to plan until...dum-da-dum...enter Great White through a damaged sea gate, and the usual havoc begins. Quaid is the constructor of this giant aquarium, Armstrong the girl obsessed with dolphins and other sea creatures; of course neither of them realises anything is afoot until people start disappearing and end up as bits and pieces floating out towards the cinema audience. Put in a baking tray, gas mark 7, and enjoy a turkey. DA

Jaws – The Revenge

(Joseph Sargent, 1987, US) Lorraine Gary, Lance Guest, Mario Van Peebles, Karen Young, Michael Caine, Judith Barsi, Lynn Whitfield, Mitchell Anderson.
100 min.
That naughty shark spoils everyone's holiday by eating a policeman (son of Scheider from *Jaws* and *Jaws 2*) on Christmas Eve. Thereafter the movie focuses on the mother and remaining son, who happens to be a marine biologist (and to have a wife and daughter), as both become obsessed by what appears to be a vendetta against the family. While it's mostly just a matter of waiting till feeding time (and some keen anticipation as to when the jaws will silence too Symbolism onto the shark: as mother and son suffer an attack of the Oedipals, the creature keeps popping up grinning. Sadly, this attempt at a bit of Art (which could have had hilarious consequences) is ditched, and the film concludes with a few people getting chewed before a messy happy ending amid chunks of exploding shark. RS

Jazz in Exile

(Chuck France, 1982, US) Dexter Gordon Quartet, Johnny Griffin Quartet, Art Ensemble of Chicago, Woody Shaw Quintet, Art Farmer, Phil Woods Quartet.
59 min.
In an earlier, shorter release (1978) this was a drag; extensive re-editing produced a delight. Too little music and too much talk – about jazzers escaping to enthusiastic Europe from a cool reception in the States (after all, the music's black) – has been rebalanced by the greatly increased concert footage. The music is mainly Hard Bop (tenorists Dexter Gordon and Johnny Griffin trading gutsy phrases, Phil Woods' sliding, striding alto, virtuoso bassist Richard Davis punching out an agile blues with Ben Sidran), but covers enough ground to include archive footage of Billie Holiday and Lester Young, and the modern histrionics of the Art Ensemble of Chicago. More could have been heard from the women (Carla Bley and Betty Carter), and sometimes the solos are cut too short. By and large, though, the film certainly delivers the goods. GA

Jazz on a Summer's Day

(Bert Stern, 1959, US) Louis Armstrong, Big Maybelle, Chuck Berry, Dinah Washington, Gerry Mulligan, Thelonious Monk, Anita O'Day, Mahalia Jackson, Sonny Stitt, Jack Teagarden.
85 min.
This documentary record of the 1958 Newport Jazz Festival is often hailed as one of the first and most influential live concert films, paving the way for later classics like 'Monterey Pop' and 'Woodstock'. A dazzling array of jazz and rock-'n'roll giants are captured on celluloid, including Chuck Berry duck-walking his way through 'Sweet Little Sixteen'. Unquestionable highlight, however, is the extraordinary Mahalia Jackson, whose soulful renditions of 'Didn't It Rain', 'Shout All Over' and 'The Lord's Prayer' send a shiver down the spine. NF

Jazz Singer, The

(Richard Fleischer, 1980, US) Neil Diamond, Laurence Olivier, Lucie Arnaz, Catlin Adams, Franklyn Ajaye, Paul Nicholas, Sully Boyar, Mike Kellin, James Booth.
116 min.
Neil Diamond, as the New York synagogue cantor's son who trades his yarmulke for the glitter of the LA music biz, makes the most cautious soft-rock superstar movie debut you'll ever get to

see. The recording and music publishing businesses are just made for clean-living folk, and guarantee almost immediate recognition and success to anyone of Diamond's obvious talent – or so the film would have you believe. But although nothing is presented to put his family-audience persona at risk, the character comes across as curiously unthinking and irresponsible. The performance is okay...but then Diamond never attempts anything so difficult as chewing gum and walking at the same time. RM

Jealousy, Italian Style

see Dramma della Gelosia

Jean de Florette

(Claude Berri, 1986, Fr/It) Yves Montand, Gérard Depardieu, Daniel Auteuil, Elisabeth Depardieu, Ernestine Mazurowna, Marcel Champel, Armand Meffre.
121 min.
In the mid-'20s, hunchback tax collector Jean Cadoret (Depardieu) inherits a Provence farm, moving there with wife and daughter to fulfil his naive city-dweller's dreams of an idyllic pastoral life. The map shows a valuable spring on his land, but the cunning Soubeyrans – Montand and son Auteuil – have stopped it up, and plan to wait for him to go broke so that they can buy up his property for a song. Depardieu, though, has some scientific knowledge up his suit sleeve, and at first his crops thrive...Berri and scriptwriter Gérard Brach brilliantly capture the rhythm of the countryside, where the pace of life is dictated by inexorable seasonal changes and the often cruel vagaries of the weather. An object lesson in literary adaptation, the film eschews mere illustration to favour an elliptical narrative which embodies, through the subtlest nuances of dialogue and the most delicate shadings of light and colour, the atmosphere and meaning of Marcel Pagnol's source novel, *L'Eau des collines*. But it is Depardieu who supplies the heart and soul of the film with a performance of towering strength and heartbreaking pathos. *Manon des Sources*, the second part of the diptych, followed in the same year. NF

Jeanne Dielman, 23 Quai du Commerce, 1080 Bruxelles

(Chantal Anne Akerman, 1975, Bel/Fr) Delphine Seyrig, Jan Decorte, Henri Storck, Jacques Doniol-Valcroze, Yves Bical.
201 min.
Chantal Akerman's feature is one of the few 'feminist' movies that's as interesting aesthetically as politically. It covers three days in the life of a bourgeois widow who supports herself and her somewhat moronic son by taking in a 'gentleman caller' each afternoon. Much of the film simply chronicles her ritualised routine, but does it in an ultra-minimal, precise style that emphasises the artifice of the whole thing...and gradually the artifice (coupled with the fact that Delphine Seyrig plays the woman) shifts the plot into melodrama, so that the film becomes a bourgeois tragedy. TR

Jeanne la Pucelle (Joan of Arc)

(Jacques Rivette, 1994, Fr) Sandrine Bonnaire, André Marcon, Jean-Louis Richard, Marcel Bozonnet, Patrick Le Mauff, Didier Sauvegrain, Jean-Pierre Lorit, Tatiana Moukhine, Jean-Luc Petit, Edith Scob.
117 min (*Les Batailles*); 121 min (*Les Prisons*). This two-part version of the great story has the space to take matters beyond the theological debate, and the agnostic, ascetic sensibility and to explore the socio-political currents which shaped an enduring popular legend. Rivette's sedulous, distanced approach is a matter of cumulative impact. The period reconstruction is undemonstrative, the screenplay (by Christine Laurent and Pascal Bonitzer) allows events to gain weight over time, and judicious bursts of Jordi Savall's soundtrack convey moments of release. All this demands a film-maker of immense confidence, but it might be said were it not for the physical presence and spiritual ambiguity of Bonnaire's performance. Unlike Dreyer's Falconetti, she's no fiery angel, but a strong, courageous, essentially human individual. Rivette refuses to underline the truth or otherwise of her holy visions; instead, he's more interested in showing the power of an idea in moulding events, and the disposability of that idea when its usefulness in Realpolitik is at

an end. He's with his heroine in showing the shock created by her explosion of gender demarcation, and in detailing the institutionalised repression of thought by a monolithic church. All this may sound the dourest of history lessons, but Rivette's mastery of the long form makes for a compelling experience; involving, thought-provoking and, as Jeanne mounts the stake, profoundly moving. TJ

Jeder für sich und Gott gegen alle (The Enigma of Kaspar Hauser/Every Man for Himself and God Against All/The Mystery of Kaspar Hauser)

(Werner Herzog, 1974, WGer) Bruno S, Walter Ladengast, Brigitte Mira, Willy Semmelrogge, Gloria Dör.
110 min.
A film that shares with *Aguirre, Wrath of God* a fascination with historical manuscripts, an uneasy laughter at human aspiration, and an awe of landscape. 19th century Germany: Kaspar arrives like a time traveller, found standing in a sleepy town square, his origins shrouded in mystery. After learning to talk, he tells of being kept in a cellar and never having seen a human being. The learned confront this enigma with the power of their logic, dissection and annotation, but Kaspar shows up the limitations of such rationalism. He departs as mysteriously as he arrived, stabbed by an unknown assailant, leaving behind a deathbed vision that he knows to be only the beginning of a story, and an enlarged liver and overdeveloped brain for doctors to ponder over. Not the same dizzy folly as *Aguirre*, but Herzog's similarly long perspective conjures as powerful a picture of man's aimless tracks through an impassive landscape. Stunning. CPea

Jefferson in Paris

(James Ivory, 1995, US) Nick Nolte, Greta Scacchi, Thandie Newton, Gweneth Paltrow, Simon Callow, Seth Gilliam, Michael Lonsdale, Nancy Marchand.
140 min.
In 1785, some ten years after he drafted the Declaration of Independence, Thomas Jefferson became America's first ambassador to the court of Louis XVI. There he observed the decadence which was to ignite the French Revolution, and there, according to this film, he twice fell in love, with the married Anglo-Italian artist Maria Cosway, and then with the half sister of his late wife, the household slave Sally Hemings. As usual with Merchant Ivory, dramatic tension, such as it is, centres on the conflict between love and convention, or, as Jefferson famously expressed it, the head and the heart. A man of reason and principle, Jefferson nevertheless embodied the contradictions of his time: he wrote that all men are created equal, yet remained a slave owner until his death; a widower who swore to remain true to his wife, he wooed Cosway (Scacchi) and had children by Hemings (Thandie Newton – very fly). Nick Nolte brings a starchy grace to Jefferson, but it's as if, regrettably, he's acting in a corset. For all the prettily embroidered rhetoric, Ruth Jhabvala's screenplay is too reticent to skewer hypocrisy, and Ivory's direction too inert to stir the passions. TCh

Jeffrey

(Christopher Ashley, 1995, US) Steven Weber, Patrick Stewart, Michael T Weiss, Sigourney Weaver, Bryan Batt, Nathan Lane, Olympia Dukakis.
94 min.
Exasperated by the stresses and contradictions of AIDS-era gay sexuality, Jeffrey (Weber), a New York waiter-cum-actor, decides celibacy is the only way forward. Next thing, of course, he meets Weiss' charming gym trainer, and is hesitating over whether he might just be The One, when a much anticipated date brings the announcement that the object of his desire is HIV-positive. Paul Rudnick's loose but often hilarious screenplay (from his play) adopts a scattershot approach to just about every aspect of the contemporary gay experience: the painful loss of friends and lovers is here, and there's a big showing for New York's Gay Pride march, though it's the sparkling comic set-pieces that leave the strongest impression. There's also a showy cameo for Weaver as the

hucksterish self-help guru of Sexual Compulsives Anonymous, and a stand-out routine in gay priest Lane's proclamation that sex and the great Broadway musicals prove the existence of God. On the debit side, not everything adds up, with stage director Ashley ill at ease at the helm, and Stewart rather uncertain as the queeny father figure coping with a crisis of his own. TJ

Jenseits der Stille
see Beyond Silence

Jenseits der Wolken
see Beyond the Clouds

J'embrasse pas (I Don't Kiss)

(André Téchiné, 1991, Fr) Philippe Noiret, Emmanuelle Béart, Manuel Blanc, Hélène Vincent, Ivan Desny, Christophe Bernard, Roschdy Zem.
116 min.
He doesn't kiss; nor, according to the subtitles laying down conditions to prospective male clients, does this Paris rent boy (Blanc) 'suck off or take it up the bum'. The innocent country boy has come a long way since arriving with high hopes of making it in the big city. His only contact (with equally vulnerable middle-aged widow Vincent) provides a bed to sleep in, but under impossible conditions. Film producer Noiret offers 'no sex' overtures of friendship, which he only later realises are more predatory than they seemed. Auditions end in humiliation and flight from his tentative ambition to become an actor. Only tart-with-a-troubled-heart Béart seems honest in this world without pity. Despite odd moments of truth and affecting scenes, Téchiné's episodic film is a downhill racer: what at first seems art house austerity reveals itself to be mere posturing. WH

Jennifer 8

(Bruce Robinson, 1992, US) Andy Garcia, Uma Thurman, Lance Henriksen, Kathy Baker, John Malkovich, Kevin Conway.
127 min.
Focusing on the dubious obsession of Garcia, a burnt-out Los Angeles cop, with an alleged serial killer – whose latest victim he dubs 'Jennifer 8' – English writer/director Bruce Robinson's first Hollywood feature fails to reconcile the conflicting demands of psychological character study and generic suspense thriller. Garcia's transfer to the small town of Eureka, California, ruffles a few feathers, especially when he starts exhuming corpses and digging into long-dead cases. The key witness, Thurman, is a young blind woman whose growing affection for Garcia and fragments of knowledge about the killer put her at risk. Garcia too is stumbling in the dark, so much so that FBI 'observer' Malkovich points the finger at *him*. The opening scene on a rain-drenched rubbish tip hints at great things, but despite strong writing and an exceptional cast, the plotting is suspect and the murderer's identity is obvious from very early on. NF

Jeopardy

(John Sturges, 1952, US) Barbara Stanwyck, Barry Sullivan, Ralph Meeker, Lee Aaker.
69 min. b/w.
Solid performances and slick direction give this thriller a certain edge, but the situation is contrived, the tension spurious. On holiday in Mexico, Sullivan is trapped by timber from a collapsing pier on a remote beach. With the tide rising, his wife (Stanwyck) drives off to seek help, leaving their young son (Aaker) to tend to his dad. She runs into an escaped killer (Meeker), who cynically appropriates the car to make good his own escape; but surprised by the way Stanwyck continues to fight him, he returns to the beach after she reminds him that he can use her husband's clothes and papers, and promises to go with him herself (as decoy for police roadblocks, or whatever he wants) provided her husband is freed. It's an MGM film, so you know that family and the love of a good woman will weigh heavily in the end. TM

Jeremiah Johnson

(Sydney Pollack, 1972, US) Robert Redford, Will Geer, Stefan Gierasch, Allyn Ann McLerie, Delle Bolton, Charles Tyner, Josh Albee, Matt Clark.
108 min.

A flawed but immensely appealing film adapted in part from Vardis Fisher's *Mountain Man*, a superb historical novel which explores the myth and the reality of the tough trappers who roamed the unconquered West in the 1850s. Shot on location in fantastically beautiful, desolate snowscapes in Utah, the first part of the film is terrific: tenderfoot Redford's first, baffled steps in the battle for survival; the weird encounter with a corpse frozen upright in the snow which provides him with his first real gun; the old man of the mountains who takes time out from hunting grizzlies to teach him how to fish, trap beaver, tell one Indian from another, and stay alive. After this things switch from documentary to picaresque adventure, and John Milius' script begins to stumble uncertainly. But it does come back on course towards the end as the Indians, half-worshipping and half-contemptuous, begin their hunt for the strange white man who has broken their taboos and disappeared into the snows – the legend of the West in the making. TM

Jeremy

(Arthur Barron, 1973, US) Robby Benson, Glynnis O'Connor, Len Bari, Leonard Cimino, Ned Wilson, Chris Bohn.
90 min.
A good example of the sucker punch. Make a nicely photographed New York boy-meets-girl story, done with the same glossy colour supplement superficiality that the boy condemns in his parents, and you too can win best first film prize at Cannes. Have Jeremy, an aspiring cellist of 16, meet aspiring ballet dancer just as shy and sensitive. Make them fall in love as they sing the theme song to each other on the soundtrack. Then one day, when it's raining and they're bored with their game of chess, get Jeremy to take off his glasses and fuck her ever so tastefully. Sew it all up by having tragedy strike three weeks and four days later. Vaguely liberal parents and moist-palmed adolescents may succumb, but most will probably emerge feeling somewhat redundant. CPe

Jericho Mile, The

(Michael Mann, 1979, US) Peter Strauss, Richard Lawson, Roger E Mosley, Brian Dennehy, Geoffrey Lewis, Billy Green Bush, Ed Lauter, Beverly Todd, William Prince.
97 min.
Made for TV, this part gritty prison movie, part equally gritty fairytale (sympathetic killer obsessively runs to Olympic standard). It's generally upbeat without being remotely wimpish or excessively naïve: the walls don't simply fall, and the optimism has to seep through a quasi-documentary context of racism and violence. It's really well acted by pros and inmates, crafted to manipulative perfection; and it beats *Rocky* every which way. See it, be suckered, be entertained. PT

Jerk, The

(Carl Reiner, 1979, US) Steve Martin, Bernadette Peters, Catlin Adams, Mabel King, Richard Ward, Dick Anthony, M Emmet Walsh.
94 min.
America's rediscovery of lame-brain comedy brought this starring debut for Steve Martin. Behind the stoned humour, it's basically a Depression romance about a sucker in the big city, boosted and updated by some pleasingly irreverent twists like his black plantation home (a foundling, he reluctantly has to accept the awful truth that he's white). The trouble with retard comedy is that it rapidly degenerates into banana-skin jokes; but at its best, *The Jerk* manages to move its central character away from the merely moronic to a truly hysterical Pollyannaism, as when he becomes ecstatic at seeing his name in the phone-book, or jumps for joy at the sight of his new home (a men's toilet: 'Like it? I love it!'). The comedy runs out of steam when the jerk makes good, but laugh for laugh it's probably a better investment than *10*. DP

Jerry Maguire

(Cameron Crowe, 1996, US) Tom Cruise, Cuba Gooding Jr, Renee Zellweger, Kelly Preston, Jerry O'Connell, Jay Mohr, Regina King, Bonnie Hunt.
139 min.
When sports agent Jerry Maguire (Cruise) writes an uncharacteristically idealistic manifesto sug-

gesting his company should opt for fewer clients and a more caring approach, he's applauded by his colleagues who, as soon as he's fired, desert him – along with all but one of his clients, mouthy footballer Rod Tidwell (Gooding). But then Jerry also has support from single mum Dorothy Boyd (Zellweger), who happens to have fallen for him. Will the prospect of failure allow him to open up to his emotions, instead of just half-hearted affairs, as before? Lauded as a witty moral fable with a revelatory performance from its star, this romantic comedy is in fact meretricious, manipulative and reactionary. Cruise is still limited to three modes of expression: anxious, determined and smugly smiling. Since Maguire never really breaks with the money-oriented definition of success favoured by the agency that fired him, his 'failure' and diatribes against cynicism are meaningless. As for his 'redemption' through the love of a good woman: she's a doting doormat who even apologises for his mistakes, and he's so peremptory about getting what he wants that the film comes over as unthinkingly sexist. Sterling performances, nevertheless, from Zellweger and Gooding. GA

Jersey Girl
(David Burton Morris, 1992, US) Jami Gertz, Dylan McDermott, Molly Price, Aída Turturro, Star Jasper, Sheryl Lee, Joseph Bologna.
95 min.
New Jersey schoolteacher Toby (Gertz) wants to trade loyal friends and the local diner for ritzy dates on Fifth Avenue. At the Mercedes showroom parking lot, she collides her battered VW into the new Mercedes belonging to Prince Charming, aka Sal (McDermott), whose vast wealth conceals his blue-collar background. His involvement with snobbish Tara (Lee) comes to an abrupt end when she makes one too many allusions to having helped him from the gutter; but can he and Toby overcome class differences and her declared ambition to look like a 'city girl'? This shamelessly contrived romance, which makes a half-hearted attempt to denigrate materialism and '80s aspirations, lurches from one predictable exchange to the next. Mind-numbing. CM

Jerusalem File, The
(John Flynn, 1971, US/Isr) Bruce Davison, Nicol Williamson, Daria Halprin, Donald Pleasence, Ian Hendry, Koya Yair Rubin.
96 min.
A slice of ill-disguised (and painfully dull) Zionist propaganda masquerading as a thriller about an idealistic American archaeology student (Davison) caught in the Arab-Israeli crossfire. Set in Jerusalem after the Six Day War, it purports to be on the side of peace and love, but in fact depicts all the violence as coming from various unspecified Arab groups, while the benevolent Israelis try to stop them fighting each other.

Jesse James
(Henry King, 1939, US) Tyrone Power, Henry Fonda, Nancy Kelly, Randolph Scott, Henry Hull, Brian Donlevy, John Carradine, Jane Darwell, Donald Meek.
105 min.
An influential, sympathetic biography of the West's most famous outlaw, 'One of the doggonedest, dad-blamedest buckaroos that ever rode across the United States of America' (not a description that immediately brings to mind Tyrone Power). Shot in new, improved Technicolor by George Barnes, the film looks well, and King directs with uncharacteristic spurts of vitality whenever Jesse gets busy, though Nunnally Johnson injects too many moral disclaimers into his script: it's all the railroad's fault. TCh

Jester, The (O Bobo)
(José Alvaro Morais, 1987, Port) Fernando Heitor, Paula Guedes, Luis Lucas, Luisa Marques, Victor Ramos, Glicinia Quartin.
127 min.
This takes patience (a degree in Portuguese studies wouldn't go amiss, either), but ultimately rewards it by pulling a dozen apparently separate threads together into a vivid picture of Lisbon's young intelligentsia in 1978, when the island roused by the Portuguese revolution finally died. Most of the central characters are involved in putting on a play (adapted from Alexandre Herculano's novel *The Jester*), and the film gets

astonishing mileage from the old device of counterpointing their on-stage and off-stage lives. The off-stage issues include gun-running, a sexually ambivalent triangle, and a murder; the on-stage scenes are designed sumptuously enough to recall the heyday of Michael Powell. TR

Jesus Christ Superstar
(Norman Jewison, 1973, US) Ted Neeley, Carl Anderson, Yvonne Elliman, Barry Dennen, Bob Bingham, Larry T Marshall, Joshua Mostel.
107 min.
It's possible that Tim Rice and Andrew Lloyd Webber originally intended their de-theologisation of Christ quite seriously, in which case they were probably nonplussed by the way the stage show generated a pop version of 'religious' awe, like an updated Miracle Play. But the whole thing was out of their hands by the time it came to the movie, and so here the contradictions are writ very large indeed. Jewison ranges a ten stone weakling Christ (Neeley) against a powerhouse black Judas (Anderson), resurrects the latter rather than the former (in a Sly Stone jumpsuit, yet), and still manages to send audiences into transports of spiritual exaltation; the final credits roll in hushed silence. Despite the 'impressive' desert locations and an array of tanks (to represent the ills of modern militarism), it's still staged like a student revue. Most notable moments are the garden of Gethsemane scene, where Jewison cuts in leering Pharisees and crucifixion details from Flemish masters to supremely kitschy effect, and the scene of Christ being flogged, shot in sadistic slow motion. TR

Jesus of Montreal (Jésus de Montréal)
(Denys Arcand, 1989, Can/Fr) Lothaire Bluteau, Catherine Wilkening, Johanne-Marie Tremblay, Rémy Girard, Robert Lepage, Gilles Pelletier, Yves Jacques, Denys Arcand.
119 min.
Unknown actor Daniel (Bluteau) is asked by the Church to revive and revitalise a version of the Passion Play. Although the result is a critical and commercial success, his employers take exception to his radical account of Christ's life – was the Messiah the bastard son of a Roman soldier? – and Daniel's reluctance to compromise sees him heading towards modern martyrdom. Thematically or tonally, few recent films have been as rich as Arcand's delicious satire on contemporary mores. If it is fundamentally a witty, free-wheeling variation on the Gospel of St Mark, it is never constrained by allegorical schematism, and manages to make deft, original swipes at a plethora of modern 'evils': media hype, advertising, hospital bureaucracy, and of course the hypocrisy of the religious establishment. But what really makes the film so enjoyable is its capacity to surprise, not least in the way that a wide variety of potentially academic issues are introduced into a classy, clever, thoroughly entertaining format. Even if you're normally scared off by things theological, this visually elegant, uncluttered movie is serious fun. GA

Je t'aime, Je t'aime
(Alain Resnais, 1967, Fr) Claude Rich, Olga Georges-Picot, Anouk Ferjac, Annie Fargue, Bernard Fresson, Yvette Étievant.
94 min.
One of Resnais' most underrated explorations of the tone of time and memory. Claude Ridder (Rich), a failed suicide, is visited by two men who invite his cooperation in an experiment (already tried with a mouse) to project him into the past to see if he can recapture a moment of his life (since he has no wish to live, and therefore has no future, he is the perfect subject). Indifferently he agrees, is whisked through a suburban no man's land to a laboratory, and – accompanied by the mouse as an experienced travelling companion – sets off on his weird, fairytale trip through time, only to become hopelessly lost. As the scientists frantically try to trace their missing guinea-pig, fragments of his past surface momentarily, recurringly. Beautiful, tranquil, but increasingly menacing clues to a love affair with a girl he may or may not have killed. The fragments remain teasingly undertain, just out of Ridder's grasp, but his feelings lead him inexorably back to the key moment of suicide; and in the present, Ridder's body – the body of a man projected into his death

– is found in the laboratory grounds. On one level a witty sci-fi adventure, on another a poetic apprehension of man's helpless entrapment by time, the film is perfectly summed up by the extraordinary last shot of the mouse, still caged by the glass dome in which it has travelled, standing with its paws spread out against the glass in mute appeal. TM

Je t'aime, moi non plus
see I Love You, I Don't

Jetée, La (The Jetty/The Pier) [100]
(Chris Marker, 1962, Fr) Hélène Chatelain, Davos Hanich, Jacques Ledoux, William Klein, Ligia Branice.
29 min. b/w.
This classic 'photo-roman' about the power of memory – 'the story of a man marked by an image of his childhood' – begins at Orly airport a few years before WWIII. That image is of a woman's face at the end of the pier; and in the post-apocalyptic world the man now inhabits as a prisoner, he is given the chance to discover its true significance as a guinea-pig in a time travel experiment. Marker uses monochrome images recognisably from the past, such as the ruins of Europe after WWII, and with a few small props and effects, subtly suggests a future environment. The soundtrack's texture is similarly sparse, and the fluid montage leads the viewer into the sensation of watching moving images. Until, that is, an extraordinary epiphany when an image genuinely does move: the man's sleeping lover opens her eyes. DT

Jet Pilot
(Josef Von Sternberg, 1957, US) John Wayne, Janet Leigh, Jay C Flippen, Richard Rober, Paul Fix.
112 min.
Turgid and risible Cold War drama enlivened only by the superb aerial footage so beloved of its producer Howard Hughes, who re-shot, re-cut and generally tinkered with the film so obsessively that it was finally released some seven years after shooting began. Clearly uninspired by the material, Von Sternberg focused all his attention on Leigh, an improbably beautiful Soviet pilot who lands in Alaska to seek political asylum and falls in love with Major Wayne. But, it transpires, she's an agent sent to turn a high-ranking officer into an informer, and he returns with her to Russia. Needless to say, she soon realises that Moscow doesn't measure up to Palm Springs, but not before some pretty daft stuff involving sexual innuendo, patriotic sentiments, and very obvious double-cross. For Von Sternberg completists only. GA

Jetsons: The Movie
(William Hanna/Joseph Barbera, 1990, US) voices: George O'Hanlon, Penny Singleton, Mel Blanc, Tiffany.
81 min.
Hanna/Barbera's futuristic follow-up to *The Flintstones* was launched on TV in 1962 and cancelled after a single season. Syndication has kept it alive for three decades, long enough for Hanna/Barbera to believe that there would be a market for a comeback in the shape of an animated feature film. Big mistake. Top-notch computer graphics, star voices and a gaggle of gadgets cannot disguise the fact that this family of the future is stuck firmly in 1962. Dad struggles for promotion while Mom remains sickeningly supportive, Sis digs shopping and dreamy rock stars, Sonny plays basketball with his robot friend, and the future is a technological Utopia where every man's need is catered for at the push of a button – Dad's job being 'digital index operator' at Spacely Space Sprockets. Not such a bad idea, but who needs it? DW

Jet Storm
(Cy Endfield, 1959, GB) Richard Attenborough, Stanley Baker, Hermione Baddeley, Bernard Braden, Diane Cilento, Paul Eddington, Megs Jenkins, David Kossoff, Virginia Maskell, George Rose, Harry Secombe, Elizabeth Sellars, Sybil Thorndike, Marty Wilde, Mai Zetterling.
99 min. b/w.
A British prototype for the *Airport* disaster

movies of the '60s and '70s, with Shepperton's version of an all-star cast among the 40 passengers and crew of a first class transatlantic flight. Attenborough is the disaster in question, a specialist in unstable compounds who is more than a little unstable himself after his daughter's death in a hit-and-run incident. It transpires that the guilty party (Rose) is also on the flight, and twitchy Dickie has a bomb stowed away. 'You think you have a plane-load of people? It's a travelling zoo!' he explains to Captain Stanley Baker – with some justification. Like its later supersonic counterparts, Endfield's film is naive and contrived, but not without interest as the alarmed passengers soon divide into groups: reactionary (advocating torture) and liberal (patience and persuasion). TCh

Jetty, The
see Jetée, La

Je tu il elle (I...You...He...She)
(Chantal Anne Akerman, 1974, Bel) Chantal Anne Akerman, Niels Arestrup, Claire Wauthion.
85 min. b/w.
The force of Akerman's disquieting and mesmeric first feature has been lost amid critical praise (for its modish sexual preoccupations) or blame (for its arrogant omission of plot). Look again. Sexually frank, coolly passionate, it's a spiritual odyssey on a low budget as we follow 'Je' (played by Akerman herself) writing a love letter ('Tu'), in a masturbatory affair with a lorry driver playing Marlon Brando ('Il'), and an unresolved encounter with her female lover ('Elle'). Minimal in style, maximum in impact, it achieves a feeling of quiet desperation most reminiscent of Fassbinder's early features; and similarly it's a daring prototype for more remarkable later work. DMacp

Jeu de l'oie, Le (Snakes and Ladders)
(Raúl Ruiz, 1980, Fr) Pascal Bonitzer
32 min.
A concise essay on maps and orientation, made in the context of a cartography exhibition at the Pompidou Centre, this is a slightly flimsy fantasy that covers some of the same ground as Greenaway's *A Walk Through H*, but with less conviction. A man finds himself embroiled in the board game 'Le Jeu de l'oie', first across Paris, then on a cosmic level. Some of Rivette's fictions, like *Le Pont du Nord*, have covered similar ground more convincingly; but the footnotes from Borges et al are informative, at least. JRo

Jeune Fille Assassinée, La
see Charlotte

Jeune Werther, Le (Young Werther)
(Jacques Doillon, 1992, Fr) Ismaël Jolé-Ménébhi, Thomas Brémond, Simon Clavière, Faye Anastasia, Pierre Mézerette, Miren Capello.
94 min.
Like the hero of Goethe's *The Sorrows of Young Werther*, on which this is based, adolescent Guillaume – much discussed but never seen – commits suicide over a love affair. Despite his death, the pangs of unrequited love that brought it about continue among his friends. Indeed, Ismaël (Jolé-Ménébhi) and Théo (Brémond), having found Miren (Capello), the object of Guillaume's love, make a move on her themselves, breaking up with girlfriends and straining their own friendship. But just as Guillaume's friends never really knew him (or, for that matter, themselves), so we never really get to understand them. AO

Jeux Interdits (Forbidden Games/The Secret Game)
(René Clément, 1952, Fr) Brigitte Fossey, Georges Poujouly, Lucien Hubert, Suzanne Courtal, Jacques Marin, Laurence Badie.
102 min. b/w.
Clément's notorious eclecticism can surely never have been so marked within a single film as in this all-purpose allegory, anti-war tract and *noir*-ish morality. Waifish children create their own secret animal cemetery and honour it

with the monuments of the human dead, while World War II holocaust and petty family feuds form a perverse backdrop to their 'innocence'...or, perhaps, a mirror to the 'perversion' of their forbidden games. Unfortunately, such a potentially fascinating patchwork is glossed over with an irritating layer of heartstring humanism, and now looks 'touching' rather than challenging. PT

Jeux sont Faits, Les
(Jean Delannoy, 1947, Fr) Marcel Pagliero, Micheline Presle, Marguerite Moréno, Charles Dullin, Jacques Erwin, Marcel Mouloudji, Howard Vernon.
91 min. b/w.
Sartre wrote this rare survivor from those Left wing movies which loomed large in Europe after 1945. English liberal critics missed their class issues and saw only poetic fatalism. Stalinist hacks punished them for lacking positive heroes and singing tomorrows. Then English Marxists fell for Cahiers' twee formalism and whored after Hollywood culture. This forgotten genre cries out for rehabilitation. In this *Heaven Can Wait* fantasy, a de luxe lady (Presle) falls in love with the workers' militia leader just before they die. The afterworld (a Tati-like bureaucracy) gives them a second chance. The Communist street-fighting man is played by Pagliero, a Gabin-Montand hybrid who also directed bleak proletarian melodramas. The plot bitterly laments the lost opportunity for a 1945 French Revolution. Though it's sapped by Delannoy's stiffish direction, it's kitted out with 'cubist Heaven' decor and a L'Herbier-type aesthetic. Compulsive for connoisseurs. RD

Je veux rentrer à la maison
see I Want to Go Home

Je Vous Salue, Marie
see Hail, Mary

Jewel of the Nile, The
(Lewis Teague, 1985, US) Michael Douglas, Kathleen Turner, Danny DeVito, Spiros Focas, Avner Eisenberg, Paul David Magid, Howard Jay Patterson.
106 min.
The end of *Romancing the Stone* found the likeable team of Turner and Douglas sailing off down a Manhattan avenue in their schooner. By *Jewel*, they are comfortably afloat in the south of France, and agreeing to go their separate ways after she is approached by a handsome sheik to write up his story and thus promote his accession to leader of some unspecified Middle Eastern kingdom. When the schooner gets blown out of the water, it's then a ripping chase, in and out of prisons, up and down the desert in an effort to locate the famous 'Jewel' which alone will restore the rightful leader to his people. The film is still as crazy and hectic as its predecessor, without ever quite coming up to the bench mark set by the original. More distressing is that, like *Indiana Jones and the Temple of Doom*, it falls into a kind of unthinking racism, in which all Arabs are seen as dishcloth-wearing fanatics, all screaming 'Aieee' and bent on murdering An infidel for Allah. CPea

Jezebel
(William Wyler, 1938, US) Bette Davis, Henry Fonda, George Brent, Margaret Lindsay, Donald Crisp, Fay Bainter, Spring Byington, Richard Cromwell.
103 min. b/w.
New Orleans, 1852, the Lympus Ball. Enter Julie Marston (Davis) dressed in scarlet. Deep shock from the maidens in white and the matrons in grey. She starts to waltz and couples shrink from the contaminating touch of her red gown. This justly famous scene from *Jezebel* (filmed, incidentally, in black-and-white) telescopes many of the film's themes. Julie is socially and sexually transgressive. Indeed her defiance of conventions threatens the very Social Order, and she is soon associated with the fever and fires that devastate the town. Preston Dillard (Fonda), engaged to Julie but already insecure in his masculinity, cannot cope with her dangerous sexuality and finds refuge with a safe woman from the North. But when Preston returns to the South, he meets Julie again and gets the fever... JCl

JFK
(Oliver Stone, 1991, US) Kevin Costner, Gary Oldman, Sissy Spacek, Tommy Lee Jones, Laurie Metcalf, Michael Rooker, Jay O Sanders, Sally Kirkland, Ed Asner, Jack Lemmon, Vincent D'Onofrio, Brian Doyle-Murray, Joe Pesci, Walter Matthau, Tomas Milian, John Candy, Kevin Bacon, Donald Sutherland.
189 min. b/w & col.
Stone goes for the gut, but the complexity of theories surrounding the Kennedy assassination might have benefited from a cooler assessment. Understandably, he is hostile to the lone assassin findings; here, Oswald (Oldman) is merely the 'patsy' of a nebulous conspiracy cover-up involving just about *everyone*; sadly, their exact roles in the *'coup d'état'* are never properly clarified. The investigation conducted between '66 and '69 by DA Jim Garrison (whitewashed as Costner) allows Stone to proffer a dazzling array of facts, hypotheses and flashbacks, intercutting archive footage, reconstructions, and more conventional dramatic material. While his logic is often murky, the data overload is forceful, if not wholly persuasive. Though the huge cast performs strongly, characterisation is minimal, and the overall structure uninspiring. Often the film seems a garbled rant, but mostly it's more complex and less flashy than Stone's other work; the urgent editing packs a powerful punch, and if the conclusions are vague and ready to see conspiracy everywhere, one can't deny the force of Stone's call for more open debate. GA

Jigsaw
(Robina Rose, 1980, GB)
67 min.
An impressive film, this sharply conceived yet sympathetic look at a group of autistic children uses formal experiment (elements of documentary, avant-garde and narrative cinema) to reflect the alienated world of its subjects. Images and sounds build up to the obsessive isolation of the film's climax: a representation of 'tunnel vision' which turns the metaphor outside in and takes you with it. HM

Jimi Hendrix
(Joe Boyd/John Head/Gary Weis, 1973, US) Jimi Hendrix, Pete Townshend, Eric Clapton, Al Hendrix, Major Charles Washington.
102 min.
Thanks mainly to the technical dexterity of producer/director Joe Boyd, this succeeds in communicating a real sense of Hendrix via his music and his friends. There are amusing and enlightening appearances from Noel Redding, Clapton, Townshend, Jagger, Little Richard, and even Lou Reed. But more importantly, the music is for once really well chosen: amazing and formerly unseen things from Monterey, Isle of Wight, Woodstock, Fillmore East, and even the Marquee Club. DP

Jimi Plays Berkeley
(Peter Pilafian, 1971, US) The Jimi Hendrix Experience.
45 min.
A record of the historic Berkeley concert on Memorial Day, 1970. For Hendrix admirers only; others are unlikely to be converted. Pilafian intercuts the concert with shots of rioting students to little effect. People flash their peace signs and say things like 'It's my country, right or wrong'. Hendrix just plays; best are 'Purple Haze' and 'Voodoo Chile'. And what did you do in the youth revolution, daddy? -

Jimmy Hollywood
(Barry Levinson, 1994, US) Joe Pesci, Christian Slater, Victoria Abril, Jason Beghe, John Cothran Jr, Rob Weiss, Chad McQueen.
109 min.
It's a sign of the times that Barry Levinson's slick, gimmicky *Disclosure* got a major theatrical release in Britain, while the same director's quirky, fascinating *Jimmy Hollywood* snuck out straight to video virtually unnoticed. Ironically (as the title implies), Hollywood is at the heart of the picture. Pesci plays an out-of-work actor, Jimmy Alto, so frustrated by his stillborn career that he turns vigilante instead. Not that he's a *Falling Down*, mad-as-hell kind of guy; he's more an accidental hero – and his media friendly alter ego, guerilla crime-fighter Jericho, turns out to be the role of a lifetime. The pacing might be tighter,

but much of the movie is a delight. With shades of *Bugsy* and *Rain Man*, as well as the verbal riffs and gender tensions which distinguished *Diner* and *Tin Men*, it's a key film in Levinson's oeuvre. TCh

Jimmy Reardon

see Night in the Life of Jimmy Reardon, A

Jimmy the Kid

(Gary Nelson, 1983, US) Gary Coleman, Paul LeMat, Walter Olkewicz, Dee Wallace, Ruth Gordon, Don Adams, Cleavon Little.
85 min.
Gary Coleman was a child star who waged a personal battle against a growth-repressing illness and the parents who spirited away the fortune he made from the hit TV series *Diff'rent Strokes*. In this indifferent comedy, however, he mugs gracelessly as the listless son of showbiz folk. LeMat is the kindly kidnapper who teaches him that life (cue retching) is worth living after all. Tell it to Donald Westlake, who must have wept when he saw what they did to one of his novels. TJ

Jingle All the Way

(Brian Levant, 1996, US) Arnold Schwarzenegger, Sinbad, Phil Hartman, Rita Wilson, Robert Conrad, Martin Mull, Jake Lloyd, James Belushi.
89 min.
Arnie's dad running round town trying to buy his son an action man toy for Christmas, but they're all sold out. And that's about it. This valiantly hypocritical, uninflected movie keeps its most cynical role for the 'good father' Ted (Hartman), a character pilloried for having the prescience to buy his son's 'Turbo Man' early. WH

Jinxed!

(Don Siegel, 1982, US) Bette Midler, Ken Wahl, Rip Torn, Val Avery, Jack Elam, Benson Fong.
103 min.
Siegel's last film, and, by all accounts, an unhappy experience. Midler conspires with blackjack dealer Wahl to kill her partner Rip Torn, which would leave her free to continue their romance and him free from the uncomfortable winning streak Torn had been enjoying at his tables. An obvious lack of rapport between Midler and Wahl doesn't help Frank D Gilroy's much rewritten script (credited to 'Brian Blessed'). TJ

Jit

(Michael Raeburn, 1990, Zim) Dominic Makuvachuma, Sibongile Nene, Farai Sevenzo, Winnie Ndemera, Oliver Mtukudzi.
92 min.
If *The Harder They Come* was a tough-nosed bus ride around Kingston, Jamaica, Raeburn's romp is a comedic scooter tour of Harare, Zimbabwe, to the lively jump of Jit music. Both are readymade tales of poor country boys in the big bad city. The main character here, UK, is an orthodontic wonder, whose only collateral (besides his teeth) is a combination of optimism and charm. He takes to following around Sofi (Nene), the local stunner, who thinks he must be kidding, and who, to add injury to insult, has a gangster boyfriend who agrees. Undeterred, UK approaches Sofi's dad for her hand, and the venal old sod suggests a wedding price of a radio-gramophone and $500 to see what happens. What happens is that the boy chases around Harare like Pee-Wee Herman on speed to earn the money, dogged at every step by the twin forces of his village 'Jukwa' (a wizened old village 'spirit' with magic powers and an alcohol problem), and the gangster's stitched-faced cronies. It's Zimbabwe's first feature, a bit of a tourist trip, with lots of musical entertainment thrown in. WH

Jitterbugs

(Malcolm St Clair, 1943, US) Stan Laurel, Oliver Hardy, Vivian Blaine, Bob Bailey, Lee Patrick, Douglas Fowley, Noel Madison.
74 min. b/w.
By far the best of the later L & H features, with the pair playing a two-man jazz band who fall foul of a gang of conmen in attempting to help singer Vivian Blaine recover the money they have swindled. Although one or two close-ups show Laurel looking distinctly ravaged, his illness never hampers the film, which is elegant, inventive, and beautifully paced by Mal St Clair. Even the musical

numbers are attractive, thanks to Vivian Blaine and the jitterbug sequence near the beginning which sees L & H handling all the instruments in the band (including trumpet in the Harry James manner). One gem of a sequence has Laurel in hilarious drag as auntie, while Hardy, masquerading as a gallant Southern colonel, exchanges wonderful sweet nothings with Lee Patrick. TM

Jo

(Jean Girault, 1971, Fr) Louis de Funès, Claude Gensac, Christiane Muller, Bernard Blier, Carlo Nell, Jacques Marin, Ferdy Mayne.
85 min.
Alec Coppel's play *The Gazebo* transposed to studio-bound France. About a writer who pretends he's writing a murder story but is in fact attempting to carry out the perfect crime, it is often predictable and sometimes repetitive. Some surprising gems, nevertheless: Bernard Blier as the Hitchcockian inspector, for instance; and de Funès, operating in that difficult area where everything is forced into the determinedly lightweight, is a unique farceur.

Joan of Arc

see Jeanne la Pucelle

Joan of Arc of Mongolia

(Ulrike Ottinger, 1989, WGer) Delphine Seyrig, Irm Hermann, Gillian Scalici, Inés Sastre, Xu Re Huor, Peter Kern.
165 min.
Thanks to on-going subsidy from German TV, Ottinger has carved out a niche for herself as the foremost lesbian adventurist film-maker in Europe. This particular farrago imagines four disparate women meeting on the Trans-Siberian Express (where their repartee falls pitifully short of the Noël Coward tone it aspires to), and then finding themselves hijacked by a nomadic Mongolian princess and dragged through a tour of 'exotic' Mongolian culture that changes their lives. The assumptions about western and eastern cultures on which this rests are every bit as repulsive as they sound, and don't stand up to a moment's thought; but the really nauseating thing about the movie is its phony reverence for Mongolian traditions, seen as a matriarchal web of ethnic ceremonies and unfathomable secrets. Shameless. TR

Joan Sees Stars

(Joan Braderman/Dana Master, 1993, US) Joan Braderman, Elizabeth Taylor, Vivien Leigh, Ava Gardner.
60 min. col & b/w.
This essay by the 'media-holic' video artist Joan Braderman is in two parts. The first ('Starsick') finds Joan –via Master's video technology – in bed with Liz Taylor (*Butterfield 8*) discoursing on friendship and shared movie passion with the stage director Leland Moss (who died of AIDS), her own illness (ulcerated colitis), and her autobiographical feminist deconstruction of the nature of the TV/video image. She mugs to the camera, breathes fire, and places herself in various physically, aesthetically and ideologically compromised positions. Thoughtful, affecting, amusing and highly consumable. Part Two ('MGM: Movie Goddess Machine') is another persuasive melange of stills, clips and images marrying *Frankenstein* with *Gentlemen Prefer Blondes*; the Vivien Leigh of *GWTW* with that of *Streetcar*; and Ava Gardner (in *On the Beach*) with Joan herself, ending with a justification of S&M ('a parody of romance') and tattooing ('our refusal written in pain, blood and skin'). A witty slap in the face to all meanie manipulators, not least 'figure fascists' and 'aerobic storm troopers'. Light-hearted and strangely moving. WH

Job, The

see Posto, Il

Jobman

(Darrell James Roodt, 1990, SAf) Kevin Smith, Tertius Mientjies, Lynn Gaines.
100 min.
Smith, the deaf and dumb son of a rural black preacher, refuses to accept the menial labour on offer in the small farming community where he's grown up. He tries to earn a living in the city, but this ends in assault, and his return home sparks off a cycle of vengeful violence. What Roodt's film

lacks in subtlety, it makes up for in dirty authenticity. A hard-hitting independent venture (the director went on to make *Sarafina!*), completed and released against the odds in apartheid South Africa. TJ

Joe Albany...A Jazz Life

(Carole Langer, 1980, US) The Joe Albany Trio.
57 min.
Carole Langer's documentary is a delight every time jazz pianist Joe Albany sits down to play, amply justifying his reference to Charlie Parker as the one influence he acknowledges in his style. The interview material, focusing almost exclusively on the Albany 'mystery', is less satisfying. After making an almost legendary name with Bird and others in the '40s, Albany became a drug addict and dropped out of sight for decades. The story of his long climb back from degradation, happily ending in renewed fame, is obviously crucially important to Albany himself, but is an almost too familiar tale. More about Parker and the 52nd Street past would have added just the right touch of cream in the coffee. TM

Joe Hill (aka The Ballad of Joe Hill)

(Bo Widerberg, 1971, Swe) Thommy Berggren, Anja Schmidt, Evert Anderson, Cathy Smith, Franco Molinari.
115 min.
Berggren plays Joe Hillstrom, a Swedish immigrant to the US in 1902, who attempts to organise the poor through speeches and songs, and is eventually executed for murder on circumstantial evidence. Like *Ådalen '31*, it's distractingly pretty to look at for a factually-inspired film about the man who became a labour songwriter and organiser with the IWW. But when Widerberg is accused of diluting his socialist message by making his films too sentimental and beautiful to look at, he argues that this attracts a wider audience than would go to a more rigorous political film, and that preaching to the converted is a waste of time...

Joe Kidd

(John Sturges, 1972, US) Clint Eastwood, Robert Duvall, John Saxon, Don Stroud, Stella Garcia, James Wainwright, Paul Koslo, Gregory Walcott.
87 min.
Photographed by the admirable Bruce Surtees, but a curiously strangled Western which can't make up its mind whether it wants to wring straight action out of the range war between poor Mexicans and a tycoon rancher (Duvall), or to explore the moral standing of the disreputable character (Eastwood) who takes law and order into his hands. Not unlikeable, but its irresolution is typified by the inappropriately rumbustious scene in which Eastwood drives a train through a saloon. TM

Joe Louis – For All Time

(Peter Tatum, 1984, US) narrator: Brock Peters.
90 min. b/w & col.
Why does boxing so consistently make for good movies? Maybe it's because the subject provides action and lurid out-of-ring lives galore, maybe because boxers always seem to be such sad figures, reliant on powerful punches for their brief period of glory and then often doomed to years of neglect and poverty. Even with as popular and long-reigning a pugilist as Louis, this element of despair is present, and along with the marvellous archive footage on view, gives this documentary its compulsive and touching quality. The only complaints, in fact, lie surprisingly with the commentary written by Budd Schulberg; not only does it never question the values of physical violence as sport, but it frequently degenerates into absurdly purple bombast. GA

Joe Macbeth

(Ken Hughes, 1955, GB) Paul Douglas, Ruth Roman, Sidney James, Bonar Colleano, Grégoire Aslan, Sidney James, Harry Green, Minerva Pious.
90 min. b/w.
A somewhat misbegotten attempt to transpose *Macbeth* as a gangster movie, though by no means the total disaster as which it was gener-

ally written off. The main problem, aside from the British studio stab at a New York '30s ambience, is the pedantically literal adaptation by Philip Yordan, which seems to be constantly inviting recognition for its daring by drawing needless attention to its source (even the names are uncomfortably echoed, Banquo becoming Banky, for instance). Some of the transpositions work (the three witches as an old flower-seller outside a nightclub), others emphatically do not (Banquo's ghost materialising unconvincingly at a country-house dinner). If the end result is disappointingly hollow, though, it is often directed with style: the gangland execution in a deserted nightclub at the beginning; the murder of 'Duncan' (Aslan) as he takes an early morning dip in a lake; the eerie self-haunting of Macbeth (Douglas, really rather good), left deserted in his castle by the defection of the two murderer-hoods and the madness of his wife. A distinct curate's egg oddity. TM

Joe Versus the Volcano
(John Patrick Shanley, 1990, US) Tom Hanks, Meg Ryan, Lloyd Bridges, Robert Stack, Abe Vigoda, Dan Hedaya, Barry McGovern, Amanda Plummer, Ossie Davis.
102 min.
Shanley's full-blown romantic fantasy, shot almost entirely on stylised sets, is a dreamlike allegory about heroism and personal fulfilment. Curiously, in a film so dependent on narrative and visual artifice, it is Hanks' multi-faceted performance as a clerk-turned-adventurer that binds the disparate elements together. After learning that he has a 'brain cloud' and only six months to live, Joe realises he has been too scared to live properly, and accepts a challenge from magnate Graynamore (Bridges): the inhabitants of a Polynesian island need a hero who will jump into a volcano to appease their gods; in return, Joe will get to live like a king and die like a man, while Graynamore gets the rights to valuable mineral deposits. Passing from the depressing grey-blue of Joe's office through LA's neon brashness to the abstract colours of the later scenes, this engaging fable builds from a slow bubble to an outright eruption of comedy, romance and tear-jerking sentiment. If you go with the flow of Joe's Capraesque journey of self-discovery, you may be swept along. NF

John and Mary
(Peter Yates, 1969, US) Dustin Hoffman, Mia Farrow, Michael Tolan, Sunny Griffin, Stanley Beck, Tyne Daly, Cleavon Little.
92 min.
Part two of Peter Yates' step-by-step demonstration of his abilities to Hollywood: first the cars (in Bullitt), here the characters (in the archetypal late '60s morning-after-the-night-before movie). Hoffman and Farrow awake to each other in a New York bed and interminably worry, via chat, fantasy, flashback and some trendy cultural reference, whether they should do it again. PT

John Carpenter's Escape from L.A.
(John Carpenter, 1996, US) Kurt Russell, Steve Buscemi, Cliff Robertson, George Corraface, AJ Langer, Stacy Keach, Peter Fonda, Pam Grier, Valeria Golino.
102 min.
When Escape from New York was released in 1981, its innovative computer graphics, satirical dystopian vision and tongue-in-cheek humour had a freshness that disguised its ramshackle narrative. Equally enjoyable was Russell's cynical anti-hero Snake Plissken, with his eye-patch and tight-lipped, Eastwood-style one-liners. After 15 years of computer-generated effects, apocalyptic sci-fi and Arnie movies with flippant kiss-off lines, the sequel feels hackneyed and pointless. In the original, Snake was sprung from prison in order to rescue the US President from Manhattan, a lawless maximum-security island populated exclusively by hardened criminals. An explosive device injected into his neck enforced safe and timely delivery. This time, the Snake's injected with a fatal virus, despatched to the earthquake-created prison island of LA, and charged with terminating the President's daughter, Utopia (Langer), a Patti Hearst-style runaway who's stolen the government's 'doomsday device' and shacked up on the island with South American drug-dealer-turned-

revolutionary Cuervo Jones (Corraface). Once ashore, he crosses the urban wasteland to Jones' fortified lair, encountering tough transsexual Hershe (Grier), weaselly tour-guide 'Map to the Stars' Eddie (Buscemi), and spaced-out surfer Pipeline (Fonda). NF

John Grisham's The Rainmaker
see Rainmaker, The

John Heartfield: Photomonteur
(Helmut Herbst, 1977, WGer)
60 min.
A documentary which looks at Heartfield primarily as a political activist working in a specific historical context. It demonstrates this relationship by the use of documentary material, such as archive footage of inter-war Germany, in juxtaposition with Heartfield's works. (These are here frequently shown, as they are rarely reproduced, in their original format as magazine or book covers.) Far from manifesting an obsequious reverence for the works, the film takes the bold step, thoroughly justified by its results, of re-using the elements of Heartfield's montages for short snippets of photo-animation. It also documents artistic influences on Heartfield's work – Berlin Dada, which was in general more immediately political in nature than its Zurich counterpart, and George Grosz in particular – and includes a detailed demonstration of how the photomontages were produced and printed. AS

Johnny 100 Pesos (Johnny Cien Pesos)
(Gustavo Graef Marino, 1993, Chile) Armando Araiza, Patricia Rivera, Willy Semler.
90 min.
A heist on a high-rise black market bank goes wrong, presenting government and police officials with a tricky prime-time hostage situation. While the gang sweat it out, the media go into a feeding frenzy, particularly regarding schoolboy crook Johnny (Araiza). Inspired by a 1990 Santiago news event, this Dog Day thriller is cynical and relatively slick, but not especially compelling or original (it perhaps seemed more daring back in Chile). TCh

Johnny Allegro (aka Hounded)
(Ted Tetzlaff, 1949, US) George Raft, George Macready, Nina Foch, Will Geer, Gloria Henry, Ivan Triesault.
81 min. b/w.
Passable thriller with Raft as a reformed criminal persuaded (mainly by the appearance of Foch as a mysterious siren) to hunt down a traitorous counterfeit gang on behalf of the Treasury Department. Things take a lift as the action shifts to an island off the Florida coast, the script begins to filch from The Hounds of Zaroff, and Macready's suavely decadent villain proceeds to hunt Raft with bow-and-arrow (he doesn't get him, sad to say). TM

Johnny Angel
(Edwin L Marin, 1945, US) George Raft, Claire Trevor, Signe Hasso, Lowell Gilmore, Hoagy Carmichael, Marvin Miller.
79 min. b/w.
A ghost ship emerges out of the fog: bulletholes, overturned chairs and broken photographs point to a perturbed past. The world of Johnny Angel is very noir indeed. Raft plays Captain Johnny Angel, who's out to avenge the murder of his father, but gets only bland sympathy from the babyish Gusty, his father's boss. Trevor, as Gusty's scheming wife, is playing a shady game of her own, while French girl Paulette (Hasso) is hunted by an unknown killer and trusts no one. They all inhabit a closed world, where even pastoral idylls reek of claustrophobia and obsession. The men struggle against the towering shadows of their fathers, ·the women are dangerously enigmatic, and the docks of New Orleans glisten under the diffuse light of a single street-lamp. Even Hoagy Carmichael sounds eerie singing 'Memphis in June'. There are no black diamonds, but Johnny Angel glitters like one. RB

Johnny Aquarius (Jancio Wodnik)
(Jan Jakub Kolski, 1993, Pol) Franciszek Pieczka, Grazyna Blecka-Kolska, Boguslaw Linda, Katarzyna Aleksandrowicz.
100 min.
Kolski's idiosyncratic blend of pantheistic mysticism and bucolic comedy is here applied to an obscure fable about a peasant blessed with mysterious healing powers who abandons his pregnant wife to tour the countryside. The fame attendant upon his miracles and the machinations of a charlatan Christ impersonator turn his head – but a curse put on his family by a crazed vagrant brings him, eventually, to his senses. Certainly Kolski's images are often startlingly eccentric, as are the shifts between 'reality', fantasy and symbolism, but quite what it all means, beyond its warning against the temptations of the flesh, remains a mystery. GA

Johnny Dangerously
(Amy Heckerling, 1984, US) Michael Keaton, Jo Piscopo, Marilu Henner, Maureen Stapleton, Peter Boyle, Griffin Dunne, Glynnis O'Connor, Dom DeLuise, Danny DeVito, Ray Walston.
90 min.
Parody of '30s gangster movies in which Michael Keaton's meteoric rise to cleanest-cut hood in town (after turning to crime at the age of 12) is matched only by his incorruptible brother's rise to fame as a crime-busting DA, complete with inevitable courtroom confrontation between the two. Some delightfully unexpected visual gags and off-the-wall one-liners, along with the good-looking period settings and a wealth of minor characters, give the film its strength. It becomes a little predictable in the middle, but the pace picks up in time for the classic final shootout. Despite lapses, infectiously good-humoured. GO

Johnny Eager
(Mervyn LeRoy, 1941, US) Robert Taylor, Lana Turner, Edward Arnold, Van Heflin, Robert Sterling, Patricia Dane, Glenda Farrell, Henry O'Neill, Barry Nelson, Charles Dingle, Paul Stewart.
107 min. b/w.
The John Lee Mahin/James Edward Grant script for this gangster movie proposes an intriguingly sleazy scenario about a cold-blooded hoodlum (Taylor), his homosexual whipping-boy (Heflin), and the masochistic society girl (Turner) who can't wait to sample his wares ('I think he'd beat a woman if she made him angry'). Given the full-gloss-and-redemption MGM treatment, it emerges as the sudsiest of soaps. Taylor seduces Turner for his own nefarious purposes, conning her into thinking she killed a man; having discovered l'amour fou, she starts going round the guilt-ridden bend; and after much prodding from the drunkenly philosophising Heflin, Taylor does the far, far better thing. LeRoy handles the grand operatics with a certain style and excellent camerawork from Harold Rosson; but nothing can salvage a film which suggests that its hero went to the bad because he never owned a dog as a boy. TM

Johnny Frenchman
(Charles Frend, 1945, GB) Françoise Rosay, Tom Walls, Patricia Roc, Paul Dupuis, Ralph Michael.
105 min. b/w.
Hands-across-the-water propaganda for the Allied effort at the end of the war, as a Cornish fishing village is eventually led, by means of true love, to abandon its hatred of a rival Breton community and realise that the French are people too. Pretty dim drama (and comedy), though it is psychologically acute in revealing Patricia Roc's romantic preference for a visiting Frenchman over the local lad who woos her by shoving pilchards down her back. GA

Johnny Got His Gun
(Dalton Trumbo, 1971, US) Timothy Bottoms, Jason Robards, Marsha Hunt, Diane Varsi, Donald Sutherland, Kathy Fields, Charles McGraw.
111 min. b/w & col.
Trumbo lays on every emotional effect and then some to get across his tale of a World War I casualty left limbless, faceless, deaf, dumb and blind, confined to a semi-existence in a hospital back room, who learns to communicate with the world

through a painful morse code tapped out with his head on the pillow, and whose final request – that people be allowed to see him or that he be allowed to die – is refused. Trumbo adapted his own novel, incredibly based on fact, some thirty years after he wrote it, and he tells the seemingly unfilmable story through a sustained interior monologue and a series of flashbacks to Johnny's childhood, his failure of a shoe-salesman father, his job in the local bakery, his first-and-last night with his girl before leaving for the front, and through a series of fantasy sequences (the most effective involving Donald Sutherland as Christ). The film is often sentimental, sometimes brilliant as well as horrifying, and it is intriguing to speculate on what Buñuel, whom Trumbo originally wanted to direct, would have made of it. VG

Johnny Guitar

(Nicholas Ray, 1954, US) Joan Crawford, Sterling Hayden, Mercedes McCambridge, Scott Brady, Ward Bond, John Carradine, Ernest Borgnine, Ben Cooper, Royal Dano.
110 min.
Emma (McCambridge) has the hots for The Dancing Kid (Brady). The Kid is wild about Vienna (Crawford). But Vienna can't drive Johnny Guitar (Hayden) out of her head. Ray's film is not a romantic comedy, but a Western. Or is it? Taking a story about two gutsy, gun-totin' matriarchs squabbling over the men they love and the ownership of a gambling saloon, Ray plays havoc with Western conventions, revelling in sexual role-reversals, turning funeral gatherings into lynch mobs, and dwelling on a hero who finds inner peace through giving up pacifism and taking up his pistols. Love and hate, prostitution and frustration, domination and humiliation are woven into a hypnotic Freudian web of shifting relationships, illuminated by the director's precise, symbolic use of colour, and strung together with an unerring sense of pace. The whole thing is weird, hysterical, and quite unlike anything else in the history of the cowboy film: where else can one find a long-expected shootout between two fast and easy killers averted by a woman's insistence that they help her prepare breakfast? Crawford and McCambridge are fallen angel and spinster harpy, while Hayden is admirably ambivalent as the quiet saddletramp with a psychopathic temper. Truffaut called the film 'the Beauty and the Beast of the Western', a description which perfectly sums up Ray's magical, dreamlike emotionalism. GA

Johnny Handsome

(Walter Hill, 1989, US) Mickey Rourke, Ellen Barkin, Elizabeth McGovern, Morgan Freeman, Forest Whitaker, Lance Henriksen, Scott Wilson.
94 min.
Part criminological essay, part revenge thriller, this adaptation of John Godey's novel *The Three Worlds of Johnny Handsome* casts Mickey Rourke as freakish villain John. Shunned even by the criminal fraternity, he's left carrying the can for a brutal robbery by ruthless associates (Barkin and Henriksen) who also kill his only friend (Wilson). At this stage the mood becomes uncertain; a surgeon (Whitaker) links recidivism with physical deformity, and decides to perform plastic surgery. But will good looks prevent Johnny's return to crime? Jaded cop (Freeman) doesn't think so; Johnny's new girlfriend (McGovern) hopes they will. The look of the film, at least, is fixed; the New Orleans backdrop assumes sinister, *noirish* hues, and the action sequences are crisp and aggressive. Barkin and Henriksen perform with relish, Whitaker and Freeman are pleasantly understated. Rourke tries harder than ever to minimise, nay obscure, his good looks, a process which merely serves to emphasise them. 'You guys did a good job' utters Johnny as he emerges from bandages with the face of a heart-throb. Hollywood can bear only so much gloom. CM

Johnny Mnemonic

(Robert Longo, 1995, US) Keanu Reeves, Dina Meyer, Ice T, Takeshi Kitano, Denis Akiyama, Dolph Lundgren, Barbara Sukowa, Udo Kier.
96 min.
He-man Johnny (Reeves, playing mannequin) has two chips, one on his shoulder, the other in his brain, the latest in data-storage enhancers. For this mnemonic courier inhabits the cyberpunk future. The banal dystopia, virtually realised

here, is a weird mix of the familar and unfamiliar: architecturally, decayed hi-tech; politically, gangster-like international neo-capitalism – an interspace between *Blade Runner* and '70s James Bond. The plot: Johnny is forced to double-load his memory to transport one last mega-program. Short of space, he's already sacrificed recall of his childhood (despite painful disjointed flashes), and now has quickly to download before his head explodes. Realising the info's importance, he joins forces with punkette Jane (Meyer) to elude Pharmakon agents and the yakuza through the streets of 'Free' New Jersey. Directing his first feature, artist Longo seems dazzled, like a rabbit, by sheer visual overload. Lundgren's arch-villain, half Visigoth, half demented Jesus freak, fits perfectly, but Takeshi's yakuza is sadly wasted. Might suit very undemanding teenagers. WH

Johnny O'Clock

(Robert Rossen, 1946, US) Dick Powell, Evelyn Keyes, Lee J Cobb, Ellen Drew, Nina Foch, Thomas Gomez, John Kellogg, Jim Bannon, Mabel Paige, Phil Brown, Jeff Chandler.
95 min. b/w.
Despite good performances and fine camerawork from Burnett Guffey, Rossen's first film as director is a disappointingly flat thriller. His script weaves a nicely complex web around Powell's Johnny O'Clock, co-owner of a gambling club who, interested only in money and women and turning a blind eye to the dubious activities of his partner (Gomez), ends up wanted for two murders and up to his ears in treachery. The trouble lies in the pacing: as director, Rossen seems so uncertain of himself that he often fails to give his actors sufficient time or space to imprint their presence on screen (true throughout, but in particular of the two murder victims: Bannon as the corrupt cop who tries to muscle in on the partnership, and Foch as the girlfriend he cruelly discards). Since they remain totally unmemorable (through no fault of the actors concerned), the subsequent action tends to become little more than a sequence of events mechanically strung together. TM

Johnny Suede

(Tom DiCillo, 1991, US/Switz/Fr) Brad Pitt, Nick Cave, Alison Moir, Catherine Keener, Calvin Levels, Peter McRobbie.
97 min.
Right from the start, it's clear that the young eponymous hero (Pitt) is madly in love with suede shoes, Ricky Nelson's songs, his plans to become a rock'n'roll idol, the romantic notion of finding a dream girl, and – most of all – himself. So when, after a flattering fling with alarmingly changeable damsel in distress Darlette (Moir), Johnny meets the more down-to-earth Yvonne (Keener), you know he'll finally have to choose between his immature fantasies and the love of a good woman. On to this slim, slightly moralistic fable, DiCillo grafts an appealing veneer of droll slow-burn humour, wacky caricature, and pseudo-hip posing. Much of what is said and done is deliberately and delightfully absurd. But the movie is saved from becoming too knowingly flip not only by DiCillo's sure sense of pace and mood, but by the performances; especially Keener, who displays a fine mix of strength, savvy and vulnerability. GA

Johns

(Scott Silver, 1995, US) David Arquette, Lukas Haas, Wilson Cruz, John C McGinley, Keith David, Elliott Gould, Arliss Howard.
96 min.
John (Arquette) wakes up homeless, shoeless and consequently resourceless in Hollywood (he'd stashed his savings in his sneakers). It's Christmas Eve, and he's set his heart on one night of luxury at the Plaza. A back-seat encounter with a cruising movie exec soon puts him back on his feet. With his sensitive friend Donner (Haas) to help out, perhaps he can still hustle up $300 in time? Former documentarist Silver's feature debut captures the acrid tang of downtown LA's sun-swept strips and telescopes some half-dozen tricks of the trade into vivid, colourful vignettes. The stories are all true, apparently, right down to the saga of the stolen shoes and an invisible bogeyman figure who haunts the street hustlers' worst nightmares, though the 24-hour time-frame is a substantial dramatic contrivance, and undercuts the on-going despair, boredom and frustration which must be central to these lives. The movie is funnier than you'd expect, and extremely well played, particularly the touching rapport

between Arquette, a meridian cowboy working overtime, and Haas, the softer new kid on the block. The excellent score is by the septuagenarian bluesman Charles Brown. TCh

Joko, Invoca Dio...e Muori
see Vengeance

Joli mai, Le

(Chris Marker, 1962, Fr)
180 min. (cut under Marker's supervision to 123 min). b/w.
A marvellous, highly influential *cinéma-vérité* examination of a specific time and place: Paris in May 1962, going through its first spring of peace since 1939 (the signing of the Evian agreement in March 1962 having finally put an end to the long-running Algerian troubles). The basic method is simple: Marker and his colleagues (unseen) elicit comments on work, money, happiness, etc, from a cross-section of Parisians. But these personal thoughts are firmly and evocatively placed within a wider socio-political context, as the film proceeds to show footage of police charges, rioters, strikers, and so forth. What distinguishes the film most, however, is its wit, both verbal and visual, so that it is simultaneously illuminating and funny. GA

Jolly Bad Fellow, A

(Don Chaffey, 1964, GB) Leo McKern, Janet Munro, Maxine Audley, Duncan Macrae, Dennis Price, Miles Malleson, Leonard Rossiter, Alan Wheatley.
96 min. b/w.
Blackish comedy about a science academic (McKern) doing away with his enemies and rivals by a new, traceless poison. It never reaches the *Kind Hearts and Coronets* level at which it was evidently pitched (it was developed by that film's director, Robert Hamer, before his death in 1963, and co-produced by Michael Balcon), but nevertheless still manages a grinning gusto. PT

Jolson Story, The

(Alfred E Green, 1946, US) Larry Parks, Evelyn Keyes, William Demarest, Ludwig Donath, Bill Goodwin, Scotty Beckett.
128 min.
Probably the most famous Hollywood showbiz biography, in which the black-faced Al (Parks) bellows his way from burlesque to Broadway and beyond, falls in love with musical comedy star 'Julie Benson' (read Ruby Keeler), but falls more in love with his audience's applause. Jolson himself sings on the soundtrack ('Avalon', 'Toot, Toot, Tootsie' and many more), Larry Parks impersonates him with studied sincerity, and the musical numbers are attractively staged by Joseph H Lewis (whose more usual territories were Westerns and *films noir*). More of the same followed, with contrived plot and without Lewis, in 'Jolson Sings Again' (1949). GB

Jonah Who Will Be 25 in the Year 2000 (Jonas qui aura 25 ans en l'an 2000)

(Alain Tanner, 1976, Switz/Fr) Jean-Luc Bideau, Rufus, Miou-Miou, Jacques Denis, Dominique Labourier, Roger Jendly, Myriam Boyer.
115 min.
Through circumstance, coincidence and necessity, eight characters find themselves drawn together. In various ways they're all irrevocably marked by the spirit of May '68, individually representative of the diverse political utopianism operating in the annus mirabilis of which Mailer wrote, 'One had the thought that the gods were back in human affairs'. Tanner gives us a Trotskyist journalist, an anarchic shopgirl who steals food, a transcendental mysticist, an educationalist; and labourer Mathieu Vernier (Rufus), who accommodates his friends' philosophies but realises that their enduringly optimistic visions can only be achieved through class struggle. Mathilde (Boyer), his wife, is pregnant with the Jonah of the title. Tanner again collaborated with John Berger, and the script is didactic and compact, though *Jonah* has a lighter and more humorous touch than *The Middle of the World*. It's a heady experience following their agile ruminations on time, language and perception, deftly superimposed on a film that pleases visually and formally. JS

Jonathan Livingston Seagull

(Hall Bartlett, 1973, US) voices: James Franciscus, Juliet Mills, Hal Holbrook, Philip Ahn.
120 min.
Richard Bach's best-selling parable for freshmen becomes on screen a very spelled-out allegory, complete with flat voice-overs and pretentious Neil Diamond soundtrack. The film's renegade seagull hero enacts the theme of spiritual development and human achievement, moving through an obsession with speed (maybe seagulls can't fly faster than 62 mph, but wouldn't it be great if they could) towards a more fashionable Oriental philosophy (perfect speed is being there), and final apotheosis as a Messiah figure. Ignore all that (admittedly difficult) and you have a finely photographed essay on birds which uses its coastal locations to good effect.

Jory

(Jorge Fons, 1972, US) John Marley, BJ Thomas, Robby Benson, Brad Dexter, Claudio Brook, Todd Martin.
97 min.
A simple and fairly strong tale about a 15-year-old kid (Benson) who turns revenge killer after watching his father murdered. But it's submerged beneath an impenetrably fruity script littered with clichés on Life with a capital L and a man finding 'a place with his name on it'. 'So what's so special about Texas?' 'It's the meanin' that's different, not the dirt'. Unremarkable direction, routine performances, and a pair of uninteresting juvenile leads finish the thing off. VG

Joseph Andrews

(Tony Richardson, 1976, GB) Ann-Margret, Peter Firth, Michael Hordern, Beryl Reid, Jim Dale, Peter Bull, John Gielgud, Hugh Griffith, Wendy Craig.
104 min.
Attempting to repeat the commercial success of *Tom Jones*, this adaptation of Fielding's first novel is little more than a middlebrow's *Carry On*. Richardson allows his photographer and designers to make pretty pictures à la 'Barry Lyndon', while himself showing little interest in Fielding's essentially moralistic themes – innocence beset by rapacious experience, physically with Joseph and Fanny, mentally with Parson Adams. Indeed he violates the novel's guts and narrative coherence, at the same time reducing it to little more than a headlong tumble of bits of knockabout bedroom farce loosely hung together. Saddest of all is the usually brilliant Michael Hordern's performance as Adams. The one potentially interesting scene, a Ken Russell pastiche – a Black Mass with Fanny as victim – merely hints at a real depravity which might have been allowed to threaten. RM

Joseph Conrad's The Secret Agent

see Secret Agent, The

Joseph Cornell: Worlds in a Box

(Mark Stokes, 1992, GB)
52 min.
Arguably one of modern art's best kept secrets, Joseph Cornell spent his life quietly creating in New York's suburbia. His best work has a curious *Alice in Wonderland* quality to it: glass-fronted boxes in which he stored 20th century detritus, from marbles and stamps to fluff. The film reveals how Cornell wanted to create a universe for his brother, who was confined to the house with cerebral palsy. Cornell later re-edited old films to entertain his brother, and these jittery, anti-narrative works bridge the gap between Dadaism and Pop Art. It's no surprise that John Lennon and Andy Warhol were among his fans. What is more surprising is prize ham Tony Curtis' in-depth knowledge of Cornell's art. The jury might still be out on whether Cornell is a Great Artist, but this reveals a man whose view of modern times is never less than fascinating. BD

Josephine (Die Ortliebschen Frauen)

(Luc Bondy, 1980, WGer) Edith Heerdegen, Libgart Schwarz, Elisabeth Stepanek, Klaus Pohl.
106 min.
After a slow and confused opening, this stylised study of claustrophobic, incestuously possessive familial repression makes compulsive viewing. Josephine assumes her late father's mantle of domestic tyranny, binding mother, sister and crippled brother to an increasingly rigid notion of respectability that shades towards sadism as outside relationships are severed and minor cruelties escalate. A fine, blackly bizarre first film from theatre director Bondy; based on the appropriately-titled novel *The Grave of the Living* by Franz Nabl, it's both co-scripted and hauntingly acted (as Josephine) by Libgart Schwarz, the wife of Peter Handke. PT

Joseph Kilián (Postava k Podpírání)

(Pavel Jurácek/Jan Schmidt, 1963, Czech) Karel Vasícek, Consuela Morávková, Pavel Bártl, Zbynek Jirmar.
40 min. b/w.
A bizarre, consciously Kafkaesque allegory in which a young man wanders the streets of Prague fruitlessly searching for a man called Joseph Kilián, of whom no one seems to have heard. Passing a state cat-shop, he impulsively hires a cat for the day, only to find, nightmarishly, that the shop is no longer there when he tries to return the cat as required. Wittily poking fun at the personality cult (a huge portrait of Stalin looms over a roomful of frayed agit-prop posters and Cold War slogans), Jurácek and Schmidt scarcely put a foot wrong in evoking the incomprehensible mazes – simultaneously absurd and terrifying – of totalitarian bureaucracy. TM

Josh and S.A.M.

(Billy Weber, 1993, US) Jacob Tierney, Noah Fleiss, Martha Plimpton, Stephen Tobolowsky, Joan Allen, Chris Penn.
98 min.
Driven to despair by his dysfunctional extended family, angst-ridden Josh Whitney (Tierney) strings his younger sibling Sam a fanciful line – Sam is not a real kid, but a Strategically Altered Mutant, sold by his parents for government warfare. Perversely, Sam embraces the lie, which miraculously explains his feelings of isolation, aggression, obsession with death, and his detachment from mom and dad. When Josh and Sam make a run for the open road, freaky coincidences conspire to prop up the delusion. Ultra-jowly newcomer Fleiss (Sam) ably portrays a child's sullen confusion when faced with the tawdry grottiness of the real world. Yet even with him, and some bitter one-liners in its favour, the overall picture is as confused and disjointed as Sam's own tortured outlook. MK

Jour de Fête

(Jacques Tati, 1948, Fr) Jacques Tati, Guy Decomble, Paul Frankeur, Santa Relli, Roger Rafal.
87 min. b/w & col.
Like Keaton before him, Tati devised gags of such sheer intricacy as to prove on occasion just too beautiful to be laughed at (it's no accident that the truly funniest talkies – Fields, the Marx Brothers – were hardly directed at all). In this, his first feature, reissued in its original 'splash colour' version (never shown at the time), an almost plotless tale of a village postman's endeavours to streamline his service *à l'américaine* is enhanced by a radiographic vision of rural minutiae which one might call hyper-realist, were it not for that term's sleek urban connotations. As for Tati the performer, he makes cycling along a tranquil country lane as spellbinding as if it were taking place on a high wire. GAd

Journal d'un Curé de Campagne

see Diary of a Country Priest

Journal d'une Femme de Chambre, Le

see Diary of a Chambermaid, The

Journal de Lady M, Le (The Diary of Lady M)

(Alain Tanner, 1993, Switz/Bel/Sp/Fr) Myriam Mézières, Juanjo Puigcorbé, Félicité Wouassi.
112 min.
It's a stormy Parisian night. Tempestuous Spanish painter Diego (Puigcorbé) shelters in a club doorway and is strangely attracted by the music within. Soon he's transfixed before girl pop-group Lady M, ogling the lead singer (Mézières) undulating in a silk slip. Their ensuing tangled affair is written up in Lady M's diary, with much pen-sucking and curling up on sofas. This project clearly meant something to Mézières and Tanner, but, like their first collaboration, *A Flame in My Heart*, it turns out to be little more than ill-written (but graphic) soft porn. When Diego's wife Nuria (Wouassi) joins the couple in bed, M pleads, 'Save me from becoming a dead tree.' Worth seeing, if at all, for the sex, but mostly just plain silly. SFe

Journey's End

(James Whale, 1930, US/GB) Colin Clive, Ian MacLaren, David Manners, Billy Bevan, Anthony Bushell, Robert Adair.
120 min. b/w.
Whale's first film, marred by some strangulated performances, is fascinating primarily as a record of his stage production of RC Sherriff's enormously successful play. The passionate sincerity of Sherriff's lament for the death of idealism in the mud of World War I still comes across with intermittent power, but is undercut by textual tampering. Though the structure of the play is respected, with opening-out limited to a prologue and brief punctuating scenes in no man's land, the speeches have all been pruned. As a result, the curiously plangent rhythms of the text (which still make it a masterpiece on stage today) are lost, with the meticulously built-up tension – in which you can almost hear the playing fields of Eton in the background as youthful veterans of the trenches mask their fear so as to live up to the hero worship of even younger schoolfellows – frittered away much of the time into an exchange of banalities. TM

Journey for Margaret

(WS Van Dyke, 1942, US) Robert Young, Laraine Day, Margaret O'Brien, Fay Bainter, Nigel Bruce, William Severn.
81 min. b/w.
MGM's weepy follow-up to the hugely successful hands-across-the sea Anglophilia of *Mrs Miniver*, this time featuring a nice, average American couple who adopt two orphaned (and disturbed, oh yes indeed) children during the Battle of Britain. Awesomely glutinous, but the fascinating thing about Margaret O'Brien is that, even at the age of five and in only her second film, she was already an accomplished actress rather than a cute personality. TM

Journey Into Autumn

see Kvinnodröm

Journey Into Fear

(Norman Foster, 1942, US) Joseph Cotten, Dolores Del Rio, Orson Welles, Everett Sloane, Agnes Moorehead, Ruth Warrick, Jack Moss.
71 min. b/w.
'Designed' rather than directed by Welles, though you wouldn't care to bet on it as things get under way with the camera craning up to a sleazy window in Istanbul and peering in – as a tinny gramophone with a stuck needle maddeningly grinds out the same phrase – for its first glimpse of the slug-like babyfaced killer played (brilliantly) by Jack Moss. Thereafter, with Cotten on the run from Gestapo agents and Welles having fun in the first of his monster roles as the Turkish chief of secret police (he directed all his own scenes), the tone veers through nightmare chases, bizarre encounters, and deflating jokes. Eminently watchable, but it does tail away. TM

Journey of a Young Composer (Akhalgazrda Kompozitoris Mogzauroba)

(Georgi Shengelaya, 1985, USSR) Giya Peradze, Levan Abashidze, Zurab Kipshidze, Rusudan Kvlividze.
105 min.
The year is 1907 and tensions are running high in the Eastern Georgian countryside, with the Tsar's cossacks seeking to crush any further insurrection. Nikusha, the young composer, drifts innocently into the area to record the music of the local peasants. Accompanied by the boisterous Leko, who's convinced that he's connected with

the underground, he makes his appointed rounds on the nobility, who go about their business like extras in a George Romero feature. Leko, swaggering and spitting, leering and swearing, stomping his feet and chewing with his mouth open (all before dinner is served), quickly inspires the wrath of his grey hosts...Shengelaya meticulously records the events of the pair's mysterious adventure, but sadly neglects the spectator. A lot is happening but there's very little to see, apart from Leko's (Peradze's) embarrassing performance. SGo

Journey of Hope (Reise der Hoffnung)
(Xavier Koller, 1990, Switz) Necmettin Cobanoglu, Nur Srer, Emin Sivas, Erdinc Akbas, Yaman Okay.
110 min.
In this moving, resolutely unglamorous drama, based on a real-life incident, a Turkish couple decide to escape their hand-to-mouth existence by upping sticks to Switzerland. Selling their possessions, they travel illegally with one of their sons, eventually getting caught up with unscrupulous smugglers who promise transport over the Swiss border. The ultimate test comes when they attempt to cross a stretch of the Alps on foot. Compelling as the unfolding horrors are, the real strength of the film rests in its strong central characterisations. Koller resists sentimentalising relationships, building up the tension slowly so that by the time their nightmare deepens the couple have built up an unspoken bond. Less satisfactory are some of the colourless depictions of the Swiss, which merely serve to throw into relief the plight of the refugees. CM

Journey of Natty Gann, The
(Jeremy Kagan, 1985, US) Meredith Salenger, John Cusack, Ray Wise, Lainie Kazan, Scatman Crothers, Barry Miller, Verna Bloom.
101 min.
Set at the time of the Depression, this suggests something like a return to form after a series of Disney disappointments. Natty's one-parent family unit is upset when daddy is forced to leave to look for work in a lumber camp in the north; subjected to the whim of a sadistic guardian landlady, she sets off to find him. On the way she has a string of adventures, runs into the obligatory wild dog whom she befriends, and you can guess the rest. Beautifully shot and well acted (Meredith Salenger in a fine performance as Natty), there's a real sense of period, even if the film does occasionally become over-sentimental. DPe

Journey to Beijing (Bei Zheng)
(Evans Chan, 1998, HK/US)
111 min.
Ostensibly a documentary about a four-month charity walk from Hong Kong to Beijing, which was timed to reach its destination on the eve of Hong Kong's reversion to Chinese sovereignty, Chan's film is in fact a wide ranging 'essay' on the narrowing – or is it? – gap between Hong Kong and the 'mother country'. Part of the film does focus on the walkers, examining their motives and their reactions to the experience, and on the people they meet on the road, but there are frequent sidetracks: for instance, a sequence examining the progress of the gay rights movement in Hong Kong and questioning its future prospects. Facing up to the inevitable sense of anti-climax which followed the hand over, Chan cuts to the heart of Hong Kong's conflicting feelings about its own way forward, and clears away all the evasions and half-truths of the full-on media coverage of the hand over itself. TR

Journey Together
(John Boulting, 1945, GB) Richard Attenborough, Jack Watling, David Tomlinson, Edward G Robinson, Bessie Love, John Justin, George Cole, Ronald Squire, Sebastian Shaw.
95 min. b/w.
Produced by the RAF Film Unit with much the same brief as Powell and Pressburger's A Matter of Life and Death, Boulting's first feature opted for semi-documentary rather than fantasy. Terence Rattigan's script follows three aspiring pilots (Attenborough, Watling, Tomlinson) through training in Britain, America and Canada, thereby paying tribute to Allied cooperation with-

out fuss or fanfare, while national idiosyncrasies are amusingly acknowledged in a scene where an American instructor (Robinson) and his wife (Love) entertain two of the trainees to dinner. The focus is on the scope and stresses of the training programme, with only one of the trio (Watling) making the grade. The script comes perilously close to convention in detailing Attenborough's tribulations (he's the working-class lad), but comes back on course with a detailed, superbly handled account of the preparations made by a crippled bomber's crew before it is ditched in the sea. With most of the cast serving in the RAF at the time, the keynote is authenticity, and the film remains surprisingly effective. TM

Journey to Italy
see Viaggio in Italia

Journey to the Centre of the Earth
(Henry Levin, 1959, US) James Mason, Pat Boone, Arlene Dahl, Diane Baker, Thayer David, Alan Napier, Peter Ronson.
132 min.
Pat Boone gives this colourful, exciting story its few nauseating moments (as when he sings 'My Heart's in the Highlands'). Otherwise it's one of the very best Hollywood adventure movies, with lots of monsters, underground oceans, sinister villains, and touches which would have delighted Jules Verne himself. James Mason as usual carries his part superbly, and there are plenty of good supporting actors like Napier and Ronson. Some of the special effects are intriguing, and believe it or not there's also quite a bit of effective sexual symbolism in typical Hollywood style, which greatly enhances the syrupy romantic subplot. Watch for the ending in which the girl is blown up on a giant funnel, with close-ups of her on her back smiling orgastically. DP

Journey to the Western Xia, The (Xi Xia Lu Tiaotiao)
(Lu Wei, 1997, China) Ni Dahong, Badema.
99 min.
The directorial debut of Lu Wei, who scripted Farewell My Concubine, is another historical drama, this time set in the eleventh century. A group of warlike 'tax-collectors' from the Tangut tribe in the province of Xixia forcibly take ten boys from a defenceless Chinese village as their tithe; when one of the infants disappears, the leader abducts a pregnant woman to avert the Emperor's wrath. But the cost of duty is high. Making splendid use of the north western landscapes (though the camerawork is raw and gutsy rather than abstract and picturesque), this is a vigorous if slightly predictable tale of barbarism modified by respect, sympathy and suffering. GA

Journey to Wisdom (Desaadanam)
(Jayaraj, 1996, Ind) Vijaya Raghavan, Kumar, Mini Nair, Soumya.
114 min.
When Pachu's chosen to become the new leader of the ashram, his grandfather's overjoyed. This is an inordinate honour for the family. Pachu's parents, however, are horrified. Dearly loving their only child, they cannot stand the thought of him being taken. Producer/director Jayaraj (from Kottayam in Kerala) explores the nature of family and duty with a keen and tender eye, probing the consequences of tradition and status without resorting to polemic: the family's elevated position in the village dissolves the intimacy of friendship, bringing an uncomfortable isolation, yet to reverse the decision would bring shame and dishonour to all. FM

Jour se lève, Le (Daybreak)
(Marcel Carné, 1939, Fr) Jean Gabin, Arletty, Jules Berry, Jacqueline Laurent, Bernard Blier, René Génin, Mady Berry.
87 min. b/w.
Possibly the best of the Carné-Prévert films, certainly their collaboration at its most classically pure, with Gabin a dead man from the outset as his honest foundry worker, hounded into jealousy and murder by a cynical seducer, holes up with a gun in an attic surrounded by police, remembering in flashback how it all started

while he waits for the end. Fritz Lang might have given ineluctable fate a sharper edge (less poetry, more doom), but he couldn't have bettered the performances from Gabin, Berry, Arletty and (as the subject of Gabin's romantic agony) Laurent. Remade in Hollywood as The Long Night in 1947. TM

Joy
(Serge Bergon, 1983, Fr/Can) Claudia Udy, Gérard Antoine Huart, Agnès Torrent, Elisabeth Mortensen, Jeffrey Kime, Claire Nadeau.
95 min.
Why is Joy acclaimed as a superstar model when she has a face like the back of a beaver? How does she get her nipples to stick out like the spikes on World War I Boche helmets? This enigmatic quality extends to the rest of the film. Okay, so she caught her parents in flagrante when she was five years old. But that's no excuse to go baring her body all over the billboards of Paris beneath the legend 'Les Droits de la Femme: l'Orgasme', a tasteless bit of filth photographed by 'a Lebanon war veteran who wanted a change of pace'. Still less is it reason for running after a revolting old roué like the architect hero, even if his doric columns do drive her crazy. Only an abrupt shock ending redeems this sub-Emmanuelle-ian piece of chic-anery. AB

Joyless Street, The (Die freudlose Gasse)
(GW Pabst, 1925, Ger) Greta Garbo, Asta Nielsen, Valeska Gert, Einar Hanson, Jaro Fürth, Werner Krauss.
11,155 ft. b/w.
Pabst's record of the process of destitution in the middle classes of Vienna in the '20s was banned in Britain when first released. As such, it later came as a major revelation, both when compared with his later work and in the context of the development of a film narrative able to accommodate a large number of characters. Its squalid realism is given conviction by a sureness of technique and a sensuousness of imagery, continually creating contrasts between the misery of the have-nots and the uncaring gaiety of the champagne-swilling affluent, the threadbare and the luxurious. RM

Joy Luck Club, The
(Wayne Wang, 1993, US) Kieu Chinh, Tsai Chin, Ming-Na Wen, Tamlyn Tomita, France Nuyen, Victor Wong.
139 min.
An intimate chronicle of the lives of three generations of Chinese-American women, this sophisticated weepy contains enough 'life events' for a season of soap operas, but it is to director Wang's credit that he never allows the tides of emotion to erode the essential truthfulness of the film's characterisations and insights. The Joy Luck Club is a mah-jong club at which four well-to-do immigrant Shanghai women swap recipes, memories and support. At one gathering – when, on the eve of a trip to China, American-born June (Ming-Na Wen) takes the place of her recently deceased mother Suyuan – the film flashes back to the critical moments in the relationships between the four pairs of mothers and daughters. Barring a lull towards the end, the film successfully sustains momentum through sensitive mise-en-scène, the all-round excellence of performance and design, its rhythmic emotional flow, and the sour-sweet blend of humour and tears. WH

Joy of Living
(Tay Garnett, 1938, US) Irene Dunne, Douglas Fairbanks Jr, Alice Brady, Guy Kibbee, Eric Blore, Lucille Ball, Franklin Pangborn, Billy Gilbert, Jean Dixon.
90 min. b/w.
Musical screwball comedy from RKO which had its title changed from Joy of Loving (naughty, naughty, said the Production Code). Dunne plays a musical comedy star driven to the brink of exhaustion by the demands of the greedy, money-grubbing family she supports; Fairbanks is the carefree hero who helps her to opt out of the rat race by showing her the joys of loving (ie. eating in romantically cosy neighbourhood restaurants and running about barefoot in the rain). Dunne sings several Jerome Kern numbers, all very stiffly staged; and the dropout message characteristic of the period hedges its bets all the way

(Fairbanks may be against money-grubbing, but with an island paradise and a small cargo business of his own he's all right). Faintly tiresome and full of flat stretches, but the excellent supporting cast helps. TM

Joy Parade, The
see Life Begins in College

Joyriders
(Aisling Walsh, 1988, GB) Patricia Kerrigan, Andrew Connolly, Billie Whitelaw, David Kelly, John Kavanagh.
96 min.
Walsh's directorial debut is the story of downtrodden Dubliner Mary Flynn (Kerrigan), who breaks away from her domineering husband and leaves her kids at the railway left luggage to go in search of something more. Something more turns out to be leather-jacketed Perky Rice (Connolly), an incorrigible car thief and desperate romantic who whisks her off on a joyride through the rolling Irish countryside. Along the way, Mary meets an ageing country and western star (Whitelaw), who organises tea-dances in a dilapidated seaside resort, and a weathered hill farmer (Kelly), whose observations bring some humour to an otherwise straight-laced film. Andy Smith's screenplay occasionally touches poignantly on the insurmountable breach between the characters' wishful flights of fancy and the reality of their cramped lives, but in the end the film suffers from a narrowness of vision: lighting, camerawork, and direction all seem bound by the constraints of the small plot, so that neither the passion nor the tragedy of the runaways is ever given full rein. EP

Juarez
(William Dieterle, 1939, US) Paul Muni, Bette Davis, Brian Aherne, Claude Rains, John Garfield, Gale Sondergaard, Donald Crisp, Gilbert Roland, Louis Calhern, Joseph Calleia.
132 min. b/w.
Only Bette Davis and Gale Sondergaard have any fire in this otherwise plodding Warner Bros costume drama about the French attempt to colonise Mexico in the 1860s, the romance between the puppet dictator (Aherne) and the Empress Carlota (Davis), and the exploits of Juarez himself (Muni), the proponent of Mexican independence. The script, by John Huston and historical researchers, was rewritten by Muni's brother-in-law. Huston commented: 'His changes did the picture irreparable damage. In Mr Muni's estimation, his contributions to the dramatic arts were for the enrichment of the world. It was heavy going around Muni'. ATu

Jubilee
(Derek Jarman, 1978, GB) Jenny Runacre, Little Nell, Toyah Willcox, Jordan, Hermine Demoriane, Ian Charleson, Orlando.
104 min.
It's almost an understatement to say that Jubilee has a lot going for it. Jarman has conceived the ingenious idea of transporting Queen Elizabeth I through time to witness the future disintegration of her kingdom as marauding girl punks roam a junky and violent urban landscape. Its patchily humorous evocation of this landscape lays the film open to criticism: several sequences stoop to juvenile theatrics, and the determined sexual inversion (whereby most women become freakish 'characters', and men loose-limbed sex objects) comes to look disconcertingly like a misogynist binge. But in conception the film remains highly original, and it does deliver enough of the goods to sail effortlessly away with the title of Britain's first official punk movie: 'Rule Britannia', as mimed by Jordan, should have 'em pogoing in the aisles. DP

Judas Was a Woman
see Bête Humaine, La

Jude
(Michael Winterbottom, 1996, GB) Christopher Eccleston, Kate Winslet, Liam Cunningham, Rachel Griffiths, June Whitfield, James Nesbitt, Vernon Dobtcheff, Freda Dowie, Dexter Fletcher.
122 min.
This determinedly non-heritage adaptation of Thomas Hardy's Jude the Obscure is an often impressive but oddly frustrating movie. Mostly, it's faithful to the story of the lowly but academically ambitious Wessex stonemason (Eccleston) who, after a disastrous marriage to Arabella (Griffiths), daughter of a pig farmer, heads off to the university town of Christminster, where he falls for his strong-willed, comparatively worldly-wise cousin Sue (Winslet). Somehow, however, the film never delivers the punch deserved by one of the 19th century's most movingly cruel English novels. Part of the trouble is that, in trying to cram Hardy's narrative into a mere two hours, Hossein Amini's brisk screenplay rarely does more than skate over the key dramatic moments. The leads, too, lack the chemistry to render the tragic outcome of Jude and Sue's socially unacceptable amour fou as devastating as it should be; Eccleston is too relentlessly 'intense' for Jude to seem a truly attractive prospect, while Winslet's Sue is such a thoroughly modern miss that she finally fails to convince. Eduardo Serra's 'Scope camerawork is eye-catching, and the film is never stilted, but it's hard to see how its emphasis on being 'modern' make the content really relevant to today. Ambitious, sensitive, but ultimately uninvolving. GA

Judex
(Georges Franju, 1963, Fr) Channing Pollack, Edith Scob, Francine Bergé, Jacques Jouanneau, Sylva Koscina, Michel Vitold.
95 min. b/w.
Franju's superbly elegant and enjoyable tribute to the adventure fanatasies of Louis Feuillade sees the eponymous righter-of-wrongs (Pollack) abduct a wicked banker in order to prevent villainess Diana (Bergé, glorious in black cat suit) laying her hands on a fortune the banker's daughter (Scob) is due to inherit. Cue for a magical clash between good and evil, with the director revelling in poetic symbolism (the opening masked ball finds our hero, with forbidding bird mask, creating a dove out of thin air), black-and-white photography that thrills with its evocation of a lost, more innocent era, and surreal set pieces. GA

Judge Dredd
(Danny Cannon, 1995, US) Sylvester Stallone, Armand Assante, Max von Sydow, Diane Lane, Rob Schneider, Jürgen Prochnow, Joanna Miles, Joan Chen, Balthazar Getty, Maurice Roëves, Ewen Bremner.
95 min.
Stallone certainly has the square jaw-line and iconic presence to play Judge Dredd, a helmeted, emotionless future-cop who dispenses summary justice on the riot-torn streets of Mega City One. When Dredd is falsely convicted of murder and, like his honest mentor Judge Fargo (von Sydow), driven out into the lifeless deserts of the Cursed Earth, the resulting vacuum is filled by corrupt Judge Griffin (Prochnow), who springs Dredd's cloned criminal brother Rico (Assante) from prison and foments social chaos. Dredd, however, is not so easily vanquished and returns to settle old family scores. Indicative of worries that Dredd's heartless, neo-fascistic persona would result in too dark a tone, the uneven script throws in femme cop Hershey (Lane) and irritating sidekick Fergie (Schneider) to add human feeling and comic relief. Despite some fuzzy flying sequences, the precocious technical mastery displayed by 27-year-old Brit director Cannon is extraordinary; but as with his flawed debut, The Young Americans, a question mark still hangs over his handling of actors and narrative fluidity. As a result, this slam-bang Stallone vehicle never quite delivers what its confident, fizzing visuals seem to promise. NF

Judgement in Stone, A
see Cérémonie, La

Judgement in Stone, A
(Ousama Rawi, 1986, Can) Rita Tushingham, Ross Petty, Shelley Peterson, Jonathan Crombie, Jessica Steen, Jackie Burroughs.
100 min.
Lord! The things that happen when you're dyslexic! Eunice (Tushingham) is thus afflicted, and according to a prologue, her inability to read causes all sorts of traumas at school. Worse, it makes her grow up into a mousy, embittered spinster, bullied by her unshaven father and given to wearing silly wigs. Dad, in fact, gets on her nerves so much (what with his ludicrous attempts at a cock-

ney accent) that she kills him and then, still concealing her disability, contrives to find a job in middle America as housekeeper with a kind and wealthy family. But what happens when she has to provide a shopping list? Yep, you guessed it: Eunice goes off her rocker, and pretty soon all hell is let loose. It's hard to tell whether this inept adaptation of Ruth Rendell's novel is meant as a straightforward psychological thriller or as a peculiarly camp black comedy. The awful acting – not merely Tushingham, all wide-eyed bathos and twitchy hysteria, but the entire cast – and the leaden direction suggest the former. GA

Judge Priest
(John Ford, 1934, US) Will Rogers, Henry B Walthall, Tom Brown, Anita Louise, Stepin Fetchit, Rochelle Hudson, Hattie McDaniel.
80 min. b/w.
A loose amalgam of Irwin S Cobb stories which Ford later reshaped, personalised and perfected as The Sun Shines Bright. This was the second of three Ford films to star Rogers, the crackerbarrel humorist perfectly cast here as the lazy gadfly who stings a small-town Southern community, still divided by prejudice and the lingering legacy of Civil War conflicts, into shamed awareness of its intolerances. A warmly funny, richly atmospheric slice of Americana, it ran some front office interference (removal of a scene involving the attempted lynching of Stepin Fetchit was one reason for the remake), and shows Ford sometimes fumbling for the touch of poetry that later came so easily (the scene in which Rogers talks to his dead wife was more fully achieved in Young Mr Lincoln and She Wore a Yellow Ribbon). But it's still terrific. TM

Judgment at Nuremberg
(Stanley Kramer, 1961, US) Spencer Tracy, Burt Lancaster, Richard Widmark, Marlene Dietrich, Judy Garland, Maximilian Schell, Montgomery Clift, William Shatner, Edward Binns.
190 min. b/w.
With his reputation for tackling only Big Issues, the Holocaust had to be on Kramer's list of cinematic 'lest we should forget' achievements. That said, this assembly of star turns in the court – including token Germans Dietrich and Schell, the latter collecting an Oscar for his efforts as the defence attorney – are often very impressive. Tracy puts in an effortlessly brilliant performance as the superjudge, and Clift as a confused Nazi victim is painfully convincing in his emotional disintegration. There are no surprises in the direction, and Abby Mann's screenplay plays the expected tunes, but there's enough conviction on display to reward a patient spectator. DT

Judgment in Berlin
(Leo Penn, 1988, US) Martin Sheen, Sam Wanamaker, Max Gail, Jürgen Heinrich, Heinz Hoenig, Carl Lumbly, Max Volkert Martens, Sean Penn, Christine Rose, Marie-Louise Sinclair, Joshua Sinclair, Jutta Speidel, Harris Yulin.
96 min.
'No one has ever been tried in the West for escaping from the East' announces Sheen early in this docudrama based upon the trial of two East German citizens who in 1978 hijacked a plane to defect to the 'free West' – or did they? Tried under American jurisdiction, their case rose to notoriety when presiding judge Herbert J Stern refused to yield to political pressure, and granted Helmut Thiele and Sigrid Radke the right to trial by jury. Penn's adaptation of Stern's book is an uncertain affair, an intriguing courtroom drama marred by heavy-handed pathos and symbolic flag-waving. Sheen hams it up as Stern, delivering Lincolnesque speeches about freedom while gazing meaningfully at newsreels of refugees. 'I'm just trying to understand these people', he tells his German-hating Jewish wife (Rose), who soon tires of the whole performance. Hoenig and Speidel are admirable as the errant Easterners, but the real surprise is Sean Penn, whose portrayal of a recently liberated, hesitant student is exemplary. MK

Judith
(Daniel Mann, 1965, US/Isr) Sophia Loren, Peter Finch, Jack Hawkins, Hans Verner, Zaharira Charifai, Joseph Gross.
109 min.

Sophia Loren, Jewish survivor of a concentration camp arriving as an illegal immigrant in Palestine on the eve of Israeli independence in 1947, steps out of the packing-case in which she has been nailed up for a taxing sea voyage looking as fresh as a film star. Yes, it's that sort of movie, and it gets worse as she searches for the Nazi husband who denounced her, a wanted war criminal now training Arabs for the coming struggle. Terminally dreary as well as totally unbelievable. TM

Ju Dou

(Zhang Yimou/Yang Fengliang, 1990, Jap/China) Li Wei, Gong Li, Li Baotian, Zheng Jian, Zhang Yi.
94 min.
A magnificent melodrama, even more visually sumptuous and emotionally draining than the same director's earlier *Red Sorghum*, even though its cruel tale of adultery and revenge constitutes, to some extent, a blatant reworking of themes. This time, it's set in and around a dyeing workshop in a remote town in the 1920s, where the young wife of the ancient, impotent and sadistic dyer decides to make the old man's adopted nephew her lover and protector. Even when she finds herself with child, their affair remains a secret; but after the dyer is left partly paralysed by an accident, they brazenly flaunt their love, so that the vengeful cuckold's only hope is to turn the child against its parents. Hardly surprising, perhaps, that the Chinese authorities virtually dissociated themselves from this Japanese-financed, less-than-rosy picture of a country given over to unfettered sexual desire and murderous hatred. But it's this vision – expressed through superbly forthright performances, and in images whose stunning colours are sure to stick in the mind – that lends Zhang's movie the stark, searing power of Greek tragedy. Its dark wit and fiery pace ensure that even the occasional overheated moments carry conviction. GA

Juge Fayard dit le Sheriff, Le

see Sheriff, Le

Juggernaut

(Richard Lester, 1974, GB) Richard Harris, Omar Sharif, David Hemmings, Anthony Hopkins, Ian Holm, Shirley Knight, Roy Kinnear, Roshan Seth, Cyril Cusack, Freddie Jones.
110 min.
Juggernaut has been stuck with a 'disaster movie' tag when in fact it bears little relation to the Hollywood crop of calamities. The potential catastrophe here is seven steel drums of amatol timed to go off and destroy 1,200 passengers unless a ransom is delivered to the mysterious Juggernaut. But Lester's movie is no glossy catalogue of modern living with a holocaust thrown in for the climax. On the contrary, it is a penetrating and sardonic commentary on a fading and troubled Britain, neatly characterised by the lumberingly chaotic ocean liner, 'The Britannic', in which everything is falling apart: newly fitted stabilisers rock the boat, the general facilities are shabby and run down, bombs keep exploding to the dismay of the stoical passengers. Anyone who's ever had to endure that peculiar form of torture, the luxury ocean liner, will find an exact description here with not a jot of misery omitted. The pace of the thriller aspect is unflagging, and the characters are unerringly drawn, from the perfect casting of Sharif as the seedy, demoralised captain, to Harris as the bomb expert (the film's research in this direction is painstaking). Without a doubt, one of the best movies of 1974. DP

Juice

(Ernest R Dickerson, 1992, US) Omar Epps, Khalil Kain, Jermaine Hopkins, Tupac Shakur, Cindy Herron, Vincent Laresca.
91 min.
This Harlem-set rap thriller examines the implosive relationship between four African-American high school 'crew' members. Q (Epps) is an aspiring scratch'n'mix DJ, holding down a relationship with an older divorcee; Raheem (Kain) has an estranged wife and child; Steel (Hopkins) is the kid, a gentle butt to their jokes; and Bishop (Shakur) is the loaded gun with no safety catch. Their average day – the light-hearted first half of the movie – is spent ditching school in favour of

playing the video-game arcades, having close encounters with rival gangs, and taking in some shoplifting of records. But an attempted hold-up instigated by Bishop goes badly wrong, and comedy turns to tragedy as fear and mutual suspicion conspire to blow the four apart. What distinguishes Dickerson's 'ghetto' movie is less the anti-violence message than the sense it gives of *inhabiting* the lives of these Harlem kids. Stylishly shot, it works well as a thriller; the result is energetic and entertaining, without the feeling of difficult truths being forgotten. WH

Jules and Jim (Jules et Jim) (100)

(François Truffaut, 1961, Fr) Jeanne Moreau, Oskar Werner, Henri Serre, Marie Dubois, Vanna Urbino, Sabine Haudepin.
105 min. b/w.
Truffaut's film about a dilettantish *ménage-à-trois* focusing around the First World War, with Moreau as the fatalistic heroine at its centre, has dated a little and the influence of Renoir is more obvious now that we are some distance from the New Wave. The lightning changes of mood from pathos to whimsy and back again still make it watchable, though. Remade by Paul Mazursky as *Willie and Phil* in 1980. RM

Jules Verne's Rocket to the Moon

(Don Sharp, 1967, GB) Burl Ives, Troy Donahue, Gert Fröbe, Terry-Thomas, Hermione Gingold, Daliah Lavi, Lionel Jeffries, Dennis Price.
101 min.
Like the rocket in question, this soppy farce has great difficulty in getting off the ground. Jules Verne had little to do with the proceedings, which involve a large star cast getting repeatedly blown up. Reminiscent of *First Men in the Moon* (even to the extent of Lionel Jeffries playing the irascible inventor in both films), but there's no comparison entertainment-wise. DP

Julia

(Fred Zinnemann, 1977, US) Jane Fonda, Vanessa Redgrave, Jason Robards, Maximilian Schell, Hal Holbrook, Rosemary Murphy, Meryl Streep, Dora Doll.
117 min.
Lillian Hellman's tight autobiographical story about memory and friendship gets the full Zinnemann gloss-wash. Julia, disaffected Anglo-American aristocrat, strides into womanhood wearing golf shoes and that brave Redgrave grin. Swept up in the anti-Fascist movement, she persuades Hellman (Fonda) to smuggle money to Berlin. One-legged and a liability to any underground movement, Julia is murdered. Hellman returns to Dashiell Hammett (Robards) for grizzled comfort. Suckers for frontier drama, trains, NY literary society and the '30s will enjoy. Zinnemann blows it most of all in the Fonda-Redgrave relationship, and no credibility is given to Hellman's ferocious talent and dominant personality. Reverential to the end, a suggestion of homosexuality is laughingly tossed off in one glittering scene. No one bothers to mention that lesbianism is central to 'The Children's Hour', the play Hellman is trying to write while, as per synopsis, 'her memory returned again and again' to Julia. JS

Julia Has Two Lovers

(Bashar Shbib, 1990, US) Daphna Kastner, David Duchovny, David Charles, Tim Ray, Clare Bancroft, Martin Donovan, Anita Olanick.
86 min.
Alone in her Californian beach apartment, Julia (Kastner) receives a call from a stranger (Duchovny). It's a wrong number, but that doesn't stop them from embarking on a revealing, lengthy conversation conducted while he shaves, she tidies. Julia only puts the receiver aside when her live-in boyfriend (Charles) arrives for lunch and demands sex. Once he's gone, the conversation is resumed, and the two agree to meet the next day. This low-budget comedy makes the most of limited means, but its resourcefulness goes beyond cautious budgeting. Long-distance intimacy exposes the characters' sense of displacement, while poking fun at life in LA. The pace picks up once there's direct interaction between the strangers, leading to the inevitable conflict between long-term security and

short-term excitement. Kastner and Duchovny offer engaging performances, and although the film could do with tightening, it's good-natured and uplifting. CM

Juliet of the Spirits (Giulietta degli Spiriti)

(Federico Fellini, 1965, It/Fr) Giulietta Masina, Mario Pisu, Sandra Milo, Valentina Cortese, Caterina Boratto, Sylva Koscina, Lou Gilbert.
145 min.
What *8½* did for its bourgeois film-director hero, *Juliet of the Spirits* does for his female opposite number, a repressed, paranoid, bourgeois housewife (played, of course, by Fellini's wife). That's to say it's a gaudy, hyperbolic pageant, in which a 'reality' composed of séances, film-star neighbours, tyrannous relatives, and a large helping of Catholic guilt is gradually invaded by 'flashbacks' and 'fantasies'. The overall charm just about carries the glibness of the psychological payoff, and the way that different veins of imagery interlock gives the film a cogency that later Fellini has woefully lacked. TR

Julius Caesar

(Joseph L Mankiewicz, 1953, US) Marlon Brando, James Mason, Louis Calhern, John Gielgud, Edmond O'Brien, Deborah Kerr, Greer Garson, George Macready.
120 min. b/w.
Although it lacks the excitement of *Macbeth* or *Othello* as imagined by Welles, a remarkably successful stab at Shakespeare. Mankiewicz, as one might expect, respects the words and films without tricks, letting the camera concentrate on performance and on preserving the rhythms of the text. Discreetly pruned, this emerges boldly and lucidly as (in producer John Houseman's words) 'a political thriller', with the motley cast pulling together surprisingly well. At least three outstanding performances (Gielgud, Calhern, Brando), the only disappointments being Mason's muffled Brutus and the two ladies on standby. TM

Jumanji

(Joe Johnston, 1995, US) Robin Williams, Bonnie Hunt, Kirsten Dunst, Bradley Pierce, Bebe Neuwirth, Jonathan Hyde.
104 min.
Young Alan Parrish lives in a postcard '60s American town. One day, he and his only friend Sarah find a Victorian jungle-based board-game, 'Jumanji'. That night, as they play, the jungle comes to life. Her throw of the dice brings bats swooping through the lounge; his takes him into the game, whence he can return only if an opponent throws a seven. Unfortunately, a terrified Sarah runs off into the night, leaving Alan trapped in 'Jumanji'. Cut to the depressed '90s. Two young orphans move into the now decrepit Parrish house and find the game in the attic. They start to play, bringing into being a marauding lion, monkeys and an older Alan (Williams), presumed murdered for over 20 years. To reverse the effects of the game, Parrish knows they must play to the end. Subsequent throws produce a psychotic Victorian hunter (Hyde, excellent), earthquakes, floods and, best of all, a herd of rhinos, zebras and elephants stampeding through the town. This is an sfx movie par excellence. Although leading actors Williams and Hunt (as the older Sarah) give competent performances, script, direction and story are all subservient to Industrial Light and Magic's extraordinary computer-generated animals and effects. Hollow, but very spectacular. NKe

Jumbo

see Billy Rose's Jumbo

Jumping for Joy

(John Paddy Carstairs, 1955, GB) Frankie Howerd, Stanley Holloway, AE Matthews, Alfie Bass, Joan Hickson, Lionel Jeffries, Richard Wattis.
88 min. b/w.
Lame, optimistically titled Britcom with young Howerd as the dog-track gopher who's sacked on suspicion of involvement in a doping scandal, but gets his own back on his old bosses by nursing a sick greyhound back to peak condition and winning the big race. Holloway's the con artist in support. TJ

Jumpin' Jack Flash

(Penny Marshall, 1986, US) Whoopi Goldberg, Stephen Collins, John Wood, Carol Kane, Annie Potts, Peter Michael Goetz, Roscoe Lee Browne.
105 min.

Funky computer operator Terry Doolittle (Goldberg) is suffering the usual terminal boredom when someone code-named Jumping Jack Flash appears on her VDU screen. The mystery man is a British agent trapped in Eastern Europe, so Terry is soon rushing around town reading contact names off the bottom of frying pans, meeting strange Dutchmen on moonlit dockside piers, gatecrashing swanky diplomatic dinners dressed as Diana Ross, and getting her slinky outfit, not to mention her nerves, well and truly shredded. Striking an effective balance between suspenseful intrigue and wacky humour, director Marshall handles both the spy-jinks and Goldberg's eccentric antics with confident panache. There are occasions when Goldberg does rather too much, arresting the action by lapsing into stand-up comic routines; fortunately, the plot soon regains its brisk momentum. NF

Jump into the Void
(Salto al Vacio)

(Daniel Calparsoro, 1994, Sp) Najwa Nimry, Roberto Shalu, Alfredo Villa, Ion Gabella.
86 min.

Raw, radical, post-*Reservoir Dogs* thriller from the Basque new wave. A portrait of the hopelessness of youth – with violent trimmings – the film centres on the character of Alex, a muttering, lovelorn punkess with the word 'Void' inscribed on her pate. This is her day: 'Shitty hopheads, shitty work, spiderman shorts, the old woman's coffeepot, Esteban's thumb, the stiff, those two bastards…who the fuck loves me?' The salty, confrontational dialogue, jumpcuts, handheld camerawork and grotesque black comic elements all signal 26-year-old writer/director Calparsoro as a significant talent, while Nimry is outstanding in the lead role. TCh

Jump the Gun

(Les Blair, 1996, UK/SAf) Baby Cele, Lionel Newton, Michele Burgers, Thulani Nyembe, Rapulana Seiphemo.
124 min.

Johannesburg, a town where a violent crime occurs every 17 seconds. This is the first film to take the lid off the new South Africa, to create a scenario around living, breathing individuals coming to terms with life in these post-Mandela times. There's poor white Clint, who thinks that the country's getting 'very black' and gun-ownership will solve his problems; there's Minnie, a white prostitute who drinks and has lost her kid; Gugu, who's black and wants to sing in a band, and will sleep with whoever it takes. There's Thabo, who studied and got out of Soweto, and Zoo, who stayed but has changed from township activist to car-hijacking gang leader – even if he is confined to a wheelchair. How these people, who've been brought up apart, get together, is a mix of sex, music and common decency. Great performances, notably from Newton's Clint and Michele Burgers' Minnie, make this a film, written and directed by one-time Mike Leigh collaborator Les Blair, that's genuinely original and genuinely magnificent. SGr

Junge Törless, Der

see Young Törless

Jungfrauenmaschine, Die

see Virgin Machine

Jungfrukällan

see Virgin Spring, The

Jungle Book, The

(Wolfgang Reitherman, 1967, US) voices: Phil Harris, Sebastian Cabot, Louis Prima, George Sanders, Sterling Holloway.
78 min.

'I thought you were entertaining someone up there in your coils,' Shere Khan the Tiger purrs malevolently (with the unmistakable voice of George Sanders) as Kaa the Snake endeavours to squeeze Mowgli the Man Cub in his horrible clutches. This animated Disney feature based on

Kipling, the last to be supervised by Big D himself, is chock-a-block with such shapely lines (with Baloo the dim-witted bear, voiced by Phil Harris, getting the best). It's also got great knockabout visual gags, mercifully little cutey-poo sentiment, and reasonable songs, including 'The Bare Necessities'. The animation has only the bare necessities, too, and the storyline is weak, but it doesn't seem to matter much. GB

Jungle Book, The
(aka Rudyard Kipling's
The Jungle Book)

(Stephen Sommers, 1994, US) Jason Scott Lee, Cary Elwes, Lena Headey, Sam Neill, John Cleese, Jason Flemying.
111 min.

In this live-action adventure, Mowgli (Scott Lee) is five before he's jungle-bred. The animals act like animals, sort of, which means that Mowgli wrestles with Baloo the bear, tumbles with wolves, but doesn't discuss philosophy with 'em. He swims in sun-shafted rivers like Johnny Weissmuller and runs like the wind. Re-entering society in proud manhood, this beautiful, innocent wild child stuns Kitty Brydon (Headey), daughter of the local divisional officer (Neill, stiff but decent), much to the consternation of a pack of snivelling subalterns led by bad-egg Elwes. Sensing that romance and animal magic won't sew up the audience, director Sommers hots up the pace with abductions and a treasure hunt in the Lost City; this seems like a loss of nerve. But Scott Lee is an unexpectedly appealing hero, partly because he's never indulged, and his dialogue is kept to a minimum. WH

Jungle Burger
(La Honte de la Jungle)

(Picha ie. Jean-Paul Walravens/Boris Szulzinger, 1975, Fr/Bel) voices: Johnny Weissmuller Jr, John Belushi, Bob Perry, Bill Murray.
85 min.

A softcore pornish cartoon Tarzan, Englished in this version to conform to the *Animal House* spirit of pre-anal comedy: the eternally adolescent class clown with the Harvard diploma stapled to his fly. There are glimpses of riotously idiosyncratic wit; but the viewer is soon left to drown in a wave of crassness while each animated participant grabs the nearest sex object and heads for the closest pile of leaves. CR

Jungle Fever

(Spike Lee, 1991, US) Wesley Snipes, Annabella Sciorra, Spike Lee, Ossie Davis, Ruby Dee, Samuel L Jackson, Lonette McKee, John Turturro, Frank Vincent, Anthony Quinn, Tyra Ferrell, Tim Robbins, Brad Dourif.
132 min.

When happily married black architect Flipper Purify (Snipes) begins an affair with his Italian-American secretary Angie (Sciorra), all hell breaks loose: his wife (McKee) throws him out, Angie leaves home after being beaten by her father, and families, friends and neighbours chip in with horrified reactions... Lee's 'joint' looks good, features a chorus of garrulous characters (most of them heavily into racial hatred), makes stirring use of music (by Stevie Wonder and others), and never allows the forgiving women a fair share of the deal. But instead of *showing* how prejudice seeps into the private intimacies of daily life, the film turns its attention to the other characters, including Flipper's junkie brother Gator (Jackson), who fuels a subplot evoking the destructive effects of crack on black society. Sadly, this aspect, which allows Lee his most unsettling and impressive scene, seems loosely tacked on to the main thrust of the film. GA

Jungle Sex

see Black Bunch, The

Jungle Story

(Kim Hong-Joon, 1996, SKor) Yoon Do-Hyun, Kim Chang-Wan, Cho Yong-Won, Kim Min-Soo.
87 min.

In this film about the struggle to establish and promote a rock band in rock-hostile South Korea, the music stands for a spirit of non-conformity and rebellion – concepts which mean something

in the country's fast-changing but still overwhelmingly feudal-Confucian society. The story elements are very familiar: endless rehearsals, dodgy contracts, 'musical differences', a bullying manager whose faith in the band never dies. But the details ring true, and there's no hint of MTV excess in the performances or visuals. Kim's taste in music seems more '70s than '90s, but he directs with real elegance and makes very smart use of vignettes like the glimpses of the girl at the pharmacy counter who measures out her life in Neil Young songs. TR

Jungle 2 Jungle

(John Pasquin, 1997, US) Tim Allen, Sam Huntingdon, JoBeth Williams, Lolita Davidovich, Martin Short, Joan Copeland, Donald Ogden Stiers.
105 min.

Allen's a top New York commodities trader dragged to the depths of the Amazon to get estranged medic spouse JoBeth Williams' signature on their divorce papers. There's a 13-year-old surprise waiting for him, however: a son (Huntingdon) he never knew about, called Mimi-Siku and raised entirely by the local Indians. Naturally, the filial bonding routine comes as something of a shock, but before long, junior and pet spider wind up back in the US, where jungle-trained blowpipe skills may just come in handy for sorting out dad's financial contretemps with a gang of dodgy Russian mafiosi. Allen is nothing if not personable, and though the material here is awfully predictable, he never makes the mistake of overplaying it into submission. No, that's left to business partner Short, who rolls his eyeballs and wrings his hands as the pair's trading balance turns life threatening. Typically for Disney, the villains aren't made of very stern stuff, nor indeed is fey spear-carrying Mimi-Siku. TJ

Junior

(Ivan Reitman, 1994, US) Arnold Schwarzenegger, Danny DeVito, Emma Thompson, Frank Langella, Pamela Reed, Judy Collins.
110 min.

Nothing is inconceivable: big Arnie's having a baby – and he's the mother. In the past, movie scientists with the hubris to play God over nature have met with thundering Gothic retribution; no such fate befalls Dr Hesse (Schwarzenegger) after experimenting on himself with a new wonder drug. Arnie has dabbled with the comic implications of genetic science before in *Twins*. This too is a one-joke movie, but at least it's a good joke. Once more director Reitman pulls the strings, slackly at first, but with ever-increasing assurance, and DeVito is back on board as Hesse's collaborator Dr Arbogast. Just as Cary Grant was once the apotheosis of masculinity and therefore ripe for humiliation, so there is something inherently, essentially funny about a feminised Arnie. He's more than matched by the hilariously dizzy Thompson as the unwitting 'father'. They must be the unlikeliest couple of 1994, but, I swear, they're great together. Call it…chemistry. TCh

Junior Bonner

(Sam Peckinpah, 1972, US) Steve McQueen, Robert Preston, Ida Lupino, Joe Don Baker, Barbara Leigh, Mary Murphy, Ben Johnson, Dub Taylor.
103 min.

Peckinpah coasting enjoyably between *Straw Dogs* and *The Getaway* with an elegiac reworking of Nick Ray's *The Lusty Men*, an alternately wistful and raucous family Western about the shrinking frontiers of the rodeo circuit and the anachronism of honour (a suited middle-class horseman rides by with *The Wild Bunch* embroidered on his saddle-blanket). Some of the symbolism's a bit heavy-handed (wild bulls: bulldozers), but the performances are finely affecting, and Peckinpah captures the contradictory flavours of the new west with a multi-camera set-up at the real Prescott, Arizona rodeo and judicious use of split screen. PT

Junk Mail (Budbringeren/
Postbudet der vidste for
meget)

(Pål Sletaune, 1997, Nor/Den) Robert Skjærstad, Andrine Sæther, Per Egil Aske, Eli Anne Linnestad, Trond Høvik.
83 min.

j

This droll Norwegian first feature shows that Aki Kaurismäki doesn't have the monopoly on deadpan Nordic humour and oddball working class characters. Lugubrious, love-struck postman Roy (Skjærstad) falls for pretty, partially deaf dry cleaning assistant Line (Sæther), whose lowlife boyfriend recently embroiled her in a mugging that left a security guard in a coma. Too shy to declare his love, Roy eavesdrops on Line's unhappy life, becoming involved in a bizarre sequence of events that unfolds like a cheap B-movie plot tinged with Nordic melancholy. The downbeat, fatalistic storyline relies a bit too heavily on ironic coincidences, but the observations are always generous and the humour never forced. NF

Jupiter's Darling
(George Sidney, 1954, US) Esther Williams, Howard Keel, Marge and Gower Champion, George Sanders, Norma Varden, William Demarest, Richard Haydn.
96 min.
Elephantine musical (literally, given that the Champions do one number with performing pachyderms), set in 218 BC and featuring Hannibal's march on Rome alongside a lavish underwater ballet for Esther Williams. Disarmingly dotty rather than good, although the Champions have one beautifully choreographed slave market routine. TM

Jurassic Park
(Steven Spielberg, 1993, US) Sam Neill, Laura Dern, Richard Attenborough, Jeff Goldblum, Bob Peck.
127 min.
Jaws with claws. Now, however, with state-of-the-art computer-generated effects, the creatures are so good you hardly care what the rest of the film is like. Unfortunately, Spielberg seems to share the disinterest. The premise is solid – scientist clones dinosaurs from blood found in insects trapped in amber, invites distinguished guest and children to his living theme park, and watches helplessly as the behemoths run amok – but the plot is full of inconsistencies and shipwrecks from Michael Crichton's novel. The performances are merely passable (save the kids and Dern), and Goldblum is ludicrous as the chaos theorist. His cod mottos are all that's left of the ethical debate, and the only discernible theme is pure Spielberg: palaeontologist Neill starts off hating children but learns to love them. But why quibble? Spielberg is still supreme as an action director, and when the T Rex makes beefburger of the jeep, or the vicious 'Raptors stalk their human prey, the film inspires wonder and awe. DW

Juror, The
(Brian Gibson, 1996, US) Demi Moore, Alec Baldwin, Anne Heche, Joseph Gordon-Levitt, James Gandolfini, Lindsay Crouse, Tony Lo Bianco, Matt Craven, Michael Constantine.
118 min.
Sculptress and single mom Annie (Moore) is thrilled to be selected for jury duty on a big Mafia trial, and even happier when an attractive art dealer (Baldwin) picks up on her work and asks her out. He's too good to be true, she tells her best friend (Heche) – and so it transpires, when he whispers these sweet nothings on the first date: if Annie doesn't swing the jury to an acquittal, then she's art history. This pappy, semi-enjoyable legal thriller (from a book by George Dawes Green) raises a number of questions, the most intriguing of which must be: is this woman the most exciting screen actress in America? No, no – not Ms Moore, though she's hit on what must be her perfect movie vocation, making sculptures you can't see (they come boxed). She's very up in the early scenes, very down thereafter, and perfectly watchable throughout, but it's still a stretch watching her persuade 11 angry jurors that black is white and 'the big spaghetti-o' should walk. No, Anne Heche is the one to look for. In just a handful of perfunctory scenes, this mercurial newcomer blows the stars off the screen and the film rings momentarily true. For the rest, screenwriter Ted Tally appears to be aiming for a low-brow companion piece to his *Before and After*, Baldwin contributes a silky, Zen hood ('If I can keep you scared, I can save you'), but director Gibson shows real bad faith by resorting to a laughably primitive climax in Guatemala, of all places. TCh

Just a Gigolo (Schöner Gigolo – Armer Gigolo)
(David Hemmings, 1978, WGer) David Bowie, Sydne Rome, Kim Novak, David Hemmings, Maria Schell, Curd Jürgens, Marlene Dietrich.
105 min.
Hemmings recut his film (reputedly the most expensive ever made in Germany to date), restoring some footage originally deleted by the producer, who radically reduced its 147 minute running time after preliminary screenings. These alterations may well have helped, but no amount of tinkering could turn it into the comedy-drama that it was clearly intended to be. Its main problem is its tone: its story of a young Prussian (Bowie) returning to a turbulent Berlin after World War I, and finding himself torn between a team of homosexual Nazis and a flotilla of wealthy widows, never finds its level, but swings wildly between coarse knockabout farce and aspirations to tragic dignity. Bowie's vacant performance reflects these uncertainties precisely, and the cluster of star names around him are reduced to delivering awkward party pieces. TR

Just a Little Whistle (Jen si Tak Trochu Písknout)
(Karel Smyczek, 1980, Czech) Michal Suchánek, Dan Sedivák, Pavel Kohout, Libuse Heczková, Renata Pokorná.
84 min.
Back to schooldays with a couple of kids from differing backgrounds forming an unholy alliance and beginning to wonder what girls are all about. Parental neglect and/or misunderstanding, a drift towards delinquency, a final betrayal. Sounds familiar? Too right, it might almost be a remake of Truffaut's *Les Quatre Cents Coups*. Competently done, with excellent performances from the two boys, but desperately predictable. TM

Just Another Girl on the I.R.T.
(Leslie Harris, 1992, US) Ariyan Johnson, Kevin Thigpen, Ebony Jerido, Chequita Jackson, Jerard Washington.
97 min.
Chantal (Johnson) lives in the Brooklyn projects. She's an A student, but her street sassiness leads to her downfall, alienating teachers and attracting Tyrone (Thigpen), a jeep-driving fly guy, who smooth talks Chantal into unprotected sex. Soon she's facing abortion or teenage motherhood. Being generous to Harris's debut would earn PC credibility, since this is the first film written and directed by an African-American woman to gain British distribution. One could dwell on Johnson's in-your-face performance, or how refreshing it is to see a black New York drama played out by home*girls*. But, facing facts, the climax is unpersuasive and the happy end a cop-out. CO'S

Just Ask for Diamond
(Stephen Bayley, 1988, GB) Susannah York, Colin Dale, Dursley McLinden, Peter Eyre, Nickolas Grace, Patricia Hodge, Saeed Jaffrey, Roy Kinnear, Bill Paterson, Jimmy Nail.
94 min.
This kiddies' private eye spoof on *The Maltese Falcon*, scripted by Anthony Horowitz from his novel *The Falcon's Malteser*, soon degenerates into superficial pastiche and becomes increasingly tiresome. Handed a box of Maltesers by a South American dwarf, teenage shamus Tim Diamond (McLinden) is soon out of his depth and forced to rely on his younger, smarter brother Nick (Dale). The Fat Man demands an audience, Inspector Snape (Paterson) and his sadistic assistant (Nail) apply the pressure, and comically inept heavies Gott and Himmell (Eyre and Grace) fall over each other to get their hands on the chocs. Sadly, only York as the drink-sodden romantic Laura Bacardi, and Patricia Hodge as the enigmatic Baroness, leave a lasting impression. NF

Just Before Nightfall (Juste avant la Nuit)
(Claude Chabrol, 1971, Fr/It) Stéphane Audran, Michel Bouquet, François Périer, Anna Douking, Dominique Zardi, Henri Attal, Jean Carmet, Marina Ninchi.
107 min.

Chabrol's tortuous, entertaining study of murder and the expiation of guilt in a small suburban town, a low-key thriller about a husband who murders his mistress (his best friend's wife), tries to confess and accept punishment, but finds a bland bourgeois unwillingness to recognise guilt from his own wife and friends. Organised in Chabrol's lurid, witty and elegant manner, this was his last productive mining of the themes of *La Femme Infidèle* before they were transmuted through repetition into the farcical intrigues of *Les Noces Rouges*. Direction, acting and script are all meticulous, and the use of subplot (the meek accountant who robs the hero's safe) is especially fine. DP

Just Between Friends
(Allan Burns, 1986, US) Mary Tyler Moore, Ted Danson, Christine Lahti, Sam Waterston, Salome Jens, Jane Greer.
120 min.
In this pseudo-sophisticated weepie, the ongoing relationships are those between two buddy seismologists, and between a loving wife and her lonely female newscaster friend who is having an affair with one of the quake-quacks, who just happens to be married to the aforesaid wife (a fit but wizened MTM). As is usual in such cases, the wife is the only person not to know what is going on, but after the adulterer's death in an auto smash while attending an anti-nuclear rally in Washington, she does find out. And the adulteress is pregnant...Even given the sensitive performances and fitfully humorous script, the end product is exactly what might be expected to eradicate stains from white-collar conscience: soap. But for those who can pause-button the mind, it works. MS

Just Cause
(Arne Glimcher, 1995, US) Sean Connery, Laurence Fishburne, Kate Capshaw, Blair Underwood, Ed Harris, Ruby Dee, Ned Beatty, Daniel J Travanti, Hope Lange, Kevin McCarthy, George Plimpton.
102 min.
There's a Hollywood dictum about not going on the floor until you've fixed the script, but it's obviously news to the makers of this picture. The novel by John Katzenbach, from which it's taken, may have been an overweight airport buy, but it did have two startling plot twists, both fumbled by the script. For some reason, Armstrong (Connery) has had a career change from investigating journalist to Harvard law professor, and this effectively destroys the humiliation of his Pulitzer backing up on him when he realises the newspaper campaign has released the wrong man from Death Row. Another no-good reason issues him with a wife (Capshaw), and to give her something to do, the script babbles about a past entanglement with the killer. Briefly, Armstrong is persuaded to take the case of black convict Bobby Earl (Underwood), railroaded for raping and killing a little girl. He was beaten into a confession by police chief Tanny Brown (Fishburne), and at the retrial is set free, after which the killings begin again. Harris as a mad serial killer is lit from under; Connery and Fishburne are adversarial along *Heat of the Night* lines, but director Glimcher makes little of the small-town Deep South locations. Pity. BC

Juste avant la Nuit
see Just Before Nightfall

Just Heroes
(John Woo, 1993, HK) David Chiang, Danny Lee, Chow Sing Chi.
93 min.
Bizarrely moralistic gangster picture in which Woo orchestrates the gunplay with customary virtuosity, but also argues that violence is wrong and 'nobody wins' in gangland feuds. As usual, the family's foregrounded. *The Godfather*-like plot charts the bloody happenings after the boss of a crime syndicate is murdered and his relatives fight to take over the reins. As in the best mobster movies, it's never quite clear who's betraying who. The director includes some self-reflexive comedy in the shape of a youngster who wants to emulate the heroes of *A Better Tomorrow* (Woo, 1986), but learns that shootouts in 'real life' are tough, unglamorous

work. Such corny moralistic humour can't help but undermine an otherwise impressive hardboiled thriller. GM

Justine
(George Cukor, 1969, US) Anouk Aimée, Michael York, Dirk Bogarde, Anna Karina, John Vernon, Philippe Noiret, George Baker, Robert Forster, Jack Albertson, Marcel Dalio, Michael Dunn, Barry Morse.
116 min.
A foredoomed attempt to compress Lawrence Durrell's *Alexandria Quartet* for Hollywood consumption, begun by Joseph Strick on location and continued by Cukor in studio sets, with the former's Tunisian exteriors cut in (irrespective of disruptive colour-matching) or back projected from time to time to make the whole thing look doubly phony. Exuding the disastrous smell of compromise in every shot, it emerges as a preposterous farrago of sex (romantic, incestuous, homosexual, nymphomaniac) and high-flown political intrigues concerning Coptic Christians and gun-running in Palestine. Only Bogarde, as the tormented Pursewarden, manages to rise above the inanities and deliver his lines as though they meant something. TM

Justine
(Stewart Mackinnon, 1976, GB) Alison Hughes, Robin Phillimore, Patrick Good, Peter Marples, Patrisha Despond.
90 min. b/w.
Who nowadays reads de Sade? His precise, logical catalogues of moral and sexual behaviour belong to a vanished time with a vanished language. If de Sade lives, it's through his present-day interpreters: de Beauvoir, Barthes, Pasolini. And the Film Work Group, whose *Justine* is an isolated and very honourable attempt to bring an important strain in contemporary European thinking into British consciousness. The film comprises a series of non-dramatic tableaux, representing incidents from the first third of the book: although the period trappings are all there, there's no attempt to 'involve' the audience by creating a 'plausible' historical reality. Instead, the visual tableaux and long speeches set out to present de Sade's book in a form that modern viewers can broach and try to come to terms with. No one could pretend that it's a complete success, but its challenge is real. RG

Justine de Sade
see Violation of Justine, The

Just Like a Woman
(Christopher Monger, 1992, GB) Julie Walters, Adrian Pasdar, Paul Freeman, Susan Wooldridge, Gordon Kennedy, Ian Redford.
106 min.
Monica (Walters) has her life turned a-tizz by the arrival of dashing city-slicker lodger Gerald (Pasdar), whose hunky eligibility only seems enhanced by fastidiously plucked eyebrows. For Gerald is happier as Geraldine; and Monica, too, soon discovers she prefers it that way. Tailored to the transatlantic *Shirley Valentine* market, the film soft-pedals shamelessly. Any sense of challenge is defused by the accent on the naughty-but-normal, and by a time-wasting 'Wall Street' subplot that allows Freeman to breeze through as a boardroom nasty, while Pasdar rides to the rescue in an embarrassing reprise of Dustin Hoffman's *Tootsie* turn. Pasdar's performance, and his suits, are straight out of a Burton's window. Walters busks it on her dependable big bright smile. And Monger stitches it all together into a slickly pedestrian TV *(sic)* movie. JRo

Just Like Weather
(Meiguo Xin)
(Allen Fong, 1986, HK) Christine Lee, Lee Chi-keung, Allen Fong, Cheng Chi-hung, Yung Man-ching.
98 min. b/w.
An object lesson in finding hidden depths in everyday material. A young Hong Kong couple are on the verge of separating, although a trip to New York might save their marriage. Fong himself interviews them about their problems, then spins them off into fictional episodes (an abortion, an arrest, an interlude with a randy vet whose chat-up line is the mating habits of dogs), and finally whisks them off to the States, where they get stuck in a New Mexican snowdrift. Underlying it all are very candid worries about the future of Hong Kong after 1997. TR

Just the Way You Are
(Edouard Molinaro, 1984, US) Kristy McNichol, Michael Ontkean, Kaki Hunter, André Dussollier, Catherine Salviat, Robert Carradine.
94 min.
Childhood polio has left musician Kristy McNichol feeling as if life hasn't treated her right, so she heads for a ski resort in the French Alps, puts her leg in a cast, and waits to see what people – particularly men – make of her now. This comedy-drama-romance, from the director of *La Cage aux Folles*, never quite hangs together and threatens to get rather spongy, but McNichol's appealing performance holds the interest throughout. TJ

Just Us
(Gordon Glen, 1986, Aust) Scott Burgess, Catherine McClements, Merfyn Owen, Gina Riley, Jay Mannering, Kim Gyngell, Marie Redshaw
95 min.
Another of those 'How I became good friends with a convict and discovered he wasn't such a bad type after all' sagas, this time based on a book by crusading Australian journalist Gabrielle Carey (played somewhat sanctimoniously by McClements). Burgess is the prisoner. Earnest, numbing fare with none of the bite of *In Cold Blood*. GM

Juvenile Court
(Frederick Wiseman, 1973, US)
144 min. b/w.
A distillation of over sixty hours of footage taken during a month in Memphis. The material that is kept is obviously that which most clearly reveals the layers of assumption and prejudice that form the basis of the entire court process, but also that which contains the most tension, irony, pathos and drama of one kind or another. All Wiseman's work has this sort of ambiguity, of apparent objectivity and latent distortion. Despite this, his films are more intelligent documentaries than you'd ever expect from the likes of the Beeb, demonstrating how much a film-maker actually robs his audience when he wants to seduce more than inform. Generally Wiseman informs. JDuC

Juvenile Liaison
(Nicholas Broomfield/Joan Churchill, 1975, GB)
97 min.
A devastating exposé of the now notorious police scheme to cope with potential young (from 7 years old) offenders. The film is a deliberately modest effort (it follows the work of one Lancashire juvenile liaison division over a seven-week period, is shot in available light, and made without TV-style window-dressing), yet it is hard to think of another British film that has so succinctly revealed the day-to-day mechanics whereby class and paternalistic authority are sustained. The collusion of the educational establishments is perhaps the hardest thing of all to take. VG

Juvenile Liaison 2
(Nick Broomfield/Joan Churchill, 1990, GB) narration: Nick Broomfield.
85 min.
Documentary film-maker Broomfield has a knack of catching life in the raw, and it's not always a pretty sight. Hence, *Juvenile Liaison* was banned fifteen years ago for undermining the image of the friendly bobby. Blackburn is the setting and some pre-teen kids are the subjects. Seven-year-old Glen, accused of stealing a cowboy suit, quakes with fear before a bullying, burly sergeant, and one little girl is given the third degree over a missing apple. The 'seen and not heard' axiom is brought disturbingly to life. This updated version includes footage shot in Blackburn in 1989 in which the original 'juveniles' are traced to discover what scars their 'liaisons' with authority may have left. Depressingly, the grown-up kids have inherited the same misguided attitudes towards children. Bristling with characteristic Broomfield tension, the film's interest goes beyond its content. Compare the anguish of the original footage with the latent irony of the additional scenes. Broomfield has picked up a black sense of humour along the way. EP

J.W. Coop
(Cliff Robertson, 1971, US) Cliff Robertson, Geraldine Page, Cristina Ferrare, RG Armstrong, RL Armstrong, John Crawford, Wade Crosby.
112 min.
Cliff Robertson's debut as director emerges as very flawed but sufficiently interesting to deserve escape from total neglect. The film's benefits are pretty much on the fringe, all the more so because it treads ground already covered by *Junior Bonner*. It's a pity, then, that the film gets hung up on its own narrative development, with Coop's efforts to win the rodeo championship (too lazy to work, too scared to steal) and his relationship (embarrassing) with a hippie girl, because Robertson's at his best with the peripheries. This comes over strongest in the first half-hour, with Coop trying to pick up the threads after ten years in prison, only to find that there aren't any. Above all he makes you understand what it's like to have been away for that long through observing his own reactions: talking to a man about his brother who has made it big; watching a couple of women going bowling; sitting drinking; realising that everything's different but that nothing much has changed. The decaying small towns have a feel that Bogdanovich, for all his painstaking efforts, never realised in *The Last Picture Show*. CPe

k

Key Largo

Kabloonak

(Claude Massot, 1994, Fr/Can) Charles Dance,
Adamie Quasiak Inukpuk, George Clisse,
Tony Vogel.
103 min.
Robert Flaherty – the 'father' of the documentary,
who died in 1951 – sits in a New York bar in 1922
like he's just been treasure hunting in the Sierra
Madre. The well-received premiere of *Nanook of
the North* has just prompted Paramount Pictures
to offer him money for another movie. Flashback
to 1919: in Port Harrison, Hudson Bay, on a snow-
stiffened whaler, Flaherty embarks on his three-
month trip to film the Eskimo way of life, under
circumstances that would have daunted even
Scott of the Antarctic. Dance makes Flaherty a
fine taciturn hero, and Jacques Loiseieux's (presumably brave) cinematography makes the film
a visual feast. Director Massot skirts the contentious issue of exactly what kind of documentary Flaherty was making (faked igloos,
stage-managed sexual manners, etc) by concentrating on the man at work – and fascinating
work it is. WH

Kafka

(Steven Soderbergh, 1991, US/Fr) Jeremy Irons,
Theresa Russell, Joel Grey, Ian Holm, Jeroen
Krabbé, Armin Mueller-Stahl, Alec Guinness.
98 min. b/w & col.
Post-WWI Prague. After the disappearance of a
colleague, Kafka (Irons), an aspiring writer and
toiling clerk, is torn between a diffident policeman (Mueller-Stahl) and an angry revolutionary
(Russell). Slowly but inexorably he's drawn into
the deadly political machinations of the times,
and an experiment in social engineering more
nightmarish than even his own imaginings. At
night, leprous, lobotomised creatures skulk in
the shadows, while anarchists conspire and the
authorities despatch body-snatchers from the
castle high above the cobbled gas-lit city streets.
Shot in inky b/w Soderbergh's follow-up to *sex,
lies and videotape* took a hammering from the
US critics. It is, however, an intriguing, idiosyncratic and often highly entertaining movie –
a biopic which conflates elements of the author's
life and writings into a fiction much bigger than
life. It takes a sluggish half hour to take shape,
and even then the absurdist comedy seems misjudged, but it's more playful than pretentious,
and it works as a genuinely eye-catching mystery thriller. TCh

Kagemusha

(Akira Kurosawa, 1980, Jap) Tatsuya Nakadai,
Tsutomu Yamazaki, Kenichi Hagiwara,
Daisuke Ryu, Masayuki Yui, Toshihiko
Shimizu.
162 min.
Though acclaimed as a magnificent return to
form, Kurosawa's first Japanese film since
Dodes'ka-den' is something of a disappointment. The basic story, clearly Shakespearean
in inspiration, is fine enough: a disreputable
thief is spared execution due to his physical
resemblance to the lord of a warring clan, in
order that the enemy might not learn of the
lord's death in battle. Ample scope, then, for the
depiction of deceitful intrigues in court, not to
mention the occasionally touching attempts of
the double to acquire the noble demeanour of
the clan chief. But for all Kurosawa's splendidly colourful recreation of 16th century Japan,
and though Nakadai's performance is impressive enough, it's all ultimately rather empty and
tedious; it could easily have been cut by almost
an hour, while the grating Morricone-like score
only serves to underline the fact that the director fails to achieve the emotional force of his
finest work. GA

Kagero-za

(Seijun Suzuki, 1981, Jap) Yusaku Matsuda,
Michiyo Ogusu, Katsuo Nakamura, Eriko
Kusuda.
129 min.
The title translates literally as 'Heat-haze
Theatre', which is a fair enough description of
these two hours of hallucinatory goings-on, in
which four increasingly abstracted men and
women wander through a series of riddles about
their identities, marital status, motives, and
indeed their very existence. Veteran director
Suzuki was idolised by Japanese students for his
outré gangster movies during the '60s. TR

Kalamazoo

(Claudia Silver, 1994, US) Adrienne Shelley,
Wally Shawn.
29 min.
Struggling actress Shelley may believe her
WASP lover broke with her due to her mom's
anti-semitism, but Jewishness hardly impinges
on this sentimental comedy about a girl's long-
term obsession with her ex. True, there are nice
scenes with shrink Wally Shawn, but this is just
as much a film about love and life on the fringes
of the New York art scene as it is about cultural
identity. Slight, light, sturdily performed, and not
without charm. GA

Kaleidoscope

(Jack Smight, 1966, GB) Warren Beatty,
Susannah York, Clive Revill, Eric Porter,
Murray Melvin, George Sewell, John Junkin,
Yootha Joyce, Jane Birkin.
103 min.
Its tricksy flashiness conjured by its title, this
Swinging London caper features Beatty as a playboy gambler (who's contrived to mark the printing plates at a playing-card factory) being
manipulated into collaring a dope smuggler for
the Yard. Down the credit list, Jane Birkin features as an 'exquisite thing': just about par for the
course from Hollywood-on-Thames. PT

Kalifornia

(Dominic Sena, 1993, US) Brad Pitt, Juliette
Lewis, David Duchovny, Michelle Forbes,
Sierra Pecheur, Gregory Mars Martin.
118 min.
Erotic photographer Carrie (Forbes) and her lover
Brian (Duchovny), a writer researching serial
murders, are not so complacent about their lives
that they don't feel the need to quit their
Pittsburgh pad, head for California and start
afresh. But their self-conscious liberalism is shak-
en when they meet the couple they've agreed to
car-share with: Early (Pitt) and Adele (Lewis),
poor white trash with few pretensions, minimal
manners and even less in the way off intellectual ability. Worse, Early is a psychopath, and even
Brian's initial voyeuristic fascination turns to fear
and revulsion when the blood starts flowing.
Many of the images from this road-thriller look
as if they're from a pop promo. More damagingly, Lewis's implausibly gullible Adele suggests
that as an actress, she's limited to a handful of
coy mannerisms. The plot is schematic, too,
loaded with stark polarities, blunt ironies and repetition. That said, however, the film is oddly
watchable. Yes, this is opportunistic, shallow and
over-extended – but somewhere behind all the
faddishness, there's a taut, pleasingly nasty B-
thriller trying to get out. GA

Kama Sutra: A Tale of Love

(Mira Nair, 1996, Ind/GB/Jap/Ger) Naveen
Andrews, Sarita Choudhury, Ramon Tikaram,
Rekha, Indira Varma.
114 min.
In 16th century India, two virgins – Princess Tara
(Choudhury) and servant girl Maya (Varma) –
play at being friends. They're destined to grow
apart, but sex, as taught by the Kama Sutra, soon
has them inextricably entwined. Tara and Maya
appear equally spoilt and pouty; meanwhile, the
objects of their affection, lecherous Raj Singh
(Andrews) and brooding sculptor Jai (Tikaram),
defy belief. Raj is the sort of man who flares his
nostrils when aroused, while Jai is prone to such
insights as, 'My work has a power even I can't
explain.' The film is visually delicious (peacock
colours nestling in a dusty postcard haze), but
that it comes from Mira Nair, director of the heart-
pummelling *Salaam Bombay!*, is dispiriting. If
there's an underlying message, it's conservative.
Even before her lessons in the art of love, Maya
is instinctively more sensuous than Tara – low
class babes, you see, have natural rhythm. And
what's behind the deluge of sex tips? Be imaginative in bed, girls, or the man in your life will
stray. Ye gods! It's like being stuck in a lift with
Jane Seymour: slave-girl chic turned nauseatingly fragrant. CO'Su

Kameradschaft

(GW Pabst, 1931, Ger/Fr) Fritz Kampers,
Alexander Granach, Ernst Busch, Gustav
Püttjer, Daniel Mandaille, Georges Charlia,
Pierre Louis.
93 min. b/w.

The absolute high-point of German socialist film-
making of its period. Pabst imagines a coal-mine
on the French-German border, where the aftermath of World War I is still being played out:
French prosperity and chauvinism hard up
against German inflation and unemployment.
There's a disaster in the French wing of the
mine...and the German miners go to the rescue.
Both the visual style and the 'message' of solidarity owe a lot to Soviet Socialist Realism, but
Pabst was a more sophisticated social critic than
any of the Russian film-makers. Only a bruised
and cynical Berlin pessimist could produce a film
as moving, sincere and committed as this. TR

Kamikaze

(Didier Grousset, 1986, Fr) Richard Bohringer,
Michel Galabru, Dominique Lavanant, Riton
Leibman, Kim Massee, Harry Cleven, Romane
Bohringer.
89 min.
When brilliant but batty boffin Galabru is fired
from his lab job, he retreats into a private world.
Incensed by the banal idiocy of the TV he endlessly watches, he invents a gizmo which can kill
the presenters, who both fascinate and repel him.
The death ray is so ingenious that no one can
fathom how the murderer operates, and investigating detective Bohringer comes into bitter conflict with the Ministry of Communications. As
co-scripted and produced by Luc Besson (who
passed it to his former assistant to direct),
Kamikaze is an ambitious if somewhat slim satire
on a society enthralled by the bland output of the
box; not only Galabru's savagely demented performance, but the sharp, sumptuous, and very
mobile widescreen photography, constitute a contemptuous attack on a medium which anybody
in their right mind will already know is inferior
to cinema. Not exactly substantial, but stylish
fun. GA

Kamikaze Hearts

(Juliet Bashore, 1986, US) Sharon Mitchell,
Tigr Mennett, Jon Martin, Sparky Vasque,
Jerry Abrahms, Robert McKenna, Jennifer
Blowdryer.
77 min.
Bashore's gritty, grimy film about the porn industry and the status of women within it continually throws the audience up against problems of
interpretation: sometimes the camera is a coolly
discriminating, independent viewpoint, sometimes a goggling, peeping eye. The peg the film
hangs on is the relationship between lithe, gorgeous porn star Sharon Mitchell and doggedly
devoted Tigr, her lover and director; the viewer's
sympathy switches nervously back and forth
between the two women. Mitch is a shameless
camera-hog, rabbiting on about joy and fulfilment through porn; Tigr is superficially less
flaky, but collapses dramatically in the harrowing last scene. There are moments of humour, and
the glimpses of the porn movie set enthral; but
the film belongs to the frighteningly blank Mitch,
who has clearly been turned inside out and torn
in the process. A tough cookie who's also a figure of supreme availability, she embodies the contradictions explored in the film. SFe

Kamikaze Taxi

(Masato Harada, 1995, Jap) Kohji Yakusho,
Kazuya Takahashi, Reiko Kataoka, Kenichi
Yajima, Mickey Curtis.
169 min.
One of the discoveries of the 1995 London Film
Festival (and let's face it, a 169-minute first film
from a Japanese director is unlikely to get a proper theatrical release in Britain). This is a young,
angry, combative movie about those endemical-
ly racist, sexist, and corrupt institutions, the
yakuza and the government. Disillusioned by the
brutal murder of his girlfriend, Tatsuo (Yakusho)
turns against the mob to rip off a wealthy minister, but the heist goes wrong, and Tatsuo finds
himself on the run – his days numbered – with
only a Peruvian-Japanese taxi-driver and a young
hooker to help him. A freewheeling original. TCh

Kanal

(Andrzej Wajda, 1956, Pol) Wienczyslaw
Glinski, Tadeusz Janczar, Teresa Izewska,
Emil Karewicz, Vladek Sheybal.
95 min. b/w.
The setting for the second film in Wajda's trilo-
gy about WWII (coming between *A Generation*

and *Ashes and Diamonds*) is the sewers of Warsaw, through which a group of partisans attempt to make their escape from the Nazis during the 1944 Uprising. This was the film that made Wajda's name in the West, and it certainly has a unique intensity and gloom, with most of the characters enduring appalling fates: two lovers reach an exit to find it sealed off with a grill, another man surfaces right into German hands. Nevertheless, scenes such as the musician playing Chopin amid the ruins have a peculiar poetry that speaks of an experience that demands to be reinvented. DT

Kanchenjungha

(Satyajit Ray, 1962, Ind) Chabi Biswas, Pahari Sanyal, Anil Chatterjee, Karuna Banerjee, Aloknanda Ray, Subrata Sen.
102 min.
Set in the beautiful hill station of Darjeeling – a point suspended in time between modern India and the past – Ray's first colour film would have delighted Henry James with its sense of the past and concern for the future. While on holiday with his downtrodden family, whose lives he has unconsciously ruined by benevolently but firmly bending them to his will, an ageing industrial tycoon finds his values shattered by a chance meeting with a young man who refuses to be ruled. As the characters converse on the circling terraces of Observatory Hill in a strictly formalised pattern of walks whose musical structure is underlined by recurring images (the paths crossed and recrossed in different circumstances; a little girl eternally circling on her pony), the themes begin to harmonise contrapuntally and subtly shape all these lives into new configurations. And over it all broods Kanchenjungha, a majestic, inscrutable éminence rose... TM

Kanehsatake (Oka) – 270 Years of Resistance

(Alanis Obomsawin, 1990, Can)
120 min.
In this passionate, affecting documentary, Alanis Obomsawin – a member of the Abenaki tribe – describes the 11-week battle fought by the Mohawks of Montreal during 1990 to stop one of their sacred burial grounds being developed into a golf course. It was a war of wills with no winners. The Mohawk 'warriors' (in army dress and with movie names like 'Psycho' and 'Freddy Krueger') and women (with real names and with their children) set up barricades, blocked off the nearby Messier bridge, and made a peace camp. They were prepared to die. Facing them were the regional police – the 'SQ' – and the Canadian Army, who weren't. An army corporal *was* killed, however, which rocketed the confrontation from local to national news. This fascinating, condemnatory document, including a historical section and interviews with politicians, captures much of the Mohawk (and native Indian) identity and struggle. It also makes clear why Canada is in the process of breaking up. WH

Kangaroo

(Lewis Milestone, 1952, US) Maureen O'Hara, Peter Lawford, Richard Boone, Finlay Currie, Chips Rafferty.
84 min.
A highly unlikely Australian Western, substituting Aborigines for Indians. Lawford and Boone plot to outwit a wealthy ranch-owner (Currie), but Lawford screws things up by falling in love with his daughter (O'Hara). Routine in all departments, it's one long yawn. DP

Kangaroo

(Tim Burstall, 1986, Aust) Colin Friels, Judy Davis, John Walton, Julie Nihill, Hugh Keays-Byrne, Peter Hehir.
110 min.
Novelist Richard Somers (Friels) and his wife (Davis) abandon the emotional and cerebral sterility of Europe in the early '20s for a new life in Australia. The couple are quickly befriended by their neighbours in Sydney; and at first captivated by the Australian couple's openness and hospitality, Somers soon come to suspect something lurking beneath the sugary surface. This adaptation of DH Lawrence's autobiographical novel (which he called his 'thought-adventure') faithfully re-examines the issue of authority as it exists on the personal and political level. Somers

finds a fresh surface in his new world, but remains contemptuous of the colonial; caught between the conflicting attractions of the all-embracing love of 'Kangaroo' (leader of a para-military movement) and the fraternity of the trade unionists, he must simultaneously resolve the ambiguity of his relationship with his wife. Burstall's characters are well defined, his exotic settings beautifully photographed (in contrast with the grim depiction of England), yet the film as a whole seems encumbered with a forced vitality. The literary origins almost inevitably serve to constrict the action rather than offer a point of departure. SGo

Kansas

(David Stevens, 1988, US) Matt Dillon, Andrew McCarthy, Leslie Hope, Alan Toy, Andy Romano, Brent Jennings.
113 min.
An uneven blend of crime thriller and rural romance, this aims for an adult complexity but misses the target by a mile. En route from LA to New York, directionless middle class kid McCarthy meets the slightly older Dillon, an insistently friendly drifter returning to his Kansas home town, and unwittingly gets caught up in an armed bank robbery. Forced to split up as they make a run for it, Dillon draws the heat and McCarthy hides the dough under a bridge. While McCarthy finds refuge on a ranch, and falls for the wealthy owner's daughter, Dillon goes on a crime spree, makes the wanted list, and subsequently turns up to demand his share of the loot...Though more morally ambivalent than the Depression era scripts it echoes, Stevens' film never follows through. McCarthy's character is distinctly unsympathetic – disloyal, opportunist, and shallow – but as Dillon becomes increasingly unhinged, the blame is clearly shifted in his direction. Like the eponymous state, this has corn for as far as the eye can see. NF

Kansas City

(Robert Altman, 1996, US) Jennifer Jason Leigh, Dermot Mulroney, Miranda Richardson, Harry Belafonte, Steve Buscemi, Brooke Smith, Michael Murphy, Jeff Feringa, Ajia Mingnon Johnson, Albert J Burnes, AC Smith.
115 min.
It's 1934, and Kansas City – the wide-open capital of jazz, gambling and crime run by 'Boss' Tom Pendergast – is hotting up, not only for the local elections, but for a 'cutting contest' between top tenors Lester Young and Coleman Hawkins. But the only thing that concerns 'Blondie' O'Hara (Leigh), apart from wanting to be like her idol Jean Harlow, is how to get back her beloved Johnny (Mulroney), a petty thief held by gang-boss and night-club owner Seldom Seen (Belafonte) after a heist gone wrong. In kidnapping laudanum-addict Carolyn Stilton (Richardson), the wife of a bigwig adviser to Roosevelt, O'Hara hopes to force an exchange. Notwithstanding a slim central narrative thread (the shifts in the relationship between O'Hara and Stilton) and a mannered performance from Leigh, Altman's film mostly succeeds as a rich tapestry of characters, subplots, themes and events. Though the structure may seem loose (the film repeatedly abandons the plotline proper for scenes of the blowing jazzers at the Hey-Hey Club), it's actually subtle and tight, with a strange, adventurous arrangement of flashbacks, and unexpected links gradually and cleverly revealed between seemingly unconnected characters. Of the many fine performances, Belafonte, Richardson and the ever dependable Brooke Smith (as Blondie's sister) are probably the standouts, while the music (from the likes of Joshua Redman, Craig Handy, James Carter, David Murray, Geri Allen and Ron Carter) is simply a blast. GA

Kansas City Bomber

(Jerrold Freedman, 1972, US) Raquel Welch, Kevin McCarthy, Helena Kallianiotes, Norman Alden, Jeanne Cooper.
99 min.
Raquel Welch is a mother-of-two neglecting her kids to get a piece of the action on the roller-derby circuit, and soon agonising over fame versus family. The derby sequences are shot with an unbelievably heavy hand – could anyone really make them this dull? The script is unspeakable. Forget it.

Kaos

(Paolo Taviani/Vittorio Taviani, 1984, It) Margarita Lozano, Omero Antonutti, Claudio Bigagli, Biagio Barone, Enrica Maria Modugno, Ciccio Ingrassia, Regina Bianchi.
187 min.
A bandit plays bowls with the head of an old woman's husband, a peasant turns werewolf, a hunchback gets trapped in an outsized olive jar, a tyrant denies tenants the right to bury their dead, and Pirandello shares his sorrows with his mother's ghosts. The common link between the stories, adapted from Pirandello, is the vast, empty Sicilian landscape harbouring a richness of dramatic tales at once emotional and elemental. This is a film of fierce sunlight, bleached rocks, dark interiors, silent stares, and dialogue as rough and sparse as the land. In the years since the Tavianis' *Padre Padrone*, naturalism has given ground to a more grotesque vision of the past, allowing black comedy to creep into the always subtle socio-historical subject matter. Exhilarating. MA

Kapo

(Gillo Pontecorvo, 1960, It/Fr) Susan Strasberg, Laurent Terzieff, Emmanuelle Riva, Didi Perego, Gianni Garko.
115 min. b/w.
Susan Strasberg is the Parisian Jewish teenager who's orphaned by the Nazis and, in order to save herself, becomes in time the heartless 'Kapo' of a Polish concentration camp. The Red Army advances and an escape is effected during which the Kapo (who has by this time fallen in love with Russian inmate Terzieff) redeems herself through self-sacrifice. Pontecorvo, a former commander in the wartime Italian resistance, who co-scripted this luridly realistic film with Franco Solinas, strives to say something about the nature of survival in the pit of degradation, but becomes mired in an overloaded plot peopled by stereotypes and filled out with signposted moral questions. Five years later, having made his mistakes here, the director executed his flawless, harrowing masterpiece, *The Battle of Algiers*. JPy

Karakter (Character)

(Mike Van Diem, 1997, Neth) Jan Decleir, Fedja van Huêt, Betty Schuurman, Victor Löw.
120 min.
Adapted from a classic novel by Ferdinand Bordewijk, this sombre, handsome costume pic set in turn of the century Rotterdam is distinguished by Jan Decleir's superb character turn as the villainous bailiff, Dreverhaven, who thinks nothing of evicting the poor, the elderly and the infirm from their homes. He's a forbidding figure with a touch of the Old Testament prophet. He seems determined to destroy his illegitimate son, a self-taught lawyer who likewise hates him. At times, the naturalistic detail is cluttering and leaves the film looking like a museum piece, but as oedipal drama, this is dark and often strangely powerful. (Winner of the 1998 foreign language Oscar.) GM

Karate Kid, The

(John G Avildsen, 1984, US) Ralph Macchio, Noriyuki 'Pat' Morita, Elisabeth Shue, Martin Kove, Randee Heller, William Zabka.
127 min.
A surprise summer hit in the States, this is another film-making-by-numbers exercise in teenage wish-fulfilment. A Jewish divorcee moves to California from New Jersey, and her son, a male Carrie called Daniel, has terrible trouble fitting in with West Coast ways. His first incipient romance runs foul of the girl's ex, a blond thug who trains at the local karate dojo run by a deranged Vietnam veteran. Fortunately his E.T. comes along in the form of an elderly Okinawan karate master, who not only becomes his special, secret friend but also handily teaches him persistence, inner strength, moral values and karate – which lead him into an apotheosis worthy of *Rocky*. This is actually director Avildsen's first hit since *Rocky*, and it has the same mixture of calculation and apparent naïveté. It borrows its formula from both East and West with good humour, and is completely free of intelligence, discrimination and originality. No wonder it was a hit. TR

Karate Kid: Part II, The

(John G Avildsen, 1986, US) Ralph Macchio, Noriyuki 'Pat' Morita, Nobu McCarthy, Danny Kamekona, Yuji Okumoto, Tamlyn Tomita, Charlie Tanimoto.
113 min.
This sequel retains the strengths of its predecessor, the gawky charm of Ralph Macchio (is he really 24?) as the cute boy-next-door turned hero, and Noriyuki 'Pat' Morita as his ever-smart, ever-wisecracking oriental mentor Miyagi. This time the action switches to Okinawa as Miyagi (with boy-next-door tagging along) returns to straighten out his dying father's estate, but also has to face up to a matter of honour that he had left unfinished. The plotline is classic Western morality-play stuff, with the goodies and baddies clearly delineated, but the set pieces are well constructed, and the whole thing is beautifully staged and shot. DPe

Karate Kid Part III, The

(John G Avildsen, 1989, US) Ralph Macchio, Noriyuki 'Pat' Morita, Robyn Lively, Thomas Ian Griffith, Martin L Kove, Sean Kanan, Jonathan Avildsen.
112 min.
Via a quick flashback, we review the Kid's triumph in the championships and his mentor Mr Miyagi's triumph over rival trainer Kreese in a car-park bust-up. Now, a year later, the title's up for grabs, but Daniel (Macchio) doesn't want to defend it – it's not important any more. Kreese wants to force him to fight Mike Barnes (Kanan), who has been trained to fight dirty; and a delightful villain, ruthless millionaire Silver (a stunning debut from Griffith) vows to help him humiliate the Kid and discredit the Master and the Way. Daniel accepts the challenge, but Mr Miyagi won't train him, and suddenly he's in deep trouble. After suffering endless abuse, Daniel wins with just a few well placed whacks: those expecting standard wish-fulfilment fantasy will be disappointed that (in tune with the philosophy, of course) he didn't give the punk a pasting. SFe

Karate Killers, The

(Barry Shear, 1967, US) Robert Vaughn, David McCallum, Curd Jürgens, Joan Crawford, Herbert Lom, Telly Savalas, Terry-Thomas, Kim Darby, Diane McBain, Jill Ireland.
92 min.
A damp *Man from UNCLE* squib, directed with pace, and hopefully throwing in a string of star cameos plus some slapstick knockabout, but still refusing to ignite. It's the one in which the redoubtable duo of Solo and Kuryakin chase clues to a secret process (extracting gold from sea-water) entrusted to the dead inventor's four daughters. TM

Karate King – On the Waterfront

see Kung Fu – Girl Fighter

Karl May

(Hans-Jürgen Syberberg, 1974, WGer) Helmut Käutner, Kristina Söderbaum, Käthe Gold, Attila Hörbiger, Willy Trenk-Trebitsch, Heinz Moog, Lil Dagover.
180 min.
The second film in Syberberg's trilogy forming, along with *Ludwig – Requiem for a Virgin King* and *Hitler, a Film from Germany*, a unique analysis of the dominant forces in German history and culture. Like a German Rider Haggard, May was an 'imperialist' novelist with a strong romantic idealism (best remembered now for his American 'noble savage' character, Winnetou), and part of Syberberg's aim is to celebrate the fragile beauty of his fantasies. But the film is structured as a kind of biography, and the long central scene of a courtroom battle marks the collapse of May's dreams as he gets more and more deeply embroiled in the realities of Prussian jurisprudence. The matter-of-fact historical framework acquires an added resonance from the fact that all the main parts are played by prominent figures from the Nazi cinema of the '30s. The mesh of fact, fiction, realism and expressionism is complex and fascinating. And the film's 'plastic' qualities are at least as sumptuous as those in *Ludwig*. TR

Kaseki

(Masaki Kobayashi, 1974, Jap) Shin Saburi, Keiko Kishi, Hisashi Igawa, Kei Yamamoto, Orié Sato, Komaki Kurihara.
209 min.
The film reveals its entire plot in its opening moments: Itsuki, widower and successful businessman, will learn in Europe that he has cancer, and reappraise his dealings with family, colleagues and friends. Dropping the element of narrative 'surprise' works as a bold distancing device, the last thing you'd expect from the director of *Kwaidan* and *Rebellion;* it enables him to view Itsuki with a kind of engaged dispassion, and to make clear-eyed points about Japanese social conventions and ethics without troubling to keep a melodrama on the boil. Despite stretches that betray its origin in a TV serial (of twice the length), the result is exceptionally innovative for a Japanese film-maker of the older generation. The web of documentary, fiction and fantasy coalesces into a commitment to change that's emotionally tough, and never for a second sentimental. TR

Kashima Paradise

(Yann Le Masson/Benie Deswarte, 1973, Fr)
110 min. b/w.
A documentary, with commentary by Chris Marker (spoken by John Atherton in the English version), which focuses on Kashima Paradise, an industrial complex some sixty miles from Tokyo. It examines the effect of total change in Japan, and the transition in one part-village from an almost medieval way of life to advanced industrial practice all within the space of a year. Japan is probably the country most susceptible to this type of rapid change at the moment, but it's something that's happening to us all.

Kaspar Hauser (Verbrechen am Seelenleben eines Menschens)

(Peter Sehr, 1993, Ger) André Eisermann, Udo Samel, Jeremy Clyde, Katharina Thalbach, Cécile Paoli, Hansa Czypionka, Hermann Beyer, Dieter Mann.
139 min.
Karlsruhe, 1812. Shortly after his birth, Kaspar, son of Crown Prince Karl of Baden, is exchanged with an ailing baby by Karl's philandering brother Ludwig, who has ambitions for the throne. The child is deposited with a nurse, but when Ludwig becomes Grand Duke and manifests hostility to Bavaria, with which Baden is in dispute, the boy is sold to a Bavarian minister, who has him hidden away for 12 years in a cellar. In 1828, Kaspar (Eisermann) is released in Nuremberg, unable to talk, walk or fend for himself; he's taken under the wing of kindly Prof Daumer (Samel), whose efforts to educate and protect the youth fail to take account of the fact that his charge is political dynamite. Whereas Herzog's *The Enigma of Kaspar Hauser* (1974) was a sorrowing, darkly comic meditation on the pitfalls of 'civilisation' and the way education destroys man's essential innocence, Sehr's Kaspar is simply a disposable pawn in Machiavellian power games between and within German states. So complex are these strategies, and so difficult is it to keep up with the narrative, that it's hard to care very much about Kaspar. A polished drama, but not much more than a rather arcane, even academic conspiracy hypothesis. GA

Katia Ismaïlova (Podmoskovnye vechera)

(Valerii Todorovsky, 1994, Rus/Fr) Vladimir Mashkov, Ingeborga Dapkounaite, Aleksandr Feklistov, Alisa Freindlikh, Natalia Shchukina.
95 min.
Adapted from Leskov's 1864 novella, this is a blend of idyll and murderous *film noir*. Set in present-day Russia, it centres on Katia (Dapkounaite), a mousy housewife reluctantly typing up the latest novel by her famous mother-in-law Irina. During a visit to the family's country house, Katia's husband Mitia abandons the women to go on a business trip, leaving his wife prey to Sergei (Mashkov), a carpenter who's been restoring the house for Irina. The affair is discovered by the tyrannical author, who insists it cease. Katia, however, has other ideas. Traditionally an icon of unbridled passion, Katia is here a muted, impassive heroine. While her later actions betoken a deep-felt desire to transform her life, her resentment against mother-in-law and husband and her longing for Sergei is barely voiced – less a consequence of Dapkounaite's sturdy performance than of the script, which vacillates between subtle allusion, unembroidered simplicity and enigmatic ellipsis. The director appears to be saying that the heated emotions of the literary classics no longer suit the modern world (or cinema) – despite plot twists that echo moments from such steamy adulterous suspensers as *The Postman Always Rings Twice* and even *Blood Simple*. Very different from most Russian movies released in Britain, this is elegant, intelligent and intriguing, even if the cool tone and languorous pace forestall deeper involvement. GA

Katinka (Ved Vejen)

(Max von Sydow, 1988, Den/Swe) Tammi Ost, Ole Ernst, Kurt Ravn, Ghita Norby.
96 min.
Von Sydow's directorial debut, an adaptation of a Herman Bang story, is as unfashionably reserved in its portrait of a woman stifled by a loveless marriage as Dreyer's *Gertrud*. Nothing happens in this triangle between Katinka (Ost), her insensitive station-master husband (Ernst), and the romantic newcomer (Ravn), but the depths of feeling are subtly pastelled in. Sven Nykvist's camera of feeling conjures up an idyllic turn-of-the-century small town atmosphere for the heroine to dream her life away in. Pressed flowers. BC

Katok i Skrypka (Roller and Violin/The Steamroller and the Violin)

(Andrei Tarkovsky, 1961, USSR) Igor Fomchenko, V Zamansky, N Arkhangelskaya, Marina Adzhuberi.
46 min.
Tarkovsky's graduation project at the VGIK film school in Moscow offers a key to all the later 'mature' work: it's his clearest statement of frustrated longing for a perfect union with an idealised father-figure. Six-year-old Sasha (Fomchenko) lives with his domineering, unsympathetic mother (Adzhuberi), and studies the violin under an even more domineering and even less sympathetic female music teacher. His idealised father-figure is Sergei (Zamansky), a butch-but-sensitive road-mender, who saves him from being bullied, gives him bread, milk and lessons in self-confidence and respect, and promises to take him to the movies – to see *Chapayev*, the venerable romantic portrait of a Communist hero. The 'romance' between man and boy receives the benediction of a prototypical Tarkovskian rainstorm, incidentally yielding a charming cine-poem about drops of water and puddles. Some ten years later, Tarkovsky reworked all of this much more elaborately in *Solaris*. TR

Katzelmacher

(Rainer Werner Fassbinder, 1969, WGer) Hanna Schygulla, Lilith Ungerer, Elga Sorbas, Doris Mattes, Rainer Werner Fassbinder, Rudolf Waldemar Brem.
88 min. b/w.
Fear and loathing in the mean streets of suburban Munich, where all behaviour obeys the basest and most basic of drives, and fleeting allegiances form and re-form in almost mathematically abstract permutations until disrupted by the advent of an immigrant Greek worker (played by Fassbinder himself; the title is a Bavarian slang term for a gastarbeiter, implying tomcatting sexual proclivities) who becomes the target for xenophobic violence. Fassbinder's sub-Godardian gangster film début, *Love is Colder than Death*, was dismissed as derivative and dilettanté-ish; this second feature, based on his own *anti-teater* play, won immediate acclaim. It still seems remarkable, mainly for Fassbinder's distinctive, highly stylised dialogue and minimalist *mise-en-scène* that transfigures a cinema of poverty into bleakly triumphant rites of despair. SJo

Kawashima Yoshiko (Chuandao Fangzi/aka The Last Princess of Manchuria)

(Eddie Fong, 1990, HK) Anita Mui, Andy Lau, Patrick Tse, Derek Yee.
111 min.

Writer/director Fong denies that he set out to parody *The Last Emperor*, but his excellent film certainly kicks the shit out of Bertolucci. It gives Anita Mui her best role since *Rouge* as the eponymous bisexual spy who sailed through some 25 years of Sino-Japanese tension and war alternately claiming Chinese and Japanese nationality and (according to Fong) covertly intervening in the politics of both sides. The film mocks all the received pieties about modern Chinese history (even the Nanking Massacre is presented in kitsch terms), subordinating them to the high-camp melodrama of Yoshiko's torrid love affairs. Variant endings exist: the one most often seen has Yoshiko executed by firing squad in 1948, but the best one shows her with her pet monkey on her shoulder in present day Tokyo, ageless and immortal. TR

Kazablan
(Menahem Golan, 1973, Isr) Yehoram Gaon, Arie Elias, Efrat Lavie, Yehudah Efroni, Joseph Graber.
114 min.
An Israeli musical directed by the dreaded Menahem Golan that manages to come off as an uncomfortable cross between *Jesus Christ Superstar*, *Fiddler on the Roof* and *West Side Story*. Probably the most interesting aspect of the film is the acknowledgment it makes of divisions in Israeli society, notably that between the 'white' or European Jews and the 'black' or non-European Jews. The analysis is somewhat blunted by making the outcast gang-leader a forgotten war hero (although it does make a valid point in a sense). The songs sound familiar. The dance routines are dismally repetitive. VG

Keep, The
(Michael Mann, 1983, US) Scott Glenn, Alberta Watson, Jürgen Prochnow, Robert Prosky, Gabriel Byrne, Ian McKellen, Morgan Sheppard.
96 min.
There is a secret buried deep within the walls of the keep, an ancient mystic shrine in the Carpathian Alps of Romania. It is an Evil so long contained that it has since been forgotten. It is an Evil more vile than the World War II German troops who have unwittingly released it, having violated the mausoleum. But there is a Man, a Man who has risen from a forgotten age who can stop the growing demon. First he must sleep with the beautiful Eva Cuza (evil demons take time to reach maturation), which he proceeds to do with infinitely more finesse than the final confrontation with the awakened Evil. Mann's film was first buried in video distribution after it flopped in the US (by that time Mann was already involved in the highly successful television series *Miami Vice*). Resurrected for cinema screening, it proves to be eerie, chilling, at times engaging. But Mann's attempt to superimpose an analysis of the emotional attraction of Fascism simply doesn't work within the Heavy Metal magazine cartoon format. SGo

Keeper, The
(Joe Brewster, 1995, US) Giancarlo Esposito, Isaach de Bankolé, Regina Taylor, Ron Brice, OL Duke, Arthur French.
90 min.
Esposito's a warder at a detention centre, A liberal studying law, he treats the prisoners with respect; his colleagues regard them as scum. When he helps bail out a Haitian baker (de Bankolé) accused of rape, whom he believes innocent, he forgets that the man will have difficulties finding a job or somewhere to live. When the man turns up on his doorstep, the warder persuades his wife (Taylor) to let him stay in their house, with alarming consequences. Fine cast, authentic early scenes, but melodrama eventually swamps the proceedings. GA

Keeper of the Flame
(George Cukor, 1942, US) Spencer Tracy, Katharine Hepburn, Richard Whorf, Margaret Wycherly, Forrest Tucker, Howard da Silva.
100 min. b/w.
Bizarre political melodrama which has its eye firmly glued on *Citizen Kane* as Tracy's reporter arrives at another Xanadu, gleans another mess of information for his biography of a Great American Citizen who has died in mysterious circumstances, and learns – having fallen for the

widow (Hepburn) whose reticence he misinterprets – that his hero had feet of Fascist clay. It works well if rather stiffly for a while, with excellent performances (Wycherly and da Silva are outstanding), but blows up into absurd histrionics and naive propaganda. TM

Keepers, The
see Tête contre les Murs, La

Keep It Up, Jack!
(Derek Ford, 1973, GB) Mark Jones, Sue Longhurst, Maggi Burton, Paul Whitsun-Jones, Frank Thornton, Queenie Watts.
87 min.
Screamingly unfunny farce in which a tenth-rate seaside quick-change artist inherits a brothel, and finds himself for some unfathomable reason acting first the part of the recently expired madam, and then that of her clients. Hence the title gag, such as it is. If you miss it the first time round, there's a chorus of voices off and even a theme song to remind you. What with performers who enunciate like rejects from a RADA elocution course, a script that must have taken all of a weekend to elaborate, a handful of arbitrary flesh shots, and a relentlessly one-note sense of humour (off-key, of course), it is hardly hyperbolic to see *Keep It Up, Jack!* as defining a whole new low in British comedy. VG

Keep the Aspidistra Flying
(Robert Bierman, 1997, GB) Richard E Grant, Helena Bonham Carter, Julian Wadham, Jim Carter, Harriet Walter, Lesley Vicerage, Liz Smith, Barbara Leigh Hunt, Bill Wallis.
101 min.
This adaptation of Orwell's '30s satire on the advertising game is a dull, timid movie, all romantic flurry, tarted-up design and chocolate box London location photography. Grant seems to fit the bill, looks and character-wise, as Gordon Comstock, the frustrated copywriter at New Albion Publicity who jacks it all in for the life of a bohemian writer in the Lambeth slums. There's a period angularity about his face and body, and his mannerisms suggest the requisite vanity and naivety. And Bonham Carter, the smart side of prim in three-quarter-length velvet coats and idiosyncratic millinery, is controlled exasperation itself as the designer who would be his bride. But Bierman, working from an uninspired script by Alan Plater, finds no way to engage with, or make relevant, the satire, and concentrates instead on routine romantic comedy. The project thus emasculated, all that remains is archaic dalliance, coy sex, tea shop chatter and laughable class caricature. Worse, the language remains flat, and – unintentionally or not – it's a reactionary reading. WH

Keiner Liebt Mich (Nobody Loves Me)
(Doris Dörrie, 1995, Ger) Maria Schrader, Pierre Sanoussi-Bliss, Michael von Au, Elisabeth Trissenaar.
104 min.
Yet another German 'comedy' that lives down to the stereotype, this centres on 29-year-old, death-obsessed Fanny Fink (Schrader), who despairs of ever meeting a man; encouraged by a gay African 'psychic' who lives in the same tenement block, she tries to get it on with her new landlord, but things go awry. Dörrie's predictable plotline, derived from the unappealing premise that her heroine's happiness depends on the company of men, relies excessively on supposedly weird and wonderful characters. Actually, it's hard to care about them, especially as it's also hard to believe Schrader – intelligent, pretty, vivacious – would be in this predicament anyway. GA

Këita! The Voice of the Griot (Këita! L'Héritage du Griot)
(Dani Kouyaté, 1994, Fr/Burkina Faso) Sotigui Kouyaté, Hamed Dicko, Abdoulaye Komboudri,Seydou Boro.
94 min.
This charming and extremely direct first feature tells the story of a 13-year-old boy's introduction to the tales and myths of his 'forgotten ancestors', when a village griot (folk teacher) 'on a mission', sets up his hammock in the garden of the boy's middle-class city home. The simplicity with which the director films both the problems that

this precipitates – the boy skips school, partly because the Western view of history seems far less relevant and engrossing than the old man's story – and the flashbacks to the magical past, pays strong dividends. Acted with appealing grace and dignity, the film is finely shot by Robert Millie and has a gentle unobtrusive score by Sotigui Kouyaté. WH

Kelly's Heroes
(Brian G Hutton, 1970, US/Yugo) Clint Eastwood, Telly Savalas, Donald Sutherland, Don Rickles, Carroll O'Connor, Stuart Margolin, Harry Dean Stanton.
145 min.
A truly silly formula World War II adventure film – lots of familiar faces, lots of explosions, and the odd 'meaningful' remark – in which Eastwood's disreputable platoon (and assorted buddies) take a time out of war to rob a bank in occupied France containing 14,000 bars of German gold. Interesting only in so far as it reveals Eastwood's nonchalant attitude to the blockbuster. Unlike Sutherland, who tries desperately to act his way out of Troy Kennedy Martin's laboured script, Eastwood just strolls through the film, along the way creating its few cinematic moments. PH

Kennel Murder Case, The
(Michael Curtiz, 1933, US) William Powell, Mary Astor, Eugene Pallette, Ralph Morgan, Helen Vinson, Jack LaRue, Robert Barrat.
73 min. b/w.
Probably the best of all the Philo Vance mysteries, with Powell as the super-suave private eye investigating a suicide that turns out to be murder. The plot is fairly preposterous, but Powell brings just enough credibility to the task to make the film at once ingenious and entertaining. In all there were a dozen Philo Vance novels, and many more films featuring the character (*The Kennel Murder Case* was remade only seven years later as Calling Philo Vance), but this one is vintage. MA

Kentuckian, The
(Burt Lancaster, 1955, US) Burt Lancaster, Dianne Foster, Diana Lynn, Ronald MacDonald, Walter Matthau, John Carradine, John McIntire, Una Merkel.
104 min.
Lancaster's only film as a director is a slow-moving, lack-lustre Western in which he plays a Kentucky frontiersman who, travelling to Texas with his young son to make a new start, becomes involved with two women and a family feud. Matthau makes an impressively villainous début (though the scene in which he bullwhips the unarmed Lancaster tends to be censor-trimmed), and Carradine is good value as a garrulous doctor; but in general the direction tends to get bogged down in not very interesting characters and relationships while neglecting to deliver the action. TM

Kentucky
(David Butler, 1938, US) Loretta Young, Richard Greene, Karen Morley, Moroni Olsen, Walter Brennan, Douglass Dumbrille.
95 min.
Romeo and Juliet meets the Kentucky Derby in this cheesy tale of hoss-breedin' folk. Sweethearts Greene and Young come from families who've been feuding since the Civil War, but he runs off, assumes a false identity and prepares his beloved's mount for victory in the big race. It's not exactly unpredictable, but Ernest Palmer and Ray Rennahan's colour camerawork displays the possibilities of the then experimental Technicolor process a year before the milestones of *Gone With the Wind* and *The Wizard of Oz*. TJ

Kentucky Fried Movie, The
(John Landis, 1977, US) David Zucker, George Lazenby, Donald Sutherland, Henry Gibson, Jerry Zucker, Evan Kim, Master Bong Soo Han, Bill Bixby, Tony Dow, Boni Enten.
90 min.
A simple case of the media munchies: a post Groove Tube variety pack offering some twenty different send-ups of American movies, TV and commercials. Sticking quite happily to the level of parody, it's full of energy, good nature, and the gross-out humour of fairly obvious targets (the tits and bums of a sexploitation trailer; the fes-

tering stiff of a TV charity appeal for the dead). The central sketch is an excellent spoof of *Enter the Dragon*. Great fun for an undemanding night out. HM

Kermesse Héroique, La (Carnival in Flanders)

(Jacques Feyder, 1935, Fr) Françoise Rosay, Louis Jouvet, Jean Murat, André Alerme, Micheline Cheirel, Lyne Clevers, Alfred Adam. 115 min. b/w.
A minor gem of pre-war French cinema, about a small bourgeois town invaded by Spanish soldiers in early 17th century Flanders. Feyder declared his intention of bringing to life Flemish painting, an end he achieves nearly perfectly through a combination of masterly use of studio sets and costumes and Harry Stradling's gorgeous photography. Faced by the cowardly reaction of their burgher husbands, the women of the town decide to save themselves by preparing a lavish welcoming feast for the bloodthirsty Spaniards. The film is distinctly ambiguous about which appetites are being satisfied and how, and about the politics of occupation – is it advocating collaboration or subversion? For this reason, Feyder found it wise to exile himself from Nazi-occupied France a few years later. Either way, though, it remains a distinctly amiable sex comedy. RM

Kerouac

(John Antonelli, 1985, US) Jack Coulter, David Andrews, Jonah Pearson, Allen Ginsberg, Lawrence Ferlinghetti, Gregory Corso, Neal Cassady.
73 min.
This feature-length documentary, narrated by Peter Coyote, reminds us that Kerouac wasn't just a handsome beatnik drifter who hung out with Burroughs and Ginsberg, and travelled across America striking moody poses. He was also a formidably talented writer. (One pundit, his biographer Ann Charters, rates him alongside Hemingway, Wolfe and Whitman.) The story is dispiriting – five unpublished novels before *On the Road* catapulted him on to the chat show circuit, then decline to a premature, drunken death at age 49. Antonelli has assembled a gallery of old rogues (Corso, Burroughs, Ferlinghetti) to reminisce about their pal Jack. He's also dug up archive footage of Neal Cassady, 'the flaming comet from the west' who inspired much of Kerouac's best work. Almost inevitably, the dramatic reconstructions of the writer's life seem dreary by comparison. GM

Kes

(Kenneth Loach, 1969, GB) David Bradley, Lynne Perrie, Freddie Fletcher, Colin Welland, Brian Glover, Bob Bowes.
113 min.
Barry Hines' novel, about a young schoolboy in Barnsley who attempts to escape the tedium and meaninglessness of his uninviting working-class future by caring for and training a kestrel that he finds, is never allowed to fall into undue sentimentality in Loach's low-key direction (his first feature). Rather than a tale of a boy and his pet, the film is a lucid and moving examination of the narrow options open to people without money, family stability and support, or education. Terrific performances, illuminated by Chris Menges's naturalistic but often evocative photography. GA

Key, The

(Carol Reed, 1958, GB) Sophia Loren, Trevor Howard, William Holden, Kieron Moore, Oscar Homolka, Bernard Lee, Beatrix Lehmann, Noel Purcell.
134 min. b/w.
Extraordinary, unwieldy World War II naval epic which fails to deliver as much as it promises, but promises so much as to be worth while none the less. Swiss waif Loren shelters and succours a succession of war-weary tugboat captains who are never quite sure whether she's a goddess or a whore, an island of love in the cold, cruel sea or a siren leading them on to their doom. Loren is excellent, and the film plays interestingly with the idea of a woman's mystery being the product of male prejudice and fear. But the dictates of the international box-office – lots of naval manoeuvres and a turgidly wooden American hero – result in a fascinatingly enigmatic melodrama being buried within a stolidly conventional war film. RMy

Keyhole, The (Noeglehullet)

(Gerhard Poulsen ie. Paul Gerber, 1974, Den) Marie Ekorre, Torben Larsen, Bent Warburg, Max Horn, Pia Larsen, Lene Andersen.
88 min.
A businessman in the opening minutes has the wonderful idea of making the first porno film to be completely realistic and believable – a notion which raised a few sniggers in the mackintoshed rows of the cinema where this epic was being screened. Nothing else in the movie, however, seemed to raise anything, although the leading couple (an aspiring movie-maker and the businessman's daughter) display a little more vivacity than one expects. According to Variety, Marie Ekorre previously appeared in the centre pages of *Penthouse*. She must have been relieved to get away from the staples. GB

Key Largo

(John Huston, 1948, US) Humphrey Bogart, Edward G Robinson, Lauren Bacall, Lionel Barrymore, Claire Trevor, Thomas Gomez, Dan Seymour.
101 min. b/w.
Reworking of a Maxwell Anderson play about a gangster under threat of deportation who holes up with his henchmen in a semi-derelict hotel on an island off Florida, holding the occupants at gunpoint and remaining blind to the menace posed by a coming hurricane. The debt to *The Petrified Forest* is obvious, but instead of wallowing in world-weary pseudo-philosophy, *Key Largo* has altogether sharper things to say about post-war disillusionment, corruption in politics, and the fact that the old freebooting ways of the gangster were about to change into something more sinisterly complex. Huston skilfully breaks up the action (basically one set and one continuous scene), working subtle variations on his groupings with the aid of superb deep-focus camera-work by Karl Freund. And although the characters are basically stereotypes, they are lent the gift of life by a superlative cast: Robinson as the truculent Little Caesar, Bogart as an embittered ex-Army officer, Bacall as the innocent who loves him, and above all Trevor as the gangster's disillusioned, drink-sodden moll. TM

Keys to Tulsa

(Leslie Greif, 1996, US) Eric Stoltz, Cameron Diaz, Randy Graff, Mary Tyler Moore, James Coburn, Deborah Kara Unger, Michael Rooker, Peter Strauss, James Spader, Joanna Going.
114 min.
Tulsa, Oklahoma, a seedy sweat-joint propped up on a little oil – Jim Thompson would know his way around here. Stoltz is a reporter, not fundamentally bad, just weak and in with the wrong crowd, who gets ever busier wallowing in trouble. His ex (Unger), a sometime femme fatale, has started batting eyelids at him again. Her brother and Stoltz's old buddy (Rooker) likes to run around drunk waving guns in the air. Her low-rent husband (Spader) looks like an Elvis impersonator in black and wants Stoltz in on a plan to blackmail the local oilman's son for the murder of a black prostitute. Meanwhile his mum (Moore) is repossessing her offspring's home. Spader and Unger make their mark, but the film's initial possibilities all close down long before the finish. Harley Peyton's screenplay (from a novel by Brian Fair Berkey) is weak on plot and motivation, and the finale – side-lining characters at its own convenience (signs of a last minute change?) – comes as a considerable anti-climax. NB

Khartoum

(Basil Dearden, 1966, US/GB) Charlton Heston, Laurence Olivier, Richard Johnson, Ralph Richardson, Alexander Knox, Johnny Sekka, Nigel Green, Michael Hordern, Zia Mohyeddin, Hugh Williams.
134 min.
A massive all-star cast and a huge budget help to make the more vacuous moments of this epic comparatively painless. It is scripted with a ponderous attention to detail by the notorious pseudo-zoologist Robert Ardrey (author of *The Territorial Imperative*), but it has some very heavyweight performances, with Heston as General Gordon and Olivier as his bloodthirsty opponent the Mahdi (the face-to-face confrontation between the two is entirely fictitious). There's also Richardson as Gladstone, Nigel Green as General Wolseley, and Michael Hordern as Lord Granville, so despite inadequacies in both direction and screenwriting, anyone interested in the period will probably find quite a lot to enjoy. DP

Kickboxer

(Mark DiSalle/David Worth, 1989, US) Jean-Claude Van Damme, Dennis Alexio, Dennis Chan, Tong Po, Haskell Anderson, Rochelle Ashana, Steve Lee.
103 min.
Kickboxing is what it says it is: fisticuffs with feet. *Kickboxer* is an upfront title, too – don't see it for psychological complexity, social comment, acting, plot or humour; go, if you nust, just for kicks. There is a story. Two brothers: Eric (Alexio), all-American asshole, is KB champion stateside; Kurt (Van Damme) is the sensitive type – mother made him take ballet lessons before he learned karate! Big brother goes on an ego-trip to Bangkok 'to kick ass', gets pulped, and ends up paralysed to boot. Given the choice of caring for his bro' or beating the shit out of his opponent, Kurt goes into training with an oriental guru and emerges 'a man'. Further motivated by the knifing of his dog, raping of his girl, and kidnapping of Eric, Kurt is not about to turn the other cheek when he finally gets into the ring. In some movies these events might suggest a dehumanising process; here they are a route to mythification. It's the facistic tale of the making of a man, the 'white warrior', virgin avenger Van Damme. At least he ain't Chuck Norris. TCh

Kicked in the Head

(Matthew Harrison, 1997, US) Kevin Corrigan, Linda Fiorentino, Michael Rappaport, James Woods, Burt Young, Lili Taylor.
89 min.
A self-consciously 'cool' US indie comedy-drama from the director of the similarly derivative *Rhythm Thief*, in which Corrigan (who co-wrote it) – horribly indulged, self-indulgent and unsympathetic in his 'cute' confusion and adolescent desires – pursues his dopey spiritual quest for truth while dealing with a petty criminal uncle (Woods), manic entrepreneur buddy (Rappaport), devoted admirer (Taylor) and the object of his desire, an improbably yielding world-weary air hostess (Fiorentino). Too determinedly offbeat, and much too perniciously flip – gunfights are funny, men's immature sexual fantasies are to be indulged by mature women – for its own good. GA

Kid

(John Mark Robinson, 1990, US) C Thomas Howell, Sarah Trigger, Brian Austin Green, R Lee Ermey, Dale Dye, Michael Bowen, Damon Bowen.
91 min.
A fairly obvious attempt to refashion *High Plains Drifter* for youthful audiences, and for about two minutes it looks like it might be fun. It isn't. A mysterious stranger rides into town on a Greyhound. When a couple of local thugs give him strife, Kid leaves them begging for mercy. He checks into an empty motel. Then people start to die strange, perverse deaths. Kid? Uh-huh. Any film that devises a murder from a tennis ball and a can of bug spray may claim some ingenuity, but *Kid* isn't just trashy enough for its own good. Instead of nihilistic exploitation, we get half-cocked teen romance and a tiresomely sentimental vigilante. Howell is no substitute for Clint Eastwood, and love interest Trigger gives an unspeakably awful performance. Such relief as there is comes from R Lee Ermey as Sheriff Luke Clanton, who extends the nice range in invective he first shared with us in *Full Metal Jacket*. 'Seems to me' he cautions 'you stuck your dick in the wrong hole, Slick'. Quite. TCh

Kid, The

(Charles Chaplin, 1921, US) Charles Chaplin, Edna Purviance, Jackie Coogan, Carl Miller, Tom Wilson, Henry Bergman, Lita Grey.
5,300 ft. b/w.
'A picture with a smile and perhaps a tear' says the opening title of Chaplin's first feature. There's no perhaps about it, what with Charlie struggling to nurture a cast-off illegitimate child in the face of unfeeling cops, doctors and orphanage workers. As always, Chaplin's opulent Victorian sentimentality is made palatable both by the amazing grace of his pantomimic skills and the balancing presence of harsh reality: the drama

and the intertwining gags are played out amongst garbage, flophouses, a slum world depicted with Stroheim-like detail. As for the smiles, they're guaranteed too, although the gags don't coalesce into great sequences the way they do in later features. GB

Kid Blue

(James Frawley, 1973, US) Dennis Hopper, Warren Oates, Peter Boyle, Ben Johnson, Lee Purcell, Janice Rule, Ralph Waite, Clifton James.
100 min.
A magical Western, this companion piece to the marvellously eccentric *Steelyard Blues* features Dennis Hopper as a one-time minor desperado, turned would-be solid citizen and failing manfully. Calmly orchestrated by Frawley, who transforms even the smallest of parts into a rounded character and allows his story-line to develop out of those characters, *Kid Blue* never strains for meaning; even the web of references to the Greece of mythology is never too pointed. Oates, Boyle, Ben Johnson and Janice Rule offer solid support. PH

Kid Brother, The

(Ted Wilde/JA Howe, 1927, US) Harold Lloyd, Jobyna Ralston, Walter James, Leo Willis, Olin Francis.
82 min. b/w.
Sources claim that half of this film was directed by Lewis Milestone, but it's a Harold Lloyd movie through and through, and perhaps only slightly less of an achievement than *Safety Last*. Lloyd's penultimate silent movie, made for Paramount, *The Kid Brother* is not an urban story (which was his trademark) but a rural one, which brings it quite close to the world of Keaton. Lloyd, like Keaton in *The Navigator*, is the living proof that every family tree must have its sap. Despised by his father and two strapping brothers, he proves he is a man after a girl catches his bespectacled eyes. The plot, of course, is just an excuse for a string of pratfalls, chases and derring-do, while the climax aboard an abandoned ship is a tour de force, and sometimes painfully violent. ATu

Kid for Two Farthings, A

(Carol Reed, 1955, GB) Jonathan Ashmore, Celia Johnson, Diana Dors, David Kossoff, Sidney Tafler, Sidney James, Alfie Bass, Brenda de Banzie, Joe Robinson, Primo Carnera, Lou Jacobi.
96 min.
Before he plunged headlong into 'international' film-making (never to be seen again), Carol Reed took this fanciful Wolf Mankowitz screenplay and tried to re-imagine Petticoat Lane in the poetic realist vein of Marcel Carné and Jacques Prévert. A young boy (Ashmore) mistakes a one-horned goat for a miraculous unicorn, and eagerly anticipates good fortune for his friends about the neighbourhood. A whimsical film, it may have seemed horribly patronising in the '50s; but from today's perspective, an intriguing, even adventurous attempt to resurrect a national cinema that had clearly lost its legs. TCh

Kid from Spain, The

(Leo McCarey, 1932, US) Eddie Cantor, Lyda Roberti, Robert Young, Ruth Hall, John Miljan, Noah Beery, J Carrol Naish, Stanley Fields.
96 min. b/w.
Eddie Cantor's talent is for those of an antique taste, but this extravagant Goldwyn production has a few other things going for it, most notably a couple of blatant routines choreographed for the Goldwyn Girls by Busby Berkeley (the chorus line is said to include Lucille Ball, Jane Wyman, Betty Grable and Paulette Goddard, but you'll need sharp eyes to spot them). The plot has Cantor and his college buddy Young innocently caught up in a bank robbery and hiding out in Mexico, where Cantor is mistaken for a famous matador. No prizes for guessing where he ends up. TCh

Kid Galahad

(Michael Curtiz, 1937, US) Edward G Robinson, Bette Davis, Humphrey Bogart, Wayne Morris, Jane Bryan, Harry Carey.
101 min. b/w.
A none too subtle exposition of the now well-worn theme of corruption in the boxing-ring, with Robinson as the go-getting manager who finds

himself a contender in the shape of a bellhop (Morris) who summarily knocks out the reigning heavyweight champion for insulting Robinson's mistress (Davis). It all boils up to a shoot-out between Robinson and racketeer Bogart when the former – having vengefully fixed a fight under the impression that Davis is cheating on him with Morris – suffers a change of heart. Actually, in one of those woozy subplots so beloved of Hollywood in the '30s, Davis has fallen for Morris all right, but he's making sheep's eyes at the innocent kid sister (Bryan) Robinson keeps in the background. Sleek direction and excellent performances keep it enjoyable. Remade in a circus setting (as *The Wagons Roll at Night*, 1941) and again as a dim Elvis Presley vehicle in 1962. TM

Kid Galahad

(Phil Karlson, 1962, US) Elvis Presley, Gig Young, Lola Albright, Joan Blackman, Charles Bronson, Ned Glass, Michael Dante, Robert Emhardt.
96 min.
A musical remake of the 1937 Warner Bros boxing drama that starred Robinson, Bette Davis and Bogart. Gig Young is OK as the trainer, but the flabby Presley, recently demobbed from the army, looks as if he couldn't survive a round with Donald Duck. His songs aren't exactly knockouts either. ATu

Kid Glove Killer

(Fred Zinnemann, 1942, US) Van Heflin, Marsha Hunt, Lee Bowman, Samuel S Hinds, Cliff Clark, Eddie Quillan, John Litel, Ava Gardner.
74 min. b/w.
Zinnemann's feature début, a neat, unpretentious and really rather enjoyable whodunit about the hunt for the killer of the town's crusading mayor. Obviously developed out of the MGM *Crime Does Not Pay* featurettes on which Zinnemann served his apprenticeship, it places the accent squarely – but not entirely seriously – on laboratory detection methods: among the gimmicks gleefully demonstrated by Heflin, as the dedicated forensic scientist, is a mini-dustette designed to collect evidence from human scalps. Likeably fresh performances, too, from Heflin, Hunt as his wisecracking assistant who despairs of his ever realising that she's a woman, and Bowman as the blandly suave killer. Ava Gardner has a tiny role as a waitress. TM

Kidnapped

(Delbert Mann, 1971, GB) Michael Caine, Lawrence Douglas, Trevor Howard, Donald Pleasence, Jack Hawkins, Vivien Heilbron, Freddie Jones, Gordon Jackson, Peter Jeffrey.
107 min.
Umpteenth adaptation of Stevenson's adventure, set in the last days of the Jacobite rebellion, and you'd have thought they might have gotten it right by now. Instead, sluggish pacing and a meandering plot, that also takes in elements from *Catriona*, kill off interest early on. Caine's Alan Breck is somewhat softened in Jack Pulman's adaptation, and the ending of the tale revised so that Breck surrenders to the English for the murder of Mungo Campbell. The cast are decent, but not much more. Filmed in Panavision and angled at children. TJ

Kidnapping of the President, The

(George Mendeluk, 1979, Can) William Shatner, Hal Holbrook, Van Johnson, Ava Gardner, Miguel Fernandes, Cindy Girling, Elizabeth Shepherd.
113 min.
Oh yeah. Verily. For it is he of Starship Enterprise (Shatner). He cometh and walketh with the American Prez in the valley of the shadow of death (a pedestrian mall in Toronto). He faceth up to the Cubans and Weathermen and psychos and he saith unto them: 'Fuck off. For we shall fear nothing. Especially not you creeps and Commies'. And they reply: 'Look upon us. We are Moloch and Satan. We come creeping forth as vermin on our bellies, the legacy of Chile and El Salvador and American imperialism. We take your Prez and hold him in our chariot (a booby-trapped armoured car), using implements of destruction from *Hawaii Five-O*, *Mission Impossible* and other halls of TV fame.' But Captain Kirk turns upon the Commies and Cubans and Weathermen, and his voice is as

thunder, saying: 'Lo. I did once (in the '70s, in fact) what you do now, and I did it well. But I look upon you and ask, is it good? It is not good'. And there is a great flashing of lightning (TNT), a beating of brows and rattling of bones, and the Prez walks on, free, down the American Way with his wife on his right hand and Kirk on his left. For although we walk through the valley of crap... CA

Kids

(Larry Clark, 1995, US) Leo Fitzpatrick, Justin Pierce, Chloe Sevigny, Yakira Peguero.
91 min.
If Clark's raw, controversial, documentary-style account of 24 hours in the lives of a group of New York early-teens is to be believed, we'd better watch and worry. Few of the kids seem bothered about *anything* except meaningless sex, whatever drugs or booze is available, and the odd bit of mindless violence. True, Clark and his writer Harmony Korine try to adopt some sort of cautionary standpoint (one girl is diagnosed as HIV-positive after just one sexual experience; drugs are not exactly glamorised), but the tone is relentlessly sordid, the view of these pubescent hedonists so hermetic, that the film-makers' 'honesty' seems exploitative and sensational. The film may not say anything new, but the way it says it does, in the end, make it some sort of landmark. Depressing. GA

Kids Are Alright, The

(Jeff Stein, 1978, US) The Who, Tom Smothers, Jimmy O'Neil, Russell Harty, Melvin Bragg, Ringo Starr, Steve Martin.
108 min.
That rare animal, a rock documentary which entertains and informs in equal quantities, *The Kids Are Alright* is a movie that comes over as a celebration of rock'n'roll itself as much as of one of its more masterful exponents. Covering The Who's 'turbulent' history from the days of sweaty Shepherd's Bush cellars to the super-technicalities required for the recording of 'Who Are You' (mercifully stopping before Moon's death), the film captures some of the most powerful rock music of the last two decades. Patching together snippets of hilarious interviews (witness the anarchic terror Moon wreaks on a panic-stricken Russell Harty) with footage of live gigs (culminating in a laser-streaked finale), plus a few fantasy sequences, the film will fascinate the under-twenties and delight the over-thirties. FL

Kids in the Hall: Brain Candy

(Kelly Martin, 1996, US) David Foley, Bruce McCulloch, Kevin McDonald, Mark McKinney, Scott Thompson.
89 min.
'Kids in the Hall', a quintet of Canadian TV comedians, hit the cinema screen with a splat. This cautionary satire is intended to showcase (in multiple roles) the protean talents of these lame gagsters. The story – forgive the word – concerns the effects of Gleemonex, a Prozac-like happiness drug sweeping the country. It's a conspiracy, of course, by Mr Big Business (McKinney), and resistance is led by an initially gullible scientist (McDonald). Irrelevant, but well done, are the special effects (a psychedelic shot of a pill's journey to the stomach) and the production design. WH

Kids of Survival: The Art and Life of Tim Rollins & K.O.S.

(Daniel Geller/Dayna Goldfine, 1996, US) Tim Rollins.
87 min.
Fly-on-the-wall documentary about artist Tim Rollins and his disciplined but productive after-school classes in modern art for the troubled, often troublesome kids of the impoverished South Bronx. The proof of the pudding is in the fact that KOS paintings – usually inspired by literary texts – show in New York's Museum of Modern Art: no bad achievement when the kids start off as truants, Nintendo addicts or worse. But the film itself, while worthy, is conservative in the extreme. GA

Kids Return

(Takeshi Kitano, 1996, Jap) Masanobu Ando, Ken Kaneko, Leo Morimoto, Hatsuo Yamaya, Mitsuko Oka, Ryo Ishibashi, Susumu Terajima.
107 min.

Masaru and Shinji are problem kids who enter society without apparent talents or prospects; their setbacks and failures as, respectively, a yakuza and a pro boxer are contrasted with the career paths of others from their school, two of whom struggle to make the grade as stand-up comics. Although it's set in the present, the indefinable retro flavour tips you the wink that these are memories and reflections from 'Beat' Takeshi's own adolescence – which doubtless explains the way the film extends such warmth to its characters without indulging or excusing their flaws. Unlike previous Takeshi protagonists, these kids don't have the easy option of 'dying well'; their quests for a viable way to survive are, however, seen with all the director's usual visual and rhythmic flair. TR

Kika

(Pedro Almodóvar, 1993, Sp) Veronica Forqué, Peter Coyote, Victoria Abril, Alex Casanovas, Rossy de Palma, Santiago Lajusticia.
114 min.
You may already know that a) this is supposed to be Almodóvar's flop; and b) you must wax all indignant over That Rape Scene. The sang froid displayed by Kika (Forqué, brilliant) during her ordeal is, if anything, the director's cock-eyed tribute to the power of women, as is the reason for the attack: a crazed ex-porn actor and escaped criminal Pablo (Lajusticia) breaks into Kika's house, finds her asleep, but can't resist sniffing her fanny. Yes, it's grotesque, but also touching, daring and very funny. Male viewers seem to resent having to recognise themselves in dim-witted Pablo. The film also fields Coyote, clinging on to youth by what appears to be false teeth and a pageboy wig. Kika's narcoleptic lover Ramón is played by cute Casanovas, and Abril's stylish Andrea Scarface presents a true-crime show which gives the film its funniest moments. When the fuss has died down, most people will agree that this is a return to form after the slightly disappointing High Heels, and is full of magic Almodóvar moments. SFe

Kikuchi

(Kenchi Iwamoto, 1990, Jap) Jiro Yoshimura, Yasuhiro Oka, Misa Fukuma, Papa Akiyama, Mama Akiyama.
68 min.
Saddled with a slavish, boring laundry job and no social life whatsoever, Kikuchi rarely leaves his bare apartment except to follow home and spy on a supermarket check-out girl. But there's no one he can tell about his secret passion, least of all his gawping, work-shy colleague. Even a stray kitten can't alleviate Kikuchi's frustration; clearly, something's got to give... This first film by a former manga illustrator, a terse and enigmatic blend of black comedy and psychodrama, has been compared to both Eraserhead and Chantal Akerman's Jeanne Dielman; another point of reference might be the slow, deceptively banal domestic dramas of Ozu, with whom Iwamoto shares a penchant for a mostly static camera, simple compositions, and an eye for the absurd details of everyday life. Only that old problem – how to show tedium without being tedious – occasionally undermines an otherwise impressive debut. GA

Killer

(Mark Malone, 1994, US) Anthony LaPaglia, Mimi Rogers, Matt Craven, Peter Boyle, Monika Schnarre, Joseph Maher.
95 min.
A professional hit-man agrees to carry out a rush job on a woman for his usual fee – plus therapy sessions. When he meets the victim, however, she's only too willing to cooperate, and of course he falls in love. Malone's directorial debut (after script credits for Dead of Winter and Signs of Life) gets a certain amount of mileage out of this little noir conceit, but conceit is all we get: the movie's all talk and no action. It's let down by the leads, LaPaglia and Rogers (both shown up by Peter Boyle's genial mob boss), who fail to generate any kind of spark. TCh

Killer, The (Da Sha Shou)

(Chu Yuan, 1971, HK) Chin Han, Wang Ping, Tsung Hua, Ching Miao, Yang Chih Ching.
93 min.
Another kung-fu assembly line gore product according to the brothers Shaw. The film exists for its fight routines, and these go to heady extremes in taking our hero out of the realm of human fallibility (dozens fall at one blow) and inching him towards complete invincibility. The plot involves heroin smuggling, romantic meetings after many years under assumed names, and so on; but the scene in which 'The Killer' confronts the head of the Black Dragon gang – a remarkable picture of sword-wielding malevolence – is a rare spark in a movie that remains routine despite its exoticism. VG

Killer, The (Diexue Shuang Xiong)

(John Woo i.e. Wu Yusen, 1989, HK) Chow Yun-Fat, Danny Lee, Sally Yeh, Chu Kong, Kenneth Tsang.
111 min.
The most dementedly elegiac thriller you've ever seen, distilling a lifetime's enthusiasm for American and French film noir, with little Chinese about it apart from the soundtrack and the looks of the three beautiful leads. It started out as a homage to Martin Scorsese and Jean-Pierre Melville, but the limitless arsenal of guns and rocket-launchers appears somehow to have got in the way. Exquisitely-tailored contract killer Jeff (Chow Yun-Fat, Honk Kong's finest actor) accidentally damages the sight of nightclub singer Jennie while blasting a dozen gangsters to kingdom come. He befriends the near-blind girl, and decides to take One Last Job to finance the cornea-graft she needs. Meanwhile he is stalked by a misfit cop (Lee), who eventually falls in love with him and winds up fighting alongside him. There are half-a-dozen mega-massacres along the way, plus extraordinary spasms of sentimentality, romance and soul-searching. The tone is hysterical from start to finish, but Woo's lush visual stylings and taste for baroque detail give the whole thing an improbably serene air of abstraction. TR

Killer!

see Que la Bête Meure

Killer: A Journal of Murder

(Tim Metcalfe, 1995, US) James Woods, Robert Sean Leonard, Ellen Green, Cara Buono, Robert John Burke, Richard Riehle, Harold Gould.
92 min. col & b/w.
1929: Two newcomers enter Leavenworth prison, Kansas. Henry Lesser, an idealistic guard, and Carl Panzram, a hard-bitten con who spits out a confession to 21 unsolved murders. The pair form a bond. Henry smuggles in paper and pen so America's first serial killer can write his memoirs – a journal so shocking it wasn't published for more than 40 years. Writer/director Metcalfe switches to b/w for the journal, but that approximates the harshness of the material, not any moral distinction. Indeed, Metcalfe holds to a liberal perspective which Panzram, for one, may not have agreed with. Woods is typecast as Panzram, but he's terrifyingly alive in the part – even double-chained and ringed by a dozen guards, he's a palpable threat. A very nasty piece of work, he none the less insists that he is a piece of work: the sum of his exposure to the indifference and sadism of others. Leonard is just an on-looker as Lesser, but he, like the film, never flinches from the disturbing truths Panzram represents. This tough, gritty movie is shot by Abel Ferrara's regular cameraman Ken Kelsch, produced by Oliver Stone and dedicated to Sam Peckinpah – so you know where it's coming from. TCh

Killer Butterfly (Salin Nabireul Cchotneun Yeoja)

(Kim Ki-Young, 1978, SKor) Kim Jung-chi, Kim Man, Kim Cha-ok.
110 min.
Not unlike one of Corman's Poe films updated to '70s Seoul (with a little Ugetsu Monogatari thrown in), this tells of a feckless, morose student torn between life and death, Eros and Thanatos, when he meets a variety of strange and supernatural beings. Some of the special effects look a little elementary, but the whole thing is extremely enjoyable, and the scene where the hero has sex with a ghost next to an automatic toaster has to be seen to be believed. GA

Killer Elite, The

(Sam Peckinpah, 1975, US) James Caan, Robert Duvall, Arthur Hill, Gig Young, Mako, Bo Hopkins, Burt Young, Helmut Dantine.
120 min.
After a brilliantly cryptic opening, The Killer Elite settles into Peckinpah's most apparently straightforward action film since The Getaway. Built around the internal politics of a San Francisco company which sidelines in dirty work that even the CIA won't touch, it concentrates on the painful recovery of an agent (Caan), wounded in knee and elbow in a double-cross, and his search for revenge. During Caan's lengthy recuperation, Peckinpah contemplates the old themes of betrayal, trust and humiliation. And through the action of the second half, Caan (like other Peckinpah heroes) comes to some sort of understanding. The set pieces (a Chinatown shoot-out, a dockland siege, the superb ships' graveyard climax) are excellent, as are so many secondary scenes. There are echoes here of Point Blank, and behind the deceits and manipulations both are essentially simple films. Unmistakable Peckinpah – not a masterpiece, but enough to be going on with. CPe

Killer Fish

(Anthony M Dawson i.e. Antonio Margheriti, 1978, Braz/Fr) Lee Majors, Karen Black, Margaux Hemingway, Marisa Berenson, James Franciscus, Roy Brocksmith, Gary Collins.
101 min.
One of the first of Carlo Ponti's exile productions, and the sort of international film-making-by-numbers tailor-made for distribution by Lew Grade, this manages to conspicuously waste more than twice the budget of New World's Piranha without approaching anything like the imagination, relevance or sense of fun of its sharp-toothed, small-fry predecessor. The piranha here guard an underwater stash of stolen jewels, and take regular nibbles from the double-crossing crooks. Majors out-machos everyone else, while Hemingway arrives halfway through for – what else? – some location modelling work. PT

Killer Inside Me, The

(Burt Kennedy, 1975, US) Stacy Keach, Susan Tyrrell, Tisha Sterling, Keenan Wynn, Don Stroud, Charles McGraw, John Dehner, John Carradine, Royal Dano.
99 min.
Not even the offices of the excellent Burt Kennedy can save this hopelessly stodgy and psychologising story about a self-consciously good cop (Keach) who finds a traumatic childhood experience catching up on him. Kennedy none the less does ensure that the film is crammed with enough pleasing incidental detail to make it watchable. But Stroud lopes through the part of a naïve and ape-ish slob with evident enjoyment; now perhaps if he and Keach had swapped roles... the pity of it is that the script by Edward Mann and Robert Chamblee wrecks a very good novel by Jim Thompson. VG

Killer is on the Phone, The (Assassino...è al Telefono)

(Alberto De Martino, 1972, It) Anne Heywood, Telly Savalas, Rossella Falk, Giorgio Piazza, Osvaldo Ruggeri.
102 min.
Crippled thriller along is-she-insane-or-are-they-trying-to-make-her-believe-it lines, shot in Ostend and featuring Savalas, in his pre-lollipop days, and Heywood, who has the knack of picking hopeless projects. De Martino rapidly forfeits interest or suspense by loading every action with equal suggestiveness.

Killer Klowns from Outer Space

(Stephen Chiodo, 1988, US) Grant Cramer, Suzanne Snyder, John Allen Nelson, Royal Dano, John Vernon.
88 min.
You'll never guess what this one is about. Funnily enough, it's about this huge circus tent that mysteriously appears up in the woods by a small American town, and then there's all these totally weird clowns who go around doing, like, gross things to people with projectile candy floss. Seems the clowns are on a mission from (surprise) outer space to collect human bodies for food. However, they are foiled by the young hero, who discovers that you can kill 'em if you knock off their big red noses. Utterly ridiculous, the dialogue exquisitely dumb, the acting sooooooooo bad, it's one for cheap laughs. DA

Killer Nun (Suor omicidio)

(Giulio Berruti, 1978, It) Anita Ekberg, Alida Valli, Massimo Serato, Lou Castel, Joe Dallesandro, Laura Nucci.
90 min.

A dated blend of softcore sleaze, routine bloodletting and explicable coyness, this stars an over-the-hill Ekberg as a nun who has given up *la dolce vita* for a life behind convent hospital walls. A secret junkie whose past sexual traumas and drug-induced hallucinations transform her from a caring angel into an avenging one, Ekberg loses her patience and starts killing patients. Given this excessive scenario, why the quaint evasions? Lesbianism is hinted at but not shown, scenes of Ekberg shooting up are filmed with her back to the camera. Isolated scenes spill over into camp humour, as when the hysterical Ekberg repeatedly stamps on an old lady's dentures. A censored version, running 81 minutes, removed two 'nasties' (the needle in the eye/scalpel to the skull sequences). NF

Killer of Killers

see Mechanic, The

Killer of Sheep

(Charles Burnett, 1977, US) Henry Gayle Sanders, Kaycee Moore, Charles Bracy, Angela Burnett, Eugene Cherry, Jack Drummond.
84 min. b/w.

A gritty, grainy slice of everyday lumpen American black struggle, marking the difficulty of maintaining slow-burn integrity – the title refers to a family breadwinner's slaughterhouse job. Shot with a telling near-documentary technique on a poverty-row budget, but lifted right out of any cinematic ghetto by the best compilation sound-track you'll hear for many a year, ranging through an unfamiliar black catalogue from Paul Robeson to electric blues. PT

Killer on a Horse

see Welcome to Hard Times

Killers, The

(Robert Siodmak, 1946) Edmond O'Brien, Ava Gardner, Burt Lancaster, Albert Dekker, Sam Levene, Charles McGraw, William Conrad, Virginia Christine.
105 min. b/w.

If anyone still doesn't know what's signified by the critical term *film noir*, then *The Killers* provides an exhaustive definition. The quality isn't in the rather average script (elaborated from Hemingway's short story) but in the overall sensibility – the casting, the use of shadows, the compositions alternating between paranoid long shots and hysterical close-ups. After the brilliant opening murder scene, what follows is a series of flashbacks as Edmond O'Brien's insurance investigator looks into the circumstances of Lancaster's death. Ava Gardner is an admirably tacky femme fatale, and her fickleness/faithfulness provides the not very surprising denouement. Worth attention as a '40s thriller, but more than that as a prime example of post-war pessimism and fatalism. TR

Killers, The

(Don Siegel, 1964, US) Lee Marvin, Angie Dickinson, John Cassavetes, Clu Gulager, Ronald Reagan, Claude Akins, Norman Fell, Virginia Christine.
95 min.

Not exactly a remake of Siodmak's film, but a very similar adaptation of Hemingway's short story, except that the old *noir* ambience has given way to broad daylight, with the two killers now characterised as corporate executives rather than as emblematic figures from the shadows. Like its predecessor, Siegel's version is at its best while setting up the chillingly ruthless detail of the opening execution (here unnervingly set in an asylum for the blind), less satisfying when it starts providing an answer to the mysterious passivity of the victim (Cassavetes). A familiar tale of robbery and betrayal unfolds, not enhanced by the glossy colour but given a terrific boost by the fact that the two killers stick around (since they now conduct the investigation themselves in the interests of better business efficiency) and are superbly characterised by Marvin and Gulager. Originally made for TV, the film was tactfully switched to cinema release following the JFK assassination. TM

Killer's Kiss

(Stanley Kubrick, 1955, US) Frank Silvera, Jamie Smith, Irene Kane, Jerry Jarret, Julius Adelman.
67 min. b/w.

Written, edited, shot, produced and directed by Kubrick for a mere $75,000, his second feature is a moody but rather over-arty B thriller whose prime pleasures lie in the high contrast black-and-white camerawork (Kubrick had been a top photographer for *Look*). The story is nothing original – a down-at-heel boxer (Smith) falls for a nightclub dancer (Kane) after saving her from being raped by her boss (Silvera), who consequently determines to put an end to their romance – but Kubrick makes the most of flashback and dream sequences, and a surreal climactic fight in a warehouse full of mannequins. The dialogue was post-synched, making for a certain stiltedness in the performances, but at least the brief running-time ensures that the film's more pretentious moments tend to flash past, rather than linger as in Kubrick's later work. (Incidentally, the film – and a fictionalised account of its making – became the subject of *Strangers Kiss* in 1983). GA

Killer Tongue (La lengua asesina)

(Alberto Sciamma, 1997, GB/Sp) Melinda Clarke, Jason Durr, Mapi Galán, Mabel Karr, Robert Englund, Doug Bradley.
99 min.

This calculatedly outrageous mix of jokey horror, road movie clichés and transvestite camp leaves a nasty taste in the mouth, but not in the way intended. Writer/director Sciamma's shambolic first feature is simply a catchy title in search of cult status. The presence of horror icons Englund (*A Nightmare on Elm Street*), Bradley (*Hellraiser*) and Clarke (*Return of the Living Dead III*) might lead you to think he's got it licked, but while Clarke looks fetching in latex bodysuit, the one-gag scenario about her talking tonsil tickler soon wears thin. To impose a spurious logic on the wayward plot, Candy (Clarke) acquires her *lengua asesina* after flakes from a crashed meteorite land in her soup. Having eaten from the same bowl, her poodles inexplicably metamorphose into a pair of screeching drag queens. Most inconvenient, since she's on the run from a bank job she's pulled with boyfriend Johnny (Durr), who himself has just escaped from a prison run by a sadistic guard (Englund). NF

Killing, The

(Stanley Kubrick, 1956, US) Sterling Hayden, Coleen Gray, Vince Edwards, Jay C Flippen, Marie Windsor, Elisha Cook Jr, Ted de Corsia, Timothy Carey.
83 min. b/w.

Characteristically Kubrick in both its mechanistic coldness and its vision of human endeavour undone by greed and deceit, this *noir*-ish heist movie is nevertheless far more satisfying than most of his later work, due both to a lack of bombastic pretensions and to the style fitting the subject matter. Hayden is his usual admirable self as the ex-con who gathers together a gallery of small-timers to rob a race-track; for once it's not the robbery itself that goes wrong, but the aftermath. What is remarkable about the movie, besides the excellent performances of an archetypal *noir* cast and Lucien Ballard's steely photography, is the time structure, employing a complex series of flashbacks both to introduce and explain characters and to create a synchronous view of simultaneous events. Kubrick's essentially heartless, beady-eyed observation of human foibles lacks the dimension of the genre's classics, but the likes of Windsor, Carey and Cook more than compensate. GA

Killing Box, The

(George Hickenlooper, 1993, US) Corbin Bernsen, Adrian Pasdar, Ray Wise, Cynda Williams, Martin Sheen.
86 min.

An arty zombie movie, this atmospheric American Civil War tale is described by director George (*Hearts of Darkness*) Hickenlooper as 'Conrad with a twist of Bram Stoker'. Confederate soldiers thought killed in an earlier skirmish are now suspected of a gruesome massacre. Forced into an alliance with Union captain Pasdar, captive Confederate colonel Bernsen finds Union soldiers crucified upside down on X-shaped crosses.

Is an army of the undead abroad in this war-torn land? Involving, with dark undertones. NF

Killing Dad

(Michael Austin, 1989, GB) Denholm Elliot, Julie Walters, Richard E Grant, Anna Massey, Laura Del Sol, Ann Way, Tom Radcliffe.
93 min.

A brief tour through the stock-room of British film comedy: seaside town out of season; mollycoddled son; overbearing neurotic mother; hopeless ventriloquist with drinking problem; faded *femme fatale* with drinking problem. Writer/director Austin's caricatures go through the motions of an Oedipal murder plot in perfunctory fashion; he seems to aspire to the satirical bite of Mike Leigh, but never achieves the accuracy, let alone the truth. Grant, struggling against being upstaged by a 1964 Beatles wig, employs his usual nose-wrinkling, eye popping mannerisms, but is unable to master the nasal tones of Harlow New Town. Elliott, object of Grant's murder mission, is wonderfully seedy. Walters brings much-needed warmth to her gin-sodden vamp: convincing, funny and sad. But Austin generally prefers to observe his characters as if they were insects under a stone: comedy needs a little more compassion. Southend looks suitably authentic and shabby, but the film is not located in real time at all, only somewhere between *Brighton Rock* and *The Punch and Judy Man*. JMo

Killing Fields, The

(Roland Joffé, 1984, GB) Sam Waterston, Haing S Ngor, John Malkovich, Julian Sands, Craig T Nelson, Spalding Gray, Bill Paterson, Athol Fugard.
142 min.

Though it gradually turns into a somewhat sentimental buddy movie, with NY journo Sydney Schanberg (Waterston) longing for news of Dith Pran (Ngor), the Cambodian aide he left behind to suffer the horrors of the Khmer Rouge after the fall of Pnomh Penh in 1975, this is still very much a superior look at one country's troubles in the wake of American involvement in South East Asia. The first hour, sprawling, chaotic and violently messy, is very good indeed, conveying both the complexity and the essential absurdity of war, while the photography by Chris Menges is stunningly convincing in detailing the scale of the carnage. The use of Lennon's 'Imagine' at the end is a severe error of judgment, but the film's overall thrust – angry, intelligent, compassionate – makes this producer Puttnam's finest movie to date. GA

Killing Floor, The

(Bill Duke, 1985, US) Damien Leake, Alfre Woodard, Clarence Felder, Moses Gunn, Jason Green, Jamarr Johnson.
117 min. b/w & col.

Black migration from the Deep South at the time of World War I, as seen through the eyes of Frank Custer (Leake), a sharecropper who comes to the 'Promised Land' of Chicago, to sweep animal remains from the floor of the slaughterhouse. Finding himself caught up in an emerging trade union movement, he attempts to convince his fellow black workers that the struggle for decent working conditions must transcend traditional racial antagonisms. Director Duke's work is like a large wooden spoon filled with gristle, blood, black and trade union history; it's kind of hard to swallow all at once. Still, it does portray an often neglected aspect of American history, while offering a less than loving glimpse at what really goes into the all-American cheeseburger. SGo

Killing of a Chinese Bookie, The [100]

(John Cassavetes, 1976, US) Ben Gazzara, Timothy Carey, Seymour Cassel, Azizi Johari, Virginia Carrington, Meade Roberts, Alice Friedland, Soto Joe Hugh.
109 min.

Cassavetes doesn't believe in gangsters, as soon becomes clear in this waywardly plotted account of how a bunch of them try to distract Gazzara from his loyalty to his barely solvent but chichi LA strip joint, the Crazy Horse West. Or rather Cassavetes doesn't believe in the kind of demands they make on a film, enforcing clichés of action and behaviour in return for a few cheap thrills. On the other hand, there's something about the ethnicity of the Mob – family closeness and family tyranny – which appeals to him, which is largely what his films are about, and which says something about the way he works with actors. The result is that his two gangster films – this one and the later *Gloria* – easily rate as his best work crisscrossed as they are by all sorts of contradictory impulses, with the hero/heroine being reluctantly propelled through the plot, trying to stay far enough ahead of the game to prevent his/her own act/movie being closed down. It's rather like a shaggy dog story operating inside a chase movie. *Chinese Bookie* is the more insouciant, involuted and unfathomable of the two; the curdled charm of Gazzara's lopsided grin has never been more to the point. (After its initial release, Cassavetes re-edited the film, adding sequences previously deleted but reducing the overall running time from 133 minutes.) MA

Killing of Angel Street, The

(Donald Crombie, 1981, Aust) Elizabeth Alexander, John Hargreaves, Alexander Archdale, Reg Lye, David Downer.
100 min.
Factually based political thriller in which a girl exposes the involvement of both government and organised crime after her father dies in mysterious circumstances while fighting attempts to 'persuade' the inhabitants of a row of terraced houses to make way for high-rise development. Not bad, though very lightweight and lumbered with a silly romance. Phillip Noyce's *Heatwave*, made the same year, did much better by the same facts. TM

Killing of Sister George, The

(Robert Aldrich, 1968, US) Beryl Reid, Susannah York, Coral Browne, Ronald Fraser, Patricia Medina, Hugh Paddick, Cyril Delevanti.
138 min.
Although one can't deny the entertainment value of Aldrich's adaptation of Frank Marcus's play about an ageing lesbian actress whose life falls apart as she loses first her job in a TV soap series and then her young lover, it could never be described as either realistic or sensitive. Rather, with its grotesque stereotyping and tour de force bitchiness and hysteria, it's like yet another instalment in the *What Ever Happened to Baby Jane?* saga. Cynical, objectionable, and fun, distinguished by Beryl Reid's marvellously energetic performance. GA

Killing Zoe

(Roger Avary, 1994, US) Eric Stoltz, Julie Delpy, Jean-Hugues Anglade, Gary Kemp, Tai Thai, Bruce Ramsay, Kario Salem.
96 min.
Zed (Stoltz) arrives in Paris to participate in a bank robbery at the invitation of an old friend, Eric (Anglade). A professional safecracker, he's swept up in a maelstrom of sex and drugs which turns to blood and guts when the robbery goes wrong. Avary's crooks make his pal Quentin Tarantino's reservoir dogs look like Cary Grant – this is a grotesquely sleazy, brutal, bloody crime flick. Not a particularly interesting one, though. Utterly unedifying. TCh

Kill Me Again

(John R Dahl, 1989, US) Val Kilmer, Joanne Whalley-Kilmer, Michael Madsen, Jonathan Gries, Pat Mulligan, Nick Dimitri.
96 min.
Desperate to evade her psychotic partner-in-crime Vince (Madsen, memorably nasty if over-Methody) after stealing money from the Mob, treacherous *femme fatale* Fay (Whalley-Kilmer) asks down-at-heel private investigator Jack Andrews (Val Kilmer) to help her fake her own death. Somewhat inevitably, Jack takes the job, loses his heart, and finds that he is wanted by cops, Mob *and* Vince. Derived from assorted Hitchcocks and *noir* classics, the tortuous storyline of writer-director Dahl's determinedly sordid thriller has its moments, but the whole thing is fatally scuppered by the Kilmer pairing. Joanne is trying far too hard and looks like it, while Val, whose pudgy baby-face makes nonsense of his world-weary, tough-guy posturing, alternates between two expressions: troubled (unsmiling) and beguiled (faintly smiling). Setting its study of betrayal and deceit in and around the gambling towns of the Nevada desert, the film sporadical-

ly achieves a truly seedy atmosphere, but there are too many symbols, too many loose ends, and too many vaguely sensationalist scenes. GA

Kill-Off, The

(Maggie Greenwald, 1989, US) Loretta Gross, Andrew Lee Barrett, Jackson Sims, Steve Monroe, Cathy Haase, William Russell, Jorjan Fox, Sean O'Sullivan, Ellen Kelly, Ralph Graff.
97 min.
For her second feature, an adaptation of Jim Thompson's novel, Greenwald *almost* gets it perfect. As she charts the sordid lives of various no-hopers struggling to make it in a seedy, wintry East Coast resort, she revels in the laconic dialogue, vicious motivations and downbeat mood beloved by Thompson fans. What these losers, each involved in activities like drug abuse, adultery, incest and so on, have in common is their hatred for Luane Devore, an elderly, bed-ridden gossip whose malicious mouth is itself a reason for killing. But which of her victims, finally, will murder her? Loretta Gross, memorably nasty as the twisted invalid, is backed up by equally efficient unknowns, while Declan Quinn's camerawork creates a vivid atmosphere of claustrophobic despair. As a thriller, however, the movie is short of real suspense: comparison with *Blood Simple* highlights Greenwald's slow pace, while *Le Corbeau*, Clouzot's misanthropic masterpiece of 1943, provides far more psychological complexity, moral rigour and nail-biting tension in its corrosive examination of paranoid corruption. GA

Killpoint

(Frank Harris, 1984, US) Leo Fong, Cameron Mitchell, Richard Roundtree, Stack Pierce, Hope Holiday, Diana Leigh.
89 min.
When a State arsenal is raided and machine-guns get into the hands of local gangs, the result is a lot of dead people. Before you can say soy sauce, a peaceful Chinese restaurant is awash in a sea of blood; but *Killpoint* caters for most tastes, ranging from simple strangulation and sexual abuse, knives and razor blades, plenty of martial arts, right through to grenades and real 'heavy metal' automatics. Dispensing with sissy things like stockings and disguises, the roaming robber gangs work on the simplistic principle of leaving no witnesses behind in colourful encounters with splashes of red everywhere. The dialogue is a bit stilted, but then most people don't last long enough to say much and the goodies win in the end anyway. Oh well, pass the ketchup. HR

Kim

(Victor Saville, 1950, US) Errol Flynn, Dean Stockwell, Paul Lukas, Robert Douglas, Thomas Gomez, Cecil Kellaway, Reginald Owen.
113 min.
Colourful location work scarcely makes up for the frequent turgid passages in this Hollywood version of Rudyard Kipling's novel. Stockwell essays the British-born, Indian-bred orphan who carves out a niche for himself as a spy for the Empire. Lukas is the Lama who teaches him a thing or two, Flynn the red-bearded spy who takes over his education. Politically indecorous, too. TCh

Kindergarten Cop

(Ivan Reitman, 1990, US) Arnold Schwarzenegger, Penelope Ann Miller, Pamela Reed, Linda Hunt, Richard Tyson, Carroll Baker.
111 min.
The trouble with comedy-thrillers is that while they are sometimes funny, they rarely thrill. If Reitman's film gets closer than most to covering the bases, there remain huge gaps in plausibility and a romantic subplot any ten-year-old could tell you is just plain icky. That the film works at all is down to Big Arnie. Far more successfully than in *Twins*, Reitman cannily exploits and debunks the Schwarzenegger screen persona. The exposition is particularly to the point, establishing him as the meanest cop on the block, a hard man who persuaded a reluctant witness to testify by threatening to hang out with her forever. Weighed down by a female partner (the delightfully cheeky Reed) and an unlikely undercover assignment as a kindergarten teacher, Macho Man looks set to become New Man. Faced with the kids from hell, Arnie has never been so

helpless or so funny. All too soon, though, the cop is backin charge; the nagging feeling that his high discipline and relentless Phys.Ed. is creating a class of *Überkinder* rather blunts the bite of the humour. TCh

Kinderspiel

see Child's Play

Kind Hearts and Coronets

(Robert Hamer, 1949, GB) Dennis Price, Alec Guinness, Joan Greenwood, Valerie Hobson, Audrey Fildes, Miles Malleson, Clive Morton, Hugh Griffith.
106 min. b/w.
The gentle English art of murder in Ealing's blackest comedy, with Price in perfect form as the ignoble Louis, killing off a complete family tree (played by Guinness throughout) in order to take the cherished d'Ascoyne family title. Disarmingly cool and callous in its literary sophistication, admirably low key in its discreet caricatures of the haute bourgeoisie, impeccable in its period detail (Edwardian), it's a brilliantly cynical film without a hint of middle-class guilt or bitterness. GA

Kind of Loving, A

(John Schlesinger, 1962, GB) Alan Bates, June Ritchie, Thora Hird, Bert Palmer, Gwen Nelson, Malcolm Patton, James Bolam, Leonard Rossiter.
112 min. b/w.
Schlesinger's first feature, an adaptation of Stan Barstow's novel directed with a quiet sympathy he subsequently lost (except for *Sunday, Bloody Sunday*) in pursuing flashy stylistics. The plot has seen sterling service (man trapped into marriage by an unplanned pregnancy), the setting is the then fashionable one of North Country factory and lower- middle- class aspirations, and the dialogue has the sort of terse, tape-recorder saltiness that scriptwriters Willis Hall and Keith Waterhouse used to churn out by the mile. Yet with all faults (which include a clumsily episodic structure), it remains keenly observant in detail and rather moving in its very unpretentiousness. TM

Kindred, The

(Jeffrey Obrow/Stephen Carpenter, 1986, US) David Allen Brooks, Rod Steiger, Amanda Pays, Talia Balsam, Kim Hunter, Timothy Gibbs, Peter Frechette.
92 min.
Geneticist John Hollins (Brooks) is shocked when his dying scientist mother refers to Anthony, a brother he never knew he had. With a crew of fresh-faced research assistants, he sets out to dismantle his old ma's cranky experiments, and discovers the mysterious Anthony in a cavernous slime-pit below stairs, the monstrous result of a hybridisation experiment. The thing shows scant regard for sibling attachments, and attempts to eat Hollins and anyone else it can lay talons on. It should be put down, but one man wants to keep the creature alive for his own devious ends. He is Dr Lloyd (Steiger in a wig resembling a pressed sparrow and looking as mean as the Ghostbusters' Stay-Puft marshmallow man). Lloyd fails and is eaten, shortly before Anthony is exploded into McNuggets of gristle and mucus. An adequate idea for a horror flick, ruined by bad pacing and a woolly plot. Not even mealy-mouthed Amanda Pays sprouting gills and fins can redeem this one. EP

King and Country

(Joseph Losey, 1964, GB) Dirk Bogarde, Tom Courtenay, Leo McKern, Barry Foster, James Villiers, Peter Copley, Jeremy Spenser.
86 min. b/w.
After three years at the front in World War I, a young soldier simply walks away from the guns; he is court-martialled, found wanting, and shot. For Losey, 'a story about hypocrisy, a story about people who are brought up to a certain way of life, who are given the means to extend their knowledge and to extend their understanding, but are not given the opportunity to use their minds in connection with it, and who finally have to face the fact that they have to be rebels in society...or else they have to accept hypocrisy.' This recasting of *The Servant* as a war film, with Courtenay playing the working-class deserter whose helplessness traps the liberal middle- class

officer (Bogarde) assigned to defend him at his court-martial, fails precisely because the sexual element in the relationship, so explicit in *The Servant*, is so repressed. Moreover, the intense questioning tone of John Wilson's source play (Hamp) is replaced with what are little more than academic debates about morality. PH

King and Four Queens, The
(Raoul Walsh, 1956, US) Clark Gable, Eleanor Parker, Jean Willes, Jo Van Fleet, Barbara Nichols, Sara Shane, Jay C Flippen.
86 min.
World-weary con artist Gable sets out to convince a quartet of widows that he was a member of their men's gang and thus throroughly deserving of a share in the lucrative stash they've buried, but he doesn't count on wily matriarch Van Fleet taking hold of the situation in the way she does. Gable's Hollywood nickname ('The King') is reflected in the title of this pared-down Western which is striking mainly for undercutting its leading man's macho authority.

King and I, The
(Walter Lang, 1956, US) Deborah Kerr, Yul Brynner, Rita Moreno, Martin Benson, Terry Saunders, Alan Mowbray.
133 min.
Over-long but visually spectacular musical version, by Rodgers and Hammerstein, of *Anna and the King of Siam*, with Kerr (dubbed for singing by Marni Nixon) as the prim widowed teacher gradually falling for Brynner's autocratic monarch. Poor songs ('Hello Young Lovers', 'Getting to Know You'), fair choreography, poor script, nice photography. GA

King and Mister Bird, The (Le Roi et l'Oiseau)
(Paul Grimault, 1980, Fr)
82 min.
The result of a long collaboration (and tortured production history) between animator Grimault and the respected screenwriter Jacques Prévert, this animated cartoon tells of the downfall of the king and kingdom of Tachycardia. Drawing upon ideas and images as different as Fritz Lang's *Metropolis* and the writings of Hans Christian Andersen, the film is distinguished by stylish graphics and an elegant visual and verbal humour that is guaranteed to appeal to all tastes and ages. The characterisations are a delight, and if the pace is occasionally as stately as the Tachycardian royal title (King Charles V-and-III-makes-VIII-and-VIII-makes-XVI), it merely allows more time to gape at the architecture of Tachycardia, a cool collage of Venetian canals, Bavarian castles, and New York tower blocks that is vast, monolithic, and truly vertiginous. FD

King Blank
(Michael Oblowitz, 1982, US) Rosemary Hochschild, Ron Vawter, Will Patton, Fred Neuman, Nancy Reilly, Peyton Smith.
72 min. b/w.
A film that perfectly captures the true spirit of Christmas. Somewhere in the vicinity of Kennedy airport, two lost souls, trapped in a web of obscenity and loathing, play out their terminal lives. All that divides the couple is the little problem of sexual difference, which of course drives the male into psychosis and leads inevitably to a destructive climax. Oblowitz charts their drift through a twilight zone of motel rooms, highways and bars in beautiful black-and-white, but pays equal attention to the sound-track, a dense collage of voices adrift from bodies, music and demented radio stations – an ice-pick for the viewer's ear. It's very funny and deeply moving, and Oblowitz's association with New York's 'New Wave' thankfully counts for nothing. Think instead of Glen or Glenda, Throbbing Gristle and Eraserhead. What the latter did for one-parent families, *King Blank* does for nice heterosexual couples. SJ

King Boxer (Tianxia Diyi Quan/aka Five Fingers of Death)
(Zheng Changhe, 1972, HK) Lo Lieh, Wang Ping, Wang Ching-Feng.
105 min.
This was the film that initiated the early '70s American craze for chop-socky. All the clichés are

already there: the young hick punching his way to star pupildom at the kung-fu school and being taught the secrets of the 'iron fist' technique (he is given an 'iron fist' manual), sweet young girlfriend versus tart-with-a-heart vying for the hero's attentions, rival martial arts schools battling it out to the death, nefarious Nips who fight dirty, and horrendous dubbing. The hero's hands get broken, but he plunges them into hot gravel and makes it to the Big Fight. All very egg fooyung, but the fight sequences are where it's at; they are splendid, and pack many a punch even by today's standards. AB

King Creole
(Michael Curtiz, 1958, US) Elvis Presley, Carolyn Jones, Dolores Hart, Dean Jagger, Walter Matthau, Liliane Montevecchi, Vic Morrow, Paul Stewart.
116 min. b/w.
Curtiz's intelligent, austere, film *noir*-ish direction provides the perfect antidote to the occasional excesses of a script based on a Harold Robbins novel (*A Stone for Danny Fisher*), and an ideal complement to Presley's performance as a street hustler who forges himself a magnetic rebel image through his music. The sequence in which he sings 'If you're looking for trouble' in a busboy's uniform in response to gangster Walter Matthau's dare is prime stuff. VG

King David
(Bruce Beresford, 1985, US) Richard Gere, Edward Woodward, Alice Krige, Denis Quilley, Niall Buggy, Cherie Lunghi, Hurd Hatfield, John Castle, Tim Woodward.
114 min.
And Richard Gere was David, a pretty unsavoury character who spent most of his time smiting the Philistines and anyone else who wore interesting hats. And Goliath of Gath got it between the eyes, and old hippy Absalom got strung up by his hair, and Gere stripped down to his nappies to do a moving Madonna-type dance. The OT, unless filmed OTT by the likes of Cecil B DeMille, is neither madly exciting nor morally sound. King David lacks spiritual uplift and amusingly dodo dialogue. It is too violent for a Sunday School audience and not violent enough for headcrushers, but fashion students will recognise it as a prime example of the Accessory Theory of Film Criticism: here are many desirable earrings, natty plaits and robes akin to Comme des Garcons out of Katharine Hamnett. AB

Kingdom, The (Riget)
(Lars von Trier/Morton Arnfred, 1994, Den) Ernst-Hugo Järegård, Kirsten Rolffes, Ghita Nørby, Søren Pilmark, Holger Juul Hansen, Annevig Schelde Ebbe.
279 min.
This mordant blend of hospital soap, occult schlocker and social satire makes David Lynch seem prim. Set in a Copenhagen hospital, it's a farce which puts a dead man's grip on the clichés of TV soap opera. The fun comes partly from the deadpan performances – from Järegård's consultant, a universally loathed Dane-hating Swede, to Rolffes' Mrs Drusse, a career patient determined to exorcise from the building the unquiet spirit of a murdered girl. No opportunity for going over the top is missed, no ethical interdict is left untransgressed, no sensibility untrammelled. As a social indictment, it's structured in tiers, from the top-floor, which houses the administrators' Masonic lodge, to the building's bowels, in which work the dishwashers, savants with Down's syndrome who function as an eerie Greek chorus. Shot in breathless *vérité*-style, and marked by von Trier's customary jaundiced tone, it's a compulsive, bizzarely plausible witches' brew of interweaving storylines, conspiracy theories and paranoiac visions, held together by manic conviction right up to its Grand Guignol finale. WH

Kingdom II, The (Riget II)
(Lars von Trier/Morten Arnfred, 1997, Den) Ernst-Hugo Järegård, Kirsten Rolffes, Ghita Nørby, Søren Pilmark, Holger Juul Hansen.
286 min.
It's back to our favourite Copenhagen hospital for another four episodes (with more to come!) of von Trier's surreal soap about medical corruption and monstrous apparitions. No recaps are supplied (some homework is necessary for the uninitiated) while further layers of plot build up with less ten-

sion and more extravagant fantasy. Little of this should be revealed in advance – be warned, however, that the emerging baby sporting Udo Kier's head was no bad dream, but a living creature who refuses to stop growing. DT

Kingdom of the Spiders
(John 'Bud' Cardos, 1977, US) William Shatner, Tiffany Bolling, Woody Strode, Lieux Dressler, David McLean, Natasha Ryan.
95 min.
The scene is Arizona, here and now. A calf mysteriously falls ill and dies, baffling local vet and Marlboro' man Shatner. Tissue samples are sent to the big-town university, and the 'liberated' Bolling (insect expert) appears, diagnosing a huge overdose of spider venom. Together they discover a spider hill, a kind of grand convention for all arachnids everywhere. Nature is up-ended. Tarantulas, usually cannibals, have become community conscious. Man's insecticides have destroyed their natural food and so they are turning to...guess what? Wooden performances, hamfisted direction, an achingly bad script, plus a grisly Country and Western sound-track amount to a must to avoid even for the diehard kitsch fan. IB

King Elephant
see African Elephant, The

King in New York, A
(Charles Chaplin, 1957, GB) Charles Chaplin, Dawn Addams, Oliver Johnston, Maxine Audley, Harry Green, Michael Chaplin, Sidney James, Jerry Desmonde, George Woodbridge.
109 min. b/w.
The Old Man's penultimate movie is very odd indeed – set in America but made in England with a cast of old lags like George Woodbridge (which never helps any film) and filled with Chaplin's loathing for the country which turned against him in the late '40s, forcing him into exile. The film reverses the real-life situation: Chaplin plays the deposed king of Estrovia who flees to the States, where he is tormented by McCarthyish investigations and more innocuous '50s phenomena (rock'n'roll, widescreen movies, TV advertising). In *Limelight*, Chaplin's acute egocentricity paid dividends, but here he seems unable to use his personal feelings for comedy: the bulk of the gags are incredibly crude. One watches the proceedings with constant interest and constant embarrassment. GB

King Kong
(Merian C Cooper/Ernest B Schoedsack, 1933, US) Fay Wray, Bruce Cabot, Robert Armstrong, Noble Johnson, Frank Reicher, James Flavin.
100 min. b/w.
If this glorious pile of horror-fantasy hokum has lost none of its power to move, excite and sadden, it is in no small measure due to the remarkable technical achievements of Willis O'Brien's animation work, and the superbly matched score of Max Steiner. The masterstroke was, of course, to delay the great ape's entrance by a shipboard sequence of such humorous banality and risible dialogue that Kong can emerge unchallenged as the most truly realised character in the film. Thankfully Wray is not required to act, merely to scream; but what a perfect victim she makes. The throbbing heart of the film lies in the creation of the semi-human simian himself, an immortal tribute to the Hollywood dream factory's ability to fashion a symbol that can express all the contradictory erotic, ecstatic, destructive, pathetic and cathartic buried impulses of 'civilised' man. WH

King Kong
(John Guillermin, 1976, US) Jeff Bridges, Charles Grodin, Jessica Lange, John Randolph, Rene Auberjonois, Julius Harris, Ed Lauter, John Agar.
135 min.
The results of this technological bonanza are pretty mixed. With the ape's human characteristics exaggerated, the new Kong lacks his predecessor's noble, yet truly alien ferocity. Seemingly too human, his relationship with the nauseating Jessica Lange is pushed to mawkish and degrading lengths. But Lorenzo Semple's script tries hard to build on its more interesting components. He is unreservedly on the side of Kong and the

anthropologist (Bridges), against the oil/sex-ploitation company who are out to exhibit the ape (and Lange) as commercial objects. And the film's spirited climax is worthy of its ancestry, while a highly ambiguous ending allows the plot to reassert its old political strength and redeem the more grotesque and sexist moments of this resurrection. DP

King Lear

(Peter Brook, 1970, GB/Den) Paul Scofield, Irene Worth, Alan Webb, Tom Fleming, Susan Engel, Annelise Gabold, Jack MacGowran, Cyril Cusack, Patrick Magee.
137 min. b/w.
Made on location in what looks like a perilously cold Denmark, Brook's only Shakespeare on celluloid found a similarly frosty reception, especially as it came out just after Kozintsev's grandly conceived Russian version. Brook's filming is graceless – looming close-ups, perverse camera moves – but there are some remarkable performances (developed from his much praised stage production a few years before with Scofield). The conception is consistent with the influential views of Jan Kott, who saw Lear as a precursor to Beckett's plays about human blindness and nothingness (a line reinforced by the casting of MacGowran as the Fool, and Magee as the Duke of Cornwall). A bleak interpretation, in every sense. DT

King Lear (Korol Lir)

(Grigori Kozintsev, 1970, USSR) Yuri Yarvet, Elsa Radzinya, Galina Volchek, Valentina Shendrikova, Karl Sebris, Regimantis Adomaitis, Oleg Dal.
139 min. b/w.
Kozintsev's lusty adaptation succeeds in finding memorable equivalents for Shakespeare's verbal imagery, although the narrative is necessarily somewhat truncated. He makes Lear and his daughters act like a conceivable family, and brings the people into the affairs of the nobility more than usual, but the women fare badly. Yarvet (whose energetic though foolish king is a far cry from the doddering dope Lear is usually made out to be) and Dal (the Fool) are incredible. Music by Shostakovich; subtitles by Shakespeare. VG

King Lear

(Jean-Luc Godard, 1987, US) Burgess Meredith, Peter Sellars, Molly Ringwald, Jean-Luc Godard, Woody Allen, Norman Mailer, Kate Miller, Léos Carax.
90 min.
Godard's dullest and least accomplished for some time. Expectedly, only the odd line of Shakespeare's text survives, mouthed by bratpacker Molly Ringwald. People wander in and out; connections are tenuous in the extreme. Mailer gets a scene or two, suggests a Mafia reading of the play, and exits. Enter Burgess Meredith to pick up the cue as an ex-hoodlum, Don Learo, bewailing to his sullen daughter Ringwald, at a lakeside restaurant, the fate of the crime barons of old at the hands of the big corporations. Godard plays a shambling 'professor', his telephone-cable dreadlocks suggesting he may be the Fool. The fragmentation of image, narrative, sound and music are familiar, but here employed to no effect. Intercut are stills of dead, great directors. Intertitles like 'C-Lear-ings' and 'No-thing' testify to Godard's continuing fidelity to the ideas of modern French existentialism. Another of his essays on the impossibility of making movies in our time, this has all the dreariness of a pathologist's dictated notes. WH

King of Alcatraz

(Robert Florey, 1938, US) Lloyd Nolan, Robert Preston, Gail Patrick, J Carrol Naish, Harry Carey, Anthony Quinn, Dennis Morgan.
56 min. b/w.
A terrific B movie from Paramount's resident backlot maestro, Robert Florey. Naish makes an unclean break from the prison island, landing up (initially in drag, accompanied by hijacking henchmen) on a tramp steamer whose wireless is manned by operators Nolan and Preston, buddies currently under disciplinary downgrading because of their perpetual brawling rivalry. They get to show their mettle to pretty Gail Patrick. The script has no time for subtleties, but the movie is extremely well put together, and it moves at a tremendous lick. TCh

King of Burlesque

(Sidney Lanfield, 1936, US) Warner Baxter, Jack Oakie, Mona Barrie, Alice Faye, Dixie Dunbar, Fats Waller.
83 min. b/w.
Backstage musical with Baxter as a burlesque producer from the wrong side of town who tries to make it big on Broadway. Mona Barrie is the leech-like socialite who marries him, then bleeds him dry of all his cash. Alice Faye is on hand to soothe him back to success in the final reel. The song and dance is chipper enough, but the storyline needs more beef. Fats Waller makes a rare (but brief) appearance. GM

King of Comedy, The

(Martin Scorsese, 1982, US) Robert De Niro, Jerry Lewis, Diahnne Abbott, Sandra Bernhard, Ed Herlihy, Lou Brown.
109 min.
Scorsese and De Niro have been pushing each other so far for so long that audience polarisation now automatically accompanies the risk of their major-league collaboration. The King of Comedy guarantees a split even at the level of expectations: it's definitively not a comedy, despite being hilarious; it pays acute homage to Jerry Lewis, while requiring of the man no hint of slapstick infantilism; its uniquely repellent prize nerd is De Niro himself. The excruciating tone is set by an early freeze-frame of fingernails frantically scraping glass. Flinch here, and you're out, because Scorsese never does while detailing fantasist Rupert Pupkin's squirmily obsessive desperation to crash TV's real-time as a stand-up comic on the Carson-modelled Jerry Langford Show. Buttonholing its star (Lewis), then rebounding from brush-offs to hatch a ludicrous kidnap plot, De Niro's Pupkin isn't merely socially inadequate; he's a whole dimension short – happily rehearsing with cardboard cut-outs, choosing the flatness of videoscreen space for his schmucky jester's tilt at being 'king for a night'. Whereas the film itself is all unexpected dimensions and unsettling excesses, with the ambiguous fulfilment of Pupkin's dream frighteningly echoing the news-headline coda of Taxi Driver. Creepiest movie of the year in every sense, and one of the best. PT

King of Hearts (Le Roi de Coeur)

(Philippe de Broca, 1966, Fr/It) Alan Bates, Geneviève Bujold, Jean-Claude Brialy, Françoise Christophe, Julien Guiomar, Pierre Brasseur, Michel Serrault, Micheline Presle, Adolfo Celi.
110 min.
One of the sleepers of all time in that, tried out in a small Boston cinema years after it flopped in the UK and in America, it became a kind of Mousetrap in student cinemas across the States. On a World War I mission, Bates discovers a town of lunatics which is due to be blown up at midnight. The fairy-tale atmosphere and carnival energy are nicely placed, but the whole excessively whimsical thing would have worked so much better if de Broca had toughened up the overall (wartime) context instead of letting everything slide towards farce. PT

King of Jazz, The

(John Murray Anderson, 1930, US) Paul Whiteman and His Orchestra, John Boles, Bing Crosby and the Rhythm Boys, Slim Summerville, Laura LaPlante.
105 min.
Jazz? Whiteman may not have been the hottest swinger in town, but this is still hugely enjoyable, partly because of the marvellous two-strip Technicolor, partly because it dispenses with story altogether to focus on a lavishly designed musical revue. Catch Joe Venuti on fiddle, and Whiteman and his boys pounding out Gershwin's 'Rhapsody in Blue'. GA

King of Kings

(Nicholas Ray, 1961, US) Jeffrey Hunter, Robert Ryan, Siobhan McKenna, Frank Thring, Hurd Hatfield, Rip Torn, Harry Guardino, Viveca Lindfors, Rita Gam.
168 min.
Despite being churlishly described at the time as 'I Was a Teenage Jesus'(in reference to the youth rebellion of Rebel Without a Cause), this is one of the most interesting screen versions of the Gospels. As so often in the work of scriptwriter Philip Yordan, the central conflict is seen in terms of political struggle and betrayal; detailing the Jews' rebellion against the oppressive power of Rome, it elevates Barabbas in particular to the status of an almost proto-Zionist nationalist leader, and the dynamics of the narrative are presented as the consequence of wide-ranging historical movements rather than the whims of charismatic individuals. As a result, some of the performances appear to lack depth, but one can't deny the effectiveness of Miklos Rozsa's fine score, and of Ray's simple but elegant visuals which achieve a stirring dramatic power untainted by pompous bombast. Despite producer Samuel Bronston's meddlesome editing, in fact, it's an intelligent, imaginative movie devoid of conventional Hollywood pieties. GA

King of Kung Fu (Shi Xiong Chu Ma/ aka He Walks Like a Tiger)

(Jiang Yixiong, 1973, HK) Alex Lung, Christine Hui, Yukio Someno, Steve Yu, Yu Lung.
93 min.
This is a straight-up Chinese actioner with no trimmings, a few decidedly graceful moments (an acrobatic group performing in slow motion), and a virtue that several of the independent productions seem to share, that of incorporating a genuine street feeling, however fleetingly, into the proceedings. Out of the same stable as Headcrusher, the film is marred by the usual rambly story-line, some sentimentality, and producer Jimmy L Pascual's continuing love affair with the police (the 'man with no name' turns out to be an investigating officer). The fights are spirited. VG

King of Marvin Gardens, The

(Bob Rafelson, 1972, US) Jack Nicholson, Bruce Dern, Ellen Burstyn, Julia Anne Robinson, Scatman Crothers, Charles Lavine, John Ryan, Sully Boyar.
104 min.
An irresistible movie, not least for its haunting vision of Atlantic City as Xanadu, a stately pleasure dome of genteelly decaying palaces, rundown funfairs, and empty boardwalks presided over by white elephants abandoned to their brooding fate. It's like some unimaginable country of the mind, and so in a sense it is as two brothers embark on a sort of game (Atlantic City provided the original place names for the Monopoly board) in which they exchange their lives, their loves and their dreams. One has retreated, like Prospero, from the pain outside into the island of his mind; the other pursues an endless mirage of get-rich-quick schemes which will let him escape to an island paradise. Their fusion is a stunningly complex evocation of childish complicity and Pinterish obsessions, inevitably leading to tragedy as the obsessions founder on reality. One of the most underrated films of the decade. TM

King of Masks (Bian Lian)

(Wu Tian Ming, 1995, HK) Chu Yuk, Chao Yim Yin, Zhao Zhi Gang, Zhang Riu Yang.
101 min.
The first film in ten years from the one-time godfather of China's 'fifth generation' directors is an eloquent and deeply felt protest against greed and inhumanity; any relevance to the state of Chinese society in the 1990s is, of course, purely coincidental. The story centres on an elderly street entertainer in the rural Sichuan of the 1930s (his act involves switching masks with uncanny speed) who realises that he risks dying without an heir to inherit the secrets of his art. He decides to adopt a son, but the boy he buys from a penniless man turns out to be a tomboy who brings him little but grief. The film's allegorical implications are almost as plain as its attacks on sexual inequalities and political misrule, but Wu lets nothing get in the way of very expressive images and a very emotive plot. TR

King of New York

(Abel Ferrara, 1989, US) Christopher Walken, David Caruso, Larry Fishburne, Victor Argo, Wesley Snipes, Janet Julian, Joey Chin, Giancarlo Esposito, Steve Buscemi.
103 min.

Quite easily the most violent, foul-mouthed and truly nasty of current gangster movies. It might be charitable to say that Ferrara, who made the reasonably decent *Cat Chaser*, is doing a *Scarface* by pointing up the designer nature of modern urban crime, its brutality and ethnic mixture, and its attempts to infiltrate the mainstream. Certainly, in the person of Walken, spare, elegant, slightly spaced and lording it over a black/hispanic gang, the film has an impressively charismatic central character: the kind of powerbroker who does favours for the poor and makes love on subway trains, but still manages the right burst of psychosis when dealing with racist rivals, Chinese nasties, or treacherous black brothers. Sadly, his performance is wasted on a film which, despite splendid location work, lurches sloppily and messily from kill to kill, orgy to orgy, coke to crack, cliché to cliché. SGr

King of the Children (Haizi Wang)

(Chen Kaige, 1987, China) Xie Yuan, Yang Xuewen, Chen Shaohua, Zhang Caimei, Xu Guoqing.
106 min.
An unschooled young man, one of the countless victims of Mao's Cultural Revolution, is labouring in the countryside when he is suddenly assigned to teach in a near-by village school. Gradually, he finds the confidence to ditch the Maoist textbook and encourage the barely literate kids to write about their own lives and feelings. At the same time, through a series of dream-like meetings with a young cowherd, he begins to sense the possibilities of a life beyond the parameters of traditional education. There are echoes here of a film like *Padre Padrone*, but Chen's film is completely free of flabby humanist sentimentality. It takes its tonality from the harsh beauty of the Yunnan landscape of soaring forests and misty valleys: a territory of the mind where hard-edged realism blurs easily into hallucination. By Chinese standards, this is filmmaking brave to the point of being visionary. By any standards, this follow-up to *Yellow Earth* and *The Big Parade* is also something like a masterpiece. TR

King of the Damned

(Walter Forde, 1935, GB) Conrad Veidt, Helen Vinson, Noah Beery, Cecil Ramage, Edmund Willard, Raymond Lovell, Percy Parsons.
76 min. b/w.
Basically just another of those penal colony movies, set in a Caribbean Devil's Island, with the convicts rebelling against a sadistic regime. Not uninteresting, though, in the Popular Front slant to its script whereby Veidt, having led a successful revolt against the cruelly oppressive (but temporary) governor, plays desperately for time before the news gets out because his main objective is to prove that the island can be run profitably and peacefully by the convicts themselves. Though too good to be true as a character (as is his bluff sidekick, played by Beery), Veidt gives his usual admirable performance; the camerawork (Bernard Knowles) is remarkably atmospheric; and Forde's direction is more than capable. TM

King of the Gypsies

(Frank Pierson, 1978, US) Sterling Hayden, Shelley Winters, Susan Sarandon, Judd Hirsch, Eric Roberts, Brooke Shields, Annette O'Toole, Annie Potts, Michael V Gazzo.
112 min.
This starts in the rematch-for-retards category – reuniting Sarandon and Shields as the selfish mother/saleable daughter team from *Pretty Baby* – then tries to filter *The Godfather* through *Fiddler on the Roof*. Result: a gypsy vernacular of incredible brayings, bleatings, and raspings painfully laced with the Bronx (where much of the action occurs), and numerous crowd scenes resembling some *Night of the Living Loviches*. Sarandon out-crasses everyone else (matched only by the scene-by-scene disintegration of Shelley Winters). The Gypsy King's young successor (Roberts) – his decline predestined by the current recession of interest in fortune-telling – tries to make it all mean something: 'This is just temporary...and it's all trashy.' If only he were right; really it's endless and doggedly in earnest. CR

King of the Hill

(Steven Soderbergh, 1993, US) Jesse Bradford, Jeroen Krabbé, Lisa Eichhorn, Karen Allen, Spalding Gray, Elizabeth McGovern, Adrien Brody.
103 min.
St Louis, 1933. The Great Depression. Twelve-year-old Aaron (Bradford) has the richest imagination in the class and the poorest parents. They board in a dilapidated hotel in the wrong part of town. Mother (Eichhorn) goes into hospital, suffering from what looks like general malaise. Father (Krabbé) sends away Aaron's younger brother to live with his aunt, and when a job finally comes his way, he has no choice but to go on the road as a travelling salesman. That leaves Aaron to fend for himself, with some help from his streetwise pal Lester (Brody), and the kindly concern of the odd sympathetic adult. If Soderbergh could be said to be playing safe here, who could blame him after the ambitious but neglected *Kafka*? True the coming-of-age scenario holds few surprises, but this beautifully played film's sensitivity speaks volumes; Soderbergh lets his camera do the talking. What seems initially a nostalgic hue eventually becomes a harder, tougher tone. The result is both heartening and astringent. TCh

King of the Roaring 20's – The Story of Arnold Rothstein (aka The Big Bankroll)

(Joseph M Newman, 1961, US) David Janssen, Dianne Foster, Jack Carson, Dan O'Herlihy, Mickey Rooney, Keenan Wynn, Joseph Schildkraut, Mickey Shaughnessy, William Demarest, Regis Toomey, Diana Dors.
106 min. b/w.
Cavalier about its facts, this biopic of the infamous, short, chubby gambling kingpin Arnold Rothstein (played by tall smoothie Janssen) contrives to suggest that all went wrong for this middle-class whizz-kid because his childhood peccadillos were dogged by a bent cop (O'Herlihy) eternally on the take. His achievement of fame, fortune and true love (Foster) comes crashing around his ears when his schemes lead to the gangland murder of his longtime buddy and partner (Rooney). Rothstein has to hold himself morally responsible; but the real culprit, we are assured, is racketeer Big Tim O'Brien (Carson), working hand-in-glove with O'Herlihy (among others) to gain control of the gambling scene by manipulating Rothstein. Terminally dreary in its convolutions, the script eventually disappears up the backside of its plodding plot, while only Jack Carson manages to invest his character with any conviction. TM

King of the Wind

(Peter Duffell, 1989, US) Frank Finlay, Jenny Agutter, Nigel Hawthorne, Navin Chowdry, Ralph Bates, Barry Foster, Anthony Quayle, Ian Richardson, Norman Rodway, Peter Vaughan, Richard Harris, Glenda Jackson, Melvyn Hayes.
102 min.
HTV's adaptation of Marguerite Henry's children's adventure story boasts the sort of cast usually reserved for Agatha Christie (a couple of lines apiece for Harris and Jackson; others guilty of accepting insupportable roles). The leads, however, go to young Navin Chowdry (from *Madame Sousatzka*) as a mute Arab orphan, and the feisty colt he grooms for the Bey of Tunis. Presented as a gift to King Louis XV of France, the pair's fortunes swing from aristocratic patronage to plebeian servitude, and back again, and back again, taking in at least six owners and locations as diverse as the French court and Newgate jail. This viewer would have been happy to trade the surfeit of plot for a touch of subtlety. But horses for courses: children will probably respond to these equestrian escapades, Chowdry makes a natural hero, and Duffell's economic direction at least ensures that the going is firm. TCh

Kingpin

(Peter Farrelly/Bobby Farrelly, 1996, US) Woody Harrelson, Randy Quaid, Vanessa Angel, Bill Murray, Chris Elliott, William Jordan, Lin Shaye.
114 min.
Harrelson's Roy Munson, the 1979 Odor Eaters

Ten-Pin Bowling Champion, has been 17 years on the skids, paying off the bubo-encrusted landlady of his verminous flophouse with vomit-inducing bouts of sex. If he's lucky. Only with the arrival of fright-wigged con artist Ernie McCracken (Murray, gleefully camp) do things look up, McCracken teaching him to make money hustling ten-pin, until he's abandoned to a bunch of rednecks who twig to him and slash off his bowling hand. Undaunted, he happens upon Quaid's Ishmael Boorg, an ingenuous Amish and fellow bowling natural, and they take off for the National Championships in Reno, pausing only to pick up mini-skirted 'personal companion' Claudia (Angel). There's something arresting in the sheer commitment the Farrelly brothers bring to the naff gags, pratfalls and ritual humiliations these three go through. More beguiling still is their warts-and-all depiction of low life, so upfront it ends up quite affectionate; equally, the keen observations quash charges of cynicism. Dumbfounding. WH

King, Queen, Knave (Herzbube)

(Jerzy Skolimowski, 1972, WGer/US) Gina Lollobrigida, David Niven, John Moulder-Brown, Mario Adorf, Carl Fox-Duering.
92 min.
Probably the most unjustly underrated of all Skolimowski's films, a surreal black comedy – based on Nabokov's novel retailing a triangle situation, with puckish overtones of obsession and perversion, between a wealthy businessman, his luscious wife, and an orphaned boy – that pushes some of the satirical extravagances of Frank Tashlin and Jerry Lewis to their most logical and deathly conclusions. Hilarious, misanthropic and disturbing, the movie amply fulfils Tom Milne's description of it as 'the most Nabokovian film the cinema has thrown up to date'. Despite reservations about its hybrid nature as an English version of a West German production, it certainly warrants a look. JR

King Ralph

(David S Ward, 1991, US) John Goodman, Peter O'Toole, John Hurt, Camille Coduri, Richard Griffiths, Leslie Phillips, Joely Richardson, Julian Glover, Judy Parfitt.
97 min.
When the entire English royal family is killed in a freak accident, a team of scholars sets about finding an heir to the throne. Meet Ralph Jones (Goodman), Las Vegas entertainer and all-round loser. The reluctant monarch makes his way to face the horrors of etiquette, corgis and entourage, and before long Buckingham Palace comes to resemble a fun-fair. Meanwhile, dastardly Lord Graves (Hurt, wonderfully hammy) plots his fall from grace. This lame hybrid of travelogue and (attempted) satire introduces the unwary American to English cuisine, cricket and newspapers, and any notions that the film is irreverent are trashed by a concluding homage to the monarchy. The ever-watchable Goodman is given no opportunity to exercise his intelligence here, while Hurt and O'Toole (impeccable as the King's private secretary) go through the paces. Laughable – without the laughs. CM

King Rat

(Bryan Forbes, 1965, US) George Segal, Tom Courtenay, James Fox, Denholm Elliott, Todd Armstrong, Patrick O'Neal, James Donald, John Mills, Alan Webb, Leonard Rossiter.
134 min. b/w.
Interesting but flawed adaptation of James Clavell's novel about a Japanese POW camp in Singapore towards the end of World War II. Taking a leaf out of Billy Wilder's *Stalag 17*, it similarly sets out to demonstrate that survival was the name of the game (with Segal taking the William Holden role as the cynical collaborator/fixer-upper), but goes a stage further to delete all notions of heroism. The trouble is that the script gets lost between too many options, setting up a number of character conflicts but taking them nowhere much. Effective performances and camera-work (Burnett Guffey), but Forbes directs with his usual lapses into overstatement. TM

Kings and Desperate Men

(Alexis Kanner, 1981, Can) Patrick McGoohan, Alexis Kanner, Andrea Marcovicci, Margaret Trudeau, Jean-Pierre Brown, Robin Spry.
118 min.

A generally inept psychological thriller, loosely taking off from the last episode of *The Prisoner* with its conflict between McGoohan and Kanner. The former's a radio phone-in host, the latter some sort of leftie who holds McGoohan hostage and demands the retrial of a recent court case over the airwaves. Pretty over the top, not to mention ill-conceived in its woolly thinking about terrorism. GA

Kings Go Forth

(Delmer Daves, 1958, US) Frank Sinatra, Tony Curtis, Natalie Wood, Karl Swenson, Leora Dana.
109 min. b/w.
Well-crafted but unconvincing mixture of war movie and melodramatic problem picture, with Sinatra and Curtis as GIs in France in 1944, falling out over Wood, an expatriate American girl who is beautiful but proves to be not entirely white. Daves, as so often, does a careful salvage job on a soapy script, but the best sequence is a brief jazz interlude with Curtis (giving the best performance in the film) grabbing a trumpet in a dive and (ghosted by Pete Candoli) sitting in with Red Norvo and group. GA

Kings of the Road (Im Lauf der Zeit)

(Wim Wenders, 1976, WGer) Rüdiger Vogler, Hanns Zischler, Lisa Kreuzer, Rudolf Schündler, Marquard Böhm.
176 min. b/w.
...or, King of the Road Movies. Wenders' epic, during which little happens, is one of the great films about men (with each other, without women), about travelling, about cinema (one of the central characters is a projection engineer visiting rundown cinemas, and about the effect of America in 'colonising' the European subconscious. The plot, such as it is, about two men meeting up, moving around Germany, and then splitting up again, is a loose framework for an investigation in various subjects that is marked by its emotional honesty, stunning visual organisation, lack of contrivance, and use of music. Marvellous. GA

Kings of the Sun

(J Lee Thompson, 1963, US) Yul Brynner, George Chakiris, Shirley Anne Field, Richard Basehart, Brad Dexter, Barry Morse, Armando Silvestre, Leo Gordon.
107 min.
An ambitious, if ludicrous, pre-Western, marking the struggles between exiled Mayan tribesmen (led by Chakiris as Prince Balam) and the native Indians (Brynner as Chief Black Eagle) in what eventually became Texas, achieving peaceful coexistence after the Mayans abandon their rites of human sacrifice. On the heels of this portentous exotica, co-writer James R Webb picked up the same year's Oscar for what might be construed as the continuing story, *How the West Was Won*. PT

King Solomon's Mines

(Robert Stevenson, 1937, GB) Paul Robeson, Cedric Hardwicke, John Loder, Roland Young, Anna Lee, Sydney Fairbrother, Robert Adams.
80 min. b/w.
Not quite Rider Haggard's ripping adventure, given that Robeson's Umbopo is required to sing (singularly soggy stuff, too, with full orchestral accompaniment) and a soppily conventional love interest has been injected. But there are two fine performances (Hardwicke as Allan Quartermain, Young as Captain Good), Stevenson keeps things moving quite briskly to the volcanic climax, and it's a damn sight better than the 1985 remake (or the 1950 Stewart Granger version for that matter). TM

King Solomon's Mines

(J Lee Thompson, 1985, US) Richard Chamberlain, Sharon Stone, Herbert Lom, Bernard Archard, John Rhys-Davies, Ken Gampu.
100 min.
Haggard's magnificently cynical Allan Quartermain gives way to Richard Chamberlain's bland incompetent, a man with the sex appeal of a sheep and the comic timing of a manatee. Sharon Stone is trapped in the role of a silly woman who needs rescuing, much like the heroine of the *Indiana Jones and the Temple of Doom* farrago, a film which this clearly imitates. The

friendly Umbopo turns out, for reasons a shade obscure, to be Twala, the book's bad number. And the feral relentlessness of tribal bloodshed is nowhere to be seen; instead there are comic Huns with pointy helmets and bad manners. It's stone cold dead on the slab. CPea

King Solomon's Treasure

(Alvin Rakoff, 1978, Can) David McCallum, John Colicos, Patrick Macnee, Britt Ekland, Yvon Dufour, Ken Gampu, Wilfrid Hyde-White.
88 min.
Credited as based on Rider Haggard's *Allan Quartermain*, but suspicions of 'poetic licence', creeping in with the appearance of the first prehistoric monster, are confirmed as full-blown travesty by the time our three bluff Victorian hearties, setting out for Solomon's legendary city, start using a pseudopod as a beast of burden. Cheapness aside (polystyrene pillars will bounce), it's the multitude of nationalities that becomes confusing (Viking vessel crewed by Romans, Queen Britt as Cleopatra, an ancient Greek and Madame de Pompadour in the space of an afternoon). But it's hard to dislike the blimpish trio, who miraculously survive rebellious priests, erupting volcanoes and tumbling cities to return to the old country with nothing but a tale to tell their grandchildren. FF

Kings Row

(Sam Wood, 1940, US) Ann Sheridan, Robert Cummings, Ronald Reagan, Betty Field, Claude Rains, Charles Coburn, Judith Anderson, Maria Ouspenskaya, Nancy Coleman.
127 min. b/w.
Question: connect President Reagan with the following quotation, 'A good town to live in. A good place to raise your children'. No, not one of Ron's election promises; it's the roadside sign that gets this glorious, maggot's-eye view of mid-town America under way, the film that made Reagan a star. Twenty years later he was back to second billing, but was busying himself as President of the Screen Actors Guild, leading and winning a strike for residual payments for non-theatrical releases. Twenty years later still, and the SAG won another deal on residuals while our Ron bid for a bigger presidency. Strange to think he'd probably protest about a contemporary *King's Row* as un-American, and that he drew up anti-union legislation. The movie, though, is one of the great melodramas (from the same Wood/Menzies stable that made *Gone With the Wind*), as compulsive and perverse as any election, a veritable Mount Rushmore of emotional and physical cripples, including a surgeon with a penchant for unnecessary amputations, a girl 'made friends on one side of the tracks and made love on the other', and best of all, a legless Reagan wondering 'Where's the rest of me?' PK

King Steps Out, The

(Josef von Sternberg, 1936, US) Grace Moore, Franchot Tone, Walter Connolly, Raymond Walburn, Elizabeth Risdon, Frieda Inescort, Herman Bing, Victor Jory.
85 min. b/w.
Exchanging Paramount and Dietrich for Columbia and Miss Grace Moore (as she is rather crassly credited), Sternberg's heart was all too obviously not in this adaptation of a Fritz Kreisler operetta. Moore, overdoing the skittish charm, plays Princess Elizabeth of Bavaria, who ends up in the arms of the Emperor Franz Josef (Tone) after intervening to save her sister (Inescort) – who loves a young officer (Jory) – from becoming his prearranged bride. Sternberg makes heavy weather of the comic opera conventions; he lumbers his star with several unflattering close-ups (notably when she sings: unusually, the songs were shot 'live'); and he gets his act together (his interest obviously captured by the bustling movement and quaint sideshow attractions of a rustic fair) only during a lengthy sequence in which the Emperor steps out incognito with the princess he believes to be a humble dressmaker. The rest is tasteless puff pastry for operetta buffs only. TM

King Ubu (Král Ubu)

(FA Brabec, 1996, Czech Republic) Marian Labuda, Lucie Bílá, Karel Roden, Boleslav Polívka, Chantal Poullain.
84 min.
A 'bawdy black farce', this downgrading of the

Scottish Play, from former Czech cameraman FA Brabec, does to Shakespeare's tragedy what Macbeth did to Duncan. Having made his military mark with army manoeuvres signalled by burps and farts, cretinous general Ubu and his lieutenant M'Nure knock off King Wenceslas at the behest of the Medusa-locked Mrs Ubu. Once enthroned, Ubu molests maidens, impose prohibitive taxes (on death, rheumatism and pickles), tours the land by motorbike, with trailing gallows rig, and declares war on Russia. It's cheerfully scattershot nonsense, but Milos Macourek's script from Alfred Jarry's play is witless, and there's a loud desperation about Brabec's direction. NB

Kini & Adams

(Idrissa Ouedraogo, 1997, Zim/GB) Vusi Kunene, David Mohloki, Nthati Moshesh, John Kani.
93 min.
Kunene and Mohloki fall out over women, work and the car they see as a passport to wealth in an Africa defined by poverty, prostitution and the corruption of traditional values. Ouedraogo uses the 'Scope frame to vivid visual effect, holds the whole ramshackle affair together through the sheer good nature of the performances, and shows us a modern, semi-industrialised Africa all too often ignored by that continent's cinema – but the fairy tale simplicity and contrived tragic climax sit uneasily together and make for a certain superficiality. GA

Kisapmata

(Mike de Leon, 1981, Phil) Vic Silayan, Charito Solis, Charo Santos, Jay Ilagan, Ruben Rustia.
90 min.
De Leon's film amply confirms the power of the work currently being done in the Filipino cinema. Based on a real- life murder scandal dating from 1961, its carefully handled story of incestuous obsession, bolstered by strong performances, builds to a climax which would be melodramatic in less skilful hands. But on the way it also paints a frightening portrait of terrible family tensions, edge-of-insanity patriarchy, and Catholic repression which makes its wider social implications abundantly and devastatingly clear. SM

Kismet

(Vincente Minnelli, 1955, US) Howard Keel, Ann Blyth, Dolores Gray, Monty Woolley, Sebastian Cabot, Vic Damone, Jay C Flippen, Mike Mazurki, Jack Elam.
113 min.
Magicians and caliphs, poets and lovers, all involved in Arabian Nights-style romantic intrigues: the ideal material, one would have thought, for a full-blown exotic musical. But despite the ripe melodies borrowed from Borodin and the expensively luscious sets, it never really takes off, thanks partly to a less than top-notch cast, partly to Minnelli's often indifferent direction. Minnelli himself has commented: 'Arthur (Freed) had already asked me to direct the picture, but I didn't relate to it, and declined. Now I was being asked again (by Dore Schary), and the implication was that I wouldn't get the Van Gogh picture (*Lust for Life*) if I didn't direct *Kismet*. I capitulated...' GA

Kiss, The

(Jacques Feyder, 1929, US) Greta Garbo, Conrad Nagel, Anders Randolf, Holmes Herbert, Lew Ayres.
5,760 ft. b/w.
Both MGM's and Garbo's last silent, this is one of the actress' most memorable films, simply because it combines characteristic studio gloss (art direction by Cedric Gibbons, luminous close-ups by William Daniels) with a genuine feeling for her mixture of erotic glamour and doomy passion. As a woman tried for the murder of a husband who refuses her a divorce, she is perfectly cast, while Ayres makes a fine show as the youngster whose kiss seals her fate. And Feyder's direction contrives to transcend the novelettish nature of the material by means of its elegance, ambiguity, and sheer commitment to the melodramatic emotions. GA

Kiss, The

(Pen Densham, 1988, US) Joanna Pacula, Meredith Salenger, Pamela Collyer, Peter Dvorsky, Mimi Kuzyk, Nicholas Kilbertus, Sabrina Boudot.
101 min.

Densham's daft and derivative 'possession' pic (his debut) starts in the Belgian Congo, with a sickly child miraculously revived when her aunt kisses her passionately, passing on an invigorating power before herself expiring. Some years later in America, soon after child-woman Salenger's religious confirmation, her mysterious aunt (Pacula) materialises at a family funeral. With the help of a blood-dripping African talisman and a bright-eyed black cat, Pacula seduces Salenger's father and incites much psychic chaos. The film soon degenerates into screeching incoherence, and – crucially – fails to explore the erotic undercurrents hinted at by Salenger's burgeoning sexuality and her aunt's corrupting desire. Salenger's tearful teen is too pathetic to elicit either sympathy or interest, Pacula hams it up as the demonic aunt, and Mimi Kuzyk provides the only shred of credible humanity as a sympathetic neighbour. Chris (*The Fly*) Walas' special effects are often more eye-catching than the inane plot deserves. NF

Kiss Before Dying, A

(Gerd Oswald, 1956, US) Robert Wagner, Jeffrey Hunter, Joanne Woodward, Mary Astor, Virginia Leith, George Macready.
94 min.
An early Ira Levin thriller, predating *Rosemary's Baby, The Stepford Wives* and *Deathtrap*, superbly adapted as an icily acute nightmare (and as a riposte to the academicism of *A Place in the Sun*) by the great Oswald, giving a criminally myopic Hollywood its first glimpse of a unique visual talent, idiosyncratically developed from that of his father, German silent director Richard Oswald. Wagner is perfect as the college kid psycho coolly removing the pregnant Woodward from his life, and both he and Hunter were picked up from here by Nick Ray to play his James Brothers the following year. PT

Kiss Before Dying, A

(James Dearden, 1991, US) Matt Dillon, Sean Young, Max von Sydow, Jim Fyfe, Ben Browder, Diane Ladd, James Russo, Martha Gehman.
95 min.
Writer-director Dearden's version of Ira Levin's novel is routine stuff, neither thrilling nor revealing as a portrait of a psychopath. Jonathan Corliss (Dillon) comes from the wrong side of the tracks and dreams of being tycoon Thor Carlsson (von Sydow). Getting that status means marrying into the family, but the first daughter (Young) gets inconveniently pregnant, so he courts and marries the second (also Young). But the fly in the ointment is her obsession with investigating her sister's death... There's an untidiness about the film that suggests something else was intended. Why those fierce opening shots of the copper furnace if we are to be denied Levin's final *Götterdämmerung?* Dillon does his best; Young doesn't seem equipped to do a lot with a woman who discovers she's nurtured a viper at her bosom; Ladd brings pathos to the role of the killer's mother. BC

Kissed

(Lynne Stopkewich, 1996, Can) Molly Parker, Peter Outerbridge, Jay Brazeau, Natasha Morley, Jessie Winter Mudie, Joe Maffei.
78 min.
This independent first feature, from story by Barbara Gowdy about a young mortician's deviant sexuality, is an edgy, challenging mix of style and content. A cross between a young Annette Bening and Isabelle Adjani, Molly Parker gives a formidable and engaging performance as an 'ordinary' woman, simultaneously chaste and sexual (she's turned on by corpses), who bravely sets out to chart her own adventurous course. The tone is, surprisingly, romantic – almost ecstatic. There are shocks (the embalming lesson is not for the faint-hearted), but overall director/co-writer Stopkevich's calm, non-judgmental approach pays rich dividends: the film is convincing, tender, and more than a little subversive. WH

Kissin' Cousins

(Gene Nelson, 1963, US) Elvis Presley, Arthur O'Connell, Glenda Farrell, Jack Albertson, Pamela Austin, Yvonne Craig, Donald Woods.
96 min.
A seventeen-day quickie, produced by Sam

Katzman as a lesson to Col. Tom Parker in how to make money, with Presley back in khaki as an air-force officer trying to move hillbillies – including himself as his blond-wigged cousin – in favour of missile bases. So thin that it barely exists. AC

Kiss Me Deadly

(Robert Aldrich, 1955, US) Ralph Meeker, Albert Dekker, Maxine Cooper, Paul Stewart, Gaby Rodgers, Cloris Leachman, Jack Lambert, Wesley Addy, Nick Dennis, Marian Carr.
105 min. b/w.
A key film from the '50s, a savage critique of Cold War paranoia bounded by two haunting sound effects: at the beginning, the desperate, panting sobs of the girl hitching a lift from Mike Hammer on the dark highway, and her despairing plea to 'Remember me' as she disappears to her death; and at the end, the strange, groaning sigh that escapes as the Pandora's box containing the Great Whatsit is finally opened to unleash an incandescent nuclear blast. Aldrich's distaste for the unprincipled brutality of Mickey Spillane's hero is evident throughout the film; but nevertheless given a sort of dumb-ox honesty by Ralph Meeker, the character acquires new resonance as an example of mankind's mulish habit of meddling with the unknown regardless of consequences. Brilliantly characterised down to the smallest roles, directed with baroque ferocity, superbly shot by Ernest Laszlo in *film noir* terms, it's a masterpiece of sorts. TM

Kiss Me Goodbye

(Robert Mulligan, 1982, US) Sally Field, James Caan, Jeff Bridges, Paul Dooley, Claire Trevor, Mildred Natwick, William Prince.
101 min.
Light fantastical comedy in which Sally Field moves into her old home and bumps into the ghost of her dead husband just as she's about to marry a new one. A *ménage à trois* with one party invisible naturally upsets her fiancé, who wonders what he is letting himself in for. *Blithe Spirit* without Madame Arcati. Noël Coward did it more entertainingly and less sentimentally years ago (though in fact it derives from the Brazilian *Doña Flor and Her Two Husbands* of 1976). JE

Kiss Me, Guido

(Tony Vitale, 1997, US/GB) Nick Scotti, Anthony Barrile, Anthony DeSandro, Molly Price, Craig Chester.
89 min.
Having found his fiancée in bed with his brother, Frankie wants out of the Bronx. He answers an ad for a roommate placed by actor Warren (Barrile), not realising that G stands for gay, not guy. Scotti's Frankie – naive and ambitious – is sweet beyond belief, and the pizza parlour where he works is portrayed as a hubbub of insular passions, where a working class man's shyness is taken for self-sufficiency. It's the gay world which, ironically, rings false. Barrile has befuddled chipmunk looks, but lacks comic timing, while Chester, as the queeny best friend, also shows a heavy hand. A first feature which goes from bad to dire as writer/director Vitale tries to hurry things on to a feel-good climax. CO'Su

Kiss Me Kate

(George Sidney, 1953, US) Kathryn Grayson, Howard Keel, Ann Miller, Keenan Wynn, James Whitmore, Tommy Rall, Bob Fosse, Bobby Van, Ron Randell.
109 min.
Cole Porter's amazing score wasn't the only standout when this tricksy backstage/onstage parallel version of *The Taming of the Shrew* first appeared. Contemporary fashion caused Sidney the headache of shooting in both 3-D and 'flat' formats, and he accentuated the planes of artifice by employing a succession of frames within frames (doors, windows, proscenia) and, for the stage scenes, shooting head-on from something like the third row of the 'audience'. The Chinese box play-within-a-play construction is worked out to a tee, and even extends to Randell playing a character called Cole Porter, scoring a Broadway musical. Brilliantly choreographed by Hermes Pan, Ann Miller's dance numbers (variously partnered by Rall, Fosse and Van) are the champagne that go with the film. PT

Kiss Me, Stupid

(Billy Wilder, 1964, US) Dean Martin, Kim Novak, Ray Walston, Felicia Farr, Cliff Osmond, Barbara Pepper, Doro Morande, Henry Gibson, Mel Blanc.
124 min. b/w.
Drawing heavily on Martin's offscreen persona, this sees him as an arrogant, sex-crazed crooner stranded in a remote Californian town and feigning interest in the songs of amateur composer Walston in return for the sexual favours of the latter's wife (Farr). Anticipating this, the desperately ambitious but possessively jealous Walston has in fact substituted a local tart-with-a-heart (Novak) for his wife; but his wife, meanwhile...Wilder's vulgar satire on greed, lust and sexual game-playing was decried as tasteless upon release; the effect is less outrageous now, but the epithet stands, particularly in the light of feminist awareness. Characteristically cynical, clever and brash, it's helped out enormously by the performances of Martin, Farr and (particularly) Novak as Polly the Pistol, but for all its ambitions it isn't really all that funny. GA

Kiss of Death

(Barbet Schroeder, 1994, US) David Caruso, Samuel L Jackson, Nicolas Cage, Helen Hunt, Kathryn Erbe, Stanley Tucci, Michael Rapaport, Ving Rhames.
101 min.
Ex-con Jimmy Kilmartin's a decent guy who'd rather babysit than hijack cars. Lured back for One Last Job – a favour to no-account cousin Ronnie – Jimmy takes a bullet and the fall. Worse, his wife, Bev, dies in an accident after a one-night stand with Ronnie. Jimmy drops the DA off against a psychotic mobster, Little Junior, to execute his revenge from behind bars, which puts him in double jeopardy on his release. Schroeder's honourable, rather onerous remake of Hathaway's gripping *film noir* is too restrained for its own good – it barely musters a climax – but it's a solid, atmospheric thriller all the same, with smart dialogue by Richard Price and a strong line-up of downbeat actors: Tucci as a DA of questionable integrity, Rhames as a scary drug-dealer, and Jackson as a cop with a weeping eye. Caruso's okay in the lead, but you can feel the weight of the movie (or is it destiny?) on his shoulders; in any case, he, along with the rest, is effectively steamrollered by Cage. 'I have an acronym for myself,' boasts Little Junior: 'Bad: Balls. Attitude. Direction'. I can't vouch for the direction, but he's definitely big on balls and attitude – no one's quite as bad as Nic when he's in this kind of mood: whether bench-pressing bargirls, confiding that he can't stand metal in his mouth, or taking another jolt of oxygen from his inhaler, this is larger-than-life villainy worthy of Elmore Leonard or Carl Hiaasen. TCh

Kiss of Death

(Henry Hathaway, 1947, US) Victor Mature, Brian Donlevy, Richard Widmark, Coleen Gray, Karl Malden, Taylor Holmes, Mildred Dunnock, Millard Mitchell.
98 min. b/w.
Late '40s Fox saw several attempts to conceal the split in the gangster film between *noir* expressionism and 'procedural' authenticity, but few as bizarre as this. Mature is the stool-pigeon torn apart by two kinds of family loyalty: the Mob and the Missus. Widmark débuts as a psycho hood with an unforgettable chuckle and a nice line in helping wheelchair-ridden old ladies down stairs. Of its period, of course, but extraordinarily modern too: nighttime New York peopled only by daylight's misfits (à la *The Warriors*); and when Mature's wife kills herself, a neighbour happily takes her place. PK

Kiss of Evil

see Kiss of the Vampire

Kiss of the Spider Woman

(Hector Babenco, 1985, Braz) William Hurt, Raúl Julia, Sonia Braga, José Lewgoy, Milton Goncalves.
121 min. b/w & col.
Flamboyant queen Molina (Hurt) and aggressive straight revolutionary Valentin (Julia) share a prison cell in an unnamed Latin American dictatorship. Molina, to Valentin's decreasing disgust, escapes the cell walls by recounting the camp French Resistance film of the title. The perfor-

mances of Hurt and Julia win votes by the minute, Babenco directs their growing relationship with subtlety and depth, and the structure – mixing flashback, arch movie fantasy and powerful cell sequences – knocks the shit out of the gimmicks in Schrader's dubious *Mishima*. A film of fine balance and tone, not least in the dramatic turnaround ending. JG

Kiss of the Vampire (aka Kiss of Evil)

(Don Sharp, 1962, GB) Clifford Evans, Noel Willman, Edward de Souza, Jennifer Daniel, Barry Warren, Isobel Black.
87 min.
A beautifully photographed film in which an English honeymoon couple are lured towards a fate worse than death by a Bavarian disciple (Willman) of the late Count Dracula. The main trouble is that some of the acting, especially from de Souza and Daniel as the young couple, is terribly stiff (against which must be set Isobel Black, playing a very fetching vampire). The use of scenery is particularly superb, giving it an almost Dreyerian quality. Ironically, the film's release was delayed until 1964 because the distributors thought that the batinfestation climax (one of the best scenes) flew dangerously close to *The Birds*, even though it was made quite some time before Hitchcock's film. DP

Kiss or Kill

(Bill Bennett, 1997, Aust) Frances O'Connor, Matt Day, Chris Haywood, Barry Otto, Andrew S Gilbert, Max Cullen.
96 min.
There's one richly absurdist scene here between two cops in a diner. There's an iota of interest in that writer/director Bennett has edited the film entirely in jump cuts (very aggravating). There's a choice quotation from Dylan Thomas to get the ball rolling ('We watch the show of shadows kiss or kill, / Flavoured of celluloid, give love the lie'). And then there's yet another ho-hum story of young lovers on the run from the law, this time through the Australian outback. TCh

Kiss the Girls

(Gary Fleder, 1997, US) Morgan Freeman, Ashley Judd, Cary Elwes, Tony Goldwyn, Jay O Sanders, Alex MacArthur, Bill Nunn, Brian Cox.
115 min.
Detective Alex Cross (Freeman) reassures a woman that she was justified in killing her abusive husband. Then we learn that the next victim of camp serial killer Casanova – if not Dr Kate McTiernan (Judd) – is no gimmicky 'new' woman. Neither saintly, nor 'GI Jane' macho, her best scenes occur in the killer's hideout, where he's collecting an array of female talent. Kate's desire to connect with these other women is palpable, and, thanks to Judd, notably moving. Nor does Kate's boldness become diluted once she joins forces with Cross. On the subject of race, the film is less impressive – its intentions are good, but it never digs deep. Why, for instance, are Freeman and Judd not allowed to develop their relationship (as they do in the James Patterson novel)? Nevertheless, a surprising, atmospheric treat. CO'Su

Kiss Tomorrow Goodbye

(Gordon Douglas, 1950, US) James Cagney, Barbara Payton, Luther Adler, Ward Bond, Barton MacLane, Steve Brodie, Helena Carter, Neville Brand.
102 min. b/w.
Excellent gangster thriller based on Horace McCoy's novel about an escaped con first ruthlessly betraying his partner, and then planning an ambitious robbery. Strong performances from a great cast and Douglas' taut, classical direction place it among the best of the post-war gangster movies, but it is of course Cagney who is most memorable: strutting, snarling, and lashing out in almost psychopathic anger at all around him, his immense energy conveys the spirit of callous violence far more effectively than the explicit acts perpetrated in later movies. GA

Kitami (Kurutta Butokai/ aka Lunatic Theatre)

(Hisayasu Sato, 1993, Jap) Takeshi Ito, Simone Kumai, Yo Suzuki, Kiyomi Ito, Koyama Hageki.
60 min.
Notorious for clearing cinemas at festival screenings, Sato's gay s/m weird-out is a direct-to-video title in Britain. Ryuzaki gets involved with Yukihiro Kitami without realising that his lover is a big-time sadist; he ends the relationship by slashing off Kitami's left arm with (what else?) a samurai sword. One year later, while scouring Tokyo for a multi-system video player to watch his Pasolini tapes, he's invited back to the 'secret theatre' where he first met Kitami. Simultaneously earnest and blackly comic, Sato's film seems less interested in either sadism or masochism as such than in the even more specialised tradition of louche psychodrama. TR

Kitchen

(Andy Warhol/Ronald Tavel, 1965, US) Edie Sedgwick.
70 min.
Drawn from a Ronald Tavel script that is frequently visible in shot, this has Edie Sedgwick and several half-undressed studs enacting a primitive psychodrama in a single set. Best seen as a documentary on non-actors struggling to cope with a script which they haven't learned. TR

Kitchen (Wo ai Chufang)

(Yim Ho, 1997, HK/Jap) Jordan Chan, Yasuko Tomita, Law Kar-Ying, Karen Mok, Lau Siu-Ming.
124 min.
Banana Yoshimoto's fey novella about a psychologically damaged girl falling in with a nice young man and his transsexual father-turned-mother was first filmed – wretchedly – by Yoshimitsu Morita in 1989. Yim Ho sensibly rethinks the book, transposing the setting to Hong Kong and focusing on the boy rather than the girl. He also gets to shoot much of it in underlit close-ups, paving the way for a real visual coup in the final scene. But he can't do anything about the fundamental lack of energy in the characters and story; elegant languor inexorably slides towards torpor. Jordan Chan is excellent as the terminally tongue-tied 'hero', but has to cope with one of the worst haircuts in screen history. TR

Kitchen, The

(James Hill, 1961, GB) Carl Mohner, Mary Yeomans, Eric Pohlmann, Tom Bell, Martin Boddey, James Bolam.
74 min. b/w.
In the steamy atmosphere of a large and insalubrious West End kitchen, chefs fight, philosophise and finally go berserk, while waitresses pout, dance and have miscarriages. An unlikely vehicle for the ACTT(the cine technicians' union) to choose for their incursion into commercial film-making, but the fact that it was the first play from socialist bright boy Arnold Wesker makes it explicable. Good intentions are perilously flimsy foundations for constructing worth-while films; Wesker and director Hill (more at home with Elsa the lioness and Worzel Gummidge) fall into the trap of making clichéd pontifications on the meaning of life, work, capitalism, the world. A strange mixture of utopian whimsicality and rather unlikely melodrama. RMy

Kitchen Toto, The

(Harry Hook, 1987, GB) Edwin Mahinda, Bob Peck, Phyllis Logan, Nicholas Charles, Ronald Pirie, Robert Urquhart, Kirsten Hughes, Edward Judd.
95 min.
Kenya, 1950. Mwangi (Mahinda) takes the job of kitchen toto or scullion in the household of police chief John Graham (Peck) after the murder of his pacifist clergyman father by Mau Mau revolutionaries. Events in the build-up to the slaughter that was to follow are presented only as they touch Mwangi, who fast becomes an embarrassment to both sides. Soon the boy is forced to take a rebel oath, swearing to take the head of a white man if required to do so, but he is already growing fond of Graham and his supremely cloying son (Pirie). The outcome of this division of loyalties is depressing, inevitable and unremarkable. All the performances are effective, particularly Peck and Mahinda – who carries the weight of the whole conflict upon his shoulders. Hook's low-key approach packs a surprisingly hard punch. He is clearly a talent to watch. RS

Kitty

(Mitchell Leisen, 1945, US) Paulette Goddard, Ray Milland, Patric Knowles, Reginald Owen, Cecil Kellaway, Constance Collier.
104 min. b/w.
One of the elegant Leisen's very best, with a lovely performance from Goddard as the 18th century London slum wench who gatecrashes society after being painted as a lady by Gainsborough. The tartly witty script (from a novel by Rosamund Marshall) owes something to *Pygmalion* as the grubby waif is taken up by Milland's raffish young man-about-town and taught the secrets of speech and deportment by his aunt. But tone and mood come closer to Renoir's *Diary of a Chambermaid*, blending sharp cynicism with shafts of tenderness as Milland seeks to capitalise on his creation, she sacrifices herself to save him from debtor's prison, and a couple of profitable marriages intervene before romance has its way. Stunningly shot by Daniel Fapp, scrupulously authentic in period detail (gorgeous sets and costumes), it's wholly delightful. TM

Klansman, The

(Terence Young, 1974, US) Lee Marvin, Richard Burton, Cameron Mitchell, OJ Simpson, Lola Falana, David Huddleston, Luciana Paluzzi, Linda Evans.
112 min.
Smalltown Alabama in the late '60s: rape, murder and rampant racism tear apart a sordid little community under the watchful, apathetic eyes of sheriff Marvin. Young directs with an alarming lack of subtlety, concentrating purely on (voyeuristically portrayed) action and rarely investigating the gradations in morality that inform the various characters. A pity, because the script by Sam Fuller and Millard Kaufman suggests the potential for something far better, a study in universal corruption pitched somewhere between Arthur Penn's *The Chase* and the inbred psychoses of Jim Thompson's novels. GA

Klassenverhältnisse

see Class Relations

Kleine Godard, Der

see Little Godard, A

Klondike Annie

(Raoul Walsh, 1936, US) Mae West, Victor McLaglen, Philip Reed, Harold Huber, Esther Howard, Soo Young.
80 min. b/w.
Action man Raoul Walsh must have been chafing at the bit as Mae West let the suggestive drawl of her dialogue dictate the film's measured pace. 'She Made the Frozen North Red Hot' said the posters, but the film could do with being a bit hotter: considering the story – Mae in the Klondike, adopting the identity of a Salvation Army missionary – the humour is tame indeed. But by 1936 censorship problems were beginning to knock the stuffing out of our heroine, though she still had her eyebrows to flutter and her blue-beat songs to sing ('I'm an Occidental Woman in an Oriental Mood for Love'). And watered down or not, Mae still remains – in the words she uses to describe her co-star McLaglen – 'no oil painting but...a fascinating monster'. GB

Klute

(Alan J Pakula, 1971, US) Jane Fonda, Donald Sutherland, Charles Cioffi, Roy Scheider, Dorothy Tristan, Rita Gam, Richard B Shull.
114 min.
Fonda's Oscar-winning performance as New York call-girl Bree Daniels is the real focus of Pakula's thriller, rather than Sutherland's Klute, the private eye whose increasingly obsessional 'protection' she reluctantly receives when menaced by a former client. Though it's obviously valid to follow the line that *Klute*, with its abstracted updates of private eye and urban *noir* conventions, initiated Pakula's string of paranoid thrillers (*The Parallax View*, *All the President's Men*), it's just as fruitful to see it as belonging to a trio of features (with *Comes a Horseman* and *Rollover*), each starring Fonda, that hinge on the contradictions of autonomy and emotional commitment facing would-be independent women. The threats of dependency and destruction here become Sutherland's investigator and Cioffi's telephone breather, and

Pakula's open ambivalence about Bree's eventual 'fate' will be repeated in Fonda's dealings with James Caan's war-hero/Western stranger and Kris Kristofferson's Wall Street cowboy. For once, a genuinely psychological thriller. PT

Knack...and how to get it, The

(Richard Lester, 1965, GB) Rita Tushingham, Ray Brooks, Michael Crawford, Donal Donnelly, John Bluthal, Wensley Pithey.
84 min. b/w.
Patchily funny but generally dated and embarrassing Swinging Sixties tale of Crawford's meek and mild school-teacher learning 'the knack' of picking up women from lecherous lodger Brooks, and trying out his technique on new-girl-in-town Tushingham. A misogynistic basis for comedy, not redeemed by the moralistic and predictable ending, and all shot in Lester's characteristically 'zany' style, with people running around all over the place for no apparent reason. Some of the tricks work; most don't; and Crawford, as always, is a pain. GA

Knave of Hearts (aka Lovers, Happy Lovers!/ Monsieur Ripois)

(René Clément, 1954, GB) Gérard Philipe, Valerie Hobson, Joan Greenwood, Margaret Johnston, Natasha Parry, Germaine Montero, Diana Decker.
103 min. b/w.
Simultaneously shot in a French version (Monsieur Ripois), Clément's first film in English proved once again that a foreign eye can often find more in a familiar setting. Philipe, in an engagingly sweet performance, plays the fickle French lover of a succession of London ladies, wooing them by playing the role they prefer to see him in. This French insight into the dreams of English womankind caused a contemporary furore, as did the use of a hidden camera on London locations to show aspects of the city rarely glimpsed in British cinema. Today it still looks remarkably authentic, with a particularly touching performance from Joan Greenwood in an unusually timid role. DT

Knickers Ahoy (Frau Wirtins tolle Töchterlein)

(François Legrand ie. Franz Antel, 1973, WGer/It) Terry Torday, Femy Benussi, Gabriele Tinti, Paul Löwinger, Marika Mindzenty.
90 min.
Period romp in which five convent girls try in turn to prove they are the daughter of Europe's greatest courtesan and heir to her fortune. Classical bawdy tales pad out a thin plot, and a number of crowd scenes sugggest a fair-sized budget. The film requires little comment beyond the mystery of its English title (not a pair to be seen), and a passing reference to the camera's lingering obsession with buttocks to the virtual exclusion of everything else.

Knife in the Head (Messer im Kopf)

(Reinhard Hauff, 1978, WGer) Bruno Ganz, Angela Winkler, Hans Christian Blech, Hans Hönig, Hans Brenner, Udo Samel.
113 min.
From a mix of classic American paranoia and German police gangsterism, Hauff weaves a disturbing and suspenseful yarn. Surviving a police bullet, scientist Berthold Hoffmann (Ganz) awakes in hospital as a stranger in his own land: without memory or speech, branded a terrorist by the police and a martyr by leftists – neither of which is 'Hoffmann' – his future depends upon retracing the events of an alien past. Shot in cold and clinical fashion, the film's drive depends upon an atmosphere so angst-laden the characters struggle for breath. Doubly disquieting – for the society it depicts, but even more for the film's own dispassion: a calculated gamble in trying to come to cool, dramatic terms with an impossibly over-dramatic reality. DMacp

Knife in the Water (Noz w Wodzie)

(Roman Polanski, 1962, Pol) Leon Niemczyk, Jolanta Umecka, Zygmunt Malanowicz.
94 min. b/w.
Polanski's first feature, a model of economic, imaginative film-making which, in many ways, he has hardly improved upon since. The story is simplicity itself: a couple destined for a yachting weekend pick up a hitch-hiker, and during the apparently relaxing period of sport and rest, allegiances shift, frustrations bubble up to the surface, and dangerous emotional games are played. Like much of Polanski's later work, it deals with humiliation, sexuality, aggression and absurdity; but what makes the film so satisfying is the tenderness and straightforward nature of his approach. With just three actors, a boat, and a huge expanse of water, he and scriptwriter Jerzy Skolimowski milk the situation for all it's worth, rarely descending into dramatic contrivance, but managing to heap up the tension and ambiguities. GA

Knight Moves

(Carl Schenkel, 1992, US/Ger) Christopher Lambert, Diane Lane, Tom Skerritt, Daniel Baldwin, Ferdinand Mayne, Katherine Isobel, Charles Bailey-Gates.
116 min.
Set during a chess championship at which widowed Grand Master Lambert is making a comeback, this irritating and over-complicated thriller features a clever opening gambit, a series of predictable moves, and a disappointing end game. A classic case of all plot and no substance, it embroils Lambert in a serial killer's sick and dangerous game of nerves: taunted by cryptic phone calls and clues written on the wall in the female victims' blood, he teams up with the police to trap the killer. But Lambert's casual sexual involvement with the first victim means the cops still regard him as the prime suspect. The film's chief difficulty is in persuading us not only that its handsome star (playing opposite his real-life wife) could be the killer, but that the chess player could have both opportunity and motive. In a vain effort to disguise this inherent implausibility, Schenkel piles on the baroque camerawork, overdesigned sets and flashy editing; but the denouement erases all the interesting and subversive possibilities at a stroke. NF

Knightriders

(George A Romero, 1981, US) Ed Harris, Gary Lahti, Tom Savini, Amy Ingersoll, Patricia Tallman, Christine Forrest, Warner Shook.
145 min.
When first shown in Britain at the London Film Festival, Knightriders was met with bewilderment, largely because it was such an anomaly within the Romero canon. In the light of his later aberrations, it looks more to the point now. The tale of a latter-day motorbiking King Arthur and his noble knights, who stage medieval jousts, it's a genuinely idiosyncratic exercise in anachronism, as well as scoring a few telling points about the nature of role-playing in modern America. Romero's regular effects man Tom Savini (later a director in his own right) features in the cast, as does scribbler Stephen King – surely the most macabre sight in the movie – in a boozy cameo. JRo

Knight Without Armour

(Jacques Feyder, 1937, GB) Marlene Dietrich, Robert Donat, Irene Vanbrugh, Herbert Lomas, Austin Trevor, John Clements, Hay Petrie, Miles Malleson.
108 min. b/w.
Reality never held much sway at Korda's Denham studios, least of all during the making of this lavishly preposterous melodrama of Russian life before and after the 1917 Revolution. Dietrich is the cool, fur-swathed Countess Vladinoff, who strips down for two titillating baths during her protracted rush to freedom organised by much-bearded Donat, who pretends to be a Russian Commissar but is actually AJ Fothergill, British secret agent. Feyder's typically stylish direction raises the film way above its subject matter, almost at times towards art. GB

K-9

(Rod Daniel, 1988, US) James Belushi, Mel Harris, Kevin Tighe, Ed O'Neill, James Handy, Daniel Davis.
102 min.
Tom Dooley (Belushi) is an unorthodox but dedicated narcotics officer, possessed of a motormouth, a battered car and an unpartnerable personality. Following a lead, he persuades a colleague to let him have a sniffer-dog so that he can investigate a suspected illegal shipment of drugs by bad guy Lyman (Tighe). The only dog available (special agent K-9, geddit?) is Jerry Lee, a good snifer but a touch unhinged after previous scrapes with malevolent hoods. From here on in it's the odd-couple scenario, with lots of jokes about disobedience, and graduation from enforced stand-off to grudging respect and finally mutual love between man and dog. Daniel directs with a light touch, clearly aimed low enough for juvenile audiences; but Belushi ain't the comic genius of all time, and it's a lot of footage to account for with a silent mutt for a foil. WH

Knock on Any Door

(Nicholas Ray, 1949, US) Humphrey Bogart, John Derek, George Macready, Allene Roberts, Susan Perry.
100 min. b/w.
Nick Romano must be the ideal name for a flawed Ray hero-victim. As embodied to vulnerable, narcissistic perfection by John Derek (long before he took up with Bo), he's the centre of a fascinating, slightly askew mix of social document and romantic agony. The basic material may be determinist melodrama – slum boy with deck stacked against him winds up on Death Row despite the efforts of a liberal lawyer (Bogart, whose Santana company made the film). But it's hard hitting in its own right, tautly crafted, and repeatedly stabbed through with Ray's impulsive generosity and anguish towards his characters. TP

Knock on Wood

(Norman Panama/Melvin Frank, 1953, US) Danny Kaye, Mai Zetterling, Torin Thatcher, David Burns, Leon Askin, Abner Biberman, Steve Geray.
103 min.
Danny Kaye's a ventriloquist with an outspoken dummy. Shrink Zetterling lays on the therapy, but a major plot device gets in her way when secret agents deposit a microfilm inside the dummy, whisking the movie into chase thriller mode, and giving the star a chance to dance with a troupe of Cossacks (choreography by Michael Kidd) and burst into balladry at an Irish convention. Funny, but a bit too much. TJ

Knots

(David I Munro, 1975, GB) Edward Petherbridge, Caroline Blakiston, Tenniel Evans, Robin Ellis, Robert Eddison, RD Laing.
62 min.
For anyone less than sold on the RD Laing cult, Munro's skilled direction of uncinematic material makes this film of the play based on his book Knots something less of an ordeal than might be expected. It centres on a series of classic double-bind situations which are personified by individual members of the Actors Company, and revealed by way of dialogue that consists entirely of a series of riddle-like verbal 'knots': 'You can't bear that I'm not interested in you being interested in me', or 'I'm afraid of the self that's afraid of the self that's afraid of the self'. It's not particularly earth-shattering, quite slight overall and a little didactic, in fact, but at least it's tackled with reasonable good humour and no psychological hair-tearing. VG

Koks i Kulissen

see Ladies on the Rocks

Kolya (Kolja)

(Jan Sverák, 1996, Czech Republic/GB/Fr) Zdenek Sverák, Andrej Chalimon, Libuse Safránková, Ondrej Vetchy.
105 min.
Prague, 1988. Since being chucked out of the Czech Philharmonic, cellist Frantisek Louka (Sverák) has been reduced to playing at funerals. With the bills mounting, the middle-aged loner agrees to a marry a Russian woman in return for enough cash to pay his debts and buy a Trabant. The bogus bride, armed with her new Czech papers, exits to join a lover in West Germany, thus threatening to land Louka in trouble with the authorities, and lumbering him with her five-year-old son Kolya (Chalimon). With each film, Czech director Jan Sverák moves ever closer to the mainstream: the oddball sci-fi parody Accumulator 1 and the dark social insights of the

road movie *The Ride* are here replaced by sentimental comedy-drama. The script (by the director's father and lead actor) is contrived, obvious and shallow, and benefits not a jot from being set during the decline of communism. That said, however, it is a polished affair, and thanks to Sverák Sr's subtle, quietly charismatic performance as the cynic softened by responsibility, it's not entirely without charm. GA

Komitas
(Don Askarian, 1988, WGer) Samuel Ovasapian, Onig Saadetian, Margarita Woskanjan, Yegishe Mangikian.
96 min.
Askarian's film attempts to find a cinematic correlative for the suffering and madness of Soghomon Soghomonian ('Komitas'), a great Armenian musician who spent his last 20 years in mental institutions, traumatised by the 1915 genocide of two million of his people. Presented in a series of eight or so sections, it has the mind-opening intensity of Tarkovsky's spiritual odysseys, the visual beauty of Paradjanov's celebrations of ethnic cultures, and an almost surreal, miraculous poetry that is Askarian's own. The images have the visionary logic of the maddened imagination: faded paintings on a ruined church wall crumble in the rain to reveal jugs foaming with colour; jam-jars are smashed, their contents left to bleed down; strange music echoes from rain drumming on a graveyard of musical instruments; a woman breast-feeds a lamb; Komitas lies on a bed of flames. The pace is leisurely, and the camera moves gently or not at all; time – too much, perhaps – is given to mediate on what is shown. At one point, Komitas says art is worthless, that only nature and light matter. This film affirms that they all matter. WH

Konfrontation Assassination in Davos (Konfrontation)
(Rolf Lyssy, 1974, Switz) Peter Bollag, Gert Haucke, Marianne Kehlau, Hilde Ziegler, Wolfram Berger.
114 min. b/w.
Based on the factual case of a young Jewish student who fled Germany and shot the leader of the Swiss Nazi party in 1936, *Konfrontation* remains unfortunately limited by its scrupulous efforts to be faithful to actual events. The quality of the film well matches the frequent insertions of newsreel footage. But beyond that, its technical limitations make the deliberate stylisation of events appear increasingly awkward. As an essay on the gradual rise and acceptance of persecution (by the oppressed in particular), it remains conscientious but unmoving, mainly because the protagonist's dilemmas (the act of political assassination grows out of personal crises rather than moral or intellectual convictions) are never satisfactorily explained. And on the question of Swiss neutrality, the film becomes increasingly hampered, ending with an interminable trial in which the film's themes are hammered out. CPe

Konga
(John Lemont, 1961, GB) Michael Gough, Margo Johns, Jess Conrad, Claire Gordon, George Pastell, Austin Trevor, Jack Watson.
90 min.
Inept, silly, and ludicrously enjoyable monster movie, with Gough as the mad boffin who injects a chimp with a growth serum, only to see it turn into an uncredited actor in a gorilla suit. Thereafter the ape grabs a Michael Gough doll and heads for Big Ben. Deeply political. GA

Korczak
(Andrzej Wajda, 1990, Pol/Ger/Fr/GB) Wojtek Pszoniak, Ewa Dalkowska, Piotr Kozlowski, Marzena Trybala, Wojciech Klata.
118 min. b/w.
The life and death of Janusz Korczak, the Polish-Jewish doctor who defied the Nazis and tended the children in the Warsaw ghetto, was first filmed (rather well, if memory serves) by Rudolph Cartier for the BBC in 1962. Wajda's version covers the same ground, and adds nothing to the sum of human knowledge of the Holocaust; since he himself has been accused of anti-Semitism in the past, it looks suspiciously like a director's heart-on-sleeve riposte to his critics. Agnieszka Holland's script starts from the German occupation of Warsaw in 1939 and the brutal herding of the city's Jews into the makeshift ghetto; it concludes with the inevitable journey to Treblinka in 1942. Korczak (more than adequately played by Pszoniak) is seen as a pugnacious academic, tough on adults – Zionist elders as well as Nazis – but soft on kids. Everything from Robby Müller's monochrome photography to Wojciech Kilar's score is a model of 'taste' and sensitivity, and all concerned work overtime to avoid sentimentality. The problem is that the film's very existence is itself a sentimental gesture. After *Shoah*, earnest humanist tracts are no longer enough. TR

Korea
(Cathal Black, 1995, Ire) Donal Donnelly, Andrew Scott, Fiona Molony, Vass Anderson.
87 min.
Ireland, 1952, and the coming of the electricity to a remote village threatens the traditional way of life forever, forcing a fisherman and his college-age son to reappraise their stagnant relationship. The death of a local lad in the Korean War, fighting for the Americans, is the metaphor for the onslaught of the outside world in this well-acted but rather stodgy rerun of familiar themes. The camerawork captures the grey dankness of the lakeside landscape, but we've been here before and insight is not forthcoming. TJ

Kotch
(Jack Lemmon, 1971, US) Walter Matthau, Deborah Winters, Felicia Farr, Charles Aidman, Ellen Geer, Arlene Stuart.
114 min.
Sentimental generational comedy, with Matthau mugging through as an irascible senior citizen, resisting all attempts made by his family to uproot him, and generally sprinkling Grey Power with sparks of a second childhood. A bit of an easy option for Jack Lemmon's debut as a director, and a strange project to involve former blacklist victim John Paxton (*Crossfire, Murder, My Sweet*) as screenwriter. PT

Koyaanisqatsi
(Godfrey Reggio, 1983, US)
86 min.
A wildly charitable viewer might describe this as an ecological documentary. Less than 90 minutes transport us from the primordial cuteness of the American South-West (a Good Thing) to the squalor of a Manhattan rush hour (a Bad Thing); and in case you still don't get the message, there's plenty of time-lapse photography to make people look like machines, and an apocalyptic score by Philip Glass to tell you off for daring to find visual pleasure in New York's skyline. At once maudlin and doggedly sarcastic, the film gives you the uncomfortable sensation of being condescended to by an idiot; it is, transparently, a product of the advanced technology it purports to despise. The title, by the way, is pilfered from the Hopi tongue and means 'vacuous hippy'. KJ

Krakatoa – East of Java
(Bernard Kowalski, 1968, US) Maximilian Schell, Diane Baker, Brian Keith, Barbara Werle, John Leyton, Rossano Brazzi, Sal Mineo.
132 min.
Originally made in Cinerama, this takes as its starting point the world's most spectacular recorded natural disaster; and then, just to make things a little more interesting, adds a mutiny, sunken hidden treasure, a new type of diving bell, balloonists galore, an orphan boy, a fire, and even a little bit of strip-tease. In short, for disaster movie addicts only; and as reviewers everywhere gleefully pointed out, Krakatoa is west of Java. PH

Kramer vs Kramer
(Robert Benton, 1979, US) Dustin Hoffman, Meryl Streep, Jane Alexander, Justin Henry, Howard Duff, George Coe, JoBeth Williams.
105 min.
A real high-class modern weepie. While Hoffman and Streep come to terms with divorce and battle over who gets the brat, Benton forsakes the eccentric and original delights of his earlier films (*Bad Company, The Late Show*) and turns in a very solid and professional domestic melodrama, helped no end by some very fine naturalistic performances. As sensitive and as unremarkable as your average Truffaut film, and as ambivalent in its sexual politics. GA

Krays, The
(Peter Medak, 1990, GB) Billie Whitelaw, Tom Bell, Gary Kemp, Martin Kemp, Susan Fleetwood, Charlotte Cornwell, Kate Hardie, Avis Bunnage, Gary Love, Steven Berkoff, Jimmy Jewel, Barbara Ferris, Victor Spinetti, John McEnery.
119 min.
Medak's biopic skirts *Sweeney*-style fair-cop-guv clichés for bolder terrain, in which the macabre beginnings of the identical angels – all chirpy cockney, poor-but-spotless nostalgia – are placed as much within womb, hearth and home as in the streets, clubs and fairground booths through which Ron and Reg came to criminal prominence between Elvis and early Beatles. If Philip Ridley's script charts most of the signposts – school, army, protection, murder – it seems keen to establish the female connection, be it through Reggie's tormented, finally destroyed wife (Hardie, magnificent), or the endless, loyal patience of the kray brood, presided over by mother (Whitelaw) and consumptive but awesome Aunt Rose (Fleetwood). Most surprising is the impressive showing of Gary and Martin Kemp (of Spandau Ballet) as the twins, despite fears that the 'youth cult' dimension might be too strong a factor in the concept; most riveting, a series of cameos including Bell (ultra-seedy as victim Jack McVitie), Berkoff (OTT as victim George Cornell), Jimmy Jewel as the tall-tale-telling grandad every young thug should have. Little about the Krays' position as social climbing roughnecks, and not in the *Badlands* league, but a lot better than one dared hope. SGr

Kremlin Letter, The
(John Huston, 1969, US) Richard Boone, Bibi Andersson, Max von Sydow, Patrick O'Neal, Orson Welles, Ronald Radd, Nigel Green, Dean Jagger, Lila Kedrova, Barbara Parkins, George Sanders, John Huston.
121 min.
Starting out as an all-star espionage saga with a state secret as the supposed Grail, this quickly reveals itself as a serpentine tale of treachery and double-dealing. What makes the film so powerful is that where before such films have generally titillated us with their stories of violence and sex in defence of one's country, Huston structures his film around such expectations, so forcing us to take account of his spies' actions. The resulting film is possibly the clearest statement of Huston's vision of a cruel and senseless world in operation. CPe

Kreutzer Sonata, The (Kreitzerova Sonata)
(Mikhail Schweitzer/Sofia Milkina, 1987, USSR) Oleg Yankovsky, Aleksandr Trofimov, Irina Seleznyova, Dmitri Pokrovsky.
135 min.
This version of the Tolstoy novel is cinematically conventional, but grips like a drowner in the writing and acting. Pozdnyshev (Yankovsky), who murdered his wife, pours out an agonised confession to a fellow-traveller on a train. His chastening tale of a relationship which stifled both parties, twisted into jealousy, and ended in violence, is explored in flashback. She (Seleznyova) first caught his eye in a drawing room entertainment by the sheer physical joy of her response to music. Life with him soon snuffed that out; and years later, he sees it again on her face as she plays the Beethoven piece with a philandering violin virtuoso. Only when she is dying does he realise what he has destroyed, and feel for another's life. Neither Albee nor Bergman dug any deeper into the pain of the loveless marriage, and Tolstoy, of course, rises to more universal levels. Yankovsky's performance is a tour de force; it invades the emotions and forces you to understand. BC

Kristina Talking Pictures
(Yvonne Rainer, 1976, US) Bert Barr, Yvonne Rainer.
90 min. b/w & col.
Rainer's third feature is arguably the closest she has yet come to the Godard wing of 'art cinema'. Like her other movies, it's a shifting collage of narrations (some visual, mostly verbal), loosely anchored in the central relationship between Kristina and her lover Raoul. Except that Kristina, generally sketched as a middle-class NYC artist concerned about the environment,

about relationships and such-like, is played by several different women...and given a personal history (archive flashbacks) as a former lion tamer in Europe who came to America to work as a choreographer. Dunno if this is 'political art', but it's certainly lively, unpredictable, and in several senses challenging. Also, it prominently features a photo of James Cagney. WW

Krug and Company
see Last House on the Left, The

Krull
(Peter Yates, 1983, GB) Ken Marshall, Lysette Anthony, Freddie Jones, Francesca Annis, Alun Armstrong, David Battley, Bernard Bresslaw.
121 min.
The main interest here lies in the fantasy world created, a cross between *Mad Max 2* and *Excalibur* in which pugnacious Celtic chieftains, on the point of making peace by marriage, are overcome by the Slayers, a warrior band ruled over by the mercurial Beast, a protean monster who makes Jabba the Hutt look like the boy next door. The story, with many romantic overtones of *The Thief of Bagdad*, is concerned with the quest of Prince Colwyn for his abducted betrothed: meeting dangers, encountering perils and helpers (including a Cyclops-style Bresslaw and several talented RSC-National Theatre stalwarts in disguise), and aided by a magical weapon, the Glaive (a jewel-encrusted starfish with prongs). Strong on stunts and special effects but often rambling and ponderously lurching into comedy, it's not the greatest of Christmas treats, but does have enough cherishable moments between the wordy longueurs; and in Lysette Anthony's Princess Lyssa, a heroine for whom many a young Turk would walk through fire and ice. SGr

Krush Groove
(Michael Schultz, 1985, US) Blair Underwood, Joseph Simmons, Sheila E, Fat Boys, Daryll McDaniels, Kurtis Blow.
97 min.
One would have thought a movie based on rap, the hip (not to say hop) sound of the mid-'80s, and featuring some of its hottest protagonists, would be sure to inspire an original story-line. But this is a Grade A stop-me-if-you've-heard-this-one-before plot. Young bloods form label, have hit, need cash to press yet more records. Enter loan shark, enter Big Deal record co, enter romance (Sheila E), entertainment. A subplot features the Three Stooges, aka the Fat Boys, attempting to make good in glamorous pop despite a noticeable lack of physical allurements. Clearly these doings are merely a device to break up the songs performed (Kurtis Blow and Sheila E are the best acts). Stick with the sound-track. EBr

Krzysztof Kieslowski: I'm So So
(Krzysztof Wierzbicki, 1995, Pol)
56 min.
As a documentary maker himself, Kieslowski was renowned for his fascination with people: the patient, sympathetic way in which he would elicit their opinions. Here, the tables are turned. He is the subject. Wierzbicki, an old friend and collaborator, quizzes him about his childhood, career and aspirations. Early on, various experts (a doctor, a priest and a clairvoyant among them) are invited to analyse Kieslowski's personality. They're all off the mark. So, perhaps, is Wierzbicki. But that's the point – Kieslowski, like the characters in his films, defies easy categorisation. Still, this documentary, made a few months before his untimely death, offers a warm, humorous profile of one of the recent cinema's greatest storytellers. GM

K2
(Franc Roddam, 1991, US) Michael Biehn, Matt Craven, Raymond J Barry, Hiroshi Fujioka, Luca Bercovici, Patricia Charbonneau, Julia Nickson-Soul.
111 min.
This abyssal action adventure details the efforts of two American buddies to scale the world's second highest peak. Roddam's intentions are made clear early on: climbing as metaphor – take risks! you've only got one shot in life! go for the dream! The film opens with drunken jock-lawyer Taylor

(Biehn) in post-party garb scaling the outside walls of his erstwhile climbing chum's apartment building. Will his scientist mate Harold (Craven) – he's the married, sensitive type – team up for the big one? Much philosophical debating later, Who's-a-Wimp Harry is *in*. The rest is snowbound, rope-and-piton daredevil drivel. On trip one (Alaska) two dorks die. Trip two involves much palaver with porters, challenges from old rivals, and beyond-the-cliché dialogue. Cinematographer Gabriel Beristain does wonders filming the mountain landscapes of Pakistan and British Columbia. WH

Kuffs
(Bruce A Evans, 1991, US) Christian Slater, Milla Jovovich, Tony Goldwyn, Bruce Boxleitner, Troy Evans, George De La Pena, Leon Rippy.
102 min.
'I'm only going to stick around until I clean up the neighbourhood,' announces reformed rebel George Kuffs (Slater). He lives on the mean streets of San Francisco where, we learn, it's customary for police districts to be sold off to private enterprise. After witnessing the death of his cop brother (Boxleitner), Kuffs inherits the family patch and sets about finding the killer. It's hard to believe that the writing team behind the beautifully understated *Stand by Me* concocted this hotch-potch, which mixes buddy-cop-thriller with rites-of-passage drama with slapstick farce. Amid the explosions and pratfalls, Evans (making his directorial debut) and Raynold Gideon throw in direct-to-camera monologues in which our hero comments on the action: this is as useful as Elmer Fudd analysing a Bugs Bunny escapade, but less funny. Granted, both characters and situations are deliberately exaggerated; but the romantic subplot, which sees Kuffs baulking at commitment (to Jovovich) also fails to ring true. CM

Kuhle Wampe
(Slatan Dudow, 1931, Ger) Hertha Thiele, Ernst Busch, Martha Wolter, Lili Schönborn, Adolf Fischer.
73 min. b/w.
Brecht scripted and participated in the making of this film, an unsentimental view of life in Kuhle Wampe, a camp for the dispossessed. Brecht saw its docile inhabitants (who struggled to maintain their dignity through an obsessive tidiness and attention to the forms of 'respectable' life) as wasting the opportunity for class solidarity and revolution. The heroine rejects this stifling of her spirit, to find moral renewal and purpose with a left wing youth movement. Brecht employs his usual mixture of didacticism (the film bears the alternative title, *To Whom Does the World Belong?*) and an almost lyrical naturalism that encourages the viewer to put across his own socio-economic analyses. What is curiously absent, however, is any treatment of the rise of the Nazis. Hitler came to power only nine months after the premiere of *Kuhle Wampe* in May 1932, and wasted little time in banning this charming and subversive film. MH

Kundun
(Martin Scorsese, 1997, US) Tenzin Thuthob Tsarong, Gyurme Tethong, Tulku Jamyang Kunga Tenzin, Tencho Gyalpo.
134 min.
Scorsese's early life of the 14th Dalai Lama is the simplest and strangest movie he has yet made. An act of self-imposed exile, it's a Hollywood film only in the production credits and language. There's minimal contextualising. The scenario (by Melissa Mathison) sticks to the Dalai Lama's point of view: his discovery by Buddhist monks searching for the reincarnation of the 13th Dalai Lama among the farming communities of northern Tibet in 1935; his upbringing and tutelage in Lhasa; through the Communist Chinese invasion of 1950, to his own exile to India nine years later. The biographical detail is honest and illuminating, be it the rodents given free range of the Potala palace, the boy's fascination with mechanics, or his wonder at the opulent religious ceremonies. The film isn't remotely slow, yet Scorsese rejects the tenets of Western melodrama and dispenses with the history in so swiftly that it's easy to get lost in the sombre raptures of red, gold and blue. Urged on by Philip Glass's throbbing, blaring score, the director conjures a phenomenal, trance-like climax, owing more to dreams, second sight and the mind's eye than conventional dramatic rhetoric. TCh

Kung Fu Fighting (Tang Shou Taiquandao/aka Crush)
(Tu Guangqi, 1972, HK) Jason Pai Piao, Chen Hung Lieh, Ingrid Hu, Kung Pei Shi.
86 min.
It is ironic that the first martial arts film to have been specially shorn (down to 60 minutes) for kiddie consumption should show every sign, even in its drastically curtailed state, of having been among the best Chinese films released here. Shooting on location in Korea, the director (a stalwart of the sword film in the '60s) balances off the weighty proportions of Korean architecture with its snow-covered courtyards and poses his figures in space to quietly dramatic effect. His use of colour and the wide screen is brilliantly controlled, and for once it looks as if the dialogue on restraint and oppression, tradition and revolt, imperialism and national identity, had found a worthy environment in a film full of incidental thematic riches. The relationship of the two children and the character played by Ingrid Wu (superb) is profoundly enigmatic and seemingly totally original; it would be interesting to see how this related to the coarser, more conventional elements. VG

Kung-Fu Gangbusters (Nanzi Han/aka Smugglers)
(John Sun i.e. Sun Jiawen, 1973, HK) Jason Pai Piau, Tommy Lu Chun, Thompson Kao Kang, Ingrid Hu, Liang Tien.
98 min. b/w.
This comprises sundry inadequate visual accompaniments to selections from *West Side Story* and *Shaft*, and finally reveals itself as a hymn to the valour of the Hong Kong police in their drug-gang busting efforts. To be avoided. TR

Kung Fu Girl, The (Tiewa/aka None But the Brave)
(Lo Wei, 1973, HK) Cheng Pei Pei, Ou Wei, James Tien, Jo Shishido, Lo Wei.
89 min.
This traces the activities of a group of revolutionaries in the period during which General Yuan Shih-kai was attempting to subvert the new republic and have himself made emperor, a move which entailed signing away North China to Japanese control. Lo Wei turns in an atmospheric film, possibly – in some of its imagery, and in its use of a 'family' as the cell which infiltrates Japanese High Command and the upper echelons of Peking government – revealing influences from Communist China. Cheng Pei Pei (from *Golden Swallow*) builds a character of muted but intense single-mindedness, wit and intelligence. Lo Wei obviously delights in his own role as a particularly unpleasant turncoat commissioner, and (directorically) cannot resist adding his familiar humorous brush-strokes. Nevertheless, the more delicate mood of encroaching horror and staunch resistance dominates the film. VG

Kung Fu – Girl Fighter (Can Nü Kongshoudao/aka Karate King – On the Waterfront)
(Hou Jing, 1970, Tai) Tang Paoyun, Chang Yu, Chen Hong Rie, Tien Yie, Hou Jing.
88 min.
A slightly haphazard film that nevertheless frequently achieves an intense visual grace as it weaves its discursive plot around the theme of China's need for national regeneration and rebirth, specifically through a wandering hero figure. It even foreshadows Bruce Lee's charismatic smashing of a 'No Dogs or Chinese Allowed' sign. Its uncertain period recreation is less important than its general description of a shady and manipulated world, laden with political innuendos which are probably more intelligible to Chinese than Western eyes. It is no doubt a clue of sorts that the film was produced by a brother of Chiang Kai Shek's personal bodyguard, and hence makes (somewhat odd) use of Taiwan's military establishments, but then again it's hardly a rabid political tract. There's a superbly sensual bath-house murder scene, sadly and with ridiculous prurience cut by the censor. VG

Kung Fu Street Fighter (Gekitotsu! Satsujinken)
(Shigehiro Ozawa, 1974, Jap) Shinichi Chiba, Goichi Yamada, Yutaka Nakajima, Tony Cetera, Tatsuro Endo. 88 min.

Japan had its Bruce Lee craze like everywhere else, and this offers a taste of the ultra-violent unarmed combat movies the Japanese started making after Lee's death in 1973. Chiba stars as Terry Tsuguri, the meanest bastard who ever gouged eyes, in an incomprehensible kidnap plot which rises to a wonderfully hysterical climax with samurai-style swordplay aboard an oil-tanker. If you can take the film's formulary nature, its rampant misogyny, and the peculiarly Japanese notion of tortured personal honour that Chiba's 'hero' represents, it's quite impressive. TR

Kung Fu – The Headcrusher (Ying Han/aka Tough Guy)

(Jiang Hong, 1972, HK) Chen Xing, Linda Ling, Henry Yue Young, Charly Chiang, Sin Lan.
90 min.
Routine stuff, taking its title from a particularly lethal grip its hero is able to administer to the skulls of those who cross his path. The unspoiled rural locations (Taiwan?) lend freshness, but otherwise this fable of a cop who goes undercover to trace a gang of smugglers lacks the spark that would have lent its perfunctorily well staged fight scenes the touch of bravura achieved only once (the climactic fight, with the hero momentarily foiled by the iron skullcap his opponent wears, but the villain nevertheless ending up hammered waist deep into the mud). Otherwise there's some fairly meretricious sex (the 'boss' suffers from ejaculatio praecox) and a fair range of physique shots. VG

Kuroneko (Yabu no Naka no Kuroneko)

(Kaneto Shindo, 1968, Jap) Kichiemon Nakamura, Nobuko Otowa, Kiwako Taichi, Kei Sato, Hideo Kanze.
99 min. b/w.
Shindo hit big with a movie called *Onibaba*, about an elderly woman and her daughter-in-law preying on lost samurai, and so it wasn't surprising that he cobbled together this variation on the earlier film. This time the two women are cat spirits (cue aerial somersaults), and the overall ambience is a great deal artier (cue eccentric 'scope compositions). Passable as a horror fantasy, but it hasn't an entrail of the gut impact of *Onibaba*. TR

Kvinnodröm (Dreams/ Journey Into Autumn)

(Ingmar Bergman, 1955, Swe) Eva Dahlbeck, Harriet Andersson, Gunnar Björnstrand, Ulf Palme, Inga Landgré, Naima Wifstrand.
86 min. b/w.
Bergman's movies in the '50s tend to lack any real perspective on their obsessive themes; each film looks like a more or less strained effort to find a 'dramatic' solution to the 'problem' of the ideas it contains. *Journey Into Autumn* tries for irony, but still ends up looking more forced than measured as fashion editor Eva Dahlbeck and model Harriet Andersson dream of reconciliation with former lovers, only to face disillusionment. TR

Kvinnorna på taket

see Women on the Roof, The

Kwaidan

(Masaki Kobayashi, 1964, Jap) Rentaro Mikuni, Michiyo Aratama, Misako Watanabe, Ganemon Nakamura, Keiko Kishi, Tatsuya Nakadai.
164 min.
Kobayashi's first independent production (after years of working under contract to a major studio) drew extensively on his own training as a student of Japanese painting and fine arts. It is a compendium of four ghost stories adapted from Lafcadio Hearn, so determinedly aesthetic in their design and style that horror frissons hardly get a look in. Very beautiful, though. One episode was removed when the film was released in Britain, reducing the running time to 125 minutes. TR

I

Legends of the Fall

La Baule-les pins
(C'est la vie)

(Diane Kurys, 1990, Fr) Nathalie Baye, Richard
Berry, Zabou, Jean-Pierre Bacri, Vincent
Lindon, Valéria Bruni-Tedeschi, Didier
Benureau, Julie Bataille, Candice Lefranc,
Alexis Derlon.
96 min.

Another autobiographical slice of life from Diane
Kurys, a bitter-sweet recollection of summer at
the seaside in 1958. Packed off with their nanny,
Frédérique (13) and Sophie (6) are happy enough
playing on the beach, but it's clear that all is not
right between their parents. Léna (Baye) joins
them only when summer is beginning to pall, and
she is alone. For the most part, Kurys concentrates on the childish hi-jinks of the sisters and
their cousins, but she subtly incorporates other
perspectives too, exploring the ramifications of
the parents' divorce through countless quietly
affecting details. This is delightfully evocative
film-making, bringing an unerringly authentic
touch to the most intangible circumstances –
childhood, memory, love gone sour – maintaining an even, unblinking vision that allows for a
great deal of humour as well as heartache, and
extracting performances from children and
adults alike that ring absolutely true. A less heroic, harsher tale than the liberating *Coup de foudre*,
but in many ways better judged. TCh

Laberinto de pasiones
see Labyrinth of Passions

Labyrinth

(Jim Henson, 1986, GB) David Bowie, Jennifer
Connelly, Toby Froud, Shelley Thompson,
Christopher Malcolm, Natalie Webster.
101 min.

Whopping great chunks of *Labyrinth* can be
traced back to the works of Carroll, Baum,
Sendak et al, but even if its main drift is repetitious and overlong, the final concoction offers
rather more incidental pleasure than 1985's
Legend. Sarah is a girl on the verge of womanhood who must tackle the mysteries of the maze
to rescue her baby brother from the evil Goblin
King, whose kooky kabuki wig and eye-catching
trousers cannot disguise the fact that he's really
David Bowie, complete with pop promo-video
interludes. Director Jim 'Muppet' Henson and
writer Terry 'Python' Jones lard Sarah's meanderings with lots of Wild Things, anthropomor-
phous landscape and animated inanimate objects.
The bittiness is relieved by some interesting conceits: an MC Escher room of gravity-defying staircases, a fart-filled Bog of Eternal Stench, and (best
of all) a grumpy gnome who sprays ickle-bitsy
fairies with insecticide before stomping them into
the ground. Thus may all cute little creatures perish. AB

Labyrinth of Dreams
(Yume no Ginga)

(Sogo Ishii, 1996, Jap) Tadanobu Asano, Rena
Komine, Kotomi Kyono, Kiriko Mano, Tomoko
Kurotani.
90 min. b/w.

Ishii's thriller, as oneiric in its way as *Angel Dust*
and *August in the Water* were, updates a story
by novelist *maudit* Kyusaku Yumeno to the
monochrome 1950s. The virginal Tomiko
(Komine) is a bus conductor in a small country
town who grows convinced that the handsome
new driver of her bus (Asano) is the man who
loved and murdered her friend in another town.
She steels herself to work with him, testing him
at every opportunity. And then she falls in love.
A Freudian fable of the night, filled with moons,
rain, dark tunnels and imminent collisions. As
Tomiko matures from repressed adolescence into
womanhood the key question is less whether the
man's a murderer, but whether it's possible for a
man to murder *with sincerity*. TR

Labyrinth of Passions
(Laberinto de pasiones)

(Pedro Almodóvar, 1982, Sp) Cecília Roth,
Imanol Arias, Helga Liné, Maria Fernández-
Muro, Angel Alcazar, Antonio Banderas,
Agustín Almodóvar, Cristina S Pascual,
Fabio McNamara.
99 min.

This is a home movie for the *Movida* set, a glamorous clash of frocks and jocks (and jocks *in*

frocks) in a Madrid peopled by drug-takers, pop
stars, wannabes, terrorists and sex maniacs.
Briefly, rock singer Sexi (Roth) is the neurotic
nympho daughter of a creepy gynaecologist
who's treating the wife of a Shah-like potentate,
whose son, bisexual Riza (Arias) also becomes a
rock singer, and is torn between the charms of
Sexi and an Arab terrorist (Banderas) with a keen
sense of smell. Meanwhile, Sexi's biggest fan, a
laundry maid, is raped continually by a father
who snorts aphrodisiac. When her heroine comes
into the dry-cleaners, the two join forces to outwit their parents, beat their beauty problems, and
fulfil their dreams. A sense of humour is the
string that will guide you through this tacky
labyrinth, which includes an appearance by legendary mini-skirted pop duo Almodóvar and
McNamara performing a rap song about fabulous
drugs. Drag till you gag. SFe

Lacemaker, The
see Dentellière, La

Lacho Drom

(Tony Gatlif, 1992/3, Fr)
103 min.

Gatlif's *Les Princes* was an impressive addition
to that small but fascinating genre, the gypsy
film; since he was Romany himself, authenticity
came easily. This film, whose title means 'safe
journey', is another invaluable contribution, an
impassioned, semi-allegorical odyssey traced,
using one group of Roms after another, from
India – by way of Egypt, Istanbul, Romania,
Hungary, Slovakia and the annual pilgrimage to
Saintes Maries de la Mer in the Camargue – to
Spain. A document of customs, craftsmanship,
costumes, faces and, most especially, song and
dance, it's a musical celebration of the gypsies'
sense of community and ability to survive in the
face of upheaval, prejudice and persecution.
Technically, the film, shot in numerous locations
in 'Scope and stereo, is a triumph, transcending
the staged nature of many sequences by means
of colour and movement. Crucial to the film's success, however, is the music, not only as an expression of the gypsies' feelings about distance, love,
exile, history and hope, but glorious in its own
right. Only the cavalier way with bird song on
the soundtrack and the sentimental use of a non-
Romany mother and child in the Hungarian
episode ring false. Otherwise, it's a joy. GA

Lacombe Lucien

(Louis Malle, 1974, Fr/It/WGer) Pierre Blaise,
Aurore Clément, Holger Lowenadler, Thérèse
Giehse, Stéphane Bouy.
134 min.

Out of school into a job, Lucien Lacombe shoots
rabbits in his spare time. Then almost imperceptibly a particular historical perspective is slipped
in behind him. World War II France is under
German occupation, and Lucien finds himself acting out his adolescent emotions, gun in hand,
within the eerie schema of Fascism. Malle's film
has two strengths: one is Lucien, Malle's answer
to the question, who becomes a Fascist? The second is the precision and total lack of histrionics
with which the mechanics of compromise are
mapped. It has one major weakness: having
drawn Lucien from the fringe of the action to the
centre of the screen, Malle seems unable to bridge
the gap between himself and the character. He
attempts to compensate with weighty (and unnecessary) symbolism, and fades out making pretty
pictures around his protagonist. Perhaps Malle's
seductive style, carried over intact from *Dearest
Love*, cannot go any further. VG

LA Confidential (100)

(Curtis Hanson, 1997, US) Kevin Spacey,
Russell Crowe, Guy Pearce, James Cromwell,
Kim Basinger, Danny DeVito, David
Strathairn, Ron Rifkin.
138 min.

Dime store detective stories have inspired more
great movies than Dostoevsky ever will, but
local-boy-made-bad James Ellroy always
seemed too tough a proposition for Hollywood
to take on. Hanson's adaptation of Ellroy's most
complex novel is a towering achievement, probably the finest mystery thriller since *Chinatown*.
Set in the '50s, this punchy cocktail of gangland
violence, police brutality, racism and sex-scan-
dal cover-ups feels torn from today's headlines.
It operates on the principles of an exposé, high-

lighting the parallax between image and reality. As Danny DeVito's muck-raising, 'Hush
Hush' magazine hack guides us on a gleeful
trawl through the seedier, sleazier aspects of
this, the last of the frontier towns, we meet three
very different lawmen: Spacey's cynical showboat Jack Vincennes; Ed Exley (Pearce), a
straight-arrow cop headed for the top; and
Crowe's Bud White, the strong arm of the law,
brawn to Exley's brains. Contrasting not only
their approaches to procedure, justice and
respect, but also their vividly etched, distinctly
volatile psycho-pathologies, Hanson inexorably
draws these three cases to one conclusion: when
the trio do take a stand, it's inspired less by idealism than self-disgust. As the emotional nexus,
a Veronica Lake lookalike trapped in a web of
male desires, Basinger is arguably the pick of a
perfect cast. Subtle, shocking, compelling and
immensely assured. TCh

Ladder of Swords

(Norman Hull, 1988, GB) Martin Shaw, Eleanor
David, Juliet Stevenson, Bob Peck, Simon
Molloy, Pearce Quigley.
98 min.

A desolate moor is the setting for murder, but
despite the hackneyed backdrop, Neil Clarke's
script for the most part creates genuinely suspenseful drama. Much of the film's credibility
stems from strong performances. Shaw plays
Don Demarco, an escaped convict who evades the
law with his travelling circus act. In his caravan
on the edge of the moor, awaiting his next
engagement, he loses a disgruntled, thieving wife
(David) and gains a caring lover (Stevenson).
Meanwhile, obsessive Detective Inspector
Atherton (Peck) takes an instant dislike to
Demarco, accusing him of one offence after another, from a local robbery to murdering his wife. It's
just a matter of time before the past catches up.
Amid the elements of kitchen-sink realism,
Atherton's character unbalances the film: as he
tracks his quarry with the refinement of a rabid
dog, it's hard to imagine him lasting two minutes
in a real police station. This has less to do with
Peck's fine performance than with misguided
efforts to inject belly laughs amid more subtle
humour. CM

Ladies and Gentlemen,
the Rolling Stones

(Roland Binzer, 1975, US)
90 min.

Documentary record of an average Stones concert (1974 repertoire), filmed by cameramen with
a Jagger fixation. With Mick in close-up eighty
percent of the time, and no visual sense of the
band as a working unit, the movie relies on the
gimmick of Dolby quad sound to make its impact.
It's not enough. TR

Ladies in Retirement

(Charles Vidor, 1941, US) Ida Lupino, Louis
Hayward, Evelyn Keyes, Elsa Lanchester,
Edith Barrett, Isobel Elsom, Emma Dunn.
92 min. b/w.

In this stage-bound yet surprisingly involving
Gothic melodrama, Lupino plays a housekeeper
who murders her ex-actress employer (Elsom) in
order to prevent her two mentally disturbed sisters (Lanchester and Barrett) from being sent to
an asylum. The blend of eccentricity and (genteel) Grand Guignol works well, though the
events portrayed are nothing like as shocking as
they must have seemed at the time of the film's
original release. Remade in 1968 as *The Mad
Room*. NF

Ladies' Man, The

(Jerry Lewis, 1961, US) Jerry Lewis, Helen
Traubel, Kathleen Freeman, Hope Holiday,
Pat Stanley, Jack Kruschen, Doodles Weaver,
George Raft.
106 min.

Jerry Lewis' second film as director is one of his
greatest, with its star almost overwhelmed by his
one major set, the split-level interior of a
Hollywood boarding hotel for aspiring actresses,
where one Herbert Heebert, practising misogynist, has been taken on in all innocence as a
houseboy. Lewis' camera performs some virtuoso movement around the rooms (Jean-Luc
Godard and Julien Temple were to borrow this
device), and the ultra-loose plotline allows for
some hilarious sequences, and even a touch of

surrealism in one entirely white interior. Highlights include Lewis breaking up a television show and dancing a tango with George Raft. DT

Ladies of the Chorus

(Phil Karlson, 1949, US) Adele Jergens, Rand Brooks, Marilyn Monroe, Nana Bryant.
61 min. b/w.
Marilyn's first sizeable role came in this Columbia programme-filler, shortly before the studio scrapped her contract after only six months. Here she steps out of the chorus and into the limelight when the star walks out on a burlesque show. Mama Jergens warns her, however, to be wary of involvement with wealthy socialite Brooks. It's formula stuff, but if you've seen all the other Monroe pictures you might want to catch this one. TJ

Ladies on the Rocks (Koks i Kulissen)

(Christian Braad Thomsen, 1984, Den) Helle Ryslinge, Annemarie Helger, Flemming Quist Moller, Hans Henrik Clemmensen, Gyda Hansen.
110 min.
The original title translates as *Chaos Behind the Scenes*, a neat summary of the lives and art of Micha and Laura, heroines of Thomsen's anti-romantic film and stars of their own comic cabaret. Abandoning loved ones, the women take to touring Denmark's damp autumnal provinces with their increasingly truculent show. The act is a success, but Micha and Laura's pleasure in their new life is spoiled by the failure of the old one, and by a suspicion that the ideals of both are largely fantasy. Although the message is unclear, it is delivered with an ingenuous vitality. And a curious optimism emerges from the film's waxy gloom: a triumph of large spirit over small aspirations, of bravura performance over pallid script. FD

Ladri di Biciclette

see Bicycle Thieves

Ladri di Saponette

see Icicle Thief

Ladro di bambini, Il

see Stolen Children, The

Lady and the Tramp

(Hamilton Luske/Clyde Geronomi/Wilfred Jackson, 1955, US) voices: Peggy Lee, Barbara Luddy, Larry Roberts, Stan Freberg.
76 min.
In 1956, when *Woof Back in Anger* was challenging perceptions on the London stage, a few critics remarked that it had all been done the year before in a Disney cartoon musical with songs by Peggy Lee. Like Osborne's play, *Lady and the Tramp* probes one of the great social fusses of the '50s: canine hypergamy – marriage or liaison above one's social caste or class – and was inspired by the tale of Walt's family spaniel. All tame stuff today; the humans are disgusting, Tramp is streetwise but sanitary, and the Lady is a wet. Happily the cameo lowlife, an excellent manic beaver, the famously villainous Siamese, and classic songs rescue the film from dumb animal sentiment. Best of these is the almost raunchy 'He's a Tramp', in which Peggy Lee shows that part of being a bitch is knowing when not to be too much of a lady. RP

Ladybird Ladybird

(Ken Loach, 1994, GB) Crissy Rock, Vladimir Vega, Sandie Lavelle, Mauricio Venegas, Ray Winstone, Clare Perkins.
101 min.
Matters start promisingly: in a pub, Maggie (Rock) belts out a ballad and transfixes Jorge (Vega), a Paraguayan exile settled in London. He's gentle and supportive, just as well, given her foul-mouthed temper and troubled life. A mother of four living in a refuge, she's persistently hounded as an unfit parent by social workers who threaten to remove her children, because of her tendency to involve herself with violent, drunken louts. Truth to tell, she's a walking disaster area, though Jorge's love and understanding finally break through her defences, encouraging her to move in with him and start their own fam-

ily. But modern Britain's an unjust place: can their fragile happiness last? Ken Loach sledgehammers his points. As social critique, the film provokes pity and anger, not thought: understandable, since it's never quite clear exactly what Loach is attacking. The methods of the social services? The bureaucracy of Tory Britain? Life itself? GA

Lady by Choice

(David Burton, 1934, US) Carole Lombard, May Robson, Roger Pryor, Walter Connolly, Arthur Hohl, Raymond Walburn.
78 min. b/w.
A sequel to Capra's Damon Runyon adaptation of the previous year, *Lady for a Day*, this helping of Hollywood hogwash has a second-hand feel. Lombard reprises her role as a fan-dancer, this time ripe for reform when she 'adopts' curmudgeonly old bag lady Robson in a Mother's Day publicity stunt. Mildly agreeable, but it would be very easy to overstate its modest quality. TJ

Lady Caroline Lamb

(Robert Bolt, 1972, GB/It) Sarah Miles, Jon Finch, Richard Chamberlain, John Mills, Margaret Leighton, Pamela Brown, Ralph Richardson, Laurence Olivier, Peter Bull.
123 min.
Bolt's debut as a director from his own script about the darling of English society who rocked the boat with her scandalous behaviour – ha, ha. She bolts through the woods in boy's clothing, marries a conscientious liberal politician (Finch), and outrages the British way of life by not being discreet (as Mother was) in who she chooses to fuck, where, when, and how often, as well as by turning up at a fancy-dress ball near-naked and blacked up as Byron's slave. Plus the film has a theme: reason versus passion. It's the end of the Age of Reason, and she is all passion while most of those around her still bow to reason. But it is impossible to take seriously on a historical or an ideas level – the 2D characters refuse to be plugged in to anything beyond the studio sets around them. On the other hand, the film won't deliver Hollywood-type glamour either. Bright spot: Richard Chamberlain as Byron gets the white-clad early 19th century ladies' knickers twisted very effectively in eye-liner and lip-colour.

Lady Chatterley's Lover

(Just Jaeckin, 1981, GB/Fr) Sylvia Kristel, Nicholas Clay, Shane Briant, Ann Mitchell, Elizabeth Spriggs, Bessie Love.
104 min.
A ghastly movie. For all his funny ideas, DH Lawrence could string a sentence together. Take away the words, leave the story and the sex, and you have something very trite indeed. Jaeckin's prissy-pretty approach in concept, direction and photography is simply the pornography of mediocrity; Lawrence needs the runaway Ken Russell touch. Kristel gives a boring performance, even allowing for the English dubbing, and she plays it with the expression of a pall-bearer – her contribution to the film's good taste pretensions. She may think she's sloughed off the *Emmanuelle* image. Wrong. This stupid movie conclusively proves that there's nothing to choose between an airplane lay and a gamekeeper's hut. JS

Lady Eve, The ▓100▓

(Preston Sturges, 1941, US) Barbara Stanwyck, Henry Fonda, Charles Coburn, Eugene Pallette, William Demarest, Eric Blore, Melville Cooper.
97 min. b/w.
A beguilingly ribald sex comedy, spattered with characteristic Sturges slapstick (Fonda can hardly move without courting disaster) and speech patterns ('Let us be crooked, but never common,' urges Coburn's conman). Fonda and Stanwyck are superbly paired as the prissy professor and the brassy card-sharp who meet on a liner for a ferociously funny battle of the sexes in which she proves triumphantly that Eve and the serpent still have the drop on poor old Adam. The glittering screwball comedy of love's labours that ensues – denounced as a brazen gold-digger and cast off, Stanwyck vengefully seeks revenge by reconquering Fonda's heart while masquerading (inimitably) as a flower of English society – is not just funny but surprisingly moving, given the tender romantic warmth of the early shipboard

scenes in which, with Stanwyck's veneer slowly melted by Fonda's vulnerability, the pair first fall irrevocably in love. Very nearly perfection, and quintessential Sturges. TM

Lady for a Day

(Frank Capra, 1933, US) Warren William, May Robson, Guy Kibbee, Glenda Farrell, Jean Parker, Walter Connolly, Ned Sparks, Nat Pendleton.
88 min. b/w.
The story (derived from Damon Runyon) is pure sentiment. A lady known as Apple Annie (Robson) is reduced to selling apples on the sidewalk for a living. She keeps the awful truth from her daughter by writing fanciful letters about high society on purloined headed notepaper...until her daughter (Parker) decides to come to New York with her fiancé, a Spanish count. What will the poor gin-soaked old body do? As it's a Capra fable, everyone from fellow street bums to the mayor is eventually galvanised in her cause. You can tell just how rich the comedy is by the fact that not even a plot like that can sink it. Robert Riskin's razor-sharp dialogue is matched by Capra's super-subtle visuals, and backed by an array of suitably Runyonesque characters. In fact it is just about worth swallowing your cynicism (and scruples) for Ned Sparks' definitive stone-faced Broadway sharpie alone. Remade by Capra himself as *Pocketful of Miracles* in 1961.

Lady from Louisiana

(Bernard Vorhaus, 1941, US) John Wayne, Ona Munson, Ray Middleton, Henry Stephenson, Dorothy Dandridge, Helen Westley, Jack Pennick.
84 min. b/w.
Wayne plays an idealistic young lawyer whose plans to clean up a rootin'-tootin' frontier town are in jeopardy as soon as he falls for alluring Southern belle Munson, whose father runs the local organised crime racket. Plodding second feature (co-scripted by Guy Endore) from German-born director Vorhaus who graduated (if that's the word) from British quota quickies to programmers like this at Republic Pictures. After *Stagecoach*, the Duke deserved better. TJ

Lady from Shanghai, The

(Orson Welles, 1948, US) Orson Welles, Rita Hayworth, Everett Sloane, Glenn Anders, Ted de Corsia, Erskine Sanford, Gus Schilling.
87 min. b/w.
Don't attempt to follow the plot – studio boss Harry Cohn offered a reward to anyone who could explain it to him, and many critics have foundered on it – because Welles simply doesn't care enough to make the narrative seamless. Indeed, the principal pleasure of *The Lady from Shanghai* is its tongue-in-cheek approach to story-telling. Welles is an Irish sailor who accompanies a beautiful woman (Hayworth, then Mrs Welles) and her husband on a sea cruise, and becomes a pawn in a game of murder. One intriguing reading of the movie is that it's a commentary on Welles' marriage to Hayworth – the impossibility of the 'boy genius' maintaining a relationship with a mature woman – and the scene in the hall of mirrors, where the temptress' face is endlessly reflected back at him, stands as a brilliant expressionist metaphor for sexual unease and its accompanying loss of identity. Complex, courageous, and utterly compelling. MA

Lady from the Shanghai Cinema, The (A Dama do cine Shanghai)

(Guilherme De Almeida Prado, 1988, Braz) Maite Proença, Antonio Fagundes, José Lewgoy, Jorge Doria, José Mayer, Miguel Falabella.
117 min.
Prado pays tribute to *film noir* in general, and to *The Lady from Shanghai* in particular; but given that Welles' mirror-play classic was itself a genre deconstruction, it's little wonder that Prado's film ends up being more labyrinthine than its play on fantasy and reality, death and desire, can quite accommodate. On a chance visit to a fleapit, seedy estate agent Lucas (Fagundes) enjoys a steamy near-encounter with *femme fatale* Suzana (Proença); the next day, he finds himself selling a flat to her sinister husband. A slave to his hormones, and intrigued by this rapidly developing

B-pic scenario, he is plunged into the customary abyss of mistaken identity, secret societies, drug runners and dead sailors. The film impresses with its hothouse look – all neon, sweat and ceiling fans – but its narrative obfuscation, spiked with Godardian distancing, is too complex to hold the attention. JRo

Lady Godiva Rides Again
(Frank Launder, 1951, GB) Pauline Stroud, Dennis Price, John McCallum, Stanley Holloway, George Cole, Diana Dors, Alistair Sim, Kay Kendall, Sidney James, Dora Bryan, Trevor Howard, Joan Collins.
90 min. b/w.
Would-be comic satire in which Pauline Stroud, winner of a local Lady Godiva contest, goes on to top a national beauty contest, the prelude to celluloid charm school training and an eventual descent into the burlesque arena. Disappointingly mundane, and done with enough discretion to claim a 'U' certificate from the censor. TJ

Lady Hamilton
see That Hamilton Woman

Ladyhawke
(Richard Donner, 1985, US) Matthew Broderick, Rutger Hauer, Michelle Pfeiffer, Leo McKern, John Wood, Ken Hutchison.
124 min.
Broderick plays a Dark Ages version of the Artful Dodger, befriending the traumatised but bold Etienne of Navarre (camp Hauer), who is eternally separated from his true love Isabeau (decorative Pfeiffer) by a horrible, nasty spell that only outrageous bravery and special effects can undo. All rather facile sword-and-sorcery stuff, of course, but at times very funny (special mention to McKern as a bumbling priest) and always beautifully photographed in the Italian Dolomites. DPe

Lady Ice
(Tom Gries, 1973, US) Donald Sutherland, Jennifer O'Neill, Robert Duvall, Patrick Magee, Jon Cypher, Eric Braeden, Buffy Dee.
92 min.
A diamond caper movie that promises well but wastes its opportunities and ends up modish and vacuous. Sutherland plays an insurance agent tracking down Jennifer O'Neill's poor little rich girl. He clearly enjoys himself, giving the complete antithesis of his silent detective in *Klute*, but she is hardly a worthy opponent. The film falls to pieces half-way through when the emphasis shifts away from the plot (which becomes too boring to follow anyway) and onto the two main characters, who spend the rest of the film in mutual admiration, eyeing each other and making half-hearted passes. CPe

Lady in Cement
(Gordon Douglas, 1968, US) Frank Sinatra, Raquel Welch, Richard Conte, Martin Gabel, Dan Blocker, Lainie Kazan, Steve Peck.
93 min.
Plodding sequel to *Tony Rome*, with Sinatra's indomitable private eye fighting his way through an unexciting collection of freaks, perverts and villains. Carbon-copy stuff, with the Florida setting and characterisation of Tony Rome recalling John D Macdonald's Travis McGee, Dan Blocker playing a variation on Chandler's Moose Malloy, and a leering attitude to sex and violence not improved by bouts of gay-baiting. A good cast and loose-limbed direction from Douglas help things out. TM

Lady in Red, The
(Lewis Teague, 1979, US) Pamela Sue Martin, Robert Conrad, Louise Fletcher, Robert Hogan, Laurie Heineman, Glenn Withrow, Christopher Lloyd, Dick Miller.
93 min.
Writer John Sayles, playing fast and loose with the known facts, inverts the gender of the Dillinger myth and backtracks with outrageous relish over the history of his scarlet companion, punching out scene after great scene of Corman New World depression sleaze. Through farm girl, sweat-shop organiser, taxi-dancer, whorehouse, slammer, Dillinger's avenging angel outguns them all in one long hard slide down the wild side. Director Teague revels in the regular motifs of

guns, money, fast cars and bizarre death, grafts on a layer of social comment lately absent in exploiters, and still slams through it all with an anarchic humour sometimes worthy of Sam Fuller. Very much the thinking person's crunch movie – chomp a cigar and see Dillinger go down again. CPea

Lady in the Car with Glasses and a Gun, The (La Dame dans l'auto avec des lunettes et un fusil)
(Anatole Litvak, 1970, Fr) Samantha Eggar, Oliver Reed, John McEnery, Stéphane Audran, Billie Dixon, Bernard Fresson, Jacques Fabbri.
105 min.
Eggar, an English secretary with an international advertising agency in Paris, is asked by her boss (Reed, so sinisterly smooth that you know he's up to no good) to work overnight at his house. Next day, she agrees to see him off at the airport with his family, then drive his car back to the house. But finding herself heading in the wrong direction, she impulsively drives on – towards the Riviera and nightmarish happenings which include encounters with various strangers who apparently recognise her, assault in the rest-room at a service station, an interlude with an enigmatic hitchhiker (McEnery), and the discovery of a body in the boot of the car. Echoes of *Psycho* proliferate (including a visit to an old dark house), but the tortuous mystifications and ponderings (shakily shored up by the revelation that she sometimes suffers bouts of amnesia) wear out their welcome long before the final gush of explanations. The presence of Stéphane Audran, as Reed's glacially neurotic wife, makes one wonder wistfully what Chabrol might have made of it all. TM

Lady in the Dark
(Mitchell Leisen, 1944, US) Ginger Rogers, Ray Milland, Warner Baxter, Jon Hall, Barry Sullivan, Mischa Auer, Gail Russell.
100 min.
A gorgeously garish adaptation of the Moss Hart musical, with songs by Kurt Weill and Ira Gershwin, in which a high-powered fashion magazine editor (Rogers) turns to psychoanalysis to resolve her inability to choose between three loves: a middle-aged backer (Baxter), an attractive but independent-minded employee (Milland), and a hunky movie star (Hall). It doesn't bear too close examination, since Hollywood got cold feet about the lady's Electra complex, leaving only hints of her competition with mommy for daddy's love, and completing the bowdlerisation by removing the haunting key song 'My Ship'. What's left is a cardboard charade, but one given a dynamic charge by Leisen's witty visual styling. The three dream sequences, in particular, are superb, with the first two coolly designed, respectively in shades of blue and gold, the third – the circus sequence in which Jenny finds herself on trial for emotional delinquency – bursting into full colour. TM

Lady in the Lake
(Robert Montgomery, 1947, US) Robert Montgomery, Audrey Totter, Lloyd Nolan, Leon Ames, Tom Tully, Jayne Meadows.
103 min. b/w.
Suffering by comparison with' *The Big Sleep* (made a year earlier), this celebrated Chandler adaptation is stubbornly loopy: shot entirely with subjective camera, it lets the audience see the world through Marlowe's eyes. Hired to track down someone's hated wife, you stumble on a dead body, and as Audrey Totter offers you her lips, darkness fills the screen: you have closed your eyes. Even novelty items like mysterious puffs of smoke from invisible cigarettes cannot disguise the high irritation factor in what Chandler himself described as a 'cheap Hollywood trick'. It really needed the magnificent panache of an Orson Welles, who had planned a '40s version of *Heart of Darkness* – about another Marlowe – in the same subjective style. DMacp

Lady in White
(Frank LaLoggia, 1988, US) Lukas Haas, Len Cariou, Alex Rocco, Katherine Helmond, Jason Presson, Renata Vanni.
113 min.
A winning, if uneven, blend of affectionate nos-

talgia and supernatural scariness, set in an idealised small town community in 1962. Haas gives a luminous performance as a young boy whose innocence is tainted when he finds himself caught between a serial child murderer, the ghost of one of the killer's victims, and the unquiet spirit of the dead girl's mother. Seen through the boy's eyes, the events have a haunting quality that is reinforced by the juxtaposition of ethereal apparitions with the more tangible terror of the child killer. An undercurrent of social reality makes itself felt, particularly when the townspeople turn on the school's black janitor, exposing an undercurrent of incipient racism. But LaLoggia is also guilty here and there of questionable excess: the cosy Italian-American family scenes tend to slip into sentimentality, while the special effects overkill of the fairytale ending threatens to drown out the more restrained character development. NF

Lady Jane
(Trevor Nunn, 1985, GB) Helena Bonham Carter, Gary Elwes, John Wood, Michael Hordern, Jill Bennett, Jane Lapotaire, Sara Kestelman, Patrick Stewart, Joss Ackland, Richard Johnson.
142 min.
A fervent supporter of the Reformation, Lady Jane Grey (Carter) was brought up at a time when England was riven with religious dissension, and to prevent the Catholic Mary ascending to the throne, was compelled to marry Guilford Dudley (Elwes), son of the Duke of Northumberland. This seemingly ill-matched marriage was unexpectedly a success, but her brief period of happiness was destroyed when, on Edward VI's death, she was forced unwillingly on to the throne for nine days and died on the scaffold a few months later. A political pawn, indeed. With a script by David Edgar and a cast including all the stalwarts of the RSC, it was not too much to expect that more would be made of her life than just another costume drama. But despite its radical gloss, this over-long, lifeless epic of doomed true love falls into all the predictable traps: excessive pageantry, Monty Python-like peasants, dialogue that drips with sentiment, and even the sight of young lovers running through rural England. JE

Lady Killer
(Roy Del Ruth, 1933, US) James Cagney, Mae Clarke, Leslie Fenton, Margaret Lindsay, Henry O'Neill, Willard Robertson, George Chandler.
76 min. b/w.
Cagney in comedy: a talent often forgotten when one thinks of this most energetically violent of actors. Here the story is tailor-made for his persona. He plays a hood who, for reasons of hiding out and making big money, goes to Hollywood; he serves his time in small parts (very funny, this), but by using the shrewdness and dishonesty he exploited in his life of crime (and writing enormous quantities of fan mail to himself), he graduates to star; whereupon his past threatens to catch up with him...The whole film is witty and fast, hurtled along by Cagney's stylish delivery, and offers a few sharply satirical swipes at Hollywood en route. GA

Ladykillers, The
(Alexander Mackendrick, 1955, GB) Alec Guinness, Cecil Parker, Herbert Lom, Peter Sellers, Danny Green, Katie Johnson, Jack Warner, Frankie Howerd.
97 min.
Mackendrick and Ealing's resident American writer William Rose had already collaborated on *The Maggie* when they came together again for this, the last, most enduring and best known of all the studio's comedies, in which the sheer blackness of the central concept is barely disguised by the accomplished farce which surrounds it. Little Katie Johnson, the innocent hostess to a gang who find it easier to silence each other than her, proves resistant to science (Guinness' fanged 'Professor'), strategy (Parker's 'Major') and all shades of brute force and ignorance as she unwittingly foils a criminal getaway that never reaches beyond St Pancras. A finely wrought image of terminal stasis, national, political (Charles Barr suggests the gang as the first post-war Labour government), and cinematic (the house as Ealing, Johnson as Balcon???). Whatever, Mackendrick immediately upped for America and the equally dark ironies of *Sweet Smell of Success*. PT

Lady L

(Peter Ustinov, 1965, Fr/It) Sophia Loren, Paul Newman, David Niven, Claude Dauphin, Philippe Noiret, Michel Piccoli, Marcel Dalio, Cecil Parker, Peter Ustinov.
124 min.
A glossy and very silly period costume piece about the life of a laundress (Loren) who dallies with international anarchists (including Newman) before marrying an English lord (Niven). Despite the impressive cast and Ustinov's attempts to emulate Max Ophüls, it looks sadly like a case of MGM having locked funds in Europe and wanting to burn them quickly. Not content with writing, directing and playing a fuddy-duddy Bavarian prince, Ustinov also dubs Philippe Noiret's voice. ATu

Lady of Burlesque (aka Striptease Lady)

(William Wellman, 1943, US) Barbara Stanwyck, Michael O'Shea, J Edward Bromberg, Charles Dingle, Frank Conroy, Gloria Dickson, Marion Martin, Pinky Lee, Iris Adrian.
91 min. b/w.
Stanwyck, as 'Dixie Daisy, the Darling of Burlesque', gets the show off to a good start with her spirited rendition of a Sammy Kahn/Harry Akst number, 'Take it off the E-String, play it on the G-String'. A strangler is loose among the showgirls in this comedy-thriller adapted from Gypsy Rose Lee's The G-String Murders (actually ghosted by Craig Rice). Although a stream of hard-boiled wisecracks keeps things amusing, the plot gets tied up in the usual dreary whodunit business of providing motives for all and sundry, and it's difficult to care very much about the jealousies, lecheries and treacheries between cardboard characters. On the other hand, one has to admire the technical skill with which Wellman choreographs the action non-stop all over the theatre, unobtrusively dovetailing it with a number of fascinatingly authentic-looking samples of old-time burlesque shtick. TM

Lady of Deceit

see Born to Kill

Lady of the Boulevards

see Nana

Lady on a Train

(Charles David, 1945, US) Deanna Durbin, Ralph Bellamy, Edward Everett Horton, George Coulouris, Allen Jenkins, David Bruce, Dan Duryea, Patricia Morison.
94 min. b/w.
Durbin plays a girl who witnesses a murder from the window of a train pulling into New York, is believed by no one, and so turns to detection herself, becoming entangled with the victim's sinisterly bizarre family (which includes the killer). With a strong supporting cast, it's surprisingly entertaining. The plot, derived from a story by Leslie Charteris previously filmed in Britain as A Window in London, doesn't delve into the dark chaos beloved of noir thrillers in the '40s so much as play it slightly tongue-in-cheek. Light, cheery and shading into darker areas for the climax, it's fun. GA

Lady Sings the Blues

(Sidney J Furie, 1972, US) Diana Ross, Billy Dee Williams, Richard Pryor, James Callahan, Paul Hampton, Sid Melton, Virginia Capers.
144 min.
A staple biopic of Billie Holiday with all the time-hallowed mundanity of the genre (its preoccupation with her heroin addiction, for instance, or the sequence that 'explains' the song 'Strange Fruit'). What it tells you most about is those kitschy concepts of 'stardom' and the like on a soap-opera/backstage drama level. Diana Ross, managing to avoid doing a Supremes-type number and keeping the songs this side of pastiche, comes out with a straightforward performance that only modulates to pure DR in an outrageous last shot which reduces Billie Holiday's death to the transience of a newspaper cutting, while holding on Diana Ross doing the pinnacle of success bit.

Lady Takes a Chance, A

(William A Seiter, 1943, US) John Wayne, Jean Arthur, Charles Winninger, Phil Silvers, Mary Field, Don Costello.
86 min. b/w.

Naive Easterner Jean Arthur takes Phil Silvers' bus trip, '14 Breathless Days in the West', but gets more than she bargained for when cowpoke Wayne shows her round some. Easygoing comic Western with the stars looking relaxed. TJ

Lady Vanishes, The

(Alfred Hitchcock, 1938, GB) Margaret Lockwood, Michael Redgrave, Paul Lukas, Cecil Parker, Dame May Whitty, Linden Travers, Naunton Wayne, Basil Radford, Mary Clare, Googie Withers.
97 min. b/w.
Critical orthodoxy has it that Hitchcock's move to Hollywood in 1940 was some kind of breakthrough in his career; that his American movies are his 'mature' work, making the earlier English ones look trivial and provincial. It's true that the qualities of his work changed in America, but a look at an early movie like this knocks the rest of the orthodox view sideways. It still looks as fresh and funny as it must have done in 1938: what does the strangling of a Tyrolean street singer have to do with the tweedy English lady in the over-crowded hotel, and why (later) does everyone on a train deny ever having seen the lady in question? There's a sheer pleasure in watching the way the plot turns so smoothly round these questions, and it's compounded by Launder & Gilliat's consistently witty dialogue and the all-round excellence of the cast. TR

Lady Vanishes, The

(Anthony Page, 1979, GB) Elliott Gould, Cybill Shepherd, Angela Lansbury, Herbert Lom, Ian Carmichael, Arthur Lowe, Gerald Harper, Jenny Runacre.
97 min.
Comparisons are odious, but this remake of Hitchcock's thriller continually begs them by trampling heavily over its predecessor. The original anticipated, with some poignancy, a Europe at war. This version uses hindsight entirely to disadvantage. In fact, its picture of 1939 Europe reflects nothing more than current market demands. Thus the plot – madcap American heiress enlists support of Life magazine photographer when cosy English nanny disappears on train in Nazi Germany – serves merely as the packaging for American stars, British support, and German villains still swaggering from the glorious victories of Cabaret and The Sound of Music. Cybill Shepherd and Elliott Gould cover their lack of chemistry with a lot of noise. The film-makers have trouble with their suspense – did she imagine it? who cares? – and it's left to Arthur Lowe and Ian Carmichael, as the cricket lovin' Blimps, to provide solid middle-order batting. CPe

Lady without Camellias, The

see Signora senza camelie, La

Lady Without Passport, A

(Joseph H Lewis, 1950, US) Hedy Lamarr, John Hodiak, James Craig, George Macready, Steve Geray, Bruce Cowling, Nedrick Young.
74 min. b/w.
Stylishly directed by the low-budget wizard who brought you Gun Crazy and The Big Combo, this is a Casablanca-type tale of European immigrants trying to get into America, and being forced to stop off in corrupt, seedy Havana en route. Lamarr is the gorgeous woman with a past who will do anything to reach the land of promise, Hodiak the immigration official who bends the rules when he falls for her. A tight little script and economically etched characters provide a strong foundation, but it is Lewis' evocative visuals that really turn this into a poverty row gem. GA

Lady With the Little Dog, The (Dama s Sobachkoi)

(Josif Heifits, 1959, USSR) Ya Savvina, Alexei Batalov, Ala Chostakova, N Alisova.
90 min. b/w.
Much to the surprise of the Mosfilm commissars, art movie buffs throughout the world took this low-key Chekhov adaptation to their hearts. An impossible love affair begins on a Black Sea holiday, and continues in snatched and furtive meetings, encounters at the theatre, and so on. Heifits' palpable nostalgia for turn-of-the-century manners and styles invests the melancholy tale with astonishing undercurrents of emotion. Until

Mikhalkov made his Unfinished Piece for Mechanical Piano, this was by far the best Chekhov movie in Soviet cinema. TR

Lair of the White Worm, The

(Ken Russell, 1988, GB) Amanda Donohoe, Hugh Grant, Catherine Oxenberg, Peter Capaldi, Sammi Davis, Stratford Johns, Christopher Gable.
93 min.
This Russell rigmarole, nominally based on the Bram Stoker novel, seems to have been made up as it went along, possibly inspired by props left over from his last. The function of much of the writing (Russell again) is to throw rickety pontoon bridges between the yawning set pieces, and you can hear it ticking. Everywhere lies the evidence of carelessness. Davis and Capaldi cower in terror, babbling about a car without its headlights on. The standard crucified Christ and raping Romans round out a nightmare. High Priestess Lady Sylvia Marsh (Donohoe) paralyses a boy scout with a bite to the willy, after leading him on in leather stockings and suspenders over snakes-and-ladders, then fits a giant dildo for an assault upon the virgin Eve (Oxenberg). Archaeologist Angus Flint (Capaldi) produces a mongoose from his sporran, and later a grenade, to combat the ancient evil of the white worm. Tiresome. BC

Lake Consequence

(Rafael Eisenman, 1992, US) Billy Zane, Joan Severance, May Karasun, Whip Hubley, Courtland Mead.
90 min.
Wealthy housewife Irene (Severance) is seeing her husband and son off on a camping trip when she spies hard-torsoed Billy (Zane), a shaven-headed, eye-kohled tree-feller. They talk by nightlight, he pulls out his blues guitar. Next day, she's fingering the objects in his caravan when it jerks into motion, and she's whipped away on a trip of sensual personal discovery. This is producer/writer Zalman King's movie for the uncertain '90s: gone is the techno-bright SM ceremonial vocabulary of his previous 91/2 Weeks. It positively drips with responsibility and eco-soundness. Director Eisenman shows his pop-promo background in a recurrent use of shock-editing, and subliminal sound and image. Despite such defects, the film has its pleasures: soporific sex scenes; Zane manfully failing to portray New Man; the amusing clichés in George Clinton's jazzy score; and the bejewelled dialogue. WH

Lalka

see Doll, The

Lamb

(Colin Gregg, 1985, GB) Liam Neeson, Harry Towb, Hugh O'Conor, Frances Tomelty, Ian Bannen, Denis Carey, Eileen Kennally.
110 min.
Lamb (Neeson), a Catholic priest teaching at a grim remand home for boys on the Irish coast, focuses his charity upon a young ten-year-old (O'Conor) who is subject to fits. When left a small legacy, he takes flight with the boy to London. Alas, as the money slowly runs out, the little good they had between them is threatened by a sordid and uncaring city. Taken from the novel by Bernard MacLaverty, the film very movingly achieves many of those things which are often so difficult in cinema. A portrait of goodness, religion at work, and a multi-faceted view of human character. CPea

Lambada

(Joel Silberg, 1990, US) J Eddie Peck, Melora Hardin, Shabba Doo, Ricky Paul Goldin, Basil Hoffman.
105 min.
A hideous mutation which combines cartoon heroism with dance-floor sex, Brazilian rhythms with Midwest (rather than West Coast) platitudes, and makes Saturday Night Fever look like class movie-making. Peck plays Kevin Laird, a 32-year-old maths teacher at the local high, whose biggest selling point is his 'nice buns' rather than his skill with a set-square, and who leaves the classroom to don leather and prowl the dance-floors of the East LA community from which he sprung (gee, he was adopted as a boy). This Clark Kent of the Dirty Dance movement uses his gift for pump-and-grind to convince the deprived that

maths can be groovy and career options more extensive than club bouncer or drug pusher. It ends not with a knife-fight but a school quiz, and of course Kevin doesn't lay a hand on posh Sandy (Hardin), who's nuts about him. It has an abysmal script, acting which makes Madame Tussaud's look like a roller disco, and some more than passable music and dancing from over 200 local beauties. SGr

Lancelot du Lac
(Lancelot of the Lake)
(Robert Bresson, 1974, Fr/It) Luc Simon, Laura Duke Condominas, Humbert Balsan, Vladimir Antolek-Oresek, Patrick Bernard.
84 min.
Malory, Tennyson, Richard Thorpe and Richard Harris wouldn't recognise Bresson's Knights of the Round Table. They clank around the Camelot area making more noise with their armour than a one-man band, confused about their purpose and even about people's identities; at the end they lie dead in a gloomy forest piled up on a scrapheap. This is the Arthurian legend stripped bare, spotlighting the characters' cruelty, pride, and the aching need for human affection. Bresson's shooting style has always been bare, and he manipulates his small inventory of images and sounds with masterful ease. The tournament provides a virtuoso example: the cameras mostly stick with the horses' feet or the jousters' weapons, and refuse to show us the whole spectacle; the tension which builds up as a result ought to make Michael Winner throw in his cards. It's stunningly beautiful, mesmerising, exhausting, uplifting, amazing – all the things you could possibly expect from a masterpiece. GB

Lancer Spy
(Gregory Ratoff, 1937, US) George Sanders, Dolores Del Rio, Peter Lorre, Joseph Schildkraut, Virginia Field, Sig Ruman, Fritz Feld.
84 min. b/w.
Sanders displaying his Prussian mannerisms for the first time in a dual role as a British naval lieutenant is required to impersonate a captured German baron for purposes of World War I espionage. You've seen it all before, what with Lorre and Ruman leading the nasty Huns, while Del Rio is mightily torn between love and duty as the siren assigned to trap Sanders. The title? That's a bit of a mystery. TM

Land and Freedom
(Ken Loach, 1995, GB/Sp) Ian Hart, Rosana Pastor, Iciar Bollain, Tom Gilroy, Eoin McCarthy.
109 min.
Loach's film charts the experiences of an unemployed young Liverpudlian (Ian Hart) when he goes to join the Republicans in the Spanish Civil War, and for the first half-hour or so it seems that Jim Allen's script is going to be a sentimental celebration of fraternal unity among the good guys. Then, mercifully, things get more complex, as Hart's confusion and divided loyalties mirror the in-fighting that plagued the Left and led to Franco's victory. The film has its shortcomings – notably the didactic discussions on, for example, the ideology of collectivism – but Loach handles what is for him an unprecedentedly large canvas with aplomb. The action scenes in particular have a raw, plausible immediacy. Nor is this just a movie which simply fills us in on fascinating historical details; thanks to muscular performances (especially from Hart), it also packs an emotional punch. GA

Land and Sons
(Land og Synir)
(Agúst Gudmundsson, 1980, Ice) Sigurdur Sigurjónsson, Jón Sigurbjörnsson, Gudny Ragnarsdóttir, Jónas Tryggvasson.
94 min.
The title tells it all – generations of hill farmers struggling to force an existence from the unyielding land, and getting ripped off by the co-operative movement set up to help them. Relationships made with sheepdogs last longer than those with women. Yet for all the bleakness (rainswept landscapes) and the occasional awkwardness in performance and editing, this is an honourable first feature on the familiar theme of country boy drifting to big city. It may not do for Iceland what The

Harder They Come did for Jamaica, but it recommends itself for its unusual setting and modest ambitions. MA

Land Before Time, The
(Don Bluth, 1988, US) voices: Gabriel Damon, Helen Shaver, Bill Erwin, Candice Huston, Pat Hingle.
69 min.
After *An American Tale*, Bluth surely had the clout to make a more adventurous animated feature than this, with its anthropomorphic espousal of American nuclear family values and its static, unimaginatively rendered backgrounds. You'd have thought, too, that a film about dinosaurs could have been mildly educational: giving the species' proper names for instance, rather than just 'Three-horns' or 'Longnecks', or – since the plot concerns a group of youngsters learning to travel together to find the Great Valley, where they'll all be saved from extinction – bringing in at least one of the theories about why the food chain became broken. Still, it has its moments: an earthquake scene is genuinely scary, the tension between the two would-be leaders should strike a chord with any kid who's ever wanted to be accepte by a gang, and some of the voices are well, if irritatingly done. DW

Landlord, The
(Hal Ashby, 1970, US) Beau Bridges, Pearl Bailey, Diana Sands, Louis Gossett, Douglas Grant, Melvin Stewart, Lee Grant, Susan Anspach.
113 min.
Ashby's first film as director – produced by Norman Jewison, whose regular editor Ashby had been – this was coolly received when first released. Presumably its anarchic satire on the mores and assumptions of the American Way of Life, which range from Sidney Poitier movies to events like the spinal meningitis summer ball, were thought to be in bad taste. Like *Leo the Last*, the film deals with the problems of a man of property once he enters into human, rather than economic, relationships with his tenants. But whereas Boorman's film is a carefully constructed whole, from its colour scheme to its casting of Marcello Mastroianni in the lead, Ashby's film (like the later and much more successful *The Last Detail*) operates through the freewheeling juxtaposition of characters in unlikely situations. Worth a look. PH

Land of Silence and Darkness (Land des Schweigens und der Dunkelheit)
(Werner Herzog, 1971, WGer) Fini Straubinger, Miss Juliet, Mr Mittermeier, Else Fährer.
85 min.
A stunning documentary about 56-year-old Fini, blind and deaf since her late teens. After 30 years of being confined to her bed by her mother, she fought to overcome her immense isolation by helping others similarly afflicted. While some of these tragically incommunicable individuals make for painful viewing, Herzog also demonstrates the humour and joys of a day at the zoo, or of a first plane flight, where touch and togetherness in suffering offer the sole but undeniable reason for living. The courage on view is astounding, and Herzog's treatment is never voyeuristic or sentimental, but sensuous and overwhelmingly moving. GA

Land of the Monsters
see Maciste Contro i Mostri

Land of the Pharaohs
(Howard Hawks, 1955, US) Jack Hawkins, Joan Collins, Dewey Martin, James Robertson Justice, Alexis Minotis, Sydney Chaplin.
106 min.
Hawks was always better with small groups of characters, but this Egyptian epic, concerning intrigue at the Pharaoh's court during the building of a massive pyramid, is far from uninteresting. Although the script (by Faulkner, among others) gets stranded with the usual slightly wooden dialogue considered necessary for ancient times, the story moves along at a stately but never sluggish pace, and is scattered with lovely moments, most notably the grim finale

when Collins gets her ironic come-uppance. With sets by Trauner and camerawork by Lee Garmes, it looks great; certainly, alongside those of Nick Ray, one of the best epics. GA

Landscape After Battle (Krajobraz po Bitwie)
(Andrzej Wajda, 1970, Pol) Daniel Olbrychski, Stanislawa Celinska, Aleksander Bardini, Zygmunt Malanowicz, Tadeusz Janczar.
111 min.
Wajda's strange, turbulent, bracing film sees him returning to his old stomping ground of World War II, but the style is far more expressionist and fragmentary, the political analysis more complex, than in his famous trilogy. The landscape in question is a former concentration camp which, after the liberation, houses Polish 'displaced persons', including the disillusioned poet Tadeusz – presumably named after the author of the film's source material, Tadeusz Borowski, who committed suicide after surviving Auschwitz. Wajda's Tadeusz (played with precision by Olbrychski) seems to have a happier time of it: his belief in humanity is rekindled by an affair with a Jewish girl escaping from Poland. But there's still no easy sentimentality here, no easy solution to the problems of national and human identity. Wajda uses his darting camera to extract endless cruel ironies from the grim setting, and even presents the final credits in an odd, unsettling manner – they're daubed up on the side of railway wagons. GB

Landscape in the Mist (Topio stin Omichli)
(Theo Angelopoulos, 1988, Greece/Fr/It) Michalis Zeke, Tania Palaiologou, Stratis Tzortzoglou.
125 min.
A small boy and his pubescent sister leave home in search of their missing father (said to be in Germany), and cross paths with various characters perhaps intended to evoke a nation in crisis; an uncle unwilling to take charge of the infant vagrants, a brute trucker, a luckless troupe of itinerant actors whose explorations of Greek history are no longer in demand. The one person to offer help is the troupe's roadie Orestes, whose own solitude, enhanced by imminent army service, prompts him to play father to the resolute waifs. A sombre, even disturbing road movie, this is no glossy Greek travelogue; endless train journeys and walks along wintry roads lead through a succession of dingy waiting-rooms, grey towns, muddy laybys, and mountains scarred by industry. But the children's slow, dreamlike odyssey also gives rise to surreal, startling epiphanies: wedding celebrants in the snow, a massive Godlike hand rising from the sea to soar over a city. If the overall tone is bleak in its portayal of betrayals, loneliness and disillusionment, Angelopoulos' assured control of mood, Giorgos Arvanitis' superb camerawork, and the kids' glowing performances provide ample pleasures. GA

Land That Time Forgot, The
(Kevin Connor, 1974, GB) Doug McClure, John McEnery, Susan Penhaligon, Keith Barron, Anthony Ainley, Godfrey James.
91 min.
The combination of a script co-written by Michael Moorcock, the largest budget Amicus has ever utilised, and director Connor (who made such a promising debut with *From Beyond the Grave*) should have added up to a lot more than this occasionally amusing Boy's Own Paper adventure. It starts off promisingly with some stylised and ridiculous heroics involving a German sub, but once the island has been occupied and a few excellent monsters vanquished, the plot settles down to some very ordinary machinations. In fact, by the time the ape-men arrive we might as well be back in one of Hammer's sub-anthropological sagas. It's better than Disney's similar attempt at family fantasy, *Island at the Top of the World*, but that's hardly a recommendation. DP

Language of Love (Kärlekens Sprak)
(Torgny Wickman, 1969, Swe) Inge Hegeler, Sten Hegeler, Maj-Brith Bergstrom, Sture Cullhed.
107 min.

Living-room-type discussion of sex, interspersed with mimed or actual illustrative sequences. Genital close-ups, at one stage including five penises in a row – sight for sore eyes. Should be shown in schools rather than to the raincoat trade. VG

La Passione

(John B Hobbs, 1996, GB) Sean Gallagher, Thomas Orange, Paul Shane, Jan Ravens, Carmen Silvera, Shirley Bassey.
106 min.
Aside from creating bland AOR rock, Chris Rea also has a passion for motor racing and cars, especially those bearing the Ferrari marque. So much so that he's committed his childhood memories to celluloid with this semi-autobiographical 'musical fantasy'. It begins well enough with a sepia-toned Rea (played by Orange and later Gallagher) showing early signs of his Grand Prix obsession, but then the whole structure goes awry as we try to make sense of the jumps back and forth through stages of the singer's youth, the weird dream sequences, the absurdity of Shirley Bassey's cabaret turn, and the fact that his music is mostly out of kilter with the surreal imagery. The Ferraris look good, though. DA

Larger Than Life

(Howard Franklin, 1996, US) Bill Murray, Janeane Garofalo, Matthew McConaughey, Keith David, Pat Hingle, Jeremy Piven, Lois Smith, Anita Gillette, Harve Presnell, Linda Fiorentino.
93 min.
Mr Cynical Chops, Murray, certainly meets his match in this buddy pic with a difference. His Jack Corcoran, motivational guru on the conference circuit, puts his success down to losing his dad at an early age, so he's in for a shock when he discovers the old man has only just passed away, bequeathing his son a circus clown's red nose and Vera, a performing elephant. Countless comic opportunities present themselves as Murray and his new pal make their way across country to settle her future: will it be with kindly researcher Garofalo, who'll return the beast to the wild, or seductive trainer Linda Fiorentino, who'll put her in a Vegas show but pay big bucks up front? Well, you don't need second sight to figure that one out. We know the elephant will knock lots of things over, tricks will be performed at significant plot points, and Bill will turn into a big softie along the way. If there's not much room for manoeuvre, Murray in curmudgeon mode is as watchable as ever. We learn, of course, to be kind to animals, though whether this sits easily with the well-trained antics of the co-star is another matter. Disgracing itself only with McConaughey's over-extended bit as a psychotic trucker, the film delivers more or less comfortably on what you'd expect, then sits down for a rest. TJ

Larks on a String (Skrivanci na niti)

(Jiri Menzel, 1969, Czech) Rudolf Hrusinsky, Vaclav Neckar, Leos Sucharipa, Jitka Zelenohorska.
90 min.
This satire was completed in 1969 and promptly banned by the authorities put in place in Czechoslovakia after the Soviet invasion of 1968. If it's easy to see why the apparatchiks weren't exactly chuffed with it, Menzel's still not the most hard-hitting of film-makers: here, as sundry bourgeois types are relocated to a '50s Stalinist factory workplace for 're-education', the focus is as much on their romantic misadventures with the women in the adjoining camp as it is on dissecting the harsh injustice of the system. For those who savour whimsy. TJ

Laserblast

(Michael Rae, 1978, US) Kim Milford, Cheryl Smith, Gianni Russo, Ron Masak, Roddy McDowall, Keenan Wynn, Dennis Burkley.
90 min.
A Jekyll/Hyde quickie rip-off, Laserblast is the epitome of what Frank Zappa once hymned as 'cheapness'. Shot in the director's front room, space creatures courtesy of Kelloggs, and a laser-gun that must have cost several dollars, it has all the sincerity of a plastic dashboard Jesus. The power that the alien laser confers on weedy Billy does allow him some vengeful destruction, but

this is stingily confined to police cars and he duly pays the dreadful price – terminal alienship ('Billy, why can't you be more ordinary?'). Brain-addling. CPea

Lásky Jedné Plavovlásky (A Blonde in Love/Loves of a Blonde)

(Milos Forman, 1965, Czech) Hana Brejchová, Vladimir Pucholt, Vladimir Mensik, Antonin Blazejovsky, Milada Jezkova, Josef Sebánek.
82 min. b/w.
Forman's second film is a small gem. The story is almost classical in its simplicity: a pretty little blonde meets a young pianist at a dance hall, and they spend a happy night of love together. But she takes the affair altogether more seriously than he does, and when she pays an unannounced call on his parents, everybody is appalled. He feels he is being trapped, she feels betrayed, and the parents see both sides in turn, until in the end nobody knows what to think because nobody seems to be playing according to any known rules. Much of Forman's humour comes from the fact that his characters peer out at the world like timid nocturnal animals, always prepared to defend themselves against attack, but constantly having the ground cut from under their feet by the discovery that people are never quite what they seem at first glance. Using mostly non-professional actors, letting them improvise, then refining, shaping and perfecting, he achieves something indescribably exact, touching and funny. TM

Lassie Come Home

(Fred M Wilcox, 1943, US) Elizabeth Taylor, Dame May Whitty, Roddy McDowall, Donald Crisp, Nigel Bruce, Elsa Lanchester, Pal.
88 min.
The daddy of dog movies has down-on-his-luck Yorkshireman Crisp reluctantly selling his son McDowall's prize collie to local aristo Bruce, but after a couple of canine escape attempts the good duke moves himself, dog and granddaughter Taylor to Scotland for some peace of mind. No sooner have they arrived, however, than Lassie's off on the arduous road to her young master. Nobody made this heart-warming fluff better than MGM. TJ

Lassiter

(Roger Young, 1983, US) Tom Selleck, Jane Seymour, Lauren Hutton, Bob Hoskins, Joe Regalbuto, Ed Lauter, Warren Clarke.
100 min.
Somewhere in the Hollywood hills there's a computer loaded with a software programme called BuildaStar. A hack punched in the script requirements for this intended star vehicle for Selleck: an action yarn pitting an American loner against evil Nazis, bent coppers, a sultry girl-friend; sardonic sex with a lashing of perversity and gratuitous nudity; dare-devil stunts and chases for excitement; pseudo-moral dilemmas for the more intellectually inclined; period London settings (1939) for a hint of authenticity. The computer duly scanned the files in its memory, notably the ones labelled James Bond, The Sting, Steve McQueen's Motor-Bike Scenes and Cary Grant/Negligée Number from Bringing Up Baby, and cobbled them all together into an Adult Entertainment. HH

Last Action Hero, The

(John McTiernan, 1993, US) Arnold Schwarzenegger, Austin O'Brien, Charles Dance, Mercedes Ruehl, F Murray Abraham, Art Carney.
131 min.
'No one likes a smart-ass,' Jack Slater (Schwarzenegger) advised young Danny (O'Brien), the kid who keeps insisting that Jack's fictional. He has a point. Here's the set-up: an elderly projectionist allows 11-year-old Danny to sneak into the midnight preview of the new Schwarzenegger action movie, Jack Slater IV. A magic ticket (!) transports him into the flick, where he helps his hero tackle the evil Benedict (Dance), until the killer in turn breaks through the screen to wreak havoc in 'reality'. It's a promising scenario but McTiernan pitches ham-fistedly at a post-modern attention span and shoots with the subtlety of a rampaging rhino. This is film-making of the 'more-is-more' school: heavy metal action, but no character, no suspense. It

may be the first action art movie but this po-mo parody is so self-reflexive it scarcely requires an audience. TCh

Last American Hero, The

(Lamont Johnson, 1973, US) Jeff Bridges, Valerie Perrine, Geraldine Fitzgerald, Ned Beatty, Gary Busey, Art Lund, Ed Lauter.
100 min.
With an absolutely top-notch cast headed by the excellent Bridges, this loose adaptation of a series of articles by Tom Wolfe could hardly fail. Telling of young Carolina hill-billy Junior Jackson (based on Junior Johnson), it traces his rise from moon-shine-runner to stock-car and demolition-derby champ, and then on to fame as a big-time racer. But this is no mere celebration of fame, since it lightly but firmly sketches in the many compromises and losses met on the road to success. Johnson directs with a keen eye for the subculture of the car tracks and the whisky brewers, so that the film emerges as a winning, intelligent portrait of an aspect of America all too rarely seen in the movies. Like a Thunder Road filtered through the perceptions of the '70s, it's an invigorating and touching movie. GA

Last American Virgin, The

(Boaz Davidson, 1982, US) Lawrence Monoson, Diane Franklin, Steve Antin, Joe Rubbo, Louisa Moritz, Brian Peck.
92 min.
Accompanied by a mediocre music score (Commodores, Cars, Blondie, etc), three moronic youths are herded through puberty and the dreary rites of passage all too familiar from endless similar films (comparing pricks, humping hookers, necking in the back of borrowed cars, spying on girls in the shower). The viewpoint is predictably phallic: fear/contempt of the female festers like a squeezed pimple; an abortion is shown more lasciviously than any sex. Puberty Blues and Porky's look positively progressive beside such sickening junk. Boaz Davidson should stick to sucking Popsicles. SJo

Last Battle, The (Le Dernier Combat)

(Luc Besson, 1983, Fr) Pierre Jolivet, Jean Bouise, Fritz Wepper, Jean Reno, Maurice Lamy, Pierre Carrive.
92 min. b/w.
That Besson previously assisted on a couple of features by the anarcho-eccentric Claude Faraldo is significant: the grim, wordless, post-holocaust humour of The Last Battle bears more than a passing resemblance to the latter's devastating Themroc. Unlike most Mad Max spin-offs, this is much more than a transplanted Western, with a hero who's as often required to be tender as he is ferocious. The result is a neat, wry, pocket-size adventure with several magic moments such as a rain-storm of fresh fish, and a touching scene where two of the most human characters manage to exchange a fragment or two of speech with the aid of a gas inhaler. The monochrome photography enhances a bare-bones atmosphere, and the small cast is splendid. A welcome addition to the post-holocaust barbarism boom. GD

Last Boy Scout, The

(Tony Scott, 1991, US) Bruce Willis, Damon Wayans, Chelsea Field, Noble Willingham, Taylor Negron, Danielle Harris, Halle Berry, Bruce McGill, Joe Santos.
105 min.
Every element is present and correct in this violent, smart-mouthed, buddy-buddy action comedy, with just enough of an ironic inflection to ensure that familiarity breeds content. Willis plays a washed-up LA private eye whose partner is killed after passing on a case. With his marriage on the rocks and his daughter under threat, he reluctantly teams up with sartorially smooth ex-football player Jimmy Dix (Wayans) to crack the case. Naturally, the initial murder is just the tip of an iceberg, which engulfs major league football, prime-time sports coverage, and the gambling interests of a ruthless businessman (Willingham). Limited though his range is, Willis was born to play this type of role; the bonus here is that his flip smarm is matched by Wayans' suave charm. Despite the testosterone-charged violence and jaw-dropping sexism, the tone is one of self-conscious excess – a strategy which constantly undercuts the film's celebration of male bonding conventions. NF

Last Challenge, The (aka The Pistolero of Red River)

(Richard Thorpe, 1967, US) Glenn Ford, Angie Dickinson, Chad Everett, Gary Merrill, Jack Elam, Delphi Lawrence, Royal Dano.
105 min.

The veteran Thorpe's last film, a Western gallantly attempting to ring the changes on an old situation, with Ford as the gunfighter turned marshal and yearning to settle down, Everett as the feisty youngster out to challenge him, and Dickinson as the saloon gal who doesn't want him dead. Watchable, thanks to solid performances, but pretty turgid. TM

Last Chance Hotel

see Emmène-moi

Last Chants for a Slow Dance

(Jon Jost, 1977, US) Tom Blair, Steve Vooheis, Jessica St John, Wayne Crouse, Mary Vollmer, John Jackson.
88 min.

The subject of Jost's excellent movie is the content of the most dirge-like Country and Western lyrics, and what that kind of indulgence leads to. His tale of a dole-queue loser, estranged from wife and kids, living an anachronistic male stud cowboy life and slowly drifting into crime, was apparently suggested by the life of Gary Gilmore. It's particularly scathing about the American macho psyche, but in a novel fashion; the music (all written and performed by Jost himself) comments on the action in a manner that's anything but the fashionably cosy way country is used in films these days. Jost shoots in long takes, relying on imaginative use of natural lighting à la early Godard. RM

Last Command, The

(Josef von Sternberg, 1928, US) Emil Jannings, Evelyn Brent, William Powell, Nicholas Soussanin, Michael Visaroff, Jack Raymond.
95 min. b/w.

The Last Command starts from a brilliant script idea: a Czarist general, defeated in the Russian revolution, finds himself down and out in Hollywood, working for peanuts as a bit-player in movies; he is spotted and hired by his former adversary, a Mayakovskian stage director turned Hollywood film-maker; and both men loved the same woman ten years earlier. Half the movie is an acid vision of the gap between success and the breadline in contemporary Hollywood, and the other half is a long flashback to revolutionary Russia, with the general seducing the woman Communist, imprisoning his rival, falling from power, and discovering abject humiliation. In other words, this is the first Sternberg masterpiece, the first of his glitteringly stylised rhapsodies of commitment and betrayal, expertly poised between satire and 'absurd' melodrama. The cast are fully equal to it; Jannings, in particular, turns the characteristic role of the general into an indelible portrait of arrogance, fervour and dementia. Even more incredible, the sheer sophistication of Sternberg's visuals makes nearly all current releases look old-fashioned. TR

Last Command, The

(Frank Lloyd, 1955, US) Sterling Hayden, Anna Maria Alberghetti, Richard Carlson, Arthur Hunnicutt, Ernest Borgnine, J Carrol Naish, Virginia Grey, Ben Cooper, John Russell, Slim Pickens.
110 min.

In the '20s and '30s, directors came no bigger than Frank Lloyd: he helmed *Cavalcade* and *Mutiny on the Bounty* and won a couple of Oscars. Hardly remembered now, his career ended with this reconstruction of the siege of the Alamo. As with the John Wayne epic of 1960, it's a travesty of history, and focuses on Jim Bowie (Hayden) rather more than Davy Crockett (Hunnicutt). The message is the same as in Wayne's film – better Tex than Mex – though the production values are considerably less impressive. This is a Republic Studios Western, so don't look for thousands of extras. But Lloyd's old professionalism produces some good battle footage. ATu

Last Crop, The

(Sue Clayton, 1990, GB/Aust) Kerry Walker, Noah Taylor.
58 min.

Ann Sweeney has a peculiar perspective on how the other half live: as charwoman to a number of Sydney apartments owned by wealthy business folk who spend months abroad, she not only cleans the trappings of financial success, but makes good use of them, letting friends take over the luxury flats in the owners' absence for romantic weekends, wedding receptions, or simply a break from routine. But not everything is rosy for Ann, burdened as she is with a delinquent son, a daughter given to bursts of moody ingratitude, and a surly father in an old peoples' home who refuses to make everyone's life easier by selling the family's derelict farm. Deceptively slight, this adaptation of Elizabeth Jolley's short story charms partly for its bitter-sweet sense of humour, partly for its beautifully convincing performances (especially Kerry Walker as the pragmatic Ann). Also impressive are the way Clayton subtly injects trenchant social and economic observations into her oblique narrative, and the crisp, clear lines of Geoff Burton's camerawork. GA

Last Dance

(Bruce Beresford, 1995, US) Sharon Stone, Rob Morrow, Randy Quaid, Peter Gallagher, Jack Thompson, Skeet Ulrich.
103 min.

A painfully earnest, painfully inadequate anti-capital punishment movie, this asks us to take pity on Stone as a butch redneck hardcase whose death-row time is all used up. And we do pity her, but for the wrong reason: because Stone gives a rigorous, unglamorous and admirably low-key performance. There's a tendency to overpraise sex symbols when they take off the make-up in roles like this, as if ugliness somehow has more integrity than beauty – it doesn't – but Stone's work here is centred and hard, as layered as anything she's done, and all the more impressive for the lack of help she gets from the script. Compelling as Stone is, the film chooses to make Morrow's lawyer the dramatic focal point – and that's its undoing, because the character never rings true. A rich kid whose brother (Gallagher) gets him on the Governor's staff as a favour, Morrow is told to assess Stone's appeal for clemency before her politically expedient execution is carried out. For reasons which remain sketchy, he throws himself into the job and soon sets about re-opening the case. This legal beagle stuff is thin and risibly melodramatic. The film isn't a travesty, but it feels uncomfortably close to one. TCh

Last Date (De Laatste Sessie)

(Hans Hylkema, 1992, Neth) Eric Dolphy, Misha Mengelberg, Buddy Collette, Han Bennink, Ted Curson, Jaki Byard.
92 min. b/w & col.

Hylkema's portrait of the late jazz multi-instrumentalist Eric Dolphy certainly talks to the right people. As well as the expected survivors of Dolphy's European and Mingus periods – said Mingus: 'Eric, I'm gonna miss ya, asshole' – we go all the way back to Roy Porter, Buddy Collette and his bride-to-be in LA, and neighbours who heard the teenage prodigy practising his eight hours a day. No wonder he told pianist Mischa Mengelberg he was lazy. Dedicated, clean-living Dolphy had diabetes – Gunther Schuller puts it down to diet deficiency, since the jazzman survived on white beans and water when broke – but when he was admitted to a Berlin hospital in 1964, the authorities, assuming he'd overdosed, left him to die. Lots of old footage of Dolphy in action, mainly on bass clarinet. BC

Last Day of Summer

(Derek Banham, 1983, GB) Annette Badland, Graham McGrath, James Gaddas, Christina Jones, Saskia Reeves.
55 min.

Adapted by Ian McEwan from one of his own stories, this is a film of moods, overheard indistinct voices, slowed hypnotic time, and particularly a troubling sense of false security and impending tragedy. In a pot-addled Thames-side commune, Tom, a 12-year-old orphan (McGrath), is befriended by Jenny, a cheerful, overweight ex-teacher (Badland, excellent), who derives a passive contentment from attending to his conventional needs (Tom likes to go to school in uniform). Their affecting idyll is played out chiefly in Tom's rowing boat on the deceptively passive river at the end of a very filmic English summer. JPy

Last Day of Winter, The (Zuihou Yige Dongri)

(Wu Ziniu, 1986, China) Li Ling, Tao Zheru, Hong Yuzhou, Zhang Xiaomin, Yu Meng.
92 min.

This is the first movie to show the Chinese Gulag, a huge labour camp in the remote north-west, and so it's no surprise that its director is one of China's ground-breaking 'fifth generation' film-makers. The stylised flashbacks to the inmates' crimes teeter on the brink of melodramatic excess, but the framing scenes in the prison are as coolly controlled and visually striking as anything in New Chinese Cinema. The movie is also startlingly candid in matters of detail, like the scene in which a woman inmate breaks down over her brother's gift – of a suitcaseful of sanitary towels. TR

Last Days of Chez Nous, The

(Gillian Armstrong, 1991, Aust) Lisa Harrow, Bruno Ganz, Kerry Fox, Miranda Otto, Kiri Paramore, Bill Hunter, Lex Marinos, Mickey Camilleri.
96 min.

Everyday routine and a long-standing relationship with her French husband (Ganz) threatens to make Beth (Harrow) cynical and complacent, and to blind her to the possibility of change. But the arrival of her lovelorn sister Vicki (Fox) causes the family to implode, with three generations forced to re-evaluate their relationships. Armstrong skilfully and gently teases out the subtexts underlying each interaction, exposing individual selfishness which insulates and provides protection against domestic insecurity. Harrow heads the strong cast with a performance of considerable power and restraint. CM

Last Days of Man on Earth, The

see Final Programme, The

Last Days of Pompeii, The

(Ernest B Schoedsack, 1935, US) Preston Foster, Basil Rathbone, Alan Hale, Dorothy Wilson, John Wood, Louis Calhern.
96 min. b/w.

Mt Vesuvius blows its top in fine fashion somewhere near the end of this sword-and-sandal spectacular, but all the molten lava the special effects team can cook up isn't enough to atone for a cool, dreary script. Marcus, an honest blacksmith (Foster), is driven by misfortune to become an amoral gladiator. He repents just in time to save Pompeii's Christians from being frazzled. The acting honours, such as they are, go to Basil Rathbone, as a memorably dapper Pontius Pilate.

Last Detail, The

(Hal Ashby, 1973, US) Jack Nicholson, Otis Young, Randy Quaid, Clifton James, Carol Kane, Michael Moriarty, Luana Anders, Nancy Allen.
104 min.

Despite Robert Towne's often sharp script – about two veteran sailors detailed to escort a young and naïve rating to prison, and showing him a sordidly 'good time' en route – and despite strong performances all round, one can't help feeling that the criticism of modern America hits out at all too easy targets in a vague and muffled manner. Also that the overlay of bleak cynicism barely conceals a troubled – and, dare one say, sometimes misogynist – sentimentality about what it means to be men together. GA

Last Dinosaur, The

(Alex Grasshoff/Tom Kotani, 1977, US) Richard Boone, Joan Van Ark, Steven Keats, Luther Rackley, Masumi Sekiya.
100 min.

Difficult to know which is the more ludicrous in this shoddy monster pic: the Joke Shop *tyrannosaurus* galumphing through the polar icecap landscape, or Richard Boone's completely erratic portrayal of Masten Thrust (yessir, that's his name) – the richest, most bored man in the world, who gathers together a little band of stereotypes (Nobel prizewinning scientist, spunky woman photographer) to track the last of the breed. With his unkempt hair, dark glasses, and habit of closing his eyes between words, Boone shows all the signs of enjoying a massive hangover; but when you have to talk about a 'forty foot monster with a brain the size of a dried pea', this is probably a distinct advantage. Japan provided the special effects and the extras who play hairy prehistoric savages; someone should complain. GB

Last Dragon, The
(Michael Schultz, 1985, US) Taimak, Vanity, Chris Murney, Julius J Carry III, Faith Prince, Leo O'Brien.
109 min.
This combines kung-fu with the current pash for pop-promo video, plus a spot of lighthearted mob violence. Chop-socker hits town, gets girlfriend, grapples with corrupt gangsters, and wins big fight. Even the klutziest of kung-fu kicks is more fun to watch than people dancing on their heads and elbows, and the determined attempt to juxtapose clashing cultures sometimes pays off. More chop-sloppy than chop-socky, but sauced up with splashes of pot-noodle charm. AB

Last Embrace
(Jonathan Demme, 1979, US) Roy Scheider, Janet Margolin, John Glover, Sam Levene, Charles Napier, Christopher Walken, Jacqueline Brookes.
101 min.
A delicious excursion into the world of Hitchcockian suspense. A taut, complex conspiracy thriller, it sees Scheider – a former 'agent' for an assassination firm – threatened by mental breakdown (guilt over his wife's death), by his former employers who find him dangerously superfluous, and by an obscure Hebraic society bent on revenge for some unknown reason. Scheider is admirably haunted as the justifiably paranoid gunman (who gets involved with a strange, duplicitous *femme fatale*), the whole thing is beautifully shot by Tak Fujimoto, and Miklos Rosza's stunning score augments Demme's careful control of atmosphere and set pieces. But what finally impresses is the way that the various references to Hitchcock and other classic thrillers are never used as an end in themselves; rather, they simply add resonance and depth to a film that works perfectly well in its own right. GA

Last Emperor, The
(Bernardo Bertolucci, 1987, China/It) John Lone, Joan Chen, Peter O'Toole, Ying Ruocheng, Victor Wong, Dennis Dun, Ryuichi Sakamoto.
163 min.
The odyssey of Emperor Pu Yi, from ruler of half the world's population to humble gardener in the People's Republic of China, is a saga of tidal historical turbulence with a small, often supine centre. Nations treated Pu Yi as a blank screen upon which they projected their ambitions, but Bertolucci's epic strives not to follow suit. The vast, gorgeous tapestry of visual delights is built around the question of one man's capacity for personal redemption, which – up to a point – transforms the puppet into protagonist. Pu Yi ascended the Dragon Throne at three but was forced to abdicate at six when China became a republic, and from then until his expulsion from the Forbidden City, his puissance was an empty charade, his palace a prison. This section of the film is sumptuously rich and strange, from the bewildering maze of the Forbidden City itself (with its 9,999 rooms) to the daily rituals surrounding the little Living God. Though courtiers indulge his every whim, but can never allow him to venture outside; to some extent his Scottish tutor (O'Toole) replaces the forfeited warmth of his mother and wet nurse, later supplemented by an Empress (Chen). Given this outlandish upbringing, it is impossible to judge his subsequent showing as playboy in exile and dupe of the Japanese – neither section memorable. The film covers over half-a-century in flashbacks, contrasting at the start the rainbow glories with the grey reality of Communist confession, and gradually monitors its spectrum as Pu Yi rejoins the human race. John Lone is superb as the sad mediocrity; and if spectacle finally triumphs over sympathy, it is not without a decent struggle. BC

Last Exit to Brooklyn
(Letzte Ausfahrt Brooklyn)
(Ulrich Edel, 1989, WGer) Stephen Lang, Jennifer Jason Leigh, Burt Young, Peter Dobson, Jerry Orbach, Alexis Arquette, Zette, Frank Military, Ricki Lake, John Costelloe.
98 min.

A violent, harrowing, but oddly tender adaptation of Hubert Selby Jr's novel about life in a working class Brooklyn neighbourhood in the '50s. In this harsh, poverty-stricken enviroment, human feeling is sacrificed to expediency as prostitute Tralala (Leigh), union leader Harry Black (Lang), and assorted workers, hustlers, wives, pimps and homosexuals struggle to survive. While a strike at a loca factory explodes into violent confrontation, Harry uses embezzled union funds to explore the homosexual desire provoked in him by transvestite Georgette (Arquette). Tralala; meanwhile, frightened by an offer of love she cannot comprehend, plunges into a rampage of self destruction. From the fragments of an experimental novel, Edel has forged a remarkably coherent whole, cross-cutting from one story to another while retaining a precise delineation of character, picking out slender, golden threads of compassion and love from a bleak tapestry of pain. Not a comfortable film, but humane and savagely beautiful. NF

Last Feelings
(L'Ultimo Sapore dell'Aria)
(Ruggero Deodato, 1978, It) Maurizio Rossi, Vittoria Galeazzi, Carlo Lupo, Angela Goodwin, Fiorenzo Fiorentini, Jacques Sernas.
105 min.
Slim, dark, good-looking teenage boy, misunderstood but eager to please, speaks dubbed English, seeks substitute family, wants sincere girl-friend and wishes to become swimming champion. Only months to live, however. Is this why my eyes swim as much as I do and why I am wetter than any swimming-pool you care to think of? Write soonest with s.a.e. CPe

Last Flight, The
(William Dieterle, 1931, US) Richard Barthelmess, Helen Chandler, John Mack Brown, David Manners, Elliott Nugent.
77 min. b/w.
A study of the Lost Generation more quintessentially Fitzgerald than anything Scott Fitzgerald ever wrote: a doomed, innocently mad-cap frolic over which hangs the aura of despair. Adapted by John Monk Saunders from his own novel *Single Lady*, it chronicles the dark night of the soul of four young aviators, invalided out as 'spent bullets' at the end of World War I and lingering on in Paris to drown their shattered nerves in dry Martinis and zany banter with a dreamily dotty rich girl in whom they instantly recognise a kindred spirit when they see her in a bar solemnly guarding someone's false teeth in her champagne glass. Nothing happens, and 'nothing matters' echoes as an ominous motif through the brilliantly racy conversations, until suddenly, within the space of a few minutes running time, three of the four have died or disappeared, and a curtain seems to fall on an era as the fourth is left to mourn the comradeship that alone survived the war. With superb dialogue that paints hell in wisecracks and an extraordinary performance by Helen Chandler as the girl, it's a small masterpiece. TM

Last Flight of Noah's Ark, The
(Charles Jarrott, 1980, US) Elliott Gould, Genevieve Bujold, Ricky Schroder, Tammy Lauren, Vincent Gardenia, John Fujioka.
98 min.
There must be a computer in the Disney studios programmed to produce live-action shooting scripts at the drop of various switches (probably labelled 'Children', 'Animals', 'Moral Homilies' and 'Some Current Cinema Fashions'). It's certainly been in use here. A plane full of two orphans, sundry animals, an evangelist (wonderful Bujold) and a hard-nosed pilot (boring Gould) crash-lands in the Pacific, with ensuing struggle back to civilisation. There's the tousle-haired faucet Schroder crying over his small zoo; an encounter with a shark; and umpteen sermons on tolerance and togetherness, with all the cast – including two Jap soldiers still fighting World War II – learning to live together in a wonderful warm glow. GB

Last Gangster, The
(Edward Ludwig, 1937, US) Edward G Robinson, James Stewart, Rosa Stradner, Lionel Stander, John Carradine.
81 min. b/w.
A typically edgy Robinson, continually threat-

ening to turn things nastier at the drop of a snarl, returns from a 10-year stretch in stir during which he's become obsessed by the time he's missed with his small son. This is bad news for ex-wife Stradner, who's since married newspaperman Stewart and watched the bond grow between the boy and his stepdad. Stewart looks much younger than his 29 years, and he's not much of a match for the headliner, but this is still an absorbing exercise in contrasting styles. TJ

Last Good Time, The
(Bob Balaban, 1994, US) Armin Mueller-Stahl, Lionel Stander, Maureen Stapleton, Olivia D'Abo, Adrian Pasdar, Zohra Lampert, Kevin Corrigan, Molly Powell.
90 min.
Very different from the ghoulish Americana of his debut, the horror-satire *Parents*, character actor Balaban's second feature is a compassionate and assured portrait of old age. Isolated in his Brooklyn apartment, Mueller-Stahl's immigrant German violinist broods on his past, haunted by sexual images of his late wife. An unlikely friendship with D'Abo's youthful stray, however, is to prove that he hasn't loosened his grip on life entirely, while the fortitude of cigar-chomping pal Stander in the face of terminal odds gives him renewed courage to continue. Adapted by Balaban and John McLaughlin from the novel by Richard Bausch, the result's a honed, if conventional testament to human resilience, delivered with unsentimental grit by the reliably excellent Mueller-Stahl, and toppped by an affecting performance from the veteran Stander – his last, and a worthy closer. TJ

Last Grave at Dimbaza
(Nana Mahomo, 1974, GB)
54 min.
A documentary shot by a British team who wanted to remain anonymous for fear of reprisals (not just against them, but the people who helped them). Most of the white South Africans they encountered were persuaded that they were simply making home movies. Consequently, and illegally, they went where camera teams had never penetrated: into the heart of the Bantustan (the tiny waste area designated for black development), the various ghettos, even into the vast houses of the white farmers. The film continually juxtaposes the two communities of South Africa to ghastly effect, and the cold statistics of its commentary are unbearable. Everyone knows that conditions in South Africa are bad. This film presents proof that they are genocidal. DP

Last Hard Men, The
(Andrew V McLaglen, 1976, US) Charlton Heston, James Coburn, Barbara Hershey, Christopher Mitchum, Jorge Rivero, Michael Parks, Thalmus Rasulala.
103 min.
Appalling tough-guy actioner, based on a novel called *Gun Down* by Brian *Death Wish* Garfield, in which Coburn and a gang of cons escape and plan revenge on sheriff Heston, whose daughter (Hershey) they kidnap and threaten to rape. The occasional elegiac tone lamenting the passing of the West seems entirely out of place. Only Michael Parks, still aping James Dean at nearly 40, provides some welcome distraction. GA

Last Hole, The
(Das letzte Loch)
(Herbert Achternbusch, 1981, WGer) Herbert Achternbusch, Gabi Geist.
92 min.
Even the fact that Achternbusch scripted the most wilfully bizarre Herzog feature – *Heart of Glass*, in which the entire cast performed under hypnosis – doesn't prepare one for the strangeness of his own films. Where Herzog has sought increasing comfort in grandiose visions and international travel, Achternbusch is less romantic and more defiantly Bavarian. However, his central character (played by himself) reminds one more of Spike Milligan than of any German: a fly-catcher and private detective, who loves only waitresses called Susan and drinks to forget the figure of six million that haunts him. As with Milligan, any attempt at synopsis is foolhardy. Suffice it to say that Achternbusch's self-elected task is to point up the absurd complacency of post-war Germany by reconnecting the raw

nerves that the Germans have tried so hard to forget, and what pulls it all together is a desperate manic seriousness. One hesitates to call this unsettling film a comedy, as its laughter is the stuff of nightmare. What right has anyone to laugh after too many are dead? But, says Achternbusch, what else can one do? CPe

Last Holiday
(Henry Cass, 1950, GB) Alec Guinness, Kay Walsh, Beatrice Campbell, Bernard Lee, Wilfred Hyde-White, Muriel George, Helen Cherry, Grégoire Aslan, Ernest Thesiger, Sidney James.
88min. b/w.
A bitter-sweet little film written by JB Priestley. Informed that he has no more than a few weeks to live, a hard-working nonentity (Guinness) collects his savings, checks into a posh hotel, and resolves to go out like a gentleman. Here his life changes beyond all recognition: he finds love and happiness, and has an equally beneficent effect on those around him. It's a charming notion, Utopia on the never-never; and while the final twist is a bit tricky, the picture is surprisingly moving, delicately handled and full of lovely vignettes. Unlikely as it may seem, this was the inspiration for Aki Kaurismäki's *I Hired a Contract Killer*. TCh

Last House on the Left, The (aka Krug and Company/ Sex Crime of the Century)
(Wes Craven, 1972, US) David Hess, Lucy Grantheim, Sandra Cassel, Marc Sheffier, Jeramie Rain, Fred Lincoln.
91 min.
Craven's first horror movie is pretty strong meat, though it never quite lives down to its infamous reputation. Two teenage girls (Grantheim and Cassel), on their way to a rock concert, are abducted, tortured and raped by a pair of psycopathic killers, Krug and Weasel, their dyke accomplice Sadie, and Krug's heroin-addicted son Junior. Then, in a twist borrowed from Ingmar Bergman's *The Virgin Spring*, the criminals ask for help when their car breaks down at a nearby house, where Cassel's parents (surprise, surprise) discover the truth and wreak brutal revenge. Rape, disembowelment and death by chainsaw are now standard horror fare, but Craven's cold, flat style of filming emphasises the fact that the violence dehumanises not only the victims but the aggressors. Craven fans will also note an early use of the domestic booby traps and dream sequences which were to be central to the later *Nightmare on Elm Street*. NF

Last Hunt, The
(Richard Brooks, 1956, GB) Robert Taylor, Stewart Granger, Debra Paget, Lloyd Nolan, Russ Tamblyn, Constance Ford.
108 min.
This bleak and impressive Western pitches ruthless, Indian-hating buffalo hunter Taylor ('One less buffalo means one less Indian') against the more sympathetic Granger, who later falls for Indian squaw Paget. The extended massacre scene is chillingly effective, and the film not only condemns the senseless slaughter of bison, but also raises questions about the Western myths of heroism and the pioneering spirit. Russell Harlan's admirably low-key cinematography complements writer/director Brooks' down-beat tone. NF

Last Hurrah, The
(John Ford, 1958, US) Spencer Tracy, Jeffrey Hunter, Dianne Foster, Basil Rathbone, Pat O'Brien, Donald Crisp, James Gleason, John Carradine, Edward Brophy, Ricardo Cortez, Jane Darwell.
121 min. b/w.
Often shrugged off as a Ford failure, but it improves with acquaintance. Sentimental, certainly, and featuring a perilously protracted death-bed scene, but with Ford superbly at ease on his Irish-American home ground in an elegiac account of the last, doomed campaign of a New England political boss (based by way of Edwin O'Connor's novel on Boston's Mayor Curley), defeated by time and new-fangled media image-making. Sidestepping the corruption inseparable from this sort of old-style politicking, Ford prints the legend with a warm, rueful (almost testamen-

tary) sense of recollection. Outstanding camera-work by Charles Lawton, and a rich gallery of performances in which Hollywood veterans and Ford's stock company are well to the fore. TM

Last Hurrah for Chivalry (Haoxia)
(John Woo, 1979, HK) Wei Bai, Liu Songren, Liu Jiang, Wei Zhuohua, Feng Ke'an.
97 min.
Dishonour among outlaws, John Woo style – except that this time the conflicts are fought out with fists, blades and spears, not guns. Woo claims it started out as a zen movie about internalised conflicts, but it plays like a regular martial arts melodrama; only the tone is darker and more cynical than usual. Kao recruits skilled fighters to exact vengeance on his old foe Pai, but is himself far from the paragon of wounded virtue he seems. The emphasis on betrayal and treachery is pretty relentless, although there's the odd visual gag and 'magic' feat to lighten the tone. Homosexual overtones are rife. TR

Last Images of the Shipwreck (Ultimas Imágenes del naufragio)
(Eliseo Subiela, 1989, Arg/Sp) Lorenzo Quinteros, Noemi Frenkel, Hugo Soto, Pablo Brichta, Sara Benítez, Andrés Tiengo.
129 min.
Ensnared in the web of the alluring Estelita (Frenkel), who repeatedly uses a suicidal charade to drum up custom for 'the oldest profession', 40-year-old insurance salesman-cum- author Robert (Quinteros) is introduced to a bizarre family whose lunatic personalities he believes will provide the inspiration for his long-dreamed-of novel: from brother José, a gun-toting psychotic thief with a grudge against God, to brother Claudio, a withdrawn obsessive who methodically removes from his lexicon words for which he no longer has use, Estelita's family is a fictional goldmine. But as the family's initial hostility towards Robert turns to acceptance, he finds his characters demanding answers to their misery, insisting that he rewrite their lives and fill the space left by their long-departed philandering father. Building on a meticulous script, Subiela crafts a finely-honed vision of society in retreat, simultaneously evoking the despair of abandonment and the joyous sparkle of salvation through error. Anchored throughout by resiliently credible performances, this is a unique blend of satirical madness and spine-tingling fantasy. MK

Last Italian Tango, The (Ultimo Tango a Zagarol)
(Nando Cicero, 1973, It) Franco Franchi, Martine Beswick, Gina Rovere, Nicola Arigliano, Franca Valeri.
98 min.
Supposedly comic adaptation of Bertolucci's *Last Tango in Paris* which has its buffoonish hero beset by dominant females. It's terribly unfunny (the butter joke is pushed for all it's worth, and predictably it ends up being spread on bread), all the worse for sticking closely to the original (whole scenes are lifted) and trying to look like Bertolucci. The dubbing is bad as well. Bertolucci's film appears a comic masterpiece by comparison.

Last Journey, The
(Bernard Vorhaus, 1935, GB) Hugh Williams, Godfrey Tearle, Judy Gunn, Eve Grey, Nelson Keys, Frank Pettingell.
66 min. b/w.
The runaway train came down the track, and the passengers on board...Vorhaus' nippiest movie demonstrates many prime cinematic virtues from an era when British film was largely theatrical. His largest cast of actors have their roles characterised with incredible economic precision. The split-second editing is superb. And as Wenders was later to discover, the emotion comes from the motion. As usual, however, it is the loco, in this case a Great Western steamer, which steals the show. CPea

Last Laugh, The (Der letzte Mann)
(FW Murnau, 1924, Ger) Emil Jannings, Mady Delschaft, Max Hiller, Emilie Kurz, Hans Unterkirchen, Olaf Storm.
7,595 ft. b/w.

A tragic tale of status and its loss, made explicit in the archetypal German symbol of uniform, the reverse of Zuckmayer's classic play *The Captain of Köpenick*. Jannings, pre-eminent in the field of gigantic pathos, gives his all as the ageing hotel doorman humiliatingly stripped of his peaked cap and epaulettes and demoted to basement lavatory attendant. Murnau makes a film of mythic resonance from almost nothing – the door motif is particularly striking – and sends up rotten the happy resolution that the studio, UFA, insisted be grafted on. SG

Last Lieutenant, The (Secondvøitnanten)
(Hans Petter Moland, 1993, Nor) Espen Skjønberg, Lars Andreaslarsen, Gard Beidsvold, Bjørn Sundquist.
100 min.
Decent, classy, rather old-fashioned drama about the confusion, divided loyalties and unadulterated fear which beset Norway in 1940 following the unexpected Nazi invasion. It centres on a retired naval lieutenant who, much to his younger colleagues' surprise, enlists in the army and then, when the government surrenders, sets up a resistance force. Nothing hugely original here, but Skjønberg's lead performance is impressive, the film avoids sentimentality, and the account of conflicting notions of collaboration and nationalism is deftly handled. GA

Last Man Standing
(Walter Hill, 1996, US) Bruce Willis, Christopher Walken, Alexandra Powers, Bruce Dern, David Patrick Kelly, William Sanderson, Karina Lombard, Ned Eisenberg, Michael Imperioli.
101 min.
Hill's remake of Kurosawa's samurai classic *Yojimbo* places the story in the Prohibition era, with Italian and Irish bootleggers clashing over Mexican liquor supplies in Jericho, Texas. 'John Smith' (Willis) takes one look at the dead horse in the middle of Main Street and gets the full measure of this godforsaken ghost town. Before long both factions are vying for his services as hired gun, and Smith cynically plays one off against the other until, steeped in blood and sickened by what he's seen, he sets about wiping out every last man. The plot will be familiar not only from *Yojimbo* but from Leone's *A Fistful of Dollars*. Hill's Tex-Mex version suggests he hasn't got the Western out of his system yet, and this highly stylised film looks like an uncomfortable exercise in cross-breeding, as if a handful of mobsters had wandered on to the wrong studio backlot. Hill goes all out for spiritual fable, with Smith bringing down the walls of Jericho, shooting for his own bloody Calvary. The conceit might have played better in a Western. As a thriller, the film tries to camouflage its lack of suspense with profligate and repetitive gunplay and a deafening barrage of noise (Ry Cooder's score is a plus, however). There's too much voice-over, and not enough for arch-nemesis Walken to do. but at least Willis has the hard-boiled hero down. An honourable failure. TCh

Last Married Couple in America, The
(Gilbert Cates, 1979, US) George Segal, Natalie Wood, Richard Benjamin, Arlene Golonka, Allan Arbus, Valerie Harper, Bob Dishy, Dom DeLuise.
102 min.
'I've heard of the sexual revolution, but I've never had it sit down so close to me,' says comfortably-married Natalie Wood, shuddering at the memory of Valerie Harper casually mentioning that she'd had her most private part tightened. But fear not for Natalie: the sexual revolution gets no closer, and America's last married couple (Wood and Segal) survive all threats and end up happily munching hamburgers with their kids. But it's a hollow victory. Throughout, the film's support for old-fashioned morality is as thinly felt as its sour ridicule of the new permissiveness. Wood's comic style always was of the galumphing kind, but even Segal loses his potency with this material. Luckily some of their friends and neighbours show more life (Richard Benjamin's manic depressive in particular), but the only word to describe the film is horrible. GB

Last Melodrama, The
(Le Dernier Mélodrame)

(Georges Franju, 1978, Fr) Michel Vitold,
Raymond Bussières, Edith Scob, Juliette Mills,
Luis Masson.
80 min.
Nostalgic, ironic, with flashes of what-might-
have-been, this film (made for TV) by master of
melodrama Georges Franju is really a prolonged
disappointment. Dealing with a touring theatre
group in a provincial French town, it's a lament
for the passing of an era of entertainment, and the
human emotions it evoked. DMacp

Last Metro, The
(Le Dernier Métro)

(François Truffaut, 1980, Fr) Catherine
Deneuve, Gérard Depardieu, Jean Poiret, Heinz
Bennent, Andréa Ferréol, Paulette Dubost,
Jean-Louis Richard.
131 min.
Once the Prince Charming of the French cinema,
Truffaut latterly carried his talent for crowd-
pleasing to the brink of turning into an Ugly
Sister. Watching this smugly hermetic tale of the
artistic pangs suffered by a French theatre com-
pany under the German Occupation in World
War II, you would never guess that films like *The
Sorrow and the Pity* and *Lacombe Lucien* had
irretrievably lifted the lid off those years. Playing
for cute nostalgia, Truffaut lets the realities go to
hell. TM

Last Moments
(Venditore di Palloncini)

(Mario Gariazzo, 1974, It) Renato Cestié, James
Whitmore, Marina Malfatti, Lee J Cobb,
Maurizio Arena, Adolfo Celi, Cyril Cusack.
106 min.
Revolting tear-jerker about a child who dies (lingeringly but sweetly) of neglect after mum runs
off and dad goes on an extended bat. A companion in awfulness to the same team's *The Last
Snows of Spring*, it doesn't miss a manipulative
trick, even ripping off the earlier film's bitter-
sweet climax: there it was a last-ditch trip to the
fairground, here it's the last-wish gratification of
a trip to a circus. TM

Last Movie, The

(Dennis Hopper, 1971, US) Dennis Hopper,
Stella Garcia, Julie Adams, Tomas Milian, Don
Gordon, Roy Engel, Donna Bacala, Samuel
Fuller, Kris Kristofferson, Sylvia Miles, Peter
Fonda, Dean Stockwell.
108 min.
Dennis Hopper's second film as director: dazzling,
chaotic, indulgent. Movie stunt-man Kansas
(Hopper), filming a Western in the Andes and
staying on with a mini-skirted Peruvian prostitute after gruff father-figure Fuller and his crew
return to Hollywood, is inextricably drawn into
the peasants' own film-making ritual with wick-
erwork cameras but real violence (and himself as
sacrificial victim). Caught within his own movie
myths – prospecting for gold with only *The
Treasure of the Sierra Madre* for guidance –
Hopper's Romantic hero obstinately refuses to
come to terms with the harsh exoticism of South
American peasant culture. The film, too, never
quite sure how the last movie should end, persistently sabotages its own resolution. But as it
disintegrates, it shoots out enough ideas to fill a
dozen movies. RMy

Last Night

(Don McKellar, 1998, Can) Don McKellar,
Sandra Oh, Callum Keith Rennie, David
Cronenberg, Sarah Polley, Geneviève Bujold,
Tracy Wright.
90 min.
This directorial debut is an apocalyptic movie
with a difference: the last six hours before the
world's end are played out on an intimate scale,
as various inhabitants of Toronto – some connected, some not – prepare for their final
moments: holding family dinners, living out sexual fantasies, trying to get home to a loved one,
finishing off a piece of work, while the world (sort
of) carries on around them. It's a witty, perceptive movie, exceptionally well structured by
writer/director McKellar, with a keen feeling for
detail, a nice line in the unexpected and a strong
sense of the wider context. Absorbing, insightful
and suspenseful from start to finish. GA

Last Night at the Alamo

(Eagle Pennell, 1984, US) Sonny Carl Davis,
Louis Perryman, Steven Mattilla, Tina-Bess
Hubbard, Amanda Lamar, Peggy Pinnell.
80 min. b/w.
The Alamo is a seedy, smoke-filled bar in contemporary Houston, populated by proud, foul-
mouthed Texans hell-bent on defending their
favourite haunt against demolition. All hopes
focus on rough, tough Cowboy (Davis), a braggart hero concealing his balding pate beneath a
ten-gallon hat and his fear of impotence beneath
boasts of high connections in the state capital.
Pennell's razor-sharp black comedy overcomes
its low budget and limited locations by means of
marvellous monochrome camerawork and a
vivid, ironic script by Kim Henkel (who co-wrote
the similarly dark and delirious *Texas Chainsaw
Massacre*) to produce a caustic comment on
filmic myths and male foibles ('A man's gotta
do...'). Yet the colourful collection of no-hope good
ole boys are never reduced to mere cardboard to
be satirised; through excellent performances, our
emotions are enlisted for these beautiful losers,
boozing and brawling their way towards a final
violent conflict that would touch the heart of John
Ford himself. GA

Last of England, The

(Derek Jarman, 1987, GB) Spring, Gerrard
McArthur, John Phillips, Gay Gaynor,
Matthew Hawkins, Tilda Swinton.
91 min. b/w & col.
'What proof do you need the world's curling up
like an autumn leaf?' Jarman's most uncompromisingly personal film is of many parts. Shots of
the man himself are accompanied by the mournful voice of Nigel Terry. Clips from home movies
are spliced with endless scenes of inner-city decay
and rent-boys throwing bricks. Pop video techniques are substituted for dialogue and linear progression. References to the Falklands War, drugs,
the Bomb and the Royal Wedding are supposed
to indicate the state of Britain today. Jarman,
however, is not engaged with his subject but
playing with it, a suspicion strengthened by continual allusions to his other work. The recurring
images of desolate beauty are poetical not polemical, mesmerising not shocking – style has subverted substance. This is art of the state. Still, no
one else could have made it. MS

Last of His Tribe, The

(Harry Hook, 1992, US) Jon Voight, Graham
Greene, David Ogden Stiers, Jack Blessing,
Anne Archer, Daniel Benzali.
90 min.
Hook's third feature (actually made for cable) has
the same fine intentions as *The Kitchen Toto* and
Lord of the Flies, and the same lack of narrative
drive and originality. It stars Greene (from
Dances with Wolves) as the 'Wild Indian', 'a free-
ranging man of nature', the last of his tribe of
Californian Native Americans, found robbing a
slaughterhouse for sustenance in 1911. Voight is
the San Franciscan museum anthropologist who
takes him in, studies, and employs him. 'That
man's soul is in your hands, Alfred,' he is told, a
message he finally takes to heart, much in the
way, presumably, Hook hopes the viewer may do.
Unfortunately, the movie is so filled with clichés,
so devoid of character development and insight,
that it's hard to see anybody sustaining interest
long enough to hang in for the film's sincere but
bathetic denouement. Never have scenes suggestive of genocide been encased in such a
vacuum. WH

Last of Sheila, The

(Herbert Ross, 1973, US) Richard Benjamin,
Dyan Cannon, James Coburn, Joan Hackett,
James Mason, Ian McShane, Raquel Welch,
Yvonne Romaine.
123 min.
The most interesting thing about this game-playing thriller seemed to be that it was scripted by
real-life puzzle-freaks Anthony Perkins and
Stephen Sondheim. The presence of an all-star
cast promised...well, something. The film itself
turned out to be heavily plotted hokum in which
a group of six unlikely Hollywood luminaries,
each with a guilty secret to hide, are brought
together on a yacht anchored off a smart
Mediterranean coast so that the film's
Machiavellian villain (Coburn) – whose wife was
killed in a hit-and-run accident after a party at

which they were all present – can wreak impossible havoc on their psyches. Campy stuff, not as
much fun as it should be.

Last of the Blue Devils, The

(Bruce Ricker, 1979, US) Count Basie, Joe
Turner, Jay McShann, Jesse Price, Eddie
Durham, Jo Jones, Baby Lovett, Speedy
Huggins.
91 min.
Ricker's delightful documentary centres on a
reunion in their old Musician's Hall of many of
the great Kansas City blues and jazzmen as they
joke and jam away a joyous time of reminiscence
and musical celebration. Ricker skilfully interlaces the proceedings with archive footage of
Basie, McShann, Charlie Parker, Dizzy Gillespie,
Billie Holiday, Coleman Hawkins and many others, in eloquent illustration of the extraordinary
influence these Kansas City men were to bring to
bear. Simply one of the best musical documentaries ever made. GA

Last of the Cowboys, The
(aka The Great Smokey
Roadblock)

(John Leone, 1976, US) Henry Fonda, Eileen
Brennan, John Byner, Robert Englund, Susan
Sarandon, Melanie Mayron, Austin Pendleton,
Dub Taylor.
106 min.
A road movie starring, not the inevitable Peter
Fonda, but Henry as a terminally ailing truck driver who steals his vehicle back after it is repossessed, picks up six evicted prostitutes during his
cross-country career, and becomes a folk hero to
the media and cheering public. Sounds kinda
familiar? Beware movies that undergo successive
title changes (it also became known as *Elegant
John and His Ladies*) and get cut to boot. TM

Last of the Dogmen

(Tab Murphy, 1995, US) Tom Berenger,
Barbara Hershey, Kurtwood Smith, Steve
Reevis, Andrew Miller, Gregory Scott
Cummins, Mark Boone Jr, Helen Calahasen.
117 min.
Kevin Costner has a lot to answer for. Take this
contemporary Western, for instance, where
tracker Berenger and anthropologist Hershey
run across a Cheyenne tribe which has managed
to survive in the mountains of Montana for a century or so without anyone noticing. The portrayal of the Native Americans seems so keen to
avoid any negative stereotyping that the
Cheyenne are reduced to benign, mystical, eco-
friendly ciphers whose all-round good-eggness
undercuts any tension in the narrative set-up.
The inference is that they've lasted so long by
killing anyone who came near, yet the reality is
more fluffy, turning an arresting B-picture action
premise into touchy-feely inanity. Berenger is a
watchable lug, but he's saddled with a routine
assignment as the boozy bounty hunter given
one last chance to redeem himself in the eyes of
sheriff Smith by locating a trio of escaped convicts in the Rockies. For 20 minutes we get *The
African Queen*, but first-time director Murphy's
screenplay works up to a slump when the
Cheyennes' cover is blown. Great landscapes,
though. TJ

Last of the Finest, The
(aka Blue Heat)

(John MacKenzie, 1990, US) Brian Dennehy,
Joe Pantoliano, Jeff Fahey, Bill Paxton,
Michael C Gwynne, Henry Stolow, Deborra-
Lee Furness, Lisa Jane Persky, Guy Boyd.
106 min.
Like MacKenzie's *The Fourth Protocol* (though
achieving greater narrative coherence), this
densely plotted cop thriller seems to be straining
for a significance that constantly eludes its grasp.
So while Dennehy gives yet another faultless performance as a veteran LA cop disillusioned by
compromise and corruption, the potentially
explosive political undercurrents fail to ignite.
Suspended after an abortive raid, Dennehy and
his undercover narcotics team pursue their own
freelance investigations. Acting on a pimp's tip-
offs, they uncover a conspiracy involving fellow
cops, drug enforcement agents and wealthy businessmen, which proves to be a front for supplying arms to right-wing rebels in Latin America.
Dennehy's relationship with his team (Pantoliano,

Fahey and Paxton) and their various blue-collar backgrounds are deftly handled, the unobtrusive camerawork leaving space for the actors to inter-act convincingly. But the filming of the action scenes is also slightly distanced, leading to some distinctly unexciting set pieces. NF

Last of the High Kings, The
(David Keating, 1995, Ire/GB/Den) Gabriel Byrne, Catherine O'Hara, Jared Leto, Christina Ricci, Colm Meaney, Stephen Rea, Lorraine Pilkington.
104 min.
Coming-of-age movie, produced and co-written by Gabriel Byrne, as fresh as a newly pulled pint of the dark stuff. Dublin, 1977: Thin Lizzy bestride the charts in black leather kecks, but for Frankie (Leto in a career-launching turn) exam results loom, girls seem unobtainable, and his mum's insistence that he's descended from the High Kings of Ireland doesn't really help. A famil-iar mix, but the fashions are suitably terrifying, and there's a neat cameo from Stephen Rea as the taxi driver who's 'had 'em all' in his cab. TJ

Last of the Mohicans, The
(Michael Mann, 1992, US) Daniel Day Lewis, Madeleine Stowe, Russell Means, Eric Schweig, Jodhi May, Steven Waddington, Wes Studi, Maurice Roëves, Patrice Chereau.
122 min.
Set in the mountainous frontier wilderness of the colony of New York in 1757, this charts the role played by Hawkeye (Day Lewis) in the complex war waged between the English and the French and their respective allies among both settlers and Indians. Adopted as a child by the Mohican Chingachgook (Means) after his white settler par-ents were killed, Hawkeye belongs to neither one culture nor the other. Similarly, he is both war-rior and peacemaker; and it is this dichotomy which simultaneously alienates him from the English military and wins him the love of the colonel's daughter (Stowe). While few would deny the impressive spectacle Mann provides in some truly magnificent battle scenes, criticisms have been levelled at the way the film changes from a historically accurate account of the war into a full-blown love story. Indeed, it is best seen as an epic romantic adventure of a sort seldom executed with much intelligence these days. As such, Mann's characteristic mix of rousing, profound-ly physical action, lyrical interludes, and strik-ingly stylish imagery, serves to create superior mainstream entertainment. GA

Last of the Red Hot Lovers
(Gene Saks, 1972, US) Alan Arkin, Sally Kellerman, Paula Prentiss, Renee Taylor, Bella Bruck.
98 min.
From a Neil Simon play about a conventionally married 40-year-old proprietor of a fish restau-rant who finds himself wanting to have an affair. He borrows his old mum's apartment and lures various ladies there, all of whom – wait for it – turn out to have 'impossible' hang-ups, and none of whom he actually screws. A few laughs are wrung out of the situation, and Sally Kellerman provides more as a raunchy lady on a fish diet, but it's all 'heart', of course. Pretty dire.

L.A. Story
(Mick Jackson, 1991, US) Steve Martin, Victoria Tennant, Richard E Grant, Marilu Henner, Sarah Jessica Parker, Susan Forristal, Kevin Pollak, Rick Moranis.
95 min.
Nothing's going right for wacky TV weatherman Harris K Telemacher (Martin): out of a job, madly in love, he pines for dippy English journalist Sara (Tennant). But she's contemplating a reconcilia-tion with her ex-husband (Grant), prompting Telemacher to embark on a hopeless affair with bimbette SanDeE* (Parker, wonderful). Steve Martin's script, a delightfully scatty account of life in the city of angels, exposes romance lurking beyond the snobbish restaurants and routine mug-gings; while British director Jackson conjures a lush vision which makes Los Angeles appear pos-itively exotic. Rising above mundane reality, Telemacher is further confused during mystical communication with the electronic freeway infor-mation sign; and after a tour of the mock period architecture, there's a strange encounter with Rick

Moranis' mock-Cockney gravedigger... Ultimately, the transforming powers of love infuse the whole with a sense of wonder. CM

Last Picture Show, The
(Peter Bogdanovich, 1971, US) Timothy Bottoms, Jeff Bridges, Cybill Shepherd, Ben Johnson, Cloris Leachman, Ellen Burstyn, Eileen Brennan, Clu Gulager, Sam Bottoms, Randy Quaid.
118 min. b/w.
Bogdanovich may have proved a wayward dis-appointment, but along with *Targets* this is a reminder that somewhere inside him the man has talent. Adapted from Larry McMurtry's novel, it tells of the problems of adolescence in a small road-side town in 1950s Texas. Sexual intrigue, the dis-illusionment of growing up, and gentle humour are common enough in many similar films. But where Bogdanovich scores is in his accurate depiction of period and place, so detailed as to be almost tan-gible, and in the unbridled sympathy he extends to his characters. The closing of the local cinema signifies the end of both personal and historical eras, but characteristically its function is never that of forced symbolism. In fact, the nostalgia for a simpler, quieter age is equally conveyed by the style of the film, which recalls nothing so much as the emotionally-draining dramas of John Ford. Superb performances all round add to the charm of this fine, if now unfashionable film. GA

Last Plane Out
(David Nelson, 1983, US) Jan-Michael Vincent, Julie Carmen, Mary Crosby, David Huffman, William Windom, Lloyd Battista.
92 min.
Produced by Dallas newspaperman Jack Cox in a bid to shoulder his way into that elite corps of journalists whose names have outlasted the Big Story that made them – in Cox's case, Nicaragua. We first see him (Vincent) on assignment in 1978, the palmy days before the storm when his friend-ship with General Somoza eases his way in a dif-ficult country. Months later he returns to the same country now frenziedly at war with itself, to discover that the same friendship makes him a target for Sandinista guerillas. Although pur-portedly based on Cox's story, what we get is largely the usual mundane journalistic fantasy of fast living and slow sex in foreign climes while the realities of the situation go hang. Somoza is shown as an avuncular nice guy pining for a plebiscite; the Sandinistas as bloodthirsty curs. Heady days for Cox, perhaps, but for us the ten-sion hardly mounts. FD

Last Princess of Manchuria, The
see Kawashima Yoshiko

Last Rites
(Donald P Bellisario, 1988, US) Tom Berenger, Daphne Zuniga, Chick Vennera, Anne Twomey, Paul Dooley, Dane Clark.
103 min.
As a priest and the son of a mob boss, Berenger is caught between 'family' codes of honour and a higher authority when he shelters a young woman (Zuniga) whose name is on a Mafia hit list. Needless to say, the pair fall in love in this contrived plod of a thriller. An MGM picture sent straight to video on both sides of the Atlantic. TJ

Last Run, The
(Richard Fleischer, 1971, US) George C Scott, Tony Musante, Trish Van Devere, Colleen Dewhurst, Aldo Sambrell.
99 min.
Scott as an ageing Chicago gangster, once an ace wheelman for the syndicate who, with wife run off and child dead, comes out of morose retirement (in Portugal) to do one last job and prove to himself, etc.etc. Huston and Boorman both opted out of directing, not surprisingly given the sententious-ly overstated script, which is always laboriously explaining things you've already guessed for your-self. But the action sequences are fine, so is Scott, and Sven Nykvist's camera-work is great. TM

Last Seduction, The
(John Dahl, 1993, US) Linda Fiorentino, Peter Berg, Bill Pullman, JT Walsh, Bill Nunn, Herb Mitchell.
110 min.

When Wendy (Fiorentino) arrives out of the blue in a small, cow-country town near Buffalo, New York, the locals – notably Mike (Berg) – don't know what's hit them. She's smart, sexy, refuses to use the customary verbal niceties, and can twist the male population round her little finger. More importantly, unknown to Mike, who soon falls in love with her, she's not Wendy but Bridget, in hiding from husband Clay (Pullman), ever since she ran out on him, taking the entire proceeds of a drug deal he'd almost died perpe-trating. And that's just the start of this tortuous, well-acted, witty, crisply photographed and immensely enjoyable thriller. GA

Last Snows of Spring, The (L'Ultima Neve di Primavera)
(Raimondo del Balzo, 1973, It) Bekim Fehmiu, Agostina Belli, Renato Cestié, Nino Segurini, Margherita Horowitz.
91 min.
A 10-year-old boy starts to die of neglect when his widowed father spends too much time for-saking his parental duties in favour of playboy activities and a jet-set life-style. With the onset of leukaemia remorse comes by the bucketful, ending with a particularly grisly final trip to the fairground. Never have the artifacts of high liv-ing seemed so unattractive, or a film looked so much like somebody's holiday snaps. More of the same was provided by *Last Moments* the fol-lowing year.

Last Starfighter, The
(Nick Castle, 1984, US) Lance Guest, Dan O'Herlihy, Catherine Mary Stewart, Barbara Bosson, Norman Snow, Robert Preston.
101 min.
Turning to his favourite video game for solace after everything's gone wrong, Alex Rogan (Guest) finds that the game is a sophisticated recruitment aid for the galactic equivalent of the RAF. By beating the high score, he gets whisked off to shoot the baddies out of the cosmos and save our sector of the universe. All pretty pre-posterous stuff, but it doesn't take itself serious-ly for one moment, and even aspires to a gentle parody of the genre. The special effects are mind-expanding: computer-generated animation that is so good it's barely distinguishable from the conventional kind. Great fun, with some truly comical moments; a must for pulp-heads and video-junkies. DPe

Last Summer
(Frank Perry, 1969, US) Richard Thomas, Barbara Hershey, Bruce Davison, Cathy Burns, Ralph Waite, Ernesto Gonzalez, Conrad Bain.
97 min.
One of those winsome, nostalgic beach movies (this one has a wounded seagull). Four gawky teenagers spend the summer on Long Island, learning the usual, bittersweet rites-of-passage lessons about life, love and loyalty. Director Perry was renowned for the way he probed human rela-tionships. He's helped here by an insightful script adapted by his wife Eleanor Perry from a novel by Evan Hunter. The acting is also a cut above the average: Cathy Burns, who's since disap-peared without trace, was Oscar-nominated for her depiction of a troubled adolescent. GM

Last Summer in the Hamptons
(Henry Jaglom, 1995, US) Victoria Foyt, Viveca Lindfors, Jon Robin Baitz, Martha Plimpton, André Gregory.
108 min.
Marginally less irritating than most of Jaglom's work, this nevertheless concerns a gallery of characters you'd probably hate to spend more than a couple of minutes with, let alone a whole weekend in the country: namely, three genera-tions of a pretentious, bitchy theatrical dynasty dominated by matriarch Lindfors, playing host to various friends, including Foyt, a successful but none too respected Hollywood actress hop-ing to make it as a serious actress. As they min-gle, fuck, discuss art and sex, and shift allegiances, Jaglom offers a few insights into family tensions and the relationship between theatre and life, but the attempts at comedy are mostly embarrassing, and the whole thing is typically indulgent. GA

Last Sunset, The

(Robert Aldrich, 1961, US) Kirk Douglas, Rock
Hudson, Dorothy Malone, Carol Lynley, Joseph
Cotten, Regis Toomey, Neville Brand, Jack
Elam, Rad Fulton.
112 min.
Aldrich's film is in some senses an attempt to
transpose to the Western genre the elements of
Sirkian melodrama – same studio, similar casting, and a plot about sexual neurosis. Kirk
Douglas is an unstable gunfighter who has murdered Sheriff Hudson's brother-in-law and wants
to revive his own love for his ex-wife (Malone).
At the same time, Douglas' daughter (Lynley)
falls in love with her estranged father, and
Malone falls in love with Hudson. Those tensions
are resolved during a cattle drive from Mexico to
Texas. The movie is more lyrical than Aldrich's
usual macho posturings, and Dalton Trumbo's
script is abrim with classical allusions. ATu

Last Supper, The

(Cynthia Roberts, 1994, Can) Ken McDougall,
Jack Nicholsen, Daniel MacIvor.
96 min.
An unflinching portrait of a man's final hours.
The camera never leaves the room where Chris,
withered by AIDS, wishes his life to be terminated after a last supper with his partner (Nicholsen).
It's a tribute to Roberts and McDougall (who died
four days after filming) that the film's power
derives less from the latter's physical condition
than from his persisting dignity. In body, Chris
looks and sounds barely human; in spirit, he transcends his affliction, particularly in two set-pieces:
a dance he performs, with white death-mask and
carnations, to 'Dido's Lament' (a riveting sequence
that puts the comparable scene in *Philadelphia* in
the shade), and the candle-lit song during which
he passes away. A simple but devastating study
of the human condition in extremis: grit your teeth
and go see. NB

Last Supper, The

(Stacy Title, 1995, US) Cameron Diaz,
Annabeth Gish, Ron Eldard, Jonathan Penner,
Courtney B Vance.
94 min.
A mordant black comedy with a sharp political
edge: If you could go back to 1919 and meet
Hitler, would you kill him? This ethical conundrum preoccupies a group of liberal grad students after an unexpected dinner guest turns
violent and ends up fertilising the tomato plants.
Why shouldn't humanists be more pro-active,
they reason, inviting a string of rightwing reactionaries to a hearty last meal. It falls apart, but
the cool cast and caustic script will leave most
right-thinking people well satisfied. TCh

Last Supper, The
(La Ultima Cena)

(Tomás Gutiérrez Alea, 1976, Cuba) Nelson
Villagra, Silvano Rey, Luis Alberto García,
José Antonio Rodríguez, Samuel Claxton.
113 min.
A brilliant Godardian parable, reflecting the contemporary Cuban situation through a tale of a
slave revolt on a sugar plantation in late 18th century Havana (historically, the moment when the
old slave-based industry was under pressure
from the new mechanised European techniques
of sugar refining, and when the heady scent of
freedom was sniffed in the air). The action takes
place over the days of Easter, culminating when
a rich, fanatically religious landowner reconstructs the Last Supper with twelve slaves. But
when the slaves' response theatens his economic
interests, the pious Christian suppresses the
uprising. This complex indictment of religious
hypocrisy and cultural colonisation reflects the
same subtlety as Alea's earlier *Memories of
Underdevelopment*. LM

Last Tango in Paris

(Bernardo Bertolucci, 1972, It/Fr) Marlon
Brando, Maria Schneider, Jean-Pierre Léaud,
Darling Legitimus, Catherine Sola, Mauro
Marchetti.
129 min.
'Even if a husband spends two hundred fuckin'
years, he's never going to comprehend his wife's
true nature,' says Brando, and in reaction to her
death he establishes an anonymous, masturbatory
relationship with Schneider in an empty Paris

apartment. The resentment of his observation suggests that the film is less about coming together
than about more private, chauvinist obsessions:
partly about Bertolucci's overriding desire to love
every image to death and indulge his doubts about
the role of director in movie-making (through the
whole Léaud subplot). But mostly the film is
Brando's, his comeback after too many bad movies.
The monumental narcissism is still there, coupled
with the inability to take himself seriously – no one
else could play a death scene concentrating on
removing the gum from his mouth. Against him,
Schneider hasn't a chance, which says a lot about
the imbalances of the film; Bertolucci doesn't seem
too interested in her either. CPe

Last Temptation
of Christ, The

(Martin Scorsese, 1988, US/Can) Willem Dafoe,
Harvey Keitel, Paul Greco, Steven Shill, Verna
Bloom, Barbara Hershey, Roberts Blossom,
Barry Miller, Irvin Kershner, André Gregory,
Harry Dean Stanton, David Bowie.
163 min.
Neither blasphemous nor offensive, this faithful
adaptation of Nikos Kazantzakis' book sees
Christ torn between divine destiny and an all too
human awareness of pain and sexuality, departing most dramatically from the gospels in the last
40 minutes, a clearly fantastic sequence in which
Jesus is led from the cross by an angel who offers
him a normal life as husband and father. The performances – especially Keitel (Judas) and Bowie
(Pontius Pilate) – are excellent; the recreation of
biblical times is effective and plausible; and the
percussive ethnic score for the most part
admirably complements the superb photography.
The dialogue, however, is often astonishingly
banal and the miracles mundane. More seriously, Scorsese fails to illuminate the soul of Christ
– essentially what the film is all about.
Nevertheless, it remains a sincere, typically ambitious and imaginative work from America's most
provocatively intelligent film-maker. GA

Last Time I Committed
Suicide, The

(Stephen Kay, 1996, US) Keanu Reeves,
Thomas Jane, Claire Forlani, Gretchen Mol,
Adrien Brody.
93 min.
The credits of this likeable, but lightweight feature, describe it as 'based on a letter by Neal
Cassady' and boasts Carolyn Cassady as consultant: indeed, it comes across as a bebop-influenced,
free-form mood piece, spun off this source, delineating the life of the guy who was later to prove
beat 'genius' Jack Kerouac's major inspiration. The
time is 1946, a period of hard readjustment, and
fresh out of Leavenworth, hipster Cassady (Jane)
is dreaming of kids and picket fences with suicidal girlfriend Joan (Forlani), but spending what
spare time is left over from the graveyard shift at
the tyre company shooting pool with dissolute
Harry (Reeves). It's a film of bits and pieces, with
the evidently talented first-time director going for
atmospheric flourishes, cutting in slo-mo
sequences and jagged hand-held shots, seemingly
modelled on jeans ads, alongside back lighting and
superimpositions. As a portrait of a 'cool dude', it's
a mite self-conscious – and sidesteps Cassady's
bisexuality – but it exudes energy and sympathy,
and the performances are winning. WH

Last Time I Saw Paris, The

(Richard Brooks, 1954, US) Elizabeth Taylor,
Van Johnson, Donna Reed, Walter Pidgeon,
Eva Gabor, Roger Moore.
116 min.
Despite a very corny script from Julius and Philip
Epstein which borrows clichés from *Casablanca* and
countless 'American in Paris' yarns, this remains
an enjoyable (if heavy-handed) melodrama. Van
Johnson wants to be the next Hemingway, but while
he's a prodigious drinker, he doesn't show much ability as a writer. Taylor, looking unbelievably glamorous, is his long-suffering wife. Pidgeon steals the
show as her father, a penniless chancer who still
manages to live the good life. (Began life as a Scott
Fitzgerald story.) GM

Last Train from Gun Hill

(John Sturges, 1959, US) Kirk Douglas,
Anthony Quinn, Carolyn Jones, Earl Holliman,
Brad Dexter, Ziva Rodann, Brian Hutton.
98 min.

Douglas as the sheriff determined to take in the
rapist who killed his wife, Quinn as the old
friend who happens to be the delinquent's father
and is equally determined to stop him. An enjoyable Western, remarkably similar but much inferior to *3.10 to Yuma*, made a couple of years
earlier. Vigorous performances, superb camerawork from Charles Lang and muscular direction
are let down by a conventional script which creates characters without any real depth or resonance. TM

Last Train from Madrid, The

(James Hogan, 1937, US) Dorothy Lamour,
Lew Ayres, Gilbert Roland, Karen Morley,
Lionel Atwill, Helen Mack, Robert Cummings,
Anthony Quinn, Olympe Bradna, Evelyn
Brent, Lee Bowman.
85 min. b/w.
The Spanish Civil War is pressganged as a backdrop for this atrocious farrago of love, duty and
tearful self-sacrifice in which assorted characters
jockey for the limited number of permits which
will enable them (or loved ones) to take the last
train out of war-torn Madrid. Roland and Quinn
are army officers, now on opposite sides, who
once swore an oath of comradeship; Lamour is
the woman they both love; Ayres is an American
journalist who falls for the daughter of a political
activist executed as he arrived to interview him;
Cummings is a callow soldier in love with a fall-
en woman, his innocence letting her hope for
redemption. And so it goes, in a torrent of tawdry
clichés, made no more palatable by inserted
newsreel shots of the bombardment of Madrid.
Roland, Quinn and Atwill give as sterling performances as their dialogue will permit; Lamour
and Cummings challenge, respectively, for most
zomboid and most embarrassing performance of
the year. TM

Last Tycoon, The

(Elia Kazan, 1976, US) Robert De Niro, Tony
Curtis, Robert Mitchum, Jeanne Moreau,
Jack Nicholson, Donald Pleasence, Ingrid
Boulting, Ray Milland, Dana Andrews,
Theresa Russell, John Carradine.
124 min.
Another episode in Hollywood's belated love
affair with Scott Fitzgerald, this takes his unfinished novel about the movie colony in the '30s
and goes for quality at the risk of squeezing the
life out of the picture. It's often pretty ponderous
despite a Pinter script, especially the protracted
central relationship between quizzically intense,
hot-shot producer De Niro and a wispy unknown
(Boulting). But De Niro proves again how well he
can carry a part, and is particularly good in
scenes dealing with the day-to-day business of
movie-making. For once a starry cast pulls its
weight; when all else fails they at least remain
interesting, mainly because Kazan's direction
favours the actors at the expense of anything else.
Although uneven, the result is still a lot better
than Hollywood's last look at itself (*Day of the
Locust*) and its last slice of Fitzgerald (*The Great
Gatsby*). CPe

Last Unicorn, The

(Arthur Rankin Jr/Jules Bass, 1982, US) voices:
Alan Arkin, Jeff Bridges, Mia Farrow, Tammy
Grimes, Angela Lansbury, Christopher Lee,
Keenan Wynn.
93 min.
Rather groovy little fable, based on Peter Beagle's
fantasy about a unicorn's search for company
(there are no singles bars in fairy-tales), that overcomes the Disney influence with some acid characterisation of the baddies (in particular Mommy
Fortuna, a warty witch, and the mythical Harpy,
whom legend or the animators have seen fit to
give three tits). Some horrific moments, too (the
mark of the best fairytales), and some sublimely
witty lines, as when a bungling magician, caught
in the branches of a tree that he has brought to
amorous life, cries, 'Oh my God, I'm engaged to
a Douglas Fir!' FD

Last Valley, The

(James Clavell, 1970, GB) Michael Caine, Omar
Sharif, Florinda Bolkan, Nigel Davenport, Per
Oscarsson, Arthur O'Connell, Madeline Hinde.
129 min.
Turgid epic set in the 23rd year of the Thirty
Years War (that's 1641, to save you looking it up)
in which Cockney Caine leads his troops into a

fertile valley which, just for once, they decide not to pillage. Reason? Caine has met refugee philosopher Omar Sharif and they've reached a mutual understanding. Clear-as-mud plotting and Tower of Babel accents don't help the allegory to make its point. A solid snore. MA

Last Voyage, The
(Andrew L Stone, 1960, US) Robert Stack, Dorothy Malone, George Sanders, Edmond O'Brien, Woody Strode, Jack Kruschen.
91 min.
Disaster for the passengers and crew of a luxury liner when an exploding boiler blows a hole in her side and it's all boats away. A certain realism is ensured by using the Ile de France on her way to the scrap-yard. But with Dorothy Malone trapped in her cabin and gurgling just above the waterline through the frenzied rescue operations, what price anything but absurdity along with the tension? TM

Last Wagon, The
(Delmer Daves, 1956, US) Richard Widmark, Felicia Farr, Susan Kohner, Tommy Rettig, James Drury, Timothy Carey, Nick Adams.
99 min.
Like Broken Arrow, a liberal Western, but contriving some complexity around the Widmark character: the son of a white missionary brought up by Comanches, he exacts revenge on the four brothers who raped and killed his Indian wife and children, falls in with the more or less racist members of a wagon train, and is left with the survivors on his hands after an Indian attack. Stylishly directed, superbly shot on location, and with a first-rate performance from Widmark, it retains a certain fascinating ambiguity: its hero, displaying an inflexible sense of purpose and charismatic qualities of leadership, could equally well be defined as an embryo Fascist. TM

Last Waltz, The
(Martin Scorsese, 1978, US) The Band, Bob Dylan, Joni Mitchell, Neil Diamond, Emmylou Harris, Neil Young, Van Morrison, Muddy Waters, Dr John, Ronnie Hawkins.
117 min.
An embellished record of The Band's farewell concert, mostly shot at San Francisco's Winterland in 1976, on a set borrowed from a local opera company. Largely wonderful music, a stage crowded with guests from Dr John to Muddy Waters, and consummately stylish filmmaking. Scorsese intersperses it with fragments of interview, shot around pool tables and in bars, treating Robbie Robertson and the others for all the world like refugees from one of his own movies. TR

Last Warrior, The
see Flap

Last Wave, The
(Peter Weir, 1977, Aust) Richard Chamberlain, Olivia Hamnett, David Gulpilil, Frederick Parslow, Vivean Gray.
106 min.
Weir up to his usual tricks with 'civilised' man coming up against an alien, apparently less rational, society. In this case it's Chamberlain's white liberal lawyer who, in defending a group of Aborigines accused of murder, stumbles across a world of ritual mysteries and prophecies of apocalyptic proportions. From the opening scene, in which an inexplicable and ferocious hailstorm hits Sydney, Weir creates an impressively unsettling atmosphere; sad, then, that all the stuff about primeval voodoo is both simplistic and patronising. Even sadder, however, is the final, climactic image, in which the threat to civilisation as we know it is presented in the form of a puddle shot through a fish-eye lens. GA

Last Winter, The
(Hakhoref Ha'Acharon)
(Riki Shelach Nissimoff, 1983, Isr) Yona Elian, Kathleen Quinlan, Stephen Macht, Zippora Peled, Michael Schneider.
89 min.
Tel Aviv, autumn, 1973. During a hiatus in the Yom Kippur war, two soldiers' wives (Quinlan, Elian) anxiously awaiting news from the front are thrown together when each identifies the same man as her husband in a blurred film of POWs.

Tracing their relationship from initial hostility to mutual support, Last Winter, filmed in English, is rather blander than its subject matter might lead you to expect. The director, himself a war veteran, carefully skirts controversy, keeping political events strictly as background colour to the human interest angle; and after teasingly suggesting an erotic attraction between the women, has Quinlan seal their bond by 'loaning' the widowed Elian her husband for a night. Still, it's tasteful, workmanlike, and a reminder that the Israeli cinema can produce something else besides Popsicles. SJo

Last Woman, The
(L'Ultima Donna)
(Marco Ferreri, 1976, It/Fr) Gérard Depardieu, Ornella Muti, David Biggani, Michel Piccoli, Renato Salvatori, Giuliana Calandra, Zouzou, Nathalie Baye.
112 min.
If Paul Morrissey's Flesh had examined any of the many questions it raised instead of simply parading them like fashions, it might well have turned into something like Ferreri's movie. Here the boyish male sex object is Depardieu, but both he and the women in his life are painfully conscious that man cannot live by his cock alone; his wife (Zouzou) has turned feminist and left him; his girl-friend (Muti) is frigid, somewhat neurotic, and very unsure of herself; and Depardieu, whose ideal is a life of eating, fucking and sleeping, is finally driven to self-mutilation in his inability to live up to his own patriarchal image of himself. It's as fraught and desperate as it sounds, and as laboriously worked out as you'd expect from the director of La Grande Bouffe; as there, though, the freshness of the performances just about makes the pessimism tolerable. TR

Last Woman on Earth, The
(Roger Corman, 1960, US) Anthony Carbone, Betsy Jones-Moreland, Edward Wain i.e. Robert Towne.
71 min.
Anybody impressed with Robert Towne's scripts for movies like Chinatown and The Last Detail will be interested to catch up with The Last Woman on Earth, his first script for Corman. Ineffably pretentious, the movie sends its three unsympathetic characters skin-diving while the nuclear holocaust breaks; they emerge from the waves to fight out a momentous ménage à trois in a deserted Puerto Rico. Most striking features are the ultra-ripe dialogue and the jaundiced view of pre-nuclear society. TR

Last Year in Marienbad
see Année Dernière à Marienbad, L'

Las Vegas Story, The
(Robert Stevenson, 1952, US) Jane Russell, Victor Mature, Vincent Price, Hoagy Carmichael, Brad Dexter, Jay C Flippen.
88 min. b/w.
A minor RKO gem showing all the preferences of its then owner Howard Hughes (aeroplanes, brunettes, breasts and disenchanted heroes). Jane Russell, with amused detachment, plays a singer returning to Las Vegas with wealthy but despicable husband Price in tow, and picking up with her erstwhile lover, hunky Mature. Initially the script relies on innuendo-laden repartee and a couple of wonderful numbers from Hoagy Carmichael. But then a man is murdered, the pace changes, and the film charges into a superb action climax with a helicopter swooping through deserted hangars and Mature making a fifty-foot leap (to save Jane, of course). It all finishes with a perfunctory nod toward family values (by marrying off an irrelevant young couple), but the film wears its intentions on its sleeve with the final shot: Hoagy looks first at the seductive Russell, then winks at us as he sings, 'My resistance is low...' HM

Late for Dinner
(WD Richter, 1991, US) Brian Wimmer, Peter Berg, Marcia Gay Harden, Colleen Flynn, Kyle Secor, Michael Beach, Peter Gallagher, Bo Brundin.
99 min.
A dusty gas-guzzler slithers along a desert road. Frank (Berg) can't drive – he's not quite right in the head – but at least he doesn't have a bullet in

his chest like his brother Willie (Wimmer). In the limbo of LA's sub-suburbs, these two hapless fugitives come to rest in the laboratory of one Doc Chilblains (Brundin), experimenter in cryonics. It is 1962. The next morning, it is 1991. Nonplussed, Frank maintains they must be late for dinner. The rest of the world supposes these defrosting hicks are simply out to lunch. This starts in quirky fashion, shifts into an amiable retread of Back to the Future, then trundles to a standstill on the home straight. Willie and Frank return to Santa Fe, an ageing wife (Harden) and grown-up child (Flynn), and suddenly it's terms of endearment time, a laborious restoration of family, hearth and home. Even if you can stomach this sentimental retardation, the film still manages to outstay its welcome. TCh

Late Show, The
(Robert Benton, 1977, US) Art Carney, Lily Tomlin, Bill Macy, Ruth Nelson, Howard Duff, Joanna Cassidy, Eugene Roche, John Considine.
93 min.
The Late Show pretty much divides its time between paying tribute to the private-eye films of the '30s and '40s, and undercutting its nostalgia with a sourer modern note. Carney plays an old, ulcerous 'eye' who gets involved in a complex plot set in modern Los Angeles. Nothing much has changed. The characters are fundamentally the same, and the story matters less than the people. Here, the central relationship develops between the laconic Carney and Tomlin's scatty, neurotic fast-talker. Benton's direction never entirely overcomes the character-acting styles of his stars (particularly Tomlin who, like many gifted impersonators, condescends towards her character). However, Benton's script hits a note of defensive humour that's just right in relation to the theme of urban loneliness. Some great lines and terrific wisecracks keep doubts at bay. All in all, maybe best seen...at a late show. CPe

Late Spring (Banshun)
(Yasujiro Ozu, 1949, Jap) Chishu Ryu, Setsuko Hara, Yumeji Tsukioka, Haruko Sugimura, Hohi Aoki, Jun Usami, Kuniko Miyake.
108 min. b/w.
A widowed professor (Ryu) and his grown-up daughter (Hara) share a life of domestic tranquillity in a Tokyo suburb, but when he is made to realise that this girl should now be married, Ryu gently overrules her reluctance and arranges a suitable match – a Gary Cooper lookalike! Some rate this simple, affecting film even above Tokyo Story. Certainly it contains passages of great beauty and humanity, and there can be no faulting the heartbreaking performances of Ryu and Hara in roles very similar to the ones they play in the later picture. It was a favourite of the director's too (Ozu lived with his own mother throughout his life) – but it must be said that while the emotions are universal, the social customs which engender them seem more 'foreign' here than in most of the oeuvre. Hara's disgust at the thought that a widower should remarry, for example. Nevertheless, this is a remarkable, piercing film, and central to an understanding of Ozu's work. He tackled much the same story in colour in 1962's An Autumn Afternoon, his last film. TCh

Latin Boys Go to Hell
(Ela Troyano, 1997, US/Ger/Sp/Jap) Irwin Ossa, John Bryant Davila, Alexis Artiles, Mike Ruiz, Jennifer Lee Simard.
70 min.
Imagine the matador sequence from Pink Narcissus mixed with all the elements of a particularly cheesy Spanish soap and you're halfway to picturing this send-up of Latin passions. A gay Mexican boy from Brooklyn falls for his straight cousin – and a hunky male model has his penis chopped off by his jealous lover and stuffed down his throat. The acting is wooden, the plot a mess, and the limits of the budget show. But the whole thing's so deliriously over the top, it hardly matters. PBur

Latino
(Haskell Wexler, 1985, US) Robert Beltran, Annette Cardona, Tony Plana, Ricardo Lopez, Luis Torrentes, Juan Carlos Ortiz.
108 min.
After the impressive but inevitably compromised

Under Fire, it's good to see a movie that deals with conflict in Central America with a real sense of commitment. Wexler's brazenly partisan film may lack the artistic sophistication of its mainstream counterparts, but it gains in power by focusing not on the familiar 'neutral' journalist/photographer figure, but on an invading American soldier, a Green Beret lieutenant (Beltran) drafted to Honduras to train a platoon of 'Contras' for secret raids on Nicaragua. There he becomes embroiled not only in the infliction of death, torture and US propaganda upon the Sandinistas, but in the contradictions of his position. First, he's a Latin American himself; second, he falls for a woman working in Honduras who hails from the village that is his prime target. Wexler's methods involve passion rather than 'balance': black-and-white moralising may occasionally be the result, but there's no denying the emotional punch dealt by the assured combination of taut narrative and intelligently researched context. GA

Laughing Policeman, The
(aka An Investigation of
Murder)
(Stuart Rosenberg, 1973, US) Walter Matthau, Bruce Dern, Lou Gossett, Albert Paulsen, Anthony Zerbe, Val Avery.
112 min.
As police clinically and methodically follow up a multiple killing on a San Francisco bus, this adaptation of the Sjöwall/Wahlöö novel looks as if it's setting the record straight on recent cop films. But in its desire to make no concessions to *Dirty Harry* et al, it destroys any potential interest with almost wilful perversity. Matthau's disgruntled cop, alienated from family and superiors, emerges as a tedious protagonist, relating to nothing, continually bored and boring. The plot hops around in an unengaging manner, while the excursions into the underworld (pimps, dopers, transvestites, Angels, etc) are patchily directed. Ironically, by the end, complete with car chase and split-second shooting, the film has become indistinguishable from all those movies it's trying so hard to disown. CPe

Laughter
(Harry D'Abbadie D'Arrast, 1930, US) Nancy Carroll, Fredric March, Frank Morgan, Glenn Anders, Leonard Carey, Diane Ellis.
82 min. b/w.
Brilliant Donald Ogden Stewart script (his first, aside from one silent credit) about an ex-Follies girl who has snared her large millionaire, finds society stifling, and happily plays with the fire of old flames from her Bohemian days. Wittily acute in its insight into Bright Young Thing nihilism, the film anticipates Cukor's marvellous *Holiday* (also scripted by Stewart) in steering a precarious path between screwball comedy and darker abysses. If D'Arrast isn't quite Cukor, he is at least Lubitsch without the nudges. TM

Laughterhouse
(aka Singleton's Pluck)
(Richard Eyre, 1984, GB) Ian Holm, Penelope Wilton, Bill Owen, Richard Hope, Stephen Moore, Rosemary Martin.
93 min.
When one of farmer Holm's pluckers loses a joint off his finger in the plucking machine and the TGWU block the transport of his Christmas geese to market, he determines to take them on foot from Norfolk to Smithfield. The anti-union stance is soon conveniently dropped as the trek turns into a protest against factory farming, with another bunch of media shits (cf. *The Ploughman's Lunch*) tagging along for the story. Presumably intended as a tribute to the continuing virtues of British pluck, the result is rather more off-putting than stirring. The main problem is that Eyre, as in the past, seems unable to invest his characters with a modicum of sympathy. That the film should have been 'inspired' by Howard Hawks's *Red River* is a point best glossed over. Comparisons are indeed odious. JP

Laughter in Paradise
(Mario Zampi, 1951, GB) Alastair Sim, Fay Compton, Beatrice Campbell, Veronica Hurst, George Cole, Hugh Griffith, Joyce Grenfell, AE Matthews, Audrey Hepburn.
93 min. b/w.

After kicking the bucket Griffith has the last laugh on his grasping relatives, each of whom stands to inherit £150,000 if, and only if, they perform the unlikely tasks designated by the deceased. Mild-mannered Sim, for instance, mercilessly hen-pecked by the priceless Grenfell, has to get himself thrown in jail. This is one of the brighter moments in a movie that's saddled with too much plot and then has to grind a way through it. Fitfully felicitous though, with a glimpse of young Audrey Hepburn. TJ

Laughter in the Dark
(Tony Richardson, 1969, GB/Fr) Nicol Williamson, Anna Karina, Jean-Claude Drouot, Peter Bowles, Sian Phillips, Sebastian Breaks.
104 min.
Despite being transplanted from the sadomasochistic gloom of the German '30s to the Swinging London of the '60s, this adaptation of Nabokov's teasingly perverse variation on the eternal triangle is not as bad as one might expect. It's shot as a series of brief, impressionistic scenes with Monteverdi tinkling tranquilly on the soundtrack: a style which works well at the beginning as the ageing art critic (Williamson, excellent) meets his cinema usherette (Karina) and finds her worming herself into his obsessions; and it serves at the end, when the critic, blinded after a lover's quarrel and believing himself alone with the repentant girl in a lonely villa, gradually realises that there is a third presence in the house, playing mocking games with him. In between times, though, the film sags horribly into all sorts of destructively non-Nabokovian vulgarities: a swinging party shot in swinging style, a surfeit of semi-nude couples cavorting on beds, etc. TM

Laura
(Otto Preminger, 1944, US) Gene Tierney, Dana Andrews, Clifton Webb, Vincent Price, Judith Anderson, Dorothy Adams, James Flavin.
88 min. b/w.
Not just another *noir* classic of '44, *Laura* almost succeeds in pulling the screen apart at the seams, if only to stitch it together again in a visibly frantic finale. The narrator's a critic, the cop a would-be necrophiliac, and the *femme fatale* a faceless corpse...or are they? Less investigative thriller than an investigation of that genre's conventions – voyeurism (looking at, and for, Laura), a search for solutions (not just whodunit but whodunwhat), and the race against time (clues and clocks, fantasies and flashbacks) – the plot is deliberately perfunctory, the people deliciously perverse, and the *mise-en-scène* radical. PK

Laura (Laura, les
Ombres de l'Eté)
(David Hamilton, 1979, Fr) Dawn Dunlap, James Mitchell, Maud Adams, Maureen Kerwin, Pierre Londiche.
100 min.
Even cut for British release, *Laura* runs for 90 minutes. Mere moments into this soft focus, softcore story of a talented sculptor and a young girl whose love overcomes her mother's objections, his blindness, and the law relating to sex with minors, you will grasp the importance of this piece of information: only paedophiles are likely to stay to the end. Priapic men and pubescent girls wrestling with Art, Love and each other in the exotic south of France may sound very merry; but wet people in an arid landscape don't add up to much more than muck, no matter how tastefully photographed. FD

Lavender Hill Mob, The
(Charles Crichton, 1951, GB) Alec Guinness, Stanley Holloway, Sidney James, Alfie Bass, Marjorie Fielding, John Gregson, Clive Morton.
78 min. b/w.
Probably not the finest Ealing comedy (although it does include an astute parody of the car chase in Ealing's own *The Blue Lamp*), but still one of the few enduringly funny movies in British cinema. Seemingly mousy bank teller (Guinness) teams up with seedy entrepreneur (Holloway) and two Cockney spivs (Bass and James) to steal gold bullion and turn it into Eiffel Tower paperweights. It won a script Oscar for TEB Clarke, who divides his satirical jibes between the police, the press and the City. Come in late and you'll miss a glimpse, in the opening scene in Rio, of a young Audrey Hepburn. TR

Law and Disorder
(Charles Crichton, 1958, GB) Michael Redgrave, Robert Morley, Elizabeth Sellars, Ronald Squire, George Coulouris, Joan Hickson, Lionel Jeffries, Brenda Bruce, John Le Mesurier, Irene Handl.
76 min. b/w.
Sub-Ealing caper from the regular team of Crichton and writer TEB Clarke (with help from Patrick Campbell): clergyman Redgrave is actually a crook who passes off his frequent spells inside as missionary trips to Africa, but when his innocent son gets a job assisting judge Morley, the swindler's underworld cronies snap into action to prevent the truth being revealed. Mild fun sustained by the usual slew of British character types. Based on the novel *Smugglers' Circuit* by Denys Roberts. TJ

Law and Disorder
(Ivan Passer, 1974, US) Carroll O'Connor, Ernest Borgnine, Karen Black, Anne Wedgeworth, Anita Dangler, Leslie Ackerman.
102 min.
Passer's first American film is an engaging and remarkably successful, if lightweight, merger of the Czech comedy of social observation with the American police vigilante genre. It's framed against the background of a disintegrating New York residential district, whose inhabitants join the Auxiliary Police unit in an attempt to preserve a veneer of civilisation. There's a deliciously broad parody performance from Karen Black (a Monroe send-up) as a hairdresser given to slanging her customers, and Passer reveals a natural delight in perceiving the comedy inherent in all forms of pomp and ceremony. The emotional judgment is more problematic, especially in the final escalation towards tragedy; but despite its unevenness the film is refreshingly entertaining, and the blue-collar ambience is stunningly well used. VG

Law and Jake Wade, The
(John Sturges, 1958, US) Robert Taylor, Richard Widmark, Patricia Owens, Robert Middleton, Henry Silva.
86 min.
A highly watchable Western – probably Sturges' best – stunningly shot by Robert Surtees, and with an excellent script by William Bowers (*The Gunfighter, Support Your Local Sheriff*) which breathes new life into the old yarn about the outlaw-turned-sheriff (Taylor) trying to resist the blandishments of a former colleague he rescues from hanging (Widmark), who then relentlessly tries all he knows to coax/force his old buddy into helping him locate the whereabouts of the buried proceeds of a bank robbery they pulled. Widmark (especially) and Taylor are both excellent, and the climactic Indian attack (with shoot-out) in a ghost town is superbly staged. TM

Law and Order
(Frederick Wiseman, 1969, US)
81 min. b/w.
One of the best of Wiseman's documentaries, an impressionistic account of the daily police routine in a predominantly black neighbourhood of Kansas City, Missouri. Although violence abounds, with a black prostitute almost strangled by a vice-squad cop, the film avoids grinding axes about police brutality. Instead, sitting back and coolly observing the situation from multiple perspectives, it suggests that any sickness in the forces of law and order is a symptom of disease in the society that breeds them. TM

Lawless, The
(aka The Dividing Line)
(Joseph Losey, 1949, US) Macdonald Carey, Gail Russell, Lalo Rios, John Sands, Lee Patrick, John Hoyt, Argentina Brunetti, Martha Hyer.
83 min. b/w.
Losey's second feature, a lynching drama set in a small Southern Californian town beset by racial tensions: local newspaper reporter (Carey), after conquering self-interest under pressure from the girl he loves (Russell), crusades on behalf of a Mexican youth (Rios) falsely accused of having raped a 'white' girl. So far, so conventional, but what gives it an edge of brilliance is Losey's eye for the smalltown locations: the shabby dance hall in the Mexican quarter, the sleepy high street,

the one-horse newspaper office, the cosy front porches and the churchgoers, all swept away in sudden primitive starkness as the fugitive is relentlessly hunted over a fantastic wasteland of rocks and rubble. The film also fairly reeks of fear, doubtless a testament to the HUAC witch-hunts, but beautifully woven into Daniel Mainwaring's script in a complex pattern (not just the racial divide, suspicion of the outsider or of anyone challenging the status quo, but the sexual anxieties that drive the 'white' youths to macho bravado in invading the Mexican dance-hall, the fear of losing his job that makes the reporter try to turn a blind eye, and so on). TM

Lawless Street, A
(Joseph H Lewis, 1955, US) Randolph Scott, Angela Lansbury, Warner Anderson, Jean Parker, Wallace Ford, John Emery, Ruth Donnelly, Michael Pate.
78 min.
The first, and better, of the two colour Westerns Lewis made with Scott, this may lack the bizarre originality of *Seventh Cavalry* but certainly makes up for it in solid craftsmanship and vivid characterisation. Scott is the marshall, about to retire, who'd like to rid the town of its rowdy, gun-totin' villains before throwing in the towel; the job is complicated, however, by his involvement with faithless music-hall *chanteuse* Lansbury, whose fickle ways weaken his resolve. Strikingly shot, tersely plotted, it's no masterwork, but once again reveals Lewis as a superior director of low-budget material. GA

Lawman
(Michael Winner, 1970, US) Burt Lancaster, Robert Ryan, Lee J Cobb, Sheree North, Joseph Wiseman, Robert Duvall, Albert Salmi, John McGiver, Richard Jordan.
99 min.
Typically ham-fisted Western from *Death Wish* Winner. Stoic lawman Lancaster arrives in the town of Sabbath on the trail of seven killers (carousing cowboys who accidentally caused the death of an old man); their protective boss, Cobb, and the town's lily-livered sheriff (Ryan) don't plan on giving him much help; neither do the townspeople. Would-be thoughtful Western which ultimately resorts to killing and ketchup to make up for its lack of style and originality. A remake of *Man with the Gun* (1955). NF

Lawn Dogs
(John Duigan, 1997, GB) Sam Rockwell, Christopher McDonald, Kathleen Quinlan, Bruce McGill, Mischa Barton.
101 min.
Rural Kentucky. Ten-year-old Devon (Mischa Barton, hypnotic) strikes up a dangerous friendship with Trent (Rockwell), a trailer-trash lawn-mower man. Their bond is established early on: Trent stripping in a traffic jam to dive off a bridge into the river; Devon stripping off her nightdress to howl naked at the moon. He's literally an outsider, exiled before dusk from the suburban fortress whose lawns he keeps from growing wild; she's a metaphorical outsider, a sickly child who dreams of Baba Yaga and the fleeing girl who drops a comb and causes an impenetrable wood to spring up behind her. While innocent, Devon's proto-sexual adoration of Trent makes their relationship as uncomfortable for the viewer as for her hypocritically straight parents. When they're dancing on the roof of Trent's truck and mooning at the security guard, they're care-free kids; when they start to compare scars, it's childhood's end. Australian director John Duigan's best films have dealt with the passage from childhood to adolescence, and here, in his first US film (from British producer Duncan *Four Weddings* Kenworthy), he maintains an atmosphere where dream is a short step from nightmare. Quirkily haunting. DW

Lawnmower Man, The
(Brett Leonard, 1992, GB/US) Jeff Fahey, Pierce Brosnan, Jenny Wright, Mark Bringleson, Geoffrey Lewis, Jeremy Slate, Dean Norris, Colleen Coffey.
108 min.
The first feature film to explore the possibilities opened up by Virtual Reality is derived in part from a Stephen King story, merged with an existing project. Using mentally retarded gardener Jobe (Fahey) as a guinea pig, mad scientist Dr

Angelo (Brosnan) exposes him to Virtual Reality teaching technology and powerful drugs which accelerate his learning ability, transforming him into a calculating genius. But tampering by a mercenary Cybertech executive produces unforeseen and dangerous side effects. Despite the hackneyed sub-Frankenstein plot, the dazzling computer-generated special effects almost carry the film. The irony is that almost nothing that matters actually depends upon, or takes place within, Virtual Reality. Until the final showdown between Jobe and his creator, what we see is merely the way Jobe's exposure to Virtual Reality affects his behaviour in the real world. Only when he and the lubricious Marnie (Wright) suit up to enjoy 'cybersex' are the storyline and computer effects fused, like their fluid bodies, together. NF

Lawnmower Man 2: Beyond Cyberspace
(Farhad Mann, 1995, US) Matt Frewer, Patrick Bergin, Austin O'Brien, Ely Pouget, Camille Cooper, Patrick le Brecque, Crystal Celeste Grant, Kevin Conway.
92 min.
Having jettisoned all but one of the original cast, this cynical sequel retreads familiar ground, provoking both disorientation and déjà vu. Simpleton gardener Jobe, last seen merging with the US phone system, has returned in physical form (instead of a virtual Jeff Fahey, we now have limbless *Max Headroom* star Frewer, who presumably came as a package with that show's director Farhad Mann). O'Brien's young, minor character Peter has been retained, however, as an identification figure for viewers who may buy the spin-off computer games. Nursed to health by Dr Cori Platt (Pouget), Jobe is then exploited by her evil boss Walker (Conway), who wants him to complete work on a powerful computer chip he's stolen from virtual reality genius Dr Benjamin Trace (Bergin). Walker plans to seize control of the Internet, but Jobe has grander ideas – to merge with, and become lord of, the virtual domain. But first he must crack the 'Egypt' code, incorporated into the chip by Trace to prevent such megalomaniac schemes. As before, almost nothing of significance takes place in cyberspace, the effects look disconcertingly artificial, and all trace of Stephen King's source story has been lost. NF

Law of Desire, The (La Ley del Deseo)
(Pedro Almodóvar,1987, Sp) Eusebio Poncela, Carmen Maura, Antonio Banderas, Miguel Molina, Manuela Velasco, Bibi Andersen, Fernando Guillén.
100 min.
Seventh feature by a Spanish writer/director hitherto unknown in this country: a lush, overblown, steamy, tragi-comedy murder thriller set in Madrid, there's something to offend and delight everyone. It opens intercutting between the filming, dubbing and première of one of fictional director/writer Pablo Quintero's homo-erotic movies. Pablo leaves the first-night party without his quasi-lover, Juan, who's straight and loves him dearly, but...desire's off his menu. Pablo sends Juan to the country to put distance between them, and a handsome stranger, Antonio, obsessed by the director, makes his move to fill the gap. Actress Tina, the director's sex-changed brother (the stupendous Carmen Maura), now a lesbian, has her own problems to deal with, plus her lover's precocious daughter. Pablo, Tina and Antonio take up their themes in a passionate fugue which accelerates fast. Wit, sex, drugs and topsy-turvy clichés abound; Almodóvar's sensuous style carries all before him. A life-affirming joy. TC

Lawrence of Arabia [100] (100)
(David Lean, 1962, GB) Peter O'Toole, Alec Guinness, Anthony Quinn, Jack Hawkins, Omar Sharif, José Ferrer, Anthony Quayle, Claude Rains, Arthur Kennedy, Donald Wolfit.
222 min.
Presented virtually as a desert mirage, this epic biopic of TE Lawrence constructs little more than an obfuscatory romantic glow around its enigmatic hero and his personal and political contradictions: Lean had obviously learned the 'value' of thematic fuzziness from the success of *Bridge on the River Kwai*, and duly garnered further Oscar successes here. Somewhere between

Robert Bolt's literariness and Freddie Young's shimmering cinematography, there should be direction: all there is is a pose of statuesque seriousness. PT

Laws of Gravity
(Nick Gomez, 1992, US) Peter Greene, Edie Falco, Adam Trese, Arbella Field, Paul Schulze, Saul Stein.
98 min.
We're back among the low-life on the mean streets of Brooklyn. Jimmy (Greene) and Jon (Trese) are two hustlers, the first under pressure from a loan-shark, the second so volatile he'll punch out anyone who annoys him, including girlfriend Celia (Field). Though hope springs eternal for the no-hoper men, Jimmy's wife (Falco) is tiring of it all, and when the guys get involved with gun-dealer Frankie (Schulze), tensions come to a head. Writer/director Gomez's first feature is nothing if not authentic. The performances are raw and itchy, the camerawork (by Jean de Segonzac) and cutting determinedly *vérité*, the script a frazzled blend of inconsequential character-chatter and aggressive outbursts. But if it's hard to fault the overall execution – the performances, especially, are solid – there's a problem that the film is so *familiar*. The pairing recalls early Scorsese, the gritty visual and verbal style Cassavetes. Efficient, but derivative. GA

Lawyer, The
(Sidney J Furie, 1968, US) Barry Newman, Harold Gould, Diana Muldaur, Robert Colbert, Kathleen Crowley.
120 min.
Remember *Petrocelli*, the mid-'70s TV series about a hip and groovy American lawyer? Well, it all started here in the movie version of the Dr Sam Sheppard murder case, where a hot shot attorney battles his way through legal technicalities and a difficult client to defend a doctor accused of killing his wife. Newman takes centre stage as the small town defence counsel grabbing his chance for national attention, though the proceedings go through some familiar moves. Watchable rather than scintillating. TJ

Laxdale Hall (aka Scotch on the Rocks)
(John Eldridge, 1952, GB) Ronald Squire, Kathleen Ryan, Raymond Huntley, Sebastian Shaw, Fulton Mackay, Prunella Scales.
77 min. b/w.
Amiable but uninvolving Ealing-esque comedy, adapted from Eric Linklater's novel, follows the clash between Hebridean car owners who refuse to cough up their road tax until the government actually builds a road on their island and the MPs who arrive to look into the matter. (Co-produced by John Grierson for Group 3.) TJ

Lazybones
(Michael Powell, 1934, GB) Ian Hunter, Claire Luce, Bernard Nedell, Michael Shepley, Sara Allgood, Bobbie Comber.
65 min. b/w.
Adapted from a play by Ernest Denny, this is a slow starter, with Hunter as an indolent baronet being urged by his impecunious family to marry an American heiress (Luce). He loves her, but scruples won't let him propose until he learns that she has lost all her money, whereupon he whisks her off to the registry office before his family can object. Complications arise, since she is led to believe he thought she was only pretending to have lost her money as a test; and her crooked cousin (Nedell) turns up to involve her in his theft of oil-related diplomatic papers from Hunter's brother-in-law (Shepley). Hereabouts, earlier moments of puckish humour escalate as Hunter rouses himself from his lethargy to resolve all problems; and graduate into dotty fantasy as he proves his ability to provide for a wife by turning his stately home into a 'Work Centre for the Wealthy Weary', where the idle rich can pay to enjoy honest toil as butlers, gardeners, etc. Modest but intelligently directed, the result is very engaging. TM

Leadbelly
(Gordon Parks, 1976, US) Roger E Mosley, James E Brodhead, John McDonald, Earnest L Hudson, Dana Manno, Art Evans, Paul Benjamin.
127 min.

The casting of Roger Mosley, with his boyish good looks, forewarns of the total blandness of yet another tragic-black-musician biopic. While pretending to stress the realism of this version of the life of Huddie Ledbetter, Parks can't disguise the fact that the details of the black folk-hero's life have been laundered for the widest possible audience. Totally inexcusable, and downright offensive to the legacy of the man's music, is the re-recording of some of Leadbelly's best-known songs (emasculated vocals, string and wood-winds even). Best moments are some early scenes involving encounters with musicians from whom he learns humility: the anonymous old-timer who introduces him to the 12-string guitar, and his early travels with Blind Lemon Jefferson (well played by Art Evans). RM

Leading Man, The

(John Duigan, 1996, GB) Lambert Wilson, Jon Bon Jovi, Thandie Newton, Anna Galiena, Barry Humphries, Patricia Hodge, Diana Quick, Harriet Walter, David Warner, Nicole Kidman.
100 min.
With Duigan directing a script by his sister Virginia, there's a whiff of indulgence about this backstage drama. A new play, *The Hit Man*, is in rehearsal in London. Its author, Felix Webb (Wilson), is conducting a clandestine affair with ingénue Hilary (Newton), and he'd leave middle-aged wife Elena (Galiena) like a shot, if he thought she could handle it. Enter American movie star Robin Grange (Bon Jovi). He's the play's lead, but slyly offers to double as the wife's lover. This is watchable, but old hat. Duigan makes only token stabs at satirising the luvvies, despite the copious egos on hand and muted support from such troupers as Warner, Humphries, Hodge and Quick. TCh

League of Gentlemen, The

(Basil Dearden, 1960, GB) Jack Hawkins, Richard Attenborough, Roger Livesey, Nigel Patrick, Bryan Forbes, Kieron Moore, Robert Coote, Melissa Stribling, Nanette Newman, Gerald Harper.
113 min. b/w.
A terrific caper movie, adapted by Bryan Forbes from a novel by John Boland. Hawkins is at his gruff best as an embittered ex-army colonel who assembles a seven-man team of similarly disgruntled former military men to execute a million pound bank robbery. Plotting and direction are as rigorously organised as the operation itself, making this a crisply enjoyable picture with typically excellent character playing from a lovable set of old lags. TJ

League of Their Own, A

(Penny Marshall, 1992, US) Tom Hanks, Geena Davis, Lori Petty, Madonna, David Strathairn, Jon Lovitz, Garry Marshall, Rosie O'Donnell, Megan Cavanagh, Tracy Reiner.
128 min.
This fictionalised account of the All American Girls' Professional Baseball League (formed in 1943, with male players lost to the war) captures heartbreaks, home runs, and little vigour. Things start promisingly as a scout (Lovitz) scours the country recruiting players, including farm-girls Dottie and Kit (Davis and Petty), dance-hall hostess 'All the Way' Mae (Madonna) and bouncer Doris (O'Donnell). As they train, rivalries emerge, focusing too heavily on Kit's jealousy over sister Dottie's physical and social advantages. Marshall piles on the sentiment, notably in framing sequences which see the film unfold in flashback and culminate in a tearful reunion; even worse, scriptwriters Lowell Ganz and Babaloo Mandel neglect the ensemble, emphasising a sense of historical occasion over character development. As the cynical manager/coach who learns to love his team, Hanks has more to wrestle with, but Madonna has do with a spot of dancing. CM

Leap into the Void (Salto nel Vuoto)

(Marco Bellocchio, 1980, It/Fr) Michel Piccoli, Anouk Aimée, Michele Placido, Gisella Burinato.
120 min.
Bellocchio's quirky subversion of bourgeois family values revives all the elements of two earlier works (*Fists in the Pocket* and *In the Name of the Father*) with its tale of a middle-aged, incestuously

puritanical judge (Piccoli) gradually destroyed by the hesitant love affair between his sister (Anouk) and a young anarchist actor. The treatment is perhaps less cruel, but Bellocchio continues the stylisation and claustrophobia of his earlier images – and with them the debt to the wise, angry, anti-patriarchal cinema of Jean Vigo. CA

Leap of Faith

(Richard Pearce, 1992, US) Steve Martin, Debra Winger, Lolita Davidovich, Liam Neeson, Lukas Haas, Meat Loaf, Philip Seymour Hoffman.
108 min.
Obviously seeking a role where he can seriously emote and turn in the goofy stuff as well, Martin has backed a loser in this confused spin on *Elmer Gantry*. His Jonas Nightengale is a cynical charlatan, whose travelling gospel revue mixes showbiz pizazz and cracker-barrel sentiment to con gullible townsfolk out of their cash. Rustwater, Kansas, is the next Bible Belt burg on the hit-list, but Mr Ultracynical has to rethink his heartless cool when perky waitress Davidovich engages his romantic attentions, and her kid brother (Haas) starts to believe the showman-preacher can actually make him walk again. Pearce's uncertain entertainment builds a conscience-impaired comic creation from Martin's sham shaman, then asks us to give credence to his part in a sudden crop of *bona fide* 'miracles' – a dumb plot development as shamelessly manipulative as his earlier slick hick schtick. This is just nonsense, and the star, whose would-be spiritual patter looks like an over-extended sketch anyway, can't save it. TJ

Lease of Life

(Charles Frend, 1954, GB) Robert Donat, Kay Walsh, Denholm Elliott, Adrienne Corri, Vida Hope, Richard Wattis.
94 min.
A Yorkshire parson (Donat) is given a year to live by his doctor, but conceals the news from his family in this tepid saga of conscience, written by Eric Ambler for Ealing. His remaining concern is to provide for daughter Corri, but the money for her musical scholarship will be harder to find when a contentious sermon loses him the opportunity of a better-paid post. Sincerity is never in doubt, but the drama's so low-key as to be almost non-existent. TJ

Leatherface: The Texas Chainsaw Massacre III

(Jeff Burr, 1989, US) RA Mihailoff, Kate Hodge, Ken Foree, Viggo Mortensen, William Butler, Joe Unger.
81 min.
Banned from general release by the BBFC on the grounds that it is excessively violent – and you'd have a hard time arguing the point. Blending the gritty, documentary quality of Tobe Hooper's original with the whacked-out psycho-comedy of Part II, Burr's darkly self-referential nightmare concerns a young couple's journey into the broiling Texan hinterlands, where Leatherface and his monstrously inbred companions await. Pursued by a jeepster from hell, covered in tanned and tortured human flesh, the 'normal' pair soon find themselves on the menu at a dinner engagement with the cannibal family: Leatherface, his two moronic brothers, feisty grandmother and corpulent grandfather, and the newest addition, a 12-year-old blond moppet who can't wait to get busy with the sledgehammer. While the on-screen gore is actually no more overt than in many mainstream horrors, what gives this its edge is the extent to which it revels in the atrocities depicted. A relentlessly sadistic and worryingly amusing movie, which will entertain and offend in equal measure. MK

Leave Her to Heaven

(John M Stahl, 1945, US) Gene Tierney, Cornel Wilde, Jeanne Crain, Vincent Price, Mary Philips, Ray Collins, Gene Lockhart, Darryl Hickman.
110 min.
Wonderful all-stops-out melodrama drawing luridly on gimcrack psychology to tell the tale of a father-fixated girl (Tierney) who picks a husband because of his resemblance to Daddy, and is then gripped by a mounting paroxysm of jealousy which inclines her to dispose violently of anyone else laying claim to his affection. The potential for

absurdity is enormous, not least in an unforgettable scene where Tierney roams the mountaintop on horseback at dawn (the colour, incidentally, is Fox-bright but exquisitely toned), scattering her father's ashes to the winds. But Stahl is totally in control, his precise pacing and compositions lending a persuasive dimension of *amour fou*, while Leon Shamroy's camera-work makes each image a purring pleasure on the eye. TM

Leaving (Bounce – Ko Gals)

(Masato Harada, 1997, Jap) Hitomi Sato, Yasue Sato, Yukiko Okamoto, Jun Murakami.
109 min.
The 'high gals' are Shibuya schoolgirls who finance their abortions, drug intake and desire for brand name fashions by hanging out – or having sex with – middle aged businessmen. Into town comes comparative innocent Lisa, about to fly off to New York the next day. After an appearance in a very softcore video goes wrong, she becomes embroiled with two high gals, not to mention a yakuza angry at the way the girls are deflecting business from his own professionals. Despite winning performances and a lively (if self-conscious) visual style, there's an air of hip posturing about this predictable, sporadically amusing urban fable. And even the bright surface can't prevent the narrative from congealing into sentimentality. GA

Leaving Las Vegas

(Mike Figgis, 1995, US) Nicolas Cage, Elisabeth Shue, Julian Sands, Richard Lewis, Steven Weber, Valeria Golino, Ed Lauter, Mike Figgis, Danny Huston, Bob Rafelson.
112 min.
Alcoholic scriptwriter Ben (Cage) is blowing his options. Our first glimpse sees his beyond-niceties collaring of an agent friend in a smart restaurant to demand drink money, a symptomatic preamble to what's staring him in the face: a 'sadly, we have to let you go' dismissal from his studio job. Figgis sets the crap game running here: the pay-off finances a one-way ticket to oblivion or, to give hell its name, Las Vegas, city of permanent after-hours. Cash the cheque, burn the past, take the freeway – we're in the booze movie, that most fascinatingly flawed form of the modern urban tragedy. This modestly budget masterpiece pools the Vegas streets with reflected neon and watches Ben drown. Shue is good as the young hooker he falls for, but Cage is extraordinary, producing an Oscar-winning performance of edgy, utterly convincing suicidal auto-destruct. In fact, Figgis makes of him something of an existential saint, a man for whom terminal self-knowledge leads to a kind of grace. If the film lacks the depth and structural sophistication of, say, *The Lost Weekend* (it was shot fast, with Declan Quinn's saturated Super-16 photography blown up, which may explain its kinetic buzz), it certainly has the courage of its convictions. WH

Leaving Lenin (Gadael Lenin)

(Endaf Emlyn, 1993, GB) Sharon Morgan, Wyn Bowen Harries, Ifan Huw Dafydd, Steffan Trevor, Catrin Mai.
90 min.
A funny and arresting portrait of a group of Welsh sixth-formers accidentally left to fend for themselves in a St Petersburg where the dissolution of the old certainties has landed the local youth in pretty much the same position. Detached from their teachers by the uncoupling of a train, these strangers in a strange land are suddenly charged with defining their emotional independence amid the emergent bohemia of a city in transition. Shooting on the hoof in the new Russia, Emlyn's camera displays an equal sense of discovery, negotiating leafy backwaters where the errant staff face ideological and marital upsets of their own. Although the film assays a grandiose overview of the relationship between artistic and personal freedoms, it works best as a witty but compassionate study of familiar types under pressure. Performed with assurance all the way, this is one to applaud. TJ

Leaving Normal

(Edward Zwick, 1991, US) Christine Lahti, Meg Tilly, Lenny Von Dohlen, Maury Chaykin, James Gammon, Patrika Darbo, Eve Gordon.
110 min.

Thelma & Louise without the turbo charge, this never seems certain where it's going. When Darly & Marianne set out on their voyage of self-discovery, their lives are a mess. Lahti's Darly is a brassy barmaid, as capable of putting her drunken customers down ('It takes more than two fingers to make me come') as of fireman's-lifting them side to side. She seems to know where she's going, especially in comparison to Tilly's little-girl-lost Marianne. But on the road from Normal (Wyoming) to Alaska, it becomes clear that both are dominated by unresolved pain and unsuccessful relationships. The script, from *Bill and Ted* writer Edward Solomon, is full of detours where we meet enjoyably surreal supporting players who seem to have wandered in from a Lynch or a Waters movie. Solomon also supplies sharp lines, mostly to Lahti, who delivers them with great style. But there is a spurious mystical element, and this shunts the film off track in the direction of sentimentality, despite its quirky charm and photogenic locations. CO'S

Lebanon...Why? (Liban...Pourquoi?)

(FN Georges Chamchoum, 1978, Leb/GB)
97 min.
Lebanon...Why? is a pertinent and necessary question, given British TV's repeated simplification of the conflict into 'leftist Moslems versus rightist Christians'. The 'why' of Chamchoum's film, however, is unfortunately little more than an index of incomprehension, not a stimulus to analysis: this irritating documentary ends with the question rather than proceeding from it. Under the production circumstances, no one could reasonably expect a structured, fully coherent, text-book presentation, but that hardly excuses the editing strategy of fragmenting every interview, cutting fast between talking heads, the repeated use of redundant footage of gesturing fighters and scarred landscapes overlaid with a melodramatic score, or the tricksy effects of emotive freeze-frames. Indeed, most information has to be gleaned from the (added) English intertitles. PT

Leben ist eine Baustelle, Das
see Life Is All You Get

Lebenszeichen
see Signs of Life

Lebewohl Fremde
see Farewell, Stranger

Le Cop (Les Ripoux)

(Claude Zidi, 1984, Fr) Philippe Noiret, Thierry Lhermitte, Régine, Grace De Capitani, Claude Brosset, Albert Simono, Julien Guiomar, Henri Attal.
107 min.
Corrupt Parisian cop René initiates naive police-academy graduate François (Lhermitte) into the advantageous corruption of the sleazy Goutte d'Or quarter in Paris, where shirts, meals, drink, whores and drugs are there for the taking – provided one turns a blind eye to certain criminal activities. Noiret is in his element as the slobbish René, Lhermitte's metamorphosis is nicely handled, and director Zidi's attention to the backstreet milieu helps to sustain a believable air of comic amorality. NF

Le Cop 2 (Ripoux contre ripoux)

(Claude Zidi, 1989, Fr) Philippe Noiret, Thierry Lhermitte, Guy Marchand, Line Renaud, Grace De Capitani, Michel Aumont, Jean-Pierre Castaldi, Jean-Claude Brialy.
108 min.
A few droll set pieces, but on the whole this disappointing sequel is wretchedly put together. Lhermitte, as painfully couth as before, wants to go straight. To prove that Paris is universally crooked, his seasoned cop partner Noiret picks up a citizen at random, and within half-an-hour, a respectable banker (Brialy) has confessed to a long-forgotten misdemeanour. Regrettably, Zidi betrays this anarchic element for a contrived corruption and conspiracy scenario. For a black comedy, the film is unconscionably sentimental about prostitutes, horses and the countryside. Worst of

all, it is maudlin towards its heroes. Noiret, a sharp fixer in the first film, looks ready to be put out to pasture, while Lhermitte proves unpersonable when asked to go beyond his straight man act. TCh

Lectrice, La

(Michel Deville, 1988, Fr) Miou-Miou, Régis Royer, Christian Ruché, Marianne Denicourt, Charlotte Farran, Maria Casarès, Pierre Dux, Patrick Chesnais.
98 min.
La lectrice, wonderfully played by Miou-Miou, is Constance, a girl who likes reading to her boyfriend in bed. One night she begins a novel by Raymond Jean called *La Lectrice*, whose leading character, Marie also likes reading...The camera follows Constance /Marie between the covers as she has social intercourse with four people who are disabled in some way: a boy in a wheelchair, a little girl whose mother is too busy to look after her, a bedridden war widow, an impotent company director. The texts chosen are appropriate (*L'Amant, Alice, War and Peace, Les Fleurs du Mal*). It becomes clear that each client is after attention of a different kind, but as soon as Marie plays along, a minor disaster ensues; only when she has to read the mucky Marquis to a geriatric judge does she begin to have doubts. This elegantly erotic and erudite games-playing has something for everyone: voyeurs will delight in the nudity, poseurs will prefer the many and various striking of attitudes, and penseurs will ponder on the way language is both a lexical and a sexual minefield. Set, too, against the beautiful wintry background of Arles as it contrasts with the colour-coded cast and the soundtrack of Beethoven sonatas. MS

Leda
see A Double Tour

Left-Handed Gun, The

(Arthur Penn, 1958, US) Paul Newman, John Dehner, Hurd Hatfield, Lita Milan, James Congdon, Colin Keith-Johnston, James Best, John Dierkes.
102 min. b/w.
Newman as Billy the mixed-up Kid, an ebullient young illiterate who takes to slinging a gun when his substitute father is killed, only to face another, sterner father figure. Endlessly fascinated by his own image, blindly following a death-wish to its logical conclusion, this Billy is very much of the rebel- without-a-cause breed, a hero unable to match up to his legend. Violent, stylised, occasionally top-heavy with symbolism (although the religious parallel is convincingly carried by Hatfield's marvellous performance as Billy's Judas disciple), *The Left-Handed Gun* is a remarkable attempt to communicate an understanding (ours of Billy, his of himself) viscerally, felt through movement and gesture. Penn's first film, it is in many ways a key stage in the development of the Western. TM

Left-Handed Woman, The (Die linkshändige Frau)

(Peter Handke, 1977, WGer) Edith Clever, Bruno Ganz, Angela Winkler, Markus Mühleisen, Bernhard Minetti, Bernhard Wicki, Rüdiger Vogler, Michel Lonsdale, Gérard Depardieu.
113 min.
A train shatters the stillness of a Paris suburb, leaves a puddle on the station platform quivering with some unsolicited, mysterious, moving energy. This Romantic metaphor is at the very centre of Handke's grave, laconic film, produced by Wim Wenders, which begins where *The American Friend* left off: in the ringing void of Roissy airport. Here, the Woman (Edith Clever, superb in the role) meets her husband (Ganz) and, for no apparent reason, rejects him in favour of a solitary voyage through her own private void. In her house, with her child, the film records a double flight of escape and exploration, her rediscovery of the world, her relocation of body, home and landscape. This emotional labour makes its own economy: silence, an edge of solemnity, an overwhelming painterly grace. Self-effacement is made the paradoxical means of self-discovery, and the film becomes a hymn to a woman's liberating private growth, a moving, deceptively fragile contemplation of a world almost beyond words. CA

Left Hand of God, The

(Edward Dmytryk, 1955, US) Humphrey Bogart, Gene Tierney, Lee J Cobb, Agnes Moorehead, EG Marshall, Benson Fong.
87 min.
Big, worthy production from Fox that looks like an all-out assault on the Oscars. In one of his last appearances, Bogart's an American pilot who crash-lands in China during WWII and goes on the run (posing as a Catholic priest) from Lee J Cobb's ruthless warlord. TJ

Left, Right and Centre

(Sidney Gilliat, 1959, GB) Ian Carmichael, Patricia Bredin, Alastair Sim, Eric Barker, Richard Wattis, Gordon Harker, Moyra Fraser.
95 min. b/w.
More a mild sitcom than a political satire, since ideological breezes are conspicuously absent from the storm which brews when the Tory by-election candidate (peer's nephew and TV panel-list) falls in love with his Labour rival (fishmonger's daughter and LSE student). Best moments come from Sim as a peer busily commercialising his stately home and counting the shekels. TM

Legacy

(Karen Arthur, 1975, US) Joan Hotchkis, George McDaniel, Sean Allen, Dixie Lee, Richard Bradford III.
90 min.
Superficially, there are resemblances to the Hollywood soap opera about the bored, anxiety-ridden wife, left alone to brood in her automated and luxurious household. However, with its edge of pain moving towards madness and suicide, and its sexual accuracy and eroticism, the film emerges as something fresher and truer. Despite being totally unsympathetic, the heroine increasingly engages our feelings with her intense frustration and rage. A small, claustrophobic work, and though the director tries to turn her heroine's anger into a metaphor for the death of an old America, its power derives from the raw image of a solitary woman, trapped and crying, 'I hate!' LQ

Legacy, The

(Richard Marquand, 1978, GB) Katharine Ross, Sam Elliott, John Standing, Ian Hogg, Margaret Tyzack, Charles Gray, Lee Montague, Hildegard Neil, Roger Daltrey.
102 min.
A typically loony English-country-house horror from the pen of Jimmy Sangster, which dumps its statutory American leads (Katharine Ross and Sam Elliott) into a hardly-stirred plot-pot of diabolic conspiracy – and slowly congeals. In other words, the legacy in question is really the British industry's continuing forlorn attempt to crack the international market with a 'nowhere' story of an England where everything stops for tea, a Rolls prowls the leafy lanes, devoted rustic retainers do little but dispose of untidy corpses, and the dark family secret resides upstairs. And the true curse is that an actor of the calibre of Ian Hogg is limited to scowling from beneath a chauffeur's cap, and Charles Gray and Lee Montague have to affect hilarious Euro-accents, while the very presence of the Hollywood 'names' (plus a dreadful Roger Daltrey cameo) turns a hackneyed script into a 'package' with 'potential'. Horror, indeed. PT

Legal Eagles

(Ivan Reitman, 1986, US) Robert Redford, Debra Winger, Daryl Hannah, Brian Dennehy, Terence Stamp, Steven Hill, John McMartin, Roscoe Lee Browne.
116 min.
Never trust a film with a character named 'Chelsea'. Here, the silly moniker belongs to Daryl Hannah, a New York boho accused of murder and saved by two crusading attorneys in the shape of Redford and Winger. The plot meanders through trial scenes, further killings, a ludicrous performance-art display by the shapely Hannah, and various tussles – sexual and otherwise – between La Winger and la Redford. It all concludes with a big fire and an even bigger courtroom drama. Everything seems to revolve around an art fraud, though that's never quite clear since this plot falls into the category kindly known as 'baggy'. RR

Legend

(Ridley Scott, 1985, US) Tom Cruise, Mia Sara, Tim Curry, David Bennent, Alice Playten, Billy Barty.
94 min.
And lo, it came to pass that the enchanted forest was filled up to here with all manner of backlighting and slow motion and starburst filters until it looked like unto a commercial for Timotei shampoo. And behold the sappy Princess Lili, who is out slumming with the peasants and the forest folk and whoops she has plunged the land into eternal darkness at minus 50 degrees centigrade. Lo, lots of snow. And who is this geek with ten tons of make-up plastered all over his mug? Lo, verily it is Tim Curry as the megalomaniac Lord of Darkness, who is threatening to do in the last horse with a horn stuck on its head, unless Jack o' the Green and a petulant Tinkerbell type who thpeaks with a lithp can get there first. And lo, this was the culmination of four years of research and preparation. And it was not good. AB

Legend of Billie Jean, The

(Matthew Robbins, 1985, US) Helen Slater, Keith Gordon, Christian Slater, Richard Bradford, Peter Coyote, Martha Gehman, Dean Stockwell.
95 min.
When brainless jocks vandalise young Binx's scooter, he and his sister Billie Jean (Helen 'Supergirl' Slater) seek compensation from the father of the chief 'fucker'; but he (Bradford) is some mean bastard, and when he starts molesting BJ, Binx accidentally shoots him in the shoulder. Bro, Sis and a coupla chums take to the road, pursued by a paternal cop (Coyote), condemned by the media, and worshipped as upholders of justice by what seems to be the entire weeny and teeny population of Texas. Robbins co-wrote Spielberg's *Sugarland Express*, to which this bears more than a passing resemblance plotwise. But there similarities end. The sentimental elevation of BJ to legendary status ('She's everywhere') is ludicrously implausible, the characterisation cardboard and cute, the humour puerile, and the squandering of the considerable talents of Coyote and Bradford criminal. Four-letter words and gags about periods fail to disguise the adolescent wish-fulfilment quality of script and direction. GA

Legend of Bruce Lee (Xi Siwang Youxi/aka The New Game of Death)

(Lin Bing, 1975, Tai) Lee Roy Lung, Lung Fei, Kus Lai, San Dus, Ronald Brown.
96 min.
Despite an opening sequence which suggests that what follows may back up the title (a collage of stills and articles, cutting to a suitably heroic training session featuring Lee Roy Lung, the film's 'lookalike' find), this sidetracks into an undistinguished contemporary kung-fu action film whose protagonist is apparently – in an odd confusion of reality and fiction – supposed to be the real-life Bruce Lee. Failing as a homage, and not aspiring to the exposé scurrility of *A Dragon's Story*, it misses out on every count. Lee Roy Lung masters only the least relevant of the star's mannerisms, and is a very boring fighter, a point underscored by the feeble-looking opponents he confronts. Heavily cut, the film is further burdened with an all-purpose soul score. VG

Legend of Frenchie King, The (Les Pétroleuses)

(Christian-Jaque, 1971, Fr/It/Sp/GB) Brigitte Bardot, Claudia Cardinale, Michael J Pollard, Micheline Presle, Georges Beller.
96 min.
This lame attempt to repeat the success of Malle's *Viva Maria* sees Bardot and Cardinale as gunfighters in the West, feuding and scratching each other's eyes out over the title-deeds to a ranch soaked in oil, with the baby-faced Pollard mugging away as the harassed sheriff. Set in a French settlement, with the characters making wiz ze ooh-la-la accents in the dubbed version. Dreadfully unfunny. GA

Legend of Hell House, The

(John Hough, 1973, GB) Pamela Franklin, Roddy McDowall, Clive Revill, Gayle Hunnicutt, Roland Culver, Peter Bowles, Michael Gough.
94 min.
Richard Matheson's disappointing adaptation of his own rather disappointing novel, a haunted-house tale in which a dying multi-millionaire (Culver) offers a physicist (Revill) £100,000 to investigate a mansion in which several psychic investigators have been killed, and to provide an answer to the perennial question about survival after death. Trivialising the theme, saddled with some terrible dialogue, needlessly tricked out with a lot of countdown-style dates, it founders into innocuous routine. Pamela Franklin, however, gives a convincing performance as the 'mental medium'. DP

Legend of Lylah Clare, The

(Robert Aldrich, 1968, US) Kim Novak, Peter Finch, Ernest Borgnine, Milton Seltzer, Valentina Cortese, Rossella Falk, Coral Browne, Gabriele Tinti, Michael Murphy.
127 min.
Hollywood picking its scabs is always a riveting sight, and never more enjoyably so than in Aldrich's supremely vulgar movie, which feeds gluttonously off movie myth and experience to create a vigorously animated Hollywood Babylon where dead stars talk and everyone's laundry is filthy. Kim Novak stars as the moulded reincarnation of Lylah Clare, whose stellar career ended in mysterious death on the night of her wedding to director Lewis Zarkan (Finch), now attempting a semi-confessional biopic on the subject, which naturally involves an outrageous gallery of grotesques and innocents in its revelatory course from concept to screen. Necrophilia, cancer, cripples, French critics, lesbianism, ignorant producers, nepotism, abortion, 'film-artists', Italian studs and TV are the tasty elements Aldrich ghoulishly (and a little masochistically) juggles into a film-fan's delight, a side-splitting charade of satire, sarcasm and sheer perverse affection. PT

Legend of the Holy Drinker, The (La Leggenda del Santo Bevitore)

(Ermanno Olmi, 1988, It) Rutger Hauer, Anthony Quayle, Sandrine Dumas, Dominique Pinon, Sophie Segalen, Jean-Maurice Chanet.
128 min.
A tramp, exiled in Paris and haunted by a criminal past, sees no way out of his predicament until, almost miraculously, he is offered 200 francs by a wealthy stranger whose only request is that, when he can afford it, he return the money to a chapel dedicated to St. Thérèse. A man of honour but weak will, the derelict takes the chance to rejoin a world to which he had become a stranger, finding work, keeping company with women, dining out and sleeping in beds; such luxuries, however, distract him from his obligation…Olmi's adaptation of Joseph Roth's novella is faithful and charming, filmed with a simplicity that mirrors the original's economy. As the alcoholic, though a tad too clean, Rutger Hauer effortlessly suggests the character's blend of pride, dignity and vunerability, while Olmi eschews prosaic realism in his evocation of Paris, seen as an oddly timeless, universal city; the lyricism matches the almost magical coincidences of the plot. Indeed the film has the resonance and innocence of a parable, its religious elements widely subordinated to a story that is told with a minimum of fuss and explanatory dialogue. Quite why the film is so affecting is hard to hard to pin down: maybe it's because Olmi is so sure of his gentle, generous touch that he feels no need for overstatement. GA

Legend of the Lone Ranger, The

(William A Fraker, 1981, US) Klinton Spilsbury, Michael Horse, Christopher Lloyd, Matt Clark, Juanin Clay, Johnn Bennett Perry, Jason Robards, Richard Farnsworth.
98 min.
The mystery is how Fraker, a gifted cameraman who made a superb directing debut in Westerns with *Monte Walsh*, could produce such a clinker as this. Purporting to be a biography of John Reid, alias the Lone Ranger, it starts with an interminable account (in gooey soft focus) of how 11-year-old John saved young Tonto from a fate worse than death, found his own parents butchered by outlaws, and took to the tepee to swear a blood pact with his Indian buddy. His adult campaign to right all wrongs is, if anything, even more flabbily inept, saddled with flavourless performances and an off-screen narrator who elucidates an already painfully limpid plot like nanny explaining to a retarded child. TM

Legend of the Lost

(Henry Hathaway, 1957, US) John Wayne, Sophia Loren, Rossano Brazzi, Kurt Kasznar.
109 min.
A lost-city desert yarn of near-classic lunacy, flecked with notions of (Christian) faith and (cinematic) illusion, as religious nut Brazzi, pragmatic guide Wayne, and wavering sinner Loren investigate mirages both Saharan and psychological. As writer Ben Hecht has Wayne put it, 'A couple of men and a dame are a strain on any civilisation.' PT

Legend of the Mountain (Shan Zhong Chuanqi)

(King Hu, 1978, HK) Hsu Feng, Sylvia Chang, Shih Chun, Tung Lin, Tien Feng.
180 min.
As long as the same director's *Touch of Zen*, but with only a quarter of the substance, this classical ghost story wanders interminably until it reaches its hugely predictable conclusion. Along the way there are some ropey performances, some ropier effects, and a lot of fabulous scenery. There are also moments of genuine delicacy and beauty, but few will have the perseverance to wade through all the self-conscious artfulness to get to them. RG

Legend of the 7 Golden Vampires, The

(Roy Ward Baker, 1974, GB/HK) Peter Cushing, David Chiang, Julie Ege, Robin Stewart, Shih Szu, John Forbes-Robertson.
89 min.
Hammer and Shaw Brothers combine to provide a fusion of kung-fu and vampirism in which Cushing's Van Helsen tracks Dracula to China, perceiving his hand behind the terrorising of a village by the malevolent undead. With early scenes that suggest a true marriage of forms as a Chinese pilgrim makes his way through Transylvanian forests to worship at Dracula's tomb, and later ones where the undead astonishingly hobble and dance their way across the screen, it is a shame that the film should muff some of the simplest set-ups, and rely for effect on some rather mechanically intercut vampire attacks. VG

Legend of the Suram Fortress, The (Legenda Suramskoi Kreposti)

(Sergo Paradjanov/Dodo Abashidze, 1984, USSR) Venerik'o Andzhaparidze, Dodo Abashidze, Sopik'o Ch'iaureli, Duduxana Ts'erodze.
87 min.
A visually striking but rather inscrutable depiction of a Georgian myth, Paradjanov's film concerns a young boy who saves the constantly crumbling Suram Fortress by allowing himself to be covered with earth and eggs and walled up alive. The undeniable visual pleasures offered by the imaginative images and rich colours are unfortunately undercut by the stylised presentation – much of the action takes place amid the ruins of the fortress as it survives today – a confusing plot and some esoteric cultural references. NF

Legend of the Werewolf

(Freddie Francis, 1974, GB) Peter Cushing, Ron Moody, Hugh Griffith, Roy Castle, David Rintoul, Stefan Gryff, Lynn Dalby, Renee Houston.
90 min.
This carries all the earmarks of a disaster-ridden project. Lurching from a hopeless opening sequence – in which a *Look at Life* voice-over 'explains' the werewolf in decidedly bland terms – into a disastrously unfocused section featuring Hugh Griffith as a travelling showman, it finally settles down to being an only faintly more coherent tale of werewolf murders, set in a grade-school version of *fin de siècle* Paris. The script is particularly preposterous, and even Cushing looks disconcerted by the shambles around him. Was everybody drunk? VG

Legends of the Fall
(Edward Zwick, 1994, US) Brad Pitt, Anthony Hopkins, Julia Ormond, Aidan Quinn, Henry Thomas, Karina Lombard, Tantoo Cardinal, Gordon Tootoosis, Paul Desmond.
133 min.
Zwick turns Jim Harrison's lean, macho novella into a purple, three-hankie Western: Mills and Daniel Boone. Set in the years around WWI, it's the story of the Ludlows: three brothers brought up in the wilds of Montana under the stern eye of their father, the Colonel (Hopkins). Alfred (Quinn), the eldest, is respectful and ambitious, as dutiful as his brother Tristan (Pitt) is rugged and untamed, but when Samuel (Thomas), the youngest, returns home from college with a beautiful wife, Susannah (Ormond), it's not long before discord blossoms. For all that it's blatantly ludicrous tosh, *Legends* performed very respectably at the American box office, and it's not hard to see why: the entire film plays like a commercial for Brad Pitt. You can imagine half the audience wondering, 'Where can I get one of those?' Every young male star should have a role like this: cowboy, soldier, adventurer, bootlegger, vigilante. He wrestles bears, scalps Jerries, sails the seven seas and nobly renounces the woman he loves (his brother's wife). Small wonder that Hopkins resorts to scene-stealing: picture Charles Laughton as Popeye out West. TCh

Leggenda del Santo Bevitore, La
see Legend of the Holy Drinker, The

Leila and the Wolves
(Heiny Srour, 1984, GB/Leb) Nabila Zeitouni, Rafiq Ali Ahmed, Raja Nehme, Emilia Fowad.
93 min.
A docudrama about the fight against victimisation of Arab women. An unlikely interlocutor garbed in a sheer white dress, Leila time-travels through the eight decades of this century, stopping here (at a time of revolution when women larded wedding invitations with news of hidden arms) and there (when young girls at the barricades are goaded into fatal action by chauvinist remarks). Visually, Heiny Srour's film is a treat, combining tinted newsreel footage with memorable images and clearly loving shots of a strife-torn nation; the acts of courage she reveals, and the example she sets to other film-makers to engage their own history, are exalting. FD

Lektionen in Finsternis
see Lessons in Darkness

Le Mans
(Lee H Katzin, 1971, US) Steve McQueen, Siegfried Rauch, Elga Andersen, Ronald Leigh-Hunt, Fred Haltiner.
108 min.
Despite a valiant attempt at editing some excitement into the repetitive spectacle of circuiting Porsches and Ferraris, this self-congratulatory advert for Steve McQueen's driving prowess really feels like it's taking the obligatory 24 hours to unwind. PT

Lemon Popsicle (Eskimo Limon)
(Boaz Davidson, 1977, Isr) Yiftach Katzur, Anat Atzmon, Jonathan Segal, Zacki Noy, Deborah Kaydar.
100 min.
A brazen and none-too-kosher attempt to transplant *American Graffiti* to 1958 Tel Aviv, where (despite the Hebrew signs in the ice-cream parlour) the juke-boxes pound out the California sound. Parading its tastelessness like a strong suit, the movie graphically follows a trio of sexually obsessed teenage boys through their first experiences of love, sex and rejection, and the classroom sweetheart through her first abortion. Were it not for their (and the camera's) fixation on private parts, the characters might be seen as taking their emotional range from the ever-present hit parade – with which the movie shares a bland indifference to the social and political climate. Lots of milk and honey, but there has to be more to the promised land than this. JD

Lemon Sisters, The
(Joyce Chopra, 1990, US) Diane Keaton, Carol Kane, Kathryn Grody, Joe Kelly, Elliott Gould, Ruben Blades, Aidan Quinn, Estelle Parsons.
93 min.
'Three lemons are just lemons. Three lemons together are a jackpot.' Atlantic City, 1959 – cue ragtime music, the seaside, boardwalks, childhood friendship. Sound familiar? This is a cheery version of the ultimate girly weepie, *Beaches*. Lifelong pals Grody, Keaton and Kane have ambitions to own a nightclub where they can perform their quirky singing act. But money isn't the only obstacle: friendship has its pressures too. A pleasing cast (including Aidan Quinn as a sleazy PR man) struggles manfully with a banal script, but there's very little here that you haven't seen before, including the mushy ending. YS

Lengua asesina, La
see Killer Tongue

Leningrad Cowboys Go America
(Aki Kaurismäka, 1989, Fin/Swe) Matti Pellonpää, Nicky Tesco, Kari Väänänen, Jim Jarmusch.
79 min.
Unable to make it big in frozen Finland, the Leningrad Cowboys, a talent-free pop group with a bizarre image and an idiosyncratic sound, head for America, where – a local promoter assures them – people will 'swallow any kind of shit'. En route to a wedding reception gig in Mexico, they drive their newly acquired Cadillac from one seedy venue to the next, taking in what Kaurismäki calls 'the steamy bars and honest folk and backyards of the Hamburger Nation'. Even without his cameo appearance as a used-car dealer, Jim Jarmusch's influence would beobvious from the tracking shots of dingy downtown areas, the stylised dialogue, and cryptic inter-titles. But Kaurismäki makes this engaging, comic road movie his own with a distinctive visual style, great running gags (the band carry with them a coffin containing their frozen bass guitarist), some memorably dreadful tunes, and his generosity towards the characters and the ordinary people they meet. Looked at superficially, it's a one-joke movie, but as with Jarmusch, the textured images and oblique nuances take priority over the wacky premise and slender storyline. NF

Lenny
(Bob Fosse, 1974, US) Dustin Hoffman, Valerie Perrine, Jan Miner, Stanley Beck, Gary Morton.
111 min. b/w.
Julian Barry's adaptation of his own stage play has all the worst faults of the Hollywood biopic: Lenny Bruce's complex life and personality are manhandled into the fable of an eager Jewish kid working second-rate clubs, who courts his future wife with flowers, rises to fame by being 'true to his art', and finds life at the top fraught with drugs, marital problems and notoriety. The monochrome photography and pseudo-documentary interpolations can't disguise the basic Harold Robbins material, and the good performances (Hoffman and Perrine) stand little chance against Fosse's withering direction: the subject matter needs far defter psychological handling than it gets. There are two powerful nightclub scenes carried by Hoffman, but otherwise Bruce emerges quite unfairly as little more than a tiresome, self-obsessed trouper. DP

Lenny Bruce Performance Film, The
(John Magnuson, 1967, US) Lenny Bruce.
68 min. b/w.
As a historical document, this is a priceless piece of celluloid; as a slice of cinema, it's a little hard-going. The visual record of his penultimate performance at the Basin Street West Club in San Francisco (at that time, August '65, just about the only city where Bruce was still kosher), it's the result of a collaboration between the 'comedian' and an educational film-maker, John Magnuson. The Bruce trademark of a whiplash wit packaged in scatological and scaldingly accurate language is in abundant evidence, even if delivered in a diction akin to Joe Strummer on speed with his jaws super-glued together. Yet for a film about a funny man, there's a disquieting air of desperation. Lit only by a single spot which gives the film a dark

and grainy feel, the car-coated figure is pinned against a dungeon-like backdrop as he reads obsessively from the transcripts of his New York obscenity trial. It makes you grimace with its truth, if not howl with its hilarity. An exhausting but still astonishing experience. FL

Lenny Bruce Without Tears
(Fred Baker, 1972, US) Lenny Bruce, Steve Allen, Malcolm Muggeridge, Kenneth Tynan, Jean Shepard, Mort Sahl, Nat Hentoff.
85 min. b/w.
Lenny Bruce would have hated this film. He would have called it sloppy, both in execution and in feeling. Although it contains some brilliant and excruciatingly funny routines from various stages in Bruce's career (and some interesting interviews), it is linked together by a moralistic continuity, hammered home by Fred Baker's heavy-voiced, humourless narration, concerned to point out how Bruce was driven to his death by a society fighting back against the vision of itself that he revealed. The moral may be true, in part; but it is too simple. Still, careless and sentimentalised as it is, the film is well worth seeing for every frame of Bruce (except the truly obscene final shots). MH

Lenny Live and Unleashed
(Andy Harries, 1989, GB) Lenny Henry, Robbie Coltrane, Jeff Beck, Fred Dread Band.
97 min.
It takes a truck-load of ego and one hell of a track record to take on 90 minutes of one-person stand-up comedy on the big screen. Richard Pryor, Eddie Murphy and Steve Martin can do it, and here Lenny Henry fulfils his aspirations to be fourth on the list with relative ease. In the Hackney Empire, Lenny keeps the live audience on their toes with a script devised by himself and his long-standing writing partner Kim Fuller. Tried and tested favourites Delbert Wilkins, Deakus and Theophilus P Wildebeeste are all pulled out of the trunk, as well as a less exposed character, blues singer Hound Dog Smith. Henry has successfully overridden the criticisms of black stereotyping (simply by ignoring the issue), but there's never been any debate over his skills as an impersonator; and here he excels as he miraculously transforms himself into mirror images of Pryor, Murphy and Martin. IA

Léolo
(Jean-Claude Lauzon, 1992, Can) Ginette Reno, Pierre Bourgault, Maxime Collin, Julien Guiomar, Giuditta del Vecchio.
107 min.
Léo is no ordinary child. Convinced that his mother was impregnated by an Italian tomato, the French-Canadian boy insists on being called Léolo; disturbed by the lunatic behaviour of his father, sisters and brother, he finds refuge in his imagination and sexual fantasy. Director-writer Lauzon pulls off a bold fusion of the mystical and the macabre. Bleak humour combines with images of startling richness; heightened by Richard Grégoire's evocative score, hallucinatory passages conjure a very real sense of childhood isolation. Dark, disturbing and utterly compelling, this is coming-of-age as the stuff of nightmare. CM

Leon (aka The Professional)
(Luc Besson, 1994, Fr) Jean Reno, Gary Oldman, Natalie Portman, Danny Aiello, Peter Appel, Michael Badalucco.
110 min.
Besson's first American movie begins promisingly with a stylish action sequence, but goes off the rails. Hitman Leon (Reno) lives in isolation in his starkly appointed New York apartment, but when a neighbouring family is massacred by corrupt cop Stansfield (Oldman) and his thugs, he becomes reluctant protector of 12-year-old Mathilda (Portman), who asks him to instruct her in the art of killing. Initial wariness between the two turns to something warmer, mutually affecting and sentimental. If this sounds familiar that's because it's so reminiscent of (but nowhere near as good as) *Gloria*. Leaving aside the question of paedophilia, the film is devoid of subtlety. Reno brings a likeably naive, quiet panache to his role; Portman is overbearingly cute and sassy; and Oldman is hammy. Besson fails to make much of New York's visual potential, and lazily asks that Leon's expertise be taken on trust. The shallowness was to be expected; the slackness is surprising. GA

Leone Have Sept Cabecas, Der

see Lion Has Seven Heads, The

Leon Morin, Priest (Léon Morin, Prêtre)

(Jean-Pierre Melville, 1961, Fr/It) Jean-Paul Belmondo, Emmanuelle Riva, Irène Tunc, Nicole Mirel, Howard Vernon, Marielle Gozzi, Patricia Gozzi.
117 min. b/w.
Melville's extraordinary excursion into Bressonian territory, set in a provincial town during the World War II German Occupation of France. With perfect formal control and an extreme emotional intensity, he forges links between the disparate themes of the Occupation, profane love, and spiritual quest. Superb performances from Belmondo as the priest with radical ideas and an eye for the women; and from Emmanuelle Riva as the young girl who, like her town, surrenders to an alien force – she is quite literally invaded by God. In exactly the same fashion as his priest, Melville uses the barest of material assets, but maximum emotional and metaphysical toughness, to inveigle the most sceptical of observers into acknowledging the operation of divine grace. With the Liberation comes a concomitant slackening of intensity; then detachment, loss, and the conclusion that even God has a sense of irony. Miraculous cinema, even for heretics. CPea

Leon the Pig Farmer

(Gary Sinyor/Vadim Jean, 1992, GB) Mark Frankel, Janet Suzman, Brian Glover, Connie Booth, David De Keyser, Maryam D'Abo, Gina Bellman, Annette Crosbie, Bernard Bresslaw.
104 min.
A polished low-budget effort, this derives its laughs from the confusion that blights a Jewish boy (Frankel) who discovers that he's the product of early experiments in artificial insemination; his biological father is not North London net-curtain king Sidney Geller (De Keyser), but one Brian Chadwick (Glover), a far from kosher pig farmer in the Yorkshire Dales. The guilt of it all! Sharply shot, cut and performed, this slight but very smart comedy proffers plenty of wittily absurd lines, a wealth of offbeat visual gags, and more than its fair share of invention. Curiously, however, it seems (for want of a better term) ideologically incoherent, or at least unreadable. Is it for or against the cosy repressions of Jewish family life? Endorsing or guying stereotypes? Are we meant to agree that personal and racial identity are defined primarily by the donor of sperm? Or that the hybridisation of farm animal species is somehow analogous to procreation between humans of different creeds? Still, it's pacy enough for its generous, mostly unsentimental humour to override more serious doubts. GA

Leopard, The (Il Gattopardo)

(Luchino Visconti, 1963, It) Burt Lancaster, Alain Delon, Claudia Cardinale, Paolo Stoppa, Rina Morelli, Serge Reggiani, Romolo Valli, Leslie French, Ivo Garrani, Mario Girotti, Pierre Clémenti.
195 min.
Prince Salina has always been the biggest cat on the block. Guys call him The Leopard. He growls, they shift ass. Now some biscuit-brain named Garibaldi wants to run the whole show from City Hall...Did 20th Century-Fox think this was the movie Visconti sold them back in 1963, the way they hacked, dubbed and reprocessed? At last, 20 years later, we have the original version in a restored Technicolor print, revealing this as one of the finest 'scope movies ever made, and Visconti's most personal meditation on history: muscular in its script, which deals with the declining fortunes of a Sicilian aristocratic clan under the *Risorgimento*, vigorous in performance, and sensuous in direction, changing moods through subtle shifts of lighting to give a palpable sense of the place and the hour. Lancaster, in the first of his great patrician roles, is superb; the rest of the players, right down to the hundreds of extras in the justly celebrated ball scene, are flawlessly cast, each of them living a moment of history for which Visconti, Marxist aristocrat himself, privately sorrowed. MA

Leopard in the Snow

(Gerry O'Hara, 1977, GB/Can) Susan Penhaligon, Keir Dullea, Jeremy Kemp, Billie Whitelaw, Kenneth More, Yvonne Manners.
94 min.
From the moment Susan Penhaligon is rescued from a dangerous blizzard in the Cumberland fells by a limping and morose racing driver (Dullea) out for a walk with his pet leopard, addicts of the Mills & Boon publishing formula will know they're on safe ground. There is the usual deft substitution of anger for sex ('You're so twisted,' cries Susan, in tears), and the careful manipulation of a colourless fiancé figure. It's fortunate that the film takes itself so seriously, since the poker-faced approach helps to define and dilute the blatant sexism of the formula. Alternatively funny or disarmingly old-fashioned. DP

Leopard Man, The

(Jacques Tourneur, 1943, US) Dennis O'Keefe, Margo, Jean Brooks, Isabel Jewell, James Bell, Margaret Landry, Abner Biberman, Ben Bard.
66 min. b/w.
Last of the three films with which Jacques Tourneur got producer Val Lewton's series of low-budget horrors at RKO off to a marvellous start, based on Cornell Woolrich's novel *Black Alibi*. Is it the leopard from a travelling zoo which has escaped after a publicity stunt, or something more sinister wreaking havoc in the Mexican border town? This slim question is transformed by Tourneur's fluent and expressive use of shadows into a stylistic tour de force. A film for lovers of pools of darkness. PH

Leo the Last

(John Boorman, 1969, GB) Marcello Mastroianni, Billie Whitelaw, Calvin Lockhart, Glenna Forster-Jones, Graham Crowden, Gwen Ffrangcon-Davies.
104 min.
Boorman's brief return to Britain, after *Point Blank* and *Hell in the Pacific* and before *Deliverance*, produced this calculatedly bizarre art movie that won him the best director award at Cannes and met with zero commercial success. A surreal vision of Notting Hill culture clash, between Mastroianni's reclusive, convalescent aristocrat and his variously deprived neighbours, it takes place in some impossible overground extension of Turner's basement from *Performance*, and yet assumes the visual and intellectual contours of a down-to-earth, contemporary *Zardoz*, by turns insightful and infuriating as it intervenes in 'social problem' areas armed only with precarious fantasy. PT

Lepke

(Menahem Golan, 1974, US) Tony Curtis, Anjanette Comer, Michael Callan, Warren Berlinger, Gianni Russo, Vic Tayback, Milton Berle.
110 min.
Weighty and uninspired attempt to do a Jewish *Godfather* that makes nothing at all of its promising material: the rise of the Syndicate and Murder Inc, and the subtle change of tack (to a corporate business ethic and image) under pressure from the clean-up campaigns of the late '30s and early '40s. VG

Les Girls

(George Cukor, 1957, US) Gene Kelly, Kay Kendall, Mitzi Gaynor, Taina Elg, Jacques Bergerac, Leslie Phillips.
114 min.
A delight to match that other Cukor musical, *A Star is Born*. With a fine score by Cole Porter, and Kelly performing some marvellous dances, it works as a highly entertaining piece of entertainment. But there is, as in the earlier film, an interesting dramatic idea: here, it's a *Rashomon*-style look at the romantic accomplishments of philanderer Kelly, seen in flashback through the eyes of three women. Great photography, too, from Robert Surtees. GA

Les Misérables

(Richard Boleslawski, 1935, US) Fredric March, Charles Laughton, Cedric Hardwicke, Rochelle Hudson, Jessie Ralph, Frances Drake, John Beal, Florence Eldridge.
109 min. b/w.
Fredric March may take the central role of Valjean, but it is Laughton's stunning performance as the sadistic Javert that really sticks in the mind. As the ruthless nemesis who hounds Valjean, from his youthful days as a galley-slave convicted for stealing bread through to respectable, wealthy middle-age, Laughton convinces with a panoply of controlled sneers, leers and ingratiating gulps, while providing the character – devoted to the law rather than to justice – with touching, credible undertones of shame and frustration. Despite occasional incursions of Hollywoodian sentimentality, the film is still perhaps the best screen version of Victor Hugo's harrowing epic of social conscience, strong on period atmosphere and endowed with fine performances. GA

Les Miserables

(Lewis Milestone, 1952, US) Michael Rennie, Robert Newton, Debra Paget, Sylvia Sidney, Edmund Gwenn, James Robertson Justice, Cameron Mitchell, Elsa Lanchester, Florence Bates.
104 min. b/w.
Rennie's Valjean is a stormy Biblical prophet (in the chiselled cinematic manner), while Newton's Javert is a puffed-up turkeycock always, it seems, about to burst his buttons. Neither the escaped convict nor the 'imprisoned' policeman holds back. In the end, however, the honours go to Newton. He knows when to lay aside the bluster and movingly touch in the details which make his character pitiable. This lavish and very carefully mounted version of Hugo's novel was scripted by Richard Murphy for Fox; it's well acted by a roster of star secondary players, all of whom rise to the dignity of the proceedings, and was shot in rich, chiaroscuro b/w by Joseph LaShelle. Notable finale in the Paris sewers; but, regrettably, somewhat lacking in passionate conviction. JPy

Les Patterson Saves the World

(George Miller, 1987, Aust) Barry Humphries, Pamela Stephenson, Thaao Penghlis, Andrew Clarke, Henri Szeps, Hugh Keays-Byrne.
94 min.
Sir Leslie Patterson, KBE – Australia's putrescent Cultural Attaché, the man who made the meat pie a fashion accessory – is one of the great comic creations of the last decade. Better, though, to chew one's foot off than spend more than ten minutes in the bugger's company, especially by way of this grotesquely charmless film, entirely devoid of mirth, wit or style. The plot is a shotgun wedding of the *Carry On Follow That Camel* with those ropey James Coburn 'spy comedies from the '60s: bad enough, but worse when the deadly virus threatening the world is a dead ringer for AIDS. Worse yet, the director is not George *Mad Max* Miller but a namesake who should be occluding dental cavities in Moonee Ponds. DAt

Lessons in Darkness (Lektionen in Finsternis)

(Werner Herzog, 1992, Fr/Ger)
52 min.
After the Gulf War, Herzog and cameraman/co-producer Paul Berriff travelled to Kuwait. What they found in the sand, besides bones, craters, rusting military debris and the shattered shells of buildings, was a blazing inferno. The bleak landscape on view was even more dramatic than the wreckage Herzog had shot in the Sahara for *Fata Morgana* (1971); small wonder, then, that as an accompaniment to the images, instead of the (ironic) creation myth he used for the earlier film, he concocted a 'narrative' to point up the apocalyptic aspects of Saddam Hussein's conflagration. The result, in 13 'chapters', is an evocation of hell on earth. Massive towers of flame and billowing black smoke transform the desert into a surreal, expressionist nightmare-world; Kuwaitis turn shocked, saddened eyes to the camera, without recrimination; fire fighters appear to be involved in bizarre, primeval rituals as they go silently about their seemingly ineffectual work. Herzog's own hushed, awestruck voice intones the poetic narration, while the likes of Wagner, Mahler, Verdi and Pärt are enlisted to furnish an epic, elegaic musical backdrop. GA

Let's Do It Again

(Sidney Poitier, 1975, US) Sidney Poitier, Bill
Cosby, Calvin Lockhart, John Amos, Denise
Nicholas, Lee Chamberlain, Jimmy Walker.
113 min.
A follow-up to *Uptown Saturday Night*, with the
acidic touches reduced to broad, Disney-like comedy. Poitier and Cosby raise money, for an organisation that bears a closer resemblance to the Elks
than the Black Muslims, by good-humouredly fixing and betting on a couple of boxing matches.
Blaxploitation 'family entertainment' with a few
genuinely funny moments. PH

Let's Get Laid!

(James Kenelm Clarke, 1977, US) Fiona
Richmond, Robin Askwith, Anthony Steel,
Graham Stark, Linda Hayden, Roland Curram,
Tony Haygarth.
96 min.
If there's anything even vaguely surprising about
this would-be comedy-thriller set in post-war
London, it's how unbelievably old-fashioned it is,
as if the geriatric former patrons of the Windmill
were being offered one last, far from great prick-
tease this side of the Reaper. The equine Ms
Richmond displays the acting abilities of a chair
and two of the most suspiciously buoyant sachets
of flesh this side of Sainsbury's. It's like a George
Formby movie with tits. GD

Let's Get Lost

(Bruce Weber, 1988, US) Chet Baker, Carol
Baker, Vera Baker, Paul Baker, Dean Baker,
Missy Baker, Dick Bock, William Claxton, Jack
Sheldon, Cherry Vanilla.
120 min. b/w.
Weber's documentary on jazz-trumpeter Chet
Baker collects an impressive number of witnesses to his con-man charm and unreliability. None
of his ex-wives finds much good to say about him
– he was bad, he was trouble, and he was beautiful – and his children scarcely knew him. Even
his Oklahoman mother takes the Fifth.
Everybody wanted to save Chet, but Chet just
wanted to get lost, and he evaporated from all
responsibilities when his habit took over. Just
about the only constant love affair over the years
was with the camera, from image-making West
Coast photographer William Claxton in the '50s
to Weber himself. The contemporary Chet in
interview takes evasive action in a zonked Bertie
Woosterish sort of way, and sings forlorn ballads
in an exhausted voice. Pity there isn't any footage
of Chet's trumpet heyday, but there are rare
extracts from terrible movies like *Hell's Horizon*
and *Love At First Sight* BC.

Let's Hope It's a Girl
(Speriamo che sia Femmina)

(Mario Monicelli, 1985, It/Fr) Liv Ullmann,
Catherine Deneuve, Giuliana De Sio, Philippe
Noiret, Giuliano Gemma, Bernard Blier,
Stefania Sandrelli.
119 min.
Men are the butt of the jokes in this gently humorous homage to sisterhood. Count Leonardo
(Noiret) returns to his ex-wife Elena (Ullmann) at
their run-down country estate with a hare-
brained scheme to turn the stables into a spa. The
plan is pipped by the Count's death, for which
senile Uncle Gugo (Blier, timing his comic bumbling impeccably) is largely responsible. Their
home threatened by bankruptcy, the female members of the household look to men for security.
But the men create more problems than they
resolve, and soon the women are scampering
back to the domestic bliss of the farmhouse,
where the mentally defused Gugo is the only tolerable male presence. It's a raggedy plot which
tries to cover too much ground; but Monicelli's
touch sets a heartening tone, and the dialogue,
though slight, carries some delightfully barbed
perceptions. EP

Let's Make Love

(George Cukor, 1960, US) Yves Montand,
Marilyn Monroe, Tony Randall, Wilfrid Hyde-
White, Frankie Vaughan, David Burns.
118 min.
A rambling romance in a backstage musical setting, with Montand as a stuffy millionaire determined to take legal action against a little revue in
which he is lampooned – until he meets Monroe.
She, starring in the show and believing him to be

an out-of-work actor, gets him a job impersonating himself; and he, trying to make good, hires
the best (Bing Crosby, Gene Kelly and Milton
Berle in cameos) to give him a showbiz polish.
The teaming of Monroe and Montand works like
a charm (the love affair was real, and you feel it),
and Cukor contrives to lend the whole thing a
witty sense of enchantment that isn't really there.
Not so much a good film as a delightful experience, with one moment of true magic: Marilyn
making her stage entrance down a fireman's pole
and purring her way into Cole Porter's 'My Heart
Belongs to Daddy'. TM

Let's Spend the Night
Together (aka Time Is
on Our Side)

(Hal Ashby, 1982, US) The Rolling Stones.
94 min.
An account of three gigs, filmed during the Stones'
1981 American tour, that rarely strays beyond the
confines of the vast stages. There's no attempt to
penetrate the carefully constructed cliché images
of 20 years – the monkishly-tonsured backroom
boy Watts, the phlegmatic Wyman, and Jagger's
posturing posterior are all present and correct.
Although one may mourn the lost opportunity to
say something about the Stones other than that
they are twenty years older than they were twenty years ago (cue 'Time Is on My Side'), a Stones
concert is still worthwhile entertainment. The
sound is of high quality, the music is as you'd
expect, and some of the helicopter shots are a
wheeze; but the relevance of those newsreel clips
of burning Buddhists and headless soldiers is
dubious – this is not Woodstock, even though
Ashby obviously wishes it was. FL

Lethal Weapon

(Richard Donner, 1987, US) Mel Gibson, Danny
Glover, Gary Busey, Mitchell Ryan, Tom
Atkins, Darlene Love, Traci Wolfe.
109 min.
In this classy all-action thriller, Mel Gibson oozes
charm the way his victims ooze blood. As a
Vietvet-turned-cop, his only talent is for killing:
since his wife's death in a road accident, he's
known to his LAPD colleagues as a man with a
death wish. After a Kim Basinger lookalike walks
off the top of a multi-storey block, investigating
detective Glover – a family man, just turned 50
and keen to see 51 – is given the dubious pleasure
of having Gibson as his new partner. However,
he soon comes to appreciate the virtues of having this 'lethal weapon' at his side when the two
unlikely buddies are faced with a murderous
gang of ex-CIA trained killers running a massive
drugs syndicate. Stylish and brutally violent, the
film escapes the usual clichés of the ex-soldier
fighting a war back home by virtue of Gibson's
blue-eyed smile. CB

Lethal Weapon 2

(Richard Donner, 1989, US) Mel Gibson, Danny
Glover, Joe Pesci, Joss Ackland, Derrick
O'Connor, Patsy Kensit, Darlene Love, Traci
Wolfe, Steve Kahan.
114 min.
This wastes no time in assuring fans that Martin
Riggs still loves getting involved in crazy things.
A high-speed chase, explosive crash and helicopter rescue all slot neatly into the opening ten
minutes. The villains are South African diplomats who run a lucrative drugs syndicate, and
it's up to Riggs (Gibson) and his long-suffering
partner Murtaugh (Glover) to throw away the
rule books and bring justice to bear. Various
trademarks of the original are repeated,
notablythe violence and the grudging affection
between the mis-matched partners. Indeed, in this
sequel their friendship has been enhanced, with
Riggs virtually a member of Murtaugh's family.
Joe Pesci makes a welcome appearance, albeit in
a silly role as a bumbling accountant who has
laundered narcotics money. By concentrating on
the often frustrating, funny relationship between
the three men, the film gains in humour but loses
some of the momentum and panache which distinguished the original. CM

Lethal Weapon 3

(Richard Donner, 1992, US) Mel Gibson, Danny
Glover, Joe Pesci, Rene Russo, Stuart Wilson,
Steve Kahan, Darlene Love, Traci Wolfe,
Gregory Millar, Damon Hines.
118 min.

This excels in the fast-paced action sequences
more than in the sometimes over-developed
buddy-gag exchanges between Gibson's manic
cop Riggs and Glover's dependable Murtaugh. An
example comes early on: Murtaugh, a perilous
week away from retirement, and Riggs, carefree
as ever, bypass the bomb squad and contrive to
blow up an entire skyscraper office block, a spectacular destructive orgasm which isn't aided by
rather crass dialogue. Following on from this is a
set-to on an ice-hockey rink, a hair-raising chase
between two speeding security vehicles, and some
typically vicious violence. Though Gibson gets a
martial arts girlfriend (Russo), Murtaugh has
asked the crazed Leo Getz (Pesci) to sell his house,
and the plot occasionally touches on the stuff of
the LA riots, what this sequel delivers is still the
kind of high-speed roller-coaster action that producer Joel Silver's films often do so well. SGr

Let Him Have It

(Peter Medak, 1991, GB) Chris Eccleston, Paul
Reynolds, Tom Courtenay, Tom Bell, Eileen
Atkins, Clare Holman, Mark McGann, Michael
Gough, Ronald Fraser, James Villiers, Clive
Revill, Michael Elphick, Murray Melvin.
115 min.
Nearly 40 years after his execution, the case of
Derek Bentley – backward, epileptic, and hanged
for a shooting committed by someone else – looks
unlikely to be shut away in the drawer of history. Medak's first film since *The Krays* shares a
concern for post-war London low-life, justice, and
– on the downside – a preoccupation with early
yoof-culture and a too gangsterish treatment of
sordid crimes. On November 2, 1952, Bentley and
his under-age mentor in criminality, Chris Craig,
were caught on the roof of a Croydon warehouse
by police, one of whom was fatally shot by 16-
year-old Craig after Bentley had uttered the
ambiguous words, 'Let him have it, Chris'.
Medak's film is an angry story told with great
force by very fine actors: notably, Courtenay as
Bentley's decently impotent dad, Atkins as his
tortured mother, Reynolds as the yobbish Craig,
and Eccleston's doomed Derek, rising manfully
to a climax that will leave only the heartless without need of a hanky. SGr

Let It Be

(Michael Lindsay-Hogg, 1970, GB) The
Beatles, Yoko Ono.
81 min.
A *cinéma-vérité* documentary of the Beatles at
work. The sycophancy of the direction notwithstanding, this survives as a fascinating record of
both the Beatles' collapse and their unending
power over their audience (us). After an hour in
which one watches the Fab Four bickering and
disintegrating before our eyes, almost magically
they reform and take us back to happier times
with their impromptu concert on the Apple
rooftop. PH

Let It Ride

(Joe Pytka, 1989, US) Richard Dreyfuss, Teri
Garr, David Johansen, Jennifer Tilly, Allen
Garfield, Mary Woronov, Robbie Coltrane.
86 min.
Although a straight-to-video special in Britain,
this quirky farce has its moments and the often
underrated Dreyfuss makes the most of them.
The plot is ripped off from an old *Bilko* episode:
a compulsive gambler has the luckiest day of his
life at the track – suddenly he can't lose – but he's
soon to find that hitting the jackpot doesn't necessarily make him any happier. One to ponder
when you shell out your weekly lottery stake.
Adapted by Nancy Dowd, under the name Ernest
Morton, from the novel *Good Vibes* by Jay
Cronley. TJ

Letter, The

(William Wyler, 1940, US) Bette Davis, Herbert
Marshall, James Stephenson, Frieda Inescort,
Gale Sondergaard, Sen Yung, Cecil Kellaway,
Bruce Lester.
95 min. b/w.
A superbly crafted melodrama, even if it never
manages to top the moody montage with which it
opens – moon scudding behind clouds, rubber
dripping from a tree, coolies dozing in the compound, a startled cockatoo – as a shot rings out, a
man staggers out onto the verandah, and Davis
follows to empty her gun grimly into his body. The
contrivance evident in Maugham's play during the

investigation and trial that follow is kept firmly at bay by Wyler's technical expertise and terrific performances (not just Davis, but Stephenson as her conscience-ridden lawyer), although Maugham's cynical thesis about the hypocrisies of colonial justice is rather undercut by the addition of a pusillanimous finale in which Davis gets her comeuppance at private hands. A pity, too, that Tony Gaudio's camerawork, almost worthy of Sternberg in its evocation of sultry Singapore nights and cool gin slings, is not matched by natural sounds (on the soundtrack Max Steiner's score does a lot of busy underlining). TM

Letter for an Angel (Surat Untuk Bidadari)

(Garin Nugroho 1994, Indon) Nurul Arifin, Aoi Furdi, Windy, Viva Westi.
118 min.
Nugroho is the one director in Indonesian cinema who is challenging taboos and opening up new ground, and so it's a pity that his movies lack for mal rigour and lapse so easily into vacuous pictorialism. Nine-year-old Lewa, motherless since infancy, but deeply attracted to his horse, writes regular letters to an angel about his problems; these include a local feud between villages, the deaths of his father and a family friend, and a suspicion that a poster of Madonna might represent his missing mother. Nugroho focuses on a tribal community caught between tradition and strong influences from outside, but loses grip when he drifts off into dime-store surrealist interludes, indulges in cheap-shot satire and gets fixated on colourful/bloody ethnic rituals. TR

Letter from an Unknown Woman (100)

(Max Ophüls, 1948, US) Joan Fontaine, Louis Jourdan, Mady Christians, Marcel Journet, Art Smith.
90 min. b/w.
Of all the cinema's fables of doomed love, none is more piercing than this. Fontaine nurses an undeclared childhood crush on her next-door neighbour, a concert pianist (Jourdan); much later, he adds her to his long list of conquests, makes her pregnant – and forgets all about her. Ophüls' endlessly elaborate camera movements, forever circling the characters or co-opting them into larger designs, expose the impasse with hallucinatory clarity: we see how these people see each other and why they are hopelessly, inextricably stuck. TR

Letters from a Dead Man (Pisma Myortvovo Chelovyeka)

(Konstantin Lopushansky, 1986, USSR) Rolan Bikov, I Riklin, V Mikhailov, A Sabinin, N Gryakalova.
87 min.
This parable of the last days of civilisation as we know it takes place mostly underground, as the survivors of what seems to have been an accidental missile exchange wait for each other to die. The letters of the title are interior monologues by an elderly scientist (Bikov), addressed to the son he knows must have perished amid the briefly glimpsed devastation on the surface. What is most remarkable to find in a Soviet film, apart from the resolutely unpartisan pessimism, is a clear religious thread. The band of silent children who represent the hope of the future are initially in the care of a priest, before the dying scientist takes upon himself their salvation. Old hands will detect shades of Tarkovsky in this; in fact, Lopushansky was assistant on *Stalker*. It may not be a masterpiece – it's often static and rhetorical – but it is a humane and timely film, and few will resist the sheer emotion of its ending. IC

Letters from the East

(Andrew Grieve, 1995, GB/Ger/Fin/Swe) Ewa Fröling, Mark Womack, Ingeborga Dapkunaite, Märta Laurent, Rein Oja, Mikk Mikiver.
107 min.
Writer/director Grieve's story of self-discovery and self-determination in occupied Estonia is a worthy take on recent Estonian history, personal and national. With a timespan book-ending 45 years of Soviet occupation, the story cuts between the 1944 exodus of thousands of refugees before the advancing Red Army, and the strengthening of the national independence movement in 1989.

In the latter year, London-based cellist Anna (Fröling) discovers among her late father's effects photographs and correspondence from Estonia which stoke her curiosity about the real fate of her mother, supposedly a casualty of the family's flight from the country when Anna was eight. Had her father been hiding something? Against advice, she returns to her birthplace; led by local film-maker Rein (Womack), she slowly, awkwardly, begins to uncover her heritage against a background of emerging nationhood. With a capable pan-European cast, Grieve's keen eye for a view, Ian McMillan's equally arresting photography, and Dvorak on the soundtrack, this has its virtues; dramatically, however, the film falls down. Anna's investigation typically involves a succession of fruitless and repetitive interviews with obscure locals; and the flashback structure is hackneyed and confusing, never fully convincing us that these are Anna's memories rather than just the film's. NB

Letters to an Unknown Lover (Les Louves)

(Peter Duffell, 1985, GB/Fr) Cherie Lunghi, Yves Beneyton, Mathilda May, Ralph Bates, Andrea Ferréol.
101 min.
Based on a story by Boileau and Narcejac (*Les Diaboliques, Vertigo*), and it shows. In occupied France, an escaped POW pretends to be his dead friend in order to take refuge with two beautiful sisters. But things, inevitably, are not what they seem. Duffell contributes strong atmosphere, disturbing nuances, and wins some fine performances (particularly from Andrea Ferréol), but the thriller aspect (not too far from T*he Beguiled*) could do with tauter direction. Interesting, nevertheless. GA

Letters to Katja

(Amber Production Team, 1994, GB/Fin)
57 min.
Finnish-born photographer Sirkka-Liisa Konttinen (a member of the estimable Amber film collective) returns after two decades in Britain to visit her family in Helsinki and at their country holiday home. Structured as a letter to her daughter (who soon gets bored of the stunning, empty landscapes her mother adores), the film is an impressionistic meditation on exile, nostalgia, nature, nationality and family. Occasionally a little too poetic, but its overall intelligence transcends purely personal concerns. GA

Letter to Brezhnev, A

(Chris Bernard, 1985, US) Alfred Molina, Peter Firth, Margi Clarke, Alexandra Pigg, Tracy Lea.
95 min.
Two girls bus it optimistically into Liverpool one night. One works as a chicken stuffer, the other is unemployed. The former rediscovers the joys of shameless rumpy-pumpy, while the other finds romance in the shape of a Russian sailor. He legs it back to Omsk, leaving matters to be fixed by 'a letter to Brezhnev'. Writer Frank Clarke and director Chris Bernard have made an escapist fantasy of cartoon-like simplicity (the love affair is, at times, ridiculously overblown) but rooted it in realistic observation which is gritty, energetic, and wonderfully funny. Exuberantly performed, the result is seductive – something like Bill Forsyth, except tougher, and taking due mileage from the fact that Liverpool is England's only mythological city. RR

Letter to Jane

(Jean-Luc Godard/Jean-Pierre Gorin, 1972, Fr) voices: Jean-Luc Godard, Jean-Pierre Gorin.
52 min.
This is a detailed, perceptive analysis of a newsphoto which shows Jane Fonda in Vietnam, looking concerned in conversation with some Vietnamese. Godard/Gorin argue very soundly that this emphasis on the concern of the West, through an image of a film star, rather than on the Vietnamese themselves and what they have to say, is only another form of the colonialism which dominates the Third World. The use of film to analyse the ideologies of still images is very effective; but by turning what should be an investigation of the photo into 'a letter to Jane' telling her off for constructing her image, Godard/Gorin fail to engage with the way meanings are constructed in news images (and other media). JWi

Letter to Three Wives, A

(Joseph L Mankiewicz, 1949, US) Kirk Douglas, Ann Sothern, Linda Darnell, Paul Douglas, Jeanne Crain, Jeffrey Lynn, Thelma Ritter, Florence Bates.
103 min. b/w.
Traditional wisdom has Mankiewicz as more writer than director, but consider the marvellously cinematic opening of *A Letter to Three Wives*: shots of a prosperous town and its stately avenues of rich men's houses, all placidly awaiting the start of the country club season, as the venomously honeyed voice of an unseen female narrator (beautifully done by Celeste Holm) begins spinning a web of speculation and suspicion round three married women, shortly to be completed by their receipt of a poisonous letter indicating that the narrator has run away with one of the husbands. With the three wives trapped for the day supervising a children's picnic, flashbacks start exploring their marital worries, perceptively probing sensitive areas of social and cultural unease. Glitteringly funny at one end of the scale (Kirk Douglas and Ann Sothern), dumbly touching at the other (Paul Douglas and Linda Darnell), it's absolutely irresistible. TM

Let the Good Times Roll

(Sid Levin/Robert Abel, 1973, US) Chuck Berry, Little Richard, Fats Domino, Chubby Checker, Bo Diddley, The Shirelles, The Five Satins, Bill Haley and the Comets.
99 min.
Shot in three days at three of Richard Nader's *Rock Revival* productions in the States, this is not the exploitative quickie you might expect but the first attempt to put rock'n'roll culture in some sort of perspective. Using split-screen, the performances at the revival concerts are set against clips of the same artists in the '50s, and against a collage of related fragments: town officials railing against beat music, Nixon appealing to the nation, the Lone Ranger ordering silver bullets, Khrushchev banging the table at the UN. Chuck Berry starts and ends the film (in duet with Bo Diddley: worth the ticket price), the Five Satins revive memories of the Moonglows and the Penguins, the Shirelles show a leg, and even the relatively talent-free interloper from the '60s, Chubby Checker, carries it off acceptably. Minor quibbles aside, the film succeeds totally. JC

Let the People Sing

(John Baxter, 1942, GB) Alastair Sim, Fred Emney, Edward Rigby, Patricia Roc, Oliver Wakefield, Annie Esmond.
105 min. b/w.
John Baxter was the British director probably least patronising and most sympathetic to the working classes and their culture during the '30s and '40s, and even if his films now often seem naïve and simplistic, it's good at least to see an honest and humorous attempt to deal with life outside Mayfair. Less scathing than *Love on the Dole* (his best known film), this adaptation of a JB Priestley novel is a spritely, vaguely Capraesque comedy about a couple of men on the run from the law, turning up in a town where the music hall is threatened with takeover, both by museum-loving dullards and by commerce. The pair join together with the locals to fight the move, while Fred Emney steals the show as a government arbitrator susceptible to the charms of alcohol. GA

Letzte Loch, Das
see Last Hole, The

Letzte Mann, Der
see Last Laugh, The

Leviathan

(George Pan Cosmatos, 1989, US/It) Peter Weller, Richard Crenna, Amanda Pays, Daniel Stern, Ernie Hudson, Michael Carmine, Meg Foster, Lisa Eilbacher, Hector Elizondo.
98 min.
Dear Hollywood: I have this astounding movie idea, so hold on to your hairpieces and picture this: an isolated group of professionals, totally cut off from the world, their deadline fast approaching, happen across an Ancient Enigma…but before they know what's going down, they are cut down to size, violently, one by one. Yeah, I know it sounds kinda like *Alien* and *The Thing*,

but that's the beauty of it, and you haven't heard the clincher. See, it ain't set in space or the Arctic, but in a Studio Preview Theatre! We get the usual motley crew of critics: the ambitious looker who really wants to pen a blockbuster (Amanda Pays could do it); the cynical old hack who is beginning to slip (a role for Richard Crenna, this); the egotist who panics as soon as the blood begins to flow; the standard no-hopers, strictly sfx fodder (we could throw in Ernie Hudson or Daniel Stern); and of course the hero, a lean, silent type who susses the Corporate Conspiracy, destroys the monster, and escapes to tell the world (how about Peter Weller?). Alternatively, you could transpose the situation to a sub-aquatic mining project, call it something imposing like *Leviathan*, and watch all those *DeepStar Six* and *Abyss* punters stay home again. TCh

Level Five
(Chris Marker, 1996, Fr) Catherine Belkhodja, Nagisa Oshima.
106 min.
Level one is reserved for Communists, Catholics, anarchists and the rest. Level two is for those with with a modicum of wit and self-awareness. That's as high as we get – except perhaps in death. Like Marker's masterpiece, *Sunless*, this is an essay film drawing on documentary and fiction techniques (crucially, aspects of correspondence); it uses the future as a conduit to the past – sci-fi as memory – a theme that takes us, naturally, to Japan. The central authorial conceit here is not without problems: Belkhodja interfacing with computer and remote-controlled camera, trying to complete a game which reconstructs the battle of Okinawa, 1945. It's easy to get lost in cyberspace. Marker goes from odd socks to military annihilation in the blink of an eye; he can be too quick to make connections, too indulgent of the muse (a toy parrot comes to mind). Yet the history of Okinawa is fascinating: 150,000 died, one third of the island's population, many by mass suicide (we meet a man who killed his entire family, rather than let them fall to the Yankee demons). Here are the foundations for Hiroshima. If ever there was a film-maker who might come up with a Theory of Everything, it's Marker. TCh

Lewis & Clark & George
(Rod McCall, 1997, US) Dan Gunther, Salvador Xuereb, Rose McGowan, Paul Bartel.
84 min.
This quirky black comedy by writer/director McCall musters more pizzazz than most contemporary crime capers. Lewis (Xuereb) and Clark (Gunther) are escaped convicts criss-crossing the West with a tricky treasure map. Lewis is an illiterate Monty Clift-lookalike with a penchant for mindless violence, Clark a white collar criminal, a useful navigator but an unreliable ally – especially after he bumps into George (Rose McGowan), a mute femme fatale with a poisonous snake in her valise. This is the kind of lark the Jonathans Demme or Kaplan might have dashed off for the drive-in market in the '70s. It both satirises and typifies Texan trailer park culture – there's a funny throwaway bit when Lewis massacres a busload of New York tourists who've come to gawp at the cowboys, and a novel scene involving the consumption of frozen beer. Cult credentials are further enhanced by the reunion of the darkly handsome Xuereb and the voluptuous McGowan from Gregg Araki's little-seen youth classic *The Doom Generation*. This is nothing like as cutting-edge, but it's fun while it lasts. Propelled by a hip, surprisingly eclectic soundtrack by Ben Vaughn, and directed with a dab hand, it isn't a second too long. TCh

Liaisons Dangereuses 1960, Les
(Roger Vadim, 1959, Fr) Jeanne Moreau, Gérard Philipe, Annette Vadim, Jean-Louis Trintignant, Jeanne Valérie, Boris Vian, Gillian Hills, Roger Vadim.
108 min. b/w.
Anyone familiar with the Frears (*Dangerous Liaisons*) and Forman (*Valmont*) versions will immediately see the problem about updating this story. The innocence and lack of guile which the preyed-upon characters must embody is not convincingly available in a contemporary setting and neither, therefore, is the cruelty which exploits those qualities; and Annette Vadim's flight into madness would surely have lacked conviction

even in 1782, when de Laclos was writing. Though this is the weakest of the three adaptations, it does have in Moreau and Philipe the choicest of scheming monsters. The Thelonious Monk score natters on, without discernible relevance; and Vadim himself appears at the start to put us right about men and women, deploying with exquisite negligence his cigarette holder, the overcoat draped around his shoulders. What did all those gorgeous women see in this noodle? BBa

Lianna
(John Sayles, 1982, US) Linda Griffiths, Jane Hallaren, Jon DeVries, Jo Henderson, Jessica Wight MacDonald, Jesse Solomon.
112 min.
Sayles is spokesman for his generation, the babies of the post-war boom who made love and fought their wars within themselves. Their growing pains came late: Lianna (Griffiths) is thirty, married and the mother of two, when she falls in love with Ruth (Hallaren), her night-school teacher. Sayles sympathetically maps the hurricane-like effects of this on Lianna's life – thrown out by her philandering husband, cold-shouldered by her straight friends, stormy scenes with her lover – his sparkling dialogue illuminating every aspect of Lianna's sexuality with a zeal that is almost proselytising. The love scenes are infused with a tender erotic glow that deepens the shadows around the titillation of *Personal Best*, and the comedy in Lianna's post-coital glee as she cruises other women and announces herself as gay to people in launderettes is irresistible. A gem, rough-hewn by Sayles and polished to perfection in peerless performances. FD

Liar
(Jonas Pate/Josh Pate, 1997, US) Tim Roth, Chris Penn, Michael Rooker, Renee Zellweger, Ellen Burstyn, Rosanna Arquette.
102 min.
Deceit, infidelity and murder. Sex, drugs and guns. Obsession, schizophrenia and psychosis. Roth, Penn and Rooker. Yup, another hard-boiled US indie offering. There's a murdered woman (Zellweger), so rich bad boy Roth sits across a polygraph machine from detective Rooker and junior trainee Penn, and tells his story. Then he tells it again. Then he tells another one. Cue flashbacks while we puzzle out what's going on: Roth's character seems to be playing power games with his interrogators, confidence tricks with the lie detector and generally misbehaving, but like everyone else he has his problems, not the least of which is that he's an alcoholic epileptic. There's fun to be had watching the three leads each turning the screw; the knotty flashback structure is handled with some lucidity; and the film often looks striking. Finally, though, the screenplay by twin writer/directors Jonas and Josh Pate fails to unearth any fresh insights into the nature of memory and duplicity. NB

Liar Liar
(Tom Shadyac, 1997, US) Jim Carrey, Maura Tierney, Justin Cooper, Cary Elwes, Anne Haney, Jennifer Tilly, Amanda Donohoe, Swoosie Kurtz.
87 min.
The father of five-year-old Max has missed one too many special occasions through alleged overwork, so when he's not there to see his son blow out the candles, a birthday wish lays down the gauntlet – daddy has to stop telling lies for one day. Since dad's in the legal profession, this obviously complicates matters, but, this being a Jim Carrey vehicle, it also provides the springboard for the usual panoply of elastic twitchery and broad knockabout. The first third of the movie pitches Carrey's aspiring attorney into professional anxieties over a career-making case, the second unleashes a 24-hour truth spell, and the rest is spent on a fairly predictable resolution. Pretty rudimentary, but it keeps Carrey's occasional over-exuberance in check and delivers likeable, effective, but decidedly mainstream comedy. TJ

Libel
(Anthony Asquith, 1959, GB) Dirk Bogarde, Olivia de Havilland, Paul Massie, Robert Morley, Wilfrid Hyde White, Richard Wattis, Millicent Martin, Kenneth Griffith, Richard Dimbleby.
100 min. b/w.

A genteel British courtroom drama, adapted from Edward Wooll's 1934 play. Aristo Bogarde's convenient amnesia prevents him from recalling anything of his life before his flight from a German PoW camp, whereupon Canadian airman Massie reveals to the press that the real baronet died during the escape and, ergo, Bogarde is an imposter. Even spouse de Havilland has her doubts in this fustian and rather creaky piece of plot-heavy fluff. TJ

Libera
(Pappi Corsicato, 1992, It) Iaia Forte, Ninni Bruschetta, Cristina Donadio.
85 min.
First-time director Corsicato has been called Naples' answer to Pedro Almodóvar, a description which might be more accurate if the Italian learned to temper his stylistic exuberance with a sense of overriding purpose. Three stories each swivel round an individual woman's misfortune at the hands of male caprice – two faithless husbands and a dope-addict son – but only the last comes up with a storyline outrageous enough to match the primary colour scheme and off-kilter wit. Here, a plucky news-vendor turns her partner's womanising to profit by taping his activities and selling the results. TJ

Libera Me
(Alain Cavalier, 1993, Fr) Annick Concha, Pierre Concha, Thierry Labelle, Christophe Turrier.
107 min.
An elegant, original and just occasionally irritating oddity, this film – from the director of *Thérèse* – consists entirely of wordless, enigmatic tableaux (many of them close-ups of faces, hands and objects). These slowly coalesce into an elliptical narrative about the spirit of resistance in an authoritarian state given over to imprisonment and torture. It looks, as one might expect, marvellous (though one can't help thinking that it rather aestheticises cruelty), and in the end it's Bressonian, in its focus on essentials, rather than gimmicky. Unlike Bresson's best, however, it remains rather soulless. GA

Liberation of L.B. Jones, The
(William Wyler, 1969, US) Lee J Cobb, Anthony Zerbe, Roscoe Lee Browne, Lola Falana, Lee Majors, Barbara Hershey, Yaphet Kotto, Arch Johnson, Chill Wills.
102 min.
A surprisingly tough-minded adaptation of Jesse Hill Ford's novel of Southern racism, with co-scriptwriter Stirling Silliphant eschewing the easy options of his earlier *In the Heat of the Night* for a grim demonstration of the inadequacies of liberal compromise over the institutional conflicts of class and colour. Wyler's final film, set in Tennessee, finds its catalyst in the divorce action brought by middle class black undertaker Browne, in which a white cop (Zerbe) is named as co-respondent. PT

Libertarias
(Vicente Aranda, 1996, Sp/Bel) Ana Belén, Victoria Abril, Ariadna Gil, Loles Leon, Laura Mañam, Miguel Bosé.
124 min.
Aranda's big number on the Spanish Civil War deserves praise for its feminist perspective on the course of the 1936-7 revolution, when women's liberation was a logical, if hardly well-recognised, constituent of the libertarian ideals that the Spanish working class rose up to assert. Seen through the eyes of Maria (Gil), an initially fragile nun driven into a female militia by the revolution in Barcelona, it also takes a thoroughly circumscribed stance on the role of religion in this history. The film crams and elides both events and characters, and, after a brave start, loses its direction and our involvement – particularly problematic is a sudden final outburst of brutal violence. NB

Libido
(John B Murray/Tim Burstall/David Baker, 1973, Aust) Jack Thompson, Max Gillies, Elke Neidhart, Byron Williams, John Williams.
92 min. b/w.
Three episodes dealing, more or less, with the theme of infidelity. *The Husband*, directed by Murray, is a depressingly flat and unimaginatively shot venture into trendy married life. *The*

Child is a studiously evocative period piece, based on a story by Hal Porter that ends up a direct crib of *The Go-Between*, with no point beyond proving that Tim Burstall can direct with a trace less vulgarity than he showed in *Stork* or *Alvin Purple*. *The Family Man*, written by David Williamson, is the best of the three, managing to at least begin to explore inter-personal tensions and latent sexual aggressions. The women picked up by the appalling male duo (cruising while the wife of one is in hospital giving birth) are drawn in a strongly idiosyncratic way; finally, though, the piece falls clumsily between TV drama, fringe theatre, and Cassavetes-style *cinéma vérité*. A fourth story, written by Thomas Keneally and directed by Fred Schepisi, has been excised. VG

Licence to Kill

(John Glen, 1989, US) Timothy Dalton, Carey Lowell, Robert Davi, Talisa Soto, Anthony Zerbe, Frank McRae, Everett McGill, David Hedison.
133 min.
Not as witty as *The Living Daylights*, but it doesn't let the audience down in the arena of effects, gadgetry, and locations. It even makes muddled concessions towards a feisty Bond girl (Lowell) – one who must prove her sincerity by splitting skulls and fingernails with equal abandon. The plot kicks off with Bond and ex-CIA friend Felix Leiter capturing billionaire drug lord Sanchez (Davi), then deftly parachuting into Leiter's wedding. But Sanchez escapes to exact bloody revenge on Leiter and his bride, leaving Bond with a personal vendetta and a revoked licence to kill. The settings range from the Florida Keys (shark attacks, spectacular aerial rescues, scuba diving) to the fictitious Isthmus City in Latin America. It's all very pacy, with the overly straightforward plotting dimmed but not obscured by the hi-tech effects. CM

License to Drive

(Greg Beeman, 1988, US) Corey Haim, Corey Feldman, Carol Kane, Richard Masur, Heather Graham, Michael Manasseri, Harvey Miller, Nina Siemaszko.
88 min.
Young Corey Haim suffers the ultimate humiliation: he fails his driving test. He's not about to let legal niceties spoil his hot date with Mercedes (Graham), however, so he lies to his parents and borrows grandfather's classic car... Everything you've ever heard about American teenagers, their music, money, fashion sense, their values, and most of all their pin-ups, in one auto-destructive movie. TCh

Lie, The (Mensonge)

(François Margolin, 1992, Fr) Nathalie Baye, Didier Sandre, Hélène Lapiower, Marc Citti, Dominique Besnéhard.
89 min.
Emma (Baye) discovers that she's both pregnant and HIV-positive – then that she was infected by her husband Charles (Sandre), a secret bisexual. Relationships with family and friends become strained as her life begins to disintegrate. Despite worthy intentions, Margolin, on his first time out as director and co-writer, sketches only a bare outline of the issues raised. AO

Liebe der Jeanne Ney, Die

see Love of Jeanne Ney, The

Liebe in Deutschland, Eine

see Love in Germany, A

Liebe ist kälter als der Tod

see Love Is Colder Than Death

Liebelei

(Max Ophüls, 1932, Ger) Wolfgang Liebeneiner, Magda Schneider, Luise Ullrich, Willy Eichberger, Paul Hörbiger, Gustaf Gründgens.
88 min. b/w.
'What is eternity?' a young girl asks her soldier lover. What indeed? As in Ophüls' *Lola Montès*, *La Ronde* and *Madame de...* this early German melodrama – which treats the passionate, whirlwind love affair between a young lieutenant and a shy, sensitive *fräulein* – acknowledges both the liberating joy of love and its sad transience. For humans are never entirely free of their past, and

young Fritz has a skeleton in his closet that makes a mockery of the pair's vows of undying love. Most similar to *Madame de...*, the film may be a little slow and ragged at times, but its final emotional power is undeniably enormous. EA

Liebestraum

(Mike Figgis, 1991, US) Kevin Anderson, Pamela Gidley, Bill Pullman, Kim Novak, Graham Beckel, Zach Grenier, Thomas Kopache, Catherine Hicks, Taina Elg.
113 min.
Figgis' temple-throbbing suspenser is a convoluted tale of lust and jealousy, moodier and more elegiac than his earlier *Internal Affairs*. Nick Kaminsky (Anderson), an architectural journalist, is summoned to the death-bed of the mother he never knew (Novak). Mooching around the unfamiliar town, he meets old friend Paul (Pullman), a property developer about to demolish a unique cast-iron department store, boarded up since a gruesome '50s murder. He becomes obsessed with the fate of the building, which Paul is sworn to destroy, and with Paul's wife Jane (Gidley), a photographer who records the ruin's final hours. And amid all the dust and debris, is a shadowy, malevolent figure who seems bent on harm towards all three. Kaminsky's adventures in the eerie small town have a Lynchian flavour: there's a paunchy, psychotic police chief, a curious doubling of whorehouse and nun scenes, and the final plot gyrations defy analysis. But the performances are great, especially Gidley's innocent and moving *femme fatale*. SFe

Lied für Beko, Ein

see Song for Beko, A

Liens de Sang

see Blood Relatives

Lies

(Ken Wheat/Jim Wheat, 1983, US) Ann Dusenberry, Bruce Davison, Gail Strickland, Clu Gulager, Terence Knox, Bert Remsen, Dick Miller.
100 min.
Out-of-work actress signs up for a very unusual role, and finds herself trapped in every paranoid's favourite nightmare – stuck in a loony bin, unable to convince anyone (except the baddies who put her there) that she's sane. Exciting first half, with a few sparky twists, but the knotty plot unravels into a straight woman-in-periller, with a bozo boyfriend brought on to rescue our hapless heroine as she struggles against the straps of her straitjacket. An amusing little body-in-the-liftshaft sequence, though. AB

Lies My Father Told Me

(Ján Kádar, 1975, Can) Yossi Yadin, Len Birman, Marilyn Lightstone, Jeffrey Lynas, Ted Allan, Barbara Chilcott.
102 min.
A distinctly warm-hearted tale of a Jewish childhood in Montreal in the 1920s. Grandfather, a rag-and-bone man, adheres to the old ways, frowning upon the brash commercial instincts of his son-in-law, and winning the favour of his grandson with his whimsical ways. Some attempt is made to sketch in ghetto life and to draw out a child's emotional reading of an adult world. But too often the film merely begs the audience's indulgence, asking it to register no more than its clucking approval or disapproval. VG

Lies to Live by (Babylon) (Babylon: la paura e la migliore amica dell'uomo)

(Guido Chiesa, 1994, It) Paolo Lorimer, Valeria Milillo, Sophie Bernhard, Bill Sage, Andrea Prodan.
100 min. b/w.
An ambitious effort to evoke the Euro-Angst movies of the '70s this starts with images in blown-up 8mm of the wringing of hands and razor-blades being run across chests, before launching into a story about a disconnected foursome in post-industrial Turin. Francesco (Lorimer) is an ex-hard-left, ex-musician, factory worker married dysfunctionally to university worker Carla (Milillo). She's recently had a fling in the States with the mysterious house detective Charles (Sage, from Hartley's *Simple Men*), who's

visiting Turin, staying at the house of her best friend Gabriella. Francesco falls into a murderous mood. With its mix of political-era Godard, '90s avant-garde anomie and Euro rock, Chiesa's film sets up a series of teasing conundrums about modern urban alienation, dopplegängers, and the like, but manages to leave them all unresolved. Photography by Gherardo Gossi gives the film an interesting surface (mainly composed of abandoned factory interiors and waste lands), but in the end the relentless lack of humour or seeming point make it a disappointing show. WH

Lieu du Crime, Le

see Scene of the Crime, The

Life, The

see Dérobade, La

Life and Death of Colonel Blimp, The 100

(Michael Powell/Emeric Pressburger, 1943, GB) Roger Livesey, Anton Walbrook, Deborah Kerr, John Laurie, Roland Culver, James McKechnie, Ursula Jeans, David Hutcheson.
163 min.
At a time when 'Blimpishness' in the high command was under suspicion as detrimental to the war effort, Powell and Pressburger gave us their own Blimp based on David Low's cartoon character – Major General Clive Wynne-Candy, VC – and back-track over his life, drawing us into sympathy with the prime virtues of honour and chivalry which have transformed him from dashing young spark of the Nineties into crusty old buffer of World War II. Roger Livesey gives us not just a great performance, but a man's whole life: losing his only love (Deborah Kerr) to the German officer (Walbrook) with whom he fought a duel in pre-First War Berlin, then becoming the latter's lifelong friend and protector. Like much of Powell and Pressburger's work, it is a salute to all that is paradoxical about the English; no one else has so well captured their romanticism banked down beneath emotional reticence and honour. And it is marked by an enormous generosity of spirit: in the history of the British cinema there is nothing to touch it. CPea

Life and Extraordinary Adventures of Private Ivan Chonkin, The (Zycie i Niezwklle Przygodv Szeregowea i Wana Czonkina)

(Jiri Menzel, 1994, GB/Fr/It/Czech Republic/Rus) Gennadij Nazarov, Zoya Burjak, Zinovij Gert, Vladimir Ilyin, Valeriy Dubrovin, Alexei Zharkov, Yuri Dubrovin.
111 min.
Menzel takes his sly mastery of the 'cinema of Occupation' to Russia for an adaptation of Vladimir Voinovich's (ex-samizdat) mega-hit novel of WWII. In the circumstances, the result is something of a miracle. The director, who has the average Czech's limited Russian vocabulary, marshals his actors very ably. He'd need to since for most of the movie they run around like chickens. His drill sergeant has Chonkin in mind when, quoting Stalin, he lectures, 'The enemy always seeks out the weakest in the chain.' When, however, the hapless, libidinous private (Nazarov) is dumped on the village of Dead End (renamed Red End), the Collective is seen in its eccentric, individualistic disarray as all weak links. Only young, fat-buttocked postmistress Nyura (Buryak), whom Menzel likes to film from the rear, to show it's a broad comedy, no doubt, proves welcoming, in and out of doors. There are some tougher swipes (the frenzy at the shop when invasion is announced, the pornographic interrogation of an old Jewish man by the NKVD), but mostly it's hayseed farce. Well shot, however, and finely acted. WH

Life and Nothing But (La Vie et rien d'autre)

(Bertrand Tavernier, 1989, Fr) Philippe Noiret, Sabine Azéma, Pascale Vignal, Maurice Barrier, François Perrot, Jean-Paul Dubois, Daniel Russo, Michel Duchaussoy.
134 min.
In 1920 in Northern France, haught Parisienne

Irène (Azéma) and local teacher Alice (Vignal) search, respectively, for the husband and fiancé they have lost in the war. They find themselves thrown on the mercy of the head of the Missing in Action office, Major Dellaplane (Noiret), whose unending efforts to identify the countless dead, shell-shocked and missing are continually being diverted by a military establishment bent on glorifying French courage with a funeral ceremony for the Unknown Soldier. The film focuses on the way these three interact, but in so doing, broaches bureaucratic hypocrisy and corruption, postwar poverty and racism, social inequality and the deceptions of romantic involvement. But it's Tavernier's careful orchestration of his medium that most expressively colours the motifs of solitude, grief and loss. Subtle, fluid camera movements explore grey fields and stark, impeccably designed sets to supply a palpable sense of time and place; unsentimental yet dignified performances (with Noiret outstanding in his hundredth film role) underline the discreet humanism of Tavernier's approach. GA

Life and Times of Allen Ginsberg, The

(Jerry Aronson, 1993, US) Allen Ginsberg, William Burroughs, Hannah Litsky, Eugene Brooks Ginsberg, Ken Kesey.
82 min.
Burroughs, Kerouac, Cassidy, Orlovsky, Huncke – there's amusement to be derived from the respectable Ginsberg family remembering their nice Jewish boy and wondering how he fell in with the wrong crowd. His Russian mother's terror of being trapped led to insanity, and drove him to a conspicuous emancipation. Protest, poetry, drugs: the best quote – 'walking on water wasn't built in a day' – came from Catholic Kerouac on the effects of LSD. Fascinating cultural history. BC

Life and Times of Judge Roy Bean, The

(John Huston, 1972, US) Paul Newman, Jacqueline Bisset, Ava Gardner, Tab Hunter, John Huston, Stacy Keach, Roddy McDowall, Anthony Perkins, Victoria Principal, Anthony Zerbe, Ned Beatty.
124 min.
A beguiling Western, even if the John Milius script got semi-strangled along the way. Hawkish mythmaker extraordinary, Milius saw Judge Bean – outlaw turned self-appointed law-giver – as an embodiment of the ambivalent virtues of the old West: evil but necessary, a robber baron achieving tragic grandeur as 'a man who comes in and builds something and then is discarded by what he built'. As such, he should have had the same outsize dimensions as the Teddy Roosevelt of The Wind and the Lion, but emerges somewhat diminished in Newman's portrayal of a winsome charmer straight out of Butch Cassidy (complete with lyrical interludes and a stickily dreadful song). Playing both ends against the middle, Huston turns it into a rumbustious, episodic lark stuffed with eccentric cameos, but still manages to invest it with his own quizzical attitude to all myths and mythmakers, so that it can be read as an allegory about the capitalistic corruptions of Nixon's America. On the whole, an underrated film. TM

Life and Times of Rosie the Riveter, The

(Connie Field, 1980, US) Lola Weixel, Margaret Wright, Lyn Childs, Gladys Belcher, Wanita Allen.
65 min. b/w & col.
'Do the job HE left behind' the wartime posters urged American women. Connie Fields' documentary explores and exposes the sexual hierarchy of labour operated during (and after) World War II as women quit their homes for the factories while the menfolk did their bit for 'Democracy'. Despite guarantees of continued work for women, the end of the war saw men resume their traditional position in the economy, and women encouraged 'Back to the stove and the marital bed'. Combining propaganda film and newsreel footage – often to hilarious effect – Field contrasts it with recollections from some of the women today in interviews that reveal the extent of sexual and racial discrimination they encountered. Consummately skilful in articulating vital political issues through a strong sense of humour. MA

Life at a Gallop (Cwal)

(Krzysztof Zanussi, 1995, Pol) Maja Komorowska, Bartosz Obuchowicz, Andrzej Zenajch, Karolina Wajda.
104 min.
A young boy arrives in the city to live with his aunt and continue his education. Aunt Idalia (Komorowska) is a determined non-conformist with a passion for riding, not exactly a recreation encouraged in Eastern bloc Europe. She and her renegade old friends seek relief from their drab lives by going for exhilarating gallops in the country. Nothing, not even tanks or stone throwing villagers, puts them off. Zanussi's autobiographical drama unfolds in the Poland of the early 1950s. Although it portrays a grim, bureaucratic society in which even schoolboys denounce each other and every sign of bourgeois individualism is frowned upon, it's also surprisingly witty and uplifting. Magnificently shot, and with an outrageously inventive ending, it belies its director's reputation as a film-maker who privileges ideas over emotions. GM

Life at the Top

(Ted Kotcheff, 1965, GB) Laurence Harvey, Jean Simmons, Honor Blackman, Michael Craig, Donald Wolfit, Margaret Johnston, Allan Cuthbertson, Robert Morley, Nigel Davenport.
117 min. b/w.
John Braine's resistible anti-hero Joe Lampton (Harvey) returns in this lacklustre sequel to Room at the Top for another double-edged demonstration of 'making it', this time in the glossier muck-'n'brass world of the swinging south. A slightly curious outsiders' view of British capital culture comes from resident Canadians Kotcheff and writer Mordecai Richler, but it's no great leap from here to the subsequent routine teleseries, Man at the Top. PH

Life Begins in College (aka The Joy Parade)

(William A Seiter, 1937, US) Ritz Brothers, Joan Davis, Tony Martin, Gloria Stuart, Fred Stone, Nat Pendleton.
94 min. b/w.
Cast for the first time without the bolster of their regular support star Alice Faye, the Ritz Brothers provide their usual second-rank comic fizz as the proprietors of Klassy Kampus Klothes, a firm of college-based tailors eager to help the local football team climb the inter-varsity league tables. It's a typically insubstantial caper with complicated plotting to the fore and the dullest juvenile leads you could imagine. TJ

Lifeboat

(Alfred Hitchcock, 1944, US) Tallulah Bankhead, Walter Slezak, John Hodiak, William Bendix, Hume Cronyn, Henry Hull, Canada Lee, Mary Anderson, Heather Angel.
96 min. b/w.
The setting is confined to a lifeboat in the Atlantic occupied by survivors from a torpedoed passenger-carrying freighter and the commander of the U-Boat responsible (Slezak). The idea was to contrast the singleminded Nazi against democracy's comparatively feeble representatives, but the script, started by Steinbeck and finished by Hitchcock, appears too calculated. It's worth seeing, though, for Hitchcock's handling of actors in a confined setting, which incidentally introduces an elusive sense of size, a perspective that is heightened by much of the film being shot in close or semi-close-up. Half the time you'd swear the lifeboat is enormous. CPe

Lifeforce

(Tobe Hooper, 1985, GB) Steve Railsback, Peter Firth, Frank Finlay, Mathilda May, Patrick Stewart, Michael Gothard, Nicholas Ball.
101 min.
A trio of dormant humanoids is spacelifted from the vicinity of Halley's Comet and brought back to earth. The female's kiss sucks vital energy from humans, turning half London into sex-crazed zombie-vampires who eventually crumble to dust. It is all an irresistible wheeze (based on Colin Wilson's Space Vampires), mixing modish Alien effects with Quatermass and the Pit-style '50s sci-fi dialogue. The overriding fear of female sexuality is so excessive as to be hilarious, and

Londoners will enjoy Chancery Lane being reduced to rubble, and St Paul's emitting a whooshy turquoise jet stream into the stratosphere. AB

Lifeguard

(Daniel Petrie, 1976, US) Sam Elliott, Anne Archer, Stephen Young, Parker Stevenson, Kathleen Quinlan, Steve Burns.
96 min.
Given direction that tends toward the same stolid beefiness as Sam Elliott's over-the-hill-at-thirty lifeguard, this still manages to perform an interesting autopsy on the psyche of the American male. The sub- (and not so sub-) text is homosexual. Heterosexual relationships, infinitely demanding and fraught with chauvinism, pale by comparison with the romantic glow of the male/male encounters; and it's every bit as haunted by the spectral fear of ageing as Death in Venice. A film that can narrow choices down to making a million as a car salesman, or drifting with alternate complacency and anxiety into middle-age as a superannuated beach bum, has something going for it in the way of cumulative obsessiveness. VG

Life in Shadows (Vida en Sombras)

(Lorenzo Llobet Gracia, 1948, Sp) Fernando Fernán Gómez.
Born in a fairground tent during a screening of films by the Lumière brothers, Carlos spends his childhood watching Chaplin, falls in love with his bride-to-be during Thalberg's Romeo and Juliet, abandons his job as critic and documentary-maker when she's killed while he's out filming political riots, and finally finds his faith again after seeing Hitchcock's Rebecca. This semi-autobiographical film, produced on a small budget as part of Spain's 'amateur cinema' movement (yet looking totally professional in execution), deals with a man whose entire life is shaped by and dedicated to the movies...for better and for worse. As it examines the twisted relationship between life and art, it includes enough references to movies to make the likes of Godard, Wenders and De Palma seem relatively uninterested in the history of their chosen medium. But this is no clever academic work: in evoking its hero's obsession for both film and his wife, it predates (appropriately) the Hitchcock of, say, Vertigo, and achieves its emotional power through a fine performance from Gómez, later to become one of Spain's most impressive actors. GA

Life Is a Bed of Roses

see Vie est un Roman, La

Life Is a Dream

see Mémoire des apparences

Life Is All You Get (Das Leben ist eine Baustelle)

(Wolfgang Becker, 1997, Ger) Jürgen Vogel, Christiane Paul, Ricky Tomlinson, Christina Papamichou, Rebecca Hessing, Armin Rohde.
118 min.
Director and co-writer Wolfgang Becker weaves a loose, wry and finally tender tale around Jan (Vogel) and his meandering negotiation of the various people in his life: enigmatic lovers, grown-up drop-outs, washed-up lonely parents, irresponsible (incomprehensible) siblings, drifting immigrants, and men with bad haircuts (for this is Germany). A neater film would have given the script another couple of drafts, but the ill-defined narrative is part of the tentative fly-by-night charm. Being about the quixotic, unpredictable paths to reconstructing a social family, it sees opening up to someone as, in the end, an affirmative act of faith and optimism. NB

Life is a Long Quiet River (La Vie est un long fleuve tranquille)

(Etienne Chatiliez, 1988, Fr) Benoît Magimel, Valerie Lalande, Tara Romer, Jérôme Floc'h, André Wilms, Daniel Gélin, Catherine Hiegel, Christine Pignet, Maurice Mons.
91 min.
Meet the Quesnoys, smugly conscious of their wealth, righteousness and impeccable taste. Meet, too, the Groseilles, a scurvy brood of slobs and

small-time criminals living at the other end of town. Their paths cross when their mutual obstetrician's nurse (and spurned lover) spitefully reveals that she once deliberately swapped the cradles of two new-born babies. Horrified by their son's life to date, the Quesnoys decide to bring Momo (Magimel) into their sheltered fold; the Groseilles agree, for a fee, but don't give a shit about retrieving their Bernadette (Lalande). Momo's habits, however, are deeply ingrained; Bernadette's curiosity about her real parents is aroused; and all hell breaks loose at the Quesnoy mansion. Chatiliez' engaging, anarchic satire on the charmless discretion of the bougeoisie revels in the downfall of the Quesnoys, charting a descent into alcoholism, drugs and easy sex with a wicked logic reminiscent of Bertrand Blier. Nor are the Groseilles glamorised: repression, racism, hypocrisy and greed are rampant. More rigour might have helped, but there is enough beadiness in Chatiliez' first feature to suggest that he may be a talent to watch. GA

Life Is Beautiful
(La Vita è Bella)
(Roberto Benigni, 1997, It) Roberto Benigni, Nicoletta Braschi, Giorgio Cantarini, Marisa Paredes, Horst Buchholz.
114 min.
Audacious but misguided, this determinedly Chaplinesque comic fable starts well enough with the innocent, childlike Guido (Benigni) arriving in a Tuscan town in 1939 to visit his uncle, and courting, in typically eccentric fashion, local teacher Dora (Braschi), whom he manages to seduce away from her Fascist fiancé. So far, so amusing – but then, when the film flashes forward to the couple and their son being sent to a concentration camp, with Guido imaginatively turning events around them into a bizarre child's game in order to protect the boy from the ugly realities of the Holocaust, the whole thing turns sickly, not to say disingenuous (how come the villains are now German rather than Italian?). Well-meaning humanistic 'charm' and a 'poetic' approach to horror (including fuzzy shots of mountains of corpses) are inadequate to the task, and soon bogs down in manipulative and maudlin sentimentality. GA

Life Is Cheap...But Toilet Paper Is Expensive
(Wayne Wang, 1989, US) Cora Miao, Victor Wong.
88 min.
As different from *Dim Sum* as one could possibly imagine, Wang's bizarre look at contemporary Hong Kong is one of the most foul-mouthed, scatological, gorily shocking and relentlessly energetic movies in years. Strung very loosely around an almost non-existent thriller plot, it continually provokes its audience into a reaction, whether it be horror, bewilderment, admiration, or simply hilarity. It is often very, very funny, and its vision of a city on the brink (of change, of an ocean, of complete social and moral breakdown) is wholly plausible. But be warned: this is not easy viewing, and whether it's a seven-minute hand-held camera chase that virtually turns into a kinetic abstract painting, ducks being killed with no pretence at humaneness, or a guy taking a shit while talking to camera, there is no question but that you'll be, shall we say, affected. GA

Life Is Sweet
(Mike Leigh, 1990, GB) Alison Steadman, Jim Broadbent, Claire Skinner, Jane Horrocks, Stephen Rea, Timothy Spall.
103 min.
A splendid follow-up to *High Hopes*, in which Leigh's improvisational method achieves symmetry in the form of two very different chefs and twin daughters who are very different from their indomitably normal parents. Andy (Broadbent), is a good-natured cook with an ambition to run his own business from a disgusting mobile snackbar flogged to him by a drunken mate (Rea), Aubrey (Spall) is a clueless fatty with a desire to be supercool, mastermind of a disastrous venture to bring gourmet cooking to Enfield. Offering such hideous fare as liver in lager and duck in chocolate sauce, Aubrey ropes in Andy's innuendo-prone wife Wendy (Steadman) as a replacement waitress. While the restaurant opening provides narrative focus, Leigh divides his interest between this and the plight of Andy and

Wendy's teenage daughters, one (Skinner) a tomboy plumber, the other (Horrocks) an antisocial anorexic whose only enthusiasms are bulimic binges and casual sex with the aid of a jar of peanut butter. Despite two performances of insufficient conviction (Spall and Horrocks), the film is magnificent, mixing enormous fun with sad, serious subjects: the enterprise rip-off, adolescent despair, parents' lost dreams for their children, role-playing, the gutsy optimism of decent, ordinary humanity (represented by Broadbent and Steadman in two stunningly unflashy performances). SGr

Life Less Ordinary, A
(Danny Boyle, 1997, GB) Ewan McGregor, Cameron Diaz, Holly Hunter, Delroy Lindo, Ian Holm, Dan Hedaya, Ian McNeice, Stanley Tucci, Tony Shalhoub, Maury Chakin.
102 min.
Not a complete write-off, the first US venture by the *Trainspotting* team is still a misfire. A screwball comedy, set in Utah, with a contemporary twist, it aims for a liberating sense of anything goes, but falters on a fantasy element that doesn't play. McGregor is Robert, a whimsical Scot, stuck in a menial job in an American corporation. Sacked, dumped and evicted in the same day, he abducts the boss's daughter Celine (Diaz), who soon takes the kidnapping in hand just to spite her dad. Meanwhile, the private detectives gunning to get her back, Hunter and Lindo, are in fact angels on a mission to ensure the couple fall for each other. Love through jeopardy is their game plan. McGregor is charming, a hopeless soft touch, easily outclassed in the brains department by the mercurial Diaz (a real livewire who jump starts the movie more than once). They make an attractive couple, doing very nicely, thanks, without the Almighty's contrived interventions – gratuitously violent scrapes which lurch the film into forced, mostly unfunny black comedy and even animation. The Coens meet Frank Capra – a mismatch made in heaven. TCh

Life of Chikuzan, The
(Chikuzan Hitori Tabi)
(Kaneto Shindo, 1977, Jap) Chikuzan Takahashi, Ryuzo Hayashi, Nobuko Otowa, Dai Kanai, Yoshie Shimamura, Mitsuko Baisho.
122 min.
Chikuzan Takahashi, in his late sixties at the time of filming, is a blind musician who has spent most of his life on the roads of Northern Japan, earning his living as a *tsugaru shamisen* player. Latterly he acquired a devoted following among Japanese students, which is why Shindo made *The Life of Chikuzan*. The movie opens with Chikuzan himself in concert, then moves into a drama-documentary reconstruction of his early years, from his impoverished parents' desperate attempts to find a livelihood for him to his successful second marriage. Shindo keeps the travelogue elements to a decent minimum, and doesn't shy away from the harshness of Chikuzan's stoicism or lapse into sentimentality. He also chooses incidents with an eye to more than his subject's biography alone. The music, of course, is sublime. TR

Life of Emile Zola, The
(William Dieterle, 1937, US) Paul Muni, Joseph Schildkraut, Gale Sondergaard, Gloria Holden, Donald Crisp, Louis Calhern, Robert Barrat, Erin O'Brien Moore.
116 min. b/w.
Plodding briefly, inaccurately and somewhat risibly through Zola's early career, this solemn biopic improves no end when it gets to its main course: an account of the Dreyfus affair and how the now prosperously ageing Zola rediscovered his youthful ideals in an impassioned fight for justice. Carefully mounted, well directed and acted, but basically the sort of well-meaning pap out of which Oscars are made. TM

Life of Oharu, The
(Saikaku Ichidai Onna)
(Kenji Mizoguchi, 1952, Jap) Kinuyo Tanaka, Tsuki Matsura, Ichiro Sugai, Toshiro Mifune, Tashiaki Konoe, Masao Shinizu.
147 min. b/w.
This chronicle of the decline of a woman, from service in the imperial court of 17th century Japan through exile, concubinage and numerous stages

of prostitution, should further enhance Mizoguchi's reputation as the cinema's greatest ever director of women, and one of the most meticulous craftsmen of the period film. To place too much emphasis on the period setting is misleading, however; for despite the historical distance from feudal Japan, the social evils exposed have an unmistakable contemporary relevance. Feminists should unequivocally applaud the narrative simplicity and the clarity with which the second-class status of women is implicitly questioned almost everywhere in the film. It's also an extremely elegant movie whichever way you look at it: tiny details of movement by the actors, beautiful compositions and photography throughout, single fluid takes often serving to state a whole scene. RM

Life on a String
(Bian Zou Bian Chang)
(Chen Kaige, 1991, China/GB/Ger) Liu Zhongyuan, Huang Lei, Xu Qing, Zhang Zhengyuan, Ma Ling, Zhang Jinzhan, Zhong Ling, Yao Erga.
108 min.
If it's hard occasionally to divine the precise meanings of Kaige's lush, mystical fable, its poetic beauty and overall clarity of purpose are impossible to deny. An old, blind master musician wanders from desert village to desert village, accompanied by his headstrong, likewise afflicted pupil and amanuensis. As a child, the master was promised by his own mentor that when he had finally broken the thousandth string on his *sanxian*, he might open up the instrument and find a prescription to restore his sight. But his teenage apprentice, sceptical of his master's ascetic beliefs, is resolved to lead his own life, and takes up with a village girl against the wishes of both the old man and her family. Chronicling the widening of the gulf between man and boy, Kaige explores the conflicts between age and youth, spirituality and physicality, discipline and disobedience, and – most movingly – the persistence and absence of faith and hope. Rarely have landscapes been photographed so sumptuously; rarely, too, has music in a film been used to such spine-tingling effect. GA

Life Size (Tamaño Natural)
(Luis García Berlanga, 1973, Sp/Fr/It) Michel Piccoli, Valentine Tessier, Rada Rassimov, Claudia Bianchi, Queta Claver, Manolo Alexandre.
100 min.
Piccoli, as a chic dentist, forsakes his 'liberated' but arid marriage for a new love. His job slides as he devotes himself entirely to her; they marry, but soon their bliss becomes contaminated and he tries to kill her...What makes *Life Size* a suitably bizarre project for Piccoli in his running battle with the bourgeoisie is that the object of his affections is a lifelike doll, complete with mucous membranes. Best are the ways in which the film tackles the problems of fantasy in an apparently permissive society, and how the doll takes on a symbolic importance beyond Piccoli's conceptions. Slightly less successful: the running gag of women as living dolls (apart from one extraordinary sequence where Piccoli's wife behaves like one in order to attract him back), and the intimations of social apocalypse at the end. CPe

Lifespan
(Alexander Whitelaw, 1975, US/Neth) Hiram Keller, Tina Aumont, Klaus Kinski, Fons Rademakers, Eric Schneider, Frans Mulders.
85 min.
Though visibly a low-budget Euro-thriller, *Lifespan* is nonetheless lent weight by its ingenious narrative and thematic audacity. In evoking and combining Faustian mythology, the modern pharmaceutical trade, Nazi medical experimentation, and Kinski's demonic search for eternal life, it perversely brings to the 'mad scientist' movie tradition a serious view of research ethics. Its horror resides in the fact of natural death, its questers after immortality working at the point where liberal science and fascist idealism collide in attempts to improve humanity by prolonging life. Its humour is equally unexpected: even what looks like a catchpenny bondage scene has Aumont tied in the knot symbolising DNA. Get past Hiram Keller's woodenness, and this is a bold and intelligent fun-movie. PT

Life Stinks

(Mel Brooks, 1991, US) Mel Brooks, Lesley
Ann Warren, Jeffrey Tambor, Stuart Pankin,
Howard Morris, Rudy De Luca, Teddy Wilson,
Billy Barty, Carmine Caridi.
95 min.
Having spent many fallow years producing sub-
standard slapstick, Brooks here returns to the
message-in-the-madness formula which once
made him great; and if the result is extremely
uneven, it's a huge leap forward from the inanities of *Spaceballs*. Selfish billionaire Goddard Bolt
(Brooks) bets rival Vance Crasswell (Tambor,
superbly slimy) that he can survive a sojourn
communing with the city's homeless.
Temporarily stripped of his wealth and taking to
the streets, Bolt is swiftly swamped by the manic
milieu of urban deprivation. Brooks plays out the
inevitable schmaltzy conclusions with predictably tepid results: Bolt finds true friendship
and love in the midst of misery, and finally turns
the tables on the money-grabbing developers.
More rewardingly, the grim, black humour of
yore sporadically breaks through the glossy
sheen, providing moments of vintage vitriol. MK

Life Story of Baal, The

(Edward Bennett, 1978, GB) Neil Johnston,
Patti Love, Jeff Rawle, Nick Edmett, Dinah
Stabb, Roger Booth.
58 min.
Brecht never produced a fully revised version of
this, his first play, and so the text can be considered fair game for further work. Bennett hasn't
simply filmed it, but has risen to the challenge of
producing a reading of it. Brecht at one level
retains sympathy for Baal; Bennett never does.
He reformulates the play as a powerful critique
of the notion of the artist as a kind of social outlaw, and resolves the sexual, moral and political
issues into urgent, provocative questions. TR

Life Upside-Down

see Vie à l'Envers, La

Life with Father

(Michael Curtiz, 1947, US) William Powell,
Irene Dunne, Jimmy Lydon, Elizabeth Taylor,
Edmund Gwenn, ZaSu Pitts, Martin Milner,
Emma Dunn, Moroni Olsen, Elizabeth Risdon.
118 min.
Clarence Day Jr's tribute to his stern philosophising dad was turned into a play (by Howard
Lindsay and Russell Crouse) that ran for more
than 3,000 performances on Broadway, a record
in its day, so it's no surprise Donald Ogden
Stewart's film adaptation should prove such a
satisfying entertainment. Powell dominates an
episodic collection of domestic vignettes, with
Dunne as the long-suffering wife, young Lydon
the future author, and teenage Taylor the intermittent romance angle. Rudimentary comic
strategies – the old boy's manful resistance to his
belated baptism can only last so long – come up
shining thanks to Powell's neatly judged inscrip-
tion of the reluctant softie behind just so much
self-important bluster and a theory on everything. Curtiz knocks it together without so much
as breaking sweat. TJ

Lift, The (De Lift)

(Dick Maas, 1983, Neth) Huub Stapel, Willeke
Van Ammelrooy, Josine Van Dalsum, Piet
Römer, Gerard Thoolen, Hans Veerman.
99 min.
This confirms all the creeping fears of those of us
who stare glassily at the ceilings of lifts...In a
Dutch high-rise building, one of the elevators suddenly gets a mind of its own, and since it is not
one of those nice, charitably disposed Otis jobs
with open grille-work, it decides to take revenge
on all the sweaty claustrophobes who have been
making its life such an up-and-down misery. The
body count is low to middling for this kind of
thing, although the methods of disposal are ingenious enough to compensate. Unfortunately, the
movie is shafted by confusions of script and execution, neither of which match up to the original
good idea. *The Shining* still holds the field among
the all-too-rare horror films which explore the
notion of an inanimate world exerting its revenge.
CPea

Lift to the Scaffold

see Ascenseur pour l'Echafaud

Light, The

see Brightness

Light Ahead, The (Fishke der Krumme)

(Edgar G Ulmer, 1939, US) Helen Beverly,
David Opatoshu, Yudel Dubinsky, Rosetta
Bialis, Tillie Rabinowitz.
120 min. b/w.
An inside job: made in Yiddish for the American
immigrant Jewish population, this celebrates the
trials and joys of being one of the 'chosen' people,
chosen to suffer, too, it often seemed. Set in a
Chagall-like Russian *shetl* near Odessa, where to
be a Jew was synonymous with being impoverished, the film combines a sentimental love story
– between a lame young man and a beautiful blind
orphan – with a conflict between the working Jews
and the village leaders over the spending of community funds. The two stories are brought together through the character of Reb Mendele, an
avuncular bookseller who spreads hope and wisdom but privately laments in passionate tones the
fate of his people. Ulmer's film touches the well-
springs of both Jewish sentimentality and hardheaded realism, exposing superstition as it praises
true faith and courageous action. MH

Light at the Edge of the World, The

(Kevin Billington, 1971, US/Sp/Liechtenstein)
Kirk Douglas, Yul Brynner, Samantha Eggar,
Jean-Claude Drout, Fernando Rey.
119 min.
1865, off Cape Horn: Lighthouse keeper Douglas
battles old seadog Brynner for the affections of
shipwrecked maiden Eggar in this less than bea-
con-bright international co-production, based on
a Jules Verne novel. Over-enthusiastic performances. TJ

Lighthorsemen, The

(Simon Wincer, 1987, Aust) Peter Phelps, Tony
Bonner, Gary Sweet, John Walton, Tim
McKenzie, Jon Blake, Sigrid Thornton,
Anthony Andrews.
131 min.
An account of a hard-fought World War I victory for the Australian mounted infantry in
Palestine, with details of place and strategy clearly delineated, captions popping up everywhere,
and much pointing at maps by moustachioed
generals. The British were at a stalemate when
the Lighthorse were summoned in 1917 to help
plan an attack on the Turco-German army at the
desert town of Beersheba, site of an 'unlimited'
water supply. A British military intelligence officer (Andrews, a smart Alec with sneering nostrils) sets up a decoy which enables the
Lighthorse to take the town by charging the
enemy artillery cannons; he also forms the link
between the facts and the fictional element. The
plot straddles *Boy's Own* action as represented
by four veterans of Gallipoli who are roped in to
assist Andrews with his undercover activities,
and *Women's Own* love interest as a fresh-faced
recruit (Phelps) discovers he is unable to kill, joins
the medical corps, and falls for a nurse
(Thornton). It's good to look at: plumed hats,
prancing thoroughbreds, and Aussie brute force
shot against the clean desert light. Should appeal
to people who like to play soldiers. EP

Light in the Piazza

(Guy Green, 1961, GB) Olivia de Havilland,
Yvette Mimieux, George Hamilton, Rossano
Brazzi, Isabel Dean, Barry Sullivan.
101 min.
Elizabeth Spencer's baroque, almost Jamesian
novel of New World corruption versus Old World
integrity is brought to the screen in the form of a
'grand tour' of North Italy. In the course of this,
Olivia de Havilland tries to marry off her mental-
ly retarded daughter (Mimieux) to a wealthy
Italian (Hamilton). Sadly, it quickly falls prey to
that most awesome of cinema's horrors – Rossano
Brazzi – as attraction develops between de
Havilland and the boy's father. A terrible film. PH

Lightning Jack

(Simon Wincer, 1994, Aust) Paul Hogan, Cuba
Gooding Jr, Beverly D'Angelo, Kamala
Dawson, Pat Hingle, Frank McRae, Roger
Daltry, Richard Riehle.
114 min.

This film, written by Paul Hogan, is essentially
a straight Western with comic touches. Lightning
Jack Kane (Hogan) is the self-styled sharpest
shooter in the West. Unfortunately, the authorities don't share Jack's high opinion of himself,
and consistently refuse to up the price on his
head. Only when Jack teams up with mute novice
desperado Ben Doyle (Gooding) do things start
going his way. Now, can he get the girl (D'Angelo)
as well? The central conceit, of two outlaws
obsessed by their 'reviews' in the press, is a nice
one, and the interplay between them is at times
mildly amusing. NKe

Lightning Over Water (aka Nick's Movie)

(Nicholas Ray/Wim Wenders, 1980,
WGer/Swe) Nicholas Ray, Wim Wenders,
Susan Ray, Tim Ray, Gerry Bamman,
Ronee Blakley.
91 min.
Fittingly made on very dangerous ground as a
celebratory last testament to an idea(l) of cinema
that died along with Nicholas Ray. Developed
haphazardly over the last two months of Ray's
life, as a roughly improvised collaboration
between the maverick Hollywood veteran and his
German Friend Wenders, it documents rawly but
honestly the paradoxes of lives devoted to conjuring the sort of privileged moments the title
alludes to. Ray, degenerating physically day by
day, sustained by an irrepressible imaginative
vitality; daily striving to reinvent cinema as
Godard long ago predicted he would. Wenders,
at an interim impasse on the protracted production of *Hammett*, constantly doubting his own
methods and motives, unsettled by his own gestures of tribute. Two exiles trying to help each
other find their ways back home, like Robert
Mitchum in *The Lusty Men*. You needn't be
steeped in film lore to appreciate the extraordinary emotions on which all this is strung. Even
with its painful contradictions and discomfitures,
it's that current rarity: one for the heart. PT

Lightning Swords of Death (Kozure Ohkami)

(Kenji Misumi, 1972, Jap) Tomisaburo
Wakayama, Akihiro Tomikawa, Goh Kato,
Yuko Hama, Fumio Watanabe.
83 min.
Originally a popular Japanese comic strip, the
Lone Wolf character in this film is the star of a
whole series of hugely successful features. The
lugubrious and podgy hero travels around, pushing his young son along in a wooden pram, journeying through a Japan where the samurai
tradition has become debased to little more than
a licence to rape and kill. It's the hero's job, of
course, to define the true code in a series of episodic adventures that end in displays of amazing
swordplay. Meanwhile, the kid just looks on. Best
is the climax in which the Lone Wolf is confronted by the Warlord's army, about 200 strong.
What to do? Start with a fusillade of rockets from
the front of the pram (yes, the kid's still sitting in
it), followed by dynamite hand grenades, the
remaining 50-odd dispatched with spears (hidden
in the pram's handles) and of course sword. Tired,
wounded and as glum as at the beginning of the
film, our hero staggers off, still pushing the pram.
One can almost forgive the appalling dubbing.
CPe

Light of Day

(Paul Schrader, 1987, US) Michael J Fox, Gena
Rowlands, Joan Jett, Michael McKean, Thomas
G Waites, Cherry Jones.
107 min.
Joe Rasnick (Fox) works in a factory. In the
evenings he plays in a group called The
Barbusters which also features his sister Patti
(Jett), a rock'n'roll rebel and mother of an illegitimate son. Their mother (Rowlands) has found
the Lord and lost the ability to communicate with
her daughter. When Joe is laid off, the group take
to the road, but Patti's light fingers in a supermarket lead to a further schism, this time with
her brother. More trauma when their mother succumbs to The Big C. What at first seems just
another dreary blue-collar melodrama turns out
to be something infinitely superior. Schrader's
strong sense of place exploits the wintry wastelands of Cleveland, Ohio, and the familiar hallmarks of alienation and resistance to repression
– in this case to religion, rammed home with a

vicious plot twist – compensate for the super-abundance of rancid rock, presumably included to titillate the teenies. The cast make the most of an intelligent script, with Rowlands and (especially) Jett providing most of the emotional punch. They create a powerful feeling of real lives being lived and lost. MS

Lightship, The
(Jerzy Skolimowski, 1985, US) Robert Duvall, Klaus Maria Brandauer, Tom Bower, Robert Costanzo, Badja Djola, William Forsythe, Arliss Howard, Michael Lyndon.
88 min.
Taken from Siegfried Lenz's dour allegorical novella about what you might do if Hitler arrived on your ship, Skolimowski's adaptation mercifully junks the more overt political dimension, and concentrates successfully on the suspense element, with sufficient metaphysical undercurrent for those who want it. Brandauer is the pacifist captain of a rusting lightship, anchored off the coast of Norfolk, Virginia in the '50s. When they rescue a drifting boat, the trio that come aboard prove to be a set of psychos, on the run to a rendezvous with their pickup boat. Their leader, a menacing dandy played by Duvall at his most wilfully extravagant, threatens to set the ship adrift, and backs it up with the cool logic that the devil always presents. Brandauer, however, continues in a kind of dumb, passive resistance. Fortunately, Skolimowski keeps the schematic struggle between good and evil sufficiently well submerged beneath an atmosphere of menace and increasing hostility, as the crew bicker and fall apart under ill-fated attempts at heroism, and Duvall enacts his increasingly bizarre *übermensch* tactics. If it puts you in mind of *Key Largo*, that is no bad thing. CPea

Light Sleeper
(Paul Schrader, 1991, US) Willem Dafoe, Susan Sarandon, Dana Delany, David Clennon, Mary Beth Hurt, Victor Garber, Jane Adams, Paul Jabara.
103 min.
A further instalment in Schrader's on-going study of confused loners, this stylish *film noir* offers yet another take on the possibility of redemption from sin and guilt in the modern world. At 40, John LeTour (Dafoe), an up-market dealer who delivers drugs to chic clubs and apartments, has hit a crisis. His boss (Sarandon) is contemplating trading in her cocaine business for herbal cosmetics; his psychic advisor (Hurt) reckons he's due for a change; and the recently re-encountered love of his life (Delany) fears that he's never quite kicked his own suicidal habit. LeTour needs a push before he can break with the past; but the requisite jolt comes in the shape of a murder. Schrader certainly has his finger on the pulse of the times, and the universally strong performances do ample justice to his sensitive ear for dialogue. But the story meanders, and it echoes *Taxi Driver* and *American Gigolo* so closely that Schrader is working less than fresh variations on over-familiar themes. For all the film's conspicuously adult intelligence, it elicits a disappointing sense of *déjà vu*. GA

Lights of Variety
see Luci del Varietà

Light Years Away
(Alain Tanner, 1981, Fr/Switz) Trevor Howard, Mick Ford, Odile Schmitt, Louis Samier, Joe Pilkington, John Murphy, Mannix Flynn.
107 min.
An abandoned petrol pump in a desolate and beautiful Irish landscape is a curiously encouraging image for the future. The year is 2000, and the central character is an intelligent, tousled vagabond called Jonas (Ford) – the product of those good-hearted socialists who nurtured him in Tanner's earlier *Jonas qui aura 25 ans en l'an 2000*. Forsaking the city, Jonas is drawn to the remote Pallas Garage and its querulous, occasionally uproarious owner Yoshka (Howard). Here, Jonas endures a pointless, arduous apprenticeship (manning the dry pump, polishing the junkheap) before he is initiated into Yoshka's wondrous secret. The themes are large – the wilderness, Icarus, the earth. The film is mysterious without being mystifying or unduly solemn. Clear as mud, in fact, with the compelling logic

of a dream. The real puzzle (though it's not a complaint) is why a politically discursive film-maker like Tanner – here working in English – has taken up this mystic and ritualistic fable. JS

Like a Bride
(Novia que te Vea)
(Guita Schyfter, 1992, Mex) Angelica Aragon, Claudette Maille, Maya Mishalska, Ernesto Laguardia.
115 min.
Having trained with the BBC in London, Schyfter returned to Mexico to make this decently crafted, undeniably sincere and slightly underwhelming portrait of the country's Jewish community. Moving through the decades, the story charts the friendship of an aspiring painter, Oshinica, from a strict Sephardic family of Turkish origin, and her more liberal-thinking pal Riffke, the daughter of refugees from the Holocaust. Spanning the currents of feminism, Zionism and socialism, the two women seek to break free from the roles assigned to them by society. The end result is more arresting as social history than drama, but the careful performances and unusual content make it worthwhile for those with an interest in the subject matter. TJ

Like a Rolling Stone
(Bo no Kanashimi)
(Tatsumi Kumashiro, 1994, Jap) Eiji Okuda, Eiko Nagashima, Reiko Takashima, Haku Ryu.
118 min.
Kumashiro's brilliant last film (based on a hard-boiled novel by Kenzo Kitakata) subverts the yakuza genre by creating a new type of anti-hero. Tanaka (Okuda, previously more associated with worthy social dramas) is a cool, high-ranking yakuza despised by his snobbish boss. Bored by his work, increasingly adrift from his own mental moorings, he debauches the girl from the local florist's shop just to give himself something to do and stitches his own stab wounds just to see what it feels like. The tension between this deeply alienated man and his job yields a film of compulsive, cumulative power, much of it shot in long, real-time takes. TR

Like Father, Like Son
(Rod Daniel, 1987, US) Dudley Moore, Kirk Cameron, Margaret Colin, Catherine Hicks, Patrick O'Neal, Sean Astin, Cami Cooper.
100 min.
A dud movie wrapping Moore's 'kid in a man's body' routine around a convenient age-swap plot. Dad (Moore) is a successful surgeon committed to good medicine for all; son Chris (Cameron) is a raunchy teenage tearaway. Dad wants Chris to follow in his footsteps and do good for others; Chris just wants to get laid. Enter a desert potion that enables 'transference of souls'. Dad drinks it, looks into son's eyes, the souls transfer, and – surprise, surprise – Dad's in Chris's body, and Chris in Dad's. This enables Dudley to play Arthur all over again with his dad's Gold Amex card. Meanwhile Chris turns up at the hospital to take patients' temperatures and shock the starchy surgeon fraternity with snazzy one-liners. The scam would have had a longer lifespan had Moore played true to the character of 16-year-old Chris instead of turning up as some generic 13-year old. As it turns out, Cameron gets most of the laughs. EP

Like Grains of Sand
(Nagisa no Sindbad)
(Ryosuke Hashiguchi, 1995, Jap) Yoshinori Okada, Kota Kusano, Ayumi Hamazaki, Koji Yamaguchi, Kumi Takada, Shizuka Isami.
129 min.
A searing drama of love, compassion and sexual identity, this is the *War and Peace* of high school romances. Shy, sensitive Ito (Okada) yearns for the love of his best friend, but though the straight Yoshida (Kusano) stands by Ito when their classmates realise he's gay, Yoshida cannot – will not – embrace him. It's an audacious, brave film, with strongly developed themes and characters (exceptionally well played by the teenage cast), but the director's narrative grasp is less impressive, and in the end, the search for a big, uncompromising statement shows signs of strain.

Like It Is
(Paul Oremland, 1997, GB) Dani Behr, Roger Daltrey, Ian Rose, Steve Bell.
92 min.
This so-so first feature gets away with casting Behr as a disco diva and Daltrey as an amoral record company boss. Amazingly, it's not camp. Rather, it's a surprisingly touching love story between a Blackpool virgin (Bell) and an up-and-coming producer (Rose) who shows him the ropes in the old smoke. Polished to the point of blandness, but sincere nevertheless. TCh

Likely Lads, The
(Michael Tuchner, 1976, GB) Rodney Bewes, James Bolam, Brigit Forsyth, Mary Tamm, Sheila Fern, Zena Walker.
90 min.
Full credit to writers Dick Clement and Ian La Frenais for trying to open out *The Likely Lads* into a feature-length story, with no need of the TV series as a constant reminder. It works a lot of the time, with a solid background of the lads' sentimental attachment to old Newcastle, and the realities of high-rise flats and married life as they increasingly look their age. And of course the characters and gags (Terry: 'I'd offer you a beer, Bob, but I've only got six cans') are terrific. Brigit Forsyth's Thelma is a genuine monster. Unfortunately, Michael Tuchner's direction is so flat that after about an hour the film does begin to seem like an extended TV special. AN

Like Water for Chocolate
(Como Agua para Chocolate)
(Alfonso Arau, 1991, Mex) Marco Leonardi, Lumi Cavazos, Regina Torne, Ada Carrasco, Yareli Arizmendi, Claudette Maille.
114 min.
Set during the Mexican revolution, this is a women's movie in that it shows the secret face of political events. Of three sisters, Gertrudis (Maille) becomes a general in the revolutionary army; Rosaura (Arizmendi) is married and has children; and the youngest, sweet-faced Tita (Cavazos), who was cheated of the chance to wed, experiences life through the disciplines of the kitchen. It might sound a bit like *Babette's Feast*, except that the rows, rapes, gunfire, ghosts and sex are a million miles from 19th century Denmark. Tita is doomed by tradition to spend her life looking after her ramrod mother (Torne), while her true love (Leonardi) perversely weds Rosaura. Director Arau doesn't linger over laborious cooking and sensual ingredients, perhaps because he has much to cover: 40 years, three generations, love wasted and renewed. Recipes are milestones as the women eat, fantasise and crave. It's overlong, but that reflects the nature of Mexican cooking: like water for chocolate, which must be brought to the boil three times, the characters continually bubble and boil over. SFe

Li'l Abner
(Melvin Frank, 1959, US) Peter Palmer, Leslie Parrish, Stubby Kaye, Howard St John, Stella Stevens, Julie Newmar, Robert Strauss.
113 min.
Having written the book for the Broadway musical based on Al Capp's comic strip featuring the hillbilly world of Dogpatch USA, Panama and Frank did it little service here with a flaccid script, even more flaccid direction, and choreography merely 'based' on Michael Kidd's original. The script, with the inhabitants shaggy-doggily resisting a plan to turn Dogpatch into an atomic testing site, could do with a nuclear blast to liven it up; but the casting is excellent, and the marvellous Johnny Mercer/Gene de Paul songs survive intact. TM

Lilac Domino, The
(Fred Zelnik, 1937, GB) June Knight, Michael Bartlett, Athene Seyler, Richard Dolman, SZ Sakall, Fred Emney, Joan Hickson.
79 min. b/w.
Hungarian fun and games perpetrated on an unsuspecting populace by Max Schach, the endearing little Viennese expatriate who charmed £2 million out of the City to make the most exhilaratingly awful extravaganzas in the history of cinema. This one involves a dashing cavalryman hero, a school-girl heiress heroine – afflicted with a neurotic need to sing and dance even when they're on the telephone – stuffed donkeys, mad

waiters, and myriads of satin-pyjama-clad star-lets. Music-hall comedian Emney adds a bit of class as an impeccably English Hungarian millionaire, while the gypsy dances and masked balls on the Denham studio backlot have the surreally exciting quality of truly bad cinema. RMy

Lili

(Charles Walters, 1952, US) Leslie Caron, Mel Ferrer, Kurt Kasznar, Jean-Pierre Aumont, Zsa Zsa Gabor.
81 min.
Perhaps too deliberately charming for its own good, but this adaptation of a Paul Gallico novel about a 16-year-old waif who falls unhappily in love with a carnival magician (Aumont), thus adding to the bitterness of the crippled puppeteer (Ferrer) who loves her from afar, is actually rather delightful, thanks to Caron's touching performance and Walters' delicately stylish direction. Caron's scenes with the puppets (through whom Ferrer talks to her, and whom she accepts as her living friends and confidants) are in fact brushed with a touch of genuine fairy-tale magic. Not really a musical (though it has one hit song, 'Hi Lili, Hi Lo'), it ends with an ambitious ballet which is attractive but seems oddly out of key with the rest of the film. GA

Lilies (Les Feluettes, ou La Répétition d'un drama romantique)

(John Greyson, 1996, Can) Brent Carver, Marcel Sabourin, Aubert Pallascio, Jason Cadieux, Matthew Ferguson.
92 min.
Quebec, 1952: a bishop's visit to a prisoner seeking confession becomes an unexpected encounter with the past. The prisoner, a boyhood friend, near the end of a life sentence, has mounted an elaborate performance by his fellow inmates, his purpose to prick the prelate's guilty conscience and pierce the passions of their hidden teenage years. It's easy to see how the theatrical artifice eliding past and present might have impressed in Michel Marc Bouchard's stage original, but on screen, for all the florid intercutting, it remains in the shadow of Robert Lepage. Still, strong performances from an all-male cast (in drag where necessary), and Mychael Danna's choral score for the Hilliard Ensemble decorate the gay melodrama with an aura of keening nostalgic melancholy. TJ

Lili Marleen

(Rainer Werner Fassbinder, 1980, WGer) Hanna Schygulla, Giancarlo Giannini, Mel Ferrer, Karl Heinz von Hassel, Erik Schumann, Hark Bohm, Rainer Werner Fassbinder.
116 min.
Fassbinder's determinedly 'tasteless' brew of sentiment and swastikas annexes the original two-way forces' favourite to a totally apocryphal cloak-and-dagger romance, camped up into a one-song musical comedy. Its basic joke is that Schygulla, required to sing 'Lili Marlene' umpteen times, can't sing; but when a variation on that has her Jewish lover (Giannini) tortured with the song by his German gaolers, one's incredulous guffaws just keep rolling. Elaborate proof that the devil really does have all the best tunes. PT

Lilith

(Robert Rossen, 1964, US) Warren Beatty, Jean Seberg, Peter Fonda, Kim Hunter, Anne Meacham, James Patterson, Jessica Walter, Gene Hackman.
116 min. b/w.
Rossen's sadly underrated last film, an ambitious reworking of legend through the emotional involvement of a trainee therapist (Beatty) with a schizophrenic girl (Seberg). Stylistically, the framework of Lilith is established by the ironic contrasts of the two walks that Vincent (Beatty) completes: the first, a purposeful one towards the asylum, and the last, a desperate zig-zag through the various corridors and stairways of the asylum itself, out into the gardens, and finally winding up where the first one began, with an exhausted and curiously childish plea for help. The irony is extended even to the cry for help, since the same social worker (Hunter) had, in the first instance, politely enquired if she could help him. It is within this framework that Rossen develops the shifting

relationship between Vincent and Lilith, beginning as patient and guide, and ending as beguiler and beguiled. CL

Lillian Russell

(Irving Cummings, 1940, US) Alice Faye, Don Ameche, Henry Fonda, Edward Arnold, Warren William, Leo Carrillo, Nigel Bruce, Claud Allister, Lynn Bari.
127 min. b/w.
Sumptuous but turgid biopic of The American Beauty – star of burlesque and light opera from the 1880s – with Fonda and Ameche as her two husbands (she had four, but who's counting?). It comes alive only when Alice Faye sings such standards as 'After the Ball' and 'The Band Plays On'. Nigel Bruce and Claude Allister appear in cameos as Gilbert and Sullivan. TM

Lily Tomlin

(Nicholas Broomfield/Joan Churchill, 1986, US/GB) Lily Tomlin, Jane Wagner, Peggy Feury.
90 min.
Not a great documentary – one learns little about Tomlin herself – but it is of interest for the way we are allowed to see how she develops her one-woman show over a period of almost two years: lines are changed, characters developed, and timing refined during 'works-in-progress' shows. But the main reason to catch this is for Tomlin's superbly funny performances, sharply satirising contemporary American stereotypes, and proving herself an actress of countless faces and voices. GA

Limelight

(Charles Chaplin, 1952, US) Charles Chaplin, Claire Bloom, Sydney Chaplin Jr, Nigel Bruce, Buster Keaton, Norman Lloyd, André Eglevsky, Melissa Hayden.
143 min. b/w.
Chaplin's final film before his exile in Europe is far and away his most personal: he recreates the London of his boyhood (a world of abject poverty, alcoholism, seedy tenement dwellings, pubs and music halls), and contemplates with supreme narcissism the onset of old age and the decline of his comic instinct. It's also Chaplin's least funny film: tears outweigh titters by several kilos (and the person who gets most laughs isn't Chaplin but Keaton, appearing briefly as his partner in a violin-and-piano routine), and there is much moralising about life's meaning and the artistic urge better suited to Reader's Digest for the back of a matchbox ('Life is splendid...it must be enjoyed...it is all we have'). It's over-long, shapeless, overblown, and...a masterpiece. Few cinema artists have delved into their own lives and emotions with such ruthlessness and with such moving results. GB

Limit Up

(Richard Martini, 1989, US) Nancy Allen, Dean Stockwell, Brad Hall, Danitra Vance, ray Charles, Rance Howard, Sandra Brogan, Luana Anders, Sally Kellerman.
88 min.
Do you have to lose your soul in order to become a success on the stock exchange? Well, yes – or maybe, in the last analysis, no… writer/director Martini can't quite make up his mind. This feeble comedy plays it both ways, lambasting the get-rich-quick mentality while showing that beneath even the meanest, dirtiest trader's chest beats a heart of gold. Runner Casey Falls (Allen) wants to become a trader, but her career path is blocked by her womanising boss (Stockwell). So she strikes a Faustian deal with a wacky, hip woman (Vance) who claims to be the devil's assistant. Casey will get the promotion, the mansion, the car, but she has to put up with endless pranks and supernatural displays from the mischievous demon. And there's the small matter of her soul…Characterisation is two-dimensional, and the intrigues fall flat. Ray Charles crops up intermittently; Sally Kellerman puts in an appearence; and it's disappointing to find Stockwell's and Allen's roles so underdeveloped. CM

Lina Braake

(Bernhard Sinkel, 1974, WGer) Lina Carstens, Fritz Rasp, Herbert Bötticher, Erica Schramm, Benno Hoffmann.
85 min.

An 'audience' movie that knows exactly what it wants. It deceptively begs respectability with its display of social concern – old people, immigrant workers – similar to Fassbinder's Fear Eats the Soul. More blatantly, the film offers a package: an art house, old folks' version of The Sting. Lina Braake, evicted from her home by the bank, is left to rot in an old people's home. Teaming up with an aristocratic old man, she swindles the bank and buys a house in Sardinia for a foreign worker family. The performances should crack even the surliest spectator; but the film's judgments and comparisons become increasingly dubious as the film moves towards its upbeat ending (like the juxtaposition of the bleak old people's home with the family celebration in Sardinia, all earthy peasant vitality and room for everyone from eldest to youngest). Does writer/director Sinkel really care for his characters? CPe

Lincoln County Incident

(Tony Brittenden, 1980, NZ) Shane Simms, Cornella Schaap, David Wright, Stephen Meyer, Grant McPhie, Pablo Rickard.
48 min.
An extremely polished comedy Western made by the students and staff of Lincoln High School in Christchurch. The pint-sized hero is Samson Peabody-Jones (Simms), whose stature stands in comic contrast to the greatness of his name and the enormity of his courage, which is severely tested by ghostly apparitions, unshaven villains, and a bar-tending floozie. The discovery of a dead prospector's map sends Jones – resplendent in green velvet knickerbockers – on his way through the contusion colours (yellow rocks, green ranges, blue skies) of 1881 New Mexico, accompanied by a chicken and a narration whose authentic American accent lets the cast concentrate on getting the action on the screen rather than the kiwi out of the voice. Full of charm, the film has the audacity to decorate its wildish west with a telephone, a Coca-Cola can, and an anarchic ending; and the aplomb to get away with it. FD

Line, The

(Robert J Siegel, 1980, US) Russ Thacker, Lewis J Stadlen, Brad Sullivan, Kathleen Tolan, Jacqueline Brookes, David Doyle, Andrew Duncan.
95 min.
Based on the true story of a Vietnam deserter who, after several suicide attempts in the army stockade, provokes a guard into killing him. As he crosses one line, fellow prisoners cross another, literally and metaphorically, by stepping out of parade in protest, and get life sentences for mutiny. Despite some powerful performances (Sullivan is outstanding as the senior stockade NCO), the film is top-heavy with a script whose painful honesty isn't always balanced: the strong story is over-compressed, notably in the media/civilian demonstration shit-storm that comes awkwardly out of nowhere into the closed world of the stockade. Well done up to a point and uncompromisingly relentless, but it makes you realise how good Costa-Gavras is at this kind of thing. JCo

Linea del cielo, La
see Skyline

Lines from the Heart (I Rollerna Tre)

(Christina Olofson, 1996, Swe) Bibi Andersson, Harriet Andersson, Gunnel Lindblom.
75 min.
The Swedish actresses Harriet Andersson, Gunnel Lindblom and Bibi Andersson spend a few days in the Provençal home of the late Mai Zetterling, the actress and director for whom they worked together in The Girls three decades before. The three discuss Zetterling, their lives and careers, Ingmar Bergman, the effects of ageing, maternity, etc, intercut are clips from Zetterling's movie. A 'fly on the wall' documentary – but the three celebrated actresses often look cramped by the camera and the need to 'perform' naturally. GA

Lineup, The

(Don Siegel, 1958, US) Eli Wallach, Robert Keith, Warner Anderson, Emile Meyer, Richard Jaeckel, Mary La Roche, William Leslie.
86 min. b/w.

Psycho-killers Julian and Dancer (Keith and Wallach) are hired to recover a heroin haul. Among their professional touches is noting down their victim's last words ('Why be greedy?'). But they can be unprofessional too – like wanting to know more about The Man who hired them. From this premise of killers rising above their station, Siegel was later to remake *The Killers*. But this black-and-white B version is the more brutal, sadistic and threatening, with its passionless killers stalking San Francisco long before existentialism was *à la mode*. DMacp

Linguini Incident, The

(Richard Shepard, 1991, US) Rosanna Arquette, David Bowie, Eszter Balint, André Gregory, Buck Henry, Viveca Lindfors, Lewis Arquette, Marlee Matlin.
98 min.
In an ultra-fashionable restaurant, Monte (Bowie) and Lucy (Arquette) are the silver-suited bar staff. Naturally they must fall in love after first disliking each other; less evident is why the bored, cynical restaurateurs should be making million-dollar bets with Monte about whether Lucy can escape from a locked mailbag in a tank of water. Presumably someone, somewhere, must have thought they could get some jokes out of the situation. They were wrong. Bowie drifts through, elegant, unconcerned and vaguely supercilious, leaching the energy from the narrative. Arquette emotes gamely as the waitress who dreams of following in Houdini's footsteps, but even she looks bored, and the sexual chemistry between the two wouldn't singe a gnat's wire. There's some amusement from the Tweedledum/Tweedledee antics of Gregory and Henry as the restaurateurs, but it's slim pickings. DW

Link

(Richard Franklin, 1985, GB) Elisabeth Shue, Terence Stamp, Steven Pinner, Richard Garnett, David O'Hara, Kevin Lloyd.
116 min.
Link is a morning-suited monkey who acts as valet for Terence Stamp, the mad professor who lives in a strange, dark mansion high on the cliffs in the middle of nowhere. Also around the house are Voodoo, and Imp, a chimp which apparently has the strength of eight men and the mind of a one-year-old. Franklin was responsible for *Psycho II*, so it's not long before, in best Hitchcock tradition, the master goes missing and the young American student assistant (Shue) is left to fight for her life against the unstoppable furry ones. Incidental pleasure comes from Link himself, a sly charmer with big paws and a penchant for cigars, who seems to have strayed in from *The Jungle Book*; but it's a slight affair which comes down to nothing more than frights in the cellars and who will survive? Too much monkey business. CPea

Linkshändige Frau, Die

see Left-Handed Woman, The

Lion, The

(Jack Cardiff, 1962, GB) William Holden, Trevor Howard, Capucine, Pamela Franklin, Makara Kwaiha Ramadhani, Paul Oduor.
96 min.
A girl's best friend is her lion in this cross-eyed savannah drama. Her game-warden stepfather (Howard) has to swallow his pride when his wife (Capucine) invites her ex-husband, Bill Holden, to come over from America to 'civilise' this wild child (Franklin). A depressing, patronising conclusion sees the original family returning to domesticity and the States. Ironically, in real life Holden liked Kenya so much that he decided to live there. TCh

Lion Has Seven Heads, The (Der Leone Have Sept Cabecas)

(Glauber Rocha, 1970, It/Fr) Rada Rassimov, Giulio Brogi, Gabriele Tinti, Jean-Pierre Léaud, Aldo Bixio, Bayak.
103 min.
Rocha's film intends to demonstrate the contradictions of imperialism in Africa and to reveal the dynamics of the revolutionary process, of struggle against it. It is filmed theatre, self-consciously and confessedly Brechtian in its method.

Seventy rather stilted, second-hand tableaux dramatise relations between a stereotypic blonde goddess (imperialism), a grotesquely posturing Léaud as Catholicism, the CIA, a black bourgeois reformist politician, and their opposition, a classic Ché figure, an African militant, and 'the people'. Very didactic and banally filmed, it tends toward a condescending populism, a rip-off analysis that doesn't seem to stem from a strong engagement with the subject, despite the clarity/accuracy of the general argument. The signs have no life. JDuC

Lion in Winter, The

(Anthony Harvey, 1968, GB) Peter O'Toole, Katharine Hepburn, Jane Merrow, John Castle, Anthony Hopkins, Nigel Terry, Timothy Dalton, Nigel Stock.
134 min.
Domestic squabbles concerning the succession at the court of Henry II in 1183. O'Toole's Henry is a grizzled, decaying old man, a continuation of the same part in Becket. Hepburn won her third Oscar for her role as his wife, Eleanor of Aquitaine. Harvey's direction is intelligent enough, though the reduction of power struggles to fits of personal pique – where the fate of nations hangs in the balance – becomes a little irritating. Enjoyable for its two lead performances, however. RM

Lion Is in the Streets, A

(Raoul Walsh, 1953, US) James Cagney, Barbara Hale, Anne Francis, Warner Anderson, John McIntire, Jeanne Cagney, Lon Chaney Jr, Frank McHugh.
88 min.
The title alludes to one assassinated overreacher, Julius Caesar; this oddball Cagney family production concerns another, Huey Long – or, as the script has it, Hank Martin. A somewhat compromised treatment of the life and political crimes of 'The Kingfish' (director Walsh advised abandonment rather than capitulation to Long family threats of legal action), this covers much the same ground as Robert Rossen's earlier feature, *All the King's Men*, and Robert Collins' later telemovie, *The Life and Assassination of the Kingfish*. In decidedly more idiosyncratic style, however, with Cagney's aggressive energy suggesting the particular populist allure of the Southern shyster-cum-demagogue. PT

Lion King, The

(Roger Allers/Ron Minkoff, 1994, US) voices: Rowan Atkinson, Matthew Broderick, Whoopi Goldberg, Jeremy Irons, James Earl Jones, Cheech Marin.
88 min.
Following the inspired *Aladdin* and the emotionally involving *Beauty and the Beast*, Disney caps a hat trick of box-office hits with this breathtaking picture. The story hews to Joseph Campbell's maxim: first act, cosy; second act, despair; third act, redemption and transfiguration. As before, the camera treats the animated material like a feature film with humans – dollies, zooms, deploying the movements you'd expect in a James Cameron movie. How's the little lion king in waiting? Not too yucky. He has to learn the responsibilities of kingship, his father (Jones) explains, but Uncle Scar (Irons) tempts him off course. Villains and irresponsibles always have more fun. The hyenas have sharp one-liners to fledge their jive-ass flight (leader Whoopi Goldberg). The layabout beasts that Simba, Lion King Jr, hangs with in the wasted years are very funny. Pumbaa the farting warthog and Timon the meerkat still offer a viable hippie alternative. Songs variable. Animation staggering. A winner. BC

Lion of the Desert

(Moustapha Akkad, 1980, US) Anthony Quinn, Oliver Reed, Irene Papas, Raf Vallone, Rod Steiger, John Gielgud, Andrew Keir, Gastone Moschin.
163 min.
Oliver Reed, the megalomaniac vanguard of Mussolini's Roman Empire, mumbles his way across Libya in 1929, decimating and concentrating and finally hanging Bedouin leader Quinn. At which, with smug hindsight, we do not blanch, knowing that everyone gets their just deserts (pronounce this either way) eventually. History furnishes an eventful plot, the film-mak-

ers supply the stereotyped characters, and the heavens (apparently) an ethereal chorus, resulting in a not un-enjoyable ripping yarn. FD

Lion's Den, The (La Boca del Lobo)

(Francisco J Lombardi, 1988, Peru/Sp) Gustavo Bueno, Toña Vega, José Tejada, Gilberto Torres, Bertha Pagaza.
116 min.
Lombardi's anti-war film is set high in the remote mountains of Peru, where the communists are in revolt against the government. A small platoon of soldiers establish a post in an Indian village. Their indecisive officer is ambushed and butchered, but none of the citizenry will admit to any knowledge of the guerillas. Career soldier Luna (Vega) is initially reassured by the arrival of tough Lieutenant Roca (Bueno), but increasingly alienated by the behaviour of his friend Gallardo (Tejada), who treats the Indians as sub-human. The enemy never surfaces, though the decimation of the army post continues, and it is this sense of impotence that finally sparks off a massacre of the villagers. *Platoon*, *The Deerhunter*, and in particular, Philip Caputo's *Rumours of War*, tap into similar psychological terrain, though continents removed. A bit more heat under the pressure cooker and a bit more characterisation would have been welcome, but the film works steadily towards its final impact. BC

Lions Love

(Agnès Varda, 1969, US) Viva, Gerome Ragni, James Rado, Shirley Clarke, Carlos Clarens, Agnès Varda, Eddie Constantine, Peter Bogdanovich, Billie Dixon, Richard Bright.
110 min.
A film bedevilled by its intellectualism. It attempts to analyse the media-*unwelt* of fringe Hollywood in June '68, the material being: avant-garde theatre (Michael McLure's *The Beard*), experimental art-film (Shirley Clarke), the hip-hype pop musical (Rado and Ragni of *Hair*), underground superstardom (Viva), and the TV news. Varda's presentation is a peculiarly confused mix of ancient Godard, clichéd surrealism, '50s pop, and a half-arsed imitation of Warholian stylistics, with some rancid cream – an embarrassingly unconvincing triangular love trip *au Bonheur* – thrown in for good measure. Set off against the love-triangle garbage is a neat doom package of assassination (Robert Kennedy), attempted murder (Andy Warhol) and attempted suicide (Shirley Clarke). A nakedly bad film, a *mélange* of incompatibles that induces embarrassment or irritation, but hardly humour or interest. JDuC

Lipstick

(Lamont Johnson, 1976, US) Margaux Hemingway, Chris Sarandon, Anne Bancroft, Perry King, Robin Gammell, John Bennett Perry, Mariel Hemingway.
90 min.
The provocative invitations of a top model (Margaux Hemingway) on lipstick advertising hoardings are taken up by a meek music teacher (Sarandon), who responds to her lack of interest by attacking and raping her. The subsequent court proceedings make much of the model's professional life as provocation: a theme reminiscent of Clint Eastwood's (superior) *Play Misty for Me*, which points to one way the subject could have been handled. In failing to reveal the model's persona as the materialisation (maintained at some cost to herself) of collective male fantasy, the script underlines its teleplay blandness. The final vision of Hemingway's flaming red-clad avenger, emerging from her sterile cocoon to line up her violator in her gun sights, seems like a gesture in search of a movie. VG

Liquid Dreams

(Mark Manos, 1991, US) Candice Daly, Richard Steinmetz, Barry Dennen, Tracey Walter, Frankie Thorn, Paul Bartel, Mink Stole, John Doe.
98 min.
In this sleekly designed, sub-Cronenbergian sci-fi pic, Candice Daly's investigations into her sister's death from an alleged drugs overdose draw her into the twilight world of Neurovid, a kinky satellite TV channel inspired by *Videodrome*. Aided by a sympathetic cop (Steinmetz), Daly tries to discover the secret of the ultimate thrill, known as

The Ritual. The sex is mildly perverse, the tone coldly cerebral, with a fine debut from the striking Daly, and strong support from Barry Dennen as The Major, Neurovid's icy supremo. NF

Liquid Sky

(Slava Tsukerman, 1982, US) Anne Carlisle, Paula E Sheppard, Bob Brady, Susan Doukas, Elaine C Grove, Otto von Wernherr.
112 min.
Director Tsukerman's personal comment on, er, the State of Western Man, magnified through a thoroughly unpleasant bunch of New York junkies, poseurs and twits. Claiming to subvert a host of Hollywood verities, Tsukerman unleashes a parasitic alien being on the New York smack-'n'sex demi-monde. Junkies and sex fiends start dropping like flies, and not even the Bruno Ganz-alike scientist can stop the voracious bug. Tsukerman stops short of his original intention of offing the whole cast, allowing for an extraordinary fairy-tale ascension at the end, but his aim of highlighting social malaise gets happily mislaid in a bizarre, often hilarious mêlée of weird drugs, weird sex and off-the-wall camp SF. *Close Encounters* for acid casualties. JG

Lisa and the Devil

see House of Exorcism, The

Lisa Theory, The

(Steven Okazaki, 1993, US) Devon Morf, Honey O Yates, Avel Sosa II, Jim Matison.
80 min.
A layabouts' movie – for layabouts even being a slacker takes too much energy – about half a dozen young dozos who share a cooperative flat. The 'theory' states that anyone named Jennifer needs a good leaving alone: a theory that seemingly applies to Lisa (Yates) who befriends Devon (Morf) then leaves him – rendering him catatonic for the rest of the movie. This is *The Young Ones* as directed by Andy Warhol, with writer/director Okazaki anatomising their relationship in flashback. These naff punk rockers, pseudo-existentialists, and non-macho dead-brains don't impress Lisa, that's for sure. If it's hard to understand quite how false-naive the director's stance is supposed to be, there's throwaway intelligence here to spare, good observation, and a nice line in self-deprecating humour. Let's hope it's not autobiographical. WH

Lisbon Story

(Wim Wenders, 1995, Fr/Port) Rüdiger Vogler, Patrick Bauchau, Vasco Sequeira, Teresa Salgueiro.
100 min.
Summoned to Lisbon by director Bauchau, who's having problems with the silent movie he's shooting there, soundman Vogler arrives late, to discover that his friend has gone missing. He determines, nevertheless, to record a soundtrack for the unfinished film and, in so doing, comes to love Lisbon (and fado/pop singer Salgueiro), falling in with various kids and crooks in the meantime. All this is both pretty (Lisbon, after all, is very photogenic) and pretty lame; Wenders has never been comfortable with the kind of gentle comedy he essays here. But it's when Vogler finally catches up with Bauchau that the movie really goes off the rails, tottering into a tedious, redundant hypothesis about the lost innocence of the cinematic edge. Wenders has escorted us around this territory before, and far more entertainingly than here. GA

Listen to Me

(Douglas Day Stewart, 1989, US) Kirk Cameron, Jami Gertz, Roy Scheider, Amanda Peterson, Tim Quill, George Wyner, Anthony Zerbe, Christopher Atkins.
110 min.
Welcome to Kenmont College and the prestigious debating team run by Professor Scheider. Among its luminaries, two scholarship students: poor country boy Tucker (Cameron) who used to make his shoes out of tyres, and bookish beauty Monica (Gertz) who doesn't date. Blonde cripple Donna (Peterson) is determined to 'dance again', but rebuffs invitations from surfer Bruce (Atkins). Topping them all is hunky Garson 'Dostoievsky' McKellar (Quill), whose writing ambitions are thwarted by a politician dad (Zerbe). Their aim to debate 'Is Abortion Immoral?' before the Supreme Court isn't helped by writer-director Stewart's supply of brainless platitudes. By the final half-hour, desperate plotting, uninspired casting and clichéd dialogue leave one student dead, another with a split lip, and Scheider lost for words. CM

Listen Up: The Lives of Quincy Jones

(Ellen Weissbrod, 1990, US)
115 min.
Quincy Jones has been at or near the centre of black music since the '40s, as player, composer, arranger and producer: hence 'Lives'. He has also had rather a hard time. Unfortunately, this film biography, though laudatory, looks like one more cross to bear. To give Weissbrod her due, she has collected some astonishing material: home movies, newsreels, low-grade video, interviews (Ray Charles, Miles, Dizzy, Sinatra, Lionel Hampton, Ella Fitzgerald, Michael Jackson and many more), and masses of still photographs, hand-written scores and printed material. But the way she has assembled the film is deplorable. Weissbrod edits with crass brutality, presumably following a half-baked analogy with musical styles and techniques. Interviewees, seldom allowed whole phrases, let alone intelligible ideas, are made to speak simultaneously. No one is captioned until the end, an utterly élitist device. More damagingly, music barely gets a look in (plenty of sounds, but no completed musical statements). A little humility (R.E.S.P.E.C.T., even) in the presence of great artistry might have been in order. JMo

List of Adrian Messenger, The

(John Huston, 1963, US) George C Scott, Kirk Douglas, Jacques Roux, Dana Wynter, Clive Brook, Herbert Marshall, Bernard Archard, Gladys Cooper, Marcel Dalio.
97 min. b/w.
Saddled with an incredibly creaky whodunit plot, this thriller should really have been set in Victorian times to accommodate its villain with a passion for disguises, its Holmesian detective in a bowler hat, its murder in a fog-bound Limehouse that is pure Griffith. As it is, archly playing the country-house game complete with drawing-room teas, fox-hunting guests, and port passed to the left, Huston never seems entirely sure whether he means to parody or play straight. Though not without *longueurs*, the result is surprisingly rich in fun, not least the insolent assurance with which Huston can give away the murderer's identity, knowing he has four guest stars (Mitchum, Lancaster, Curtis and Sinatra) also prancing around in disguise to act as mystificatory red herrings. TM

Lisztomania

(Ken Russell, 1975, GB) Roger Daltrey, Sara Kestelman, Paul Nicholas, Fiona Lewis, Veronica Quilligan, Nell Campbell, John Justin, Ringo Starr.
104 min.
Since *Tommy* was Ken Russell's first real commercial hit, it's not surprising that *Lisztomania* should be a blatant attempt to repeat the formula. But without Pete Townshend behind him, Russell has to fall back on his own notion of a 'rock opera'...which means casting the hapless Daltrey as yet another Messiah and Ringo (ho ho) as the Pope, and hiring Rick Wakeman to play garbled rearrangements of Liszt and Wagner. The result is not only catastrophically wide of the mark as a 'sense experience', but misogynist, addled and grandiosely witless. The most pitiable aspect is that Russell is here patronising his collaborators as much as he's always patronised his audience. TR

Litany for Survival: The Life and Work of Audre Lorde, A

(Michelle Parkerson/Ada Gay Griffin, 1995, US) Audre Lorde.
90 min.
'It is the work of the poet within us to bridge contradictions.' Audre Lorde – black, lesbian, feminist warrior – knew plenty about that. Though determined to survive as who she was, it wasn't an easy option: she suffered a backstreet abortion, married a white man and had two children along the way. Griffin and Parkerson interviewed the poet extensively in the eight years before her death by cancer in 1992: Lorde tells her story eloquently, too involved in the evolutionary struggle to waste time on regrets and bitterness, too involved in life to fear death. At the forefront of liberation movements in America, Lorde did not shrink from the political at home. In a revealing interview her son talks about having to define his own version of what manhood meant – one that wouldn't repulse his mother. An inspirational figure who believed her poetry was a means rather than an end – 'The power you feel is a power you own' – Lorde is well remembered here. FM

Little Angel (Engelchen)

(Helke Misselwitz, 1996, Ger) Susanne Lothar, Cezary Pazura, Sophie Rois, Herbert Fritsch, Kathrine Angerer.
89 min.
Something of a caged bird, Ramona (Lothar) works in a lipstick factory and lives alone near the Ostkreuz station in East Berlin. One day a stranger, Andrzej (Pazura), grabs and kisses her. He's a Pole working the black market, avoiding the police. Ramona sees him again, then some more. She becomes pregnant, and happy – then she loses the baby. Something of a downer, this quiet, sombre film has its heart in the right place, but never finds the devices to engage its audience. Given that the protagonist is (apparently) psychologically unbalanced, the realist method (writer/director Helke Misselwitz has a documentary background) of slowly recording her ups and downs isn't enough to help us get inside her head. A sense of helpless Central European melancholia percolates through, but as drama it's all too grey and worthy. NB

Little Big League

(Andrew Scheinman, 1994, US) Jason Robards, Ashley Crow, Luke Edwards, Timothy Busfield, John Ashton, Dennis Farina, Ken Griffey Jr, Sandy Alomar Jr, Carlos Baerga, Lou Piniella.
119 min.
Twelve-year-old Billy Heywood (Edwards) has a problem: what to do when super-rich Grandpa (Robards) leaves him an entire major league baseball team of his own. When faced with the impending school vacation and the prospect of handling the day-to-day running of the Minnesota Twins, his response is to rekindle among the primadonna players a sheer love of the sport, resurrect their hopes of making the play-offs, and hope that Mom (Crow) doesn't get too upset over the odd cuss-word emanating from his lips due to big game tension. Making his directorial debut after producing such improving fare as *The Princess Bride* and *Stand by Me*, Scheinman is so keen to pile on the moral precepts, that the proceedings never really take on an imaginative life of their own. The film does, however, avoid tub-thumping triumphalism and manages better than most Hollywood sports movies to integrate its roster of real-life players within the contrivances of the storyline. TJ

Little Big Man

(Arthur Penn, 1970, US) Dustin Hoffman, Faye Dunaway, Martin Balsam, Richard Mulligan, Chief Dan George, Jeff Corey, Amy Eccles, Kelly Jean Peters.
147 min.
Penn's adaptation of Thomas Berger's novel is an epic post-Western that sets out to demythologise its subject-matter through the eyes of Jack Crabb (Hoffman), either a 121-year-old hero who's seen it all or a phenomenal liar. Ambiguity, both towards fact and character, is the keynote, as Hoffman's protagonist is orphaned, adopted by Indians, returned to the whites as a conman, and finally acclaimed as the sole white survivor of Custer's downfall at Little Big Horn. It's a shaggy, picaresque tale, laden with off-beat but pertinent observations as Crabb exchanges cultures and bears witness to the white man's genocidal treatment of 'the human beings'. Parallels with Vietnam naturally abound, but finally it's a wryly ironic re-writing of American history that makes up for its occasionally facile debunking of heroic targets by means of vivid direction and effortless performances. Funny, humane, and a work of brave intelligence. GA

Little Buddha

(Bernardo Bertolucci, 1993, Fr/GB) Keanu Reeves, Ying Ruocheng, Alex Wiesendanger, Chris Isaak, Bridget Fonda, Raju Lal.
140 min.

Nine-year-old Jesse (Wiesendanger), son of Seattle teacher Fonda and architect Isaak is identified as a possible reincarnation of a Tibetan Buddhist lama. On a visit to their apartment, dying lama Norbu (the sympathetic Ying Ruocheng) gives Jesse a picture-book of the life of Siddhartha/Buddha and suggests a visit to his monastery. Facing bankruptcy, Jesse's father accepts, and on the subcontinent Jesse witnesses Siddhartha's cosmic battle to banish evil, the multi-form Lord Mara, and finds he is just one of three candidates from whom Norbu must choose. Bertolucci's epic is a disappointment. With its once-upon-a-time structure, it has the feeling of a beautiful but very expensive kids' movie, intercut with a '50s 'Scope sandal-saga. Reeves makes a pretty, exotic, bare-breasted icon as the damask-cloaked prince turned rasta-style ascetic. On a deeper level, the film seems not to be specifically about Buddha, but about resistance and acceptance, weirdly resolving itself into an confusing essay on the deification of children. WH

Little Caesar

(Mervyn LeRoy, 1930, US) Edward G Robinson, Douglas Fairbanks Jr, Glenda Farrell, Stanley Fields, Sidney Blackmer, Ralph Ince, William Collier Jr.
80 min. b/w.
Though it looks somewhat dated now, there's no denying the seminal importance of this classic adaptation of WR Burnett's novel. Robinson – vain, cruel, jealous and vicious – is superb as the ruthlessly ambitious mobster Rico Bandello, determined to gain sole control of the city's criminal empire, anxious that his dancing-gigolo sidekick Massara (Fairbanks) should not leave him for a woman, and ending in bland astonishment that death should have overtaken him ('Mother of God, is this the end of Rico?'), despite the cautionary opening title assuring one and all that those who live by the sword, etc. Like many early talkies, the film often in fact errs on the slow side, at least in terms of dialogue; but the parallels with Capone, Tony Gaudio's photography, and LeRoy's totally unrepentant tone ensure that it remains fascinating. GA

Little Darlings

(Ronald F Maxwell, 1980, US) Tatum O'Neal, Kristy McNichol, Armand Assante, Matt Dillon, Krista Errickson, Alexa Kenin, Maggie Blye.
94 min.
Setting out as a rough-edged youthsploiter (factions at summer camp take bets on whether Tatum O'Neal or Kristy McNichol will lose her virginity first), it soon becomes apparent that the real message is that 'growing up' is not to be achieved by the simple act of defloration. *Little Darlings* proceeds to hammer the point home, till you emerge from its setting of woods, handy boathouses and the boys' camp across the lake, head ringing with the maxim, 'At 15, sex is bad, friendship good, and clean fun the answer'. If you can get over the moralising, there's a treat from Kristy McNichol as the tough-talking, Marlboro-smoking kid who can deliver a kick to the cobblers to rival Paul Newman, while Matt Dillon as her 'gentle giant' initiator and the sound-track (Blondie, Bonnie Raitt) also provide some welcome relief. FF

Little Dorrit

(Christine Edzard, 1987, GB) Derek Jacobi, Alec Guinness, Eleanor Bron, Michael Elphick, Joan Greenwood, Sarah Pickering, Miriam Margolyes, Max Wall, Cyril Cusack, Patricia Hayes, Roshan Seth, Bill Fraser.
176 min (Part I)/181 min (Part II).
'Make money, sir. Be as rich as you honestly can, sir.' *Little Dorrit* is about lucre – filthy and otherwise – so Christine Edzard's masterful two-part adaptation of Dickens' novel has a peculiar relevance for today. Part I (*Nobody's Fault*) tells the tale of fortunes lost and found, of secrets buried and unearthed, from the viewpoint of Arthur Clennam (Jacobi), who in his attempts to help the Dorrits abandons wealth and is brought to The Marshalsea, a debtors' prison. Part II (*Little Dorrit's Story*) relates the same story through the eyes of Little Dorrit herself (Pickering), the dutiful daughter of the 'Father of The Marshalsea' (Guinness), who forms a deep love for the oblivious Clennam. In the first part

the powerful momentum of the narrative is broken by abrupt shifts back in time, but in the second the events ingeniously begin to overlap. Besides the excitement of the story, the chief delight of this epic production lies in the superb performances, which manage to convey Dickens' penchant for the grotesque while suggesting the inner life that many critics deny exists in the novel. Impressive camera-work and Verdi's music help make the six hours roll by far too quickly. MS

Little Drummer Girl, The

(George Roy Hill, 1984, US) Diane Keaton, Yorgo Voyagis, Klaus Kinski, Sami Frey, Michael Cristofer, David Suchet, Anna Massey, Thorley Walters.
130 min.
Keaton stars as Charlie, a right-on actress recruited by Israeli intelligence to help winkle out a top Palestinian terrorist. The film's misfortune is that it captures all too faithfully the tortuous, pretentious and rather unimaginative approach of John Le Carré's more recent work. Kinski is allowed a few show-stealing scenes as the officer who masterminds the seduction, both mental and physical, of the reluctant Charlie, but Keaton is altogether too much the star to portray effectively a woman who is supposed to be without qualities, a blank sheet who allows herself to be written all over by a bunch of strangers. This process of character is the most interesting idea. As for the rest of the film, there's just too little action, too much talk. RR

Little Foxes, The

(William Wyler, 1941, US) Bette Davis, Herbert Marshall, Teresa Wright, Patricia Collinge, Dan Duryea, Charles Dingle, David Richardson, Carl Benton Reid.
116 min. b/w.
Lillian Hellman's play about the malevolence of human greed, as displayed in the internecine machinations of a wealthy Southern family, now creaks audibly. But you are unlikely ever to see a better version than this, caressed by Gregg Toland's deep-focus camera-work, embalmed by Wyler's direction and Goldwyn's sumptuous production values, galvanised by some superlative performances. The sulphurous Davis, her face a livid mask as she dispenses icy venom behind feline purrs, outdoes herself to provide the proceedings with a regally vicious centre; even so, she is in constant danger of being upstaged by Duryea, Dingle and Collinge. TM

Little Girl...Big Tease

see Snatched

Little Godard, A
(Der kleine Godard)

(Hellmuth Costard, 1978, WGer) Hellmuth Costard, Jean-Luc Godard, Rainer Werner Fassbinder, Andrea Ferréol, Hark Bohm.
81 min.
Costard here contrasts two approaches to film-making practice. In the red corner, Costard himself and Jean-Luc Godard, the former struggling to set up a Super-8 Co-op, the latter running rings around cultural officials in Hamburg Council. In the blue corner, Fassbinder shooting *Despair* on a huge tax-shelter budget, and Hark Bohm shooting his supremely idiotic movie about kiddie rebellion, *Moritz, lieber Moritz*. What emerges most strongly is a sense of the political and aesthetic chaos that Costard has made of his life. How do you take a movie whose director stages a scene showing himself leaping out of bed to answer a doorbell in order to display his own erection? TR

Little Hut, The

(Mark Robson, 1957, US/GB) Stewart Granger, David Niven, Ava Gardner, Walter Chiari, Finlay Currie, Jean Cadell.
90 min.
A neglected wife (Gardner), her husband (Granger) and an admirer (Niven) are shipwrecked on a desert island. André Roussin's stage farce ran for two years in Paris, and almost three in London (in an adaptation by Nancy Mitford), but this screen version is unbelievably bad; all talk, no action, and utterly superficial. These three layabouts wouldn't survive five minutes on a traffic island. TCh

Little Ida (Liten Ida)

(Laila Mikkelsen, 1981, Nor/Swe) Sunniva Lindekleiv, Howard Halvorsen, Lise Fjeldstad, Arne Lindtner Naess, Ellen Westerfjell.
79 min.
A return to the theme of childhood innocence spoiled by the rigours of war which has recently seen distinguished service in *Spirit of the Beehive* and *Muddy River*. Here the setting is Northern Norway, 1944-5, and the child seven-year-old Ida, cruelly ostracised for her mother's liaison with a German soldier. Mikkelsen mostly stays the right side of the line between sensitivity and sentimentality, delicacy and dullness, supported by Sunniva Lindekleiv's winning performance as a mercifully un-cute child, and by some stunning cinematography, all in muted tones of grey and brown which suddenly explode, in the final victory procession, into a proud flurry of red Norwegian flags. In its own unassuming way, a small gem of miniaturist observation. SJo

Little Lord Fauntleroy

(Jack Gold, 1980, GB) Ricky Schroder, Alec Guinness, Eric Porter, Colin Blakely, Connie Booth, Rachel Kempson.
103 min.
Basically unacceptable advertisement for the concepts of philanthropy practised by an oppressive aristocracy in capitalist Victorian England. Presented with such intractable material, director Jack Gold conspires with a cast of British character actors (immaculate) against the unacceptable face of American child acting (Schroder, wondrous). Zzzzzz. CPe

Little Malcolm and His Struggle Against the Eunuchs

(Stuart Cooper, 1974, GB) John Hurt, John McEnery, Raymond Platt, David Warner, Rosalind Ayres.
110 min.
This film would probably be produced by C4 or Handmade now. Back then it was financed by the Beatles' crumbling Apple empire, with George Harrison as fledgling executive producer. It won an award in Berlin, died in the West End, and vanished. In fact, David Halliwell's stage satire on Fascism, in the form of an art student's revolt against authority, translated fairly well to the screen, and the themes of paranoia and impotence are handled with enough kick for it to have deserved more success. There are particularly strong performances from the men (admittedly rather old for students), but it is Ayres as the only woman who steals the show. CPe

Little Man Tate

(Jodie Foster, 1991, US) Jodie Foster, Dianne Wiest, Adam Hann-Byrd, Harry Connick Jr, David Pierce, Debi Mazar, PJ Ochlan, Celia Weston, George Plimpton, Josh Mostel.
99 min.
Fred Tate (Hann-Byrd) is a gifted child: by age seven, he can play the piano backwards, paint like a master, and solve complex maths problems. But at school he's bored in lessons, and left doodling Da Vinci-style while other pupils frolic in the playground. Single parent mother Dede (Foster) comes into conflict with child psychologist Jane Grierson (Wiest), who takes the boy under her wing: tough-talking Dede is ready with the hugs, while Jane serves up macrobiotics and disciplinary lectures. Foster's directorial debut is a worthy attempt to explore a little-understood subject, but the film is bogged down by an approach to Wiest and Foster's characters which polarises intellect and emotion. Hann-Byrd has more to grapple with, and perfectly conveys Fred's jumbled motives and acute sensitivity. Tackling a difficult project, Foster draws good performances from her cast, but could have done with a better script. CM

Little Man, What Now?

(Frank Borzage, 1934, US) Margaret Sullavan, Douglas Montgomery, Alan Hale, Muriel Kirkland, Alan Mowbray, Mae Marsh, Catherine Doucet.
90 min. b/w.
One of Borzage's remarkable romantic weepies, dealing – like *A Farewell to Arms*, *Three Comrades* and *The Mortal Storm* – with the tran-

scendent power of love to survive in times of horrific spiritual and economic poverty. Here the couple – Sullavan, at her most radiant, and Montgomery – manage to stay together whatever the '20s depression in post-war Germany can throw at them. Beautiful, committed, and deeply moving, it's the sort of film that's virtually impossible to make today without falling into trite banality; that, however, speaks less of the film's age than of the saddening cynicism of modern-film viewing habits. GA

Little Matchgirl, The
see Petite Marchande d'allumettes, La

Little Mermaid, The
(John Musker/Ron Clements, 1989, US) voices: René Auberjonois, Christopher Daniel Barnes, Jodi Benson, Pat Carroll, Buddy Hackett, Kenneth Mars.
83 min.
Hans Christian Andersen is given the update in Disney's animated fairytale, the action punctuated by calypso and sweeping ballads as 16-year-old rebellious mermaid Ariel follows her one true, human love, handsome Prince Eric. When the affair is thwarted by her domineering father Triton, sea-witch Ursula offers to turn Ariel into a human for three days; but if she fails to secure a royal kiss at that time, she becomes Ursula's property. This return to traditional Disney territory is geared to captivate children while allowing them to maintain their street cred, largely by combining extravagant animated technique with ranging musical styles. The underwater scenes are spectacular: shimmering, illusory images set behind bold, primary sea life. Why, given this kind of creative care, do the film-makers resort to racial stereotyping for Ariel's crustacean servant? CM

Little Miss Marker
(Walter Bernstein, 1980, US) Walter Matthau, Julie Andrews, Tony Curtis, Sara Stimson, Bob Newhart, Lee Grant, Brian Dennehy, Kenneth McMillan.
102 min.
A calculated line-up: Matthau as a tight-fisted bookie, Julie Andrews as an English Rose, Tony Curtis as a camp hoodlum, and the doe-eyed Sara Stimson as Damon Runyon's Little Miss Marker. The setting is some hack's idea of '30s Depression New York, depressing all right in its complete lack of conviction, and the story is as contrived as the set: a father hands his daughter over as surety for a $10 racing debt, and proceeds to disappear into the river. Matthau, landed with the child and regretting the lost money, is gradually softened up by Childish Charms – though any audience, one suspects, would be left stone cold by this cynical attempt to engage their emotions. A film which aspires to a heart of gold, but is clearly alloy all the way. JCl

Little Mother
see Don't Cry for Me Little Mother

Little Murders
(Alan Arkin, 1971, US) Elliott Gould, Marcia Rodd, Vincent Gardenia, Elizabeth Wilson, Jon Korkes, John Randolph, Donald Sutherland, Lou Jacobi, Alan Arkin, Doris Roberts.
110 min.
A wryly funny parable, scripted by Jules Feiffer from his own play, about a photographer living in a metropolis where murder, rape and arson are so commonplace that nobody notices any more. Happily spending his days shooting shit in all shapes and sizes ('Harper's Bazaar wants me to do its Spring issue'), he naturally gets beaten up from time to time (but the muggers, he says, soon get tired and go away). Into his life comes a happy, beautiful girl who insists that everyone should wake up with a smile in the mornings; and just as he begins to discover what it is to have feelings, a sniper's bullet intervenes. Some of the fun poked at the nervous disintegration of Establishment authority (judge, cop, clergyman) is done in blatantly extraneous revue-type sketches. But the performances are perfection, and at the end you are left with a haunting image of the Feiffer world, where little daily murders done to man's soul have made feeling not merely dangerous but impossible. TM

Little Nellie Kelly
(Norman Taurog, 1940, US) Judy Garland, George Murphy, Charles Winninger, Douglas McPhail, Arthur Shields, Forrester Harvey.
100 min. b/w.
Sentimental tosh based on an old George M Cohan musical, about a young girl striving to placate her bilious old grandfather (Winninger, obviously meant to be charmingly-cutely Irish but emerging as truly obnoxious) when he objects to her marriage to a sworn enemy. Lots of irritating Irish blarney, with only Garland's clear tones leavening the brew in a number of songs (naturally including 'It's a Great Day for the Irish'). GA

Little Night Music, A
(Harold Prince, 1977, Aus/WGer) Elizabeth Taylor, Diana Rigg, Len Cariou, Lesley-Anne Down, Hermione Gingold, Laurence Guittard, Christopher Guard, Chloe Franks.
125 min.
Stephen Sondheim's adaptation of Ingmar Bergman's Smiles of a Summer Night is an elaborate musical homage-cum-variation. It still centres on a yearn-of-the-century country house party, at which virginities are lost, adulteries are floated, and True Love wins through. Sondheim muffles the Freud but constructs some wonderful contrapuntal duets and trios, with characters in different places singing on top of each other. Harold Prince's film version is devoid of filmic ideas, but does give Elizabeth Taylor her least ridiculous part in a decade, and generally has decent performances. However, it also cuts the original score in a way that reduces the emotional credibility, and crassly highlights the weakest (because most conventional) song, 'Send in the Clowns'. Not offensive, just silly. TR

Little Nikita (aka Sleepers)
(Richard Benjamin, 1988, US) Sidney Poitier, River Phoenix, Richard Jenkins, Caroline Kava, Richard Bradford, Richard Lynch, Loretta Devine, Lucy Deakins.
98 min.
Despite a screenplay by the esteemed Bo Goldman (One Flew Over the Cuckoo's Nest, Scent of a Woman), this lacklustre espionage thriller is bogged down with the sort of clichés you'd expect from the height of the Cold War. It's none too credible either, with River Phoenix as a typical American teen who discovers that his parents are in fact dormant Soviet spies. Phoenix and Poitier (as the FBI man who sets him straight) invest the material with more emotional authenticity than you'd think possible, but it's an uphill struggle. TJ

Little Odessa
(James Gray, 1994, US) Tim Roth, Edward Furlong, Moira Kelly, Vanessa Redgrave, Maximilian Schell, Paul Guilfoyle.
98 min.
Josh (Roth) can't enter the Russian-Jewish area of Brighton Beach, New York, where he grew up, so he makes his hits elsewhere. A contract on a jeweller, nevertheless, forces him back. There he fences with his kid brother, who loves him; his father, who certainly doesn't; his ailing mother, whom he loves beyond words; and a girl... The film has a thesis: hitmen must have psychopathy on their CVs; but even bad guys have souls. It's Roth's tough job to illustrate this, which, in his finest performance to date, he does magnificently. James Gray, aged 25, directs this dark, spare piece – his first feature – as to the manor born. WH

Little People
(Thomas Ott/Jan Krawitz, 1982, US)
88 min.
Although the term 'dwarf' is now acceptable in the US when referring to people of short stature, in this country it still conjures up images of circus freaks and Snow White, and remains part of the vocabulary of prejudice. It is this prejudice that this piquant documentary undermines by introducing us through interviews to people of short stature. FD

Little Prince, The
(Stanley Donen, 1974, US) Richard Kiley, Steven Warner, Bob Fosse, Gene Wilder, Joss Ackland, Clive Revill, Victor Spinetti, Graham Crowden.
89 min.
A sad disaster for Donen with what was surely a misconceived project from the beginning. At each scene change, The Little Prince intrusively fractures the delicate mood of Saint-Exupéry's allegorical fable about a crashed pilot's encounter with a being from another planet. The book linked its simple line drawings to its text in a way that avoided both cuteness and sentimentality; the film frequently amazes with its grossness, notably in the planet sequence, where a nuance-less distorting lens technique is heavily overworked. Frederick Loewe's music is unmemorable (with Richard Kiley belting through the desert bawling out particularly un-singable lyrics) and the sentimentality often outrageously glutinous. Only Bob Fosse's Snake comes off in a regulation classic dance routine. VG

Little Princess, A
(Alfonso Cuarón, 1995, US) Eleanor Bron, Liam Cunningham, Liesel Matthews, Rusty Schwimmer, Arthur Malet, Vanessa Lee Chester, Errol Sitahal.
97 min.
This exemplary version of Frances Hodgson Burnett's novel has been updated to WWI by Richard LaGravenese and Elizabeth Chandler. When her father, an army captain and a widower, is posted to France from India, young Sara (Matthews, excellent) is lodged in the New York boarding school of Miss Minchin (Bron). No sooner has her classmates' resentment at her wealth abated (Sara keeps them spellbound with accounts of the Hindu myths) than news arrives of father's death in the trenches. The ogreish Miss Minchin casts off her hypocrite's cloak and dispatches Sara to the school's Gothic attic, her only solace being secret meetings with the black servant Becky. Director Cuarón transforms these elements of Victorian melodramatic contrivance with skill and sensitivity into a humanist rites-of-passage story, both moral and spiritual, where courage, trust and faith prove their own reward. He's audacious, too: the Bollywood pastels of the myth sequences; an exciting, Lean-like rooftop escape; a magical snow-shake which is a moment of sheer cinematic élan. And when Sara offers her passionate, outraged response – 'Every little girl is a little princess!' – to Miss Minchin's scorn, she turns the declaration into a defiant defence of dignity and dreams. WH

Little Rascals, The
(Penelope Spheeris, 1994, US) Travis Tedford, Bug Hall, Brittany Ashton Holmes, Kevin Jamal Woods, Zachary Mabry, Whoopi Goldberg, Mel Brooks, Daryl Hannah.
83 min.
This feature version of the old Hal Roach 'Our Gang' comedy series plays so young we could be watching another species. None of the cast is over three feet tall, and what they lack in acting ability they make up in freckles. Smarmed-down hair with spikes, sideways caps, bowlers and bow-ties give an old-fashioned look to the diminutive members of the He-Man Woman-Haters Club, and speeded-up sequences and venerable visual gags give the token nod to the original series. There's plot: Alfalfa (Hall) falls for a cutesy girl and incurs the ire of club president Spanky (Tedford), who pronounces the death sentence; and their rocket-shaped little car is threatened with its first defeat in the Go-Kart Derby. Director Spheeris (Wayne's World) seems to have taken her obsession with youth culture beyond the limit, including a scene of dancing teenies in pink leotards that would make John Waters blush. Many reaction shots feature Petey the dog covering his heart-branded eye with his paws. WH

Little Romance, A
(George Roy Hill, 1979, US) Laurence Olivier, Diane Lane, Thelonious Bernard, Sally Kellerman, Broderick Crawford, David Dukes.
108 min.
Hard to dismiss completely a film in which Broderick Crawford turns up as 'Brod', but with Olivier overdoing it dreadfully as the crinkly old ne'er-do-well who persuades misfit American teen Lane and French youth Bernard to run off to Venice and consolidate their love by the Bridge of Sighs, it's not one that'll win over hardened cynics either. Georges Delerue's delightful score won an Oscar. Adapted from a novel by Patrick Cauvin. TJ

Little Shop of Horrors, The

(Roger Corman, 1960, US) Jonathan Haze, Jackie Joseph, Mel Welles, Dick Miller, Myrtle Vail, Leola Wendorff, Jack Nicholson.
70 min. b/w.
Made by Corman – with Daniel Haller credited as art director, though you have to see it to appreciate that joke – on a sheer nothing budget in one dust corner of a studio, complete with re-used cardboard and paste sets, this is worth seeing if only for Jack Nicholson's definitive role as a masochistically-inclined dental patient named Wilbur Force. A suitably Freudian story about a demanding plant that just keeps on growing, it's dressed up with *Dragnet* takeoffs as well. Its spoofy comedy keeps you tittering, sniggering and occasionally laughing out loud right to the last ridiculous frame. PG

Little Shop of Horrors

(Frank Oz, 1986, US) Rick Moranis, Ellen Greene, Vincent Gardenia, Steve Martin, Tichina Arnold, Tisha Campbell, Michelle Weeks, James Belushi, John Candy, Bill Murray.
94 min.
In the basement of Mushnik's Skid Row florist's, weedy shop-boy Seymour pines for bubbly-blonde shop-girl Audrey. But the basement is also home to a strange and unusual plant, a growing, bloodthirsty demon determined to devour mankind. It's hard to pinpoint just what makes this surreal saga such a delight. There's the music, a wonderful doowop score from the off-Broadway hit based on Corman's 1960 cult classic. There's the antics of Second City veteran comedians (Murray, Candy, Belushi). There's Steve Martin as 'The Dentist', Audrey's biker-boyfriend, a happy-go-lucky sadist who nearly steals the show. And finally there's the plant, a 50-ft jiving, root-stomping, vegetable from whose 49-ft lips comes the voice of Levi Stubbs of the Four Tops. Though Frank Oz will be damned for changing the play's original ending – let them eat carrots – this wild and witty musical is great fun. SGo

Little Sister (Zusje)

(Robert Jan Westdijk, 1995, Neth) Kim van Kooten, Hugo Metsers III, Roeland Fernhout, Ganna Veenhuysen.
91 min.
Low budget pseudo-documentary about a film-maker's return to Amsterdam and the troubled relationship he shared with his little sister, now a fashion design student. Using a subjective camera – shots of the floor when the film-maker gets drunk, etc – it self-consciously explores themes of voyeurism and real-time film-making, but without much insight. As intimations of an incestuous relationship between the two become more explicit, so do the film's faults. Everything's sign-posted, from the name of the hotel to which he's forced to go, to the sub-Freudian resolution. A discomforting exercise in self-therapy, about a film-maker's exercise in self-therapy. WH

Little Soldier, The

see Petit Soldat, Le

Littlest Horse Thieves, The

see Escape from the Dark

Littlest Rebel, The

(David Butler, 1935, US) Shirley Temple, John Boles, Jack Holt, Karen Morley, Bill 'Bojangles' Robinson, Willie Best, Guinn Williams.
70 min. b/w.
A sentimental and none too enlightened Civil War picture, painting our Shirl as the heroine of the hour. She lives with her ma, her 'Uncle Billy' (Robinson), and her other happy slaves while pop (Boles) is fighting for the Confederacy. He returns when ma starts ailing, but Shirl persuades the nice Yankee colonel (Holt) to let him escape. Mr Lincoln is not impressed and executions seem in order, but a tug on his beard from the littlest rebel and all is back to rights. The problem with this picture is that it's still charming, despite all of the above. The tap routines with Robinson are the highlights, and go at least some way towards absolving the inherently patronising attitudes. TCh

Little Theatre of Jean Renoir, The

see Petit Théâtre de Jean Renoir, Le

Little Vera (Malenkaya Vera)

(Vasili Pichul, 1988, USSR) Natalya Negoda, Liudmila Zaitseva, Andrei Sokolov, Yuri Nazarov, Alexander Alexeyev-Negreba.
134 min.
The film that shocked the Soviets with its depiction of yer average Russian family as a squalid, sottish, violent bunch of amoral no-hopers. Filtered through Western eyes, the sex scenes seem mild, the foul language blunted by subtitles, and the rebellious stance tame. But the film's message is still subtly affecting. The circumscribed sadness of life in a dull industrial town; the inability of the generations to understand each other; the hard-eyed look at love as an explosive and divisive, not redemptive force; these themes are mercilessly delineated. There's also a welcome anarchic humour at work: when stolid Sergei bemoans Vera's lack of purpose, she writhes on top of him purring: 'You and I share the same goal. *Communism*'. You can feel the shock waves from here. The film's chief revelation is Negoda's searing performance as Vera, a feisty, mean-minded hellcat who injects chaos into every life that touches hers. The booze-fuelled tale is wildly melodramatic, but the performances, pitilessly shot in gritty, realistic settings, are excellent. SFe

Little Women

(George Cukor, 1933, US) Katharine Hepburn, Joan Bennett, Paul Lukas, Frances Dee, Jean Parker, Edna May Oliver, Douglass Montgomery, Henry Stephenson, Spring Byington.
115 min. b/w.
Surely the definitive version of Louisa May Alcott's novel, sweet, funny, perfectly cast, and exquisitely evocative in its New England period reconstruction. Cukor rightly emphasises the seasons, starting with a winter of discontent as, with father serving in the Civil War, the four March girls face the prospect of growing up in reduced circumstances. But as the seasons change, so do joys return, and the film offers an endlessly pleasurable series of vignettes: the breaching of the ogre's castle next door (to find it inhabited by a very kind old man and a very personable young one); the disastrous performance of Jo's play; the business of Beth's piano, and the fluttering alarms of her bout with scarlet fever; the first stirrings of romantic interests. The cement that holds all this together is Hepburn's miraculous performance as the tomboy Jo, angrily resisting the approach of womanhood ('Why can't we stay as we are?'). Cukor mines a rich vein of sentiment, never over-stepping the mark into slush, but it is Hepburn's Jo, making a subversive *choice* of what she wants her life to be, who ensures that the cosiness isn't everything. TM

Little Women

(Gillian Armstrong, 1994, US) Winona Ryder, Gabriel Byrne, Trini Alvarado, Susan Sarandon, Samantha Mathis, Kirsten Dunst, Claire Danes, Mary Wickes, Eric Stoltz, John Neville, Christian Bale.
118 min.
Hard times in New England during the Civil War, again. Winona Ryder's Jo is full of puppyish enthusiasm, brimming with enthusiasm and the thrill of anticipated passion, with Byrne's Professor Bhaer; Trini Alvarado is gentle Meg; newcomer Claire Danes is fragile Beth; and Kirsten Dunst's precocious Amy is suitably adorable. Presiding over Louisa May Alcott's family is Susan Sarandon's long-suffering Mrs March, going some way to cut through the sweetness. Gillian Armstrong resists the urge to revel in period detail, offering a somewhat clouded vision of the family, paying attention, for example, to their Transcendental beliefs. Be prepared, however, for a large beaker of the milk of human kindness. SFra

Live a Life

(Maxim Ford, 1982, GB) The Beat, Black Slate, Tom Robinson, Barry Ford, OK Jive, Martin Besserman, Alexei Sayle.
78 min.
A documentary that takes the Rainbow concerts at the end of the Jobs Express march as its springboard. The musical interludes lighten an otherwise relentless parade of disaffected youth whose hopes of getting a job are as low as the interest shown in them by the Tory Government. Videoed off the TV screen, the rhetoric of such government bods as Tebbit is set against that of the country's young as they outline their grievances. Perhaps their over-familiar points of argument would be more incisive and less repetitive with a bit of judicious editing; and perhaps if the makers had tried to provide a concrete answer to their problems, this film would be more than the worthy but – alas – boring piece of work it is. FL

Live and Let Die

(Guy Hamilton, 1973, GB) Roger Moore, Yaphet Kotto, Jane Seymour, Clifton James, Julius W Harris, Geoffrey Holder, David Hedison, Gloria Hendry, Bernard Lee.
121 min.
Destructive tomfoolery on a typically grand scale, with Moore – trying on 007's white jacket for the first time – matched against a battery of colourful villains (blacks are the baddies this time) and voodoo chiles. Two hours long and anti-climactic, but Bond fans won't be disappointed. VG

Live Flesh (Carne Trémula/ En chair et en os)

(Pedro Almodóvar, 1997, Sp/Fr) Francesca Neri, Javier Bardem, José Sancho, Angela Molina, Liberto Rabal, Penelope Cruz, Pilar Bardem.
101 min.
This free but sensitive adaptation of Ruth Rendell's thriller is Almodóvar's most impressive film to date – darker, straighter and far more controlled than his camp extravaganzas. A story of obsession, hatred, jealousy and revenge, it concerns a young man sent to prison for his accidental involvement in a police raid that went disastrously wrong. He comes out – and he wants the crippled cop who helped to put him away. The performances are spot on, the control of pace, mood and narrative is assured, the visuals are crisp, stylish and imaginative, and the whole film has, for Almodóvar, an unprecedented weight and substance. GA

Live for Life

see Vivre pour Vivre

Live in Peace

(Hu Binliu, 1997, China) Pan Yu, Bai Xueyun.
97 min.
Despite a promising fragmented start, which suggests a wide ranging look at familial and generational tensions in contemporary China, this soon settles into a heartwarming tale of a curmudgeonly crone, who makes unreasonable demands of her work-exhausted son and his wife, but is finally won over by the country girl the couple hires as her maid and companion. Very pedestrian. GA

Lives of Performers

(Yvonne Rainer, 1972, US) John Erdman, Valda Setterfield, Shirley Soffer, Fernando Torm, Yvonne Rainer.
90 min. b/w.
Yvonne Rainer's characteristically witty and episodic first feature draws together the different strands of her own work (as dancer, choreographer, director) in a multi-faceted reflection of and on the elements of role-playing within role-playing. Three dancers, whose emotional triangle provides the film's narrative centre, are observed – from one another's points of view, in rehearsal and performance, public and private, expressing their own feelings and other people's – with Babette Mangolte's tightly choreographed camera-work visually equating Rainer's zig-zagging approach to a central theme. JD

Living

see Ikiru

Living Daylights, The

(John Glen, 1987, GB) Timothy Dalton, Maryam d'Abo, Jeroen Krabbé, Joe Don Baker, John Rhys-Davies, Art Malik, Robert Brown.
131 min.
Confused plot and digressive globe-trotting

notwithstanding, the best Bond in years. A radical rethink on 007 accommodates the new man; Dalton brings a positive emotional commitment to tight spots and courtship, and emerges as a Buchanite romantic hero. The pre-credits sequence on the Rock of Gibraltar grips like wet rope; the murderous milkman's raid on HQ is a chiller; the final shoot-out with Joe Don Baker's arms dealer amid toy soldiers and model battlefields is a fruitful metaphor. Lethal gizmos and digital countdowns are kept to the minimum, which leaves more room for the acting. On the debit side, in place of the usually globally ambitious mastermind, the writers have given us a couple of seedy dealers who keep moving the goalposts: arms, drugs, diamonds. That and unmemorable events in Afghanistan apart, enjoy. BC

Living Dead, The (Unheimliche Geschichten)

(Richard Oswald, 1932, Ger) Paul Wegener, Eugen Klöpfer, Harald Paulsen, Roma Bahn, Roger Wisten, Victor De Kowa.
89 min. b/w.
Paul (*Golem*) Wegener's first talkie is a glorious horror comic that plays like *Great Moments of Expressionist Fantasy*. Poe and RL Stevenson are so much grist to its pulp-fiction mill: it knocks off a creditable *Black Cat* in the first ten minutes, and then races through a waxwork chamber of horrors and an insane asylum to put *Charenton* in the shade, before climaxing breathlessly in *The Suicide Club*. Villainous Wegener storms through mass murder, incitement to murder, alchemy, sedation, a guillotining, and even a den of sci-fi gadgetry on the way; the amusingly stolid hero never knows what hit him. Incredibly, the film has virtually no reputation. TR

Living Dead at the Manchester Morgue, The (Fin de Semana para los Muertos)

(Jorge Grau, 1974, Sp/It) Ray Lovelock, Christine Galbo, Arthur Kennedy, Aldo Massasso, Giorgio Trestini.
93 min.
Although made in the Lake District with a mainly dubbed cast, Arthur Kennedy as a very American English policeman, and a plot indebted to *Night of the Living Dead*, this works against all the odds. Through intelligent handling of locations, England becomes a very bleak place indeed, full of sinister quietness. Hero and heroine, thrown together by chance, find themselves pursued by both police and an army of cannibalistic living dead through this increasingly nightmarish landscape. It's a film of unrelieved blackness, from the seedy photographer who snaps his junkie wife cowering in the bath to homicidal babies, from mongol child at a petrol station to Kennedy's brutal sergeant. It's all the more absurdly fatalistic for refusing to draw political, moral or social conclusions. VG

Living Doll

(Peter Litten/George Dugdale, 1989, GB) Gary Martin, Katie Orgill, Mark Jax, Freddie Earlle, Eartha Kitt.
92 min.
Shy adolescent Martin can't find nobody to love, least of all the attractive young woman (Orgill) who runs the flower concession at the hospital where he works. Until, that is, her nubile body turns up on the mortuary slab, whereupon Martin steals it and takes it home to his seedy bed-sit. Then, while Orgill's body decomposes on the sofa, he tries to woo her with gooey talk and silky underwear. Nosey landlady Eartha Kitt, meanwhile, keeps threatening to discover her lodger's rotten secret. There's the seed of an idea here, but this necrophiliac romance never germinates, let alone flowers. Sensitively handled, as in Dominique Deruddere's *Crazy Love*, it might have smelled quite sweet; instead, it gives off the sickening whiff of unimaginative exploitation. NF

Living End, The

(Gregg Araki, 1992, US) Craig Gilmore, Mike Dytri, Darcy Marta, Mary Woronov, Johanna Went, Paul Bartel.
84 min.
Araki sought to make fumbling anti-dramas about the flotsam of Los Angeles: depressed, ambivalent, uncommitted. This is really different. It's a

queer 'couple-on-the-lam' movie, crammed with genre memories but closer to a bent *Pierrot le Fou* than to anything out of Hollywood. Two body-positive guys, a raunchy hustler and a passive movie critic, fall violently in love and flee a caricatured LA together after the hustler carelessly shoots a cop. Their aimless, fuck-the-world rampage through the void of Middle America has the same weight and impact as a good Act-Up slogan or a solid punk thrash. Groovy. TR

Living in Oblivion

(Tom DiCillo, 1995, US) Steve Buscemi, Catherine Keener, James LeGros, Dermot Mulroney, Danielle Von Zerneck.
90 min. b/w & col.
DiCillo's second feature gets great mileage out of the simple, familiar premise of an idealistic filmmaker struggling to complete his movie. The director is Nick (Buscemi), an arty tyro believed by some to be 'tight with Tarantino' and by himself to be in love with leading lady Nicole (Keener). Nick's main headache, however, is leading man Chad Palomino (LeGros), a petulant hunk whose vanity outweighs his doubtful commitment, and whose philandering inflames rivalries between various women on set, notably Nicole and producer Wanda, whose lover Wolf was never too fond of Chad in the first place. And then, as further irritants, there are the errant booms and malfunctioning smoke-machines, the eye-patches and goatees, the senile mothers, psycho-analysing drivers and hypersensitive extras – a total nightmare. The ingenious narrative, told from differing perspectives and incorporating tales within tales and teasing elisions between 'film' and 'reality', is actually informative about the nuts and bolts of shooting a movie, and not only as a catalogue of technical disasters – through the shamefully under-rated Keener, we get a real insight into screen acting and the way fatigue, memory, stress and surroundings can take their toll. Hers, however, is merely the finest of a whole host of spot-on performances. A treat. GA

Living It Up (La Bella Vita)

(Paolo Virzi, 1994, It) Claudio Bigagli, Sabrina Ferilli, Massimo Ghini, Giorgio Algranti.
97 min.
Lightly likeable study of a marriage in decline, set against a backdrop of widespread unemployment and a shift from socialism to free-market get-up-and-go. Bigagli's steelworker gets laid off, suffers poor health, and sees his hitherto faithful wife (the somewhat stunning Ferilli) have an affair with a smarmy local TV celeb. What's interesting is that she's viewed at least as sympathetically as the film's nominal hero; indeed, it's unfathomable why such a lively, intelligent, resourceful woman would be attracted to a lazy, depressive, self-pitying ugly-mug like Bigagli in the first place. A minor but promising first feature. GA

Living on the Edge

(Michael Grigsby, 1987, GB)
86 min.
A documentary examining the lives and attitudes of working-class Britons: a Devon farming family forced through bankruptcy to abandon their land after 40 years; a jobless family imprisoned on a Birkenhead housing estate; members of a South Wales mining community, bemoaning their reputation during the strike as 'the enemy within'; young Glaswegians travelling to London in search of work. Keenly analytical and wide-ranging, Grigsby's film presents an impressionistic mosaic of the sundry intertwined forces that have wrecked the lives of these intelligent, articulate people. Political history, increasingly rampant consumerism, popular songs, archive radio and film material, all serve to illuminate the feeling that a massive portion of the population has been sold down the line. Poetic, perceptive and often profoundly moving as it monitors the sine wave from the Depression of the '30s to that of the present, the film's illustration that 'in the '30s people had principles; now they've got mortgages and cars' would be totally depressing, were it not for the sheer resilience of these people about whom the government barely cares. GA

Lizards, The (I Basilischi)

(Lina Wertmüller, 1963, It) Toni Petruzzi, Stefano Sattaflores, Sergio Farrannino, Luigi Barbieri, Flora Carabella.
85 min. b/w.

The Lizards is that perennial Italian favourite, the portrait of small-town loafers constantly hatching half-hearted plans but hopelessly trapped in their own lethargy. Wertmüller's first feature, it's not fundamentally very different from Fellini's *I Vitelloni* of a decade earlier, with Morricone's score a definite plus. Later, in the mid-'70s, Wertmüller became a dubious arthouse smash hit in America with films like *Love and Anarchy, Swept Away* and *Seven Beauties*. TR

Loaded

(Anna Campion, 1994, GB) Oliver Milburn, Nick Patrick, Catherine McCormick, Thandie Newton.
98 min.
In this feature debut by Jane Campion's sister, a party of English school-leavers travels to a remote country house to shoot a low-budget horror movie. But during filming, and especially during a videotaped collective acid trip, tensions surface threatening to tear the group apart. The writer/director's sympathy for her characters is, regrettably, not matched by her understanding of them. Emotional revelations that should explode in the tranquil silence of the forest are curiously muffled. NF

Local Hero

(Bill Forsyth, 1983, GB) Burt Lancaster, Peter Riegert, Denis Lawson, Peter Capaldi, Fulton Mackay, Jenny Seagrove, Jennifer Black, Christopher Rozycki, Rikki Fulton.
111 min.
For all the ballyhoo about *Chariots of Fire*, Forsyth's is the more significant film because it rediscovers a genre that was once among the British cinema's proudest achievements. *Local Hero*, which concerns the frustrations of a Texas oilman's attempts to buy up an idyllic Scottish village, ranks as a lyrical anti-urban comedy in the great tradition of films like I *Know Where I'm Going* and *Whisky Galore*; and its essential triumph is to prove that comedy can still contain a gentle, almost mystical, aspect without necessarily being old-fashioned. The film achieves this best in its superb sense of location and the haunting contrast between Texas and Scotland. Forsyth cannot quite tease out of his characters the kind of strange subtlety that Powell and Pressburger delivered, but it is enough that he and producer David Puttnam succeed in making you realise just how badly this kind of film has been missed. DP

Locataire, Le

see Tenant, The

Loch Ness

(John Henderson, 1994, GB) Ted Danson, Joely Richardson, Ian Holm, Harris Yulin, James Frain, Keith Allen, Nick Brimble, Kirsty Graham, Harry Jones, Julian Curry, John Savident.
101 min.
While the digitised wonders of *Jurassic Park* and *Jumanji* show it's possible to put just about anything on screen these days, this charming, modestly budgeted Anglo-American offering confirms there's still a special glow to be enjoyed when screenplay, characters and performers just seem to click together. Expect wall-to-wall effects, and you'll be disappointed. Here's a jaunty family fable where the power of legend and imagination, and the affection for people and place vanquish all-comers. Rarer than a sighting of Nessie is, of course, a sparkling movie performance from Danson, but that's what we get, self-deprecating and sympathetic as the has-been LA zoologist sent to disprove the existence of the mythic beastie once and for all. John Fusco's witty script sticks to the formula in confronting him with Richardson's no-nonsense lochside innkeeper (to supply the romance) and her lively daughter (Graham, agreeably unprecocious). No, it's not particularly original, but with terrific support from wax-jacketed water bailiff Holm, bright-eyed expedition helper Frain, a handful of perfectly judged shock moments from John Henderson (directing his first features after the children's TV series *The Borrowers*), and a lush, classy, folk-tinged score from Trevor Jones, it's a compact winner that hits the bull's eye in almost every department. TJ

Locket, The

(John Brahm, 1946, US) Laraine Day, Brian Aherne, Robert Mitchum, Gene Raymond, Ricardo Cortez, Sharyn Moffet, Henry Stephenson, Katherine Emery.
85 min. b/w.

One of the many émigrés to Hollywood who gave a distinctively Germanic twist to established genres, Brahm hit a winning streak of baroque melodramas in the mid-'40s which are all visually remarkable and emotionally supercharged. Virtually all action in *The Locket* is contained in the ever-receding flashbacks that present an imminent bride and 'hopelessly twisted personality' almost exclusively through the eyes of her past lovers. A psychodrama, definitely, complete with analyst, but strangely ambivalent about its own insights, right up to the mesmerising finale of the bride meeting her traumatic Calvary on her way up the aisle. NA

Lock Up

(John Flynn, 1989, US) Sylvester Stallone, Donald Sutherland, John Amos, Sonny Landham, Tom Sizemore, Frank McRae, Darlanne Fluegel, Larry Romano.
109 min.

Although reviled for his macho roles, Stallone is a shrewd star who knows his limitations; the problem is that he tends to give his audienc exactly what they expect, and no more. In this tough prison drama, he plays Frank Leone, a model prisoner with only six months to serve. Suddenly transferred to a maximum security hell-hole presided over by sadistic warden Drumgoole (Sutherland) – whose custody he previously escaped – he is pushed to the edge by a systematic campaign of harrasment and beatings. Leone at first resists, but finally cracks when a psycho about to be released says he's been hired by Drumgoole to rape and kill Leone's girlfriend (Fluegel). Always at his best when smouldering before the burn, Stallone makes the most of a tailor-made role, with useful support from a gallery of multi-ethnic archetypes. Effectively cast against type, Sutherland sports a fearsome haircut and spits out hackneyed hate with more conviction than it deserves. A competent action picture, directed with considerable kinetic power. NF

Lock Up Your Daughters!

(Peter Coe, 1969, GB) Christopher Plummer, Susannah York, Glynis Johns, Ian Bannen, Tom Bell, Elaine Taylor, Jim Dale, Kathleen Harrison, Roy Kinnear, Georgia Brown.
103 min.

An amalgam of Fielding's *Rape Upon Rape* and Vanbrugh's *The Relapse*, based on the stage musical version, translated to the screen without the Laurie Johnson/Lionel Bart score. It's terrible. Life in lusty 18th century London, rife with innuendo and much elbow-digging humour. Certainly one of the worst films of the year. CPe

Loco de Amor

see Two Much

Lodger, The

(Alfred Hitchcock, 1926, GB) Ivor Novello, June, Marie Ault, Arthur Chesney, Malcolm Keen.
7,685 ft. b/w.

'In truth you might almost say that The Lodger was my first picture.' Indeed, what makes the film so fascinating is the way it dissolves into pre-echoes of Hitchcock's later work. His concern with the uncertain line between guilt and innocence, his confident dismissal of the minutiae of the plot, the disturbing intrusions of fetishistic sexuality, are as apparent here as they are in *Psycho*. The tone is lighter (despite the Ripper-esque story) and the tone more superficial, but the film has its own vigorous identity, and there are moments – Novello coming out of the fog to make the lights dim and the cuckoo clock go berserk – which are memorably effective. RMy

Lodger, The

(John Brahm, 1944, US) Merle Oberon, George Sanders, Laird Cregar, Cedric Hardwicke, Sara Allgood, Doris Lloyd, Aubrey Mather, Queenie Leonard.
84 min. b/w.

One of the great evocations of that strange lost city of Hollywood imagination, the fogbound London of *Jack the Ripper*. It might almost be a continuation of *Pandora's Box* as a blind man haltingly taps his way through Whitechapel past posters announcing a reward for the Ripper's capture, a hulking figure prowls in the obscurity, a woman's screams are accompanied by animal panting while the camera stares blindly into a dark hole in the wall. Huge, feline, softly obscene as he builds his sonorous facade of biblical quotations and secretly rinses his bloody hands in the waters of the Thames, Laird Cregar gives a remarkable portrayal of perverted sexuality, at once horrific and oddly moving. Stunningly shot by Lucien Ballard, this is one of those rare films – like *Casablanca* – in which everything pulls together to create a weirdly compulsive atmosphere. TM

Lodz Ghetto

(Kathryn Taverna/Alan Adelson, 1988, US)
103 min. b/w & col.

Six months after Hitler's troops marched into the Polish city of lodz to the welcoming salutes of German Poles in 1939, all the city's jews were rounded up and either locked up in the slums or shot. After the 'de-Jewing' of Prague, another large contingent of Jews was sent to the Lodz ghetto as slave labour, swelling the population fighting for survival there to 200,000. This chilling photo-documentary reconstructs the horrors of the imprisoned, from starvation to separation as many were carted off to concentration camps towards the end of the war, using rare colour and other archive footage and heart-wrenching photographic stills. The commentary is taken from diaries and monographs of the ghetto people, from scrupulously traced documents of the period. After a confused beginning (where is Lodz? How many were locked up?), the film's powerful drive and lack of sentiment challenge you to continue watching, and leave you wondering about the strength of human resilience. Only 800 survived in the ghetto until liberation. JGl

Logan's Run

(Michael Anderson, 1976, US) Michael York, Richard Jordan, Jenny Agutter, Roscoe Lee Browne, Farrah Fawcett-Majors, Michael Anderson Jr, Peter Ustinov.
118 min.

Logan (York) is a security guard in a computer-controlled bubble civilisation whose hedonistic inhabitants are compelled to die at 30. His job is to hunt the fugitives, but one day outside the bubble he discovers 'new' emotions with Jenny Agutter. The lavish production has some good effects sequences, but its plot is as corny as the dreadful lurex drape costumes and Jerry Goldsmith's slushy score. Fundamentally, this is just further proof of Hollywood's untiring ability to reduce all science fiction to its most feeble stereotypes. DP

Loin des Barbares
(Far from the Barbarians)

(Liria Bégéja, 1993, Fr) Dominique Blanc, Timo Flloko, Sulejman Pitarka, Ronald Guttman.
93 min.

An impressive thriller-style investigation into the realities of exile for Paris's Albanian community. Zana (Blanc), a painter, spirited out of Albania as a baby, receives a call from a compatriot refugee at the airport saying he has news of the father she assumed was dead. She helps the man escape and embarks on an eye-opening tour through a little-seen side of Paris – the refugee camps, hotels and places of political asylum. Shot in a dark, frenetic style, the movie doesn't pull its punches, and nor does it offer any simplistic insights. Fine performances. WH

Loin du Viêt-nam

see Far From Vietnam

Lola

(Jacques Demy, 1960, Fr) Anouk Aimée, Marc Michel, Jacques Harden, Elina Labourdette, Margo Lion, Alan Scott.
91 min. b/w.

Simultaneously a tribute to Max Ophüls (to whom it is dedicated), Nantes (its setting), American musicals, and the joyous but always glorious romantic roundelay centred on the allur-ing and enigmatic presence of Aimée's eponymous cabaret-dancer, forced to choose between a trio of lovers. Its breezy tone, narrative coincidences, circling camera, and overall *brio* suggest a certain superficiality, but at its heart lies a wistful awareness that happiness in love is both transient and largely dependent on chance. Very beautifully shot, in widescreen and luminous black-and-white, it is also formally astonishing, with all the minor characters serving as variations on the central couple. GA

Lola

(Rainer Werner Fassbinder, 1981, WGer) Barbara Sukowa, Armin Mueller-Stahl, Mario Adorf, Matthias Fuchs, Helga Feddersen, Karin Baal, Ivan Desny.
115 min.

A wonderfully upfront narrative rendered in garish primary colours, this discursive update of *The Blue Angel* poses Lola (Sukowa) and the blue-eyed trembling-pillar-of-rectitude building commissioner who helplessly falls for her (Mueller-Stahl) as barometers of the moral bankruptcy at the heart of Germany's post-war 'economic miracle'. Lola (owned, like most of the city, by Mario Adorf's bluffly sleazy building profiteer) threads sinuously through the civic corruption of reconstruction, accruing sufficient manipulative credit to buy a slice of the status quo, seductively scuttling several shades of idealism with the oldest of come-on currencies. Business as usual. The prostitution metaphors come undiluted from early Godard, the poster-art visuals from the magnificent melodramas of Sirk and Minnelli; the provocations are all Fassbinder's own. PT

Lola Montès

(Max Ophüls, 1955, Fr/WGer) Martine Carol, Peter Ustinov, Anton Walbrook, Ivan Desny, Will Quadflieg, Oskar Werner, Lise Delamare, Paulette Dubost.
140 min.

A biography of the celebrated 19th century adventuress, but not a biography in the conventional sense: the lady's life is chronicled in a highly selective series of flashbacks, framed by scenes in a New Orleans circus where she allows herself to be put on show to a vulgar and impressionable public. The space between her memories and her circus appearance is the distance between romantic dreams and tawdry reality, or between love and the knowledge that love dies. Ophüls conjures that space into life – indeed, makes it the very subject of his film – by means of the most sumptuous stylistic effects imaginable: compositions unmatched in their fluidity, moving-camera-work that blurs the line between motion and emotion. If ever a director 'wrote' with his camera, it was Ophüls, and this still looks like his most sublime work. TR

Lolita

(Stanley Kubrick, 1961, GB) James Mason, Sue Lyon, Shelley Winters, Peter Sellers, Diana Decker, Jerry Stovin, Gary Cockrell, Marianne Stone.
153 min. b/w.

Less genuinely ecstatic in its portrait of paedophiliac obsession than Nabokov's novel – Kubrick is too cold and distanced a director ever to portray happiness, it seems – but nevertheless far more satisfying than his later works (one hesitates to call them mere movies). Mason is highly impressive as Humbert Humbert – all repressed passion and furrowed brow – and Winters contributes just the right amount of vulgarity as Lo's mother. Kubrick manages to handle the moral and psychological nuances with surprising lucidity, but the decision to indulge Peter Sellers' gift for mimickry in the role of Quilty tends to scupper the movie's tone. Fascinating, nevertheless. GA

Lolita

(Adrian Lyne, 1997, Fr/US) Jeremy Irons, Melanie Griffith, Frank Langella, Dominique Swain, Suzanne Shepherd, Erin J Dean, Ronald Pickup.
137 min.

This deploys body doubles, mostly avoids anything more explicit than a kiss, and is unlikely to foment paedophile activity, especially as it goes out of its way to stress the wretched consequences of Humbert Humbert's poisoned/poisonous infatuation with teenage nymphet Lo. One might, perhaps, concede that it's so concerned to make us understand Humbert at the same time as recognising his guilt that we learn little of Lolita's feelings, but the same is essentially true of Nabokov's novel. Moreover, the acting is spot on: Swain is excellent as Lo; Irons suitably impassioned, befuddled and tormented as Humbert; Griffith well cast as Charlotte Haze; and Langella's Quilty infinitely preferable to Peter Sellers' grandstanding in the Kubrick version. If the film has a problem, it's that its moral circumspection renders it a touch dull. Here, what humour there is consists largely of clumsy slapstick; any irony is generally heavy-handed; and the few moments of more florid mise-en-scène still evoke the fast-and-flashy aesthetic of an ads director. Nevertheless, the movie is neither sensationalist nor unintelligent, and some may even find the performances finally achieve a genuine poignancy. GA

e'Lollipop

(Ashley Lazarus, 1975, SAf) José Ferrer, Karen Valentine, Bess Finney, Muntu Ben Louis Ndebele, Norman Knox.
93 min. b/w.
An all-stops-out tale of the undying friendship of two boys – one white, the other coloured – raised by a Catholic mission in a small South African village. The main message of the film is a liberal one about the need for tolerance and harmonious coexistence. More difficult to understand is the unquestioning attitude towards the American presence in South America. When the chips are down, it's US knowhow and technology that saves the day. CPe

Lolly-Madonna XXX (aka The Lolly-Madonna War)

(Richard C Sarafian, 1973, US) Rod Steiger, Robert Ryan, Scott Wilson, Jeff Bridges, Season Hubley, Katherine Squire, Ed Lauter, Randy Quaid.
105 min.
This moves in on Peckinpah/Boorman territory, and comes adrift through lack of the singleness of purpose those directors' obsessive preoccupations might have given it. It starts as a kind of thriller, with a gang of backwoodsmen capturing a girl at a lonely bus stop, then moves on to take in inter-family feuding (the Feathers headed by Steiger versus the Gutshalls led by Ryan), rape, mental deficiency, illicit moonshining, revenge killings, and some flashbacks to the death of the wife of one of the kidnappers. Sarafian can bring off the odd key scene in a fresh and convincing way, but seems unable to establish the drive the film needs to take it past its complicated plot and on to a satisfactory climax. Basically, rather overdecorated backwoods mayhem, memorable for the sequence where Ed Lauter fantasises himself as a Country & Western star and goes out to die like Elvis waving to his cheering fans. VG

Lolo

(Francisco Athié, 1991, Mex) Lucha Villa, Roberto Sosa, Damian Alcazar, Alonso Echanove.
88 min.
A Mexican slum melodrama and a very pale shadow of Buñuel's Los Olvidados, Lolo (short for Dolores) loses his job when he's hospitalised after a mugging; the shock screws up his sense of personal mortality, and when he causes the accidental death of an old woman his only instinct is to grab his girlfriend and run. Unpersuasive in all departments. TR

London

(Patrick Keiller, 1994, GB) voice: Paul Scofield.
85 min.
This lies in that fertile territory between fiction and documentary. Everything you see is actually there, but as Scofield's anonymous Narrator takes us through his 'journal' of 1992, what we hear goes way beyond the mere facts to embrace meditative reflection, political satire, erudite literary anecdote, mythification and offbeat humour. The 'story' is structured round three journeys undertaken by the Narrator and his friend/ex-lover Robinson (also unseen) to research the source of English Romanticism. But as the pair attempt to get a grip on the city's history, contemporary events distract them from their planned route and their focus on the past.

Both a fascinating study of a culture in decline, and a scathing commentary on the effects of more than a decade of Conservatism, the film touches on figures as diverse as Baudelaire, John Major and the Chippendales. One of the most original British features in a long time. GA

London Belongs To Me (aka Dulcimer Street)

(Sidney Gilliat, 1948, GB) Alastair Sim, Stephen Murray, Richard Attenborough, Fay Compton, Wylie Watson, Susan Shaw, Joyce Carey, Hugh Griffith, Gladys Henson.
112 min. b/w.
A shabby London lodging-house has the usual assortment of oddballs, including Alastair Sim – that staple of eccentricity – as a phony medium. Most particularly, there is garage-hand Attenborough, who lives with his mum (Henson). For a while, the picture looks like out-takes from This Happy Breed, but it swerves into thrillerdom, and then into something else again when Attenborough steals a car and his former girlfriend is killed in a hit-and-run accident. Attenborough is sentenced to hang for murder, and his fellow-lodgers march to Whitehall demanding a reprieve. Gilliat handles the thematic lurching very ably, even if it does look like a filmed play, and Attenborough's performance uses the left-over menace and panic of Brighton Rock. ATu

London Connection, The (aka The Omega Connection)

(Robert Clouse, 1979, GB) Jeffrey Byron, Larry Cedar, Roy Kinnear, Lee Montague, Mona Washbourne, Nigel Davenport, David Kossoff.
84 min.
When Walt was alive, Disney films were great: fifteen-Kleenex tearjerkers, lots of monkey business with Hayley Mills, and the promise of Annette Funicello if only you'd Stay in School. But since their presiding genius copped it, the studio's films have developed increasingly terminal 'cute plots': flying beds, cars that think faster than they run, brontosauri that get shunted around town by stuntmen in drag. This one features the clean-cut British boy and a fellow-American he visits in London; together they help a defected East European scientist save his 'unique energy formula' from the clutches of a dubious syndicate. Back home, our jock hero works for his 'uncle' (Uncle Sam – geddit?), and things are made pretty easy by his array of sub-Bond defence devices. There is one impressive stunt, but the plot is such a bland-out you may be asleep when it happens. CR

London Kills Me

(Hanif Kureishi, 1991, GB) Justin Chadwick, Steven Mackintosh, Emer McCourt, Roshan Seth, Fiona Shaw, Brad Dourif, Tony Haygarth, Garry Cooper, Gordon Warnecke.
107 min.
20, unemployed and tired of being in debt, Notting Hill drugs dealer Clint (Chadwick) decides to go straight. Trouble is, friend and posse boss Muffdiver (Mackintosh) is reluctant to let him go. Worse, Clint not only rivals Muff for the affections of junkie Sylvie (McCourt), but he lacks the shoes he needs to become a waiter at a local diner. Ready to beg, steal or borrow from anyone, Clint embarks on a quest for footwear. Kureishi's directing debut means well, but wayward plotting, charmless performances and flat direction ensure that tedium sets in early. Evidently intended as an authentic look at Notting Hill life, it rarely rings true; and Kureishi buries the flaws beneath sporadic bursts of running about to music (hoary clichés for showing the wild, irresponsible joys of youth). It's hard, finally, to know exactly what it's all about, or even whether it's meant as a comedy. GA

London Rock and Roll Show, The

(Peter Clifton, 1973, GB) Mick Jagger, Chuck Berry, Little Richard, Bill Haley and the Comets, Jerry Lee Lewis, Bo Diddley.
84 min.
A spotty record of the 1972 Wembley concert, this is finally worth it for the performances. The twitchy style is of the zoom-in-and-cut-away variety, and secondary content offers sparse interviews with performers and too much crowd

'atmosphere'. There could have been more talk, because the interviews provide some lighter moments: Bill Haley theorises on fraternity, while Jerry Lee Lewis and Little Richard squabble for the title of king; Little Richard supports his claim with an impromptu, quivering solo of 'I Believe' as proof of his range. Darkness brings some relief from the overall restlessness as cameras concentrate more on performers and less on crowds. Chuck Berry's triumphant climactic set is shot in a thankfully straightforward manner. CPe

Loneliness of the Long Distance Runner, The

(Tony Richardson, 1962, GB) Tom Courtenay, James Bolam, Avis Bunnage, Michael Redgrave, Alec McCowen, James Fox, Joe Robinson, Topsy Jane, Julia Foster.
104 min. b/w.
Alan Sillitoe's fiction fuelled the excellent Saturday Night and Sunday Morning, but this one started life as a short story and grew flabbier for the screen. Courtenay's Borstal boy is crabbed and corroded by class hatred, and his only moment of satisfaction comes when he throws a cross-country race against a local public school to spite the upper class Governor (Redgrave). Chariots of Bile. Even in this softened-up version, Time found the hero 'prolier-than-thou'. Most of the period hallmarks of the British New Wave are paraded here. The disaffected hero treats us to Hoggartian interior monologues and climbs the nearest hill so that we can see the hopeless urban sprawl – Nottingham, in this case – laid out like his future. He gets the obligatory lyrical day off, a bracing trip to Skegness. Courting couples snog beside the barbed wire, and there's no shortage of editing between lads being flogged and choirs singing 'Jerusalem'. The general thrust is that Britain provides no sustenance for the working class soul, and consumerism spearheaded by telly comes in for some stick. It all seems a long time ago. BC

Lonely Are the Brave

(David Miller, 1962, US) Kirk Douglas, Gena Rowlands, Walter Matthau, Michael Kane, Carroll O'Connor, George Kennedy, William Schallert.
107 min. b/w.
A striking modern Western, with Douglas' ex-con cowboy pitting his horse and wits against technocrat sheriff Matthau and the world of 'progress', in an attempt to hold on to his dream of freedom and the pioneering spirit. The message of Dalton Trumbo's script is often a little too heavily underlined, with Douglas' martyrdom buttressed by some rather obvious symbols, but Miller directs with an eloquent feeling for landscape, making excellent use of Philip Lathrop's monochrome photography as the cowboy is pursued by helicopters into the mountains. Beautifully acted by a superb cast, it's a gripping, elegiac movie, imbued with a very real nostalgia for a vanished world. GA

Lonely Hearts

(Paul Cox, 1981, Aust) Wendy Hughes, Norman Kaye, Jon Finlayson, Julia Blake, Jonathan Hardy.
95 min.
As crankily bizarre in its own way as the later Man of Flowers, this is a sort of neo-realist comedy with a touch that Buster Keaton would have admired, not least the opening funeral sequence in which hearse and solitary mourner's car, befuddled by traffic lights, engage in a startled pas de deux of overtaking before settling down again in dignified procession. Pushing 50, alone for the first time with his mother now dead, Peter the piano-tuner (Kaye) is free at last to find out if there's life in the old dog yet. Splashing out on a new toupee, amusing himself by pretending to be blind as he goes about his work, he acquires a girl (Hughes) through a lonely-hearts agency, hesitantly suspecting that she may be rather too young but not that over-protective parents have induced in her a pathological fear of sex. Tenderly and wittily, Cox nurses their relationship along through assorted ups and downs, in particular their involvement in a production of Strindberg's The Father (a wickedly accurate satire of amateur dramatics). Beautifully observed and beautifully acted, it's a small gem. TM

Lonely Hearts Club
(Jimo Fangxin Julebu)
(Yee Chih-Yen, 1995, Tai) Pai Yueh-O, Yang
Kuei-Mei, Denys Hsieh, Gao Chien-Guo.
110 min.
Former critic Yee's debut feature traces an intricately linked network of romantic dreams, delusions and desires across half a dozen well-drawn
and superbly acted characters. At its core, a middle-aged office accountant (played against type
by the woman who is Taiwan's answer to Oprah),
endlessly frustrated by her daughter, husband
and mother-in-law, starts imagining that she
could have an affair with the new office boy. He,
of course, is gay, and has more than enough problems of his own. Yee reveals the complexities of
the characters bit by bit, and maintains a sense
of humour even when things start to go badly
wrong for them. TR

Lonely in America
(Barry Alexander Brown, 1990, US) Ranjit
Chowdhry, Adelaide Miller, Tirlok Malik,
Robert Kessler.
96 min.
Indian immigrant Arun (Chowdhry) arrives in
New York with little to his name besides a
turquoise suit, computer literacy and boundless
optimism. 'I feel I own the place already!' he
declares. He dumps the largesse – a job on Max's
newsstand, an apartment and extended-familial
support – offered by his uncle, in favour of
embracing the American dream (and white girlfriend) in his own inimitable fashion. Tirlok
Malik's script contains some comic gems, but
what insights it offers into the experience of New
York's Asian community are largely travestied
by Brown's inexperienced, clumsy direction and
his over-forced atmosphere of naive triumphalism. This low-budget romantic comedy oscillates
like a metronome between likeable and naff. WH

Lonely Lady, The
(Peter Sasdy, 1982, US) Pia Zadora, Lloyd
Bochner, Bibi Besch, Joseph Cali, Anthony
Holland, Jared Martin.
92 min.
Hollywood on Hollywood again: Harold Robbins'
sleazy little yarn features Pia Zadora as a wide-
eyed ingénue in a slashed dress, fresh out of high-
school creative-writing courses, and learning
about Beverly Hills on the wrong side of a very
nasty rape with a garden hose. In no time at all
she is scrabbling her way to a screenwriting
Oscar through the land where every Mercedes
convertible has a toupee. It's hardly her talent
with a pen that knocks them horizontal, but apart
from a curious tendency to shower all the time
with her dress on, such rogueries threw this spectator into a deep state of lacquered composure.
CPea

Lonely Passion of
Judith Hearne, The
(Jack Clayton, 1987, GB) Maggie Smith, Bob
Hoskins, Wendy Hiller, Marie Kean, Ian
McNeice, Alan Devlin, Prunella Scales.
116 min.
Brian Moore's novel makes for a depressing experience in Clayton's hands. Everything seems congealed in a time warp,and if the forlorn,
shabby-genteel dreams of a Dublin boarding-
house conjure up the feeling of '40s Rattigan, the
treatment could be a late '50s Room at the Bottom.
Judith Hearne's lonely passion is for being loved,
and failing that, the hard stuff. Neither of her
amulets – a photo of her late aunt and a picture of
The Lord – can save her from the bottle, and she
regularly loses her piano students and her lodgings. It's a hermetic story in which hope springs
eternal despite the treadmill of character, and
Maggie Smith calibrates her suffering to a nicety,
rising to ferocious anguish before an uncommunicative altar shrine. The landlady's brother,
James Madden (Hoskins), returned from the States
and full of bull, appears to be a romantic contender, but is only interested in her putative savings. The landlady's lecherous son (McNeice) is
grotesque beyond the call of duty. A downer. BC

Lonely Wife, The
see Charulata

Lonely Woman, The
see Viaggio in Italia

Lonesome Cowboys
(Paul Morrissey, 1968, US) Viva, Taylor Mead,
Tom Hompertz, Louis Waldon, Joe
Dallesandro, Eric Emerson, Julian Burroughs,
Francis Francine.
110 min.
Fans of Warhol's work, with its complete disregard for logic, characterisation and chronology,
will revel in this 'Western'. It encapsulates the
essence of '60s decadence, with all of the cast (and
probably the crew) high on acid and passing the
joints around, but it does raise several interesting questions about the early pioneering days.
The naturalness of sex between men who were
living together, riding together and dying together on the lonesome trail is a concept not even hinted at in conventional Westerns, let alone
explored. The film is by turns hilarious, camp,
aggravating and bizarre; no awards for the acting, however, which varies between the incompetent and the amateur. MG

Lone Star
(John Sayles, 1995, US) Chris Cooper, Matthew
McConaughey, Elizabeth Peña, Joe Morton,
Kris Kristofferson, Stephen Mendillo, Clifton
James, Miriam Colon, Frances McDormand.
135 min.
A skeleton's discovered in the desert just outside
the Tex-Mex bordertown of Frontera, and sheriff Sam Deeds (Cooper) soon concludes that the
dead man – 'bribes 'n' bullets' lawman Charlie
Wade (Kristofferson), reputedly run out of town
40 years ago by Sam's late, legendary father
Buddy (McConaughey) – was murdered. But who
killed him, and why? It may, of course, be connected with the racial tensions that have always
divided Frontera's population. After all, his own
teenage romance with Pilar Cruz (Peña), now a
teacher with a troubled son of her own, was
frowned on by their parents; and even now the
blacks are still marginalised: if they're not unemployed, most are stuck out at the army base headed by Delmore Payne (Morton), a by-the-book
colonel whose faith in rugged individualism has
alienated him from both his father and his son.
Writer/director Sayles's witty, vividly demotic
dialogue knocks even Tarantino for six, the
characterisations are uniformly colourful and
credible, the soundtrack and the widescreen camerawork exemplary, and the sense of a living,
working, interrelating community is superbly
realised. All this – and one of the most quietly
subversive endings in American cinema. GA

Lone Wolf McQuade
(Steve Carver, 1983, US) Chuck Norris, David
Carradine, Barbara Carrera, Leon Isaac
Kennedy, Robert Beltran, LQ Jones, RG
Armstrong.
107 min.
As senseless violence goes, this is very senseless
and very violent. Norris is a Texas Ranger,
Carradine an oily senator smuggling weapons to
'Central American terrorists', but the story-line
has more non-sequiturs than bodies, which is saying something. The problem with martial-arts
movies is that the villains never do anything sensible, like blow the hero away; they stand around
doing nothing while their buddies get wasted,
waiting for their turn. Films like this are the adult
version of those wonderfully witless movies we
used to love so much at the ABC Minors'. JCo

Long Ago, Tomorrow
see Raging Moon, The

Long and the Short
and the Tall, The
(Leslie Norman, 1960, GB) Laurence Harvey,
Richard Todd, David McCallum, Richard
Harris, Ronald Fraser, John Meillon,
Kenji Takaki.
105 min. b/w.
Keith Waterhouse and Willis Hall's play, about a
British patrol in Burma intent on killing an innocent Japanese prisoner in hysterical retribution
for atrocities committed against British soldiers,
was a hit at the Royal Court Theatre as directed
by Lindsay Anderson, with Peter O'Toole in the
key role of the doubter. Michael Balcon, when he
produced the film, replaced Anderson with Leslie
Norman, an Ealing veteran, and junked O'Toole
in favour of Laurence Harvey. The result was
suitably meretricious. PH

Long Arm, The
(aka The Third Key)
(Charles Frend, 1956, GB) Jack Hawkins,
Richard Leech, John Stratton, Dorothy Alison,
Geoffrey Keen, Ursula Howells, Sydney Tafler.
96 min. b/w.
The last Ealing film actually made at the famous
studios before the move to Borehamwood, this
paean to the middle-class copper's lot (with
Scotland Yard 'tec Hawkins harassed at home
and at work) was, like The Blue Lamp of six years
before, highly influential on British TV cop
shows of the '60s. As if to stress the genre's development, a close viewing reveals Stratford Johns
as a mere constable in those days. PT

Long Day Closes, The
(Terence Davies, 1992, GB) Marjorie Yates,
Leigh McCormack, Anthony Watson,
Nicholas Lamont, Ayse Owens, Tina Malone,
Jimmy Wilde.
85 min.
Like Distant Voices, Still Lives, Davies' final autobiographical film rings wholly true, due to the
richness and the rightness of the allusions he
makes through sets, costumes, dialogue, music,
radio and cinema itself. Such is Davies' artistry
that he shapes his material (an impressionistic
series of brief, plotless scenes recalled from 1955-
6, when he was about to leave junior school) into
a poignant vision of a paradise lost. While economic constraints, school bullies, religious terror
and barely-felt sexual longing are present, the
accent is on the warmth 11-year-old 'Bud' receives
from his family and neighbours. Indeed, it's primarily about the small, innocent but very real
joys of being alive, recreated with great skill and
never smothered by sentimentality. The stately
camera movements; the tableaux-like compositions; the evocative use of music and movie dialogue; the dreamy dissolves and lighting – all
make this a movie which takes place in its young
protagonist's mind. Beautifully poetic, never contrived or precious, the film dazzles with its stylistic confidence, emotional honesty, terrific wit
and all-round audacity. GA

Long Day's Dying, The
(Peter Collinson, 1968, GB) David Hemmings,
Tom Bell, Tony Beckley, Alan Dobie.
95 min.
A clumsy adaptation of Alan White's fine novel
about four lost soldiers – three British paratroopers and a German who becomes their prisoner –
wandering around a World War II battlefield in
Europe which becomes a private hell. The novel's
rather interesting argument, that a highly-trained
soldier can revel in his skill as a killer and yet
remain a pacifist, gets lost in hysterical overstatement, much camera trickery, insistent soft-
focus photography, and a script by Charles Wood
which is unwisely cast as a poetic stream-of-con-
sciousness monologue. Excellent performances,
though, especially from Tom Bell. TM

Long Day's
Journey Into Night
(Sidney Lumet, 1962, US) Katharine Hepburn,
Ralph Richardson, Jason Robards, Dean
Stockwell, Jeanne Barr.
174 min. b/w.
A straightforward transposition which captures
much of the claustrophobic cannibalism of Eugene
O'Neill's autobiographical play about a family
tearing itself to pieces in a chain of quarrels, with
love and hatred describing vicious circles around
the self-centred parsimony of the actor father, the
nervy drug-addiction of the mother, the incipient
alcoholism of the elder son, and the tubercular condition of the younger one. Described by him as 'a
play of old sorrow, written in tears and blood', it
imposes itself by sheer weight of emotion. Terrific
performance from Robards as the drunk, good
ones from Hepburn (despite miscasting),
Richardson (his mannerisms for once in character)
and Stockwell (though a bit lightweight to represent O'Neill the future writer). TM

Longest Day, The
(Ken Annakin/Andrew Marton/Bernhard
Wicki/Darryl F Zanuck, 1962, US) John
Wayne, Robert Mitchum, Henry Fonda, Robert
Ryan, Mel Ferrer, Robert Wagner, Eddie
Albert, Edmond O'Brien, Richard Burton,
Kenneth More, Peter Lawford, Richard Todd,

Leo Genn, Bourvil, Jean-Louis Barrault, Arletty, Curd Jürgens, Hans Christian Blech, Peter Van Eyck.
180 min. b/w.
Four directors, five writers (including Romain Gary and James Jones), a block-buster source novel by Cornelius Ryan, and one of the biggest all-star casts of all time (many of them with damn all to do) make this one of the last true war epics. High on noise, spectacle and heroism as the Allies invade Normandy, generally strong on performances and humour, but still over-long and laden with the usual national stereotypes. GA

Longest Yard, The (aka The Mean Machine)
(Robert Aldrich, 1974, US) Burt Reynolds, Eddie Albert, Ed Lauter, Michael Conrad, Jim Hampton, Harry Caesar, Bernadette Peters, Mike Henry, Richard Kiel.
122 min.
A fiercely anti-authoritarian parable mixing broad, black comedy and fast action, this portrays the conflict between prison inmate Reynolds and head warden Albert when a football game is organised between prisoners and guards; the inmates see it as their chance to take revenge for all the brutality they've suffered, while the guards are pressurised by Albert into playing dirty and humiliating their opponents. The themes are dignity and compromise, freedom and betrayal; if it all gets bogged down occasionally in its macho-violence trip, it's nevertheless very exciting, very witty, and elevated above its action-movie status by Aldrich's deliberate references to Nixon in Albert's characterisation of the warden. GA

Long Goodbye, The
(Robert Altman, 1973, US) Elliott Gould, Nina Van Pallandt, Sterling Hayden, Mark Rydell, Henry Gibson, David Arkin, Jim Bouton, Warren Berlinger.
111 min.
Despite cries of outrage from hard-line Chandler purists, this is, along with Hawks' *The Big Sleep*, easily the most intelligent of all screen adaptations of the writer's work. Altman in fact stays pretty close to the novel's basic narrative (though there are a couple of crucial changes), but where he comes up with something totally original is in his ironic updating of the story and characters: Gould's Marlowe is a laid-back, shambling slob who, despite his incessant claim that everything is 'OK with me', actually harbours the same honourable ideals as Chandler's Marlowe; but those values, Altman implies, just don't fit in with the neurotic, uncaring, ephemeral life-style led by the 'Me Generation' of modern LA. As Marlowe attempts to protect a friend suspected of battering his wife to death, and gets up to his neck in blackmail, suicide, betrayal and murder, Altman constructs not only a comment on the changes in values in America over the last three decades, but also a critique of *film noir* mythology: references, both ironic and affectionate, to Chandler (cats and alcoholism) and to earlier private-eye thrillers abound. Shot in gloriously steely colours by Vilmos Zsigmond with a continually moving camera, wondrously scripted by Leigh Brackett (who worked on *The Big Sleep*), and superbly acted all round, it's one of the finest movies of the '70s. GA

Long Good Friday, The
(John MacKenzie, 1979, GB) Bob Hoskins, Helen Mirren, Dave King, Bryan Marshall, Derek Thompson, Eddie Constantine, Brian Hall, Stephen Davis.
114 min.
Overrated thriller, often ludicrously compared to the only superficially similar *Performance*. About an East End gangland leader, with plans to develop the Docklands with the help of organised crime from overseas, who sees his empire threatened with extinction after a number of disasters are inflicted on him by mysterious rivals, it certainly manages to create a more convincing and contemporarily relevant London underworld than is usually seen in movies; and there's no denying the charismatic quality of Hoskins' slightly mannerised and stereotypical characterisation of yer typical Cockney 'ood. But the gangsters' connections with Mafia, IRA, big business and so on, are paraded like the latest fashions rather than examined, and the admittedly well-constructed set pieces are all too often diminished in effect by the uninspired camera-work. GA

Long Gray Line, The
(John Ford, 1955, US) Tyrone Power, Maureen O'Hara, Ward Bond, Donald Crisp, Robert Francis, Betsy Palmer, Phil Carey, Harry Carey Jr, Peter Graves.
138 min.
A beautifully crafted film, every image composed with graceful simplicity, but all that emerges is a lame 'Goodbye Mr Chips of West Point'. As a clumsy young man fresh off the boat from Ireland, hired by West Point Military Academy as a waiter, Marty Maher (Power) enlists to escape the mounting bill for breakages set against his wages, and becomes an instructor despite his ineptitude. Fifty years later, he is still there, a living monument to West Point, revered (he and his wife O'Hara having lost their only child at birth) as a beloved surrogate father to generations of cadets. The placid endorsement of military tradition (a straw dummy doubt about raising boys up to be cannon-fodder is easily disposed of) would be easier to take were it not for the rampant Irishry (jigs and pseudo-poetic blarney at every opportunity) that makes the sentimentality flow in buckets. Good performances, nevertheless. TM

Long Holidays of 1936, The (Las Largas Vacaciones del 36)
(Jaime Camino, 1976, Sp) Amalia Gadé, Ismael Merlor, Angela Molina, Vincente Parra, Francisco Rabal, José Sacristán.
107 min.
Breaking with the defensive, allegorical style imposed by Franco's regime, Jaime Camino burst into the brightening days of the post-Franco era with this oblique but compelling study of the Spanish Civil War. Set in a middle-class resort outside Barcelona during 1936-39, his film charts the social, sexual and personal transformations which those momentous yet tragic revolutionary events brought in their wake. Through the alert and radicalised children and the impotent, squabbling adults, trapped on permanent 'vacation' by the Fascist uprising of 1936, we are made to understand in microcosm the wider political canvas. Using up till now 'forbidden data', trivial events are drawn large in humorous and tragic detail as the Civil War pervades everything. CG

Long, Hot Summer, The
(Martin Ritt, 1958, US) Paul Newman, Joanne Woodward, Orson Welles, Anthony Franciosa, Lee Remick, Angela Lansbury.
117 min.
A steamy, Freudian tale of family intrigue set in the deep South, based on a compilation of stories by William Faulkner. Welles is the tyrannical Varner, whose rejected weakling son (an excessively neurotic performance from Franciosa) seeks consolation in bed with his sexy wife (Remick). A suspected 'barn burner' and definite troublemaker, Ben Quick (Newman) arrives in town, and is welcomed by Varner as a suitable heir to his empire. The sparks fly between Quick and Varner's schoolmistress daughter (Newman and Woodward together for the first time), but under her cold exterior beats a passionate heart, and predictably they are in each other's arms by the final shot. The ending is an unconvincing cop out, but it can't spoil the film's compulsive dramatic tension (or a marvellous comic cameo from Angela Lansbury as Welles' long-suffering mistress). JE

Long Kiss Goodnight, The
(Renny Harlin, 1996, US) Geena Davis, Samuel L Jackson, Patrick Malahide, Craig Bierko, Brian Cox, David Morse, GD Spradlin, Tom Amandes.
120 min.
Samantha Caine's an amnesiac suburban wife. Her violent past surfaces, however, when rogue US intelligence agents recognise her as sometime assassin Charly Baltimore, missing for years and believed dead. By amazing coincidence, just as her ex-colleagues decide to protect their current dirty-tricks scam by terminating her, Sam/Charly starts having flashbacks to her former self. She's also nudged along by fragments of evidence uncovered by low-rent private eye and reluctant sidekick Mitch Hennessey (Jackson). So when the bad guys' sadistic henchman (Bierko) kidnaps her 8-year-old daughter, Sam hacks off her long dark hair and emerges with a dyed blonde bob, a really bad attitude and a weapons training that's second to none. The film's unconventional only in the sense that, as visualised by Harlin, the $4m script by Shane

Black dispenses entirely with traditional storytelling techniques. Instead, this violent escapist fantasy detonates a string of atomised action sequences so knowingly ironic that they aspire to the condition of post-modern pastiche. The only saving graces are Davis's stripped-down, mean-as-a-wildcat portrayal of the Uzi-toting Charly, and Jackson's engagingly ineffectual turn. Like Charly's alter ego, however, you may have trouble remembering what happened once it's all over. NF

Long Live the Lady! (Lunga Vita alla Signora!)
(Ermanno Olmi, 1987, It) Marco Esposito, Simona Brandalise, Stefania Busarello, Simone Dalla Rosa, Lorenzo Paolini.
106 min.
A slight but charming comedy set in a remote château, to which come six catering-school teenagers to wait at a banquet. Seen largely through the watchful eyes of shy, solemn Libenzio (Esposito), the absurdly militaristic preparations, the meal, and the post-prandial relaxation away from the silent stare of the stern, cadaverous hostess, become as magically tantalising and dreamily sinister as the transition from childhood to adulthood. The often unpredictable, faintly surreal satire is distinguished by Olmi's subtle eye for detail; while the exact significance of relationships and events is left intriguingly ambiguous, a wealth of emotion is conveyed not by the remarkably sparse dialogue but by faces, glances and gestures momentarily caught by the camera's serene and tender gaze. GA

Long Memory, The
(Robert Hamer, 1953, GB) John Mills, John McCallum, Elizabeth Sellars, Eva Berg, Geoffrey Keen, Thora Hird.
96 min. b/w.
One of the marker posts of Hamer's decline after *Kind Hearts and Coronets*, this revenge thriller has John Mills, trying hard to summon up some grit, as a vengeful convict who's just spent 12 years inside for a crime he didn't commit. Hamer makes the most of the marshes and mud flats of the Thames Estuary, but the over-familiar plotting never springs to life. TJ

Long Night, The
(Anatole Litvak, 1947, US) Henry Fonda, Barbara Bel Geddes, Vincent Price, June Duprez, Queenie Smith, Elisha Cook Jr, Howard Freeman.
97 min. b/w.
Hollywood's cannibalisation (sometimes shot for shot) of Carné's *Le Jour se lève*. Bowdlerised and tricked out with a silly happy ending, but a better film than critics allowed at the time with Carné's film under threat of definitive suppression to make way for it. Excellent performances (with Price at his smarmiest, and Fonda only a shade self-pitying where Jean Gabin gave the role sheer, mutinous power), but above all a wonderful *noir* sheen from Sol Polito's camera-work. TM

Long Ride, The
(Pál Gábor, 1983, US/Hun) John Savage, Kelly Reno, Ildikó Bánsági, László Mensáros, Ferenc Bács.
93 min.
A US pilot bales out over Hungary during World War II, and the Resistance helps him to flee to freedom across the Yugoslavian border. There being no cars, and with the Germans watching the trains, our hero (Savage) escapes on horseback, and *The Long Ride* becomes an excuse for lavish tracking and helicopter shots over the great Hortobagy plain. Not a hugely expensive picture, but co-production with Hollywood bought Gábor chopper shots and an indifferent American star. It also saddled him with a compromised script — just to keep the ideology straight, the pilot first considers fleeing East to join the advancing Red Army — and a sentimental ending whereby the plucky peasant lad who helps the hero to flee dies on reaching the border. MA

Long Riders, The
(Walter Hill, 1980, US) David Carradine, Keith Carradine, Robert Carradine, James Keach, Stacy Keach, Dennis Quaid, Randy Quaid, Nicholas Guest, Christopher Guest.
99 min.
Hill's film holds its head high in a distinguished

company of movies about the Jesse James/Cole Younger gang, refusing to bother too much about historical facts or psychological motivation, instead serving up a potted commentary on the conventions of the genre itself. Concentrating on familiar rituals – the funeral, the hoe-down, the robbery (a stunning tour de force in slow motion) – Hill pays tribute to such directors as Ford, Hawks and Ray, emphasises the mythic aspects of the Western, and focuses on the subjects of kinship and the land (probably suggested by Scotsman Bill Bryden's screenplay). This last theme is emphasised by Hill's coup of casting real-life brothers as the members of the gang. A beautiful, laconic and unsentimental film. GA

Long Ships, The

(Jack Cardiff, 1963, GB/Yug) Richard Widmark, Sidney Poitier, Rosanna Schiaffino, Russ Tamblyn, Oscar Homolka, Beba Loncar, Colin Blakely, Gordon Jackson, Lionel Jeffries.
124 min.
Awful international Technirama hodge-podge, adapted from a novel by Frank G Bengtsson, in which the Vikings wrestle with the Moors to lay hands on the legendary Golden Bell of St James (rather an anti-climax when it finally appears). Chief North African Poitier seems to be taking matters seriously, while Scandinavian rival Widmark clearly does not. Homolka overplays the role of Krok, a Viking shipbuilder, quite enjoyably. TJ

Long Shot

(Maurice Hatton, 1978, GB) Charles Gormley, Neville Smith, Ann Zelda, Wim Wenders, Stephen Frears, Jim Haines, Alan Bennett, John Boorman, Susannah York.
85 min.
An incestuous, half-hoax docu-farce, largely set against the background of the Edinburgh Festival, on the travails of setting up a British feature film. Scots producer Gormley hustles to package Neville Smith's commercial-sounding script about Aberdeen oilmen (called Gulf and Western), fighting to retain some semblance of meaning for the words 'independent' and 'British' in the face of temptations to grab an American director, Euro-market stars, and even the remotest whiff of Québecois finance. If you can imagine a picaresque comedy being forged from the repeated lament for a native cinema, this is it – and its hard-knocks humour probably succeeds in carrying it beyond an in-joke. PT

Longtime Companion

(Norman René, 1990, US) Stephen Caffrey, Patrick Cassidy, Brian Cousins, Bruce Davison, John Dossett, Mark Lamos, Dermot Mulroney, Mary-Louise Parker, Michael Schoeffling, Campbell Scott.
99 min.
Like much of the AIDS-related art now coming out of New York, this anodyne, apolitical movie about the impact of the virus on a group of well-heeled, white New Yorkers seems curiously remote from British experience. Longtime Companion (the euphemism for 'lover' in the obit columns of NY papers) opens on a Fire Island beach in the halcyon summer of 1981, just as news breaks of rare cancers in the gay community, and then leapfrogs through the following decade, taking one day from each year as a spot-sample of the HIV epidemic's grisly progress. Headed by Davison, Lamos and Caffrey, a stalwart cast of theatre actors attacks the bitty, anecdotal script with fair gusto and considerable conviction, building up an affecting picture of the collapse of a network of friends and lovers. But director René and scriptwriter Craig Lucas spend all their energy avoiding sentimentality and pushing 'positive attitudes', when what the movie desperately needs is some larger perspective on the issues and the characters. The film is decent, no less but no more. TR

Long Voyage Home, The

(John Ford, 1940, US) John Wayne, Thomas Mitchell, Ian Hunter, Ward Bond, Barry Fitzgerald, John Qualen, Arthur Shields, Mildred Natwick, Wilfrid Lawson.
104 min. b/w.
Adapted from four one-act plays by O'Neill,

Ford's tribute to the plight of plucky seamen aboard a British freighter as WWII begins features his usual mixture of romanticised camaraderie and courage, boisterous braggadocio and brawling, and banal homespun philosophy. Beginning with an erotic skirmish with exotic island maidens, and ending with the death of Mitchell, shanghaied while drunkenly rescuing Wayne (oddly cast as an innocent Swedish farmlad) from the clutches of another crew, the film is chiefly noted for Gregg Toland's remarkable high-contrast camerawork which even manages to alleviate Ford's most maudlin excesses. None the less, a strong cast of risibly mixed accents copes gamely. GA

Long Weekend

(Colin Eggleston, 1977, Aust) John Hargreaves, Briony Behets, Mike McEwen, Michael Aitkens, Roy Day.
97 min.
The message here is: mess with the primeval forces of Nature, and Nature will get you in the end. It seems that if you wife-swap, have abortions, or run over a kangaroo, you are going to have a lousy weekend. You won't be able to find the beach; ants will mess up your picnic; the chicken will go off pong, the spear-gun will go off ping; and God knows how the lager will stay cold. These and many other 'mysterious' events are so heavily laden with symbolism that any possibility of suspense or credibility is sunk even before Nature can start to get really raw. Walkabout and The Last Wave did it much better. DSi

Look Back in Anger

(Tony Richardson, 1959, GB) Richard Burton, Mary Ure, Claire Bloom, Edith Evans, Gary Raymond, Glen Byam Shaw, Donald Pleasence, George Devine.
100 min. b/w.
Archetypal squalid British realism in an effectively scripted and well acted version of John Osborne's now dated play about the miseries induced by angry young graduate Jimmy Porter, railing against society and taking out his frustrations on his long-suffering wife (Ure). Burton is too old for the part, and Richardson's turgidly literal approach is none too involving. GA

Looker

(Michael Crichton, 1981, US) Albert Finney, James Coburn, Susan Dey, Leigh Taylor-Young, Dorian Harewood, Tim Rossovich, Darryl Hickman.
94 min.
This tediously convoluted sci-fi thriller combines elements from Westworld and Coma, with Coburn as a tycoon experimenting with subliminally hypnotic TV commercials featuring replicated holograph models (the original girls, 'perfected' by Finney's plastic surgeon, are subsequently murdered for no apparent reason). Mostly pretty silly and uncertain whether to be tongue-in-cheek, it has one or two good scenes and some intriguing hardware, including the Looker (Light Ocular Oriented Kinetic Energetic Responsers) disorientation gun. TM

Looking for Langston

(Issac Julien, 1988, GB) Ben Ellison, Matthew Baidoo, John Wilson, Akim Magaji.
45 min. b/w.
A poetic visual fantasy of the lives of black gay men in '20s Harlem, shot in beautiful monochrome and packed with startling images of dream and desire. Scenes alternate between a dark, smoky club where men in formals dance and cruise, windswept beaches, secluded bedrooms, and scary alleyways where the same men make love, while the poetry of Langston Hughes and contemporary black gay writer Essex Hemphill meditates on the aesthetics of sexual desire. It may sound painfully arty, but the images are fresh and exciting enough to sweep away any such reservations. RS

Looking for Mr Goodbar

(Richard Brooks, 1977, US) Diane Keaton, Tuesday Weld, William Atherton, Richard Kiley, Richard Gere, Alan Feinstein, Tom Berenger.
136 min.
Judith Rossner's calculated bestseller, about a contemporary woman's sexuality and her

'descent' into the world of New York singles bars, gets what it deserves in this old-fashioned adaptation. Behind the apparent sexual frankness lurks the familiar spectre of moral puritanism, while Brooks' script disastrously employs two standard Hollywood bulwarks as major reference points: cod Freud and American Gothic. Theresa (Keaton) hangs out in bars cruising for men, fuelled with the certain knowledge that, starting with her father, all men are pricks. Her dislocated sexuality is clumsily related back to her family: with cartoon loud-mouth Irish bigot cop for a father, Tuesday Weld as an air-hostess sister, memories of a crippled childhood and suspicions of hereditary illness, it could hardly be otherwise. As a result, Theresa is merely acted upon, an American Emmanuelle whose dreary promiscuity is driven on guilt. Only Diane Keaton's performance counters the overall heavy-handedness. CPe

Looking for Richard

(Al Pacino, 1996, US) Al Pacino, Kevin Spacey, Winona Ryder, Alec Baldwin, Harris Yulin, Aidan Quinn, John Gielgud, Vanessa Redgrave, Kenneth Branagh, Kevin Kline, Peter Brook, James Earl Jones, Rosemary Harris, Estelle Parsons.
112 min.
Pacino's first film as writer/director is a marvellously intelligent, witty and imaginative exploration of the problems faced by anyone wishing to act in Shakespeare or translate the plays to film. The movie's part documentary, part adaptation of Richard III: Pacino scours the streets of New York for vox-pop comments on the playwright; elicits opinions from academics, critics and celebrated thesps on questions of performance, the text and the history behind it; holds readings and rehearsals; and provides dramatic renditions of key scenes. Besides offering an enthralling abridged account of the play, Pacino's film is a hugely informative and entertaining attempt to measure Shakespeare's accessibility and value to the modern world. Whether visiting Stratford, arguing with co-writer Frederic Kimball or producer Michael Hadge, allowing a derelict to wax lyrical about Shakespeare's poetry, or staging a sparsely populated but impressively cinematic version of the climactic battle on Bosworth Field, Pacino seduces us with his enthusiasm, energy and passion. GA

Looking Glass War, The

(Frank R Pierson, 1969, GB) Christopher Jones, Pia Degermark, Ralph Richardson, Anthony Hopkins, Paul Rogers, Susan George, Ray McAnally, Robert Urquhart, Maxine Audley, Anna Massey.
107 min.
Typically convoluted Cold War espionage antics from Le Carré. Fine and quirky while the young Polish defector (Jones) selected as a pawn in the espionage game is guided through his training process by a series of bored eccentrics, with delicious performances from Rogers and Richardson (one nursing a permanent cough, the other a mad glint in his eye) as the Blimpish security chiefs hankering for the good old days when they weren't just a Civil Service backwater, and dreaming of the grand come-back they are busily setting in motion. But with the mission itself comes a swift descent into banal action, totally tedious as the sense of authenticity is dissipated in a welter of incredibly silly dialogue spoken by incredibly silly characters. TM

Look Me in the Eye

(Nick Ward, 1994, GB) Caroline Catz, Seamus Gubbins, Barnaby Stone, Mat Patresi.
80 min.
A woman allows herself to be picked up by a mysterious photographer. She strips slowly for his camera, but he walks out when she tries to consummate the relationship. A schoolteacher, recently married, Ruth is both exhibitionist and voyeur, a fantasist driven to act out her desires. Returning to the photographer's studio, she spies on him making love to a prostitute and, when they've gone, recreates the scene by seducing an estate agent. Alone, she tears the place apart. Ward's second film mines female sexual psychology in the guise of enigmatic melodrama. The result is intriguing, but not entirely convincing. Despite a bold central performance from Catz (who doubles as the prostitute), it's hard to see what triggers the teacher's increasingly reck-

less behaviour, while Stone's photographer remains a cipher, perhaps a figment of Ruth's over-heated imagination. Ward is good on the seedy hotels and sex shops around Kings Cross. There's almost a surfeit of texture – you can practically sniff the wall-paper, taste the chemical skin of Seamus McGarvey's cinematography. Ultimately, though, the film proves too tricky for its own good. A heady, enigmatic brew all the same. TCh

Looks and Smiles
(Kenneth Loach, 1981, GB) Graham Green, Carolyn Nicholson, Tony Pitts, Roy Haywood, Phil Askham.
104 min. b/w.
Sheffield, 1980: the evening paper warns of yet more redundancies in the steel industry, and the choice before school leavers Alan and Mick is either the forces or the dole. Alan (Pitts) enlists and is posted to Belfast, where he develops a taste for duffing up Catholics. Mick (Green) stays at home, tinkers with his bike, scours the sits vac, and takes up with shop-girl Karen (Nicholson) amid rising despair. Familiar Loach territory, and presented in characteristically spartan documentary style. Excellent performances from the three principals (all amateurs), resolutely unfussy black-and-white photography by Chris Menges, and a complete absence of self-consciousness on either side of the camera add up to a quietly devastating portrayal of human waste. JP

Look Who's Talking
(Amy Heckerling, 1989, US) John Travolta, Kirstie Alley, Olympia Dukakis, George Segal, Abe Vigoda, Louis Heckerling.
96 min.
From the opening shots of wriggling white tadpoles swimming through a neon womb, Amy Heckerling tackles motherhood humorously and head on, alternating between mucky-diaper realism and bright fantasy. Baby Mikey comes complete with snappy personality and the streetwise voice of Bruce Willis. Slapdash mum Mollie (Alley, a convincingly falliable parent) falls out with the already married father (Segal) just before the birth, and is tended instead by a taxi-driver who ferries her to hospital. Baby instantly likes the look of feckless cabbie James (Travolta), but Mollie is resistant to true love, especially when *her* mum (the admirable Dukakis) is striving to fix her up with someone more respectable. It's what-is-a-good-father time. Of course, we know it's the guy that's poor but *fun*. Heckerling directs this dippy but delightful film with a light, zany touch and a reasonably low yuck-factor (dribbles notwithstanding). Particularly cute is the way Travolta sends up his most famous role in a parodic disco dance routine. SFe

Look Who's Talking Now
(Tom Ropelewski, 1993, US) John Travolta, Kirstie Alley, Olympia Dukakis, Lysette Anthony, David Gallagher, Tabitha Lupien, George Segal.
95 min.
Travolta and Alley return as doting parents James and Mollie Ubriacco, their two kids now firmly ensconced in infanthood and the household recently extended by the arrival of mongrel Rocks – whose innermost thoughts are voiced by gruff Danny DeVito. The plot arrives in the shape of Lysette Anthony's power businesswoman Samantha, perky pilot James's new boss and keen to do more than fly with him. The action cranks itself up into a dilemma: Will 'work' prevent dad from spending the Yuletide period with the family? Comic interest is sustained by the entrance of prissy poodle Daphne (voice-over: Diane Keaton), but the preponderance of nudging innuendo was enough to earn the film a '12' certificate, thus excluding the audience of younger children who might otherwise have enjoyed the movie. TJ

Look Who's Talking Too
(Amy Heckerling, 1990, US) John Travolta, Kirstie Alley, Olympia Dukakis, Elias Koteas, Twink Kaplan; voices: Bruce Willis, Roseanne Barr, Damon Wayans, Mel Brooks.
80 min.
Mikey, the tot with the Bruce Willis voice-over, is about to acquire a sister (thoughts by Roseanne Barr). 'Don't you just hate it when you get your head caught in your placenta?' muses the yet-to-be-born sprog. That's about as good as the gags

get in this uninspired sequel to 1989's blockbuster. The story picks up with accountant Mollie (Alley) and cabbie James (Travolta) semi-settled in domestic bliss. But after the birth of their daughter, problems start to escalate: will James ever realise his dream to become an airline pilot and thus earn a decent salary? Will Mikey make it through toilet training? And when will Mollie stop giving money to her no-good, gun-crazy brother (Koteas)? This is formulaic stuff as the once-happy couple bicker incessantly, with a fire and rainstorm thrown in to lend a sense of danger when complacency threatens to become overwhelming. Crucially, this forgettable sequel lacks its predecessor's lively pace and comic tension. CM

Loophole
(John Quested, 1980, GB) Albert Finney, Martin Sheen, Susannah York, Colin Blakely, Jonathan Pryce, Robert Morley, Alfred Lynch, Christopher Guard.
105 min.
This pedestrian bank heist 'thriller', with its resolutely old-fashioned air bolstered by the token presence of an American star (Sheen) and the crushing earnestness with which everyone else approaches their hackneyed roles as if they were fresh-minted, was released to critical and box-office responses of consensual indifference. London's sewers (though which the bank is approached, and which are of course menaced by a rainstorm flood) don't have quite the cinematic resonance of LA's storm drains, and only tend to throw the mind even further back and off course to numerous POW tunnel movies. PT

Loose Cannons
(Bob Clark, 1990, US) Dan Aykroyd, Gene Hackman, Ronny Cox, Nancy Travis, Robert Prosky, Paul Koslo, Dick O'Neill, Jan Triska, David Alan Grier.
94 min.
A reeking stinker of a comedy: Aykroyd and Hackman are Washington, DC, cops searching for a Nazi sex film in which a West German politician is caught with his pants down. Mossad agents, pornographers and rabbis all cross their path, without eliciting a laugh between them. From the director of *Porky's* I and II, but this one didn't hit pay dirt. GM

Loose Connections
(Richard Eyre, 1983, GB) Lindsay Duncan, Stephen Rea, Carole Harrison, Frances Low, Jan Niklas, Gary Olsen, Robbie Coltrane.
96 min.
A welcome attempt to revive and update – steering clear of crass stereotypes – the bitter-sweet romance of classics like *I Was a Male War Bride* and the Tracy-Hepburn vehicles. Having built her own car, dogmatic feminist Sally drives off to Munich, accompanied by mild chauvinist Harry, who fits none of her requirements that her co-driver be vegetarian, gay and German-speaking. As their odyssey turns into a series of disasters, their differences (in class, education and attitudes to sex) flare up and then fizzle out under the benevolent influence of Glenfiddich. Maggie Brooks's script, from her own novel, may be a mite too schematic, and in the first half creates a Sally too cold and condescending to win much sympathy, but Duncan and Rea are both impressive. Best of all, however, is the portrayal of the English abroad: Bedford boozers in Rhineland bierkellers, Liverpool loonies celebrating after a soccer victory, and fleeting bonhomie between strangers stranded in strange lands are all wittily and subtly observed. GA

Loot
(Silvio Narizzano, 1970, GB) Richard Attenborough, Lee Remick, Hywel Bennett, Milo O'Shea, Roy Holder, Dick Emery, Joe Lynch.
101 min.
A sad example of the process of literary castration. By the time Ray Galton and Alan Simpson's script (which adds 'comic' scenes like a police bulldozer destroying a garden of gnomes and removes the more outrageous lines from Joe Orton's play) has passed through Narizzano's hands, all that is left is a caricature of the original. In place of the absurdity and emotional intensity, a collection of British character actors and a couple of stars go through their paces while Narizzano milks Orton's story of misplaced affection and an elusive corpse for all it's worth. PH

Lord Jim
(Richard Brooks, 1964, GB) Peter O'Toole, Paul Lukas, Daliah Lavi, Eli Wallach, Curd Jürgens, James Mason, Akim Tamiroff, Jack Hawkins, Ichizo Itami, Jack MacGowran, Christian Marquand.
154 min.
Hands up those who know that the real Dith Pran – the Cambodian hero of *The Killing Fields* – worked as a translator on this movie while it was on location at Angkor Wat, and that Juzo Itami, director of *Tampopo*, played a major role. Another fact is that Brooks' adaptation of Conrad's novel is immeasurably better than its reputation, and a scene towards the end – on a raft in the middle of a fog-bound river as O'Toole's Jim and Mason's Gentleman Brown discuss the age of the world and the price of evil – is an extraordinary attempt to convey Conradian metaphysics. 'Attempt', because Brooks is not entirely successful, with a major structural flaw (as in the novel itself) when the story ends two-thirds of the way through and has to start up again. Nevertheless, the film's pleasures far outweigh its inadequacies: Freddie Young's photography does for the Asian jungles what he did for the desert in *Lawrence of Arabia*, and the same might be said in praise of O'Toole's all-aquiver, neurotic performance. ATu

Lord Love a Duck
(George Axelrod, 1965, US) Roddy McDowall, Tuesday Weld, Lola Albright, Martin West, Ruth Gordon, Max Showalter, Harvey Korman, Martin Gabel.
105 min. b/w.
Axelrod's patchy but often brilliant first attempt at direction: a kooky fantasy, very funny in its satire of contemporary teen morals and mores. McDowall plays a high school student of enormous IQ and fabulous powers, which he exercises in order to grant a pretty co-ed (Weld) her every heart's desire, starting with the thirteen cashmere sweaters she requires to join an exclusive sorority, and ending with a husband whom he obligingly murders to leave her free to realise her true dream of movie stardom. Whereupon, realising he did it all for love, he ends up in the booby-hatch, happily dictating his memoirs. Taking in some delicious side-swipes at the 'Beach Blanket' cycle, Axelrod reveals much the same penchant (and talent) for cartoon-style sight gags as Tashlin, and coaxes a marvellous trio of variations on the American female from Tuesday Weld, Lola Albright and Ruth Gordon. Daniel Fapp's stunningly cool, clear monochrome camerawork is also a distinct plus. TM

Lord of Illusions
(Clive Barker, 1995, US) Scott Bakula, Kevin J O'Connor, Famke Janssen, Vincent Schiavelli, Daniel Von Bargen, Barry Del Sherman, Sheila Tousey.
122 min.
Barker's full-blooded adaptation of his story *The Last Illusion* arrives in Britain on video as a 'director's cut', with an extra 12 minutes, but since it's not letter-boxed, half the film's missing anyway. Hired by the enigmatic Dorothea (Janssen) to look out for her illusionist husband, Philip Swann (O'Connor), private eye Harry D'Amour (Bakula) enters a world where magic and illusion imperceptibly mingle. At the heart of the mystery is another of Barker's Faustian pacts: having learned his craft from religious cult leader Nix (Von Bargen), Swann recanted and sent Nix into temporary limbo. Now another Nix acolyte, the effete Butterfield (Sherman), has engineered his vengeful mentor's resurrection. Barker feels that the extra scenes flesh out the characters and explain their motivations, but much of this expository detail could be inferred from the studio's shorter cut. More fascinating are the imaginatively perverse images, the parallels between magic and cinematic illusion, and a gay subtext that presents the central struggle as a sexual/professional ménage à trois involving Nix, his heir apparent, Swann, and the aspiring Butterfield. NF

Lord of the Dance
(Richard Kohn, 1985, Fr/Switz/WGer)
113 min.
An excellent documentary, filmed at the Thubten Choling Monastery, high on the remote northern slopes of Everest, where in a form unchanged for

over 400 years, the followers of the Tibetan Buddhist 'Diamond Path' have performed their spectacular and beautiful religious dance festival known as 'Mani-Rimdu': a three-week ceremony of empowerment, ritual and celebration wherein the initiates assume the form of 'Lord of the Dance' and annually banish the destructive spiritual forces of the universe. WH

Lord of the Flies

(Peter Brook, 1963, GB) James Aubrey, Tom Chapin, Hugh Edwards, Roger Elwin, Tom Gaman.
91 min. b/w.
An underrated adaptation of William Golding's 1954 novel about a gang of English schoolboys stranded on a desert island after a nuclear holocaust. At first their unscheduled outward bound adventure is a great wheeze. But then things degenerate into tribal warfare based on class differences – the public school chaps are the hunters, and the oicks are virtual slaves. Golding's novel took Darwin's theories of natural selection to their ultimate conclusion, and while the apocalyptic parable is hardly the subtlest ever devised, the imagistic prose made it a devastating one. Brook knows he can't have his 10-12-year-olds mouthing philosophical and poetic paragraphs, so he shoots it like a documentary, overcoming the starvation budget, the location problems, and the sometimes awkward performances. However, the principals are excellent: Aubrey's Ralph, who just about keeps his dignity while all around are losing theirs, Chapin's beastly Jack, and Edward's tragic Piggy, who loses his glasses and then his life. ATu

Lord of the Flies

(Harry Hook, 1990, US) Paul Balthazar Getty, Chris Furrh, Danuel Pipoly, Andrew Taft, Edward Taft, gary Rule.
90 min.
In this second version of William Golding's novel, a group of cadets from an American military school are stranded on a desert island, along with the wounded pilot, after their plane crashes. Eventually the camp divides; Ralph (Getty) and Piggy (Pipoly) represent the values imposed by adults and civilisation; while they struggle to maintain a signal fire, Jack (Furrh) and his band of hunters, giving way to more primitive impulses, run rampage and turn murderous. The film, simplistically assuming the book's central metaphor to be imperialism – hence the military slant – retains the bare bones of Gollding's narrative, but that's all. There's little attempt to hint at the deeper issues, while the revelatory moment when the impaled pig's head looms in the clearing to reveal man's inner darkness, is merely flat. Executive producer Lewis Allen also produced Peter Brook's superior 1963 version; he took on the project after learning that TV producers planned a remake with an 'upbeat ending'. This is better than that, but not nearly good enough. CM

Lord of the Rings, The

(Ralph Bakshi, 1978, US) voices: Christopher Guard, William Squire, Michael Scholes, John Hurt, Simon Chandler, Dominic Guard, Norman Bird.
133 min.
Disney first held the rights to Tolkien's epic in the late '50s, so it's surprising that we had to wait so long, particularly since Kubrick and Boorman both tried unsuccessfully to set up productions. Mercifully, the book has escaped the typical Disney demolition; Bakshi's version, using animation and live-action tracings, is uniformly excellent, sticking closely to the original text and visually echoing many of Tolkien's own drawings. Use of British voices, together with the sensitive Leonard Rosenman sound-track, augments the impression of authenticity; and Bakshi wisely chose to leave Vol.3 for a later date, which allows him to avoid simplification to the point of superficiality. NFe

Lords of Discipline, The

(Franc Roddam, 1982, US) David Keith, Robert Prosky, GD Spradlin, Barbara Babcock, Michael Biehn, Rick Rossovich, John Lavachielli.
103 min.
Another in that most unlikely of 1980s genres: the US military college saga, this time a liberal conspiracy thriller, pitting its hero against the

racist secret society which controls the college. If the blend doesn't quite work, it is no fault of Roddam, who gives the film the pace, energy and excitement he instilled into the action sequences of *Quadrophenia*. In the first half, Roddam admirably conveys the notion of an enclosed world with its own insane rules and rituals; but as the conspiracy format becomes more obvious, the sheer confinement of the setting and period begins to work heavily against the film, closing down its narrative options precisely at the point when, in this kind of thriller, you want them to open up. DP

Lords of Flatbush, The

(Stephen F Verona/Martin Davidson, 1974, US) Perry King, Sylvester Stallone, Henry Winkler, Paul Mace, Susan Blakely, Maria Smith.
88 min.
A small masterpiece that places the mood and general ethos of the '50s with absolute precision and total affection. The Lords are a teenage high school leather gang in Brooklyn – or as they winningly call themselves, 'a social and athletic club'. The film observes their relationships and muffed sexual encounters over some months in 1958, the year one of their number gets married. Verona and Davidson direct superbly – the film's silences are every bit as telling as the perfectly judged dialogue – and it is shot and edited with a welcome degree of wit. Above all, the characters are all real, rather than academic or sentimental recreations. VG

Lorenzo's Oil

(George Miller, 1992, US) Nick Nolte, Susan Sarandon, Peter Ustinov, Kathleen Wilhoite, Gerry Bamman, Margo Martindale, James Rebhorn, Ann Hearn, Maduka Steady.
135 min.
Miller's 'true story' medical drama is based on the case of the Odones, an economist and his linguist wife, whose five-year-old son Lorenzo was diagnosed as having ALD, a degenerative, quickly fatal, and little understood brain disease. The couple (Nolte and Sarandon) refuse to accept the inevitable, abandon work to care for their son at home, and set about learning biochemistry to find a cure, in so doing taking on the medical profession and the received wisdom of the charity organisations. The film comes over as a *tour de force* version of the disease-of-the-week TV movie: half scientific detective story, half domestic drama, replete with scenes of suffering. Throughout, Miller points up every least thing: religious symbolism, snow-dusted Christmas windows for pathos, spinning news headlines, and swirling, diving camera movements. Finally, it begins to seem a little dishonest and self-conscious, as if Miller were trying to make an AIDS movie with hope and a positive ending. The night of San Lorenzo, after all, is the night when wishes come true. WH

Loser

(Erik Burke, 1991, US) Brendan Kelly, John Salemmo, Bernice De Leo, Nadine Miral.
83 min.
This punchy, low-rent New York comedy turns the yuppie nightmare genre on its head by taking a lunkheaded blue-collar no-hoper and dropping him into the heat of Manhattan glitzery. Hank (the amiably lumbering Kelly) is at the bottom of the heap – out of work, out of money, out of love – with only his klutz of a wide-boy buddy for comfort. Then his number comes up in the lottery, and everyone wants to know him. You know from the start that there has to be a sting in store, but while you wait it's a very enjoyable ride. Crammed with larger-than-life stereotypes – hopheads, hustlers and ludicrous hipsters – it treads a narrow line between cracker barrel humanism and gleeful misanthropy, but mainly it exudes delight at its own cheap and cheerful sense of fun. JRo

Loser Takes All

(Ken Annakin, 1956, GB) Rossano Brazzi, Glynis Johns, Tony Britton, Robert Morley, Albert Lieven, Felix Aylmer, AE Matthews, Joyce Carey, Geoffrey Keen.
88 min.
Graham Greene adapted his own least interesting novella for the screen, but later admitted that the result was 'a disaster'. The film is stymied by the miscasting of Rossano Brazzi as the middle-aged accountant who loses his fiancée Johns when he breaks the bank at Monte Carlo (under-

standably, Greene wanted Alec Guinness for the part). Filmed in 'Scope for no apparent reason; remade almost as indifferently in 1990 as *Strike It Rich*. TCh

Losin' It

(Curtis Hanson, 1983, US) Tom Cruise, Jackie Earle Haley, John Stockwell, John P Navin Jr, Shelley Long, Henry Darrow, Hector Elias.
104 min.
Take a trio of high-school boychicks setting out in their red Chevy convertible for a rooty-tooty time in south-of-the-border Tijuana. The year is 1963. Their aim, of course, is 'losin' it', and no prizes for guessing what 'it' is. So far, so familiar, but add a kid who's a wizard wheeler-dealer, and Long as a wronged wife who rides along for a quickie divorce, and you've got a *Porky's* with real meat on it. Cruise road-tests the prototype of his *Risky Business* ingénu, while Haley recycles his runt from *Breaking Away* with a sock stuffed into his crotch as he combs the town for spurious Spanish Fly. AB

Los Olvidados

see Olvidados, Los

Loss of Innocence

see Greengage Summer, The

Lost and Found

(Melvin Frank, 1979, GB) George Segal, Glenda Jackson, Maureen Stapleton, Hollis McLaren, John Cunningham, Paul Sorvino.
105 min.
A belated and redundant re-teaming of Touch of Class pair Segal and Jackson has them sparring interminably through married life, to increasingly wearying effect. She gets soft-focus close-ups; both get witless lines. If life is indeed the 'crock of shit' that well-read taxi-driver Sorvino helpfully explains it to be, this movie's the perfect mirror.

Lost Angels
(aka The Road Home)

(Hugh Hudson, 1989, US) Donald Sutherland, Adam Horovitz, Amy Locane, Don Bloomfield, Celia Weston, Graham Beckel, Patricia Richardson, Kevin Tighe, Nina Siemaszko.
116 min.
In Hudson's characteristically flashy foray into the cinema of delinquency, Horovitz (of the Beastie Boys) plays an LA brat repeatedly driven to commit antisocial acts of violence by his middle class folks: mom and stepdad are assholes, the brother he idolises is already well on the road to ruin, and dad naturally is an ex-cop. No wonder the boy's a nihilist. Girls, for once, offer scant succour, since Locane, met at a corrective centre, is not only into drugs but suffers from hammily mobile facial grimaces. Salvation is at hand, however, in the hapless form of Dr Sutherland, the traditionally troubled good guy, a shrink forever at odds with the money-obsessed psychotherapy establishment. For all Hudson's determination to tell it like it is (inmates eat own shit – shock!), and his evident love of bombastic flourishes (craning camera, lotsa loud music, weirdo slo-mo), the film serves up only trite melodrama and hackneyed moral homilies. GA

Lost Boys, The

(Joel Schumacher, 1987, US) Jason Patric, Corey Haim, Dianne Wiest, Barnard Hughes, Edward Herrmann, Kiefer Sutherland.
97 min.
This pathetic attempt at comic horror (deriving from an initial project to rework *Peter Pan* in vampiric terms) not only plays fast and loose with vampire mythology but also fails to deliver either frights or laughs. Soon after moving to the coastal town of Santa Clara with his mother (Wiest) and elder brother Michael (Patric), young MTV addict Sam (Haim) is warned against vampires by the two Goonies who run the local comic shop. Lured to a wild cave party, Michael gets his first taste of blood (out of a bottle?). Forewarned is forearmed, however, and when Michael starts wearing shades, sleeping all day and flying around, Sam and the comic kids reach for the holy water, garlic and wooden stakes. Directed with a cavalier disregard for intelligibility, this has to be one of the most anaemic vampire flicks ever made. NF

Lost Continent, The

(Michael Carreras, 1968, GB) Eric Porter, Hildegard Knef, Suzanna Leigh, Nigel Stock, Tony Beckley, Neil McCallum, Benito Carruthers, Jimmy Hanley.
98 min.
Outrageously plotted (after Dennis Wheatley's novel *Uncharted Seas*), garishly shot and played poker straight, this Hammer masterwork mutates the Gothic into the surreal as Porter's potentially explosive ship drifts into the uncharted nightmare world of the Sargasso, where the seaweed bites and the natives live in a time warp. Sad that since Carreras took over control of Hammer from his father, his sole directorial credit should have been on *Shatter* following Monte Hellman's sacking. PT

Lost Highway

(David Lynch, 1996, US) Bill Pullman, Patricia Arquette, Balthazar Getty, Gary Busey, Robert Blake, Richard Pryor, Robert Loggia.
134 min.
Jazz saxophonist Fred (Pullman) is haunted by anxiety about the fidelity of his wife Renee (Arquette) and the mysterious arrival of video recordings shot inside their house. Fred sees himself, on one tape, next to his wife's battered body, and is arrested for murder. Overnight, Fred vanishes, to be replaced by garage mechanic Pete (Getty), who hasn't a clue how he ended up in jail. To make matters more mystifying, Pete presently becomes involved with Alice (Arquette again), mistress of his gangster pal Mr Eddy (Loggia), leading him into a nightmarish intrigue which only gradually begins to connect, obscurely, with Fred. The plotting, with its inexplicably metamorphosed protagonist and its various doubles, makes one suspect Lynch may be having us on. It's ironic, then, that narrative is the most intriguing thing about the film, leading us either to dismiss it as pretentious rubbish or to try to make sense of it on a metaphorical level. Fortunately, Lynch's mastery of mood through sound, space, decor and lighting means that we're more or less engrossed throughout, even though some of the sillier moments – not to mention the uncharacteristically clumsy use of music – try one's patience. GA

Lost Honour of Katharina Blum, The (Die verlorene Ehre der Katharina Blum)

(Volker Schlöndorff/Margarethe von Trotta, 1975, WGer) Angela Winkler, Mario Adorf, Dieter Laser, Heinz Bennent, Jürgen Prochnow.
106 min.
A disturbingly powerful version of Heinrich Böll's novel about the irresponsibility of the gutter press and their ability to destroy lives. Winkler is excellent as the shy, apolitical young woman who sleeps with a man she meets at a party, unaware that he's a terrorist; next morning, after he's gone, armed police burst in, arrest her, and the nightmare begins. A smear campaign is started against her character, her privacy is repeatedly violated, and the links between single-minded, right-wing police and news-hungry press are made clear. It's a frightening account of how external, arbitrary forces can ruin lives, which simultaneously portrays the heroine as a courageous, dignified upholder of her freedom. Sometimes surreal, always intelligent and menacing, it's far superior to Schlöndorff's later *The Tin Drum*. GA

Lost Horizon

(Frank Capra, 1937, US) Ronald Colman, Jane Wyatt, John Howard, Edward Everett Horton, Margo, Sam Jaffe, HB Warner, Thomas Mitchell, Isabel Jewell.
117 min. b/w.
Classic fantasy epic based on James Hilton's novel, with a number of air-passengers hijacked after leaving war-torn China, and ending up in Tibet's Shangri-La, where peace, good health and longevity are the rule. Colman is torn between staying and returning to normal 'civilisation', and the result is a full-blown weepie, complete with kitschy sets, admirable if incredibly naïve sentiments, and fine acting from Colman. Not at all the sort of film one could make in these considerably more jaundiced times, as was evident with the appearance of the atrocious remake in 1973. GA

Lost Horizon

(Charles Jarrott, 1972, US) Peter Finch, Liv Ullmann, Sally Kellerman, George Kennedy, Michael York, Olivia Hussey, Bobby Van, James Shigeta, Charles Boyer, John Gielgud.
143 min.
A disastrous remake of James Hilton's novel that replaces the old-fashioned hokum and wish-fulfilment of the Capra version with a melodramatic confrontation of the 'real' (the plane and its passengers are refugees from an unnamed Asian war) with the worst of recent cultural mythology (Shangri-La is little more than Disneyland with beads, and is overseen by a very Maharishi-like Charles Boyer). PH

Lost in America

(Albert Brooks, 1985, US) Albert Brooks, Julie Hagerty, Michael Green, Tom Tarpey, Raynold Gideon, Maggie Roswell.
91 min.
Brooks is the co-writer, director and star of this film, which deserves recognition as a perfectly judged satire on the well-travelled upwardly mobile couple who opt out of the rat race. They go horizontally mobile by pooling their assets and taking to the not-so-*Easy Rider* road, only to find they have swapped their *American Dream* for a dead-end nightmare. Characterisation and comic timing are faultless, and Brooks is brilliant, soaring ever so neatly OTT in his boss' office or throwing an apoplectic fit when he discovers his wife's secret vice. AB

Lost in Siberia (Zateriannyi v Sibiri)

(Alexander Mitta, 1991, USSR/GB) Anthony Andrews, Yelena Mayorova, Vladimir Ilyin, Ira Mikhalyova, Yevgeni Mironov, Alexei Zharkov, Nicolas Chagrin, Elena Secota.
108 min.
This co-production describes the horrors of Stalin's camps and Arctic gulags in the '40s from the perspective of a British archaeologist falsely arrested for spying. Andrei Miller, a Brit of Russian grandparentage, is pulled off his dig and cattle-trucked to Siberia, where an escape attempt adds 25 years to his sentence. Living down in life's base camp, his identity stripped to bare bone, he finds only love and friendship can save the spirit. This is basically a journey-through-hell movie, with scenes of Doré-like torment, dehumanising injustice, hunger, privation and terror. Most harrowing is the depiction of violence among prisoners. Here the film's style veers closer at times to the visceral expressionism of Alan Parker's *Midnight Express* than, say, to that of Caspar Wrede's *One Day in the Life of Ivan Denisovich*; what holds it back is the acrid whiff of authenticity. Despite the excesses, it's an impressive effort, with a strong, committed performance from Andrews as Miller. WH

Lost in the Stars

(Daniel Mann, 1974, US) Brock Peters, Melba Moore, Raymond St Jacques, Clifton Davis, Paula Kelly.
114 min.
One of the weakest of the American Film Theatre's 'stage records', this adaptation of Alan Paton's *Cry the Beloved Country* was the last musical scored by Kurt Weill. Opened up by screenwriter Alfred Hayes to little effect, and ploddingly directed by Daniel Mann, Paton's story of a black clergyman (Peters), who discovers the horrors of repression and racism when he travels to Johannesburg in search of his son, is transformed into a series of well-intentioned clichés. Weill's music is marvellous. PH

Lost in Transit

see Tombes du Ciel

Lost in Yonkers (aka Neil Simon's Lost in Yonkers)

(Martha Coolidge, 1993, US) Richard Dreyfuss, Brad Stoll, Mike Damus, Irene Worth, Mercedes Ruehl, David Strathairn, Robert Guy Miranda.
114 min.
Movies of Neil Simon plays never seem to be *directed by* anyone – and this film is a case in point. Two little brothers (Stoll and Damus) are dumped on Grandma by their father, a recent widower, and find themselves unwelcome.

Grandma (Worth) runs her candy store and her family on an inhumanly tight rein. Her inability to show love has turned her son, the boys' Uncle Louie (Dreyfuss), into a feckless crook on the run, and daughter Bella (Ruehl) into a near retard, forever thwarted in her dreams of marriage and children. This sounds like a Jewish take on *The Glass Menagerie*, though Simon leaves one feeling faintly furtive about the odd manipulated tear. Irene Worth is outstanding as the matriarch, rising to the soundless scream that reveals the cost of her regime upon herself. Dreyfuss is in finger-popping mode, but Ruehl seems to have strayed in from the Broadway stage. BC

Lost Moment, The

(Martin Gabel, 1947, US) Robert Cummings, Susan Hayward, Agnes Moorehead, Joan Lorring, Eduardo Ciannelli, John Archer.
89 min. b/w.
A remarkably effective adaptation of Henry James' *The Aspern Papers*, closer to the shivery ambience of *The Innocents* than to the oh-so-discreet charm of *Daisy Miller* or *The Europeans*. An opportunist publisher (Cummings) lodges incognito in the Venetian house of a long-dead poet's lover, hoping to find the literary treasure-trove of letters hidden there, and gradually comes under the spells of the past incarnate – the 105-year-old former loved one (Moorehead) and her schizophrenic niece (Hayward). The ghostly web of shifting identities and sexual tensions is superbly spun, making one regret that Martin Gabel subsequently confined himself to an acting career. PT

Lost One, The

see Verlorene, Der

Lost Paradise, The (Het Verloren Paradijs)

(Harry Kümel, 1978, Bel) Willeke van Ammelrooy, Hugo van den Berghe, Bert André, Gella Allaert, Stephen Windross.
94 min.
This may have little of the fantastic frenzy which dominated *Malpertuis* or *Daughters of Darkness*, but it's just as peculiar. A Flemish village is threatened by a motorway, whose siting provokes full-scale battle between the nature-loving burgomaster, the boorish but aspiring seed merchant, two *dummkopf* surveyors, and a crowd of stammering, vacillating, bewildered villagers. Then in strides Willeke van Ammelrooy, stately lady with a past, red hair, red mac and red fingernails, who adds a dose of arty sex to the buffoonery and broad satire. If Kümel hadn't such a heavy hand with everything the mix might have been quite explosive. But it remains one for curiohunters: there can't be that many ecological-political-sex-comedy-dramas around. GB

Lost Patrol, The

(John Ford, 1934, US) Victor McLaglen, Boris Karloff, Wallace Ford, Reginald Denny, Alan Hale, JM Kerrigan, Billy Bevan.
74 min. b/w.
At first glance, a fairly commonplace war-in-the-desert picture (with Yuma standing in for Mesopotamia), about a British patrol stranded during World War I falling prey to Arab snipers. Three main things distinguish it: Ford's adroit avoidance of 'Foreign Legion' clichés in the characterisation and plotting; Max Steiner's excellent score, which won an Oscar; and Karloff's extraordinary 'expressionist' performance as a soldier convinced that doom is at hand. The latter, in particular, represents an aspect of Ford's work that is often forgotten: a bold use of visual and dramatic stylisation, often associated with religious themes and characters. TR

Lost Sex (Honno)

(Kaneto Shindo, 1966, Jap) Hideo Kanze, Nobuko Otowa, Eijiro Tohno, Yoshinobu Ogawa, Kaori Shima.
103 min. b/w.
Given Shindo's predilection for either pretentious symbolism or heady sex'n'violence, you might well fear the worst for this study of a middle-aged man who lost his virility at Hiroshima, regained it, lost it again after Bikini, and is patiently coaxed back to vim and vigour by his obliging widowed housekeeper. Surprisingly, it turns into an engaging character study, coloured by a wry wit more characteristic of Ichikawa. Few other

directors could have brought the correct serio-comic touch to a scene in which the housekeeper, seeking to stimulate her master, stage manages an 'ancient custom' in which three masked males besiege her house by night, miaowing like rampant toms. Adding greatly to the pleasure are some marvellously melancholy (and beautifully photographed) snowy mountain locations. TM

Lost Squadron, The

(George Archainbaud, 1932, US) Richard Dix, Mary Astor, Erich von Stroheim, Joel McCrea, Dorothy Jordan, Robert Armstrong, Hugh Herbert.
79 min. b/w.
With a cynically acidic script by Herman J Mankiewicz, this early talkie is one of the most enjoyably scabrous examples of Hollywood on Hollywood. Veteran airmen from World War I, desperate for work, get jobs as stuntmen on a movie (cue for some fine aerial photography), but they don't reckon with their director, an egotistical and obsessive (not to mention homicidally jealous) tyrant who'll stop at nothing in his desire to make a great film. Von Stroheim was perfect for the part: not only does he have a whale of a time strutting around in jodhpurs, snapping his whip and snarling through the megaphone, the role is also wonderfully reminiscent of his own reputed past as a sadistically cruel and inspired film-maker. GA

Lost Weekend, The

(Billy Wilder, 1945, US) Ray Milland, Jane Wyman, Philip Terry, Howard da Silva, Doris Dowling, Frank Faylen.
99 min. b/w.
A scarifyingly grim and grimy account of an alcoholic writer's lost weekend, stolen from time intended to be spent on taking a cure and gradually turning into a descent into hell. What makes the film so gripping is the brilliance with which Wilder uses John F Seitz's camera-work to range from an unvarnished portrait of New York brutally stripped of all glamour (Milland's frantic trudge along Third Avenue on *Yom Kippur* in search of an open pawnshop is a neo-realist *morceau d'anthologie*) to an almost Wellesian evocation of the alcoholic's inner world (not merely the justly famous DTs hallucination of a mouse attacked by bats, but the systematic use of images dominated by huge foreground objects). Characteristically dispassionate in his observation, Wilder elicits sympathy for his hero only by stressing the cruelly unthinking indifference to his sickness: the male nurse in the alcoholic ward gleefully chanting, 'Good morning, Mary Sunshine!', or the pianist in the bar leading onlookers in a derisive chant of 'somebody stole my purse' (to the tune of 'Somebody Stole My Gal') after he is humiliatingly caught trying to acquire some money. A pity that the production code demanded a glibly unconvincing ending in which love finds a way. TM

Lost World, The

(Irwin Allen, 1960, US) Michael Rennie, Jill St John, Claude Rains, David Hedison, Richard Haydn, Fernando Lamas.
98 min.
Dreary version of Conan Doyle's yarn about an expedition to a prehistoric enclave in the South American jungle (the silent version of 1925 was at least fun). The characters are insufferable, the dialogue abominable, and Willis O'Brien's special effects are hamstrung by Allen's decision to use real reptiles disguised as monsters. TM

Lost World: Jurassic Park, The

(Steven Spielberg, 1997, US) Jeff Goldblum, Julianne Moore, Pete Postlethwaite, Arliss Howard, Vince Vaughn, Richard Attenborough, Peter Stormare.
129 min.
Despite the tighter script, this sequel suffers by provoking a sense of déjà vu: crucially, our wonder at the dinosaurs – the first film's trump card – is severely diminished second time around, while the suspense set-pieces are simply more of the same. Story and characterisation, such as they are, are contrived; it now turns out there's a second secret island populated by the beasts, which Goldblum reluctantly visits with a 'good' research expedition, and Postlethwaite leads a 'bad' team of hunters hired to transport them to a San Diego theme park. There's much hiding from T Rexes on the rampage after the baddies have messed with their young; indeed, there's much stuff about parenting, too, with Goldblum now lumbered with an (inexplicably black) daughter – presumably an identification figure for younger viewers, who may find some of the nastier attacks (men torn in two, faces bitten by initially sweet-seeming mini-monsters) hard to take. And the eco message is pap, an excuse for a climactic scene of a T Rex terrorising the LA suburbs (when, oddly, the model work is most conspicuous and unreal). In short, what you'd expect, and no more. GA

Lost World of Sinbad, The (Daitozoku)

(Senkichi Taniguchi, 1963, Jap) Toshiro Mifune, Makoto Satoh, Jun Funato, Ichiro Arishima, Miye Hama.
97 min.
So little of the Japanese popular cinema reaches this country that it's been hard to judge whether the movies are as fanatically Americanised as most of the other Japanese mass media. Here is Exhibit A for the Prosecution: a Western-style swashbuckling fantasy which the dubbers have been able to turn into a Sinbad story without missing a beat. Although it's by no means rank, it remains the kind of film that gives a 'formula' a bad name. All the ingredients are there, including decent, if limited, special effects, but the emphases are curiously misjudged: there's too much plot, Mifune's presence goes for nothing, the comedy is hopelessly non-integrated, and the Gothicisms are too perfunctory. But the saddest thing is the bland rejection of the entire Oriental fantasy tradition. TR

Louise

see Chère Louise

Louisiana Story

(Robert Flaherty, 1948, US) Joseph Boudreaux, Lionel Le Blanc, E Bienvenu, Frank Hardy, CT Guedry.
78 min. b/w.
Flaherty's last work, like his first, *Nanook of the North*, was the product of one of those fluke occasions when a sponsor (in this case, the Standard Oil Company) offers money with no strings attached. With no disciplining 'purpose', Flaherty's totally intuitive method was tested to its limits – and his editor Helen Van Dongen has recorded the extraordinary convolutions of plot and readings that his material underwent en route to its ravishing conclusion. As an account of oil exploration, Flaherty's narrative may seem slightly naive; but his vision of a child's mythworld, and the oilmen's intrusion and acceptance into it, is perhaps his greatest achievement. DC

Loulou

(Maurice Pialat, 1980, Fr) Isabelle Huppert, Gérard Depardieu, Guy Marchand, Humbert Balsan, Bernard Tronczyk.
105 min.
Pialat's film boasts France's two currently most important film stars: Depardieu as the slobbish drifter Loulou, and Huppert as the bright, rather aimless Nelly, who abandons her lover-boss and bourgeois friends for better sex and a simpler life (drink and TV, inarticulate tenderness and lost opportunities). With its combination of storytelling and social observation, *Loulou* sketches a portrait of France in the '70s (blue collar, big-bellied, chauvinist); and in its pessimism about social and sexual revolution, the film mocks the prosperity wrought by Giscard. At the end, as Nelly and Loulou stumble, drunk, out of the bar and into the Parisian suburbs, this really is 'darkness on the edge of town'. CA

Love (Szerelem)

(Károly Makk, 1971, Hun) Lili Darvas, Mari Törőcsik, Iván Darvas.
92 min. b/w.
Two women from different worlds whose lives have become rituals around an absent man: Makk catches the nuances of their relationship. One is the man's bedridden mother, who believes her imprisoned son is hitting the big time in America. The other is his wife, carefully sustaining the illusion in the old lady. The film is set in 1953, and shades of the consequences of the cult of the personality hang in Makk's references to the extravagant exploits of the son in the States. Finely shot by János Tóth, the film exhibits a concern for the quality of people's lives that stays this side of the nostalgic, and seems a characteristic of current Hungarian cinema. It may sound grim, it isn't in the least.

Love Among the Ruins

(George Cukor, 1975, US) Katharine Hepburn, Laurence Olivier, Colin Blakely, Richard Pearson, Joan Sims, Leigh Lawson, Robert Harris.
102 min.
Cukor's last really impressive film was, ironically, made for television, and as such is stylistically rather less ambitious than his finest work. That said, his strengths were always his way with actors and his interest in the nuances of the battle between the sexes, and this remains a minor gem on both counts. Hepburn is the Edwardian dowager being sued for breach of promise by a much younger man (Lawson); Olivier is the eminent barrister whose course of defence – born of outrage at her inability to remember their brief affair years previously – is to portray her (falsely) as a senile old duffer incapable of passion. A gently sentimental comedy that never patronises the aged, the film charms with its subtle insights, quiet generosity, and sympathy for the plight of women in a repressive, male-dominated society. In short, it's a Cukor film through and through. GA

Love and a .45

(CM Talkington, 1995, US) Gil Bellows, Renee Zellweger, Peter Fonda, Rory Cochrane, Jeffrey Combs, Jace Alexander, Michael Bowen.
101 min.
Bellows pulls a hold-up with an empty pistol before toddling home to TV and girlfriend Zellweger, but soon a botched heist forces them to abandon their mobile-home for the open road, pursued by various cops and robbers. Plenty of excessive, derivative violence, but anyone desperate for a fix of style and sassiness will be disappointed. Fonda has a daft cameo as a trippy hippy who speaks through a device on his neck. AO

Love and Bullets

(Stuart Rosenberg, 1978, US) Charles Bronson, Jill Ireland, Rod Steiger, Henry Silva, Strother Martin, Bradford Dillman, Michael V Gazzo.
103 min.
Bronson sheds his enigmatic rough-tough persona, dons suit, and coifs hair to join Jill Ireland (impersonating Tammy Wynette) and Rod Steiger (taking off Brando) in this routine tale of witness wanted by FBI and mobsters alike. Characterisation becomes caricature, dialogue is diabolic, and with the whole of Switzerland to frolic in, the ability of both hunter and hunted to arrive in the same place at the same time transcends the realms of coincidence and enters those of ESP. *Love and Bullets*, my eye; embarrassment and tedium is more like it. FF

Love and Death

(Woody Allen, 1975, US) Woody Allen, Diane Keaton, Olga Georges-Picot, Harold Gould, Jessica Harper, Alfred Lutter, James Tolkan.
85 min.
On the same inspired wavelength as the Mel Brooks *2000 Year Old Man* routines, Stephen Leacock's parodies of the Russian novel, and any number of insane SJ Perelman dialogues. It's another episode in Allen's New-neurotic romance with Diane Keaton, this time with Napoleon's invasion of Russia interfering. This allows a string of terrific visual gags using battles, Death the Grim Reaper, swords, grand opera, village idiots, snow, Napoleon and Olga Georges-Picot: 'Are you in the mood?' 'I've been in the mood since the late 1700s'. Less stylised than *Sleeper*, it's somehow not as satisfying to watch: in the cod-Russian manner, there are a lot of dark interior conversations between the lovers which tend to indulgence. But the running metaphor of Wheat is excepted honourably from this criticism, and as less than half-a-dozen lines are bum, *Love and Death* is an almost total treat. AN

Love and Death on Long Island

(Richard Kwietniowski, 1997, GB/Can) John Hurt, Jason Priestley, Fiona Loewi, Sheila Hancock, Maury Chaykin.
93 min.
Kwietniowski's feature debut, a marvellous adap-

tation of Gilbert Adair's novel, tells the hilariously unlikely tale of the obsession harboured by reclusive old fart London novelist Giles De'ath (Hurt) for hunky but not very talented American teen pin-up Ronnie Bostock (Priestley) after seeing him in an appalling movie. Unquestionably hetero until his wife died, and barely cognisant of the modern technological world, let alone Long Island (where he fetches up in an attempt to meet his unwitting beloved), De'ath is simultaneously embarrassed, confused, tormented and rejuvenated by his infatuation. A genuinely literate, affectionate fish-out-of-water comedy, which never overplays its *Death in Venice* references, the film benefits hugely from Hurt's superb performance and from Kwietniowski's lovely parodies of straight-to-video fare. GA

Love and Duty
(Lian'ai yu Yiwu)

(Richard Poh, i.e. Bu Wancang, 1931, China) Ruan Lingyu, Raymond King (i.e. Jin Yan), Chen Yanyan, Li Ying.
152 min. b/w.
Believed lost until a near-pristine tinted print was discovered in Uruguay (!) in 1994, this epic-length melodrama is something of a revelation: a sophisticated account of love as the force most likely to upset a 'well ordered' society. The legendary Ruan Lingyu (21 at the time) plays a woman from adolescence to old age and doubles as the character's teenage daughter in the climactic scenes. Nai-Fan marries on the orders of her stern, traditional father and gives her rich, boring husband two children; but she runs away to be with the struggling writer she really loves, only to face a life of disappointment, hardship and poverty. Recent (1997) screenings confirm the film's lasting power to move audiences – and to make them laugh, thanks to the witty sketch of a shy courtship and the dream-sequence parody of a Douglas Fairbanks movie. TR

Love and Human Remains

(Denys Arcand, 1993, Can) Thomas Gibson, Ruth Marshall, Cameron Bancroft, Mia Kirshner, Joanne Vannicola, Rick Roberts.
100 min.
Brad Fraser's *Unidentified Human Remains and the True Nature of Love* was praised as a play, but here, adapted for the screen, it seems much ado about very little. It's full of big issues, but what's said about them is less substantial, provocative or witty than in Arcand's previous attempt to monitor the contemporary pulse, *Jesus of Montreal*. The film centres on two flat-sharing friends: actor/writer David (Gibson), a manipulative bisexual cynic, and book-reviewer Candy (Marshall), whose quest for romance leaves her torn between a barman and a woman met at the gym. Add a dominatrix, a teenage busboy with a crush on David, a transvestite and others, and you have a fashionable cross-section of young Montreal – but which, if any, is the serial killer terrorising the city? Unfortunately, it's a half-hearted mystery. The characters are so unsympathetic, and the tone so determinedly cool, that the movie ends up as cautious and emotionally tepid as the behaviour it depicts. Not bad, but certainly not very likeable or illuminating. GA

Love and Music

see Stamping Ground

Love and Other Catastrophes

(Emma-Kate Croghan, 1996, Aust) Frances O'Connor, Alice Garner, Radha Mitchell, Matt Day, Matthew Dyktynski, Suzi Dougherty.
79 min.
Made on a shoestring by a bunch of film school graduates (director and co-writer Croghan was 23 at the time), this sweet, brisk campus comedy has a refreshingly current feel. For once, you believe the actors are the age they're playing. The romantic musical chairs are routine, but Croghan has a light touch, and a shrewd eye for the rules of attraction. It's too unassuming to be brattily obnoxious. Film buffs will doubtless enjoy the frequent in-jokes (and come out numbering their three favourite films, and why). TCh

Love at First Bite

(Stan Dragoti, 1979, US) George Hamilton, Susan Saint James, Richard Benjamin, Dick Shawn, Arte Johnson.
96 min.

A camp and knowing spoof along the lines of Rowan and Martin's *Laugh-In*, in which Count Dracula (Hamilton), dispossessed by the People's Commissar in his native Transylvania, moves to New York to have a bite out of the Big Apple and Susan Saint James. Atrociously directed and full of groan-making jokes, but the cast are having such a good time that it's difficult not to respond in a similar way. See it when you feel at your silliest.

Love at Large

(Alan Rudolph, 1990, US) Tom Berenger, Elizabeth Perkins, Anne Archer, Kate Capshaw, Annette O'Toole, Ted Levine, Ann Magnuson, Kevin J O'Connor, Ruby Dee, Barry Miller, Neil Young.
97 min.
Rudolph regularly pitches his movies somewhere between reality and unreality, which makes his work very uneven: either charming or frustratingly whimsical. Sadly, this foray into *film noir* territory, despite delightful moments, is mostly dispiritingly inconsequential. When Harry Dobbs (Berenger) – a PI about to break with his jealous girlfriend (Magnuson) – is asked by mysterious Miss Dolan (Archer) to keep tabs on a guy named Rick, the down-at-heel dick finds himself trailing a bigamist to a ranch, while being trailed in turn by a novice shamus, Stella (Perkins), hired by his jealous lover. Harry and Stella eventually join forces to right marital wrongs; but what they – and everyone else – really seek is love, a fleeting, indefinable emotion that Rudolph appears to be making his life's study. Because he can't decide whether his romantic comedy is also a thriller, it lacks suspense and memorable gags. If Berenger and Archer are unconvincing, the rest of the women – notably Perkins – hint at depths unexplored by the script. But hints are not enough, and unless the film's elusive, brittle mood traps you in the first few minutes, you may well find it much ado about nothing. GA

Love Ban, The

see It's a 2'6" Above the Ground World

Love Bewitched, A
(El Amor Brujo)

(Carlos Saura, 1986, Sp) Antonio Gades, Cristina Hoyos, Laura Del Sol, Juan Antonio Jimenez.
98 min.
The third collaboration between Saura and choreographer Gades, once again teeming with hot gypsy passions. But this one suffers from high-styled pretensions, and is short-circuited by non-musical scenes that have all the subtlety of old-fashioned, flaring-nostrils melodrama. The story is a supernatural love triangle about a woman possessed by the soul of her dead husband and pursued by the man who murdered him. The camera-work is straightforward and strong, the dance sizzling and authentic; but as with most series, *Flamenco III* isn't quite as satisfying as its predecessors. AR

Love Bug, The

(Robert Stevenson, 1968, US) David Tomlinson, Dean Jones, Michele Lee, Buddy Hackett, Joe Flynn, Benson Fong, Joe E Ross, Pedro Gonzalez-Gonzalez.
107 min.
The first instalment in the long-lived Disney series, based on Gordon Buford's story *Car-Boy-Girl*, reveals how Jones, an unsuccessful San Francisco racing driver, discovers that his Beetle has rather more personality than he expected. 'Herbie' and his plucky stunt drivers steal the show in this agreeable family entertainment. TJ

Love, Cheat & Steal

(William Curran, 1993, US) John Lithgow, Eric Roberts, Mädchen Amick, Richard Edson, Donald Moffat.
96 min.
Not exactly bad, but in no way notable. When Roberts reads that old flame Amick – whose evidence put him away in the Ravensville State Prison, Nevada, seven years ago – has married wealthy banker Lithgow, he breaks out of stir together with cellmate Edson and straight for the newly-weds' California love nest, where he passes himself off as her brother. Not that he

wants to kill her, understand: rather, he's set on robbing Lithgow's bank (with her reluctant help, naturally). Meanwhile honest John has other problems since he's uncovered a money-laundering scam perpetrated by bank officials in cahoots with Colombian drug barons. Lithgow does a decent turn, of course, but Edson seems to have picked up Roberts' taste for ham, and Amick is as shallow as those other youngsters who emerged from *Twin Peaks*. GA

Love Child

see Child Under a Leaf

Love Child, The

(Robert Smith, 1987, GB) Sheila Hancock, Peter Capaldi, Percy Herbert, Lesley Sharp, Alexei Sayle, Arthur Hewlett, Stephen Frost, Steven O'Donnell.
100 min.
If Bill Forsyth teamed up with the Comic Strip, the result might be something like this: a determinedly whimsical, slightly-too-surreal look at working-class life on a Lambeth housing estate. Neither quite funny enough for comedy nor realistic enough for satire, but some strong cameos, warmth and wry wit make it enjoyable. Capaldi is a wide-eyed, gangling delight as an orphaned love child of the '60s (his father played with cult rock group the Pink Frogs) who fails to develop the 'bijou little killer streakette' required by his accounting-firm boss, and instead discovers magic 'shrooms and free love with an artist from the local squat. Meanwhile, in an amusing reversal, his dope-smoking gran (Hancock) plans to leave him for a place of her own. Though these two, by sheer force of personality, flesh out their stereotypes, the over-casting of alternative TV comedians (particularly Frost and O'Donnell as bully-boy policemen) was a mistake. DW

Lovecraft
(aka Cast a Deadly Spell)

(Martin Campbell, 1991, US) Fred Ward, David Warner, Julianne Moore, Clancy Brown, Alexandra Powers.
92 min.
An engagingly left-field brew of gumshoes and ghouls, originally made for cable. The premise is that in Los Angeles in 1948, everyone is using magic – except, that is, for Marlowesque private eye H Philip Lovecraft (Ward). The plot, in this slapdash homage to Cthulhu, Yog-Sothoth and all the other unspellable regulars of horror writer HP Lovecraft's demonology, is the thinnest of McGuffins: the sinister Amos Hackshaw (Warner in prime eye-rolling mode) wants Lovecraft to get back his copy of the notorious grimoire, The Necronomicon, and to watch over the virtues of his virginal daughter. Distractions are added by the mandatory *femme fatale*, a nefarious club-owner and his sorcerous stooge, and a malevolent beastie. The narrative founders precariously between *film noir* verisimilitude and total cloud nine daffiness, with lurid but ultimately tame special effects, and a disappointing apocalyptic showdown. But there's much jaw-dropping flipness to be savoured on the way. JRo

Love Crazy

(Jack Conway, 1941, US) William Powell, Myrna Loy, Gail Patrick, Jack Carson, Florence Bates, Sidney Blackmer, Sig Ruman, Vladimir Sokoloff, Elisha Cook Jr, Donald MacBride.
99 min. b/w.
One of Conway's better movies, thanks to perfect casting and a brightly inventive script. Powell and Loy, both in cracking form, are blissfully celebrating their fourth anniversary when he gets stuck in a lift with an old flame (Patrick). Complications ensue, mother-in-law (Bates) gleefully smells a rat, and Loy sues for divorce. Powell obtains a postponement on the grounds of insanity (which he demonstrates at every opportunity). Loy retaliates by having him committed; he escapes disguised as his sister; and... well, it all comes out in the wash. This is screwball territory, so questions of implausibility or tastelessness don't really come into it; besides, it really is very funny, with every member of the cast contributing. Highlights include Powell's wonderfully refined drag act, and his efforts to explain, for the benefit of a lunacy commission, what a runaway cockatoo and playing boats with top hats in the swimming-pool had to do with his falling naked out of a tree onto a patio full of party guests. TM

Loved

(Erin Dignam, 1997, US) William Hurt, Robin Wright Penn, Amy Madigan, Joanna Cassidy, Jennifer Rubin, Sean Penn.
102 min.
Writer/director Dignam's film is part earnest TV movie and part that elusive beast, the American Art Film. Hurt's a DA trying to convince Robin Wright Penn to testify against her abusive ex-husband. Trouble is, she still loves him. More ambitious than it sounds, this elliptical, superbly acted film aims for spiritual intangibles. The tone is set by Sean Penn's haunting cameo as a man tormented by the fences we put up around us. TCh

Loved One, The

(Tony Richardson, 1965, US) Robert Morse, Anjanette Comer, Jonathan Winters, Rod Steiger, Dana Andrews, Milton Berle, James Coburn, Ayllene Gibbons, John Gielgud, Tab Hunter, Margaret Leighton, Liberace, Roddy McDowall, Robert Morley, Lionel Stander.
119 min. b/w.
Evelyn Waugh's satirical novel about the British in Hollywood and Californian funeral practices was long a Buñuel project, but it finally fell to Richardson and a potentially riotous cast. Morse, unfortunately, as the British poet who ends up in the pet cemetery business, is no match for the expert wackiness on display, in particular Ayllene Gibbons as Steiger's bedridden (and food-bound) mother, and Liberace as a casket salesman. Sadly, the script, by Terry Southern out of Christopher Isherwood, just tries too hard to pack too much in, and the frenetic pacing becomes tiresome very quickly. DT

Love, etc.

(Marion Vernoux, 1996, Fr) Charlotte Gainsbourg, Yvan Attal, Charles Berling, Thibault de Montalembert, Elodie Navarre, Marie Adam.
104 min.
A Georges Delerue-like Gallic version of Julian Barnes' novel *Talking It Over*, about a ménage à trois, this second feature from Vernoux (director Jacques Audiard's partner) is a self conscious attempt, complete with its 'Scope visuals and 180° circling camera, to refract modernity through a period lens – with one eye on the '60s New Wave, and the other on the more contemplative '70s. Gainsbourg, in fashionably mismatched outfits, plays strong-headed Marie, who marries orthodox Benoît (Attal) but becomes more and more intrigued by his 'crazier' lecturer pal of 20 years, Pierre (Berling). Attal and Berling give strong performances, notably in a passionate, confrontational head to head, but despite the evident intention to examine 'a man's world', it's Gainsbourg's lively gamine who provides the most compelling portrait. The film's retro chic aesthetic admits a certain waywardness and the odd longueur (the early pacing is variable, to say the least), but it grows considerably in interest and confidence as it progresses. WH

Love Eternal

see Eternel Retour, L'

Love Field

(Jonathan Kaplan, 1992, US) Michelle Pfeiffer, Dennis Haysbert, Stephanie McFadden, Brian Kerwin, Louise Latham, Peggy Rea.
104 min.
Lurene (Pfeiffer), a Dallas housewife infatuated with Jackie Kennedy, puts her marriage at risk when she takes the Greyhound to Washington to see the President's funeral. On the bus, she makes friends with a black fellow passenger (Haysbert) and the daughter he may or may not be abducting. This affecting romantic comedy probes the gradations of racial prejudice still prevalent in the South despite JFK's best efforts. Kaplan has a light touch throughout (the assassination itself is evocatively understated) and Pfeiffer gives a marvellously touching, funny and credible performance. Unaccountably denied a theatrical release in Britain, this is a most impressive and enjoyable work. GA

Love Goddesses, The

(Saul J Turell/Graeme Ferguson, 1965, US) narrator: Carl King.
87 min. b/w & col.
A fascinating but maddeningly snippety compilation of clips purporting to trace the changing face of the vamp and Hollywood's treatment of sex. The thesis is negligible, and not helped by the evident non-cooperation of some studios (notably MGM), so that Garbo is represented only by an early Swedish short, and Hedy Lamarr by the nude bathing scene from *Ecstasy*. But after its splendid opening coup (Dietrich emerging from the gorilla skin in *Blonde Venus*), it does offer pleasing glimpses, from Louise Glaum to Monroe, Taylor et al. Pity the print quality is variable and the silent footage printed at the wrong speed. TM

Love Happy

(David Miller, 1949, US) The Marx Brothers, Ilona Massey, Vera-Ellen, Marion Hutton, Raymond Burr, Eric Blore, Marilyn Monroe.
91 min. b/w.
A depressing final bow for the Marx Brothers. Groucho has about ten minutes of screen time, one or two of them in the company of Marilyn Monroe, and there is a decent rooftop chase amongst advertising hoardings for Harpo. But it's a dead duck as a comedy, and the brothers look ill, old and jaded. ATu

Love Hurts

(Bud Yorkin, 1990, US) Jeff Daniels, Cynthia Sikes, Judith Ivey, John Mahoney, Cloris Leachman, Amy Wright, Mary Griffin.
115 min.
Paul Weaver (Daniels) gets his divorce papers on the eve of his sister's wedding, and rather than seek oblivion in another one-night stand, he decides to attend the ceremony. Guess who else is there? But Weaver's attempts at impressing his wife (Sikes) and two children are distracted by the presence of scatty Susan (Ivey), who has marriage problems of her own. By and large, Ron Nyswaner's script (written nearly a decade earlier) refuses the easy sympathies which affect too many such films; as Weaver confronts an unforgiving wife and daughter, his situation becomes progressively irredeemable. When it works, this relatively unpredictable approach is very effective – as when Weaver and his wife make a desperate attempt at reconciliation – but other sequences are too indulgent and unfocused. CM

Love Hurts (Hartverscheurend/ Heart-Rending)

(Mijke de Jong, 1993, Neth) Marieke Heebink, Mark Rietman.
85 min.
Well-meaning, not unintelligent, but rather tiresome look at the volatile relationship of two ill-matched lovers: a fully paid-up member of 'alternative Amsterdam' (she sings, helps out Kurdish refugees, worries about her HIV-positive friend, gets smashed, and laughs and screams a lot), and a comparatively strait-laced lawyer. Intended, surely, as a realistic study of the fragility of love in a divided, crumbling world, the film not only takes a few unnecessary turns into melodrama, but is relentlessly PC as its heroine, even more than her sullen lover, soon becomes an acute pain in the arse. GA

Love in a Fallen City (Qingcheng zhi Lian)

(Ann Hui, 1984, HK) Cora Miao, Chow Yun Fat, Keung Chung Ping, Chiu Kao.
97 min.
Using the masks and hieratic gestures of Peking Opera as a governing metaphor, Ann Hui describes the social and familial plight of a young divorcée in wartime China. The film centres on her nervous romance with a self-assured, westernised playboy in the Hong Kong of 1941, as the city falls to the Japanese. The loving reconstruction of the period tends to run away with itself, and there are some cloying romantic clichés. An interesting, ambitious failure. TR

Love in a Women's Prison (Diario Segreto da un Carcere Femminile)

(Rino Di Silvestro, 1972, It) Anita Strindberg, Eva Czemerys, Olga Bisera, Jenny Tamburi, Paolo Senatore.
100 min.
Unimaginative and ludicrously inept offering, consisting of flatly directed examples of a variety of turn-ons (lesbians, fighting femmes, mild bondage and spanking), and a schoolboy plot involving drug smuggling, the Mafia, and intergang rivalry. Dull and unerotic, and the hit-and-miss dubbing doesn't help. CGi

Love in Germany, A (Eine Liebe in Deutschland)

(Andrzej Wajda, 1983, WGer/Fr) Hanna Schygulla, Marie-Christine Barrault, Armin Mueller-Stahl, Elisabeth Trissenaar, Daniel Olbrychski, Piotr Lysak, Bernhard Wicki.
107 min.
Of the many films on the nature of Nazism, very few scrutinise its manifestation in the daily lives of ordinary people. Adapted from Rolf Hochhuth's novel, this may be framed as a particular historical enquiry into the events surrounding an illicit love affair between a small-town shopkeeper (Schygulla) and a Polish POW (Lysak), but their predicament is so movingly embodied that it lifts the film out of semi-autobiographical dredging and into the realm of tragedy. Their love is destroyed by the local petit bourgeoisie, so infected with political disease that the village is rotten with gossip, greed, suspicion. Alongside Schygulla's aching gravity, Mueller-Stahl weighs in a tremendous performance as the perplexed and irritable Gestapo chief. CPea

Love in Las Vegas

see Viva Las Vegas

Love in Limbo

(David Elfick, 1992, Aust) Aden Young, Craig Adams, Russell Crowe.
102 min.
Perth, 1957: a bespectacled adolescent (Young) is expelled from school for marketing his highly detailed drawings of naked women among his innocent classmates, whereupon he's parcelled off into a job in his uncle's clothing firm, and real life begins. Taken under the wing of the office rake (Adams), the lad is introduced to drink, women, cigarettes, etc, but his reactions are complicated when his widowed mum and his mentor begin to take an interest in each other. Assembling the story in a mosaic of kitsch furnishings and dayglo colours, Elfick finds both humour and pathos in the material, piecing events together with a rollercoaster rhythm. Most enjoyable. TJ

Love in the Afternoon

(Billy Wilder, 1957, US) Gary Cooper, Audrey Hepburn, Maurice Chevalier, John McGiver, Van Doude, Paul Bonifas, Lise Bourdin.
126 min. b/w.
An over-long and only spasmodically amusing romantic comedy, clearly made as a tribute to Lubitsch. Set in Paris, it concerns the predictably blooming love between wealthy American playboy Cooper and Hepburn, the innocent but determined daughter of Chevalier's private detective, whose cuckold client (McGiver) intends to take revenge on Cooper with a pistol. The script – Wilder's first with IAL Diamond – has its moments, but by and large it's conspicuously lacking in insight or originality, while Hepburn's fresh-faced infatuation for her all too visibly ageing guide to the adult, sensual world comes across as faintly implausible. GA

Love in the Afternoon (L'Amour, l'Après-midi)

(Eric Rohmer, 1972, Fr) Bernard Verley, Zouzou, Françoise Verley, Daniel Ceccaldi, Malvina Penne, Babette Ferrier.
97 min.
The last of Rohmer's *Six Moral Tales* sees its hero married – in contrast to the protagonists of the earlier films, who were merely contemplating marriage – and resisting the temptation of an affair, almost out of perversity. Equally, the film is a homage to the late afternoon – seen by Rohmer as a sunny parallel to 3am and the dark night of the soul – the time Bernard Verley eccentrically chooses as his regular lunch time. A formal, elegant examination of someone puzzled by marital fidelity, *Love in the Afternoon* is a wonderfully cool and lucid exposition of the twists and turns of its hero's thoughts. PH

Love in the Strangest Way (Elles n'oublient pas)

(Christopher Frank, 1994, Fr) Thierry Lhermitte, Maruschka Detmers, Nadia Fares, Patrick Timsit, Umberto Orsini.
107 min.
Light leading-man Lhermitte gets the chance to open up his emotional range as Julien, a hard-nosed operator for a debt-collection agency. He comes a cropper when tangling with seductive Angela (Detmers) whose blatant come-on is conveniently timed to coincide with the wife and kids' annual holiday. One seedy fling later, we find Julien beating a retreat, but, after spouse Anne's return, Angela continues to seek his help in waiving her boyfriend's overdue loan, and soon turns up again as the family's new child-minder. So far, so perfunctory; but where writer/director Frank really hits the rocks is in trying to raise the passion level when murder enters the fray. TJ

Love Is a Ball (aka All This and Money Too)

(David Swift, 1963, US) Charles Boyer, Glenn Ford, Hope Lange, Ricardo Montalban, Telly Savalas, Ruth McDevitt, Ulla Jacobsson.
111 min.
A syrupy Michel Legrand score, European locations and much Hollywood Franglais mark this disposable filler (from Lindsay Hardy's novel *The Grand Duke and Mr Pimm*) as society matchmaker Boyer hopes to fix up penniless duke Montalban with Lange's American heiress, who of course falls for Ford's dashing racing driver. Neither film title quite hits the mark. TJ

Love Is a Many-Splendored Thing

(Henry King, 1955, US) Jennifer Jones, William Holden, Isobel Elsom, Torin Thatcher, Jorja Curtright, Virginia Gregg.
102 min.
East meets West for some lush tripe based on a novel by Han Suyin, who had company in disliking it. Set in a full deck of CinemaScope Hong Kong postcards as an American journalist and a Eurasian doctor lady wallow in an ill-fated romance conducted in pidgin poetry ('Sadness is so ungrateful'). With that title and an Oscar-winning theme song, what did you expect? TM

Love Is Colder than Death (Liebe ist kälter als der Tod)

(Rainer Werner Fassbinder, 1969, WGer) Ulli Lommel, Hanna Schygulla, Rainer Werner Fassbinder, Hans Hirschmüller, Katrin Schaake.
88 min. b/w.
A restless and sombre foray into the black-and-white world of the Hollywood gangster film as interpreted by B-movie mavericks such as Sam Fuller, and ex-Cahiers iconoclasts such as Godard, here stripped bare by Fassbinder to reveal the cold underlying mechanism of love, death, loneliness, friendship, hate, betrayal and manipulation. Shot on a *pfennig* budget, this – his first feature – is both an assured 'revolutionary' critique of genre, and at the same time a constantly searching experiment in style and treatment. The plot? For what it is worth, the worn-leather-jacket-and-boots, chain-smoking ex-con and pimp (Fassbinder) refuses the brutal 'persuasions' of the Syndicate, befriends a felt hat and raincoat (Lommel), only to be betrayed by a jealous prostitute lover (Schygulla) in an attempted bank robbery. In this bleak world of bare sets, static camera shots, and stylised acting, was awkwardly born one of the greatest 'lives in film' the cinema has seen. WH

Love Is Like a Violin

(Jana Bokova, 1977, GB)
54 min.
Jana Bokova's observational portraits (her NFS films *Jokey* and *Militia Battlefield*; her TV films on Don McCullin and Marevna and *Marika*) have been highly achieved and entertaining examples of *cinéma-vérité* that engage with character through 'performance'; a film about a community theatre group would seem a natural progression. Yet the film emerges as an intriguing bundle of contradictions. In attempting to document how the Common Stock theatre company creates a performance for, and with material gathered from, pensioners in Hammersmith, Bokova appears torn between an analysis of a process and a series of contrasted group portraits of actors and OAPs. PT

Love Is My Profession

see En Cas de Malheur

Love Is the Devil

(John Maybury, 1998, GB) Derek Jacobi, Daniel Craig, Tilda Swinton, Anne Lambton, Annabel Brooks.
90 min.
Maybury's film about Francis Bacon (Jacobi) focuses on the slow but inexorable downward spiral of his seven-year relationship with his lover, model and muse George Dyer (Craig), a smalltime villain whom the painter first met burgling his house. It's the tale of a charged but uncomfortable encounter, not only between two very different personalities, but between two different (but both very English) worlds: the arty, boozy Soho set and, ironically rather less amoral and more sympathetic, the East End criminal fraternity. At its heart is a raw, painful, even cruel love affair based on dominance, submission, snobbery and sadism, which is brought vividly to life by images often (but never excessively) reminiscent of Bacon's paintings. The performances are terrific, with Jacobi particularly astonishing as Bacon. GA

love jones

(Theodore Witcher, 1997, US) Larenz Tate, Nia Long, Isaiah Washington, Lisa Nicole Carson, Khalil Kain, Leonard Roberts.
109 min.
Disappointed in love, twenty-something Nina Mosley (Nia Long) plays it cool when publicly courted by Darius Lovehall (Tate) at Chicago nightspot The Sanctuary. With further effort, subterfuge, wit, charm and a spot of dancing, Darius and Nina finally come together. The pair duly make a splendid hash of things. By the way, she's a promising photographer; he's a promising writer – so much in common. A shame to split up, no? Both, probably, have much to learn about themselves and love: Sorry, please try again later. They do. A very (self-consciously) adult love story of temperate disposition, sage demeanour and protracted passage. Kudos to first-time writer/director Witcher for his level-headed attempt to tackle well trodden subject matter with a modern black twist. Unfortunately, a relationship has to be pretty special if the couple are going to pair up thrice over. The script seems to lose interest in its latter stages and Witcher never evinces a depth of insight such that you sit up and take notice. NB

Loveless, The

(Kathryn Bigelow/Monty Montgomery, 1981, US) Willem Dafoe, Robert Gordon, Marin Kanter, J Don Ferguson, Tina L'Hotsky, Lawrence Matarese.
84 min.
'Man, I was what you call ragged ... I knew I was gonna hell in a breadbasket' intones the hero in the great opening moments of *The Loveless*, and as he zips up and bikes out, it's clear that this is one of the most original American independents in years: a bike movie which celebrates the '50s through '80s eyes. Where earlier bike films like *The Wild One* were forced to concentrate on plot, *The Loveless* deliberately slips its story into the background in order to linger over all the latent erotic material of the period that other films could only hint at in their posters. Zips and sunglasses and leather form the basis of a cool and stylish dream of sexual self-destruction, matched by a Robert Gordon score which exaggerates the sexual aspects of '50s music. At times the perversely slow beat of each scene can irritate, but that's a reasonable price for the film's super-saturated atmosphere. DP

Love Lessons (Laererinden/ Lust och fägring Stor)

(Bo Widerberg, 1996, Swe/Den) Johan Widerberg, Marika Lagercrantz, Tomas von Brömssen, Karin Huldt, Björn Kjellman, Nina Gunke.
130 min.
Sweden, 1943: six months in the life of 15-year-old Stig (Bo's son Johan Widerberg), who's come to the attention of his wispily carnal teacher Viola (Lagercrantz). She's dissatisfied with her salesman husband Frank (von Brömssen), and an affair duly begins. At first, Stig thinks Frank's the enemy; as it turns out, however, Viola's the one to watch. All starts well enough. Shot with mouth-watering crispness, the early scenes between Viola and Stig are tinglingly erotic and oddly authentic. Von Brömssen, too, is wonderful as a man so full of tears and alcohol he's all but leaking. But what next? Wirter/director Widerberg's baffled. In the baggiest of second halves, he plies us with bland new characters and increasingly wordy monologues, labouring at humour like a tired man with a shovel. He even has a go at war, reducing real-life horrors to winsome marginalia. Stig himself is too good to be interesting, while Viola proves far too bad. And so, as dappled light plays on yet another of her silky suspender-belts and a crashing concerto swells for the umpteenth time, you find yourself stiff with indifference. CO'Su

Love Letter

(Shunji Iwai, 1995, Jap) Miho Nakayama, Etsushi Toyokawa, Bunjaku Han, Katsuyuki Shinohara, Miki Sakai.
117 min.
Japan's Fuji Television produced this glossy exercise in adolescent longing, and it looks it. A vehicle for pop idol Miho Nakayama to sigh and offer melancholy looks aplenty, it gives her a double role as Hiroko, the prim, grief-stricken young woman who sends a letter to her dead boyfriend's old address, and Itsuki, the rather feistier type who (happening to share a name with the chap in question) gets this unexpected missive, and whose initially tentative response is to send both girls on a voyage of discovery. TJ

Love Letters

(William Dieterle, 1945, US) Jennifer Jones, Joseph Cotten, Ann Richards, Cecil Kellaway, Gladys Cooper, Anita Louise, Reginald Denny.
101 min. b/w.
A florid romantic melodrama about an amnesiac cured – and cleared of her husband's murder – by the love of a soldier (Cotten) who had earlier dreamed up the letters supposedly written by his buddy (whom she then married). Never mind the dottily contrived plot and the tiresomely fey Jones; the superlative camera-work (Lee Garmes) and Dieterle's brooding direction make it a really rather ravishing experience. TM

Love Letters

(Amy Jones, 1983, US) Jamie Lee Curtis, James Keach, Amy Madigan, Bud Cort, Bonnie Bartlett, Matt Clark.
89 min.
Put together in the corner of the Corman factory reserved for 'art', this proves once more that Corman can beat Hollywood mainstream in any genre. After the death of her mother, Jamie Lee Curtis discovers a cache of love letters which point to an affair of the heart indulged by her mother after she was born. They trigger the need, and soon she is knee-deep in a similar heartbreaker with a professional photographer (Keach), who is married but not about to leave. Just another triangle, perhaps, but this one is distinguished on several fronts. The passion is strong; the strength is hers; the obsession is not comfortable; and the treatment is uncompromising in its head-on stare at the sweet sickness. The last film to have sufficiently encompassed the derangement of love unto death was Truffaut's *The Woman Next Door*, and this film is very much more in the European tradition of *Last Tango in Paris* than in the Hollywood one of soft-focus romance. CPea

Love Letters from Teralba Road, The

(Stephen Wallace, 1977, Aust) Bryan Brown, Kris McQuade, Gia Carides, Joy Hruby, Kevin Leslie.
50 min.
A working-class marriage is on the rocks: the partners separate, move in with their respective families, and then tentatively try to make amends. The strength of this modest movie, financed by the Sydney Filmmakers Co-operative, largely derives from what writer/director Stephen Wallace has chosen to leave unstated,

and the way in which what seems at first an intolerable bind – especially from the point of view of the wife, authoritatively played by Kris McQuade – is finally revealed to be something much more complex and less pessimistic. Constructed from a series of real letters found in a Sydney flat, the film is unlikely to find favour in feminist quarters, but is strongly recommended as an illustration of the labyrinthine byways of the married state. JPy

Love Lottery, The

(Charles Crichton, 1953, GB) David Niven, Peggy Cummins, Anne Vernon, Herbert Lom, Gordon Jackson, Felix Aylmer, Theodore Bikel, Sebastian Cabot, Hattie Jacques, Humphrey Bogart.
89 min.
Worn down by the pressures of Hollywood stardom and the attentions of his female fans, Niven, a British movie star, flees Hollywood for the sanctuary of Italy, only to allow Lom, the head of a gambling syndicate, to put him up as the prize in a so-called 'Love Lottery'. Thereafter, Vernon buys up hundreds of tickets to boost her chances, while London typist Cummins hopes the real thing will measure up to her daydreams. Humphrey Bogart – in his only film for Ealing Studios! – pops up unbilled in the final reel of this misfiring satire. TJ

Lovely to Look at

see Thin Ice

Lovely Way to Die, A (aka A Lovely Way to Go)

(David Lowell Rich, 1968, US) Kirk Douglas, Sylva Koscina, Eli Wallach, Kenneth Haigh, Sharon Farrell, Gordon Peters.
103 min.
Douglas as a tough New York cop who turns in his badge after being ticked off for roughing up a crook or two in the cause of justice. He is promptly hired as a private eye by a lawyer friend (Wallach) who has a pretty client (Koscina) accused of murdering her wealthy husband and in need of protection. The attraction is very mutual, and soon Douglas is busy warding off assorted thuggish intruders with one hand, while romancing the lady with the other. A lumbering mixture of screwball romantic comedy and tortuously-plotted thriller, trying desperately to be 'with it' (lots of swinging New Wave stylistics), it relies on a relentlessly jolly score to keep things going and avoid flying off in all directions at once. TM

Lovely Way to Go, A

see Lovely Way to Die, A

Love Machine, The

(Jack Haley Jr, 1971, US) John Phillip Law, Dyan Cannon, Robert Ryan, Jackie Cooper, David Hemmings, Jodi Wexler, Shecky Greene.
110 min.
The love machine isn't a sex aid (unless you like your sex sleek, ruthless and sadistic), it's television, and its embodiment the glacier-profiled person of newscaster Robin Stone (Law). We're taken, courtesy of Jacqueline Susann's novel, on a picaresque trip of the American television industry, in hot pursuit of Robin's rise to fame and power over the bodies of various ladies, including the network chief's wife (who gives him a final boost to the top in exchange for a key to his apartment) and a top model who commits suicide when he rejects her love. The world is the glossy ideal of Western consumer society (silk, models, fashion, even a camp photographer), and the film works on the crudest level possible. Pernicious crap. MV

Love Maker, The

see Calle Mayor

Love Match

see Partie de Plaisir, Une

Love Me or Leave Me

(Charles Vidor, 1955, US) Doris Day, James Cagney, Cameron Mitchell, Robert Keith, Tom Tully, Harry Bellaver, Veda Ann Borg.
122 min.
The story of torch singer Ruth Etting and her involvement with racketeer Gimp Snyder, who used his muscle to launch her career, was rewarded with marriage, and ran into trouble when she hit the big time and outgrew his adoring but bullying machinations. Cagney, hovering constantly on the verge of *White Heat* mania, plays well off Doris Day's girl-next-door persona, lending a genuinely explosive edge to their relationship as, finding his demands increasingly inhibiting both personally and professionally, she begins to yearn for the less complicated devotion of her piano-player (Mitchell). Not quite as tough as it thinks it is – the script contrives to skirt the notion of any pre-marital sex deal – the film nevertheless has more substance than most musical biopics. And the stream of standards sung by Day, often used with dramatic point – 'You Made Me Love You', 'Mean to Me', 'Shaking the Blues Away', 'Ten Cents a Dance' – are a treat. TM

Love Me Tender

(Robert D Webb, 1956, US) Richard Egan, Debra Paget, Elvis Presley, Robert Middleton, William Campbell, Neville Brand, Mildred Dunnock, Bruce Bennett.
89 min. b/w.
Presley's debut film. It's basically a standard Western, about three Confederate brothers who steal a Union payroll and take it back to the family farm when the war is over. This is where Elvis comes in and the Western opts out – he's the younger, fourth brother, who has married the older brother's girl. A feud ensues, Presley gets filled with lead (but not before his pelvis and voice-box have had a workout), and finally reappears as a ghost, reprising the title number over his own grave. From debut to necropolis all in the space of a single movie. ATu

Love Me Tonight

(Rouben Mamoulian, 1932, US) Maurice Chevalier, Jeanette MacDonald, Charles Ruggles, Myrna Loy, C Aubrey Smith, Charles Butterworth, Robert Greig, Elizabeth Patterson.
96 min. b/w.
A superb musical, outstripping the possible influences of René Clair and Lubitsch, to whose work this has been compared. A tale of the gradual dawn of romance between 'the best tailor in Paris' (Chevalier) and a haughty princess (MacDonald), the film is a stylish masterwork of technical innovations, and a delirious result of Mamoulian's desire to incorporate movement, dancing, acting, music, singing, décor and lighting into a cogent cinematic whole. The songs develop the action and characters, the dialogue is witty and rhythmic, and the entire film, with its fine score by Rodgers and Hart, is a charming, tongue-in-cheek fantasy that never descends into syrupy whimsy. GA

Love, Mother (Csók, Anyu)

(János Rózsa, 1987, Hun) Dorottya Udvaros, Róbert Koltai, Kati Lajtai, Simon G Gévai, Sándor Gáspár.
97 min.
The Kalmars, a remarkably affluent Budapest family, are united only by brief communications on a kitchen blackboard. Secret affairs and even more secret depressions are observed through an ingenious telescopic device by their young son, a mute witness to this domestic parade of follies. Rózsa's film is a virtuoso piece of tiresome whimsy, which collapses when the general air of circumspection turns to serious moralising. DT

Love of Jeanne Ney, The (Die Liebe der Jeanne Ney)

(GW Pabst, 1927, Ger) Edith Jeanne, Brigitte Helm, Fritz Rasp, Hertha von Walther, Uno Henning, Vladimir Sokoloff.
8,671 ft. b/w.
Pabst's adaptation of a novel by Ilya Ehrenburg is in many ways a trial run for his masterpiece *Pandora's Box*, made the following year. Its German heroine flees from the Crimea after her Bolshevik lover has assassinated her diplomat father; the main part of the film finds her in Paris, struggling to maintain her integrity amid sundry corruptions and betrayals. The characters are not drawn with the depth of the later film, and the sheer density of plot tends to dominate everything else. The extraordinary richness of Pabst's visual articulation, however, turns this into an advantage: the narrative courses along vigorously, taking both Pabst's social insights and his aesthetic effects in its stride without wavering. TR

Love on the Dole

(John Baxter, 1941, GB) Deborah Kerr, Clifford Evans, Joyce Howard, Frank Cellier, Mary Merrall, George Carney.
100 min. b/w.
Despite the relevance of its theme, Walter Greenwood's sentimental tragedy remains very much a '30s period piece. The Salford slums look as irredeemably picturesque as the surrounding Pennine countryside, and 'Honest' Sam Grundy in his big car and check suit looks more like a teddy bear than a repulsive villain. Kerr is ideally the archetypal Lancashire millgirl, but her mixture of coolness and fragility works surprisingly well in the scenes with the grumbling, bullying father she 'disgraces' and the fawningly lecherous bookie she pawns her body to. The real bite, though, comes from the gaggle of black-coated gossips – Mrs Dorbell, Mrs Nattle, Mrs Jike and Mrs Bull – who, Greek-chorus-like, pronounce judgment over their hap'orth of gin. RMy

Love on the Ground

see Amour par terre, L'

Love on the Run

(WS Van Dyke II, 1936, US) Clark Gable, Joan Crawford, Franchot Tone, Reginald Owen, Mona Barrie.
80 min. b/w.
Ducking out on the brink of her marriage to a European prince, American heiress Crawford enlists Gable's help in making her getaway, not knowing he's a journalist assigned to cover the nuptials but more interested in tracking down shady flying ace Owen. Busy, inconsequential romantic comedy with too much exposition for the stars to make much of it. TJ

Love on the Run (L'Amour en Fuite)

(François Truffaut, 1978, Fr) Jean-Pierre Léaud, Marie-France Pisier, Claude Jade, Dani, Dorothée, Rosy Varte, Julien Bertheau.
95 min.
Fifth and final instalment in the saga of Truffaut's narcissistic hero, Antoine Doinel, who hardly seems to have matured at all in this piece of whimsy. Encounter follows encounter in (ho hum) picaresque fashion, while Antoine remains bewildered at the vicissitudes of both women and life. There are welcome moments of irony and some sharply handled scenes, but they don't succeed in lifting the film above the most self-indulgent level of sentimentality. HM

Lover, The (L'Amant)

(Jean-Jacques Annaud, 1992, Fr/GB) Jane March, Tony Leung, Frédérique Meininger, Arnaud Giovaninetti, Melvil Poupaud, Lisa Faulkner, Xiem Mang.
115 min.
Late '20s Indo-China. A 15-year-old schoolgirl leans wistfully on the rail of a ferryboat crossing the Mekong. Observing her is an elegant, rich Chinese. With exquisite Parisian manners he offers her a lift to her lowly Saigon boarding-house. Thus meet cute the Young Girl (March) and the Chinaman (Leung) referred to in Marguerite Duras' assumedly autobiographical '80s novel (controversially, Annaud opted for a Gerard Brach script rather than Duras' own). For all the footage of glistening flesh – most of the film takes place in a darkened room where the two explore the realm of the senses – this is basically a melancholic piece about the remembrance of times, places and passions lost (with voice-over narration by Jeanne Moreau). The Young Girl, altogether too complex for the inexperienced March to do more than simply embody, was then in the process of taking her life into her own hands. She will become a writer, and has developed the strength to avoid both the predatoriness of her mother and the romantic dependence of her lover. But at a price. This sombre quality dignifies an otherwise shoddily directed movie. WH

Loverboy

(Joan Micklin Silver, 1989, US) Patrick Dempsey, Kate Jackson, Kirstie Alley, Carrie Fisher, Robert Ginty, Nancy Valen, Charles Hunter Walsh, Barbara Carrera, Vic Tayback.
99 min.

Continuing in his niche as put-upon teen stud, Dempsey plays hopeless student randy (who else?). Dumped by his disillusioned girlfriend (Valen), he's also in imminent danger of having college funds cut off by angry Dad (Ginty). A summer job delivering pizzas introduces him to rich, sophisticated Barbara Carrera, and before long he's on call to her friends, all wealthy, frustrated wives who pay handsomely for his services (wild sex, cosy chats, dancing sessions). By some strange logic, the accumulated sums are supposed to get Randy back to college, and thus back into the arms of his girl. But that's if deceived husbands remain ignorant. This is very silly stuff, but mildly engaging none the less. Silver adeptly juggles the set pieces, orchestrating a frantic, slapstick climax; and the likeable Dempsey is supported by a dependable cast, including Kirstie Alley as a vengeful doctor and Carrie Fisher as a body-builder's cynical wife. CM

Lovers (Amantes)

(Vicente Aranda, 1991, Sp) Victoria Abril, Jorge Sanz, Maribel Verdú, Enrique Cerro, Mabel Escaño, José Cerro.
103 min.

Madrid in the '50s. Young soldier Paco (Sanz) is courting his major's maid Trini (Verdú), the only tension between them being her determination to preserve her virginity until they are married. When Paco is discharged from the army and takes a room in the home of beautiful young widow Luisa (Abril), he is delighted at the happy 'resolution' to his ferocious sexual frustration: he has a passionate affair with Luisa, while Trini remains pure. But he had not bargained on the mad jealousy which both women develop, and is soon faced with an impossible choice. Aranda focuses tightly on his three principals, effectively conveying the dreadful, consuming power of passion. But he fails to imbue this true story with enough depth for the grand tragedy to which he aspires. We are never given any reason to care about these lovers, and Franco's Spain serves merely as a richly photographed backdrop. CO'S

Lovers, The

see Amants, Les

Lovers!, The

(Herbert Wise, 1972, GB) Richard Beckinsale, Paula Wilcox, Susan Littler, Nikolas Simmonds, Anthony Naylor, Rosalind Ayres.
89 min.

Spin-off from a TV comedy series, but better than average because someone has bothered to think of it as a film, not just prolonged television. The boy and girl of the title, surrounded by the myth of the permissive society, find the reality of living at home with the parents in middle-class Manchester somewhat different. The film gains from being set in specific locations, so the characters acquire a degree of reality that the lot in *Coronation Street* will never have. It also creates the right degree of gaucheness in the protagonists without ever becoming condescending. Not recommended, really, just put together and acted with a surprising degree of conscientiousness. CPe

Lovers, Happy Lovers!

see Knave of Hearts

Lovers in Woomuk-Baemi (Woomuk-Baemi ui Sarang)

(Jang Sun-Woo, 1989, SKor) Park Joong-Hoon, Yu Hae-Ri, Choi Myong-Gil, Lee Dae-Kun, Choi Ju-Bong, Shin Chung-Sik.
110 min.

The nearest Jang has ever come to straight social realism, this describes a stormy sexual triangle in the outer city suburb of the title. A male supervisor in a small sewing factory consoles one of the workers, a woman battered by her impotent husband, and they find themselves having an affair. Trouble is, he already has a steady partner, a former bargirl who won't give him up without a fight. Jang doesn't take sides (each of the characters has his/her reasons) but relishes the spontaneity of the emotions and the impossibility of concealing the scandal from the rest of the community. There's no symbolism, but the film's verve prefigures the imminent renaissance in Korean cinema. TR

Lovers of Verona, The

see Amants de Vérone, Les

Lovesick

(Marshall Brickman, 1983, US) Dudley Moore, Elizabeth McGovern, Alec Guinness, John Huston, Wallace Shawn, Gene Saks, Alan King, Ron Silver.
96 min.

Moore's a Manhattan psychiatrist who falls for one of his patients (McGovern). This comedy-romance, with the emphasis firmly (and often unbearably) on the latter, smacks more than a little of Woody Allen: no surprise when you consider that Brickman collaborated on *Sleeper*, *Annie Hall* and *Manhattan*. Unfortunately, the Allen trademarks are only superficially exploited; where Woody might have gloried in uncovering and lampooning the psychiatrist's guilt, Brickman avoids any real conflicts, and has the ghost of Sigmund Freud make frequent appearances as a mixed guardian angel/agent provocateur. Guinness fleshes out the role somewhat stiffly, and the result is nothing to compare with the similar function served by Gielgud in *Arthur*. What's left is a love story slightly less moving than an 'Interflora' ad. GD

Lovesick on Nana Street (Hole ahava be'shikun gimel)

(Savi Gabizon, 1995, Isr) Moshe Ivgi, Hannah Azulai Hasfari, Avigail Arieli.
94 min.

Chauvinist braggart Victor (Ivgi) has a reputation around his Israeli estate as the local lewd boy, so it's nothing unusual when he propositions a good-looking stranger in town, Michaella (Hasfari), inviting her to a supposed orgy with two Norwegian girls. She's not interested, but the days pass and Victor won't move on, dreaming up an affair and so losing his grip that he is incarcerated in the local asylum, alongside a host of similarly lovelorn fellows. This is one odd number: certainly captivating in its vision of unrequited love en masse, the town a cuckoo's nest of personal breakdown and pandemia. It's also highly problematic, given the director's evident yet obscure identification with Victor's plight: in particular, it's hard to unravel the congruence or otherwise of the character's sexist erotomania with his sudden fit of helpless amour fou. Intriguing, none the less. NB

Loves of a Blonde

see Lásky Jedné Plavovlásky

Loves of Liszt, The (Szerelmi Almok – Liszt)

(Márton Keleti, 1970, Hun/USSR) Imre Sinkovits, Ariadne Shengelaya, Klara Lutchko, Igor Dmitriev, Sándor Pécsi.
185 min.

A film with all the grace of a dinosaur and the liveliness of a dodo. For two and a half hours (mercifully, 32 minutes were cut for British release) we're treated to a childishly reverential biography which outdoes even Hollywood biopics in its horde of clichés and name-dropping. The settings, both interior and exterior, are attractive in their holiday-brochure way, yet they are never treated with any imagination (the director's main trick is to make the camera pirouette round the piano during Liszt's recitals, which only makes it seem as though he's performing on ice). And while the dollops of music are finely performed (mostly by György Cziffra and Sviatoslav Richter), the selection signally fails to support the script's claim that Liszt is a key figure in the development of modern music. GB

Love Story

(Leslie Arliss, 1944, GB) Margaret Lockwood, Stewart Granger, Patricia Roc, Tom Walls, Moira Lister, Reginald Purdell.
108 min. b/w.

If you thought the Erich Segal *Love Story* was a bit much, then try this one for size. Lockwood is a pianist dying of heart trouble, Granger a mining engineer going blind. Down in Cornwall where English movie passions bloom, she's composing a swan-song ('The Cornish Rhapsody') while he dickers over an operation that may restore his sight (but thereby hangs much soul-searching and self-sacrifice). Fulsome, indeed. TM

Love Story

(Arthur Hiller, 1970, US) Ali MacGraw, Ryan O'Neal, John Marley, Ray Milland, Russell Nype, Katharine Balfour.
100 min.

The bland mating of love and leukaemia which brought a box-office bonanza. 'What can you say about the girl you loved, and she died?' muses O'Neal before looking back to his days of clichéd happiness with Ali MacGraw. 'Very little of any interest,' replies Arthur Hiller, as he leads us through a turgid, trauma-ridden tale of young students falling in lerv, making it financially, and then separating, thankfully, for ever. Dated before it was made. GA

Love Streams

(John Cassavetes, 1984, US) Gena Rowlands, John Cassavetes, Diahnne Abbott, Seymour Cassel, Margaret Abbott, Jakob Shaw.
141 min.

As so often in Cassavetes' work, there's little plot: desperate attempts at a sexual life from a boozy, middle-aged writer staving off loneliness; a divorced woman's struggles to hang on to her husband, daughter and sanity. Half-way through, when the woman takes refuge in the writer's chaotic household, the nature of their relationship (they're brother and sister) gradually unfolds. Very little else happens; but sparks fly throughout as the characters, guided firmly by the director's customary emphasis on spontaneous, naturalistic performance, search for closeness, warmth and self-definition. It's a long and wayward path, but humour, aching sadness, and sensitivity to the inner lives of people deemed eccentric, mingle to produce a rich, impressionistic tapestry. The oblique treatment occasionally leads to infuriating obscurity, but the movie's sense of 'real life', dynamic performances, and admirable lack of moralising make it compulsive. GA

Love Test, The

(Michael Powell, 1934, GB) Judy Gunn, Louis Hayward, David Hutcheson, Googie Withers, Morris Harvey, Bernard Miles, Eve Turner.
63 min. b/w.

A romantic comedy set in a chemistry lab up against a deadline to produce a formula for fireproof celluloid. Hoping to be made department head, Thompson (Hutchinson) stirs up chauvinist resentments when the appointment goes provisionally to Mary (Gunn), a serious young woman with no time for men; and he ensures that John (Hayward), already interested in Mary, is elected in a plot to distract her from her work. With the pair soon head-over-heels in love, Thompson throws another spanner in by telling Mary that John is actually making a play for her job, meanwhile ensuring that work comes to a standstill. Only John, though repulsed by the angry Mary, goes on working selflessly to find the formula... Scripts like this were the bread-and-butter of British movies, the difference being that Powell's stylishness, invention and impeccable direction of actors turn this one into a real charmer. Hayward and Gunn are touchingly sincere as the lovers, and Googie Withers (among several fine supporting performances) contributes a gem of a cameo as a pertly predatory secretary. TM

Love Unto Waste (Dixia Qing)

(Stanley Kwan, 1986, HK) Tony Leung, Chow Yun-fat, Irene Wan, Elaine Jin, Ts'ai Ch'in.
97 min.

Here, at last, are images of Hong Kong life that readers of *The Face* and *i-D* would recognise. Four smart young things spend their time dressing, bonking, and getting smashed – until one of them is brutally, arbitrarily murdered in a burglary. The survivors come under the scrutiny of an eccentric cop, and their underlying fears and regrets slowly but surely emerge. Thanks to ace performances, the effect is surprisingly fresh and moving. TR

Love! Valour! Compassion!

(Joe Mantello, 1997, US) Jason Alexander, Stephen Spinella, Stephen Bogardus, Randy Becker, John Benjamin Hickey, Justin Kirk, John Glover.
114 min.

Forget the title. Adapted by Terrence McNally from his own play, this is the stinging tale of eight gay friends and their trysts and tangles over three holiday weekends. Technically, rookie director Mantello is desperate to play straight. And, at times, the savoured tastefulness of the setting (a New York country house), not to mention the clothes, makes you want to rush out and hug something ugly. *Seinfeld*'s Alexander shines as Buzz, a stage show fan as flamboyant as Liza Minnelli and twice as depressed. This is a man who's played phoney so long he doesn't feel real even to himself. Glover is also marvellous as John, the cynical Brit. He looks perfect, and even when he goes through the standard cathartic revelation, he manages to remain stiff with mistrust. Strangely, Glover's atrocious in a second part, as John's twin James. Certainly it's an uneven ride, with many of the emotional climaxes drifting into bathos. What saves the film is that its theme – that most sexual relationships don't last a lifetime – is a bomb which explodes with absolute quiet. When the kiss-off finally comes, it leaves the neck hairs standing. CO'Su

Love With the Proper Stranger

(Robert Mulligan, 1963, US) Natalie Wood, Steve McQueen, Edie Adams, Herschel Bernardi, Tom Bosley, Harvey Lembeck.
102 min. b/w.

Charmingly bitter-sweet tale of the carefree jazz musician and the romantic shop-girl he gets pregnant, leading her to a back-street abortionist as a preferable alternative to facing her strict Italo-American family. Familiar in theme, but given a delightfully fresh flavour by Mulligan's atmospherically low-key direction, excellent performances from Wood and McQueen, and vivid location shooting in New York's Little Italy (the musician's union hall at the beginning, the amusement park, the sad and shabby street of the abortionist). Edie Adams is outstanding as the quizzically cynical stripper with whom McQueen is shacked up, but who is given a characteristically raw deal by a script working its way toward the obligatory happy ending. TM

Loving

(Irvin Kershner, 1970, US) George Segal, Eva Marie Saint, Sterling Hayden, Keenan Wynn, Nancie Phillips, Janis Young, Roland Winters, Roy Scheider.
89 min.

Brilliantly observed comedy, somehow at once screwball, satirical and sensitive, taking a refreshingly cynical angle on the clichés of Misunderstood Artist vs The Rest. Segal is the commercial illustrator turned egotistically Angry, scattering contracts, colleagues, wife and mistress in the wake of his empty 'bohemian' anarchy; a less easily indulged figure than Sean Connery's rebel poet in Kershner's earlier *A Fine Madness*, ending up as nakedly absurd as the institutions he takes such glee in attacking. A timely reminder of Kershner's true (major) worth, subsequently dimmed by a series of faceless 'projects' like *Return of a Man Called Horse* and *The Empire Strikes Back*. PT

Loving Couples

(Jack Smight, 1980, US) Shirley MacLaine, James Coburn, Susan Sarandon, Stephen Collins, Sally Kellerman.
98 min.

Flat champagne has nothing on this drearily predictable sitcom about a marriage crisis, solved when each partner seeks temporary refuge with a younger mate. Handsome young stud Collins, in other words, whisks MacLaine into a rejuvenating bout of disco dancing. Meanwhile Coburn, faced with the self-doubts of Sarandon's insecure young career girl, relearns the male prerogative of bolstering the feminine ego. Described as an irreverent romantic comedy about morality in the '80s, the film in fact subscribes to conventions as old as the hills and twice as rocky, burying any hints of feminist awareness beneath the routines of macho courtship. Faced with direction paced

at a lethargic crawl and dialogue of inconceivable banality, the cast respond with performances of glazed charm. TM

Lovin' Molly

(Sidney Lumet, 1973, US) Blythe Danner, Anthony Perkins, Beau Bridges, Edward Binns, Susan Sarandon.
98 min.

A slow and rambling replay of threads from *The Last Picture Show*, similarly based on a Larry McMurtry novel (*Leaving Cheyenne*) and seen through the same misty eyes. The film attempts to trace the relationship of its three protagonists over some forty years, overcome with a deepening sense of loss as youthful rural idyll turns sour with age and material success. Perkins is the withdrawn Gid; Bridges the placid brother; and Blythe Danner the woman intermittently shared by the brothers but refusing to marry either of them. It is her character the film has most difficulty with, battling to cope with her conscious quest for independence but sliding back into earth-mother cliché. While Lumet elicits very watchable performances, he doesn't really manage to imbue the film's sentimental fabric with enough insight to sustain its weighty format. VG

Loving the Dead

(Mira Hamermesh, 1991, GB)
52 min.

Mira Hamermesh's film about her return to Poland to search for her mother's grave yields a wider picture of the Holocaust. Poland was the killing floor for most European Jews under the Nazis, and few, understandably, have moved back since the war. The culture is kept marginally alive through the efforts of various custodians; one craftsman makes clay models of traditional *stetl* figures, a group stages re-enactments of village life, and Auschwitz has its ghastly museum. Those who escaped return to pore over the ghetto photos. Most Poles, however, seem indifferent. BC

Loving Walter

see Walter

Low Down Dirty Shame, A

(Keenan Ivory Wayans, 1994, US) Keenan Ivory Wayans, Charles S Dutton, Jada Pinkett, Andrew Divoff, Salli Richardson, Corwin Hawkins, Gary Cervantes.
108 min.

Having profitably ransacked the '70s blaxploitation genre for the jaunty send-up *I'm Gonna Git You Sucka*, writer/director/star Wayans comes up with a few clichés of his own in this contemporary action-comedy. Turned out of the LAPD, Andre Shame is a struggling PI whose street wisdom and rough charm win him no new cases – until DEA agent Rothmiller (genre stalwart Dutton) offers him a lucrative covert job, tracking down $20m in drug money from narcotics baron Mendoza (Divoff, courtesy of Scumbags Inc). So far, so hackneyed, but when Shame's perky assistant Peaches (Pinkett) starts overdoing the enthusiastic incompetence in a vain bid to up the humour quotient, and the gumshoe's old flame Angela (Richardson) turns up on Mendoza's arm to add a dash of romantic rivalry, the plot starts running on tramlines. Although bassman Marcus Miller's thumping score delivers the requisite kick, and young Pinkett shows enough enterprise to suggest she might be quite appealing with a better script, it's a moderate, undistinguished movie all round, despite Wayans' basic affability in the star role. Next time, perhaps he shouldn't try to do it all himself. TJ

Lower Depths, The

see Bas-Fonds, Les

Lower Depths, The (Donzoko)

(Akira Kurosawa, 1957, Jap) Toshiro Mifune, Isuzu Yamada, Ganjiro Nakamura, Kyoko Kagawa, Bokuzen Hidari.
137 min. b/w.

It's difficult to get too worked up these days over Gorky's classic proletarian drama (one of the showpieces of Stanislavsky realism) about the human flotsam washed up in a Moscow dosshouse and living on illusions: very much of its period in its sturdy affirmation of life amid deprivation and degradation, it has dated as awk-

wardly as most social documents. But Kurosawa's very faithful transplant to the Tokyo slums, pre-rehearsed and shot with three cameras in long takes, makes astonishingly skilful use of space within the constricted main set (there are in fact only two), and is fascinating simply as a tour de force. Marvellous performances, too, mining a rich vein of ironic humour amid all the misery. TM

L.627

(Bertrand Tavernier, 1992, Fr) Didier Besace, Charlotte Kady, Philippe Torreton, Nils Tavernier, Jean-Paul Comart, Jean-Roger Milo, Lara Guirao, Cécile Garcia-Fogel, Claude Brosset.
146 min.

Parisian drugs-squad detective Lulu (Besace) has an obsessive mission, born of a hatred for the way drugs waste lives, as in the case of his junkie-prostitute friend Cécile (Guirao). But the department is underfunded; he's saddled with several colleagues who are incompetent, naive or racist; and his various relationships, with his superiors, his wife (Garcia-Fogel), addicts and informants, merely serve to muddy his idealistic code. Tavernier's documentary-style *policier* is admirable, intriguing, and finally something of a disappointment. On the credit side, it never pulls its punches, it's unsentimental in its depiction of both law enforcers and breakers, it acknowledges that both the system and racial inequality exacerbate the drugs problem, and its raw, rambling narrative makes for an impressively authentic alternative to the slick, heroic clichés produced by the Hollywood mainstream. But the film – engrossing enough in any ten-minute excerpt – lacks dramatic drive, frequently slipping into tedious procedural detail. GA

L-Shaped Room, The

(Bryan Forbes, 1962, GB) Leslie Caron, Tom Bell, Brock Peters, Cicely Courtneidge, Bernard Lee, Avis Bunnage, Patricia Phoenix, Emlyn Williams.
142 min. b/w.

A queasy sample of the 'new British realism' of the early '60s, based on a novel by Lynne Reid Banks, with Caron as a pregnant French girl who holes up in a Notting Hill bedsit. The house, of course, is peopled by a surefire stockpot of picturesque characters, from seedy doctor and gay black to lesbian actress and chatty tart, not forgetting the tyro writer (Bell) who falls for Caron and draws literary inspiration from their story. Good performances, but it's all a bit like a po-faced trial run for TV's *Rising Damp*. TM

Lucas

(David Seltzer, 1986, US) Corey Haim, Kerri Green, Charlie Sheen, Courtney Thorne-Smith, Winona Ryder, Thomas E Hodges, Ciro Poppiti.
100 min.

Refreshing teen movie that takes the side of the dweebs. Lucas (Haim) is an awkward 13-year-old, more Adrian Mole than Luke Perry. He befriends and falls in love with an 'older' woman – 16-year-old Kerri. But she betrays him for the school football hero, attractively played by Charlie Sheen. More subdued and much more honest than any of John Hughes' egregious forays into adolescence, the film's only drawback is an artificially upbeat ending.

Lucia

(Humberto Solas, 1969, Cuba) Raquel Revuelta, Eslinda Nuñez, Adela Legra, Eduardo Moure, Ramón Brito, Adolfo Llaurado.
161 min. b/w.

Easily the finest film to come out of Cuba in the '60s, Solas' powerful triptych depicts three stages in his country's – and his countrywomen's – struggle for liberation. Using a different idiom and visual style for each era (high-contrast melodrama for the 1890s, nostalgic irony for the 1930s, carnival slapstick for the 1960s), he manages, without any political simplifications, to bring the historical process palpably, and humanly, to life. The film was way ahead of its time in linking sexual and political oppression: interest stays focused on the three heroines, but part of that interest lies in the extent to which they take their political colour from the men they love. Free from dogmatic orthodoxy, the film also observes how contradictions and imperialist emotions survive even the best-programmed revolutions. In an upbeat ending, the struggle is seen to continue. JD

Luci del Varietà (Lights of Variety/Variety Lights)

(Alberto Lattuada/Federico Fellini, 1950, It) Carla Del Poggio, Peppino De Filippo, Giulietta Masina, John Kitzmiller, Folco Lulli, Franca Valeri.
94 min. b/w.
Despite the shared directorial credit, there's no doubt into whose filmography this cherishable oddity fits; and more than just the parade of eccentric dreamers and melancholy misfits identifies it. In the margin of its brash and tolerably sentimental story of the punctured pretensions of a troupe of second-rate travelling music-hall players, is examined a tension between 'artist' and 'showman' that not only anticipates the subsequent polarity of critical attitudes to Fellini, but also chimes perfectly with the elements of reflexive stock-taking in *Casanova*. PT

Lucie Aubrac

(Claude Berri, 1997, Fr) Carole Bouquet, Daniel Auteuil, Patrice Chéreau, Eric Boucher, Jean-Roger Milo, Heino Ferch, Jean Martin, Pascal Greggory.
116 min.
Based on the true story of two Resistance heroes, Berri's typically meticulous WWII drama concerns the efforts of Lucie Aubrac to liberate her husband Raymond from Gestapo incarceration. While Bouquet and Auteuil are dependably solid, they never really achieve the chemistry that might have made this into a more moving love story; the real problem, however, lies in the leaden pacing, and Berri's superficial, somewhat repetitive screenplay, which offers no particularly revealing insights, let alone dramatic excitement. Not exactly bad, the film is rather dull, and serves mainly as a reminder of how grippingly Melville's *L'Armée des Ombres* treated similar material. GA

Lucifer Rising

see Anger Magick Lantern Cycle, The

Luck of Ginger Coffey, The

(Irvin Kershner, 1964, Can/US) Robert Shaw, Mary Ure, Liam Redmond, Tom Harvey, Libby McClintock, Leo Leyden.
99 min. b/w.
A quiet, compellingly probing adaptation of Brian Moore's novel about a man's painful growth into self-realisation. Shaw is excellent as the eponymous hero, a blarneying Irish immigrant who comes to the land of opportunity (Canada) convinced that he is the man it has been waiting for. Told of a vacancy as sub-editor on a newspaper, he immediately sees himself as becoming the editor within weeks; offered a good job as assistant to the owner of a diaper-cleaning service, he turns it down as beneath his dignity; and it is only after successive disappointments, when his despairing wife (Ure, equally good) has left him to take a job in order to support their teenage daughter, that Ginger begins to take realistic stock. Kershner's even, penetrating direction makes marvellous use of the Montreal locations, perfectly capturing the weird beauty of the city's mixture of gleaming skyscrapers and tall, old-fashioned houses festooned with iron staircases, all draped under a layer of snow and ice. TM

Luck, Trust & Ketchup: Robert Altman in Carver Country

(Mike Kaplan/John Dorr, 1994, US) Robert Altman, Tess Gallagher, Anne Archer, Bruce Davison, Robert Downey Jr, Peter Gallagher, Buck Henry, Jennifer Jason Leigh, Jack Lemmon, Huey Lewis, Lyle Lovett, Andie MacDowell, Frances McDormand, Matthew Modine, Julianne Moore, Christopher Penn, Tim Robbins, Annie Ross, Lori Singer, Madeleine Stowe, Lili Taylor, Lily Tomlin, Tom Waits, Fred Ward.
90 min.
Kaplan has been an associate of Robert Altman since the mid-'70s, so you'd hardly expect his documentary on the making of *Short Cuts* to be in any way critical. That said, it avoids the sort of hagiographic gush that mars most on-set promos, while one evident advantage of his friendship with Altman was that he had unprecedented access to cast, crew and director alike. True, long-term admirers of the great man won't learn very

much they didn't already know, but more recent converts should find this movie-on-the-movie intelligent and illuminating. Kaplan's prime achievement is his film's clarity; it's structured chronologically, charting the production from inception to wrap party, and interviewing each member of the large cast in sequence while they were on set. GA

Lucky Break

(Ben Lewin, 1994, Aust) Anthony LaPaglia, Gia Carrides, Sio Bantuke, Jacek Koman.
94 min.
Bizarre semi-black comedy charting the on-off relationship between Carrides (a polio victim whose erotic fantasies fuel her novels) and shady jeweller LaPaglia, who's torn between his wealthy fiancée and the woman whose leg he believes is only temporarily broken. The film, which occasionally gets rather too broad to work as properly romantic comedy, is frank about the difficulties of physical impairment, and even seems to celebrate it here and there.

Lucky Jim

(John Boulting, 1957, GB) Ian Carmichael, Terry-Thomas, Hugh Griffith, Sharon Acker, Maureen Connell, Jean Anderson, Clive Morton.
95 min. b/w.
Kingsley Amis' novel about redbrick university life turned into likeable but harmless knockabout farce by the Boulting Brothers. The situation of accident-prone, caustic-minded young lecturer Jim Dixon having problems with his girlfriend and his professor – he was promptly annexed as an example of 'Angry Young Man' protest – here lacks all sense of satire, not surprisingly given the casting of the wet Carmichael in the central role. Cosy, undemanding, and quite forgettable. GA

Lucky Lady

(Stanley Donen, 1975, US) Gene Hackman, Liza Minnelli, Burt Reynolds, Geoffrey Lewis, John Hillerman, Robby Benson, Michael Hordern.
118 min.
The only vaguely remarkable thing about *Lucky Lady* is that it presents an overtly troilist relationship to its family audience with so little fuss: Hackman, Reynolds and Minnelli share a bed in '30s America, and make their living by running booze across the Mexican border. Unfortunately, the film's originality stops there, which is surprising since it was scripted by the talented Huyck/Katz partnership (*American Graffiti*, *The Second Coming*). Donen's determined 'lightness' is typified by the ghastly, insistent score which punctuates almost every action with a corny tune. The story is virtually non-existent, the period detail coyly derivative, and much of the comedy would be shamed even by the most meagre Anna Neagle vehicle of the '40s. DP

Lucky Luciano

(Francesco Rosi, 1973, It/Fr) Gian Maria Volonté, Rod Steiger, Edmond O'Brien, Charles Siragusa, Vincent Gardenia, Charles Cioffi, Silverio Blasi.
115 min.
Rosi's characteristic dossier on power and corruption tracks the enigmatic figure of repatriated Mafioso gangster Luciano through the web of political/criminal complicity that set the course of Italy's post-war 'recovery'. While specific judgment on Luciano himself is open-endedly reserved, the evidence adduced from a variety of sources (mosaic-style, with Siragusa, for instance, playing himself as a US Narcotics Bureau investigator) is damningly clear on the way the Americans established the Mafia as a 'friendly' buffer against communist influence, only to later have the worm turn vengefully with a flood of drugs back to the States. *Film noir* meets the conspiracy thriller in a flurry of masterful set pieces, operatic intensity segues into documentary-like observation of the complex machinery of manipulable power, and Rosi provides a context for the *Godfather* films which threatens to outdo their own cinematic forcefulness. PT

Lucky Luke

(René Goscinny, 1971, Fr/Bel) voices for English version: Rich Little.
76 min.
The animated adventures of the popular

European comic-strip cowboy, rendered in cheap and listless graphics, but augmented on the English version's soundtrack by Rich Little's verbal imitations of a host of Hollywood Western stars. PT

Lucky Mascot

see Brass Monkey, The

Lucky Star

(Roy Del Ruth, 1938, US) Sonja Henie, Richard Greene, Cesar Romero, Joan Davis, Buddy Ebsen, Arthur Treacher, Elisha Cook Jr, Louise Hovick.
84 min. b/w.
To boost sales in the sports department, Sonja Henie, a parcel-wrapper at a Fifth Avenue store, agrees to become an advertising mannequin at snowy Plymouth University, never suspecting this will rile her fellow co-eds. Skating, sleigh rides, and romance in the sweetshop (with Richard Greene) ensue. Mournful racoon-skin support from Buddy Ebsen and a notable ice finale, 'Alice in Wonderland Through the Looking Glass'. JPy

Lucky Texan, The

(Robert N Bradbury, 1933, US) John Wayne, Barbara Sheldon, Lloyd Whitlock, George Hayes, Yakima Canutt, Ed Parker, Gordon Demaine, Earl Dwire.
53 min. b/w.
Jerry Mason (Wayne) goes prospecting with Jake, his father's old pardner (Hayes), but is duped by a couple of assayers. Charley's aunt saves the day when Jerry is had up for murdering Jake. One of Lone Star's more lively Westerns, with a gold-seeking dog, a somnolent sheriff (Canutt), an above-average final chase (automobile, horse, train), and Wayne somewhat flummoxed by the details of lady's underwear. Pretty primitive, none the less. JPy

Ludwig

(Luchino Visconti, 1972, It/Fr/WGer) Helmut Berger, Romy Schneider, Trevor Howard, Silvana Mangano, Helmut Griem, Nora Ricci, Gert Fröbe, John Moulder Brown.
255 min.
Interested only in Ludwig of Bavaria as a neurotic individual, Visconti centres everything on the king's fears, sublimations and fantasies. He therefore produces a loving, uncritical portrait of a mad homosexual recluse, whose passions are opera, fairy-tale castles, and exquisite young men. Nothing is more sumptuous than Helmut Berger's performance in the lead, the brooding mad scenes, the deliberately contrived hysterical outbursts, and it takes only a flicker of scepticism to find the whole charade risible. But suspension of disbelief has its own rewards: Visconti's connoisseurship of historical detail and manners is as acute as ever, and his commitment to his subject is total. The film was originally released in cut versions ranging between 186 and 137 minutes; this uncut one, obviously more coherent, simply doubles the interest/boredom rate. TR

Ludwig – Requiem for a Virgin King (Ludwig – Requiem für einen jungfräulichen König)

(Hans Jürgen Syberberg, 1972, WGer) Harry Baer, Balthasar Thomas, Peter Kern, Peter Moland, Günther Kaufmann, Ingrid Caven.
139 min.
The first part of Syberberg's remarkable trilogy (followed by *Karl May* and *Hitler, a Film from Germany*), this takes the legend of Ludwig II of Bavaria (Wagner's patron, virgin homosexual, mad visionary, builder of impossible castles, aesthetic recluse) and filters it through the subsequent chaos of German history: the rise of Bismarck and the Prussians at the turn of the century, and the rise of Hitler in the '30s. It's constructed as a series of 28 tableaux, which makes it more like a pageant than a conventional drama: it's full of deliberate disjunctions and contradictions (both Wagnerian stage designs and modern video footage are used as back-projections, for instance), and it feels free to use elements of kitsch (a Nazi rhumba) alongside moments of 'high art' (Isolde's *Liebestod*) without apparent distinction. The slow pace and ultra-mannered staging compel either fascination or outright

rejection. Those fascinated are rewarded with constant surprises and delights, because it's one of the most beautiful and defiantly original movies of the '70s. TR

Ludwig's Cook (Theodor Hierneis oder wie man ein ehemaliger Hofkoch wird)
(Hans Jürgen Syberberg, 1973, WGer) Walter Sedlmayr.
84 min.
Made by Syberberg immediately after *Ludwig – Requiem for a Virgin King*, *Ludwig's Cook* sets out to deal with some of the historical 'truths' about the fairytale monarch that the earlier film ignored. But Syberberg's approach is typically sly and oblique: Walter Sedlmayr (best known here as the grocer in *Fear Eats the Soul*) starts by taking us on a guided tour of Ludwig's castle, but soon slips into the role of Theodor Hierneis, who became Ludwig's head cook in 1882. And so everything that we learn about Ludwig comes from the (literal or metaphorical) perspective of his kitchens. The approach is a wonderfully subversive corrective to the orthodox histories, and at the same time a starting-point for a fascinating reflection on fact and fiction as opposite sides of the same coin. In its unmomentous way, a major film. TR

Lullaby of Broadway
(David Butler, 1950, US) Doris Day, Gene Nelson, SZ Sakall, Billy de Wolfe, Gladys George, Florence Bates.
92 min.
Amiable backstage Warners musical with Doris Day as an up-and-coming British comedienne and singer who goes to New York in the mistaken belief that mum is a huge star on the stage there. Thanks to sweetie-pie millionaire 'Cuddles' Sakall, the truth is hidden long enough for her to launch her own crack at Broadway. A handful of Gershwin and Porter tunes include 'Please Don't Talk About Me When I'm Gone', but the stuff in between is just so much fluff. TJ

Lulu Belle
(Leslie Fenton, 1948, US) Dorothy Lamour, George Montgomery, Otto Kruger, Albert Dekker.
87 min. b/w.
Lamour vamps in a none too persuasive attempt to extend her range, playing an ambitious chanteuse who's also something of a femme fatale. Yes, we know, Dottie dallied with Bob Hope's affections when she only ever had eyes for Bing, but this is ridiculous. Where's Rita Hayworth when you need her? From a play by Charles MacArthur and Edward Sheldon. GM

Lumière Noire (Black Night)
(Med Hondo, 1994, Fr) Patrick Poivey, Ines de Medeiros, Roland Bertin, Pascal Legitimus, Charlie Bauer, Gilles Sagal.
107 min.
Med Hondo made an international breakthrough in 1968 with his Burkina Faso-based warrior-queen epic *Sarraounia*. Here he brings an outsider's eye to a Parisian thriller: Poivey's an airport technician caught up in a terrorist attack who has to fight police bureaucracy to clear his name when he's suspected of involvement in the violence.

Luna, La
(Bernardo Bertolucci, 1979, It) Jill Clayburgh, Matthew Barry, Laura Betti, Veronica Lazar, Renato Salvatori, Fred Gwynne, Alida Valli, Tomas Milian, Franco Citti.
142 min.
An Oedipal parable, in which Matthew Barry's young junkie falls in love with his opera-singer mother (Clayburgh). Ravishing to look at, but the movie's real curiosity is the way it fails to reverse Bertolucci's usual preoccupations: it emerges that the boy's real problem is the lack of a father and need for a family – an emphasis that Bertolucci himself vehemently denies. CA

Luna e l'Altra
(Maurizio Nichetti, 1996, It) Iaia Forte, Aurelio Fierro, Luigi Burruano, Ivano Marcesetti, Maurizio Nichetti, Eraldo Turra.
100 min.
Nichetti's characteristically broad, sentimental comedy concerns a well-meaning but strait-laced

teacher living with her disenchanted father in mid-'50s Milan. A magic lantern which she confiscates from some kids from a travelling circus liberates the teacher's free-spirited shadow. The shadow takes a room in the local bordello and generally scandalises the town (still partly inhabited by fascist sympathisers), causing much embarrassment to the woman's more stolid self. It's winsome and ingratiating, and not helped by all the obligatory circus and brass-band stuff, or by the director's own performance as the school janitor in love with the heroine. Technically clever, though. GA

Luna en el Espejo, La
see Moon in the Mirror, The

Lunatic, The
(Lol Creme, 1990, US) Julie T Wallace, Paul Campbell, Carl Bradshaw, Reggie Carter, Winston Stona, Linda Gambrill.
94 min.
This mind-boggling, often boring comedy/drama sex romp presents a disarmingly naive view of Jamaican life. It's centred on gentle lunatic Aloysius (Campbell) and the *ménage à trois* he sets up with blonde German tourist Inga (Wallace) and mad, machete-wielding goat-butcher Service Johnson (Bradshaw). They take to sex, then to crime, thence retribution. You could read the movie as a kind of upbeat reggae satire-cum-parody. It dances through all the major social and cultural themes: poverty, education, magic and animism, racism, class, religion, sexual politics, and finally cricket! The music score is by Wally Badarou, and the soundtrack sports such as Black Uhuru and Toots and the Maytals. The *patois* is easier to understand than in *The Harder They Come*, and Jamaica looks stunning in a touristy kind of way. A movie that asks to be laughed at. WH

Lunatic Theatre
see Kitami

Lunch on the Grass
see Déjeuner sur l'Herbe, Le

Lune dans le Caniveau, La
see Moon in the Gutter, The

Lune et le téton, La
see Tit and the Moon, The

Lunes de fiel
see Bitter Moon

Lunga Vita alla Signora!
see Long Live the Lady!

Lured (aka Personal Column)
(Douglas Sirk, 1947, US) George Sanders, Lucille Ball, Charles Coburn, Boris Karloff, Cedric Hardwicke, Joseph Calleia, Alan Mowbray, George Zucco, Robert Coote.
102 min. b/w.
A remake of Siodmak's *Pièges*, transposed to London, with Lucille Ball as the taxi-dancer recruited by the police to help trap a serial killer preying on girls by way of lonely hearts ads. The ambience is strangely indeterminate – contemporary London wavers between Edwardian Gothic and transatlantic chic), and the script – mostly a slavish copy of the original, with all its faults – is not helped by a fatuous 'inspiration' (doubtless intended to add a bit of French decadence) whereby the killer is said to be inspired by Baudelaire's poetry. The lighter scenes work well enough, with Ball's heroine turned into a chorus-line Nancy Drew, and the ambivalently debonair Sanders (a vast improvement on Chevalier) more plausible as both romantic interest and chief suspect. But the darker corners are sadly neglected: Siodmak's superb depiction of the killer's slow, hapless self-betrayal goes for very little here; and the wonderfully sinister, yet touching sequence involving von Stroheim's mad couturier (now played by Karloff) is truncated into crude stereotype. TM

Lush Life
(Michael Elias, 1993, US) Jeff Goldblum, Forest Whitaker, Kathy Baker, Tracey Needham, Lois Chiles.
96 min.

A middlebrow take on the life of two jobbing jazzers in contemporary New York. Goldblum (stretching for louche) is a married-but-improvising sax player, Whitaker (far more credible) is his trumpet-blowing buddy. It meanders along quite happily, until 'untimely death' intervenes, somewhat unpersuasively. TCh

Lust and Desire (Le Désir et la Volupté)
(Julien Saint-Clair, 1973, Fr) Claire Gregory, Denise Roland, Alan Scott, Vania Vilers, Catherine Lafont, Francis Lax.
84 min.
A hot title masking cool exploitation, this is an identikit example of the French sex cinema, down to the last chic ensemble and piano arpeggio. Flagging eroticism, with the married protagonists suffering from sexual estrangement, is given a typically contrived boost by the introduction of a night-club stripper. The only point in the film's favour is that it does pay a wee more attention than usual to the sexual needs of its female characters, even allowing that lesbianism and bisexuality may offer liberating potential rather than being just another variation. VG

Lust for Life
(Vincente Minnelli, 1956, US) Kirk Douglas, Anthony Quinn, James Donald, Pamela Brown, Everett Sloane, Niall MacGinnis, Jill Bennett, Henry Daniell.
122 min.
In contrast to the normal Hollywood biopic of 'The Great Artist', in which Art forever takes second place to the Man, Minnelli here offers an account of the developing intensity of Van Gogh's art. Throughout *Lust for Life*, Van Gogh, brilliantly portrayed by Kirk Douglas as a man forever on a knife-edge, struggles to explain himself to his family and to Anthony Quinn's Gauguin. However, Minnelli, with the colours he chooses – which follow those of the paintings – and with his dramatic counterpointing of events in Van Gogh's life with his canvases, undermines all explanations. Minnelli neither explains Van Gogh's art in terms of his life or vice versa, but celebrates both. PH

Lustful Amazon, The (Maciste contre la Reine des Amazones)
(Clifford Brown ie. Jesús Franco, 1973, Fr) Val Davis, Alice Arno, Robert Woods, Montie Prolis, Lina Romay, Chantal Broquet.
65 min.
Unrelievedly unimaginative offshoot from the Italian strong-man series, with a distinctly European garden standing in for the Amazonian jungle as Maciste sets off in quest of lost treasure, only to be pressed into service as a stud by the Amazon queen. Bored robot actresses walk through their non-roles in an understandable daze; and to cap it all, far from being staunchly independent, the Amazons are depicted as woeful figments of a chauvinistic male ego. VG

Lust in the Dust
(Paul Bartel, 1985, US) Tab Hunter, Divine, Lainie Kazan, Geoffrey Lewis, Henry Silva, Cesar Romero, Gina Gallego, Woody Strode.
84 min.
Bartel's outrageous and affectionate spoof of the B Western puts the oats back into the horse opera genre with its *Duel in the Sun*-style heaving bosoms, and some heavy-drinking dames vieing for the attentions of Clinty-eyed Tab Hunter. Divine, as a lascivious barroom bint, gets a bit tiresome after a while, but script, songs ('Let me take you south of my border...') and Henry Silva are all excellent. AB

Lust Seekers, The
see Good Morning...and Goodbye

Lusty Men, The
(Nicholas Ray, 1952, US) Susan Hayward, Robert Mitchum, Arthur Kennedy, Arthur Hunnicutt, Glenn Strange, Lane Chandler.
113 min. b/w.
Nick Ray understood character and psychological pressures better than almost any of his contemporaries, and *The Lusty Men* was one of his

happiest breaks: sympathetic producers, a great cameraman (Lee Garmes, who shot Sternberg's Dietrich movies), and one of Robert Mitchum's finest performances. The story isn't much (the security of family life versus the rootlessness and danger of working as a rodeo rider), but the situation is rich in emotional resonances which Ray conjures into life convincingly. TR

Luther

(Guy Green, 1973, US/GB/Can) Stacy Keach, Patrick Magee, Hugh Griffith, Robert Stephens, Alan Badel, Julian Glover, Judi Dench, Leonard Rossiter, Maurice Denham.
112 min.
At school history classes, Luther emerged as one of the more interesting figures of history because of his constipation, the type of detail that posterity often overlooks. But even Fifth Formers should be disappointed with this version of John Osborne's scatological account of Luther, the bowel movements of history, and the rupture with the Catholic Church. Although Stacy Keach occasionally conveys Luther's intensely felt, near physical relationship with Mother Church, the proceedings are mounted in a totally undynamic manner. This leaves Osborne's dialogue in the lurch, either sounding stupidly matey ('Here's the man who did in four of the sacraments') or downright silly ('Look at Erasmus. He never really gets into serious trouble'). What remains is a few tormented ramblings and a sweating, tonsured cast.

Luv

(Clive Donner, 1967, US) Jack Lemmon, Peter Falk, Elaine May, Nina Wayne, Eddie Mayehoff, Paul Hartman, Severn Darden.
96 min.
A dire kooky farce (based on a play by Murray Schisgal) about contemporary sexual lunacy. The characters behave like berserk idiots, jumping in and out of love like so many rabbits, getting rid of unwanted partners by pushing them off the Brooklyn Bridge, and generally falling about in incoherent ecstasy. One sits bemused as joke after joke misfires, and the hapless actors are left mugging in a vacuum of chic settings. Some sense of comedy timing in the direction might have helped; and the cast could have been introduced to the atrociously post-synchronised dialogue which trails disconsolately behind them. TM

Lydia

(Julien Duvivier, 1941, US) Merle Oberon, Edna May Oliver, Alan Marshal, Joseph Cotten, Hans Yaray.
104 min. b/w.
This seductive Hollywood remake of Duvivier's earlier *Carnet du Bal* can't quite compete with the swoony romantic pessimism that engulfed the '30s French cinema, but as an ersatz exercise in old-school charm it has its moments. Oberon is at the centre of another episodic structure as a New England grande dame reflecting over the string of various lovers life turned up for her. TJ

m

The Mummy (1932)

M (100)

(Fritz Lang, 1931, Ger) Peter Lorre, Otto Wernicke, Ellen Widmann, Inge Landgut, Gustav Gründgens, Theodor Loos.
118 min. b/w.
Lang's first sound film was based on the real-life manhunt for the Düsseldorf child-murderer (an extraordinary performance by Peter Lorre). A radical, analytical film that entertains many of Lang's fascinations: innovative use of sound; the detail of police procedure; the parallels drawn between organised police behaviour and the underworld...a construction which carries Lang's own view of the arbitrariness of the Law. A subversive film, or more simply a movie brimming over with the ferment of Lang's imagination at its height? You choose. RM

M

(Joseph Losey, 1951, US) David Wayne, Howard da Silva, Luther Adler, Martin Gabel, Steve Brodie, Raymond Burr, Glenn Anders, Karen Morley, Norman Lloyd.
88 min. b/w.
Losey's remake of Lang's most famous film was inevitably subjected to invidious comparisons when it was first released. The main problem, as Losey admitted ('I couldn't believe myself in the idea of the whole underworld ganging up against the killer') is the weak ending. Where Lang achieved a double knockout with Lorre's great speech in which he turns the accusation against his accusers – effecting a complete turnabout in sympathies, not just because we understand that he is helpless to combat his sickness, but because he has turned into a victim of persecution – Losey manages only a sucker punch because the setting is no longer Nazi Germany. This said, the first half of the film is excellent, with the Los Angeles locations wonderfully used as a strange and terrifying concrete jungle, and a remarkable performance from David Wayne that bears comparison with Lorre. TM

Maborosi (Maboroshi no Hikari)

(Hirokazu Koreeda, 1995, Jap) Makikio Esumi, Takashi Naito, Tadanobu Asano, Goki Kashiyama, Naomi Watanabe, Midori Kiuchi.
109 min.
Documentarist Koreeda's quietly devastating first fiction feature is about a young woman deeply troubled by the fear that she brings death to her nearest and dearest. Having lost her grandmother (to old age) and her first husband (to an inexplicable suicide), she lives happily in a fishing village with her second husband, but something inside remains frozen. Made under the benign influence of Hou Xiaoxian, the tale is told in contemplative wide-angle shots; the absence of any spurious, unearned intimacy with the characters makes the climactic scenes profoundly moving. TR

Mac

(John Turturro, 1992, US) John Turturro, Katherine Borowitz, Michael Badalucco. Carl Capotorto, Ellen Barkin, John Amos, Olek Krupa.
118 min.
Queens, New York, 1953. Mac (Turturro) and his younger brothers Vito (Badalucco) and Bruno (Capotorto) work together in the building trade. Mac's obsessive perfectionism brings him into constant conflict with foreman Polowski (Krupa), who is only interested in cutting corners. Eventually Mac persuades his brothers that they should go into business for themselves, but the intensity of work inevitably takes its toll. Turturro's directorial debut is – appropriately – a labour of love. It's an ambivalent portrait of a Willy Loman figure, a man whose pride in his craft verges on egomania. There are strong performances throughout. The psychodrama which emerges towards the end infringes Cassavetes territory, but without the essential rigour. This, however, is a serious, likeable effort, not always successful, perhaps, but shot through with insight and conviction. TCh

Macabre

(William Castle, 1957, US) William Prince, Jim Backus, Christine White, Jacqueline Scott, Philip Tonge, Ellen Corby.
73 min. b/w.
The cheapo horror king's first venture in the genre. Not as good as *The Tingler*, though it gets a good start by being set predominantly in a foggy cemetery, where a frantic search is going on for a child supposedly buried alive in one of the graves. But then rather laborious flashbacks start explaining the whys and wherefores of the mystery with small town 'revelations' in the Peyton Place manner. TM

Macadam Tribu

(José Laplaine, 1996, Fr/Zaire) Lydia Ewandé, Hassane Kouyaté, Sidy Camara, Habibou Dembélé, Djibril Kouyaté, Djénéba Diawara.
87 min.
Centred on two brothers – one a womanising wastrel, the other an upcoming boxer – and their anxieties about their mother, heavily into the booze since her husband abandoned her, this funny, racy, pacy and poignant debut feature (from a Zairean-born writer/director now based in Europe) is full of vitality, in terms of both performances and cinematic style. It's an unpretentious but dazzling, deceptively loose-structured portrait of a community (the setting is non-specific 'urban Africa') obsessed with sex, money and social standing. It treats adultery, neighbourly rivalries and political posturing with an admirably light touch while offering serious food for thought on such issues as unemployment and the erosion of local communities. GA

Mac and Me

(Stewart Raffill, 1988, US) Christine Ebersole, Jonathan Ward, Tina Caspary, Lauren Stanley, Jade Calegory, Vinnie Torrente, Martin West.
99 min.
First the good news: Jade Calegory, who plays the boy-hero in this cuddly alien yarn, was born with spina bifida, and the film is neither sentimental nor exploitative in dealing with its wheelchair-confined star. Unfortunately, there's little else to commend. Unless you missed *E.T.*, you know the story: an alien, separated from its family and hunted by nameless agents, hides in suburban California, befriends a boy, and is saved by the neighbourhood kids. Directed by Raffill with no hint of wit, personality or invention, the film soon degenerates into a litany of product placements: every frame is littered with Coke cans, and the invitation to interpret 'Mac' as 'Mysterious Alien Creature' is unlikely to fool anyone even before the song-and-dance number that pops up in a well-known junk-food chain. Mind-blowingly, the last item on the shopping list of hard sells is America itself: the alien no longer wants to go home, he's found a better life in LA. Give the kids a break; take them to something else. TCh

Macao

(Josef von Sternberg/Nicholas Ray, 1952, US) Robert Mitchum, Jane Russell, William Bendix, Gloria Grahame, Thomas Gomez, Brad Dexter, Philip Ahn, Vladimir Sokoloff.
81 min. b/w.
Not an entirely happy production – Sternberg, according to Mitchum, shot and cut it in such a way that characters kept walking into themselves, with the result that Nick Ray was called in to reshoot many of the action scenes – but still a delightful bit of RKO exotica. The thin story, set in the port of the title, sees Mitchum's drifter joining up with Russell's sultry singer and helping the local cops catch a criminal bigwig. But what is so enjoyable, apart from Harry Wild's shimmering camerawork, is the tongue-in-cheek tone of the script and performances, best evidenced in the sparkling banter and innuendo between Mitchum and Russell. GA

Macaroni (Maccheroni)

(Ettore Scola, 1985, It) Jack Lemmon, Marcello Mastroianni, Daria Nicolodi, Isa Danieli, Maria Luisa Santella.
106 min.
Forty years after World War II, an American executive (Lemmon) returns to Naples on business, only to be confronted by an amiable eccentric (Mastroianni) who over the years has been writing to his own sister, pretending to be Lemmon, in order to console her for being wooed and abandoned by Lemmon as a GI. A loopy enough premise for a crazy farce, but Scola avoids the obvious and turns in a touching comedy about friendship and the importance of imagination. While Lemmon is as effectively professional as ever as the surly grouch regenerated by the Neapolitan way of life, it is Mastroianni who steals the show. Perfectly attuned to the film's easygoing examination of the gulf between reality and fantasy, hopes and disillusionment, Mastroianni manages to make convincing a man stricken with a singularly fertile form of insanity and blessed with a heart as huge and warm as Vesuvius. Gently ironic, remarkably relaxed, he is Lancaster-like in his effortless ability to demonstrate pathos, humour and dignity. GA

MacArthur – The Rebel General

(Joseph Sargent, 1977, US) Gregory Peck, Ivan Bonar, Ward Costello, Nicolas Coster, Marj Dusay, Ed Flanders, Dan O'Herlihy.
130 min.
Typical Hollywood biopic which, despite proclamations of objectivity, tilts in the direction of hagiography. Inadvertently, the movie mirrors MacArthur in its own hubris: epic ambitions way beyond all budgetary control. The script is sprinkled with walking-on-the-water jokes in a half-hearted attempt to have its MacArthur and demystify him as well, but these merely enhance the image of the Perfect American General ('40s vintage) – a commodity which, as can be seen here, should never be exported. SM

Macbeth

(Orson Welles, 1948, US) Orson Welles, Jeanette Nolan, Dan O'Herlihy, Roddy McDowall, Edgar Barrier, Alan Napier, Erskine Sanford, John Dierkes, Gus Schilling.
107 min. b/w.
Not entirely successful, hardly surprisingly in that it was shot in 23 days on a cheap Western backlot at Republic Studios. Also, Ms Nolan's Lady Macbeth is something of a disaster. That said, though, the film – unlike so many adaptations of the Bard – is pure cinema: moodily magnificent photography by John L Russell reinforces the sense of a nightmarish world before time, where primitive emotions hold sway with absolute, compelling simplicity. Adventurous film-making that takes risks, and full of imaginative flourishes. GA

Macbeth

(Roman Polanski, 1971, GB) Jon Finch, Francesca Annis, Martin Shaw, Nicholas Selby, John Stride, Stephan Chase.
140 min.
The opening shot of a yellow, withering moonscape stretching away to infinity – revealed to be a desolate sea-shore on which the three witches proceed to the ritual burial of a noose, a severed arm and a dagger – effortlessly establishes the cold, barbarous climate of Shakespeare's play. Polanski's imagery, evoking a characteristically cruel, irrational and blood-boltered world, is often magnificently strange and hieratic: the death of the Thane of Cawdor, for instance, hanged by way of a massive iron collar and chain from a high tower in a courtyard ringed by cloaked soldiers; or the almost pagan ritual of Macbeth's coronation, starting with his bare feet stepping into the huge footprints embedded in the sacred stone. The relative weakness is that Polanski's evident desire to elicit understated, naturalistic performances from his cast also underplays the poetry of the play, which as a result never quite spirals into dark, uncontrollable nightmare as the Welles version (for all its faults) does. TM

McCabe and Mrs Miller

(Robert Altman, 1971, US) Warren Beatty, Julie Christie, Rene Auberjonois, Hugh Millais, Shelley Dumas, Michael Murphy, John Schuck, William Devane, Keith Carradine.
121 min.
One of the best of Altman's early movies, using classic themes – the ill-fated love of gambler and whore, the gunman who dies by the gun, the contest between little man and big business – to produce a non-heroic Western. McCabe (Beatty) hasn't the grand dimensions of a Ford, Fuller or Leone hero; he is an amiable braggart, a bungling lover, a third-rate entrepreneur with chronic indigestion and a penchant for bad jokes. Mrs Miller (Christie) is a whorehouse madame who prefers her opium pipe to McCabe's amorous overtures. Their relationship is to a large extent a mournful background to Altman's central concern of chronicling the harsh conditions of life in a rawly devel-

oping mining town in the Northwest. His vision of the role of the individual represents another removal from genre tradition. Confronted with the primitive character of social organisation and the brutality of nature, Altman's Westerner is insignificant, isolated and vulnerable; his survival is chancy, a question of luck rather than skill. JdeG

Macchina Ammazzacattivi, La
see Machine That Kills Bad People, The

McGuire Go Home!
see High Bright Sun, The

Machine Gun Kelly
(Roger Corman, 1958, US) Charles Bronson, Susan Cabot, Morey Amsterdam, Jack Lambert, Wally Campo, Barboura Morris, Connie Gilchrist.
80 min. b/w.
Corman's first gangster movie is one of the most ambitious and rewarding of his '50s quickies: not because it transcends any of its inherent limitations, but rather because it indulges them recklessly. Apparently modelling itself on Siegel's *Baby Face Nelson*, it sees Kelly (Bronson) as a child-like thug with a pathological fear of death, helplessly dominated by his moll Flo (Cabot, Corman's favourite *femme fatale* until Barbara Steele came along). The post-Freudian motifs aren't imposed on the dime-novel material; they grow with a hysteria all of their own from the sleazy settings and one-note performances. The movie reveals Corman as a director entirely in touch with his audience, and Floyd Crosby as one of the most prodigiously resourceful cameramen in Hollywood history. TR

Machine That Kills Bad People, The (La Macchina Ammazzacattivi)
(Roberto Rossellini, 1948, It) Gennaro Pisano, Giovanni Amato, Marilyn Buferd, Bill Tubbs, Helen Tubbs, Pietro Carloni.
83 min. b/w.
Minor but mildly pleasing Rossellini, set in a small town in Southern Italy thrown into a tizzy by the machinations of a mysterious old man. Saint or devil, he endows a camera with the power not merely to kill people, but to ferret out sources of wealth. Cue for a flurry of treachery and greed, all casually swept under the carpet in a final pirouette. The neo-realist techniques don't always mix too comfortably with the fantasy, making it an Ealing comedy with an edifying bent. TM

Maciste Contro i Mostri (Colossus of the Stone Age/Fire Monsters Against the Son of Hercules/Land of the Monsters)
(Guido Malatesta, 1962, It) Reg Lewis, Margaret Lee, Luciano Marin, Myra Kent, Andrea Aureli.
82 min.
Dreadful muscle-man epic featuring some prehistoric monsters which look as though they were created by Harryhausen's third junior assistant stand-in. The human battle scenes are atrociously choreographed (you can almost imagine The Anvil Chorus over the penultimate one), and Malatesta shows no signs of being able to direct his way out of a paper bag, let alone Reg Lewis act his way out of one. The dubbing is above-par stupid. PM

Mackenna's Gold
(J Lee Thompson, 1968, US) Gregory Peck, Omar Sharif, Telly Savalas, Camilla Sparv, Keenan Wynn, Julie Newmar, Ted Cassidy, Eduardo Ciannelli, Eli Wallach, Edward G Robinson, Raymond Massey, Burgess Meredith, Anthony Quayle, Lee J Cobb.
136 min.
Matinee adventure material blown up to deliciously absurd proportions, as the gold-lust clichés tumble from Carl Foreman's typewriter to be treated by the assembled stellar multitudes as if they were fresh-minted bullion. Peck's sheriff has The Map, everyone else wants it. Everyone double-crosses everyone else. And in the Lost Canyon of Gold there's...(wait for it)...an ironic Conclusion. Treasure of the Sierra Madness. PT

McKenzie Break, The
(Lamont Johnson, 1970, GB) Brian Keith, Helmut Griem, Ian Hendry, Jack Watson, Patrick O'Connell, Horst Janson.
106 min.
Rare reversal of the POW camp formula, with Germans the potential escapees from a Scottish internment. Keith and Hendry do ideological battle with fanatical Nazi Griem, who is willing to sacrifice half his less politicised men to cover his planned breakout. Elaborated with unusual care for authenticity, it's tautly handled by Johnson (better known for abrasive telemovies), and adapted from Sidney Sheldon's novel by William Norton (father of *Convoy* adaptor and *More American Graffiti* director BWL Norton). PT

Mackintosh Man, The
(John Huston, 1973, GB) Paul Newman, Dominique Sanda, James Mason, Harry Andrews, Ian Bannen, Michael Hordern, Nigel Patrick, Peter Vaughan, Roland Culver.
99 min.
Reasonably entertaining old-fashioned thriller, with British intelligence hiring a freelance agent (Newman) to expose Communist infiltration in high places. A quick stretch inside to gain credibility with the opposition, then a well-handled break-out leads Newman to a remote and mysterious house in Ireland. A spot of bother, another nicely handled escape across the moors; a resumé of the plot for Dominique Sanda, who can't work it out; then everyone's off to Malta for the climax. If you can accept Newman as a totally unconvincing Australian (thankfully only for about 20 minutes), an appalling array of accents (mainly Irish), and Dominique Sanda as an unlikely member of the British Secret Service, then it whiles away the time pleasantly enough. CPe

Macomber Affair, The
(Zoltan Korda, 1947, US) Gregory Peck, Joan Bennett, Robert Preston, Reginald Denny, Carl Harbord.
89 min. b/w.
Archetypal Hemingway tale of the rich dilettante on safari (Preston) – tormented by his own cowardice, taunted by his wife (Bennett), and finally rendered superfluous as she turns to their white hunter guide (Peck). Surprisingly persuasive (considering the stars stayed in Hollywood while three second unit cameramen shot the backgrounds), thanks to an admirably terse script and excellent performances. But it gradually begins to fall apart in the last third as courage is put to the test among the big game. TM

Macon County Line
(Richard Compton, 1973, US) Alan Vint, Cheryl Waters, Geoffrey Lewis, Joan Blackman, Jesse Vint, Max Baer.
89 min.
Alan Vint and his brother Jesse form an agreeable duo, playing roistering brothers on a spree in Macon County, Georgia, in the '50s. They pick up a girl, fool around some, and run up against a redneck cop (Baer), who warns them on their way, then mistakenly goes on the rampage after them when he finds his wife raped and murdered. As the film moves from rompish comedy into something altogether darker, its moral tone becomes more overbearing, and the blood-spattered ending (the script is based on fact, but fails to prepare its ground adequately) seems to come from a different movie altogether. CPe

McQ
(John Sturges, 1974, US) John Wayne, Eddie Albert, Diana Muldaur, Colleen Dewhurst, Clu Gulager, David Huddleston, Julie Adams, Al Lettieri.
111 min.
Perhaps the first commercial film to show the indirect influence of Watergate. It's also the best of the current spate of cop movies, despite the presence of an overage and cumbersome Wayne. He plays a Seattle lieutenant who goes on the rampage when his best friend gets killed, only to discover that it's the force itself that is corrupt, even to the point where they can double-cross the local crime syndicate in a dope deal. Wayne comes over not so much the lone crusader as an anachronism in a world of institutionalised crime. Rather than solve the plot, Wayne merely reveals that everything he has

stood for is corrupt. The accusing finger even rests on him for a while; a pity, then, that he's too thick-skinned to let it register. CPe

Macunaima
(Joaquim Pedro de Andrade, 1969, Braz) Grande Otelo, Paolo José, Dina Sfat, Milton Gonçalves, Rodolfo Arena.
108 min.
De Andrade's film has a plot of fairytale simplicity. Macunaima, born black and middle-aged in the Brazilian jungle, turns into a young white on his way to the city. There, he and his stooge-like brothers, wide-eyed but their native shrewdness still intact, are buffeted around by the Marx Brothers-type logic that dominates the plot, while the film takes constant delight in visual incongruities. Macunaima takes up with a girl revolutionary, but she is killed by her own time bomb; the villain is the local industrial magnate, the Cannibal Giant, who feeds his guests to man-eating fish. The film, the introduction tells us, is about consumerism as cannibalism, about a Brazilian devoured by Brazil. It's a bizarre and often very funny comedy that applies its central thesis with unerring accuracy.

McVicar
(Tom Clegg, 1980, GB) Roger Daltrey, Adam Faith, Cheryl Campbell, Billy Murray, Georgina Hale, Ian Hendry.
112 min.
Despite excellent teamwork between Daltrey and Faith, a cracking cast, and inspiring raw material, this musical version of *Scum*-meets-*Out* somehow buries these advantages deep inside a saucy action thriller format. Having read the headlines, bought the book etc, few surprises are left: why no mention of the real-life characters (Charlie Richardson, Ian Brady) of the prison inmates? Though it's good to see someone Escape from Durham rather than Alcatraz, the dependable British fascination with villains is played out once too often for anyone to care, and leaves McVicar's unique insights into crime more or less untouched. If you want to see Daltrey prove himself a straight actor, see it; otherwise read the book. DMacp

Madadayo (Not Yet)
(Akira Kurosawa, 1993, Jap) Tatsuo Matsumura, Kyoko Kagawa, Hisashi Igawa, George Tokoro.
120 min.
Kurosawa's thirtieth film is, sadly, as trite and embarrassing as its immediate predecessors, *Dreams* and *Rhapsody in August*. About Hyakken Uchida, a teacher who retires, in 1943, to concentrate on his writing career, and abandons his reclusive ways, once a year only, to welcome his adoring former students to his birthday celebrations, it's a maudlin, fulsomely nostalgic affair. The turgid narrative consists almost entirely of static, predictable, repetitive scenes in which the grown students, after reminiscing with the prof about the good old days, are overcome by tearful emotion and told by their mentor to shape up. 'Humanism' at its mushiest. GA

Mad Adventures of 'Rabbi' Jacob, The (Les Aventures de Rabbi Jacob)
(Gérard Oury, 1973, Fr/It) Louis de Funès, Suzy Delair, Marcel Dalio, Claude Giraud, Claude Piéplu.
100 min.
As the name implies, one big Jewish (not to mention Moslem and Catholic) joke in which Rabbi Jacob (de Funès) becomes inadvertently entangled with inefficient Arab terrorists and various other neurotic characters. The script is so banal and full of the most appalling jokes (to an Arab: 'You bet on the wrong *camel*'), that the film's success (if any) depends on reactions to de Funès' brand of humour (a mixture of slapstick and idiotic facial expressions). It might appeal to kids who like to see their protagonists wallowing in vats of green chewing-gum. GSa

Madagascar Skin
(Chris Newby, 1995, GB) John Hannah, Bernard Hill, Mark Anthony, Mark Petit, Danny Earl.
93 min.
This playful second feature is a world away from

the medieval meditations of *Anchoress*. A virtual two-hander, it's a disarming love stories featuring a very odd couple: Hannah's young gay
man, a fugitive from the club scene where the
Madagascar-shaped birthmark on his face makes
him feel ill at ease; and Hill's slightly shady
Harry, a thumping heterosexual whose sheltered
coastal hideaway may indicate that he too is running away from a past he'd rather not have to
deal with. There's plenty of quirky humour, much
that's the unexpected, and a gleeful eye for the
absurd, as the film quizzically picks its way
towards the triumph of their affections. TJ

Madame Bovary

(Jean Renoir, 1934, Fr) Valentine Tessier,
Pierre Renoir, Daniel Lecourtois, Max Dearly,
Fernand Fabre, Robert Le Vigan.
117 min. b/w.
Butchered by its original distributor (who cut it
by an hour), surviving in a merely adequate print,
this is nevertheless superb early Renoir. Valentine
Tessier, mannered and theatrical – though not
inappropriately so – is something of an acquired
taste as Flaubert's unfortunate provincial lady,
dreaming of romance while trapped in marriage
to a bovine village doctor (magnificently played
by Pierre Renoir), but the direction is masterly.
Making systematic (and stunning) use of deep
focus, Renoir captures perfectly the eternally irreconcilable beauty and boredom of the provinces,
rooting Emma squarely in lovely Norman landscapes which her pathetic yearnings for a fantasy world turn into a bleak desert. TM

Madame Bovary

(Claude Chabrol, 1991, Fr) Isabelle Huppert,
Jean-François Balmer, Christophe Malavoy,
Jean Yanne, Lucas Belaux.
140 min.
Chabrol's long-delayed adaptation of Flaubert's
novel is as suffocating as its heroine's predicament. Emma, the ambitious farmer's daughter
taken for a wife by arch-mediocrity Dr Bovary
(Jean-François Balmer in a perfectly controlled
performance), has been the subject of see-sawing
literary interpretations since the 1860s. Chabrol
sticking to the letter of the text avoided the temptation to cast her in a modernised feminist role and
stressed instead her stifling limitation of choices
in provincial 19th century France. Isabelle
Huppert, often a blood-drained, internalised
actress, outdoes herself here, playing Emma in a
distracted, half-comatose state, resuscitated
briefly by the odd gowned ball or the lifeline to
passion proffered by heart-breaker Rodolphe
(Malavoy). The birth of a child fails to bring light
into her eyes. A classical art movie saturated with
Chabrol's dark romantic pessimism. WH

Madame Butterfly

(Frédéric Mitterrand, 1995, Fr/Jap/Ger/GB)
Ying Huang, Richard Troxell, Ning Liang,
Richard Cowan, Jing Ma Fan.
134 min.
A few snippets of archive footage from turn-of-
the-century Japan provide the most arresting
moments in this rarely more than adequate film
of the Puccini warhorse (routine accompaniment
from the Orchestre de Paris under James Conlon).
What we get is a realist, meat-and-two-veg rendition in picture postcard 'Japanese' settings
rigged up for the occasion on the coast of Tunisia,
where the chief location is the heroine's unhappy
home. Mitterrand's camera moves in and out
from behind the paper screens with a certain nim-
bleness, but you'd be forgiven if you wanted a bit
more cinematic flair from a movie billed as 'A
Martin Scorsese Presentation'. TJ

Madame Claude

(Just Jaeckin, 1976, Fr) Françoise Fabian,
Murray Head, Dayle Haddon, Klaus Kinski,
Robert Webber, Marc Michel, Maurice Ronet.
111 min.
Jaeckin, the man to blame for initiating the deadly rash of Emmanuelliana, has a knack for making movies in which sex appears about as much
fun as a trip to the launderette. Perhaps realising
this, he has bolstered the regulation softcore sighs
with a purportedly 'political' thriller plot.
Unfortunately the latter is equally inane, and one
can only surmise that Jaeckin has a knack for
making movies about as interesting...etc. Klaus
Kinski looks like he'd give anything to be on a
raft up the Amazon. PT

Madame Curie

(Mervyn LeRoy, 1943, US) Greer Garson,
Walter Pidgeon, Henry Travers, Albert
Bassernan, Robert Walker, C Aubrey Smith,
Dame May Whitty, Reginald Owen.
124 min. b/w.
Medical history MGM-style as the on-screen husband and wife who battled through the Blitz in
the Oscar-winning *Mrs Miniver* roll up their
sleeves in the lab and get on with the dogged
business of discovering radium. Actually, the pop
science angle is done rather well, but Garson's
evident sanctity brings an air of portentousness
to the film that it could clearly do without. If you
want the basics on where X-ray technology came
from, you could do worse. From the book by Eve
Curie. TJ

Madame de... (The Earrings
of Madame de...)

(Max Ophüls, 1953, Fr/It) Danielle Darrieux,
Charles Boyer, Vittorio De Sica, Jean
Debucourt, Lia de Léa, Mireille Perrey,
Jean Galland.
102 min. b/w.
Ophüls's penultimate film, indulging a characteristically tender irony in its adaptation of Louise
de Vilmorin's novel, is – even by his standards –
exceptionally elegant in its rendering of its *fin de
siècle* Paris *milieu* of ballrooms, the opera, and
dashing young military officers paying their
attentions to the unnamed heroine (Darrieux) of
the title. The story concerns this beautiful
woman's adulterous affair with an Italian diplomat (De Sica), with a pair of earrings playing an
implausible and extraordinary role in their relationship. What is particularly brilliant about the
film is the way Ophüls constantly draws attention to this improbable plot device, to allow a distanced and unmoralistic meditation on actions
and their consequences. Also fine is the sumptuous decor, photographed in superb monochrome,
and there is a particularly good performance from
Boyer as the discreet 'wronged' husband. RM

Madame Rosa
(La Vie devant Soi)

(Moshe Mizrahi, 1977, Fr) Simone Signoret,
Claude Dauphin, Samy Ben Youb, Gabriel
Jabbour, Michal Bat Adam, Costa-Gavras.
120 min.
Badly adapted from a rather good novel by Emile
Ajar, this is art cinema at its artless, exploitative
worst. An essentially simple tale – of a prostitute's child, Momo, brought up with a bevy of
similar kids by professional foster-mother/aged
ex-prostitute Madame Rosa – is used to screw the
audience for every ounce of its social conscience,
with Signoret evidently (and mistakenly) convinced that she's in a 'political' film. Far from
reflecting the realities of streetwalking in Pigalle,
or of childhood in the ghetto of Belleville, the film
trades instead on Rosa's memories of Auschwitz
(to which she refers with objectionable facility)
and the boy's Algerian background to fabricate
a pretentious allegory on Israeli/Arab conflict.
Eventually, thank God, Rosa dies and doe-eyed
Momo is 'rescued' – in a crowning example of
nauseating, complacent sentimentality – by a
chic young couple. CA

Madame Sin

(David Greene, 1972, GB) Bette Davis, Robert
Wagner, Denholm Elliott, Gordon Jackson,
Dudley Sutton, Catherine Schell.
90 min.
Lips a venomous scarlet slash, hair in Gorgonic
braids, eyes popping ad lib, Bette Davis is a criminal arch-fiend plotting to hijack a Polaris sub
('Just one'). Lots of exotic sets and outlandish
secret weapons, just a pity it's all rather old hat
Bond stuff. Still, with Denholm Elliott giving sterling support as her sycophantic aide, Davis has
a ball with some genuinely monstrous lines. 'Poor
quality photography,' she rasps apologetically
while showing Robert Wagner some footage of
his fiancée being tortured to death, 'but we can't
always choose the best camera positions'. TM

Madame Sousatzka

(John Schlesinger, 1988, GB) Shirley MacLaine,
Peggy Ashcroft, Twiggy, Shabana Azmi,
Leigh Lawson, Geoffrey Bayldon, Lee
Montague, Navin Chowdhry.
122 min.

Schubert, Chopin, Beethoven, Schumann – the
music moves the emotions, though nothing else
does in this pedestrian version of Bernice Rubens'
novel. Let's hear it again for the faded rooming-
house full of types: the ageing osteopath queen
(Bayldon), the ageing no-hope pop singer
pushover in the attic (Twiggy), the aged, distracted, aristocratic owner in the basement
(Ashcroft). And, in cloak and comic walk, severe
but mush underneath, the ageing, imperious
piano teacher of the title (MacLaine). Into this
overworked literary armature arrives 14-year-old
Manek (Chowdhry), a talented Indian lad with a
domineering mother in back, for lessons. Madame
soon has him in her grip, reining him in from concert exposure – though he is obviously mustard
– before heading him off from the inevitable rite-
of-passage in the attic. Probably conceived as
more dislikeably monomaniacal than MacLaine
plays her, this teacher has to get used to the
painful fact that her chicks will fly the coop. Who
could blame them? Fusty stuff. BC

Madame X

(Ulrike Ottinger, 1977, WGer) Tabea
Blumenschein, Roswitha Jantz, Irena von
Lichtenstein, Yvonne Rainer.
141 min.
A militant film, albeit one of a highly unorthodox
kind. Ulrike Ottinger's lesbian feminist pirate
adventure deliberately flouts every rule of orthodox film syntax, and is so uneventful and repetitive that many may well find it impossible to
take. The evident aim is a destruction of traditional spectacle, and a construction of a new way
of presenting women on film. The pirate plot is a
high-camp pretext (and not in any sense a vehicle) for 'heroic' new images of women. The most
obviously impressive scenes are those involving
Yvonne Rainer as an artist disillusioned with the
artocracy around her, who takes off for the high
seas on roller skates, pausing only to declaim her
disillusionment (as recorded in her notebooks) to
a passing TV interviewer. TR

Mad Bomber, The

(Bert I Gordon, 1972, US) Vince Edwards,
Chuck Connors, Neville Brand, Cristina Hart,
Faith Quabius, Ilona Wilson, Ted Gehring.
95 min.
Detective Vince Edwards hunts Los Angeles for
dynamiter Chuck Connors (a nicely quirky characterisation), who is writing to the papers to
explain that his bombs are punishments meted
out to society. The victims include a high school,
a hospital, a Women's Lib group...and aid comes
from the unlikely quarter of a pathetic rapist
(Brand, another fine performance). Shoddily
assembled, but brightly conceived and very well
acted, it has a genuine B movie vitality. VG

Mädchen in Uniform (Girls in
Uniform/Maidens in Uniform)

(Leontine Sagan, 1931, Ger) Dorothea Wieck,
Hertha Thiele, Ellen Schwannecke, Emilia
Unda, Hedwig Schlichter.
98 min. b/w.
A key early German talkie: a powerful melodrama about life in a Prussian boarding school for
the daughters of the bourgeoisie – a bastion of
the ideology of 'strength through suffering'. The
plot mechanics are predictable – unhappy pupil
with crush on housemistress is driven to attempt
suicide – but the atmosphere and sensitivity to
teenage fears are not: stage actress Leontine
Sagan brings an exceptionally warm touch to her
depiction of female friendships, and her denunciation of the Prussian orthodoxy is more a matter of subtle imagery than shrill accusations.
Whether it adds up to a precursor of militant lesbianism is another question... TR

Mädchen Rosemarie, Das
(The Girl Rosemarie)

(Rolf Thiele, 1958, WGer) Nadja Tiller, Peter
van Eyck, Carl Raddatz, Gert Fröbe, Mario
Adorf, Horst Frank.
100 min. b/w.
The murder of Rosemarie Nitribitt, callgirl, on
which Rolf Thiele based this film was one of
those events which stir popular imagination for
a long time because they seem to sum up an era.
The mixture of provincial pettiness, ruthless
money-making, and post-war shabbiness which
propelled Rosemarie, her poodles and her white
Mercedes to something more poignant than noto-

riety proved lethal in the end. Thiele's sharply directed film provides a more direct account of the grotty side of the economic miracle than Fassbinder, who was to portray it as belonging to such a remote and giddy past. RB

Mad Doctor of Market Street, The
(Joseph H Lewis, 1942, US) Lionel Atwill, Una Merkel, Claire Dodd, Nat Pendleton, Anne Nagel, Noble Johnson.
61 min. b/w.
Lewis at his low-budget looniest, and barely the worse for that. The material is preposterously absurd. It begins with mad boffin Atwill chased out of a recognisably modern American city for his sinister experiments, shifts to a swish ocean liner for a quick dash of social comedy (Merkel) and disaster movie, then ends up on a ludicrously unexotic desert island where the few shipwreck survivors are menaced by Atwill's desire to take up his old work again. *Everything* is cheap, tacky and infantile, but you can't help but admire the way Lewis balances his evident, slyly humorous disdain for the script and production values with a surprisingly professional pretence at some sort of commitment. Zomboid fun. GA

Mad Dog and Glory
(John McNaughton, 1992, US) Robert De Niro, Bill Murray, Uma Thurman, Kathy Baker, David Caruso, Mike Starr.
97 min.
This intriguing but not wholly successful blend of thriller, comedy and romance is essentially a buddy movie. It's concerned more with the friendship between Chicago forensic detective Wayne 'Mad Dog' Dobie (De Niro) and loan-shark Frank Milo (Murray), than the feelings between De Niro and Glory (Thurman), a salesgirl sent by the gangster as a gift after the cop saves his life. Just as Glory is merely a prize to be won, so Richard Price's script and McNaughton's direction relegate her to the function of a catalyst. Sexual politics aside (the film also avoids acknowledging its gay dimensions), it nevertheless exerts a quirky charm. Back on form, De Niro seems committed to the part of the sensitive loner, while Murray all but succeeds in mixing smooth and sinister, heartfelt and hot-tempered. But the film's real strength lies in incidentals: marginal characters; Dobie's love of photography and Louis Prima records; the drugs-murder which gets the whole thing started. Here, Price's street savvy and McNaughton's taut pacing bind the disparate elements impressively. GA

Mad Dog Morgan (aka Mad Dog)
(Philippe Mora, 1976, Aust) Dennis Hopper, Jack Thompson, David Gulpilil, Frank Thring, Michael Pate, Wallas Eaton, Bill Hunter, John Hargreaves.
110 min.
An excellent early example of the Australian revival, this is a pacy, violent bushranger saga; basically a Western in all but locale, with the same sort of critical kinship to its US models as *Backroads*. Hopper's hirsute Irish outlaw (a first-rate performance) is the victim of social barbarities inflicted at the behest of bald, bullish policeman Thring, and David Gulpilil again represents the unknowable forgotten option like some 'good injun'. PT

Mad Dogs and Englishmen
(Henry Cole, 1994, GB) Elizabeth Hurley, C Thomas Howell, Joss Ackland, Jeremy Brett, Claire Bloom, Frederick Treves, Patrick Lichfield.
97 min.
Rich bitch Antonia Dyer's heroin habit has led her into a dangerous world where crime and punishment easily become confused. The audience, too: Ackland's Insp Stringer of the the Yard, a bent copper struggling with incestuous desires and imminent retirement, seems more like a decent actor who's wandered into the wrong thriller. Bike messenger Mike is so infatuated with Antonia he'll pick up smack at 3 am on her whim, but Howell is so inexpressive his behaviour might as well be motivated by suicidal impulses. Antonia fits Hurley like 'that dress', but despite her plummy, punky credentials, she can do little to humanise a Sloane who spends most

of her time lolling in silk lingerie, burning tin foil. The handling is clumsy, the moralising dire, and gestures towards genre movie-making are laughable. TCh

Mad Dogs and Englishmen
(Pierre Adidge, 1971, US) Joe Cocker, Leon Russell, Rita Coolidge, Claudia Linnear.
118 min.
Leon Russell organised the caravan tour of the States in the spring of 1970 which featured Joe Cocker, the Greaseband and about forty others, and which this film documents. A team of 16mm cameramen followed them around, concentrating on simple, multi-camera coverage of concert numbers, and filling in the touring gaps with ungimmicky shots of the troupe in buses, hotels and streets. The sound recording for the first few numbers leaves something to be desired; but considering the pleasantly chaotic formation of the 'family' onstage, this is perhaps understandable, and is made up for in the unpretentious appearance of the movie as a whole. So it comes down to whether you like the music of the Cocker/Russell team. If you do, you won't be disappointed. JC

Mad Dog Time (aka Trigger Happy)
(Larry Bishop, 1996, US) Ellen Barkin, Gabriel Byrne, Richard Dreyfuss, Jeff Goldblum, Diane Lane, Larry Bishop, Gregory Hines, Kyle MacLachlan, Burt Reynolds, Michael J Pollard, Angie Everhart, Paul Anka, Rob Reiner, Richard Pryor, Joey Bishop.
93 min.
Writer/director Bishop, son of the old Rat Pack member Joey Bishop, looks set on founding his own pack with this spoof of gang warfare. Whereas Sinatra's pack made sneery, slick movies together, Bishop can organise his material and he shares his jokes. Gang boss Vic (Dreyfuss) is released from mental hospital, but finds his turf threatened with ambitious weeds like mortician MacLachlan, who longs to see everyone professionally, and his own once-faithful caretaker, Byrne. The new blood presents him with a commemorative straitjacket at his welcome home party, so the chances of détente are slim. Vic is also preoccupied with settling scores with his former hitman Nicky (Goldblum), who took up with his mistress once the boss was banged up. There's byzantine plotting, trade-offs and double-bluffs aplenty, plus an amusing trial in which rival hitmen duel to the death from facing executive desks. The leads play up enthusiastically with the brass ring shared by Goldblum and Barkin's shifty moll Rita. There's a conveyor belt of faded or fuddled walk-ons from the likes of Pollard, Pryor, Reynolds and Anka, while the soundtrack is vintage cuff-shooting crooner. Fair fun. BC

Made
(John MacKenzie, 1972, GB) Carol White, Roy Harper, John Castle, Margery Mason, Doremy Vernon.
104 min.
Rather dated already, MacKenzie's film swerves uneasily between social realism and melodramatic clichés as it follows a girl's attempts to find a way out from her miserable life looking after her illegitimate child and an invalid mother. Salvation is offered by a do-gooding priest and a boring old folksinger (Harper playing himself, quite well actually). It has its moments of acute perception, but much of the time is content with a typically British glamorisation of seedy lives. Ken Loach, one feels, would have handled it far better. GA

Made for Each Other
(Robert B Bean, 1971, US) Renee Taylor, Joseph Bologna, Paul Sorvino, Olympia Dukakis, Helen Verbit, Louis Zorich.
107 min.
Jewish girl from the Bronx meets an Italian boy from Brooklyn at an emergency encounter group on Christmas Eve. From there develops an erratic relationship that continually erupts into near-sadistic confrontations: the girl wants to be loved but not possessed, the guy wants to possess but not love (explicitly anyway). Much of the film is taken up by the couple's violent exchanges, which at times come over as childishness; but the chauvinistic attitudes and the film's unresolved

tensions make it just about worth a look (although you have to sit through a lot of ego-shit before getting your head into the overall trip). JPi

Made in America
(Richard Benjamin, 1993, US) Whoopi Goldberg, Ted Danson, Will Smith, Nia Long, Frances Bergen, Phyllis Avery.
110 min.
Director Benjamin makes amiable but bland comedies, and here's another. The pitch is ebony (Goldberg) meets ivory (Danson) as bio-chemical parents of, well, a light-brown daughter (Long) when they belatedly discover she was the fruit of a sperm-bank mix-up. Whoopi's a successful, politicised, single working-mother; Danson's a lovable, reconstructable cowpoke. After the first half sets up intriguing racial/political/biological conundrums, the second simply lets them go hang. Energetically directed with a fair smattering of funny lines. WH

Made in Heaven
(Alan Rudolph, 1987, US) Timothy Hutton, Kelly McGillis, Maureen Stapleton, Ann Wedgeworth, James Gammon, Debra Winger, Ellen Barkin, Don Murray, Timothy Daly.
102 min.
Back in the '50s, Mike (Hutton) dies saving a family from a car accident. In heaven he falls in love with Annie (McGillis), a new soul waiting to be born, and he's forced to gamble on 30 more years on earth in order to search out his lost love. Will they meet again? Unlikely; he's reincarnated as under-achieving would-be musician Elmo, she as wealthy, talented Ally, spliced to an ambitious film-maker. Offbeat and very imaginative, Rudolph's movie displays the same absolute control of atmosphere – both celestial and worldly – that made his earlier work so tantalising. The narrative drifts a little as Elmo and Ally make their separate ways through the '60s, and the ending taxes credibility. But the film looks a treat, the performances are convincing and charismatic, and the result, as they say, is a real charmer. GA

Made in Hong Kong (Xiang-gang Zhizao)
(Fruit Chan, 1997, HK) Sam Lee, Neiky Yim, Wenbers Li, Amy Tan.
107 min.
Bad things start happening to Moon, a kid from a housing estate, when he comes into possession of two bloodstained letters left behind by a schoolgirl suicide: his mother walks out, he starts having pesky wet dreams, his mentally handicapped best friend gets into trouble – and he falls for a girl who turns out to be seriously ill. The irresistibly named Fruit Chan, a long-serving assistant director in the film industry, got this indie feature made on a wing and a prayer: various industry figures (notably Andy Lau) helped out, hardly anyone got paid and the non-pro cast was recruited on the street. Much of it is fresh, truthfully observed and touching in its honesty, but the climactic escalation into triad melodrama and the several false endings suggest that old industry habits die hard. None the less, a striking achievement. TR

Madeleine
(David Lean, 1949, GB) Ann Todd, Leslie Banks, Elizabeth Sellars, Norman Wooland, Ivan Desny, Ivor Barnard, Andre Morell, Edward Chapman.
114 min. b/w.
One of three films Lean made virtually as star vehicles for his wife Ann Todd. Here she manages to extend the range of her semi-hysterical screen personality into a flimsily forceful character who pits her amoral deviousness against the rigid hypocrisy of Victorian Glasgow. Lean strongly emphasises her vulnerability: her French lover (Desny) is a preening bully, her father (Banks) a fire-eating patriarch, and her passage to the courtroom (accused of poisoning the lover) is marked by the furious rantings of a male mob. Where the film is remarkable, though, is in never allowing her to become simply a victim. She dares to expose and enjoy her sensuality, and cunningly exploits the prim reticence expected of a Victorian miss to avoid submission to marriage, deflecting the hostile gaze of outraged society with a proudly enigmatic vanity. RMy

m

Mademoiselle

(Tony Richardson, 1966, GB/Fr) Jeanne
Moreau, Ettore Manni, Keith Skinner, Umberto
Orsini, Jane Berretta.
103 min. b/w.
After *Tom Jones*, Tony Richardson launched into
a series of extremely ambitious films (*The Loved
One*, *The Sailor from Gibraltar* and *Mademoiselle*)
which were all lambasted by the critics for their
pretentiousness. This one boasts a script by Jean
Genet which was partially rewritten by no less
than four writers (David Rudkin, Michel Cournot,
Oscar Lewenstein, and Richardson himself), and
the results were understandably mixed, though
not nearly as awful as *The Sailor from Gibraltar*,
which deserves its reputation as the most meaningless movie of the '60s. Here, Jeanne Moreau
plays a strung-up French schoolteacher who is
driven by her lust for a woodcutter to commit a
series of atrocities, but the whole thing suffers
from Richardson's terrible addiction to artistic
overstatement (not to mention the difficulty of
making an intimate drama with an international
cast speaking several languages). DP

Mad Genius, The

(Michael Curtiz, 1931, US) John Barrymore,
Marian Marsh, Donald Cook, Carmel Myers,
Charles Butterworth, Mae Madison, Luis
Alberni, Boris Karloff.
81 min. b/w.
Barrymore enjoys himself immensely in this ripe
horror effort as a demented and crippled
Svengali figure who takes over the running of a
ballet company. Alberni is way, way over the top
as the drugged dancing master, and Boris Karloff
pops up as the sadistic dad. The finale, which
involves a brutal murder in the middle of a ballet performance, is well worth waiting for. In
short, a stonker. TJ

Madhouse

(Jim Clark, 1974, GB) Vincent Price, Peter
Cushing, Robert Quarry, Adrienne Corri,
Natasha Pyne, Linda Hayden,
Catherine Willmer.
92 min.
Basically an actor's revenge plot in the wake of
Theatre of Blood, but reasonably witty in its use
of inter-penetrating fantasies born of the Dream
Factory. The film has its faults, not least a tendency to allow things to go over the top; but the
interweaving of the character of Paul Toombes,
fictional veteran star of the *Doctor Death* series
who is no longer able to tell fantasy and reality
apart (he is glimpsed roaming Sunset Boulevard
in his Doctor Death costume), with the real-life
career of Vincent Price (who plays the part), is
quite inspired and lends the film some sharp
moments. Sequences from *The Fall of the House
of Usher*, *The Raven* and other Price movies add
a deeper piquancy to the mixture. A number of
small parts are nicely filled, and in-jokes include
the total dispensability of the TV series director:
his death goes all but unnoticed. VG

Madhouse

(Tom Ropelewski, 1990, US) John Larroquette,
Kirstie Alley, Alison LaPlaca, John Diehl,
Jessica Lundy, Bradley Gregg, Dennis Miller,
Robert Ginty.
90 min.
Mark (Larroquette) and Jessie (Alley) are an LA
couple on the threshold of their dreams. The
money they earn – he as a finance manager, she
as a TV journalist – just about enables them to
mortgage their futures away on a cramped
starter-home a mile from Venice Beach. Both eye
their very own bedroom with delicious expectation, but – this being a comedy – coitus is forever interrupted. First, cousin Fred (Diehl), a
newly-redundant sewage treatment operative,
arrives with his wife (Lundy), who is pregnant,
neurotic, and owner of a murderable cat; they
take over the bedroom. Then Jessie's sister (La
Placa), a rich bitch who has left her oil-sheik husband, gets the spare room. Having the neighbour
(Ginty) about the place when his house burns
down ain't so bad, but his kids have seriously bad
attitudes. Then there's the elephant...A run-of-the-
mill extremist farce, lazily written and fum-
blingly directed. WH

Madigan

(Don Siegel, 1968, US) Richard Widmark,
Henry Fonda, Inger Stevens, Harry Guardino,

James Whitmore, Susan Clark, Michael Dunn,
Steve Ihnat, Don Stroud, Sheree North.
101 min.
A film that marks a crossroads in Siegel's career.
The methods of the two strongarm cops
(Widmark and Guardino), given seventy-two
hours to find a killer, invite comparisons with
those of the two professional gunmen in Siegel's
earlier *The Killers*. But the film also looks forward
to *Coogan's Bluff* and *Dirty Harry* as the first to
exploit the ambivalent enforcer/protector role of
the police in society, with Fonda as the martinet
police commissioner enforcing strict public morality while practising marital infidelity at home.

Mad Little Island

see Rockets Galore

Mad Love

(Antonia Bird, 1995, US) Drew Barrymore,
Chris O'Donnell, Joan Allen, Matthew Lillard,
June Ciccolella, Kevin Dunn, Liev Schreiber.
96 min.
When Matt (O'Donnell) gets a load of Casey
(Barrymore), he has no idea what he's looking at.
She's wild and impetuous and just a little crazy.
A lot crazy, her father says, forbidding the relationship and putting her in psychiatric care when
things get heavy. The young lovers hit the road,
and the radio is their compass ('If the next song's
country, we go north, if it's rock, we go south'),
guiding them from watery Seattle to dusty New
Mexico (rock'n'roll all the way). Things get heavier. Written by Paula Milne (*The Politician's Wife*)
and directed by Antonia Bird (*Priest*), Brit interlopers in Hollywood, this has the elements of a
'90s *Splendor in the Grass*, even a *Lilith*. When
Barrymore says she likes 'rudeness, noise, honesty, danger' you tend to believe her, but sadly
this movie has been Disneyed along the way, it's
altogether too polite, quiet, false and safe. A disappointment. TCh

Mad Love
(aka The Hands of Orlac)

(Karl Freund, 1935, US) Peter Lorre, Frances
Drake, Colin Clive, Isabel Jewell, Ted Healy,
Sara Haden, Edward Brophy.
70 min. b/w.
A classic slab of Grand Guignol, with Lorre in
great form – bald, bulging-eyed and blessed with
a magnificent leer – as the insane surgeon who
lusts after the gorgeous Ms Drake, and in order
to win her, operates on her concert pianist husband (Clive) after his hands are mutilated in an
accident, deliberately grafting on the hands of a
guillotined, knife-throwing murderer. The usual
Gothic motifs, in fact – dismemberment, murder,
madness, and the threat of rape – all played out
in semi-serious fashion with some delirious set
pieces, atmospherically shot by Gregg Toland
and performed (with the exception of the wood-
en Clive) with gleeful abandon. Great fun. GA

Mad Magician, The

(John Brahm, 1954, US) Vincent Price, Mary
Murphy, Eva Gabor, John Emery,
Patrick O'Neal.
72 min. b/w.
Originally shown in 3-D, this vigorous little
shocker has another psychotic role for Price as a
magic-trick inventor who goes over the edge
when fellow magicians rip off his act and his wife
runs off with a younger rival. There's much play
with Vincent's latest gizmo (a chainsaw that
seems to behead its victims) but the piece as a
whole is a few notches down in content and style
from the previous year's *House of Wax*. TJ

Mad Max

(George Miller, 1979, Aust) Mel Gibson, Joanne
Samuel, Hugh Keays-Byrne, Steve Bisley, Tim
Burns, Roger Ward, Vince Gill.
100 min.
George Miller's film is an outrageous exploiter
drawing intelligently on everything from *Death
Race 2000* to *Straw Dogs* for its JG Ballard-ish
story about a future where cops and Hell's Angels
stage protracted guerrilla warfare around what's
left of a hapless civilian population. The tone
sometimes wavers into self-parody, and there are
occasional crude patches, but overall this edge-
of-seat revenge movie marks the most exciting
debut from an Australian director since Peter
Weir. DP

Mad Max 2

(George Miller, 1981, Aust) Mel Gibson, Bruce
Spence, Vernon Wells, Emil Minty, Mike
Preston, Kjell Nilsson.
96 min.
Set a few years after *Mad Max* (which looks primitive by comparison), *Mad Max 2* concerns a
strange post-industrial future where motorised
warlords scour the deserts for fuel. Max, played
in proper Eastwood style by Gibson, comes upon
an oil fortress beleaguered by hordes of biker barbarians. The simple plot has the macho inspiration of a 2000 AD comic strip, and though the film
can't quite sustain its length, it's kept alive by its
humour and the sheer energy of its visuals. In
fact, Miller's choreography of his innumerable
vehicles is so extraordinary that it makes
Spielberg's *Raiders of the Lost Ark* look like a kid
fooling with Dinky toys. DP

Mad Max Beyond
Thunderdome

(George Miller/George Ogilvie, 1985, Aust) Mel
Gibson, Bruce Spence, Tina Turner, Helen
Buday, Angelo Rossitto, Frank Thring,
Rod Zuanic.
107 min.
Mad Mel is back on the job, cleaning up the dust-
bowls of post-apocalyptic Aussie. This time
around, he's matched against Auntie (Turner)
and the denizens of the pig-shit powered
Bartertown in a rather erratic plot which rambles
around the Outback before finally pulling itself
together for the usual stunning chariots of fire
and brimstone chase scene. En route, however,
Miller unveils some marvellously original cinematic snaps (the lost city of the feral children;
Master Blaster, the dwarf-powered giant;
Thunderdome itself); and if the thrills and special
effects lack a little of the punch of *Mad Max 2*,
there's still enough imagination, wit and ingenuity to put recent Spielberg to shame. DAt

Mad Miss Manton, The

(Leigh Jason, 1938, US) Barbara Stanwyck,
Henry Fonda, Sam Levene, Frances Mercer,
Stanley Ridges, Whitney Bourne, Hattie
McDaniel, Penny Singleton.
80 min. b/w.
Gilt-edged performances from the two stars display something of the chemistry that exploded
between them in *The Lady Eve*. Stanwyck's madcap heiress stumbles across a murder, only to
have the body vanish and a dyspeptic cop
(Levene) shrug it off as one of her notorious
pranks, while journalist Fonda denounces her as
an obnoxious example of the idle rich. Instantly
on her mettle, Stanwyck rounds up her circle of
equally scatty girlfriends and, ignoring a death
threat or two, proceeds to solve the mystery with
some help from the repentant Fonda. The whodunit tangles tend to overstay their welcome, but
Nick Musuraca's dark-toned camerawork leavens the screwball comedy with genuine menace;
and Philip G Epstein's dialogue provides a witty
undertow of fun poked at the class war (what
with Hattie McDaniel playing an anything but
downtrodden black maid: 'In my home, the revolution is here', Stanwyck grumbles). The final
clinch even manages a neat subversion of 'correct' attitudes, when Fonda suggests an extended honeymoon since Stanwyck can afford it: 'I
wanted to live on your income' she coos meltingly; 'That's foolish,' he retorts, 'who's going to live
on yours?' TM

Mad Monkey, The
(El Mono loco)

(Fernando Trueba, 1990, Sp) Jeff Goldblum,
Miranda Richardson, Anemone, Dexter
Fletcher, Daniel Ceccaldi, Liza Walker,
Arielle Dombasle.
108 min.
Relying more on atmosphere and serpentine plot
twists than on button-pushing shock effects, this
psychological thriller builds inexorably to a disturbing climax. Goldblum plays an American
scriptwriter whose marital difficulties are exacerbated when he gets involved in a European
movie project financed by a Paris-based producer (Ceccaldi). The precocious young English
director (Fletcher) has only the flimsiest of outlines, a brief quotation from one of Goldblum's
favourite books, *Peter Pan*. Nevertheless, after
the writer's initially reluctant agent (Richardson)
cuts him a good deal, he starts work with the

director on an abstract, almost avant-garde script. Surrounding the project is a compelling web of sexual intrigue, at the centre of which is the director's androgynous 16-year-old sister (Walker), an adolescent *femme fatale* who catalyses all the participants' selfish desires. As the plot coils ever tighter, handled with smooth assurance by Trueba, sexual fantasy and hallucinatory dream sequences give way to a frighteningly complex psychological reality. NF

Mad Monster Party
(Jules Bass, 1967, US) voices: Phyllis Diller, Boris Karloff, Gale Garnett, Ethel Ennis.
94 min.
Horror spoof using stop-motion animation: the first meeting of the World Organisation of Monsters is attended by Frankenstein's creature, the Wolf Man, Dracula, King Kong and the Mummy. Not often removed from the vaults.

Madness of King George, The
(Nicholas Hytner, 1994, GB) Nigel Hawthorne, Helen Mirren, Amanda Donohoe, Rupert Everett, Ian Holm, Rupert Graves, Julian Wadham, Jim Carter, Geoffrey Palmer, Alan Bennett.
110 min.
The late 1780s: George III (Hawthorne), already disturbed by the loss of the American colonies, finds his ebullience further eroded by the onset of alarming mood swings: he jumps his wife's lady-in-waiting (Donohoe), disrupts concerts, and goes generally gaga. While doctors argue over stools and methodology, a wider crisis arises: Prime Minister Pitt vainly assures Parliament that the King is healthy; but his Whig rival Fox throws in with the disaffected Prince of Wales. The Queen (Mirren) alone remains absolutely loyal, and when Wales denies her access to her spouse, the monarch's only hopes lie with an equerry (Graves), a few wary courtiers, and Willis, an unconventional parson-turned-medic (Holm). This elegant adaptation by Alan Bennett of his own stage success is the best of his contributions to the big screen to date: sturdily performed and persuasively detailed, and with a beady delight in political in-fighting. The semi-heroic role afforded the disciplinarian Willis is perhaps a touch reactionary, and there's a nagging feeling that there's less here than meets the eye. But it's funny and moving. GA

Madonna of the Seven Moons
(Arthur Crabtree, 1944, GB) Phyllis Calvert, Stewart Granger, Patricia Roc, Peter Glenville, Jean Kent, Nancy Price, John Stuart, Dulcie Gray.
110 min. b/w.
One of the main attractions of the early Gainsborough melodramas (*The Man in Grey*, *Fanny by Gaslight*) is Arthur Crabtree's atmospheric lighting. His touch is evident here, too, but doesn't really compensate for the mess he makes of directing this tale of schizoid sexuality and Florentine low-life. Calvert, the epitome of '40s respectability, displays a surprising sensuality as the woman raped in adolescence by a gypsy and subsequently developing a split personality, but the emotional impact of the scenes in the *Seven Moons* and its seedy environs is dissipated in subplots that are silly, clumsy and grindingly boring. Crabtree's melodrama collapses around his ears, but there are real gems among the debris. Just think of England while you wait for them to turn up. RMy

Madre Muerta, La
(Juanma Bajo Ulloa, 1993, Sp) Karra Elejalde, Ana Alvarez, Lio, Silvio Marsó, Elena Irueta.
111 min.
This follow-up to Ulloa's little-seen *Butterfly Wings* displays a notable aesthetic rigour and intellectual clarity. Without such formal discipline, this psychological thriller might have spilled over into dubious exploitation, but like his haunted protagonist, the director/co-writer always pulls back from the brink. Entering a house late one night, a thief shoots dead the mother of a child, who stares in silent witness to his crime. Ten years later, the thief, Ismael (Elejalde), spots a mute, seemingly autistic teenage girl in the garden of a Madrid hospital. Gripped by an irrational fear of disclosure, he abducts Leire (Alvarez) and holds her prisoner in the semi-derelict house he

shares with his possessive girlfriend Maite (Lio). Jealous of their captive's womanly body, Maite favours walking her in front of a train, but the initially resolute Ismael suggests blackmail instead. The fact that Leire, a helpless child trapped in a woman's body, is fetishistically manacled to a bed lends a dangerous, almost perverse erotic edge to some scenes. Bound to her by guilt, however, Ismael is also paralysed by her innocence, a purity he cannot defile, which he believes may yet redeem him. Twisted and tender. NF

Madron
(Jerry Hopper, 1970, US/Isr) Richard Boone, Leslie Caron, Paul Smith, Gabi Amrani, Chaim Banai, Avraham Telya.
93 min.
There's Westerns, dull Westerns, and dull Richard Boone Westerns – here Boone joins up with gung-ho nun Caron to take on the Apaches. Shot in the Negev. TJ

Mad Room, The
(Bernard Girard, 1968, US) Stella Stevens, Shelley Winters, Skip Ward, Carol Cole, Severn Darden, Beverly Garland.
93 min.
American Gothic: a remake of *Ladies in Retirement*, rather disastrously renovated for contemporary consumption. Shelley Winters is the wealthy widow, Stella Stevens the companion whose teenage brother and sister (released after years in a mental institution, suspected of hacking their parents to bits) come to stay. Skeletons in the cupboard, hacked-up bodies, and severed hands still can't make it anything more than routine. CPe

Mad Wednesday
see Sin of Harold Diddlebock, The

Maestro de Esgrima, El
see Fencing Master, The

Maestro, Il (The Maestro/ Double Game/Conductor)
(Marion Hänsel, 1989, Bel) Malcolm McDowell, Charles Aznavour, Andrea Ferréol, Francis Lemaire.
90 min.
Shot in English, writer/director Hänsel's moody drama from the higher echelons of the European music scene has lots of ambition, but not quite the artistic clout to make the best of potentially interesting material. McDowell's a famous Jewish conductor who suffers a nervous breakdown when he returns to Italy for the first time in many years to work on a production of *Madame Butterfly*. It's left to impresario Lemaire to ferret out the his dark secret, tracing the maestro's life back to a wartime flight from the Nazis and a series of events that tied his destiny to charlatan Aznavour. Engrossing for classical music buffs, but finally somewhat superficial. TJ

Maeve
(Pat Murphy/John Davies, 1981, GB) Mary Jackson, Mark Mulholland, Brid Brennan, Trudy Kelly, John Keegan.
109 min.
'Men's relationship to women is just like England's relationship to Ireland'. This assertion made to an ex-boyfriend by the eponymous heroine, on a return visit to her Catholic minority family in her native Belfast after a period of self-chosen exile in the (for her) liberating atmosphere of cosmopolitan London, signposts just what's wrong with this film. For, ambitious though it is, and largely successful in portraying the lived detail of the banality of bigotry operating in British Army-occupied Belfast, what *Maeve* conspicuously fails to do is to convincingly conflate its heroine's feminist concerns with those of the committed Republican boyfriend. Their dialogues finally find no point of intersection, and the film, like Maeve, seems to settle for its 'right not to know what (it's) doing'. An important effort, therefore, but a missed opportunity. RM

Mafu Cage, The
(Karen Arthur, 1977, US) Lee Grant, Carol Kane, Will Geer, James Olson, Will Sherwood.
101 min.

A foray into the incestuous lives of two sisters, Karen Arthur's second feature is a slow, visually beautiful tale of sexuality and madness, with a haunting score by Roger Kellaway. Cissy (Kane, excellent) is creative and crazy. She's in love with her dead father and her doting older sister Ellen (Grant), and has turned their living-room into a claustrophobic jungle (they were brought up in Africa). At one end is 'The Mafu Cage', a home for primates – and a coffin if they go too far. For neither man nor ape (there's a lovely orang-utan involved) may touch her, Ellen, or their father's collection of phallic African treasures without violent consequences...At which point the film becomes problematic; the pace starts to drag; Ellen's relationship with a man is unconvincing; the two women's attitudes toward their own sexuality evolves in very unliberated fashion. Despite this, the hot-house aura remains enticing, and although the narrative comes close to exploitation, there's a surprisingly loving depth to the characters. HM

'Maggie', The (aka High and Dry)
(Alexander Mackendrick, 1953, GB) Paul Douglas, Alex Mackenzie, Tommy Kearins, James Copeland, Abe Barker, Geoffrey Keen, Dorothy Alison.
92 min. b/w.
Here Ealing's foremost director was ostensibly making his statutory contribution to the studio's 'old crock' cycle that had begun the previous year with *The Titfield Thunderbolt*. But the cruel comedy of a rich Yank being slowly tormented by the canny crew of an ancient Scots cargo boat – it's transporting his furniture to a new holiday home, a commission undertaken only to save the boat from the scrapyard – gave Mackendrick and Ealing's resident American writer William Rose latitude to explore, in both autobiographical and wider cultural terms, the contradictions of the Old World and the New. Tradition and continuity become questionable values, the battle lines are blurred in comparison with those of *Whisky Galore*, and typically of the director of the subsequent *High Wind in Jamaica* and *Sammy Going South*, it is the young cabin boy who is the most ambivalent character. PT

Magic
(Richard Attenborough, 1978, US) Anthony Hopkins, Ann-Margret, Burgess Meredith, Ed Lauter, Jerry Houser, David Ogden Stiers.
107 min.
A hammed-up version of the old chestnut about the ventriloquist who is 'taken over' by his dummy, clumsily adapted by William Goldman from his own novel and infinitely better done in *The Great Gabbo* and *Dead of Night*. Hopkins starts over the top and soars even higher. Ann-Margret is wasted, and only Burgess Meredith (as the ventriloquist's ill-fated agent) comes out of the farrago with any honours. This is not a genre that suits Attenborough's 'epic' approach to movie-making. MA

Magic Bow, The
(Bernard Knowles, 1946, GB) Stewart Granger, Phyllis Calvert, Jean Kent, Dennis Price, Cecil Parker, Felix Aylmer.
106 min. b/w.
The life and loves of violin virtuoso Paganini, heavily fictionalised to include a duel and the pawning of his beloved Stradivarius. Hokum, of course, but lent bravura by Knowles' vivid direction and camerawork (he also made the wonderful *Jassy* for Gainsborough), and just a touch of authenticity by having Yehudi Menuhin ghost the fiddling. GA

Magic Box, The
(John Boulting, 1951, GB) Robert Donat, Margaret Johnston, Maria Schell, John Howard Davies, Robert Beatty, Laurence Olivier, Michael Redgrave, Eric Portman.
118 min.
Written by Eric Ambler as a cinematic pageant for the 1951 Festival of Britain, this tale of William Friese-Greene, the British inventor who first patented a commercially viable motion picture camera (or did he?), is mainly of parochial interest for the cavalcade of household names. Lord Olivier turns up under a policeman's helmet to stare suspiciously at Donat's – 'But it moved!' – first triumphant screen projection. Then there's

(among others) Jack Hulbert, Kathleen Harrison, Margaret Rutherford, Peter Ustinov, Stanley Holloway, Robertson Hare, Emlyn Williams, Ronald Shiner, Cecil Parker and most of the cast of *Radio Fun*, who all deferred most of their salaries. Dull stuff, though. BC

Magic Christian, The

(Joseph McGrath, 1969, GB) Peter Sellers, Ringo Starr, Richard Attenborough, Laurence Harvey, Christopher Lee, Spike Milligan, Yul Brynner, Roman Polanski, Raquel Welch, Dennis Price, John Cleese.
95 min.
An extravagant, undisciplined adaptation of Terry Southern's biting satire on the power of money – the plot is little but a stringing together of various hoaxes and practical jokes perpetrated by an eccentric multi-millionaire (Sellers) on a greedy populace – *The Magic Christian* is all too clearly representative of the impasse independent mainstream film-making found itself in when given its head by the industry in the '60s. The result is a variety concert of a film in which most of the acts/jokes fall flat. PH

Magic Donkey, The

see Peau d'Ane

Magic Flute, The (Trollflöjten)

(Ingmar Bergman, 1974, Swe) Josef Köstlinger, Irma Urrila, Håkan Hagegård, Elisabeth Eriksson, Ulrik Cold, Birgit Nordin.
135 min.
The utopian imagery of Mozart's opera has pervaded Bergman's recent films; the 'ideal' couple Tamino and Pamina, united in the dawn of enlightenment and triumph over adversity, have haunted his angst-ridden couples since *Hour of the Wolf*. Made for Swedish TV, his film of the opera itself was obviously intended to popularise it. His strategy was to stage it in an 18th century theatre, complete with quaintly spectacular stagecraft, in front of a modern audience looking like delegates from a UNESCO conference; he introduces a few backstage gags, and lots of audience reaction shots, but mostly just films close-ups of the singers (doing their stuff in Swedish, incidentally). The trouble is that Bergman's ostensibly supportive tactics tend actually to subvert Mozart's conception, and so the result is a good deal less momentous than Bergman thinks. But it's still much livelier than most TV versions of operas. TR

Magician, The

(Rex Ingram, 1926, US) Paul Wegener, Ivan Petrovich, Alice Terry, Firmin Gémier, Gladys Hamer, Stowitts.
77 min. b/w.
Adapted from the Somerset Maugham novel inspired by the life of Aleister Crowley, a bizarre melodrama which starts in Paris and moves to the Riviera: the sinister Dr Haddo (Wegener) uses hypnotism to kidnap a young woman (Terry) on the eve of her wedding, because he needs the blood from a virgin's heart to complete the formula for a homunculus. Ingram's strengths were mainly pictorial, and he here delivers plenty of high-flown images. Best of all is the sequence in which Haddo transports his victim into a Bosch-like vision and hands her over to a naked satyr for his nameless pleasures. Of great historical interest as the missing link between German expressionism and Hollywood fantasy. Michael Powell worked on it as assistant director. TR

Magician, The

see Ansiktet

Magician of Lublin, The

(Menahem Golan, 1978, WGer/Isr) Alan Arkin, Louise Fletcher, Valerie Perrine, Shelley Winters, Lou Jacobi, Warren Berlinger, Maia Danziger.
114 min.
Turn-of-the-century Warsaw: Yasha, an itinerant Jewish magician (Arkin), pursues the world, the flesh and the devil, and has enough spare hubris left over to want to fly; clearly the subject matter is rare enough to be beguiling. Unfortunately Golan's treatment, with its mixture of art house pretensions and vulgarity, founders at precisely those points where it departs from Isaac Bashevis Singer's original Yiddish novel. Where that used

clear-eyed tender realism to point toward ambiguity of experience and mystery, Golan over-dramatises, tips into hysteria, and substitutes a specious mysticism that is sadly literal. What survives (filmed in English) is sufficiently removed from mainstream cinema to be of interest – but not for Singer fans. CPea

Magic Night

see Goodnight Vienna

Magic of Lassie, The

(Don Chaffey, 1978, US) James Stewart, Mickey Rooney, Pernell Roberts, Stephanie Zimbalist, Michael Sharrett, Alice Faye, Gene Evans, Mike Mazurki.
99 min.
'She's something that came from God!' James Stewart croaks in this monstrous musical adventure, which marks Lassie's comeback to the big screen after many years in TV. And he might be right, since everyone treats the dog with utmost sentimental reverence: when she's taken from her vineyard home by a nasty city slicker, even the sight of her empty food bowl makes people weepy. Diabetics and animal-haters should avoid, but for schlock addicts the film boasts Alice Faye (first film in 17 years) preparing eggs while singing a terrible song about roses and their 'scratchy, catchy thorns'. Unbelievable. GB

Magic Town

(William Wellman, 1947, US) James Stewart, Jane Wyman, Kent Smith, Ned Sparks, Wallace Ford, Regis Toomey, Ann Doran, Donald Meek.
103 min. b/w.
A fascinating companion piece (some would say antidote) to the films Robert Riskin wrote for Frank Capra. Riskin writes and produces here, and Capraesque elements seem well to the fore: Stewart's 'too much of a dreamer' hero, hoping for a 'miracle'; an idyllic small town called Grandview; a newspaper editor heroine (Wyman) trying to bring about positive change. But in fact there's an almost total reversal of Capraesque values, for director 'Wild Bill' Wellman is no old softie. Thus Stewart's dream (he's an independent opinion pollster) is to find the 'mathematic miracle' of a small town which will exactly represent America as a whole, and thus help him make a million at the expense of his big rivals with their cross-country sampling methods; while Wyman's idea of change might turn the idyllic community into another part of the rat race. There's a feeling of reserve and none of Capra's heart-rending; which of course makes for a less obviously involving experience, though Wellman's way of visually orchestrating his themes without drawing didactic attention to them is unique. CW

Magic Toyshop, The

(David Wheatley, 1986, GB) Tom Bell, Caroline Milmoe, Kilian McKenna, Patricia Kerrigan, Lorcan Cranitch, Gareth Bushill.
107 min.
Like *The Company of Wolves*, an Angela Carter period piece. After the death of her parents, pubescent Melanie (Milmoe) is sent, along with younger brother and sister, to live with her tyrannical Uncle Philip (Bell), a toymaker who doesn't like children playing with his toys. The central relationship between the girl and her coeval Uncle Finn (McKenna) is touching and funny, but juvenile fantasy is an excuse for numerous not so special effects: a block of wood sprouting into leaf, a stone statue springing tears. These seem incongruous, which is not the same as being surreal. In sad contrast to *The Company of Wolves*, the nastiness is tame, the pace too laid-back, the laid-back not laid-back enough, and a magical atmosphere singularly lacking. MS

Magnetic Monster, The

(Curt Siodmak, 1953, US) Richard Carlson, King Donovan, Jean Byron, Leonard Mudie, Byron Foulger.
76 min. b/w.
One of the earnest 'menace to mankind' movies so beloved of sci-fi in the '50s, about an experimentally developed radioactive isotope that keeps consuming energy and doubling in size until it becomes a veritable monster. Crisply done and not at all bad, even though the climax is largely constructed out of footage borrowed from a 1934 German film, *Gold*. TM

Magnificent Ambersons, The 100 (100)

(Orson Welles, 1942, US) Joseph Cotten, Dolores Costello, Agnes Moorehead, Tim Holt, Anne Baxter, Ray Collins, Richard Bennett.
88 min. b/w.
Hacked about by a confused RKO, Welles' second film still looks a masterpiece, astounding for its almost magical recreation of a gentler age when cars were still a nightmare of the future and the Ambersons felt safe in their mansion on the edge of town. Right from the wryly comic opening, detailing changes in fashions and the family's exalted status, Welles takes an ambivalent view of the way the quality of life would change under the impact of a new industrial age, stressing the strength of community as evidenced in the old order while admitting to its rampant snobbery and petty sense of manners. With immaculate period reconstruction, and virtuoso acting shot in long, elegant takes, it remains the director's most moving film, despite the artificiality of the sentimental tacked-on ending. GA

Magnificent Doll

(Frank Borzage, 1946, US) Ginger Rogers, Burgess Meredith, David Niven, Stephen McNally, Peggy Wood, Robert Barrat.
95 min. b/w.
Novelist Irving Stone scripted this stately pseudo-historical melodrama. Ginger Rogers is thoroughly miscast as the Virginia belle and Quaker widow Dolley Payne, who (unwittingly) held America's future in the balance as she prevaricated over her suitors Aaron Burr (Niven) and James Madison (Meredith). Fortunately, she chooses the latter, Thomas Jefferson's Secretary of State, destined to become the fourth President of the United States, while the cynical Burr tries and fails to declare himself Emperor. One of those biopics that substitute arrant nonsense for much more dramatic fact. TCh

Magnificent Obsession

(Douglas Sirk, 1954, US) Jane Wyman, Rock Hudson, Barbara Rush, Otto Kruger, Agnes Moorehead, Paul Cavanagh.
108 min.
Sirk directed a number of films which say an awful lot about '50s America. A European who saw Americans more clearly than most, he found, in the 'women's weepies' producers often gave him, a freedom to examine contemporary middle class values. This one has a preposterous plot: playboy Hudson takes up medicine again after being indirectly responsible for the death of a philanthropic doctor and directly responsible for his widow's blindness. Assuming the dead man's role, Hudson starts practising the same kind of secretive Christianity, but has to resort to an alias to win the widow herself. Sirk turns all this into an extraordinary film about vision: sight, destiny, blindness (literal and figurative), colour and light; the convoluted, rather absurd actions (a magnificent repression?) tellingly counterpointed by the clean compositions and the straight lines and space of modern architecture. Sirk's films are something else: can Fassbinder even hold a candle to them? CPe

Magnificent Seven Deadly Sins, The

(Graham Stark, 1971, GB) Harry Secombe, Spike Milligan, Bruce Forsyth, Harry H Corbett, Ronald Fraser, Leslie Phillips, Ian Carmichael, Alfie Bass, June Whitfield.
107 min.
A pitiful collection of burlesque sketches so laboriously scripted that Graham Stark's crude direction is like a kindly act of euthanasia. The comic talents involved, harping on their TV personalities with deadly monotony, hardly manage to raise a smile from beginning to end. At a pinch, one might make an exception for Ian Carmichael and Alfie Bass, mildly amusing as a couple of motorists illustrating the sin of pride when they meet bumper-to-bumper in a narrow lane, but it hardly seems worth while. TM

Magnificent Seven, The

(John Sturges, 1960, US) Yul Brynner, Steve McQueen, Robert Vaughn, Charles Bronson, Horst Buchholz, James Coburn, Eli Wallach, Brad Dexter.
138 min.
Sturges' remake of Kurosawa's *The Seven Samurai*

is always worth a look, mainly for the performances of McQueen, Bronson, Coburn and Vaughn. The theme of the group of professionals coming together to defend a cause or undertake a useless task, mainly as an exercise for their narcissistic talents, was one that would be constantly reworked during the '60s. Numerous set pieces, like Coburn's knife fight, Vaughn's fly-catching and McQueen's jokes, stay in the mind even years later. CPe

Magnificent Seven Ride!, The

(George McCowan, 1972, US) Lee Van Cleef, Stefanie Powers, Mariette Hartley, Michael Callan, Luke Askew, Pedro Armendariz Jr, James B Sikking, Ed Lauter.
100 min.
Fifth outing for the mercenary heroes who originated as *The Seven Samurai*, lagging a long way behind 1 and 2 (Kurosawa, Sturges), but a marked improvement on 3 and 4 (Kennedy, Wendkos). Set a little laboriously in 'changing times', with Chris now ageing, married and law-abiding, while likely candidates for his team are either dead or languishing in jail. But the characterisations are sharp, the script economical, and the strategy of the final confrontation set out almost as intriguingly as in *The Seven Samurai*. TM

Magnificent Two, The

(Cliff Owen, 1967, GB) Eric Morecambe, Ernie Wise, Margit Saad, Cecil Parker, Isobel Black, Virgilio Teixeira.
100 min.
Take Morecambe and Wise away from the stand-up TV routine and what do you have? A lame spoof adventure about travelling salesmen in a South American state torn by revolution (Eric, of course, resembles the revolution's dead figurehead and is persuaded to pose in his place, unaware of an assassination in the offing), in which the comedians' special talents are woefully misused. At least Cliff Owen keeps it pacy, making it the least awful of the trio of movies in which the duo failed to take the cinema by storm. GA

Magnifique, Le

see How to Destroy the Reputation of the Greatest Secret Agent.

Magnum Force

(Ted Post, 1973, US) Clint Eastwood, Hal Holbrook, Mitchell Ryan, David Soul, Felton Perry, Robert Urich, Kip Niven, Tim Matheson.
124 min.
Scripted by John Milius and Michael Cimino, this second *Dirty Harry* episode is both less violent and less morally ambivalent than its superb predecessor. Harry's back on the force after throwing away his badge in recognition of his illegal methods at the end of Siegel's movie, and here he's using his tough, no-nonsense approach to track down some rookie cops who, in emulation of his earlier vigilante deeds, are blasting the usual assortment of 'criminal scum'. While never as disturbing as the first film, it fails to convince because of the turnaround in Harry's character, and because it posits in facile fashion degrees of taking the law into one's own hands: Harry's acceptable, the gun-crazy kids aren't. That said, it has some fine action sequences, and is far less objectionable than the later *Sudden Impact*. GA

Magus, The

(Guy Green, 1968, GB) Michael Caine, Anthony Quinn, Candice Bergen, Anna Karina, Paul Stassino, Julian Glover, Takis Emmanuel.
116 min.
A starry cast and flashily glossy location photography can't disguise the fact that this version of John Fowles' novel (from a screenplay by the author himself) is a muddled disaster. The rather silly, semi-mystical tale of humans on a Greek island being manipulated by Quinn's mysterious Doctor Conchis may have worked well enough in print, but on film (and only about half of the book is actually used) it seems pretentious, insubstantial, and sometimes barely comprehensible. GA

Mahabharata, Le
(The Mahabharata)

(Peter Brook, 1989, Fr) Urs Bihler, Ryszard Cieslak, Georges Corraface, Mamadou Dioumé, Miriam Goldschmidt, Jeffrey Kissoon.
171 min.
Based on a complex and subtle anonymously written Indian narrative 3,500 years old, *The Mahabharata* – originally adapted by Jean-Claude Carrière and Peter Brook for the latter's inspirational, widely praised stage production, also seen in a longer TV version – attempts nothing less than to tell the epic story of mankind. A fiery explosion of such rich Indian colours as saffron, ochre, crimson and white, the film is not just a record of the stage production, but a fine piece of work that has been completely rethought for the screen. Strangely, whereas in the theatre one was impressed with the *way* the story was told, on film the gripping tale – of the developing rivalry between the Pandavas and Kauravas, who provoke a war that brings the world to the brink of total destruction – comes over with greater intensity. Brook has created a film fantasy, a fascinating combination of the earthy and the spiritual which is never remotely folksy, and which is enriched by the vitality and diversity of its international cast. JE

Mahanagar (The Big City)

(Sayajit Ray, 1963, Ind) Madhabi Mukherjee, Anil Chatterjee, Haradhan Banerjee, Haren Chatterjee, Vicky Redwood.
131 min. b/w.
A funny and ambiguously ironic account of a young woman's progress from subdued, traditional housewife to wage earner, finally achieving equality when she resigns her job – a gesture of solidarity for a sacked friend – and joins her husband among the ranks of the lower middle class urban unemployed. Set in 1955 in a bank crash-ridden Calcutta, Ray's Ozu-like comedy about anglicised Indians who sprinkle their conversation with English phrases marks a step forward from the famous pastorales which made his name in the West. PW

Mahjong (Majiang)

(Edward Yang, 1996, Tai) Virginie Ledoyen, Tang Congsheng, Ke Yulun, Zhang Zhen, Wang Qizan, Elaine Jin, Carrie Ng, Wu Nianzhen.
121 min.
Edward Yang's brilliant dark comedy weaves together many characters in present-day Taipei. One desperate businessman faces ruin; another opts out of the rat race and finds a kind of serenity with a woman not his wife. A gang of street-smart boys breaks up. A lost French girl, looking for a man who said he loved her, get a crash course in emotional truths and lies. And one confused boy tries to figure out whether he should love his father or kill him. The various strands of plot are interwoven with phenomenal mastery, and Yang's images are as effortlessly precise as ever. It's his sharpest funny/sad vision of city life yet. TR

Mahler

(Ken Russell, 1974, GB) Robert Powell, Georgina Hale, Richard Morant, Lee Montague, Rosalie Crutchley, Benny Lee, Miriam Karlin, Angela Down.
115 min.
This musical biography, Russell-style, comes over like a cross between a comic strip and Life with the Mahlers (or the trials of bringing up and living with a genius). All the usual brashness and obsessions are there, which may well offend the purists, especially as the film is very much a reply to Visconti's *Death in Venice*. What he gives us is in fact one of the more successful excursions into the cinema of pantheism, a series of tableaux interpreting Mahler's music. Powell is suitably impressive as the composer, and Georgina Hale excellent as his wife (on its most serious level, the film is about her stifled creativity). Despite the low budget (maybe because of it), Russell has produced his most appealing work since his BBC *Omnibus* days.

Mahogany

(Berry Gordy, 1975, US) Diana Ross, Billy Dee Williams, Anthony Perkins, Jean-Pierre Aumont, Beah Richards, Nina Foch, Marisa Mell.
109 min.
Much of the blame for the decline of Tamla-Motown as a source of great pop records has been allotted to founder Berry Gordy's ceaseless struggle for mainstream mass acceptance. The same glossy decadence permeates this Gordy pro-duced/directed movie, wherein Motown's Diana Ross is the poor little black girl who achieves her fashion designer ambitions via a Rome-based modelling career – plus a golden-hearted sugar daddy – only to throw it all away for a return to the ghetto and Commitment in the form of her First Love. Total sacrifice to commerciality and the ethics of Dreamerica leave only the script's very occasional flash of wit and Anthony Perkins' deliciously loony fashion photographer on the credit side. GD

Maidens in Uniform

see Mädchen in Uniform

Maid for Pleasure
(Filles Expertes en Jeux Clandestins)

(Guy Maria, 1974, Fr) Marcel Charvey, Olivier Mathot, Valérie Boisgel, Brigitte de Borghers, Bob Askloff.
91 min.
Maybe the maid was, but the movie isn't: it's liable to give a great deal of pain, particularly in the ear-drums. The heroine is a 'nurse' at an eerie château, full of ticking clocks, creaking doors and chirping crickets. She also has to contend with her master's leers, a major-domo with a hypnotic stare and a groping hand, and a 15th century witch. It's consistently repellent: ponderous, pretentious, and almost deafening. GB

Maids, The

(Christopher Miles, 1974, GB/Can) Glenda Jackson, Susannah York, Vivien Merchant, Mark Burns.
95 min.
An appallingly castrated version of Genet's closeted, claustrophobic play about sado-masochistic fantasies. Besides some silly attempts to 'open out' the proceedings (meaningless given the original's intention), the direction displays a disarming British sang-froid and literalness towards the Gallic masterpiece. Worst offenders, however, are Jackson and York, prancing around like a couple of *Grande Dames* of the theatre, and playing out their games of dominance and submission with all the conviction of a vicar's sisters feeling up the parrot.

Maidstone

(Norman Mailer, 1970, US) Norman Mailer, Rip Torn, Beverly Bentley, Robert Gardiner, Carolyn McCullough.
110 min.
Mailer plays a 'character' called Norman T Kingsley, an avant-garde film-maker (he's also running for President) who harangues, provokes and debates with a number of people gathered as he's preparing his next movie. Despite a thin try at a story, some bluff spouting about exploring the nature of different 'realities', or about creating whirlpools of energy and then following them through, it's not really worth treating this farrago – in which the name of the game is 'let's play football with other people's psyches' – seriously as a film. Lawrence Durrell has treated the 'reality' theme much better in novel form; Cassavetes has coped far more honestly and delicately with the fine line between people acting themselves and projecting their abilities on to 'characters'; this is simply 110 minutes of pure Megalomailer. MV

Main Actor, The
(Der Hauptdarsteller)

(Reinhard Hauff, 1977, WGer) Mario Adorf, Vadim Glowna, Michael Schweiger, Hans Brenner, Rolf Zacher, Akim Ahrens.
91 min.
This has something of the same hard-edged documentary authenticity as Hauff's earlier *Brutalisation of Franz Blum*, though a tone of autobiographical self-flagellation adds a slightly mawkish element. A teenage boy and his brutal father act in a film about their no-hope lives; at the end of the shooting, the boy runs away to the anguished middle class director, who unsuccessfully tries to help him start a new life. Hauff, it seems, actually had this experience with a non-professional actor he used in an earlier film. The movie doesn't get very deep beneath the skin of its wayward adolescent protagonist, but it registers as a thoroughly competent (if somewhat crude) example of second division New German Cinema. JPy

Main Event, The

(Howard Zieff, 1979, US) Barbra Streisand, Ryan O'Neal, Paul Sand, Whitman Mayo, Patti D'Arbanville, James Gregory.
112 min.
This 'romantic screwball comedy/glove story', in which zany Streisand rescues failed boxer O'Neal, is awful – unless you're a devotee of the strident Streisand, who does at least deliver her lines with some punch. The script, however, assumes that the most powerful women are those who can beat men at their own game – a failed cosmetics queen, Streisand sets out to manipulate O'Neal so as to recoup her losses – but would be only too happy to throw in the towel to the right man.

Main Street

see Calle Mayor

Mairi Mhor

(Mike Alexander, 1993, Scotland) Alyxis Daly, Ceit Kearney, Sim Mac Coinnich.
63 min.
In 1871, 'tired of the speakers of English', Mairi Mhor began writing resistance songs in Gaelic, protesting at the displacement of the Scottish Highland and Island folk by the Southern landlords. Unjustly imprisoned in Inverness at the age of 51, she expresses her anger in song, discovering a talent for music; these songs became central to the identity of the region and are still sung today. The achingly beautiful landscape of Skye, and the music it inspired, provide a haunting canvas for this valuable piece of historical research. FM

Maison de Jade, La

(Nadine Trintignant, 1988, Fr) Jacqueline Bisset, Vincent Perez, Véronique Silver, Yves Lambrecht, Serge Marquand.
98 min.
Older woman falls for younger man and – we could have warned her – ends up alone, swigging from the Martell bottle as she sobs through their old camcorder footage. An adaptation by Trintignant and Madeleine Chapsal of the latter's allegedly autobiographical bestseller, this is all relentlessly subjective. In the early snog 'n' bonk stages, young Perez is presented as the epitome of charm and desirability, though many will yearn to see a custard pie collide with that wouldbe brooding pan. But after splitting, he is portrayed as a contemptible little coward, and again audience sympathies may reverse, with the reflection that no such all-round wonderful person as Bisset ever walked the earth. BBa

Maître de musique, Le

see Music Teacher, The

Maîtresse

(Barbet Schroeder, 1976, Fr) Gérard Depardieu, Bulle Ogier, André Rouyer, Nathalie Keryan, Roland Bertin, Tony Taffin, Holger Löwenadler.
112 min.
Schroeder's classic of underground love sits well alongside the masochistic undertones of Last Tango in Paris. Ogier is the professional maîtresse (or dominatrix) who conducts a straight romance with Depardieu at ground level, but has a dungeon below stairs where she entertains her compliant clients. The trick, of course, is that overground comes to mirror underground, but the whole thing is lent more than a little frisson from the knowledge that some of those clients were real. A wickedly funny fable on the more demanding side of love. CPea

Majdhar

(Ahmed A Jamal, 1984, GB) Rita Wolf, Tony Wredden, Feroza Syal, Andrew Johnson, Sudha Bhuchar, Tariq Yunus.
76 min.
Rita Wolf has a fine profile. Director Jamal thinks so too: any excuse serves for a close-up of her as Fauzia, a young middle class Pakistani who's caught in an uncomfortable midstream ('majdhar') when her husband deserts her for an Englishwoman. Fauzia copes, and emerges as a strong person after pensively staring at the wall and having an affair with a TV researcher who's after a bit of exotica. The film is an interesting 'worthy' experiment by Retake, an Asian collective anxious to redress the media stereotype image, etc. As collective efforts go, this is not bad. The plot is rich and full of possibilities, but the script is unfortunately thin and full of missed opportunities. Embarrassingly awkward (as opposed to meaningful) silences are broken by laborious and unnatural dialogue, which is rescued slightly by Ustad Imrat Khan's moving music. Both Wolf and Feroza Syal (playing her friend) are good, but more experienced direction would help. BB

Major and the Minor, The

(Billy Wilder, 1942, US) Ginger Rogers, Ray Milland, Rita Johnson, Robert Benchley, Diana Lynn, Frankie Thomas, Norma Varden.
100 min. b/w.
Wilder's first film as director begins brilliantly with Rogers as a New York career woman disillusioned to find her house calls offering scalp massage unsubtly subject to male misinterpretation – in particular from a lecherous Benchley pursuing 'a little drinkypoo, biteypoo, rhumbapoo' – who masquerades as a pigtailed 12-year-old innocent in order to avoid paying full adult fare on the train home to Iowa. Very funny stuff as she meets Milland's protective major, and finds ambiguous refuge in his sleeping compartment, although it later proves to be a one-joke situation as she is forced to accompany him to the military academy where he instructs, and becomes mascot to a horde of hopefully lecherous cadets. Pretty irresistible, nevertheless, with Rogers doing a beautiful job of dovetailing sexual provocation and demure innocence. TM

Major Barbara

(Gabriel Pascal/Harold French/David Lean, 1941, GB) Wendy Hiller, Rex Harrison, Robert Morley, Robert Newton, Emlyn Williams, David Tree, Marie Lohr, Sybil Thorndike, Deborah Kerr.
121 min. b/w.
George Bernard Shaw collaborated on the screenplay of this straightforward adaptation of his 1905 comedy about the daughter of a munitions tycoon (Hiller) who joins the army – the Salvation Army, that is – pursued by an amorous professor of Greek (Harrison). There is plenty to relish, notably Roberts Newton and Morley hamming it up (as, respectively, the rumbustious Bill Walker and the overbearing tycoon), and Deborah Kerr in her debut; but it does tend to just sit there. It was David Lean's first shot at directing, but producer Pascal helmed the bulk of it. TCh

Major Dundee

(Sam Peckinpah, 1964, US) Charlton Heston, Richard Harris, Jim Hutton, James Coburn, Michael Anderson Jr, Senta Berger, Mario Adorf, Brock Peters, Warren Oates, Ben Johnson, RG Armstrong.
134 min.
Formally, this is barely recognisable as a Peckinpah movie (producers hacked out 20 minutes, distributors 14 more); yet many of his major thematic preoccupations (loyalty, betrayal, redemptive death) are clearly emerging here as Major Dundee, a Federal officer relegated to command of a prison camp, sets out to subdue a band of marauding Apaches at the head of a ragtag volunteer troop of thieves, renegades and paroled Confederate prisoners (the latter ambivalently headed by Harris). Of the many debts to Ford, the largest is Heston's Dundee, trading on his image of epic man of action but propelled, like Wayne in The Searchers, by racial hatred, wormeaten by divided loyalties, and finally found wanting at the crunch. A fine if fractured Western, more subversive of conventional mythologies than it seems. CPea

Major League

(David S Ward, 1989, US) Tom Berenger, Charlie Sheen, Corbin Bernsen, Margaret Whitton, James Gammon, René Russo, Wesley Snipes, Charles Cyphers, Dennis Haysbert.
106 min.
A baseball movie which crosses schoolboy fantasy with Police Academy slapstick and lockerroom in-jokery. Its tale of a rags-to-riches rise by one of the sport's longest-standing jokes, the Cleveland Indians, is chock full of variably amusing gags and bit players, with Sheen as a wild punk pitcher raised in a series of prisons, and Berenger as an over-the-hill catcher who wins back the girl he loves. Whitton plays the new ex-showgirl owner, desperate to move the team to sunny Florida and herself to an exotic condo, who gathers together a bunch of players so ropey that their failure will enable her to convince the commissioners that the move is justified. Like so much of the film it's a daft but not too daft proposition; and what redeems it is that the action sequences are superbly filmed, climaxing with Sheen's bullish entry into the arena at make-orbreak time, the crowd singing 'Wild Thing' in clamouring unison. SGr

Major League II

(David S Ward, 1994, US) Charlie Sheen, Tom Berenger, Corbin Bernsen, Dennis Haysbert, James Gammon, Omar Epps.
105 min.
The original Major League brought high jinks and low comedy to the baseball movie genre, and showcased the immense talents of Wesley Snipes. This sequel didn't cut it in the States, and it's hard to see why British audiences should show it any more respect, given that it's formula and lacks Snipes. True, most of the regulars return to the plate: Sheen as delinquent pitcher Rick 'Wild Thing' Vaughn; Berenger as Jake Taylor, the ageing catcher with dodgy knees; and the rest of the Cleveland Indians. RJ Stewart's screenplay highlights one of the great-in jokes of American team sports – how players are transformed during the close season by fame, fortune or adversity; here, the team is split asunder when Vaughn attempts to clean up his image and when Pedro Cerrano (Haysbert) switches bafflingly from voodoo to Buddhism. SGr

Make Mine a Million

(Lance Comfort, 1959, GB) Arthur Askey, Sidney James, Dermot Walsh, Olga Lindo, Bernard Cribbins, Kenneth Connor.
82 min. b/w.
Flimsy, dated, but not unenjoyable British farce. James is a soap-powder magnate. He wants promotion on the advert-free National Television service and hires Askey to interrupt transmissions with promo spots for his detergent, the delightfully named Bonko.

Making It

(John Erman, 1971, US) Kristoffer Tabori, Marilyn Mason, Bob Balaban, Joyce Van Patten, Lawrence Pressman, Louise Latham, Sherry Miles.
97 min.
The best thing about this piffling cautionary tale for teens is Tabori's cool and witty performance (his debut) as a 17-year-old high school kid (pushing drugs looms high on the curriculum) whose penchant for making it with anything in skirts stores up a load of grief for him. The unbelievably silly climax has Tabori procuring an abortion for his girlfriend (Miles) on a false alarm, finding the appointment coming in handy because his widowed mum (Van Patten) has got herself knocked up, and being forced to sit in on the operation because the doctor feels the experience may make a man of him. Cue for classic kitsch as mother and son gaze at each other with fond new understanding, murmuring 'It's been 17 years and I feel I'm just beginning to know you'. TM

Making It

see Valseuses, Les

Making Love

(Arthur Hiller, 1982, US) Michael Ontkean, Kate Jackson, Harry Hamlin, Wendy Hiller, Arthur Hill, Nancy Olson, John Dukakis.
112 min.
Zack and Claire love Rupert Brooke, Gilbert & Sullivan, and each other. Till one day Zack meets Bart. Arthur Love Story Hiller, it seems, is a director possessed of what the French call a thématique. Note the subtle cultural references, substituting for the earlier film's Mozart and the Beatles, as well as the abiding interest in incurable conditions, whether leukaemia or, as here, homosexuality. Luckily, his hapless protagonists are deeply caring souls: Zack finds eventual fulfilment with a handsome, sensitive hunk; Bart, a novelist of the runny softboiled school, will write a sensitive bestseller about the affair; while Claire manages to land an overwhelmingly sensitive second husband (and even christens their son Rupert). This is a three-handkerchief movie, all right, but for the nose. It stinks. GAd

Making Mr Right

(Susan Seidelman, 1987, US) John Malkovich, Ann Magnuson, Glenne Headly, Ben Masters, Laurie Metcalf, Polly Bergen.
98 min.

Seidelman's follow-up to *Desperately Seeking Susan* is a stylish, offbeat romantic comedy but lacks its predecessor's loopy charm. When PR consultant Frankie (Magnuson) is hired to create a human image for the Chemtech Corporation's latest android, Ulysses, she doesn't reckon on him losing his head over her, and vice versa, and ends up clashing with the android's maker, Dr Peters, who fears that Ulysses' exposure to love's irrationality will jeopardise his forthcoming space mission. Seidelman handles the romance with great sensitivity, contrasting Ulysses' innocent, non-manipulative affection with the self-centred immaturity of Frankie's senator boyfriend. Crucial weaknesses, however, are the miscasting of Malkovich as both Peters and Ulysses (he lacks charisma as the romantic lead), and the numerous distracting subplots. The flat, garish photography conjures up the shiny-clean future of '50s sci-fi movies, but the film's magpie borrowings are poorly integrated, resulting in inconsistencies of tone and pacing. Much to enjoy, though, not least the audaciously happy ending. NF

Making of Maps, The

(Endaf Emlyn, 1995, Wales) Gavin Ashcroft, Catherine Tregenna, Waldwyn Pate, Abigail Creel, Lara Ward.
90 min.

Endaf Emlyn's third Welsh-language feature is a not entirely successful mood-piece set on the remote Welsh coast in the Cold War early '60s. An adolescent boy (Ashcroft, good) recalls the fateful months following the disappearance of his dancer sister. In the large family house by the dunes live his ex-ballerina mother, a bedridden 'hysteric'; his munitions-worker father, 'a bad man' who may have played too free with the young charges of the family dance school; and his other sister, 'all pain and no beauty'. The boy makes maps to hide his secrets and befriends an oddball Pole with secrets of his own. The story meanders on, meditating on unseen events (an accidental death, a suicide and a rape) to the neo-classical strains of Mark Thomas's score and the noise of sea birds, but to no discernible purpose. WH

Making Up (Abgeschminkt)

(Katja von Garnier, 1992, Ger) Katja Riemann, Nina Kronjäger, Gedeon Burkhard, Max Tidof, Daniela Lunkewitz.
54 min.

An offbeat, sassy look at female friendship. Its 55 minutes tell a very slight story: Maischa (Kronjäger), a boy crazy nurse, has a dreary married boyfriend, but flips for a hunk at a party. The hunk, René, suggests a date, but has visitor Mark in tow. Maischa calls on her scruffy friend Frenzy (Riemann), whose despairing attempts to draw a newspaper comic-strip about a mosquito named Rubi are the backbone of the film, to find her suffering as usual from a creative block. Sulky Frenzy is paired off with Mark, facetious and childish, while Maischa swans off for dinner with gorgeous René. But things are not that simple. The two girls have a brilliant, silly chemistry. SFe

Mala Noche

(Gus Van Sant, 1985, US) Tim Streeter, Doug Cooeyate, Ray Monge, Nyla McCarthy, Sam Downey, Bob Pitchlynn.
78 min. b/w & col.

Van Sant's winning feature debut (made on 16mm for an incredible $25,000) tells the tale of a shabby store-boy's brief encounter with two desperate wetbacks. Walt (Streeter, excellent) spends most of his time selling liquor to the bums of Portland, Oregon. He becomes obsessed with 16-year-old cock-tease Johnny, who doesn't speak a word of American but knows the difference between 15 and 25 dollars. Walt pursues him in his dreams and through the rainy nights, but only manages to put up (yes, that way too) his gun-toting friend Pepper, who is in his turn pursued by the cops. Walt's pawky commentary brings out the equivocal nature of his fragile relationship with the two boys: he may nurse Pepper when he's ill, let Johnny swipe food when he's hungry, but as a comparatively wealthy gringo Walt is nevertheless exploiting the situation. Even so – as one sweaty scene reveals – a Mexican can still

make 'white butt squeal'. Offbeat, offhand, and at times off-the-wall, this sad and funny film recalls *Streetwise* and *Stranger Than Paradise*, but in its own unabashed way is better than either. MS

'Mala' Ordina, La

see Manhunt in Milan

Malaya (aka East of the Rising Sun)

(Richard Thorpe, 1949, US) Spencer Tracy, James Stewart, Valentina Cortese, Sydney Greenstreet, Lionel Barrymore, Gilbert Roland, John Hodiak.
98 min. b/w.

A murky World War II actioner in which James Stewart and Spencer Tracy further the Allied cause by smuggling rubber out of Jap-infested Malaya with the help (sometimes given under 'persuasion') of the planters. Tracy does the rough stuff as an uncommitted adventurer; Stewart handles the message as a man with a score to settle (his brother was killed fighting in the Pacific). You'd think the film was still fighting the war, the way Stewart carries on, getting himself killed (Tracy too) while indomitably waving the flag. It's made, such as it is, by the excellent supporting cast which seems to have *Casablanca* vaguely in mind. TM

Malcolm

(Nadia Tass, 1986, Aust) Colin Friels, Lindy Davies, John Hargreaves, Chris Haywood.
85 min.

A would-be comic caper movie from the land of Oz. A wordly-witless but highly inventive simpleton (Friels) persuades his roomers, a laconic ex-con (Hargreaves) and his breasty 'sheila', to make use of his technical talents in a series of remote-controlled heists. If the set pieces don't exactly have you splitting your sides with mirth, the movie does engagingly stay true to its childlike vision, all gadgets and gleeful immorality, more than helped along by the perfectly pitched playing of Friels and Hargreaves. WH

Malcolm X

(Spike Lee, 1992, US) Denzel Washington, Angela Bassett, Albert Hall, Al Freeman Jr, Delroy Lindo, Spike Lee, Theresa Randle, Kate Vernon, Lonette McKee.
201 min.

Lee's labour of love is arguably his most anonymous film to date, with fewer in-your-face stylistic flourishes or confrontational ideological statements than his earlier works. True, the scenes of young Malcolm (Washington) and his pal Shorty (Lee) at a Boston dance hall exhibit a fizzy choreographic flair; true, too, that the opening credits footage of the Rodney King beating hints at an anger none too shy of courting controversy. But mostly, while the film glides from Malcolm's early years as a hustler and petty criminal to his emergence in the Nation of Islam, it plays surprisingly safe as a solidly crafted trawl through the didactic/hagiographic conventions of the mainstream biopic. In short, it's a familiar tale of a man up against prejudice coming to see the light. If the first hour contains most of the drama, it's the later scenes that constitute the lesson: how to achieve black pride, power and dignity in the face of white oppression. Were it not for Washington's charismatic performance and the abiding fire of Malcolm's oratory, this didacticism might be tedious; but Lee's skill at playing to his strengths ensures that only the whitewashing of NOI's attitude to women, and odd scenes such as Malcolm's prison visit by an apparition of Elijah Muhammad, come over as major flaws. GA

Malena Is a Name from a Tango (Malena es un Nombre de Tango)

(Gerardo Herrero, 1996, Sp) Ariadna Gil, Marta Belaustegui, Carlos López, Luis Fernando Alvés, Isabel Otero, Marina Saura.
109 min.

A strangely detached and self-conscious, but surprisingly involving melodrama, which follows Malena (Gil) from childhood, through her adolescent obsession with a girl-chasing German cousin, and a raunchy but uncommitted rela-

tionship with a macho womaniser, to marriage to a loving but dull husband. Malena thinks there's bad blood in the family, and she's got it, unlike her well-behaved twin Reina. Is she too non-conformist ever to find happiness? An arresting take on the social and psychological obstacles faced by free-spirited women in a patriarchal world, it's helped no end by Ariadna Gil's versatile, charismatic performance. GA

Malevil

(Christian de Chalonge, 1981, Fr/WGer) Michel Serrault, Jacques Dutronc, Robert Dhéry, Jacques Villeret, Hanns Zischler, Jean-Louis Trintignant.
119 min.

Vaguely reminiscent in mood of Polanski's *Cul-de-Sac*, this is a weird – but not weird enough – post-nuclear survival drama, with assorted members of a strong cast gathering at the eponymous castle and trying to keep civilisation going. After a decent start, the movie soon drifts into the usual set of dramatic options: illness, reproduction, farming, and of course the fascists in the forest. ATu

Malice

(Harold Becker, 1993, US) Alec Baldwin, Nicole Kidman, Bill Pullman, Bebe Neuwirth, George C Scott, Anne Bancroft, Peter Gallagher, Josef Sommer.
107 min.

All appears normal in a tranquil college town in Massachusetts. Newly-weds Tracy and Andy Sarafian (Kidman and Pullman) are restoring their dream house. He teaches English, she does voluntary work at the hospital. Andy meets old chum, arrogant but brilliant surgeon Jed Hill (Baldwin) – who, to Tracy's chagrin, insinuates himself into their home. Surely he isn't the local serial rapist. A melodramatic thriller which did surprisingly well in the US given its implausible straight-to-video scenario. Undistinguished. TCh

Malicious

(Ian Corson, 1996, US) Molly Ringwald, Patrick McGaw, John Vernon, Sarah Lassez.
90 min.

When sweetheart Laura departs for the weekend, Doug (McGaw) agrees against his better judgment to drop into a party. Slack teen fare thriller in the *Pacific Heights* and *Single White Female* mode (that is, psychopath in the midst of cosy, homey perfection). Molly Ringwald has honed her rich-bitch routine since *The Breakfast Club*, but doesn't quite convince as Doug's malicious seductress. EP

Malizia

(Salvatore Samperi, 1973, It) Laura Antonelli, Turi Ferro, Alessandro Momo, Angela Luce, Pino Caruso.
97 min.

Really no more than an extended joke revolving round the attitudes of Italian men towards *La Mama* and women in general. With the death of his wife, a businessman and his three sons find their lives disrupted by the arrival of a beautiful new maidservant. While father is trying to lay to rest the ghost of his wife and woo the maid into marriage, his middle son, aged 14, forces the girl through a series of sexual humiliations that culminate one stormy night on the eve of her wedding. Next day, after the ceremony, in front of a proud and unsuspecting father, he dutifully calls her 'Mother' and wishes every happiness. An Italian idyll: knocking off mother before father can. In spite of good moments, the film remains muddled and unsure, dividing itself between sharp observations and a 14-year-old's wet dream. CPe

Mallrats

(Kevin Smith, 1996, US) Shannen Doherty, Jason Lee, Jason Mewes, Kevin Smith, Renee Humphreys, Michael Rooker, Stan Lee.
100 min.

A depressing mess. Like *Clerks*, Smith's first film, it centres on a bunch of teen no-hopers, their lives dominated by sex and pop culture, but unlike *Clerks*, it never makes them seem any more interesting than the brats you'd find in a John Hughes' flick, just more obscene. 'Truth or Dare' is the TV show which provides the plot with an ostensible climax, but Smith seems to think they're synonymous – this is all dare, and precious little truth.

The callow, sub-John Waters shock-comedy might be less tiresome if Smith didn't botch the timing so relentlessly. The funniest bit involves a topless palm reader with three nipples. TCh

Malou

(Jeanine Meerpfel, 1980, WGer) Ingrid Caven, Helmut Griem, Grischa Huber, Ivan Desny, Peter Chatel, Marie Colbin.
94 min.
Meerpfel's first feature is a meandering but delicately engaging study of belonging and female self-discovery. The plot is deliberately simple, indeed almost non-existent. Spurred by the unearthing of certain glittering family heirlooms, a woman seeks out her family past. This device is used to create a tandem narrative, with her story of present marital uncertainty being set alongside the previous tragedy of her mother, Malou. Born around the turn of the century, Malou led a life entirely defined by men. When her husband leaves her, she is left without identity and even nationality, adrift in a strange country. With a hypnotic central performance from Dietrich lookalike Caven as the mother, Meerpfel's film makes its feminist points in ambiguous, even teasing fashion, and moves easily to a conclusion neatly poised between liberation and alienation. RR

Malpertuis

(Harry Kümel, 1971, Bel/Fr/WGer) Orson Welles, Susan Hampshire, Michel Bouquet, Mathieu Carrière, Jean-Pierre Cassel, Sylvie Vartan, Walter Rilla.
124 min.
A fresh-faced blond sailor (Carrière) is shanghaied from a '20s port full of sleazy bars and artnouveau mansions, and held captive in the endless corridors of a crumbling Gothic pile called Malpertuis: we don't discover why until the end, in a *denouement* as outrageous and devastating as any ever filmed. Kümel elaborates the mystery like a master, drawing much of his design and composition from Surrealist painting (Magritte, de Chirico), and weaving serpentine patterns from the intrigues between the many characters. Welles is at his most mountainous as the house's patriarch; Hampshire is a revelation, playing three contrasted women. This English dialogue version is better than the French/Flemish originals. TR

Malpractice

(Bill Bennett, 1989, Aust) Caz Lederman, Bob Baines, Ian Gilmour, Pat Thomson, Janet Stanley.
90 min.
This uncompromising, 'fly on the wall' Australian piece confronts medical malpractice and the aftermath suffered by an 'ordinary' family. Coral Davis goes into hospital to give birth to her third child, and misjudgments by the junior doctor who undertakes the delivery result in a brain-damaged baby. Bennett has produced an immensely impressive film which explores the emotional and legal consequences. Documentary camera techniques combine skilfully with credible performances, and dialogue which appears improvised underscores moments of great vulnerability. Strong and compelling. CM

Maltese Falcon, The (100) (aka Dangerous Female)

(Roy Del Ruth, 1931, US) Bebe Daniels, Ricardo Cortez, Dudley Digges, Una Merkel, Robert Elliott, Thelma Todd, Dwight Frye.
80 min. b/w.
The first film version of Hammett's *The Maltese Falcon* (retitled *Dangerous Female* for TV): if it's not quite the solid classic of the Huston version (1941), the two adaptations are still remarkably similar, and it's fun to watch the earlier cast run through the characterisations that Bogey, et al, have made so familiar. Cortez, for instance, is a slightly sleeker Sam Spade, Daniels not quite as viper-ish as Mary Astor, while Digges makes good as 'the fat man', even if he doesn't really have the waistline. TJ

Maltese Falcon, The

(John Huston, 1941, US) Humphrey Bogart, Mary Astor, Sydney Greenstreet, Peter Lorre, Elisha Cook Jr, Barton MacLane, Lee Patrick, Ward Bond, Gladys George.
100 min. b/w.
Huston's first film displays the hallmarks that were to distinguish his later work: the mocking attitude toward human greed; the cavalier insolence with which plot details are treated almost as asides; the delight in bizarre characterisations, here ranging from the amiably snarling Sam Spade ('When you're slapped, you'll take it and like it') who opened a whole new romantic career for Bogart, to Lorre's petulant, gardenia-scented Joel Cairo, Cook's waspishly effete gunsel, and Greenstreet's monstrously jocular Fat Man ('By gad, sir, you are a character'). What makes it a prototype *film noir* is the vein of unease missing from the two earlier versions of Hammett's novel. Filmed almost entirely in interiors, it presents a claustrophobic world animated by betrayal, perversion and pain, never – even at its most irresistibly funny, as when Cook listens in outraged disbelief while his fat sugar daddy proposes to sell him down the line – quite losing sight of this central abyss of darkness, ultimately embodied by Mary Astor's sadly duplicitous siren. TM

Mama

(Zhang Yuan, 1991, China) Qing Yan, Huang Haibo, Pan Shaquan.
90 min.
Released in China only after a two-year ban, Zhang Yuan's debut feature looks at first glance like a Ken Loach 'social problem' movie. It centres on the plight of a woman librarian in Beijing who struggles to bring up her teenage son (retarded since a childhood accident) without help from her absent husband or the state, and juxtaposes that fiction with relevant documentary material. But Zhang isn't content with showing street-level realities for their own sake; he pushes his material towards expressionism, using the mother's inevitable mood swings as keys to the tone and texture of the images, a strategy that brings him within breathing distance of *film noir* by the end. China's 'Sixth Generation' film-makers couldn't have got off to a stronger start. TR

Maman et la Putain, La

see Mother and the Whore, The

Mama's Dirty Girls

(John Hayes, 1974, US) Gloria Grahame, Paul Lambert, Sondra Currie, Candice Rialson, Christopher Wines, Dennis Smith.
80 min.
For a while this looks promising, with Gloria Grahame laying down a fair and acrid parody of the bourgeois marriage ethos for the benefit of her daughters. 'When I was your age, I just wanted a man, but a man can go just as easy as a man can come. A man is only a man, but property is security'. Having murdered her husband with the aid of the two eldest girls, only to discover that he was unfortunately penniless, she tries again, but this time picks a man with the same idea. Meanwhile the daughters find men of their own...At which point the whole thing peters out into the drab flats of routine misogyny: the women become malevolent schemers, and it's up to the men to right things (violently). VG

Mamba

see Fair Game

Mambo Kings, The

(Arne Glimcher, 1992, US) Armand Assante, Antonio Banderas, Cathy Moriarty, Maruschka Detmers, Roscoe Lee Browne, Desi Arnaz Jr, Célia Cruz.
105 min.
A spirited evocation of the mambo craze which swept post-war America, adapted from Oscar Hijuelos' Pulitzer Prize-winning novel. Cuban musicians César and Nestor Castillo (Assante and Banderas) arrive in New York to find love, greed and, ultimately, fame. César thrives on the success of their band, and relentlessly pursues sex and the Yankee dollar, while his mournful brother laments his lost love and homeland. First-time director Glimcher establishes a restless pace, from the opening violence through to the energetic, swirling musical sequences, while screenwriter Cynthia Cidre tones down some of the book's flamboyance and machismo, emphasising the eroticism of sudden passion and repressed desire; and there's a sure feel for period in both tone and technique. CM

Mame

(Gene Saks, 1974, US) Lucille Ball, Beatrice Arthur, Robert Preston, Bruce Davison, Kirby Furlong, Jane Connell.
131 min.
Starving fans of musicals won't live long on *Mame*, another paean to American matriarchy, or rather auntiarchy, and the swansong of the Queen of the B movie and TV sitcom. Lucille Ball, cast 20 years younger than she is, simply hasn't the drive and steel of a Rosalind Russell, an Angela Lansbury or a Ginger Rogers, all of whom played the part before her. And Mame is the Life-Force. She can declare Christmas a month early and get snow with it. When he's not ogling his star in perpetual soft focus and a $300,000 fashion parade, Saks fails to get enough retakes, match his shots, or inject the essential vim. There's a preposterously smug put-down of the bourgeoisie, and some dull songs. SG

Mamma Roma

(Pier Paolo Pasolini, 1962, It) Anna Magnani, Ettore Garofolo, Franco Citti, Silvana Corsini, Luisa Loiano, Paolo Volponi.
114 min. b/w.
Pasolini's second feature jumps a class from the sub-proletarian milieu of *Accattone*, following the efforts of a prostitute, 'Mamma Roma' (Magnani), to make a petty-bourgeois life for herself and her teenage son in suburban Rome. It combines formal audacity, unflinching candour and heart-breaking compassion to produce a work of shattering beauty. Pasolini's was a cinema of contradictions. Nobody before – or since – had tried to marry stories about the underclass with a religious cinematic style normally reserved for the adoration of saints or the mysterious workings of God. The film is composed in the form of a lament, employing classical music (the 'populist' Vivaldi), painterly compositions (shot by Tonino Delli Colli to echo works by Caravaggio among others) and processional camera movements (a track through an apartment arch that suggests anything from a triumphal return to a descent through the gates of hell), in order to counterpoint the tragic trajectory of his story. For this Marxist sympathiser, radical poet and novelist, the peasantry was the fount of pre-religious grace, inevitably to be broken on the wheel of bourgeois conformity. Whatever Pasolini's intentions, what makes the film so distinctive is the passion he brings to the screen. Magnani is the only professional actress, but her iconic, larger-than-life persona, far from unsettling the film, balances it. WH

Man About Town

see Silence est d'Or, Le

Man Alive

(Ray Enright, 1945, US) Pat O'Brien, Ellen Drew, Adolphe Menjou, Rudy Vallee, Fortunio Bonanova, Jonathan Hale, Jack Norton.
70 min. b/w.
A quite funny and charming minor comedy, with O'Brien as a neglectful husband who, reported drowned in a car accident while drunk, takes to posing as a ghost to prevent his wife from marrying an old flame. One particularly good sequence has O'Brien reviving after being fished out of the river, unaware that he is aboard a showboat, to be confronted by a 'Green Pastures'-style representation of heaven; convinced he is dead and distractedly going to the door, he this time finds himself in hell (the stokehold, given an added touch of conviction by the fortuitous presence of Menjou, sporting his Mephistopheles costume from the show). Invention flags latterly, though, as the lies and deceptions he gets up to instead of owning up (at Menjou's meddlesome suggestion) lead to rather tiresome complications. TM

Man Alone, A

(Ray Milland, 1955, US) Ray Milland, Mary Murphy, Ward Bond, Raymond Burr, Lee Van Cleef.
96 min.
A lone gunslinger stranded in the desert (Milland) comes upon the corpse-strewn wreck of a stagecoach. With the finger of suspicion firmly pointed at him, he then holes up in town to play a lone hand (more or less, since he is befriended by sheriff's daughter Mary Murphy) against the corrupt citizen (Burr) using him as a cover-up for nefarious activities. At the film's heart is a persuasive though

clumsily inserted consideration of the nature of corruption, occasioned when Ward Bond's sheriff, hitherto in Burr's pay, does some soul-searching on finally declaring himself on the side of the angels. Milland's direction (his debut) is sometimes a little too ponderously deliberate, but – like the performances – eminently watchable. TM

Man and a Woman, A
see Homme et une Femme, Un

Man, a Woman and a Bank, A
(Noel Black, 1979, Can) Donald Sutherland, Brooke Adams, Paul Mazursky, Allan Magicovsky, Leigh Hamilton, Nick Rice.
101 min.
Oddly enough, the almost total failure to create suspense, laughs or even a credible technological heist (in what is supposed to be a comedy-suspense movie about a computer bank raid) doesn't matter much. A certain whimsical, old-fashioned charm refuses to be squashed by microchips or '80s cynicism; the relationship between the two men is touching; and the self-conscious 'romance' that develops for Sutherland and Adams provokes indulgent grins all round, not least from the principals themselves. There is also a truly sizzling scene involving Leigh Hamilton as a carefully luscious gameshow hostess demonstrating to lover Mazursky 'how Redford and Nicholson kiss' which is almost worth the price of a ticket alone. A difficult movie to get het up about: inoffensive, charming, and a bit like Banana Instant Whip. DSi

Man Between, The
(Carol Reed, 1953, GB) James Mason, Claire Bloom, Hildegard Neff, Geoffrey Toone, Ernst Schroeder.
101 min. b/w.
Very much a return to the world of Harry Lime, with the ruins of edgy, divided Berlin standing in for the sewers of Vienna. The drab, snow-clad city finds its human counterpart in Mason's sardonic, disreputable double agent, who stalks and then succumbs to the provocatively virginal Bloom. Cold war dogmatism is refreshingly muted, with free world heroes and Stalinist heavies merely a backcloth to the complexly ambiguous relations centred on Mason. The film's rambling, ramshackle construction drew unfavourable comparisons with The Third Man, but despite thematic similarities, it is more fruitfully seen as a forerunner to the down-at-heel spy stories of John Le Carré. RMy

Man Bites Dog (C'est arrivé près de chez vous)
(Rémy Belvaux/André Bonzel/Benoît Poelvoorde, 1992, Bel) Benoît Poelvoorde, Rémy Belvaux, André Bonzel, Jacqueline Poelvoorde-Pappaert, Nelly Pappaert, Jenny Drye, Malou Madou.
96 min.
Mostly, Ben (Poelvoorde) is an ordinary sort of guy. One passion, however, is unusual: he regularly commits murder, not exactly at random, but certainly without malice or provocation. So intriguing is Ben's deadly charm that a film crew decide to make a documentary about him; and come to like him so much that they start facilitating, then collaborating in, his crimes. This spoof fly-on-the-wall documentary is funny, scary, provocative, and profoundly disturbing. While the body count is sky high and the violence explicit, it's neither a thriller nor, finally, a psychological study. Rather, it's a witty, uncompromising acknowledgment of both film-makers' and audiences' often unhealthy fascination with the spectacle of violence. Even as you admire its bravura, intelligence and seeming authenticity, such is its rigour that you are also forced to question just why you are watching it. Purely on a gut level, it may offend; but as an exploration of voyeurism, it's one of the most resonant, caustic contributions to the cinema of violence since Peeping Tom. GA

Man by the Shore, The (L'Homme sur les Quais)
(Raoul Peck, 1992, Fr) Jennifer Zubar, Toto Bissainthe, Jean Michel Martial, Patrick Rameau.
105 min.
Political and social ferment in '60s Haiti as recalled by an innocent young girl. Initially too

fragmented and arty – it comes on at times like a Caribbean Spirit of the Beehive – the film slowly settles down into an effectively understated portrait of a society beset by betrayal, fear and violence. Generally sturdy performances (though one character, wrecked after torture, seems a grotesque, metaphorical caricature) and sustained control of the unsettling mood make for a minor but intelligent entertainment. GA

Man Called Horse, A
(Elliot Silverstein, 1970, US) Richard Harris, Judith Anderson, Jean Gascon, Manu Tupou, Corinna Tsopei, Dub Taylor.
114 min.
First of a series of Westerns in which Richard Harris seemed determined to outdo Brando's penchant for situations permitting a bit of sadomasochistic suffering. Here, as an English lordling captured by Sioux, he undergoes the particularly nasty trial-by-torture of the Sun Vow. Self-touted as an authentic picture of Sioux manners and customs, the film to some extent delivers the goods (despite sacrificing a great deal of credibility by absurdly casting Judith Anderson as a malevolent old crone). But the Sun Vow sequence, lingered on in enervatingly gloating detail, ultimately defines it as exploitative.

Man Called Noon, The
(Peter Collinson, 1973, GB/Sp/It) Richard Crenna, Stephen Boyd, Rosanna Schiaffino, Farley Granger, Patty Shepard, Aldo Sambrell.
95 min.
Instantly forgettable Western about a Dryden-quoting gunfighter who suffers from amnesia until he falls down a ravine at the end and – surprise, surprise – remembers where the gold is and that he's not the villain everyone has accused him of being. The whole thing would be preposterous enough without Collinson's direction. He continually makes his actors compete with the flapping doors, wagon wheels, bites of driftwood and rock that he insists on placing between them and the camera. The only other shots in his repertoire are excessive close-up, zoom, and ground shots angled upwards at 45 degrees. Hardly surprising that you come out exhausted. CPe

Man Called Peter, A
(Henry Koster, 1955, US) Richard Todd, Jean Peters, Marjorie Rambeau, Jill Esmond, Doris Lloyd, Emmett Lynn.
119 min.
Scots-born, American-trained Presbyterian minister Peter Marshall, who was to gain national prominence as the Chaplain to the US Senate, is the subject of this unstoppably earnest CinemaScope biopic, where faith is unshaken even by a heart attack in the pulpit. The combination of Richard Todd and Hollywood religiosity makes a potent argument for descaling the kettle. TJ

Manchurian Candidate, The
(John Frankenheimer, 1962, US) Frank Sinatra, Laurence Harvey, Janet Leigh, Angela Lansbury, Henry Silva, James Gregory, Leslie Parrish, John McGiver, Khigh Dhiegh.
126 min. b/w.
Korean War veteran Major Marco (Sinatra) is troubled by a recurring nightmare in which Congressional Medal of Honor hero Raymond Shaw (Harvey) carries out Communist instructions to shoot fellow American POWs. Working for Intelligence, Marco unravels a cunning Red plot to brainwash his old platoon and to turn Shaw into an assassin. Shaw's father-in-law is the ranting McCarthyite Senator Iselin (Gregory), a mouthpiece for Shaw's ambitious mother (Lansbury), a political background which gives the killer access to the highest in the land. Who is Shaw's American control, when and where are they going to aim him? Frankenheimer's version of Richard Condon's tragically prophetic novel looks even better now than it did then. It's greatest virtue lies in its brilliant balancing acts: political satire and nail-biting thriller, the twin lunacies of the Right and Left, and the outrageously funny dialogue during the parallel courtships set against the sadness of the unloveable Shaw's predicament. Among a marvellous cast – star-wattage Sinatra, hilariously dumb Gregory, the giggling Peking Institute brainwasher Khigh Dhiegh – Lansbury stands out. An Iron Lady to savour, for a change. A masterpiece. BC

Mandala
(Im Kwon-Taek, 1981, SKor) Chun Moo-Song, Ahn Song-Gi, Pang Hui, Ki Jong-Su.
105 min.
This breakthrough film by South Korea's best-known director is a leisurely, chiefly lyrical account of the friendship between two notably different Buddhist monks – Pobun, a somewhat pessimistic young ascetic fleeing the commitment demanded by his girlfriend, and the old Jisan, whose unorthodox preference for alcohol and an active sex life belie an easy-going wisdom repressed by his stricter, seemingly more devout peers. The film also works as an unexpectedly tough appraisal of the tenets and practices of a living philosophy. Woolly-mindedness and poetic overkill are, on the whole, avoided, while enlightenment is presented as often resulting from – or leading to – loneliness, masochism and self-denial. A film whose spiritual integrity is reflected in the mantric calm of its measured rhythms and elegant imagery, it's nevertheless rooted in a recognisably modern, material world, so that you don't need a special interest in Buddhism for its quiet virtues to work their spell. GA

Mandat, Le
see Money Order, The

Mandela
(Jo Menell/Angus Gibson, 1995, US) Nelson Mandela, Mabel Mandela, Mandla Mandela, Walter Sisulu, Anthony Sampson, Joe Matthews, Evelyn Mandela, Nomzamo Winnie Mandela, Desmond Tutu.
123 min.
This two-hour 'official' biography, co-produced by Jonathan Demme, serves a double purpose. It's a populist résumé of the life of one of the 20th century's most remarkable men, tracing Mandela's days from his Xhosa village at the end of WWI to his Nobel Peace Prize in 1993 and his inauguration as President of South Africa in 1994. Mandela gives extensive studio and on-location interviews and narrates much of the film himself. Second, as a political work, it serves as a celebratory, if far from hagiographic tribute to the man, echoing to the sound of the 'revolutionary' voices and music, ancient and modern, of South Africa. WH

Mandingo
(Richard Fleischer, 1975, US) James Mason, Susan George, Perry King, Richard Ward, Brenda Sykes, Ken Norton, Lillian Hayman.
126 min.
The tedious, emasculated stereotype of the Deep South circa 1840, with its stoical slaves and demure southern belles, is effectively exploded here. Fleischer utilises the real sexuality and violence behind slavery to mount a compelling slice of American Gothic which analyses, in appropriately lurid terms, the twists and turns of a distorted society. The plot explores the declining years of a slave-breeding family, whose slaves are treated not so much like animals as humanoids: their physical intimacy with the master-race is total. Finally it is the sheer absurdity and incongruity of the various women's roles in this crazy set-up which cracks the society wide open. The story is basically Victorian melodrama with more than an echo of the Brontes, but it is acted with enormous gusto, by Perry King especially; and Richard Kline's highly atmospheric pictorialisation of the Falconhurst domain adds a great deal. Good to see Fleischer returning to the kind of psychopathological thriller that he can handle so well. DP

Mandragora
(Wiktor Grodecki, 1997, Czech Republic) Mirek Caslavka, David Sveck, Pavel Skripal, Kostas Zedraloglu, Jiri Kodes.
130 min.
Notwithstanding the elegant opening shot (of a shop window smashed and looted to the strains of choral music), this account of a teenage runaway who leaves his bullying father and boring home town for the streets of Prague, only to be pushed immediately by a ruthless pimp into a squalid, violent, druggy world of male prostitution and pornography, is pretty hackneyed by Western European standards. Despite the sombre tone, the film tends towards sensationalism, so that its manifest good intentions seldom result in anything more than trite stereotyping. GA

Mandy (aka Crash of Silence)

(Alexander Mackendrick, 1952, GB) Phyllis Calvert, Jack Hawkins, Terence Morgan, Mandy Miller, Godfrey Tearle, Marjorie Fielding, Patricia Plunkett, Dorothy Alison, Edward Chapman.
93 min. b/w.

The only avowedly 'serious' film of Mackendrick's superb Ealing quintet, *Mandy* is also the first expression of his abiding fascination with the psychology and revealingly distorted perception of a child, developed later in *The Maggie* and, triumphantly, in *Sammy Going South* and *A High Wind in Jamaica*. Nevertheless, the director focuses as tightly on the emotional traumas and narrowed perspectives of the parents as he does on the deaf-and-dumb little girl of the title, revealing their senses to be almost as numbed as hers. Paradoxically, but with much justification, it has often been pointed out that the film's true theme is blindness. PT

Manèges (The Wanton)

(Yves Allégret, 1949, Fr) Simone Signoret, Bernard Blier, Jane Marken, Frank Villard, Jacques Baumer.
90 min. b/w.

A cynically sharpish script about a gold digger (Signoret) who marries a doting riding-master (Blier), leads him a wretched dance while bleeding him dry, then gets hoist with her own petard while looking for another rich sucker. Fussily structured as a complex of flashbacks sometimes covering the same scene from different viewpoints (with Allégret resorting to some irritatingly mannered optical effects to string them together), it's all pretty superficial. But the performances, especially Jane Marken as Signoret's brassily mercenary mother, are superb. TM

Man Escaped, A

see Condamné à mort s'est échappé, Un

Man for All Seasons, A

(Fred Zinnemann, 1966, US) Paul Scofield, Robert Shaw, Wendy Hiller, Leo McKern, Orson Welles, Susannah York, Nigel Davenport, John Hurt, Corin Redgrave, Colin Blakely, Cyril Luckham.
120 min.

An agonisingly respectable, sincere film of Robert Bolt's literate play, with Scofield as Sir Thomas More, endorsing the divine right of the Pope over and above his King. McKern is Thomas Cromwell; Shaw, Henry VIII; Hiller, Mrs More. They're all fine, but Orson Welles alone relieves the boredom in a marvellous cameo as Cardinal Wolsey. If only they'd let him loose with the whole sorry history... TCh

Man Friday

(Jack Gold, 1975, GB) Peter O'Toole, Richard Roundtree, Peter Cellier, Christopher Cabot, Joel Fluellen.
115 min.

Turning the familiar Crusoe/Man Friday story on its head, this version becomes a straightforward confrontation between instinctive, spontaneous, lithe and beautiful Black versus repressed, guilt-ridden and mottled White: a fable for our times. Crusoe's imperialism, individualism, competitiveness and other cornerstones of Western civilisation also fail to measure up alongside Man Friday's natural grace. But too seldom does this Crusoe become anything more than a one-dimensional, knock-down figure, and O'Toole's noisy, strangled performance is disastrously wide of the mark. The simple tone would be more acceptable if the general level of satire owed less to stock British comedy, and if attempts to leaven the message hadn't included interludes like the one where Crusoe and Friday go hang-gliding. CPe

Man from Africa and Girl from India

(Harbance Mickey Kumar, 1982, Trin) Sanam Sun Bhalinder, Michael Walker.
145 min.

Sexual repression, cultural alienation and religious fanaticism are only some of the ingredients in the extraordinary 'melting pot' of this movie from Trinidad. Parallel plots, stuck together with lots of calypso music, illustrate contrasting examples of extremism, with the black, virile machoman Michael not getting enough, and his friend

Shaam, the sensitive Indian boy, unable to kiss his beautiful bride without seeing devils. The complicated plot falls over itself trying to explain every moral twist and turn, while the actors (none of them professional) are endearingly theatrical. Apparently a huge success in the West Indies and parts of America, it's being aimed at an ethnic audience here who may be better able to appreciate its style and cultural intricacies. HR

Man from China

(Zhang Tielin, 1990, GB) Yang Ying Sheng, Marina Baker.
45 min.

A short feature by Zhang Tielin, a former movie star in China, now an exile in Britain. It charts the experiences of a young Chinese painter who comes to London soon after the Beijing massacre and decides to stay. His initial difficulties in adjusting and the misunderstandings are sketched succinctly, but the meat of the film is the account of the boy's psychological blocks: his determination to go it alone, and his almost pathological inability to accept help and affection. In other words, not the usual anecdotal guff, but an intense and demanding study of the 'inner wounds' that afflict so many Chinese from the PRC. A more than impressive debut. TR

Man from Colorado, The

(Henry Levin, 1948, US) William Holden, Glenn Ford, Ellen Drew, Ray Collins, Edgar Buchanan.
99 min.

An uncredited King Vidor allegedly shot some of this intriguing but not wholly achieved psychological Western, which has twitchy cavalry officer Ford transformed by his Civil War experiences into a disturbed killer. The outlook is not good when he's appointed a noose-happy judge, leaving former adjutant Holden to rebel against his subsequent reign of terror. The scenario alludes to the homecoming traumas of WWII combatants, but the characterisation, regrettably, lacks the deftness to give the movie real punch. TJ

Man from Hong Kong, The

(Brian Trenchard Smith, 1975, Aust/HK) Jimmy Wang Yu, George Lazenby, Ros Spiers, Hugh Keays-Byrne, Roger Ward, Rebecca Gilling, Frank Thring.
103 min.

Wang Yu's Hong Kong super-cop arrives in Sydney on a case, mercifully not reduced to Chinese caricature status. Otherwise this is imitation late Bond stuff, larded with all the predictable ingredients: girls, car chases, less than pointed wit, fights (kung-fu and otherwise), hanggliding as the novel twist, and a number of statutory Chinese martial arts movie ingredients lurking under the Western veneer. Directed with basic bash-and-smash competence. VG

Man from Island West, The (Xibu Lai de Ren)

(Huang Ming-Chuan, 1990, Tai) Wu Hongming, Chen Yiwen, Xiao Cuifen, Sharman Lanporan.
96 min.

Made on a shoestring, Taiwan's first ever indie feature breaks a lot of new ground: it focuses attention on the sad plight of survivors from Taiwan's aboriginal tribes (most of whom are now manual labourers or prostitutes), and it superimposes an ancient myth on its modern story to create an innovative twin-level structure. A stranger from Taipei turns up in a coastal village, founded by the Atayal tribe, in search of something he won't divulge. His visit catalyses contradictory local feelings about the place, but also mysteriously echoes an Atayal myth about the redeemer Yawi, who once led the tribe to deliverance. Strong elemental imagery plus startlingly raw emotions equals a minor classic. TR

Man from Laramie, The

(Anthony Mann, 1955, US) James Stewart, Arthur Kennedy, Donald Crisp, Cathy O'Donnell, Aline MacMahon, Wallace Ford, Alex Nicol, Jack Elam.
101 min.

A magnificent, if slightly over-ambitious Western. Cattle baron Crisp, who is going blind, is obsessed with who will inherit his ranching

empire: his psychopathic natural-born son Nicol, or the more reliable Kennedy, adopted by the old man to keep Nicol in line. Into this morass of sibling rivalry bursts a vengeful Stewart, bent on finding the gunrunner responsible for selling weapons to the Indians who slaughtered his younger brother's cavalry detachment. Visually impressive, psychologically complex and sometime brutally violent, it suffers slightly from the emphasis on the familial machinations at the expense of Stewart's tortured psyche. Otherwise, it's 24-carat stuff. NF

Man from Majorca, The (Mannen från Mallorca)

(Bo Widerberg, 1984, Swe/Den) Sven Wollter, Tomas von Brömssen, Håkan Serner, Ernst Günther, Thomas Hellberg.
105 min.

A pair of Swedish vice cops stumble onto 'something big' when a routine post office raid turns out to be connected with a subsequent hit-and-run accident and the murder of a garrulous wino. They are beginning to get a whiff of high-level corruption, centering on the Minister of Justice's cavortings with a high-class prostitute, when their phlegmatic superior is ordered to drop the case. Widerberg keeps the action tight, dealing smoothly with the details of police routine and framing the most mundane objects in such a way as to lend them a strangely sinister aspect. The opening post office raid is a slickly handled set piece, setting the tone for a cleverly constructed script which contains enough suspense and red herrings to keep one gripped almost to the end. Unfortunately, the government cover-up having proved all too successful, there's no gratifying pay-off, leaving one with a slight sense of anti-climax. A neat thriller, but more satisfying than electrifying. NF

Man from Snowy River, The

(George Miller, 1982, Aust) Kirk Douglas, Jack Thompson, Tom Burlinson, Sigrid Thornton, Lorraine Bayly, Terence Donovan, June Jago.
115 min.

Same name, but this movie based on an epic poem by one AB 'Banjo' Paterson, about a young mountain boy's efforts to tame a stallion, is not the work of the *Mad Max* director. This other Miller dolls up a routine passage-to-manhood saga with widescreen mountain locations and a camera that only moves to show off the expensive production values. The presence of Kirk Douglas in two roles (his scallywag performance and his gritted one) attempts to give the film the gloss of an American Western, fooling no one. CPe

Manganinnie

(John Haney, 1980, Aust) Mawuyul Yathalawuy, Anna Ralph, Phillip Hinton, Elaine Mangan, Buruminy Dhamarrandji, Reg Evans.
90 min.

The last survivor of a doomed Aboriginal tribe goes walkabout with a little white girl, initiating her into the mysteries of the Dreamtime before finally falling victim to the guns of early European colonists in the infamous Black Drive. A Disney insistence on cute baby wombats and other assorted fauna mar the film, although the narrative itself is aeons away from the fresh-faced vigour of those ripping adventure yarns, at first seeming maddeningly slow, then assuming a dreamy, languid rhythm of its own. And despite the facile nature/culture clash turning on a Noble Savage stereotype of long lineage in Australian cinema, the fact that *Manganinnie* echoes history (the brutal 19th century genocide of the Tasmanian aboriginal race) lends this first project from the Tasmanian Film Corporation a curious poignancy as a small act of contrition. SJo

Mangler, The

(Tobe Hooper, 1994, US) Robert Englund, Ted Levine, Daniel Matmor, Jeremy Crutchley, Vanessa Pike.
106 min.

One would expect a horror movie about a possessed laundry-press to put the audience through the wringer. Instead, this tedious Stephen King adaptation takes the two-dimensional characters of the source story and squashes them even flatter. Englund and Hooper last teamed up on the abysmal straight-to-video *Nightmare* (aka *De Sade*), on which this is no improvement. Levine fails to get inside the skin of his jaded cop, investigating a series of industrial accidents at the grim Blue Ribbon Laundry. The bone-crushing, limb-severing mayhem centres on an ancient machine jealously guarded by irascible owner Bill Gartley (Englund), who clanks around on stainless-steel leg braces following an earlier mishap of his own. Although the mechanical beast is a fearsome creation, and some of the mangling is gratifyingly gory, the bizarre ranting of the cop's veggie, mystic neighbour – about Faustian pacts and the sacrifice of 16-year-old virgins – takes some swallowing, as indeed do the stodgy plotting, scenery-chewing performances and dodgy sfx. NF

Mango Tree, The
(Kevin Dobson, 1977, Aust) Christopher Pate, Geraldine Fitzgerald, Robert Helpmann, Gerard Kennedy, Gloria Dawn, Diane Craig.
93 min.
Written and produced by former Hollywood actor Michael Pate, and starring his son, this is yet another slice of Aussie nostalgia, with the wide-eyed lad about to come to manhood as he and the century move into their late teens. The inevitable acquisition of wisdom is aided by a collection of veteran Queensland small-town eccentrics, notably grandma (Fitzgerald) and a professor (former ballet star Helpmann). PT

Manhattan (100)
(Woody Allen, 1979, US) Woody Allen, Diane Keaton, Michael Murphy, Mariel Hemingway, Meryl Streep, Anne Byrne, Karen Ludwig.
96 min. b/w.
A milestone in Woody Allen's career as he dropped (temporarily, at least) the slavish imitation which undermined 'Interiors' and found a tone of his own. The note of tragi-comedy is nicely judged as his hero, a TV comedy writer nervously contemplating a switch to serious literature, equally nervously frets over the women in his life and a pending betrayal of his best friend. An edgy social comedy framed as a loving tribute to neurotic New York, overlaid with an evocative Gershwin score, it's funny and sad in exactly the right proportions. Allen could well strive vainly ever to better this film. TM

Manhattan Melodrama
(WS Van Dyke, 1934, US) Clark Gable, William Powell, Myrna Loy, Leo Carrillo, Isabel Jewell, Mickey Rooney, Nat Pendleton.
93 min. b/w.
The last movie John Dillinger ever saw (he was fingered by the lady in red and shot as he left the cinema), this is an archetypal gangster movie of the period, a product of the moral backlash instigated by Hoover and the Hays Office in response to the dangerous ambivalence of *Little Caesar* and its ilk. Clark Gable (who was said to resemble Dillinger) is a thoroughly affable kind of gangster – not averse to a little wager, but essentially a good type who stumbled on to the wrong track when he was a lad (played by Mickey Rooney). Powell is his old pal from those bygone days, now a district attorney. Clark doesn't think twice about putting his life on the line if it will help Bill get elected governor. This Oscar-winning scenario inspired a hail of imitators over the next five years, and was thoughtfully resurrected by John Gregory Dunne in his novel *True Confessions*. TCh

Manhattan Murder Mystery
(Woody Allen, 1993, US) Alan Alda, Woody Allen, Anjelica Huston, Diane Keaton, Jerry Adler, Joy Behar, Ron Rifkin.
107 min.
Like the Bob Hope movies which it alludes to, *Manhattan Murder Mystery* is as light and brazenly generic as Allen's early work. As a result, it is both unusually insubstantial and, at least in the second half, extremely funny. Hope-like in his panicky cowardice, Larry worries not only about the feelings of his wife Carol (Keaton, refreshing) for his old friend Ted (Alda), but about her determination to investigate the death of a neighbour. At first, Larry thinks Carol is fantasising, but then he starts to witness strange events. Cue to a fast, ramshackle, thrill comedy as entertaining as it is removed from the realities of contemporary New York. A movie inspired by movie escapism. Minor, but surprisingly, almost defiantly upbeat. GA

Man Hunt
(Fritz Lang, 1941, US) Walter Pidgeon, Joan Bennett, George Sanders, John Carradine, Roddy McDowall, Ludwig Stossel, Heather Thatcher.
105 min. b/w.
While far from Lang's finest, definitely a superior thriller, set on the eve of World War II. Sadly but inevitably jettisoning much of Geoffrey Household's superb novel ('Rogue Male'), it follows Pidgeon's big game hunter from his arrest by the Gestapo (after taking a 'practice' shot at Hitler), through his escape back to England, to his final, brutal conflict in the Dorset Hills where he has been pursued by Sanders' marvellously sinister Quive-Smith. The evocation of England is pure Hollywood nonsense, Bennett's prostitute is too coy and saddled with an atrocious Cockney accent, and the sequence with McDowall's cabin boy the stuff of Boy's Own. But the basic theme of hunter-and-hunted survives intact, beautifully expressed in taut scenes like Carradine's stalking of Pidgeon through the London Underground. Forget the shortcomings and the propagandistic finale, and you have a gripping *noir* thriller, bleak, complex and nightmarish. GA

Manhunt
see From Hell to Texas

Manhunter
(Michael Mann, 1986, US) William Peterson, Kim Greist, Joan Allen, Brian Cox, Dennis Farina, Stephen Lang, Tom Noonan, David Seaman.
120 min.
Mann hits top form with this splendidly stylish and oppressive thriller adapted from Thomas Harris' Red Dragon. The plot is complex and ingenious: FBI forensics expert Will Graham (Peterson), blessed (and tormented) by an ability to fathom the workings of the criminal mind through psychic empathy, is brought back from voluntary retirement to track down a serial killer, the 'Tooth Fairy'. Focused on the anxiety and confusion of the hunter rather than his psychotic prey, the film functions both as a disturbing examination of voyeurism, and as an often almost unbearably grim suspenser. Mann creates a terrifying menacing atmosphere without resorting to graphic depiction of the seriously nasty killings: music, designer-expressionist 'Scope photography, and an imaginative use of locations, combine with shots of the aftermath of the massacres to evoke a world nightmarishly perceived by Graham's haunted sensibility. The performances, too, are superior, most memorably Cox's intellectually brilliant and malevolent asylum inmate. One of the most impressive American thrillers of the late '80s. GA

Manhunt in Milan (La 'Mala' Ordina)
(Fernando Di Leo, 1972, It/WGer) Mario Adorf, Henry Silva, Woody Strode, Adolfo Celi, Luciana Paluzzi, Sylva Koscina, Cyril Cusack.
92 min.
Typically derivative Italian paranoid thriller about Mafia inter-gang feuding. A mishmash of formulary devices, decorated with the usual high ratio of lethal encounters, is perambulated around the statutory handful of 'thriller' locations: topless bar, hippie commune, boss' suite, prostitute-haunted roadside. The sole point of interest lies in the rise, some half way through, of one Luca Canalli, self-styled small-time pimp and Mafia stooge, to hero status. As played by Mario Adorf, Canalli is a character of literal bone-headedness – useful for smashing telephones, people and car windscreens – and patently soft-centred despite his profession. Adorf's two-dimensional performance gives the character a certain conviction; not enough to turn the film into a viable proposition, though. VG

Mania
see Flesh and the Fiends, The

Maniac Cop
(William Lustig, 1988, US) Tom Atkins, Bruce Campbell, Laurene Landon, Richard Roundtree, William Smith, Robert Z'Dar, Sheree North, Erik Holland.
85 min.

Had writer/producer Larry Cohen directed this low-budget thriller himself, it might have displayed more vitality and wit. As it is, despite abundant action and a start involving a fistful of murders, the overall effect is sluggish. There's a psycho killer in police colours terrorising New York. Detective McCrae (Atkins) reckons he's a member of the force, but his boss disagrees, until the wife of young officer Jack Forrest (Campbell) is found dead, leaving a diary and cuttings that implicate her faithless spouse. While Forrest and his policewoman girlfriend (Landon) struggle to establish his innonence, subplots snowball, peripheral characters proliferate, and the killings culminate in a none too imaginatively staged car chase. Only the odd line of dialogue and occasional bizarre detail hint at Cohen's quirky signature; performances and camerawork are solid enough, but both cutting and direction are formulary and flabby. EA

Maniac Cop 2
(William Lustig, 1990, US) Robert Davi, Claudia Christian, Michael Lerner, Bruce Campbell, Laurene Landon, Robert Z'Dar, Leo Rossi.
88 min.
Again scripted by Larry Cohen, this sequel is a lively if predictable romp, with unashamedly low-brow ambitions and a budget to match. Returning from his watery grave to wreak further vengeance on the police force that stitched him up, zombiefied cop Matt Cordell (Z'Dar) teams up with serial killer Turkell (Rossi), a crazed degenerate on 'a crusade against the whores of the world'. Enter the sublimely acne-scarred Davi, stepping into Campbell's shoes (the star of the original is blown away after ten minutes) as substitute hero Lt McKinney, a gun-toting cynic who doesn't believe in the walking dead, psychiatrists, or guilt. Directed with workaday deftness by Lustig, who squeezes in a couple of rattlingly good car chases and some spectacular fiery special effects, the movie is notable mainly for the quirky black comedy of Cohen's script. Boasting some incredibly cheap gags about casually slaying traffic cops on parking patrol, this is bound to keep the exploitation cognoscenti more than happy. MK

Maniacs on Wheels
see Once a Jolly Swagman

Manifesto
(Dusan Makavejev, 1988, US) Camilla Soeberg, Alfred Molina, Simon Callow, Eric Stoltz, Lindsay Duncan, Rade Serbedzija.
96 min.
Makavejev's adaptation of a Zola short story has a vague period setting – Central Europe, 1920 – which augurs badly for the ensuing fuzziness of this self-conscious black comedy. Svetlana (pouting Danish discovery Soeberg) arrives in the village of Waldheim (well, one wonders...) with gun in garter ready for the assassination of the visiting King. Revolution may be in the air, but a lecherous police chief, a doting postman and an uptight schoolmistress all conspire to make her plans less well laid than her own person. Despite the presence of Molina, Stoltz and Duncan respectively in these roles, their various crazy performances render them both unrecognisable and oddly ineffective. There are glimpses of Makavejev's past exuberance, with dollops of wild sex and delicious photography, but the final impression is of a project too long delayed and heavily compromised. DT

Manila by Night (aka City After Dark)
(Ishmael Bernal, 1980, Phil) Charito Solis, Johnny Wilson, William Martinez, Rio Locsin, Bernardo Bernardo.
160 min.
Banned from export at the time by Imelda Marcos herself, this was Ishmael Bernal's masterpiece: a deeply truthful celebration of the night street-life he knew and loved in all its squalor, pain and joy. The characters are authentic flaming creatures (fags, dykes, bisexuals, hookers of all genders, dopers, plus assorted petty criminals), some played by big stars like Solis and Martinez, others by friends or bit-player favourites of Bernal's. There's no doubt that the fashions and lifestyles have dated, but it remains impressive for its honesty and candour, its daringly original structure, its Cassavetes-worthy improvisations and its complete lack of phoney compassion for its fraught and wasted characters. TR

Manila: In the Claws of Darkness (Maynila, sa mga Kuko ng Liwanag)

(Lino Brocka, 1975, Phil) Rafael Roco Jr, Hilda Koronel, Lou Salvador Jr, Lily Gamboa-Mendoza, Juling Bagabaldo.
125 min.

Gripped in the film's subtitular 'claws of darkness', country-boy Julio seeks his lost village sweetheart, lured to the big city by a procuress. Slitting the underbelly of Manila (Brocka's true protagonist), he moves through shanty towns, street markets, building sites, brothels, and cheap Chinese cafés, all throbbing with poisonous life: the sin and cynicism of poverty under President Marcos' regime, captured with a raw immediacy against which the golden, sun-splashed flashbacks of pastoral romance seem like the flimsiest of painted veils. SJo

Man I Love, The

(Raoul Walsh, 1946, US) Ida Lupino, Robert Alda, Bruce Bennett, Andrea King, Martha Vickers, Alan Hale, Dolores Moran, Warren Douglas, Don McGuire.
96 min. b/w.

At an after-hours session in a New York jazz club, resident singer Lupino joins in a heartfelt rendition of 'The Man I Love'. Homesick after an unhappy affair, she decides to visit her family in California: a married sister (King) and two younger siblings (Vickers, Douglas). All of them, not to mention the young married couple across the hall (Moran, McGuire), are either in or heading for trouble, mostly emotional, and much of it traceable to a lecherous night-club owner (Alda). Impulsively, driven by an awareness of her own bleak isolation, Lupino tries to help: with some success, but in the process getting snared in Alda's greasy clutches, while simultaneously grasping at the mirage of happiness with a former jazz pianist (Bennett) running away from an unhappy marriage and a burned-out talent. The dialogue is a mite pretentious at times, and the plot comes perilously close to soap at the end. But the performances are excellent, and Walsh's sympathetic direction, wonderfully flexible in negotiating the pinball effect as characters and problems interact, gives the whole thing the touching, kaleidoscopic flavour of a prototype Alan Rudolph movie. TM

Man I Married, The (aka I Married a Nazi)

(Irving Pichel, 1940, US) Joan Bennett, Francis Lederer, Lloyd Nolan, Anna Sten, Otto Kruger, Maria Ouspenskaya.
77 min. b/w.

One of the movies that looks as though it was trying to prepare the American public for entry to the war in Europe, Fox's drama (from the novel Swastika by Oscar Shisgall) grafts a propaganda element on to a story of domestic discord. Bennett is the American wife left to battle for custody of her son when German husband Lederer's trip home winds him over to the Nazis and he decides to stay on. Although simplistic, the film's portrait of life under the Third Reich (where Czechs sweep the streets and beating drums whip up the crowds at public meetings) is unquestionably persuasive. TJ

Man in a Dream, A

see Homme qui Dort, Un

Man in Grey, The

(Leslie Arliss, 1943, GB) Margaret Lockwood, Phyllis Calvert, James Mason, Stewart Granger, Harry Smith, Martita Hunt.
116 min. b/w.

Mason was in fine caddish fettle for this Gainsborough bodice-ripper, a Regency romp (from Lady Eleanor Smith) chronicling the fortunes of old school chums Calvert and Lockwood, the latter eventually to seduce her pal's roguish husband, Mason's glacial Lord Rohan. The strangled vowels and heaving sighs play like the highest Cartland camp, but in its day this was raunchy stuff for the British screen. In fact, the low-cut dresses distressed the Americans so much, they asked for portions of the film to be reshot so they could get it past the censor.

Man in Love, A (Un Homme Amoureux)

(Diane Kurys, 1987, Fr) Peter Coyote, Greta Scacchi, Jamie Lee Curtis, Claudia Cardinale, Peter Riegert, John Berry, Vincent Lindon, Jean Pigozzi.
111 min.

Coyote plays an American film star, Steve Elliott, who falls for his young co-star (Scacchi) while in Rome to play the lead in a film about the writer Cesare Pavese. She, infatuated, walks out on her French fiancé, Elliott's suspicious wife (Curtis) threatens to turn up, the director throws tantrums, and Elliott's assistant (Riegert) engineers escape routes for his boss. It sounds farcical, but the opulent interiors, rousing score by Georges Delerue, and the embarrassment of unrestrained petting, give this tale of adultery a heavyweight romanticism it can't carry. The film (shot in English, incidentally) wins points on other scores: Riegert's wry detachment from the drama is wonderfully appropriate and often hilarious, and Pigozzi's bombastic director is perfect. EP

Man in My Life, The

see Homme de ma Vie, L'

Man in the Glass Booth, The

(Arthur Hiller, 1975, US) Maximilian Schell, Lois Nettleton, Luther Adler, Lawrence Pressman, Henry Brown.
117 min.

One of the unhappy 'American Film Theater' attempts to embalm theatrical performances. This version of Robert Shaw's play (from whose credits he requested his name be removed) works up a certain weight in its exploration of themes of guilt and forgiveness as a wealthy New York Jew is placed on trial, accused of being a former Nazi concentration camp commandant. But it still emerges as stagily verbose, with a self-indulgent performance from Schell. TM

Man in the Iron Mask, The

(James Whale, 1939, US) Louis Hayward, Joan Bennett, Warren William, Joseph Schildkraut, Alan Hale, Walter Kingsford, Bert Roach, Marion Martin, Albert Dekker.
110 min. b/w.

A stylish swashbuckler from the flamboyant James Whale, with Louis Hayward sharply distinguishing his twin roles, the tyrannical Louis XIV and his identical 'lost' brother. Warren William lends fine support as the fourth musketeer, D'Artagnan, and the film has a fine romantic arc to it, although it hasn't the bizarre wit of the director's most memorable pictures (except perhaps in the bizarre comeuppance that awaits the bad twin when he has to don the iron mask in his turn, and imagines himself strangling to death on his own ever-growing whiskers). TCh

Man in the Iron Mask, The

(Randall Wallace, 1998, US) Leonardo DiCaprio, Jeremy Irons, John Malkovich, Gérard Depardieu, Gabriel Byrne, Anne Parillaud, Judith Godrèche.
132 min.

The draw is fresh-faced DiCaprio in the dual role of the youthful despot Louis XIV and his wronged twin Phillippe, wearer of the cruel headgear. It then falls to older weightier thesps, Depardieu (Porthos), Irons (Aramis), Malkovich (Athos) and Byrne (D'Artagnan), to carry the action, as the standard ageing Musketeers. However, unable to impose any consistency of tone, writer/director Wallace (the scriptwriter of Braveheart) fails to reconcile the actors' diverse styles, leaving everyone costumed up but with no place to go. More comfortable with the emotional vulnerability of the imprisoned Phillippe than the vain cruelty of the tyrant monarch, DiCaprio again fails to convince as a worldly womanising adult. As the Musketeers who hatch a plot to replace the hated King with his identical twin, the others fare somewhat better. Only Depardieu, drunken and self-pitying, overplays his hand, his performance sliding into annoying farcical excess. NF

Man in the Moon, The

(Robert Mulligan, 1991, US) Sam Waterston, Tess Harper, Gail Strickland, Reese Witherspoon, Jason London, Emily Warfield, Bentley Mitchum.
99 min.

For this rites-of-passage drama, screenwriter Jenny Wingfield draws on personal recollections; but while she brings intelligence to the depiction of teen angst, her attempt to follow formula means that the heart-warming tone steadily becomes overheated. It's the late '50s, and 14-year-old Dani (Witherspoon) is on the verge of major discoveries about sex and family ties. There's a handsome new boy (London) in the neighbourhood who leaves both Dani and her older sister (Warfield) weak-kneed. As though uncertain of her material's quiet strengths, Wingfield resolves this tension and follows it up with a clichéd love scene, tear-jerking tragedy, and a chastening heart-to-heart on Dad's boat. More consistent are the fine performances which Mulligan draws from his cast: Harper as the level-headed mother, Waterston as the taciturn father, and Witherspoon in a striking debut. CM

Man in the Road, The

(Lance Comfort, 1956, GB) Derek Farr, Ella Raines, Donald Wolfit, Lisa Daniely, Karel Stepanek, Cyril Cusack.
84 min. b/w.

Cold War spy thriller with a stale storyline about communist agents trying to prise a secret formula from a brilliant amnesiac scientist (young writer Ella Raines to the rescue). Guy Morgan, who adapted the script from a popular novel of the day (Anthony Armstrong's He Was Found in the Road), was a former secretary of the British Screenwriters' Association and habitually complained about the lack of recognition screenwriters received. He protested too much, perhaps. GM

Man in the Street, The (Sokaktaki Adam)

(Biket Ilhan, 1995, Tur) Metin Belgin, Suna Yildizoglu, Selda Özer.
89 min.

Sailing into Istanbul harbour, smuggling goods after a long sojourn away, come Yakub and Hasan. While Yakub's straight into the drinking dens and brothels, Hasan's losing control of the deal; except he hardly seems to care – he can't put away thoughts of Ayhan, his real love whom he abandoned here once before. There's an air of drunken melancholy about this film. At heart it seems to be a languorous dissertation on personal disquiet and disconsolation – there's some, slight sense of context (the dislocations of modern life and transient work, perhaps; every once in a while strangers stop as if in recognition of the camera, and regale us with observations, musings and wry remarks), but it makes little impression. Like a drunkard, Hasan seems governed by some foreign stimulus that we're not party to. NB

Man in the White Suit, The

(Alexander Mackendrick, 1951, GB) Alec Guinness, Joan Greenwood, Cecil Parker, Michael Gough, Ernest Thesiger, Vida Hope, Howard Marion Crawford, Patric Doonan.
85 min. b/w.

Certainly one of Guinness' best performances as the laboratory dishwasher in a textile mill who invents a fabric that never wears out and never gets dirty, thus incurring the wrath of both management and labour, satirically depicted as being hand-in-glove in their conservative reliance on restrictive practices. Typically, the Ealing formula for goodnatured whimsy prevents Mackendrick from pushing the darker aspects of the theme (eminently present in Thesiger's brooding old vulture of an industrialist) to their logical conclusion. But as David Thomson acutely observed, in a note about the extent to which the acid disenchantment of Sweet Smell of Success was already apparent in Mackendrick's earlier work, there is enough of Kafka in the film to lift it right out of the Ealing comedy tramlines. TM

Man in the Wilderness

(Richard C Sarafian, 1971, US) Richard Harris, John Huston, Henry Wilcoxon, Percy Herbert, Dennis Waterman, Prunella Ransome, Norman Rossington.
105 min.

The team that had such a success with A Man Called Horse decided to try their luck again with this sensationalist bit of cod anthropology based on a true story. In the 1820s, the guide to a fur-trapping expedition in the great North West is left by his captain to die after being savaged by a grizzly. His desire for revenge is expiated after he faces the violence of nature and several gruelling Indian tribal rituals. Explicit, simplistic, and if you've seen *A Man Called Horse*, highly predictable. GA

Man Is Not a Bird
(Covek nije Tica)
(Dusan Makavejev, 1965, Yugo) Milena Dravic, Janez Vrhovec, Eva Ras, Stojan Arandelovic, Boris Dvornik.
80 min. b/w.
Makavejev's first feature is a delightful, typically eccentric concoction, centred very loosely indeed around a story about an engineer who visits a new town to assemble mining machinery. There his devotion to work fouls up his relationship with his beloved, while a fellow worker encounters problems when his wife discovers he has a mistress. A freewheeling kaleidoscope mixing comedy and social comment as it deals with both labour and sexual politics, not to mention many seemingly unrelated topics such as hypnotism and culture (there's a marvellous climactic scene with Beethoven performed in an enormous foundry while the heroine conjures her own ode to joy), it defies description but is extremely entertaining. GA

Man Is Ten Feet Tall, A
see Edge of the City

Mani sulla Città, Le
(Hands Over the City)
(Francesco Rosi, 1963, It) Rod Steiger, Guido Alberti, Carlo Fermariello, Salvo Randone, Dany Paris, Angelo D'Alessandro.
105 min. b/w.
Rosi on property development rackets and political manoeuvring in the Naples city council is every bit as tough and forthright as Rosi on Sicily (*Salvatore Giuliano*) and on oil diplomacy (*The Mattei Affair*). His film follows the irresistible rise of the speculator Nottola (Steiger, excellently cast) as he channels the public building programme on to his own land, shrugs off the collapse of a slum tenement in an area that needs redevelopment, and cold-bloodedly shifts the balance of power in the council to his own advantage. It's not only totally convincing as an analysis of civic corruption, but also one of the very few left wing movies that one can imagine actually reaching the mass audience it's aimed at. TR

Manitou, The
(William Girdler, 1977, US) Tony Curtis, Michael Ansara, Susan Strasberg, Stella Stevens, Jon Cedar, Ann Sothern, Burgess Meredith, Paul Mantee, Jeanette Nolan.
105 min.
Burgess Meredith's splendid cameo of an eccentric anthropologist almost justifies the price of a seat for this *Exorcist* spin-off. The victim this time (Strasberg) develops a nasty lump on her neck which, growing at an astonishing rate, turns out to be the foetus of a 400-year-old medicine man. Medical science proves impotent, Indian magic a mere half-measure, requiring good old 'love' to weigh in on the final cosmic shootout. The special effects are superb, easy winners in an engaging inter-denominational free-for-all that blends Marvel Comics' Doctor Strange with Corman's *The Raven*. A successful excursion, spoiled only by the director's habit of plopping in postcard views of the Golden Gate Bridge instead of exteriors. GD

Man Like Eva, A
(Ein Mann wie Eva)
(Radu Gabrea, 1983, WGer) Eva Mattes, Lisa Kreuzer, Werner Stocker, Charles Regnier, Carola Regnier, Charly Muhamed Huber.
89 min.
That a woman plays the late German director Fassbinder is this film's trump card. For one thing, Mattes manages, miraculously, to look, talk and walk like the great man; for another, it lends the movie a psychosexual complexity that is highly suitable for dealing with Fassbinder's tortured bisexuality. Sexual power-games are the driving force behind both film and director as the Fassbinder figure's tormented jealousy and cruel whims play off friends, lovers, and actors against one another to disastrous effect. The movie's greatest strength is its manifest sincerity. You may not believe much of what happens here, but

Fassbinder's life really was a chaotic can of worms, and this tells it like it was (though it is fiction, not documentary). No conventional biopic entertainment, it's a sad film about a sad man. GA

Man-Made Monster
(aka The Electric Man)
(George Waggner, 1941, US) Lionel Atwill, Lon Chaney Jr, Anne Nagel, Frank Albertson, Samuel S Hinds.
68 min. b/w.
Minor but efficient little chiller, with Atwill doing his usual mad scientist bit and experimenting on the hapless Chaney who, after an accident, finds he is immune to electricity. Needless to say, things get nastily out of control as Chaney goes on the rampage. Nothing special, really, although Chaney (in his first horror movie) lends a touch of pathos to his role, and John Fulton's special effects are as good as ever. GA

Man Named John, A
(E Venne un Uomo)
(Ermanno Olmi, 1965, It) Rod Steiger, Adolfo Celi, Rita Bertocchi, Pietro Gelmi.
94 min.
Not so much a biography of Angelo Roncalli as an attempt to evoke the aura of his life and the paths that led to his becoming the much-loved Pope John XXIII, Olmi's film uses Rod Steiger as a 'mediator'. Steiger, in other words, lends his presence as commentator, occasionally stands in for the Pope, gazes benignly at the small boy who represents the pontiff as a small boy. With Steiger reflecting a sort of conventional awe, it is perhaps small surprise that what emerges from this jigsaw portrait is pretty much a pious homage. Olmi's quirkish hand and eye as a film-maker are really evident only in the early sequences, shot in delicate colours almost like fairytale illustrations, which conjure the quaintly rustic surroundings in which the future Pope grew up. TM

Manneken Pis
(Frank Van Passel, 1994, Bel) Antje de Boeck, Frank Vercruyssen, Ann Petersen.
90 min.
With its carefree blend of the off-beam and the everyday, this game Belgian first feature seems to tap the same vein of oddball whimsy mined by *Toto the Hero* and *The Sexual Life of the Belgians*. Sweet, bald, shy Harry is a humble dishwasher hiding a dark secret (his family were run over by a train while he was out of their car taking a leak), all of which makes him uncertain in his wooing of a comely Brussels tramdriver, whose elderly confidant pours scorn on the whole proceedings. Unafraid to switch from farce to grim foreboding in an instant, director Van Passel throws in a vibrant colour palette, but doesn't quite have the discipline to achieve the emotional impact intended. Refreshing, though. TJ

Mannequin
(Michael Gottlieb, 1987, US) Andrew McCarthy, Kim Cattrall, Estelle Getty, James Spader, GW Bailey, Carole Davis.
90 min.
This pitifully unfunny comedy has only two things going for it: its theme song, Starship's 'Nothing's Gonna Stop Us Now', is a hit single; and it is short. Cattrall plays an Egyptian princess who, back in 2514 BC, is saved by the Gods from being married off to a dung-dealer, and turns up as a dummy in a Philadelphia department store window. McCarthy, a frustrated artist who had a hand in her fashioning, is enchanted to discover that she comes alive at night. In between dressing-up and undressing one another, the pair also dress a few of the ailing store's windows, thereby reviving its fortunes and thwarting the takeover plans of avaricious rivals. Incidental 'humour' is provided by a screaming gay black stereotype, a Rambo-fixated security guard and his cowardly bulldog, and McCarthy's jealous ex-girlfriend. A film about, by and for dummies. NF

Mannequin Two: On the Move (aka Mannequin on the Move)
(Stewart Raffill, 1991, US) Kristy Swanson, William Ragsdale, Meshach Taylor, Terry Kiser, Stuart Pankin, Cynthia Harris.
95 min.

This unwelcome sequel to *Mannequin* has neither the stars nor the director of the original. Only Taylor returns, reprising his offensive camp black stereotype. A thousand years ago in Hauptmann-Koenig, a prince's sweetheart is turned to wax by an evil enchanter (hooray!). Cut to the present: the girl awakens (boo!) in a department store, to be reunited with her inexplicably reincarnated lover. Young stars Swanson and Ragsdale are bland beyond belief, but worse still are the antics of the fiendish Count Spretzle's 'amusingly foreign' bodyguards. Raffill's heavy-handed direction is jam-packed with product placement, and interrupted every ten seconds with yet another plug for a boring MOR rock song. MK

Manny & Lo
(Lisa Krueger, 1995, US) Mary Kay Place, Scarlett Johansson, Aleksa Palladino, Paul Guilfoyle, Glenn Fitzgerald, Cameron Boyd.
97 min.
After mom dies, 11-year-old Manny's abducted by her 16-year-old sister Lo, an aggressively nihilist, petty criminal. They take off on a spree, ending up in a remote, deserted ski chalet. Trouble is, Lo's pregnant (though barely admits it), so they kidnap former nurse Elaine (Place), herself rather less stable than first appears. This sweet if somewhat implausible first feature is a gentle, occasionally dark comedy-cum-coming-of-age drama, held together by strong interplay between the conflicting leads (Place is particularly good) and by a wry, pleasingly understated sense of humour. GA

Man of Africa
(Cyril Frankel, 1953, GB) Frederick Bijurenda, Violet Mukabureza, Mattayo Bukwirwa, Butensa.
74 min.
A real oddity, shot by Frankel in deepest Uganda with an eight-man crew. Frequently revealing the shortcomings of the Flaherty/Grierson approach to fictionalised documentary, its story – about a tribe of Africans who resettle in pygmy country and face danger from malaria, elephants and internal strife – is thin, melodramatic and more than a little trite. But the film's curiosity value, plus the endearing grace and energy of the pygmies, make it worth a look. GA

Man of Aran
(Robert Flaherty, 1934, GB) Colman King, Maggie Dirrane, Michael Dillane, Pat Mullin, Patch Ruadh.
75 min. b/w.
Flaherty was neither the documentary purist nor the victim of movie commerce that he has so often been called – more a talented exoticist. Here he quite happily places the Aran fishermen in a preconceived *mise en scène* of spartan struggle in order to arrive at his intended goal: images of stylised heroism. A film which remains – especially in its elemental images of sea and storm – mightily impressive. PT

Man of Flowers
(Paul Cox, 1983, Aust) Norman Kaye, Alyson Best, Chris Haywood, Sarah Walker, Julia Blake, Bob Ellis.
91 min.
A lonely, middle-aged art collector pays a young artist's model to ritually strip for his voyeuristic pleasure every week (to an aria from Donizetti's 'Lucia di Lammermoor'). Gradually he becomes unwillingly involved in her messy private life, and as his psychotherapy continues, we learn about the relationship of his fantasies to his obsession with his dead mother. Cox's film, handsome indeed for its modest budget, and not at all the dirty-old-man-buys-sex-object story the above suggests, is quite unlike any film to have emerged from Australia. Cox achieves a difficult balance between a quirkily individual sense of humour, and a more poignant, serious sense of purpose about the privacy of our fantasy lives and our essential loneliness, which is right on target. A genuine oddity. RM

Man of Iron
(Czlowiek z Zelaza)
(Andrzej Wajda, 1981, Pol) Jerzy Radziwilowicz, Krystyna Janda, Marian Opania, Irena Byrska, Wieslawa Kosmalska.
152 min. b/w & col.

Wajda's remarkable sequel to *Man of Marble* welds newsreel footage of the Solidarity strike to fiction in a strong investigative drama. A disillusioned, vodka-sodden radio producer is bundled off to Gdansk in a black limousine. His mission: to smear one of the main activists – who also happens to be the son of the hapless 'Marble' worker-hero. But, tempered by bitter experience of the failed reforms of '68 and '70, these new men of iron are more durable than their fathers, not as easily smashed. Media cynicism, censorship and corruption are again dominant themes, this time anchored through the TV coverage of the strike, though the conclusion hints with guarded optimism at a possible rapprochement between workers and intelligentsia. An urgent, nervy narrative conveys all the exhilaration and bewilderment of finding oneself on the very crestline of crucial historical change; and for the viewer, all the retrospective melancholy of knowing that euphoria shattered by subsequent events. SJo

Man of Marble (Czlowiek z Marmur)
(Andrzej Wajda, 1976, Pol) Jerzy Radziwilowicz, Krystyna Janda, Tadeusz Lomnicki, Jacek Lomnicki, Michael Tarkowski.
165 min. b/w & col.
A jaundiced regard for documentary practice pervades Wajda's slice of Polish history, which takes the form of an inquiry conducted by a young, aggressive film-school graduate into the fate, after reward, repudiation and rehabilitation, of a '50s Stakhanovite shock-worker, a record-breaking bricklayer. Film-as-evidence (monochrome flashbacks represent propagandist archive footage) is stripped of its authority just as inexorably as the investigative process meets an impasse at the point where preconceptions and actuality intersect. Wajda builds his own 'detection' story with complete assurance, though it's often difficult to decide whether his visual style is a parody of TV's (an ageing cameraman bemoans the constant use of hand-held shots and the wide-angle lens) or an accommodation of it. PT

Man of No Importance, A
(Suri Krishnamma, 1994, GB/Ire) Albert Finney, Rufus Sewell, Tara Fitzgerald, Brenda Fricker, Michael Gambon, Patrick Malahide, Anna Manahan.
99 min.
A modest attempt at retelling the life of Oscar Wilde through the parallel experiences of a Dublin bus conductor. 1963: Alfie Byrne (Finney) enlivens the passengers on the Number 34 route by reciting poetry, but decides to stage Wilde's *Salome* after punching the ticket of a beautiful provincial girl, Adele (Fitzgerald). Alfie's sister (Fricker) senses matrimony in his new infatuation, though this is hardly likely as Alfie refers to his bus driver as 'Bosie' (Sewell), and diffidently frequents gay pubs. It isn't long before the stage production is threatened by the local Queensberry in the form of a butcher (Gambon) outraged at being cast as Herod, and by Aubrey Beardsley's illustrations for the play. Rehearsals grind comically on while various hetero and homosexual revelations provoke a green carnation, an assault, a suicide attempt and a cautious, sexless entente. If the basic premise is far-fetched, the dialogue is often deftly literate. Finney is in fine form, but his accent is all over the place. BC

Man of the House
(James Orr, 1994, US) Chevy Chase, Farrah Fawcett, Jonathan Taylor Thomas, George Wendt, David Shiner, Art LaFleur.
97 min.
Excruciating Disney comedy in which Chase is a top DA and would-be step-dad to pubescent moppet Thomas. Junior doesn't want the newcomer disrupting the happy home he shares with artist mom Farrah Fawcett and a battle ensues to see just who's the real 'Man of the House'. On a YMCA programme father and son don Native American costumes to raindance together. Male bonding occurs. Come home, Herbie. TJ

Man of the Moment
(John Paddy Carstairs, 1955, GB) Norman Wisdom, Lena Morris, Belinda Lee, Jerry Desmonde, The Beverley Sisters.
88 min. b/w.

Foreign Office filing clerk Wisdom drops a washbasin on the head of one of the delegates to a Geneva conference and is forced to take his place. His unwitting efforts on behalf of a small island make him a major diplomatic figure and he is invited to visit the grateful islanders. Wisdom's cretinous humour is an acquired taste: fans speak highly of this one. NF

Man of the West
(Anthony Mann, 1958, US) Gary Cooper, Julie London, Lee J Cobb, Arthur O'Connell, Jack Lord, John Dehner, Royal Dano, Robert Wilke.
100 min.
A superb Western, exemplifying Mann's capacity for integrating his interest in spectacle with a resonant narrative fully deserving the adjective 'classic', in which Gary Cooper's ex-outlaw is under constant, ranting pressure from Cobb's gang-leader father-figure to return to the fold. The odyssey of Cooper (playing the emblematically named Link Jones) from pasture to desert to ghost town and back, and from settled present to tormented past and back, bridges the traditions of classical tragedy and classic Hollywood. Mann's synthesis of archetypal characters and generic iconography is seamless; and he manages to inscribe landscape, anxious voyeurism and fratricide within his narrative resolution. Textbook cinema, maybe, but Mann's work will remain rich for discovery and celebration. PT

Man of the Year
(Dirk Shafer, 1995, US) Dirk Shafer, Vivian Paxton, Deidra Shafer, Michael Ornstein, Claudette Sutherland, Calvin Bartlett, Beth Broderick, Fabio, Mary Stein
86 min.
In 1992, Dirk Shafer was voted *Playgirl* magazine's man of the year. He was the incredible hunk, handsome, buff, built, yet sensitive and intelligent, sympathetic to the modern woman. Dirk worked *Playgirl* like he knew it was his big break, and *Playgirl* worked Dirk. They knew he was the best spokesman they could hope for. He manned the phone hotlines, and he did the TV talk show circuit. Only one problem. Dirk Shafer is, was and surely always will be...gay. A semi-documentary, this purports to be the work of filmmakers who only stumble across Shafer's deception mid-shoot. This conceit doesn't come off: we never believe in the team behind the camera, let alone the eccentrics in front of it. The fake interviewees are fairly easy to spot, but the film gets the tone about right, touching lightly and wittily on issues of sexual orientation, pornography, 'outing' and popular self-deception. Dirk emerges as charming, naive and a little manipulative. He also wrote and directed this playful mea culpa. TCh

Man on a Tightrope
(Elia Kazan, 1953, US) Fredric March, Gloria Grahame, Terry Moore, Cameron Mitchell, Adolphe Menjou, Richard Boone, Robert Beatty.
105 min. b/w.
Cold War parable, decently acted and directed, but inevitably disappointing when compared to Kazan's other films of the era. There's no Brando or Dean to lift it above the ordinary – only Fredric March trying too hard to impress. The screenplay, by Robert E Sherwood from a story by Neil Paterson, concerns a struggling circus troupe in Communist Czechoslovakia who dream of escape to freedom in Austria. Apparently based on fact, but with little of the colour or energy of most big top tales. GM

Manon des Sources
(Claude Berri, 1986, Fr/It/Switz) Yves Montand, Daniel Auteuil, Emmanuelle Béart, Hippolyte Girardot, Margarita Lozano, Elisabeth Depardieu.
120 min.
Essential viewing for anyone who enjoyed *Jean de Florette*. Ten years after Jean's death (in this continuation of Pagnol's novel *L'Eau des collines*), his 18-year-old daughter Manon (Béart) still haunts the hills overlooking the farm stolen from her father by the canny Soubeyran (Montand) and his dim-witted nephew Ugolin (Auteuil). Thousands of red carnations now flower there, but the Soubeyrans' blossoming fortunes are about to wither and die. Paradoxically, Ugolin has fallen in love with Manon, though his decla-

rations fall on stony ground, leading in the end to tragedy. There is a satisfying symmetry to events, with Manon able to take her revenge on the Soubeyrans by stopping up the main village spring. However, in the final scenes, the film slides into a Hardyesque fatalism, with the loose ends tied up a little too neatly, resulting in an air of literary contrivance. It nevertheless succeeds, like the earlier film, in tapping the well-springs of one's emotions. NF

Man on Fire
(Elie Chouraqui, 1987, Fr/It) Scott Glenn, Jade Malle, Joe Pesci, Brooke Adams, Jonathan Pryce, Paul Shenar, Danny Aiello, Lou Castel.
92 min.
A thriller without a spark of imagination. As he is zipped into a body-bag, ex-CIA agent Creasy (Glenn) recalls how he was hired to babysit Sam (Malle), 12-year-old daughter of an Italian businessman. Sam's a cute kid, but she reminds him (in slo-mo flashback) of a dead child in war-torn Beirut. So he wants out, but things pick up when she compares him with Lenny in Steinbeck's *Of Mice and Men*, then serenades him with 'Someone to Watch Over Me'. Of course she gets kidnapped by reptilian criminals anyway; but with a subtlety typical of the film, he crashes a cement-mixer into the kidnappers' hideout and dies – or does he? – in his rescue bid. Borrowing wholesale from Scorsese, this inept thriller adds insult to injury with a risible voice-over, a sickly soundtrack, atrocious dubbing (though 'filmed in English'), and corny freeze frames. NF

Man on the Flying Trapeze, The
(Clyde Bruckman, 1935, US) WC Fields, Mary Brian, Kathleen Howard, Grady Sutton, Vera Lewis, Carlotta Monti, Walter Brennan.
65 min. b/w.
A rich example of middle period Fields, when his films were squarely centred on the nightmare of American small town life and all the jokes had an extra edge. Fields' Ambrose Wolfinger suffers a termagant wife, a rude mother-in-law, her sponging son, and a job where he hasn't had any time off in 25 years. His only blessings are a very lovely daughter and a stock of applejack in the cellar. Director Clyde Bruckman worked on *The General*, but don't expect any cool control: it's just the usual helter-skelter style of all unpretentious comedies, with the kind of blatant back projection that only adds to the fun. GB

Man on the Roof, The (Mannen på Taket)
(Bo Widerberg, 1976, Swe) Carl Gustaf Lindstedt, Gunnel Wadner, Håkan Serner, Sven Wollter, Eva Remaeus, Thomas Hellberg.
109 min.
A Swedish box-office hit, and a far cry from Widerberg's earlier *Adalen '31*: the lyrical feeling for landscape is replaced by the occasional aerial view of downtown Stockholm, and the visionary socialism by some trite sociologising. Based on a novel by Sjöwall and Wahlöö, it starts tough with a police inspector disembowelled in his hospital bed. But it swiftly undercuts its own suspense, with lengthy sections illustrating the equal tedium of police routine and cops' domestic lives. The idea of corruption on the force is evidently a shocking novelty in Sweden: the film is so busy explaining what turns a loyal civil servant into a psychopathic sniper that it's left without a villain. Keeping the killer's face off-camera causes more irritation than suspense. The few tense moments – like the helicopter lurching into a busy street – just aren't enough to make a thriller. JD

Manpower
(Raoul Walsh, 1941, US) Marlene Dietrich, Edward G Robinson, George Raft, Alan Hale, Walter Catlett, Eve Arden, Frank McHugh, Barton MacLane, Ward Bond.
105 min. b/w.
An overheated, *noir*-ish melodrama about a sexual triangle: stolid power-line worker Robinson has plucked Marlene Dietrich from a dance-hall dive and married her, but his sexier fellow-worker Raft fools around with her. The conflict naturally comes to a head on the power lines during a thunderstorm. This is the only American movie that doesn't label Dietrich as a foreigner, but its overall 'Frailty, thy name is woman' tone pre-

serves her status as an object to be feared. Arcane fact: it's an unofficial remake of a 1932 Mervyn LeRoy film called *Two Seconds*, which starred Robinson in the same role. TR

Man's Best Friend
(John Lafia, 1993, US) Ally Sheedy, Lance Henriksen, Robert Costanzo, John Cassini, Fredric Lehne.
87 min.
Mad scientist Henriksen transforms a cuddly Tibetan mastiff into MAX 3000, a genetically engineered 'psycho mutt' that can only be controlled with stabilising drugs. When scoop-seeking TV reporter Sheedy and her camerawomen break into the EMAX lab and escape with the pooch, the time bomb starts ticking. The police have no leads (ho ho), MAX is headed for a 'psychotic episode', and paperboys, mailmen and neighbourhood moggies are on the menu. Swerving arbitrarily from cute dog stuff that should carry an adult health warning to toned-down gore scenes that fail to deliver the necessary slavering savagery, this mongrel project lacks a pure horror pedigree. So by the time the genetically hybrid MAX starts camouflaging himself as a pile of garage junk, or scaling buildings with the agility of a gravity-defying leopard, you too may be climbing the walls. Hard to credit. NF

Man's Castle
(Frank Borzage, 1933, US) Spencer Tracy, Loretta Young, Marjorie Rambeau, Arthur Hohl, Glenda Farrell, Walter Connolly.
75 min. b/w.
Borzage was responsible for some of the oddest Hollywood films of the '30s, and few can be more bizarre than *Man's Castle*, a heated Depression melodrama with Tracy and Young as a pair of incurably optimistic lovers attempting to set up house together in shantytown. Their amoral romantic passion for each other is sufficient in Borzage's eyes to justify theft, even murder. The film ends with one of the director's most poetic images: the couple lying in each other's arms in a boxcar, she still in her wedding-dress. RM

Man's Favourite Sport?
(Howard Hawks, 1963, US) Rock Hudson, Paula Prentiss, Maria Perschy, John McGiver, Charlene Holt, Roscoe Karns, Norman Alden.
120 min.
Dismissed by Robin Wood in his monograph on Hawks as 'tired' but championed by the French, *Man's Favourite Sport?* is in many ways the quintessential Hollywood auteur movie. Seen in isolation from the rest of Hawks' work, it seems to be merely an out-of-time slapstick comedy. Seen in context, it effortlessly demonstrates the auteur's ability to stamp his artistic identity on anything – in this case, the travails of an armchair expert (Hudson) forced to enter a fishing contest and confronted with a typically Hawksian superior woman (Prentiss). A marvellous film. PH

Man's Hope
see Espoir

Mansion of the Doomed
(aka The Terror of Dr Chaney)
(Michael Pataki, 1975, US) Richard Basehart, Trish Stewart, Gloria Grahame, Lance Henrikson, Al Ferrara, Vic Tayback.
89 min.
Hand a Franju-esque plot to an American Exploitation film maker, and you have to be prepared for pritty dire consequences. It's a pleasant surprise, therefore, to find that this rehash of *Les Yeux sans Visage* is a modest gem of pulp horror. Casting helps tremendously: Basehart is the eminent eye-surgeon whose daughter loses her sight when his car crashes; Grahame the devoted assistant who helps him kidnap victims for transplant purposes, and acts as keeper to the unfortunates caged in the cellar, robbed blind. Pataki's direction has the courage of the script's grisly convictions, and he turns in a strong shocker, its relentless assault on the eyes aided by video close-ups of ocular surgery and some excellent make-up work. It's good to see an example of the genre without apocalyptic pretensions, and which doesn't feel the insecure need to send itself up. PT

Manson
(Robert Hendrickson/Laurence Merrick, 1972, US) Charles Manson, members of his 'Family', DA Vincent Bugliosi.
93 min.
This documentary compilation stretches a little material an awful long way (it's padded out with 'lyrical' song sequences and redundant multi-screen opticals), but it does include all the extant footage of Manson himself, and some fairly lengthy interviews with those members of the 'Family' who weren't arrested for the Sharon Tate/La Bianca killings. The approach of the reporting is earnestly middlebrow; the commentary is tendentious when it takes statements at face value (like Squeaky Fromm's bland assertion that she was influenced by TV violence), but it's thankfully never sensational. In truth, the material adds up to nothing very much, but it's undeniably discomforting to see acid-scarred hippies insisting on their continuing reverence for Manson, or discussing the experience of having a lover blow out his brains at the moment of climax as if it were nothing out of the ordinary. Many people won't need to see the film to come to terms with the fact of Manson's 'philosophy', and the compilers do very little to compel attention; a fictional treatment of the subject like Barry Shear's *The Todd Killings* works out a good deal more provocative and suggestive. TR

Man to Respect, A
(Un Uomo da Rispettare)
(Michele Lupo, 1972, It/WGer) Kirk Douglas, Giuliano Gemma, Florinda Bolkan, Reinhard Kolldehoff, Wolfgang Preiss.
108 min.
The old story of the professional thief pulling the ultimate job before getting out for good. The cast act like robots, and look as if they've been told to speak with their mouths shut to make dubbing easier. Underneath all the mechanics and violence lurks a shred of human feeling: Douglas' wife, understandably aggrieved by his behaviour, double-crosses him at the end, but it's the only human gesture in the whole film.

Man Trouble
(Bob Rafelson, 1992, US) Jack Nicholson, Ellen Barkin, Harry Dean Stanton, Beverly D'Angelo, Michael McKean, Saul Rubinek, Viveka Davis, Veronica Cartwright, David Clennon, John Kapelos, Lauren Tom, Paul Mazursky.
100 min.
The last time Nicholson appeared in a film written by Carole Eastman and directed by Rafelson, the result was one of the definitive pictures of the early '70s, *Five Easy Pieces*. Here Nicholson is Harry Bliss, proprietor of the 'House of Bliss' guard-dog agency. A scuzzy charmer down on his luck, Harry isn't about to let a rich, beautiful and vulnerable client like Joan Spruance (Barkin) slip away from him. Her sister Andy (D'Angelo) owns the luxury mansion in the Hollywood hills, but she's been kidnapped by her boyfriend, one of the most powerful men in America (Dean Stanton); so Joan is all alone, and someone is trying to kill her. The trouble is, the film never seems to know where it's headed. Not quite a romance, a thriller or a comedy, it's a movie with an on-going identity crisis. Barkin, playing against type, produces a shrill caricature of femininity, while Rafelson indulges Nicholson's familiar soft-spoken laxity, another of his personable rogues. TCh

Manuela
(aka Stowaway Girl)
(Guy Hamilton, 1957, GB) Trevor Howard, Elsa Martinelli, Pedro Armendariz, Donald Pleasence, Warren Mitchell, Jack McGowran.
95 min. b/w.
From the opening scene of ribaldry over a dead shipmate's coffin to the brutally off-hand dismissal of easement and affection at the end, this may prove too bleak a prospect for many temperaments. That such a despairing work emerged from where and when it did is one of the minor wonders of the cinema. The setting is a ramshackle freighter hauling cheap cargo around the Med, Howard the washed-up captain with a crew of averagely vicious malcontents, and Martinelli the fugitive teenager with whom Howard doesn't find love and redemp-

tion, though such is on offer. The treatment of religion as a silly nuisance is likewise unexpected, though adding to the general impression of hopelessness. The closing dialogue might have become one of the standard quotes of the movies, had not the tone of pervasive bitterness consigned the film to an isolation almost as complete as that of its hero. BBa

Manufacturing Consent: Noam Chomsky and the Media
(Peter Wintonick/Mark Achbar, 1992, Can) Noam Chomsky.
165 min.
The natural audience for this long but thoroughly engrossing documentary is North America, since it was made to give Chomsky and his radical ideas the kind of profile the US press and broadcast media routinely deny him. None the less, this is useful as an introduction to the man himself (his Depression childhood, his rise in linguistics, his radical activism) and even more valuable as an anthology of his political campaigns and major debating skirmishes. The film-makers avoid a 'voice-of-authority' commentary, allowing cutting and juxtapositions to carry the arguments and dialectics forward. More's the pity, then, that they sometimes fall back on tabloid-style gimmickry to get points across, none of which is necessary to bolster Chomsky's largely incontrovertible arguments. A decent, civilised piece of work. TR

Ma Nuit chez Maud
see My Night with Maud

Man Upstairs, The
(Don Chaffey, 1958, GB) Richard Attenborough, Bernard Lee, Donald Houston, Dorothy Alison, Kenneth Griffith, Patricia Jessel, Maureen Connell, Virginia Maskell.
88 min. b/w.
Attenborough as the quiet lodger who blows his cork, shoves a policeman down the stairs, and barricades himself into his room at the top. Very obviously a second-hand variation on *Le Jour se lève* but quite grippingly done, although Alun Falconer's script tends to run to stereotype in trying to extract significance from the reactions of police, welfare officer, and other tenants. The resolution, brought about by a sympathetic young mother (Alison), is dismayingly inadequate, to say the least. TM

Man Who Broke the Bank at Monte Carlo, The
(Stephen Roberts, 1935, US) Ronald Colman, Joan Bennett, Colin Clive, Nigel Bruce, Montagu Love, Frank Reicher, Ferdinand Gottschalk.
66 min. b/w.
Brisk romantic comedy, co-scripted by Nunnally Johnson, with the debonair Colman as a White Russian aristocrat: at first, he earns his daily bread as a cabbie, but then strikes lucky on the Riviera gaming tables. Bennett's the vamp assigned to lure him back to the casino and make sure he loses what he's just won. GM

Man Who Came to Dinner, The
(William Keighley, 1941, US) Monty Woolley, Bette Davis, Ann Sheridan, Billie Burke, Jimmy Durante, Reginald Gardiner, Grant Mitchell, Mary Wickes.
112 min. b/w.
Scripted by Julius and Philip Epstein from Kaufman and Hart's play, a delightful comedy about a radio host (Woolley) and his chaotic sojourn, after accidental injury while on a lecture tour, at the suburban home of Billie Burke and family (who are expected to wait on him hand and foot while suffering a stream of insults). Based loosely on the character of theatre critic Alexander Woollcott, and thus peppered with caricatures of stage celebrities like Noël Coward (Gardiner), Harpo Marx (Durante) and Ann Sheridan's voracious actress (Gertrude Lawrence? Tallulah?), it's rather unimaginatively directed, but the performers savour the sharp, sparklingly cynical dialogue with glee. GA

Man Who Changed His Mind, The (aka The Man Who Lived Again)

(Robert Stevenson, 1936, GB) Boris Karloff, Anna Lee, John Loder, Frank Cellier, Donald Calthrop, Cecil Parker, Lyn Harding.
66 min. b/w.
Stevenson's career followed exactly the same trajectory as that of Alfred Hitchcock – he was discovered by Michael Balcon, feted at home and then lured off to Hollywood by David O Selznick. (He went on to direct *Mary Poppins* and *The Love Bug*.) In the '30s, he was considered one of the most promising British talents around. This risible horror pic (co-scripted by Sidney Gilliat) does little to explain why. It's a far-fetched yarn about a scientist with an unlikely ability to transplant brains from one body to another. Stiff performances and creaking dialogue. GM

Man Who Could Work Miracles, The

(Lothar Mendes, 1936, GB) Roland Young, Ralph Richardson, Ernest Thesiger, Joan Gardner, Edward Chapman, Sophie Stewart, George Zucco, George Sanders.
82 min. b/w.
Less well known than the other Korda/HG Wells collaboration *Things to Come*, this stands the test of time far better. Alexander Korda's anglophilia allows an endearing seriousness to settle round Wells' now clichéd visions, and the film's cosy view of the world doesn't entirely conceal a coldly pragmatic estimation of man's limitations. Roland Young, as a Mr Polly-like shop assistant, the unwitting guinea-pig in a divine experiment, succeeds marvellously in conveying the power-lust of the meek and righteous, and the wooden performances of the rest of the cast fail to rob the film of its resonance and charm. Certainly it's pedantic and disjointed, but its concerns for world peace, and meditations on the dangers and attractions of absolute power, make it a moving epitaph for Baldwin's Britain. RMy

Man Who Died Twice, The

see Silencieux, Le

Man Who Fell to Earth, The [100]

(Nicolas Roeg, 1976, US) David Bowie, Rip Torn, Candy Clark, Buck Henry, Bernie Casey, Jackson D Kane.
140 min.
Roeg's hugely ambitious and imaginative film transforms a straightforward science fiction story into a rich kaleidoscope of contemporary America. Newton (Bowie), an alien whose understanding of the world comes from monitoring TV stations, arrives on earth, builds the largest corporate empire in the States to further his mission, but becomes increasingly frustrated by human emotions. What follows is as much a love story as sci-fi: like other films of Roeg's, this explores private and public behaviour. Newton/Bowie becomes involved in an almost pulp-like romance with Candy Clark, played out to the hits of middle America, that culminates with his 'fall' from innocence. Roeg, often using a dazzling technical skill, jettisons narrative in favour of thematic juxtapositions, working best when exploring the clichés of social and cultural ritual. Less successful is the 'explicit' sex Roeg now seems obliged to offer; but visually a treat throughout. CPe

Man Who Had His Hair Cut Short, The (De Man die Zijn Haar Kort Liet Knippen)

(André Delvaux, 1966, Bel) Senne Rouffaer, Beata Tyszkiewicz, Hector Camerlynck, Hilde Uitterlinden.
94 min. b/w.
This moving and remarkably original first feature from Delvaux (based on a novel by Johan Daisne) makes his subsequent excursions into 'Vogue' surrealism (*Un Soir...un Train, Rendezvous à Bray*) look decidedly mechanical. The man who has his hair cut short is Govert Miereveld (Rouffaer), a hopeless schoolteacher who develops a crush on a mature female pupil; the experience unhinges him, and his involuntary attendance at an autopsy is enough to push him right over the edge. Delvaux's main feat is to

take his audience into Miereveld's manias without pretending to explain them, but he also manages to maintain an unsentimentally detached view of his character as an outsider, especially through the recurrent use of the Kurt Weill-esque 'Ballad of Real Life' on the soundtrack. The result is a mixture of psychological thriller and *noir* love story, and it's more than a little wonderful. TR

Man Who Had Power Over Women, The

(John Krish, 1970, GB) Rod Taylor, Carol White, James Booth, Penelope Horner, Charles Korvin, Alexandra Stewart, Keith Barron, Clive Francis.
90 min.
A Swinging London PR man (Taylor), having marital problems, gets so sickened by adulteries and abortion after shepherding round a nasty bisexual pop idol (Francis) that he punches the idol and quits his slick agency. It's a heavily obvious Awful Warning to all those teenyboppers with too much stardust in their eyes. Disappointing, as Krish's earlier work looked good. RD

Man Who Knew Too Little, The

(Jon Amiel, 1997, US/Ger) Bill Murray, Peter Gallagher, Joanne Whalley, Alfred Molina, Richard Wilson, Geraldine James, John Standing.
94 min.
When dumb video store assistant Murray arrives unexpectedly and inconveniently at the London home of his banker brother, Gallagher, the latter gets him out of the way for the evening by signing him up for an interactive role playing game – a fake thriller scenario – called 'Theatre of Life'. Trouble is Murray mistakenly answers a phone call intended for a hired killer, and is soon up to his neck in a real plot involving blackmail, murder, and a conspiracy engineered by Wilson to blow up a banquet held to mark an Anglo-Russian peace agreement. Cue misunderstandings, as Murray unwittingly finds himself in a life-threatening farce featuring callgirl Whalley, assassin Molina, cops, torturers, Morris dancers and Russian dolls. Despite the title, this fitfully very funny vehicle spoofs not Hitchcock but those tortuously silly British spy thrillers of the '60s, its depiction of London as risibly unreal as that of the movies it's guying. Unsophisticated but fun. GA

Man Who Knew Too Much, The

(Alfred Hitchcock, 1934, GB) Leslie Banks, Edna Best, Peter Lorre, Nova Pilbeam, Frank Vosper, Hugh Wakefield, Pierre Fresnay.
75 min. b/w.
Vintage Hitchcock, with sheer wit and verve masking an implausible plot that spins out of the murder of a spy (Fresnay) in an equally implausible Switzerland (all back-projected mountains), leaving a pair of innocent bystanders (Banks and Best) to track his secret – and their kidnapped daughter – in a dark and labyrinthine London. Where the remake had Doris Day maternally crooning with fateful foreboding, sharpshooting Best simply grabs a rifle and gets after the villains. Pacy, exciting, and with superb settings (taxidermist's shop, dentist's chair, mission chapel complete with gun-toting motherly body, shootout re-enacting the Sidney Street siege, terrific climax in the Albert Hall), it also has nice villainy from a scarred, leering Lorre (here making his British debut). At two-thirds the length of the remake, it's twice the fun. TM

Man Who Knew Too Much, The

(Alfred Hitchcock, 1956, US) James Stewart, Doris Day, Brenda de Banzie, Bernard Miles, Ralph Truman, Daniel Gélin, Alan Mowbray.
120 min.
The sole instance of Hitchcock actually remaking one of his earlier movies, this replaces the British version's tight, economic plotting and quirky social observations with altogether glossier production values and a typically '50s examination of the family under melodramatic stress. Stewart and Day are the complacent cou-

ple whose son is kidnapped by spies, and who wend their way through a characteristically Hitchcockian series of suspense set pieces (including a virtuoso crescendo at the Albert Hall) in their attempts to recover him. Starting slowly amid colourful but rather superfluous travelogue-style Moroccan footage, the film improves no end as it progresses, with anxiety about the boy's safety steadily undermining the apparent happiness of a marriage founded on habit and compromise. GA

Man Who Left His Will on Film, The (Tokyo Senso Sengo Hiwa)

(Nagisa Oshima, 1970, Jap) Kazuo Goto, Emiko Iwasaki, Sugio Fukuoka, Keiichi Fukuda.
94 min. b/w.
This is Oshima's post-1968 analysis of the failure and disillusionment of the student Left, and it's among his most biting and cautionary films. Like *Death by Hanging* and other movies, it starts with a riddle (the real or imaginary disappearance of a student militant), and then follows through all the implications with a remorseless logic. Another student sets out to trace the missing boy, fearing that he committed suicide; his only leads are conversations with the militant's estranged girlfriend and a roll of film shot by the boy just before he vanished. But it's less a mystery thriller than a series of provocative questions. What is militancy? Does 'struggle' mean violence? Is it really possible for an individual to identify with the interests of a group? And what part do sexual problems play in determining the feelings and actions of young people? TR

Man Who Lived Again, The

see Man Who Changed His Mind

Man Who Lived Twice, The

(Harry Lachman, 1936, US) Ralph Bellamy, Marian Marsh, Thurston Hall, Isabel Jewell, Nana Bryant, Ward Bond.
73 min. b/w.
Promising Columbia second feature in which Bellamy's the killer on the run who seeks refuge in a hospital, undergoes an op courtesy of neurosurgeon Hall, and begins a new career as a successful doctor. But can the past be far behind? Implausible, perhaps, but there was enough in the idea to merit a 3-D remake, *Man in the Dark*, with Edmond O'Brien. TJ

Man Who Loved Cat Dancing, The

(Richard C Sarafian, 1973, US) Burt Reynolds, Sarah Miles, Lee J Cobb, Jack Warden, George Hamilton, Bo Hopkins, Robert Donner.
114 min.
At first, after a chance encounter saddles a gang of train robbers with a refined lady, this looks as though it might develop into a reasonably engaging tale. But as the going gets harder and the gang fall out among themselves, the film reveals itself to be a thoroughly routine love story. The killing factor, however, is the supreme indifference that Burt Reynolds and Sarah Miles display towards their roles. CPe

Man Who Loved Women, The (L'Homme qui Aimait les Femmes)

(François Truffaut, 1977, Fr) Charles Denner, Brigitte Fossey, Leslie Caron, Nelly Borgeaud, Geneviève Fontanel, Nathalie Baye, Sabine Glaser.
119 min.
Charmless tale of a man whose one interest in life is looking at, pursuing, and making love to women, an obsession leading him to a premature (for him, if not for the audience) death. Seen by some as a misogynist catalogue, by others as a mature, detached examination of an unsympathetic character's fatal passion for largely indifferent females, either way it irritates by its overwrought sense of literary-style paradox, by its insistence on eccentricity as its source of humour, and by its haphazard and gratuitous form: constructed largely in flashbacks, it nevertheless fails to explain or illuminate its central character's behaviour. GA

Man Who Loved Women, The

(Blake Edwards, 1983, US) Burt Reynolds, Julie Andrews, Kim Basinger, Marilu Henner, Cynthia Sikes, Jennifer Edwards, Sela Ward, Ellen Bauer.
110 min.

Edwards' muddled remake of one of Truffaut's less than happy movies involves a Hollywood lay-about sculptor (Reynolds) whose sack-count seems about par for the course in LA. Far from his obsession with women seeming strange, his psycho-babble accounts of womanising to his shrink (an unlikely Andrews) sound like no more than the usual Anna Raeburn phone-in whingeing. But while the movie desperately lacks humour, and the right touch, it yet manages to be very good-natured in an unmalicious sort of way. CPea

Man Who Mistook His Wife for a Hat, The

(Christopher Rawlence, 1987, GB) Emile Belcourt, Frederick Westcott, Patricia Hooper.
75 min.

Michael Nyman's 'chamber opera' is based on neurologist Oliver Sacks' case history of a man suffering from agnosia: the inability to recognise everyday objects. As the Neurologist (Belcourt) questions and conducts tests upon music lecturer Dr P (Westcott), the story proper takes time out for interviews with both Sacks himself and a neurological surgeon, allowing librettist and director Rawlence to transform an individual case study into an investigation of problems of perception. Thanks to sensitivity and wit and to a subtle, sympathetic use of close-ups, the film finally becomes very moving. And Nyman's shimmering music, crisply sung by the three leads, is not only entirely appropriate to mood and meaning, but also memorable in its own right. GA

Man Who Shot Liberty Valance, The

(John Ford, 1962, US) James Stewart, John Wayne, Vera Miles, Lee Marvin, Edmond O'Brien, Andy Devine, Woody Strode, Jeanette Nolan, John Carradine.
121 min. b/w.

Ford's purest and most sustained expression of the familiar themes of the passing of the Old West, the conflict between the untamed wilderness and the cultivated garden, and the power of myth. Stewart plays a respected senator who returns on a train (in an opening echoing that of 'My Darling Clementine') to attend the funeral of his old friend Wayne. In one scene, Stewart wipes the dust off a disused stagecoach, marking in a simple gesture the distance between the Old West inhabited by Wayne and the new West which he himself represents. In the central flashback sequence, it is revealed that it was not Stewart who shot the outlaw Liberty Valance (Marvin) but Wayne, the gun law of the Old West paving the way for the development of a new civilisation. For Ford, the passing of the Old West is also the passing of an age of romantic heroism. The only link between the two worlds is the desert rose, a flowering cactus hardy enough to survive the harshness of the desert and humanise the wilderness. NF

Man Who Watched Trains Go By, The (aka Paris Express)

(Harold French, 1952, GB) Claude Rains, Marius Goring, Herbert Lom, Marta Toren, Ferdy Mayne, Anouk Aimée, Eric Pohlmann, Felix Aylmer, Lucie Mannheim.
80 min.

Rains is perfectly cast as Simenon's mousy Dutch shipping clerk outraged to find, after meticulously keeping the books for 18 years, that his boss (Lom) has besmirched his integrity by cooking those books, intending to make off with the proceeds. Unable to resist his wanderlust when fate takes a hand – Lom falls accidentally to his death – Rains skips impulsively out on his family with the loot and heads for Paris, romance and adventure. On the same train is his old chess crony from the police (Goring), sympathetic but suspicious and asking awkward questions. So far so good, even if the dialogue does make rather too free with pregnant chess metaphors. But when Rains gets away, to find not the Paris of his dreams but a sordid nightmare of greed and murder, the film degenerates into crude, predictable melodrama (with Toren and Mayne hamming up the villainy, and Rains overdoing the naive bumpkin bit). TM

Man Who Would Be King, The

(John Huston, 1975, US) Sean Connery, Michael Caine, Saeed Jaffrey, Christopher Plummer, Karroum Ben Bouih, Jack May, Shakira Caine.
129 min.

Huston first mooted his Kipling adaptation in the '40s (for Gable and Bogart), but the wait proved more than worthwhile, with the imperialist parody of two conmen's rise to Kafiristan kingship gaining in resonance from its director's maturity. Connery and Caine (both excellent) become classic Huston overreachers, and echoes of *The Treasure of the Sierra Madre* and *Moby Dick* permeate the mythic yarn. Almost too lively to be dubbed a meditation on power. PT

Man With a Cloak, The

(Fletcher Markle, 1951, US) Barbara Stanwyck, Joseph Cotten, Louis Calhern, Leslie Caron, Jim Backus, Margaret Wycherly, Joe DeSantis.
81 min. b/w.

Intriguing period melodrama/Gothic thriller set in 1840s New York, with Caron as a young Frenchwoman arriving from Paris to beg a financial favour of her curmudgeonly grandfather (Calhern), and discovering that his housekeeper and butler (Stanwyck and DeSantis) are planning to kill the old man for his money. But dashing stranger Cotten steps in to help. Peppered with literary allusions (Poe in particular), shot on elegant MGM sets, highly atmospheric, and endowed with fine performances from a strong cast, it's well worth a watch. GA

Man With a Million

see Million Pound Note, The

Man With a Movie Camera (Chelovek s Kinoapparatom)

(Dziga Vertov, 1929, USSR)
6,004 ft. b/w.

An analytical account of the State of the (Soviet) Union at a crucial transitional stage, this is one of the most seminal and therefore controversial films in the history of cinema. Vertov's exhilarating and often hilarious exploration of the relations between cinema, actuality and history opened up all the issues Godard, the avant-gardes, and political film-makers have been wrestling with ever since. The film cannot easily be slotted into any single tradition, because it poses all the questions about the status of representation which dominant cinema represses. A truly radical and liberating work. PW

Man Without a Face, The

(Mel Gibson, 1993, US) Mel Gibson, Nick Stahl, Margaret Whitton, Fay Masterson, Gaby Hoffman, Geoffrey Lewis.
115 min.

A solidly crafted if ultimately unexceptional family film about the mentor-pupil relationship of a disfigured outcast and a fatherless 12-year-old boy. 'Hamburger Head' McLeod (Gibson) lives on an island, keeping visitors at bay with his Alsatian dog and his surly manner. Desperate to get into the military college attended by his missing father, Chuck Norstadt overcomes his fear and asks the former teacher to tutor him for the entrance exam. Nick Stahl is fine as the boy, but director Gibson could, perhaps, have dispensed with the redundant extracts from *Red River* and *The Merchant of Venice*. NF

Man Without a Star

(King Vidor, 1955, US) Kirk Douglas, Jeanne Crain, Claire Trevor, Richard Boone, Jay C Flippen, William Campbell, Mara Corday.
89 min.

A fine, edgy Western, handsomely shot by Russell Metty and beautifully paced by Vidor. A conventional range war plot is lent some of the sweaty unpredictability of *Duel in the Sun* by the love-hate relationship between Douglas, the cowboy with a pathological hatred of barbed wire, and Crain as the cattle baroness whose cause he eventually abandons in defence of individual liberties. Fine performances, not least from Claire Trevor as the good-hearted saloon girl, and Boone as the villainous gunslinger. TM

Man With the Deadly Lens, The

see Wrong Is Right

Man With the Golden Arm, The

(Otto Preminger, 1955, US) Frank Sinatra, Kim Novak, Eleanor Parker, Arnold Stang, Darren McGavin, Robert Strauss, Doro Merande.
119 min. b/w.

The first major Hollywood film on heroin addiction, a subject totally proscribed by the Hays Code. Sinatra is excellent as the ex-con junkie trying to make it as a jazz drummer but pulled into a world of pushing, and Kim Novak convinces as his enigmatic mistress; but the casting of Eleanor Parker as his supposedly wheelchair-ridden wife is miscalculated, and Preminger's evocation of the social milieu of the drug user/pusher shows little sign of first-hand observation. There are some great scenes, though, notably Sinatra's audition for a make-or-break drumming job, and the later scene where he suffers cold turkey in Novak's apartment. Notable for its jazz score, too. RM

Man With the Golden Gun, The

(Guy Hamilton, 1974, GB) Roger Moore, Christopher Lee, Britt Ekland, Maud Adams, Hervé Villechaise, Clifton James, Marc Lawrence, Bernard Lee.
125 min.

Formula film-making that relies entirely on its set piece chases (land and water), fights (gun, fist and karate), and stunted gestures toward glamorous romance, played off against a variety of travel poster Far Eastern locations. The script is banal, the gags and double entendres barely up to *Carry On* standard, and the whole dismally lacking in the style that the 007 series so desperately needs. Roger Moore's interpretation of Bond is blandness personified. It is left to Christopher Lee, playing a kind of Westernised, Dracula-esque Fu Manchu, to lend some semblance of style and suavity as Scaramanga, the man with a hideout in Red China and a hankering after the status of gentleman. VG

Man With the Green Carnation, The

see Trials of Oscar Wilde, The

Man with the X-Ray Eyes, The

see X – the Man with X-Ray Eyes

Man With Two Brains, The

(Carl Reiner, 1983, US) Steve Martin, Kathleen Turner, David Warner, Paul Benedict, Richard Brestoff, James Cromwell.
93 min.

Played by Steve Martin with the mixture of flat cynicism and crazed childishness which makes him a near successor to Jerry Lewis, brilliant brain surgeon Dr Hfuhruhurr falls foul of a wicked husband-collector (Turner), while still carrying on an affair with the talking brain of his dead wife, conveniently stored in a jar of purple fluid. Also in there somewhere are the crazed 'elevator' killer who turns out to be a very famous American TV chat-show host, the even more crazed Dr Necessiter (Warner, on his usual bonkers form transferring human brains into gorillas), and a condo apartment with an interior as large as Frankenstein's castle. It's a patchy affair, often hilarious, often thin, but it does contain a bewildering array of underwear adorning Ms Turner which would make a corpse sit up and steam. And any movie which contains the line 'Into the mud, scum-queen' is surely not totally devoid of cultural merit. CPea

Man, Woman and Child

(Dick Richards, 1982, US) Martin Sheen, Blythe Danner, Sebastian Dungan, David Hemmings, Craig T Nelson, Nathalie Nell.
100 min.

Drawn from an Erich *Love Story* Segal novel, this gives a predictably romantic account of the impact on a self-styled 'perfect marriage' of the existence of a 'love child'. The film is given an old-fashioned quality by making the child the progeny of a French dalliance by the husband, and falls into line by reserving the full weight of its carefully orchestrated poignancy for the 'lost' relationship of father and son. Sheen, as the père more or less manqué, bears up manfully. As the put-upon wife, Danner, a keenly stylish performer, is always a whole lot more than just watchable, and Hemmings is pudgily satyric as her chief temptation (she's a sucker for a Brit accent). VG

Manxman, The

(Alfred Hitchcock, 1928, GB) Carl Brisson, Anny Ondra, Malcolm Keen, Randle Ayrton, Clare Greet.
8,163 ft. b/w.
A distinctly un-Hitchcockian melodrama (his last real silent, since *Blackmail* came next), based on a best-selling novel by Hall Caine written in the 1890s. Its story is accordingly old-hat (a love triangle that reaches crisis when the woman's fisherman husband – wrongly believed dead – returns to find her pregnant with his best friend's child; but Hitch makes the most of his fine Isle of Man locations, while the frequent use of shots taken through windows anticipates the interest in voyeurism in his later work. GA

Mapantsula

(Oliver Schmitz, 1988, SAf) Thomas Mogotlane, Marcel Van Heerden, Thembi Mtshali, Dolly Rathebe, Peter Sephuma.
104 min
At last, a South African movie about Panic in the streets! The streets are those of the suburbs, shanty-towns and shopping-malls of Johannesburg, and Panic is a small-time crook who keeps his nose out of politics. The trouble is that politics touches everyone on the streets of Jo'burg, as Panic discovers when he is picked up by the police for questioning and dumped in a cell with a bunch of township militants, precisely the people he most despises and fears. White director Schmitz and black co-writer/star Mogotlane wisely leave Panic's future to our imagination, and concentrate instead on getting inside the skin of a scuzzy but not dislikeable criminal. (The title, incidently, is the township argot for 'spiv'.) The result has much the same energy that Lino Brocka brings to his Filipino slum melodramas, and it gets far closer to the sights, sounds, smells and rhythms of Soweto life than an entire Attenborough of white liberal movies. Needless to say, it's banned from SA cinema screens. TR

Map of the Human Heart

(Vincent Ward, 1992, GB/Aust/Fr/Can) Jason Scott Lee, Patrick Bergin, Jeanne Moreau, Anne Parillaud, John Cusack.
109 min.
Ward's ambitious epic love story covers two continents and three decades and, its execution apart, could have sprung from one of those fat romantic chronicles written for the typing pool. But Ward has an extravagant visual imagination so that even the more outlandish scenes, like the hero and heroine finally consummating their passion on a half-deflated barrage balloon, linger in the mind. Where lack of money cramps his vision of WWII bombing raids on Germany, the director achieves a pleasing shorthand with lighting. Map-maker Bergin lands his biplane in Canada's Arctic Circle and befriends an Inuit boy with TB, flying him to a Montreal hospital, where he becomes best friends with a half-caste Indian girl on Moreau's ward. Ten years later, the friendship has blossomed into love. Fate intervenes at an indecent rate, serving up plenty of misunderstandings, but the mise-en-scène is stunning. Go with the floe. BC

Marat/Sade, The

see Persecution and Assassination of Jean-Paul Marat...

Marathon Man

(John Schlesinger, 1976, US) Dustin Hoffman, Laurence Olivier, Roy Scheider, William Devane, Marthe Keller, Fritz Weaver, Richard Bright, Marc Lawrence.
126 min.
Adapted by William Goldman from his own novel, this thriller is quite effective in its basic set pieces, even if the overall thrust seems a trifle ponderous. Hoffman plays a graduate student catapulted into a confrontation with grim former concentration camp Jew-killer Szell (Olivier, giving a rather circumscribed if impeccable performance). The pointlessly obscure construction and numerous loose ends make the triviality of the plot all the more annoying, and Schlesinger should have resisted the grossly over-used Central Park locations. Best moment is a compelling night sequence centering on the use of dentistry as a grisly method of torture. DP

Maravillas

(Manuel Gutiérrez Aragón, 1980, Sp) Fernando Fernan Gomez, Cristina Marcos, Enrique Sanfrancisco.
An abrasive curio that begs anything but art-movie reverence from its audience, this slyly surreal patchwork stitches together 'problem pic' incidentals with provocative glee and no hint of a moralistic message. The culture-clash incongruity of Nina Hagen's 'African Reggae' and an image of walking along a precipice sets the tone for a narrative that attaches itself to a 16-year-old girl's encounters wth casual crime, a corrupt church, a charmed circle of godfatherly Jews, a father lazily resigned to porn and yoghurt, and a Judas identified with electric-chair icons Caryl Chessman and Gary Gilmore. Its inconsequentiality appearing alternately savage and absurd, with even the apocalypse conjured only in a kids' TV cartoon, the result is admirably irresponsible. PT

March Comes in Like a Lion (San-Gatsu no Lion)

(Hitoshi Yazaki, 1990, Jap) Yoshiko Yura, Bang-Ho Cho, Koen Okumura, Shoko Saito, Meika Seri, Takeshi Naito.
118 min.
Or, perhaps, love among the ruins. In present-day Tokyo, a waste land of tenements prey to decrepitude and demolition, 'Ice' (Yura) decides to collect Haruo (Cho), the young man she's set her heart on, from the hospital where he's being treated for amnesia. A little lie is needed to entice him back to the apartment she's found for them: she tells him she's his lover, neglecting to add that she's also his sister. With no recollections to suggest otherwise, he goes along with her – but how long before his memory returns? With its long, static, carefully composed takes, taciturn script and tantalisingly ambivalent tone, Yazaki's beautifully matter-of-fact study of incestuous longing is an engrossing, sexy and remarkably tender movie. Crucially, it eschews both easy judgments and fake sentimentality; indeed, there's a droll, deadpan humour at work, most noticeably in the frequent sight gags. At the same time, however, the evocative use of metaphors ensures that the general air of detachment makes not for a dry, academic exercise, but a poetic tale of a fragile, blossoming romance that's finally both subtly subversive and, thanks to the charismatic central performances, deeply affecting. GA

March or Die

(Dick Richards, 1977, GB) Gene Hackman, Terence Hill, Catherine Deneuve, Max von Sydow, Ian Holm, Marcel Bozzuffi, Jack O'Halloran.
107 min.
An inconsistently-toned conflation of *Morocco*, *Beau Geste* and *The Four Feathers* that can't decide whether to take its Foreign Legion clichés at face value or to parody them. Hill's hard luck hero is OK, and Holm refines his oily Arab party piece, but as in so many Lew Grade confections, most of the cast are pure window-dressing. Despite Richards' helmsmanship, a yarn which obstinately refuses to rip. PT

Marge, La (The Streetwalker)

(Walerian Borowczyk, 1976, Fr) Sylvia Kristel, Joe Dallesandro, Mireille Audibert, Denis Manuel, André Falcon, Louise Chevalier.
91 min.
Saddled with an ungainly English title – even ignoring Barthes' specific use of *la marge* to denote the erotic midriff margin between two items of clothing, 'the edge' or 'on the fringe' would have been closer – Borowczyk's adaptation of an André Pieyre de Mandiargues novel works hard to create a private hallucinatory world out of modern Paris and the twilight district of the Rue St Denis. An unexpectedly well-groomed Dallesandro plays a happy husband who, learning of the sudden death back home of his wife and child, turns to the obsessive pursuit of a beautiful Dutch whore (Kristel). It's a frustrating battle of extraordinary details – the prostitutes' glistening wardrobe, the remarkable '70s soundtrack – over an unconvincing narrative and flat acting. Borowczyk delivers palpable moments of erotic fascination, but they surface fitfully in an environment over which the director clearly had insufficient control. DT

Margaret's Museum

(Mort Ransen, 1995, Can/GB) Helena Bonham Carter, Clive Russell, Craig Olejnik, Kate Nelligan, Kenneth Walsh, Andrea Morris.
100 min.
Nova Scotia, the late '40s: Margaret MacNeil (Bonham Carter), a child-woman, struggles against the inexorable pull of the coal mines. With father and one brother already gobbled up, Margaret and her mother (Nelligan) vow to preserve the youngest male in the family (Olejnik). And when Margaret falls in love with Neil (Russell) – a fiddle-tickling, Gaelic-crooning giant – she makes it her mission to safeguard him, too. Clearly attracted by all things Celtic, writer/director Ransen makes much of the siren call of the dead, Margaret's primitive wedding and Cape Breton's boozy yarn-spinning locals. Too much: he rubs our nose in lots of carefully placed grit, but essentially this is 'pixies skipping in the moonlight' territory. All in all, the enterprise seems embarrassingly amateurish. But lo! Half-an-hour before the end comes a miracle. As intricately Gothic, as sexually bizarre as a Leonora Carrington dreamscape, Margaret's final attempt to preserve her loved ones dismembers the emotions. Is she damned or blessed? You're too stunned to tell. Visceral details float glutinously and all the while a feverishly numb Bonham Carter finally achieves a level of concentration that makes the scenes between her and Nelligan electric. Having been dismally slight, the film then becomes almost too complex and dark to bear, for it's hard to imagine a more exhilarating testament to the reality of poverty and the utter impotence of love. CO'Su

Margie

(Henry King, 1946, US) Jeanne Crain, Glenn Langan, Lynn Bari, Esther Dale, Hobart Cavanaugh, Alan Young, Barbara Lawrence, Conrad Janis.
94 min.
Harmless nostalgia as Crain passes on to her daughter tales of her own high school years in the Ohio of the late '20s, when the arrival of handsome French teacher Langan sent every girl's hormones into a tizzy. An unfortunate running gag involving knicker elastic, a crucial meeting at the skating rink, and much use of the popular songs of the time ease all and sundry towards an upbeat final reel. TJ

Maria's Lovers

(Andrei Konchalovsky, 1984, US) Nastassja Kinski, John Savage, Robert Mitchum, Keith Carradine, Anita Morris, Bud Cort, Karen Young.
109 min.
Soldiers returning from the wars is a perennially hardy theme for revealing not only the mental ruinations of conflict, but also the way in which home is never quite the place you left behind. Savage, as the Slav soldier returning to his rural Pennsylvania home after World War II, is unable to face the reality of the woman he has kept stored in his dreams (Kinski), and he has to undergo further exile and debasement before he can return to his community once more whole. It may be Konchalovsky's own exile which makes some scenes waver on an edge of uncertainty, but there is still much to admire: filming the American heartlands so that they look like the Steppes is no mean achievement, nor is conjuring a very moving love scene between Mitchum and Kinski. CPea

Mariachi, El

see El Mariachi

Mari de la Coiffeuse, Le

see Hairdresser's Husband, The

Marie

(Roger Donaldson, 1985, US) Sissy Spacek, Jeff Daniels, Keith Szarabajka, Morgan Freeman, Fred Thompson, Lisa Banes.
112 min.
Marie is a single parent who supports her three kids and invalid mum through college, and braves the medical establishment in diagnosing her youngest child's illness; then, zooming to speedy prominence as chairwoman of the Tennessee parole board, she single-handedly purges the body politic of the sweaty parasites in

its bosom. And it's all true. Blessed are the pure in heart, but also deadly dull. Spacek is competent as her usual embattled heroine, but Marie could use a few warts, and as hot political exposés go, local corruption in Tennessee seems of less than pressing concern. However, Donaldson directs with fluid, docudramatic urgency, and there are further compensations in the support performances. SJo

Marie – a Hungarian Legend
see Tavaszi Zápor

Mariée était en Noir, La
see Bride Wore Black, The

Marie in the City
see Marie s'en va-t-en ville

Marie, légende hongroise
see Tavaszi Zápor

Marie s'en va-t-en ville (Marie in the City)
(Marquise Lepage, 1987, Can) Frédérique Collin, Geneviève Lenoir, Denis Lavasseur.
75 min.
A 13-year-old runaway holes up in the garish Montreal apartment of an out-of-luck, coke-addicted hooker: no surprises here, but Lenoir, the tomboy determined not to show the knocks of life, and Collin, the middle-aged professional determined not to hang up her wigs, add a dash of vinegar to a very sentimental script. JPy

Marigolds in August
(Ross Devenish, 1979, SAf) Winston Ntshona, John Kani, Athol Fugard, Joyce Hesha, Abel Ntshinga.
87 min.
An examination of the 'invisibility' of blacks in South Africa caused by conditioned white indifference; an invisibility which means poverty and unemployment. The film is set in and around Schoenmakerskop, an opulently sleepy, immaculately manicured whites-only seaside hamlet just outside Port Elizabeth, scriptwriter Athol Fugard's home town. Its central characters all have their real-life counterparts: Daan (Ntshona), the crafty, suspicious but fundamentally good-natured jobbing gardener, jealously protecting his economic lifeline; Melton (Kani), desperately and stubbornly courageous as he searches for work; and Paulus Olifant (Fugard), a nomadic snake-catcher, scavenger and bush-philosopher. All, in one way or another, are outlawed by white society, and gradually realise that this makes them brothers. A powerful, pessimistic, but bracing film. SC

Marilyn
(No director credited, 1963, US) commentary: Don Medford; narrator: Rock Hudson.
83 min. b/w & col.
A Fox compilation in which Rock Hudson turns up at a Hollywood projection room to show himself some clips from Marilyn Monroe's films. It's reasonably comprehensive, but there's one snag: Fox could use only their own material, so you won't see (or even hear any reference to), for example, UA's Some Like It Hot or MGM's The Asphalt Jungle. You will see All About Eve, Monkey Business, Niagara, Gentlemen Prefer Blondes, River of No Return, Bus Stop, and the unfinished Something's Got to Give (released with Doris Day as Move Over, Darling).

Marilyn – The Untold Story
(John Flynn/Jack Arnold/Lawrence Schiller, 1980, US) Catherine Hicks, Richard Basehart, Frank Converse, John Ireland, Viveca Lindfors, Jason Miller, Sheree North.
120 min.
This made-for-TV movie (originally running 150 minutes) offers few fresh insights into the well-worn topic of Monroe's life and character. The depressingly familiar treatment portrays the stereotypical helpless dumb blonde, in search of a family she never had, vainly attempting to become a serious actress, with little suggestion either of her intelligence and courage, or of the destructive condescension of the men she lived and worked with. Catherine Hicks' performance is proficient enough, if woefully lacking in charis-

ma. But the plodding script rarely transcends banality and ludicrous name-dropping ('Did Mr Kennedy ring?'), while many of the supporting cameos are downright embarrassing. GA

Marius
(Alexander Korda, 1931, Fr) Raimu, Pierre Fresnay, Orane Demazis, Alida Rouffe, Fernand Charpin, Robert Vattier.
125 min. b/w.
The first of a trilogy set in Marcel Pagnol's home town of Marseilles (to be followed by Fanny and César), this centres on the decision of Marius (Fresnay) to answer the call of the sea, despite opposition from his father César (Raimu), and despite his love for Fanny (Demazis). Some sniffy critics thought that playwright Pagnol shouldn't have dabbled in celluloid at all: Richard Griffith, in The Film Since Then, considered his output 'not part of a purposeful cinema'. In place of purpose, these films display such old-fashioned virtues as truth to life and boundless humanity; they also contain some of the fruitiest acting under the sun, particularly from Raimu. This first instalment, notably more boisterous than the others, was directed by Korda on a whistle-stop tour of France; by the end of the year he had crossed the Channel, and the rest, as they say, is history. GB

Marius et Jeannette
(Robert Guédiguian, 1997, Fr) Ariane Ascaride, Gérard Meylan, Pascale Roberts, Jacques Boudet, Frédérique Bonnal, Jean-Pierre Darroussin.
102 min.
Set in l'Estaque, an impoverished, industrialised area of Marseilles, this funny, tender, enchanting film starts as if it's going to be a familiar misfits-meeting-cute romance. Soon after her feisty temper costs her her supermarket job, single mother Jeannette (Ascaride, the writer/director's wife) embarks on a relationship with the equally wacky Marius (Meylan), a taciturn security guard at a disused cement works. He's accepted by her kids and friends, but when he disappears for a few days, Jeannette suspects his no-show is simply another example of male unreliability, and it's left to her neighbours to investigate. In fact, while the faltering central romance gives the film a semblance of narrative structure, Guédiguian's prime concern is how community and friendship make economic and emotional hardship bearable. That Marius is called 'Marius' is probably no accident, since the celebratory account of working class life in all its variety recalls Pagnol's classic Marseilles trilogy, albeit without the overheated theatricality and pathos. Less love story than love letter to a particular, Mediterranean way of life, this is peopled with credible individuals as proud, perverse and needy as they are brave, tolerant and likeable. GA

Marjoe
(Howard Smith/Sarah Kernochan, 1972, US) Marjoe Gortner, Sister Allie Taylor, the Rev. Ray Boatwright, Mrs Ruby Boatwright.
88 min.
Marjoe Gortner – the name's an amalgam of Mary and Joseph – began his career as a revivalist preacher at the age of four, broke off in his teens, but returned to the Church some years later, both eyes open and on the make. This documentary reveals that Marjoe really wants to belong to the Deity of Showbiz Rock; each night he preaches the word of the Lord to blue-rinsed motherly matrons who shudder in ecstasy and reach for their purses because he moves so sexily in the name of the Lord. Marjoe talks frankly, even cynically, to the camera about his profession: the gimmicks, the money, the qualms, the hypocrisy involved. Only gradually do we realise that he is manipulating us and the film-makers just as readily as he used his congregations. Marjoe wants to be famous and a star (he did get started, but never really made it). What better way of advertising than in this documentary where he shows himself the Lord's hipster putting down the squares, rejecting preaching and declaring himself up for offer? CPe

Marked for Death
(Dwight H Little, 1990, US) Steven Seagal, Basil Wallace, Keith David, Tom Wright, Joanna Pacula, Elizabeth Gracen, Bette Ford, Jimmy Cliff.
93 min.

'I've become what I most despise,' opines action-man Seagal in the risibly philosophical opening to this sub-standard bash-'em-up pic. A former narc agent, he makes a spiritual voyage home in search of his 'good side'. Unsurprisingly, his fascination for all things dark soon overwhelms his new-found pacifism, and he renews his struggle against the forces of evil: black dealers under the satanic influence of blue-eyed rasta Screwface (Wallace). The film is wretchedly incoherent; unable to orchestrate action sequences, Little leaves the knock-kneed nihilist flailing in impotent rage to a hideous score. As the climax approaches, the entire shebang ups stumps to Jamaica, where Jimmy Cliff makes a cameo appearance, and the hero's buddy (David) delivers a conciliatory speech about the native kids being driven to crime by their deprived upbringing. An ugly movie, with lousy wardrobe to match. MK

Marked Woman
(Lloyd Bacon, 1937, US) Bette Davis, Humphrey Bogart, Lola Lane, Isabel Jewell, Jane Bryan, Eduardo Ciannelli, Allen Jenkins, Mayo Methot.
99 min. b/w.
A markedly different sort of gangster movie, this is a film à clef, 'torn from the headlines' in the best Warners tradition. In 1936, Special Prosecutor Thomas E Dewey put Lucky Luciano behind bars on prostitution charges. The case hinged on the testimony of three 'working girls' who tied the mob boss directly to the vice operation. The names have been changed, and the less salubrious details swept under the carpet, but to all intents and purposes Bogart plays Dewey (a rare appearance on the right side of the law), Ciannelli is Luciano, and Davis is the prostitute 'Cokey Flo' (here, nightclub hostess Mary Dwight). What really makes the film stand out is its focus on the women, identifying Davis and her girlfriends as the unsung heroines of a cruel economic and social trap; even at their moment of triumph, the girls' future is defined by an uncertain and unsettling fog. Davis shows her mettle, smartly directed by Bacon, and there is strong support, right down to Bogie's wife at the time, Mayo Methot. The hardboiled screenplay is by Robert Rossen and Abem Finkel, who couldn't know that a year later Flo and the others would admit they had perjured themselves for money and legal protection. TCh

Mark of the Vampire
(Tod Browning, 1935, US) Lionel Barrymore, Elizabeth Allan, Bela Lugosi, Lionel Atwill, Jean Hersholt, Carol Borland, Donald Meek.
61 min. b/w.
A remake of Browning's own silent London After Midnight (transported to Czechoslovakia), this semi-parodic vampire thriller creaks here and there, but still has enough style to warrant an honoured place among early horror films. Lashings of lore and atmosphere (strange noises, dancing peasants, bats, spiders and cobwebs) embellish a far-fetched but amusing tale of strange deaths at a sinister castle. It's hard to decide who overacts the most, with Barrymore, Atwill and Lugosi all candidates, though the 'surprise' denouement provides Lugosi with an excuse of a sort. But a real touch of class is present in James Wong Howe's magnificent photography, not to mention Carol Borland's stunning apparition as a vampire. GA

Mark of Zorro, The
(Rouben Mamoulian, 1940, US) Tyrone Power, Linda Darnell, Basil Rathbone, Gale Sondergaard, Eugene Pallette, J Edward Bromberg, Montagu Love.
93 min. b/w.
A superb swashbuckler, less athletic than the silent Fairbanks version but making up for it on the romantic side, and cleverly choreographing its action scenes until they whisk along like a ballet. Above all it looks terrific, with Mamoulian indulging his passion for shadows, while Arthur Miller's camerawork makes striking use of the contrasting white Spanish architecture and black of Zorro's cape and costume. Rathbone, rarely without a rapier in his hand and forever ferociously limbering up ('He's always stabbing at something' someone wearily complains) until he is summarily skewered in the magnificent final duel, is outstanding as Zorro's malevolent adversary. TM

MARKS (MARKS no Yama)

(Yoichi Sai, 1995, Jap) Kiichi Nakai, Masato Hagiwara, Masato Furuoya, Ittoku Kishibe, Takuzo Kakuno.
139 min.
Bafflingly complex but totally assured in tone, style and pace, this adaptation of a celebrated novel by Kaoru Takamura starts out visceral, turns political and winds up metaphysical. The plot conflates a series of seemingly random murders in Tokyo with two dark histories: the fate of a young man orphaned when his parents killed themselves, and the secrets of a college mountaineering club which served as the front for a cell of gay right-wing fanatics. Nakai's down-at-heel detective gives it a very likeable centre. Full of images and scenes which stick in the mind, this is Korean-Japanese director Sai's best film to date. TR

Marian

(Petr Václav, 1996, Czech Republic) Stefan Ferko, Milan Cifra, Radek Holub, Jaroslava Vyslouziklová.
105 min.
This moving first feature observes the institutionalisation of a gypsy boy, taken from his mother at the age of three, with a sharp realist's eye. Ferko (as the young Marian) and Cifra (as the older) give superb performances as 'the different boy' whose experiences made him first attempt suicide, and then the murder of a warden (who treated him as a temporary pet), before reform school, prison and then faltering steps into the equally cruel, outside world. The documentary roots of director and co-writer Václav are evident, but his emotionally expressionist use of landscape (the torrential river, the snow-bound woods) and mature, if demanding, use of narrative shorthand show him to be a film-maker of all-round talent. WH

Marlene

(Maximilian Schell, 1983, W Ger) Annie Albers, Bernard Hall, Marta Rakosnik, Patricia Schell, William von Stranz.
94 min.
How do you make a documentary about a legendary star who will talk but not be filmed (presumably because time has not been altogether kind to the celebrated image)? Schell takes no easy routes, and if the result borders on the pretentious, it rewards repeated viewings. As a starting point, he had twelve hours of taped conversations in which he and Dietrich can be heard arguing, eventually coming to verbal blows: throughout, Dietrich responds with defiant assertions, frequent dismissals of the past and her own performances, a reluctance to reveal much new. Schell supplies the necessary biography and film clips – plus some cruelly revelatory footage of her later stage performances – while brilliantly turning the documentary into a reflection on its own creation. DT

Marlowe

(Paul Bogart, 1969, US) James Garner, Gayle Hunnicutt, Carroll O'Connor, Rita Moreno, Sharon Farrell, William Daniels, Jackie Coogan, HM Wynant, Bruce Lee.
95 min.
Quite surprising that Chandler's *The Little Sister* – if memory serves, the only Marlowe novel to deal at all with the Hollywood film colony – had never been filmed before. This snappy and stylish update is certainly watchable, even if it lacks the definitive status of *The Big Sleep* (first version) and *The Long Goodbye*. Garner's rumpled charm is engaging enough as he takes on a missing persons case and finds himself sinking into ever more murky waters, while Paul Bogart's solid direction and some fine supporting performances (particularly O'Connor) help to create an atmosphere of almost universal corruptibility. Surprisingly, even the inclusion of some fashionable martial arts – courtesy of Bruce Lee – actually works rather well. GA

Marnie

(Alfred Hitchcock, 1964, US) Sean Connery, Tippi Hedren, Diane Baker, Martin Gabel, Louise Latham, Alan Napier, Mariette Hartley, Bruce Dern.
130 min.
Often criticised for its lack of suspense – a quality that underlines its similarity to *Vertigo* – this is neither thriller nor psychodrama, even though it deals with wealthy Connery's marriage to frigid, kleptomaniac Hedren. Rather, it's a perverse romance which seeks less to explain its eponymous heroine's 'problems' than to examine a relationship based upon extraordinary motivations: Connery, in deciding to marry the woman who has stolen from him and betrayed his trust, is clearly as emotionally confused and unfulfilled as the woman whose mind and past he attempts to investigate. As such, it's as sour a vision of male-female interaction as *Vertigo*, though far less bleak and universal in its implications. That said, it's still thrilling to watch, lush, cool and oddly moving; though the claims of some devotees, arguing that the obviously artificial backdrops are a Brechtian device to make plain Marnie's alienation, are hard to swallow. GA

Marooned

(John Sturges, 1969, US) Gregory Peck, Richard Crenna, David Janssen, James Franciscus, Gene Hackman, Lee Grant, Nancy Kovack, Mariette Hartley, Scott Brady.
133 min.
One of Sturges' better films, an extremely realistic space movie about a NASA accident, which had the misfortune to go out on release at precisely the time when the astronauts of Apollo 13 were battling with an exactly similar emergency. Faced with this real-life competition, the film was undeservedly buried. The widescreen effects are first-rate, as is Peck as the embattled controller, and the suspense builds remorselessly to a neat conclusion. DP

Marquis

(Henri Xhonneux, 1989, Bel/Fr) Philippe Bizot, Bien de Moor, Gabrielle Van Damme, Olivier Dechaveau, Bernard Cogneaux, Pierre Decuypère.
83min.
In this tribute to the Marquis de Sade, the original Mr Whippy of *belles lettres* is a dreamy-eyed spaniel who spends his time in the Bastille engaging in dispute with his winsome willy, an amiably philosophical member called Colin. French satirist and cartoonist Roland Topor designed and co-wrote this strange Revolutionary romp with Xhonneux. With the cast performing in half-animal, half-human panto drag, the film's principal novelty is to stage the events leading up to the fall of the Bastille as 'Carry On Beatrix Potter'. This the makers do very well, with disarmingly gruesome masks and atmospheric period décor. It's perhaps too burlesque to be disturbing, and there's a weary Gallic saltiness to the dream sequences. De Sade gets a rather easy ride, too, portrayed as content to scribble his sprawling libertine yarns rather than yield to Colin's priapic promptings. But it's a considerable oddity that manages to be witty, thoroughly obscene, and rather endearing all at once. JRo

Marquise von O..., Die (The Marquise of O)

(Eric Rohmer, 1976, WGer/Fr) Edith Clever, Bruno Ganz, Peter Lühr, Edda Seippel, Otto Sander, Ezzo Huber, Bernhard Frey.
107 min.
Based on a novella by Heinrich von Kleist set at the time of the Napoleonic Wars. A virtuous widow (Clever), saved from rape and then, while asleep, raped by her rescuer (Ganz), is cast off by her family when she gives birth to a child and proclaims her innocence, only to be then courted by her 'heroic rescuer', whom she doesn't know is the father of her child. In the course of the story, Kleist sets out in a most ironically literary fashion a series of arguments about the place of women in society. Rohmer's great achievement is that it is this, rather than merely the story, that he has brought to the screen, recreating and making even more ironic Kleist's literary written conversations, and opting, in his colour scheme, sets and camerawork, for a style that hovers between formalism and realism, and so further distances the viewer from the characters. PH

Marriage of Maria Braun, The (Die Ehe der Maria Braun)

(Rainer Werner Fassbinder, 1978, WGer) Hanna Schygulla, Klaus Löwitsch, Ivan Desny, Gottfried John, Gisela Uhlen, Günther Lamprecht.
119 min.
Knowing in advance that Fassbinder considers the institution of marriage to be the most insidious trap that mankind has yet devised for itself doesn't prepare you for *The Marriage of Maria Braun*. It opens in 1943 as an air raid hits Maria and Hermann Braun's wedding ceremony, and closes with another explosion, highly ambiguous in effect and implication. In between, Hermann goes missing on the Russian front, serves years in jail, and emigrates to the States, while Maria sails through unruffled, acquiring wealth and position pending his return. It is at once Fassbinder's most conventional and elusive film: that final explosion keeps ricocheting long after it's over. TR

Marriage Story (Kyolhon Iyagi)

(Kim Ui-Seok, 1992, SKor) Choi Min-Su, Shim Hye-Jin.
101 min.
The 'honeymoon period' ends the night he asks her to give him a blow-job in the car. She realises that she's been getting less than him from the sex, and the marriage starts going downhill. Her professional progress (she graduates from dubbing foreign movies – Kim Novak in *Vertigo*! – to working in radio plays) boosts her self-assurance. In Korea, though, a wife who puts herself at the same level as her husband is effectively ending the marriage. A key film for Korea's 'new cinema' (a huge domestic hit, it inspired a flood of imitations), this is an unerringly accurate account of feminist stirrings in a very patriarchal society. It's also really funny. TR

Married Couple, A

(Allan King, 1969, Can) Billy Edwards, Antoinette Edwards, Bogart Edwards.
112 min.
Cinema not quite *vérité* as a camera crew camp out in a couple's house and watch their not quite every move. A frightening picture of the acquisitive society, but on the whole the bland camera fails to probe deep enough to make either good documentary or interesting escapism.

Married to the Mob

(Jonathan Demme, 1988, US) Michelle Pfeiffer, Mathew Modine, Dean Stockwell, Mercedes Reuhl, Alec Baldwin, Trey Wilson, Joan Cusack.
104 min.
When philandering Mafia hit-man 'Cucumber' Frank de Marco is killed by his boss Tony 'The Tiger' Russo, his widow Angela (Pfeiffer) decides to abandon her stockbroker-belt home (bursting with stolen goods) and start anew with a job and a dingy room on the Lower East Side. Easier said than done: obsessively amorous Tony (Stockwell) courts her with a vengeance, while FBI agent Mike Downey (Modine) suspects that she planned Frank's death with Tony. If the slim plot of Demme's romantic black comedy lacks the outrageous panache and exhilarating twists of *Something Wild*, the film nevertheless delights through its sheer good-humoured glee in all that is kitschy or off-the-wall, and its wealth of inventive incidental details. While it's all relentlessly shallow, the performances, music and gaudy visuals provide a fizzy vitality for which many other directors would give their right arm. Amazingly, for all its hip anarchy, it's finally an oddly old-fashioned slice of entertainment. Preston Sturges might have approved.GA

Married Woman, A

see Femme Mariée, Une

Marrying Kind, The

(George Cukor, 1952, US) Judy Holliday, Aldo Ray, Madge Kennedy, Mickey Shaughnessy, Griff Barnett.
93 min. b/w.
A poignant little tragi-comedy, scripted by Ruth Gordon and Garson Kanin, about a lower middle-class couple (Holliday and Ray) whose marriage cannot withstand the pressures against them. The divorce court listens first to the husband's story, then to the wife's, and then the judge arrives at some notion of 'the truth'. It's contrived, but the film's critique of traditional gender roles within marriage is still sharp, and Judy Holliday shows an unexpected depth. TCh

Marrying Man, The
(aka Too Hot to Handle)

(Jerry Rees, 1991, US) Kim Basinger, Alec
Baldwin, Robert Loggia, Elizabeth Shue,
Armand Assante, Paul Reiser, Fisher Stevens.
116 min.
Handsome playboy Charley Pearl (Baldwin) has
finally opted for stability, and is set to marry the
respectable daughter (Shue) of a movie mogul.
But on the way to his bachelor party, he is smitten by sultry nightclub singer Vicki (Basinger),
and they embark on a tempestuous, on-off relationship which encompasses four marriages. It's
hard to spot vintage Neil Simon in his screenplay
for this indulgent comedy, which exhaustively
examines the premise that no one lover can provide both passion *and* emotional security. The
action kicks off in 1948, a period which throws
up various characters supposed to remind us of
real-life celebrity counterparts; such comparisons, however, are lost amid the clichéd dialogue
uttered by Charley's adoring entourage of showbiz buddies, whose apparent function is to make
the not-so-loving couple appear more exciting
and glamorous. Alas, to little effect. CM

Marry Me! Marry Me!

see Mazel Tov ou le mariage

Mars Attacks!

(Tim Burton, 1996, US) Glenn Close, Michael J
Fox, Pierce Brosnan, Danny DeVito, Annette
Bening, Jack Nicholson, Martin Short, Sarah
Jessica Parker, Rod Steiger, Tom Jones, Lukas
Haas, Sylvia Sidney, Paul Winfield, Pam Grier,
Joe Don Baker, Jerzy Skolimowski, Barbet
Schroeder.
106 min.
Earth's in peril, yet again, and the US President
must call the shots. This time, though, we're
rooting for the space invaders. Tim Burton's film
is the most subversive big-budget Hollywood
production in years, a splenetic satire which gleefully trashes contemporary culture – politics, science and religion, the army, TV, food, music, even
money. Unfortunately, it's not very good. The
tacky design undoubtedly cost a fortune, and
there's a real perversity in casting superstars to
ham it up in homage to Ed Wood. The anarchy
is sometimes inspired (Burton incinerates
Congress, movie stars and doves with equal
abandon – he loves playing Godzilla), but much
of the film is flat and cripplingly indulgent. It
feels nearly half an hour too long, and Nicholson,
in a double role, is just too much. It's a personal
work, but not a mature one. It didn't hit home at
the US box-office, but the reviews have been surprisingly accommodating. In that sense, this sour,
prefabricated cult movie has the last laugh – and
I'm afraid the joke's on us. TCh

Marseillaise, La

(Jean Renoir, 1937, Fr) Pierre Renoir, Lise
Delamare, Andrex, Edmond Ardisson, Nadia
Sibirskaia, Louis Jouvet, Léon Larive, Gaston
Modot, Julien Carette.
145 min. b/w.
A heroically romantic interpretation of the events
leading up to the French Revolution; its postula-
tion of an alternative to nationalism vs monar-
chism is obviously closely related to the Popular
Front period during which the film was made.
But this is also something that, along with
Renoir's sweeping emotional populism, tends to
distance us from much of the film. However, even
if you're not particularly attuned to Renoir's values (simplicity, nature, etc), he is always sufficiently shrewd in his analysis of the aristocracy
for those sections of the film to have an air of
authentic and haunting decadence. It is a relief,
too, to see the lingering archaism of the earlier
sections of the film swept away in an astonishing last third of quiet power.

Marseille Contract, The

(Robert Parrish, 1974, GB/Fr) Michael Caine,
Anthony Quinn, James Mason, Alexandra
Stewart, Maureen Kerwin, Marcel Bozzuffi,
Catherine Rouvel, Maurice Ronet.
90 min.
The old routine: tough cop, bent colleagues, dope
shipment, hired killer...varied by moving the location to Paris and Marseille, by making Quinn a
top US Embassy official, and by making his best
buddy the contract killer out to get the untouch-

able 'respected member of society'. Despite the
routine situation and the routine casting of Quinn,
Caine and Mason (Caine actually perking the film
into some semblance of interest), Parrish does
manage to infiltrate a little intelligence into the
proceedings from time to time. But he can't shift
the nagging sense of numbing over-familiarity.
VG

Martha

(Rainer Werner Fassbinder, 1973, WGer)
Margit Carstensen, Karlheinz Böhm, Gisela
Fackeldey, Adrian Hoven, Peter Chatel.
95 min.
The everyday fascism Fassbinder dissects often
rests on the simple observation that there are elements of sado-masochism even in such
respectable bourgeois relationships as true
romance and happy-ever-after marriage. Here he
takes the staples of the Sirk melodrama (love at
first sight, a ferris wheel courtship, a honeymoon
drive) and stands them on their heads, combining '40s costumes and movie references with
recognisably real locations and high colour photography. He forces to their logical extremes the
attitudes implicit in the woman's weepie and the
little woman's traditional craving for a strong and
competent man, pushing a sentimental romance
into a high camp study of s-m, full of images of
vampirism, claustrophobia and haunted house
genre movies. With no explicit references to a
world beyond the screen, with indulgently aesthetic settings and outlandishly theatrical performances (notably from Carstensen as the
perennially hapless victim), he creates a dazzling
baroque abstraction with unsettling relevance to
even the most mundane domestic partnerships.
JD

Martha & Ethel

(Jyll Johnstone, 1993, US)
77 min. b/w & col.
The nannies profiled in director Johnstone and
co-writer Barbara Ettinger's absorbing documentary – Ethel, a black woman born in the
Deep South, who worked for the Ettingers; and
Martha, Johnstone's mother substitute, a former
Rhine maiden who emigrated to the US in the
mid-'30s – couldn't come from more different
worlds, or embody more polarised values. Yet
their lives ran curiously parallel. The film cuts
between both them, incorporating archive
footage (*Mädchen in Uniform* for Martha), photographs and contemporary music, together
with extensive interviews and reflections from
the nannies' now grown-up charges and employers. Ettinger takes Ethel back to South Carolina;
Martha, likewise, is taken back to Oberkirch
where, in an open carriage, she's feted by the
mayor and dances a jig of joy that was a long
time coming. The two women were born a couple of years apart in the first decade of the century; each struck out alone in her 30s, almost
single-handedly raising someone else's large
family. Seeing them in their 90s brings home
very powerfully what can only be described as
the workings of destiny in our lives. WH

Martha – Meet Frank, Daniel
and Laurence

(Nick Hamm, 1998, GB) Monica Potter, Rufus
Sewell, Tom Hollander, Joseph Fiennes, Ray
Winstone, Deborah Weston.
88 min.
A love story in which three men take just two
days to fall for the same woman. Martha (Potter),
a blonde American, flies into London almost
empty-handed, ready to start the rest of her life.
The lads are childhood friends, now grown somewhat apart. Daniel (Hollander) is an unconvincingly successful but convincingly brazen music
executive with a jet setting lifestyle and ego.
Frank (Sewell) is an unemployed actor seemingly more motivated to spite Daniel than to find
work. Caught in the middle, Laurence (Fiennes)
is the shy, sensitive type, who teaches bridge to
old ladies, finds his pals frustratingly self-
absorbed, and generally looks flushed and
uncomfortable as if wondering quite how he got
into all this. Nothing special. NB

Martin

(George A Romero, 1976, US) John Amplas,
Lincoln Maazel, Christina Forrest, Elyane
Nadeau, Tom Savini, George A Romero.
95 min.

A dazzling opening sequence (not for the squeamish) as a teenage vampire of today (Amplas) satisfies his bloodlust in a railway sleeper
compartment. Thereafter, Romero plays fascinating games with myth and reality as he balances traditional vampire lore against medically
certifiable psychosis. Fundamentally a quite serious movie, relevant to contemporary personality
problems and stresses, but shot through with a
wicked streak of black humour. It doesn't always
come off, but Romero makes stunning use of his
Pittsburgh locations to create a desolate suburban wasteland, and at its best it is rivetingly raw-
edged. TM

Marty

(Delbert Mann, 1955, US) Ernest Borgnine,
Betsy Blair, Joe De Santis, Esther Minciotti,
Karen Steele, Jerry Paris.
91 min. b/w.
Sentimental tale of a butcher from the Bronx,
afraid he is too ugly to attract girls, who takes
pity on a plain jane schoolteacher at a dance, then
finds love sidling up crabwise. Overrated at the
time, largely because its teleplay origins (by
Paddy Chayefsky) brought a veneer of naturalism and close-up intimacy to the Hollywood of
the day. But it does have doggy charm and a certain perceptiveness (the butcher's continuing
doubts as to what his mates will think; his mother's jealousy despite constant nagging about marriage). TM

Marvin's Room

(Jerry Zaks, 1996, US) Meryl Streep, Diane
Keaton, Leonardo DiCaprio, Robert De Niro,
Hume Cronyn, Gwen Verdon, Hal Scardino,
Dan Hedaya.
98 min.
Hairdresser and single mum Lee (Streep), struggling with rebellious teenager Hank (DiCaprio),
gets an invitation to visit – after some 20 years
– from her estranged sister Bessie (Keaton). On
arrival in Florida, Lee finds that ditzy Dr Wally
(De Niro) has not only diagnosed Bessie as having leukaemia, but her sister is also facing decisions about the care of their stroke-ridden father
Marvin (Cronyn) and elderly aunt Ruth
(Verdon), with whom Bessie shares her home.
The movie's subject is how need and the imminence of death can be catalysts for growth, closer family feeling and love. First-time director
Zaks has fashioned a restrained weepie, adapted by Scott McPherson from his own stage play,
which doesn't so much open up the text as harness it to strong ensemble performances, with
the actors investing power in restricted, even
staple, roles: Streep gives her most credible blue-
collar performance to date; Keaton sidesteps
saintliness to mix vulnerability and small heroics. In concert with this, the film is shot with discreet professionalism, while Rachel Portman
confirms her mastery of mildly melodramatic
mood music. WH

Mary of Scotland

(John Ford, 1936, US) Katharine Hepburn,
Fredric March, Florence Eldridge, John
Carradine, Donald Crisp, Douglas Walton,
Robert Barrat, Moroni Olsen.
123 min. b/w.
A better film than its reputation would suggest,
marvellously shot by Joe August, and with Ford
making striking use of the imposing RKO sets
even while remaining strangled by the arty ambitions of Maxwell Anderson's play (which contrives to reduce history to a novelette chronicling
the jealous rivalry that drove Elizabeth Tudor to
destroy Mary Stuart). One electric sequence – a
hellfire sermon delivered by Moroni Olsen as
John Knox – shows the extent to which Ford
remained uninvolved elsewhere by the polite conventions of historical costume drama, but the performances are fascinating in their careful, slightly
stilted way, and it looks terrific. TM

Mary Poppins

(Robert Stevenson, 1964, US) Julie Andrews,
Dick Van Dyke, David Tomlinson, Glynis
Johns, Hermione Baddeley, Karen Dotrice, Elsa
Lanchester, Arthur Treacher, Reginald Owen,
Ed Wynn.
139 min.
Compared to even 'sophisticated' juvenile fodder,
the sheer exuberance of Disney's adaptation of
PL Travers' children's classic should tickle the

most jaded fancy. Indeed, the film can hardly contain itself with its catalogue of memorable songs, battery of dance routines, and strong supporting cast. As for the leads, Julie Andrews, after beating off other pretenders to the role (in part because Walt liked the way she whistled), produced an Academy Award-winning portrayal of the Edwardian nanny whose mad magic seethes beneath a patina of respectability that is, as Mary Poppins' references state, 'practically perfect in every way'. But oh, Dick Van Dyke's Cockney accent! You can hardly understand him with his mouth open – but you probably wouldn't recognise him with his mouth closed. FD

Mary, Queen of Scots

(Charles Jarrott, 1971, GB) Vanessa Redgrave, Glenda Jackson, Patrick McGoohan, Timothy Dalton, Nigel Davenport, Trevor Howard, Ian Holm, Daniel Massey.
128 min.
Meticulously schoolmarmish, John Hale's script lays out all the power plays behind Elizabeth Tudor's battle to keep Mary Stuart off her throne, but fails to provide much else. Redgrave (melting) and Jackson (tetchy) are head girls on the opposing teams, while Jarrott, who made a small corner for himself in this sort of coffee-table kitsch (*Anne of the Thousand Days*, *Lost Horizon*) before walking on the wilder side (*The Other Side of Midnight*), never lifts it much above the level of a village pageant. TM

Mary Reilly

(Stephen Frears, 1996, US) Julia Roberts, John Malkovich, Glenn Close, George Cole, Michael Gambon, Michael Sheen, Linda Bassett, Ciaran Hinds, Moya Brady.
109 min.
Coppola's *Dracula*, Branagh's *Frankenstein*, Jordan's *Vampire*, and now Frears' *Jekyll and Hyde*. Will these horrors never cease? A more modest failure than the others, this lacks the vaulting artistic hubris to compensate for its over-produced, over-determined inertia. The film, adapted by Christopher Hampton from a novel by Valerie Martin, approaches Stevenson's characters from a new angle: the point of view of a scullery maid in Dr Jekyll's household. Such nifty cultural repackaging sounds intriguing, but comes a cropper as soon as it's apparent that Mary (Roberts) is missing all the action: she cleans up after the murders, watches while Jekyll goes into his lab and Hyde comes out, flirts timidly with both – and that's just the highlights. It's not all bad: cinematographer Philippe Rousselot enshrouds everything in a fine Victorian fog, and George Fenton contributes an atmospheric score, but Frears never seems to get a fix on the material. If her accent is all over the place, it's hardly Roberts' fault that her pale, gaunt Mary seems to have been sampling the doctor's concoctions. Columbia have grafted on a panicky blood-and-thunder climax, with a belated transformation scene, but the film remains obstinately decorous, about as scary as an episode of *Upstairs, Downstairs*. TCh

Mary Shelley's Frankenstein

(Kenneth Branagh, 1994, US) Robert De Niro, Kenneth Branagh, Helena Bonham Carter, Tom Hulce, John Cleese, Richard Briers, Aidan Quinn, Ian Holm, Robert Hardy, Celia Imrie, Cherie Lunghi.
123 min.
In returning to Mary Shelley's novel, Kenneth Branagh presumably intended to give his version of the much-told tale authenticity and depth. But the finished film, regrettably, for all it's romantic bombast, lacks the poetry and pathos of James Whale's 1931 classic, let alone the wit of the later *Bride of Frankenstein*. De Niro, as the hapless creature, is dependably sympathetic, eyes expressive beneath *Elephant Man*-style make-up. The rest of the cast, however, are pretty dismal: chestbaring Branagh, too earnest and dashing, as the obsessive Victor; Bonham Carter, an inappropriately modern miss, as the doc's beloved Elizabeth; Cleese, ever the Python, a morose medical lecturer with a murky past; Briers as a blind peasant devoted to the good life. Equally uninspired is Steph Lady and Frank Darabont's often gratingly modern script and Branagh's far from light direction. Continuity seems all over the shop. Not frightening, just silly. GA

Masada
(aka The Antagonists)

(Boris Sagal, 1980, US) Peter O'Toole, Peter Strauss, Barbara Carrera, Anthony Quayle, David Warner, Clive Francis, Giulia Pagano, Denis Quilley, Timothy West.
121 min.
A boiled down – but still interminable – version of the four-part TV series adapted from Ernest K Gann's novel, this is a sort of would-be Biblical epic with Zionist overtones. Set in Judea during the first century AD, it tells the tale of Masada, the fortress defiantly held against the might of Rome by a handful of Jews fighting to retrieve their freedom – and their homeland – after the sack of Jerusalem by Roman colonialists. In between lengthy bouts of scuffling, with rhubarbing Jews and Romans prodding each other with tinny swords, the Jewish leader Eleazar (Strauss) is as strong and silent as a good Zionist guerilla should be, while the Roman commander (O'Toole) ponders the ironies of good government and the loneliness of the long-distance colonial administrator. Terrible stuff, irretrievably scuttled by O'Toole's hollow, ranting performance. TM

Ma Saison Préférée
(My Favourite Season)

(André Téchiné, 1993, Fr) Catherine Deneuve, Daniel Auteuil, Marthe Villalonga, Jean-Pierre Bouvier, Chiara Mastroianni, Carmen Chaplin, Jean Bosquet, Ingrid Caven.
127 min.
Here is Gallic star power saving a standard-issue domestic drama from mediocrity. Emilie (Deneuve) is a notary public in a small town in south-western France, her younger brother Antoine (Auteuil) a top Toulouse neurologist, while their widowed mother Berthe (Villalonga) lives alone, causing both offspring no little concern. Their ongoing confrontation over care plans for the old girl reveals the emptiness in their own personal lives. The performances bring these emotional entanglements to vivid, awkward life: Auteuil, as in *Un Coeur en Hiver*, manages to warm our sympathy for a fundamentally detached, even dislikeable character; and Deneuve glides elegantly through another two hours of screen time desired by all, but incapable of love herself. Before you know it you're affected. TJ

Masala

(Srinivas Krishna, 1991, Can) Srinivas Krishna, Sakina Jaffrey, Zohra Segal, Saeed Jaffrey, Heri Johal, Madhuri Bhatia.
106 min.
From the opening of Srinivas Krishna's vibrant directorial debut, you know you're in for something different as an obviously model plane explodes and brightly coloured saris float down. Aboard are an Indian family returning home after emigrating to Canada, and the film recounts a bizarre chain of events among the extended family they leave behind. Rebel son Krishna (played by the director) returns to the fold, introducing one cousin to magic mushrooms, another to sex; his rich uncle harbours suspected terrorists in his sari shop while hobnobbing with the Minister of Multi-Culturalism; Grandma Tikkoo (the wonderfully expressive Segal) communicates with Lord Krishna via her video recorder; and Mounties ride around Toronto trying to keep the chaos under control. An uplifting, extremely funny film, this has some serious things to say about sexuality, race, religion and politics. It takes risks – drawing on Hindi musicals to convey the characters' inner lives isn't an unqualified success – but without them, *Masala* wouldn't be nearly as spicy. CO'S

Mascara

(Patrick Conrad, 1987, Bel/Neth/Fr/US) Charlotte Rampling, Michael Sarrazin, Derek De Lint, Jappe Claes, Herbert Flack, Harry Cleven, Eva Robbins.
98 min.
At a performance of Gluck's *Orpheus and Eurydice*, twisted police chief Sanders (Sarrazin) and his incestuously beloved sister Gaby (Rampling) befriend the costume designer (De Lint). Gaby is enamoured of the designer's good looks, Sanders of one of his slinky creations, which he fancies for someone at a subterranean dive, where he and his cronies (straight off Genet's Balcony) amuse themselves listening to transvestite divas miming to Bellini, or watching chain-mailed leather boys swapping oysters mouth-to-mouth. Later discovering that the old (but unconsummated) flame for whom he had acquired the dress has something(s) in her panties, Sanders strangles her/him in disgust. The whole sordid affair dribbles on headlong to such a bathetic climax that even ardent searchers after nefarious enjoyment should draw seven veils over this one. WH

Maschera, La
see Mask, The

Maschera del Demonio, La (Black Sunday/Mask of the Demon/Revenge of the Vampire)

(Mario Bava, 1960, It) Barbara Steele, John Richardson, Ivo Garrani, Andrea Cecchi, Arturo Dominici.
84 min. b/w.
A classic horror film involving Barbara Steele as a resurrected witch who was burned to death in a small medieval town and seeks revenge on her persecutors. The exquisitely realised expressionist images of cruelty and sexual suggestion shocked audiences in the early '60s, and occasioned a long-standing ban by the British censor. The visual style still impresses, but the story beneath it has become too formularised for the film to retain all its original power. DP

Masculin Féminin (Masculine Feminine)

(Jean-Luc Godard, 1966, Fr/Swe) Jean-Pierre Léaud, Chantal Goya, Catherine-Isabelle Duport, Marlène Jobert, Michel Debord, Birger Malmsten, Eva Britt Strandberg, Brigitte Bardot.
110 min. b/w.
Godard offers '15 precise facts' about the children of Marx and Coca-Cola: a series of scattershot observations of young people in Paris in 1965. This is pre-political Godard, which means that it attacks on all cylinders without having any strong line of its own. But its parodies and satires are recklessly inventive, and its fundamental pessimism isn't as flip as it may at first seem. TR

M*A*S*H

(Robert Altman, 1969, US) Donald Sutherland, Elliott Gould, Tom Skerritt, Sally Kellerman, Robert Duvall, Jo Ann Pflug, Rene Auberjonois, Gary Burghoff, Fred Williamson, John Schuck.
116 min.
Altman's idiosyncratic career received a dramatic boost when he took Ring Lardner Jr's script (already turned down by a dozen directors) and turned it into a box-office smash. Dealing with the crazily humorous activities of a Mobile Army Surgical Hospital's staff and the carnage of the Korean (read Vietnam) war, it shows Altman's stylistic signature in embryonic form: a large number of fast-talking eccentric characters, a series of revealing vignettes rather than a structured plot, comparisons of real life with media versions purveyed by the camp's radio, and semi-audible, overlapping dialogue. It's frantic, clever fun, but in comparison with later works such as *Thieves Like Us* and *The Long Goodbye*, its cynical stance often rings hollow; its targets – military decorum, religious platitudes and sexual hypocrisy – are too easy, and there's little of the director's muted, unsentimental humanism in evidence. GA

Mask

(Peter Bogdanovich, 1985, US) Cher, Sam Elliott, Eric Stoltz, Estelle Getty, Richard Dysart, Laura Dern, Harry Carey Jr.
120 min.
Rocky Dennis (Stoltz), a boy with an appallingly deformed skull, at 16 has already far outlived doctors' predictions. The most effective scenes deal with Rocky's determined attempt to confront everyday problems: school, rows with parents and friends, growing up. Elsewhere the film becomes mawkish: the bike gang who act as Rocky's friends/occasional bodyguards seem idealised, while the romance between bike jock

Gar (Elliott) and Rocky's mother (Cher) tends to curdle the stomach. Still, Bogdanovich invests the story with warmth, generosity and considerable power. RR

Mask, The (aka The Eyes of Hell)

(Julian Roffman, 1961, Can) Paul Stevens, Claudette Nevins, Bill Walker, Anne Collings, Martin Lavut.
83 min. b/w & col.

A totally banal murder plot is enlivened by sequences depicting the psychedelic nightmares induced by a magical burial mask, which impel first an archaeologist (Lavut), then the psychiatrist who refuses to believe him (Stevens), to murderous frenzies. When the mask is put on, the audience gets the cue to put on the cardboard specs. The 3-D process is tacky in the extreme, but some of the graphic effects (credited to Slavko Vorkapich) are quite unusual.

Mask, The (La Maschera)

(Fiorella Infascelli, 1988, It) Michael Maloney, Helena Bonham Carter, Feodor Chaliapin Jr, Roberto Herlitzka, Michele de Marchi.
90 min.

Lush, if not mushy romance, in the 18th century Italian style, as playboy Maloney falls hard for travelling-player Bonham Carter. She promptly cold-shoulders him, but soon becomes fascinated by the enigmatic stranger who appears in her life. Decorative trappings, but the moth-eaten plot, regrettably, comes straight from the give-me-a-break file. TJ

Mask, The

(Charles Russell, 1994, US) Jim Carrey, Cameron Diaz, Peter Riegert, Peter Greene, Amy Yasbeck, Richard Jeni.
101 min.

Stanley Ipkiss is a likeable schmuck, a bank teller who wouldn't say 'boo' to a goose. Men don't give him a second glance, women look right through him – until, one night, Stanley happens across an ancient mask. Wearing it, he's transformed into a lime-faced bundle of mischievous energy, part man, part loony tune. 'I could be a superhero,' he muses, 'a force for good…' But first for some fun: he wreaks vengeful havoc at his local garage, robs the bank where he works, and sweeps lovely nightclub chanteuse Tina (Diaz) off her feet. This is a treat, a classic Jekyll and Hyde story for the '90s. Director Russell brings a lowbrow pulp rigour to the material that's reminiscent of vintage Roger Corman and pays lavish homage to animator Tex Avery. The design is bright as a button and the transformation scenes real eye-poppers, but the film's best special effect is putty-faced Carrey with his razzle-dazzle star turn as the affable Stanley and his manic alter ego. Hip, flip and fly. TCh

Mask of Dimitrios, The

(Jean Negulesco, 1944, US) Zachary Scott, Peter Lorre, Sydney Greenstreet, Faye Emerson, George Tobias, Victor Francen, Eduardo Ciannelli, Steve Geray, Florence Bates, Kurt Katch.
95 min. b/w.

A fine *noir*-ish thriller, adapted from Eric Ambler's novel (*A Coffin for Dimitrios*), and respecting its *Citizen Kane* structure as a mousy little mystery writer (Lorre), intrigued by the reported murder of a seedily nasty international criminal (Scott), begins to reconstruct his story by talking to people from his past. The result is superficial but stylishly atmospheric, with vivid characterisations (notably Greenstreet as a genial blackmailer who ambiguously and rather movingly befriends Lorre) and low-key lighting effects that bring subtle echoes of *The Maltese Falcon* (Arthur Edeson shot both films). TM

Mask of Fu Manchu, The

(Charles Brabin/Charles Vidor, 1932, US) Boris Karloff, Lewis Stone, Karen Morley, Myrna Loy, Charles Starrett, Jean Hersholt.
72 min. b/w.

Highly engaging if none too classy tale of Sax Rohmer's sophisticated and fiendishly brilliant Oriental villain, battling against Scotland Yard in an attempt to obtain Genghis Khan's mask and sword, which he needs to conquer the world. Much depends on Karloff's tongue-in-cheek por-

trait of the sinister, sadistic anti-hero, although Tony Gaudio's camerawork, the surprisingly imaginative sets, the ingenious tortures, and Myrna Loy's gleeful performance as Fu Manchu's sado-nymphomaniac daughter help no end. GA

Mask of Fury

see First Yank into Tokyo

Mask of the Demon

see Maschera del Demonio, La

Masque of the Red Death, The

(Roger Corman, 1964, GB) Vincent Price, Hazel Court, Jane Asher, Skip Martin, David Weston, Patrick Magee, Nigel Green, John Westbrook.
89 min.

Less polished than *The Tomb of Ligeia*, but still the best and most ambitious of Corman's Poe cycle. Apart from a scruffy opening scene, it looks stunningly handsome, with Nicolas Roeg's camera providing alluring effects like the sudden switches from white to yellow, purple to black, as Jane Asher scurries through a sequence of rooms each designed in a different colour. It is also graced by an intelligent script (the admirable Charles Beaumont) which probes the concept of diabolism with considerable subtlety, even though the black magic scenes were removed in Britain by the censor. Where most films of this nature tend simply to pile on the blood, here there is a genuine chill of intellectual evil in the philosophical speculations of Price's 12th century Italian Prince Prospero, 'safely' immured in his castle while the plague rages outside, dreaming up fiendish ways of entertaining/tormenting his prisoner-guests. TM

Masquerade

(Basil Dearden, 1964, GB) Cliff Robertson, Jack Hawkins, Marisa Mell, Christopher Witty, Bill Fraser, Michel Piccoli, Tutte Lemkow, Charles Gray.
102 min.

An early script collaboration from William Goldman produces a nicely understated satire on the spy movie boom, in which the Foreign Office despatch Hawkins and Robertson (old wartime buddies, not very up on the espionage thing) to kidnap a young Arab prince for his own protection prior to his coronation. The plot convolutions of Victor Canning's novel *Castle Minerva* are given a wryly cynical edge, and Dearden copes surprisingly well with the spectacle. PT

Masquerade

(Bob Swaim, 1988, US) Rob Lowe, Meg Tilly, Kim Cattrall, Doug Savant, John Glover, Dana Delany, Erik Holland, Brian Davies.
91 min.

Tilly (achingly vulnerable) plays a fragile young heiress who returns from college to find her loath-some stepfather (Glover) and his girlfriend monopolising her swanky Hamptons pile. She takes up with Lowe, whose professional yachts-man front masks his activities as a gigolo, and they marry, Tilly believing that he loves her for herself; but she is the target of a long-term conspiracy that results in double murder. Swaim has pulled together a dense, stylish, Hitchcockian thriller in *noir* vein which turns on the moral and sexual ambiguity of the Lowe character, beautifully shot in crisp, pristine tones that contrast effectively with the sordid goings-on. However, Swaim's analysis of American class structures is limited: the film finally sides with the rich as innocent victims of the criminally-embittered less privileged. EP

Masquerade (Marattom)

(G Aravindan, 1989, Ind) Urmilla Unni, Sadanam Krishnan Kutty, Pulluvan Narayanan, Keshavan.
90 min.

Financed by Indian national TV, Aravindan's film is a weird and sometimes wonderful meditation on the realities that may or may not underpin traditional Kathakali theatre. It centres on the climax of the play *Keechaka Vadham* – where the disguised protagonist Bhima kills the antagonist Keechaka – and posits a bumbling police investigation into the 'crime': was it the character who died or the actor? Or was it something *represented* by the character? And who actually carried out

the killing? Despite helpful captions dividing the film into chapters, most western viewers will be too baffled by the forms of Kathakali itself to unravel these Brechtian complexities. Fortunately, the 'illusion' side of the conundrum is well served by the costumes and choreography of the original play, and so there's plenty to fill the eye. TR

Masques

(Claude Chabrol, 1987, Fr) Philippe Noiret, Robin Renucci, Bernadette Lafont, Monique Chaumette, Anne Brochet, Roger Dumas, Pierre-François Duméniaud.
100 min.

'I'd kill my sister for a good pun' says the hero of Chabrol's murder mystery; but it looks as if smarmy TV show host Christian Legagneur (Noiret) may already have knocked his chances, and his sister, on the head. Dressed in the sheep's clothing of biographer Roland Wolf, the hero insinuates himself into Legagneur's country house, where the latter's goddaughter (Brochet) languishes in a state of narcolepsy. Everyone in the house has a double identity, from the allegedly mute chauffeur/chef to the amorous masseuse/fortune-teller (Lafont). But it is what lies behind his host's polite mask that interests the snooping Roland. Noiret's slobbish screen persona is ill-suited to his role as a bourgeois manipulator with a gift for cerebral word games, and it is only when the facade cracks at the end that his more corporeal style of nastiness seems appropriate. Chabrol frames the verbal sparring with characteristic precision, but the subtle plot suffers from a surfeit of *politesse* and a dearth of red-blooded passion. NF

Massacre (Mueda – Memoria e Massacre)

(Ruy Guerra, 1980, Moz) Filipe Gunoguacala, Romao Canapoquele, Baltasar Nchilem.
80 min. b/w.

Mueda was a massacre. The name is that of the village in Northern Mozambique where in 1960 it took place. The Portuguese colonial regime did the killing. In independent Mozambique, those inhabitants of Mueda who survived regularly re-enact the massacre *in situ*. They themselves play the roles of victims, assassins, and spectators. Ruy Guerra, now a Brazilian but born in Lourenço Marques (now Maputo, the capital of Mozambique), filmed this extraordinary creation of liberated popular culture, intercutting it with first-hand interviews on the massacre. The mix is compelling, and the grave yet joyous spectacle unique. SH

Massacre at Central High (aka Blackboard Massacre)

(Renee Daalder, 1976, US) Derrel Maury, Andrew Stevens, Kimberly Beck, Robert Carradine, Ray Underwood.
88 min.

An intriguing, diagrammatic example of subversive cinema. The action takes place in a lavish LA high school where authority is noticeable by its total absence, and where life exists only in the gaps between classes. This teen exploiter goes for nothing less than an entire allegory on society, power structures, and the failure of revolution. Despite a deceptively laid back style, the film's ambition, knowingness and surefootedness make it worth a look. VG

Massacre in Rome (Rappresaglia)

(George Pan Cosmatos, 1973, It/Fr) Richard Burton, Marcello Mastroianni, Leo McKern, John Steiner, Robert Harris, Delia Boccardo, Peter Vaughan, Anthony Steel.
104 min.

Rome's Gestapo chief (Burton) and a Catholic priest (Mastroianni) size up over the problem of reprisals during the last days of the Nazi occupation in World War II. Although based on fact, the film invents Mastroianni's character for the dramatic purposes of face-to-face confrontation. The ensuing debate, cumbersome and full of doughty moralising about non-involvement and complicity, results in a hands down victory for Burton's well-modulated vowels over Mastroianni's limited machine-gun English. Cosmatos' cripplingly emphatic direction reveals every creak in the plot and displays no whit of faith in an audience's intelligence. CPe

Master and Margarita, The (Majstori i Margarita)

(Aleksandar Petrovic, 1972, Yugo/It) Ugo Tognazzi, Mimsy Farmer, Alain Cuny, Bata Zivojinovic, Pavle Vujisic.
101 min.
An intriguing but rather half-baked adaptation of Mikhail Bulgakov's novel. The Master (Tognazzi) is a much revered writer whose new play about the life of Christ is threatened with withdrawal during rehearsals because it is considered ideologically unsound. He finds solace in Margarita (Farmer), a beautiful girl who mysteriously crosses his path, but becomes tortured to the point of insanity by conflicting hopes and fears when the sinister Professor Woland (Cuny, excellent) – the Devil, no less – uses his magical powers to ensure that rehearsals go forward, but also enlivens the première with a horrific display of illusions which drives the audience from the theatre in panic. Some pleasure is to be had from the loving recreation of Moscow in the '20s, and from the fantasy elements (though pedestrian by comparison with the novel). But despite literary allusions which dress up the narrative (evoking the tale of Faust and Marguerite, for example), the novel is still so boiled down that it emerges, anti-climactically, as just a plodding allegory about the repression of dissident artists. TM

Master Gunfighter, The

(Frank Laughlin ie. Tom Laughlin, 1975, US) Tom Laughlin, Ron O'Neal, Lincoln Kilpatrick, Barbara Carrera, Geo Ann Sosa, Victor Campos.
121 min.
The *Billy Jack* series (featuring a disillusioned half-breed Indian Vietnam veteran) was sufficiently successful in the States to produce this spin-off Western. Set in Spanish California, it has Laughlin alone in challenging a decadent aristocracy for exploiting the peaceful local Indians. The film could have worked but for an excess of formula ingredients and muddled preachings. Adapted from a Japanese film, the transposition dubiously retains much samurai swordfighting and semi-Oriental costumes. Meanwhile, the over-mannered camerawork pays its dues to the Italian Western. In the resulting cultural hash, the plot with its strong anti-religious theme is too often disregarded. Laughlin is spectacularly uncharismatic, his doughy features laughable in brooding close-up. Best are the superb Monterey coast locations, reminiscent of *One-Eyed Jacks*; a pity nothing else is. CPe

Master Musician, The

see Born of Fire

Master of Kung Fu, The

see Death Kick

Master of Love (Racconti Proibiti di Nulla Vestiti)

(Brunello Rondi, 1973, It) Rossano Brazzi, Magali Noël, Arrigo Masi, Ben Eckland, Barbara Bouchet, Janet Agren, Tina Aumont.
109 min.
Carry On Decameron, with Pasolini's innocent doodlings sabotaged by a more leery, exploitative approach: nuns jump up and down in bathtubs, wearing just their wimples, and excruciating puns abound as the Master initiates his younger, more spiritual apprentice with the help of a number of tales. Tina Aumont makes a beguiling appearance as a witch in an otherwise silly episode, injecting more sense of fun into her role than the other ladies. The film does have its aspirations: stylistic references range as far afield as *Tom Jones*, and the church is lampooned rather heavy-handedly in a sketch about a 'miraculous' conception (the priest is behind a wooden screen doing his stuff). Another has the Master as a flagellating Christ in an amusing attempt to seduce a legendary virgin. The end sees the Master and Lady Death leaping through the fields, off for that Last Great Coupling in the sky.

Master of the World

(William Witney, 1961, US) Vincent Price, Charles Bronson, Mary Webster, Henry Hull, Wally Campo, Richard Harrison.
104 min.
A pleasantly ludicrous children's fantasy movie, with a talented production team making the most of a low budget (Roger Corman produced, and the adaptation from Jules Verne is by Richard Matheson, who was obviously making a bit of a holiday of this one). Vincent Price plays Robur, a mad inventor who has much the same anti-war hang-ups as Captain Nemo, but who captains a giant flying-machine rather than a submarine, and flies around the world trying to end war by the threat of mass destruction. Although the final message is pretty sickening, the film's imaginative use of stock shots and its garish line in 19th century hardware are admirable. DP

Master Race, The

(Herbert J Biberman, 1944, US) George Coulouris, Stanley Ridges, Osa Massen, Nancy Gates, Lloyd Bridges.
96 min. b/w.
This wordy curiosity, made after D-Day in anticipation of a swift end to the war, serves mostly as a propaganda vehicle for the allied civilian rehabilitation programme. However, beneath the surface appeal to fundamentally decent values (and for a forgiveness amounting to an almost total eradication of memory), fear, hatred, suspicion and disruption are all conveyed with more conviction than the fragile brave new world for which the Americans (with help from the British and Russians) hope. A German general, aware that the war is lost, has gone undercover to stir up World War III, and even in the moment of victory, violence erupts again. CPe

Masters of the Universe

(Gary Goddard, 1987, US) Dolph Lundgren, Frank Langella, Meg Foster, Billy Barty, Courteney Cox, James Tolkan.
106 min.
It must have seemed like a good idea at the time – to re-animate in live action the cartoon characters from the popular tots' TV series *He-Man*. Most of the action takes place on Earth, where the anorexic Skeletor (Langella) pursues with evil intention the squeaky clean He-Man (Lundgren). Each craves possession of the Cosmic Key, which – like a platinum Amex card – gets you wherever you want to go. A couple of dumb-ass kids become involved with the goodies and, in addition to some feeble lovey-dovey, provide the wherewithal for the stranded aliens to return to Eternia. There are lots of flashes and bangs, but the effects are neither special nor camp enough to be more than vaguely amusing. MS

Matador

(Pedro Almodóvar, 1985, Sp) Assumpta Serna, Antonio Banderas, Nacho Martínez, Eva Cobo, Julieta Serrano, Chus Lampreave, Carmen Maura.
106 min.
Ai No Corrida, literally. Death and Desire are inextricably linked in this Hispanic mix of sex, symbolism, violence and very chic design. A trainee bullfighter is driven by his guilt as a failed rapist to confess to the murder of a number of young men and women; but his maestro (retired from the corrida after being gored) and his lady lawyer are far guiltier than he, since the ultimate orgasm can only be achieved through killing. Not so much a maelstrom as a mess of ludicrously contrived eroticism, pretentious dialogue, and reprehensibly voyeuristic sensationalism, Almodóvar's silly, cod-philosophical whodunit impresses only for its bravado (fans of Paul Verhoeven may love it). GA

Mata Hari

(George Fitzmaurice, 1932, US) Greta Garbo, Ramon Novarro, Lionel Barrymore, Lewis Stone, C Henry Gordon, Karen Morley.
90 min. b/w.
Set in World War I France, the film is Garbo's even before she appears on screen to dazzle her willing audience; once there, it becomes impossible to dissociate the legend of the star from the myth of Mata Hari. Beautiful, charismatic and sublimely inaccessible, the miserable figure of history has become an irresistible spy, slavishly aided by her eager admirers. Staged almost entirely indoors and at night, the twilight melodrama of her mission is heightened by cinematographer William Daniels' stunning visuals: shadows and lines which contrast her total strength with the pale imitations who surround her. And even when (romantically, inevitably) she's destroyed by the love of a young Russian pup, she remains as ever, laconic and riveting. HM

Mata Hari

(Curtis Harrington, 1984, GB) Sylvia Kristel, Christopher Cazenove, Oliver Tobias, Gaye Brown, Gottfried John, William Fox.
108 min.
There are few things that Kristel is good at, and exotic dancing is not one of them. It could be argued, then, that she is miscast as the terpsichorean temptress who moonlight as a double agent in World War I. But this is a radical reworking of the legend. 'What I have done' breathes Sylvia, 'I have done for lurve', mostly for Cazenove, but also for Tobias, a German lady doctor, a man on the train, and some old codger in the next hotel room. But Sylvia is good at wearing hats trimmed with pampas grass, simulating orgasm during thunderstorms, and wielding her foil in a topless fencing match. This avails her not. She is trotted out into the early morning dry ice for one last big bang, out of the barrels of Frenchmen wearing fezzes. AB

Mata-Hari, Agent H.21

(Jean-Louis Richard, 1964, Fr/It) Jeanne Moreau, Jean-Louis Trintignant, Claude Rich, Franck Villard, Albert Rémy, Georges Riquier.
99 min. b/w.
The first half is really rather irresistible, with period Paris lovingly recreated and Jeanne Moreau not afraid to present Mata Hari as a bourgeois homebody in between her bouts of glamorous slinkiness. Tongue at least partly in cheek, she is insidiously funny, not least while performing an idiotic Oriental dance in which the finger movements transmit a coded message. Then love raises its head (after some delightfully outrageous vamping): a drearily routine affair in which she and Trintignant are even subjected to the TV ad indignity of a rapturous romp in the country; and as the film founders, it becomes increasingly apparent that Richard's plodding direction has no way of keeping up with Truffaut's script. TM

Match Factory Girl, The (Tulitikkutehtaan Tytto)

(Aki Kaurismäki, 1990, Fin/Swe) Kati Outinen, Elina Salo, Esko Nikkari, Vesa Vierikko, Reijo Taipale, Silu Seppälä.
69 min.
This final part of Kaurismäki's 'Working Class Trilogy' (which began with *Shadows in Paradise* and *Ariel*), has an affecting, fable-like simplicity. The tone is set by striking, almost abstract shots of the factory where shy, unattractive Iris (Outinen) sits checking matchbox labels on a production line. After handing over her hard-earned wages to her selfish mother and stepfather, Iris whiles away her spare time in a coffee bar, or waiting in vain to be asked to dance at the local disco. Her one attempt to break out – buying a pink dress, meeting a rich man, spending the night with him – inevitably ends in pregnancy and humiliation. Cheques, not feelings, are the currency of emotional exchange, left on bedside tables or sent with cursory notes saying 'Get rid of it'. Finally pushed over the edge, Iris plots a calm, methodical revenge on those who have poisoned her dreams. Despite the Bressonian overtones, the film has more in common with the radical proletarian pessimism of Fassbinder. Influences notwithstanding, Kaurismäki remains one of a kind. NF

Maternale

(Giovanna Gagliardo, 1978, It) Carla Gravina, Anna Maria Gherardi, Maria Masè, Francesca Muzio.
95 min.
An affluent Italian family, an idyllic summer's day, a sumptuous villa, a destructive struggle for power between mother and daughter. *Maternale* is an intimate and – in its adherence to the unities of time, place and action – highly formalised exploration of 'female' themes: frustrated desires, mother-child rivalry, the regime of the domestic, manifested here in an almost sensual obsession with food. But despite Gagliardo's experimental intentions, it all seems curiously old-fashioned, with the luscious imagery, dreamlike mood, mannered *mise en scène*, and perhaps partly the 1960 setting, overlaying the film with the faded bloom of art cinema. SJo

Matewan

(John Sayles, 1987, US) Chris Cooper, Mary McDonnell, Will Oldham, David Strathairn, Ken Jenkins, Kevin Tighe, Gordon Clapp, James Earl Jones, Josh Mostel.
133 min.

A lone stranger arrives in town to unite the locals against the heavies with guns: a scenario familiar from countless Westerns. When the Stone Mountain Coal Company, which owns virtually everything in the West Virginian town of Matewan, reduces its workers' pay and begins employing blacks and Italians against the wishes of the local whites, ex-Wobbly union rep Joe Kenehan (Cooper) is sent in to overcome dissidence and prevent violent conflict with the armed strike-breakers recently hired by the company. But tempers run high, racial contempt is rife, and betrayal looms. Set in the 1920s, Sayles' marvellously gripping movie never compromises its political content in its deployment, or up-ending, of Western conventions. It possesses a mythic clarity, yet there's also a welcome complexity at work, in the vivid characterisations and the unsentimental celebration of community and collective action. The result is witty, astute, and finally very moving. GA

Matilda

see Roald Dahl's Matilda

Matinee

(Joe Dante, 1993, US) John Goodman, Cathy Moriarty, Simon Fenton, Omri Katz, Lisa Jakub, John Sayles.
99 min.

In Key West during the 1962 Cuban Missile Crisis, 14-year-old Gene (Fenton) is preoccupied with the forthcoming visit by B-movie king Lawrence Woolsey (Goodman) to promote Mant, his new bargain-basement exploiter about a chap mutating into an ant. Plotwise that's about it in this engagingly affectionate satire on small-town American fears. As Gene, his brother and buddies prepare for the riotous excitement of Woolsey's Saturday matinee preview, it's the details of the string of visual and verbal gags that make the film so enjoyable. The clips from Mant are spot on, what with the cod-scientific expository dialogue, dreary design, deathless hamming and Cold War clichés. Goodman's schlock merchant displays just the right mix of con-man materialism and childlike glee at his own bogus movie magic; the customary in-jokes and cameos reinforce the mood of loving, wryly amused hommage, and the kids' stuff never cloys. Inspired chaos, and for anyone into the delirious absurdities of '50s sci-fi, a must. GA

Matinee Idol, The

(Frank Capra, 1928, US) Bessie Love, Johnnie Walker, Lionel Belmore, Ernest Hilliard, Sidney D'Albrook, David Mir.
65 min. b/w.

Long believed lost, until a print turned up in France and was beautifully restored with the aid of high definition video, Capra's silent comedy contains much that anticipates his later flair. A Broadway star stumbles on a travelling theatrical troupe of hilarious ineptitude, and hires them for a cheap laugh to appear in the big city. The cruelty of the conceit is happily defused by the exuberant playing of Bessie Love, one of the screen's great comediennes of the '20s and '30s. DT

Mattei Affair, The
(Il Caso Mattei)

(Francesco Rosi, 1972, It) Gian Maria Volonté, Luigi Squarzina, Peter Baldwin, Franco Graziosi, Gianfranco Ombuen.
115 min.

An astonishingly powerful conspiracy thriller. Enrico Mattei, head of the state-owned oil firm AGIP and president of ENI, the man Time dubbed 'the most powerful Italian since Caesar Augustus', died in 1962 in a highly suspicious air crash. His death was followed by a wall of silence. In the light of his championship of the Italian economy against the machinations of international cartels, his death – in fact and in Rosi's masterful film – carries a sickening political inevitability. Rosi casts the film along the lines of an inquest, and pieces together not simply a picture of the man himself (Volonté, brilliantly cast), but of the dynamics of capital, the role of the media, and the traps to which the individualist hero can't help but fall prey. The Mattei Affair is Point Blank played out at the level of power politics and monopolistic economic intrigue. Essential viewing. VG

Matter of Heart

(Mark Whitney, 1983, US) Marie-Louise von Franz, Barbara Hannah, Liliane Frey-Rohn, Laurens van der Post.
106 min.

A bio-doc about Jung, the man who took the sex out of psychoanalysis, put the supernatural in, and rechristened it Analytical Psychology. After brooding shots of Alpine mists and waterfalls, the stuff of Teutonic fairytale, the film is mostly well-heeled talking heads reminiscing about the man and expounding his teachings. Jung comes over like Dr Shorofsky in Fame – a loveable old grouch. For anyone coming from psychiatry, psychoanalysis, or just plain old messed-up common sense, the Jungian message may seem quite weird. But weird or not, it is quite well explored here as Jung's disciples, all quite old now of course, circle round selected themes – among them the role of the anima and animus in psychic life, the liberating and initiatory aspects of Jung's relationship with Toni Wolff, the power of the shadow side in human affairs, and Jung's apocalyptic visions of the end of the world. RI

Matter of Honour, A
(Técnicas de duelo)

(Sergio Cabrera, 1988, Col/Cuba) Frany Ramirez, Humberto Dorado, Florina Lemaître, Vicky Hernández, Edgardo Roman.
92 min.

A film more about humour than honour. Set in a small town in the Colombian Andes, it concerns a feud between the local schoolteacher and the butcher – each of whom has a healthy and affectionate regard for the other, but is urged on by the differing factions determined not to spoil the chance of a fight. All the local characters and bureaucracies have their part to play: the mayor and the military, the priest and the police. They help to raise the temperature for the final duel, which is naturally assumed to settle every personal difference and show that might is right. But the scores the protagonists have to settle are those accumulated by long friendship and common politics, and these are the virtues that finally triumph. A touchingly funny film in the mould of post-war Italian cinema, pressing that most sensitive of Latin nerves, machismo. AH

Matter of Life and Death, A
(aka Stairway to Heaven) 100 (100)

(Michael Powell/Emeric Pressburger, 1946, GB) David Niven, Kim Hunter, Roger Livesey, Raymond Massey, Marius Goring, Robert Coote, Abraham Sofaer, Kathleen Byron, Richard Attenborough, Bonar Colleano.
104 min. b/w & col.

One of Powell and Pressburger's finest films. Made at the instigation of the Ministry of Information, who wanted propaganda stressing the need for goodwill between Britain and America, it emerges as an outrageous fantasy full of wit, beautiful sets and Technicolor, and perfectly judged performances. The story is just a little bizarre. RAF pilot Niven bales out of his blazing plane without a chute and survives; but – at least in his tormented mind – he was due to die, and a heavenly messenger comes down to earth to collect him. A celestial tribunal ensues to judge his case while, back on earth, doctors are fighting for his life. What makes the film so very remarkable is the assurance of Powell's direction, which manages to make heaven at least as convincing as earth. (The celestial scenes are in monochrome, the terrestial ones in colour: was Powell slyly asserting, in the faces of the British documentary boys, the greater realism of that which is imagined?). But the whole thing works like a dream, with many hilarious swipes at national stereotypes, and a love story that is as moving as it is absurd. Masterly. AH

Matti di Slegare

see Fit To Be Untied

Mau Mau

(Uwe Schrader, 1992, Ger) Marlen Diekhoff, Peter Franke, Catrin Striebeck.
92 min.

Schrader's third feature is a hand-held, low-budget post-Fall-of-the-Wall slice of low life, set in the immigrant area of a German city and following three interconnected couples. As city centres have filled with marginals, so Schrader makes marginals the centre of his extremely well acted film. Its focal point is the Mau Mau, a pastel kitsch, sleazy strip bar. Anyone old enough to have lost their way in life can drink here and toast their hard-won communality of defeat. Like a drink-sodden realist, Schrader hangs around and observes the pimps, gangsters, night-owls and lonely old bar flies. After an hour or so, you've got to know them, their interlocking destinies, and there you have it: a functioning model of a demi-monde! This is like a post-Fassbinder Fassbinder movie. It's non-judgmental and lacking in nihilism – but it also lacks Fassbinder's political acuity and gutter poetry. WH

Maurice

(James Ivory, 1987, GB) James Wilby, Hugh Grant, Rupert Graves, Denholm Elliott, Simon Callow, Billie Whitelaw, Ben Kingsley, Judy Parfitt, Mark Tandy.
140 min.

In this adaptation of EM Forster's posthumously published novel, a gay man in Edwardian England is seen to have three choices. Like Durham (Grant), he can opt for frigid, respectable marriage; like Viscount Risley (Tandy), he can solicit soldiers in bars and be grateful for six months' hard labour; or, most bravely, like Maurice (Wilby), he can risk everything for requited love. It takes a long time for Maurice to reach this point; only in the arms of his game-keeping bit of rough (Graves) does he realise that he's been taught 'what isn't right'. The initial stages, set in Brideshead country, are jerky, but thereafter the original's social comedy and serious passion are superbly evoked. The performances are excellent, the period trappings, like the love scenes, in the best possible taste. MS

Mauvaise Conduite

see Improper Conduct

Mauvais Sang
(The Night Is Young)

(Léos Carax, 1986, Fr) Michel Piccoli, Juliette Binoche, Denis Lavant, Hans Meyer, Julie Delpy, Carroll Brooks, Hugo Pratt, Serge Reggiani.
119 min.

In his second feature (following Boy Meets Girl), Carax combines his personal concerns – young love, solitude – with the stylised conventions of the vaguely futuristic romantic thriller. Loner street-punk Alex (Lavant) joins a gang of elderly Parisian hoods whose plan to steal a serum that will cure an AIDS-like disease is complicated by the deadly rival strategies of a wealthy American woman, and by Alex falling for the young mistress of a fellow gang-member (Piccoli). Again Carax's virtues are visual and atmospheric rather than narrative; while the script may occasionally smack of indulgent pretension, there is no denying the exhilarating assurance of individual sequences, and the consistency of Carax's moodily romantic vision. Certainly he would do well to create stronger female characters and avoid lines lumbered with laconic poeticism. But the film is, finally, affecting, thanks to a seemingly intuitive understanding of colour, movement and composition, and to an ability to draw from earlier films without ever seeming plagiaristic. GA

Maverick

(Richard Donner, 1994, US) Mel Gibson, Jodie Foster, James Garner, Graham Greene, Alfred Molina, James Coburn, Dub Taylor, Geoffrey Lewis, Denver Pyle.
127 min.

Richard Donner's big-screen offshoot of the old TV Western series, from a Butch Cassidy-meets-The Sting script by William Goldman, is slick, cute, formula, and full of lazy gags. Gibson lobs in a narcissistic performance as card-sharp Brett Maverick, up to his neck in oater shenanigans with the likes of con-woman Annabelle (Foster, not a natural comic), 'Marshal' Zane Cooper (Garner, the original TV Maverick), bandido Angel (Molina), and Indian chief Joseph (Greene, in a turn that comes on as PC but seems somehow offensive). A financially successful exercise in target-marketing, but not much of a movie. GA

Ma Vie en Rose

(Alain Berliner, 1997 Fr/Bel/GB/Switz)
Georges Du Fresne, Michèle Laroque, Jean-Philippe Ecoffey, Hélène Vincent, Daniel Hanssens.
89 min.
Seven-year-old Ludovic's determined to grow up a girl, which is hard on his family, who face the scorn of locals made uneasy by a sudden outbreak of non-conformism. This Belgian first feature evolves into a domestic battle of wills. Will Ludo deny his feelings and put the household back on an even keel, or can the grown-ups find the courage to accept their child, even if it makes them the black sheep of the community? Child actor Georges Du Fresne's projection of innocence and absolute certainty drains away any suspicion that the film-makers might be using him to tell a story that's fundamentally about adult sexual confusions. It isn't. It's about a child's pre-sexual intimations of gender identity, as influenced by his favourite TV show, a pink extravaganza starring a sort of live-action Gallic Barbie doll. Wry comedy is certainly not precluded, while Laroque and the excellent Ecoffey make the parents' emotional confusion tell, but it's the film's combination of compassion and whimsical charm that makes it utterly disarming. TJ

Ma vie sexuelle (Paul Dedalus' Journey) (Comment je me suis disputé... ('ma vie sexuelle'))

(Arnaud Desplechin, 1996, Fr) Mathieu Amalric, Emmanuelle Devos, Emmanuel Salinger, Marianne Denicourt, Thibault de Montalembert, Chiara Mastroianni, Roland Amstutz.
180 min.
This subtle and startlingly imaginative film concerns the intersecting relationships between a group of 20 and 30-year-old Parisians, notably assistant university professor Paul (Amalric), who's torn between his long-term girl Esther (Devos), his best friend's girl (with whom he guiltily had a fling a couple of years ago), and another woman he meets at a party. Paul's problem is indecision, which is of little use to his friends, colleagues and lovers, and even more damaging to himself. What makes this intimate epic so fascinating is the depth of characterisation – it's beautifully acted – and the way both script and direction use small details to offer telling insights into the lives, emotions and aspirations of the group. Loneliness is economically but expertly evoked with a cup of coffee and Ravel on the soundtrack; a bizarre but highly original scene featuring a monkey, a radiator and an arrogant academic brilliantly blends black humour and psychological unease. GA

Maxie

(Paul Aaron, 1985, US) Glenn Close, Mandy Patinkin, Ruth Gordon, Barnard Hughes, Valerie Curtin, Googy Gress.
98 min.
Adapted from a novel by Jack Finney, who wrote *Invasion of the Body Snatchers*, this is about another sort of body snatcher: the ghost of a flapper floozie who periodically takes over the body of bishop's secretary Jan. What Maxie wants is a chance to prove herself as a movie star, an ambition that was curtailed back in the '20s by a fatal crash on the eve of her big chance. It's a dream of a role for Close, who gets to play both nice girl and tart with a heart, but unfortunately she hasn't quite got the light comic touch required for this sort of whimsy. Much mileage is made out of Jan unexpectedly behaving very badly at parties, and there is a lot of farcical bedroom business as Jan's husband (played fairly charmlessly by Patinkin) wonders whether it is adultery when you bonk with your wife while her body is being occupied by someone else. It is all staggeringly lightweight; now had it been made forty years ago with Ginger Rogers and Cary Grant...AB

Maximum Overdrive

(Stephen King, 1986, US) Emilio Estevez, Pat Hingle, Laura Harrington, Yeardley Smith, John Short, Ellen McElduff, JC Quinn.
97 min.
Horror institution Stephen King's first shot at directing is a loud, obnoxious, single-idea schlocker. A malicious comet passes too close to Earth and sets all the mechanical objects in Wilmington, North Carolina, off on a bloody killing spree. Lawnmowers turn nasty, vending machines fire killer cans, and at the Dixie Boy Truck Stop only Emilio Estevez stands between the maniac rigs gathering force outside and the end of civilisation as we know it. There's carnage galore, but minimal interest. King himself described it as a 'wonderful moron picture', and he was half-right. TJ

Maximum Risk

(Ringo Lam, 1996, US) Jean-Claude Van Damme, Natasha Henstridge, Jean-Hugues Anglade, Zach Grenier, Stéphane Audran, David Hemblen.
101 min.
A standard Van Damme pic, competently assembled but with little of the manic edge found in director Lam's Hong Kong movies. In the tradition of *Double Impact*, we get two action heroes for the price of one. Retired French soldier Alain discovers his unknown twin dead on the streets of their home town on the Côte d'Azur. The corpse, for reasons too convoluted to explain, is Mikhail, a runner for the gang bosses of New York's Russian community. To find the killer, Alain poses as Mikhail and probes the underworld of Little Odessa. Along for the ride is Henstridge, taking care of titillation as Mikhail's girl, while the likes of French law enforcer Anglade and Russian Mafia kingpin Hemblen ensure we never want for over-ripe supporting performances. TJ

Max Mon Amour (Max My Love)

(Nagisa Oshima, 1986, Fr/US) Charlotte Rampling, Anthony Higgins, Bernard-Pierre Donnadieu, Victoria Abril, Ane-Marie Besse, Nicole Calfan, Pierre Etaix, Fabrice Luchini, Diana Quick.
97 min.
Finding that his wife Margaret (Rampling) has been lying about her afternoon activities, Peter (Higgins) – a Brit diplomat in Paris – begins to suspect her of infidelity. But when he discovers that her lover is a chimpanzee, he is so taken aback that, instead of yielding to jealousy, he insists on Max moving into the plush apartment the couple share with their young son and a maid. As scripted by frequent Buñuel collaborator Jean-Claude Carrière, Oshima's film bears more than a passing resemblance to the late master's sly, surreal satires on the charmless discretion of the bourgeoisie: eager to hide his shock and anger beneath a mantle of liberal sophistication, Peter merely engineers a situation of futile impasse, while Margaret's *amour fou* (or is it *amour bête*?) seems motivated less by passion than by a boredom born of indolence. That said, lumbered with stilted performances from Rampling and Higgins, clearly ill at ease with Anglo-French dialogue, Oshima never achieves Buñuel's cool but mordant tone: despite the potentially subversive material, the film frankly lacks bite. On one level, however, it succeeds: our sympathies rest throughout with Max who, despite his touchy irritability, deserves neither Peter's tolerant condescension nor – and this is arguably more destructive – Margaret's love. GA

Max Wall – Funny Man

(Jon Scoffield, 1975, GB) Max Wall, Anne Hart, Bob Todd.
40 min.
An unfortunate title, for the great Max – 'man's answer to the peacock' – has to be seen in the flesh to be seen at his best. In this little movie (filmed with video cameras at the Richmond Theatre before a well-lubricated audience) he seems at his second best, simply because he relies so heavily on live audience response; when his gags and bits of business are edited together and framed in darkness on a cinema screen, they seem pale imitations of the originals. Still, this is a valuable celluloid record of Prof Wallofski doing his stuff, searching for the piano stool, swatting a fly, measuring up his arms, and pulling faces that you never knew existed. GB

Maxwell Street Blues

(Linda Williams/Raul Zaritsky, 1981, US) Jim Brewer, Blind Arvella Gray, Coot 'Playboy' Venson, John Henry Davis, Pat Rushing.
56 min.
Blind ageing blacks playing the streets for a living and recounting hobo days seems like the stuff of Uncle Tom cliché; but it's a very real life for the musicians on Chicago's Maxwell Street, a poor Jewish market and blues buskers' venue since the beginning of the century. Williams and Zaritsky capture the blues as it was and still is played on the sidewalks which once hosted Big Bill Broonzy, Muddy Waters, Sleepy John Estes, Homesick James and others. Acoustic or electric, religious or rude, Maxwell Street is the untouched roots of the blues (although the absence of any youth on the street would seem to have set its expiry date). A heartening film, and a chastening experience for any rock fans who think their rock heroes thought up those licks themselves. JG

Maybe Baby

see For Keeps

Maybe...Maybe Not

see Bewegte Mann, Der

Mayerling

(Anatole Litvak, 1935, Fr) Charles Boyer, Danielle Darrieux, Suzy Prim, Jean Debucourt, Vladimir Sokoloff.
96 min. b/w.
A voluptuous romance, with Boyer as the Archduke Rudolf, tragically smitten with Darrieux' Maria Vetsera. Litvak is equally good at conveying the tidal wave of passion that drowned the heir to the throne, and the moral opprobrium that consumes the Hapsburg court. Of course it is novelettish, Barbara Cartland rubbish, but done with extraordinary skill and commitment. Boyer is ideal as the doomed and dissolute romancer who was never up to ruling anyway; and Darrieux is not only exquisitely beautiful, she's alive as well. The visual opulence rivals anything in Hollywood, where Litvak, a Jewish-Russian refugee, was hastily whisked, to produce wartime propaganda movies. This is his one really estimable picture, which he remade in 1957 for TV. ATu

May Fools

see Milou en mai

Mayor of Hell, The

(Archie Mayo, 1933, US) James Cagney, Madge Evans, Dudley Digges, Frankie Darro, Allen Jenkins, Arthur Byron, Harold Huber.
90 min. b/w.
Cloud nine tosh from the days when Warner movies preached that delinquents were just good kids in need of a helping hand. Cagney plays a ward-heeler rewarded with a political sinecure as Deputy Commissioner of a reform school. Up from the slums himself, horrified by the sadistic brutality of the director (Digges), Cagney takes over. Improving the food, relaxing the discipline, and replacing the warders with a system of self-government, he soon has the boys eating out of his hand. But unrest back in the ward ends with Cagney shooting the trouble-maker (Huber) in self-defence; and while he's in hiding, Digges restores his old regime. Jeopardising his freedom, Cagney rushes back in time to end a riot by the boys (a tubercular kid died after being locked in an unheated cell), though not before Digges falls to his death. The good angel Happy Ending tidies away all awkward questions, and Cagney is asked to stay on as director. Despite the risible script, Cagney is as watchable as ever, and Mayo directs sleekly. Remade as vehicles for the Dead End Kids: *Crime School* (1938) and *Hell's Kitchen* (1939). TM

Mazel Tov ou le mariage (Marry Me! Marry Me!)

(Claude Berri, 1968, Fr) Claude Berri, Elizabeth Wiener, Luisa Colpeyn, Grégoire Aslan, Régine, Prudence Harrington, Betsy Blair.
90 min.
A comedy of manners which cocks a wryly amused eye at the pomp and circumstance attending preparations for the marriage of a nice Jewish boy (Berri himself) to a nice Jewish girl (Wiener). He is French, poor, a bit of a dreamer; she is Belgian, rich, practical and pregnant. Complications set in when she realises she truly loves him, but he goes starry-eyed about an English teacher (Harrington). All comes out in the wash, of course, though not without the caustic

implication that a happy Jewish family in the hand is worth two grand passions in the bush. What makes the film, really, is its refusal to fall back on stereotypical characters and situations. Its constant alertness to eccentricities of behaviour make it both engaging and often very funny. TM

M. Butterfly
(David Cronenberg, 1993, US) Jeremy Irons, John Lone, Barbara Sukowa, Ian Richardson, Annabel Leventon, Vernon Dobtcheff.
101 min.
Despite initial surprise that Cronenberg was to film David Henry Hwang's play about an affair between a French diplomat and a she-male Chinese opera singer, links with the horrormeister's earlier work soon become clear. It's disappointing, however, that Cronenberg's dissection of the extremities of desire and the slippage of sex roles is less radical than in, say, *Dead Ringers* or *The Naked Lunch*. In pre-Cultural Revolution Beijing of the early '60s, René Gallimard (Irons), inspired by a performance of *Madame Butterfly*, projects on to singer Song Liling (Lone) a cultural imperialist fantasy of compliant Chinese womanhood. For reasons that remain obscure, he/she responds by recreating him/herself in this image, acting out a parody of submissive femininity and initiating a bizarre but mutually fulfilling charade. Blackmailed by a party official into obtaining political secrets, Song Liling later draws her lover into playing his own double role as a spy. Only when their espionage is revealed in a Paris court does Gallimard discover his lover's best-kept secret. NF

Me
see *Enfance nue, L'*

Me and Marlborough
(Victor Saville, 1935, GB) Cicely Courtneidge, Tom Walls, Barry Mackay, Alfred Drayton, Iris Ashley, Cecil Parker.
84 min. b/w.
A costume comedy which, despite the efforts of urbanely professional Saville, looks more like an English pantomime than the breakthrough to Hollywood it was intended as. Wooden old Tom Walls hasn't much to do as Marlborough, and his hangdog ragbag of an army is no match for ebullient Principal Boy Courtneidge. Strutting, pouting, singing, brawling, her woman soldier Kit Ross reduces the ruffianly riff-raff around her to a pack of sulky schoolboys. If the anti-patriotic populism of music-hall songs like 'I'm Colonel Coldfeet Of The Coldstream Guards' is missing, there's still a slimy villain of a recruiting sergeant, and the film's cynicism about martial valour and the glories of war is refreshing. RMy

Me and My Brother
(Robert Frank, 1968, US) Julius Orlovsky, Joseph Chaikin, Peter Orlovsky, John Coe, Allen Ginsberg, Roscoe Lee Browne.
95 min. b/w & col.
Frank's confusing, complex and ultimately exhilarating movie was one of the cinema's first serious attempts to deal with mental illness. It started out as a *cinéma-vérité* portrait of Julius Orlovsky, a catatonic schizophrenic removed from hospital by his poet brother Peter, and dragged along on a tour of campus poetry gigs with Allen Ginsberg. Partly because of Julius' own unresponsiveness (he's tranquillised up to the eyeballs), Frank decided during the shooting to introduce a second, fictional Julius (played by Chaikin) to act out some hypotheses about the real man's state of mind. The result is a daring mixture of fact and fiction, as Laingian as Peter Robinson's documentary *Asylum*: no statement is made or situation explored without immediately being challenged or confronted with an alternative reading. It's as sprawling and chaotic as it sounds, but it remains firmly (and movingly) anchored in its concern for Julius himself. TR

Me & My Matchmaker
(Mark Wexler, 1996, US) Irene Nathan.
55 min.
When documentarist Mark Wexler (son of cinematographer Haskell) decided to make a film about traditional Jewish matchmaker Irene Nathan, he did not expect to find himself going out with some of her clients, whom he was inter-

viewing, or to have Irene take such an interest in his own love life. The film's funny, fascinating, and finally faintly disturbing. How far is Wexler prepared to exploit the women he meets in order to 'improve' his movie? Or is he making it partly to meet women? And for all Irene's wit, charm and good intentions, one can't help feeling by the end that she's something of a meddler and control freak. Creepily intriguing. GA

Mean Dog Blues
(Mel Stuart, 1978, US) Gregg Henry, Kay Lenz, George Kennedy, Scatman Crothers, Tina Louise, Felton Perry, James Wainwright.
109 min.
Just an everyday story of an everyday prison farm containing the usual ingredients: sadistic guards, underfed Doberman, and the obligatory framed innocent (Henry) whose survival rests with his choice to either 'Kiss ass, haul ass, or haul ass'. Guess what – he legs it. FF

Mean Machine, The
see *Longest Yard, The*

Mean Season, The
(Phillip Borsos, 1985, US) Kurt Russell, Mariel Hemingway, Richard Jordan, Richard Masur, Joe Pantoliano, Richard Bradford, Andy Garcia.
104 min.
A crime reporter is sucked deep into the story he is covering when the murderer chooses him as confidant. Russell is commanding as the burnt-out hack, but Hemingway (as his menaced girlfriend) is given no chance to do more than glow weakly beneath the darkening skies that herald Miami's 'mean season' of hurricanes. It is Jordan as the psychopath whose presence precipitates the gripping atmosphere already half achieved by Frank Tidy's photography of the humid closing of the weather. Based on the novel *In the Heat of the Summer* by one-time crime reporter John Katzenbach, and filmed in the actual newsroom of the 'Miami Herald', the film lacks nothing in verisimilitude. Only, perhaps, something in meaning: all the ingredients are assembled, but one leaves the cinema still waiting for someone to hand over the recipe. FD

Mean Streets 100 (100)
(Martin Scorsese, 1973, US) Harvey Keitel, Robert De Niro, David Proval, Amy Robinson, Richard Romanus, Cesare Danova, Robert Carradine, David Carradine.
110 min.
The definitive New York movie, and one of the few to successfully integrate rock music into the structure of film: watch Keitel waking to the sound of the Ronettes, or De Niro dancing solo in the street to 'Mickey's Monkey'. *Mean Streets* is also pure Italian-American. Charlie (Keitel), a punk on the fringes of 'respectable' organised crime, ponders his adolescent confusions and loyalties. Beneath the swagger, he's embarrassed by his work, his religion, and by women and his friends, particularly Johnny Boy (De Niro), who owes everyone money. Scorsese directs with a breathless, head-on energy which infuses the performances, the sharp fast talk, the noise, neon and violence with a charge of adrenalin. One of the best American films of the decade. CPe

Meat
(Frederick Wiseman, 1976, US)
112 min. b/w.
Here Wiseman's normally astute and intelligent handling of documentary material for once falters. *Meat* never attempts to match Franju's descent to the slaughterhouse in *Le Sang des Bêtes*, it is true; but whatever one might expect from the director of *Hospital* and *Primate*, it surely would not be the bland and unenquiring advertisement for the US meat industry that emerges. The film does offer one eerie spectacle, however, as what Wiseman calls 'the Judas Goat' leads the other beasts to the slaughter before swiftly sidestepping the death chamber itself. VG

Meatballs
(Ivan Reitman, 1979, Can) Bill Murray, Harvey Atkin, Kate Lynch, Russ Banham, Kristine DeBell.
94 min.
Apparently written by a Corman PR man about

a poignant moment he once had watching *Animal House*! Filmed as light entertainment in the Canadian backwoods, *Meatballs* features a cast in search of a good time at summer camp. Camp counsellor Tripper (Murray) is a John Belushi clone whose 'charisma' dominates the film's production-line wackiness and sentimental story (of a kid who doesn't fit). Learning to fit is what this dodo of a camp is all about, showing that the American Way is big and blowsy enough to take a few off-the-wall-style persons, once the ol' sexuality is straightened out. RP

Mechanic, The (aka Killer of Killers)
(Michael Winner, 1972, US) Charles Bronson, Jan-Michael Vincent, Keenan Wynn, Jill Ireland, Linda Ridgeway, Frank de Kova.
100 min.
In this case, mechanic means hired assassin. A glossy, violent, pointless movie from the team who later perpetrated *Death Wish*; mildly entertaining if you want to watch Bronson suggesting silent, brooding menace for the umpteenth time. VG

Medea
(Pier Paolo Pasolini, 1970, It/Fr/WGer) Maria Callas, Giuseppe Gentile, Laurent Terzieff, Massimo Girotti.
118 min.
It's worth stressing the position of *Medea* in Pasolini's work, since it makes much the most sense when seen in context: it followed *Pigsty* (whose twin-level structure it duplicates, this time within a single narrative), and preceded the much-abused trilogy (whose rumbustious humour and sexuality were apparently a reaction against the outright nihilism evident here). That said, the film stands as Pasolini's most bizarre exploration of Freudian themes through Marxist eyes: a retelling of Medea's story (elopement, marriage, desertion, revenge) as a mixture of social anthropology and ritual theatre, with every incident given both a 'magic' and a 'rational' reading. Its splendours crystallise in the casting of Callas as Medea, a virtual mime performance with her extraordinary mask of a face bespeaking extremes of emotion; its weaknesses, equally, in the casting of Gentile as Jason, blandly butch, whose presence does nothing to fill out an ill-sketched, passive role. But the real achievement is that Pasolini's visual discourse is every bit as eloquent as the verbal one he puts in the mouth of Terzieff's centaur. TR

Medicine Man
(John McTiernan, 1992, US) Sean Connery, Lorraine Bracco, José Wilker, Rodolfo de Alexandre, Francisco Tsirene Tsere Rereme.
105 min.
Deep in the heart of the rainforest, Dr Campbell (Connery) has discovered then lost a cure for cancer, so it's back to the drawing board in his rickety hut. Ignorant of his (near) findings, the university funding the research sends fellow biochemist Dr Crane (Bracco) to pull the plug. Once informed of the situation, she joins with Campbell in an attempt to repeat the formula *and* to beat the developers threatening the rainforest (which contains the crucial ingredient). Our couple argue and yell, in exchanges lent a humorous edge; national differences and eccentricities are endlessly flaunted (Connery as irascible Scot, Bracco as hard-nosed New Yorker); but the script utterly fails to create engaging sexual tension. A maestro of the action movie, McTiernan effectively captures the horrors of a climactic jungle fire, but at other times, the setting merely provides an exotic backdrop to bolshie posturing and feats of derring-do. If only they'd cast Schwarzenegger. CM

Mediterraneo
(Gabriele Salvatores, 1991, It) Diego Abatantuono, Claudio Bigagli, Giuseppe Cederna, Claudio Bizio, Gigio Alberti, Vanna Barba.
92 min.
Eight mismatched, unwilling Italian combatants and a donkey land on a tiny Greek island in 1941 in order to capture it for Mussolini. If the film hadn't been made by Italians, you might have thought it racist: the eight are alternately stupid, cowardly, lazy and libidinous. They scream, overreact, and fire at chickens by mistake. One night

m

they shoot the donkey when it won't say the password. The wireless operator, whose beast it is, smashes the radio. Their battleship is blown up in the bay. No one knows where they are, and for them the war is over. Gradually, Attic transformation takes place. The hidden islanders emerge: compliant shepherdesses disrobe, the artistic lieutenant restores the frescoes in the church, breasts are bared physically and emotionally, and everyone tries Greek dancing. It isn't really together enough to be an anti-war film: there's no historical or philosophical background, no depth, nothing but sun, sand, saccharine and a stirring bouzouki score, and the surprisingly bitter epilogue doesn't begin to redress the balance. SFe

Medium, The
(Gian Carlo Menotti, 1951, US) Marie Powers, Anna Maria Alberghetti, Leo Coleman.
84 min. b/w.
The composer Menotti wandered only once into the world of cinema, splendidly directing (with the probable help of Alexander Hammid) this version of his tragic opera about a fake spiritualist thrust into spiralling madness by an unseen hand at her throat. This magnificent chimera, although without progeny, is perfectly realised as an eerie, claustrophobic chamber piece, with a musical style that exists somewhere between Beat and Bartok. With monstrous characters and images only conceivable in a fevered or an operatic mind (where else would one find Toby the deaf mute gypsy boy, or defiant eyelids sealed with hot candle wax), yet fully realisable nowhere else but the cinema, Menotti sucks one into his world of overwrought emotions, heightened by a libretto that makes the film as accessible as *West Side Story* yet perfectly demonstrates the power of the spoken word. FD

Medium Cool
(Haskell Wexler, 1969, US) Robert Forster, Verna Bloom, Peter Bonerz, Marianna Hill, Harold Blankenship, Peter Boyle.
111 min.
Focusing on a news cameraman's responses and responsibilities to the world framed through his lens – in particular, the 1968 Chicago Democratic Convention and its attendant political riots, during which parts of the film were shot – ace liberal cinematographer Wexler's feature debut as director is a fascinating though not wholly successful fusion of *cinéma-vérité* and political radicalism. Already under the FBI's gaze for his civil rights and socialist documentaries, Wexler was actually accused of inciting the Chicago riots (the script was registered a year before); later he would again be subpoenaed over Emile de Antonio's film on the Weather Underground, which he shot. Recent movies owing a sizeable debt to *Medium Cool* include *Newsfront* and *Circle of Deceit*. PT

Medusa Touch, The
(Jack Gold, 1978, GB/Fr) Richard Burton, Lino Ventura, Lee Remick, Harry Andrews, Alan Badel, Marie-Christine Barrault, Jeremy Brett, Michael Hordern, Gordon Jackson.
109 min.
Gold's Midas touch with prestige TV material here for once transfers to the big screen with a full-blooded approach to the most implausible hokum. A skilful blend of the familiar (casting, English locations) and the outrageous (the script's mix of whodunit, disaster movie and telekinetic thriller) produces a beguiling entertainment in which half the fun's to be had from constructing a coherent synopsis out of the loony mess of flashback, foresight, eccentricity and even ecology. Ventura's a French sleuth on Common Market secondment to the Yard; Burton's a mysteriously troubled author with murderous mental powers. Watch for the bouncing cathedral bricks at the end. PT

Mee Pok Man
(Eric Khoo, 1995, Singapore) Joe Ng, Michelle Goh, Lim Kay Tong.
105 min.
Hard to say if Khoo's splendid debut feature is an authentic tragedy of erotic obsession or the blackest of black comedies; either way, it scores brownie points for demolishing the vision of Singapore life put about by the island's tourist board. The Mee Pok Man (named after the flat noodles he makes and sells from a market stall) lives in the

stern shadow of his late father and dotes from afar on the world-weary hooker Bunny. He gets his chance to 'save' this tarnished angel when he finds her bleeding after a hit-and-run accident and takes her home to nurse her. The plot may be *The Collector* with a twist, but the style is all Khoo's own: cool, tender and stoic, even in the face of extreme perversity. TR

Meetings of Anna, The
see Rendez-vous d'Anna, Les

Meeting Venus
(István Szabó, 1990, GB) Glenn Close, Niels Arestrup, Moscu Alcalay, Macha Méril, Ildikó Bánsági, Dorottya Udvaros, Erland Josephson, Johanna Ter Teege, Maria de Medeiros.
120 min.
When Hungarian conductor Zoltan Szanto (Arestrup) arrives in Paris for rehearsals of Wagner's *Tannhäuser*, he is optimistic that this will be a big career break. The lavish production has brought together top European and American talent, and though this might mean that he is misunderstood in six different languages, Szanto hopes that everyone will share his dedication. Instead, passion among the musicians is confined to bedrooms and kitchens, and spirited debate saved for union meetings. Szabó based this story on his own experiences, along with producer David Puttnam's at Columbia, and personal affinities may have blinded both to the project's indulgences. Petty in-fighting might stir the creative juices, but the endless nationalistic jibes and egocentric displays do little to endear the characters. There's too much chaos and not enough comedy; if this is meant to mirror the new Europe, the future looks grim. CM

Meet John Doe
(Frank Capra, 1941, US) Barbara Stanwyck, Gary Cooper, Edward Arnold, Walter Brennan, James Gleason, Spring Byington, Regis Toomey, Ann Doran, Gene Lockhart.
132 min. b/w.
Stanwyck causes a sensation with an invented newspaper story about a tramp promising to kill himself to protest at the state of the world – and then she auditions plain-speaking hick Gary Cooper for the part. His goodwill campaign takes the nation by storm, but proves ripe for political manipulation. After a bright start, this hunkers down to serious hand-wringing... Coop's hick (none too convincingly hinted at as the new Messiah) turns out to be a bore, and Capra strains to accommodate political chicanery and his own half-baked idealism. TCh

Meet Me at the Fair
(Douglas Sirk, 1952, US) Dan Dailey, Diana Lynn, Hugh O'Brian, Scatman Crothers, Carole Mathews, Chet Allen.
87 min.
The second of Sirk's 'trilogy' of witty, light-hearted musicals nostalgically evoking small-town America around the turn of the century, blessed with an engaging and lively performance from Dan Dailey as the travelling medicine show proprietor who hides out a runaway orphan (Allen) and woos the pretty delegate from the orphanage board (Lynn) who is supposed to bring him back. The song-and-dance numbers are adequate rather than inspired (although the backstage routine involving Dailey and Carole Mathews is staged and shot with astonishing virtuosity); but Sirk's customary concern with hypocrisy and intolerance is, given the genre and overall tone of the piece, surprisingly to the fore in a subplot about corrupt politicians (admirably headed by the darkly handsome O'Brian). GA

Meet Me in St Louis
(Vincente Minnelli, 1944, US) Judy Garland, Margaret O'Brien, Leon Ames, Mary Astor, Tom Drake, Lucille Bremer, Marjorie Main, June Lockhart, Harry Davenport.
113 min.
Minnelli's captivating musical still comes up fresh as paint with each successive viewing, as charmingly, romantically nostalgic as an old valentine. One reason, quite apart from the wit and warmth of the characterisations or the skill with which Minnelli integrates the numbers, is that the seismic little shudders of dismay that shake the St Louis family of 1903 – threatened with a move to New York, where father has a bet-

ter job waiting – seem to hint at the end of an era and the disappearance of a world where such uncomplicated happiness can exist. It's a feeling which the self-enclosed formality of the film encourages, with its division into four acts, each introduced by a filigreed tintype from the family album which gradually springs to life. One of the great musicals. TM

Meet Mr Lucifer
(Anthony Pelissier, 1953, GB) Stanley Holloway, Peggy Cummins, Jack Watling, Joseph Tomelty, Barbara Murray, Humphrey Lestocq, Kay Kendall, Gordon Jackson.
81 min. b/w.
Interesting more for its attitudes than for its execution, this satire on television sees Holloway as an unsuccessful panto actor taking out his grievance on the medium by dreaming he is the Devil, turning TV sets all over the country into a source of unhappiness for viewers. The attack is bluntedged and the humour thin, though it does offer a chance to see a fascinating gallery of personalities from days long past (including such luminaries as Gilbert Harding, Philip Harben and MacDonald Hobley). GA

Meet the Applegates
(Michael Lehmann, 1990, US) Ed Begley Jr, Stockard Channing, Dabney Coleman, Bobby Jacoby, Cami Cooper, Glenn Shadix, Susan Barnes, Adam Biesk.
89 min.
The Applegates are highly evolved giant insects forced out of their Brazilian rain forest home by greedy land developers. With only a Dick and Jane school reader as guide, they show up in Median, Ohio, posing as a typical American family. Their plan is to infiltrate and blow up a nuclear power plant, irradiating the planet and making it safe again for bugs. But life in small-town Ohio is fraught with dangers: sonic bug repellents, date rapists, lethal Grasshopper cocktails, roaches of the marijuana variety. So while Jane Applegate (Channing) discovers hedonistic consumerism, neglected husband Dick (Begley) succumbs to fleshier pleasures, and the kids (Jacoby and Cooper) do the teenage thing. Soon they're your average, screwed-up American family, their mission forgotten, until fearsome Aunt Bea (Coleman in drag) turns up determined to kick some *homo sapiens* butt. While it never quite matches the sardonic bite, visual stylishness and ear-catching language of Lehmann's earlier *Heathers*, this wacky eco-comedy delivers plenty of laughs. NF

Meet the Feebles
(Peter Jackson, 1989, NZ) voices: Danny Mulheron, Donna Akersten, Stuart Devenie, Mark Hadlow, Ross Jolly.
97 min. b/w & col.
This deliberately gross movie uses mangy muppets to send up the backstage musical. As the cast of the 'Meet the Feebles' variety show lurch towards a live performance that may land them a syndicated TV series, we are party to the egomaniac excesses, tribulations and jealousies that beset corrupt producer Bletch the Walrus, star singer Heidi the Hippo, star-struck new boy Robert the Hedgehog, and a host of talentless performers and backstage johnnies. Tacky song-and-dance numbers punctuate the action, but despite the attention to set and puppet design, the penning of seven original songs, and Murray Milne's often inventive camerawork, the question remains: why bother to go to all this trouble in order to make a string of gags about vomiting, pissing, shitting, jissom pressure, bunnilingus, and knicker-sniffing anteaters? More generous observers might cite the parallel with bad taste guru John Waters; but compared to this shallow crap, even the Baltimore Bard's offerings run deep. NF

Meet Whiplash Willie
see Fortune Cookie, The

Meilleure Façon de Marcher, La
see Best Way to Walk, The

Mein Krieg
see My Private War

Me Ivan, You Abraham
(Moi Ivan, Toi Abraham)

(Yolande Zauberman, 1993, Fr) Roma
Alexandrovitch, Sacha Iakovlev, Maria
Lipkina, Vladimir Machkov.
105 min. b/w.
The first feature by documentary-maker
Zauberman conjures up the culture of the
Yiddish-speaking Jewish communities of pre-war
Eastern Europe – specifically that of a schtetl
near the Polish border, where two couples, a 12-
year-old Orthodox Jew and his Gentile friend, and
the Jew's sister and her communist boyfriend, are
forced to flee the disintegrating town. These two
friendships are examined with a strange, exultant mix of intimate lyricism and abstract physicality. The Jews' vanished world is seen through
a glass darkly, with its ancient wooden interiors,
markets, wild landscapes, and clashing generational, cultural and religious conflicts. The mood
is hard to define – part gloomy pessimism, reminiscent of early Wajda, part the complex char-
acter-weaving of Alexei Gherman. Finally,
perhaps, it has echoes of a Tarkovskian spiritual quest – but everything harmonises: Jean-Marc
Fabre's saturated b/w imagery, the expressive
acting, the evocative use of music (Arvo Pärt's
'Cantus'). A haunting auspicious film. WH

Melancholia

(Andi Engel, 1989, GB) Jeroen Krabbe,
Susannah York, Ulrich Wildgruber, Jane
Gurnett, Kate Hardie, Saul Reichlin.
87 min.
Like writer/director Andi Engel, the hero (or
anti-hero) of this elegant existential/political
thriller – successful art critic David Keller
(Krabbe) – is a product of the radical '60s, a
German now living in Britain. But his success
is hollow: Dürer's engraving 'Melancholia' on
his upmarket apartment wall, vodka on his
desk, abandoned relationships (most notably
with old flame York), angst and melancholy in
his heart. This moral inertia is catalysed by an
unexpected phone call: a voice from the German
past tells him he has been chosen as the assassin of a Chilean ex-torturer, coming to London
for a conference. Can he stay true to the ideals
of his youth? Could he, should he, kill? Krabbe,
rugged and taciturn (the clipped dialogue of the
opening sounds echoes of the B thriller) gives an
excellent performance, personalising moral and
political issues with facial sensitivity, a palpable intellect, and physical restraint. There is
much to enjoy: Hitchcockian tension and invention in the action sequences, a contemplative but
fluid visual style and an evocative use of music.
Good, too, to see London and Hamburg filmed
as expressively as they are here by cameraman
Denis Crossan. WH

Melinda

(Hugh A Robertson, 1972, US) Calvin
Lockhart, Rosalind Cash, Vonetta McGee, Paul
Stevens, Rockne Tarkington, Ross Hagen,
Renny Roker.
109 min.
Directorial debut for the editor of Midnight
Cowboy and Shaft. An entry in the short-lived
blaxploitation genre, it features a hip, fast-jiving
black DJ (Lockhart) who trains nights on karate
at the Panther HQ and gives out ultracool sounds
by day. He finds himself picking up lovely
Melinda (McGee). They have two days of bliss
before she's carved up. Turns out it's the
Syndicate, an all-white band of nasties, and she
has a tape incriminating the big boss which she
has passed to our hero. Some scenes suggest that
there's a strong eye somewhere behind the camera, but mostly the plot just meanders awkwardly along, not helped by similarly plodding
dialogue.

Mélo

(Alain Resnais, 1986, Fr) Sabine Azéma, Fanny
Ardant, Pierre Arditi, André Dussollier,
Jacques Dacqmine, Hubert Gignoux, Catherine
Arditi.
110 min.
Resnais has preserved the theatrical conventions
of Henry Bernstein's 1929 period piece, complete
with interval curtains, stage lighting and
enclosed sets. Why he chose this particular vehicle becomes clear as female anguish and the corrosive power of memory move centre stage.
Settled hubby and violinist Pierre (Arditi) invites

his more celebrated recitalist friend Marcel
(Dussollier) to dinner. Pierre's wife Romaine
(Azéma) falls for Marcel as he delivers a melancholy speech about faithless mistresses and the
depths of his soul, and during their ensuing affair
determines to prove him wrong. The grandly
swooning passion, the petals of a rose pressed in
a diary – the matter may be dated but the delivery is compelling. There is real pain and cruelty
here among the Brahms duets. BC

Melvin and Howard

(Jonathan Demme, 1980, US) Paul Le Mat,
Jason Robards, Mary Steenburgen, Elizabeth
Cheshire, Chip Taylor, Michael J Pollard,
Denise Galik, Gloria Grahame, Elise Hudson.
95 min.
A beautifully observed, beautifully performed
offbeat comedy. The story is slim: milkman
Melvin Dummar (Le Mat) picks up a grouchy old
hobo in the Nevada desert one night, lends him a
quarter while disbelieving his claim to be Howard
Hughes, and then returns to a mundane life of
work, divorce, remarriage, and failed songwriting attempts, until eight years later he appears to
have been left a fortune by the dead tycoon. But
this remarkable (factually based) plot is merely a
hook on which to hang an unglamorous account
of American working class life. Melvin and his
wives' experiences are double-edged examples of
the allure and failure of the American dream of
success, fame and wealth, although Bo
Goldman's script and Demme's understated
direction never become overly serious or 'significant'. And the film's delightful humour derives
– unusually in these days of brainless Animal
House spoofs and one-liners – from the characters, who are affectionately observed but never
patronised. GA

Memed My Hawk

(Peter Ustinov, 1984, GB) Peter Ustinov,
Herbert Lom, Denis Quilley, Michael Elphick,
Simon Dutton, Leonie Mellinger, Rosalie
Crutchley, Michael Gough.
110 min.
Set in Turkey in the 1920s, this tells the tale of
young Memed (Dutton), a peasant who, to win his
childhood sweetheart, heroically takes to the
mountains as a brigand, incurring the wrath of
his feudal master Abdi Agha (Ustinov) and the
authorities. Beyond these bare bones, little
remains of Yashar Kemal's fine novel (a stirring
adventure and a persuasive indictment of injustice). Hopelessly mangled and confused, the film
is little more than a vehicle for Ustinov (who
stars, directs and wrote the screenplay) and his
capacity for funny accents/camp comedy. It is left
to Freddie Francis' photography of sun-bleached
Yugoslavia (permission to film in Turkey was
refused) to hold the attention during a trying two
hours. FD

Mementos
(Doea Tanda Mata)

(Teguh Karya, 1985, Indon) Alex Komang,
Jenny Rachman, Hermin Chentini, Eka
Gandara.
93 min.
Karya's film suffers from the Hamlet syndrome:
a hero who spends the whole movie doing nothing but go through agonised introspections. The
script problem (compounded by the shortcomings of Komang's performance in the lead) finally works the film into an impasse that no amount
of beautiful period set-direction can relieve. Karya
cunningly invests his story (of anti-colonial resistance in the 1930s) with contemporary resonances, but his daring counts for little when the
material is so uncompelling. TR

Mémoire des Apparences
(Life Is a Dream)

(Raúl Ruiz, 1986, Fr) Sylvain Thirolle, Roch
Leibovici, Bénédicte Sire, Laurence
Cortadellas, Jean-Bernard Guillard,
Jean-Pierre Agazar.
105 min.
Ruiz at his densest and most oblique. Ostensibly
a version of Calderón's Spanish Golden Age
drama Life Is a Dream, it starts as a psychological detective story about a former Resistance
fighter attempting to reconstitute the play and
the details it conceals about an underground
resistance network. Despairing, he ends up hanging around the local cinema, which doubles as a

police station, as well as a playground for the
excesses of memory and the imagination. The
most explicitly dreamlike of Ruiz's fictions, with
Magritte and Borges allusions foremost, it's also
a good example of his tendency to overstate, to
booby-trap his fictions with more false bottoms
than the conscious mind can properly assimilate.
But bearing in mind that sleep forms the main
agenda here, you're probably safe to doze off from
time to time. JRo

Memoirs of an Invisible Man

(John Carpenter, 1992, US) Chevy Chase, Daryl
Hannah, Sam Neill, Michael McKean, Stephen
Tobolowsky, Jim Norton, Pat Skipper.
99 min.
Carpenter's sci-fi comedy is essentially a $40 mil-
lion B movie, with remarkable special effects
compensating for a thin storyline. A noir-ish
opening, complete with voice-over and flashback,
hints at a darker tone more in keeping with HF
Saint's source novel. But once Chase has been rendered invisible, the plot consists of one endless
chase scene, punctuated by inventive sight gags
and the odd romantic interlude. After a freak accident at a research laboratory, Nick Halloway discovers that being invisible isn't the voyeur's
dream he fantasised about as a child. Now 'the
most exotic intelligence asset' available, he
becomes the subject of a huge manhunt led by
cynical CIA man Jenkins (Neill). Aided by anthropologist Alice (Hannah), he tries to evade his pursuers and find time to adjust to his invisibility.
When played for laughs, this works well, while
the action scenes generate an atmosphere of paranoia and menace; but failing to explore the pathos
of Nick's predicament, the film becomes an inflated lightweight comedy whose shortcomings are
all too visible. NF

Memoirs of a Survivor

(David Gladwell, 1981, GB) Julie Christie,
Christopher Guard, Leonie Mellinger, Debbie
Hutchings, Nigel Hawthorne.
115 min.
Christie plays the diarist of Doris Lessing's novel,
surviving in a not-too-distant future Britain
resembling nothing so much as the landscape of
Derek Jarman's 'Jubilee'. The depressing picture
carefully detailed by Gladwell of a nation spiritually, politically and economically bankrupt –
Thatcher's Britain, in fact – is one in which people queue in the streets for water rations, the corner newsvendor with no papers to sell speaks the
news to impassive listeners, horses and dogs are
set upon for food, packs of wild children huddle
in the underground. Through all this Christie
wanders with the comfort of her fantasies, too
familiar by half to arthouse regulars. RM

Memories

(Katsuhiro Otomo/Koji Morimoto/Tensai
Okamura, 1995, Jap)
113 min.
Not counting Roujin Z, for which he came up with
a story and some designs, this is Otomo's first
animation feature since Akira: a portmanteau
film (based on three of his graphic short stories)
which fully represents his range and at the same
time fulfils his dream of providing real creative
opportunities to young artists stuck in TV animation hell. Magnetic Rose, the first episode, is
spectacular space opera: two intrepid scouts, a
ghost ship and the story of a love without end,
set in a cosmic Sargasso Sea. Stink Bomb is cautionary sci-fi comedy: a guy takes an untested
drug in mistake for a cold cure and turns into a
maximum security risk. And Cannon Fodder,
directed by Otomo himself, is a bizarre parable
of war, peace and expendability. All three
episodes are cogent, provocative and superbly
designed. TR

Memories of Duke

(Gary Keys, 1980, US) Duke Ellington, Cootie
Williams, Russell Procope, the Duke
Ellington Band.
85 min.
Black producer/director Gary Keys' monument
to Ellington consists of concert footage of the
band's 1968 tour, intercut with interview comments from long-time sidemen Cootie Williams
and Russell Procope. If the sound quality of the
numbers leaves something to be desired, the
inclusion of Ellington-composed classics like
'Take The A Train', 'Satin Doll' and 'Black And

Tan Fantasy' (and information about long and satisfying sojourns of individual musicians with the band) more than attests to the Duke's stature as Jazz Giant. RM

Memories of Me
(Henry Winkler, 1988, US) Billy Crystal, Alan King, JoBeth Williams, Janet Carroll, David Ackroyd, Phil Fondacaro.
105 min.
Unreleased in the UK, this typical Billy Crystal offering, co-written and produced with fellow comic Alan King, is an uneasy blend of neurotic comedy and mawkish sentimentality. Its story of a heart surgeon whose recent coronary forces him to reassess his life and rebuild his relationship with his estranged dad is too eager to please, but Crystal mugs away with consummate professionalism and nightclub veteran King brings acerbity to the role of the curmudgeonly father.

Memories of Underdevelopment (Memorias del Subdesarrollo)
(Tomas Gutiérrez Alea, 1968, Cuba) Sergio Corrieri, Daisy Granádos, Eslinda Nuñez, Beatriz Ponchora, Omar Valdés.
104 min. b/w.
The Cuban Film Institute (ICAIC) was founded in 1959, only months after Castro came to power. It was some years, however, before its fruits were exposed to European and US audiences; Alea's film, his fifth feature, was the breakthrough. The story is related in the form of a diary by a prosperous bourgeois who chooses to stay in Havana when his family leaves for the States in 1961. While he rejects many of the bourgeois ideals of his upbringing, he is unable to shake off either sexual neurosis or his European-based intellectual paralysis, continuing to live uncertainly as a rent-drawing property-owner. The 'underdevelopment' of the title is a complex pun describing both individual and national problems of the revolution in its infancy, though the film is anything but literary in its attack: Alea proceeds with dazzling and highly accomplished technique towards a perceptive and witty analysis. Many critics at the time were surprised by the strain of self-criticism running through a film produced by what is virtually a government ministry in a Marxist country. RM

Memories Within Miss Aggie
(Gerard Damiano, 1974, US) Deborah Ashira, Patrick L Farrelly, Harry Reems, Kim Pope, Mary Stuart.
69 min.
Around 1974, US hardcore film-makers were getting over their first flush of triumph at simply putting the sex act on screen, and Damiano turns to psychological horror for this tale of a demented old woman reminiscing through a lifetime of romantic fantasy to a predictably macabre final revelation. In its hardcore form (running 78 minutes), the film's small momentum was generated by various sexual acts which served to disguise the sheer wretchedness of everything in between. This softcore version, from which the British censor removed nine minutes to eradicate any lingering traces, looks like some meandering American fringe theatre production in which everyone has swallowed too much Valium. Even the most diehard porno audience will be panting…to get out of the cinema. DP

Memory of Justice, The
(Marcel Ophüls, 1975, GB/WGer/US) Yehudi Menuhin, Daniel Ellsberg, JK Galbraith, Albert Speer, Marcel Ophüls.
278 min. b/w & col.
An investigation of the impact of the Nuremberg trials on the German conscience, and a study of the implications of the moral and legal principles established there for events like Hiroshima and Vietnam, The Memory of Justice operates by steadily drawing the viewer into a situation that is forever expanding, as new ramifications and contexts are found by Ophüls in the course of his interviews and in the use he makes of library footage. The film is, accordingly, as important for its method of investigation as for the facts it reveals. In contrast to the tight narrative and fixed viewpoint of the run-of-the-mill TV documentary, Ophüls' film is so structured as to force

the viewer to involve himself in the arguments presented in the actual process of watching the film, thus transforming a passive viewing into an active reading. PH

Memphis Belle
(Michael Caton-Jones, 1990, GB) Matthew Modine, Eric Stoltz, Tate Donovan, DB Sweeney, Billy Zane, David Strathairn, John Lithgow, Jane Horrocks.
102 min.
In East Anglia, 1943, the crew of an American B17 bomber prepare for their 25th daylight mission: if they return alive, it'll be a record and they'll be whisked back to the States for a propaganda tour. Inspired by real-life events covered in Wyler's WWII documentary The Memphis Belle, this David Puttnam production may not be the most original movie around, but at least Caton-Jones steers through the stock situations with verve and panache. Aided by uniformly sturdy performances (Modine and Strathairn are particularly fine as the pilot and commanding officer), he even carries off such Hawksian moments as Modine's moonlit monologue to his plane, and achieves a genuine mood of claustrophobia, vulnerability and danger in the airborne scenes, while never giving way to bogus jingoism. Admittedly, one could do with less of the dog and 'Oh Danny Boy'; and towards the end, the story's sheer eventfulness risks tipping the tone into self-parody. For the most part, though, this is sensitive, gripping, oddly old-fashioned cinema. GA

Men (Männer)
(Doris Dörrie, 1985, WGer) Heiner Lauterbach, Uwe Ochsenknecht, Ulrike Kriener, Janna Marangosoff, Dietmar Bär.
99 min.
Love me, love my double standards, that's what Julius (Lauterbach), a power-hungry German packaging magnate and habitual seducer of secretaries, expects from his wife. He gets it too, until their 12th anniversary, when a love bite on her neck suggests that an equaliser is at work. At this early point in Doris Dörrie's concise and sharply observed satire, you might be forgiven for thinking that a feminist attack is under way. Not so. Julius, who hasn't come to own a Maserati simply by waiting for things to happen, takes leave of absence to strike back. Concealing his identity, he persuades his wife's lover (Ochsenknecht) to accept him, first as a lodger in his squalid bachelor apartment, then as a partner in his low-achieving hippy life. It's the start of an unpredictable friendship that puts both men's motivation under the microscope. Dörrie's screenplay requires a certain suspension of disbelief – would a wife be so easily deceived by a gorilla suit? – but she turns the tables neatly so that each gets his just deserts. Hers not to stick in the knife, rather to entertain with insight and mirth. MCR

Men, The
(Fred Zinnemann, 1950, US) Marlon Brando, Teresa Wright, Everett Sloane, Jack Webb, Richard Erdman, Howard St John.
85 min. b/w.
Even in his first movie, Brando's ability to transcend mediocre material is very much in evidence. The Men, a ward full of war-veteran paraplegics under the stern but loving care of Doctor Everett Sloane, struggle to come to terms with their predicament, hoping eventually to exchange their own tough bonhomie for the world outside. Although Stanley Kramer's typically soapy production focuses attention on Brando's tempestuous relationship (wrecked by his feelings of shame and inadequacy) with devoted fiancée Teresa Wright (all syrupy sincerity), the film timidly skirts problems of sexual frustration and impotence. It also almost totally ignores the cause of the paraplegics' disabilities: not one of them ever expresses regret at having ruined life and limb for Uncle Sam. Despite the worthy wetness, however, young Marlon manages to sidestep sentimentality; even confined to a wheelchair, the raw power underlying his controlled gestures and brooding glances is charismatic. GA

Menace II Society
(Allen Hughes/Albert Hughes, 1993, US) Tyrin Turner, Jada Pinkett, Larenz Tate, Arnold Johnson, MC Eiht, Marilyn Coleman.
97 min.

Another tale from the 'hood, but, regrettably, the Hughes brothers' first feature is a compendium of clichés. Beginning with the murder of a Korean shopkeeper by two Watts teenagers, the film focuses on the dilemma faced by Caine (Turner), torn between the members of his 'posse' and his good girl Ronnie (Pinkett), who tries to persuade him from his violent ways. Photographed, scored and performed with more flair than the material deserves. GA

Men Are Children Twice
see Valley of Song

Men Are Not Gods
(Walter Reisch, 1936, GB) Miriam Hopkins, Gertrude Lawrence, Sebastian Shaw, Rex Harrison, AE Matthews, Val Gielgud, Laura Smithson, Lawrence Grossmith, Wally Patch.
90 min. b/w.
Producer Alexander Korda roped in Walter Reisch, an old pal from his Viennese days, to direct; hired top US cameraman Charles Rosher (who'd worked on Murnau's Sunrise); lured over Hollywood luminary Hopkins, and bolstered the cast with British stage stalwarts, but to no avail – this yarn about a stenographer who falls for a married actor (he contemplates strangling his wife during a performance of Othello) remains throwaway, novelettish nonsense. GM

Men at Work
(Emilio Estevez, 1990, US) Charlie Sheen, Emilio Estevez, Leslie Hope, Keith David, Dean Cameron, John Getz, Hawk Wolinski, John Lavachielli, John Putch, Tommy Hinkley, Darrell Larson.
98 min.
Estevez scripted, directed and stars, alongside brother Sheen, in this comic thriller about two Californian garbage collectors who find a dead body in one of their bins. Estevez must take the blame for the overall cheery incompetence, although the film, like the average dustbin of affluence, contains many fresh elements amid the trash. There's a gruesome conservation theme (toxic dumping off a premier surfing beach), and an amazingly lively corpse (Darrell Larson doesn't let a little detail like rigor mortis inhibit a performance of extraordinary animation). This snigger-snigger attitude to death is matched by a general tastelessness. Sheen gloatingly spies on the woman living opposite, and there's a nasty running gag whereby the boys outwit, disarm, strip and handcuff pairs of policemen in compromising positions. But the grotesque practical jokes perpetrated against two interfering bumblers are genuinely funny, while Estevez and Sheen remain cutely goofy even when indulging themselves in this adolescent idiocy. SFe

Men Don't Leave
(Paul Brickman, 1990, US) Jessica Lange, Arliss Howard, Joan Cusack, Kathy Bates, Tom Mason, Chris O'Donnell, Charlie Korsmo.
114 min.
When her husband dies in an explosion, leaving her with massive debts, two young sons and no visible means of support, Beth Macauley (Lange) moves to a cramped apartment in the city, where she lands a thankless job in a gourmet foodstore. While her younger son (Korsmo) takes to petty burglary, and teenage Chris (O'Donnell) finds solace with a young nurse (Cusack), Beth starts an affair with a musician (Howard); but progress is impeded as she gives way to delayed shock and declines into depression. What distinguishes this weepie is its deglamorised approach: all-consuming angst is anchored in the minutiae of everyday life and wry observation. While not without its occasional lapses into over-long sob sessions, Barbara Benedek and Brickman's intelligent script offers strong characterisations, and the performances – particularly from Lange and Korsmo – are excellent. Absorbing, truthful, and full of tender insight. CM

Ménilmontant
(Dimitri Kirsanoff, 1924, Fr) Nadia Sibirskaia, Yoland Beaulieu, Guy Belmont.
50 min. b/w.
Time has dealt much more kindly with Kirsanoff than with most of his contemporaries. A Russian émigré in Paris who enjoyed little contact with other film-makers, his extraordinary montages, dissolves and narrative ellipses nevertheless echo

the tricks that became tics in so many early avant-garde experiments. But in Kirsanoff's work, such devices are overridden and firmly welded together by the romantic impressionism which casts a haunting aura of malevolent beauty over *Ménilmontant* and its suburban axe-murderer.

Men in Black
(Barry Sonnenfeld, 1997, US) Tommy Lee Jones, Will Smith, Linda Fiorentino, Vincent D'Onofrio, Rip Torn, Tony Shalhoub.
98 min.
They're here – and they have social security numbers. Aliens are everywhere, just trying to get along like the rest of us, mostly, under the watchful eyes of an extra-governmental police agency, the Men in Black. Agent K (Jones) picks out a New York cop (Smith) to become his new partner, J, initiating him into the secrets of the universe: galactic weaponry, memory erasers and power dressing. At the same time, an unintegrated alien bug takes residence in the (loose-fitting) body of farmer D'Onofrio, with a plan that might mean curtains for the planet. Sonnenfeld's film is just good enough to remind us how lazy most blockbusters have become in the decade since *Gremlins* and *Ghostbusters* – hits with a similar hip, relaxed vibe.The personable well-paired stars make the most of a superior script by Ed Solomon ('He said the world was coming to an end.' 'Did he say when?'), and, taking eye-popping special fx in his stride, the director makes adroit use of out-of-this-world NY locations. It's so much fun, in fact, that it's almost over before you realise that you've been watching a great idea for a movie in desperate search of a plot. TCh

Men in War
(Anthony Mann, 1957, US) Robert Ryan, Aldo Ray, Robert Keith, Phillip Pine, Nehemiah Persoff, Vic Morrow, James Edwards, LQ Jones, Scott Marlowe.
104 min. b/w.
One of the best of the lost patrol movies, set in Korea in 1950, bleakly anti-heroic and prefiguring Milestone's *Pork Chop Hill* in the bitter irony of its climactic assault on a hill. Beautifully staged by Mann with his usual eye to landscape, and an intriguing sub-theme querying the nature of military authority as Ryan's lieutenant, wearily devoting himself to shepherding his men through alive, comes into conflict with – while forced to rely on the battle skills of – Aldo Ray's sergeant, whose sole interest, pursued with doglike devotion, lies in trying to save a shellshocked colonel (mad but still a symbol of authority). TM

Men of Respect
(William Reilly, 1990, US) John Turturro, Katherine Borowitz, Dennis Farina, Peter Boyle, Rod Steiger, Lilia Skala, Steven Wright, Stanley Tucci.
113 min.
Macbeth as a mobland drama is no sillier than *The Tempest* in deep space; but the Scottish Play is so obviously a prototype for tales of young wiseguys slaying their way to *capo*-dom that to rewrite the original is simply stating the obvious. Young hood Mike Battaglia (Turturro), egged on by ambitious wife Ruthie (Borowitz), kills gang boss Steiger and gets to be *padrino*. But no sooner is the deed done than he starts hallucinating visits from slain buddy Bankie Como (Farina). Reilly rewrites the original in fustian *noir*, but shows too much respect for it, bending over backwards to fit in touches like catatonic comic Steven Wright in a slouch-on part as the Porter, pathetic fallacy galore, and lines like 'Not a man of woman born can do shit to me'. Turturro acts as though he can't believe what he's got into but is determined to have a field day anyhow; and Borowitz gives Ruthie a slinky gravitas, although she doesn't look the kind to freak out with the Ajax. JRo

Men of Two Worlds
(Thorold Dickinson, 1946, GB) Eric Portman, Phyllis Calvert, Robert Adams, Cathleen Nesbitt, Orlando Martins, Cyril Raymond.
107 min.
Three years in the making, Dickinson's film survived the loss of filmstock and equipment when a U-Boat sunk their ship en route to locations in Tanzania. What remains is a well-intentioned, slightly musty drama exploring the clash of science and superstition in colonial East Africa,

where a witch doctor refuses to let commissioner Portman evacuate his tribe to escape the sleeping sickness sweeping his village. These days though, it all looks a bit patronising. TJ

Menschen am Sonntag
see People on Sunday

Men's Club, The
(Peter Medak, 1986, US) Roy Scheider, Harvey Keitel, Richard Jordan, Craig Wasson, Frank Langella, Treat Williams, David Dukes, Stockard Channing, Marilyn Jones.
101 min.
Californication. Six men meet in the home of a buddy psychotherapist to talk about themselves and women. The real estate agent (Keitel) remembers one who put her tongue in his mouth. The doctor (Williams) remembers the one who came between him and his strawberry dessert – he kicked her. Attorney Langella's wife, thanks to analysis, discovered herself and scarpered with the furniture. Blah blah blah. When they have eaten all the food, drunk all the wine, and wrecked the place throwing knives, they move on to an up-market San Francisco brothel, where they all make out/up/mistakes. All, that is, except the shrink, rapped over the head with a casserole by his irate spouse. Flashes of genuine intelligence and wit in the writing only render the moral nihilism of the whole high-tack enterprise all the more inexcusable. MS

Men's Lives
(Josh Hanig/Will Roberts, 1975, US)
43 min.
With the rise of the women's movement in America, men have been forced to question, to some extent, male stereotypes and the roles they're expected to play. This rather twee documentary never gets much beyond asking very general questions, alternating between half-baked theorising and studying a variety of male groups, from the children's playground through to the student dance. The film largely ignores the gap between a male ideal and various interpretations of that ideal, and also skates over the implications of language and its emotional charges. When there's the curious contradiction of an 'effeminate' young male dancer defending himself in classic macho terms – 'A man is someone who will stand up for what he thinks is right' – the film fails to even notice the wires crossing. CPe

Mensonge
see Lie, The

Men Who Tread on the Tiger's Tail, The
see Tora no Oo Fumu Otokotachi

Men, Women: User's Manual (Hommes femmes Mode d'emploi)
(Claude Lelouch, 1996, Fr) Fabrice Luchini, Bernard Tapie, Alessandra Martines, Pierre Arditi, Ticky Holgado, Daniel Gélin, Anouk Aimée, Claude Lelouch.
123 min.
After the international acclaim for his revisionist update of *Les Misérables* comes this offering from Lelouch, far more typical of the maverick filmmaker's run of convoluted all-star melodramas that regularly boost the French box office and which, equally regularly, receive frosty treatment from the Paris critical elite. His major coup here, however, is casting business magnate Tapie, who served a prison sentence for tax evasion. He seems more or less to be playing himself, a charismatic rogue who receives his comeuppance from doctor Martines, a vengeful old flame who switches his unblemished medical reports with the gloomy verdict on twitchy undercover cop Luchini. The sick one soon comes over all glad-to-be-alive, and his perfectly healthy counterpart's on his way to Lourdes for a 'miracle' cure. Ever intent on gilding the lily, Lelouch weaves in some rather tiresome teenage romantic asides, and detains us further with the rags-to-riches story of a falsetto street singer. The main diversion is Lelouch's characteristically virtuoso camerawork, with sweeping helicopter shots and a luscious, blue-tinged Paris captivating the atten-

tion while you try to work out how elegant, sixty-something con-artist Anouk Aimée fits into the mazy grand design. Tapie is a surprisingly personable screen presence, but the film itself is decorative, mercurial and really rather mystifying. TJ

Mephisto
(István Szabó, 1981, Hun) Klaus Maria Brandauer, Ildikó Bánsági, Krystyna Janda, Rolf Hoppe, György Cserhalmi, Péter Andorai, Karin Boyd.
144 min.
For all the retro art movie gloss recently applied to the cautionary spectacle of the pre-war rise of Nazism, there has been precious little incisive appraisal of the precise seductive allure of fascism, and certainly none to match that offered by Szabó's remarkable film. Adapted from Klaus Mann's more hysterically vindictive 1936 novel, Szabó's film delineates the self-deceiving ease with which a talented actor may rationalise the sort of radical careerist compromises that lead from committed exponency of Brecht towards impeccably Aryan readings of Goethe, and even the personal betrayals that doom friends and lovers to exile or elimination. A superbly modulated, fruitfully ambivalent central performance by Brandauer carries the emotional and intellectual weight of the political dilemma, while Szabó happily refuses to overstress the Faustian parallels of the perverse power-pact between the cultural icon and his Goebbels-like puppeteer. PT

Mephisto Waltz, The
(Paul Wendkos, 1971, US) Alan Alda, Jacqueline Bisset, Barbara Parkins, Curd Jürgens, Bradford Dillman, William Windom.
109 min.
A tale of diabolism with a plot familiar from *Rosemary's Baby*; but where Polanski's film developed into a complex investigation of doubt and fear as well as evil, this is anything but subtle. Alda plays an ex-musician turned writer of music ready to trade wife and child for a career, Bisset his down-to-earth, fearful wife who follows her man even into Satanism. The Devil-worshipping couple are a world famous concert pianist (Jürgens) dying of leukemia, and his daughter (Parkins), whose incestuous relationship is continued after her father's death through his usurping of the younger man's personality and hands. Wendkos seems prone to script troubles with his movies, and this is no exception; he goes all out to kill it, shooting with heavily greased lens from every conceivable angle, exiling normality to periphery. Bizarre and vulgar, certainly, but also very hard to follow. VG

Mépris, Le (Contempt)
(Jean-Luc Godard, 1963, Fr/It) Brigitte Bardot, Michel Piccoli, Jack Palance, Fritz Lang, Giorgia Moll.
103 min.
A film about – among other things – integrity. The basic situation, faithfully adapted from Moravia's novel *A Ghost at Noon*, concerns a young woman (Bardot) who is gradually possessed by an overwhelming contempt for her husband (Piccoli), a writer beset by doubts when he is called in as script-doctor to a film of *The Odyssey*, being made by a director (Lang) who wants to capture the reality of Homer's world, and a crass producer (Palance) who just wants more mermaids. Yes, she agrees that the money will be useful; no, she doesn't feel he is selling out since he is interested in the subject; and which ever way he decides to jump is perfectly all right by her. But there still remains that tight knot of contempt which she won't explain and he doesn't understand. Around this Godard weaves subtle parallels with Homer's tale of patient Penelope, the statues of Minerva and Neptune which brood over the modern tragedy, locations which paradoxically set the airy spaces of a flat in Rome against the confines of the Homeric landscapes of Capri, and for good measure a stream of cinematic jokes. Magnificently shot by Raoul Coutard, it's a dazzling fable. TM

Mercedes Mon Amour (Fikrimin Ince Gulu)
(Tung Oken, 1992, Tur) Iylas Salman, Valeria Lemoine, Micky Sebastian.
90 min.
Bit of a broad comedy with Bayram (Salman) as

the nerd Everyman, a Munich street cleaner, who achieves his dream of buying a yellow 350SE Mercedes to show off at home. It's a long drive (believe me!): scratches, scrapes, troubles with hippy vans, aggressive lorry drivers and thieving parking-lot attendants dog his every kilometre. Turkey seems like bad car trouble: there's more crashed vehicles here than in Godard's French weekend. The music is French-style too: ding-dong disco seemingly from one of their '60s commercials. The film has a moral ('thinking about No 1' German-style can leave you stranded), but it's more interested in the drive. WH

Mercenaries, The
(aka Dark of the Sun)
(Jack Cardiff, 1967, GB) Rod Taylor, Yvette Mimieux, Peter Carsten, Jim Brown, Kenneth More, Andre Morell, Olivier Despax, Guy Deghy, Calvin Lockhart.
100 min.
The Congo, 1960: soldier-of-fortune Taylor braves rebel-held territory to rescue the white folk and retrieve a fortune in diamonds for President Ubi. The political backgound is skated over so we can get on with a crude variation on the cowboy-and-injuns schtick and plenty of lip-smacking carnage. Tricked out with an ex-Nazi (Carsten) still sporting a swastika, a disheveled blonde Belgian refugee (Mimieux), a loyal African sergeant (Brown), and a dipso English doctor (More) who sacrifices himself for a woman in labour, the film has an exceptionally unsympathetic hero and a preposterous moral turn-round at the close. Adapted from a novel by Wilbur Smith. TJ

Mercenario, Il
(The Mercenary/ A Professional Gun)
(Sergio Corbucci, 1968, It/Sp) Franco Nero, Tony Musante, Jack Palance, Giovanna Ralli, Eduardo Fajardo, Bruno Corazzari, Remo De Angeles, Joe Camel.
105 min.
During the Mexican Revolution, Nero, the mercenary Sergei Cowalski, is hired to transport silver to a mine in Texas, only to find that Musante and his co-workers have taken control. Switching sides, the hired gun finds himself teaching the rebel leader how to put his revolutionary ideas into practise, but his idealistic fervour is tested when the men's firepower gathers them a personal fortune. Plenty of baroque touches in this spaghetti Western, including Palance as Curly, a white-suited gay gunman (looking like 'a bewigged Burgess Meredith' as one contemporary reviewer had it). TJ

Mercenary, The
see Mercenario, Il

Merchant of Four Seasons, The (Händler der vier Jahreszeiten, Der)
(Rainer Werner Fassbinder, 1971, WGer) Hans Hirschmüller, Irm Hermann, Hanna Schygulla, Andrea Schober, Gusti Kreissl, Kurt Raab, Klaus Löwitsch.
89 min.
Made before Fear Eats the Soul, which it resembles in many respects, this deceptively muted melodrama chronicles the 'rubbing out' of a character found oddly irrelevant by those around him: a man who dreamed of being an engineer, but had to settle for a fruit and vegetable stall, his aspirations constantly frustrated by his social circumstances. The film builds with remarkable power towards a concluding scene in which the process of Hans' destruction is revealed to be blindly self-perpetuating. Fassbinder's regular ensemble perform with enormous precision, and there's a remarkable dinner party scene in which, in a kind of mesmeric shorthand, the mechanics of destruction are revealed, working like clockwork. VG

Merci la vie (Thank You, Life)
(Bertrand Blier, 1991, Fr) Charlotte Gainsbourg, Anouk Grinberg, Gérard Depardieu, Michel Blanc, Jean Carmet, Catherine Jacob, Jean-Louis Trintignant, Annie Girardot.
118 min. b/w & col.

Wheeling a supermarket trolley full of seagulls, shy, sexually inexperienced Camille (Gainsbourg) comes across Joëlle (Grinberg), a none-too-virginal abandoned bride seen by Camille as a gift from heaven. The pair embark on a series of raucous, sometimes violent and often funny (mis)adventures with variously exploitative, lecherous and pathetic men: fathers, film-makers, a doctor (Depardieu), a Nazi officer (Trintignant). Is it all really happening, or just a movie, or simply Camille's dream? Snazzily shot, wittily performed and structured, Buñuel-fashion, according to the logic of a dream, this bizarre blend of road movie, comedy, psychodrama and various other genres shifts with wayward glee not only between times – the present (?) and WWII – but between colour, black-and-white and monochrome tints. Lending some coherence is a sense that every age has its crises (AIDS, the Holocaust), that life is shit; but Blier's precise intentions are finally unfathomable. GA

Mercury Rising
(Harold Becker, 1998, US) Bruce Willis, Alec Baldwin, Miko Hughes, Chi McBride, Kim Dickens, Peter Stormare.
111 min.
Autistic kid and washed-up FBI agent on the run from out-of-control government security outfit: such is the not very high concept which the fitfully interesting Becker has to dumb himself down to the point of ignominy to put over. Withholding wit, invention and style, he barely acknowledges life in the real world. John Barry's score, with its reiterated 'autistic kid' theme, would have sounded corny to Ivor Novello, though it's in keeping with the general principle of patronising the audience. BBa

Merlusse
(Marcel Pagnol, 1935, Fr) Henri Poupon, André Pollack, Thomeray, Rellys, Jean Castan.
66 min. b/w.
Merlusse, his face disfigured by shrapnel, is a mutilé de guerre – an everyday sight of the period. He's a teacher, cold and correct, as a defence against the routine nastiness of his boarding school charges. The substance of the film – Merlusse assigned to supervise those pupils with nowhere to go for the Christmas holidays – is strong enough to fuel a Disney melodrama or a grand, emotional Lloyd Webber aria. What's extraordinary is not that Pagnol declines the melodrama (a villain in a Pagnol movie is anyway unthinkable) but that he only casually dramatises the situation, making this perhaps the first do-it-yourself weepie. Discretion, a refusal to indulge poignant detail, to ironise or to produce a big finish – here's a film that clearly never imagined postmodernism. BBa

Mermaids
(Richard Benjamin, 1990, US) Cher, Bob Hoskins, Winona Ryder, Michael Schoeffling, Christina Ricci, Caroline McWilliams, Jan Miner.
110 min.
Charlotte (Ryder) has upped sticks 18 times in her young life, and she's hoping to settle down with her mother and sister in Eastport, Massachusetts. Their new house borders a convent, allowing the Jewish teen to indulge in fantasies about handsome handyman Joe (Schoeffling) and, perversely, about life as a nun. Loopy Mom (Cher) has neglected to tell her daughter about the facts of life, leaving Charlotte stranded between desire and fears of pregnancy. This self-conscious, eccentric comedy is set in 1963, a year which sees Charlotte's innocence fade in the wake of both sexual discovery and Kennedy's assassination. The film is burdened by curious details and observations, and its preoccupation with all things aquatic (little sister is an ace swimmer, Mom dresses up as a mermaid for New Year's Eve, etc) is overworked. Characterisation suffers, with Charlotte and her mother too self-absorbed to engage our sympathies. Crucially, they just aren't funny. CM

Merrill's Marauders
(Samuel Fuller, 1962, US) Jeff Chandler, Ty Hardin, Peter Brown, Andrew Duggan, Will Hutchins, Claude Akins.
98 min.
Fuller's superb patrol movie – taut, bleak and damning – was a self-confessed 'rehearsal' for his

long-gestating The Big Red One, following a World War II American platoon in Burma on a suicidal trek, suffering from what the unit doctor diagnoses as AOE – 'accumulation of everything' – and burdened by madness, exhaustion, and the demonstrable irrationality of their wasted energies. Fuller draws potent ironies from his casting of young cowboy 'heroes' (including Bronco and Tenderfoot), and mobilises his camera in violent sympathy with the men's physical and psychological effort. PT

Merrily We Go to Hell
(Dorothy Arzner, 1932, US) Fredric March, Sylvia Sidney, Adrienne Allen, Skeets Gallagher, Kent Taylor, Cary Grant, Esther Howard.
78 min. b/w.
Part voguish 'sophisticated' satire, part domestic melodrama, this film from the Lubitsch era at Paramount is a curious but highly entertaining hybrid. March, a journalist and would-be playwright with a heartbreak in his past and a liking for the bottle, woos and weds Sylvia Sidney's heiress, and we follow their 'matrimony modern style' through better and worse, richer and poorer, sickness and health, up to a dubiously happy ending of which Sirk would have been proud. As befits a film by Hollywood's foremost female 'auteur', all the male characters are hopelessly immature; yet the women rarely transcend movie types. PT

Merry Christmas Mr Lawrence
(Nagisa Oshima, 1982, GB) David Bowie, Tom Conti, Ryuichi Sakamoto, Takeshi, Jack Thompson, Johnny Okura.
124 min.
For all the praise heaped upon Oshima's admittedly ambitious film about East-West relations in the microcosm of a Japanese POW camp during World War II, it's far less satisfactory than most of his earlier work. It may go against Japanese taboos as it deals with commandant Sakamoto's obsessive love for prisoner Bowie, it may be stylishly shot, it may seem uncompromising in its depiction of the Japanese war ethic and the insistence on harakiri as a more honourable reaction to defeat than submission to imprisonment. But the web of relationships between English and Japanese is too schematic in its polarisation of characters, Oshima's handling of the narrative is not so much elliptical as awkward, and Bowie's performance is embarrassingly wooden. Add to that Sakamoto's turgid score and posing narcissism, some horrendous symbolism, and some pretty shoddy technical work (several of the pans are hurried and blurred), and you have a fair old mess. GA

Merry-Go-Round
(Erich von Stroheim/Rupert Julian, 1922, US) Norman Kerry, Dorothy Wallace, Mary Philbin, Cesare Gravina, Edith Yorke, George Siegmann, Dale Fuller.
12 reels. b/w.
Stroheim was sacked by Irving Thalberg only a little way into the shooting of his last film for Universal, and it was completed by Rupert Julian. Sets and screenplay, however, remain Stroheim's personal achievement; and from the opening sequence, where his Viennese Count hero (Kerry) is observed going through his daily rituals in his leisured environment, it's possible to imagine what Stroheim himself would have done with the rest of the film. The fairground scenes, where the Count meets and falls for the heroine (Philbin), are mostly blown by Julian's direction of his actors. What remains, though, is a strong sense of contrast between the lavish Viennese court and the fairground low-life. If the contrived narrative lacks the conviction Stroheim's attention to detail might have given it, at least his sense of design remains dominant. RM

Merry Widow, The
(Erich von Stroheim, 1925, US) John Gilbert, Mae Murray, Roy D'Arcy, Tully Marshall, George Fawcett, Josephine Crowell, Dale Fuller.
12 reels. b/w.
Commissioned by MGM to film Franz Lehar's operetta, Stroheim characteristically tried to bury it within a larger framework of his own devising. He added a prologue that finally occupied more

than half the total running time. Stroheim makes everything possible out of the grotesqueries, most notably the baron's foot fetishism and the sadist's ignominious death, but his elaborate scheme of erotic contrasts is finally engulfed by the frivolous artifice of the original operetta. The result is stylish and spasmodically witty, but rarely more. TR

Mery per sempre
see Forever Mary

Mes Petites Amoureuses
(Jean Eustache, 1975, Fr) Martin Loeb, Ingrid Caven, Jacqueline Dufranne, Dionys Mascolo, Henri Martinez, Maurice Pialat.
123 min.
After *The Mother and the Whore*, Eustache turns his attention here to pubescence in provincial France. The tone is somewhat reminiscent of *Malle* (*Le Souffle au Coeur*, *Lacombe Lucien*) in its attempt at an unsentimental depiction of the sexual awakening of a 13-year-old boy; but ultimately it's more tough-minded, recognising as it does the effects of class and social status on the boy's development. More important is the continual stress on his essential aloneness in coming to terms with sexual experience; he rarely smiles, and finally comes across somewhat like a Bresson protagonist. A minor irritation is the relentless accumulation of short scenes, some with very little to add. RM

Message, The
see Al-Risalah

Message to Love: The Isle of Wight Festival
(Murray Lerner, 1994, US) Jimi Hendrix, The Doors, Free, Kris Kristofferson, The Who, Miles Davis, Jethro Tull, Joni Mitchell, Ricki Farr.
126 min.
'I just woke up about two minutes ago,' quips Jimi Hendrix. He then launches into the title track of Lerner's often hilarious documentary on the biggest, grubbiest, most colourful, chaotic gathering of the masses since Jesus dished out the loaves. Shot on both 16 and 35mm, the film spends as much time rummaging through the backstage shenanigans as it does covering the sounds of the multitude of 'dadrockers' on the bill. And thank goodness it does, because here we have an event so haphazard and disorganised, you can only wonder how it continued to function beyond even the first few bars of music. Six hundred thousand 'brothers and sisters' rowed, shipped, and hitched their way across the watery divide, yet the organisers had sold just 50,000 tickets. 'The fence must die,' proclaimed graffiti painted by destitutes on 'desolation row'. The corrugated sheeting collapsed, and it was left to financially strapped MC/promoter Ricki Farr to cool things down, and to Joni Mitchell to lose her head by telling the rowdy crowds to 'stop behaving like tourists, man.' The music is exemplary stuff to anyone who heard it the first time around – The Doors, Free, Kris Kristofferson (who eventually stormed off stage), The Who, Miles Davis (silhouetted against the dusk), Jethro Tull – but it's the hilarity of the sound-bites that makes this *really* worth catching. DA

Messer im Kopf
see Knife in the Head

Messidor
(Alain Tanner, 1978, Switz/Fr) Clémentine Amouroux, Catherine Retoré, Franziskus Abgottspon, Gérald Battiaz, Hansjorg Bedscard.
123 min.
A comparison between this and Terrence Malick's *Badlands* makes for an interesting contrast between American and European concepts of the cinema. Both films deal with a couple in flight, and the way in which a puzzled society becomes engrossed in their one-way journey. But there the similarities end. In Malick's film, the violence is within the central characters themselves. Tanner uses the progress of his female travellers to examine, not them but the harsh logic that underpins an 'exemplary' capitalist state like Switzerland. Thus, once Clémentine Amouroux and Catherine Retoré choose to become margin-

al characters – when they meet, they decide for a lark to see how long they can survive without money – they soon find that society has no place within it for them. PH

Metalstorm: The Destruction of Jared-Syn
(Charles Band, 1983, US) Jeffrey Byron, Mike Preston, Tim Thomerson, Kelly Preston, Richard Moll, R David Smith.
83 min.
A dire cross between *Mad Max* and *Star Wars*, set on the futuristic desert planet of Lemuria, where a padded-leather-clad nasty called Jared-Syn (Mike Preston) is taking over the planet with the aid of a deadly crystal. Hero Jack Dogen (Byron), a Peacekeeping Ranger, sets out to destroy Jared-Syn, accompanied by a knowledgeable desert nomad (Thomerson, putting in the only decent performance). They stumble upon an ancient crystal mask which will give Jack sufficient power, but must first face Jared-Syn's son Baal, a half man/half machine that squirts green hallucinatory gunk at its victims. With vehicles and ideas left over from the *Mad Max* set, not even the 3-D effect can deflect attention from the naff performances and excruciatingly dull script. DA

Meteor
(Ronald Neame, 1979, US) Sean Connery, Natalie Wood, Karl Malden, Brian Keith, Martin Landau, Trevor Howard, Richard Dysart, Henry Fonda.
107 min.
Shoddy, unspeakably inept sci-fi disaster movie, with America and Russia combining forces when a meteor on collision course threatens to destroy the earth. Shored up by tacky effects and a predictable hands-across-the-Iron-Curtain romance between Yank scientist (Connery) and Red interpreter (Wood). See it on peril of death by boredom. TM

Meteor Man, The
(Robert Townsend, 1993, US) Robert Townsend, Marla Gibbs, James Earl Jones, Robert Guillaume, Luther Vandross, Bill Cosby.
100 min.
Meek black teacher (Townsend) is transformed into a green-garbed warrior after being struck by an emerald meteor. The teacher is the sort who tells pupils to run away from bullies. 'Meteor Man' walks the Washington, DC, 'hood and attends to gangsters who've spent too long at the hair salon – whenever you see a blond crop, trouble is never far away. Regrettably, writer/director Townsend spoils a promising idea (there aren't *that* many black masked avengers) by shamelessly milking every tear-jerking moment. RDo

Métisse (Cafe au Lait/Blended)
(Mathieu Kassovitz, 1993, Fr) Julie Mauduech, Mathieu Kassovitz, Hubert Koundé.
101 mins.
Métisse, the first film from the director of *La Haine*, is a (surprisingly) breezy and (unsurprisingly) brash comedy about a mulatto Parisienne torn between two boyfriends: a wealthy black (Koundé) and a laddish Jew (Kassovitz). The rivals reluctantly put their mutual antipathy on hold when their lover announces that she's pregnant, and won't reveal which of them's the father. If *La Haine* owed a debt to *Do the Right Thing*, here the key influence is *She's Gotta Have It* (at one point Koundé accuses the bike-mad Kassovitz of believing he's in a Spike Lee movie). This is a more benign than *La Haine*, and less assured, but it raises pertinent questions about gender and racial politics. TCh

Metro
(Thomas Carter, 1997, US) Eddie Murphy, Michael Rapaport, Michael Wincott, Carmen Ejogo, Kim Miyori, Art Evans.
117 min.
An adept turn from Murphy as San Francisco hostage negotiator Scott Roper knits together a functional assembly of stock cop-movie elements. This is probably the closest to a genuine dramatic part Murphy's ever played, and his snappy patter is persuasively integrated into Roper's daily routine. It's a tailor-made role, balancing action

highlights and the usual bit of lip. Unfortunately, there's little to be done with Randy Feldman's by-the-book plotting. Rapaport's SWAT team rookie proves his mettle as the main man's new partner; Wincott's ruthless jewel thief supplies the villainy; and Ejogo is the hero's vaguely feisty girlfriend-in-peril. TJ

Metropolis
(Fritz Lang, 1926, Ger) Alfred Abel, Gustav Fröhlich, Brigitte Helm, Rudolf Klein-Rogge, Fritz Rasp.
13,743 ft. b/w.
UFA's most ambitious production, intended to rival Hollywood in its spectacular evocation of the 21st century city of Metropolis and its mechanised society founded on slavery. Thea von Harbou's script is a bizarre mixture of futuristic sci-fi and backward-looking Gothic horror; it's at best garbled, and its resolution is, to say the least, politically dubious. Fritz Lang's direction, on the other hand, is tremendously inventive and exhilarating: no director before (and not that many since) had worked so closely with cameramen and designers to achieve such dynamic visual and spatial effects. TR

Metropolis
(Fritz Lang/Giorgio Moroder, 1926/1984, Ger/US) Alfred Abel, Gustav Fröhlich, Brigitte Helm, Rudolf Klein-Rogge, Fritz Rasp.
83 min.
Some balk in horror at Moroder's reduction in length of Lang's film, and the addition of mushrock songs (Pat Benatar, Adam Ant, Freddie Mercury et al). Others praise the beautifully restored print, superb tinting, and the tautening induced by the removal of unnecessary intertitles and occasional substitution of subtitles. The political narrative – the city ruler's son reconciling his father's 'brain' with the 'hands' of the oppressed workers – remains highly suspect. But the swift tempo of Moroder's re-editing, combined with his feverish, disco-based score (the awful songs may prove easy to ignore), create the impression of a strip cartoon adventure directed by a genius. DT

Metropolitan
(Whit Stillman, 1989, US) Carolyn Farina, Edward Clements, Christopher Eigeman, Taylor Nichols, Allison Rutledge-Parisi, Dylan Hundley, Isabel Gillies, Will Kempe, Elisabeth Thompson.
98 min.
When Tom (Clements), a quiet, middle class student with a distaste for privileged wealth, is unexpectedly adopted by a group of debs and escorts calling themselves the Sally Fowler Rat Pack, his pride and prejudice are rapidly eroded, not only by the glam sophistication of the soirées he attends in hired tux, but by the articulate, contentious conversations in which he takes part. Audrey (Farina), especially, seems a soul-mate, but Tom still nurses secret feelings for old flame Serena (Thompson), a socialite with too many strings to her beaux. Will he ditch the deb scene, find true love, or merely make it through the season unscathed? Writer-director Stillman's first feature is that rarity, a literate comedy of drawing-room manners which is at once civilised and *very* funny. Its nicely underplayed allusions to Jane Austen are wholly in keeping with Stillman's deft dialogue, ironic but sympathetic characterisations, and gentle probing of emotional and social nuance. The performances from a young, unknown cast are perfectly gauged, and wintry Manhattan is used as a gloriously seductive backdrop to the adolescent anxieties on view. GA

Mexico: The Frozen Revolution
(Raymundo Gleyzer, 1970, US/Arg)
60 min. b/w & col.
Gleyzer's documentary analyses the betrayal of the 1910 revolution, incorporating rare newsreel footage of Villa and Zapata, not as historical decoration but as part of a dialectic that culminates in the massacre by troops of the present regime of some 400 students in one day during the Mexican Olympics. By being at all times specific, the film gains reverberations that reach well beyond its immediate subject, without letting that subject slide into second place. It's genuinely informative about Mexico as well as being a very gracefully made film. It also makes almost a

virtue of the narrative voice-over, balancing it whenever possible against interviews with individuals – and if the level of political awareness of those individuals seems impressive, it's surely a comment on our own media. VG

Miami Blues

(George Armitage, 1990, US) Fred Ward, Jennifer Jason Leigh, Alec Baldwin, Nora Dunn, José Perez, Charles Napier, Paul Gleason, Martine Beswicke, Obba Babatunde.
99 min.
Armitage's adaptation of Charles Willeford's *Miami Blues* is a movie introduction to Hoke Moseley of the Miami Police Department, a middle-aged Homicide sergeant harried by alimony and sporting a set of dentures made for him on the cheap by the technician who makes false teeth for the Miami Dolphins. Like Elmore Leonard's, Willeford's world is very precise about economics; when Hoke is hospitalised by the blithe psychopath Junior Frenger (Baldwin) – who steals his gun, badge and, cruelly, his teeth – he has trouble settling his medical bill. Meanwhile Junior plays cop in the metropolis and house with an infantile hooker, while Hoke tries to trap him. Ward is physically fine for Hoke, Baldwin a wired Junior, and best of all is Leigh's hooker, but it doesn't quite translate to the screen. Willeford didn't write genre, and the film washes about a bit finding a tone. BC

Miami Rhapsody

(David Frankel, 1995, US) Mia Farrow, Paul Mazursky, Sarah Jessica Parker, Antonio Banderas, Gil Bellows, Naomi Campbell, Kevin Pollak.
97 min.
We are in tropical Miami, but from the opening strains of Satchmo, Mia Farrow gabbling to her analyst, the infidelities, the talk and the whole damn *ronde*, we can sense that Woody Allen woz 'ere. Age has prompted ad-copywriter Gwyn (Parker) to accept the proposal of connubial whatsit from zoo-keeper Matt (Bellows), but the evidence of her family constitutes a caveat. First, dad tells her he suspects mum of a fling, and she finds mum (Farrow) is indeed romancing a nurse (Banderas); but then she finds dad (Mazursky, a director who cues another raft of associations) is himself sleeping with his secretary; brother Jordan is bonking Kaia (Campbell). As written, directed and produced by Frankel, this is a highly consumable product, a talky, breezy romantic comedy without particular insight, but filmed with pleasing brio. Mark Isham's score and the song soundtrack (mambo and jazz classics of the Porter/Ellington pedigree) give it the Rolls-Royce touch. But the acting's the thing. Parker's a sparky enough actress to hold the storm centre, and there are a half-dozen highly watchable performances, notably from Mazursky and Pollack. WH

Micha

(Gerard Michael MacCarthy, 1992, Ire/Rus) Genya Korhin, Victoria Korhina, Igor Kostolesvsky, Andrew Urgant.
97 min.
Filmed in St Petersburg and the old LenFilm Studios, Irish writer/director MacCarthy's ambitious debut feature attempts to explore the harsh changing realities of living in that city through the experiences and mind of a young boy, Micha, whose father is in exile in Germany. It follows him from his anglophile school (where he's nevertheless chastised for reading American *Premiere*) and through the hours he spends exploring the city until his waitress mother finishes work. He is taken under the wing of the film crew surrounding the enigmatic Borodin (who plays a gangster in a TV soap), but everyday reality on the street seems equally unreal. Truth and fiction meld. Floating unsettlingly from stylisation to naturalism, from realism to expressionism, from dream to tough reality, the film is at times obscure, but it has a surreal, compulsive quality and is acted with melancholy conviction. WH

Michael

(Nora Ephron, 1996, US) John Travolta, Andie MacDowell, William Hurt, Bob Hoskins, Robert Pastorelli, Jean Stapleton, Teri Garr, Calvin Trillin.
105 min.
Hollywood's perennial fascination with Earthbound angels gets a cornball comic twist in Ephron's shaggy-dog story about a pair of Chicago hacks and a self-professed 'angel expert' dispatched to *Field of Dreams* country to find a dotty old lady who claims the Archangel Michael is living at her Iowa motel. And yes, he has wings. What they find is a portly, stubble-chinned seraph (Travolta) who, in the course of a cross-country car journey to Chicago, reveals his God-given wisdom by smoking, drinking, brawling and seducing women. Since they work for a tabloid obsessed with alien invaders and human freaks, washed-up cynic Frank Quinlan (Hurt) and his feckless partner Huey Driscoll (Pastorelli) are unimpressed. But Michael isn't going to waste his last trip to Earth trying to convert non-believers. Instead, he redeems thrice-divorced, former romantic Dorothy (MacDowell) and ex-alcoholic Frank by helping them to fall in love with one another. Which leaves Huey to do what he does best: look after the paper's mongrel mascot Sparky and feed off the scraps of dialogue thrown to him by the other characters. One senses a tension between the original screenplay, by reporter Jim Quinlan and novelist Pete Dexter, and the whimsical gloss given it by Ephron and her sister/co-writer Delia. The result's a series of funny, sentimental, self-contained turns. The storyline, meanwhile, wanders aimlessly. NF

Michael Collins

(Neil Jordan, 1996, US) Liam Neeson, Julia Roberts, Stephen Rea, Alan Rickman, Aidan Quinn, Ian Hart, John Kenny, Gerard McSorley, Michael Dwyer, Owen Roe.
132 min.
Writer/director Jordan's film tracing the career of Irish Republican hero Michael Collins, from the Easter Rising to his death in 1922, depicts a man whose belief in violence is finally transformed by the horrors of civil war into a desire for peace. It's a dense, stirring tale, with Collins (Neeson) under threat from both the English and his compatriots. Is Ned Broy (Rea) a spy or an ally working from within Dublin Castle? How serious is his split with Eamon De Valera (Rickman), who prefers to fight on for a Republic than settle temporarily for the Free State brokered by Collins? And what of bosom pal Harry Boland (Quinn), who feels personally betrayed when his girl Kitty (Roberts) transfers her affections to Collins? This is Jordan's most ambitious and satisfying movie a thriller with a real sense of scale, pace, menace and moral import. With the exception of Rickman's awesomely mannered De Valera, the performances are top notch (even Roberts makes a decent stab at the romantic interest, incarnating the ideological fall-out between Collins and Boland), while Chris Menges' camerawork and Anthony Pratt's designs perfectly evoke a country falling apart with no one, it seems, able to halt the tragedy. GA

Michael Kohlhaas

(Volker Schlöndorff, 1969, WGer) David Warner, Anna Karina, Relia Basic, Anita Pallenberg, Inigo Jackson, Michael Gothard, Anton Diffring.
95 min.
Schlöndorff's bizarre third feature was the first of a spate of adaptations from Kleist. Edward Bond wrote it (it's in English), and laboured mightily over the contemporary parallels in the story of a 16th century horse-dealer whose stand against a criminal landowner takes him outside the law himself. Schlöndorff films it as all-stops-out melodrama, complete with rioting peasants, rioting students, contrasts between righteous and non-righteous rebellion, and one of David Warner's least restrained performances. If the result evokes Ken Russell, it's because it shares some of Russell's visual strength as well as some of his dramatic weakness. TR

Michael Shayne Private Detective

(Eugene Forde, 1941, US) Lloyd Nolan, Marjorie Weaver, Elizabeth Patterson, Joan Valerie, Walter Abel, Donald MacBride, Douglas Dumbrille.
77 min. b/w.
Nolan's 'keyhole dick' is ludicrously quick with his fists and has an annoying habit of twirling a keychain round his finger, he's also not above faking a murder (with a mickey finn and a bottle of catsup) to frighten the sense back into the headstrong girl (Weaver) he's supposed to be chaperoning. Based on a novel by Brett Halliday, *Dividend on Death*, this is the first in a series of 12 produced by Fox between 1940 and '47. It's an extremely convoluted betting and horse-swapping mystery, with a mildly diverting subplot featuring an elderly Ellery Queen fan (Patterson) who helps Shayne with this not terribly diverting 'baffle book' case. Nolan is a reliable player, and Bogart's Marlowe may have learned something from him, but he lacks ingrained world-weariness. JPy

Michael Strogoff

see Adventures of Michael Strogoff, The

Mickey One

(Arthur Penn, 1964, US) Warren Beatty, Alexandra Stewart, Hurd Hatfield, Franchot Tone, Jeff Corey.
93 min. b/w.
Mickey (Beatty) is a successful nightclub comedian, confused and neurotic about his life in general, and possibly suffering from a persecution complex: someone or something is threatening him, for something he may have done in the past. Exactly what he is afraid of – the Mob, America at large, his conscience? – and why remains all too obscure in Penn's most European movie, made with almost total artistic freedom; the result, at once his most infuriating and one of his most intriguing films, is a rather vague allegory about alienation, guilt and despair, structured as an elliptical narrative complete with jump-cuts and bizarre, symbolic images. A few scenes are truly disquieting – as when Beatty is auditioned in a silent, darkened auditorium – but the overall effect is too cerebrally self-conscious to be genuinely gripping. GA

Micki + Maude

(Blake Edwards, 1984, US) Dudley Moore, Amy Irving, Ann Reinking, Richard Mulligan, George Gaynes, Wallace Shawn, John Pleshette.
117 min.
After Edwards' hopeless *The Man Who Loved Women* comes this altogether more successful piece which might be subtitled 'The Man Who Loved Two Women'. Moore is married to careerist lawyer Micki (Reinking), and yearns for a child which she will not provide. He takes cellist Maude (Irving) for a mistress, impregnates and marries her, only to find Micki too is pregnant. The film's greatest moments of comedy spring from the bigamous Moore's escalating panic in the face of keeping two marriages together but separate, culminating in a double delivery in adjacent hospital wards of frantic delirium; Keystone cops meet *The Hospital*. It is none the worse for being resolutely old-fashioned in its virtues, and – in its compassion towards all parties – marked by a complete absence of the sour element which distinguished previous Edwards comedies like *10* and *S.O.B.* CPea

Microcosmos (Microcosmos: Le Peuple de l'herbe)

(Claude Nuridsany/Marie Pérennou, 1996, Fr/Switz/It)
75 min.
The close-up photography is stunning in this slightly (but not too cutely) anthropomorphic documentary on the lives of the inhabitants of a summer meadow. All insect and invertebrate life is here (ladybird with seven spots, swallowtail butterfly, burgundy snail, ang spider, rhinoceros beetle, red ants) in the daily round of sex, violence, work and conspicuous food consumption, but while the film's technically superb, the mainly wordless format ultimately wears a little thin. GA

Midaq Alley (El Callejon de los Milagros)

(Jorge Fons, 1994, Mex) Ernesto Gomez Cruz, Maria Rojo, Salma Hayek.
140 min.
Transposing a novel of Egyptian street life by the Nobel Prize-winning author Naguib Mahfouz to contemporary Mexico, director Fons splits the story into four episodes each told from a separate point of view: from the macho bar owner who seemingly turns gay in an afternoon, to the beautiful Alma (Hayek, star of Robert Rodriguez's

Desperado), whose impatience for love leads her quickly to the local brothel. Although everything teeters on the edge of soap opera, and the intertwining of the stories reveals few surprises, the film scores with its strong pacing and gutsy humour. DT

Midas Run
(aka A Run on Gold)
(Alf Kjellin, 1969, US) Richard Crenna, Anne Heywood, Fred Astaire, Roddy McDowall, Ralph Richardson, Adolfo Celi, Cesar Romero, Maurice Denham.
106 min.
A crime-of-the-century caper, not high in the credibility stakes at the best of times, but pushed several rungs lower by the casting of Fred Astaire as a member of an aristocratic English family (his accent explained away by recalling that Sir Winston Churchill, too, had an American mother). A British secret service chief, Astaire masterminds a gold bullion robbery, then solves the crime himself, all in order to secure the knighthood that has so far escaped him. Crenna plays an expert in military strategy duped into helping (but ingeniously exculpated afterwards), and Richardson contributes a characteristic civil service cameo. Script, acting and direction are equally laboured. TM

Middle Age Crazy
(John Trent, 1980, Can) Bruce Dern, Ann-Margret, Graham Jarvis, Deborah Wakeham, Eric Christmas.
95 min.
Loosely based around a weepie sung by Jerry Lee Lewis, this should have you cringing in the aisles. Dern's Joe Suburbia appears to have everything – a wife (Ann-Margret) whose only consideration is her husband's satisfaction; a son who wants to be an architect; a business (building taco stands) that's thriving; and a ranch-styled villa with a jacuzzi. But in every dream home is a heartache, and Dern gets neurotic when he crosses the middle-age dateline of 39 to 40. All the popular US taboos suddenly strike: the quest for eternal youth ('The future sucks. Stay 18 for the rest of your lives'), the fear of death (Jessica Mitford for the '80s), male menopause (virility means you can score with a younger girl). Although Dern and Ann-Margret struggle valiantly, the cloying sentimentality, the repressive morality, the flabby direction and the scabrous script result in a slice of irredeemable cod. IB

Middleman, The
(Jana-Aranya)
(Satyajit Ray, 1975, Ind) Pradip Mukherjee, Satya Bannerjee, Dipankar Dey, Lily Chakravarti, Aparna Sen, Utpal Dutt.
131 min. b/w.
Although Ray's later films saw him moving away from his early gentle humanism towards something more concerned with the political and economic problems facing modern India, they remain primarily descriptive rather than works of intense political commitment. Here he deals with a university graduate forced to enter the world of commerce: his confidence eroded by the experience of being interviewed for jobs for which there are literally thousands of applicants, he eventually sets himself up as someone who buys and sells anything. Meanwhile he finds himself reduced to compromising his ideals more and more. Beautifully performed, blessed with Ray's customary sense of balance, and wittily satirising the absurdity of bureaucracy run riot, it makes absorbing viewing. GA

Middle of the World, The
(Le Milieu du Monde)
(Alain Tanner, 1974, Switz/Fr) Olimpia Carlisi, Philippe Léotard, Juliet Berto, Denise Perron, Jacques Denis, Roger Gendly.
117 min.
Tanner's most achieved film to date is also his most apparently conventional, the story of a love affair between a café waitress and an ambitious (married) local politician which comes to a catastrophic end. But the subject matter (a woman struggling for independence) and formal structure (including 'empty' shots of a bleak winter landscape) come together with breathtaking lucidity. The tone is compassionate, and for a truly '70s tragedy the ending is curiously upbeat. CA

Middleton's Changeling
(Marcus Thompson, 1997, GB) Ian Dury, Amanda Ray-King, Colm Ó Maonlaí, Billy Connolly, Campbell Morrison, Moya Brady, Richard Mayes, Guy Williams, Vivian Stanshall.
96 min.
Attempting a radical update of Middleton's Jacobean tragedy, with the iconoclastic intentions, but without the discipline or sense of Baz Luhrmann's *Romeo & Juliet*, writer/producer/director/editor Thompson throws in incongruous modern trappings amid a general sense of gothic medievalism. At court in Alicante, Beatrice (Ray-King) betrothed by her father Vermandero (Mayes) to marry Alonso (Williams), falls for dashing Alsemero (Ó Maonlaí). Their trysts are witnessed by Vermandero's servant De Flores (Dury), a toad-like villain who lusts after her and whom she abhors. In desperation she accepts his offer to dispose of Alonso; then, before she can marry Alsemero, De Flores reveals his price – Beatrice's virginity. Intercut are lengthy scenes of Connolly running a slave-trade circus of lunatics. Gary Moore's monotonous guitar lines soar across the soundtrack, attempting to evoke grand tragedy, while Thompson's camera indulges in similarly grandiloquent swoops. NB

Midnight
(Mitchell Leisen, 1939, US) Claudette Colbert, Don Ameche, John Barrymore, Mary Astor, Francis Lederer, Hedda Hopper, Monty Woolley.
94 min. b/w.
An enchanting comedy which starts with Colbert, as an American chorine on the make, stranded in Paris in a gold lamé evening gown (what else?). She is befriended on the one hand by a poor taxi-driver who is really a Russian count (Ameche), and on the other by a wealthy socialite (Barrymore) who 'introduces' her to society so that she can oblige by luring a gigolo away from his wife. Uncanny coincidental parallels with *La Règle du Jeu* abound, and although the film echoes Renoir's bark more than his bite, it has a superbly malicious script by Brackett and Wilder, gorgeous sets and camerawork, and a matchless cast. All in all, probably Leisen's best film. TM

Midnight Clear, A
(Keith Gordon, 1992, US) Peter Berg, Kevin Dillon, Arye Gross, Ethan Hawke, Gary Sinise, Frank Whaley, John C McGinley.
108 min.
As the end of World War II approaches, a group of American soldiers settle in a deserted house on the French-German border in order to report on enemy movements. But their foe remains elusive, and after making contact with these young, nervous men, the Germans prove strangely unwilling to attack. Less war movie than psychological thriller, screenwriter-director Gordon's absorbing, stylised adaptation of William Wharton's novel explores issues of faith and morality. The performances are uniformly excellent as the film moves inexorably towards bloody confrontation and spiritual reckoning. CM

Midnight Cowboy
(John Schlesinger, 1969, US) Jon Voight, Dustin Hoffman, Sylvia Miles, Brenda Vaccaro, John McGiver, Barnard Hughes, Jennifer Salt.
113 min.
Outrageously overrated at the cynical end of the Swinging Sixties, when the seedy New York milieu in which the pathetic buddy-buddy story takes place was thought to be truthfully depicted. Instead, as Voight's likeably dumb Texan hick hustler teams up with limping guttersnipe Hoffman in an effort to make enough money from the wealthy women of New York to fulfil dreams of living in sunny Florida, the film indulges in bland satire, fashionable flashiness, and a sodden sentimentality that never admits either to its homosexual elements or to the basic misogyny of its stance. Add to that a glamorisation of poverty and an ending that makes *Love Story* seem restrained, and you have a fairly characteristic example of Schlesinger's shallow talent. GA

Midnight Dancers (Sibak)
(Mel Chiongjo, 1994, Phil) Alex Del Rosario, Gandong Cervantes, Lawrence David, Luis Cortez.
100 min.

A sequel of sorts to Lino Broca's botched *Macho Dancer*, Chiongjo's likeable melodrama offers a moral (but not moralistic) panorama of gay life in Manila. Young footballer Sonny, new in town from the sticks, is introduced to gay prostitution by his two elder brothers, both of whom already perform as G-stringed macho dancers in a gay bar and support their mother by turning tricks. The film is let down by some weak performances and feeble fight choreography, but its feeling for the vagaries of rent-boy life is palpably sincere. Its best scenes centre on eldest brother Joel, who has a wife and child and a male lover and manages to keep all of them happy. TR

Midnight Express
(Alan Parker, 1978, GB) Brad Davis, Randy Quaid, John Hurt, Irene Miracle, Bo Hopkins, Paolo Bonacelli, Paul Smith.
121 min.
A meaty anecdote, heavily fictionalised from a factual source, about an American kid on a dope charge going through Hell in a Turkish jail. Some of the performances (Hurt, Davis) give it an illusion of depth, but it's mostly expert in avoiding moral resonance and ambiguity: everything is satisfyingly clear-cut, just as every shot and every cut are geared to instant emotional impact. Political, moral and aesthetic problems arise when you try to superimpose the film on the 'truth' it purports to represent. As a head-banging thriller, though, it makes some of Hollywood's hoariest stereotypes seem good as new, and it panders to its audience's worst instincts magnificently. TR

Midnight Fear
(Bill Crain, 1990, US) David Carradine, Craig Wasson, August West, Page Fletcher, Evan Richards.
85 min.
Sheriff Carradine comes to the rescue in this minor shocker, a cheap variation on ye old psychos-menace-single-woman-in-remote-shack routine. There's a diabolically fiendish plot device (watch for it), but it's insufficient to make a proper movie out of nasty junk. TJ

Midnight in the Garden of
Good and Evil
(Clint Eastwood, 1997, US) Kevin Spacey, John Cusack, Jack Thompson, Irma P Hall, Jude Law, Alison Eastwood, Paul Hipp, The Lady Chablis.
155 min.
When New York journalist John Kelso (Cusack) arrives in Savannah, Georgia, to cover one of the lavish Christmas parties held by wealthy antique dealer Jim Williams (Spacey), he doesn't expect to get caught up in a murder trial. But after his host shoots volatile young employee Billy Hanson (Law), Kelso finds himself following the case with a view to writing a book, and making enquiries that might help substantiate Williams' self-defence plea – an investigation which, in introducing him to such locals as the transvestite nightclub artiste Lady Chablis and voodoo queen Minerva, uncovers a whole new world beneath the colourful but in many ways conservative veneer of Savannah society. Elegantly directed and beautifully performed, Eastwood's film of John Berendt's non-fiction best-seller is a warm, witty, consistently intriguing character study. Particularly successful are the funny, touching scenes shared by Cusack and the flirtatious Chablis, typical of the movie's fascination with questions of pretence, trust and tolerance. Also engaging, however, is the quirky wit and Eastwood's readiness, whenever the occasion arises, to deflect focus away from the crime on to other details in the social tapestry, subtly nudging at divisions involving race, class, gender and sexuality. GA

Midnight Man, The
(Roland Kibbee/Burt Lancaster, 1974, GB) Burt Lancaster, Susan Clark, Cameron Mitchell, Morgan Woodward, Harris Yulin, Robert Quarry, Joan Lorring, Ed Lauter, Nick Cravat.
119 min.
Lancaster joins forces with screenwriting friend Kibbee (*The Crimson Pirate*, *Vera Cruz*) on an adaptation of David Anthony's thriller *The Midnight Lady and the Mourning Man*. The narrative is as abbreviated as the title, and for all the sense the plot makes, they might as well have

called it 'The and The'. Even so, there's enough incident crammed in to fill columns. Suffice it to say that prominent parts are played by an ex-cop working as a college nightwatchman (Lancaster), a pretty parole officer with a taste for garish lipstick (Clark), the murdered daughter of a corrupt senator, a stolen tape of intimate confessions, an unfinished poem laced with Greek mythology, and a volume of Krafft-Ebing. Non-prominent parts are played by the two directors, who stage events with little flair. GB

Midnight Run

(Martin Brest, 1988, US) Robert De Niro, Charles Grodin, Yaphet Kotto, John Ashton, Dennis Farina, Joe Pantoliano, Richard Foronjy.
126 min.
That old formula, handcuffed captor and captive who become buddies on the run, gets an injection of new life from the playing of the cast. Bounty hunter Jack Walsh (De Niro) captures bail-jumping accountant Jon Mardukas (Grodin) in New York, but his problems really start when he tries to deliver him to the bail bondsman in LA. Mardukas, learning that his employer was a Mafia mobster, stole millions which he distributed among the poor, and Walsh has to run the gauntlet of the FBI, the Mob and a rival bounty hunter (Ashton), besides putting up with his captive's concern about smoking and morality. Both actors get off on each other, improvising routines and inhabiting the standard Odd Couple teaming so interestingly that at times the film touches a profundity. Here and there, director Brest succumbs to the car chase, but overall the movie is way above average for the genre. BC

Midnight Sting

see Diggstown

Midsummer Night's Dream, A

(Max Reinhardt/William Dieterle, 1935, US) James Cagney, Dick Powell, Olivia de Havilland, Joe E Brown, Mickey Rooney, Jean Muir, Verree Teasdale, Ian Hunter, Anita Louise, Victor Jory, Hugh Herbert.
132 min. b/w.
Perhaps not the most faithful of screen adaptations of Shakespeare, but certainly one of the most charming. The performances are surprisingly superb – notably Cagney as Bottom and a young Rooney as Puck – while visually the movie is a triumph of art direction (by Anton Grot) and luminous photography (by Hal Mohr). And although accusations of kitsch are perfectly justified, the scenes of the fairies wafting through the forest are beautiful enough to bring tears to the eyes. No wonder that the infant Kenneth Anger, playing the Changeling, would later turn to high camp and magic in his own movies. GA

Midsummer Night's Dream, A

(Celestino Coronado, 1984, GB/Sp) Lindsay Kemp, Manuela Vargas, The Incredible Orlando, Michael Matou, François Testory, Neil Caplan.
77 min.
This axes at least 75% of Shakespeare's text and lets the images and score do the talking. It derives from a Kemp stage production, but is never stagy in the bad sense: its origins simply enhance the overall texture of the artifice, making it like a Richard Dadd painting come to life. Modest liberties are taken with the plot, so that the feuding couples switch sexual proclivities as well as partners, but it's surprisingly faithful to the spirit of the play. through lustrous photography and a memorably refined performance from Jack 'Orlando' Birkett as Titania. TR

Midsummer Night's Dream, A

(Adrian Noble, 1996, GB) Lindsay Duncan, Alex Jennings, Desmond Barrit, Barry Lynch, Howard Crossley, Robin Gillespie, John Kane, Mark Letheren, Kenn Sabberton.
103 min.
Sadly, this cross-over to the screen of an acclaimed stage production by Adrian Noble, the Royal Shakespeare Company's artistic director, is a nightmare. What impressed about the original was the colour and energy. Here, the colours are chocolate-box garish. The women seem to be refugees from the wedding-gift counter at Peter Jones, and the men look like waiters in a haplessly themed King's Road restaurant.

An attempt has been made to open the play out (and unify it) by letting loose a schoolboy in the action. The result's a baffling mix that leaves the action panting behind arch cinematic references to everything from *Peter Pan* and *The Wizard of Oz* to *ET*. SGr

Midsummer Night's Sex Comedy, A

(Woody Allen, 1982, US) Woody Allen, Mia Farrow, José Ferrer, Julie Hagerty, Tony Roberts, Mary Steenburgen.
88 min.
Monogamous at heart, Woody Allen has ended his brief affair with Fellini (*Stardust Memories* out of *82*) and gone back to his first love Bergman. Allen's version of *Smiles of a Summer Night* keeps the period country house setting but reduces the characters to six: two medical swingers, an elderly academic and his much younger fiancée, and a long-married couple whose sex-life has ground to a halt. Allen, of course, plays the frustrated husband (he redirects his energies towards inventing flying bicycles, astral lamps and the like), and gives himself nearly all the funny lines. He spends the rest of the movie satirising the men and adoring the changing moods of the women. His best invention remains his own screen persona, and the Bergman borrowings here provide it with a warm, romantic and old-fashioned setting. TR

Midway
(aka Battle of Midway)

(Jack Smight, 1976, US) Charlton Heston, Henry Fonda, James Coburn, Glenn Ford, Hal Holbrook, Toshiro Mifune, Robert Mitchum, Cliff Robertson.
132 min.
'This is the way it was', drones the introduction to this massively extravagant account of America's WWII naval victory, a sure indication of the film's probable untrustworthiness. 'Dad, I've fallen in love with a Japanese girl. I need your help' – 'Six months after Pearl Harbor! You have one lousy sense of timing!'. Saddled with such crass dialogue, the 'human' interest and the array of stars make predictably little impact against all the weaponry wheeled out to recreate the battle. Small wonder that Fonda wanders through the film looking as though he's holding a royal flush to Mifune's pair of twos. The rest is noisy, incomprehensible and lumberingly irrelevant, complete with shell-schlock Sensurround.

Miei Primi 40 Anni, I

see My First 40 Years

Mi Familia

see My Family

Mighty Aphrodite

(Woody Allen, 1995, US) Woody Allen, Mira Sorvino, Helena Bonham Carter, Peter Weller, F Murray Abraham, Olympia Dukakis, Jeffrey Kurland, J Smith Cameron, Steven Randazzo, Claire Bloom, Michael Rapaport.
95 min.
Three years after sports writer Lenny (Allen) allowed his art dealer wife Amanda (Bonham Carter) to persuade him that they should adopt a child, a nagging curiosity about where young Max's brains came from leads Lenny to seek out the boy's natural mother, hooker Linda Ash (Sorvino), marginally better known as actress 'Judy Cum'. Horrified by, but sympathetic to Linda's plight, Lenny tries to better her life, pursuing his mission with such zeal that he barely notices when Amanda, encouraged by smooth Jerry Bender (Weller), starts to drift away from him. Lenny's another of Allen's nervy, intellectual, middle-class heroes, and most of the gags centre on the clash of social and cultural aspirations arising from his encounter with the dumb-blonde tart-with-a-heart. A make-weight Greek chorus is thrown in to comment on Lenny's hubristic do-gooding. Sorvino does her able best to transform her caricature into someone to care about; Bonham Carter copes respectably with a relatively minor role; and Rapaport contributes a fair turn as an unbelievably stupid boxer. But Allen's familiar device of juxtaposing sentiments and language, the lofty and the banal (one moment the Olympians, the next the nebbish protagonist), rapidly palls. GA

Mighty Barnum, The

(Walter Lang, 1934, US) Wallace Beery, Adolphe Menjou, Virginia Bruce, Rochelle Hudson, Janet Beecher, Herman Bing.
87 min. b/w.
The mighty Wallace Beergut was an elephant trainer at the age of 16, so here he's at home in the blustering, larger-than-life role of 19th century showman Phineas Taylor Barnum, who starts off by collecting a few freaks (including Tom Thumb), and graduates to the Greatest Show on Earth, with the help of his partner Bailey Walsh (Menjou). His wife, meanwhile, is understandably upset when he dallies romantically with Swedish Nightingale Jenny Lind. A blustering, larger-than-life biopic. AB

Mighty Ducks, The
(aka Champions)

(Stephen Herek, 1992, US) Emilio Estevez, Joss Ackland, Lane Smith, Heidi Kling, Josef Sommer.
103 min.
Very lame ice-hockey flick. Estevez is arrogant hot-shot lawyer Gordon Bombay, condemned to community service for drink-driving. He reckons he can go one-on-one with his troubled past and get back at his boss by coaching a team of little league no-hopers (cast from a cupboard marked 'brats, assorted'). Ackland lingers embarrassingly as a kindly sports-store owner. TJ

Mighty Joe Young

(Ernest B Schoedsack, 1949, US) Terry Moore, Ben Johnson, Robert Armstrong, Frank McHugh, Douglas Fowley, Paul Guilfoyle.
94 min. b/w.
King Kong for kids, with the great ape shorn of myth, tamely housebroken, and even required to be the hero of an orphanage fire. But he does have an engagingly dotty showbiz act, holding up a platform on which Terry Moore sits strumming 'Beautiful Dreamer' at a grand piano. The whole 'Golden Safari' nightclub show is rather a splendid piece of kitsch, complete with voodoo dancers, ten circus strongmen in leopard-skins pitted against Joe in a tug-of-war, and a spiritedly destructive rampage when three drunken revellers go backstage to ply the already resentful ape with a bottle. For all the sneers cast at the film, it's in fact surprisingly well crafted, with position of tongue in cheek perfectly judged. TM

Mighty Morphin Power Rangers: The Movie

(Bryan Spicer, 1995, US) Paul Freeman, Nicholas Bell, David Yost, Amy Jo Johnson, Jason David Frank, Karan Ashley, Johnny Yong Bosch, Steve Cardenas.
95 min.
The story goes thus: Angel Grove, California, is menaced by Ivan Ooze (Freeman), an ugly mug with a propensity for creating buckets of purple slime. Can the six all-American teenage superheroes overcome their new rubbery adversary? The TV series from which this is derived is notorious for its indifferent B-movie sfx; matters are improved here with some notably effective computer-generated graphics. The comic-book fight sequences, too, are a little more imaginative. But, like the series, the film is also corny as hell, with glaring continuity lapses, cringeworthy performances, silly monsters and laughable set-pieces. (Why, for instance, do the Rangers always perform somersaults diagonally across the screen whenever they yell, 'Okay, it's morphin' time'?) Kids will love it. DA

Mighty Mouse in the Great Space Chase

(Ed Friedman/Lou Kachivas/Marsh Lamore/Gwen Wetzler/Kay Wright/Lou Zukor, 1983, US) voices: Allen Oppenheimer, Diane Pershing.
87 min.
Harry the Heartless, fiendish feline with a line in scintillating repartee, is threatening democracy with his Doomsday Machine in this animated cartoon. Mighty Mouse is a musclebound thicko who hangs around keeping the cosmos tidy and divulging vital stellar secrets at the drop of a hanky, which is possibly why he takes an entire full-length feature to save the solar system. You will thrill to gadgets like the Atomic Brain Switcher: watch Harry swap bodies with plucky

heroine Pearl Pureheart, see him putting on make-up and fluttering eyelashes at his first lieutenant! Okay, this is no mousterpiece – the animation lacks all kinds of depth – but it ain't no mousetrap either. AB

Mighty Quinn, The

(Carl Schenkel, 1989, US) Denzel Washington, James Fox, Mimi Rogers, M Emmet Walsh, Sheryl Lee Ralph, Art Evans, Esther Rolle, Robert Townsend.
98 min.
When a rich American is murdered on a Caribbean isle, the white community pins the blame on local ne'er-do-well Maubee (Townsend). They reckon without the new black Chief of Police Xavier Quinn (Washington), crusader for Justice and Truth. The focus is firmly on the black cast: Townsend's deadpan patois, Washington playing the white man in a world gone sour, plus a posse of gutsy, gorgeous black gals. Which leaves a couple of stars with little to do: James 'Ice ay, get ite of hyar' Fox, and Rogers, who eschews acting and merely opens her eyes very wide to express intense sensuality. As if the plot weren't perfunctory enough (bags of Yankee dollars, corruption in high places, CIA asassins), we take extended breaks from it to contemplate Quinn's gradual recovery of his roots, culminating in the grateful islanders serenading him with a reggae version of the title song. SFe

Mignon Has Left (Mignon è partita)

(Francesca Archibugi, 1988, It/Fr) Stefania Sandrelli, Jean-Pierre Duriez, Leonardo Ruta, Céline Beauvallet, Francesca Antonelli, Lorenzo De Pasqua.
90 min.
The posh Parisian life of 14-year-old Mignon (Beauvallet) is disrupted when her father is jailed and she is dispatched to Italy to visit relatives. Chaos reigns in the Forbicioni family: Dad is having an affair, Mum is pursued by her brother-in-law, and the five children are suffering growing pains. Particularly afflicted, Giorgio (Ruta) becomes infatuated with his snooty French cousin, neglects his schoolwork, and makes a botched suicide attempt. While the conflicts in Francesca Archibugi's first feature tend to soap opera (unrequited love, rebellion, teen pregnancy, terminal illness), there are compensations in the casual, affectionate portrayal of family life. More satisfying are the enfolding adult dramas, which receive less emphasis yet capture the sort of impulsiveness that eludes the depiction of teen angst. This has a great deal to do with Stefania Sandrelli's sensitive performance as the mother. CM

Mikado, The

(Victor Schertzinger, 1939, GB) Kenny Baker, Jean Colin, Martyn Green, Constance Willis, Sydney Granville, John Barclay.
91 min
England's answer to The Wizard of Oz proved to be another costly mistake for the man with the gong. Why shrewd businessmen CM Woolf and J Arthur Rank expected America to welcome this very English operetta is one of the unsolved mysteries of Wardour Street. Of course it's good, but casting an American crooner (the engaging and very pretty Baker) as Nanki-Poo hardly mitigates Gilbert & Sullivan's impenetrable insularity. For those with vague memories of 'Three Little Maids From School Are We' echoing through their childhood, however, this is a real treat. Enchantingly subtle Technicolor and the splendid ensemble playing of the D'Oyly Carte company make it a strangely evocative experience. RMy

Mike's Murder

(James Bridges, 1984, US) Debra Winger, Mark Keyloun, Darrell Larson, Paul Winfield, Brooke Alderson, William Ostrander.
97 min.
Shy bank worker Winger (Winger – shy?) is drawn out of her shell by a new romance, and, when the man of her dreams is brutally murdered, she turns 'tec to track down the culprits – uncovering some unpalatable home truths in the process. Two years in the editing, the makers' struggle to get the thing to make sense certainly shows. The dusty Joe Jackson soundtrack album is sometimes found in second-hand record stores. TJ

Mikey and Nicky

(Elaine May, 1976, US) Peter Falk, John Cassavetes, Ned Beatty, Rose Arrick, Carol Grace, William Hickey, Sanford Meisner, Joyce Van Patten, M Emmet Walsh.
119 min.
Nicky (Cassavetes), cooped up in a dingy hotel room, dreading lethal reprisals from a mobster he's betrayed, calls upon Mikey (Falk) for help. But as they search the city's backstreets for sanctuary, it becomes clear that his buddy is less saviour than Judas (and that the sacrificial victim is no saint either). May's script simply observes the way old wounds are reopened as the pair reminisce about their past friendship, while allowing her actors ample space to emote with adolescent exuberance and paranoia. The vérité style, complete with itchy focus finger and rambling narrative, often seems less assured than in Cassavetes' own films. But with an imaginative use of locations, carefully controlled atmosphere, and superb performances all round, it's an often impressive, always watchable modern noir thriller, based on credible human motivations. GA

Milagro Beanfield War, The

(Robert Redford, 1987, US) Ruben Blades, Richard Bradford, Sonia Braga, John Heard, Carlos Riquelme, Daniel Stern, Chick Vennera, Christopher Walken, M Emmet Walsh.
118 min.
A New Mexican handyman (Vennera), by a mix of magical intervention and carelessness, kicks down the sluice gate of a privatised water supply, which converts his parched ancestral patch into a potentially fertile field of beans. But a developer (Bradford) in cahoots with all the men-with-no-smiles from State Governor (Walsh) down, wants the water for a planned leisure valley. Battle is enjoined. Which cues stormy domestic quarrels, riotous community meetings, the re-illusionment of a hack (Heard), a chance for the local conscience (Braga) to look vital in jeans and crisp white blouse, and for the sheriff (Blades) to display his lopsided grin. A tragic accident threatens the happy ending, but hang on in. Ostensibly a celebration of the triumph of community over exploitation and injustice, Redford's film sustains a slow mood of simpatico amiability and photographs the landscape with moony or golden washes that are perhaps hard to dislike, but is slain by its adherence to an outdated populist mythology. WH

Mildred Pierce

(Michael Curtiz, 1945, US) Joan Crawford, Jack Carson, Zachary Scott, Eve Arden, Ann Blyth, Bruce Bennett, George Tobias.
113 min. b/w.
James Cain's novel of the treacherous life in Southern California that sets housewife-turned-waitress-turned-successful restaurateur (Crawford) against her own daughter (Blyth) in competition for the love of playboy Zachary Scott, is brought fastidiously and bleakly to life by Curtiz' direction, Ernest Haller's camerawork, and Anton Grot's magnificent sets. Told in flashback from the moment of Scott's murder, the film is a chilling demonstration of the fact that, in a patriarchal society, when a woman steps outside the home the end result may be disastrous. PH

Miles from Home

(Gary Sinise, 1988, US) Richard Gere, Kevin Anderson, Brian Dennehy, Penelope Ann Miller, Helen Hunt, John Malkovich.
108 min.
Sinise's opening sequence of Khrushchev paying an official visit to Iowa's most productive farm, shaking hands with the proud owner (Dennehy), and rumpling his small sons' hair, is so singular and promising that the film never really recovers from it. It settles for being the story of the two sons disillusionment as they are disinherited by the march of financial speculation, and forced into rebellion. In many ways, it's a late straggler in the brief farm genre, but the presence of Gere as the older brother, Frank, unbalances any attempt at airing agricultural grievances. Prompt to resort to the gun, a hell-raising outlaw in a black hat, Frank is the stuff of Hollywood, and his relationship with his idolising brother, sensitive, circumspect Terry (Anderson), is practically a screen syndrome. The final shot of Frank's hat lying on a country road being taken up by another kid gives some idea of the deterioration that has taken place. BC

Milestones

(Robert Kramer/John Douglas, 1975, US) Grace Paley, Mary Chapelle, Sharon Krebs, Jim Nolfi, Susie Solf, Joe Stork.
206 min.
Shot as 'fictional' documentary, Milestones amounts to a three-and-a-half hour testament to a generation. Despite the cinéma-vérité style, the scope of the project is epic: the interconnecting lives and lifestyles of various young people scattered across America as a generation of white activists or dropouts ponder 'where they're at'. Milestones is almost entirely about people talking. Sometimes this compulsion to talk everything through – and an obsessive need for reassurance –amounts to moving in circles, not forward; what optimism there is seems almost wilfully naive and painfully fragile. The film refrains from judging its characters, which is why some may find it boring. But, as with Kramer's Ice it's a film that will doubtless gain with age: posterity is left to decide whether the generation on view found a new future or lost its way. CPe

Milieu du Monde, Le

see Middle of the World, The

Militia Battlefield

(Jana Bokova, 1975, GB)
61 min.
Jana Bokova's unusual documentary scores in two ways. One, it reveals a genuinely bizarre subculture of gay clubs and expatriate entertainers in London. Two, it builds its endearingly rambling philosophy into its own structure, so its focus remains suitably diffuse. A very promising debut. TR

Milk Money

(Richard Benjamin, 1994, US) Melanie Griffith, Ed Harris, Michael Patrick Carter, Malcolm McDowell, Anne Heche, Casey Siemaszko, Philip Bosco.
109 min.
Melanie Griffith is V, a big-city tart with a heart, who's discovered by a group of schoolboys who've cycled in from the suburbs with the intention of paying a woman to take her clothes off. Motherless 12-year-old Frank (Carter) decides that V could be matched with his father, an absent-minded professor (Harris), and the girl finds herself strutting through the lawned suburbs of fictitious Middleton. Here no house has less than five bedrooms, and everyone says hello in the street. 'It looks like TV,' she observes. This feelgood romantic comedy is short on laughs, sexual chemistry, and the thriller subplot won't produce any white knuckles (McDowell is a pimp intent on tracking down his working girl). Like Pretty Woman, the major excitement comes from the wardrobe department. What'll V look like when gets out of that tacky brazen outfit? Answer: Jane Asher in a floral frock. JBa

Milky Way, The

see Voie Lactée, La

Millennium

(Michael Anderson, 1989, US) Kris Kristofferson, Cheryl Ladd, Daniel J Travanti, Robert Joy, Lloyd Bochner, Brent Carver, David McIlwraith, Maury Chaykin.
105 min.
Sci-fi writer John Varley adapted his own short story Air Raid for this screenwriting debut, but an intriguing concept ends up with all the credibility of speculation that the moon is made of green cheese. Plane crash expert Bill Smith (Kristofferson) is called in to investigate the mid-air collision of a 747 and a DC-10. But this is no ordinary catastrophe: watches found in the wreckage run backwards, and a futuristic stungun is unearthed. Bill soon meets Louise (Ladd), who heads a commando team from a thousand years in the future. These time travellers have urgent business in the 20th century, which helps sustain life among a dying race of humanoids subsisting on infusions of fluorocarbons. The film never really overcomes obvious budgetary constraints, with important moments drained of impact because the effects lack imagination. Kristofferson and Travanti (as a physicist) are effectively true to form, but Ladd is woefully inadequate. CM

m

Miller's Crossing (100)

(Joel Coen, 1990, US) Gabriel Byrne, Albert Finney, Marcia Gay Harden, John Turturro, Jon Polito, JE Freeman, Mike Starr, Al Mancini, Richard Woods, Steve Buscemi.
115 min.

Like *Blood Simple* and *Raising Arizona*, this works both as a crime thriller and as an ironic commentary on that genre. With fast, sharp, witty dialogue and Byzantine plotting, it charts the gang war between Leo (Finney) and Caspar (Polito) in an American city during Prohibition. Tom (Byrne), Leo's loyal right-hand man, is the lover of Leo's mistress (Harden), whose brother (Turturro) Caspar wants killed. Exactly how this and other complications are sorted out forms the hugely inventive, enjoyable narrative core of the film. But it is also a tribute to the crime literature (notably Hammett) and movies of the '30s, artfully poised between 'realism' and a subtle acknowledgment of its own artifice. And there's yet another level, since it is composed – visually, verbally and structurally – as a series of variations on the themes of 'Friendship, character, ethics'. At times the criss-crossing of abstract motifs recalls the formal complexity of a Greenaway film. It's arguably the US mainstream's first art movie since *Days of Heaven*; and quite wonderful. GA

Millhouse, a White Comedy

(Emile de Antonio, 1971, US)
92 min. b/w.

Millhouse follows the form of Antonio's earlier films in that it is almost entirely composed of carefully selected newsreel material that is allowed to speak for itself. Only the context in which the extracts are presented, and the occasional use of music to satirise a sequence, indicate Antonio's actual manipulation of his material. *Millhouse* is entirely concerned with Nixon's political career, backing up the early material with interviews with some of his opponents at the time. Most of the speeches he made then were terrifying in their implications, not merely for the content itself but for the cold-blooded way in which Nixon can be seen to support only those policies he reckons most popular (the death penalty for dope peddling, nuclear war as preferable to an American defeat in South East Asia, etc). It's certainly a funny film (commie-baiting Nixon 'discovering' microfilm in a bed of pumpkins), but the strength with which it reveals the full horror of Nixon's personality is devastating. JDuC

Million, Le

(René Clair, 1931, Fr) René Lefèvre, Annabella, Louis Allibert, Vanda Gréville, Paul Olivier, Raymond Cordy.
89 min. b/w.

Classic early René Clair, this is the one about a hunt for a lost lottery ticket which ends in a football scrimmage on an opera stage, foreshadowing *A Night At The Opera*. It features asynchronous sound and other experimental devices of the time. Luckily it's lively enough to survive the worst textbook bromides: the playing, the delightful music, and the dialogue (half-sung, half-spoken) all mesh together in a way no one but Clair ever quite matched. GB

Millionairess, The

(Anthony Asquith, 1960, GB) Sophia Loren, Peter Sellers, Alastair Sim, Dennis Price, Vittorio De Sica, Gary Raymond, Miriam Karlin.
90 min.

Absurd casting of Loren at the hands of husband Carlo Ponti and indifferent scripting by Wolf Mankowitz were poor beginnings for this turgid adaptation of Shaw's play. Millionairess in search of husband lights on poor humanitarian Indian doctor played by Sellers. The Shavian wit is dissipated somewhere between the glamorisation of Loren and the 'funny' Indian accent of Sellers which serves as mouthpiece for the familiar socialist message-mongering. RM

Million Pound Note, The (aka Man With a Million)

(Ronald Neame, 1954, GB) Gregory Peck, Jane Griffiths, Ronald Squire, Wilfrid Hyde-White, Joyce Grenfell, AE Matthews, Maurice Denham.
91 min.

An adaptation of Mark Twain's yarn about two wealthy brothers who pick on a penniless seaman to settle their bet as to whether someone could live on a million without spending anything. Scripted by Jill Craigie (Mrs Michael Foot), it emerges as a bland Technicolor sitcom that overstretches the short story ironies of everything coming to he who has. Squire and Hyde-White are the brothers, Peck the holder of the paper-money fortune who (initially) can't spend it for trying. PT

Millions Like Us

(Frank Launder/Sidney Gilliat, 1943, GB) Eric Portman, Patricia Roc, Gordon Jackson, Anne Crawford, Joy Shelton, Basil Radford, Naunton Wayne, Valentine Dunn, Megs Jenkins.
103 min. b/w.

Launder and Gilliat's portrait of a family at war is remarkable not only for its breadth of social detail – Dad joins the Home Guard, Mum goes back to her old job as a telephonist, daughter joins the ATS, and son is sent overseas to fight – but also for its perceptive observation of the youngest daughter's experiences as a factory worker. Patricia Roc's life on the factory floor, and her relationships with the girls who share the dormitory accommodation, don't shy away – as many other films of the period did – from the class conflicts which still riddled wartime English society. The ending, too, with the working class foreman (Portman) rejecting the rich society girl (Crawford) who has fallen for him, and looking forward instead to a new kind of society (one with a Labour government), raises pertinent questions about what exactly is being fought for. Is it the restoration of the old order, or the foundation of a new one? Intelligent entertainment at its best. NF

Milou en mai (May Fools/Milou in May)

(Louis Malle, 1989, Fr/It) Michel Piccoli, Miou-Miou, Michel Duchaussoy, Dominique Blanc, Harriet Walter, Bruno Carette, François Berléand, Martine Gautier, Paulette Dubost.
108 min.

Although this gentle country-house comedy is farcical in structure (with the various members of the Vieuzac family lapsing into indiscretion and conflict as they strive to sort out the estate after the death of the mother of Piccoli's sexagenarian aristocrat), genuine black humour is held at bay by Malle's refusal simply to condemn his characters' wealth, blinkered conservatism or selfishness. His huge, unsentimental affection for both bucolic milieu and characters is perhaps surprising given that the time is May 1968. Stranded by strikes and unable to hold a proper funeral for the corpse, the clan philander, fall out, and finally flee for the hills in absurd fear of Commie atrocities. It's less political satire, though, than a partly nostalgic evocation of an era; *La Règle du Jeu* and *Weekend* may be ancestors, but the tone is more akin to Goretta or Truffaut. The script (by Malle and Jean-Claude Carrière) never lives up to its promising premise, and the gags wear thin towards the end; but the performances and photography offer considerable pleasures, and the result has the same slight, poignant lyricism as its Stéphane Grappelli score. GA

Mimic

(Guillermo Del Toro, 1997, US) Mira Sorvino, Jeremy Northam, Alexander Goodwin, Giancarlo Giannini, Charles S Dutton, Josh Brolin, F Murray Abraham.
102 min.

The first US picture from the Mexican director of *Cronos* is a sci-fi thriller, fusing a dark, poetic allegory about the perils of genetic manipulation with grim, relentless, subterranean horror. Three years after scientists Sorvino and Northam save New York's children from a polio-like epidemic – by tampering with the DNA structure of the disease's main carrier, the ubiquitous cockroach – the results of their arrogant experiments come back to haunt them. Giant fast-evolving insects now lurk in the subway tunnels beneath the city, mimicking and preying upon their sometime predators, human beings. Uncompromising, subversive and occasionally perversely comic. NF

Minamata

(Noriaki Tsuchimoto, 1971, Jap).
155 min. b/w.

A documentary on the appalling tale of the Japanese village of Minamata, whose inhabitants were systematically poisoned by effluent from a nearby factory. It strips away the trendiness from the pollution issue, but makes it all too easy to localise the problem by concentrating on the victims of one primitive fishing village. What becomes plain is that the necessary area for investigation must be the firms and individuals who live off this degree of human agony, rather than primarily the victims.

Mina Tannenbaum

(Martine Dugowson, 1993, Fr) Romane Bohringer, Elsa Zylberstein, Florence Thomassin, Jean-Philippe Ecoffey, Nils Tavernier, Stéphane Slima, Hugues Quester.
128 min.

Cutting a swath through the personal histories of two young Jewish Parisians, aspiring painter Mina (Bohringer) and media wannabe Ethel (Zylberstein), this stylish, perceptive and wise film chronicles a friendship formed in childhood, strengthened by the romantic yearnings of adolescence, and tested by adulthood's inevitable parting of the ways. Reflective Mina is filled with anxiety, while Ethel can turn on the brash exterior – and though the mutual reliance forged in their teenage years has given these women shelter from their insecurities, it may not survive their common interest in the arrogant art dealer Dana (Ecoffey), whose own designs are cloaked beneath an abrasive exterior. Bohringer and Zylberstein work wonders, the chemistry of their relationship laying the foundation for the film's cumulative emotional impact. Its themes are the inescapable weight of the past, the damage unwittingly inflicted by the family's embrace; the betrayal involved when one dear friend who has been with you all your life is suddenly no longer there. TJ

Minbo Woman – Or the Gentle Art of Japanese Extortion (Minbo No Onna)

(Juzo Itami, 1992, Jap) Nobuko Miyamoto, Akir Takarada, Takehiro Murata, Yasuo Daichi.
125 min.

After *Death Japanese Style*, *Tampopo* and *A Taxing Woman* had taken a freewheeling satiric approach to such established Japanese institutions as the family funeral, the quest for the perfect bowl of noodles, and the national tax agency, the internationally successful director Juzo Itami turned his attention to the country's yakuza in this courageous comic exposé. The film-maker's spouse Nobuko Miyamoto again features as a female lawyer who teams up with an anti-extortion expert to expel the gangster's influence from a luxury hotel business they threaten to overwhelm. Itami treats it all like the familiar genre story of the samurai coming to rescue the put-upon villagers, but his bravery was not without a price, for real-life yakuza stabbed the director near his home shortly after the film's release. TJ

Mind Games

see Agency

Mindwarp

(Steve Barnett, 1990, US) Bruce Campbell, Angus Scrimm, Marta Alicia.
92 min.

A post-apocalyptic gore-fest funded by *Fangoria* magazine. Frustrated by the antiseptic underground environment of Inworld, with its narcotic, computer-induced fantasy images, Judy (Alicia) flees to the ravaged wasteland above. There, she teams up with post-apocalyptic Jeremiah Johnson figure Stover (Campbell), and together they confront The Seer (Scrimm), crazed leader of a religious cult based on salvaged scrap materials and human sacrifice. Eye-gouging, blood-spurting nastiness compensates for some ramshackle plotting. NF

Miners' Film, The

(Cinema Action, 1975, GB).
45 min.

Cinema Action describe themselves as a non-profit-making collective of trade unionists dedicated to working class films. *The Miners' Film*, made around the 1974 strike, although necessarily partisan, avoids the distortions of so many seemingly 'honest' documentaries through its refusal to impose an overall viewpoint via a commentary. The miners are allowed to articulate for themselves the hardships of their recurring struggle and their strengthening solidarity. As a Welsh miner puts it: 'We're gradually understanding now that the greatest power, the most important people, are the people that produce. And I believe that 1974 was the turning point, when this power was realised for the first time'. CPe

Miniskirted Dynamo, The

(Rivka Hartman, 1996, Aust) Dora Bialestock.
55 min.
Rivka Hartman's highly personal portrait of her late mother, Dora – a leading pathologist-turned-pioneer in matters of child care and abuse – reveals a strong willed, self-motivated, immensely energetic Jewish woman whose warmth and generosity fell far short of reaching her daughter. Some of the family adored her, but they never stood up to her – for Rivka, who may end up as domineering as mom, it was an endless battle. Home movies, interviews with family and friends, and Hartman's reminiscences make for a surprisingly engrossing hour. GA

Ministry of Fear

(Fritz Lang, 1944, US) Ray Milland, Marjorie Reynolds, Carl Esmond, Hillary Brooke, Dan Duryea, Alan Napier, Percy Waram, Erskine Sanford.
86 min. b/w.
Forget the phony studio settings and the script's hesitancies in adapting Graham Greene's novel about a spy hunt in wartime London. This is a wonderfully atmospheric, almost expressionistic thriller, packed with memorable moments: the jolly village fête ominously taking place at night; the open door of the railway carriage and the muted tapping which heralds the arrival of the blind man out of a cloud of steam; the rat-like tailor using an enormous pair of cutting-shears to dial his call of warning moments before they are found plunged into his stomach. And right from the opening shot of Milland waiting alone in a darkened room for the stroke of midnight – the magic hour which will release him from one paranoiac nightmare (the mercy killing of his wife) into another – Lang sets his characteristic seal of fatality on the action. TM

Minnie and Moskowitz

(John Cassavetes, 1971, US) Gena Rowlands, Seymour Cassel, Val Avery, Timothy Carey, Katherine Cassavetes, Elizabeth Deering.
115 min.
An idiosyncratic romance, and a far lighter movie than is usual from Cassavetes. Detailing the problems that background and character bring to a relationship, he creates a captivatingly witty and sympathetic picture of a pair of misfits deciding to make a go of it together despite numerous incompatibilities and adversities. As always, it is the performances that dominate, with their sensitively-felt, naturalistic speech patterns and gestures; and for all its optimism, the film is still centred around a core of loneliness, while Cassavetes also contrasts the difficulties of real life with the idealised glamour purveyed by Hollywood (an attack on the system that could barely accommodate him?). The result is an understated and intimate view of two unexceptional people that is only sentimental when the characters themselves are sentimental. GA

Minotaur

(Dan McCormack, 1993, US) Michael Faella, Ricky Aiello, Holley Chant, Willo Hausman.
55 min.
In a baroque room dominated by a champagne glass-shaped bath and the giggling beauty queen in it, the Minotaur, a balding, overweight, burnt-out '50s entertainer (Elvis with shades of John Belushi?), injects and ingests an insane cocktail of drugs and drink. The expensive camp setting points up the tawdriness of his behaviour, but his raw hysteria and explosive violence are punctuated by quieter reminiscences of his heyday and childhood. Stunningly designed, fluidly filmed and boldly acted, this provocative meditation on celebrity is both terrifying and exhilarating. NF

Miracle, The

(Neil Jordan, 1990, GB) Beverly D'Angelo, Donal McCann, Niall Byrne, Lorraine Pilkington, JG Devlin, Cathleen Delaney, Tom Hickey, Mikkel Gaup.
97 min.

In the small, nun-swept Irish seaside town of Bray, teenage would-be writers Rose (Pilkington) and Jimmy (Byrne) – the latter enjoying a strangely fraternal relationship with his saxophonist Dad (McCann), an alcoholic since his wife died before Jimmy could get to know her – spend their time speculating about the lives of the townsfolk. But only when glamorous American actress Renee (D'Angelo) turns up, do they really enter a world of romance and mystery, with Jimmy determining to seduce the older woman. But why is she holding back, and what is her interest in Jimmy's dad? Back on home ground after his spectacularly poor stabs at the American market, Jordan throws together, with some success, quite a few themes in this small-scale drama: the importance of memory, the problematically varied nature of love, issues of faith, and the relationship between reality, desire and literature. Although the film is overly literary in its use of symbolism and analogy, the performances are direct and affecting (D'Angelo, Byrne and Pilkington especially), and Jordan's affection for both characters and milieu is conspicuous throughout. GA

Miracle in Milan (Miracolo a Milano)

(Vittorio De Sica, 1950, It) Francesco Golisano, Brunella Bovo, Paolo Stoppa, Emma Gramatica, Guglielmo Barnabo.
101 min. b/w.
Made the year after *Bicycle Thieves*, this is a less coherent but more exuberant film, with De Sica injecting a stiff dose of fantasy into what could have been another plangent tale of gentleman tramps and shantytown life: the humble down-and-outs threatened with eviction by business speculators escape – thanks to angelic intervention – to their reward in heaven. Outrageous sentimentality undercut by outrageous cheek. CA

Miracle in the Rain

(Rudolph Maté, 1956, US) Jane Wyman, Van Johnson, Peggie Castle, Fred Clark, Eileen Heckart, Barbara Nichols, Alan King.
107 min. b/w.
Weepie in which plain Jane Wyman finds sweet romance with Johnson's wholesomely cheerful Southern soldier, only to have him killed in (WWII) action. Not a patch on Minnelli's *The Clock*, though much better than one might expect, thanks to a similar concern for humble detail and a nice array of New York locations. But the final 'miracle' – one of scriptwriter Ben Hecht's follies as Wyman is granted spiritual uplift in a vision of her late love – is a tough lump of goo to swallow. TM

Miracle Mile

(Steve DeJarnatt, 1989, US) Anthony Edwards, Mare Winningham, John Agar, Lou Hancock, Mykel T Williamson, Kelly Minter, Kurt Fuller, Denise Crosby, Robert Doqui.
88 min.
A nuclear thriller with a devastating narrative hook. Having arranged to meet a new girlfriend (Winningham) after her night shift at an LA diner, trombone-player and shy romantic Harry (Edwards) oversleeps and misses her. At 4.05 am, he picks up a ringing pay-phone outside the diner, and a voice screams 'It's happening! I can't believe it. We're locked into it...50 minutes and counting'. Is this some late-night freak's joke, or has a chance crossed line given Harry warning of impending nuclear Armageddon? With one deft stroke, writer-director DeJarnatt taps into the nightmare of being the first to know about the (possible) end of the world, and the awesome responsibility of having to communicate this news to others. The patrons of the Miracle Mile diner are understandably sceptical, but with less than an hour to live, Harry's personal priorities come sharply into focus. Cleverly written, authentically staged and sympathetically played, it's brave, uncompromising, and above all, frighteningly believable. NF

Miracle of Morgan's Creek, The

(Preston Sturges, 1944, US) Betty Hutton, Eddie Bracken, William Demarest, Diana Lynn, Porter Hall, Jimmy Conlin, Almira Sessions, Brian Donlevy, Akim Tamiroff.
99 min. b/w.
Characteristically hectic Sturges amalgam of

satire and slapstick, hitting out at such sacred cows as Momism and religion as it tells of the predicament of Hutton, a lively smalltown girl who finds herself pregnant after a drunken binge during which she married one of six unknown soldiers. Enter the stuttering oaf Bracken who loves her, to help out as stand-in father and watch agog as the town itself gets caught up in an inexorable whirl of chaos. Great verbal gags and non-sequiturs, fast-paced action, and a thorough irreverence for all things deemed respectable – politicians, policemen and magistrates included – make it a lasting delight, not least when the lady finally gives birth...to sextuplets. GA

Miracle of the Bells, The

(Irving Pichel, 1948, US) Fred MacMurray, Frank Sinatra, Alida Valli, Lee J Cobb, Charles Meredith.
120 min.
This over-extended and uncertain satire (adapted by Ben Hecht from a novel by Russell Janey) on fake religiosity has an ill-at-ease Sinatra as the priest persuaded by press agent MacMurray into offering his church for the funeral of late-lamented actress Valli, whose final film is due for imminent release. After three days of bell ringing, however, the girl is restored to life: Miracle or stunt? It's very hard to care. TJ

Miracle on 34th Street

(Les Mayfield, 1994, US) Richard Attenborough, Elizabeth Perkins, Dylan McDermott, JT Walsh, Joss Ackland, James Remar.
114 min.
Padding the deluxe avenues of Manhattan, kindly gentleman Kriss Kringle (Attenborough) is first seen confirming to a child that he is in fact the real Father Christmas. Mr Reassuring he may be, but he's also possessed of a medieval guildsman's pride: seeing the Santa from Cole's department store swigging whisky on a street parade, he wrests the reins away from him and takes over his sleigh, so impressing a Cole's executive (Perkins) that she hires him for the duration. The queues grow legion, until finally he's charged with being an impostor. That's not his only trial: he also has to convince Perkins' precocious daughter, which means delivering her Christmas list of a father, a house and a brother. This is a philosophical movie. How do you prove Santa's existence? It's a shaky business – like this movie – based on trust. All the kids I took loved it. The appeal must lie in the Santa-as-fantasy-grandfather-figure – with bottomless pockets. WH

Miracles

(Jim Kouf, 1985, US) Tom Conti, Teri Garr, Paul Rodriguez, Christopher Lloyd, Adalberto Martinez.
87 min.
Conti and Garr have just got divorced when they both, yes both, collide with a Mexican bankrobber on the run from the cops. He takes them hostage and flies off to his homeland, only to bale out when the plane runs out of fuel, leaving them to crash-land in the desert. But that's only the start of the non-stop, near-fatal disasters afflicting the couple. It's hard to win laughs with a script that is sitcom predictable; that aims for thrills with widespread destruction without ever making you care about its imperilled characters; that thinks kooks of all kinds saying 'sonofabitch' every half-minute and screaming at full volume are actually amusing. GA

Miracle Woman, The

(Frank Capra, 1931, US) Barbara Stanwyck, David Manners, Sam Hardy, Beryl Mercer, Russell Hopton.
90 min. b/w.
Fascinating cautionary tale loosely inspired by the Aimee Semple Macpherson affair, with Stanwyck as a minister's daughter – seeking revenge against the faithful who hounded her father to his death – who teams up with a wily conman (Hardy) to become big business as an evangelist. Stunning camerawork from Joseph Walker makes a joy of the evangelistic razzmatazz (climaxed when Stanwyck does her preaching from a lion's cage), but is equal to the more delicate shading of the comeuppance in which Stanwyck sees the true light after bringing illumination to a blind songwriter. The end

sees her a humble soldier in the Salvation Army, but – so beautifully do Stanwyck and Manners play out the love affair, and so perfectly does Capra direct it (with the tenderness, almost, of Borzage) – that you don't feel at all like laughing. TM

Miracle Worker, The

(Arthur Penn, 1962, US) Anne Bancroft, Patty Duke, Victor Jory, Inga Swenson, Andrew Prine, Beah Richards.
107 min. b/w.
Penn's remarkable screen version of William Gibson's play about Helen Keller, which he directed on Broadway. It's a stunningly impressive piece of work, typically (for Penn) deriving much of its power from the performances. Patty Duke as the young girl born deaf and blind, and Anne Bancroft as the stubborn Irish governess who helps her overcome her inability to speak, spark off each other with a violence and emotional honesty rarely seen in the cinema, lighting up each other's loneliness, vulnerability, and plain fear. What is in fact astonishing is the way that, while constructing a piece of very carefully directed and intelligently written melodrama, Penn manages to avoid sentimentality or even undue optimism about the value of Helen's education, and the way he achieves such a feeling of raw spontaneity in the acting. GA

Miracolo a Milano

see Miracle in Milan

Mirage

(Edward Dmytryk, 1965, US) Gregory Peck, Diane Baker, Walter Matthau, Leif Erickson, Kevin McCarthy, George Kennedy, Robert H Harris, Jack Weston, Walter Abel.
109 min. b/w.
Peck as an amnesiac in New York who traces his past back into the middle of a murder plot. Although the two leading players, Peck and Diane Baker, are shown up by their supporting cast, this remains one of the better thrillers of the '60s. The harsh black-and-white photography, the various levels of reality, and the use of urban landscape, all contribute to the feeling of unease, building up an atmosphere that is perhaps better than the mechanics of the plot deserve. CPe

Miroir a deux faces, Le (Lo Specchi a due facce/The Mirror Has Two Faces)

(André Cayatte, 1958, Fr/It) Michèle Morgan, Bourvil, Gérard Oury, Ivan Desny, Sandra Milo, Sylvie, Carette, Pierre Brice, Elisabeth Manet.
97 min. b/w.
Interesting to re-view this in the light of the Streisand 'remake', though any resemblance are so superficial as to appear coincidental. Bourvil, in one of his occasional dramatic roles, plays a mean, penny pinching, spoiled child of a man who deliberately seeks out a plain woman to marry, on the grounds she'll be less bother. Ten years later, a chance encounter with a cosmetic surgeon transforms the wife into Michèle Morgan, newly confident and socially in demand, whereupon Bourvil, deprived of his conveniently arranged world, goes spectacularly berserk. Cayatte shows his customary relish for the unpleasant: the nightmare honeymoon in Venice is richly detailed and Sylvie sketches in the quietly venomous mother-in-law with her usual economy. If Streisand's film was quintessential '90s Hollywood feel good, this is equally characteristic '50s French astringency. BBa

Mirror (Zerkalo) 100 (100)

(Andrei Tarkovsky, 1974, USSR) Margarita Terekhova, Philip Yankovsky, Ignat Daniltsev, Oleg Yankovsky, Nikolai Grinko.
106 min. b/w & col.
Tarkovsky goes for the great white whale of politicised art – no less than a history of his country in this century seen in terms of the personal – and succeeds. Intercutting a fragmented series of autobiographical episodes, which have only the internal logic of dream and memory, with startling documentary footage, he lovingly builds a world where the domestic expands into the political and crisscrosses back again. Unique its form, unique its vision. CPea

Mirror, The (Der Spiegel/Ayna)

(Erden Kiral, 1984, WGer/GB) Nur Sürer, Suavi Eren, Hikmet Celik, Vasilis Tsaglos, Nikos Skiadas.
91 min.
Based on The White Ox by Osman Sahin, this unrelenting Turkish moral tale (punctuated with many charged silences) was shot in Greece as a German-British co-production. Its theme is the mind-bending effects of extreme poverty. A rich young aga leaves the love gift of a mirror for the wife of a peasant. The husband murders the shy suitor with his wife's forced compliance, and buries his remains beneath the impacted earth of his ox's byre, which is half the couple's one-room home. However, the memory of the gift remains immovably lodged in the woman's mind. Spare, disquieting, and other-worldly. JPy

Mirror Crack'd, The

(Guy Hamilton, 1980, GB) Angela Lansbury, Edward Fox, Rock Hudson, Kim Novak, Elizabeth Taylor, Geraldine Chaplin, Tony Curtis, Charles Gray, Nigel Stock.
105 min.
Though it's obvious after five minutes that this is a complete no-no, the cinema equivalent of a bellyflop, it exercises a perverse fascination. You couldn't ask for a weirder exercise in whimsical English fantasy than a Miss Marple mystery masquerading as a Royal Command Performance in which all the American stars look stoned. Hingeing on death threats sent to the star (HRH Liz Taylor) of a visiting US movie, we are plunged into a timeless zone of the Home Counties, village lawns and pickled English character players where murders occur as inexplicably and as regularly as teatime. The main highlight is not the cheating plot but the rollcall of puffy, under-rehearsed stars: Hudson and Taylor as a neurotic couple in search of their cue cards, Tony Curtis stealing scenes as a bug-like movie producer, while a pink-clad, souped-up Kim Novak reappears as the legendary Kim Novak. The overall effect is of a holographed Madame Tussaud's. DMacp

Mirror Has Two Faces, The

see Miroir a deux faces, Le

Mirror Has Two Faces, The

(Barbra Streisand, 1996, US) Barbra Streisand, Jeff Bridges, Pierce Brosnan, George Segal, Mimi Rogers, Brenda Vaccaro, Lauren Bacall, Austin Pendleton.
126 min.
You want love against the odds? You've got it. Rose (Streisand) and Gregory (Bridges) are two brainy Columbia professors who will like lettuce in the presence of beauty. Greg hits on a plan. He and Rose will enter into a romance of the mind. He won't have to fight temptation, because Rose is homely as sin: no beauty, no sex, no worries. The only problem? Rose has already fallen in lust with Gregory and can't scramble out. The mirror may have two faces, but Streisand's happy with the one, still employing that riot of eye-rolls and lip-chews so disarming (once) in Funny Girl. Bridges does well as the bumbling nerd, his gulpingly shy exterior hiding a darkly fastidious core; and Bacall runs up and down the scale as Rose's haughty mother. Camp, but not much fun. CO'Su

Mirror Phase

(Carola Klein, 1978, GB) Leonie Klein, Carola Klein, Ewan Klein.
47 min.
When the child first catches sight of her image in a mirror, she sees herself as though she were another person. The 'recognition' of this framed coherent being as oneself is the first step in the creation of that fiction which is the Ego: the infant, as yet without full motor co-ordination, nonetheless perceives herself as a fully expressive whole. Carola Klein filmed her daughter Leonie in the process of such 'recognitions' in the early months of childhood. Mirror Phase is literally an analysed home movie, the 8mm print blown up into a perceptible 16mm grain. Choral voice-overs, dual camerawork, and the fractioning of the screen suggest that we also can misrecognise our relation to film: that cinema too can function as a 'specular ego'. Such work has obvious debts to Laura Mulvey's writing and film-making; and Mirror Phase is something like Riddles of the Sphinx from the child's perspective. But where Riddles attempted to question film's use of narrative and character, Mirror Phase is fixed within the actual fact of Leonie's development and her parents' evident personalities – a return to the charm of the home movie, but a crucial restraint on the film's analysis. MM

Miserables, Les

see Les Misérables

Misérables, Les

see Les Misérables

Misérables, Les

(Jean-Paul Le Chanois, 1957, Fr) Jean Gabin, Bernard Blier, Bourvil, Gianni Esposito, Serge Reggiani, Danièle Delorme, Silvia Monfort.
187 min.
A glossy CinemaScope classic, a film for all the family which does Victor Hugo proud. Back in 1957, directors didn't count for much, and it relies on clumsily edited, sluggish shots of an all-star cast, headed by a superb Gabin as the ex-convict turned do-gooding businessman struggling to atone for his past. In 1958, Truffaut made his first film. Les Misérables is, in other words, one of the last of the dinosaurs. For dinosaur, read splendidly moralistic melodrama, guaranteed to kill those Sunday afternoon blues. Bet it makes you cry. PHo

Misérables, Les (aka Les Misérables du vingtième siècle)

(Claude Lelouch, 1995, Fr) Jean-Paul Belmondo, Michel Boujenah, Alessandra Martines, Salomé (Lelouch), Annie Girardot, Philippe Léotard, Philippe Khorsand, Jean Marais, Micheline Presle.
174 min.
Following fate-tossed Henri Fortin's progress through unjust imprisonment, the boxing ring and two world wars, this vast and vastly enjoyable epic demonstrates how the hero's obsession with reaching the end of Hugo's novel makes him compare his plight to that of Jean Valjean, both men sticking to their moral integrity to get them through the very worst of times. In Fortin's case, he helps a Jewish family escape both the Gestapo and the anti-Semitic collaborators all too keen to sell them out, and it's Lelouch's unflinching depiction of France's shoddy wartime treatment of the Jews that puts a little iron in the movie's abundant soul. You could argue that such hard-edged drama sits ill beside the generally light-hearted tone of Belmondo's picaresque adventures and the imaginative dips in and out of Hugo, but it's part of the magic Lelouch has worked that his story-of-all-stories theme matches the catch-all inclusiveness of his old-fashioned celluloid showmanship. Although Boujenah's portrayal of the hard-pressed Jewish father Ziman sails close to caricature, elsewhere Léotard and Girardot make a marvellously grizzled rural couple, while Belmondo's performance sweeps the whole thing along with undemonstrative charisma. TJ

Misery

(Rob Reiner, 1990, US) James Caan, Kathy Bates, Richard Farnsworth, Frances Sternhagen, Lauren Bacall, Graham Jarvis.
107 min.
The gore is toned down and the psychology played up in this darkly humorous adaptation of Stephen King's novel. Paul Sheldon (Caan) is a successful author of romantic fiction, but public demand for his heroine Misery Chastain has stifled his creativity; so after killing her off in a forthcoming final adventure, he writes a long-neglected personal novel. When a blizzard sends his car off the road on the drive home from his mountain retreat, his life is saved by nurse Annie Wilkes (Bates), who soon has the invalid tucked up in her home. It's a bonus that as his number one fan she's extremely attentive; and a definite minus that she's a psychopath who's looking forward to his next 'Misery' novel... William Goldman's intelligent script operates both as psycho-thriller and as sly comment on the sort of attitude towards celebrity which can enshrine and – in this case, literally – imprison the object of devotion. The casting is inspired: Caan oozes frustration at his physical disability, while Bates brings authority and an eerie

m

naturalness to her demented character, her home-spun expressions ('oogie', 'dirty birdy') providing a bizarre counterpoint to her increasingly cruel actions. Reiner captures *just* the right level of physical tension, but for the most part wisely emphasises the mental duels. Terrific. CM

Misfits, The
(John Huston, 1960, US) Clark Gable, Marilyn Monroe, Montgomery Clift, Eli Wallach, Thelma Ritter, Estelle Winwood, James Barton.
124 min. b/w.
A superbly shot anti-Western, constantly dragged down by Arthur Miller's verbose, cloyingly glib script about emotional cripples searching for a meaning to life in the twilight of the American frontier, with Monroe as the Reno divorcee who becomes a sort of earth mother/conscience to a group of ex-cowboys scratching an unhappy living around the rodeos. Lent a testamentary (almost prophetic) gloss when it proved to be the end of the line for both Gable and Monroe, with Clift – giving the best performance in the film – to follow soon after. But it really comes good only in the mustang round-up at the end, an overly symbolic but nevertheless magnificent sequence. TM

Mishima: A Life in Four Chapters
(Paul Schrader, 1985, US/Jap) Ken Ogata, Masayuki Shionoya, Junkichi Orimoto, Naoko Otani, Go Riju.
120 min. b/w & col.
A fantasist recreating himself in his own image to perfection; a narcissist building his puny body into a muscled samurai; an ultra-rightist patriot raising a private army to restore Japan to its former glory; an artist achieving his spiritual redemption through the ritual disembowelling of *seppuku*. Schrader may have finally achieved the violent transfiguration that he seeks along with his protagonists: the movie has all the ritual sharpness and beauty of that final sword. Moreover it has a unique structure. Three of Mishima's most autobiographical novels are dramatised on sets of incandescent colour designed by Eiko; flashbacks to Mishima's early life are in serene black-and-white; and the whole is bracketed by a Costa Gavras-style recreation of the last day of his life. Confusing as it sounds, Schrader's grip never falters. Finally Philip Glass' insistent score virtually transforms the whole thing into opera. There is nothing quite like it. CPea

Miss Firecracker
(Thomas Schlamme, 1989, US) Holly Hunter, Mary Steenburgen, Tim Robbins, Alfre Woodward, Scott Glenn, Veanne Cox, Ann Wedgeworth, Trey Wilson, Amy Wright, Bert Remsen.
103 min.
This adaptation of Beth Henley's play *The Miss Firecracker Contest* abounds with idiosyncratic detail and such familiar Henley ingredients as family madness; but the interplay is more emotionally complicated, the perspective less wilfully detached than, say, *Crimes of the Heart*. Carnelle Scott (Hunter) is known as the loosest lady in her small Mississippi town. She plans to redeem her reputation by winning the Miss Firecracker beauty/talent contest (which, since she was orphaned as a child, assumes enormous importance as a sign of social acceptance), forging ahead with her ambitions both helped and hindered by her cousins, one-time Miss Firecracker Elaine (Steenburgen) and tormented Delmount (Robbins). Despite touches of enforced eccentricity, the story is redeemed by its observation of bittersweet relationships and self-deceptions. Amid notions of self-determination and individual enterprise, Henley is graciously compassionate, embracing human limitations and self-acceptance. Performances are carefully modulated, but this is Holly Hunter's movie. Her show-stopping tap dance to the strains of 'The Star-Spangled Banner' is worth the price of admission alone. CM

Missing
(Costa-Gavras, 1981, US) Jack Lemmon, Sissy Spacek, Melanie Mayron, John Shea, Charles Cioffi, David Clennon, Richard Bradford, Janice Rule.
122 min.

As darkness falls on a terrified city, taxis and buses refuse all passengers, trapped pedestrians beg strangers for sanctuary, even an earthquake cannot drive people onto the street. It may sound like apocalyptic science fiction, but it's Costa-Gavras' extraordinary first American movie, based on true events during the Chilean coup of 1973. It explores the disappearance of a young American writer, and prompted a furious rebuttal from the US State Department. Spacek and Lemmon are fine as the missing man's wife and father, but what makes the film so overwhelming in places is its unending night-time imagery of a society coming apart at the seams. Costa-Gavras underpins his campaigning content with all the electric atmosphere of a paranoid conspiracy thriller, and ensures that *Missing* will remain the cinematic evocation of a military coup for years to come. DP

Missing in Action
(Joseph Zito, 1984, US) Chuck Norris, M Emmet Walsh, Davis Tress, Leonore Kasdorf, James Hong, Ernie Ortega.
101 min.
On some occasions, sitting through a real stinker of a movie is perversely entertaining. This is so bad it defies belief. Norris, veteran of trashy but fun martial arts movies, plays Colonel James Braddock, a self-appointed gook-zapping 'Nam vet. Taking off his shirt at every available opportunity, Norris hunks his way through the jungle to rescue a gang of unofficial POWs, GIs imprisoned long after the end of the war. Cue lots of explosions, perfunctory action sequences, transparent gore, and 'all gooks are baddies' propaganda. Xenophobic, amateurish and extraordinarily dull, it nevertheless grossed 26 million dollars in the States. JCo

Missing Link
(David Hughes/Carol Hughes, 1989, US) Peter Elliott.
90 min.
Michael Gambon's gruff tones lend weight to this offbeat Hollywood venture into pre-history, a slow quasi-documentary saga of the last ape-man left alone to confront the African landscape after his family is wiped out. Arresting location camerawork by the directors, and much hairy make-up by Rick (*American Werewolf in London*) Baker fail to fill the credibility gap. From *Batman* producers Peter Guber and John Peters. TJ

Mission, The
(Parviz Sayyad, 1983, US/WGer) Parviz Sayyad, Mary Apick, Houshang Touzie, Mohammad B Ghaffari, Hedyeh Anvar, Hatam Anvar.
108 min.
A neat little thriller set in New York; the twist is that the hitman is a young Iranian (Touzie) who has been ordered by 'His Eminence' (representative of otherwise faceless superiors) to terminate 'The Colonel', ex-SAVAK (secret police under the Shah) and therefore enemy of the Khomeini regime. The hunter homes in on his prey, but by a quirk of kismet ends up rescuing him from a couple of muggers. Apart from satisfying the straightforward requirements of its genre, *The Mission* embraces extra dimensions: as a study of blind fanaticism, as religious polemic, as a portrait of the stranger in a strange land. And there are some lovely touches of black humour, like the would-be assassin sneaking up on his jogging quarry with a lethal-looking skipping rope at the ready. The Colonel is played by the film's writer/producer/director, who fell foul of the Iranian censor under both the Shah and the Ayatollah, so he should know. AB

Mission, The
(Roland Joffé, 1986, GB) Robert De Niro, Jeremy Irons, Ray McAnally, Aidan Quinn, Cherie Lunghi, Ronald Pickup.
125 min.
In the 18th century, Spain and Portugal were at each other's throats over rights to territory in South America. Neither side suffered a great deal, the real victim being the native Indians. Here their only protection comes in the form of a Jesuit priest intent on giving God to the jungle (Irons), and a slave trader warring with the Jesuits who later joins their order (De Niro). The theme of Robert Bolt's script is the conflict between compassion and politics, at its moral centre the pow-

erful church official (McAnally, marvellous) sent by the King of Portugal to decide whether the Jesuit missions, and the native communities which surround them, should survive. Enacted against the stunning backdrop of the Amazon jungle, the action has a rousing, epic quality. What it doesn't have, however, is passion. The climax is brutal, De Niro and Irons are impressive as the opponents who become soul mates; yet *The Mission* manages to be both magnificent and curiously uninvolving, a buddy movie played in soutanes. RR

Missionary, The
(Richard Loncraine, 1981, GB) Michael Palin, Maggie Smith, Trevor Howard, Denholm Elliott, Graham Crowden, David Suchet, Michael Hordern, Roland Culver.
86 min.
Along with *Local Hero*, this marks a return to the kind of gentle comedy drama that has more in common with the old Ealing films than with the zaniness of Monty Python. A naive missionary returns from colonial Africa to be sent among the Fallen Women of Edwardian London. From them he learns that missionary has another meaning, which he embraces with the fervour of a man finding his true vocation. Affectionate treatment of English eccentrics – choleric general (Howard), aristocratic nympho (Smith), dotty butler (Hordern), keep-fit bishop (Elliott) – maintains interest between the rather meagrely distributed comic set pieces. But despite stylish direction, Palin's artless vicar is too familiar and too supine to carry a full-length film, a personal project in which he seems oddly self-effacing. MB

Mission Impossible
(Brian De Palma, 1996, US) Tom Cruise, Jon Voight, Emmanuelle Béart, Henry Czerny, Jean Reno, Ving Rhames, Kristin Scott-Thomas, Vanessa Redgrave, Ingeborga Dapkunaite.
110 min.
Twenty minutes into this big-budget update of the '70s spy series, half the cast has been wiped out, and Cruise's Ethan Hunt has been 'disavowed' by his employers, the CIA. To clear his name and avenge the death of his mentor Jim Phelps (Voight), Hunt assembles a crew of rogue agents to break in to CIA headquarters, playing a precarious double game with breathless self-assurance. 'Mission: Impenetrable': a bewildering, ludicrous, but mostly fun, sometimes even smart postscript to a genre that went out of fashion with the Cold War. There's more and less here than meets the eye. More, because De Palma, the cinematographer and the screenwriters have concocted an elaborate series of conceits and deceits, masks and trompe l'oeils, which slyly undermine the paranoid imperatives of the original series – and, indeed, the Cold War itself. Less, because De Palma is the most hermetic of American filmmakers; combine that with the pressure to deliver a mainstream blockbuster and you've got a recipe for superficiality. Despite the snags, De Palma remains a virtuoso puppet-master, pulling the strings taut in a nail-biting robbery sequence, switching from micro to macro with Hitchcockian panache, and finally letting rip with a hell-for-leather climax. TCh

Mission to Moscow
(Michael Curtiz, 1943, US) Walter Huston, Ann Harding, Oscar Homolka, George Tobias, Gene Lockhart, Eleanor Parker, Helmut Dantine, Victor Francen.
123 min. b/w.
Interesting either as an expressive object or as pure movie. Based on a bestselling memoir by Joseph E Davies, US ambassador to the USSR from 1936 to 1938, it makes an impassioned plea to John Doe to forget his fears about commies and embrace Russia as a comrade in arms against the Nazi peril. Subsequently an embarrassment, it was called in question by HUAC in 1947 (when studio head Jack Warner slid from under, since the film had seemingly been made at the request of the White House, but scriptwriter Howard Koch was thrown to the wolves). Presenting Stalin as everybody's favourite uncle, the infamous purges as mere matters of national security, and Reds as all-American Joes in furry hats sharing the same utopian dream, its thesis was rightly slated by Agee as 'a great glad two-million dollar bowl of canned borscht'. On the other hand, it's quite beautifully put together by Curtiz. TM

Mississippi Blues

(Robert Parrish/Bertrand Tavernier, 1993, Fr/US)
96 min.

Tavernier, in pursuit of some Southland of the mind constructed from bits of Faulkner, Minnelli and Nick Ray, joins up with Parrish, whose own agenda has more to do with re-experiencing and communicating the flavour of his 1920s Georgia boyhood. Inevitably friction ensued, traces of which we are allowed to glimpse, but the fascinatingly lopsided result of the collaboration is really three overlapping movies, Parrish's, Tavernier's and the inadvertent one that emerges out of the obdurate individuality of the various interviewees. Those with low tolearance for gospel/blues should be aware that an awful lot of it goes on here – although we do get to see the director of *Saddle the Wind* sing 'Shall We Gather at the River', if that's your idea of a collector's item. BBa

Mississippi Burning

(Alan Parker, 1988, US) Gene Hackman, Willem Dafoe, Frances McDormand, Brad Dourif, R Lee Ermey, Gailard Sartain, Stephen Tobolowsky.
127 min.

Parker's film, loosely based in fact, goes for the gut rather than the head in its assessment of Deep South racism. When three civil rights activists disappear from a small Mississippi town in 1964, the FBI responds (two of the missing men were white) by sending in agents Dafoe and Hackman, the former a by-the-book Yankee determined never to violate the rights of the interrogated, the latter a local boy who opines that to deal with scum you must sink to gutter level. Scum the villains certainly are: ugly, ignorant rednecks devoted to the Klan, and all too happy to punish blacks who protest against injustice or blab to interfering outsiders. In the film, the blacks are almost without exception seen as mute victims, and typically for a film by an Englishman, race hatred is defined in terms of class and economic envy. But Hackman is excellent, especially in his surprisingly tender scenes with McDormand, wife of sadistic deputy Dourif; and for once, Parker directs without depending on flashy visual tropes. The relative anonymity is a plus; only the end falls foul of hyperbole, and it's arguably the director's most controlled film to date. GA

Mississippi Masala

(Mira Nair, 1991, US) Denzel Washington, Sarita Choudhury, Roshan Seth, Sharmila Tagore, Charles S Dutton, Joe Seneca, Ranjit Chowdhry, Mira Nair.
118 min.

Nair's ambitious film examines a burdensome plurality of subjects associated with race and migration within the confines of a more-or-less conventional love story. Four-year-old Mina, her lawyer father and family, of Indian origin, are among those expelled from Uganda in 1972. Eighteen years later, we find them in Greenwood, Mississippi. Mina (Choudhury) has become, unlike her father (Seth), acclimatised if not entirely assimilated to her new country, and is employed as a cleaner at the local motel, hopeful but not impatient for greater things. She meets Afro-American Demetrius (Washington), a clean-cut, self-employed contract carpet cleaner, and their relationship unleashes the submerged rivalries, resentments and prejudices of their respective communities. An interesting if poorly constructed and self-contradicting drama, directed with something less than assurance, but given some appeal by the honesty of its performances. WH

Mississippi Mermaid

see Sirène du Mississipi, La

Miss Mary

(Maria Luisa Bemberg, 1986, Arg/USA) Julie Christie, Nacha Guevara, Eduardo Pavlovsky, Luisina Brando, Gerardo Romano, Iris Marga.
110 min.

Miss Mary (Christie) is a lonely, starchy English governess whose recollections of her time in the employ of a wealthy Buenos Aires family provide insights into the type of spiritual malaise which is induced by an excess of cash. The father (Pavlovsky) spends much of the time at the billiard table; the mother (Guevara) is a fixture at

the piano, playing melancholy Satie. The period is the late '30s/early '40s, and some acknowledgment of the shifting political scene as the Peron regime approaches filters through in after-dinner conversations or in the street disturbances which interrupt Miss Mary's thoughts. There's a sense of impending doom for the family, but the camera maintains a distance inhibiting our involvement, and even Miss Mary's testimony is thrown into question by the Catholic/Victorian upbringing which has left her almost as emotionally sterile as her employers. It's not an enjoyable film, rambling at times, but it deserves attention for its faithful reflection of the suffocating emptiness of a repressive way of life. EP

Miss Nobody (Panna Nikt)

(Andrzej Wajda, 1996, Pol) Anna Wielgucka, Anna Mucha, Anna Powierza.
98 min.

A diffident 15-year-old girl from the countryside moves with her family to a high-rise apartment in Warsaw. As she tries to adjust to city life, she's befriended first by a wild, gypsy-like classmate, and then by the teenage daughter of entrepreneurial Poles. Miss Nobody clearly stands for Poland-in-miniature, caught between eastern mysticism and western materialism, but as political allegory, this is crude and heavy-handed. Wajda, seemingly taking his cue from Kieslowski, concentrates on the emotional lives of his characters, rather than on the social changes occurring around them. The strongest scenes are those in which the elements themselves seem torn by the heroine's anxieties (a climactic scene in the woods); but Wajda is no miniaturist by nature, and one suspects he'd prefer a much more epic canvas than this. Adapted from a novel by Tomas Tryzna. GM

Missouri Breaks, The

(Arthur Penn, 1976, US) Marlon Brando, Jack Nicholson, Randy Quaid, Kathleen Lloyd, Frederic Forrest, Harry Dean Stanton, John McLiam, John P Ryan, Richard Bradford.
126 min.

A wonderfully quirky Western, brilliantly scripted by Thomas McGuane, which strips all the cute whimsy away from the *Butch Cassidy* theme (outlaws on the run from a relentless lawman), replacing it with a kind of pixillated terror. Playing the 'regulator' as a camp Buffalo Bill with an Irish accent, Brando makes his entrance playing peekaboo from behind his horse, and at one point even stalks his prey in a dress and poke bonnet. But he is also a legalised killer, expert with a rifle but preferring (as the flail of God) to use a harpoon shaped like a crucifix. And as his gloating sadism shades into hints of bizarre perversion when he dedicates a love song and a kiss to his horse, the tone gradually darkens to a kind of horror. It's one of the few truly major Westerns of the '70s, with a very clear vision of the historical role played by fear and violence in the taming of the wilderness. TM

Miss Pinkerton

(Lloyd Bacon, 1932, US) Joan Blondell, George Brent, John Wray, Ruth Hall, C Henry Gordon, Elizabeth Patterson, Holmes Herbert.
66 min. b/w.

Potboiling whodunit set in an old dark house, crammed with shots of menacing silhouettes and characters all behaving sinisterly. Blondell, as lively as usual, is the best thing in the film as a nurse sent to tend to Elizabeth Patterson, prostrated by the suicide – possibly murder – of her nephew. When Patterson goes the same way, done in by hypodermic, Blondell helps Brent's police inspector – for whom she naturally falls – uncover a dastardly legal plot. The supporting performances are indifferent. TM

Miss Robin Hood

(John Guillermin, 1952, GB) Margaret Rutherford, Richard Hearne, James Robertson Justice, Edward Lexy, James Robertson Justice, Michael Medwin, Sidney James, Dora Bryan, Peter Jones, Reg Varney.
78 min. b/w.

Sub-Ealing whimsy finds shy children's writer Hearne unwittingly embroiled in a life of crime when eccentric youth club leader Rutherford enlists his help to swipe a whisky formula she claims was stolen from her ancestors. A jaunty but rather inane little number (co-written by

Patrick Campbell), largely notable as one of the few films made by the short-lived Group 3 Productions, set up by the National Film Finance Corporation with the specific remit of making low-budget pictures. TJ

Miss Sadie Thompson

(Curtis Bernhardt, 1953, US) Rita Hayworth, José Ferrer, Aldo Ray, Harry Bellaver, Charles Bronson, Russell Collins.
91 min.

A dire, updated, absurdly bloated 3-D version of Somerset Maugham's *Rain* – a tale of sin and redemption in the tropics – completely missing out on the dark, brooding intensity of Raoul Walsh's silent *Sadie Thompson*. Conviction never gets a look in, what with Ferrer wandering zombie-fashion through acres of pious platitudes as the religious bigot who turns out (surprise, surprise) to be a closet rapist, while Hayworth, mouthing a string of dubbed songs and cheerfully revving her motor as the good-time gal who is no better (and not much worse) than she should be, seems to be moulding her characterisation on Doris Day. Only Aldo Ray, as the bovine marine who falls for Sadie, and in so doing discovers the meaning of tolerance, emerges from the affair with any credit. TM

Miss Shumway jette un sort

see Rough Magic

Mr and Mrs Bridge

(James Ivory, 1990, US) Paul Newman, Joanne Woodward, Margaret Welsh, Robert Sean Leonard, Kyra Sedgwick, Saundra McClain, Blythe Danner, Gale Garnett, Simon Callow, Austin Pendleton.
125 min.

In this adaptation of Evan S Connell's twin novels, Newman plays Mr Bridge, a distinguished Kansas City lawyer, and Woodward plays Mrs Bridge. It is not a marriage of like minds: India is all caring and sharing, but hidebound Walter, though full of love for his family, dare not speak its name. The first World War is over and the second one coming, but Walter refuses to move with the times. In many ways the film is about disappointment: the disappointment children cause parents – fast-and-loose Ruth (Sedgwick) goes to New York to become an actress, and fails; Carolyn (Welsh) ends in divorce; Douglas (Leonard) cannot even bring himself to kiss mother – and the disappointment felt when spouses, friends and life itself fail to live up to expectation. The episodic outcome is disappointing, too. Newman is good and Woodward superb, but their moving portrayals exist in a vacuum of overpowering beauty. Stunningly photographed interiors and exteriors take the breath away, but their inhabitants seem almost irrelevant. MS

Mr and Mrs Smith

(Alfred Hitchcock, 1941, US) Carole Lombard, Robert Montgomery, Gene Raymond, Jack Carson, Betty Compson, Philip Merivale.
95 min. b/w.

A gentle crazy comedy, with Lombard and Montgomery as a couple who discover that their marriage wasn't legal and go through courtship all over again. Less Hitchcock, however, than writer Norman Krasna, who at his best could twist conventional characters and plot patterns in such beguiling ways that you'd almost forget their antiquity. This comes near his best. GB

Mr Arkadin
(aka Confidential Report)

(Orson Welles, 1955, Sp/Fr) Orson Welles, Paola Mori, Robert Arden, Akim Tamiroff, Michael Redgrave, Patricia Medina, Mischa Auer, Katina Paxinou.
100 min. b/w.

Long unavailable for theatrical screening but finally resurfacing on TV in a version edited closer to Welles' cut than that originally released here, *Mr Arkadin* assumed an equivalent patina of myth and legend to that cultivated by its central character, non-naturalistically posited somewhere between Kane and God. Arkadin is the powerful financier who employs his own researcher to piece together his apparently forgotten past, to find a shabby Rosebud to dramatise his by-now bored puppeteering. Flamboyantly melodramatic, it's a playfully egocentric display of egocentrism and a magician's perverse revelation of his own trickery. Failure or not, it's irresistible. PT

Mr Baseball
(Fred Schepisi, 1992, US/Jap) Tom Selleck, Ken Takakura, Aya Takanashi, Toshi Shioya, Dennis Haysbert.
113 min.
Hardly one of Schepisi's finest hours: Selleck mugs his way through the usual 'fish out of water' routine as a lippy American ball-player who joins a Japanese team, but, somewhat predictably, has difficulty adjusting to the confines of group mentality. It's fairly tame stuff, but Matsushita's take-over of Universal dumped the production into controversy, with the Japanese reckoning the script was anti-Japanese and the Yanks reckoning it anti-American. We Brits took one look and called it 'straight to video'. TJ

Mr Billion
(Jonathan Kaplan, 1977, US) Terence Hill, Valerie Perrine, Jackie Gleason, Slim Pickens, William Redfield, Chill Wills, Dick Miller, RG Armstrong, Kate Heflin.
93 min.
Chase comedy without the glamour of *Silver Streak* but with much pleasant and well-handled action. Italian garage mechanic (spaghetti Western star Hill in his American debut) inherits billion dollars from financier uncle in California; company hires Perrine to seduce him into handing over power of attorney; she falls for him instead, so the pair must be ambushed, shot at, handcuffed together etc, to prevent Hill claiming inheritance by specified date. He escapes, and naturally tangles with a whole crowd of eccentrics on his way across America. Like other Corman colts, Kaplan opts for a '30s approach, whose soft-centre no amount of flashy cutting can hide; but there is a nice tongue-in-cheek air ('Perverts are people too'), and a lot of Hollywood clichés are delivered fresh and with relish. AN

Mr Blandings Builds His Dream House
(HC Potter, 1948, US) Cary Grant, Myrna Loy, Melvyn Douglas, Reginald Denny, Sharyn Moffet, Connie Marshall, Louise Beavers.
94 min. b/w.
'Mr Dreamings Builds His Bland House' would be a more accurate title for this distinctly quaint RKO comedy of Cary Grant's advertising man from Manhattan trying to set up a rural haven for his family in Connecticut, despite dry rot and all kinds of neighbourhood shysters. Naturally the dream comes true, and Blandings is probably the world's happiest commuter. The sweet, flimsy charm of all this would no doubt be indigestible without the personable performances of the stars, or the smug confidence of the script (Panama and Frank) and direction. GB

Mister Cory
(Blake Edwards, 1956, US) Tony Curtis, Charles Bickford, Martha Hyer, Kathryn Grant, Henry Daniell, William Reynolds, Russ Morgan.
92 min.
Made just before *Sweet Smell of Success*, serving almost as a run-up to Curtis' characterisation as Sidney Falco, this mines the same vein of guttersnipe, braggart ambition, but to comic and rather less successful effect. Curtis plays a Chicago slum kid who, while employed as a waiter, makes it rich as a gambler among the country-club set, and ends up having to choose between classy Hyer (who likes him for his body) and her sister Grant (who likes him for himself). A glossy, almost-black comedy, it never really works as sharp social satire, despite the pointed irony of the sexually ambiguous relationship between Curtis and the ageing gambler (Bickford) with whom he goes into lucrative partnership. But Curtis' sense of timing, coupled with Edwards' solid professionalism, make for breezy if forgettable entertainment. GA

Mr Deeds Goes to Town
(Frank Capra, 1936, US) Gary Cooper, Jean Arthur, George Bancroft, Lionel Stander, Raymond Walburn, Walter Catlett, Douglas Dumbrille, HB Warner.
115 min. b/w.

Before Capra got down to Christmas card morals, he perfected the screwball comedy technique of pursuing common sense to logical ends in a lunatic situation. *Mr Deeds Goes to Town* is one of the best, with Cooper saying nope to a $20 million inheritance, and newshound Jean Arthur going for his 'inside story': and if you've seen *The Electric Horseman*, you'll see where it borrowed its ludicrous charm. DMacp

Mr Drake's Duck
(Val Guest, 1950, GB) Douglas Fairbanks Jr, Yolande Donlan, AE Matthews, Jon Pertwee, Reginald Beckwith, Wilfrid Hyde-White.
85 min. b/w.
Complications mount in this adaptation of a vintage radio play (by Ian Messiter) when nice American couple Fairbanks and Donlan start a new life in England and discover their recently purchased duck is laying solid uranium eggs. A light-hearted frolic from another age. Uranium eggs? Ho, ho, ho! TJ

Mr Forbush and the Penguins (aka Cry of the Penguins)
(Al Viola, 1971, GB) John Hurt, Hayley Mills, Dudley Sutton, Tony Britton, Thorley Walters, Judy Campbell, Joss Ackland.
101 min.
Filmed on location with the assistance of the Argentinian army and navy, and with Arne Sucksdorff responsible for the Antarctic animal sequences. Viola's version (Forbush alone in the Antarctic wastes) was pruned to make way for the inconsequential framing story (directed by an uncredited Roy Boulting) deemed necessary to get people into the cinema. So Graham Billing's novel emerges as a trite romantic fable about a rich young biologist who leaves home and his frigid girlfriend (Mills) for the warm-hearted beasties of the frozen South. There's a single sequence during the arrival of the penguins that makes the rest of the film just about worth sitting through.

Mister Freedom
(William Klein, 1968, Fr) John Abbey, Delphine Seyrig, Jean-Claude Drouot, Philippe Noiret, Catherine Rouvel, Sami Frey, Serge Gainsbourg, Donald Pleasence, Yves Montand.
110 min.
The colossal Mr Freedom (Abbey) wears baseball gear, feverishly decorated – like so much else in this heavy-handed romp – with stars, stripes, red, white and blue. His mission is to rid France of America's ideological enemies, represented by Red-China-Man (a smoke-breathing yellow-tailed monster) and Moujik-Man (Noiret in a rather fetching inflated red costume). But Freedom overplays his hand, and blows up the whole country along with himself. Klein shows a parallel lack of restraint, going all out to slay American imperialism with sledgehammer irony and a comic strip style which soon becomes tiresome. Isolated things remain among the debris: a shot of a smiling girl with two boiled eggs and a strip of bacon on her chest in a heady montage on the delights of American life; the sight of Christ silencing the Virgin Mary with 'Mom, please!'; and of course Delphine Seyrig as a drum majorette/whore double agent. GB

Mister Frost
(Philippe Setbon, 1990, Fr/GB) Jeff Goldblum, Alan Bates, Kathy Baker, Roland Giraud, Jean-Pierre Cassel, Daniel Gélin, Henri Serre, Charley Boorman.
104 min.
Setbon's second film as director, in a career which has encompassed cartoons, comics and the screenplay for Godard's *Détective*, is an odd affair. The eponymous anti-hero (Goldblum) is apprehended for a particularly hideous series of murders after a would-be burglar breaks into his garage and discovers a corpse with its throat cut. The question is: is Mister Frost, as detective Felix Detweiller (Bates) believes, the Devil himself; is he a vibrant, sexy, all-powerful healer in an institution for the helpless and insane; or is he just another heavy-duty nutter? The film does grip, despite the sometimes below-par quality of both the camerawork and the acting. The real weakness lies in the performance of Bates, who leaves much to be desired both as cop and as putative lover of a doctor played by the excellent Kathy Baker. Much of the narrative, moreover, is mean-

dering, trying too hard to reconcile romance with horror pic and with theatre of the intellect. Different, though. SGr

Mr Hobbs Takes a Vacation
(Henry Koster, 1962, US) James Stewart, Maureen O'Hara, Fabian, John Saxon, Marie Wilson, Reginald Gardiner, Lauri Peters, John McGiver.
115 min.
A wholesome family comedy with Stewart and O'Hara as a couple whose quiet vacation becomes a noisy free-for-all for the kids. Fabian, one of the first rock singers to be created overnight by publicity hype (with hit songs like 'Tiger' and 'Turn Me Loose'), apart from singing one song, gives a performance so wooden it has to be seen to be believed. DP

Mr Holland's Opus
(Stephen Herek, 1995, US) Richard Dreyfuss, Glenne Headly, Jay Thomas, Olympia Dukakis, WH Macy, Alicia Witt, Terrence Howard.
143 min.
It's Glenn Holland's first day at school: he's the reluctant new music teacher at John F Kennedy High. It's 1965, and Mr Holland (Dreyfuss) is anxious to get back to his real work, composition, but as time passes he rechannels his passion into the students, until one day he wakes up, 30 years later, and wonders what happened to his life. Although the avowed inspiration here is *It's a Wonderful Life*, this tear-jerker shares plenty of old school ties with such British counterparts as *The Browning Version* and *Goodbye, Mr Chips*. Screenwriter Patrick Sheane Duncan has created a dramatic arc that's also a learning curve: Holland starts off a stiff-shirt disciplinarian, but comes to realise that he gets better results when he mixes up the Ludwig Van with a little Ray Charles. The film soft-pedals the uglier realities of contemporary schools and Holland's last, most sentimental lesson is to appreciate his own worth. But sentimentality can have its heart in the right place and, in any case, this isn't the film's only message: Dreyfuss' exemplary performance shows how selfishly Holland neglects his own family in favour of his pupils, and it's clear how conservative politics impinge even on music classes. A middle-brow melodrama which functions as the thinking person's *Forrest Gump*. Music to my ears. TCh

Mr Hulot's Holiday
see Vacances de M. Hulot, Les

Mister Johnson
(Bruce Beresford, 1990, US) Maynard Eziashi, Pierce Brosnan, Edward Woodward, Beatie Edney, Femi Fatoba, Denis Quilley, Bella Enaharo, Nick Reding.
102 min.
Another film about a white master and a black servant from the director of *Driving Miss Daisy*. Colonial West Africa, c.1920: Rudbeck (Brosnan) is a fastidious English District Officer, Johnson (Eziashi) his chief clerk, a native more English than the English. William Boyd, who adapted Joyce Cary's novel for the film, has compared Johnson to Falstaff and Candide; but a character who lived in his own right on the page picks up all kind of social baggage when projected on to the screen. Here, despite Eziashi's droll performance, Johnson comes to embody an offensive, regressive racial stereotype. A colonial sensibility runs through the film, despite the trite disavowals that pepper the script. It misfires drastically, but Beresford's anonymous direction at least apes some received notion of 'quality'. He photographs the landscape prettily, and the film is neatly turned. Eminently respectable, in fact. TCh

Mr Jolly Lives Next Door
(Stephen Frears, 1987, GB) Adrian Edmondson, Rik Mayall, Peter Cook, Nicholas Parsons, Peter Richardson, Gerard Kelly, Granville Saxton.
52 min.
TV's Comic Strip in a niagara of blood, booze, saliva and sick, this has Edmondson and Mayall as a pair of bored escorts who, while taking no care of Nicholas Parsons, become involved with a hit-gang and an axe-man (Cook). The abuse is so gratuitous, the pace so riotous, that a kind of

obscene serenity hovers over the mayhem. It's funny. Comic Strippers will adore it, and after a six-pack, so will anybody else. MS

Mr Jones

(Mike Figgis, 1994, US) Richard Gere, Lena Olin, Anne Bancroft, Tom Irwin, Delroy Lindo, Bruce Altman, Lauren Tom.
114 min.
Mike Figgis's film began as a brooding account of the affair between Mr Jones (Gere), an erratic depressive, and Libbie (Olin), his dedicated, love-struck psychiatrist. But Gere, it seems, resisting typecasting and attempting to give his role some depth, started panic bells ringing in Hollywood executive offices. With the result that post-production tampering reduced an apparently sombre film – about (among other matters) whether the psychiatrist has the right to deprive Jones of his sometimes dangerous 'highs' – to an essentially empty, over-hyped, feel-good movie. In its present state, the film veers unsteadily between overblown romance and a portrait of a disturbed and pained man as a wacky guy who's fun to be with. Small wonder that the director has disowned the release version. NF

Mr Klein

(Joseph Losey, 1976, Fr/It) Alain Delon, Jeanne Moreau, Suzanne Flon, Michel Lonsdale, Juliet Berto, Francine Bergé, Jean Bouise, Louis Seigner.
123 min.
The action of Losey's film takes place against the Nazi deportation of French Jews – a set of circumstances which the film doesn't so much explore as get lost in. Klein (Delon), a Parisian art dealer, is delivered a copy of a Jewish newspaper. Investigating this, he becomes aware of a mysterious Jewish alter-ego bearing the same name. Though they do not meet, Klein finds the other impinging increasingly on his life, even living in his flat when he's not there. The confusion of identities forces Klein to defend himself against a charge of being Jewish. Predictably, the film ends with his deportation; quite unaccountably, Losey makes this a deliberate choice, as Klein purposely avoids the lawyers bringing the evidence which can release him, a piece of fatalism which resolves nothing whatsoever. Sadly, Losey's determinedly enigmatic treatment turns a potentially very interesting theme into cheap mystification. AS

Mr Lord Says No

see Happy Family, The

Mr Love

(Roy Battersby, 1985, GB) Barry Jackson, Maurice Denham, Margaret Tyzack, Linda Marlowe, Christina Collier, Helen Cotterill, Julia Deakin.
91 min.
Set in crumbling Southport-on-Sea, where one Donald Lovelace (Jackson), a mild-mannered, fiftyish landscape gardener sows his wild oats among the town's lonely womenfolk in a last-ditch quest for romance and nooky. Both of which he reaps with astounding ease from a range of eccentric Lancastrian matrons, though poor Donald Juan ends up getting dumped on by all the ladies in his life from Queen Victoria downwards. An unashamedly old-fashioned little film with a dash of nostalgia and a touch of Ealing comic whimsy. SJo

Mr Majestyk

(Richard Fleischer, 1974, US) Charles Bronson, Al Lettieri, Linda Cristal, Lee Purcell, Paul Koslo, Taylor Lacher, Frank Maxwell, Alejandro Rey.
103 min.
Charles Bronson, his eyes just about open, strides through this film as a paternalistic melon-grower in Colorado, anti-racist, tolerant of unions (well, you can tell, he gets the melon-picking union girl in the end; how does Cristal keep her hair so black and shiny after all that sweaty work?), who falls foul of local crooks and labour racketeers. The melon-grower beats ruthless psychopath, casting aspersions at the police force en route. Fleischer handles a heavy script and most of the acting like no one should handle a melon; but he really soars into competence at moments of tension, car chases, and general cinematic escapism. MV

Mr Mom
(aka Mr Mum)

(Stan Dragoti, 1983, US) Michael Keaton, Teri Garr, Martin Mull, Ann Jillian, Christopher Lloyd.
91 min.
In these post-feminist times, you might have thought that the spectacle of men doing housework was a little played out as a subject for comedy. But this – in which unemployment forces Keaton to swop roles with his wife Garr – plays the usual trick of taking a '30s formula and pushing it far further than it has gone before. Keaton visibly disintegrates into an alcoholic, pill-popping soap opera addict, until he screams the final admission to his wife: 'My brain is like oatmeal. I never knew it was like this'. Written by ex-Lampoon regular John Hughes, the film is funniest when it is detailing the psychological horrors of housework, notably the awful pull of the soap opera which begins to merge with Keaton's domestic reality. The various props, like the voracious vacuum cleaner, are less successful, but Hughes still manages to play on the anxieties of middle America with fairly devilish skill. DP

Mr Moto's Gamble

(James Tinling, 1938, US) Peter Lorre, Lynn Bari, Keye Luke, Dick Baldwin, Harold Huber, Douglas Fowley.
71 min. b/w.
Starting with Think Fast, Mr Moto in 1937, Lorre (sporting steel-rimmed glasses and buck teeth) starred eight times in an engaging characterisation as John P Marquand's inscrutable Japanese sleuth – expert in disguise, master of ju-jitsu – in a series discontinued in 1939 because of deteriorating relations between America and Japan. Fast, formulary and quite fun, the films are much of a muchness, and not unlike poor relations to the Charlie Chan series. Mr Moto's Gamble (third in the series) in fact started life as a Chan film, taken over (along with Keye Luke) on Warner Oland's death. Despite an equally engaging characterisation by Henry Silva, The Return of Mr Moto, an attempt to revive the series in 1965, remained a one-off. TM

Mr Mum

see Mr Mom

Mr Music

(Richard Haydn, 1950, US) Bing Crosby, Nancy Olson, Charles Coburn, Ruth Hussey, Marge and Gower Champion, Groucho Marx, Peggy Lee, Claude Curdle (i.e. Richard Haydn).
113 min. b/w.
Okay-ish Burke/Van Heusen musical has knitwear-clad Bing as a talented tunesmith who'd rather have another round of golf than write a hit Broadway show, but who, when the money runs low, has to turn to impresario Coburn for help. There are two conditions to the latter's offer of a substantial loan: that he come up with some new numbers, and that he take on super-secretary Olson. Crooning and romancing inevitably follow, but it's all a bit too relaxed to go down as one of the greats.

Mr Nanny

(Michael Gottlieb, 1992, US) Hulk Hogan, Austin Pendleton, Sherman Hemsley, David Johansen, Robert Gorman, Madeline Zima.
84 min.
Cross Home Alone with Kindergarten Cop and you get 'Home Cop', which is basically what we have here. An American wrestling champ with two or three films under his belt, Hogan has an unusual combination of assets: brawn and an authentic American accent. He doesn't take himself too seriously either, which could prove his downfall – that and excruciating movies like this. He plays a genial ex-wrestler who accepts a job as a bodyguard, only to find that the bodies in question – Alex and Kate (Gorman and Zima), sorely neglected by his scientist father (Pendleton) since their mother's death – are both pre-pubescent and exceptionally vindictive. As the title implies, gender identity is at the heart of the movie. Kate teaches Hulk to be dainty by dressing him in a tutu; but come the crunch, the H-man – 'one tough mother' – helps father and son to bond by vanquishing their enemies. TCh

Mr North

(Danny Huston, 1988, US) Anthony Edwards, Robert Mitchum, Lauren Bacall, Harry Dean Stanton, Anjelica Huston, Mary Stuart Masterson, Virginia Madsen, Tammy Grimes, David Warner.
93 min.
Danny Huston's first feature owes more to Frank Capra than to his dad John. Adapted from the Thornton Wilder novel Theophilus North, it's a gently moral fable about a young man (Edwards) who cycles into 1920s Newport (sun-dappled Gatsby territory) and roots out evil by virtue of his good nature, good sense and mysterious knack of dispensing static electricity at will. Kids call it magic, while adults call it faith healing and plague him with requests. Prime beneficiaries of Mr North's special powers are the town's wealthy elder (Mitchum), a shy debutante (Masterson), and a lively housemaid (Madsen). Also drifting in and out of the whimsical plot are Bacall's local madam, Stanton's fraudulent Cockney valet, and Anjelica Huston as Mitchum's loving daughter and North's heart's desire. Apart from a minor hiccup where sceptics initiate a witch hunt against our hero, there's never a moment's doubt that Good Will Out. Although delicately acted and lovingly shot, it adds up to little more than candy floss. EP

Mr Peabody and the Mermaid

(Irving Pichel, 1948, US) William Powell, Ann Blyth, Irene Harvey, Andrea King, Cliton Sundberg.
89 min. b/w.
Amorous amphibian antics as a staid Boston banker goes fishin' and catches comely mermaid Blyth. Inoffensive timepasser written by Nunnally Johnson. TJ

Mister Quilp

(Michael Tuchner, 1974, GB) Anthony Newley, David Hemmings, David Warner, Michael Hordern, Paul Rogers, Jill Bennett, Sarah-Jane Varley.
119 min.
'I may be simple-hearted but I think the world is grand' trills winsome Little Nell in the opening minutes of this musical version of The Old Curiosity Shop sponsored by Reader's Digest. Well, the film is terrible: two solid hours of excruciating overacting from Newley as the vile and dwarfish Quilp, phony sets and costumes which look as though they've only just been removed from the wrapping-paper, botched songs (by Newley) and choreography, lackadaisical direction, and lots of good character actors going to waste. GB

Mr Reliable (a True Story)

(Nadia Tass, 1996, Aust) Colin Friels, Jacqueline McKenzie, Paul Sonkkila, Frank Gallacher, Lisa Hensley, Aaron Blabey, Geoff Morrell, Neil Fitzpatrick.
113 min.
Recently released from prison, Wally Mellish (Friels) drives back into Sydney in the long hot summer of 1968. Having fallen for spunky single parent Beryl (McKenzie), Wally wins praise for his home-building skills in sleepy Glenfield, until he lets off a warning shotgun blast at a cop, who is hounding him unnecessarily, and finds himself at the centre of a lengthy siege – an open-air concert of emergency police squads, sniper units, back-up reserves with canteen facilities, journalists, camps of spectators, barbecue stalls – which becomes nationwide news. Ordinary and none too bright Wally may be, but his tenacity, self-awareness and inventive, if unconventional, manner make him suitable material for the media to fashion into a people's hero. An access of nostalgic affection for the Australian Summer of Love results in a slight archness; and despite Friels' sympathetic performance and some engaging cameos (notably Sonkkila's sublimely second-rate Police Commissioner), a fluid pace and deft comic touches, the film ends up somewhat overloaded with whimsy and benevolence. WH

Mister Roberts

(Mervyn LeRoy/John Ford, 1955, US) Henry Fonda, James Cagney, William Powell, Jack Lemmon, Betsy Palmer, Ward Bond, Nick Adams, Harry Carey Jr.
123 min.
Trouble-bound adaptation of Thomas Heggen's

Broadway hit about a WWII supply ship, its martinet captain, and the junior officer who finally makes the symbolic gesture required to liberate the pent-up tensions in the crew. Ford became diplomatically ill, LeRoy took over, and an uncredited Joshua Logan (responsible for the original stage show) directed bits as well. The fact that the picture is seamlessly anonymous testifies to the power of star performances rather than to any directorial engagement. The acting is the only reason to watch it: Fonda as the frustrated lieutenant who craves a go at the Japs; Cagney as the tyrannical captain; Powell as the cynical medico; and Lemmon as Ensign Pulver, the joker in the pack. ATu

Mr Saturday Night
(Billy Crystal, 1992, US) Billy Crystal, David Paymer, Julie Warner, Helen Hunt, Mary Mara, Jerry Orbach, Ron Silver, Sage Allen.
119 min.
A dream project for star, co-writer and first-time director Crystal, in which his affection for the characters and familiarity with the material sometimes prevent him from achieving sufficient distance. Stand-up comic Buddy Young Jr (Crystal), managed by his brother Stan (Paymer), was a household name in the '50s and '60s. Now he's just another has-been trying for a comeback, struggling to retain his dignity in the face of humiliating auditions and demeaning bit-parts in TV commercials. Flashbacks to Buddy's childhood and heyday strike the right balance between nostalgia and realism. Scenes of Jewish family life, jokes about food, and lovingly recreated borscht-belt shows evoke the atmosphere of the time; while the egocentric comic's difficult relationships with the self-sacrificing Stan and estranged daughter Susan (Mara) reveal a darker side to showbiz and familial ties. By contrast, the modern scenes are cloyingly sentimental. Even so, there are probably enough sharp one-liners, hilarious routines and clever mimicry to see most people through the soggier patches. NF

Mister Skeeter
(Colin Finbow, 1985, GB) Peter Bayliss, Louise Rawlings, Orlando Wells, Rodney Dodds, Richard Bartlett, Rose Hill.
78 min.
Jamie and Lisa, on the run from a children's home, meet eccentric vaudevillian Mr Skeeter (Bayliss) in a seaside shelter; they exchange confidences, watch the sun rise, and share stolen food. As the police close in on the two runaways, the film focuses on the brief encounter of this oddly innocent yet worldly-wise trio, and is closely observed, funny, and excellently photographed, with memorable performances and dialogue. Made by the Children's Film Unit. SMcA

Mr Skeffington
(Vincent Sherman, 1944, US) Bette Davis, Claude Rains, Walter Abel, Richard Waring, George Coulouris, Jerome Cowan, Charles Drake.
146 min. b/w.
Take a large stock of hankies with you: this monumental soaper drips interminably on. It's a simple tale of a vain society gal (Davis, who else?) who secures a financially wonderful but loveless marriage to a Jewish stockbroker (Rains). After a stay in a concentration camp, he goes blind; then she catches diphtheria, and realises that he loves her after all, and... oh well, for the rest you can use your imagination, which is more than writers Julius and Philip Epstein (ex-*Casablanca*) did. Vincent Sherman cradles this arrant tosh with the tenderest of loving camera movements, and almost smothers it to death in the process. GB

Mr Smith Goes to Washington
(Frank Capra, 1939, US) James Stewart, Jean Arthur, Claude Rains, Edward Arnold, Guy Kibbee, Thomas Mitchell, Eugene Pallette, Beulah Bondi, Harry Carey.
129 min. b/w.
Stewart's young Wisconsin senator exposing corruption and upholding true American values in a Senate House riddled with graft is quintessential Capra – popular wish-fulfilment served up with such fast-talking comic panache that you don't have time to question its cornball idealism. Scriptwriter Sidney Buchman's crackling dialogue is also lent sharp-tongued conviction by

Rains, as the slimy senior senator, Jean Arthur as the hard-boiled dame finally won over by Stewart's honesty, and Harry Carey as the Vice President. NF

Mr Vampire
(Lau Kun Wai, 1986, HK) Ricky Hui, Moon Lee, Chin Suit Ho.
92 min.
A ditsy rewrite on vampire mythology as we know it. When a Chinese family is menaced by blood-craving zombies, they discover that the thing the creatures really hate is sticky rice, and that by holding your breath it's possible to stop the fiends in their tracks. How all this new-found knowledge filters into the narrative is wild, funny, and not a little strange.

Mr Wonderful
(Anthony Minghella, 1992, US) Matt Dillon, Annabella Sciorra, Mary-Louise Parker, William Hurt, Vincent D'Onofrio.
97 min.
Writer/director Minghella's second feature brings ambivalence and a touch of realpolitik to the stuff of candyfloss romance as it charts the relationship between New York electrical worker Gus (Dillon) and his former wife Lee (Sciorra). Having achieved her long-suppressed wish to go to college, she's now the recipient of maintenance payments from her financially strapped ex-husband. If he could find someone to marry her pronto, it would solve all his money problems and let him pursue his new flame Rita (Parker) – but where to find such a Mr Wonderful? The answer, of course, is staring him in the mirror each morning, but the awkward corners of these emotional lives refuse to be subjugated within conventional movie plotting. Against an assured Italian-American background, Dillon adeptly conveys the inarticulate longings and confusion of a repairman who can't fix his own life, and the film's generosity of spirit is touching in itself. TJ

Mistress
(Barry Primus, 1991, US) Robert Wuhl, Martin Landau, Jace Alexander, Robert De Niro, Danny Aiello, Eli Wallach, Christopher Walken, Laurie Metcalf, Sheryl Lee Ralph, Jean Smart, Tuesday Knight, Ernest Borgnine, Stefan Gierasch.
109 min.
Despite sturdy acting from a starry cast, actor Barry Primus' directorial debut is a lacklustre affair, unsure of whether it's a satire or a morality play as it tells of down-at-heel producer (Landau) and has-been director (Wuhl) fighting to get the latter's movie script off the ground, intact and untainted by the financiers' desires to see their various mistresses become stars. The gags are too obvious; the conflict between art and money is hackneyed; and the plot goes badly off the rails in the later reels. De Niro, who produced, is surprisingly weak; Landau alone is excellent. GA

Mrs Brown
(John Madden, 1997, GB/US/Ire) Judi Dench, Billy Connolly, Antony Sher, Geoffrey Palmer, Richard Pasco, David Westhead, Gerard Butler.
104 min.
Madden's film owes its existence to the success of *The Madness of King George*, a period vehicle for a superb but cinematically under-appreciated actor. For Farmer George, substitute Widow Victoria, still immersed in grief four years after the death of Albert. For Nigel Hawthorne, substitute Judi Dench. Like Nicholas Hytner's film, *Mrs Brown* documents a period during which the monarchy was in crisis due to the government's unpopularity and the sovereign's emotional instability. For madness, substitute grief: Victoria was so inconsolable that she became known as the Widow of Windsor. Enter John Brown, a no-nonsense Highlander and devoted servant to Her Majesty; only he has the guts to wean her out of her sadness, to talk to her like a woman. Dench is magnificent as Victoria, a toy-sized, black-suited, dough girl of despair, a woman slowly recovering her wits and her expectations. But Connolly's Brown is hardly less fine, a cast-iron portrait of a man teetering on the edge of ridicule and disgrace but wishing to go the whole nine yards for the cause he serves. SGr

Mrs Dalloway
(Marleen Gorris, 1997, US/GB/Neth) Vanessa Redgrave, Natascha McElhone, Michael Kitchen, Alan Cox, Sarah Badel, Lena Headey, John Standing, Rupert Graves, Margaret Tyzack.
97 min.
Clarissa Dalloway (Redgrave), the beautiful wife of an eminent MP, loves to give parties. A day in her life, however, is a serious affair, interwoven with the experiences of a WWI veteran, Septimus (Graves), and a flood of painfully pleasant memories. Eileen Atkins' adaptation of Virginia Woolf's novel concentrates exclusively on Mrs Dalloway's ruminations. Thus, although we sympathise with Septimus, the originality of his experience is lost; and cousin Ellie, the 'invisible' spinster, brought so spikily to life in the novel – in the film remains a voiceless nobody. Unfortunately Redgrave chews up the scenery, and when she's meant to be ecstatic appears merely unhinged. The characters of Sally (Clarissa's best friend), and Peter (her first and most ardent suitor), make more sense and are well served by both young (Headey/Cox) and old (Badel/Kitchen) sets of actors. Peter's wimpish arrogance is wonderfully caught, as is Sally's casual, fox-like intelligence. Fascinated by Clarissa and also resentful, these two alone make us understand her appeal. Sue Gibson's visuals are excellent, and the depiction of London is perfect. CO'Su

Mrs Doubtfire
(Chris Columbus, 1993, US) Robin Williams, Sally Field, Pierce Brosnan, Harvey Fierstein, Polly Holliday.
125 min.
It's built like a Volvo, wears floral print dresses and affects a faint Scots burr: Robin Williams as Mrs Doubtfire – or, more accurately, divorced father-of-three Daniel as Mrs Doubtfire – is the sort of prosthetic-aesthetic nightmare you'd expect to encounter wielding a kitchen knife in a slasher movie. Not that this stops Daniel's ex-wife Sally Field from placing their winsome ones in his/her charge. Indeed, Mrs D soon begins to look like the perfect nanny, a hairy Poppins even the kids take a shine to. Williams has always been uncommonly in touch with his 'feminine', caring, nurturing side, so Daniel's all dressed up with no place to go. Instead, he/she has to learn some tried and trite lessons about parental responsibility and emotional maturity. Sit-com stuff, then, with laboured farcical interludes, and a mushy post-feminist sensibility. Funny notwithstanding. TCh

Mrs Miniver
(William Wyler, 1942, US) Greer Garson, Walter Pidgeon, Teresa Wright, Dame May Whitty, Reginald Owen, Henry Travers, Henry Ney, Henry Wilcoxon, Helmut Dantine.
134 min. b/w.
Hollywood's multi-Oscared tribute to the home front in wartime Britain. See Mrs Miniver disarm a German parachutist and hide his gun behind the teacups. See gallant hubby stiffen the old upper lip before sailing off to help with the Dunkirk evacuation. An average English couple, practising their little economies but housed in gracious splendour, they live in an England which may be at war but where the local flower show soldiers on. Classic soap opera in which good old British understatement has a field day, everybody is frightfully nice, and sentimentality is wrapped up in yards of tasteful gloss. TM

Mistress Pamela
(Jim O'Connolly, 1973, GB) Julian Barnes, Ann Michelle, Dudley Foster, Anna Quayle, Anthony Sharp, Rosemarie Dunham, Derek Fowlds, Jessie Evans, Fred Emney.
91 min.
Richardson's 18th century classic *Pamela* clearly dredged up for its bawdy possibilities. The self-satisfied and calculated middle class morality of his treatise on female virtue is transformed with much heavy-handed winking and nudging into an obsolete sitcom about the efforts of a beautiful servant (Michelle) to preserve her maidenhead from the insistent Lord Devenish (Barnes). A few wheezy jokes and some ripped clothing later, true love and a happy ending prevail. The supporting cast, notably Dudley Foster and Fred Emney, give some relief, but the two leading play-

ers offer little beyond their prettiness. About all
the film has in common with the original is a
notable lack of humour. CPe

Mrs Parker and
the Vicious Circle
(Alan Rudolph, 1994, US) Jennifer Jason Leigh,
Campbell Scott, Matthew Broderick, Andrew
McCarthy, Tim McGowan, Nick Cassavetes,
Matt Malloy, Sam Robards, Wallace Shawn,
Keith Carradine.
124 min. b/w & col.
Alan Rudolph's *The Moderns* celebrated the
American away team of the '20s – Hemingway
and pals. This companion biopic of the mistress
of the bon mot, Manhattanite Dorothy Parker,
paints a similar mass portrait of the wits, wags
and writers of the home team. All the Rudolph
trademarks are here: the improvisatory feel, the
overlapping dialogue, the ironic but celebratory tone, the vital performances from leads
(Jennifer Jason Leigh as Parker and Broderick
as Charles MacArthur, in particular) and
cameos. Then there's the delight in design
(François Séguin's low-lit speakeasies and hotel
rooms), and the roving camera style (Jan
Kiesser); the interest in art and artifice, genius
and suffering. Rudolph and JJL manage to make
this 'brilliant bitch' entirely fascinating, if not
completely sympathetic. In perhaps the one
scene where she looks radiantly happy, Parker
says to MacArthur, 'Oh, Charlie, I'm going to
wear my heart on my sleeve like a red wet
stain.' She could be speaking for Rudolph.
Absolutely superb. WH

Mrs Pollifax – Spy
(Leslie Martinson, 1970, US) Rosalind Russell,
Darren McGavin, Nehemiah Persoff, Harold
Gould, Albert Paulsen, Dana Elcar.
110 min.
Witless, worthless spy comedy about a middle-
aged matron's enlistment in the CIA. Martinson,
a long-time TV series toiler who'd provided the
drive-in market in the '50s with such treats as Hot
Rod Girl and Hot Rod Rumble, had recently had
his head turned by the unaccustomed success of
the big-screen Batman and similar spy-spoof
material in the Raquel Welch-starring Fathom.
Ros Russell, pseudonymously scripting as well
as starring, was old enough to have known better, but did the honourable thing and retired
immediately after. PT

Mrs Soffel
(Gillian Armstrong, 1984, US) Diane Keaton,
Mel Gibson, Matthew Modine, Edward
Herrmann, Trini Alvarado, Jennie Dundas.
111 min.
Mrs Soffel (Keaton), a good woman but victim of
a cool marriage to the warden of Allegheny
County jail in turn-of-the-century Pittsburgh,
spends her days dispensing Christian comfort to
the inmates: during the first hour there is more
praying than regular dialogue. The answer to the
lady's prayers turns up in Mel Gibson, a condemned murderer; they go on the run together,
but without much success. It's a handsomely
mounted period piece, but can't shake off a certain air of good manners; like the lady herself, stifled by law, custom and breeding, and unable to
let rip on a bid for freedom. CPea

Mrs Winterbourne
(Richard Benjamin, 1996, US) Ricki Lake,
Shirley MacLaine, Brendan Fraser, Loren
Dean, Miguel Sandoval, Paula Prentiss.
106 min.
This adaptation of Cornell Woolrich's novel *I
Married a Dead Man* (previously filmed as *No
Man of Her Own*) begins with a seedy room, a
corpse on the bed and an evangelist on the
unwatched TV assuring of an astonishing future.
The arrival of the cops trigger the flashbacks...so
far, so *noir*. But then something truly nightmarish happens. The movie transforms somewhat
unsuccessfully into a comedy about a loveable
kook to whom awful things keep happening. It's
as though ten minutes into *Phantom Lady*, June
Allyson had entered the picture and staged a
takeover. In principle, there's certainly no reason
why a retro-*rosé*-*noir*, postmodern genre
stew shouldn't amuse, intrigue or innovate, but
this crashes early on when it becomes clear that
Lake is a rather chilly and distinctly unpersuasive presence. BBa

Mitchell
(Andrew V McLaglen, 1975, US) Joe Don
Baker, Martin Balsam, John Saxon, Linda
Evans, Merlin Olsen, Morgan Paull.
97 min.
Baker's the big lumpy cop who won't take no and
another assignment for an answer when he's told
to lay off the gun-happy lawyer (Saxon) he suspects of cold-blooded murder, and to concentrate
on the businessman with the coke connection
(Balsam). He realises that in such a sparsely-pop-
ulated cheapie they just have to be in collusion,
as he punches and shoots his way to the final
credits accompanied by vocal encouragement
from one of those country singers with terminal
cancer. Balsam and Saxon contribute no more
than their required quota of urbane sneers before
being bulldozed into oblivion by the golem hero
of this irredeemably routine potboiler. GD

Mi Vida Loca
see My Crazy Life

Mixed Blood
see Cocaine

Mixed Company
(Melville Shavelson, 1974, US) Barbara Harris,
Joseph Bologna, Lisa Gerritsen, Tom Bosley,
Dorothy Shay, Ruth McDevitt.
109 min.
A typically trite and sickly concoction by
Shavelson, whose funnybone seemed much
firmer when he was scripting Paramount comedies in the '40s. You can easily gauge its quality
by the plot: when a basketball coach is rendered
sterile through mumps, his wife urges the adoption of three cute but problematical kids – a semi-
delinquent black, a Vietnamese orphan, and a
Hopi Indian. All prejudices are ultimately overcome, and the result is a runaway victory for the
upper class American liberal. The performers are
far superior to their material, particularly
Barbara Harris; but on the whole this movie gives
a whole new meaning to the word 'yuck'. GB

Mixed Nuts
(Nora Ephron, 1994, US) Steve Martin, Rita
Wilson, Madeline Kahn, Juliette Lewis,
Anthony LaPaglia, Adam Sandler, Rob Reiner.
97 min.
Oh, dear. Anyone who didn't appreciate the polished sophistication of *Sleepless in Seattle* should
be made to watch Ephron's third outing as writer
and director...until they submit. This remake of
a French farce, *Le Père Noël*, est une Ordure, is a
disaster. Ephron's timing and sensitivity have
deserted her, leaving behind only the sentimentality. It's Christmas Eve at Martin's suicide hot-
line service – Lifesavers – but it's the staff
(Wilson, Kahn) who seem most desperately in
need of help. Ephron pitches for zany, which
means we have to endure a pregnant Lewis at her
most hysterical, LaPaglia as a gun-toting Santa,
Sandler as a ukulele-playing tee-shirt writer
('Save the Dolphins – that's one of mine'), a
lovelorn transvestite and a serial killer, while the
leads alternately scream and faint, as well they
might. TCh

Mob, The
(aka Remember That Face)
(Robert Parrish, 1951, US) Broderick Crawford,
Betty Buehler, Richard Kiley, Otto Hulett,
Matt Crowley, Neville Brand, Ernest Borgnine,
Charles Bronson.
87 min. b/w.
Familiar gang-busting stuff set in On the
Waterfront territory, with Crawford as a cop who,
inadvertently goofing on duty, is officially reported as suspended and sent undercover to make
good the damage by finding out who is masterminding the brutal extortion racket among longshoremen. William Bowers' script manages one
or two genuine surprises – with Crawford at one
point being hired to eliminate himself – but its
main contribution is a nice line in sharp, waywardly witty dialogue. Given fast, flexible direction by Parrish, excellent camerawork (Joseph
Walker) and a full house of vivid performances,
the result is an unusually tense and enjoyable
genre piece. Pity about the last reel, when everything collapses (though not too destructively) into
routine histrionics. TM

Mo' Better Blues
(Spike Lee, 1990, US) Denzel Washington,
Spike Lee, Wesley Snipes, Giancarlo Esposito,
Robin Harris, Joie Lee, Bill Nunn, John
Turturro, Dick Anthony Williams, Cynda
Williams, Nicholas Turturro.
129 min.
It's clear from the opening that the way Lee sees
jazz is as Art, sanitised and consequently a mite
gutless. Indeed, as obsessive trumpeter Bleek
(Washington) advances on his inevitable comeuppance – you know he's gotta get it – Lee's
earnest parable proceeds to hit whole clusters
of bad notes. First, the music is wrong: ghosted by Branford Marsalis, Terence Blanchard et
al, Bleek's gigs range through an anachronistic
array of styles, while Lee's underlining of mood
with a handful of classics (Coltrane, Ornette,
Miles) comes over as a showy hip parade of his
own cultural credibility. But more damagingly,
plot and characterisation are trite, perhaps even
reactionary. If Bleek's errant attitude to his two
lovers (Joie Lee, Cynda Williams) is symptomatic of an arrogant devotion to his art, the
women rarely rise above schematic stereotypes
(the Jewish club-owners fare even worse).
Moreover, Lee's coda advocates submissive
motherhood for a neglected lover and patriarchal domesticity for all concerned. Ideology
apart (no drugs here), a messy, meandering
script ensures that, despite stylish camerawork
and sturdy acting, this lengthy indulgence succeeds neither as jazz movie nor as cautionary
tale. GA

Mobster, The
see I, Mobster

Mobsters (aka Mobsters –
The Evil Empire)
(Michael Karbelnikoff, 1991, US) Christian
Slater, Patrick Dempsey, Richard Grieco,
Costas Mandylor, F Murray Abraham, Lara
Flynn Boyle, Michael Gambon, Christopher
Penn, Anthony Quinn.
121 min.
This youth movie sees Slater leading a group of
apprentice gangsters to the top of the bloody
heap: *Young Guns* meets *The Untouchables* with
a vengeance. But it has all the morals of the aver-
age clam: Slater plays the young Charlie 'Lucky'
Luciano who, along with charming pals like
Grieco's Bugsy Siegel and Dempsey's bookish
Meyer Lansky, was a far more loathsome mobster than the Moustache Petes from the Old
Country who came before him and his pals. In
order to show these charmers in an attractive
light as they scheme and plot and fight,
Karbelnikoff makes sure that their wrinkly rivals,
Don Masseria (Quinn) and Don Faranzano
(Gambon) are depicted as, respectively, sadistic
and pig-like, racist and rapacious. This is ageism
with knobs on. A noisy, silly, rather immature
film. SGr

Moby Dick
(John Huston, 1956, GB) Gregory Peck,
Richard Basehart, Leo Genn, Harry Andrews,
Orson Welles, Friedrich Ledebur, Edric
Connor, Bernard Miles.
116 min.
Easy to pick holes in Huston's brave stab at
Melville's masterpiece, which opens with
breathtaking boldness as a solitary wanderer
appears over the brow of a hill, comes to camera to proclaim his 'Call me...Ishmael', then
leaves it to follow in the wake of his odyssey.
Granted the great white whale is significantly
less impressive when lifting bodily out of the
sea to crush the Pequod than when first
glimpsed one moonlit night, a dim white mass
of menace lurking in a black sea. Granted, too,
a lightweight Ahab (Peck) and a pitifully weak
Starbuck (Genn). But there are marvellous
things here: Ishmael's alarming initiation into
the whaling community at the tavern; Father
Mapple's sermon (superbly delivered by
Welles); Queequeg's casting of the bones and
his preparation for death; nearly all the whaling scenes. Lent a stout overall unity by Ray
Bradbury's intelligent adaptation, by colour
grading which gives the images the tonal quality of old whaling prints, and by the discreet
use of a commentary drawn from Melville's
text which imposes the resonance of legend, it
is often staggeringly good. TM

Model

(Frederick Wiseman, 1980, US)
125 min. b/w.
Models pose; Wiseman shoots. Photographers
pose; Wiseman shoots. Wiseman shoots photographers shooting models. How objective can you
get? Model intervenes in an image-making
process whose variable components are objecti-
fication, exhibitionism and voyeurism: instead of
analysis it offers us mere duplication. Not so
much New York anthropology as a chic lifestyle
commercial. Wiseman poses...PT

Model Shop

(Jacques Demy, 1968, US) Anouk Aimée, Gary
Lockwood, Alexandra Hay, Carole Cole,
Severn Darden, Tom Fielding, Neil Elliot.
95 min.
Demy's only – and underrated – American film
may lack the fairytale charm of his finest French
work, but the bitter-sweet delicacy of tone and
acute feeling for place are at once familiar.
Aimée's Lola, abandoned by her lover Michel, has
now turned up in LA where, older and sadder, she
works in a seedy photographer's shop, and brings
brief respite to a disenchanted young drifter
(Lockwood) with whom she has a one night
stand. Unlike Antonioni with Zabriskie Point,
Demy never even tries to deal with the malaise
afflicting American youth in the '60s, but gives
us yet another (relatively plotless) tale of transient happiness and love lost. It's also one of the
great movies about LA, shown for once as a ramshackle, rootless sprawl, where movement on the
freeways (accompanied by the sounds of West
Coast band Spirit) is seemingly endless. GA

Modern Love

(Robby Benson, 1990, US) Robby Benson,
Karla DeVito, Burt Reynolds, Rue
McClanahan, Burt Reynolds, Frankie Valli,
Louise Lasser.
109 min.
Producer/director/star Benson added this would-
be comic tale of modern married life to his undistinguished screen canon while teaching a
university film-making class in Southern
Carolina. Karla DeVito, the shrink he visits to sort
himself out then ends up marrying, is his real-life
wife, and their daughter, too, ends up somewhere
down the cast list. A vanity production with nothing to recommend it. TJ

Modern Romance

(Albert Brooks, 1981, US) Albert Brooks,
Kathryn Harrold, Bruno Kirby, Jane Hallaran,
James L Brooks, George Kennedy,
Bob Einstein.
93 min.
Writer/director Brooks casts himself as a neurotic, workaholic film editor who, unable to cope
with his obsessive love for the beautiful Harrold,
forces himself to give her up. He then adopts an
equally compulsive regime of trying to forget her:
taking up jogging, looking up old flames, and
immersing himself in the editing of a low-budget
sci-fi movie – made by his namesake James L
Brooks (director of Broadcast News). None of this
works, of course, but having wooed Harrold once
more, he again falls prey to this perverse, self-
destructive syndrome. Extremely funny, ultra-
hip and alarmingly insightful. NF

Moderns, The

(Alan Rudolph, 1988, US) Keith Carradine,
Linda Fiorentino, Genevieve Bujold, Geraldine
Chaplin, Wallace Shawn, John Lone, Kevin J
O'Connor, Elsa Raven.
126 min.
Rudolph's full-blown and unashamedly romantic evocation of the artistic life of '20s Paris - a
playful, ironic, and affirmative meditation on
life, love, and art - shows him at his most delightfully accessible. He relocates his resident ensemble players within the lusciously recreated cafés,
galleries and salons of Montmartre and the
Latin Quarter - truly 'a Paris of the mind' - where
nothing can be taken at face value. Poor painter-
cum-Chicago Tribune-caricaturist Nick Hart
(Carradine, dazzlingly good) clashes with fellow
American-in-Paris and rich art collector Stone
(Lone, monolithic) over Rachel (Fiorentino, beautiful). His integrity is called into question when,
thinking that money will enable him to reunite
with Rachel, he is persuaded by predatory and
fickle Nathalie de Ville (Chaplin), a wealthy col-

lector of lovers, to forge a series of paintings.
Hemingway is there, as are Gertrude Stein,
Picasso et al. It's Rudolph's most entertaining
movie, elating, erotic, and full of life, colour,
music, games, romance, dreams, and humour.
Carradine could be Gary Cooper, and Rudolph
turns fakery into an authenticated masterwork.
WH

Modern Times

(Charles Chaplin, 1936, US) Charles Chaplin,
Paulette Goddard, Henry Bergman, Chester
Conklin, Tiny Sanford, Allen Garcia,
Hank Mann.
85 min. b/w.
The last appearance of the Chaplin tramp, before
Hitler, Monsieur Verdoux and other personae
took over. Antics and situations from the earliest
shorts are revived in a narrative framework
designed to portray 'humanity crusading in the
pursuit of happiness', as the opening title puts it;
the tramp faces the perils of factory machinery,
poverty, starvation and Depression unrest – and
just about survives. Chaplin's political and philosophical naivety now seems as remarkable as his
gift for pantomime. GB

Modesty Blaise

(Joseph Losey, 1966, GB) Monica Vitti, Dirk
Bogarde, Terence Stamp, Harry Andrews,
Michael Craig, Scilla Gabel, Clive Revill,
Rossella Falk.
119 min.
Coolly received by comparison with the more
immediately accessible James Bond films which
were then at the height of their popularity,
Modesty Blaise is, like Rolls-Royces, built to last.
Modelled on the cartoon strip, it plays the game
up to the hilt with its op-art sets, its extravagant
conceits, its outlandish violence, and its arch-
fiend Gabriel (Bogarde having a ball in silvery
wig and sinister glasses) daintily dreaming up
ever more monstrous fancies. But under the non-
stop stream of jokes lies a bitter edge of malice,
directed not only against the genre itself but
against a society which trusts its politicians and
its generals. TM

Mogambo

(John Ford, 1953, US) Clark Gable, Ava
Gardner, Grace Kelly, Donald Sinden, Eric
Pohlmann, Philip Stainton, Laurence Naismith.
116 min.
Gable's performance in Red Dust alongside Jean
Harlow had been one of his earliest hits; 21 years
later he was still big enough at the box-office to
star in this remake, re-scripted by original
screenwriter John Lee Mahin, and re-sited from
a studio-set Saigon to African locations. The
insolent sex talk of the original is here toned
down, and the relaxed rumbustiousness of the
safari love triangle is wholly in keeping with
Ford's holidaying inclinations at the time. Half-
hearted, half-baked, and at least half-watchable.
PT

Mogliamante

see Wifemistress

Mohammad,
Messenger of God

see Al-Risalah

Mohawk

(Kurt Neumann, 1956, US) Scott Brady, Rita
Gam, Neville Brand, Lori Nelson, Allison
Hayes, John Hoyt, Vera Vague, Mae Clarke,
Ted de Corsia.
79 min.
One of only a handful of films that deal with New
England's Mohawk Indians, this duff B Western
re-uses battle and background footage from John
Ford's Drums Along the Mohawk, and might
have done well to borrow more, because the rest
is quite ludicrous. Brady plays an artist whose
charm captivates women as diverse as his fiancée
Lori Nelson, barmaid Allison Hayes (the original
50-foot woman) and Native American Rita Gam.
In between dalliances, he is instrumental in avert-
ing a wicked landowner's plot to provoke Indians
and settlers into wiping each other out. TCh

Moi Ivan, Toi Abraham

see Me Ivan, You Abraham

Moindre des Choses, La

see Every Little Thing

Moine, Le (The Monk)

(Ado Kyrou, 1972, Fr/It/WGer) Franco Nero,
Nathalie Delon, Nicol Williamson, Nadja
Tiller, Eliana De Santis, Elisabeth Wiener,
Denis Manuel.
92 min.
Buñuel had plans to film Matthew Gregory Lewis'
controversial masterpiece, but finally handed the
project over to his friend Kyrou. Buñuel is still
credited as co-screenwriter (with Jean-Claude
Carrière), and the production remains comparatively faithful to Lewis both in atmosphere and
intention. The ending is more cynical (though
much less horrific) in the film, while there are
many simplifications and one very perverse interpolation; but the character of Ambrosio (a pious
clerical superstar who is damned by a sudden all-
engulfing sexual passion) remains the centrepiece.
The problem with the film is that nobody can
shoot a Buñuel script quite like Buñuel, and elements that might have become gold in the hands
of the master tend to be flat. Still, there are few
enough adaptations of Gothic novels, and this one
is more intricate and intelligent than most. DP

Moi, Pierre Rivière

(René Allio, 1975, Fr) Claude Hébert,
Jacqueline Millière, Joseph Leportier, Antoine
Bourseiller, Jacques Debary.
130 min.
A naturalistic reconstruction of a 19th century
peasant crime in Normandy: the young Pierre
Rivière's 'inexplicable' murder of his mother, sister and brother. Rivière left behind a 50-page
prison testament, recently published by Michel
Foucault, and the film locates itself squarely within Foucault's questions about 'history' – about
what is explicable and what is not. It's less
impressive for Allio's quaintly French belief that
nothing has changed in Normandy in the last 150
years (and that 'truth' in all its ambiguity was
therefore waiting for the camera) than for the psychopathology of the case itself, and the interesting non-professional performances. TR

Mojo

(Jez Butterworth, 1997, GB) Ian Hart, Ewen
Bremner, Aidan Gillen, Martyn Gwynn-Jones,
Hans Matheson, Andy Serkis, Ricky
Tomlinson, Harold Pinter.
90 min.
Jez Butterworth's viciously funny play (the Royal
Court, 1995) had the critics throwing Tarantino
references like confetti. The movie, scripted by Jez
and his brother Tom, is reminiscent of Absolute
Beginners. It's set in 1958, in a Soho music club,
the owner of which is killed by a rival gangster
muscling in on a hot new singing sensation.
Designed in bold, bright strokes, this has the kind
of dizzy verve that mixes toffee apples with murder and revenge – a rock'n'roll freneticism that's
never less than diverting. But the pinball structure may be too clever (the group power dynamics are unclear), and, for all the gloss, the movie
still exists in the stunted half-world of theatrical
adaptation. Fab performances, exuberance and
style ensure that it works, but only in spurts. TCh

Mole, The

see Topo, El

Moll Flanders

(Pen Densham, 1996, US) Robin Wright,
Morgan Freeman, Stockard Channing, John
Lynch, Brenda Fricker, Geraldine James,
Aisling Corcoran.
122 min.
As Robin Wright's (hardly unglamorous) Moll
overcomes poverty, abuse, prostitution, drink,
rich people's spite and the loss of her loved ones,
her journal is recounted by Moll's fellow servant
and ally Hibble (Freeman) to her orphaned
daughter Flora (Corcoran). Many cut-out characters, and direction consisting largely of putting
pictures against the words: a very basic historical tour of 18th century England. NB

Molly Maguires, The

(Martin Ritt, 1969, US) Richard Harris, Sean
Connery, Samantha Eggar, Frank Finlay,
Anthony Zerbe, Bethel Leslie, Art Lund.
125 min.

Less simplistic than most Ritt movies, this is set in the Pennsylvania of 1876, where the miners, Catholic Irish and surly, are at the mercy of their predominantly Protestant employers after an ineffectual strike to improve conditions. The nub of the film comes in the odd, abrasive friendship which springs up between Connery, leader of a secret organisation committed to acts of terrorism until the bosses submit, and Harris as an informer equally disgruntled but out for his own interests. Essentially two facets of the same personality, the pair are cunningly used to explore areas of ambivalence in the extent to which the actions of each are justified. The trouble, as so often with Ritt films, is that the situation remains interesting rather than involving. But at least this detachment means that one has the leisure to savour the textures of Wong Howe's magnificent camerawork. TM

Moment by Moment

(Jane Wagner, 1978, US) Lily Tomlin, John Travolta, Andra Akers, Bert Kramer, Shelley R Bonus, Debra Feuer.
105 min.
Ostensibly a vehicle for John Travolta, the film documents a love story between an older woman and a young drifter. With totally unsympathetic characters set against a background of shrink-riddled, over-privileged Marin County society, and accompanied by some of the worst easy-listening muzak LA could dredge up. Yuk.

Moment d'Egarement, Un (In a Wild Moment/One Wild Moment/A Summer Affair)

(Claude Berri, 1977, Fr) Jean-Pierre Marielle, Victor Lanoux, Christine Dejoux, Agnès Soral, Martine Sarcey.
100 min.
Computerised comedy: find two unappetisingly overweight hams (Marielle and Lanoux), cast them as a pair of menopausal mates adrift in St Tropez, let one of them be seduced by the other's nubile daughter. Should the need arise, through miscalculation, for an atom of real narrative invention (as here, with the film's denouement), just leave it fashionably 'open-ended' by resorting to a freeze-frame. Its sole interest is as a choice specimen of the complacent obsession of French film-makers with near-incestuous, near-paedophiliac liaisons. Remade equally blandly by Stanley Donen as Blame It On Rio. GAd

Moment of Truth, The (Il Momento della Verità)

(Francesco Rosi, 1964, It/Sp) Miguel Mateo Miguelin, José Gomez Sevillano, Pedro Basauri Pedrucho, Linda Christian.
110 min.
The glare of the sun, the surge of flamenco, the roar of the crowd: Rosi's film about bullfighting is all this and more. Onto a 'Blood and Sand'-style story of an Andalusian boy abandoning his arid, poverty-stricken home for the supposed glamour of the urban corridas, is grafted an ambivalent, subtle analysis of the thorny byways bordering on the road to fame and fortune; exchanging hardship for the manipulative deals of entrepreneurial Dons and the contempt of bourgeois socialites, the hero's resolve to make good finally results in a blurred nightmare of disillusionment and death. Without glorifying the 'sport', the magnificent 'scope compositions nevertheless display the matador's mesmeric grace and daring, while admitting the frenzied brutality that delights the bloodthirsty, callous crowds. It's a colourful, cruel world of senseless exploitation (of animals and humans alike) and tyrannical traditions, rendered with vivid brilliance by this uncommonly unsentimental director. GA

Moments

(Peter Crane, 1973, GB) Keith Michell, Angharad Rees, Bill Fraser, Jeannette Sterke, Donald Hewlett.
92 min.
Figuratively, the story about the length of drop on the rope: a man in an Eastbourne hotel is seemingly rescued from suicide by a young girl. With the Grand Hotel setting, intermingling of past and present (real or imagined), shifting levels of 'reality', and the use of the out-of-season resort as a symbol for inner desolation, it is not hard to see the influence of Resnais. And such pretensions

are surprisingly welcome after the sub-11 plus level of most British movies. It's all the more pity that the film's central relationship cannot sustain credibility: the plot depends on too much verbal exposition; explanations are too predictable for an essay on uncertainty; and the characters move from clichéd stodgy middle-age and freewheeling youth to stereotyped fugitives from deadening routine. CPe

Mommie Dearest

(Frank Perry, 1981, US) Faye Dunaway, Diana Scarwid, Steve Forrest, Howard da Silva, Michael Edwards, Jocelyn Brando.
129 min.
Good intentions to redress the balance of Christina Crawford's vengeful mother-fucker of a bestseller bio are in evidence aplenty; but how else than as camp can you take Faye Dunaway's waxwork Joan Crawford screeching for an axe, or throwing a scenery-chewing fit over her daughter's use of wire coathangers in the wardrobe? Perry doesn't help, with his credit sequence tease withholding our first glimpse of the stellar visage, and his determination to pose 'Joan' in geometrical symmetry with the lines of her spotless deco domestic mausoleum. Really no dafter, perhaps, than some of Joanie's own Warner Bros melodramas; the trouble is, it thinks it's Art. PT

Mo' Money

(Peter Macdonald, 1992, US) Damon Wayans, Stacey Dash, Joe Santos, John Diehl, Harry J Lennix, Marlon Wayans, Mark Beltzman.
90 min.
This comedy-romance-thriller has the substance of a midnight snack. Writer and co-executive producer Wayans plays Johnny Stewart, a scam artist who works with his brother Seymour (Marlon Wayans), much to the despair of their dead father's ex-partner on the police force. Along strolls Amber (Dash), a glamorous careerist with a credit card company, and smitten Johnny lands a job in her firm's mailroom to pursue his courtship. His efforts to impress involve stealing credit cards with which to finance a fancy lifestyle; but once caught, he finds himself embroiled in blackmail and violence. Director Macdonald is comfortable with the action sequences, but tension dissipates well before the final bone-crunching shoot-out. Damon and Marlon are at their best in the opening comic sequences, which allow their chemistry to operate, but their pacing is disrupted by the ensuing formulaic thrills. CM

Mona Lisa

(Neil Jordan, 1986, GB) Bob Hoskins, Cathy Tyson, Michael Caine, Robbie Coltrane, Clarke Peters, Kate Hardie, Zoe Nathenson.
104 min.
An assured London-set thriller about the need to love. An old friend (Caine, looking like a man who sweats horribly into his pyjamas) gives minor-league villain Hoskins a job as chauffeur to a dauntingly elegant prostitute (Tyson). This triggers one of the most affecting love stories in recent cinema, between a short, overweight racist and the 'thin black tart' who helps him adjust to a world he finds alien and asks him to find her friend, who has vanished in the mire of big city vice. Plotting a slow descent towards hell, the film deliberately invites comparison with Taxi Driver, though Hoskins, unlike Scorsese's solipsistic avenger, is an utterly ordinary hero, romantic, lost among the pimps and hoods, at ease only when listening to old Nat King Cole numbers. A wonderful achievement, a dark film with a generous heart in the shape of an extraordinarily touching performance from Hoskins. RR

Monde du Silence, Le (The Silent World)

(Jacques-Yves Cousteau/Louis Malle, 1956, Fr)
86 min.
'The latest precision cameras…the deepest dive yet filmed…' Things change, though. Whereas this was regarded at the time as irreproachable, improving, suitable for classroom bookings, the good Captain Cousteau and his all-male ensemble come across now, in 1998, as an aggravating lot, in their once natty '50s swimwear, amusing themselves by straddling giant turtles and turning them into agonising 'comic relief', or filling the screen with torrents of blood as they slaugh-

ter a passing school of sharks ('All sailors hate sharks'). On the other hand, the film-makers' intermittent poetic ambitions are strikingly justified as the cameras explore the wreck of a torpedoed freighter, the commentary becoming an elegy for the lost ship and her crew. The movie has acquired a further dimension as an apprentice work by co-director Louis Malle, though students of his oeuvre will need ingenuity to relate this to anything he made subsequently. BBa

Monde sans pitié, Un (Tough Life/A World Without Pity)

(Eric Rochant, 1989, Fr) Hippolyte Girardot, Mireille Perrier, Yvan Attal, Jean-Marie Rollin, Cécile Mazan, Aline Still, Paul Pavel, Anne Kessler, Patrick Blondel.
88 min.
Jobless, womanising Hippo (Girardot), who lives off his drug-dealing younger brother, is cynically devoted to no one but himself. Falling for Nathalie (Perrier), a rather bookish, professionally get-ahead woman, is the last thing he expects or thinks he needs. When Nathalie invites Hippo over for tea, his endless round of parties, poker games, petty crime and sleeping late suddenly seems less attractive. A simple story, this, but for his excellent feature debut, Rochant adopts a pacy, elliptical narrative style to create an enormously witty and likeable study of emotional alienation and commitment. Though dealing with 'serious' themes (the gulf between classes and generations, responsibility through influence, the need to be honest with oneself as well as with others), it never bogs down in solemn moralising, but paints a vivacious, uncommonly plausible portrait of the preoccupations of contemporary Parisian youth. Stylishly shot, it also benefits from very affecting performances by Perrier and Girardot. GA

Mondo Trasho

(John Waters, 1969, US) Divine, David Lochary, Mink Stole, Mary Vivian Pearce, Mark Isherwood.
95 min. b/w.
Everyone should see at least one early Waters film (this was his first feature); whether you can take two is a matter of personal bad taste. From the moment the picture wobbles reluctantly onto the screen, this clearly demonstrates that the Baltimore boy was ahead of his time when it came to punk aesthetics and desire for shock's sake. Especially in his next epic, Multiple Maniacs, inspired by the Sharon Tate killing, which has the obscene Divine as a mass murderer, delayed on her way to her final carnage by the Religious Whore (Mink Stole) who gives her a 'rosary job' before the altar. Less blasphemous, Mondo Trasho finds Divine lugging round the lifeless body of Mary Vivian Pearce, whom she has run over with her Cadillac convertible, all to the accompaniment of a tinny medley of '60s tunes. Both films are dreadful; bet they had a few laughs making them, though. JS

Money

see Argent, L'

Money Movers

(Bruce Beresford, 1978, Aust) Terence Donovan, Ed Devereaux, Tony Bonner, Lucky Grills, Alan Cassell, Frank Wilson, Candy Raymond, Bryan Brown.
94 min.
Tautly paced and unpretentiously punchy, Beresford's heist thriller is an object lesson in mainstream narrative confidence and economy, detailing the ironic convergence of underworld, undercover and under-suspicion around a security firm vault containing $20 million. The question of who polices the police runs like a black comedy subtext through the film, but is never allowed articulation until the complex business at hand is out of the way in a generically inevitable blood-bath; while the prevalent assumption of universal corruption begins to play havoc with audience sympathies. PT

Money Order, The (Le Mandat)

(Ousmane Sembene, 1968, Fr/Sen) Makuredia Guey, Yunus Ndiay, Issen Niang, Mustafa Ture, Farva Sar.
90 min.

A political film criticising the type of bureaucracy that has arisen in post-colonial Senegal. A money order is sent to an unemployed, illiterate relative by a hard-working lad seeking his fortune in Paris. But all attempts to cash the money order are frustrated: the man's illiteracy and ignorance of finance allow him to be exploited by those with education. The power is in the hands of the clerks and intellectuals, who use their knowledge for private advantage. Although the film can be criticised for the relative gentleness of its attack, Sembene succeeds in pointing up the divisiveness created by the colonial heritage. The French-colonised elite are now busy oppressing and colonising their own people. Shot in Wolof, the local language, the film asserts Senegalese culture against the rapacious way of the West. Not surprisingly it proved popular with the 'people', but was ignored by the bourgeois when originally released. JDuC

Money Pit, The
(Richard Benjamin, 1985, US) Tom Hanks, Shelley Long, Alexander Godunov, Maureen Stapleton, Joe Mantegna, Philip Bosco, Josh Mostel.
91 min.
As a yuppie nightmare, this is much safer than After Hours but no less funny. Hanks is a successful lawyer, most of whose clients are 16-stone, transvestite rock bands with names like 'The Cheap Girls'. When his girlfriend's ex-husband reappropriates their love nest, he is forced to buy a large amount of real estate out in the suburbs of New York. This is the money pit. Part of the pleasure is watching the house fulfil your worst expectations: doors come off hinges, wiring burns up like a powder trail, baths crash through ceilings, roofs leak. You can see it coming, but it still has the delicious anticipation of the slow burn. And it all gets much worse. Director Richard Benjamin has the rare gift of knowing just where the funnybone lies, a certain taste for Keatonesque slapstick, and a very fine comic performer in Hanks. CPea

Money Talks
(Brett Ratner, 1997, US) Chris Tucker, Charlie Sheen, Heather Locklear, Gerard Ismaël, Damian Chapa, Veronica Cartwright, David Warner, Paul Sorvino.
96 min.
Tucker is an LA street hustler on the run from French diamond smugglers, and Sheen an ambitious TV journalist on the brink of an advantageous marriage, who has everything to gain (or lose) from helping him. Tucker's great in straight parts, but has modelled his funny man routine too closely on Eddie Murphy. Meanwhile, Sheen seems comfortable in a role that has only one angle (everything his character sees reminds him of an item he did for TV). Diversions are provided by the script, which comes from Alec Sokolow and Joel Cohen of Toy Story: Tucker makes a 'speech' at a posh, all-white gathering, which is in fact one long quote from a Barry White song, and (wrongly) assumes the palefaces won't recognise it. What we're being alerted to, over and over, is the cultural apartheid at work in America and the power to be gained from sneaking across the divide. CO'Su

Money Train
(Joseph Ruben, 1995, US) Wesley Snipes, Woody Harrelson, Jennifer Lopez, Robert Blake, Chris Cooper, Joe Grifasi, Scott Sowers.
110 min.
Ever since their successful teaming in White Men Can't Jump, Hollywood has wanted to reunite Snipes and Harrelson for a buddy picture. Directed with routine efficiency, this loco action comedy plays a one-joke, high-concept plot to the hilt, squandering cash and energy on a subway heist that takes forever to arrive and then goes nowhere. The comic twist is that Snipes and Harrelson are foster brothers; the set-up that they're New York transit cops who end up robbing the Money Train to pay Woody's gambling debts. With a fortune in fares at stake and hardass Money boss (Blake) on their case, Snipes once again digs his irresponsible white brother out of a hole. The pair obviously enjoyed ragging one another, and director Ruben finally puts the money on the screen with a Taking of Pelham One Two Three-style climax. As Snipes and Harrelson's fellow transit cop and mutual love interest, the smouldering Lopez mostly just stands around waiting for the boys to make up their minds about her. Hardly worth the four-year wait. NF

Mon Homme
(Bertrand Blier, 1996, Fr) Anouk Grinberg, Gérard Lanvin, Valéria Bruni-Tedeschi, Olivier Martinez, Dominique Valadié, Aurore Clément, Jean-Pierre Léaud, Sabine Azéma.
99 min.
This could be Blier's masterpiece, and/or his most disparaging work. For 25 years, he's been serving up provocative satirical dissections of French social, sexual and cultural mores. Here, again, he goes just too far. The pert Grinberg, the muse of his most recent films, is the tart with a heart: a $1,000-a-day girl, this woman has the gift and the appetite. Meeting homeless tramp Jeannot (Lanvin), she brings him to her apartment for succour and offers herself in a gesture of submission. She takes him as her pimp, shaving, suiting and smartening him, and enjoys the conventional (and conventionally ugly) life of the oldest profession, until 'her man' over-reaches himself, prostituting her neighbour (Bruni-Tedeschi), and the cops send him down. The merciless simplicity of Blier's method breaks the heart. His inscrutable stance and ironic distance from his characters is now so firmly entrenched that he feels free to blend moments of lyricism (a beautiful, dreamy drift of snowflakes worthy of Demy), jaundiced poetry (nodding toward Pialat) and melodrama, without teetering off the razor-edge path between offence and pathos. The Barry White songs and the 'Scope photography further emphasise the feeling of alienation. One senses an almost inhuman objectivity at work, which makes Blier seem more and more a compatriot of that arch misanthrope Henri-Georges Clouzot. WH

Monika
see Sommaren med Monika

Monk, The
see Moine, Le

Monkey Business
(Norman Z McLeod, 1931, US) The Marx Brothers, Thelma Todd, Ruth Hall, Harry Woods, Rockcliffe Fellowes, Tom Kennedy.
77 min. b/w.
The four Marx Brothers as stowaways trying to bull their way through immigration by pretending to be Maurice Chevalier (each hopefully doing an impersonation to prove it), then crashing a Long Island society party to sow havoc. With Monkey Business, their first screen original, the team cast caution to the winds, helped by a perky script ('Tell me, has your grandfather's beard got any money?' – 'Money? Why it fell hair to a fortune') and some lunatic sight gags. Thelma Todd provides Groucho with his most delectable and intelligent foil. GB

Monkey Business
(Howard Hawks, 1952, US) Cary Grant, Ginger Rogers, Charles Coburn, Marilyn Monroe, Hugh Marlowe, George Winslow.
97 min. b/w.
Immaculate screwball comedy by its greatest practitioners, in which Cary Grant polishes up at least three previous roles as an absent-minded chemist in search of a youth drug. The chaos starts when a mischievous monkey accidentally mixes the magic formula into the water cooler, whereupon Grant and wife Ginger Rogers take turns to regress into childhood. For Grant, that means sex, speed, a crew-cut, checked jacket and socks, while Rogers wants to dance the hoochie-coochie in their honeymoon hotel. Monroe is on hand as the typist who can't type, while the timing of the gags can put most Hollywood comedies, never mind TV sitcoms, to shame. The classic inverted-world comedy, where kids and animals bring sexual anarchy into the demure adult world, leaving all inhabitants much refreshed and highly amused. DMacp

Monkey Grip
(Ken Cameron, 1981, Aust) Noni Hazlehurst, Colin Friels, Alice Garner, Harold Hopkins, Candy Raymond, Michael Caton, Tim Burns.
102 min.
Gloom settles quickly as Nora (Hazlehurst) launch-es into a portentous account of her emotional ups-and-downs. Thirtyish, separated from the father of her child, she is suffering almost stoically as a single parent in Sydney but still hoping to get fulfilled. Prospects look slim when, after discarding junkie number one, she falls for Javo (Friels), the sort of guy who needs a day's notice to tie his shoelaces. After much airing of thick-eared romantic problems in swimming-pools, squats and studies, Nora emerges, so she informs us, an older but infinitely wiser woman. What seems extraordinary is that this should have been held up (and apparently applauded) as the story of a woman fighting to control her life, when she's clearly making a dreadful mess of it. It's also unrelieved by the faintest glimmer of humour, except for one (unintentionally?) quite hilarious scene in which Javo's acting ambitions take a tumble when he heaves all over the footlights on his debut. Noni Hazlehurst is excellent, but it's an unrewarding plod. JP

Monkey Shines
(George A Romero, 1988, US) Jason Beghe, John Pankow, Kate McNeil, Joyce Van Patten, Christine Forrest, Stephen Root, Stanley Tucci, Janine Turner.
113 min.
Moving away from the apocalyptic horror of his 'Living Dead' trilogy, Romero reaffirms his equal aptitude for controlled chills, previously evident in Martin. Paralysed in a road accident, Allan Mann (Beghe) is provided with a trained Capuchin monkey, Ella, as home help. A research specimen before training, Ella had been injected with human brain tissue by Allan's mad scientist pal (Pankow) in the hope of increasing her learning ability. Now, as a result of a mysterious mind-meld, Ella responds to Allan's moods, violently enacting his frustrated rage against his bossy nurse (Forrest), fussing mother (Van Patten) and ex-fiancée (Turner), in nocturnal rampages which he experiences as hallucinatory nightmares seen through the monkey's eyes. Things build to a nasty climax when Allan falls in love with Ella's trainer Melanie (McNeil), triggering a violently jealous reaction from Ella. What sets this apart from most modern horror movies, besides a sparing use of special effects, is Romero's careful development of a credible emotional context for the pyromaniac madness and razor-wielding terror. Romero's is a formidable talent which others can only hope to ape. NF

Monkey Trouble
(Franco Amurri, 1994, US) Harvey Keitel, Mimi Rogers, Thora Birch, Christopher McDonald, Kevin Scannell, Alison Elliott.
96 min.
Like any nine-year-old, Eva (Birch) wants a dog. Stepdad is a cop with allergies to animal hair, and so he's no help. Mommy (Rogers) reckons that Eva isn't ready for the responsibility of a pet, since her room's a mess. Issues of trust, autonomy and self-realisation are at stake. Meanwhile, gypsy organ-grinder Shorty (Keitel) and his capuchin have attracted the attention of a pair of hoods who want the light-fingered monkey for a heist. The creature goes AWOL, hides in a tree and falls in Eva's lap. She keeps him, hides him, loves him, even puts a nappy on him. Very annoying. WH

Monolith
(John Eyres, 1993, US) Bill Paxton, Lindsay Frost, Louis Gossett Jr, John Hurt.
91 min.
Two mismatched Los Angeles detectives, thrown together after witnessing a Russian scientist shoot down an apparently 'possessed' child, discover a mysterious alien life-force that inhabits human bodies and shoots fireballs from their eyes. Ho-hum. NB

Monolith Monsters, The
(John Sherwood, 1957, US) Lola Albright, Grant Williams, Les Tremayne, Trevor Bardette, William Flaherty, Linda Scheley.
77 min. b/w.
The original 'rocky horror': a Jack Arnold-originated, quite effective Universal sci-fi paranoia yarn featuring the alien-induced metamorphosis of men to stone, and a subsequent stampede of towering crystal structures across small-town America. Grant Williams (The Incredible Shrinking Man) is again dwarfed by his adversaries, though he plays the only possible hero: a geologist. PT

Mono loco, El

see Mad Monkey, The

Mon Oncle (My Uncle)

(Jacques Tati, 1958, Fr) Jacques Tati, Jean-Pierre Zola, Adrienne Servantie, Alain Bécourt, Yvonne Arnaud.
116 min.
Tati's first film in colour. Yes, his contrast of the glorious awfulness of the Arpels' automated Modernistic house with Hulot's disordered Bohemianism is simplistic. Yes, Hulot as champion of the individual is oddly de-personalised. And one might even conclude that Tati is a closet misanthrope. Such text-book reservations come and go as this extraordinary film meanders like the Arpels' concrete garden path. But while some episodes are protracted, many are unforgettably funny, wonderfully observed, and always technically brilliant. Insane gadgets slam and roar, high heels click like metronomes, and even a depressed dachshund in a tartan overcoat obligingly submits to Tati's meticulous direction. JS

Mon Oncle Antoine (My Uncle Antoine)

(Claude Jutra, 1971, Can) Jacques Gagnon, Lyne Champagne, Jean Duceppe, Olivette Thibault, Lionel Villeneuve, Claude Jutra.
110 min.
Taking a French-Canadian mining town, with all its feelings of dead-endedness, Jutra shows with some sympathy why people stay on. Events centre round one Christmas in the life of young Benoît (Gagnon), who works for his uncle, also the undertaker, in the general store. Against the background of communal festivities and the death of a boy, he becomes aware of the complexity of his own feelings and the fallibility and unhappiness of adults. A film of moments: Benoît's reaction to a girl first wearing make-up; glimpsing the notary's wife trying on a girdle; realising his uncle (Duceppe) is little more than a drunken sot; his revulsion at the dead boy's naked legs. Although sometimes lacking subtlety, the film avoids most of the clichés about adolescence and resists drawing conclusions. CPe

Mon Oncle d'Amérique (My American Uncle/My Uncle from America)

(Alain Resnais, 1980, Fr) Gérard Depardieu, Nicole Garcia, Roger Pierre, Marie Dubois, Nelly Borgeaud, Pierre Arditi, Henri Laborit.
126 min.
After the disappointments of Stavisky and Providence, Resnais here retrieves his position as a great film innovator. My American Uncle takes three middle class characters (two of them from well-defined working class backgrounds) and leads them through a labyrinth of 'stress' situations. The tone hovers between soap opera and docudrama, consistently pleasurable if hardly gripping. Then it introduces its fourth major character, Henri Laborit, a bona fide behavioural scientist, who discusses his theories of biological and emotional triggers. Shortsighted critics seem to imagine that the fictional material merely illustrates what Laborit says, although Resnais inserts some jokey shots of 'human' mice to demolish any such notions. His triumph is to create a new kind of fiction: a drama that not only leaves room to think, but opens up fissures that thoughts flood into, some prompted by Laborit, others by personal reflections, yet others by dreams. Inevitably, it ends in a riddle, and one which proves that surrealism lives. TR

Mon Père, ce héros

(Gérard Lauzier, 1991, Fr) Gérard Depardieu, Marie Gillain, Patrick Mille, Catherine Jacob, Charlotte de Turckheim, Eric Berger.
104 min.
Proof positive that Depardieu is a star of international magnitude: even a pedestrian comedy like this warrants theatrical release in Britain. André (Depardieu), a divorced middle-aged businessman, takes daughter Véronique (Gillain) away for Christmas, but her bathing-suit makes him wonder whether Mauritius was such a good idea. At 14, she is not his little girl any more. Much smitten with one particular youth, Véronique impresses him with a tapestry of lies: she is a runaway, and André her sugar-daddy

lover. Only when André is enveloped in the deceit do things perk up momentarily, and still the picture lumbers from laborious farce to shameless sentiment with all the grace of a beached whale (an image Depardieu brings to mind). The bovine sensibility of this tacky, tasteless blague is underscored with misogyny and a scurrilous hint of racism. TCh

Mon Premier Amour

(Elie Chouraqui, 1978, Fr) Anouk Aimée, Richard Berry, Gabriele Ferzetti, Nathalie Baye, Jacques Villeret.
100 min.
A young man falls in love with his mother (not hard if she's as agelessly radiant as Anouk) when he learns that she is dying of leukaemia. Not a case of necrophilia, alas, nor even of incest. Director Chouraqui obviously learned to distill pure mush with glitter sauce as assistant to Lelouch. TM

Monsieur Hawarden

(Harry Kümel, 1968, Neth/Bel) Ellen Vogel, Hilde Uitterlinden, Johan Remmelts, Dora Van Der Groen, Senne Rouffaer, Xander Fisher.
106 min. b/w.
Kümel's first feature is not much like his subsequent Daughters of Darkness or Malpertuis, although all three films centre on questions of sexual identity, and all three are bravura exercises in style. Monsieur Hawarden is an artily restrained melodrama about a Viennese lady around the turn of the century who kills one of her lovers and then retreats into hiding in masculine drag. It is hubristically dedicated to Sternberg, but in fact closely resembles Bergman's The Face in both its black-and-white chiaroscuro photography and its plotting. Relentlessly beautiful and sensitive, it clearly gave Kümel the chance to work a lot of 'art cinema' ideas out of his system before launching into his more commercial (and more imaginative) horror/fantasy films. TR

Monsieur Hire

(Patrice Leconte, 1989, Fr) Michel Blanc, Sandrine Bonnaire, Luc Thullier, André Wilms.
79 min.
Prime suspect in the murder of a young girl, Monsieur Hire – a quiet, balding, middle-aged tailor – spends much of his time secretly gazing from his window at Alice, who lives in the apartment opposite. His solitude, however, is broken when Alice, having glimpsed his face in the light of a storm, visits him in his room and bluntly asks why he spies on her. In this oddly touching, enigmatic adaptation of Simenon's novel, Leconte focuses less on the murder mystery – Hire repeatedly proclaims his innocence, but how sinister is his voyeurism? – than on the unexpectedly tender relationship that develops between watcher and watched, gently manipulating audience sympathies to create a poignant study of amour fou. Appropriately in a film concerned with voyeurism and loneliness, restraint is the keynote, with Michel Blanc's playing of Hire especially intriguing in its cool, sensitive understatement. But it is Leconte's direction that steals the show. Opting for subtlety rather than suspense, slowly but surely piecing together a jigsaw of brief elliptical scenes which mirror the nervy hesitancy of Hire's emotions, Leconte's narrative economy contrives to say a great deal about his hapless protagonist. GA

Monsieur Hulot's Holiday

see Vacances de M. Hulot, Les

Monsieur Ripois

see Knave of Hearts

Monsieur Verdoux

(Charles Chaplin, 1947, US) Charles Chaplin, Martha Raye, Isobel Elsom, Marilyn Nash, Mady Correll, Irving Bacon, William Frawley, Charles Evans.
123 min. b/w.
Chaplin's self-styled 'comedy of murders' about a gent who marries short-lived wealthy women was generally disliked on its first appearance: people found it slow, cold, bitter and insufficiently funny. Now it shapes up as Chaplin's most startling, most invigorating movie: its icy tem-

perature is positively bracing after the hot syrup of his earlier work (though a dollop of that survives in the waif character played by Marilyn Nash). Chaplin uses his customary fastidious gestures to emphasis human nastiness – typified by the brassy Martha Raye, who plays the most vulgar woman ever created, chattering away with her mouth full of croissant and laughing not like one drain but ten. GB

Monsignor

(Frank Perry, 1982, US) Christopher Reeve, Genevieve Bujold, Fernando Rey, Jason Miller, Joe Cortese, Adolfo Celi, Leonardo Cimino, Robert Prosky.
121 min.
A movie seemingly predicated on the naive belief that audiences will be surprised that priests sleep with nuns, kill people (or Germans in World War II, at least), profit from the black market, and make deals with the Mafia to help the Vatican's cash flow problem. To its credit, there is commendably little wrestling with conscience over these minor doctrinal points; Christopher Reeve pauses only to square that mighty jaw and brush off his soutane, before plunging into the world of high finance, low sex, toppling dynasties, and Machiavellian in-fighting. Indeed, the movie's flat, TV-style matter-of-factness might even be said to correspond with a certain Pelagian pragmatism. Producer Frank Yablans was also guilty of The Other Side of Midnight, a 20-Hail Mary slice of epic schlock in roughly the same league as this: mortal sins, true confessions, purple stuff. CPea

Monster

see Humanoids from the Deep

Monster and the Girl, The

(Stuart Heisler, 1941, US) Ellen Drew, Robert Paige, Paul Lukas, Joseph Calleia, George Zucco, Rod Cameron, Onslow Stevens.
65 min. b/w.
No masterpiece, but an unusually lively B shocker, engagingly mixing ingredients as Drew, a girl tricked into white slavery prostitution by gangsters, is avenged by a gorilla into which her brother's brain has been transplanted (he was framed by the gang for murder and duly executed) by Zucco's mad doctor. It sounds wild and it is, but opening with a mesmerising shot of Drew looming up out of the mist to tell her story in flashback ('I'm Susan, the bad luck penny; I bought a million dollars' worth of trouble...for everybody'), it generates a bizarre conviction. Surprisingly well acted, it is also directed with real flair, notably in a sequence where the gorilla (constantly threatened with betrayal by a puzzled dog who recognises his master somewhere in there) stalks the rooftop in parallel with his gangster-prey strolling in the deserted nighttime street below. TM

Monster Club, The

(Roy Ward Baker, 1980, GB) Vincent Price, John Carradine, Donald Pleasence, Stuart Whitman, Richard Johnson, Britt Ekland, Patrick Magee, Barbara Kellerman, Simon Ward.
97 min.
Scrapings of the horror-omnibus barrel in the Amicus tradition. The famous horror writer R Chetwynd-Hayes (Carradine), having donated some blood, is taken along by the grateful vampire (Price) to his club so that fellow-monster-members may provide him with material for future books. There follow three witlessly routine tales (adapted from stories by Chetwynd-Hayes), drearily executed and graced not at all by such luminaries as Pleasence, Magee and Whitman. Stultification is completed by assorted pop groups, presumably hired by the Monster Club to capture the teenage market, who are on hand to introduce each story with discordant squalls. TM

Monster from Green Hell

(Kenneth Crane, 1957, US) Jim Davis, Robert E Griffin, Barbara Turner, Eduardo Ciannelli, Vladimir Sokoloff, Joel Fluellen.
71 min. b/w.
A test rocket carrying various animals and insects goes off course and crash-lands in deepest Africa. Soon, scientists Davis and Griffin hear tell of giant wasps on the loose in the very area where the rocket went down. Could cosmic rays

have brought about these grotesque mutations? Of course they could! Crane's monstrous film incorporates ingenious trick photography, model work and stop-motion animation, as well as extensive footage culled from the 1939 Spencer Tracy picture *Stanley and Livingstone*. The result is not so much a movie as a patchwork. TCh

Monster in a Box
(Nicholas Broomfield, 1991, US/GB) Spalding Gray.
96 min.
As in *Swimming to Cambodia*, this is one man and his mouth, given free range; and again, against all odds, it's riveting. Here, Gray addresses the intimate business of writing a novel. Or not writing it. The opus in question – a huge, unwieldy chunk of his life, and the monster of the title – sits reproachfully on the table throughout, as Gray tells how he set out to write it in an attempt to exorcise the trauma of his mother's death. Gray's mastery of the art of digression is so compelling that the trimmings added by Broomfield are almost superfluous. Gray himself provides plenty to look at – the unearthly glow of his hair, his regrettable choice of shirt, those mystifyingly shaped eyebrows, and a repertoire of hand signals that makes it quite clear why he found it so hard to sit down and type. Whether you'd want to be stuck in a railway carriage with him is another matter, but on screen he is – as they say – unputdownable. JRo

Monster of Terror
(aka Die, Monster, Die!)
(Daniel Haller, 1965, GB/US) Boris Karloff, Nick Adams, Suzan Farmer, Freda Jackson, Terence de Marney, Patrick Magee, Leslie Dwyer.
81 min.
Haller's highly enjoyable debut as a director is a slow, moody, loose adaptation of HP Lovecraft's marvellous story *The Colour Out of Space*, with Karloff (excellent, as usual) as the scientist attempting, with the aid of a strange meteorite (it causes plant life to grow monstrously and organisms to mutate) to invoke the Dark Powers to return to rule the earth again. Not surprisingly, given that Haller served as art director on Corman's Poe cycle, his film features much the same battery of ground fogs, dank passageways, and vaulted stone chambers. He uses these effectively enough, but adds some even better effects of his own, notably the vision of desolate wasteland which surrounds the warlock's domain, and the greenhouse in which he secretes the monstrous, throbbing organisms he has created. TM

Monster on the Campus
(Jack Arnold, 1958, US) Arthur Franz, Joanna Moore, Troy Donahue, Whit Bissell, Judson Pratt, Helen Westcott, Eddie Parker.
76 min. b/w.
'Is this fish really one million years old?' asks Troy Donahue, pointing at the new specimen at Professor Donald Blake's lab. It sure is, and what's more, if you get infected then you revert to primitive instinctual behaviour. With that in mind, Jack Arnold's hijacking of the Wolf Man plot onto a campus terror tale needs all his talent for making the incredible seem possible: giant dragonflies and million-year-old fish don't quite look so strange as the '50s finned creatures known as automobiles that glide down the campus and suburban avenues. DMacp

Monster Squad, The
(Fred Dekker, 1987, US) André Gower, Robby Kiger, Stephen Macht, Duncan Regehr, Tom Noonan, Brent Chalem.
82 min.
More of a clever comic parody than a jokey pastiche, this lively kiddies' horror pic delivers frights and laughs which are rooted in a sure and sympathetic grasp of Monster Movie mythology. To take advantage of a confluence of evil that occurs only once every hundred years, Count Dracula (Regehr) flies to America, then summons the Wolfman, Gill-Man, Mummy and Frankenstein's monster. Alerted to Dracula's evil plan, The Monster Squad – a gang of pre-teen kids and their slightly older tough-guy pal – fashion stakes in woodwork class, melt down their parents' cutlery to make silver bullets, and give the monsters hell. Confirming the promise of his

debut feature *Night of the Creeps*, Dekker plays around imaginatively with the genre while delivering several nice touches. NF

Montagna del Dio Cannibale, La (Prisoner of the Cannibal God/Slave of the Cannibal God)
(Sergio Martino, 1978, It) Ursula Andress, Stacy Keach, Claudio Cassinelli, Antonio Marsina, Franco Fantasia.
99 min.
Kicking off with such gastronomic delights as the ingestion of live iguanas, snakes, toads and other wriggly things, this climaxes rather tamely with a main course of very dead human. In between, with Ursula Andress in New Guinea looking for her missing ethnologist husband, there is a fair helping of native bashing, alligator mauling, and the many ways Ursula can fall into the river, render her safari suit transparent, and display her waterproof mascara to full advantage. The flimsiest of plots and the crassest of ecological messages (uranium and capitalism versus nature and cannibalism) surround this general desire to disrobe the Andress form. FF

Montalvo et l'enfant (Montalvo and the Child)
(Claude Mourieras, 1988, Fr) Mathilde Altaraz, Christophe Delachaux, Robert Seyfried, Jean-Claude Gallotta, Michel Ducret, Marceline Bertolot.
76 min. b/w.
De Sica with a difference; a gem that successfully wears its heart on its neo-realist sleeve, this coming-of-age tale is shot in a radiantly glowing black-and-white filled with deep shadows and pearly iridescence. Revolving around a boisterous working-class family's get-together, it links the separate stories of the Child (Ducret) and his hero Montalvo (Delachaux) through a series of short, telling incidents that are emotionally heightened by the subtle, imaginative choreography of Jean-Claude Gallotta, which integrates dance into the narrative with such skill that the dividing line between naturalism and stylisation seems to evaporate. Few such films allow us to believe so completely in the truth of their performers as real people; it is as if Mourieras and Gallotta just happened to stumble across this family one Sunday afternoon. AR

Montand
(Jean Labib, 1994, Fr) Yves Montand.
135 min.
An 'auto-biopic' in that the commentary consists of the actor/singer's own reminiscences, recorded as he prepared material for his book, *You See, I Haven't Forgotten*, this is, inevitably, an affectionate look at a great French cultural icon. Moving from his impoverished childhood in Marseille, through music-hall and movies, and relationships with Piaf and Monroe, to his final disenchantment with communism and his sorrow and loneliness after the death of his wife Simone Signoret. Fascinating partly for the archive footage, and partly for the apparent honesty of Montand's revelations. GA

Monte Carlo
(Ernst Lubitsch, 1930, US) Jeanette MacDonald, Jack Buchanan, ZaSu Pitts, Claude Allister, Tyler Brooke, Lionel Belmore.
90 min. b/w.
What can a penniless countess do when faced with the dilemma of true love versus class and financial expediency? She (Jeanette MacDonald) dithers: between Count Rudolf (Buchanan), known to her only in his masquerade as her hairdresser, and the monocled Prince Otto (Allister), who is 'Rich, wealthy, and has nothing but money'. Sumptuous sets, costumes, and a plethora of the titled and the wealthy combine to give *Monte Carlo* a fairytale quality which takes all the sting out of its assumptions about the mercenary nature of women, while preposterous songs and foolish romanticism make it gay, frivolous and thoroughly charming. FF

Montenegro
(Dusan Makavejev, 1981, Swe/GB) Susan Anspach, Erland Josephson, Bora Todorovic, Per Oscarsson, John Zacharias, Svetozar Cvetkovic.
96 min.

If it begins deceptively, as though setting out to be your typically angst-ridden Swedish art movie, by the time it's reached its set of climaxes – fireworks exploding, couple orgasming, narrative resolving – Makavejev's film could not have strayed further from the beaten track. Anspach is the frustrated housewife taking her pleasure where she can find it; and where she finds it, after airport body searches and missed flight connections, is, Makavejev suggests, in an increasingly unstable landscape which may be interior (psychological) or exterior (the tacky, exotic Club Zanzi-Bar, local hangout for a community of immigrant workers). Funny, bizarre and horny, *Montenegro* may not be as extreme in conception as the suppressed *Sweet Movie*, but it certainly lives up to its producer's brief to Makavejev: 'high quality comedy with a popular appeal and measured eroticism'. What more do you want from a film? RM

Monterey Pop
(DA Pennebaker, 1968, US) Janis Joplin, Jefferson Airplane, The Who, Jimi Hendrix, Otis Redding, Ravi Shankar, The Mamas and the Papas.
88 min.
Quite simply one of the best rock concert films ever (distilling the 1967 International Pop Festival at Monterey, California), thanks not only to some great performances (towards the end, with Joplin, Redding, Hendrix, things really start cooking), but also to the way it sums up the spirit of the times (the summer of love) while never sentimentalising. Hang on to the end, however, when a small Indian man appears nursing a sitar: Ravi Shankar's exhilarating twenty-minute finale is the best thing in the entire movie. GA

Monte Walsh
(William A Fraker, 1970, US) Lee Marvin, Jack Palance, Mitch Ryan, Jeanne Moreau, Jim Davis, Bo Hopkins, Michael Conrad, Allyn Ann McLerie.
108 min.
A stunning debut Western for cameraman-turned-director Fraker, chronicling the death of an era as two cowboys (Marvin and Palance) ride into town to find that a bleak winter has brought hard times. Eastern capital has moved in with new methods, jobs are hard to come by, and the pair buckle down to the only work they can get, watching morosely as more and more men are laid off. Gradually the mood darkens. An old cowboy, ending his days in the humbling task of fence-mending, rides his horse crazily over a cliff. Old friends disappear, to return with the law on their heels as desperation drives them to rustling or robbery. Palance (brilliantly cast against type) decides to quit and become a storekeeper; and Marvin, after proving something to himself by taming a bronc no one else could handle, proves something else by rounding on the owner of a Wild West show who offers him a job ('I ain't spittin' on my whole life'). Thus far the film is relatively naturalistic, gently elegiac in tone; but after Marvin's nocturnal encounter with the horse, a strange twilight falls (the twilight of the gods, no less). Fate strikes twice at his life; he is forced to assume the traditional role of gunman; and in settings formally drained of colour, he embarks on his revenger's tragedy...A rare treat. TM

Month by the Lake, A
(John Irvin, 1994, US/GB) Vanessa Redgrave, Edward Fox, Uma Thurman, Alida Valli, Carlo Cartier, Alessandro Gassman, Natalia Bizzi.
91 min.
Adapted from a romantic interlude by HE Bates, this is so flat and passionless that, without the warm glow of the cinematography and the deliriously romantic Italian settings, it would almost certainly have been consigned to video. Lake Como, 1939. Miss Bentley (Redgrave) is holidaying with her Italian friends on the shore of her favourite lake. Lonely and bored, she soon perks up when she notices the rugged looks of the only other English visitor present, Fox's starchy Major Wilshaw. The two meet, chat, play tennis, and romance might have blossomed, were it not for the arrival of fickle, flirtatious American nanny Miss Beaumont (Thurman, twitchy). Still, even though Miss Bentley feels rejected by the major's lack of interest in her, she's chuffed when she in turn attracts the attention of local youth Vittorio (Gassman). Thus unfolds a four-way tangle, age difference the theme. This day-by-day account of

month-long holiday romances does not fit comfortably into 91 minutes, and after the fourth al fresco breakfast, your eyes wander past the characters to focus on the views behind. DA

Month in the Country, A
(Pat O'Connor, 1987, GB) Colin Firth, Kenneth Branagh, Natasha Richardson, Patrick Malahide, Richard Vernon, Elizabeth Anson.
96 min.
In the summer of 1920, two traumatised victims of World War I meet in a Yorkshire village: Birkin (Firth), who stutters, has come to restore a mural in the local church, and Moon (Branagh), still tormented by nightmares, has come to excavate the land around it. Birkin falls for the beautiful wife (Richardson) of the uncharitable vicar (Malahide), and Moon falls for Birkin. Neither gets what he wants, but together they succeed in solving a minor mystery. O'Connor directs Simon Gray's script with great sensitivity. It's all taken at a gentle pace, but dullness is averted by a sly humour. The pretty-prettiness of Hovis commercials is not always avoided, and recurrent images of the apocalyptic painting, intended to give the rather pat plot a mystical resonance, don't; but all the performances are accomplished, and that of Firth is brilliant. MS

Montreal Main
(Frank Vitale, 1974, Can) Frank Vitale, John Sutherland, Dave Sutherland, Ann Sutherland, Allan Bozo Moyle.
88 min. b/w.
Vitale's first feature was the most honest film about male sexuality made to date...which is to say that it's both troubled and troubling, in the most positive sense. It centres on a character called Frank Vitale, an unemployed artist-photographer, and his circle of (predominantly gay) friends. Frank's closest friend is Bozo; they have a disastrously furtive attempt at sex together at one point, although neither considers himself gay. But their friendship, and Frank's life in general, threatens to fall apart when Frank meets the 12-year-old Johnny and in some sense falls in love with him. It's impossible to be more explicit about it, since the film itself isn't. In fact, hardly anything happens in the way of reportable incident: it plays as a stream of modest encounters and conversations, which seem like improvisations. Brilliant casting, photography, and especially editing, however, give the whole movie an acute psychological focus. TR

Monty Python and the Holy Grail
(Terry Gilliam/Terry Jones, 1974, GB) Graham Chapman, John Cleese, Terry Gilliam, Eric Idle, Terry Jones, Michael Palin.
90 min.
Python's delightful and, on the whole, consistent reductio ad absurdum of the Grail legend, in which the Knights forsake their chorus line can-can dancing at Camelot for a higher aim. The Pythons set up a 'historical' tale as the sum total of modern anachronisms and misconceptions about it, a format repeated in The Life of Brian. CPe

Monty Python's Life of Brian
(Terry Jones, 1979, GB) Terry Jones, Graham Chapman, Michael Palin, John Cleese, Eric Idle, Terry Gilliam, Carol Cleveland.
93 min.
The Three Wise Men go to the wrong manger, thus foisting upon Brian Cohen a role for which he is eminently unprepared. More Carrying On than usual from the Pythons, but the use of a tried and tested storyline (Cleese: 'Yes, it has got a bit of shape, hasn't it?') results in their most sustained effort to date. Python successfully lampoon religious attitudes rather than religion itself, while the comedy relies mainly on memories of the classroom; which is apt enough, considering that most of the audience is likely to associate knowledge of the Holy Writ with schooldays too. Jokes about Great Profits must have been hard to resist. CPe

Monty Python's The Meaning of Life
(Terry Jones, 1983, GB) Graham Chapman, John Cleese, Terry Gilliam, Eric Idle, Terry Jones, Michael Palin, Carol Cleveland.
90 min.
The Python swansong, a nostalgic return to the

sketch format of the original TV shows, garnished with the 'explicit' sex and violence jokes that are deemed necessary to get bums on seats in cinemas in these depraved times. This is the one with the exploding Mr Creosote, the parody of Zulu, and the sketch about organ-snatching from live donors. The highpoint comes early, when a Catholic family in Yorkshire burst into song with 'Every Sperm is Sacred'. TR

Moon 44
(Roland Emmerich, 1989, WGer) Michael Paré, Lisa Eichhorn, Malcolm McDowell, Dean Devlin, Brian Thompson, Stephen Geoffreys, Leon Rippy, Jochen Nickel.
99 min.
Intergalactic hijackers are zapping our planets, and the next target is Moon 44, to be exploited for mineral wealth and already used as a training ground for hi-tech 'copter pilots. The mining corporation sends up investigator Felix Stone (Paré), who's deep undercover, pretending to be a fighter pilot while hunting a saboteur. The plot contains one potentially intriguing idea: the musclebound pilots, most of whom are criminals, are hamstrung without their navigators, weakling teen geniuses to a boy. The boys are beaten up and sexually abused by the pilots, who then wonder why they keep getting directed into cliff faces. A silly subplot concerns library books; and our worst fears are realised when McDowell bumbles into view as Major Lee, enigmatic station commander. The film looks nice but unoriginal (blue light, dry ice, flashing instrument panels); the model work is okay but laboured; the acting is stunningly mediocre. SFe

Moon and Sixpence, The
(Albert Lewin, 1943, US) George Sanders, Herbert Marshall, Steve Geray, Doris Dudley, Elena Verdugo, Eric Blore, Florence Bates.
85 min. b/w & col.
Somerset Maugham's Gauguin-inspired novel is well and faithfully served by Lewin's characteristically literary direction; Sanders, especially, savours the elegant dialogue and cool ironies in his role as the quiet suburban broker who suddenly throws it all in, and leaves London and his family to embark upon a painting career in Paris. Indeed, the actor was the perfect choice for the part, his impeccably supercilious intelligence conveying both the self-centredness and the determination of a man with a private mission which he believes transcends social niceties. If the studio sets weaken the final scenes in Tahiti, Lewin's sensitivity to Maugham's moral nuances ensures unusually sophisticated Hollywood entertainment. GA

Moon and the Sledgehammer, The
(Philip Trevelyan, 1971, GB) Mr Page, Jim Page, Peter Page, Kathy Page, Nancy Page.
65 min.
Engaging documentary about an eccentric family (old man, two sons, two daughters) living wild in a tumbledown house in the Sussex woods and doing their own thing (mainly music and tinkering with steam engines and other ancient machinery). Their lifestyle, expounded in fascinatingly wayward conversation which is allowed to make its own pace, embodies a weird cautionary logic about the miracles of modern technocracy. TM

Moonfleet
(Fritz Lang, 1955, US) Stewart Granger, Jon Whiteley, George Sanders, Viveca Lindfors, Joan Greenwood, Melville Cooper, Jack Elam, Dan Seymour, Ian Wolfe.
87 min.
A young boy and a rakish smuggler search for a legendary lost diamond in a wonderfully stylised version of 19th century Cornwall. The characters are linked and haunted by the memory of the boy's dead mother, and their 'romance' is a journey through a dark world of gallows and graveyards. Lang disliked working in CinemaScope, a ratio he described in Le Mépris as 'only good for funerals and snakes', but uses it brilliantly. SJ

Moon Has Risen, The (Tsuki wa Noborinu)
(Kinuyo Tanaka, 1955, Jap) Mie Kitahara, Shoji Yasui, Chishu Ryu, Hisako Yamane, Kinuyo Tanaka.
90 min. b/w.

A charming and vivid family drama, scripted by Ozu and directed by actress Tanaka, who also makes a cameo appearance as a put-upon servant. Kitahara plays spoilt and imperious Setsuko Asai, youngest daughter of a wealthy family from Nara. Together with handsome lodger Shoji, she plots to marry off her elder sister to a family friend who has long admired her; in a comic interlude, the inspired lovers begin to correspond in code, to the frustration of the plotters. But when Setsuko herself falls in love, she is not quite so adroit at manipulating matters. The relationship between the three sisters (the eldest a shy, widowed stay-at-home) is delicately drawn, as is the growing attraction between Setsuko and Shoji, which at first threatens to spoil their free-and-easy friendship. A delicate fable of growing up. SFe

Moon in the Gutter, The (La Lune dans le Caniveau)
(Jean-Jacques Beineix, 1983, Fr/It) Gérard Depardieu, Nastassja Kinski, Victoria Abril, Vittorio Mezzogiorno, Dominique Pinon, Bertice Reading, Milena Vukotic.
137 min.
Like Beineix's debut feature Diva, this is a film of dazzling surface and equally dazzling superficiality; but where Diva was taut and full of action, The Moon in the Gutter is slow and portentous. Based on David Goodis' thriller about a bloodstain on a street and a stevedore obsessed with finding the man who raped his sister and prompted her suicide, the film expands the compressed plot of the novel into a catalogue of glossy images, all of it shot in the studio. The crux of the story is the relationship between the hulking stevedore (Depardieu) and a rich femme (Kinski) who, far from being fatale, represents the impossible dream at the end of his investigative quest. Beineix does manage to charge the affair with a sense of fierce anticipation; that aside, the film seems like an exercise in the non-development of narrative. In the end, though it's not the disaster the French press cracked it up to be, only the images stay in the memory as the Fabergé egg lies smashed on the floor, a pile of glittering fragments. RR

Moon in the Mirror, The (La Luna en el Espejo)
(Silvio Caiozzi, 1990, Chile) Gloria Munchmeyer, Rafael Benavente, Ernesto Beadle.
105 min.
A slight, but charming piece about a cantankerous, bedridden old bully and the deleterious effect he has on his shy, corpulent son's wooing of a neighbouring widow. At first the tone is light and semi-comic. Later, however, it shifts to a darker acknowledgement of complicitous emotional enslavement. Imaginatively shot, sensitively acted. GA

Moon Is Blue, The
(Otto Preminger, 1953, US) William Holden, David Niven, Maggie McNamara, Dawn Addams, Tom Tully.
99 min. b/w.
Despite the fuss at the time, there's little blue about this except the title: a stage-bound adaptation of F Hugh Herbert's mildly amusing and mildly naughty romantic comedy – typical Broadway 'sophistication'– about a girl retaining her honour while snaring her man. McNamara is the pixie picked up by Holden on top of the Empire State Building (that's the 'opening out' bit), accepting a dinner invitation to his flat, and causing some tiresome altercations when the middle-aged and lecherous Niven (father of Holden's ex-fiancée Addams) happens to drop in. Amazing to think that the power of the Hollywood Production Code (not to mention the League of Decency) was effectively broken because Preminger insisted on retaining such shocking obscenities as 'virgin', 'seduce' and 'mistress' in the dialogue. TM

Moonlight and Valentino
(David Anspaugh, 1995, US) Elizabeth Perkins, Whoopi Goldberg, Kathleen Turner, Gwyneth Paltrow, Jon Bon Jovi, Jeremy Sisto, Josef Sommer, Shadia Simmons.
104 min.
A women's film, '90s style. When her husband

dies, Rebecca (Perkins) can't bring herself to pronounce the W-word, but she's immediately surrounded by an ad hoc support group – neighbour Goldberg, sister Paltrow, and mother-in-law Turner – all too ready to put her in her weeds. Each woman comes with a badge denoting her own special interest group: the widow, the wife, the virgin and the divorcee. It's like a convention. Grudges and recriminations surface, the inevitable 'intimacy issues', but nothing too disruptive, nothing that can't be put right with a cathartic group hug. You can gauge the sensitivity factor from Rebecca's creative writing assignment: write a poem without words. The film has a neat line in neat lines, gets a lift from Paltrow's palpable sexual anxiety, but works much too hard for its tears. In his first major role, Jon Bon Jovi plays a sex object, and he's every bit as anaemic as the rest. Based on an autobiographical play by Ellen Simon (Neil's daughter). TCh

Moonlighting
(Jerzy Skolimowski, 1982, GB) Jeremy Irons, Eugene Lipinski, Jiri Stanislaw, Eugeniusz Haczkiewicz, Denis Holmes, Jenny Seagrove, Jerzy Skolimowski.
97 min.
Conceived and made with an urgency appropriate to the December 1981 military clampdown on Skolimowski's native Poland, this film is a characteristically oblique and quirky response. Displacement rather than confrontation is the key, with a group of Polish builders busy renovating their boss' London house when the axe falls at home. Irons plays their leader, the only English speaker, who is forced into a parody of twisted labour relations when he decides to conceal the news from his co-workers. But the tendency towards allegory is pleasingly offset by an alienated vision of the English daily round: a farcical and surreal mixture of frustration, deception and shoplifting. The result is as much about 'us' as 'them';, and constitutes a quietly disturbing, often sharply amusing, flip side to Wajda's men of marble and iron. SJ

Moon Over Parador
(Paul Mazursky, 1988, US) Richard Dreyfuss, Raul Julia, Sonia Braga, Jonathan Winters, Fernando Rey, Sammy Davis Jr, Paul Mazursky.
104 min.
This broad farce set in a fictional Latin American country has actor Dreyfuss, having finished work on a movie shot on location in Parador, expressing his desire to find the part of a lifetime. He little bargains for what follows: bearing a resemblance to the country's dictator, he is abducted by Chief of Police Julia and forced to impersonate the recently deceased tyrant in order to forestall revolution. Inevitably, after initial stage nerves, he takes to the part, revelling in deception and falling for the dead man's mistress (Braga), who persuades him to disobey his captors and involve himself in social reforms. Cameos by Mazursky himself (as the late dictator's mother) and Sammy Davis Jr only increase the impression that the whole thing is a lazy, self-indulgent home movie born of its creator's taste for theatricality. For one brief moment, with a malignant CIA introduced, the film looks a little more promising, but all too soon it slips back into soppy sentimentality. GA

Moon Over the Alley, The
(Joseph Despins, 1975, GB) Doris Fishwick, Peter Farrell, Erna May, John Gay, Sean Caffrey, Sharon Forester.
102 min. b/w.
About the lives of a number of dwellers in a rooming-house just off the Portobello Road, well within the Loach/Garnett tradition of environmental realism, but at the same time managing the infusion of poeticism implicit in the title by means of Kurt Weill-esque songs (music by Hair arranger Galt MacDermot). Though the characters initially come across as well-trodden kitchen sink stereotypes – frustrated adolescents, suspicious middle-aged parents, a young Jamaican couple, an Irish bartender, reclusive 'dirty old man' – the film quickly disarms with its quirky humour. Laughs aside, it's a far from complacent look at the problems of an increasingly squalid London. RM

Moonraker
(Lewis Gilbert, 1979, GB/Fr) Roger Moore, Lois Chiles, Michel Lonsdale, Richard Kiel, Emily Bolton, Toshiro Suga.
126 min.
After one bravura *Superman* parody, one space battle, half-a-dozen seductions, and a host of gags, you feel that Bond has turned into a one-man variety show. But *Moonraker* is mercifully much better than recent Bondage, with fantastic special effects, some excellent buffery (cracks at *Star Wars*, *Close Encounters*, Clint Eastwood, to name but a few), and the usual location-hopping style that makes Versailles feel like Disneyland. The space-age plot is spread dangerously thin, the fights all tend to slapstick, and the wanton destruction has become rather too predictable. But it's held together by likeable performances (Kiel as 'Jaws', Lonsdale as a suitably urbane villain) and, above all, an overwhelming level of tongue-in-cheek. CA

Moonrise
(Frank Borzage, 1948, US) Dane Clark, Gail Russell, Ethel Barrymore, Allyn Joslyn, Harry Morgan, Rex Ingram, Lloyd Bridges, Selena Royle.
90 min. b/w.
Perhaps Borzage's greatest film, *Moonrise*, a brooding tale of a murderer's son (Clark) driven to violence by others harping on his past, is the perfect answer to those critics who have derided Borzage as a 'mere' romantic, a mere celebrator of the magic of love. Deeply melancholic, the film creates a sense of physical reality with its low-key lighting and harsh compositions that Borzage's lovers on the run cannot defeat: their 'Seventh Heaven' in an abandoned mansion is only temporary. PH

Moonrunners
(Gy Waldron, 1974, US) James Mitchum, Kiel Martin, Chris Forbes, Arthur Hunnicutt, Joan Blackman, George Ellis, Waylon Jennings, Spanky McFarland.
102 min.
Essentially an extended car chase laced with nuggets of wisdom dispensed by a moonshiner from way back (played by Arthur Hunnicutt, creating an island of watchability in the surrounding mishmash). *Moonrunners* assembles a grateful crate of familiar ingredients – the banjo-picking accompaniment, the car chases, some thick-ear rough stuff, a plot that makes gestures toward supporting the rugged individualist against the syndicate – all articulated with minimum atmosphere and maximum country-style mugging. It lacks even the slightly redeeming oddness of *The Lolly-Madonna War*; and James Mitchum gives an especially charmless performance in the lead, making his final words about 'going to Nashville to become a star' ring extremely hollow. VG

Moonshine War, The
(Richard Quine, 1970, US) Patrick McGoohan, Richard Widmark, Alan Alda, Lee Hazlewood, Joe Williams, Will Geer, Melanie Johnson.
100 min.
Amiable caper adapted by Elmore Leonard from his own novel about whisky hijackers in hillbilly country just before the repeal of Prohibition, with McGoohan's scarecrow ex-revenue agent and Widmark's Rabelaisian struck-off dentist joining forces to lay siege to Alda's hidden cache of moonshine when money, guile and threats get them nowhere. Directing with one eye very much on *Bonnie and Clyde*, Quine makes heavy weather of the tone and style, but the characterisations – abetted by nice dialogue – make it more enjoyable than not. TM

Moonstruck
(Norman Jewison, 1987, US) Cher, Nicolas Cage, Vincent Gardenia, Olympia Dukakis, Danny Aiello, Julie Bovasso, John Mahoney, Feodor Chaliapin.
102 min.
Jewison's Italo-American movie mainly comprises the look of things: the family table, the homely Italian restaurant, Cher, the moon over Brooklyn Bridge. Widowed Loretta (Cher), engaged to dull Johnny (Aiello), contacts his brother Ronny (Cage) to invite him to the wedding; they fall in love. Her father (Gardenia), too, is having an affair. Both adulterer and suitor seem driven to passion by depression, though Cage's hammy performance convinces less than Gardenia's glooming over his glasses. Jewison gently mocks the old ways of formal respect and sexism. Stronger on mores than amore, a half smile for a summer night. BC

Moonwalker
(Colin Chilvers/Jerry Kramer, 1988, US) Michael Jackson, Joe Pesci, Sean Lennon, Kellie Parker, Brandon Adams.
93 min.
What begins like a concert movie and ends with the dull whimper of a moralising fairytale for TV kids is, startlingly enough, a long and expensive pop video. The fact that it is a cut-and-paste job, interpolating chunks of Jackson history in with a sequence of rather feeble cartoon-dominated 'episodes', lends the whole adventure the distinctly un-cinematic ambience of a fanzine, which is great for the fans. Mum and Dad and baby sibling, however, will be alarmed and bored by the spectacle – the former alarmed by the vast displacement of cash on so witless a project, and bored because it's boring, the latter frustrated because a human version of *My Little Pony* is not as entertaining as the real thing. Altogether a ghastly experience, which even the rabid 11-year-old in your life might well find patronising and unimaginative. NC

Moon Warriors (Zhan Shen Chuanshuo)
(Samo Hung, 1992, HK) Andy Lau, Maggie Cheung, Anita Mui, Kenny Bee.
86 min.
A mythic tale of crossed swords and double-crossed allegiances, princes, peasants and killer bamboo, Samo Hung's film is a visually splendid, dramatically rich, but somewhat rarefied martial arts yarn. Andy Lau (*Days of Being Wild*) is Fei, a peasant fisherman who finds himself protecting the beautiful princess Yueh (Mui) and her betrothed, the rightful heir to the kingdom, who has been usurped by his evil younger brother. Taking refuge in an ancient subterranean palace, it becomes clear there's a traitor in their midst. Much imaginative staging, even if the romanticism sometimes topples into kitsch (Hei Wei the whale seems to have swum out of a Disney picture). The highly acrobatic fights, however, are oddly uninvolving. TCh

Mord und Totschlag
see Degree of Murder, A

More About the Language of Love (Mera ur Kärlekens Språk)
(Torgny Wickman, 1970, Swe) Inge Hegeler, Sten Hegeler, Maj-Brith Bergström-Walan, Ove Arström.
97 min.
A follow-up to *The Language of Love* which is just as clumsily directed – all those round-the-coffee-table sex chats and unrelated street scenes! Stonily serious, the film is clearly informational (if on a grade school level) rather than exploitative, with the most detailed and basic demonstrations being the most successful sequences. Problems considered are homosexuality (male and female, superficially); VD (also superficially); sex and the handicapped; and impotence. One sequence deals with a repressive commune whose exploitation of its female members goes without comment by the pundits. VG

More American Graffiti
(BWL Norton, 1979, US) Candy Clark, Bo Hopkins, Ron Howard, Paul Le Mat, Mackenzie Phillips, Charles Martin Smith, Cindy Williams, Anna Bjorn.
111 min.
Richard Dreyfuss' price proved too high, otherwise the whole gang returns for a sequel which builds its highly episodic narrative around a last reunion at a New Year's Eve drag race in 1964, used as an anchor from which to flash forward through the '60s; but the film's problems arise less from the confusing time structure than from the misguided determination to preserve the tone of the original at all costs. In the world of Vietnam, drugs and revolution, what was genuine innocence becomes glib farce, and Norton's refusal to register the darkening of the kids' world quickly makes that world itself less real. DP

More Bad News

(Adrian Edmondson, 1987, GB) Adrian
Edmondson, Rik Mayall, Nigel Planer, Peter
Richardson, Jennifer Saunders, Dawn French.
53 min.

A spoof rockumentary from TV's Comic Strip.
It's 1987, four years after Bad News, the heavy
alloy outfit, broke up in a welter of bitterness,
apathy and prawn tandoori. Since then, Colin
(Mayall) has become a bank clerk, Spider
(Richardson) has retreated to rural hippiedom,
and Den (Planer) has been getting by as a painter
and decorator. Only Vim (Edmondson) has kept
the faith, playing Mary Hopkins numbers in wine
bars and lovingly transcribing songs sent to him
from beyond the grave by John Lennon. Now
they've been acrimoniously reunited to play the
Castle Donnington Monsters of Rock festival,
alongside Motorhead, Def Leppard et al. If you
like the Comic Strip, and want to know what 100
pints of lager in the local Indian does to your
deportment, this is for you. DAt-

More the Merrier, The

(George Stevens, 1943, US) Jean Arthur, Joel
McCrea, Charles Coburn, Bruce Bennett,
Richard Gaines, Ann Savage, Ann Doran.
104 min. b/w.

The housing shortage in wartime Washington
provides the pretext for this engaging post-screw-
ball comedy, remade some two decades later as
Walk, Don't Run. Prim Jean Arthur reluctantly
agrees to take Coburn as a boarder, and the next
thing she knows he has sublet his half of the
apartment to handsome McCrea. Their ménage à
trois is innocent enough, but inevitably Arthur's
marriage plans come in for modification. Coburn
won an Oscar for his supporting role as the mischievous old matchmaker Mr Dingle, but the real
pleasure lies in the sympathetic ensemble playing: the trio trying to stick to Arthur's farcical
morning schedule; sunbathing on the roof reading Dick Tracy; or the young lovers necking on
the front steps. Shooting through and around
doors, windows and paper-thin walls, Stevens
achieves a credible sense of what it's like living
in someone else's space. Despite a belated drift
towards sentimentality, this remains a refreshingly intimate movie. TCh

Morgan, a Suitable
Case for Treatment

(Karel Reisz, 1966, GB) David Warner,
Vanessa Redgrave, Robert Stephens, Irene
Handl, Newton Blick, Nan Munro, Bernard
Bresslaw, Arthur Mullard, Graham Crowden.
97 min. b/w.

Because it struggles to combine the Royal Court
world of Anger and After playwrights (fantasising artist with Communist mother and rich wife
in Kensington) with what Lester and Antonioni
were doing to British cinema at the time, this version of David Mercer's TV play all but loses the
theme of genuine madness underneath. Morgan,
a part that suits David Warner down to the
ground, sabotages his wife's second marriage,
dressing up as a gorilla, rewiring her house, etc;
but the character is itself short-circuited by being
surrounded with eccentrics (Handl, Bresslaw,
Mullard) as dotty as he is. Morgan sticks in the
memory as a collection of funny moments, with
the fatal habit (shared by If..., among others) of
confronting issues, then farting around when the
going gets rough. AN

Morning After, The

(Sidney Lumet, 1986, US) Jane Fonda, Jeff
Bridges, Raúl Julia, Diane Salinger, Richard
Foronjy, Geoffrey Scott.
103 min.

Sometime promising actress turned lush Fonda
wakes up to find, in her bed, a dead man with a
knife through his heart. She panics and tries to
flee the state, but thwarted by airport bureaucracy, ends up taking her chances with redneck ex-
cop Bridges. Focusing on the central character's
struggle towards a tentative moral redemption,
Lumet creates a film more intense than tense,
more low-key character study than thriller. Fonda
captures the duplicity of an actress playing a role,
while Bridges' restraint provides the perfect foil
for her neurotic mannerisms. But Lumet's narrative economy, sympathetic handling of actors, and
superb eye never quite jell. It's as if a talented
director has made the most of what he had, when
what he had was never quite enough. NF

Morning Departure
(aka Operation Disaster)

(Roy Baker, 1949, GB) John Mills, Helen
Cherry, Richard Attenborough, Lana Morris,
Nigel Patrick, George Cole, Bernard Lee, James
Hayter, Kenneth More.
102 min. b/w.

Hit by a mine, a crippled submarine sinks to the
sea floor, killing all but twelve of its crew – only
eight of whom can escape. Stiff upper lips are
brandished for'ard, aft and amidships, except by
the always emotional Attenborough, who is
reduced to a hysterical wreck by the thought of
his slow demise. If the claustrophobia gets a bit
too much for you, you might like to speculate
upon the fact that this was originally a stage
play. NF

Morocco

(Josef von Sternberg, 1930, US) Marlene
Dietrich, Gary Cooper, Adolphe Menjou, Ulrich
Haupt, Juliette Compton, Francis McDonald.
92 min. b/w.

Sternberg's first Hollywood film with Dietrich
looks like a deliberate reversal of their first collaboration on The Blue Angel the year before in
Germany. Dietrich plays another sumptuous
vamp, but this time one who is retreating from
her past by taking a one-way ticket to Morocco…
as although she runs delicately cruel rings around
Menjou's affection for her, she ultimately sacrifices everything for the man she truly loves,
legionnaire Gary Cooper. It's been customary to
dismiss Sternberg's 'absurd' plots as mere vehicles for his experiments with lighting and decor,
and his loving explorations of Dietrich's visual
and emotional possibilities. The truth is that films
like Morocco are completely homogeneous: the
plotting and acting are in exactly the same
expressionist register as everything else. Here,
the highly nuanced portraits of men and a woman
caught between the codes they live by and their
deepest, secret impulses, remain very moving and
100 per cent modern. TR

Morons from Outer Space

(Mike Hodges, 1985, GB) Mel Smith, Griff
Rhys Jones, Joanne Pearce, Jimmy Nail, Paul
Bown, James B Sikking, Dinsdale Landen.
97 min.

This ineptly combines lamebrain comedy and
sci-fi adventure, two of Hollywood's most popular genres of the last decade. Four dimwitted
aliens get lost in space, crash on the M1, and are
adopted by Rhys Jones, who immediately recognises their potential as pop stars and chat show
persons. The whole mess ends with the rock
concert now obligatory in a certain type of
British movie. Both Hodges (Get Carter, Pulp)
and Smith & Jones (Not the Nine O'Clock News),
who also scripted, have promising track
records; but here, despite straining every sinew
desperately, they provide a minimal quotient of
chuckles. RR

Mortal Kombat

(Paul Anderson, 1995, US) Christopher
Lambert, Robin Shou, Linden Ashby, Cary-
Hiroyuki Tagawa, Bridgette Wilson, Talisa
Soto, Trevor Goddard.
101 min.

As video-game-inspired movies go, this
remains leagues ahead of last year's Street
Fighter. Of course, there's only so much one can
do with a game that never leaves the fighting
arena, but British director Anderson does a fair
job with what he was given: four good-looking
leads, some very impressive sfx, Babylonian
sets, a bone-crunching soundtrack, and a battery of well-choreographed fights. That the plot
occasionally reaches areas so ambiguous as to
be unfathomable is beside the point; this is
about hand-to-hand combat, pure and simple.
Lambert plays Rayden, a highly-charged
friendly God from the mystical Outworld. Not
so friendly to sorcerer Shang Tsung (Tagawa),
host of Outworld's infamous tournament where
groups of humans go into battle against
unearthly combatants and generally wind up
getting thrashed. With Earth as the main prize,
it's finally left to the skills of Rayden's three
new hopefuls – Liu Kang (Shou), Johnny Cage
(Ashby), and Sonya Blade (Wilson) – to wrest
the fate of the planet from Outworld's grasp.
DA

Mortal Kombat 2:
Annihilation

(John R Leonetti, 1997, US) Robin Shou, Talisa
Soto, Brian Thompson, Sandra Hess, Lynn
Red Williams, Irina Pantaeva, Deron McBee.
95 min.

The ruler of Outworld, Shao-Khan, attempts yet
again to merge his planet with Earth. It's a toss
up which aspect of this drivel is worst: the pre-
school performances; the elementary fantasy-
speak; the design (purple and more purple); the
lack of continuity (characters miraculously
cleaned up following mud fights in the middle of
nowhere); the action scenes (the cast spend most
of their time somersaulting); the editing; the camerawork… DA

Mortal Storm, The

(Frank Borzage, 1940, US) Margaret Sullavan,
James Stewart, Robert Young, Frank Morgan,
Irene Rich, Robert Stack, Bonita Granville,
Maria Ouspenskaya, Dan Dailey.
100 min. b/w.

One of Hollywood's invariably slightly embarrassing attempts to get to grips with the Nazi
peril. Set in an all-American small town in
Germany on the eve of Hitler's appointment as
Chancellor of the Third Reich, with the narrator
pontificating about 'the mortal storm in which
man finds himself today', it constantly teeters on
the brink of absurd naiveté, kept more or less on
balance by skill, sincerity and good intentions.
The film is almost retrieved by the touching
Sullavan/Stewart love affair, shaping up to be one
of those incandescent romantic visions transcending reality that is the mark of a Borzage
film. The fact that it doesn't quite work that way
is probably because almost the entire film was
directed, uncredited, by Victor Saville. TM

Mortal Thoughts

(Alan Rudolph, 1991, US) Demi Moore, Glenne
Headly, Bruce Willis, John Pankow, Harvey
Keitel, Billie Neal, Frank Vincent.
103 min.

This intricate, intellectually satisfying and emotionally involving murder mystery risks falling
between two stools. Neither an 'Alan Rudolph
Film' nor a glossy star vehicle, it has a naturalistic tone, a conventional plot, measured pacing,
and a serpentine narrative. It opens powerfully:
Moore, giving evidence on her own free will, is
questioned by detective Keitel. We flash back and
forth in time as she relates events leading to an
as yet unknown crime. Headly, who plays the
happy-go-lucky owner of a hairdressing salon
where Moore works, has a drunken, violent husband (Willis) whom she constantly jokes about
bumping off. But Keitel senses that Moore's
account of their volatile three-way relationship
doesn't add up: who is she protecting, and from
what? Rudolph makes excellent use of video technology, and coaxes outstanding performances
from the three leads. NF

Mort de Mario Ricci, La

see Death of Mario Ricci, The

Morte a Venezia

see Death in Venice

Morte di un Operatore

see Death of a Cameraman

Mortelle Randonnée

see Deadly Run

Mort en ce Jardin, La
(Evil Eden)

(Luis Buñuel, 1956, Fr/Mex) Georges Marchal,
Simone Signoret, Charles Vanel, Michèle
Girardon, Michel Piccoli, Tito Junco.
97 min.

Buñuel uses an interesting genre: The Wages of
Fear inspired left wing French film-makers to join
Mexican producers and make very violent melo-
dramas with Third Worldish themes. Here, in a
Bolivia-type state, clashes between troops and
striking miners force a jungle trek on an ill-
starred gang: a prostitute (Signoret), a priest
(Piccoli), a trader (Vanel), an adventurer
(Marchal), a deaf-mute beauty (Girardon). Jungle
hazards include snakes, thirst, toilet-paper prob-

lems, and the bourgeois joys of looting a wrecked plane. Its garish, vicious action beats Sam Fuller at his own game, and adds philosophical suspense, as jungle paranoia makes Marxist fraternity look as delirious as a Surrealist dream. Co-writer is Raymond Queneau, the Picasso of avant-garde writing. RD

Mortgage
(Bill Bennett, 1989, Aust) Brian Vriends, Doris Youanne, Bruce Venables, Andrew Gilbert.
90 min.
Australian director Bennett drafted in real solicitors and architects to play themselves, while leaving his actors to stand in for the unsuspecting would-be home-owners in this documentary-style drama, which will draw groans of recognition from those who've been through the war zone of the housing market themselves. Bennett used the same technique in Malpractice to explore the legal and medical ramifications following the delivery in hospital of a brain damaged baby. TJ

Moscow Distrusts Tears (Moskva Slezam ne Verit)
(Vladimir Menshov, 1979, USSR) Vera Alentova, Alexei Batalov, Irina Muraveva, Alexandr Fatiushin, Raisa Ryazanova.
152 min.
Moscow Distrusts Tears, maybe, but not Hollywood: incredibly, Menshov's jejune melodrama was awarded an Oscar for Best Foreign Language Film. By *The Three Sisters* out of *How to Marry a Millionaire* (or rather, in the Workers' State, a hockey champion or TV cameraman), its rambling plot involves a trio of provincial factory girls descending on the capital and setting their caps at every eligible member of the local intelligentsia. Twenty years later, predictability has set in with a vengeance: divorce, loneliness, intimations of mortality, as well as the providential apparition of a nice, virile hyper-sensitive mate for the most obviously sympathetic of the three. Well acted, occasionally amusing, but at over two hours, quite interminable. Heartwarming assurance that escapism is the same the world over. GAd

Moscow on the Hudson
(Paul Mazursky, 1984, US) Robin Williams, Maria Conchita Alonso, Cleavant Derricks, Alejandro Rey, Savely Kramarov.
117 min.
When Russian saxophone player Vladimir (Williams) visits New York, his experiences back home lead him to defect, leaving family, friends and a familiar culture for the pursuit of pleasure and freedom. But after the initial delirium, he slowly finds that the Big Apple is rife with poverty, racism, unemployment, and mugging. Mazursky's comedy may not exactly be politically profound, with its suggestion that freedom and happiness are relative concepts. But where it scores so highly is not only in its ability to evoke Vladimir's astonishment at the bizarre, sometimes brutal texture of New York life, but also in the generosity it extends to the musician's sad predicament. Even the absurdity and chaos of his department store defection (treated by the surrounding Americans as yet another media spectacle) becomes in Mazursky's hands a heroic moment of private, victorious self-assertion. Romantic humanism may not be fashionable in these cynical cinematic times, but few directors reveal the tragicomic lives of ordinary people with such sensitivity and humour. GA

Moses
(Gianfranco De Bosio, 1975, It/GB) Burt Lancaster, Anthony Quayle, Ingrid Thulin, Irene Papas, Aharon Ipale, Yousef Shiloah, Marina Berti, Laurent Terzieff.
141 min.
'We must follow' – 'Follow? Where to?' – 'To the Promised Land – where else?' This long collection of edited highlights from the 360-minute Lew Grade TV series is sunk right from the start by some of the most pathetic 'epic' dialogue since Victor Mature said, 'Bring in a woman and you bring in trouble' during *Samson and Delilah*. But at least DeMille's splurges had cohesion and some sort of visual unity; *Moses* jumbles up half-formed ideas (the Egyptians as emaciated and verbose intellectuals, for example) with patches of realism, to produce something that is totally

without style. The special effects are cut-price (directed by Mario Bava, so we might have expected better) and compare poorly with those of *The Ten Commandments*. So when the script finally becomes interesting, pitting Moses against an implacable God, the effect has already been sabotaged – by the second-rate manifestations of His vengeance, by an unsympathetic gang of Israelites/extras, and by Lancaster's wooden performance ('The punctilious observance of the Sabbath, as you so grandiloquently term it...'). AN

Moses and Aaron (Moses und Aron)
(Jean-Marie Straub/Danièle Huillet, 1975, WGer/Fr) Günter Reich, Louis Devos, Werner Mann, Eva Csapó, Roger Lucas, Richard Salter.
110 min.
As in Straub/Huillet's *Chronicle of Anna Magdalena Bach*, the soundtrack comes first: a performance, sung live on location, of Schönberg's passionately dialectical opera. The original is notoriously difficult to stage adequately, and Straub's 'materialist' approach serves it better than any theatrical production is ever likely to; the precise, ultra-concrete images are simple enough to permit concentration on the score, and (again like the Bach film) sufficiently charged to generate a passionate intensity of their own. TR

Mosquito Coast, The
(Peter Weir, 1986, US) Harrison Ford, Helen Mirren, River Phoenix, André Gregory, Dick O'Neill, Martha Plimpton, Conrad Roberts.
119 min.
Given that Paul Theroux's harrowing tale of jungle craziness is one of the least filmable properties of recent years, Weir's river journey to the heart of darkness works considerably better than one might imagine. Meticulously translated from the book, *Mosquito Coast* charts the mental decline and fall of idealistic inventor Allie Fox, who drags wife and family to the jungles of Central America in a doomed effort to bring ice to the natives. Although it's too long, with Weir attempting to negotiate too many psychological bends in Theroux's *River of No Return*, the director still manages to conjure out of the breathtaking landscape a genuine whiff of mental and physical hell, and in so doing draws from Harrison Ford a tour de force performance as mad Allie. Indeed, this is Ford's movie: Helen Mirren's flower-child-gone-to-seed wife and son Charlie (Phoenix), the heart and voice of the novel, are mere jungle shadows in comparison. Wherein lies the film's major flaw; for try as he might, after a lifetime playing the ultimate hero, Ford finally fails to convince as the ultimate villain, particularly when he's back battling natives à la Indiana Jones. A brave and serious piece of film-making, nevertheless. DAt

Mosquito Squadron
(Boris Sagal, 1968, GB) David McCallum, Suzanne Neve, David Buck, David Dundas, Dinsdale Landen, Charles Gray, Vladek Sheybal, Robert Urquhart.
90 min.
One of those WWII movies you'd thought they couldn't possibly make any more, with stiff-upper-lip quota filled to bursting as our brave boys in blue embark on low-level bombing raids to destroy V3 and V4 development installations in Germany. It means well, and stages the action competently enough, but that doesn't weigh much against the balance of a preposterously contrived script. McCallum is the squadron leader who falls for Neve, wife of his best friend (Buck) after the latter is reported missing, presumed killed in action. Then news comes that Buck is alive and being held hostage in the very château the squadron has orders to destroy. Cue for moral decision-making of the Boy's Own Paper variety. TM

Moss Rose
(Gregory Ratoff, 1947, US) Peggy Cummins, Victor Mature, Ethel Barrymore, Vincent Price, Margo Woode, George Zucco, Patricia Medina.
82 min. b/w.
Don't look too closely at the plot of this slice of Edwardian Gothic about a chorus girl (Cummins, not yet immortalised by *Gun Crazy*) who worms

her way into an olde English household by blackmailing an invitation out of the young master (Mature, no less) who supposedly murdered her friend. Soon, silly girl, she is next in line to be done away with. Motivation is nobody's strong point, and poor Price's police inspector has to play singularly dumb (sitting on the fact that two murders are linked by a Bible and a pressed rose) to keep the pot boiling. Enjoyable, though, and beautifully shot by Joe MacDonald, with Ethel Barrymore rather splendidly doing her thing as a possessive matriarch. TM

Most Dangerous Game, The (aka The Hounds of Zaroff)
(Ernest B Schoedsack/Irving Pichel, 1932, US) Joel McCrea, Fay Wray, Leslie Banks, Robert Armstrong, Noble Johnson.
63 min. b/w.
By far the most chilling version of Richard Connell's much adapted and imitated short story, boasting an authentic touch of de Sade in Leslie Banks' performance as the world-weary big game hunter and connoisseur of arcane pleasures, possessor of a remote island fortress to which he ensures that passing ships are attracted and then wrecked on the reefs. 'First the hunt, then the revels' he purrs – with Fay Wray clearly destined to be the reluctant object of those revels – as he suavely entertains his guests while outlining the rules of the hunt against a human quarry he has devised to tickle his jaded palate, highly delighted to discover a worthy opponent in McCrea, a hunter almost his equal in celebrity. Still one of the best and most literate movies from the great days of horror, it is particularly effective in its measured graduation from words to action with the long, ferocious, beautifully choreographed hunt sequence, in which the human prey ironically wins the day by drawing on all his reserves of animal cunning. TM

Most Dangerous Man Alive
(Allan Dwan, 1961, US) Ron Randell, Debra Paget, Elaine Stewart, Anthony Caruso, Gregg Palmer, Morris Ankrum.
82 min. b/w.
For the range and quantity of his output, Dwan has frequently been compared to Howard Hawks, and like Hawks he made one science fiction movie late in his career (his last film, in fact). But despite an interesting theme about a mobster who survives an atomic explosion to become a fugitive of steel, it's no *Thing from Another World*. Its bleak, uncompromising narrative and austere visuals are closer to a gangster B picture than sci-fi, and only three sequences (including a semi-nightmarish episode in which the heroine tries to arouse the metallic villain) are really memorable. The film does, however, contain one classic moment. The villain has been horribly mutilated by a nuclear explosion, has murdered five people, and is about to be incinerated by flame-throwers: 'If you tell the truth', the heroine shouts to him, 'there won't be anything to worry about'. This, incidentally, was the film being remade in Wim Wenders' The State of Things. DP

Most Desired Man, The
see Bewegte Mann, Der

Most Terrible Time in My Life, The (Waga Jinsei Saiaku no Toki)
(Kaizo Hayashi, 1993, Jap/Tai/China) Masatoshi Nagase, Yang Haitin, Kiyotaka Nanbara, Shiro Sano.
92 min.
To Sleep, So As to Dream and *Circus Boys* marked Kaizo Hayashi as an expert pasticheur of old movie styles, but this loving tribute to 'Scope thrillers of the Seijun Suzuki kind (complete with a Joe Shishido guest appearance) is something else again. Masatoshi Nagase stars as Yokohama private eye Mike Hama tangling with a gang of Chinese/Korean immigrants who call themselves 'The New Japs' and uncovering a plot to rearrange crime in East Asia. Cutting hard from laughs to gut-wrenching violence, featuring a cast of exceptionally beautiful hitmen and revelling in wicked subtexts, this is a rapturous entertainment. It comes with a recommendation from the Japan Detective Agency Association, so you know it makes sense. TR

Most Wanted

(David Hogan, 1997, US) Keenen Ivory Wayans, Jon Voight, Jill Hennessy, Paul Sorvino, Robert Culp, Wolfgang Bodison.
99 min.
Facing the hot seat after killing his commanding officer in a fight during the Gulf War, decorated marksman Sgt James Dunn (Wayans) is given one last, covert opportunity to redeem himself. Col Grant Casey (Voight) recruits him for the elite 'Black Sheep' hit squad, his first assignment being one Donald Bickhart (Culp), a biotechnology magnate accompanying the First Lady to a public dedication. Or so it seems. At any rate, Dunn doesn't have much choice. When another gun fires, however, just as he's taking aim, and the President's wife drops dead, he realises he's the fall guy for a political assassination. 'The First Lady...Wow!' surmises the CIA Deputy Director (Sorvino). Written by Wayans, this unexceptional chase movie takes itself rather seriously, but at least it knows the ground. NB

Motel

(Christian Blackwood, 1989, US/WGer)
86 min.
Blackwood's free-wheeling documentary is actually a series of mini-films that suggest everything from Fred Wiseman to *Raising Arizona*. The first pitstop is The Silver Saddle, New Mexico, run by three redoubtable women. The most conventional of the sequences, it's still marked with expansive curiosity and grotesque humour. The guests at The Blue Mist – situated opposite the Arizona State Prison – are mostly wives of the inmates, and include a former guard, staying in the infamous room 22. Here a con on furlough chopped up his mother, before making the fundamental error of trying to sell the pieces to the local grocer. Then there's The Amargosa, complete with its own theatre, in a ghost town, pop. 4, and The Movie Manor, which backs on to a drive-in cinema. And why not? TCh

Mother

(Albert Brooks, 1996, US) Albert Brooks, Debbie Reynolds, Rob Morrow, Lisa Kudrow, John C McGinley, Isabel Glasser.
104 min.
Brooks is a sorely under-rated movie-maker in Britain. Andrew Sarris called *Mother* the best film of 1996, but here it is, a year later, sneaking out straight to video. That said, it doesn't lose much on the small screen, where its subtle, quietly devastating observations on dysfunctional families and male neuroses look right at home. In *Lost in America* Brooks hit the road in a camper van to 'touch Indians'; here, twice divorced, but still intrepid, he moves back in with mom to get to the root of his problems with women. He's aggressive; she's impassive. 'The Experiment' isn't very scientific, but it gradually gets (rather pat) results. There aren't many films which tackle the generation gap between middle-aged kids and their old folks with such unsentimental comic acuity – and Reynolds essays her best role in three decades with delectable good grace and charm. TCh

Mother (Mat)

(Vsevolod Pudovkin, 1926, USSR) Vera Baranovskaya, Nikolai Batalov, A Chistyakov, Ivan Koval-Samborsky, Anna Zemtzova.
5,906 ft. b/w.
A major work from the heroic age of radical experiment in Russian cinema, this is a much altered reworking of Gorki's novel, about a peasant woman becoming a political militant after betraying her son's cache of arms to the police. Pudovkin tightened the overall structure, introduced the character of the drunken reactionary husband, and drew masterly performances from members of the Moscow Art Theatre. TR

Mother Alone, A (Duwata Mawaka Misa)

(Sumitra Peries, 1997, Sri Lanka) Sangeetha Weeraratne, Tony Ranasinghe, Sanath Gunathilake, Wasanthi Chathurani, Sriyani Amarasena.
130 min.
Jilted by her boyfriend as soon as she becomes pregnant, young Thushari is sent away to stay with her aunt; obviously, she can't now marry as her parents had arranged. It's pre-Independence Sri Lanka, and Thushari has already tried to induce a miscarriage. The problem is not all's well between aunt and uncle; Thushari comes home and is sent to another aunt. Adapted from a story by GB Senanayake, this rigidly episodic film conveys the stigma, confusion, helplessness and even tedium of being a single, young, disenfranchised mother. But for all its humanism, the plain storytelling never works in the film's favour; and at over two hours, it's very very slow. NB

Mother and Son (Mat i Syn/ Mutter und Sohn)

(Aleksandr Sokurov, 1997, Rus/Ger) Gudrun Geyer, Aleksei Ananishnov.
71 min.
Aleksandr Sokurov's previous films have borne such titles as *The Lonely Voice of Man*, *The Degraded* and *Sad Insensitivity*, accompanied by documentary 'elegies' – *Elegy*, *Russian Elegy*, and *Simple Elegy*. 'Why can't America make cinema like this?' Scorsese has asked. The answer is not hard to find. This is not only slow (lyrical), serious (ambitious) and sombre (unironic), it's almost entirely free of narrative, conflict and character development, and manifests such a fundamental disengagement from the dramatic conventions of the medium as to make Peter Greenaway, or even Robert Bresson, look like naturals for the next Hollywood dinosaur picture. In other words, not a lot happens. In a stone cottage, the mother (Geyer) lies dying, old and hushed and frail, tended by her son (Ananishnov). They speak of shared dreams and fears, and he picks her up and carries her through the countryside; the next day he takes another such walk, alone. In place of drama, Sokurov's recourse and inspiration is art, landscape painting in particular. The walks take us through beach, forest and mountain country; Sokurov and his cameraman Aleksei Fedorov compose it in serene, stylised tableaux, sometimes hazy or luminous, sometimes stretched or skewed, emphasising the surface of the film until the locations resemble painted studio backdrops. As a pastoral tone poem, the film is stunning; there are images here as remarkable as any in cinema. NB

Mother and the Whore, The (La Maman et la Putain)

(Jean Eustache, 1973, Fr) Jean-Pierre Léaud, Françoise Lebrun, Bernadette Lafont, Isabelle Weingarten, Jacques Renard, Pierre Cottrell, Bernard Eisenschitz, Jean Eustache.
219 min. b/w.
Three-and-a-half hours of people talking about sex sounds like a recipe for boredom; in Eustache's hands, it is anything but. There is no 'explicitness': the film is about attitudes to, and defences against, sex and the body. Using dialogue garnered entirely from real-life conversations and sticking entirely to a prepared script (no improvisation), Eustache has provided us with a ruthlessly sharp-eyed view of chic, supposedly liberated sexual relationships, revealing them to be no less a disaster area of tragic dimensions than their 'straighter' counterparts. Veronika (Lebrun) cripples herself by regarding herself entirely through male eyes; Alexandre (Léaud, playing a character eerily close to his standard screen persona) is revealed to be the victim of a greedy, self-regarding, and desperate chauvinism; Marie (the superb, strong Lafont) is a less fully delineated character, sadly allowed only two fierce rejoinders to Alexandre's blind demands. Each of the three holds part of the 'truth' about their situation; none can put the pieces together. *The Mother and the Whore* is an icy comment on the New Wave, informed throughout by Eustache's striking visual intelligence. VG

Mother, Jugs & Speed

(Peter Yates, 1976, US) Bill Cosby, Raquel Welch, Harvey Keitel, Allen Garfield, Dick Butkus, Bruce Davison, LQ Jones, Larry Hagman, Valerie Curtin.
98 min.
A totally inconsequential 'comedy-thriller' about rival freelance ambulance companies in LA. The film squanders its resources, both human (Cosby gets two funny lines, Keitel gets nothing) and automotive (the ambulances look like ice-cream vans) via a rambling, episodic excuse for a storyline and sub-minimal characterisation that makes *Crossroads* look like Ibsen. Incredible to think that Yates did *Bullitt* all those years ago, lamentable that a potential urban *M*A*S*H* should end up such an irredeemable, awesomely yawnsome farce. GD

Mother Küsters' Trip to Heaven (Mutter Küsters Fahrt zum Himmel)

(Rainer Werner Fassbinder, 1975, WGer) Brigitte Mira, Ingrid Caven, Margit Carstensen, Karl-Heinz Böhm, Irm Hermann, Gottfried John.
108 min.
One of Fassbinder's most provocative films, *Mother Küsters' Trip to Heaven* sets out to nail political exploitation on the left rather than the right. Factory worker Küsters, faced with the threat of redundancy, kills his boss and commits suicide. His widow (Mira) finds herself deserted by her family and friends...until a wealthy communist couple (Böhm and Carstensen) decide to make political capital from her plight. The film achieved the distinction of being banned from both the official Berlin Festival and its fringe event, the Forum. TR

Mother Night

(Keith Gordon, 1996, US) Nick Nolte, Sheryl Lee, Alan Arkin, John Goodman, Kirsten Dunst, David Strathairn, Norman Rodway, Kurt Vonnegut.
114 min.
This stylish adaptation of Kurt Vonnegut's novel is an idiosyncratic mix of historical realism, rapt fantasy and offbeat humour. Nolte is Howard W Campbell Jr, an apolitical American playwright in Nazi Germany whose work as a conduit for US intelligence, concealing encoded communiqués in his Jew-baiting broadcasts on German radio, yields widely inspirational Nazi propaganda. Living incognito in New York after the war, his eventual exposure gathers a storm of interested parties – Israeli war-crimes investigators, white supremacists, his supposedly dead wife. An ambivalent meditation on deception, personal responsibility and commitment in an enigmatic world; some may find the studied, circumspect style unaffecting, but there's no denying the fascination of the material. NB

Mother's Boys

(Yves Simoneau, 1993, US) Jamie Lee Curtis, Peter Gallagher, Joanne Whalley-Kilmer, Vanessa Redgrave, Luke Edwards, Joss Ackland.
95 min.
Just when you thought every conceivable permutation of the 'home invasion' plot had been worked, along comes this flashy, vapid variation. The twist here is that the 'happy family' consists of Gallagher, his three kids, and his schoolmarm girlfriend Whalley-Kilmer. And the intruder is not some scheming psycho home-wrecker but the children's 'natural' mother, Curtis, who walked out on them all three years earlier. Her revived claim on the family's affections at first seems genuine, but soon she's poisoning the boys' minds with lies about their father and surrogate mother. Curtis also makes a play for Gallagher and it's his refusal of her advances that precipitates the final all-out attack. Director Simoneau fills the screen with artificially lit images, over-dressed sets and immaculately designed costumes, while neglecting such essentials as pacing and suspense. NF

Mother Wore Tights

(Walter Lang, 1947, US) Betty Grable, Dan Dailey, Mona Freeman, Connie Marshall, Vanessa Brown, Senor Wences.
107 min.
First teaming of Grable and Dailey, no Astaire-Rogers but the next best thing, and making the most of a nostalgic score ('Put Your Arms Around Me, Honey', 'Rolling Down to Bowling Green', 'You Do', 'Kokomo Indiana') as a pair of turn-of-the-century vaudevillains. Warm, colourful and a real charmer, despite tiresome complications latterly when the couple's eldest daughter grows up a snob ashamed of her background. TM

Motion and Emotion: The Films of Wim Wenders

(Paul Joyce, 1990, GB) Wim Wenders, Hanns Zischler, Samuel Fuller, Robby Müller, Dennis Hopper, Harry Dean Stanton, Peter Falk, Ry Cooder, Kraft Wetzel.
90 min.
Paul Joyce and producer Chris Rodley's thorough, intelligent documentary manages to celebrate

Wenders' work, to contextualise it, and to question some of the assumptions he makes in his films. They use interviews (with Wenders, his actors, collaborators, and German critic Kraft Wetzel), clips, and music to explain and explore his output of the last two decades. Fuller is funny and colourful; Hopper, Falk, Stanton and Ry Cooder are anecdotal but perceptive; Zischler is Teutonically serious; and Wetzel provocative but often spot-on in his unsentimental assessment of Wenders' strengths and weaknesses (on his faintly adolescent attitude towards those he doesn't understand, for instance: 'Aren't women mysterious? Aren't kids wonderful in their innocent wisdom? Let's put on another record!'). The film, while justifiably admiring, never slips into hagiographic excess, and a judicious use of songs provides an uplifting, paean-like tone. GA

Motocyclette, La
see Girl on a Motorcycle

Motorist
(Chip Lord, 1989, US) Richard Marcus, Jo Harvey Allen, Jules Backus, Sumi Nobuhara, Phil Garner, Toshi Onuki.
70 min.
Part fiction, part documentary essay, this wry, wacky road movie takes a driver (Richard Marcus) through the American Southwest to LA as he delivers a grey '62 Ford Thunderbird to a young Japanese. A Ford man with a respect for Cadillac, Richard talks to himself, the traffic, the radio and the car, lamenting the end of the Mechanical Age, offering an anecdotal history of himself and US dream cars, and commenting on the massive, mythic landscape around him. The few characters he meets – a mystic waitress, a gas attendant with a passion for franchise history – add vivid colour, but it's Richard's droll musings that fuel the film, providing a fascinating, often very funny semiology of '50s car culture to accompany ancient ads and documentary clips. The many references range from Henry Ford and Diego Rivera to McDonald's and UFOs, but the whole thing is lent coherence by Marcus' charismatic presence and Lord's assured control of mood. A small gem of a film. GA

Motor Psycho
(Russ Meyer, 1965, US) Alex Rocco, Haji, Stephen Oliver, Holle K Winters, Joseph Cellini.
Three evil Californian bikers go on an orgy of rape and murder before savagely mistreating the wife of 'horse croaker' veterinarian Cory Maddox (Rocco). The vengeful Maddox gets on the delinquents' tail, linking up en route with the shapely Ruby (Haji), widow of their latest victim. These two characters achieve something quite extraordinary in a Meyer film – a platonic relationship between a man and a woman, only threatened when a rattler sinks its fangs into the vet's leg and he forces Ruby's reluctant head down onto the wound with repeated hysterical shrieks of 'Suck it!' AB

Mouchette
(Robert Bresson, 1966, Fr) Nadine Nortier, Marie Cardinal, Paul Hébert, Jean Vimenet, J-C Guilbert.
90 min. b/w.
Bresson's wholly austere study of the miseries of an inarticulate teenage peasant girl in provincial France, which culminates with her apathetic suicide, achieves an intense purity of a kind that few directors essay, let alone achieve. The simplicity is radical, not facile, and the result is an extraordinary spiritual meditation, not an exercise in gratuitous depression. TR

Moulin Rouge
(John Huston, 1952, US/Fr) José Ferrer, Colette Marchand, Suzanne Flon, Zsa Zsa Gabor, Eric Pohlmann, Christopher Lee.
123 min.
Lumpish biopic, historically laughable as it pursues Hollywood's perennial view of the artist as solitary and star-crossed in both life and love. What taste can do, Huston does, abetted by Paul Sheriff's set designs and some fine colour camerawork from Oswald Morris. But playing Toulouse Lautrec on his knees, Ferrer could equally well be begging for mercy from the script. Best bit is the first reel, which evokes the spirit of Paris in the Naughty Nineties in a swirling mass of colour and movement. TM

Mountains of the Moon
(Bob Rafelson, 1989, US) Patrick Bergin, Iain Glen, Richard E Grant, Fiona Shaw, John Savident, James Villiers, Adrian Rawlins, Peter Vaughn, Delroy Lindo, Bernard Hill, Anna Massey, Leslie Phillips.
136 min.
Because Rafelson's idiosyncratic account of Burton and Speke's search for the source of the Nile is concerned not with the destination but with the journey, he allows the narrative to be sidetracked by a series of colourful vignettes: a lion attack, the placating of wary tribesmen with swathes of cloth, and a menacing brush with camp Lord Ngola and his scheming advisor. These episodes reveal much about the Victorian explorers: Burton (Bergin) is a womanising adventurer and anthropologist; Speke (Glen) a shallow opportunist aristocrat with a book contract in his back pocket; and their relationship is further complicated by a hint that Speke harbours an unrequited love for his manly partner. Like any journey, it is more exciting going than coming back, a problem compounded here by a coda about Speke claiming full credit for their joint discoveries (though a lighter note is struck when Burton and Bernard Hill's Dr Livingstone strip off to compare battle scars). Unbounded praise for Roger Deakins' photography, equally at home with the sun-baked African vistas and the dark wood tones of the Royal Geographic Society. Despite longueurs, this handsome epic has a spark of intelligence and a pleasing wit. NF

Mourir à Tue-Tête
(A Scream from Silence)
(Anne Claire Poirier, 1979, Can) Julie Vincent, Germain Houde, Paul Savoie, Monique Miller, Micheline Lanctôt.
96 min.
Harrowing rape movie (based on fact) in which the victim's life disintegrates as a result. It's dreadful as cinema (over-acted, obsessed with realism), but excellent as a case-example of Brownmiller's thesis – that rape is never the product of desire but a brutal and symbolic assertion of sexual oppression. Uncomfortable viewing for any man. CA

Mouse and His Child, The
(Fred Wolf/Charles Swenson, 1977, US) voices: Peter Ustinov, Neville Brand, Andy Devine, Sally Kellerman, Cloris Leachman.
83 min.
London crime figures are Toy-Town statistics compared to the frog-mugging, mouse-napping and brazen treacle brittle heists in this animated feature based on author/illustrator Russell Hoban's fantasy classic. The graphics slog of more than 30 US animartistes is worth it, especially in the opening toyshop scene where we meet our heroes – a bland duo of wind-ups spot-welded together in an eternal last tango. The clockwork rule of 'doing what you're wound to do, not what you want to do' is topsy-turvied after the magic midnight hour; and the adventures of the mice meander to the rubbish dump empire of Manny the Rat (spivvy unctuous voice by Ustinov), their escape aided by a stagestruck parrot (high camp beak-work from Leachman). Hoban won't thank directors Wolf and Swenson for laying naff hands all over the finale of his whimsy and turning it into a homily. BPa

MouseHunt
(Gore Verbinski, 1997, US) Nathan Lane, Lee Evans, Maury Chaykin, Christopher Walken, Vicki Lewis, Eric Christmas.
98 min.
Ernie and Lars Smuntz (Lane and Evans) are going through a bad patch. Their dying father's string factory is making a loss; Ernie's position as a chef has just been terminated; and dimwit Lars couldn't hold down a job even if he tried. Then father dies, leaving them the factory and a decrepit country mansion. As luck would have it, though, the house is worth a fortune, so the pair set about restoring it for auction. There's just one obstacle: a territorial mouse with an attitude problem. This film comes over as a mix of Laurel and Hardy, Home Alone and Tom and Jerry, and it works very well. Lane is especially funny, his deadpan Hardy-esque mannerisms working perfectly against Evans' winsome Laurel-inspired character, and there's a memorable cameo from Walken as a manic exterminator. It looks good, too, the generous use of wood and autumnal colours giving it an earthy, almost timeless appearance. Exceptional effects. DA

Mouse on the Moon, The
(Richard Lester, 1963, GB) Margaret Rutherford, Bernard Cribbins, Ron Moody, David Kossoff, Terry-Thomas, June Ritchie, Michael Crawford, Roddy McMillan, John Le Mesurier.
85 min.
Slightly desperate sequel to The Mouse That Roared, with the Duchy of Grand Fenwick beating the major powers in the space race, thanks to the happy discovery that the local wine is an excellent substitute for rocket fuel. No longer present in his triple role, Sellers is replaced by a busy horde of character actors, while Lester (just prior to his first Beatles film) works overtime on the jokes. TM

Mouse That Roared, The
(Jack Arnold, 1959, GB) Peter Sellers, Jean Seberg, David Kossoff, William Hartnell, Leo McKern.
90 min.
Engaging Ealing-ish comedy about the Duchy of Grand Fenwick, a Lilliputian state which declares war on America on the principle that losers always boom economically. Sellers is brilliant as the graciously melancholy Duchess (less good in his other two impersonations as prime minister and army chief), but the script veers wildly between satire and slapstick. Taking it pretty much as it comes, Arnold (Creature from the Black Lagoon, Incredible Shrinking Man) seems most at home with moments of fantasy like the ten-man invading army's triumphal progress in clanking chain-mail through New York's deserted streets. TM

Mouth Agape, The
(La Gueule Ouverte)
(Maurice Pialat, 1974, Fr) Monique Mélinand, Hubert Deschamps, Philippe Léotard, Nathalie Baye, Alain Grestau.
82 min.
Pialat's third feature takes up a theme which, on the face of it, could not seem more uninviting: a middle-aged woman dying of cancer, and how this affects her husband and son. But what Pialat makes of this is so recognisable, embarrassing and moving – even, on occasion, funny – that he more than justifies his use of a forbidding subject. He has ideas about how emotions involving sex and death are intimately related – and about the clarity and lack of it that they shed on everything else, as son and father each go lusting after every woman in sight. He has ideas about cinema, too, and an expressive style that can encapsulate a lifetime of memories in a single shot. Without a trace of sentimentality or easy effect, this seemingly semi-autobiographical work is as intense in its way as The Mother and the Whore, and unforgettable. JR

Mouth to Mouth
(Boca a Boca)
(Manuel Gómez Pereira, 1995, Sp) Javier Bardem, Josep Maria Flotats, Aitana Sánchez-Gijón, Maria Barranco, Myriam Mézières.
96 min.
Bardem's a would-be Hollywood actor hoping to make it as a stereotype Spanish hunk, who falls for Sánchez-Gijón when she calls him up at the Madrid phone-sex company where he works. Things are difficult: she tells him she got his number from her husband, another of his clients, who's just decided he's gay. Complications ensue. Strangely similar in places to Girl 6, this is a stylish but none too funny slice of sub-Almodóvar farce, full of teasing, chic eroticism and absurd plot twists. GA

Movers and Shakers
(William Asher, 1985, US) Walter Matthau, Charles Grodin, Vincent Gardenia, Tyne Daly, Bill Macy, Gilda Radner, Steve Martin, Penny Marshall.
79 min.
Written and produced by Charles Grodin, this is a flat look at Hollywood madness from an insider who might have been expected to muster a little more sardonic zest for the occasion. There's some mild fun to be had as mogul Matthau buys the rights to best-selling how-to guide Love in

Sex, then hands hack writer Grodin the unenviable task of turning it into a movie. Cameos from Martin and Radner, but straight to video in the UK. TJ

Movie Crazy

(Clyde Bruckman, 1932, US) Harold Lloyd, Constance Cummings, Kenneth Thomson, Sydney Jarvis, Robert McWade.
84 min. b/w.
Patchy Lloyd talkie in which he rather drags out his all-American boy characterisation as an aspiring actor summoned to Hollywood by mistake but winning out in the end (discovered as a natural comedian during his disaster-prone attempts at being a heart-throb). Improving after a slow start, it has some fine sight gags, notably a cleverly sustained 10-minute elaboration of the magician's coat routine, inadvertently worn by Lloyd to a party and producing things that cause endless embarrassment. TM

Movie Days
(Biodagar)

(Fridrik Fridriksson, 1994, Ice) Orvar Jens Arnarsson, Jon Sigurbjörnsson, Gudrún Asmundsdottir, Rurik Haraldsson.
90 min.
A semi-autobiographical film from the director of *Children of Nature* about a young movie addict banished for the summer to a relative's farm. There he is rewarded for his chores with an initiation into the ways of nature, and tales of trolls and ghosts from old man Toni. Stylised, but never particularly stylish, this is quiet, reflective and somewhat flimsy. TCh

Movie Movie

(Stanley Donen, 1978, US) George C Scott, Harry Hamlin, Rebecca York, Trish Van Devere, Eli Wallach, Barbara Harris, Barry Bostwick, Art Carney, Red Buttons, Jocelyn Brando.
106 min. b/w & col.
Donen takes us back to the days 'when the only four-letter word in movie houses was EXIT' – to quote George Burns' explanatory prologue, nervously tacked on to this pastiche double feature of the 1930s in case any thickheads didn't get the joke. It's a useful word to know, too, considering the dire nature of Larry Gelbart and Sheldon Keller's script, the flatness of the performances from George C Scott and entourage, and the pointlessness of the entire exercise. The concluding Busby Berkeleyesque *Baxter's Beauties of 1933* at least homes in on its genre far more sharply and sympathetically than the opening boxing melodrama *Dynamite Hands* (in black-and-white), which loses its focus in a welter of cheap jokes. GB

Moving

(Alan Metter, 1988, US) Richard Pryor, Beverly Todd, Randy Quaid, Dave Thomas, Dana Carvey, Rodney Dangerfield.
89 min.
Pryor, in his unfunniest role to date, has just lost his long-standing engineering job, but has the good fortune to be offered the career opportunity of a lifetime. Less fortunately for his family, who like it where they are, it involves a 2,000 mile trek to relocate in Boise, Idaho. Still, anywhere to escape the wrath of neighbour Quaid, a manic slob who takes great pride in his postage-stamp lawn, trimming it – and everyone else – with a souped-up industrial lawn-mower. The shit really hits the fan when the removal men finally turn up and proceed to demolish the family's possessions, and when Pryor discovers that the delivery driver of his shiny new Saab is a schizo. A couple of funny moments, and that's it. DA

Moving
(Ohikkoshi)

(Shinji Somai, 1993, Jap) Kiichi Nakai, Junko Sakurada, Tomoko Tabata, Tsurubei Shofukutei.
117 min.
There are two unavoidable problems at the core of this film about the psychological impact of a couple's separation on their 11-year-old daughter. First, the 45-year-old male director seems to have no point of entry into the mind of his young protagonist, so that the entire film rings hollow. Second, the girl herself (newcomer Tomoko

Tabata) is a most obnoxious spoiled brat, which makes it hard to care. TR

Moving Target, The
see Harper

Mozart in Love

(Mark Rappaport, 1975, US) Rich La Bonte.
99 min.
Funnier and altogether more assured than its predecessor, Rappaport's second feature respectfully lays waste to the inflexibility of grand opera. WA Mozart's casual/intense relations with the three Weber sisters are the pretext; Mozart's own arias are the soundtrack; the actors wear costumes, stand in front of backdrop projections, and mime to perfection. Inspired. TR

Ms .45
(aka Angel of Vengeance)

(Abel Ferrara, 1980, US) Zoë Tamerlis, Albert Sinkys, Darlene Stuto, Helen McGara, Nike Zachmanoglou, Jimmy Laine ie. Abel Ferrara, Peter Yellen.
84 min.
After having been raped twice in one day, Thana (Tamerlis), a mute garment worker, steps out each night to shoot cross-sections of male chauvinist scum, blowing them away with an assured panache. Ball-breaking entertainment which Abel Ferrara directs with a wit, flair and pace that belie his low budget, using sleazy locations for a spot-on evocation of everyday violence in the Big Apple. AB

Much Ado About Nothing

(Kenneth Branagh, 1993, GB) Kenneth Branagh, Emma Thompson, Michael Keaton, Ben Elton, Keanu Reeves, Denzel Washington.
111 min.
If nothing quite matches the teeming, joyful, acrobatic opening high in the hills of Tuscany, there's much to commend in Branagh's pruned, international version of Shakespeare's troubling comedy. Washington is the well-meaning Duke to Reeves' splendidly imperious John the bastard, while Keaton and Elton are a suitably clueless Dogberry and Verges. Branagh and Thompson, as Beatrice and Benedick, seem on the whole happier with the romance than the comedy – but do a fair job with some of the best verbal jousting in the language. SGr

Muddy River (Doro no Kawa)

(Kohei Oguri, 1981, Jap) Nobutaka Asahara, Takahiro Tamura, Yumiko Fujita, Minoru Sakurai, Makiko Shibata,
105 min. b/w.
The story of a necessarily short-lived friendship between children, set in a riverside suburb of Osaka in the mid-1950s, not yet witness to Japan's Economic Miracle. A war widow and her two kids moor their houseboat opposite a small restaurant, and the kids befriend Nobuo, the shy young son of the restaurateur. The woman surreptitiously carries out the only trade she can to support herself and her children. The film centres on Nobuo, the lower middle class boy, and observes (without undue sentimentality) his discoveries in rapid succession of class difference and sex. The movie is based on a novel, whence doubtless the metaphor that underpins the tale (the mud of experience), but Oguri's direction is not in the least literary: he trusts his sharp black-and-white images to dramatise the spaces between the characters, and gets performances of natural maturity from his young actors. Oguri's first feature, it's one from the heart. TR

Müde Tod, Der
see Destiny

Mudlark, The

(Jean Negulesco, 1950, GB) Alec Guinness, Irene Dunne, Andrew Ray, Anthony Steel, Finlay Currie, Wilfrid Hyde-White.
99 min. b/w.
This British-made Fox production wheels on a heavily made-up Irene Dunne as Queen Victoria and cuts in a lot of touristy footage in the service of a whimsical story about a young scamp who inveigles his way into Windsor Castle and gives the gloomy old monarch a good laugh in the process. Guinness is all fuss and business as

Prime Minister Disraeli, pouncing on the incident to push his new Reform Bill through Parliament, but it's the boy, played by the 11-year-old son of comedian Ted Ray, who steals the movie.

Mueda – Memoria e Massacre
see Massacre

Muerte de un Burocrata
see Death of a Bureaucrat

Mule Train

(John English, 1950, US) Gene Autry, Pat Buttram, Sheila Ryan, Robert Livingston, Frank Jaquet.
60 min. b/w.
When his pal's partner is killed in a dispute over mineral rights, Autry enters the fray by rigging up a wagon train to bring supplies to a dam under construction. The Museum of Modern Art, NY, chose this moderately pacy B-Western to represent Autry's homespun fare in their collection. TJ

Mulholland Falls

(Lee Tamahori, 1995, US) Nick Nolte, Melanie Griffith, Chazz Palminteri, Michael Madsen, Chris Penn, Andrew McCarthy, Treat Williams, John Malkovich, Ed Lauter, Daniel Baldwin, Bruce Dern.
107 min.
Meet the 'Hat Squad', a free-ranging unit of the LAPD comprising Detectives Hoover (Nolte), Coolidge (Palminteri), Hall (Madsen) and Relyea (Penn). It's the early '50s. A good-time gal is found embedded in six inches of sand, like a steamroller had a crush on her. Who knew her? Gay filmmaker Jimmy Fields (McCarthy), for starters; the chairman of the Atomic Energy Commission, General Timms (Malkovich), more intimately; and then there's the very married, very motivated detective Max Hoover. With cinematography by Haskell Wexler, production design by Richard Sylbert and a cast fleshed out with the likes of Treat Williams, Daniel Baldwin and Bruce Dern, this has the look down pat, but when it comes to substance, emotional complexity or narrative authority, forget it, Jake, this isn't Chinatown. Director Tamahori caught the eye with *Once Were Warriors*, but his first Hollywood feature falls flat with a hollow thud. It doesn't help that, after an intriguing opening, Pete Dexter's screenplay fails to construct a mystery which really connects, that too many supporting characters never come to life, and that Malkovich invests a pivotal role with his peculiar brand of terminal lethargy. TCh

Mugshot

(Matt Mahurin, 1996, US) Robert Knepper, Michael Williams, Belinda Becker, Robert Walker, Willie Lassic, Maxine Joyner, Shevonne Tucker.
87 min.
Visually stylish it may be (like his two principal characters, writer/director Mahurin was a photographer), but this first feature is arty and pretentious as it explores the enigmatic relationship between an amnesiac white holed up in a derelict Harlem building, and the black guy ('Rumor') who offers to help in return for payment, but insists he stay put. As Rumor starts discovering aspects of his charge's life (including his black girlfriend), the film becomes increasingly stilted, symbolic and stultifying. New York is shot like some bleak sci-fi cityscape. GA

Mullaway

(Don McLennan, 1988, Aust) Nadine Garner, Bill Hunter, Sue Jones.
92 min.
Mull, also confusingly known as Phoebe, has to leave school when her mother falls terminally ill, to look after her three siblings and her father who works nights. Her problems are just starting: she discovers her elder brother, who is trying to set up a rock band, shooting up; her younger sister is hair-wrenchingly precocious; and the younger brother, with a preference for the library rather than the beach like ordinary boys, has been inculcated into the ways of the Lord by their born-again father, who seems incapable of communicating with his children other than by reading them biblical quotes. Veering between the absorbing and the gauche, this is a gentle and at times poignant representation not only of

teenagers and family life, but of someone young learning how to cope the hard way. JGl

Multiplicity

(Harold Ramis, 1996, US) Michael Keaton, Andie MacDowell, Harris Yulin, Richard Masur, Eugene Levy, Ann Cusack, John deLancie, Brian Doyle-Murray.
117 min.
Doug Kinney (Keaton) is running out of time. He's working all hours, barely sees the kids, and now wife Laura (MacDowell) wants to split domestic duties so she can return to her career. It seems too good to be true, then, when genetic scientist Dr Leeds (Yulin) offers to double Doug's capacity by making a clone, a facsimile identical in appearance and experience. Safely housed away above the garage, Doug 2 can handle business, while the original devotes himself to quality time with the family and the pursuit of happiness. Not quite a *Groundhog Day* replica, but a near-relative none the less, this is a mid-life crisis comedy about masculinity, mortality and the roads not taken. The development is funny and smart. Doug 2 has a mind of his own, and a libido, so he's soon dating his (their) secretary, eyeing the wife, and cloning himself for some additional home help. If Doug 2 embodies the original's repressed machismo, Doug 3 is his feminine side, swapping cooking tips with the bewildered, uncomprehending Laura. With the inevitable, infantile Doug 4 – a failed experiment, a third-generation copy – the movie comes close to genuinely anarchic subversion, even daring triple adultery in one night of passion. Unfortunately, in trying to rein in the material and impose some kind of closure, the film-makers plump for an inadequate, bourgeois sit-com mode and the movie evaporates before your eyes. Oh well, it was fun while it lasted, and hats off to Michael Keaton, Michael Keaton, Michael Keaton and – very funny in a supporting turn – Michael Keaton. TCh

Mummy, The

(Karl Freund, 1932, US) Boris Karloff, Zita Johann, David Manners, Edward Van Sloan, Arthur Byron, Noble Johnson.
72 min. b/w.
Hardly a horror film in that it refuses to go for shock effects, this tale of Im-ho-tep, an ancient Egyptian priest brought back to life by an archaeologist, is a sombre and atmospheric depiction of eternal passion and occult reincarnation. The script throws up a heady mixture of evocative nonsense that bears little relation to the realities of Egyptian religion and history, but the whole thing is transformed by Karloff's restrained performance as the mummy who becomes, in his new life, an Egyptian archaeologist stalking Cairo in search of his beloved, a reincarnated princess; and by Freund's strong visual sense (he had previously been cameraman on Murnau's *The Last Laugh*, Lang's *Metropolis*, and the original *Dracula*). Not as great as Universal's earlier *Frankenstein*, but a fascinating instalment in the studio's series of classic fantasies. GA

Mummy, The

(Terence Fisher, 1959, GB) Peter Cushing, Christopher Lee, Yvonne Furneaux, Eddie Byrne, Felix Aylmer, Raymond Huntley.
88 min.
One of the most fetching of Fisher's early Hammer movies, the third in the trilogy which comprises *The Curse of Frankenstein* and *Dracula*. Its qualities are almost entirely abstract and visual, with colour essential to its muted, subtle imagery. Christopher Lee looks tremendous in the title role, smashing his way through doorways and erupting from green, dream-like quagmires in really awe-inspiring fashion. Yvonne Furneaux plays one of Fisher's most crucial heroines, Isobel Banning, who has to let her hair down (literally) and become sensual in order to free her husband (Cushing) from the curse he invokes by opening an Egyptian tomb. DP

Mummy's Hand, The

(Christy Cabanne, 1940, US) Dick Foran, Peggy Moran, Wallace Ford, George Zucco, Eduardo Ciannelli, Cecil Kellaway, Tom Tyler.
67 min. b/w.
First of four '40s revivals for Universal's dreariest monster, who could do little but lurch around swathed in bandages, arms outstretched for another bout of mayhem. Western star Tom Tyler, dragging one useless leg behind him, at least brought a certain baleful menace to the role, whereas Lon Chaney Jr, taking over for *The Mummy's Tomb* (1942), *The Mummy's Ghost* (1944) and *The Mummy's Curse* (1944), merely looked incongruously overweight. The sense of déjà vu is not helped by the cost-cutting habit of incorporating the famous flashback sequence from Freund's 1932 film explaining the historical circumstances of the mummy's fate (*The Mummy's Tomb* also includes a flashback to its predecessor, plus stock footage of torch-brandishing villagers from Frankenstein!). *The Mummy's Hand* and *The Mummy's Ghost* are the best in an uninspiring quartet. TM

Mummy's Shroud, The

(John Gilling, 1966, GB) Andre Morell, John Phillips, David Buck, Elizabeth Sellars, Maggie Kimberley, Richard Warner, Catherine Lacey, Dickie Owen.
84 min.
Writer/director Gilling collaborated on some of Hammer's most imaginative pictures (*The Plague of the Zombies* and *The Gorgon* among them), but this old bag of tricks does neither him nor the studio justice. In 1920 Stanley Preston, the usual swaggering imperialist (Phillips), orders the desecration of an Egyptian tomb and unleashes ancient evil. Vengeance comes in the shape of Prem (Owen), slave to a mummified pharaoh, occupant of the tomb. First to die is Sir Basil Walden (Morell), the honourable archaeologist committed to a lunatic asylum by Preston. Catherine Lacey performs entertainingly as a soothsayer. GM

Muppet Christmas Carol, The

(Brian Henson, 1992, US) The Muppets, Michael Caine, Steven MacKintosh, Meredith Braun, Robin Weaver, Donald Austen.
86 min.
Acted to the parsimonious hilt by the human Scrooge (Caine), and framed by author-narrator Charles Dickens (the Great Gonzo) addressing his rodent audience (Rizzo the Rat), the story survives. Well, it would: it's the same story of redemption that powers Stallone movies. All the pen-pushing glovesters in Scrooge's office run on fear of dismissal, a topical note, with Bob Cratchit (Kermit the Frog) negotiating but nervous. Not so his wife Miss Piggy, ready to have a go at Scrooge, but mindful of the needs of their family, a brood as mixed as you would expect from pigs and frogs, which explains the medical condition of Tiny Tim, a froglet with a cough on crutches. The three ghosts of Christmas are wonderful. Elsewhere, Fozzie Bear bears a resemblance to Francis L Sullivan in the David Lean Dickens adaptations, and there's a shop called Micklewhite. As an actor, Kermit can corrugate his forehead vertically. Good fun. BC

Muppet Movie, The

(James Frawley, 1979, GB) Charles Durning, Austin Pendleton, Milton Berle, Mel Brooks, James Coburn, Elliott Gould, Bob Hope, Steve Martin, Richard Pryor, Orson Welles.
97 min.
First of the big-screen spin-offs, this unwisely ignores the successful formula of the TV shows. The Muppets travel to Hollywood and stardom; aimless aerial and American location footage replace the tight studio format; and Kermit is no longer a stand-up comic but a star in the making. Numerous guest stars make brief appearances instead of contributing to whole sketches built around their willingness to be lampooned by a bunch of puppets. Slapstick chases and weak movie references look tired, while the attitude towards Miss Piggy and Camilla the Chicken is, well, less than progressive. Somewhere the film loses sight of its origins and its audience (mainly children, one presumes); Mel Brooks' sinister, crazed Jewish Nazi surgeon looks particularly out of place. Even adults will have difficulty following the murky soundtrack. CPe

Muppets Take Manhattan, The

(Frank Oz, 1984, US) Art Carney, James Coco, Dabney Coleman, Gregory Hines, Linda Lavin, Joan Rivers.
94 min.
After setting Hollywood alight, the Muppets take on another enduring rags-to-riches American myth: let's do a Broadway show. Only this time it's Frogway and, the musical, written and starring our own Kermit (natch), is only lacking one till-busting ingredient: there aren't enough frogs. During the 94 minutes of this delightful movie, the Muppets graduate from college, hit New York, are parted and reunited minutes before curtain-up, with Kermit saved from amnesia by a right hook from Miss Piggy. SGr

Muppet Treasure Island

(Brian Henson, 1996, US) Tim Curry, Jennifer Saunders, Kevin Bishop, Billy Connolly, The Muppets.
100 min.
After the delightful *Muppet Christmas Carol*, this fourth Kermit and pals star vehicle comes as a slight disappointment, but it's a treat all the same. The format's unchanged. The pre-puppet warm-up, with black-toothed Saunders, slovenly 'kerchiefed Connolly and the rest of the sea dogs, is all slopped ale, menacing curses and roisterous yo-ho-ho, served up just short of Python-esque pastiche. The heart only leaps with the dockside arrival of Kermit's Capt Smollett and his kaleidoscopic crew of woolly friends as the movie sets sail for the usual ahistoric musical extravaganza. There's bad news. Kermit's role is upsettingly minor and underwritten. Worse, Miss Piggie's superstar status is becoming a crashing bore: her South Sea queen of the warthogs (Benjamina Gunn) favours ostentation over dignity. Yet Barry Mann and Cynthia Weil's musical numbers have more than enough goofy lyrics to cheer the cockles. Bishop comes off well, too, with his contemporary Jim Hawkins, sensible, winsome but thankfully not cute. The new star, and about time, is Rizzo the Rat. He's not as bright, witty or charismatic as Kermit, but what courage, what staying power! WH

Mur, Le

see Wall, The

Murder

(Alfred Hitchcock, 1930, GB) Herbert Marshall, Nora Baring, Phyllis Konstam, Edward Chapman, Miles Mander, Esmé Percy, Donald Calthrop.
108 min. b/w.
Perhaps the most provocative of all early British Hitchcocks, a whodunit that transcends the limitations of its mystery plot by focusing on theatrical mediations of reality (courtesy of *Hamlet*). A girl silently accepts her prosecution for murder; the lone juror who believes in her innocence starts an investigation of his own; and winds up confronting the first negative gay stereotype in popular cinema. TR

MURDER and Murder

(Yvonne Rainer, 1996, US) Joanna Merlin, Kathleen Chalfant, Catherine Kellner, Isa Thomas, Jennie Moreau, Rod McLachan.
113 min. b/w & col.
Doris, 63 and a grandmother, has recently fallen in love for the first time with a woman, Mildred, a life-long lesbian and well-to-do professor. Rainer's film examines the women's relationship in characteristically wide-ranging and often playful terms: it's about identity, memory, communication breakdown, role-playing, power-struggles, stereotypes, and performance. It's also not nearly as funny as it would like to be – much of the 'slapstick' is painfully tedious – and some of the vaguely experimental formal conceits seem a little pointless or dated. GA

Murder at 1600

(Dwight Little, 1997, US) Wesley Snipes, Diane Lane, Alan Alda, Daniel Benzali, Ronny Cox, Dennis Miller, Diane Baker, Tate Donovan, Harris Yulin.
107 min.
That's 1600 Pennsylvania Avenue. A woman's found murdered at the White House and detective Snipes (average) is soon at loggerheads with secret service chief Benzali over jurisdictional privilege. Circumstantial evidence points to a cleaner, but Snipes knows a fall guy when he sees one, and special agent Lane reluctantly concurs. The script has President Cox trying to tough out a hostage crisis in North Korea without recourse to the military, while Snipes is understandably more concerned with the local bureaucracy about to flatten his house. Passable, but punches are

pulled, and all suspense jettisoned some 20 minutes from home. TCh

Murder at the Vanities

(Mitchell Leisen, 1934, US) Carl Brisson, Victor McLaglen, Jack Oakie, Kitty Carlisle, Dorothy Stickney, Gertrude Michael, Jessie Ralph, Duke Ellington.
89 min. b/w.
Delightfully offbeat mixture of whodunit and musical, with McLaglen's cop called to the theatre to investigate the attempted murder of a singer during a run of Earl Carroll's 'Vanities' revue, then lingering to find the killer when a murder occurs. The mystery is merely conventional, but it's alternated with superbly staged musical sequences, spectacular but respecting the proscenium's limits and notable for their cheekily bizarre nature (scantily clad girls in suggestive routines, with the murder discovered when blood drips onto a posing chorine's bare shoulder during a rendition of 'Sweet Marijuana'). Duke Ellington makes a welcome appearance, and Leisen handles the whole thing with witty, typically lavish style. GA

Murder by Confession
see Absolution

Murder by Contract

(Irving Lerner, 1958, US) Vince Edwards, Phillip Pine, Herschel Bernardi, Caprice Toriel, Michael Granger, Cathy Browne.
81 min. b/w.
A terrific, no-nonsense B movie which comes on like something by Jean-Pierre Melville: cool, calm and dispassionate. Edwards is Claude, a technician who goes into crime as a career move, to 'improve himself'. A series of hits later, he looks every inch the professional assassin, confident enough to take his time, competent enough not to fear detection. It isn't *entirely* his fault if something goes wrong on the big contract... Lerner and his superb cameraman, Lucien Ballard, make the most of a shoestring budget to produce a taut, spare, amoral film; it doesn't look restricted, it looks restrained. Well ahead of its time, too. TCh

Murder by Death

(Robert Moore, 1976, US) Eileen Brennan, Truman Capote, James Coco, Peter Falk, Alec Guinness, Elsa Lanchester, David Niven, Peter Sellers, Maggie Smith, Nancy Walker, Estelle Winwood.
95 min.
Essentially a filmed play (the world's most famous fictional sleuths summoned for a weekend by Capote's eccentric electronics wizard and invited to solve a murder due to happen at midnight), *Murder by Death* is entertaining enough, even though the joke wears a little thin. As plot loses importance and parody reigns supreme, Falk and Maggie Smith get the best lines. However, unlike *Murder on the Orient Express* – so stylised as to be virtually a parody – here director Moore and writer Neil Simon seem to have no real affection for either the characters they plunder mercilessly for laughs, or the locked room puzzle they turn on its head. Introductions over, the film slides downhill. PH

Murder by Decree

(Bob Clark, 1978, Can/GB) Christopher Plummer, James Mason, David Hemmings, Susan Clark, Anthony Quayle, John Gielgud, Frank Finlay, Donald Sutherland, Genevieve Bujold.
112 min.
Not entirely successful, but still an imaginative and ambitious attempt to combine historical speculation, conspiracy thriller, and the world of Conan Doyle. Treading much the same territory as Stephen Knight's book *The Final Solution*, it sees Sherlock Holmes and Dr Watson investigating the Jack the Ripper murders, and coming up with an answer that involves royalty, Parliament and the Masons. For a full account of the theory – largely convincing – read Knight's book; but this will give you an idea of what may have prompted the murder of five prostitutes in Victorian London. The different threads are neatly interwoven, suspense and explanation being carefully balanced, and the horror of the crimes evoked in suitably nightmarish images. The only drawbacks, in fact, lie in Sutherland's appearance as a loony visionary, and in Plummer's occasional adoption of ludicrous disguises. GA

Murderer Lives at Number 21, The
see Assassin Habite au 21, L'

Murder, He Says

(George Marshall, 1945, US) Fred MacMurray, Helen Walker, Marjorie Main, Jean Heather, Porter Hall, Peter Whitney, Mabel Paige.
94 min. b/w.
A black farce with MacMurray as a public opinion pollster trapped in the backwoods home of a crazed hillbilly family while looking for a colleague who has disappeared. The family is alarming enough, with whip-cracking Ma (Main), half-witted twin giants with a gleeful taste for torture (Whitney), and murderous shenanigans which make *Cold Comfort Farm* look like child's play; but there's also a ferocious pistol-packin' mama newly busted out of jail (Walker), only she turns out to be a nice girl looking for the loot everyone is fussing about so that she can clear her innocent dad. Not always as subtle as it might be, but beautifully acted (MacMurray especially), nicely timed by Marshall, and really very funny. TM

Murder, Inc.
see Enforcer, The

Murder in the First

(Marc Rocco, 1994, US) Christian Slater, Kevin Bacon, Gary Oldman, Embeth Davidtz, Bill Macy, Stephen Tobolowsky, Brad Dourif, R Lee Ermey, Kyra Sedgwick, Ben Slack.
122 min.
In Alcatraz on a minor charge, gentle, granite-willed Henri Young (Bacon) ends in hellish solitary confinement for three punishing years that all but break his body yet leave him thirsting for revenge on the duplicitous inmate who put him away. Soon, there's a murder in the mess hall, and Young looks to be going down again for an even longer stretch. Yet when tyro lawyer Stamphill discovers the truth of his client's previous treatment, he decides to plead on the killer's behalf, thus shaking the prison service to the core. Bacon's extraordinary physical commitment powers this heartfelt, occasionally bombastic portrait of institutionalised injustice, compellingly adapted by Dan Gordon from a true story. A hyperactive camera and Chris Young's thunderous score lay on the emphasis. Slater's good as the lawyer and Oldman chilling as the razor-cropped associate warden, but it's Bacon's picture – and if he doesn't win an Oscar, there ain't no justice in the world. TJ

Murder in Thornton Square, The
see Gaslight

Murder Is a Murder...Is a Murder, A (Un Meurtre est un Meurtre)

(Etienne Périer, 1972, Fr/It) Jean-Claude Brialy, Stéphane Audran, Robert Hossein, Michel Serrault, Catherine Spaak, Claude Chabrol.
103 min.
In a seemingly undistinguished career, Périer at last came up with a fascinating thriller, a pure Hitchcock-Chabrol pastiche. The theme is essentially a reworking of *Strangers on a Train*, concerned with guilt rather than murder: guilt over the accidental death of the insufferable wife (Audran) of Paul Kastner (Brialy) which could so easily have been murder, and which a stranger (Hossein) subsequently claims his reward for arranging. Périer appears totally at ease with the Chabrol-like nuances: a sinister sister-in-law (also Audran) like a reincarnation from Poe's 'Ligeia', but who in reality is just nutty; or the carefully planned alibi that degenerates into pure farce when the railway commissionaire (Chabrol) breaks his glasses. Added to which he has set the protagonists in a sea of familiar Hollywood paraphernalia – rambling houses, wheelchair lifts, living-room chests – enhancing the gleefulness without destroying the menacing atmosphere. GSa

Murder My Sweet
see Farewell, My Lovely

Murder on Monday
see Home at Seven

Murder on the Orient Express

(Sidney Lumet, 1974, GB) Albert Finney, Lauren Bacall, Martin Balsam, Ingrid Bergman, Jacqueline Bisset, Jean-Pierre Cassel, Sean Connery, John Gielgud, Wendy Hiller, Anthony Perkins, Vanessa Redgrave, Rachel Roberts, Richard Widmark, Michael York.
131 min.
The formula can't fail: a first class journey on the '30s Orient Express, meticulous detail, a murder with all suspects aboard. In fact, the most suspect thing is the comfortable complacency of it all, threatened only by the flashback beginning, a Lindbergh-type kidnapping recalled with dreamlike intensity, and Richard Widmark's haunted performance. The script copes with the silliness of Agatha Christie's plot (whodunit is disappointingly obvious), and works best as an essay on the use of the English language by foreigners: the train's full of them, and their quirky phrases help provide the solution to the mystery. Lumet ensures a smooth ride, but as usual takes too long to say what he means and brings the Express in 20 minutes late. CPe

Murders in the Rue Morgue

(Robert Florey, 1932, US) Bela Lugosi, Sidney Fox, Leon Ames, Arlene Francis, Noble Johnson, Brandon Hurst.
75 min. b/w.
Very loosely based on a tale by Poe, this is a pedestrian but still highly enjoyable account of a mad scientist (Lugosi) scouring Paris for young female victims to prove his rather unusual theory of evolution: experiments involve mixing the blood of the women with that of a gorilla. The perverse and sordid sexual implications of the story are rarely made explicit, although there are a couple of genuinely unpleasant scenes. Stylistically (it's beautifully shot by Karl Freund) the whole thing owes more to *The Cabinet of Dr Caligari* than to Poe. GA

Murders in the Rue Morgue

(Gordon Hessler, 1971, US) Jason Robards, Herbert Lom, Christine Kaufman, Adolfo Celi, Lilli Palmer, Maria Perschy, Michael Dunn.
87 min.
Chris Wicking's script takes the basic premise of a Grand Guignol theatre in Paris which is running an adaptation of Poe's story, and whose leading actress (Kaufman) is afflicted by weird nightmares involving elements of the play. The action slips back and forth bewilderingly from the play she is in to her dreams and then to her waking experience. It's a bold and complex structure for a horror film, and at times the thematic depth of the story doesn't hold up dramatically. But there's enough fascination and style in the dream sequences alone to hold the attention, and the action builds to a pleasingly obsessional – and genuinely Poe-like – climax, with the heroine completely isolated from reality. DP

Murders in the Zoo

(A Edward Sutherland, 1933, US) Lionel Atwill, Charlie Ruggles, Randolph Scott, Gail Patrick, Kathleen Burke, John Lodge.
64 min. b/w.
In a splendidly fiendish opening sequence, Atwill's millionaire sportsman disposes of a rival for his wife's affections by leaving him to die in the Indochinese jungle, having first carefully stitched up his lips. 'What did he say?' asks the anxious wife (Burke), told that her lover went on alone. 'He didn't say anything,' Atwill blandly replies. Back in America, Atwill carries on the good work, using the zoo to which he supplies animals as a convenient disposal ground: another rival succumbs to green mamba poison, and the suspicious Burke ends up in the alligator pit. Instead of exploring its Sadian motifs (the erotic charge Atwill gets from 'protecting' his wife, for instance), the script unfortunately opts for comedy (capably handled by Ruggles) and a slightly tiresome detection motif (Scott as a toxicologist who discovers that the mamba wasn't the culprit). Fine, macabre fun for all that, beautifully shot by Ernest Haller, and very capably directed (although a little more extravagance would have helped the finale: Atwill setting the big cats free to cover his escape, but ending in a boa constrictor's coils). TM

Muriel (Muriel, ou le Temps d'un Retour)

(Alain Resnais, 1963, Fr/It) Delphine Seyrig, Jean-Pierre Kérien, Nita Klein, Jean-Baptiste Thierrée, Claude Sainval, Jean Champion.
116 min.

Not the easiest of Resnais films, but certainly his wittiest exploration of the vagaries of memory (teasingly set in Boulogne, a city largely lost under post-war urban developments). A spell-binding mosaic of images preserving, destroying, falsifying or testifying to the past, it sets two attitudes in opposition. A woman (Seyrig) attempts to ward off present tedium by conjuring the memory of her first love. Her stepson (Thierrée), treasuring some film of an atrocity he witnessed in Algeria in which a girl called Muriel was tortured to death, is determined to allow no escape from actuality. What both forget is that things change, that memory must feed on reality and vice versa. If her remembered love proves disappointingly remote from actuality, so his celluloid actuality turns out to need memory to bring it alive again. Impasse. TM

Muriel's Wedding

(PJ Hogan, 1994, Aust) Toni Collette, Rachel Griffiths, Bill Hunter, Jeanie Drynan.
106 min.

Rather too obviously aimed at the *Strictly Ballroom* feel-good market, this is nevertheless an engaging, funny and sometimes surprisingly tough romantic comedy about one Muriel Hislop, an unsophisticated plain Jane (Collette), who'll do anything – including lie – to leave her dull home-town of Porpoise Spit in pursuit of dreams fuelled by ABBA songs. It could do with a little more irony, not to say originality, but the perkiness of the script, production design and performances (notably Griffiths as Muriel's pal) carry it through with flying, gaudy colours. GA

Murmur of the Heart

see Souffle au Coeur, Le

Murmur of Youth (Meili zai Chang-ge)

(Lin Cheng-Sheng, 1997, Tai) René Liu, Tseng Tsing, Tsai Chin-Hsin, Lin Hsui.
105 min.

Two girls, coincidentally both named Meili, work side-by-side in a movie theatre box office and have a brief romantic fling – which means more to one of them than the other. Director/co-writer Lin (*A Drifting Life*) takes his time getting them to this point; he spends more than an hour contrasting their home lives (one is from a middle-class family and gets no emotional support from her parents, the other is from an impoverished working-class family with a senile grandmother who was once a prostitute), turning the film into a meditation on changing values and morals in the ever-more-urbanised 1990s. Cool, calm and very assured. TR

Murphy's Law

(J Lee Thompson, 1986, US) Charles Bronson, Kathleen Wilhoite, Carrie Snodgrass, Robert F Lyons, Richard Romanus, Angel Tompkins, Lawrence Tierney.
100 min.

Murphy's Law, if you recall, states that if anything can go wrong it will. For Bronson's Murphy, however, far more goes right than wrong. When reminded of that law, in fact, he snarls back his own variation: Don't fuck with Jack Murphy. It's a warning to be well heeded. Murphy's a tough LA cop, victim of a frame-up. So he goes on the run from his own colleagues, accompanied by a wily, recalcitrant gamine (Wilhoite) who happens to be handcuffed to his wrist, and who hot-wires cars and spews out more foul phrases than you may ever have heard at one time. Might and right ultimately prevail, of course, but not before nigh on a dozen reasonably inventive killings, the bulk of them utterly gratuitous. JCoh

Murphy's Romance

(Martin Ritt, 1985, US) Sally Field, James Garner, Brian Kerwin, Corey Haim, Dennis Burkley, Georgann Johnson.
108 min.

The bridge drives and soda fountains of picturesque small-town Arizona offer interminable pretexts for meetings cute and heartwarming romance between Field's divorced mum and Garner's corner-store pharmacist who dispenses homespun advice along with his prescriptions. From the same writer/director/star team responsible for *Norma Rae*, this cornball comedy comes on more as a depressing barometer of contemporary Hollywood. Boo to Field's ex-husband (Kerwin), a no-good boyo who roars into town on an Easy Rider bike, strums '60s folk songs, enjoys *Friday the 13th*. Hooray for Murphy (Garner) with his purse-lipped work ethic, blue grass fiddle, and solid old jalopy (adorned with no-nukes stickers as a token nod to liberalism). Field ploughs her now over-familiar furrow of plucky independence, and it's only the abrasive charm of Garner and Kerwin that redeems the film from terminal whimsy. SJo

Murphy's War

(Peter Yates, 1971, GB) Peter O'Toole, Sian Phillips, Philippe Noiret, Horst Janson, John Hallam, Ingo Mogendorf.
106 min.

Sole survivor of a British merchant vessel, sunk by torpedoes off the coast of Venezuela during the last days of World War II, conducts a one-man war against the U-Boat responsible, all the way to a kamikaze end. But the potential of the storyline breaks down into a series of cliché scenes, characters and relationships, and neither Yates nor his lead actor Peter O'Toole has the inspiration to boost the level higher than mere competence. TR

Musicals Great Musicals: The Arthur Freed Unit at MGM

(David Thompson, 1996, US) Leslie Caron, Cyd Charisse, Betty Comden, Stanley Donen, Adolph Green, Michael Kidd, Ann Miller, Andre Previn, Mickey Rooney.
85 min.

This lucid, lively and informative account of the lyricist-turned-producer who transformed the movie musical (from revue fare with contemporary hits and tap-dancing chorines, to lavish stories in which songs and dance furthered plot and characterisation) features terrific clips from all his hits and a raft of revealing interviews. Rare highlights include footage from the abandoned version of *Annie Get Your Gun* starring a less than capable Garland, and of the Broadway version of *On the Town*, with songs cut from the film. Best clip: the amazingly erotic blues section of the *American in Paris* ballet. GA

Music Box

(Costa-Gavras, 1989, US) Jessica Lange, Armin Müller-Stahl, Frederic Forrest, Donald Moffat, Lukas Haas, Cheryl Lynne Bruce, Mari Töröcsik.
126 min.

Was Mike Laszlo (Müller-Stahl), a retired Hungarian blue-collar worker living in Chicago these last 37 years, once head of an SS death squad? War crimes investigator Burke (Forrest) thinks he was, and in the light of eye-witness reports of Nazi atrocities in Hungary, takes him to court to face extradition charges. Mike's attorney daughter Ann (Lange), defending him, successfully undermines the prosecution by suggesting that its Hungarian witnesses have been sent by a government keen to discredit anti-Commie Europeans…The film is a polished enough blend of courtroom thriller, domestic melodrama and political pot-boiler that asks us, like Ann, to judge Mike's claims of innocence for ourselves; but in its attempts to probe more deeply the gulf between filial loyalty and moral integrity, and the problem of how and why we serve justice on crimes committed half a century ago, it is often overly shallow and cautious. Costa-Gavras wisely avoids facile flashbacks, but the cool tone, fascination with architecture and visual symmetry, and sluggish pacing of the trial scenes preclude real emotional and intellectual involvement, sturdy performances from a solid cast notwithstanding. GA

Music for the Movies: Bernard Herrmann

(Joshua Waletzky, 1992, US)
58 min.

A fascinating documentary. A member of Aaron Copland's circle, Herrmann – after a stint in radio – made an auspicious start with the music for *Citizen Kane*, and went on to compose some fifty more scores before his last for Scorsese's *Taxi Driver*. In that time, he made his 'anti-Hollywood style' – he was all for the primacy of the expression of interior psychological states – a standard option. There are testimonies from his ex-wife and various other composers and critics (including Scorsese and Chabrol), and lots of his unforgettable music. Personally, he seemed to be an arsehole: irascible, egocentric and cold. He considered his film work second-rate by nature. He wanted to be a conductor of a major symphony orchestra, something he got to do only as an actor for Hitchcock in The Man Who Knew Too Much. WH

Music for the Movies: The Hollywood Sound

(Joshua Waletzky, 1995, US/Fr/Jap) David Raksin, Fred Steiner.
85 min.

With the aid (and occasional cheeky interference) of David Raksin, one of the few survivors of Hollywood's 'Golden Age' and the BBC National Orchestra of Wales under conductor John Mauceri playing to a big screen, this loving tribute to the great studio composers underlines the importance of their contribution to the success of so many classics. Such names as Alfred Newman, Max Steiner and Erich Wolfgang Korngold are mulled over and a number of key sequences recreated with live music for the camera (notably *The Adventures of Robin Hood*), but the real gem is Raksin's account of how he came to compose the *Laura* theme. Educational and really rather thrilling. DT

Music for the Movies: Toru Takemitsu

(Charlotte Zwerin, 1994, US) Hiroshi Teshigahara, Masaki Kobayashi, Masahiro Shinoda, Nagisa Oshima.
58 min.

Described by one of his co-workers as having a face 'like Jean-Louis Barrault with diarrhoea', Japan's Toru Takemitsu commands a unique position as a leading contemporary composer who also works prolifically on film soundtracks. Deploying well-chosen clips and a number of distinguished interviewees (directors Teshigahara, Kobayashi and Oshima), Zwerin's film concentrates on Takemitsu's association with the '60s new wave of Japanese cinema, introducing new freedom in musical form and breaking the mould with his use of traditional Japanese instruments. Sound stuff. TJ

Music Lovers, The

(Ken Russell, 1970, GB) Richard Chamberlain, Glenda Jackson, Max Adrian, Christopher Gable, Izabella Telezynska, Kenneth Colley.
123 min.

Little more than distorted *Omnibus* portraits, Russell's 'outrageous' musical musings have dated badly. This bombastic reading of Tchaikovsky as a guilty gay, disastrously overcompensating something approaching a patina of period charm. The '1812' sequence is pure Monty Python. PT

Music Machine, The

(Ian Sharp, 1979, GB) Gerry Sundquist, Patti Boulaye, David Easter, Michael Feast, Ferdy Mayne, Clarke Peters.
90 min.

Obviously produced on a skin-tight budget, yet designed to contain every possible ingredient for mass commercial teen appeal. Its major source is *Saturday Night Fever*, transposed to Camden's Music Machine and its environs (with, incidentally, quite a good sense of location). The disco fairytale is pursued, with young hero (Sundquist) aided by two 'fairy godparents' (Boulaye and Peters) who embody the ideal qualities of the beautiful disco-person. They're black, Americanised, and act rich. What disappoints is the limping naturalism of the style (which regrettably extends to the dancing), and the predictable bits of 'social realism' slotted in to explain the hero's disco-dream, like the scene at the Job Centre. JS

Music Man, The

(Morton Da Costa, 1962, US) Robert Preston, Shirley Jones, Buddy Hackett, Hermione Gingold, Pert Kelton, Paul Ford.
151 min.

Overlong but generally faithful and entertaining screen version of Meredith Willson's Broadway hit, with Preston in fine form as the conman whose bogus music professor enlivens a small Iowa town by convincing the inhabitants they need a uniformed brass band, with himself on expenses. Zestily performed and choreographed, beautifully shot by Robert Burks, full of standards like '76 Trombones' and 'Till There Was You', and endowed with a warming nostalgia for old-fashioned ways. GA

Music of Chance, The

(Philip Haas, 1993, US) James Spader, Mandy Patinkin, Charles Durning, Joel Grey, M Emmet Walsh.
95 min.
When fireman-turned-drifter Jim Nashe (Patinkin) offers to finance the next poker game of Jack Pozzi (Spader), a cardsharp he's found wandering dazed by a country road, he little bargains for the strange turn of events that follows. Pozzi looks a sure bet against old farts Bill and Willie (Durning and Grey), but suddenly his luck changes, and Jim and Jack, deep in debt, are forced to construct a medieval wall in the victors' garden, overseen by groundsman Calvin (Walsh). The first feature of documentarist Haas may be rather literary in tone, but for all its slightly studied air, it has many virtues. Most obviously, the actors are terrific, with Spader very successfully cast against type as a sleazeball, and Patinkin a small wonder of understatement. For the most part, Haas handles his droll, resonant parable admirably, balancing its philosophical and dramatic dynamics with assurance and wit. Crucially, he has a good eye for an element of mystery. Minor, but unexpectedly engrossing. GA

Music Room, The

see Jalsaghar

Music Teacher, The
(Le Maître de musique)

(Gérard Corbiau, 1988, Bel) José Van Dam, Anne Roussel, Philippe Volter, Sylvie Fennec, Patrick Bauchau, Johan Leysen, Marc Schreiber.
98 min.
Van Dam (Leporello in Losey's Don Giovanni) plays a great baritone who retires at the height of his powers to teach two young pupils in his château: dewy-eyed Sophie (Roussel) and vulnerable street-thief Jean (Volter). Not since James Mason whisked schoolgirl Ann Todd to pianistic stardom in what seemed six months flat (The Seventh Veil) has the training of musical genius slipped by so smoothly, thanks to lyrical landscapes, sumptuous pre-WWI social swish, and doses of soundtrack Mahler. A showdown with the protégé of Van Dam's old enemy gives the chance of hearing tenors duel in a rare Bellini aria, well timed for a public apparently insatiable for the Domingo/Pavarotti/Carreras sound. Jerome Pruett's dubbed voice isn't in that league, and the film won't do for song competitions what Breaking Away did for bicycle races. MHoy

Mustang Country

(John Champion, 1976, US) Joel McCrea, Nika Mina, Robert Fuller, Patrick Wayne.
79 min.
Fourteen years on from Peckinpah's Guns in the Afternoon, McCrea's last movie was this mundane family Western in which a rancher comes out of retirement, teams up with Indian boy Mina and tames Montana's last wild mustang. Pleasant to see the old boy up and about, but there's little to it. TJ

Mustang...The House that Joe Built

(Robert Guralnick, 1975, US) Joe Conforte, Sally Conforte.
85 min.
This does practically everything wrong. It's an extremely low-budget documentary (one man and a hand-held camera) filmed inside the Mustang Ranch in Storey County, Nevada, which in 1970 became America's first legalised brothel. Guralnick tracks after Mustang boss Joe Conforte long after it becomes painfully obvious the guy's sayin' nuttin'; and there's little in the way of hard information. But it doesn't matter. The extreme sleaziness of the environment (a prison-like compound surrounded by ten-foot wire), in contrast to the collective persona revealed by the women, is so evident that all Guralnick has to do is keep the camera rolling. There's no doubt about the women being exploited, or about their resilience; and it is they who manage to give the film its subversive force. Women will probably be surprised at how much they recognise in what they see; men will probably dismiss it. VG

Mutant

see Forbidden World

Mutant

(John 'Bud' Cardos, 1983, US) Wings Hauser, Bo Hopkins, Jody Medford, Lee Montgomery, Marc Clement, Cary Guffey, Jennifer Warren.
99 min.
A modest but diverting addition to the Greenpeace Horror Subgenre, which begins with brothers Josh and Mike (Hauser, Montgomery) searching for some relaxation away from the big city. What they find is Goodland, a sticksville where the hicks are being transformed into bloodthirsty blue-tinted zombies (with veins full of caustic zinc chloride) by the googoo muck dumped from a nearby chemical plant. The story is the usual slobbery stuff, lifted out of the rut by characters who are actually quite likeable, and given a further fillip by a couple of splendid set pieces. Cop a load of the schoolteacher trapped in the toilet by a washroomful of zombified infants, or the doctor who is earnestly examining a mutated corpse, unaware that her assistant is turning into a slavering ghoul behind her. AB

Mutations, The

(Jack Cardiff, 1973, GB) Donald Pleasence, Tom Baker, Brad Harris, Julie Ege, Michael Dunn, Scott Antony, Jill Haworth.
92 min.
Tired sci-fi horror in which students live in Prince of Wales Drive and drive Jaguars, while their professor (Pleasence) uses human beings, procured for him by a grotesquely deformed Tom Baker, to further his experiments in plant-animal mutations. Shades of Tod Browning's Freaks as the results get hived off into Michael Dunn's sideshow. The moral stretches no further than don't carve up your own students: two in a week and everything starts to go wrong, including the plot. Scott Antony ends up a cross between a lizard and a Venus Flytrap; Julie Ege has a fair bash at acting, gives up in face of all the silliness, and takes off her clothes instead.

Mute Witness

(Anthony Waller, 1995, GB/Ger/Rus) Marina Sudina, Fay Ripley, Evan Richards, Oleg Jankowskij, Igor Volkov, Alec Guinness.
96 min.
Billie (Sudina), the make-up artist on an American slasher-movie, is accidentally locked overnight in the rambling Moscow studio where the film is being made. She wanders into the basement looking for someone to let her out. What she finds, however, is a cameraman shooting a scene in which a masked actor stabs a woman to death – and it looks for real. Billie flees, though since she's mute, she can't scream or phone for help. What's more, will anyone ever believe her story? Waller's witty, action-packed thriller seldom lets up. He milks the murky Moscow locations and the heroine's isolated predicament for all they're worth – only Billie's sister Karen (Ripley) attempts to understand her sign-language, while brother-in-law Andy (Richards) is too obsessed by the film he's directing to attend to anyone but himself – while switching rapidly back and forth between straight suspense and black comedy, ironic excess and tiny telling details. Scary and great fun. GA

Mutiny on the Bounty

(Frank Lloyd, 1935, US) Charles Laughton, Clark Gable, Franchot Tone, Herbert Mundin, Eddie Quillan, Dudley Digges, Donald Crisp, Movita.
132 min. b/w.
An exotic and gripping piece of Hollywood mythology, made with all the technical skill and gloss one associates with Irving Thalberg's MGM. Frank Lloyd's direction and the literate screenplay constantly juxtapose the notions of 18th century naval service as an aristocrat's high adventure and an ordinary seaman's press-ganged misery, underlying the central clash between Captain Bligh and Fletcher Christian with a surprisingly sharp examination of British breadfruit imperialism. Unlike the 1962 remake, this version virtually deserts Christian after the mutiny, concentrating on Bligh's amazing 4,000 mile open boat voyage and the subsequent court-martial. Laughton scowls magnificently, and paints a remarkable portrait of Bligh's humourless character, while Gable injects a startling (and unintentional) bisexuality into the Tahitian sequences. ATu

Mutiny on the Bounty

(Lewis Milestone, 1962, US) Marlon Brando, Trevor Howard, Richard Harris, Hugh Griffith, Richard Haydn, Tim Seely, Percy Herbert, Tarita, Gordon Jackson.
185 min.
Milestone's overlong and frequently leaden version of the classic tale of sadism and revolt, set in the high-adventure world of a 18th century ship sailing to the South Pacific, is not a patch upon the 1935 Laughton and Gable version. Brando makes a total mess out of his English accent, the romantic interlude in Tahiti goes on endlessly, and the visuals (perhaps the main point of interest in the movie) too often resort to travelogue-style vistas and picture-postcard lighting. GA

Mutiny on the Buses

(Harry Booth, 1972, GB) Reg Varney, Doris Hare, Anna Karen, Michael Robbins, Bob Grant, Stephen Lewis, Bob Todd.
89 min.
Much lower than these cretinous larks among London's bus crews comedy cannot get. The sole interest in this truly appalling spin-off from the TV sitcom series lies in wondering why the sweaty Varney – trying to play half his age as he gets engaged against his family's wishes – never got a better haircut to stop the greasy locks falling over his face. GA

Mutter und Sohn

see Mother and Son

Mutters Courage

see My Mother's Courage

My Ain Folk

see My Childhood

My American Cousin

(Sandy Wilson, 1985, Can) Margaret Langrick, John Wildman, Richard Donat, Jane Mortifee.
95 min.
A 12-year-old girl (Langrick) is stuck on a remote ranch in British Columbia in 1959 with her parents and five siblings. Her hormones play up when her American cousin (Wildman), 18, beautiful and very bored, comes to stay. The crunch comes when his folks turn up to take him home. A detailed, witty and highly sympathetic foray into the realm of adolescent sexuality, winner of six Genie awards in Canada. TJ

My American Uncle

see Mon Oncle d'Amérique

My Apprenticeship

see Childhood of Maxim Gorki, The

My Beautiful Laundrette

(Stephen Frears, 1985, GB) Saeed Jaffrey, Roshan Seth, Daniel Day Lewis, Gordon Warnecke, Derrick Branche, Shirley Anne Field, Rita Wolf.
97 min.
Not content with setting itself in London's Asian community, this also tells a gay love story. Daniel Day Lewis gives a luminous performance as the white ex-National Front hoodlum who befriends an Asian (Warnecke) and helps him create his commercial dream, a laundrette which glitters like a Hollywood picture palace. The fact that Lewis finds himself demoted in the ensuing suds war is typical of Hanif Kureishi's script, which refuses to push Asians into their customary dramatic role as victims. Instead, they're seen as rapacious businessmen, pedalling furiously on

their Tebbitite cycles, and therefore puzzled, as well as angered, by the vicious prejudice they suffer at the hands of the establishment. Saeed Jaffrey is marvellous as the smoothest of the smooth operators, and Frears directs in his customarily unfussy style. But the strength of the film is its vision – cutting, compassionate and sometimes hilarious – of what it means to be Asian, and British, in Thatcher's Britain. RR

My Best Friend's Girl
(La Femme de Mon Pote)
(Bertrand Blier, 1983, Fr) Coluche, Isabelle Huppert, Thierry Lhermitte, Farid Chopel, François Perrot.
100 min.
Blier's films are a continuing chronicle of the male psyche, getting to the parts even Howard Hawks didn't often reach. Arriving at a ski resort in search of a new steady and the home that goes with him, Huppert seizes on the local romantic (Lhermitte). The latter's best buddy (Coluche), a slob heading towards a middle-age of confirmed bachelorhood, is designated as her daytime minder, and is disarmed by her guilt-free desire for an affair. Appalled at the discovery of his own vulnerability, he finds himself agonisingly torn between male loyalties and the emotional crutch of an affair. As ever, Blier's script is out of the top drawer, and French comic Coluche, atypically cast, is excellent as the racked 'mec'. A simple storyline belies a thoughtful film with more than a hint of Buñuel's wit. BG

My Best Friend's Wedding
(PJ Hogan, 1997, US) Julia Roberts, Dermot Mulroney, Cameron Diaz, Rupert Everett, Philip Bosco, M Emmet Walsh, Rachel Griffiths.
105 min.
When Julianne (Roberts) hears that her best friend Michael (Mulroney) is getting married – this weekend! – she's horrified. The bride, Kimmy (Diaz), is beautiful, wealthy, smart, tasteful and sensitive. Obviously she'll have to go. Installed as maid of honour, Julianne has four days to win back her man and prevent the marriage. In *Muriel's Wedding*, director Hogan orchestrated sympathy for a perennial underdog obsessed with marriage; here, we're meant to empathise with a Machiavellian anti-hero – as Julianne humiliates her rival at a karaoke club, re-routes the honeymoon, and generally comes on like Glenn Close in *Fatal Attraction*. Roberts' fragile charm keeps it going for longer than you might imagine, but Mr Mulroney's magnetism must be taken entirely on faith, and the film's brazen amorality gradually freezes the smile on your face. Whenever invention fails, Hogan resorts to forced pratfalls, songs or camp farce – Everett easily steals the show as Julianne's gay colleague. TCh

My Blue Heaven
(Herbert Ross, 1990, US) Steve Martin, Rick Moranis, Joan Cusack, Melanie Mayron, William Irwin, Carol Kane, William Hickey, Deborah Rush, Ed Lauter.
95 min.
In this truly mind-numbingly awful movie, Steve Martin plays a mobster forced to move to San Diego from his New York stomping ground as part of a witness protection programme rap-beating deal. San Diego takes on the aura of some Pacific version of Milton Keynes: all little leagues, little boxes and little gardens, populated by so many of Martin's erstwhile criminal colleagues that life on the run turns into a nostalgic round of petty felonies and made-member hugs. Further dismay looms not only in co-star Rick Moranis' continuing obsession with misusing his talents by trying to play a straight man, but in the normally loveable Martin's gross and tedious portrayal of Mafia slobdom. If we must have parodies and comedies of crime, let them be funny, *capisce*? SGr

My Bodyguard
(Tony Bill, 1980, US) Chris Makepeace, Adam Baldwin, Matt Dillon, Ruth Gordon, Martin Mull, John Houseman, Craig Richard Nelson.
96 min.
Alan Ormsby's script, about a new kid in a Chicago high school who hires the biggest guy in school to fend off a lunch money protection racket, is (unusually) directed not for nostalgia value but from a perspective of adolescent insecurity,

and helped along by fresh performances from a cast of inexperienced young actors. Finally, though, the message that accompanies the central theme – Kids are basically Nice – is that Brute Force Rules. The only real refinement of that great American truth offered here is that it's likely to be most effective when employed intelligently.

My Brilliant Career
(Gillian Armstrong, 1979, Aust) Judy Davis, Sam Neill, Wendy Hughes, Robert Grubb, Max Cullen, Pat Kennedy.
100 min.
Overrated though attractive slice of nostalgia, based on a novel published in 1901 about a girl from a poor farming family, stuck in the outback and undecided between expectations that she will marry a local landowner and her own resolve to become a writer. The period atmosphere is evoked with careful delicacy, but the characters rarely become more than stereotypes with performances (Judy Davis excepted) to match. TM

My Brother's Wedding
(Charles Burnett, 1983, US) Everette Silas, Jessie Holmes, Gaye Shannon-Burnett, Ronald E Bell, Dennis Kemper, Sally Easter.
116 min.
A young working class black living in one of LA's seedier ghettos is having problems with his sense of duty to others, bothered by his brother's forthcoming marriage to a wealthy doctor's daughter, and hanging around with his wastrel ex-con pal against his family's wishes. Somewhere between domestic soap and *Mean Streets*, Burnett's low-budget film confronts a number of universal dilemmas without ever becoming turgidly heavy. Overlong, perhaps, but the witty script and generous characterisations often work wonders. GA

My Brother Talks to Horses
(Fred Zinnemann, 1946, US) 'Butch' Jenkins, Peter Lawford, Beverly Tyler, Charlie Ruggles, Edward Arnold, Spring Byington.
93 min. b/w.
An 11-year-old boy who converses with horses is popular with racetrack gamblers. Whimsical comic canter, drawn from a novel titled *Joe the Wounded Tennis Player*. NF

My Childhood/
My Ain Folk/My Way Home
(Bill Douglas, 1972/1973/1978, GB) Stephen Archibald, Hughie Restorick, Jean Taylor-Smith, Bernard McKenna, Paul Kermack, Helena Gloag.
48/55/78 min. b/w.
Bill Douglas' trilogy succeeds in evoking a genuine sense of compassion for the characters in these harsh tales of his childhood in a Scottish mining village in the '40s, without tipping the scales into mawkishness. Pared down to essentials, the stark black-and-white images restore some freshness to a tired, unfashionable aesthetic. And shot over eight years, the cruelty and compulsiveness of the 'memories' still haunt the finished work. DMacp

My Cousin Rachel
(Henry Koster, 1952, US) Olivia de Havilland, Richard Burton, John Sutton, Audrey Dalton, Ronald Squire.
98 min. b/w.
This Daphne du Maurier adaptation rather pales beside the earlier *Rebecca*, although the ingredients – death and a mysterious femme fatale – are not dissimilar. Burton was Oscar-nominated for his Hollywood debut as the young Englishman both distrustful of and attracted to de Havilland, the woman who may have fatally poisoned his foster father. Thick with studio atmospherics, but the resolution is weak. TJ

My Cousin Vinny
(Jonathan Lynn, 1992, US) Joe Pesci, Ralph Macchio, Marisa Tomei, Mitchell Whitfield, Fred Gwynne, Lane Smith, Austin Pendleton, Bruce McGill, Maury Chaykin.
119 min.
Pesci plays Vincent La Guardia Gambini, proud Brooklyn attorney-at-law, who gets called South to Wahzoo City to defend his college-kid cousin (Macchio) and pal (Whitfield), falsely accused of a convenience store murder. Trouble is, Vinny

ain't no expert on criminal law, having just completed his bar exams. Still, the majesty of the law doesn't over-impress this self-made guy; but then his shades, white shoes and total ignorance of procedure don't exactly impress by-the-book Judge Haller (Gwynne). Vinny fears he's gonna get found out, the kids fear they're gonna fry. Pesci's variation on New Jersey machismo (vulnerable in this case) isn't enough to fill a comedy; but Dale Launer's script luckily provides some fine routines for the supporting cast, notably the scene-stealing Marisa Tomei as Mona Lisa Vito, Pesci's sharp-tongued girlfriend. It's a small, surprisingly gentle affair, prone to fits and starts, but fun. WH

My Crasy Life
(Jean-Pierre Gorin, 1992, US)
92 min.
This portrait of Samoan street gangs in LA may appear to conform to fly-on-the-wall documentary criteria, but in fact it's highly manipulated, scripted and shaped by Gorin together with the gang members. There's little glamour or action: Gorin films the self-styled Original Gangsters sitting around, playing cards, reminiscing about getting stabbed, or talking chillingly about the revenge ethic. Essentially, they are playing their own parts, which casts an interesting light on their monotonous, almost ritualistic rhetoric: a language Gorin has called 'the music of survival'. As befits the co-founder with Godard of the radical Dziga Vertov Group, Gorin shakes up the structure by interspersing scenes that don't strictly integrate – notably, a LA patrol cop being talked at by his computer. Anti-*vérité* in the extreme, this is a hard film to watch, sometimes verging on the inscrutable; but at the very least it offers an antidote to the glamour that can seep into even the toughest Hollywood street fictions. JRo

My Crazy Life (Mi Vida Loca)
(Allison Anders, 1993, US) Angel Aviles, Seidy Lopez, Jacob Vargas, Marlo Marron, Jessie Borrego, Magali Alvarado, Julian Reyes.
95 min.
With their men dead or in jail, a group of young Hispanic women from Echo Park, Los Angeles, struggle to raise their children, resorting to gangland tactics only to introduce some sense of identity or purpose into their difficult lives. The action revolves round five of these locas each with her own story to tell. Writer/director Anders mixes real gang members with up-and-coming Latin American actresses, but this ploy fails to lend the film authenticity or vitality. The tone seems, to put it kindly, misguidedly romantic. SFra

My Darling Clementine `100`
(John Ford, 1946, US) Henry Fonda, Victor Mature, Linda Darnell, Walter Brennan, Cathy Downs, Tim Holt, Ward Bond, Alan Mowbray, John Ireland.
97 min. b/w.
Like many Hollywood directors, Ford's claims for his films are very modest. For him the key thing about *My Darling Clementine* is its authenticity: 'I knew Wyatt Earp...and he told me about the fight at the OK Corral. So we did it exactly the way it had been'. For viewers, however, the film's greatness (and enjoyability) rests not in the accuracy of the final shootout, but in the orchestrated series of incidents – the drunken Shakespearean actor, Earp's visit to the barber, the dance in the unfinished church – which give meaning to the shootout. Peter Wollen's comment on the significance of Earp's visit to the barber's and its outcome makes clear just how complex the ideas contained in these incidents are: 'This moment marks the turning point of Earp's transition from wandering cowboy, nomadic savage, bent on revenge, unmarried, to married man, settled, civilised, the sheriff who administers the law'. PH

My Dear Tom Mix
(Carlos García Agraz, 1992, Mex) Ana Ofelia Murguia.
120 min.
A boy befriends his 60-year-old great aunt Joaquin in the Mexican town where she lives with her nephew and his wife. She a kind, generous soul, but somewhat crazy, with a fixation on Tom Mix Westerns. When bandits drive into town in a Model T, help comes from an unexpected quarter...well, not *that* unexpected, actually. A

charming conceit, well acted but sluggishly paced, and as sentimental as the B Westerns it holds dear – developed through the Gabriel Garcia Marquez script workshop. TCh

My Dinner with André
(Louis Malle, 1981, US) Wallace Shawn, André Gregory, Jean Lenauer, Roy Butler.
111 min.
Bring two New York intellectuals together and they'll beat each other's ears off swapping stories about their psychoanalysts. Here Malle celebrates just such an encounter, recreated by the original participants: a sad, never-quite-made-it playwright (Shawn) and a brilliantly successful director (Gregory) who dropped out to 'find himself' in a quest ranging from Grotowski in Poland to Tibet, the Sahara and remoter Scotland. Just two people talking, shot mostly in close-up. But hammering against the wall of Shawn's pragmatism, sometimes pulled up short in awareness of its own absurdity, Gregory's account of his spiritual odyssey becomes a magical mystery tour of thoughts, dreams, fantasies and emotions. Riveting, exhilarating stuff. TM

My English Grandfather (Robinsonada anu Chemi Ingliseli Papa)
(Nana Dzhordzhadze, 1986, USSR) Zhanri Lolashvili, Nineli Chankvetadze, Guram Pirtskhalava, Tiko Eliosidze.
76 min. b/w & col.
Wacky and whimsical versions of the Russian revolution by Russians were hardly thick on the ground before glasnost, and if Nana Dzhordzhadze's film is sometimes too Comic Cuts to hold together, it tickles like a Flann O'Brien essay. A contemporary composer recalls his English grandfather, a telegraph engineer called Hughes who was stranded in Georgia by events in 1917. Legally, the three-metre circumference of soil at the base of the telegraph posts belonged to Britain, so Hughes moved his brass bed and belongings away from the upheavals of history and became a species of Robinson Crusoe. Whether boxing with Bolsheviks, laying out rapists with flower vases, or courting the local leader's sister, our hero remains a rampant individualist of bumbling charm. A diverting curiosity. BC

My Fair Lady
(George Cukor, 1964, US) Audrey Hepburn, Rex Harrison, Stanley Holloway, Wilfrid Hyde-White, Gladys Cooper, Jeremy Brett, Mona Washbourne.
175 min.
Lerner and Loewe's musical version of Shaw's *Pygmalion* transferred effectively to the screen by Cukor, the director who, thematically if not stylistically, would seem to be the perfect choice for the project (many of his films deal with the relationship between real life and assumed appearances, and *Born Yesterday* is a beautifully funny update of the story). The sets, costumes (by Cecil Beaton), photography, and Hermes Pan's choreography are all sumptuously impressive, and Harrison makes a fine, arrogant Professor Higgins; but Hepburn is clearly awkward as the Cockney Eliza in the first half, and in general the adaptation is a little too reverential to really come alive. GA

My Family (Mi Familia/aka East LA)
(Gregory Nava, 1994, US) Jimmy Smits, Edward James Olmos, Esai Morales, Eduardo Lopez Rojas, Elpidia Carrillo, Jenny Gago, Mary Steenburgen, DeDee Pfeiffer.
126 min.
Nava's first film since *A Time of Destiny*, written with his wife and collaborator Anna Thomas, and produced under the auspices of Francis Coppola, is an ambitious saga charting 60 years and three generations of the Sanchez family. Nava exacerbates the structural problems posed by the time-frame by relying too heavily on a folksy voice-over and by adapting his mise-en-scène to the decades, so that the 1920s sequence, in which paterfamilias Jose walks from Mexico to Los Angeles, is relayed in a mystic, misty-eyed style, complete with DW Griffith optical effects. Survive this (and it's a chore), and things come into sharper focus in the '50s, where scenes of teen angst – the death of young tearaway Chucho

(Morales) at the hands of the police – are rendered in bold, saturated compositions which inevitably recall gang movies of the period. By the late '70s, the film's fragments of love, pain, anger and injustice are really beginning to add up, particularly in impassioned scenes between youngest son Jimmy (Smits) and illegal immigrant Isabel (Carrillo, a revelation here). It's shapeless, but there's iron in its soul. TCh

My Father Is Coming
(Monika Treut, 1991, Ger/US) Alfred Edel, Shelley Kästner, Annie Sprinkle, Mary Lou Graulau, David Bronstein, Michael Massee.
81 min.
Treut – a German director whose sex-pol essays like *Virgin Machine* and *Seduction: the Cruel Woman* have earned plenty of controversy and cult acclaim – here spins a tale of sexual awakening, presided over with ecstasy-aunt jollity by 'post-porn sex goddess' Sprinkle. Vicki (Kästner) is a sexually confused actress holding down a waitress job, and trying to persuade her visiting Bavarian papa (the marvellously shambling Edel) that she's happily married, although her 'husband' is fully occupied with vogueing Latin boys. Happily, La Sprinkle is on hand to distract papa with tender mercies and household appliances while Vicki makes her mark as a nightclub diva. A low-rent, loosely structured lesbian coming-out story that entertains a range of sexual orientations, Treut's film enshrines an engaging worldview – SoHo chic seen from a sort of polysexual Teutonic 'Carry On' perspective. JRo

My Father's Glory
see Gloire de mon père, La

My Father, the Hero
(Steve Miner, 1994, US) Gérard Depardieu, Katherine Heigl, Emma Thompson, Dalton James, Lauren Hutton, Stephen Tobolowsky.
90 min.
A Hollywood remake of the French comedy *Mon Père, ce héros* in which Depardieu reprises his role as the discomforted father of a pubescent girl. André arrives at the apartment of his ex-wife (Hutton) to whisk daughter Nicole on a get-to-know-you vacation. In Nassau, Nicole (Heigl) is mortified at the idea of anyone suspecting he's her father and starts fabricating a lifestyle to impress heart-throb Ben (James). Meanwhile lonely André falls for the local manhunter Diana. Makes *Baywatch* seem intellectual. WH

My Favourite Blonde
(Sidney Lanfield, 1942, US) Bob Hope, Madeleine Carroll, Gale Sondergaard, George Zucco, Victor Varconi, Edward Gargan, Dooley Wilson.
78 min. b/w.
Along with the later *My Favourite Brunette*, one of the funnier Hope vehicles, in which he plays a vaudeville entertainer (working with a trained penguin) who inadvertently becomes pulled into the world of espionage by British agent Carroll. With much cowardice and braggadocio in reaction to the threat of the pursuing Nazis, it's routine Hope, but the script sparkles with bright lines ('You got relatives out there?' he mutters when the penguin steals his applause, 'You and me will have to have a talk with a taxidermist') delivered with plenty of flair and gusto. GA

My Favourite Brunette
(Elliott Nugent, 1947, US) Bob Hope, Dorothy Lamour, Peter Lorre, Lon Chaney, John Hoyt, Reginald Denny, Charles Dingle.
87 min. b/w.
Likeable parody of the hardboiled world of Hammett and Chandler. Hope goes through his familiar routine as a craven photographer, a specialist in baby portraiture, who takes over from an absent private eye (Alan Ladd in a trench-coated cameo appearance) to help out Lamour's damsel in distress. The wisecracks are a little thin on the ground, but the *noir* atmosphere is handled with a nice mixture of bizarrerie (Lorre, Chaney) and deadpan (such iconographic figures as Jack LaRue and Anthony Caruso). TM

My Favourite Season
see Ma Saison Préférée

My Favourite Wife
(Garson Kanin, 1940, US) Cary Grant, Irene Dunne, Gail Patrick, Randolph Scott, Ann Shoemaker, Donald MacBride, Scotty Beckett.
88 min. b/w.
Originally planned for Leo McCarey, but a car accident intervened. Directed by the mercurial Garson Kanin, it remains a relatively formulaic (though beautifully produced) bedroom comedy, with Grant as the husband whose wife, presumed dead after a shipwreck, returns to their Californian home only to find him remarried. Grant's habitual skill at playing the faint-hearted prig is such that one can almost overlook the moments of mawkish sentiment and gentle complacency about the country-club milieu. The film was remade in 1963 as a Doris Day/James Garner vehicle (*Move Over, Darling*): some indication, perhaps, that it never really achieved the satirical bite of *Adam's Rib* (scripted by Kanin) or the giddy sexual risk-taking of Grant and Ginger Rogers in *Once Upon a Honeymoon*. CA

My Favourite Year
(Richard Benjamin, 1982, US) Peter O'Toole, Mark Linn-Baker, Jessica Harper, Joseph Bologna, Bill Macy, Lainie Kazan, Lou Jacobi, Cameron Mitchell.
92 min.
Fond nostalgia for that golden and not altogether mythical age (1954) when American television was live and innovative and came from New York City. Finding his feet in this buzz of hard work and talent is a young scriptwriter (Linn-Baker), suddenly assigned the heady task of nursemaiding an uproarious guest star through rehearsals and away from drink and trouble. The guest is a former screen idol in the Errol Flynn mould – a very funny performance from O'Toole, who throws himself into the drunk's pratfall routines like a lanky rag doll, coming up ever serene, debonair and with a suspicion of eye-liner. Richard Benjamin directs the smartish script and the chaotic tomfoolery quite brilliantly; but all concerned mishandle the soppy section where O'Toole gets misty-eyed about his discarded daughter. Still, the pace picks up for the magnificent comic climax. JS

My First 40 Years (I Miei Primi 40 Anni)
(Carlo Vanzina, 1987, It) Carol Alt, Elliott Gould, Jean Rochefort, Pierre Cosso, Massimo Venturiello, Riccardo Garrone, Capucine.
107 min.
This glitzy tale of ambition and sex Italian-style is like Fellini's *La Dolce Vita* re-written by Jacqueline Susann on acid. It follows the beautiful Marina (Alt) in her sexual conquests and social climbing, from an early marriage to a handsome but penniless duke, through a spell as a millionaire's plaything, to a tempestuous affair with a mercurial communist artist who likes to slap her around. A romantic affair with married journo Nino (Gould) begins with champagne and roses, but also ends in disillusionment. The characters are vapid, the dubbing ludicrous, and the would-be evocative soundtrack merely bizarre (Paul Anka, Gilbert O'Sullivan, Mungo Jerry and '70s bubble gum pop). What it lacks in substance, it tries to make up for in sartorial accessories and exotic locations, achieving a perversely compelling trashiness. High camp fun or 24 carat kitsch, depending on your tolerance level. NF

My First Wife
(Paul Cox, 1984, Aust) John Hargreaves, Wendy Hughes, Lucy Angwin, David Cameron, Anna Jemison, Charles Tingwell, Betty Lucas.
98 min.
John (Hargreaves) introduces classical music over the late-night Melbourne air waves to pay his way as a composer. His wife Helen (Hughes) meanwhile indulges in some close harmony with a fellow choir member. One long painful night she comes clean about her adultery, and decides to leave John, taking their daughter with her. But John cannot cope with the separation. Standard soap on paper, but Cox fills the screen with luminous images of desires and anguish, and encourages his actors to portray emotional states of an almost embarrassing intensity. Rarely has the naked human body seemed so vulnerable, so raw; rarely has a simple shot – a girl and a dog – com-

bined with a phrase of music seemed so potent. With its teasing, semi-autobiographical title, this is not always a comfortable film, but its compassion, wit and vigour are undoubtedly the real thing. DT

My Foolish Heart
(Mark Robson, 1949, US) Susan Hayward, Dana Andrews, Kent Smith, Lois Wheeler, Jessie Royce Landis, Gigi Perreau, Robert Keith.
98 min. b/w.
Loosely based on a short story by JD Salinger (*Uncle Wiggily in Connecticut*, so travestied that it's no wonder Salinger subsequently kept Hollywood at arm's length), this Goldwyn production is a finely polished but drearily turgid example of the '40s weepie. Hayward plays a fallen college girl: cynical, selfish, alcoholic, married to a man she doesn't love, and expecting the child of a playboy pilot. The melodramatic situation is wrung for all it's worth and more, with the woman's final, inevitable realisation of the error of her ways only adding to the disaster of Robson's pedestrian direction and the mediocrity of the performances. GA

My Forbidden Past
(Robert Stevenson, 1951, US) Robert Mitchum, Ava Gardner, Melvyn Douglas, Janis Carter, Lucile Watson.
81 min. b/w.
A Hughes RKO production dismissed as soapy claptrap by most critics, this steamy tale, set in 1890s New Orleans, of Ava Gardner's desperate plans to lure Mitchum away from his wife when she inherits a fortune, is terribly underrated. Nonsense it may be, and Mitchum's low-key style is certainly at odds with the overheated emotionalism of the plot. But it is extremely entertaining, largely thanks to a marvellously cynical script which insists from start to finish on the basic selfishness of human interaction. Nasty fun. GA

My Friend Flicka
(Harold Schuster, 1943, US) Roddy McDowall, Preston Foster, Rita Johnson, Jeff Corey, James Bell.
89 min.
Archetypal boy 'n' his hoss story (from the novel by Mary O'Hara), a Technicolor hit during the war and held in affection ever since. McDowall begs Foster, his rancher pa, for a colt of his own, then faces the trials and responsibilities of looking after it. All at once now, 'Aaah.' TJ

My Friend Ivan Lapshin
(Moi Drug Ivan Lapshin)
(Alexei Gherman, 1981, USSR) Andrei Boltnev, Nina Ruslanova, Andrei Mironov, A Zharkov, Z Adamovich.
99 min. b/w & col.
Gherman's masterly film (his third) is framed as an autobiographical reminiscence of the 1930s, just before the Stalinist terror began to bite. Through the eyes of a 9-year-old kid we watch episodes from the life of a small-town police chief: his home life in a ludicrously overcrowded apartment, his unsuccessful courtship of a glamorous actress, and his rather more successful campaign to hunt down the criminal fraternity of the Soloviev gang. There is nothing sinister about this Ivan, but the film is crammed with tiny suggestions of the horrors to come, designed to provoke disquieting speculations about the eventual fate of this potentially dangerous man. Gherman's methods are resolutely observational and low-key, and his subject is the lull before the storm; the drama emerges as if by accident from a collage of resonant and deeply felt scenes from day-to-day life. Wonderfully vivid performances and amazingly original camerawork (mostly in elegantly faded monochrome) bring a vanished world to life with complete conviction. TR

My Girl
(Howard Zieff, 1991, US) Dan Aykroyd, Jamie Lee Curtis, Macaulay Culkin, Anna Chlumsky, Richard Masur, Griffin Dunne, Ann Nelson, Peter Michael Goetz.
102 min.
It's 1972, and 11-year-old Vada (Chlumsky) lives with her dotty granny and widowed mortician father (Aykroyd) in a house which doubles as a funeral parlour. Daily contact with corpses has

produced a very odd child, given to pranks around the caskets, hypochondria and death-obsession, but shy Thomas (Culkin) proves a true and tolerant friend. Their knockabouts won't last forever, though: cosmetologist Shelly (Curtis) arrives to divide Dad's affections, and Vada experiences her first period, a make-up session, and bereavement... Zieff's direction is uninspired, but the film is considerably redeemed by screenwriter Laurice Elehwany's dark humour. Chlumsky gives a lively performance, which is more than can be said for Culkin. CM

My Girl 2
(Howard Zieff, 1994, US) Dan Aykroyd, Jamie Lee Curtis, Anna Chlumsky, Austin O'Brien, Richard Masur, Christine Ebersole, John David Souther.
99 min.
After kissing Macaulay Culkin only to see him stung to death by killer bees in *My Girl*, Pennsylvania waif Vada Sultenfuss (Chlumsky) takes her pubertal traumas to Los Angeles. Assigned to write a school essay on 'someone very special...someone you've never met', mortician's daughter Vada opts for another stiff: her mother, who expired shortly after giving birth. She lived in Los Angeles, but nobody (including super-rotund dad Aykroyd) can remember anything about her. Maybe amiable Uncle Phil (Masur) and his unwed partner Rose (Ebersole) can help. It's hard to pinpoint what's so grisly about this film. Zieff's direction is far from his worst, Janet Kovalcik's script side-steps the mawkish, Chlumsky has shed her moppet-mouthed ghastliness and new boyfriend O'Brien is one up on Culkin. Perhaps it's that the obsession with death sits so uneasily against the young-love backdrop. MK

My Girlfriend's Boyfriend
(L'Ami de Mon Amie)
(Eric Rohmer, 1987, Fr) Emmanuelle Chaulet, Sophie Renoir, Anne-Laure Meury, Eric Viellard, François-Eric Gendron.
103 min.
The sixth in Rohmer's glorious series of *Comédies et Proverbes*. As ever, the plot is slight: shy civil servant Blanche escapes the loneliness of her new life in a Parisian suburb through her friendship with self-assured computer programmer Léa. When Léa goes on holiday, Blanche, who initially fancies herself enamoured of handsome engineer Alexandre, finds herself growing closer to her friend's lover Fabien. Questions of fidelity and betrayal, delusion and deceit lie at the film's heart, which is large indeed, extending ample compassion to the characters. Once again the performances of the young cast are miraculously naturalistic, and equally impressive is Rohmer's mastery of mood: a chaste and silent stroll along a canal towpath is tense with gentle eroticism, a summer party becomes fraught with embarrassment and unspoken feelings. Funny, moving, and full of insights that other directors barely dream of, it is quite simply an absolute charmer. GA

My Heroes Have Always Been Cowboys
(Stuart Rosenberg, 1991, US) Scott Glenn, Kate Capshaw, Ben Johnson, Balthazar Getty, Tess Harper, Gary Busey, Mickey Rooney, Dub Taylor.
106 min.
Battered but unbowed, rodeo-rider Glenn returns from the circuit dismayed to find pa Johnson in an old folks home, and running straight up against the rest of the family who reckon the old bastard should stay there. Glenn's world-weary performance brings a glimmer of real heart to this sagebrush saga, though the rekindling of romance with former high-school sweetheart Capshaw and his eventual return to the bull ring are such contrivances that the characters don't stand much of a chance. TJ

My Hustler
(Andy Warhol, 1965, US) Paul America, Ed Hood, Joseph Campbell, John MacDermott, Genevieve Charbon, Dorothy Dean.
70 min. b/w.
Made on Fire Island beach, this is vintage Warhol, with rather more structure than usual. The camera pans between a bronzed, blond hustler, statuesque on the sand, and an ageing queen talking on the verandah of a beach house. The

queen provides most of the soundtrack: part monologue, part conversation in best New York camp style, witty, vicious, outrageous, etc. Dramatic interest of sorts is provided by the arrival of a female neighbour intent on seducing the hustler, and shortly after of the Sugar Plum Fairy, another hustler, also with a lustful eye on the beach. The three have a bet as to which one will succeed; and the second half is filmed with a static camera in the bathroom while they wash and shave. At the end, after they've all tried to pull him, offering variations on the wealth/possessions theme, we never get to know who wins out. But that's unimportant: the myth of the ending is a literary hangover. JB

My Learned Friend
(Basil Dearden/Will Hay, 1943, GB) Will Hay, Claude Hulbert, Mervyn Johns, Ernest Thesiger, Charles Victor, Hy Hazell, Lloyd Pearson.
76 min. b/w.
A slightly desperate but surprisingly funny farce, agreeably tinged with black. Will Hay's last film, in which, as an incompetent barrister being kept till last as a bonne bouche by a criminal (Johns) determined to eliminate everyone connected with his trial, he frantically tries to forewarn the other victims in an attempt to stave off his own end. The dizzy climax, courtesy Harold Lloyd and/or Hitchcock, is a pursuit over the face and hands of Big Ben. TM

My Left Foot
(Jim Sheridan, 1989, GB) Daniel Day Lewis, Ray McAnally, Brenda Fricker, Ruth McCabe, Fiona Shaw, Eanna MacLiam, Alison Whelan, Declan Croghan, Hugh O'Conor, Cyril Cusack.
103 min.
Day Lewis' recreation of writer/painter Christy Brown's condition is so precise, so detailed and so matter-of-fact that it transcends the carping about casting an actor without cerebral palsy. He couldn't have done it better. More to the point, he does it with so little show that the character of Christy – cussed, frustrated, indulged, immature – comes through powerfully. Writers Shane Connaughton and Jim Sheridan take extraordinary liberties with Brown's autobiography, but they've caught the spirit of the man, and satisfied the family, who are presented as saintly, if chaotic. Brenda Fricker, wonderfully eloquent in her silences, and Ray McAnally, in his last screen role, make an utterly convincing Mam and Dad, stopping just the right side of sentimentality. Less happy is Fiona Shaw as the fictional Eileen Cole, an amalgam of several characters in the book. Sheridan gives us an atmospheric Dublin and the economy of the best TV drama; and 13-year-old Hugh O'Conor, playing Christy as a boy, makes an admirable job of holding the ring before the arrival of the main act. JMo

My Life
(Bruce Joel Rubin, 1993, US) Michael Keaton, Nicole Kidman, Bradley Whitford, Queen Latifah, Michael Constantine, Haing S Ngor.
116 min.
Bob and Gail Jones (Keaton and Kidman) are expecting their first child. Bob, though, has cancer and may not live to see the baby, so he starts to make a video journal about his life – thus embarking on a journey of self-discovery into the density of the human heart and the expansiveness of the human soul. The only thing dense and expansive, however, is the sentimentality. Ironically, we don't know much more about Bob after he's discovered himself than we knew before. He's angry and ashamed of his family, and angry and ashamed of himself because of it. Indeed, rather than examine Bob's life in any depth, the film chooses in the end to become the celebration of a baby. AO

My Life and Times with Antonin Artaud
see En Compagnie de Antonin Artaud

My Life as a Dog (100)
(Mit Livsom Hund)
(Lasse Hallström, 1985, Swe) Anton Glanzelius, Manfred Serner, Anki Lidén, Tomas von Brömssen, Melinda Kinnaman.
101 min.
This charming, bitter-sweet evocation of child-

hood is something of a minor gem. Set in the Sweden of the 1950s, it describes the 400 blows suffered by a resourceful, twitchy and energetic 12-year-old boy who is farmed out to country relatives when his antics and demands for attention prove too much for his ailing mother. Hallström nurtures from his young star (Glanzelius) a performance of remarkable range and maturity, presenting a poignant picture of youthful tenacity struggling to come to terms with disappointments and events that may be beyond his comprehension, but which he manages to negotiate with his quirky, open-eyed optimism intact. Witty, touching and perceptive as he contrasts the rural village and its strange but generous-hearted eccentrics with the harsher realities of the city, Hallström makes it a seamless mix of tragedy and humour. WH

My Life's in Turnaround

(Eric Schaeffer/Donal Lardner Ward, 1993, US) Eric Schaeffer, Donald Lardner Ward, Dana Wheeler Nicholson, Lisa Gerstein, John Sayles. 84 min.
Schaeffer and Ward (writers, directors and stars of this first feature) play two struggling young film-makers scraping together the wherewithal to make a movie. Very droll, or it would be if the script had a bit more horsepower and the players a bit more screen presence. The best moment comes from John Sayles as a dodgy financier railing against so-called 'independent' movie-makers, but it's a very mild diversion. TJ

My Life to Live

see Vivre sa Vie

My Life Without Steve

(Gillian Leahy, 1986, Aust) voice: Jenny Vuletic.
53 min.
Alone in a Sydney bedsit, a woman meditates on the loss of her lover to another woman. It's the usual thing: confusion, recrimination, guilt, fear, anger, loneliness. Finally, however, she takes a few tentative steps towards a rediscovery of her sense of self. It's structured as a monologue accompanied by crisp, painterly images of the narrator's apartment and its view over a bay, the rambling digressions (bursting with cultural references) clearly meant to represent an intensely relevant essay on romantic love and loss. But for all its worthy intentions, the movie suffers from fashionable, dilettante pretensions and from a dearth of humour that turns its narrator's liturgy of misery into a self-piteous wallow that fails to stir the emotions. Not a little irritating. GA

My Little Chickadee

(Edward F Cline, 1940, US) Mae West, WC Fields, Joseph Calleia, Dick Foran, Ruth Donnelly, Margaret Hamilton, Donald Meek. 83 min. b/w.
Pairing West and Fields in one film was probably one of those ideas that seemed good at the time. But the two iconoclasts just don't mix. Fields has easily the best of it, working from his own script (though he diplomatically shared screen credit with his prickly co-star). He's in his element tossing off lunatic stories and choice aphorisms at the bar and card table of Greasewood City, a parody Western town, but time hangs heavy in his exchanges with the buxom Mae, who marries him for his non-existent money. And it hangs even heavier when Mae's by herself. GB

My Little Girl

(Connie Kaiserman, 1986, US) James Earl Jones, Geraldine Page, Mary Stuart Masterson, Anne Meara, Pamela Payton Wright.
117 min.
16-year-old Franny (Masterson) is a poor little rich girl who spends some of her time as a volunteer helper at a centre for children in care. She befriends a pair of black sisters, but when one is transferred to a more secure institution, she become involved in helping her to escape. Connie Kaiserman's sententious debut aims to show the plight of criminal brats and circumstantial orphans and to reveal the dangers of do-gooding; as a director, unfortunately, she shares her central character's naivety and lack of judgment. The final half-hour is taken up with a wholly unnecessary and wholly awful talent night given by the centre's inmates. Still, the performances are good. MS

My Little Pony

(Michael Jones, 1986, US) voices: Danny DeVito, Madeline Kahn, Cloris Leachman, Rhea Perlman, Tony Randall.
100 min.
An animated feature hopefully plugging the *My Little Pony* line in toys. Pretty Ponyland is threatened with manic monochrome by the wicked witch Hydia and her evil slime, Smooze. Utter Flutter provides salvation, but don't ask what it is, because the queasy colours, screeching voices, and songs of staggering banality make paying attention difficult. Jejune in conception, devoid of talent in realisation, this painful dross perpetrates its own critique when Reeka (or was it Draggle? One of the witch's daughters, anyway) remarks on seeing her spell fail, 'How embarrassing, I'm going home'. MS

My Love Has Been Burning (Waga Koi Wa Moenu)

(Kenji Mizoguchi, 1949, Jap) Kinuyo Tanaka, Mitsuko Mito, Kuniko Miyabe, Ichiro Sugai, Koreya Senda.
84 min. b/w.
A film that deserves the same kind of praise as *Ugetsu Monogatari* and *Sansho Dayu*. Drawn from the autobiography of a late 19th century pioneer for women's rights in Japan, the film is one woman's journey through an extremely complex, contradiction-laden phase of modern Japanese history: when notions of democratic party politics were cohering, for instance, although – as is devastatingly demonstrated – not even the most liberal-thinking male politician thought to extend the freedoms for which he was fighting to his own wife. Undoubtedly one of Mizoguchi's most violent films – the scenes in the silk mill and prison show some horrific brutalities – it's also notable for a wonderful performance from Mizoguchi's favourite actress, Kinuyo Tanaka. RM

My Man Godfrey

(Gregory La Cava, 1936, US) William Powell, Carole Lombard, Gail Patrick, Eugene Pallette, Alice Brady, Mischa Auer, Alan Mowbray.
93 min. b/w.
Heartless screwball classic, directed with clinical glee by the still undervalued La Cava and scripted by the mysterious Morrie Ryskind, who began with the Marx Brothers and later drifted into weepies and right wing politics. Godfrey (Powell) is the high-minded tramp found during a society 'scavenger hunt' and led back by the more than lovely Lombard into her household, full of profligate madcaps who duly become a little more civilised. The film has lost some of its allure over the years, but it's still streets and streets ahead of the addled whimsy favoured by latter-day Hollywood. GB

My Man Godfrey

(Henry Koster, 1957, US) June Allyson, David Niven, Jessie Royce Landis, Robert Keith, Martha Hyer, Eva Gabor, Jay Robinson.
92 min.
Wretched remake of La Cava's stinging screwball comedy about a scatterbrain socialite who 'collects' one of the Depression's forgotten men and adopts him as her butler. Apart from deficiencies on all other glitzy Ross Hunter fronts, the script tries to update by turning the down-and-out into an illegal immigrant. With the part of an ex-Luftwaffe pilot played by OW Fischer, as originally planned, it just might have worked; with Niven, it's disastrously bland. TM

My Memories of Old Beijing (Chengnan Jiushi)

(Wu Yigong, 1983, China) Shen Jie, Zheng Zhenyao, Zhang Min, Zhang Fengyi, Yan Xiang.
93 min.
Wu Yigong's almost dream-like recreation of a young girl's Beijing childhood is often like memory itself, impressionistic, anecdotal and resonant in its initially disassociated detail; and because this framework eschews a direct, linear narrative, Wu neatly sidesteps the melodramatic conventions of much Chinese cinema. The result is an immensely accessible and often tender film, sometimes betrayed by its visual and stylistic ambition but nonetheless consistently evocative, and full of a diffuse, affecting melancholy. SM

My Mother's Castle

see Château de ma mère, Le

My Mother's Courage (Mutters Courage)

(Michael Verhoeven, 1995, Ger/GB/Aus) Pauline Collins, Ulrich Tukur, Natalie Morse, Robert Giggenbach, Günter Bothur, George Tabori.
90 min.
In 1994 the playwright George Tabori visits the set of a film being made from his mother's diaries. An encounter with the leading actress whisks him back to the past to place the story in context – a distancing framework that challenges us to consider our own connection with these images of terror. There's more time for reflection as the action moves on to Tabori's mother, a middle-aged housewife arrested while doing her shopping and dispatched to Budapest's main railway station, where the Gestapo punctiliously marshal hundreds of her fellow Jews into freight wagons. Surprising, maybe, to see Pauline Collins as Mrs Tabori (the film's shot in English), but she's superb as an essentially cheery woman numbed by the events around her and driven to make a stand for the first time in her life. Determined to avoid displaying emotion in front of her captors, Collins, in a key moment, chokes back the tears in a straining, desperate attempt to retain her dignity. A remarkable scene, and it says a lot for the power and intelligence of the film and its central performance, that its most haunting image is of a woman trying not to cry. TJ

My Name Is Joe

(Ken Loach, 1998, GB) Peter Mullan, Louise Goodall, David McKay, Anne Marie Kennedy, Gary Lewis, David Hayman.
105 min.
After coming into conflict over a young couple troubled by debt and drug-dependency, amateur soccer coach and recovering alcoholic Joe (Mullan) and health service worker Sarah (Goodall) find themselves embarking on a mutually wary but fulfilling romance; the trouble is, they have different ideas about how to deal with the problems posed by the unforgiving world around them. Very funny, typically insightful and authentic, and surprisingly sexy (for a Loach movie), this also proceeds to an emotionally quite devastating conclusion, where Renoir's thesis that 'everyone has their reasons' is put painfully to the test. The performances are uniformly superb (though Mullan is especially charismatic), and the direction discreet but wonderfully telling. GA

My Name is Julia Ross

(Joseph H Lewis, 1945, US) Nina Foch, George Macready, Dame May Whitty, Roland Varno, Anita Bolster.
64 min. b/w.
Having toiled industriously on nonsense for years, B-movie king Lewis was at last given a chance, by Columbia's Harry Cohn, with a slightly higher budget and infinitely more malleable material. Taking a job as secretary to Whitty, Foch soon finds herself in deadly peril: drugged and removed to a remote Cornish manse, she awakes to discover that she has been given another woman's name, not to mention a husband in the shape of Whitty's psychotic son Macready. So far, so bad, but things worsen when she hears her incarcerators plotting her demise as a fake suicide. Handling the various plot twists with ease and eliciting superior performances from his three leads, Lewis repeatedly displays his ability to convey mood and meaning through visuals: Burnett Guffey's camera prowls nervously through shadowy interiors, Macready's madness is vividly evoked by his endless knife-playing. A small, dark gem in the *Rebecca* tradition, it may not be as startlingly original or adventurous as Lewis's later *Gun Crazy* or *The Big Combo*, but it knocks Penn's remake *Dead of Winter*, for six. GA

My Name Is Nobody (Mio Nome è Nessuno)

(Tonino Valerii, 1973, It/Fr/WGer) Henry Fonda, Terence Hill, Jean Martin, Piero Lulli, Leo Gordon, RG Armstrong, Remus Peets.
130 min.
Produced by Sergio Leone and very much bear-

ing his stamp, a Western which takes as its theme the alchemy whereby life is turned into legend. The year is 1899, and feared but fading gunfighter Jack Beauregard (Fonda) lives for the day he can lay down his deposit on a steamer berth to Europe. Instead he meets his angel of death, a young gunfighter calling himself Nobody who, in turn, lives for the legend of Beauregard and an obsessive vision of the ultimate confrontation: between Beauregard, alone on an immense plain, and the 150 men of the Wild Bunch. With superbly handled action sequences, excellent cinematography, and a Morricone score worthy of his *Man With No Name* efforts, it's a film to be seen. VG

My New Friends
(Wo Xin Renshi de Pengyou)
(Tsai Ming-Liang, 1995, Tai) Tsai Ming-Liang.
56 min.
Tsai interrupted his pre-production for *The River* to make this pioneering documentary for Taiwan's nascent AIDS-awareness campaign. Ignoring instructions to 'play down the gay angle', he centres the film on his own very candid conversations with two HIV+ young men. Sadly the identities of the interviewees have to be concealed, and so the freewheeling camerawork focuses most often on Tsai himself; but the sense of rapport between the director and his 'new friends' is palpable and very moving, even to Western viewers already only too familiar with these issues. TR

My New Gun
(Stacy Cochran, 1992, US) Diane Lane, James LeGros, Stephen Collins, Tess Harper.
95 min.
A deceptive, quirky and amusing black comedy from the independent sector. Set in upmarket wood-clad suburban New Jersey, it follows events when a housewife (Lane, in her best performance to date) is given a pearl-handled revolver by her nerd husband for her protection (and against her wishes). Attractive next door neighbour Skippy (Collins) asks to borrow the gun for unexplained reasons, she agrees, and the two become implicated. There are many questions. What, for instance, has Skippy's strange mother (Harper), a Country & Western singer, to do with all this? Cinematographer Ed Lachman gives it all a bright look, to augment the feeling of unsettling disingenuousness. For this is a film without explanations, more 'screw-loose' than 'screwball', with a pinch of Lynch. WH

My Nights with Susan, Sandra, Olga and Julie (Mijn Nachten med Susan Olga Albert Julie Piet & Sandra)
(Pim de la Parra, 1975, Neth) Willeke Van Ammelrooy, Hans Van der Gragt, Nelly Frijda, Franulka Heyermans, Marya de Heer, Jerry Brouwer.
100 min.
The biggest mystery about this psycho-sex-drama is why it took five writers (including Harry Kümel, who should have known better) to cobble together dialogue that consists mainly of characters calling out the names in the title. Blond biker stays at farmhouse full of assorted weirdos, namely two murderous nymphets (Sandra and Olga), troubled heroine (Susan), sleeping beauty (Julie) and simpleton hag (Piet) who collects dead bodies and watches everyone spying on each other. Presumably intended as an adult fairytale, it takes itself ludicrously seriously but never overcomes the fundamental problem of so what and who cares.

My Night with Maud (Ma Nuit chez Maud)
(Eric Rohmer, 1969, Fr) Jean-Louis Trintignant, Françoise Fabian, Marie-Christine Barrault, Antoine Vitez.
113 min. b/w.
The third in Rohmer's series of *Moral Tales* (though shot out of sequence after *La Collectionneuse*) was the film that sealed his international reputation. Exquisitely shot by Nestor Almendros in a chill and wintry Clermont-Ferrand, it tells – lightly, wittily and amazingly perceptively – of the long night of the soul of a Catholic engineer (Trintignant), smugly secure in his acceptance of Pascal's wager (it pays to believe

in God, because if you win, you win eternity; if you lose, you lose nothing), who makes up his mind he is going to marry a girl (Barrault) he has seen only in church. His philosophy comes in for a rude shaking up during the teasing, tantalising, and ultimately chaste night he spends with the free-thinking divorcee Maud (Fabian), who opens his eyes to the fact that 'a choice can be heartbreaking'. Still one of Rohmer's best films. TM

My Own Private Idaho
(Gus Van Sant, 1991, US) River Phoenix, Keanu Reeves, James Russo, William Richert, Rodney Harvey, Chiara Caselli, Udo Kier, Grace Zabriskie, Tom Troupe
104 min.
Van Sant's impressive third feature has enough ideas to fill three movies, a plenitude that threatens to blow the film apart (but never does). It's a road movie filmed mainly from the point of view of gay hustler Mike (Phoenix, superb), a narcoleptic who falls unconscious without warning at moments of stress. As Mike tours the Pacific Northwest doing 'dates', he meets up with mayor's son Scott (Reeves), and together they set off in search of Mike's mother. The disconcerting realities of the situation are punctuated by sequences of surreal, dreamlike beauty, 'documentary'-style inserts, and playful variations on Shakespeare, with Scott still playing Prince Hal to the Falstaffian Bob (Richert), a thief and exhustler, in the knowledge that he will soon be 'King'. Stunning to look at – the dawn and dusk landscapes are sublime – and seductively scored, the film's uniqueness lies in its remarkable emotional open-heartedness. WH

My Private War (Mein Krieg)
(Harriet Eder/Thomas Kufus, 1990, Ger)
90 min. b/w & col.
The German army on the Russian front boasted six amateur cameramen in the ranks, whose footage comprised a fascinating blend of the ordinary and the horrendous. In place of the heel-clicking automata of war films, we see a young soldier in a swastika armband embarrassed by a visit from his mum; a Christmas tree stabbed into the frozen earth beside a machine-gun emplacement; the joy of shooting down a Russian plane with a rifle. In interview, the veterans display extreme agitation on the subject of the execution of peasants and Jews, and great pride in their old German cameras which performed so well at temperatures below zero. BC

Myra Breckinridge
(Michael Sarne, 1970, US) Mae West, John Huston, Raquel Welch, Rex Reed, Farrah Fawcett, Roger C Carmel, Jim Backus, John Carradine.
94 min.
As an adaptation of Gore Vidal's novel, this is a major travesty. As a Hollywood comedy, it's a major disaster. As a 20th Century-Fox movie, it's the best argument yet for employing a director who can direct. But as a Raquel Welch movie, it's better than most. TR

My Sister Eileen
(Richard Quine, 1955, US) Janet Leigh, Jack Lemmon, Betty Garrett, Robert Fosse, Kurt Kasznar, Richard Yorke, Horace McMahon.
108 min.
Two spirited Ohio girls, plain, forbearing Ruth (Garrett) and blonde, head-turning Eileen (Leigh), take a 30-day let on a Greenwich Village basement, determined to make their mark on Manhattan. Good-looking wide-screen musical (by Jule Styne and Leo Robin), with Bob Fosse as the unprepossessing soda jerk who wins Eileen against the opposition of a shipload of Brazilian naval cadets, and Jack Lemmon, as the magazine editor, an old-school sexual predator (essentially idiotic), who finally recognises Ruth for what she is, a real writer and a real stunner. Funny, innocent and light on its toes. JPy

My Sons (Musuko)
(Yoji Yamada, 1991, Jap) Rentaro Mikuni, Emi Wakui, Masatoshi Nagase.
121 min.
Yamada, director of the endless 'Tora-san' series, called this his homage to Ozu, and it's true that the focus on parental expectations and filial obligations is Ozu-esque, as are a few of the images. Grizzled veteran Mikuni plays a cantankerous

tobacco farmer from a village in Iwate Prefecture; his wife died a year ago, and he's getting too old to carry on. His two contrasted sons have moved to the outskirts of Tokyo, and the core of the film is the old man's visit to the capital to assess their futures and his own. This is not an example of what's happening in contemporary Japanese cinema, and it has the usual Yamada problem of being all surface and no depths; but it has sincere affection for its characters, and is very well acted and directed. Genuinely touching, its qualities make it Yamada's best film by far. TR

My Son the Fanatic
(Udayan Prasad, 1997, GB) Om Puri, Rachel Griffiths, Stellan Skarsgård, Akbar Kurtha, Gopi Desai, Moya Brady.
87 min.
Combining affecting romance with sharp political and psychological insights, Hanif Kureishi's script (from his own short story) centres on Pakistani cabbie Parvez (Om Puri), whose respect and love for most things English – including local prostitute Bettina (Griffiths) – brings him into terrible conflict with his teenage son, an Islamic fundamentalist who contemptuously views the ways of his family's adopted northern English city as decadent, depraved and disposable. Thematically rich, and never opting for simplistic polarities in its exploration of the clash of cultures, generations and ethical beliefs, the film overcomes its initial uncertainties of tone to mount a very moving study of a man in crisis; Puri is terrific, especially in his scenes with the excellent Griffiths. GA

My Stepmother Is an Alien
(Richard Benjamin, 1988, US) Dan Aykroyd, Kim Basinger, Jon Lovitz, Alyson Hannigan, Joseph Maher, Seth Green.
108 min.
In a last-ditch attempt to save her planet from imminent destruction, alien Celeste (Basinger) arrives on earth to seek the help of widowed scientist Steve (Aykroyd). Her identity is a secret, which results in confusion when Steve falls for and marries what he believes to be a beautiful and naive European; his teenage daughter (Hannigan) is none too pleased with her conniving stepmother, particularly after catching her slurping on battery fluid and talking to an ugly creature in her handbag. The film offers several entertaining sequences, but *Splash* it ain't, for while that film took a similar scenario and beautifully conveyed romantic notions of innocence, this is marred by cruel and juvenile gags. Hence an overlong scene which introduces Celeste to the experience of kissing. Worse still, comedian Lovitz plays Steve's truly tedious playboy brother. With earthlings like him, intelligent forms of life would be better advised to stay in their own galaxy. CM

Mystère Picasso, Le
(Henri-Georges Clouzot, 1956, Fr)
Pablo Picasso.
90 min.
Picasso was famously reluctant to be filmed at work. But when persuaded in 1955 to sketch before the camera of Henri-Georges Clouzot, master (and miserabilist) film director, he evidently took to it with relish. Stripped to a pair of shorts, parading his square torso, the 75-year-old Pablo plays up to the camera, even turning out a sketch to a five-minute deadline. Because he was asked to work on transparent screens, allowing the camera fully to frame the emerging picture instead of having to peep over the artist's shoulder, we get to see the work develop, with Picasso's different styles accompanied by a soundtrack that moves from bebop to flamenco. RY

Mysterians, The (Chikyu Boeigun)
(Inoshiro Honda, 1957, Jap) Kenji Sahara, Yumi Shirakawa, Takashi Shimura, Akihiko Hirata.
89 min.
The Mysterians come from an exploded planet and aren't the friendliest aliens: they start forest fires and landslides, and send up a galumphing robot monster. They ask for three kilometres of Japan, but really want the whole earth; most ghastly of all, they kidnap women to propagate their kind. Still, we humans aren't very nice in return, and it's not long before this lively sci-fi extravaganza from Inoshiro *Godzilla* Honda has

turned into an out-and-out war film, with tanks and ray guns trundling and blasting away in the midst of lavish but variable special effects. GB

Mysterious Island
(Cyril Endfield, 1961, GB) Joan Greenwood, Michael Craig, Herbert Lom, Michael Callan, Gary Merrill, Percy Herbert, Dan Jackson, Nigel Green.
100 min.
Ray Harryhausen's stop-motion animation effects are the best thing about this version of the oft-filmed Jules Verne yarn. Craig leads a gang of Union soldiers who flee a Confederate jail by balloon, only to be washed up on the isolated isle where Lom's Capt Nemo has been experimenting to solve the world's food crisis (hence the giant hen, huge bees and over-sized crabs which test the plucky escapers). Scripted by several hands, but Bernard Herrmann's score a decided plus. TJ

Mystery Date
(Jonathan Wacks, 1991, US) Ethan Hawke, Teri Polo, Fisher Stevens, Brian McNamara, BD Wong, Tony Rosato, Victor Wong.
93 min.
Darker humour than you might anticipate raises this erratic teen comedy out of the usual rut. Hawke thinks he's got it made when brother McNamara sets him up with siren next door Teri Polo, but he's about to become an unwitting pawn in his brother's dodgy business dealings as a corpse turns up in the back of the car. Straight to video in Britain. TJ

Mystery in Mexico
(Robert Wise, 1948, US) William Lundigan, Jacqueline White, Ricardo Cortez, Tony Barrett, Jacqueline Dalya, Walter Reed.
66 min. b/w.
You've seen every twist in this routine caper a thousand times before. Lundigan is the insurance agency detective sent to Mexico on the trail of a fellow-employee (Reed) who has disappeared along with a valuable necklace. White is the pretty blonde singer who may be an accomplice, but obviously isn't since Lundigan falls for her. She is actually Reed's sister, so he's obviously innocent too; and it only remains for Cortez' villain (who owns a nightclub, naturally) to get his comeuppance after demonstrating his nastiness. Wise directs neatly enough, but the half-hearted romantic byplay and wisecracking dialogue cry out for Mitchum and Russell. Only Dalya, as Cortez' disillusioned, man-hungry mistress, manages to give her lines any bite. TM

Mystery of Alexina, The (Mystère Alexina)
(René Féret, 1985, Fr) Philippe Vuillemin, Valérie Stroh, Véronique Silver, Bernard Freyd, Marianne Basler, Philippe Clévenot.
90 min.
Set in mid-19th century provincial France, this tells of a young woman who arrives to teach at a girls' boarding school and falls in love with a colleague, only to discover to her own astonishment that she is in fact a man. It's excellently performed and shot, and Féret teases out the ironies of Alexina's predicament, denied the right to love either as woman or man, with sure, steady clarity. Finally, however, it never entirely escapes a certain dullness, while its portrait of oppression born of ignorance and fear is unduly one-dimensional. Fascinating, nevertheless, as a sensitive account of an extraordinary story based in historical fact. GA

Mystery of Edwin Drood, The
(Timothy Forder, 1993, GB) Robert Powell, Jonathan Phillips, Rupert Rainsford, Michelle Evans, Finty Williams, Freddie Jones, Peter Pacey, Nanette Newman, Ronald Fraser, Glyn Houston, Andrew Sachs, Gemma Craven.
112 min.
Dickens' final, tantalisingly unfinished novel, as adapted and directed by Forder, and filmed on a shoestring around the environs of Rochester Cathedral, hasn't supplied a particularly apt or satisfying development (in fact, there's a touch of Hammer about the finale). Too many scenes simply wobble about without registering much of pith or moment, and the absence of editing skills compounds the air of amateurism. The pity is that the central character of choirmaster John

Jasper, who may or may not have done away with his eponymous nephew, is given great, brooding weight by Powell. Most Dickensian of all is Freddie Jones as local dignitary Mr Sapsea, a man both orotund and snuff-taking; while Finty Williams as Rosa presents the usual pale purity that Dickensian men pine after. BC

Mystery of Kaspar Hauser, The
see Jeder für sich und Gott gegen alle

Mystery of Rampo, The (Ranpo)
(Kazuyoshi Okuyama, 1994, Jap) Masahiro Motoki, Naoto Takenaka, Michiko Hada, Mikijiro Hira.
100 min.
This became a cause célèbre in 1994 when producer Okuyama objected to the work of director Rintaro Mayuzumi and remade it the way he wanted. The two versions were released side-by-side in Tokyo; the 1995 London Film Festival, predictably, is showing only the producer's cut. Edogawa Ranpo ('Edgar Allan Poe') was the pen name of Hirai Taro (1894-1965), writer of erotic/fantastic mystery fiction; the wheeze behind this imaginary episode from his life is to trap him inside one of his own bizarre and enigmatic stories. Okuyama has cast and designed it expensively, and the animated prologue is quite cute. But it's basically piffle, founded on a lamentably dated idea of what images of Japan foreign suckers might pay to see. TR

Mystery of the Wax Museum
(Michael Curtiz, 1933, US) Lionel Atwill, Fay Wray, Glenda Farrell, Allen Vincent, Frank McHugh, Arthur Edmund Carewe.
78 min.
In the early '30s, when Universal were riding high with Frankenstein and Dracula, Warners hunted round for their own horror subject, and found one in the idea of a sculptor who murders his models and embalms them in wax to achieve death-in-life. It's an interesting Poe-like theme, full of bizarre implications, and has since been remade several times (once in 3-D); but this remains the classic. Filmed in one of the earliest two-tone Technicolor processes, it is beautiful to look at, full of muted green compositions and stunningly modulated colour effects. Interesting, too, to note that its tough, wisecracking girl reporter (Farrell) and newspaper setting bear the unmistakable stamp of the Warner house style. There's a slightly cruel, almost fascist streak throughout, especially in the police's handling of things, and the shocks are a little sparse by present standards. But it holds up amazingly well, and its pale, shimmering images linger in the mind. DP

Mystery Street
(John Sturges, 1950, US) Ricardo Montalban, Sally Forrest, Marshall Thompson, Bruce Bennett, Elsa Lanchester, Jan Sterling.
93 min. b/w.
A neat thriller, despite getting itself a little hung up on the contemporary vogue for documentary trimmings. The opening sequences, set in Boston for a change and magnificently shot by John Alton, are classic film noir, detailing the circumstances leading inexorably to the murder of Jan Sterling, a girl on the make and not above a bit of blackmail. Next comes the police procedural bit, featuring a didactic (but not uninteresting and cleverly integrated) sequence set in the Harvard Department of Legal Medicine. The temperature never fully recovers, although Sturges handles the rest (caught up in his own lies, the wrong man (Thompson) lands in the net; stoutly maintaining his innocence, his wife (Forrest) gets increasingly distraught; sympathetic cop (Montalban) begins to wonder if he could possibly have got it all wrong) with considerable deftness and some subtlety. Nice performances, too, especially from Montalban as the zealous but still self-questioning cop, while Elsa Lanchester revels in one of her inimitably batty, gin-swilling landladies. TM

Mystery Train
(Jim Jarmusch, 1989, US) Masatoshi Nagase, Youki Kudoh, Screamin' Jay Hawkins, Cinqué Lee, Nicoletta Braschi, Elizabeth Bracco, Tom Noonan, Joe Strummer, Rick Aviles, Steve Buscemi.
110 min.

A trilogy of off-beat, Beat-besotted tales, shot in gorgeous colour, set in and around a seedy Memphis hotel. On one level it's about passers-through: a Japanese teenage couple on a pilgrimage to Presley's grave and Sun studios; an Italian taking her husband's coffin back to Rome, forced to share a room with a garrulous American fleeing her boyfriend; and an English 'Elvis', out of work, luck in love and his head as he cruises round town with a black friend, a brother-in-law, and a gun. But on a deeper level, the film is about storytelling, about how we make connections between people, places, objects and time to create meaning, and how, when these connections shift, meaning changes. Only halfway through do we begin to grasp how the stories and characters relate to each other. Happily, Jarmusch's formal inventiveness is framed by a rare flair for zany entertainment: Kudoh and Nagase make 'Far From Yokohama' delightfully funny; Braschi brings the right wide-eyed wonder to 'A Ghost'; and Strummer proffers real legless menace in 'Lost in Space', which at least explains the cause and effect of a mysterious gun shot heard in the first two episodes. Best of all are Screamin' Jay Hawkins and Cinqué Lee as argumentative hotel receptionists hooked on Tom Waits' late night radio show. They, and Jarmusch's remarkably civilised direction, hold the whole shaggy dog affair together, turning it into one of the best films of the year. GA

Mystic Pizza
(Donald Petrie, 1988, US) Vincent Philip D'Onofrio, Annabeth Gish, William R Moses, Julia Roberts, Adam Storke, Lili Taylor, Conchata Ferrell.
104 min.
Jojo, Daisy and Kat are pizza-pushers who live in Mystic, on the Connecticut coast. Jojo (Taylor) is carrying on a stormy romance with a redneck fisherman. Daisy (Roberts), a bit of a social climber, is having an affair with the owner of a throbbing red Porsche. And good old Kat (Gish), soon to start studying astronomy at Yale, is about to have a bad case of babysitter blues. Each of these women, through being used and abused by men, achieves some kind of self-realisation. If the plot (by Amy Jones) sounds pedestrian and pat, it is. However, thanks to sensitive direction by Petrie, the result is a thoroughly involving movie that doesn't resort to violence, sex or schmaltz to pack an emotional punch. Petrie imbues the Portuguese-dominated fishing village with a real sense of place, and the three female leads (Gish in particular) are excellent. MS

My Sweet Lady
see Sunshine Part II

My Sweet Little Village (Vesnicko má Stredisková)
(Jiri Menzel, 1985, Czech) János Bán, Marian Labuda, Rudolf Hrusinsky, Petr Cepek, Milena Dvorská.
100 min.
In the village in question, a cooperatively-run community, live Pavek – who is short and fat – and his workmate Otik, who is long and thin. Because Otik's teeth outnumber his IQ, he is more hindrance than help, so when he directs the long-suffering Pavek's truck into a gatepost, their fraught friendship is threatened. As if this weren't catastrophic enough, a party bureaucrat sets his heart on Otik's cottage, and arranges for him to be rehoused in a high-rise honeycomb in Prague. Menzel directs a good-natured comedy in which pleasure is derived from such innocent pursuits as consuming beer and bangers in the sun, riding through the unremarkable countryside, and watching the desperate home-produced TV. The optimism, if indulgent, is infectious, and the Laurel and Hardski relationship is ultimately moving. MS

Myth of Fingerprints, The
(Bart Freundlich, 1996, US) Noah Wyle, Roy Scheider, Julianne Moore, Blythe Danner, James LeGros, Arija Bareikis, Hope Davis, Laurel Holloman, Brian Kerwin, Michael Vartan.
90 min.
Warren (Wyle) hasn't been home to Maine in three years, partly because he still hasn't got over being dumped by the love of his life. When he does turn up for Thanksgiving, however, it's

not Daphne who's the problem, but his dad Hal (Scheider), who welcomes Warren, his other children – persistently angry Mia (Moore), non-committal Jake (Vartan), easy-going Leigh (Holloman) – and their various partners with an indifference verging on outright hostility. Somehow, Warren's mum Lena (Danner) keeps a fragile peace, though Mia's tantrums and Hal's icy disapproval repeatedly threaten to turn the reunion into an emotional bloodbath. While writer/director Freundlich's serio-comic study of a dysfunctional family is hardly original, it is a remarkably mature, assured and perceptive first feature. A superior cast give their best in a faintly old-fashioned, carefully crafted, very enjoyable movie from a young talent to watch. GA

My Tutor
(George Bowers, 1982, US) Caren Kaye, Matt Lattanzi, Kevin McCarthy, Clark Brandon, Bruce Bauer, Arlene Golonka, Crispin Glover.
97 min.
Poor little rich kid (Lattanzi) flunks his graduation French, so his father hires an attractive 29-year-old tutor (Kaye) who initiates him into rather more than the mysteries of *la plume de ma tante*. Both flap their eyelashes and flash their toothpaste smiles, but are insipid and boring as they go through the motions of nude swimming, clinging wet T-shirts, shared bubble baths and lyrical love scenes. Puerile dross which dares to speak with feeling of the value of sex while making such an obvious play for the soft porn market. JE

My 20th Century
(Az én XX századom)
(Ildikó Enyedi, 1989, Hun/WGer/Cuba) Dorothea Segda, Oleg Yankowski, Paulus Manker, Peter Andorai, Gábor Máté.
104 min. b/w.
East European whimsy is usually heavy-going, especially when most of the women are played by the same actress, and this feminist frolic through the political and technological birth-pangs of the present century has all the poetry of a dodo on downers. At the exact moment that Edison unveils the electric light bulb in a New York park, twin sisters are born in Budapest. This arbitrary conjunction leads into a collage of very loosely related scenes (crammed with allusions to movies, pulp fiction, etc. etc) in which the sisters' lives diverge and faithfully reconverge via a trip on the Orient Express. Chic black-and-white photography and relentless 'cleverness' won this wearying charade the Best First Feature prize at Cannes. TR

My Uncle
see Mon Oncle

My Uncle Antoine
see Mon Oncle Antoine

My Uncle from America
see Mon Oncle d'Amérique

My Universities
see Childhood of Maxim Gorki, The

My Way Home
see My Childhood

My Way Home (Igy Jöttem)
(Miklós Jancsó, 1964, Hun) András Kozák, Sergei Nikonenko.
109 min. b/w.
This early (pre-*Round-Up*) Jancsó movie is apparently autobiographical in spirit if not in letter. Its young Hungarian protagonist wanders through the Russian-occupied Hungary of the final months of WWII, suffering a pointedly arbitrary round of arrests, internments and accusations. In a way that foreshadows Jancsó's later choreographic effects, he is sometimes the focus of our attention, and sometimes lost in larger patterns of landscape and movement. The film's centrepiece is its study of the one period when he comes to rest: he is assigned to help a wounded Russian soldier tend a herd of cows. Jancsó's portrait of the warm, doomed relationship between the two men is one of the most moving and clear-sighted analyses of male sensibilities and friendship in all cinema. TR

My Young Auntie (Zhangbei)
(Lau Kar-Leung aka Liu Jialiang, 1981, HK) Hui Yinghong, Lau Kar-Leung, Wang Longwei, Xiao Hou, Gordon Liu.
121 min.
The Shaw Bros policy of selling dubbed-only versions of their productions does no favours to Lau's over-extended kung fu comedy, first and foremost a showcase for the talents (martial and otherwise) of his then girlfriend Hui Yinghong. She plays an upright young widow from the Chinese hinterland, who finds herself in the 'cosmopolitan' Canton of the 1930s, trying to protect an inheritance from the black sheep of the family she married into. One set of repetitive jokes springs from her youth (she could be the daughter of her elderly nephew, played by Lau himself), and another from her joshing relationship with her nephew's son (played by Lau's real-life star pupil Xiao Hou), a boy her own age who has been 'westernised' by studying in Hong Kong. The dubbing kills all the 'Chinglish' language gags, and so the entertainment value rests squarely on the fight scenes – which are expectedly brilliant in choreography and execution. The UK video release is correctly letterboxed. TR

n

Nikita

n

Nada

(Claude Chabrol, 1974, Fr/It) Fabio Testi, Michel Duchaussoy, Maurice Garrel, Michel Aumont, Lou Castel, Didier Kaminka, Viviane Romance.
134 min.

A chillingly cool political thriller, all the better for its non-partisan stance. No attempt is made to whitewash the activist group in Paris, calling themselves Nada in memory of the Spanish anarchists, who kidnap the American ambassador (at an exclusive brothel) in a welter of functional violence. A motley collection of malcontents and seasoned professionals, driven by absurd ideological confusions, they are for that reason a doubly dangerous time bomb likely to explode at any random moment. But against them Chabrol sets the cold calculation of the forces of order, wheeling, dealing, finally engineering a politic holocaust, and emerging as even less concerned with human life than the terrorists they are hunting down as a threat to society. Right is on their side, but it is the members of Nada, groping desperately to build little burrows of viable living in a world of expediency and corruption, who become the heroes in spite of everything. Powerful, pure *film noir* in mood, it's one of Chabrol's best films. TM

Nadia

(Alan Cooke, 1984, US) Talia Balsam, Jonathan Banks, Joe Bennett, Simone Blue, Johann Carlo, Conchata Ferrell, Carrie Snodgress.
99 min.

Let's hear it for the baby gymnasts, whose patron saint is now enshrined in the true story (made for TV) of the rise and fall and rise again of Nadia Comaneci, first spotted at the age of six showing her knickers in a Romanian playground. After eight years training under the watchful eye of coach Bela Karolyi, Nadia scoops three golds at Montreal and becomes the first Olympic gymnast ever to score a Perfect 10. But the strain of being the most famous person in Romania takes its toll. Nadia gets too tubby; her parents divorce; she quarrels with her best friend; she drinks bleach. Triumphing over adversity, an infected hand, and the Russians – in a tale to inspire another generation of little girls in leotards – she leads her team to victory with a 9.95 on the balance beam. AB

Nadine

(Robert Benton, 1987, US) Jeff Bridges, Kim Basinger, Rip Torn, Gwen Verdon, Glenne Headly, Jerry Stiller.
83 min.

Benton's lightweight romantic comedy has Nadine Hightower (Basinger) witness the murder of a photographer while trying to recover some candid nude pics. Having escaped with photos of a proposed road development instead, she tricks her soon-to-be-ex husband Vernon (Bridges) in helping her recover the right ones. However, when Vernon discovers the map photos, he decides to cash in on them. But first they must deal with their rightful owner, a ruthless businessman (Torn) and his two henchmen. Despite a plot with more twists than a rattlesnake, Benton plays the crime caper for laughs, concentrating on the couple's nervous edging towards a romantic reconciliation. Basinger is excellent as the flaky heroine, while Bridges exudes vulnerable charm as her two-bit loser of a husband. NF

Nadja

(Michael Almereyda, 1994, US) Suzy Amis, Martin Donovan, Peter Fonda, Karl Geary, Galaxy Craze, Elina Löwensohn.
100 min. b/w.

Highly stylised b/w camerawork and Pixelvision, moody poeticism, and farcical genre parody merge to tantalising if not altogether coherent effect in Almereyda's quirky New York update on the Dracula story. The heavily Mittel-European persona of Löwensohn is used effectively as the Count's enigmatic, doomy daughter who hopes to tempt Lucy (Craze) away from her husband (Donovan), while desperately trying to get in touch with her own estranged twin brother. About blood, blood ties and breakdown (of families, relationships and, perhaps, an entire society), it's an idiosyncratic film, admired by many for its strong atmosphere, and by this writer for its absurd(ist) casting of a barely recognisable Fonda as Donovan's mad uncle Van Helsing. GA

Naked

(Mike Leigh, 1993, GB) David Thewlis, Lesley Sharp, Katrin Cartlidge, Greg Cruttwell, Claire Skinner.
131 min.

Mike Leigh's film explores a form of male self-loathing manifesting itself in misogynist insults and violence. When Johnny (Thewlis), an out-of-work twenty-something given to manic rants and rough sex, visits ex-girlfriend Louise (Sharp) in London, it's hard to know whether or not he aims to persuade her to return with him to Manchester. Getting stoned and sleeping with her spaced-out flatmate Sophie (Cartlidge) is unlikely to endear her to such a prospect, as is his sudden decision to roam the streets of the capital, waxing philosophical to anyone he meets. But is he any worse than Jeremy (Cruttwell), a smooth sadist who claims a landlord's right to invade the girls' house and subject them to sexual humiliation? Hilarious, but sometimes hard to stomach, Leigh's picaresque tale is his most troubling and intriguing work since *Meantime*; it's also by far his most cinematic. The cast is outstanding – Thewlis, in particular, whose virtuoso performance gives the film its cruel energy, wit and power. GA

Naked and the Dead, The

(Raoul Walsh, 1958, US) Aldo Ray, Cliff Robertson, Raymond Massey, William Campbell, Richard Jaeckel, James Best, Joey Bishop, LQ Jones, Robert Gist, Barbara Nichols.
131 min.

Just as Joseph Heller's *Catch-22* was to virtually defeat Hollywood a decade later, Norman Mailer's mighty (and mightily important) novel defeated director Walsh and screenwriters Denis and Terry Sanders. In fact, it owes hardly anything to Mailer, except for one or two episodes and the title. What we have is a routine war adventure about a platoon behind enemy lines, directed in Walsh's normal manner (he cares about the action and lets the rest dawdle). The tropical scenery is fine, and only Massey's performance as the fascist-minded general is memorable. ATu

Naked Are the Cheaters

(Derek Ashburne, 1971, US) Angela Carnan, Robert Warner, Vickie Carbe, Douglas Frey, Neola Graef.
62 min.

Absolutely dire, farcically amateurish non-film about a Washington wheeler-dealer who runs a callgirl service on the side. Possibly stripped at some point of most of whatever rudimentary sex footage it contained; at any rate, tricked out with some incomprehensible flash-cutting, the perfunctoriness of the proceedings is impossible to describe. VG

Naked Cell, The

(John Crome, 1987, GB) Vicky Jeffrey, Richard Fallon, Jacquetta May, Yvonne Bonnamy, Jill Spurrier.
90 min.

'Ere, wanna see a film about a woman who goes mad 'cos she can't get enough sex? Forget *Fatal Attraction* and all that glossy stuff, this is the real thing – serious bonking, filthy talk, you know, realistic. She's a career woman, see, and a bit of a lush, and we first meet her in the mental home where she's remembering episodes like this bloke with designer stubble giving her one on the sink. The guards question her repeatedly about why she keeps picking up strange blokes, but much of her memory is a blank. Known only as The Prisoner (Jeffrey), she spends much of her time f-ing and blinding and taking leaks in a bucket. We finally learn that she strangled a stranger while he was on the job. In short, she seems to be a Woman Trapped by her Desires. Crude, exploitative rubbish. NF

Naked Childhood

see Enfance nue, L'

Naked City, The

(Jules Dassin, 1948, US) Barry Fitzgerald, Howard Duff, Dorothy Hart, Don Taylor, Ted de Corsia.
96 min. b/w.

Despite its reputation, a rather overrated police procedure thriller which has gained its seminal status simply by its accent on ordinariness and by its adherence to the ideal of shooting on location. In organising the hunt for a brutal murderer, Fitzgerald's detective is too winsome and hammy, Taylor's assistant merely wooden; thanks be then to Ted de Corsia as the killer, adding a touch of real nastiness and urgency to the admittedly well-constructed final chase. GA

Naked Dawn, The

(Edgar G Ulmer, 1955, US) Arthur Kennedy, Betta St John, Eugene Iglesias, Roy Engel, Charita.
82 min.

From the master of the B movie quickie, a rather studio-bound but compellingly tense Western. Kennedy plays a marauding bandit who, after the death of his sidekick, invades the home of a Mexican farmer (Iglesias), draws him into crime, and falls for his wife (St John). Unusually for Ulmer, it was shot in Technicolor, which is employed for some tellingly expressionistic effects. The film's romantic triangle was even an inspiration for Truffaut's *Jules and Jim*. DT

Naked Face, The

(Bryan Forbes, 1984, US) Roger Moore, Rod Steiger, Elliott Gould, Anne Archer, David Hedison, Art Carney, Ron Parady.
106 min.

Big Rog puts aside his James Bond image and dons a cardigan to play a wimpy psychiatrist who thinks that he's next on the list of those responsible for the murder of an ex-patient. Sidney Sheldon's pulp novel gets the Cannon treatment: numerous guest stars, shabby production values, and nil credibility. NF

Naked Gun, The

(David Zucker, 1988, US) Leslie Nielson, Priscilla Presley, Ricardo Montalban, George Kennedy, OJ Simpson, Susan Beaubian, Nancy Marchand, John Houseman.
85 min.

Fans of the *Airplane* team (and especially of their short-lived TV series *Police Squad!*, by which this gloriously tacky spoof cop-thriller is inspired) will know that corny old gags, hoary clichés, and downright silliness can, if delivered in the right spirit, provide far more fun than any amount of Merchant-Ivory *bons mots* or Woody Allen witticisms. As ever, sophistication is conspicuously absent as tactless, dim-witted Lt Frank Drebin (Nielsen) investigates the shooting of a cop during a ludicrously audacious drugs bust. One hesitates even to attempt a synopsis of the admirably perfunctory plot, other than that suspects include a deliriously plastic Priscilla Presley and a magnificently corseted Montalban. Ineptitude rules throughout. Finally, though, it's Nielsen's show: with an unaccountable flair for the needlessly dramatic, he holds the entire shambling absurdity together by treating everything as if it were a matter of life or death. The endlessly tasteless juvenilia should make you ashamed of laughing yourself into a stupor. GA

Naked Gun 2½: The Smell of Fear, The

(David Zucker, 1991, US) Leslie Nielsen, Priscilla Presley, George Kennedy, OJ Simpson, Robert Goulet, Richard Griffiths, Jacqueline Brookes, Lloyd Bochner, Anthony James.
85 min.

In this deliriously silly sequel to the marvellously tasteless juvenilia of Lieutenant Frank Drebin's first chaotic outing on the big screen, Drebin (Nielsen) is out to foil a conspiracy designed to prevent wheelchair-bound conservationist Dr Meinheimer (Griffiths) from influencing George Bush's energy policy. The fact that the plotters' leader Hapsburg (Goulet) is dating Drebin's old flame Jane (Presley) only complicates matters further. Thus is the scene set for romantic agony, moral dilemma, profound ecological controversy, and the most tuneless caterwauling heard in a movie since the last instalment. A corny cornucopia of cop-saga clichés, Zucker's film is a sublimely free-wheeling parody of every ridiculous matter-of-life-and-death scene ever to appear in a crime thriller. A minor masterpiece of infantile idiocy. GA

Time Out Film Guide **619**

Naked Gun 33⅓: The Final Insult

(Peter Segal, 1994, US) Leslie Nielsen, Priscilla Presley, George Kennedy, OJ Simpson, Fred Ward, Kathleen Freeman, Anna Nicole Smith.
83 min.

For all those fans desperate to find out what the Statesville Prison actually looks like, here's your chance. It's where Lt Frank Drebin (Nielsen) goes very conspicuously undercover when he's brought back from retirement, and a rough ride at the sperm bank, to monitor the activities of Rocco (Ward), a terrorist with grand plans. That's about it in terms of story (except for the usual heart-rending subplot detailing Drebin's efforts to win back the beloved Jane), but who cares? The spoof-policier series is about non-stop gags, pure and simple, and this third instalment, for all its lax plotting and ludicrous characterisation, remains infinitely more pleasurable than sticking you face in a fan. Indeed, the five minutes of the pre-credits sequence are quite possibly the funniest since the talkies came in. Thereafter, it's hit and miss, but the hits are so frequent and spot-on, you'd have to be dead (and buried) not to find the film painfully hilarious. Inspired, inspirational, gloriously inane. GA

Naked in New York

(Dan Algrant, 1994, US) Eric Stoltz, Mary-Louise Parker, Ralph Macchio, Kathleen Turner, Tony Curtis, Timothy Dalton, Jill Clayburgh, Roscoe Lee Brown, Eric Bogosian, Quentin Crisp, William Styron.
91 min.

This pseudo-autobiographical comedy, from a first-time writer/director, concerns a youthful playwright Jake Biggs (Stoltz), an aspiring angry young man with a Woody Allen line in romantic-neurotic confession straight to camera. Spurred by the absence of his father and the remoteness of his mother (Clayburgh), Jake's creativity wows his college classmates. But after graduation the spark falters when he settles down with Joanne (Parker). Picked up by a producer (Curtis), Jake hits the big time when a Broadway star (Turner) expresses interest in his work. The film begins brightly, but its agile, astute voice begins to flag as the plot becomes steadily more conventional, and the tone of wry self-effacement veers dangerously close to self-congratulation. An assured debut, nevertheless, scoring some satiric hits against the New York art scene, with Curtis and Turner enlivening matters no end. TCh

Naked Jungle, The

(Byron Haskin, 1954, US) Charlton Heston, Eleanor Parker, William Conrad, Abraham Sofaer, John Dierkes, Douglas Fowley.
95 min.

A weird and wonderful combination of melodrama, sexual symbolism and exotic adventure. At the turn of the century, South American plantation-owner Heston battles both with an army of red ants and with his feelings of impotence and disgust towards the red-haired beauty he has married by proxy (Parker). Produced by George Pal, sumptuously shot by Ernest Laszlo, intelligently and literately scripted by Philip Yordan, it somehow, miraculously, holds absurdity at bay.

Naked Kiss, The

(Samuel Fuller, 1964, US) Constance Towers, Anthony Eisley, Michael Dante, Virginia Grey, Patsy Kelly, Betty Bronson.
93 min. b/w.

Not altogether the best of Fuller, despite an electrifying opening sequence in which a statuesque blonde (Towers) advances on her pimp, flailing out with her handbag as he staggers drunkenly until her wig falls off, revealing her to be totally bald. Subsequently seeking fresh fields in a small American town where vice is kept carefully screened behind locked doors, she instead becomes ministering angel in a children's orthopaedic hospital. It takes a little swallowing, but Fuller's grasp of character and milieu is so sure that the film gradually imposes itself as a scathing exposé of hypocrisy, unforgettable for the sharp savagery of scenes like the one in which Towers calmly marches into the local bordello and stuffs the madam's mouth full of dollar bills as retribution for trying to corrupt an innocent. TM

Naked Lunch

(David Cronenberg, 1991, GB/Can) Peter Weller, Judy Davis, Ian Holm, Julian Sands, Roy Scheider, Monique Mercure, Nicholas Campbell, Michael Zelniker, Robert A Silverman, Joseph Scorsiani.
115 min.

Cronenberg's film of William Burroughs' novel fleshes out the plot with details from the junkie author's life. He casts Weller as Burroughs' alter ego, Bill Lee, a cockroach exterminator who experiments with injecting his own bug powder. An appointment with the sinister Dr Benway (Scheider), Lee's meeting with a strange creature, and the murder of his wife (Davis) precipitate Lee's flight to Interzone, more mental state than actual place, a decadent, nightmare world run by bureaucrats who control the market in a rare drug, The Black Meat. Under the hallucinatory influence of the drug, Lee's grasp of reality disintegrates as he uses a speaking insect typewriter to file obscure reports. Through his most complex and brilliant cinematic metaphor to date, Cronenberg links these drug-induced images with Lee's eventual salvation, as he comes to terms with his repressed homosexuality and discovers another, more permanent way of altering reality – the writing of his novel 'The Naked Lunch'. Burroughs purists may be disappointed, but this dark distillation of the novel's themes gets closer to its essence than any 'straight' adaptation could hope to do. NF

Naked Night, The

see Gycklarnas Afton

Naked Runner, The

(Sidney J Furie, 1967, GB) Frank Sinatra, Peter Vaughan, Derren Nesbitt, Nadia Gray, Tony Robins, Edward Fox.
102 min.

One of the complex spy games which proliferated in the mid-'60s: more Cold War crises of conscience in East Germany, with Sinatra as the wartime crack shot unwillingly reactivated for an assassination plot. A tortuously hollow narrative is further obfuscated by Furie's customarily flashy direction, which fragments the looking glass to the point of impenetrability. PT

Naked Spur, The

(Anthony Mann, 1953, US) James Stewart, Robert Ryan, Janet Leigh, Ralph Meeker, Millard Mitchell.
91 min.

The third Mann/Stewart Western was the simplest yet most effective of their collaborations, with the actor giving one of his most hysterical performances as a bounty hunter driven by naked greed. Unable to capture and bring back outlaw Ryan without help, Stewart enlists old-timer Mitchell and dishonourably discharged cavalryman Meeker. But having captured Ryan – who, they discover, is looking after a friend's young daughter (Leigh) – the ill-matched trio are played off against one another by the manipulative Ryan. Through strong, clear story-telling and tremendous use of landscape, Mann infuses the familiar scenario with a remarkable psychological complexity. NF

Naked Tango

(Leonard Schrader, 1990, US) Vincent D'Onofrio, Mathilda May, Esai Morales, Fernando Rey, Cipe Lincovski, Josh Mostel, Constance McCashin.
92 min.

1924. Sailing to Buenos Aires, tired of her ageing, possessive husband (Rey), Stephanie (May) impulsively exchanges identities with a suicide. The girl gone overboard was a mail-order bride, and Stephanie – now Alba – happily marries handsome Jewish groom Zico (Morales), only to find herself enslaved in a hellish world of prostitution, sexual abuse and murderous violence presided over by her hubby's underworld chum Cholo (D'Onofrio). As ever in such films, the heroine both abhors and comes to adore her captor-tormentor, mainly because of his passion for, and expertise in, the tango. The directing debut of screenwriter Leonard Schrader (brother of Paul) may be a slick study in baroque set design, costume and lighting; but the script's stilted clichés serve only to turn what was evidently intended as a homage to the films of Valentino and Louise Brooks into a sexist fantasy so inept it comes over as camp parody. GA

Naked Truth, The (aka Your Past is Showing!)

(Mario Zampi, 1957, GB) Terry-Thomas, Dennis Price, Peter Sellers, Peggy Mount, Shirley Eaton, Joan Sims, Miles Malleson, Kenneth Griffith, Wilfrid Lawson.
92 min. b/w.

Simply spiffing comedy about scandal-mongering, with smarmy Dennis Price playing a gutter press baron who plans to blackmail a number of public figures or smear them across page one unless they hand over their House of Lords luncheon vouchers. Much miffed, Terry-Thomas contacts other victims – Peggy Mount's romantic novelist, Peter Sellers' TV celeb – and lays plans to undo the beastly rotter. A period piece, maybe, but much funnier and arguably more authentic than Scandal. ATu

Naked Under Leather

see Girl on a Motorcycle

Name of the Rose, The (Der Name der Rose)

(Jean-Jacques Annaud, 1986, WGer/It/Fr) Sean Connery, Christian Slater, Helmut Qualtinger, Elya Baskin, Michel Lonsdale, Volker Prechtel, F Murray Abraham.
131 min.

As intelligent a reductio of Umberto Eco's sly farrago of whodunnit and medieval metaphysics as one could have wished for. Just who is killing the monks of an isolated monastery in a variety of vile ways, and why? William of Baskerville is the Franciscan Holmes called upon to point the finger: a complex man, at once the great detective delighted with his own powers of deduction, and a man both defeated by the brutality of his age and enthralled by its mysteries (and it's to Sean Connery's credit that he portrays as much and more). In addition, the film simply looks good, really succeeds in communicating the sense and spirit of a time when the world was quite literally read like a book, with impressively claustrophobic sets, particularly the Escher-like labyrinth of a library with its momentous secret. The monks themselves are marvellous, a gallery of grotesques straight out of Brueghel, and if the film has faults, they are quibbles: the murder mystery is solved too soon, and rather too much plot is crammed into the available space. AMac

Namu, The Killer Whale

(Laslo Benedek, 1966, US) Robert Lansing, John Anderson, Lee Meriwether, Richard Erdman, Robin Mattson, Joe Higgins.
89 min.

The usual 'boy and his killer whale' tale receives a slightly different spin in this superior family offering, with Lansing as the naturalist who gives sanctuary to the eponymous ocean-going predator in his own cove, only to meet strong opposition from fishermen worried about their salmon stocks. Not as glossy as the latter-day Free Willy, but it passes – quite attractively and unsentimentally. Laslo Benedek who began his career as a camera assistant at UFA in the early '30s is best remembered as the director of Marlon Brando's The Wild One (he was also responsible for a Frank Sinatra musical titled The Kissing Bandit). TJ

Nana

(Jean Renoir, 1926, Fr) Catherine Hessling, Jean Angelo, Werner Krauss, Valeska Gert, Pierre Philippe, Claude Autant-Lara, Pierre Champagne, André Cerf, Pierre Lestringuez, Raymond Guérin-Catelain.
144 min. b/w.

Renoir's rare 1926 adaptation of Zola's novel about a gamine's rise to riches and notoriety during the Second Empire, and widely regarded as the director's finest silent. True, the lead performance of Hessling is at the very least broad, eccentric and at odds with the overall naturalism of the piece, while for the first hour or so the film is rather static, mostly content simply to tell the story, record the performances, and lavish attention on Claude Autant-Lara's sumptuous sets. As the movie proceeds, however, with the amoral courtesan gleefully taking every opportunity to humiliate her various, rival suitors, the initially light-hearted satire gives way to a bleaker mood, admirably incarnated by the increasingly dark, shadowy images. Renoir's subtle way with detail, coupled with a beautifully restrained performance from Krauss as the Count Muffat, makes for an accumulation of psychological and emotional nuance that anticipates his (superior) later films. GA

Nana

(Dan Wolman, 1982, It) Katya Berger, Jean-Pierre Aumont, Yehuda Efroni, Massimo Serato, Mandy Rice-Davies, Debra Berger.
92 min.
More Erogenous Zone than Emile Zola, this 'loose' adaptation of his novel about a coquette's rise to fame and riches is updated from Second Empire to the can-can age of Lautrec, and introduces Nana as the porno-protégée of a certain bleu film-maker called Méliès. It also lends weight to the theory that Zola was not a Naturalist but a Nudist, occasioning nude rollicking and a pivotal scene of huntsmen pursuing naked ladies through the dingles. Artistic licence also extends to the book's downbeat ending (Nana expiring in a mass of suppurating smallpox sores); in this ridiculous piece of fluff she goes off in a balloon to India for a bit of quiet meditation. AB

Nana (aka Lady of the Boulevards)

(Dorothy Arzner, 1934, US) Anna Sten, Phillips Holmes, Lionel Atwill, Muriel Kirkland, Richard Bennett, Mae Clarke, Reginald Owen.
89 min. b/w.
Conceived by Sam Goldwyn as a vehicle to launch his protégée Anna Sten, this is a very loose and inevitably bowdlerised version of Zola's classic novel about a gamine from the gutters who becomes the most celebrated whore in Paris. With the sex and syphilis gone, it becomes a somewhat stolid if sumptuously designed romantic melodrama about a music-hall actress torn apart by her liaisons with brothers Holmes and Atwill. But Arzner treats her heroine sympathetically, while Gregg Toland's lustrous photography makes a fair stab at exoticising her into a Garbo/Dietrich figure. And her lacklustre reputation notwithstanding, Sten – albeit rather too wholesome for the part – is surprisingly affecting. GA

Nanny, The

(Seth Holt, 1965, GB) Bette Davis, Wendy Craig, Jill Bennett, James Villiers, William Dix, Pamela Franklin, Jack Watling, Maurice Denham, Alfred Burke.
93 min. b/w.
A spirited pot-boiler from the almost forgotten ex-editor Seth Holt (his Station Six Sahara is a stunner that deserves revival), with Davis as Nanny to a houseful of neurotics. In particular, there is a 10-year-old boy (Dix), just released from a psychiatric hospital, who believes Davis wants to murder him. Made for Hammer Films (with whom Davis subsequently starred in The Anniversary), it capitalises on the star's performance in What Ever Happened to Baby Jane?, and while no one will have any trouble figuring out what's going on, Holt's atmospheric direction and Davis' performance keep one thoroughly hooked. ATu

Nanou

(Conny Templeman, 1986, GB/Fr) Imogen Stubbs, Jean-Philippe Ecoffey, Christophe Lidon, Valentine Pelka, Roger Ibanez, Daniel Day Lewis, Lou Castel.
110 min.
Nanou (Stubbs) is an awfully nice English rose, bent on adventure and experience during a summer in France. She takes up with political activist slob Luc (Ecoffey, clearly a would-be Depardieu), much to the dismay of old flame Max (Day Lewis, all brooding eyebrows and twitchy lips). Not only does Luc involve Nanou in dangerous acts of terrorism, he also treats her like a dog. Quite why the masochistic miss is so taken with him is unclear; first love never seemed so boring or unattractive. Conny Templeman's first feature is one of the most horrendously middle class movies in years. Seen through Nanou's irritatingly naive eyes, the French unemployed are a sorry bunch: unshaven, grubby male chauvinists who all eat like pigs. Only the evocation of place – the grim, grey villages and plains of Northern France – holds any interest, thanks no doubt to the work of production designer Andrew Mollo. GA

Naples Connection, The (Un Complicato Intrigo di Donne, Vicoli e Delitti)

(Lina Wertmüller, 1985, It) Angela Molina, Francisco Rabal, Harvey Keitel, Daniel Ezralow, Vittorio Squillante, Paolo Bonacelli.
106 min.
A back street sleaze job: someone is putting the frighteners on the Rocco clan by wasting their menfolk. The victims are found with their balls pricked by the needle of a syringe. Meanwhile an epicene bum-boy prances around in his redundant church dance studio with nothing on save a jockstrap. A bathetic script provides some unsavoury delicacies – 'let's take a walk in the drains'; 'the awesome vagina'; 'let's make hate' – and Harvey Keitel's gangster comes to a spectacular end. But at the conclusion, Wertmüller's ingenuous fem-moral cop-out fails to redeem this violent slapdash. As in all soft porn, the prurience is ultimately prudish, but even so this dip into depravity, with its druggery and buggery, its flirtations with lesbianism and transvestism, has something for everyone. Only dog-lovers will be disappointed. MS

Napoléon 100

(Abel Gance, 1927, Fr) Albert Dieudonné, Wladimir Roudenko, Gina Manès, Nicolas Koline, Annabella, Antonin Artaud, Edmond Van Daële, Alexandre Koubitsky, Abel Gance.
270 min. b/w.
To see Napoléon with a full orchestra performing Carl Davis' score is an almost unimaginably thrilling experience. The 'concert' aspect heightens the sense of occasion, and the Beethoven-based score fully equals Gance's own grandiloquent poetry. The film itself is a paradox. Presumably nobody applauds it for its politics: it offers a crudely psychologised vision of Bonaparte as a 'man of destiny' (said to have inspired De Gaulle in 1927), and ends on a note of fascistic triumph with the invasion of Italy. It is nonetheless a great film, the work of a man with a raving enthusiasm for cinema. Purely visual storytelling had reached a peak of sophistication by the mid-1920s, but Gance pushed the 'language' of cinema further than anyone else: he moved easily between lyricism, bombast, intimacy and dementia, mixed vivid performances with daring montage experiments. No superlative is enough. TR

Napoleon and Samantha

(Bernard McEveety, 1972, US) Michael Douglas, Will Geer, Arch Johnson, Johnny Whittaker, Jodie Foster.
91 min.
Two kids, orphaned Whittaker and sidekick Foster (her first movie, aged nine), get the title roles in this mild Disney live-action offering: they embark across country (the Strawberry Mountains, Oregon) with their elderly pet lion, Major, to join college student pal Douglas, who's doing some goat-herding over the summer. Melodramatic 'kidnapping' angle (in the second half) fails to fire up the plot. TJ

Narrow Margin

(Peter Hyams, 1990, US) Gene Hackman, Anne Archer, James B Sikking, JT Walsh, M Emmet Walsh, Susan Hogan, Harris Yulin, Nigel Bennett, BA Smith.
97 min.
A remake of Richard Fleischer's superb 1952 train thriller must be artistically redundant. But Hyams has always had a magpie tendency to borrow from the best, daring to make a sequel to 2001, remaking High Noon as Outland, even fitting his original screenplays (Capricorn One, Running Scared) into prevailing cycles. Given this reliance on proven formula, Hyams is an ingenious craftsman who makes supremely watchable movies, and this one is a case in point. District Attorney Hackman is escorting a reluctant witness (Archer) to testify in a murder trial, but assassins are on the same train to make sure she doesn't. Hyams boosts the set-up with some heavy-duty action, but the journey follows essentially the same tracks as in '52 for an exciting ride. Hackman is boringly good, but Archer (like Marie Windsor before her) enjoys the more ambivalent role. Very good indeed, she offers sufficient reason to check out this update, even if it does run out of steam before the end of the line. TCh

Narrow Margin, The

(Richard Fleischer, 1952, US) Charles McGraw, Marie Windsor, Jacqueline White, Queenie Leonard, Jack Maxey, Don Beddoe.
70 min b/w.
Fleischer has yet to have his critical day: with Blake Edwards, he is one of the last surviving classically-trained American directors. Here is classic pulp premise (cops escorting hoodlum's widow to Grand Jury trial with a pack of killers bent on eliminating her before she talks); essence of B movie casting (the malevolently magnificent McGraw and the sleazy siren Windsor); and classic setting (transcontinental express train with every passenger, every stop a possibly malign menace). Teeming with incident, it is fashioned into a taut, breathtakingly fast and highly suspenseful 'sleeper' par excellence. CW

Nashville

(Robert Altman, 1975, US) Ned Beatty, Karen Black, Ronee Blakley, Keith Carradine, Geraldine Chaplin, Shelley Duvall, Allen Garfield, Henry Gibson, Barbara Harris, Michael Murphy, Lily Tomlin, Keenan Wynn.
161 min.
Altman's country music epic, intertwining the lives and longings and lonelinesses of its twenty-four protagonists with exquisite free-form grace, can be faulted for trying to bring everything together at the end with an assassination making an arbitrarily resounding statement about showbiz and politics. Forget this and the film is a wonderful mosaic which yields up greater riches with successive viewings, not least in the underrated songs, the superlative performances, and the open-mindedness of Altman's approach to direction. Immensely, exhilaratingly enjoyable. TM

Nasty Girl, The (Das schreckliche Mädchen)

(Michael Verhoeven, 1989, Ger) Lena Stolze, Monika Baumgartner, Michael Gahr, Robert Giggenbach, Elisabeth Bertram.
94 min.
Sonja (Stolze), a bright schoolgirl from a middle class Bavarian family, wins a Euro-essay prize and becomes the pride of her small town. Spurred by success, she embarks on a follow-up essay: 'My Town in the Third Reich'. Doors start slamming before anyone has time to formulate the usual lies and evasions, and Sonja is forced to abandon her project – although not before her parents suffer unpleasant social reprisals. Sonja grows up, marries her beloved teacher (Giggenbach) and has kids, but never forgets the time she was barred from access to the civic archives. Now a very determined adult, she picks up her old project...Verhoeven is far too smart to focus his movie on guilty secrets from the Nazi past; his target is the Germany of the present, and in particular the cosy way church and state work arm-in-arm to maintain a facade of bland social order. His script is based on a real-life woman, but his method couldn't be further from docudrama. He uses several types of stylisation to keep banality at bay, matching visual wit with scalpel-sharp dialogue. Stolze's highly engaging performance is the icing on the cake. TR

Nasty Habits

(Michael Lindsay-Hogg, 1976, GB) Glenda Jackson, Melina Mercouri, Geraldine Page, Sandy Dennis, Anne Jackson, Anne Meara, Susan Penhaligon, Edith Evans, Rip Torn, Eli Wallach.
92 min.
The appeal of this adaptation of Muriel Spark's novel The Abbess of Crewe rests precariously upon one slim idea: resetting Watergate in a nunnery. Once the initial idea has been planted – Glenda Jackson out to get elected abbess at all costs – the audience is made to look awfully hard for laughs. The 'political' gags, like Mercouri's Kissinger-type roving nun, are often abysmal (only Sandy Dennis' impersonation of John Dean deserves to escape criticism); and with increasing desperation, the humour depends on the nuns' monotonous displays of venal ways (smoking, swearing, boozing, even shacking up with the Jesuits down the road). It's all terribly predictable and tame. CPe

Nathalie Granger

(Marguerite Duras, 1972, Fr) Jeanne Moreau, Lucia Bosé, Luce Garcia Ville, Gérard Depardieu.
85 min.

Duras' early feature gains much in atmosphere from the house where it was shot, the author's own home outside Paris (where, among other things, she wrote *Hiroshima, Mon Amour* with Resnais). It's the setting for a typically indefinable 'narrative' bringing together the brooding presence of two women, Moreau and Bosé, a sense of crisis surrounding daughter Nathalie's abandonment of her piano lessons and violent conduct at school, and a rather daffy tyro turn from Depardieu as a flailing washing machine salesman. The effect is as diffuse as it is compelling, a celluloid equivalent of atonal music or free verse, but Duras' avowedly instinctive approach pays dividends for the patient viewer. TJ

National Health, The

(Jack Gold, 1973, GB) Lynn Redgrave, Eleanor Bron, Sheila Scott-Wilkinson, Donald Sinden, Jim Dale, Colin Blakely, Clive Swift, Mervyn Johns, Bob Hoskins.
97 min.

A would-be blackly comic *Carry On Doctor* that never manages to work itself free from the deadly grip of Peter Nichols' script (from his own stage play) about Britain as a terminal ward. Jack Gold really ought to be up there with Nicolas Roeg. His BBC films (*The World of Coppard, Mad Jack, Arturo Ui, Stocker's Copper*) show real style and finesse. But his features have either lacked the identity to leap from a genre (*The Reckoning*), or been constricted by theatrical origins (*The Bofors Gun*, in the taut, burly mould of British film-making, and *The National Health*, too diffuse and fussy to satisfy). All three films betray TV's main bad influence – too much respect for the sanctity of the script. SG

National Lampoon Goes to the Movies

(aka National Lampoon's Movie Madness)

(Henry Jaglom/Bob Giraldi, 1981, US) Peter Riegert, Diane Lane, Candy Clark, Teresa Ganzel, Ann Dusenberry, Robert Culp, Robby Benson, Richard Widmark, Christopher Lloyd, Elisha Cook, Julie Kavner, Mary Woronov.
89 min.

A National Lampoon movie deemed unfit for US theatrical release. Dumb parodies of 'hard-boiled' Robbins-like soaps, cop movies and 'personal growth' educational fare. Very poor. TJ

National Lampoon's Animal House

(John Landis, 1978, US) John Belushi, Tim Matheson, John Vernon, Verna Bloom, Tom Hulce, Cesare Danova, Peter Riegert, Donald Sutherland.
109 min.

Beer barrels shatter windows, rock'n'roll blares out, havoc rules in this sharp, college-campus-of-'62 crack at American Graffiti. An unashamed sense of its own fantasy is coupled with classically mounted slapstick; nostalgia mixes with cynicism in seductive proportions; and John Belushi's central performance as brain-damaged-slob-cum-Thief-of-Bagdad is wonderful. CA

National Lampoon's Class Reunion

(Michael Miller, 1982, US) Gerrit Graham, Michael Lerner, Fred McCarren, Miriam Flynn, Stephen Furst, Marya Small, Shelley Smith.
85 min.

It's a dark and stormy night when a high school class reassembles in the now deserted classrooms of their alma mater. A murder is committed, and a mysterious doctor appears announcing that it's 'all about...mental illness'. A psychopath is lurking in the shadowy corridors of Lizzie Borden High: wimpish Walter seeking revenge upon his old classmates for a cruel joke once played on him. The characterisations and jokes remain as hackneyed as the plot and as primary as the film's garish colours. FD

National Lampoon's Loaded Weapon 1

(Gene Quintano, 1992, US) Emilio Estevez, Samuel L Jackson, Jon Lovitz, Tim Curry, Kathy Ireland, William Shatner, F Murray Abraham, Charlie Sheen.
83 min.

A new low in lame spoofery, this half-cocked cop claptrap conjures up even fewer laughs than the *Lethal Weapon* series it's meant to be sending up. With Estevez and Jackson in the buddy-buddy Mel'n'Danny roles, we look set for a more contemporary spin on the *Naked Gun* routine, but this trigger-happy, chortle-shy effort is severely hampered by lack of comic invention. The mix isn't far from the similarly dismal fly-boy skit *Hot Shots!*: there ain't enough plot to sustain the action, so it's heigh-ho and on we go with embarrassed guest stars and meaningless sketches. Hence, rent-a-ham Shatner is a scenery-chewing Mr Big, Abraham lurks behind bars as Dr Hannibal Lecher, and Sheen wanders around under the impression that simply appearing uncredited with his bruv will just slay them out there. Wrong, wrong and wrong again; this *Loaded Weapon* fires only dumb-dumb bullets. TJ

National Lampoon's Movie Madness

see National Lampoon Goes to the Movies

National Lampoon's Vacation

(Harold Ramis, 1983, US) Chevy Chase, Beverly D'Angelo, Imogene Coca, Randy Quaid, Anthony Michael Hall, Dana Barron, John Candy, Eddie Bracken.
98 min.

National Lampoon takes on another stereotype of middle America: the family vacation. Chevy Chase, his face pinkened by the strain of having to be in control, plays the affluent suburban patriarch who leads his family on a summer jaunt from Chicago to Disneyland (here rechristened Walleyworld). The result is not so much a comedy about American values as a 2,500 mile skid on a banana skin. The visual gags come thick and fast, and are about as subtly signposted as the exit markers on a freeway. An exercise in the comedy of humiliation which is the stuff of shamefaced giggles. RR

National Velvet

(Clarence Brown, 1944, US) Mickey Rooney, Elizabeth Taylor, Donald Crisp, Anne Revere, Angela Lansbury, Reginald Owen, Norma Varden.
125 min.

Two children train a sorrel gelding, won in a village raffle, to win the Grand National. This is a charmer for boys and girls of all ages, with a captivating performance from the young Liz Taylor as Velvet, the butcher's daughter, and graceful, fluent direction by Clarence Brown. The National was actually filmed on a Pasadena golf course. TCh

Nattvardsgästerna (The Communicants/Winter Light)

(Ingmar Bergman, 1962, Swe) Ingrid Thulin, Gunnar Björnstrand, Max von Sydow, Gunnel Lindblom, Allan Edwall.
80 min. b/w.

The middle part of Bergman's trilogy about God's silence – it is flanked by *Through a Glass Darkly* and *The Silence* – and the most austere, *Winter Light* focuses on a small group of parishioners found at the beginning of the film attending Holy Communion. The village pastor (Björnstrand) is realising he has become an atheist since his wife's death. His faith is further tested by an offer of marriage from a schoolteacher (Thulin) tortured with eczema, and the solace demanded by a man (von Sydow) suicidally depressed by the threat of nuclear war. The pastor fails on both counts, and Bergman gives us an ambiguous ending back in the church service – what he himself called 'certainty unmasked'. Never a comfortable film, it's finely acted by a familiar Bergman ensemble, and the awesomely cold vistas form a perfect counterpoint to the spiritual freeze. DT

Natural, The

(Barry Levinson, 1984, US) Robert Redford, Robert Duvall, Glenn Close, Kim Basinger, Wilford Brimley, Barbara Hershey, Robert Prosky, Richard Farnsworth, Joe Don Baker.
137 min.

This upbeat adaptation of Bernard Malamud's gritty allegory of the world of baseball is one of those test cases for the mood or generosity of the spectator: give yourself over completely to its wide-eyed brand of mythologising, and it will reward you with a tidal wave of emotion, hero-worship and strange medieval morality tale; a flicker of disbelief, however, and you'll see nothing but its faults. The Arthurian basis to Redford's rise to baseball stardom means that the narrative can include very un-Hollywoodlike devices such as an unexplained 16-year gap when he is out in the cold, expiating his fall from grace with a murderous femme fatale. Moreover, this mythological basis releases the cast from the necessity for naturalism (despite the title). There are also other things to enjoy: a great line up of supporting actors (especially Brimley and Farnsworth doing their grouchy old man double act), Caleb Deschanel's photography, Randy Newman's score. Let yourself go and be rewarded by the sight of a hero running home to victory through clouds of fire. CPea

Natural Born Killers

(Oliver Stone, 1994, US) Woody Harrelson, Juliette Lewis, Robert Downey Jr, Tommy Lee Jones, Tom Sizemore, Rodney Dangerfield.
119 min. b/w & col.

Mickey (Harrelson) and Mallory (Lewis) are white-trash low-lifes who get their kicks from killin' just about anybody who gets in their way. Their antics are covered by scumbag talkshow host Wayne Gale (Downey) whose reports turn the pair into folk heroes. Meanwhile, detective Jack Scagnetti (Sizemore) is determined to put them behind bars. Trailing hype and tabloid hysteria in its wake, Stone's film is at once a phenomenon and unremarkable. True, it's technically extraordinary; with the director resorting to a frantic collage of film and video, b/w and colour, back- and front-projection, fast and slow motion to develop his thesis that crime and violence are fanned by sensationalist media attention. At least that's what he seems to be saying. Basically, the story is just a tarted up variation of the *Badlands/Wild at Heart* scenario, with ultra-broad swipes at media and authority figures tossed in for good measure. The actors are given no space to build up characters, and the film's main 'virtue' is that it's nowhere near as explicit as the tabloids suggested. Turgid. GA

Nature of the Beast, The

(Franco Rosso, 1988, GB) Lynton Dearden, Paul Simpson, Tony Melody, Freddie Fletcher, Dave Hill, Roberta Kerr, David Fleeshman.
96 min.

The beast is unemployment. There have been eight years of Thatcherism since Franco Rosso's *Babylon*, and as he turns from what it was to be working-class, black and British in Brixton to what it is to be working class, white and unemployed in the distressed North of England, the effect of the intervening years can be detected in both the change of location to the colder, stonier climes of Lancashire, and the quieter but more desperate responses of his characters. The plainly allegorical tale is from the same school, if not the same class, as *Kes*. Fletcher (the hero's brother in Loach's film) plays the father of another troubled teenager and school truant, motherless wild-child Bill (Dearden), from whose point of view the narrative unfolds. There's trouble't mill. Grandad (Melody) is sacked, Dad joins the picket. Meanwhile a beast roams the moors, descending on the town to kill at night. Superstition is rife, and Bill takes a gun to kill it. The results may be uneven, but the restrained performances are truthful, and the sense of pain and frustration is genuinely moving. WH

Naufragos, Los (Shipwrecked)

(Miguel Littin, 1992, Chile) Marcelo Romo, Valentina Vargas, Bastian Bodenhofer, Patricio Bunster.
119 min.

Extraordinary dark and poetic movie about a man who returns home to Chile after 20 years and finds himself in the cold grip of his own maddening ghost story. Littin layers his descent into the maelstrom in a series of scenes akin to Dante's

Divine Comedy as retold by Edgar Allan Poe: all the people he encounters (old lovers, household retainers, his brother, who have stayed through the hurricane) reflect through a glass darkly his own guilt and despair. Here there's no boundary between the real and the imaginary. Hans Burmann's evocative camerawork suffuses the film in smoky mists and indelible images that achieve the same eery, alienating quality that Edmond Richard did in Welles's *The Trial*. Except for the over-allegorical ending, it's a work of considerable power and originality. WH

Naughty but Nice
(Ray Enright, 1939, US) Ann Sheridan, Dick Powell, Gale Page, Helen Broderick, Ronald Reagan, ZaSu Pitts.
90 min. b/w.
Its title may make it sound like one of those saucy British sex comedies from the early 1970s, but in fact this is a squeaky clean Warner Bros musical. Powell's an ingenuous, clean-cut music professor from out in the sticks who heads for Manhattan hoping to sell his symphony. Smooth but untrustworthy shyster Ronald Reagan buys it, but then bowdlerises it, turning it into a popular song for oomph girl, Ann Sheridan. Wittily scripted by the prolific Jerry Wald, this takes a few sly digs at the world of music publishing before dribbling off into a conventional romantic ending. GM

Naughty Marietta
(WS Van Dyke, 1935, US) Jeanette MacDonald, Nelson Eddy, Frank Morgan, Elsa Lanchester, Douglas Dumbrille, Edward Brophy, Akim Tamiroff.
106 min. b/w.
The first MacDonald-Eddy vehicle, enormously popular in its day so somebody must have been able to stand this simpering duo. An adaptation of Victor Herbert's 1905 operetta (which perpetrated *Ah! Sweet Mystery of Life*), set in New Orleans, with MacDonald as the French princess running out on an arranged marriage, kidnapped by pirates, and falling for the stalwart backwoods scout who rescues her. Eddy, believe it or not, addresses her as 'Bright Eyes'. The fine supporting cast is a relief. TM

Navigator, The
(Buster Keaton/Donald Crisp, 1924, US) Buster Keaton, Kathryn McGuire, Frederick Vroom, Noble Johnson, Clarence Burton.
5,702 ft. b/w.
Gag for gag, one of the funniest of all Keaton's features as he copes with the snags involved in running a deserted ocean liner single-handed, philosophically accepting the fact that machinery has a malevolent will of its own. Prevented from becoming one of his best only because it (necessarily) lacks the lovingly detailed backgrounds and incredibly beautiful visual textures of films like *Our Hospitality*, *The General* and *Steamboat Bill Jr*. TM

Navigator: A Medieval Odyssey, The
(Vincent Ward, 1988, Aust) Bruce Lyons, Chris Haywood, Hamish McFarlane, Marshall Napier, Noel Appleby.
91 min. b/w & col.
A bold fusion of history, myth, and futuristic fantasy, Ward's imaginitive medieval odyssey ravishes the eye, challenges the mind, and stirs the eart. When young Griffin's older brother Connor returns to their 14 century Cumbrian mining village with horrifying tales of the Black Death, the elders fear the small community is doomed. But in a prophetic dream, Griffin sees a religious pilgrimage by which a resolute band may triumph over the pestilence through an act of religious faith. Their quest, to erect a new spire on a distant church steeple, will take them deep into the bowels of the earth and make them strangers in a strange land, because they emerge from their tunnels into the glass towers, monstrous machinery and religious scepticism of modern-day New Zealand. There is a powerful allergorical undercurrent, too, which draws a parallel between the plague-threatened village and the modern city, itself living under the spectre of a nuclear Armageddon. NF

Navy Heroes
see Blue Peter, The

Navy Seals
(Lewis Teague, 1990, US) Charlie Sheen, Michael Biehn, Joanne Whalley-Kilmer, Rick Rossovich, Cyril O'Reilly, Bill Paxton.
114 min.
Popularised by *The Abyss*, the Navy Sea, Air and Land commandos here go into action against an Arab terrorist who has his hands on a consignment of Stinger missiles. The film nevertheless avoids all mention of politics by pitching diligent team-leader Biehn, crazy Sheen and the other all-American sea-mammals against a fanatical splinter group dedicated to senseless violence rather than any specific ideological goal. Tipped off by half-Lebanese TV journalist Whalley-Kilmer, the SEALS parachute into the sea off Beirut and prepare to kick some Arab butt. Having played a psychotic SEALS officer in *The Abyss*, Biehn this time leaves the loony stuff to Sheen. Teague, meanwhile, is far too busy orchestrating the large-scale action sequences to make anything of the cardboard characters, episodic plotting, or clunking dialogue. NF

Nazarín
(Luis Buñuel, 1958, Mex) Francisco Rabal, Marga López, Rita Macedo, Ignacio López Tarso, Ofelia Guilmain, Luis Aceves Castañeda, Rosenda Monteros.
94 min. b/w.
One of the least sardonic of all Buñuel's films. Father Nazarín, a non-denominational journeyman priest, wanders through the plagues, sins and poverty of the secular world, experiencing a number of episodes that echo incidents in the gospels...until he learns the momentous lesson that he can receive charity as well as give it. Buñuel never ridicules Nazarín's efforts to follow Christ's teachings, but instead stresses the priest's fundamental detachment, and observes how irrelevant most of his work is to the sinners he tangles with. To the extent that the open ending is optimistic, Nazarín is a true Buñuel hero. TR

Néa (A Young Emmanuelle)
(Nelly Kaplan, 1976, Fr/WGer) Sami Frey, Ann Zacharias, Nelly Kaplan, Françoise Brion, Micheline Presle, Heinz Bennent, Ingrid Caven.
105 min.
Absurdly and opportunistically released here as *A Young Emmanuelle*, Nelly Kaplan's film in fact hovers in tone in the same range as Rohmer's moral fables, but its plot reveals the sexual-political drive that runs through all her work. The spoilt child of a rich Geneva family writes an erotic novel (for her own fantasy life). Oppressed by her bigoted father and by a hypocritical family life, she becomes wilfully determined – publishing the novel anonymously, encouraging her (gay) mother to leave home for her lover, and taking a lover herself to acquire the experience that she feels she lacks. The film's insistence on sexual liberation in itself makes it curious; but after a hesitant opening, the subject matter is matched by an enchanted tone, hanging between humour and cruelty, slim snatches of parody, heartache and eroticism. For once, a radical film that is generous, ingenious and alive. CA

Neapolitanische Geschwister
see Reign of Naples, The

Near Dark
(Kathryn Bigelow, 1987, US) Adrian Pasdar, Jenny Wright, Lance Henriksen, Bill Paxton, Jenette Goldstein, Joshua Miller.
94 min.
A full-blooded vampire movie which gives the well-worn mythology a much-needed transfusion by stripping away the Gothic trappings and concentrating instead on a pack of nocturnal nomads who roam the sun-parched farmlands of the modern Midwest. Kissed by a pale, mysterious girl from out of town, it soon dawns on farmboy Caleb that Mae's love-bite has infected him with a burning desire – for blood. Subsequently snatched by Mae's vagabond pals, Caleb is gradually seduced by their exciting night-life. So, despite his reluctance to make a 'kill', Caleb is soon caught between his blood sister and his blood relatives – father and younger sister – who are in hot pursuit. Western iconography, *noir*-ish lighting, and visceral horror are fused with an affecting love story in this stylish 'Vampire Western', which (unlike Bigelow's rather static debut feature *The Loveless*) is driven forward at a scorching pace, a subtle study in the seductiveness of evil and a terrifying ride to the edge of darkness. NF

Nearly Wide Awake
(David Hutt/Martin Turner, 1977, GB) Alex Cox, Suzy Gilbert, Liz Salom, Niven Boyd.
65 min.
A wild and woolly tapestry woven from incidents in the novels of Knut Hamsun (including *Hunger*), this was shot on a frayed shoestring by two postgraduate film students at Bristol University – and looks very much like a student movie. Deliberately flouting any formal discipline and passing up no opportunity for visual or aural display inseeking to conjure up an outcast's hallucinating vision, it is often maddeningly uncoordinated, but intermittently packs a visceral punch. Budgetary limitations mean that the period setting sometimes goes awry, and the copper who appears at one point seems to have strayed in from Dock Green.

Near Room, The
(David Hayman, 1995, GB) Adrian Dunbar, David O'Hara, Julie Graham, Emma Faulkner, David Hayman.
89 min.
This Scottish thriller, developed by British Screen and written by Robert Murphy, is regrettably no advert for the future of small-budget, big-screen British product. Dunbar's a Glaswegian journo-turned-investigator whose search for a young girl (his daughter, unbeknownst to her) leads him into heavy-duty pressure, caught between hard-nosed editors, bent cops, prostitutes, paedophiles and power-hungry lawyers. 'The machinations of the secret state have been exposed,' says a character, but it's only a ruse. Hayman's stylised TV direction, the sountrack atmospherics, the over-use of red filters and circling overhead camera, and the formula performances detract from what could have been a topical *noir* drama. WH

Necessary Roughness
(Stan Dragoti, 1991, US) Scott Bakula, Hector Elizondo, Robert Loggia, Harley Jane Kozak, Larry Miller, Sinbad, Fred Dalton Thompson.
108 min.
This tale of a 34-year-old quarterback's return to college football is marginally less funny than wearing a jock-strap on your head, and less original than putting Ralgex down your opponent's shorts. In Texas, former university league bigtimers The Fighting Armadillos are decimated by charges of corruption, and forced to replenish their numbers with anaemic no-hoper academics. Only geriatric drop-out Paul (Bakula) can save the day, but to do so he must return to college and get his degree. Cue endless football montages, interspersed with a load of drivel about finding fulfilment, making real friends, and rediscovering the joys of pure sporting endeavour. Even the presence of reliably grimy stalwarts Elizondo and Loggia, and the inclusion of a naff sexual-equality subplot, can't alleviate the boredom. MK

Necronomicon (aka H.P. Lovecraft's Necronomicon)
(Christophe Gans/Shu Kaneko/Brian Yuzna, 1993, US) Jeffrey Combs, Tony Azito; Bruce Payne, Richard Lynch, Belinda Bauer; David Warner, Bess Myer, Millie Perkins; Signy Coleman, Obba Babatunde, Don Calfa.
97 min.
A three-part portmanteau movie based on tales by the horror author HP Lovecraft. With its fluid camera style and lush score, French director Gans' 'The Drowned' is the most stylish segment, in which the inheritor of a 1920s clifftop hotel, Payne, tries to resurrect his dead girlfriend. Gans' sure build-up emphasises atmosphere and character rather than effects, but the gloopy finale certainly makes up for it. By contrast, Japanese film-maker Kaneko's 'The Cold' is a torpid affair in which mad doctor Warner uses his victims' spinal fluid to sustain eternal life. Capping things off nicely is *Society* director Yuzna's 'Whispers', which makes a bloody spurt for the gorier end of the horror picture spectrum. Having pursued the furtive driver of a speeding car into a subterranean world, a male and female cop are lured to their fate by a sly old bum and his blind, religious-fanatic wife, who feed them to some flying flesh-eaters. While neither as subtle or stylish as Gans' segment, this certainly delivers old-fashioned gore-a-plenty. NF

Necropolis

(Franco Brocani, 1970, It) Viva Auder, Tina
Aumont, Carmelo Bene, Pierre Clémenti, Paul
Jabara, Louis Waldon.
120 min.
Brocani conjures together all your favourite
European cultural and historical myth figures in
order to attack the centuries of 'sublimation' that
have produced our cities and their inhabitants.
The gang's all here: Frankenstein's monster
gropes towards the awareness that his mind is a
universe; Attila, naked on a white horse, liberates
his people from their ignominy; the ultra-caustic
Viva bemoans the frustrations of married life and
drifts into the elegiac persona of the Bloody
Countess Bathory; Louis Waldon is a hip
American tourist searching for the (missing)
Mona Lisa. The range is extraordinary, from
stand-up Jewish comedy to a kind of flea-market
expressionism. Brocani's approach is contemplative rather than agitational, which confounds
the impatient; Gavin Bryars' lovely Terry Riley-
esque score matches the ambience exactly. TR

Ned Kelly

(Tony Richardson, 1970, GB) Mick Jagger,
Allen Bickford, Geoff Gilmour, Mark
McManus, Serge Lazareff, Peter Sumner, Ken
Shorter, Frank Thring.
103 min.
Richardson's bushranger biopic merely applies a
simplistic gloss to the 'outlaw' image already projected onto Jagger by the British media, and his
role as the legendary Australian anti-hero
emerges as little more than an uncomfortable displacement of his tabloid notoriety. The beard and
iron mask Jagger assumes for the part obscure
his specific rock/cultural persona as effectively
as they do his features; and overall this outback
Western comes a poor second to *Mad Dog*, the
later Philippe Mora/Dennis Hopper outlaw movie
also shot down under. PT

Needful Things

(Fraser C Heston), 1994, US) Max von Sydow,
Ed Harris, Bonnie Bedelia, Amanda Plummer,
JT Walsh, Ray McKinnon, Duncan Fraser.
120 min.
Better than most Stephen King adaptations,
mainly because an exceptionally strong cast adds
substance to the facile storyline about a mysterious stranger, Leland Gaunt (von Sydow), who
opens the antique shop of the title in Castle Rock,
Maine, and, by tapping into the inhabitants'
acquisitive desires, sets them at one another's
throats. As Fraser C Heston has observed, there
are no supernatural beings here – the only monster is avarice. Little more than an EC Comics-
style morality tale about the greedy getting their
comeuppance, but the director has a strong eye
for visual detail and expansive composition. NF

Neige était sale, La
(The Stain on the Snow/
The Snow Was Black)

(Luis Saslavsky, 1953, Fr) Daniel Gélin, Marie
Mansart, Daniel Ivernel, Nadine Basile, Jean-
Pierre Mocky.
104 min. b/w.
The setting is a Nazi-occupied country (explicitly *not* France – *quelle suggestion!*) where Frank,
the son of a blowsy brothel keeper, spends his
days hanging out with the girls and their German
clients, and his nights hanging out with the boys,
stealing and black marketeering. Mired in self-
disgust, he proceeds to ever greater atrocities –
murdering an old lady who was kind to him as a
child, arranging the rape of a naive neighbour
who's in love with him – and finally, the depths
plumbed, getting himself executed. The tone is
non-sensational; indeed, from the start, the film
seems as exhausted as its hero is by the finish:
you wonder if the director even bothered to show
up. Mostly, it induces gloom to no useful end. BBa

Neighbors

(John G Avildsen, 1981, US) John Belushi,
Kathryn Walker, Dan Aykroyd, Cathy
Moriarty, Igors Gavon, Dru-Ann Chukron.
96 min.
Belushi's final appearance, scripted by Larry
Gelbart from Thomas Berger's novel, and detailing the purportedly hilarious chaos that befalls a
quiet suburban couple (Belushi and Walker)
when a pair of uninhibited nutters (Aykroyd,

Moriarty) move in next door. In fact, ruthlessly
ironing out Berger's subtleties of tone in favour
of a rumbustious *Animal House* collision between
Belushi and Aykroyd, it becomes increasingly
tiresome, with few funny moments to leaven the
proceedings. GA

Neil Simon's Lost in Yonkers

see Lost in Yonkers

Neither By Day Nor By Night

(Steven Hilliard Stern, 1972, US/Isr) Zalman
King, Miriam Bernstein-Cohen, Dalia
Friedland, Edward G Robinson, Mischa
Asheroff, Chaim Anitar.
95 min.
'When I waited for light there came the darkness',
the pretty nurse reading from the Book of Job
reminds us. And indeed it does in the shape of
this peculiarly awkward story of a bitter-sweet
relationship formed in hospital between a cynical expatriate American, a veteran of the Israeli
war who is about to go blind, and a short-sighted old girl who mistakes him for a reincarnation
of her former lover. Good intentions and a
Yiddish flavour abound, but emotional toughness
soon gets sacrificed for the sake of a good wallow. Strange that a film which preaches the
virtues of 'insight' should handle the theme with
such obtuseness. All that pulling in and out of
focus, plus a particularly crass sub-Simon and
Garfunkel soundtrack, and it's difficult to say
whose trials are more gruelling, the characters'
or the audience's. CPe

Neither the Sea Nor the Sand

(Fred Burnley, 1972, GB) Susan Hampshire,
Michael Petrovitch, Frank Finlay, Michael
Craze, Jack Lambert, Anthony Booth.
94 min.
Must qualify as one of the worst films of the
decade. Girl, married, goes to Jersey in winter to
'work things out'. Bumps into enigmatic chap
who keeps saying urgent things like 'Reality is
truth...can you understand that?' She leaves her
husband for him, but his prim brother objects.
'Let's go to Scotland'. They arrive at the cottage.
'It used to be the old bakery, you know'. Not
before time, Adonis succumbs to a heart attack,
and the film veers into ghost territory. The girl's
love somehow keeps him alive (but at least he's
dumb, so can't trot out any more pearls of wisdom). Eventually, back in Jersey, she accepts that
decomposition can no longer be put off, and they
wander into the sea to drown. And be together.
Which is no more than they deserve. Gordon
Honeycombe scripted this awful effort from his
own novel.

Nela

(Hans Conrad Fischer, 1980, WGer) narrators:
Paul Rogers, Judi Dench.
99 min.
Far from being the great unmentionable, death
seems to be a topic about which most people will
witter on interminably at the drop of an armband.
This death belongs to Nela (Cornelia), a painter
of naive pictures in bold colour, and the daughter of the director (an Austrian documentary film-
maker). She died of leukemia at 22 – a death in
itself no different from anyone else's (normal,
tragic), but whose circumstances here prompt a
panegyric of bland mediocrity. It tells us nothing
about her whatever. Her paintings remain; they
can stand or fall on their own merits. Here death
were better honoured by a decent silence. CPea

Nell

(Michael Apted, 1994, US) Jodie Foster, Liam
Neeson, Natasha Richardson, Richard
Libertini, Nick Searcy, Robin Mullins.
113 min.
Deep in the mountains of North Carolina, Dr
Jerome Lovell (Neeson) discovers a grown wild
child, Nell (Foster). She's had no contact with the
outside world, having been raised entirely by her
invalid mother, and can speak only in a strange
onomatopoeic language. But can Nell continue to
live her own life, as Lovell hopes, or is she too
important for that, a unique subject for a scientific study, as psychologist Paula Olsen (Richardson)
would have it? With a court hearing in the offing,
the rival scientists camp out in the backwoods.
This metaphor-movie is both touching and tasteful. It allows Foster to play scared and alone, traumatised and neurotic, and, most importantly, free

and inspirational. She gets to 'commune with
nature', speak in tongues, and bring Neeson and
Richardson together. Nice photography; nonsensical courtroom speech at the close. TCh

Nell Gwyn

(Herbert Wilcox, 1934, GB) Anna Neagle,
Cedric Hardwicke, Jeanne de Casalis, Muriel
George, Esmé Percy, Moore Marriott, Miles
Malleson.
85 min. b/w.
With King Charles II putting into practice his
promise to restore the country 'to its old good
nature, its old good manners and its old good
humour' by leading a rollicking chorus in a 17th
century musical hall, it is difficult not to warm to
Wilcox's very democratic brand of royalism.
Neagle is rather too hoydenish to be truly sexy,
but she has a zest and brazenness breathtaking
in its disregard for the conventions of polite society, and Hardwicke's king almost convinces one
that there was a time when royalty wasn't synonymous with lily-livered mediocrity. Despite a
script which is rather too hesitant at improving
upon history, this is a worthy example of disreputable costume drama, a genre British cinema
occasionally excelled in. RMy

Nelly & Monsieur Arnaud
(Nelly and Mr Arnaud)

(Claude Sautet, 1995, Fr) Emmanuelle Béart,
Michel Serrault, Jean-Hughes Anglade, Claire
Nadeau, Françoise Brion, Michel Lonsdale.
106 min.
When Nelly (Béart) informs husband Jérôme that
a certain Monsieur Arnaud (Serrault), an elderly
friend of a friend, has offered her a fortune to help
ease their financial troubles, Jérôme seems so
unsurprised at her acceptance that she ends their
relationship. Only then does she actually take the
money, along with temp work typing up
Arnaud's memoirs of his life as judge and businessman. A barely acknowledged intimacy
grows between the young woman and her generous but temperamental employer, an intimacy
threatened by jealousy when she begins seeing
his publisher Vincent (Anglade). An exquisitely
witty, beautifully moving film, Sautet's follow-up
to *Un Coeur en hiver* is a similarly understated
study in adult emotions. As the film proceeds quietly towards its unsentimental, but piercingly sad
conclusion, Sautet's sure, light touch even allows
for comic scenes (Lonsdale provides a splendidly morose cameo as a mysterious visitor to
Arnaud's apartment). Béart is subtle and
restrained, Serrault fastidious, moody, waspish,
but given to moments of startling warmth and
honesty; together they produce a fragile mood of
humour and heartbreaking melancholy. Classical
French film-making par excellence. GA

Nelly's Version

(Maurice Hatton, 1983, GB) Eileen Atkins,
Nicholas Ball, Anthony Bate, Barbara Jefford.
100 min.
An amnesiac with a suitcase full of cash checks
in at a Home Counties hotel. A Michael Nyman
score propels her wanderings with edgy B movie
insistence. Her wake becomes littered with cross-
purpose conversations, crime, accidents and
arson. Is she an escapee or an escapist? A con-
spirator or a conspiracy victim? Is she Nelly Dean
(who, remember, used to sit and dream) or is she
really this Eleanor Wilkinson whom strangers
claim as friend, mother and wife? Is *Nelly's
Version* a feminist thriller, or a fiction about fiction? It's a mystery, certainly, and a damn good
one; inventively playful in the filmic ambiguities
piled on those of Eva Figes' novel by director
Maurice Hatton. And all, of course, to be taken as
seriously as the Freudianism of Hitchcock's
Spellbound, which strays on screen here amid
umpteen wryly allusive nods to the *cinéma d'auteur*. As the railway porter helpfully explains,
apropos of plot, psychology or maybe just trains,
it's all a matter of connections. PT

Nel Nome del Padre

see In the Name of the Father

Nel segno di Roma

see Sign of the Gladiator

Nelson Affair, The

see Bequest to the Nation

Nelson Touch, The

see Corvette K-225

Nénette et Boni

(Claire Denis, 1996, Fr) Grégoire Colin, Alice Houri, Valéria Bruni-Tedeschi, Jacques Nolot, Vincent Gallo, Alex Descas, Jamila Farah.
103 min.
Boni (Colin) is a pizza cook who harbours obscene, even sociopathic fantasies about the local baker's wife; Nénette (Houri) is his younger sister who runs away from boarding school and asks the embarrassed, reluctant Boni to give her shelter. This fragmented, often overly enigmatic film is a study of the two siblings' mostly aggressive relationships with each other, their friends and their estranged father. There are odd, rather contrived fantasy scenes here which sit uneasily with the generally downbeat naturalism of the rest of the film; and since the script seems determined to tease rather than inform, it's a little hard in the end to fathom exactly what director and co-writer Denis is really getting at. The performances, however, are good, and the music appealing. GA

Neon Bible, The

(Terence Davies, 1995, GB) Gena Rowlands, Diana Scarwid, Denis Leary, Jacob Tierney.
92 min.
This adaptation of John Kennedy Toole's novel returns to the concerns of Terence Davies' acclaimed autobiographical work: the joys and agonies of family life; the onset of adulthood; the oppressive hypocrisy of organised religion. Here, however, instead of Liverpool, the setting is small-town Georgia in the '40s: life is quiet for young Tierney, son of struggling farmer Leary and hypersensitive Scarwid, until the sudden and not entirely unwelcome arrival of his aunt (Rowlands), a has-been but eternally optimistic nightclub singer whose devil-may-care ways sit awkwardly with the town's conservatism. Though the writer/director is working abroad and telling a linear story, it's immediately apparent – from the measured pacing, the immaculate compositions and elegant camera movements, the audacious ellipses and the inspired use of music – that this is a hallmarked Davies film. As such, it is extraordinarily moving, notably in a simple, underplayed death scene. Gena Rowlands' performance is a marvel of subtle nuances. GA

Neptune Factor, The

(Daniel Petrie, 1973, Can) Ben Gazzara, Yvette Mimieux, Walter Pidgeon, Ernest Borgnine, Chris Wiggins, Donnelly Rhodes.
98 min.
An extremely half-hearted attempt to make an undersea 2001 and a film of monumental dullness. Leaden submarine sequences that are too slow to be funny finally begin to alternate, about an hour into the film, with unconvincing blow-ups of harmlessly attractive goldfish, anemones, sea eels and so forth, all supposedly deadly creatures ready to destroy the craft at a single wrong move from her crew. One to avoid.

Nest, The (El Nido)

(Jaime de Armiñán, 1980, Sp) Héctor Alterio, Ana Torrent, Luis Politti, Agustín González, Patricia Adriani. 97 min.
Don Alejandro is a courtly, quixotic figure on a white steed, stigmatised as 'eccentric' for daring, at sixty, to harbour sexual desires. 13-year-old Goyita (Ana Torrent from Spirit of the Beehive), firstseen as a school-play Lady Macbeth, is a sensual child-woman but no simple Hispanic Lolita, for she lives literally in the shadow of the law at the station of the local Guarda Civil. The story tells of their chaste but erotic love, with nothing of the whimsical or lubricious: it's the 'tragic show' of stifled dreams, illicit longings, acted out intricately by all the characters, male and female, old and young, and interwoven with a dense web of symbolic allusions – suggestively haunting bird imagery, exultant use of music (Haydn's Creation) and the Macbeth motif that ominously mirrors the main plot. A film of infinite tenderness, lyricism and passion. SJo

Nest of Gentlefolk, A (Dvorianskoe Gnezdo)

(Andrei Mikhalkov-Konchalovsky, 1969, USSR) Leonid Kulagin, Beata Tyszkiewicz, Irina Kupchenko, A Kostomolotsky, V Sergachov.
106 min.
The first thing you notice about Konchalovsky's film is the vulnerability of its characters. Based on one of Turgenev's stories, it's all there – the travels abroad to remote and seductive but unsatisfying foreign capitals, the continuing dialogue on the meaning of Russianness, the feeling of gentlemanly melancholy...and those women. A man, a gentleman (even if his mother was a servant), reopens his old estate, a servant girl bobbing ahead of him opening doors, drawing back curtains – an excuse for some superb camerawork. Shown sumptuous portraits of his father's family, he asks to see his mother's portrait. In a sense the rest of the film is an attempt to piece together the picture, first of one woman – the wife who left him – then another, and to paint himself into their world. Not a bad aim, and one that isn't given a falsely easy solution either.

Nest of Vipers (Ritratto di Borghesia in Nero)

(Tonino Cervi, 1978, It) Senta Berger, Ornella Muti, Capucine, Christian Borromeo, Giuliana Calandra, Stefano Patrizi.
105 min.
A heated sex melodrama set in Fascist Italy just before World War II, this isn't bad at all. About a provincial innocent who comes to Venice to study music, befriends a fellow student (gay), has an affair with the friend's mother (attractive), then casts her aside in favour of a millionaire's daughter (attractive and rich), it boasts handsome production values recalling the sunbathed settings of Bertolucci and of The Garden of the Finzi-Continis. The Fascist context may be incidental, but Cervi makes some headway against the sexploitation elements in his tale of a passionate and jealousy-driven bourgeoisie, keeping things the right side of interesting up to his Chabrol-style climax of brutal murder and complicity in its cover-up. RM

Net, The

(Irwin Winkler, 1995, US) Sandra Bullock, Jeremy Northam, Dennis Miller, Diane Baker, Wendy Gazelle, Ken Howard, Ray McKinnon.
115 min.
A cod Hitchcockian thriller with Internet knobs on. Babe-next-door Bullock plays Angela, a nerdy freelance computer analyst who, after a top politician blows his brains out, gets caught up in a worldwide web of intrigue, murder and corruption. The night before she goes on holiday, a colleague mails her a mystery virus that provides access to reams of top-secret classified information; however, neither his plane crashing, nor a total computer meltdown at LA airport alerts Angela to danger. While sunning herself in Mexico, she meets an Englishman (Northam), who shares her love of computers and can quote lines from her favourite film, Breakfast at Tiffany's. This immediately alerts us to the fact that Jack is either (a) married, (b) gay, or (c) the bad guy. Angela, however, who doesn't get out much, misses all this. Pretty soon she's fleeing from her gun-wielding seducer, trying to recover an identity that's being systematically erased through alteration of her personal computer records, and dodging bullets on spinning carousels. NF

Network

(Sidney Lumet, 1976, US) Faye Dunaway, William Holden, Peter Finch, Robert Duvall, Wesley Addy, Ned Beatty.
121 min.
Washed-up news anchorman (Finch) flips on air, finds God, and is gleefully exploited by his TV company to boost the ratings with his epileptic evangelic revivalism. Network gives a rather old-fashioned plot the '70s treatment: the result is slick, 'adult', self-congratulatory, and almost entirely hollow. Paddy Chayefsky's entrenched but increasingly desperate script parades its middle-aged symptoms to little effect: it's ulcerous, bilious, paranoid about youth, and increasingly susceptible to fantasy. Above all, it's haunted by fear of failing powers; presumably people telling each other what lousy lays they were is to be taken as indication of the film's searing honesty. Lumet's direction does nothing to contain the sprawl, and most of the interest comes in watching such a lavishly mounted vehicle leaving the rails so spectacularly. CPe

Never Cry Wolf

(Carroll Ballard, 1983, US) Charles Martin Smith, Brian Dennehy, Zachary Ittimangnaq, Samson Jorah, Hugh Webster, Martha Ittimangnaq.
105 min.
Sent to the desolate northern reaches of Canada to prove that the wolves are destroying the herds of caribou, Tyler (Martin Smith) might be any one of us left to fend for ourselves in a bleak landscape. Ballard's film, produced by Disney and resembling the old nature films, tells of an engaging, fearful scientist who grows to admire the wolves he is sent to condemn, adopts their diet (mouse stew minus the tails), and learns from an ancient, mystical Inuit (the furclad local inhabitants) that in true Darwinian fashion the wolves only cull the weaker members of the herd. For the most part very absorbing, the film suffers from some embarrassingly obvious symbolism. JE

NeverEnding Story, The (Die unendliche Geschichte)

(Wolfgang Petersen, 1984, WGer) Barret Oliver, Noah Hathaway, Moses Gunn, Tami Stronach, Patricia Hayes, Sydney Bromley.
94 min.
A fairytale of the very best kind, with luscious effects which include a flying dragon, a rock monster, a fairy princess (mercifully grave and untwee), and a threat in whose vanquishing lies hope. Made at Munich's Bavaria Studios, the film concerns a withdrawn schoolboy, ignored by his businessman father and bullied at school, who steals a book and finds himself in thrall to the point where he is called upon to enter its world and save the magic land of Fantasia. Adapted from the novel by Michael Ende, the film is a mix of German Romanticism (complete with Wagnerian sets and a score in part by Giorgio Moroder) and Syberberg by way of Disney, or perhaps vice versa. There are even moments of moralising which give the twin heroes' quest someting of the steely tone of a Pilgrim's Progress. VG

NeverEnding Story II: The Next Chapter, The

(George Miller, 1989, Ger) Jonathan Brandis, Kenny Morrison, Clarissa Burt, John Wesley Shipp, Martin Umbach, Alexandra Johnes.
90 min.
This sequel to Wolfgang Petersen's ambitious film finds young Bastian (Brandis) returning to the dream world of Fantasia to save the Childlike Empress and her kingdom from an expanding and engulfing 'Emptiness'. Reunited with his alter ego Atreyu, and aided again by a menagerie of creatures (flying dog Falkor and the mountainous Rockbiter are joined by man-sized twitchy bird Nimbly), Bastian is lured into the deceitful web of sorceress Xayide (Burt), unknowingly selling his soul as he trades memories for miracles. Directed with pedestrian ease by Miller (of Man from Snowy River not Mad Max fame), this lacks the clumsy charm of its predecessor, its ropey narrative woefully failing to lash together the visual set pieces. While the intriguing themes are present and correct – the death of imagination, the loss of memory and identity – they are so swathed in cynical schmaltz as to be rendered all but sterile. MK

NeverEnding Story III: Escape from Fantasia, The

(Peter Macdonald, 1994, Ger) Jason James Richter, Melody Kay, Jack Black, Tony Robinson, Carole Finn, Ryan Bollman, Freddie Jones, Julie Cox.
95 min.
This further instalment reverses the worlds: here Fantasia comes to earth. Troubled by a new step-sister (Kay) and the taunts of the 'Nasties', led by crop-haired Slip (Black), Bastian (Richter) slopes off to Fantasia, leaving behind his copy of the empowering NeverEnding Story. The interactive book falls into the hands of Slip and his gang, who use it to foment chaos. Bastian is ordered back to the real world by the Child Empress, but accidentally takes his Fantasia pals with him. They are scattered all over the US. Can he reunite them? The animatronic characters from the Henson Creature Shop are looking familiar by now, but this new old-fashioned feel is part of the charm. It's a weak story, but the sfx, sets, opticals, humans and product-placements are orchestrated with a light touch. WH

Never Give an Inch

see Sometimes a Great Notion

Never Give a Sucker an Even Break (aka What a Man!)

(Edward Cline, 1941, US) WC Fields, Gloria Jean, Leon Errol, Susan Miller, Franklin Pangborn, Margaret Dumont.
70 min. b/w.
WC Fields' last starring vehicle has to be seen to be believed, and even then it probably won't be; it's constructed like one of his tallest stories, drunkenly veering from improbability to improbability, and produced with loving carelessness as Fields' hopeful scriptwriter tries to sell a story to the long-suffering Franklin Pangborn. The itinerary takes in the Esoteric Film Studios, a Russian colony in Mexico, and a neighbouring mountain top inhabited by the man-eating Mrs Hemogloben, played by a very raucous Margaret Dumont. But Fields' true co-star is the horrid singing moppet Gloria Jean, and for all the master's visual and verbal nonsense, the total result is more perverse than funny. GB

Never Let Go

(John Guillermin, 1960, GB) Richard Todd, Peter Sellers, Elizabeth Sellars, Adam Faith, Carol White, Mervyn Johns, John Le Mesurier.
91 min. b/w.
Cosmetics salesman Todd has his car stolen and, without insurance or much assistance from the police, decides to track it down himself. The trail leads through youthful thug Faith (his first screen role) to gang boss Sellers (taking a rare tilt at a villainous role) in this stolid homegrown crime caper, considered very brutal in its day, with a self-consciously strident use of 'adult' language. Quite persuasive turns from Todd and Sellers. TJ

Never Say Die

(Elliott Nugent, 1938, US) Bob Hope, Martha Raye, Andy Devine, Gale Sondergaard, Alan Mowbray, Sig Ruman, Monty Woolley.
80 min. b/w.
One of Bob Hope's best early films, in which he plays a millionaire hypochondriac led to believe he is slowly digesting himself (his acidity test has been mixed up with a dog's) and who therefore disposes of the rest of his life with the usual complicated results. Scripted originally by Preston Sturges, with Hope's regular gagmen Hartman and Butler brought in to add trademark wisecracks; the familiar Hope persona is already evident but not entirely fixed, so the mix works quite well, with enough of the original surviving (the European health spa, the philosophical butler, the delight in verbal eccentricities) to make it something of an embryo Sturges film. Martha Raye is excellent, even rather touching, as the girl he marries when he thinks he has only two weeks to live, and the supporting cast is admirable. TM

Never Say Never Again

(Irvin Kershner, 1983, GB) Sean Connery, Klaus Maria Brandauer, Max von Sydow, Barbara Carrera, Kim Basinger, Bernie Casey, Alec McCowen, Edward Fox, Rowan Atkinson.
134 min.
For all of us whose adolescence was entwined around a vision of a coral beach and Ursula Andress emerging from the foam in a white bikini, it's very comforting to return to the ambience; as the admirable Q has it, 'I hope this is a return to more gratuitous sex and violence, Commander Bond'. The plot is a *Thunderball* retread – the underwater hijacking of nuclear weapons, the holding of the world to ransom; routine stuff if your name is 'Bond...James Bond'. As usual, a hefty slice of the pleasure in watching late Bondage comes from the villains, in this case Bergman's chief angst-master von Sydow as the man with the fluffy white cat, Brandauer proving that a man may smile and smile and be a villain, and Carrera, she of the pneumatic balcony. The action's good, the photography excellent, the sets decent; but the real clincher is the fact that Bond is once more played by a man with the right stuff. Civilisation is safe in the hands of he who has never tasted quiche, and who, on the evidence here, at least, can perform a very passable tango. CPea

Never So Few

(John Sturges, 1959, US) Frank Sinatra, Gina Lollobrigida, Peter Lawford, Steve McQueen, Richard Johnson, Paul Henreid, Brian Donlevy, Dean Jones, Charles Bronson.
124 min.
Capt Sinatra (plus facial hair in the opening scenes) finds himself leading a handful of Kachin guerillas against Burma's 40,000 Japanese invaders in this slack WWII picture, adapted from Tom T Chamales' novel, which somehow manages to include his romance with La Lollo, the mistress of an oily profiteer (Henreid). Most of the novel's moral issues are sidestepped, while much is made of the Himalayan scenery. McQueen joined the cast when Sinatra fell out with Sammy Davis Jr, a fortunate break for the youngster who went on to make both *The Magnificent Seven* and *The Great Escape* with action specialist Sturges. Shot in 'Scope. TJ

Never Talk to Strangers

(Peter Hall, 1996, Can/US) Rebecca DeMornay, Harry Dean Stanton, Antonio Banderas, Dennis Miller, Len Cariou, Eugene Lipinski, Martha Burns, Beau Starr.
86 min.
An adequate psychological thriller on a topical theme – Repressed Memory Syndrome – but with little special quality, few frills or thrills, and a relaxed, almost languid exposition. DeMornay is a New York criminal psychologist, traumatised in childhood by the death of her mother, and currently engaged on the examination of a serial killer (Stanton) to determine whether or not he has Multiple Personality Disorder. Despite a desire to avoid romantic attachment, she's seduced into a passionate affair with mysterious stranger Tony Ramires (Banderas), a sensitive charmer with a darker side. She has a darker side, too, or at least a risk-taking sexual appetite, staying with her Puerto Rican amour despite his suspicious lies and his tampering with her personal property. When a series of threats come her way, she becomes more certain of his guilt, though viewers might plump for the grudge-taking serial killer, her creepy father or even a seemingly innocent 'friend' suffering from unrequited passion. Peter Hall's vocabulary of suspense rarely goes beyond the shock increase in volume or the quick edit, and the belated rendering of threatening atmosphere betokens a more subtle analytical approach which never arrives. WH

Never Too Young to Rock

(Dennis Abey, 1975, GB) Peter Denyer, Freddie Jones, Sheila Steafel, Joe Lynch, Peter Noone.
99 min.
Update of those putting-on-a-show escapades of the '40s, featuring Scott Fitzgerald, Mud, The Glitter Band, The Rubettes, Slick. All are top of the pops, with the exception of Bob Kerr's Whoopee Band, who seem a race apart and predictably get the least exposure. For the first hour, unfunny comedy dominates, as Denyer and a reluctant Freddie Jones track down famous groups for a 'Pick of the Hits' concert; the final 30 minutes is music, music, music. Despite the title, it makes you feel at least 102. GB

New Adventures of Don Juan, The

see Adventures of Don Juan

New Age, The

(Michael Tolkin, 1994, US) Peter Weller, Judy Davis, Samuel L Jackson, Patrick Bauchau, Corbin Bernsen, Jonathan Hadary, Patricia Heaton, Audra Lindley.
110 min.
Peter Witner (Weller) quits his mega-salaried job as a Los Angeles copywriter at the same time that his wife Katherine (Davis), a graphic designer, loses a major account. Their marriage on the rocks, the couple follow the advice of a New Age guru (Bauchau) and stake everything on opening a super-luxurious shop, 'Hip-ocracy'. Though filled with its fair share of diverting ideas, Tolkin's film seems half-seduced by the surfaces it attempts to penetrate. Cinematographer John F Campbell ably captures the ritzy, elegant, but unrewarding milieu of art-bedecked apartments, Petronius-like SM clubs, and spiritual retreats, and Weller and Davis suggest well the psychological panic and brittle suffering, respectively, of these two emblematic victims of modern American materialism. As a moral fable, however, it loses its way, chiefly due to the use of heavy-handed symbolism and an unenlightening play with confusing psycho-sexual ideas of opposing male-female principles. A brave stab, nevertheless, with a finely executed finale as Peter sets about his ironic salvation. WH

New Babylon, The (Novyi Vavilon)

(Grigori Kozintsev/Leonid Trauberg, 1929, USSR) Yelena Kuzmina, Pyotr Sobolevsky, D Gutman, Sophie Magarill, Sergei Gerasimov.
7,218 ft. b/w.
One of the very few great Soviet silent directors to re-establish a reputation after the intervening years of social-realist dogma, Kozintsev first made his mark as a pioneer of the 'Eccentric' movement, co-directing with Trauberg a series of extravagant entertainments and satires. *The New Babylon* represented one of the most controversial examples: muting the formal anarchy, and almost iconoclastically viewing the fate of the 1871 Paris Commune through the eyes of a department store shopgirl. TR

New Barbarians, The (I Nuovi Barbari)

(Enzo G Castellari, 1983, It) Fred Williamson, Timothy Brent ie. Giancarlo Prete, George Eastman ie. Luigi Montefiore, Anna Kanakis.
91 min.
The minestrone version of *Mad Max 2*. The new Barbarians rule the post-holocaust desert with a doddery death-cult philosophy, an inexhaustible arsenal, a fleet of tackily customised dune buggies, and a fetching SM wardrobe eventually explained away by the revelation that they're all gay. They kill Christians (a new Moses included) and rape our hero – an insipid automaton with all the charisma of Mel Gibson's big toe – before being blown away by Fred Williamson's exploding arrows, a wild-child's slingshot, and our buggered road warrior's instrument of poetic revenge, a massive corkscrew up the rear. For aficionados of true dreck only. PT

New Centurions, The (aka Precinct 45: Los Angeles Police)

(Richard Fleischer, 1972, US) George C Scott, Stacy Keach, Jane Alexander, Scott Wilson, Rosalind Cash, Erik Estrada, Clifton James, James B Sikking, William Atherton, Ed Lauter.
103 min.
A hack adaptation of Joseph Wambaugh's novel which makes you see why he subsequently bulldozed into control of his own work on the screen. Every symbol of social unease is grabbed and used with unbelievable crudity in throwing together a series of all-in-a-day's-work episodes: battered baby, rent extortionists, marital strife, gay entrapment (for a giggle), it's all there, except that the more you're supposed to sympathise with the cops, the more sympathy you in fact feel for their victims. It's sort of bound together by a strange initiation theme, in which an older cop teaches the young one all he knows before blowing his own head off.

New Face in Hell

see PJ.

New Game of Death, The

see Legend of Bruce Lee

New Jack City

(Mario Van Peebles, 1991, US) Wesley Snipes, Ice T, Allen Payne, Chris Rock, Judd Nelson, Mario Van Peebles, Michael Michele, Bill Nunn, Russell Wong, Thalmus Rasulala.
100 min.
Touted as a ground-breaking addition to the crime-on-the-streets genre, Van Peebles' thriller is far more modest: a high-tech update on that old warhorse, a mobster's rise and fall. Ruthless Nino Brown (Snipes) lords it over a New York neighbourhood with an empire built on crack and violence. It's only when two disenchanted streetwise officers come together – African-American Scott Appleton (Ice T) and Nick Peretti (Nelson) – that his domain is effectively threatened. The movie pays lip service to social analysis while delight-

ing in the paraphernalia of violence. As such, it's a superior example of what used to be called blaxploitation, with Van Peebles piling on corruption and carnage for all he's worth. GA

New Jersey Drive
(Nick Gomez, 1995, US) Sharron Corley, Saul Stein, Gabriel Casseus, Gwen McGee, Andre Moore, Donald Adeosun Faison.
95 min.
After his over-rated debut, *Laws of Gravity*, writer/director Gomez comes down to earth with a thud in this dispiriting slice-of-life-in-the-projects picture. The film (executive producer Spike Lee) does have an authentic tedium about it (monotonous dialogue, repetitive dramatic situations) which mirrors the hopelessness of its young characters' predicament. Gomez is good with actors (Corley is a find), but his naturalistic, hand-held style only takes you so far; there's none of the insight or passion which ignites such films as, say, *La Haine* and Lee's own *Clockers*. TCh

New Kind of Love, A
(Melville Shavelson, 1963, US) Paul Newman, Joanne Woodward, Thelma Ritter, Eva Gabor, Maurice Chevalier, George Tobias, Marvin Kaplan, Robert Clary.
110 min.
Director Shavelson cut his teeth as a writer for Bob Hope and Danny Kaye. He could have done with either of those comedians in this laboured, overdressed Parisian comedy. Instead, he ended up with Mr and Mrs Method, the always earnest Newman and Woodward. She's a fashion buyer, he's a lout of a journalist. He can't stand her short hair, but ends up falling for her when she's fitted with a wig. Saint-Laurent, Cardin and Dior provided the costumes, but the script could have been written by Andy Capp. GM

New Leaf, A
(Elaine May, 1970, US) Walter Matthau, Elaine May, Jack Weston, George Rose, William Redfield, James Coco.
102 min.
Browning a little round the edges, not least because Paramount subjected the film to fairly drastic re-editing, Elaine May's directorial debut still makes for cherishable comedy viewing precisely because she eschewed the modish flash her former cabaret partner Mike Nichols brought to his movie-making. May herself plays the frumpishly eccentric but wealthy botanist pursued with murderous intent by Matthau's ageing, financially embarrassed playboy. PT

New Life, A
(Alan Alda, 1988, US) Alan Alda, Ann-Margaret, Hal Linden, Veronica Hamel, Mary Kay Place, John Shea, Beatrice Alda.
104 min.
After 20 years of marriage, middle-class New Yorkers Alda and Ann-Margaret decide to call it a day, leaving each of them free to enter anew the wild and wonderful world of the single life – which has altered somewhat since last they encountered it. This is deep Woody Allen territory, and despite something of a change of image for Alda the actor (bearded, permed and obnoxious), Alda the writer/director isn't quite able to ring the changes on a familiar routine. Smoothly done, though. TJ

New Lot, The
(Carol Reed, 1943, GB) Bernard Miles, Peter Ustinov, Raymond Huntley, John Laurie, Philip Godfrey, Geoffrey Keen, Robert Donat.
42 min. b/w.
This was produced by the Army for in-house consumption only, then remade for the general public as *The Way Ahead*. Believed to be lost until a print turned up in India in the mid-'90s, it deals with the training of five conscripts and their transformation from truculent civilians into efficient soldiers and team members. The comparison has to be with the first half of *Full Metal Jacket*: the films collide at every point, e.g. the antithetical depictions of authority (Keen here compared to Lee Ermey there). Both movies take as central the business of schooling people to kill (a theme displaced in *The Way Ahead*) – what has naively been called 'dehumanisation' in Kubrick's film. With a brisk tenderness, Reed represents the process as the conscious, willing

sacrifice of something precious. Nothing less gung-ho could be imagined than this affecting, invaluable work. BBa

Newman's Law
(Richard Heffron, 1974, US) George Peppard, Roger Robinson, Eugene Roche, Gordon Pinsent, Abe Vigoda, Louis Zorich.
99 min.
Hardnosed but rigorously honest detective (Peppard) finds himself framed and suspended when he gets too close to the big dope king. Despite the routine plot, Anthony Wilson's script (for the first half anyway) manages to establish with some feeling the routine and bureaucratic nature of policework. Unfortunately, Heffron's direction is incapable of sustaining the necessary momentum. Although he manages well enough with a supermarket shoot-up, things fall to pieces once Peppard goes on the rampage. Peppard's downbeat performance survives along with a few other fringe benefits: a gangster with a nice line in Nixonian answers; the all-pervasive, slightly suspect masculine relationships; and the way the film ends up somewhere between *Dirty Harry* and *Serpico*. CPe

New Moon
(Robert Z Leonard, 1940, US) Jeanette MacDonald, Nelson Eddy, Mary Boland, George Zucco, HB Warner, Grant Mitchell, Stanley Fields.
105 min. b/w.
The Romberg-Hammerstein operetta with its setting switched from Tsarist Russia to New Orleans in the hope that audiences would identify it with the hugely successful (and remarkably similar) *Naughty Marietta* as MacDonald's haughty aristocrat falls for Eddy's gallant bondslave (but he's really a French Duke, exiled for his egalitarian beliefs since the year is 1789). The score isn't bad, otherwise the mixture is as before, only stodgier. TM

New One-Armed Swordsman, The (Xin Dubi Dao)
(Chang Cheh, 1970, HK) Li Ching, David Chiang, Ti Lung, Ku Feng, Chen Hsing.
102 min.
Chang Cheh had been the leading director of swordplay and martial arts movies at Shaw Brothers for ten years or more before this. A few years later, especially since the break-up of his partnership with the martial arts choreographer Liu Chia-Liang, his career would be on the wane. But there's no denying that he has knocked off a number of minor classics over the years, and this is one of the best: a sombre, Gothic-toned saga of chivalry, denied but finally confirmed. Excellent performances from David Chiang (as the hero who severs his own right arm when he loses a duel), Ti Lung (as his utterly charming buddy), and Ku Feng (as the relishably villainous baddie). TR

News Boys, The
see Newsies

News from Home
(Chantal Akerman, 1976, Fr/Bel) narrator: Chantal Akerman.
90 min.
Akerman explores the disjunction between European myths about New York – with its monumental cityscapes and cinematic glamour – and the reality, a place of hopeless ghettos and monotonous suburbs. In counterpoint to cinema-photographer Babette Mangolte's powerful images of the city, the soundtrack consists of banal letters from a petit bourgeois Belgian mother to her daughter in New York. A considerable contribution to the hinterland area between narrative cinema and the avant-garde. LM

News from Nowhere
(Alister Hallum, 1978, GB) Timothy West, Kika Markham, John Cater, Clive Swift, Dave Hastings.
53 min.
An attractive little film sponsored by the Arts Council. William Morris, wife, friend, dog and boatman travel up the Thames in 1880, their journey interrupted by champagne breakfasts, expostulations on matters aesthetic and socialist, flashbacks to Rossetti and the Pre-Raphaelites, and glimpses

of Morris stomping about Iceland. By filtering facts and quotations through a fictional framework, Alister Hallum and his co-writer Philip Henderson have brought their fascinating subject painlessly and vividly to life, retaining all his ambiguities. And Timothy West has all the beard and fire required for a convincing impersonation. GB

News from the Good Lord
see Des Nouvelles du Bon Dieu

Newsfront
(Phillip Noyce, 1978, Aust) Bill Hunter, Chris Haywood, John Dease, Wendy Hughes, Gerard Kennedy, John Ewart, Angela Punch, Bryan Brown.
111 min. b/w & col.
An ambitious attempt at capturing the social history of a generation through the experiences of a newsreel cameraman, with brilliantly mounted set pieces, including debates finely tuned to fluctuations in a bigoted, rapidly changing sociopolitical climate. Easy to overlook such shortcomings as the lack of a strong narrative, the failure to develop the women characters adequately, and the risk of degenerating into mere nostalgia. It's never less than terrific to look at, and the seamless matching of new material with actual newsreel footage is truly remarkable. RM

Newsies (aka The News Boys)
(Kenny Ortega, 1992, US) Christian Bale, Bill Pullman, Ann-Margret, Robert Duvall, David Moscow, Ele Keats, Kevin Tighe, Michael Lerner, Charles Cioffi, Marc Lawrence.
125 min.
Directed by choreographer Ortega, this Disney musical is based on a strike of 1899, in which New York's newsboys rallied against press baron Joseph Pulitzer (Duvall). It espouses the Great Man theory of history, with dynamic young tearaway Jack Kelly (Bale) galvanising the masses with his sheer charisma, sullen jeans-ad looks, and middling ability to carry a tune. If you have a soft spot for feisty, back-talking *bambini* with cute squints, backwards caps and names like Crutchy, Dutchy and Bumlets, your heart will melt. Frighteningly adept attention-grabbers to a lad, these *nouveaux* Dead End Kids gambol to a brassy, forgettable score; the anachronistic proto-hip-hop touches rankle, though Jack Feldman's lyrics provide the odd witty touch. Not quite *Matewan* with tunes; more like *Oliver!* without them. JRo

New Tales of the Taira Clan
see Shin Heike Monogatari

New Year's Day
(Henry Jaglom, 1989, US) Maggie Jakobson, Gwen Welles, Melanie Winter, Henry Jaglom, David Duchovny, Milos Forman, Michael Emil, Donna Germain, Tracy Reiner.
92 min.
Drew (Jaglom), wrestling with mid-life crisis, has left LA for a new life in New York. He arrives on New Year's Day, only to find that the lease allows the previous tenants an extra day in his apartment. By the time he's argued his way into the living-room, he knows their most intimate problems: Lucy (Jakobson) has a womanising boyfriend, Annie (Welles) is giving up 'compulsive behaviour', and childless Winona (Winter) is feeling broody. They're joined by Lucy's parents, boyfriend and psychiatrist, as well as mutual friends (including Milos Forman) and a psychosexologist (Emil, wonderful). Jaglom's opening monologue gives way to a loosely structured series of revelations, his camera roving among conversations which are by turns banal, touching and funny. Some characters are appealing, but there's not much emotional depth as Jaglom raises complex themes only to conclude that they leave him feeling 'moody and weird'. By the end, you'll know what he means. CM

New York, New York
(Martin Scorsese, 1977, US) Liza Minnelli, Robert De Niro, Lionel Stander, Barry Primus, Mary Kay Place, Georgie Auld, George Memmoli, Dick Miller.
153 min.
Scorsese's tribute/parody/critique of the MGM musical is a razor-sharp dissection of the conventions of both meeting-cute romances and rags-to-riches biopics, as it charts the traumatic love

affair between irresponsible but charming jazz saxophonist De Niro (dubbed by George Auld) and mainstream singer Minnelli. On an emotional level, the film is a powerhouse, offering some of the most convincingly painful rows ever shot; as a depiction of changes in American music and the entertainment world, it is accurate and evocative; and as a commentary on showbiz films, it's a stunner, sounding echoes of Minnelli's own mother's movies and career (particularly *A Star Is Born*) as well as other classics like *On the Town* and the first *A Star Is Born* (in which Stander also appeared). Superbly scored, beautifully designed by Boris Leven to highlight the genre's artificiality, and performed to perfection. GA

New York Nights
(Simon Nuchtern, 1983, US) Corrine Alphen, George Ayer, Bobbi Burns, Peter Matthey, Missy O'Shea.
111 min.
Arthur Schnitzler's cunning form from *La Ronde* blagged to display a group of daisy-chaining demi-mondaines indulging in ten kinds of rumpy-pumpy all over town. All vile stuff, of course, but as usual there is a certain recherché pleasure to be had from incidentals: 1 Sample dialogue: 'I am 18' – 'Yeah? And I'm Roman Polanski'. 2 A husband who decks his wife up in a moustache and makes talent from the local gay club have her on the sofa while he plays martial music on a baby grand. 3 Plato's Retreat: a place where Socratic dialogues take place in a sauna. 4 The NY skyline with a dirigible above it. Warning: the Surgeon General has determined that watching this film will give you herpes. CPea

New York Stories
(Martin Scorsese/Francis Coppola/Woody Allen, 1989, US) Nick Nolte, Rosanna Arquette, Steve Buscemi, Patrick O'Neal, Deborah Harry, Heather McComb, Talia Shire, Giancarlo Giannini, Carole Bouquet, Woody Allen, Mia Farrow, Mae Questel, Julie Kavner.
124 min.
Three directors, three featurettes. Co-written with his teenage daughter, Coppola's centerpiece, 'Life Without Zoe', is quite simply a mess. The story (poor little rich girl plots to reunite her separated parents and return a bangle to an exotic princess) is nonsense, nothing more than a maudlin, self-indulgent excuse to have horrid brats and members of the Coppola clan prance about in funny clothes to the strains of Francis' favourite music. Scorsese's opener, 'Life Lessons', which does make sense, centres on a muscular performance from Nolte as an immature, egocentric artist obsessed with assistant Arquette. The plot, inspired by Dostoievsky, seems meant as some sort of personal reflection on the links between artistic productivity and sexual/emotional frustration. The visuals, performances and superb music provide many pleasures, but the slight, anecdotal inevitability of the tale is a drawback, since the material promises something richer and deeper. Only Woody Allen seems to have understood what is possible in a featurette. Although 'Oedipus Wrecks' is only an extended variation on nagging Jewish momma gags, it's not only his funniest film in years, it also works beautifully: as it should in a short, every moment counts. GA

Next of Kin
(John Irvin, 1989, US) Patrick Swayze, Liam Neeson, Helen Hunt, Adam Baldwin, Andreas Katsulas, Bill Paxton, Michael J Pollard.
109 min.
When his brother is killed in a mob-style hit, Truman Gates (Swayze), an Appalachian hillbilly turned Chicago cop, is torn between his duty and family loyalty which requires that he opt for Old Testament revenge. But even if he can locate a black witness to the slaying, or prove that a smooth mobster's ambitious son (Baldwin) was implicated, can he do so before vengeful brother Briar (Neeson) takes the law into his own hands? On the loose with a shotgun and a belly full of hate, Briar is unwittingly setting the scene for a showdown between the urban mobsters, with their state-of-the-art firepower, and the good ol' country boys who favour crossbows, axes and snakes. Together with *Hamburger Hill*, this illustrates that Irvin probably couldn't stage an action scene if you held a gun to his head. Even more turgid and unconvincing are the quieter 'dramatic' scenes, which serve only to arrest the plot's minimal momentum and prolong the agony. NF

Next of Kin, The
(Thorold Dickinson, 1942, GB) Mervyn Johns, John Chandos, Nova Pilbeam, David Hutcheson, Stephen Murray, Phyllis Stanley, Charles Victor, Basil Radford, Naunton Wayne.
102 min. b/w.
Originally intended as an army training film advising that 'Careless Talk Costs Lives', this was expanded by Ealing into a feature thriller. The switch shows in the didactic pacing, especially at the beginning, but like Cavalcanti's *Went The Day Well?* (though not as good), the film has a chillingly casual authenticity as it noses into seedy byways to uncover the chain of fifth columnists that includes an antiquarian bookseller (Murray), a stripper (Stanley) and an Irish sailor (Victor). Although the ending was softened when Churchill wanted to have the film banned as a threat to morale (the 'betrayed' commando raid succeeds, though only at the cost of heavy casualties), it still stands up pretty well. TM

Next Stop, Greenwich Village
(Paul Mazursky, 1976, US) Lenny Baker, Shelley Winters, Ellen Greene, Lois Smith, Christopher Walken, Dori Brenner, Antonio Fargas, Lou Jacobi.
111 min.
A middlebrow *American Graffiti*, minus the music and set in Greenwich Village, 1953. Aspiring young actor moves into the Village, thereby allowing writer/director Mazursky to render into clichés all the obvious ingredients of the period: coffee bars, suicide bids, Actors' Studio classes, cheap parties, the Rosenbergs, uncertain contraception, illegal abortions. Add Shelley Winters as a Jewish momma to give the movie heart, and Antonio Fargas as a misunderstood black gay to give it pathos, and you have a fair idea of the film's efforts to win its audience. Sadly, the pretensions of most of the characters are matched by Mazursky: pointed homages to 'Gadge' Kazan and Marlon, unnecessary dream sequences, and continuous endorsement for his rather tedious characters; one is only surprised that there wasn't a kid called Jimmy Dean at the party.

Next Voice You Hear…, The
(William Wellman, 1950, US) James Whitmore, Nancy Davis, Gary Gray, Lillian Bronson, Art Smith, Tom D'Andrea, Jeff Corey.
83 min. b/w.
Beautifully scripted (Charles Schnee) and directed, the first half of this Dore Schary production is a persuasive minimalist portrait of a lower middle-class small-town family (factory-worker Whitmore, wife Davis, and young son Gray): loving and reasonably contented, but showing signs of stretch-marks where the struggle to make ends meet doesn't quite match consumer aspirations. Much of it is both funny and pointed; and the moments of unease, escalating into a vague sense of guilty panic, are equally well handled as the voice on the radio (heard only in reported speech, since the divine voice doesn't record) proves to be God announcing a visit. The trouble is that God's message turns out to be the usual guff (love one another, count your blessings, nature and all that); and the only way the film can drum up any suitable conflict is by waxing melodramatic about the mother's pregnancy ('Talk about your miracle!' cries delighted dad when all goes without a hitch). Schnee's dialogue and Wellman's direction deserve better than this crowd-pleasing scenario. TM

Nez au Vent, Le
(Dominique Guerrier, 1995, Fr) Yves Robert, Philippine Leroy-Baulieu.
90 min.
An ingenious if not entirely satisfying fantasy in which elderly perfume-boffin Robert commits suicide, is admitted to the wrong neighbourhood of the beyond, and returns to this world, where he relives key moments from his life and helps sort out his grown son's troubled existence. The film shifts between past and present, makes some telling points about love, selfishness and commitment, but never quite manages to balance its black comedy with its more serious moments. GA

Niagara
(Henry Hathaway, 1953, US) Marilyn Monroe, Joseph Cotten, Jean Peters, Casey Adams, Don Wilson, Richard Allan.
90 min.
Marilyn's first real starring vehicle, a steamily

melodramatic thriller into which she fits a trifle uncomfortably: unbecomingly costumed, uneasy with dialogue, and exposed to acres of footage designed to ram her down the audience's throat as a heartless, lusting bitch, a sexpot honeymooner scheming to kill her husband (Cotten), a mentally disturbed war veteran who has his own ideas. Odd to realise (this was after all her eighteenth film) that Hollywood took so long to discover the vulnerability that became Monroe's distinctive quality. Worthseeing for Hathaway's superbly crafted direction, even if it needed a Hitchcock to merge the symbolism of the location (the falls, the belltower) with the themes of sexual domination and envy. TM

Nibelungen, Die
(Fritz Lang, 1924, Ger) Paul Richter, Margarete Schön, Hanna Ralph, Gertrud Arnold, Theodor Loos, Hans Adalbert von Schlettow, Bernhard Goetzke, Rudolf Klein-Rogge.
10,551 ft (Part 1)/11,732 ft (Part 2). b/w.
Siegfried, the first part of Lang's epic, based on the same myth cycle that inspired Wagner's *Ring*, is a slow, grave pageant in the form of a ballad. The visual style is as monumental as the narrative, with forests and castles modelled on 19th century Romantic paintings, and the whole is based upon an intense pleasure in spectacle, compounded by the inspired trick-work: a magical dragon, fiery landscapes for Brunhilde's Northern home, and Walter Ruttmann's interpolated *Dream of the Hawks*. In the second part, *Kriemhild's Revenge*, as Kriemhild and the Huns destroy the Burgundians who have murdered Siegfried, so the emphasis on fatalistic design, plotting and architecture is replaced by the furious, crowded movement of the battle which comprises most of this half. The mix of desire, death and revenge is common in Lang, but here, with the distance of myth, the concentration on violent spectacle, and – most important – the woman as focal point, the impression is of pure, passionate nihilism running riot. SJ

Nicaragua – No Pasarán
(David Bradbury, 1984, Aust)
74 min.
A detailed account of the inability of America to accept Nicaragua's non-client status. The Sandinistas emerge as well short of perfect, but clearly no sane Nicaraguan would trade them for the vile Somoza, and the whole atmosphere of the country is clearly different from its neighbours. Even the soldiers smile. JCo

Nicholas and Alexandra
(Franklin J Schaffner, 1971, US) Michael Jayston, Janet Suzman, Harry Andrews, Tom Baker, Timothy West, Jack Hawkins, Laurence Olivier, John McEnery, Eric Porter, Michael Bryant, John Wood, Ian Holm, Michael Redgrave, Curt Jürgens.
189 min.
Old-fashioned, overlong costume epic, comfortably reactionary in its view of the Tsar Nicholas as a saint who knew not what he was doing to the Russian people, and of the revolutionaries as potential tyrants reaching hungrily for power. The first part is elegant and surprisingly affecting in detailing the love story of Nicholas and Alexandra (beautifully played by Jayston and Suzman), blighted when their son turns out to be a haemophiliac and Rasputin (Baker) erupts into their lives. The revolutionaries get shorter shrift. Two comrades exchange recollections of Siberia before introducing themselves – 'Josef Stalin...''My name is Lenin' – with the name-dropping becoming decidedly Goonish when Lenin then turns to a bystander to cry, 'Trotsky, you've been avoiding me!' Much cameo role-playing around here; and in the last part of the film, devoted to the decline and fall of the Romanovs, they seem to take an unconscionable time a-dying. TM

Nicholas Nickleby
(Alberto Cavalcanti, 1947, GB) Derek Bond, Cedric Hardwicke, Alfred Drayton, Aubrey Woods, Jill Balcon, Bernard Miles, Sally Ann Howes, Stanley Holloway, Sybil Thorndike, Fay Compton, Cathleen Nesbitt.
108 min. b/w.
For a director who dabbled in the avant-garde, Cavalcanti makes surprisingly little of the surreal possibilities of this convoluted Dickensian nightmare. As in *Champagne Charlie* he collaborated with art director Michel Relph to create an

impressively atmospheric Victorian London, but stylish visuals hardly compensate for the flat, cursory rendering of some of Dickens' best drawn characters. Only Bernard Miles as Noggs and Cedric Hardwicke as wicked Uncle Ralph are given enough space to establish a proper presence. Meagre and one-dimensional, the film is finally smothered by Ealing's cosy sentimentality. RMy

Nicht Versöhnt (Not Reconciled)

(Jean-Marie Straub, 1965, WGer) Heinrich Hargesheimer, Carlheinz Hargesheimer, Martha Ständner, Danièle Straub, Henning Hermssen.
53 min. b/w.
Fifty years of German social and political history, from the anti-Communism of 1910 through the anti-semitism of the '30s to a political reprisal in 1960. Explored a-chronologically, in vignettes from the lives of three generations of a middle class family. Taken from Heinrich Böll's novel *Billiards at Half Past Nine*, but with all the mechanics of storytelling and the frosting of 'style' removed. Read the novel for the narrative; see Straub's movie for the steely precision of its ideas and images, enhanced by Brechtian acting and the absence of all redundancies. Difficult in ways that few films are, but necessarily difficult. TR

Nick Carter in Prague (Adela Jeste Nevecerela)

(Oldrich Lipsky, 1977, Czech) Michal Docolomansky, Rudolf Hrusinsky, Milos Kopecky, Lasislav Pesek, Neda Konvalinkova.
102 min.
A whimsical, hopelessly leaden comedy about American private eye Nick Carter breezing into Prague to foil legendary master criminal The Gardener. The central problems are the script, which lacks even a glimmer of mystery, suspense or poetry, and the direction, which reduces every gag and every baroque extravagance to the same bland level. TR

Nick Carter – Master Detective

(Jacques Tourneur, 1939, US) Walter Pidgeon, Rita Johnson, Henry Hull, Donald Meek, Stanley Ridges, Milburn Stone, Sterling Holloway.
60 min. b/w.
The first of MGM's three Nick Carter B movies, in which he (not the period creation but a private eye in the contemporary mould) investigates espionage in an aircraft factory. Tourneur's second film in Hollywood, it's briskly and competently done, but the best thing about it is Donald Meek's performance as Bartholomew the Bee Man, a mousy little apiculturist who fancies himself as a private eye, keeps following Nick Carter (Pidgeon) around, and more than once proves to be the man on the spot. TM

Nickelodeon

(Peter Bogdanovich, 1976, US/GB) Ryan O'Neal, Burt Reynolds, Tatum O'Neal, Brian Keith, Stella Stevens, John Ritter.
122 min.
To make a clinker out of a gift of a subject like silent movie-making is some feat, yet Bogdanovich manages it with honours. Set between 1910 and 1915, *Nickelodeon* spends ages muddling the protagonists' lives and their suitcases before they settle down to make pictures. Despite some comic intentions, the film takes itself far too seriously as a *hommage* to the movie pioneers. But with Bogdanovich's yearning nostalgia totally lacking in perspective, this dreary recreation becomes entirely a work of the past tense; certainly there's no wit, pace or enthusiasm to suggest that it's alive. The direction is agonisingly pedantic for a comedy, and leaves O'Neal and Reynolds totally exposed, mugging away in charmless and clumsy fashion. CPe

Nickel Queen

(John McCallum, 1971, Aust) Googie Withers, John Laws, Alfred Sandor, Ed Devereaux, Peter Gwynne, Joanna McCallum.
89 min.
Totally appalling piece of Australiana, with hippies and socialites and nickel in them thar hills, and banality by the spadeful all around. Makes *The Adventures of Barry Mackenzie* look like a can of Fosters (which it isn't).

Nick of Time

(John Badham, 1995, US) Johnny Depp, Christopher Walken, Marsha Mason, Charles S Dutton, Roma Maffia.
89 min.
No sooner has accountant Depp disembarked at the Los Angeles railway station than he's separated from his infant daughter and presented with a gun, a photograph and a schedule. If he hasn't killed the woman in the picture – Governor of California Marsha Mason – within the next 80 minutes, then he'll never see his child again. It's a nifty pretext for a nail-biting thriller, but even on this abbreviated timescale the movie nags at your credulity. Given that the conspiracy ripples out alarmingly wide, it seems improbable that head honcho Walken should have concocted quite such a whimsical plan, and it's a long wait before the impassive Depp takes any resolute action. Written by the prolific, old-fashioned Patrick Sheane Duncan, the film's passably ingenious, but director Badham fluffs its central gimmick, the notion that the action is played out, *Rope*-style, in real time, by cutting away from his hard-pressed protagonist at convenient intervals. Even so, it's not a bad effort. Badham's sub-De Palma, not Hitchcock, but he's still fractionally above average. TCh

Nick's Movie

see Lightning Over Water

Nicky and Gino

see Dominick and Eugene

Nico

see Above the Law

Nico Icon

(Susanne Ofteringer, 1995, Ger) Alan Wise, James Young, Helma Wolff, Nico Papatakis, Carlos de Maldonado-Bostock, Edith Boulogne, Billy Name, Paul Morrissey, Jonas Mekas, John Cale, Viva, Sterling Morrison.
72 min.
One of those figures who elevate ennui into an art form, or at least a way of life, Nico had a kind of night-of-the-living-dead glamour which fascinated anyone (mostly men) who spent time with her. A teen model for *Vogue*, she landed a bit part in *La Dolce Vita*, had a son by Alain Delon, and hooked up with Andy Warhol and the Velvet Underground to cut one classic album. As a chanteuse, she made Marlene Dietrich sound girlish. As a performer, she was utterly opaque – but then that seems to have been her way off stage, too. She didn't have a career, she had an addiction. It was the only thing she shared. Bonding with her son, she introduced him to heroin, and later, when he was hospitalised in a drug-induced coma, she recorded the sound of the life-support machine as a backing track for one of her songs. This is a compelling portrait of an unlovely beauty, a fascinating void. Using extensive home movies, especially from the Factory period, interviews with the survivors (John Cale, Paul Morrissey, Sterling Morrison), and clips painfully contrasting the glacial ingenue with the elegantly ravaged junkie, writer/director Ofteringer probes the enigma without finding much of substance behind the surface. But what surface! The film's formal inventiveness – games with framing and superimposition – gives it some of the texture of '60s underground film, and there's a strong sense of that whole pseudo-bohemian scene. You don't come out feeling any warmer towards Nico, necessarily, or desperate to dig out those solo albums, but there's something haunting about her; she didn't so much make her mark as leave us the scars to remember her by. TCh

Nido, El

see Nest, The

Night After Night

(Archie Mayo, 1932, US) George Raft, Constance Cummings, Wynne Gibson, Mae West, Roscoe Karns, Alison Skipworth, Louis Calhern.
70 min. b/w.
It seems strange to find the stately Mae West playing a jolly character called Maudie Triplett, and even stranger to find her fourth in the cast list, but after all this was her first film.

Her scenes are few, yet she throws so much into them that the leading players in this comedy drama (cool Constance Cummings and icy George Raft, the Archie Andrews of gangsters) momentarily fade into oblivion. They soon come back, though, along with the muddled story about a speakeasy proprietor's love for a Park Avenue dame. GB

Night Ambush

see Ill Met By Moonlight

Night and Day

(Michael Curtiz, 1946, US) Cary Grant, Alexis Smith, Monty Woolley, Mary Martin, Ginny Simms, Jane Wyman, Eve Arden, Victor Francen, Dorothy Malone, Alan Hale.
128 min.
Weak biopic of Cole Porter in which Curtiz fights a losing battle with a conventional, highly sanitised, thoroughly sentimental script. Though unadventurously chosen, the songs (staged lushly if none too imaginatively by LeRoy Prinz) are at least worth listening to, especially when sung by Ginny Simms (though some swear by Mary Martin's rendition of *My Heart Belongs to Daddy* as the highlight of the film). TM

Night and Day (Nuit et Jour)

(Chantal Akerman, 1991, Fr) Guillaine Londez, Thomas Langmann, François Negret.
100 min.
Akerman's lyrical chronicle of a heterosexual ménage-à-trois looks banality straight in the face. New to Paris, youngsters Julie (Londez) and Jack (Langmann) experience a summer of love broken only by his nightly taxi round, which leaves her free to wander the streets and strike up an equally sexual relationship with Joseph (Negret), who drives the same cab during the day. Without conscience, Julie flits between lovers, but her willingness to flaunt every morality threatens both liaisons. The performers are attractive, in an androgynous way, but their lack of distinctiveness typifies the film's anonymity. TJ

Night and the City

(Jules Dassin, 1950, GB) Richard Widmark, Gene Tierney, Googie Withers, Francis L Sullivan, Herbert Lom, Hugh Marlowe, Mike Mazurki.
95 min. b/w.
Bizarre *film noir* with Widmark as a smalltime nightclub tout trying to hustle his way into the wrestling rackets, but finding himself the object of a murderous manhunt when his cons catch up with him. Set in a London through which Widmark spends much of his time dodging in dark alleyways, it attempts to present the city in neo-expressionist terms as a grotesque, terrifyingly anonymous trap. Fascinating, even though the stylised characterisations (like Francis L Sullivan's obesely outsized nightclub king) remain theoretically interesting rather than convincing. Inclined to go over the top, it all too clearly contains theseeds of Dassin's later – and disastrous – pretensions. TM

Night and the City

(Irwin Winkler, 1992, US) Robert De Niro, Jessica Lange, Cliff Gorman, Alan King, Jack Warden, Eli Wallach, Barry Primus, Gene Kirkwood, Richard Price.
104 min.
Nothing to write home about in this remake. Richard Price's script is typically funny-tough, but the structuring is aimless and the characters psychologically nowhere. Motormouth shyster lawyer Harry Fabian (De Niro) is humiliated in court by big shot boxing promoter Boom Boom (King), and decides to take revenge by recruiting Boom Boom's retired brother Al (Warden) and promoting some bouts of his own. He turns to his married mistress, bartender Helen (Lange), for the financing, but everything he touches plunges him deeper into trouble. None of this makes any sense (Fabian cheats Helen with a bogus liquor licence, for instance, and she doesn't complain). Worst of all, Fabian is issued with all the inner depths of a DJ, and we're expected to care about his ambitions. The hopes of no-hopers in *film noir* rendered up a piteous bouquet, but there's none of that here. Even De Niro can't do much with the role, beyond yammering and dancing on the spot like a warmed-over version of his Johnny Boy in *Mean Streets*. BC

Night at the Opera, A

(Sam Wood, 1935, US) The Marx Brothers, Kitty Carlisle, Allan Jones, Margaret Dumont, Sig Ruman, Walter Woolf King.
92 min. b/w.
The Marx Brothers at the turning point, just before their gradual descent into mediocrity at the hands of MGM, who wanted their comedy to be rationed and rationalised. It's a top budget job, opulent and meticulous, with its fair share of vices: this is the first Marx Brothers film where you really feel like strangling the romantic leads. But it has even more virtues: there's no Zeppo, the script's generally great (Kaufman and Ryskind), Dumont's completely great, and the Brothers get to perform some of their most irresistible routines – the stateroom scene and all. GB

Night Beauties

see Belles de nuit, Les

Nightbreed

(Clive Barker, 1990, US) Craig Sheffer, Anne Bobby, David Cronenberg, Charles Haid, Hugh Quarshie, Hugh Ross, Doug Bradley, Oliver Parker, Nicholas Vince.
102 min.
Psychotic shrink Decker (Cronenberg) and racist police chief Eigerman (Haid) are icons of modern evil; the Nightbreed are a variegated tribe of shape-shifters, whose subterranean lair is attacked and overrun by the genocidal forces of law and order. Caught in the cultural crossfire are confused, colourless hero Boone (Sheffer) and transparently doomed love interest Lori (Bobby). Convinced by Decker that he is a serial killer, Boone panics, escapes from custody and heads for Midian, a mythical necropolis to which he feels drawn by an inexorable fate. Pursued by Decker's homicidal alter ego, Boone unwittingly fulfils an ancient prophecy... In adapting his own novella *Cabal*, Barker aims for a carnival feel, a breathless ghost-train ride through a fantastical world of grotesquely glamorous monsters. For all their dangerous exoticism, however, none of the myriad monsters has an identity that is more than skin deep. Barker calls his shambolic, uninvolving narrative 'scattershot'; put less kindly, it's explosive and directionless as a blunderbuss. NF

Night Caller, The (aka Blood Beast from Outer Space)

(John Gilling, 1965, GB) John Saxon, Maurice Denham, Patricia Haines, Alfred Burke, John Carson, Warren Mitchell, Robert Crewdson.
84 min. b/w.
Minor but not unintelligent British sci-fi thriller (from a novel by Frank Crisp) with imported star Saxon looking as though he hasn't quite found his bearings yet. The plot involves a UFO (an energy valve for transmuting matter), a female scientist (Haines, persuasive) who succumbs at the close to chief alien Medra (Crewdson), and sundry young women who answer the advertisements of Medra's modelling agency, only to be spirited away to planet Ganymede for genetic jiggery-pokery. TJ

Night Caller (Peur sur la Ville)

(Henri Verneuil, 1975, Fr/It) Jean-Paul Belmondo, Charles Denner, Catherine Morin, Adalberto-Maria Merli, Lea Massari, Jean Martin.
125 min.
Belmondo plays super-cop on the tops of Paris buildings and underground trains, piling stunt on daredevil stunt and risking his neck for a particularly silly story. Like *The Eiger Sanction*, there's some mileage in seeing a star so blatantly performing his own stunts, crashing through plate-glass windows of high rise buildings while suspended from a helicopter, etc. But desperately little of the film's energy goes into a plot that combines a settling of an old score with a hunt for a one-eyed killer who strangles loose women. CPe

Nightcleaners

(Berwick Street Film Collective, 1975, GB)
90 min.
This documentary started out as a conventional agit-prop project in support of the 1972 campaign to unionise women nightcleaners in London. In the three years that it took to complete, it turned into something very much more complex and challenging: a film that places the nightcleaners' campaign within a series of broader political discussions formulated as an 'open text' which asks as many questions about its own status as a film as it does about the socio-political issues that are its subject. No engaged person should overlook its challenge. TR

Nightcomers, The

(Michael Winner, 1971, GB) Marlon Brando, Stephanie Beacham, Thora Hird, Harry Andrews, Verna Harvey, Christopher Ellis, Anna Palk.
96 min.
A film crass enough to have the outraged ghost of Henry James haunting Wardour Street with flashing eyes and gnashing teeth. Purporting to explain how Peter Quint and Miss Jessel became the ghostly presences of *The Turn of the Screw*, it has Brando mumbling endless Irish blarney, and Stephanie Beacham roped naked to her bed at frequent intervals, as the pair corrupt the two innocents in their care with sado-masochistic goings-on. Michael Hastings' dialogue is evidently designed to echo the hieratic Jamesian flavour, but tends to sound embarrassingly like a Cockney nanny doing her best to be genteel. TM

Night Crossing

(Delbert Mann, 1982, US) John Hurt, Jane Alexander, Beau Bridges, Glynnis O'Connor, Ian Bannen, Klaus Löwitsch, Kay Walsh.
106 min.
Scrapings of the Disney barrel in this true story of two East German families (supplied in best Disney tradition with two kids apiece) perilously escaping to the West in a flimsy, homemade hot-air balloon. Despite valiant efforts by the cast to overcome unimaginative stereotyping, didactic moralising makes the film largely unpalatable, and the excitement, although piled on, never really mounts. It's hard to care whether the families make it or not. FD

Nightfall

(Jacques Tourneur, 1956, US) Aldo Ray, Brian Keith, Anne Bancroft, James Gregory, Jocelyn Brando, Frank Albertson, Rudy Bond.
78 min. b/w.
In this superb adaptation of David Goodis' novel, a man (Ray), evidently on the run in California, befriends a girl (Bancroft) in a bar, but thinks (wrongly) she has set him up for two men on his tail. Dogging his footsteps for some months now, an insurance investigator (Gregory) wearily mulls over the case with his wife (Brando): the man is wanted for murder back in Chicago, but... 'he grows on you; it's almost like he needs protection'. A series of flashbacks, as beautifully placed and paced as in *Out of the Past*, prove the aptness of this description of the characteristic Goodis hero, perfectly incarnated by Ray as a large, friendly dog baring its teeth under threat. He was, we learn, an innocent bystander framed for murder by two bank-robbers – one sadistically trigger-happy (Bond), the other curiously ambivalent (Keith) – who think he knows the whereabouts of the $350,000 which went astray somewhere in the mountains of Wyoming. With nicely unforced symbolism (Burnett Guffey's camerawork is terrific throughout), the dark urban streets give way to wide open snowscapes as he embarks on a desperate quest for his lost innocence. A minor film compared to *Out of the Past*, perhaps, but no less gripping. TM

Night Falls on Manhattan

(Sidney Lumet, 1996, US) Andy Garcia, Richard Dreyfuss, Lena Olin, Ian Holm, James Gandolfini, Colm Feore, Ron Liebman, Sheik Mahmud-Bey.
113 min.
Lumet has made 40-odd films, some classic, some lousy. This isn't by any means the biggest Lumet dog (it's from Robert Dailey's novel *Tainted Evidence*), but it's definitely barking in the big one at Cruft's. Promising Assistant DA Casey (Garcia) is son of veteran cop Liam (Holm). Liam's seriously injured during a raid on brutal drug dealer Washington (Mahmud-Bey). With the deranged New York DA at risk of losing his job, Casey prosecutes his father's assailant. He mysteriously acquires, within seconds, the hand of a beautiful, well connected woman (Olin) and is catapulted from crappy little Assistant DA to head of the whole shebang. Dreyfuss shines as a radical defence attorney. SGr

Night Games

(Roger Vadim, 1979, US) Cindy Pickett, Barry Primus, Joanna Cassidy, Paul Jenkins, Mark Hanks, Gene Davis.
107 min.
Cindy Pickett plays an ageing anorexic narcissist, freaked by flashbacks to a childhood rape whenever her Hollywood tycoon husband attempts to penetrate one of her Janet Reger negligees. He soon departs, leaving our heroine to her fantasies, which concern a very silly lesbian *thé dansant* and a succession of square-jawed chaps in feather boas. In no way funny or erotic, the only nice thing about it is that after 107 minutes, it ends.

Night Hair Child

(James Kelly, 1971, GB) Mark Lester, Britt Ekland, Hardy Krüger, Lilli Palmer, Harry Andrews, Conchita Montez.
89 min.
The sight of kids in adult situations is unfailingly embarrassing, and *Night Hair Child* (whatever that means) is no exception. In it Mark Lester plays a 12-year-old voyeur who touches up Britt Ekland, and later joins her for some purpose or other (even he seems uncertain) between the sheets. Everyone involved blunders along, seemingly unaware of the sensitivity necessary to develop this story of a young newlywed who finds that she is living in the same house as a pubescent sex maniac, who may also be plotting to murder her. The casting is crazy, with Ekland hardly the actress for this sort of thing; and the script meanders all over the place, with a long psychiatric interview and a dream sequence seemingly interpolated just for the hell of it, before finally falling to bits. Still, at least Lester gets his deserts, the little brat. DMcG

Night Has a Thousand Eyes

(John Farrow, 1948, US) Edward G Robinson, Gail Russell, John Lund, Virginia Bruce, William Demarest, Jerome Cowan, John Alexander.
81 min. b/w.
Aside from the fine opening sequence – Lund's rescue of Gail Russell from the brink of suicide, and discovery of her mortal terror of the stars – a disappointing adaptation of Cornell Woolrich's superb novel, which is systematically emasculated and stripped of its darkly obsessional drive. On its own more conventional level, though, a reasonably gripping psychological thriller, with a fine performance from Edward G Robinson as a man haunted by his ability to foresee the future. Farrow makes it reasonably atmospheric (abetted by very fine camerawork from John F Seitz), but the script is marred by tiresome discussions as to whether extrasensory perception is rationally or scientifically accountable, and by a silly plot twist which allows for a (partly) happy ending. TM

Night Has Eyes, The (aka Terror House)

(Leslie Arliss, 1942, GB) James Mason, Joyce Howard, Mary Clare, Wilfrid Lawson, Tucker McGuire, John Fernald.
79 min. b/w.
Mason is his usual interestingly ambivalent self as a shellshocked composer in this unremarkable but efficient little thriller in which he plays host one dark and stormy night to a young woman (with whom he falls in love) searching for her missing friend, presumed murdered on the foggy Yorkshire Moors. No more than a question of did he or didn't he, but handled with gusto and some style. GA

Nighthawks

(Ron Peck/Paul Hallam, 1978, GB) Ken Robertson, Tony Westrope, Rachel Nicholas James, Maureen Dolan, Stuart Craig Turton, Clive Peters.
113 min.
Undoubtedly worthy, Britain's first major gay movie is nevertheless often excruciatingly dull, and in many ways highly pessimistic. Dealing with a schoolteacher who cruises the discos endlessly but remains in the closet at work – until, that is, a revelatory discussion with his pupils – the film fails through its sluggish pace and awkward amateur performances. Worst of all, however, is that it presents its hero as such a miserable sod; anyone tempted toward his own sex would surely be deterred after watching Robertson's endlessly unsmiling face. GA

Nighthawks

(Bruce Malmuth, 1981, US) Sylvester Stallone, Billy Dee Williams, Rutger Hauer, Lindsay Wagner, Persis Khambatta, Nigel Davenport.
99 min.

A ruthless terrorist hijacking a cable car, even in New York, is a mildly ludicrous idea – were no 747s handy? The plot of *Nighthawks* makes no sense. Its thrills are strictly visual: the thriller as TV commercial? Stallone (the cop) gives a restrained performance for once, and Rutger Hauer (the terrorist) shows why he was to make it big in Hollywood. MB

Nighthawks II

see Strip Jack Naked

Night Holds Terror, The

(Andrew L Stone, 1955, US) Jack Kelly, Hildy Parks, Vince Edwards, John Cassavetes, David Cross, Edward Marr, Jack Kruschen, Joel Marston.
86 min. b/w.

Tense thriller, based on an actual incident, follows husband and wife Kelly and Parks as they're held hostage by a gang led by Edwards and an especially nasty Cassavetes. Low-key and unsensationalised, it takes an effective grip on the nerves and predates the likes of *In Cold Blood* by a decade or more. TJ

Night in Casablanca, A

(Archie Mayo, 1946, US) The Marx Brothers, Sig Ruman, Lisette Verea, Charles Drake, Lois Collier, Dan Seymour.
85 min. b/w.

'I'm Beatrice Reiner, I stop at the hotel' says Verea as the slinky spy; 'I'm Ronald Kornblow, I stop at nothing' leers Groucho, manager of the said hotel in Casablanca mainly because previous incumbents have been mysteriously murdered. Independently produced, the Marx Brothers' penultimate vehicle is a vast improvement on their last four rapidly degenerating efforts for MGM. Lightweight, saddled with too much plot about spies and a hunt for hidden loot; but with Groucho enjoying a liberal supply of one-liners and Harpo very much at the heart of things, it is funny if hardly as subversive as their best work. Frank Tashlin contributed some of the brighter ideas, notably the opening gag of the building collapsing when Harpo obligingly stops leaning against it in response to a cop's enquiry as to whether he thinks he's holding it up, and the sequence in which all three Marxes delay spymaster Ruman's getaway by surreptitiously emptying his trunks as fast as he packs them. TM

Night in Havana: Dizzy Gillespie in Cuba, A

(John Holland, 1989, US) Dizzy Gillespie.
84 min.

John Birks ('Dizzy') Gillespie, trumpeter, be-bop confederate of Charlie Parker, champion of Afro-Cuban rhythms in the American jazz mainstream, in Cuba to headline Havana's Fifth International Jazz Festival, is filmed at official receptions (including an audience with Castro), walkabouts, interviews, rehearsals, jam sessions and in performance. The result is an entertaining mixture of documentary, travelogue, concert and historical music lesson. The last is fascinating, illustrating the difference in the development of rhythm in the Caribbean and South America and in the US (slaves shipped to South America and the Caribbean were allowed to keep their percussive instruments – the common 'language' – and those sold to the US were not). The music is a unifying thread. He plays 'A Night in Tunisia', duets with fast and flashy Cuban trumpeter Arturo Sandoval, rehearses a big band, finales with 'Manteca'. In view of the current hipness of Cuban music, a timely film. GBr

Night in the Life of Jimmy Reardon, A (aka Jimmy Reardon)

(William Richert, 1988, US) River Phoenix, Ann Magnuson, Meredith Salenger, Ione Skye, Louanne, Matthew L Perry, Paul Koslo, Jane Hallaren.
93 min.

William (*Winter Kills*) Richert's rites of passage movie is based on a novel he wrote 20 years ago when he was 19. Set in Chicago in 1962, it's narrated by the eponymous hero (Phoenix), a socially-ambitious 17-year-old from the wrong side of the tracks, who models himself on Dean, Kerouac and Casanova. The film charts a crucial few days, between school and college, in which his boyhood illusions of a glittering campus career, and an idyllic romance with virginal Ivy Leaguer Salenger, succumb to a manly assumption of responsibility. The trouble starts when he is conned by an ex into paying for her abortion with money intended for college; then, planning to elope with Salenger, he falls foul of his own libido, bedding everyone from his best friend's girl to a divorcee acquaintance of his mother. While the film has the charm of rose-tinted retrospect and is often very funny, the pacing is wrong (it seems much longer than it is) and the sex scenes fail to convince. EP

Night in Versailles, A

see Versailles rive gauche

Night Is Ending, The

see Paris After Dark

Night Is Young, The

see Mauvais Sang

Night Journey (Gece Yolculugu)

(Ömer Kavur, 1987, Tur) Aytaç Arman, Macit Koper, Zuhal Olcay, Sahika Tekand.
107 min.

Sombre (possibly cautionary) tale of a man's retreat from the world. Director Ali and his writer scout locations for their next feature. They find the perfect set, an archaic ghost town abandoned in 1923, whereupon Ali, already feeling uncommunicative, is so struck by the forsaken buildings that he withdraws from the film project and moves in to the empty church with just a candle and his typewriter, to the bewilderment of everyone who knows him. The town's an arresting presence, but Ali's a real mystery. NB

Nightmare

(Tim Whelan, 1942, US) Brian Donlevy, Diana Barrymore, Gavin Muir, Henry Daniell, Hans Conreid, Arthur Shields.
81 min. b/w.

Based on a story by Philip MacDonald, a cheap but reasonably effective little Universal thriller, with gambler Donlevy stumbling across a murder, getting involved with a girl (of course), and finding himself up against Nazi agents. George Barnes' photography of a Hollywoodian London is nicely atmospheric, while Daniell is as marvellously sour and sinister as ever. GA

Nightmare

(Maxwell Shane, 1956, US) Edward G Robinson, Kevin McCarthy, Connie Russell, Virginia Christine, Rhys Williams.
89 min. b/w.

Everyone knows the dream from which you wake up convinced you've committed a murder. Here Kevin McCarthy finds evidence that suggests the nightmare was in fact reality, and brings his detective brother-in-law (Robinson) in to investigate. McCarthy's good at paranoia – remember him in *Invasion of the Body Snatchers*? – and Robinson is as dependable as ever as the sleuth. The story is by Cornell Woolrich, and the superb *noir* atmosphere is the work of cinematographer Joseph Biroc. A jumpy jazz score by Herschel Burke tightens the strings on this taut little thriller. Shane had nevertheless filmed the same story before, to greater effect, as a 1947 cheapie, 'Fear in the Night'. MA

Nightmare

(Freddie Francis, 1963, GB) David Knight, Moira Redmond, Jennie Linden, Brenda Bruce, George A Cooper, Irene Richmond, John Welch, Clytie Jessop.
82 min. b/w.

The fourth of Hammer's psychological thrillers, made to capitalise on the success of films like *Psycho* and *Les Diaboliques*. It is one of Freddie Francis' most imaginative films, making the most of a patchy Jimmy Sangster script. Knight (a faceless Hammer lead) is the suspect hero, and Linden the tormented young heroine haunted by the fear of hereditary insanity who, as the film begins, is plagued by a recurring nightmare in which her mother lures her into a mental asylum. Normally the Hammer psychological strain has a disconcertingly contemporary tone, but here the apparatus (who is trying to drive the girl out of her mind?) is truly Gothic: old country house, absent guardian, white phantom, etc. DP

Nightmare Alley

(Edmund Goulding, 1947, US) Tyrone Power, Joan Blondell, Colleen Gray, Helen Walker, Mike Mazurki, Taylor Holmes, Ian Keith.
111 min. b/w.

Though perhaps it tries too hard to be 'respectable' and downplays its tawdry trash vulgarity a little too much (the film is tough, but William Lindsay Gresham's superb novel is even tougher), this is still a mean, moody, and well-nigh magnificent melodrama. Power excels as the hick fairground huckster who rises to society celebrity as a fake spiritualist, only to have fickle fortune arc him back to the midway as the boozed-up, live-chicken-eating geek. Blondell, Gray and the strange Helen Walker are the women he uses/abuses to grease his path. Lee Garmes' camerawork, Jules Furthman's script, and Goulding's direction make this one of the most oddball and enduring of the decade's Hollywood highspots. CW

Nightmare Before Christmas, The (aka Tim Burton's The Nightmare Before Christmas)

(Henry Selick, 1993, US) voices: Danny Elfman, Chris Sarandon, Catherine O'Hara, William Hickey, Glenn Shadix.
76 min.

A treat from Hollywood's most unlikely Midas: an original fairy tale, screenplay by Caroline Thompson from a story and characters created by Tim Burton, adapted by Michael McDowell and told in stop-motion animation with a lively score by Danny Elfman. Jack Skellington, the Pumpkin King, is bored with his annual Halloween triumph. A chance visit to nearby Christmastown gives him an idea: he and his spooky friends will stand in for Santa this Christmas! This beautifully realised confection will delight grown-ups of all ages. TCh

Nightmare on Elm Street, A

(Wes Craven, 1984, US) John Saxon, Ronee Blakley, Heather Langenkamp, Amanda Wyss, Nick Corri, Johnny Depp, Robert Englund.
91 min.

There's a mad slasher on the rampage, but this guy is dead already and he's going after teenagers in their dreams. The trick is to stay awake; the resourceful heroine fights off drowsiness with pills and coffee, and as the border between dream and reality blurs, so the slightest nod can send her into a nightmare where the rules are stacked. The ending is laughable, but so what? Craven has played his ace, and it's a screamer. AB

Nightmare on Elm Street Part 2: Freddy's Revenge, A

(Jack Sholder, 1985, US) Mark Patton, Kim Myers, Robert Rusler, Clu Gulager, Hope Lange, Marshall Bell, Robert Englund.
85 min.

An adequate follow-up, although Freddy the freak's claw-flexing is nowhere near as gory. This time he possesses the body of young Jesse Walsh (Patton), a lad who moves into that house five years on from the earlier killings. The plotline has more holes than a tea bag, and is essentially no more than an excuse for a series of well executed special effects. Nevertheless, the film hangs reasonably well together, not least because of good performances from all concerned. DPe

Nightmare on Elm Street 3: Dream Warriors, A

(Chuck Russell, 1987, US) Heather Langenkamp, Patricia Arquette, Larry Fishburne, Priscilla Pointer, Craig Wasson, Brooke Bundy, John Saxon, Robert Englund.
96 min.

This time, Old Pizza Face terrorises a bunch of 'sleep-disturbed' kids whose doctors believe they share a group delusion. Langenkamp, heroine of the original film and now a specialist in dream disorders, helps sceptical psychiatrist Wasson wake up to the truth. A particularly nice touch is the ability of one of the teenagers to pull people into her dreams, allowing Langenkamp and the threatened kids to gang up against Freddie. The neat script also fills in a little more of the Freddie mythology, including a suitably tasteless account of his conception. A creepy score and Russell's sure grasp of the skewed logic of nightmares helps to sustain the ambiguity between the 'real' and 'dream' worlds, while Englund's Freddie now fits like a glove. NF

Nightmare on Elm Street, 4: The Dream Master, A
(Renny Harlin, 1988, US) Robert Englund, Rodney Eastman, Danny Hassel, Andras Jones, Tuesday Knight, Toy Newkirtk, Lisa Wilcox.
93 min.
The dislocated nightmare logic of Wes Craven's original has now been reduced to a black comic carnival ride designed to showcase cult-hero Freddy's stand-up act and some variable special effects. Before that, the negligible script has to explain how Old Pizza Face can extend his stalking-ground to a new generation of kids. In brief, he reaches out into the darkness to embrace shy, teenage Alice (Wilcox) who, once tainted by her knowledge of Freddy's existence, unwittingly forms a link between the two generations. There are a few genuinely inspired moments – notably the Roach Motel joke, and the extraordinary body-ripping climax. But while some of the monotonous effects are strikingly surreal, Harlin's direction creates an atmosphere which is more morbid than scary. NF

Nightmare on Elm Street 5: The Dream Child, A
(Stephen Hopkins, 1989, US) Robert Englund, Lisa Wilcox, Kelly Jo Minter, Danny Hassel, Erika Anderson, Nick Mele, Whitby Hertford.
89 min.
A flimsily plotted but visually impressive addition to the endless Freddy Krueger saga, with an unsavoury gynaecological flavour. Teenage Alice (Wilcox) is terrorised by a reborn Freddy (Englund), who is attempting to massacre her Springwood High chums by stalking them through the dreams of Alice's unborn child. Retreading old ground, the chaotic storyline flashes back to the now legendary rape of Amanda Krueger by a throng of maniacs, and the subsequent birth of Old Pizza Face. 'It's a breech-birth...It's backwards!' screams a nurse as a flat-legged Freddy foetus (courtesy David Miller) hightails it out of the womb. Later, director Hopkins goes one step further and takes us *inside* Alice's womb, where her unborn child is being fed the souls of Krueger's victims by a flesh-faced Freddy, functioning as a decidedly suspect intrauterine device. The rest is a series of disjointed but nevertheless diverting special effects set pieces. Leslie Bohem's script dishes up the requisite helping of one-liners, and all the usual quasi-religious mythical tosh is present and correct. MK

Nightmares
(Joseph Sargent, 1983, US) Cristina Raines, Emilio Estevez, Lance Henriksen, Richard Masur, Veronica Cartwright.
99 min.
A portmanteau of four stories, three of them scripted by Christopher Crowe, the fourth by Jeffrey Bloom, hopefully in the *Twilight Zone* manner. The best of them has Emilio Estevez as a computer whizkid, obsessed with a space combat game, who finds himself engaged in a real battle that alarmingly ends in another world. Here Sargent makes effectively febrile use of the bustling activity of the arcades and the rock pouring from the hero's walkman in counterpoint to the video game imagery. In general, though, the scripting is unimaginative, derivative, and desperately predictable as the film limps through its jokily cautionary tales of a housewife who narrowly escapes a homicidal maniac when she insists on a late-night shopping trip because she's out of cigarettes, a priest restored to his faith and duty by an encounter

with a demonic car, and a suburban family busy exterminating rats who find themselves confronted by a monster looking for its baby. TM

'Night, Mother
(Tom Moore, 1986, US) Anne Bancroft, Sissy Spacek, Ed Berke, Carol Robbins.
96 min.
Overwrought adaptation by Marsha Norman of her own Pulitzer Prize-winning play which fails to make the most of its leading ladies. Bancroft in her familiar role as the long-suffering mother is dignified, severe and utterly humourless, and her character sets the movie's tone. Spacek likewise seems a little self-important as her suicidal middle-aged daughter. Director Moore presumably thought his main task was simply to provide a platform for his bravura stars. Unfortunately, by plumping for an inert shooting style, he leaves the actresses looking smug and stolid. GM

Night Moves
(Arthur Penn, 1975, US) Gene Hackman, Jennifer Warren, Edward Binns, Harris Yulin, Kenneth Mars, Janet Ward, James Woods, Anthony Costello, John Crawford, Melanie Griffith, Susan Clark.
99 min.
A truly enigmatic thriller and a key film of the '70s, brilliantly scripted by Alan Sharp. Hackman is the private eye torn apart from within, unable to come to terms either with his father or his errant wife, but doggedly, almost pointlessly, pursuing a wayward daughter for an equally wayward mother. Sharp's elusive, fragmented script precisely catches the post-Watergate mood, while Penn's direction brilliantly parallels the interior/exterior investigation. A very pessimistic film, it ends exactly at the moment that Hackman understands what has happened but can do nothing about it. Essential viewing. PH

Night Must Fall
(Richard Thorpe, 1937, US) Robert Montgomery, Rosalind Russell, Dame May Whitty, Alan Marshal, Kathleen Harrison, EE Clive, Beryl Mercer.
117 min. b/w.
Montgomery, skilfully suggesting a sickly veneer that belies his matinée idol charm, is surprisingly effective as the psychopathic pageboy with a hat-box in which he treasures the grisly trophies of his penchant for decapitation. The trouble with Emlyn Williams' stage play is that, having established Danny's character and the basic situation – Danny closeted with the rich old lady he wants as his next victim (Whitty, wonderfully skittish and foolish), and the frustrated young companion who wants *him* (Russell, miscast) – it resorts to pure melodramatic contrivance. The creakiness is exacerbated in this fairly opened-out adaptation, with a series of stagy exits and entrances conveniently helping the plot along, but frittering away what tension there is as the consummation of Danny's desire is forever delayed while the police bumble absurdly and Russell agonises as she realises the truth. TM

Night Must Fall
(Karel Reisz, 1964, GB) Albert Finney, Mona Washbourne, Susan Hampshire, Sheila Hancock, Michael Medwin, Martin Wyldeck, Joe Gladwin.
105 min. b/w.
Mindful, perhaps, of the way a straightforward approach exposed the limitations of Emlyn Williams' play in 1937, this adaptation by Clive Exton and Reisz not only adds a good deal of flummery psychological detail, but abandons the narrative approach in favour of a choppy, static style, with jagged direct cuts between scenes and the emphasis often on close-ups of heads awkwardly (symbolically ?) poised at the edge of the screen. The idea, it seems, is to evoke the *aura* of the psychopath rather than the narrative excitements of his story. But with old-fashioned cross-cutting coming back with a vengeance to provide some suspense for the climax, nothing really hangs together. Finney brings off a few memorable moments (notably a hypnotically horrible little ritual with the hat-box), but the one unqualified success of the film is Freddie Francis' dreamy yet diamond-sharp camerawork. TM

Night My Number Came Up, The
(Leslie Norman, 1954, GB) Michael Redgrave, Alexander Knox, Sheila Sim, Denholm Elliott, Ursula Jeans, Michael Hordern, Nigel Stock, Bill Kerr, Alfie Bass, Victor Maddern.
94 min.
RC Sherriff turned a newspaper article by Air Marshal Sir Victor Goddard (a leading spiritualist and communicator with the Other Side) into this suspenseful Ealing aerial drama. Redgrave grows progressively more uptight on a long-haul flight to Japan as events in a nightmare he's experienced begin to come true. Clever plot construction, a plane-load of top British thesps, and smooth handling from director Leslie Norman (Barry's dad) all give good value. TJ

Night Nurse
(William Wellman, 1931, US) Barbara Stanwyck, Ben Lyon, Joan Blondell, Clark Gable, Charlotte Merriam, Charles Winninger, Blanche Frederici.
72 min. b/w.
A wonderfully pacy thriller, with sparkling dialogue, a nice line in blackish humour, an undertow of pre-Hays Code eroticism, and Stanwyck in full-hard-bitten cry as a nurse foiling a plot to kill two little girls for their inheritance. With neither she nor Gable (in support as a villainous chauffeur; Lyon makes little impact as the nominal hero) worrying about niceties of image, it's tough, taut and fun. TM

Night of Counting the Years, The (El Mumia)
(Shadi Abdelsalam, 1969, UAR) Ahmed Marei, Zouzou El Hakim, Ahmad Hegazi, Nadia Loutfy, Gaby Karraz.
102 min.
An impressive directorial debut by ex-art director Shadi Abdelsalam, *The Night of Counting the Years* is an examination of cultural imperialism in reverse: instead of selling Coca-Cola to Egypt, Western merchants are stealing rarities from Egyptian tombs. At first posed in moral terms – should the new chief of an Egyptian tribe allow his people to earn money by selling the antiquities from 'officially' undiscovered tombs, or stop the trade at the cost of stopping the flow of money to his poverty-stricken people – the film develops into a study of the importance of defending the past from would-be cultural exploiters. Slow-moving but absorbing, and quite beautifully shot. PH

Night of San Juan, The
see Coraje del Pueblo, El

Night of San Lorenzo, The (La Notte di San Lorenzo)
(Paolo Taviani/Vittorio Taviani, 1981, It) Omero Antonutti, Margarita Lozano, Claudio Bigagli, Massimo Bonetti, Norma Martelli, Enrica Maria Modugno.
107 min.
On the Night of San Lorenzo, the night of falling stars when wishes come true, a woman recalls for her loved one another such night long ago, when a group of peasants fled the Nazis through the Tuscan countryside and exploding shells shot through the sky instead of stars. The Taviani brothers have transformed this story from their own childhood into a collective epic handed down orally through the decades, but wildly embellished in the re-telling. It's at once more ambitious in its sweep and more Utopian than their previous *Padre Padrone*, more romantic in its desire to recapture a lost, breathless intensity of experience. SJo

Night of the Big Heat
(Terence Fisher, 1967, GB) Christopher Lee, Peter Cushing, Patrick Allen, Sarah Lawson, Jane Merrow, William Lucas.
94 min.
Hammer mainstay Terence Fisher made three movies for the cheapjack Planet outfit of which this (from a sci-fi novel by John Lymington) was the last. It's mighty hot for winter on the small island of Fara where scientist Lee has rigged up a lab in the security of the White Swan hotel. He believes the heat's caused by energy starved aliens. Cushing, the local doctor, is frazzled to

death. Dynamite proves ineffective against the invaders, but as all seems lost a saving thunderstorm breaks. Even less exciting than it sounds. TJ

Night of the Comet
(Thom Eberhardt, 1984, US) Robert Beltran, Catherine Mary Stewart, Kelli Maroney, Sharon Farrell, Mary Woronov, Geoffrey Lewis, Peter Fox.
95 min.
When the citizens of Earth take a break to gaze skyward at a passing comet, it comes as no surprise when they all turn into little piles of paprika. At first, apart from a few flesh-eating 'freak-dog zombies', the only survivors appear to be two gum-chewing teenage sisters with an ability to operate submachine guns and who still find time to bicker over the last boy in the world. Hot on their trail is a labful of deranged scientists, only partially exposed to the comet's rays and now eager for healthy young blood to decelerate their own gradual desiccation. High on humour but low on gore (though not without the occasional effective frisson), this comes as a welcome relief after the increasingly formulaic splash'n's-platter in horror and sci-fi movies. AB

Night of the Creeps
(Fred Dekker, 1986, US) Jason Lively, Steve Marshall, Jill Whitlow, Tom Atkins, Wally Taylor, Bruce Solomon.
88 min.
Egged on by frat house jock Brad, nerds Chris and JC thaw out the freeze-dried body of a guy who got 'slugged' back in 1959. Meanwhile, the axe-man who offed his girlfriend on the same night comes up through the floorboards and starts cutting people down to size. The careworn cop on the case thinks he's Hammett, the kids just ham it. Neither Dekker's sloppy direction nor the cheapo make-up and effects do justice to the hand-me-down but sporadically lively script. Not the most sophisticated or scary horror film of the year, perhaps, but enjoyable enough in a ramshackle sort of way. NF

Night of the Demon
(aka Curse of the Demon)
(Jacques Tourneur, 1957, GB) Dana Andrews, Peggy Cummins, Niall MacGinnis, Maurice Denham, Athene Seyler, Reginald Beckwith.
82 min. b/w.
One of the finest thrillers made in England during the '50s, despite the fact that the final cut was tampered with against the director's wishes. Tourneur had used MR James' short story *Casting the Runes* as the basis for a marvellous cinematic dialogue between belief and scepticism, fantasy and reality. His intrepid rational hero (Andrews) is a modern scientist who is gradually persuaded that his life is threatened by a black magician. The director employed a number of enormously skilful devices to ensure that the audience experiences the hero's transition from confident scepticism to panic, and the process is observed with such subtlety that, in the original version at least, the interpretation of the plot was left open (ie. the hero may simply be the victim of a conspiracy and/or his own imagination). The producer decided that the film lacked substance (in fact it was far more terrifying than most horror films), and added special effects of the 'demon' very near the beginning, which of course missed the whole point of what Tourneur had been attempting. Even so, the rest is so good that the film remains immensely gripping, with certain sequences (like the one where Andrews is chased through the wood) reaching poetic dimensions. DP

Night of the Demons
(Kevin S Tenney, 1988, US) Lance Fenton, Cathy Podewell, Alvin Alexis, Hal Havins, Mimi Kinkade, Linnea Quigley.
89 min.
A gang of thoroughly objectionable teenagers party Halloween away in a haunted house. Some of them get possessed by evil spirits, and the frequent foulness of language is then replaced by nastiness of a different sort. A girl dances around a room with a bodiless arm clamped to her ankle (severed while a couple copulate in a coffin); a boy gets his eyes squished out by the bimbo who's putting him up; but the best bit is when a somewhat distraught young lady pushes her lipstick *inside* her left breast. You feel for her. MS

Night of the Eagle
(aka Burn, Witch, Burn!)
(Sidney Hayers, 1961, GB) Janet Blair, Peter Wyngarde, Margaret Johnston, Kathleen Byron, Anthony Nicholls, Colin Gordon, Reginald Beckwith.
87 min. b/w.
Made on a comparatively low budget and adapted from Fritz Leiber's novel *Conjure Wife*, this is about a hardheaded psychology lecturer in a provincial university who gradually discovers that his wife Tanzie and some of his closest colleagues are practising witchcraft (in furtherance of campus politics). From the opening sequences in which Tanzie (Blair) scrambles frantically round her house searching for a witch-doll left by one of the faculty wives, the whole thing takes off into a kind of joyous amalgam of *Rosemary's Baby* and *Who's Afraid of Virginia Woolf?*. There are one or two irritations in the phony Americanised look of the college students, and in the miscasting of Janet Blair; but Sidney Hayers shoots the whole thing with an almost Wellesian flourish, and the script (by Charles Beaumont and Richard Matheson) is structured with incredible tightness as the sane, rational outlook of the hero (Wyngarde) is gradually dislocated by the world of madness and dreams. DP

Night of the Following Day, The
(Hubert Cornfield, 1968, US) Marlon Brando, Richard Boone, Rita Moreno, Pamela Franklin, Jess Hahn, Gérard Buhr.
93 min.
Cornfield is one of the more enigmatic film-makers of post-war Hollywood, an industry insider from an early age, whose occasional movies are quirky, innovative and well worthseeking out. This one is a gripping account of a kidnapping that goes wrong, and the script takes its dream-like narrative structure from – of all things – Ealing's *Dead of Night*. Its other major asset is an expert cast, with Brando giving one of his most gutsy, enjoyable, least mannered performances of the '60s, and Boone outstanding as a sadistic thug. DP

Night of the Generals, The
(Anatole Litvak, 1966, GB/Fr) Peter O'Toole, Omar Sharif, Tom Courtenay, Donald Pleasence, Joanna Pettet, Philippe Noiret, Charles Gray, Coral Browne, Harry Andrews, Christopher Plummer.
147 min.
Outraged Nazi general to German major: 'Are you wearing perfume?' 'I occasionally wear a light after-shave, sir'. O'Toole and Sharif utter lines like these with absolutely straight faces in what is ostensibly about the generals' plot to assassinate Hitler. There's also a subplot involving a prostitute murderer (quite obviously O'Toole, since he's nutty as a fruitcake). O'Toole's performance is as over the top as it was in *The Ruling Class*, but this film (also an analysis of the élite) is far funnier since it takes itself so seriously. Ignore the plot, just revel in the clichés. CPe

Night of the Ghouls
(aka Revenge of the Dead)
(Edward D Wood Jr, 1959, US) Criswell, Tor Johnson, Keene Duncan, Valda Hansen, Maila 'Vampira' Nurmi, Duke Moore.
69 min. b/w.
If you thought cult 'artiste' Edward D Wood Jr's ironically celebrated astro-turkey *Plan 9 from Outer Space* was transcendently awful, you'd better brace yourself for this, deemed too shambolic to unleash upon unsuspecting cinema audiences. Scenery-chewing psychic Criswell and majestically talentless ex-wrestler Johnson return in this no-budget farrago about a fake medium unwittingly resurrecting the dead. Expect yet more of the 'neo-Brechtian panache' (ie. complete technical incompetence) that secured Wood his rep as the very worst of the worst. TJ

Night of the Hunter, The 100 (100)
(Charles Laughton, 1955, US) Robert Mitchum, Lillian Gish, Shelley Winters, Billy Chapin, James Gleason, Sally Ann Bruce, Peter Graves.
93 min. b/w.
Laughton's only stab at directing, with Mitchum as the psychopathic preacher with

'LOVE' and 'HATE' tattooed on his knuckles, turned out to be a genuine weirdie. Set in '30s rural America, the film polarises into a struggle between good and evil for the souls of innocent children. Everyone's contribution is equally important. Laughton's deliberately old-fashioned direction throws up a startling array of images: an amalgam of Mark Twain-like exteriors (idyllic riverside life) and expressionist interiors, full of moody nighttime shadows. The style reaches its pitch in the extraordinary moonlight flight of the two children downriver, gliding silently in the distance, watched over by animals seen in huge close-up, filling up the foreground of the screen. James Agee's script (faithfully translating Davis Grubb's novel) treads a tight path between humour (it's a surprisingly light film in many ways) and straight suspense, a combination best realised when Gish sits the night out on the porch waiting for Mitchum to attack, and they both sing 'Leaning on the Everlasting Arms' to themselves. Finally, there's the absolute authority of Mitchum's performance – easy, charming, infinitely sinister. CPe

Night of the Iguana, The
(John Huston, 1964, US) Richard Burton, Ava Gardner, Deborah Kerr, Sue Lyon, Skip Ward, Grayson Hall, Cyril Delevanti.
118 min. b/w.
Films of Tennessee Williams' plays now often look very artificial and overwrought, but with this Huston came up with one of the best. Williams is treated with respect rather than reverence, and Huston injects his own sly humour. The film, which perambulates around Burton as the clergyman turned travel courier after a sex scandal, and the effects of his various crises of faith on the coachload of women teachers he is escorting (with assorted provocations from Lyon's nymphet, Gardner's blowsy hotel proprietor, Kerr's artist) is all the more interesting in the light of *Wise Blood*, Huston's later descent into the maelstrom of religious obsessions. PH

Night of the Lepus
(William F Claxton, 1972, US) Stuart Whitman, Janet Leigh, Rory Calhoun, DeForest Kelley, Paul Fix, Melanie Fullerton.
88 min.
Down on the ranch, a couple of scientists start tampering with nature. They shoot some rabbits full of hormones, and next thing you know the bunnies are four foot high, weighing 150 lbs, and rampaging through Arizona. Whoever thought up this particular movie monster should have their head examined. You can film a rabbit from a low angle, place it against a miniature set, smear red paint on its muzzle, and it will still look like your average, cuddly, nose-twitching bunnikins. One for Beatrix Potter buffs. AB

Night of the Living Dead
(George A Romero, 1969, US) Judith O'Dea, Duane Jones, Karl Hardman, Keith Wayne, Judith Ridley, Marilyn Eastman, Russell Streiner.
96 min. b/w.
With its radical rewriting of a genre in which good had always triumphed over evil, Romero's first feature shattered the conventions of horror and paved the way for the subversive visions of directors like David Cronenberg, Tobe Hooper and Sam Raimi. The film's opening scene immediately signals its own subversiveness. In broad daylight, a brother and sister visit their father's grave; seeing a tall man lumbering towards them, Johnny tries to frighten Barbara with a daft Boris Karloff impersonation; suddenly the figure lurches forward and kills him. With the presumed hero dead within the first few minutes, the inexorable logic of the modern 'nightmare movie' is set in motion, and from this moment on the terror never lets up. Together with a small group of fellow survivors, Barbara holes up in a nearby farmhouse, besieged by an ever-swelling tide of flesh-eating zombies. Trapped inside the house, they fight for their lives, but nothing works out as it should; whenever it seems there might be a glimmer of hope, Romero cruelly reverses our expectations. The nihilistic ending, in particular, has to be seen to be believed. Chuckle, if you can, during the first few minutes; because after that laughter catches in the throat as the clammy hand of terror tightens its grip. NF

Night of the Living Dead

(Tom Savini, 1990, US) Tony Todd, Patricia
Tallman, Tom Towles, McKee Anderson,
William Butler, Katie Finnerman.
96 min.
This surprisingly successful colour remake of
George Romero's seminal zombie movie, scripted by Romero himself and directed by make-up
effects man Savini, uses the audience's familiarity with the original to indulge, frustrate and subvert its expectations. Savini himself has said: 'It's
not a remake so much as retelling... There are lots
of twists and turns that aren't in the original.
And, in a way, it's almost a sequel: sixty minutes
into this movie you're getting, in a way, another
film'. Yet despite its knowingness, there is genuine horror here, as a party of terrified survivors
are trapped in a remote country house by a relentless horde of flesh-eating zombies. NF

Night of the Party, The

(Michael Powell, 1934, GB) Leslie Banks,
Malcolm Keen, Jane Baxter, Ian Hunter, Ernest
Thesiger, Viola Keats, Muriel Aked.
61 min.
'The script was a stinker,' was Powell's justifiable comment in his autobiography. A whodunit
in the most antiquated sub-Agatha Christie mode,
it has a lecherous newspaper baron (Keen) try to
blackmail an indiscreet girl (Keats), daughter of
the Commissioner of Police (Banks), into submitting to his unwelcome attentions. During a game
of 'Murder' at a society party, the lecher, unsurprisingly, is murdered. The routine expository
labour of setting everybody up with a motive
(there's even a sinister butler) is leavened by
Powell's willingness to give the actors time and
space; he makes a mini bravura triumph of the
party sequence by shooting the 'Murder' game in
darkness, with intermittent illumination by fire-
light and a flickering neon sign; and the final
court scene, after the usual routine of police interrogation and politic confessions, is enlivened by
a magnificently dotty performance from Ernest
Thesiger at his most malignantly epicene. The
end result is much more fun than it has any right
to be. TM

Night on Earth

(Jim Jarmusch, 1991, US) Winona Ryder, Gena
Rowlands, Giancarlo Esposito, Armin Müller-
Stahl, Rosie Perez, Isaach De Bankolé, Béatrice
Dalle, Roberto Benigni, Paolo Bonacelli, Matti
Pellonpää.
129 min.
LA, 7.07pm: chain-smoking Ryder gets movie
agent Rowlands in the back of her cab, and inadvertently persuades her she'd be right for a role
Rowlands is casting. At the very same time, taxi
drivers across the world are also having seemingly inconsequential encounters with passengers: in New York, inept East German exile
Müller-Stahl hands over the wheel to young black
Esposito; in Paris, Ivory Coaster De Bankolé discusses sight and sex with blind, belligerent Dalle;
in Rome, raving Benigni confesses a carnal past
to priest Bonacelli; and in Helsinki, melancholy
Pellonpää calms three drunks with a tale of infinite sadness. As ever with Jarmusch, as the five
sequential stories proceed toward their unexpectedly poignant conclusion, there's a touch of
the experimental at play; but it's also a film of
great warmth. Character prevails throughout,
and with the exception of a miscast Ryder, the
performances are terrific. Though it may take a
while to get Jarmusch's gist, hang in there; by the
time Tom Waits growls his lovely closing waltz
over the credits, Jarmusch has shown us
moments most film-makers don't even notice. GA

Night on the Town, A

see Adventures in Babysitting

Night Passage

(James Neilson, 1957, US) James Stewart,
Audie Murphy, Dan Duryea, Brandon de
Wilde, Dianne Foster, Elaine Stewart.
90 min.
This minor (and obscurely titled) Stewart
Western was to have been directed by Anthony
Mann, who pulled out at the last minute because
he felt Borden (Winchester '73) Chase's script
wasn't up to scratch. Stewart plays a railroad
worker who discovers that the robbers bent on
stealing the payroll with which he has been
entrusted are being led by his brother (Murphy).

Neilson wades through the good brother/bad
brother plot like an ox through mud, Stewart
whiling away the time by playing accordion. NF

Night Paths
(Wege in der Nacht)

(Krzysztof Zanussi, 1979, WGer) Mathieu
Carrière, Maja Komorowska, Horst Frank,
Zbigniew Zapasiewicz.
97 min.
Working for German TV in exile from his native
Poland, Zanussi seems curiously uninvolved in
this return to the well-worn theme of uneasy relationships between victor and vanquished during
World War II. A Polish baroness (Komorowska),
whose estate has been commandeered, at first
resists the attentions of a young German officer
(Carrière), then exploits them on behalf of the partisans. Mournfully attractive visually (the
chateau, the lowering forest), but the conflict
remains largely theoretical. TM

Night Porter, The
(Il Portiere di Notte)

(Liliana Cavani, 1973, It) Dirk Bogarde,
Charlotte Rampling, Philippe Leroy, Gabriele
Ferzetti, Giuseppe Addobbati, Isa Miranda.
118 min.
Like Last Tango in Paris, an operatic celebration
of sexual disgust, set in 1957 in a Viennese hotel
where Bogarde (maintaining a low profile as a
porter) and Rampling (a guest while her conductor husband embarks on a concert tour) meet and
recreate their former relationship as sadistic SS
officer and child concentration camp inmate; a
sexuality that can only end in degradation and
self-destruction. Somewhere along the way, the
film's handling of serious themes, and its
attempts to examine the Nazi legacy in terms of
repression and guilt, both sexual and political, get
lost amid all the self-conscious decadence. The
English language version is terrible. CPe

Night Shift

(Ron Howard, 1982, US) Henry Winkler,
Michael Keaton, Shelley Long, Gina Hecht, Pat
Corley, Bobby DiCicco, Nita Talbot.
106 min.
All credit to Howard, Winkler and scriptwriter
Lowell Ganz for bucking their Happy Days TV
formula to cast Winkler as a shy, sad sack Wall
Street wizard who runs away from the pressures
into a job as night attendant at the morgue. Very
funny he is too, whether cosseting his pet rubber
plant, fighting a running duel with a ferociously
neighbourly dog, or trying to make love with a
girlfriend whose neuroses make coitus interruptus a way of life. Even brighter is his odd couple
pairing with Michael Keaton in the Fonz role as
a manic ideas man who bounces in, takes one look
round at the mortuary drawers – 'What's in here?
Stiffs and stuff? Neat!'– and soon has the bewildered Winkler turning his sanctum into a cooperative sanctuary for harassed prostitutes.
Thereabouts the script begins to lose momentum,
opting for frantic farce rather than pointed satire.
Likeable, though. TM

Nightshift

(Robina Rose, 1981, GB) Jordan, Anne Rees-
Mogg, Mitch Davies, Jon Jost, Max Handley,
Mike Lesser, Heathcote Williams.
67 min.
An evocation of Resnais' Marienbad in a West
London hotel where the nocturnal residents inexplicably walk and talk in slow motion and the
receptionist sits silently watching the world drift
by from behind an impassive white Noh mask.
Heathcote Williams does a conjuring trick, Jon
Jost impersonates an American (movie?) tycoon,
and three girls re-enact the pillow fight from Zéro
de Conduite. A few odd arresting images fail to
stifle the tedium of watching a succession of post-
punk Knightsbridge poseurs going through their
art film number. MA

Night Sun
(Il Sole anche di notte)

(Paolo Taviani/Vittorio Taviani, 1990,
It/Fr/Ger) Julian Sands, Charlotte Gainsbourg,
Nastassja Kinski, Massimo Bonetti, Margarita
Lozano, Patricia Millardet, Rüdiger Vogler.
113 min.
In 18th century southern Italy, favoured by the
king, promising young soldier Baron Sergio

Giuramondo (Sands) is to marry a duchess
(Kinski), but finds that she was previously the
monarch's lover. Proudly turning his back on
court life, he becomes a monk; but such is his disillusionment with society, that he presently elects
to live alone in a desolate hermitage on Mount
Petra. Even there, however, his quest for truth
and spiritual perfection comes under threat, both
from an adventuress bent on seducing him, and
from the priests and pilgrims who believe him a
worker of miracles. In their characteristically sensitive, imaginative adaptation of Tolstoy's Father
Sergius, the Tavianis again address philosophical and political questions (the value and perils
of retreat, the place of pride in idealism) in a simple, lucid style that lends the story the magical
power of myth. Though Giuseppe Lanci's camerawork is consistently elegant, the way the
Tavianis pare down composition, dialogue, narrative and performance to essentials ensures a
clarity of purpose and effect rarely encountered
in contemporary cinema. GA

Night to Remember, A

(Roy Baker, 1958, GB) Kenneth More,
Laurence Naismith, Michael Goodliffe, Frank
Lawton, David McCallum, Honor Blackman.
123 min. b/w.
It's going to be years before this can be watched
in a spontaneous way, without measuring pro
and con against Titanic (1997). This earlier
account of the sinking differs first in methodology: declining to superimpose any trivial business
about unsuitable marriages or missing jewels, it
proceeds via a series of vignettes to relate the
facts as researched in Walter Lord's best-seller –
although still retaining a few unshakeable myths
(the cowardly transvestite, the playing of 'Nearer
My God to Thee'). Some artfully carpentered ply-
wood in the Pinewood tank (with extras bussed
to the local lido for jumping-in-the-water shots)
can hardly compare with the prodigiousness of
Cameron's reconstruction, although the mere
sight of the actors' breath, an effect available free
of charge to Baker, is arguably more eloquent
than all the digital composition in the world.
Certainly, this is the version for grown-ups. The
characterisation of the ship's officers, for example, as representatives of an indefensible system,
yet individually honourable and brave, proved
too tough a concept for Cameron, strictly a heroes
and villains man. And much is made here (and
nothing there) of the role of the Californian, the
Mr Magoo of maritime history, which lay a few
miles off the wreck, her crew perfectly unable to
grasp what was happening in front of them.
Kenneth More may not measure up to Leonardo
DiCaprio in terms of erotic impact, but his personification of brisk, cheerful efficiency is just the
job. BBa

Night Train to Munich

(Carol Reed, 1940, GB) Margaret Lockwood,
Rex Harrison, Paul Henreid, Basil Radford,
Naunton Wayne, Felix Aylmer, Raymond
Huntley.
95 min. b/w.
In terms of cast, plot and scriptwriters (Launder
and Gilliat), this bears a deliberate resemblance
to Hitchcock's The Lady Vanishes as it merges
comedy and thrills with propaganda in its tale of
a Czech scientist's daughter escaping from a concentration camp, only belatedly to discover that
she's been allowed to get away to reveal the
whereabouts of her father. And though the action
bats along at a furious pace, especially during the
train scenes and the cable-car climax, the film
only serves to show the importance of the director in the film-making process; the cast and script
are fine, but Reed fatally lacks Hitchcock's light,
witty touch and his effortless ability to create suspense out of ordinary circumstances. GA

Night Watch

(Brian G Hutton, 1973, GB) Elizabeth Taylor,
Laurence Harvey, Billie Whitelaw, Robert
Lang, Tony Britton, Bill Dean.
98 min.
Tired, old-fashioned thriller, with Elizabeth
Taylor as that old stand-by: a woman recovering
from a nervous breakdown who sees dead bodies in the boarded-up house across the garden,
but naturally they have disappeared by the time
the police arrive. Based on a stage play, it has a
gratuitously bloody climax and a kick-yourself
ending, but its amoebic plot is stretched almost
to snapping point over 98 min. DMcG

Nightwatch (Nattevagten)

(Ole Bornedal, 1994, Den) Nikolai Coster Waldau, Ulf Pilgaard, Kim Bodnia, Sofie Graaboel, Lotte Andersen, Ulf Pigaard.
107 min.
Danish writer/director Bornedal exploits the peculiarly horrifying and portentous atmosphere of a hospital mortuary to the full in this classy psychological thriller. While law student Martin (Waldau) moonlights as a nightwatchman at the city's hospital morgue, a sex killer stalks the streets, leaving behind a string of scalped female bodies. Martin has barely started his new job when one of the victims is brought in and laid out between the serried ranks of corpses. The sly insinuations of Chief Insp Wörmer (Pilgaard) increase his edginess, as the policeman implicates first his old friend Jens (Bodnia) and then Martin himself in the murders. Tightly scripted, with just a drop of wicked black humour, the film delivers creepy hints of necrophilia, visceral shocks and heart-racing suspense. The one unconvincing note is the parallel between these murderous events and rehearsals for an amateur theatrical production of *Mephisto*. Otherwise, this is the kind of superior genre movie-making where the eerie fluttering of moths in a glass lampshade is as chilling as the screaming, hysterical violence that follows. NF

Night Watch, The

see Trou, Le

Night We Never Met, The

(Warren Leight, 1993, US) Matthew Broderick, Annabella Sciorra, Kevin Anderson, Jeanne Tripplehorn, Justine Bateman.
89 min.
You can live with someone without knowing them, but in most cases at least the co-habitants have been properly introduced. Not so in writer/director Leight's first film. When stock-broker Brian (Anderson) moves in with his fiancée, he assures his drinking buddies he'll keep his Greenwich Village bachelor pad for a couple of nights a week. He instructs his secretary to sublet it on the free days. That suits Sam (Broderick) just fine. He can't afford a place of his own, but craves escape from his crowded flat-share, even if only at weekends. Then there's Ellen (Sciorra), a frustrated housewife looking for a pied-à-terre in the city. She gets Mondays and Fridays. Brian and Sam swap nights, unbeknown to Ellen, who assumes that the former is the sensitive, tasteful gourmet who leaves her presents, and that Sam is the slob who treats the flat like a tip. When she decides to have an affair, she chooses the wrong man. The film has three amiable leads and doesn't overstay its welcome. TCh

Nightwing

(Arthur Hiller, 1979, Neth) Nick Mancuso, David Warner, Kathryn Harrold, Steven Macht, Strother Martin, George Clutesi, Ben Piazza.
105 min.
Despite the fluttering efforts of its many thousand leathery predators, *Nightwing* (based on Martin Cruz Smith's first novel) never really takes off. It does inspire one or two moments of nausea, as the itinerant vampire bat colony emerges from a canyon on an American Indian reservation to dine on the living bodies of local campers. But Hiller's direction simply plods to a corny and unsatisfactory ending after getting bogged down in subplots concerning whale-oil prospectors, Indian religious mumbo-jumbo, and inter-tribal rivalries. MPl

Night Zoo (Un Zoo la Nuit)

(Jean-Claude Lauzon, 1987, Can) Gilles Maheu, Roger Le Bel, Lynne Adams, Lorne Brass, Germain Houde, Corrado Mastropasqua, Jerry Snell.
115 min.
This unconvincing French-Canadian thriller is a dawdler, with outbreaks of nastiness followed by listlessly arty longueurs. Marcel (Maheu) gets out of prison and goes to retrieve his loot, but a couple of bent cops are determined on their cut. Meanwhile, Marcel's girl Julie (Adams) has gone on the game, and his dad Albert (Le Bel) has a weak ticker which makes family reconciliation yet another priority, and our hero spends a lot of time blasting about on his motorbike. Dad's birthday party apart, it is determinedly sleazy. We are treated to Marcel getting forcibly sodomised in prison at the start, blown in an insanitary lav by one of the cops, Marcel's labouring rump as he attempts to reunite with Julie, and an improbable scene in a porno peep show in which the bad guys threaten Julie with a syringe. There are lots of empty threats featuring gunshots across the bows, and Marcel's loft is so spacious you wonder why he needs the money anyway. BC

Nijinsky

(Herbert Ross, 1980, US) Alan Bates, George de la Peña, Leslie Brown, Alan Badel, Carla Fracci, Colin Blakely, Ronald Pickup, Ronald Lacey, Jeremy Irons, Anton Dolin.
125 min.
At the very least, *Nijinsky* is the best gay weepie since *Death in Venice*. It chronicles the last fraught year or so in the dancer's romance with Ballets Russes impresario Diaghilev, and is thus the first major studio film to centre on a male homosexual relationship (albeit a doomed one) without being moralistic. Director Ross and writer Hugh Wheeler betray their subject by presenting Nijinsky's choreographic experiments as deranged, and by associating his madness with Stravinsky's discords; they also give short shrift to the one woman involved, Romola de Pulsky, the go-getting heiress who seduced and married Nijinsky, thereby alienating Diaghilev from his protégé forever. But they do right by their male characters (Alan Bates, in particular, is a plausibly adult Diaghilev), their grasp of the historical reconstructions seems more than competent, and their dialogue and exposition are unusually adroit. Best of all, they never show ballet for its own sake, and have the courage to keep decorous dynamics in the forefront throughout. TR

Nikita

(Luc Besson, 1990, Fr/It) Anne Parillaud, Jean-Hugues Anglade, Tchéky Karyo, Jeanne Moreau, Jean Reno, Roland Blanche, Jean Bouise.
117 min.
Starting with a bloody tour de force – a drugstore robbery – this seldom lets up. The eponymous heroine, a punk-junkie sociopath, is given a life sentence for killing a cop, but after being drugged by her captors, wakes up believing herself dead. And so she is, officially: held in a secret government establishment which trains undercover assassins, she is given a new identity; and on her eventual release, she turns her violent tendencies to patriotic use, sporadically abandoning both her new-found respectability and her law-abiding lover to earn her keep with a gun. While Besson's relentlessly stylish *noir*-thriller suffers from occasionally implausible plotting and an increasing lack of clarity in its later scenes, it benefits enormously from a memorably assured, intense performance from Anne Parillaud. Her scenes with her prison boss/Svengali (Karyo) and her gullible lover (Anglade) are surprisingly touching, so that there is for once an emotional undertow to Besson's visual pyrotechnics, even if the film finally doesn't add up to anything very profound. GA

Nil by Mouth

(Gary Oldman, 1997, GB) Ray Winstone, Charlie Creed-Miles, Kathy Burke, Edna Dore.
124 min.
The actor Gary Oldman's debut as writer/director is so uncompromisingly honest, it makes other portraits of working-class life look like sour caricature or misplaced idealism. Oldman grew up in south east London, the setting for this tale of macho violence, drunkenness, drug addiction and petty crime, and very clearly knows what he's talking about. He's helped, of course, by stunning performances from his entire cast, most notably Winstone as the volatile but self-pitying Ray, given to beating up his long-suffering wife (Burke) and threatening her irresponsible junkie brother (Creed-Miles). There's no sermonising or romanticising here, just a sad, clear-eyed acknowledgement that domestic abuse and crime create a vicious circle from which many barely even try to escape. Shot and scripted in a deceptively casual, bleakly 'realist' style, it's the closest Britain has produced to a Cassavetes film, and as such, profoundly humane. GA

Nina Takes a Lover

(Alan Jacobs, 1993, US) Laura San Giacomo, Paul Rhys, Cristi Conway, Fisher Stevens.
100 min.
Bored and neglected, Nina (San Giacomo) falls under the spell of a Welsh photographer (Rhys) she meets in a San Francisco park. Their affair is revealed in flashbacks, a series of confessions and confidences, as a journalist investigating 'marriage in the '90s' gently probes the whys and wherefores. The device is a little obvious, but director Jacobs gives the film an ingenious structure, and it's charmingly played by two attractive leads. 'This story is different than what you've heard before,' Nina promises at the start, and within the familiar confines of the sex-and-lies genre, she's absolutely right. TCh

9 1/2 Weeks

(Adrian Lyne, 1985, US) Mickey Rourke, Kim Basinger, Margaret Whitton, David Margulies, Christine Baranski, Karen Young.
117 min.
After *Flashdance* Lyne's steamy saga of *amour fou* hardly bears up to the inevitable *Last Tango* comparisons. He, a slimline, ultracool Mickey Rourke, is a self-satisfied commodities broker. She, sultry yet sweet Kim Basinger, is a recently divorced art gallery gal. She believes love is unimportant until meeting him, and then his teasing request, 'Will you do this for me?', cues a decorative series of sexual variations in search of a theme. Lyne works hard to give their naughty games a glossy veneer – streams of light and water, jagged editing, rock music to seduce by – but prefers to leave the audience to work out the psychology. The film has evidently gone through innumerable revisions, and little remains that is truly daring for the jaded '80s. Bump and grind for the Porsche owner. DT

Nine Lives of Fritz the Cat, The

(Robert Taylor, 1974, US) voices: Skip Hinnant, Reva Rose, Bob Holt, Robert Ridgley.
76 min.
Without director Ralph Bakshi, and now bearing almost no resemblance to Robert Crumb's original, this animated sequel to *Fritz the Cat* is woefully inept. A stoned Fritz fantasises his way out of his welfare and retirement existence. Kissinger makes a telling appearance; but Hitler as an unfortunately anaemic-looking Pink Panther, and a time-filling photo montage sequence are better indications of the film's true level. CPe

Nine Months

(Chris Columbus, 1995, US) Hugh Grant, Julianne Moore, Tom Arnold, Joan Cusack, Jeff Goldblum, Robin Williams, Mia Cottet.
103 min.
An extraordinarily naff concoction from writer/director Columbus, which confirms the near certain perils of remaking French comedies (here *Neuf mois*, 1994). Grant plays Englishman Sam Faulkner who's happily coupled with Moore's Rebecca – until, that is, she announces she's pregnant. His painful memories of their would-be romantic tryst on the beach being broken up by the noxious kids of the parents-from-hell, car-trader Marty (Arnold) and wife Gail (Cusack), the philosophical counsels of confirmed bachelor Sean (Goldblum, the only vaguely recognisable human in the film), and his fear of trading in his beloved Porsche for a four-wheel drive, push Sam the way of the true cad: off out of it. But, of course, being a Columbus movie, transgression is only a learning curve, here a pretty reactionary one, and smug to boot. When Williams did his turn as an émigré Russian gynaecologist facing his first delivery, I felt a chuckle building. But by the time Grant emotes before the ultrasound scan, my goodwill had been all used up. WH

Nine Months (Kilenc Hónap)

(Márta Mészáros, 1976, Hun) Lili Monori, Jan Nowicki, Gyula Szersén, Roszich Dzsoko, Kari Berek, Géza Bodó.
93 min.
Márta Mészáros is the wife of Miklós Jancsó, though it is hard to see any family resemblance in this direct, appealing and humanly-complex account of a young woman's quest for (or rather, gradual acceptance of) independence. The options, between marriage to a likeable but repressive foundry foreman and life on her own with a child by a former lover, are presented in equally unenviable light. The film's case comes to rest, in the end, on which kind of life the hero-

ine is most prepared to sacrifice herself to. Crisply filmed and politically less a matter of special pleading than much recent East European cinema. MA

976-Evil
(Robert Englund, 1988, US) Stephen Geoffreys, Patrick O'Bryan, Sandy Dennis, Jim Metzler, Maria Rubell, Robert Picardo, Lezlie Deane.
100 min.
The directorial debut of *Nightmare on Elm Street* anti-hero Robert ('Freddie') Englund is a sloppily scripted horror pic which takes far too long to get started and then fails to deliver the goods. 976-Evil is a toll-free phone number providing a daily horrorscope, an offer which connects with rebellious teenager Spike (O'Bryan); but it's his nerdy cousin Hoax (Geoffreys) whose attention is really engaged. Hooked up to the diabolical forces on the other end of the line, Hoax undergoes a physical and mental transformation. Little happens for the first hour, after which Hoax starts taking revenge on his religious fanatic Aunt Lucy (Dennis), Spike's new girlfriend (Deane), and the school bully. Englund says the film is about filial envy and the dangers of hero worship, but really it's just a reworking of the revenge-of-the-nerd scenario, with an underdeveloped familial twist. So by the time the Ice and Fire pits open up inside and outside Aunt Lucy's house, it's difficult to care about who will plummet into the frozen abyss or plunge to a fiery death. Odd scenes suggest that Englund has a good eye for visual set pieces. NF

1988: The Remake
(Richard R Schmidt, 1978, US) Ed Nylund, Skip Kovington, Carolyn Zaremba, Willie Boy Walker, Dickie Marcus, Bruce Parry.
97 min. b/w & col.
Bizarre, overlong low-budget independent depicting the auditions held by a dying librarian who wants to remake *Showboat* as 'a musical comedy with the stench of death'. Patchily amusing as it wheels on freaks, eccentrics and talentless no-hopers – with all references to the MGM classic bleeped out (resulting in a dreadful Gong Show-style cacophony) – it's all a little indulgent. GA

Nineteen Eighty-Four
(Michael Radford, 1984, GB) John Hurt, Richard Burton, Suzanna Hamilton, Cyril Cusack, Gregor Fisher, James Walker.
110 min.
Sensibly realising that science fiction is always a distortion of the time at which it was written rather than a prediction of the future, Radford aligns himself with Anthony Burgess's suggestion that the book only makes sense as *1948*, with its food rationing, its housing shortages, bad cigarettes and Churchillian slogans. The look of the film certainly achieves the right rubble-strewn, monochrome period feel with precision and genuinely cinematic scope. Perhaps the greatest hurdle cleared, however, is the problem of incident. Radford's achievement is to have incorporated the impossible preaching and crazed ideas into the fabric with hardly any loose threads. The locations look very like modern Britain; and Burton at last found the one serious role for which he searched all his life. CPea

1941
(Steven Spielberg, 1979, US) Dan Aykroyd, Ned Beatty, John Belushi, Lorraine Gary, Murray Hamilton, Christopher Lee, Tim Matheson, Toshiro Mifune, Warren Oates, Robert Stack, Treat Williams, Nancy Allen, Bobby DiCicco, Slim Pickens.
118 min.
Spielberg's extravagant *folie de grandeur*, a madcap comedy recreation of an allegedly true story, with Hollywood suffering from mass panic when it's thought that a Japanese submarine is about to lead an invasion force into California. The period sets are wonderful, the cast full of bright talent, and Spielberg's expertly choreographed slapstick is wondrous to behold. There is a problem, however, in that it isn't actually very funny: one feels that Spielberg was concentrating his powers so much on the mechanics of timing, cause and effect, that he forgot that what makes the best comedies funny is human reaction. Here the characters are too cartoon-like ever to win our attention (though Stack's military bigwig obsessed with Disney's *Dumbo* is the touching exception who proves the rule). GA

1900 (Novecento)
(Bernardo Bertolucci, 1976, It/Fr/WGer) Burt Lancaster, Robert De Niro, Gérard Depardieu, Dominique Sanda, Donald Sutherland, Sterling Hayden, Stefania Sandrelli, Francesca Bertini, Alida Valli.
320 min.
International tensions and discords are often mainsprings of interest in a film, and the fundamental contradiction between political line and status as glossy commodity might have made Bertolucci's *1900* fascinating. But whether one takes the two-part movie as a glamorous epic or as a lengthy advertisement for the Italian communist party, it still looks like a major catastrophe. Even leaving aside the questions about its sexual politics, the film is crippled by its ineptitude as 'popular' drama (the dynastic rivalries spanning the years, the convulsive deaths, the messy marriages are all strictly sub-Jacqueline Susann) and its manifest inadequacy as political argument (Donald Sutherland is established as Fascism incarnate and then metamorphosed into something like a Disney cartoon villain). The mannered elegance of the camerawork and lighting cocoons the whole sad mess within a veneer of utterly spurious 'style'. TR

Nineteen Nineteen
(Hugh Brody, 1984, GB) Paul Scofield, Maria Schell, Frank Finlay, Diana Quick, Clare Higgins, Colin Firth, Sandra Berkin.
99 min.
For Sophie (Schell), the past is literally a foreign country; when she flies from New York to Vienna to see Alexander Scherbatov (Scofield), it is to explore that forgotten territory. For in 1919 they were both patients of Dr Freud. Together they dredge their memories, and map out not only the confessions of the couch, but also the huge historical shifts that separated them; like Freud himself, they were victims of the Nazi arrival. The film operates in much the same way as the talking cure itself; Freud's skilful probings are heard (Finlay's voice) though he is never seen; and the film makes sense of the past by the same shifting, organic, inexplicable process. A sensitive, interior film, with all the restorative power that Freud must have hoped for. CPea

1969
(Ernest Thompson, 1988, US) Robert Downey Jr, Kiefer Sutherland, Bruce Dern, Mariette Hartley, Winona Ryder, Joanna Cassidy.
95 min.
Thompson's evocation of the spirit of the '60s protest is most moving when it abandons the soapbox and concentrates on domestic discord. We follow the fortunes of college buddies Ralph (Downey) and Scott (Sutherland), opposed in temperament but united in ideals. They both despise American involvement in Vietnam, but Scott's is the one with a social conscience, while Ralph likes to get stoned and strip down to his underwear. Inevitably the two rebels clash with their parents, inspiring support from their mothers (splendid performances from Cassidy and Hartley) and hostility from Scott's gung-ho father (played with conviction by Dern). The film effectively recreates the fear and defiance which accompanied Nixon's support of the draft lottery, with 19-year-olds designated as the first for the slaughter. CM

Nine to Five
(Colin Higgins, 1980, US) Jane Fonda, Lily Tomlin, Dolly Parton, Dabney Coleman, Sterling Hayden, Elizabeth Wilson, Henry Jones, Lawrence Pressman.
109 min.
Despite an excellent and promising cast, this Hollywood attempt at a mainstream feminist comedy is flabby and bland. Fonda is the new secretary in the office, Tomlin and Parton are the veterans who teach her to cope with and combat chauvinistic male oppression, incarnated by embezzling boss Coleman. As one might expect, the three club together in a plot to exact revenge; but as soon as their plans get underway, the film degenerates still further into toothless satire and wish-fulfilment slapstick (notably a fantasy involving Coleman's death). And the climax simply underlines the film's lack of courage in its convictions: the trio's tangle of problems are resolved (happily, of course) by a man. Complacent, and even worse, not very funny, despite the efforts of the ever-excellent Tomlin. GA

90 Days
(Giles Walker, 1985, Can) Stefan Wodoslawsky, Christine Pak, Sam Grana, Fernanda Tavares, Daisy De Bellefeuille.
99 min.
Blue is shy, sincere, a little surly; his friend Alex, conversely, is a full-blooded philanderer, ludicrously unable to comprehend why his wife has thrown him out and his mistress won't see him. So far so simple, but Giles Walker's gently probing comedy of masculine manners soon breaks away from such polarities. The self-centred Blue invites over from Korea a woman he's never met, courtesy of a mail-order catalogue, but is too hung-up to come clean about their relationship; while Alex's macho pride softens into confusion and fear as soon as he is approached by a mysterious young woman offering $10,000 for his sperm. *90 Days* – the visa period the Canadian authorities allow Blue and Hyang-Sook to make up their minds about marriage – avoids making judgments; Walker is content simply to observe his creations with warmth and honesty. It is all largely charming, and the quiet performances ensure involvement. GA

99 and 44/100% Dead
(aka Call Harry Crown)
(John Frankenheimer, 1974, US) Richard Harris, Edmond O'Brien, Bradford Dillman, Ann Turkel, Chuck Connors, Constance Ford.
98 min.
A further chapter in the decline of a brilliant '60s director, with Frankenheimer here aping the more surefire gangland milieu treats of Siegel and Boorman. Harris, with O'Brien and Dillman as rival gang bosses, plays a hitman contracted to sort out a gangland war in a coyly futuristic environment of urban decay. Snappily edited chase and crash sequences, shot with Frankenheimer's familiar command of distorting lenses, make for the best sequences in a film which looks as if it had been designed by Hugh Hefner, inflatable women and all. Harris goes through his usual long-suffering trauma as the peerless protagonist. RM

92 in the Shade
(Thomas McGuane, 1975, US) Peter Fonda, Warren Oates, Margot Kidder, Burgess Meredith, Harry Dean Stanton, Sylvia Miles, Elizabeth Ashley.
93 min.
Adapted from his own superb, blackly comic novel of eastern seaboard eccentrics, macho mythology and the ultimate Florida face-off, McGuane's sole film as director is one of the most enjoyable messes ever to be suppressed as unsaleable. His literary talent lionised and his film reputation secure on scripts for *Rancho Deluxe*, *Missouri Breaks* and *Tom Horn*, McGuane here exhibits a totally appealing incompetence as director: the movie's got all the coherence of an amiable narrative jam-session. Storywise, Fonda wants to set up as a Key West fishing guide; Oates claims a monopoly and threatens to kill him if he does. That's it...except for the crazy-quilt interaction of cultishly-cast fringe characters, mouthing idiosyncratically lively dialogue and obviously having a ball. Jimmy Buffet's songs might give you some hook for what's going on, but the fun's infectious anyway. PT

'92 The Legendary La Rose Noire (Heimeigui dui Heimeigui)
(Joe Chan, 1992, HK) Tony Leung, Maggie Shiu, Bo Bo Fung, Wan Sze Wong.
100 min.
As its ineffably pretentious Anglo-French title suggests, this looks back to the '60s, when costumed crime-busters, mysterious private eyes and vicious master criminals crowded the screen in low-budget Cantonese movies. Joe Chan (with substantial uncredited assistance from Wong Kar-Wai's then partner Jeff Lau) lifts characters, dialogue and sometimes entire scenes from these movies in parody of material that was pretty far gone to begin with. Highbrow critics in Hong Kong and Taiwan were charmed out of their pants and raved about post-modernism. Westerners may be reminded of Losey's *Modesty Blaise*. TR

Ninja III – The Domination

(Sam Firstenberg, 1984, US) Sho Kosugi, Lucinda Dickey, Jordan Bennett, David Chung, Dale Ishimodo, James Hong, Bob Craig.
95 min.
In this sequel to *Enter the Ninja* and *Revenge of the Ninja*, a Ninja (a skilled, almost superhuman Japanese warrior) crops up in California and kills off a couple of hundred extras, prior to being riddled with police bullets. His spirit passes into Lucinda Dickey, telephone engineer and part-time aerobics teacher. Keeping his sword in her airing cupboard, she develops a tendency to go slanty-eyed, crushing billiard balls with her bare hands, and knocking off the cops who killed her predecessor. The plot incorporates a nifty hot-tub murder and some oriental poltergeist effects, before the arrival of another Ninja. Thus the scene is set for a spiffing finale complete with deranged Buddhist monks and a Ninja zombie. Unbelievable! AB

Niños Abandonados, Los

(Danny Lyon, 1975, US)
63 min.
Although its obvious point of reference is *Los Olvidados*, there are few similarities between Lyon's film and Buñuel's, other than the subject: the homeless children of South America. *Los Niños Abandonados* is the simplest and most basic documentary, avoiding embroidery, refusing commentary, and largely choosing to avoid judgment or easy answers. Its observation of the children in their pathetic round of begging and cruel games, ignored by the world around them, is essentially pictorial (Lyon was a photographer before he started making films). If Lyon opts for compassion rather than analysis, it is nevertheless hard to sidestep an awareness of the church's impotence and hypocrisy. SM

Ninotchka

(Ernst Lubitsch, 1939, US) Greta Garbo, Melvyn Douglas, Ina Claire, Bela Lugosi, Sig Ruman, Felix Bressart, Alexander Granach.
110 min. b/w.
This was the first time since 1934 that Garbo had been seen in the 20th century, and the first time ever that her material was predominantly comic (though it was hardly the first time she'd laughed, as the ads insisted). But her character still had an icy aura, at least at the outset – she plays a Russian comrade staying in Paris on government business, a situation providing writers Wilder, Brackett and Walter Reisch with rich material for impish political jokes ('The last mass trials were a great success. There are going to be fewer but better Russians'). Then she meets the acceptable face of Capitalism in the form of Melvyn Douglas, and like many a lesser MGM star before her, succumbs completely to his suave looks and honeyed voice. The film's not quite the delight history says it is – by the late '30s, the famed Lubitsch touch was resembling a heavy blow, the elegant sophistication turning crude and cynical. Yet it's still consistently amusing, and Garbo throws herself into the fray with engaging vigour. GB

Ninth Configuration, The (aka Twinkle, Twinkle, Killer Kane)

(William Peter Blatty, 1979, US) Stacy Keach, Scott Wilson, Jason Miller, Ed Flanders, Neville Brand, George DiCenzo, Moses Gunn, Robert Loggia, Tom Atkins.
118 min.
It's easy to see why *Exorcist* author William Peter Blatty's debut effort as a director stayed on the shelf for a year. This unfathomable yarn about an ace US Army psychiatrist, at work in an isolated military nuthouse populated by a gallery of service fruitcakes (from cowardly astronauts and Congressional Medal winners to Vietnam war malingerers) has the same tortured Christian iconography as Blatty's bestseller, but is altogether more pretentious on the level of reflection about the Problem of Evil and the question Is God Dead (or is he just living in sin?). A kind of *Invasion of the Body Snatchers* meets *Catch-22*, or maybe Fuller's *Shock Corridor* set as an episode from *The Twilight Zone*. Sounds interesting enough, but isn't. RM

Nixon

(Oliver Stone, 1995, US) Anthony Hopkins, Joan Allen, Powers Boothe, Ed Harris, Bob Hoskins, EG Marshall, David Paymer, Robert Hyde Pierce, Paul Sorvino, Mary Steenburgen, JT Walsh, James Woods, Kevin Dunn.
192 min.
Centred on a storm-tossed night in 1973, with President Nixon slipping into embittered reverie and recollection as he sits in the Lincoln Room at the White House listening to the tapes that may prove his undoing, Stone's film flashes back to Nixon's childhood in '20s California before meandering on to modern times and ending with his funeral. Though fragmented and using various styles and filmstocks, this is more engrossing than most of the duds in the director's ambitious but frustrating career, partly because it focuses squarely on such a tantalising protagonist. As played (not mimicked) by Hopkins, Tricky Dick is a maelstrom of emotions: convinced he's universally misunderstood and hated; haunted by guilt over the dead Kennedys and his own TB-afflicted brothers; alternating between idealism and despair, honesty and lies; scared, stubborn, erratic. It's a rich conception, well supported by muscular performances from Boothe (Al Haig), Sorvino (Kissinger), Hoskins (Hoover) and, especially, Allen (Nixon's wife Pat). With Watergate dominating the third and final hour, however, the narrative becomes more familiar, predictable and prone to bathos and bombast: as wayward and self-regarding as its subject, the film long overstays its welcome. GA

Noah's Ark

(Michael Curtiz, 1929, US) Dolores Costello, George O'Brien, Noah Beery Sr, Louise Fazenda, Guinn Williams, Paul McAllister, Myrna Loy.
135 min. b/w.
A spectacular and ambitious part-talkie epic which marries a Biblical theme (the Flood) with a romance set on the eve of the Great War. Each actor doubles parts in the Biblical and contemporary stories, and the Warners special effects department has a beano: train wrecks, battles, deluges, and a cast of thousands. Whether it makes any sense as an historical parallel seems somehow beside the point. What matters is that they spent $1,500,000 on the production, and the money, as they say, is on the screen. A much-trimmed version running 75 minutes (the intertitles and dialogue sequences were eliminated, and a new sound effects track added) was issued in 1957. MA

No Answer from F.P.1 (F.P.1 antwortet nicht)

(Karl Hartl, 1932, Ger) Hans Albers, Paul Hartmann, Peter Lorre, Sybille Schmitz, Georg August Koch.
115 min. b/w.
F.P.1 is an artificial island in mid-Atlantic, and it's not answering because there's a saboteur on board: the designer has been shot, the crew have been gassed, and the structure is sinking...This German sci-fi melodrama aspires to something of the grandeur of *Metropolis*, but its roots really lie in penny dreadful comics and early movie serials. As such, it's rather pedestrian in its exposition (it takes forever to get the plot moving), but fair value once the panics and alarms start multiplying. The stock performances are rather good, especially from Albers as the aviator-hero soaked in booze and self-pity, and Lorre as a bizarrely masochistic photographer. And Curt Siodmak's storyline manages to cross the epic adventure elements with a romantic triangle without either getting in the way of the other. Specialists may care to note the early associations of flying with sexual virility. TR

No Blade of Grass

(Cornel Wilde, 1970, GB) Nigel Davenport, Jean Wallace, John Hamill, Lynne Frederick, Patrick Holt, Anthony May, Wendy Richard, George Coulouris.
96 min.
An account of an English family's struggle for survival in the new world created by a virus that has destroyed virtually all earth's crops, *No Blade of Grass* lacks the primitive power of Wilde's earlier films *The Naked Prey* and *Beach Red*. Moreover, in its social attitudes and theorising, it exposes the shallowness of Wilde's conception of man as an animal dressed in civilised trappings that can, all too easily, be slipped off. PH

Nobody's Fool

(Evelyn Purcell, 1986, US) Rosanna Arquette, Eric Roberts, Mare Winningham, Jim Youngs, Louise Fletcher, Gwen Welles, Stephen Tobolowsky.
105 min.
The opening track on Cassie (Arquette), in drifty Thrift shop layers puffing at a dandelion clock, may activate fears that Frodo is in the offing, but hang in there. Buckeye Basin – motto: to be or not to be ain't much of a choice – is a cartoon of tank-town half-life. Seen through this perspective, Cassie's kookiness is a touching attempt to keep her dreams alive. Happily, a travelling Shakespeare theatre comes to town, along with hunky set designer Riley (Roberts, improved). The film, full of extraordinary images, seldom slips off its playful perch, and when it does there's always Arquette to cope with the Brautigans. A Shelley Duvall for the '80s, her blend of vulnerability and physical comedy could charm you into believing anything. Delightful. BC

Nobody's Fool

(Robert Benton, 1994, US) Paul Newman, Melanie Griffith, Bruce Willis, Jessica Tandy, Dylan Walsh, Pruitt Taylor Vince, Philip Bosco, Josef Sommer.
110 min.
Around North Bath, upstate New York, Don 'Sully' Sullivan (Newman) is notorious as something of a wastrel. He left his family years ago, he's not averse to a spot of petty crime – especially in his run-ins with construction boss Carl (Willis), with whose wife (Griffith) Sully has a barely platonic relationship – and his cronies include the town idiot and a one-legged lawyer who's never won Sully a case. Only his landlady (Tandy) really believes in him. Still, Sully is a die-hard optimist, and when his estranged son and grandson turn up, a chance arises to make amends to his family. Benton's quietly superb adaptation of Richard Russo's novel is one of those movies you thought they didn't make any more. It succeeds on several levels: as a wry hymn to community and long-term familiarity, a Hawksian fable about responsibility, an elegiac portrait of an endangered way of American life, and a quixotic celebration of unfounded optimism as embodied in Newman's supremely easy playing. GA

Nobody Lives Forever

(Jean Negulesco, 1946, US) John Garfield, Geraldine Fitzgerald, Walter Brennan, Faye Emerson, George Coulouris, George Tobias.
100 min. b/w.
Garfield is the New York con-man, semi-reformed by wartime service as an army NCO, who goes to Los Angeles to 'rest', but is there tempted to swindle the innocent Fitzgerald of the inheritance left to her by her late husband. Predictable but well-acted Warners yarn, scripted by WR Burnett, with a horribly sugary conversion scene in a chapel at Capistrano, but a memorable finish on a fogbound pier in which the radiantly beautiful Fitzgerald, kidnapped by jibberingly psychotic Coulouris, seems somehow to transcend her oil-stained surroundings. JPy

Nobody Loves Me

see Keiner Liebt Mich

Nobody Ordered Love

(Robert Hartford-Davis, 1971, GB) Ingrid Pitt, Judy Huxtable, John Ronane, Tony Selby, Peter Arne, Mark Eden.
87 min.
Dreadful 'exposé' of the movie scene, involving a hustling opportunist (Selby) who wheels and lays his way through a completely phony version of the British film industry. The film in production that all the fuss is about, a challenging anti-war epic that supposedly ends up as a big success, looks every bit as abysmal as the rest.

Nobody Runs Forever (aka The High Commissioner)

(Ralph Thomas, 1968, GB/US) Rod Taylor, Christopher Plummer, Lilli Palmer, Camilla Sparv, Daliah Lavi, Clive Revill, Lee Montague.
101 min.
Limp Rank thriller from Jon Cleary's novel *The High Commissioner*, with Taylor as the Aussie cop

who tracks the eponymous diplomat (Plummer) to London to investigate his first wife's murder, and finds himself involved in a political assassination intrigue. A lamentable waste of a good cast. PT

Nobody Will Speak of Us When We're Dead (Nadie Hablará de Nosotras cuando Hayamos Muerto)
(Agustín Díaz Yanes, 1995, Sp) Victoria Abril, Federico Luppi, Pilar Bardem, Daniel Giménez Cacho, Ana Ofelia Murgia.
105 min.
This breathtakingly assured film begins in Tarantino mode with Abril caught in the crossfire between Mexican gangsters and DEA agents. She heads back to Spain with details of the Mob's local money-laundering operation; unfortunately, she's a total flop as a cat burglar, and falls off the wagon with a bump. A thriller with a difference: we're concerned, for instance, as much about Abril's fish dinner as the gangsters' reprisals. An acute, witty dissection of machismo in Spanish culture, a disquisition on the existence of God, and an advertisement for adult education. TCh

Noce blanche
(Jean-Claude Brisseau, 1989, Fr) Vanessa Paradis, Bruno Crémer, Ludmila Mikael, François Negret, Jean Dasté, Véronique Silver.
92 min.
This pessimistic romance, a vehicle for teenage French pop star Paradis, is a self-conscious and occasionally nauseating tale of *amour fou*, assembled with some skill from a collection of clichés both banal and exploitative. Paradis plays a troubled (but brilliant) 17-year-old school truant who becomes passionately involved with a 50-year-old married philosophy teacher. There are reasons for her moody, distracted personality: her psychiatrist dad has absented himself to Paris, leaving her alone amid the soulless concrete modernity of St Etienne; her mother is suicidal; her brothers are hardened delinquents; and she herself has a murky history of child prostitution. Paradis doesn't have to act much: the emphasis is on penetrating glances, pulling on jeans, coquettish pawing and petulant tantrums. Crémer provides the film's backbone, bringing intelligence and feeling to the role of a man swamped by an impossible, unwanted, but irresistible passion. WH

Noces de Papier, Les
see Paper Wedding, A

Noces Rouges, Les (Blood Wedding/Red Wedding/ Wedding in Blood)
(Claude Chabrol, 1973, Fr/It) Michel Piccoli, Stéphane Audran, Claude Piéplu, Eliana De Santis, Clotilde Joano, François Robert.
98 min.
Coinciding with the French elections, *Les Noces Rouges* was banned ostensibly because it was about a real murder case, but obviously also for the broad portrayal of its Gaullist villain – a man with a sly plan for expropriating property and developing it as factory-workers' high-rise dwellings plus plastics factory which, while benefiting the town, will end up pouring a small fortune into his own pocket. Sadly, although there is more positive vulgarity around than ever, Chabrol doesn't seem to know how to take his errant couple. As more or less critically approached figures of fun, they're great; it's when he falls in love with them that the film goes awry. Should have been sly and funny, or dark and tragic; ends up neither one nor the other. VG

Nocturna
(Harry Tampa ie. Harry Hurwitz, 1978, US) Yvonne De Carlo, John Carradine, Nai Bonet, Brother Theodore, Sy Richardson, Tony Hamilton.
83 min.
And now, suckers – Dracula...disco version. The Count's statuesque granddaughter Nocturna (played with unusual zomboid quality by executive producer Nai Bonet) runs away to the New York disco scene with what she calls 'my boyfriend', a friendly blond hulk who had been doing a gig in Transylvania. There are a few ideas which wouldn't disgrace a Mel Brooks movie: Dracula (Carradine) wearing dentures, a lady vamp sleeping in curlers and coffin, and her exasperated complaints about the quality of urban blood through 'pollution, drugs and preservatives'. It's all terrible, but there's no indication that it's meant to be anything else. Only see it when you feel very, very silly. JS

Nocturne
(Edwin L Marin, 1946, US) George Raft, Lynn Bari, Virginia Huston, Joseph Pevney, Myrna Dell, Mabel Paige.
88 min. b/w.
Scripted by Jonathan Latimer and treading similar ground to *Laura*, *Nocturne* turns investigation (the search for a composer's murderer) into obsession, largely through Raft's understated performance. He follows a typically fetishistic trail: spurred on by photographs of the victim's lovers, and looking for 'Dolores', just a name in a song by a dead man...SJ

No Deposit, No Return
(Norman Tokar, 1976, US) David Niven, Darren McGavin, Don Knotts, Herschel Bernardi, Barbara Feldon, Kim Richards, Brad Savage, Charlie Martin Smith.
112 min.
Lukewarm Disney comedy about two kids – plus pet skunk, natch – mistakenly kidnapped by a pair of bungling crooks. Millionaire grandpa Niven, normally pestered out of his life at hols time, is highly delighted and does his best to see they stay kidnapped. The kids/crooks scenes are fair enough, with Darren McGavin milking his part for every resigned look it's worth. There are also some good Harold Lloyd antics in pursuit of the skunk, and a funny car chase. But the rest is sacrificed to the bland presence of Niven, looking throughout as if he's doing everyone a favour. He isn't. AN

No Drums, No Bugles
(Clyde Ware, 1971, US) Martin Sheen, Davey Davison, Rod McCary, Denine Terry.
85 min.
Virtually a solo piece for Sheen, as the legendary Ashby Gatrell, sitting out the Civil War in a Virginia cave. Surprisingly watchable for what boils down to a long interior monologue, and retrospectively resonant as one of Sheen's trio of key military portraits: his pacifist here shading into his deserter in *The Execution of Private Slovik* and his uncomprehending Willard in *Apocalypse Now*. Sheen and Ware later reunited on the telemovie *Story of Pretty Boy Floyd*. PT

No End (Bez Konca)
(Krzysztof Kieslowski, 1984, Pol) Grazyna Szapolowska, Maria Pakulnis, Aleksander Bardini, Jerzy Radziwilowicz, Artur Barcis, Michal Bajor.
107 min.
A film not seen outside Poland until 1986 because of its pro-Solidarity stance. It opens with its hero (Radziwilowicz) explaining that he is already dead; he spends his time, unseen, patiently observing the actions of his wife, child and lawyer colleagues, and just occasionally intervening from his spirit world. He was a lawyer who specialised in representing victims of Poland's martial law, but now he watches helpless as one of his clients is persuaded by his survivors to renounce his principles in order to remain free. Interwoven in the knotty debates on law, freedom and *realpolitik*, is the growing despair of his wife, who discovers too late that she loved him more than she thought. Western cinema has the luxury of being politically apathetic if it wishes; it is heartening to find that a film burning with a passionate engagement with the system can still emerge from a closed world. And one, moreover, which still has space for tenderness, quiet, and an excursion into the realms of the spirit. CPea

No Escape
(Martin Campbell, 1994, US) Ray Liotta, Lance Henriksen, Stuart Wilson, Kevin Dillon, Kevin J O'Connor, Don Henderson, Jack Shepherd.
115 min.
This futuristic prison movie takes place on an island where civilisation has broken down, to be replaced by a violent struggle between two primitive factions. The anarchic Outsiders, led by the charismatic Marek (Wilson), have 'gone native', wearing fearsome masks and launching repeated attacks on the peace-loving Insiders' fenced-off commune. Presided over by their spiritual leader, the Father (Henriksen), these born-again New Age hippies grow crops, wear hand-knits and try to recover their self-esteem. Meanwhile, the prison island's sadistic warder rubs his hands at the prospect of the factions wiping each other out. Ex-Marine Captain Liotta is the wild card who may shift the balance of power. Impressive production values, but, regrettably, the robust action scenes and human drama are too often dwarfed by the stunning landscapes and imaginative sets, or clouded by the script's baggy philosophising. NF

No Fear, No Die
see S'en fout la mort

No Highway (aka No Highway in the Sky)
(Henry Koster, 1951, GB) James Stewart, Marlene Dietrich, Glynis Johns, Jack Hawkins, Elizabeth Allan, Janette Scott, Ronald Squire, Niall MacGinnis, Kenneth More.
99 min. b/w.
Flying to Labrador to investigate an air crash, scientist Jimmy Stewart works out that the plane he is travelling in (with Dietrich as a glamorous fellow-passenger) is due to disintegrate at any minute. The drama (based on Nevil Shute's novel) strains credibility; but sly comic touches from the leads effectively give us a nod and a wink, while Koster milks the suspense for all it's worth. TCh

Noire de..., Une
see Black Girl

Noir et Blanc
(Claire Devers, 1986, Fr) Francis Frappat, Jacques Martial, Joséphine Fresson, Marc Berman, Claire Rigollier.
80 min. b/w.
Accountant Antoine (Frappat) is so shy that his health club boss suggests a massage to reduce tension. Thus he takes his first steps into a secret life of self-discovery, shame and pain. Devers' debut, adapted from Tennessee Williams' short story *Desire and the Black Masseur*, is a compelling look at an asexual sado-masochistic relationship between two utterly ordinary men. Shot, rightly, in black-and-white, the film never romanticises the tender emotions that grow in a climate of sinister ritual and silent desire, nor does it fall prey to easy moralising or racial stereotypes. Until the enigmatic final scene, Devers' quiet observations are lucid, often touching and funny. Most impressively, the handling of potentially sensationalist subject matter is discreet but tough. The performances, too, are admirably understated. GA

Noises Off
(Peter Bogdanovich, 1992, US) Carol Burnett, Michael Caine, Denholm Elliott, Julie Hagerty, Marilu Henner, Mark Linn-Baker, Christopher Reeve, John Ritter, Nicollette Sheridan.
104 min.
Another theatrical metaphor fails to transfer to the screen. This adaptation of Michael Frayn's stage hit undoubtedly has its moments, but will still disappoint those who laughed themselves silly at the original. Frayn's play is literally a set piece: the humour derives from the way his cast of *farceurs* eminently succeed in tripping over the furniture, and suffering havoc from every prop, every technical and personal nightmare known to the business. Bogdanovich's film neither reproduces the tableau immediacy of the original, nor opens it up sufficiently as Peter Yates did with *The Dresser*. The result is almost always frustrating, the camera often cutting away from the point of a scene or an exchange, and the early part of the film flags badly before the giddy mayhem of the climax. Reeve (as a squeamish matinee idol) and Elliott (as the veteran drunk) turn in top-rate performances. Not good or fun enough, though. SGr

Noi Tre (The Three of Us/ We Three)
(Pupi Avati, 1984, It) Christopher Davidson, Lino Capolicchio, Dario Parisini, Carlo Delle Piane, Gianni Cavina, Ida Di Benedetto.
90 min.

It's idyllic summer-interlude time for the 14-year-old Mozart. To prepare for examinations for Bologna's Accademia Filarmonica, spunky young Amadé comes with his father to the country villa of Count Pallavicini. It is not a welcoming household: the Count is a curmudgeon with a distant young wife, a diffident son Giuseppe (who pisses on their bed) and a mad cousin. Avati's interest is in showing Mozart as a common-or-garden spotted youth, sneaking in a quick adolescence (fights with local roughnecks, romance with a neighbour's daughter, bonding with Giuseppe) between music lessons, exam pressure, overbearing parental encouragement, and the damnable, insistent call of genius. It's not an engaging tale, shot with the restraint of Straub but with hardly a note of music to relieve the deathly monotony. Framed as a poetic imagining, in the present, of two old men taking a walk in the woods, the film is entirely true to their dull inspiration. WH

Noi vivi

see We the Living

No Man's Land

(Alain Tanner, 1985, Switz/Fr/WGer/GB) Hughes Quester, Myriam Mézières, Jean-Philippe Ecoffey, Betty Berr, Marie-Luce Felber.
110 min.
A very inconsequential yarn about a group of disenchanted small-time smugglers (a cowman, an Algerian girl, a couple who run a club with a small dance-floor) in a village somewhere on the frontier of France and Switzerland. A gold run seems to offer the prospect of the freedom they all crave, but oddball characters, some torrid clinical sex and a lot of coming and going through the woods and across the mountains fails, regrettably, to add up to anything either significant or diverting. JPy

No Man's Land

(Peter Werner, 1987, US) DB Sweeney, Charlie Sheen, Lara Harris, Randy Quaid, Bill Duke, RD Call, Arlen Dean Snyder, M Emmet Walsh.
106 min.
Great to watch experts at work, but one of the things that militates against this portrait of professional car thieves is that they daren't show you how they do it (after Rififi, there was a rash of burglars sticking umbrellas through ceilings to catch falling plaster). Beyond carrying a posh shopping-bag to allay suspicion, there are no tips about ripping off Porsches. Rookie cop Benjy (Sweeney) is sent to infiltrate a bent garage owned by Ted Varrick (Sheen), who may have been implicated in the killing of a cop. Varrick lives the high life, and is so personable that Benjy falls for his spell and his sister (Harris, toneless and wilting), besides getting off on stealing cars. Will the cop in him rise up in time to intercept the evil in Varrick? Surface stuff, with neither actor up to the ambiguities, but entertaining enough around the car chases. BC

No Man of Her Own

(Mitchell Leisen, 1949, US) Barbara Stanwyck, John Lund, Jane Cowl, Phyllis Thaxter, Richard Denning, Lyle Bettger, Henry O'Neill, Milburn Stone.
98 min. b/w.
Based on a Cornell Woolrich novel (I Married a Dead Man) that bears many similarities to his Waltz Into Darkness (filmed by Truffaut as La Sirène du Mississipi), this is an excellent little thriller, tautly directed by Leisen and with a powerhouse performance from Stanwyck as a pregnant woman who assumes the identity of a young bride killed with her husband in a train crash. Just as she is enjoying the fiscal fruits of deception, her lover (Bettger) shows up and blackmails her. Apart from John Lund's predictable performance as the romantic lead – he's as anaemic here as in Wilder's A Foreign Affair – the film is constantly surprising and deliriously implausible. ATu

No Maps on My Taps

(George T Nierenberg, 1979, US) Chuck Green, Sandman Sims, Buster Brown, Bunny Briggs.
60 mins.
Can blue men sing the whites? Can Fred Astaire tap dance? Well – yes; but the top-hat-and-tails routine, like the Clapton solo, sho' nuff got black roots. This lively showcase for veteran Harlem

hoofers delightedly lets them show. A spirited tap 'contest' in front of the Lionel Hampton Band and an enthusiastic audience caps a unique retrospective portrait of the art, featuring amazing clips from both mainstream and 'race' movies of the '30s heyday, and fixing tap as another enduring expression of black American culture. PT

No Mercy

(Richard Pearce, 1986, US) Richard Gere, Kim Basinger, Jeroen Krabbé, George Dzundza, Gary Basaraba, William Atherton.
108 min.
His partner murdered by hoodlums, tough Chicago cop Eddie Jillette (Gere) takes a trip to New Orleans on a mission of vengeance against gangster Losado (Krabbé). Trouble is, the sole witness to the crime – a sultry, pouting blonde named Michel (Basinger) – is also Losado's slave-cum-mistress. To complicate matters, they do things different down South, and pretty soon Eddie's at loggerheads not only with Losado's lot but with the New Orleans cops. What matter, though, when a sweaty stint fleeing through the Bayou swamps with Michel brings at long last love into Eddie's life? Richard Pearce's thriller suffers from near-total predictability, with a script that careers headlong through clichéd situations, calculatedly coarse dialogue, and cardboard characters. That said, Pearce reveals a strong feel for lurid locations and spectacular set pieces, and makes the film look stylish, too much so in the case of the three leads. Indeed, taken straight it's all a little risible; but as fast-paced hokum pitted with plot-holes, it's polished fun – no more, no less. GA

No Mercy, No Future (Die Berührte)

(Helma Sanders-Brahms, 1981, WGer) Elisabeth Stepanek, Hubertus von Weyrauch, Irmgard Mellinger, Nguyen Chi Danh, Erich Koitzsch-Koltzack.
108 min.
Based on a letter received from a schizophrenic woman, this is not about treatment or clinical causes, but – as Sanders-Brahms puts it – about 'madness from within'. Called Veronika, the woman trudges through Berlin, lank-haired and grey faced, giving herself to society's castoffs (the old, the disabled, the immigrants) in the hope of finding Christ. Elisabeth Stepanek's performance is faultless, her heavy yet mobile face always interesting. But it's questionable whether the film is successful at exploring emotions 'from within'. The hallucinations are mere effects, the stroboscopic sequence is physically unbearable; while the sex and suicide attempts are more curious than moving. But detachment is continually challenged by urgent evidence of the madness on the outside: the tawdriness of Berlin (the paradigmatic schizoid city), the radio news reports, the shadowy figures of the girl's crabby parents living in uncomfortable, rococo splendour. If it's miserable being mad, it's pretty tough being ordinary. JS

None But the Brave

(Frank Sinatra, 1965, US/Jap) Clint Walker, Tatsuya Mihashi, Frank Sinatra, Tommy Sands, Brad Dexter, Takeshi Kato, Tony Bill.
105 min.
Sinatra's sole attempt at direction prefigures Boorman's Hell in the Pacific by stranding a World War II planeload of American marines on the same tiny island in the Solomons as a band of marooned survivors from a Japanese battalion. The carefully constructed mood as the two groups warily circle each other – spasmodically clashing in battle, tentatively setting up lines of contact, gradually establishing an all too brief time out of war – is stupidly fractured by two flashbacks obviously designed to provide a love interest; and the anti-war message is naively overplayed. Nevertheless, Sinatra displays great competence as an action director, and a sequence where the Americans attempt to capture a boat laboriously built by the Japanese is beautifully choreographed, ending with a memorable shot of both sides staring in silence as a hand-grenade destroys their only means of escape. Excellent performances, too (with the Japanese mercifully allowed to speak Japanese). TM

None But the Brave

see Kung Fu Girl, The

None But the Lonely Heart

(Clifford Odets, 1944, US) Cary Grant, Ethel Barrymore, June Duprez, Barry Fitzgerald, Jane Wyatt, Dan Duryea, George Coulouris.
113 min. b/w.
A fascinating but dissatisfying adaptation by Odets of Richard Llewellyn's tale of a Cockney wastrel, living in the London slums of the '30s, who mends his selfish ways when he realises that his mum (Barrymore) is dying. Bogus poetry wrecks the Cockney dialogue, dripping sentimentality and a distinctly Hollywoodian East End soften the darker shadows of the piece. The performances, however, and George Barnes' camerawork are worth watching. GA

None Shall Escape

(André De Toth, 1944, US) Alexander Knox, Marsha Hunt, Henry Travers, Richard Crane, Dorothy Morris, Trevor Bardette.
85 min. b/w.
Scripted by Lester Cole (later one of the HUAC 'Hollywood Ten'), this anticipates the end of WWII and the Nuremberg Trials to stage an International War Crimes Commission in Warsaw. The case under consideration is that of Wilhelm Grimm (Knox), former Reichs Commissioner of the Western Region of Poland. Fascinatingly, although 'leniency' is not the order of the day (as the title suggests), and no punches are pulled in detailing his crimes (the term 'extermination camp' is not used, but the script is unique for the period in making it quite clear that Grimm's regime in Warsaw is to implement the final solution), the film is not concerned with zomboid Nazis and their horrors. Rather, tracing Grimm's career in flashback from 1919, when he returned after WWI minus a leg and plus a bitter resentment of Germany's humiliation in defeat, it attempts to probe the psychology of the man; and in so doing, without in any way condoning or sympathising, it manages to elicit a glimmer of understanding. There are naiveties, and the film now suffers from a certain déjà vu; but script, direction and acting all remain impressive. TM

No Nukes

(Julian Schlossberg/Danny Goldberg/Anthony Potenza, 1980, US) James Taylor, Carly Simon, Bonnie Raitt, Graham Nash, John Hall, David Crosby, Bruce Springsteen.
103 min.
First the good news: 20 minutes of Springsteen. The bad news is a further 80 minutes of concert and behind-the-scenes footage which, unless you're a fan of the soft rock icons of the late '60s, looks like a catalogue of aged hippies reliving their former glory. Filmed during five concerts performed for free and organised by Musicians United for Safe Energy (MUSE), it's a pity that the movie builds so obviously towards Springsteen's appearance, defusing the very real political message of the MUSE team (Nuclear Energy is BAD for you) and turning Springsteen into nothing more than a crowd-puller. FF

No Orchids for Miss Blandish

(St John L Clowes, 1948, GB) Jack LaRue, Linden Travers, Hugh McDermott, Walter Crisham, Lily Molnar, Zoe Gail.
104 min. b/w.
'The most sickening exhibition of brutality, perversion, sex and sadism ever to be shown on a cinema screen' squawked the Monthly Film Bulletin. 'Nauseating muck', 'about as fragrant as a cesspool', 'a wicked disgrace to the British film industry' echoed the national press. The film's 'hero' – a down-at-heel newspaperman – is indeed a nasty piece of work, and as insensitive as his colleagues in the real world to the fondly passionate relationship between Miss Blandish and her morbidly introverted kidnapper. But the critical hysteria over this confident, well-crafted homage to Hollywood is puzzling. The sets, the acting, the smoothly effective direction are all remarkably good, redolent of a short-lived maturity attained by British cinema in the late '40s. James Hadley Chase's novel was remade in 1971 as The Grissom Gang. RMy

Noose

(Edmond T Gréville, 1948, GB) Carole Landis, Joseph Calleia, Derek Farr, Stanley Holloway, Nigel Patrick, Ruth Nixon, Carol Van Derman, Hay Petrie, John Slater.
95 min. b/w.

Richard Llewellyn's adaptation of his own play is something of a transatlantic compromise. Calleia, a vicious Mafia-style gangster nastier than Edward G Robinson ever was in his heyday, heads a profitable black market racket in postwar Soho, throwing vicious tantrums and pursuing his hedonistic pleasures (ex-girlfriends get knuckledustered and dumped in the Thames) while his partner, a cheery Cockney wide-boy (Patrick), takes care of the business end. His comeuppance – brought about when an intrepid girl reporter (Landis) stirs up trouble, and her ex-army husband (Farr) leads troops of local workers in a pugilistic rescue – is very British and slightly risible. But taking the whole thing by the scruff of the neck, the talented Gréville turns it into something rich, strange and rather wonderful. His boldly stylised direction, backed by Hone Glendining's expressionistic lighting and the daringly over-the-top performances (Calleia and Patrick are both marvellous), gives this grippingly black yet bleakly funny thriller an almost Wellesian edge. TM

No Pets

(Tony Buba, 1994, US) John Amplas, Lori Cardihle, Ben Tatar, Rick Applegate.
79 min.
Shot on a shoestring budget in Pittsburgh, this is a perceptive, unpatronising and compassionate study of a blue-collar worker struggling through in the face of inevitable disappointments. Episodic in structure, it follows Eddie (Amplas), a factory machinist, a single man, and owner of a mongrel that his landlady wants shot of. What happens to a guy like this, stuck in a dead-end job when his high-school pals went off to college, left to contemplate the might-have-beens over a beer with the guys from work? There are no false promises or fake uplift here, just an honest stare into the face of some uncomfortable home truths. TJ

Nora Helmer

(Rainer Werner Fassbinder, 1973, WGer) Margit Carstensen, Joachim Hansen, Barbara Valentin, Ulli Lommel, Klaus Löwitsch.
101 min.
Fassbinder's version of Ibsen's *A Doll's House* for television develops a radical yet scrupulous reading of the play. Stripped of sentimentality and giving Nora (Carstensen) self-assurance from the start, this studio production delivers its critique of bourgeois marriage with a force rarely matched even in the theatre. The brutal prose, harshly delivered, is complemented by the unique visual spectacle which Fassbinder manages to wring from a videotape studio. Achieving effects of lighting and framing which British TV directors have never dreamed of, he makes the oppressiveness of Nora's home as concrete as a tank-trap. Almost every scene is shot through latticework, net curtains, cut glass, ornate mirrors, so that the characters are perhaps visually obscured but always intellectually focused. All the BBC's producers of tele-classics should be chained to chairs and forced to watch it. JW

Nord (North)

(Xavier Beauvois, 1991, Fr) Xavier Beauvois, Bulle Ogier, Bernard Verley, Agnès Evrard.
96 min.
Despite an (acknowledged) debt to the films of Maurice Pialat, Beauvois's feature debut is a pretty distinctive achievement, not only for the authenticity of its observations (it's set in Calais, where the writer/director/lead actor grew up), but for the raw honesty of its emotional content. At first you think it's Beauvois, as the teenager bored out in his box by provincial life, who's on the slippery slope; then it transpires it's his pharmacist dad (Verley) who's into substance abuse; then mum (Ogier), hitherto apparently the voice of reason, gets in on the dysfunctional act. Aided by superb performances, Beauvois shows us the potential (and all too common) horrors of everyday family life without moralising or sensationalism; as in his even more ambitious follow-up (*Don't Forget You're Going to Die*), there's real depth, insight and truth here. GA

No Retreat, No Surrender

(Corey Yuen, 1985, US) Kurt McKinney, Jean-Claude Van Damme, JW Fails, Kathie Sileno, Kim Tai Chong, Kent Lipham.
84 min.

McKinney, a Bruce Lee freak, is disappointed when his karate instructor dad opts out of a confrontation with some dumb heavies and moves the family to Seattle. There McKinney chums up with break dancer RJ (Fails), who shows him the town's most famous slab of marble, covering the grave of the late Bruce Lee; and as the new boy in town, he becomes a choice victim for the bully boys who frequent the hamburger bars. Drawing upon the spirit and skills of his deceased mentor to quell the local populace, he also gets even with the bad guys who chop-sueyed his father. *No Retreat, No Surrender* borrows heavily from the likes of *The Last Dragon, Karate Kid* and even *Rocky IV*, but makes them look like masterpieces by comparison. Some fancy dan karate and a good cameo performance from Van Damme as a Russian heavy might have made an enthralling ten-minute video; otherwise it's just more proof that the real thing died with Bruce Lee in 1973, even though the corpse keeps twitching. CB

No Return Address
(Sin Remitente)

(Carlos Carrera, 1994, Mex) Tiare Scanda, Fernando Torre Laphame.
95 min.
An impressive and melancholy drama, finely lit in dark tones by Xavier Perez Grobet, which sees an old bachelor postal clerk teased into a sad last go at love by an equally 'lost' upstairs neighbour, a twenty-something female photo-journalist who writes him anonymous notes, supposedly from an admirer. It's fascinating to watch Carrera's mordant humanism at work: no character – the clerk, the prostitutes, the modern neighbour, the clerk's unreconstructed friend, especially – is without faults, delusions or reasons. It's this attention to detail, observation and even-handedness that distinguishes the movie. The mood is ably sustained and Laphame (as the clerk) gives a performance that recalls the master Emil Jannings in its old-fashioned pathos. WH

Normal Life

(John McNaughton, 1995, US) Luke Perry, Ashley Judd, Bruce Young, Jim True, Dawn Maxey, Scott Cummins, Kate Walsh.
102 min.
This 'true life' crime drama may not view love as a form of pathological delusion, but it sure paints a cynical portrait of suburban alienation, particularly within marriage. The film straddles the territory between freewheeling 'couple on the lam' actioner and darker domestic drama, but isn't settled in either. There are three main characters. Perry is rookie cop Chris, a neat and sober, military moustachioed man who falls for star-gazing, self-mutilating, probably suicidal wild card Pam (Ashley Judd, playing it like she's in an Abel Ferrara movie). The third character (as in *My New Gun*) is an automatic weapon, introduced to Pam by Chris on their first date at the Chicago cops' indoor shooting range. As the film traces the arc of Chris and Pam's relationship – an at times bloody battle of diametrically opposed aspirations, coursing through credit card debt, housekeeping arguments and bank-robbing methods – the gun increasingly becomes the third member in a destructive *ménage à trois*, not least in terms of sexual symbolism. The flattened non-judgmental style pays dividends in some highly evocative scenes – the cold discomfort of a marriage ceremony echoing to the sound of Pam's dying father's cough – but in most it seems clumsy and over-emphatic. WH

Norman... Is That You?

(George Schlatter, 1976, US) Redd Foxx, Pearl Bailey, Dennis Dugan, Michael Warren, Tamara Dobson, Vernée Watson, Wayland Flowers.
92 min.
Betrayed by his wife, the boorish manager of an Arizona dry-cleaning establishment is dealt a second blow when he discovers his son Norman living in a hideous Los Angeles apartment with a camp boyfriend. After ninety minutes of shouting, pouting, door-slamming and homespun philosophising – adapted with a black cast from a Broadway flop – one can only marvel at the continuing, condescending, sitcom attitude to homosexuality. Foxx and Bailey bluster helplessly as the parents; the statuesque Dobson, as a hooker brought in to straighten Norman out, looks on in saucer-eyed incomprehension; only Wayland

Flowers, a manic puppeteer, manages to transcend the material with an energetic demonstration of the nice but limited art of self-parody. JPy

Norman Loves Rose

(Henri Safran, 1982, Aust) Carol Kane, Tony Owen, Warren Mitchell, Myra De Groot, David Downer, Barry Otto.
98 min.
An ill-conceived Frankenstein's monster of second-hand jokes and worn-out caricatures, this is a disappointment after Safran's earlier *Storm Boy*. While preparing for his bar mitzvah, Norman discovers sacred encouragement for his profane interest in sister-in-law Rose, and seizes the opportunity presented by his mother's absence and his brother Michael's low sperm count. Rose becomes pregnant, but refuses to reveal Norman as the father. Norman is not happy. Only Warren Mitchell's unerring sense of comic timing instils any humour into this banal film; the other characters cast only pale shadows upon the stifling Sydney suburbs. FD

Norma Rae

(Martin Ritt, 1979, US) Sally Field, Beau Bridges, Ron Leibman, Pat Hingle, Barbara Baxley, Gail Strickland, Morgan Paull.
114 min.
Ritt's usual simplistic liberalism certainly dampens the labour relations angle to this tale of a Southern millworker finding herself as a union activist protesting against working conditions. Sentimental and facile, the film allows her far too easy a path to success in terms of her almost universal acceptance by fellow-workers, give or take a few token blacklegs. But far more successful is the way the film stresses her development as an independent woman; finding it painful as she undermines her husband's expectations of her simply as a washing, cooking, ironing, maternal sex-machine, she nevertheless ploughs firmly ahead, while never being portrayed as in any way an incomplete, irresponsible mother and wife. Nicely performed by a strong cast, especially Field and Leibman, it's often mawkishly soft, but surprisingly touching. GA

Norseman, The

(Charles B Pierce, 1978, US) Lee Majors, Cornel Wilde, Mel Ferrer, Jack Elam, Christopher Connelly, Kathleen Freeman.
90 min.
'Wizard, what say your signs about this New Land?' asks Lee Majors – playing a permed Bionic Bjorn of a Viking prince – of soothsayer Jack Elam in AIP's idea of Norsespeak. The New Land is Vineland (America), and the Six Million Dollar Viking and his crew have rowed across in 1006 AD in search of his father who, it turns out, has been captured and blinded by cartoon Indians who resemble Grateful Dead roadies given the freedom of the make-up department. From then on, even Mel Brooks couldn't have improved on it: hilarious dialogue, eccentrically filmed battle scenes, Cornel Wilde and Mel Ferrer both in beards behind which to hide their embarrassment. AC

North

see Nord

North

(Rob Reiner, 1994, US) Elijah Wood, Matthew McCurley, Dan Aykroyd, Kathy Bates, Kelly McGillis, Bruce Willis.
87 min.
Tired of suffering neglect and endless rows, bright, popular, eight-year-old North (Wood) makes history by divorcing his parents; the catch is he has to find acceptable replacements by Labor Day, or he'll end up in an orphanage or back with Mom and Dad. Cue a frantic odyssey to Texas, Hawaii, Alaska, Africa where sundry would-be parents fail to live up to his dreams. And what if he decides to go home? Would his pal Winchell (McCurley), riding high on the nationwide fervour he's whipped up in kids against their folks, allow North to abandon the cause? Reiner is undecided just how fantastically he should treat this ludicrous plotline. Added to which there's a dire musical number, a silly thriller subplot, and much maudlin didacticism from narrator Willis in various guardian angel (dis)guises. Misery. GA

North Avenue Irregulars, The (aka Hill's Angels)

(Bruce Bilson, 1978, US) Edward Herrmann, Barbara Harris, Susan Clark, Karen Valentine, Michael Constantine, Cloris Leachman, Patsy Kelly.
99 min.
The British release title, *Hill's Angels*, may be misleading but it's no misprint: the hero is Presbyterian minister Mike Hill, the angels are his nutty female parishioners, and they all have some cutesy, badly-plotted fun battling against a horrid crime syndicate. The style is the norm for late '70s Disney: low on kids and animals, high on limp satire of contemporary fads (citizens' radio) and car-mangling. The cast is a weird mixture of Hollywood veterans and younger talents who deserve far better parts; the director's a recruit from TV; the result is just about bearable. GB

North by Northwest 100 (100)

(Alfred Hitchcock, 1959, US) Cary Grant, Eva Marie Saint, James Mason, Leo G Carroll, Jessie Royce Landis, Martin Landau, Philip Ober, Josephine Hutchinson.
136 min.
From the glossy '60s-style surface of Saul Bass' credit sequence to Hitchcock's almost audible chortle at his final phallic image, *North by Northwest* treads a bizarre tightrope between sex and repression, nightmarish thriller and urbane comedy. Cary Grant is truly superb as the light-hearted advertising executive who's abducted, escapes, and is then hounded across America trying to find out what's going on and slowly being forced to assume another man's identity. And it's one of those films from which you can take as many readings as you want: conspiracy paranoia, Freudian nightmare (in which mothers, lovers, gays and cops all conspire against a man), parable on modern America in which final escape must be made down the treacherous face of Mount Rushmore (the one carved with US Presidents' heads). All in all, an improbable classic. HM

North Dallas Forty

(Ted Kotcheff, 1979, US) Nick Nolte, Mac Davis, Charles Durning, Dayle Haddon, Bo Svenson, John Matuszak, Steve Forrest, GD Spradlin.
118 min.
Something of a mess, both in terms of the wayward plot which rambles all over the place, and in terms of the rather muddled juggling of audience sympathies. Nolte is the pro-football player who is disgusted on the one hand by the ruthless machinations of the team management, and on the other by the brute macho behaviour of his fellow-players. The trouble is that his confusion is mirrored by the film-makers in that they seem undecided as to whether the sports biz and the hulks it enlists are charismatically exciting or morally bankrupt. But Nolte ambles through it all with naturalistic conviction, and Durning is his usual reliable self. GA

Northerners, The (Der Noorderlingen)

(Alex Van Warmerdam, 1992, Neth) Leonard Lucieer, Jack Wouterse, Rudolf Lucieer, Alex Van Warmerdam, Annet Malherbe, Loes Wouterson.
107 min.
Van Warmerdam's bizarre but not unappealing comedy inhabits a world of its own. Set in a remote village in the latter half of 1960, the film observes the oddball antics of the few villagers through the eyes of a 12-year-old boy so obsessed with news from the Congo that he wanders the woods in blackface calling himself Lumumba. Evidently, this is a form of escape from his parents' bickering: his fanatically religious mother is unhappy about the sexual demands made by his butcher father. The neighbours, meanwhile, are a woman desirous of a child and her infertile forest-warden husband, arch-enemy of the postman, who habitually steams open everyone's mail. What all this signifies is unclear. Certainly, the village is presented as a hotbed of hypocrisy, veiled racism, dysfunctional sexuality, and all-round nosiness, but Van Warmerdam isn't one for the explicit touch. That said, there are moments of deadpan charm, and the offbeat tone holds the attention surprisingly well. GA

Northern Lights

(John Hanson/Rob Nilsson, 1978, US) Robert Behling, Susan Lynch, Joe Spano, Marianne Astrom-DeFina, Ray Ness, Helen Ness.
93 min. b/w.
Extraordinary film-making: vast, looming close-ups of faces in black-and-white, a landscape gripped by winter, and behind it all a fictional re-creation of the struggle by a handful of Dakota farmers toward political organisation during World War I. The pseudo-documentary tone is maddeningly naive, but the stubborn, passionate images survive. CA

Northern Star, The

see Etoile du Nord, L'

North of Vortex

(Constantine Giannaris, 1991, GB)
58 min.
A superbly composed and strikingly evocative film. Skyscrapers, freight trains, desert roads: we are in the midst of an American mood piece distilled from road movies, Kerouac, junk and all that jazz. A (gay) poet picks up a (bi) sailor and a (desperate) waitress. Taking turns behind the wheel, they drive west across the radio dial. Shot in a grainy monochrome you could get lost in, the film never quite arrives at the ironic nonchalance Giannaris is aiming for, but his cool eye for emotional byways makes it a proposition worth exploring. TCh

North Sea Hijack

(Andrew V McLaglen, 1979, GB) Roger Moore, James Mason, Anthony Perkins, Michael Parks, David Hedison, Jack Watson, George Baker, Jeremy Clyde, David Wood, Faith Brook.
100 min.
It's a wonder that the SNP ('It's Scotland's oil') never thought of this one, it's so simple: hold HM Government to ransom by threatening to blow up a drilling rig and a production platform. Where *North Sea Hijack* fails is that it takes a potentially convincing idea, then completely undermines it by subjecting it to shallow treatment. The Navy, represented by tired Admiral James ('I wish I sailed') Mason, is beaten before it starts, and it's left to free enterprise (Moore) to save the coffers of the nation. He is a freelance commando chappie, against whose ice-cool nerve (he does petit-point) the hijackers haven't a chance...and neither does the film. With more imagination, more of Faith Brook's send-up of a well-known lady PM, and less of Moore's excruciatingly smug misogyny, this might just have made it to comic levels. FF

North Star, The (aka Armored Attack)

(Lewis Milestone, 1943, US) Anne Baxter, Dana Andrews, Walter Huston, Ann Harding, Erich von Stroheim, Farley Granger, Walter Brennan.
105 min. b/w.
Heroic Russian villagers fight off Nazi invaders in this hokey pro-Soviet flag-waver, which was later to embarrass the Goldwyn studio and just about everybody who'd worked on it, when McCarthy's commie-hunting investigators started prying. Lillian Hellman wrote the dire screenplay – and, yes, that is Walter Brennan as a Russky.

North to Alaska

(Henry Hathaway, 1960, US) John Wayne, Stewart Granger, Fabian, Capucine, Ernie Kovacs, Mickey Shaugnessy, Karl Swenson.
122 min.
Wayne's on good-natured, cussin' and brawlin' form for this frontier adventure in which he and partner Granger strike gold in Alaska, then spend the rest of the movie fighting over Capucine and battling it out with swindler Kovacs. Two-fisted CinemaScope barnstormer. TJ

North West Frontier (aka Flame Over India)

(J Lee Thompson, 1959, GB) Kenneth More, Lauren Bacall, Herbert Lom, Wilfrid Hyde-White, IS Johar, Ursula Jeans, Ian Hunter.
129 min.
An excellent adventure film which turns the Raj into an apposite backdrop for the British equivalent of a Western. Kenneth More is a British officer who must aid the escape of a Hindu prince from a city besieged by the Muslims. This he does by means of a decrepit steam train, with a handful of Western passengers on board, one of them an enemy agent. It's exciting stuff, with reams of incident, confident dialogue, and impeccable 'Scope photography by Geoffrey Unsworth. TCh

Northwest Passage

(King Vidor, 1940, US) Spencer Tracy, Robert Young, Ruth Hussey, Walter Brennan, Nat Pendleton, Robert Barrat, Lumsden Hare, Donald MacBride.
125 min.
Subtitled 'Roger's Rangers' and intended as the first instalment in a two-part true-life adventure (the second film was never made because Tracy and Vidor didn't get on), this 18th century frontier saga follows Tracy's Major Roger and mapmaker Young into Canada to quell the Indian tribes who'd been striking across the border at the colonists. Vidor certainly plays up the hardships they endure en route, but it's hard for modern viewers to look on in approval as Tracy and his men set fire to a sleeping Indian village, treated as just another testing obstacle like the torrential river bridged by the teamwork of a human chain. It's never suggested that his heroes emerge from all this unscathed, but they are certainly made stronger and wiser by the experience. The early Technicolor gives the film the look of a children's storybook. TJ

No Sad Songs for Me

(Rudolph Maté, 1950, US) Margaret Sullavan, Wendell Corey, Viveca Lindfors, Natalie Wood, John McIntire, Ann Doran, Richard Quine, Jeanette Nolan.
89 min. b/w.
In her last film, Margaret Sullavan plays a housewife diagnosed as suffering from terminal cancer. Keeping the news from her husband (Corey), at first because she is panicky, later because he is at a crucial stage in his career as a surveyor, she gradually starts putting her house in order: teaching her small daughter (Wood) to be self-reliant, and befriending her husband's assistant (Lindfors) – whom he has hovered on the brink of falling in love with while working together – in the hope that the gap she leaves behind will soon be filled. Despite the soapy scenario, and a cosmetic illness that allows Sullavan to fade out as gracefully as the Lady of the Camellias, this is a much better film than it sounds. Howard Koch's script is a miracle of delicacy, psychological insight and quiet humour; the performances are superb; and Maté's precise, perfectly controlled direction obstinately refuses to indulge any slush. TM

No Secrets! (aka Touch of the Sun)

(Peter Curran, 1982, GB) Oliver Reed, Sylvaine Charlet, Peter Cushing, Keenan Wynn, Bruce Boa, Edwin Manda, Wilfrid Hyde White.
80 min.
Dismal would-be comedy laden with patronising post-colonial attitudes. When an American spacecraft crash lands in Africa and its crew members are held captive by local tribesmen, officer Reed and commissioner Cushing (looking particularly weary) are the bumbling response despatched by the West. From the lost battalion of unreleased British features, it seems. TJ

Nosferatu a Venezia

see Vampires in Venice

Nosferatu the Vampyre (Nosferatu: Phantom der Nacht)

(Werner Herzog, 1979, WGer/Fr) Klaus Kinski, Isabelle Adjani, Bruno Ganz, Roland Topor, Walter Ladengast, Dan Van Husen.
107 min.
Stylish, sombre, owing little to the Murnau classic and nothing to Hammer or Hollywood, Herzog's foray into Dracula territory is the story of an inhabitant of 18th century Delft (Ganz, striving hard to expand the limits of his part), whose encounter with the weary, jealous Count (Kinski, indescribable) brings doom to his marriage, home town and self. Unfortunately, Herzog's inspired

seriousness creates serious problems, for the film is too aware of its cultural dimensions (the Plague, Faust, Freud), too lacking in narrative drive, to work as a horror story. And the impressively detailed historical recreation tends to undermine – not underline – the deliberate silent-screen formality of acting and (minimal) dialogue. It's an error of conception which clouds over the luminous photography and excellent performances with an intermittent failure of style: fascinating, but flawed. CA

Nosferatu – eine Symphonie des Grauens

(FW Murnau, 1922, Ger) Max Schreck, Alexander Granach, Gustav von Wangenheim, Greta Schröder, GH Schnell, Ruth Landshoff.
6,453 ft. b/w.
Murnau's classic vampire movie, though not his best film, remains one of the most poetic of all horror films. Its power derives partly from Schreck's almost literally sub-human portrayal of the Count, resplendent with long ears and fingers and a wizened, skeletal face, partly from the sexual undercurrents coursing through the movie which suggest that the vampire is a threat not only to bougeois society and its emphasis upon scientific rationality, but also to the very marriage of the Harker couple. A film that survives repeated viewings. GA

No Skin Off My Ass

(Bruce LaBruce, 1990, Can) Klaus von Brucker, Bruce LaBruce, GB Jones.
75 min. b/w.
A punk hairdresser (LaBruce) takes time off from watching Altman's *That Cold Day in the Park* on TV and picks up a surly skinhead (von Brucker), taking him home to bed, board and bondage fantasies. The sullen object of his desire isn't about to stick around and listen to the Carpenters, though, and hightails it to the apartment of his lesbian film-maker sister (Jones), who's busy casting for her new production, 'Girls of the SLA'. Jones is undoubtedly the star of this exceptionally cut-price venture, with the sassiest delivery and by far the best lines ('I wonder if this is how Agnès Varda got started?' she sighs). LaBruce's film has been compared to Kuchar and Warhol, but both would be hard pressed to beat the longueurs and economy measures. One of the tackier highlights of the new wave of Queer Cinema, it's patchily enjoyable and pretty endearing. JRo

No Smoking

see Smoking/No Smoking

Nostalgia (Nostalghia)

(Andrei Tarkovsky, 1983, It) Oleg Jankovsky, Erland Josephson, Domiziana Giordano, Patrizia Terreno, Laura De Marchi, Delia Boccardo, Milena Vukotic.
126 min. b/w & col.
Another of Tarkovsky's strange, hauntingly beautiful meditations on man's search for self. The film may forsake the run-down space station of *Solaris* or the miraculous Zone of *Stalker* for the hilltop villages of Tuscany, but its framework is familiar (flashbacks in spectral black-and-white, the use of rich sepia alongside pastel colour to blur distinctions between dream and reality), and so are its themes (memory, melancholia, disenchantment with the material world, dogged stumbling after salvation). An appropriately haggard academic, Gorchakov (Jankovsky), has come to Italy to research the life of an obscure Russian composer. Brooding over familial traumas and his compatriot's eventual suicide, he's incapable of communicating with his statuesque young interpreter (Giordano), let alone having an affair with her. In the meantime he meets Domenico (Josephson), a recluse whom the locals dismiss as mad. Each man recognises something of himself in the other, and they embark upon the most absolute of alliances...Tarkovsky remains as much a metaphysician as anything else, and *Nostalgia* isn't an entertainment but an article of faith. AMac

Nostalgia for Countryland (Thuong Nho Dong Que)

(Dang Nhat Minh, 1995, Vietnam/Jap) Ta Ngoc Bao, Thuy Huong, Le Van.
116 min.

With four excellent movies behind him, there's no doubt that Dang Nhat Minh is Vietnam's foremost director and one of the best in South-East Asia as a whole. But this Japanese-financed film about a farm boy's crush on a woman émigrée who revisits her home village in North Vietnam lacks almost all the qualities which have distinguished his early work: it's soft-edged, easily sentimental, poorly acted and full of obvious padding. This is not the first time that money from NHK (Japan's BBC) has thrown a talented director off course, but it's the saddest example of recent years. The single most interesting moment – the young hero's astonishment when he has his first spontaneous orgasm in the fields – was too much for the Vietnamese censor. TR

Nostradamus

(Roger Christian, 1993, GB/Ger) Tchéky Karyo, F Murray Abraham, Rutger Hauer, Amanda Plummer, Julia Ormond, Assumpta Serna, Anthony Higgins, Diana Quick, Michael Gough.
120 min.
As the millennium approaches, interest in the writings of the 16th century visionary Nostradamus has revived. Played with effective restraint, Karyo's Nostradamus is a man tormented by dreams and drug-fuelled visions, frustrated by the ignorance of his fellow medical practitioners, and persecuted by religious zealots. Although the film hedges its bets regarding the veracity of Nostradamus's predictions, there is much to admire here. Director Christian successfully evokes the historical period, and Karyo conveys the intellectual turmoil of a religious man driven by a hunger for truth. The only off-key note is sounded by Hauer's eccentric turn as a mystic monk. NF

No Surrender

(Peter Smith, 1985, GB) Michael Angelis, Avis Bunnage, James Ellis, Tom Georgeson, Bernard Hill, Ray McAnally, Mark Mulholland, Joanne Whalley, JG Devlin.
104 min.
An acerbic, frequently very funny farce scripted by Alan Bleasdale, here bringing with him Angelis, Hill and Ellis from *The Boys from the Black Stuff*. It's the same slightly surreal allegory on contemporary Britain: a seedy Liverpool nightclub, where Angelis takes over as manager to find that his predecessor – a practical joker – has booked a gaggle of appalling acts to perform at a New Year's Eve binge, attended by two parties of OAPs, one Protestant, the other devout Irish Catholics. Mayhem ensues, of course, amid a collection of excellent performances and witty one-liners. No masterpiece, to be sure, but highly enjoyable, for all its underlying bleakness. GA

Not a Love Story

(Bonnie Sherr Klein, 1981, Can) Bonnie Sherr Klein, Linda Lee Tracey, Marc Stevens, Ed Donnerstein, Kate Millett.
68 min.
A crusading attack on pornography by concerned mother Klein, seconded by a Montreal stripper (Tracey) with a cute comedy act and increasing doubts about her profession. Klein's pretty depressing view that porn is not culturally determined, but born of some 'inherently male' drive to hurt and defile, seems almost oblivious to basic and much-debated questions such as how to find the thin blue line between hardcore and misogyny in 'respectable' representations of women, or the potentially enlightening effect of porn's explicitness about female sexuality (both points raised by Kate Millett in an all-too-brief sequence). Most disturbing of all is that Klein's own camera is itself often compulsively and rather unpleasantly voyeuristic. SJo

Not a Pretty Picture

(Martha Coolidge, 1975, US) Michele Manenti, Jim Carrington, Anne Mundstuk, John Fedinatz, Amy Wright, Stephen Laurier.
83 min.
Written, directed and produced by Coolidge, this is a film within a film. Part narrative reconstruction of her own rape at 16, part documentary footage of director and actors, it seems more of a cathartic exercise for those participating than an instruction to its audience (Michele Manenti, who plays Martha, was also an adolescent rape victim). Their tremendous emotional involvement

proves inadvertently alienating: watching the director's distress at seeing her narrative self being raped is disturbing, not because of what it says about rape, but because it's so intensely personal. Also, the 1962 high school scenario is culturally distancing, particularly for a British audience. A film which never really manages to confront us with the enormity of its subject, nor with any kind of analysis as to why rape occurs. HM

Not As a Stranger

(Stanley Kramer, 1955, US) Robert Mitchum, Olivia de Havilland, Frank Sinatra, Charles Bickford, Gloria Grahame, Broderick Crawford, Lee Marvin, Lon Chaney.
135 min. b/w.
Typically well-meaning slice of Kramerkitsch, based on a bestseller (what else, with that title?) about a medical student (Mitchum) driven by a sense of vocation which makes him use people – notably de Havilland's improbably blonde Swedish nurse – with the kind of alienating selfishness that means his comeuppance is on the way. The exceptional cast helps to while away the platitudes and pieties, provided you can accept the likes of Mitchum, Sinatra and Marvin as somewhat wrinkly students. TM

Notebook on Cities and Clothes (Aufzeichnungen zu Kleidern und Städten)

(Wim Wenders, 1989, WGer) Yohji Yamamoto, Wim Wenders.
81 min.
After the dizzy heights of *Wings of Desire*, Wenders came down to earth with this scribble-pad of a documentary, comprised of sundry video doodles and 16mm jottings. Invited by the Georges Pompidou Centre to make a film 'in the context of fashion', he overcame his initial scorn, and decided to fly from Berlin to Paris and Tokyo on the trail of clothes designer guru Yohji Yamamoto. There is footage of the black-clad genius of the cutting-shears spluttering about his love for cities from the roof of the Pompidou, circling and snipping in his Tokyo studio, and sitting with Buddha-like serenity amid the chaos of his Paris show. Through it all, Wenders drones on with a series of either banal or tenuous links and meditations on the similarities between film-making and clothes-designing, the suitability of video to the ephemerality of fashion, and how he had been *aching* to meet Yamamoto ever since purchasing one of his creations. The result has all the panache of a hastily-assembled jumble of out-takes from a *Clothes' Show* filler. WH

Not for Publication

(Paul Bartel, 1984, US) Nancy Allen, David Naughton, Laurence Luckinbill, Alice Ghostley, Barry Dennen, Richard Paul, Paul Bartel.
87 min.
Lois (Allen), personal assistant to the Mayor of New York, works nights moonlighting for *The Informer*, a sleazy little rag which specialises in shock-horror sensations like 'Frog Baby Ax Murders', while she waits impatiently for the day when she can turn the paper back into the august journal that her father used to edit. After the wayward perversity of *Eating Raoul*, Bartel has turned out a surprisingly tame and curiously old-fashioned comedy, a rather charming tale spiced with naughty black undertones. Highlight among these is the scene where Lois and her photographer (Naughton), clad in cuddly costumes, perform a cheery barnyard song about bestiality in front of a leering audience of kinky animal lovers. AB

Nothing But the Best

(Clive Donner, 1964, GB) Alan Bates, Denholm Elliott, Harry Andrews, Millicent Martin, Pauline Delany, Godfrey Quigley, Alison Leggatt.
99 min.
An echo from a time when social mobility looked easy and 'A-type ladies in E-type Jags' were the goal of every bright young man. If, despite Nic Roeg's lush photography, the glittering prizes look horribly tarnished, that only deepens the black comedy. Jimmy Brewster's climb to the top comes without angst or guilt or tragic sacrifice; he doesn't sell his working class soul, but merely steals one with a better pedigree. Frederic Raphael's

witty script and Donner's tricksy direction superbly capture a world where image is everything. Trumpeting that robust contempt for the establishment that was the essence of 'TW3' satire, they hack their way through social conventions to expose the grubbily materialist heart of 'swinging London'. Salutarily un-nostalgic. RMy

Nothing But the Night

(Peter Sasdy, 1972, GB) Christopher Lee, Peter Cushing, Diana Dors, Georgia Brown, Keith Barron, Gwyneth Strong, Fulton Mackay.
90 min.
Strange tale of a series of murders of trustees of an orphanage on a Scottish island, revealed as having supernatural causes. Something has obviously come fatally adrift with the film, which wavers between Chabrol-like touches, a bit of Truffaut in his *Bride Wore Black* mood, and some straight British MI5 stuff. The script seems mostly at fault, and often the acting is just that little bit over-emphatic, which doesn't help. Not Sasdy at his best. DP

Nothing in Common

(Garry Marshall, 1986, US) Tom Hanks, Jackie Gleason, Eva Marie Saint, Hector Elizondo, Barry Corbin, Bess Armstrong, Sela Ward.
119 min.
Hanks plays David Basner, slick creative director of an advertising agency. Trying to land a lucrative account, he negotiates with the irascible client while unwittingly falling into bed with his daughter. Meanwhile, David's grouchy father (Gleason) announces that David's mother (Saint) has left him after 33 years of marriage. As the familial crisis becomes increasingly intrusive, it not only affects David's work but forces him to reassess his relationship with his parents. This curiously broken-backed film begins as a hilarious satire on high-power advertising, but ends as a *Terms of Endearment*-style weepie about intergenerational conflicts. Thanks to Hanks and a razor-sharp script, the early scenes make the most of the frenetic, cutthroat action. When the film slips into a more serious vein, however, it simply treads water while threatening to drown in its own tears. NF

Nothing Lasts Forever

(Tom Schiller, 1984, US) Zach Galligan, Apollonia van Ravenstein, Lauren Tom, Dan Aykroyd, Imogen Coca, Eddie Fisher, Sam Jaffe, Paul Rogers, Mort Sahl, Bill Murray.
82 min. b/w & col.
Saturday Night Live alumnus Schiller wrote and directed this oddball first feature, a glimpse of a future where the Port Authority now rules New York City with an iron hand, and where young Galligan, having failed the regulatory artist's test, is sent to the traffic department. The film soon descends underground (where veteran Sam Jaffe holds sway) before heading to the moon for further adventures. Not all of the invention hits the target, but the film's determination to go its own way is not unendearing, and there's a succession of star cameos to prick the interest. TJ

Nothing Personal

(Thaddeus O'Sullivan, 1995, Ire) Ian Hart, John Lynch, James Frain, Michael Gambon.
85 min.
One dark night in Belfast, 1975. Trapped on the wrong side of the sectarian divide, Liam (Lynch) finds himself at the mercy of a Loyalist paramilitary group, while his young daughter roams the streets looking for him. Confidently mounted by O'Sullivan, working in a very different register from his mainstream feature debut, *December Bride*, this humanist drama is engaging enough, and very well acted with a tooth-and-nails psycho turn from Ian Hart, but it's too schematic, one of those films where you can read the third act in the first ten minutes. TCh

Nothing Sacred

(William Wellman, 1937, US) Carole Lombard, Fredric March, Charles Winninger, Walter Connolly, Sig Ruman, Maxie Rosenbloom, Frank Fay.
75 min.
Irresistible performance from Lombard as the small-town girl, supposedly dying of radium poisoning but well aware that she isn't, who determines to grab all she can get when a newspaper brings her to New York for a last fling as a pub-

licity stunt. Ben Hecht's sparkling script occasionally loses its way between the satire and the screwball romance, but is even more caustic about newspapermen than *The Front Page* ('The hand of God reaching down into the mire couldn't elevate one of 'em to the depths of degradation'), and provides a welcome antidote to Capracorn in its view of small towns as hellholes to be got out of where an intruder is likely to be stoned or bitten by small boys. Some marvellous digs at the morbid sentimentality of the crowd, too, in particular a scene where a wrestling match is held up for ten seconds in tribute to the doomed girl while the bell solemnly tolls ten times. Quite attractively shot in colour, although prints tend to be suffused by an unpleasant pinkish wash. TM

Nothing to Lose

(Steve Oedekerk, 1997, US) Tim Robbins, Martin Lawrence, John C McGinley, Giancarlo Esposito, Michael McKean, Susan Barnes, Kelly Preston, Steve Oedekerk.
98 min.
Nick (Robbins) and Ann (Preston) play husband-and-wife games in bed. He thinks she's a fat pig; she wants a divorce. Who can spin it out longest? Anyway, next day Nick gets off a late working assignment, only to catch Ann in bed with his boss (McKean). Stunned, he drives away, anywhere – to a hold-up at a red light in slumtown. It's T Paul (Lawrence) wanting Nick's wallet, waving a gun in his face. With a manic laugh and his foot on the gas, Nick defenestrates the money and drives the hapless sometime criminal to the Arizona desert for a round of mismatched comic capers. No surprises here. There are nods to the race issue, but this isn't exactly Tom Wolfe, and though some jokes work, more don't. NB

No. 3

(Song Neung-Han, 1997, SKor) Han Suk-Kyu, Lee Mi-Yeon, Choi Min-Sik.
108 min.
A brilliantly inventive, off-the-wall satire on the gangster mentality. Tae-Ju (Han) joins a gang in 1990, when economic times are hard, and finds himself stuck at No 3 in the hierarchy – essentially a low grade hatchet man. His efforts to get ahead are not helped by his wife's infidelity (she aspires to a literary career and starts taking lessons) or by the attentions of a cynical, bad mannered prosecutor who dogs his steps. The action leapfrogs through the years until Tae-Ju finally settles his rivalry with the gang's No 2 (Ashtray, named after his weapon of choice) in a night-club called Chaos; a coda whisks the characters into the future to see what becomes of them after the millennium. First-time director Song, previously best known as the writer of *Taebaek Mountains*, reportedly based it on his encounters with a real-life gang boss. TR

No Time for Tears

(Cyril Frankel, 1957, GB) Anna Neagle, George Baker, Sylvia Syms, Anthony Quayle, Flora Robson, Michael Hordern, Joan Hickson, Rosalie Crutchley, Joan Sims, Angela Baddeley.
86 min.
Maybe there's a note of irony in the title, for this children's hospital drama spends nearly all its efforts bathing us in sentimentality of the starchy, received-pronunciation Home Counties kind. Anna Neagle's the all-seeing matron who saves two slum kids from their slovenly mother, while doctor Baker tries out his bedside manner on nurse Syms. Predictable and fairly patronising, but it certainly gives an insight into prevailing health attitudes of the day. TJ

Not Now, Comrade

(Harold Snoad/Ray Cooney, 1976, GB) Leslie Phillips, Lewis Fiander, Carol Hawkins, Roy Kinnear, Windsor Davies, Don Estelle, Michele Dotrice, June Whitfield, Ray Cooney, Ian Lavender.
90 min.
Or ever. Leslie Phillips capers as one Rimmington of the Defence Ministry (in naval beard and yellow Bentley), hot on the trail of defecting Russian ballet dancer Fiander, the KGB who're tailing him, and accompanying stripper Hawkins whose purpose seems to be to add a whiff of titillation. From the darkest days of British cinema, a farrago which began life as Cooney's Whitehall farce, *Chase Me, Comrade*. TJ

Not of This Earth

(Roger Corman, 1956, US) Paul Birch, Beverly Garland, Morgan Jones, William Roerick, Jonathan Haze, Dick Miller, Ann Carroll.
67 min. b/w.
Low budgets give little reason for regret when the often tacky effects are surrounded by so much imagination, good humour, and sheer joy in film-making as here. *Not of This Earth* is a minor sci-fi gem, with an alien (Birch; you can tell he's an ET by his briefcase and dark glasses, establishing him as infinitely superior to the moronic middle Americans on view) terrorising Earth (or a small backlot) in his quest for blood for the folks back home. GA

Not on Your Life

see Verdugo, El

Notorious 100

(Alfred Hitchcock, 1946, US) Cary Grant, Ingrid Bergman, Claude Rains, Louis Calhern, Leopoldine Konstantin, Reinhold Schunzel, Moroni Olsen.
102 min. b/w.
One of Hitchcock's finest films of the '40s, using its espionage plot about Nazis hiding out in South America as a mere MacGuffin, in order to focus on a perverse, cruel love affair between US agent Grant and alcoholic Bergman, whom he blackmails into providing sexual favours for the German Rains as a means of getting information. Suspense there is, but what really distinguishes the film is the way its smooth, polished surface illuminates a sickening tangle of self-sacrifice, exploitation, suspicion, and emotional dependence. Grant, in fact, is the least sympathetic character in the dark, ever-shifting relationships on view, while Rains, oppressed by a cigar-chewing, possessive mother and deceived by all around him, is treated with great generosity. Less war thriller than black romance, it in fact looks forward to the misanthropic portrait of manipulation in *Vertigo*. GA

Notorious Gentleman

see Rake's Progress, The

Not Quite Jerusalem

(Lewis Gilbert, 1984, GB) Joanna Pacula, Sam Robards, Kevin McNally, Selina Cadell, Zafrir Kochanovsky.
114 min.
In the play from which this is adapted, the tough desert life of the kibbutzniks lent them an air of curt self-sufficiency, while the working class English volunteers who had come for a working holiday displayed a vicious, heartfeld hatred for England. Here, this strong material (adapted by playwright Paul Kember himself) has been caramelised. Gilbert has created a toffee-apple with the apple removed: bite through the sweet crust of romantic Holy Land locations, handsome Israelis, dashing Arab terrorists and corny jokes, and what remains is sheer emptiness. The characters are caricatures, the situations clichés, and the production leaden. One saving grace: Polish actress Joanna Pacula, who alone manages to invest her role with a patina of plausibility, radiates a heat that marks the ascension of a star. MH

No Trees in the Street

(J Lee Thompson, 1958, GB) Sylvia Syms, Herbert Lom, Joan Miller, Melvyn Hayes, Stanley Holloway, Liam Redmond.
96 min. b/w.
Released at a time when kitchen sink drama was all the rage, this is an unremarkable 'we had it tough' chronicle from another age (Ted Willis adapted his own play), set in the backstreets of 1938 London. Joan Miller's the desperate mum who tries to get sultry daughter Sylvia Syms married off to crooked turf accountant Lom, while young Melvyn Hayes – latterly remembered for his stint on TV's *It Ain't Half Hot Mum* – tries hard to convince as the ne'er-do-well son. TJ

Not Reconciled

see Nicht Versöhnt

Notre Histoire (Our Story/ Separate Rooms)

(Bertrand Blier, 1984, Fr) Alain Delon, Nathalie Baye, Michel Galabru, Geneviève Fontanel,

Jean-Pierre Darroussin, Gérard Darmon, Sabine Haudepin.
111 min.
Blier kicks off with a dream that must be uppermost in the male psyche: Nathalie Baye entering your railway carriage and demanding a fast one from the luggage rack. The trouble here is that she picks on Delon, a drunken old romantic, who just won't let her go. She is intent on being a short story; he clearly prefers Russian novels. There are glorious scenes of the town's male population shuttling from house to house in dressing gowns, their coitus forever interrupted, which bring to mind the anarchy and nightmare of Buñuel. But the ending looks like a shaky conclusion to a film with nowhere to go. However, Baye grows more and more beautiful, while at 50 Delon looks like he hasn't slept for years. CPea

Notte, La
(Michelangelo Antonioni, 1961, It/Fr) Jeanne Moreau, Marcello Mastroianni, Monica Vitti, Bernhard Wicki, Maria Pia Luzi.
121 min. b/w.
The middle section of Antonioni's trilogy on bourgeois alienation, La Notte covers twenty-four hours in the breakdown of a 'typical' middle class marriage. The husband (Mastroianni) is a novelist with a block, spineless, out of touch with his own instincts; the wife (Moreau) is a bored socialite who understands her own predicament but doesn't know how to get past it. Scene after scene is introduced solely to make laboured points about their emotional/social/philosophical problems; Antonioni's intimations of a broader political context are startlingly shallow. It's impossible to discern the relevance of this kind of film-making, which is doubtless why nobody (including Antonioni) practises it any more. TR

Notte di San Lorenzo, La
see Night of San Lorenzo, The

Notti Bianche, Le
see White Nights

Not Without My Daughter
(Brian Gilbert, 1990, US) Sally Field, Alfred Molina, Sheila Rosenthal, Roshan Seth, Sarah Badel, Mony Rey, George Corraface.
116 min.
According to her Iranian-born husband Moody (Molina), Moody's family reunion is as American as apple pie. Certainly Moody's family reunion in Tehran ain't her idea of a holiday, and no sooner have they stepped on foreign soil than Betty is accosted by shrieking women beseeching her to cover her head. Things get worse. She's informed that Moody plans to stay in Iran and raise their little girl as a Muslim. The law strips Betty of all her rights, while Moody prevents her from leaving the house. Based on Betty Mahmoody's real-life story, the film emphasises her isolation, surrounded by an incomprehensible language and culture, and by vehement anti-American sentiments. Field captures the sense of outrage to perfection, puffy-eyed, screaming and plotting escape. Appropriately enough, the film is strictly deglamorised; combined with the lack of sympathetic characters, it all adds up to difficult, compelling viewing as we're drawn into the deepening nightmare. CM

Not Yet
see Madadayo

N'oublie pas que tu vas mourir (Don't Forget You're Going to Die)
(Xavier Beauvois, 1995, Fr) Xavier Beauvois, Roschdy Zem, Chiara Mastroianni.
118 min.
Xavier Beauvois won admirers for Nord, his memorable debut; here, in his even better and more unsettling follow-up, he plays an art student whose desperate attempts to avoid military service reveal that he's HIV positive, whereupon he begins systematically to immerse himself in the realm of the senses. Despite a finished technique, there's a rawness here – evident not only in the explicit scenes of sex and drugs, but in the dark, edgy humour that repeatedly and unexpectedly bubbles to the surface – that lends the film an emotional punch. Great performances and a strong John Cale score. GA

Nous Etions Tous des Noms d'Arbres
see Writing on the Wall, The

Nous Etions un Seul Homme
see We Were One Man

Nous Irons Tous au Paradis
see Pardon Mon Affaire, Too

Nouvelle Vague
(Jean-Luc Godard, 1990, Fr) Alain Delon, Domiziana Giordano, Roland Amstutz, Laurence Cote.
90 min.
As the rather obvious storyline progresses – a woman kills a lover, whose exact double (his brother?) comes back to haunt her – Godard's script and soundtrack make interminable use of quotations to offer thoughts (?) on almost everything under the sun. It looks nice enough, in an elegant, posh-car-commercial kind of way, but Delon, in the dual role, looks unhappily as if he had strayed in from another movie, and the whole thing comes over as inconsequential intellectual wank. Stillborn stuff from a former *enfant terrible* who seems to be suffering from terminal regression, it is vague rather than *nouvelle*. GA

November 1828
(Teguh Karya, 1979, Indon) Slamet Rahardjo, Jenny Rachman, Miruli Sitompul, El Manik, Rahmat Hidayat.
135 min.
Celebrations of anti-colonial struggles are par for the course for cinema from emerging countries, but Teguh Karya's mini-epic about the Javan resistance against the Dutch in the early 19th century isn't just another 'worthy' Third World entry. Apart from the fact that it looks and sounds very accomplished, the movie displays an intelligent grasp of the dynamics of melodrama (there are 'family' tensions on both sides of the clash), and presents traditional Javan culture without recourse to folksy stereotypes. TR

November Men, The
(Paul Williams, 1993, US) James Andronica, Leslie Bevis, Beau Starr, Robert Davi.
98 min.
Following the 1992 Bush/Clinton presidential campaign with an unauthorised (and undetected) camera, Paul Williams' thriller draws on the legacy of 1960s assassinations, fusing conspiracy fact and fiction. An egotistical guerilla film-maker (Andronica) recruits a seriously disaffected band of citizens to film a fake assassination attempt on a very real George Bush. The stakes appear to be raised when individual factions emerge and are incorporated into an ever-changing script, to the point where the camerawoman (Bevis) alerts the Secret Service. Shot as low-budget realism with an improvised air, the film unsettles, using dreams and shifting narrators, while exploring the reality behind the 'seeing is believing' myth. A multi-layered, twisting denouement supports Lyndon Johnson's belief that there's no need to worry about the left, they'll never pick up a gun – 'It's the right you have to worry about; it they don't get what they want, they'll blow you fucking head off.' FM

November Moon (Novembermond)
(Alexandra von Grote, 1984, WGer/Fr) Gabriele Osburg, Christiane Millet, Danièle Delorme, Stéphane Garcin, Bruno Pradal, Louise Martini.
107 min.
A wartime romance in which the two lovers just happen to be women. When November, a German Jewess, arrives in Paris in 1939, she captures the heart of a young man, but falls for his sister Férial. As the Occupation looms, November is forced to flee into the countryside, where she is sheltered by gentle peasants, but is shopped to the authorities and set to work in an officers' brothel. She manages to return to Paris, the bottom of the sofa acting as hidey-hole when anyone comes to call. With another mouth to feed, Férial has no choice but to work for the collaborationist press, bringing the mistaken but inevitable peacetime retribution. Both Osburg (November) and Millet (Férial) give powerful performances, and

thanks to von Grote's sensitive direction, this gripping slice of herstory achieves a quiet grandeur. MS

November Plan, The
(Don Medford, 1976, US) Wayne Rogers, Elaine Joyce, Philip Sterling, Clifton James, Diane Ladd, Meredith Baxter Birney, Laurence Luckinbill, Jack Kruschen, Dorothy Malone, Lloyd Nolan.
103 min.
Occasionally interesting private eye thriller, set in '30s LA, with Rogers investigating the murder of a starlet's lover and uncovering a plot to overthrow Roosevelt's government. With the film cobbled out of three episodes of a TV series called *City of Angels*, the weakly wisecracking, sub-Chandleresque script poses problems, as does Rogers' bland performance. But the political insights are intriguing in their tentative equation of the more conservative elements in American society with similar tendencies in Fascist Italy. GA

Novia que te Vea
see Like a Bride

Now and Then
(Lesli Linka Glatter, 1995, US) Demi Moore, Melanie Griffith, Rosie O'Donnell, Rita Wilson, Christina Ricci, Thora Birch, Gaby Hoffmann, Ashleigh Aston Moore, Willa Glen, Bonnie Hunt.
102 min.
Producer Demi Moore intended, it seems, a coming-of-age tale in the *Stand by Me* mould. What she ended up with was a syrupy dose of boyfriends and female bonding – in short, yet another uninspired 'women's film'. Fulfilling a childhood promise to 'always be there for each other', bohemian writer Samantha (Moore), actress Teeny (Griffith), and doctor Roberta (O'Donnell) return to their hometown, the bizarrely named Gaslight Addition, as Chrissy (Wilson) prepares for the birth of her first child. As they reflect on the pact which brought them together, the film reverts to 1970 and the start of their friendship. Director Glatter cut her teeth on *NYPD Blue*, but she brings none of that TV series' realism and punch to her feature debut, favouring instead a pastel-hued mise-en-scène. For a film which defines its characters entirely in relation to each other, there's a curious lack of chemistry between the leads. Only in the childhood sequences are the undercurrents and tensions of the various relationships explored. KM

No Way Home
(Buddy Giovinazzo, 1996, US) Tim Roth, James Russo, Deborah Kara Unger, Joseph Regno, Catherine Kellner, Saul Stein, Bernadette Penotti.
93 min.
As Joey Larabito leaves prison, we glimpse the scars cut into his back: cue flashback to the moment they were inflicted. In the same way, what develops as a subtle low-key character piece eventually descends into an OTT criminal melodrama. Six years in arrears – his wits ravaged by a childhood accident – Joey (Roth) arrives home to see his older brother Tommy (Russo). His knock is answered by a dishwater blonde, Lorraine, a sister-in-law he knew nothing about (Unger). She's reluctant to let a murderer stay, but Joey's quiet manner wins her over, and he becomes a useful ally as her husband digs himself ever deeper into debt. Roth negotiates the tricky business of mental deficiency with unsentimental deliberation. Unger – so cool and distant in *Crash* – emerges as a fine actress, shading from suspicion of Joey to trust with real emotional delicacy, going the opposite route with Russo, and hinting at a suburban fatigue that's eating away at her insides. Writer/director Giovinazzo gives us an authentic whiff of the sunny, slummy streets of Staten Island, but undercuts the good work which has gone before with an ill-judged bloody dénouement. TCh

No Way Out
(Joseph L Mankiewicz, 1950, US) Richard Widmark, Sidney Poitier, Linda Darnell, Stephen McNally, Ruby Dee, Ossie Davis.
106 min. b/w.
Poitier's first – and best – film, *No Way Out* is also one of the most honest films dealing with

racial conflict. Widmark plays the bigoted petty criminal who holds Poitier's doctor responsible for the death of his friend, and nearly incites a race riot in his search for revenge. While undoubtedly it fudges some of the issues, Mankiewicz's literate script makes this one of the few movies from the past dealing with racial issues that are still viewable today. PH

No Way Out
(Roger Donaldson, 1986, US) Kevin Costner, Gene Hackman, Sean Young, Will Patton, Howard Duff, George Dzundza, Jason Bernard.
115 min.
A gripping update on John Farrow's 1947 *The Big Clock*, its parallel duplicities relocated to the Pentagon. The mistress (Young) of devious Secretary of Defence Brice (Hackman) has been murdered, and Lt Farrell (Costner) is called in to catch the killer without stirring up the headlines. The problem is that Brice himself did the deed accidentally, while Farrell is the unknown man who had roused his jealousy by sharing her favours. Farrell's mission becomes a quicksand of double bluffs, concealments, and attempts to sabotage the clues in order to avoid the Pentagon fingering him for the murder. A very convincing nightmare, and if Hackman gives too rounded a performance to approach the omniscient evil of Laughton's original, Patton assumes the mantle as Brice's henchman, while Costner confirms his arrival as a star. Clearly, they can remake 'em like that any more. BC

No Way to Treat a Lady
(Jack Smight, 1967, US) Rod Steiger, George Segal, Lee Remick, Eileen Heckart, Michael Dunn, Murray Hamilton, Barbara Baxley.
108 min.
A scathingly funny black comedy satirising movie psychopathology. Steiger is brilliant as a sort of Boston strangler, son of a great actress who has left her boy with a mother fixation, a taste for impersonation, and a thirst for applause. Genuinely funny as he sets out to satisfy all three urges through murder, meanwhile making a special telephone confidant out of a reluctant cop (Segal, also brilliant) with Jewish momma problems of his own. Smight directs uncertainly, especially in some statutory love scenes, but the script (based on William Goldman's novel) is unstoppably witty. Difficult to resist a film in which a dwarf hopefully confesses to the killings, only to be told that eye-witness accounts point to a taller killer. 'See what I mean?' he cries, 'I'm a master of disguises!' TM

Nowhere
(Gregg Araki, 1996, US/Fr) James Duval, Rachel True, Nathan Bexton, Chiara Mastroianni, Debi Mazar, Kathleen Robertson, Scott Caan, Christina Applegate, Shannen Doherty, Rose McGowan.
82 min.
Araki's previous film, *The Doom Generation* (1994), never got a release in Britain. A lurid orgy of sex and violence, it was genuinely provocative, shocking and erotic, and it would have been sport watching the censor trying to grapple with it. *Nowhere* does have a UK distributor, but it's a piece of shit. Teen nihilism of the cheapest kind, it's as pretentious as Jean-Luc Godard, as tacky as one of those Z grade turkeys by Ted V Miklas, and at least twice as boring as that sounds. The hero (Duval) is a confused bisexual called 'Dark'. Araki persuaded a bunch of hot young actors to appear around him – True, Caan, Applegate, Mastroianni, Doherty, McGowan, an Alien Bodysuit – but he forgot to give them anything to do or say. TCh

Nowhere Man (Muno no Hito)
(Naoto Takenaka, 1991, Jap) Naoto Takenaka, Jun Fubuki, Kotaro Saito.
110 min.
Adapted from an avant-garde comic-strip by Yoshiharu Tsuge, this debut feature by the actor Naoto Takenaka is like a Japanese answer to the average 'Film on Four': earnest, quirky, over-emphatic and a little preachy. The meandering plot, a shaggy-dog story without the punchline, follows a down-at-heel comic-strip author whose work no longer sells; he tries to support his family by selling 'aesthetic' stones, tangles with the crook who controls the stone market, gets new inspiration from a mysterious bird-man, and

winds up doing the lowliest work he can think of. As protests against materialism and the Japanese work ethic go, this is on the weak side, but it has a certain languorous charm. TR

Nowhere to Run
(Robert Harmon, 1993, US) Jean-Claude Van Damme, Rosanna Arquette, Kieran Culkin, Joss Ackland, Ted Levine, Tiffany Taubman.
95 min.
When fugitive jailbird Van Damme holes up with widowed mother Arquette, he not only charms his way into her kids' affections and her bed, but ends up protecting her from avaricious speculator Ackland. Based on a story by Joe Eszterhas and Richard Marquand, this ham-fisted thriller from Mark (*The Hitcher*) Harmon was clearly intended to transform Van Damme from muscle-bound action star to mainstream Hollywood hero. When Van Damme is doing what he does best – narcissistically displaying his body and thumping the bad guys – the film works reasonably well. By contrast his attempts to lighten up and play quieter dramatic scenes offer an embarrassing array of boyish smiles, dumb looks and stilted dialogue. NF

Now, Voyager
(Irving Rapper, 1942, US) Bette Davis, Paul Henreid, Claude Rains, Bonita Granville, Gladys Cooper, John Loder, Ilka Chase, Lee Patrick, Janis Wilson, Franklin Pangborn.
117 min. b/w.
Davis, impeccable as usual, turns the sow's ear of Hollywood's notion of a repressed spinster (remove the glasses and lo! a beauty) into something like a silk purse. Great stuff as a worldly-wise psychiatrist (Rains at his smoothest) recommends a cruise, and bitter-sweet shipboard romance soars with an unhappily married architect (Henreid, suavely performing the archetypal two-cigarette trick). The women's weepie angle gets to be a bit of a slog later on, but it is all wrapped up as a mesmerically glittering package by Rapper's direction, Sol Polito's camerawork, and Max Steiner's lushly romantic score. TM

Nude Bomb, The (aka The Return of Maxwell Smart)
(Clive Donner, 1980, US) Don Adams, Sylvia Kristel, Vittorio Gassman, Rhonda Fleming, Dana Elcar, Pamela Hensley, Andrea Howard, Norman Lloyd, Bill Dana.
94 min.
From the production team that gave us TV's *Get Smart* – part of that post-McCarthy tradition in spy series intent on demonstrating that the individualist bungling West could defeat the starkly mechanical East. For the big screen, though, the producers have turned post-Watergate: corporate business is now the object of paranoia. The flimsy plot is built around a Mafia-style designer (Dana) whose organisation (KAOS) broadcasts worldwide the fact that it has the power to destroy all known fabrics. Unless ransom is paid it will unleash its device: will Agent 86 (Adams) and his female companions be able to save the world from nakedness? 'From a character conceived by Mel Brooks', reads the blurb, and there are various nods to his style of humour throughout this bitty spoof. But the rest relies more on technology than style, and on mediocre effects that can't carry the plot. RW

Nuit Américaine, La
see Day for Night

Nuit de Varennes, La
see That Night in Varennes

Nuit du Carrefour, La
(Jean Renoir, 1932, Fr) Pierre Renoir, Winna Winfried, Georges Koudria, Dignimont, GA Martin, Jean Gehret, Michel Duran.
73 min. b/w.
The screen's first Simenon adaptation, a wonderfully impenetrable mystery in which a series of murders and murder attempts gradually unravel a tale of star-crossed love and stolen diamonds, centreing on a lonely crossroads, a sleazy garage, and a semi-derelict house harbouring an enigmatic, drug-stupefied femme fatale. Shot almost entirely on location and in direct sound, with most of the action taking place at night or in permanently shrouding mists, the whole film

is seen and heard as through a glass, darkly. Myth (perpetuated by Godard) has it that three reels were lost; in fact nothing is missing, except that the money ran out and undoubtedly left gaps and rough edges. The mystification is an integral part of Renoir's conception: scenes are constantly being shot past Maigret or over his shoulder, as if to focus concentration on the mysterious person or object he is contemplating, but which is seen only hazily in the background, leaving us intrigued, tantalised and little the wiser until Pierre Renoir's Maigret ('Simple! Why didn't I think of it before?') condescends to explain. Weird, hallucinating and oddly poetic, it prefigures the treacherous perspectives of the later *film noir*. TM

Nuit et Jour
see Night and Day

Nuit fantastique, La (The Fantastic Night)
(Marcel L'Herbier, 1942, Fr) Fernand Gravey, Micheline Presle, Saturnin Fabre, Charles Granval, Bernard Blier.
89 min. b/w.
Better known for his silent films, L'Herbier here essayed a wartime escapist fantasy. A young man (Gravey) prefers his dream world to daytime reality, where he pursues his obsession, a mysterious goddess in white named Irène (Presle), who inhabits a small surreal world dominated by her father, a conjuror (Fabre). As in Woody Allen's *Purple Rose of Cairo*, the dreamer remains conscious of his edifying fiction, preferring it to reality. A bit rough around the edges: let's call it a semi-precious jewel. SGo

Nuits de la Pleine Lune, Les
see Full Moon in Paris

Nuits Fauves, Les
see Savage Nights

Nuits Rouges (Shadowman)
(Georges Franju, 1973, Fr/It) Jacques Champreux, Gayle Hunnicut, Gert Fröbe, Ugo Paglai, Josephine Chaplin, Patrick Préjean, Raymond Bussières.
105 min.
This is the movie version of *L'Homme sans Visage*, a pilot for a TV series shot simultaneously but separately: a hugely beguiling tribute to the world of the pulp thriller, in which bizarre and ornate secret societies emerge from their mysterious labyrinths to do battle on the streets and rooftops of contemporary Europe. Feuillade, the early master of the French serial, is a major visual influence, but *Shadowman* broadens to take in the twilit worlds of Sax Rohmer (signalled by the character Petrie, the English antiquarian) and Jean Ray, with nods even in the direction of Von Daniken and *The Dawn of Magic*. The plot feasts itself on remote contol taxis piloted by waxworks, occult ceremonies, staring zombies, ancient charts, and mass assassinations: no one uses a revolver when a poison blowpipe or an animated sculpture will do, and Franju leavens the brew with his own style and wit, achieving some effects of startling visual beauty. DP

Number One
(Les Blair, 1984, GB) Bob Geldof, Mel Smith, Alison Steadman, PH Moriarty, Phil Daniels, Alfred Molina, James Marcus.
106 min.
Lots of street cred, low-rent locations, a plot based around snooker, and a nice big dollop of London villainy; add an unlikely, bumpy love story between Geldof's budding Hurricane Higgins and Steadman's tart with heart of gold, plus Smith on top form, and you could almost shout 'Frame and Match!' to all concerned. Sadly, though, what lets the film down is its preposterous ignorance of the game in question, which goes so deep that it will appal or amuse anyone who has managed two consecutive editions of *Pot Black*. When it steers clear of snooker, there's much to enjoy, but any film which lurches from grainy realism to outrageous cartoon with such abandon simply can't be number one. SGr

Number One (aka Pro)

(Tom Gries, 1969, US) Charlton Heston, Jessica Walter, Bruce Dern, John Randolph, Diana Muldaur.
105 min.

As his fortieth year approaches, American footballer Heston finds his marriage falling apart and his playing career with the New Orleans Saints in its twilight, an odd role for one of the monolithic heroes of the Hollywood screen, and one that he doesn't seem to be able to do much with. Pretty banal, for Heston completists only. TJ.

Number Seventeen

(Alfred Hitchcock, 1932, GB) Leon M Lion, Anne Grey, John Stuart, Donald Calthrop, Barry Jones, Garry Marsh.
64 min. b/w.

Based on a play and conceived by Hitch as a spoof on the dark house type of thriller, this is actually a fairly creaky affair in which a detective (Stuart) joins forces with Leon M Lion's charmless Cockney to track down a gang of jewel thieves, one of whom (female, natch) falls in love with him. The action culminates in a race between a train and a Green Line bus: quite obviously model-work, but nevertheless exciting. AB

Number 3

See No. 3

O

On the Waterfront

O Amor Natural

(Heddy Honigmann, 1996, Neth)
76 min.
This feature length documentary was inspired by the erotic poetry of the Brazilian writer Carlos Drummond de Andrade. The poetry was never published during Drummond's lifetime – he was worried that readers would find it pornographic. The director interviews elderly Brazilians from all walks of life, inviting them to recite Drummond's verse and to reminisce about their own erotic adventures. The poetry itself is tremendous – full of ripe, carnal imagery – and there's something touching and humorous in seeing the dessicated old timers read it aloud. The film works both as a social document, charting a generation's attitudes toward love, sex and marriage, and as a lyrical celebration of Drummond's life and work. GM

Oberwald Mystery, The (Il Mistero di Oberwald)

(Michelangelo Antonioni, 1980, It/WGer)
Monica Vitti, Franco Branciaroli, Luigi Diberti, Elisabetta Pozzi, Amad Saha Alan, Paolo Bonacelli.
129 min.
An oddly misjudged attempt by the master of Italian alienation to film Jean Cocteau's melodramatic play *The Eagle Has Two Heads*, previously filmed by Cocteau himself (*L'Aigle à Deux Têtes*, 1948). Ten years after the assassination of her husband Prince Ferdinand, the lonely internal exile of the queen (Vitti) of a middle European country is broken when she gives refuge to a fugitive anarchist poet. Shot on video and then transferred to film, this features muddy visuals and suffers badly from the predictable mismatch of Cocteau's flamboyant aestheticism and Antonioni's emotionally distanced formalism. NF

Objective, Burma!

(Raoul Walsh, 1944, US) Errol Flynn, William Prince, James Brown, George Tobias, Henry Hull, Warner Anderson.
142 min. b/w.
A classic Hollywood platoon movie, with Flynn and his men parachuting into Burma to wipe out a key Japanese radio station. The taut action, sparse dialogue, and faultless technique keep things moving so fast that there's no time to reflect upon the morality of war or the miraculous way in which Flynn and his men survive against such overwhelming odds. Very much in the time-honoured 'war is hell' tradition, with plenty of gritty detail but the implicit suggestion that those who survive such carnage are somehow ennobled by it. Prickly reading of the film as suggesting that Errol Flynn and the Americans won the Burma Campaign single-handed provoked a massive outburst of popular and critical vilification when the film was first released in this country, and following a full-scale diplomatic incident it was banned until 1952. NF

Object of Beauty

(Michael Lindsay-Hogg, 1991, US/GB) John Malkovich, Andie MacDowell, Lolita Davidovich, Rudi Davies, Joss Ackland, Bill Paterson, Ricci Harnett, Peter Riegert, Jack Shepherd.
103 min.
An enervated American couple in London, Jake (Malkovich) and Tina (MacDowell) find their funds running out and their hotel bill mounting. He pressures her to sell her valuable Henry Moore sculpture, she resists, and its disappearance widens the mistrust between them. In fact, it has been stolen by deaf-mute chambermaid Jenny (Davies), who appreciates it for its beauty. This, on paper, contrasts with the futility of their values. Few who sit through the film will need the signpost, though they may wonder why Jenny, her punk brother, and their milieu seem to have strayed in out of Mayhew. Lindsay-Hogg wrote and directed this dull, static flounder, which exposes both MacDowell's limitations and Malkovich's withdrawal of labour. Shepherd, Ackland and Paterson go for little in cameo roles. BC

Oblomov (Neskolko Dnei iz Zhizni I.I. Oblomova)

(Nikita Mikhalkov, 1979, USSR) Oleg Tabakov, Yuri Bogatyryov, Elena Solovei, Andrei Popov.
140 min.

Cross the two-hour barrier with a film about inertia and ennui – albeit a gentle period comedy – and you've automatically got a problem: how to convey the feelings without inducing them? Mikhalkov can't totally stave off drooping eyelids, but this engagingly adapted parable (from Goncharov's novel) of a privileged recluse being reluctantly dragged towards light, life and love produces its share of helpful wry nudges. Still, it has to be admitted that as the tardily socialised, eternally indecisive Oblomov, Tabakov invests sloth with a winning seductiveness. PT

Oblong Box, The

(Gordon Hessler, 1969, GB) Vincent Price, Christopher Lee, Alastair Williamson, Hilary Dwyer, Peter Arne, Maxwell Shaw, Rupert Davies.
91 min.
A loose adaptation of Poe's story *The Premature Burial*, set in 19th century England, with Price as the lord of the manor whose brother (Williamson) kept locked away after being mysteriously mutilated in Africa, escapes and seeks revenge after being inadvertently buried alive in an attempt to spirit him away from prying eyes. The first half-hour or so has a really enigmatic quality as Hessler's camera prowls through the sombre mansion, using subjective camera to convey the alienated and animal-like existence of the strange Sir Edward. By keeping Sir Edward behind the camera for so long, his evil is exaggerated enormously, giving him a kind of sub-human aura long after the device has been discontinued. After this cryptic opening, however, the script rapidly begins to disintegrate (Chris Wicking, alas, is confined to 'additional dialogue'). Begun by Michael Reeves, the film was taken over by Hessler after the former's death.

Obsession (aka The Hidden Room)

(Edward Dmytryk, 1948, GB) Robert Newton, Phil Brown, Sally Gray, Naunton Wayne, Olga Lindo, Ronald Adam.
98 min. b/w.
Certainly Dmytryk's best British film, made after his blacklist exile and before freedom from the Hollywood system led him into the pretensions of *Give Us This Day*. Adapted by Alec Coppel from his own novel, it's an intriguing 'perfect murder' thriller in which an obsessively jealous husband lures his rival to a cellar on a bomb site, keeping him chained there until the coast is clear and his own grimly meticulous preparations for disposing of the body in an acid bath are complete. Perhaps only Buñuel could have done justice to the flavour as the avenger sadistically torments his victim during the wait, and an odd intimacy starts to spring up between them. Here both dialogue and performances (with Newton doing much less eye-rolling than usual) stay a little too close to the surface, but it has much the same narrative grip as Dmytryk's earlier Hollywood movies like *Murder My Sweet*, *Cornered* and *Crossfire*. TM

Obsession

(Brian De Palma, 1976, US) Cliff Robertson, Genevieve Bujold, John Lithgow, Sylvia Williams, Wanda Blackman, Patrick McNamara.
98 min.
Schrader and De Palma's tribute to Hitchcock's *Vertigo* may lack the misogyny and bloodbath sensationalism of De Palma's later work, but it's still dressed up in a mortifyingly vacuous imitation of the Master's stylistic touches. Virtuoso gliding camera movements do not necessarily a good film make. The main problem with the film, in fact, is the excruciatingly slow pace; although if you've seen *Vertigo*, the story itself – of a businessman haunted by guilt about his wife's death, and getting involved years later with her lookalike – will fail to yield the narrative surprises and suspense required in a thriller. GA

Obsession, An (Tsumetai Chi)

(Shinji Aoyama, 1997, Jap) Ryo Ishibashi, Kazuma Suzuki, Kyoko Toyama.
109 min.
Cool, distinctive, borderline pretentious thriller about a cop who loses his gun, a lung, his wife and his grip in a shooting incident. The case itself

is frankly mystifying, but the manner in which the director layers and textures the film is reward in itself, especially the highly expressive use of sound. Not quite in the Takeshi Kitano league, however. TCh

O.C. & Stiggs

(Robert Altman, 1987, US) Daniel H Jenkins, Neill Barry, Paul Dooley, Jane Curtin, Jon Cryer, Ray Walston, Dennis Hopper, Melvin Van Peebles.
109 min.
Altman's one major studio picture between *Popeye* and *The Player* was a complete misfire. As scripted by *National Lampoon*'s Tod Carroll and Ted Mann, it's a peculiarly juvenile foray into teen anarchy, as the two pranksters of the title set about harassing Phoenix, Arizona, in general, and the Schwab family (racist, materialistic, dumb and ugly) in particular. As satire, it falls flat, partly because Altman gets the sub-*Popeye* comic-strip tone all wrong (with the notable exception of Dooley's Randall Schwab), partly because the kids are so snide and smart-ass. Small wonder it only achieved video release. GA

Occasional Work of a Female Slave (Gelegenheitsarbeit einer Sklavin)

(Alexander Kluge, 1973, WGer) Alexandra Kluge, Franz Bronski, Sylvia Gartmann, Traugott Buhre, Ursula Dirichs.
91 min. b/w.
That rarest of movies: a left wing comedy which doesn't hang itself up in questions of 'realism' but does involve itself very closely with the everyday flux of political and social pressures. Alexandra Kluge (the director's sister) plays a young housewife and mother who works as a part-time abortionist; her cynical complacency gives way to a bright-eyed 'activism' when she's forced out of the job and starts waging a one-woman war against the authorities, the bosses, and the tyranny of the family. Kluge charts her hopeless campaign through documentary (an unblinking look at the fact of abortion) and witty fiction alike, his methods recalling both Brecht and Godard; everything is informed by a kind of wry humour that keeps the plot in perspective without tempering its immediacy. It's hard to think of another film that's as honest, relevant and yet not disillusioned as this. TR

Occupation in 26 Pictures, The (Okupacija u 26 Slika)

(Lordan Zafranovic, 1978, Yugo) Frano Lasic, Boris Kralj, Milan Strljic, Stevo Zigon.
116 min.
An exquisitely photographed, excessively 'choreographed' picture-book study of the impact, on three initially gilded youths (Jew, radical and staunch patriot) of Yugoslavia's fascist occupation. It progresses at a dreamlike pace from idyll to nightmare – indeed, to scenes of unwatchably sadistic repression. JD

Occupied Palestine

(David Koff, 1981, US)
86 min.
The opening credit on this documentary reads 'Vanessa Redgrave Productions presents...', but those expecting the cause-mongering propaganda of a crank will be disappointed. For Koff's film does allow the opposition's apologists to defend Israel and Zionism. *Occupied Palestine* has sufficient perspective to be able to see the 'repossession' of land by the Israelis both as a cultural fulfilment of Zionism and as an economic strategy since, as one witness shrewdly observes, 'the separation of the Arab from his land provided a mobile labour force in the service of the Zionist economy'. The catalogue of atrocities attributed to the Israeli army makes it very difficult to dismiss the Palestinian case out of hand. RM

Occupy!

(Gael Dohany, 1976, GB) CG Bond, Allan Dosser, Bernard Dunleavy, Clive Odom.
55 min.
'You can't fight redundancy with strike action. It can't be done'. So the Fisher-Bendix factory workers in Kirkby, near Liverpool, occupied – twice, both times literally chasing management off the premises. Their struggle against a succession of asset-stripping owners, grotesque

mismanagement, and their own gender and occupational divisions, is unusually well portrayed here. Three media are interwoven – the workers' own recollections on film; the Liverpool Everyman's theatrical reconstruction of the work-in; and Granada TV's news footage – enabling the film to avoid the turgidity of British documentary exegesis and to counterpoint different styles of 'reality'. The strategy gives the agitational work an ironical portent, and links it wonderfully well with another Kirkby film, *Behind the Rent Strike*. MM

Ocean's 11
(Lewis Milestone, 1960, US) Frank Sinatra, Dean Martin, Sammy Davis Jr, Peter Lawford, Angie Dickinson, Richard Conte, Cesar Romero, Patrice Wymore, Akim Tamiroff, Henry Silva, Joey Bishop, Ilka Chase.
128 min.
The Rat Pack plus sundry others, playing ex-army buddies, plan a grand heist in Las Vegas, relieving five casinos simultaneously of their loot. The antics of Sinatra & Co (complete with guest spots for the likes of Shirley MacLaine, George Raft and Red Skelton) become rather hard to bear, and the evocation of Las Vegas as a neon nightmare may possibly be unintentional, since the film was made by Sinatra's own company as an extended advertisement for the Clan's shows there. The heist itself, though, is a superb piece of movie-making. ATu

October
see Oktyabr

October Man, The
(Roy Baker, 1947, GB) John Mills, Joan Greenwood, Kay Walsh, Edward Chapman, Joyce Carey, Felix Aylmer, Catherine Lacey, Patrick Holt.
98 min. b/w.
Good old amnesia has another outing, with Mills as a murder suspect none too sure of his own innocence when a model (Walsh) to whom he has lent some money is found strangled, but eventually able to unmask the (glaringly obvious) real killer. Lethargically paced, stiffly adapted by Eric Ambler from his own novel, the film's most attractive features are Joan Greenwood as the girl who believes in our hero, and the setting in a gently decaying hotel. TM

Octopussy
(John Glen, 1983, GB) Roger Moore, Maud Adams, Louis Jourdan, Kristina Wayborn, Kabir Bedi, Steven Berkoff, David Meyer, Anthony Meyer, Vijay Amritraj.
131 min.
This finds Bond on better form than he's been for some time. The action sequences are tighter, the visual gags more inventive, and if the plot is no great shakes, the whole thing is served up with a decent approximation to the old panache. Predictably, the Red Menace is hammered even harder than usual. No mileage in hanging around dreary old East Berlin though, so quick switch to the exotic sunbaked vistas of India, where Maud Adams presides over an international smuggling gang. Hot in pursuit via balloon, folding mini-jet and supercharged rickshaw comes Bond to try to tie up a few plot strands. If age has done nothing to sap Old Moore's ability to emerge shamelessly into close-up once the stunt double has done his stuff, his potency is showing signs of wear and tear with only two cursory scenes *en sack*. He even looks vaguely abashed when Ms Adams calls him a hired assassin. Could Bond finally be falling prey to the superspy's most dreaded malady – introspection? JP

Odd Angry Shot, The
(Tom Jeffrey, 1979, Aust) Graham Kennedy, John Hargreaves, John Jarratt, Bryan Brown, Graeme Blundell, Richard Moir, Ian Gilmore.
92 min.
The odd angry shot was just about all the Aussies managed in their own ignominious Vietnam war adventure. The film's title, though, might as well refer to the barbed sentiments the 'poor bloody infantry' reserve for the local politicos who sent them there and then conveniently forgot them. The movie, like the slim autobiographical novel on which it's closely based, raised something of a ruckus at home.

But away from the controversy, its message of class-conscious disenchantment sits uneasily atop an episodic, post-*M*A*S*H* tragi-comedy featuring everybody's stereotype of the boozy, brawling, macho Aussie group. A brave gesture, maybe (and one in terms of narrative economy from which *Gallipoli* could have learned), but hidebound by its respect for generic clichés. PT

Odd Couple, The
(Gene Saks, 1967, US) Jack Lemmon, Walter Matthau, John Fiedler, Herbert Edelman, Monica Evans, Carole Shelley.
105 min.
An irresistible double act from Lemmon and Matthau as a pair of divorced husbands who set up house together for companionship, and in so doing discover exactly what it was that made them impossible to live with in the first place. Lemmon is the neurotic one who tries to throw himself out of a window but can't get it open, and who clears his sinuses by barking like a seal in the middle of the night; Matthau is the placid slob determined on a good time who can't understand why his flatmate threatens to burst into tears if he suggests a bit of fun and female companionship. Chief bone of contention is the apartment itself, which Matthau likes to keep swilling in a poker-playing atmosphere of ash and empties, while Lemmon rushes home each evening to wield an obsessively fastidious vacuum-cleaner. Saks takes Neil Simon's play pretty much as it comes, but with Lemmon and Matthau to watch, and a generous quota of one-liners, who needs direction? TM

Odd Job, The
(Peter Medak, 1978, GB) Graham Chapman, David Jason, Diana Quick, Simon Williams, Edward Hardwicke, Bill Paterson, Michael Elphick, Richard O'Brien.
87 min.
The preconceptions surrounding the Monty Python team and their particular brand of lunacy do not marry well with this solo venture from Graham Chapman. Playing the straight man Arthur, who hires a bungling odd job man (Jason) to perpetrate his 'suicide', Chapman is in need of an outrageous cast in order to reduce the plot to the level of absurdity that this type of humour demands. From his opposite number Diana Quick (as the wife whose desertion provokes the quest for – and subsequent flight from – suicide), all he gets as a foil is over-dramatic acting without the required degree of parody. Hardly rolling in the aisles stuff, but there are some chuckles. Watch for a brilliant performance from Bill Paterson as Morningside Mull of Scotland Yard, and Richard O'Brien's cameo as a gay/bike leather heavy. FF

Odd Man Out
(Carol Reed, 1947, GB) James Mason, Robert Newton, Robert Beatty, Kathleen Ryan, Cyril Cusack, FJ McCormick, William Hartnell, Fay Compton.
116 min. b/w.
Mason's wounded, haunted, hunted IRA gunman staggers through expressive and suspenseful encounters with the pavement saints, barroom poets and angel artists of the urban landscape of Guinness-soaked legend; through a *noir*-ish, nightmarish purgatory whose heady atmosphere was conjured by Reed out of the (oh so) thin air of British cinema and reconstructed two years later for the better-known *The Third Man*. Based on the novel by FL Green; an eccentric masterpiece. PT

Odds Against Tomorrow
(Robert Wise, 1959, US) Harry Belafonte, Robert Ryan, Shelley Winters, Ed Begley, Gloria Grahame, Will Kuluva.
96 min. b/w.
A taut, downbeat, New York-shot bank heist thriller, with the traditional dishonour among thieves revolving around the openly racial conflict between Ryan and Belafonte. Developed originally by Belafonte's own company after he'd picked up the rights to the William McGivern novel, the script was rewritten at Wise's suggestion to turn around the optimistic 'kin-under-the-skin' conclusion and provide a stunning shootout finale (in which the two corpses, ironically, become indistinguishable). PT

Odessa File, The
(Ronald Neame, 1974, GB/WGer) Jon Voight, Maximilian Schell, Maria Schell, Mary Tamm, Derek Jacobi, Peter Jeffrey, Klaus Löwitsch.
129 min.
Adapted from Frederick Forsyth's bestseller, a straightforward slice of investigative journalism that has Young Germany trying to reconcile itself to the evils of Nazism as Voight hunts down a protected war criminal (Schell) now high up in industry. Voight's performance gives credibility to his character's obsession, but even that cannot overcome the discrepancy between the deeper themes (mass execution and the expiation of guilt) and the routine nature of this piece of box-office action adventure.

Ode to Billy Joe
(Max Baer, 1976, US) Robby Benson, Glynnis O'Connor, Joan Hotchkis, Sandy McPeak, James Best, Terence Goodman.
Based on Bobbie Gentry's caustic pop classic, *Ode to Billy Joe* fleshes out the narrative ambiguities and implications of the song with surprising success. Through sensitive use of some beautiful locations (Tallahatchie Bridge is always central to, but never overwhelms, the proceedings), sympathetic attention to the flavour of the period (like the excited reaction to a first flush toilet), and an unusually sinewy script from Herman Raucher (it only dissolves into slushy Rod McKuen territory towards the close), Baer convincingly depicts the smalltown mores of a Mississippi backwater in the early '50s. Virtually all the performances are winners, but most impressive are the star-crossed teenage lovers, Benson and O'Connor, who catch the joys, fears and fantasies of adolescence with ingenuous authenticity. Only the last half-hour becomes laboured, and in one sequence hideously sentimental, which is not improved by the intrusively slushy score from Michel Legrand. IB

Odette
(Herbert Wilcox, 1950, GB) Anna Neagle, Trevor Howard, Peter Ustinov, Marius Goring, Bernard Lee, Alfred Shieske, Gilles Quéant.
123 min. b/w.
Neagle portraying another Great Lady, this time Odette Churchill, the French wife of an Englishman, who spied for the French Resistance during World War II, was captured and tortured by the Nazis, but survived to be awarded the George Cross. Neagle acquits herself reasonably well, but the whole film is bogged down by a surfeit of respect and patriotism. The kind of film in which you know in advance exactly what will happen next. GA

Odeur de la Papaye Verte, L'
see Scent of Green Papaya, The

Oedipus Rex (Edipo Re)
(Pier Paolo Pasolini, 1967, It) Franco Citti, Silvana Mangano, Carmelo Bene, Julian Beck, Alida Valli, Ninetto Davoli.
104 min.
Pasolini's working of the Sophoclean tragedy, though not wholly successful, has its very definite strengths. Citti's Oedipus is intuitive and primitive rather than intellectual; the myth itself is treated as a dream set in the Moroccan desert in parenthesis between 'Oedipal' scenes in modern Bologna; and visually it's often astonishing, the harsh desert sunlight and dry buildings isolating the characters effectively. RM

Oedipus the King
(Philip Saville, 1967, GB) Christopher Plummer, Lilli Palmer, Richard Johnson, Orson Welles, Cyril Cusack, Roger Livesey, Donald Sutherland, Friedrich Ledebur.
97 min.
Screamingly tedious version of the Sophocles tragedy in which the cast progress from poetic mouthing to ferocious ranting as they shuffle around the ruins of a Greek amphitheatre. Even Welles, looking like Santa Claus on leave from a disreputable department store in woolly wig and sackcloth nightie, seems subdued in his brief appearance as Tiresias. TM

Oeufs de l'Autruche, Les
see Ostrich Has Two Eggs, The

Of a Thousand Delights
see Vaghe Stelle dell'Orsa

Off and Running
(Edward Bianchi, 1991, US) Cyndi Lauper,
David Keith, Johnny Pinto, David Thornton,
Richard Belzer, José Perez, Hazen Gifford.
90 min.
Although not up to the standard of Madonna in
Desperately Seeking Susan, Cyndi Lauper (in
her second feature) isn't bad at playing a version of herself: a tough cookie with a soft centre. Would-be actress Cyd (Lauper) has got as
far as playing a mermaid in a Miami Beach
hotel bar. After witnessing her boyfriend's murder, she hightails it out of town and hooks up
with an unlikely lover (Keith) and a streetwise
kid (Pinto). With the killer on their trail, the mismatched family jumps the Manhattan train for
a predictably madcap adventure. For Lauper
fans only. CO'S

Off Beat
(Michael Dinner, 1986, US) Judge Reinhold,
Meg Tilly, Cleavant Derricks, Joe Mantegna,
Jacques D'Amboise, James Tolkan, Amy
Wright, John Turturro, Anthony Zerbe,
Harvey Keitel, Fred Gwynne, Austin
Pendleton, Penn Jillette, Mark Medoff.
92 min.
Librarian Reinhold (moonlighting for a cop friend)
falls for law-enforcer Tilly in this impossibly mel-
low-yellow comedy: writer Mark Medoff (*Children
of a Lesser God*) turns up as a police sergeant, min-
gling with a first-division supporting cast, which
includes illusionist Penn Jillette. Did they show
Mantegna, Keitel, Gwynne, et al, another script?
TJ

Offence, The
(Sidney Lumet, 1972, GB) Sean Connery,
Trevor Howard, Vivien Merchant, Ian Bannen,
Derek Newark, Peter Bowles, John Hallam.
113 min.
Adaptation of a stage play (*This Story of Yours*)
by John Hopkins (of *Z Cars*). Discreet as it is, the
opening-out process (effected by Hopkins himself)
has sabotaged the strange, claustrophobic duel in
which a suspected child-molester (Bannen) and the
cop obsessively convinced of his guilt (Connery)
find themselves subtly changing places during the
course of interrogation. Embedded in a 'realistic'
police scene, dialogue and situations now have a
ring of arty melodrama. Fascinating, nevertheless,
with outstanding performances from Connery and
(especially) Bannen. TM

Officer and a Gentleman, An
(Taylor Hackford, 1981, US) Richard Gere,
Debra Winger, Louis Gossett Jr, David Keith,
Robert Loggia, Lisa Blount, Lisa Eilbacher.
124 min.
Pace all those swooning fans of gorgeous Gere,
but Hackford's hymn to rampant individualism
in Reagan's America is an exploitative no-no.
While the immaculately garbed and coiffed hero
goes through the paces of training under a sadistic black (natch) sergeant to be a military pilot (we
all find it admirable to want to drop bombs and
kill, don't we?), he discovers that self is the sole
person worth bothering about, and that women
are really only after men for their status and
money. Macho, materialistic, and pro-militarist,
it's an objectionable little number made all the
more insidious by the way Hackford pulls the
strings and turns it into a heart-chilling weepie.
GA

Official Version, The
(La Historia Oficial)
(Luis Puenzo, 1985, Arg) Héctor Alterio,
Norma Aleandro, Chela Ruiz, Chunchuna
Villafañe, Hugo Arana.
115 min.
Alicia (Aleandro) happily disseminates doctored
Argentinian history to her pupils, and dutifully
tolerates a husband who unashamedly boasts of
his entrepreneurial expediency. But the suspicion
begins to grow that her adopted daughter might
be the child of one of 'The Disappeared', which
prompts not only a reappraisal of her non-politi-
cal stance, but also of her marriage. Surprisingly
muted and not without lapses into sentimentality, the result nevertheless packs a massive emotional punch. JP

Off Limits (aka Saigon)
(Christopher Crowe, 1988, US) Willem Dafoe,
Gregory Hines, Fred Ward, Amanda Pays,
Kay Tong Lim, Scott Glenn, David Alan Grier,
Keith David.
102 min.
Not another Vietnam War film but a pacy, violent thriller set in the sleazy red light district of
Saigon in 1968. Two US Army cops (Dafoe and
Hines) think a serial prostitute killer may be one
of their own top brass. A previous investigator
and key witnesses have been frightened into
silence or simply killed off. Backed up by their
staff sergeant (Ward), they whittle the suspects
down to five, but pressure from above squashes
the investigation, forcing them to go it alone.
Later, with the help of a streetwise nun (Pays),
they locate a vital eye-witness who has disappeared into the VC tunnel complex on the outskirts of the city. Like these labyrinthine tunnels,
the plot twists and turns, but Crowe never loses
his sense of direction, sustaining the suspense
and staging the action scenes with admirable
vigour; the result, although the Saigon setting is
simply a seedily exotic backdrop, is an auspicious
first feature. NF

Of Great Events and Ordinary People (De Grands Evénements et des Gens Ordinaires)
(Raúl Ruiz, 1978, Fr)
60 min.
Ruiz has the gaze of an exile and a mind brimming with Cartesian wit. Detached, demanding,
often scintillating, his films are conundrums
without simple answers. But in *Of Great Events*
(which starts out as a documentary on the '78
French presidential elections), Ruiz seems curiously uninterested in the documentary discourse
he uses and confronts. Its meanderings are, none
the less, a pleasing antidote to the moral fervour
of the Griersonian documentary tradition. SH

Of Mice and Men
(Lewis Milestone, 1939, US) Lon Chaney Jr,
Burgess Meredith, Betty Field, Charles
Bickford, Bob Steele, Roman Bohnen, Noah
Beery Jr.
107 min. b/w.
Impressive adaptation of Steinbeck's novel, made
at the same time as *The Grapes of Wrath* (though
released earlier) and matching Ford's harsh lyricism in its evocation of the Depression, the desperation of the migrant farmworkers, their
pipedreams of a little place of their own some day.
Terrific performances mask much of the novel's
naive social philosophy: Chaney as Lenny, the
half-witted gentle giant with a fondness for soft,
furry things and a tendency to pet too hard when
panicked; Field as the bored young farmer's wife
who provokes tragedy by playing the sex kitten;
Meredith as Lenny's friend and minder, who is
forced to turn executioner rather than let society's
notions of justice loose on his charge. TM

Of Mice and Men
(Gary Sinise, 1992, US) John Malkovich, Gary
Sinise, Ray Walston, Casey Siemaszko,
Sherilyn Fenn, John Terry, Joe Morton, Noble
Willingham.
111 min.
Sinise's second crack at directing, with a Horton
Foote adaptation of the John Steinbeck
Depression era novel – about innocently lethal
retard Lennie (Malkovich) and his increasingly
despairing protector George (Sinise) – which
seems doomed to remain a period piece. Big
Lennie likes stroking soft things, and nags
George to describe life on their fantasy farm while
they labour as ranch-hands under the tyrannical
Curly (Siemaszko). Lennie crunches Curly's fist
to pulp in his paw, and over-responds to the
come-ons from Curly's wife (Fenn). It's hard not
to snigger at her arching about and complaining
of the heat, and harder still to believe Malkovich's
shamble and gape, a simian variant on Dustin
Hoffman's Rain Man. Both are strictly Dogpatch
caricatures, while Sinise seems plain vain. BC

O for Oblomov (O wie Oblomov)
(Sebastian C Schroder, 1982, Switz) Erhard
Koren, Olga Strub, Daniel Plancherel,
Sebastian C Schroder.
85 min.
Almost a documentary about a documentary,
which cleverly avoids the tedium often inherent
in film about film and fiction about fiction (the
reference point is Goncharov's novel about a well-
intentioned but slothful Russian nobleman). Two
film crews (documentary and TV live show)
arrive simultaneously to interview a likeable but
pseud eccentric, Niklaus Nepro, whose chaotic
disposition proves infectious: the crews each
shoot each other, the live show disintegrates into
utter muddle. Witty and intelligent, the film
preaches something; but peeling away the fragile layers of irony, sparing no one, it's hard to see
quite what. SFr

Oggi a me...domani a te!
see Today It's Me...Tomorrow You!

Ohayo (Good Morning)
(Yasujiro Ozu, 1959, Jap) Chishu Ryu, Kuniko
Miyake, Yoshiko Kuga, Koji Shidara,
Masahiko Shimazu.
94 min.
An enchanting update of Ozu's own silent *I Was
Born, But...*, dedicated to the proposition that small
talk, however tedious and repetitious, is a necessary lubricant for the wheels of social intercourse.
The setting is a residential suburb of Tokyo, in the
process of transition to Western consumerism,
where two small boys send the entire world to
Coventry because their parents, fearing TV will
breed idiocy (killing the conversation that the boys
cruelly dismiss as small talk), refuse to have a set
in the house. Radiating out from the resulting tensions and resentments in the community comes an
extraordinary cross-section of tragi-comic incident.
An old man gets drunk because he cannot get a
job; a middle-aged man is brought face to face with
his approaching retirement; a young couple are
inspired to declare their love entirely in terms of
the weather; an unwanted grandmother broods
about filial ingratitude; a kindly woman is forced
to move by neighbourly doubts as to her morals.
A brimming sense of life, in other words, gradually transforms the small talk into a richly devious
portrait of humanity being human. TM

Oh! Calcutta!
(Jacques Levy, 1972, US) Raina Barrett, Mark
Dempsey, Samantha Harper, Patricia
Hawkins, Bill Macy, Mitchell McGuire.
100 min.
An unqualified disaster, repudiated by Kenneth
Tynan as a travesty of his censor-challenging
stage revue. Sketches contributed by Jules Feiffer,
John Lennon, Robert Benton and Sam Shepard,
among others, are staged by Levy on a stage, complete with canned audience reactions; and one
watches in bemusement and mounting boredom
as theatrical timing and delivery kill what little wit
there is. Even worse are the 'opened out' passages
where the cast coyly assemble in the nude by a
lake, there to prance amid the pastoral scene. TM

O. Henry's Full House (aka Full House)
(Henry Koster/Henry Hathaway/Jean
Negulesco/Howard Hawks/Henry King, 1952,
US) Charles Laughton, David Wayne, Marilyn
Monroe; Richard Widmark, Dale Robertson;
Anne Baxter, Jean Peters; Fred Allen, Oscar
Levant; Jeanne Crain, Farley Granger.
117 min. b/w.
John Steinbeck, looking and sounding disconcertingly like Ward Bond, hosts five tales by O Henry,
of which only Hathaway's segment is devoid of
interest. Negulesco and King both contribute sentimental valentines in which love transcends the
miseries of illness and poverty respectively. Hawks'
'The Ransom of Red Chief' is about two child-kid-
nappers who end up paying their victim's dad to
take the little horror off their hands. It's noteworthy for the casting of the two most mournful comics
of the day as a double act; and for the fact that the
adventures of such unprofessional no-hopers interested someone like Hawks in the first place. At the
front of the movie, Laughton characteristically generates his own atmosphere of benign fantasy, playing a bum trying to get himself jailed for the winter.
This episode also includes an encounter between
two sacred monsters – Laughton's hobo and
Monroe's hooker meeting on a windy street corner
for a brief demonstration of the virtues of kindli-
ness and respect. BBa

Oh! For a Man

see Will Success Spoil Rock Hunter?

Oh, God!

(Carl Reiner, 1977, US) George Burns, John Denver, Teri Garr, Donald Pleasence, Ralph Bellamy, William Daniels, Barnard Hughes, Paul Sorvino, Barry Sullivan, Dinah Shore.
104 min.
The title's no idle blasphemy, for God really does feature in Reiner's highly bizarre, mostly delightful comedy – and in the avuncular shape of George Burns, too, dressed for the golf course. He appears before supermarket manager Denver (more weird casting), determined to tell mankind that he's still around and watching. The result plays like an over-extended version of the Reiner/Mel Brooks 2000-Year-Old Man sketches, where world history is seen through the eyes of a grouchy Jewish old-timer. So here we have God's views on most things from TV to avocados, all enunciated in Burns' inimitably crisp'n'dry manner. Fun ultimately falters with some routine satire, but when the Devil's having such a time at the box-office, this comes as a welcome comic riposte from the other side. Two indifferent sequels followed: Oh, God! Book II (1980) and Oh, God! You Devil (1984). GB

Oh, Men! Oh, Women!

(Nunnally Johnson, 1957, US) Ginger Rogers, David Niven, Dan Dailey, Barbara Rush, Tony Randall.
90 min.
Oh, crikey! Debonair shrink Niven finds his personal and professional life in a spin when he learns from patient Rogers that his fiancée Rush is carrying on with her movie-star husband Dailey. His feelings of shock and dismay are further compounded when no-hoper Randall announces from the couch that he too is having a much-anticipated fling – also with Rush, of course. Writer/director Johnson's jolly farce isn't what you'd call challenging, but thanks to willing performers it's very light on its feet. Niven's as elegant as ever, Randall's suitably klutzy in his first screen bow. Shot in CinemaScope, because there's a whole lot of reclining going on.

Oh, Mr Porter!

(Marcel Varnel, 1937, GB) Will Hay, Moore Marriott, Graham Moffatt, Dave O'Toole, Dennis Wyndham.
84 min. b/w.
You either love or loathe Will Hay, though this is by far his finest moment and might well convert unbelievers. As the garrulous, officious and totally incompetent station master of the isolated and sleepy Irish village of Buggleskelly, he tries desperately to modernise facilities and meanwhile gets involved with gun-runners. Some of the humour is rather dated now, but the atmospheric creation of a quaintly antiquated rural Britain – that never in reality existed – holds plenty of charm. GA

O.H.M.S.
(aka You're in the Army Now)

(Raoul Walsh, 1937, GB) Wallace Ford, John Mills, Anna Lee, Grace Bradley, Frank Cellier, Frederick Leister.
86 min. b/w.
A brisk Warners-style gangster thriller rapidly turns into a plodding British military drama: Wallace Ford is the American hoodlum who flees the States after being tagged for a murder he didn't commit in a Chinese gambling den. Arriving in Britain, he pretends he's Canadian and enrols in the army. Fresh-faced recruit John Mills becomes his best friend, and they both vie for the attention of the Sgt-Major's daughter. Some neat jokes about the differences between Yank and Limey culture don't atone for all the shots of British military parades and postcard village scenes. Nor does the Boy's Own ending carry anything like the charge of one of director Walsh's Hollywood thrillers. GM

Oh Rosalinda!!

(Michael Powell/Emeric Pressburger, 1955, GB) Anton Walbrook, Michael Redgrave, Anthony Quayle, Ludmilla Tcherina, Dennis Price, Mel Ferrer, Anneliese Rothenberger.
101 min.
'They should have been forcibly suppressed' spluttered one early review of Powell and Pressburger's update of the Strauss operetta Die Fledermaus, set in four-power occupied Vienna; even the title's two exclamation marks betrayed an unseemly excess. The blatant artifice, sugar-candy sets, and preposterous plot, once deplored by the critical establishment, are now cherished by connoisseurs: what better way to pass a disgracefully self-indulgent Sunday afternoon? SJo

Oh! What a Lovely War

(Richard Attenborough, 1969, GB) Joe Melia, Colin Farrell, Paul Shelley, Angela Thorne, Mary Wimbush, Corin Redgrave, Maggie Smith, Michael Redgrave, Laurence Olivier, John Mills, Vanessa Redgrave, Ralph Richardson, John Gielgud, Dirk Bogarde, Kenneth More.
144 min.
Theatre Workshop's play on the excesses and follies of war got misplaced in transition, and producer Len Deighton ended up removing his name from the credits. It remains an often too-clever, sometimes moving piece which never effectively reconciles its lampooning of the World War I General Staff (Haig playing leapfrog; conducting battles from a helter-skelter; losses reflected on cricket scoreboards) with its sincerity towards the salt-of-the-earth working class who were the ones who copped it. Lots of contemporary songs, scores of well-known faces. CPe

Oh, You Beautiful Doll

(John M Stahl, 1949, US) June Haver, Mark Stevens, SZ Sakall, Charlotte Greenwood, Jay C Flippen, Gale Robbins.
93 min.
Purporting to be a biopic of Fred Fisher, composer of such '20s song hits as 'Come Josephine in My Flying Machine' and 'Who Paid the Rent for Mrs Rip Van Winkle', this is a stock Fox musical featuring Cuddles Sakall as a would-be classical composer distressed to have his operatic efforts turned into popular songs. Stahl's last film, it's something of a come-down from the glories of Leave Her to Heaven, made four years earlier; full of charm and attractive touches, all the same. TM

Okaeri

(Makoto Shinozaki, 1995, Jap) Sasuma Terajima, Miho Uemura, Shoichi Komatsu.
99 min.
Shinozaki's debut feature (the deliberately Ozuesque title is the set expression for welcoming someone home) argues speciously that it takes something as grave as a mental crack-up to bring warmth and sincerity into a 'typical' Japanese marriage. Kitazawa is a primary school teacher, an average neglectful husband; his childless wife Yuriko has a part-time job but spends most of her days pining for her lost career as a concert pianist...until she slips into paranoid delusions and starts to behave with alarming oddity. The woman's unexplained lack of relatives or friends to turn to tips you the wink that this version of Japanese home life is phoney from the word go, and the endless elaboration of her schizophrenia is a repellently cruel way of conveying her need for tenderness and love. Pretentious and ugly. TR

O-Kay for Sound

(Marcel Varnel, 1937, GB) Bud Flanagan, Chesney Allen, Jimmy Nervo, Teddy Knox, Charlie Naughton, Jimmy Gold, Graham Moffatt, Fred Duprez, Enid Stamp-Taylor.
85 min. b/w.
The Crazy Gang (street buskers) are signed up as extras for a film, but when they arrive on set in natty pinstripes and bowlers they're mistaken for the financier's emissaries and given control of the production. Chaos ensues plus some of the boys' favourite stage routines. Made in the same year as Oh, Mr Porter!, director Marcel Varnel's best-remembered British picture. TJ

Oklahoma!

(Fred Zinnemann, 1955, US) Gordon MacRae, Shirley Jones, Charlotte Greenwood, Rod Steiger, Gloria Grahame, Eddie Albert, James Whitmore, Gene Nelson.
145 min.
Rodgers and Hammerstein's musical about the growth of love in the farmlands where the corn stands as high as an elephant's eye, transferred to the screen with stolid respect rather than verve. The story's threadbare (and rather overbalanced by Steiger's Method intensity as the sinister Jud), the visual aspects are uninspired; but some of the performances are delightful (notably Gloria Grahame singing 'I Cain't Say No'), and the choreography by Agnes DeMille is suitably ebullient. GA

Oklahoma Crude

(Stanley Kramer, 1973, US) George C Scott, Faye Dunaway, John Mills, Jack Palance, William Lucking, Harvey Jason, Cliff Osmond.
111 min.
Crude oil, that is, with Faye Dunaway back in 1913 – hair dyed black and talking so like Jane Fonda that Kramer could be excused for thinking he had perhaps signed her up – reluctantly allowing Pa John Mills and hobo George C Scott to defend her one oil well against the big and nasty Pan Okie oil company, led by Jack Palance. Dunaway, a rabid man hater, nevertheless determined for some reason to succeed in a man's world, fights them all off with a virginal intensity before implausibly succumbing to Scott's embraces in the face of box-office demands. In spite of a couple of attempts (thanks mainly to the script) to venture outside routine comedy-adventure, things remain hampered by the curious casting, blatant overacting, and Big Country theme music. However if the sight grabs you of Scott delivering the 'message' of the film by literally pissing on Palance, with the news that it's what businessmen do to each other all the time, then this might be your movie. CPe

Oklahoma Woman, The

(Roger Corman, 1956, US) Richard Denning, Peggie Castle, Cathy Downs, Tudor Owen.
72 min. b/w.
Corman made four lively B-Westerns at the start of his career as a producer/director, of which this is probably the best. Peggie Castle, 'queen of the outlaws', stands between reforming ex-con Denning and his dubious past, so Cathy Downs grabs the reins and sets her man back on the straight and narrow. TJ

Okoge

(Takehiro Nakajima, 1992, Jap) Misa Shimizu, Takehiro Murata, Takeo Nakahara, Atsushi Fukazawa.
120 min.
The best of a sudden surge of gay movies from Japan, this second feature by veteran scriptwriter Nakajima is all about compromise and accommodation. Two gay men, with nowhere to go to make love, avail themselves of a bedroom offered by an obliging young woman. But one of them is married with a family, and his vengeful wife tears his secret life to shreds, along with his designer shirts. With its emotional cataclysms, its graphic sex scenes, and its chorus of drag queens, Okoge is one of the year's prime guilty pleasures. TR

Oksutan
(3pm Paradise/Bath House)

(Kwak Kyung-Taek, 1997, SKor)
90 min.
A somewhat tiresome and predictable allegorical 'satire', with representatives of a microcosmic contemporary Korea – a monk, a hood, whores, a politician's wife, a voyeur, a soldier – hanging out at a bath house with lame comic consequences. The humour is generally flabby, the humanism soggy, and the only notable element is the (within limits) frank depiction of human anatomy. GA

Oktyabr (October/Ten Days That Shook the World)

(Sergei Eisenstein/Grigori Alexandrov, 1927, USSR) Vasili Nikandrov, N Popov, Boris Livanov, Eduard Tissé, Nikolai Podvoisky.
9,272 ft. b/w.
Commissioned to celebrate the tenth anniversary of the 1917 revolution, Eisenstein came up not with a rousing spectacle that might please the proletariat, but with an experimental film aimed at exemplifying his theory of 'intellectual montage'. The result, for all its spectacular set pieces (notably the raising of the Petrograd bridges and the storming of the Winter Palace), is sometimes hard to follow, since human actions and motivations tend to be neglected in favour of the overall, rather abstract design of the film, and the

narrative is regularly interrupted by montage shots of metaphorical and symbolic value. As a result, the film remains an interesting oddity rather than entertaining or illuminating. Indeed, watching it today can seem hard work. GA

Old Acquaintance

(Vincent Sherman, 1943, US) Bette Davis, Miriam Hopkins, John Loder, Gig Young, Dolores Moran, Roscoe Karns, Phillip Reed.
110 min. b/w.
Based on a play by John Van Druten, remade by Cukor in 1981 as *Rich and Famous*, this has Davis (sweet) and Hopkins (sour) as two novelists maintaining a professional and personal love-hate rivalry over twenty years. Arrant nonsense, with Davis (though Hopkins is the despicable one who writes for money) living in fabulously opulent circumstances and required to carry her noble self-sacrifice on into the next generation. Sherman and the stars somehow contrive to make it riveting. TM

Old and New

see General Line, The

Old Boyfriends

(Joan Tewkesbury, 1978, US) Talia Shire, Richard Jordan, John Belushi, Keith Carradine, John Houseman, Buck Henry, Bethel Leslie, Joan Hotchkis, Gerrit Graham.
103 min.
First feature for Joan Tewkesbury, an Altman associate who scripted *Thieves Like Us* and *Nashville*. Hesitating between its Old Hollywood ambitions and soap opera climax, it definitively blows a promising road movie story – of fucked-up West Coast psychologist Dianne Cruise (Shire) visiting three old boyfriends on a compulsive trip down memory lane. The failure owes something to slack direction, and probably more to the misogyny of Paul and Leonard Schrader's script, which contrives a distinctly reactionary mix of sentiment, morality, and melodrama. CA

Old Curiosity Shop, The

(Thomas Bentley, 1934, GB) Ben Webster, Elaine Benson, Hay Petrie, Beatrix Thompson, Gibb McLaughlin, Reginald Purdell.
95 min. b/w.
Thomas Bentley built his entire career out of Dickens: prior to 1921, he had filmed *Oliver Twist*, *David Copperfield*, *Hard Times*, *The Pickwick Papers*, and even managed a remake of his 1914 version of *The Old Curiosity Shop*. His third version of the novel, photographed by Claude Friese-Greene (the son of the bankrupted camera inventor) is a lovingly butchered rendition of the story of the moneylender Quilp (Petrie) and the tragic Little Nell (Benson). It's cloyingly sentimental, and in its style still shows the primitive glow of early British movie-making of the 1910s. More of an artifact than an adaptation. ATu

Old Dark House, The

(James Whale, 1932, US) Boris Karloff, Melvyn Douglas, Charles Laughton, Gloria Stuart, Ernest Thesiger, Raymond Massey, Lilian Bond, Eva Moore.
71 min. b/w.
Alongside *The Bride of Frankenstein*, Whale's greatest film, a masterly mixture of macabre humour and effectively gripping suspense. A very simple story – a group of travellers stranded by a storm take shelter in the sinister, unwelcoming Femm household, a gloomy mansion peopled by maniacs and murderers – allows Whale to concentrate on quirky characters (Laughton's brash, boorish Yorkshire mill-owner, blessed with a near-incomprehensible accent, is particularly delightful) and thick Gothic atmosphere to stunning effect. But what is perhaps most remarkable is the way Whale manages to parody the conventions of the dark house horror genre as he creates them, in which respect the film remains entirely modern. GA

Old Dracula

see Vampira

Old Enough

(Marisa Silver, 1983, US) Sarah Boyd, Rainbow Harvest, Neill Barry, Alyssa Milano, Danny Aiello, Susan Kingsley, Roxanne Hart.
92 min.

An exceptional delight, this first feature from Joan Micklin Silver's daughter brings together two girls during a hot New York summer: Lonnie (Boyd), twelve, well-behaved, a little innocent, from a wealthy, sophisticated family; and Karen (Harvest), fourteen, seemingly more mature, sassy in the knowledge of the streets handed down from working class parents and elder brother. Little happens: but with its precise, perceptive observation and performances, and wry, gently ironic humour, the whole thing rings remarkably true. GA

Old-Fashioned Way, The

(William Beaudine, 1934, US) WC Fields, Judith Allen, Joe Morrison, Jan Duggan, Baby LeRoy, Jack Mulhall.
74 min. b/w.
Old-fashioned indeed: this wonderful Fields vehicle, set at the end of the last century, includes the song 'A Little Bit of Heaven Known as Mother' and a performance of the renowned melodrama *The Drunkard*. For all his pose of misanthropy, Fields has a heart as wide as the Grand Canyon, and he poured into this one film all his love for the gaslight era and the vaudeville life. As the Great McGonigle, leader of a travelling theatre troupe, he fights heroically against a sea of troubles, including an interfering sheriff and a doting old ham called Cleopatra Pepperday. Beaudine's direction is on the slow side, but this at least allows the laughs to be fully savoured. GB

Old Flames

(Christopher Morahan, 1989, GB) Simon Callow, Stephen Fry, Miriam Margolyes, Clive Francis.
86 min.
Simon Gray's dark spoof in which sundry fucked-up ex-public school yuppies 'disappear', features those noble stalwarts of the system, Fry and Callow, battling to stop their middle age being wrecked by an old 'Amplesider' with an obscure grudge. Full of the usual social-sexual frumpery that lends itself so admirably to that unremarkable genre of London-based thrillers in which smarmy city types get their comeuppance. Morahan's film, made for the BBC, will no doubt carve some morbid niche for itself on late night television. The moral? Don't lock up a promising violinist in the school music rooms if he's going to turn up 25 years later as an asthmatic, toupee-troubled neurotic by the name of Mr Quass. JCh

Old Gringo

(Luis Puenzo, 1989, US) Jane Fonda, Gregory Peck, Jimmy Smits, Patricio Contreras, Jenny Gago, Gabriela Roel, Sergio Calderon, Pedro Armendariz Jr.
120 min.
Novelist Carlos Fuentes' speculation about what actually befell writer Ambrose Bierce when he joined Pancho Villa's revolution down Mexico way in 1913 makes a fascinating story, rich in character, relationships and cultural clashes. The film, though it doesn't look particularly good and often sounds rather literary, certainly bulges with content, and the principals, Bierce (Peck), middle-aged spinster Harriet Winslow (Fonda) and revolutionary general Arroyo (Smits) grab the dramatic opportunities with both hands. Bierce's predicament, cynical, self-disgusted and seeking a meaningful death, echoes that of the hero in *The Petrified Forest*. In the autumn of his years, he finds a surrogate family, a daughter, and a satisfying quietus. The Fonda part – besides carrying the voice-over – is something of a stereotype, initially brittle and later melted by love. The film can't substantiate its claim to play out the personal drama in terms of this turbulent period of history, but it's a worthy project, and will probably send people back to the book and – even better – to Bierce. BC

Old Lady Who Walked in the Sea, The (La Vieille qui Marchait dans la Mer)

(Laurent Heynemann, 1992, Fr) Jeanne Moreau, Michel Serrault, Luc Thuillier, Géraldine Danon, Jean Bouchaud.
94 min.
Moreau is growing old disgracefully – and clearly enjoying every minute of it. That famously haughty countenance is somewhat weather-beaten now, but the imperious demeanour is still very much intact. As inveterate con-artist and incorrigible jewel thief Lady M, Moreau combines instinctive class with learned disdain for

social convention, elegant diction with a singularly vituperative tongue, rampant egoism with painful infirmity. She enjoys challenging the conceits of the world, she says. Heynemann's mainstream comedy has surprisingly dark undercurrents – it's a caper movie which dares to ebb from time to time. Given her head, Moreau wrings every drop of pathos, pride and passion from the proceedings. Serrault just about holds up his end as her antiquated accomplice Pompilius, but Thuillier is out of his depth as the bronzed toyboy she adopts as her *dauphin*. Fleetingly, Moreau makes you think of an earlier ménage-à-trois, when she consorted with Jules and Jim so happily. But things are more complicated in old age and neither man is really a match for her. TCh

Old Man and the Sea, The

(John Sturges, 1958, US) Spencer Tracy, Felipe Pazos, Harry Bellaver.
86 min.
A painfully sincere, meticulously faithful, and pitifully plodding adaptation of Hemingway's novel about the symbolic struggle between an old Mexican fisherman and a giant marlin. At its most embarrassing in the endless monologues where Tracy has to mouth Hemingway's notion of a poetic patois ('You're a fine fish, Fish, you fight a brave good fight'). The pity of it is that some fine camerawork (from a team that included James Wong Howe and Floyd Crosby) is sabotaged by clumsy back-projection and hideous colour-matching. Hemingway himself can be briefly glimpsed in a bar scene towards the end. TM

Old Well (Lao Jing)

(Wu Tianming, 1987, China) Zhang Yimou, Liang Yujin, Xie Yan, Lu Liping.
130 min.
This chronicles decades of ill-fated attempts to dig for water in an arid village in the Taihang mountains, and like some Chinese answer to *Padre Padrone*, tells the story of the village's first college graduate and his struggle to bring a measure of rationality to a bizarre and backward community. The result is not the standard tract on Third World problems, but a quite remarkable warts-and-all portrait of the strengths and weaknesses of the Chinese people, shot through with memorable characters and moments of heart-stopping intensity. At its core is a stunning performance from first-time actor Zhang Yimou, the brilliant young cinematographer of *Yellow Earth*. TR

Oleanna

(David Mamet, 1994, US/GB) William H Macy, Debra Eisenstadt.
89 min.
Mamet's film of his controversial play sensibly resists the temptation to 'open out' the material for the screen; it stays a two-hander and the focus remains on the switchback of argument and counter-argument. Macy's slightly pompous college professor accused by angry student Eisenstadt of sexual misconduct, yet the issue is directed less toward the actual physical detail of the incident, rounding more on the whole male/female nexus of elitism, authority and power that's almost a given in our everyday experiences. Are the conventions of social interaction harmless, or are they to be picked apart by the revisionist ethics of political correctness? Mamet shows both sides of the coin and allows the audience to continue to argue it out among themselves – which they did, frequently, in theatre foyers. Expect this straightforward, compelling adaptation to provoke just the same level of domestic debate. As ever, the writing is rich, flexible, masterly. TJ

Oliver!

(Carol Reed, 1968, GB) Ron Moody, Shani Wallis, Oliver Reed, Harry Secombe, Hugh Griffith, Jack Wild, Clive Moss, Mark Lester, Peggy Mount, Leonard Rossiter.
146 min.
From *The Third Man* to *Oliver!* is a pretty vertiginous collapse, even for twenty years in the British film industry. Reed is craftsman enough to make an efficient family entertainment out of Lionel Bart's musical, but not artist enough to put back any of Dickens' teeth which Bart had so assiduously drawn. SG

Oliver & Company

(George Scribner, 1988, US) voices: Joey Lawrence, Billy Joel, Cheech Marin, Richard Mulligan, Roscoe Lee Browne, Sheryl Lee Ralph, Dom DeLuise, Taurean Blacque, Robert Loggia, Bette Midler.
74 min.

This animation feature from Disney is a bestial rehash of *Oliver Twist*, wherein cute kitten Ollie, abandoned in New York, falls into 'baaaad' (ie. good) canine company. Swindled out of a meal by streetwise hound Dodger, our hero asserts his virility by debunking the rogue mutt in front of his comrades. Accepted as 'one of the boys', Ollie is sent out with his new chums as they scavenge for pickings with which their amiable master Fagin can pay off a debt to fiendish Mr Sykes. Much cornball adventure ensues, punctuated by healthy helpings of singing, dancing and general merriment. Billy Joel provides the voice of Dodger, and despite having made some unpleasant records, turns in a few tolerable foot-tapping numbers. Midler's larynx is its usual gargantuan self, handling the steamy vocal chores for pampered pooch Georgette, but top marks go to Cheech Marin as Tito, the diminutive chihuahua with a man-sized ego who wins Georgette's heart by challenging everything that moves to a fight. MK

Oliver's Story

(John Korty, 1978, US) Ryan O'Neal, Candice Bergen, Nicola Pagett, Edward Binns, Benson Fong, Charles Haid, Kenneth McMillan, Ray Milland, Josef Sommer, Sully Boyar, Swoosie Kurtz.
90 min.

It's been a whole 18 months since Jenny's death (nearer 8 years for the paying public). A decent enough period for mourning, but now Oliver must 'get out and meet people'. Equally manipulative in its intentions, the sequel to *Love Story* is less *Oliver's Story* than a neo-conservative tribute to 'life involvement'. 'Tangible incentive' murmurs his therapist when O'Neal's permanent angst at last fetches up against Candice Bergen (beautiful...liberated...rich), and his musings turn once more to love and exploitation. As far as it goes, all perfectly competently handled, aside from the occasional masochistic hilarity ('Is that how you know it's good? When it hurts?'). What really hurts is that the prodigal's final return to his father's wealth and business is seen as more life-enhancing than his community law practice. CPea

Oliver Twist

(David Lean, 1948, GB) John Howard Davies, Alec Guinness, Robert Newton, Kay Walsh, Francis L Sullivan, Henry Stephenson, Mary Clare, Anthony Newley, Kathleen Harrison, Diana Dors.
116 min. b/w.

Lean's second Dickens adaptation, perhaps marginally less beguiling than *Great Expectations*, but still a moving and enjoyable account of Dickens' masterpiece, which gets off to a memorable start with Oliver's pregnant mother battling through the storm to reach the safety of the workhouse. The film tellingly recreates the horrors of Victorian slum life (the attractive if artificial sets atmospherically lit and shot by Guy Green), and is particularly noteworthy for Guinness' striking Fagin.

Oliver Twist

(Clive Donner, 1982, GB) George C Scott, Tim Curry, Michael Hordern, Timothy West, Eileen Atkins, Cherie Lunghi, Oliver Cotton, Richard Charles, Martin Tempest.
102 min.

Yet another helping of *Oliver Twist*, all too clearly showing its TV origins? What the Dickens could it possibly have to offer that Lean's 1948 version or Reed's all-singing, all-dancing *Oliver!* haven't already given us? Not a lot, unless it's a timely illustration of the Return to Victorian Values that everyone's going on about. (Gin at a penny a pint? We should be so lucky). George C Scott, as Fagin, gives an interesting new transatlantic flavour to the proceedings, but otherwise fails to generate anything other than total disbelief. A dollop of dirt on the face of some precocious brat does not make for a really convincing waif; and an *Oliver Twist* that leaves one sympathising with Bill Sykes must surely have taken a wrong turning somewhere. AB

Olivia

(Jacqueline Audry, 1950, Fr) Edwige Feuillère, Simone Simon, Claire Olivia, Yvonne de Bray, Suzanne Dehelly, Marina de Berg.
96 min. b/w.

Based on the novel by Dorothy Bussy (originally published pseudonymously), *Olivia* is set in a French girls' boarding school late in the 19th century, and deals with suppressed love, idolatry and inner conflict, a million miles away from infantile crushes on 'Miss'. Perhaps a little long, it narrowly misses being maudlin and hammy thanks to the performance by Edwige Feuillère as the charismatic head teacher, Mademoiselle Julie, on whom Olivia more than dotes. Although the main theme is self-control and self-will, references and innuendoes point to lesbian love, and it's not hard to imagine that in the '50s the censors' eyebrows would have shot up (eleven minutes were in fact cut on its first release in this country). Today it seems perfect viewing for a quiet Sunday afternoon. LS

Olivier Olivier

(Agnieszka Holland, 1991, Fr) François Cluzet, Brigitte Roüan, Jean-François Stévenin, Grégoire Colin, Marina Golovine, Frédéric Quiring.
109 min.

Olivier, the coddled nine-year-old son of a provincial French family, disappears; and despite the promises of a well-meaning police inspector (Stévenin), fails to reappear. The loss breaks up his already tension-torn family – older sister Nadine, vet father (Cluzet) and over-protective mother (Roüan) – and in a storm of recriminations, Papa hightails it to Africa. Then, six years later, the unthinkable happens... Based, unimaginably, on a true story, the film begins with a picture of rural bliss, but then turns the conventions upside-down. Six years on, the drama focuses on the older Nadine (a sensitive, fiery performance by Golovine) and the young seed of discord who enters the family nest, played with disarming charisma by Colin. Cluzet, Roüan and Stévenin are excellent too. Part intimate melodrama, part mystery story, the film delves with confidence into some dark areas, and takes the scalpel to the nuclear family as pitilessly as anything since Bergman's heyday. JRo

O Lucky Man!

(Lindsay Anderson, 1973, GB) Malcolm McDowell, Ralph Richardson, Rachel Roberts, Arthur Lowe, Helen Mirren, Mona Washbourne, Dandy Nichols, Graham Crowden, Peter Jeffrey, Anthony Nicholls.
174 min.

A modern *Pilgrim's Progress*, with Malcolm McDowell (reprising the name, if not the character, of the hero of *If...*) as the young man in search of fame and the better things of life, *O Lucky Man!* is a disappointment. Lacking the specificity of either *If...* or *This Sporting Life*, it's an undisciplined (at nearly three hours long) humanist shriek of anger at what 'They' are doing to 'Us', lashing out wildly without purpose. The result is a film that approaches its material not in the manner of a Swift or an Orwell, but as the *Carry On* team might under the temporary influence of surrealism. In short, all puff and no thought. None the less interesting, with Alan Price's songs punctuating and informing the film's episodic action. PH

Olvidados, Los
(The Young and the Damned)

(Luis Buñuel, 1950, Mex) Alfonso Mejía, Roberto Cobo, Estela Inda, Miguel Inclán, Alma Delia Fuentes.
88 min. b/w.

Buñuel's return to the public eye after nearly 20 years in the critical wilderness came with this superbly caustic account of poverty, delinquency and crime in the slums of Mexico City. Basically he took a then popular genre, a major force in both Hollywood and Italian neo-realism – the liberal social conscience picture – and transformed it into a brilliantly acidic vision of human desires, fears and foibles. The story concerns the tragedies that befall a couple of members of a violent gang of kids who go round mugging, robbing and generally inflicting cruelty on everyone around them. But Buñuel, unlike his peers, is not content to lay all the blame for their acts and predicament on an abstract society: individuals

also have inner motivations. Thus there is a poetic and precise emphasis on dreams and sexuality, and characters are far from being stereotypes: a blind man, frequently tormented by the kids, can hardly arouse our pity when Buñuel also shows him to be a hypocrite and a paedophile. A wonderfully lucid film that refuses to allow us to indulge in blinkered sentimentality or narrow ideology. GA

Olympische Spiele 1936 (Olympiad)

(Leni Riefenstahl, 1938, Ger).
118 min (Part I)/107 min (Part II). b/w.

Masterwork – or vicious propaganda for the master race? Riefenstahl's films haunt the liberal imagination and its belief in the ennobling function of Art. Orchestrated like *Triumph of the Will* around a historical mass gathering, this record of the 1936 Berlin Olympics is another display of epic showmanship, where documentary information is placed a very poor second to sheerly spectacular effects. Here, though, the human body is eroticised in a paean to physical beauty that suggests how compatible fetishism and fascism can be. SJo

Ombre du Doute, L' (A Shadow of Doubt)

(Aline Issermann, 1992, Fr) Mireille Perrier, Alain Bashung, Sandrine Blancke, Emmanuelle Riva, Michel Aumont, Roland Bertin, Thierry Lhermitte, Josiane Balasko.
106 min.

Questioned by a teacher over her tendency to rewrite fairy-tales with unhappy endings, 12-year-old Alexandrine (Blancke) timidly admits that her father Jean (Bashung) has been sexually abusing her. Unsurprisingly, he denies the accusation, rightly confident that, like the sceptical legal authorities, his wife Marie (Perrier) will believe him rather than her daughter. Nevertheless, social worker Sophia (Balasko) feels sure the girl isn't lying or even the victim of an over-ripe imagination, and goes ahead with the investigation...Happily resorting neither to stale Hollywood-style homily, nor to the dour grainy 'realism' of most British social-problem movies, this fictional case-study blends a cool, almost scientifically objective approach to a notoriously difficult issue with a visual and narrative style that's distinctly poetic. Crucially, writer/director Issermann avoids sensationalism and sentimentality, allowing for a dramatic balance that's enhanced by the uniform excellence of the performances. Tough, intelligent, compelling and – remarkably – not at all grim. GA

Omega Connection, The

see London Connection, The

Omega Man, The

(Boris Sagal, 1971, US) Charlton Heston, Anthony Zerbe, Rosalind Cash, Paul Koslo, Lincoln Kilpatrick, Eric Laneuville.
98 min.

This second screen adaptation of Richard Matheson's classic sci-fi novel *I Am Legend* (the first was *The Last Man on Earth*, 1964) still doesn't succeed in conveying the exultant paranoia of its original as effectively as (for example) *Night of the Living Dead*. In Matheson's story, the last man on earth was besieged by vast numbers of vampires, the victims of an apocalyptic plague; but this version substitutes a few albino mutants for the vampires, and reduces the original's brilliant cross-fertilisation of Gothic myth and doomsday fantasy to an averagely competent exercise in comic strip sci-fi. DP

Omen, The

(Richard Donner, 1976, USA) Gregory Peck, Lee Remick, David Warner, Billie Whitelaw, Harvey Stephens, Leo McKern, Patrick Troughton.
111 min.

Although this tale of a satanic child was as successful at the box-office as *The Exorcist*, there's not a drop of green vomit in sight. Instead, this apocalyptic movie mostly avoids physical gore to boost its relatively unoriginal storyline with suspense, some excellent acting (especially from Warner and Whitelaw), and a very deft, incident-packed script. There is not a single original theme in *The Omen*, but its makers are so resolute in avoiding padding, and so deceptively accomplished in their use of emotional triggers, that you come out wondering how the film succeeds so well. The secret lies partly in the hermetically tight construction which, among other things, veers the action to a spooky chase across Europe just when other horror movies are getting bogged down in what dumb effect to produce next. DP

Omen IV: The Awakening

(Jorge Montesi/Dominique Othenin-Girard, 1991, US) Faye Grant, Michael Woods, Michael Lerner, Madison Mason, Ann Hearn, Jim Byrnes, Asia Vieira.
97 min.
'You have won... *nothing!*' gurgled Antichrist Damien Thorn ten years ago, as he expired at the feet of a gigantic Jesus in *The Final Conflict*. No idle threat, for Damien had a child (surprise!) in whose hands rests the future of evil. Adopted by a rising statesman and his twitchy wife, young Delia is soon enjoying all the fiendish fun befitting the devil's daughter (throwing nannies out of windows, etc). Directed in workaday fashion by Montesi (who was dragged in to sort out the mess made by Othenin-Girard), this misguided TV mini-series turned big-screen blow-out boasts the silliest script since *Exorcist II: The Heretic*. 'I couldn't believe we had two strange deaths in one day,' mumbles Mom with completely straight face, before launching into yet another tiresome tirade about the apocalypse, intercut with baffling footage of ex-nuns frolicking with live snakes. MK

On a Clear Day You Can See Forever

(Vincente Minnelli, 1970, US) Barbra Streisand, Yves Montand, Bob Newhart, Larry Blyden, Simon Oakland, Jack Nicholson, John Richardson, Pamela Brown, Irene Handl, Roy Kinnear.
130 min.
Fashioned from a Broadway half-success of 1965, this can be strongly recommended to all who like curate's eggs, good tunes, and nice colours. On the surface, Alan Jay Lerner's libretto could have been made to measure for Minnelli, with its emphasis on lavish imagined worlds juxtaposed with reality (under hypnosis a Brooklyn girl reveals a past life as a Regency dazzler called Melinda – and guess who the hypnotist falls in love with?). And Minnelli is able to decorate his material with beguiling visual conceits – the opening time-lapse photography, the colour contrasts between past and present. But he can do nothing to combat the script's length and shallowness, and there are some thumb-twiddling moments in between Burton Lane's delightful songs. The two star performers make an odd team, with their varying kinds of professionalism and vowel sounds. GB

On Any Sunday

(Bruce Brown, 1971, US) Mert Lawwill, Steve McQueen, Malcolm Smith, Bruce Brown.
91 min.
A bike movie with a difference: no Hell's Angels, no sex, no drugs. Instead, director/ producer/narrator/writer Brown (who made the surfing documentary *The Endless Summer*) has come up with a feature-length commercial for good, clean motorcycling fun depicting just about every conceivable permutation of motorised two-wheel sport from ice-racing, enduro, moto-cross and road racing to the spectacular, crash-ridden American speciality, dirt-track racing. Spending some time following the progress of Mert Lawwill, one of America's top dirt-trackers, the film also has considerable footage of Steve McQueen playing at moto-cross and desert racing. It abounds with intelligently applied stop-frame, slow motion and colour treatment knick-knacks which heighten the excitement and visual impact. Though a schlocky Country 'n' Western soundtrack and over-simplistic narration irritate after a while, this is an imposing essay compared to which the outlaw biker pics are tame travesties of what the two-wheel trip's all about. MW

On Approval

(Clive Brook, 1944, GB) Clive Brook, Beatrice Lillie, Roland Culver, Googie Withers, OB Clarence, Hay Petrie.
80 min. b/w.
Though plays dealing with the amorous and other vagaries of the idle rich may no longer dom-

inate the West End stage, the species is by no means extinct, and with this version of Frederick Lonsdale's hit of the '20s we have a good opportunity to examine the animal. Brook plays a penurious duke wooing an American pickle heiress (Withers), but – after a twin 'trial marriage' on a remote Scottish island – being rejected in favour of his dog-eared companion (Culver) and ending up with Beatrice Lillie, whose selfish cynicism dwarfs even his own. Though Brook's deliberately 'cinematic' approach was highly praised at the time (according to Lindsay Anderson it was 'the funniest British comedy ever made'), it is the performances, Lonsdale's deft craftsmanship, and the presence of the semi-mythical Lillie which now holds interest. RMy

On Boys, Girls and the Veil (Sobyan Wa Banat)

(Yousry Nasrallah, 1995, Egypt) Bessem Saura.
72 min.
This documentary on contemporary attitudes to the wearing of the *hijab* (the veil) among Egypt's youth seems deceptively simple at first: he follows Bessem Saura, a 24-year-old teacher and would-be actor, as he chats to friends, family and colleagues about their lives. However these relaxed discussions constantly throw up fragments of historical, social, and political information which gradually fit together to present an image of a non-fundamentalist Islamic society which undermines and challenges many of the assumptions too easily vocalised in the West. Not only that, but the interaction between the members of the Saura family provides a wonderfully engrossing central narrative. FM

Once a Jolly Swagman (aka Maniacs on Wheels)

(Jack Lee, 1948, GB) Dirk Bogarde, Renee Asherson, Moira Lister, Bill Owen, Bonar Colleano, Thora Hird, James Hayter, Patric Doonan, Cyril Cusack, Sidney James.
100 min. b/w.
In America, in anticipation of Roger Corman, this twee little film was called *Maniacs on Wheels*. Bogarde plays a factory worker who becomes a speedway star. His Aussie mate (Owen) flies off the handlebars and suffers brain damage (hence the original title). But this does not deter Dirk from racing – and enlisting for WWII – while fiancée Renee Asherson gets all worried for his safety. ATu

Once Around

(Lasse Hallström, 1991, US) Holly Hunter, Richard Dreyfuss, Danny Aiello, Laura San Giacomo, Gena Rowlands, Roxanne Hart, Danton Stone, Tim Guinee, Griffin Dunne.
115 min.
Hallström's first Hollywood feature went belly-up at the US box office (it opened the weekend the Gulf War erupted) and emerged gingerly on video in Britain, but this rather overbearing romantic comedy is by no means a disaster. Hunter's the inexperienced heroine who travels to the Caribbean for a much-needed break after being dumped by her boyfriend, but the rebound brings brash salesman Dreyfuss her way, sweeping her off her feet and soon causing a deep rift with her close-knit family. Dreyfuss is even more obnoxious here than he was in *Tin Men*, but intentionally so, his eagerness to please driving everyone but Hunter nuts. TJ

Once a Thief (Zongheng Sihai)

(John Woo, 1991, HK) Chow Yun Fat, Leslie Cheung.
104 min.
Lighter in tone than most Woo thrillers, this begins – disconcertingly – far away from the mean streets of Hong Kong as three master thieves plan to steal a Modigliani masterpiece outside Paris. The opening stunt, involving car, motorcycle and parachute, is slickly handled but bloodless. Only when the thieves become involved in an epic seafront shoot-out does Woo really get into his customary kinetic groove. Back in Hong Kong, the pace quickens, but the attempt to combine comedy with hardboiled action doesn't convince. Nor do the director's usual musings on friendship and family loyalty carry much resonance. GM

Once in Paris...

(Frank D Gilroy, 1978, US) Wayne Rogers, Gayle Hunnicutt, Jack Lenoir, Clément Harari, Tanya Lopert, Doris Roberts.
100 min.
No more and no less than a tale of American-alone-in-Paris seducing the lady in the hotel room next door. All the ritual stages of courtship are trotted out, on down to a bitter-sweet parting. A certain gay undertone in the subplot (concerning the roguish chauffeur who comes between them) does little to rescue the film from being absolutely average. CPea

Once Is Not Enough

see Jacqueline Susann's Once Is Not Enough

Once There Was a War (Der var engang en Krig)

(Palle Kjaerulff-Schmidt, 1966, Den) Ole Busck, Yvonne Ingdal, Kjeld Jacobsen, Astrid Villaume, Katja Miehe Renard.
94 min. b/w.
A calm, doggily funny study of a young boy growing up in the suburbs of Copenhagen during WWII. In this child's eye view of war, there is scarcely a German to be seen, except for the odd embarrassed sentry, considered as fair game for mockery. RAF bombers fly overhead, eagerly watched because they drop mysterious strips of tinfoil, to be collected and hoarded away as treasures. Adults, huddled in corners muttering about the Gestapo, impinge chiefly as nuisances because they worry, they forbid excursions. There are airy fantasies of heroism ('Hello, Winston' begins his report to London, 'it's me'), and occasional nightmares in which his family is tortured to death. Mostly, though, he is too busy poring over dirty books and worrying about girls to think too much about the war. Beautifully shot on location in soft, naturalistic tones, with witty high-contrast lighting for the fantasy sequences, it's a strangely haunted and haunting film, all the more effective for its insouciant air of being miles removed from the realities of war. TM

Once Upon a Forest

(Charles Grosvenor, 1992, US) voices: Michael Crawford, Ben Vereen, Ellen Blain.
71 min.
Toxic gas contaminates an idyllic wood. Three youngsters – woodmouse, mole and hedgehog – seek a rare herbal remedy for their irradiated badger friend. Sage Cornelius (Crawford) watches over the sick infant. Eco-friendly animated co-production between Hanna-Barbera and HTV Cymru/Wales which makes one long for animals whacking each other with sticks of dynamite. MK

Once Upon a Honeymoon

(Leo McCarey, 1942, US) Ginger Rogers, Cary Grant, Walter Slezak, Albert Dekker, Albert Basserman.
117 min. b/w.
The year is 1938, the setting a beleaguered Europe in which Cary Grant plays roving radio reporter to Ginger Rogers' Bronx-born golddigger (with Viennese baron Slezak for a husband). A nonsense plot and bizarre soundtrack (continuous waltzes) can't disguise the fact that this is really three movies in one (love story, spy drama, anti-Nazi polemic), but the whole thing is saved by its irreverence, mixing the romance (and newsreel footage) with moments of outrageously tasteless kitsch: Rogers' Nazi husband cutting up a cake-map of Czechoslovakia, clocks with swastika hands. Splendid, eccentric tragi-comedy. And the erotic undertow of the Grant-Rogers partnership is just incredible. CA

Once Upon a Time

(Alexander Hall, 1944, US) Cary Grant, Janet Blair, James Gleason, Ted Donaldson, William Demarest, Howard Freeman, Art Baker.
89 min. b/w.
Light-hearted Hollywood fairytale (adapted from Norman Corwin's radio play *My Client Curley*) has Broadway producer Grant looking for new talent after mounting three flops in a row, and hitting pay-dirt with young Donaldson's dancing catterpillar, a remarkable creature that performs only to 'Yes Sir, That's My Baby' on the harmonica. Success beckons, a deal with Disney is struck...and then our many-legged friend vanishes without trace. That's showbiz, huh? TJ

Once Upon a Time in America (100)

(Sergio Leone, 1983, US) Robert De Niro, James Woods, Elizabeth McGovern, Treat Williams, Tuesday Weld, Burt Young, Joe Pesci, Danny Aiello.
229 min.
In 1968, Noodles (De Niro) returns to New York an old man after 35 years of exile, ridden by guilt. His cross-cut memories of the Jewish Mafia's coming of age on the Lower East Side in 1923, their rise to wealth during Prohibition, and their *Götterdämmerung* in 1933, provide the epic background to a story of friendship and betrayal, love and death. While Leone's vision still has a magnificent sweep, the film finally subsides to an emotional core that is sombre, even elegiac, and which centres on a man who is bent and broken by time, and finally left with nothing but an impotent sadness. CPea

Once Upon a Time in China (Huang Feihong)

(Tsui Hark, 1991, HK) Jet Li, Yuen Biao, Jacky Cheung.
135 min.
Tsui Hark has been trawling his childhood memories of Hong Kong for years, looking for stories to remake and heroes to revive, and this is his most impressive catch to date. It brings back one of South China's perennial favourites, martial artist and bone-setter Wong Fei Hung, and imagines him as a young man in 1875, battling renegade Chinese in cahoots with the unscrupulous British. Tsui spends far too much time trying to freshen up the mythology surrounding the character (he has a rather tiresome stable of disciples); as usual, he comes into his own in the action set pieces, especially a fight atop flailing ladders. Underlying it all is a Peckinpah-esque lament for dying traditions and values, but its real strengths are its choreography, its flashes of wit, and its all-round exuberance. TR

Once Upon a Time in China II (Huang Feihong zhi Er: Nan'r Dang Zi Qiang)

(Tsui Hark, 1992, HK) Jet Li, Rosemond Kwan, Max Mok, Zhang Tielin, David Chiang.
123 min.
Episode Two in Tsui Hark's project to do for late 19th century China what Sergio Leone did for the American West is a blast. This is the best action-adventure-comedy that Tsui has ever made, hence one of the year's most exhilarating entertainments. Young hero Wong Fei Hung travels from Hong Kong to Guangzhou in 1895 to attend a medical conference, and finds himself caught between Sun Yat-Sen's struggle to overthrow imperial rule and the hysterical xenophobia of the White Lotus Clan, a mystical 'boxer' sect. The entire film is a riff on East-West relations, and it implicitly questions China's present-day political competence and stability, but choreographer Yuen Woo-Ping's action set pieces are its true *raison d'être*. TR

Once Upon a Time in the West (C'era una Volta il West) 100 (100)

(Sergio Leone, 1968, It) Henry Fonda, Claudia Cardinale, Jason Robards, Charles Bronson, Frank Wolff, Gabriele Ferzetti, Keenan Wynn, Paolo Stoppa, Lionel Stander, Jack Elam, Woody Strode.
165 min.
The Western is dead, they tell us. Long live Leone's timeless monument to the death of the West itself, rivalled only by Peckinpah's *Pat Garrett and Billy the Kid* for the title of best ever made. We're talking favourite films here, so only superlatives will do. Worth starting at the beginning: a stakeout at a deserted station, Jack Elam and a fly – the most audacious credit sequence in film history. A soundtrack never bettered by any Dolby knob-twiddlers – unnatural sounds of 'silence' and Morricone's greatest score, handing Bronson his identity with a plangent, shivery harmonica riff, carrying Leone's crane shots upwards over a railhead township, clip-clopping Robards into the rigorous good/bad/ugly schema. Countercasting (sadist Fonda) and location choice (Monument Valley) that render an iconic base for Leone and collaborators

(Bertolucci and Argento, no less) to perform their revisionist/revolutionary critique of the Classic American (ie. Fordian) Creation Myth. And more, too. Critical tools needed are eyes and ears – this is Cinema. PT

Once Upon a Time in Triad Society (Wangjiao Cha-fit-ren)

(Cha Chuen-Yee, 1996, HK) Francis Ng, Lee Lai-Chun, So Chi-Wai, Allen Ting, Chan Wai-Man, Pauline Chan.
92 min.
Knocked off in ten days by an ex-TV director with nine previous quickies to his credit, this is a spirited and remarkably witty demolition of the myth of 'righteousness' in triad gangs as expressed in the hit *Young and Dangerous* series. Kwan (Francis Ng, villain in the first *Young and Dangerous* movie) is a housing estate kid who sets out to become 'the worst guy in triad society' after suffering a series of let-downs, betrayals and beatings. Director Cha provides alternative versions of his story (one Kwan's idealised fantasy, the other supposedly real), but both are full of parodies of other movies and cynical subversions of cops-and-robbers conventions. Pitched somewhere between Monty Python and Roger Corman, this shows what can be achieved by a film-maker with more talent than money. TR

Once Upon a Time in Triad Society 2 (Qu ba! Cha-fit-ren Bingtuan)

(Cha Chuen-Yee, 1996, HK) Francis Ng, Roy Cheung, Cheung Tat-Ming, Ada Choi.
92 min.
Less a sequel – it has the same director, writer and star as the first movie, but new characters and an unrelated storyline – than an even more inventive follow-up. This time Ng plays a compulsive gambler and congenital coward; unluckily for him, his need to present a macho front wins him a starring role in a battle to save control of Mongkok from a marauding Mainland China gang. His bathetic exploits (mostly with a gay prostitute friend getting in the way) are intercut with the lives of a tough-but-sensitive triad footsoldier (Roy Cheung) and an out-of-his-depth cop (Cheung Tat-Ming) whose pregnant wife goes shopping in the wrong place at the wrong time. Funny, emotive and really quite exciting, this was one of the best Hong Kong movies of its year. TR

Once Upon a Time – the Revolution

see Giù la Testa

Once Upon a Time...This Morning (Kala Krangnung Mua Shao Ni)

(Bhandit Rittakol, 1994, Thai) Santisuk Promsiri, Jintara Sukkapat, Ronnarong Buranat, Martang Jantranee.
35 min.
Ex-critic and screenwriter Bhandit Rittakol updates a Thai fairy tale about a family in peril into the terms of a mid-1990s thriller. Mum and Dad are divorced and the three kids (much to their disgust) live with Mum in her new Bangkok apartment. After one of their frequent rows with Mum, the kids run away to look for Dad – unaware that the baby's cot contains a bag of pure heroin hidden there by a kid courier on the run. Cue an extended chase in which the fast-learning kids are pursued by both their distraught parents, the police and the drug lords and their hired street kids. A lot happens on the way to the admirably unsentimental climax, much of it genuinely gripping. TR

Once Upon a Time...When We Were Colored

(Tim Reid, 1996, US) Al Freeman Jr, Phylicia Rashad, Paula Kelly, Leon, Richard Roundtree, Salli Richardson, Isaac Hayes, Polly Bergen.
111 min.
This adaptation of Clifton Taulbert's novel details a young boy's post-WW2 rites of passage in the segregated Mississippi Delta. Basically anecdotal – the Joe Louis title defeat; the 'ice wars' as the NAACP campaign began to bite – it celebrates a community who were 'never beat down',

surviving days in the cotton fields on a diet of pride, resolution, family and community solidarity and sweet potato pie. The period reconstruction is flawless, the camerawork glowing, and the affirmation of the progressive role of education effulgent and endearing. WH

Once Were Warriors

(Lee Tamahori, 1993, NZ) Rena Owen, Temuera Morrison, Mamaengaroa Kerr-Bell, Julian Arahanga.
99 min.
An emotionally raw, visually stylish first feature, with the intensity of the best social melodrama, about the indomitable spirit of battered Maori wife Beth Heke (Owen) as she struggles to hold together her disintegrating family. Husband Jake (Morrison) is a violent yet charismatic bully, the sullen eldest son is already a gang member, the youngest is in care, and only gifted daughter Grace (Kerr-Bell) offers hope for the future. A gritty human drama evoking the residual vibrancy of a threatened culture. NF

On Company Business

(Allan Francovich, 1980, US) Phillip Agee, James Wilcott, William Colby, Victor Marchetti.
180 min.
Francovich's three-hour documentary on the CIA may seem a daunting prospect, but don't be put off: it's an exemplary piece of documentary construction which makes full use of archive material and rarely loses its sense of pace or humour. The film's real strength lies in its interviews with CIA personnel and ex-personnel – from bureau chiefs to mercenaries – who behave increasingly like the cast of a Hollywood film about the CIA. It's frightening on several counts: the openness of those involved in naked political aggression and interference, and the overwhelming feeling that everyone interviewed is telling only part of the truth. An indictment of American foreign policy, of several administrations, and of an entire social structure, the film also raises the interesting speculation that a similar examination would never be possible in this country. SM

On connaît la chanson

see Same Old Song

On Dangerous Ground

(Nicholas Ray, 1951, US) Robert Ryan, Ida Lupino, Ward Bond, Ed Begley, Cleo Moore, Charles Kemper, Sumner Williams.
82 min. b/w.
A superb *noir* thriller with a difference. Ray's second film with producer John Houseman (the first being *They Live By Night*) starts off in the sinister urban jungle, with Ryan's cop increasingly brutalised by the 'garbage' he is forced to deal with. Finally, his methods become so violent that he is sent to cool off in snowy upstate New York, where his search for a sex killer brings him into contact with Lupino's blind woman and her mentally retarded brother (Williams). It's a film about the violence within us all, about the effects of environment and family upon character (Lupino, peaceful and a healing force, even has a tree in her living room), and about the spiritual redemption of a fallen man. If it sometimes seems a little schematic, there is no denying the power of the performances (Ryan in particular is ferociously effective, a true precursor to Siegel's *Dirty Harry*), nor the eloquence of Ray's poetic but tough direction. Aided enormously by George Diskant's high contrast camerawork and by Bernard Herrmann's stunning score, which emphasises the hunt motif in Ryan's quest, it's a film of frequent brilliance. GA

On Dangerous Ground

see Choke Canyon

On Deadly Ground

(Steven Seagal, 1994, US) Steven Seagal, Michael Caine, Joan Chen, John C McGinley, R Lee Ermey, Shari Shattuck.
100 min.
Seagal has made a name for himself knocking the stuffing out of low-life scumbags – here, in his directorial debut, his victims are rich ecologically-unsound scumbags. Caine's snaked-eyed, snakeskin-booted oil magnate knows he must get his rig on-line, or drilling rights will revert to the

'Eskimos'. Following the death of the rig foreman and an oil spill, trouble-shooter Forest Taft (Seagal) is set up as the fall guy for an alleged sabotage plot. Through contact with the Inuits, Taft learns he is a spirit warrior who must teach the oil men to 'fear the bear.' When the crud hits the fan, however, Taft eschews cosmic dream energy in favour of 'cold, hard reality' – ie a familiar arsenal of weapons. In contrast to his short, sharp fighting style, Seagal's presentation of the human conflicts and underlying issues consists of vague, sweeping gestures. NF

Ondeko-za on Sado, The
(Masahiro Shinoda, 1975, Jap)
55 min.
The 'Ondeko-za' is an extraordinary group of young Japanese who have exiled themselves to virtually complete isolation on Sado Island in the Japan Sea in order to preserve and/or recreate various Japanese folk arts, especially so-called 'demon drumming'. Shinoda's documentary provides a good deal of useful background information about their motives and the range of their activities. Founder/leader Tagayasu Den turns out to be a veteran of the '50s student riots, and many of the 17-strong group are dropouts or otherwise alienated kids; it's clear that the strenuous physical discipline of training for and performing in the Ondeko-za programme provides all of them with more constructive solutions to contemporary problems than most self-willed exiles achieve. TR

One and One (En och En)
(Erland Josephson/Sven Nykvist/Ingrid Thulin, 1978, Swe) Ingrid Thulin, Erland Josephson, Björn Gustafsson.
90 min.
One and one makes two: the message of this study of the social relationship between an odd couple (middle-aged woman artist and her bachelor cousin) is that good maths is bad psychology. From a script by Josephson, shot by Nykvist, and directed by Josephson, Nykvist and Thulin, the package just oozes prestige made in Bergmanland, but the film is full of silences and whispers signifying nothing, except perhaps Bergman's absence. In this case, one and one and one make zero. SH

One and Only, The
(Carl Reiner, 1977, US) Henry Winkler, Kim Darby, Gene Saks, William Daniels, Harold Gould, Hervé Villechaize, Richard Karron.
98 min.
The One and Only is Andy Schmidt, a hopeful actor setting out in the '50s with a Texas-sized ego, a bottomless barrel of jokes, and a WASP wife called Mary Crawford, only to find himself in the wrestling branch of showbiz, his fighting persona variously a hypnotist, Adolf Hitler, and an outrageous gay. And Andy Schmidt is Henry Winkler, whose ingratiating style certainly helps to make this comedy flabby round the edges. However, Reiner obviously loves the subject, and his direction is pointed but unfussy, while Steve Gordon's script balances the soppy looks and exchanges with many lunacies and acid cracks, often aimed at Winkler's dwarf sidekick ('Why don't you take three months off and change a light bulb?'). If only the madcap strain had been strengthened, the film might have achieved more momentum; as it is, with good performances all round, it's pleasant but so-so. GB

One Armed Boxer (Dubi Quan Wang)
(Wang Yu, 1973, HK) Wang Yu, Tang Shin, Tien Yeh, Lung Fei, Wu Tung Choo.
97 min.
Here the tournament-dominated martial arts film intersects interestingly with the more folkloric magic aspects of the sword film. Wang Yu, directing with an eye to the Italian Western, plays his own hero, perhaps the most masochistic, impetuous and fight-loving of the lot, subjecting himself to the ultimate in dispossession before, through pain and self-punishment, coming back from the as-good-as-dead to wreak havoc. Wang Yu pits his hero against a genuinely fantastic array of fighters, including a fanged karate expert with a lank black mane, given to perching in the corners of rooms between the wall and ceiling like some malevolent bat, and two inflatable Tibetan lamas (who

are able to arrest their own circulation). Distributor cuts make nonsense of the care taken to build up to the fight scenes by paying scrupulous attention to the rites attached to the various arts. VG

One Born Every Minute
see Flim-Flam Man, The

One by One
(Claude DuBoc, 1974, US) Jackie Stewart, Mike Hailwood, Peter Revson, François Cevert; narrator: Stacy Keach.
94 min.
A very boring documentary indeed about Grand Prix racing: you don't know what dullness is until you've been talked round the Nurburgring by Jackie Stewart. Everything in it is touched with banality, from the camera being pointed at everything in range, to Stacy Keach's narration, which gives every bromide the ring of Eternal Truth ('The car is a thoroughbred with a soul of its own, brought to life by sorcerers' apprentices called...Mechanics'). But the main complaint is more fundamental: it's impossible to tell what's going on, as we cut from Monaco to the pile-up at Silverstone (good footage of the latter, but the BBC's was better). And a lot of the title's irony is thrown away, as it's never made clear to the less informed that the interviews with Revson and Cevert are being shown after their deaths. AN

One Day in the Life of Ivan Denisovich
(Caspar Wrede, 1971, GB/Nor) Tom Courtenay, Espen Skjonberg, James Maxwell, Alfred Burke, Eric Thompson, John Cording.
100 min.
Worthy, faithful version of Solzhenitsyn's novel about the difficulties of life in a Siberian labour camp. Courtenay is superb as Ivan, struggling to survive to the end of his ten-year sentence, and the whole thing is conscientiously put together – shot in sub-zero temperatures near the Arctic Circle in Norway, with gaunt, haunted faces and the drab buildings and landscapes evocatively shot by the great Sven Nykvist (Bergman's regular cameraman). The problem, however, is that in his efforts to be accurate and restrained, Wrede forsakes passion, and creates a film as cold and clinical as the environment it observes. GA

One Deadly Summer (L'Eté Meurtrier)
(Jean Becker, 1983, Fr) Isabelle Adjani, Alain Souchon, Suzanne Flon, Jenny Clève, Michel Galabru, François Cluzet, Manuel Gélin.
133 min.
For the first twenty minutes or so, this looks like an all too familiar chirpy French rural comedy: wiggly, pert-buttocked coquette-cum-slut Adjani arrives in a small French village and sets the local manhood afire with lust and rumour. Then the tone shifts and we're all set to discover that she's out for revenge for some outrage inflicted on her in childhood. Things still look predictable, but as the film progresses, become more and more complex; events are related in differing ways by the various characters, and Adjani's role takes on deepening and more disturbing perspectives. Just as beneath the glossy visuals there lie murky and enigmatic themes of exploitation, treachery and falsehood, so the initial stereotypes are gradually peeled away to reveal confused characters played with an increasing intensity by a fine cast, none more so than Adjani herself. Directed with verve, the film rarely departs from the commercial mainstream, but within those conventions it operates with assurance, subtlety and plenty of surprises. GA

One Eight Seven
(Kevin Reynolds, 1997, US) Samuel L Jackson, John Heard, Kelly Rowan, Clifton Gonzalez Gonzalez, Tony Plana, Karina Arroyave.
119 min.
Brooklyn. Teacher Trevor Garfield (Jackson) finds '187' scrawled across his notebook – the California penal code number for homicide. It's a death threat from (he thinks) a pupil he's just failed, but the principal won't take heed. Garfield's stabbed by an unseen assailant in the school corridor. A year later and physically healed, he takes a job in South Central LA, with fellow teachers Rowan and Heard. It's another rundown institution. Goaded by another macho

homeboy, Cesar (Gonzalez), Garfield decides to play it Cesar's way. Thus far, that Hollywood rarity: an intelligent issue film with a social conscience and a sense of dramatic control. Echoing the trip-hoppy soundtrack, the visuals owe too much to pop video, yet exercise a certain pull. Jackson bears the weight of the film in a constrained, introverted role (terrorised, pertinacious, innocent passion squandered), but a grand resolution and some melodramatic twists and set-pieces undercut the hard-nosed tone. NB

One-Eyed Jacks
(Marlon Brando, 1961, US) Marlon Brando, Karl Malden, Pina Pellicer, Katy Jurado, Ben Johnson, Slim Pickens, Timothy Carey, Elisha Cook Jr.
141 min.
Fascinating to see Brando directing this revenge Western – double-crossed by Malden, his outlaw partner, he erupts from the past to haunt the older man, now a lawman and proud father – exactly as he acts, so that the whole movie smoulders in a manner that is mean, moody and magnificent. At its origin is a novel by Charles Neider which, though changing the names, retold the story of Pat Garrett and Billy the Kid. Brando's further changes (Rio/Billy now kills rather than is killed by Dad Longworth/Garrett) were evidently made with a view to indicting shifty, mendacious society as the real villain. The Freudian intentions lurking in the character conflicts and the card symbolism, the homosexual and Oedipal intimations, are underpinned by the extraordinary settings. Surely uniquely in a Western, the key scenes are played out against the rocky Monterey sea coast, with waves crashing portentously in the background, so that nature echoes the Romantic agony of a hero much given to brooding in corners or gazing out into space shrouded in his Byronic cape. The result, laced with some fine traditional sequences and stretches of masochistic violence, is a Western of remarkable though sometimes muddled power. TM

One False Move
(Carl Franklin, 1991, US) Bill Paxton, Cynda Williams, Billy Bob Thornton, Jim Metzler, Michael Beach, Earl Billings.
106 min.
A superb modern thriller in the ultra-hardboiled Jim Thompson mould, in which a trio of criminals, wanted for a brutally murderous drugs heist, converge on a small, quiet Arkansas township where the local cop, treated with contempt by the LA officers in charge of the case, looks forward to a High Noon-style showdown. The asides on racial and sexual inequality are made subtly and succinctly; the performances and pacing are nigh perfect; the violence is explicit, disturbing but never gratuitous; and Franklin – a black actor whose directing debut this is – achieves a consistency of mood that other far more experienced film-makers would give their right arms for. One of the finest American movies in recent years. GA

One Fine Day
(Michael Hoffman, 1996, US) Michelle Pfeiffer, George Clooney, Mae Whitman, Alex D Linz, Charles Durning, John Robin Baitz, Ellen Greene.
109 min.
More a mobile-phone movie than an old-fashioned romantic comedy, this irksomely frenetic love story sees single mother Melanie (Pfeiffer, not glamorous but with all modern Hollywood's ersatz PC trimmings) and divorced weekend dad Jack (arch-mugger Clooney) meeting cute all over touristy New York City. It's a tease. Melanie falls in hate at first sight, as Jack's lateness at the school gates means their respective five-year-olds will miss the Circle Line ferry trip. But necessity makes strange bedfellows – though it could hurry up! – as the two are forced to care for each other's kids in rotation while she races to close an architectural project and he hurtles about to support a City Hall corruption piece he's written. WH

One Flew Over the Cuckoo's Nest (100)
(Milos Forman, 1975, US) Jack Nicholson, Louise Fletcher, William Redfield, Will Sampson, Brad Dourif, Sydney Lassick, Christopher Lloyd, Danny De Vito, Scatman Crothers.
134 min.
A strictly realistic approach to Ken Kesey's novel

confines the horizons of the original into a saner, less delirious tragi-comedy. Set in an insane asylum, the film involves the oppression of the individual, a struggle spearheaded by an ebullient Nicholson, turning in a star performance if ever there was one as he leads his fellow-inmates against the sinisterly well-meaning Nurse Ratched (Fletcher). For all the film's painstaking sensitivity and scrupulous chartings of energies and repressions, one longs for more muscle, which only Nicholson consistently provides. CPe

One From the Heart
(Francis Coppola, 1982, US) Frederic Forrest, Teri Garr, Raúl Julia, Nastassja Kinski, Lainie Kazan, Allen Garfield.
107 min.
Apparently Coppola got his inspiration while wandering the back streets of Tokyo with a copy of Goethe's *Elective Affinities*, pondering the Kabuki and his alimony payments. He saw a sequence of brilliant tableaux: a hoary yarn about love lost and refound, spun with high-tech artifice and elaborate theories about colour. Fortunately the movie outgrew its origins with barely a stretch mark in sight, to become a likeable, idiosyncratic musical, its few remaining pretensions (dud symbolism just when you most expect it) so bare-faced they're almost winning. The human element keeps the film modest. Coppola shows an affection for the commonplaceness of his new romantic couple (Forrest and Garr) surprising after his previous ones from the heart of darkness: they smooch, quarrel, cheat on each other (respectively with Kinski and Julia), and live to smooch again over a long Fourth of July weekend in a Las Vegas confected entirely in the sets and mixing-boards of Zoetrope studios. The result, crafted with the help of cinematographer Vittorio Storaro, looks terrific: walls dissolve, scenes play in wry tandem, and the dance routines move nimbly into neon-tinged fantasies. At times the project seems in danger of being scuppered by its own lavishness; the saving grace is a light heart. KJ

One Full Moon
(Un Nos Ola Leuad)
(Endaf Emlyn, 1991, GB) Dyfan Roberts, Tudor Roberts, Betsan Llwyd, Delyth Einir, Cian Ciaran, Dilwyn Vaughn Thomas, Robin Griffith.
98 min.
This subtitled Welsh language drama, the second feature from Ffilm Cymru, is based on a novel by Caradog Prichard dealing with a harrowing remembered childhood in a remote slate-mining community in the 1920s, and is essentially of the poetic naturalism school. It cuts back and forward from the '50s to the '20s as a man (D Roberts) revisits the village where he spent his traumatic, fatherless adolescence with his hard-pressed mother. Past and present begin to meld. The film shows their hard daily lives, conducted under the vigilant, sin-watching eye of the church, with matter-of-fact honesty and no little humour. The bright, imaginative boy (T Roberts) – angels are no strangers to him – has a warm relationship with his mother. But she is vulnerable: when she is assaulted by a mad itinerant tinker, her frenzied need for expiation pushes her over the edge, and unbalances the boy. Emlyn's attitude to redemption is as enigmatic as the recurring images – scudding skies over green hills, cleansing water, the impassive face of the Virgin. How much does heaven allow? WH

One Generation of Tattoos
(Irezumi Ichidai)
(Seijun Suzuki, 1965, Jap) Hideki Takahashi.
87 min.
A somewhat more straight-ahead yakuza yarn than Suzuki was later to come up with, but still a perfect example of how gangster histrionics can be wedded with flights of emotional and spiritual fancy. A mob executioner, desperate to protect his sensitive younger brother from his treacherous boss, takes him on the road, only to find endless moral complications and divided loyalties, all of which culminate in a chance to make the supreme sacrifice. The climactic fight, filmed through a battery of sliding doors, offers all the aesthetic brilliance you'd desire, but the film's real strength lies in its depiction of a cathartic confrontation with destiny. AP

One Good Cop
(Heywood Gould, 1991, US) Michael Keaton, Rene Russo, Anthony LaPaglia, Kevin Conway, Rachel Ticotin, Tony Plana, Benjamin Bratt, Charlaine Woodard.
114 min.
Out of the Batsuit, Keaton has run up and down the register, playing a drug addict (*Clean and Sober*), succumbing to a fatal illness (*My Life*), or Relating to Children, which he does in a big way here as a caring NYC police officer. When his partner's killed in the line of duty, Keaton adopts his offspring. Still time, though, to track down the bad guys in this bland, uninvolving thriller, one of those films that seems to be speaking to two mutually exclusive audiences: the junior schmaltz crowd and cop movie completists. Straight to video in Britain. TJ

One Hamlet Less
(Un Amleto di Meno)
(Carmelo Bene, 1973, It) Carmelo Bene, Lydia Mancinelli, Alfiero Vincenti, Luigi Mazzanotte, Franco Leo.
A parody of Shakespeare with Hamlet as a frustrated playwright, Polonius as a bumbling Freudian psychologist, Ophelia and Gertrude as half-naked fantasy figures. Carmelo Bene's film (derived from one of Jules Laforgue's *Moralités Légendaires*) begins with some striking visual ideas – pure white backdrops, outlandishly overblown and opulent costumes – and then proceeds to repeat these motifs ad infinitum, to the point of monotony and way beyond. JR

One Heavenly Night
(George Fitzmaurice, 1931, US) Evelyn Laye, John Boles, Leon Errol, Lilyan Tashman, Hugh Cameron, Henry Kolker, Marion Lord.
82 min. b/w.
Hopes for this Goldwyn musical are raised by a stylish opening in which Tashman – as Fritzi, toast of Budapest night life – belts out her number, then gleefully provokes a riot among her admirers. Alas, she is rusticated by the police for scandalous behaviour; and Laye, making her Hollywood debut as a flower-seller with dreams of stardom, is persuaded to serve Fritzi's stint of rustic exile while she holes up with her current lover. Some very sub-Stroheim sex-play ensues as Count Mirko (Boles), the country magistrate responsible for Fritzi's good behaviour, confidently expects to bed the pseudo-Fritzi, while the dismayed innocent sets a romantic snare intended to leave him panting with frustration. True love naturally brings matrimonial bliss, and boredom for the viewer. The songs are standard operetta stuff, moonily sung; there are acres of unfunny comedy for Errol and Cameron (in servant/confidant roles); but the camerawork (George Barnes and Gregg Toland) is gorgeous. TM

One Hour With You
(Ernst Lubitsch/George Cukor, 1932, US) Maurice Chevalier, Jeanette MacDonald, Genevieve Tobin, Roland Young, Charlie Ruggles, George Barbier.
80 min. b/w.
Directed first by Cukor under Lubitsch's supervision, and then largely re-shot by the latter, this is in many ways a typical piece of sophisticated, smug fluff from Lubitsch and his regular screenwriter Samuel Raphaelson. A remake of the 1924 *The Marriage Circle*, it presents Chevalier as a philandering Paris doctor, flaunting his thick-accented charm at MacDonald. Songs, verse, snappy dialogue, and asides to the audience make it likeable and clever. But Cukor, interviewed about the film's authorship, put his finger on its problem: 'It's really a Lubitsch picture, and if you think you can detect what I did in it, you're imagining things. Lubitsch's pictures were brilliant, even if they lacked feeling. He didn't want his comedies to have any feeling. Now, my idea of comedy is that they should always touch you unexpectedly'. GA

One Hundred and
One Dalmatians
(Wolfgang Reitherman/Hamilton Luske/Clyde Geronimi, 1960, US).
79 min.
One hundred and one little bundles of fun; enormous quantities of bog-roll spring to mind. This is Disney at his finest, and not until *The Prisoner*

was there a work of such intense numerological significance. Sure it's wonderful to see spots on the screen, but why so many spots and why 101 Dalmatians? This version of Dodie Smith's dog-napping classic has a voice-over by Pongo the Dog to keep a tight lead on the activities of his cute human pets, the screechingly evil Cruella de Vil and her voguishly Cockney minions, Jasper and Horace. Beyond this sublimely simple alienation effect, deeper thematic concerns are run with theological significance: when to start a litter, the slaughter of animals for fur coats, the deadly opiate of TV commercials, and even a pre-echo of the cable debate (the 'twilight bark') turn and re-turn to the conclusion that we're all in some sense 'spotted', if not actually Dalmatians. There is probably not enough violence for it to be a profoundly moral film, but it is brilliant entertainment none the less. RP

101 Dalmatians
(Stephen Herek, 1996, US) Glenn Close, Jeff Daniels, Joely Richardson, Hugh Laurie, Mark Williams, Tim McInnerny, Joan Plowright.
103 min.
Live-action remake of Disney's enduring classic scripted by John Hughes – and the final act is pretty much a retread of *Home Alone*. Pongo starts well, turning on the shower for his 'pet' human (Daniels) and engineering his meeting with an attractive member of the opposite sex (Richardson), but soon abandons any pretence of being an intelligent protagonist. The film has two main things going for it: Glenn and Close, whose outlandish, cartoonish, monstrously coiffed performance as Cruella gives it life and breath. Plaudits are also due to McInnerny's sadly under-used flunky, a breathtaking dalmatian-powered bike chase around London, and the first-rate costume designs. Delightfully dotty in places, but mostly patchy. DW

100 Days Before the
Command (Sto Dnei
Do Prikaza...)
(Khusein Erkenov, 1990, Rus) Armen Dzhigarkhanian, Elena Kondulainen, Aleksandr Chislov, Vladimir Zamanskii, Oleg Vasilikov, Roman Grekov.
68 min.
Shot in 1990, but not seen outside Russia until the director took a print to the 1994 Berlin Film Festival, this expressive anti-militarist collage must have come as quite a shock to the Gorky studio which funded it and to the local army barracks which offered manpower and facilities. Both were apparently duped by a fake script, concealing the film's swingeing assault on the brutality, dehumanisation and outright despair that was the ordinary Russian soldier's lot. The film's non-linear narrative encompasses a wider field of concern, however, than the strictly political. While one might rank director Erkenov's work beside that of such mavericks as Tarkovsky and Paradjanov, the Uzbeki-born director is more directly confrontational in using the Russian realist tradition to his own ends, revealing harsh poetic truths about a country whose troops have served in the Afghan war and a recent series of internal conflicts. If the obfuscatory construction makes it hard-going at times, the film has a burning commitment and a forthright individuality that's hard not to admire. Recommended to those with a strong constitution. TJ

One Hundred Men and a Girl
(Henry Koster, 1937, US) Deanna Durbin, Adolphe Menjou, Leopold Stokowski, Eugene Pallette, Mischa Auer, Alice Brady, Billy Gilbert.
84 min. b/w.
Tugging at conductor Stokowski's sleeve a few years before the Mickey Mouse of *Fantasia* pulled the same trick, Universal teen-star Durbin here had the object of getting him to lead her orchestra of unemployed musician friends, including papa Menjou, in a programme of suitably cloying classics. By happy circumstance, those friends happen to comprise the Philadelphia Symphony Orchestra. PT

100 Years of Polish Cinema
(100 Lat w Kinie)
(Pawel Lozinski, 1996, Pol)
61 min.

Conceived by Kieslowski and executed by his assistant on *Three Colours: White*, this is the only film in the British Film Institute's 'Century of Cinema' series which focuses on the viewer rather than the cinéaste: film-goers of all ages are invited to recall the Polish movies which have meant most to them. The conjunction of their words and their favourite images not only brings the film clips to life but also says a lot about the fundamental appeal of cinema itself. Highly engaging throughout, it becomes immoderately moving when two of the interviewees explain how Kieslowski films changed their lives. TR

One in a Million
(Sidney Lanfield, 1937, US) Sonja Henie, Adolphe Menjou, Don Ameche, Ned Sparks, Jean Hersholt, the Ritz Brothers, Borrah Minevitch, Arline Judge.
95 min. b/w.
Sonja Henie figure skates to victory for her Swiss papa (Hersholt) at the 1936 Garmisch Winter Olympics (only one uniformed German soldier in sight). At the 1908 Games father was stripped of *his* title for naively taking money for a new pair of skates. The Norwegian world champion skater made her unaffected US debut for Fox in this musical concoction enlivened by Ned Sparks' lugubrious asides and a robust showstopper by Borrah Minevitch and his Harmonica Rascals. JPy

One Lost Year
(Gerardo Lara, 1993, Mex) Vanessa Bauche, Tiare Scanda, Marco Munoz.
100 min.
Sensitive if somewhat drawn-out account of the sentimental education of a 16-year-old girl from a Mexican village, who, against the wishes of father and childhood sweetheart, goes to high school in the city of Toluca. Strong on her friendship with another girl, fine, if a tad predictable, on her experiences with various macho types, the film is weakest in its pretensions at wider social comment. GA

One Man Mutiny
see Court-Martial of Billy Mitchell, The

One Man's War (La Guerre d'un Seul Homme)
(Edgardo Cozarinsky, 1981, Fr/WGer)
109 min. b/w.
A representation of Occupied France through the diaries of Ernst Jünger, German military commandant in Paris, *One Man's War* brings World War II into focus not with the lying lens of the deadpan documentary, but through a series of highly original techniques which gain all the more brilliance by their obliqueness. The diaries are not accompanied by pictures representing the events Jünger describes, but by contemporary newsreels, and by painstakingly chosen music which challenges words, images and their assumptions. The effect is to produce a moving, gripping document which raises profound questions about the war, and indeed all wars: the interaction of individuals and events; the definitions of propaganda and collaboration; and the weakness of ideologies in the face of gigantic forces equipped with their own superhuman logic. Jünger's beliefs, a strange mix of futurism and Junker chivalry, start by imposing a bizarre, philosophical unity on the film, but they end in dissolution. A genuine *tour de force*. DRo

One Million Years B.C.
(Don Chaffey, 1966, GB) John Richardson, Raquel Welch, Percy Herbert, Robert Brown, Martine Beswick.
100 min.
A loose remake of the 1940 special effects extravaganza with Victor Mature, Hammer's version of the life and times of cavemen and women again cheerfully neglects a few million years of evolution and has our antecedents living side by side with the brontosauri. There's a simple story about lovers from different tribes, and Welch grunts beautifully clad only in a few bits of bunny fur, but the real stars are Ray Harryhausen's superbly animated dinosaurs. It was Hammer's biggest box-office hit and inaugurated a cycle, but the more cheaply made sequels were no match for the ferocious reptile fights on display here. DT

One Minute to Zero
(Tay Garnett, 1952, US) Robert Mitchum, Ann Blyth, William Talman, Richard Egan, Charles McGraw, Margaret Sheridan.
105 min. b/w.
RKO didn't waste much time in getting this Korean War drama on screen, and the documentary footage used to fill in the background is far more striking than anything the scriptwriters could come up with. Mitchum's strictly on autopilot as the US colonel charged with evacuating all American citizens from Korea, which means persuading comely UN official Blyth that she has to go too. The blend of action and romance never amounts to much. TJ

One More River
(aka Over the River)
(James Whale, 1934, US) Diana Wynyard, Colin Clive, Frank Lawton, Mrs Patrick Campbell, Jane Wyatt, Reginald Denny, C Aubrey Smith, Lionel Atwill.
90 min. b/w.
A glowing example of how to turn English drawing-rooms and stiff upper lips into the stuff of tragedy, adapted by RC Sherriff from the last volume in Galsworthy's *Forsyte Saga* (which made a forceful plea for a change in the divorce laws). Wynyard and Lawton are perfect as the unhappily married lady and the nice young man kept apart by the barriers of convention, and finding their love for each other cruelly put through the wringer when (though blameless) they are dragged through the mire by her odious husband (Clive). It's not unlike *Brief Encounter*, raised a couple of rungs in the social ladder to the milieu of noblesse oblige and the proper thing, pride, privilege and Tory victories at the polls; but what astonishes is the skill and sensitivity with which Whale manages to suggest the still waters of passion slowly coming to the boil under the surface. A polished, elegant gem of a movie. TM

One More Time
(Jerry Lewis, 1969, GB) Sammy Davis Jr, Peter Lawford, Maggie Wright, Leslie Sands, John Wood, Esther Anderson.
93 min.
A film to leave egg on the faces of Jerry Lewis' staunchest admirers is this London-set Rat Pack farce in which the man himself doesn't appear. A sequel to Richard Donner's equally inept *Salt and Pepper*, it shifts Davis and Lawford from Soho clubland into the criminal environs of the landed gentry when Lawford undertakes the impersonation of his late, lorded twin brother. Absolutely appalling. PT

One Night Stand
(Mike Figgis, 1997, US) Wesley Snipes, Nastassja Kinski, Kyle MacLachlan, Ming-na Wen, Robert Downey Jr, Amanda Donohoe, John Ratzenberger.
103 min.
On a trip to New York, commercials director Snipes bumps into and spends the night with UN employee Kinski. Thus is set in train a series of feelings, emotions and events driven by a logic of their own. Figgis has refashioned a bonkfest outline by Joe Eszterhas into a script focused evenly on the experience and motivations of its five main characters. Snipes, cast against type, is notable as a decent guy, happily married with two kids, for whom the affair constitutes a trigger for a quiet reassessment of both his marriage and his lost '60s idealism. Downey is affecting as the gay choreographer, still idealistic and still suffering for his art (AIDS, inevitably), with whom Snipes rekindles a friendship; and Kinski enlivens all her scenes. WH

One of Our Aircraft Is Missing
(Michael Powell/Emeric Pressburger, 1942, GB) Godfrey Tearle, Eric Portman, Hugh Williams, Bernard Miles, Hugh Burden, Googie Withers, Pamela Brown, Emrys Jones, Robert Helpmann, Peter Ustinov.
102 min. b/w.
Though not top-notch Powell & Pressburger, an ambitious low-key wartime thriller that totally transcends any propaganda considerations, thanks to sharp characterisation and imaginative scripting. The crew of a British bomber sent out on a mission to Europe (by air controller Powell,

making a symbolically revealing guest appearance) are forced to bale out and make their way back overland through the Low Countries. No simple task, given that – as so often in Powell's movies – the enemy is not merely external but also internal: tensions mount among the Brits, while distrust abounds in their dealings with apparently sympathetic Dutchmen. Rather like *49th Parallel* without the epic sweep, an impressively directed and beautifully performed piece of work. GA

One of Our Dinosaurs Is Missing
(Robert Stevenson, 1975, US) Peter Ustinov, Helen Hayes, Clive Revill, Derek Nimmo, Joan Sims, Andrew Dove, Max Harris, Bernard Bresslaw, Roy Kinnear, Joss Ackland.
94 min.
A delight: old pro Stevenson invests a sketchy story with the same flair for mysterious smoky visuals he brought to the neglected *Bedknobs and Broomsticks* and to *Jane Eyre* twenty-seven years earlier. This is a further Disney return to the picturesque England of fog, milords and crimped nannies, with every foreigner a villain – it's the Chinese this time, led by Peter Ustinov, who turns a straightforward part into an acting showcase. The English cast, too, bats right down in a way happily reminiscent of Ealing comedy. Given all these assets, the plot hardly matters. AN

One of Those Things (Haendeligt Uheld)
(Erik Balling, 1970, Den) Roy Dotrice, Judy Geeson, Zena Walker, Frederick Jaeger.
80 min.
Watchable Danish thriller, shot in English for the international market, has Dotrice as a car company exec who tries to conceal that he ran over and killed a cyclist. Geeson is the minx who uses her knowledge of the incident to worm her way into a job and threaten his marriage, but are her motives sexual, or financial: or mere perversity? The complications are well worked out, and there's even a trip to Japan to test a new car and make love on the train from Tokyo to Fujiyama. TJ

One of Us (Echad Mi'Shelanu)
(Uri Barbash, 1989, Isr) Sharon Alexander, Alon Aboutboul, Dahlia Shimko, Dan Toren.
110 min.
Conflicting loyalties come to the boil in this passionately felt Israeli drama when military policeman Alexander has to investigate his former pals in an elite paratroop unit, accused of murdering the Arab who blew up one of their comrades. The treatment is well-judged, pointed but never hectoringly didactic, in a screenplay by the director's brother Benny Barbash, a soldier in the Yom Kippur War, who later turned peace activist and playwright. TJ

One on One
(Lamont Johnson, 1977, US) Robby Benson, Annette O'Toole, GD Spradlin, Gail Strickland, Melanie Griffith, James G Richardson, Lamont Johnson.
97 min.
Attractive if soft-centred basketball story, a sort of junior *Rocky*. High-school star Benson is wooed with a sports car into taking an athletics scholarship, finds himself chased by the randy college secretary, falls hopelessly for his teacher, is persecuted by a tyrannical coach, almost flunks, resolves to make the team, gets the (right) girl, wins the match, then tells the coach where to stick his scholarship. The most interesting scene involves Lamont Johnson himself, as the mysterious alumnus who sponsors Benson, and who stands for the corrupt recruiting dwelt on at greater length in the original script (written by Benson and his father) which caused two universities to forbid filming on their premises. AN

One Plus One (aka Sympathy for the Devil)
(Jean-Luc Godard, 1968, GB) The Rolling Stones, Anne Wiazemsky, Iain Quarrier, Frankie Dymon Jr, Danny Daniels.
99 min.
Like *Le Gai Savoir*, though more extreme in its

abandonment of narrative forms, one of Godard's attempts to 'start again at zero'. Originally conceived literally as one plus one: a theme of construction (the Rolling Stones rehearsing 'Sympathy for the Devil'), and one of destruction (the suicide of a white revolutionary when her boyfriend deserts to Black Power). Endless production problems and disgruntlement on Godard's part turned it into a random collage which the viewer is supposed to 'edit' himself. A daunting task, but the images are often riveting. In the version called 'Sympathy for the Devil', producer Iain Quarrier tacked the completed recording of the Stones' number on to the end of the film (and in an incident at the 1968 London Film Festival that has become legend, was assaulted by an infuriated Godard for his pains). TM

1 + 1 = 3

(Heidi Genée, 1979, WGer) Adelheit Arndt, Dominik Graf, Christoph Quest, Helga Stock, Dietrich Leiding.
85 min.
A modestly engaging, low-key feminist movie about an unmarried actress in Munich who becomes pregnant but decides against marrying the child's father, and eventually moves in with a more agreeable man she meets on a winter sports holiday. In the end she determines to live and raise her child alone, a decision which, considering the men in the movie, seems eminently reasonable. Don't get the impression that this movie has it in for men; it's much harder on the parental generation, and very sympathetic to kids who find themselves unwitting victims of middle class domestic unrest. Heidi Genée worked as an editor with the first wave of new German directors (Kluge, Sinkel), and has a keen eye for the absurdities of domestic life as well as a good ear for comic lines. MA

One PM

(DA Pennebaker, 1969, US) Jean-Luc Godard, Richard Leacock, Eldridge Cleaver, Tom Hayden, Jefferson Airplane, LeRoi Jones, Tom Luddy, Rip Torn, Anne Wiazemsky.
90 min.
In 1968, Godard began work on a film in America (One AM or One American Movie) dealing with aspects of resistance and revolution. Dissatisfied with what he had shot, he abandoned the project. Pennebaker here assembles the Godard footage, together with his own coverage of Godard at work (One PM standing for either One Parallel Movie or One Pennebaker Movie). Although it may be dubious to show stuff that Godard had rejected, the film does manage to convey how he got his results. You can draw your own conclusions about his approach and why he abandoned the film.

One Rainy Afternoon

(Rowland V Lee, 1936, US) Francis Lederer, Ida Lupino, Hugh Herbert, Mischa Auer, Erik Rhodes, Roland Young.
79 min. b/w.
Lederer causes consternation when he arrives in a cinema after the show has started, sits in the wrong seat, and kisses Lupino (very much the wrong girl) who isn't at all happy about it. That's the set-up in this bubble-headed piece of tosh which needed a higher voltage cast than the one on offer to charm the viewer in the manner intended. Quite sweet though. TJ

One Sings, the Other Doesn't (L'Une Chante, l'Autre Pas)

(Agnès Varda, 1976, Fr/Bel/Cur) Valérie Mairesse, Thérèse Liotard, Gisèle Halimi, Ali Raffi, Jean-Pierre Pellegrin.
120 min.
Varda's film about the changing but deep friendship between two women from 1962 to 1976 is also the story of the transformation of their attitudes towards being women in a patriarchal culture. But two distinct elements – a stylistic approach and a sense of nostalgia – make this a very different kind of feminist film, in which reality, though present, never leaves any real scars on an essentially romantic fable. The film's ambience remains that of the '60s dream rather than the harsh reality of the '70s; but as such, it at least provides a considered escapist identification that mainstream cinema has traditionally denied women in its male-dominated fantasies. SM

One That Got Away, The

(Roy Baker, 1957, GB) Hardy Krüger, Michael Goodliffe, Terence Alexander, Alec McCowen, Colin Gordon, Stratford Johns.
111 min. b/w.
Here's the seemingly authentic story of Oberleutnant Franz von Werra, shot down in 1940, author of two unsuccessful attempts to escape from England and a third, successful one from Canada. In national terms one can read this as British self-abasement (hard to imagine the Germans making The Wooden Horse), as self-confidence (no problem about acknowledging a resourceful enemy) or as unblushing commercialism (Rank determined to crack the German market). But the strongest impression is of an incredibly glamorous Krüger, with Dean haircut and black leather jacket, against whom the home side have fielded such dubious sexpots as McCowen and Alexander – this no doubt a token of the self-image of the British male in 1957. Worth noting that the film was regarded as piquant rather than as offensive; it's still worth watching, despite too many scenes of Krüger lurching across muddy fields and frozen rivers. A laconic end title states that von Werra was killed in action a few months after getting back to Germany. BBa

1,000 Plane Raid, The

(Boris Sagal, 1968, US) Christopher George, Laraine Stephens, JD Cannon, Gary Marshall, Michael Evans, James Gammon, Henry Jaglom.
94 min.
George has the task of training up a thousand new pilots for a massed raid on a Nazi aeronautics factory in this routine WWII actioner. Along the way he begins to wonder whether saturation bombing is justified…but by that time the mission is fixed. Doubtful whether the budget actually stretched to the demands of the title. TJ

One Touch of Venus

(William A Seiter, 1948, US) Ava Gardner, Robert Walker, Dick Haymes, Eve Arden, Olga San Juan, Tom Conway.
81 min. b/w.
Despite the rude deletion of over half the score and less than ecstatic renditions of the remaining songs, a pleasantly witty adaptation of the Kurt Weill/SJ Perelman/Ogden Nash musical. The gaps are only patchily filled by zany comic business presumably supplied by Frank Tashlin as co-screenwriter; but Robert Walker, excellent as the timid store clerk in love with a statue of Venus which comes alive as the predatory Gardner (dubbed in the songs by Eileen Wilson) is backed by a sterling cast. TM

One-Trick Pony

(Robert M Young, 1980, US) Paul Simon, Blair Brown, Rip Torn, Joan Hackett, Lou Reed, Allen Goorwitz (Garfield). The Lovin' Spoonful, The B-52's, Sam and Dave, Tiny Tim.
98 min.
Shambling, self-obsessed and extremely irritating bleat of a film, written and starring Paul Simon, about how terrible it is to be a huge rock star when your personal life is falling apart. Plenty of muso spotting to be done. TJ

One, Two, Three

(Billy Wilder, 1961, US) James Cagney, Arlene Francis, Horst Buchholz, Pamela Tiffin, Lilo Pulver, Howard St John, Hans Lothar.
115 min. b/w.
Coarse Cold War satire, structured largely as farce, with Cagney as the aggressive Coca-Cola executive in West Berlin, trying desperately to win advancement by selling the beverage to Russia, and simultaneously required to prevent his boss from discovering that the latter's birdbrained daughter has married a rabid Commie from East Berlin. Marvellous one-liners, of course, and Cagney, spitting out his lines with machine-gun rapidity in his final film until his belated appearance in 'Ragtime', is superb (and superbly backed by a fine cast). But the targets of Wilder's satire – go-getting, up-to-the-minute, consumer America versus the poverty and outdatedness of Communist culture – are rather too obvious. GA

1, 2, 3, Sun

see Un Deux Trois Soleil

One Way or Another (De Cierta Manera)

(Sara Gomez Yera, 1977, Cuba) Mario Balmaseda, Yolanda Cuéllar, Mario Limonta, Isaura Mendoza.
73 min. b/w.
The ostensible subject of this remarkable film is the jive-talking, toe-tapping, good-for-nothing class of slum-dwelling lumpens known as 'marginals': 'a worldwide economic stratum of very defined characteristics – principally unemployment'. But the actual subject turns out to be a rather different delinquency: the misogyny and anti-social codes of Cuban machismo. Back in '74, the year of her tragic death (left unfinished, the film was completed by Tomás Alea and Julio García Espinosa), Sara Gomez Yera was already combining documentary, fiction, samba music and droll voice-over lectures to examine the transformations wrought by revolution on a generation of Cuban men. As the title indicates, contradiction is the name of the game, and the film brilliantly counterposes macho cruelties and loyalties, socialist change and intractable traditions, revolutionary fervour and political authoritarianism. MM

One Wild Moment

see Moment d'Egarement, Un

One Woman's Story

see Passionate Friends, The

On Golden Pond

(Mark Rydell, 1981, US) Katharine Hepburn, Henry Fonda, Jane Fonda, Doug McKeon, Dabney Coleman, William Lanteau, Chris Rydell.
109 min.
Generation gap tearjerker with Fonda and Hepburn as a septuagenarian married couple visiting their lakeside New England bungalow for their 48th summer together. When middle-aged daughter Jane arrives with boyfriend and his teenage son in tow, the scene is set for the artificial befriending across the generations – Fonda teaches the boy to fish, to read Treasure Island (a 'real' life alternative to chasing girls and television). This adaptation of Ernest Thompson's immensely calculated 1978 play leaves you wishing Jane Fonda's IPC production company had never become involved as she regrets (the relationship she never had with her father), Hepburn flutters, and the elder Fonda mutters (the four-letter words that are supposed to endear him to us as a salty old 'character'). Two of Hollywood's best-loved veterans deserved a far better swan song than this sticky confection. RM

On Her Majesty's Secret Service

(Peter Hunt, 1969, GB) George Lazenby, Diana Rigg, Telly Savalas, Ilse Steppat, Gabriele Ferzetti, Yuri Borienko, Bernard Horsfall, George Baker.
140 min.
The Bond films were bad enough even with the partially ironic performances of Connery. Here, featuring the stunning nonentity Lazenby, there are no redeeming features. The 'plot' (a series of glossy set pieces) is the one about 007 tracking down a loony Swiss villain (Savalas) who's...guess what?...threatening the world with some scientific thingamyjig. GA

Onibaba (The Hole)

(Kaneto Shindo, 1964, Jap) Nobuko Otowa, Jitsuko Yoshimura, Kei Sato, Taiji Tonomura, Jukichi Uno.
105 min. b/w.
A tale, apparently based on legend, about two women, one elderly and the other her daughter-in-law, who survive by killing samurai and selling their armour to buy rice. When the girl begins to lust after a neighbour, the older woman becomes jealous, and tries to frighten the girl by wearing a demon mask at night. No masterpiece by any means, it's at times overplayed, but it's striking visually, handling swift horizontal movement – and using the claustrophobic body-high reeds among which the women live – very well. It's also genuinely erotic, and the treatment in detail of the women's lives as essentially bestial is interesting so long as Shindo stops short of portentous allegorising about the human condition. RM

Onion Field, The

(Harold Becker, 1979, US) John Savage, James Woods, Franklyn Seales, Ted Danson, Ronny Cox, David Huffman, Christopher Lloyd.
126 min.
An expertly performed adaptation of Joseph Wambaugh's novel, based on the real-life case history of an LA Cop (Danson) murdered by two hijackers he tries to arrest (Woods, Seales), and the effect of the killing on his partner (Savage). It's the usual heavy Wambaugh brew: police procedure closely observed without a trace of romanticism, suggesting simply that life in the force is psychological hell. So far, so good. But that very insistence on authenticity is followed by the film to the detriment of the narrative's dramatic structure; half way through, the whole thing begins to ramble badly. Engrossingly sordid, nevertheless. GA

Only Angels Have Wings

(Howard Hawks, 1939, US) Cary Grant, Jean Arthur, Richard Barthelmess, Rita Hayworth, Thomas Mitchell, Sig Ruman, John Carroll, Allyn Joslyn, Noah Beery Jr.
121 min. b/w.
Take Hollywood's idea of a small banana republic in Central America, move in on its bar cum rooming-house cum airstrip, focus on the group of people living and working there, and you've got the basic elements of Hawks' terrific Only Angels Have Wings, or Only Mad People Want to Fly Mail Planes Over the Andes. Hemmed in by impassable mountains (all the time) and fog and blizzards (most of the time), the personal and work ethics of this little crew become magnified to epic proportions. But it's an epic played out in the confined space of the Dutchman's bar; the more claustrophobic because these men are flyers and need the open sky. If it sounds improbable, it is. Mythical cinema at its best. JCl

Only Game in Town, The

(George Stevens, 1969, US) Elizabeth Taylor, Warren Beatty, Charles Braswell, Hank Henry, Olga Valéry.
113 min.
Stevens' last film, a hoarily old-fashioned romantic comedy about a Las Vegas chorus girl and a compulsive gambler who find the courage to face life in their love for each other. Based on a play and always looking the part, it has occasional moments of life injected by Taylor and Beatty. Characteristic of the general soft-centredness is the fact that the title evidently refers not to gambling or prostitution – as one might expect of the Las Vegas setting – but to marriage. TM

Only the Brave

(Anna Kokkinos, 1995, Aust) Elena Manadalis, Dora Kaskanis.
60 min.
Four girls smoke joints and torch trees. Another saga of wild, nihilistic teenagers? Not quite. While her friend Vicki is disruptive at school, seemingly an easy score for the local blokes, and keen to try her luck as a singer, Alex is more introspective: wary of losing her virginity, fascinated by literature, and haunted by the fact that her mum abandoned herself and her dad to go and live in Sydney. Neither girl has much of a life; both, in the end, are determined to get out of town, separately or together, depending on whether their friendship can withstand the tensions that arise when Alex develops an interest in the woman who teaches her English. Tough and unsentimental, the film nevertheless suffers from slightly awkward performances and from the fact that, for the first half at least, its two leads are not as sympathetically drawn as they might be. GA

Only the Lonely

(Chris Columbus, 1991, US) John Candy, Maureen O'Shea, Ally Sheedy, Kevin Dunn, Milo O'Shea, Bert Remsen, Anthony Quinn, James Belushi.
104 min.
Chicago policeman Danny Muldoon (Candy) is bored. His working day is spent with a loutish partner (Belushi), while evenings are devoted to his cantankerous mother (O'Hara). Even this is more exciting than the existence suffered by Theresa (Sheedy), who spends her day making-up corpses in the local morgue. She overcomes painful shyness, and the unlikely couple fall in love, much to the annoyance of Danny's mother. It's ultimatum time: move with Mom to Florida,

or marry his girlfriend. Writer-director Columbus never really hits his stride (is this a drama about overcoming loneliness, or a comedy about a domineering mother?). Worse, he can't resist indulging in overwrought fantasy sequences which, far from being funny, serve to undermine the prevailing tender mood. The performances, at least, are fine, particularly the exchanges between O'Hara and Quinn as her patient suitor. CM

Only the Strong

(Sheldon Lettich, 1993, US) Mark Dacascos, Stacey Travis, Geoffrey Lewis, Paco Christian Prieto, Todd Susman, Jeffrey Anderson Gunter.
99 min.
A paean to the Brazilian martial art of capoeira harks back to those break-dancing quickies. The plot is the usual. Louis (kung-fu champ Dacascos) learns kicking ass to samba in Brazil with the US Army Special Forces, returns to Miami to find drug-dealers all over his old high school, kicks ass, converts a squad of delinquents to capoeira, takes on bossman Silverio (Prieto) in an ass-kick-up, and gets the green light for ass-kicking to samba on the syllabus. This martial art requires chaps to go into slow motion a lot and to be ethnically vague about the moves. In this context an average actor like Geoffrey Lewis, playing the defeated old schoolteacher, hums like a dynamo. Avoid like El Plagueo. BC

Only Two Can Play

(Sidney Gilliat, 1961, GB) Peter Sellers, Mai Zetterling, Virginia Maskell, Richard Attenborough, Kenneth Griffith, John Le Mesurier, Raymond Huntley.
106 min. b/w.
Peter Sellers is at his most controlled in this biting, rather sad farce, adapted from the Kingsley Amis novel That Uncertain Feeling. He's embarrassingly good as an anxiously lecherous Welsh librarian, married with kids, living in a gloomy apartment with peeling wallpaper and the plumbing up the spout. Enter Mai Zetterling, the delicious, bored wife of a local dignitary... It's well-observed, dry, and just a tad smutty. TCh

Only When I Larf

(Basil Dearden, 1968, GB) Richard Attenborough, David Hemmings, Alexandra Stewart, Nicholas Pennell, Melissa Stribling, Terence Alexander, Edric Connor.
103 min.
Richard Attenborough dons assorted disguises and is sometimes brilliant – notably as a manically jolly psychiatrist. Otherwise this is a plodding adaptation of Len Deighton's jokey novel about a trio of confidence tricksters (Attenborough, Hemmings, Stewart), which opens with a lengthy pre-credits sequence detailing their method of operation, repeats this twice over with variations, and ends on a note of hollow laughter. TM

Only When I Laugh (aka It Hurts Only When I Laugh)

(Glenn Jordan, 1981, US) Marsha Mason, Kristy McNichol, James Coco, Joan Hackett, David Dukes, John Bennett Perry.
120 min.
Expertly reworked by Neil Simon from his play The Gingerbread Lady, Only When I Laugh is positively profligate with its witty dialogue, yet resolves itself into something of dramatic weight. In his first film as producer, Simon assembles a trio of New Yorkers who, like all his best characters, are smart enough to know which part they are playing, and support each other via a droll orgy of facetious self-mockery. Coco is the fat, gay actor who feels he should be a star but is turned down for haemorrhoid commercials; Hackett, the placid beauty anxiously approaching her fortieth birthday; Mason, the central character, a Broadway actress who comes home from the boozers' clinic, a little wan but puckish glamour restored. Though full of good intentions re daughter (McNichol) and career, we know she's going to take that fatal drink sometime in the next three reels. JS

Only Yesterday

(John M Stahl, 1933, US) Margaret Sullavan, John Boles, Edna May Oliver, Billie Burke, Benita Hume, Reginald Denny, George Meeker.
106 min. b/w.

An incredible opening sequence, offering a crash course on the Wall Street disaster of October 29, 1929 as the camera cruises lingeringly from stock exchange through society party, shows Stahl at his very best. On the day that ruins him, the dispirited tycoon hero (Boles) has his conscience coincidentally prodded by a letter from the girl (Sullavan) he ruined in the days of his youth, and he remembers...A pleasing conceit, reminiscent of Letter from an Unknown Woman, but developed on lines that run more to sentimentality than to the incandescent romantic despair of Ophüls' film. Some remarkable sequences, nevertheless, with unfailingly elegant direction from Stahl and a radiant performance from Sullavan (her debut) making up for the stodgy Boles. TM

Only You

(Norman Jewison, 1994, US) Marisa Tomei, Robert Downey Jr, Bonnie Hunt, Joaquim de Almeida, Fisher Stevens, Billy Zane.
108 min.
Though convinced by a childhood ouija game that she's destined to marry a man named 'Damon Bradley', incorrigible romantic Faith Corvatch (Tomei) is now betrothed to a dull podiatrist. Until, that is, she answers a phone call from one of her fiancé's school chums who's passing through Pittsburgh en route to Venice, Italy – his name, Damon Bradley. She dashes to the airport, misses him, then sets off in quest of her soulmate. Damon, however, proves elusive, and in Rome Faith is wooed by shoe-salesman Peter (Downey), who tries to persuade her that he, Mr Wright, is a better bet than her fantasy Mr Right. With smitten Peter now in pursuit, Faith persists in her quest, scouring the Tuscan countryside and coastline for the man of her dreams. For a veteran director, Jewison is surprisingly light on his feet, though he tends to wander off forgetfully at times, leaving the plot to advance without him. Even so, the ravishing visuals, some swooning love songs, and the strains of Verdi should see you through to the predictably moist ending. NF

On Moonlight Bay

(Roy Del Ruth, 1951, US) Doris Day, Gordon MacRae, Leon Ames, Rosemary DeCamp, Mary Wickes, Billy Gray.
95 min.
A pleasantly nostalgic period musical, set in small town Indiana on the eve of America's involvement in WWI, based on Booth Tarkington's marvellous Penrod stories but largely ditching his monstrously funny small boy to provide a vehicle for big sister Doris Day and her budding romance with MacRae. Very much in the manner of Meet Me in St Louis, though nowhere near as good. The charming golden oldie score, featuring an array of hummable standards to go with the title song, is a definite plus. TM

On ne Meurt que 2 Fois

see He Died with His Eyes Open

On Our Land

(Antonia Caccia, 1981, GB)
55 min.
As a catalogue of the officially sanctioned iniquities and inequities of the Israeli government against the state's one in six citizens who are Palestinian Arabs, Antonia Caccia's documentary is efficient enough. What it achieves by means of its conventional interviews with dispossessed Palestinians (in Arab villages on the West Bank and Gaza Strip) is a persuasive profile of a state pursuing welfare policies which, whether intentionally or by default, amount to racism. Housing, employment, education and medicine are all areas where the Arabs are shown as suffering blatant discrimination. But most telling of all are laws which forbid Arabs to own or build on land they've occupied for generations. What diminishes the film's value to the viewer who is not so much uncommitted to either side as simply uninformed, is a partisanship which doesn't even allow the official Israeli position the opportunity to condemn itself out of its own mouth. RM

On purge Bébé

(Jean Renoir, 1931, Fr) Louvigny, Marguerite Pierry, Michel Simon, Olga Valéry, Sacha Tarride, Nicole Fernandez, Fernandel.
62 min. b/w.
Undertaken by Renoir to prove his efficiency as a

director of talking pictures, this droll adaptation of a slight, one-act farce by Feydeau is chiefly memorable for the relaxed performances and the then revolutionary sound effect of a flushed toilet. The plot revolves around a porcelain manufacturer (Louvigny) vainly trying to sell a supposedly unbreakable line in chamber-pots to a supplier (Simon) for the French army. Meanwhile, the manufacturer's idle wife (Pierry), drifting casually about their apartment in her dressing-gown, struggles to persuade their son to take a laxative. Aside from the inimitable Michel Simon as the slow-witted supplier, the film also features the first screen performance by Fernandel. DT

On the Beach
(Stanley Kramer, 1959, US) Gregory Peck, Ava Gardner, Fred Astaire, Anthony Perkins, John Meillon, Donna Anderson.
133 min. b/w.
Heavy going indeed as Mr Liberal Conscience himself, Stanley Kramer, wades turgidly through Nevil Shute's story of the aftermath of nuclear apocalypse. Set in Australia, where the radiation effects of war in the Northern hemisphere have still to take effect, it follows a group of characters as they wait for death to arrive. Fine photography, but the script is a typically numbing affair, and the cast, aside from Peck and Meillon (whose part was considerably cut), seem totally out of their depth. GA

On the Beat
(Robert Asher, 1962, GB) Norman Wisdom, Jennifer Jayne, Raymond Huntley, David Lodge, Esma Cannon, Eric Barker, Eleanor Summerfield.
105 min. b/w.
You may not believe this, but an otherwise totally sensible and widely respected British film director, not altogether unconnected with *Time Out's* past, has a soft spot for Norman Wisdom. Phooey! The man's humour is of the most cretinous nature imaginable. Here he appears as a dimwit car park attendant at Scotland Yard who sees his dream of becoming a copper like dad come true after he accidentally catches a bunch of crooks. Embarrassingly unfunny, it just shows that being a film comic is a most unsuitable job for a moron. GA

On the Black Hill
(Andrew Grieve, 1987, GB) Mike Gwilym, Robert Gwilym, Bob Peck, Gemma Jones, Jack Walters, Nesta Harris.
117 min.
Our countryside, in this adaptation of Bruce Chatwin's novel which crams 80 years into less than two hours, hasn't looked so ravishingly lovely since *Far From the Madding Crowd*. Hardy, without his overview, crops up a bit in Chatwin's characters too, with Amos Jones (Peck), a stubbly and splenetic son of the soil, belonging to the same bloodline as the Mayor of Casterbridge ('wrong-headed as a buffalo'), and further enraged by being a Welsh tenant on marcher land. His tender courtship of English middle class Mary (Jones) leads to a miserable marriage. They rent a farm, he's out in all weathers, and only fiddle-playing granddad (Walters) provides much companionship for gifted Mary. Twins are born (Mike and Robert Gwilym) who prove constitutionally inseparable, World War I conscription and the possibilities of romance notwithstanding. Amos feuds irreconcilably with his neighbour, and dies regretting his expulsion of a pregnant daughter. The bachelor twins celebrate their 80th birthday with a flight over the terrain they have toiled so long upon. Grieve's film may portray baffled lives in which chances of joy are stifled by a mixture of stiff-necked pride and chapel religion, but it is the look of it all you remember. BC

On the Bridge
(Frank Perry, 1992, US)
95 min.
A documentary account, surprisingly non-depressing, of veteran director Perry's own reaction to being diagnosed as having prostate cancer and, perhaps, other related, possibly terminal symptoms. We see him trying out various treatments (both conventional and alternative), arguing with his doctor, visiting counsellors and faith-healers, and generally coping with an admirable blend of courage, wit and determination. Still fighting the disease with an unexpect-

ed degree of success, he has made a film which, besides being fascinating in its own right, may well give heart to other sufferers and their loved ones. GA

On the Buses
(Harry Booth, 1971, GB) Reg Varney, Doris Hare, Michael Robbins, Anna Karen, Stephen Lewis, Bob Grant.
88 min.
Dire spin-off from the stultifyingly unfunny TV series, with the lads at the local bus depot peeved to find women being brought in as drivers, and cracking a lot of awful sexist jokes as a result. Just to add to the insult, the film is extraordinarily badly made: flat, paceless and technically shoddy. GA

On the Game
(Stanley Long, 1973, GB) Pamela Manson, Charles Hodgson, Suzy Bowen, Nicola Austine, Allen Morton.
87 min.
Listless 'documentary' about prostitution through the ages, with lots of hammy recreations from different periods (presumably a follow-up to Long's *Naughty!* of 1971, a 'report on pornography and erotica through the ages'). It is neither informative nor provoking on any level. All the women have exceptionally large breasts.

On the Nickel
(Ralph Waite, 1979, US) Ralph Waite, Donald Moffat, Penelope Allen, Hal Williams, Jack Kehoe.
96 min.
Waite, himself openly a former alcoholic, took time off from playing Dad in TV's 'The Waltons' to produce, write, direct and star in this hopelessly sentimentalised picture of life on Los Angeles' Skid Row. Most of the cast came from Waite's own Los Angeles Actors' Theatre company. TR

On the Town
(Stanley Donen/Gene Kelly, 1949, US) Gene Kelly, Frank Sinatra, Jules Munshin, Betty Garrett, Ann Miller, Vera-Ellen, Alice Pearce.
98 min.
In 1948, Jules Dassin used New York as one big location for *The Naked City*. The following year, to Louis B Mayer's incredulity, producer Arthur Freed turned the city into a sound stage for the movie of the Broadway musical of the Leonard Bernstein/Jerome Robbins ballet *Fancy Free*. Taking as its premise 'New York, New York, it's a wonderful town', the show looses three 'gobs' on the women (including the imperishable Alice Pearce), the sights, and the nightlife of the town. The most cinematic of film musicals and the one most given to dance, *On the Town* is exhilarating, brash spectacle, all rip-snorting, wisecracking attack, and maybe just a teensy bit unlikeable. SG

On the Waterfront
(Elia Kazan, 1954, US) Marlon Brando, Eva Marie Saint, Karl Malden, Lee J Cobb, Rod Steiger, Leif Erickson, Martin Balsam.
108 min.
Superb performances (none more so than Brando as Terry Malloy, the ex-boxer unwittingly entangled in corrupt union politics), a memorably colourful script by Budd Schulberg, and a sure control of atmosphere make this account of Brando's struggles against gangster Cobb's hold over the New York longshoremen's union powerful stuff. It is undermined, however, by both the religious symbolism (that turns Malloy not into a Judas but a Christ figure) and the embarrassing special pleading on behalf of informers, deriving presumably from the fact that Kazan and Schulberg named names during the McCarthy witch-hunts. Politics apart, though, it's pretty electrifying. GA

On the Wire
(Elaine Proctor, 1990, GB) Michael O'Brien, Aletta Bezuidenhout.
85 min.
In this riveting study of mental and social disintegration, Michael O'Brien plays Wouter Fourie, an Afrikaner major in the South African Defence Force, desperately trying to equate his experiences in the bush with the strict God-fearing Calvinist community at home. The fences are going up around him, while he and his wife fall prey to a

frankly dangerous sexuality. Provocatively linking sex, repression and violence with the forces of religion and apartheid, this is powerful film-making, an immensely bold, accomplished debut for writer-director Elaine Proctor of the National Film School. TCh

On Top of the Whale
(Het Dak van de Walvis)
(Raúl Ruiz, 1981, Neth) Willeke van Ammelrooy, Jean Badin, Fernando Bordeu.
90 min. b/w & col.
The most minimalist of Ruiz's extended fictions, this is a linguistic fantasy set – supposedly – in the depths of Patagonia, although the action is quite patently shot in a nondescript house in Holland. Some time in a barely recognisable future, a couple visit a mysterious socialist millionaire on an island where only two members remain of a legendary tribe. As the action unfolds, so does the Indians' strange, paradoxically limited language. One of Ruiz' most Babel-like fictions, hopping from language to language almost arbitrarily, it's also among his richest in visual terms. Not altogether convincing as the disquisition on colonialism that it's been seen as, it's more of a scrambled shaggy dog story, but austere with it. Apparently it's also Jim Jarmusch's third favourite film ever; make of that what you will. JRo

Onze Mille Verges, Les
see Bisexual

Ooh...You Are Awful
(aka Get Charlie Tully)
(Cliff Owen, 1972, GB) Dick Emery, Derren Nesbitt, Ronald Fraser, Pat Coombs, William Franklyn, Brian Oulton, Norman Bird, Liza Goddard, Ambrosine Phillpotts.
97 min.
All TV comic Emery's favourite creations (the naughty vicar, the gay stereotype, the thick-as-a-plank skinhead) are present and correct in this tawdry screen adventure, where he plays a con-man in line for a fortune if he can locate the mystery woman who has the combination to a Swiss bank account tattooed on her bottom. TJ

Open City
see Roma, Città Aperta

Open Doors (Porte aperte)
(Gianni Amelio, 1989, It) Gian Maria Volonté, Ennio Fantastichini, Renato Carpentieri, Renzo Giovampietro.
109 min.
Fascist Palermo, 1937. Scalia (Fantastichini), sacked accountant of the Confederation of Workers and Artists, slips a bayonet into its chief, Councillor Spadafora, and leaves him face down on a bloodied map of Italy. In the accounts office, he similarly despatches his successor. Then he rapes his wife and shoots her dead in front of an altar to her blessed Virgin. At home with his young son, he calmly awaits arrest. The heart of the film consists of the efforts of a liberal judge (Volonté) to investigate, despite pressure, the facts behind the case – a tale of all-pervasive corruption – in order to save the entirely unsympathetic Scalia. Despite the period trappings – it's adapted from a factually based book by Leonardo Sciascia – the left wing Amelio is more interested in universal concerns, especially the role of a cultured mind in societies where political expediency is the order of the day. The film's glory, accordingly, is Volonté's massive, remarkably sensitive performance: he makes thought palpable. A leisurely, thoughtful political drama, its sophistication and depth rewardingly confound expectations at every turn. WH

Opening Night
(John Cassavetes, 1977, US) Gena Rowlands, Ben Gazzara, John Cassavetes, Joan Blondell, Paul Stewart, Zohra Lampert, Laura Johnson.
143 min.
Since *Minnie and Moscowitz*, Cassavetes has pre-occupied himself with qualifying traditional genre material through emphasis on the intuitive and improvised aspects of the actor-as-auteur. In *Opening Night*, this essentially stylistic approach takes on an additionally playful thematic resonance. For here we are in the realm of backstage drama; the casting of Joan Blondell and distant echoes of *All About Eve* locate the film squarely

within that tradition. And Cassavetes gives us several levels of 'performance' to contend with as he parallels the 'real' problems of ageing star Gena Rowlands with those of the character she plays onstage in the appropriately titled *The Second Woman*. Overlong, but intelligent and intriguing. PT

Open Season
(Los Cazadores)
(Peter Collinson, 1974, Sp/Switz) Peter Fonda, Cornelia Sharpe, John Phillip Law, Richard Lynch, Albert Mendoza, William Holden, Helga Line.
104 min.
A cross between *Straw Dogs* and *Deliverance*, although its references are considerably wider and the plot itself is another reworking of *The Hounds of Zaroff*. Fonda, Law and Lynch – three clean-cut American boys who played football and served in Vietnam together – like to prove they are men two weeks in the year by going into the mountains to indulge in a little swimming, hunting, drinking, comradeship, murder and rape. Unfortunately Collinson is no Peckinpah or Boorman; so he has to rely on self-indulgent camerawork (soft focus and telephoto), ironic music, and overstressed dialogue ('Your licence to kill ran out after the war...but they forgot to tell you') to make sure the message gets across. And the hamfisted structure – fatal to this type of movie – makes even the Hitchcockian techniques fall flat. But there is plenty of nastiness, if that's what turns you on. GSa

Opera (Terror at the Opera)
(Dario Argento, 1987, It) Christina Marsillach, Ian Charleson, Urbano Barberini, Daria Nicolodi, Antonella Vitale.
90 min.
The Visconti of Violence goes straight for the throat (and eyes) in this stylishly sick thriller about a young diva – the setting is a production of *Macbeth* at La Scala opera house –terrorised by a psycho killer. All the trademarks are here: minimal plot, striking set pieces, baroque camera movements, misogynist violence. As always, though, the most horrific thing is the dubbing. See it, if you must, on the big screen, because its swirling camerawork and imaginative nastiness will be completely lost on video. NF

Opera do Malandro
(Ruy Guerra, 1986, Fr/Braz) Edson Celulari, Claudia Ohana, Elba Ramalho, Ney Latorraca, Fabio Sabag.
108 min.
Take *The Threepenny Opera*, relocate in Rio, replace Kurt Weill's score with Brazilian sambas, and embellish with dancing and dreamy decor...In this loose adaptation of Brecht's classic, Guerra tells a tale of fairytale simplicity: the year is 1941, and the Brazilian government is backing the Nazis against the wishes of the US-obsessed population at large, one of whom – white-suited pimp Max – is developing his own capitalistic practices. Between pool-room rumbles, black-market deals, and living off the earnings of faithful Margot (ex-mistress of corrupt cop Tiger), Max devises a plan to seduce the apparently innocent daughter of his arch-enemy, nightclub-owner Otto Strüdell, which has unexpected consequences. The pleasure to be had from Guerra's elegant, robustly physical movie derives not only from Chico Buarque's lilting, swinging score and the colourfully extravagant dancing, but from Guerra's deceptively playful tone, bewitchingly pitched somewhere between realism and filmic fantasy. Hollywood ancestors – notably Hawks' *Scarface* and Gene Kelly musicals – are refracted through a double prism of Brechtian modernism and traditional Brazilian culture. Political satire and lusty melodrama are imaginatively merged, with Guerra's camera deftly juggling various tropes of cinematic illusion. All in all, an astonishing offering of wit, verve and imagination. GA

Operation Amsterdam
(Michael McCarthy, 1959, GB) Peter Finch, Eva Bartok, Tony Britton, Alexander Knox, Malcolm Keen, Melvyn Hayes.
104 min. b/w.
Brisk, no-nonsense British war movie (from Rank), tersely directed by McCarthy (whose background was in documentary) and full of unfussy, businesslike endeavour. Tony Britton leads a mission to Amsterdam in the summer of 1940 (the eve

of the Nazi invasion) to prevent a valuable stash of industrial diamonds falling into enemy hands. Time is short – the Germans are only hours from town – but Britton and his crew make sure they get the job done. The one real casualty here is characterisation – there's such an onus on keeping the narrative moving that we get precious little chance to learn what makes the heroes tick. Adapted by the director and John Eldridge from the book *Adventure in Diamonds* by David E Walker. GM

Operation Crossbow
(Michael Anderson, 1965, GB/It) George Peppard, Jeremy Kemp, Tom Courtenay, Sophia Loren, Trevor Howard, John Mills, Richard Johnson, Anthony Quayle, Helmut Dantine, Richard Todd, Lilli Palmer, Paul Henreid, Sylvia Syms.
116 min.
Standard World War II 'mission impossible' adventure in which three Allied officers with scientific training (Peppard, Kemp, Courtenay) are parachuted into Holland, posing as Dutch or German scientists reported missing, in order to locate – and help destroy, at the cost of their lives – the V2 rocket base at Peenemunde. Much ado about background authenticity is nullified by the cardboard characters, but the starry cast makes it all relatively painless. A Carlo Ponti production, so Sophia Loren came with the package and gets shot for her pains: TM

Operation Daybreak
(Lewis Gilbert, 1975, US) Timothy Bottoms, Martin Shaw, Joss Ackland, Nicola Pagett, Anthony Andrews, Kika Markham, Anton Diffring, Carl Duering.
119 min.
As with other war films around this time, the problems of dramatic reconstruction are never reconciled with those of historical perspective. Based on the assassination in 1941 of Reinhard Heydrich (the Nazi leader in Czechoslovakia) and the subsequent German reprisals, the film unhappily mixes scrupulous accuracy with too much shoddily-rendered suspense. Apart from Anton Diffring's Heydrich, the characters are painted in black and white, so that the film falls apart when one of the freedom fighters unconvincingly becomes a turncoat. Only in the last ten minutes or so, with the final shootout and death of the last two assassins, does the film get to grips at all. Otherwise an over-routine journey.

Operation Disaster
see Morning Departure

Operation Petticoat
(Blake Edwards, 1959, US) Cary Grant, Tony Curtis, Dina Merrill, Gene Evans, Arthur O'Connell, Joan O'Brien.
124 min.
Despite the fortuitous teaming of Grant and Curtis – as the commander of a creaking World War I submarine determined to get it back in action by fair means or foul, and as the conman lieutenant who obligingly wheels, deals and steals the necessary materials – this is a very thin comedy indeed. Not unpleasant, but the situations (including the inevitable invasion of women aboard the sub) are horribly familiar, and the dialogue none too inspired. GA

Operation Thunderbolt
(Menahem Golan, 1977, Isr) Yehoram Gaon, Assaf Dayan, Ori Levy, Arik Lavi, Klaus Kinski, Sybil Danning, Mark Heath.
125 min.
Who needs another Entebbe raid film? Following *Raid on Entebbe* and *Victory at Entebbe*, this official Israeli version does rather have the look of yesterday's news despite Golan's efforts to build an immediacy through use of reaction shots and fast editing. The script wisely concentrates on the general plight of the hijacked instead of opting for the usual disaster movie composition of individual experiences. The result at least has more cohesion than *Victory at Entebbe*. Two strikes against it are its dreadful score and Mark Heath's Idi Amin; compensation comes with Kinski's haunted, cryptic performance as the hijack leader, giving the film a much-needed dramatic centre. CPe

Operation Undercover
see Report to the Commissioner

Opposite Sex, The
(David Miller, 1956, US) June Allyson, Joan Collins, Dolores Gray, Ann Sheridan, Leslie Nielsen, Agnes Moorehead, Joan Blondell.
117 min.
Cukor's 1939 sparkling conversation piece, *The Women*, had an all female cast. This low voltage remake adds songs, CinemaScope and (gulp) men, in the shape of philandering Nielsen, who's married to ex-chanteuse Allyson but fooling around with chorine Collins. 'Young Man With a Horn' remains the most memorable title from an undistinguished set of tunes. TJ

Optimists of Nine Elms, The
(Anthony Simmons, 1973, GB) Peter Sellers, Donna Mullane, John Chaffey, David Daker, Marjorie Yates.
110 min.
Two kids form a quirky relationship with an eccentric old busker (Sellers). Despite there being a host of things (like songs and music by Lionel Bart) that should have crippled this venture, it has, on the contrary, a lot going for it. With the help of the two kids and some fine location work, Simmons sketches a suitably hard-edged and realistic portrait of a drab existence south of the river. Father is aggressive and mother run-down, reduced to having a quick one Sunday mornings when the children are out. Conditions at home are poor and crowded, but the 'better life' of a promised new council flat is shown up for what it is. At least you feel that Simmons has continually avoided the easy way out, and that should be enough to counteract any feelings of unease. CPe

Orca (aka Orca...
Killer Whale)
(Michael Anderson, 1977, US) Richard Harris, Charlotte Rampling, Will Sampson, Bo Derek, Keenan Wynn, Scott Walker, Robert Carradine.
92 min.
Yet another attempt to poach in the profitable waters of *Jaws*. The threat this time is the eponymous whale, supposedly a killer species. The threatened include Richard Harris in a one-dimensional performance as the shark hunter turned whale-killer, Charlotte Rampling as a marine biologist studying the species, and a townful of fisherfolk. There is some startling footage, but Anderson's direction dithers perceptibly, and finally opts for an unpleasant mish-mash of phony ecological concern and meretricious sensationalism. The ultimate indignity the beast suffers is to become a simple extension of Harris' threadbare macho image. VG

Orchestra Rehearsal
(Prova d'Orchestra)
(Federico Fellini, 1978, It/WGer) Balduin Baas, Clara Colosimo, Elisabeth Labi, Ronaldo Bonacchi, Ferdinando Villella.
72 min.
Too much art, too little substance, kills Fellini's modern parable of an orchestra intent on anarchy – confessing their passions, protesting their individuality, and collectively dismissing their boss conductor. A satirical made-for-TV vignette, it makes you marvel at what can be done with one gag, one set, and a swollen reputation. DMacp

Orchestra Wives
(Archie Mayo, 1942, US) George Montgomery, Ann Rutherford, Cesar Romero, Lynn Bari, Carole Landis, Jackie Gleason, Glenn Miller and his Band.
98 min. b/w.
Second and by far the best of (surprisingly) only two movies graced by the Glenn Miller band, with some great numbers strung out on a slender plot enlivened by bright dialogue as the wives do a lot of loving and bitching while following the band tour. A moment to treasure is the specialty dance to 'I've Got a Gal in Kalamazoo' by the marvellous Nicholas Brothers. TM

Ordeal by Innocence
(Desmond Davis, 1984, GB) Donald Sutherland, Faye Dunaway, Christopher Plummer, Sarah Miles, Ian McShane, Diana Quick, Annette Crosbie, Michael Elphick.
88 min.
In this adaptation of what was reputedly Agatha Christie's favourite among her own novels, a sci-

entist (Sutherland) turns up with evidence which would have cleared a tried murderer. Alas, the boy has been hanged, and the family seems more interested in covering up the past than rehabilitating his reputation. Set in the '50s, the film succeeds admirably in catching a feeling of repression and social conformity, and the idea of murder as a means of maintaining respectability rather than for gain or passion. Agatha Christie's creation is finally recovered from Cluedo territory, and provides British cinema with a genuine '50s black thriller. CPea

Order of Death (aka Corrupt)
(Roberto Faenza, 1983, It) Harvey Keitel, John Lydon, Nicole Garcia, Leonard Mann, Sylvia Sidney, Carla Romanelli.
101 min.
Keitel is a cop whose secret world of high living (financed by illicit side-dealing) is invaded by Lydon, who not only confesses to a spate of cop-killings, but seems to know more about Keitel than is comfortable. Two little balls of poison, they become locked together in sadistic games in which the captor needs his victim as much as the victim needs his confessor. The film (shot in English) is very much in line with the Continental habit of turning genres around – like Leone with the Western, this is a spaghetti thriller – and it uses the hard-nosed framework as a prop for its greater interest in the moral complexities of guilt, punishment and transference, rather than the traditional gestures of its US models. Keitel is his usual ineffable self, his features glassy with repressed anxiety and violence; the only miscalculation is the casting of Lydon (aka Johnny Rotten), who seems as threatening as a wet poodle. CPea

Orders
see Ordres, Les

Orders Are Orders
(David Paltenghi, 1954, GB) Margot Grahame, Maureen Swanson, June Thorburn, Raymond Huntley, Bill Fraser, Peter Sellers, Brian Reece, Sidney James, Tony Hancock.
78 min. b/w.
Crude farce in which an American film unit descends on an army barracks to make a sci-fi movie, with the buxom actresses sowing predictable havoc. Based on a 1932 play, previously filmed (as *Orders Is Orders*) in 1933, with jokes just as antiquated. Just about worth suffering to see Tony Hancock in his film debut as the harassed bandmaster. TM

Orders to Kill
(Anthony Asquith, 1958, GB) Paul Massie, Irene Worth, Lillian Gish, Eddie Albert, Leslie French, James Robertson Justice, John Crawford, Lionel Jeffries, Sandra Dorne, Jacques Brunius.
111 min. b/w.
A way above average Asquith film, this is a WWII drama, with Massie sent to Occupied Paris to kill a Resistance leader (French) suspected of being a Nazi collaborator. But his target turns out to be a mild-mannered family man with Lillian Gish for a mother. Despite his doubts (later proved to be well-founded), the deed is done, and the movie starts to focus on Massie's later life. Working well in the first half as a thriller, it then turns into a Graham Greene-like, intensely Catholic study of the conflict between conscience and duty. ATu

Order to Kill
(El Clan de los Inmorales)
(José G Maeso, 1973, Sp/It/Dom) Helmut Berger, Sydne Rome, José Ferrer, Kevin McCarthy, Elena Berrido.
95 min.
This extraordinarily tacky offering does at least have some interesting undercurrents. Shot in Santo Domingo (of all places), and featuring Helmut Berger (of all people) toting a machine-gun (of all things), the film on one level is a catalogue of ineptness: crude establishing shots, irrelevant music, jerky editing, and a plot (which has Berger blackmailed into working for a renegade police chief) that warrants little attention. What holds it together beneath the surface mess is a distinctly homosexual aura of sadism and masochism. Since this has nothing to do with the

plot, one is surprised at the relentlessness of the smouldering looks and rippling torsos. In addition to some crude emphasis on phallic gunplay, the utter disposability of the women, and trials of strength and endurance, the film goes to outrageous lengths to have its star look disarranged or be beaten up.

Ordet (The Word) [100]
(Carl Dreyer, 1954, Den) Henrik Malberg, Emil Hass Christensen, Preben Lerdorff Rye, Cay Kristiansen, Birgitte Federspiel.
125 min. b/w.
Dreyer's penultimate feature (*Gertrud* followed a full decade later) is another of his explorations of the clash between orthodox religion and true faith. Based with great fidelity on a play by Kaj Munk, it's formulated as a kind of rural chamber drama, and like most of Dreyer's films it centres on the tensions within a family. Its method is to establish a scrupulously realistic frame of reference, then undercut it thematically with elements of the fantastic and formally with a film syntax that demands constant attention to the way meaning is being constructed. The intensity of the viewer's relationship with the film makes the closing scene (a miracle) one of the most extraordinary in all cinema. TR

Ordinary People
(Robert Redford, 1980, US) Donald Sutherland, Mary Tyler Moore, Judd Hirsch, Timothy Hutton, M Emmet Walsh, Elizabeth McGovern, Dinah Manoff, James B Sikking.
124 min.
Any movie starring the all-American dream mum Mary Tyler Moore as a neurotic, domineering mother, papering over the cracks as her husband and son go to pieces, should get ten out of ten. Unfortunately, Robert Redford's super-tasteful *Ordinary People* uses her pixie grin as its only effective irony. For the rest, it's a scrupulously observed affluent American psychodrama that wishes it was Chekhov: tinged with autumn leaves, and following the cocktail party, the golfing holiday, the school swimming race, it peels away the happy smile of these 'ordinary people', plunged into misery after the death of one son and the breakdown of another. An actors' movie and an advert for therapy, extremely bitter, but handsomely directed in its elegant pretentiousness, it leaves you the impression that Redford is, despite it all, as cuddly as a teddy-bear. DMacp

Ordinary Tenderness
see Tendresse Ordinaire

Ordres, Les (Orders)
(Michel Brault, 1974, Can) Jean Lapointe, Hélène Loiselle, Claude Gauthier, Louise Forestier, Guy Provost.
107 min. b/w & col.
Brault's film not only doesn't provide answers to the political questions it throws up in its reconstruction of the effects of Canada's 1970 War Measures Act, it scarcely even seems aware of the true questions. Brault's sifting of the case histories of 450 Quebec citizens, arrested and detained without charge under virtual martial law which arose from two political kidnappings, is absorbing enough as 'Kafkaesque' dramatic reconstruction. And the persecution of five of them invites all of the expected audience empathy. But ultimately the film merely becomes a prolonged liberal wank over the summary loss of civil liberties, when it should be getting at the question of how this state of authoritarian paranoia became possible in a supposedly democratic society. RM

Orfeu Negro
see Black Orpheus

Organ
(Kei Fujiwara, 1996, Jap) Kimihiko Hasegawa, Kenji Nasa, Kei Fujiwara, Ryo Okubo, Shozo Tojima.
105 min.
Diminishing returns hit splatter movies faster than most other genres, and this starts straining for effect and repeating itself within its first hour – with a turgid 45 minutes of blood-letting and grotesquerie to go. Director/writer/star Fujiwara (she played the mutilated girlfriend in *Tetsuo*) kicks it off in neo-*noir* mode: undercover cops

investigate a yakuza-financed trade in body parts ripped from murder victims for transplant surgery. But the weird brother and sister doing the murdering and organ-extractions turn out to have histories as hideously abused kids, which twists the film in the direction of pop psychodrama. TR

Organization, The
(Don Medford, 1971, US) Sidney Poitier, Gerald S O'Loughlin, Barbara McNair, Sheree North, Raúl Julia, Ron O'Neal, Allen Garfield.
107 min.
Poitier's third (and final) appearance as Lt. Virgil Tibbs, now risen beyond the good black cop idea to regular good cop, with all the hagiography this implies (good looks, boyish charm, nice wife, happy kids; against him the villains are unpleasant, faceless, childless, ruthless). The organization is a world-wide heroin combine operating behind the façade of big business. None too convincing (since the film is torn between the need to make them ridiculous and the need to have us rooting for them) is the group of good-hearted liberals who, distressed by the fuzz's lack of action, decide to take on the organization themselves. Tibbs, needless to say, does an exemplary job. In spite of everything, the climactic action sequences are genuinely intriguing and totally involving. VG

Organized Crime and Triad
Bureau (Zhong'an Shilu O-ji)
(Che Kirk Wong, 1993, HK) Danny Lee, Anthony Wong, Cecilia Yip.
90 min.
The perennial bad boy of Hong Kong cinema, Kirk Wong (trained in Croydon) has left behind the SM perversities of his early movies and found a niche directing hard-man thrillers much closer to street-level realities than anything John Woo ever did. This one's about an oddball cop (Danny Lee, who also produced) tracking a villain to his island hideaway to arrest him, only to lose him in a break-out. The fact that the bad guy was about to flee into Mainland China hints at political references, but what this is really about is staging running battles between cops and criminals in everyday locations, from the island backwater to the crowded streets of central Kowloon. As such, it's a blast. TR

Orgasmo
see Paranoia

Orgueilleux, Les
(The Proud Ones)
(Yves Allégret, 1953, Fr/Mex) Gérard Philipe, Michèle Morgan, Carlos L Moctezuma, Victor M Mendoza, Michèle Cordoue.
104 min. b/w.
One of those sub-Graham Greene tales of redemption in exotic climes (actually based on a story by Sartre, *L'Amour Rédempteur*), with Morgan as a chic tourist stranded in a Mexican village when her husband suddenly dies of meningitis, and Philippe as the drink-sodden doctor regaining his self-respect in the ensuing epidemic (not to mention her arms). Busily atmospheric, it strains mightily after a sort of sweaty eroticism (a key scene being one in which Philippe has to give Morgan an extremely painful lumbar injection), with the bleak and dusty locations often strikingly shot by Alex Phillips; but despite the valiant efforts of both leads, the central relationship and redemption theme are ludicrously spurious. TM

Original Gangstas
(Larry Cohen, 1996, US) Fred Williamson, Jim Brown, Pam Grier, Paul Winfield, Richard Roundtree, Ron O'Neal, Isabel Sanford.
99 min.
Gary, Indiana: a dying steeltown. A young basketball hopeful is killed by hoodlums. An elderly cornerstore proprietor tells the cops who did it. The Rebels shoot him. The man's football-coach son (Williamson) returns from LA and, with the help of angry oldies, including the dead boy's mum (Grier) and estranged, ex-boxer father (Brown), sets about cleaning up the town. He declares war on the Rebels – ironic, given that two decades earlier he'd been a founder of the gang. Despite its standard formula, this belated blaxploitation picture is something of an oddity. First, it attempts to

frame its story of ghetto warfare within an economic and political context; second, it pits '70s stars against the kind of younger, more heavily armed and more nihilistic characters familiar from '90s fare. In siding so explicitly with the old-timers in their outrage at mindless murder, it flirts with sentimentality, but at least it's not seduced by the gangstas' macho posturing; moreover, Williamson and Brown's own former irresponsibilities – abandoning families and struggling communities – are presented as being at least partly to blame for the chaos and carnage now on the streets. As an action-thriller the film never quite delivers; sociologically, however, it's not without interest. GA

Orion's Belt (Orions Belte)

(Ola Solum, 1985, Nor) Helge Jordal, Sverre Anker Ousdal, Hans Ola Sorlie, Kjersti Holmen.
103 min.
A Norwegian thriller, and it ain't half bad. Actually, it's half pretty good, and the rest is average. Three sailors, who make a living doing less than legal things with their broken-down boat, are quite happy roaming the stormy Arctic seas until they stumble on a secret Russian surveillance post. Chaos ensues as the Russians discover them and try to kill them off, notably in a fine helicopter attack. Towards the end, the suspense drops a little as the film becomes more conventional, but the first hour is gripping, intelligent, and unusual, both in terms of characterisation and story. And the location shooting, predictably, is superb. GA

Orlando

(Sally Potter, 1992, GB/Rus/Fr/It/Neth) Tilda Swinton, Billy Zane, John Wood, Lothaire Bluteau, Charlotte Valandrey, Heathcote Williams, Quentin Crisp, Dudley Sutton.
93 min.
There are lots of intellectual traditions vying for ascendancy in Potter's adaptation of Virginia Woolf's 1928 modernist novel, but the joy is that the film comes over simply: a beautiful historical pageant of 400 years of English history, full of visual and aural pleasures, sly jokes, thought-provoking insights, emotional truths – and romance. It begins at the opulent court of Virgin Queen Elizabeth (Crisp), where the male immortal Orlando receives favour and an estate; and thence follows his quest for love in 50-year jumps through the Civil War, the early colonial period, the effete literary salons of 1750 (by which time Orlando is a woman), the Victorian era of property, and finally a 20th century postscript added by Potter. The fine, stylised performances from an idiosyncratic international cast are admirably headed by Swinton's magnificent Orlando, who acts as the film's complicitous eyes and ears; and there's little to fault in Alexei Rodionov's cinematography, which renders the scenes with rare sensitivity. It's a critical work – in the sense that it comments wryly on such things as representations of English history, sexuality/androgyny and class – but made in the spirit of a love poem to both Woolf and the England that made us. WH

Orlovs, The (Suprugi Orlovy)

(Mark Donskoi, 1978, USSR) Nina Ruslanova, Anatoly Semyonov, Seryozha Tegin, Danil Sagal, Yuri Kamorny.
85 min.
A friend of Gorki, Eisenstein's assistant, Civil War Red soldier: Mark Donskoi's extraordinary career spans a century of Russian history, and includes making the three famous *Gorki* films in the '30s which more recently influenced Bill Douglas in his own autobiographical trilogy. *The Orlovs*, taken from another Gorki story, is fashioned in the same style as his earlier films: a close Dickensian focus on everyday village life which pre-dates the later unacceptable face of Soviet Social Realism. The central couple are given the chance of transcending the general misery of their lives by working in a hospital during a cholera outbreak. The poem, he regresses, they part; a moral tale with its typical Gorkian emphasis on the necessity of striving for a better existence. Heartening to find a social vision of such clear-eyed optimism from a 78-year-old. CPea

Ornette: Made in America

(Shirley Clarke, 1985, US) Ornette Coleman, Demon Marshall, Gene Tatum.
80 min.

Not surprisingly, the musical content in this documentary about modern jazz's greatest iconoclast is superb: much of it revolves around a 1983 performance of Ornette Coleman's 'Skies of America' suite, with orchestra and the harmolodic Prime Time band. Clarke's film, however, is something else: with updated psychedelic visual tricks, and little info on the master's life or career, it fails to do him or his music justice. But for the sight and sound of the man in action (including some fine archive footage from the early '70s), it's essential viewing for any jazz aficionado. GA

Orphans

(Alan J Pakula, 1987, US) Albert Finney, Matthew Modine, Kevin Anderson, John Kellogg, Anthony Heald.
120 min.
Adapting his own play, Lyle Kessler has ventured out from the clapped-out clapboard in Newark where Phillip (Anderson) is kept in thrall to his brother Treat (Modine). An opening sequence, showing Treat as a compassionate mugger, establishes the violent conflict of emotions within the robbing hood, but otherwise the few external excursions don't add much. Fortunately, the pressure-cooker atmosphere of the central arena is by no means dissipated. Phillip believes he will die if he goes outside, so while his keeper is out providing for them, he prowls the house like a mangy caged animal or (though Treat thinks he's illiterate) reads in the attic. This precarious state of interdependence is upset when Treat brings back Harold (Finney), a gangster who is drunk and rolling in dodgy dollars, in a ransom bid defeated when Harold, a fellow-orphan, offers these dead end kids his affection. Under Harold's munificent guidance, the lonesome sons rehabilitate both their home and themselves...until Treat's inability to control his feelings precipitates disaster. Pakula's direction extracts every ounce of energy from this ferocious tragedy, with Finney and Anderson, repeating their acclaimed performances from the London stage production, eclipsed by Modine, in stunning form. It's funny, fearsome, and finally very moving. MS

Orphans of the Storm

(DW Griffith, 1921, US) Lillian Gish, Dorothy Gish, Creighton Hale, Joseph Schildkraut, Frank Losee, Catherine Emmett, Morgan Wallace.
143 min. (21 fps). b/w (tinted).
Griffith's neglected epic stars the Gish sisters as victims of the chaos that hits Paris during the French Revolution. Authentic down to real champagne at an aristocratic bacchanal, the film depicts the storming of the Bastille with spectacular flair. While the director's handling of humour (clumsy) and pathos (heavily milked) demands some generosity from the audience, the eternal radiance of Lillian Gish shines through everything. The restored print under review (in 1998), from New York's Museum of Modern Art, is fine on detail but suffers from excessive tinting. DT

Orphée (Orpheus)

(Jean Cocteau, 1950, Fr) Jean Marais, Maria Casarès, François Périer, Marie Déa, Edouard Dermithe, Juliette Gréco, Henri Crémieux.
112 min. b/w.
Marais (Cocteau's companion) plays the '40s poet (alias Cocteau) who's won fame, fortune and the hatred of Left Bank youth. Desperate for inspiration, he follows an imperious Princess flanked by Fascist (or 'Cruising') type police. Her rubber-gloved hand leads through the looking-glass to a slow-motion night kingdom...This *Sur-Noir* fantasy has more meanings than the Book of Revelations. It's an allegory for Poetry. It's the Confessions of a Gay Opium-Eater. Its mirrors and misogyny, optical tricks and enigmatic phrases, mark it as prime meat for Lacanians and feminists. With its Resistance Band radios and brutal militiamen it catches the terrors of Occupation life. Its tight cross-lacing of paranoid dreaming and poetic realism grips like a bondage corset. When Resnais in Japan couldn't get his *Hiroshima, Mon Amour* crew to understand, he'd refer to *Orphée*, whose weird myth fascinated them all. RD

Ortliebschen Frauen, Die

see Josephine

Osaka Story

(Toichi Nakata, 1994, GB)
75 min.
A compulsive account of Toichi Nakata's return to Osaka to tell his Japanese-Korean family, who want him home and married, that he plans to stay in the West as a film-maker. An illuminating look at Japanese family life (dad is misanthropic tyrant) and a study of the difficult relationship between Japanese and Koreans, the film has an almost confrontational frankness that belies some of the conventionally polite behaviour on view. GA

Oscar

(John Landis, 1991, US) Sylvester Stallone, Ornella Muti, Kirk Douglas, Peter Riegert, Vincent Spano, Marisa Tomei, Chazz Palminteri, Harry Shearer, Martin Ferrero, Tim Curry, Don Ameche, Richard Romanus, Kurtwood Smith, Eddie Bracken, Yvonne De Carlo, William Atherton.
109 min.
Landis transposes Claude Magnier's French farce to Prohibition-era America in homage to the screwball comedies of the '30s. The script is sharp, if formulaic, but the film suffers from several contradictions: this is a farce without sexual tension, a family film with Stallone in the lead, a Landis comedy without vulgarity. At the centre of a deliciously convoluted plot involving mislaid suitcases and never-laid suitors is the plight of Snaps (Stallone), a gangster who promised his dying father to go straight, only no one believes him. Which is the reverse of Stallone's plight: he's trying to go into comedy, only we can't quite believe him. It's a demanding role which calls for more than he can give. Only an eye-poppingly camp Tim Curry, and Harry Shearer and Martin Ferrero's bickering Finucci Brothers, inject life into the proceedings. Landis orchestrates the action with military precision, but forgot to tell his troupe to go over the top. DW

Oscar, The

(Russell Rouse, 1966, US) Stephen Boyd, Elke Sommer, Tony Bennett, Eleanor Parker, Milton Berle, Joseph Cotten, Jill St John, Edie Adams, Ernest Borgnine.
121 min.
Tacky Tinseltown soaper, logging the unscrupulous rise to stardom of an Academy-nominated actor in a succession of flashbacks, featuring numerous stellar walk-ons and dreadful dialogue. Co-scripted by sci-fi hero Harlan Ellison, based on the novel by Richard Sale, and directed by gimmick-master Rouse, whose *The Thief* contains not one line of dialogue, but who himself had a moment of true glory in co-scripting *DOA*. PT

Oscar and Lucinda

(Gillian Armstrong, 1997, US/Aus) Ralph Fiennes, Cate Blanchett, Ciaran Hinds, Tom Wilkinson, Richard Roxburgh, Clive Russell, Bille Brown.
132 min.
In this exquisite adaptation of Peter Carey's novel, gambling is more than an obsession – it's a leap of faith. For eccentric Anglican cleric Oscar Hopkins, winning on the horses is God's way of providing financial support for him and the Oxford poorhouse, while Australian heiress Lucinda Leplastrier's evenings around the card table are just one expression of the scandalous individualism that has already seen this single woman running her own glass factory. As we follow their personal histories from troubled childhood to awkward maturity, the pair seem destined to meet, even though they have grown up on opposite sides of the world. An ocean voyage from Portsmouth to Sydney allows fate to play its hand, but can such emotionally fragile individuals take advantage of their chance combination? Fiennes and Blanchett's expertly judged performances stand at the centre of this tantalising narrative, which conjures a touching love story from the silences of its protagonists' halting vulnerability. For director Armstrong, it marks another wise portrait of resilient Victorian womanhood to match even *My Brilliant Career*, but here she goes beyond her usual classical economy. Everything a costume drama should be. TJ

Ososhiki (Death Japanese Style/Funeral Rites)

(Juzo Itami, 1984, Jap) Tsutomu Yamazaki, Nobuko Miyamoto, Kin Sugai, Shuji Otaki, Ichiro Zaitsu.
124 min. b/w & col.
Another film about food, sex and death from Itami, inspired by his own participation in the funeral of his wife's father. Yamazaki and Miyamoto play a married couple who are hauled out of their dopey work in a TV studio and plunged into the exceedingly expensive business of co-ordinating the burial rites of the wife's cantankerous father. The three-day wake turns out to be a succession of absurd mishaps, family squabbles and unwelcome surprises, reaching its spiritual nadir when an uninvited woman guest drunkenly insists on having sex with Yamazaki before she'll agree to leave. A light-black satire, this is less a Japanese *The Loved One* than a rather feebly wishful attempt to revive the Ozu spirit in Japanese cinema. Invoking Ozu (and there are direct visual quotes from *The End of Summer* and other movies) is to invite comparisons, and that's unwise, given the film's uncertainty of tone and structure. The stand-out sequence is probably also the most realistic: the head of the family struggling to master funeral etiquette from an instructional video. TR

Ossessione

(Luchino Visconti, 1942, It) Clara Calamai, Massimo Girotti, Juan De Landa, Dhia Cristiani, Elio Marcuzzo.
139 min. b/w.
Visconti's stunning feature debut transposes *The Postman Always Rings Twice* to the endless, empty lowlands of the Po Delta. There, an itinerant labourer (Girotti) stumbles into a tatty roadside trattoria and an emotional quagmire. Seduced by Calamai, he disposes of her fat, doltish husband (De Landa), and the familiar Cain litany – lust, greed, murder, recrimination – begins. *Ossessione* is often described as the harbinger of neo-realism, but the pictorial beauty (and astute use of music, often ironically) are pure Visconti, while the bleak view of sexual passion poaches on authentic *noir* territory, steeped, as co-scriptwriter Giuseppe De Santis put it, 'in the air of death and sperm'. SJo

Osterman Weekend, The

(Sam Peckinpah, 1983, US) Rutger Hauer, John Hurt, Meg Foster, Dennis Hopper, Craig T Nelson, Helen Shaver, Cassie Yates, Burt Lancaster, Chris Sarandon.
105 min.
Adapted from Robert Ludlum's thriller, this trails a McGuffin about an un-American spy ring, but really revolves around a top brass CIA man with his eye on dictatorship (Lancaster), a disgruntled agent whom the aforesaid bastard has double-crossed (Hurt), and a flag-waving investigative reporter (Hauer) whom Hurt manipulates into a game of unmask the spy from three candidates (Hopper, Nelson, Sarandon) that has a much more sinister purpose. It all raises the question: who needs another mess of espionage and post-Watergate paranoia? Not Peckinpah, certainly, since he shows scant interest in the convolutions of the plot (neatly enough set out in Alan Sharp's script). Instead, he toys with the agent's name (Fassett) as an excuse to explore facets of reality, fascinatingly turning the screen into a multi-purpose surveillance device. There's a neat trick involving a prerecorded 'live' TV show, a precision-timed shootout round a swimming-pool, some flickers of dark humour. Not a hell of a lot to come away with, except that (sadly, Peckinpah's last film) it is directed with such dazzling skill. TM

Ostrich Has Two Eggs, The (Les Oeufs de l'Autruche)

(Denys de la Patellière, 1957, Fr) Pierre Fresnay, Simone Renant, Georges Poujouly, André Roussin, Yoko Tani.
82 min. b/w.
'My wife's cheating on me, my son's got a boyfriend…*Vive la famille!*' ironises Fresnay in the gruff bark he favoured for comedies. This adaptation of a play by André Roussin (who also fancied himself as an actor) has zero entertainment value or cinematic interest, but it remains significant sociologically for having, mid-century, a leading character who is gay *and* sympa-thetic. Not only that, but the traditional 'heavy' figures (e.g. the womanising younger brother) all accept Lolo's gayness and try to help him; even Dad comes around when one of his son's frock designs wins a big cash prize. Who plays this phenomenon? No one. In a virtuoso job of construction, Lolo is kept off-screen from start to finish, evidently on the calculation that audiences would be more inclined to accept an abstract sympathetic gay. Still, as incremental progress goes, this counted as a moderate increment. BBa

Otello

(Franco Zeffirelli, 1986, It) Placido Domingo, Katia Ricciarelli, Justino Diaz, Petra Malakova, Urbano Barberini.
123 min.
Opera puritans will no doubt find much to carp about in this *Otello*, but they can go stuff themselves. Antiquated art forms need jiffing up, and Zeffirelli has cut the pack of cards at his disposal, inserted a couple of ballet numbers (composed by Verdi for the opera's Paris première), and reshuffled it all into something that is cinema instead of mere filmed performance. Distracting flashbacks during the love duet, and a tendency to dwell on the faces of handsome young actors, do not detract from the story's punch; and the cuts, although obscuring Roderigo's fate, enable the tragedy to unfold with a brio more acceptable to audiences weaned on Hollywood rather than Glyndebourne. The three principals are magnifico in both the warbling and the thespian stakes. AB

Othello

(Orson Welles, 1951, Mor) Orson Welles, Michael MacLiammoir, Suzanne Cloutier, Robert Coote, Hilton Edwards, Fay Compton.
91 min. b/w.
Welles's sixth feature (made directly after his avant-garde *Macbeth*) was shot in fits and starts over a period of four years, on a dozen locations in Morocco and Italy, often without money. Naturally, Welles turned the limitations into strengths. When the costumes didn't show up, he filmed in a Turkish bath. When an actor couldn't make it, he used a stand-in and changed his camera angle. When challenged to match footage shot in Mogador and Venice, he contrived dazzling webs of montage. This is Shakespeare filmed with love and powerhouse enthusiasm, never with reverence. The visual rhetoric is synchronised with the verbal imagery: they hit sensory overload together. A very great *film noir*. TR

Othello

(Stuart Burge, 1965, GB) Laurence Olivier, Maggie Smith, Frank Finlay, Joyce Redman, Derek Jacobi, Robert Lang, Kenneth Mackintosh, Anthony Nicholls, Sheila Reid.
166 min.
Fortunately, Shakespeare's most compressed, most domestic tragedy is here not 'opened out', but kept in its place as a claustrophobic chamber piece. But the basic, very evident fault of the film lies in its initial conception: an apparent desire simply to record Olivier's justly famous stage performance (at the National Theatre, directed by John Dexter). His bravura 'school of semaphore' style will not translate to a subtler, less literary medium, and comes across as such gross hamming as to leave a lingering impression of Othello as some demented nigger minstrel. Yet further evidence (as if more were needed) of the fundamental differences between theatre and film. Great theatre performances need great critics; not some enthusiast with a camera and an eye for posterity. CPea

Othello

(Oliver Parker, 1995, GB) Laurence Fishburne, Irène Jacob, Kenneth Branagh, Nathaniel Parker, Michael Maloney, Anna Patrick, Indra Ove, Nicholas Farrell, Michael Sheen.
123 min.
Though purists may decry the number of textual excisions and accent-watchers balk at the mix of French, Italian, English and tidied-up Brooklyn on offer here, Parker's first feature is a highly engaging attempt at Shakespeare's most domestic tragedy. Set in various Italian locations, the film obeys the cardinal rule which helps Iago to ensnare the jealous Moor and allows us to forget much of the play's innate absurdity: speed in all things. Using the camera well to explore reactions from onlookers and the main participants, Parker allows Branagh to assume the ring-master role in what is the actor's finest screen performance to date: an Iago rooted in reality, torn and muddied by the art of warfare, but still determined to work his poisonous will; a villain inspired by sexual jealousy but also by a banal, inexplicable malice, superbly hinted at in several perky asides. Fishburne is exotic, proud, bald and more than usually violent. The flashbacks and bed-scenes work, and the idea of having Cassio (Nathaniel Parker) slip Othello his suicide weapon is typically intelligent. But most importantly, everyone gets better as the film progresses, especially Fishburne whose early reserve explodes into passion, violence and moving sorrow. SGr

Other, The

(Robert Mulligan, 1972, US) Uta Hagen, Diana Muldaur, Chris Udvarnoky, Martin Udvarnoky, Norma Connolly, Victor French, John Ritter.
100 mins.
Scripted by Tom Tryon from his own novel, Mulligan's supernatural foray into the troubled world of childhood mercifully avoids the gory excesses of superficially similar films like *The Exorcist*, made the following year. It might have been mere mumbo-jumbo: his already fertile imagination further stimulated by the promptings of a wise old Russian-born grandmother (Hagen), who teaches him how to empathise totally with other creatures (human and animal), a young boy refuses to believe in the death of his twin brother, whom he blames for a series of mysterious killings. If the level of suspense is lowered by the fact that we soon realise who is responsible, Mulligan none the less produces a genuinely unsettling atmosphere, undermining the idyllic veneer of his '30s pastoral setting by refusing to romanticise his characters and stressing the claustrophobic elements of living in a close-knit community. As so often with this director's work, the film is craftsmanlike rather than brilliant, but the performances, Robert Surtees' lush camerawork, and Mulligan's solid psychological insights make for thoughtful, sometimes even chilling, entertainment. GA

Other Halves

(John Laing, 1984, GB) Lisa Harrow, Mark Pilisi, Fraser Stephen-Smith, Paul Gittins, John Bach, Clare Clifford.
105 min.
Laing deserves a medal for his attempts to negotiate the minefield of sensibilities laid by fellow-New Zealander Sue McCauley in this adaptation of her controversial novel: the tale of a despairing, middle class Auckland housewife (Harrow) who falls in love with a teenage Polynesian offender (Pilisi) while receiving psychiatric care for attempted suicide. Treating every taboo, not to mention cliché, associated with race, class and age, it could so easily have led to disaster. But Laing's documentarist's eye, used so effectively in his earlier *Beyond Reasonable Doubt*, manages to give enough sense of the reality behind the contrasted urban nightmares experienced by the two principals to make up for the inevitable infelicities involved. Using a quiet, unemphatic style, he concentrates on the fine performances of Harrow and Pilisi; and what emerges is an honest and affecting tribute to the courage of two outsiders struggling to find some private place of their own in the hostile world. WH

Other Men's Women

(William Wellman, 1931, US) Grant Withers, Mary Astor, Regis Toomey, James Cagney, Joan Blondell.
70 min. b/w.
Reminiscent of Renoir's *La Bête Humaine* (and not shamed by the comparison), this kicks off as fast, fluid, wisecracking comedy, then unexpectedly turns into a touching little tragedy about three people caught up in an unhappy triangle. The outcome is familiar, even conventional, with one rival being heroic and the other outdoing him; but the treatment is so rooted in reality and the acting so good (a bizarre trio of Astor, Withers and Toomey) that the result is a small masterpiece. Above all it is a film to be revelled in for its documentary detail: the sleepy little town with its quiet suburbia, its grimy hash-joint and steamy dance hall (where Cagney, in a supporting role, has a characteristically marvellous moment), and its vast, smoky complex of railway lines, shunting yards and railway sheds, always a major character in the film and swelling to malevolent proportions for the dark, rain-soaked finale. TM

Other One, The
(Conversa Acabada)

(Joao Botelho, 1981, Port) Cabral Martins, André Gomes, Juliet Berto, Jorge Silva Melo.
100 min.
'I am neither I nor the other one/I am something in between'. So wrote the Portuguese poet Mário de Sá-Carneiro, whose friendship with fellow-poet Fernando Pessoa during 1912-1916 forms the 'documentary' material of this Syberbergian first feature by Botelho. The political and moral crisis in early 20th century Portugal, the impasse of exile and the seduction of death, are the key themes in this richly stylised, quasi-theatrical attempt to put poetry on the screen. Stylish, and not short of substance. MA

Other People's Money

see Argent des Autres, L'

Other People's Money

(Norman Jewison, 1991, US) Danny DeVito, Gregory Peck, Penelope Ann Miller, Piper Laurie, Dean Jones, RD Call, Mo Gaffney, Tom Aldredge.
101 min.
The wiles of Wall Street may have been the stuff of '80s entertainment, but this adaptation of an off-Broadway play seems distinctly dated. Still, DeVito gives a wonderfully hammy, vindictive performance as wheeler-dealer 'Larry the Liquidator', whose latest target is a family-run, debt-free company. But chief executive Peck, his companion (Laurie) and her lawyer daughter (Miller) are determined to fight tooth and nail against the onslaught. Jewison does an impressive job with the sexually-charged scenes between DeVito and Miller. Other passages fall flat: the relationship between Peck and Laurie lacks impetus, and there's a sense of déjà vu about the constant references to Japanese knowhow. What Peck is doing in such an underwritten role is something of a mystery. CM

Other Side of Midnight, The

(Charles Jarrott, 1977, US) Marie-France Pisier, John Beck, Susan Sarandon, Raf Vallone, Clu Gulager, Christian Marquand, Sorrell Booke.
166 min.
The Other Side of Midnight gloriously restores the era of Now, Voyager – right down to the nonsense title; expert schlocksmiths Daniel Taradash (Doctors' Wives) and Herman Raucher (Summer of '42) have adapted Sidney Sheldon's bestseller into the movie equivalent of a good long bad read. Pisier aborts herself with a (wire) coathanger as World War II breaks out, sleeps her way across Europe, winds up mistress to a Greek tycoon, and deviously hires the pilot who jilted her back in 1940...The only let-downs are Jarrott's usual stuffy direction and John Beck's boring performance as the pilot. AN

Other Side of Sunday, The
(Søndagsengler)

(Berit Nesheim, 1996, Nor) Marie Theisen, Hildegunn Riise, Bjørn Sundquist.
97 min.
Rural Norway, 1959: Maria (Theisen), eldest of three children born to a stern parson, finds there's little of God's love in either her own life or the town's conformist Christian ethos; everything remotely pleasurable – lipstick, cafés, rock'n'roll, boys – is out of bounds. Only the verger, Mrs Tunheim, seems to share Maria's frustration and love of nature. Slight, but well-observed and ably performed. GA

Other Side of the
Mountain, The
(aka A Window to the Sky)

(Larry Peerce, 1975, US) Marilyn Hassett, Beau Bridges, Belinda J Montgomery, Nan Martin, William Bryant, Dabney Coleman.
102 min.
Embarrassing tearjerker wrung out of the real-life tragedy of a girl paralysed by a fall on the eve of selection as an Olympic skier. Shaken out of her self-pity by another skier (Bridges), she (Hassett) finds that she can still live a useful life (teaching in an Indian reservation school), and at last feels able to accept the love offered by Bridges – only to have fate tragically intervene once more. Accompanied by a slushy number

sung by Olivia Newton-John, ending on a note of bitter-sweet resignation, it's as unbearably fulsome as its sequel (The Other Side of the Mountain Part 2, 1978). TM

Other Sister, The

see Otra, La

Othon (Les Yeux ne peuvent pas en tout temps se fermer)

(Jean-Marie Straub/Danièle Huillet, 1969, WGer/It) Adriano Aprà, Anne Brumagne, Ennio Lauricella, Olimpia Carlisi.
83 min.
Straub examines the process by which events enter our cultural mainstream, and the process by which their use as part of a communications system is transformed into Culture. Corneille's play of political intrigue in Late Empire Rome is used as a base. The text speaks of individual power games outside of any social context. Straub perches his actors in togas on the Capitoline Hill in broad daylight. He treats Corneille's words as an undifferentiated block of sound (the actors gabble expressionlessly), and interweaves it with birdsong, traffic noises, the loud splashing of a fountain. A dialectic is set up between the abstraction of the actors' speech and the intimacy of their presence on screen; and between the actors as actors and the actors as play characters, between the actuality of the past and our use of it, with light and colour changes taking on some of the functions of intonation in speech. The film can be mesmeric or irritating: irritating if one tries to force it into fulfilling preconceived notions of plot and character, mesmeric if one trusts the film-maker to lead one into fresh areas of perception.

Otley

(Dick Clement, 1968, GB) Tom Courtenay, Romy Schneider, Alan Badel, James Villiers, Leonard Rossiter, James Bolam, Fiona Lewis, Freddie Jones.
91 min.
Scripted by Clement and Ian La Frenais, this vastly entertaining – if occasionally bewildering – comedy thriller stars Courtenay as the cowardly Otley, an innocent (though none too honest) Portobello Road layabout caught in a muddle of murder, mayhem and espionage. The plot never stops in its search for new ways to embarrass Otley: in one scene he seeks refuge in a crowd, only to find himself the only white man in a Black Power demonstration. More importantly, Otley's petty but human wheeling-and-dealing (lifting the odd art object for resale to the antique stalls) is consistently counterpoised to the slick inhumanity of his forever changing allies/friends, who only think of him as a tool to be used and then thrown away. PH

Otra, La (The Other Sister)

(Roberto Gavaldón, 1946, Mex) Dolores del Rio, Agustín Irusta, Victor Junco, José Baviera.
104 min. b/w.
If it weren't for the frequent pauses for morbid pseudo-poetic philosophising, this might be a Warners melodrama, Bette Davis vintage. (Indeed, it bears some resemblance to Bernhardt's A Stolen Life.) Desperate, impoverished del Rio murders her wealthy, unsympathetic, identical twin sister, and adopts her identity, only to experience doubts over abandoning her own loyal lover and confusion over the hitherto unknown facets of her sibling's existence. Fine noir-style camerawork and a taut if over-schematic narrative are let down by clumsy dialogue and the star's hammy double performance. Hitchcock might have enjoyed the fascination with guilt and its transference, but not, probably, the execution. GA

Our Daily Bread

see City Girl

Our Girl Friday (aka The Adventures of Sadie)

(Noel Langley, 1954, GB) Joan Collins, Kenneth More, George Cole, Robertson Hare, Hermione Gingold, Walter Fitzgerald, Hattie Jacques.
87 min.
Shipwrecked on an island in the Pacific with jolly Irish stoker More, hardbitten journo Cole and

stuffy economics lecturer Hare, millionaire's daughter Joan Collins clung to her 'U' certificate in this British sex comedy of 1954 (from Norman Lindsay's novel The Cautious Amorist). TJ

Our Hospitality

(Buster Keaton/John Blystone, 1923, US) Buster Keaton, Natalie Talmadge, Joe Roberts, Joe Keaton, Leonard Chapman, Craig Ward.
6,220 ft. b/w.
The main reason why Keaton is funnier and infinitely more 'modern' than Chaplin is that his movies are written, directed and shot as movies, never as excuses for comedy and/or pathos. This was his second feature and first full-length masterpiece, a story about the innocent inheritor of an old feud between Southern families, who carelessly starts dating the girl from the other family. The period setting (1831, the early days of rail travel) is made integral to the action, and all the laughs spring directly from the narrative and the characters. Buster's climactic rescue of his sweetheart from a waterfall is one of his most daringly acrobatic (and most celebrated) gags. TR

Our Man in Havana

(Carol Reed, 1959, GB) Alec Guinness, Burl Ives, Maureen O'Hara, Ernie Kovacs, Noël Coward, Ralph Richardson, Paul Rogers, Jo Morrow, Grégoire Aslan.
111 min. b/w.
A real 'winds of change' film, with traditional values visibly crumbling in the heat of pre-revolutionary Cuba. Guinness is wonderful. Discovering an unexpected ability to recognise the real in the game of make-believe, he emerges as master of the situation through the boldness of his fantasies. This mad world, where fictional characters die real deaths and even the Clean-Easy man can't be trusted, has little in common with Le Carré's Circus, but as Guinness' vacuum-cleaner salesman/spy sheds his innocence, he becomes dimly recognisable as an early incarnation of mole-catcher Smiley. Graham Greene's 'entertainment' is only gently macabre and the threats never quite materialise, but the film cleverly captures the confusion of optimism, cynicism and money-grubbing greed of the 'never had it so good' years. RMy

Our Man in Marrakesh

see Homme de Marrakesh, L'

Our Mother's House

(Jack Clayton, 1967, GB) Dirk Bogarde, Margaret Brooks, Pamela Franklin, Louis Sheldon Williams, John Gugolka, Mark Lester, Sarah Nicholls, Gustav Henry, Parnham Wallace, Yootha Joyce.
105 min.
In this matter of fact tale of the macabre, seven children, the eldest aged 13, stick together to carry on as normal after their mother's death. With the old girl safely buried in the garden, all looks to be going smoothly, until ne'er-do-well Bogarde turns up claiming he's their long-lost dad. Intriguing material (adapted by Jeremy Brooks and Haya Harareet from the novel by Julian Gloag), but it's not quite as persuasive as it could have been since all the brats seem to speak with different accents and Bogarde is notably uneasy as the passing Cockernee rogue. TJ

Our Relations

(Harry Lachman, 1936, US) Stan Laurel, Oliver Hardy, Sidney Toler, James Finlayson, Daphne Pollard, Iris Adrian, Alan Hale.
74 min. b/w.
The first of only two of their films produced by Stan Laurel – the other is Way Out West – Our Relations is a key Laurel and Hardy movie, polished in its production values and spared any interference from Hal Roach. Stan and Ollie play two respectable citizens confronted with their disreputable and irresponsible twin brothers in the most tightly plotted and structured of their films. Abounding in comic moments, it has been both praised as a masterpiece (by Borde and Perrin) and attacked (by Charles Barr) for being too neat and structured. PH

Our Republic

see Repubblica Nostra

Our Story

see Notre Histoire

Our Town

(Sam Wood, 1940, US) Thomas Mitchell, Fay Bainter, Frank Craven, William Holden, Martha Scott, Guy Kibbee, Beulah Bondi.
90 min. b/w.
An amiable, slightly expurgated adaptation of Thornton Wilder's play celebrating the home-spun values of a 'typical' small town in New Hampshire. Kicking off with a senior citizen (Craven) buttonholing the camera to act as our guide, it proceeds (by way of some hokey philosophising) to a tolerably banal account of humble humanity facing up to the everyday experience of living, loving and dying. Set in a studio-built town, attractively designed by William Cameron Menzies but not exactly conducive to the required 'realistic' atmosphere, the film is rescued from insufferable cosiness by pleasant performances, Aaron Copland's score, and Wood's meticulous attention to detail. TM

Our Twisted Hero (Urldleui llgureojin Youngung)

(Park Chon-Won, 1992, Korea) Kyung In Hong, Jung Il Ko, Min Sik Choi.
119 min.
Park Chon-Won began his career with a dire pseudo-Marxist agit-prop movie about workers' rights. This second feature is a considerable improvement, but the director hasn't yet fully outgrown a reliance on melodramatic cliché or a tendency to hammer home elementary lessons. His subject here is a school in 1959–60 (a microcosm of the state) and the focus is on a new boy's discovery of the collusion between the class bully and the corrupt teacher. TR

Our Vines Have Tender Grapes

(Roy Rowland, 1945, US) Edward G Robinson, Margaret O'Brien, James Craig, Agnes Moorehead, Butch Jenkins, Frances Gifford.
105 min. b/w.
Hollywood was never at its best describing rustic simplicities and folksy values, as in this account of the humble lives of a Norwegian farming community in Wisconsin. Good performances (Moorehead in particular) and a fair feel for the pace of country life, but the film's better moments (the kids squabbling over a pair of roller-skates, the arrival of the circus in town) have to be offset against the crampingly studio-bound atmosphere and an intrusively conventional love interest. TM

Our Wall (Duvarimiz)

(Panicos Chrysanthou, 1993, Cyp)
112 min.
The Berlin Wall may be gone, but Europe still endures its wire-mesh curtains: 22 years after Turkey's invasion, Cyprus is yet a nation divided. This grand-standing documentary conveys the history at a multiform, personal level, capturing the individual tragedies on both sides with accounts of Greek and Turkish speakers, friends and families, riven by the partition. Memories and archive footage recall 40 years of disintegration since – surprise! – the colonial machinations of British rule, and there are troubling allusions to other, contemporary outbreaks of nationalist madness ('Cyprus Will Not Become Yugoslavia,' peace marchers proclaim). NB

Out

(Eli Hollander, 1982, US) Peter Coyote, O-Lan Shepard, Jim Haynie, Danny Glover, Scott Beach, Semu Haute.
83 min.
Coyote sets off on a spiritual odyssey through a series of explosive and paranoid scenarios which, as well as providing him with a bewildering range of different identities (terrorist, drugs dealer, vice squad agent, healer), serve to parody both movie genres and 'significant' situations. Taken seriously, this offbeat road movie looks like so much late '60s counter-culture codswallop. But what saves the film from accusations of horrendous pretentiousness is its bizarre and often very funny sense of the absurd (presumably intentional). Political plotters derive plans from letters fished out of alphabet soup; intensely meaningful dialogues degenerate into hilariously banal banter; a wise old Indian intersperses words of cosmic insight with glowing appreciations of his new boots. Infuriating and amiable at the same time, it's so far out it's almost in. GA

Outback

(Ted Kotcheff, 1970, Aust) Donald Pleasence, Gary Bond, Chips Rafferty, Sylvia Kay, Jack Thompson, John Meillon.
109 min.
A sadly confused film, shot with something like a social realist's eye for accurate documentation – clothes, faces, sex habits, furniture, buildings, language. Into this very precise context, however, is dropped the melodramatic tale of a schoolteacher from the city (Bond) who goes to pieces in a remote desert township (a favourite piece of Australian mythology) under the impact of the hard-drinking, gambling, nihilistic pressures of life there, and is finally raped by Pleasence's renegade doctor. The end result is crudely exploitative.

Outbreak

(Wolfgang Petersen, 1995, US) Dustin Hoffman, Rene Russo, Morgan Freeman, Kevin Spacey, Cuba Gooding Jr, Donald Sutherland, Patrick Dempsey.
128 min.
Imagine a disease that makes the bubonic plague look like measles, and is spread in the air like a common cold: so deadly, so rapacious that within a matter of days a sub-continent the size of America is consumed. It's rather too easy to see the film as a metaphor for AIDS panic in the same way that '50s alien B-movies mirrored fears of the Red Menace: viruses as deadly as the one in this film already exist, and apocalyptic non-fiction best-sellers like Laurie Garrett's *The Coming Plague* have already softened up audiences for a film that its makers have touted as a *Jaws* for the '90s. Petersen's thriller does have its moments, most of them in the first half, which shows the painstaking methods by which such viral monsters are tracked and identified, and touches on the ethical problems presented by military intelligence and germ warfare, represented here by Sutherland's beribboned baddie, Gen McClintock. It's a pity, then, that the second half degenerates somewhat into a barely credible rescue mission involving dinky Hoffman and his estranged wife Russo. Entertaining, but not fatally attractive. SGr

Outcast of the Islands

(Carol Reed, 1951, GB) Trevor Howard, Ralph Richardson, Kerima, Wendy Hiller, Robert Morley, George Coulouris, Wilfrid Hyde-White, Frederick Valk, Betty Ann Davies.
102 min. b/w.
With all its faults, still one of the cinema's sharpest stabs at Conrad. Chief problem is the script, which tends to turn the whole thing towards picaresque tropical adventure by introducing character after character without ever quite pinning down the moral conflicts illuminated by their interaction. The recurring Conrad theme (clash between noble and ignoble) was probably doomed anyway, since Richardson gives a bizarrely stilted performance as Lingrad, thereby depriving Willems (superbly played by Howard) of the sounding-board that measures his descent into moral degradation. A pity, since individual scenes have a power rare in Reed's work, and the last shot – of Aissa, the sultry beauty who both destroys and is destroyed by Willems, squatting balefully in the rain and seeming to melt back into the earth – perfectly encapsulates Conrad's ambivalent view of the man who is hopelessly wrong in all his actions yet represents a bold gesture towards life. TM

Outcasts, The

(Robert Wynne-Simmons, 1982, Eire) Mary Ryan, Mick Lally, Don Foley, Tom Jordan, Cyril Cusack, Brenda Scallon.
104 min.
Mystery and magic from the mists of Erin in which a shy and awkward girl, Maura (Ryan), finds friendship and maybe more with an itinerant, half-legendary fiddler called Scarf Michael (Lally) on the night of a rural wedding. Thereafter, Maura is no longer a figure of fun and abuse, but a woman suspected of black magic by the superstitious villagers. The film is strong on 'atmosphere' (which means it pisses with rain most of the time and everyone struggles through the bog on their way to various dramatic encounters), but predictably slack in dialogue and characterisation. Mary Ryan works hard at making Maura a sympathetic central character, but this is another 'romantically Irish' film that has little of the power and articulacy of Neil Jordan. MA

Outer Way, The (Gedo)

(Rokuro Mochizuki, 1998, Jap) Haku Ryu, Amiko Kanetani, Akaji Maro, Atsushi Narasaka, Shiro Shimomoto.
99 min.
Only Mochizuki could have come up with a Buddhist deconstruction of the yakuza movie. Himuro (Haku Ryu at his best since Kitano's *Violent Cop*) is fired by his police superiors as a scapegoat for their complicity with *sokaiya* racketeers. This pale rider fetches up in a small town by the sea and soon figures out what makes the community tick: a mix of bent politics, dodgy religion, Internet porn, disorganised crime and a little marijuana cultivation on the side. He befriends the mysterious local 'garbageman' Kuwata (*butoh* star Maro) and the self-hating Mika (Kanetani), who becomes his lover. With an assist from Kuwata, Himuro does weed the yakuza patch and sort out the scumbag politician who is the centre of the local moral vacuum. But he's no angelic scourge, being as mired in corruption as anyone else. As ambiguous moral fables go, this is in the same league as Pasolini's *Theorem*. The amazing score (based on Buddhist music and chants) is by Koji Endo. TR

Outfit, The

(John Flynn, 1973, US) Robert Duvall, Karen Black, Joe Don Baker, Robert Ryan, Timothy Carey, Richard Jaeckel, Sheree North, Marie Windsor, Jane Greer, Elisha Cook.
103 min.
Excellent adaptation of a novel by Richard Stark (Donald E Westlake), who also provided the source material for *Point Blank*, *The Split* and Godard's *Made in USA*. A taut, grim thriller, it sees Duvall, just out of prison and with revenge burning in his heart for the murder of his brother, taking on the Syndicate with the help of heavy Joe Don Baker. Tightly scripted by Flynn himself, sharply shot by Bruce Surtees, it's a cool, exciting thriller in the Siegel tradition, paying more than passing reference to classic *film noir* with its host of character actors (Cook, Windsor, Greer, Carey), a cruel performance from Ryan as the mob leader, and its vision of people caught up in a chaotic, confused and treacherous world. GA

Out for Justice

(John Flynn, 1991, US) Steven Seagal, William Forsythe, Jerry Orbach, Jo Champa, Shareen Mitchell, Sal Richards, Gina Gershon.
91 min.
Hollywood bodyguard turned producer/star, Seagal sees this as a progression from the foundation of his action films (*Above the Law*, *Hard to Kill*, *Marked for Death*) to the higher ground of 'art'. If his career wasn't built on brawn and *aikido* skills, it would be tempting to challenge him on this. Okay, so the plot is 'character-driven' to the extent that his tough New York cop Gino has a problem: he's too busy beating up the baddies who whacked his best friend/partner to find a moment to patch up his rocky marriage. But if you cut the beatings, you wouldn't be left with much. Fans of unnecessarily graphic violence will love it, but if you're looking for 'art', look elsewhere. CO'S

Outland

(Peter Hyams, 1981, GB) Sean Connery, Peter Boyle, Frances Sternhagen, James B Sikking, Kika Markham, Clarke Peters, Steven Berkoff, John Ratzenberger.
109 min.
High Noon re-located on sunless Io, Jupiter's third moon, with Connery as the upright federal marshal posted to the mining base where a death-dealing black market in drugs is tacitly sanctioned by the profiteering authorities. Because both dialogue and direction are none too exciting, one's tired eyes wander endlessly over the space base sets, where they see the plot as an overuse of that potent sci-fi movie convention which conveys 'realism' by showing that life on the outer limits will be as dingy and badly lit as a suburban subway, with all the usual vices. JS

Outlaw, The

(Howard Hughes, 1943, US) Jane Russell, Jack Beutel, Walter Huston, Thomas Mitchell, Joe Sawyer, Mimi Aguglia.
121 min. b/w.
A film more joked about than seriously considered after its notorious production problems (Hawks walked off the set), censorship difficulties (centering on Jane Russell's cleavage), and Hughes' usual obsessive tinkering with details. By no means as bad as its detractors would have it, it remains a fascinating (if minor) Western with a determinedly offbeat story about Doc Holliday, Pat Garrett and Billy the Kid coming to conflict over Holliday's stolen horse and half-breed Russell. Jules Furthman's script is often disarmingly tongue-in-cheek, Gregg Toland's photography is characteristically ravishing, and there is a quirky eroticism to the proceedings, manifest in Russell's performance and in some surprising undertones suggesting homosexuality. GA

Outlaw and His Wife, The (Berg-Ejvind och hans Hustru)

(Victor Sjöström, 1917, Swe) Victor Sjöström, Edith Erastoff, John Ekman, Nils Arehn, Jenny Tchernichin-Larsson.
9,124 ft. b/w.
Sjöström's lead performance may disappoint those familiar with his marvellous contribution many years later to Bergman's *Wild Strawberries*, but there is still much to admire in this tale, set in 19th century Iceland, of a sheep-stealer finding work and love with a rich widow (the director's wife), and then being hounded by society into the freezing wilderness. If the story tends to aim too self-consciously for grand passions (often resulting in an unfortunately melodramatic tone), there is no denying the film's visual beauty, with Sjöström's use of the sparse farm sets and the monumental landscape serving to ensure that Nature, as opposed to the humans on view, takes precedence as the most forceful character. GA

Outlaw Blues

(Richard T Heffron, 1977, US) Peter Fonda, Susan Saint James, John Crawford, James Callahan, Michael Lerner, Steve Fromholz.
101 min.
'You'll never catch me alive – except on KVET' boasts country-singing ex-con Peter Fonda in a tone both romantic and expedient, which sums up the genial anecdote that is *Outlaw Blues*. His song is ripped off after a prison visit by the local Johnny Cash, so the paroled Fonda goes after him, shoots him in the leg, and hides out in Susan Saint James' shed. She sees the main chance, negotiates a recording contract, and makes Fonda a celebrity by smuggling him into record stores and radio stations and then calling the cops. Heffron and writer BWL Norton might have taken the story to its logical conclusion (posthumous superstardom) instead of spending so much time on chase sequences. But as it is there are many interesting ironies, not least that an indifferent title song, poorly sung by Fonda, can be made so effective by judicious use. AN

Outlaw Josey Wales, The

(Clint Eastwood, 1976, US) Clint Eastwood, Chief Dan George, Sondra Locke, Bill McKinney, John Vernon, Paula Trueman, Sam Bottoms, Geraldine Keams, Royal Dano.
134 min.
A remarkable film which sets out as a revenge Western: Eastwood sees his family massacred and joins the Confederate guerillas; after the Civil War, he is hunted by Union soldiers while he pursues his family's slayer and a friend apparently turned traitor. But slowly the film changes direction, until through a series of comic interludes it becomes the story of a man who (re)discovers his role as family man, as he befriends Indians and various strays and leads them to a paradise of sorts where they can forget their individual pasts. If that seems like a rewrite of Hawks' *Red River*, visually *The Outlaw Josey Wales* is closest to Anthony Mann in its breathtaking survey of American landscapes (and seasons). Most importantly, after a period of directorial uncertainty, the film demonstrated Eastwood's ability to recreate his first starring role, as the mythic Man with No Name of the Italian Westerns, and to subtly undercut it through comedy and mockery. PH

Out of Africa

(Sydney Pollack, 1985, US) Meryl Streep, Robert Redford, Klaus Maria Brandauer, Michael Kitchen, Malick Bowens, Joseph Thiaka, Michael Gough, Rachel Kempson.
162 min.
Aptly described in *TO* as a Safari Park movie; it's hard to imagine how even an untalented director could make the landscape here look less than ravishing, and Pollack is certainly better than untalented. As to the rest: Meryl gets to try a Danish accent this time as Karen Blixen, the author whose accounts of farming in Africa are the basis of the film. In Brandauer, as her pox-ridden husband, she has met her match in the ham stakes. And in Redford, as the Etonian adventurer who becomes her lover, she is bettered by the 'blank sponge' effect; for once his bland charm actually has a use. For all that it may come out of Africa, the film's final destination is not many miles from Disneyland. CPea

Out of an Old Man's Head (I Huvet på en Gammal Gubbe)

(Tage Danielsson, 1968, Swe) Hasse Alfredson, Fatima Ekman, Monica Nielsen, Ernst Günther, Gus Dahlström, Rolf Bengtsson.
76 min.
Recuperating from an injury in an old folk's home, widower Johan Björk (the comedian Hasse Alfredson) runs through the incidents of his life: from childhood japes in the countryside, through his first visit to a whore house, to the running-away to sea of his son Erik – all expressed in a curious dreamlike mix of animation and live action. The tone and content of Per Åhlin's often inventive animation styles (two-dimensional cut-outs, crayon drawings, photographic collages, realist line-drawings, etc) veers between sophisticated erotic surrealism, notably in the whore house episode, and the standard sentiments of a children's cartoon. Over-extended and uneven, but a genuine oddity none the less. JPy

Out of Life

see Hors la vie

Out of Order (Abwärts)

(Carl Schenkel, 1984, WGer) Götz George, Renee Soutendijk, Wolfgang Kieling, Hannes Jaenicke, Klaus Wennemann.
88 min.
Being stuck in a lift in a high-rise office block, when everyone else has gone home and your fellow-stuckees are wigging out, is sheer hell. Schenkel has captured all the claustrophobic intensity of such a nightmarish predicament, complete with horrible scrunching metal sounds. The four imprisoned protagonists are a smarmy besuited businessman, a Walkman-packing punk, a mysterious man with a suitcase, and Renee Soutendijk, who retouches her lipstick. Cables fray and so do tempers – they're stranded 300 feet up the shaft and two of the blokes are squabbling over the girl. One or two strands of the plot strain credibility, but the basic situation does not, resulting in lift-hanging suspense and sweaty palms all round. AB

Out of Order

(Jonnie Turpie, 1987, GB) Sharon Fryer, Gary Webster, Pete Lee-Wilson, Cheryl Maiker, The Wee Papa Girl Rappers, George Baker, Peter Cellier, Glynn Edwards.
98 min.
Jaz (Fryer) and Anthony (Webster) are a couple of layabout lovebirds roosting in the telegenic town of Telford. Glynis and Kerry (The Wee Papa Girl Rappers) run pirate station Radio Giro. When Anthony decides to climb out of the rut and become a rookie rozzer, teenage trauma looms. Meanwhile Billy (Lee-Wilson), a BT phone fetishist, gets fired but discovers that he has the ability to tap into the network without using the receiver, ie. he is tele-pathic. One way or another they all end up in the cells, and Anthony has to decide which side he's on. This offering from the Birmingham Film and Video Workshop gleefully rips off the good bits of TV, video and cinema techniques, and stirs them up into a tangy salmagundi of styles. The soundtrack, a basic mix of Rap, Disco and Funk, manages to splice The Smiths, Robert Palmer and Smiley Culture with Frank Sinatra. The result

doesn't say anything new about the joys of living in Thatcher's Britain, but the means by which the message is put across is both witty and wacky. MS

Out of Rosenheim

see Bagdad Café

Out of Season

(Alan Bridges, 1975, GB) Vanessa Redgrave, Cliff Robertson, Susan George, Edward Evans, Frank Jarvis.
90 min.
After relishing the nuances of the master-servant relationship in *The Hireling*, the super-smooth Alan Bridges finds himself landed with an impossible project. The dire script wrings every possible cliché out of the situation (mother and daughter while winter away in their deserted seaside hotel, until they're interrupted by the arrival of an intruder from the past). The biggest mystery is why this stagey stuff (all brooding desire, jealousy and intimations of incest) was filmed at all, and why a cast of this calibre should have bothered. VG

Out of the Blue

(Dennis Hopper, 1980, Can) Linda Manz, Dennis Hopper, Sharon Farrell, Raymond Burr, Don Gordon, Eric Allen.
93 min.
From its horrific opening moments – truckdriver Hopper drunk at the wheel with daughter Manz ploughs into the town's school bus full of screaming children – you're left in no doubt that you're in for an edgy experience. The teenage Manz, in a quite sensational performance under Hopper's direction, embodies the nihilistic ethos of punk in a way that other mainstream projects (*Foxes*, *Times Square*) couldn't begin to achieve. Manz impassively (and why not, with mum a junkie and dad an incestuous paedophile) observes life in small-town America's roadhouses and bowling alleys, embittered by the death of Elvis and Sid Vicious, and interested only in the drum kit at which she flails away in her bedroom. If ever there was a movie about Sex and Drugs and Rock'n'Roll, this is it, a film of and about extremes, directed by an extremist. Extraordinary. RM

Out of the Dark

(Michael Schroeder, 1988, US) Cameron Dye, Karen Black, Lynn Danielson, Karen Witter, Starr Andreeff, Karen Mayo-Chandler, Angela Robinson, Teresa Crespo, Tracey Walter, Silvana Gallardo, Bud Cort, Geoffrey Lewis, Divine, Paul Bartel.
89 min.
A straight re-run of those '70s slasher pics in which a string of attractive young women are bludgeoned, strangled or stabbed to death by a mystery assailant whose identity is obvious after about ten minutes. This time, it's the employees of the Suite Nothings phone-sex business (presided over by Karen Black) who are being terrorised by a killer in a clown mask. As a gesture towards sexual equality, a Hispanic male gets a spade through his head, while the sleaze quotient is constantly upped by the woman's breathy phone-talk about throbbing love muscles (what's never explained is why they dress and make-up like hookers to talk on the phone). Candidates for whodunit include the hunky photographer (Dye) with a previous conviction for assaulting his girl, the dorky assistant (Cort) with a stash of SM mags, and the prostitute-killer whom LA cop Divine (in his last film) is tracking in a parallel investigation. NF

Out of the Fog

(Anatole Litvak, 1941, US) Ida Lupino, John Garfield, Thomas Mitchell, Eddie Albert, John Qualen, George Tobias, Aline MacMahon, Leo Gorcey.
93 min. b/w.
Oddly atmospheric mixture of *noir* melodrama and semi-comic parable (based on Irwin Shaw's play *The Gentle People*), in which Garfield's tin-pot Dillinger terrorises a small wharfside community by extracting protection money. Problems arise when Lupino, daughter of Mitchell – who eventually plots with Qualen to combat their oppressor – falls for the hood. Originally intended by Shaw as an anti-fascist statement, the film's message is inevitably confused by the fact that

Mitchell and Qualen finally take the law into their own hands. Nevertheless, the vivid performances, the occasionally poetic dialogue (by a team of writers that included Jerry Wald and Robert Rossen), and James Wong Howe's excellent moody photography lend it a professionalism that the story barely warrants. GA

Out of the Past 100
(aka Build My Gallows High)
(Jacques Tourneur, 1947, US) Robert Mitchum, Jane Greer, Kirk Douglas, Rhonda Fleming, Richard Webb, Steve Brodie, Virginia Huston.
96 min. b/w.
The definitive flashback movie, in which our fated hero Mitchum makes a rendezvous with death and his own past in the shape of Jane Greer. Beguiling and resolutely ominous, this hallucinatory voyage has two more distinctions: as the only movie with both a deaf-mute garage hand and death by fishing-rod, and as one of the most bewildering and beautiful films ever made. From a traditionally doomed and perversely corrupt world, the mood of obsession was never more powerfully suggestive: Mitchum waiting for Greer in a Mexican bar beneath a flashing neon sign sums it up – nothing happens, but everything is said. Superbly crafted pulp is revealed at every level: in the intricate script by Daniel Mainwaring (whose credits for *Phenix City Story* and *Invasion of the Body Snatchers* need no further recommendation), the almost abstract lighting patterns of Nick Musuraca (previously perfected in *Cat People* and *The Spiral Staircase*), and the downbeat, tragic otherworldliness of Jacques Tourneur (only equalled in his *I Walked with a Zombie*). All these B movie poets were under contract to RKO in the winter of 1946, and produced the best movie of everyone involved – once seen, never forgotten. DMacp

Out-of-Towners, The
(Arthur Hiller, 1969, US) Jack Lemmon, Sandy Dennis, Anne Meara, Ann Prentiss, Ron Carey, Sandy Baron, Phil Bruns, Carlos Montalban, Paul Dooley, Billy Dee Williams.
97 min.
Lemmon and Dennis undergo the unexpurgated Manhattan melodrama: arriving from Iowa for a job interview, the couple run into a transit strike, a blizzard, a hotel which hasn't honoured their reservation, a mugging, and other New York specialities. Then, when they are flying home again happily, their plane is hijacked by Cuban revolutionaries. Neil Simon cranks out this kind of fluff before breakfast, but it *is* enjoyable. Lemmon suffers the mounting indignities with the skill acquired from playing urban neurotics for most of his career. Sandy Dennis, whose 'Oh my Gards' punctuate the film like fingernails on a blackboard, gets everything she asks for. ATu

Out 1: Spectre
(Jacques Rivette, 1972, Fr) Jean-Pierre Léaud, Bulle Ogier, Michel Lonsdale, Juliet Berto, Françoise Fabian, Bernadette Lafont, Jean Bouise.
255 min.
Rivette's grandest and boldest experiment to date enrages some spectators because it gives them so much to cope with: 255 minutes of improvisation by at least half of the best New Wave actors, edited and arranged so that sometimes it's telling a complex mystery story – about thirteen conspirators, two theatre groups, and a couple of crazed outsiders – while the rest of the time it's telling a realistic story about the same people that deliberately makes no sense at all. Not so much a digest of Rivette's legendary 12-hour version (hardly ever screened, its title is *Out 1: Noli Me Tangere*) as a ghost and a reworking of some of the same material ('a critique', Rivette himself says), it's a challenging and terrifying journey for all who can bear with it. As Richard Roud put it:'Cinema will never be the same, and neither will I'. JR

Outrageous!
(Richard Benner, 1977, Can) Craig Russell, Hollis McLaren, Richert Easley, Allan Moyle, David McIlwraith, Helen Shaver.
100 min.
'Isn't anybody straight any more?' wonders Robin (Russell) as he arrives in New York to make his club debut as a drag artiste, having left his flatmate Liza (McLaren) back in Toronto struggling with her schizophrenia and an awkward pregnancy. As in the best vintage Warhol

movies, everything rests on the characters, and hence the performances: McLaren's inwardness connecting improbably with Russell's brashness in a funny/serious relationship that is often touching. Plus, of course, the wicked drag impersonations of Dietrich, the Bettes (Davis and Midler), Garland, Streisand and others. It's technically very rough-and-ready, but consistently very funny in its off-the-wall humour. CPe

Outrageous Fortune
(Arthur Hiller, 1987, US) Bette Midler, Shelley Long, Peter Coyote, Robert Prosky, John Schuck, George Carlin, Anthony Heald.
99 min.
Lauren (Long) and Sandy (Midler) share the same two-timing lover (Coyote), a fact they only discover after he has skipped town, hotly pursued by the CIA over some stolen toxin. The stick-sisters join the chase, the script's mistaken assumption being the more the merrier. Lauren is classy and cultured, Sandy ain't, and their initial rivalry resembles a duet for the disdainful nostril and the gob. As a vehicle for their considerable comic talents, the enterprise is wheelclamped by type casting. Both identify a mutilated corpse as not being their man, but of course it is Bette who gets to spell out in clear that the clue was the size of his dick. Once the chase is on, there are reels of escapes down laundry chutes and madcap rides on baggage carts and motorbikes, and no shortage of threshing gams. It's the sort of comedy in which captives' bonds are thick and new as ropes aboard pirate films, while outbursts of C & W underline the fun of the chase. BC

Outside In
(Steve Dwoskin, 1981, GB/WGer) Olimpia Carlisi, Steve Dwoskin, Merdelle Jordine, Derek O'Connor, Tony Haygarth, Marie Manet.
115 min.
For his eighth feature, Dwoskin focuses on his own disablement by polio, and its hazards to his emotional and sexual life. It's a strange, riveting mixture of Hal Roach slapstick, vivid confessions, open-hearted self-reflexivity, and Dwoskin's own highly formalist aesthetic of the unblinking look (which had some English feminists hopping mad but reached their European sisters). Dwoskin reinvents the cinema from where Straub left off. The cast ranges through Carlisi from Fellini-land to Jordine from *Crossroads*. A haunting documentation of a strange, difficult life; its pratfalls and fetishes, triumphs and disasters. Crutches of fire? RD

Outside Man, The
(Un Homme est Mort)
(Jacques Deray, 1972, Fr/It) Jean-Louis Trintignant, Ann-Margret, Roy Scheider, Angie Dickinson, Georgia Engel, Michel Constantin, Ted de Corsia.
104 min.
Perfect casting for Trintignant as a French hit man imported to America and efficiently executing his contract, only to discover that there appears to be a contract out on him. Deray's thrillers often go sadly astray, but this one was co-scripted by Jean-Claude Carrière (Buñuel's latter-day collaborator), and wittily fashions a dark variation on *Through the Looking-Glass* out of the hit man's bafflement as he becomes the hunted in a country where he doesn't understand the language (the dialogue is in English, with occasional subtitled French) and where tribal customs seem alarmingly bizarre. Los Angeles becomes the quirky central character, and although Dickinson is rather wasted, there are memorable supporting performances from Ann-Margret, Scheider, Engel and de Corsia (the latter summarily rubbed out as subject of the contract, but presiding – embalmed and seated on a funeral parlour throne) over a shootout at his own wake. TM

Outsider, The
see Guinea Pig, The

Outsider, The
(Tony Luraschi, 1979, Neth) Craig Wasson, Sterling Hayden, Patricia Quinn, Niall O'Brien, TP McKenna, Elizabeth Begley, Ray McAnally.
128 min.

Grimly authentic by all accounts about life in 1973 Belfast, this first feature about Northern Ireland still seems more a piece of crusading Americana: a young, war-scarred American idealist enlists in the IRA only to find he is worth more to them dead than alive. From there it trades on the sensationalism and realism of its material: torture, bitterness, and sudden violent death. More confusing than illuminating, it's a film which will rely most on its reputation than its achievement; at a time when 'anything goes', is this one of the limits? DMacp

Outsiders, The
see Bande à part

Outsiders, The
(Francis Coppola, 1983, US) C Thomas Howell, Matt Dillon, Ralph Macchio, Patrick Swayze, Rob Lowe, Emilio Estevez, Tom Cruise, Glenn Withrow, Diane Lane, Tom Waits.
91 min.
Like the Corleones, like Kurtz in *Apocalypse Now*, and like Hank and Frannie in *One From the Heart*, the kids in *The Outsiders* (adapted from SE Hinton's novel) are looking for a better world. The street life of teenage Tulsa is divided into the 'socs' (pronounced soches) who go to college and wear Brut, and the greasers from the other side of the tracks, who don't. When a soc is knifed, three greasers go on the run to a rural idyll, turn tragic heroes, and finally return to try to cement a tenuous truce: like so much teenage Americana, it's about the rites of passage from adolescence to adulthood. Surprisingly for Coppola, it's a modest, prosaic, rather puritan drama with a MORAL, which, if you want to be uncharitable, is a last-ditch attempt to prove he can turn in a well-crafted piece without contracting elephantiasis of the budget. Lightly likeable, but the kids at whom it's aimed would probably rather be leaping in the aisles to Duran Duran, while their parents would opt for a rerun of *Rebel Without a Cause*. CPea

Outsiders, The
(Oka Oorie Katha)
(Mrinal Sen, 1977, Ind) Vasudeva Rao, Narayana Rao, Mamata Shankar, AR Krishna, Pradeep Kumar.
114 min.
Though Sen is often touted as the more corrosively political counterpart of his compatriot Satyajit Ray, the evidence of a film like this tends to suggest that he merely draws from a deeper well of despair. A study of 'marginals' – a low-caste father and son whose response to rural poverty is an extremist passivity, shading into idle parasitism – it manages a modicum of black humour from the old man's half-baked self-justifications, but slides inexorably towards tragedy and into a deadlock position of presenting defeatism as revolt. The anger's real enough, but its direction is uncertain, and sadly ineffectual. PT

Outward Bound
(Robert Milton, 1930, US) Leslie Howard, Douglas Fairbanks Jr, Helen Chandler, Beryl Mercer, Alec B Francis, Alison Skipworth, Dudley Digges.
84 min. b/w.
An allegorical Broadway play (by Sutton Vane) from the mid-'20s became a mildly intriguing early talkie. Howard's a passenger on a sombre ocean liner bound who-knows-where, lost souls heading for their final destination. The dialogue is heavy going and primitively recorded, but Hal Mohr did an evocative job with the ghostly visuals. TJ

Overboard
(Garry Marshall, 1987, US) Goldie Hawn, Kurt Russell, Edward Herrmann, Katherine Helmond, Michael Hagerty, Roddy McDowall.
112 min.
This hilarious and touching romantic comedy recalls the integrated plotting and sophisticated dialogue of '30s Hollywood. Spoiled heiress Joanna (Hawn) and her husband (Herrmann) sail their luxury yacht into a tiny Oregon fishing village to effect some repairs. Joanna hires hunky local carpenter Dean Proffitt (Russell) to fit some cupboards, but when his handiwork fails to satisfy, tosses him overboard and sails

away. Shortly after, Joanna herself falls overboard and lands in hospital with amnesia. Seizing his chance, Dean claims the rich bitch as his lost wife, mother to four uncontrollable kids... Russell is excellent as overgrown kid Dean; Hawn gives her best performance to date as the hapless heiress turned gutsy wife and mother (the kids aren't just cutely naughty, they're truly obnoxious); and Marshall's faultless timing makes the most of Leslie Dixon's neatly contrived situations and snappy dialogue. NF

Over Her Dead Body

see Enid Is Sleeping

Overlanders, The

(Harry Watt, 1946, GB) Chips Rafferty, Daphne Campbell, John Nugent Hayward, Jean Blue, Helen Grieve, John Fernside.
91 min. b/w.
Ealing's plans to dramatise the Australian contribution to the war effort didn't mature until after hostilities ceased, but the success of this epic reconstruction of a 1942 cattle-drive (virtually a displaced Western, in fact, given an emphatic political context – the drive is occasioned by a 'scorched earth' policy in face of the advancing Japanese threat – at odds with a counterpart like 'Red River') ensured a continuity of antipodean production that lasted until the home studio itself folded in 1959. Watt brought both a documentarist's research and eye to the project, exposing the outback as a viable location and incidentally elevating Rafferty to the status of a national icon. PT

Overlord

(Stuart Cooper, 1975, GB) Brian Stirner, Davyd Harries, Nicholas Ball, Julie Neesam, Sam Sewell, John Franklyn-Robbins.
83 min. b/w.
Set against the build-up to D-Day, a grainy fictional account of a young man's call-up, his life on and off duty while training, and the final vindication of his premonitions of death on the beaches of Normandy, is juxtaposed with contemporary footage. Made with the cooperation of various military establishments, the result is predictably restricted. With a script of little beyond stock phrases, and uninspired handling of the well-worn tale of the private's progress, the film does little to allay its endorsement of a passive acceptance of death to a point where it's elevated into a falsely poetic notion. More problematic is the handling of documentary footage, edited in such a way as to convey a hallucinatory and grotesque beauty: shots of a night raid intercut with daylight dead; a plane's camera recording the strafing of a train; the pattern of exploding bombs. Such aerial scenes are disturbing for their eerie remoteness, but they also bear little relation to the leaden-footed human story. CPe

Over Our Dead Bodies

(Stuart Marshall, 1991, GB)
84 min.
Marshall's documentary (an extended version of the one televised in Channel 4's Out series) traces the response to AIDS of gay activist groups in America and Britain. The film itself is also activist, giving platform to ACT UP, Queer Nation and Outrage, organisations fighting to keep AIDS and all the issues surrounding the disease in the public consciousness. Interviews are intercut with footage of meetings, demos and kiss-ins. The messages come hard and fast, with serious allegations levelled at church, state and health bodies. British lesbians and gays are criticised for failing to use grief and anger as political weapons for change. The opinions and statistics that dominate the film provoke a detached, intellectual response; only the few personal stories, and the scenes of demos where AIDS sufferers are manhandled by butch NYPD officers, encourage emotional involvement. CO'S

Over the Brooklyn Bridge

(Menahem Golan, 1983, US) Elliott Gould, Margaux Hemingway, Sid Caesar, Burt Young, Shelley Winters, Carol Kane.
106 min.
Golan bases his concept of comedy on the fact of the Jewish family as intrinsically funny and fascinating, especially when it features Shelley

Winters in her Yiddishe Momma incarnation. Gould, as her boy, is aiming to shift upmarket from his scuzzy diner, but his rich uncle (Caesar) won't advance the necessary spondulicks unless he kisses off his gentile girlfriend (Hemingway) and marries Cousin Cheryl (Kane). Clever Mr Golan realises that an audience is best kept amused by such stock comic clichés as uncle's poofy son, his friend's nagging wife, Cousin Cheryl's aggressive seduction technique. His masterstroke is to underline the essential transience of his project by naming it after a landmark well known as a high spot for the potential suicide. One can only wish the entire cast and crew had taken the plunge. AB

Over the Edge

(Jonathan Kaplan, 1979, US) Michael Kramer, Matt Dillon, Pamela Ludwig, Vincent Spano, Tom Fergus, Harry Northrup, Andy Romano, Ellen Geer.
94 min.
New Granada: a typically neat and neighbourly new town for middle class families, offering all mod cons. Except, that is, for the kids, left to find the usual entertainment of drugs, drink and sex in a run-down prefab 'rec'. When this last haven is threatened with demolition, adolescent high spirits and bad behaviour result in nihilist rage and rebellion. Kaplan's terrific movie – nervously held back from distribution here for five years – is one of the best movies to date about the generation gap. Although the parents and teachers are never reduced to uncaring stereotypes, their blind, status-oriented decisions and actions provide adequate fuel for the justly frustrated kids, who must be the most credible bunch of youngsters to make it onto celluloid. Script, photography and performances (including Dillon before he decided to become a teenage Stallone) are all top notch, and Kaplan directs with pace, imagination, and a fine ear for dialogue and music. GA

Over the Hill

(George Miller, 1992, Aust) Olympia Dukakis, Sigrid Thornton, Derek Fowlds, Pippa Grandison, Bill Kerr.
110 min.
Imported leading lady Dukakis takes centre stage in this well-meaning but uninspired road movie. A 60-year-old widow flies back from America to stay with her daughter in Sydney. Unfortunately, the welcome there isn't as warm as she'd hoped, so she makes an escape with her granddaughter and heads off across country in a flashy '59 Chevvy. TJ

Over the Top

(Menahem Golan, 1986, US) Sylvester Stallone, Robert Loggia, Susan Blakely, Rick Zumwalt, David Mendenhall, Chris McCarty.
93 min.
Machismo with schmaltz. Stallone plays some dumb trucker, into arm-wrestling, whose cab is a mobile gym. Twelve years ago – for some never-explained reason – he deserted his wife and kid, and now that his spouse is dying, he comes to collect his son from a military academy. An evil plutocratic grandfather doesn't like it; neither does the stuck-up cadet, but gradually his standoffishness turns to love. Pop-promo tactics are resorted to only some of the time, and this enables the persistent humour and compassion of the script to shine through. Inevitably there is a bicep-bursting climax in Vegas, and even though he does wear clip-on ties, it is impossible not to root for the New Yorkie Bar man. What next, caber-tossing? MS

Owd Bob (aka To the Victor)

(Robert Stevenson, 1938, GB) Will Fyffe, John Loder, Margaret Lockwood, Moore Marriott, Graham Moffatt, Elliott Mason, Edmund Breon, Wally Patch, Alf Goddard.
78 min. b/w.
One of the great sheepdog trial films and a clear hint that Stevenson (who went on to make many similar saccharine fables for Disney) was obsessed with sentimental comedy even in his British days. Fyffe is tremendous value as the wheezing avaricious Cumberland shepherd whose prize-winning dog attacks other folk's sheep. John Loder is the handsome newcomer to the valley with the temerity to challenge Fyffe's authority. Margaret Lockwood, soon to become Gainsborough's brightest light, is largely wast-

ed as Fyffe's sweet natured daughter, but many of the studio's most rambunctious character actors (including Will Hay's two stooges, Moffatt and Marriott) are on parade. Hearty, rustic fun. GM

Owl and the Pussycat, The

(Herbert Ross, 1970, US) Barbra Streisand, George Segal, Robert Klein, Allen Garfield, Roz Kelly.
96 min.
Buck Henry's skilful adaptation of Bill Manhoff's Broadway hit about the abrasive encounter (mental and physical) between an illiterate tart and an intellectual pseud. Neil Simon territory, sometimes tiresomely raucous and treading well-worn paths, but any tendency to sentimental whimsy is kept firmly at arm's length by the verbal fireworks. Brilliant performances from Streisand and Segal, each timing their lines with the knife-edge precision that used to be the glory of the Tracy-Hepburn partnership. TM

Ox, The (Oxen)

(Sven Nykvist, 1992, Swe) Stellan Skarsgard, Ewa Fröling, Lennart Hjulström, Max von Sydow, Liv Ullmann, Erland Josephson.
92 min.
A subtitle introduces this harrowing, but finally uplifting film as 'a true story as told by Sven Nykvist'. This is rural southern Sweden, in the middle of the catastrophic crop failures and famine of the late 1860s. Skarsgard, his wife Fröling, and their young child face certain starvation; ox meat is the only desperate solution. Without the beast, the man's employer's smallholding cannot function, and the penalty for its slaughter is as harsh as that for murder. Disconcertingly straightforward, veteran cinematographer Nykvist's film is an essentialist delineation of a society under severe strain, held together only by the strictest religious and social codes. By focusing on the couple's story, themes of crime and punishment, suffering and redemption, suspicion and fidelity, are made manifest. The acting (not least von Sydow's pastor) matches the overall mood, restrained and expressive; and shot with varying colour tones to reflect inner states of mind, the film unfolds like the four seasons, ending with a spring-like scene of reconciliation. WH

Ox-Bow Incident, The (aka Strange Incident)

(William Wellman, 1943, US) Henry Fonda, Dana Andrews, Anthony Quinn, Henry Morgan, Jane Darwell, Mary Beth Hughes, William Eythe, Frank Conroy, Francis Ford.
75 min. b/w.
A sombre, somewhat simplistically liberal Western in which three drifters (Andrews, Quinn and Ford), lynched as rustlers on the flimsiest of evidence, are posthumously proven innocent by good guy Fonda (interestingly, the film's dynamics and characterisations can be seen to prefigure Twelve Angry Men). But for all the obviousness of its 'message' (which once made it seem a landmark in the genre), the movie is impressively taut, not merely because of Wellman's tersely economic pacing of his material, but because Fox's decision to cut costs by shooting it entirely on a studio set serves, ironically, to increase the mood of claustrophobic tension. Indeed, its affinity to film noir is evident not only in the dark shadowy photography, but in the gallery of grotesques that populates this decidedly uncelebratory portrait of the frontier spirit. GA

Oxford Blues

(Robert Boris, 1984, US) Rob Lowe, Ally Sheedy, Amanda Pays, Julian Sands, Julian Firth, Alan Howard, Gail Strickland, Michael Gough.
97 min.
Or 'A Wank in Oxford'. An obtuse, obsessed Las Vegas car lot attendant (Lowe), thanks to a little computer hacking, gets to go to an Oxford of perpetual wintry sunrises and sunsets and where, God help us, cicadas still chirp at night. He manages to take the virginity of fellow-student Lady Victoria (Pays, beautiful), but not her hand in marriage. His American brashness riles fuddy-duddy academia and the mafia of the Oriel Rowing Club. They instil him with 'character'. He rows and grows up to indulge in such adult activities as wrecking rooms and sloshing Moet &

Chandon everywhere. Funny and moral? Nah. Tiresome? You bet. MS

Oyster and the Wind, The (A ostra e o vento)

(Walter Lima Jr, 1997, Braz) Leandra Leal, Lima Duarte, Fernando Torres, Floriano Peixoto.
115 min.

This reverie-cum-mystery (beautifully shot by Pedro Farkas) concerns the inhabitants of one of Brazil's remote Downed Islands – 'where the days go backwards and forwards like the waves' – populated only by a 60-year-old lighthouse keeper, his jealously guarded daughter Marcela, and a crew of sailors who bring provisions once a month. Unfolding through flashbacks (Marcela is played by three actresses), it's a tale of troubled sexual awakening, repressed passions and mysterious pasts, in which nothing is made explicit. Marcela's disembodied voice is invoked as one sailor reads her journal, conjuring up the story of the mysterious Saulo and 'The Idiot' boy Roberto – but what's truth? what fiction? A mature, distinctively directed work, oneiric and powerful, but also a touch warped and darkly obsessive. WH

p

Il Postino

Pacific Heights

(John Schlesinger, 1990, US) Melanie Griffith, Matthew Modine, Michael Keaton, Mako, Nobu McCarthy, Laurie Metcalf, Carl Lumbly, Dorian Harewood, Luca Bercovici, Tippi Hedren, Sheila McCarthy, Dan Hedaya, Miriam Margolyes, Beverly D'Angelo.
104 min.
Carter Hayes (Keaton) is *not* the ideal tenant: he trifles with razor blades, cultivates cockroaches, and doesn't pay the rent. It's a sign of the times when the landlord gets all our sympathy, but that's the general idea. Live-in lovers Drake and Patty (Modine and Griffith) buy a sprawling Victorian house in San Francisco. To pay for renovations, they rent out apartments to a quiet Japanese couple and to the psychopathic Hayes, who proceeds to strip the fittings and terrorise everyone in the house. But the law is firmly on his side. Schlesinger stages the action with smooth assurance, gradually building tension until Hayes goes completely round the bend. The problem lies in Daniel Pyne's script: the relationship between Drake and Patty is half-realised, while Hayes' motivations remain strangely muddled. That said, Keaton is chillingly convincing. CM

Pack, The

(Robert Clouse, 1977, US) Joe Don Baker, Hope Alexander-Willis, Richard B Shull, RG Armstrong, Ned Wertimer.
99 min.
Dogs left by summer vacationers gang together, run wild, and terrorise an out-of-season island resort. Somewhere inside *The Pack* a modestly good movie struggles to find expression. But Robert Clouse's script (from Dave Fisher's novel) is almost indecently hasty in turning the characters into dog food, and his direction is monotonously relentless in its pursuit of the requisite thrills. Occasional set pieces work – a woman trapped in a car, for instance – but little is done to string them together. It's a pity that Joe Don Baker's strangely reticent hero isn't allowed greater dimension, and that stalwarts like Shull and Armstrong are given so little to do. CPe

Package, The

(Andrew Davis, 1989, US) Gene Hackman, Joanna Cassidy, Tommy Lee Jones, John Heard, Dennis Franz, Reni Santoni, Pam Grier, Chelcie Ross, Ron Dean, Kevin Crowley, Thalmus Rasulala.
108 min.
Soviet intelligence has nasty plans for the American President. This time their plot is assisted by neo-Nazis who are none too happy with feelings of East-West accord, but they haven't reckoned on Sergeant Johnny Gallagher (Hackman), an army veteran at loggerheads with young(ish) Colonel Whitaker (Heard). A court-martialled serviceman (Jones) escapes from Gallagher's custody, and it transpires that the man had adopted a false identity. Gallagher gets his ex-wife (Cassidy), a personnel officer, to help his private investigation, which uncovers military and police corruption… The plot is reasonably entertaining, and Davis handles the action sequences well, but where the film transcends a lingering sense of *déjà vu* is in its intelligent performances: Hackman and Cassidy make a strong, unsentimental couple, hints of romance and reconciliation lurking beneath their businesslike exchanges. But this is hardly ground-breaking stuff, the main difference from earlier Red Threat thrillers being that the enemy is less clearly defined. CM

Package Tour, The (Társasutazás)

(Gyula Gazdag, 1985, Hun)
73 min.
A documentary which follows a coach party of former inmates on a trip to Auschwitz. As a subject it has a certain built-in success factor; the uncontained grief of these people is inevitable, though none the less moving. But while the camera's presence often proves unbearably intrusive upon its subjects' emotions, there is a far more telling interview, intercut with the journey, from a woman who was forced to stay at home, thanks to a recurrent illness brought on by the attentions of the camp doctor. She speaks in tranquil recollection about the arbitrary nature of the death

queues, and who might or might not survive the ovens. Because of her cool and her distance, it is her one remembers when the agony of the visitors is long forgotten. CPea

Pack Up Your Troubles

(George Marshall/Raymond McCarey, 1932, US) Stan Laurel, Oliver Hardy, Donald Dillaway, Mary Carr, Charles Middleton, Tom Kennedy, Billy Gilbert, James Finlayson, George Marshall.
68 min. b/w.
The second Laurel and Hardy feature, admittedly patchy but generally underrated. Perhaps because, after the rumbustious army farce of the beginning, it switches to a quieter vein of sentimental comedy as the boys fulfil a promise to deliver a dead comrade's little daughter to the care of her wealthy grandparents (only clue, the family name is Smith). Best moment is when Stan tries to tell the child a bedtime story and finds himself sleepily on the receiving end. Look out for director Marshall's cameo as a bad-tempered army cook. TM

Padre Padrone

(Paolo Taviani/Vittorio Taviani, 1977, It) Omero Antonutti, Saverio Marconi, Marcella Michelangeli, Fabrizio Forte, Marino Cenna.
113 min.
A Sardinian shepherd manages to free himself from his family, educate himself, then return home to fight an overdue battle with the figure who oppressed him, his father. *Padre Padrone* is a terrific subject, a true story that illuminates a universal problem: how can one man make a positive stand against his own patriarchal society? The boy's acquisition of language is a key factor, and the film's triumph is that it actualises this in an extraordinarily emotive way: after a consciously theatrical introduction, it presents fragments of experience (landscape, sounds, routines) which cohere into a vision of nature and human society as the boy matures. TR

Pagemaster, The

(Maurice Hunt/Joe Johnston, 1994, US) Macaulay Culkin, Christopher Lloyd, Ed Begley Jr, Mel Harris.
75 min.
Mediocre, really, this mixture of real actors and animation. Richard (Culkin) is a kid who learns courage after being exposed to the world of books. Sheltering from a storm in the library, Richard encounters the Merlin-like librarian (Lloyd), slips and is knocked unconscious, after which he's conducted on a tour of Adventure fiction (voice of Patrick Stewart), Horror (Frank Weller) and Fantasy (Whoopi Goldberg). These three are books with arms, and are as imaginatively drawn as Mr Sugar Lump. Dr Jekyll and Mr Hyde, Moby Dick and Ahab, Long John Silver and Alice in Wonderland thrust their more visceral moments at the lad, forcing him to overcome his fear of heights and confrontation. BC

Page Miss Glory

(Mervyn LeRoy, 1935, US) Marion Davies, Pat O'Brien, Dick Powell, Mary Astor, Frank McHugh, Patsy Kelly, Barton MacLane.
90 min. b/w.
Although more famous for being newspaper tycoon William Randolph Hearst's mistress than an actress in her own right, Marion Davies gives a fair performance here as a small-town girl who comes to New York and works as a chambermaid. Until, that is, con-men O'Brien and McHugh, who've won a beauty contest with a fake composite photo, talk her into putting flesh on their latest scam. NF

Page of Madness, A (Kurutta Ippeiji)

(Teinosuke Kinugasa, 1926, Jap) Masao Inoue, Yoshie Nakagawa, Ayako Iijima, Hiroshi Nemoto.
60 min. b/w.
Acted by an avant-garde theatre group, conceived and directed by one-time kabuki female impersonator Kinugasa, *A Page of Madness* remains one of the most radical and challenging Japanese movies ever seen here. An old sailor works as a janitor in an asylum to stay close to his insane wife and help her to escape, except that she doesn't want to go...Kinugasa deploys a

battery of expressionist distortions and otherwise stylised images to plunge his audience into 'irrational' experience, always withdrawing to a 'saner' perspective, and then undercutting that with another visual or dramatic shock. This version has music added by Kinugasa when he rediscovered the print in 1970. TR

Pagliacci (aka A Clown Must Laugh)

(Karl Grune, 1936, GB) Richard Tauber, Steffi Duna, Diana Napier, Arthur Maggetson, Esmond Knight, Jerry Verno, Gordon James.
92 min. b/w & col.
Rudimentary screen adaptation of Leoncavallo's one-act opera, which gives brawny Austrian tenor Tauber (who'd emigrated to England in 1933) the chance to belt out the big number (in English) 'On with the Motley'. Duna's the unfaithful spouse, Knight (who lost much of his sight during WWII but successfully continued his screen career right up until Lars von Trier's startling 1984 debut *Element of Crime*) her soldier lover. It switches to experimental Chemicolour for a couple of scenes. TJ

Pain in the A**, A

see Emmerdeur, L

Painted Boats

(Charles Crichton, 1945, GB) Jenny Laird, Robert Griffith, Bill Blewett, May Hallatt, Grace Arnold, Harry Fowler.
63 min. b/w.
Ealing docu-drama portrait of English canal life, modestly charting the lives of two boat families with the aid of a Louis MacNeice commentary, and examining the demands of tradition and change in the immediate postwar world. The sole product of a proposed studio series to consolidate the wartime fusions of fiction and documentary, elsewhere sustained only intermittently until TV stepped wholeheartedly into the breach. PT

Painted Desert

(Masato Harada, 1993, Jap) James Gammon, Kazuya Kimura, Nobu McCarthy.
96 min.
The Shochiku company's first English-language production has the slightly clammy air of something pulled out of a film buff's closet (that's what comes from getting Hollywood obsessive Masato Harada to direct and co-write it), but it plays remarkably well. A heavily guarded Mafia *capo* holes up in a desert villa fearful of assassination. The only visitor allowed in is the chef from the run-down local diner – a handsome young Japanese man recently found dying in the desert, who turns out to have his own secret agenda. Some of the plot's Japanese baggage is clumsily integrated, but the dialogue is witty and the playing absolutely charming. Best of all is James Gammon, plucked from character-actor obscurity and pushed centre stage as a grizzled, seen-it-all gangster with old-time manners out of a John Ford movie. TR

Painted Heart

(Michael Taav, 1992, US) Will Patton, Bebe Neuwirth, Robert Pastorelli, Casey Siemaszko, Mark Boone Jr, Jayne Haynes.
90 min.
Taav's first feature occupies the same setting and psychological territory as David Lynch's visions of small-town America. About a love triangle, involving house painter Wesley (Patton), his boss Willie (Pastorelli) and Willie's sensitive, vulnerable wife Margaret (Neuwirth), the film turns into a picture of hidden desires, romantic dreams and dangerous obsessions. A boy is saved from his drunken father by his mother's offer of sex; using her lipstick he colours a newspaper ad that reads, 'With these clothes you'll have no problems.' Thirty years later, an agitated Wesley breaks into Margaret's house and, before leaving lipstick as a present, tells her, 'I've got some ideas I don't know what to do with.' An affair develops: Margaret projects years of romantic longing on to her new lover, while the paranoid Wesley, fearing discovery, spies on Willie's own clandestine activities. At this stage, it's not clear whose disturbing childhood we've seen. The consequences, though, are alarmingly clear – 'The Lipstick Killer' is on the loose. An unsettling film in which ideas, tone and texture unite with quietly confident storytelling. NF

Painted Veil, The
(Richard Boleslawski, 1934, US) Greta Garbo,
Herbert Marshall, George Brent, Warner
Oland, Jean Hersholt, Keye Luke.
83 min. b/w.
Typically lush MGM vehicle for Garbo, drawn
from Somerset Maugham's novel and set in
Hollywood's China, in which she manages to sail
through a clichéd plot – neglected by overworked
medical missionary husband (Marshall), she succumbs to unworthy diplomat lover (Brent), but
redeems herself during a cholera epidemic – and
still light up the screen with her ever-sensuous,
charismatic presence. The production values are
characteristically sumptuous, William Daniels'
photography is lustrous, and Boleslawski directs
with suitable flair, although his interest in the acting theories and practices of Stanislavsky is hardly apparent from the performances. GA

Painters Painting
(Emile de Antonio, 1972, US) William de
Kooning, Helen Frankenthaler, Hans Hoffman,
Jasper Johns, Bob Rauschenberg, Andy
Warhol.
116 min. b/w & col.
Uncharacteristically for de Antonio, this takes the
form of a homage rather than a critique. An
apparently non-evaluative selection of auspicious
interviewees (long-time friends of the film-maker,
we're told) holding forth on postwar American
art and its fashionable New York heyday, in fact
take their validity as spokespeople from the commercial terms of the art market, and the only analytical correlatives invoked are those of the
contemporary critics, dealers and buyers who
decreed their 'importance' in the first place. The
interviews are almost conspiratorially cosy,
although still mystificatory next to the colour
shots of the paintings in question, and one is left
grasping at anecdotal material to sustain interest. While fans of Rauschenberg, Stella, Johns,
Koons, de Kooning et al might love it, it's a decided aberration in de Antonio's important oeuvre.
PT

Paint Your Wagon
(Joshua Logan, 1969, US) Lee Marvin, Clint
Eastwood, Jean Seberg, Harve Presnell, Ray
Walston, Tom Ligon.
165 min.
Logan's rotund version of Lerner and Loewe's
musical Western may lack actors (Presnell
excepted) who can actually sing, but that's compensated for by a solid plot involving a farcical
discovery of gold, and the growth of a mining
town (No Name City) that develops from amoral
shantydom to respectability and a holocaust.
When the novelty wears off of watching
Eastwood (as one of Seberg's two husbands in a
variant on a Mormon ménage) singing *I Talk to
the Trees* like a cross between Roy Rogers and
Bobby Vee, you'll have a wavering but consistently interesting performance from Marvin,
hamming away as the other husband. VG

Paisà
(Roberto Rossellini, 1946, It) Maria Michi, Gar
Moore, Carmela Sazio, Dots M Johnson, Harriet
White, Bill Tubbs, Dale Edmonds.
124 min. b/w.
Rossellini recounts the liberation of Italy during
WWII in six distinct episodes. The film's style is
the foundation on which the whole aesthetic of
neo-realism was built: endless establishing shots,
and long 'neutral' takes that allow each viewer to
make up his own mind about the characters. But
the choked-back sentimentality of much of the
action (GI doesn't recognise prostitute as the girl
he once loved, etc) belongs to a very much older
tradition than the visual style. Only the long, final
episode in the Po Valley remains wholly impressive: its view of the sheer arbitrariness of warfare
anticipates some of Jancsó's abstractions. TR

Pajama Game, The
(George Abbott/Stanley Donen, 1957, US)
Doris Day, John Raitt, Carol Haney, Eddie Foy
Jr, Barbara Nichols, Reta Shaw.
101 min.
A truly joyous screen adaptation of the
Broadway musical, with Doris Day heading the
union in a clothing factory. The real star of the
show is arguably Bob Fosse's stunning choreography, in particular the *tour de force* sequence of
the workers' picnic. No opportunity to use the

bright colours and props offered by the setting is
missed, and the songs by Richard Adler and Jerry
Ross are memorable ('Hey, There' and 'There
Once Was a Man'). An enthusiastic young Jean-
Luc Godard dubbed it 'the first left-wing
operetta'. DT

Pakeezah
(Kamal Amrohi, 1972, Ind) Ashok Kumar,
Meena Kumari, Raaj Kumar, Veena, Kamal
Kapoor.
150 min.
This popular musical suggests that, at its best,
the much-scorned commercial product of
'Hollywood-Bombay' is equally extraordinary in
its own way. A byzantine story (of star-crossed
lovers) that proceeds fitfully through the fabulous logic of dreams; luscious colour-scope photography, and a febrile camera craning and
tracking restlessly through fairytale locations
and sets; and never even a single screen kiss, but
instead some of the most brazenly erotic songs
and dances you'll ever see on film. SJo

Paleface, The
(Norman Z McLeod, 1948, US) Bob Hope, Jane
Russell, Robert Armstrong, Iris Adrian, Robert
Watson, Clem Bevans.
91 min.
Hope in perhaps his finest role as Painless Potter,
a quack dentist travelling the Old West and getting into deep waters when he meets and is married by the trouble-shooting Calamity Jane as a
cover for her secret activities as a government
agent. The gags centre as always around his bluff
bravado, but he was rarely given a better script
(to which Frank Tashlin contributed) or a more
responsive partner than the wittily seductive, sardonic and deceitful Jane Russell. GA

Pale Rider
(Clint Eastwood, 1985, US) Clint Eastwood,
Michael Moriarty, Carrie Snodgrass,
Christopher Penn, Richard Dysart, Sydney
Penny, Richard Kiel, John Russell.
116 min.
One of the oldest Western themes: an enigmatic
knight errant rides into town, sides with the poor
but decent folk against the robber barons, then
rides back to the horizon leaving the West won
for the forces of good. This is shot in classical
style, with much less of the baroque, mystical
flourish which characterised *High Plains Drifter*.
But there are sufficient question-marks inserted
to lift it out of the routine: Eastwood's preacher
man seems to carry the stigmata of a ghost; and
he arrives as the answer to a maiden's prayer.
Furthermore, his care for the landscape puts him
in the Anthony Mann class. It's good to be back
in the saddle again. CPea

Palermo or Wolfsburg
(Palermo oder Wolfsburg)
(Werner Schroeter, 1980, WGer/It) Nicola
Zarbo, Calogero Arancio, Padre Face,
Cavaliere Comparato, Brigitte Tilg, Gisela
Hahn.
175 min.
The story of a Sicilian boy from Palermo who
arrives as a guest-worker at the Volkswagen factory in Wolfsburg. He meets a pretty German girl,
settles a debt of honour by murder, and as a final
surprise becomes a Christ-like martyr at his trial.
Operatic and naturalistic in turn, Schroeter's tale
of helplessness and outrage seems too convinced
of its own importance to really work; and after
nearly three hours, that matters. DMacp

Pal Joey
(George Sidney, 1957, US) Frank Sinatra, Kim
Novak, Rita Hayworth, Barbara Nichols,
Elizabeth Patterson, Bobby Sherwood.
111 min.
Columbia's Harry Cohn snapped up the rights to
the Rodgers and Hart musical on its first appearance, no doubt feeling a strong kinship with its
heel of a hero, and then had a pig of a job casting
the leads. By the mid-'50s he'd got it nailed –
showing off his new sex symbol Kim Novak as
the young innocent eyed by Sinatra's nightclub
entertainer, and providing a final chance for his
old sex symbol Rita Hayworth to sing (dubbed)
and shake those legs as her experienced rival. In
other films, George Sidney cultivated his dubious
taste to the point of a fine art, but here his glossy

vulgarity ultimately serves to smother the bite of
the original material. The result is a musical
externally lavish but somehow hollow inside; a
musical with electric moments but dull scenes.
GB

Pallieter
(Roland Verhavert, 1978, Bel) Eddy Brugman,
Jacqueline Rommerts, Sylvia De Leur.
90 min.
Plot is nothing and atmosphere is all in this
Belgian oddity based on a famous novel by Felix
Timmermans. A turn-of-the-century degenerate
townie transforms himself into a childlike rural
hero who blows soap-bubbles, puts mirrors round
the outside of his house, champions nature
against the bespoilers ('Oh tree, my brother' he
declaims), marries a charming girl, and sets out
round the world in a cart to avoid the century's
horrid future. All of which is captured in radiant
photography, accompanied by the inevitable
bursts of Vivaldi's *Four Seasons* (eat your heart
out, *Elvira Madigan*). It's far too simpering and
flaccid for lasting pleasure, but there is something
relaxing about the film's relaxed pace and indulgent moods. Provided you're in an indulgent
mood yourself, of course. GB

Palm Beach Story, The
(Preston Sturges, 1942, US) Claudette Colbert,
Joel McCrea, Rudy Vallee, Mary Astor, Sig
Arno, Robert Warwick, William Demarest,
Franklin Pangborn.
90 min. b/w.
Sturges was riding high in the early '40s, writing
and directing comedies of such density and wit
that a moment's inattention might make an audience miss six great one-liners, five amazing bits
of business, four eight-syllable words, and three
crowd scenes. And few of his films were as
smoothly accomplished as *The Palm Beach Story*,
a knowing satire on the driving forces of sex and
money, with Colbert fleeing from her righteous
and penniless husband into the ridiculous arms
of yachtsman billionaire Rudy Vallee. Hilarious,
irresistible, impeccably cast. GB

Palookaville
(Alan Taylor, 1995, US) William Forsythe,
Vincent Gallo, Adam Trese, Gareth Williams,
Lisa Gay Hamilton, Bridgit Ryan, Kim
Dickens, Frances McDormand.
92 min.
Russ, Sid and Jerry are at wit's end: they're broke,
unemployed, and prepared to turn a blind eye to
legal niceties. Yet burglary may not be for them.
They over-shoot the local jewellery store and
break into the pastry shop next door – a sticky
situation, especially for Russ, whose brother-in-
law's a cop. An armoured car robbery suggests
itself, if only they can work up the necessary
gumption, but these guys may be too good to be
bad – or just too bad at being bad. A gentle comic
fable, this follows the trials of three not-so
wiseguys and finds them fundamentally innocent. It's hardly an original idea – that criminal
negligence can be funny – but Taylor, his screenwriter David Epstein and a winning cast headed
by Gallo (Russ), Trese (Jerry) and Forsythe (Sid)
find a fresh angle on it, fruitfully exploiting the
discrepancy between a macho gun culture and
the impotence of these men's lives. The film
makes time for a handful of delicious, delicately
observed comic digressions; and Taylor captures
an eloquent slice of New Jersey lowlife:
Springsteen with laughs. All very nice. But
Gallo's charged, explosive presence spikes the
punch – he gives the whimsy some kick. TCh

Paltoquet, Le
(Michel Deville, 1986, Fr) Fanny Ardant,
Daniel Auteil, Richard Bohringer, Philippe
Léotard, Jeanne Moreau, Michel Piccoli, Claude
Piéplu, Jean Yanne, An Luu.
93 min.
There's been a death in a French flophouse, but
virtually all of the film takes place in a deserted
factory which Moreau has turned into a gloomy
café of sorts. Here four men play bridge while the
Dior-draped Ardant languishes in a hammock.
One of them is a killer. The barman (Piccoli in fine
whimsical form) is the 'nonentity' of the title; he
presides over the game-playing, and cues bursts
of loud music: Janacek, for example, serves to herald the entrance of the detective (Yanne) determined to unravel the murder mystery. When not

being abused by the customers, Piccoli reads a copy of the thriller by Franz-Rudolph Falk on which the film is based: its subject, in other words, is nothing but itself. This is Robbe-Grillet intertextualised with Greenaway, and the result is an enthralling tediousness. MS

Pandemonium (Shura)

(Toshio Matsumoto, 1970, Jap) Katsuo Nakamura, Yasuko Sanjo, Juro Kira, Masao Imafuku, Tamotsu Tamura.
134 min. b/w.
Conceived as a lacerating attack on the Japanese film industry's typical 'heroic' samurai movies, this Japanese independent adapts an 18th century kabuki play to remarkably provocative effect. The plot, as schematic and stylised as a Jacobean tragedy, deals with a would-be samurai's descent into a hell of his own making as he seeks revenge on a couple who trick him. Matsumoto couldn't have realised the psychological passions or the violence with more terrifying force, but his aim is exorcism, not indulgence: the reflective, ultra-formal shooting style, and strategies like the use of captions as 'chapter headings', force the audience to read the film as a complex web of metaphors. The integrity and aesthetic daring of the result are doubtless what caused the British censor to ban it. TR

Pandora and the Flying Dutchman

(Albert Lewin, 1950, UK) James Mason, Ava Gardner, Nigel Patrick, Sheila Sim, Harold Warrender, Mario Cabré, Marius Goring, John Laurie.
122 min.
Lewin's extraordinary film is based on the story of the unfortunate sailor doomed to travel the oceans for all time until he finds a woman who loves him so much that she will sacrifice her own life for his salvation. The legend is updated to a Spanish village in the '30s where various men compete for the affections of Pandora, a beautiful young American (Gardner), and where Mason's mysterious yacht puts into harbour. Lewin combines a script of exuberant literacy with a visual splendour often bordering on the surreal. Mason is his usual impeccable self, while Gardner is gloriously believable as a woman for whom any man would be prepared to suffer eternal damnation. Occasionally absurd, always bold, the film tells a lushly romantic story so skilfully that it possesses the inevitability of myth. RR

Pandora's Box (Die Büchse der Pandora) [100]

(GW Pabst, 1928, Ger) Louise Brooks, Fritz Kortner, Franz Lederer, Carl Goetz, Krafft Raschig, Alice Roberts, Gustav Diessl.
10,676 ft. b/w.
A masterful adaptation/compression of Wedekind's Lulu plays, the most humanely tragic portrait of obsession that the cinema has to boast. Lulu's guilelessly provocative sexuality leads her from a gaggle of Berlin lovers and admirers (a lesbian countess, a newspaper editor, the latter's son, etc) to a squalid garret in London, where she finds her Thanatos in the shape of Jack the Ripper. Louise Brooks' legendary performance and Pabst's brilliantly acute direction both remain enthralling. TR

Pane e Cioccolata

see Bread and Chocolate

Panic in Needle Park, The

(Jerry Schatzberg, 1971, US) Al Pacino, Kitty Winn, Alan Vint, Richard Bright, Kiel Martin, Michael McClanathan, Warren Finnerty, Marcia Jean Kurtz, Raúl Julia.
110 min.
A gruelling but highly responsible film about the influence of heroin on a New York street romance. Schatzberg moves with considerable force over the urban territory of Midnight Cowboy, using handheld cameras and a sustained editing rhythm to convey the couple's gradual descent into hell as mercilessly as he shows the needles entering his characters' veins (in close-up). Pacino, as the boy, proves that he didn't need Coppola to make him act, but Kitty Winn is less satisfactory, and the film is finally subject to an iron law of diminishing returns after its plot plumbs the depths and can

find nothing to do except batter us some more. In fact, the anti hard drugs message comes on so strong and so realistically that the British censor's ban (lifted in 1975) seems positively malicious: it's precisely this kind of suppression of information which results in junkie mythologies. DP

Panic in the Parlor

see Sailor Beware

Panic in the Streets

(Elia Kazan, 1950, US) Richard Widmark, Paul Douglas, Barbara Bel Geddes, Jack Palance, Zero Mostel, Alexis Minotis.
93 min. b/w.
A classy thriller, much less laden with significance than most Kazan movies. Film noir and the Method go remarkably well together as the panic-stricken manhunt gets under way when a victim of a gangland killing is found to be riddled with pneumonic plague. Explicitly identified as rats to be exterminated, the menace – two killers (Palance, Mostel) who may be plague-carriers – is tracked through a pullulating garbage dump marvellously conjured out of some sweaty dockland locations in New Orleans. Some awkward psychologising early on about the police chief (Douglas) and his obstructive attitude as Widmark's Public Health Service officer tries to get things moving, otherwise it's all go, heightened realism, and first-rate performances. TM

Panic in Year Zero

(Ray Milland, 1962, US) Ray Milland, Jean Hagen, Frankie Avalon, Mary Mitchell, Joan Freeman, Richard Garland, Richard Bakalyan.
95 min. b/w.
Panic in Year Zero, about the aftermath of the devastation of Los Angeles by nuclear attack, stands as an extraordinary reminder of just how close avant-garde and popular movies can get in times of social upheaval. The first half-hour, consisting of an endless series of half-wrecked cars streaming across the screen, close-ups of a meaningless radio dial, and the characters' frantic attempts to think the 'unthinkable', could almost be an experimental short rather than an AIP exploitation movie. Frankie Avalon is about the only difference. There are perhaps some naivetés as Milland (actor) realises that the law of the jungle now holds sway in trying to protect his family, but a remarkable effort from Milland (director) all the same. DP

Panther

(Mario Van Peebles, 1995, US) Marcus Chong, Courtney B Vance, Kadeem Hardison, Bokeem Woodbine, James Russo, Tyrin Turner.
124 min.
1966. The Disunited States of America. Huey Newton (Chong) and Bobby Seale (Vance) form the Black Panther Party for Self-Defense. Initially little more than a community self-help programme, the organisation soon becomes a popular movement with a radical political agenda, and enough militancy to terrify J Edgar Hoover, who labels the Panthers 'Public Enemy Number One'. When Judge (Hardison) is approached by the FBI, the Panther leadership convinces him to act as a double agent, and the stakes become a matter of life and death, for Judge himself and for subsequent generations of black Americans. Working from a screenplay by his father Melvin (taken from his own novel), Mario Van Peebles recreates the turbulence of the period, and makes a convincing case on behalf of the Panthers. Less happily, fictional paranoia-thriller elements are clumsily integrated: Judge's story doesn't ring true, and it distracts from more absorbing, documented facts. Time will tell whether the Van Peebles' theory that the FBI collaborated with the Mob to flood the ghettos with drugs holds up as history, but here it's a hysterical, dramatically suspect conclusion to an often stimulating, stylish movie. TCh

Paolozzi Story, The

(Al Lauder, 1980, WGer/GB) Eduardo Paolozzi.
120 min.
Just as collage is central to Eduardo Paolozzi's art, so this fascinating documentary about the rebellious, versatile Italo-Scot interprets his life and work through a collage of disparate but carefully juxtaposed references. Figures invoked in illuminating his style and ideas include (to name but a few) Léger, Disney, Wittgenstein, Icarus and St Sebastian; while his mixed cultural inher-

itance, his love of nature and distaste for industrialised society, are lucidly demonstrated as we view his creations and are led through his varied history. If Paolozzi's verbal abilities are rarely as eloquent as the enormous range of his vividly intelligent castings, graphics and totems to mechanised man, the film nevertheless successfully presents his work in a socio-political as well as an aesthetic context. And it's good, too, to see in detail the physical processes of artistic work, rather than simply its finished products. GA

Papa, les Petits Bateaux...

(Nelly Kaplan, 1971, Fr) Michel Bouquet, Sheila White, Michel Lonsdale, Sydney Chaplin, Pierre Mondy, Marcel Dalio, Bernard Musson.
92 min.
Very much a film of its time, this is Nelly Kaplan's oblique tribute to Tex Avery and Betty Boop (and Jerry Lewis), a comedy melodrama that aspires to animation with its utterly improbable fantasy of an incorrigible millionaire heiress kidnapped by comic strip gangsters, and held to ransom in a suburban house where she picks them off one by one, seeding little squabbles, encouraging greed, and carrying out the occasional murder (funniest of these: a Corsican mobster, inflamed by lust for the heroine, demonstrates his macho tour de force, the Death Leap, only to be impaled on his own knife). It's Snow White and the Seven Dwarfs as much as anything, with all seven eventually laid to rest in the garden and she their wide-eyed victor. The tone (insistent fake-naïveté) is occasionally irritating, but at its best rather resembles the charmed craziness of Céline and Julie. CA

Paperback Hero

(Peter Pearson, 1972, Can) Keir Dullea, Elizabeth Ashley, John Beck, Dayle Haddon, Franz Russell, George R Robertson.
94 min.
Not at all a bad film, Pearson's portrait of a small-town Midnight Cowboy is precise and convincing. The background of the wheat and cattle town in Saskatchewan is drawn with a conscientiousness that gives the film a rare three-dimensionality; and Dillon (Dullea) is a persuasive hero/victim, a totally unsympathetic character who has swallowed the Big Country myth whole, and is increasingly puzzled to find the world around him oddly out of phase with his 'Marshal Dillon' self-image. Pearson has expertly judged the distance between Dillon in his circumscribed world and the townsfolk in their not unattractive one, never falling into the trap of caricature; his faults are a tendency towards over-explicitness, plus a certain lack of emotional directness and vitality. Visually, the film is almost too seductive, but Elizabeth Ashley is excellent as the ever-waiting girlfriend, and all the smaller parts are uniformly well filled. VG

Paperback Vigilante

(Peter Davis/Steffan Lam, 1975, US) Howard Hunt.
75 min.
Howard Hunt was a crook. His biggest job was the break-in at the Democratic Party headquarters in the Watergate building, a crime which eventually toppled a President. He was also a prolific writer of spy stories in which the agents of Western capitalism blackmail and subvert – and don't get caught. The Paperback Vigilante is a documentary which exploits this paradox, tracing Hunt's life from university to White House against the fantasy backdrop of his novels. The film isn't just biography, though. Hunt's career in the CIA, through the Guatemala coup ('a clean and surgical-like operation'), the ill-fated Bay of Pigs invasion of Cuba, to his plucking from retirement to join Nixon's 'plumber's unit', is shown as a classic example of a son of the American ruling class being heavily financed to subvert 'international communism'. 'If you cut off the head of a chicken, you can do with the body what you will' says Hunt about his own plan to assassinate Castro (the interview which interlaces the film is excellent). EPr

Paper, The

(Ron Howard, 1994, US) Michael Keaton, Glenn Close, Robert Duvall, Marisa Tomei, Randy Quaid, Jason Robards, Spalding Gray.
112 min.

Director Howard's attempt to recycle the classic '30s newspaper comedy is busy, busy, busy. Keaton's in his element as Henry Hackett, city editor of the New York *Sun*. Today's top story is the controversial arrest of two black youths in a race murder. But while Henry and his bitchy colleague Alicia (Close) debate tabloid semantics, he's equally preoccupied with a job offer from a rival, editor Duvall's health, and his wife's great expectations (Tomei, eight and a half months pregnant)…the suspects' rumoured innocence is almost an afterthought. A perennial innocent himself, Howard responds to the blunt professionalism of the hack pack with as much enthusiasm as Billy Wilder and Howard Hawks before him – but spoils it by insisting that somehow the tabloids have integrity. He likes his sincerity straight. It's come to something when a newspaper movie casts the cynical journalist as the villain, and the big moral dilemma here would scarcely support a sit-com. Even so, quite watchable, with whip pans and fast tracks, and one eye constantly on the clock. TCh

Paper Chase, The
(James Bridges, 1973, US) Timothy Bottoms, Lindsay Wagner, John Houseman, Graham Beckel, James Naughton, Edward Herrmann, Craig Richard Nelson.
111 min.
A muddled and slick 'youth' film. Worth seeing because it says a lot more than the makers intended about how hustlers like John Mitchell and Ehrlichman were turned out by the 'best' law school. Bottoms plays a small-town Minnesota kid who wants to make it into the upper echelon via Harvard Law School. Excellent sequences of his quarrelsome study group tearing one another apart under fierce competitive strain – and a fine performance by Houseman as their olympian, sadistic professor – make the film watchable. Writer-director Bridges seems totally unaware that his ambitious young hero, not the professor, is the villain. CSi

Paperhouse
(Bernard Rose, 1988, GB) Charlotte Burke, Ben Cross, Glenne Headly, Elliot Spiers, Gemma Jones, Sarah Newbold.
92 min.
An 11-year-old girl succumbs to fainting fits, is put to bed, and draws an imaginary house with an imaginary friend. Through dreams, she enters this otherworld of her own creation. Down these Elm Streets a young girl must go, you might think, but Bernard Rose's striking movie debut has more art (and heart) up its sleeve than the usual bogeyman/teenagers routine. This time the monster is the girl's estranged father, and the shocks are more to do with primary fears of a violent adult world. Matthew Jacobs' script also manages to convey atmospheric banality without dealing with naturalistic characters, while the design department succeeds in turning infantile sketches into near-apocalyptic landscapes, often to shattering effect. Ultimately, where the film scores over the current gore market is in its return to the values of emotion and psychology within fantasy. There are production compromises (an over inflated score, a miscast Glenne Headly); but Rose, veteran of that banned Frankie Goes To Hollywood video, directs with exhilarating assurance, and Charlotte Burke makes an excellent heroine. DT

Paper Marriage
(Krzysztof Lang, 1992, Pol/GB) Gary Kemp, Joanna Trepechinska, Rita Tushingham, Richard Hawley.
90 min.
Alicjia (Trepechinska) comes from Warsaw to Newcastle to marry an accommodating Englishman, only he isn't so accommodating this side of the channel. Being, she says, resourceful and emancipated, she sets about finding work and a husband. Aiden (Kemp) fits the bill: he's a British citizen and desperate for money. Although their marriage is a sham, circumstances contrive to keep the couple together, for richer, for poorer, for better, for worse. Peter Weir made essentially the same story with a New York setting and a French star; but in contrast to *Green Card*'s lush romanticism, this is cold and depressing. Lang and his Polish crew obviously felt no compulsion to prettify Newcastle, and it's no surprise when Alicjia starts to gaze longingly at flight offers to the US. By the same token, there's

no warmth in the relationship. Trepechinska gives a fair account of herself without ever reconciling the contradictions inherent in the role, while Kemp proves so soft-spoken he barely registers. That's one trouble with a marriage of convenience: there's no meaningful long-term engagement. TCh

Paper Mask
(Christopher Morahan, 1990, GB) Paul McGann, Amanda Donohoe, Frederick Treves, Tom Wilkinson, Barbara Leigh-Hunt, Jimmy Yuill, Mark Lewis Jones.
105 min.
Dissatisfied as a lowly hospital porter, Matthew Harris (McGann) decides to step into the shoes of a recently deceased doctor in an attempt to up his social status, and bluffs his way into a job in a Bristol hospital. One disastrous night in casualty later, the administrators are on his case, and Harris is ready to give up. However, inspired by lust for lithesome nurse Christine (Donohoe), he decides to bash on, resulting in fatal blunder, grand illusions, and murderously misguided covert operations. Written with flair by ex-medic John Collee, this competent thriller-cum-melodrama is held together by Donohoe's endearingly edgy performance as the love-struck Christine. There are equally rewarding scenes set in the world of dinner parties and of boorish professional bonhomie. Where the screenplay falls down, however, is in its failure to establish Harris' ability to carry off such an audacious hoax, leaving the movie with a major credibility problem. MK

Paper Moon
(Peter Bogdanovich, 1973, US) Ryan O'Neal, Tatum O'Neal, Madeline Kahn, John Hillerman, PJ Johnson, Randy Quaid.
102 min. b/w.
A charming mixture of Hawksian comedy and Fordian lyricism imbues Bogdanovich's not-too-sentimental meeting-cute between a conman (Ryan O'Neal) busy bamboozling widows into buying bibles during the Depression, and the 9-year-old wily brat who may or may not be his daughter (Tatum O'Neal). Modern cynicism and efficient acting hold the potential mushiness at bay, and the pair's picaresque odyssey through the Kansas dustbowl, during which they vie for control over their increasingly bizarre partnership, is admirably served by Laszlo Kovacs' marvellous monochrome camerawork. After *Targets* and *The Last Picture Show*, Bogdanovich's best movie. GA

Paper Tiger
(Ken Annakin, 1974, GB) David Niven, Toshiro Mifune, Hardy Kruger, Ando, Ivan Desny, Irene Tsu, Ronald Fraser.
99 min.
Niven does an ageing Billy Liar with a wavering upper lip, spinning tall stories to the crushingly winsome little brat, son of a Japanese diplomat, whom he tutors in some unspecified Far Eastern country plagued with cretinous revolutionaries. In so far as the film has any serious themes, they are entirely retrospective, with their roots in WWII: Kruger (the German), Mifune (the Jap) and Niven (the Englishman) all conform to desperate type. Niven, of course, despite all his blustering, still proves capable (it's that Dunkirk spirit) of acquitting himself when the chips are down (in the form of a listless kidnapping plot). CPe

Paper Wedding, A (Les Noces de Papier)
(Michel Brault, 1990, Can) Genevieve Bujold, Manuel Aranguiz, Dorothée Berryman, Monique Lepage.
90 min.
Claire (Bujold) is 39 and, despite the matchmaking efforts of her mother, still a spinster, with only a (married) lover for security. When her lawyer sister asks her to marry political exile Pablo Torres (Aranguiz) to prevent his deportation, Claire grudgingly agrees, only to find herself under investigation by the Immigration Department. With only three days to spare before the official hearing to determine whether the marriage is genuine, the newly-acquainted newly-weds set about discovering enough about each other to present a passable imitation of *bona fide* lovers. Less overtly political than his previous work, Brault's gently observed drama still manages to tackle the corruption of immigration laws

while wistfully fantasising about the productive coalition of alien cultures. The elfin-like Bujold is excellent, and the interesting use of stop-frame and flashback make this an intriguing cinematic exercise. MK

Papillon
(Franklin J Schaffner, 1973, US) Steve McQueen, Dustin Hoffman, Victor Jory, Don Gordon, Anthony Zerbe, Robert Deman, Woodrow Parfrey, Bill Mumy, George Coulouris.
150 min.
Based on Henri Charrière's bestselling epic about life imprisonment in a French penal colony, *Papillon* begins atmospherically with the heat and deprivation well conveyed. But with Schaffner unable to find the necessary perspective to prevent the film from becoming unevenly episodic, it ends up looking as if it were tacked together by at least three different directors. Jerry Goldsmith's insistent music doesn't help much either. Consequently McQueen's escape bids and subsequent doses of solitary take on the proportions of a masochist's marathon. He battles manfully against miscasting and a script that remains content merely to celebrate his prowess. He almost carries it off, apart from one romantic dalliance, true Hollywood South Seas style, and the totally perfunctory final half-hour. CPe

Parade
(Jacques Tati, 1974, Fr/Swe) Jacques Tati, Karl Kossmayer and His Mule, Les Williams, Les Vétérans, Les Sipolo.
85 min.
An eccentric slice of light entertainment ringmastered by Tati. He contributes a couple of superlative mime routines, and even briefly resurrects Hulot as a klutzy angler battling with slippery fish and a folding stool. But the show, and its host, are not the main thing. Les clowns, c'est vous announces Tati: contributions from the floor are invited and (thanks to judicious plants) are forthcoming, with scuffles erupting in the orchestra, a hatcheck girl surrounded by crash helmets, and a myriad other behind-the-scenes incongruities and calamities. This was Tati's valediction, made for Swedish TV the year he went bankrupt. Shot live, and on video, it can't aspire to the meticulous *mise en scène* of his big screen work; and one feels saddened that this great director should have found no other outlet for his genius. SJo

Parade of the Planets (Parad Planyet)
(Vadim Abdrashitov, 1984, USSR) Oleg Borisov, Sergei Nikonenko, Sergei Shakurov, Alexei Zharkov, Pyotr Zaichenko.
96 min.
A strangely dreamlike tale, perhaps symbolic. The narrative is straightforward enough: a group of Red Guard veterans are unexpectedly 'killed' during a weekend of manoeuvres, and finding themselves with ample free time, set off on an odyssey into an increasingly disturbing landscape: a town populated only by women, deserted lakeland forests, a sinister old people's home. Some of it is almost embarrassingly reminiscent of Hollywood's hippy '60s allegories (notably the skinny-dipping to the strains of Beethoven); other moments have an elusive poetry. It's supposedly about the ghosts that haunt the contemporary Russian psyche: quite what they are isn't exactly clear. GA

Paradine Case, The
(Alfred Hitchcock, 1948, US) Gregory Peck, Alida Valli, Ann Todd, Louis Jourdan, Charles Laughton, Charles Coburn, Ethel Barrymore, Leo G Carroll.
115 min. b/w.
In no sense a 'wronged innocent' thriller, *The Paradine Case* sets out to be a morality tale on the dangers of Strong Emotion. A happy marriage is threatened when rising young barrister Peck falls hopelessly in love with the woman (Valli) he is defending on a murder rap. Blinded by passion, he can see neither her guilt, nor that her obsession lies elsewhere – with the man (Jourdan) whom he would destroy in her stead. Bleak in its message (those who love passionately inevitably destroy the object of their desire), the movie only half works; Peck is rather half-hearted, Valli coldly cat-like, Ann Todd as the rejected wife too self-sacri-

p

ficing and loyally forgiving to be true. And the intricate, triangular plot is finally overburdened by the courtroom setting from which it tries to draw a laborious analogy between the perversion of love and justice. FF

Paradise

(Mary Agnes Donoghue, 1991, US) Melanie Griffith, Don Johnson, Elijah Wood, Thora Birch, Sheila McCarthy, Eve Gordon, Louise Latham, Greg Davis.
111 min.
This Hollywood remake of *Le Grand Chemin* is altogether slicker, revelling less in strange and simple provincial goings-on than in the star pairing of real-life couple Johnson and Griffith. Unhappily married, Ben and Lily Reed are plunged into bitter reflection on the death of their son when they are left in charge of ten-year-old Willard (Wood). The city boy has his own problems: he's uncertain why his pregnant mother (Gordon) has dumped him with country bumpkins, and bewildered about his father's prolonged absence from home. Amid the domestic dramas, sentimentality is never very far away. Johnson is nowhere near as flawed or interesting as his French counterpart, but at least he and Griffith are credibly loveless and joyless. They're helped by writer-director Donoghue's jaded observations and sensitive direction, though such attention is at the expense of the children, who are sometimes painfully stilted in their exchanges. Alas, the quirks which enlivened the original are missing: no peeing into gargoyles here. CM

Paradise Alley

(Sylvester Stallone, 1978, US) Sylvester Stallone, Lee Canalito, Armand Assante, Frank McRae, Anne Archer, Kevin Conway, Aimée Eccles, Tom Waits.
109 min.
Nominally set in 1946, in the poverty-trap of Hell's Kitchen, but pitched waveringly between *Rocky*, *Guys and Dolls*, and some prototype Warner Brothers Depression drama of the preceding decade, Stallone's hit-and-miss directorial debut (he also writes, stars and sings the theme song) maps the classic escape route via the ring (wrestling this time) with a unique style of baroque excess. The plot (Stallone scheming himself and his two brothers uptown on the tails of ambitious gimmickry) is shot full of sentimental holes; but the creation of a floridly fantasticated netherworld of low-life high-rollers and their inevitably multi-coloured circumlocutions is irresistible. PT

Paradise – Hawaiian Style

(Michael Moore, 1965, US) Elvis Presley, Suzanna Leigh, James Shigeta, Donna Butterworth, Marianna Hill, Irene Tsu, Linda Wong.
91 min.
A desperate attempt to revive Presley's by then flagging film career with a brazen action replay of *Blue Hawaii*. Irredeemably awful, it displays an enervated, paunchy Elvis ambling through familiar locations against which dreary adolescent tiffs are played out. AC

Paradise Road

(Bruce Beresford, 1997, US/Aust) Glenn Close, Frances McDormand, Pauline Collins, Cate Blanchett, Jennifer Ehle, Julianna Margulies, Wendy Hughes, Elizabeth Spriggs.
121 min.
The Fall of Singapore. A boat evacuating women and children is strafed and sunk. The survivors swim ashore to be met by the Japanese forces in Sumatra and herded into a remote internment camp. For the various women – a dignitary's wife (Close), a missionary (Collins), a model (Ehle), a grande dame (Spriggs), an Aussie nurse (Blanchett), and a lone American (Margulies) – those who can endure will face three years' hard labour. A feminised PoW movie, writer/director Beresford's ensemble film describes downbeat, recalcitrant heroism: the loss of family, serfdom, disease, the threat of rape and prostitution. The 'twist' is the women's choice of succour. Based on Betty Jeffrey's diaries *White Coolies*, the film documents how inmates formed a 'vocal orchestra' and performed their own arrangements of symphonic classics. Finely acted, opulently produced, old-fashioned, unadventurous and emotionally hidebound. NB

Paradis Perdu

(Abel Gance, 1939, Fr) Fernand Gravey, Micheline Presle, Robert Pizani, Elvire Popesco, Robert Le Vigan, Alerme, Jane Marken.
88 min. b/w.
Napoléon made Gance, at 38, the youngest Grand Old Man of French cinema. Thereafter his career, a sequence of theatrical adaptations and historical romances relieved only by some grandiose (and mostly doomed) projects, described a precipitously downward spiral similar to that of L'Herbier. Not much extravagance, then, in this film, the sentimental chronicle of a World War I widower overly troubled by his daughter's physical resemblance to her late mother. Academic and impersonal, its sole asset is a youthfully ingenuous Micheline Presle. GAd

Parallax View, The

(Alan J Pakula, 1974, US) Warren Beatty, Paula Prentiss, William Daniels, Walter McGinn, Hume Cronyn, Kelly Thordsen, Chuck Waters.
102 min.
A thriller about a journalist, alerted to the mysterious deaths of witnesses to the assassination of a presidential candidate, who embarks on an investigation that reveals a nebulous conspiracy of gigantic and all-embracing scope. It sounds familiar, and refers to or overlaps a good handful of similar films, but is most relevantly tied to *Klute*. Where *Klute* was an exploration of claustrophobic anxiety, *The Parallax View* is inexorably agoraphobic. Its visual organisation is stunning as the journalist (Beatty) is drawn into an increasingly nightmarish world characterised by impenetrably opaque structures, a screen whited out from time to time, or meshed over with visually deceptive patterns. It is some indication of the area the film explores that in place of the self-revealing session with the analyst in *Klute*, *The Parallax View* presents us with the more insecurity-inducing questionnaire used by the mysterious Parallax Corporation for personality-testing prospective employees. Excellent performances; fascinating film. VG

Paranoia (Orgasmo)

(Umberto Lenzi, 1968, It/Fr) Carroll Baker, Lou Castel, Colette Descombes, Tino Carraro, Lilla Brignone.
91 min.
Luridly dotty yarn in which an American lady (Baker) holes up in a remote Italian villa, suffering from drink and some sort of guilt complex about the elderly husband who died in a car crash leaving her a sizeable fortune. Enter a smooth young man (Castel), calling to her from the bushes and holding out dirt-encrusted arms into which she ecstatically rushes ('Oh, yes! Dirty me!'). Joined by his so-called sister (Descombes) and getting rid of the Mrs Danvers-like housekeeper (Brignone), Castel proceeds to inveigle the poor lady into a mad-making programme of swinging music, drugs and three-way sex. No prizes for guessing that money is the root of all evil, and that the victim, reduced to crawling haggardly from one empty whisky bottle to the next, wends her way to the attic for an agreeably ruthless finale. Good performances keep it watchable, but Lenzi's swinging direction (a mass of hideous mannerisms) keeps it well short of achieving orgasmo. TM

Parapluies de Cherbourg, Les (The Umbrellas of Cherbourg)

(Jacques Demy, 1964, Fr/WGer) Catherine Deneuve, Nino Castelnuovo, Anne Vernon, Ellen Farner, Marc Michel, Mireille Perrey, Jean Champion.
92 min.
A novelettish story that in the hands of most directors would be no more than trivial is transformed by Demy into something rather wonderful: a full-scale all-singing musical whose inspiration is Hollywood but whose tone and setting are resolutely Gallic. Shopgirl Deneuve loves a poor mechanic who leaves her pregnant when he departs for military service. During his absence, she is courted by a diamond merchant and nudged into marriage by her ambitious mother...This bittersweet romance – whose underlying message would seem to be that people invariably marry the wrong person – is lavished with affection. Vivid colours and elegant

camera choreography are bound together by Michel Legrand's sumptuous score. And never has an Esso station looked so romantic. CPe

Para Recibir el Canto de los Pajaros

see Bird's Singing, The

Parasite

(Charles Band, 1982, US) Robert Glaudini, Demi Moore, Luca Bercovici, James Davidson, Al Fann, Cherie Currie, Vivian Blaine.
85 min.
When a scientist arrives in an arid, futuristic landscape largely inhabited by 'Fickies' (predictably resembling Hell's Angels), he unfortunately brings with him two lethally ravenous lumps of slime: one in his stomach, one in a thermos. These of course attack all and sundry in repetitively gory set pieces which lack any of the intelligence, wit or style of Cronenberg's superficially similar *Shivers*. Uninspired actors intone a banal script, reduced by clumsy pacing to a minimum of suspense. The use of 3-D is presumably meant to lift this cinematic sludge above its peers; but apart from the obligatory objects placed in the foreground or – just occasionally – hurled at the camera, it's visually as uninteresting as a cat-food commercial. GA

Parasite Murders, The (aka Shivers/They Came from Within)

(David Cronenberg, 1974, Can) Paul Hampton, Joe Silver, Lynn Lowry, Allan Migicovsky, Susan Petrie, Barbara Steele.
87 min.
This first commercial feature by a former underground film-maker offers a heady, if finally muddled, combination of globs of horror and social criticism. Despite its exploitation format, even the British censor discerned a moral to the tale and passed it uncut. Best is the way Cronenberg deliberately manipulates his synthetic cast and bland visuals, whose plastic surfaces erupt to reveal their repressions and taboos beneath; slug-like parasites (a mix of aphrodisiac and venereal disease) rampage through a luxury tower block, turning the inhabitants into sex-craving zombies. But exactly what is its moral? One suspects Cronenberg is laughing up his sleeve, as some (like the censor) read *Shivers* as an attack on permissiveness, while others take it as an indictment of the whole of modern society. Often, however, the film stops little short of wholesale disgust at the human condition. Misanthropic, indeed, but the black humour and general inventiveness place it high above most contemporary horror pictures. CPe

Par-delà les Nuages

see Beyond the Clouds

Pardners

(Norman Taurog, 1956, US) Dean Martin, Jerry Lewis, Lori Nelson, Jackie Loughery, Agnes Moorehead, John Baragrey, Jeff Morrow, Lon Chaney Jr.
90 min.
Despite the title, the Martin and Lewis partnership was nearing breaking point on this spoof Western, a loose remake of Taurog's *Rhythm on the Range*, made 20 years earlier with Bing Crosby. Lewis is the especially maladroit millionaire son of a former rancher, who is persuaded to go west once again by the saddle-happy son (Martin) of his father's old partner, to regain the family seat and clean up the town. There is more singing than gunslinging, and Lewis is at his most worryingly infantile; but overall it's an amiable enough romp scripted by, of all people, bestseller Sidney Sheldon. DT

Pardon Mon Affaire, Too (Nous Irons Tous au Paradis)

(Yves Robert, 1977, Fr) Jean Rochefort, Claude Brasseur, Guy Bedos, Victor Lanoux, Danièle Delorme, Marthe Villalonga, Jenny Arasse.
112 min.
Sprawling comic saga of four middle-aged lads about Paris; and very typical fare from Yves Robert, who bestrides MOR French cinema like a colossus, at least in terms of quantity and popularity. Robert isn't short of good gags; unfortu-

nately he isn't short of bad ones, either, and seems unable or unwilling to fit his horde into any coherent shape or maintain any coherent tone. Rochefort is always watchable as the would-be rake, while Danièle Delorme's performance as his spirited wife saves the film from being unpleasantly chauvinist. All in all, it's bearable. Loosely remade by Gene Wilder as *The Woman in Red* GB

Pardon Us

(James Parrott, 1931, US) Stan Laurel, Oliver Hardy, Wilfred Lucas, June Marlowe, James Finlayson, Walter Long.
55 min. b/w.
The first Laurel and Hardy feature (if one excludes *Rogue Song*, in which they were merely featured), shot on the sets of *The Big House* and parodying prison breakout movies. Too slow and rambling to rank with their best, but full of things to treasure like Laurel's raspberry-blowing tooth, and the wonderful blackface musical interlude when the boys hide out in a cotton-picking shantytown. TM

Parenthood

(Ron Howard, 1989, US) Steve Martin, Mary Steenburgen, Dianne Wiest, Jason Robards, Rick Moranis, Tom Hulce, Martha Plimpton, Keanu Reeves, Harley Kozak, Dennis Dugan, Leaf Phoenix.
124 min.
The first ten minutes of this comedy about families is terrific, but after that it's hit-and-miss peppered with very funny one-liners. Probably only Robert Altman has the narrative grip to keep such a mosaic moving, and several stories here merely take up space. Steve Martin's manically over-conscientious dad steals the film, whether chewing the pitch as his small son fumbles at baseball, or entertaining a kids' party as an unconvincing cowboy. All this is in reaction against his own dad (Robards), who neglected him in favour of ever-feckless Hulce. Divorcee Wiest's fruity teenage offspring (Plimpton and Phoenix) barely communicate with her, except to hurl insults about her vibrator, while Rick Moranis' toddler is force-fed a flash-card education in Kafka and karate. At bottom, it's squashy old Dodie Smith's *Dear Octopus* with a top dressing of hard, smart-ass gags – very much the American TV sitcom formula. But if it's all a bit of a cop-out, there's enough to chortle at, and Martin at least is bang on. BC

Parents

(Bob Balaban, 1988, US) Randy Quaid, Mary Beth Hurt, Sandy Dennis, Bryan Madorsky, Juno Mills-Cockell, Kathryn Grody, Deborah Rush.
82 min.
Balaban's grisly feature debut deals with both the stultifying bad-taste conformism of Eisenhower's America and the theme of mutual distrust between adults and offspring, and turns them into the stuff of everyday horror. Nick and Lily Laemle (Quaid and Hurt) are new arrivals in a small Indiana town; everything about their life together stresses their normality. If there is a fly in the ointment, it's their young son Michael (Madorsky), a moody, introspective brat who has macabre fantasies derived from his horrific Oedipal nightmares. As the film progresses, however, we come to wonder whether it's the adults, rather than the progeny, who are loopy and cruel...If the film finally fails to shock or surprise, it's nevertheless both imaginatively shot and wittily scripted, and strikes a nice balance between gentle parody and a queasy unease associated with *bona fide* genre suspense. Superior performances by Quaid, Hurt and Madorsky. GA

Parents Terribles, Les (The Storm Within)

(Jean Cocteau, 1948, Fr) Yvonne de Bray, Jean Marais, Gabrielle Dorziat, Marcel André, Josette Day.
98 min. b/w.
Les Parents Terribles is the opposite pole to a film like *Orphée*: Cocteau the airy purveyor of fantasy proving that he could keep his feet on the ground with the best of them in a gut-wrenching tale of incestuous emotional rivalries destroying a family from within. Simply transposing his play intact (two sets, five characters, no exteriors), stressing the theatricality (credits imposed on a stage curtain; the *trois coups* sounded; the division into acts

marked), Cocteau nevertheless translates it into claustrophobically cinematic terms. Subtle changes in perspective, metronomically precise editing, clinical use of close-up (like the justly famous shot – his smiling mouth, her agonised eyes – as the son confidingly whispers into possessive mum's ear that he has fallen in love), make this not only an astonishingly dynamic film, but melodrama of the highest order. Stunning ensemble performances, but Yvonne de Bray (the mother) is out of this world. TM

Parfait Amour! (Perfect Love!)

(Catherine Breillat, 1996, Fr) Francis Renaud, Isabelle Renauld, Laura Saglio, Alain Soral, Delphine de Malerbé.
115 min.
Breillat's provocative drama charts how an idyllic affair between a divorcee – an optician with two kids – and a feckless, womanising twenty-something leads to brutal murder. Though some may find the woman's increasingly masochistic reactions to her young lover's behaviour questionable, the film is psychologically astute; just watch how the boy's early curiosity about the woman's greater experience slowly turns to insecurity and a determination to take control. The performances are unsentimental, the tone uncompromising, and if the film ends up too schematic for its own good, there's no denying its emotional punch or the intelligence of its dark insights. GA

Parfum d'Yvonne, Le

(Patrice Leconte, 1994, Fr) Jean-Pierre Marielle, Hippolyte Girardot, Sandra Majani, Richard Bohringer, Paul Guers, Corinne Marchand.
89 min.
Summer on Lake Geneva in the '50s finds Girardot's would-be writer hiding out from military service and the Algerian War. For a youthful wastrel of enigmatic means, the holiday atmosphere keeps the rest of the world at bay, perfectly setting the scene for a moment of sensual adventure when into his life walks glacial beauty Yvonne (Majani), and fez-wearing associate, the mysterious Dr Meinthe (Marielle). Erotic fascination and a giddy whirl of socialising fill the days that follow, all of it undercut by the realisation of life's fleeting evanescence. Typically succinct and joyously using the 'Scope format, Leconte's film is diaphanous in content but rich in visual and aural atmospherics. There's a heady whiff of pleasure to be gained from its piquant bouquet. TJ

Paris After Dark (aka The Night Is Ending)

(Leonide Moguy, 1943, US) George Sanders, Philip Dorn, Brenda Marshall, Madeleine LeBeau, Marcel Dalio, Robert Lewis, Henry Roland.
85 min. b/w.
Stock WWII tub-thumper about the need for resistance to Nazism. Dorn plays a factory worker who limps home to occupied Paris. Having suffered terrible brutality while a PoW (he is in fact dying), he is determined to keep his nose clean; but his wife (Marshall) is helping the society doctor (Sanders) for whom she works as a nurse to organise sabotage at the factory. Instead of exploring this dilemma (or the hint of class conflict between factory worker and aristocratic doctor), Howard Buchman's script opts for a woozy plot in which Dorn thinks Marshall and Sanders are lovers. After young brother shows that it's better to die than live as a slave, Dorn comes round and makes the good sacrifice to get the Gestapo off his wife's tail. Dalio hovers as the local barber, a perfumed poodle who – to no one's surprise but the cast's – turns out to be a collaborator. TM

Paris Awakens

see Paris s'éveille

Paris Belongs to Us

see Paris Nous Appartient

Paris by Night

(David Hare, 1988, GB) Charlotte Rampling, Michaeal Gambon, Robert Hardy, Iain Glen, Jane Asher, Niamh Cusack, Robert Flemyng.
103 min.

Writer/director Hare could hardly have anticipated the topicality of this study in Thatcherite morality released amid Tory debate over a 'united' Europe. The heroine of this thriller is ambitious Euro MP Clara Paige (a riveting performance by Rampling), whose swift rise within the Conservative ranks has been paralleled by growing neglect of her relationships with drink-sodden MP husband (Gambon) and young son. On assignment in Paris, Clara's life is devastated by hitherto untapped emotions. She has a passionate affair with entrepreneur Wallace (Glen), and – suspecting a blackmail attempt – commits murder with horrifying efficiency. For all her advocacy of self-determination, Clara is quick to try to evade the consequences of her misdeed. Hare avoids preachiness, thanks largely to taut, sparse dialogue, and brooding visuals from cinematographer Roger Pratt; the look and themes are those of a modern-day *film noir*, with the plot conjuring a nightmarish world of deception, sexual manipulation, and extortion. CM

Paris Does Strange Things

see Eléna et les Hommes

Paris Express

see Man Who Watched Trains Go By, The

Paris France

(Gérard Coccoritti, 1993, Can) Leslie Hope, Peter Outerbridge, Victor Ertmanis, Dan Lett.
105 min.
Blocked wife and bored writer Lucy Quick (Hope) is an acolyte of Anaïs Nin's brand of author-erotica, so when she finds Sloan, the latest discovery of Michael, her publisher husband, rifling through her drawers, she of course invites him in for a closer look. Sloan (Outerbridge) is a hot young bisexual with a book on serial killer Ed Gein under his belt. His arrogant, ambiguous pose also excites Michael's business partner William (Lett). This movie resembles a nightmare collaboration between Philip Kaufman's shrink and the National Film Board of Canada: lots of liberal, literary huffing and puffing interspersed with recherché avant garde-ism. The stew is overcooked and then some. TCh

Paris Is Burning

(Jennie Livingston, 1990, US)
78 min.
Made over three years (and also seen in Britain on TV in a shortened version in the BBC's *Arena* slot in 1990), Jennie Livingston's documentary is the original fly-on-the-ball vogueing spectacular. Long before Madonna tightened up that basque, the black and Hispanic queens of Harlem and Brooklyn were striking all manner of poses. Bound by poverty and prejudice, these material girls staged their own world of high fashion and fantasy, costume and competition. 'Giving good face' is only part of the challenge; it's whether you can pass as something other than your 'real' self that determines how well you score. This is queer culture's revenge on the world that surrounds and excludes it. Drag queens compete for the accolade of Real Woman, butch queens for the title of Real Man, which would all be rather tiring were it not for the varying combinations of enthusiasm and irony the competitors invest in the proceedings. 'If everyone did more balls and less drugs, it would be a sweet world,' proclaims one. Now who could possibly throw shade at that? PBur

Paris 1900

(Nicole Védrès, 1947, Fr)
91 min. b/w.
A charming compilation which broke new ground in its day with its breezily impressionistic portrait of *La Belle Epoque*, all fun and frolic but ending with a trainload of fodder setting off for the front in 1914. It may have been overtaken by more recent efforts on TV, but the marvellous footage is wittily used: Blériot's triumph after flying the channel, Eiffel and his tower (plus the birdman who sadly plopped from the top), the great flood of Paris, a street round-up of anarchists, snippets of a whole host of personalities from Monet, Renoir and Rodin to Bernhardt, Réjane, Melba, Mistinguett, Colette, Willy and Buffalo Bill. Pity that in the English version Monty Woolley's phrasing of the commentary is so archly facetious. TM

p

Paris Nous Appartient
(Paris Belongs to Us)
(Jacques Rivette, 1960, Fr) Betty Schneider, Gianni Esposito, Françoise Prévost, Daniel Crohem, François Maistre, Jean-Claude Brialy.
140 min. b/w.
Ex-*Cahiers du Cinéma* critic Rivette now makes stupendously long (and good) films that tend to get shown only at festivals. This was his first, made with the traditional shoestring budget and Claude Chabrol's camera. As in most Rivette films, the action centres around a ritual or theatrical event: here, a troupe of actors rehearse *Pericles*, only to fall apart under the burden of various kinds of angst. It's a bracing experience, though the movie is ultimately too hermetic and mysterious for its own good; when he gives himself a longer time span – as in the magnificent four-hour *L'Amour Fou* – Rivette shows he can orchestrate his themes to perfection. GB

Paris qui Dort
(The Crazy Ray)
(René Clair, 1923, Fr) Henri Rollan, Madeleine Rodrigue, Marcel Vallée, Albert Préjean, Charles Martinelli.
5,500 ft. b/w.
The first feature of director-writer-novelist-Dadaist René Clair resembles his better-known short 'Entr'acte' in its manic comic invention and its all-round energetic absurdity. It starts out with a crazed inventor perfecting a ray that suspends animation throughout Paris, and then has a great deal of fun tracing the paths of a handful of 'survivors' through the frozen city. The prolific jokes about motion and stasis are fundamentally movie concept gags, and they relate directly to contemporary avant-garde film concerns. TR

Paris s'éveille
(Paris Awakens)
(Olivier Assayas, 1991, Fr) Judith Godrèche, Jean-Pierre Léaud, Thomas Langmann.
95 min.
This third feature by former *Cahiers du Cinéma* critic Assayas is his best to date, and one of the few French movies about middle-class relationships that is neither precious nor airily detached from social realities. It's essentially a triangle drama: father (Léaud, playing his real age, for once), much younger second wife (Godrèche, fetching), and semi-estranged son (Langmann, son of Claude Berri). Fluently written and played with palpable enthusiasm by the entire cast, it works outwards from small details. Everything is precisely judged, from the hang of an art-class model's scrotum to the bearing of a waitress in a Chinese restaurant. TR

Paris, Texas (100)
(Wim Wenders, 1984, WGer/Fr/GB) Harry Dean Stanton, Dean Stockwell, Aurore Clément, Hunter Carson, Nastassja Kinski, Bernhard Wicki.
148 min.
A man in a red baseball cap comes stumbling over the Mexican border and into the Texan desert, mute, bowed but driven by an obsessive quest. When his brother (Stockwell) drives him (Stanton) home to LA, the shards of his broken life are painfully pieced together in fits and starts of talk. Four years ago he 'lost' his family; now he has returned to find them. Reunited with his 7-year-old son, he travels to Houston, where he finds his wife (Kinski) working in a peep-show. Wenders once more finds himself on the borders of experience, finally achieving an unprecedented declaration of the heart, even if man and wife can only perceive each other through a glass darkly. Wenders' collaboration with writer Sam Shepard is a master-stroke, wholly beneficial to both talents; if Wenders' previous film, *The State of Things*, was on the very limits of possibility, this one, through its final scenes, pushes the frontier three steps forward into new and sublime territory. CPea

Paris Trout
(Stephen Gyllenhaal, 1991, US) Dennis Hopper, Barbara Hershey, Ed Harris, Ray McKinnon, Tina Lifford, Daratha Henry, Eric Ware, Ronreaco Lee, Gary Bullock.
99 min.
The eponymous protagonist of Gyllenhaal's rather superb first feature is a repellent, racist

loan-shark (played to the tight-lipped hilt by Hopper) who rules the roost in a late '40s Southern community. When a young black (Ware) welshes on the agreement after borrowing money to buy a car, Trout dispenses the only kind of justice he feels comfortable with; then, confronted by his wife (Hershey) about his crime, he starts down a road to total insanity by first humiliating, then subjecting her to horrible sexual abuse. Pete Dexter's script from his own novel is tough, often disturbing stuff, with a whiff of small-town Southern life that takes in everything from a John Lee Hooker TV commercial to William Faulkner and Harper Lee. Sometimes the pace is as slow as watching cotton grow, but at others the rage and bigotry on Hopper's face spills out dreadfully across the screen. Excellent performances from Hopper, Hershey and Ed Harris (as Hershey's lawyer-lover), some languorous photography from Robert Elswit, and a package of big issues inside a small frame, make this a film not to be missed. SGr

Paris vu par...(Six in Paris)
(Jean Douchet/Jean Rouch/Jean-Daniel Pollet/Eric Rohmer/Jean-Luc Godard/Claude Chabrol, 1964, Fr) Joanna Shimkus, Nadine Ballot, Barbet Schroeder, Micheline Dax, Claude Melki, Claude Chabrol, Stéphane Audran.
98 min.
A disappointingly lightweight collection of sketches, filmed in 16mm (blown up to 35mm) in an attempt to encourage experiment by reducing costs. Godard's contribution elaborates a story told in *Une Femme est une Femme* (about a girl who posts letters to her two lovers, then agonises that she got the envelopes mixed), interestingly but not very successfully told as *cinéma-vérité* style with Albert Maysles as cameraman. Rohmer and Rouch are desperately cramped for space; Douchet's episode is routine *Nouvelle Vague* sexual sparring; Pollet's is neatly observed but conventional. By far the best sketch is Chabrol's ruthlessly funny caricature of a bourgeois couple (played by himself and Audran) whose constant nagging, quarrelling and platitudinising drive their young son to resort to earplugs, with the result that he is blithely unaware of his mother's desperate cries for help when...TM

Paris Was a Woman
(Greta Schiller, 1995, GB)
75 min.
Greta Schiller is best known for her 1986 documentary on early women jazz musicians, *International Sweethearts of Rhythm*. Ten years may have passed, but this appraisal of the women involved in the Left Bank scene shares a similar mix of marvellous archive footage and testimony. Schiller contends that the creative women living in Paris during the early decades of this century have been overlooked in favour of their more famous male contemporaries, and that Gertrude Stein, Sylvia Beach, Adrienne Monnier, Janet (Genet) Flanner and Djuna Barnes deserve recognition for their contributions to the modernist movement. The problem is that, with the possible exception of Stein, the achievements of the group compared to those of, say, Picasso, Hemingway or Joyce do seem relatively minor. In fact, it soon becomes clear that it's the way these women led their lives, as much as what they chose to do, that interests Schiller. The obvious, if never overtly stated connection is that they were all lesbians (the commentary's constant use of the term 'friends' grates horribly) who, by distancing themselves sexually from contemporary mores, also released themselves from other conventional expectations. FM

Parker
(Jim Goddard, 1984, GB) Bryan Brown, Cherie Lunghi, Kurt Raab, Bob Peck, Beate Finkh, Gwyneth Strong, Hannelore Elsner.
97 min.
An Australian toy manufacturer (Brown) has a charming English wife (Lunghi), a high-class German whore as mistress (Elsner), and a suitably comfortable life-style which crumbles after he is kidnapped and then mysteriously released on a business trip to Germany. Parker's experiences begin to obsess not only him, but also the German investigator (Raab) and the wife, who suspects the worst, and whose loyalty finally cracks as her husband bizarrely returns to images of the crime while recuperating back in

London. Though arrestingly shot on location and with a tense, restless performance from Brown, both direction and script are just too fussy for their own good, more interested in lots of confusing and enervating cutting about than in establishing the initial premise of the story: a man suddenly at odds with both himself and all he surveys. SGr

Parking
(Jacques Demy, 1985, Fr) Francis Huster, Keiko Ito, Hugues Quester, Marie-France Pisier, Jean Marais.
95 min.
Demy's career peaked early, the references, tone, sentiments all fixed and fully explored by the end of the '60s. His later movies all seemed to misfire in one way or another, not least this passing strange musical adaptation of Greek myth, in which Orpheus is represented as a French pop star of Eurovision-esque vapidity, performing a Michel Legrand score which veers from the characteristically inventive to the characteristically saccharine. The scenes in the Underworld (reached via doward spiralling car park) have some force, and it would be worth knowing whether the director, who died in 1990, had already felt the touch of mortality when he embarked on this project. The hero's upfront bisexuality indicates a buried motif running through much of Demy's work. BBa

Park Row
(Samuel Fuller, 1952, US) Gene Evans, Mary Welch, Bela Kovacs, Herbert Heyes, Tina Rome, JM Kerrigan.
83 min. b/w.
This early Fuller drama matches his tabloid style to the story of a newspaper war between two proprietors in 1886. It's compulsive for its insider's knowledge, and passion for the press, but is mostly memorable for a roller-coaster type tracking shot of a fight scene that is pure cinema. The mood is set early: a guy in a bar jumps off Brooklyn Bridge to provide a front page story. When he returns from the jump (alive), the journalist in question has been sacked. A tough world. DMacp

Parlor, Bedroom and Bath
(aka Romeo in Pyjamas)
(Edward Sedgwick, 1931, US) Buster Keaton, Charlotte Greenwood, Reginald Denny, Cliff Edwards, Dorothy Christy, Joan Peers, Sally Eilers, Edward Brophy.
75 min. b/w.
After a marvellous start with *The Cameraman*, Keaton's features for MGM went steadily downhill. Convinced that slapstick was not only finished but infra dig for a major star, Thalberg saddled him here with a Broadway farce from 1917, ploddingly handled in the 'photographed stage play' manner. Buster plays a gormless billposter who stumbles into a household of rich young things, and in a plot to further romance, is persuaded to pretend to be a mysterious Lothario. Hopelessly backward with girls, he is sent to an experienced female tutor (Greenwood), but a mix-up finds him closeted instead with the young wife (Peers) of a violently jealous man. Bogged down in acres of plot and witless dialogue that prevents him from developing a single gag (slapstick or otherwise), Keaton simply goes through the motions. Pitiful to watch. TM

Parole de Flic
see Cop's Honour

Parsifal
(Hans-Jürgen Syberberg, 1982, Fr/WGer) Michael Kutter, Karin Krick, Edith Clever, Armin Jordan, Robert Lloyd, Aage Haugland.
255 min.
Set in medieval times, around the temple of the Holy Grail, *Parsifal* offers its director more than just the possibility of interpreting Wagner's seductive last opera. He reduces the central Christian theme and refocuses it on a decaying Europe, while simultaneously confronting past with present, myth with reality, the rational with the romantic. Filmed exclusively within a studio – a practice which Syberberg has practically reinvented – it's all staged within a gigantic set of Wagner's death mask, with constantly shifting projected backgrounds. Among a mixed cast of actors and

singers, Edith Clever gives a particularly impressive expressionist performance as Kundry (sung by Yvonne Minton). Wagner, as the most radical dramatist of his age, is matched by Syberberg's vision, confirming that he is one of the most visually distinctive film-makers of his time. Continually surprising, provocative, probably infuriating for purists, *Parsifal* is compulsive viewing for both music and movie enthusiasts. KG

Partie de Campagne, Une 100

(Jean Renoir, 1936, Fr) Sylvia Bataille, Georges Darnoux, Jane Marken, André Gabriello, Jacques Brunius, Paul Temps, Jean Renoir.
45 min. b/w.
Supposedly left unfinished, but filming was in fact completed, except that the producers wanted Renoir to expand to feature length; he was reluctant, other things intervened, then the war, and the film was finally released in 1946 with the addition of a couple of titles. It may be only a featurette, but this masterly adaptation of a Maupassant story is rich in both poetry and thematic content. On an idyllic country picnic, a young girl leaves her family and fiancé for a while, and succumbs to an all-too-brief romance. The careful reconstruction of period (around 1860) is enhanced by a typically touching generosity towards the characters and an aching, poignant sense of love lost but never forgotten. And, as always in Renoir, the river is far, far more than just a picturesque stretch of water. Witty and sensuous, it's pure magic. GA

Partie de Plaisir, Une (Love Match)

(Claude Chabrol, 1974, Fr/It) Paul Gégauff, Danièle Gégauff, Paula Moore, Michel Valette, Pierre Santini, Giancarlo Sisti, Clémence Gégauff.
101 min.
One of Chabrol's most maligned films. A cool and elegiac study of the canker destroying a family from within, it is given bizarre overtones – part confession, part game – as well as a peculiar poignancy by the fact that the script is modelled by Chabrol's regular scriptwriter Paul Gégauff, who plays the lead opposite his former wife Danièle, on his own marital troubles. Accusations galore of chauvinism were levelled at the film, of course, as the man, having fashioned the woman in his image of perfection, then simultaneously encourages and resents her independence to the point of brutality and even murder. But what emerges from the heart of the film, undercutting the Pavlovian response, is the sense of bitter despair underlying the man's full awareness that he had found paradise, but because of his own intransigently idealistic nature, was unable to find peace and harmony there. TM

Parting Glances

(Bill Sherwood, 1985, US) Richard Ganoung, John Bolger, Steve Buscemi, Adam Nathan, Kathy Kinney, Patrick Tull.
90 min.
On the surface, Sherwood's first feature looks like the Gay Yuppie Movie it was rumoured to be. Its beautiful characters inhabit covetable NY apartments and lofts, and Fire Island and the Area club are on their social circuit. Yet crucially they lack the cocaine-charged solipsism which renders such things Yuppoid. Sherwood brings a notable grace and droll humour to his story of two male lovers parting against the backdrop of a friend dying of the Big A. At times it errs towards MGM production values, but it has a tenderness, warmth, humour and, despite that looming Big A, a lightness of heart that will win it many friends. The romantic close stretches belief, but it's a film of subtle and elegant musicality. JG

Partner

(Bernardo Bertolucci, 1968, It) Pierre Clémenti, Stefania Sandrelli, Tina Aumont, Sergio Tofano, Giulio Cesare Castello.
105 min.
In all of Bertolucci's movies, there's a central conflict between the 'radical' impulses and a pessimistic (and/or willing) capitulation to the mainstream of bourgeois society and culture. It's a contradiction that takes on juggernaut proportions in '1900', but it stands as a major source of tension and interest in many of the earlier films. Both *Before the Revolution* and *Partner* try to examine it head-on. *Revolution* is about a middle class 20-year-old who 'discovers' Marxism and tries – for a while – to change his life; *Partner* is

an exuberant response to the student riots of '68, with Clémenti as a timid drama student confronting his anarchic revolutionary alter ego. The first is mostly 'classical' in style, the second aggressively 'new wave', but both are full of interruptions and digressions: they throw out ideas and allusions (usually to other movies) with reckless enthusiasm, and they remain invaluable aids to an understanding of the '60s. TR

Partners

(James Burrows, 1982, US) Ryan O'Neal, John Hurt, Kenneth McMillan, Robyn Douglass, Jay Robinson, Denise Galik, Rick Jason.
98 min.
Sent into the decadent underworld in a lilac VW convertible, odd couple O'Neal (womanising cop masquerading – unconvincingly – as a dumb gay stud) and Hurt (given a bum deal as his partner, an unhappy closet case) skid to a halt in a welter of stupidly sexist stereotypes and a scrappy murder investigation plot. The way O'Neal is confirmed in his macho piggishness, and Hurt finds fulfilment in proving himself an ideal housewife, suggests that the average American male, his privileges eroded by feminism, can still get his dinner cooked and his slippers warmed by the fire if he turns gay. But the film seems less interested in exploring this intriguing (if offensive) idea than in setting up situations where we can ogle O'Neal's body. RMy

Parts: the Clonus Horror (aka Clonus)

(Robert S Fiveson, 1978, US) Tim Donnelly, Dick Sargent, Peter Graves, Paulette Breen, Keenan Wynn, David Hooks.
90 min.
Competent and engrossing sci-fi thriller in the *Coma* vein, concerning a human transplantation top-security unit, in which clones of top people are carefully nurtured before being suspended in plastic bags to await their medical fate. Interesting on ethics, and boasting nice cameos from Hollywood vets Keenan Wynn (as a retired journalist) and Peter Graves (a corrupt senator). SGo

Party, The

(Blake Edwards, 1968, US) Peter Sellers, Claudine Longet, Marge Champion, J Edward McKinley, Fay McKenzie.
98 min.
Sellers gets to do his funny accent as an accident-prone Indian actor brought to Hollywood, fired for inadvertently sabotaging the movie (a briefly hilarious parody of *Gunga Din*), and invited in error to a posh party at the studio chief's home. From there on, Blake Edwards flexes his Jacques Tati muscles, spinning an elaborate garland of gags around one rather drawn-out situation as Sellers – seconded by a drunken waiter and a baby elephant – innocently reduces the party by degrees to an apocalyptic shambles and his hosts to gibbering wrecks. Quite a few very funny moments, but one doesn't laugh so much as admire the ingenuity. TM

Party and the Guests, The (O Slavnosti a Hostech)

(Jan Nemec, 1966, Czech) Ivan Vyskocil, Jan Klusák, Jiri Nemec, Zdenka Skvorecká.
71 min. b/w.
An acute piece of historical foresight, with a marvellous basic idea. A group of picnickers wandering in a summery wood change into evening-dress, emerge into the grounds of a stately mansion, and are rescued from a band of roving thugs by their host, who ushers them to a magnificent banquet laid out under the stars. Then a man is reported to have left the party; the urbanity vanishes; tracker dogs can be heard howling in the distance. The allegory is obvious, of course, with the avuncular dictator mouthing platitudes, his brutish minions straining at the leash, and the guests submitting like patient sheep to the pointless show of the party. But once one has grasped the message and admired the glittering camerawork, that's about it (although the dialogue may well have carried more hidden charges for Czech audiences). TM

Party Girl

(Nicholas Ray, 1958, US) Robert Taylor, Cyd Charisse, Lee J Cobb, John Ireland, Kent Smith.
99 min.

Or the optimistic version of *Johnny Guitar*, set in Prohibition Chicago. Robert Taylor has the limp, Cyd Charisse is the dancer, and both are prostitutes of a kind (he a gangster's lawyer, she a party girl) who use each other as emotional crutches before achieving mutual independence and trust. Although the script is poor, Ray's handling of colour and scope is as masterful as ever. Too often consigned to the 'fabulous but flawed' bin, *Party Girl* is far better than that. As in all Ray's films, ideas and emotions are transformed into stunning visuals, as when Lee J Cobb's gangster shoots up a portrait of Jean Harlow after he discovers that she's recently got married. PH

Party – Nature Morte, The

(Cynthia Beatt, 1991, Ger) Tilda Swinton, Féodor Atkine.
89 min. b/w.
Beatt's first feature centres on a staggering performance from Swinton: part Diva, part Harpy, part woman struggling to cope and make sense of it all. She plays Queenie, married to a German and living in Germany; the marriage has reached one of its periodic crises, and Queenie's way out of the impasse is to throw a big all-night party. During it, she humiliates her husband by flirting with a handsome French stranger (Atkine). She succeeds in making a drama out of a crisis. Shot in steely monochrome, this is a small triumph for high-concept film-making. It's structured as a flow of vignettes, with an ever-changing cast of party guests in the background; dozens of people get their minute or two of prominence, but everything turns around the central triangle of wife, husband and potential lover. The only real weakness is the dialogue, far too much of which is quoted from literature and poetry. But the grasp of mood and rhythm is spot on. TR

Party Party

(Terry Winsor, 1983, GB) Daniel Peacock, Karl Howman, Perry Fenwick, Sean Chapman, Phoebe Nicholls, Gary Olsen.
98 min.
Sold as a sassy young British film ('lotta skirt, lotta geezers, lotta class...') with a passable compilation soundtrack, and directed/co-scripted by National Film School graduate Winsor, this comedy of adolescent errors and angst comes across as disappointingly arthritic. The plot – New Year's Eve jollities, expanded from a student short – seems too insubstantial for a full-length feature. It's impossible to sympathise or identify with this charmless assembly of wimps, vamps, wallflowers, fast flash womanisers, piss artists, comic bobbies, vicars, and – that ultimate figure of *Carry On* hilarity – the horny middle-aged male. You feel Winsor doesn't much like his desperate party people; and that, surely, is unforgivable. SJo

Pascali's Island

(James Dearden, 1988, GB) Ben Kingsley, Charles Dance, Helen Mirren, Stefan Gryff, George Murcell, Nadim Sawalha, TP McKenna.
104 min.
Set during the death throes of the Ottoman Empire on an island uneasily divided between Greeks and Turks, Barry Unsworth's tragic tale of deceit makes an ambitious subject for Dearden's debut. Pascali (Kingsley) is a Turkish spy increasingly troubled that his reports are unread. Into this stalled society of spies and lies comes a new development when Bowles (Dance), a bogus English archaeologist, unearths an ancient bronze statue, risks all to bear it off, and places Pascali in a position where he has to initiate action. Fez, Levantine shiftiness and all, Kingsley strips away the facile associations with Lorre, Ustinov, Greenstreet & Co, and justifies a tragic destiny for his character. The milieu may seem remote but the performances illuminate, and the story has an originality that compensates for the modest budget. BC

Pasolini's 120 Days of Sodom

see Salò o le Centoventi Giornate di Sodoma

Pasolini, un Delitto Italiano (Pasolini, an Italian Crime)

(Marco Tullio Giordana, 1995, It/Fr) Carlo de Filippi, Nicoletta Braschi, Tony Bertorelli.
100 min.

Driven by a pulsing Morricone score, this forthright investigative thriller re-examines the murder of the great Italian director and poet Pier Paolo Pasolini in Ostia in 1975, and the subsequent, inadequate police inquiry (the case was reopened in light of the evidence presented in the film and the book which inspired it). While Giordana's comparatively conventional style has nothing in common with Pasolini's, the film's mode of address serves as a powerful, moving testament to the esteem in which the film-maker was (and still is) held, and a devastating critique of the society which couldn't accommodate his integrity. TCh

Pasqualino Settebellezze
see Seven Beauties

Passage, The
(J Lee Thompson, 1978, GB) Anthony Quinn, James Mason, Malcolm McDowell, Patricia Neal, Kay Lenz, Christopher Lee, Michel Lonsdale, Marcel Bozzuffi.
98 min.
Anthony Quinn, in yet another portrait from his gallery of craggy, loveable peasants, plays a Basque shepherd who ferries an escaping scientist and his family across the Pyrenees into Spain during WWII, pursued by a tenacious SS officer (Malcolm McDowell with supercilious swagger). McDowell's comically histrionic performance is, in fact, the single redeeming feature in this lamentably simplistic and unpleasant piffle. File under Carry On Garrotting and forget. AC

Passage Home
(Roy Baker, 1955, GB) Anthony Steel, Peter Finch, Diane Cilento, Cyril Cusack, Geoffrey Keen, Hugh Griffith, Duncan Lamont, Gordon Jackson, Michael Craig.
102 min. b/w.
This is the one about the martinet captain (Finch) and the mutinous crew. But given that the setting is the Depression year of 1931, that the captain of the merchant ship feeds his crew rotten potatoes to cut down on expenses, and that the film is told in flashback from the moment when the merchant company offers a grateful eulogy on his retirement, it is by no means uninteresting. Brightly scripted and well acted (aside from the colourless Anthony Steel), it takes some sharpish digs at exploitation and the class system, only partly negated by the cop-out ending. MA

Passager de la Pluie
see Rider on the Rain

Passagers, Les
see Shattered

Passage to India, A
(David Lean, 1984, GB) Judy Davis, Victor Banerjee, Peggy Ashcroft, James Fox, Alec Guinness, Nigel Havers, Richard Wilson, Antonia Pemberton, Saeed Jaffrey.
163 min.
This proves a curiously modest affair, abandoning the tub-thumping epic style of Lean's late years. While adhering to perhaps 80 percent of the book's incident, Lean veers very wide of the mark over EM Forster's hatred of the British presence in India, and comes down much more heavily on the side of the British. But he has assembled his strongest cast in years. Particularly fine is Judy Davis as the foolish hysteric, Miss Quested, who gives the crux of the film (was she or was she not raped in the Marabar caves by her Indian host?) its strongest moments. And once again Lean indulges his taste for scenery, demonstrating an ability with sheer scale which has virtually eluded British cinema throughout its history. Not for literary purists, but if you like your entertainment well tailored, then feel the quality and the width. CPea

Passage to Marseille
(Michael Curtiz, 1944, US) Humphrey Bogart, Michèle Morgan, Claude Rains, Philip Dorn, Sydney Greenstreet, Peter Lorre, George Tobias, Helmut Dantine, John Loder, Victor Francen, Eduardo Ciannelli.
110 min. b/w.
Something of a follow-up to Casablanca, but without that movie's deft and evocative script. Bogart plays Jean Matrac, a journalist converted, by a confrontation at sea with Greenstreet's elegant fascism (shades of Huston's Across the Pacific), from

bitterness against a France that has wronged him to self-destructive patriotism with the Free French. The movie is brought to earth by its unnecessary complexity – at one point we're in a flashback from a flashback from a flashback – but the central scenes on Devil's Island have a cogency and atmosphere, particularly Bogart's spell in solitary, which demonstrate the movie it might have been. The last reel quivers with the sort of emotionalism that wartime audiences adored. Bogart hasn't much to do beyond gritting his teeth, Rains typically holds the plot together, and Michèle Morgan is thanklessly cast as the wife waiting at home 'till we meet again'. SG

Passenger, The (Professione: Reporter)
(Michelangelo Antonioni, 1975, It/Fr/Sp) Jack Nicholson, Maria Schneider, Jenny Runacre, Ian Hendry, Steven Berkoff, Ambrose Bia.
119 min.
Despite the burdensome presence of Runacre in a relatively minor role, this is Antonioni's finest film for years. With a terse, imaginative script by Peter Wollen (betraying both his interest in structure/structuralism and his past experiences as a political correspondent abroad) that delves into Graham Greene-ish territory, it concerns a TV reporter (Nicholson) who exchanges identity with an acquaintance he finds dead in a North African hotel room, only to find himself hunted not just by mystified wife and friends, but by some rather threatening strangers. At times obscure, the relationship Nicholson strikes up with Schneider in his bid to escape to a new life seems both a little perfunctory and gratuitous to the central theme. But the film's opening, charting the burnt-out journalist's progress through an endless desert, and the final twenty minutes – including a virtuoso seven-minute single take – are stunning. GA

Passenger 57
(Kevin Hooks, 1993, US) Wesley Snipes, Bruce Payne, Tom Sizemore, Alex Datcher, Bruce Greenwood, Robert Hooks, Elizabeth Hurley.
84 min.
This routine hijack drama lacks the budget and class to match the Die Hard films it seeks to emulate. It's lifted, however, by a top-flight performance by Wesley Snipes, whose fast-talking airline security expert enlivens the plot with his screen presence, physical grace and devastating martial arts skills. 'Always bet on black,' Snipes advises feisty flight attendant Datcher, after Payne, freed from his FBI captors by fellow terrorists, takes over a domestic flight to Los Angeles. The plot soon nose dives; but what it lacks in logic, it makes up for in relentless action. An efficient, entertaining time-waster, but Snipes deserved better for his first solo starring role. NF

Passe ton bac d'abord
(Maurice Pialat, 1979, Fr) Sabine Haudepin, Philippe Marlaud, Bernard Tronczyk, Anik Alane, Michel Caron.
80 min.
Best known in Britain for La Gueule Ouverte and Loulou, Pialat is a major, though unfortunately marginalised, French talent whose realist eye here lights on provincial teenage life, producing something like a cross between Ken Loach and a Gallic Gregory's Girl. The non-professional kids, on communal holiday from the title's exhortation to concentrate on their school exams, show a lively disregard for any notion of adolescent angst, despite dead-end prospects, while Pialat never indulges the exploitative clichés of the native genre of 'nostalgic' teen-sex low comedy. PT

Passion
(Jean-Luc Godard, 1982, Fr/Switz) Isabelle Huppert, Hanna Schygulla, Jerzy Radziwilowicz, Michel Piccoli, Laszlo Szabo, Jean-François Stévenin.
88 min.
For the '60s generation, Godard effectively reinvented cinema, but for many who came to movies in the '70s he trailed a reputation as a brusque, didactic, doctrinaire apologist for the 'lost causes' of May '68. Passion brought a chance to (re)discover what all the fuss was about. Reunited with cameraman Raoul Coutard after 16 years, and with a trio of great actors (Huppert, Schygulla, Piccoli), he orchestrates his personal passions for classical music, romantic painting, and the busi-

ness of film-making around his favourite theme of how life relates to love. In a film studio, a Polish director is recreating in tableaux vivants a series of celebrated paintings by Goya, Ingres, Delacroix, Rembrandt and El Greco (breathtakingly lit and framed by Coutard), but the backers complain that there's no story. Outside, at the hotel, are many stories, but none is allowed to assume centre stage and focus your vision on a single narrative. Godard asks you to look everywhere at once, offering sounds and images that astonish the senses and tease the mind. It's a film you'll need – and want – to see several times. MA

Passion, A (En Passion)
(Ingmar Bergman, 1969, Swe) Liv Ullmann, Bibi Anderson, Max von Sydow, Erland Josephson, Erik Hell, Sigge Forst.
100 min.
All Bergman's films in the late '60s centre on isolated social groups (often the partners of a marriage) and show them under attack from both inside and out: Laingian fissures and cracks open up between the characters, and their precarious security is challenged by irruptions from the outside world. Bergman preserves and extends his private mythologies (witness the way that images and names recur from film to film), but in a broader (less precious, more honest) context. Liv Ullmann says it all in The Shame when she dreams of 'living in the truth'. Here, another bold step forward in Bergman's analysis of human isolation, the public and private manias of Hour of the Wolf are brought down to earth among middle class intruders in an island community. TR

Passionate Friends, The (aka One Woman's Story)
(David Lean, 1948, GB) Trevor Howard, Ann Todd, Claude Rains, Betty Ann Davies, Isabel Dean, Arthur Howard, Wilfrid Hyde White.
95 min. b/w.
Adapted by Eric Ambler from the novel by HG Wells, this triangular romance is one of three films Lean made in the late '40s with his then wife Ann Todd and reckoned by critic David Thomson as his piece 'most deserving rediscovery'. Todd and husband Rains are on holiday in Switzerland when she runs into her former lover Howard for the first time in nine years, causing a rift in her present relationship when her other half misreads the by-now platonic relationship between the two old pals. As ever the craft of the piece (an intricate flashback structure, Guy Green's beautiful cinematography) seems to carry all before it, but there's a degree of emotional subtlety here that often went missing in the director's later work. TJ

Passione, La
see La Passione

Passion de Jeanne d'Arc, La (The Passion of Joan of Arc) [100]
(Carl Dreyer, 1928, Fr) Renée Jeanne Falconetti, Eugène Silvain, Maurice Schutz, Michel Simon, Antonin Artaud.
7,251 ft. b/w.
Dreyer's most universally acclaimed masterpiece remains one of the most staggeringly intense films ever made. It deals only with the final stages of Joan's trial and her execution, and is composed almost exclusively of close-ups: hands, robes, crosses, metal bars, and (most of all) faces. The face we see most is, naturally, Falconetti's as Joan, and it's hard to imagine a performer evincing physical anguish and spiritual exaltation more palpably. Dreyer encloses this stark, infinitely expressive face with other characters and sets that are equally devoid of decoration and equally direct in conveying both material and metaphysical essences. The entire film is less moulded in light than carved in stone: it's magisterial cinema, and almost unbearably moving. TR

Passione d'Amore
(Ettore Scola, 1981, It/Fr) Bernard Giraudeau, Valeria D'Obici, Laura Antonelli, Jean-Louis Trintignant, Massimo Girotti, Bernard Blier.
119 min.
An Italian costume drama set in the 19th century, about a dashing young cavalry officer and his love. Senso, alas, it is not. After interminable mopings when the lovers are separated by his transfer to a remote frontier post, things brighten up momen-

tarily with the appearance of a mysterious woman bearing a marked resemblance to Murnau's *Nosferatu*. Her looks apparently suffered in an illness following an early amorous deception. Now, requiring to be treated with the forbearance befitting an officer and a gentleman, she battens onto our hero's affections like a vampire on heat. Probably only Buñuel could have got away with the grotesque romantic tushery whereby the enormity of her passion finally conjures a response, and the pair soar together in a bout of *amour fou*. Po faced nonsense with cardboard characters, it has excellent camerawork and nicely dry supporting performances from Trintignant and Blier. TM

Passion Fish

(John Sayles, 1993, US) Mary McDonnell, Alfre Woodard, Vondie Curtis-Hall, Angela Bassett, David Strathairn.
135 min.
Tetchy and bitter after a car crash which has left her paralysed from the waist down, daytime soap star May-Alice (McDonnell) returns to her late parents' Louisiana home to drown her sorrows. Only with the arrival of Chantelle (Woodard), a determinedly unservile black from Chicago, does the reluctant patient meet her match in obstinacy. It's a spiky, volatile relationship, but when Chantelle helps May-Alice get rid of some unwelcome visitors, a fragile link is forged between the two equally proud but very different women. Sayles' most warmly perceptive, touching movie to date, *Passion Fish* delivers far more than its generic roots would suggest. The director's witty, understated script and relaxed, classical direction may touch on issues of sickness, race and sexual politics, but do so in ways that are never laboured, schematic or sentimental. Marvellously nuanced performances, effortlessly superior film-making. GA

Passion of Darkly Noon, The (Die Passion des Darkly Noon)

(Philip Ridley, 1995, GB/Ger/Bel) Brendan Fraser, Ashley Judd, Viggo Mortensen, Loren Dean, Grace Zabriskie, Lou Myers, Kate Harper.
101 min.
Ridley's slow-burning fable builds to a shocking finale, part apocalyptic religious vision, part intellectual slasher movie. Darkly Noon (Fraser), sole survivor of a Waco-like siege, is given refuge by beautiful forest dweller Callie (Judd), whose lover Clay (Mortensen) later returns for a passionate reunion. Egged on by crazy hermit Roxy (Zabriskie), Darkly cranks himself up into a state of violent delirium. As the vengeful innocent wraps barbed wire around his chest, one recalls the disturbing weirdness of *The Reflecting Skin* and fears the worst. NF

Passion of Remembrance, The

(Maureen Blackwood/Isaac Julien, 1986, GB) Anni Domingo, Joseph Charles, Antonia Thomas, Carlton Chance, Jim Findley, Ram John Holder.
82 min.
This montage of documentary footage and representational dramatic episodes from London's Sankofa Collective offers a series of individual reflections, each bearing a potential for further development. The focal point is the confrontation between a young man and woman, attempting to rationalise the gap which has separated them as they stand before a barren landscape. 'Man' is accused of forsaking 'Woman' in his struggle to raise the consciousness of the black community. Over-extended in scope and tied down by its own rhetoric, the film nevertheless succeeds as it catches the conflicts of gender and generation within the community itself, with visions of a 'black experience' giving way to the more nominal insights of black experiences. SGo

Passport to Fame

see Whole Town's Talking, The

Passport to Pimlico

(Henry Cornelius, 1948, GB) Stanley Holloway, Margaret Rutherford, John Slater, Barbara Murray, Betty Warren, Hermione Baddeley, Paul Dupuis, Raymond Huntley, Jane Hylton, Basil Radford, Naunton Wayne.
85 min. b/w.

Perhaps the most Ealingish of the Ealing comedies, celebrating the cosy sense of wartime togetherness recaptured when the inhabitants of Pimlico, discovering their hereditary independence from Britain, set up a restriction-free (but soon beleaguered and ration-hit) state. A brilliant idea whose satirical possibilities are never really explored. The film is nevertheless carried along on a wave of zany inventiveness (hit by sanctions, the 'Burgundians' promptly respond by having customs officers patrol the tube trains passing through their territory), while an amiable cast does well by TEB Clarke's genial script (especially Margaret Rutherford as the history don quivering with ecstasy over the historical significance of the discovery of the ancient Burgundian charter). TM

Password Is Courage, The

(Andrew L Stone, 1962, GB) Dirk Bogarde, Maria Perschy, Alfred Lynch, Nigel Stock, Reginald Beckwith, Richard Marner, Ed Devereaux, Colin Blakely, Ferdy Mayne.
116 min.
Although frequent sticklers for authenticity (they sank a real ship for *The Last Voyage*), writer/director Andrew Stone and his producer wife Virginia turned English villages into enemy Germany in this unexpected take on the true-life WWII heroism of a certain Sgt-Maj Coward, the scourge of Nazi PoW camps (he bartered, at one point, to save prisoners in Auschwitz). Often played for fun, it doesn't quite come off, but at least it's a variation on the usual stiff-upper-lip routine. Based on John Castle's biography of Charles Coward. TJ

Pasternaks, The

(Nick Gifford, 1978, GB) Josephine Pasternak, Lydia Pasternak.
50 min.
Nick Gifford's fine, slow-burning documentaries all work by the same set of principles: to get as close to the subjects as possible, but not to use them; and to allow them to speak for themselves – no spurious manufacture of narrative or 'telling' structuralising. *The Pasternaks* is an extended interview with Boris Pasternak's two surviving septuagenarian sisters, who share a house in Oxford. They reminisce wonderfully about their father Leonid (a painter who seems to have crossed the subject matter of Millet with Impressionist techniques) and the family, via a collection of photographs, paintings and drawings. What emerges from Gifford's most 'conventional' documentary subject is a Jamesian pastel portrait of a rather respectable artistic family, living through extra-ordinary times. The description of Boris' funeral, where thousands flocked to the unannounced ceremony, is most moving. CPea

Pasteur

(Sacha Guitry, 1935, Fr) Sacha Guitry, Jean Périer, José Squinquel, Henry Bonvallet.
74 min. b/w.
Guitry was meticulous about his credits, and when this movie announces itself as *'réalisé par Sacha Guitry, sous la direction de Fernand Rivers'* – Rivers was the producer – we may assume that Guitry expects us to infer he was not entirely a free agent here. And indeed, it is all rather uncharacteristic. The film is a series of highlights from a brilliant life: experiments, obstruction by pigheaded establishment, rabid child cured, ideas embraced, venerated old age. Guitry could never be dull, but this is undemanding stuff by his standards. However, it's notable for the opening, in which the author summarises Pasteur's career, shows us some photos, analyses his handwriting and reads the admirable letter by the scientist that moved him to make the film. A common sense biopic opening, but can anyone think of another film-maker who's had the self-confidence to attempt anything similar? BBa

Pastorale

(Otar Iosseliani, 1975, USSR) Rezo Tsarchalachvili, Lia Tokkadse-Djiegueli, Marina Kartzevadse, Tamara Gabarachvili, Nana Iosselliani.
95 min.
A turgid and occasionally twee account of a string quartet holidaying in (Soviet) Georgia. A hint of romance, a touch of the travelogues, a surfeit of lyrical shots, and a lot of chamber music. Running into trouble, apparently because of its

'formalist aesthetic', it was not released to the West until 1982, when it was shown at the Berlin and London festivals: not the best of choices, even considering the generally dismal contemporary output of Soviet cinema. MA

Pastoral Hide-and-Seek (Denen ni Shisu)

(Shuji Terayama, 1974, Jap) Kantaro Suga, Hiroyuki Takana, Chigusa Takayama, Keiko Niitaka, Kaoru Yachigusa.
102 min.
Terayama's second feature recapitulates some of the main themes of *Throw Away Your Books* in more directly personal terms: it's a film about a film-maker's re-examination (and attempted revision) of his own childhood. His boyhood self is an unprepossessing lad who lives with his monstrous, widowed mother, fantasises about the desirable girl-next-door, and finds the visiting circus a touchstone for his dreams of escape. With passion, wit and a genuinely engaging charm, Terayama poses the burning question: Does murdering your mother constitute a true liberation? The autobiographical stance and the circus motif have evoked countless comparisons with Fellini, but they're very wide of the mark: the film isn't burdened with bombast or rhetoric, but it is rich in (authentically Japanese) poetry, and its modernist approach is challenging in the best and most accessible sense. TR

Pastor Hall

(Roy Boulting, 1940, GB) Nova Pilbeam, Seymour Hicks, Wilfrid Lawson, Marius Goring, Percy Walsh, Brian Worth, Bernard Miles.
97 min. b/w.
Although its production was halted for reasons of political expediency by the censors during the Chamberlain era, after war erupted this treatment of Pastor Martin Niemöller's principled stand against the Nazis in 1934 reached the screen with its portrayal of camp atrocities intact. Roy Boulting turns rural Germany into a mirror for little England, which ups the propaganda factor. Adapted by Leslie Arliss, Haworth Bromley and Anne Reiner from the play by the German revolutionary poet and dramatist Ernst Toller. A bit creaky, but fascinating. TJ

Past Tense

(Graeme Clifford, 1994, US) Scott Glenn, Anthony LaPaglia, Lara Flynn Boyle.
87 min.
A hardbitten cop has dreams (and dreams within dreams) about a mysterious femme fatale, the sort of stuff parodied in Altman's *The Player*. Director Clifford strains for psychological symbolism, but the stylised photography and design are simply silly, as is the script. And with Glenn and Flynn Boyle failing to be James Stewart and Kim Novak, that leaves a 'thriller' which is very vaguely Hitchcockian, but lacks an ounce of the Master's art – though making sex and violence this tedious is, perhaps, an art in itself. AO

Pat and Mike

(George Cukor, 1952, US) Spencer Tracy, Katharine Hepburn, Aldo Ray, William Ching, Jim Backus, Sammy White, Charles Bronson, Chuck Connors.
95 min. b/w.
Written, like several other Cukor films of the period, by Ruth Gordon and Garson Kanin, and charting the conflict between what Carlos Clarens called 'the redneck paternalism of Spencer Tracy and Katharine Hepburn's outraged liberal sensibilities', this is a lazy, episodic, conventional but strangely charming variation on the old comedy formula of initially hostile misfits falling in love (here platonic). Hepburn gets to show off her considerable athletic talents as the bright, upper middle class sporting all-rounder; Tracy gets to be gruffly loveable as the rough-diamond promoter-manager who finally becomes her protector. There are far too many shots featuring real-life sports stars, but the sparring leads, and Ray's dim boxer, work superbly together under Cukor's deceptively effortless, always elegant direction. GA

Patch of Blue, A

(Guy Green, 1965, US) Sidney Poitier, Shelley Winters, Elizabeth Hartman, Wallace Ford, Ivan Dixon.
105 min. b/w.

Shelley Winters won an Oscar for being perfectly horrible as the harridan mom in this dated, but not too sentimental fable in which blind daughter Hartman is brought out of her shell and given a sense of self-worth by her burgeoning friendship with Poitier, unaware throughout that he's a black man. In hindsight, it all looks like a rather tentative Hollywood essay at the race angle, but the actors do mesh together convincingly despite the obvious narrative contrivances, and debut girl Hartman's persuasive account of the everyday travails of the sightless is engrossing without overdoing the self-pity. That, unfortunately, is left to Jerry Goldsmith's insistently 'sensitive' score, plaintive woodwinds to the fore. TJ

Paternity

(David Steinberg, 1981, US) Burt Reynolds, Beverly D'Angelo, Norman Fell, Paul Dooley, Elizabeth Ashley, Lauren Hutton, Juanita Moore.
93 min.
Reynolds tones down the Southern accent that goes with his popular redneck image for the part of New York's most eligible bachelor, just turned 44 and realising that his life is empty without progeny. The decision that he wants to be a father, and the recruitment of waitress Beverly D'Angelo as the mother (she needs the money for her music studies), sets the scene for a lightweight sex comedy, with her whiling away her pregnancy in his luxurious Manhattan apartment while he continues to womanise. Any notion that a topical social issue will be taken as seriously as it deserves is decisively scotched long before the thoroughly predictable romantic ending; but *Paternity* is difficult to actually dislike, largely because of its engaging duo of stars. RM

Pat Garrett and Billy the Kid

(Sam Peckinpah, 1973, US) James Coburn, Kris Kristofferson, Bob Dylan, Richard Jaeckel, Katy Jurado, Slim Pickens, Chill Wills, Jason Robards, RG Armstrong, Luke Askew, Jack Elam, Charlie Martin Smith, Harry Dean Stanton, Barry Sullivan.
121 min.
Restored and reassembled, this is the full and harmonious movie that Peckinpah wanted to be remembered by before the butchers at MGM got their hands on it. Starting with a framing sequence from 1909 which shows Coburn's aged Garrett being gunned down by the same men who hired him to get Billy the Kid back in 1881, the additional 15 minutes introduce the menacing figure of Barry Sullivan's Boss Chisum, a frolicsome brothel scene ('Last time Billy was here it took four to get him up and five to get him down again'), some engaging Wild West cameos, and a less obtrusive use of Bob Dylan's soundtrack. All in all the film is more playful, more balanced, and very much an elegy for the old ways of the West, rather than a meandering bloodthirsty battle between Kristofferson's preposterously likeable outlaw and Coburn's ambivalent survivor, Garrett. Like Ford's *The Man Who Shot Liberty Valance*, it both records and condemns the passage of time and the advent of progress; and there is a sombre, mournful quality which places the film very high up in the league of great Westerns. SGr

Pather Panchali 100

(Satyajit Ray, 1955, Ind) Kanu Bannerjee, Karuna Bannerjee, Uma Das Gupta, Subir Bannerjee, Chunibala Devi.
115 min. b/w.
Ray's first film, and the first instalment of what came to be known as *The Apu Trilogy*, completed by *Aparajito* (*The Unvanquished*, 1956, 113 min, b/w) and *Apur Sansar* (*The World of Apu*, 1959, 106 min, b/w). The first Indian film to cause any real stir in Europe and America, it is still something to wonder at: a simple story of country folk told with all the effortless beauty, drama and humanity which seem beyond the grasp of most Western directors. The plot is nothing more than a string of ordinary events, focused on the experiences of Apu, child of a small family eking out an existence in a ramshackle Bengal village: a train thunders by across the plains, a frugal meal is prepared, the rains and the wind flatten and drench the landscape, someone dies. The two later films show Apu's development in more 'civilised' societies – particularly Calcutta, where he pursues his studies until money runs out, falls into an arranged marriage, painfully lives through the deaths of his parents and wife, loses

direction, and pulls through chastened but undefeated. There are three changes of actor (Apu at different ages), and Ray's narrative methods sometimes veer distractingly from the episodic to the linear. What doesn't change is his remarkably natural way with symbolism (spot all those trains!), his eye for the visual poetry of both raw nature and industrial squalor, and his faith in the human ability to grow with experience. *Pather Panchali*, in particular, retains a fresh and pellucid beauty. GB

Pathfinder (Veiviseren)

(Nils Gaup, 1987, Nor) Mikkel Gaup, Ingvald Guttorm, Ellen Anne Buljo, Inger Utsi, Svein Scharffenberg.
86 min.
An epic adventure set in Lapland a thousand years ago, this fuses the mythic simplicity of a folk tale with the kind of lean action that would not disgrace a Kurosawa film. The battle between Good and Evil here involves the peace-loving Lapps and savage black-clad invaders, the Tchudes. When 16-year-old Aigin (Mikkel Gaup) sees his family wiped out by a Tchude raiding party, he flees to a nearby village. The villagers make for the safety of the coastlands, but the vengeful Aigin stays to confront the raiders, only to be captured and forced to act as their pathfinder. Will he lead them to the Lapp settlement, or will he succeed in tricking them into a vital mistake? Shot against a frozen landscape of breathtaking beauty, Nils Gaup's film is supported by a strangely appropriate electronic soundtrack, and although the sudden climax doesn't quite fulfil expectations, has a rivetingly economical narrative development. NF

Path of the Brave
(Vittee Khon Kla)

(Euthana Mukdasanit, 1991, Thai) Narin Tongkum, Thisawan Suwanpho, N-hatai Pichitra, Puthichai Amatayakul.
133 min.
The handsome young Jopa is inspired by the legends of heroes past to challenge what he sees as the declining virility of his people (a hill-tribe in Northern Thailand). He claws his way to victory in the tribe's ritual tests of strength and then demands to choose his own bride rather than accepting the reigning 'Earth Mother'. Before long, having trampled on rivals and critics, he is making warlike noises at a neighbouring tribe. Euthana's folk epic is an Orwellian political fable with up-to-date resonance in Thailand. It's a touch didactic, but interestingly stylised performances and a great score make it impressive overall. TR

Paths of Glory

(Stanley Kubrick, 1957, US) Kirk Douglas, Adolphe Menjou, Ralph Meeker, George Macready, Wayne Morris, Timothy Carey, Joseph Turkel, Richard Anderson.
86 min. b/w.
Unusually trenchant for its time, adapted from Humphrey Cobb's factually based novel, Kubrick's first 'prestige' movie bitterly attacks the role of the French military authorities in World War I through an account of the court-martial and execution of three blameless privates. The critique of military hypocrisy and misguided strategy is laid out in an ultra-lucid exposition, full of almost diagrammatic tracking shots that are much more self-consciously virtuoso in camera style than anything in later Kubrick. The film is politically and emotionally anchored in Kirk Douglas' astonishingly successful performance as the condemned men's defender. One measure of the film's effectiveness is that it was banned in France on political grounds for eighteen years. TR

Patrick

(Richard Franklin, 1978, Aust) Susan Penhaligon, Robert Helpmann, Rod Mullinar, Bruce Barry, Julia Blake, Helen Hemingway, Robert Thompson.
110 min.
An Australian thriller concerning a comatose patient with telekinetic powers (Thompson) who looks a lot like Marty Feldman. There are a few interesting ideas, and at least one good shock, but they're buried by some dreadful script and production errors: the setting is a hospital in which everyone spends their time shouting at each other

for no reason at all except the writer's eccentric idea of dramatic construction, and even the shock sequences are interrupted by long phone calls discussing what's happened so far. DP

Patriot Game, The

(Arthur Mac Caig, 1978, Fr) Rev Ian Paisley, Bernadette Devlin, Lord Chichester Clark, Brian Faulkner, Joe Austin.
97 min.
By denying the premise of the British media's treatment of Ulster as an insoluble religious conflict, Mac Caig's documentary restores a historical and political context to Republican struggle for a united, socialist Ireland. Unashamedly propagandist, it gives a coherent voice to the Provisionals, and re-runs the TV headlines of the past eleven years to frame rare scenes of contemporary life in the nationalist ghettos. Not only does it succinctly analyse the roots of the 'troubles' (Britain's economic and military oppression) and offer a rationale for Republican strategy (from the Civil Rights movement to IRA bombing campaigns), but it presents a 'hidden', and in many ways inspirational, portrait of life under occupation, of a besieged but organised working class, and of pervasive grass roots resistance. PT

Patriot Games

(Phillip Noyce, 1992, US) Harrison Ford, Anne Archer, Patrick Bergin, Sean Bean, Thora Birch, James Fox, Samuel L Jackson, Polly Walker, James Earl Jones, Richard Harris.
117 min.
So duff that you wonder why they didn't ask Roger Moore to star. Jack Ryan (Ford) has retired from his CIA job as an analyst, but finds himself dragged back into that world after foiling an IRA assassination attempt on a Brit royal. He kills a terrorist, whose brother Sean (Bean) vows vengeance on Ryan and his family. In fact, Sean becomes an uncontrollable menace to terrorist organiser Kevin (Bergin), though this is sabotaged by plaintive Irish jigs whenever he dons the ski-mask. Attempts on the lives of Ryan's wife (Archer) and daughter (Birch) force him to sign up again with avuncular Admiral Greer (Jones). Between the implausibilities – Lord Holmes (Fox) decorates Ryan on behalf of Britain in Ryan's front room – the loose ends, and the climactic speedboat duel, one might be forgiven for seeing it as a Saturday Morning Picture Club serial. BC

Patriot, The (Die Patriotin)

(Alexander Kluge, 1979, WGer) Hannelore Hoger, Alfred Edel, Alexander von Eschwege, Hans Heckel, Beate Holle.
120 min. b/w & col.
The mocking intelligence which has pricked so many German bubbles in Kluge's films for once seems to have overreached itself. *The Patriot* is Gabi Teichert (Hoger), the history teacher first seen excavating the past in *Germany in Autumn*. Here her symbolic quest for a counter-history, expanded to inordinate length, is presented as a whimsical collage of documentary footage, interview material, and fairytale interludes, all supposedly seen from the viewpoint of a knee belonging to a German corporal who died at Stalingrad. Itself a joint but unable to make connections, the knee leaves the spectator to draw his own conclusions while remembering that the casualties of war still deserve their say. The idea is that reading between the lines of these impressions of Germany past and present might – as in Syberberg's *Hitler* – yield a new concept of history. But Kluge's lesson, muffled by some laborious humour, emerges as pretty banal. TM

Patrullero, El

see Highway Patrolman

Patsy, The

(Jerry Lewis, 1964, US) Jerry Lewis, Ina Balin, Everett Sloane, Keenan Wynn, Peter Lorre, John Carradine, Phil Harris, Hans Conreid.
101 min.
Who but Jerry Lewis would have dreamed up this pot-pourri of comic fears as a bellboy is chosen to take the place of a dead comedian by his scriptwriters? Explicitly quoting Chaplin-style routines, Lewis bends the sentimentality into shape to produce a witty and magical essay on comedy, illusionism and fear. DMacp

Patsy, The
see Addition, L'

Patterns
(aka Patterns of Power)
(Fielder Cook, 1956, US) Van Heflin, Everett Sloane, Ed Begley, Beatrice Straight, Elizabeth Wilson.
83 min. b/w.
Adapted by Rod Twilight Zone Serling from his own TV play, this is a tense and claustrophobic melodrama which demonstrates the price of professional ambition. Heflin is the recently hired company man who is forced, by his boss Sloane, to come into conflict with ageing executive Begley, the man he is supposed to replace. Reminiscent of Executive Suite (though much less sleek and slick), it's a little dated now, but the well-crafted performances of the strong cast (especially Begley as the disintegrating man) work wonders. GA

Patterns of Power
see Patterns

Patti Rocks
(David Burton Morris, 1987, US) Chris Mulkey, John Jenkins, Karen Landry, David L Turk, Stephen Yoakum.
87 min.
More sex, lies and celluloid. Morris' independent feature is less conspicuously smart and neat than Soderbergh's sex, lies and videotape, delivering instead a confrontational, dirty, blue-collar realism. In the first of two clearly opposed halves, Billy (Mulkey) convinces Eddie (Jenkins) to accompany him on a long journey to meet his mistress; he wants to persuade her to have an abortion. They drive through the night, Billy sustaining an endless tirade of pussy jokes and cock fantasies, while his more mature, lonely friend laughs, argues, listens. This provocative glimpse of 'real men' at large, written and acted with rare conviction, proved too much for some; but rest assured, further up the road waits Patti Rocks. Played with enormous affection by Karen Landry, she is compassionate, responsible, and much more than a match for the guys. It is a beautifully judged, stimulating film, full of risks and verve, and worked through with rare intelligence and humour. TCh

Patton (aka Patton: Lust for Glory)
(Franklin J Schaffner, 1969, US) George C Scott, Karl Malden, Michael Bates, Stephen Young, Michael Strong, James Edwards, Frank Latimore.
171 min.
As a study of power, neither Coppola's script nor Schaffner's direction are precise enough to merit the praise that has been heaped upon them. As an exercise in biography, however, Schaffner and Coppola's character study of General George S Patton is marvellous, especially in its sideways debunking of the American Hero. The film lays bare the roots of Patton's lust for power in his willingness to sacrifice everything to his vaunting ego, a trait which is mirrored in George C Scott's superb performance. PH

Patty Hearst
(Paul Schrader, 1988, US/GB) Natasha Richardson, William Forsythe, Ving Rhames, Frances Fisher, Jodi Long, Olivia Baraash, Dana Delany, Marek Johnson.
108 min.
Schrader's biopic covers well-documented events: the kidnapping of newspaper heiress Hearst by the Symbionese Liberation Army, her transformation into an urban guerrilla, her capture by the FBI, and subsequent trial. Schrader, interested in how she survived, accepts her version and stands clear of the nagging doubts that most of us entertained at the time. There's a Bressonian rigour to this portrayal of the process of brainwashing. Bound, gagged, and blindfolded, Patty is kept in a tiny cupboard for days, after which sensory deprivation is gradually reduced, so that her impressions grow from voices and changes in light to distinctions between her captors. And what a Spartist crew they are – all revolutionary claptrap and middle clas guilt. Reborn as Tania, she takes part in a bank raid, during which she is photographed on security video, gun in hand.

Later she takes part in a shootout at a sports store. The SLA are wiped out in a police swoop, but she escapes, living with underground groups till her arrest. It's a lot for trauma to account for. Richardson brings terrific dedication to the role including a perfect American accent, but it's an airless, exhausting film. BC

Patu!
(Merata Mita, 1983, NZ)
112 min.
A record of the anti-apartheid protests against the South Africans' 1981 rugby union tour of New Zealand. The received image of the country as a land in which harmonious interracial relationships have been worked out is profoundly undermined by this documentary (its director is a Maori woman; its title is a Maori word for 'kill' or 'hit'). Their police, looking identical to the British copper, turn out to be expert at cracking the skulls of unarmed, peaceful protesters as the extent and determination of the protests increase (it comes as a relief when they eventually don crash helmets). And the sport itself is represented not by players, but by supporters who are rampantly racist (they really do say 'Would you want your sister to marry one?'). As a record of mobilisation of public opinion in the face of immense propaganda (through the collusion of the media with Muldoon's right wing government in misrepresenting the aims of the protest), it's a wholly successful and convincing tribute. GBr

Paul and Michelle
(Paul et Michelle)
(Lewis Gilbert, 1974, Fr/GB) Anicée Alvina, Sean Bury, Keir Dullea, Ronald Lewis, Catherine Allégret.
105 min.
Sequel to the soppy Friends (1971), in which a pair of neglected Parisian kids (aged 15 and 14) mooned through a romantic idyll in the Camargue which ended in the birth of a child. Now, leaving school three years later, Paul sets off in search of Michelle and their young daughter, and wins her away from an American airline officer (Dullea). Summer together, followed by life at the Sorbonne, conjures up flashbacks from the earlier film, much gamboling, a contrived student riot, and a gratuitous abortion. Claude Renoir's photography and Alvina's looks help some, but Dullea's air of constant embarrassment is comment enough on this extremely awkward film.

Paulina 1880
(Jean-Louis Bertuccelli, 1971, Fr) Eliana de Santis, Olga Karlatos, Maximilian Schell, Michel Bouquet, Sami Frey, Romolo Valli.
As a result of a highly repressive upbringing, super-sensual Paulina is brought to the extreme pitch of murdering her married lover. The critique of Catholicism and the late 19th century haute bourgeoisie intended by Bertuccelli (who made his debut the previous year with the impressive Ramparts of Clay) is unfortunately smothered by a blandly 'beautiful' treatment and an insistent glamorisation of victim Paulina. It hovers on the edge of good film-making, but never quite makes the grade. VG

Pauline à la Plage
(Pauline at the Beach)
(Eric Rohmer, 1982, Fr) Arielle Dombasle, Amanda Langlet, Pascal Greggory, Feodor Atkine, Simon de la Brosse, Rosette.
95 min.
Rohmer, in the third of his 'Comedies and Proverbs', may still be tiptoeing delightfully through the same verbose ground that he's covered for years, but no other director so clearly reveals the distances between words and meaning, thought and action. Here his 15-year-old heroine (Langlet) goes on holiday, and instead of fun finds a perverse, sometimes painful lesson in the emotional games of the adult world: as her older cousin (Dombasle) rejects a boring old flame and lurches into an affair with a sly advocate of freedom in relationships, she witnesses the trio's discussions, double standards, and deceit. Dispensing with heavy plotting as he coolly observes and dissects well-meaning but frequently cruel human interaction, Rohmer yet again proves his ability to merge poignancy and humour by means of delicately nuanced performances and naturalistic but pointed dialogue. GA

Paura, La
see Fear

Paura e amore
see Three Sisters

Paura nella Città dei Morti Viventi (City of the Living Dead/The Gates of Hell)
(Lucio Fulci, 1980, It) Christopher George, Janet Agren, Katriona MacColl, Carlo De Mejo, Antonella Interlenghi.
93 min.
Low-grade actors wander Salem and one by one become victims, then members, of a group of mouldy, maggotty corpses performing motiveless murders. It's laughably awful; though with its nonsensical 'plot' randomly constructed according to the illogic of fear, and its grotesque emphasis on physical mutability, fragmentation and decay, it could just conceivably be the sort of disreputable movie the Surrealists would have loved. GA

Pavlova – A Woman for All Time (aka Anna Pavlova)
(Emil Lotianou, 1983, GB/USSR) Galina Beliaeva, James Fox, Sergei Shakourov, Vsevolod Larionov, Martin Scorsese, Bruce Forsyth, Roy Kinnear.
133 min.
Before bodypopping, people used to dance on their toes. This was called ballet and Pavlova did it from 1882 to 1931. When she wasn't pretending to be a dying duck or a falling maple leaf, Anna was romping on her Hampstead lawn, accompanied by gardener Roy Kinnear. Or she was having her hand kissed by impresario Bruce Forsyth. Meanwhile, the world was changing – 'There's been a revolution in Russia!' A hagiopic down to the last frill of its tutu, this Anglo-Russian coproduction was supervised by Michael Powell, but don't expect another Red Shoes. There's enough swanning around en pointe to keep the little rats happy, but Anna (the woman, the bird, and the maple leaf) remains an enigma. AB

Pawnbroker, The
(Sidney Lumet, 1964, US) Rod Steiger, Geraldine Fitzgerald, Jaime Sanchez, Brock Peters, Thelma Oliver, Baruch Lumet, Juano Hernandez, Raymond St Jacques.
115 min. b/w.
An uneasy mixture of European art movie (the Resnais-like flashbacks that punctuate the narrative) and American ciné-vérité (it was shot on the streets of New York), The Pawnbroker never achieves the intensity its subject matter threatens. It's almost as though Lumet was unsure as to whether he wanted to shock or move his audience with the story of a Jewish pawnbroker (Steiger) who is finally forced to leave the world of his concentration camp memories as the pressures of living in Harlem force themselves upon him. PH

Paws
(Karl Zwicky, 1997, GB/Aust) Billy Connolly (voice), Nathan Cavaleri, Emilie Francois, Joe Petruzzi, Caroline Gillmer, Rachael Blake, Sandy Gore.
84 min.
Connolly's voice-over is the one redeeming feature of this Australian oddity. 'PC' is a Jack Russell with above-average intelligence – when connected to a crude portable computer system (old circuit boards, elastic bands and a plastic lunch box), he's able to speak. After the mysterious murder of his elderly owner, PC shows up at the Feldman household in suburban Sydney and types commands into the computer of teenage Zac (Cavaleri). It transpires that the dog's former owner had salted away a fortune, leaving clues to its whereabouts on a floppy disk. DA

Payday
(Daryl Duke, 1972, US) Rip Torn, Ahna Capri, Elayne Heilveil, Michael C Gwynne, Jeff Morris, Cliff Emmich.
103 min.
For the most part this is an accurate and observant movie about a country and western singer on the road. Doubts about the commercial viabil-

ity of such a project are reflected in the introduction of overly dramatic elements into the script (a manslaughter and a last-scene death). But it remains one of those welcome movies made by people with genuine knowledge of their subject, on the assumption that their audience is going to be reasonably knowledgeable and interested in the first place. Rip Torn makes a credible middleweight country star...petulant, arrogant and vulnerable; and the support players are well cast (particularly Gwynne as the band's manager, whose job involves immediately converting every incident into commercial terms). Not a total success, but anyone in any way fascinated by the music business should be stimulated. JC

Payroll
(Sidney Hayers, 1961, GB) Michael Craig, Françoise Prévost, Billie Whitelaw, Kenneth Griffith, William Lucas, Tom Bell, Barry Keegan, Joan Rice.
105 min. b/w.
Treading Tyneside territory a decade before Get Carter, this crime thriller features a gang of unlikely Geordies as the target of the vengeance-seeking widow of a security guard killed in a factory payroll heist. Nerve-ends snap a little too patly on cue as the noose tightens, but the fresh use of provincial backdrops (part of the British cinema's belatedly sudden discovery of 'the North') and the oddly assorted casting exercise their own fascination. PT

Peacemaker, The
(Mimi Leder, 1997, US) George Clooney, Nicole Kidman, Armin Mueller-Stahl, Marcel Iures, Alexander Baluev.
124 min.
When an explosive train-collision in deepest Russia results in radioactive fallout, spunky boffin Kidman and shit kickin' Colonel Clooney (briefly at odds) are despatched East to trace terrorists suspected of smuggling Soviet nuclear weapons into countries less stable, safe and, dammit, less civilised and cherishable than the USA. The ultimate horror arises when the man behind it all (Iures), seemingly a meek Bosnian music professor, arrives armed and dangerous in NY. If this sounds cynical, maybe that's unfair on the action sequences, mostly well directed (albeit often at excessive length) by Mimi Leder, an ER veteran whose first feature this is. It's also a little harsh on the efficient, attractive Kidman and Clooney; on Iures, who lends the prof a modicum of dignity (though his principles are explained only in terms of vengeful grief); and on Mueller-Stahl, whose good Russian – the movie's best performance – disappears all too soon. But Michael Schiffer's half-hearted liberal script remains riddled with the xenophobic stereotyping mistaken by Hollywood fat cats for an accurate depiction of the world. That said, fair fireballs. GA

Peach-Blossom Land, The (Anlian Taohuayuan)
(Stan Lai, 1992, Tai) Brigitte Lin, Jin Shijie, Li Lijun, Ismene Ting.
107 min.
Based on his own stage play, Stan Lai's feature debut is a textbook lesson in finding cinema within and beyond theatre. A rehearsal space has been double booked. One troupe wants to work on Hidden Love, a sob story about an old man's memories of his one great love in old Shanghai. The other is shambling through a farcical parody of the classical Peach-Blossom Land, in which a cuckolded peasant stumbles into utopia but cannot get past his earthly woes. It's predictable that the two plays will intersect to produce new meanings, but not so obvious that those meanings turn out to be working notes for an analysis of key problems in modern Chinese culture. Lai sensibly hired the creative team from Days of Being Wild (cameraman Chris Doyle, designer William Chang) to help him hone a credible cinematic style. TR

Pearl of Death, The
(Roy William Neill, 1944, US) Basil Rathbone, Nigel Bruce, Evelyn Ankers, Miles Mander, Dennis Hoey, Rondo Hatton.
69 min. b/w.
Holmes and Watson on the trail of the Borgia pearl, hastily hidden after its theft in a plaster bust of Napoleon, and simultaneously sought by the criminal's horrific henchman, the Creeper. Neill does his usual neat job on this adaptation of The Six Napoleons, with the atmosphere considerably enhanced by the introduction of the monstrous, silently prowling Creeper. Rondo Hatton, who played the part, suffered from a rare glandular deformity and became a sinister horror movie heavy before his disease killed him in 1946. PT

Pearls of the Crown, The
see Perles de la Couronne, Les

Pearls of the Deep (Perlicky na dne)
(Jiri Menzel/Jan Nemec/Vera Chytilová/Jaromil Jires/Evald Schorm, 1965, Czech) Pavla Marsálková, Ferdinand Kruta, Josefa Pecháltová, Vera Mrázková.
107 min. b/w & col.
This episode film from the days of the New Wave, based on stories by the writer of Closely Observed Trains (Bohumil Hrabal), provides a heady reminder of Czech fashions. The thing closely observed here is death, seen at work in locations like a geriatric hospital (Nemec's episode), a Grand Prix motor race (Menzel), and a self-service restaurant (Chytilová). But the mood is the customary one of ironic contemplation, shading into overt fantasy; sometimes the mixture is clumsily handled (Chytilová and Schorm are the main culprits), yet it's mostly successful. GB

Peasants of the Second Fortress, The (Sanrizuka: Daini Toride no Hitobito)
(Shinsuke Ogawa, 1971, Jap)
143 min. b/w.
The fourth film of six devoted to the peasant communities of Sanrizuka, giving a complete documentation of an important political struggle in Japan. Excellently photographed, it records a six-year battle (thus far successful) between peasants and the State over farmland which the government wished to take over for a new airport: a useful reminder that the forces of pollution can be stemmed by concerted action. Ogawa has the fortunate ability to let people and events speak for themselves, while remaining evidently compassionate, curious, and carefully selective in his handling of the material. An admirable political film. JDuC

Peau d'Ane (The Magic Donkey)
(Jacques Demy, 1970, Fr) Catherine Deneuve, Jean Marais, Jacques Perrin, Delphine Seyrig, Micheline Presle, Fernand Ledoux, Sacha Pitoeff, Henri Crémieux.
89 min.
Even on paper this couldn't have seemed such a terrific idea, and Demy's attempt to fuse Cocteau with Disney via one of Perrault's less endearing conceits (a gold-shitting donkey) contrives to be both garish and coyly tasteful. Deneuve sings four Michel Legrand ballads whose resemblance to each other is matched by their resemblance to the composer's earlier work, while a soppy Perrin emerges as more Prince Charles than Prince Charming. To its credit are Delphine Seyrig as a chic, malicious Fairy Godmother, and Marais as the genuinely Cocteau-esque King. GAd

Peau Douce, La (Silken Skin/The Soft Skin)
(François Truffaut, 1964, Fr) Jean Desailly, Françoise Dorléac, Nelly Bénédetti, Daniel Ceccaldi, Laurence Badie, Jean Lanier.
118 min. b/w.
A superb tragi-comedy of adultery in which a middle-aged intellectual ducking out from under a demanding wife tries to turn a casual affair with an air hostess into the love of his life, but succeeds only in triggering a calamitous crime passionel. Wry, disenchanted, directed with an astonishingly acute eye for the disruptions of modern urban living (the film is punctuated by gears changing in cars, lights being switched on and off), it is rather as though the airily fantastic triangle of Jules and Jim had been subjected to a cold douche of reality. Between the two films, Truffaut had been preparing his book on Hitchcock, and the lesson of the master, evident in the rigour of Truffaut's direction, is even more pleasingly applied in the irony whereby the hero's chosen mistress turns out to be a cool, teasingly uninvolved blonde, while all the passion lurks in the dark wife's libido. TM

p

Pebble and the Penguin, The
(Don Bluth, 1995, US) voices: Martin Short, James Belushi, Tim Curry, Shani Wallis.
74 min.
The bold, Technicolor palette used against Antarctic white is pleasurable, and the film fair rattles through its formula set-pieces. And if the coat-tailed penguins resemble puff-cheeked (Yogi) bears and (Minnie) mice more than true sphenisciformes, that's par for the cartoon course. But the romantic plot is excruciating. Dork penguin Hubie falls for flutter-eyed babe Marina in the run-up to the match-making 'Full Moon Ceremony', but nasty Drake pushes him out of the way – into a half-hour of escapades on the high seas. Can he make it back with the requisite pebble (part of the real-life mating ritual of the Adeli penguins, it seems) before she meets a fate worse than death? The characterisations are weak and unendearing. Worse, the big 'action' sequences turn up with the pacing and predictability of clock chimes. And, in what is perhaps the last great medium for musicals, the perfunctoriness of Barry Manilow's songs and arrangements seem guaranteed to put off yet another generation. WH

Peccato Veniale
see Venial Sin

Peddler, The (Dastforoush)
(Mohsen Makhmalbaf, 1987, Iran) Zohreh Saramadi, Esmail Saramadian, Morteza Zarrabi, Behzad Behzadpoor.
95 min.
A trilogy of low-key misery set in the poor quarters and shanty suburbs of modern Teheran, The Peddler plumbs depths of unhappiness usually the territory of David Lynch, with none of his redeeming humour. From the title shot – of a pickled foetus revolving slowly in a bottle – onwards, the stories are grisly viewing. Babies are abandoned to the mercies of grinning lunatics; sheep are slaughtered in protracted detail; the elderly are left to rot. Mankind lives in terror, courting death; the overall effect is numbing. RS

Pedestrian, The (Der Fussgänger)
(Maximilian Schell, 1973, WGer/Switz) Gustav Rudolf Sellner, Maximilian Schell, Peter Hall, Gila von Weitershausen, Peggy Ashcroft, Elisabeth Bergner, Lil Dagover, Françoise Rosay
97 min.
A strange excursion into writing, producing and directing for actor Schell, with a depressing tale of an elderly German industrialist whose life falls apart after he is banned from driving due to an accident in which his son is killed. The press claims he is a war criminal, workers at his factory get restless, and confusion sets in with a vengeance. Notable mainly for its weird casting: the gaggle of grandes dames; Sellner, in the lead part, was head of the Berlin Opera; and yes, it is the Peter Hall, playing a scandal-mongering newspaper editor. GA

Peeper
(Peter Hyams, 1975, US) Michael Caine, Natalie Wood, Kitty Winn, Thayer David, Liam Dunn, Dorothy Adams, Timothy Carey.
87 min.
A lame spoof of the '40s private eye thriller. Doubts set in with the credits, read off by 'Humphrey Bogart' (impersonator Jerry Lacy) standing in a dark alley, although what follows could have worked if only the director and cast had found the right pace and inflection for WD Richter's script, a satisfying pastiche which has the nice touch of not having anyone killed. In addition, the depth of the sets, period detail, and richly dark photography all conspire against the film's stars. Wood makes a distinctly un-fatale contribution, and Caine looks totally miscast as a Cockney private eye in California; even Segal and Audran, so disappointing in The Black Bird, outclass them. Like that film, this comedy reworking of the detective thriller, a type of film that often carried enough wit of its own, invites only detrimental comparisons. CPe

Peeping Tom

(Michael Powell, 1960, GB) Karl Böhm, Anna Massey, Maxine Audley, Moira Shearer, Esmond Knight, Michael Goodliffe, Shirley Anne Field, Brenda Bruce.
109 min.

In the early '60s, there was one brave film (which had nothing to do with kitchen sinks or working class tragedies) which struggled single-handed to drag the British cinema into the present tense: Michael Powell's phenomenal *Peeping Tom*. It centres on scoptophilia (voyeurism, or the morbid desire to watch), and so the central character naturally works in movies; but his obsessions are compounded by his childhood experiences at the hands of his father, a psychologist interested in the mechanisms of human fear, and he grows up with a helpless compulsion to kill. Mark Lewis (Böhm, later rediscovered by Fassbinder for *Fox*) is the most gentle of psychopaths, an eternal victim whose crimes are cries of rage against his father and stepmother, and at the same time pathetic rehearsals for his own inevitable death. A Freudian script of notable maturity teases limitless implications from this premise, while maintaining a healthy sense of humour. First-timers may care to note that Daddy in this Oedipal riddle is played by Michael Powell. TR

Pee-Wee's Big Adventure

(Tim Burton, 1985, US) Paul Reubens, Elizabeth Daily, Mark Holton, Diane Salinger, Judd Omen, Tony Bill, James Brolin.
91 min.

Fed by comic tributaries perhaps, but Pee-Wee Herman comes over as a delightful original. It's a balancing act, and he doesn't put a '50s preppy white buckskin wrong. He lives in a house which is a Heath Robinsonish turn in itself, and responds to his environment with all the restraint of a streaker in a carwash. A nasty boy steals his beloved bicycle. Pee-Wee gives chase, taking in a lot of America's tourist map and winding up in Hollywood (which buys his adventure, and we see their version too). Dreamlike situations hover on the edge of unease (a meeting with a waitress in the mouth of a model dinosaur, pursuit by her giant boyfriend waving a caveman's bone), and there's a wonderfully sustained gag in which Pee-Wee rescues animals from a burning pet shop, nervously stalling the snakes. The score works edgily against the comedy, and the dream sequences are just this side of Dali. Pee-Wee himself comes from the school of acting that usually sits under a bubble – Rage, Foiled, Idea – in a cartoon. Truly weird and wonderfully addictive. BC

Peggy Sue Got Married

(Francis Coppola, 1986, US) Kathleen Turner, Nicolas Cage, Barry Miller, Catherine Hicks, Joan Allen, Barbara Harris, Don Murray, Maureen O'Sullivan, Leon Ames, Jim Carrey.
103 min.

More relaxed – sloppy, even – than any of Coppola's usual busy films, this explores that universal fantasy of getting a second chance at your youth: a 40-year-old Turner faints at her high school reunion, and wakes 20 years earlier in 1960 during her last schooldays. The crux of her return is to sort out what later became a less-than-successful marriage to her feckless husband (Cage in endearingly dopey form). The movie is unfortunately bound to be compared with the much slicker *Back to the Future*. Ignore the ridiculous happy ending of this film, and you have a much more fatalistic exercise in which Coppola eschews easy laughs in favour of the exposure of feeling and the fact that these people's lives, however empty, matter to them. Turner is in the Oscar class. CPea

Peg of Old Drury

(Herbert Wilcox, 1935, GB) Anna Neagle, Jack Hawkins, Cedric Hardwicke, Hay Petrie, Margaretta Scott, Mairie O'Neill, Arthur Sinclair, Sara Allgood.
77 min. b/w.

Biopic of 18th century Irish actress Peg Woffington. With curly hair, gypsy earrings and an excruciating Irish accent, Neagle's Peg is intended as a warm earthy hussy. 'That David Garrick, sure he's the broth of a man,' is typical of her banter (script by Miles Malleson from the play *Masks and Faces* by Charles Reade and Tom Taylor). But there's not a hint of spontaneity or passion about her performance. Even when she's swilling beer with the male members of the Steak and Kidney Club, or dressed as a young swell, fighting a duel in the Vauxhall Gardens, there's always a Home Counties reserve, a coldness, about her. When she sings, she sounds suspiciously like Vera Lynn. Even stiffer is Sir Cedric Hardwicke as Garrick, a pompous, porcine figure with a ridiculous bellow of a voice. Wilcox is so determined to remind us of his high art credentials that he continually slows up the action with dreary static scenes of his stars reciting Shakespeare on stage. GM

Peking Opera Blues (Dao Ma Dan)

(Tsui Hark, 1986, HK) Brigitte Lin, Cherie Chung, Sally Yeh, Mark Cheng, Wu Ma.
105 min.

You need a fairly thorough-going grasp of the political and factional fall out from China's 1911 revolution to make nonsense of the plot (in which two undercover revolutionaries set out to foil warlord Yuan Shikai's plan to expand his territory), not to mention a working knowledge of traditional Peking Opera. Happily, the plot doesn't matter. The film is a speed-crazed riff on what happens when a spy melodrama meets a backstage comedy: Feydeau with blood at 150 beats per minute. Everyone in it is sparky (especially Brigitte Lin, in male drag for the first time), and most of the gags are pretty funny. But Tsui's kinetic dazzle is the main thing. TR

Pelican Brief, The

(Alan J Pakula, 1993, US) Julia Roberts, Denzel Washington, Sam Shepard, John Heard, Tony Goldwyn, James B Sikking, Robert Culp, John Lithgow.
141 min.

The assassination of two Supreme Court justices has bewildered the nation, but not coltish, flame-haired law student Darby Shaw (Roberts), whose unofficial conspiracy theory is shockingly vindicated by anonymous hitmen. Exit Darby's sozzled mentor Callahan (Shepard), enter crusading reporter Grantham (Washington). Writer/director Pakula's adaptation of John Grisham's potboiler is a classy but transparent reintroduction to Roberts' sympathetic spunky/vulnerable screen presence (and also, regrettably, to her limited range). Washington, on the other hand, breathes composure and self-assurance, despite finding himself fighting with his impatient news editor, clarifying the plot with a sketchy flow-diagram, and other clichés from the thriller-hack's manual. An old hand at this sort of thing, Pakula goes through the motions, but not much more. TCh

Pelle the Conqueror (Pelle Erobreren)

(Bille August, 1988, Den/Swe) Max von Sydow, Pelle Hvenegaard, Astrid Villaume.
150 min.

The moralistic plot of August's literary adaptation (it's based on the first part of Martin Andersen Nexo's four-volume novel) revolves around the adventures of turn-of-the-century Swedish emigrants Lasse (von Sydow) and his son Pelle (Hvenegaard), who seek their fortunes in Denmark. But life's no better abroad, with employment and lodgings secured under back-breaking conditions at a large farm. Underdog labourers find comfort in each other's company, while their rich employers in the big house can trust no one. Against the backdrop of the changing seasons, wide-eyed Pelle is on hand to witness relationships form and flounder. Despite occasional lapses into sentimentality, the film is saved by its performances and its uncluttered depiction of harsh impoverished lives. Von Sydow towers above the rest of the cast with an immensely moving, tender depiction of a man cowed by age and servitude. Some dramatic intensity is nevertheless dissipated by the sheer number of conflicts contained within the two-and-a-half hours running time. CM

Pelvis

(RT Megginson, 1977, US) Luther 'Bud' Whaney, Mary Mitchell, Cindy Tree, Bobby Astyr, Billy Pagett.
83 min.

Hick musician Purvis (Whaney) leaves his Southern sweetheart Betty-Lou (Mitchell), comes to New York, and meets up with agent Suzie Starmonger (Tree), who changes his name to Pelvis and puts him on the road to success: he sings bad-taste songs like 'Nazi Lady' and ends up dressed completely in silver (face and all), flying as high as a kite. This crude, frantic parody has very little to do with Presley himself (though the star won fame as an impersonator), and concentrates instead on giving the whole myth of showbiz success a swift and childish kick below the belt. There are a few dotty moments, and Pelvis himself has a certain gormless charm, but in general – fergettit! GB

Penelope 'Pulls It Off'

(Peter Curran, 1975, GB) Linda Marlowe, Anna Bergman, Nicholas Day, George Murcell, Horst G Fleck, Benno Hummer, Ron Kitchen Jr, Judith de la Couronne.
84 min.

Lady Charterley (Marlowe) and daughter Penelope (Ingmar's sprog Anna) meet the debts of the ancestral pile by selling forged Old Masters, and taking their clothes off (quite cheerfully). 'It's rubbish, it's rubbish,' a green parrot squawks. Filmed in West Germany. JPy

Penitentiary

(Jamaa Fanaka, 1979, US) Leon Isaac Kennedy, Thommy Pollard, Hazel Spears, Donovan Womack, Floyd Chatman.
99 min.

A second wave blaxploitation flick, *Penitentiary* is still bedevilled by the uncomfortable contradictions of its mucho macho forebears. It's basically the serviceable yarn of the young stranger on a bum rap, sentenced to an institutional hell-hole, and eventually bucking the terror regime with two righteous fists. And daubed onto the screen with the vitality of all-round excess, teetering crazily between heavy gore and outright farce, it works effectively as back row cheer-a-minute stuff. But its assumptions stink. Stomp the gays, screw the women, and everyone else make way for the super-spade swagger. Black cinema's standing still while it merely swaps one stereotype for another, and any brothers'n'sisters routine will just have to wait till a man's done what a man's gotta do. Consciousness here is as low as the budget. A sequel, *Penitentiary II*, followed in 1982. PT

Pennies from Heaven

(Herbert Ross, 1981, US) Steve Martin, Bernadette Peters, Christopher Walken, Jessica Harper, Vernel Bagneris, John McMartin, John Karlen, Tommy Rall.
108 min.

Dennis Potter's remarkably intelligent transatlantic adaptation of his BBC serial turns the pitfalls of 'Hollywoodisation' into profit, now stressing the 'pennies' over the 'heavenly' symbolism by specifically locating Arthur Parker's grubby melodrama in the Chicago of the Depression, and culling his liberating daydreams from not only the era's popular music, but its even more culturally resonant musicals, recreated with both MGM opulence and biting Brechtian wit. Parker's search for sexual and spiritual silver linings takes him (Martin) through the dark worlds of Edward Hopper and Walker Evans, as he and fallen angel Bernadette Peters become true nighthawks whose epiphanies are those of the glitzy sound-stage production number, and who re-problematise every earnest thesis on the evils of escapism by confronting economic and emotional recession with Hollywood's eternal currency. Let's face the music and dance, indeed. PT

Penny Gold

(Jack Cardiff, 1973, GB) Francesca Annis, James Booth, Nicky Henson, Una Stubbs, Joseph O'Conor, Joss Ackland.
90 min.

A brilliant opening sequence, otherwise this flat-footed British thriller is hampered by something like the world's worst script, including flashbacks no one would ever conceivably flash back to, and by a cumbersome storyline about big league stamp trading. A couple of incipient themes are visible: one lingers in the juxtaposition of travel-oguish footage (shot round Windsor Castle) with the *Blow-Up* style investigation into the jet set life of a girl found dead in a studio; the other is the air of evil alter ego that hangs about the dead girl's twin sister, and is dismissed in one badly written scene.

Penny Serenade

(George Stevens, 1941, US) Irene Dunne, Cary Grant, Edgar Buchanan, Beulah Bondi, Ann Doran.
125 min. b/w.

A classic 'women's picture' in every sense: an emotional/sentimental switchback, nostalgically framed (Dunne, on the point of leaving Grant, reminisces the family-romance narrative to gramophone accompaniment), and a construction of the 'ideal' woman (fulfilled in motherhood, naturally) so upfront as to be almost disarming – though not, as in similar work by Douglas Sirk, pushed quite so far that it might be construed as being critical. Either with it or at it, or more likely both, you'll weep. PT

Penthesilea: Queen of the Amazons

(Laura Mulvey/Peter Wollen, 1974, GB) Northwestern University Mime Company, Peter Wollen, Grace McKeaney.
99 min.
Mulvey and Wollen's film opens with a mime performance of Kleist's play about the Queen of the Amazons, and then proceeds through a suite of four further sequences designed to tease out some of the main implications in this opening 'statement'. Feminist issues loom large, not surprisingly, but the film embraces many other things, from Kleist's bizarre personal history to the way an actor feels in assuming a role. It's constructed as an exploration of relationships, real or potential, rather than as an argument or a single line of thought: it's interested in the link that may exist between a Greek vase-painting of a warrior woman and the Suffragettes, or, more formally, between a specific sound and a specific image. As such, it's a kind of scrapbook with a polemic kick. And it's also something of a milestone in dragging the moribund British cinema into an era long inhabited by Godard and Straub. TR

People Next Door, The

(David Greene, 1970, US) Eli Wallach, Julie Harris, Deborah Winters, Stephen McHattie, Hal Holbrook, Cloris Leachman, Nehemiah Persoff.
93 min.
Heartless soap opera with good actors given no time to develop any character in depth as they are hurtled on from crisis to crisis to crisis. Much soul-searching among the over-thirties about where they went wrong as they try to bridge the generation gap. Much is made of the question of just who is the nigger in the staid, suburban woodpile – organ-playing son, tripped-out daughter, killer father, chainsmoking mum? There's even a mum-knows-best miracle cure.

People of France, The

see Vie est à nous, La

People on Sunday (Menschen am Sonntag)

(Robert Siodmak/Edgar G Ulmer, 1929, Ger) Erwin Splettstosser, Wolfgang von Waltershausen, Brigitte Borchert, Christl Ehlers, Annie Schreyer.
89 min. b/w.
There are two reasons why a modest, silent German movie like this is still in circulation today. One is a matter of its authorship: all four of the unknown young men who wrote and directed it (Fred Zinnemann and Billy Wilder in addition to Siodmak and Ulmer) went on to have more or less distinguished careers in Hollywood. The other is a matter of style: it was one of the earliest movies to renounce stars, drama and the other paraphernalia of commercial cinema in favour of a non-professional cast and an unmomentous, everyday storyline. Amazingly, its variety of 'realism' has hardly dated at all. Most of it centres on a Sunday excursion from the bustle of Berlin to a countryside lake, where a bachelor and his married friend drift in and out of flirtations with two young women. Hardly anything happens, but the play of gazes, emotions and counterpoints becomes deeply engrossing. You end up not only learning a lot about life in 1929, but also realising how little sexual mores have changed. TR

People That Time Forgot, The

(Kevin Connor, 1977, GB) Patrick Wayne, Sarah Douglas, Dana Gillespie, Thorley Walters, Shane Rimmer, Doug McClure, Tony Britton.
90 min.
A lame sequel to Connor's earlier Edgar Rice Burroughs adaptation, The Land That Time Forgot, which was at least occasionally lively. This time it's a dreary trudge through perfunc-

tory adventures (prehistoric monsters, hostile natives, erupting lava) as Patrick Wayne leads an expedition back to the mysterious island where Douglas McClure has been stranded since last time. Even the dinosaurs seem dozy.

People Under the Stairs, The

(Wes Craven, 1991, US) Brandon Adams, Everett McGill, Wendy Robie, AJ Langer, Ving Rhames, Sean Whalen, Bill Cobbs.
102 min.
Craven aims for an archetypal confrontation between childlike innocence and wicked step-parent cruelty, but the results are more grim than Grimm. Black ghetto child Fool (Adams) joins a pair of neighbourhood burglars planning to steal a legendary hoard of gold coins from the Old Dark House of weirdo couple McGill and Robie. Once inside, things go badly wrong: Rottweilers go for the throat, mutant children lurk beneath the stairs, and while maniacal Robie invokes the wrath of the Lord, wigged out McGill rampages in leather fetish gear, firing a shotgun at the brats in the walls. Trapped with tongue-less mutant Roach (Whalen) and abused stepdaughter Alice (Langer), Fool barely escapes being fed to the voracious People Under the Stairs. There are a few push-button frights, but a total dearth of mind-disturbing terror; the humour, too, is broad, crowd-pleasing stuff. NF

People vs. Larry Flynt, The

(Milos Forman, 1996, US) Woody Harrelson, Courtney Love, Edward Norton, James Cromwell, Crispin Glover, James Carville, Brett Harrelson, Donna Hanover.
130 min.
When Larry Flynt (Woody Harrelson), a Cincinnati strip-club proprietor, decides to improve business by putting out an explicitly illustrated newsletter, even his shrewd business sense can't predict that, as publisher of Hustler magazine, he'll end up a millionaire. Nor does he foresee the trials and tribulations his notoriety will bring in the shape of prosecutions for obscenity, contempt of court and libel. Fortunately, Flynt has the support of both his wife Althea (Love) and his lawyer Alan Isaacman (Norton) whose devotion to civil liberties outweighs his distaste for his client's life style. Since Flynt's real-life saga is colourful enough to ensure compelling drama, Forman's film is never less than fun: the irrepressible pornographer's courtroom antics make lively comedy. The performances, too, are winning: Love, gradually succumbing to drug-addiction and AIDS, is all too credible; Harrelson engagingly roguish; and Norton steals the show. But Forman and scriptwriters Scott Alexander and Larry Karaszewski are so keen to render Flynt a populist hero that they skate over the issues: the exploitative misogyny of Flynt's output is never examined, the prurient hypocrisy and intolerance of his persecutors seriously overplayed, plus Larry and Althea's odd romance lacks bittersweet conviction. GA

People Will Talk

(Joseph L Mankiewicz, 1951, US) Cary Grant, Jeanne Crain, Walter Slezak, Finlay Currie, Hume Cronyn, Sidney Blackmer.
110 min. b/w.
A bracingly bilious and loquacious Mankiewicz film that turns a highly esteemed gynaecologist (Grant) into a mouthpiece for the director's State of the Union address. The US of A is in a terrible state, and Grant's treatment of an unmarried mother (Crain) is heavily symbolic: her apparent immorality (Mankiewicz was amazed that the Hays Office approved the script) is set against the darker crimes and hypocrisies of American society. The man who made Crain pregnant dies in Korea; a university professor (Cronyn) stands in for Senator McCarthy; and there are pungent swipes at tax evasion and the crass materialism of the postwar boom. The fact that Mankiewicz can contain all this within the context of a romantic comedy testifies to his immense sophistication, and Grant's performance is one of his very best. ATu

Pépé le Moko

(Julien Duvivier, 1936, Fr) Jean Gabin, Mireille Balin, Line Noro, Lucas Gridoux, Fernand Charpin, Saturnin Fabre, Marcel Dalio, Gaston Modot.
93 min. b/w.

A touchstone film for cinema historians trading in literary labels like 'poetic realism' and often mistakenly said to be a transposition of the Hollywood gangster movie, Pépé le Moko deserves to be reassessed for what it is – a vigorous thriller about a French gangster hiding out in the Algiers Casbah. Full of sinuous camerawork, dingy sets, deep shadows, and even darker motives, this is also the film that fixed Gabin's image for keeps as the outsider condemned to a life in the underworld. See it for the edgy, suspenseful climax where Gabin, tempted out of hiding by his femme fatale, runs to meet death. Film noir as we know (and love) it is just around the corner from here. MA

Pepi, Luci, Bom... (Pepi, Luci, Bom y otras chicas del montón)

(Pedro Almodóvar, 1980, Sp) Carmen Maura, Félix Rotaeta, Olvido 'Alaska' Gara, Eva Siva, Diego Alvarez, Pedro Almodóvar.
80 min.
Almodóvar's first feature shows how many of his obsessions and themes sprang fully formed from the start. Some scabs he feels compelled to pick at: drugs, adverts, musical numbers, sexual violence, and that dodgy topic, female masochism. Pepi (Maura), after inviting a neighbouring cop to fondle rather than bust her, is raped in her trashy flat and vows revenge, introducing the policeman's wife to the pleasures of golden showers and lesbian SM. Set during Madrid's punk era, the film shows in embryo Almodóvar's technique of alternating pleasurable humour with wanton offensiveness. Some scenes are hard to stomach, plotting is chaotic, and the budget and film quality are so low that the king of kitsch can make only a brave stab at his favourite acid colours and tacky interiors. The costumes are fab. SFe

Peppermint Frappé

(Carlos Saura, 1967, Sp) Geraldine Chaplin, José Luis López Vásquez, Alfredo Mayo, Emiliano Redondo.
94 min.
Vertigo via Buñuel. Saura's ambitions may have been a bit loftier than his talent back in 1967, but this slice of art house surrealism insinuated itself past Franco's censors to give a welcome glimpse of a Spanish film culture dominated by the shadow of its absent master. The engagingly provocative yarn of erotic obsession, in which plain-Jane Chaplin is 'remoulded' by her unhinged boss into the image of his brother's foxy wife (also Chaplin) isn't obstructed overmuch by Saura's reverential 'homages', and its roots in a script by Rafael Azcona (subversive plotsmith for Berlanga and Ferreri) ensure that sufficient black comedy incisiveness penetrates the flashy surface. PT

Peppermint Freedom (Peppermint Frieden)

(Marianne SW Rosenbaum, 1984, WGer) Peter Fonda, Saskia Tyroller, Hans Brenner, Hans Peter Korff, Cleo Kretschmer.
112 min. b/w & col.
Marianne Rosenbaum's first feature returns to the well-thumbed time of Germany, year zero, as seen through the eyes of a little girl (Tyroller), living in US-occupied Bavaria, for whom postwar freedom is as palpable as the tastes of peppermint and fresh-ground coffee. Her fantasies focus on Mr Frieden/Freedom (Fonda), a larger-than-life American soldier with a great big black sedan, a huge toothpaste ad grin, infinite supplies of Wrigley's spearmint gum, and the hots for one of the local women. All streng verboten by the village priest, whose awful warnings of the red peril, hellfire and nuclear holocaust blur and balloon in the little girl's mind to the point of nervous breakdown. The kids emerge, refreshingly, not as cute moppets but as beings with a sense of wonder, scepticism and implacable logic that shows up the adult world as absurd and impoverished. And while Rosenbaum comes to some melancholy conclusions, her arresting, grainy images and sharp eye for the incongruous take her there with considerable astringency and wit. SJo

Peppermint Soda

see Diabolo Menthe

Perceval le Gallois

(Eric Rohmer, 1978, Fr) Fabrice Luchini, André Dussollier, Marc Eyraud, Gérard Falconetti, Arielle Dombasle, Clémentine Amouroux, Michel Etcheverry, Marie-Christine Barrault.
138 min.

Rohmer's adaptation of Chrétien de Troyes 12th century Arthurian poem is a unique film, combining cinema, theatre, medieval music, iconography, mime and verse to create a stylised and surprisingly coherent spectacle: shot totally in the studio, its sets alone are worth the price of a ticket. But more astonishing, perhaps, is the way in which Rohmer translates the text into a moral investigation which frequently resembles his contemporary comedies as selfish young innocent Perceval, whose very naïveté literally disarms his enemies, undergoes a sentimental education in the codes of Chivalry, Courtship, and Faith. His odyssey is observed with ironic wit and revealing distance; not surprisingly for Rohmer, a key stage in his development occurs when he learns the dangers of talking too much or too little. Far more accessible and entertaining than Bresson's *Lancelot du Lac* or Syberberg's *Parsifal*, and relevant in a sense undreamed of by *Excalibur*, the film marries medieval passion with modern perspective and sires its own special magic. GA

Percy

(Ralph Thomas, 1971, GB) Hywel Bennett, Denholm Elliott, Elke Sommer, Britt Ekland, Cyd Hayman, Janet Key, Adrienne Posta.
103 min.

Excruciating comedy in the *Carry On* mould, with Bennett as the hapless recipient of the world's first penis transplant. When it isn't leeringly dragging in nudge-nudge images (like the Post Office Tower) or dredging up every phallic gag known to schoolboy smut, the film laboriously records the bemused hero's attempts to come to terms with 'Percy' by tracing the donor (a notorious philanderer killed in the accident that caused his own dismemberment) and interviewing the female witnesses to its prowess.

Percy's Progress

(Ralph Thomas, 1974, GB) Leigh Lawson, Elke Sommer, Denholm Elliott, Judy Geeson, Harry H Corbett, Vincent Price, Adrienne Posta, Julie Ege, Barry Humphries.
101 min.

One would have thought that *Percy* had pretty well worn out the already thin gag about the man who has a nine-inch penis transplant. But no, we are regaled with a second episode in which, with Lawson taking over the lead from Hywel Bennett, Percy is left (temporarily) the sole sexually active organ on the planet. British sex comedies are nothing if not prurient, and Percy (the name is now the hero's) isn't allowed so much as a bulge in his trousers. Incredibly, someone has blackmailed all sorts of big names into appearing in cameo parts. VG

Père Goriot, Le

(Robert Vernay, 1944, Fr) Pierre Renoir, Georges Rollin, Pierre Larquey, Claude Genia, Sylvie, Jean Desailly.
96 min. b/w.

Balzac's 1835 novel was allegedly the first, but not the last, to use a boarding house setting to present a cross section of humanity. This crowded canvas is made more intricate for the adaptor by several characters whose histories were developed in later Balzac tales. In the event scriptwriter Charles Spaak opts to focus on Rastignac, gauche young man on the make at the start, disillusioned opportunist at the end. His rough handling by jovial corrupter Vautrin and by the two poisonous daughters of Old Goriot are the substance of the film. Sometimes the staging seems rather flat, while other sequences are startlingly good, a discrepancy explained by the film's date. But it's further confirmation, along with *Fantômas contre Fantômas*, that Vernay deserves better than the obscurity into which he's fallen. The acting is uneven, ranging from mesmerising (Renoir) to amateurish (Larquey). BBa

Perez Family, The

(Mira Nair, 1995, US) Marisa Tomei, Anjelica Huston, Alfred Molina, Chazz Palminteri, Trini Alvarado, Celia Cruz, Bill Sage.
113 min.

There's something about Hispanic culture which has film-makers swinging their hips. Although based on the Mariel boatlift of 1980, this is no less a rose-tinted spectacle than, say, *Don Juan DeMarco* or *The Mambo Kings*. It's crammed with histrionic performances and ersatz *mise-en-scène*, and it looks like a musical after all the songs have been cut out. Tomei is Cuban prostitute Dottie Perez, Molina political prisoner Juan Raul Perez (they're erroneously recorded as husband and wife by US immigration officials); Huston is his real wife Carmela, who escaped to Miami 20 years before, and token Hispanic Alvarado their daughter Teresa. Tomei gets the worst of it. Coming to the States with a passion for Elvis, a long line in cocktail dresses, and the ambition to 'fok' John Wayne, she shakes her money-maker, amasses an extended misfit family, and generally carries on like Rita Moreno with ants in her pants. TCh

Perfect

(James Bridges, 1985, US) John Travolta, Jamie Lee Curtis, Jann Wenner, Anne De Salvo, Stefan Gierasch, Laraine Newman, Marilu Henner.
120 min.

Co-scripted by Rolling Stone writer Aaron Latham, featuring Rolling Stone editor Jann Wenner effectively playing himself, this stars John 'Snakehips' Travolta as a Rolling Stone reporter forced to rethink his journalistic ethics while in pursuit of two stories. Is he man enough to go to jail rather than surrender tapes of his interview with a businessman on a trumped-up coke-dealing charge? Is he unscrupulous enough to take advantage of his romantic liaison with aerobics teacher Curtis to spice up his exposé of Californian health clubs as the singles bars of the day? Aerobics being a sexual surrogate for the '80s, the film gets hung up on endless scenes of grinding groins and pumping loins set to a bonking disco beat. AB

Perfect Alibi

(Kevin Meyer, 1994, US) Teri Garr, Hector Elizondo, Charles Martin Smith, Kathleen Quinlan, Alex McArthur.
96 min.

Your basic *Hand That Rocks the Cradle* knock-off. French au pair, employed by wealthy Americans, takes charge of kids, husband, house and car, edging the wife and mother out of the picture and rubbing out anyone in the way. Family friend Garr investigates, helped by sympathetic cop Elizondo and sleazy private eye Smith, leading to a highly uninteresting conclusion. With its boring, high-key TV-movie look, banal script, and comatose performances, it makes Curtis Hanson's creaky Rebecca De Mornay vehicle seem the pinnacle of the genre. AO

Perfect Circle (Savresni Krug)

(Ademir Kenovic, 1997, Fr) Mustafa Nadarevic, Almedin Leleta, Almir Podgorica, Josip Pejakovic, Jasna Diklic.
108 min.

This is the Bosnian Muslim take on the siege of Sarajevo. Quieter than *Welcome to Sarajevo* (and a million miles from *For Ever Mozart*), it adopts a low key, humanist perspective which might be termed 'old fashioned', both in a pejorative and complimentary sense. A little like *Kolya*, it has an older man reluctantly adopting a couple of orphaned boys, one of them a deaf mute. There's a strong feeling for ordinary life in extraordinary circumstances (circumstances shared by the film-makers), which renders the occasional explosions of senseless horror all the more effective. TCh

Perfect Couple, A

(Robert Altman, 1979, US) Paul Dooley, Marta Heflin, Titos Vandis, Belita Moreno, Henry Gibson, Dimitra Arliss, Ted Neeley, Heather MacRae.
112 min.

Altman hits a note of surprising magic here, commenting on cinematic traditions of romantic comedy even as he updates them. The lovers (Dooley, Heflin) meet through an LA video-dating service. He's an ageing antique dealer, driven to the bureau by his entombment in a repressive Greek-American family; she's an aimless waif who lives and sings in a communal rock group tyrannised by its lead singer. Music is as focal as it was in *Nashville*: the classics in which Dooley's family are steeped, versus the Easy-Listening raunch which Heflin peddles. Though both commune and traditional family are shown to be equal parts alluring and lethal, the search for togetherness is treated with a satirical sympathy, so that the happy ending – clearly recognised when it comes as a slyly structured fantasy – works as a real reward for both lovers and audience. CR

Perfect Friday

(Peter Hall, 1970, GB) Ursula Andress, Stanley Baker, David Warner, Patience Collier, TP McKenna, David Waller.
95 min.

Straightforward thriller in which a staid bank clerk (Baker) becomes aware of brighter horizons when he meets the invitingly luscious Andress, who is more or less estranged from her impecunious husband, a layabout peer of the realm (Warner). He therefore evolves a plan, in which all three members of the triangle take part, to rob his own bank. Familiar stuff, right down to the airport finale in which all foregather for a last ironic flourish; but it's competently staged (after a queasily 'stylish' beginning) and well performed. TM

Perfect Love!

see Parfait Amour!

Perfectly Normal

(Yves Simoneau, 1990, GB/Can) Robbie Coltrane, Michael Riley, Deborah Duchene, Eugene Lipinski.
105 min.

Coltrane plays garrulous con-man-cum-chef Turner. Arriving in an Ontario town, he inveigles his cab driver into sharing a meal. Five minutes of fast food and patter later, the driver – a retiring brewery-operative, hockey-player and all-round nonentity named Renzo (Riley), clearly a soupçon less than the full salami himself – finds Turner has invited himself back to his flat, where he takes over the spare room, prepares a lavish Italian meal, and proceeds to elaborate his grandiose scheme to open a restaurant with a grand opera theme. Before you can shout Puccini, shy Renzo – throw off those inhibitions! – is donning prima donna outfit and warbling with the best of them down at the packed-out Ristorante Bel Canto. Canadian director Simoneau plays out this liberationist tosh with ne'er a qualm of self-consciousness. His uneasy mix of Capra-esque whimsy, camp sensibility and oddball romance is so absolutely ingenuous that words fail. The lead performances, both curiously winning, hold the film together, after a fashion. WH

Perfect Murder, The

(Zafar Hai, 1988, Ind) Naseeruddin Shah, Stellan Skarsgard, Amjad Khan, Madhur Jaffrey, Ratna Pathak Shah, Sakina Jaffrey.
93 min.

Someone tries to bump off Mr Perfect, you see, private secretary to a bustling tycoon. He survives – which is more than can be said for this Bombay duck. Inspector Ghote (Shah) is called in to investigate. The malignant millionaire (Khan) doesn't like it; nor does his wife (Madhur Jaffrey); nor, for that matter, does anybody else. Ghote's wife wants him home with her; his boss wants him to solve the case of a Minister's missing ring; and he is expected to look after a visiting Swedish criminologist. Nothing goes according to plan. HRF Keating's adaptation of his own novel, though shot in English, must surely have been originally intended for home consumption in India. A mixture of cack-handed slapstick and schmaltz, it seems primarily a tribute to *Carry On Up the Khyber*. An Indian throwaway. MS

Perfect Strangers (aka Vacation from Marriage)

(Alexander Korda, 1945, GB) Robert Donat, Deborah Kerr, Glynis Johns, Ann Todd, Roland Culver, Elliot Mason.
102 min. b/w.

Meet the Drabs – Donat and Kerr – and watch how the war gives their marriage a little excitement and a well-deserved holiday: he goes into the Navy, she becomes a Wren, and each enjoys a fling. The movie was made by MGM British in the manner of *Mrs Miniver*, and was to have been directed by Wesley Ruggles. Divided into three 'acts', with a script by Clemence Dane, it is a reasonably acted, authentically staged evocation of British resolve under stress. The eagle-eyed may spot Roger Moore in a walk-on. ATu

Perfect Weapon, The

(Mark DiSalle, 1991, US) Jeff Speakman, John Dye, Mako, James Hong, Dante Basco, Mariska Hargitay, Seth Sakai.
112 min.
On the sliding scale of high-kicking action heroes, Jeff Speakman chops in a long way beneath the Chuck Norrises and Jean-Claude Van Dammes of the martial arts world. He's a nifty enough mover, but boasts rather less charisma than the average PE instructor. Here, he's one of those quiet loner types. When his spiritual guru is murdered by a rampaging gang of Koreans, he takes instant revenge in the usual fashion. GM

Perfect Woman, The

(Bernard Knowles, 1949, GB) Patricia Roc, Stanley Holloway, Nigel Patrick, Miles Malleson, Irene Handl, Anita Sharp-Bolster, Fred Berger.
89 min. b/w.
When Prof Malleson models a revolutionary robot on niece Roc, Messrs Patrick and Holloway take the creation to the West End to prove just how convincing 'she' is. Unfortunately, the tin woman's flesh-and-blood counterpart gets wind of the wheeze, leading to much complication when the boys book 'her' into the bridal suite of a snazzy hotel. Hardly your PC vision of womanhood, but this British farce breezes along happily enough on its own terms. TJ

Perfect World, A

(Clint Eastwood, 1993, US) Kevin Costner, Clint Eastwood, Laura Dern, TJ Lowther, Keith Szarabajka, Leo Burmeister.
138 min.
While this lacks the class and assured blend of genre traditions and subversion that marks Eastwood's best work, it *is* very entertaining. In some respects, the film looks formulaic: an escaped con (Costner) flees with a child hostage (Lowther), pursued by Texas Ranger Eastwood, criminologist Dern, a trigger-happy FBI sniper and assorted redneck assistants. To an extent, all goes predictably. Costner gets to like the kid, his essential goodness underlined by contrast with the psycho sadist who is briefly his fugitive partner, while Clint's conservative but well-meaning law enforcer discovers a measure of empathy with both the pragmatic Dern and his prey. Among the familiar stuff, however, there are very fine moments. It's just a pity that Costner never really comes alive. That said, the director manages mostly to avoid the enormous maudlin pitfalls of his material, at least until the over-extended final scene. As usual with Eastwood, little is overstated – and the accent is on humour. GA

Performance 100 (100)

(Nicolas Roeg/Donald Cammell, 1970, GB) James Fox, Mick Jagger, Anita Pallenberg, Michèle Breton, Ann Sidney, Johnny Shannon, Anthony Valentine.
105 min.
Roeg's debut as a director is a virtuoso juggling act which manipulates its visual and verbal imagery so cunningly that the borderline between reality and fantasy is gradually eliminated. The first half-hour is straight thriller enough to suggest a Kray Bros documentary as Fox, enforcer for a London protection racket, goes about his work with such relish that he involves the gang in a murder and has to hide from retribution in a Notting Hill basement. There, waiting to escape abroad, he becomes involved with a fading pop star (Jagger) brooding in exile over the loss of his powers of incantation. In what might be described (to borrow from Kenneth Anger) as an invocation to his demon brother, the pop star recognises his lost power lurking in the blind impulse to violence of his visitor, and so teases and torments him with drug-induced psychedelics that the latter responds in the only way he knows how: by rewarding one mind-blowing with another, at gunpoint. Ideas in profusion here about power and persuasion and performance ('The only performance that makes it, that makes it all the way, is one that achieves madness'); and the latter half becomes one of Roeg's most com-

plex visual kaleidoscopes as pop star and enforcer coalesce in a marriage of heaven and hell (or underworld and underground) where the common denominator is Big Business. TM

Péril en la Demeure

see Death in a French Garden

Péril Jeune, Le (Good Old Daze)

(Cedric Klapisch, 1994, Fr) Romain Duris, Julien Lambroschini, Nicolas Koretzky, Vincent Elbaz, Joachim Lombard.
101 min.
Four thirty-something men await the birth of a child fathered by their dead pal; as they reminisce, we're taken back to their schooldays in the early '70s, when picking up girls, political demos, squats and drugs seemed more important than settling down or thinking about the future. The film's a bitter-sweet tribute to the trials and joys of friendship, distinguished less by its final stance on drugs and irresponsibility than by its energetic, wry and affectionately vivid re-creation of what now, 20 years on, seems an unfashionable decade. It could be tougher and subtler, but it's highly watchable all the same. GA

Period of Adjustment

(George Roy Hill, 1962, US) Jane Fonda, Tony Franciosa, Jim Hutton, Lois Nettleton, John McGiver, Mabel Albertson, Jack Albertson.
112 min. b/w.
Light comedy mixes with more intimate material in Isobel Lennart's adaptation of the Tennessee Williams play, with newly-wed Fonda dismayed to find that macho Korean vet husband Jim Hutton won't be winning any medals for services between the sheets, and taking their problem to more established couple Franciosa and Nettleton, who have in-law trauma of their own. All in all, it's an appealing mix, even if the shifts in tone seem to unsettle cast and director alike. First-rate performances, though, especially from Fonda, as a wide-eyed Southern belle. TJ

Perles de la Couronne, Les (The Pearls of the Crown)

(Sacha Guitry/Christian-Jaque, 1937, Fr) Sacha Guitry, Raimu, Jacqueline Delubac, Arletty, Jean-Louis Barrault, Lyn Harding, Marguerite Moréno, Renée Saint-Cyr, Marcel Dalio, Claude Dauphin, Cécile Sorel.
118 min. b/w.
Guitry's trilingual (French, English, Italian) toast to the *Entente Cordiale* is a tale of the adventures of seven pearls, four of them safe in the English crown, three of them lost from a necklace at the time of Mary Queen of Scots. Perhaps little more than the sum of its parts – but what parts! Raimu, Marguerite Moréno (Giraudoux's *Madwoman of Chaillot*), Arletty as an Abyssinian snake-charmer, Jean-Louis Barrault as Napoleon, and the maestro himself in a quintet of roles. Irresistibly effervescent dialogue, a sprightly 'modern' visual style – one could go on forever about a film that comes to an end all too soon. GAd

Permanent Record

(Marisa Silver, 1988, US) Alan Boyce, Keanu Reeves, Michelle Meyrink, Jennifer Rubin, Pamela Gidley, Richard Bradford, Barry Corbin, Kathy Baker.
91 min.
This second feature from the director of *Old Enough* must be counted a disappointment. A well-intentioned study of high-school kids coping (and not coping) with the pressures of adolescence, its naturalistic style only makes the more overt dramatic elements look forced and clichéd. Basically a non-starter, it does showcase a sympathetic performance from the very happening Keanu Reeves. The music is by Joe Strummer, and Lou Reed has a cameo, but it's par for the course that Gilbert and Sullivan get more of a look in. TCh

Permanent Vacation

(Jim Jarmusch, 1981, US) Chris Parker, Leila Gastil, Maria Duval, John Lurie.
65 min.
Jim Jarmusch's 16mm feature debut, made not long after the writer/director graduated from film

school, is an oblique study of a young man (Parker) adrift on the streets of New York. As he roams, he has chance encounters with a car thief, a saxophone player and a grizzled war veteran, among others. Learning their stories, he begins to seem more and more isolated. Even his relationship with his girlfriend (Gastil) is coming under strain. Perhaps the film doesn't have quite the charm of its successor, *Stranger Than Paradise*, but Jarmusch's freewheeling episodic approach to storytelling is already evident. GM

Permis de Conduire, Le (The Driving Licence)

(Jean Girault, 1974, Fr) Louis Velle, Pascale Roberts, Sandra Julien, Jacques Jouabbeau.
90 min.
Appalling Gallic sitcom about a provincial bank manager's automotive and amorous misadventures when posted to Paris. The insulting script and slap-happy direction stall as often as Velle's ingratiating *naif* on their collective way through every second-hand learner-driver/driving test gag you've ever seen before, and the going actually gets harder as the film goes further downhill with our 'hero' plunging into a 'misunderstood' affair. *Merde*, in any language. PT

Permission to Kill

(Cyril Frankel, 1975, US/Aus) Dirk Bogarde, Ava Gardner, Bekim Fehmiu, Timothy Dalton, Nicole Calfan, Frederic Forrest.
97 min.
This limp spy story should have been prefaced by a caption saying: actors at work. A goodish cast demonstrates little more than the fact that actors, too, sometimes have to take on jobs to pay the rent. The film also indulges Bogarde's weakness for inferior espionage thrillers. At his most fastidious (the pursed lips vs the raised eyebrow), he plays a security officer attempting to prevent a political exile (Fehmiu) from returning to lead his people. Various skeletons from the hapless man's past are manipulated into Bogarde's service and wheeled on in an attempt to make him stay. As one of them says towards the end: 'There are no words adequate to describe what we've just seen'. A fair demonstration of the script's lack of any awareness. CPe

Per Qualche Dollari in più

see For a Few Dollars More

Persecution

(Don Chaffey, 1974, GB) Lana Turner, Ralph Bates, Olga Georges-Picot, Suzan Farmer, Mark Weavers, Patrick Allen, Ronald Howard, Trevor Howard.
96 min.
Routine attempt at a psychological thriller, given more weight than it deserves by a good performance from Ralph Bates as the pawn in his pathologically domineering mother's game. Lana Turner, as the rich American widow living in London and haunted by a richly murky past, labours to hold her head high and bear up despite the Grand Guignol all round her tipping into embarrassing silliness. Trevor Howard makes a fleeting guest appearance, and Chaffey's direction lapses into the tic of concealing the camera behind whatever comes to hand (leaves, a balustrade, fire...). VG

Persecution and Assassination of Jean-Paul Marat as Performed by the Inmates of the Asylum of Charenton Under the Direction of the Marquis de Sade, The

(Peter Brook, 1966, GB) Ian Richardson, Patrick Magee, Glenda Jackson, Michael Williams, Robert Lloyd, Clifford Rose, John Steiner, Freddie Jones.
116 min.
Straightforward 'theatrical' version of Peter Weiss' fascinating play, a brilliantly analytical Brechtian epic with tortuous play-within-play convolutions. In the asylum, de Sade (Magee) has written a play, to be performed by inmates under his own direction and staged before an invited audience: a dialectic on revolution argued between Marat (Richardson) and de Sade himself,

its performance continually interrupted by the director of the asylum (Rose) demanding certain excisions. There was much critical hostility to the film when it was first released, based on the premise that Brook had ruined his own stage production by isolating details for emphasis at the expense of an overall tableau effect. In fact the film works very well, right up to the audience-entrapping finale. RM

Persona 100

(Ingmar Bergman, 1966, Swe) Liv Ullmann, Bibi Andersson, Margaretha Krook, Gunnar Björnstrand, Jörgen Lindström.
81 min. b/w.
Bergman at his most brilliant as he explores the symbiotic relationship that evolves between an actress suffering a breakdown in which she refuses to speak, and the nurse in charge as she recuperates in a country cottage. To comment is to betray the film's extraordinary complexity, but basically it returns to two favourite Bergman themes: the difficulty of true communication between human beings, and the essentially egocentric nature of art. Here the actress (named Vogler after the charlatan/artist in *The Face*) dries up in the middle of a performance, thereafter refusing to exercise her art. We aren't told why, but from the context it's a fair guess that she withdraws from a feeling of inadequacy in face of the horrors of the modern world; and in her withdrawal, she watches with detached tolerance as humanity (the nurse chattering on about her troubled sex life) reveals its petty woes. Then comes the weird moment of communion in which the two women merge as one: charlatan or not, the artist can still be understood, and can therefore still understand. Not an easy film, but an infinitely rewarding one. TM

Personal Best

(Robert Towne, 1982, US) Mariel Hemingway, Scott Glenn, Patrice Donnelly, Kenny Moore, Jim Moody, Kari Gosswiller.
127 min.
The sort of nerve required to produce an excellent screenplay like *Chinatown* seems to have deserted Towne in this, his directorial debut. A hesitation in dealing fully with the central relationship, coupled with an over-reliance on slow-motion photography, finds the film losing momentum almost before it leaves the starting blocks. Having set up a lesbian relationship between two athletes preparing for the Olympics (Hemingway and Donnelly) which promises to explore the effect of competition and rivalry in the context of physical surrender and gentle intimacy, it trickles away, foundering on such scenes as a first evening spent arm-wrestling, boozing, belching and farting, too reminiscent of the rugby locker room to be a convincing prelude to any sort of love affair. The thesis collapses into banal presumptions as jarring as the superfluous close-ups of undulating thighs and quivering crotches. HR

Personal Choice

see Beyond the Stars

Personal Column

see Lured

Personal History of the Australian Surf, A

(Michael Blakemore, 1981, Aust) Michael Blakemore, Leaf Nowland, Mathew Watkin, Daniel Matz, Michael Shearman.
52 min.
Basically a home movie in which theatre director Blakemore traces his graduation from Bondi Beach to National Theatre. Wryly subtitled 'the confessions of a straight poofter', it focuses on what seems to be Australia's national hang-up: dad's macho indoctrinations versus sonny's artistic leanings. Engaging enough, and mercifully (or sadly, depending on point of view) short on surfing spectacle. TM

Personal Services

(Terry Jones, 1987, GB) Julie Walters, Alec McCowen, Danny Schiller, Shirley Stelfox, Victoria Hardcastle, Tim Woodward, Dave Atkins.
105 min.
Waitress Christine Painter (Walters) sublets seedy bedsits to local prostitutes, by whose lifestyle she is at once appalled and fascinated. Inevitably, one thing leads to another, and pretty soon CP is catering to the oddly innocuous fantasies of middle-aged, middle class clients. The opening disclaimer, offering safe assurance that the film is not about, only inspired by Cynthia Payne, seems symptomatic of its overall timidity. For although one can applaud the emphasis on everyday ordinariness and the almost matter-of-fact portrait of sexual diversity, what begins as a sporadically astute examination of one woman's drift into a secret and forbidden life, soon degenerates into cliché (what she truly wants is a real man) and an embarrassingly celebratory 'all the world's a pervert' stance. Some good performances (notably Walters, McCowen and Stelfox), but the film itself finally remains toothless, cosy, and (in the saddest sense) very, very English. GA

Persons Unknown

see Soliti Ignoti, I

Persons Unknown

(George Hickenlooper, 1996, US) Joe Mantegna, Kelly Lynch, Naomi Watts, JT Walsh, Xander Berkeley, Jon Favreau.
99 min.
Jim Holland (Mantegna), an ex-cop nursing an ailing Long Beach security business, knocks the beautiful Amanda (Lynch) off her feet, but has no idea what he's getting into. He wakes to find she's made herself at home in his filing cabinet. Next time they meet, Amanda's ripped off a sackful of drugs money, and he's stolen it right back. By now he's more interested in her sister Molly (Watts). There's something about a woman in a wheelchair. The breezy set-up promises a thriller in the Elmore Leonard vein: snappy dialogue, strong sense of place, quirky character detail. It's a shame that an hour in, just as everything's shaping up nicely, Hickenlooper's film regroups, resettles and rethinks. In essence, this consists of throwing away the plot and getting to know Jim, Amanda and Molly a whole lot better as they hole up in the High Sierras. Worse, the longer we spend in their company, the less interesting they seem, but at least JT Walsh is on hand with his trademark brand of shameless opportunism. TCh

Persuasion

(Roger Michell, 1995, GB) Amanda Root, Ciaran Hinds, Sam West.
107 min.
A TV Jane Austen which enjoyed considerable theatrical success in the US. Anne Elliot (Root, working wonders with an array of awkward, furtive glances) is the one sensible, unselfish member of the family of a foolish baronet, forced by debt to abandon their mansion for Bath. A decade earlier, she suffered an enduring 'disappointment': she reluctantly gave up her intended, deemed by her family and friends to have few prospects or connections. Now, however, Capt Wentworth (Hinds) is back in England, having made his fortune on the high seas; society being what it is, their paths soon cross. But will he succumb to the young Musgrove girl who's set her cap at him? And what of Anne's hitherto estranged cousin (West), whose charm, money and affections would seem to make him a perfect catch? Overall, the film, adapted by Nick Dear, is strong on psychological insights, feminist asides and the social relevance of place; if the dominant look remains televisual, John Daly's fluid camera (particularly mobile in the whirl of Bath), and some careful colour coding lend a level of invention seldom seen in TV costumers. GA

Per un Pugno di Dollari

see Fistful of Dollars, A

Pétain

(Jean Marboeuf, 1992, Fr) Jacques Dufilho, Jean Yanne, Jean-Pierre Cassel, Jean-Claude Dreyfus, Antoinette Moya, Julie Marboeuf, Ludwig Haas.
135 min.
Marboeuf's meticulous history lesson on Vichy France is unlikely to win fans anywhere. The French won't thrill to his re-creation of their shameful period of collaboration with the Nazis, while foreigners will prate about moral fibre. Having lost the war, most Frenchmen wanted to keep in with the victors to limit the damage, and this meant obeying orders and rounding up the Jews. The aged WWI hero Marshal Pétain (Dufilho) was wheeled on-stage as the fig leaf of Third Reich absolutism, but the political running was made by Laval (Yanne) who managed to trick the octogenarian into a public handshake with Hitler. Most of the action occurs in the Hôtel du Parc in Vichy where the French puppet government trim and twist their principles. It's an extraordinarily hermetic work. None of the stuff going on outside the hotel room is involving. Dufilho is wonderfully cast, while Yanne chiefly picks on Laval's cartoon characteristic and smokes incessantly as he signs away his nation. A plod. BC

Petal, A (Kkotyip)

(Jang Sun-Woo, 1996, SKor) Moon Sung-Kuen, Lee Jung-Hyun, Lee Young-Ran, Sul Kyoung-Ku, Park Chul-Min, Nah Chang-Jin.
101 min.
The first mature attempt in Korean culture to come to terms with the Kwangju Massacre of 1980, an unhealed wound comparable with the Tiananmen Square massacre in the minds of Chinese. A young woman, nameless and mentally disturbed, wanders the countryside looking for her brother; she runs into a heavy-drinking labourer and starts tagging along behind him. He tries to get rid of her by insulting, abusing and finally raping her, but she stays with him. Through flashbacks (two of them animated) we learn what the man doesn't know: how the girl's brother and mother died, why she cracked mentally. The girl is perhaps too fragile a symbol to personify the entire nation's trauma, but Jang's shattering film none the less sets a new benchmark for the serious treatment of politics and sex in Korean cinema. TR

Pete Kelly's Blues

(Jack Webb, 1955, US) Jack Webb, Janet Leigh, Peggy Lee, Edmond O'Brien, Andy Devine, Lee Marvin, Ella Fitzgerald, Martin Milner, Jayne Mansfield.
95 min.
Opens stunningly with a New Orleans jazz funeral which puts the similar sequences in *Young Man with a Horn* and *Imitation of Life* to shame both musically and atmospherically. Perhaps a little too pedantic in its recreation of Kansas City speakeasies during Prohibition days, and inclined to strain after effect in its depiction of gangster violence (the final shootout in a deserted dance hall, with coloured lights flashing and player piano rattling away, is just a shade too much). Enormously likeable all the same as one of the few films to take jazz seriously. The soundtrack, with Ella Fitzgerald a real knockout as she sings 'Hard Hearted Hannah' and the title song, is a treat. TM

Pete 'n' Tillie

(Martin Ritt, 1972, US) Walter Matthau, Carol Burnett, Geraldine Page, Barry Nelson, Rene Auberjonois, Lee H Montgomery, Henry Jones, Kent Smith.
100 min.
This starts out as one of those hard-boiled romances in which Matthau and Burnett, performing with characteristic professionalism, graduate from affair to marriage while Julius J Epstein's script supplies them with suitably grudging wisecracks. But then it gets taken over by a series of soap-style catastrophes: he screws his secretary, their baby dies, they separate, she's in a 'rest home'...but everything's really all right, of course. There's even a moment when you think she's going to marry campy Rene Auberjonois – unfortunately not. Often incidentally funny, though.

Peter and Pavla (Cerny Petr)

(Milos Forman, 1964, Czech) Ladislav Jakim, Pavla Martinková, Jan Ostrcil, Bozena Matusková, Vladimir Pucholt.
85 min. b/w.
Like *Il Posto*, Forman's first film is about a boy's bemused encounter with the world in his first job, in this case as a trainee supermarket detective; and like Olmi, Forman displays a sympathetically quizzical eye for human failings. Urged by pompous dad to make good, the slow-witted Peter doggedly shadows a suspect (the wrong man, as it happens) through the shelves and the streets, but never quite summons up the resolution to do anything; prodded by fond mum about marriage

prospects, he falls for the adorable Pavla, but remains too bashfully hesitant to realise how available she is. No messages here, simply an irresistibly wry and witty look at life's little pitfalls, full of affection for every last one of the characters. TM

Peter Ibbetson
(Henry Hathaway, 1935, US) Gary Cooper, Ann Harding, Ida Lupino, John Halliday, Douglas Dumbrille, Virginia Weidler, Dickie Moore.
88 min. b/w.
Reputedly 'discovered' by Paul Eluard in a suitably aleatory fashion by following a woman into the Paris cinema at which it was playing, this adaptation of George du Maurier's novel was hailed by André Breton and other Surrealists as the cinematic embodiment of their magnificent obsession with *l'amour fou* – the love that transcends all known obstacles. In fact it is a gentler and more romantic channelling of the libidinal surges of *L'Age d'Or*. A young architect, played with understated intensity by Cooper, meets in adult life his lost childhood love, and is subsequently falsely imprisoned for the murder of her husband. Undeterred by physical separation, the couple continue to meet in their own world, preserved in their youth, until the lasting reunion of death. The film's boldness and continuing appeal lie in its unhesitating and exultant acceptance of the primacy of love, and in its seamless transitions between the worlds of reality and dream. NA

Peter Pan
(Hamilton Luske/Clyde Geronimi/Wilfred Jackson, 1953, US) voices: Bobby Driscoll, Kathryn Beaumont, Hans Conried.
76 min.
Having annoyed Carroll purists in 1951 with his cartoon version of *Alice in Wonderland*, Disney went on to exasperate Barrie fans by using American boy star Bobby Driscoll's voice for Peter Pan, modelling the usually unseen Tinkerbell on Marilyn Monroe, and employing the Sammys Cahn and Fain to compose songs like 'What Makes the Red Man Red'. If you can view it without thinking of Disney fucking about with yet another children's classic and relax in the studio's last great use of Technicolor, then you're in for a treat. PM

Peter Rabbit and Tales of Beatrix Potter
see Tales of Beatrix Potter

Petersen
(Tim Burstall, 1974, Aust) Jack Thompson, Jacki Weaver, Joey Hohenfels, Amanda Hunt, George Mallaby, Arthur Dignam, Wendy Hughes.
107 min.
Petersen (Thompson), another in the *Alvin Purple* brigade of Australian superstuds, is a peculiarly repulsive anti-hero who grunts his way acquiescently through various encounters and a baffling mish-mash of middle class observation and incident. The fact that the film has some well-observed moments (the script is by David Williamson) only makes its overall effect all the more inconsequential. We are whirled from the sterility of academic life, via the hypocrisy of marriage, to the crude vulnerability of a lower middle class party menaced by Hell's Angels. But each reasonable scene is promptly knocked on the head by idiotic drinking bouts and repulsive leers in the direction of women's lib, abortion, etc. The fact that the softcore sex is less tedious than usual remains something of an achievement in view of the hero's corpse-like demeanour. DP

Peter's Friends
(Kenneth Branagh, 1992, GB) Hugh Laurie, Imelda Staunton, Stephen Fry, Emma Thompson, Kenneth Branagh, Alphonsia Emmanuel, Rita Rudner, Tony Slattery, Richard Briers.
101 min.
Six old friends from the Cambridge Footlights are reunited after a decade for New Year's Eve, and take stock of what happened to their dreams, characters and relationships. The witty script isn't pitched much above a sitcom, but a couple

of the turns are terrifically good. Maggie (Thompson) is in publishing, palpably lonely, and so desperate for a lover that she bounds at prospects like a puppy, while Sarah (Emmanuel) has a turnover rate that approximates Catherine the Great's. Peter (Fry), now a Lord and hosting the party at his stately home, never fulfilled his literary promise, nor did Andrew (Branagh), who sold out to Hollywood and has returned with a laminated LA wife (Rudner). Roger (Laurie) and Mary (Staunton) live lives of quiet desperation after the death of a child. Acting honours go to Staunton for her extraordinary emotional depths, and to Thompson for her super-gawky eccentricity. Branagh's drunk scene doesn't work, and most will guess the pay-off, but it's an amiable enterprise. BC

Pete's Dragon
(Don Chaffey, 1977, US) Sean Marshall, Helen Reddy, Jim Dale, Mickey Rooney, Red Buttons, Shelley Winters, Jim Backus.
134 min.
Pete (Marshall) is orphaned and freckly; the dragon is animated and pale green. As a pair they're technically unconvincing and emotionally unpalatable, particularly when they snuggle together in close-up or when the dragon uses a gentle finger to lift a tear from his pal's eye. But the film's sentimentality is mostly contained in the trite and foolish songs; the remainder is familiar Disney knockabout comedy, depending for much of its appeal on the mugging of mountebank Jim Dale, his assistant Red Buttons, and Mickey Rooney's cuddly drunk of a lighthouse keeper. The dragon itself grunts, grins and goofs around, but isn't half as appealing as its creators obviously hoped. More character and better animation would have helped. GB

Petite Marchande d'allumettes, La (The Little Matchgirl)
(Jean Renoir/Jean Tedesco, 1928, Fr) Catherine Hessling, Jean Storm, Manuel Raaby, Amy Wells.
29 min. b/w. (Sonorised version; the considerably longer silent original has been lost.)
All too often, Renoir has been simplistically characterised as a 'realist', poetic or otherwise. This little gem from his silent period, based on the Hans Christian Andersen story, gives the lie to both that categorisation and to the director's own oft-quoted assertion that he had only made one film over and over again. For here, as the little match girl (Hessling, then his wife) lies dreaming in the snow – her would-be customers and a gendarme become toy soldiers and a jack-in-the-box – Renoir revels both in various optical effects and in the fantastic nature of the dying girl's delirium. The imagery, an extraordinarily potent blend of impressionism and expressionism, creates a genuinely poignant magic, confirming the director's origins in the avant-garde. GA

Petite Voleuse, La
(Claude Miller, 1988, Fr) Charlotte Gainsbourg, Didier Bazace, Simon de la Brosse, Raoul Billerey, Chantal Banlier.
109 min.
Originally a project nurtured by Truffaut over many years, this also had some late input from Claude de Givray. The array of authors could in part account for the somewhat uneven quality of the film's opening third, which focusses at length upon the heroine's delinquency and her stumbling attempts to lose her virginity. Gradually, however, a greater sense of direction emerges. The setting is post-war France, and precocious teenager Janine (Gainsbourg) is keen to enter the adult world. Initial successes are thwarted when a background in petty theft catches up with her. From provincial tolerance to punitive austerity, the mood shifts to encompass Janine's fortunes. It's difficult not to become interested in the perverse twist of her life, but her strange detachment divests the film of some emotional impact. Given such constraints, Gainsbourg delivers an appropriately low-key performance which boasts maturity way beyond her years. References to the romantic allure of cinema, and Janine's blossoming interest in photography (read film-making), add up to something of a homage to Truffaut. CM

Petit Matin, Le (The Virgin and the Soldier)
(Jean-Gabriel Albicocco, 1970, Fr) Catherine Jourdan, Mathieu Carrière, Madeleine Robinson, Jean Vilar, Christian Baltauss, Margo Lion.
115 min.
A coyly maudlin romance set in Occupied France during WWII, all about an adolescent girl, much given to riding dreamily around on a white horse, and her love affairs – of varying degrees of intensity and fulfilment – with said horse, a childhood playmate who turns out to be gay (Baltauss), and a handsome young German soldier (Carrière), also much addicted to galloping about. Always a prettifier, Albicocco drenches the whole thing in a pale green tint, so that even shots of Jewish deportees look like chocolate-box tops. There's a fulsome Francis Lai score to match the decoratively swirling mists prevailing in the area, and despite a would-be tragic ending, the whole thing is marshmallow through and through. TM

Petit Prince a dit, Le
(Christine Pascal, 1992, Fr/Switz) Richard Berry, Anémone, Marie Kleiber, Lucie Phan, Mista Prechac, Claude Muret.
106 min.
This movie treats with restraint the emotive subject of a little girl diagnosed with a fatal illness – and its effect on her parents. But don't turn the page yet. The film is no horror ride, and watching it is by no means depressing. Violette (Kleiber) is a pudgy, well-adjusted, rather awkward ten-year-old, whose recent blackouts and lack of manual co-ordination arouse concern in her mother Mélanie, a divorced actress (Anémone), who arrives on a visit while the girl's father Adam (Berry) is away on a trip. On his return, Mélanie berates him: how can he, a medical man, be so blind to his daughter's problems? After seeing scans of Violette's brain and overhearing the diagnosis of a tumour, he whisks her away in an effort to forestall the truth. For Violette the trip is just an unexplained holiday, and much of the film's specialness resides in its invitation to reflect anew on the everyday pleasures and pastimes of life, and on the moving father-daughter relationship. WH

Petit Soldat, Le (The Little Soldier)
(Jean-Luc Godard, 1960, Fr) Michel Subor, Anna Karina, Henri-Jacques Huet, Paul Beauvais, Laszlo Szabo, Georges de Beauregard, Jean-Luc Godard.
88 min. b/w.
Godard introduces his 'little soldier' as a man turning from action to reflection: Bruno Forestier (Subor) is some kind of secret agent working against Algerian terrorists in France, but he doesn't believe in his fight, and his mind is full of aesthetic and philosophical questions. In fact, he's in many ways a prototype for *Pierrot le Fou*. Bruno, too, falls in love with Anna Karina, and worries whether her eyes are Velazquez-grey or Renoir-grey; he suffers torture for her, and is finally betrayed, not by her but by the lousy political machine, in which Left and Right are mirror faces of each other. Looked at in the context of Godard's later, militant work, this film's analysis is at once naive and fascinating. TR

Petit Théâtre de Jean Renoir, Le (The Little Theatre of Jean Renoir)
(Jean Renoir, 1969, Fr/It/WGer) Fernand Sardou, Jeanne Moreau, Françoise Arnoul, Jean Carmet, Marguerite Cassan, Milly, Nino Formicola, Andrex, Dominique Labourier.
100 min.
Renoir's last film, made for TV, displays all the effortlessness of a master, with Renoir introducing his four sketches as anecdotes that have amused him. In lesser hands, they might have become sentimental or misguided, rather than the light, deft pieces they are, full of charm and an awareness of civilised virtues. An old tramp and his wife retain their dignity and love in the face of hardship; a husband falls victim of his wife's electric waxer in a satire on some of the dehumanising aspects of city life; Jeanne Moreau sings a song from the *Belle Epoque*; an old man learns to accept his young wife's infi-

delity in a piece that affirms the positive virtues of country life as strongly as the second episode condemns city ways. Renoir proves once again that he is among the easiest and most relaxing of directors to watch. CPe

Petomane, Il (The Windbreaker)

(Pasquale Festa Campanile, 1983, It) Ugo Tognazzi, Mariangela Melato, Vittorio Caprioli, Riccardo Tognazzi, Gianmarco Tognazzi, Flavio Colusso.
101 min.
Joseph Pujol, *Le Pétomane*, was a real-life character who had an astonishing range of bowel sounds: 'not every zephyr is alike'. In *Belle Époque* Paris, he earned a fortune with his show at the Moulin Rouge, where he performed to musical accompaniment by his sons and blew smoke-rings from both ends at once. He is shown mixing with the likes of Gide and Satie, and Schönberg writes a piece for his sphincter (which, if true, says a lot about 'the great dodecaphonist'). Tognazzi, in marvellous form, plays the fartiste as a fastidious, rueful man who falls in love with an orphaned countess cellist, and goes to great lengths to conceal his profession, with predictable results. He also rouses the wrath of moralists who, having failed to deter him with heckling, brand 'TACI' (silence) on his right buttock. Festa Campanile's leisurely film includes the obscenity trial where Dante, no less, is cited in his defence ('And he made of his arse a trumpet'), and a bum-blasting finale in front of royalty. It's entirely inoffensive, and such handsome light comedy is not to be sniffed at. MS

Petrified Forest, The

(Archie Mayo, 1936, US) Leslie Howard, Bette Davis, Humphrey Bogart, Genevieve Tobin, Dick Foran, Charley Grapewin, Porter Hall.
83 min. b/w.
Based on a play by Robert Sherwood rather than Maxwell Anderson, but otherwise astonishingly similar to *Key Largo*, and for a time almost as good as the setting is established (a rundown desert roadhouse) and the characters introduced (dissatisfied girl dreaming of escape, her garrulous grandfather, pouter pigeon father, ox-like hired hand admirer). But all too soon the insufferable literary pretensions creep in, mainly centering on Howard's vagrant poet, who stumbles in from the desert nursing some sort of existential grievance against a world which has no place for Art; and who begs the on-the-run gangster who turns up to hold them hostage ('the last great apostle of rugged individualism') to put him out of his misery. 'Sure I'll do it', Bogart laconically drawls (thereby earning the audience's gratitude). As the darkly brooding Duke Mantee, spared the speechifying because his lines are monosyllabic, Bogart wipes the floor with Howard, and the rest of the cast are fine. TM

Pet Sematary

(Mary Lambert, 1989, US) Dale Midkiff, Fred Gwynne, Denise Crosby, Brad Greenquist, Michael Lombard, Miko Hughes, Blaze Berdahl, Susan Blommaert.
103 min.
Like its predecessors (though this time scripted by the author himself), Lambert's leaden, morbid, rather nasty adaptation of Stephen King's novel fails to solve the problem of visualising his complicated internal narratives: stripped of inner lives, the ordinary people who populate his books take on a flat cartoon-like quality. The story of Dr Louis Creed (Midkiff) and his efforts to revive his three-year-old son (Hughes), killed by one of the giant trucks that thunder past their new Maine home, is more like a sketchy outline than a finished work. No film about a scalpel-wielding three-year-old psycho zombie could be entirely devoid of shocks. But reams of tedious exposition, about a children's pet 'sematary' and the magical resurrecting properties of an Indian burial ground, stretch patience and credulity to their limits, while Lambert fails to exploit the potential of the novel's best set pieces. The stories told in flashback by Creed's wife (Crosby) and their elderly neighbour (Gwynne) also seem hopelessly contrived, arresting the book's page-turning plot without adding emotional or psychological depth. NF

Petticoat Pirates

(David MacDonald, 1961, GB) Charlie Drake, Anne Heywood, Cecil Parker, John Turner, Maxine Audley, Thorley Walters, Victor Maddern, Dilys Laye, Anton Rodgers, Murray Melvin.
87 min.
Undistinguished British farce (in Technicolor and CinemaScope). Stoker Charlie (the diminutive Drake) helps 150 Wrens under Superintendent Maxine Audley, who've hijacked a frigate, HMS 'Huntress', to prove they're the equal of their male counterparts. Hardly a feminist masterpiece, but fans will relish the nightmare court-martial in which Drake plays all the parts. TJ

Petulia

(Richard Lester, 1968, GB) Julie Christie, George C Scott, Richard Chamberlain, Arthur Hill, Shirley Knight, Pippa Scott, Joseph Cotten, Kathleen Widdoes, Richard Dysart.
105 min.
Did Nicolas Roeg have a hand in directing *Petulia*? He's credited as the cinematographer, and the visual style is unmistakably his, but the film's 'Roegian' currents run deeper than that. There's the splintered narrative, full of cuts back and forward through time. There's the structure based on visual 'rhymes' and other correspondences. There's the mixture of muted melodrama and neurotic psychology. There's even a 'psychic' association between Julie Christie and a child in danger, like a flash-forward to *Don't Look Now*. The actual subject remains typical of Dick Lester, with its funny/sad storyline (the 'kooky' Petulia is torn between her bizarre in-laws and her own whims, the latter including a flirtation with a divorced doctor) and its backdrop of 'psychedelic' San Francisco (complete with the Grateful Dead and Janis Joplin). Overall, though, the film leads into *Performance* much more than it harks back to *Help* and *The Knack*. TR

Peu de Soleil dans l'Eau Froide, Un (Sunlight on Cold Water)

(Jacques Deray, 1971, Fr) Claudine Auger, Marc Porel, Bernard Fresson, Barbara Bach, Judith Magre, Gérard Depardieu, Jean-Claude Carrière.
110 min.
A fatuous tale (adapted from a novel by Françoise Sagan) about a young journalist, on the verge of nervous breakdown, who is sent away to the country to recuperate. There he meets – wouldn't you know? – a married lady who falls in love with him at first sight. Complications follow, merely multiplying the incredulity. Porel gives one of the most boring, suburban, asexual performances imaginable, and Auger comes on with all the discretion of a Kotex ad. How did Jean-Claude Carrière come to get mixed up in this as co-scriptwriter? VG

Peur sur la Ville

see Night Caller

Peyton Place

(Mark Robson, 1957, US) Lana Turner, Hope Lange, Arthur Kennedy, Lloyd Nolan, Lee Philips, Terry Moore, Russ Tamblyn, Betty Field, Mildred Dunnock, Diane Varsi.
162 min.
Tasteful adaptation of Grace Metalious' best-selling novel detailing the lives and loves of 'ordinary folk' in a small New England town. It comes with its full quota of sex, conspiracy and violence, but the story is told in such circumspect fashion that next to nobody was offended. Turner, whose own private life was one long soap opera, plays a widow with a teenage daughter. Nobody knows why she treats the lass quite so sternly. Nor can they understand why she doesn't want to marry the dashing new high school principal. Nominated for just about every Oscar going, the film spawned a dreary sequel and an immensely popular TV series. GM

Phaedra

(Jules Dassin, 1961, US/Greece) Melina Mercouri, Anthony Perkins, Raf Vallone, Elizabeth Ercy, Olympia Papadouka, Jules Dassin.
116 min. b/w.
A risibly misbegotten attempt to update Euripides' *Hippolytus*, and not a patch upon Dassin's best Hollywood work. Mercouri is characteristically overbearing as the wife of a shipping magnate (Vallone) who falls in love with her stepson (Perkins, hopelessly miscast). But the main problem is that the transposition from ancient to modern Greece simply won't wash: gone are the poetry, psychological insights, and dramatic single-mindedness of the original, while the horror of incest seems horribly overblown when applied to a stepson in the modern world. Thus the final car crash is less tragic than wholly unnecessary, and what one takes away from the film is the impression of a classic travestied. GA

Phantasm

(Don Coscarelli, 1978, US) Angus Scrimm, Michael Baldwin, Bill Thornbury, Reggie Bannister, Kathy Lester, Terrie Kalbus.
89 min.
A film that somehow manages to disregard all known standards of suspense and narrative without paying the price. For twenty minutes it's recognisable horror pic stuff, with a flimsy youngster-discovers-shady-doings-up-at-funeral-parlour plot. But that's before the revelation that the local morgue is actually an assembly line for some incredibly mixed-up creatures who stop living, get crushed to a height of 3ft 2in, packed in garbage cans, and shipped off as dwarf slaves to somewhere in outer space. Simply has to be seen to be (dis)believed.

Phantasm II

(Don Coscarelli, 1988, US) James Le Gros, Reggie Bannister, Angus Scrimm, Paula Irvine, Samantha Phillips, Kenneth Tigar.
97 min.
The only valid reason for seeing this belated sequel is that it goes some way towards explaining the incomprehensible plot of its predecessor. Now 19, Mike (Le Gros) emerges from seven solid years of psychoanalysis to discover – surprise, surprise – that it wasn't all in his disturbed mind. The ensuing action again pits Mike and 'bald, middle-aged ex-ice cream vendor Reg' (Bannister) against the cadaverous Tall Man (Scrimm) and his malevolent dwarf slaves. Clammy stuff, with a few spirited gore sequences, such as flying spheres which attach themselves to the victim's forehead and drill their way into the brain. There are a few good jokes, and patches of gruesome inventiveness, but no cumulative tension. NF

Phantom, The

(Simon Wincer, 1996, US/Aust) Billy Zane, Treat Williams, Kristy Swanson, Catherine Zeta Jones, James Remar, Casey Siemaszko, Samantha Eggar, Patrick McGoohan.
100 min.
Created by cartoonist Lee Falk in 1936 and still running, The Phantom has some claims to being the original comic-strip superhero, but this belated, albeit decorative adaptation looks tamely second-hand. Deep in the jungle island of Bengalla, the Ghost Who Walks is an immortal masked figure who watches over the native tribespeople, but closer inspection reveals that this purple-clad crusader is actually 21st in a family line whose mission has remained constant through the generations: revenge against the Sengh pirate brotherhood, now vying with power-crazed magnate Xander Drax to reunite the four deadly Skulls of Touganda and unleash an ancient and deadly force of evil. Little expense has been spared in putting this adventure fantasy on screen, with vintage planes and automobiles by the yard, striking Art Deco production design and breathtaking Thai coastal locations. A pity that the performers are so uncharismatic, with leading man Billy Zane plastic and soulless in Lycra, and not much more winning when he switches to playboy mode to woo free-spirited politico's daughter Kristy Swanson (pertly anonymous). Treat Williams barks as bully-boy Drax to numbing effect and Catherine Zeta Jones proves remarkably boring as a dyke-vixen villainess. TJ

Phantom Baron, The

see Baron Fantôme, Le

Phantom India (L'Inde Fantôme)

(Louis Malle, 1968, Fr) narrator: Louis Malle.
378 min (7 parts, each 54 min).

A very personal labour and a densely informative account of its subject. Though the film opens with the avowed intention of 'not making up one's mind...of just following the camera', Malle's own commentary continually betrays a need to interpret what he sees, to tease out symbols from his visual impressions (a blinkered horse endlessly circling a mill as an image of a society unchanging and blind to the necessity of change, for instance). This compulsion seems limiting, but is always counteracted by a deliberate sense of irony at Malle's own expense, and the reminder that in India there are always at least two ways of looking at things. Seen together, the seven episodes provide an excellent picture of a very complicated society in its several aspects: the religion, predominantly Hindu but accommodating 50 million Muslims, as well as minority sects; the caste system, officially abolished in 1947 but still all-pervasive; the rival cultures of the North and South, Aryan and Dravidian; and political differences, ranging from xenophobic and racist minority groups preaching persecution of the Muslims to Communist parties operating in societies without trade union consciousness even in industrialised communities. Well worth seeing if you've any interest in India at all. RM

Phantom Lady

(Robert Siodmak, 1944, US) Ella Raines, Franchot Tone, Alan Curtis, Thomas Gomez, Elisha Cook Jr, Aurora, Fay Helm, Andrew Tombes, Regis Toomey.
87 min. b/w.
Siodmak's first American success, a moody thriller from a Cornell Woolrich novel which set the mould for a string of dark classics. The wife of an engineer (Curtis) is murdered, his female alibi's very existence is denied by every witness, and he faces the chair. His secretary (Raines) and a curious off-duty cop (Gomez) investigate...Siodmak's angled compositions and dramatic lighting might be uncharitably ticked off as genre staples, but his manipulation of the film's key motif is masterly. He concentrates on the tangible and psychological evidence – the 'records' – of absence: the wife's portrait, the messages on the office dictaphone, the court transcript, the dead witness' typed address, the hat that recalls a dead fiancé. And the film's quest is for a woman who exists only in the memories of the condemned man and the audience. PT

Phantom Light, The

(Michael Powell, 1934, GB) Gordon Harker, Ian Hunter, Binnie Hale, Milton Rosmer, Donald Calthrop, Reginald Tate.
75 min. b/w.
A creaky stage play is transformed by Powell into a cheap but splendidly atmospheric comedy thriller. Gordon Harker stars as a Cockney lighthouse-keeper who, with the aid of an insurance investigator (Hale) and a naval officer (Hunter), sees off a gang of wreckers intent on no good. The leader of the wreckers is one 'Dr Carey', the setting is Wales, and the climactic confrontation is intercut with a ship heading for the rocks. Any party, even the Welsh Nationalists, could interpret this allegory to their own ends. TCh

Phantom Lover, The
(Xin Yeban Gesheng)

(Ronny Yu, 1995, HK) Leslie Cheung, Wu Qian Lian, Huang Lei, Liu Lin.
102 min.
This grandiose vehicle for Leslie Cheung was intended to launch his comeback from a few years of 'retirement' as a singer, but neither the movie nor the soundtrack CD impressed the justifiably cynical HK public. Shot in China and based on a much more interesting 1937 melodrama made in Shanghai, it's a thinly plotted riff on the Phantom of the Opera story: Cheung plays the acid-scarred tenor who's reduced to warbling to his true love from behind a curtain while a surrogate beau mimes his words on stage. Awesomely insincere, the film piles on the romantic imagery and hopes the anachronistic score will glutinise the viewer's natural resistance. TR

Phantom of Liberty, The

see Fantôme de la Liberté, Le

Phantom of the Opera, The

(Rupert Julian, 1925, US) Lon Chaney, Mary Philbin, Norman Kerry, Snitz Edwards, Gibson Gowland, Arthur Edmund Carewe.
8,460 ft. b/w & col.
There were many fingers in this pie during production, most of them no longer on the credits, which doubtless accounts for its hobbling exposition and the pathetic scenes that separate its highpoints. But the highs are way up there with the best in the tradition of Gothic fantasy: Chaney's best ever phantom, his face scarred to hell by acid, unmasked at the organ by the timorous heroine; the phantom stopping a costume ball when he appears as the Red Death; the phantom shrouded in the most romantic cape ever seen, perched on top of the statue of Apollo to eavesdrop on the lovers. And the sustained crescendo of the end is still unrivalled. TR

Phantom of the Opera

(Arthur Lubin, 1943, US) Claude Rains, Susanna Foster, Nelson Eddy, Edgar Barrier, Jane Farrar, J Edward Bromberg, Hume Cronyn, Leo Carrillo, Miles Mander.
92 min.
Very pretty to look at, with lush Technicolor, handsome sets, and even a fetchingly sculptured mask to give Claude Rains' rather benign Phantom the look of a contented feline. The accent is more on musical extravaganza than horror, with endless operatic snippets for Eddy and Foster to warble, making it all a somewhat tiresome waste of Rains' performance. TM

Phantom of the Opera, The

(Terence Fisher, 1962, GB) Edward de Souza, Heather Sears, Herbert Lom, Michael Gough, Thorley Walters, Ian Wilson, Martin Miller, Renee Houston, Miles Malleson.
84 min.
A peculiarly low-keyed film, containing very little violence by Hammer's standards (it didn't even get an X certificate), with the whole Phantom theme handled remarkably tamely (and Lom suffering from a particularly unimaginative make-up and mask). But Fisher's direction is as accomplished as ever, and there are several good flourishes in the opera house auditorium. Because of its restraint and a fairly thin plot, the overall effect of the film is curiously abstract, evolving into a series of nice sets and compositions. DP

Phantom of the Opera

(Dwight H Little, 1989, US) Robert Englund, Jill Schoelen, Alex Hyde-White, Bill Nighy, Terence Harvey, Stephanie Lawrence.
93 min.
Knocked unconscious while auditioning for a Broadway musical, aspiring starlet Christine Day (Schoelen) awakens to find herself mysteriously transported to Victorian London, where she is understudying for objectionable prima donna Carlotta (Lawrence). When Carlotta is struck dumb by the discovery of a freshly peeled stagehand in her wardrobe, Christina is manoeuvred into the spotlight by the shadowy figure of deformed and demented composer Erik Destler (Englund). Soon the temporally displaced diva finds herself the centre of a murder investigation as all who slight her are swiftly and stickily dispensed with by her pathological paramour. Little's rehashing of the well-worn melodrama (with added sub-Faustian angle) pays half-hearted visual homage to Hammer's 1962 Herbert Lom vehicle. It also chucks in gruesome skin-grafting special effects for good measure. Englund romps around doing his standard 'hideously deformed anti-hero' routine, but the rest of the cast remain resolutely wooden. Sporadically interesting, occasionally inept, and not a little uncalled for. MK

Phantom of the Paradise

(Brian De Palma, 1974, US) Paul Williams, William Finley, Jessica Harper, George Memmoli, Gerrit Graham.
91 min.
Despite the dread MOR dirges given to Harper's crooning ingenue, arguably De Palma's finest film. A highly inventive updating of the Phantom of the Opera story to the rockbiz world – complete with borrowings from Faust and The Picture of Dorian Gray – it tells of rock composer Finley's desire for revenge after he is cheated by a nightclub and record label mogul (Williams). Nothing that remarkable about the plot in itself, but De Palma employs his love of gadgetry to imaginative effect (making terrific use of split screens and video technology), and casts a satirically beady eye upon the money-hungry foibles of the music industry. Best, in fact, is the cameo by Gerrit Graham as the camp, 'Producers'-style glamrock star, although Memmoli's world-weary manager and the piss-take of Alice Cooper are also memorable. GA

Phantom President, The

(Norman Taurog, 1932, US) George M Cohan, Claudette Colbert, Jimmy Durante, George Barbier, Sidney Toler.
78 min. b/w.
Not exactly sharp political satire, this tells of a stodgy banker who's running for the American presidency, and of the lookalike silver-tongued medicine man who is drafted in to take his place and add zest to the campaign. But it does offer a rare chance to see Cohan ('Mr Broadway') in action. Whether he's as wonderful as Cagney's impersonation of him in Yankee Doodle Dandy is a matter of opinion, but the double role certainly allows him ample space to demonstrate his versatility. Not, however, his song-writing skills: the mediocre tunes were supplied, surprisingly, by Rodgers and Hart. GA

Phantom Strikes, The

see Gaunt Stranger, The

Phantom Tollbooth, The

(Chuck Jones/Abe Levitow, 1969, US) voices: Mel Blanc, Laws Butler, Candy Candido, Hans Conreid.
89 min.
MGM's first feature-length cartoon is about a bored child who drives through a magic turnpike and learns from the (too) many strange characters he meets that the world is really a very interesting place. The Norton Juster book it's based on obviously aspired to become a children's classic, being a very moral tale indeed. But although all its teaching is sensible (learning words and numbers can be useful, mistakes don't matter as long as you try), there are just too many lessons here for most kids to take in, and not enough conventional cartoon humour to sugar the pill. But there are some very nice ideas to get older children's imaginations working, particularly the professor who conducts the sunrise from a podium, and a well-directed live action prologue and epilogue.

Phar Lap

(Simon Wincer, 1983, Aust) Tom Burlinson, Martin Vaughan, Judy Morris, Celia de Burgh, Ron Liebman, Vincent Ball, John Stanton.
118 min.
Reluctant sportsters may empathise with Phar Lap, the ugly duckling of the 1930s Australian horse-racing scene. Despite a pedigree bloodline, the horse is unwilling to put any effort into racing, until a young 'strapper' dishes a little love into training sessions and hey presto, a winner is born. Trouble follows when he becomes too big to race in Australia and is shipped abroad, where disaster strikes...Based on fact, Wincer's film leaves a lot of unanswered questions concerning Phar Lap's fate, and echoes the horse's pace: slow start, pick up in the middle, a blinkered rush to the finishing post. The sight of the animal racing, shot in slow motion, fully reveals the beauty of the power and effort needed to win; less enjoyment, however, is to be had from the human characters, with only Leibman and Vaughan standing out as a pair of stubborn toughs. JWil

Phase IV

(Saul Bass, 1973, GB) Nigel Davenport, Lynne Frederick, Michael Murphy, Alan Gifford, Helen Horton, Robert Henderson.
84 min.
The ants is coming! Anyone who has ever watched an army of ants streaming back and forth along their 'motorways', defying the elements to accomplish their world-conquering task, knows this story well. Too well. Humankind's fate is left in the hands of several unusually inept and colourless scientists, the ants get the works from the special effects department, and original ideas (so often a casualty in sci-fi cinema) take a back seat. Only the opening titles really grab you, but then they should: Bass is the man who gave you the cat crawl for Walk on the Wild Side. As a director he's still got a lot of bugs to iron out. MA

Phenix City Story, The

(Phil Karlson, 1955, US) Richard Kiley, Edward Andrews, John McIntire, Kathryn Grant, Biff McGuire, John Larch, James Edwards.
100 min. b/w.

Behind the bland title lies a barnstorming semi-hysterical thriller which pulls few punches in its attempt to chronicle the true story of an Alabama town which was founded in the early 1800s by runaway blacks and renegade whites, and by the 1950s had become a kind of supermarket for every conceivable criminal activity, from black market babies to elections rigged by crime syndicates. Eventually the military moved in and laid waste most of the vice area. Karlson's film follows this extraordinary story with newsreel-type relish, and the militaristic ending may be the closest any American film ever got to advocating a domestic coup. DP

Phenomena

see Creepers

Phenomenon

(Jon Turteltaub, 1996, US) John Travolta, Kyra Sedgwick, Forest Whitaker, Robert Duvall, David Gallagher, Ashley Buccille.
124 min.

Despite an intriguing premise and a strong opening, this allegory about the limits of human intelligence goes seriously pear-shaped in the middle. Struck by heavenly (or is it alien?) light, auto mechanic George Malley acquires a voracious intellect and an ability to absorb facts and ideas. At first these gifts provide trivial entertainment and practical solutions to everyday problems, but once the novelty wears off, his small-town neighbours start to worry. As with his Jamaican bob-sled comedy, Cool Runnings, director Turteltaub's film soon slips into inspirational mode, allowing subtle performances to be overshadowed by a hyperbolic score and a desperate straining for cosmic significance. Not even Travolta's bold performance as the brilliant but bewildered George, skillfully treading the line between affecting naivety and cloying sentimentality, can survive this deluge of mawkishness. NF

Philadelphia

(Jonathan Demme, 1993, US) Tom Hanks, Denzel Washington, Jason Robards, Mary Steenburgen, Antonio Banderas, Ron Vawter.
125 min.

Hollywood's first major movie about AIDS is, at the very least, as good as we had any right to expect. The plot is simple: Andrew Beckett (Hanks), a gay lawyer with AIDS, is fired for 'incompetence' and sues his bosses, hiring a homophobic attorney (Washington) to represent him. Less a portrait of gay life or the effects of AIDS, the story serves as a framework to examine associated issues. Why do Beckett's bosses sack him and not a woman employee with AIDS? Should people with fatal or contagious diseases tell their employers about their condition? Is there any occasion when we don't have the right to remain silent about our sexuality? Such questions constitute the film's backbone. More importantly, most of the 'big' emotional scenes we'd expect to see are omitted. Thus, we never feel we're being manipulated into shedding easy tears. The movie is defined by a tone of quiet restraint. Safe and apolitical it may be, but Philadelphia succeeds as a deeply affecting humanist drama. GA

Philadelphia Experiment, The

(Stewart Raffill, 1984, US) Michael Paré, Nancy Allen, Eric Christmas, Bobby DiCicco, Louise Latham, Kene Holliday, Joe Dorsey.
101 min.

Did you know that in 1943 the US Navy was conducting experiments with a view to rendering its fleet invisible to enemy radar? And did you know that one of these experiments went horribly wrong, flinging crew members David and Jim (Paré and DiCicco) into a time warp, so that they fetched up in the Nevada Desert 41 years later? At this point the stage sci-fi fan will sit back to soak up the hokum. Which gets hokier as the heroes flee from the military, tangle with their own future, and cope with the problem of 'drifting molecules'. Meanwhile, a raging vortex threatens to engulf not only Nevada, but...Forget Twilight Zone – the Movie. This is the true cinematic successor to the TV series, helped by deadpan delivery of dopey lines. AB

Philadelphia Story, The 100

(George Cukor, 1940, US) Katharine Hepburn, Cary Grant, James Stewart, Ruth Hussey, Roland Young, John Howard, Virginia Weidler, Henry Daniell.
112 min. b/w.

Cukor and Donald Ogden Stewart's evergreen version of Philip Barry's romantic farce, centreing on a socialite wedding threatened by scandal, is a delight from start to finish, with everyone involved working on peak form. Hepburn's the ice maiden, recently divorced from irresponsible millionaire Grant and just about to marry a truly dull but supposedly more considerate type (Howard). Enter Grant, importunate and distinctly sceptical. Also enter Stewart and Hussey, snoopers from Spy magazine, to cover the society wedding of the year and throw another spanner in the works. Superbly directed by Cukor, the film is a marvel of timing and understated performances, effortlessly transcending its stage origins without ever feeling the need to 'open out' in any way. The wit still sparkles; the ambivalent attitude towards the rich and idle is still resonant; and the moments between Stewart and Hepburn, drunk and flirty on the moonlit terrace, tingle with a real, if rarely explicit, eroticism. GA

Philosoph, Der

see 3 Women in Love

Philosopher's Stone, The (Paras Pathar)

(Satyajit Ray, 1957, Ind) Tulsi Chakraverty, Kali Bannerjee, Rani Bala.
111 min. b/w.

A comic fantasy about an elderly clerk who finds a stone which has the property of turning base metals into gold, this was something of a potboiler slipped into Ray's schedule because of delays on The Music Room. Losing out against the promptings of conscience, the downtrodden hero decides to use the stone to acquire the comforts he and his wife have never known, only to find his troubles merely beginning as he is swept into a wealthy social whirl. Shot in the neo-realist style, it has something of the same doggy charm as Rossellini's Miracle in Milan, though much more crudely made. If the political and social satire sometimes seems a little obvious, it is also evident that there are many allusions which tend to escape Western audiences. TM

Phoelix

(Anna Ambrose, 1979, GB) Philip Beaumont, Angela Coles, Amber Teran, Cozey Fanni Tutte, Robert Hornery.
47 min.

An aged art connoisseur (Beaumont) and his young female neighbour (Coles), who has a job posing naked in a club, meet and exist in fantasy and reality. Although this raises certain much-discussed questions about the nature of representation, and about the construction of narrative and daydreams in films, 'Phoelix' tends to treat these as just pretty and pertinent issues, opting instead for a mannered concentration on detail. HM

Phone Call from a Stranger

(Jean Negulesco, 1952, US) Shelley Winters, Gary Merrill, Keenan Wynn, Michael Rennie, Bette Davis.
96 min. b/w.

A decent, but hardly outstanding dramatic compendium. Having survived an air crash, Merrill visits the bereaved families of three of the fellow passengers with whom he had become friendly during the fateful flight. Davis, then Merrill's husband, appears in a subordinate role as Wynn's bedridden spouse, and moves things up a gear or two. Written and produced by Nunnally Johnson. TJ

Photographing Fairies

(Nick Willing, 1997, GB) Toby Stephens, Emily Woof, Frances Barber, Phil Davis, Ben Kingsley, Rachel Shelley, Edward Hardwicke.
106 min.

Devastated by the death of his true love, photographer Charles Castle (Stephens) withdraws into a life of rational scepticism, calmly plying his trade through the trenches of WWI and its aftermath. When a woman brings him a photograph of her two girls playing with little winged crea-tures, it seems genuine; and upon investigation, Charles awakens to new possibilities and discovers a flower which, when consumed, provides sensory access to a world of fairies. This first feature (from the book by Steve Szilagyi) is a resolutely modern period drama, a grown-up fairytale for the '90s. One can quibble with the overly precise, determined dialogue, and the dramatic weight Emily Woof's character (Charles' potential real-world lover) must bear in a secondary but pivotal role, but these are minor failings, and director Nick Willing otherwise shows a sure sense of judgment. Aided by a fine cast (notably Kingsley as the girls' vicar father) and, appropriately, stunning photography by John de Borman, it's a fresh, rewarding film, intelligent and very beautiful. (See also FairyTale – A True Story.) NB

Physical Evidence

(Michael Crichton, 1988, US) Burt Reynolds, Theresa Russell, Ned Beatty, Kay Lenz, Ted McGinley, Tom O'Brien, Kenneth Welsh, Ray Baker.
99 min.

Reynolds used to snap out a smart line, hold the audacity for a close-up, then cinch a zip or slam in a magazine. In this hopelessly muddled thriller, he is denied his routine, and what his fans make of the resulting penny-plain actor is anybody's guess. Script-heavy, improbable, and with a thrown-together plot, the movie doubtless started out as a gloss on the complications of '40s film noir. Framed for a killing, drunken cop Joe Paris (Reynolds) is assigned up-market attorney Jenny Hudson (Russell) to defend him. He can't remember what he did on the night in question, won't implicate his married lover (Lenz), and they go through the usual period of mutual resentment. Jenny lives with a bracered yuppie (McGinley) who says things like 'I thought we were gonna spend some quality time together'. The case is crazy with clues, fights, new characters who fail to detain the attention, and all-important tapes containing something or other. The resolution is rubbish. BC

Piaf (aka Piaf – The Early Years/The Sparrow of Pigalle)

(Guy Casaril, 1974, Fr) Brigitte Ariel, Pascale Christophe, Guy Tréjean, Pierre Vernier, Jacques Duby, Anouk Ferjac.
105 min.

She was born in a gutter (literally) and raised in a brothel, went blind in infancy and 'miraculously' recovered her sight, lost her own child to tuberculosis, and ultimately triumphed on the music hall stage: Edith Piaf's early life, as potential biopic material, is simply too crude to be true. Yet, if rendered as a popular song by a director like Demy, it could have been extraordinarily poignant. By infallibly homing in on every available cliché, and dubbing the lugubrious Ariel with the voice of an imitator rather than Piaf's own, Casaril has made a movie worthy of inclusion in the catalogue of indignities which befell its subject during her lifetime. GAd

Piano, The 100 (100)

(Jane Campion, 1993, Aust) Holly Hunter, Harvey Keitel, Sam Neill, Anna Paquin, Kerry Walker, Tungia Baker.
120 min.

Nineteenth century Scotland: Ada (Hunter) hasn't spoken since she was six. She communicates with hand signs, and doesn't consider herself silent, thanks to the joy she takes in playing her piano. But when she arrives in New Zealand for an arranged marriage, her husband (Neill) insists the piano is too unwieldy to be carried from the beach. So, when Baines (Keitel), a neighbouring settler turned half-Maori, buys it, Ada agrees to give him piano lessons, unaware that he intends eventually to give her the instrument in return for small but illicit sexual favours. Campion's Gothic romance is notable for its performances and Michael Nyman's score. The writer/director offers something more starkly, strangely beautiful than most costume dramas, and the whole film puts a fresh spin on the traditional love story. The characters are stubborn and inward-looking, and it's the refusal to sentimentalise that makes this harsh tale of obsession so moving. Campion never underestimates the power physical obsession exerts over human souls, and, for once, a modern film treats erotic passion honestly. GA

Piccadilly

(EA Dupont, 1929, GB) Anna May Wong, Jameson Thomas, Gilda Gray, Cyril Ritchard, King Ho Chang, Charles Laughton, Ellen Pollock, Ray Milland.
106 min. b/w.
Big silent buses, spilling light out onto an incongruously familiar West End, display the film's credits and introduce us to Dupont's glitteringly sinister London. Descending from the palatial dance-floor of a Piccadilly nightclub, we pass through the kitchen and the scullery to a world of roughhouse pubs and seamy Chinese emporia. Anna May Wong has a wiry strength which belies expectations of lotus-flower passivity. She distracts the dishwashers with her table-top dancing, and snares her all-powerful boss (Thomas) with her serpentine sensuality. The melodramatic machinations of the plot may be weak, but Dupont's assured direction, Alfred Jünge's art direction, and Werner Brandes' lighting create an atmosphere so hauntingly evocative as to be satisfying in itself. RMy

Pickpocket 100

(Robert Bresson, 1959, Fr) Martin Lassalle, Marika Green, Pierre Leymarie, Jean Pelegri, Kassagi, Pierre Etaix.
75 min. b/w.
Bresson is the dark Catholic of French cinema. Here a young man, unwilling/unable to find work, flirts with the idea of pickpocketing: an initial, almost disastrous attempt leads him on. Theft follows theft, on the Paris Métro, in the streets. for the activity occupies an obsessive, erotic position in his daily life. Increasing skill leads to increasing desire, and so to alienation from his only friend, and from the moral counsel of the detective who watches over him with paternal concern. Black-and-white images in the summer sun...of hands flexing uncontrollably, of eyes opaque to the camera's gaze...all part of a diary/flashback that is in the process of being 'written' by the thief himself in prison. Read it as an allegory on the insufficiency of human reason; as a tone poem on displaced desire; as Catholic first cousin to Camus' *The Outsider* (written about the same time): one of the few postwar European films that is both cerebral (an essay on The Human Condition) and resolutely sensual (the constant, restless evaporation of our daily lives). CA

Pickup on South Street

(Samuel Fuller, 1953, US) Richard Widmark, Jean Peters, Thelma Ritter, Richard Kiley, Murvyn Vye, Willis Bouchey.
80 min. b/w.
A superb thriller dismissed by many critics as a McCarthyist tract on its first appearance. Nominally about the hunting of Commie spies, it broadens to probe the hysterical New York underworld of the '50s, effortlessly capturing the feel of the milieu. The character Fuller seems to admire most is Widmark's pickpocket, a petty criminal who finally helps the FBI not because of any political commitment, but to settle a personal score; and although there are patriotic lines in the film, like Ritter's 'What do I know about Commies? Nothing. I just know I don't like them', they usually have an ironical slant in that they stem from private rather than public motives. Perhaps finally flawed by its overt political assumptions, but the film remains a desperate kind of masterpiece.

Picnic

(Joshua Logan, 1955, US) William Holden, Rosalind Russell, Kim Novak, Betty Field, Cliff Robertson, Susan Strasberg, Arthur O'Connell, Nick Adams.
113 min.
An enormously tedious and overblown adaptation of William Inge's successful play about a drifter (Holden) who arrives in a Kansas town, a brawny sexual presence who changes some of the people's lives. It is typical of the kind of histrionic, slightly daring, small-town stories which always got rave reviews in the '50s on account of their 'dramatic authenticity'. There are admittedly some reasonable performances (Holden, Robertson and Strasberg, in particular), but Kim Novak in a crucial central role is completely flat. DP

Picnic at Hanging Rock

(Peter Weir, 1975, Aust) Rachel Roberts, Dominic Guard, Helen Morse, Jacki Weaver, Vivean Gray, Kirsty Child, Margaret Nelson.
115 min.
Three girls and a teacher from an exclusive Australian academy unaccountably vanish while visiting a local beauty spot. Set in the Indian summer of the Victorian era, the film is dominated in turns by vague feelings of unease, barely controlled sexual hysteria, and a swooning lyricism. As for the mystery, we're left to conclude that it can only be explained in terms beyond human understanding. As such, the film is rooted in a tradition of sci-fi and horror cinema, depicting the school as a privileged elite, gradually contaminated and destroyed from within by its inability to understand the mystery which confronts it. But in the final count, nothing is satisfactorily resolved because tensions remain unexplored. while the atmospherically beautiful images merely entice and divert. The result is little more than a discreetly artistic horror film. CPe

Picnic on the Grass

see Déjeuner sur l'Herbe, Le

Picture Bride

(Kayo Hatta, 1995, US) Youki Kudoh, Tamlyn Tomita, Akira Takayama, Toshiro Mifune, Yoko Sugi.
95 min.
The sugar trade with the US brought many Japanese labourers to the fields of Hawaii from the later part of the 19th century on. The most they could look forward to was saving enough for a mail-order wife from back home, and suitable payment brought thousands of single young 'picture brides' to the new frontier. The first feature of Hawaiian-born Kayo Hatta is drawn from an amalgam of real-life testimony and follows the fortunes of Riyo (Kudoh from *Mystery Train*), who arrives in Honolulu in 1918 to find that her husband Matsuji (Takayama) is 20 years older than his photo, and that she faces a married life dominated by toil on the plantation. We're left in no doubt as to the fortitude of these women or the burden placed on their menfolk, yet the film-makers' determination to see the best in everyone feels forced. Tamlyn Tomita is sound as the heroine's supportive best friend and there's a noteworthy cameo from Mifune as a silent-cinema narrator, but a subplot about industrial agitation is left unresolved and a sidestep into the supernatural misfires. TJ

Picture of Dorian Gray, The

(Albert Lewin, 1945, US) Hurd Hatfield, George Sanders, Angela Lansbury, Peter Lawford, Donna Reed, Lowell Gilmore, Richard Fraser, Morton Lowry.
110 min. b/w & col.
Generally underrated version of Oscar Wilde's Faustian tale about a young Victorian gentleman who sells his soul to retain his youth, directed with loving care by the equally underrated Lewin (best known, perhaps, for *Pandora and the Flying Dutchman*). Hatfield – cool, beautiful, and effortlessly suggesting the corruptibility of Dorian's dark soul – is excellent, though even he is overshadowed by the cynical, epigrammatic brilliance of Sanders as Lord Henry. With elegant *fin de siècle* sets superbly shot by Harry Stradling, and the ironic Wildean wit understated rather than overplayed, it's that rare thing: a Hollywoodian literary adaptation that both stays faithful and does justice to its source. GA

Picture Perfect

(Glenn Gordon Caron, 1997, US) Jennifer Aniston, Jay Mohr, Kevin Bacon, Olympia Dukakis, Illeana Douglas, Kevin Dunn, Anne Twomey.
102 min.
Aniston's a thrusting advertising exec who gets passed over for promotion because she doesn't quite fit in with the corporate ethic – married is good, married and mortgaged even better. Best pal Illeana Douglas reckons that if she can at least pretend to be engaged to some rich Bostonian, then the bosses might change their minds. The only Bostonian she can lay hands on, however, is Jay Mohr, a bloke who videotapes weddings. She wants to pay him to pose as her fiancée, but he has already fallen in love with her. And so on, until the director suddenly has one more sub-plot than he knows what to do with. Still, Aniston (from TV's *Friends*) has the rare gift of getting you to root for her in the most trying of circumstances, a quality that will stand her in good stead when she progresses to better material. TJ

Pictures

(Michael Black, 1981, NZ) Kevin J Wilson, Peter Vere-Jones, Helen Moulder, Elizabeth Coulter, Terence Bayler, Matiu Mareikura, Ron Lynn.
87 min.
A pensive, oddly querulous tribute to New Zealand's 19th century pioneer stills photographers, the Burton Brothers, this is weighed down with a gravely simple lesson in political history that sacrifices both character and drama to sketchy schematics. In the aftermath of the Maori wars, idealistic settler Walter Burton (Vere-Jones) documents the misery of a dying culture while becoming increasingly estranged from his own: he's less the misunderstood artist, though, than one all too well understood by the colonial authorities bent on censoring him. Brother Alfred (Wilson) arrives later, trading on his reputation as a society portraitist and landscape romanticist to give the governmental patrons the images they want. Supporting stereotypes abound, and the ironies are trowelled on. It's handsome and well-meaning enough, but there's hardly a spark of cinema to it. PT

Picture Show Man, The

(John Power, 1977, Aust) Rod Taylor, John Meillon, John Ewart, Harold Hopkins, Judy Morris, Sally Conabere, Garry McDonald, Patrick Cargill.
98 min.
A cutely nostalgic portrait of the early years of movie exhibition in Australia, charting the tragicomic rivalries of travelling film showmen in the '20s. If the scenery and period 'charm' don't grab you, you could try reading the narrative as a metaphor on the contemporary Aussie cinema's production boom, and the conflicting demands for an indigenous or 'international' focus (the latter represented by Taylor's outsider/competitor). Not, however, particularly recommended. PT

Picture Snatcher

(Lloyd Bacon, 1933, US) James Cagney, Ralph Bellamy, Patricia Ellis, Alice White, Ralfe Harolde, Robert Emmett O'Connor, Robert Barrat.
77 min. b/w.
Cagney's in typically ebullient shape for this zippy little melodrama as an ex-con who turns Weegee-style 'picture snatcher', grabbing shots of camera-shy underworld figures and selling them to the newspapers. He uses his skills to get in with the police lieutenant father of latest flame Patricia Ellis, but his copybook is soon severely blotted when he smuggles a camera in up his trouser leg to snap a notorious murderer in the electric chair. Cagney's energy keeps it going, though there's also an early bow for Ralph Bellamy as a feisty newspaper editor. TJ

Piece of the Action, A

(Sidney Poitier, 1977, US) Sidney Poitier, Bill Cosby, James Earl Jones, Denise Nicholas, Hope Clark, Tracy Reed, Titos Vandis, Frances Foster, Jason Evers, Marc Lawrence.
135 min.
Poitier and Cosby, successful thieves and pointedly more honest than the organisations they rob, suddenly acquire a social conscience when blackmailed by a retired cop (Jones) into doing time at the local community centre and using their knowhow to prepare a bunch of dead end kids for society. Instead of usefully contemplating the subversive implications of such an arrangement, *A Piece of the Action* abandons the idea that society's there for the taking in favour of wholesale sincerity and homespun philosophy. The result is best described as integration comedy: a kind of black version of Dale Carnegie's *How to Win Friends and Influence People*. CPe

Pieces of Dreams

(Daniel Haller, 1970, US) Robert Forster, Lauren Hutton, Will Geer, Ivor Francis, Richard O'Brien, Edith Atwater.
99 min.
Soapy melodrama about a priest who gives up the priesthood after meeting Hutton's long-legged and embarrassingly rich social worker divorcee. Sole surprise is the presence as director of Haller, who almost manages to erect quite another kind of film within the general skeleton of this smooth escapist vehicle by having our Father fall victim to the very 'vice' against which he is seen holding forth – 'Beware the flesh, above all beware the flesh' – in the confessional. VG

Pied Piper, The
(Irving Pichel, 1942, US) Monty Woolley,
Roddy McDowall, Anne Baxter, Peggy Ann
Garner, Otto Preminger, J Carrol Naish.
86 min. b/w.
A world-weary misanthrope (Woolley, an unlikely star) finds himself escorting young master
McDowall and his brattish sister across France
by train to escape the Nazi occupation. Baxter falters as the mademoiselle who comes to their aid,
but the film does well by an obviously contrived
scenario. Highlight: Woolley squaring up to Nazi
major Preminger in the interrogation room.
Scripted by Nunnally Johnson from a Nevil Shute
novel. TJ

Pied Piper, The
(Jacques Demy, 1971, GB) Donovan, Donald
Pleasence, Jack Wild, Michael Hordern, John
Hurt, Cathryn Harrison, Roy Kinnear, Peter
Vaughan, Diana Dors.
90 min.
Pleasence, as the *nouveau riche* burgomeister of
Hamelin, attempts to evade the plague of rats by
perching his chair of office in tubs of boiling
water; behind him – pulling the strings? – the
Church struggles on a knife edge for power. *The
Pied Piper* has everything wrong with it; yet over
and over again it will toss up images that take it
towards what must have been Demy's intentions.
The film is strongest when dealing in his characteristic language of images: the corpse left by
the Black Death nestling in the midst of apparent
rural bliss, the cathedral-shaped cake that
explodes obscenely with live rats. Too often
Demy has seemed to be doing little but produce
cinematic candy floss; this admittedly imperfect
film of Browning's poem is at least trying for
more. VG

Pied Piper, The (Krysar)
(Jiri Barta, 1985, Czech/WGer)
57 min.
Barta's cruel Gothic version of the classic
medieval legend once again demonstrates the
continuing excellence of Czech animation.
Hamelin is a grey Caligariesque mountain of slop-
ing hovels and palaces, its burghers obscene figures whose sole motivation is the acquisition of
filthy lucre; the Piper, cheated by the corrupt
council after clearing the city of rats, is a gaunt
incarnation of Death whose flute conjures idyllic
visions of verdant landscapes totally at odds with
Hamelin's stony monotones. An impressive film,
notable not only for its richly imaginative juxtapositions of visual textures, but for its resolutely
grotesque account of a society's lemming-like
race towards self-annihilation. GA

Pièges (Personal Column/Snares)
(Robert Siodmak, 1939, Fr) Maurice Chevalier,
Pierre Renoir, Marie Déa, Erich von Stroheim,
André Brunot, Jean Temerson,
Jacques Varennes.
115 min. b/w.
A likeable *policier*, with Déa as a taxi-dancer persuaded by the police to act as a decoy when a
friend falls victim to a serial killer who snares his
prey through lonely hearts ads. Her adventures
while responding to likely ads are a trifle too
picaresque (they include taking down a gang of
white slavers); but they do hang together in mood
and manner until Chevalier turns up as romantic
lead and chief suspect: in effect playing himself
with repellent complacency, indulged with *two*
trademark songs, he very nearly destroys the
ambience. At its best, though, the film captures
the same sense of brooding menace as Siodmak's
later work in *film noir*, with terrific performances
from Stroheim (as a pathetically batty couturier,
ruined by a rival, who stages fashion shows for
imaginary audiences) and Pierre Renoir (as the
enigmatic *éminence grise* behind Chevalier's business interests). TM

Pierrot le Fou [100]
(Jean-Luc Godard, 1965, Fr/It) Jean-Paul
Belmondo, Anna Karina, Dirk Sanders,
Raymond Devos, Graziella Galvani, Samuel
Fuller, Laszlo Szabo, Jean-Pierre Léaud.
110 min.
'Put a tiger in my tank' says Belmondo to an out-
raged Esso pump attendant...and the voyage
begins. *Pierrot le Fou* was a turning-point in

Godard's career, the film in which he tried to do
everything (and almost succeeded). It's the tragic tale of a last romantic couple fleeing Paris for
the South of France. But then again it's a painting by Velazquez (says Godard); or the story of a
bourgeois hubby eloping with the babysitter; a
musical under the high-summer pine trees; or a
gangster story (with Karina the moll and
Belmondo the sucker). She was never more cautious about her love; he was never more drily self-
aware; and the film agonises for two hours over
a relationship that is equal parts nonsense and
despair. In desperation he finally kills her and
himself while the camera sweeps out over a
majestic Mediterranean sea. And a voice mockingly asks: 'Eternity? No, it's just the sun and the
sea'. CA

Pier, The
see Jetée, La

Pigs
(Cathal Black, 1984, Eire) Jimmy Brennan,
George Shane, Maurice O'Donoghue, Liam
Halligan, Kwesi Kay, Joan Harpur.
79 min.
'Home Sweet Home' mutters Jimmy (Brennan),
screwing a bulb into a naked socket in the derelict
Georgian pile where he has decided to take up residence, soon joined by a motley crew of other
squatters. Set on the subcultural fringes of
Dublin's not-so-fair inner city, *Pigs* starts out as
everyone's worst nightmare of house-sharing,
with the inhabitants variously subsisting on diets
of cider and Complan, a pair of false teeth pressed
into service as pastry cutters, and a pan of pigs'
trotters festering on the stove. Gradually it darkens into a sardonic comedy of despair as the little household falls apart under the pressures of
violence, harassment and urban decay. Black's
first feature is a small film and a bit raggedy
round the edges, but possessed of an angry and
pungent eccentricity that carries the day. SJo

Pigskin Parade
(David Butler, 1936, US) Stuart Erwin, Judy
Garland, Patsy Kelly, Jack Haley, Johnny
Downs, Betty Grable.
93 min. b/w.
Grid-iron musical caper in which Texas college
no-hopers take on Yale's finest. Major train-spot-
ting points if you already knew that 15-year-old
Judy Garland made her big screen entrance here,
billed ninth and singing 'It's Love I'm After', but
that the Oscar-nominated Erwin stole the show
as a hick melon-thrower who comes in handy
when the Southerners' quarterback gets injured.
TJ

Pigsty (Porcile)
(Pier Paolo Pasolini, 1969, It/Fr) Pierre
Clémenti, Jean-Pierre Léaud, Alberto Lionello,
Ugo Tognazzi, Anne Wiazemsky, Margarita
Lozano, Marco Ferreri, Franco Citti,
Ninetto Davoli.
100 min.
To accompany screenings of Buñuel's short feature *Simon of the Desert*, Pasolini wanted to make
Orgy, a fairytale about an 'innocent' (Clémenti)
who roams the volcanic wastes of Etna devouring people. But then he added a second story mirroring the themes of *Orgy*, called *Pigsty*. A savage
parody of Godard, Resnais and...Pasolini, ironically chronicling the 'existential anguish' of the
children of the bourgeoisie, it features Léaud as
a mystic youth whose being finally merges with
'nature': he gets eaten by the pigs he loves. *Porcile*
is not only an exquisitely revolting satire, it is
also Pasolini's most fascinating piece of cinema.
PW

Pill, The
see Test Tube Babies

Pillars of Society (Stützen der Gesellschaft)
(Detlef Sierck ie. Douglas Sirk, 1935, Ger)
Heinrich George, Maria Krahn, Horst
Teetzmann, Albrecht Schoenhals, Suse Graf,
Oskar Sima.
84 min. b/w.
Hypocrisy, opportunist exploitation, small-town
gossip and greed: the ills infecting the bourgeoisie
in the sublime '50s weepies of Douglas Sirk were
already deliciously apparent in his German films

of the '30s. Characteristically dissecting a decadent middle-class family, his *Pillars of Society* –
adapted from Ibsen – employs the homecoming
of black sheep brother-in-law Johann
(Schoenhals) to exhume the buried sins of corrupt
capitalist Councillor Bernick (George). Just as
illicit desire and deceit fester beneath Bernick's
respectable facade, so lucid detachment and acute
psychological detail underlie Sirk's smooth, shimmering visuals: Brechtian songs and discreet
symbolism keep things cool and clear until the
repressed passions finally erupt in a cathartic sea-
storm. GA

Pillow Book, The
(Peter Greenaway, 1995, Neth/Fr/GB) Vivian
Wu, Yoshi Oida, Ken Ogata, Hideko Yoshida,
Ewan McGregor, Judy Ongg, Ken Mitsuishi,
Yutaka Honda.
126 min.
A Japanese calligrapher marks his daughter
Nagiko's every birthday with two rituals: he
paints a greeting on her face, and then his sister
reads from Sei Shonagon's 'Pillow Book', a 10th
century diary of reminiscences, observations, and
list upon list of exquisite, precious and graceful
things. Nagiko (Vivian Wu) grows up with a
fetish for calligraphy – demanding that her lovers
paint hieroglyphics on her flesh. She keeps a pillow book, too, but her lists reflect a growing frustration. Then an affair with a bisexual British
translator, Jerome (McGregor), opens up possi-
bilites. Jerome's scribbling cannot satisfy her, but
he offers his own body as her canvas. They fall
in love, and he strips to present her texts to his
gay lover, a publisher. This is as defiantly esoteric as any of Greenaway's films, and as visually dense as *Prospero's Books*, with frames within
frames, computer graphics, subtitles, projections
and superimpositions all vying for the eye in a
sumptuous, seamless collage of gold, red and
black. The result is ravishingly gorgeous, but
such aestheticism is itself a kind of perversion,
an idea embodied in Nagiko. The actors are models, fetishised objects, and sometimes they seem
utterly at a loss, but, by way of counterpoint, this
is also both a very intimate, sensual film, and a
torrid, lurid melodrama, full of passion, jealousy,
hatred and revenge. TCh

Pillow Talk
(Michael Gordon, 1959, US) Doris Day, Rock
Hudson, Tony Randall, Thelma Ritter, Nick
Adams, Marcel Dalio, Allen Jenkins, Lee
Patrick.
105 min.
Long disparaged as a reactionary, prudish symbol
of virginal womanhood, Doris Day was hopefully
reclaimed by certain British feminist film critics as
a woman who chose to say no to the manipulations
of Don Juans. A fair point, but did she have to be
quite so clean and wholesome, verging on the
stereotype of the 'good girl'? At any rate, this, the
first of her romantic comedies with Rock Hudson
– chaste Doris shares a party line with philandering Rock and with predictable results – is frothily
enjoyable, although in comparison with (say) the
battle-of-the-sexes comedies of Hawks, it often
seems complacent and shallow. GA

Pimpernel Smith
(Leslie Howard, 1941, GB) Leslie Howard,
Francis L Sullivan, Mary Morris, Hugh
McDermott, Raymond Huntley, Manning
Whiley, David Tomlinson.
121 min. b/w.
Leslie Howard was among the British actors
based in Hollywood who returned home during
World War I to do their bit for the war effort, and
this tale of a reincarnated Scarlet Pimpernel
smuggling people out from under the Nazi's
noses typifies the star's attitude to traditionally
English values. Deftly directed and imaginatively edited, the film may nevertheless be just too
restrained and Anglo-Saxon for its own good
(especially Howard's characterisation of the
absent-minded archaeology professor setting out
to disprove the existence of an Aryan civilisation). Stiff-upper-lip it ain't, though. MA

Ping Pong
(Po Chih Leong, 1986, GB) David Yip, Lucy
Sheen, Robert Lee, Lam Fung, Victor Kan,
Barbara Yu Ling, Ric Young.
100 min.
At last a Chinatown movie, distinguished by its

lively pace and quirky humour, that's about Gerrard Street, not San Francisco: the British-born director has made a dozen or more features in Hong Kong, but this is his first on home ground. It's about Elaine Choi (Sheen, excellent), a junior clerk in a law office, who is plucked from the typing pool to execute a Chinese will she can't even read. But there are strings attached to restaurateur Sam Wong's bequests that the beneficiaries cannot accept; and Elaine finds herself at the centre of a mystery thriller – or is it a farce? Finally, inspired by the legend of the Woman Warrior, she begins to discover reserves of inner strength she never knew she had. Aside from the ever-reliable David Yip, most of the faces are unfamiliar. Not in the least inscrutable, though: these are engaging characters whose confusions and doubts testify to the problems of being foreigners in a strange (but largely benign) land. TR

Pink Flamingos

(John Waters, 1972, US) Divine, David Lochary, Mary Vivian Pearce, Mink Stole, Danny Mills, Edith Maney, Channing Wilroy, Cookie Mueller.
95 min.
Waters' exercise in deliberately appalling taste is not for the sensitive, needless to say, offering a series of more or less disgusting gags (a messy copulation involving the killing of a chicken, loads of scatological references, a close-up of a scrawny youth spectacularly flexing his anus) deployed around a plot in which a villainous couple attempt to wrest from Divine 'her' claim to be the most disgusting person alive. The cast camp it up as if auditioning for some long-gone Warhol project. Waters raids de Sade in pursuit of extremes, but the difference between him and Warhol (or that other arch-exponent of extreme disgust, Otto Muehl) is that Waters' grotesquerie is decidedly trivial. VG

Pink Floyd Live at Pompeii (Pink Floyd à Pompéi)

(Adrian Maben, 1971, Fr/Bel/WGer) David Gilmour, Roger Waters, Richard Wright, Nick Mason.
85 min.
Technically excellent, this raises the question whether documentary is the most suitable cinematic form in which to present rock music. Although Pompeii and its geography are used along with split screen and rhythmic editing to evoke atmosphere, the unnecessary interviews with the group – and even the images of the band playing – tend to detract from the pleasure the music arouses, simply because the music is constructed not to conjure images of musicians but to provide scope for the listener's imagination. The film may be a brilliant visual record of the Floyd playing, but sadly the music works on you more if you just close your eyes. SM

Pink Floyd: The Wall

(Alan Parker, 1982, GB) Bob Geldof, Christine Hargreaves, James Laurenson, Eleanor David, Kevin McKeon, Bob Hoskins.
95 min.
'We don't need no education' – cue inevitable shots of blank-faced schoolkids on a conveyor-belt to the dead-end mincer. It's hard to see where the much-rumoured creative clashes between Floydian self-analyst Roger Waters and director Parker arose, since the movie is a matter of such stunning literalism: it's little more than kinetic sleeve art keyed slavishly to a slim concept-album narrative. Neither Parker's bombastic live action sequences (carrying Geldof's mute Pink from a war-baby context of military carnage towards neo-fascist rallying, via the turbulence of rock stardom) nor Gerald Scarfe's animation offer more than pictorial italicising of Waters' lyrics; and the autobiographical pain is laid on so thick it emerges looking more like misogynist petulance. Crossing Privilege with Tommy couldn't result in anything shallower. All in all, it's just another flick to appal. PT

Pink Narcissus

(Anonymous, 1971, US) Jim Bidgood.
70 min.
For years, Pink Narcissus was a film shrouded in mystery, known only to the most ardent fans of underground/gay cinema after a brief outing in

the early '70s, and from a few awed reviews in the press. Now that it has resurfaced in a rediscovered print, it's pleasing to report that the film's wicked reputation is fully justified. It's a hugely overblown sexual fantasy centering around one boy, a dark-haired, pouting young thing who drifts through various sets (sleazy street, club, Arabian Nights-style orgy), dressing up and dressing down, cruising and being cruised. It's all massively erotic, healthily funny and visually impressive, reminiscent of Lindsay Kemp, Kenneth Anger and their ilk. The fact that the identity of the film-maker still remains unknown only enhances the pleasure. RS

Pink Panther, The

(Blake Edwards, 1963, US) David Niven, Peter Sellers, Robert Wagner, Capucine, Claudia Cardinale, Brenda de Banzie, John Le Mesurier.
114 min.
First in the popular series that has repeatedly side-tracked Edwards ever since, with Sellers' death not even staunching the flow. Live action cartoonery had been underworked since Tashlin mapped its possibilities with Jerry Lewis, but the novelty value of Sellers' disaster-prone Inspector Clouseau, funny French accent and all, wore off quicker than its commercial value. The eponymous diamond, which reappeared in 1974's The Return of the Pink Panther – and was here sought by suave thief Niven – was symptomatically forgotten in subsequent efforts which still bore its name. PT

Pink Panther Strikes Again, The

(Blake Edwards, 1976, GB) Peter Sellers, Herbert Lom, Colin Blakely, Leonard Rossiter, Lesley-Anne Down, Burt Kwouk, André Maranne, Richard Vernon.
103 min.
The fifth Pink Panther effort might seem marginally disappointing even to diehard Clouseau fans, with slapstick gags for the pratfalling clown hung very loosely on increasingly implausible jet-setting plot antics. Lom's former Chief Inspector Dreyfus, driven mad by Clouseau's bungling and now a master criminal plotting manic, twitching revenge, shifts the series into the realm of mad scientist fantasy, full-scale exploding Bavarian castle finale and all. Added to a score of movie references, it's just enough to keep one's critical faculties anaesthetised. RM

Pink String and Sealing Wax

(Robert Hamer, 1945, GB) Googie Withers, Mervyn Johns, Gordon Jackson, Sally Ann Howes, Mary Merrall, Garry Marsh, John Carol, Catherine Lacey.
89 min. b/w.
Hamer spins his melodrama between two parallel worlds in Victorian Brighton: a suffocating middle-class household dominated by bullying patriarch Johns, and a glitteringly sordid tavern queened over by the magnificently bosomed Withers. As Johns' repressed son (Jackson) becomes infatuated with Withers and implicated in a plot to poison her husband, Hamer unfortunately dissipates the central conflict between these two worlds in a plethora of marginal subplots. Brilliant scenes round the bourgeois dinner table, bitchy confrontations in the bar, add some classy realism to the film, but the parallel between Johns' repressive sadism and Withers' destructive amorality is not pursued. In a distinctly hurried denouement, arrogant Googie is reduced far too easily to a crumpled mass of guilt and tears while the bourgeois family lives happily ever after. RMy

Pink Telephone, The (Le Téléphone Rose)

(Edouard Molinaro, 1975, Fr) Mireille Darc, Pierre Mondy, Michel Lonsdale, Daniel Ceccaldi, Gérard Hérold, Françoise Prévost.
93 min.
A sadly predictable satire about the French small businessman: a naive, middle-aged and paternal managing director (Mondy), subject to takeover by a wily American conglomerate, becomes besotted with Darc, supposedly the PR man's niece but actually a callgirl hired as an inducement for the night. Unfortunately, the film follows the man's lumbering innocence through to its logical conclusion (he decides to give up everything for her), ignoring the more interesting implications of his ruined marriage and strik-

ing work force. Even the humour at the expense of business ethics isn't as sharp as it might have been.

Pinocchio

(Ben Sharpsteen/Hamilton Luske, 1940, US) voices: Dickie Jones, Christian Rub, Cliff Edwards, Evelyn Venable, Walter Catlett, Frankie Darro.
88 min.
Disney's second cartoon feature is a rum old mixture of the excellent and the awful. The story itself has the harsh morality and cruelty of Victorian children's literature, but Disney orchestrates his queasy material with some stunning animation of a monster whale thrashing about and much delightful background detail (the candle-holders and clocks in the toymaker's shop). However, one also has to suffer the cavortings of a cute goldfish called Cleo, and several appearances of an odious fairy. Pinocchio, in fact, probably shows Disney's virtues and vices more clearly than any other cartoon. GB

Pinocchio and the Emperor of the Night

(Hal Sutherland, 1987, US) voices: Edward Asner, Tom Bosley, Scott Grimes, James Earl Jones, Rickie Lee Jones, Don Knotts.
87 min.
Likeable, if predictably pale, sequel to Disney's Pinocchio, which replaces Jiminy Cricket with a glowbug called Gee Willikers. Pinocchio is whisked off to sea on a passing magic carnival ship commanded by the Emperor of the Night, who gets his power from living puppets like Pinocchio or he dies. The music is cheerful and bouncy although it was very loud, and the voices are good too, particularly the Good Fairy, who reminded me of Margaret Thatcher. Overall, I'd say it was an enjoyable film' (Keiron Pim, aged 8). DA

Pin Up Girl

(Bruce Humberstone, 1944, US) Betty Grable, John Harvey, Martha Rae, Joe E Brown, Eugene Pallette, Mantan Moreland, Skating Vanities, Condos Brothers, Charlie Spivak and His Orchestra.
83 min.
A peppy Washington stenographer (Grable) becomes entangled by chance with a Navy hero of Guadalcanal (Harvey), and to maintain the romance takes a night job as a singer in a swanky new club (run by Brown). Her fantasising past catches up with her, however, in the shape of one of her 500 'fiancés', a soldier to whom she gave a pin-up photo of herself when she was a service waitress back home in Missouri. Harvey's a vapid hero, and the script is nothing special (it's one of those stories where the hero fails to recognise his true love when she puts on a pair of spectacles and looks at him cross-eyed), but Grable and singing rival Rae, both engaging troupers despite the mugging, do their best to liven up the proceedings, and there's a rousing uniformed finale in which Sgt Grable puts the female chorus through their parade ground paces. JPy

P.I. Private Investigations

(Nigel Dick, 1987, US) Clayton Rohner, Ray Sharkey, Paul LeMat, Talia Balsam, Phil Morris, Martin Balsam, Anthony Zerbe, Robert Ito, Vernon Wells.
91 min.
First feature from pop video impresario Nigel Dick, keeping an eye on the critical success of After Hours and Something Wild. Joey (Rohner) is the uncool yuppie who stumbles into someone else's trauma and emerges a more together person, his tormentors this time a gang of bent cops. The humour stems from a series of seemingly fated coincidences. After being unfairly passed over for promotion at work, he returns to his apartment to find a body in the shower and an alien tape on his answering machine, which contains information that could help Joey's journalist father (Zerbe) expose police corruption, and turns Joey into a marked man. Razor-faced Ryan (Sharkey) is the crooked detective assigned the job, but he consistently bungles his opportunities and degenerates into a cop of the Keystone variety. Similarly, as our hero is relentlessly pursued against a soundtrack of Dick's video hits, the film slides into self-parody, despite some outrageous moments and inspired twists. EP

Piranha

(Joe Dante, 1978, US) Bradford Dillman, Heather Menzies, Kevin McCarthy, Keenan Wynn, Dick Miller, Barbara Steele, Belinda Balaski, Melody Thomas, Bruce Gordon, Barry Brown, Paul Bartel.
94 min.
Engaging tongue-in-cheek exploitation pic from the Corman stable, in which Menzies and Dillman stumble upon an army camp where mad scientist McCarthy has been developing a mutant strain of man-eating piranha fish for use in the Vietnam war. Things get worse when the finned flesh-eaters escape into a local river. John Sayles' witty script plays the action for laughs rather than chills, stealing wholesale from the plot of Spielberg's *Jaws*, while director Dante piles on the cinematic in-jokes and cheap shock effects. NF

Piranha II: Flying Killers

(James Cameron, 1981, Neth) Tricia O'Neil, Steve Marachuk, Lance Henricksen, Ricky G Paull, Ted Richert.
95 min.
A copy rather than a sequel, this has none of the intelligence, wit or tempo that graced the first swarm of hungry fish. With ruthless resort-owners again refusing to jeopardise their dollars for the sake of their guests' safety, the film relies unimaginatively on the puritanical notion that pleasure invites punishment. Tanned flesh is appetisingly displayed, to be torn to shreds by appallingly squeaky fish-models, and the drunken lechery of the holidaymakers seems far more responsible than profit lust for the final bloodshed. That bare-breasted women and a young black deaf-mute are on the menu makes it very clear who is considered fit to survive and who isn't. RB

Piranha Women in the Avocado Jungle of Death

see Cannibal Women in the Avocado Jungle of Death

Pirate, The

(Vincente Minnelli, 1948, US) Judy Garland, Gene Kelly, Walter Slezak, Gladys Cooper, Reginald Owen, George Zucco, the Nicholas Brothers.
102 min.
A dazzling Caribbean cod-swashbuckler of a musical, with acting as its very theme and the imaginative projection of illusionism its self-referential life-blood. Strolling player (Kelly) woos sheltered but romantic girl (Garland) in the guise of the notorious pirate Macoco, while her dull fiancé (Slezak) desperately hangs on to his own concealed identity. Cole Porter songs, a choreographed camera, vivacious performances, and Minnelli's customarily camp colour scheme and decor are wonderfully seductive vehicles for the themes that run obsessively through almost all the director's films, be they musicals, comedies or melodramas. PT

Pirates

(Roman Polanski, 1986, Fr) Walter Matthau, Cris Campion, Damien Thomas, Ferdy Mayne, David Kelly, Charlotte Lewis, Richard Pearson, Olu Jacobs, Roy Kinnear, Bill Fraser.
124 min.
A rollicking, raunchy, rumbustious romp on the 17th century high seas, neither more nor less amusing than the standard Hollywood swashbuckler, and lacking the zest of the best (such as Curtiz' *Captain Blood*). Matthau, spewing cock-eyed Cockney accent and timber-shivering oaths, has the role of his career as the peg-legged Captain Red, whose unassuageable greed for gold propels him and his footling French sidekick through a series of adventures; and through it all runs evidence of Polanski's infantile sense of humour, mostly involving excrementa, enemas, rat-eating and big-toe biting. Campion (a wimpy French pop singer) can do little as the sidekick, a role originally intended for Polanski himself; and latest Polanskiette Charlotte Lewis merely pouts and points her bosom. The film belongs to Matthau; it's just a pity that his star vehicle doesn't do him justice. AB

Pirates of Penzance, The

(Wilford Leach, 1982, GB) Kevin Kline, Angela Lansbury, Linda Ronstadt, George Rose, Rex Smith, Tony Azito.
112 min.
Not so much a movie as a straight lift from Joe Papp's Broadway stage production, this should of course be awful – a couple of Yankee pop stars (Ronstadt, Smith) camping up Gilbert and Sullivan. In fact, taken on its own terms, it's a near unqualified success, ironically because the camera illuminates the parts footlights fail to reach. Consequently, the show is strewn with throwaway sight gags absent from the stage version which, while mercifully never quite sliding into camp, serve to apply a much needed cattle prod to Messrs G & S. The sets are superb. La Ronstadt – despite a more than casual resemblance to Miss Piggy – makes Pamela Stephenson sound like Arthur Mullard; and Pirate King Kline is definitely the most dashing thing since Errol Flynn swung from his last chandelier. DAt

Piravi (The Birth)

(Shaji, 1988, Ind) Premji, SV Raman, Chandran Nair, Mullaneyi, Kottara Gopalakrishnan.
110 min.
An unusual first film in many ways, centered around an absent hero, an engineering student at the state capital. His father, who lives in a remote coastal village, expects his son's imminent return, and journeys each evening to the bus stop, only to be disappointed. Following a report of police arrest, the old man makes a painful trip to the city, but discovers nothing.It becomes clear that the son will not be coming back. Writer/director Shaji and his 83-year-old star Premji make the father's pain and confusion heartbreakingly authentic in what is a profoundly sensual film: the sheer effort of walking, the abrasive physical presence of the elements. At the same time, it addresses current political concerns: the infringement of the modern world on traditional beliefs; establishment corruption; the role of women; education. A master of nuance and mood, Shaji values grace and the human spirit, but the film ends on a tragically ambivalent note. Quiet and contemplative in conception, it is deeply moving in effect. TCh

Pirosmani

(Georgy Shengelaya, 1971, USSR) Avtandil Varazi, David Abashidze, Zurab Kapianidze, Teimuraz Beridze.
85 min.
A slow and sensitive portrait of the great Georgian primitive artist who died in 1918 and whose work is still not widely known outside Russia, *Pirosmani* effectively keeps its distance from the central character. Proud and lonely, Pirosmani forsakes all security to paint, exchanging his work in city bars for food, drink and a bed. His isolation is conveyed through composition and image, while his private life (alcoholism and an inability to make contact with a singer he silently worships) is hinted rather than stressed. A restrained film, possibly too non-involving for some, beautifully shot in muted colours, and composed of studies with the subjects often looking posed and self-conscious, as the artist must have seen them. It's not often that an artist gets the film he deserves. CPe

Pistol, The (Pistolen)

(Jiri Tirl, 1973, Swe) Inga Tidblad, Gunnar Björnstrand, Håkan Westergren, Nils Eklund, Berndt Lundquist, Bertil Norström.
79 min.
A spry old lady (Tidblad), tired of living alone for 30 years in a servantless but immaculately clean mansion, decides to commit suicide. Setting about repairing an antique pistol which is a family heirloom, she temporarily regains the will to live through the friendship of a gentlemanly antique-dealer (Westergren), and in gratitude makes him a present of the now fully-functioning pistol. When he unaccountably puts the piece up for sale, she smashes his shop window and steals it back...Written and directed by Tirl, a Czech-born cameraman, *The Pistol* aspires to the tone of a Chekhov chamber-drama, but turns out as little more than a pretty, but essentially empty, photo-essay on an old lady and a stately home. JPy

Pistolero of Red River, The

see Last Challenge, The

Pit and the Pendulum, The

(Roger Corman, 1961, US) Vincent Price, Barbara Steele, John Kerr, Luana Anders, Anthony Carbone, Patrick Westwood.
85 min.
Corman at his intoxicating best, drawing a seductive mesh of sexual motifs from Poe's story through a fine Richard Matheson script. Vincent Price is superbly tormented as the 16th century Spanish nobleman obsessed by the fear that his wife was entombed alive in his castle's torture chamber, a repetition of family history that entails his takeover by the personality of his dead father, the Inquisitor who built the fiendish dungeon. And Barbara Steele, as the faithless wife who faked her own death, embodies all the contradictions of Poe's quintessential female to perfection.

Pit and the Pendulum, The

(Stuart Gordon, 1990, US) Lance Henriksen, Roma de Ricci, Jonathan Fuller, Francis Bay, Mark Margolis, Jeffrey Combs, Tom Towles, Oliver Reed.
92 min.
A gruesome adaptation of Edgar Allan Poe's classic horror story which, while lacking the subtlety of Richard Matheson's script for Roger Corman's 1961 version, lays on the cruelty and horror with relish. During the Spanish Inquisition, the pious fiancée of a baker attends an *auto-da-fe* and unwittingly incurs the wrath of Henriksen's ruthless Grand Inquisitor. While Maria is interrogated and tortured, her lover sneaks into the castle and tries to rescue her, only to end up on the wrong end of a razor-sharp pendulum. The scene in which inquisitor Henriksen willingly surrenders himself to a whipping by a man he previously crucified as a heretic – meanwhile enjoying erotic visions of the Virgin Mary's face superimposed onto the heroine's voluptuous body – is especially memorable, perversely combining violent spectacle, religious asceticism, masochism and blasphemy. Sadly, Gordon throws away the poorly staged pendulum scene at the end, resulting in a slight anticlimax. NF

Pitfall

(André De Toth, 1948, US) Dick Powell, Lizabeth Scott, Jane Wyatt, Raymond Burr, Byron Barr, John Litel, Ann Doran.
86 min. b/w.
Rather flatly scripted, but a not uninteresting clash between moral tale and *film noir*. Powell plays the archetypal suburban man, blessed with family, home and job, but suffering a vague itch of awareness that life hasn't lived up to expectations. His work as an insurance claims agent lures him into involvement with a siren (Scott) and the inevitable aftermath of violence, deceit, and sudden death. From this he is rescued by the exercise of a double standard (Scott pays for her murder, Powell gets away with his); but the film still contrives a troubled intimation that things ain't quite what they used to be in suburbia. Burr, modelling himself on Laird Cregar (who would have made more of the role), gives one of his better performances as the hulking yet oddly pathetic private eye who digs the pitfall in trying to pursue his own hopeless infatuation. TM

Pit of Darkness

(Lance Comfort, 1961, GB) William Franklyn, Moira Redmond, Bruno Barnabe, Leonard Sachs, Nigel Green, Anthony Booth, Nanette Newman.
76 min. b/w.
British B-pic, adapted by director Lance Comfort from Hugh McCutcheon's novel *To Dusty Death*, spinning a tortuous yarn about a honest man with memory loss who seems to have done something villainous in the past. Moira Redmond's the concerned wife trying to get husband Franklyn (as smooth as he always is) to remember the details of a jewel heist from a safe he personally designed. TJ

Pixote (Pixote a lei do mais fraco)

(Hector Babenco, 1981, Braz) Fernando Ramos da Silva, Jorge Juliao, Gilberto Moura, Edilson Lino, Zenildo Oliveira Santos, Marilia Pera.
127 min.
Not since Buñuel's *Los Olvidados* has the plight of kids in Third World urban poverty been so acutely affecting; and not since Truffaut's *400 Blows* has a child actor (da Silva) so etched his tragic delinquency on the memory of middle-class audiences. Even allowing for the institutional horrors depicted in *Scum*, nothing in recent cinema comes close to the devastating

account of brutalisation and exploitation offered in Babenco's film about a 10-year-old boy who somehow survives the vicious oppression of the reform school, to escape and find his way into dope-dealing, prostitution and murder in the Brazilian underworld. Originally labelled a 'denunciation' film in Brazil for its critique of a social system that fails to prevent the majority of the country's three million homeless kids from turning to crime, *Pixote* arrived here laden with art cinema awards for its exposé of a problem which, for all its cultural remoteness, carves into your conscience with the sudden thrust of a flick knife in a street fight. MA

Pizza Triangle, The
see Dramma della Gelosia

P.J. (aka New Face in Hell)
(John Guillermin, 1967, US) George Peppard, Raymond Burr, Gayle Hunnicutt, Coleen Gray, Susan Saint James, Brock Peters, Jason Evers, Wilfrid Hyde-White, Severn Darden, Bert Freed.
109 min.
Peppard plays PJ Detweiler, down-at-heel shamus, in this unmemorable addition to the largely unmemorable private eye cycle of the late '60s. Hired (after undergoing a toughness test) by tycoon Raymond Burr – you know *he's* up to no good because he hoards his cigar butts – PJ gets to go to a murkily exotic island in the Bahamas as bodyguard to the tycoon's mistress (Hunnicutt) because someone has been trying to kill her. Beatings-up, attempted murders and red herrings proliferate before he solves the case. Gracelessly directed with a huge close-up to underline every plot point, it goes through the routine motions, offering very little apart from the odd wisecrack and a lot of thick-ear violence. TM

Place, The
see Platz, Der

Place in the Sun, A
(George Stevens, 1951, US) Montgomery Clift, Elizabeth Taylor, Shelley Winters, Anne Revere, Keefe Brasselle, Raymond Burr, Fred Clark.
122 min. b/w.
Typically slow and stately in the later Stevens manner, this is a shameless travesty of Theodore Dreiser's monumental (if ponderous) *An American Tragedy*. Most of the book's acid social comment is elided, turning Dreiser's hero's attempt to better himself by latching onto a snobbish society girl into something like a starry-eyed romance; what is left is rendered meaningless by being ripped out of period context into a contemporary setting. Although all three leads are excellent, only the scenes with Winters (the pregnant mill girl who gets in the way, and of whose murder – willed if not actually committed – Clift is found guilty) really work. TM

Place in the World, A
(Adolfo Aristarain, 1992, Arg) Jose Sacristan, Federico Luppi, Leonor Benedetto, Cecilia Roth.
120 min.
An entirely winning and deceptively unassuming portrait of life in a 'frontier' town – some hundreds of miles down the railway tracks from the Argentine capital – with an only son revisiting the small sheep-rearing community of his late adolescence and recalling both his remarkable family and the turn of events during a particular autumn some eight years before. His father, a one-time sociology professor, his mother, a doctor, and a no-nonsense nun in civvies are the three 'progressive' figures who minister to the families of the local collective they've fought to set up. But when a mysterious Spanish geologist arrives to work for the town's venal landowner, it slowly emerges that radical change is on the way. Director Aristarain lavishes this unremarkable scenario with highly nuanced attention to character, mood and structure, and produces a film of quiet profundity, laced with gentle regret and something of the elegiac glow of some late Westerns. Evocative camerawork from Ricardo de Angelis, a fine Copland-esque score by Patricio Kauderer, and highly impressive performances. Thoughtful, informed, perfectly judged. WH

Place of One's Own, A
(Bernard Knowles, 1945, GB) Margaret Lockwood, James Mason, Barbara Mullen, Dennis Price, Dulcie Gray, Ernest Thesiger, Helen Haye, Moore Marriott.
92 min. b/w.
Tame but occasionally effective ghost story (an adaptation from Osbert Sitwell), set in Edwardian times, with Lockwood as the young secretary haunted by a murdered woman when she goes to live with an elderly couple (Mason and Mullen) in an elegant country house. Not a patch upon Knowles' loony but marvellous *Jassy*, although Lockwood and Mason are as effortlessly professional as ever. GA

Places in the Heart
(Robert Benton, 1984, US) Sally Field, Lindsay Crouse, Ed Harris, Amy Madigan, John Malkovich, Danny Glover, Lane Smith, Bert Remsen.
111 min.
A winner in the cardiac stakes. Field is the small-holding farmer, recently widowed, who takes in a blind veteran (Malkovich) and desperately tries to farm her cotton crop with the help of a black itinerant farmhand (Glover). Friendships quicken, love hardens, the constant toil is made endurable by the small town ethic of communal feelings. Much is unemphatic, but all of it carries the moving weight of conviction. And it ends on a healing grace-note which passeth all understanding. CPea

Plaff! or Too Afraid of Life (Plaf – Demasiado miedo a la vida)
(Juan Carlos Tabio, 1988, Cuba) Daisy Granados, Thais Valdés, Luis Alberto Garcia, Raúl Pomares.
110 min.
Tabio's screwball soap opera takes us into the lives and loves of a family in the middle-class suburbs of Havana. It's tacky, it's wacky, it's, well, serious too. Widowed Concha (Granados) distrusts the alliance of brawn and brain when her beloved baseball-player son marries a girl engineer with her own ideas (about bureaucratic impedimenta, the role of women, and Concha). Concha has problems enough: made wary of men by the philandering of her dear departed, she distrusts the charms of taxi-driver Tomas, so is forced to take comfort in the spells of a Santeria-cult priestess. When the young marrieds move in, splat! – eggs start to fly. Tabio leaves no doubt that this is *farce*, not so much admitting the presence of the camera as flaunting it. Every mirror reveals the camera crew, props are thrown onto the set, the film cranks to a halt for apologies about missing scenes. The sight gags, absurd histrionics and hyperbolic use of sound communicate an infectious sense of fun, but the film can't quite hide a deathly conventional morality which, sadly, hauls it back into sanity and nauseating good faith. WH

Plague Dogs, The
(Martin Rosen, 1982, US) voices: John Hurt, Christopher Benjamin, James Bolam, Nigel Hawthorne, Warren Mitchell, Bernard Hepton.
103 min.
The uncharitable might claim that the same heavy hands which mauled *Watership Down* four years earlier have beaten *The Plague Dogs* back into the dreary pack of animal tales that Richard Adams' books towered head and shoulders above. Certainly the story of Snitter (a pathetic fox terrier who believes himself responsible for the death of his master and much else besides), his friend (an embittered Labrador), and their escape from an animal research centre into the Lake District and the company of a worldly fox, gains nothing from animation more closely resembling painting-by-numbers than the Disney-type high quality it aspires to. Similarly, Adams' succinct complaint about animal exploitation is reduced to a mute whine. However, the point is at least made, and the sugary coating may make it easier for some to swallow. FD

Plague of the Zombies, The
(John Gilling, 1966, GB) Andre Morell, Diane Clare, Brook Williams, Jacqueline Pearce, John Carson, Alex Davion, Michael Ripper.
91 min.
Perhaps a little tame these days, compared with modern gore-shock, but Gilling's Hammer chiller about zombies being exploited by a Cornish tin-mine owner (echoes of the classic *White Zombie*) is highly atmospheric. Often imaginatively directed (in particular a splendid, nightmarishly green-tinted vision of the undead rising from the graveyard earth), it boasts really classy photography (Arthur Grant) and an outstanding performance from Jacqueline Pearce (the admirable snake-woman from *The Reptile*, here being beheaded to save her from untimely zombification). GA

Plainsman, The
(Cecil B DeMille, 1936, US) Gary Cooper, Jean Arthur, James Ellison, Charles Bickford, Porter Hall, Victor Varconi, John Miljan, Gabby Hayes, Anthony Quinn.
113 min. b/w.
A little too self-consciously epic (it begins with Mrs Lincoln reminding the President that they'll be late for the theatre) and much too reliant on back-projection, but still an enjoyably spectacular Western which rambles through the familiar parade of gun-runners, Indian uprisings and figures from history (ruthlessly telescoped to get them all in, including a nobly heroic Custer). Cooper's fine, sombre portrayal of Wild Bill Hickok (lumbered with a skittishly romantic Calamity Jane, but nevertheless allowed to meet his death at the hands of Jack McCall) seems to come from another, altogether less trivial movie. TM

Plaisir, Le (House of Pleasure)
(Max Ophüls, 1951, Fr) Claude Dauphin, Gaby Morlay, Madeleine Renaud, Danielle Darrieux, Ginette Leclerc, Jean Gabin, Pierre Brasseur, Daniel Gélin, Simone Simon.
95 min. b/w.
Ophüls' second French film following his return from the USA was adapted from three stories by Maupassant. *Le Masque* describes how an old man wears a mask of youth at a dance hall to extend his youthful memories. *La Maison Tellier*, the longest episode, deals with a day's outing for the ladies from a brothel, and a brief romance. In *Le Modèle*, the model in question jumps from a window for love of an artist, who then marries her. Although Ophüls had to drop a fourth story intended to contrast pleasure and death, these three on old age, purity and marriage are shot with a supreme elegance and sympathy, and the central tale in particular luxuriates in the Normandy countryside. The whole is summed up by the concluding line, that 'happiness is no lark'. DT

Plan 9 from Outer Space
(Edward D Wood Jr, 1956, US) Gregory Walcott, Mona McKinnon, Bela Lugosi, Maila 'Vampira' Nurmi, Tor Johnson, Lyle Talbot, Tom Keene, Criswell.
79 min. b/w.
Crowned 'The Worst Film Ever Made' at New York's Worst Film Festival in 1980, this deserves its niche in history for featuring the last screen performance of Bela Lugosi, as a ghoul resurrected by space visitors for use against scientists destroying the world with their nuclear tests. Two minutes of Lugosi in his Dracula outfit, shot for another Wood film abandoned when Lugosi died, are supplemented by footage of an unemployed chiropractor hired as a double; a good foot taller than Lugosi, he of course keeps his face wrapped in a cape. But that's nothing: we also learn that top-level Pentagon offices are furnished with one lamp and two telephones each, while the bedroom furniture of one character is exactly the same as his patio furniture of the previous scene. It all ends with famous psychic Criswell asking the audience, 'Can you prove it didn't happen? God help us in the future'. Prophetic. CR

Planes, Trains and Automobiles
(John Hughes, 1987, US) Steve Martin, John Candy, Laila Robbins, Michael McKean, Larry Hankin, Edie McClurg.
92 min.
When their flight is grounded by snow, suave advertising exec Neal Page (Martin) finds himself stuck with travelling shower-curtain-ring salesman Del Griffith (Candy), the human equiv-

alent of a Double Whopper. Griffith offers the benefit of his wide-ranging travel experience, and the pair set off overland on an odyssey of disasters. Sympathy, initially with the exec, shifts to the salesman, who is revealed as a vulnerable and lonely misfit, while his companion proves an intolerant bully and foul-tempered snob. A couple of overgrown brats seems an appropriate focus for John *The Breakfast Club* Hughes first adult movie, but if his direction is slick, his script lacks wit and perception. Essentially, it's the stars' keenly observed nuances of character that make this comedy amiable enough. EP

Planète Sauvage, La

see Fantastic Planet

Planet of the Apes

(Franklin J Schaffner, 1967, US) Charlton Heston, Roddy McDowall, Kim Hunter, Maurice Evans, James Whitmore, James Daly, Linda Harrison.
112 min.
Four sequels and a TV series bred contempt, but this first visit to Pierre Boulle's planet, bringing a welcome touch of wit to his rather humourlessly topsy-turvy theory of evolution, remains a minor sci-fi classic. The settings (courtesy of the National Parks of Utah and Arizona) are wonderfully outlandish, and Schaffner makes superb use of them as a long shot chillingly establishes the isolation of the crashed astronauts, as exploration brings alarming intimations of life (pelts staked out on the skyline like crucified scarecrows), and as discovery of a tribe of frightened humans is followed by an eruption of jackbooted apes on horseback. The enigma of the planet's history, juggled through Heston's humiliating experience of being studied as an interesting laboratory specimen by his ape captors, right down to his final startling rediscovery of civilisation, is quite beautifully sustained. TM

Platinum Blonde

(Frank Capra, 1931, US) Jean Harlow, Loretta Young, Robert Williams, Reginald Owen, Walter Catlett, Halliwell Hobbes.
98 min. b/w.
Although finally saddled with a somewhat banal message about the value of good hard work and the evils of inherited wealth, this lively comedy is infinitely preferable to the turgid, reactionary sermonising of the director's later Capracorn epics (*Mr Deeds Goes to Town, Mr Smith Goes to Washington*, etc). The plot – Williams' journalist falls for a wealthy but fickle socialite, rather than his tough colleague, only to discover the error of his ways – is predictable but fast-moving, with some delightfully cynical wisecracks contributed by Capra's regular writer Robert Riskin. But it's finally Williams, in his last performance before dying from a ruptured appendix, who steals the show; though both Harlow and Young are efficient and ravishing, they are strangely miscast – Harlow as the heiress, Young as the down-to-earth news hound. GA

Platoon

(Oliver Stone, 1986, US) Tom Berenger, Willem Dafoe, Charlie Sheen, Forest Whitaker, Francesco Quinn, John C McGinley, Richard Edson.
120 min.
Stone's Vietnam film is a savage yet moving account of a 19-year-old's baptism under fire: clambering out of a transport plane, Sheen is soon plunged into the bloody chaos of combat. The use of his letters home as a commentary establishes personal experience as the core of the film; but broader political issues do manifest themselves when, unable to make any headway against the elusive Vietcong, the grunts turn their anger and weaponry on one another, the platoon splitting into warring factions that reflect peacetime social divisions. Two conflicting impulses appear in the movie: a desire to assault the audience with searing images that will cauterise the Vietnam wound once and for all; and a wish for a more artistically distanced elegy, given its purest expression in Georges Delerue's plaintive score. Perhaps it is this unresolved tension that allows *Rambo* fans to relish the violence while concerned liberals ponder the horror. That said, Stone's eye-blistering images possess an awesome power, which sets the senses reeling and leaves the mind disturbed. NF

Platz, Der (The Place)

(Uli M Schüppel, 1997, Ger)
52 min.
A video documentary about a German building site may not sound exciting. Rest assured: it isn't. I suppose you could say Schüppel's film draws on the tradition of Walter Ruttmann's 1927 *Berlin, Symphony of a Great City* and Wenders' *Wings of Desire*, but all it really boils down to is monochrome footage of construction work at the Potsdamer Platz, with voice-over reminiscences from the labourers, reflecting on their own special places – pastoral, to a man. Music by former Einstürzende Neubauten musician FM Einheit. TCh

Playbirds, The

(Willy Roe, 1978, GB) Mary Millington, Glynn Edwards, Gavin Campbell, Alan Lake, Windsor Davies, Derren Nesbitt.
94 min.
Tatty sex thriller named after the magazine of the same title and characteristics, a down-market 'Men Only' competitor. It's not surprising, then, that the movie – featuring mascot Mary as the policewoman who becomes bait for the centre-spread murderer – is dreary yawn-a-minute stuff. GD

Playboys, The

(Gillies MacKinnon, 1992, GB) Albert Finney, Aidan Quinn, Robin Wright, Milo O'Shea, Alan Devlin, Niamh Cusack, Ian McElhinney, Adrian Dunbar.
109 min.
In a remote Irish border village in 1957, unwed mother Tara (Wright) is lectured by the women-folk and priest on the wages of sin, while the men, notably Police Sergeant Hegarty (Finney) hover like moths around a flame, only to meet with rejection. The situation worsens when she finally yields to Tom (Quinn), tale-spinning member of a troupe of travelling players led by the irrepressibly optimistic Freddie (O'Shea)... Directed by MacKinnon with great pace and a minimum of moralising or sentimentality, Shane Connaughton and Kerry Crabbe's tale of passion makes for a superior period drama, as tough, touching and witty as Connaughton's *My Left Foot*. Much credit is due to the cast, particularly Finney, who brings a melancholy gravity to a film which elsewhere steers sensibly clear of solemnity (the troupe's hammy renditions of *Othello* and *Gone With the Wind* are especially funny). With time, place and mood sensitively evoked, this is solid, intelligent entertainment, mercifully free of the usual 'Oirish' clichés. GA

Play Dirty

(André De Toth, 1968, GB) Michael Caine, Nigel Davenport, Nigel Green, Harry Andrews, Bernard Archard, Daniel Pilon.
117 min.
A workmanlike rip-off of *The Dirty Dozen*, with Caine leading a group of ex-criminals in an attack on a German supply dump in North Africa during WWII. The script, by Lotte Colin and a certain Melvyn Bragg, aims for grand anti-war rhetoric. De Toth keeps the action going well, and the end is great – forgetting that they are wearing German uniforms, our surviving lads break cover to take a bow and get mown down by friendly fire. Ironic, huh? ATu

Player, The

(Robert Altman, 1992, US) Tim Robbins, Greta Scacchi, Fred Ward, Whoopi Goldberg, Peter Gallagher, Brion James, Cynthia Stevenson, Vincent D'Onofrio, Dean Stockwell, Richard E Grant, Sydney Pollack, Lyle Lovett, Dina Merrill.
124 min.
Shrewd Hollywood exec Griffin Mill (Robbins) is already paranoid that a rival may join the studio; but what of the anonymous postcards he's getting from a scriptwriter whose pitch he hasn't followed up? Rattled by the death threats, he decides (wrongly) that the likely sender is David Kahane (D'Onofrio). But when Kahane is found dead after a meeting with Mill and it becomes known that Mill is dating the writer's ungrieving lover (Scacchi), his troubles multiply... Altman turns Michael Tolkin's thriller into the most honest, hilarious Hollywood satire ever, even persuading some 60 celebs to play themselves. Besides the

superb performances, photography, music and seamless blend of comedy and tension, what's finally so special about the film is its form. Altman refines his open, 'democratic' style of the '70s, to show an untidy world from numerous shifting perspectives, yet the film is far from chaotic. With its many movie references and film-within-a-film structure, it's forever owning up to the fact that it's only a movie. Only? Were more films as complex and revealing about people, society and the way we watch and think about films, today's Hollywood product would be far more interesting than it is. GA

Players

(Anthony Harvey, 1979, US) Ali MacGraw, Dean-Paul Martin, Maximilian Schell, Pancho Gonzáles, Steve Guttenberg, Melissa Prophet, Guillermo Vilas.
120 min.
At Wimbledon's Centre Court, the men's singles finalists emerge, Dan Maskell's commentary sets the scene, and the heartaches (ie. flashbacks) begin. Finalist Martin, we learn, likes having sex beside Mexican swimming-pools with MacGraw, the wealthy designer he rescued from a burning car; but she keeps jetting to the side of her Italian millionaire/yachtsman (Schell), who in turn seems to be quite into his glamorous secretary. The soapy plot is so incredibly old-fashioned that it might be forgiven if the script didn't keep hitting so many lines straight into the net: exchanges like 'How old are you?' – 'Don't ask' are only matched by unashamedly pulpy love scenes ('Tell me everything...like how you got so beautiful'). A pity, because the tennis relationships, including a cameo from Pancho Gonzáles, ring far more true; and the last set of the Wimbledon final, when we are allowed to get to it, comes close to Hollywood adrenalin-pumping at its best. DP

Playing Away

(Horace Ové, 1986, GB) Norman Beaton, Robert Urquhart, Helen Lindsay, Nicholas Farrell, Brian Bovell, Gary Beadle, Sheila Ruskin, Patrick Holt.
102 min.
Monocle, pipe in clenched jaw, retired colonel and vicar showing slides of the Masai in the village hall for Third World Week – all this lacks is Basil Radford and Naunton Wayne for a picture of the Home Counties in the '30s according to Agatha Christie. The trouble is, it's set in the present. The annual cricket match between a Suffolk village and Brixton begins with a phone call from Derek (Farrell) – almost lockjawed with good breeding – to Willie Boy (Beaton), loveably demonstrative captain of the partying Brixton XI. Willie Boy dreams of returning to Jamaica, and his experiences in chilly Sneddington help him make up his mind. Most of the cultural exchanges are on the obvious level of introducing the whites to the herb, a bit of fancying, and the odd racist remark. The cricket match turns into a shambles, Brixton wins, but Sneddington discourteously fails to lay on an end-of-play 'Spot of lunch, old boy?' celebration. Miss Marple would have served tea and Osbornes at least. BC

Playing for Keeps

(Bob Weinstein/Harvey Weinstein, 1984, US) Daniel Jordano, Matthew Penn, Leon W Grant, Mary B Ward, Marisa Tomei, Jimmy Baio, Harold Gould.
106 min.
Danny (Jordan) inherits an old run-down estate, and with the help of his friends, sets out to build the first hotel run by and for teenagers. The townsfolk oppose their plans, but Chloe Hatcher (Ward), Farmer Hatcher's daughter, decides to help them out – she's fallen for Danny. Disappointingly, Danny's opening night festivities at the Rock Hotel do not include a surprise performance by the ever-loveable Einstürzende Neubauten. SGo

Playing from Plates (Grajacy Z Talerza)

(Jan Jakub Kolski, 1995, Pol/Fr) Dojnica Paladiuk, Krzysztof Pieczynski, Mariusz Saniternik, Franciszek Pieczka, Grazyna Blecka-Kolska.
107 min.
Kolski's enigmatic mix of fantastic allegory, mystic fairytale, and bucolic comedy tosses together a crew of peasant weirdos – an elderly farmer vis-

ited by the Angel of Death, a dwarf would-be nurse whom he saves from suicide, a two-faced 'monster' who lives at the bottom of his well, and a mad fiddler who 'reads' shards of crockery as inspiration for his fatally hypnotic rhapsodies – to create a meandering Beauty and the Beast-style parable about the transforming power of love. Ludicrous, for sure, and not, as far as one can gather, politically correct or progressive; still, the sheer, wayward inventiveness of the whole thing ensures a certain oddball appeal. GA

Play It Again, Sam

(Herbert Ross, 1972, US) Woody Allen, Diane Keaton, Tony Roberts, Jerry Lacy, Susan Anspach, Jennifer Salt, Joy Bang, Viva.
86 min.
Allen's neurosis is not to everyone's taste, but this movie – based on his own stage play about a film critic with seduction problems who takes Bogart as a role model – shows him at his best, exploring the gap between movie escapism and reality. It's not really as pretentious as that, and anyway, in contrasting his chaotic life with the Bogart image, Allen forgets the contrast between his chaos and our prosaic lives. No doubt someone somewhere takes Woody as his mentor and fails to be funny, just as Woody here stumbles after Bogey's cool. Still, the working out of the parallels with *Casablanca* are masterly, and there are plenty of good sight gags and one-liners. Much better than Allen's previous self-directed effort, *Everything You Always Wanted to Know About Sex*. SG

Play It Cool

(Michael Winner, 1962, GB) Billy Fury, Michael Anderson Jr, Dennis Price, Richard Wattis, Anna Palk, Maurice Kaufmann, Peter Barkworth, Helen Shapiro, Shane Fenton, Bobby Vee, Danny Williams, Lionel Blair.
81 min. b/w.
Rich business type Price is the titled old square who wants to keeps daughter Anna Palk out of the clutches of dodgy popster Kaufmann, but is powerless to prevent romance spawning when she meets up with hunky singing sensation Billy Universe (Fury) and embarks on a tour of London nightlife. Minor fresco of '60s Britpop frippery: Helen Shapiro, Shane Fenton and The Fentones, an imported Bobby Vee and Lionel Blair all in the same movie. Blimey, pass the Tizer. TJ

Playmaker, The

(Yuri Zeltser, 1993, GB) Colin Firth, Jennifer Rubin, John Getz.
91 min.
On advice from barman Eddie (Getz), aspiring actress Jamie (Rubin) takes on a $5,000 one-to-one acting course with Talbert (Firth) in his isolated Los Angeles eyrie (like the pad in *North by Northwest*). First, she undergoes a bit of personality stripping, then he dresses her as a harridan/femme fatale and ropes her into a wheelchair. And that's only lesson two. The tables are later turned by some very implausible plot twists. A movie veering unsteadily from psycho-sexual power play to naturalistic horror thriller, with some finely achieved, but far from saving moments of tension and sexual *frisson*. WH

Play Me Something

(Timothy Neat, 1989, GB) Lucia Lanzarini, Charlie Barron, John Berger, Hamish Henderson, Tilda Swinton, Stewart Ennis, Robert Carr.
72 min. b/w & col.
John Berger here collaborates with Neat to bring one of his own short stories to the screen, also appearing as the mysterious story teller. A handful of men and women await the plane for Glasgow on the Hebridean island of Barra: visitors, a girl (Swinton) setting off for a job on the mainland, locals who have charge of the airport, and in their midst, Berger. Jaunty, vibrant and expansive, he makes a mesmerising storyteller; and his tale, on the face of it a simple yarn of a peasant (Brumo) on a weekend trip to Venice, becomes a complex exploration of people and places, factories and farms, sex, politics, music…ways of being. The film quite naturally takes on myriad textures: colour and black-and-white, 35mm and blown-up 16mm footage, and for the story-within-the-story, still photographs by the exemplary Jean Mohr. Berger and Neat have discovered that there is a useful application for post-modernism after all, the better to tell a tale. TCh

Play Misty for Me

(Clint Eastwood, 1971, US) Clint Eastwood, Jessica Walter, Donna Mills, John Larch, Jack Ging, Irene Hervey, Donald Siegel.
102 min.
Eastwood's first film as director, and first exploratory probe for the flaws in his macho image as outlined in Siegel's *The Beguiled*. A highly enjoyable thriller made under the influence of Siegel (who contributes a memorable cameo as a bartender), it casts Eastwood as a late-night Californian DJ who, flattered by the persistent attentions of a mysterious fan (Walter), lets himself be picked up for a one night stand before going back to his true love (Mills). Before long, blandly assuming an on-going relationship, Walter reveals herself to be a suicidal hysteric who won't take no for an answer; and poor Eastwood is driven into a corner like a mesmerised rabbit, unable to find a way out of the impasse without driving one of his two jealous women over the edge. From there it's but a step to the watcher in the bushes, the carving knife glittering in a darkened room, and a splendid all-stops-out finale. TM

Playtime

(Jacques Tati, 1967, Fr) Jacques Tati, Barbara Dennek, Jacqueline Lecomte, Valérie Camille, France Rumilly.
152 min.
Tati's Hulot on the loose in a surreal, scarcely recognisable Paris, tangling intermittently with a troop of nice American matrons on a 24-hour trip. Not so much a saga of the individual against an increasingly dehumanised decor, it's more a semi-celebratory symphony to Tati's sensational city-set, all reflections and rectangles, steel, chrome, gleaming sheet metal and *trompe l'oeil* plate glass. Shot in colour that looks almost like monochrome, recorded in five-track stereo sound with scarcely a word of speech (the mysterious language of objects echoes louder than words), this jewel of Tati's career is a hallucinatory comic vision on the verge of abstraction. SJo

Plaza Suite

(Arthur Hiller, 1970, US) Walter Matthau, Maureen Stapleton, Barbara Harris, Lee Grant, Jennie Sullivan, Tom Carey.
114 min.
Harmless piece of Neil Simon fluff, rather flattened by Hiller's steamroller direction: three playlets, set in the same hotel room, with the gimmick that all three male leads are played by Matthau. The first is the best, with Matthau beautifully partnered by Maureen Stapleton as a couple celebrating their 24th wedding anniversary, she waxing all nostalgic, he itching to get away to his mistress, and a history of marital irritation charted by their absurdist dialogue. The rest is thumb-twiddling time, with Matthau as a Hollywood producer seducing a happily married old flame (the delightful Harris, wasted) with his big-time act, and as the father of a hysterical bride (Sullivan) who has locked herself in the loo with the wedding waiting. TM

Please Don't Eat the Daisies

(Charles Walters, 1960, US) Doris Day, David Niven, Janis Paige, Spring Byington, Richard Haydn, Patsy Kelly, Jack Weston.
111 min.
Urbane, thoroughly frivolous comedy about a drama critic, his wife, their four squabbling sons, and pet sheepdog (adapted by Isobel Lennart from Jean Kerr's best-seller about life with the *NY Herald-Tribune*'s Walter Kerr). There's not much in the way of plot (a slap in the face from an actress he's panned precipitates a family move from New York to the safety of the country), but the interplay between the stars is mildly diverting: Doris Day, prim and fragrant, bustles around the house; Niven smiles and wriggles his tache in his usual louche way. And that's about it. Good performance from the dog. GM

Pleasure Principle, The

(David Cohen, 1991, GB) Peter Firth, Lynsey Baxter, Hadyn Gwynne, Lysette Anthony, Sara Mair-Thomas, Ian Hogg.
100 min.
Freelance journalist Dick (Firth) can't resist dames, and dames can't resist him. Causing him varying degrees of hormonal distress are Sammy (Baxter), a dippy divorcee just waiting for Dick to come and free her sexuality; ex-wife

Anne (Mair-Thomas), now a born-again radical lesbian; and two women whose elegance and sophistication are signalled by their coffee-ad eyebrow-arching: brain surgeon Judith (Gwynne) and lawyer Charlotte (Anthony). The theme of the improbable Don Juan has been thoroughly overhauled by the likes of Truffaut and Woody Allen, and this adds nothing new. It knee-jerks smugly at all the right themes, acknowledging its hero's new-man machismo, but the voice-over continually invites the male viewer to share its wide-eyed bewilderment at the Mystery That Is Woman. The women are stereotyped and manipulative, perverse harridans or cuddlesome love-bunnies. More pain than pleasure. JRo

Pleasure Seekers, The

(Jean Negulesco, 1964, US) Ann-Margret, Tony Franciosa, Carol Lynley, Gardner McKay, Pamela Tiffin, Gene Tierney, Vito Scoti, Brian Keith, Antonio Gades.
107 min.
The box-office recipe for *Three Coins in the Fountain* (three American gals, a glitzy European location, romantic complication) doesn't quite hold good the second time around when director Negulesco tries to repeat the trick in Madrid instead of Rome. Ann-Margret gets most screen time (and has a socko dance number, 'Everything Makes Music When You're in Love', on a Spanish beach) as she pines for a local medic, while Lynley falls for her boss and Tiffin makes a play for aloof playboy Franciosa. Smoothly done in lush CinemaScope, but so contrived its sundry dramatic crises exist in an emotional vacuum. TJ

Pleins Feux sur l'assassin

(Georges Franju, 1960, Fr) Pierre Brasseur, Pascale Audret, Jean-Louis Trintignant, Jean Babilée, Dany Saval, Marianne Koch, Philippe Leroy-Beaulieu.
88 min. b/w.
Characteristically, Franju's adaptation of a story by Boileau-Narcejac (the creators of *Vertigo* and *Les Diaboliques*) negates suspense in favour of a highly pleasurable succession of strange images. An eccentric château-owner (Brasseur) dies, peacefully encased with his favourite wind-up miniature ballerina behind a mirror. With his body unaccounted for, the greedy heirs are legally obliged to wait five years, and devise a *son-et-lumière* to raise funds for the upkeep of the expensive château. Meanwhile, a murderer in their midst begins eliminating future rivals… Franju creates some wonderfully atmospheric monochrome textures, extracts another haunting score from Maurice Jarre, and throws in plenty of absurd humour, as well as a typically fetishistic line-up of doll-like women. The actors are encouraged into striking attitudes, so that emotional conviction is sacrificed for surreal effect. With its unconventional blend of narrative pulp and visual sophistication, the film was a commercial flop, rarely to be seen outside France, until eventually the rediscovery of the original negative gave it a new lease of life. DT

Plein Soleil (Delitto in pieno sole/Blazing Sun/Purple Noon)

(René Clément, 1959, Fr/It) Alain Delon, Marie Laforêt, Maurice Ronet, Elvire Popesco, Erno Crisa, Frank Latimore, Bill Kearns, Romy Schneider.
119 min.
René Clément and Chabrol's collaborator Paul Gégauff got hold of Patricia Highsmith's *The Talented Mr Ripley* decades before Wim Wenders laid hands on the novelist's psychopathic protagonist in *The American Friend*. In his third film appearance, 24-year-old Delon exudes icy charm as Ripley, the emissary sent by an American industrialist to rescue his son (Ronet, sublimely dissolute) from yachting decadence. Delon, though, has a killer scheme of his own – murder the guy, pocket the loot, and steal his girl (Laforêt). Easy. It just takes a thread of steel in the nerves – and a director with the stealth and patience to wind up the tension and avoid rushing the pay-off. Audiences weaned on switchback cutting and adrenalin pace will have to adjust, but even the admittedly clunky first 30 minutes make sense in retrospect. Delon's determined chill aside, there's much to enjoy: a

narrative stitched together with old school expertise; vivid marine camerawork by Henri Decaë; a startling rinky-dink piano score by Nino Rota. TJ

Plenty

(Fred Schepisi, 1985, US) Meryl Streep, Sam Neill, Charles Dance, John Gielgud, Tracey Ullman, Sting, Ian McKellen, André Maranne.
124 min.
David Hare has been laying into the British for so long now, one begins to wonder what they ever did to him. When *Plenty* was first produced on the stage, its compelling vision of our postwar decline, seen through the eyes of a wartime heroine, had its edge dulled by a hectoring moral righteousness. Balance is restored in Schepisi's film, largely by the obvious filmic process of shifting the point of view among the characters. The life of Susan Traherne (Streep) suffers a steady decline alongside the more retrograde incidents of our history (Festival of Britain, Suez), until her only option is to take to the road as a vagrant to try and recapture her former glory as a spy in World War II France, when the world seemed young. Performances all round are excellent, especially Dance as her long-suffering boyfriend, and Gielgud as the last exponent of decency at the Foreign office. Whether or not you buy the message, it's a work that qualifies as epic, and reveals Hare as a great Romantic. CPea

Pleure Pas la Bouche Pleine

see Spring into Summer

Plot

see Attentat, L'

Plot Against Harry, The

(Michael Roemer, 1970, US) Martin Priest, Ben Lang, Maxine Woods, Henry Nemo, Jacques Taylor, Jean Leslie.
81 min. b/w.
Described by the *Village Voice* as 'a deadpan, post-Jarmusch comedy made when Jarmusch was still in grammar school', shot on the streets in black-and-white with sly camera movements and naturalistic sound, Roemer's film is comedy out of *cinéma-vérité*. It looks and feels like Jarmusch, a seriously oblique, cool look at Jewish aspirations and social morality: this perhaps explains why it was shelved until 1989, since no one in 1970 thought it merited release. A two-bit New York Jewish racketeer, Harry Plotnick is released after a 12-month 'vacation' to find his affairs in disarray. The Mob has muscled in on his turf, the tax man is auditing his books, a parole officer is hovering, and his sister's staying over...all this before Harry has even crashed into his ex-wife's car and met a daughter he didn't know he had. It may sound frantic, but in fact the plot takes a back seat to ironic observation. Through it all wanders Martin Priest's magnificently nonplussed Harry, an outsider stoically trying to work his way back in. TCh

Ploughman's Lunch, The

(Richard Eyre, 1983, GB) Jonathan Pryce, Tim Curry, Rosemary Harris, Frank Finlay, Charlie Dore, David De Keyser, Nat Jackley, Bill Paterson.
107 min.
Ian McEwan must have whooped for joy when the Falklands war erupted, transforming his script from an examination of the Suez affair into a much spicier story of shabby English values, set during the Falklands crisis but filtered through the perspective of Suez. Sadly, the resulting film veers wildly in quality, and fails to cast much illumination on either past or present. Pryce turns in a creepingly accurate performance as an ambitious BBC newsroom hack who is commissioned to write a book on Suez while the Falklands war is in progress; but much of the film is concerned with his pursuit of a rich bitch (Dore), whom he fancies precisely because she is (literally) out of his class. It all culminates neatly, but with typically facile signposting of its political analysis, at the 1982 Conservative Party Conference, with the old guard (for which read resurgent Tory traditionalism) triumphing over the middle class upstart (opportunistic liberalism). It's all far too literary for its own good (McEwan indulges himself by including portraits of his bookish mates), and these aren't people you love to hate, they're just people you hate. RR

Plumbum, or a Dangerous Game(Plyumbum, ili opasnaya igra)

(Vadim Abdrashitov, 1986, USSR) Anton Androsov, Yelena Yakovleva, Aleksandr Feklistov, Elena Dmitrieva.
90 min.
A Soviet teenager adopts a code name based on the Latin word for lead, worms his way into the city's underworld gangs, and sets himself up as a supergrass. The special police squad to which Plumbum attaches himself are happy to use him, but when he turns in his own father for poaching, the zealousness with which he is pursuing his clean-up campaign raises some perplexing questions about his methods and motives. Is Plumbum an exemplary citizen, or simply the product of a repressive regime, which delegates only a distorted image of power to one who, like his fellow citizens, had so long been denied it? This was the subject of much controversy and heated debate when first released in the USSR. GA

Plunder

(Tom Walls, 1930, GB) Tom Walls, Ralph Lynn, Robertson Hare, Winifred Shotter, Mary Brough, Doreen Bendix.
98 min. b/w.
Ben Travers' farces, which were immensely popular in the '20s, were filmed at the time with the original casts. *Plunder* (revived at the National Theatre in 1978) is as fine an example of the farceur's art as you will find anywhere, though unusually it contrives to include a violent death. Filmically naive, it nevertheless offers considerable pleasure, not only as the historical recreation of a '20s Aldwych farce, but principally as a showcase for the exemplary acting of Ralph Lynn as the monocled ass, and Tom Walls as a Raffles-type jewel thief of unusually sombre suavity. As the plotting escalates to the correct pitch of frenzy, their interplay and timing remain consistently immaculate. There's also a neat Art Deco set. CPea

Plutonium Circus, The

(George Ratliff, 1994, US)
73 min.
A documentary canvassing opinion on the safety, or otherwise, of the Pantex Plant outside Amarillo, Texas, a Cold War nuclear weapons factory – now devoted to dismantling the weapons. As in Errol Morris's work, what's fascinating here is the sheer eccentricity of so many of Ratliff's subjects: best, probably, is Stanley Marsh III, owner of the Cadillac ranch, crackpot conceptual artist and acerbic wordsmith. GA

Poachers (Furtivos)

(José Luis Borau, 1975, Sp) Lola Gaos, Ovidi Montllor, Alicia Sánchez, Ismael Merlo, José Luis Borau, Felipe Solano.
83 min.
A local Spanish governor, still impetuous and spoilt in middle age, hunts with his cronies in a forest where his former nurse runs an inn. Such insolences as seeing this figure of authority in relation to his childhood nanny underlie much of this muted and beautifully observed film. Spanish publicity for *Furtivos* challenged Franco's description of Spain as 'a peaceful forest' by asking 'What is rotting beneath the silence of a peaceful forest?' Thus, the family tragedy at the film's centre is related on several levels: individual, generational, political, and religious. The nurse, bitter and perhaps incestuous, is usurped by a runaway girl brought to stay by her only son. After years of repression and forced servility, she finally cracks when presented with her son's spontaneous, guilt-free relationship with the girl. Strong performances, photographed with beautiful precision. CPe

Pocahontas

(Mike Gabriel/Eric Goldberg, 1995, US) voices: Irene Bedard, Mel Gibson, David Ogden Stiers, Billy Connolly, Christian Bale, Linda Hunt.
81 min.
Disney's *Pocahontas* can't get stirred dramatically for political correctness, the finale will please nobody, and the songs are duff. That said, there are enough incidental felicities to pass the time pleasantly. A great deal of care went into the depiction of the Native Americans, in particular the gorgeous heroine, but the whites and various pet animals – Meeko the racoon, Flit the hum-

mingbird – come from stock. Given the pompous colonialist views that John Smith has to express, it's just as well they requisitioned the endearingly jivey tones of Gibson for the hero. Pocahontas shows him that the natives live harmoniously in primitive Paradise. He takes her point and they fall in love. The British settlers only want gold, but whether they're all as villainous (Connolly voices one) as mustachioed Gov Ratcliffe and his decadent pug isn't clear. Smith is captured by Pocahontas' father, Chief Powhatan, but she saves his life by offering hers. He then stops a British bullet intended for the Chief. All this self-abnegation carries over into a *Casablanca*-style ending. BC

Pocket Money

(Stuart Rosenberg, 1972, US) Paul Newman, Lee Marvin, Strother Martin, Wayne Rogers, Christine Belford, Kelly Jean Peters, Fred Graham, Hector Elizondo, Terrence Malick.
102 min.
Third of the Rosenberg/Newman collaborations, and a wry, leisurely relief after the heavyweight experiences of *Cool Hand Luke* and *WUSA*. The lazily incongruous character studies of naive Newman, hard-drinking, slow-witted Marvin, and a strong support cast, come from a script by Terrence Malick, revving up on this and the equally off-the-wall *Gravy Train* for his own *Badlands*; while the barest bones of plot (the ill-suited pair stumble through Mexico on a crooked cattle-dealing assignment) are down to the source novel, JPS Brown's *Jim Kane*. PT

Po di Sangui

(Flora Gomes, 1996, Fr/Port/Guinea-Bissau) Ramiro Naka, Bia Gomes, Edna Evora. Dadu Cissé.
90 min.
When the nomad Dou returns to his Guinea-Bissau village to find his twin has died, he's reluctant to take on, according to tradition, his brother's widow and daughter. Things get worse: the village is stricken by drought, and the witch doctor advises his people to abandon their birthplace. Though visually elegant (even if the slow, ornate camera-movements soon begin to irritate), Gomes' film is too obscure for non-African audiences. Included somewhere as an ecological message about the need to preserve trees (which, apparently, contain the villagers' souls), but quite what some scenes in the snail-paced narrative actually mean is likely to remain, for most, a mystery. GA

Poetic Justice

(John Singleton, 1993, US) Janet Jackson, Tupac Shakur, Khandi Alexander, Regina King, Joe Torry, Maya Angelou, Ché J Avery, Lloyd Avery II, Lori Petty.
109 min.
Singleton's follow-up to *Boyz N the Hood* is an honorable failure, a flawed attempt to take black film out of the macho gangsta ghetto. It's the tale of a hairdresser, Justice (Jackson), and a mailman, Lucky (Shakur). Fate throws them together with mutual friends, bickering lovers Iesha (King) and Chicago (Torry), on a road trip up the coast from LA to Oakland. In classic Hollywood style they loathe each other at first, but slowly come to fall in love. Singleton has a feel for the rhythms of black lives and the movie begins promisingly. Intermittent forays into subjectivity are, however, less persuasive: notably the interior monologues in which we hear Justice's poetry. Actually the work of Maya Angelou, these mature, proud declamations don't belong in Justice's mouth: the nadir finds the camera ogling Jackson's curves as she 'writes' Angelou's 'Phenomenal Woman'. But it's when the movie hits the road that trouble really starts. The stop-go motion of the mail van is an appropriate image for the film's lack of momentum, as both couples repeatedly fight and make up, with an alternative image of black experience at each pit stop. Too much cultural baggage for so slight a scenario. TCh

Point, The

(Fred Wolf, 1970, US) voices: Alan Barzman, Mike Lookinland, Paul Frees, Lenny Weinrib.
75 min.
A patchy one-man-band attempt by rock-'n'crooner Harry Nilsson at a children's animated musical fantasy, about a father who tears his son away from watching TV by reading a story

about the Pointed Village, where everything has a point until the birth of a round-headed boy...Made originally for TV, the animation is excellent, and many of the images are given a shot in the arm by a tailor-made score ('the pointless forest' especially), but the whole thing is weighed down by the doughy morality (dare one say 'point'?). Adults who ferret out readings in Puffins will love it; children will probably be reasonably entertained. IB

Point Blank

(John Boorman, 1967, US) Lee Marvin, Angie Dickinson, Keenan Wynn, Carroll O'Connor, Lloyd Bochner, Michael Strong, John Vernon, Sharon Acker, James B Sikking.
92 min.
One of the definitive films to emerge from Hollywood in the late '60s, this hard-nosed adaptation of Richard Stark's The Hunter owed much to the European influences that Boorman brought with him from England. People have noted the influence of Resnais behind the film's time lapses and possible dream setting, but Godard's Alphaville offers a more rewarding comparison. Both films use the gangster/thriller framework to explore the increasing depersonalisation of living in a mechanised urban world. Just as Constantine's Lemmy Caution was a figure from the past stranded in a futuristic setting, so Marvin's bullet-headed gangster is an anachronism from the '50s transported to San Francisco and LA of the '60s, a world of concrete slabs and menacing vertical lines. Double-crossed and left to die, Marvin comes back from the dead to claim his share of the money from the Organization, only to become increasingly puzzled and frustrated when he finds there is no money, because the Organization is the world of big business run by respectable men with wallets full of credit cards. CPe

Point Break

(Kathryn Bigelow, 1991, US) Patrick Swayze, Keanu Reeves, Gary Busey, Lori Petty, John McGinley, James Le Gros, John Philbin.
122 min.
Undercover FBI agent Reeves strips for action and gets into some serious male bonding when he infiltrates the Californian surfing fraternity in search of a gang of bank robbers who call themselves the Ex-Presidents. During the course of the investigation, however, Reeves is seduced by 'spiritual' surfer Swayze's cosmic talk about oneness with the sea, and becomes addicted to the adrenalin rush of life on the edge. Despite this theme of Faustian redemption, the distinction between good and evil is far from black and white, Swayze's reckless craving for danger filling an elemental void in Reeves' hollow soul. There are times when the dialogue is a shade comic, others when the brilliantly staged action set pieces become almost abstract. Plausibility, though, has never been director Bigelow's strong suit, and there's precious little to be found here. Even so, there's enough high-octane, heart-racing excitement for a dozen movies. NF

Point Is to Change It, The (Es Kommt drauf an, sie zu verändern)

(Claudia Alemann, 1973, WGer)
54 min.
A documentary made at a time when feminist theory on unequal pay was in its infancy, this gets at the heart of the problem with considerable precision. For instance: why are women workers often employed in declining industrial sectors? Answer: cheap labour and minimal plant investment go together. 'It's more profitable to employ women than to automate a plant. It's cheaper to sack a woman than to keep a machine idle' With Britain in the throes of 'de-industrialisation', there are lessons here for more than just women. MM

Point of No Return (aka The Assassin)

(John Badham, 1992, US) Bridget Fonda, Gabriel Byrne, Dermot Mulroney, Anne Bancroft, Harvey Keitel, Geoffrey Lewis.
108 min.
Bland Hollywood remake of Luc Besson's Nikita: Fonda plays Maggie, a junkie who kills a cop and is offered the choice of dying or selling her soul to the Government. She chooses the latter, and

under the eye of agent Bob (Byrne) retrains as a killer with feminine wiles. Bob is infatuated with his creation, but can't mix business with pleasure, so, when Maggie emerges as a glamorous hit-woman, he has to stand by while she falls for photographer JP (Mulroney). In the original, stylish direction and committed acting diverted attention from the espionage hocus-pocus. Here we have MTV slickness, bigger-budget action and a Nina Simone soundtrack. CO'S

Point of Order

(Emile de Antonio, 1963, US)
97 min. b/w.
Rejected by the 1963 New York Film Festival because it wasn't 'a real film', de Antonio's debut feature is perhaps the purest expression of his analytical approach to documentary and the 'media-event'. To the raw material of hours of video footage of the 1954 US Army-McCarthy hearings, he brought a radical collagist's technique: constructing an inquiry into the phenomenon of McCarthyism without moving from his editing bench, taking up a camera, or adding a word of commentary; re-democratising the historical documents once dominated by the authority of McCarthy's 'performance'; and opening up an early oppositional direction to cinéma-vérité. PT

Pointsman, The (De Wisselwachter)

(Jos Stelling, 1986, Neth) Jim Van Der Woude, Stéphane Excoffier, John Kraaykamp, Josse De Pauw, Ton Van Dort.
96 min.
Accidentally stepping off a train in the remote Scottish Highlands, a chic Frenchwoman finds herself stranded with a Dutch railway points-operator who leads a lonely, basic existence. Winter falls; as the pair become increasingly isolated, lacking a common language, an intricate, near-silent mating ritual is enacted. The woman, sophisticated and worldly, wears her most provocative clothes to tease never-felt emotions from her virgin acquaintance, until she becomes a captive of his awakened passion. Taking no account of plausibility, Stelling's exploration of the uses and abuses of power is art house fare, but neither obscure nor elitist. Enthralling performances generate a claustrophobic tension, but there's humour too. The director is merciless with the pointsman's few visitors: a leering, randy postman with transparent courtship tactics, an engine driver whose scepticism about the whole affair anticipates that of the audience. EP

Poison

(Todd Haynes, 1990, US) Edith Meeks, Scott Renderer, James Lyons, John R Lombardi, Larry Maxwell, Susan Norman.
85 min.
Inspired by Jean Genet, Haynes' enigmatic movie interweaves three apparently unconnected stories. In 'Hero' (shot in the style of a vox-pop TV documentary on suburban life), a young boy's mother (Meeks), schoolmates and neighbours relate how he disappeared, miraculously, after killing his father; in 'Horror' (reminiscent of '50s B movie sci-fi fantasies), a scientist (Maxwell) isolates the human sex-drive in a serum which turns him into a lethally infectious, grotesque mutant; and 'Homo', a mix of pastoral lyricism and claustrophobic grittiness, portrays the cruel, obsessive love felt by an imprisoned thief (Renderer) for an inmate he first met at reform school. The disparate styles and the absence of clear links between the stories make for unusually provocative viewing, because their shared themes (deviancy, alienation, persecution, monstrousness) are merely implied through the cutting. Compelling and quirkily intelligent; Genet, one feels, would have been impressed. GA

Poison Ivy

(Katt Shea Ruben, 1992, US) Drew Barrymore, Sara Gilbert, Tom Skerritt, Cheryl Ladd.
89 min.
Although marketed as a 'home invasion' thriller in the Single White Female vein – teenage nymphette Ivy (Barrymore) wreaks havoc in the home of rich kid Cooper (Gilbert) by seducing her ex-alcoholic father (Skerritt), supplanting her ailing mother (Ladd), and generally ruining Coop's

life – there is more to Poison Ivy than meets the eye. Distanced from the over-heated emotions and events by Coop's naive voice-over narration – 'I guess you have to give up certain things when you take on a friendship' – we witness much of what happens at one remove. In this and other ways, Ruben subverts the salacious subject matter, while exploring the dangerously ambiguous relationship between anarchic wild child Ivy and emotionally neglected rich kid Coop (an understated, moody performance from Gilbert). Its willingness to take risks, and its insights into the frailties and confusions of teenage friendships ('She might have been lonelier than I was', reflects Coop at the end), lift the film right out of the rut. NF

Police

(Maurice Pialat, 1985, Fr) Gérard Depardieu, Sophie Marceau, Richard Anconina, Pascale Rocard, Sandrine Bonnaire, Franck Karoui, Jonathan Leina.
113 min.
A superficially genial cop (Depardieu) cross-examines a Tunisian drug-dealer. The can of worms is opened, and Depardieu plunges in, laying about the Parisian Arab community, doing deals with their corrupt lawyer, and with a woman (Marceau) who has stolen a suitcase of money. It is all going tougher and more furious than any other recent policier, when the film abruptly changes gear and becomes the chronicle of Depardieu's ill-fated amour for Marceau, a chronic liar, and deep in sin. Pialat is heir to the misanthropic strain in French culture, and dwells at great length on the uncomfortably real. There is no one else who pushes his actors to such uncomfortable extremes. If you want a thriller, then you're in for a rough ride; this is about tension, conflict and hostility, and almost all of it between man and woman. CPea

Police Academy

(Hugh Wilson, 1984, US) Steve Guttenberg, Kim Cattrall, GW Bailey, Bubba Smith, Donovan Scott, George Gaynes, Andrew Rubin, David Graf, Michael Winslow.
96 min.
When entry restrictions to the force are waived by the new mayor of an American city, all manner of kooky cadets flood the cop training shop. This collection of misshapen oddballs and outcasts is put through its paces, and the result is a lot of ideologically unsound humour: women, blacks, gays, fatties, rednecks, psychopaths and nymphomaniacs all get the crass comic stereotype treatment. For this reason, New Puritans should avoid it like the plague; but the crude Carry On charm will delight filmgoers who are in a relaxed and infantile state of mind, and who will lap up the fast-paced flow of cod set pieces. AB

Police Academy 2: Their First Assignment

(Jerry Paris, 1985, US) Steve Guttenberg, Bubba Smith, David Graf, Michael Winslow, Bruce Mahler, Marion Ramsey, Colleen Camp, Howard Hesseman, Art Metrano, George Gaynes, Bobcat Goldthwait.
87 min.
Lacks the unbridled vulgarity of its predecessor, though gags about superglue and enforced anal inspection are naturally allowed to intrude. Six inept rookies are transferred to the 16th Precinct, where they have to contend with both the unscrupulous Lieutenant Mauser (Metrano), whose promotion depends on their flunking, and the local gang of street sociopaths led by a raving loony whose strangulated psychobabble attains pitches of sublime apoplexy (Goldthwait). This will sort out the taste freaks from the trash fans: may the Force be with you. AB

Police Academy 3: Back in Training

(Jerry Paris, 1986, US) Steve Guttenberg, Bubba Smith, David Graf, Michael Winslow, Marion Ramsey, Leslie Easterbrook, Art Metrano, Bobcat Goldthwait, George Gaynes.
84 min.
Due to budget cuts, one of the two police academies in the state has to close, so Lassard's graduates come back to help out. The slim plot is a feeble excuse for a series of set pieces, some of which can be seen coming even before the open-

ing credits roll, and a handful that are genuinely funny. Guttenberg (who cut his teeth on *Diner*) is a natural comedian, but it's Goldthwait who impresses most with a truly awesome performance as Zed, the acid casualty cadet. DPe

Police Academy 4: Citizens on Patrol

(Jim Drake, 1987, US) Steve Guttenberg, Bubba Smith, Michael Winslow, David Graf, Tim Kazurinsky, Sharon Stone, Leslie Easterbrook, Marion Ramsey, GW Bailey, Bobcat Goldthwait, George Gaynes.
87 min.
More of the same from the wackiest police force on the streets, and their newly recruited civilian helpers. Goldfish-loving Commandant Lassard institutes a new community policing programme, and slimy Captain Harris (Bailey) tries to sabotage the operation. Plenty of pigeon-shit, superglue and squirting ketchup sight gags, plus the usual smutty verbal innuendo. Highlights again include Goldthwait's strangulated vocal ejaculations, a couple of Ninja movie naff-dubbing jokes, and a signpost life-saving gag featuring the chesty Easterbrook in a wet T-shirt. NF

Police Academy 5: Assignment Miami Beach

(Alan Myerson, 1988, US) Bubba Smith, David Graf, Michael Winslow, Leslie Easterbrook, Marion Ramsey, Janet Jones, GW Bailey, George Gaynes, Rene Auberjonois.
90 min.
With Guttenberg and Goldthwait having taken their engaging charm and strangulated vocal chords elsewhere, this plumbs new depths of puerile humour. Commandant Lassard having reached retirement age, the devious Captain Harris wants to step into his shoes. Meanwhile, the whole gang flies to Miami to see Lassard receive an award. *En route*, Lassard unwittingly swaps bags with a trio of bungling jewel thieves, and is later kidnapped by them. The *Apocalypse Now*-style Wagnerian soundtrack that accompanies the air boat chase across the Everglades almost raises a smile. Otherwise it's business as usual: fart jokes. NF

Police Academy 6: City Under Siege

(Peter Bonerz, 1989, US) Bubba Smith, David Graf, Michael Winslow, Leslie Easterbrook, Marion Ramsey, Lance Kinsey, Matt McCoy, Bruce Mahler, GW Bailey, George Gayns, Kenneth Mars, Gerrit Graham.
84 min.
Surely the nadir of the rehash genre, a string of unconnected party pieces by a cast whose world weariness would imply that they know exactly how cynical this whole venture has become. With Guttenberg long gone and his space duly filled by a lookalike cutie, the gang are hot on the trail of a mastermind villain knee-deep in burglary and real estate fraud. One by one, the scriptwriters manoeuvre each wacky funster into position to perform his or her zany turn. The finest moment features a rap performed by three 'dudes' who have clearly recorded the vocals *a cappella*, over which the Neanderthals in post-production have dubbed some backing music. The fact that said music is in a different time signature to the rapping hasn't occurred to anyone, so we are treated to a surrealist fusion of rap and morse code: the only arresting moment in a mind-numbingly tedious film. MK

Police Academy 7: Mission to Moscow

(Alan Metter, 1994, US) George Gaynes, Michael Winslow, David Graf, GW Bailey, Leslie Easterbrook, Christopher Lee, Ron Perlman.
82 min
Maybe the stringent environmental protection laws in the States prevented the producers from filming their dirty work on home territory, but this time they fled to Russia, where the boys and girls in blue have been called in by Lee's desperate Moscow cop to take on Perlman's rampant Mafia mobster and generally kick butsky. Lame, sloppy, cackhanded, utterly redundant – put succinctly, the very worst of the series. TJ

Police Story

(William Graham, 1973, US) Vic Morrow, Edward Asner, Diane Baker, Sandy Baron, Chuck Connors, Harry Guardino, Ralph Meeker, John Bennett Perry, Ina Balin.
100 min.
LA cop Joseph Wambaugh turned writer to tell it like it was/is, and his first books, *The New Centurions* and *The Blue Knight*, quickly became movie and (award winning) TV mini-series respectively. Wooed some more by the small screen, he created *Police Story* and served on the often marvellous series as consultant. This is the pilot, released here as a movie. Directed with his usual authority by Graham, arguably the most subtle and mature of small screen specialists, it offers a chance to see Asner in pre *Lou Grant* days, teamed with such excellent but unsung actors as Morrow, Guardino and Meeker. Disturbed by the way Hollywood treated his novels, Wambaugh turned producer for *The Onion Field*, but the result was more meaningful than muscular. CW

Police Story (Jingcha Gushi)

(Jackie Chan, 1985, HK) Jackie Chan, Briget Lin, Maggie Cheung, Chua Yuen, Bill Tung, Kenneth Tong.
100 min.
A Hong Kong pot-noodle-boiler which nevertheless manages to stir-fry a mixture of chop-socky, slapstick and stunts into a heavier *Dirty Harry*-ish framework. As the cop assigned to protect a gangster's moll turned prosecution witness, Jackie Chan – part Bruce Lee and part Michael Crawford – has to contend with an impatient girlfriend, bent cop, and sue-happy lawyer, as well as the bad guys. He also performs some eye-popping stunts, such as hanging from the top of a speeding double-decker by a walking stick. The climactic chop-out amidst the shattering glass of a shopping mall is fairly well done, but it's a measure of the story's weakness that the most fascinating moments arrive in the form of an end-credits montage of outtakes and behind-the-scenes set-ups of the action sequences. Chan, however, is poetry in motion. AB

Pollux et le Chat Bleu

see Dougal and the Blue Cat

Poltergeist

(Tobe Hooper, 1982, US) JoBeth Williams, Craig T Nelson, Beatrice Straight, Dominique Dunne, Oliver Robbins, Heather O'Rourke, Michael McManus, Zelda Rubinstein.
114 min.
Credited to Hooper, but every inch a Spielberg film, this is a barnstorming ghost story, set in one of the small suburban houses Spielberg knows and loves, where the family canary is called Tweety, and the kids read Captain America comics and eat at the Pizza Hut. Gradually this impossibly safe world is (in a truly ingenious plot development) invaded by something inside the family television. Soon the plot takes off into a delirious fight with demonic forces suggestive of nothing so much as a Walt Disney horror movie; and although the sub-religious gobbledegook (including a tiresome midget medium) is hard to take, it is consistently redeemed by its creator's dazzling sense of craft. For this one, Spielberg has even contrived a structural surprise which leaves the audience spinning like one of his house's haunted rooms, and arguably matches the opening of *Psycho* in its impudent virtuosity. DP

Poltergeist 2: The Other Side

(Brian Gibson, 1986, US) JoBeth Williams, Craig T Nelson, Heather O'Rourke, Oliver Robins, Zelda Rubinstein, Will Sampson, Julian Beck, Geraldine Fitzgerald.
91 min.
Some people never learn. The Freeling family sensibly quit their hole in the ground at Cuesta Verde and take refuge with Granma Jess, who recognises a fellow clairvoyant in little Carol Anne. Soon the psychic forces are shaking up their domestic life, and a cadaverous stranger seems determined to take the blonde moppet back into the other world. Enter Munchkin medium Tangina (Rubinstein) and an all-wise Red Indian (Sampson) to join in the battle, and the old tug-of-war is noisily enacted again. This sequel, *sans* Spielberg but obedient to his spirit, simply

fails to regenerate the original's gut-grinding fears that make you dread ever scratching a spot again. And the contribution of Giger's design work has only added one near-unwatchable sequence. DT

Poltergeist III

(Gary Sherman, 1988, US) Tom Skerritt, Nancy Allen, Heather O'Rourke, Zelda Rubinstein, Lara Flynn Boyle, Kip Wentz, Richard Fire, Nathan Davis.
98 min.
A low-budget sequel which tries, and fails, to make a virtue out of adversity by substituting cheap mechanical effects for the expensive light and magic of I and II. Little Carol Anne (O'Rourke), now living with her uncle (Skerritt) and aunt (Allen) in an ultra-modern Chicago condominium, attends a school for exceptionally gifted but emotionally disturbed children. But the Preacher of Pain is still on her trail, so her guardians team up with diminutive psychic Tangina (Rubinstein), who says it's all done with mirrors. Small consolation for those trapped in the iced-over swimming pool or the building's increasingly erratic lifts! A couple of choice moments cannot compensate for a threadbare scenario bereft of attention-grabbing visual effects. Sadly, talented young O'Rourke passed over to the other side herself shortly after the film was completed: a shame that this mundane movie will be her celluloid epitaph. NF

Polyester

(John Waters, 1981, US) Divine, Tab Hunter, Edith Massey, Mink Stole, David Samson, Joni Ruth White, Mary Garlington, Ken King.
86 min.
Likely to be criticised for being less than murky Waters, even with its 'Odorama' card to scratch for olfactory pleasures/displeasures; but then it's clear from an opening helicopter shot that bad taste has found the budget to go middle of the road. Divine, as a Baltimore housewife with the cultural aspirations of Mary Whitehouse on speed, is now virtually indistinguishable from the Liz Taylor of *The Mirror Crack'd*. Spurned in family life by an unfaithful husband, a contemptuous disco-queen daughter, and a glue-sniffing son with a vicious bent towards foot fetishism – but undeterred by her dog's suicide – she relives the dreams of all '50s queens and finds solace in the arms of Tab Hunter. OK, so it's not *The Cherry Orchard*, but who can resist a film where a massive drive-in billboard proclaims 'Now showing – Three Great Marguerite Duras Hits'. SM

Polygraph, The (Le Polygraphe)

(Robert Lepage, 1996, Can/Fr/Ger) Patrick Goyette, Marie Brassard, Peter Stormare, Maria de Medeiros, Josée Deschênes.
104 min.
Do memories – or lie-detectors – always reveal the truth? That's just one of questions raised by Lepage's ambitious but occasionally clumsy follow-up to *The Confessional*. Did François murder his lover two years ago? His neighbour, Lucie – playing, as it happens, the dead woman in a film being made by the latter's friend – finds him gentle and supportive, but then she's too busy with her own new, mysterious lover (Stormare, the psycho from *Fargo*) to realise that François was once a prime suspect. If this complex, visually adventurous exploration of memory, guilt and the strange connections between apparently unconnected people and events may be seen as another oddball Hitchcockian pastiche, it's also rather too contrived for its own good. Very watchable, nevertheless. GA

Pont du Nord, Le

(Jacques Rivette, 1981, Fr) Bulle Ogier, Pascale Ogier, Jean-François Stévenin, Pierre Clémenti, Mathieu Schiffman.
131 min.
A movie that pushes the conspiratorial playfulness of Rivette's *Céline and Julie* in directions both maddening and magical. Ogier and her daughter Pascale are here the crossed-paths comrades impulsively taking up the silent challenge of the city's codes: hopscotching the map of Paris' arrondissements and turning it into a life-size outdoor board game. As ever in Rivette's labyrinthine re-imaginings of the urban obstacle

course, the rules and goals are obscure while the allusive clues, keys and signposts multiply alarmingly. Underworld and wonderland merge in the open air; joyous whimsy blurs with justified worry; and Rivette risks exploring the scarifying powers of fantasy and paranoia with a panning, punning documentary eye. With so many oblique strategies, a little irritation is inevitable...but if you could possibly imagine a pre-micro *Tron*, the leaps of faith needed here shouldn't be difficult. PT

Pony Soldier
(Joseph M Newman, 1952, US) Tyrone Power, Cameron Mitchell, Thomas Gomez, Robert Horton, Penny Edwards.
82 min.
Unexceptional Western with Power as the Mountie on a mission to the US to stop Mitchell and his Cree Indians from launching an all out attack. There are white captives to be rescued, too, in a movie that builds to a finale patched together from borrowed bits of Wellman's *Buffalo Bill* (1944). TJ

Pookie
see Sterile Cuckoo, The

Pool of London
(Basil Dearden, 1950, GB) Bonar Colleano, Susan Shaw, Renee Asherson, Earl Cameron, Moira Lister, Max Adrian, Joan Dowling, James Robertson Justice, Alfie Bass, Leslie Phillips, George Benson, Victor Maddern.
85 min. b/w.
After the success of the police drama *The Blue Lamp* (1949), Basil Dearden and Ealing studios continued in what passed for a realist vein with this tale of merchant seaman Colleano's involvement in a diamond smuggling racket and his subsequent flight when he becomes chief suspect in a murder investigation. Few surprises in the story, but the location work in the bustling Docklands captures a time and place now gone forever. TJ

Poor Cow
(Kenneth Loach, 1967, GB) Carol White, Terence Stamp, John Bindon, Kate Williams, Queenie Watts, Geraldine Sherman.
101 min.
Not a patch upon Loach's best work, largely because he falls into all the usual traps of kitchen sink realism as he follows the fortunes of a dismal teenage waif (White), saddled with a criminal husband (Bindon, typecast), living with a prostitute aunt (Watts) while he's inside, falling for the husband's mate (Stamp), then going back to the aunt and further troubles when he gets nicked too. Relentlessly sordid, and not helped by the unusual move (for Loach) of using name actors. GA

Popdown
(Fred Marshall, 1968, GB) Diane Keen, Jane Bates, Zoot Money, Carol Rachell, Debbie Slater, Bill Aron.
98 min.
An embarrassingly dated and tedious tour of Swinging '60s London (mini-skirts and Hank Marvin glasses everywhere), as bizarrely undertaken by two camera-clicking aliens, Aries and Sagittarius (Bates, Money). Crazy, man. Though not enough so to prevent it from being rapidly cut down to 54 minutes for release. IB

Pope Joan
(Michael Anderson, 1972, GB) Liv Ullmann, Olivia de Havilland, Lesley-Anne Down, Trevor Howard, Jeremy Kemp, Patrick Magee, Franco Nero, Maximilian Schell.
132 min.
Based on a legend about a woman who became Pope in the 9th century in the guise of a man, and who was torn apart by an angry crowd when her deception was discovered, this was stripped free of the contemporary frame (shown in America) in which Joan reappears as a modern lass who believes herself to be the reincarnation of the 9th century Pope. What's left is a rough and often painfully clumsy costume epic with the usual love story underneath it all, and chauvinistic presumptions abounding. Against all odds, Ullmann gives a remarkable performance, and it could have been a gem of a subject had it been handled by a woman director. VG

Pope Must Die, The
(Peter Richardson, 1991, GB) Robbie Coltrane, Beverly D'Angelo, Herbert Lom, Alex Rocco, Paul Bartel, Balthazar Getty, William Hootkins, Robert Stephens, Annette Crosbie, Salvatore Cascio, John Sessions, Peter Richardson, Adrian Edmondson.
99 min.
Coltrane plays a portly priest appointed Pope due to a clerical mix-up: Father Albini is a smiling front-man for the masons, mafiosi and gunrunners who run the Vatican Bank, while Father Albinizi (Coltrane) is a rock'n'rolling, really rather useless priest holed up in a rural orphanage filled with photogenic *bambini*. Like John Goodman's King Ralph, Pope Dave I must locate reserves of greatness beneath his unpromising exterior; discover that the love of a good woman is incompatible with his office; and finally waddle back to obscurity. The Vatican he inherits is staffed by chain-smoking, poker-playing prelates with hip-flasks under their robes. Coltrane manages his few moments of Papal grandeur with something approaching true dignity, whether it's sweeping out the money-lenders from the Bank, delivering an impromptu sermon on the hellfire awaiting a jobsworth, or administering extreme unction. There are many good laughs, albeit of a rather simple-minded nature, but even by its own ludicrous standards the plot unravels helplessly towards the end. A pontiff's egg. SFe

Pope of Greenwich Village, The
(Stuart Rosenberg, 1984, US) Eric Roberts, Mickey Rourke, Daryl Hannah, Geraldine Page, Kenneth McMillan, Tony Musante, M Emmet Walsh, Burt Young, Val Avery.
120 min.
A sad re-run of the *Mean Streets* idea (awkwardly adapted by Vincent Patrick from his own admirable novel): the excellent Mickey Rourke, dipping in and out of the New York Italian underworld, just can't keep tabs on his wild young protégé (Roberts, in a performance about five miles over the top). It lacks virtually everything that made Scorsese's film great, although there is a characteristically fine performance from Burt Young as Bedbug Eddie, the local Mafia boss. The final confrontation, in which Bedbug threatens to remove Rourke's right hand, gives the right chill, which the rest can't match. CPea

Popeye
(Robert Altman, 1980, US) Robin Williams, Shelley Duvall, Ray Walston, Paul Dooley, Paul L Smith, Richard Libertini, Donald Moffat.
114 min.
With neither production companies (Paramount and Disney, for Heaven's sakes!) nor critics able to make up their minds what a maverick iconoclast like Altman was doing turning EC Segar's comic strip into a live-action musical, this film was virtually doomed to failure and neglect. Certainly, with Williams giving a virtuoso fast-mumbling performance as the hero, and gags ranging from expertly choreographed slapstick to subtle verbal infelicities (Popeye muttering about 'venerable disease'), it is far too sophisticated to function merely as kids' fodder. Nor is its story – in which Popeye searches for his lost Pappy while courting Olive Oyl – any less discursive, fragmented or off-the-wall than Altman's finest work. Indeed, the film may be seen as a weird and wonderful variation on the *McCabe and Mrs Miller* theme, with the immaculately designed township of Sweethaven, the vividly drawn characters, and Harry Nilsson's songs of inarticulacy all contributing to a portrait of a bizarre society at once recognisably human and fantastically dreamlike. Often, watching the actors contorting themselves into non-human shapes, you wonder how on earth Altman did it; equally often, you feel you are watching a wacky masterpiece, the like of which you've never seen before. GA

Pop Gear
(Frederic Goode, 1965, GB) Matt Monro, Susan Maughan, The Animals, The Honeycombs, The Rockin' Berries, Herman's Hermits, The Nashville Teens, The Four Pennies, Billy J Kramer and the Dakotas.
68 min.
An end-of-'64 round-up of fab numbers introduced by Jimmy Savile, sung one after another under

conditions of extreme commercial duress, and bookended with Beatles clips. It's the moment when the Beat Boom has just been co-opted: each pancake-encrusted group pouts and plays to the camera, allowed only neutered movement and looking confused all round. For hipster and historian alike it's fascinating (The Four Pennies perform Leadbelly's *Black Girl*, which they've obviously just discovered for themselves; Tommy Quickly does a novelty version of early ska classic *Humpty Dumpty*; Eric Burdon looks menacing among the Christmas decorations; and Stevie Windwood is obviously under the age of consent). It also demonstrates to the rock fashionmonger of today the reactionary context from which those stilettoes and stretch pants really evolved. CR

Porcile
see Pigsty

Pork Chop Hill
(Lewis Milestone, 1959, US) Gregory Peck, Harry Guardino, George Shibata, Woody Strode, Rip Torn, James Edwards, George Peppard, Robert Blake.
97 min. b/w.
A film that might have been an only slightly lesser echo of Milestone's marvellous *A Walk in the Sun* in its concern for the individual soldier and the collective pointlessness of war (Korea in this case). It details (quite brilliantly) the bloody assault on a hill of no particular strategic value (no sooner taken than it's abandoned) except that winning it will mean that the general staff will be speaking from strength at the truce talks already under way. Compromise is evident in the way Peck plays the lead as a gung-ho John Wayne (in the real action on which the story is based, the lieutenant commanding the assault was apparently untried and more than fallible); but pre-release tampering also introduced a note of jingoism into Peck's final voice-off after the carnage ('Millions live in freedom today because of what they did') which was contrary to Milestone's intentions and contrary to the tone of the film itself. Impressive, nevertheless, and with fine performances. TM

Porky's
(Bob Clark, 1981, Can) Dan Monahan, Mark Herrier, Wyatt Knight, Roger Wilson, Cyril O'Reilly, Tony Ganios, Kaki Hunter, Kim Cattrall, Susan Clark, Alex Carras.
98 min.
Writer/director Clark shifts the *American Graffiti* formula to a '50s Florida high school to mount a runaway farce fuelled by the agonies of adolescent sexual frustration. The resulting American box-office bonanza made it the *Animal House* of 1982, and Clark convincingly captures a tone of masochistic agony as his randy kids are derided, exploited and generally humiliated by the adults around them. There are plenty of sexual gags, but the basic plot is as innocently Oedipal as *Jack the Giant Killer* as the gang desperately attempt to defeat nightclub owners, parents, and policemen armed with glistening truncheons in their quest for sexual experience. Despite its thinly liberal veneer, it's as reactionary as a smash-and-grab raid, but it's vulgar enough to be fascinating even while you hate it, and it's certainly the most revealing American success since *Taps*. DP

Porky's II: The Next Day
(Bob Clark, 1983, Can) Dan Monahan, Wyatt Knight, Mark Herrier, Roger Wilson, Cyril O'Reilly, Tony Ganios, Kaki Hunter.
98 min.
The students from the Florida high school are putting on an evening of Shakespeare – cue for much Pucking around – but they run up against the Righteous Flock (who condemn the Bard as obscene) and the Ku Klux Klan (who object to Romeo being played by a Seminole). Matters are resolved in a mess of grotesque caricature, knicker standing, and four-letter filth. This is the perfect film for puerile people who fall about at the merest hint of big dicks, big tits, snakes in the toilet, fairies, foreskins and men in drag. In short, it's a load of old garbage...and shamefully funny. AB

Porky's Revenge
(James Komack, 1985, Can) Dan Monahan, Wyatt Knight, Tony Ganios, Mark Herrier, Kaki Hunter, Scott Colomby, Nancy Parsons.
92 min.
It's graduation time, and the oldest bunch of high

school kids since *Grease*, still in search of the true nature of sex, are together again in a series of witless capers, tenuously linked with attempts to win the interstate basketball championship and put one over on their old adversary, den-of-vice owner Porky. It's all surprisingly tame, with raunch and humour conspicuous by their absence; and structurally it's a mess, nothing more than a series of unconnected events thrown together in no particular order. GO

Porridge
(Dick Clement, 1979, GB) Ronnie Barker, Richard Beckinsale, Fulton Mackay, Brian Wilde, Peter Vaughan, Julian Holloway, Geoffrey Bayldon, Christopher Godwin.
93 min.
'I'm used to this kind of food, I went to Harrow' admits a disgraced dentist over his lunch. Prison life as conceived in *Porridge* is indeed about as punishing an ordeal as boarding school, and because links with a tougher and nastier reality are very, very tenuous, the film is in fact unobjectionable and quite funny. Far funnier and better constructed than the dread phrase 'TV spin-off' would imply, and still firmly under the control of screenwriters Dick Clement and Ian La Frenais (also credited, respectively, as director and producer). Beckinsale and Barker are excellent as the Laurel and Hardy duo of cons who find themselves breaking in, rather than out of the nick. Another definite plus is the use of Chelmsford Prison (empty since a fire the previous year) as principal location. JS

Portaborse, Il
see Footman, The

Porte aperte
see Open Doors

Porte des Lilas (Gates of Paris/Gate of Lilacs)
(René Clair, 1957, Fr) Pierre Brasseur, Georges Brassens, Henri Vidal, Dany Carrel, Raymond Bussières, Annette Poivre.
95 min. b/w.
An alcoholic stumblebum (Brasseur) befriends a dashing but amoral young hoodlum (Vidal) with predictably sombre results. The absolute last gasp of French poetic realism, engulfed only two years later by the tidal New Wave, whose airy location shooting made Clair's suffocating studiobound 'realism' hard to differentiate from the socalled 'poetry'. Of interest, though, as the sole venture into film of the bardic guitarist Brassens. GAd

Portes de la Nuit, Les (Gates of the Night)
(Marcel Carné, 1946, Fr) Pierre Brasseur, Yves Montand, Nathalie Nattier, Serge Reggiani, Jean Vilar, Saturnin Fabre, Mady Berry, Raymond Bussières, Julien Carette.
106 min. b/w.
Perhaps unwisely, despite Vilar's fine performance, Destiny is personified in this tail-end example of the Carné-Prévert collaboration, offering doom-laden warnings which the characters ignore as they rush to meet their fates. Carné wasn't too happy about Prévert's dated populism, evident here in the suggestion that France's legacy from the Occupation was a heroic working class and a bourgeoisie of collaborators or profiteers. Stemming from this, the film's main problem is its contrived characters, only helped by Brasseur at his most hysterical, with Montand and Nattier hopelessly inadequate in roles written for Gabin and Dietrich. Only Reggiani really impresses as a young collaborator tormented by self-loathing. The evocation of nocturnal Paris (the action takes place from dusk to dawn) is hauntingly beautiful, but this is a hollow film. TM

Portes tournantes, Les
see Revolving Doors, The

Portland Street Blues (Hongxing Shisan Mei)
(Raymond Yip, 1998, HK) Sandra Ng, Kristy Yeung, Alex Fong, Shu Qi, Ng Mang-Tat, Noel Chik.
114 min.
A spin off from the *Young and Dangerous* series, telling the life story of Sister 13 (Sandra Ng, terrific), the Hung Hing gang's lesbian branch leader in Mongkok, a character introduced in *Young and Dangerous IV*. Sister 13 has 'felt like a boy' since childhood, but went through a quasi-hetero phase when she and a girlfriend had to flee into China and found themselves rivals for the attention of gang-member/boxer Coke (Fong, authentically dishy). But the constant struggle to compensate for her father's endless mistakes and a friendship with the vengeful junkie prostitute Scarface (Shu, amazing) helped her to realise her true sexuality – and won her status in the gang. The flashback structure and back-story elements are a touch over complicated, but nothing matters much other than Sister 13 herself: a plausible, non-iconic dyke at the centre of a broadly realistic thriller. Three cheers. TR

Port of Shadows
see Quai des Brumes, Le

Portrait of a Lady, The
(Jane Campion, 1996, GB/US) Nicole Kidman, Barbara Hershey, John Malkovich, Martin Donovan, Mary Louise Parker, Shelley Winters, Richard E Grant, Shelley Duvall, Christian Bale, Viggo Mortensen, John Gielgud.
144 min.
Henry James' masterpiece has long been deemed impossible to translate successfully into film; Jane Campion and screenwriter Laura Jones have, however, produced an adaptation as cinematically intelligent as it is faithful to the original. Beginning, adventurously but wisely, with Isabel Archer (Kidman) rejecting Lord Warburton's proposal of marriage, the film charts the changes in its young American heroine's fortunes when, after inheriting a fortune put her way by ailing English cousin Ralph Touchett (Donovan), she travels to Italy, where she's introduced by her mentor Madame Merle (Hershey) to widowed aesthete Gilbert Osmond (Malkovich). Though a friend advises her to wed a long-time admirer who's followed her from America, and Ralph would prefer her to remain true to her free-spirited ideals, Isabel is tempted by Osmond's courtship. Besides the uniformly fine performances, what makes the film so rewarding – and challenging – is its refusal to soften or sentimentalise James' study of New World innocence unprotected against Old World experience. With Stuart Dryburgh's stunning 'Scope camerawork, and a number of audaciously imaginative sequences (notably Isabel's erotic fantasy, and a Dali-esque, b/w 'silent' short to evoke her Grand Tour), this is as far from heritage flummery as you can get. GA

Portrait of a '60% Perfect' Man: Billy Wilder (Portrait d'un Homme 'à 60% Parfait': Billy Wilder)
(Annie Tresgot, 1980, Fr) Billy Wilder, Jack Lemmon, Walter Matthau, IAL Diamond, Michel Ciment.
58 min.
This is Wilder on Wilder, really, even though he's intelligently interviewed by Michel Ciment (film critic from *Positif*), affectionately talked about by Lemmon and Matthau, and the whole is filmed with style by Annie Tresgot. Because the cunning old professional knows exactly where he wants the film to go: he's as capable of directing, with humour, from in front of as from behind the camera. Lovely stuff. HM

Portrait of a Young Girl at the End of the '60s in Brussels
(Chantal Akerman, 1993, Fr) Circé, Julien Rassam, Joelle Marlier, Cynthia Rodberg.
59 min.
A semi-autobiographical portrait of a young girl's final day at school – she quits, that is – in 1968, which she spends playing hookie with a young army deserter she meets at a cinema, and later partying with him and her best pal Danièle (who may be her secret love). It's a talky movie, shot on the hoof through the streets of Brussels. Fresh, gentle and touching – and not at all 'minimalist'.

Portrait of Jason
(Shirley Clarke, 1967, US) Jason Holliday i.e. Aaron Paine.
100 min. b/w.
Shirley Clarke's third feature is almost as straightforward as its title. It picks up the passionate interest in ghetto subcultures that Clarke established in *The Connection* and *The Cool World*, but this time without feeling any need to create a fiction: *Portrait of Jason* is simply a two-hour conversation with a middle-aged, black, homosexual prostitute. The new simplicity of approach reflects the enormous influence of Andy Warhol on independent film-making in the '60s: a new trust in basic film-making techniques, and a new distrust of 'artifice' like editing. Jason himself certainly provides enough artifice to keep any audience engrossed: his colourful, self-mocking account of his life reveals a great deal about the situation of a ghetto boy with 'whiteboy fever'. The moral catch is that by fulfilling Jason's dreams of himself as a 'performer', the movie deliberately pushes him out of his own control...TR

Portrait of Jennie
(William Dieterle, 1948, US) Jennifer Jones, Joseph Cotten, Ethel Barrymore, Lillian Gish, Cecil Kellaway, David Wayne, Henry Hull, Florence Bates.
86 min. b/w & col.
A companion piece to the Dieterle/Selznick *Love Letters*, also starring Jones and Cotten; but where the earlier film remained rooted in superior romantic hokum, this one takes wing into genuine romantic fantasy through its tale of a love that transcends space and time as Cotten's struggling artist meets, falls in love with, and is inspired by a strangely ethereal girl (Jones) whom he eventually realises is the spirit of a woman long dead. Direction and performances are superb throughout, but the real star is Joseph August's camera, which conjures pure magic out of the couple's tender odyssey, from the gravely quizzical charm of their first encounter in snowy Central Park (when she is still a little girl, strangely dressed in clothes of bygone days) through to the awesome storm at sea that supernaturally heralds their final parting. Buñuel saw it and of course approved: 'It opened up a big window for me'. TM

Portrait of Teresa (Retrato de Teresa)
(Pastor Vega, 1979, Cuba) Daisy Granados, Adolfo Llaurado, Alina Sanchez Alberto Molina.
103 min.
Havana housewife and mother, textile worker and convener of her factory's cultural group: Teresa has to balance the demands of an exhausting triple day, coping all the while with conspicuous lack of cooperation from her husband and other Cuban heels. Notable among their number is a television interviewer whose oily machismo is an acute indictment of the female image projected by the media. The archaic attitudes and insulting assumptions that confront working women, even after a revolution, are sketched in with a skilful lightness of touch. Vega directs in bright primary colours, and with a fine eye for the minute but revealing moments and movements of daily life. SJo

Portrait of the Artist as a Young Man, A
(Joseph Strick, 1977, GB) Bosco Hogan, TP McKenna, John Gielgud, Rosaleen Linehan, Maureen Potter, Niall Buggy, Brian Murray.
92 min.
A prosaic and reverential treatment of the didactic high points of James Joyce's novel, which provides at best an occasional reminder of his gleeful contempt for that uniquely Irish blend of political and religious duplicity. But Strick's view of Ireland as the subject of a coffee table movie gives no sense of 'the sow that eats her farrow'. JPy

Portraits Chinois
(Martine Dugowson, 1996, Fr/GB) Helena Bonham Carter, Romane Bohringer, Marie Trintignant, Elsa Zylberstein, Yvan Attal, Jean-Philippe Ecoffey, Miki Manojlovic, Jean-Claude Brialy.
123 min.

A flat-warming party on the Left Bank brings together design assistant Bonham Carter, her partner, screenwriter Ecoffey, vain movie director Attal, his womanising producer Manojlovic, shy couture assistant Bohringer, and even more neurotic Zylberstein, who winds up tearful in the loo. The presence of the last two reminds us of writer/director Dugowson's startling debut *Mina Tannenbaum*, but her approach here takes in a wider ensemble, eases up on the melodrama, and develops its insights cumulatively. We see how these friends and co-workers negotiate their relationships through a swath of infidelities, creative rivalries and secret romances, each remaining true only to him or herself. While the tone's predominantly light, some of the actors take their chances better than others. Unfortunately, Bonham Carter's central performance (in creditable French) is too busy and bitty, in the process filleting the emotional core from the film. Even so, Dugowson's deft attentiveness to her characters' inner lives shows the instinctive flair of a film-maker who will doubtless continue to get better and better. TJ

Portuguese Goodbye, A (Um Adeus Português)
(Joao Botelho, 1985, Port) Rui Furtado, Isabel de Castro, Maria Cabral, Fernando Heitor, Cristina Hauser.
85 min. b/w & col.
In Portuguese Africa in 1973, a small platoon of soldiers is stranded, prey both to an unseen guerrilla enemy and to their own doubts about the war they are waging. Twelve years on, an elderly couple, still mourning the death of their son in the African campaign, make one last visit to their surviving children, now grown up and living in Lisbon. Botelho's delicately mesmerising film interweaves these two simple stories, and achieves a contemplative serenity not unlike that of Ozu; hardly surprising or inappropriate in that the contemporary story is indeed a Portuguese update of the Japanese master's *Tokyo Story*. As the reunion gives rise to painful memories and barely expressed tension, the film charts the family's disappointments and losses with a dry-eyed melancholy, gently proposing a stoic resignation as a response to life's vicissitudes. Botelho never quite matches the emotional power of his mentor. Nevertheless, this is one fine film; watch it peacefully and patiently, and be moved. GA

Poseidon Adventure, The
(Ronald Neame, 1972, US) Gene Hackman, Ernest Borgnine, Red Buttons, Carol Lynley, Roddy McDowall, Stella Stevens, Shelley Winters, Jack Albertson, Leslie Nielsen.
117 min.
The Big Upturned Ship film, with God and the Rev Gene Hackman leading a motley crew to the top – no, sorry, to the bottom – of the SS *Poseidon*, capsized by high waves in one of Irwin Allen's sea-tanks. They mount an outsize Christmas tree, clamber through kitchens, wriggle along ventilator shafts, battling all the while with personal crises and water, water, water. It's a terrific piece of junk: the top-notch screenwriters (Stirling Silliphant and Wendell Mayes) never let a cliché slip through the net, and Neame's anaemic direction ensures that every absurdity is treated at face value. GB

Positively True Adventures of the Alleged Texas Cheerleader-Murdering Mom, The
(Michael Ritchie, 1993, US) Holly Hunter, Beau Bridges, Swoosie Kurtz, Gregg Henry, Matt Frewer, Fred Koehler, Frankie Ingrassia.
105 min.
This sharply satirical slice of true-life Americana is a gift for *Smile* director Ritchie, whose films and themes it uncannily parallels. Hunter is by turns charming, chilling and oddly sympathetic as the ambitious Baptist mother ruthlessly promoting her daughter's ill-fated campaign to become a high-school cheerleader. Flatly lit TV interview footage after the incident is intercut with dramatisations of the lead-up to Hunter's arrest and trial for solicitation to murder her daughter's rival. Ritchie captures the texture of small-town Texan life and the mad scramble for TV rights to the story. (Made for cable.) NF

Posse
(Kirk Douglas, 1975, US) Kirk Douglas, Bruce Dern, Bo Hopkins, James Stacy, Luke Askew, David Canary, Alfonso Arau, Katharine Woodville.
93 min.
A post-Watergate Western reflecting a profound mistrust of the motives of politicians, and framing its story within the ironic cry: 'To the polls, ye sons of freedom!' The small township is shown to be as much a prey to Douglas' ambitious, uptight marshal, bucking for the US Senate, as it is to the man he's tracking down, a 'ruthless' outlaw (Dern, being generously allowed to steal the film). With its picture of America in the making (on the make) – early baseball, carefully conspicuous ads for Bulova and Schlitz, and the ubiquitous photographer recording everything for posterity – the film painstakingly attempts to locate the roots of contemporary malaise. That it doesn't work, as such, is a result of the general *naiveté* of its reversals of the standard good guy/bad guy format. But what emerges is a likeable Western, pleasantly subversive, crisply photographed, and despite some padding, engagingly put together. CPe

Posse
(Mario Van Peebles, 1993, US) Mario Van Peebles, Stephen Baldwin, Billy Zane, Charles Lane, Salli Richardson, Melvin Van Peebles.
111 min.
This 'New Jack' Western shoots off in all directions but never hits home. There's much historical revisionism on offer – one third of cowboys were black, apparently – but the only source material that really counts here is old movies (*The Wild Bunch*, *The Magnificent Seven*, and, especially, Leone). A refugee from the Spanish-American war, Mario Van Peebles' Jessie Lee leads a band of deserters west to Cutter's Town, where he has a score to settle. On his tail is sadistic Colonel Graham (Zane) and his 'Iron Brigade'. The jarring 1990s sensibility of this over-directed, under-written movie extends to style as well as content. Worst of all is the blatantly fetishistic attitude the director adopts towards his posturing macho star. TCh

Possessed
(Curtis Bernhardt, 1947, US) Joan Crawford, Van Heflin, Raymond Massey, Geraldine Brooks, Stanley Ridges, John Ridgely, Moroni Olsen.
108 min.
Crawford may play a nurse, but she'd need a warehouse of Phensics to clear up her troubles in this one. Madly in love with *nogoodnik* Heflin, she chooses to marry her wealthy employer (Massey) after his own ailing wife has tottered into insanity and suicide. Joan totters the same way soon after, and no one in the '40s could do it with such steely eyes or tautened shoulders. And she's helped every inch of the way by the Warners melodrama machine, working at fever pitch under the direction of German *émigré* Bernhardt, revelling in the expressionist tradition of morbid fantasy and psychological anguish. Compelling viewing, then, and a film even madder than most of its characters. GB

Possession
(Andrzej Zulawski, 1981, Fr/WGer) Isabelle Adjani, Sam Neill, Margit Carstensen, Heinz Bennent, Johanna Hofer, Shaun Lawton, Carl Duering.
127 min.
Self-exiled Polish directors – like Walerian Borowczyk – who wind up doing art movies in Paris tend over the years to go over the top in the sex/horror stakes. But Zulawski goes Grand Guignol in one leap with an outrageously sick story, filmed in English, about a schizoid housewife (Adjani, acting like a terminal rabies victim) who deserts husband and lover for an affair in a deserted Berlin apartment with a piece of fungus that grows into a many-tentacled monster and eventually metamorphoses into her husband's *doppelgänger*. Confused? Don't look for logic, don't ask why Adjani mutilates herself with an electric knife, or why Carstensen (playing a hooker) affects a clubfoot, don't expect any relief from the miscarriage scene (buckets of oozing blood and pus), and above all don't see this on a full stomach. Turkey of the year, even though the main ingredient is pure ham. MA

Possession of Joel Delaney, The
(Waris Hussein, 1971, US) Shirley MacLaine, Perry King, Michael Hordern, David Elliott, Lisa Kohane, Barbara Trentham, Lovelady Powell, Miriam Colon.
108 min.
MacLaine plays a wealthy New York divorcée who is beastly to her Puerto Rican maid, and gets her comeuppance when her brother (King) – whom she dotes on with more than sisterly warmth – becomes possessed by the spirit of a Puerto Rican sex murderer. There is some slick racial moralising (rich white New Yorkers shouldn't be beastly to their less privileged neighbours). But stir in some mumbo-jumbo in which shrieking Puerto Ricans try to exorcise the devil, and a climax in which MacLaine and her children are tortured at knife-point by the spirit of racial vengeance, and what you come away with is an alarmist message saying 'Keep New York White'. Even as melodrama it's distinctly sluggish. TM

Postcards from America
(Steve McLean, 1994, GB/US) Olmo Tighe, Michael Tighe, James Lyons, Michael Imperioli, Michael Ringer, Maggie Low.
93 min.
New York multi-media artist and gay activist David Wojnarowicz died in 1992, but his faith in writer/director McLean, the adapter of his autobiographical writings, is vindicated by this arresting first feature. Framing three periods in the life of an American outsider, the film moves nimbly between a troubled New Jersey childhood as young David (Olmo Tighe) finds himself caught between an abusive father and long-suffering mother; an adolescence spent on sidewalks where the teenage David (Michael Tighe) hustles for a living; and anguished maturity in which the adult David (Lyons) discovers the thrill of anonymous sex on the open road, before facing the shadow of AIDS. With its feel for the American landscape pitched between Kerouac and Gus Van Sant, the film's immersion in low-life Americana seems so authentic it's a surprise to learn that this is the work of a British movie-maker – McLean's background in music video and art direction tells in the sheer visual assurance. Piercing and provocative, McLean's determinedly cinematic vision announces him as, potentially, a key British independent of the '90s. TJ

Postcards from the Edge
(Mike Nichols, 1990, US) Meryl Streep, Shirley Maclaine, Dennis Quaid, Gene Hackman, Richard Dreyfuss, Rob Reiner, Mary Wickes, Conrad Bain, Annette Bening, Simon Callow, Gary Morton, CCH Pounder.
101 min.
Carrie Fisher has successfully adapted her semi-autobiographical novel about a Hollywood actress' battle with drug addiction, broadening the conflict in order to accommodate family strife between brassy showbiz all-rounder Doris Mann (MacLaine) and her addictive daughter Suzanne (Streep). While the film works partly on the level of exposé, this relationship dominates; as a result, Dreyfuss (kindly doctor), Quaid (unreliable lover) and Hackman (avuncular director) have an almost functional status. Fisher's intelligence and humour turn what might have been movie brat indulgence into something much sharper and involving. Nichols has a sure feel for the material, and he's blessed with two great performances from his leads (particularly a gutsy MacLaine). Despite the serious themes, the film remains essentially lightweight, with an uplifting resolution. This is Hollywood, after all. CM

Postino, Il (The Postman)
(Michael Radford, 1995, It/Fr) Massimo Troisi, Philippe Noiret, Maria Grazia Cucinotta, Linda Moretti, Renato Scarpa, Anna Bonaiuto.
108 min.
When, in 1952, the exiled Chilean poet and diplomat Pablo Neruda (Noiret) takes up residence in a house on a quiet little island off the Neapolitan coast, the fan mail he receives is so copious that the postmaster hires Mario (Troisi), the none too bright son of a local fisherman, to deliver the celebrity's mail. At first, Mario is simply starstruck by Neruda, who responds with understandable wariness to the postman's gauche attempts at conversation; soon, however, he's teaching Mario about metaphors, and when the postman falls for Beatrice (Cucinotta), a lovely

p

but rather aloof barmaid, the poet agrees to try to help him win her with words. Inspired by an incident in Neruda's life, the story's engaging blend of easy humour and sunny romance takes hold from the start and never lets go. Much of its seductive charm derives from the excellence of the leads: Noiret does his gruff but malleable turn to perfection, while Troisi (who died soon after filming finished) exudes a simplicity of heart, mind and soul that never seems excessively sentimental. Mercifully, Radford avoids making the small peasant community too glamorously Arcadian. Old-fashioned it may be, but it knocks the spots off pap like *Cinema Paradiso*. GA

Postman (Youchai)

(He Jianjun, 1995, China) Feng Yuanzheng.
90 min.
The second independent film by He Jianjun (aka He Yi) marks a new level of achievement for Beijing's seemingly uncrushable independent film-makers. The introverted Xiao Dou is promoted from installing post-boxes to the job of delivering mail when an old postman is arrested for stealing letters. Before long he too is intercepting other people's mail, a habit that makes him privy to their secrets and leads him to make furtive sorties into their lives. He comes to know a woman who was sucked into prostitution when her singing career stalled, a gay junkie pining for his dead lover, and an elderly lover whose son has decided to kill himself. Meanwhile Xiao Dou's relationship with his own sister begins to shift from emotional to sexual intimacy. Nothing here can be reduced to symbolism or allegory, but the *Dekalog*-like story yields any number of provocative implications for Chinese urban society in the 1990s. The core issues here are privacy (a concept so alien it's hard to express in Chinese) and the way that people's inner lives remain beyond the reach of even the most rigorous state control. TR

Postman, The
see Postino, Il

Postman, The

(Kevin Costner, 1997, US) Kevin Costner, Will Patton, Larenz Tate, Olivia Williams, James Russo, Tom Petty.
178 min.
A sense of déjà vu pervades this self-directed, over long and outsized Costner project. In a post-apocalyptic, anarchic wilderness, a semi-fascist goon squad terrorises the surviving populace. Costner, a loner scavenging on the fringe of society, instigates and leads a just and glorious resistance. The film aims for an uncomfortable compromise between the dramatic sincerity of *Dances with Wolves* and the epic spectacle of *Waterworld*, but lacks the explanatory detail and narrative fluency to achieve either. It's his charlatan side that switches on the story: chancing across a crashed mail truck, he assumes the dead postman's uniform and talks his way into the next walled town, improvising a tale in which a reconstituted US government is slowly re-establishing its infrastructure. He gets his food, and thus inspires a true, rookie mail service – an audacious social enterprise which outrages Patton's feudal tyrant. There's no discernible irony in the eventual glorification of the hero. NB

Postman Always Rings Twice, The

(Tay Garnett, 1946, US) Lana Turner, John Garfield, Cecil Kellaway, Hume Cronyn, Audrey Totter, Leon Ames, Alan Reed.
113 min. b/w.
In many ways a more striking reading of Cain's novel than the Rafelson remake, even though required to pussyfoot on the sexual side. With the opening shot of a sign announcing 'Man Wanted', and Turner's first appearance heralded by a lipstick teasingly rolling across the floor to Garfield's feet, no bed is needed to show what she is selling. A drifter passing through, paralysed by her black widow sting, Garfield becomes a man without a will, immobilised in the bleak little California backwater and gradually mired in a cesspit of lust, betrayal and murder that turns too late into love. The plot gathers slack latterly; but this is only a minor flaw in a film, more grey than *noir*, whose strength is that it is cast as a bleak memory in which, from the far side of paradise, a condemned man surveys the age-old trail through sex, love and disillusionment. TM

Postman Always Rings Twice, The

(Bob Rafelson, 1981, US) Jack Nicholson, Jessica Lange, John Colicos, Michael Lerner, John P Ryan, Anjelica Huston, William Traylor.
123 min.
An honourable effort to be faithful to James M Cain's novel about a hobo and a waitress who murder her husband in Depression-era America. Nicholson and Lange make a class act, and the film does restore the overt sexuality missing from the 1946 version. But, disappointingly given his excellent track record with films like *Five Easy Pieces*, *The King of Marvin Gardens* and *Stay Hungry*, Bob Rafelson tries to make art out of high-grade pulp, with a resultant loss of energy. MB

Posto, Il (The Job/The Sound of Trumpets)

(Ermanno Olmi, 1961, It) Sandro Panzeri, Loredano Detto, Tullio Kezich.
90 min. b/w.
Olmi's modern classic, his second feature, has a hero of Keatonesque ingenuousness – a Candide loosed on the big city (Milan), and surviving in spite of the roaring alienation and enclaves of privilege apparently designed to defeat him. Olmi keeps the scenario firmly anchored in a humane realism, and builds a comedy of feeling based upon the implicit observation of the minutest detail, the subtle shifts of emotion on the human face, the shared memories of adolescent embarrassment. If exercises in applied sadism like *10* pall, go and see a genuine master extract as much sexual charge from the sharing of a coffee spoon, and then real humour from the problem of how to dispose of the cups. A delight, no less acute for being gentle. CPea

Pot Luck

(Tom Walls, 1936, GB) Tom Walls, Ralph Lynn, Robertson Hare, Diana Churchill, Gordon James, Martita Hunt, Sara Allgood.
71 min. b/w.
The 'funniest team of comedians on any screen today' have aged less well than contemporaries like Claude Hulbert and Will Hay. Hare is still marvellous as the incarnation of timid bourgeois respectability, but Walls – here afflicted by an awful Oirish brogue – is terribly hammy, and the appeal of Lynn's silly-ass antics defies comprehension. That said, the Aldwych farces, enormously popular in the inter-war years, are a part of English history, and this one is a relatively painless introduction to their standard routines and characterisations. Walls is an appalling director, but with one of Ben Travers' few original screenplays, and the photography of Arthur Crabtree and Roy Kellino – two of Britain's most gifted cameramen – the moonlit meanderings around Wrotten Abbey look refreshingly un-stagebound. RMy

Poto and Cabengo

(Jean-Pierre Gorin, 1979, WGer/US) Grace Kennedy, Virginia Kennedy, Jean-Pierre Gorin, Dr Elissa Newport.
73 min.
A fascinating if only partly successful film by Godard's former collaborator. A documentary about six-year-old twins, Grace and Virginia Kennedy, who for years spoke in their own private, impenetrable language, it frustrates partly because, by the time the film was being made, the girls were already losing their own language and beginning to speak in broken English. But Gorin's open depiction of his own effect on the girls' lives while making the film, his portrait of sterile lower middle class American family life, and the innate interest of his subject still make it highly absorbing. GA

Poulet au Vinaigre
see Cop au Vin

Poussière d'Ange
see Angel Dust

Powaqqatsi

(Godfrey Reggio, 1988, US)
99 min.
Like its predecessor *Koyaanisqatsi*, Reggio's wordless eco-doc is visually stunning, but undermined by a fairly serious flaw. Where *Koyaanisqatsi* looked at the madness of First World civilisation,

and ended up criticising the very technology that enabled the film to be made, *Powaqqatsi* (Hopi for a parasitic life force) directs the same technology at the Third World. The result is even more dubious than its predecessor. Once again Philip Glass supplies the soundtrack, infiltrated here by choirs and Third World instrumentation; and where *Koyaanisqatsi* was edited into a progressively steeper climax, this has little sense of rhythmic flow. At best the message is a fairly obvious criticism of First World domination of the Third, and at worst a hippy celebration of the Dignity of Labour. JG

Powder

(Victor Salva, 1995, US) Sean Patrick Flanery, Mary Steenburgen, Lance Henriksen, Jeff Goldblum, Brandon Smith, Bradford Tatum, Susan Tyrrell.
112 min.
When his guardian grandparent cops it, 'Powder' (Flanery), a traumatised, telepathic teenage albino, is dragged from his cellar into the unknown world of rural Texas. His frightened-rabbit appearance is only intensified by the hostile reception he encounters. Still, some folk are kindlier: Jessie (Steenburgen), for instance, principal of the kids' home he is taken to, or Sheriff Barnum (Henriksen), converted to the cause after Powder provides a medium to his comatose mother's final wishes. Then there's Goldblum's chipper science teacher, sufficiently intrigued to make reference to Einstein's forecast of a more evolved, more enlightened future humankind. It's astonishing how far writer/director Salva's film takes its ideas of innocence, beauty and goodness versus all that is false and ugly: thoroughly OTT and yet apparently straight-faced, with nary a wink of self-recognition. Impassioned nonsense, really, but something to behold. NB

Power

(Sidney Lumet, 1986, US) Richard Gere, Julie Christie, Gene Hackman, Denzel Washington, Kate Capshaw, EG Marshall, Beatrice Straight, Fritz Weaver, Michael Learned, JT Walsh.
111 min.
What Lumet did for American broadcasting in *Network*, he tries to do here for the political campaign trail, with Gere – media consultant to American political hopefuls – to personify the transference of power from candidates and parties to those experts who can best manipulate the tube. Although it puts him in direct competition with his former mentor (Hackman), Gere takes up a suspicious newcomer (Walsh) at the request of a Washington lobbyist (Denzel Washington) whose underhanded dealings eventually reawaken his own political convictions. Despite making use of Hackman, Christie and Marshall in supporting roles, and actual US newscasters to cover the election results, the film is still a complete mess. Barely held together by Cy Coleman's powerful score, it finally falls apart thanks to the embarrassing amateurism of the party political broadcasts the characters produce, and the Vidal Sassoon world they inhabit. SGo

Power, The

(Byron Haskin, 1967, US) George Hamilton, Suzanne Pleshette, Michael Rennie, Nehemiah Persoff, Earl Holliman, Arthur O'Connell, Aldo Ray, Barbara Nichols, Yvonne De Carlo, Richard Carlson, Gary Merrill.
108 min.
An underrated sci-fi thriller, based on the novel by Frank M Robinson. Set in a research institute, the plot concerns the hunt for a mysterious, murderous super-brain who is evidently one of the scientists. The investigation, led by Hamilton, whose mind becomes increasingly tampered with by his quarry's power, takes him through a cross-section of contemporary America in search of the killer's past. More than once the film seemingly goes off at a tangent, only to return chillingly to the matter at hand: as when a woman kisses one of the researchers during a party into which the film has become sidetracked, only to discover that he's dead. George Pal's special effects are excellent, and Hamilton's performance is surprisingly good. DP

Power and the Glory, The

(William K Howard, 1933, US) Spencer Tracy, Colleen Moore, Ralph Morgan, Helen Vinson, Clifford Jones, Henry Kolker, Sarah Padden.
76 min. b/w.

As scripted by Preston Sturges (who impressed the producers at Fox so much they ordered director Howard to shoot his screenplay word for word), this story of a railway tycoon's rise and fall looks like a dry run for *Citizen Kane*, even though Sturges allows himself a little more sentiment on the matter than Welles ever did. Tracy, previously a villainous supporting player, grabbed his first lead and never looked back, but the movie as a whole is more significant for its place in the history books than as a living, breathing, viewing experience. TJ

Power of Kangwon Province, The (Kangwon-do ui Him)
(Hong Sang-Soo, 1998, SKor) Paik Jong-Hak, Oh Youn-Hong, Kim You-Suk, Jun Jae-Hyun, Park Hyun-Young, Im Sun-Young.
109 min.
Less assertively 'new' than *The Day a Pig Fell into the Well* but more complex in structure and subtler in effect, Hong's second film tells two seemingly distinct stories (one after the other) and leaves the viewer to grapple with two disconcerting revelations: first, that the two protagonists are ex-lovers who have never got over each other, and second, that their stories happen *not* sequentially but within the *same* time frame. The first centres on Jisook, a young woman from Seoul who takes a trip to Kangwon with two girlfriends and meets a nice-but-married cop with whom she stays in touch. The second centres on Cho, a between-jobs teacher with a wife and kid; he, too, takes a short break in Kangwon with an old schoolfriend, who already has tenure in a university teaching post. The twist of lemon is that the two stories are also virtual mirror images of each other, as if both were variations on some larger meta-narrative. Virtuoso film-making, but not in the least high flown; Hong's targets are the ways people trap themselves in routines of all kinds, and the ways people hide truths from themselves and each other behind desultory small talk. TR

Power of Men Is the Patience of Women, The (Die Macht der Männer ist die Geduld der Frauen)
(Cristina Perincioli, 1978, WGer) Elisabeth Walinski, Eberhard Feik, Dora Kürten, Christa Gehrmann.
80 min.
A docudrama on battered wives, reconstructing the very painful experiences of Addi (Walinski), a young working mother, at the hands of her husband (and of the patriarchal powers-that-be). A strange hybrid of narrative and documentary realism, the film is sometimes hard to watch, but the use of Addi's voice-over, commenting and analysing her situation, widens it out to demand involvement. Made on a slim budget by a largely female crew, it's a sincere if distressing film which contrives to end on a positive note: women can be strong, especially when they act together. HM

Power of One, The
(John G Avildsen, 1991, US) Stephen Dorff, Armin Müller-Stahl, Morgan Freeman, John Gielgud, Fay Masterson, Robbie Bulloch, Clive Russell, Alois Moyo, Marius Weyers.
127 min.
A glossy adaptation of Bryce Courtenay's novel, set in '30s South Africa, where orphaned PK (latterly played by Dorff) experiences both the privileges and privations of his strife-ridden society. Set upon in boarding-school because he is the only English boy among Afrikaners, he falls back on the friendship of kindly German composer/botanist Doc (Müller-Stahl). But the outbreak of war brings further conflict: the British imprison Doc, and PK's visits introduce him to the brutality inflicted on black prisoners. It's there that proud, resourceful Geel Piet (Freeman) takes the boy in hand, teaching him to box and transforming him into a champion. Avildsen draws good performances from the three actors who play PK, as well as from the ever-reliable Freeman and Müller-Stahl, but subtlety is abandoned when he focuses on the ring and teen romance. The climax is a slugging match between PK and a former school bully which would make Rocky proud. CM

Power Play
(Martyn Burke, 1978, Can/GB) Peter O'Toole, David Hemmings, Donald Pleasence, Barry Morse, Jon Granik, Marcella Saint-Amant, Dick Cavett.
102 min.
Tedious, glib, and reactionary, this hovers in CIA fantasy land (*Mission Impossible* time warp). In an anonymous European banana republic, an idealistic young WASP military junta overthrow a corrupt and fascistic civilian government of Balkan villains. Despite O'Toole's endearingly ironic performance as the double-crosser in the pack, the moral remains objectionably circular: 'change breeds reaction, so join the reactionaries'. Miss it. CA

Powwow Highway
(Jonathan Wacks, 1988, GB) A Martinez, Gary Farmer, Joanelle Nadine Romero, Geoff Rivas, Roscoe Born, Wayne Waterman.
91 min.
In Santa Fe, a Cheyenne woman is arrested on a trumped-up drugs charge. A few hundred miles north, her brother, Buddy Red Bow (Martinez), leaves the land hearings he is contesting for his tribe and sets off to bail her out. By chance, he meets old schoolmate Philbert Bono (Farmer) in his 'war pony', a beat-up '64 Buick. Together, they head down the Powwow Highway. Martinez makes Buddy an urgent, charismatic militant, but the thrust of the movie – like *Kiss of the Spider Woman* – is to deepen the activist's understanding of his own people and undercut his assumptions of superiority. Farmer's Philbert is a wonderful creation: a huge, lumbering totem-pole of a man whose heart matches his enormous appetite, and whose easygoing nature softens a determination quite as strong as Buddy's. They drive through wintry Montana, Philbert quietly digressing to do homage at spiritual picnic spots, until the open space gives way to 'condo-land' and the end of their quest comes into view. It's an odd, breezy picture, crisply directed by *Repo Man* producer Wacks; Farmer and Martinez are funny and warm, though their sensitivity is too often swamped by a wailing rock score, and the ideas, finally, are replaced by movie clichés. TCh

Prague
(Ian Sellar, 1991, GB/Fr) Alan Cumming, Sandrine Bonnaire, Bruno Ganz, Raphael Meiss, Henri Meiss, Hana Gregorová.
89 min.
The opening scenes of Sellar's film – in which young Scot Alex Novak (Cumming) arrives in Prague in search of a snippet of film that supposedly shows his family swimming in the river back in 1941 – suggest a distinct improvement upon the indulgent, woolly poeticism of *Venus Peter*. Unfortunately, the sub-Forsythian comedy of this prologue soon gives way to arty obscurantism. As the increasingly unsympathetic Alex becomes embroiled in a bizarre *ménage à trois* with film archive clerk Elena (Bonnaire) and her boss Josef (Ganz), the script degenerates into frustratingly enigmatic dialogue and a series of scenes whose precise import is unclear. Characters are insufficiently fleshed out, and Prague is reduced to a picturesque backdrop to a story that doesn't seem to be able to decide whether it's a full-blown romance, a satire on East European bureaucracy, a comedy of errors, or a meditation on the legacy of time, memory and history. The cast does its best, to no avail, with a portentous, contrived script. GA

Praise Marx and Pass the Ammunition
(Maurice Hatton, 1968, GB) John Thaw, Edina Ronay, Louis Mahoney, Anthony Villaroel, Helen Fleming.
90 min.
Very much a product of the revolution in the air of 1968, Hatton's first feature has rather dated in its attempts to state a case for radical social change in Britain. More than a little muddled anyway when trying to be serious, it was always much better at digging satirically into areas of bad faith as its hero, a 30-year-old Marxist-Leninist of working class origins (sharply played by a pre-*Sweeney* Thaw), seduces a string of bourgeois beauties in the hope of also impregnating them with his revolutionary message. As in *Long Shot*, Hatton's quirkish sense of humour is the thing. TM

Pram (Barnvagnen)
(Bo Widerberg, 1963, Swe) Inger Taube, Thommy Berggren, Lars Passgard.
95 min.
Bo Widerberg had just scandalised his native industry with a book criticising Ingmar Bergman's domination of the Swedish cinema when he turned out his first feature as writer/director. This story of a female drifter vacillating between two lovers, an intellectual and a pop singer, has, it could be said, a more contemporary feel than Bergman's work from the same period. But really – a mouse scraping at the cathedral door. TJ

Pravda
(Jean-Luc Godard/Dziga Vertov Group, 1969, Fr)
58 min.
Put together as crudely and urgently as an agit-prop poster, this analysis of Czechoslovakia after Dubcek finds Godard's Dziga Vertov Group beginning its struggle to formulate an uncompromised, revolutionary, theoretical film practice. On the soundtrack, the voices of 'Vladimir' and 'Rosa' argue dialectically in an attempt to arrive at the 'truth' about Dubcek revisionism and Russian imperialism. Meanwhile the images are what Godard has since called 'political tourism' in post-'68 Czechoslovakia, giving way to a blank screen whenever the country cannot furnish a politically correct signifier. A self-confessed failure on its own terms, the film is none the less vital as a step towards a valid form of political cinema. TR

Prayer for the Dying, A
(Mike Hodges, 1987, GB) Mickey Rourke, Bob Hoskins, Alan Bates, Sammi Davis, Christopher Fulford, Liam Neeson, Leonard Termo.
108 min.
It would be nice to say that Hodges' movie about an IRA man – chopped about by other hands, laden with opprobrium after Enniskillen – is a noble ruin. Actually, it is so preposterously melodramatic that you can relish every minute. Sickened by killing, IRA hit man Fallon (Rourke, great accent) flees to England, contacting crime boss Meehan (Bates, camp) to get a new passport. Meehan's price is one more hit, but in carrying out the contract Fallon is seen by Father Da Costa (Hoskins, ludicrously miscast). To silence the priest, Fallon tricks him into hearing his confession, but the police and an IRA hit team are closing in. There is still time, however, for Fallon to fall in love with the priest's blind, organ-playing niece, and for ex-SAS Father DaCosta to go berserk and flatten three heavies with a dustbin lid. Will Fallon manage to rescue priest and niece, who are tied to the top of the belfry tower with a time-bomb, and thereby save his soul, if not his ass? BC

Prayer of the Rollerboys
(Rick King, 1990, US) Corey Haim, Patricia Arquette, Christopher Collet, JC Quinn, Julius Harris, Devin Clark, Mark Pellegrino, Morgan Weisser.
94 min.
A tame, teen-movie rip-off of – among others – *Red Dawn*, *A Clockwork Orange* and *Surf Nazis Must Die*, this is a sci-fi pic for the computer-games generation. *RoboCop*-style media images present a paranoid vision of a future where the economic superpowers of Germany and Japan have bankrupted the United States, decimating its adult population and forcing the abandoned children to live in camps. Teen heart-throb Haim plays Griffin, a pizza delivery boy dedicated to saving both his country and his impressionable younger brother from the fascist New Order promised by Gary Lee (Collet) and his racist Rollerboy army (with the aid of an addictive drug). The only opposition is from the Freaks, a motley collection of Blacks, Hispanics and bikers, unsuitable allies for our clean-cut hero. Instead, he teams up with an adult cop (Quinn) and a young, attractive undercover agent (Arquette). The violence is toned down, the sex innocuous, the interest level zero. NF

Preacher's Wife, The
(Penny Marshall, 1996, US) Whitney Houston, Denzel Washington, Gregory Hines, Courtney B Vance, Jenifer Lewis, Loretta Devine, Lionel Ritchie.
124 min.

Christmas is here, but for the Rev Henry Biggs (Vance) it's hard to be jolly. A life-long do-gooder, he's reached a mid-life crisis of faith: he's no longer convinced he's making a difference to his community, is failing to put in that quality time with his gospel-singing wife Julia (Houston) and son Jeremiah, and is tempted to sell up the run-down church he inherited from Julia's father to a smarmy property developer (Hines). Not only that, but he's even disbelieving when the Lord answers his prayers by sending down the Angel Dudley (Washington). A surprisingly tolerable remake of the 1947 Cary Grant vehicle *The Bishop's Wife*, thanks chiefly to the casting of Washington, who lends a vital blend of wit, pathos and self-effacement. A pleasingly uncynical film, too, about halfway real people and problems, however two-dimensional and trite. But, beware, if you can't abide Hollywood platitudes, if you're allergic to syrup, and if you object to a movie designed partly to showcase Whitney's new album. NB

Preaching to the Perverted
(Stuart Urban, 1997, GB) Guinevere Turner, Christien Anholt, Tom Bell, Julie Graham.
100 min.
Pity poor Peter (Anholt). A virginal computer boffin, he thinks he's bound for glory when Henry Harding MP (Bell) sends him undercover, on a mission from God to infiltrate the House of Thwax fetish club. The idea is to record evidence for a public prosecution, but for Peter this entails gross private humiliation at the hands of American dominatrix Tanya Cheex (Turner). She's only too happy to whip this puppy lover into shape, but when he comes clean, will she turn the other Cheex? Writer/director Urban is known for his BBC TV work, including the BAFTA-winning Falklands drama *An Ungentlemanly Act*, but his first feature is more in line with late-night satellite broadcasting at its starkest. The shock tactics, however, are nowhere near as offensive as the tissue-thin characterisation, stiff performances, anticlimactic script, and a half-cocked stylisation – play-school Almodóvar – which basically boils down to pink and purple production design. A movie for masochists. TCh

Precinct 45: Los Angeles Police
see New Centurions, The

Predator
(John McTiernan, 1987, US) Arnold Schwarzenegger, Carl Weathers, Elpidia Carrillo, Bill Duke, Jesse Ventura, Kevin Peter Hall.
106 min.
Big Arnie straps on the fetishistic military hardware for a rumble in the jungle with a merciless, camouflaged alien (Hall). A routine operation to rescue a cabinet minister captured by South American guerrillas turns into a fight to the death when Arnie's crack platoon is picked off one by one by an invisible adversary, which then makes itself visible, removes its protective helmet, and challenges him to a fair (!) fight. With its stilted dialogue and hammy acting, the film has the look of an expensive production but the feel of a B movie, delivering the sort of undemanding monster mayhem Arnie's fans have come to expect. NF

Predator 2
(Stephen Hopkins, 1990, US) Kevin Peter Hall, Danny Glover, Gary Busey, Ruben Blades, Maria Conchita Alonso, Bill Paxton, Adam Baldwin, Robert Davi, Calvin Lockhart.
108 min.
Showing little of the flair that distinguished its predecessor, this sequel lacks two winning ingredients: a suspenseful plot and Schwarzenegger. It's 1997, ten years since the invisible alien's last appearance, and the conflict has shifted to a different kind of jungle: futuristic Los Angeles, where the police battle against powerful drug lords. The law enforcers get unexpected help from the predator (Hall), who shimmers into view and rips out a villain's spinal column. Maverick cop Harrigan (Glover) is on his trail, but so is Federal Agent Keyes (Busey), heading a special task force. Attempting an uneasy alliance of genres, the film ends up rudderless, leaving the bewildered heroes with merely functional roles as they chart the indiscriminate behaviour of their foe. Harrigan and Keyes clash wardrobes and fall to ceaseless bickering over jurisdiction. CM

Prejudice
(Ian Munro, 1989, Aust) Patsy Stephen, Grace Parr, Vic Hawkins, Penny Stehli, Robert Burns, Allan McFadden.
115 min.
Docu-drama exposing the discrimination faced by two women. Jessica is a photographer on a daily paper. She's good at her job, but her Barry McKenzie-like colleagues harass and denigrate her. Letitia's a highly qualified Filipino nurse, ostracised by her patients and passed over for promotion because of her race. The women fight back. Earnest, self-righteous, but powerful in patches. GM

Prelude to a Kiss
(Norman René, 1992, US) Alec Baldwin, Meg Ryan, Kathy Bates, Ned Beatty, Patty Duke, Sydney Walker, Stanley Tucci.
106 min.
Straight-as-a-die Peter (Baldwin) and ditzy bartender Rita (Ryan) are introduced at a party, fall swiftly in love and, despite differences, marry after a few months. At the wedding things start to go really wrong, for the couple and for us: after a congratulatory kiss from an old codger (Walker), Rita undergoes a massive personality change which first manifests itself on the honeymoon. For Peter, it's almost as if the body-snatchers have invaded, but when he bumps into the mysterious old buffer in the bar, it becomes clear that the scenario is less a study in sci-fi paranoia, more a matter of maudlin hokum. Very sticky. GA

Premature Burial, The
(Roger Corman, 1961, US) Ray Milland, Hazel Court, Richard Ney, Heather Angel, Alan Napier, Dick Miller.
81 min.
The third of Corman's generally impressive Poe cycle suffers from the fact that Milland, rather than Vincent Price (lead in most of the other entries in the series), stars as the cataleptic medical student haunted by fantastic fears of being buried alive like his father before him. Needless to say, nightmare becomes reality and revenge is meted out; indeed, the predictability of the plotting clearly led Corman to focus his attention, somewhat decoratively, on conjuring up a gloomy Gothic atmosphere that, while effective, too often seems an end in itself, rather than a means of creating horror. The film does have its macabre moments, however, notably Milland proudly showing friends around a tomb he has devised for himself, complete with a variety of exits should his worst dreams come true. GA

Premonition, The (Svart Lucia)
(Rumle Hammerich, 1992, Swe) Tova Magnusson, Figge Norling, Lars Green, Björn Kjellman, Niklas Hjulström, Malin Berghagen.
114 min.
This slow-burning and finally rather unsatisfying genre offering teases the viewer with a smorgasbord of doomy portentousness. Having confided numerous sexual fantasies to her diary and a subsequent, rather daring academic assignment, schoolgirl Mikaela (Magnusson) is understandably alarmed when the bespectacled Swedish teacher (Green), who's the object of her adolescent desire, appears to act out her innermost sado-masochistic dreams. The narrative looks set to burst into carnage when Mikaela's mind conjures an ominously threatening set of images. Hammerich keeps us waiting an age before anything definitively bloody occurs and his movie hits the rocks as soon as he has to put away the fancy flummery and come up with a pay-off. TJ

Prénom Carmen
see First Name: Carmen

Préparez Vos Mouchoirs (Get Out Your Handkerchiefs)
(Bertrand Blier, 1977, Fr/Bel) Gérard Depardieu, Patrick Dewaere, Carole Laure, Riton, Michel Serrault, Sylvie Joly, Eléonore Hirt.
109 min.
An inspired attack on 'real life' melodramas of the soppy kind capped by *Kramer vs Kramer*.

Depardieu, all solicitude and whispers, is the ham-fisted husband, worried by his wife's elusive 'dizzy spells'; Dewaere is the first of several men he invites into their marriage to 'cheer her up'; Riton is the schoolboy-lover she finally adopts to complete a bizarre *ménage-à-quatre*. Somewhere in all this chaos, the movie firmly puts the boot into mainstream French comedy, substituting absurd and amiable bad taste for the intellectual rigor mortis of which Parisians are so proud. An erratic, often hilarious movie. CA

Présence réelle, La
(Raúl Ruiz, 1984, Fr) Franck Oger, Nadège Clair, Camila Mora, Catherine Oudin, Louis Castel, Jean-Loup Rivière.
60 min.
A good example of how Ruiz, given a perfectly straightforward commission, will deliver anything but the expected. Ostensibly an essay on the Avignon Festival, it starts off with an actor puzzling over his 'virtual' presence on a videodisc about a Festival that hasn't happened yet, but where he can nevertheless be seen. If this sort of meditation on real and imaginary presence – on the differences between film, theatre, filmed theatre and theatrical cinema – had been developed more cohesively, it would have been a much more gripping film. But then it wouldn't have been Ruiz. As it is, the Gothic horror imagery, run-of-the-mill Magritte allusions, and staggeringly cut-rate special effects – felt pen on glass – are so many prodigal throwaways from a man who's often plagued with too many ideas for his own good. JRo

President's Analyst, The
(Theodore J Flicker, 1967, US) James Coburn, Godfrey Cambridge, Severn Darden, Joan Delaney, Pat Harrington, Barry McGuire, Eduard Franz, Will Geer, William Daniels, Joan Darling.
103 min.
A neglected satire whose premise is the secrets to which the US President's shrink is privy, and the ways in which these endanger him. Pursued by everyone from foreign agents to security organisations like the FBI and the CIA, Coburn quickly becomes a picaresque hero on the run through an America whose psychological landscape is every bit as absurd as Hunter Thompson's Las Vegas. Inevitably, in a paranoid conspiracy-theory movie about ten years before its time, some sequences – like a psychedelic sojourn with a hippy group – are now badly dated. But overall it's hilarious stuff, held together by Coburn's tongue-in-cheek performance, one of his best. RM

Presidio, The
(Peter Hyams, 1988, US) Sean Connery, Mark Harmon, Meg Ryan, Jack Warden, Mark Blum, Dana Gladstone, Jenette Goldstein.
98 min.
Hyams' *Running Scared* was a crime thriller about a pair of ill-matched cops, one black, the other white; this one is a crime thriller about a pair of ill-matched cops, one military, the other civilian: one can have too much of a goodish thing. Set on the eponymous San Francisco military base, it opens promisingly with a break-in at an officers' club culminating in the killing of a military policewoman, a car chase, and the shooting of a civilian cop. The resulting joint investigation teams seasoned, by-the-book military policeman Connery and young civilian cop Harmon. They have crossed swords before, and just to complicate things, Connery's daughter (Ryan) starts making advances to Harmon to wind up her dad. Meanwhile, the investigation dribbles along, with links between former CIA agents, Vietnam veterans, and a missing water bottle pointing to some kind of criminal conspiracy. As usual, Hyams makes good use of the locations, and stages the stunt sequences with great skill, but his handling of the romance and father/daughter conflicts is at best uncertain, at worst embarrassing. NF

P..... Respectueuse, La (The Respectful Prostitute/The Respectable Prostitute)
(Marcel Pagliero/Charles Brabant, 1952, Fr) Barbara Laage, Ivan Desny, Walter Bryant, Marcel Herrand.
97 min. b/w.
Is Sartre still taken seriously (in 1998)? This bar-

p

barous melodrama (based on his play, which he helped adapt) should sow misgivings in the heart of even the staunchest admirer. It's set in an American South where all the blacks are saintly and passive and all the whites, except the title *putain*, do nothing but seethe with racist venom. Enter the movie at any point and it offends – musically, via Auric's whining arrangement of 'Swing Low Sweet Chariot', and dramatically through the author's inability even to compose a scene in which two people in a room behave plausibly. Camerman Shuftan does his best to reproduce Dixie in the Courbevoie studios, but is hampered by Laage's willowy mannequin looks, as wrong here as the signs telling motorists to 'honck' for service. BBa

Press for Time
(Robert Asher, 1966, GB) Norman Wisdom, Derek Bond, Angela Browne, Derek Francis, Noel Dyson, Frances White, Peter Jones, Allan Cuthbertson.
102 min.
Gormless Norman is the Prime Minister's grandson, a newspaper-seller kicked upstairs (because grandfather is embarrassed) to a journalist's post in a seaside town (where he wreaks much havoc). Based on a novel by *Evening Standard* hack Angus McGill, this features Wisdom in three roles, spreading his creepy persona too thinly for comfort. His humour was very much a product of the conscription years; by 1966, it had worn hopelessly thin, and after this film, he attempted to update his style with Swinging Sixties fare like *What's Good for the Goose* – a disastrous step, it transpired. JRo

Pressure
(Horace Ové, 1975, GB) Herbert Norville, Oscar James, Frank Singuineau, Lucita Lijertwood, Sheila Scott-Wilkinson, Ed Devereaux.
110 min.
Britain's first 'black' feature, co-scripted by Ové and Samuel Selvon, deals honestly and realistically with what life is like for a school-leaver who is black: the futile job interviews, the patronising platitudes, people's simple inability to comprehend that black can be not only beautiful but also English. Although it fudges its ending, there's enough honesty and entertainment along the way to place the Dickensian jokes of 'Black Joy' firmly back in their fairytale. SM

Presumed Innocent
(Alan J Pakula, 1990, US) Harrison Ford, Brian Dennehy, Raúl Julia, Bonnie Bedelia, Paul Winfield, Greta Scacchi, John Spencer, Joe Grifasi, Tom Mardirosian.
127 min.
Pakula and Frank Pierson faced a difficult task in adapting Scott Turow's novel. The dense, first-person narrative – told from the perspective of an alleged murderer – has been simplified and tightened, its psychological subtleties jettisoned, the emphasis shifted to legal and forensic investigation. Rusty Sabich (Ford) is a prosecuting attorney whose life is thrown into turmoil after a colleague (Scacchi) is raped and murdered. They had enjoyed a brief affair, and suspicion falls on Sabich, who finds himself hiring a defence attorney (Julia). Even stripped down, the plot provides suspense and intellectual fascination, but the film quickly runs into problems of characterisation. In Turow's novel, the victim is viewed from Sabich's vantage point; here, the emotional distortion has been lost, and her role is merely functional. To a lesser degree, Sabich also loses in the translation, but he's given dimension via his relationship with his tormented, mathematician wife (Bedelia, excellent) and through Ford's earnest intensity. In a welcome return to suspense, Pakula effectively conveys the claustrophobia of domesticity and courtroom procedure. CM

Prêt-à-Porter
see Ready to Wear

Pretty Baby
Louis Malle, 1977, US) Brooke Shields, Keith Carradine, Susan Sarandon, Frances Faye, Antonio Fargas, Matthew Anton, Diana Scarwid, Barbara Steele, Gerrit Graham.
110 min.
Despite the scandalised yelps about child pornography, a film of disarmingly subversive innocence, set in a New Orleans bordello (1917

vintage) where the pretty baby of the title eagerly awaits her twelfth birthday and the deflowerment which will inaugurate her career. All red plush, ragtime and Renoir nudes, it would be candy confection except that vice is viewed here partly through the enchanted eyes of the child (Shields), partly through the candid camera of a photographer (Carradine) who sees flesh and its desires as the stuff of art and beauty. The Nabokovian relationship between these two asks some very pertinent questions about the hypocrisy of conventional morality. TM

Pretty in Pink
(Howard Deutch, 1986, US) Molly Ringwald, Harry Dean Stanton, Jon Cryer, Annie Potts, James Spader, Andrew McCarthy.
97 min.
A pretty superior teen angst movie, with John Hughes (producing and scripting but not directing this time) completing the series he began with *Sixteen Candles* and *The Breakfast Club*. Being young, Hughes tells us, isn't easy. Red-haired Ringwald has no mother in sight, Harry Dean Stanton for a downbeat father, and an unfortunate high school rep. She wears odd clothes, tools round in a clapped-out Beetle, and works in a record store at weekends (cue Psychedelic Furs, The Smiths, etc). Still, she's got lots of spirit, and by the end even the Nice, Unbelievably Rich Kid with the BMW is beginning to recognise what we've known all along: that she's the best thing around. It's a plea on behalf of upward mobility, and – more remarkable – revolves around a single question: will Molly make it to the high school prom? To be able to give this kind of stuff new and sympathetic twists is a tribute to Hughes' skill with narrative, and to Ringwald's magnetism as a performer. RR

Pretty Maids All in a Row
(Roger Vadim, 1971, US) Rock Hudson, Angie Dickinson, Telly Savalas, John David Carson, Roddy McDowall, Keenan Wynn, William Campbell.
95 min.
Somebody's knocking off girls at the high school in this sex-comedy-thriller, which doesn't get far in any of these directions. The sex is an updated equivalent of the kind indulged in by Rock Hudson in innumerable bedroom comedies. The comedy consists largely of Telly Savalas wearing his dark glasses on the top of his bald head, plus a few gags about embarrassing erections. And the thriller aspect derives from a couple of close-ups of Hudson looking dangerously manic. In one shot, the boom microphone hovers in full view for several seconds; an indication of the general sloppiness and pointlessness of Vadim's first American-made feature.

Pretty Poison
(Noel Black, 1968, US) Anthony Perkins, Tuesday Weld, Beverly Garland, John Randolph, Dick O'Neill, Clarice Blackburn.
89 min.
Ever since this corrosive tale of insidious madness and deceptive innocence in Small Town USA, buffs have sought out Noel Black's other work (mainly for TV), vainly hoping to find something as good. The film is blithely written by Lorenzo Semple Jr, who suddenly proved at a stroke that he was worthy of more than the script consultant's job on *Batman*.And the performances are great. Perkins' role, as a dedicated fantasist employed at a chemical factory, treads on *Psycho* ground without ever causing the usual feelings of *déjà vu*; but Tuesday Weld is the film's linch-pin, brilliantly playing a girl whose drum-majorette demeanour hides the most amazing emotions. In a word, recommended. GB

Pretty Village, Pretty Flame (Lepa sela lepo gore)
(Srdjan Dragojevic, 1996, Serbia) Dragan Bjelogrlic, Nikola Kojo, Velimir Bata Zivojinovic, Dragan Maksimovic, Zoran Cvijanovic.
129 min.
A harrowing response to the Bosnian conflict, this war drama disarms preconceptions and prejudices by adopting a strategy of temporal dislocation. Cutting from 1980 to 1992 (the first day of the war) and to 1994 (a bloody hospital ward), and back again, it reveals its secrets with no little care. A Muslim and a Serb grow up and work togeth-

er, but inevitably find themselves on opposite sides when a Serb unit is trapped inside a disused tunnel with no food or water. Boldly shot and edited, the film quite rightly puts you through the wringer. TCh

Pretty Woman
(Garry Marshall, 1990, US) Richard Gere, Julia Roberts, Ralph Bellamy, Jason Alexander, Laura San Giacomo, Alex Hyde-White, Hector Elizondo.
119 min.
Vivian (Roberts) is not a happy hooker. She looks the part, but unlike her feisty friend Kit (San Giacomo) she retains a *core of vulnerability*. So does workaholic Edward (Gere), even though he's a multi-millionaire take-'em-and-break-'em tycoon. In LA for the week, he hires Vivian to act as a beautiful, disarming escort while he dines the opposition, grooming and schooling her in the process. Before you know it, she's discovering a sense of self-worth, while he's taking shoes and socks (and time) off to stroll in the park and overhaul his ethics. This is predictable *Pygmalion* stuff, but with plenty of laughs along the way. Roberts can act, and Gere, though not renowned for his comic skills, is more than a smoochy foil to kooky Vivian, and just about manages to look like a man who has channelled all his sexual energy into corporate ball-crushing. Retch-making moments (he thinks she's doing drugs in the bathroom, she's really – *aaawww!* – flossing her teeth) are kept to a minimum and the sex scenes sweetly restrained. But for a film that attempts to satirise snooty materialism, it focuses too pantingly on the designer labels, and comes down firmly on the side of 'rich is better'. SFe

Prey of the Chameleon
(Tex Fuller, 1991, US) James Wilder, Alexandra Paul, Daphne Zuniga.
85 min.
The Hitcher with a twist. A dumb psychological suspense picture in which ex-mercenary Wilder, back home in middle America, picks up a housewife stranded by her broken-down car. His passenger (Zuniga, best known for Rob Reiner's *The Sure Thing*) is not what she seems; in fact, she's an escapee from a mental institution, who befriends her victims, kills them, and then assumes their identities. TJ

Prick Up Your Ears
(Stephen Frears, 1987, GB) Gary Oldman, Alfred Molina, Vanessa Redgrave, Wallace Shawn, Lindsay Duncan, Julie Walters, James Grant.
110 min.
Artists have usually had a cardboard time of it on film. What writers do is not cinematic, so Frears' film on Joe Orton concentrates elsewhere. The finally tragic 16-year relationship between Orton (Oldman) and his lover Kenneth Halliwell (Molina), and their defiant isolation from conventional society are the central themes here, but neither is particularly illuminating. The clumsy distancing device of a narrative by literary agent Peggy Ramsay (Redgrave) prevents one from caring about the doomed pair, or from feeling Halliwell's anguish. Orton was formed in opposition to the prevailing moral climate, and his plays were his revenge. They were distinguished by a gleeful vindictiveness that seems disproportionate to the Establishment targets presented here as caricatures. The main failure to get to grips with the subject lies in Alan Bennett's script: his familiar comic cadences and inspired mismatches hijack the proceedings. Line by line, it's outrageously funny, but like the collage on the wall of the Islington flat, it doesn't add up to more than the sum of its parts. BC

Pride and Prejudice
(Robert Z Leonard, 1940, US) Greer Garson, Laurence Olivier, Edna May Oliver, Edmund Gwenn, Mary Boland, Maureen O'Sullivan, Melville Cooper, Marsha Hunt, Heather Angel, Ann Rutherford, Karen Morley.
119 min. b/w.
An adaptation of the Helen Jerome play based on Jane Austen's novel, which may well make Austenites quiver at its infidelities and occasional insensitivities (not to mention the perhaps inevitable blurring of the subtler social ironies), but is surprisingly dry and droll. Aldous Huxley's contribution to the script undoubtedly helped, but

it is the cast which carries it: marvellous performances all round, with Garson's cool prejudice perfectly matched against Olivier's chill pride, and only minor reservations (Mary Boland's Mrs Bennett is a little too tiresomely tiresome). TM

Pride and the Passion, The
(Stanley Kramer, 1957, US) Cary Grant, Frank Sinatra, Sophia Loren, Theodore Bikel, John Wengraf, Jay Novello.
132 min.
Spectacularly solemn and silly epic based on CS Forester's novel about Napoleon's Iberian campaign (*The Gun*), full of sound and fury (and heaving bodies) signifying nothing. If you can believe in Sinatra as an 1810 vintage Spanish guerrilla, you can believe anything, but it's still a slog through a platitudinous script as (with Grant and Loren looking on while providing the love interest) he struggles to lug a vast cannon within range of the Napoleonic invaders. TM

Pride of St Louis, The
(Harmon Jones, 1952, US) Dan Dailey, Joanne Dru, Richard Hylton, Richard Crenna, Hugh Sanders, James Brown, Chet Huntley.
93 min. b/w.
Full enjoyment of this sports biopic depends on actually having heard of baseball giant Dizzy Dean, the hillbilly pitcher who won stardom with the St Louis Cardinals before injury almost ended his involvement with the sport. Dailey, usually seen in Hollywood musicals, makes him a cheerily sympathetic type, but it's one for the aficionados of the game and *Citizen Kane* obsessives looking for another movie where screenwriter Herman J Mankiewicz gives a real-life figure fictional treatment. TJ

Pride of the Marines
(aka Forever in Love)
(Delmer Daves, 1945, US) John Garfield, Eleanor Parker, Dane Clark, John Ridgely, Rosemary DeCamp, Ann Doran.
120 min. b/w.
The true story of Al Schmid, a young soldier blinded by a Japanese grenade in the heroic defence of Guadalcanal, allows Garfield to produce a performance of well-modulated intensity that draws upon his understanding of ordinary people, their eager but simple ambitions, and the courage they often find in adversity and despair. The cloying patriotism – although mitigated in part by a confrontation of the social problems facing the US in the aftermath of World War II – is hard to stomach. But the thoughtful script (notice in particular the characters' reaction to the news of Pearl Harbor), the fine direction (you'll either love or hate the bizarre dream sequence), and above all Garfield, make this a film that's always watchable, sometimes riveting. FD

Priest
(Antonia Bird, 1994, GB) Linus Roache, Tom Wilkinson, Cathy Tyson, Robert Carlyle, James Ellis, Lesley Sharp, Robert Pugh.
109 min.
When Father Greg (Roache) arrives at his new Liverpool parish, he's appalled at what he regards as the lax morals of his more experienced colleague, Father Matthew (Wilkinson), who shares a bed with their housekeeper Maria (Tyson). The priests are utterly at odds, temperamentally, politically and doctrinally. However, it soon emerges that Greg's fierce conservatism covers a turmoil of self-doubt: one evening he swaps his dog collar for a leather jacket and picks up a lover in a gay bar (Carlyle). The film calls on the traditions of the best radical TV drama. Wickedly sardonic and very moving, with an outstanding performance from Roache at the centre of a fine cast, it clearly works a treat for cinema audiences. In the opening sequence a priest uses a large crucifix as a battering ram, which gives a fair idea of the level of ecclesiastical debate. The film's true subject, however, is emotional courage, and that it has in spades. TCh

Priest of Love
(Christopher Miles, 1980, GB) Ian McKellen, Janet Suzman, Ava Gardner, Penelope Keith, Jorge Rivero, Maurizio Merli, John Gielgud, James Faulkner, Sarah Miles.
125 min.
High in the running for the year's dumbest art

movie, opening on a shot of burning books, this launches into the life story of DH Lawrence with all the naive lyricism of an early Ken Russell biopic. Suzman struggles to toughen up the role of Frieda, but succumbs to the script early on when required to describe sex as 'the only way to reach the soul of man'. McKellen has the 'look of genius' in his eyes, the twang of Nottingham in his speech, and TB in his lungs. On the interminable route to his deathbed, Lawrence experiences lurid sunsets and a generous helping of flashbacks, and sees his manuscripts blown away in the wind so often you wonder how he ever published a single word. Directed like the most twee of travelogues, it's not worth staying with even for the closing moment of sublime silliness when the remains of the dead novelist return to New Mexico in a terracotta chicken brick. Desperate...although subsequent re-editing down to a 99 minute version did help slightly. MA

Prima della Rivoluzione
see Before the Revolution

Primal Fear
(Gregory Hoblit, 1996, US) Richard Gere, Laura Linney, Frances McDormand, Edward Norton, John Mahoney, Alfre Woodard, Terry O'Quinn, Joe Spano, Tony Plana.
129 min.
Suave, womanising top Chicago attorney Martin Vail (Gere) is arrogant enough to demand the cover for any magazine interview he grants. In fact, he's such a publicity fiend, that when he catches a newsflash of young Aaron Stampler (Norton) attempting to escape from the scene of an ugly murder, he drops everything to be the first to offer his services – gratis. The stuttering Southern ex-hobo's accused of killing his guardian, the city's beloved archbishop. The DA, an old foe of Vail, and a friend of the victim, is insisting on the death penalty; and, to spice things up, Vail's embittered ex (Linney), a prosecutor in the DA's department, is detailed to the case. Despite a talky script (based on a book by William Diehl) full of hanging ethical, procedural and social conundrums, first-time director Hoblit seems at ease in this two-act movie. The first hour, detailing the city's scummy realpolitik, is a smooth, predictable preamble to the ably executed trial-scene second half. There are twists, but few surprises. Gere dashes grandly, and dashes around manfully in his tailor-made role, and Norton shows notable range, but unfortunately in an environment too mechanical for it to prove much. WH

Primary Colors
(Mike Nichols, 1998, US) John Travolta, Emma Thompson, Adrian Lester, Kathy Bates, Billy Bob Thornton.
143 min.
Travolta looks the spitting image of Bill Clinton – from the rear. This *film à clef* about Clinton's 1990 campaign for the Democratic Presidential nomination offers plenty of food for thought on the corruption of the political process, but despite the absorbing material – Elaine May sticking close to the novel by Anonymous (actually political correspondent Joe Klein) – Nichols comes off as the perennial wavering voter. As satire, it's toothless and indulgent; as drama of conscience, it's not a patch on real life (see DA Pennebaker's documentary *The War Room*). The performances are pitched all over the place, but the real problem is Travolta's avowedly sympathetic, yet electractingly uncharismatic, intellectually lightweight impersonation of the President – Bill gives much better sincerity than this. TCh

Primate
(Frederick Wiseman, 1974, US)
105 min. b/w.
'We get erection at one frequency, and ejaculation at another' a researcher says to a colleague. In this case the scientists are talking about apes, but as behaviour researchers discover and refine new methods of electronic control, it's perhaps only a matter of time before human beings are routinely implanted with electrodes and their sexuality controlled by electronic impulses. Wiseman spent a great deal of time filming these types of investigations at a well-known primate research centre in America. Unfortunately, his style is not to inform but simply to record. We are shown an endless series of experiments on chim-

panzees, orang-utangs and gorillas, executed with cold, heartless efficiency; but the images of operations and dissections, as brutal as they sometimes appear, are meaningless unless we are provided with basic information on why this particular research is being conducted. This lack of viewpoint is particularly disappointing in a slow, rambling documentary that could have given us a purposeful look into the mechanics of behaviour and the frightening implications suggested by scientific research. LR

Prime Cut
(Michael Ritchie, 1972, US) Lee Marvin, Gene Hackman, Angel Tompkins, Gregory Walcott, Sissy Spacek, Janit Baldwin, William Morey.
86 min.
Ritchie's inexplicably underrated second feature is a superb amalgam of pulp gangster thriller and fairytale, in which white knight/ Chicago syndicate enforcer (Marvin) visits recalcitrant black knight/Kansas boss (Hackman), rescuing damsel in distress (Spacek, making her debut) while there. Underneath a surface that constantly juxtaposes opposites, *Prime Cut* concerns a curious, fundamental *naiveté* underlying America's corruption: that allows Hackman to give the country the dope and flesh it wants; that permits Marvin to attempt to live out his Beauty and the Beast romance; that implies, in the fairground shootout, an America totally oblivious to what is going on in front of its eyes. In his round-trip of bars, hotels, flophouses, ranches, cities and countryside, Ritchie demonstrates a truly fine handling of locations, best realised in two classic Hitchcock-like chases, through the fairground, and across a cornfield pursued by a combine harvester. CPe

Prime of Miss
Jean Brodie, The
(Ronald Neame, 1968, GB) Maggie Smith, Robert Stephens, Pamela Franklin, Gordon Jackson, Celia Johnson, Diane Grayson, Jane Carr, Shirley Steedman, Helena Gloag.
116 min.
Muriel Spark's wonderful slip-sliding novella is narrowed down and heightened in Jay Presson Allen's adaptation for Fox of her own stage play (drawn from Spark's book), which omits much sense of the wider, crueller world of the '30s outside the Marcia Blaine School for Girls in Edinburgh, where Miss Brodie imparts her own rarefied, romantic view of life to her chosen 'set'. Nevertheless, Maggie Smith is handed a part in the eccentric, trite, purposeful and finally pathetic Jean Brodie which allows her to play to all her considerable strengths. Her performance is ably counterpointed by Stephens as the knowing, married art teacher Teddy Lloyd (to whose bed she attempts to send one of her girls, in her own place), and Celia Johnson as the pursed headmistress determined to sack her. Good support, too, from the girls, notably Jane Carr, as Mary McGregor, the new girl who dies on her way to fight against Miss Brodie's hero Franco, and Pamela Franklin, as Sandy, who finally puts paid to her teacher by denouncing her fascism. JPy

Primrose Path, The
(Gregory La Cava, 1940, US) Ginger Rogers, Joel McCrea, Marjorie Rambeau, Miles Mander, Henry Travers, Joan Carroll.
93 min. b/w.
A likeable social comedy from the talented La Cava (for whom Rogers had given such a fine performance in the earlier *Stage Door*). Ginger's the girl from the wrong side of the tracks – morally rather than financially, coming as she does from a family of prostitutes and drunkards – who loses her respectable hubby McCrea, ambitious proprietor of a hamburger stand, when he finally gets to meet her parents. The romance and the attempts at seamy realism don't really mesh smoothly enough, but the performances and civilised direction make the unusual subject highly watchable. GA

Prince and the Pauper, The
(aka Crossed Swords)
(Richard Fleischer, 1977, Pan) Oliver Reed, Raquel Welch, Mark Lester, Ernest Borgnine, George C Scott, Rex Harrison, David Hemmings, Charlton Heston, Harry Andrews, Murray Melvin, Sybil Danning.
121 min.

Produced under the same flag of convenience as the Salkinds had employed for their earlier pair of Dick Lester *Three Musketeers* films, this hid its status as a redundant remake (of a Warners/Errol Flynn romp of 1937, which cast genuine twins in the double-lead role) under the title *Crossed Swords* in America. Fleischer's anonymous direction and Mark Lester's lack of range (as the urchin/prince lookalikes) throw the weight of Mark Twain's cross-cut yarn of confused identities onto a series of lumbering star cameos (Heston as Henry VIII, Scott as a Cockney villain, etc). Princely sets, but a debilitating poverty of wit and imagination. PT

Prince and the Showgirl, The
(Laurence Olivier, 1957, GB) Laurence Olivier, Marilyn Monroe, Sybil Thorndike, Richard Wattis, Jeremy Spenser, Jean Kent, Esmond Knight, Maxine Audley.
117 min.
Flimsy Ruritanian whimsy adapted from Terence Rattigan's damp coronation year divertissement, *The Sleeping Prince*. A rather condescending vehicle for Monroe, who had demonstrated astonishing range and skill the previous year in *Bus Stop*, with Olivier's leaden direction constantly conveying the impression that real actors are graciously propping up the pretty novice. Few sparks fly, but Olivier's Teutonically humourless Regent of Carpathia – in Britain for the 1911 coronation of George V – is nicely played off against Marilyn's innocently saucy showgirl. TM

Prince of Darkness
(John Carpenter, 1987, US) Donald Pleasence, Jameson Parker, Victor Wong, Lisa Blount, Dennis Dun, Susan Blanchard, Anne Howard.
101 min.
Carpenter's first low-budget horror pic for some time. Summoned to an abandoned church by a frightened priest (Pleasence), Prof Birack (Wong) finds a basement shrine dominated by a canister of green fluid. A manuscript reveals the existence of the Secret Brotherhood of Sleep, worshippers of Satan, who was entombed in the canister by his father, the evil anti-God, millions of years ago. Birack is sceptical until jets of liquid from the canister transform some of his team into malevolent zombies. Meanwhile, the embryonic Satan is struggling to release himself, and his father's power has begun to manifest itself. Refracting the traditional conflict of Good and Evil through quantum mechanics and sub-atomic physics, the sometimes talky script remains engrossing thanks to Carpenter's chilling atmospherics. The claustrophobic terror generated by fluid camerawork and striking angles is reinforced by a narrative which builds slowly but surely towards a heart-racing climax. NF

Prince of Foxes
(Henry King, 1949, US) Tyrone Power, Wanda Hendrix, Orson Welles, Everett Sloane, Felix Aylmer, Marina Berti, Katina Paxinou.
107 min. b/w.
In one of his enforced breaks from filming *Othello*, Welles contributed a bold outline sketch for Cesare Borgia to this strikingly handsome historical drama, filmed in Italy on actual locations wherever possible. Alas, his is virtually a cameo performance, and the plot focuses less happily on Power as a soldier of fortune, determined to bury his peasant origins, who agrees to serve as Cesare's ruthless hatchet man. Much of the film is given over to his drearily prolonged crisis of conscience, resolved when he is taught a lesson in selfless humanity by the elderly duke (Aylmer) whose domain he is committed to destroy and whose young wife (Hendrix) he is busily seducing. It nevertheless remains visually splendid throughout; there's a fascinatingly detailed siege sequence (courtesy of Leonardo Da Vinci); and Everett Sloane chips in with a lively display of roguishly amoral villainy. TM

Prince of Homburg, The (Il Principe di Homburg)
(Marco Bellocchio, 1997, It) Andrea Di Stefano, Barbora Bobulova, Toni Bertorelli, Anita Laurenzi.
89 min.
A staid, uninvolving adaptation of Kleist's story about a high-born cavalry general (Di Stefano) who faces execution after disobeying orders and leading a charge that results in victory. As the

film proceeds to examine his crisis of faith, it confronts questions of honour, courage, heroism and responsibility with clarity but little dramatic force. It's a slow, elegant, lifeless costume drama, and its stylistic conservatism only adds to its aura of redundancy. GA

Prince of Jutland
(Gabriel Axel, 1994, Fr/GB/Den/Neth/Ger) Gabriel Byrne, Helen Mirren, Christian Bale, Tom Wilkinson, Brian Cox, Freddie Jones.
110 min.
A major disappointment after the delightful *Babette's Feast*, Axel's version of the Hamlet story (in English) is taken not from Shakespeare but an earlier source. Bale is the prince who goes literally barking mad (or does he?) after witnessing the murder of the king his father (Wilkinson). By the time we reach the scene in which the murderer (Byrne) 'consoles' the coveted queen (Mirren), the stilted script, half-hearted acting and overall poverty (financial and imaginative) raise the question: Is it some sort of parody? Indeed the later skirmishes are so small and scrappy they look not unlike the Pythons' glorious sketch of famous battles staged by the Batley Townswomen's Guild. GA

Prince of Pennsylvania, The
(Ron Nyswaner, 1988, US) Fred Ward, Keanu Reeves, Bonnie Bedelia, Amy Madigan, Jeff Hayenga, Tracey Ellis.
93 min.
The problem with small town movies is that story and characters can seem as inconsequential as the place itself. Nyswaner's episodic script counters this by playing up the idiosyncrasies of his horizontally mobile mining family, presided over by domineering patriarch Ward. Oppressed by Ward's narrow pursuit of the American Dream, his wife (Bedelia) turns to obsessive consumerism and clandestine nookie with Ward's best pal, while his eldest son (Reeves) indulges in Heath Robinson inventions and unrequited love for the world-weary ex-hippy owner of a run-down ice-cream joint (Madigan). Determined to avoid a life of quiet desperation, Reeves hatches a bizarre plot to kidnap his own father and split the ransom (a jealously-guarded family nest-egg) with his mother. The quirky charm soon wears thin as the shrewd observations of small town frustration give way to a more strained oddball humour. By the time Reeves dons a Freddy Krueger mask to abduct his father, one feels the desperation has begun to affect the film itself. NF

Prince of the City
(Sidney Lumet, 1981, US) Treat Williams, Jerry Orbach, Richard Foronjy, Don Billett, Kenny Marino, Carmine Caridi, Tony Page, Lindsay Crouse, Bob Balaban, James Tolkan.
167 min.
Dealing with drugs, cops and corruption, this is *Serpico* all over again, but revised, enlarged and immeasurably improved. All moral certainties have gone, leaving instead a can of worms where questions of friendship, loyalty and honesty are redefined in the ambiguous light of corruption as a NY police officer (Williams), inspired by an indefinable mixture of reformist zeal, guilty self-loathing, and sheer delight in the opportunity for headline exploits, turns informer on behalf of the DA's commission of enquiry. An astonishing in-depth portrait of the interlocking worlds of police and hoodlum results, with no punches pulled and no easy solutions. Lumet isn't noted as the most cinematic of directors; but here the intricate mosaic structure he developed in *Dog Day Afternoon* generates a dynamism entirely its own, with the invisible *mise en scène* guaranteed by the galvanising interplay of New York locations and a brilliant ensemble cast. TM

Prince of Tides, The
(Barbra Streisand, 1991, US) Nick Nolte, Barbra Streisand, Blythe Danner, Kate Nelligan, Jeroen Krabbe, Melinda Dillon, George Carlin, Jason Gould, Brad Sullivan.
132 min.
Pat Conroy's novel of tears, treacle and trauma cries out for the Sirk treatment, but gets, thanks to Streisand, the sort of over-the-top endorsement Joan Crawford brought to *Mildred Pierce*. South Carolina football coach Tom Wingo (Nolte) is called to New York by his suicidal sis-

ter's shrink, Dr Lowenstein (Streisand), to help unearth the childhood trauma. He's been bent out of shape by it, too, and can't get in touch with his love centres. During psychoanalytical sessions, his trauma surfaces in flashbacks. These are yeasty indeed. We glimpse Tom, his sister and brother underwater, where they congregate to avoid their parents. Dad (Sullivan) could give Freddy Kreuger a run for his money; Mom (Nelligan, brilliant) plays all emotional ends against the middle; but the capper comes when a pack of slavering convicts descends upon the household. Better at last, Tom makes it with Lowenstein, who seems to get a costume change in every frame. They do make 'em like it any more. BC

Princes, Les (The Princes)
(Tony Gatlif, 1982, Fr) Gérard Darmon, Muse Dalbray, Dominique Maurin, Hagop Arslanian, Tony Gatlif, Tony Librizzi, Céline Militon.
100 min.
Inhabiting a squalid slum, along with his obstinate old mother and his daughter, Nara (Darmon) has problems. He is forever threatened with eviction; his job, to say the least, is less than secure; and he is the constant victim of contempt and prejudice emanating from 'respectable' society, whose guardians are the surly gendarmes. For Nara is a gypsy, and as such is automatically relegated to the lower echelons of French society. Gatlif's episodic study of the *gitanes* of modern France carries plentiful conviction, thanks no doubt to the fact that the director is himself of Romany stock. The grim options afforded his nomadic heroes are depicted with grainy realism (Jacques Loiseleux's muted, sombre photography providing countless evocative images of a France rarely shown on film), and Gatlif rarely sentimentalises: the gypsies' macho, patriarchal culture is viewed critically, while moments of humour alleviate the film's downbeat thrust. GA

Prince – Sign o' the Times
(Prince, 1987, US) Prince, Cat, Sheila E, Sheena Easton.
85 min.
It's obvious to say, but this is a better-than-average film of a show because a Prince show is a better-than-average show. The one that didn't make it to Wembley, based around the last-but-one-album, filmed in Rotterdam and at the Paisley Park Studios, it also includes the video for *U Got The Look*, which features Easton, who is obviously a trouper but a loser in the raw sex/pure energy stakes to Cat, Prince's co-star in the sexual slapstick routines that constitute a good part of the film's visual appeal. Musically, it's a matter of opinion, but from the sparse funk of the title tune to the bebop blow-out around Charlie Parker's *Now's the Time*, this guiltless grooving in Eden fizzes with brilliantly choreographed wit and invention. MC

Prince Valiant (Prinz Eisenherz)
(Anthony Hickox, 1997, Ger/GB/Ire/US) Stephen Moyer, Katherine Heigl, Thomas Kretschmann, Edward Fox, Udo Kier, Joanna Lumley, Ron Perlman, Anthony Hickox.
91 min.
The Camelot squire Segue (Moyer) jousts in the armour of Sir Gawain (Hickox) in defence of his fallen master's reputation: watching the display is King Arthur (Fox) and his charge, slender Princess Ilene of Wales (Heigl). Bu then villains escape with Excalibur. Blaming the Scots, Arthur dispatches his lieutenants to do battle, and entrusts Segue with Ilene's safe passage home. The real culprits, however, are the Barbarians of Thule, in league with exiled Morgan Le Fey (Lumley), who's hell-bent on world domination. Directed by horror specialist Hickox with his customary visual panache – the opening is a marvel of heady whip pans, close-ups and jump cuts – this is a very contemporary, '90s timepiece. Characters and language are given a modern, revisionist sheen. Sources are sported like a coat of arms, from the story's origins (comic-strip frames interrupt/develop the narrative), to a Pythonesque pseudo-*Jabberwocky* and a *Lancelot du Lac*-like focus on detail. That said, this is hardly junior Bresson. Very silly towards the end. NB

Princess, The
(Adj Király Katonát!)
(Pál Erdöss, 1982, Hun) Erika Ozsda, Andrea Szendrei, Dénes Diczházi, Árpád Tóth.
113 min. b/w.
Fresh from school, 15-year-old Jutka and several friends leave rural Hungary for what they hope will be a better life in Budapest. But alongside the joys of boys, coffee-bars, concerts and a little money, they also discover a harsh adult world of betrayal, violence and endless compromise. With its catalogue of disasters that turn the girls' dreams into nightmares, *The Princess* might seem like a resolutely pessimistic foray into *vérité*-style naturalism; the overwhelming final impression, however, is of its characters' ability to survive against all odds. Central to the movie's faith in humanity is Erika Ozsda's glowing performance as Jutka, as she slowly but steadily is transformed from surly orphan to responsible, worldly-wise young woman. For once the realist style illuminates rather than irritates. GA

Princess Bride, The
(Rob Reiner, 1987, US) Cary Elwes, Mandy Patinkin, Chris Sarandon, Christopher Guest, Wallace Shawn, Andre the Giant, Robin Wright, Peter Falk, Carol Kane, Peter Cook, Mel Smith.
98 min.
A fairytale as told to a bedridden boy: the willowy Buttercup (Wright), destined as consort to the wicked Prince Humperdinck (Sarandon), is abducted and whisked through a series of life-threatening exploits and miscast comic cameos. The story, adapted from William Goldman's book, is partly a traditional fantasy, with a damsel in distress, dashing lover, evil villains, and lotsa monsters and swordfights, but also a knowing commentary on the conventions of all such tales. The tone falls disconcertingly between straight action adventure and anachronistic Jewish spoof; the leads are vacuous; the absurdities sometimes forced and obvious. Only Guest's sadistic Count Rugen and Patinkin's vengeful Spanish swordsman inject any real enthusiasm into the proceedings; but the film does exude a certain innocent, unassertive charm, and kids will probably love it. GA

Princess Caraboo
(Michael Austin, 1994, US) Phoebe Cates, Jim Broadbent, Wendy Hughes, Kevin Kline, John Lithgow, Stephen Rea, John Sessions, John Wells, Roger Lloyd Pack, Murray Melvin.
97 min.
Based on a true story, this decorative social satire relates the case of a beautiful vagabond picked up near Bristol in 1817, who claims to be Princess Caraboo, escaped from a slave ship. Roundly mocked as an impostor, she winds up in court, but her composure commands respect and a wealthy woman takes her in. While insecure Mrs Worrall (Hughes) detects true quality, her husband (Broadbent) is more sceptical, but once dreams of lucrative trade beckon, he's as ready as his wife to parade their enigmatic guest. Caraboo lives it up in Regency society, but the servants, convinced that 'one of them' is pulling a fast one, plot to unmask her. Phoebe Cates's intriguing Caraboo transcends all tests. Called on to convince an ethnographer, she flunks badly, but he leaves in tears, touched by her grace. An everyday story of social-climbing and neo-classicism, this is a winner. SFe

Princess Charming
(Maurice Elvey, 1934, GB) Evelyn Laye, Henry Wilcoxon, Yvonne Arnaud, Max Miller, George Grossmith, Finlay Currie, Ivor Barnard, Francis L Sullivan.
78 min. b/w.
As a princess escaping from revolutionaries, in disguise and married to the handsome captain of the guard (although already promised to a neighbouring ruler), Laye finds her singing brutally curtailed by a bunch of ersatz Bolsheviks and Max Miller's machine-gun humour. Elvey's direction is, to say the least, erratic; but the Gainsborough emphasis on speed and economy prevents the film from plunging into embarrassing longueurs. Continuity and plot plausibility become increasingly irrelevant as Miller indelicately tramples upon the conventions of Ruritanian musical romance, in the end galvanising the rest of the cast enough to transform the film into a gloriously funny pantomime. RMy

Principe di Homburg, Il
see Prince of Homburg, The

Prinz Eisenherz
see Prince Valiant

Prise de Pouvoir par Louis XIV, La (The Rise to Power of Louis XIV)
(Roberto Rossellini, 1966, Fr) Jean-Marie Patte, Raymond Jourdan, Silvagni, Katharina Renn, Dominique Vincent, Pierre Barrat.
102 min.
'Power is shared by too many hands': the Sun King ponders problems of maintaining monarchic strength in the face of hungry peasants and conniving nobility. Rossellini displays the king's bizarre but effective methods of minimising the threat of insurgence: reserving every governmental decision for himself, assembling the aristocrats full-time at Versailles away from parliament, and forcing them into debt through emulation of his own extravagant tastes in fashion. Brilliantly marshalling performance, colour, dialogue, and above all claustrophobic space, Rossellini reveals the customs, atmosphere and ideology of Louis' reign with an unrivalled lucidity and honesty; at the same time he creates a new moral cinema of history. Draining his account of distracting dramatic artifice, he constructs a cinema of ideas, didactic without being propagandistic, cerebral but highly accessible. It's as inventive as Syberberg's tableaux, but endowed with infinitely greater clarity. GA

Prison
(Renny Harlin, 1987, US) Viggo Mortensen, Chelsea Field, Lane Smith, Lincoln Kilpatrick, Tom Everett, Ivan Kane, Andre De Shields.
103 min.
Way out in the Wyoming wastes, a rotting concrete hell-hole, once Creedmore Penitentiary, condemned these 20 years, is re-commissioned to ease overcrowding. It has a guilty secret: back then an innocent man was given a 60,000 volt goodbye in the execution chamber, and Sharpe kept stumm. Unluckily for Sharpe, the victim's spirit decided to hang around to exact gruesome revenge. With an assured visual style, Harlin stokes up the temperature to near-riot conditions before exploding the screen with electrifying special effects mayhem – floors glow red hot, barbed wire is vivified, the very pipes take on murderous life. The staple array of cons and screws are interestingly characterised, and the woman-reformer-to-the-rescue plot is neatly integrated with the supernatural effects. A tough, entertaining, intelligent hybrid of hard-ass prison drama and horror-shocker exploiter from Charles Band's Empire Pictures. WH

Prisoner, The
(Peter Glenville, 1955, GB) Alec Guinness, Jack Hawkins, Raymond Huntley, Wilfrid Lawson, Jeannette Sterke, Ronald Lewis, Kenneth Griffith.
91 min. b/w.
Bridget Boland's play has been opened out slightly to emphasise a context of social unrest in an unspecified totalitarian (Eastern bloc?) state, but as with other works about inquisition, the suspect's ordeal becomes the audience's. Glenville stands back from time to time so that we can really appreciate the performances of Guinness, as a Cardinal subjected to torture for his beliefs, and Hawkins as his inquisitor; but in boxing parlance, he might have broken up more of the clinches. TCh

Prisoner of Rio
(Lech Majewski, 1988, Braz) Steven Berkoff, Paul Freeman, Peter Firth, Florinda Bolkan, José Wilker, Zezé Mota, Desmond Llewelyn.
105 min.
The fact that Ronnie Biggs co-wrote this fiasco (filmed in English) may explain the portrait of the Great Train Robber as a sharp-witted charmer, his sole real concern in life his son. The story recounts the less-than-legal efforts of cop Berkoff (macho, variable accent) to bring Biggs (Freeman, larger-than-life Londoner) back to Blighty and prison. The intrigue is messily and murkily conceived, involving undercover agents, swarthy thugs, shady fixers, and much predictable ado about

Carnival. Majewski renders entire scenes devoid of dramatic point or meaning by the sort of editing that makes you wonder what's happening, why, and where; the pacing is listless, the camera invariably wrongly placed, the whole stitched with leering shots of skimpily clad revellers and travelogue padding. Risible throughout. GA

Prisoner of Second Avenue, The
(Melvin Frank, 1975, US) Jack Lemmon, Anne Bancroft, Gene Saks, Elizabeth Wilson, Florence Stanley, Maxine Stuart, Ed Peck, Sylvester Stallone.
105 min.
A promising opening, with Lemmon pitting his nervous energy against a New York heat wave. But a glance at the credits gives rise to a stifling feeling of over-familiarity: director from *A Touch of Class*, author (Neil Simon) of numerous well-oiled Broadway hits, guest actor (Saks) better known for directing film versions of those hits. It all adds up to one of those wisecracking comedies that move smoothly and predictably through set pieces dwelling on the frustrations of urban life and the toll exacted on Lemmon and Bancroft's middle class marriage. At least it confirms Anne Bancroft's latent talent for comedy, but otherwise there's little more than routine jokes like the day in the country, the relations, the buckets of water, the burglary, the TV dinners, and the glib touches of sentimentality that warn you the ending's coming up. CPe

Prisoner of Shark Island, The
(John Ford, 1936, US) Warner Baxter, Gloria Stuart, Joyce Kay, Claude Gillingwater, Harry Carey, Paul Fix, John Carradine.
95 min. b/w.
One of Ford's least dated films from the '30s, even though its attitude towards the blacks it portrays is (understandably, given the times) undeniably racist. Inspired by historical reality, it begins with the assassination of the director's beloved, almost Godlike Lincoln by John Wilkes Booth, before proceeding to focus on the harsh fate dealt by destiny and an unforgiving America to Dr Samuel A Mudd, imprisoned for treating Booth's wounded leg. If the quasi-liberal message is undermined not only by a nostalgia for the Old (ie slave-owning) South but also by the over-emphatic assertions of Mudd's innocence, the film is nevertheless for the most part tautly scripted (by Dudley Nichols), vividly shot, and blessed with muscular performances. Baxter excels himself as the good doctor whose selfless integrity finally ensures his pardon, while Carradine's sadistic prison guard is terrific. GA

Prisoner of the Cannibal God
see Montagna del Dio Cannibale, La

Prisoner of the Mountains (Kavkazski Plennik)
(Sergei Bodrov, 1996, Kazakhstan/Rus) Oleg Menshikov, Sergei Bodrov Jr, Djemal Sikharulidze, Susanna Mekhralieva, Alexei Zharkov, Valentina Fedotova.
99 min.
Two Russian soldiers (one experienced, one a rookie) are ambushed and taken hostage by a Chechen village chieftain who intends to trade them for his son, imprisoned by the Russian authorities. That's about it in terms of plot, with the two soldiers falling out and getting to know each other, trying to work out a means of escape, and coming to some sort of uneasy, suspicious understanding of their captors. Bodrov's clear-eyed, unsentimental, but engrossing film is impressive for many reasons: its genuinely unromanticised sympathy for the Chechens, its awareness of the absurd futility of war, its insistence that despite cultural differences we share a common humanity, the use of landscape, and the marvellous performances (with the director's son terrific as the novice Russian). GA

Prisoner of Zenda, The
(John Cromwell, 1937, US) Ronald Colman, Madeleine Carroll, Douglas Fairbanks Jr, Raymond Massey, Mary Astor, C Aubrey Smith, David Niven, Montagu Love.
101 min. b/w.
Easily the best version of Anthony Hope's perennial Ruritanian adventure, often cited as one of the great swashbucklers. It's certainly impeccably cast, with Colman at his dashingly romantic

best doubling as the King and the English looka-like who helps to save his throne, while Fairbanks revels in Rupert of Hentzau's charming villainy, Carroll provides a sweetly melting princess, and Massey is iconographically perfect as Black Michael the usurper. Lots of pomp and splendour (especially in the over-indulged Coronation sequence) make Cromwell's elegant direction incline to stateliness, but the swordplay is ripping and Wong Howe's camerawork superb. TM

Prisoner of Zenda, The

(Richard Thorpe, 1952, US) Stewart Granger, Deborah Kerr, James Mason, Louis Calhern, Jane Greer, Lewis Stone, Robert Douglas, Robert Coote.
100 min.
Lush but rather leaden remake of Anthony Hope's Ruritanian romance, establishing some sort of continuity by casting Lewis Stone, star of the 1922 version, in a supporting role as the Cardinal. Entertaining enough, though Granger is merely competent by comparison with Colman in the 1937 version, and Thorpe hasn't a tenth of Cromwell's style. Mason, though basically miscast, runs away with the acting honours as a Teutonically villainous Rupert of Hentzau, and Joseph Ruttenberg contributes some attractive Technicolor camerawork.

Prisoner of Zenda, The

(Richard Quine, 1979, US) Peter Sellers, Lynne Frederick, Lionel Jeffries, Elke Sommer, Gregory Sierra, Jeremy Kemp, Catherine Schell, Norman Rossington, John Laurie.
108 min.
A limp and shoddy farce in which neither Sellers' lifeless double-role mugging, nor a dire fish-out-of-water script by Dick Clement and Ian La Frenais, encourage anything more than a deepening nostalgia for the straightfaced swashbuckling of previous adaptations of Anthony Hope's novel. Here the intrigues of Ruritanian royalty are conveyed with all the comic panache of an overlong Christmas variety show sketch on TV. PT

Prison Girls

(Thomas de Simone, 1973, US) Robin Whitting, Angie Monet, Tracy Handfuss, Maria Arrold, Liz Wolfe.
94 min.
Various girls undergo sexual rehabilitation during a two-day parole from prison (a plot is hastily added at the very end: the authorities have let the girls out in the hope that one of them will lead the police to a notorious hoodlum). Thanks to the censor, the episodes range in quality from the pretty dire to the abysmal. An Angels' gang-bang survives more or less intact, while a sequence involving a woman being brought to climax for the first time is cut almost into non-existence. Two points of interest: no one makes it as far as a bed (sofas and floors draw at two apiece); and although characters drag hard on the occasional joint, no one thinks of actually lighting it.

Prison Stories: Women on the Inside

(Donna Deitch/Joan Micklin Silver/Penelope Spheeris, 1990, US) Rae Dawn Chong, Lolita Davidovich, Annabella Sciorra, Talisa Soto, Rachel Ticotin, Silvana Gallardo, Grace Zabriskie, Francesca Roberts.
90 min.
Made for cable, this three-part film by women, about women in prison and its effect upon their families, is less convincing than the average TV documentary. Outwardly swaggering but inwardly crushed, the subjects gradually progress towards rehabilitation and remorse to save their children. Prison authorities come across as tough but fair, with the exception of the members of Silver's 'Parole Board' – easily the best of the trio – who have trouble understanding that a pregnant battered wife who sees her daughter attacked might resort to firearms. BC

Private Affairs of Bel Ami, The

(Albert Lewin, 1947, US) George Sanders, Angela Lansbury, Ann Dvorak, Frances Dee, Albert Basserman, Hugo Haas, Katherine Emery, Warren William, John Carradine.
112 min. b/w.
A lovingly literate adaptation of Maupassant's novella about a soldier (Sanders) returning from

the wars without prospects, persuaded to capitalise on the good looks that seem irresistible to women, and finding it difficult to get off the roundabout even when he falls genuinely in love (with the wonderful Lansbury). Set in a stylish evocation of 19th century Paris partly based on contemporary paintings, and partly (like the London of *The Picture of Dorian Gray*) a vivid product of the imagination, the film fascinatingly refuses to stigmatise its hero as he becomes increasingly and tragically mired. If there is a villain, it is a society so dependent on the appearances of success that everyone in it is encouraged to adopt a facade to reap their just rewards. In a series of elliptical asides that combine into a wry comment on the non-status of the career woman at that time, Lewin even contrives to suggest that the widow of a distinguished journalist who helps Sanders on his way to success not only secretly writes his copy, but had done the same for her husband for years. A sadly neglected film. TM

Private Benjamin

(Howard Zieff, 1980, US) Goldie Hawn, Eileen Brennan, Armand Assante, Robert Webber, Sam Wanamaker, Barbara Barrie, Mary Kay Place, Harry Dean Stanton, Albert Brooks.
110 min.
Before he fell victim to the debilitating Hollywood law that demands comedy star vehicles be written by committee, Zieff showed in *Slither* and *Hollywood Cowboy* a real flair for enhancing off-the-wall fun material. But *Private Benjamin*, concocted by no less than three scribes from a collective semi-consciousness bounded by re-runs of *M*A*S*H* and *No Time for Sergeants*, lodges gracelessly alongside *House Calls* and *The Main Event* as an anonymous chore for its director. Another depressing example of the big-screen gag-string sitcom, it turns exclusively on a plot that grew from a concept that developed from an idea that somebody should never have had – Goldie Hawn joins the army. PT

Private Club (Club Privé pour Couples Avertis)

(Max Pécas, 1974, Fr) Philippe Gasté, Eva Stroll, Patrick Lachaume, Chantal Arondel, Michel Vocoret.
90 min.
Sometimes funny, often inept story of a Parisian taxi-driver who goes over the top when he discovers that his fiancée works in an exclusive brothel (whose wares he nevertheless samples without scruple). Some characterisation seeps in at the edges, and there's even a twist to the plot, such as it is. But it of course turns out that the fiancée was being blackmailed, so a rather abrupt true-love ending wins out over the 'liberated' hedonism preached elsewhere in the film. It's notable mainly for the curious blessing given by implication to the audience in one scene: as the bushes fill up with snoopers trying to see what's going on with a trio on the back seat of a taxi, someone announces that such people are quite harmless, being there only to pay 'their respects to these lovely goddesses – it's a time-honoured ritual'. Which is one way of putting it.

Private Conversation, A (Bez Svidetelei)

(Nikita Mikhalkov, 1983, USSR) Irina Kupchenko, Mikhail Ulyanov.
93 min.
An ex-husband unexpectedly returns to his former wife's flat. He is boozy and belligerent, elated with the success of his daughter's concert; she timid, dowdy and anxious about their son. Appearances are inevitably not what they seem, and an intricate power game commences to the ironic accompaniment of romantic schmaltz on the TV. Worth seeing for the acting alone, especially for Ulyanov as he exposes the pathetic justifications of a paranoid failure who knows he has gone off the rails. JE

Private Enterprise, A

(Peter K Smith, 1974, GB) Salmaan Peer, Marc Zuber, Ramon Sinha, Yehye Saeed, Diana Quick, Subhash Luthra.
78 min.
A nicely quirky and human-scaled study of a young Birmingham Asian undergoing cultural dislocations as he tries to come to terms with trade union activity at work and the prospect of a prearranged marriage within his ethnic com-

munity. Smith's occasionally absurdist eye, and Peer's performance as the low-key hero determined to become an individual citizen rather than an immigration statistic, lift this low-budget first feature out of the problem pic rut. PT

Private Files of J Edgar Hoover, The

(Larry Cohen, 1977, US) Broderick Crawford, José Ferrer, Michael Parks, Ronee Blakley, Rip Torn, Celeste Holm, Michael Sacks, Dan Dailey, Raymond St Jacques, Howard da Silva, June Havoc, Lloyd Nolan, John Marley.
112 min.
Rattling compulsively along through myth and history like some factoid TV mini-series, but constantly informed by a radical intelligence and humour, Cohen's analytical biopic surprisingly resolves into a complex investigation of the forces of realpolitik and sexual politics which created an arch-villain/monster from a moralist boy-scout lawyer. The movie may have the look of tabloid sleaze, but it never trades in the simplistic put-down or facile political optimism. If the idea of Hoover as a tragic figure hardly squares with the '70s consensus, then the playing, especially of Broderick Crawford as Hoover, does much to shift the prejudice; while at the point where post-Watergate cinema would usually present us with a revelatory crusader, Rip Torn's uptight FBI agent (our narrator) peters out into confused impotence. Genre fans can take comfort, however, since some expectations are happily served...Dillinger dies again. PT

Private Function, A

(Malcolm Mowbray, 1984, GB) Michael Palin, Maggie Smith, Denholm Elliott, Richard Griffiths, Tony Haygarth, John Normington, Bill Paterson, Liz Smith, Alison Steadman.
94 min.
Set in a small Yorkshire town in 1947, this first feature scripted by Alan Bennett is a pig-movie, about the smells they make and the lengths to which people went to steal one in austerity Britain, when there really was an illicit trade in the animals. Onto this thin premise, Bennett and Mowbray layer a subplot of middle class social warfare as timid chiropodist Palin and his wife Maggie Smith, a Lady Macbeth of the aspidistras, try to scale the heights of Northern society by nicking a porker secretly earmarked for the town's celebration of the coming marriage of Princess Elizabeth. Too downbeat for farce, too whimsical to be an effective observation of the reality of ration-book Britain, the movie seems a mess, despite fine performances. RR

Private Hell 36

(Don Siegel, 1954, US) Ida Lupino, Steve Cochran, Warren Duff, Dean Jagger, Dorothy Malone.
81 min. b/w.
Minor by Siegel standards, but still an admirably neat, tight B thriller from Lupino's Filmakers company (she also co-scripted), with Cochran and Duff as two LA cops who accidentally stumble on the loot during a robbery investigation, the latter reluctantly playing along with the former's impulsive decision to keep it for themselves. Familiar stuff, with conscience and comeuppance dogging their every move (the title refers to the trailer park where their guilty secret is stashed), but given a vivid edge by the characterisations (Cochran the likeable good-timer, Duff the dour family man) and the plausible motivations. A fellow cop is killed in the line of duty, and the latent resentment of men risking their lives for too little pay is given a turn of the screw because Duff now has a baby to provide for, and Cochran falls hard for a singer (Lupino) who loves him but asks for the moon. Siegel's direction (the opening sequence in particular, with an off-duty Cochran stumbling perilously in on a store robbery while on his way home, is a gem) is impeccable. TM

Private Lesson, The (Lezioni Private)

(Vittorio De Sisti, 1975, It) Carroll Baker, Renzo Montagnani, Rosalina Cellamare, Leonora Fani, Emilio Lo Curcio, Leopoldo Trieste.
93 min.
Determined not to let personal feelings hamper her career, matronly music teacher Carroll Baker grits her teeth and submits to the unconventional demands of a teenage homosexual blackmailer. De Sisti opts for an over-familiar evocation of

the '50s and a conventional loss-of-virginity sex-ploiter, hampered by the customary contrivances and caricatures of the genre. JPy

Private Lessons
(Alan Myerson, 1980, US) Sylvia Kristel, Howard Hesseman, Eric Brown, Patrick Piccininni, Ed Begley Jr, Pamela Bryant.
87 min.
Anyone who enjoyed *Steelyard Blues* and waited patiently for Myerson's second big screen venture, might be tempted by this; but unless you're also a 15-year-old male virgin dreaming of being sexually initiated by your father's housekeeper, who just happens to be Sylvia Kristel, then forget it. This particular wet dream is wrapped in a vacuous blackmail plot (which enables the young hero to fantasise that he's fucked Sylvia to death, and her to reveal her heart of gold) and padded with lots of horrible Golden Oldie soft-centred Rock (Clapton, Rod Stewart, etc). But Teen Oriented Voyeurism rules as the protagonist (Brown) stalks his prey (and her stand-in) armed with cameras, binoculars, and an overtly Oedipal mix of fear and desire. SJ

Private Life (Chastnaya Zhizn)
(Yuli Raizman, 1982, USSR) Mikhail Ulyanov, Iya Savvina, Irina Gubanova, Tatyana Dogileva, Aleksei Blokhin.
104 min.
About the spiritual desolation of a workaholic factory manager (Ulyanov) who finds himself retired early, and finds suddenly that he has no friends and can no longer talk to anyone in his family. The languorous pace and utter obviousness of every point encourages the mind to wander, and it ultimately runs for the cover of easy sentimentality. Hard to dislike, though, since its main quality is its burning sincerity. TR

Private Life, A
(Francis Gerard, 1988, GB) Bill Flynn, Jana Cilliers, Kevin Smith, Ian Roberts, Anthony Fridjhon, Joanna Weinberg.
93 min.
Based on the true story of Jack and Stella Dupont, who waged a 30-year fight against South African apartheid and its laws forbidding marriage across the colour bar. Gerard's film traces the couple's relationship from their first meeting, when policeman Jack wanders into the café where Stella (of mixed race background but untraced birth registration) works; after he leaves the force, the emphasis is on their efforts to maintain domestic harmony while contesting Stella's classification as coloured. The focus is almost exclusively on tension within the family rather than the broader context of confrontation, which produces an emotional force that is direct and uncluttered; but Jack's position as a solid, stable force is too literally conveyed, a fault due in part to the fact that Bill Flynn offers only modest support to Jana Cilliers' sensitive performance. Worthy and at times moving, but with a soppy and intrusive score. CM

Private Life of Henry VIII, The
(Alexander Korda, 1933, GB) Charles Laughton, Binnie Barnes, Robert Donat, Elsa Lanchester, Merle Oberon, Wendy Barrie, Everley Gregg, John Loder.
96 min. b/w.
'Am I a king or a breeding bull?' Laughton sulkily roars down the dinner table in what is probably the most commercially successful British film ever made. Throughout the film, he manages to hold in tension Henry's greedy enjoyment of the trappings of power and his weary loathing for a life where everything, especially his sexual performance, is a matter of public interest. Laughton's transformation from bullying womaniser to henpecked glutton is a masterly study of a man's decline into dotage, but it is still only the icing on the cake of an amazing exploration of the morbid doubts and fears underlying a seemingly virile masculinity. RMy

Private Life of Sherlock Holmes, The
(Billy Wilder, 1970, GB) Robert Stephens, Colin Blakely, Irene Handl, Christopher Lee, Tamara Toumanova, Genevieve Page, Clive Revill, Catherine Lacey, Stanley Holloway.
125 min.
A wonderful, cruelly underrated film. Although there are some terrifically funny moments, and on

one level the Wilder/Diamond conception of Conan Doyle's hero does tend to debunk the myth of the perfect sleuth (there are allusions to his misogyny and cocaine addiction), this alternative vision of Holmes sets up a stylish and totally appropriate story (concerning dwarves, dead canaries, and the Loch Ness monster) as a context in which to explain the reason for Holmes' forsaking of his emotional life to become a thinking machine. Betrayal and lost love are the elements that catalyse this process, turning Holmes from a fallible romantic into a disillusioned cynic. With a stunning score by Miklos Rozsa, carefully modulated performances, lush location photography, and perfect sets by Trauner, it is Wilder's least embittered film and by far his most moving. GA

Private Lives of Elizabeth and Essex, The
(Michael Curtiz, 1939, US) Bette Davis, Errol Flynn, Olivia de Havilland, Donald Crisp, Vincent Price, Henry Daniell, Nanette Fabray, Alan Hale, Robert Warwick, Leo G Carroll.
106 min.
Not so much a swashbuckler as a costume romance, kept high-toned (not to say strangled) by its source in a Maxwell Anderson play. Dominated by historical inaccuracies and a tightly controlled performance from Davis as the waspish queen, all too conscious of her fading charms and her favourite Flynn's roguishly roving eye. Some spectacular pageantry too in what was, oddly enough, the only colour film in which Davis appeared until the '50s. TM

Private Parts
(Paul Bartel, 1972, US) Ayn Ruymen, Lucille Benson, John Ventantonio, Laurie Main, Stanley Livingstone, Charles Woolf, Ann Gibbs.
87 min.
Bartel's first feature is a version of his perennial theme: caricatured straight middle class values brought up against caricatured sexual excesses. The heroine is a teenage runaway (straight out of a *Beach Party* movie) who takes refuge in a seedy San Francisco hotel populated with freaks, perverts, and nuts. The funniest of the latter is the guilty leather queen with a secret phallic shrine in his room; the most inventively conceived is the transvestite photographer who uses a hypo as a phallic substitute and has a thing about dirty bath-water. Bartel himself doesn't remember it too fondly, probably because the plot's demands sometimes get in the way of the humour, but it is in exceptionally poor taste, and the tone is quintessential Bartel. TR

Private Parts
(Betty Thomas, 1997, US) Howard Stern, Robin Quivers, Mary McCormack, Fred Norris, Michael Murphy.
109 min.
Given US 'shock jock' Howard Stern's most conspicuous qualities – the ultra-nerdy appearance, the unrepentant egotism, the arrested adolescent obsession with breast and penis size – you'd be forgiven for expecting this loose adaptation of his best-selling 'autobiography' to be embarrassing and annoying in equal measure. Nor do the opening scenes bode well. But once the film flashes back to trawl through his life and career – from staging salacious puppet shows for OAPs as a kid, through the endless battles with station bosses angered by his determination to say and do whatever he wants on-air, to his final vindication, in 1985, as America's top radio personality – it's hard to resist his rude, gleeful determination to rid himself of the taboos, predictability and tedium of conventional radio. Though Betty Thomas's movie tones down some of Stern's more troubling takes on sensitive issues and plays up his enduring relationship with his astonishingly supportive wife (McCormack), it still has more than enough outrageous moments to sustain hilarity until the end credits. No one could seriously take Stern for a people's hero – he's too crass, conceited and self-serving – but here at least, as a non-PC mirth-monger, he has what it takes, no shit. GA

Private Pleasures (I Lust och Nöd)
(Paul Gerber, 1976, Swe) Elona Glenn, Ulf Brunnberg, Per-Axel Arosenius, Marie Ekorre, Caroline Christensen.
96 min.

This somewhat pretentious Swedish sex offering about a young woman's discovery of her 'duality' displays a lot of ostentatious camerawork and arty editing which will probably go unnoticed by most patrons. Essentially a rather stolid reworking of the *Emmanuelle* themes, the film nevertheless makes some effort with its psychological mystery plot and attention to detail. Occasional sequences deserve a place in a much better movie (a drowsy conversation in the bright sun, for instance), and Elona Glenn adds distinction. The rest scarcely lives up to its rather over-inflated estimation of its own 'significance'.

Private Popsicle (Sapiches)
(Boaz Davidson, 1982, Isr/WGer) Iftach Katzur, Zachi Noy, Jonathan Segal, Sonia Martin, Menache Warshawsky.
100 min.
Or, 'Carry On Up the Golan Heights'. The fourth episode in the seemingly inexhaustible spew of puerile sexual antics, scatological language, and inappropriately used '50s pop soundtrack, has the *Lemon Popsicle* trio called up for National Service. Amid tried, tested and worried-to-death clichés of the army training camp (including ignorant ranting sergeant, visiting dignitaries, and mistaken rank identities), Eckel, Meckel and Schmeckel descend beyond the limits of bad taste to literally end up covered in excreta. The plot is as fresh as an Italian's armpit, the dubbing was seemingly done by a blind deaf mute, and the jokes are as funny as bubonic plague. FL

Private Road
(Barney Platts-Mills, 1971, GB) Susan Penhaligon, Bruce Robinson, Michael Feast, George Fenton, Robert Brown, Kathleen Byron, Patricia Cutts.
89 min.
Platts-Mills' second feature steps up a class from working to middle, but remains as quietly and sympathetically observant as *Bronco Bullfrog*, though this time using professional actors and a bolder visual stylisation. Very much of its time in its account of a girl's attempt to escape the cosy suburbanism of her family in Esher – by way of an affair with a classless writer who introduces her to the dropout world – it remains as engagingly unclassifiable as *Bronco Bullfrog*. Well worth a look for its odd mixture of romanticism and scepticism about society's future. TM

Privates on Parade
(Michael Blakemore, 1982, GB) John Cleese, Denis Quilley, Michael Elphick, Nicola Pagett, Bruce Payne, Joe Melia, David Bamber, Simon Jones, Patrick Pearson.
113 min.
An adaptation of Peter Nichols' play which continues the strange British love affair with National Service, the Far East, and tatty theatrical camp, rolling them all together in a thin excuse for a plot: a troupe of virgin soldiers trek around up-country Malaysia, doing Carmen Miranda impressions to audiences of blank-faced Gurkhas, and getting caught in the crossfire between Communists, the locals, and their own sergeant's gun-running activities. A few laughs, a few tears; something palatable is being said about the state of the nation. Through it all strides Cleese, barking his familiar brand of pop-eyed, cheerful racism to cover the unmistakable air of a man fighting a losing battle. But it's all rather wan; the sensibilities remain stubbornly theatrical, and the English countryside resolutely refuses to stand in for the Malaysian jungle. CPea

Private's Progress
(John Boulting, 1956, GB) Ian Carmichael, Richard Attenborough, Dennis Price, Terry-Thomas, William Hartnell, Peter Jones, Victor Maddern, Jill Adams, Thorley Walters, Ian Bannen, Jon Le Mesurier, Kenneth Griffith, George Coulouris.
102 min. b/w.
A delightful Boulting Brothers comedy about a mild, innocent undergraduate (Carmichael) drafted into the army, falling in with a bunch of spivs, and being sent to Germany disguised as a Nazi to steal art treasures. The absurdly irreverent attitude towards everything – army routines,

class snobbery, official protocol, and corruption – is the stuff of amiable, nostalgic farce rather than biting satire, but it's beautifully performed by a host of character actors and often very funny. GA

Private Vices & Public Virtues (Vizi Privati, Pubbliche Virtù)

(Miklós Jancsó, 1976, It/Yugo) Lajos Balázsovits, Pamela Villoresi, Franco Branciaroli, Teresa Ann Savoy, Laura Betti.
104 min.
This continues Jancsó's attack on paternalist authority, but its dreamily languorous pace is about all it has in common with its predecessors. Filmed in Italy, it uses the Mayerling story as the basis for a political fable about an act of rebellion: a young prince refuses to bend to his father's will, by staying on his country estate and by debauching the sons and daughters of local landowners to create a scandal in the capital. Apart from the cruel but inevitable pay-off, that's really all that happens, but Jancsó elaborates it into an extraordinary multi-sexual erotic rhapsody, using dancers rather than actors to turn the pastoral drama into something like an Elizabethan masque. The sexual aspect manages to be completely forthright (it centres on the figure of a hermaphrodite) but not at all prurient; as if Freud's 'polymorphous perversity' were the ultimate weapon against patriarchal tyranny. TR

Privilege

(Peter Watkins, 1967, GB) Paul Jones, Jean Shrimpton, Mark London, Max Bacon, Jeremy Child, William Job, James Cossins.
103 min.
There's no denying Watkins' ambition and intelligence in this satire of the rock world being used by the Establishment as a force for keeping the masses quiet in times of hardship and fascism; but much of the acting is poor, while the tone is frequently far too hysterical for its own good. That said, Johnny Speight's story, of an enormously successful pop idol (Jones) being manipulated by the government for their own devious purposes, did allow Watkins to make some pertinent points anticipating both the Festival of Light, and the way that rock culture has been absorbed and rendered harmless by the society it is supposed to be rebelling against. GA

Privilege

(Yvonne Rainer, 1990, US) Alice Spivak, Novella Nelson, Blaire Baron.
103 min. b/w & col.
Rainer's meditative film on the menopause has a mock-documentary framework: 'Yvonne', a black American film-maker, conducts a series of interviews with middle-aged women. Interspersed are clips from hilarious black-and-white educational films with pompous male doctors. The camera also watches a computer screen, scrolling up provocative texts, messages from the real or the fictional documentary-maker. The menopause is rather left behind as we follow the story of Jenny, a white friend of the fictional Yvonne. Her experiences with a lesbian neighbour and two repellent local men serve to muddle the central issue. In the end the message seems simply to be that we often disparage people who are older or darker-skinned than us, and that men in general aren't very nice to women. SFe

Privileged

(Michael Hoffman, 1982, GB) Robert Woolley, Diana Katis, Hughie Grant, Victoria Studd, James Wilby.
96 min.
The story of the making of Privileged would make a good film: a group of Oxford students under the avuncular eye of John Schlesinger make a film. Instead, the students have opted for undergraduate melodrama, which rather tiresomely echoes Schlesinger's '60s-style narcissism. Edward (Woolley), who's generously endowed with arrogance, leads an attractive quartet of fellow-students through the travails of love, during rehearsals for a production of The Duchess of Malfi which acts as an arena and a mirror for their emotional ups and downs. Curiously, for a first film, this is well acted, well paced, and made with considerable style (per-

haps too much, as punts float by lazily and all too familiarly), but the content is so light that it has all but blown away before the credits roll. LU

Prize of Arms, A

(Cliff Owen, 1961, GB) Stanley Baker, Tom Bell, Helmut Schmid, John Westbrook, John Phillips, Fulton Mackay, Patrick Magee, Geoffrey Palmer.
105 min. b/w.
Cashiered army officer Baker, dismissed from the service for black marketeering, teams with Tom Bell and Polish explosives expert Schmid to steal a military payroll bound for North Africa in this watchable selection of heist-goes-wrong plot manoeuvres. Atmospheric and authentic army camp-life photography by Gilbert Taylor; based on a story co-credited to Nicolas Roeg. TJ

Prize of Peril, The (Le Prix du Danger)

(Yves Boisset, 1983, Fr/Yugo) Gérard Lanvin, Michel Piccoli, Marie-France Pisier, Bruno Cremer, Andréa Ferreol, Jean Rougerie.
98 min.
A desperately dumb variation on the thesis that all the world's a telly channel, life (and death) just another game show. Unemployment is rising, ratings are falling, when a TV executive comes up with a show that pits a solitary volunteer contestant against a team of armed hunters in a once-a-week chase across the city, filmed live up to and including the moment of death. The show wins Christians vs Lions popularity. Everyone is happy: the producer (Pisier, just bitching it in the absence of a scripted character), the presenter (Piccoli, in Daz-white suit and slipping hair-piece), and the advertisers. Until Lanvin, playing The Hero (remember heroes? they're supposed to win), makes his bid for the million-dollar prize and discovers (you don't say) the game is rigged. Plot weaknesses apart, there's something culturally unreal about this cheapie Paris production with second-rate stuntwork that tries to be (the dubbing doesn't help) mid-Atlantic or universal. MA

Prizzi's Honor

(John Huston, 1985, US) Jack Nicholson, Kathleen Turner, Robert Loggia, John Randolph, William Hickey, Lee Richardson, Michael Lombard, Anjelica Huston, Lawrence Tierney, CCH Pounder.
129 min.
When hit man Nicholson, a thick lieutenant for the Prizzi mob, falls for unknown beauty Turner, it's bad luck that she too turns out to be a highly paid, if freelance, assassin. She's also brainy enough to take the Prizzi clan for a financial ride; so it's only a matter of time before it's a case of till death do them part. The movie's success lies in Huston's very sure manipulation of mood and tone, somehow connecting black comedy, tongue-in-cheek acting, heavy irony, and even high camp into a coherent story. For all the coast-to-coast jetting, the action is largely composed of faces talking in rooms; the period could be '50s, could be '80s; and Nicholson's thick-upper-lip impersonation of Burt Young has him moving perilously close to Brando, both in mannerism and sheer size. It is, however, a very stylish walk with love and death. CPea

Pro

see Number One

Problem Child

(Dennis Dugan, 1990, US) John Ritter, Jack Warden, Michael Oliver, Gilbert Gottfried, Amy Yasbeck, Michael Richards.
81 min.
For this story to work (wealthy, shallow but well-meaning parents adopt nightmare child), the audience should identify with the boy, or at least feel a sneaking admiration for his antics. But Michael Oliver's snotty, fakesy-cutesy, grating, whining brat is a fatal turn-off. A film this bad just has to have a mushy message, and it's this: unloved and unwanted, it isn't until he meets Ben Healy (Ritter) and experiences unconditional love, that the unspeakable Junior attains a sense of self-worth. This isn't so much a film about parenting as fathering; the bitch-wife who wants a child purely as a lifestyle accessory is finally and humiliatingly removed from the scene so that Dad and his lad

can march off into the happy sunset of mutual regard. Enough to make you gag. SFe

Problem Child 2

(Brian Levant, 1991, US) John Ritter, Michael Oliver, Jack Warden, Laraine Newman, Amy Yasbeck, Ivyann Schwan, Gilbert Gottfried.
91 min.
The sorry crew are back again, except that Amy Yasbeck, unable to reprise her role as the humiliated mother, plays the simpering school nurse who steals Ritter's heart. The wicked witch here is heiress LaWanda Dumore (Newman), who improbably sets her Calvin Klein cap at pop-eyed, pudgy Ritter. A faint heh-heh might escape your lips at the antics of an Ellen Barkin lookalike tot (Schwan), but mostly it's predictable, hopelessly over-extended stuff: the pissing-in-lemonade joke, the lengthy projectile vomit scene, fun with farts, and the exploding toilet gag. SFe

Procès de Jeanne d'Arc (Trial of Joan of Arc)

(Robert Bresson, 1962, Fr) Florence Carrez, Jean-Claude Fourneau, Marc Jacquier, Roger Honorat, Jean Gillibert.
65 min. b/w.
Based on the minutes of Joan of Arc's trial, this can be seen as Bresson's essay in sado-masochistic voyeurism. Joan (Carrez) is manacled, spied at through peepholes, genitally scrutinised, and forced (by the director) to squat on a wooden stool as if on a toilet seat. The tension generated by juxtaposing such humiliation with the serenely beautiful text (from the transcription of the trial) resolves itself in the unforgettable final image of Joan's charred remains like a burnt-out firework. GAd

Producers, The

(Mel Brooks, 1967, US) Zero Mostel, Gene Wilder, Kenneth Mars, Estelle Winwood, Renee Taylor, Dick Shawn, Lee Meredith.
88 min.
Brooks' first feature, an absolutely hilarious and tasteless New York Jewish comedy about Broadway. Mostel plays a producer determined to clean up by staging the worst flop in history, first making sure that it's over-backed by all of the rich widows hot for him. Mostel and Wilder (as his bumbling Portnovian accountant) ham outrageously, and some of the humour falls flat. But the all-time flop itself could serve as a definition of kitsch, its centrepiece being the number 'Springtime for Hitler', all tits, pretzels and beer steins, in the best tradition of gaudy American burlesque. RM

Professional Gun, A

see Mercenario, Il

Professional, The

see Leon

Professionals, The

(Richard Brooks, 1966, US) Burt Lancaster, Lee Marvin, Robert Ryan, Jack Palance, Claudia Cardinale, Ralph Bellamy, Woody Strode, Joe De Santis.
123 min.
Bellamy: 'You bastard!' Marvin: 'In my case an accident of birth, but you, sir, are a self-made man'. Brooks could certainly write a line and direct action, but his taut and disillusioned yarn of American mercenaries intruding into the Mexican revolution to 'rescue' Cardinale had only a couple of years in critical favour before it was comprehensively eclipsed by Peckinpah's ostensibly similar The Wild Bunch. PT

Professione: Reporter

see Passenger, The

Profundo carmesí

see Deep Crimson

Proiezionista, Il

see Inner Circle, The

Project A (A Jihua)

(Jackie Chan, 1984, HK) Jackie Chan, Samo Hung, Yuen Baio, Dick Wei, Mars, Isabela Wong.
102 min.

Famous for the scene in which the acrobatic Chan, cornered by pirates, is left hanging by a clock's minute hand, this is a rumbustiously entertaining caper set in Hong Kong at the turn of the century. Chan's a navy daredevil up against the most ruthless buccaneers and con artists of the South Seas. There's little sign of the effort it took to achieve the startling and always fluid effects. It's reported that after one vertiginous stunt went wrong writer/director/star Chan landed head first and was lucky to escape with his life. GM

Projected Man, The
(Ian Curteis, 1966, GB) Bryant Halliday, Mary Peach, Norman Wooland, Ronald Allen, Derek Farr, Sam Kydd.
90 min.
British sci-fi yarn cloned from *The Fly*. A push-back-the-frontiers-of-knowledge scientist uses himself as a guinea pig in a laser-power experiment. He emerges a frazzled monster. Anyone who touches his electrically charged body dies. Low voltage. GM

Projectionist, The
(Harry Hurwitz, 1970, US) Chuck McCann, Ina Balin, Rodney Dangerfield, Jara Kohout, Harry Hurwitz, Robert Staats.
88 min.
An affectionately scatty though uneven low-budget independent chronicling the numerous fantasies of a slobbish projectionist (McCann), given to retreating into movie-inspired fantasies and meanwhile waging a running battle against his tyrannical theatre manager (Dangerfield). The film is unhappiest in its attitude towards its hero, the archetypal fat man whom we're half-expected to sympathise with, half-expected to laugh at. But anyone with a fondness for Hollywood will find much to enjoy: trailers for *The Terrible World of Tomorrow*, the Judeo-Christian Good-Guy kit, impersonations of Bogart, Wayne and Greenstreet. Less successful are the collages using contemporary footage, the visit to Rick's Café in *Casablanca*, and the running battle involving Captain Flash (McCann's alter ego) and The Bat which culminates with the heroes of Hollywood (Errol Flynn, Sergeant York, Flash Gordon etc.) pounding the forces of Fascism, Hitler and Mussolini included.

Project X
(Jonathan Kaplan, 1987, US) Matthew Broderick, Helen Hunt, Bill Sadler, Johnny Ray McGhee, Jonathan Stark, Robin Gammell.
108 min.
Broderick is assigned to work on a US military programme using chimps to test flight simulators, but becomes so attached to the primates that he's soon railing against their treatment. Disneyish drama with a conscience.

Promesse, La
see Promise, The

Promise
(Ningen no Yakusoku)
(Yoshihige Yoshida, 1986, Jap) Rentaro Mikuni, Sachiko Murase, Choichiro Kawarazaki, Orie Sato, Tetsuta Sugimoto.
123 min.
An old woman is found dead: hubby confesses to murdering her. What starts out as a whodunit thriller evolves into a flashback meditation on the effects of senility, both on the victim and on the family that tries to support its elders. All very sensitive, and quite powerful in its tentative argument in support of euthanasia, but it's relentlessly grim, over-reliant on symbolism (water, mirrors), and often tediously repetitive. But the performances and imaginative, precisely composed photography work wonders in counteracting boredom. GA

Promise, The
(Das Versprechen/
La Promesse)
(Margarethe von Trotta, 1994, Ger/Fr) Meret Becker, Corinna Harfouch, Anian Zollner, August Zirner, Susann Ugé, Eva Mattes, Hark Bohm.
116 min.
In tracing the love affair of two bright young East

Germans – Konrad (played in gauche youth by Zollner, in soulful maturity by Zirner) and Sophie (Becker in her rock'n'rollin' days, Harfouch in her svelte designer mode) – separated from the outset when she escapes to the West, Margarethe von Trotta, a doyenne of the leftist New German Cinema of the '70s and '80s, seems to be attempting too much: a history, in personal terms, of the two Germanys from the building of the Wall, in 1961, to its fall. When the couple meet up in Prague, in the spring, you know the tanks of '68 will crush their chances of being re-united; their son's sole function seems to be as a symbolic bond between the two states; and when Konrad becomes an eminent scientist, specialising in the periodicity of sunspots, one wearily suspects yet another ironic metaphoris on offer. On the plus side, there's a bold, eclectic blend of *vérité*-style footage, still photographs and straightforward narrative, while Jürgen Knieper's sub-Georges Delerue strings often evoke a sympathetic mournfulness. WH

Promise, The
(La Promesse)
(Jean-Pierre Dardenne/Luc Dardenne,1996, Belg/Fr/Luxembourg) Jérémie Renier, Olivier Gourmet, Assita Ouedraogo, Olivier Gourmet, Rasmané Ouedraogo.
93 min.
An impressively tough, raw realist drama, set in and around the drabber areas of Liège, in which a 15-year-old comes into conflict with his single parent father after a tragedy forces the boy to confront the moral implications of the pair's exploitative business in smuggling and housing illegal immigrants. Having made a promise to a dying African that he'll look after his wife and kid, young Igor is torn between filial duty and growing affection for his impoverished 'charges', between fear of his dad's bouts of drunken violence and his desire to keep his word. The performances are superb, the interplay between father and son extraordinarily well observed, and the whole thing at once wholly unsentimental and deeply moving. GA

Promised Land
(Michael Hoffman, 1987, US) Jason Gedrick, Tracy Pollan, Kiefer Sutherland, Meg Ryan, Goofy Gress, Deborah Richter, Oscar Rowland, Sandra Seacat.
102 min.
The American Dream hasn't a prayer in the small town of Ashville. Of the four teenage protagonists, Hancock (Gedrick) slides from the pinnacle of high school basketball hero to local cop, and looks like losing his cheerleader girlfriend (Pollan) to college as well; and sensitive Danny (Sutherland) drops out and takes off, but returns with nothing but a prison record and a delinquent tattooed wife (Ryan). Friends at school, sweet Danny and soured Hancock are manipulated into a tragic confrontation, but it hardly proves the case against American ethics. On the debit side – 'Look Homeward Angel'? – winged symbols abound, Ryan's zany Bev is a spin-off from *Something Wild*, and the police force seems altogether too young. The film has a lot going for it though, with its beautiful snowy landscapes, empty highways, and committed playing from the cast. BC

Promised Lands
(Susan Sontag, 1974, Fr)
87 min.
A marked advance on Sontag's first two films (*Duet for Cannibals* and *Brother Carl*) in terms of imagination and cogency, this personal essay about contemporary Israel reflects much of the same passion and intelligence to be found in her non-fictional prose. Addressing itself to tragic and contradictory elements in the state of Israel itself rather than a broader consideration of the Arab-Israeli conflict, it intermittently suggests the influence of Russian documentary film-maker Dziga Vertov in its use of sound and grasp of visual syntax. But while many of Vertov's works are songs of celebration, *Promised Lands* – through statements by a novelist, physicist, psychiatrist, and a harrowing final sequence of a soldier being 'treated' for shock – is closer to the feeling of a scream. Like some of Sontag's other work, it may suffer from an attraction to morbidity that detracts from a wholly lucid exposition. JR

Promise Her Anything
(Arthur Hiller, 1965, GB) Warren Beatty, Leslie Caron, Robert Cummings, Hermione Gingold, Keenan Wynn, Lionel Stander, Cathleen Nesbitt, Bessie Love.
97 min.
Shot in Britain but set in the supposedly wacky Bohemian world of Greenwich Village, this dull attempt at an offbeat and sophisticated romantic comedy falls flat on its face, thanks largely to the usual sluggish direction from Arthur *Love Story* Hiller. Opportunistically cast (Beatty had just been cited as co-respondent in the Peter Hall-Leslie Caron divorce), Beatty and Caron try hard as the down-at-heel 'adult' movie-maker and the French widow looking for a father for her baby son, while the rest of the cast do their best; but a dismal script by William Peter Blatty leaves them flailing in the dark. GA

Prom Night
(Paul Lynch, 1980, US) Leslie Nielsen, Jamie Lee Curtis, Casey Stevens, Eddie Benton, Antoinette Bower, Michael Tough, Robert Silverman.
95 min.
It looks promising: a sincere *Halloween* rip-off which takes time out to milk *Carrie*, *Saturday Night Fever*, and all those B feature 'lust and rivalry' high school sagas. The masked axeman terror here coincides with the anniversary of the death of a small girl, caused accidentally by four older kids who swear to keep their guilty secret. Corny, but not enough for Lynch, who also throws in the escape of a homicidal maniac wrongly imprisoned for the child's murder, and a confusion of red herring conflicts which mark the plot as a poor imitation of John Carpenter's patient terrorism of good by evil. But if you forget motivation, the visual trick-or-treat of slow revenge is entertaining enough: a weirdo janitor dribbling at the window; the victim's year book photos pinned with shards of shattered mirror. Jamie Lee Curtis is superb as Miss Naturally Popular and Prom Queen-to-be, isolated in empty high school corridors: if you like your psychologising loose and edited to that unstoppable disco beat, it's a night out, just.

Promoter, The
see Card, The

Proof
(Jocelyn Moorhouse, 1991, Aust) Hugo Weaving, Genevieve Picot, Russell Crowe, Heather Mitchell, Jeffrey Walker.
90 min.
Writer-director Moorhouse's striking first feature deals with blindness, but the opening shot of dark glasses, a white stick and a camera immediately signals its unorthodox approach. Although its main character is a blind photographer, its true subject is emotional security, the need to have faith in what we cannot see, to trust without proof. When 32-year-old Martin (Weaving) befriends amiable kitchen-hand Andy (Crowe), he asks him to describe photographs he has taken but never seen. In this way, he uses his photographs to test people's honesty. But his young housekeeper Celia (Picot), secretly in love with Martin and fiercely jealous, seduces Andy, thereby forcing him to lie to Martin... Moorhouse's deceptively simple snapshot aesthetic, and bold juxtaposition of harrowing and humorous scenes, are both powerful and original. Like the Hockney-style collage Celia creates from photo fragments of Andy's body, the edges don't fit neatly, but a truth emerges from the composite whole. As Andy says, 'Everybody lies, but not all the time'. NF

Prophecy
(John Frankenheimer, 1979, US) Talia Shire, Robert Foxworth, Armand Assante, Richard Dysart, Victoria Racimo, George Clutesi.
102 min.
Based on the intrinsically arresting idea that mercury poisoning has populated a huge area of American wilderness with numerous rampaging mutations, but somehow no one has noticed. Unfortunately, the film never integrates its eco-horror plot with the cardboard shocks, and the whole venture stops dead with the script's inane assumption that the heroine will put motherhood above all to nurse an ailing monster. It's a small relief when it finally turns round and bites her.

Prophecy, The
see God's Army

Proposition, The
(Y Fargen)
(Strathford Hamilton, 1996, Wales) Nicola
Beddoe, Aneirin Hughes, Richard Lynch,
Richard Harrington, Jennifer Jones, Owen
Garmon.
100 min.
Made-for-Welsh-TV period drama, with a recently widowed (and recently indebted) bourgeois
wife forced to take her herd of cattle south-east
to Gloucester to sell them to the army to save her
ancient pile. It was billed as a Wales-ian Western
and, true, the shots of the landscape are impressively handled, but its Napoleonic War background is just so much red-coated colour. The
dramatic triangle (she takes brawling and boozing bastard Rhys along as drover; his legit brother Huw, the sheriff, a demented and murderously
insane man, clearly suffering from unrequited
love, follows on) is too standard to generate genuine emotion or frisson. WH

Proprietor, The
(Le Propriétaire)
(Ismail Merchant, 1996, US/GB/Fr) Jeanne
Moreau, Sean Young, Sam Waterston, Nell
Carter, Austin Pendleton, Pierre Vaneck,
Christopher Cazenove, Jean-Pierre Aumont,
Marc Tissot.
113 min.
This long, intricately woven film concerns
Adrienne Mark, a famous French writer, long
resident in New York, who renews her flagging
self-belief through the reacquisition of her old
family house in Paris, stolen by a Nazi collaborator whom her mother had trusted. On its deepest level this is an oblique tribute by Ismail
Merchant to his scriptwriter of 35 years, the
author Ruth Prawer Jhabvala, who as a child quit
her native Cologne, as the earth began to shake
in the prelude to WWII, for the start of what was
to become a life marked by a sense of 'dispossession'. Written by George Trow, who worked
on the surreal Savages for Merchant Ivory in
1972, and Jean-Marie Besset, the story discourses on the necessity of not standing still, following your heart and not compromising your
principles. Above all, however, it's about the
duties of friendship, which take precedence over
even the custodianship of true works of art:
exemplified here by a portrait of Adrienne as a
child, given by the author to her New York maid
(Carter, superb), as a parting present and then
returned to enable Adrienne to reclaim her past.
The film is unified by the calm, regal presence
of Jeanne Moreau, who keeps her head while all
about her seem close to losing theirs in a scrabble of intrigue, crossed love affairs, and the hurly
burly of a contentious film remake of one of
Adrienne's books. Delightful and, at the close,
very affecting. JPy

Prospero's Books
(Peter Greenaway, 1991, Neth/Fr/It) John
Gielgud, Michael Clark, Michel Blanc, Erland
Josephson, Isabelle Pasco, Tom Bell,
Kenneth Cranham.
120 min.
Though faithful to the text of Shakespeare's The
Tempest, Greenaway's characteristically dense
film could hardly differ more from literal adaptations like Branagh's Henry V. Structuring its
motifs around the 24 books Prospero took into
exile (as imagined by Greenaway), they dealt with
water, cosmology, pornography, ruins, hell,
music, etc), the director conveys the arcane
knowledge the Duke needs to take his magical
revenge. By having Prospero 'invent' the other
characters and their lines (all spoken by Gielgud
until the final act), he equates him with the Bard,
lending the play a modernist dimension as an
exploration of creative processes. The movie
serves not only as an acknowledgment of the
imminent end of Gielgud's career, but as a demonstration of how new technology has expanded
film's potential, its superimposed images offering an almost unprecedented complexity of information. To some degree, the relentless
proliferation of ideas smothers the dramatic
highs and lows, but this is a minor quibble compared to the sheer ambition and audacity of the
overall conception. GA

Prostitute
(Tony Garnett, 1980, GB) Eleanor Forsythe,
Kate Crutchley, Kim Lockett, Nancy Samuels,
Richard Mangan, Phyllis Hickson.
98 min.
Producer Tony Garnett's first stab at direction
was obviously made for the best of motives: a
concern about the harassment of prostitutes by
police and courts. But his style (TV docu-drama)
and line of argument (prostitution is a job like any
other) leave a lot to be desired. Just as important
as the day-to-day reality of sex for sale is the
imaginative role that it plays in the Western
world; and with his tale of a Birmingham prostitute and her unhappy move to London, Garnett
seems determined to exclude that whole area of
debate. Fine as a campaign film; but a major disappointment as anything else.

Prostitution Racket, The
(Storie di Vita e Malavita)
(Carlo Lizzani, 1975, It) Cinzia Mambretti,
Cristina Moranzoni, Lidia Di Corato, Danila
Grassini, Anna Curti.
91 min.
Sad to see Lizzani, a not inconsiderable talent from
the days of Italian neo-realism, reduced to scripting and directing this standard exploitation-exposé
stuff. On the basis of 'research' (that dead hand),
we are subjected to gritty but uniformly overheated episodes purporting to show how poverty
and boredom force women to turn tricks. Quite so,
but the relentless villainy of all the pimps, and the
submissive foolishness of all the women, makes
the whole exercise woefully implausible. JPy

Proteus
(Bob Keen, 1995, GB) Craig Fairbrass, Toni
Barry, William Marsh, Jennifer Calvert, Doug
(Pinhead) Bradley.
97 min.
A sci-fi action picture based on the novel Slimmer
by John Brosnan (alias Harry Adam Knight), this
first feature by sfx wizard Keen wisely allows
only glimpses of its mutant creature before delivering a monstrous finale. Stranded on an oil rig,
six shipwrecked drug smugglers stumble on a
secret DNA manipulation lab. Roaming the rig is
the resultant abomination, a protean creature that
absorbs its victims and their characteristics.
Gung-ho hero Fairbrass plays the action scenes
to the hilt; scary atmosphere sustained by watery
images and gloopy effects. NF

Protocol
(Herbert Ross, 1984, US) Goldie Hawn, Chris
Sarandon, Richard Romanus, André Gregory,
Gail Strickland, Cliff De Young, Keith
Szarabajka, Ed Begley Jr, Kenneth Mars,
Kenneth McMillan.
95 min.
Hawn plays 35-year-old peabrain Sunny, who
waits on tables in a Washington DC cocktail bar
dressed as an emu. Stopping a bullet meant for a
Middle Eastern potentate, she winds up a national heroine with a job in the State Department,
where the cynical politicos find her easy meat to
tempt that same potentate into granting permission for a US military base. Base humour, too,
which pits Sunny's screwball (fucknut?) mentality against the strict social mores of Capitol, it all
ends in a 'Sunnygate' scandal, but Goldie recovers enough marbles to see that the tenets of the
Declaration of Independence are upheld.
Innocence triumphs over corruption, and the
dizzy blonde proves that fucknuts can make it
into Congress. Hawnsville yawnsville. AB

Proud and Profane, The
(George Seaton, 1955, US) William Holden,
Deborah Kerr, Thelma Ritter, Dewey Martin,
William Redfield, Marion Ross.
111 min. b/w.
Lucy Hendon Crockett's turbulent novel of WWII
romance, The Magnificent Bastards, underwent
a title change on its way to the screen, though the
producers almost settled for The Magnificent
Devils before ending up with this one. Nurse Kerr
is a widow who tangles emotionally with colonel
Holden while on a mission to visit the place where
her husband died, but her ensuing pregnancy and
his invalid wife complicate matters. The ghost of
From Here to Eternity is never far away, but in
this instance the credibility factor is a good deal
lower. TJ

Proud Ones, The
(Robert D Webb, 1956, US) Robert Ryan,
Jeffrey Hunter, Virginia Mayo, Robert
Middleton, Walter Brennan.
94 min.
Unusual Western in which the oedipal themes are
writ large. Ryan's a marshall trying to keep order
in a violent frontier town, but he's prey to recurring fits of blindness. Moreover, the son of a desperado has vowed to kill him, and Mayo, tired of
life in a lawless backwater, won't wait for him forever. 'Scope photography by Lucien Ballard. GM

Proud Ones, The
see Orgueilleux, Les

Proud Ones, The
see Cheval d'Orgueil, Le

Proud to Be British
(Nicholas Broomfield, 1973, GB)
40 min. b/w & col.
A National Film School documentary in which
residents of the small town of Beaconsfield reveal
appallingly ingrained attitudes on such subjects
as Britain's imperialistic benevolence, the natural superiority of the British race, the necessity of
class and the status quo. Interviewees range over
several generations, and from working to ruling
class. Broomfield has eschewed all commentary
and allowed the subjects to speak for themselves.
The irony is blunt but effective. RM

Prova d'Orchestra
see Orchestra Rehearsal

Providence
(Alain Resnais, 1977, Fr/Switz) John Gielgud,
Dirk Bogarde, Ellen Burstyn, David Warner,
Elaine Stritch, Denis Lawson, Samson
Fainsilber.
107 min.
At the centre of David Mercer's tendentious, scatological and wordy screenplay is the figure of a
dying writer (Gielgud), a protean spider weaving his final malevolent fiction from the tangled
fabric of patriarchal feelings and retributive fantasies about his family's independent lives. In the
gentler and more sensitive hands of Resnais,
eschewing as always absolutes and glib moral
equations, this hackneyed central device leads,
not into a predictable reality vs fantasy narrative, but into a haunted, haunting journey
through the corridors of the unconscious mind.
A painted backdrop against which real waves
break; Saint Laurent-clothed characters posed
theatrically in rooms so totally given over to deco
chic that their three-dimensional reality seems
cardboard; scrambled identities (one character
taking on another's dialogue or face): through
such devices Resnais creates the steps and sets
of a kind of Freudian ballet that is also pure cinema. Past and future dissolved into a totally compelling present tense that can, paradoxically,
only be approached through memory and imagination. JD

Provinciale, La
see Girl from Lorraine, A

Prowler, The
(Joseph Losey, 1951, US) Van Heflin, Evelyn
Keyes, John Maxwell, Katherine Warren,
Emerson Treacy, Madge Blake.
92 min. b/w.
A rivetingly cool, clean thriller about the trap
which inexorably closes on a woman unhappily
married to a rich husband, and the cop on the
make for the better things in life who, summoned
to deal with a prowler, lingers to get rid of the
husband and take both wife and money for himself. Superb performances from Evelyn Keyes
and Van Heflin, equally superb art direction (with
the white Spanish house, a symbol of affluence
and its emptiness, surrounded by the night of the
hunter), and direction which grips like a steel
claw, loosening only in the rather melodramatic
final sequences. Even here, with the lovers guiltily holed up in a derelict shack to keep her pregnancy secret from awkward questioning, and
their relationship boiling to a fraught climax over
the difficult birth, Losey rises magnificently to
the occasion in his use of the Mojave Desert ghost
town location. TM

Prowler, The
(aka Rosemary's Killer)
(Joseph Zito, 1981, US) Vicky Dawson, Christopher Goutman, Lawrence Tierney, Farley Granger, Cindy Weintraub, Lisa Dunsheath.
88 min.
Don't despair if you missed *Friday the 13th* and its offspring; here's another chance to see a lot of well-fed youngsters foolishly ignoring all the Rules for Characters in Horror Movies and getting themselves carved up by a marauding maniac. Hours and hours (or so it seems) of witless wanderings through sparsely populated dorms, acres and acres of exposed female flesh pierced by pitchforks and knives, and kissy kissy scrunch till the cows come home. You've seen it all before; and if you haven't, then you certainly won't want to start seeing it now. AB

Psychic Killer
(Raymond Danton, 1975, US) Paul Burke, Jim Hutton, Julie Adams, Nehemiah Persoff, Neville Brand, Aldo Ray, Whit Bissell, Rod Cameron, Della Reese.
89 min.
Although not up to sophisticated John Carpenter standards, *Psychic Killer* – with Hutton released from an asylum in possession of a mysterious medallion which enables him to wreak revenge on those responsible for his wrongful commitment – wouldn't disgrace the Corman stable. A good, cheap, diverting horror exploiter with a reasonably developed sense of its own ridiculousness (a couple of funny, bloody murders), and a cast of old hands (Adams, Ray, Brand) who know a hilt when they see one, and boy, do they play up to it. Ray Danton used to act in films just like this, and if not inspired, his handling of the grotesque is both sure-footed and fun. SM

Psycho (100)
(Alfred Hitchcock, 1960, US) Anthony Perkins, Janet Leigh, Vera Miles, John Gavin, Martin Balsam, John McIntire, Simon Oakland, John Anderson.
109 min. b/w.
No introduction needed, surely, for Hitchcock's best film, a stunningly realised (on a relatively low budget) slice of Grand Guignol in which the Bates Motel is the arena for much sly verbal sparring and several gruesome murders. But it's worth pointing out that Hitch was perfectly right to view it as fun; for all its scream of horror at the idea (and consequences) of madness, it's actually a very black comedy, titillating the audience with its barely linear narrative (the heroine disappears after two reels), with its constant shuffling of audience sympathies, and with its ironic dialogue ('Mother's not quite herself today'). Add the fact that we never learn who's buried in Mrs Bates' coffin, and you've got a stunning, if sadistic, two-hour joke. The cod-Freudian explanation offered at the conclusion is just so much nonsense, but the real text concerning schizophrenia lies in the tellingly complex visuals. A masterpiece by any standard. GA

Psycho II
(Richard Franklin, 1983, US) Anthony Perkins, Vera Miles, Meg Tilly, Robert Loggia, Dennis Franz, Hugh Gillin, Claudia Bryar.
113 min.
With Norman Bates judged sane and released from mental hospital 22 years after the Crane shower murder, things revert to abnormal at the old Gothic house: Norman takes in a sweet young house guest (Tilly), and jealous Mother rears her murderous head again. But who's the real killer? Norman? Marion Crane's revenge-mad sister (Miles)? The fired motel manager (Franz), incensed by Norm's puritan attitude to his turning the place into a vice-house? While the film lacks the thematic depth and darkness – and the virtuoso style – of Hitchcock's, it does a fair job of recreating the exhilarating blend of horror and black humour, with a fair quota of outrageous narrative digressions and perplexing twists along the way. Franklin manages to pay homage to the Master's style without ever falling into the redundantly baroque excesses of, say, De Palma. Scary and fun, it's as worthy a sequel as one might reasonably expect. GA

Psycho III
(Anthony Perkins, 1986, US) Anthony Perkins, Diana Scarwid, Jeff Fahey, Roberta Maxwell, Hugh Gillin, Lee Garlington, Gary Bayer.
96 min.
Business as usual at the Bates motel as a runaway nun with the same initials as Marion Crane triggers Norman first into a mental replay of the shower-bath murder, then to a tender case of mooncalf love. Nice idea to revive Norman's taxidermy hobby, so that his real mum of *Psycho II* (an impostor, it transpires) is now stuffed and directing operations from upstairs just as Mother used to, ensuring that the course of true love is anything but smooth. Sadly, the slashings have become distinctly déjà vu, and the plot is as full of holes as Janet Leigh's corpse. As Norman, Perkins gives another superb exhibition of controlled hysteria, with the fetching hint of a macabre wink lurking in the background; but in his role as director (his debut), he sets too much store by Hitchcock's Catholic apologists. Kicking off with a suicidal nun in a recreation of the belltower scene from *Vertigo*, he lumbers the film with some religious ironies which simply get in the way. It's not unenjoyable, but it isn't half the pastiche that *Psycho II* was. TM

Psycho-Circus
see Circus of Fear

Psycho Killers
see Flesh and the Fiends, The

Psychomania
(Don Sharp, 1972, GB) George Sanders, Beryl Reid, Nicky Henson, Mary Larkin, Roy Holder, Robert Hardy, Patrick Holt.
91 min.
The first British Hell's Angels pic, and just about the blackest comedy to come out of this country in years. It features a bike gang called The Living Dead, whose leader (Henson) discovers the art of becoming just that. So he kills himself and is buried along with his bike, until he guns the engine and shoots back up through the turf; two victims later, he drives to a pub and calls his mother (Reid), a devil worshipper ensconced in her stately old dark house with Sanders as her sinisterly imperturbable butler, to say he's back. This level of absurdity could be feeble, but Sharp knows how to shoot it straight, without any directorial elbows-in-the-ribs. Consequently, much of the humour really works, even though the gang as individuals are strictly plastic. DP

Psychotherapy
see Don't Get Me Started

Psych-Out
(Richard Rush, 1968, US) Susan Strasberg, Dean Stockwell, Jack Nicholson, Bruce Dern, Adam Roarke, Max Julien, Henry Jaglom, Barbara London.
88 min.
A typical AIP quickie put together in an instant bid to cash in on the 'Summer of Love', its action eventually amounting to a slam-bang compendium of every hippy cliché from the bad trip to the redneck rumble. The plot, which has a deaf girl (Strasberg) scouring San Francisco's Haight Ashbury for her missing brother (a crazed Dern), is hard to take. But if you can accept the clichés and archaisms, as well as some third-rate acid rock from The Seeds and Strawberry Alarm Clock, there are compensations: some beautifully baroque performances (Dern and Stockwell in particular), Laszlo Kovacs' effective visualisation of Strasberg's bad STP trip, the spectacle (as irresistible as it is preposterous) of Jack Nicholson sporting lead guitar at the Filmore. DP

P'Tang, Yang, Kipperbang
(Michael Apted, 1982, GB) John Albasiny, Abigail Cruttenden, Maurice Dee, Alison Steadman, Mark Brailsford, Robert Urquhart.
80 min.
The first in Channel 4's *First Love* telemovie series (unwisely given a theatrical release after being seen on TV), this has its roots in the boyhood memories of writer Jack Rosenthal. We're back in postwar England, an age of unbounded optimism buoyed by the prospect of peace and the promises of a Labour government. Our schoolboy hero, 'Quack Quack' Duckworth (Albasiny) has only two ambitions: to score the winning run for England in a test match against Australia, and to kiss a girl in his class (the enchanting Cruttenden). Such is the flimsy premise of this all-too-easily nostalgic movie, whose production values and period detail are overstated to the point of cliché. Apted's direction is precise but unremarkable, and though Rosenthal's script triggers some long-buried memories, like classroom catchwords (hence the title) and furtive fumblings towards sexual awareness, it's an empty film that leaves you with little besides a Heinz soup glow. MA

PT Raiders
see Ship That Died of Shame, The

Puberty Blues
(Bruce Beresford, 1981, Aust) Nell Schofield, Jad Capelja, Geoff Rhoe, Tony Hughes, Sandy Paul, Leander Brett.
87 min.
Nothing more than the overrated *Getting of Wisdom* updated and transposed to beach-movie territory, this replaces period prettiness with an equally crass teenage formula imported from countless cheap Californian quickies. The trouble is that Beresford is determined both to have his cake and to eat it, as he adopts the viewpoint of two schoolgirl surfer-gang apprentices on the codes and rituals of their Aussie peers, parading the sex'n'drugs'n'sand staples of the genre at gratuitous length before finally turning round with his heroines to dismiss it all as boys' play kidstuff. And even then the message comes down to a wimpy 'don't beat 'em, join 'em' compromise. PT

Public Access
(Bryan J Singer, 1994, US) Ron Marquette, Dina Brooks, Burt Williams.
90 min.
An impressive debut from writer/director Singer, this chilly little parable taps into the poisonous well-springs of the middle-American psyche. When Whiley Pritcher (Marquette) arrives in Brewster, it's a quiet, complacent, no-account kind of place. He rents a room by the week and then sets about booking four slots of prime-time public access TV on the local cable TV station: Sunday, 7pm, 'family hour'. He calls the show 'Our Town' and asks, 'What's wrong with Brewster?' Before too long it's '*Who's* wrong?' It's obvious from the way Whiley scrubs the bath naked that something's amiss, but as Singer probes his soft-spoken anti-hero, it becomes clear he'll stop at nothing to achieve his enigmatic ends. The film is overly measured, with lots of slow zooms and slow motion (even the actors seem to be on go-slow), but it's engrossing, and Marquette is a genuinely scary customer, a dry-cleaned all-American sociopath. TCh

Public Enemy, The
(William Wellman, 1931, US) James Cagney, Jean Harlow, Edward Woods, Donald Cook, Joan Blondell, Mae Clarke, Beryl Mercer.
84 min. b/w.
Hard to believe that it was the aptly named Woods and not Cagney who was originally slated for the lead role of Tom Powers, the part that rocketed Cagney to stardom and typecast him as a trigger-happy punk. Now, of course, the film seems the archetypal Cagney vehicle as he graduates from petty theft to big-time bootlegging and murder, but it's fairly seminal for other reasons: the acknowledgment that crime is at least partly the product of poor social conditions, the emphasis on booze as the mainspring for the Mob's illegal income, the deployment of events and characteristics from the lives of real-life gangsters (in this case Hymie Weiss) to create myth from fact. Best known for the rampantly misogynist scene in which Cagney plunges a grapefruit into Mae Clarke's nagging face over the breakfast table, the film is badly let down by the performances of Harlow as a classy moll, and Cook and Mercer as Cagney's brother and mother (the latter coming across as a simpering moron). But Cagney's energy and Wellman's gutsy direction carry the day, counteracting the moralistic sentimentality of the script and indelibly etching the star on the memory as a definitive gangster hero. GA

Public Enemy Number One
(David Bradbury, 1980, Aust) narrator: Richard Oxenburgh.
58 min.

A documentary on Australia's veteran radical journalist Wilfred Burchett. Returning to his beloved SE Asia in the wake of Pol Pot's holocaust and in the midst of a war between former comrades, Burchett exhibits much the same devastated incomprehension he had to conquer as the first Western newsman to file a report from Hiroshima. Burchett's unique experience between these two cataclysms – 30 years of reporting from the communist position on Korea, Vietnam and Cambodia, which earned him close friendship with Ho Chi Minh and an 'enemy's' exile from his Australian homeland – more happily form the major focus of this remarkable inspirational film memoir. PT

Public Eye, The
(Howard Franklin, 1992, US) Joe Pesci, Barbara Hershey, Stanley Tucci, Jerry Adler, Jared Harris, Richard Riehle.
99 min. b/w & col.
The main virtue of screenwriter Franklin's debut as director is Pesci's portrayal of Weegee, the famous low-life tabloid photographer of urban disaster, lightly concealed as Bernstein, The Great Bernzini. Watching this isolated character in his nocturnal environment, cursing and kicking corpses into patterns for the shot, seeing the scene freeze into black-and-white for the famous photo – this is the heart of the film. When we track the uncouth artist to a publisher where his work is rejected again, leaving his ego undented, veterans may be reminded of the painter Gulley Jimson in The Horse's Mouth, with the swearing left in. Pesci is unstoppably on throughout. Both the tentative romance with nightclub-owner Kay Levitz (Hershey) – though finely played – and the plot, which concerns a government gas-rationing scandal, seem uneasily grafted on in an attempt to qualify for film noir, though Bernstein does get an incredible live action shot out of it. Good dialogue, nice period recreation, great performances. BC

Puen-Paeng
(Cherd Songsri, 1983, Thai) Sorapong Chatri, Kanungnit Rerksasarn, Chanuteporn Visitsophon.
131 min.
Quite unlike the mainstream of Thai movies (but a little too similar to the same director's masterly The Scar), this is an elegiac rural melodrama about two contrasted sisters in love with the same cowherd. It's set in the '30s, and lovingly detailed period touches strike an optimum balance between nostalgic escapism and serious reconstruction of traditions that are already almost extinct. At its heart are magical images of life in a Thai village: a brazen girl propositioning a naked boy as he bathes in the river, a romance pursued on the backs of water buffalo. TR

Puerto Escondido
(Gabriele Salvatores, 1993, It) Diego Abatantuono, Valeria Golino, Claudio Bisio, Renato Carpentieri.
110 min.
Surprisingly, from the maker of Mediterraneo, this opens with an edgy comic menace as self-important Milan banker Mario (Abatantuono) is blasted at close range by a smiling serial killer. He survives, but is visited in hospital by his assailant – a police commissioner investigating the case. It's like The Trial meets Man Bites Dog until Mario, having anxiously befriended the killer cop, dumps him and flees to South America. As his designer suit frays and money fails, he falls in with fellow Italians, a peyote-loving beach bum (Bisio) and his girl (Golino), who find their already incompetent scams hopelessly compromised by their lazy, cowardly house guest. The film's all over the place and has its longueurs, but succeeds thanks to Abatantuono's performance. Full marks, too, for the dark, unpatronising picture of Mexico, throwing into deeper relief the merry antics of the protagonists. SFe

Pugni in Tasca, I
see Fists in the Pocket

Pull My Daisy
(Robert Frank/Alfred Leslie, 1958, US) Allen Ginsberg, Jack Kerouac, Larry Rivers.
50 min.
Those who know Frank's stark, dispassionate pictures of blank-faced Americans will be surprised by the zany humour of this film. A group of Frank's friends (Ginsberg and painter Larry Rivers) loon about in a New York loft improvising round a scene from a Kerouac play about the Beat Generation. Straight society is represented by the bishop, his disapproving mother and prim sister, who are entertained with drinking, cussing, poetry and jazz. Kerouac provides an insane voice-over commentary which distances the audience by emphasising the artificiality and self-parody of the play-acting. The uneasy mix of informality and posturing makes the film a forerunner of Warhol's 'home movies'.

Pulp
(Mike Hodges, 1972, GB) Michael Caine, Mickey Rooney, Lionel Stander, Lizabeth Scott, Nadia Cassini, Al Lettieri, Dennis Price.
95 min.
Writer-director Hodges took his abrasive, mordant style from the Newcastle of Get Carter to the Mediterranean for this, his second feature. Caine plays a pithy author of pulp fiction hired to ghost some secret memoirs. So inevitably he becomes an amateur sleuth, a wisecracking sore thumb in the impenetrable murk of fringe mafioso. There's a touch of hommage here, a dash of indulgence there, but Pulp deserved a kinder critical reception than it received, if only for Rooney's exuberant send-up of himself. One of those movies that's a laugh a line after a pint or three. SG

Pulp Fiction ⓒ
(Quentin Tarantino, 1994, US) John Travolta, Samuel L Jackson, Uma Thurman, Bruce Willis, Harvey Keitel, Tim Roth, Rosanna Arquette, Amanda Plummer, Eric Stoltz, Steve Buscemi.
154 min.
A sprawling, discursive fresco: three stories bookended by a prologue and epilogue. In the first story, a mobster (Travolta) is charged with looking after the irresponsible wife (Thurman) of his vengeful boss. In the second, a washed-up boxer (Willis) tries to trick the Mob by failing to throw a fight. And in the third, two hitmen (Travolta and Jackson) carry out a job, only to call on the services of a 'cleaner' (Keitel) when it gets messier than planned. It's the way Tarantino embellishes and, finally, interlinks these old chestnuts that makes the film alternately exhilarating and frustrating. There's plenty of sharp, sassy, profane dialogue, and there are plenty of acute, funny references to pop culture, though the talk sometimes delays the action, and the references sometimes seem self-consciously arch. And there are, too, the sudden lurches between humour and violence – shocking, but without moral depth. What writer/director Tarantino lacks, as yet, is the maturity to invest his work with anything that might provoke a heartfelt emotional response to his characters. Very entertaining, none the less. GA

Pulse
(Paul Golding, 1988, US) Joey Lawrence, Cliff De Young, Roxanne Hart, Charles Tyner, Myron Healey.
91 min.
This tense little thriller with a touch of the Stephen Kings shows what happens when a series of power surges turns an ordinary Los Angeles household into a death-trap. An uneasy exposition with well-handled effects gives way to a disappointing resolution. As tends to be the case in these affairs, the film-makers can't think up much of a reason why the electrics should go berserk in the first place. TJ

Pumping Iron
(George Butler/Robert Fiore, 1976, US) Arnold Schwarzenegger, Louis Ferrigno, Matty Ferrigno, Victoria Ferrigno, Mike Katz, Ken Waller.
86 min.
'Pumping iron is a great feeling...like coming, but coming continuously' smiles Arnold Schwarzenegger, relaxed in the confidence that he's demolishing another popular prejudice against bodybuilding. Pumping Iron in fact starts knocking preconceptions sideways in its opening moments – with a sequence showing Schwarzenegger taking ballet lessons to improve his posing style – and it goes on to demonstrate convincingly that bodybuilders are as 'normal' in their vanities, foibles and rivalries as any other group of nuts. The movie is a very shrewd mixture of documentary and realistic fiction, put together with both eyes and ears on entertainment value; it has, for example, an extremely agreeable LA session-rock score. Its strongest card is the outrageously charismatic Schwarzenegger, but its view of musclemen and physique contests in general has a charm not unlike Rocky. TR

Pumping Iron II: The Women
(George Butler, 1984, US) Bev Francis, Rachel McLish, Lori Bowen Rice, Carla Dunlap, Steve Michalik.
107 min.
A drama doc on the run-up and final for the 1983 Caesar's Cup in Las Vegas which proves even more engaging than Pumping Iron. The line-up of well-oiled beauties includes one controversial Australian, Bev Francis, who powerlifts 500 pounds for breakfast, and whose musculature defies rational analysis. The crux of the tournament then comes down to whether the judges, blind fools to a man, will accept something so obviously superior or opt for the safety of a body more 'traditionally feminine' such as gorgeous pouting Rachel McLish, who is discovered to have illegal padding in her unmuscled bits, oh the shame of it all. Ironically, the winner turns out to be the one with the firmest grasp of the political undercurrents. Huge fun. CPea

Pumpkin Eater, The
(Jack Clayton, 1964, GB) Anne Bancroft, Peter Finch, James Mason, Cedric Hardwicke, Rosalind Atkinson, Richard Johnson, Maggie Smith, Eric Porter.
118 min. b/w.
Harold Pinter penned one of his superior scripts in this fastidious adaptation of Penelope Mortimer's novel about a compulsive child-bearer and her unfaithful screenwriter husband. The influence of European cinema (in particular Antonioni) is evident in the delineation of despair among the middle classes, and there is something peculiarly self-parodic in the heroine enduring a nervous breakdown in Harrods. Fine performances notwithstanding, the world of the Hampstead soap opera now seems so far away as to almost rate as science fiction. DT

Pumpkinhead (aka Vengeance, the Demon)
(Stan Winston, 1987, US) Lance Henriksen, John DiAquino, Jeff East, Florence Schauffler, Kimberly Ross, Joel Hoffman, Cynthia Bain.
86 min.
When Pennsylvanian country-dweller Ed Harley's kid gets (accidentally) killed by a group of marauding young townies on motorbikes, the aggrieved father (Henriksen) seeks justice, or more precisely, vengeance. Aided by the mythically wizened old crone from Black Ridge (Schauffler), he invokes the rampaging form of Pumpkinhead, a 15-foot monstrosity who doesn't believe in penal reform and with whom one does not mess lightly. From there on it's stiff-city for the unfortunate kids, as well as some hellish rewards for Harley himself. Having established himself in make-up before moving to directing, Winston eschews the usual frustratingly fleeting glimpses of 'monster-in-very-poorly-lit-surroundings', and – with the help of the creature-effects team that brought you Aliens and Predator – delivers more than ample amounts of full-bodied fantasy. Henriksen is superbly anguished throughout, his pectorals and cheek-bones competing for the most exciting on-screen spectacle award. MK

Pump Up the Volume
(Allan Moyle, 1990, US) Christian Slater, Scott Paulin, Ellen Greene, Samantha Mathis, Anthony Lucero, Andy Romano, Annie Ross.
102 min.
By night, shy student Mark Hunter (Slater), resentful because his family has moved from New York to an Arizona backwater, retires to the basement to become pirate radio DJ Hard Harry, so named because he pretends to masturbate on air. Mixing outrage, Leonard Cohen and social commentary, his show becomes compulsory for the youngsters at Hubert Humphrey High School. They phone and write in with problems ranging from teen pregnancy to loneliness, but when one listener commits suicide, Hard Harry is charged with criminal solicitation. Now all they have to do is find him... Writer-director Moyle turns what could have been a wallow in teen angst into some-

thing altogether more forceful. The perfectly cast Slater effectively propels the film, his intensity and dry delivery giving it a definite edge, as does a soundtrack which includes Ice T, Concrete Blonde and the Cowboy Junkies. CM

Punch and Judy Man, The

(Jeremy Summers, 1962, GB) Tony Hancock, Sylvia Syms, Ronald Fraser, John Le Mesurier, Hugh Lloyd, Barbara Murray, Hattie Jacques.
90 min. b/w.
Hancock's finest celluloid hour-and-a-half has the doleful comic as a seaside children's entertainer whose marriage to ambitious Syms is under threat due to his continuing lowly rank in the town's social strata. Written by Hancock and Philip Oakes, it's an understated, melancholy tale with a rather personal tone, and good work from the likes of Le Mesurier and Hugh Lloyd as Hancock's fellow beach-front artistes. TJ

Punchline

(David Seltzer, 1988, US) Sally Field, Tom Hanks, John Goodman, Mark Rydell, Kim Greist, Paul Mazursky.
122 min.
One problem here is that the jokes aren't funny; another is that Sally Field is funny by mistake. It's saved by Tom Hanks' portrayal of Steven Gold, flunking seedy medical student by day and ambitious trainee stand-up by night. Admiration (hero worship) arrives in the shape of Lilah Krytsick (Field), a downtrodden housewife so sweetly caring, so maternally smothering, that even boiling oil couldn't be good enough. Lilah, alas, wants to be a comic too. Under Gold's tutelage she becomes one; the rule, he explains, is that you don't get on by telling someone else's haggard gags, but by spieling from experience. Her experience consists of Polish roots and her husband's personal habits, and the punters learn to love it. Worse, Krytsick learns to love Gold, and vice versa. The talent contest climax is the equivalent of a badly engineered courtroom drama, tantrums, tears and all. It's to Hanks' credit that *Punchline* remains grimly watchable. SGa

Punch Me in the Stomach

(Francine Zuckerman, 1996, NZ/Can) Deb Filler.
72 min.
A barely cinematic 'opening out' of stand-up comic Deb Filler's one-woman show, inspired by her own experiences growing up as a Jew in New Zealand, and those of her father, a survivor of the death camps. A bold attempt to turn unlikely material into comedy, but really, it just ain't funny. GA

Punisher, The

(Mark Goldblatt, 1989, Aust) Dolph Lundgren, Louis Gossett Jr, Jeroen Krabbé, Kim Miyori, Bryan Marshall, Nancy Everhard, Barry Otto.
89 min.
Renegade cop Frank Castle (Lundgren) goes underground after his wife and kiddies are killed by the Mafia, emerging leather-clad and steel-eyed as the Punisher. After offing 125 hoods in five years, a feat he describes as 'work in progress', it looks like he can hang up his crossbow when the Yakuza muscle in on New York to finish off the rest of the Family. But when the fiendish Japs kidnap the cack's children, soft-hearted Mr P intervenes on behalf of his erstwhile enemies. Villains are offed, guns go blam, and inarticulate Oriental cries fill the air. Almost worse than the storyline's hackneyed idiocy is the psychological improbability of the characters (though Krabbé wrestles heroically with his numb role as the head Don). A little more fetishism wouldn't go amiss, and we get nowhere near enough kinky weaponry, crotch shots and masochism (despite a neat bit of auto-cauterising). Set against this is the blithe humour of the proceedings, a welcome shortage of love interest, Dolph's minimalist wit, and two arch-villainesses attired in black plastic and other form-fitting fabrics. Destructive, reprehensible, and marvellous fun. SFe

Punishment Park

(Peter Watkins, 1971, US) Carmen Argenziano, Stan Armsted, Jim Bohan, Frederick Franklyn, Gladys Golden, Sanford Golden.
89 min.
A futuristic pseudo-documentary in which political dissenters can choose Federal prison or the

three-day ordeal of Punishment Park. Watkins reconstructs Greening of America political confrontations with a granny realism and a pretence of impartiality. The trouble is that as the film progresses, his own political intentions become increasingly obscure, unless what we have here is merely an indulgence of the naive polarisation of the American left in the late '60s – Us (the righteous) versus Them (the pigs), with nothing in between. RM

Punk and the Princess, The (aka The Punk)

(Mike Sarne, 1993, GB) Charlie Creed-Miles, Vanessa Hadaway, David Shawyer, Jess Conrad, Jacqueline Skarvellis.
96 min.
An adaptation of 14-year-old Gideon Sams' cult novel *The Punk*, made 15 years after publication by 53-year-old singer/sometime-director Mike Sarne (who also co-produced and wrote the screenplay). David (Creed-Miles), the disaffected son of an odious copper, wanders the streets of Notting Hill. One day he stumbles backstage during rehearsals for a fringe production of *Romeo and Juliet*. There he meets spoilt rich-girl Rachel (Hadaway), and amid the sniffing, spliffing, squalor and squats of West London, the star-cross'd lovers experience the usual coming-of-age problems. Very poor in all departments. NF

Punk in London

(Wolfgang Büld, 1977, WGer) The Sex Pistols, Stranglers, Clash, X-Ray Spex, Boomtown Rats, Adverts, Jolt, Electric Chairs, Subway Sect, Jam.
106 min.
Earnest young German TV director: 'Why don't you want to appear in our movie?' Jean-Jacques Burnel: 'Because I'm not a prostitute'. *Punk in London* makes all the mistakes that visiting film crews with sociological briefs usually make, especially when they're headed by earnest young directors. It pretends that its superficial observations are in-depth analyses; it contents itself with interviewing peripheral figures because it can't get near the nazz. Büld doesn't help himself by worrying about the sound quality, and sometimes dubbing recorded versions of songs over images of the same song in performance, to absurd effect. No musical highlights, but a couple of the interviews are fun: one with the disarmingly honest roadie Rodent, the other with The Lurkers' bassist and his elderly parents, conducted in their home over a TV set relaying a disco track on *Top of the Pops*. TR

Punk Rock Movie, The

(Don Letts, 1977, GB) The Sex Pistols, Clash, Siouxsie and the Banshees, Generation X, X-Ray Spex, Heartbreakers, Subway Sect.
The directness of the title sums it up sweetly: after nine years this still emerges as the most faithful and wittiest punk documentary ever made. Filmed largely during the famed 100 days of the Roxy in early '77 by resident DJ Letts, it captures the smell and rush of the phenomenon at its chaotic peak, and the jitter of Super-8 shoots most of the prime movers as the spirit of the thing befits; video would have been disastrous. Priceless and highly embarrassing highlights include pre-Pogue Jam fan Shane McGowan pogoing fitfully during the opening credits, a confused Siouxsie applauding herself at the end of 'Bad Shape', assorted Clash persons making dicks of themselves outside a cafe (reminiscent in part of Dezo Hoffman's home movies of the Beatles), and a splendidly explicit Wayne County sticking his head into the bass drum at the end of 'Cream in My Jeans'. Best of all, Rotten's performance on stage and off is magnificent. In pre-punk terminology, it's all eminently groovy.

Puppetmaster, The (Ximeng Rensheng)

(Hou Xiaoxian, 1993, Tai) Li Tianlu, Lin Qiang, Chen Kuizhong, Zuo Juwei, Hong Liu, Bai Minghua.
114 min.
This hallucinatory biopic covers the first 36 years of Li Tianlu's life story. The film shows a life buffeted every which way by family, work and politics (Taiwan was a Japanese colony for the whole period shown here, and things got rough in the war years), but Li survived each chapter of accidents by turning himself into a true folk-artist, retelling

myths and legends on his puppet theatre stage. Li appears several times as a funny and very laid-back raconteur, but mostly we see reconstructed episodes from his memoirs. The film covers much ground, from the collapse of feudal society to the defeat of the Japanese, but the overall pace is slow and contemplative, and the focus is deliberately narrow. Hou Xiaoxian has been moving towards this storytelling style for years, and it's probably too minimalist to make new converts. But long-term admirers (and dope heads) will come out of the film with a vivid sense of Chinese folk-culture and an agreeably blurred vision of the relations between an individual and his society. TR

Puppet Masters, The (aka Robert A. Heinlein's The Puppet Masters)

(Stuart Orme, 1994, US) Donald Sutherland, Eric Thal, Julie Warner, Will Patton, Richard Belzer, Tom Mason.
109 min.
Aliens land in Iowa and take over humans. Sutherland has been this way before (*Invasion of the Body Snatchers*, 1978) and it shows. There's no suspense (ETs rampage from the word go); no frissons (loud hailers telegraph the shocks); and it's insufficiently bright to be an *hommage*. AO

Puppet on a Chain

(Geoffrey Reeve, 1970, GB) Sven-Bertil Taube, Barbara Parkins, Alexander Knox, Patrick Allen, Vladek Sheybal, Ania Marson.
98 min.
A half-baked thriller set in Amsterdam, and wearily flaunting the familiar backdrop of canals and barrel-organs while struggling to extract some excitement from a limp Alistair MacLean adventure about an American narcotics agent (Taube) and a drug ring whose nastiest habit is getting rid of meddlers by hanging them from meathooks. Reeve's direction serves up spasmodic lumps of violence in lieu of suspense, and the one tolerable sequence – an extended speedboat chase through the canals – was contributed by Don Sharp. TM

Pure Formality, A (Una Pura Formalità)

(Giuseppe Tornatore, 1994, It/Fr) Gérard Depardieu, Roman Polanski, Sergio Rubini, Nicola di Pinto.
108 min.
Essentially a stagey two-hander in which, in a strangely sinister, seemingly timeless police station, inspector Polanski interrogates the partly amnesiac Depardieu, who claims he's a famous author but who may in fact be responsible for a murder committed near the novelist's home. Emphatically metaphorical and full of thumpingly obvious symbolism, Tornatore's film depends heavily on the two leads for effect – Polanski's sly, shrewd performance outshines Depardieu's broader turn – but even they can't distract from the ludicrous contrivance of the film's threadbare central conceit. GA

Pure Hell of St Trinian's, The

(Frank Launder, 1960, GB) Cecil Parker, Joyce Grenfell, George Cole, Thorley Walters, Eric Barker, Irene Handl, Dennis Price, Liz Fraser, Sidney James.
94 min. b/w.
Third in the Ronald Searle series. After they have burned down the school, the girls are shipped off to the Middle East, where – with the inevitable harem and secret agents lurking – inspiration seems to have deserted the St Trinian's scriptwriters. Some bright moments, but on the whole very disappointing. Irene Handl replaced Alastair Sim as the headmistress, otherwise the crew remained the same. DMcG

Pure Luck

(Nadia Tass, 1991, US) Martin Short, Danny Glover, Sheila Kelley, Sam Wanamaker, Scott Wilson, Harry Shearer, Jorge Russek.
96 min.
Hollywood remake of a French farce has private eye Glover on the trail of klutzy heiress Kelley, who's been kidnapped on vacation in Mexico. Concerned dad Wanamaker comes up with the notion of unleashing accountant Short on the case, a man so encumbered by ill fortune he's somehow bound to stumble across the girl. A misfire. TJ

Puritan, The (Le Puritain)
(Jeff Musso, 1937, Fr) Jean-Louis Barrault, Pierre Fresnay, Viviane Romance.
87 min. b/w.
Apparently the centre of considerable controversy when it was made, *The Puritan* still looks cogently argued and provocative. Based on a novel by Liam O'Flaherty, it's basically the old chestnut about puritanism masking an inferno of repressed lusts. What makes it interesting is partly Barrault's terrific performance as the moral vigilante who kills a girl and clumsily tries to frame her lover; and partly the plotting, which leaves the police in no doubt about Barrault's guilt from the start, and allows Barrault to understand his own problems as the effect of his crime sinks in. The result is a rather well-crafted study of a pathetic figure who achieves personal freedom only at the moment that the cell door closes on him. Musso isn't another Buñuel, and nobody could consider the film especially subversive; but its fundamental intelligence is nicely complemented by the warmth of Musso's feeling for his characters, especially in the low-life bars and clubs. TR

Purple Haze
(David Burton Morris, 1982, US) Peter Nelson, Chuck McQuary, Bernard Baldan, Susanna Lack, Bob Breuler, Joanne Bauman.
104 min.
Magenta Fogg writes: 'Sometimes life is really too much, I mean, I just saw this incredibly deep and meaningful movie about this guy called Caulfield (like in *Catcher in the Rye*) who gets thrown out of school back in 1968, and he trucks on home to Straight City, and his mum and dad lay a heavy trip on him, and his chick freaks out over *The Graduate*, and everyone is giving off very negative vibes, except these two amazing friends, one's into frying his brains on all kinds of dynamite stuff, and the other is this really cool disc jockey who spins Procul Harum and Steppenwolf and The Byrds and other beautiful sounds into the universe, and they all go to this party full of groovy flower girls flashing their titties and making good karma, but then the first friend gets drafted and freaks out and the whole scene turns very, very heavy, I mean, a load of straights think this movie is a total and complete bummer full of stupid clichés about the 'Age of Aquarius', and only for 'Book of the Dead' heads and other geriatric hippies, but they are just part of the breadhead conspiracy and should be left inside their boring fascist reality.' SJo

Purple Noon
see Plein Soleil

Purple Rain
(Albert Magnoli, 1984, US) Prince, Apollonia Kotero, Morris Day, Olga Karlatos, Clarence Williams III.
111 min.
Since Prince first appeared on stage caressing the long neck of his guitar and sucking at its quivering head, he has been a man to watch. And if at first it was just to check that he did not creep up from behind, it burgeoned into something else...respect, earned by his raunchy, inventive brand of funk and the sense that here was someone who could be truly great. The considerable appeal of the film depends upon his presence, and luckily the man sweats charisma, for the plot is at best predictable, at worst incomprehensible. Partly autobiographical, part fiction, it tells of The Kid (Prince), product of a broken home and an impregnable ego, struggling to the top of the rock heap. His girlfriend Apollonia loves him but is attracted by his arch-enemy, lead singer with rival band The Time (it gets very reductionist). But this is all no more than fancy padding around the film's heart, which only starts to really pump when Prince is up on stage: a teasing, hot amalgam of Marc Bolan, Nijinsky and the Scarlet Pimpernel, as electric as his guitar. FD

Purple Rose of Cairo, The
(Woody Allen, 1985, US) Mia Farrow, Jeff Daniels, Danny Aiello, Irving Metzman, Stephanie Farrow, Van Johnson, Dianne Wiest, Zoe Caldwell, John Wood, Milo O'Shea, Edward Herrmann.
82 min.
During the Depression, downtrodden housewife Farrow so inflames a film's leading man (an explorer-poet) that he climbs down from the screen, and entices her into a chaotic but charming love affair. Woody Allen's deft script investigates every nook and cranny of the couple's bizarre relationship, the irate Pirandellian reactions of the illusory characters left up on the screen, and the bewilderment of the actor whose movie persona has miraculously gone walkies. As the star-struck couple, Farrow and Daniels work wonders with fantastic emotions, while Allen's direction invests enough care, wit and warmth to make it genuinely moving. GA

Purple Taxi, The (Le Taxi Mauve)
(Yves Boisset, 1977, Fr/It/Eire) Peter Ustinov, Charlotte Rampling, Fred Astaire, Philippe Noiret, Eddie Albert, Agostina Belli.
120 min.
Filmed in Ireland, with Boisset not the only French director of his generation to be seduced into making a mystery movie with a whimsical flavour, this is one of the worst French movies of the decade: a confused attempt at creating intrigue out of the lives of several expatriates trying to escape their past. None of the English-speaking stars look like they know what's going on, especially Astaire, bowling round the Irish countryside in the taxi of the title. Thank God the best French film-makers have realised that making an English-language movie is not as easy as it seems; pity it took a disaster like this to ram home the message. MA

Pursued
(Raoul Walsh, 1947, US) Robert Mitchum, Teresa Wright, Judith Anderson, Dean Jagger, John Rodney, Alan Hale, Harry Carey Jr.
101 min. b/w.
A superb Western *film noir*, with Mitchum pursued through near-epic landscapes of the mind by the indistinct demons of childhood trauma, and the narrative boldly structured around flashback insights which gradually provide both a key to his identity and the inexorable impetus for a violent catharsis. Walsh's intelligent handling of Oedipal themes here and in *White Heat* gives the definitive lie to his self-cultured image as merely an adventuresome Hollywood primitive, while the film proves that the late '40s *noir* sensibility spread way beyond the bounds of the urban crime thriller. PT

Pursuit of Happiness, The
(Robert Mulligan, 1970, US) Michael Sarrazin, Barbara Hershey, Robert Klein, Sada Thompson, Ralph Waite, Arthur Hill, EG Marshall.
98 min.
Too shapeless, too drawn out, too much reliance on symbols – that is part of what is wrong with Mulligan's entry in the youth movie stakes. The plot is melodramatic but not incredibly so: the hero (Sarrazin) finds himself college boy one moment, prisoner (by virtue of a collision with an old lady who steps out in front of his car on a dark and rainy night) and prosecution witness in a prison murder trial the next. Mulligan seems to have intended exploring his innocent hero's 'pursuit', or rather flight, on a physical level – his opting out of student politics to indulge his model boat hobby is merely the first step – but instead the subject escapes, losing itself in getting Sarrazin from A to B rather than really looking at why. There is a serious point to it all – it shouldn't look faintly silly, but it does. VG

Pursuit of the Graf Spee
see Battle of the River Plate, The

Pursuit to Algiers
(Roy William Neill, 1945, US) Basil Rathbone, Nigel Bruce, Marjorie Riordan, Rosalind Ivan, Martin Kosleck, John Abbott, Frederick Worlock, Morton Lowry.
65 min. b/w.
Twelfth in the Rathbone/Bruce Sherlock Holmes series, with only two more to go and energies beginning to flag. After an intriguingly mysterious opening in a typically foggy London, Holmes and Watson are bogged down in a shipboard adventure, fending off would-be assassins of the young European monarch they are escorting. Pretty stale stuff, through Nigel Bruce makes his singing debut with 'Loch Lomond'. GA

Pusher
(Nikolas Winding Refn, 1996, Den) Kim Bodnia, Zlatko Buric, Laura Drasbæk, Slavko Labovik.
110 min.
This is the worst week in Frank's life – and very possibly the last. Deep in debt, he fixes up a complicated heroin deal involving his skinhead pal Tony and Balkan dealer Milo. The exchange is a bust, and Frank loses both the money and the merchandise. By Thursday, Tony's out of the picture and Milo's putting on the squeeze. By Friday, Saturday might never happen. Using available light, spasmodic handheld camerawork, and improvised dialogue, write/director Refn goes out of his way (in his first feature) to create an everyday world of extraordinary circumstance – then piles on a pounding thrash guitar score and punchy editing to create a kind of electric realism. Scorsese is a touchstone, but it's a long time since he achieved this kind of blistering intensity. It's a rough ride, for sure: Tony's idea of small talk scorches the ear; the music's loud enough to feel; and a series of violent confrontations are so near-the-knuckle it's a relief not to come out bleeding. Yet this is much more than an assault on the senses. As Frank, Bodnia's baleful tough guy stoicism masks an emotional constipation which even precludes physical contact with his hooker girlfriend (Drasbæk). Wheeling and dealing for all he's worth, he can only conclude that he's not worth much; and if Copenhagen comes to resemble hell on earth, it's definitely a hell of Frank's own making. TCh

Pushing Hands (Tui Shou)
(Ang Lee, 1991, Tai) Sihung Lung, Lai Wang, Deb Snyder, Bo Z Wang.
105 min.
This first feature by a Taiwanese graduate from the NYU Film School has a crippling central flaw. The film is about an elderly tai chi master from Beijing who clashes with his all-American daughter-in-law when he retires to his son's home in upstate New York. The culture gap is so extreme (and on her side, so vehemently expressed) that you wonder why on earth she married a Chinese guy in the first place – a question the script blithely ignores. That said, this is a reasonably amiable comedy-drama with a strong streak of sentimentality. It falls a long way short of Wayne Wang's Chinatown movies. TR

Push! Push! (San-bu In-gwa)
(Park Chul-Soo, 1997, SKor)
95 min.
After a technically smart but seemingly uninvolving first 20 minutes, this ambitious, fragmented comedy drama, charting the experiences of doctors, patients, family and friends in a busy maternity ward, kicks in with a vengeance. Covering all manner of medical, ethical, political and psychological issues to do with pregnancy, the film embraces slapstick, satire, social comment, suspense, melodrama and even documentary footage, as it mounts an unexpectedly affecting tribute to the courage and determination of women, whatever their take on motherhood. GA

Pussy Talk (Le Sexe qui Parle)
(Frédéric Lanzac, 1975, Fr) Pénélope Lamour, Béatrice Harnois, Sylvia Bourdon, Ellen Earl-Coupey, Nils Hortzs.
91 min.
Men! Are you afraid of women? Are you weighed down by their insatiable sexual demands? Are you embarrassed by their behaviour in public? Do they humiliate you? Do you have nightmares about their furry little snatches concealing vicious little teeth? Then here at last is a film made with you, only you, in mind! And all those nasty hardcore sex scenes have been cut out in the 65 minute British release version, so you won't be distracted from the message you want to hear! TR

Putney Swope
(Robert Downey, 1969, US) Arnold Johnson, Antonio Fargas, Laura Greene, Eric Krupnik, Pepi Hermine, Ruth Hermine, Allen Garfield, Mel Brooks.
88 min. b/w & col.
A satire on American ways of life, written and

directed by Downey and misfiring on most cylinders. The idea is promising enough: the token black member of a big business board of directors is elected chairman because everybody votes for him on the assumption that no one else will. After some good lines in the opening scene, however, it all fizzles out in a series of damp squibs aimed indiscriminately at capitalism, Black Power, TV commercials, etc. TM

Puzzle of a Downfall Child

(Jerry Schatzberg, 1970, US) Faye Dunaway, Barry Primus, Viveca Lindfors, Barry Morse, Roy Scheider.
104 min.
Written by Adrian Joyce, who scripted the infinitely superior *Five Easy Pieces*, this emerges as an overwrought and soapy psychodrama in which top fashion model Dunaway, in an attempt to recover from a nervous breakdown, retires to a beach cottage and looks back into the events, both real and imaginary, that have caused her predicament. Vacuously stylish, pretentious, and poorly performed, this dud marked the debut of the often overrated Schatzberg, a former fashion photographer. GA

Pygmalion

(Anthony Asquith/Leslie Howard, 1938, GB) Leslie Howard, Wendy Hiller, Wilfrid Lawson, Marie Lohr, Scott Sunderland, Jean Cadell, David Tree, Everley Gregg, Esmé Percy.
96 min. b/w.
While the British film industry tumbled into one of the more serious of its periodic crises, an unlikely bunch of radicals and adventurers set out to breathe life into George Bernard Shaw's pre-(1914-18)war excursion into language and materialism. They produced a very radical – if still very male – film. Unlike the later *My Fair Lady*, the stress here is on Higgins' creation of a princess from 'a heap of stuffed cabbage leaves'. There is no Cinderella story: Eliza's transformation is forced and painful, and Higgins' final 'Where the devil are my slippers?' a refusal to forget, sentimentally, the enduring reality of patriarchy. Above all, the film is remarkable in that it strengthens rather than dilutes Shaw's insistence on language as the vital instrument of power and oppression. RMy

Pyrates

(Noah Stern, 1991, US) Kevin Bacon, Kyra Sedgwick, Bruce Martin Payne, Kristin Datillo, Buckley Norris.
95 min.
Groovy photographer Bacon and free-spirited cellist Sedgwick find their passions causing havoc when fires keep breaking out as they do the nasty. The first time a lava lamp explodes, the second time round though, and the joke's already gone too far. Presumably, real-life couple Kev 'n' Kyra had a few giggles making it, but a match carefully placed under the script would have saved everyone a lot of trouble. TJ

Pyromaniac's Love Story, A

(Joshua Brand, 1995, US) William Baldwin, John Leguizamo, Sadie Frost, Erika Eleniak, Joan Plowright, Armin Mueller-Stahl, Mike Starr, Julio Oscar Mechoso.
94 min.
Be warned by the 'once upon a time' opening: this film serves up sugar and ham in a reduced-plot dressing, and has the nerve to call it cute salad. Sergio (Leguizamo) is the pastry boy with the light and fluffy head whose hopeless love for the waitress across the street (Frost) is to be edged towards fruition by the mysterious fire that destroys the cake shop where he works. His fate at the hands of a convoluted plot is exacerbated by a stupidity so infuriating that that you begin to find the very sight of him intensely annoying. Enter the other young lovers. Baldwin, almost overwhelmed by his kook-signifiers (walking stick, beard, overcoat), plays the real pyromaniac, who's burnt down the shop in a fit of pique with his own object of desire. Outrageouly overdone, this character arrives far too late to add much interest or shed much light; and by the time Eleniak (the super-rich super-bitch Baldwin's in love with) enters the fray to sort out the nonsense from the rubbish, you're long since ready to wash your hands of the lot of them. LMu

q

The Quiet Man

Q & A
(Sidney Lumet, 1990, US) Nick Nolte, Timothy Hutton, Armand Assante, Patrick O'Neal, Lee Richardson, Luis Guzman, Charles Dutton, Jenny Lumet, Paul Calderon.
132 min.
Few film-makers have dealt with American police corruption as effectively as Lumet; but while this tough, fundamentally sound New York thriller has its moments, it's no *Prince of the City*. Ambitious, idealistic assistant DA Reilly (Hutton) investigates a homicide case in which Lt Mike Brennan (Nolte), one of the NYPD's finest, shot a Hispanic dope dealer. The focus shifts towards racial tension as the Irish fall prey to old animosities against blacks and Hispanics, including crime baron Texador (Assante). Despite a redundant romantic subplot, much of the film is tightly written and directed, embellishing its conflicts with a wealth of telling detail; but it does remain earnest and faintly predictable. Although the performances are mostly solid (Assante particularly fine throughout), it never quite achieves the harsh, convincing tone it aims for. GA

Q – the Winged Serpent
see Winged Serpent, The

Quadrophenia
(Franc Roddam, 1979, GB) Phil Daniels, Leslie Ash, Philip Davis, Mark Wingett, Sting, Raymond Winstone, Toyah Wilcox, Michael Elphick.
120 min.
Fine as long as it sticks to recreation of period and place, and stays with a simple enough plot – 1964 mod Daniels' Brighton beach battles with the Rockers, and his on/off love affair with Ash. But as the film progresses, it becomes bogged down in silly moralising and metaphysics, struggling to accommodate itself to the absurd story of The Who's rock opera. Good performances, though, and directed with admirable energy for the first half. GA

Quai des Brumes, Le (Port of Shadows)
(Marcel Carné, 1938, Fr) Jean Gabin, Michèle Morgan, Michel Simon, Pierre Brasseur, Robert Le Vigan, Aimos, Marcel Pérès.
89 min. b/w.
One reason the French picked up on American *film noir* so quickly in the late '40s was that they'd had their own *films noir* a decade earlier: romantic crime thrillers in low-life settings, fatalistic in mood and fog-grey in atmosphere. *Pépé le Moko* launched the cycle in 1937 and made Gabin a star. *Quai des Brumes* clinched every last detail of the genre the following year. Gabin plays an army deserter who tries to protect Morgan from the criminal intentions of Simon and Brasseur. Shot almost entirely on its main studio set, a waterfront bar, the visuals have the same downbeat poetry as Jacques Prévert's dialogue. Those who know Gabin's glowering silences only from the clips in *Mon Oncle d'Amérique* have a revelation in store. TR

Quai des Orfèvres
(Henri-Georges Clouzot, 1947, Fr) Louis Jouvet, Suzy Delair, Bernard Blier, Simone Renant, Charles Dullin, Pierre Larquey.
105 min. b/w.
It's unfortunate that *The Wages of Fear* is virtually the only Clouzot film that anyone remembers, since his real background lies in a much more traditional French thriller vein, of which *Quai des Orfèvres* is a fine example. The plot is suitably marginal: a hard-times couple (Blier, Delair) whose marriage is crumbling find themselves implicated in a murder. Clouzot doesn't waste a moment over the rampant implausibilities, but devotes all his energies to a romantically bleak evocation of the low-life settings: run-down music-halls, squalid apartments and gloomy police stations, peopled with lonely hookers, lesbians and pornographers. Jouvet's Maigret-esque cop gets all the best lines, and gives the film its human, tragic focus. TR

Quantrill's Raiders
(Edward Bernds, 1958, US) Steve Cochran, Diane Brewster, Leo Gordon, Gale Robbins.
68 mins.
Brisk little Western. Bernds has a knack for action and keeps matters galloping along. Set in Kansas during the Civil War, the story concerns a Confederate outlaw's attempt to blow up a Yankee ammunition dump. Gordon, fresh from playing Dillinger in *Baby Face Nelson*, is as mean a varmint as anybody could wish to find on the open plains. Cochran, who'd just appeared in Antonioni's *Il Grido*, is the Gary Cooper-like hero. GM

Quartet
(Ralph Smart/Harold French/Arthur Crabtree/Ken Annakin, 1948, GB) Basil Radford, Jack Watling, Mai Zetterling, Dirk Bogarde, Françoise Rosay, George Cole, Susan Shaw, Mervyn Johns, Hermione Baddeley, Cecil Parker, Nora Swinburne.
120 min. b/w.
First of three Somerset Maugham portmanteaux (its success engendered *Trio* and *Encore*), introduced by the old boy himself. Predictably enough, the beady-eyed Maugham cynicism has been smoothed away in RC Sherriff's adaptation of the four carefully assorted stories, leaving 'civilised' entertainment that is rescued from typically glossy but indifferent Gainsborough packaging (sets and music are particularly bad) by the performances. Parker and Swinburne are outstanding in the last (and best) story, directed by Annakin, about a pukka colonel baffled by the discovery that his placid wife has a reputation as a passionate poetess. TM

Quartet
(James Ivory, 1981, GB/Fr) Isabelle Adjani, Anthony Higgins, Maggie Smith, Alan Bates, Pierre Clémenti, Daniel Mesguisch, Suzanne Flon.
101 min.
An adaptation of Jean Rhys' semi-autobiographical novel (for another angle on the affair, see Ford Madox Ford's *The Good Soldier*, in which a victim of circumstances, stranded in the Paris of the '20s when her con-man husband is jailed, becomes subject to the predatory help of a hedonistic upper class English couple. Maggie Smith and Alan Bates successfully personify the cold spirit that Rhys held to be pre-war England, but Adjani manages merely to reduce Marya's fatalism to spinelessness. The direction, intimate yet retaining a sense of distance, is true both to Rhys and to Ivory. FD

Quatermass Experiment, The
(Val Guest, 1955, GB) Brian Donlevy, Richard Wordsworth, Jack Warner, Margia Dean, David King-Wood, Gordon Jackson, Harold Lang, Thora Hird, Lionel Jeffries.
82 min. b/w.
It was the enormous success of this Hammer version of Nigel Kneale's TV series which began the whole horror boom in Britain. As a result of its popularity, the company decided to tackle the Frankenstein monster, and subsequently discovered that the public's appetite for myth and fantasy was practically insatiable. The theme of the film (man returns from space as a kind of monster) is by now fairly stereotyped, but it's amazing how impressive Richard Wordsworth's performance remains. Phil Leakey's make-up manages to convey the idea of a whole body in the process of decomposition; and staggering over bombsites, his deformed arm wrapped pathetically in an old overcoat, Wordsworth's Victor remains one of the most sympathetic monsters in movie history. Perhaps the most remarkable thing about the film, in retrospect, is the way in which its opening sequence mirrors so precisely the intrusion of Hammer into the cosy middle class domesticity of British cinema in the late '50s. Two insipid lovers are sent screaming from their haystack bower as a huge tubular rocket ship (looking less like a spacecraft than an enormous phallus) plunges into the ground where they have been lying...DP

Quatermass II
(Val Guest, 1957, GB) Brian Donlevy, John Longden, Sidney James, Bryan Forbes, Vera Day, William Franklyn, Charles Lloyd Pack, Michael Ripper.
85 min. b/w.
An eerie political fable on the lines of Siegel's *Invasion of the Body Snatchers*, and despite some clumsy moments that have not worn well, it remains one of the more bizarre and impressive of the early British horror pictures. Photographed by Gerald Gibbs in a sombre monochrome that nicely evokes an aura of muted hysteria and despair, it describes Quatermass' discovery that virtually the whole of Britain has been taken over by things from another world, and that the government has already begun laying waste the countryside. Provided you steel yourself against the familiar faces (like Bryan Forbes and Sidney James), the chill is still there. CPe

Quatermass and the Pit
(Roy Ward Baker, 1967, GB) James Donald, Andrew Keir, Barbara Shelley, Julian Glover, Duncan Lamont, Bryan Marshall, Peter Copley, Edwin Richfield.
97 min.
The third and most interesting of Nigel Kneale's *Quatermass* parables, scripted without interference by Kneale himself from his original TV series, so that his richly allusive web of occult, anthropological, religious and extraterrestrial speculation emerges intact as excavations at a London underground station turn up what appears to be an unexploded Nazi bomb, but proves to be a mysterious space craft. Hammer unfortunately delayed filming for several years, partly because of the sheer elaborateness of the subject matter, and partly because the plot did not lend itself to instant monster treatment. By the time the project came to be filmed, the company had moved from Bray and much of the atmosphere of their productions had been lost; but the brilliant pre-Von Daniken anthropological theme of Kneale's script still guarantees interest. DP

Quatre Aventures de Reinette & Mirabelle
see 4 Adventures of Reinette & Mirabelle

Quatre Cents Coups, Les (The 400 Blows) 100
(François Truffaut, 1959, Fr) Jean-Pierre Léaud, Albert Rémy, Claire Maurier, Patrick Auffay, Georges Flamant, Guy Décomble.
101 min. b/w.
Truffaut's first feature, and although not his best, infinitely better than the self-indulgent, increasingly compromised work he was turning out towards the end of his career. Revealing a complicity with downtrodden, neglected and rebellious adolescence that is intensely moving but never mawkish, shot on location in Paris with a casually vivid eye that is almost documentary, it still has an amazing freshness in its (quasi-autobiographical) account of 13-year-old Antoine Doinel's bleak odyssey through family life, reform school, and an escape whose precarious permanence is questioned by the final frozen image of the boy's face as he reaches the sea – freedom or point of no return? Still one of the cinema's most perceptive forays into childhood, and fun for spotting the guest appearances of such *Nouvelle Vague* luminaries as Jeanne Moreau, Jean-Claude Brialy, Jacques Demy and (in the funfair scene) Truffaut himself. TM

Quatre Nuits d'un Rêveur
see Four Nights of a Dreamer

Quattro dell'Ave Maria, I (Ace High/Revenge in El Paso)
(Giuseppe Colizzi, 1968, It) Eli Wallach, Terence Hill ie.Mario Girotti, Bud Spencer ie. Carlo Pedersoli, Brock Peters, Kevin McCarthy, Livio Lorenzon.
137 min.
Second pairing of the Hill/Spencer team (later to sustain the 'Trinity' series) in a spaghetti spoof that has Wallach parodying his 'Ugly' persona as a roguish Mexican bandit, playing cat-and-mouse with Hill and Spencer over some stolen money while plotting revenge against the four men who framed him into jail. In a suitably cockeyed homage to Leone and Morricone, the climactic Wallach/McCarthy confrontation uncoils to the strains of a waltz. Apparently nothing but coincidentally, the Hill character is named Cat Stevens. PH

Queen, The
(Frank Simon, 1968, US) Jack Doroshow, Richard Finochio, Crystal, Andy Warhol, Larry Rivers, Edie Sedgewick, Terry Southern.
68 min.
An outlandish documentary which follows the arrival, preparation for, and participation in the 1967 Drag Miss All American Beauty Queen

Contest of a bunch of international hopefuls. The men come into town, lounge about, then dress up and sally out on stage as girls. Breasts created by flesh-cramping sellotape squeeze out of swimsuits; rivalries created by a pursuit for the title shriek around backstage; Sylvia goes bananas and the audience go wild. A rocky horror show indeed. HM

Queen Christina

(Rouben Mamoulian, 1933, US) Greta Garbo, John Gilbert, Ian Keith, Lewis Stone, Elizabeth Young, C Aubrey Smith, Reginald Owen, Gustav von Seyffertitz, Akim Tamiroff.
100 min. b/w.
On the face of it, this is the usual historical hogwash, made to the traditional recipe (prepare a literate but daft script around the concepts of love, honour and duty; stir in two gooey-eyed stars, one of whom may be miscast and a bad wearer of costumes; bring to the boil, stirring in teaspoonfuls of C Aubrey Smith, rhubarbing peasants, snow, ducks, and Gothic lettering; serve with naive music). But *Queen Christina* is lifted far above its origins, partly by Mamoulian (who moulds potentially stodgy scenes with his finicky regard to detail), and partly by Garbo herself: she turns her character into a living entity, extracts real emotion from the script's purple clumps ('Snow is like a wild sea. One can go and get lost in it...'), and glides through Mamoulian's winding camera movements with grace, wit and beauty. She plays the 17th-century Queen of Sweden, whose career comes unstuck when she falls for the Spanish Ambassador (a touching but inadequate performance from John Gilbert, her old cohort from the silents). GB

Queen Kelly

(Erich von Stroheim, 1931/1985, US) Gloria Swanson, Walter Byron, Seena Owen, Wilhelm von Brinken, Madge Hunt, Tully Marshall, Florence Gibson.
100 min. b/w.
Bearing even less resemblance, as it stands, to Stroheim's original conception than did his earlier masterpieces, this tale of an innocent convent girl courted and corrupted by a dissolute prince engaged to a Ruritanian queen, simultaneously delights and frustrates. Transforming the hackneyed melodramatic plot into an audaciously slow spectacle of lush decor and delirious lighting, the Von conjured up a sensuously detailed world of misguided romanticism and seductive cynicism, where monarchs wield jealous whips and kindness conceals cunning strategies. But with only half the script filmed, and a dissatisfying ending tacked on by other, insensitive hands, Swanson's original 1931 release inevitably betrayed the balance, epic scope and tragic irony one would expect from this giant among filmmakers. The present version, deleting the tacked on 'suicide' ending, incorporates the two edited reels of African footage (on which Stroheim was working when he was fired) which were rediscovered in 1965, fleshed out by the use of titles and stills. The result is a profoundly flawed vision of what might have been, but riveting none the less. GA

Queen of Hearts

(Jon Amiel, 1989, GB) Vittorio Duse, Joseph Long, Anita Zagaria, Eileen Way, Vittorio Amandola, Roberto Scateni, Ian Hawkes.
112 min.
A winning debut for Amiel, working from a script by Tony Grisoni about the experience of Italian immigrants to London circa the '50s (although it seems to waver in period). It's told from the point of view of imaginative ten-year-old Eddie (Hawkes), son of Rosa and Danilo (Long, excellent), elopers from Central Italy (where the first section is set). It's a family affair, centering on the East End café where waiter Danilo buys after a gambling windfall. Relatives arrive; the four children quarrel and grow up; grandma grumbles about the old ways; a shining new Espresso machine arrives; a wedding is celebrated; Eddie's brother takes to crime. Then jilted Barbariccia, 'King of the Knives', to whom Rosa was promised back in Italy, arrives bent on revenge. It's a modest film, but rich in human relationships – their scams, aspirations and myths – and true to the fantastic spirit of the boy narrator. The strong cast (some of the actors unprofessional) makes up for the rough edges. It plays like a mix of Ealing kid's fantasy and a gentle, naive pastiche of *The Godfather*. WH

Queen of Outer Space

(Edward Bernds, 1958, US) Zsa Zsa Gabor, Eric Fleming, Laurie Mitchell, Paul Birch, Barbara Darrow, Dave Willock.
80 min.
Standout 'Best Worst' movie in which astronauts crash-land on Venus and discover that women are ruling the planet. It takes the earthlings a while to grasp the feminine superiorities ('Even if a woman could build a gizmo like that, she'd never know how to aim it!'), and rather longer to locate the leader (Gabor) of those subversives who feel that 'vimmin cannot live vizout men'. The Place may be Venus, but the Time looks more like cocktail hour than the future; everyone's wearing vintage Swanky Modes and ice-skating skirts. There's also a fine display of '50s sublimated sexuality in the endless kissing scenes – which may have you pondering, along with the expedition's professor, 'How ironic that our lives and the lives of millions on Earth should depend on the sex appeal of our Captain'. CR

Queen of Spades, The

(Thorold Dickinson, 1948, GB) Anton Walbrook, Edith Evans, Yvonne Mitchell, Mary Jerrold, Ronald Howard, Anthony Dawson, Miles Malleson, Athene Seyler, Michael Medwin.
95 min. b/w.
A pleasingly macabre fantasy, brilliantly designed by Oliver Messel, whose sets show rare imagination in evoking the suffocating decadence of imperial Russia. Expansion of Pushkin's short story, about an impecunious young officer's obsessive attempts to wrest the secret of winning at cards from a diabolical old countess, means that the first half never seems to be getting anywhere (there are cast problems, too, with Walbrook at his most sibilantly melodramatic, Evans coated in rubberised make-up, and the support variable to say the least). Yet Dickinson's elegantly prowling, darting camera, and his marvellously eerie sound effects (like the rustle of silk and the tapping stick that herald the ghostly presence of the countess) pull it all together in an impressive crescendo. TM

Queen's Guards, The

(Michael Powell, 1961, GB) Daniel Massey, Robert Stephens, Raymond Massey, Ursula Jeans, Judith Stott, Elizabeth Shepherd, Duncan Lamont, Ian Hunter, Jess Conrad, Jack Watling, Andrew Crawford, Nigel Green.
110 min.
Powell's sad farewell to British features was, by his own admission, crippled by lack of any conviction in the script. In a series of flashbacks from a Trooping the Colour ceremony, a young officer (Daniel Massey) remembers the abiding family problem: his dead brother is forever held up to him as an example by their military father, who is totally obsessed with the pride of the service. Despite an imposing performance by Raymond Massey in this role, neither the period frolics (which include a visit to a 'beat' club) nor the ponderous heroics carry much conviction, with only the faintest whiff of the flair or emotion that infused *The Life and Death of Colonel Blimp*. DT

Queens of the Big Time

(Adriana Trigiani, 1996, US)
74 min.
Roseto, Pennsylvania, is a small town populated almost entirely by people of Italian stock, whose forefathers recreated their hometown, Roseto Valforte, in Foggia, upon emigrating to America in the 1890s. 'The Big Time' is the annual festival honouring the town's patron saint, Our Lady of Mt Carmel, and begins with a car procession of teenage 'princesses' and the crowning of the new 'queen'. This first film, complete with the home movies of the director's grandfather, covers the centennial celebration, when all the living queens (from the most recent to her 1926 counterpart) gathered together. A warm, amusing, uncritical look at tradition, friendship and community. GA

Queens Logic

(Steve Rash, 1991, US) Kevin Bacon, Linda Fiorentino, John Malkovich, Joe Mantegna, Ken Olin, Tony Spiridakis, Chloe Webb, Tom Waits, Jamie Lee Curtis, Ed Marinaro, Kelly Bishop.
112 min.
Fabulous cast, so-so idea. This is yet another post-*Big Chill* way-we-were movie: a bunch of buddies hang out remembering the good times, the bad times, the godawful records. What's testing their communal ability to grow up here is marriage: the impending one between painter Olin and hairdresser Webb, and the crumbling one between Mantegna's mouthy fishmonger and Fiorentino. The rest of the gang is on hand to provide moral or alcoholic support. Steve Rash handles the slightly diffuse business with sensitivity, but the film coasts mainly on the acting. Mantegna stands out for sheer bravado; Chloe Webb just about contrives to steal the show with a lipful of feistiness. But, as usual, it's really a boys' film, about leering, beering and losing your swim-shorts, and for straight boozy larking, *Hangin' with the Homeboys* has it licked by a mile. JRo

Queer Story, A (Jilao Sishi)

(Shu Kei, 1997, HK) George Lam, Jordan Chan, Francis Ng, Christine Ng, Fredric Mao.
112 min.
Marriage guidance counsellor Law Kar-Sing (Lam) has a stable relationship with his younger boyfriend Sonny (Chan), but remains so deeply closeted that he has never broken the news to his childhood sweetheart that he's gay. Nor has he ever told his ultra-conservative father. The crunch comes when Sonny tires of his lover's evasions and walks out, forcing Law to rethink his life. The only real problem with Shu Kei's enjoyable comedy-drama is its insufficiently hidden agenda: too many scenes seem designed solely to set up common Chinese homophobic prejudices, only to knock 'em down. As Hong Kong's first overtly pro-gay movie, though, it's a credible piece of work. Its biggest asset is Jordan Chan, clearly a huge star-to-be. TR

Queimada! (Burn!)

(Gillo Pontecorvo, 1968, It/Fr) Marlon Brando, Evaristo Marquez, Renato Salvatori, Norman Hill, Tom Lyons.
132 min.
Pontecorvo's memorable sequel to *Battle of Algiers* sees Brando in finely ambiguous form as the drunken, cynical Sir William Walker, a British agent sent to the Caribbean island of Queimada in the mid-1800s to stir up a native rebellion against the Portuguese sugar monopoly; ten years later, he is forced to return there to destroy the leader he himself created, in order to open up trade with Britain. Falling between epic adventure and political allegory, the film is occasionally clumsily structured and poorly focused; but Pontecorvo, working from a script by Franco Solinas, provides a sharp, provocative analysis of colonialism, full of telling irony, bravura set pieces, and compelling imagery, while Brando's stiff-lipped performance, emphasising his character's confused mixture of dignity and deceit, intelligence and evil, determination and disillusion, never allows the allegory to dominate the human content. A flawed but fascinating film. GA

Que la Bête Meure (Killer!)

(Claude Chabrol, 1969, Fr/It) Michel Duchaussoy, Caroline Cellier, Jean Yanne, Anouk Ferjac, Marc Di Napoli, Maurice Pialat, Guy Marly, Lorraine Rainer, Dominique Zardi.
110 min.
Chabrol's most Langian film – the end is a virtual recreation of that of *Moonfleet* – *Que la Bête Meure*, like Lang's *Rancho Notorious* and *The Big Heat*, is dominated by the themes of revenge and destiny. However, in contrast to those films, whose heroes are trapped within their desire for revenge, Chabrol's protagonist (Duchaussoy), at first determined to kill the murderer (Yanne) of his son in a hit-and-run accident, finds his self-imposed task less and less appealing as he closes in on his prey. Finally, after Yanne's son kills his boorish, tyrannical father, Duchaussoy claims responsibility for the murder in order not to lose this second, substitute son. A masterful film, all the more powerful for the fact that so much of its meaning is contained in the camera's perspective of what happens rather than simply what happens. PH

Que la Fête Commence (Let Joy Reign Supreme)

(Bertrand Tavernier, 1975, Fr) Philippe Noiret, Christine Pascal, Jean Rochefort, Jean-Pierre Marielle, Marina Vlady.
120 min.

Tavernier's second film, made during the period when the rewriting of history on film was the key issue in French cinema, never released in Britain but a hit in the US under the ironic title *Let Joy Reign Supreme*. Spectacular as French costume movies go, but never extravagant for its own sake, this is a subtle exploration of power politics in the court of the Regent Philippe of Orleans in 1719, taking in the revolutionary cause of Breton secessionists and the commerce in sex that provokes intrigues. Noiret is compelling as the Regent, and Pascal fleshes out the peasant girl from whose perspective the narrative is argued. Here 'Winstanley' meets 'Casanova', and it works. MA

Quentin Durward

see Adventures of Quentin Durward, The

Querelle

(Rainer Werner Fassbinder, 1982, WGer/Fr) Brad Davis, Franco Nero, Jeanne Moreau, Günther Kaufmann, Laurent Malet, Hanno Pöschl.
108 min.

More a dream about than a dramatisation of Genet's novel, this is glorious and infuriating in equal parts. The port of Brest is built and lit more like one of Burroughs' Cities of the Red Night, murderous deity Querelle's ambisexual encounters are suffused with a sweaty, tangible eroticism, and Fassbinder's 'version' stays faithful to Genet's nightmare poetry. But its narrative detachment, weighty monologues, Resnais-like anachronisms, and (most irritating of all) listless rationale turn it into a lurid hymn to teenybop nihilism. All in all, perhaps an entirely appropriate parting shot from a drug-crazed German faggot. JG

Quest, The

(Jean-Claude Van Damme, 1996, US) Jean-Claude Van Damme, Roger Moore, Janet Gunn.
95 min.

Lord Edgar Dobbs (Moore), a roguish con-man, first rescues fugitive New York street criminal Chris Dubois (Van Damme) from sea-borne gunrunners, then sells him into bondage. But all this 1920s *Boy's Own* stuff is just window-dressing for the main event, the Ghan-gheng, a winner-takes-all contest featuring the world's greatest fighters. Dobbs' bumbling efforts to steal the prize, a Golden Dragon, are no more diverting than the drippy romance between Dubois and society-girl reporter Carrie (ex-stuntwoman Janet Gunn who, like first-time director Van Damme, should have stuck to her day job). The risible fight scenes showcase the stereotyped sartorial and imaginary fighting styles of the international contestants: the Orientals are treated with some respect, but the Spanish contestant prances Flamenco-style in frilly shirts and bum-hugging trousers, while his Scottish counterpart sports a kilt and eschews the traditional head-butt for a similarly terpsichorean approach. NF

Qu'est-ce qui fait courir David?

see What Makes David Run?

Quest for Fire

(Jean-Jacques Annaud, 1981, Can/Fr) Everett McGill, Ron Perlman, Nameer El-Kadi, Rae Dawn Chong.
100 min.

'Body Language and Gestures by Desmond Morris; Special Languages Created by Anthony Burgess'. With these eye-catching credits, *Quest for Fire* boldly states its claims to dance along the abyss of the ridiculous. That it manages not to fall in is something of an achievement, but not a sufficient one to justify 100 minutes of grunts and hand-waving in the service of an otherwise unremarkable story. What watchability the film does have is probably due to a screenplay by Gerard Brach, Polanski's regular co-writer. Still, if you have a weakness for exotic scenery (filmed in Canada, Scotland, Kenya), and some curiosity

about the everyday life of prehistoric humankind, you will probably take some mild pleasure in this saga of the Ulam tribe's search for a way to light their fire. MH

Quest for Love

(Ralph Thomas, 1971, GB) Joan Collins, Tom Bell, Denholm Elliott, Laurence Naismith, Lyn Ashley, Neil McCallum, Ray McAnally.
91 min.

An adaptation of a story by John Wyndham, but as directed by Ralph Thomas and 'acted' by Joan Collins, it emerges as a puerile sci-fi romance in which a scientist (Bell) is transported into a parallel world. The year is the same, but in his new world, Vietnam hasn't happened, nor the conquest of Everest, nor the surgery of heart transplants. Making little of this premise, the film plunges forthwith into a moony romance where his lady of the camellias (Collins) dies of a heart condition, and he races off in search of her counterpart in the other world to save her from a similar fate. TM

Question of Silence, A (De Stilte Rond Christine M)

(Marleen Gorris, 1982, Neth) Edda Barends, Nelly Frijda, Henriette Tol, Cox Habbema, Eddy Brugman, Hans Croiset.
96 min.

Three strangers brutally murder the inoffensive manager of an Amsterdam boutique, but the case is less straightforward than it seems. Told in flashback via the investigation of a criminal psychiatrist brought in to certify insanity, the film convincingly shows the motive behind the killing as intolerable male oppression of various kinds, the twist in this thriller/courtroom drama being that the muggers – and their psychiatrist – are very ordinary women and their victim a man. The story is told with an astonishing assurance and visual flair that belie the small budget and debutant director Gorris' lack of experience. Her feminism is uncompromising, but of a disarmingly undogmatic kind. The result is at once accessible and deeply unsettling: the upbeat ending, for instance, has the male way of looking at the world literally laughed out of court, with a cathartic laughter that explodes out of the women's earlier silent isolation, and goes on echoing long after the film is over. SJo

Quick and the Dead, The

(Sam Raimi, 1995, US) Sharon Stone, Gene Hackman, Russell Crowe, Leonardo DiCaprio, Lance Henriksen.
108 min.

This engagingly OTT homage to the style and revenge fantasies of the spaghetti Western centres on a deadly tournament – organised by Hackman, boss of the township Redemption – to find the fastest gun in the West. Enter a motley crew, among them Sharon Stone's Eastwood-like interloper, who has a secret agenda of her own...A deadpan black comedy, Sam Raimi's fast-paced movie looks and sounds like a Leone oater but more so. The violence is heightened by an intelligent, often hilarious use of special effects. Stone, who co-produced, is surprisingly effective in the lead, and Hackman's Herod is wonderfully, unrepentantly villainous. Terrific fun. GA

Quick Change

(Howard Franklin/Bill Murray, 1990, US) Bill Murray, Geena Davis, Randy Quaid, Jason Robards, Bob Elliott, Philip Bosco, Phil Hartman, Jack Gilpin.
88 min.

New York is the central character in this quirky comedy, which brings Murray, Davis and Quaid together as an unlikely trio of bank-robbers, pulling off the neatest heist imaginable before going adrift on the rocks of Big Apple chaos. It's Murray and screenwriter Franklin's joint first directorial effort – based on Jay Cronley's novel – and does have much to recommend it, notably some superb set pieces from a collection of redoubtable character actors (particularly cherishable is a scene with a hopelessly lost Central American cab driver), a feisty show from Robards as the cop who has to crack the case, and a tailing-down of Murray's usual smart-ass character into someone who has to achieve a cool equilibrium under pressure. There are also some useful street locations, climaxing with a very accurate conjuration of all the hell that is Times Square. Not likely to set the world alight, but a neat and engaging little comedy of bad manners. SGr

¿Quién Puede Matar a un Niño? (Death Is Child's Play/Island of the Damned/Would You Kill a Child?)

(Narciso Ibáñez Serrador, 1975, Sp) Lewis Fiander, Prunella Ransome, Maria Druille, Lourdes de la Cámara, Roberto Nauta.
112 min.

Horror films are almost by definition so full of plagiarism and revamped ideas that it's always exciting to find real originality in a plot. While this is influenced by *Night of the Living Dead* and *Lord of the Flies*, its twist is inventive and, potentially, highly relevant: the children of a remote Spanish island are afflicted by a kind of supernatural plague, and slaughter the adult population. Finally, though, the film fails to take advantage of its own idea. Hints over the credits that the children of the human race may be exacting revenge for war atrocities are undercut by a gratuitous *Rosemary's Baby* subplot. DP

¿Quién sabe?

see Bullet for the General, A

Quiet American, The

(Joseph L Mankiewicz, 1958, US) Audie Murphy, Michael Redgrave, Claude Dauphin, Giorgia Moll, Bruce Cabot, Richard Loo.
120 min. b/w.

Graham Greene was incensed by the way his novel's anti-American bias was shifted into anti-Communism as his quiet American arrives in Indo-China in 1952 with naive notions about a moral 'third force' helping to resolve the conflict. Vietnam history may have proved Greene right, but this remains a superior, strikingly intelligent film. Locations in Saigon help in lending an amazingly convincing atmosphere, and Mankiewicz is very nearly at his best in probing the murky relationship between Murphy's American Candide and Redgrave's tormentedly cynical British war correspondent, with sexual rivalry and unwanted personal obligations providing a quicksand basis for their ideological clash. Much underrated at the time. TM

Quiet Days in Clichy (Stille Dage i Clichy)

(Jens Jorgen Thorsen, 1969, Den) Paul Valjean, Wayne John Rodda, Ulla Lemvigh-Müller, Avi Sagild, Susanne Krage.
96 min. b/w.

Joey and Carl fuck, suck and eat their way through Henry Miller's Paris, the last frontier for the American hero to conquer. There's lots of women, and the studs waste no time getting them on the bed, in the bath, on the floor, anytime, anywhere, anyhow. Cartoon bubbles, subtitles, and Country Joe's music fill in the thoughts and keep it moving. Rodda's bad acting defies description. You might dismiss the whole thing as a superior skinflick; nevertheless it goes a long way towards conveying what Miller was about, giving the feel of Paris behind the feel of the crack. It's also often quite funny, which should be sufficient recommendation for those who have sat through one dour sex film too many. CPe

Quiet Earth, The

(Geoffrey Murphy, 1985, NZ) Bruno Lawrence, Alison Routledge, Peter Smith, Anzac Wallace, Norman Fletcher, Tom Hyde.
91 min.

Zac Hobson finds himself the planet's sole reluctant survivor of a catastrophic error in the secret energy project on which he's been engaged, and the combination of guilt and self-delusion soon sends him off his rocker. Murphy starts to develop this idea with a series of delightfully inventive scenes, with Zac proclaiming himself world dictator, trying a little transvestism, and finally challenging God to a duel. But what promises initially to become an SF spoof of genuine oddity, soon degenerates into a merely conventional thriller with the arrival of two fellow survivors. Still, compensation is provided by desolate Auckland locations, some fine sight gags, and the ebullient Lawrence as Zac. The moral: 'Don't fuck with the infinite'. WH

Qui êtes-vous Polly Maggoo?

see Who Are You Polly Maggoo?

Quiet Man, The [100]

(John Ford, 1952, US) John Wayne, Maureen
O'Hara, Victor McLaglen, Barry Fitzgerald,
Mildred Natwick, Arthur Shields, Ward Bond,
Jack MacGowran.
129 min.
Ford's flamboyantly Oirish romantic comedy
hides a few tough ironies deep in its mistily nostalgic recreation of an exile's dream. But the illu-
sion/reality theme underlying immigrant boxer
Wayne's return from America to County Galway
– there to become involved in a *Taming of the
Shrew* courtship of flame-haired O'Hara, and a
marathon donnybrook with her truculent, dowry-
withholding brother McLaglen – is soon
swamped within a vibrant community of stage-
Irish 'types'. Ford once described it gnomically
as 'the sexiest picture ever made'. PT

Quiet Please, Murder

(John Larkin, 1942, US) George Sanders, Gail
Patrick, Richard Denning, Sidney Blackmer,
Lynne Roberts, Kurt Katch.
70 min. b/w.
Cheapo thriller enhanced by an unusual plot and
location, with Sanders as a manic book collector
who will do anything to get his hands on rare editions. Mainly set in a library, it takes off when
Sanders kills while stealing a Shakespeare folio,
and becomes more complicated when an evil Nazi
art collector gets in on the act. Lively, blessed by
a typically cool performance from Sanders, and
helped no end by Joe MacDonald's stylish camerawork. GA

Quiet Room, The

(Rolf de Heer, 1996, Aust) Chloe Ferguson,
Phoebe Ferguson, Paul Blackwell, Celine
O'Leary.
90 min.
The fascination with perception and communication that characterised de Heer's *Bad Boy
Bubby* again dominates this look at a couple's
deteriorating relationship as witnessed (with confusion and misunderstanding) by their 7-year-old
daughter, who simply refuses to speak – though
we hear her thoughts in voice-over. Without ramming the point home, de Heer shows the well-
meaning parents' insensitivity, their desperation
and their occasional readiness to use the child as
a pawn in their power games; and while it's basically a one-idea movie, and perhaps too concerned with formal originality, as opposed to
emotional content, it still offers acute insights into
a child's inner world. GA

Quigley Down Under

(Simon Wincer, 1990, US) Tom Selleck, Laura
San Giacomo, Alan Rickman, Chris Haywood,
Ron Haddrick, Tony Bonner, Jerome Ehlers.
120 min.
To date, the '90s Westerns suggest a return to the
revisionist oaters of 20 years earlier: anti-Westerns,
or at any rate anti-colonial. If this Selleck vehicle
about an American cowboy in Australia is hardly
'Dances with Dingoes', it is a pleasant surprise to
see the predictably jokey signs of dislocation –
koalas and roos – make way for the moral issues
the genre thrives on. Sharpshooter Quigley goes
down under to shoot dingoes for rancher Marston
(Rickman) – or so he thinks. When it transpires
that he is to eliminate aborigines, a feud develops,
and he becomes a champion of the native tribes.
Unfortunately, his status as righter of wrongs is
mirrored to some extent by the script, which shows
a particularly heavy hand in exposition. But
Selleck's easy charm carries it through the sticky
patches. Aussie director Wincer handles the action
convincingly, and Rickman's splendidly snide villain is a real treat. TCh

Quiller Memorandum, The

(Michael Anderson, 1966, GB/US) George
Segal, Alec Guinness, Max von Sydow, Senta
Berger, George Sanders, Robert Helpmann,
Robert Flemyng, Peter Carsten.
103 min.
The thinking man's spy thriller, in as much as
Harold Pinter wrote the script. Although the whole
thing is ill-served by Michael Anderson's direction,
it remains perversely likeable precisely because it
is rather long-winded and enigmatic: it gets clos-

er to the feel of Len Deighton's novels far better
than any of the three Harry Palmer films. The acting, with George Segal versus neo-Nazi Max von
Sydow, is excellent, the Berlin locations so-so. CPe

Quince Tree Sun, The
(El Sol del Membrillo)

(Victor Erice, 1992, Sp) Antonio López, María
Moreno, Enrique Gran, José Carrtero.
139 min.
A truly magnificent film from the maker of *Spirit
of the Beehive* and *The South*, which effortlessly transcends the term 'documentary'. Basically,
it follows Madrileño painter Antonio López as he
meticulously and slowly labours over a painting
of a quince tree in his garden. That the task takes
him months is of interest in itself, but where the
film scores is in its fleshing out of its subject
through conversation with friends, wife, admirers, and builders at work on his house, a strategy that simultaneously contextualises López and
puts his bizarre, even limited conception of artistic endeavour into perspective. Don't worry
about a lengthy, fairly banal dialogue about half-
an-hour into the film; the rest is visually extraordinary, funny, touching, and quite unlike
anything else. GA

Quintet

(Robert Altman, 1979, US) Paul Newman,
Vittorio Gassman, Fernando Rey, Bibi
Andersson, Brigitte Fossey, Nina Van
Pallandt, David Langton.
118 min.
While certainly not one of Altman's most successful movies, this excursion into the sci-fi genre
was unfairly criticised or neglected upon release.
Set in a bleak landscape during a tough, inhospitable ice-age, it concerns a seal trapper
(Newman) and his wife (Fossey) who wander into
a strange, desolate city where they meet a group
of people playing a mysterious game, for which
the stakes gambled are life and death. Slow,
humourless, and occasionally over-emphatic in
its use of symbolism, it's nevertheless a fascinating film, which manages to work thanks to its
absolute mastery of atmosphere. GA

Quiz Show

(Robert Redford, 1994, US) John Turturro, Rob
Morrow, Ralph Fiennes, Paul Scofield,
Elizabeth Wilson, Mira Sorvino, Martin
Scorsese, Barry Levinson.
132 min.
In America in the '50s, TV quiz shows were
watched by more than half the viewing public.
When handsome Ivy League lecturer Charles Van
Doren became reigning champ of *Twenty One*, he
found himself a national celebrity. Then a defeated former champion, Herbie Stempel, a working-
class Jew from Queens, New York, claimed the
show was fixed. Redford has fashioned (from
Paul Attanasio's brilliant screenplay) an impeccably nuanced Faustian drama which aspires to
capture America's fall from grace: that point at
the end of the '50s when the country first lost faith
in itself. Poised, patrician and with a genius IQ,
Van Doren (Fiennes) appears to be the perfect role
model. Instead, he is a victim of the values of the
times and his own greed for approval. In an investigation which evokes (or prefigures) *All the
President's Men*, Congressional agent Dick
Goodwin (Morrow) sniffs out the conspiracy. He's
intent on putting television on trial, but deeply
reluctant to believe that Van Doren could be
implicated. Perfectly pitched, the film brims with
insight and wit. Highly recommended. TCh

Quo Vadis?

(Mervyn LeRoy, 1951, US) Robert Taylor,
Deborah Kerr, Peter Ustinov, Leo Genn,
Patricia Laffan, Finlay Currie, Abraham
Sofaer, Buddy Baer, Marina Berti, Felix
Aylmer.
171 min.
At the time, *Quo Vadis?* was the highest grosser
for MGM after *Gone With the Wind*. Between the
acres of heaving muscle in the arena, half of Italy
starring as the Roman troops, and sets that dwarf
even Ustinov, you may detect a story about a
Roman commander under Nero who falls in love
with a Christian girl and gets them both thrown
to the lions. It does last virtually three hours, and
along the way does have stretches of tedium, but
LeRoy invests most of it with pace, true spectacle, and not a little imagination (like the camera

craning acrobatically over thousands of festive
Romans before coming to rest on Robert Taylor's
face; or an 'orgy' viewed by Nero through a piece
of red glass). They won't make them like this any
more. MSu

r

Ran

r

Rabid

(David Cronenberg, 1976, Can) Marilyn Chambers, Frank Moore, Joe Silver, Howard Ryshpan, Patricia Gage, Susan Roman, J Roger Periard
91 min.
As a maker of sci-fi/horror movies, Cronenberg seems obsessed with the links between sex and violence as well as the *Body Snatchers* theme of a possessed community. His earlier combination of the two strains in *Shivers* was too mechanically lurid and derivative to be very effective, but *Rabid* is far more successful. This time Cronenberg has opened up his story so that it literally portrays the panic and slow devastation of a whole Canadian city: a new strain of rabies reduces its victims to foaming murderous animals, and Cronenberg examines the mysterious sexual agency behind the plague with bewitching ambiguity. *Rabid* is also far better staged than its predecessor, and the best scenes, including one classic episode in a chicken takeaway, are pitched ingeniously between shock and parody, never quite succumbing to farce. None of the other recent apocalypse movies has shown so much political or cinematic sophistication. DP

Rabid Grannies

(Emmanuel Kervyn, 1989, Bel) Elie Lison, Catherine Aymerie, Danielle Daven, Anne-Marie Fox, Jack Mayar, Françoise Moens.
88 min.
An opportunistically retitled Belgian horror pic, courtesy of Troma Inc, in which a group of mercenary nephews and nieces gather for their aged aunts' annual birthday party. Half way through dinner, the two old girls are transformed by a surprise present into grotesque, vengeful crones, who vomit green slime and are a little short on familial affection. Crucifixes, holy water and pump-action shotguns prove useless as the vicious oldsters rip, slice and hack their way through the assembled relatives. The cheapskate special effects are reasonably effective, but the characters are cardboard, the plot negligible, and the dubbed 'English' dialogue literally unspeakable. The fact that the old ladies are neither rabid nor grannies – they are in fact Possessed Aunties – is conveniently ignored. NF

Racconti di Canterbury, I

see Canterbury Tales, The

Racconti Proibiti di Nulla Vestita

see Master of Love

Race for Life

see Si tous les gars du monde…

Race for the Yankee Zephyr

(David Hemmings, 1981, NZ/Aust) Ken Wahl, Lesley Ann Warren, Donald Pleasence, George Peppard, Bruno Lawrence, Grant Tilly, Robert Bruce.
108 min.
The Yankee Zephyr of this amiable treasure hunt yarn is a US Navy cargo plane, missing since 1944, with a shipment of medals, a crate of Old Crow, and 50 million dollars in gold bullion aboard. The race to claim the salvage rights involves jet boats, beat-up helicopters, and mechanical abortions of the latter's parts, with Pleasence as a wheezy old sot who discovers the wreck. Pitting him and his macho partner (Wahl) against the suave penthouse chic of Peppard's businessman, Hemmings operates the race at a stop/start pace that leaves you feeling genial enough to forgive the stereotyping and the thin running jokes. It's all so lightweight that the action has to be anchored into place by a picaresque script involving crocodiles and their various genitalia. FL

Race, the Spirit of Franco (Raza,el Espíritu de Franco)

(Gonzalo Herralde, 1977, Sp).
80 min. b/w & col.
A fascinating demolition operation on Franco's imaginatively autobiographical exercise in cinematic myth-making, the 1941 *Race*, this juxtaposes sections of that notorious piece of melodramatic propaganda with the more prosa-ic testimonies of Franco's surviving sister, Pilar, and the actor Alfredo Mayo, who incarnated the role of the Franco surrogate 36 years earlier. The distance between fact and the romantic image is naturally comic, and the inherent interest of the previously inaccessible film is immense. The whole goes entertainingly beyond mere posthumous point-scoring. PT

Race with the Devil

(Jack Starrett, 1975, US) Peter Fonda, Warren Oates, Loretta Swit, Lara Parker, RG Armstrong, Clay Tanner, Jack Starrett, Wes Bishop.
88 min.
Less a race than a chase, with holidaymaking Fonda, Oates and wives fleeing a bunch of Texas Satanists whose human sacrifice they've barged into. A crescendo of near-miss car smashes, horrible discoveries in the caravan, and out-of-order telephones, convinces the quartet that the whole state's bent; by which time we think so too, and dread the outcome. A wittily efficient quickie, the film is a winner all the way – a surprise, since Starrett's career thus far had been the movie director's equivalent of a criminal record. But it was scripted by Lee Frost and Wes Bishop, who produced another jolly horror, *The Thing with Two Heads* and who started classically by making sex films in a garage. AN

Rachel and the Stranger

(Norman Foster, 1948, US) Loretta Young, William Holden, Robert Mitchum, Gary Gray, Tom Tully, Sara Haden.
93 min. b/w.
A film about homesteaders which has the lazy rhythm of a ballad in telling its tale of the widower (Holden), the bondswoman (Young) he marries but treats as a servant, and the roving cowboy friend (Mitchum) who opens his eyes by seeing – and treating – her as a woman. Although slightly marred by an Indian raid dragged in as an unnecessary catalyst (but very well done), it's a real charmer, held together by Mitchum's electric presence as the laconic interloper with a gently roving eye and a winning way with his guitar and songs. TM

Rachel Papers, The

(Damian Harris, 1989, GB) Dexter Fletcher, Ione Skye, Jonathan Pryce, James Spader, Bill Paterson, Shirley Anne Field, Michael Gambon, Lesley Sharp.
95 min.
Despite certain changes – it is updated from the early '70s to the late '80s, for instance – Martin Amis' clever, shallow first novel, the tale of teenager Charles Highway, eager to sleep with an older woman before he is 20, is rendered with some fidelity. The book's first person narrative finds a clumsy correlative in the brat's direct-to-camera confessions; and the humour is as smug, adolescent and misogynist as it was in the novel. The flaws lie less in the performances (Fletcher's Highway and Skye's Rachel, primary object of his self-serving affections, are both insubstantial, overshadowed by Pryce's crowd-pleasing cameo as Highway's irreverent hippy brother-in-law) than in the direction. Working from his own script, Harris shows no sense of detail; characters barely develop, London becomes a topographical mess, and each time the plot falters, we get long '60s-style interludes with no dialogue, cut to bland pop. The result is without dramatic or moral weight, despite Highway's contrived comeuppance, and it's impossible to care about the characters. GA

Rachel, Rachel

(Paul Newman, 1968, US) Joanne Woodward, Estelle Parsons, James Olson, Kate Harrington, Bernard Barrow, Donald Moffat, Geraldine Fitzgerald, Nell Potts.
101 min.
An impressive directorial debut for Newman, *Rachel, Rachel* stars his wife, Joanne Woodward, and their daughter Nell Potts. An account of a spinster striving to break out of her frustrating job as a teacher and her demanding home life, looking after her mother, the film's virtues lie in the wry observation of Rachel's slipping into a second childhood when James Olson appears on the scene as a possible saviour. While in no way as powerful as Barbara Loden's Wanda, Newman's film none the less captures the quiet desperation of enforced life in sleepytown America. PH

Rachel's Man

(Moshe Mizrahi, 1975, Isr) Mickey Rooney, Rita Tushingham, Leonard Whiting, Michal Bat-Adam, Avner Hiskiyahu, Dalia Cohen.
111 min.
The biblical saga of Jacob (Whiting), who received his father's blessing instead of Esau, ran away and fell in love with Rachel (Bat-Adam), courted her for seven years, but then got fobbed off with her elder sister (Tushingham). Lots of simple sunny visuals, combined with some flashy photography, make the film look like a cross between a Russell Flint watercolour and a Pirelli calendar. Attempts to beef up a desperately slim story include much emphasis on Jacob and Rachel's love story, some discreet nudity, a couple of songs 'Smother Me With Kisses For Ya Love Is Sweeter Than Wine', and an outrageously hammy (but thankfully diverting) performance from Rooney, offering his interpretation of the original Jewish businessman. Overall, the film's attempts to capture the measured pace of the Old Testament are terribly laboured, making it seem twice as long as it actually is.

Racing with the Moon

(Richard Benjamin, 1984, US) Sean Penn, Elizabeth McGovern, Nicolas Cage, John Karlen, Rutanya Alda, Max Showalter, Crispin Glover.
108 min.
Yuletide 1942 in a small Californian coastal town, and local boy Penn is hoping to step out with McGovern (who, unlike him, comes from the right side of the tracks) before induction into the Marines. This conflates a number of currently modish themes: coming of age in small-town USA; the last fling before manhood and possible death; nostalgia; and the crossing of social barriers. What it doesn't do, however, is give sufficiently dramatic incident; very little seems to happen in this social vacuum, and none of it is memorable. CPea

Racket, The

(John Cromwell, 1951, US) Robert Ryan, Robert Mitchum, Lizabeth Scott, William Talman, Ray Collins, Joyce MacKenzie, Robert Hutton, Virginia Huston, William Conrad.
89 min. b/w.
The omens were good. Howard Hughes had produced the silent version of *The Racket* which sparked Hollywood's gangster cycle. John Cromwell had won his first movie chance with his performance in a Broadway revival of the original play. Mitchum plus Ryan looked a failsafe powerhouse confrontation. But...Hughes' RKO was slowly running down; Cromwell was under greylist pressure from HUAC; and Mitchum got himself cast as a cop – representing goddam Society, no less! Softer than it should have been, then, but still dark enough to lose yourself in. PT

Radio Days

(Woody Allen, 1987, US) Seth Green, Julie Kavner, Michael Tucker, Dianne Wiest, Josh Mostel, Mia Farrow, Wallace Shawn, Kenneth Mars, Jeff Daniels, Danny Aiello, Tony Roberts, Diane Keaton.
88 min.
Woody Allen is always weakest when nostalgic; indulgence leads to caricature and overstatement. Set at the start of World War II, the film follows the fortunes of a family of Jewish underachievers. Against the backdrop of their predictably colourful obsessions, a glimmer of a story charts the progress of Farrow from Manhattan nightclub cigarette-girl to celeb of the airwaves. The real star, however, is radio itself, that pre-TV purveyor of everyday unreality against which wartime America measured its dreams. It's a great idea for a movie, but Allen fatally opts for a *Fellini: Amarcord* approach of formless narrative, larger-than-life coincidence, and rambling ruminations on what times there used to be. GA

Radio Flyer

(Richard Donner, 1993, US) Lorraine Bracco, John Heard, Elijah Wood, Joseph Mazello, Adam Baldwin, Ben Johnson.
101 min.
'History is all in the mind of the teller; the truth is in the telling' – so Tom Hanks instructs his young son by way of a preamble to this fanciful coming-of-age tale, which failed to find a the-

atrical distributor in Britain after bombing in the States. You can see why the script attracted big bucks: it has an accentuated literary air that must have read like 'class', a serious angle – child abuse – and it's all couched in the magic juvenilia of a Spielberg (Donner directed *Goonies*). It's the story of two brothers, their mother (Bracco), and the violent alcoholic who becomes their stepfather (Adam Baldwin in a pitiless role, photographed Spielberg-style from the waist down). It's not a total loss, but the voice-over is infuriatingly overdone, as if the film-makers didn't trust the visuals, the kids are resistible and the tone's discomfortingly cute. TCh

Radioland Murders

(Mel Smith, 1994, US) Mary Stuart Masterson, Brian Benben, Ned Beatty, Michael Lerner, Christopher Lloyd, Scott Michael Campbell, Corbin Bernsen, Candy Clark, Rosemary Clooney.
112 min.
It's 1939 and Radio WBN Chicago is on air, but amid the melee of performers and technicians lurks a dastardly killer. Did anyone control this cross between *Radio Days* and *Rocketeer*, or was it just left to freewheel? George Lucas, once the director of *Star Wars*, now an effects guru and shadowy executive producer, apparently had the idea long long ago. As an *hommage* to the screwball comedies of yesteryear it fails, with obvious one-liners and mistimed pratfalls, but as kitsch farce it succeeds, with an attractive cast, breathless pace, and lavish visuals. AO

Radio On

(Christopher Petit, 1979, GB/WGer) David Beames, Lisa Kreuzer, Sandy Ratcliff, Andrew Byatt, Sue Jones-Davies, Sting, Sabina Michael.
102 min. b/w.
A first feature written and directed by Petit, this is an apparently simple road movie (with an extraordinary soundtrack that runs from Bowie to Kraftwerk and Wreckless Eric) in which a man travels from London to Bristol by car to clarify the mysterious death of his brother. But his private journey also stands for an excursion back into the sour '70s, and his failure to communicate with those he meets on the road – an army deserter, a garage mechanic, a woman in search of her child – becomes a rambling commentary on the obsessive, ironic disenchantment of living in Britain now. A rare, almost eerie attempt at mythic British cinema, which ends with its hero stalled in his battered old Rover at a quarry edge, his questions still unanswered, forced to move on (into the '80s). '*We could be heroes, just for one day...*' – and the time is up. CA

Rafferty and the Gold Dust Twins

(Dick Richards, 1975, US) Alan Arkin, Sally Kellerman, Mackenzie Phillips, Alex Rocco, Charlie Martin Smith, Harry Dean Stanton, John McLiam, Arch Johnson.
91 min.
A road movie which teams three unlikelies – two female vagrants, one of them a spiky 15-year-old, and a washed-up ex-sergeant – and gives them no particular destination. As with many similar films, it substitutes character study for narrative. At first the film's low-key approach is deceptive. But for all the oblique humour, engaging peripheries, and surface toughness, *Rafferty* is a fundamentally warm-hearted movie which gradually beseeches us to love its oddball characters. During the last third, by which time the film has started to wear its heart on its sleeve, it all starts to come together; it's a long wait, though. Mackenzie Phillips, as the girl, gives a strong natural performance which offsets Arkin's studious acting. Really the entire film should have been about their relationship, rather than just the ending, which has them exiting for Uruguay just as things were getting interesting. CPe

Raffles

(Harry D'Abbadie D'Arrast/George Fitzmaurice, 1930, US) Ronald Colman, Kay Francis, Bramwell Fletcher, Frances Dade, David Torrence, Alison Skipworth.
72 min. b/w.

EW Hornung's 'Raffles' helped fix the ideal of the gentleman amateur, the handsome urbane sportsman with a hankering for illicit adventure. In this caper, scripted by Sidney Howard, Raffles romances Lady Gwen Manders (Francis), hobnobs with royalty, and pinches a priceless necklace for a suicidal friend who can't honour a debt. John Barrymore had played the hero a few years before, David Niven was to play him a few years later, but neither matched Colman's effortless, brilliantined charm. GM

Raga

(Howard Worth, 1971, US) Ravi Shankar, Alla Rakha, Yehudi Menuhin, Lakshmi Shankar, Usted Allaudin Khan, George Harrison.
96 min.
A very reasonable documentary about Ravi Shankar, very uncritical about him and very critical about some of the ways the West has assimilated his music. Full rein is given to Shankar's belief in the importance of authority, tradition, the guru in music, with some good footage of Indian 'culture' to back it all up. Thankfully you get to hear a sizeable amount of music in different contexts, from Western pop and classical to Indian traditional. All in all, an adequate delve into a musician who deserves a lot of respect. The clichés are there, but are pleasantly unobtrusive. George Harrison can't be too happy with the way he comes over, though. JDuC

Ragazza di Trieste, La

see Girl from Trieste, The

Rage in Harlem, A

(Bill Duke, 1991, GB/US) Forest Whitaker, Gregory Hines, Robin Givens, Zakes Mokae, Danny Glover, Badja Djola, John Toles-Bey, Screamin' Jay Hawkins.
115 min.
Duke's snappy, stylish, relentlessly pacy comedy-thriller, lighter than Chester Himes' source novel, is mostly very enjoyable. It charts the farcical situation that develops when Imabelle (Givens) arrives in mid-'50s Harlem with bullion stolen by her presumed-dead lover Slim (Djola). Hoping to do a deal with fence Easy Money (Glover) and needing a hideaway, she moves in with naive, pious undertaker's assistant Jackson (Whitaker), who reluctantly enlists the help of his criminal brother Goldy (Hines) when Slim turns up to regain both loot and Imabelle. The scene is thus set for funny, bloody intrigue involving hoodlums, cops, club-owners, and other cartoon-thin inhabitants of an improbably colourful Harlem; but for all the explicit violence, the film is less gritty *noir* than ebullient, good-natured fantasy. GA

Rage in Heaven

(WS Van Dyke, 1941, US) Robert Montgomery, Ingrid Bergman, George Sanders, Lucile Watson, Oscar Homolka.
85 min. b/w.
Co-scripted by Christopher Isherwood from a novel by James Hilton, but still boasting a plot as murkily unconvincing as the English setting. Montgomery, blandly repeating his *Night Must Fall* characterisation (though further up the social scale), is a wealthy scion who goes all funny at full moon, marries his mama's companion (Bergman in her third Hollywood movie), and conceives a dotty revenge plot when he thinks he has grounds for jealousy. Even a strong cast can't make much headway on such soggy ground. TM

Raggedy Man

(Jack Fisk, 1981, US) Sissy Spacek, Eric Roberts, Sam Shepard, William Sanderson, Tracey Walter, RG Armstrong, Henry Thomas.
94 min.
Spacek's extraordinary ability to portray a specific kind of American innocence gives life to a fairly ordinary plot about a frustrated 1940s rural telephonist – the mother of two children – who becomes involved with a passing sailor. Eventually the film erupts into small-town violence, but it is essentially a period piece directed with quiet impressiveness by Spacek's husband, former art director Fisk, who has extracted good performances from all of the principals (including Thomas as one of the kids, soon to appear as the boy in *E.T.*). Spacek herself is given free rein, and turns in all that you'd expect and more, including a number of marvellous little insights

from her own Texas childhood. Something as slight as this could never have got off the ground without her, but she makes you glad it did. DP

Raggedy Rawney, The

(Bob Hoskins, 1987, GB) Bob Hoskins, Dexter Fletcher, Zoe Nathenson, Zoe Wanamaker, Dave Hill, Ian Dury, Ian McNeice, Veronica Clifford.
103 min.
Hoskins' first outing as a director, a World War I tale of Romany folk, is set somewhere unspecific in the East European theatre. Fletcher plays a drafted boy soldier who escapes the carnage by donning woman's clothing and taking to the countryside. Port in a storm is provided by a passing band of gypsies, led by the ever-the-cockney Hoskins, who mistake Fletcher for a rawney – a traveller's word meaning a kind of vagabond female fortune-teller – and take him/her into their company. From here on in, Hoskins' darkening tale focuses on the lives of this less than merry band, with various set pieces – a traditional wedding, a ritual burial – strung together by a meandering plot concerning the group's various sexual and social rivalries and problems. The film suffers from disconcerting shifts of tone, mood, and focus, and threatens to become a case of paving over with good intentions; but its themes – the warts-and-all humanity of the travellers culture, the all pervasive destructiveness of war, the survival instinct – are delivered with sufficient sympathy and commitment to overcome the doubts. WH

Raging Bull 100 (100)

(Martin Scorsese, 1980, US) Robert De Niro, Cathy Moriarty, Joe Pesci, Frank Vincent, Nicholas Colasanto, Theresa Saldana, Mario Gallo.
129 min. b/w & col.
With breathtaking accuracy, *Raging Bull* ventures still further into the territory Scorsese has mapped in all his films – men and male values; in this case through the story of 1949 middleweight champion Jake La Motta. De Niro's performance as the cocky young boxer who gradually declines into a pathetic fat slob forces you to question the rigid and sentimental codes of masculinity which he clings to even as they destroy him, like a drowning man clutching a lead weight. The anti-realism of the fights prevents them sinking back into the narrative, and instead creates a set of images which resound through Jake's personal confrontations: their smashing, storyless violence is relentlessly cut with domestic scenes until you learn to flinch in anticipation. This film does more than make you think about masculinity, it makes you see it – in a way that's relevant to all men, not just Bronx boxers. JWi

Raging Moon, The (aka Long Ago, Tomorrow)

(Bryan Forbes, 1970, GB) Malcolm McDowell, Nanette Newman, Georgia Brown, Barry Jackson, Gerald Sim, Michael Flanders, Bernard Lee.
111 min.
A sincere attempt to portray a love affair between two paraplegics without undue sentimentality. It's not quite as awful as it sounds, mainly because McDowell and Newman perform well, convincingly scoffing at do-gooders. Meanwhile, Bryan Forbes' screenplay often has an acid joke up its sleeve to cut the cuteness. ATu

Ragman's Daughter, The

(Harold Becker, 1972, GB) Simon Rouse, Victoria Tennant, Patrick O'Connell, Leslie Sands, Rita Howard, Brenda Peters, Brian Murphy, Jane Wood.
94 min.
A sloppy slice of social realism, adapted from Alan Sillitoe's novel but not bothering to reproduce the period detail that goes with its archetypal '60s message about regional dead ends. Good performance by Rouse as the working class chap with council flat, two kids, and no job after being fired from the cheese factory for pilfering, who looks back in nostalgia to his youth of carefree petty criminality in the company of a nouveau riche girlfriend. But the already rootless narrative is further sabotaged by camerawork which drains all character from the Nottingham locations. TM

Ragtime

(Milos Forman, 1981, US) James Cagney, Brad Dourif, Moses Gunn, Elizabeth McGovern, Kenneth McMillan, Pat O'Brien, Donald O'Connor, James Olson, Mandy Patinkin, Howard E Rollins, Mary Steenburgen.
155 min.

EL Doctorow's overrated bestseller, a panoramic epic of the melting-pot America of 1906, made its way to the screen shorn of Doctorow's central conceit, that his 'Ordinary People' warrant equal time alongside major historical figures: Henry Ford, J Pierpont Morgan, Emma Goldman, Harry Houdini, all are written out of the script. It's also clear that the dementia which animates each of the important fictional characters in the novel simply doesn't work when rendered in flesh-and-blood. Forman nevertheless handles the diverse strands of the complicated plot well enough to suggest that the film's central weakness – black pianist Coalhouse Walker's attempt to obtain satisfaction for the racially-motivated vandalism of his shining new car – is inherent in the novel. The siege of the Pierpont Morgan Library which ensues is protracted and boring. Good performances, though, from Cagney as the persuasively authoritative police chief Waldo, and (especially) James Olson, a pillar of quiet Waspish dignity as the self-appointed conscience interceding between the massing police and the militant Coalhouse. RM

Raid, The

(Hugo Fregonese, 1954, US) Van Heflin, Anne Bancroft, Richard Boone, Lee Marvin, Peter Graves, Tommy Rettig, James Best, John Dierkes, Claude Akins.
83 min.

Excellent, factually-based Civil War Western, in which Heflin's Confederate officer leads a group of soldiers, with whom he has escaped from a Union prison camp, in a plan to avenge the destruction of Southern communities by first taking over, and then sacking, a Northern town close to the Canadian border. Tension is slowly but surely built up as the men try to infiltrate the township; conflicting emotions arise with Heflin's growing respect for the widow with whom he lodges (Bancroft); and the final, savage massacre is powerfully staged by Fregonese, who makes superb use throughout of Lucien Ballard's typically moody photography. This was the film that served as a springboard for John Arden in writing his play *Serjeant Musgrave's Dance*. GA

Raiders of the Lost Ark

(Steven Spielberg, 1981, US) Harrison Ford, Karen Allen, Paul Freeman, Ronald Lacey, John Rhys-Davies, Denholm Elliott, Alfred Molina, Wolf Kahler.
115 min.

Hollywood's chutzpah whizzkids Spielberg and Lucas team up to bring the audiences who flocked to *Star Wars* and *Close Encounters* a replay of the innocent pleasures of Saturday serials, but done at two hours length with a much larger budget than the old cliffhangers could command. Spielberg's evasion of present day realities in an effort to recapture the sheer childlike fun of moviegoing is as perverse as was his previous film, *1941*. What he offers is one long, breathtaking chase of a plot as his pre-World War II superhero, outsize and Bogartian, races to prevent the omnipotent Ark of the Covenant from falling into the hands of Hitler's Nazis. Whether you swallow it or not, see it for a handful of totally unexpected visual jokes, worth the price of admission alone. RM

Raid on Entebbe

(Irvin Kershner, 1976, US) Peter Finch, Martin Balsam, Horst Buchholz, John Saxon, Sylvia Sidney, Jack Warden, Yaphet Kotto, Charles Bronson, Tige Andrews, Eddie Constantine, Warren Kemmerling, Robert Loggia, David Opatoshu, James Woods.
118 min.

Heroic jingoism and some sentimental moments aside, this version of the Israeli raid on Entebbe airport (shot as a TV special and considerably better than *Victory at Entebbe*), catches a good deal of the breathless excitement of the first media reports of that made-for-the-movies military operation. Predictably, no time is wasted on the PFLP's version of events, though suave Horst Buchholz, leader of the unattractive kidnappers, is allowed one moment of humanity when he finally declines to blow up the prisoners. Resisting his recent propensity for effects, Kershner adopts a sensibly straightforward approach to Barry Beckerman's boiled-down and politically low-key narrative. In this he is self-effacingly assisted by his well-cast stars (avoiding caricature, Yaphet Kotto gives a notably intelligent and charismatic impersonation of Amin). JPy

Railway Children, The

(Lionel Jeffries, 1970, GB) Dinah Sheridan, Bernard Cribbins, William Mervyn, Iain Cuthbertson, Jenny Agutter, Sally Thomsett, Peter Bromilow, Gordon Whiting.
108 min.

Jeffries displays miraculous tact in adapting E Nesbit's children's classic as an affectionate homage to those golden Edwardian days when God was in his heaven and all right with the world. Christmas festivities are under way at a cosy suburban home when Father (Cuthbertson) is spirited away by two suspiciously flat-footed visitors; it's all right really, of course, but meanwhile, Mother (Sheridan) and her three children are exiled to genteel poverty in a cottage on the Yorkshire moors. There the children take over, forming a secret pact with the railway which runs sleepily past the bottom of the garden, and responding gravely to wryly funny encounters with such characters as the portly businessman from the train (Mervyn) who is delighted to be adopted as 'the nicest old gentleman we know', or the stationmaster (Cribbins) who never quite manages to shed his air of stuffy resentment while becoming their best friend. Events are not lacking – mother falls ill, they save the train from derailment, they harbour an unhappy Bolshevik refugee – but above all the film perfectly captures the timeless, magical world of childhood where grief, joy and adventure are solemn, entirely personal affairs, quite unexplainable to adults. It is...almost...another *Meet Me in St Louis* TM

Rain

(Lewis Milestone, 1932, US) Joan Crawford, Walter Huston, William Gargan, Beulah Bondi, Matt Moore, Guy Kibbee, Walter Catlett.
93 min. b/w.

Crawford was released by MGM to United Artists for this second screen adaptation of Somerset Maugham's steamy short story about a missionary bigot and prostitute Sadie Thompson, locked in an implacable battle of wills amid the pounding of tomtoms and tropical rain. Feeling herself in the shadow of distinguished previous Sadies on both stage and screen, Crawford was later to pronounce herself 'lousy', as did contemporary critics and fans. Their judgment in retrospect seems unkind: Crawford's Sadie is a mature, gutsy performance; she and Huston, as the repressed zealot, strike sparks off each other, an electricity that Milestone's stolid direction is seldom able to match. SJo

Rainbow

(Bob Hoskins, 1995, GB/Can) Willy Lavendal, Bob Hoskins, Saul Rubinek, Dan Aykroyd, Jacob Tierney, Jonathan Schuman.
101 min.

Plants need light to photosynthesise; rainbows give colour (thence light) to the world; without rainbows the world would turn monochrome and everyone would suffocate. Circulating within the rainbow are gold nuggets providing energy. If the nuggets are removed the rainbow will feel sick and lose interest. Were someone to find a way into the rainbow, one brief moment of greed could trigger global apocalypse – a harsh, fading world ravaged by fatal illness and social breakdown, where hordes of incompetent supporting actors roam the streets. That's the scenario envisioned in Hoskins' geo-fable. Bob's an 'offbeat' magician whose 10-year-old son Mike (Lavendal) discovers the end of the rainbow behind Hudson Harbor, NJ, and jumps in, only to be followed by sulky adolescent brother Steven (Tierney), who pockets the gold. There's comic relief with Aykroyd's paedophobic Kansan police chief, before matters enter the realm of pre-millennial kids' apocalypse movie. Despite sterling cinematography, the special effects look like computer games. NB

Rainbow, The

(Ken Russell, 1988, GB) Sammi Davis, Paul McGann, Amanda Donohoe, Christopher Gable, David Hemmings, Glenda Jackson, Dudley Sutton.
111 min.

Russell's second bash at DH Lawrence is either evidence of a fizzled-out talent or a sad, cliché-ridden attempt to make his film subservient to (part of) the text. He focuses on the later chapters: the story of Ursula Brangwen, wilful, intelligent and independent daughter of Anna (Jackson, who played an older Ursula in *Women in Love*) and artisan Will (Gable). Ursula engages in an uninhibited, exploratory relationship with her swimming teacher Winifred (cue skinny-dipping and intimate, glowing rub-downs on the hearth rug); falls for the dashing, if rough, charms of army officer Skrebensky (McGann); and, breaking the familial bonds, strives to make her way as a teacher in a school stifled by sexual harrassment and formality. The film reeks of mediocrity, floundering in banal imagery (kisses against boughs, rushing waterfalls, etc). Many essentials in what is a masterful three-generation novel have been jettisoned, and Carl Davis' score is formulary in the extreme. Saving graces are Sammi Davis' earthy, matter-of-fact portrayal of Ursula, and Amanda Donohoe's sensitive Winifred. WH

Rainbow Jacket, The

(Basil Dearden, 1954, GB) Bill Owen, Fella Edmonds, Kay Walsh, Edward Underdown, Robert Morley, Wilfrid Hyde-White, Charles Victor, Honor Blackman, Sidney James.
99 min.

The first collaboration between Dearden and TEB Clarke after *The Blue Lamp* follows the career of a middle-aged jockey (Owen) who, having forfeited his own career by taking a bribe, lives again through the success of a young protegé (Edmonds), whom he rescues from corruption at the vital moment. Despite its intriguing subject, the film offers little but the cosy, sentimental view of life that is typical of late Ealing films. PH

Rainclouds Over Wushan (Wushan Yunyu/aka In Expectation)

(Zhang Ming, 1995, China) Zhang Xianmin, Zhong Ping, Wang Wenqiang, Yang Liu, Li Bing, Xiu Zongdi, Wang Shengguo.
96 min.

Shot as an unauthorised indie production but finally released under the Beijing Film Studio banner, Zhang's excellent first feature has been in trouble with the Film Bureau ever since it began winning prizes abroad. Wushan is a small town on the Yangtze which will be submerged when the Three Gorges Dam comes into service. In this doomed setting, Zhang traces three disparate but intersecting lives: a river-station watchman, a hotel clerk and a young cop, all currently single but two expecting to marry soon. All three central characters are selfish but lack self-awareness; Zhang's funny/sad emphasis is on their sexual desires, frustrations and (often misplaced) hopes. TR

Raining in the Mountain (Kong Shan Ling Yu)

(King Hu, 1978, HK) Hsu Feng, Sun Yueh, Shih Chun, Tien Feng, Tung Lin.
120 min.

Stylised gesture, pantomime humour, flurries of colour and fighting: King Hu's tale of a power struggle in a Ming dynasty monastery has all the abrupt magic of a fairy story, with its villains, good guys, and secret treasure. An immaculately made, inscrutable, and eventually frustrating play of forms. CA

Raining Stones

(Ken Loach, 1993, GB) Bruce Jones, Julie Brown, Gemma Phoenix, Ricky Tomlinson, Tom Hickey.
91 min.

Despite the unemployment, petty crime and crack that afflict their Lancashire housing estate, Bob (Jones) and wife Anne (Brown) remain staunch Catholics. Bob does odd jobs to put food on the table, but also because he's determined to buy

Time Out Film Guide **737**

their daughter her communion dress, rather than accept a loan from the priest. He's soon in hock to loan-sharks. Though the subject of Loach's film is as dark as ever, the movie is funnier than *Riff-Raff*, thanks to another delicious performance from Ricky Tomlinson as Bob's pal Tommy. The gags range from deadpan Northern banter to slapstick and scatology, but they don't overshadow the political acuity of Jim Allen's script , or the narrative's inexorable progress into the stuff of everyday nightmare. This is no rant, but a warm, unsentimental tribute to the working-class spirit. Superbly acted, as always, and a hugely enjoyable example of the cinema of commitment. GA

Rainmaker, The (aka John Grisham's The Rainmaker)

(Francis Ford Coppola, 1997, Ger/US) Matt Damon, Claire Danes, Jon Voight, Mary Kay Place, Mickey Rourke, Danny DeVito, Dean Stockwell, Teresa Wright, Virginia Madsen, Johnny Whitworth, Danny Glover.
135 min.
This competent, anonymous legal drama (scripted by Michael Herr) is the best John Grisham adaptation yet. We're back in ingenue Southern lawyer territory, following law school grad Rudy Baylor (Damon) through his inaugural case to a mercurial triumph against the odds. So far, so insipid; thankfully, the story is less the usual addled potboiler than a diary of civil litigation – centring on Rudy's pursuit of a giant insurance company accused of stalling on health claims arising from policies marketed to the poor and unrepresented, such as his client Donny Ray Black (Whitworth). Rudy describes the dilemma of his calling in voice-over, musing over ideals and corruptions, compromises and lawyer jokes. His pilgrim's progress leads us through an entertaining gallery of lawyerly archetypes. There's the cynic, Rudy's long sold-out adversary Leo F Drummond (Voight); the corrupt, his low-life employer Bruiser Stone (Rourke); and the merely ignoble, his 'paralawyer' assistant Deck Schifflet (DeVito). There's a wider perspective on the legal action, too, counterpointing Rudy's 'rainmaking' lawsuit with both a damp squib of another case, and a subplot involving Danes's abused wife which suggests the limitations of the law. NB

Rain Man

(Barry Levinson, 1988, US) Dustin Hoffman, Tom Cruise, Valeria Golino, Jerry Molen, Jack Murdock, Michael D Roberts, Ralph Seymour, Lucinda Jenney.
133 min.
Seeing the finished product, you can see why there was such a turnover of directors and writers. There is no story, no motor, and given the nature of the premise, nothing much can happen; so it's lucky that Levinson, a fine observer of human behaviour washing about, was signed to make this increasingly costly dramatic standoff look busy. Hoffman does a self-contained turn, Cruise does Handsome Classes, though people say he's getting better. Charlie Babbitt (Cruise), a two-bit hustler trading cars, learns that Raymond (Hoffman), the brother he's forgotten, is to inherit three million dollars, and zones in to chisel him out of it. Raymond is autistic and institutionalised, but in their time together on the road, Charlie learns Raymond's limitations and windfall gifts – he can memorise numbers – and discovers his own decency. Raymond is a fixed point for Charlie to develop against, and just to amplify that Charlie is a stranger in a strange land, even his girlfriend Susanne (Golino) exists more fully in another language. Basically, it is a two-hander in which one side is stalled and stays stalled, devoid of an overview which might illuminate. Hard to do, though. BC

Rain or Shine

(Frank Capra, 1930, US) Joe Cook, Louise Fazenda, Joan Peers, William Collier Jr, Dave Chasen, Tom Howard.
92 min. b/w.
Capra's early sound effort was intended as a showcase for Broadway comic Cook, whose mercurial slapstick talent made him a top draw on stage, but rarely translated into screen craft. Here he's running a circus hit by bad weather, declining audiences, a recalcitrant owner and performers about to go on strike. He manages to keep the show on the road, however, with a one-man display of clowning that (literally) brings the house

down. Capra upped his directorial reputation by filming the climactic conflagration in one take, a risky undertaking given rudimentary early talkie technology, even if he did use several cameras for coverage. TJ

Rain People, The

(Francis Ford Coppola, 1969, US) Shirley Knight, James Caan, Robert Duvall, Tom Aldredge, Marya Zimmet, Laurie Crews, Andrew Duncan.
101 min.
Coppola's fourth feature, a fascinating early road movie made entirely on location with a minimal crew and a constantly evolving script. Never very popular by comparison with *Easy Rider* probably because it suggested that dropping out was mere escapism, it has far greater depth and complexity to its curious admixture of feminist tract and pure thriller. Knight is outstanding (in a superb cast) as the pregnant woman who runs away in quest of the identity she feels she has lost as a Long Island housewife, and finds herself increasingly tangled in the snares of responsibility through her encounters with a football player left mindless by an accident (Caan) and a darkly amorous traffic cop (Duvall). Symbolism rumbles beneath the characterisations (Caan as the baby she is running from and with, Duvall as the sexuality and domination she is trying to deny) but it is never facile; and the rhythms of the road movie (leading through wonderfully bizarre locations to a resonantly melodramatic finale) confirm that Coppola's prime talent lies in choreographing movement. TM

Rains Came, The

(Clarence Brown, 1939, US) Myrna Loy, Tyrone Power, George Brent, Brenda Joyce, Nigel Bruce, Maria Ouspenskaya, Joseph Schildkraut, HB Warner, Laura Hope Crews.
104 min. b/w.
Skilful direction, superlative camerawork from Arthur Miller, but the script is precious twaddle about a strangled romance between a titled English coquette (Loy) and a bashful Hindu doctor (Power in tasteful brownface). Honour is saved when the monsoon comes (with spectacular earthquake to boot), bringing self-sacrifice and redemption among the suffering plague victims. TM

Rains of Ranchipur, The

(Jean Negulesco, 1955, US) Richard Burton, Lana Turner, Fred MacMurray, Joan Caulfield, Eugenie Leontovich, Michael Rennie.
104 min.
Redundant colour/'Scope remake of Clarence Brown's overrated *The Rains Came* (itself not much more than a transposition of Ford's *The Hurricane*), with forbidden interracial romance (memsahib Turner and unlikely Hindu Burton) metaphorically stirring the monsoon and worse as the elements turn censorious. PT

Raintree County

(Edward Dmytryk, 1958, US) Elizabeth Taylor, Montgomery Clift, Eva Marie Saint, Nigel Patrick, Lee Marvin, Agnes Moorehead, Rod Taylor, Walter Abel, Tom Drake.
168 min.
MGM's attempt to repeat the success of *Gone With the Wind* turned out to be an elephantine bore. Set in the Civil War, with Taylor as a tough Southern belle doing anything to win Yankee teacher Monty Clift for a husband, only to get bored with him, it offers up the usual stew of sordid goings on, but never brings it to the boil. The performances, surprisingly given the cast, don't help either; even Clift, wrecked by drink and the emotional problems (the car accident came during production), fails to convince. GA

Raise Ravens

see Cria Cuervos

Raise the Red Lantern (Dahong Denglong Gaogao Gua)

(Zhang Yimou, 1991, HK) Gong Li, Ma Jingwu, He Caifei, Cao Cuifeng, Jin Shuyuan, Kong Lin.
125 min.
Northern China, the 1920s. Having agreed – to spite both her stepmother and fate – to become

the fourth wife of an ageing, wealthy clanleader, 19-year-old Songlian (Gong Li) finds herself immured in a palatial complex plagued by paranoia, jealousy and intrigue. The red lanterns, hung outside the suite of whichever wife is currently the object of the master's attentions, are an index of power; and Songlian, determined to wrest control from her rivals, feigns pregnancy. But the real power, of course, lies with the master, and the women's in-fighting yields tragic results. Dealing, like *Red Sorghum* and *Ju Dou*, with a young woman married to an older man and struggling to survive in a society defined by oppressive patriarchal tradition, Zhang's film elicits a strong sense of *déjà vu*. The lavish, schematic colours hold considerable appeal, while the atypical symmetry and stillness of the compositions stress the strait-jacket mores of a stagnant feudal culture. The acting is excellent, too, but one can't help but feel that Zhang has said it all before and more imaginatively. GA

Raise the Roof

(Walter Summers, 1930, GB) Betty Balfour, Maurice Evans, Jack Raine, Sam Livesey, Ellis Jeffreys, Arthur Hardy.
77 min. b/w.
A refreshingly unpretentious backstage musical, set among the lower reaches of the theatre world, where a tatty revue company that makes Hamlet seem like a perishing pantomime battles valiantly against the catcalls and rotten tomatoes. Fortunately it has the inestimable advantage of silents star Betty Balfour, trembling on the brink of love with a bizarre mixture of worldly vulgarity and little girl charm. Like a ruffled cockatoo, she bullies her fellow players into dropping their costumes and their actorly aspirations and giving the public what it wants: 'Laughter and legs...mostly legs'. Nice to know Britain has a musical tradition to be proud of. RMy

Raise the Titanic!

(Jerry Jameson, 1980, US) Jason Robards, Richard Jordan, David Selby, Anne Archer, Alec Guinness, Norman Bartold, M Emmet Walsh.
114 min.
One of the floppiest of Lord Grade's expensive flops, a would-be blockbuster limply adapted from Clive Cussler's bestseller about a secret operation to recover a haul of 'byzanium', reportedly in the hold of the 'Titanic' when it sank in 1912, and now urgently sought to fuel a defence system codenamed 'The Sicilian Project'. Naturally the Commies get in on the act, and apart from a brief perk-up during the actual raising of the ship, the whole thing founders dismally in a welter of ludicrous dialogue, routine love triangle, and desperately dull action. PG

Raising Arizona

(Joel Coen, 1987, US) Nicolas Cage, Holly Hunter, Trey Wilson, John Goodman, William Forsythe, Sam McMurray, Randall 'Tex' Cobb, M Emmet Walsh.
94 min.
The superbly labyrinthine plotting of *Blood Simple* must have been a hard act to follow; praise be, then, to the Brothers Coen for confounding all expectations with this fervently inventive comedy. Sublimely incompetent convenience-store robber Hi McDonnough (Cage, at his best yet) seems doomed to return repeatedly to the same penitentiary until true love hoves in view in the form of prison officer Edwina (Hunter). Spliced in a trice, the frustratedly infertile couple kidnap one (surely he won't be missed?) of the celebrated Arizona quintuplets, heirs to an unpainted-furniture fortune. But happiness being evanescent, complications ensue when a pair of Hi's old cellmates turn up in search of sanctuary; and then there's the problem of a rabbit-shooting biker of hellish hue, hired by Arizona Senior to find his missing brat. What makes this hectic farce so fresh and funny is the sheer fertility of the writing, while the lives and times of Hi, Ed and friends are painted in splendidly seedy colours, turning Arizona into a mythical haven for a memorable gaggle of no-hopers, halfwits and has-beens. Starting from a point of delirious excess, the film leaps into dark and virtually uncharted territory to soar like a comet. GA

Raising Cain

(Brian De Palma, 1992, US) John Lithgow, Lolita Davidovich, Steven Bauer, Frances Sternhagen, Gregg Henry, Tom Bower, Mel Harris, Teri Austin.
92 min.
Dealing here with the potentially juicy subject of multiple-personality disorder, De Palma provides an irresistible vehicle for Lithgow in a variety of parts stemming from child psychologist Dr Carter Nix. The first half-hour is deliberately unnerving and confusing before the plot settles down to examine why and how a number of children and a few adults have disappeared. There's a great deal of humour, not least in the persons of Carter's evil alter ego Cain, and their equally nasty father, a psycho-scientist who thinks nothing of driving his own kin completely round the twist in the name of research. And Sternhagen is superb as a cancer-stricken doctor who first sparks off suspicions about the aforementioned Lithgow brood. More to the point, De Palma, as an avowed disciple of Hitchcock, is back at his chilling best with a series of real seat-ejectors. Lithgow is consistently brilliant, while Davidovich makes a good fist as his wife. A really exciting 90 minutes worth, so long as you don't take it too seriously. SGr

Raising the Wind

(Gerald Thomas, 1961, GB) James Robertson Justice, Leslie Phillips, Kenneth Williams, Sidney James, Liz Fraser, Paul Massie, Eric Barker, Jennifer Jayne.
91 min.
Ponder that title for a moment. Peruse the cast list. Yes, in everything but name it's a *Carry On* up the Music College, with a load of penniless students forced to fiddle for a living. James Robertson Justice does his Sir Lancelot Spratt thing as Draconian conductor Sir Benjamin Boyd. You can guess the rest. AB

Rake's Progress,The (aka Notorious Gentleman)

(Sidney Gilliat, 1945, GB) Rex Harrison, Lilli Palmer, Griffith Jones, Margaret Johnston, Jean Kent, Godfrey Tearle, Guy Middleton, Marie Lohr.
123 min. b/w.
A memorable performance from Harrison as the quintessential upper class cad, scion of a family which traditionally breeds Tories for Westminster. Sent down from Oxford after crowning the Martyr's Memorial with a chamberpot, he is packed off to a South American coffee plantation, rebels against the idiocies of the colonial way, and returns for a brief period of glory as a racing driver. From there on it's downhill, pursuing a shabby love 'em and leave 'em attitude to women, causing his father's death with his drunken driving, and drifting from selling used cars to selling himself as a professional dancing partner. Consistently enjoyable and often caustically witty; but the satirical overview of upper class decadence is rather undercut by the script's implication that all the boy needs is a good war to make him pull his socks up. With his sins already excused by his reckless courage and devilish charm, he naturally redeems himself by getting blown up in WorldWar II. TM

Rally 'round the Flag, Boys!

(Leo McCarey, 1958, US) Paul Newman, Joanne Woodward, Joan Collins, Jack Carson, Dwayne Hickman, Tuesday Weld, Gale Gordon, Murvyn Vye.
106 min.
A roundly botched farce about the uproar in a small community when a missile base is planned in the area. A good example of Hollywood's hesitant efforts to get with it in the late '50s, with fashionable subject matter (sex and the bomb), hip stars (Newman, struggling in the days before he learned to play comedy), and unwarranted CinemaScope fittings. It backfires grandly, of course. TCh

Rambling Rose

(Martha Coolidge, 1991, US) Laura Dern, Robert Duvall, Diane Ladd, Lukas Haas, John Heard, Kevin Conway, Robert Burke, Lisa Jakub.
112 min.
Though her employers, the ever-genteel Daddy and Mother (Duvall and Ladd) welcome her with open arms, 19-year-old housekeeper Rose (Dern) proves a difficult addition to their household. Thirteen-year-old Buddy (Haas) is hopelessly smitten; and Rose develops a crush on Daddy. She's out to find Mr Right, which involves wearing skimpy dresses and sleeping with one boyfriend after another. Calder Willingham's adaptation of his own novel is set in the pre-war South of his youth; instead of prompting jealousy, Rose's promiscuous behaviour causes Mother to rail against the South's tradition of oppression; and when the terrible truths of Rose's past are revealed, Mother's defence of the girl provides an electrifying climax. The performances are first-rate as emotions shift between confusion and confrontation; and Willingham's intelligent script combines humour, idiosyncratic observation, and lingering tenderness. CM

Rambo: First Blood, Part II

(George Pan Cosmatos, 1985, US) Sylvester Stallone, Richard Crenna, Julia Nickson, Charles Napier, Steven Berkoff, Martin Kove, Andy Wood.
96 min.
Culture slips back into a comic strip mode for retarded schoolboy types. Rambo is a man of big biceps but very little brain. He is assigned to prove that American PoWs are no longer being held by the Vietcong, but instead finds a cageful of his fellow fighters. Left to undergo protracted torture by pig manure and electrified bedspring, he breaks out to rescue the PoWs and blast all the Commies and Gooks to kingdom come. It may be mindless escapism, but one would prefer a hero who is less of a machine, and a plot which refrains from indulging the sort of MIA/PoW myths likely to convince audiences that the Americans are still at war in SE Asia. AB

Rambo III

(Peter MacDonald, 1988, US) Sylvester Stallone, Richard Crenna, Marc de Jonge, Kurtwood Smith, Spiros Focas, Sasson Gabai, Doudi Shoua.
102 min.
Stallone, up against the Soviet Union, caught in a casuistical interchange between good guy Crenna and Red hammer of Afghanistan de Jonge about the unwisdom of superpowers attempting to crush freedom-loving peasant patriots. Huh? Not for Rambo such abstractions. He is only persuaded to break off his crash course in Buddhist meditation by the capture of his buddy, and his commitment to liberating Afghanistan comes after a manly variant of polo with the tribesmen and a dead goat. Then there's spunky orphan Hamid, though quite what depths of empathy their lingering looks are meant to imply remains a tantaliser. Rambo fights his way into the Russian fortress, fights his way out, and fights his way in again. He doesn't award pay-off lines, but he does explain that he's no tourist, and displays risible stoicism in removing a spike from his stomach and cauterising the hole with a charge of gunpowder. Saturday Morning Picture Club stuff, only dearer. BC

Rampage

(Phil Karlson, 1963, US) Robert Mitchum, Elsa Martinelli, Jack Hawkins, Sabu, Cely Carillo.
98 min.
On assignment in the Malaysian jungle at the behest of a German zoo, hunters Mitchum and Hawkins tussle over female prey Martinelli as they stalk the trail of a fearsome feline. Standard action romp amid variably convincing greenery. Sabu, who died later that year, looks especially weary, a shadow of his younger self. TJ

Ramparts of Clay (Remparts d'Argile)

(Jean-Louis Bertuccelli, 1970, Fr/Alg) Leila Schenna, the inhabitants of the village of Tehouda, Algeria.
86 min.
A slow, often fascinating, documentary-like study of an alien and primitive existence in a remote North African village, based on the book *Change at Shebika* by Jean Duvignaud. Only gradually, as the ways of 'civilisation' intrude, does the theme of rebellion emerge. The village men strike over their wages, bringing in the military; on a more personal level, an illiterate orphan girl's frustrations increase. At the film's centre lies an awareness both of the villagers' simple dignity (endorsed by almost every shot) and of the hopelessly stulti-fying impositions of a primitive culture upon the individual. Civilisation does offer knowledge, but with it comes exploitation and destruction.

Ramrod

(André De Toth, 1947, US) Joel McCrea, Veronica Lake, Donald Crisp, Don DeFore, Preston Foster, Arleen Whelan, Charlie Ruggles, Lloyd Bridges.
94 min. b/w.
Despite an enigmatic opening reel, the issues soon sort themselves out in this striking 'psychological' Western. Veronica Lake (excellent) is the strong-willed daughter of a rancher (Ruggles) who wants her to marry the man *he* admires, a ruthless, up-and-coming cattle baron (Foster). Clearly opting for a man she can dominate, Lake rebelliously elects to marry an out-of-town sheepman provided he re-locates on land she owns, careless of the fact that a range war will probably ensue. When the sheepman is scared off by Foster's threats, Lake defiantly decides to go it alone; and violence escalates as Foster, with her father's tacit blessing, sets out to bring her to heel. Caught in the middle as her reluctant ramrod is McCrea, just emerging from a bout of alcoholism after losing his wife and child. McCrea insists on doing things by the law, but finds himself sucked in as evil breeds evil, with Lake gradually emulating Foster, dirty trick for dirty trick. The stark little tragedy whereby Lake wins her war but forfeits McCrea's love is surprisingly persuasive; and all the performances are first-rate, with several minor characters (Crisp's ageing but indomitable sheriff, DeFore's happy-go-lucky opportunist, Whelan's patient 'other woman') adding their strands to the complex moral weave. TM

Ran 100 (100)

(Akira Kurosawa, 1985, Fr/Jap) Tatsuya Nakadai, Akira Terao, Jinpachi Nezu, Daisuke Ryu, Mieko Harada, Yoshiko Miyazaki.
160 min.
Kurosawa established himself as the best cinematic interpreter of Shakespeare with his recasting of Macbeth as a samurai warlord in *Throne of Blood*. That he should in his later years turn to *King Lear* is appropriate, and the results are all that one could possibly dream of. *Ran* proposes a great warlord (Nakadai), in a less than serene old age, dividing his kingdoms up between his three sons. True to the original, the one he dispossesses is the only one faithful to him, and *ran* (chaos) ensues as the two elder sons battle for power, egged on by the Lady Kaede (an incendiary performance from Mieko Harada). The shift and sway of a nation divided is vast, the chaos terrible, the battle scenes the most ghastly ever filmed, and the outcome is even bleaker than Shakespeare's. Indeed the only note of optimism resides in the nobility of the film itself: a huge, tormented canvas, in which Kurosawa even contrives to command the elements to obey his vision. A Lear for our age, and for all time. CPea

Rancho Deluxe

(Frank Perry, 1974, US) Jeff Bridges, Sam Waterston, Elizabeth Ashley, Charlene Dallas, Clifton James, Slim Pickens, Harry Dean Stanton, Richard Bright, Patti D'Arbanville.
94 min.
Despite a preoccupation with puncturing the myths of the modern West, *Rancho Deluxe* operates most noticeably, and in the main successfully, as a slickly packaged youth movie. Although given a narrative about cattle rustling, the film is just as much a present day generation gap comedy, about the romps of two 'cowboys' (one white, one Indian), whose disdain of establishment values and notions of the 'freedom' of the West bring them into perpetual confrontation with reactionary elders. In keeping with the audience it is aimed at, the film is self-consciously cynical and insolent, and at the same time fundamentally romantic and seeking to be liked. The combination works surprisingly well, thanks to good ensemble acting, even if Thomas McGuane's script sometimes veers towards sentiment and smart-ass observations. CPe

Rancho Notorious

(Fritz Lang, 1952, US) Marlene Dietrich, Arthur Kennedy, Mel Ferrer, Lloyd Gough, Gloria Henry, Jack Elam, William Frawley, Dan Seymour.
89 min.

The old Lang story of Hate, Murder and Revenge...this time in the form of his last and most unusual Western. Arthur Kennedy, obsessed with avenging his murdered fiancée, falls in with gunslinger Ferrer and crime queen Dietrich, and gradually, inexorably, becomes indistinguishable from the men he was hunting. The fateful moral, the complete avoidance of naturalism, and the integration of an ongoing ballad into the plot, all make the movie quintessential Lang; add an overt political stance and it would be quintessentially Brechtian too. TR

Random Harvest

(Mervyn LeRoy, 1942, US) Ronald Colman, Greer Garson, Susan Peters, Philip Dorn, Reginald Owen, Henry Travers, Margaret Wycherly, Edmund Gwenn.
124 min. b/w.
Colman is a shell-shocked WW I amnesiac who meets and marries music hall singer Garson; a collision in a taxi makes him forget he's married to her and return to his pedigreed family background; but she becomes his secretary, and eventually another shock...Eclipsed at the time only by the adjacent Garson-starring *Mrs Miniver* for both tosh-value and box-office receipts, this remarkably contrived delve into the here-today-gone-tomorrow memory of lovelorn Colman drew from critic James Agee the oft-quoted but irresistible line: 'I would like to recommend this film to those who can stay interested in Ronald Colman's amnesia for two hours and who could with pleasure eat a bowl of Yardley's shaving soap for breakfast'. Of course, you get froth both ways, but it doesn't taste that bad. PT

Randy Rides Alone

(Harry Fraser, 1934, US) John Wayne, Alberta Vaughn, George Hayes, Yakima Canutt, Earl Dwire, Arthur Artego, Tex Phelps.
53 min. b/w.
Marvin Black (Hayes), a desperado, otherwise a mild, hunch-backed storekeeper known as 'Matt the Mute', is determined to gain control of Peyote Pass by murdering the owner of the Half-Way House saloon and buying the property from his niece (Vaughn). Wayne, speaking his few lines with the dry tone and slow inflection which was to be his trademark as a star, puts matters right and blows the blackhat to smithereens with his own dynamite. (Poor sound recording on the print under review, from the UCLA Film Archive.) JPy

Ranpo

see Mystery of Rampo, The

Ransom

(Casper Wrede, 1974, GB) Sean Connery, Ian McShane, Norman Bristow, John Cording, Isabel Dean, William Fox, Richard Hampton, Robert Harris.
98 min.
A modest British thriller, in the same mould as *The Internecine Project*, which seems similarly intent on dealing with issues of contemporary relevance. The action is set in Scandinavia, and concerns two terrorist actions: the kidnap of the British ambassador at his residence; and the hijack of a passenger plane on the tarmac of a nearby airport. Law and order security chief Colonel Tahlvik (Connery) is given the task of handling the situations – only to discover that all is not what it seems. Although Wrede and his photographer Sven Nykvist are more than competent, the movie nevertheless has a distinct air of triviality, due mainly to the made-for-TV ethos that seems to surround the whole production. Some stock characters and formula dialogue don't help either. GSa

Ransom

(Ron Howard, 1996, US) Mel Gibson, Rene Russo, Brawley Nolte, Gary Sinise, Delroy Lindo, Lili Taylor, Liev Schreiber, Donnie Wahlberg.
121 min.
They want $2m – chump change to a NY entrepreneur like Tom Mullen (Gibson) when his son's life is on the line. He goes to the FBI, and they advise him to pay. But the drop-off is botched, and Mullen's not so sure he can trust these kidnappers to hold up their end of the bargain. To pay or not to pay? Such dilemmas make for edgy suspense, if not equitable marital relations, and

Mullen's audacious solution here only ups the ante, leaving wife Russo hoarse with rage and horror. Unless you're familiar with an obscure 1957 Glenn Ford movie, also called *Ransom*, you'll likely be quite taken aback too. Yet this twist is as nothing compared to the truly mind-boggling claim in the credits, that this tough, penetrating thriller was directed by Ron Howard. In popular, sentimental movies from *Splash* through *Apollo 13*, Howard has proved himself a reliably competent but unerringly fatuous craftsman. How he's grown up overnight! Much of the credit must go to screenwriter Richard Price, who brings an insidious, vitriolic class-consciousness to bear. The film doesn't just trade on Gibson's dangerous, lunatic machismo, it unearths a colder, more callous and more complex narcissism. His nemesis knows him so much better than his wife. Howard pushes and probes this rich tension with expert casting, restless camerawork and a fractured editing style. The result is overwrought, but riveting. TCh

Rapa Nui

(Kevin Reynolds, 1994, US) Jason Scott Lee, Esai Morales, Sandrine Holt, George Hanares, Eru Potaka-Dewes, Rena Owen.
106 min.
Rapa Nui is what the natives call Easter Island: 'the navel of the world'. Here the Long Ears lord it over the Short Ears, forcing them to carve huge, monolithic statues – the *moai* – for the gods. Noro (Lee), the Long Ears' champion, will compete against his childhood friend Make (Morales) to decide who will be clan 'birdman' this year – and for the hand of a Short Ear, Ramana (Holt). A labour of love for director Reynolds (*Robin Hood*), and co-produced by Kevin Costner, this is a curious Hollywood project, but not a successful one. The leads are okay, but the English-language Polynesian dialogue, containing such lines as, 'I don't need this, I have chicken entrails to read,' does not help matters; and the script settles for the kind of cod anthropology found in Disney animations. Shot on Easter Island, the movie looks impressive – the *National Geographic* in 'Scope – but perhaps the makers should have followed the example of the *moai* and kept their mouths shut. TCh

Rape, The
(Niet voor de Poesen)

(Fons Rademakers, 1973, Neth/Bel) Bryan Marshall, Alexandra Stewart, Alex Van Rooyen, Leo Beyers, Martin Van Zundert, George Baker, Sylvia Kristel, Edward Judd.
93 min.
An interesting little movie adapted from Nicolas Freeling's novel *Because of the Cats, Rape* is an intelligent thriller masquerading as a sex film. The sex is there – in an extended rape sequence and a bit of underwater fucking – but the thrust of the film is the investigation by Inspector Van der Valk (Marshall) of a series of senseless robberies, culminating in a rape and a murder, that leads him to a confrontation with the Ravens, a group of adolescent rich kids. A Dutch/Belgian co-production shot in English, the stilted conversations meld perfectly with the static, non-dramatic visuals which forever have Van der Valk's slightly puritanical presence calling into question the luxurious surroundings he is caught up in. PH

Rape of Malaya, The

see Town Like Alice, A

Rape Squad

see Act of Vengeance

Rapid Fire

(Dwight H Little, 1992, US) Brandon Lee, Powers Boothe, Nick Mancuso, Raymond J Barry, Kate Hodge, Tzi Ma, Tony Longo.
95 min.
The kicks and jinks are high in this jolly martial arts movie. Jake Lo (Lee), brought up in the States, is briefly at Tiananmen Square when his Chinese father, working for the US Government, is run over by a tank. Back at college in the States, he angrily refuses to endorse the Democracy movement (the depiction of Chinese immigrants is thoughtful and unstereotypical), then witnesses a Mafia hit against a Chinese drug baron. He chops his way outta that one, but the FBI want

him to testify, and suddenly everyone's on his tail... The fight scenes are brilliant, and though Lee lacks the animal grace of his father Bruce or the comic skills of Jackie Chan, he has cheerful wit and timing, plus the bod of a Chippendale. Like a good spring roll, this is crisp, tasty, and full of good things. SFe

Rappin'

(Joel Silberg, 1985, US) Mario Van Peebles, Tasia Valenza, Charles Flohe, Eriq La Salle, Kadeem Hardison, Richie Abanes, Leo O'Brien.
92 min.
John 'Rappin' Hood (Van Peebles) and his band of merry poets take on the baddies, a stop-at-nothing property development corporation and the gang recruited to terrorise the tenants they wish to evict; it seems that all Hood & Co have to do is break into verse and everything is suddenly right as rain. Peppered with offensive stereotypes, the only light relief comes when the hip crew succumb to another rapattack. It's not an unmitigated disaster, but the absurd grand finale, at the crucial public hearing where the power of rap conquers all, pushes it irrevocably over the edge. PG

Rappresaglia

see Massacre in Rome

Rapture, The

(Michael Tolkin, 1991, US) Mimi Rogers, David Duchovny, Patrick Bauchau, Kimberly Cullum, Terri Hanauer, Dick Anthony Williams, Will Patton.
102 min.
Directorial debut for Tolkin, best known as the novelist who wrote *The Player*. Unfortunately, it is loony stuff, rising to a cherishable risibility in the final third. Sharon (Rogers) is a telephone operator who spends her nights partying with three-in-a-bed pick-ups until self-disgust turns her to God, after which disgustingness becomes the least of her problems. When her husband is randomly murdered, she takes her little daughter into the desert to await the Last Trumpets of Armageddon. A caring cop (Patton) turns up with food, but is unable to prevent an almost unwatchable tragedy. In jail, the prophecies of the Book of Revelations come to pass, the bars fall away, and she scoots off on the cop's motorbike pursued by the First Horseman of the Apocalypse, after which the shit gets plenty astral. Disquietingly, America seems to be leaping with these evangelistic Born Agains, but quite where Tolkin stands is obscured by shoddy plotting. Rogers puts her all into it. BC

Rapunzel Let Down Your Hair

(Susan Shapiro/Esther Ronay/Francine Winham, 1978, GB) Margaret Ford, Suzie Hickford, Jessica Swift, Laka Koc, Lydia Blackman.
78 min.
From the Grimm Brothers' story (immediate inquiry into the nature of fairytales – eternal truths or patriarchal fantasies?) emerges a very attractive, perceptive film which happily encompasses several knotty problems relevant to feminism today. Breaking with a traditional narrative, Rapunzel's story is retold and reinterpreted, each version using a different movie genre accompanied by a wonderful music score. Thus the super-seductive animation of dream and symbolism; the opportunist male voyeur as *film noir* detective; a raunchy cartoon Venus, her roots firmly in witchcraft; the family melodrama of menopausal angst; and finally Rapunzel's own tale, a live-action narrative which completes the film's substructure of the stages of womanhood, and leads firmly out of an urban desert to a finale of feminist celebration. Fairytales were always appealing, but they never made quite so much sense. HM

Rare Breed, The

(Andrew V McLaglen, 1965, US) James Stewart, Maureen O'Hara, Brian Keith, Juliet Mills, Don Galloway, David Brian, Jack Elam, Ben Johnson, Harry Carey Jr.
108 min.
Born into the Ford/Wayne axis as the son of Victor, McLaglen was steeped in Western lore from an early age, and graduated through tele-series like *Gunsmoke* and *Have Gun – Will Travel*

to a string of features hymning the old generic simplicities in their twilight. His features with Wayne tended to be as reactionary as the Duke himself (a predilection subsequently confirmed in work like *The Wild Geese*), but this effort about O'Hara's attempts to cross a Hereford bull with Texas longhorn stock is innocuously banal. And the human supporting cast just about make it worthwhile. PT

Rashomon 100

(Akira Kurosawa, 1951, Jap) Toshiro Mifune, Machiko Kyo, Masayuki Mori, Takashi Shimura, Minoru Chiaki, Fumiko Homma.
88 min. b/w.
If it weren't for the closing spasm of gratuitous, humanist optimism, *Rashomon* could be warmly recommended as one of Kurosawa's most inventive and sustained achievements. The main part of the film, set in 12th century Kyoto, offers four mutually contradictory versions of an ambush, rape and murder, each through the eyes of one of those involved. The view of human weaknesses and vices is notably astringent, although the sheer animal vigour of Mifune's bandit is perhaps a celebration of a sort. The film is much less formally daring than its literary source, but its virtues are still plentiful: Kurosawa's visual style at its most muscular, rhythmically nuanced editing, and excellent performances. TR

Raskolnikow

(Robert Wiene, 1923, Ger) Gregory Chmara, Maria Germanowa, Sergei Kammissaroff, Pawel Pawloff, Maria Krishanovskaja.
b/w. 6,992 ft.
The Cabinet of Dr Caligari is almost unique among silent 'classics' in that nobody attributes its qualities to its director; Robert Wiene has never seemed more than a peripheral figure, and his later attempts to repeat his one-off success never won him any real reputation. He both directed and scripted this adaptation of Dostoievsky's *Crime and Punishment*, and seems to have had grandiose artistic ambitions for the project, drawing his cast from Stanislavsky's Moscow Art Theatre, and commissioning 'expressionist' sets from Andrei Andreiev. The result poses fascinating questions. Was the disjunction between the naturalistic acting and the artificial decor deliberate, or simply inept? And was the 'expressionism' (the sets and a scattering of dream sequences) an attempt to visualise the moral/theological dimension of the novel, or simply a matter of fashion? There are no ready answers, but the film certainly sustains the questions. TR

Rasputin and the Empress

(Richard Boleslawski, 1932, US) John Barrymore, Ethel Barrymore, Lionel Barrymore, Diana Wynyard, Ralph Morgan, Edward Arnold, Gustav von Seyffertitz, Jean Parker.
133 min. b/w.
The one and only time that the Barrymore family appeared together on screen, Lionel as Rasputin, Ethel as the Tsarina, John as Prince Chegodieff (ie. Youssoupoff). This curio – the subject of litigation brought against MGM by the Prince and Princess Youssoupoff, who claimed it was historically inaccurate – is often strangely dull in its depiction of the last days of the Czar's court, although one can't deny the attraction of its impressive sets and costumes. GA

Rat, The

(Graham Cutts, 1925, GB) Ivor Novello, Mae Marsh, Isobel Jeans, Robert Scholtz, James Lindsay, Marie Ault.
7,323 ft. b/w.
Swaggering adaptation of Novello's own play, co-written with Constance Collier. Novello plays Pierre Boucheron, a 19th century Parisian jewel thief and vagabond. The picture opens in exhilarating fashion, with Boucheron leading the gendarmes on a chase through the back streets before escaping down a manhole. Much of the story unfolds in the White Coffin, a demi-monde bar full of sultry looking prostitutes, all of them in love with Boucheron, and assorted knife brandishing ruffians. (At one stage, in an attempt to show he's easily a match for Valentino and Novarro, the star dances a tango, ripping his partner's skirt at the hip so she can move more easily.) The subplot, about his fling

with a bored aristocratic woman whose diamonds he steals, is purely routine. But Cutts directs the chases and fights with verve, the Gallic underworld is imaginatively evoked, and Novello makes a suitably louche, charismatic anti-hero. GM

Ratboy

(Sondra Locke, 1986, US) Sondra Locke, Robert Townsend, Christopher Hewett, Larry Hankin, Sydney Lassick, Gerrit Graham, Louie Anderson, SL Baird.
104 min.
Once upon a time in Hollywood a young actress, with the help of her friend Clint Eastwood and his Malpaso company, made a modern fairytale about a little boy who looked like a rat. Locke plays the good ol' country girl who rescues the bewhiskered rubbish-tip recluse to transform him into a star. Unfortunately, however, Locke's 'very black, funny and sad comedy' is neither funny nor sad, and the only thing black about it is its stereotypical depiction of Blacks as conmen and Uncle Toms. Give it a miss. SGo

Rate It X

(Paula de Koenigsberg/Lucy Winer, 1985, US)
93 min. b/w & col.
In what the production notes describe as 'a bitingly funny and disarming journey through the landscape of American sexism', the (women) film-makers have collated some fifteen or so interviews with men involved in some way or another in what is called the 'consumer zone'. Quite what this grisly assortment of wits and raconteurs thought they were letting themselves in for is a mystery. It is not a pretty sight. The interviews range from 'Ugly George', he of the successful cable TV show – the travelling Mr Camera who persuades passing 'pieces of ass' to strip in alleyways for a quiet bit of nationwide exposure – through Madison Avenue lingerie execs boasting of overcoming the bra-burning threat, to a gang of gaga war vets, given the opportunity to enlarge on their perception of traditional sex roles. Sexism? Nah, we can't spell it, but heck, we's can do it anyway! There's ample evidence in this film to confirm that some 15 years after what has been called the 'second feminist wave', the nasty extremes of sexism are only too alive and well. But what of the ethics of documentary filmmaking? The poor damn fools who people this document may have been too obtuse to comprehend the intentions of its makers if it was spelled out to them. But was it? And does it matter? WH

Rats, The (aka Deadly Eyes)

(Robert Clouse, 1982, US) Sam Groom, Sara Botsford, Scatman Crothers, Lisa Langlois, Cec Linder.
93 min.
Silly film about a plague of giant cat-size rats that can gnaw through a human hand more viciously than a Great Dane. Hunky schoolteacher (Groom) falls for the local public health inspector (Botsford), who is concerned about the frequent sightings of rats in and around the sewage system. With the opening of a new public subway system under way, she orders the sewers to be fumigated, but these tough critters are immune to such trivial things. From then on, it's rodent on the rampage. Clouse uses the Steadicam technique (as employed by Carpenter in *Halloween*), but unfortunately it doesn't work for rats, and only gives the impression that they are huge, slow-moving creatures. A short but wonderful performance from Scatman Crothers is the only thing that lifts the film out of the sewers for a few moments. DA

Rat-Trap (Elippathayam)

(Adoor Gopalakrishnan, 1981, Ind) Karamana, Sarada, Jalaja, Rajam K Nair, Prakash, Sonan.
121 min.
A middle-aged rural landowner, who has never had to do a thing for himself, loses the female relatives who wait on him, one after another, and watches helplessly as his estate, already ravaged by thefts and mismanagement, falls into decay. Not a fresh subject, but the treatment is extraordinary: using rats as his governing metaphor, Gopalakrishnan constructs his film like a cinematic rondo, making every composition and every camera movement count. TR

Raven, The

(Louis Friedlander i.e. Lew Landers, 1935, US) Bela Lugosi, Boris Karloff, Irene Ware, Lester Matthews, Samuel S Hinds.
62 min. b/w.
A second teaming for Karloff and Lugosi after the success of *The Black Cat*. This time round Bela has the upper hand as a surgeon obsessed by Poe, frustrated in his passion for a beautiful dancer (Ware) after repairing the damage when her face is scarred in a car crash, and mutilating Karloff's ugly criminal even further when he arrives for a face job, in order to force his cooperation in pursuing his ugly designs on the girl. An absurd script, without a hint of self-parody, and a nicely equipped set (moving walls, a razor sharp pendulum that slowly lowers itself on to victims) make for entertaining if undemanding viewing. GA

Raven, The

see Corbeau, Le

Raven, The

(Roger Corman, 1963, US) Vincent Price, Boris Karloff, Peter Lorre, Hazel Court, Olive Sturgess, Jack Nicholson, Connie Wallace.
86 min.
The humour of Richard Matheson's well-calculated send-up of Poe's gruesome *The Black Cat* – as the middle story in Corman 's *Tales of Terror* – went down so well that Matheson here used Poe's poem *The Raven* as the basis for a full-length parody. With Price, Karloff and Lorre superbly funny as rival magicians – and Jack Nicholson turning up to give the most atrocious performance of his career as the juvenile lead – *The Raven* is one of the few fantasy comedies that hangs together as happily as a fairytale, and it climaxes with a suitably splendid duel of marvels between Karloff and Price. DP

Raw Deal

(Anthony Mann, 1948, US) Dennis O'Keefe, Claire Trevor, Marsha Hunt, Raymond Burr, John Ireland, Chili Williams, Curt Conway, Whit Bissell.
79 min. b/w.
A fine *noir* thriller, product of the dream marriage between Mann's direction and John Alton's camera. O'Keefe's escape from jail is arranged by the racketeer (Burr) for whom he is serving a rap, and who confidently expects him to be killed, thus shutting his mouth and eliminating the need to pay him off. Along for the ride is Trevor, who loves him, and as hostage, the girl from the lawyer's office (Hunt) who has become interested in his case. The action is sharp, the characterisation vivid (Burr gets to anticipate *The Big Heat* by hurling a bowl of flaming brandy over a girl who annoys him; Ireland is memorable as a cool hood who gets his kicks by needling the nervous Burr while patiently building card houses). But what gives the film its wholly distinctive flavour is the voice-over narration by Trevor. 'She's getting under his skin,' she sadly comments as Hunt's initial flirtatiousness turns to disgust, thereby sparking a yearning in O'Keefe for his own lost innocence; throughout, her despairing efforts to understand the romantic ramifications in which the three of them get caught lend the film an unusual emotional depth. TM

Raw Deal

(John Irvin, 1986, US) Arnold Schwarzenegger, Kathryn Harrold, Sam Wanamaker, Paul Shenar, Robert Davi, Ed Lauter, Darren McGavin, Joe Regalbuto.
105 min.
Schwarzenegger only takes his shirt off twice. Even Kathryn Harrold, as female bazooma interest, never reveals more than a partially-clad bosom, which she repeatedly points at Arnie in an unsuccessful attempt to woo him away from his alcoholic wife and his mission in life – to wipe out all the gangsters in Chicago. Single-handedly. Big Arnie is approached by his former FBI boss and asked to infiltrate the brotherhood of Mr Big in order to beat the organisation apart from the inside. Mr Big, failing to recognise the ex-Mr Universe, takes him on as a bodyguard, and Arnie gets to repeat all of his major set pieces, like driving a truck through the side of a building, toting several machine-guns in each fist, and the now obligatory arming-up-in-a-vest sequence. Unfortunately there is none of the self-deprecating humour of *Commando*, just mindless action. AB

Rawhide
(aka Desperate Siege)

(Henry Hathaway, 1950, US) Tyrone Power, Susan Hayward, Hugh Marlowe, Dean Jagger, Edgar Buchanan, Jack Elam, George Tobias, Jeff Corey.
86 min. b/w.

A competent Western, not improved by a redundant voice-over and a corny score, very similar in plot to the later *The Desperate Hours* (actually, it's based on a 1935 gangster movie, *Show Them No Mercy*). Power is a young Easterner, sent by his father to learn the Overland Mail business, who finds himself fighting for survival – along with a woman (Hayward) and her dead sister's little daughter – when four escaped convicts, led by the well-bred but ruthless Marlowe, take over his way station to wait for the stage carrying a shipment of gold. The action follows pretty predictable lines, but Marlowe's three henchmen are nicely characterised and played: Tobias, bovine and stolidly obedient; Jagger, grizzled and amiable, forever muttering crazily into his beard; Elam, leering, lecherously sadistic, gleefully potting off shots at the child (he misses, of course). By contrast, the three leads tend to declaim Dudley Nichols' stiff dialogue as though it were holy writ. TM

Raw Meat
see Death Line

Rayon Vert, Le
see Green Ray, The

Razor's Edge, The

(Edmund Goulding, 1946, US) Tyrone Power, Gene Tierney, John Payne, Anne Baxter, Clifton Webb, Herbert Marshall, Elsa Lanchester, Fritz Kortner.
146 min. b/w.

A kind of *Lost Horizon* for the Lost Generation as a soldier returning from the First World War shrugs off his wealthy background to search for spiritual fulfilment. Starting among the smart set in Europe (Paris and the Riviera created in the studio), it then moves rather less persuasively to India. Classic Hollywood kitsch, with the shallow sophistication of Somerset Maugham's novel well matched by the glossiest glitter that Fox could buy. But somehow Goulding (an erratic but underrated director) manages to dominate it all with an almost Premingerian *mise en scène*, aided by some superb performances (Tierney in particular). TM

Razorback

(Russell Mulcahy, 1984, Aust) Gregory Harrison, Arkie Whiteley, Bill Kerr, Chris Haywood, David Argue, Judy Morris, John Howard, John Ewart.
95 min.

An American animal rights activist (Morris) arrives in the Australian outback to investigate the slaughter of kangaroos. She encounters much male chauvinist piggery and a couple of swinish psychopaths before being taken to tusk by the biggest boar of the lot, a death-dealing piece of pork which eats people and makes off with babies in dingo fashion. The activist's husband (Harrison) starts sniffing at a trail which leads all the way to the Petpak Cannery, a noisome inferno of half-hacked carcasses and hissing pipes. Bill Kerr pops up looking suitably grizzled in the Captain Ahab role, but is madly out-acted by Haywood and Argue as the psychopathic Baker brothers. Mulcahy directs with all the wit and subtlety previously evident in his pop promo videos for the likes of Duran Duran, utilising all manner of surrealist landscaping and moody great moon shots to evoke the mysterious Walkaboutism of the outback. But the razorback itself, when it finally emerges, resembles nothing so much as a stuffed pig being pushed around by propmen. AB

Reach for the Sky

(Lewis Gilbert, 1956, GB) Kenneth More, Muriel Pavlow, Lyndon Brook, Lee Patterson, Alexander Knox, Dorothy Alison, Sydney Tafler.
135 min. b/w.

Chocks away, Smithy. Maudlin, overlong, hero-worshipping stuff, with More waddling pathetically around on artificial legs impersonating Douglas Bader, symbol of everything stiff-upper-lipped and jolly good show about Britain and the RAF boys during the war. If you haven't seen this, you're probably the saner for it. GA

Ready to Wear
(aka Prêt-à-Porter)

(Robert Altman, 1994, US) Kim Basinger, Richard E Grant, Tim Robbins, Julia Roberts, Marcello Mastroianni, Sophia Loren, Anouk Aimée, Tracey Ullman, Michel Blanc, Jean-Pierre Cassel, Linda Hunt.
133 min.

One of the world's finest film-makers, Robert Altman is also one of the most erratic, with an alarming tendency to aim his satirical barbs at easy targets. It's no surprise, then, that he should opt for this smug, unfocused, facile swipe at the follies of the fashion world. Much has been made of the authentic location shooting and the starry cast, but there's a world of difference between the carefully interwoven vignettes and deft portraiture of *Nashville* and *Short Cuts* and what passes for narrative and characterisation here. There's no story to speak of and no centre. Ironically, the only halfway decent moments involve the emotional sparring between journos Robbins and Roberts, and the gentle comic style of Mastroianni's furtive fugitive. Otherwise, it's a meaningless, meandering babble of broad grotesquerie. GA

Real Blonde, The

(Tom DiCillo, 1997, US) Matthew Modine, Catherine Keener, Daryl Hannah, Maxwell Caulfield, Elizabeth Berkley, Buck Henry, Christopher Lloyd, Denis Leary, Steve Buscemi.
105 min.

This attempt at combining satirical comedy with deeply felt emotional drama is only fitfully successful. One minute, he's mocking the inanities of the New York film, fashion and music industries. The next, he's scratching over the relationship between his antagonists, struggling actor Modine and make-up artist Keener, with Bergman-like intensity. There are some wonderful moments along the way – Keener beating up her martial arts tutor (Leary) or Modine as a pimpled, white-skinned extra in a Madonna video. Caulfield is sardonic and funny as the louche young seducer/soap opera star who shrivels up when he has the chance to make love with a real blonde (Hannah). Modine is enjoyably sanctimonious as the Arthur Miller-spouting young thesp, but, bizarrely, director DiCillo, while mocking everybody else, seems to take him at face value. GM

Real Genius

(Martha Coolidge, 1985, US) Val Kilmer, Gabe Jarret, Michelle Meyrink, William Atherton, Patti D'Arbanville, Robert Prescott, Louis Giambalvo, Jonathan Gries, Ed Lauter.
106 min.

This is for real: in the heart of Reagan's America there is an institute of technology populated by whizz kids in their teens and twenties who spend their time dreaming up hi-tech zap guns of a Star Wars nature. Now Coolidge has made a film about them, and it's not very real at all, probably because the screenwriters are veterans of stuff like *Police Academy* and *Bachelor Party*. So what we get is a load of teenage Einsteins playing hi-tech pranks in the passageways of Pacific Tech. There's a hippyish ex-student hanging out in a cupboard because he doesn't approve of what's being done with his inventions, but the rest of the little eggheads are unaware that the results of their laser experiments are being swiped by an unscrupulous professor so that a covert government agency can enhance its stock of death-dealing 'peacetime' weaponry. There's a great film in there somewhere, but this isn't it. It's good-natured, it's well-meaning, but only the opening scenes catch anything of the subject's potential for black comedy. AB

Real Glory, The

(Henry Hathaway, 1939, US) Gary Cooper, David Niven, Broderick Crawford, Reginald Owen, Andrea Leeds, Kay Johnson, Vladimir Sokoloff, Henry Kolker.
95 min. b/w.

Shades of *Gunga Din* and *Lives of a Bengal Lancer* as three soldiers of fortune (Cooper also being an army doctor) join a suicide mission to stamp out Moro terrorism in the Philippines in 1906. Dubious historically and politically, and inclined to overdo the heroism (especially when the colonel's daughter bravely joins the fight against cholera after refusing to leave for safety). But Hathaway is second to none at this sort of boy's own adventure. The action, virtually non-stop, is terrific. TM

Reality Bites

(Ben Stiller, 1994, US) Winona Ryder, Ethan Hawke, Ben Stiller, Janeane Garofalo, Steve Zahn, Swoosie Kurtz, Joe Don Baker, Harry O'Reilly.
99 min.

Almost inevitably, as the first mainstream Hollywood movie to focus on post-college 'Generation X'-ers, actor Stiller's directorial debut sets up all sorts of youth-cred expectations it then has a hard time fulfilling. Ryder plays recent graduate Lelaina Pierce, given the heave-ho by a Houston TV station and left to fend for herself in the harsh economic climate of the '90s. Luckily, though, love is there – but can she choose between muso Troy (Hawke), a goatee-sporting wastrel, or will it be smarmball MTV executive Michael (Stiller)? There's probably a moderate little romantic comedy crying to get out here, but the film's vain striving for casual hip proves suffocatingly obtrusive. TJ

Real Life

(Francis Megahy, 1983, GB) Rupert Everett, Cristina Raines, Norman Beaton, Warren Clarke, Isla Blair, James Faulkner, Catherine Rabett.
93 min.

Calling a film *Real Life* and subtitling it *A Romantic Comedy* suggests a certain coyness of approach, which as it turns out is not far wrong. The material is such that, in comparison, Mills & Boon look positively Wagnerian. A young man of faultless profile (Everett – no prizes for guessing) is given to much whimsical fantasising, something that renders him inept both professionally and personally, until he meets an older woman (Raines) and, the richer for the experience, gets his girl. Paper-thin, and sadly lacking either the brittle/crisp scripting or the lightness of touch needed to make it acceptable escapism. Megahy, veteran of TV's *Minder* and *The Professionals* as well as numerous documentaries, signally fails to suggest that he has found a new vocation. VG

Real McCoy, The

(Russell Mulcahy, 1993, US) Kim Basinger, Val Kilmer, Terence Stamp, Gailard Sartain, Zach English.
105 min.

Part old-fashioned caper, party vanity project for Basinger, this yarn about a reformed cat burglar trying to go straight aims for the lightweight appeal of something like *To Catch a Thief* but is burdened with a sentimental subplot about the heroine's relationship with her estranged son. Having served six years for an aborted bank robbery, Karen McCoy (Basinger) returns to Atlanta, Georgia, where sometime associate Schmidt (Stamp) coerces her into one last job. Kilmer is the getaway driver (and love interest). Pretty lifeless. NF

Realm of the Senses, The
see Ai No Corrida

Re-Animator

(Stuart Gordon, 1985, US) Jeffrey Combs, Bruce Abbott, Barbara Crampton, David Gale, Robert Sampson, Gerry Black.
86 min.

Brilliant young brainiac Herbert West (Combs) announces that he has conquered brain death. Top neuro-surgeon Dr Hill (Gale) doesn't believe him. Fellow-student Dan Cain (Abbott) does believe, after West moves in with him and with some dayglo green serum makes his dead cat come back to life, sort of. Lovecraft is the brains behind the original six-part story, published in 1922. Gordon's first film is pure splatstick, a knockabout zombie gorefest played dead straight by its actors, which revitalises the bit that other horror films can't reach, namely the funnybone. AB

Re-Animator 2

(Brian Yuzna, 1989, US) Jeffrey Combs, Bruce Abbott, Claude Earl Jones, Fabiana Udenio, David Gale, Kathleen Kinmont, Mel Stewart.
96 min.

Five years after the 'Miskatonic Massacre', mad scientist West (Combs) conducts Frankensteinian experiments in creating human life: mixing re-animating serum with an iguana's amniotic fluid, he bypasses the brain to inject new life into autonomous body parts. Sadly, the film has the same quality, its spastic, sloppily assembled plot jerking around with no hint of governing intelligence. After an hour, some semblance of direction is achieved as West and his partner Cain (Abbott) graduate from limb grafts to produce a splendidly ghoulish 'bride' (dead patient's head, metal-clasped torso, dancer's feet, hooker's legs, the heart of Cain's dead lover) as the object of Cain's perverse desire. Meanwhile a maniac cop, assorted loons and hordes of mausoleum mutants besiege the basement lab, and West's arch-rival Dr Hill (Gale) – undeterred by the loss of his body – plans a flying visit. The excessive blood-spurting gruesomeness and cartoonish stop-motion effects trivialise the horror and undercut the would-be black humour in this travestied sequel to Stuart Gordon's hugely enjoyable film. NF

Rear Window 100 (100)

(Alfred Hitchcock, 1954, US) James Stewart, Grace Kelly, Wendell Corey, Thelma Ritter, Raymond Burr, Judith Evelyn.
112 min.

Of all Hitchcock's films, this is the one which most reveals the man. As usual it evolves from one brilliantly plain idea: Stewart, immobilised in his apartment by a broken leg and aided by his girlfriend (Grace Kelly at her most Vogue-coverish), takes to watching the inhabitants across the courtyard, first with binoculars, later with his camera. He thinks he witnesses a murder...There is suspense enough, of course, but the important thing is the way that it is filmed: the camera never strays from inside Stewart's apartment, and every shot is closely aligned with his point of view. And what this relentless monomaniac witnesses is everyone's dirty linen: suicide, broken dreams, and cheap death. Quite aside from the violation of intimacy, which is shocking enough, Hitchcock has nowhere else come so close to pure misanthropy, nor given us so disturbing a definition of what it is to watch the 'silent film' of other people's lives, whether across a courtyard or up on a screen. No wonder the sensual puritan in him punishes Stewart by breaking his other leg. CPea

Reason Over Passion (La Raison avant la Passion)

(Joyce Wieland, 1969, Can)
82 min. b/w & col.

Not quite a structural film, *Reason Over Passion* nevertheless aggressively incorporates its own sense of space (the film almost literally traverses the vast expanse of Canada) and time (80 minutes metronomically click by as computer-generated anagrams of the title flash across the screen). As in all basically formalist work, the political sympathies remain ambiguous, but the film is clearly grounded in an ironic attitude toward the colonial status of Canada (the title is a phrase invoked by Pierre Trudeau), and perhaps even the colonial status of women. The way those sympathies are formulated – re-situating the subject in space, playing on language versus image, raising the notion of a patriotic (sic) ideology – is what gives the film a continuing freshness and surprising relevance. DD

Reason to Live, a Reason to Die, A (Una Ragione per Vivere e Una per Morire)

(Tonino Valerii, It/Fr/Sp/WGer, 1972) James Coburn, Telly Savalas, Bud Spencer, Ralph Goodwin, Joseph Mitchell, Robert Burton.
96 min.

One of the worst Westerns in years, curious only for the way it mixes standard motifs from Western and war film. The beginning owes everything to *The Dirty Dozen;* and the finale, the attack on the fortress (after an extremely plodding journey across familiar terrain) has commander Telly Savalas' uniform looking more like field grey than Confederate blue. There's some wholesale carnage at the end, but even this fails to revive flagging spirits. CPe

Rebecca

(Alfred Hitchcock, 1940, US) Laurence Olivier, Joan Fontaine, George Sanders, Judith Anderson, Nigel Bruce, Gladys Cooper, Reginald Denny, C Aubrey Smith, Florence Bates, Melville Cooper, Leo G Carroll.
130 min. b/w.

Hitchcock's first Hollywood film (made for David O Selznick) was also his only one to receive a 'best picture' Oscar: all the financial advantages of America meant that for the first time he could really explore his technical imagination and create a gripping blend of detective story, gothic romance, and psychological drama. Daphne Du Maurier's fairly lightweight bestseller (about a naive young woman who marries an aristocratic patriarch, then finds her life dominated by his dead wife Rebecca) became a tale of fear and guilt, power and class. What makes the film doubly interesting is Hitchcock's fear of women, and the way it goes beyond the simple limits of narrative. The blindly loyal Mrs Danvers (Rebecca's former maid) is an almost immobile, leech-like figure. Rebecca, as malevolence personified, is never seen and therefore more dangerous. The 'pure' innocent central character (Fontaine, excellent by being totally infuriating) is treated as a pathetic victim of circumstance, her *gaucherie* and anguish trapped by a circling camera whose measured, taunting pace revels in her 'female' masochism. A riveting and painful film. HM

Rebecca's Daughters

(Karl Francis, 1991, GB/Ger) Peter O'Toole, Paul Rhys, Joely Richardson, Keith Allen, Simon Dormandy, Dafydd Hywel, Sue Roderick.
97 min.

Based on a screenplay by Dylan Thomas, with updatings by Guy Jenkin, this rural romp is *The Scarlet Pimpernel* out of Gainsborough Studios via Ealing. Set in Wales in 1843 and drawing upon historical fact, it has handsome heir Anthony Raine (Rhys) joining forces with a rabble of local farmers and labourers against avaricious drunk Lord Sarn (O'Toole) and the Turnpike Trust. Called in to protect the owners' interests, priggish Captain Marsden (Dormandy) and his dragoons are outwitted by Rebecca's Daughters, marauding gangs of men who dress as women to attack the hated turnpikes. Anthony's fiancée (Richardson) naturally prefers the cross-dressed avenging Rebecca to the seemingly ineffectual Anthony. Hints of an underlying seriousness are reinforced by Welsh director Francis' obvious affinity with both the material and the locations. For the most part, though, the tone is set by the fist fight between Anthony and a 'son of the soil' (Hywel) which predictably spills over into a pigsty. NF

Rebel

(Michael Jenkins, 1985, Aust) Matt Dillon, Debbie Byrne, Bryan Brown, Bill Hunter, Ray Barrett, Julie Nihill, John O'May, Kim Deacon.
93 min.

The year is 1942: the Japanese are on the run at Guadalcanal, and Matt Dillon's libido is advancing on Sydney, Australia. The well-defined object of his desire is Kathy (Byrne), lead singer of an all-girl band, who's doing her bit by entertaining the troops on leave. Persistence pays off, and though married, Kathy is won over by young Sgt Rebel's humanity, sensitivity and high cheek bones: he's a deserter determined never to fight again, and willing to sock several people in the jaw to emphasise the point. With an anti-war stance at heart, *Rebel* deserves some praise amid the current onslaught of bellicose films. But instead of confronting the complex issues and emotions plausibly inherent in the scenario, it falls back on clichés and one-dimensional characters, less a musical than a comic strip punctuated by verse. SGo

Rebel, The

(Robert Day, 1960, GB) Tony Hancock, George Sanders, Dennis Price, Irene Handl, John Le Mesurier, Paul Massie, Margit Saad, Grégoire Aslan, Liz Fraser.
105 min.

The first and best of two attempts to turn Hancock into a screen star, scripted by his regular TV writers Ray Galton and Alan Simpson, this is an only partially successful film. The first half, with Hancock turning from a bowler hat and

the City to an artist's beret and the Left Bank – and ordering 'snails, egg and chips' as a compromise – is fine. But Day labours over Hancock's unexpected success as the leader of the Infantile school of painting, and breaks the golden rule of Hancock's comic art by allowing him an unqualified victory over life's circumstances. PH

Rebellion (Joi-Uchi)

(Masaki Kobayashi, 1967, Jap) Toshiro Mifune, Takeshi Kato, Yoko Tsukasa, Tatsuya Nakadai, Tatsuyoshi Ehara, Michiko Otsuka.
121 min. b/w.

A fine movie from the team that gave you *Harakiri,* though this is much easier on the stomach. Again the spotlight is on Japan's code of honour – the rebellion is Mifune's, tired of having his family life mucked around by his Shogun overlords (the date is 1725). Characters spend much time talking, sitting cross-legged and frozen while their passions rise to boiling-point; everything erupts, however, in the finale, in which long grass, glistening sword blades and bloody bodies elegantly fill the Tohoscope frame. Compare or contrast with the French classical drama of Corneille and Racine (and don't write on both sides of the paper). GB

Rebel Nun, The (Flavia la Monaca Musulmana)

(Gianfranco Mingozzi, 1974, It/Fr) Florinda Bolkan, Maria Casarès, Claudio Cassinelli, Antony Corlan, Spiros Focas.
99 min.

Most Italian movies dealing with naughty nuns are fairly decorous (like *The Nun and the Devil*, which wouldn't make anyone's wimple flutter), but here is an exception: it's packed to bursting with naughty happenings, and all beautifully photographed too. The heroine, moreover, is portrayed as a fervent Women's Libber, born five centuries too early, who is enraged that Father, Son, Holy Ghost and all twelve apostles are masculine. To prove that women can outdo males in senseless brutality, she joins forces with an invading army of Moslems, and takes revenge by aiming a spiked ball at the eyes of her convent's male patron saint. Any sign of intelligence or serious thinking is welcome in this cesspool realm of cinema, but the results here seem very hollow. GB

Rebel Rousers

(Martin B Cohen, 1970, US) Cameron Mitchell, Jack Nicholson, Bruce Dern, Diane Ladd, Harry Dean Stanton.
78 min.

Shot in 1967 and shelved for three years before it was allowed to escape, this dim entry in the '60s slew of biker pictures is as tawdry as they come, but at least the makers had the good fortune to catch a young cast on the cusp of bigger and better things. When Nicholson's gang rides into town, architect Mitchell's girlfriend becomes a race trophy. TJ

Rebels of the Neon God (Qing Shaonian Nezha)

(Tsai Ming-Liang, 1992, Tai) Chao-Jung Chen, Yu-Wen Wang, Kang Sheng Lee, Chang-Bin Jen.
106 min.

Hsiao Kang doesn't really believe his superstitious mother's notion that he might be a reincarnation of the mischievous god Nezha, but it does give him ideas: he drops out of cram school, pockets the refund and gets hung up on the slightly older crook Ah Tze. His confused feelings for Ah Tze find suitably confused expression – he tries to get to know him by vandalising his motorbike and daubing it with the word 'AIDS'. No director since Fassbinder has such insight into the lives of lost young men in crumbling inner cities as Tsai Ming-Liang delivers in this devastating first feature. Brilliantly observed, with dialogue kept to a minimum, and as tender as a Lou Reed elegy. TR

Rebel Without a Cause

(Nicholas Ray, 1955, US) James Dean, Natalie Wood, Sal Mineo, Jim Backus, Ann Doran, Corey Allen, Edward Platt, Dennis Hopper, Nick Adams, William Hopper.
111 min.

Dean's finest film, hardly surprisingly in that Ray was one of the great '50s directors. The story, much imitated since, might sound like nothing much – unsettled adolescent from good home can't keep himself out of trouble, and gets involved with bad sorts until tragedy takes over – but what makes the film so powerful is both the sympathy it extends towards all the characters (including the seemingly callous parents) and the precise expressionism of Ray's direction. His use of light, space and motion is continually at the service of the characters' emotions, while the trio that Dean, Wood and Mineo form as a refuge from society is explicitly depicted as an 'alternative family'. Still the best of the youth movies. GA

Reckless Moment, The [100]
(Max Ophüls, 1949, US) James Mason, Joan Bennett, Geraldine Brooks, Henry O'Neill, Shepperd Strudwick.
81 min. b/w.
Having concealed her daughter's accidental killing of her seedy older lover, upper middle class housewife Bennett finds herself being blackmailed by a loan shark; fortunately for her, the man he sends – small-time crook and loner Mason – becomes infatuated with Bennett, and ends up killling his partner. Ophüls' noir melodrama, like his previous film, Caught, can be seen as a subtle, subversive critique of American ambitions and class-structures: in committing the moral and legal transgression of concealing a corpse, Bennett is merely protecting the comfort and respectability of her family life, and the irony is that Mason's self-sacrifice, made on her behalf, simply serves to preserve the status quo that has relegated him to the role of social outcast. This sense of waste, however, is implied rather than emphasised by Ophüls' elegant, low key direction, which counterpoints the stylisation of Burnett Guffey's shadowy photography with long, mobile takes that stress the everyday reality of the milieu. A marvellous, tantalising thriller, it also features never-better performances from Mason and Bennett. GA

Recollections of the Yellow House (Recordacões da Casa Amarela)
(João César Monteiro, 1989, Port) Manuela de Freitas, João César Monteiro, Sabina Sacchi, Inéz de Medeiros, Teresa Calado.
122 min.
The impoverished tenant of a Lisbon boarding-house, João de Deus (played to perfection by the writer-director) is one of the great miseries of the movies. He muses, in a dispassionate but doomy voice-over, on death, illness, solitude, and the bedbugs that make a nightly attack on his testicles. As the seedy, sexually frustrated, but occasionally kindly protagonist proceeds towards a pathetic, cracked assault on his harridan landlady's daughter, it's hard to know whether to laugh, weep or simply slit your wrists. In the end, it's that wry, detached sense of comic absurdity that saves the film from plunging into maudlin miserabilism. Using long, often static takes, an elliptical narrative, and stark but stylish compositions, Monteiro sidesteps psychodrama to produce something altogether cooler, more thought-provoking, and more perverse. The film makes its slow way towards the appallingly run-down mental hospital of the title, and a denouement as fantastic as it is subversive. A fascinating, quietly caustic critique of the outmoded mores of Portugal's petite bourgeoisie. GA

Record of a Tenement Gentleman (Nagaya Shinshiroku)
(Yasujiro Ozu, 1947, Jap) Choko Iida, Hohi Aoki, Eitaro Ozawa, Mitsuko Yoshikawa, Sokichi Kawamura, Hideko Mimura, Chishu Ryu.
72 min. b/w.
A widow, Tane, reluctantly shelters a young boy for the night when her neighbour discovers him lost and alone in the city. On further investigation, it seems that the boy's father, a carpenter, has abandoned him out of poverty. Tane tries to do the same, but the boy will have none of it. They strike a deal – as long as he stops wetting his bed, he can stay. This is Ozu in optimistic mood, which is not to say that loss and resignation don't figure in large part (no film-maker ever

had a surer grasp of the melancholy of everyday things), just that here the generosity of spirit seems irresistible – and irresistibly comic. (And Chishu Ryu sings!) TCh

Recuperanti, I (The Scavengers)
(Ermanno Olmi, 1969, It) Antonio Lunardi, Andreino Carli, Alessandra Micheletto, Pietro Tolin, Marilena Rossi.
94 min.
A curiously exact echo of Olmi's first feature, Time Stood Still, with its quietly funny exploration of the relationship between two men, one young and one old, who have nothing in common but their work. High up in the mountains, amid past battlefields, they scavenge for old shells and hidden ammunition dumps, dreaming of the day of El Dorado when they will find the armoured car which supposedly lies buried somewhere, lost and forgotten. Shot in documentary style, with amateur actors and a minimum of plot, it may not sound too enticing; but one has to reckon with Olmi's extraordinary ability to make bricks without straw, and here he constructs an entire drama out of the conflict between two lifestyles. Deceptively simple, it speaks volumes about our rat-race civilisation in its vivid, quizzically funny way. TM

Red and the White, The (Csillagosok, Katonák)
(Miklós Jancsó, 1967, Hun/USSR) József Madaras, András Kozák, Tibor Molnár, Jácint Juhász, Anatoli Yabbarov.
90 min. b/w.
The setting is the aftermath of the Russian Revolution: the 'reds' are the revolutionaries, the 'whites' the government forces ordered to suppress them. Jancsó focuses on a young Hungarian fighting with the reds, and charts the arbitrary pattern of arrests, imprisonments and escapes that he goes through. As in The Round-Up, Jancsó is here primarily interested in the mechanisms of power, seen as virtual abstractions: the characters have political status, not personal identity, and the lengthy arabesques described by the camera classify their struggles for supremacy as an endless cycle of gain and loss. The effect is a precise ambivalence: a celebration of revolutionary heroism, and an icily detached recognition that both sides in a war can be mirror images of each other. TR

Red Badge of Courage, The
(John Huston, 1951, US) Audie Murphy, Bill Mauldin, Arthur Hunnicutt, John Dierkes, Royal Dano, Andy Devine, Douglas Dick.
69 min. b/w.
By the time MGM had finished chopping and re-editing Huston's footage in quest of a more conventional war movie, the interior logic of Stephen Crane's account of a terrified boy's baptism of fire during the American Civil War had been rudely cast overboard. The fragments that remain, linked by a voice-over commentary drawn from the novel, nevertheless exhibit a remarkable delicacy and depth of feeling that sometimes (as in the death of the Tall Soldier) approximates the visionary quality of the novel. And visually, with Harold Rosson's camerawork lovingly recreating the harsh, dustily faded textures of Matthew Brady's Civil War pictures, it looks absolutely superb. TM

Red Baron, The
see Von Richthofen and Brown

Red Beads (Xuan Lian)
(He Yi, 1993, HK/China) Liu Jiang, Shi Ke.
90 min.
He Yi (aka He Jianjun) raised money privately to make this underground feature without official approval, and the film fully reflects the resulting freedom from constraints. A pallid guy waiting for his date in a noisy restaurant daydreams a situation in which he works as a lonely orderly in a mental hospital. He grows obsessed with the young woman patient who is already dreaming of red beads and gradually enters her delusions – if that's what they are. Hard to say if this is jet-black comedy or expressionist nightmare. Either way, it's an amazingly provocative vision by Chinese standards. It's also highly atmospheric, persuasively felt and eerily erotic. TR

Red Beard (Akahige)
(Akira Kurosawa, 1965, Jap) Toshiro Mifune, Yuzo Kayama, Yoshio Tsuchiya, Tatsuyoshi Ehara, Reiko Dan, Kyoko Kagawa, Takashi Shimura.
185 min. b/w.
A monumental hospital soap opera which looks exactly as though Kurosawa had taken a long look at Ben Casey and Dr Kildare, and decided that anything they could do he could do better. One has to reckon, however, with the fact that the Japanese Dr Gillespie, alias Red Beard, is played by Toshiro Mifune, and that Kurosawa really can do things better than most. While Red Beard busily demonstrates to his reluctant young intern that caring for the poor is more rewarding than a society practice, the film bowls along magnificently in a weird mixture of genuine emotion, absurdity and poetic fantasy. Perhaps only Kurosawa could have brought off the scene in which Red Beard, thwarted in one of his good works, erupts into a samurai frenzy, knocks out some 20 men, breaks arms and legs like matchsticks, and ends with a gravely shamefaced mutter: 'I think I've gone too far'. TM

Red Circle, The (Le Cercle Rouge)
(Jean-Pierre Melville, 1970, Fr/It) Alain Delon, André Bourvil, Yves Montand, François Périer, Gian Maria Volonté, André Eykan, Pierre Collet, Paul Crauchet.
150 min.
Melville's special achievement was to relocate the American gangster film in France, and to incorporate his own steely poetic and philosophical obsessions. He described this, his penultimate film, as a digest of the nineteen definitive underworld set-ups that could be found in John Huston's picture of doomed gangsters, The Asphalt Jungle. Darker, more abstract and desolate than his earlier work, this shows, set piece by set piece, the breakdown of the criminal codes under which Melville's characters had previously operated. Even in the butchered version distributed in Britain (dubbed and cut to 102 minutes) it's worth seeing: the mood remains, as does the film's central sequence, a superbly executed silent jewel robbery in the Place Vendôme. CPe

Red Corner
(Jon Avnet, 1997,US) Richard Gere, Bai Ling, Peter Donat, Byron Mann, Tsai Chin, Bradley Whitford, Robert Stanton.
122 min.
A fundamental circumstance of the 20th century: the unjustly accused prisoner shut up in some vast, unknowable totalitarian penal system. Not really a predicament to be exploited as a vehicle for a film star (Gere, playing a media executive under arrest in contemporary China), nor one to be crudely decked out as melodrama, complete with heroine, bad guy and final courtroom shoot-out that puts everything to rights. But if you're curious to see what Darkness at Noon might have been like had Koestler written it for Mills & Boon... BBa

Red Dawn
(John Milius, 1984, US) Patrick Swayze, C Thomas Howell, Lea Thompson, Charlie Sheen, Darren Dalton, Ben Johnson, Harry Dean Stanton, Powers Boothe, Ron O'Neal, Vladek Sheybal.
114 min.
This imagines a Russo/Cuban invasion of the American heartland by crack airborne troops. Despite scrupulously reconstructed tank battles and partisan raids, its military thesis is patently ridiculous: why would the Russians ignore the massive lessons they learned against Napoleon and Hitler to instigate a suicidal conventional invasion of the American mainland? They wouldn't, but any other scenario, including the obvious nuclear one which Milius ducks, leaves no room for the patriotic struggle he wants to show. Paranoia can of course be an excellent dynamic for movie-makers, and within its own dream-like structure, Red Dawn is both compelling and witty (the town's drive-in becomes a 're-education camp'). But it also contains moments that are repulsive in the grand right wing tradition, all the more so since Milius, who once held the fascination of a rebel, is here voicing sentiments that the Reagan administration actually believes. DP

Red Desert, The (Deserto Rosso)

(Michelangelo Antonioni, 1964, It/Fr) Monica Vitti, Richard Harris, Carlo Chionetti, Xenia Valderi, Rita Renoir, Aldo Grotti.
116 min.

Perhaps the most extraordinary and riveting film of Antonioni's entire career; and correspondingly impossible to synopsise. Monica Vitti is an electronics engineer's neurotic wife, wandering in bewilderment through a modern industrial landscape (the film is set in Ravenna) which Antonioni has coloured in the most startling and original way imaginable. The film is an aesthetic feast, but don't let that distract you from the haunting intricacy of the plot and the performances. Only Richard Harris, as Corrado, the mining engineer who becomes her refuge but who is just passing through, seems uneasy; despite what so many critics said at the time, Vitti's portrayal of the confused girl, alienated from the stark technological landscape around her, is among her very best. DP

Red Detachment of Women (Hongse Niangzijun)

(Xie Jin, 1960, China) Zhu Xijuan, Wang Xin'gang, Xiang Mei, Jin Naihua, Wang Li, Tie Niu.
113 min.

The original tropical-gothic melodrama whose storyline was co-opted during the Cultural Revolution for both a dance drama and a 'model revolutionary opera'. Apparently there really was a women's militia which rebelled against local tyrants in Hainan Island in the 1930s. But this script is an outright fantasia, part *Caged Heat* (women in chains in torture dungeons) and part Maoist dogma (underground communists guide the uprising and the heroine's greatest moment is signing her application for Party membership). Xie Jin delivers the propaganda but doesn't disguise his nostalgia for an older current in romantic film-making; the film looks like a cousin of *Black Narcissus*, complete with the dishy Wang Xin'gang in the David Farrar role. TR

Red Detachment of Women (Hongse Niangzijun)

(Collective, 1970, China) Ching Ching-hua, Lo Sing Siang, members of the China Ballet Troupe.
105 min.

This showpiece of the Cultural Revolution now functions as a virtual documentary of an ideological 'moment'. Objectively it's a straightforward transposition from the stage of a balletic narrative detailing the heroic exploits of a peasant's daughter with a women's battalion of Communist guerillas during the '30s. But the staging, score and shooting together stridently attest to a highly specific, transparently limited view of the parameters of revolutionary art. PT

Red Dust

(Victor Fleming, 1932, US) Clark Gable, Jean Harlow, Mary Astor, Donald Crisp, Gene Raymond, Tully Marshall, Willie Fung.
83 min. b/w.

The archetypal steamy melodrama, with Gable as the boorish-but-sexy manager of a rubber plantation in Indo-China who falls for platinum prostitute Harlow, despite a moment of adulterous lust for cool-but-I'm-burning-up-inside Mary Astor. So excessive that some of it turns camp, and rampantly sexist, but you can see why the Depression audiences flocked. CA

Red Firecracker, Green Firecracker (Paoda Shuang Deng)

(He Ping, 1994, HK/China) Ning Jing, Wu Gang, Zhao Xiarui, Gao Yang.
111 min.

He Ping's overdue follow-up to *The Swordsman in Double-Flag Town* is one of the few Chinese films to have absolutely no subtext: all its phallic play, gender subversion and castration fantasies are right up there on screen. Set in the 1920s, it's about a macho painter hired to produce New Year pictures for a fireworks company headed by a woman who's been forced to dress and behave like a man. She, however, finds the pres-

ence of a louche male in the house curiously disturbing and starts paying him private visits. Ructions of the explosive sort ensue, culminating in a hair-raising fireworks contest orchestrated by the vengeful elders of the clan. No great leap forward for Fifth Generation cinema, but a lot of fun. TR

Redheads

(Danny Vendramini, 1992, Aust) Claudia Karvan, Catherine McClements, Alexander Petersons, Sally McKenzie, Anthony Phelan.
107 min.

This thriller, set in Brisbane, kills two good ideas with one movie. The first is to tell a real-ist story of the developing relationship between two young women from either side of the tracks: of how sisterly friendship gives them the courage to face up to the chauvinistic, corrupt and unjust system surrounding them. The other is to deliver a slick crime thriller with a high paranoia factor. The one elbows out the other. The script has its origins in a play directed by Vendramini, where the main characters were a Maori girl and a female social worker. Here they've been replaced by a teenage white offender, Lucy (Karvan), and a rookie legal-aid lawyer, Diana (McClements). Lucy has been secretly sleeping with Diana's boss, and when he's gunned down by an anonymous assailant, she fears for her life as the web of cops, lawyers and detention-centre employees close in. A ponderous script is not helped by self-conscious video and sound effects and jarring *noir* lighting. A plus is Karvan's sparky performance. WH

Red Heat

(Walter Hill, 1988, US) Arnold Schwarzenegger, James Belushi, Peter Boyle, Ed O'Ross, Larry Fishburne, Gina Gershon, Richard Bright.
104 min.

A partial return to form for slam-bang Hill, this is the *48 HRS* formula crossed with *Gorky Park*. Unstoppable unorthodox Russian cop Danko (Schwarzenegger) arrives in the US on the trail of Soviet pusher and cop-killer Viktor (O'Ross), and is assigned to reluctant, wisecracking, unorthodox Chicago cop Ridzik (Belushi). 'We're parked in the Red Zone, no offence' says Ridzik at the airport: perhaps the only passably witty line in a canon of crass national jibes. Big Arnie plays the Soviet the way he plays all his juggernauts, only more taciturn again, but the relationship grows as he breaks a suspect's fingers and generally bypasses Miranda-Escobedo. 'Who is Dirty Harry?' goes a gag, after the cops have compared firepower. The most visually interesting stuff occurs in Moscow; hugely amplified biffs accompany the pell-mell punch-ups; and the ending, a suicidal confrontation between large vehicles, may be intended as a parody of *Rambo III*. Surface stuff, moderately contemptuous, but entertaining enough. BC

Red House, The

(Delmer Daves, 1947, US) Edward G Robinson, Lon McCallister, Allene Roberts, Judith Anderson, Rory Calhoun, Julie London, Ona Munson.
100 min. b/w.

If you go down to the woods today, you're bound for a big surprise: you won't find a picnic, however, but necrophilia, madness, incestuous longings, tyrannical possessiveness, and murder. Impossible to give an effective synopsis of the incredibly heavy plotting; but basically, when one-legged farmer Robinson's adopted daughter brings home a potential boyfriend, all manner of mysteries, scandals and sinister goings-on are let loose as Robinson resorts to violence to keep the young ones away from his nasty secret down in the nearby forest. Warped relationships are the norm in his weird but hardly wonderful world, and indeed even the film itself boasts a perverse pedigree: it's a pastoral, *noir*-inflected psychodrama with supernatural overtones, dealing chiefly with the thin line between healthy and sick sexuality. All very Freudian, in fact, and often very frightening, with Robinson in superb form as the patriarch tormented by his past. GA

Red Inn, The

see Auberge Rouge, L'

Red Line 7000

(Howard Hawks, 1965, US) James Caan, Laura Devon, Gail Hire, Charlene Holt, John Robert Crawford, Marianna Hill, James Ward, Norman Alden.
110 min.

Hawks' most *maudit* film: a motor-racing melodrama with a cast of then-unknowns who have (with the exception of Caan) remained unknown. There is undoubtedly a certain classical finesse to Hawks' dovetailing of thrills on the track with spills in the boudoir. But even the most devoted Hawksians have acknowledged that this rehash of favourite characters and situations is strictly Formula One...and non-Hawksians were thinking out their emotional problems in rather different terms by the mid-1960s. TR

Red Lotus Society, The (Feixia A-Da)

(Stan Lai, 1994, Tai) Ying Zhaode, Chen Wenming, Na Weixun, Li Tongcun, Li Lijin.
120 min.

More cinematic but less sure-footed than Lai's first film *The Peach-Blossom Land*, this anatomy of the Chinese obsession with keys to 'secret knowledge' suggests that the whole city of Taipei has lost the plot. A young language tape salesman decides to find someone to teach him 'vaulting' – the art of achieving weightlessness, as described in countless martial arts movies and novels – and scours the city for three surviving masters from the legendary Red Lotus Society who are rumoured to be living ordinary lives under assumed identities. Very beautifully shot by Chris Doyle, but not persuasive enough as a vision of reality for the characters' superstitions and paranoias to seem justified. TR

Red Monarch

(Jack Gold, 1983, GB) Colin Blakely, David Suchet, Carroll Baker, Ian Hogg, Jean Heywood, David Threlfall, Nigel Stock, Brian Glover.
100 min.

In this jet black comedy about the end of Stalin, scripted by Charles Wood from stories by the well-placed Kremlin-watcher Yuri Krotkov, the dictator (Blakely) is a ghastly paranoid prankster, while Beria (Suchet), his lecherous police chief, rolls with the jokes and abuses himself like a terrified jester when his master seems about to dispense with his services. This quick-silver double act is a tour de force (the two Georgians are represented as distrustful Ulstermen), and the film runs confidently up and down the comic scale, from the absurdity of Mao Tse-tung's visit for Stalin's 70th birthday (unable to communicate, the two dictators stuff themselves on hard-boiled eggs), to the macabre finale when the Politburo gathers outside Stalin's door hoping against hope he may be dead (opening his eyes to see his marionettes jigging for joy, the tyrant spits out the one word 'Idiot!' – a judgment on himself perhaps – before Beria sinks to his knees and throttles him). The film ends with a line from Yevtushenko: the poet will never feel safe until Stalin's heirs cease to occupy the Kremlin. JPy

Red Nightmare

(George Waggner, 1962, US) Jack Webb, Jack Kelly, Jeanne Cooper, Peter Breck, Robert Conrad.
18 min.

This slice of Hollywood paranoia, never actually released, dates from the Red Scare period following the Cuban missile crisis, and was 'personally supervised' by Jack L Warner for the Department of Defence, to remind every American not taking sufficient interest in their local PTA that 'responsibilities are a privilege'. With an omnipresent Jack Webb acting as thought-control personified, the film hilariously scuttles its own thesis all the way down the line. The uniformed Reds who actually turn up in some poor Mid-Town Joe's dream not only take over his community, but turn his family into automatons, march his daughter off to work farm, close the Sunday School, up his piecework quota, and – final straw – claim to have invented the telephone! Tantrums inevitably lead to a show trial and a quick bullet. Awakening, on the other hand, brings everyday American sweetness and light – and just as inevitably, another cautionary lecture from Webb. Hysterical, indeed. PT

Red Planet Mars

(Harry Horner, 1952, US) Peter Graves, Andrea King, Herbert Berghof, Marvin Miller, House Peters, Vince Barnett.
87 min. b/w.
A candidate for the nuttiest sci-fi pic of all time, this incredible Cold War relic rolls out a barnstorming plot in which TV transmissions from Mars, revealing that the planet's ruled by a godlike supreme being, cause global revolution on Earth. But that's just the set-up. It then transpires that the messages were faked by a mad scientist hoping to topple capitalism. But that's just the twist. There follows a further bona fide transmission from Mars, proclaiming that its leader is God himself, which stirs up a worldwide religious revival and a resolve for all to live in harmony. From another age, if not another planet. TJ

Red Psalm (Még Kér a Nép)

(Miklós Jancsó, 1971, Hun) Lajos Balázsovits, András Bálint, Gyöngyi Bürös, Andrea Drahota, József Madaras.
88 min.
Where Jancsó's *Agnus Dei* was opaque and difficult, this is crystal clear and involving: looking for a language in that film, he found it here and uses it with dazzling precision. Like his earlier films, *Red Psalm* is centred on a specific period in Hungarian history: the turn-of-the-century uprising of landless agricultural workers. It was a socialist uprising, and songs of the period – including a remarkable socialist *Lord's Prayer* – are woven into the film. A work of amazing and totally uncosmetic beauty, it's a folk tale around the belief of the people in their own ultimate victory, and the symbol Jancsó has chosen is the wounded palm that's also a rosette of hope. VG

Red Rings of Fear (Enigma Rosso)

(Alberto Negrin, 1978, It/Sp/WGer) Fabio Testi, Christine Kaufmann, Ivan Desny, John Taylor, Fausta Avelli, Brigitte Wagner.
85 min.
A dire cheapo thriller which relies on confusion for suspense, schoolgirl nymphets for titillation, and Fabio Testi's five o'clock shadow for a sense of adventure. A girl gets murdered, Testi's the flat-footed gumshoe who investigates, convent school inmates are under siege and suspicion, and there's a complicated sideline about a jeans shop. The *denouement* is just about discernible from the surrounding detail – abortions, arson, art forgeries – but hardly worth waiting for. HM

Red River

(Howard Hawks, 1948, US) John Wayne, Montgomery Clift, Walter Brennan, Joanne Dru, John Ireland, Noah Beery Jr, Paul Fix, Coleen Gray, Harry Carey Jr, Harry Carey Sr.
133 min. b/w.
Hawks' leisurely adaptation of Borden Chase's story about the establishing of the Chisholm Trail by Wayne and Clift's cattle train is a sheer delight that works on many levels. Firstly, it's an examination of Wayne's heroic image, here shown to be needlessly authoritarian and stubborn as he comes into conflict with his more liberal surrogate son Clift, gradually coming in for more and more criticism from garrulous Greek-chorus figure Brennan for his repeated killing of deserters. Secondly, it's yet another variation on Hawks' perennial concern with the theme of self-respect and professionalism, and being part of 'the group'. Finally, it's an intimate epic celebrating the determination to establish civilisation in the wilderness, with Clift's refusal to resort to the gun viewed as an essential improvement upon Wayne's trigger-happy rough justice. Immaculately shot by Russell Harlan, perfectly performed by a host of Hawks regulars, and shot through with dark comedy, it's probably the finest Western of the '40s. GA

Red Rock West

(John Dahl, 1992, US) Nicolas Cage, JT Walsh, Lara Flynn Boyle, Dennis Hopper, Craig Reay.
98 min.
When Michael Williams (Cage) drifts into the hick town of Red Rock, he's surprised when bar-owner Wayne Brown (Walsh) assumes he's a hit-man and hands over five grand as down payment on killing his wife Suzanne (Boyle). Having told Suzanne about the contract, Williams accepts

$10,000 from her to kill Brown. Free to skedaddle, he thinks he's struck lucky. But fate steps in when he runs over a man, takes him back to hospital and finds that *sheriff* Brown wants to nail him. And that's just the first 20 minutes of this well-played, highly entertaining and playfully ingenious thriller. GA

Red Rose, White Rose (Hong Meigui Bai Meigui)

(Stanley Kwan, 1994, HK/Tai) Winston Chao, Joan Chen, Veronika Yip.
110 min.
Stanley Kwan, director of the sublime *Rouge* and *Actress*, has adapted the most famous Chinese account of the war between men and women, a novella by the late Eileen Chang, preserving every ounce of the book's irony and sarcasm. In pre-communist Shanghai a western-educated man (Chao) runs away from his torrid mistress (Chen, never better) and marries a traditionally submissive girl (Yip)…and proceeds to turn her into a neurotic wreck. Easy to imagine Fassbinder liking this story, and he'd have loved the way Chris Doyle's hallucinatory cinematography accentuates the plot's twists of the knife. TR

Reds

(Warren Beatty, 1981, US) Warren Beatty, Diane Keaton, Edward Herrmann, Jerzy Kozinski, Jack Nicholson, Paul Sorvino, Maureen Stapleton, Nicolas Coster, M Emmet Walsh, Gene Hackman, Ian Wolfe, Bessie Love.
196 min.
Maybe not 3 hours to shake the world, but mightily impressive in its creative grasp of the inbuilt contradictions of 'epic' political cinema and historical representation, *Reds* intriguingly yokes romance and revolution to produce a timely monument to dissent. While veteran witnesses to the lives and impact of activist journalists John Reed and Louise Bryant offer conflicting memories in documentary inserts, Beatty and co-writer Trevor Griffiths construct a heroic love story textured as a dialectical biopic. The Russian October stands as an emotively agitational centrepiece, but the film's focus remains on the American socialist heritage and radical tradition: a deliberately patterned weave that acknowledges provocative contrasts – between Greenwich Village intellectualism and the rank-and-file labour struggles of the Wobblies, between organisation and 'culture', between vying CP factions, between enlightened patriarchy and early feminism. Beatty's Reed and Keaton's Bryant observe, criticise, swim against and participate in their times, maintaining a steady fascination through the plausibility of their erratically developing relationship, emphasising that history begins at home, in every sense. PT

Red Shoes, The ☐100☐

(Michael Powell/Emeric Pressburger, 1948, GB) Anton Walbrook, Moira Shearer, Marius Goring, Leonid Massine, Albert Basserman, Robert Helpmann, Esmond Knight, Ludmilla Tcherina, Frederick Ashton.
133 min.
In outline, a rather over-determined melodrama set in the ballet world: impresario (Walbrook) 'discovers' dancer (Shearer), and makes her a slave to her art, until young composer (Goring) turns up to offer her a lifeline back to reality. But in texture, it's like nothing the British cinema had ever seen: a rhapsody of colour expressionism, reaching delirious heights in the ballet scenes, but never becoming too brash and smothering its own nuances. And if the plot threatens to anchor the spectacle in a more mundane register, it's worth bearing in mind the inhibition on which it rests: the central impresario/dancer relationship was modelled directly on Diaghilev and Nijinsky, and its dynamic remains 'secretly' gay. TR

Red Sky at Morning

(James Goldstone, 1970, US) Richard Thomas, Catherine Burns, Desi Arnaz Jr, Richard Crenna, Claire Bloom, John Colicos, Harry Guardino, Strother Martin, Nehemiah Persoff, Victoria Racimo.
112 min.
1944, and off Dad (Crenna) goes into the Navy after taking wilting Southern Mum (Bloom), slipping into Vivien Leigh's shoes') and son

(Thomas) to a Mexican hideaway mansion. From there develops an unusually blatant mixture of voyeuristic wish-fulfilment as teeny high school petting and chicken games are laid aside by sons who follow their fathers, unquestioning, to the battlefront. As if by sympathetic magic, for instance, the moment Thomas actually screws his girlfriend, the moment he takes over his father's ritual manly tasks (such as helping an artist friend lug yet another of his hero-busts up to his private Mount Rushmore where Bogart, Chuchill and DiMaggio rub shoulders), comes the news that Dad has been blown up. Any number of loving, lying shots of tousselled heads windblown against the sky, gamely tearful faces saying goodbye. The only good thing is that Vilmos Zsigmond's photography manages to wring a grain or two of realism from those faces.

Red Sonja

(Richard Fleischer, 1985, US) Arnold Schwarzenegger, Brigitte Nielsen, Sandahl Bergman, Paul Smith, Ernie Reyes Jr, Ronald Lacey, Pat Roach.
89 min.
Dim *Conan* style comic strip adventure about some prehistoric bint from Hyborea (Nielsen) wandering around seeking revenge on the evil Princess whatsername (Bergman), who's nicked some powerful talisman and is bent on destroying the world as rotten set designers know it. Big Arnie flexes his muscles but not his thespian talents, Nielsen (Stallone's friend) delivers her lines at two words a minute, and poor Ronald Lacey is forced to reprise his *Raiders of the Lost Ark* Nazi villain bit in exceedingly silly costumes and hats. Worst of all, there's a charmless brat prince for Sonja to take under her wing. Pap, and Fleischer – who at least brought a touch of humour to *Conan the Destroyer* – should know better. GA

Red Sorghum (Hong Gaoliang)

(Zhang Yimou, 1987, China) Gong Li, Jiang Wen, Teng Rujun, Liu Ji, Qian Ming, Ji Chunhua.
92 min.
The stuff of legend, Zhang Yimou's film satisfies both as straight folk tale and as a subversive tribute to the vitality and endurance of Chinese peasant culture. Set in a remote Northern province in the '20s and '30s, the story is narrated by a man who remembers the lives and times of his grandparents. A girl is waylaid and ravished in a field, en route to an arranged marriage with an elderly, leprous winemaker. He mysteriously dies, and her ravisher eventually lives with her so that together they make the red sorghum wine. As the film develops, the tone shifts from light to dark, humour giving way to horror and sacrifice with the arrival of Japanese forces. Formerly a cameraman, Zhang fills the 'Scope screen with rich, sensuous images that illuminate and celebrate peasant life (waving sorghum fields, an eclipse of the sun), and uses actors, music and colour in a deeply expressive way. This, his debut as a director, confirms him as one of the finest and most versatile of China's 'Fifth Generation' film-makers. WH

Red Squirrel, The (La Ardilla Roja)

(Julio Medem, 1993, Sp) Nancho Novo, Emma Suárez, Maria Barranco, Carmelo Gómez, Karra Elejalde, Cristina Marcos.
104 min.
Abandoned by his girl, washed up as a rock singer, Jota (Novo) is on the brink of suicide when he sees a biker skidding off the road. First on the scene, he discovers a young woman (Suárez), physically unharmed, but without memory or ID. Improvising wildly, Jota claims she is his girlfriend Lisa and steals her away from hospital to a remote campsite ('The Red Squirrel') where, he says, they will become reacquainted. As 'Lisa's' old personality begins to reassert itself, events take a dark turn, and it becomes clear Jota's got a lot more than he bargained for. Funny in both senses, the movie is improbable, melodramatic and overblown, yet utterly compelling and entirely persuasive. The Basque writer/director Julio Medem (*Vacas*) addresses psycho-sexual power plays, the nature of identity, lies and surprises. A fervid romantic mystery, forever flying off in new and unexpected directions. TCh

Red Sun (Soleil Rouge)

(Terence Young, 1971, Fr/It/Sp) Charles
Bronson, Toshiro Mifune, Alain Delon, Ursula
Andress, Capucine, Bart Barry,
Lee Burton.
112 min.
Samurai (Mifune) meets gunslinging hero
(Bronson) meets black-gloved fascist (Delon) in
the old West, with touches of the *Dollar* syndrome. Young, of *Dr No*, *Thunderball* and
Mayerling, can't keep the over-inflated production values together, and it all disintegrates into
individual performances. A wasted opportunity.

Red Wedding

see Noces Rouges, Les

Reed: Insurgent Mexico
(Reed: México Insurgente)

(Paul Leduc, 1971, Mex) Claudio Obregón,
Eduardo López Rojas, Ernesto Gómez Cruz,
Juan Angel Martinez, Carlos Castañón.
106 min. b/w.
American journalist John Reed became world
famous through his reporting of the Russian
Revolution in *The Ten Days That Shook the
World*. This deals with his earlier conversion to
the cause of social upheaval, a result of his observation of the Mexican Revolution. The strength
of Paul Leduc's dramatised reconstruction lies in
its authenticity (the sepia wash is suitably appropriate) and its refusal to indulge in myth-making. Instead, the struggle is presented in terms
of the people involved, and reflected in Reed's
own crisis of conscience and gradual commitment (via a somewhat Hemingway-like path) to
the uprising.

Reefer and the Model

(Joe Comerford, 1988, Ire) Ian McElhinney, Eve
Watkinson, Carol Scanlan, Birdy Sweeney,
Sean Lawlor, Ray McBride.
93 min.
Reefer, Spider and Badger eke out a living on a
dilapidated trawler, having renounced (provisionally, at least) their lawless past. When the
homeless, pregnant 'Model' (Scanlan) – returning from London to kick a heroin habit – joins
the crew and begins a hesitant relationship with
Reefer (McElhinney), the men's complacent
beliefs and faded ideals come in for reappraisal...but one last caper proves inevitable.
This sharp thriller sparks with vitality and wit,
artfully playing its macho hero off against the
innate authority of the pregnant Model, and discovering refreshing variations on the 'underdogs against the world' formula. Comerford is
strong on spiky characterisation and political
nuance, but uneasy when it comes to the
mechanics of narrative development (the time
scale is particularly erratic) and stylistic treatment. Disarmingly balancing elements of
Ealing-esque whimsy and violent realism, the
ending comes perilously close to incoherence,
arguably romanticising the very mentality it
attempts to undercut. Even so, the film has a relevance and resonance you won't find in many a
more polished effort. TCh

Reefer Madness

(Louis Gasnier, 1936, US) Dave O'Brien,
Dorothy Short, Kenneth Craig, Carleton
Young, Lillian Miles, Thelma White, Pat
Royale.
67 min. b/w.
Vintage camp in the form of an outrageous anti-
dope film, this begins with a pompous teacher
warning his startled parents' association that the
killer weed, more dangerous than any other drug,
is spreading through the land like an evil disease,
sapping the cream from our upstanding youth.
An exemplary tale unfolds, where maniacal creatures seduce a handsome lad, with the best grades
and a fine eye for the tennis ball, into the abhor-
rent looseness of the reefer game. Horror of horrors, he fucks a lady of ill virtue, and ends
accused of murdering his girlfriend. Another
murder and a suicide later, the villain is caught,
justice vindicated, and the drug gang cleaned up.
It's basically a lousily made film, but the one-
dimensional 'vice' and portentous didacticism
more than make up for that. One of the most
absurdly earnest exercises in paranoia you'll ever
have the good fortune to see. JDuC

Ref, The
(aka Hostile Hostages)

(Ted Demme, 1994, US) Denis Leary, Judy
Davis, Kevin Spacey, Glynis Johns, Robert J
Steinmiller Jr, Raymond J Barry, Christine
Baranski.
97 min.
It's Christmas Eve in Connecticut and for the
Chasseurs (Davis and Spacey), Santa arrives a
few hours early in the unconventional form of cat
burglar Gus (Leary), an armed desperado who
takes them hostage when his get-away falls
apart. This is a vindictive affair, a truly nasty-
minded black comedy at the expense of your
upper-middle-class dysfunctional American family. Director Ted Demme (Jonathan's nephew)
never applies the scalpel where a blunt instrument will do, and the screenplay by Richard
LaGravenese and Marie Weiss does become a
mite repetitive. Nevertheless the film has a caustic edge and energy which keeps the laughs flowing. In his first starring role, comedian Leary
makes his ranting career criminal strangely sympathetic, but he's more than matched in the vitu-
peration stakes by Spacey, Davis, and especially
Glynis Johns, as a demurely monstrous mother-
in-law. Naturally, the ordeal gravitates towards
gun-point group therapy, but there's bite here as
well as bark. TCh

Reflecting Skin, The

(Philip Ridley, 1990, GB) Viggo Mortensen,
Lindsay Duncan, Jeremy Cooper, Sheila Moore,
Duncan Fraser, Evan Hall.
95 min.
Set amid the golden corn of the '50s Midwest,
Ridley's directorial debut (he scripted *The Krays*)
confronts 'the nightmare of childhood'. Virtually
ignored by his neurotic mother and ineffectual
father, eight-year-old Seth (Cooper) creates a
world of his own, imagining that reclusive
English-woman Dolphin Blue (Duncan) is a vampire, and that the foetus he finds in a barn is his
dead friend transformed into an earth-bound
angel. Reality begins to seep in when Seth's father
is accused of murdering children who have gone
missing in the area, and Seth's older brother
(Mortensen) returns from the Pacific with tales of
a bomb that explodes like a second sun. The complex, non-linear narrative is almost operatic in its
visual and emotional excess, employing exaggerated camera angles, saturated colours and an
ultra-loud soundtrack to create a heightened,
sometimes dangerously portentous reality.
Admirably ambitious but, one suspects, a little
overripe for English sensibilities. NF

Reflections

(Kevin Billington, 1983, US) Gabriel Byrne,
Donal McCann, Fionnula Flanagan, Harriet
Walter, Gerard Cummins, Niall Tobin.
100 min.
A pompous young academic (Byrne) rents a cottage on a dilapidated Irish estate in order to finish off his book on Isaac Newton. The days are
hot, the grass is high, and the folks in the Big
House soon prove a whole lot more interesting
than Newton: drunken stumblebum husband
(McCann), valiumed-up wife (Flanagan), and
exceedingly playful niece (Walter). Scripted by
novelist John Banville, Billington's film certainly
looks engaging enough, but it gets increasingly
bogged down in its own languor. Art and Life
grapple rather solemnly, and the surface gloss
only points up the lack of dramatic bite. Yet
almost all reservations pale beside Harriet
Walter's superb performance as the niece.
Tender, understated, generous, this is film acting
of a very high calibre, and makes the film well
worth a spin. JP

Reflections in a Golden Eye

(John Huston, 1967, US) Marlon Brando,
Elizabeth Taylor, Brian Keith, Julie Harris,
Robert Forster, Zorro David.
109 min.
A veritable hothouse of strange desires and
bizarre fancies, what with Taylor and Brando
brooding moodily, brandishing whips, and galloping round on symbolic stallions. Stuck in the
married quarters of a Deep South army base, she
is carrying on with another officer (Keith), while
he hopefully dogs a virginal young soldier
(Forster) with a penchant for riding nude in the
woods. The soldier meanwhile takes to sneaking
into Taylor's room to watch her sleep, and Keith's

neurotic wife (Harris) consoles herself in a motherly affair with a cuddly Filipino houseboy. It all
ends predictably in murder, but isn't nearly so
risible as it sounds. For one thing, Huston's quirkish sense of humour is way ahead of anybody,
while the unusually literate script (based on the
Carson McCullers novel) manages to lend genuine depth and credibility to the characters. For
another, the sense of tranquil summer stagnation
is beautifully sustained: the lectures on military
history in stifling classrooms, the afternoons
spent riding in the forest, the evening drinks and
endless card games, and at night the boredom,
the frustrations, and the loneliness which make
anything possible. All in all, a superbly controlled
exercise in the malevolent torments of despair.
TM

Refrigerator, The

(Nicholas De Jacobs, 1991, US) Julia McNeal,
David Simonds, Angel Caban.
86 min.
A wry slice of domestic horror, in which Ohio
newlyweds Eileen and Steve Bateman move into
a seedy New York apartment and dream of making it in the big city. But the apartment's ancient
refrigerator exerts a strange influence over their
lives. Steve is consumed by a desire to consume,
while Eileen is haunted by memories of her mother's domestic enslavement. The malevolent appli-
ance also frustrates her efforts to start an
independent career as an actress. The cheapo special effects (a man-eating fridge, flying fans, and
a foot-eating pedal-bin) are perfectly suited to an
offbeat, Kafkaesque horror comedy which, while
sympathetic to Eileen's female plight, satirises
her husband's yuppie aspirations. NF

Refusal, The
(Die Verweigerung)

(Alex Corti, 1972, Aus) Kurt Weinzierl, Julia
Gschnitzer, Hugo Gottschlich, Helmut Wlasak,
Fritz Schmiedl.
94 min. b/w.
A dramatised documentary about Franz
Jägerstetter, perhaps the least understandable
type of our times: the man who dies for his religious principles. Austria, 1943: the Catholic
Church and the local community have adopted the
line of least resistance towards the Nazis. Against
everyone's advice, Jägerstetter refuses to do military service, accepting execution rather than serve
a country in which he has no rights, only obligations. Only secondarily, however, is the film concerned with one man's martyrdom; primarily it
deals with the very ordinary people party to it.
Much has been made of the human body's capacity for deprivation and abuse (reinforced by a soldier talking of Stalingrad) at the expense of the
mind's faculty for the same. Jägerstetter's exception points to the rule: crises like living under Nazi
regimes do little to formulate people's attitudes.
Life is a matter of prevarication and endurance,
and afterwards forgetting. Thirty years later, the
villagers interviewed in this film had little opinion either way about the whole business.

Regarde les hommes tomber
(See How They Fall)

(Jacques Audiard, 1993, Fr) Jean Yanne, Jean-
Louis Trintignant, Mathieu Kassovitz, Bulle
Ogier.
100 min.
The first feature of the screenwriter Jacques
Audiard is a clever thriller that fascinates as
much for its ingenious, elliptical structure as for
its *noir*-derived insights into obsession, loyalty
and betrayal. Yanne's the salesman whose mid-
life crisis coincides with his inadvertent involvement in the murder of a cop; as he sets out to trace
the killer, his life begins to fall apart. At the same
time, we witness the faltering growth of the
friendship between seedy, aggressive con-man
Trintignant and slow-witted innocent Kassovitz.
Inexorably, but in surprising ways, the two stories gradually converge. And because it ends up
admitting to the homo-erotic dynamics of the
Trintignant-Kassovitz relationship, it's also,
finally, rather more moving than the enigmatic
early scenes lead one to expect. GA

Regarding Henry

(Mike Nichols, 1991, US) Harrison Ford,
Annette Bening, Bill Nunn, Mikki Allen, Donald
Moffat, Aida Linares, Elizabeth Wilson.
108 min.

This contrived, custom-built drama for the caring '90s seeks to manipulate every cliché about the greedy '80s. Henry Turner (Ford) is a rich New York lawyer who has pursued his career at the expense of relationships with his wife (Bening) and young daughter (Allen). He throws tantrums over petty domestic details, bolsters wealthy clients, and kicks the underdog when he's down. Then one night he is shot during a robbery, and the resulting brain damage renders him utterly dependent on the goodwill of others. He learns to read again, re-evaluates relationships, and upon returning to work, realises his old, evil ways. There's no subtlety of characterisation, and despite the severity of Henry's injuries, little to disconcert the viewer. Bening and Ford give the material all they've got, but they're fighting an uphill battle. CM

Regeneration

(Raoul Walsh, 1915, US) Rockliffe Fellowes, Anna Q Nilsson, Carl Harbaugh, William A Sheer, James A Marcus.
6 reels. b/w.
The problems and pitfalls of film history are well illustrated by the case of Walsh's feature debut for Fox. Long feared lost until rediscovered by the Museum of Modern Art, this first feature-length gangster picture emerges as a fast-moving melodrama; an energetic account of the rise of a slum kid (Fellowes) to gang leader, and his subsequent dilemma when torn between the code of loyalty of his gang and his good, mission-running sweetheart (Nilsson). Intriguingly, its eventful plotline is revealed as flatly contradicting the accepted synoptic account provided by Walsh in his autobiography. There the eventual fates of Nilsson and Fellowes are reversed, and an ending is transposed from another film entirely. None the less, a distinctly major rediscovery, distinguished by a remarkable approach to physical casting, a robust treatment of violent action, and a sheer narrative pace to shame contemporary ponderousness. PT

Regeneration

(Gillies MacKinnon, 1997, GB/Can) Jonathan Pryce, James Wilby, Jonny Lee Miller, Stuart Bunce, Tanya Allen, David Hayman, Dougray Scott, John Neville.
114 min.
Near the end of WWI, the poet Siegfried Sassoon (Wilby) arrives at Craiglockhart Castle, Edinburgh, a military hospital where pioneering psychiatrist William Rivers (Pryce) tends shell-shocked victims of the trenches. Not that Sassoon needs treatment: having published a pamphlet opposing the war, he's been diplomatically dispatched to hospital rather than prison. His 'convalescence' brings him into contact with another writer, Wilfred Owen (Bunce), whose poetry Sassoon encourages. Rivers, meanwhile, is heading for a breakdown of his own, brought on less by overwork than his empathy with traumatised patients like Billy Prior (Miller), a working class officer rendered mute by his battlefield experiences. Adapted by Allan Scott from Pat Barker's acclaimed novel, MacKinnon's film is subtle, elegant and sharply intelligent. Aided by marvellous performances all round, MacKinnon has fashioned a profoundly moving film that never resorts to manipulative cliché. The trenches are impressively recreated in flashback, but even more affecting are those intimate scenes which suggest that such horrors will never lose their grip on those who have survived them. GA

Reggae

(Horace Ové, 1970, GB) The Pyramids, Pioneers, Maytals, Desmond Dekker, Black Faith, John Holt, Count Prince Miller, Millie.
60 min.
Ové's documentary record of the 1970 Caribbean Music Festival at Wembley is now inevitably dated by somewhat sententious political and social claims. Nevertheless, it remains a fascinating and indispensable key to understanding this originally very derivative form. And latterday converts, uninterested in anything but the excitement generated by the music itself, will want to catch the movie for individual performances. RM

Reggae Sunsplash II

(Stefan Paul, 1979, WGer) Burning Spear, Third World, Peter Tosh, Bob Marley and the Wailers, Clancy Eccles.
109 min.

A travel-fodder tableau of young lovers silhouetted against a Caribbean beach, with an accompaniment of 10cc's *Dreadlock Holiday*, strikes the first discordant note. Nearly two hours and much well-intentioned but naive politicising later, all credibility is gone. The film chronicles the Reggae Sunsplash II festival at Montego Bay, with the proceedings interrupted by apparently random interviews with Rastafarians and by unguarded shots of locals where the prying camera produces a distinctly uncomfortable air. Unfortunately there is little here for the reggae connoisseur: a passable performance from Marley; some flaccid disco from Third World; and probably the best of the bunch, silken vocals from one of reggae's gentlemen, Winston Rodney (Burning Spear). LW

Règle du Jeu, La [100] (100) (The Rules of the Game)

(Jean Renoir, 1939, Fr) Marcel Dalio, Nora Gregor, Jean Renoir, Roland Toutain, Mila Parély, Gaston Modot, Julien Carette, Paulette Dubost, Pierre Magnier.
110 min. b/w.
Banned on its original release as 'too demoralising', and only made available again in its original form in 1956, Renoir's brilliant social comedy is epitomised by the phrase 'everyone has their reasons'. Centreing on a lavish country house party given by the Marquis de la Chesnaye and his wife (Dalio, Gregor), the film effects audacious slides from melodrama into farce, from realism into fantasy, and from comedy into tragedy. Romantic intrigues, social rivalries, and human foibles are all observed with an unblinking eye that nevertheless refuses to judge. The carnage of the rabbit shoot, the intimations of mortality introduced by the after-dinner entertainment, and Renoir's own performance are all unforgettable. Embracing every level of French society, from the aristocratic hosts to a poacher turned servant, the film presents a hilarious yet melancholic picture of a nation riven by petty class distinctions. NF

Reigen

see Dance of Love

Reign of Naples, The (Neapolitanische eschwister)

(Werner Schroeter, 1978, WGer/It) Liana Trouché, Roméo Giro, Tiziana Ambretti, Antonio Orlando, Renata Zamengo.
125 min.
Most films show people's personal lives as if they were outside history, and History as a dry document of political events. *The Reign of Naples* breaks down this comfortable separation in its telling of history – Naples from 1944 to '69 – as everyday existence. And not, as in so many Italian art films (*The Damned* for example) as the everyday existence of the upper middle class; Schroeter follows the lives of a few families in the poor quarter, and shows us post-war Italy in the flesh. The young girl trying to keep her dignity and earn a living, her brother working for the Party, the woman whose daughter dies from lack of penicillin – all are shown with as much passion as if this were a romantic melodrama. In contrast, standard historical information is cursorily sketched in at intervals over shots of posters, documentary footage, old stills: standard images for 'History'. It is rare that politics is shown to be the substance of real life: this film achieves it. JWi

Reign of Terror (aka The Black Book)

(Anthony Mann, 1949, US) Robert Cummings, Arlene Dahl, Richard Basehart, Richard Hart, Norman Lloyd, Arnold Moss, Charles McGraw, Jess Barker, Beulah Bondi.
89 min. b/w.
Co-scripted by Philip Yordan – who wrote *Johnny Guitar* as well as Mann's two great epics, *El Cid* and *The Fall of the Roman Empire* – this is a French Revolutionary drama made on the lines of Mann's *film noirs* like *T-Men*, with atmospheric camerawork by John Alton and ambitious art direction (the producer was William Cameron Menzies, who made *Things To Come* and designed *Gone With the Wind*). History is thrown to the wolves as Robert Cummings impersonates a public prosecutor and tries to overthrow the dictatorship of Robespierre (Basehart), whose incriminating 'Black Book' (furnishing the British

release title) has been stolen. Historians will scoff and the casting is hardly French, but on its own terms the movie works very well. ATu

Reincarnation of Peter Proud, The

(J Lee Thompson, 1974, US) Michael Sarrazin, Jennifer O'Neill, Margot Kidder, Cornelia Sharpe, Paul Hecht, Tony Stephano.
104 min.
A psychical sex thriller totally lacking in thrills, sex or psychic phenomena, this takes its proud place in that tiny elite of features with scenarios so atrocious that their entire action has to unfold before the title premise can even be established: in other words, that the reincarnation of Peter Proud is indeed Peter Proud's reincarnation. Sarrazin moves prosaically through the proceedings as the man whose recurring nightmare turns out to be a memory of his former life, but the plot is so minimal that the proceedings constantly have to be padded out with hideous travelogue footage and emoting-by-numbers from a shifting and evidently uncertain cast. At one point, in what is supposed (God help us) to be a climactic suspense sequence involving cross-cutting, Thompson interpolates lengthy footage of Sarrazin and girlfriend doing a lolloping square dance to a vocal which endlessly intones 'Better is to come'. This is by far the film's most fantastic assertion. DP

Reine Margot, La

(Patrice Chéreau, 1994, Fr/Ger/It) Isabelle Adjani, Daniel Auteuil, Jean-Hugues Anglade, Vincent Perez, Virna Lisi, Pascal Greggory, Jean-Claude Brialy, Barbet Schroeder.
162 min.
Centred on the intrigues leading up to and following the St Bartholomew's Day Massacre of 1572, this historical drama begins with the arranged, loveless wedding of the Roman Catholic Marguerite de Valois (Adjani) – sister to eccentric King Charles IX (Anglade), daughter of the scheming Catherine de Medici – and the Huguenot Henri de Navarre (Auteuil). Despite Catherine's hope that the marriage may unite France, the mutual hatred felt by Catholics and Protestants soon degenerates into carnage; and Margot, who has learned to tolerate her husband while falling for young Huguenot La Môle (Perez), finds herself caught in a deadly trap. Chéreau's film is a fast-moving and savagely ironic yarn. It's also visceral, with a high gore-factor, a pervasive whiff of filth, and a compelling percussive score. The performances are top-notch, while the dark, rich photography is painterly but never lifeless. GA

Reise der Hoffnung

see Journey of Hope

Reise nach Lyon, Die

see Blind Spot

Reivers, The

(Mark Rydell, 1969, US) Steve McQueen, Sharon Farrell, Will Geer, Rupert Crosse, Mitch Vogel, Michael Constantine, Lonny Chapman, Juano Hernandez, Clifton James, Dub Taylor, Allyn Ann McLerie.
111 min.
Period charm accounts for much of the mild enjoyment to be had from this sunnily nostalgic adaptation of William Faulkner's novel about an unholy trio – small boy (Vogel), dimwitted young buck (McQueen) and wily black (Crosse) – who 'borrow' a 1905 Winton Flyer and drive triumphantly off to Memphis for three days of illicit pleasure. The message about how his experiences help the boy to grow up is a little hard to take in this winsome reading of Faulkner, but the settings are first rate and so are the performances, though Rydell's direction tries just too hard, drenching itself in 'style'. TM

Réjeanne Padovani

(Denys Arcand, 1973, Can) Luce Guilbeault, Jean Lajeunesse, Roger Lebel, Margot MacKinnon, René Caron.
94 min.
Municipal corruption vaguely echoing *Hands Over the City* led some critics to align Arcand's second feature with the political dossiers of Francesco Rosi. In fact, Arcand uses a more

detached, observational style, rooted in the documentary background he shares with better-known Quebecois directors like Perrault and Brault, and his finely-nuanced portrait of capitalist conspiracy is strained only by some belated, over-wrought melodrama. By which time you'll believe anything, anyway. PT

Relentless
(William Lustig, 1989, US) Judd Nelson, Robert Loggia, Leo Rossi, Meg Foster, Patrick O'Bryan, Ken Lerner.
93 min.
Nelson, the coolly rebellious type from *The Breakfast Club*, turns psycho in this unimaginative serial-killer number. Abused as a child and turned down for entry to the police force, he becomes the randomly motivated 'Sunset Killer', leaving buddy cop duo Loggia and Rossi to track him down. Straight to video in Britain, but successful enough on homeground to spawn a couple of sequels. TJ

Relic, The
(Peter Hyams, 1996, US) Penelope Ann Miller, Tom Sizemore, Linda Hunt, James Whitmore, Clayton Rohner, Chi Muoi Lo, Thomas Ryan.
110 min.
This surprisingly nasty horror picture fuses elements of the haunted-house, serial-killer and monster-mayhem sub-genres into a hybrid creature that grabs you and won't let go. A gala evening is disrupted and police lieutenant Vincent D'Agosta (Sizemore) clashes with the director of the Chicago natural history museum when a violent murder suggests a psycho killer is loose in the building. Evolutionary scientist Margo Green (Miller) shares the cop's fears, but her investigations suggest that a genetically mutating mythical creature, Kothoga (effects Stan Winston), is about to chew its way through some of the city's wealthiest benefactors. It's not hard to spot who'll be next to suffer the beast's wrath, but it's difficult to resist the relentless bombardment of knee-jerk shocks, genetic gobbledygook, South American mythology and head-ripping gore. NF

Remains of the Day, The (100)
(James Ivory, 1993, US) Anthony Hopkins, Emma Thompson, Peter Vaughan, James Fox, Ben Chaplin, Christopher Reeve.
134 min.
Who else but Merchant Ivory to give the big-screen treatment to Ishiguro's Booker Prize-winning novel about class, fascism and the stiff upper lip? Hopkins plays Mr Stevens the butler, a man so fanatically devoted to selfless service that he carries on pouring the port while his father lies dying, and refuses to question the Nazi sympathies of his titled master (Fox). Yet love steals unawares into even the hardest of hearts, and his stern warnings to female staff cannot protect him from falling slowly for the new housekeeper, Miss Kenton (Thompson). That the film works is down to Hopkins, who plays his face like a lyre – a tic here, an inflected eyebrow there. It's an astonishing performance, but the viewer is still hard-pressed to commit to him emotionally. It's Thompson we really feel for, trying to get some reaction from the man she too comes secretly to love. In these scenes of repartee, where politeness is a weapon and every honorific twists in the gut like a knife, the film finally comes alive. DW

Rembrandt
(Alexander Korda, 1936, GB) Charles Laughton, Elsa Lanchester, Gertrude Lawrence, Edward Chapman, Walter Hudd, Roger Livesey, John Clements, Marius Goring.
85 min. b/w.
Less successful at the time than the earlier *Private Life of Henry VIII*, but a far better film, thanks to a subtle, touching performance from Laughton as the ageing painter coming to terms with both the death of his beloved Saskia (Lanchester) and an increasing hostility to his work. Surprisingly sombre, it lacks a tight plot, but appeals through its vivid characterisation, superb Vincent Korda sets, and Georges Périnal's lovely camerawork. GA

Remember Last Night?
(James Whale, 1935, US) Edward Arnold, Robert Young, Constance Cummings, Sally Eilers, Arthur Treacher, Edward Brophy, Robert Armstrong, Reginald Denny, Gustav von Seyffertitz.
81 min. b/w.

Delightful screwball parody of the detective thriller, where the discovery of a corpse among inert revellers after a wild party triggers a sparkling cascade of gags eventually taking off into surrealist fantasy. Cheerfully annexing ice-cubes from the packs on their hungover heads to mix a hair of the dog, faltering only momentarily as they discover another body sleeping it off ('Steady! They can't all be dead'), the hero and heroine (beautifully played by Young and Cummings) are clearly derived from the Nick and Nora Charles of *The Thin Man*. But Whale's use of elisions, non-sequiturs and unexpected stresses creates what is virtually a blueprint for the style developed by Robert Altman in and after '*M*A*S*H*'. TM

Remember Me?
(Nick Hurran, 1996, GB) Robert Lindsay, Rik Mayall, Imelda Staunton, Brenda Blethyn, James Fleet, Haydn Gwynne.
77 min.
Mired in suburbia and a stale marriage, and engaged in a vicious territorial dispute with her two teenagers, Lorna (Staunton) hates her life. So when old college beau Jamie (Lindsay) shows up on the doorstep, well, it has to be an improvement. He has a Rolls outside, but no petrol and no ready cash. Perhaps Lorna could spare a few bob? She can't, but she will, if Jamie stays for dinner – and never mind her sadsack husband Ian (Mayall), he's just feeling sorry for himself. This is essentially a modest British domestic comedy remoulded as Chekhovian farce. Screenwriter Michael Frayn doesn't let the mechanics overshadow character; the humour here springs from heartfelt hope and despair. Wisely resisting the temptation to caricature, the actors retain straight faces even as their world is invaded by gangsters, rampaging ex-wives and preposterous in-laws. Restrained, sour and stooped, Mayall is all grey defeat; and you can see how Lindsay's blithe charm rekindles something in Staunton's breast. The film's melancholy hysteria couldn't be more British – it is subtle but exact on the unwitting effrontery of the rich, and the sorry, ingrained subservience of the rest. And very funny too. TCh

Remember My Name
(Alan Rudolph, 1978, US) Geraldine Chaplin, Anthony Perkins, Moses Gunn, Berry Berenson, Jeff Goldblum, Timothy Thomerson, Alfre Woodard, Marilyn Coleman.
94 min.
Largely successful update of the noir-inflected melodramas of the '40s, with Chaplin playing the Stanwyck-style role as the vengeful but sympathetic woman who gets out of prison and returns to her former husband (Perkins) to wreak havoc upon his new marriage. What really distinguishes the film are the tremulous, nervy performances, although Rudolph's direction – while occasionally too arty – is imbued with an admirable generosity towards the characters. Also endowed with a fine blues score by (and performed by) Alberta Hunter, and crisp photography from Tak Fujimoto, it's well worth seeing. GA

Remember That Face
see Mob, The

Remember the Day
(Henry King, 1941, US) Claudette Colbert, John Payne, John Shepperd, Ann Todd, Anne Revere, Douglas Croft.
85 min. b/w.
Somewhat reminiscent of a female American *Goodbye, Mr Chips*, this expertly crafted school story has Colbert as the teacher who inspires future presidential candidate Croft during his formative years, but who shatters his youthful crush on her by falling for fellow tutor Payne. It's all told in nostalgic flashback, and controls the ebb and flow of laughter and tears with old-school command. TJ

Remember the Night
(Mitchell Leisen, 1940, US) Barbara Stanwyck, Fred MacMurray, Beulah Bondi, Elizabeth Patterson, Sterling Holloway, Georgia Caine.
94 min. b/w.
Taken from a script by Preston Sturges (his last before he graduated to directing), a winning romantic comedy-drama from the ever-elegant Leisen, who elicits a superb performance from

Stanwyck as the hardboiled shoplifter faced with staying in jail over Christmas, but given bail by prosecuting attorney MacMurray and taken to visit his family for the holiday. Playing superbly on the personae of his leads, Leisen creates a movie of warmth and immense style, which never quite trips over into excessive sentimentality. GA

Remembrance
(Colin Gregg, 1982, GB) David John, Gary Oldman, Martin Barrass, Kenneth Griffith, Ewan Stewart, John Altman, Sally Jane Jackson.
117 min.
An episodic slice-of-life drama (the last 24 hours in port of a group of young naval ratings) cut with muted suspense (a search for the identity of the comatose victim of a disco bouncer's brutality), this Channel 4-commissioned feature occupies an unhappy middle ground between the distinctive approaches of Loach and Hines (*Looks and Smiles*) and Frears and Poliakoff (*Bloody Kids*). Opportunistically and inappropriately lumbered with a 'Falklands factor' promotional emphasis during its cinema release, the film subsequently took a major prize at the Taormina festival – presumably awarded more for good intentions than achievements. PT

Remembrance (Kyoshu)
(Takehiro Nakajima, 1987, Jap) Hiroshi Nishikawa, Sairi Komaki, Masahiro Tsugawa, Takaki Enomoto, Masashi Fujita.
115 min.
This plotless movie, obviously autobiographical in origin, charts a young man's coming-of-age in a small country town in the early 1950s: familiar territory for anyone who has seen films like *Muddy River* and *Warming Up for the Festival* (the latter scripted by Nakajima, here a first-time director at the age of 53). It's thoroughly amiable, and persuasively acted by its young lead Nishikawa, but fatally lacks the underlying toughness and sense of larger perspectives found in an equivalent Chinese movie like *The Time to Live and the Time to Die*. TR

Reminiscences of a Journey to Lithuania
(Jonas Mekas, 1972, US)
82 min.
In 1972, Jonas and Adolfas Mekas returned to visit their family in Lithuania for the first time since they had emigrated to America 27 years earlier. Both brothers made films of the event. Jonas Mekas' version is his most formally ambitious work to date: a film in three dissimilar parts designed to explore the relationship between residence, exile, and the experience of visiting a 'foreign' place. It begins somewhat like a conventional documentary, with material examining the ghettoes of New York in the '50s, where the Mekas immigrants first made their homes, then shifts into a less predictable 'diary' mode for the reunion with the family in Lithuania itself, and then moves on to self-questioning footage shot in Europe on the way back to America. The basic romanticism is patently sincere, but sometimes looks like a defensive pose, which makes it all the more poignant. TR

Remo Williams: The Adventure Begins (aka Remo – Unarmed and Dangerous)
(Guy Hamilton, 1985, US) Fred Ward, Joel Grey, Wilford Brimley, JA Preston, George Coe, Charles Cioffi, Kate Mulgrew, Patrick Kilpatrick, Michael Pataki.
121 min.
Korean martial arts veteran Chiun (Grey under several tons of slap) is assigned to re-educate Makin (Ward), a NYC cop who has been mugged, kidnapped, facelifted and rechristened Remo Williams by a secret government organisation. After learning to dodge bullets and dangle from Ferris wheels, Remo is unleashed to investigate the iffy armament activities of a bigwig industrialist (Cioffi). Based on *The Destroyer* pulp books, this turns out to be a jokey Action Man affair, but although the hero spends much of his time hanging off high places such as the Statue of Liberty, the film itself never gets off the ground. AB

Rempart des Béguines, Le (The Beguines)

(Guy Casaril, 1972, Fr/It) Nicole Courcel, Anicée Alvina, Venantino Venantini, Jean Martin, Ginette Leclerc, Harry-Max, Yvonne Clech.
90 min.

A self-consciously 'artistic' film about lesbianism, so coy that one spends much of the time wondering whether the older woman is 'bohemian' – she wears kimonos and has a taste for black Russian cigarettes – or just a high class tart. The story's about a poor little rich girl, only child of a widowed politician, whose furtive emotions blossom at the hands of his mistress, around which Casaril is content merely to weave pretty pictures. They're such an unsympathetic bunch – cold fish of a father (Martin), the mistress (Courcel) overbearing and tetchy, and the daughter (Alvina) spoilt – that with Casaril prepared to take them at face value, it's difficult not to lose interest fast and resign oneself to yet another sex movie. CPe

Remparts d'Argile

see Ramparts of Clay

Renaissance Man

(Penny Marshall, 1994, US) Danny DeVito, Gregory Hines, Cliff Robertson, James Remar, Lillo Brancato Jr, Stacey Dash, Kadeem Hardison, Richard T Jones, Khalil Kain.
128 min.

Unemployed ad exec Bill Rago (DeVito) lands a civilian posting at a US Army base. He's to teach basic comprehension to eight 'squeakers' – the slowest new recruits. Armed only with an intuitively unmilitary intelligence and a well-thumbed copy of *Hamlet*, he does just that. Penny Marshall's film couldn't be more sincere. But don't let the poster fool you: this is no comedy, it's a two-hour-plus English lesson. Very much a product of the Clinton era, the movie has serious political intentions. It's an exhortation to America to face up to her social and spiritual malaise with a sense of responsibility, discipline and humanity. Too bad the director's such a lousy propagandist. In essence, a painfully earnest sit-com. TCh

Renaldo & Clara

(Bob Dylan, 1977, US) Bob Dylan, Sara Dylan, Joan Baez, Ronnie Hawkins, Ronee Blakley, Jack Elliott, Harry Dean Stanton, Bob Neuwirth, Mel Howard, Allen Ginsberg, Helena Kallianiotes, Joni Mitchell, Sam Shepart, Arlo Guthrie.
235 min.

Dylan's endlessly long attempt at a personal feature intercuts excellent concert footage from the Rolling Thunder tour with some pretentious but quite enjoyable play-acting from his retinue (Baez, wife Sarah, Allen Ginsberg) which capitalises on the rumours and mysteries surrounding Dylan's love life. Not nearly as bad as its vitriolic US reception suggested, but if you don't like Dylan you won't be converted. DP

Rendez-vous à Bray (Rendezvous at Bray)

(André Delvaux, 1971, Fr/Bel/WGer) Anna Karina, Bulle Ogier, Mathieu Carrière, Roger Van Hool, Martine Sarcey, Pierre Vernier.
93 min.

On the surface, Delvaux's excursions into the ambiguous territory lying between fact and fantasy, past and present, may appear similar to the dry and difficult puzzles offered in the films of Resnais. But the Belgian seems a much warmer director, concerned with the emotional impulses behind dreams, combining dread and desire in both images and narrative. The result is a genuinely beautiful surrealism exploring the pains and joys of the human mind. Here the setting is a lonely country house during the First World War. Summoned to a rendezvous there by the owner, a friend serving at the front in the air-force, a young pianist (Carrière) arrives to find the friend mysteriously absent and no explanation forthcoming from the enigmatically beautiful housekeeper (Karina). Fearing his friend dead, he relives their relationship, stimulated by erotic yearnings that span past (the friend's girl, Ogier) and present (the housekeeper), conjuring ghostly shadows of guilt...GA

Rendez-vous d'Anna, Les (The Meetings of Anna)

(Chantal Akerman, 1978, Fr/Bel/WGer) Aurore Clément, Helmut Griem, Magali Noël, Lea Massari, Hanns Zischler, Jean-Pierre Cassel.
127 min.

A quietly moving odyssey: an itinerary of train journeys, hotel rooms, and chance meetings that relates the past to a present lack of confidence among Europeans. A series of train rides, a series of tales. Only once do film and central character overcome their emotional reticence: when Anna (hitherto a passive listener), in a scene both surprising and logical, lies in bed with her mother and 'confesses' her love for another woman. A chaste refusal to supply easy answers means that the film is primarily descriptive; what emerges most strongly is a moving eroticism stemming from the everyday. HM

Rendez-vous de Paris, Les (Rendez-vous in Paris)

(Eric Rohmer, 1995, Fr) Clara Bellar, Antoine Basler, Mathias Megard, Judith Chancel, Malcolm Conrath, Cécile Pares.
98 min.

Three short stories chart the effects of chance encounters of the amorous kind in contemporary Paris. In the first, a student, doubtful of her lover's fidelity, is chatted up in a market by a youth who may or may not be a thief; in the second, a teacher's attempts to seduce a woman already in a long-term relationship are both stimulated and frustrated by her feelings about the public places in which they are forced to meet; in the third, an artist playing host to a Swedish visitor decides to ignore her in favour of a woman he follows through the streets to the Picasso Museum. Slight tales, perhaps, but Rohmer turns a seemingly inconsequential confection into yet another of his subtle studies of modern love. What gives this particular piece a lift is that Rohmer shot it so casually, on 16mm and a minimal budget, so it's something of a return to the ideals of the Nouvelle Vague; and that it's very much a love-letter to Paris. The acute feeling for milieu is not decorative but crucial, in that the relationships we see are profoundly affected by the mood, population and topography of the places in which they develop. Witty, touching, perceptive, this is a film that belies Rohmer's 70-odd years. GA

Renegades

(Jack Sholder, 1989, US) Kiefer Sutherland, Lou Diamond Phillips, Clark Johnson, Peter MacNeill, John Di Benedetto, Joe Griffin, Floyd Westerman, Jami Gertz, Rob Knepper, Bill Smitrovich.
106 min.

Young guns Sutherland and Phillips team up again, this time as a renegade cop and a Lakota Indian thrown together by tangentially related crimes. Working undercover to expose a bent cop, Sutherland participates in a heist that goes wrong; the fleeing gang members duck into a museum, where they kill Phillips' brother and make off with a priceless Lakota spear. Subsequently left for dead, Sutherland is saved by Phillips, and the two embark on a joint quest, suppressing their mutual hostility as they pursue the murderers down Philadelphia's mean-ish streets. Sholder's robust staging of the car chases, punch-ups and shootouts recalls the kinetic energy of his earlier *The Hidden*. His handling of the quieter familial and buddy-buddy realtionships, on the other hand, is hopelessly leaden, serving only to stop the action-packed narrative in its tracks. The sadly under-used Jami Gertz turns up briefly as a beauty parlour bimbo with 'disposable love interest' written all over her. NF

Rentadick

(Jim Clark, 1972, GB) James Booth, Richard Briers, Julie Ege, Ronald Fraser, Donald Sinden, Tsai Chin, Kenneth Cope, John Wells, Richard Beckinsale, Michael Bentine, Spike Milligan.
94 min.

Written by John Cleese and Graham Chapman, with help from satire-generation veterans John Wells and John Fortune, and produced by Ned Sherrin, this ought to be a cut above the level suggested by the 'oo-er missus' title and the presence of a character called Madame Greenfly. It isn't quite, but a fairly scattershot approach to its

spoof spy formula – inept 'tec Booth caught up in a nerve gas scam – at least keeps it moving briskly. A touch of exotic strangeness comes from the likes of Sinden, Bentine, Milligan, and that tackiest of early '70s sex symbols, Julie Ege. But the film's single weirdest asset has to be the theme song by Dave Dee and the Kings Singers. JRo

Repentance (Monanieba)

(Tengiz Abuladze, 1984, USSR) Avtandil Makharadze, Iya Ninidze, Merab Ninidze, Zeynab Botsvadze, Ketevan Abuladze.
150 min.

A Soviet movie about the traumas of the Stalinist years: the tyranny, the betrayals, the persecutions, and the unexplained disappearances, mounted by Georgian director Abuladze as a weird phantasmagoria of dreams and nightmares, absurdist drama and black comedy. He starts from the ceremonial burial of a town mayor, and the subsequent repeated disinterment of the corpse by the daughter of two of the late tyrant's victims. Flashbacks show his rise to power and growing megalomania. Varlam the mayor was a paranoid secret policeman, a brutal bully-boy. The character is not just an amalgam of Stalin and Beria, but a compendium of every conceivable fascistic trait; and Abuladze tries to underline this desperately literal 'universality' by setting him in a context outside history and culture, where knights in armour stand alongside black-shirted thugs and Boney M vies with Debussy on the soundtrack. The result is neither as minatory nor as moving as it thinks it is, despite some arresting surreal images and the performance of Makharadze as Varlam. TR

Replacement Killers, The

(Antoine Fuqua, 1998, US) Chow Yun-Fat, Mira Sorvino, Michael Rooker, Jürgen Prochnow, Carlos Gomez, Frank Medrano, Kenneth Tsang.
87 min.

With his looks, easy charm and devastating close combat skills, Chow Yun-Fat became one of the world's coolest stars, despite never having made an American movie. He was iconic in John Woo's *The Killer* and *Hard-Boiled*; and perhaps inevitably, the US majors signed him up in the wake of Woo's Hollywood success. Several English lessons later, with Woo as watchful exec producer, Chow gets his big break, but, regrettably, it's a lifeless copy of his HK pictures. In a virtual rerun of *The Killer*, he plays a hitman, whose debt to the Chinese mob will be paid off if he carries out one last job on detective Rooker. Lining up his sights, he finds himself unable to eliminate his target in front of the man's small son, and soon the mob are out to replace him with someone who can. The formula is so wearisome, the viewer has plenty of time to muse on the incidentals: Chow's uncanny facility for returning fire in mid-dive; Mira Sorvino's no nonsense re-invention of the clichéd squealing bimbo role; director Antoine Fuqua's striking repertory of sinuous camera moves. Next time maybe they'll trust the star with more than three words of dialogue at a time. TJ

Repo Man

(Alex Cox, 1984, US) Harry Dean Stanton, Emilio Estevez, Tracey Walter, Olivia Barash, Sy Richardson, Susan Barnes, Fox Harris, Tom Finnegan, Vonetta McGee.
92 min.

When LA punk Otto (Estevez) loses both girl and job, he's hardly prepared for an adventure of mind-blowing proportions when he's conned into helping out a repo man (Stanton). Not only does he find himself in mortal danger while repossessing cars from irate owners, he also gets caught up in a manic world populated by knitting cops, CIA clones, lobotomised nuclear scientists, drippy hippies, UFO freaks, and the roguish Rodriguez Brothers, all in search of a '64 Chevy carrying a lethal cargo. Cox's weird and wonderful first feature defies description, with a plot and characters at once grounded in the seedy reality of Reagan's America and effortlessly enhanced by flights of pure, imaginative fantasy. What distinguishes the movie is its offbeat, semi-satirical sense of humour, seamlessly woven into its wacky thriller plot. But there are endless things to enjoy, from Robby Müller's crisp camerawork to a superb set of performances, from witty movie parodies to a tremendous punk soundtrack. GA

r

Report to the Commissioner (aka Operation Undercover)

(Milton Katselas, 1974, US) Michael Moriarty, Yaphet Kotto, Susan Blakely, Hector Elizondo, Tony King, Michael McGuire, Dana Elcar, William Devane, Richard Gere.
112 min.
'It's happened – they've sent us a hippy' Yaphet Kotto cries on sighting his latest recruit, the zombie-like Bo (Moriarty) framed in the precinct doorway. And one's heart goes out to him, for nothing is quite as stodgy (even obnoxious) as a slice of basic Hollywood action that tries to persuade us of its social concern. Cursed with a weighty script by Abby (*Judgement at Nuremberg*) Mann and Ernest Tidyman based on James Mills' novel, the film makes very heavy weather indeed of its inane tale about a hippy-liberal who joins the (undercover) force. Katselas injects what sentimentality he can into the patently contrived affair. VG

Repossessed

(Bob Logan, 1990, US) Linda Blair, Ned Beatty, Leslie Nielsen, Susan Blakely, Anthony Starke, Thom J Sharp, Lana Schwab, Robert Fuller.
84 min.
Suburban housewife Nancy Aglet's childhood ordeal of demonic possession is becoming a recurring nightmare. Beset by demons emerging from her TV set, Nancy (Blair) starts spewing green vomit over her children, writhing on vibrating beds, and threatening the neighbourhood priest in a gruff voice. The kids suspect PMT, but Nancy knows better, as does retired exorcist Father Mayii (Nielsen). Originally conceived as a spoof of *The Exorcist*, this was extensively re-edited when test screenings showed that 15-year-olds simply didn't understand the references. Afraid of losing the teen market, writer/director Logan excised the subtler humour and pasted in a batch of unrelated and (supposedly) crowd-pleasing bawdy gags, notably a lengthy gym sequence wherein Father Mayii gets fit to fight the devil, allowing Nielsen to wander into women's showers, gaze at women pumping up their bosoms, play with brassières, etc. The result may be worth a few cheap pubescent laughs, but *Exorcist* fans will doubtless feel cheated. MK

Reptile, The

(John Gilling, 1966, GB) Noel Willman, Jennifer Daniel, Ray Barrett, Jacqueline Pearce, Michael Ripper, John Laurie, Marne Maitland.
91 min.
Down in remoter Cornwall, courtesy of Hammer horror, a doctor is busily experimenting and villagers are foaming at the mouth, turning black, and dying of snake venom. Made back-to-back with 'Plague of the Zombies' and shot on the same sets, it's slower and moodier than its companion-piece but strikingly Conan Doyleish in its stately costume horrors. Jacqueline Pearce is terrific as the unfortunate cobra-girl, victim of her father's pursuit of forbidden knowledge. TM

Repubblica Nostra (Our Republic)

(Daniele Incalcaterra, 1995, It)
78 min.
A skilfully edited documentary with minimum of directorial intervention about the 'charismatic' media tycoon Silvio Berlusconi, his foundation of Forza Italia (which swept to power in February 1994), his rise to become Italy's prime minister, and his fall from power. The film cross-cuts, primarily, between two political candidates, one from the broad left Progressive Alliance, the other a Berlusconi employee (a director of the Diakron polling company); the 'clean hands' investigating magistrates Davigo and Di Pietro; and various media representatives. For those who like to draw their own conclusions. WH

Republic of Sin

see Fièvre Monte à El Pao, La

Repulsion

(Roman Polanski, 1965, GB) Catherine Deneuve, Yvonne Furneaux, John Fraser, Ian Hendry, Patrick Wymark, Valerie Taylor, Helen Fraser, Renee Houston, James Villiers.
104 min. b/w.
Still perhaps Polanski's most perfectly realised film, a stunning portrait of the disintegration, mental and emotional, of a shy young Belgian girl

(Deneuve) living in London. When she's left alone by her sister in their Kensington flat, she becomes reclusive and retreats into a terrifying world of fantasies and nightmares which find murderous physical expression when she is visited by a would-be boyfriend (Fraser) and her leering landlord (Wymark). Polanski employs a host of wonderfully integrated visual and aural effects to suggest the inner torment Deneuve suffers: cracks in pavements, hands groping from walls, shadows under doors, rotting skinned rabbits, and – as in *Rosemary's Baby* – the eerie, ever-present sound of someone practising scales on a piano. And despite the fact that the girl's manically destructive actions derive from a terror of sexual contact, Polanski never turns his film into a misogynist binge: the men she meets are far from sympathetically portrayed, and we are led to understand her fear and revulsion by the surreal expressionism used to portray her mental state. All in all, one of the most intelligent horror movies ever made, and certainly one of the most frighteningly effective. GA

Requiem for a Vampire

see Requiem pour un Vampire

Requiem for a Village

(David Gladwell, 1975, GB) Vic Smith, the villagers of Witnesham and Metfield, Suffolk.
68 min.
Here the dead quite literally arise, and an old man follows them into church where, his youth regained, he relives his wedding in a sleepy Suffolk village, now under siege from ice-cream vans, motorcycles and excavators. The film proceeds, within the framework of the old man's working day, slowly and with scrupulous detail, to build a picture of the village as it was in his youth. What separates the movie, however, from a mere wistful lament for happier times, is the way in which its parts cohere around the central conceit that, through memory, the past and present merge to form a bond which proves stronger than death itself. JPy

Requiem for Dominic

(Robert Dornhelm, 1990, Aus) Felix Mitterer, Viktoria Schubert, August Schmölzer, Angelica Schütz.
91 min.
Not since *Circle of Deceit* – perhaps even *Battle of Algiers* – have the deadly chaos and white-knuckled fear of political turmoil been as convincingly conveyed as in this docu-thriller about the lies, violence and anger of the 1989 Romanian revolution. Shot on location in Timisoara just months after Ceausescu's demise, it interweaves newsreel and video footage with fictional material inspired by the fate of Dornhelm's childhood friend Dominic Paraschiv, with a fictional Paul Weiss (Mitterer) standing in for Dornhelm as an exile returning to seek out the truth behind Paraschiv's arrest and imprisonment as a Securitate terrorist allegedly guilty of murdering 80 factory workers. Despite its autobiographical aspects, the factually-based investigative plot serves primarily not to clear the late Paraschiv's name, but to demonstrate how the paranoia and bloodlust born of such a repressive regime merely serve to produce further fear and mindless brutality: humane ideals are in short supply, and anyone who threatens to expose the deceptions of an already unstable system finds his life in peril. Dornhelm films with a gut-wrenching immediacy, but never sinks to simplistic agit-prop. GA

Requiem pour un Vampire (Requiem for a Vampire/ Virgins and Vampires)

(Jean Rollin, 1971, Fr/Ger) Marie-Pierre Castel, Mireille D'Argent, Philippe Gasté, Dominique, Louise Dhour.
95 min.
Although rarely seen, this faintly surreal sex-vampire movie achieved a minor cult reputation thanks to its blend of vampirism and sado-eroticism. With almost all of the latter removed at the censor's behest (cut running time, 78 minutes), what remains is a mildly distracting tale of two fugitive teenagers who stumble upon a castle inhabited by an aged vampire and his cohorts. Attempts to initiate the girls conveniently entail the loss of their virginity, but when one fails to follow through and the other refuses to reveal the whereabouts of her handsome seducer, their captors threaten cruel reprisals. Much sought in its original form. NF

Rescuers, The

(Wolfgang Reitherman/John Lounsbery/Art Stevens, 1977, US) voices: Bob Newhart, Eva Gabor, Geraldine Page, Joe Flynn, Jeanette Nolan, John McIntire.
77 min.
Two members of the all-mouse Rescue Aid Society go to the help of an orphan girl being held captive by the horribly evil Medusa in her riverboat home at the Devil's Bayou. But the people who need rescuing are the Disney animators and storymen, who seem uncertain whether to keep up the old studio traditions of cute characters and plush settings, or to branch out into contemporary urban satire. *The Rescuers* dabbles in both styles, most unsatisfyingly, and the handful of sappy songs don't improve things. There is one lovely character, though – Orville the albatross, who runs an airline service armed with goggles, scarf, and a sardine tin for his passengers to sit in. GB

Rescuers Down Under, The

(Hendel Butoy/Mike Gabriel, 1990, US) voices: Bob Newhart, Eva Gabor, John Candy, Tristan Rogers, Adam Ryan, George C Scott, Peter Firth.
77 min.
Thirteen years after the Mouse Rescue Aid Society packed off Bernard and Bianca on their first mission, they're back. A young boy has been kidnapped, deep in the Australian outback: an evil poacher is holding him until he reveals the whereabouts of a rare eagle's nest, so this is a double quest – to save the child and the eagle eggs. It's surprising that *The Rescuers* should be the first Disney animated feature to merit a sequel. Inoffensive as they are, humble Bernard and the aristocratic Bianca are not the studio's most memorable creations; and for all the quaintly old-fashioned romance and desperately broad comedy, this is nothing if not an adventure film (clearly testifying to the influence of Spielberg). As for the animation, computer technology invests contemporary features with sometimes breathtaking dynamism, but outback flora being what it is, this isn't the most colourful Disney movie. TCh

Reservoir Dogs ⑩⑩

(Quentin Tarantino, 1991, US) Harvey Keitel, Tim Roth, Michael Madsen, Chris Penn, Steve Buscemi, Lawrence Tierney, Randy Brooks, Kirk Baltz, Eddie Bunker, Quentin Tarantino.
99 min.
Tarantino's powerful homage/reworking of the heist-gone-wrong thriller – stealing ideas from Kubrick's *The Killing* and Scorsese's *Mean Streets*, among others – is probably the final word (or frame) on the subject. A bunch of colour-coded crooks (Mr White, Mr Pink, etc), previously unknown to each other, chosen and named by ageing *capo* Joe Cabot (Tierney) and his son Nice Guy Eddie (Penn), execute a jewellery robbery. The job done, the getaway fucked up, they reassemble at a warehouse to get what's coming to them. Tarantino engineers their demise from the interaction of their character flaws – there is certainly no honour among these talkative thieves – with the inexorable logic of a chess grandmaster. Despite the clockwork theatrical dynamics – most of the action is restricted to the warehouse – the film packs a massive punch. It's violent, intelligent, well written (by Tarantino) and acted (Buscemi, Roth and Penn take the prizes). A *tour de force*. WH

Respectable Prostitute, The

see P..... Respectueuse, La

Respectful Prostitute, The

see P..... Respectueuse, La

Restless Breed, The

(Allan Dwan, 1957, US) Scott Brady, Anne Bancroft, Jay C Flippen, Rhys Williams, Jim Davis, Scott Marlowe, Evelyn Rudie.
81 min.
Dwan made his first picture in 1911, invented the dolly shot around 1915, and was still working in his seventies on a series of low-budget Westerns, much admired by connoisseurs like Martin Scorsese for their supreme economy of form, the gesture of a true master. In this instance, money was obviously tight, but Dwan's craftsmanship is well in evidence in the simplest of revenge stories, with Brady as the lawyer out to get his

father's killer, Davis the villainous gun-runner, and a youthful Bancroft as the half-breed Indian who proves her mettle along the way. Roundly satisfying. TJ

Restless Natives
(Michael Hoffman, 1985, GB) Vincent Friell, Joe Mullaney, Teri Lally, Ned Beatty, Robert Urquhart, Bernard Hill, Rachel Boyd, Mel Smith, Bryan Forbes.
89 min.
Truly dire attempt to reproduce the whimsical charm of Bill Forsyth, in which two Edinburgh teenagers tackle the problem of unemployment by turning to highway robbery, relieving coachloads of tourists of cash and jewellery as they buzz around the Highlands on a moped, disguised in joke-shop masks and armed with toy guns loaded with sneezing powder. Dreadfully unfunny, it soon becomes embarrassing as fantasy takes over, and the pair are lauded as modern-day Rob Roys, legends in their own lifetime. Syrupy, silly, and not a mite objectionable in its closet patriotism. GA

Restoration
(Michael Hoffman, 1996, US) Robert Downey Jr, Sam Neill, Polly Walker, David Thewlis, Meg Ryan, Ian McKellen, Hugh Grant.
118 min.
This adaptation (by Rupert Walters) of Rose Tremain's brilliant Booker-shortlisted novel is a lot better than rumours about its frantic, lengthy post-production might have suggested. Downey is Robert Merivel, a rakish physician invited to the court of Charles II and favoured for curing one of the king's spaniels. He's a callow, hedonistic young man torn between the rigours of knowledge, the wealth of preferment, and the sexual intemperance of an age quickly forgetting the puritanism of the Cromwells. He weds one of the king's best mistresses in a lavish court ceremony, but is deflated to find Charles ready to take his place in the marriage bed. Out of favour and tricked by court painter Finn (Grant), Merivel journeys through 1660s England, taking refuge in a Quaker community that includes his sickly friend Pearce (Thewlis) and mad, Irish Katharine (Ryan). Ryan, with legs waxed and lipstick in place, is a striking example of how the film goes astray as soon as it plays the star casting game; but at least the doomed Katharine and the survivor Merivel have their baby, the major stepping stone on the physican's path to maturity and virtue. Engaging if uneven. SGr

Resurrected
(Paul Greengrass, 1989, GB) David Thewlis, Tom Bell, Rita Tushingham, Michael Pollitt, Rudi Davies, William Hoyland, Ewan Stewart, Christopher Fulford, David Lonsdale.
92 min.
Combining a Falklands story with the broader theme of institutionalised bullying within the armed forces, this provocative and punchy drama attacks both issues with fierce intelligence. The basis is the true story of a young British soldier who went missing during battle, was presumed dead, and accorded a memorial service with full military honours. Some weeks later, Private Deakin (Thewlis) turned up alive. The name has been changed, but fiction takes over properly when Deakin, an awkward embarrassment for his Lancashire village community, returns to barracks. Their hatred fuelled by tabloid stories of Deakin's alleged desertion, two fellow soldiers (Fulford, Lonsdale) organise a kangaroo court martial. Although Greengrass' direction is a shade televisual, Martin Allen's tough, polemical screenplay confronts the core issues without losing sight of the characters' individual psychology. Most tellingly, Allen demonstrates that the soldiers' systematic brutalisation of Deakin is provoked partly by their own insecurity, their realisation that the dividing line between heroism and desertion is wafer thin. Thewlis is superb as the confused Deakin, with excellent support from Bell (his father) and Fulford. NF

Resurrection
(Daniel Petrie, 1980, US) Ellen Burstyn, Sam Shepard, Richard Farnsworth, Roberts Blossom, Clifford David, Pamela Payton-Wright, Eve LeGallienne, Lois Smith.
103 min.

Despite strong performances, particularly from Burstyn and Shepard, a rather embarrassing look at the subject of faith-healing, with Burstyn finding she has the power after she survives a car crash which kills her husband. Problems develop with her Bible-thumping parents (she insists it's love, not God, that helps her heal), and with Shepard, a beneficiary of her gift who treats her with erratic, tormented reverence after romance develops between them. The film is let down by Petrie's bland, prettified direction, and by a script from Lewis John Carlino which is forever going on hippy-style about the Power of Love. GA

Resurrection Man
(Marc Evans, 1997, GB) Stuart Townsend, Geraldine O'Rawe, James Nesbitt, John Hannah, Brenda Fricker, James Ellis, Sean McGinley.
102 min.
Notwithstanding a sterling central performance from the up-and-coming Townsend, this account of the deeds of the Shankhill Butchers (adapted by Eoin McNamee from his book) leaves a pretty nasty taste in the mouth. The problem lies in the film-makers' seeming inability to decide whether it's a political work, a genre thriller, or a study of violent psychopaths (in which case it doesn't tell us much about them). Regardless of the fact that the killers' contribution to the Belfast Troubles of the '70s was not politically motivated (though their capacity for carnage was used by the terrorists), and despite director Marc Evans' insistence that this is a fiction, the makers seem to want to have their cake and eat it, leaving the movie open to charges of sensationalist exploitation. Polished but dodgy. GA

Resurrection of Zachary Wheeler, The
(Bob Wynn, 1971, US) Leslie Nielsen, Bradford Dillman, James Daly, Angie Dickinson, Robert J Wilke, Jack Carter.
100 min.
Yesterday's sci-fi meets today's 'heart-snatchers' headlines in this pre-Coma medical thriller. As dogged reporter Nielsen searches for the senator he's seen whisked away from hospital after a near-fatal car crash, the politician himself (Dillman) wakes in a New Mexico clinic with a whole new set of internal organs, plundered from clone-like captive 'somas', bred specifically as transplant donors. This low-budget curio (itself seamlessly transferred from video to film) treads an engaging path through the genre clichés and asks most of the right questions about the selective application of medical high-tech, without ever quite sparking. But if it ends with an evasive whimper, at least it's a politically outrageous one. PT

Retour d'Afrique, Le (Return from Africa)
(Alain Tanner, 1973, Switz/Fr) Josée Destoop, François Marthouret, Juliet Berto, Anne Wiazemsky, André Schmidt.
109 min. b/w.
Stifled by the alienating dead weight of Genevan conventions, a young Swiss couple hatch heady plans to move to Africa and 'work for the Third World'. A last-minute hitch, however, leaves them stuck in their own stripped flat, to come to terms with their own world. Their articulate self-awareness precludes the sort of instinctive, freewheeling revolt of Tanner's La Salamandre, but never leads them into the mere cypher roles of Godard's analogous couple in Le Gai Savoir. Instead, they explore a claustrophobic environment of ideas which is the landscape of Messidor in miniature, and emerge with an optimistic vision of personal politics of the sort worked through later in Jonah Who Will Be 25 in the Year 2000. Surprisingly warm didacticism. PT

Retour de Martin Guerre, Le (The Return of Martin Guerre)
(Daniel Vigne, 1982, Fr) Gérard Depardieu, Nathalie Baye, Stéphane Peau, Sylvie Méda, Bernard-Pierre Donnadieu, Maurice Barrier, Isabelle Sadoyan, Roger Planchon, Maurice Jacquemont.
123 min.
Rural France, 1542: after several years of unhap-

piness in his village, a young man suddenly disappears, leaving his wife and farm. Nine years later he returns from the war, a changed man; his story is convincing, his wife accepts him wholeheartedly, and his farm prospers. But doubts about his true identity are sown. The storyline is a legend which the French hold dear, and even inspired Montaigne to write an essay on its curiosity. For quite aside from the obvious interest over a possible impostor in the wrong bed, the story strikes deep at a philosophic knot: what constitutes human identity, or soul? And is a woman's love necessarily exclusive? Unfortunately the film lets the questions go hang, in favour of some admittedly successful courtroom drama, in which Depardieu reprises his role from Danton, where he has to talk as if his life depended on it (which it does). The decor is dripping with research from some university's medieval department: mud-caked codpieces and pigs rooting among the worzels, all filmed in glorious Squalorama. But there are enough courtroom reversals to keep Perry Mason fans more than happy. CPea

Retreat, Hell!
(Joseph H Lewis, 1952, US) Frank Lovejoy, Richard Carlson, Russ Tamblyn, Anita Louise, Ned Young, Lamont Johnson.
95 min. b/w.
A curious Korean War propaganda assignment, perversely hymning the American art of attacking in the wrong direction. Lewis can't (for once) do a great deal with the well-worn yarn of an army unit being blooded and battling forth-and-back to rearguard heroism. But beyond his characteristically telling handling of violence, several incidentals push up the interest quotient: the most capable soldier is played by McCarthy blacklist victim Ned Young, while Lamont Johnson, later a director of note, is also in the cast. PT

Retribution
(Guy Magar, 1987, US) Dennis Lipscomb, Leslie Wing, Suzanne Snyder, Jeff Pomerantz, George Murdock, Pamela Dunlap.
109 min.
Though often scary, this patchy horror pic is handicapped by embarrassment about its tawdry terror tactics, its hyperventilated hysteria all too often tempered by an undue attention to redundant 'human interest' stuff. Tortured artist (Lipscomb) takes a dive from a high window, but his suicidal impulses are frustrated when his body is possessed at the moment of death by the vengeful spirit of a murdered gambler, and he is transformed into a telekinetic maniac hunting down the culprits (and subjecting them to grisly deaths). Tart-with-a-heart (Snyder) tries to console him with soppy romantic love, while psychiatrist (Wing) wrestles with his schizophrenia. Hampered by some hideous dialogue, it's about 20 tedious minutes too long, though Magar's stylish handling of the telekinetic mayhem just manages to sustain one's wavering interest. NF

Retroactive
(Louis Morneau, 1997, US) Shannon Whirry, Jesse Borrego, Jim Belushi, Kylie Travis, Frank Whaley, M Emmet Walsh.
90 min.
Returning to Texas after a botched hostage crisis, police psychologist Travis crashes her car in the middle of nowhere. Accepting a lift from redneck Belushi and his girl Whirry, she little suspects he's a petty criminal with a murderous temper. When the ride turns into a nightmare, with corpses scattered across the desert, Travis takes refuge in a government lab where lone boffin Whaley is experimenting in time reversal. Trouble is, when Travis travels back to forestall the havoc wreaked by Belushi, the situation deteriorates. With its explosive action, black comedy and far-fetched sci-fi imposed on an otherwise vaguely plausible crime thriller, this modest indie film is reminiscent of such low budget '80s exploiters as Tremors and the work of Charles Band. Like the most memorable of these, it's lifted out of the rut by a quirky, imaginative script. True, Belushi's performance is overbearing and M Emmet Walsh turns in yet another sweaty cameo; true, too, that the frequent visual emphasis on Travis' cleavage flags the movie's compromised ambitions. Nevertheless, there's more than enough energy, bravado and invention to engage the attention throughout. GA

Return, The

(Phil Mulloy, 1988, GB) Tony Guilfoyle,
Oengus Macnamara, Lesley Nightingale.
85 min.
First feature in ages (since *Give Us This Day* in
1982, in fact) from one of Britain's most talented
independent film-makers: a powerful, claustrophobic drama that uncovers Oedipal passions in
the mind of a desperate Irishman facing eviction
from his docklands slum. Literate writing and
magnificent performances wring maximum intensity from a plot sprung on flashbacks and fantasies. It sounds like the usual social-realist guff,
but it plays more like a Borges conundrum. TR

Return, The (Tro' Vé)

(Dang Nhât Minh, 1994, Vietnam) Nguyên Thu
Hiên, Tran Luc, Manh Cuong, Duong Viêt Bát,
Minh Tiêp.
110 min.
Using the idiom of melodrama but not the clichés,
Dang explores the regrets and contradictions provoked by the new materialism which has swept
Vietnam with the government's economic
reforms. As a schoolteacher, Loan lost the man
she loved; already married, he left on an illegal
boat to seek his fortune overseas. Three years
later she's unhappily married to a go-getting nouveau riche businessman when her first love
comes back. Vastly more accomplished than
most Vietnamese films, this is original and sincerely felt. And its ending is a real surprise. TR

Return Engagement

(Alan Rudolph, 1983, US) Dr Timothy Leary, G
Gordon Liddy, Carol Hemingway.
89 min.
'You sound like an old married couple' a journalist tells acid guru Timothy Leary and Watergate
master-plumber G Gordon Liddy, as they squabble drunkenly over supper between engagements.
Leary? Liddy? Engagements? America really is
a wonderful country: two of the wildest cards in
its pack became the highest-paid act on the college lecture circuit, debating each other. Liddy is
the straight man – patriotism, loyalty, law &
order, guns and the flag; Leary is the soft-shoe-
shuffling joker – youth, consciousness expansion,
evolution, the individual. *Return Engagement* –
Liddy arrested Leary 16 years before – follows
them on the road, on and off stage, with their
wives, Liddy with a Hell's Angels chapter, Leary
lecturing alfresco at Esalen. By the end it's hard
to decide which is flakier than the other, though
some of the debate audiences are weirder than
either. A fascinating portrait of seeming opposites locked together by mutual self-interest, and
in some twisted way, by history. JCo

Return from Africa

see Retour d'Afrique, Le

Return from the River Kwai

(Andrew V McLaglen,1988,GB) Edward Fox,
Denholm Elliott, Christopher Penn, Tatsuya
Nakadai, George Takei, Nick Tate, Timothy
Bottoms, Michael Dante, Richard Graham
101 min.
This definitive 'non-fictional' account of the rescue of Allied troops from a Japanese PoW camp
features an unspectacular line-up of actors whose
sole point of reference is the implicit understanding that they've all had better parts. Leading our
heroes is well-known American fighter pilot
Christopher Penn, followed hotly by Edward Fox,
commander of the Brit contingent of the prisoners, the Australian Commander Nick Tate, and
Colonel Denholm Elliot, who makes a virtue of
playing the fall guy in life's rich tapestry of war
films. Pitted against these awesome odds are evil
Lieutenant Tanaka (played with traditional sadistic relish by George Takei) whose plan is to ship
the PoWs to various Japanese car factories, and a
thinly disguised Hirohito-style Major Harada
(Nakadai). A tacky lager lout view of war. JCh

Return from Witch Mountain

(John Hough, 1978, US) Kim Richards, Ike
Eisenmann, Bette Davis, Christopher Lee, Jack
Soo, Denver Pyle.
93 min.
With its early scenes set in LA's urban wasteland
and superior music from Lalo Schifrin, Disney's
belated sequel to *Escape to Witch Mountain*
seems promising for a while. But it rapidly gets

stuck in the same groove as the original: the two
kids with supernatural powers fall prey to Lee's
villainous scientist, and constantly display their
gift for 'molecular mobilisation', levitating
(among many other things) wine casks, museum
exhibits, gold bars, trash cans, security guards,
and the Board of Education's bus for rounding
up truants. There's also a helpful goat called
Alfred, and it's a moot point who does the most
bleating – the goat or Bette Davis as Lee's sidekick. OK family fun, at a pinch. GB

Return of a Man Called Horse, The

(Irvin Kershner, 1976, US) Richard Harris, Gale
Sondergaard, Geoffrey Lewis, Bill Lucking,
Jorge Luke, Claudio Brook, Enrique Lucero,
Jorge Russek.
129 min.
Surprisingly, this sequel eclipses *A Man Called
Horse* in every way. The action resumes six years
on, with Lord John Morgan (Harris, as ardently
inscrutable as ever) chafing against a lame aristocracy in England. He returns to Dakota and his
Yellow Hand Indians, only to find them routed
from their sacred burial grounds by unscrupulous
trappers and living, physically and spiritually
blighted, in the badlands. By painfully rediscovering his own sense of identity, he helps bring
about the rebirth of the tribe. The sumptuous locations and seasonal variations skilfully complement
this meticulous recreation of the early 19th century Indian lifestyle. Interestingly, the emotional
peak comes half way through with the harrowing
Sun Vow ritual, which culminates in a cathartic
thunderstorm of epic proportions. Thereafter the
film shifts into a lower but still effective key. IB

Return of Captain Invincible, The

(Philippe Mora, 1982, Aust) Alan Arkin,
Christopher Lee, Kate Fitzpatrick, Bill Hunter,
Michael Pate, David Argue, John Bluthal,
Chelsea Brown, Arthur Dignam, Chris
Haywood.
91 min.
Is it a billabong? A dingo? A dead kangaroo? No,
just a drink-sodden superhero who in the '50s was
accused by the UnAmerican Activities investigators of flying without a pilot's licence and wearing tights in public. Now he's washed up down
under, and it takes a threat the magnitude of
Operation Ivory, a plan by the evil Mr Midnight
to rid New York of its entire immigrant population, before the President thinks to call for *The
Return of Captain Invincible*. Packed with unexpected musical numbers by *Rocky Horror*
Richards O'Brien and Hartley, stuffed with one-
liners and sideswipes at big-budget fantasy films,
crammed with Australian actors in kinky cameos,
this is an irresistible blend of farce, satire and
sheer Antipodean idiocy. Arkin brings just the
right touch of grounded superheroism to the role
of 'Vince'; and Christopher Lee, sending himself
up something rotten, almost steals the show as the
malevolent Midnight, belting out his songs in a
rich baritone while half-naked henchwenches
cavort lewdly around his leather-clad thighs. AB

Return of Captain Marvel, The

see Adventures of Captain Marvel, The

Return of Captain Nemo, The

see Amazing Captain Nemo, The

Return of Count Yorga, The

(Bob Kelljan, 1971, US) Robert Quarry,
Mariette Hartley, Roger Perry, Yvonne Wilder,
George Macready.
97 min.
Witty and suspenseful sequel to *Count Yorga,
Vampire*, with Quarry's ruthless, hypnotic, modern-day bloodsucker offing a family in order to
lay his fangs into a new bride, only to meet resistance from the girl's fella. Moments of inventively chilling horror. TJ

Return of Doctor X, The

(Vincent Sherman, 1939, US) Wayne Morris,
Rosemary Lane, Dennis Morgan, Humphrey
Bogart, John Litel, Lya Lys, William Hopper,
Huntz Hall.
62 min. b/w.

A brisk B horror, not so much a sequel to *Dr X*
as an imitation of *The Walking Dead*, with
Bogart replacing Karloff as the executed man
brought back to zombie life, this time with vampiric lusts to boot, by a doctor (Litel) made up to
look like Leslie Banks in *The Most Dangerous
Game*. Directed with some style by Sherman (his
first film), but saddled with the usual lame script
and designed too much as a vehicle for the routinely breezy reporter hero (Morris), it's worth
watching mainly for Bogart's baleful performance. The best moment is his unsettling first
appearance, emerging from the depths of Litel's
laboratory, pallid in pince-nez, with a white
streak in his hair and a white rabbit in his arms.
TM

Return of Dracula, The (aka The Fantastic Disappearing Man)

(Paul Landres, 1958, US) Francis Lederer,
Norma Eberhardt, Ray Stricklyn, Jimmie
Baird, John Wengraf, Virginia Vincent.
77 min. b/w.
Little known, apparently (since Carlos Clarens
and Les Daniels both ignore it in their key books
on the horror genre), but a surprisingly 'deep'
piece of schlock, ignoring most of the drive-in
requirements of the time and building up a flat,
grey, joyless picture of vampire Lederer searching for 'love' in Middle America – and thus the
regeneration which only the New World can give
his dying 'culture'. Mucho cheapo, and probably
for devotees only, but they ought to find it quietly remarkable. CW

Return of Frank James, The

(Fritz Lang, 1940, US) Henry Fonda, Gene
Tierney, Jackie Cooper, Henry Hull, John
Carradine, Donald Meek, J Edward Bromberg.
92 min.
Fox's follow-up to *Jesse James* was Lang's first
Western and his first film in colour; if it's more
conventional than the later *Rancho Notorious*, it
nevertheless displays the director's interest in
the psychology (and indeed the pitfalls) of
revenge. At the start of the film, Frank (Fonda)
is happy to let the law pronounce sentence on
the Ford brothers, who killed Jesse; but when
they are pardoned, he begins a deadly hunt that
alienates him from society, imperils not only his
own life but those of his friends, and threatens
to destroy his long-held ideas of justice. For all
its fine photography and sturdy performances,
the film is finally little more than efficient and
routine, with Lang rarely probing beyond the
ironic if superficial twists of the narrative.
Though it bears some slight thematic resemblance to the earlier *Fury* and *You Only Live
Once*, he's clearly not as comfortable with dusty
townships and baked landscapes as with the
noir-like ambience of his contemporary crime
movies. GA

Return of Martin Guerre, The

see Retour de Martin Guerre, Le

Return of Maxwell Smart, The

see Nude Bomb, The

Return of Sabata (E'Tornato Sabata...Hai Chiuso un' Altra Volta)

(Frank Kramer i.e. Gianfranco Parolini, 1971,
It/Fr/WGer) Lee Van Cleef, Reiner Schöne,
Annabella Incontrera, Gianni Rizzo, Gianpiero
Albertini.
107 min.
Standard Italian Western starring an invincible
Van Cleef, armed with a gutter of fancy
weapons, up against an over-complicated plot
and a cast that shows a lot of teeth in an unsuccessful attempt to cover up some appalling dubbing. As usual, greed and hypocrisy are the
themes, and gold is the real reason for a ruthless
Irishman's exploitation of the local people. Until
Van Cleef rides into town, that is. He recruits his
assistants from a travelling circus; lots of sleight-
of-hand and acrobatics, therefore, but the rest is
routine.

Return of the Big Cat

(Tom Leetch, 1974, US) Jeremy Slate, Pat Crawley, Jeff East, Kim Richards, Christian Juttner, David Wayne.
70 min.

In a homestead in the timberland of Northern California, a small part (Richards) has not spoken since encountering a cougar two years before. Now the mountain lion's back. Amy's two brothers have tamed a wild yellow dog, Boomer, which at the Thanksgiving Day climax sees justice done. A Disney programmer (little seen after its initial release) in which ageless old timers enact an undiluted fundamentalist parable and a graceful big cat is regarded as nothing less than a 'heathen devil'. JPy

Return of the Cisco Kid, The

(Herbert I Leeds, 1939, US) Warner Baxter, Lynn Bari, Cesar Romero, Henry Hull, Kane Richmond, C Henry Gordon, Robert Barrat.
70 min. b/w.

Baxter won an Oscar as the do-gooding bandit the Cisco Kid ten years previously for *In Old Arizona*, and here he's back under the sombrero for a third time, falling for Bari and helping her old dad get back at the swindler who cheated them out of their nest-egg. Pretty creaky, but the public enjoyed it enough to warrant a string of sequels with sidekick Romero assuming the title role. TJ

Return of the Dragon

see Way of the Dragon

Return of the Dragon (Qisha Jie/aka Infernal Street)

(Shen Jiang, 1973, Tai) Yu Tien Lung, Chao Chien, Wang Yen Pin, Miao Tien, Sun Yueh.
93 min.

An example of the middle phase martial arts film. No longer attached to the depiction of tournaments, it retains from those earlier films the teenage rebel hero chafing against the restraints of a compromised adult world paying its dues to imperialism. The film is set around an opium rehabilitation clinic (in the early '30s), whose doctors notice a dramatic increase in patients following the opening of a club as an underhand means of paving the way for a Japanese invasion. Yu Tien Lung, looking all of 17, plays the adopted helper at the clinic with exemplary directness, illustrating the concept of the everyman protagonist who can assume heroic dimensions, even – as a kind of gag – invincibility. Formula stuff that runs like clockwork. VG

Return of the Fly

(Edward Bernds, 1959, US) Vincent Price, Brett Halsey, David Frankham, John Sutton, Danielle De Metz.
80 min. b/w.

Virtually a re-run of the original shocker, with surviving brother Price issuing dire warnings before young master Halsey reassembles his late dad's matter transference equipment and swiftly ends up in the same half-man/half-fly state himself. Passable enough for genre addicts, but watching it straight after the first film probably isn't a good idea. TJ

Return of the Jedi

(Richard Marquand, 1983, US) Mark Hamill, Harrison Ford, Carrie Fisher, Billy Dee Williams, Anthony Daniels, Peter Mayhew, Sebastian Shaw, Frank Oz, Dave Prowse, Alec Guinness, Kenny Baker.
132 min.

At the opening of this third instalment of the *Star Wars* saga in the States, an audience rioted, convinced that someone had switched reels on them, so baffled were they by the shifts in the narrative. It is confusing. All the old gang are there, older, wiser and tireder: Luke Skywalker is looking more like Han Solo, who is looking more like Ben Kenobi; Princess Leia seems almost Queenly; and in the concentration on sub-Muppet gothic, impressive aerial combat effects, and occasional attempts at 'love me, love my monster' humour, it's not surprising that Billy Dee Williams' Lando Calrissian has little chance to re-establish his *Empire Strikes Back* persona in all the toing-and-froing. But try telling that to the kids and the parents who have come, not to riot, but to wonder. To wonder at the teddy-bear tribes, the monstrous Tennielstyle Jabba the Hutt, and the way in which heroes and heroines can fall off high-speed motorbikes without a stain on their 25th century jockstraps. The rest of us might be wondering if it isn't about time George Lucas tried his hand at universes new. SGr

Return of the Jedi: Special Edition

(Richard Marquand, 1983/1997, US) Mark Hamill, Harrison Ford, Carrie Fisher, Billy Dee Williams, Anthony Daniels, Peter Mayhew, Sebastian Shaw, Frank Oz, Dave Prowse, Alec Guinness, Kenny Baker.
132 min.

This reissue accentuates the film's disengaged, almost perfunctory air. Tonal continuity isn't at fault. Director Marquand surrendered most of his post-production responsibilities to executive producer George Lucas, so the result isn't exactly idiosyncratic. It's just that in scope and ambition, *Jedi* resembles nothing so much as the next level of a computer game, with a new environment, new gadgets and new creatures. The first hour is deathly slow, a problem the 'Special Edition' compounds by inserting new footage into the singing-and-dancing scenes at Jabba's palace, where Leia, Lando and the droids have gone to rescue the carbon-frozen Han. Things liven up once Luke, having reached the peak of his Jedi powers, tries to coax his father, Darth Vader, from the dark side of the Force. Their subsequent confrontation, culminating in the removal of Vader's mask, is the film's strongest moment. Most people's biggest *Jedi* gripe can be summed up in one word: Ewoks. Do you think they're cute lickle lifesavers? Or do you, like me, simply wonder what they taste like barbecued? The debate will run and run. JO'C

Return of the Living Dead, The

(Dan O'Bannon, 1984, US) Clu Gulager, James Karen, Don Calfa, Thom Mathews, Beverly Randolph, John Philbin, Jewel Shepard.
91 min.

Any film which features a dead, bald and very hungry punk lurching towards the camera screaming '*More Brains!*' gets my vote. Directed by O'Bannon courtesy of George Romero, this is an energetic cross-referencing of genre: not just a horror movie, but a comic apocalyptic zombie horror movie. O'Bannon has his cake, eats it, and then throws it up in the face of the audience. Warehousemen unwittingly release a zombie interred by the CIA (of course) along with a nifty gas which ensures that local graveyards are bursting at the seams with brain-peckish corpses. Most of the film froths and bubbles merrily: there is a deeply artistic sequence where a punkette dances naked on a tombstone before being transformed into a zombie, and another moving bit where para-meds get their heads munched. Finally, however, O'Bannon runs short on the bad taste gags. Matters conclude, anti-climactically, with the death of civilised life as we know it. RR

Return of the Living Dead Part II

(Ken Wiederhorn, 1987, US) James Karen, Thom Mathews, Dana Ashbrook, Marsha Dietlein, Suzanne Snyder, Philip Bruns, Michael Kenworthy.
89 min.

Not even a nuclear explosion, it seems, can prevent a sequel to a tongue-in-cheek zombie pic. A surviving canister of zombiefying fumes rolls off an army truck and is punctured by a pair of teenage meatheads, once again releasing a weird fog that revives the occupants of an adjacent graveyard. The rest is a virtual re-run, with 12-year-old Jesse (Kenworthy), his older sister Lucy (Dietlein), and handsome cable TV-installer Tom (Ashbrook) enjoying such edifying experiences as a bunch of zombies turning a pet shop into a brain emporium. Karen and Mathews, heroes of Part I, are also resurrected for guest appearances as a pair of grave-robbers; fortunately they get theirs early on. Unlike O'Bannon's film, this is merely repetitive and dull, the tedium relieved only by the graphic brain-eating and Philip Bruns' deliciously OTT performance as the mad Doctor Mandel. NF

Return of the Living Dead III

(Brian Yuzna, 1993, US) J Trevor Edmond, Mindy Clarke, Kent McCord, Sarah Douglas, Mike Moroff, Sal Lopez.
97 min.

Retaining the jokiness of Dan O'Bannon's original, and a marked improvement on Ken Weiderhorn's lame sequel, Yuzna gets back to basics with a mutated Romeo and Juliet storyline, an anti-military theme, some fetishistic zombie make-up, and a surprisingly bleak ending. Unable to cope with the death of new girlfriend Julie (Clarke), army brat Kurt (Edmond) employs the experimental methods developed by his scientist father for use on captive zombies to bring her back from the dead. Yuzna and fx maestro Steve Johnson put human flesh on the plot's bare bones, without ever losing sight of the central offbeat romance. NF

Return of the Magnificent Seven

see Return of the Seven

Return of the Musketeers, The

(Richard Lester, 1989, GB/Fr/Sp) Michael York, Oliver Reed, Frank Finlay, C Thomas Howell, Kim Cattrall, Geraldine Chaplin, Roy Kinnear, Christopher Lee, Philippe Noiret, Richard Chamberlain, Eusebio Lazaro, Alan Howard, Bill Paterson, Jean-Pierre Cassel.
101 min.

Those boisterous idealists are back behind the reins, and despite the prolonged rest since the last in Lester's series of Dumas adaptations, they're looking pretty saddle-sore. Twenty years on, after a parting of ways, the musketeers are reunited – following initial skirmishes which divide loyalties – by France's Queen Anne (Chaplin) in a bid to save King Charles (Paterson) from the chop. Laying siege to their plan is the avenging Justine (Cattrall), daughter of their old enemy Milady. Howell acquits himself well enough as the bookish adopted son of Athos (Reed), while old troopers York, Finlay, Chamberlain and Kinnear (his last performance) coast lazily through their roles. The most glaring weakness lies in the needless complexity of the action, which at times threatens to overwhelm what little coherence exists as subplots tumble into each other until a speedy resolution in the final frames. Only undemanding fans of preceding instalments will find something to enjoy. CM

Return of the Pink Panther, The

(Blake Edwards, 1974, GB) Peter Sellers, Christopher Plummer, Catherine Schell, Herbert Lom, Peter Arne, Peter Jeffrey, Grégoire Aslan, David Lodge, Graham Stark, Eric Pohlmann, Burt Kwouk, Victor Spinetti, John Bluthal, Peter Jones.
113 min.

Fourth in the series, promisingly reuniting Edwards and Sellers with their respective careers not exactly buoyant since *A Shot in the Dark* ten years earlier, *The Return of the Pink Panther* delivers a good deal of that promise, from Richard Williams' ultra-ritzy animated credits to the four or five brilliantly timed set pieces of Clouseau-engineered mayhem. Things are shakier whenever Sellers is off-screen, and especially whenever Plummer's debonair jewel thief is on; and the movie wastes time on its jet-set locations, has too many British character actors in unfunny bit parts, and cries out for a devastating finale which never comes. But the occasional misfires, with the verbal gags rarely as inspired as the visual ones, are forgiveable in the context of Clouseau's running battles with swimming pools, a vacuum cleaner, false moustaches, gear levers that come away in the hand, and his oriental factotum-cum-sparring partner. TR

Return of the Secaucus Seven

(John Sayles, 1979, US) Bruce MacDonald, Adam Lefevre, Gordon Clapp, Karen Trott, David Strathairn, Maggie Renzi, Maggie Cousineau, Jean Passanante, Mark Arnott, John Sayles, Amy Schewel.
110 min.

A motley group of '60s survivors reunite ten

years on in a New Hampshire cottage to mull over the implications of reaching thirty – shuffling counter-culture nostalgia and fragmenting future perspectives between themselves during a weekend of low-key stocktaking, love-making and laughter. Sayles' fascinating debut as a writer/director, produced independently on the modest earnings from his witty genre screenplays for Roger Corman, returns him to the naturalistically observed world and characters of his fiction. Intelligently applying the virtues of necessity, Sayles concentrates on dialogue and editing to construct a spider's web of intricate personal politics and emotions, and a warm, unmannered comedy of character and connections. No amens, no emblems, and no excess; just a variant on Alain Tanner's *Jonah Who Will Be 25 in the Year 2000* which laughs with its 'greened' Americans rather than at them. PT

Return of the Seven (aka Return of the Magnificent Seven)
(Burt Kennedy, 1966, US) Yul Brynner, Robert Fuller, Julian Mateos, Warren Oates, Jordan Christopher, Claude Atkins.
96 min.
Actually, only Brynner returns for this okay-ish sequel in which the requisite number of gunslinging types, among them a pre-Peckinpah Warren Oates, saves another Mexican village, though this time Larry Cohen's script has the unfortunate peasants toiling under the yoke of a crazed visionary. Bubblegum stuff. TJ

Return of the Soldier, The
(Alan Bridges, 1982, GB) Alan Bates, Ann-Margret, Glenda Jackson, Julie Christie, Jeremy Kemp, Edward De Souza, Frank Finlay, Jack May, Ian Holm.
102 min.
Coming home. Ulysses, Napoleon, Travis Bickle, they all suffered from the same problem of returning from the wars to a prosaic home life, which is not quite the place they left behind them. In this adaptation of Rebecca West's novel, Bates returns from the First World War, his mind in ruins, to a starchy wife (Christie), an adoring female cousin (Ann-Margret), and his modest Palladian pile. After the trenches, what he now faces is the pain of an arid marriage and the weight of the past, so he opts for an old and dowdy flame (Jackson) and leaves the trick cyclist (Holm) to sort out the *ménage à quatre*. It's a glossy, respectful costume drama about the upper class habit of strangling the heart, but over it all hovers that certain, unmistakable air of irrelevance. Now, if it had been a soldier returning from Ulster, that would have been something. CPea

Return of the Swamp Thing, The
(Jim Wynorski, 1989, US) Louis Jourdan, Heather Locklear, Sarah Douglas, Dick Durock, Joey Sagal, Ace Mask, Chris Doyle.
87 min.
Having accidentally created his own arch-enemy in Wes Craven's 1982 *Swamp Thing*, Dr Arcane (Jourdan) is now perfecting an immortality serum, in which his late wife's rare blood group was to be a vital ingredient. Enter estranged daughter Abigail (Locklear), full of questions about mother, and, more importantly, full of the requisite red stuff. Soon the only thing standing between dad and daughter's main artery is the vegetating form of Dr Alec Holland (Durock), victim of a 'bio-restorative' chemical accident which turned his body into Hampstead Heath on legs. 'You're a plant, aren't you?' Abigail observes astutely as she's whisked to safety by the he-man hedgerow, with whom she soon falls in love. Apprenticed under Corman, Wynorski is well-versed in double-bluffing his audience, denying them the chance of balking at dreadful special effects by implying that the ineptitude is deliberate. He opts for cheap nostalgic laughs and camp '50s sci-fi scenery; depending on whether you find this funny, you'll either smile knowingly or gasp in disbelief. MK

Return of the Vampire, The
(Lew Landers, 1943, US) Bela Lugosi, Nina Foch, Frieda Inescort, Matt Willis, Gilbert Emery, Miles Mander, Roland Varno.
69 min. b/w.
Verbose but appealingly tatty little horror movie which is given a facelift by excellent performances (Foch did well enough in this debut to earn a starring role as the splendidly lycanthropic gypsy queen in *Cry of the Werewolf*). Dracula (Lugosi in his first genuine vampire role since the original *Dracula*), now known as Armand Tesla since Columbia had filched him from Universal, is unearthed by a bomb during the London blitz, and goes about his usual depredations with the aid of a werewolf (Willis) whose presence was obviously inspired by *Frankenstein Meets the Wolf Man*. Soon after, monster rallies assembling all the old favourites became two a penny as the ailing horror genre went into almost terminal decline. MA

Return to Oz
(Walter Murch, 1985, US) Nicol Williamson, Jean Marsh, Fairuza Balk, Piper Laurie, Matt Clark, Michael Sundin, Tim Rose.
109 min.
Dorothy (Balk) whiles away Kansas days yearning for her lost wonderland. A traumatic flight from a nightmarish ECT clinic sees her washed up in the otherworld with an irksome talking chicken, but Oz ain't what it used to be. The Yellow Brick Road is rubble, the Emerald City dilapidated, and its citizens marmarised effigies. Finding allies in a Pumpkinhead and a rotund robot, Dorothy fends off the evil Wheelers, eludes the terrifying Princess Mombi (Marsh), and infiltrates the mountain stronghold of the Nome King (Williamson) before Oz is restored to its former glory. Without musical numbers, the narrative seems a perilously thin journey- with-no-particular-purpose. But a shadowy side looms large in the scary clinic scenes, and with such splendidly malevolent creations as Mombi. Not for nervous children, heh heh heh. AB

Return to the Blue Lagoon
(William A Graham, 1991, US) Milla Jovovich, Brian Krause, Lisa Pelikan, Courtney Phillips, Garette Patrick Ratliff.
98 min.
Having touched a voyeuristic nerve with *The Blue Lagoon*, H de Vere Stacpoole promptly banged out a few follow-ups, one of which (*The Garden of God*) inspired this movie sequel in which the infant son of the deceased couple from *The Blue Lagoon* is castaway along with a girl child whose mother (Pelikan) dies of pneumonia after raising both kids to puberty. This spectacularly contrived plot allows director Graham to put his strapping stars (Krause and Jovovich) through their pubescent paces while simply re-running the sexy set pieces for which Randal Kleiser's tacky 1980 movie was famed. Things begin boldly, with bloody evidence of menstruation and talk of masturbation and copulation; but when mating time arrives, the pair merely snog, simper, fall writhing to the ground, then proceed to an impromptu wedding ceremony, perpetuating the myth that babies come from marriage. Like a sex education film made by semi-liberated nuns, the movie keeps its sticky truths hidden beneath a veneer of leering cleanliness. MK

Return to the Edge of the World
see Edge of the World, The

Reuben, Reuben
(Robert Ellis Miller, 1982, US) Tom Conti, Kelly McGillis, Roberts Blossom, Cynthia Harris, E Katherine Kerr, Joel Fabiani, Lois Smith.
101 min.
With his crumpled tweed suit and his apparently irresistible Highland brogue, writer Gowan McGland is soon worming his way into the pants of neighbourhood New England wives while mourning the expiry of his muse. Since the stuff he wrote when he was on top form sounds like Patience Strong in especially lyrical vein, this might not be too much of a blow. Nevertheless, McGland/Conti is a worried man, and well he might be as he has to try to straddle a plot cannibalised out of a Peter DeVries novel and an unrelated Broadway play, which threatens constantly to come apart at the seams. Director Miller seems quite unable to decide whether he's making a portrait of maudlin self-absorption or an eccentric-on-the-loose comedy, and has a habit of turning glutinous whenever the cracks start to appear. Conti is impressively dissolute, and turns on the charm with great gusto, but against odds like these all he can do is go down fighting. JP

Reunion (L'Ami retrouvé)
(Jerry Schatzberg, 1989, Fr/WGer/GB) Jason Robards, Christian Anholt, Samuel West, Françoise Fabian, Maureen Kerwin, Barbara Jefford.
110 min.
This moving rendition of Fred Uhlman's novel, about boyhood friendship betrayed under the destructive momentum of Nazism, shows Schatzberg at his (albeit limited) best. Jewish New York lawyer Henry Strauss (Robards) revisits Stuttgart to claim the remaining effects of the family he left in 1933. Cue a flashback to the body of the film: his time at the elite Gymnasium and his deep but never easy friendship with a fellow outsider, the aristocratic Konradin. The film is dominated by remembrance: the tricks it plays, the pain it involves. Schatzberg encourages his young actors – Anholt as the adolescent 'Hans', West as Konradin – to personalise, and thus to universalise – their relationship. It's a staple situation, but their sharing (Konradin proudly showing a coin collection in his grand house on the hill; Hans introducing his politically naive parents; the soon-to-be-shattered idyll of trips to the Black Forest) speaks volumes of cumulative small truths. Harold Pinter's tight and unobtrusive script, Trauner's fine production design and Philippe Sarde's muted but expressive score ensure a feeling of all-round professionalism. WH

Revenge
(Tony Scott, 1989, US) Kevin Costner, Anthony Quinn, Madeline Stowe, Tomas Milian, Sally Kirkland.
124 min.
Recently retired fighter pilot Cochran (Costner) enjoys an idyllic break at the Mexican ranch of old friend and tennis partner Tibey Mendez (Quinn). Despite a sense of loyalty and hints of Tibey's ruthlessness, Cochran becomes involved in a passionate affair with his beautiful wife Miryea (Stowe). When their treachery is discovered, Tibey's revenge is cold, calculated and vicious; but Cochran survives to even the score…Scott manages the shift from tremulous romance to violent retribution very well, but his efficient handling of some surprisingly tough action scenes is compromised by a surfeit of pop promo clichés: billowing net curtains, clouds of fluttering doves, an excessive use of coloured filters. What emotional intensity there is therefore derives from the two central performances. Always comfortable as a romantic lead, Costner here displays a more menacing side, his obsession laced with a dangerously uncontrolled violence; and his conviction is matched by Quinn's formidable portrayal of the autocratic Mendez. With more dramatic depth and less visual flash, this might have captured some of the poetic fatalism of Jim Harrison's original novella. NF

Revenge (aka Inn of the Frightened People)
(Sidney Hayers, 1971, GB) Joan Collins, James Booth, Ray Barrett, Sinead Cusack, Tom Marshall, Kenneth Griffith, Zuleika Robson, Donald Morley, Patrick McAlinney.
89 min.
A barnstorming melodrama in which two grieving fathers (Booth and Barrett) kidnap the slimy recluse (Griffith) they suspect of being the rapist who murdered their pre-teen daughters. Having beaten him up somewhat over-enthusiastically, they stash the corpse in the cellar of Booth's pub pending disposal, only to find that he is still alive and an acute embarrassment, since they dare neither let him go nor despatch him in cold blood. Cue for some wild loony tunes as everybody concerned gets hysterically caught up in rape and violence. 'I don't know what's come over us' says Booth's wife (Collins), as she eagerly submits to sexual assault by her stepson. Done with deadly solemnity and a truly atrocious script (the characters are forever asking each other if they're all right, suggesting nice cups of tea, and saying 'I'll think of something' as the problems escalate), it's almost as hilarious as a Joe Orton farce. Poor Sidney Hayers can do nothing but go along for the ride. TM

Revenge in El Paso

see Quattro dell'Ave Maria, I

Revenge of Frankenstein, The

(Terence Fisher, 1958, GB) Peter Cushing, Michael Gwynn, Francis Matthews, Eunice Gayson, John Welsh, George Woodbridge, Lionel Jeffries, Oscar Quitak, Richard Wordsworth, Michael Ripper.
89 min.

A strange, blackly comic reworking of the Frankenstein myth, which was Fisher and Hammer's follow-up to their initial *The Curse of Frankenstein* of 1956. In one of his best performances, Cushing plays on the ambiguity of the central character, so that the Baron becomes a kind of Wildean martyr, alternating between noble defiance and detached cruelty. Much of the action is set in a poor hospital reminiscent of *The Marat/Sade*, and there is an extraordinary climax which irresistibly suggests the forces of chaos erupting into a repressive community as a monstrously deformed experimental subject crashes through a window into a smart society ball. DP

Revenge of the Creature

(Jack Arnold, 1955, US) John Agar, Lori Nelson, John Bromfield, Nestor Paiva, Grandon Rhodes, Robert B Williams, Ricou Browning, Clint Eastwood.
82 min. b/w.

The official sequel to *The Creature from the Black Lagoon*, also shot in 3-D, this is a quirky fusion of subterranean imagery and social anxiety which has weathered as well as its predecessor. Here the Amazon gill-man is captured by a research team and taken to a huge tank in Marineland, Florida, from which it eventually escapes. Far from being a monster, it emerges as a strange, beautiful alien which the humans torment with crude behavioural experiments. The story of captivity and the creature's gradual reassertion of its identity is arresting enough, but in a flash of unconscious insight, the film also throws up a link between the creature's otherness and the identity confusion of the heroine. This is not just a question of beauty-and-the-beast sexual suggestion (though there's plenty of that). The two keep staring at each other through the glass tank as she begins to express doubts about abandoning science for motherhood; although fleeting, this notion of creature and woman as strangers in a male colony is something you won't find in *King Kong*. If the monster hunt at the end proves a little disappointing, it's only because, unlike so much of the rest, it has become familiar through imitation. DP

Revenge of the Dead

see Night of the Ghouls

Revenge of the Dead

(Evan Lee, 1975, US) Larry Justin, J Arthur Craig, James Habif, Robert Clark, Doug Senior, Christopher Lee.
87 min.

This wreck could best be summarised as a really bad episode of *Night Gallery*, endlessly protracted. The makers appear to have dabbled in cinema in much the same way that their characters dabble in the occult: ineptly, and with horrendous results. Christopher Lee has been enlisted to give a pre-credits pep talk, but surely he couldn't have seen what follows: a cut-rate catalogue of amateur acting, botched continuity, mismatched footage, and all-embracing incompetence. Purporting to portray a paralysis victim's psychically-conjured monster, the filmmakers feel obliged to spike the mess with derivative, adolescent 'humour' and a dose of prurient sex. Not even the aesthetic of trash could be used to defend this saddening spectacle. PT

Revenge of the Nerds

(Jeff Kanew, 1984, US) Robert Carradine, Anthony Edwards, Tim Busfield, Andrew Cassese, Curtis Armstrong, Julie Montgomery.
90 min.

Of all movie genres, the Yankee hi-jinks college comedy, populated by nauseating stereotypes (the hunky super-bonker sportsman, the outrageous but loveable slob, the token black man with riddim, girls with huge busty substances) is surely one of the most expendable. Kanew's film takes

a timely hatchet to them all, with a bunch of nerds, fed up with being dumped on by the star fraternity, deciding on all-out confrontation to seek retribution. The resulting mêlée occasionally degenerates to utter filth (the belching contest has to be heard to be believed), but most of the time is a fine balance of send-up and superior slapstick. The only worthy successor to *Animal House*. DPe

Revenge of the Pink Panther

(Blake Edwards, 1978, GB) Peter Sellers, Herbert Lom, Dyan Cannon, Robert Webber, Burt Kwouk, Paul Stewart, Robert Loggia, Graham Stark, Alfie Bass.
100 min.

The best things about the previous two Clouseau movies were brilliantly orchestrated set pieces of Clouseau's mechanical incompetence, and Herbert Lom's psychotic Chief Inspector Dreyfus. In this, the sixth in the series, Edwards forsakes these two strengths almost completely in favour of a flurry of lame racial jokes (inscrutable Chinese, Italian mafiosi, that outrageous French accent), and a plot which has Clouseau involved with the French connection, resorting to a string of strictly one-joke disguises. The part of the Chinese manservant Cato (Kwouk) is built up to little effect, and Dyan Cannon is mostly wasted. The laughs come, but they're pretty hollow. RM

Revenge of the Vampire

see Maschera del Demonio, La

Revengers, The

(Daniel Mann, 1972, US/Mex) William Holden, Ernest Borgnine, Woody Strode, Susan Hayward, Roger Hanin, Jorge Luke, Warren Vanders.
112 min.

Respectable rancher (Holden) hires six convicts from a Mexican chain gang to help track down the renegade white man (Vanders) who led the raiding party of Indians which massacred his family. The body of the story concerns the highly dubious relationship between the rancher, who is rapidly becoming corruptible, and the ex-cons, expressing varying degrees of corruption, integrity and loyalty. All of which culminates in a morally-charged confrontation with the comanchero; but relying heavily on (useless) action for want of ideas, it's mainly a matter of guys galloping through forests, over mountains, and through blizzards to the point of exhausting boredom. JPi

Reversal of Fortune

(Barbet Schroeder, 1990, US) Glenn Close, Jeremy Irons, Ron Silver, Annabella Sciorra, Uta Hagen, Fisher Stevens, Jack Gilpin, Christine Baranski.
111 min.

Claus von Bülow's trial in 1982 for the attempted murder of his wealthy wife Sunny had it all: sex, drugs, nobility and betrayal. She had lapsed into an irreversible coma and her husband was found guilty; but an appeal, in which his case was handled by Alan Dershowitz (from whose book the film is adapted), led to acquittal. *Reversal of Fortune* intersperses flashbacks of the von Bülow marriage with a reconstruction of legal investigations for the second trial. Under Schroeder's direction, the social comparisons are by no means subtle; and a detached approach to characterisation is most acute in the case of comatose Sunny (Close) – whose 'brain dead, body never better' – whose disembodied voice provides commentary. That said, the performances from Irons (as von Bülow) and Silver (Dershowitz) hit the right pitch within a rather difficult scenario. But this is a strange, unsatisfactory mixture of satire and docudrama which engages the mind and leaves the emotions intact. CM

Revolt of Mamie Stover, The

(Raoul Walsh, 1956, US) Jane Russell, Richard Egan, Joan Leslie, Agnes Moorehead, Jorja Curtright, Jean Willes.
93 min.

William Bradford Huie's novel about the production-line life of a Honolulu prostitute came to the screen (adapted by Sidney Boehm) virtually unrecognisable thanks to the good offices of the Production Code. Here the emphasis is on Russell's romantic travails as a dance hall 'hostess' and her ill-starred relationship with wealthy writer Egan, though Agnes Moorehead does inject a sliver of

hard reality as the madam who runs the joint. The star looks good in CinemaScope and Technicolor, but as a movie it rarely convinces. TJ

Revolution

(Hugh Hudson, 1985, GB) Al Pacino, Donald Sutherland, Nastassja Kinski, Joan Plowright, Dave King, Steven Berkoff, John Wells, Annie Lennox, Richard O'Brien.
125 min.

An almost inconceivable disaster which tries for a worm's eye view of the American Revolution, the worm in question being Pacino as a son of the good earth who is pushed into the fight by the taunts of Kinski and motivated by the sadism of British sergeant Sutherland. Maybe the original script had a shape and a grasp of events. If so, it has gone. There has clearly been drastic cutting, and nothing is left but a cortege of fragments and mismatched cuts. It's also the first 70 mm movie that looks as if it was shot hand-held on 16 mm and blown up for the big screen. Director? I didn't catch the credit. Was there one? TR.

Revolutionary, The

(Paul Williams, 1970, US) Jon Voight, Jennifer Salt, Seymour Cassel, Robert Duvall, Collin Wilcox-Horne, Lionel Murton.
101 min.

Adapted from Hans Konigsberger's novel, this is the classic story of a youth (Voight, excellent) seeking change but unsure how to bring it about, set within the context of revolutionary politics in a seedy and deliberately anonymous London that might be taken as any major city. Paul Williams' film is a masterful piece of social observation. Although the issues raised by *The Revolutionary* are the age-old ones of means-versus-ends, it achieves a certain integrity by its determinedly low-key approach to its subject. PH

Revolving Doors, The (Les Portes tournantes)

(Francis Mankiewicz, 1988, Can/Fr) Monique Spaziani, Gabriel Arcand, Miou-Miou, François Méthé, Jacques Penot.
102 min.

From New York, sensitive Quebecoise Celeste (Spaziani) sends her memoirs – spanning 50 years or so in her journey from provincial '20s immaturity to Big City jazz life – to her abandoned middle-aged son, taciturn painter Blaudelle (Arcand). Most of the action, or inaction, takes place in his flat as he stares into space – ah, memory! Blaudelle's son Antoine (Méthé) is a lonely, bright boy, disturbed by his parents' estrangement (there are explanatory scenes in parks with Miou-Miou as his mother); intrigued, he sets off to find his grandmother in the mean bars of New York. Mankiewicz directs this dull essay on memory and generational separation with an enervating sensitivity that borders on obscurity. Symptomatic is a lengthy, central flashback set in and around a local silent cinema where Celeste, a classically-inclined musician, takes a job providing piano accompaniment; presumably intended to illuminate the broadening of her musical, intellectual and emotional horizons, it explains nothing. WH

Reward, The

(Serge Bourguinon, 1965, US) Max Von Sydow, Gilbert Roland, Emilio Fernandez, Yvette Mimieux, Efrem Zimbalist Jr, Henry Silva.
91 min.

French director Bourguinon won the Oscar for Best Foreign Language Film with 1962's *Sundays and Cybele*, his first feature, then went to Hollywood and swiftly blew his chances with this lackadaisical South-of-the-Border thriller. The price on accused killer Zimbalist's head becomes the source of much friction between Von Sydow, the crop-duster who fingers him, and Roland, the cop leading the hunt. The point about the malign influence of money is made early on, leaving the rest of the film to fizzle to a surprisingly underwhelming conclusion. 'Where's the beef?' you're tempted to ask. TJ

Rhapsody in August (Hachigatsu no Kyoshikyoku)

(Akira Kurosawa, 1990, Jap) Sachiko Murase, Hisashi Igawa, Narumi Kayashima, Tomoko Ohtakara, Mitsunori Isaki, Toshie Negishi, Richard Gere.
97 min.

If Kurosawa's execrable *Dreams* ended up as a

moron's guide to the Green manifesto, here we are presented with a child's primer to the evils of war. Four children are spending the summer at their grandma's home near Nagasaki while their parents are visiting the old lady's long-lost brother in Hawaii. Thanks to grandma's tales of 1945, when America's atomic bomb killed her husband, the kids learn the importance of never forgetting the lessons of the past, and of blaming war itself rather than foreigners. All's well until Clark (Gere) – the old lady's Japanese-American nephew – announces his imminent arrival: will he imagine that his Japanese cousins hate him for the Bomb, and so dash the kids' parents' dreams of an easier life? Who cares would be a tempting response, were it not for the often touching performances. There's more narrative movement here than in *Dreams*, but the pedagogic humanism still gets bogged down in facile simplification. GA

Rhapsody in Blue

(Irving Rapper, 1945, US) Robert Alda, Joan Leslie, Alexis Smith, Oscar Levant, Charles Coburn, Julie Bishop, Albert Basserman, Al Jolson, Paul Whiteman, Hazel Scott.
139 min. b/w.
Biopic with all the usual faults plus Alda, as George Gershwin, at one point looking hilariously like a Frankenstein monster as he sits at the piano while protruding arms clearly not his own tinkle the ivories. Still, it's something of a musical feast, with a slew of old favourites and an outstanding all-black number on 'Blue Monday Blues'. When the music fails, there's always Sol Polito's lushly impressive camerawork. TM

Rhubarb

(Arthur Lubin, 1951, US) Ray Milland, Jan Sterling, Gene Lockhart, William Frawley, Elsie Holmes, Taylor Holmes, Donald MacBride.
95 min. b/w.
An eccentric millionaire (Lockhart), soured by his daughter's lack of affection, leaves his empire – including a baseball team – to a stray cat called Rhubarb, appointing the team's publicity manager (Milland) as the cat's guardian. A nice opening sequence has Lockhart watching gleefully as the disrespectful stray drives the VIP members of an exclusive golf club crazy by stealing balls from under their noses. After that it's downhill all the way as Milland fights off escalating problems: the disgruntled daughter (Elsie Holmes) tries to discredit Rhubarb in court as an impostor, then to have him eliminated; Milland's wedding has to be postponed several times because his fiancée (Sterling) seems to be allergic to Rhubarb; and worried bookies kidnap the cat when the baseball team, convinced he is a good luck charm, unexpectedly starts winning. Laboriously written, directed and acted (apart from Lockhart and the splendid cat), the comedy obstinately refuses to fizz. TM

Rhythm Thief

(Matthew Harrison, 1995, US) Jason Andrews, Kimberley Flynn.
84 mins. b/w.
Simon (Andrews) plays his cards close to his chest and seems to think he's in control: since arriving in New York from the sticks, he's built a kind of career selling bootleg music tapes on the streets, embarked on a casual relationship with a woman who, despite herself, can barely resist him, and his cool demeanour has earned the respect of local low-lifes. Well, not quite all. The musos whose sounds he steals are ready to get heavy, while Marti (Flynn), a dreamy girl with mystical-poetic pretensions who's followed him from back home, seems quietly determined to crack his tough emotional shell. Maybe city life isn't all it's made out to be. Harrison's grainy b/w, $11,000 second feature may have won the Best Director Prize at 1995's Sundance festival, but that doesn't mean it's not a pretty trite tale of redemption. True, the direction has a certain raw energy and terse economy, but the slim, stretched-out storyline is laden with clichés both ancient (the waifish would-be saviour, a seaside idyll) and modern (endless inarticulate street talk, seedily offbeat behaviour). Hard going. GA

Riaba Ma Poule
(Ryaba My Chicken)

(Andrei Konchalovsky, 1993, Rus/Fr) Inna Churikova, Alexander Surin, Guennadi Iegoritchev, Guennadi Nazarov.
117 min.

O tempora! O mores! Not only has Russian peasant life altered somewhat since Konchalovsky made *Asya's Happiness* back in '67, his talent has changed dramatically too – and not for the better. Here, he returns to the kolkhoz of the earlier and far superior film (featured, unwisely, in brief clips), and uses the same villagers to act out a bizarre, supposedly comic fable about the moral and social turmoil caused when Asya's chicken lays a golden egg. A broad, sour farce, that seems to argue that democracy can't succeed because the Russian peasants are so idle, greedy and stupid. Which wouldn't be so bad if it were funny or touching. But it's not. Awful. GA

Ricco (Un Tipo con una Faccia Strana Ti Cerca per Ucciderti)

(Tullio Demicheli, 1973, It/Sp) Christopher Mitchum, Barbara Bouchet, Arthur Kennedy, Malisa Longo, Paola Senatore.
93 min.
New Turin Mafia chief Don Vito enjoys immersing enemies in caustic soda and turning them into bars of soap, but this won't wash with Ricco, whose dad, the previous chief, was rubbed out in Vito's bid for top position. Back in 1962, Demicheli tried to launch Sean Flynn in *The Son of Captain Blood* as natural swashbuckling successor to dad Errol, and failed miserably. Here he tries the same trick with Robert Mitchum's second son Chris and succeeds, if only because it's far easier to walk around half-asleep than it is to leap up a ship's mast. Arthur Kennedy as Vito lends a small measure of reliable respectability, but it's not enough to get this superordinary revenge movie off the rocks. PM

Rice People

see Gens de la rizière, Les

Rich and Famous

(George Cukor, 1981, US) Jacqueline Bisset, Candice Bergen, David Selby, Hart Bochner, Steven Hill, Meg Ryan, Matt Lattanzi, Daniel Faraldo.
117 min.
Considering neither Bisset nor Bergen had ever shown the slightest acting ability before in movies, their performances in the Bette Davis/Miriam Hopkins roles in this loose reworking of *Old Acquaintance* are very capable. They play two college friends in a story spanning the years 1959-81. Liz (Bisset) develops into a formidable, prickly New York literary figure (Calvin Klein wardrobe, Algonquin, Greenwich Village), while southern belle Merry Noel (a surprisingly comic Bergen) turns from Malibu housewife into wealthy trash novelist (Chanel, gold-chain handbags, Waldorf Astoria, Beverly Hills). Of course much of the credit must go to Cukor, the veteran 'woman's director'; but the film disappoints in its unconfident handling of the secondary characters: the Rolling Stone journalist who lays Liz, Merry's daughter, and the daughter's unsuitable Puerto Rican boyfriend. So many young people in a very old man's film (his last, in fact). JS

Rich and Strange

(Alfred Hitchcock, 1932, GB) Henry Kendall, Joan Barry, Betty Amann, Percy Marmont, Elsie Randolph, Aubrey Dexter.
92 min. b/w.
Hitchcock's career is full of unexpected patterns and internal correspondences, but none are more bizarre than the comparison between this modestly ambitious drama of 1932 and his Cold War spy movie. *Torn Curtain* of 1966. Both are about couples abroad (in this case, middle class suburbanites who come into money and take a disastrous world cruise), and both are extraordinarily scathing about the timidity and emotional reserve of their central characters: innocence, of the most banal and compromised kind confronts experience in the form of exotic strangers and risks, and responds by retreating further into its shell. It wasn't well received at the time, but Hitchcock himself retained enthusiasm for it. TR

Richard Pryor Here & Now

(Richard Pryor, 1983, US) Richard Pryor.
95 min.
Filmed in front of a wildly partisan crowd in New Orleans who are clearly going to crease themselves at every 'motherfucker' he utters, Pryor

tries to swing into his accustomed groove and finds it eluding him at every turn. The material is weak, the delivery uncertain, and the manic depressive behind the quickfire patter is more clearly revealed than ever. Interspersed with variations on the old routines are plaintive assurances that he's straightened himself out, with Pryor seeming pathetically eager to immerse himself in the glow of goodwill emanating from the faithful. While the general embarrassment is not entirely untempered by flashes of brilliance, the abiding memory is of a once great comedian brought (literally) to his knees. JP

Richard Pryor Live in Concert

(Jeff Margolis, 1979, US) Richard Pryor.
78 min.
The film that introduced British audiences to Richard Pryor's real forte – acidic and self-damning humour – after his appearance in a relatively straight role in *Blue Collar*, and his 'clean' parts in *California Suite* and *The Wiz*. This record of one of his gigs in 1978 at Long Beach, California, may be technically imcompetent, but it just can't mar his vulgar and ebullient attacks on everything from Richard Pryor to police brutality, from God to sexual chauvinism. Politics, humour and sex in a great combination.

Richard Pryor Live on the Sunset Strip

(Joe Layton, 1982, US) Richard Pryor.
81 min.
Pryor is a one-man comic circus: mime artist, piss artist, wisecracker and, briefly in 1981, human firecracker. His freebasing accident gives him the chance to get one back at his fans when he strikes a match at the end of his gig and waves it at the audience: 'Richard Pryor running down the street, huh? I know all that shit you have been saying while I was away'. But nothing's burned out inside him. The jokes still go off like repeater fireworks, a second punchline catching you unawares just when you thought your sides were splitting for real. Pryor's act (and the filming of it) is so smoothly articulated , one subject detouring into another, that it's impossible to isolate favourite individual routines. But you have to see it – a couple of times – to savour the satire and relish the wit of the solo stand-up comic who's so slick and smartassed he makes Alexei Sayle look like a glove puppet and George Burns a dinosaur. MA

Richard III

(Laurence Olivier, 1955, GB) Laurence Olivier, John Gielgud, Claire Bloom, Ralph Richardson, Cedric Hardwicke, Stanley Baker, Alec Clunes, Norman Wooland, Laurence Naismith, Pamela Brown, John Laurie, Michael Gough.
161 min.
Olivier's third film as actor/director, and his third 'personal' Shakespeare adaptation. Whether you take his central performance on its own terms (as a 'definitive' reading of the part) or as high camp, it's undoubtedly interesting as a phenomenon. Less debatable, unfortunately, is his ability as a director: his approach is for the most part tediously staid and conservative, and it becomes almost laughable when it tries to transcend its own timidity in the dramatic climaxes. TR

Richard III

(Richard Loncraine, 1995, GB) Ian McKellen, Annette Bening, Kristin Scott-Thomas, Jim Broadbent, Robert Downey Jr, Maggie Smith, Nigel Hawthorne, Jim Carter, Dominic West, Bill Paterson, Adrian Dunbar, Edward Hardwicke, Michael Elphick.
104 min.
This triumphant take on the Crookback king is as different from Olivier's '50s historical pageant as chalk is from malmsey. It starts in some vague, post-WWI civil-war period: a ritzy function, a jazz band, a crooner belting out lines from the wrong author – Marlowe! But the ambience soon assumes the fractured pomp of the original, superbly realised in the remastered southern landscapes: Brighton Pavilion, St Pancras turned into a seaside palace, the Armageddon of Bosworth Field played out with Battersea Power Station as a backdrop. The reasoning behind the film was to bring classical actor McKellen together with a director who has avoided the Bard; the result is a fresh, unified vision which may add lines and make cuts, but does a fine job of turn-

ing Shakespeare's grand design into a veritable world at war. With Scott-Thomas' loveless Lady Anne fixing up in the back of a Rolls; Downey and Bening as out-of-favour American Nevilles; Broadbent as a pucker, pissed-off Buckingham; and Hawthorne as a sonorous Clarence pacing his last steps amid rain and concrete, the piece is awash with talent and imagery. McKellen is a marvellous demon king: unctuous, snarling, taking the throne like Hitler at a Nuremberg rally. A seamless, high-octane thriller of power and politics, one for today and tomorrow. SGr

Richie Rich
(Donald Petrie, 1994, US) Macaulay Culkin, Jonathan Hyde, John Larroquette, Michael McShane, Edward Herrmann, Christine Ebersole, Claudia Schiffer.
94 min.
Richie, heir to billions, must defeat villainous Van Dough (Larroquette) who's taken over the benevolent family business and plans to murder the parents. Happily, Richie (Culkin) is a rebellious Little Lord Fauntleroy, and has buddied with a bunch of tough ethnically mixed street kids. Aided by a laser gun and inventor Prof Keenbean (McShane), the youngsters rout the baddies. Richie's faithful British butler (Hyde) does the usual with the role and, like Gielgud before him, is demoted to leathers. Unendurable. BC

Rich in Love
(Bruce Beresford, 1992, US) Albert Finney, Jill Clayburgh, Kathryn Erbe, Kyle MacLachlan, Piper Laurie, Ethan Hawke, Suzy Amis, Alfre Woodard.
105 min.
Another sub-literary Deep South coming-of-age snoozer, in which 17-year-old Lucille (Erbe) has a bit of growing up to do when Mom (Clayburgh) leaves to start 'a second life'. There's bullish paterfamilias Warren (Finney) to guide through the trauma of being on his own again, a task so time-consuming that Lucille has to put her own life (upcoming exams, tentative steps towards romance) on hold a while. Then the surprise return of vivacious, pregnant, married sister Rae (Amis) with her Yankee husband Billy (MacLachlan) livens up the whole household, particularly when that little glint in Billy's eye starts to do strange things to a girl's adolescent hormones. We've been here many times before, but rarely with such an unprepossessing junior heroine: Erbe's such a prissy li'l missy that the sympathy vacuum at its core kills the movie stone dead. For the rest, reuniting Beresford and writer Alfred Uhry from Driving Miss Daisy, it's all lengthy vaawel sounds, Charleston summer sun, Georges Delerue firmly in the key of saccharine, and absolutely no surprises. TJ

Rich Kids
(Robert M Young, 1979, US) Trini Alvarado, Jeremy Levy, Kathryn Walker, John Lithgow, Terry Kiser, David Selby, Roberta Maxwell, Paul Dooley.
101 min.
Produced by Robert Altman but set in Woody Allen country, this is the mild-mannered story of a 12-year-old boy and girl whose friendship is strengthened by the common bond of screwed-up, wealthy, divorcing parents. What at first looks like a critical and obsessively detailed chronicle of the families' lifestyle (high energy consumers), opts instead for a faintly funny, more than faintly stereotyped treatment of anxious and well-meaning child/parent relations – and is consequently less interesting. Alvarado and Levy, as the wise pre-teens, have much the best scenes, and sense exactly what is expected of children pretending to be children. JS

Ricochet
(Russell Mulcahy, 1991, US) Denzel Washington, John Lithgow, Ice T, Kevin Pollak, Lindsay Wagner, Mary Ellen Trainor, Josh Evans, Victoria Dillard.
102 min.
Mulcahy's slasher-thriller manages to be as entertaining as it is improbable and violent. Washington, in a refreshingly unpolitical role, plays Nick Styles, a cop who becomes a hero when he pulls down his pants in order to arrest a street psycho. The event, recorded on amateur video, catapults Styles into the big time as an assistant district attorney and role model, but

also makes him an implacable enemy in the shape of the demonic psycho (Lithgow). He is the stuff of which nightmares are made, and Washington's mental and physical destruction is the driving force behind his escape from prison and assumption of a new identity. Ricochet has some dodgy moments – a scene where Washington is doped and then infected with VD by a hired prostitute leaves a nasty taste in the mouth – but it runs a fascinating line between cartoon fantasy and big city chiller. If you don't take it seriously, it's a lot of fun. SGr

Riddle of the Sands, The
(Tony Maylam, 1978, GB) Michael York, Jenny Agutter, Simon MacCorkindale, Alan Badel, Jürgen Andersen, Michael Sheard, Hans Meyer.
102 min.
First published in 1903, Erskine Childers' novel is one of the great adventure classics of English fiction, a tour de force (long a favourite project of Michael Powell's) in which two eccentric young Englishmen manoeuvre a 30-foot yacht around the North Sea German coastline and stumble on a demonic Hun scheme for the invasion of England. Rank's version is faithful enough, but founders on the considerable production difficulties involved: without the resources of Jaws, how do you portray violent storms, wrecks, sea chases, and the whole eerie desolation of dangerous coastal navigation? Although it works hard for authenticity (locations rather than a studio tank), the film is just too pretty to convey a real sense of danger, and too glossy to capture subtleties of atmosphere and characterisation. DP

Riddles of the Sphinx
(Laura Mulvey/Peter Wollen, 1977, GB) Dinah Stabb, Merdelle Jordine, Rhiannon Tise, Clive Merrison, Marie Green, Paula Melbourne.
92 min.
Mulvey and Wollen's second film places the simple story of a mother/child relationship in the wholly unexpected context of the myth of Oedipus' encounter with the Sphinx; its achievement is to make that context seem both logical and necessary. First off, the story: a broken marriage, an over-possessive mother, a growing awareness of feminist issues, a close female friend, and a newly questioning spirit of independence. Then, underpinning it, the myth, which introduces a set of basic questions about the female unconscious. The mixture of feminist politics and Freudian theory would be enough in itself to make the film unusually interesting, but various other elements make it actively compelling: the beautiful, hypnotic score by Mike Ratledge, the tantalising blend of visual, aural and literary narration in the telling of the story, and the firm intelligence that informs the film's unique and seductive overall structure. TR

Ride, The (Jísda)
(Jan Sverák, 1994, Czech) Anna Geislerová, Radek Pasternák, Jakub Spalek.
88 min.
Mercifully less obscure – and indeed less ambitious – than Sverák's previous Accumulator 1, this is a good-looking road movie in which two friends buy a second-hand car (from a shady dealer, natch), drive out into the country, and give a lift to strange, distracted woman whose presence fuels tensions between the two men. Snappily edited and consummately stylish, it's nevertheless a somewhat hollow, formula affair, interesting more for what it shows of the current mindset of the Czech Republic than for any inherent drama. GA

Ride a Wild Pony
(Don Chaffey, 1975, US) Robert Bettles, Eva Griffith, Michael Craig, John Meillon Sr, Alfred Bell, Melissa Jaffer, John Meillon Jr.
91 min.
A Disney film set in Australia with two kids (one rich, paralysed and pampered, the other poor, gap-toothed and cheeky) fighting for the ownership of a wild white pony. Sounds irredeemably yucky? Well, you're wrong – the pony gets very few close-ups, and the script makes a point of presenting the paralysed girl as a real toffee-nosed stinker, thus giving a welcome acerbic tinge to the drama. Jack Cardiff's photography is radiantly crisp, and all the actors, young or old, seem to believe in what they're doing. Even the moral

homilies ('If you keep running away from the big people, you just make yourself small') ring true. The only blight is provided by Chaffey's mannered direction, liable to induce vertigo or a permanent squint. GB

Ride in the Whirlwind
(Monte Hellman, 1966, US) Cameron Mitchell, Jack Nicholson, Millie Perkins, Harry Dean Stanton, George Mitchell, Tom Filer.
82 min.
Shot back-to-back with The Shooting, this Jack Nicholson-scripted effort is considerably less ambiguous and weird than its celebrated sibling Western. Most of the action takes place in a ranch-house, where three cowboys wrongly accused of being outlaws wait out their fate. Incidental laughs aside, the resulting ennuis don't always seem intentional. DT

Ride Lonesome
(Budd Boetticher, 1959, US) Randolph Scott, Karen Steele, Pernell Roberts, James Coburn, James Best, Lee Van Cleef.
73 min.
One of the best of the Boetticher/Scott Westerns, bleaker but not too distant in mood from the autumnal resignation of Peckinpah's Ride the High Country, as Scott's ageing lawman lets time catch up with him and foregoes (even as he achieves) the vengeance he had planned on the man who hanged his wife so long ago that the killer, taxed with it, says 'I most forgot'. It's deviously structured as an odyssey of cross-purposes in which Scott captures a young gunman (Best) and proceeds to take him in, ostensibly for the bounty on his head. Actually, Scott hopes to lure Best's brother (Van Cleef), the man who killed his wife, into a rescue bid; two outlaw buddies (Roberts and Coburn) tag along, biding their time, desperate to collect the amnesty that goes with Best's capture; the presence of a pretty widow (Steele) stokes a measure of sexual rivalry; and there are Indians about. Beautifully scripted by Burt Kennedy, with excellent performances all round as the characters evolve through subtly shifting loyalties and ambitions, it's a small masterpiece. TM

Rider on the Rain
(Passager de la Pluie)
(René Clément, 1969, Fr/It) Marlène Jobert, Charles Bronson, Annie Cordy, Jill Ireland, Gabriele Tinti, Jean Gaven, Corinne Marchand, Marika Green.
119 min. b/w.
A promising start with a girl going home to a lonely house, unaware that she has a sex maniac in the boot of her car. He rapes her, she shoots him, and the film spirals into a mad Hitchcockian mystery (the dead man's name is finally revealed, in tribute to the Master, to be MacGuffin), which is rather nullified by the fact that nobody behaves with any sort of credibility. Good performances from Jobert and Bronson, though, and glossy direction from Clément. TM

Riders of Destiny
(Robert North Bradbury, 1934, US) John Wayne, Cecilia Parker, George Hayes, Yakima Canutt.
60 min. b/w.
First of the 16 Westerns produced by the Lone Star outfit for the B-studio Monogram Pictures and starring the young John Wayne, this has particular curiosity value because the Duke's undercover agent Singin' Sandy does just that (though the voice is dubbed by the director's son). Stuntman Canutt wears the black hat, pilfering the water supply from beneath the noses of honest farmers, while he and Wayne worked out between them the slick fight choreography. Surprisingly good, considering. TJ

Riders of the Storm
see American Way, The

Ride the High Country
(aka Guns in the Afternoon)
(Sam Peckinpah, 1961, US) Randolph Scott, Joel McCrea, Ronald Starr, Mariette Hartley, James Drury, RG Armstrong, Edgar Buchanan, LQ Jones, Warren Oates.
93 min.

Peckinpah's superb second film, a nostalgic lament for the West in its declining years, with a couple of great set pieces (the bizarre wedding in the mining camp, the final shootout among the chickens). Affectionately funny as Scott and McCrea, once more hired and temporarily in harness, creak rheumatically while climbing off their horses, turn aside from the trail to bathe aching feet, and sport long woolly combinations for bed. But also achieving an almost biblical grandeur as the two oldtime lawmen, fallen upon hard times and suddenly realising that the world has left them behind, contrive not to fall from grace and self-respect when a tempting gold shipment comes between them. Truly magnificent camerawork from Lucien Ballard. TM

Ridicule
(Patrice Leconte, 1996, Fr) Fanny Ardant, Charles Berling, Bernard Giraudeau, Judith Godrèche, Jean Rochefort, Carlo Brandt, Bernard Dhéran, Albert Delpy.
102 min.
Leconte's costumer, detailing the deceit and moral destitution of pre-Revolutionary Versailles, is an idiosyncratic, but never self-indulgent caricature of aristocratic *belle esprit*, as the 18th century lobbying system secures political advancement through finely wrought dirty gibes. To the court comes Ponceludon de Malavoy (Berling), a hydrologist seeking royal sponsorship for a scheme to drain his marshes. Though struck by the alien ways of the courtly class, with his rapier tongue he could profit in a world where 'wit opens every door'. He finds an ally in the Marquis de Bellegarde (Rochefort), and in Bellegarde's daughter, the buxom Mathilde (Godrèche). But does he have the force of character to survive the self-serving designs of his competitors, typified by the Comtesse de Blayac (Ardant) and her lover, the Abbé de Vilecourt (Giraudeau)? And can he preserve his sense of mission amid the temptations of self-glory? Leconte was never in danger of succumbing to the trappings of period drama, but it's remarkable how distinct in tone this is from such flamboyant extravagances as *The Hairdresser's Husband* or *Tango*. Rather than indulging the eccentric rebelliousness of his characters, this is a more sober, mature work, a disquisition on personal corruption, the duplicity of social graces and the malignancy of self-enclosed elites. Rather deliberately paced, and mired in archaic and abstruse puns, the film is perhaps more interesting than enjoyable. Still, Leconte's customary zest and mordant humour are there, lurking behind the claustrophobic production design and free-spirited camerawork. NB

Riff-Raff
(Ken Loach, 1990, GB) Robert Carlyle, Emer McCourt, Jimmy Coleman, George Moss, Ricky Tomlinson, David Finch, Richard Belgrave, Derek Young.
95 min.
Loach lightens up for this documentary-style comedy about the scams, laughs, dangers and camaraderie of work on a London building site. Newcomer Carlyle plays Stevie, a Scottish ex-con teenager who gets a job tearing the guts out of a closed-down hospital. His workmates are a mixed bunch: Irishmen, West Indians and Scousers with a healthy disrespect for their idle ganger, a talent for ducking and diving, and a keen eye for the main chance. The company's cavalier disrespect for basic safety standards eventually brings tensions on the site to a head. Bill Jesse's pointedly funny script skilfully evokes the texture of working life; Loach's handling of Stevie's tentative romance with would-be singer Susan (McCourt), on the other hand, wavers between the touchingly simple and curiously off-key. There are times, too, when the lively spontaneity of the improvised scenes slips into inaudible chaos. Sadly, Bill Jesse died without seeing the finished film, but this is as good an epitaph as he could have hoped for. NF

Rififi
see Du Rififi chez les Hommes

Rififi in Paris
see Du Rififi à Paname

Rift, The (La Grieta)
(Juan Piquer-Simon, 1988, Sp) Jack Scalia, R Lee Ermey, Ray Wise, Deborah Adair.
89 min.

A by-the-numbers submarine pic which steals its every idea and re-floats the usual stuff about a missing craft, a government conspiracy, an on-board saboteur (*Alien*), and a big mother of a monster (*Aliens*). The captain (Ermey) is a hardass, the crew is multi-ethnic, and the hero's estranged wife is on board (*The Abyss*) to up the tension level. When Siren One, a state-of-the-art nuclear sub, goes missing at a depth of 27,000 feet, the vessel's hunky designer (Scalia) joins a NATO team sent down to investigate. Tracking a 'black box' signal to the deep Dannekin rift, the crew discovers a vast underwater cavern populated by mutant life forms, apparently the result of some secret government experiments in gene splicing and accelerated evolution. Pretty soon, the seaweed hits the fan, and the crew are faced by monsters without and an enemy within. The wooden characterisations are predictably shallow, but the dodgy monster effects and model work plumb new depths of ineptitude. NF

Right Out of History: The Making of Judy Chicago's Dinner Party
(Johanna Demetrakas, 1980, US)
75 min.
A documentary about the creation of an elaborate work of art: 'The Dinner Party', made not only by Judy Chicago but by 400 volunteers, is an immense table with place settings designed to commemorate great women from history whose achievements have been pushed 'right out of it' (hence the title). The film is perhaps even more interesting than the finished 'Dinner Party', since it raises some tricky questions about the relations of production on this 'cooperative project', and reveals the complexity of its history. Skilled women with no pretensions to being 'artists', such as china painters and embroiderers, slave away on a labour of love; but even more fascinating than the vast and detailed organisation of traditionally feminine skills is the enormity of Judy Chicago's ego, as she hectors mild-looking coworkers about their ignorance, clinging to her authorship to the end. JWi

Right Stuff, The
(Philip Kaufman, 1983, US) Sam Shepard, Scott Glenn, Ed Harris, Dennis Quaid, Fred Ward, Barbara Hershey, Kim Stanley, Veronica Cartwright, Pamela Reed, Scott Paulin, Mary Jo Deschanel, Levon Helm, Scott Wilson, Jeff Goldblum.
193 min.
From the opening moments it is clear that we have the nearest modern equivalent to a Western: men of quiet virtue going skyward, leaving the tawdry world of log-rolling politicians behind. John Ford might have made it, and director Kaufman matches up to the master of this kind of poetic hero worship. Beginning with Chuck Yeager's breaking of the sound barrier in the late '40s, he uses the great test pilot as a counterpoint to the training and eventual missions of the seven astronauts chosen for America's first space programme. Kaufman (like Tom Wolfe, whose book *The Right Stuff* this is taken from) is well enough aware of the media circus surrounding the whole project, but still celebrates his magnificent seven's heroism with a rhetoric that is respectful and irresistible. CPea

Rigolboche
(Christian-Jaque, 1936, Fr) Mistinguett, Jules Berry, André Lefaur.
90 min. b/w.
Aged 61, gallantly described as a young lady and supposedly capturing the heart of a noticeably bored Jules Berry, the fabled Mistinguett delivers all her close-up lines gazing soulfully skywards (presumably it helped to keep the dewlaps from sagging). Fleeing from a shady past in Dakar, she becomes a star in Paris, finding time to croon to her boarded-out child along the way. Gracelessly tedious, but there is one nice thing about the film: it was solemnly banned during the WWII Occupation because the Germans thought the title (actually the name of Mistinguett's character) was making fun of 'les Boches'. TM

Rigoletto
(Jean-Pierre Ponnelle, 1989, It) Luciano Pavarotti, Ingvar Wixell, Edita Gruberova; Vienna Philharmonic conducted by Riccardo Chailly.
118 min.

Guzzling dwarves, bedizened courtesans, Pavarotti draped in gilded fruit and garlands: Ponnelle's film of Verdi's melodious blood-and-thunder – about a hunchbacked jester, his ravished daughter, and vengeance that goes terribly wrong – is taken at full-frontal face value. Marvellous locations – mouldering palaces, riverside slums – make up for Ponnelle's filmic clumsiness and occasional over-emphasis. As Rigoletto, Wixell is spiteful, tender and ferocious, Gruberova sings like an angel except when stretched by the 'Tremenda vendetta' duet, and Pavarotti's libertine Duke photographs well, acts dashingly, and ends 'La donna è mobile' with a ringing high B. Riccardo Chailly conducts the Vienna Phil in a sleek, surging performance. Handsome to see and hear. MHoy

Ring, The
(Alfred Hitchcock, 1927, GB) Ian Hunter, Carl Brisson, Lillian Hall-Davies, Forrester Harvey, Gordon Harker, Billy Wells.
8,007 ft. b/w.
Arguably the finest of Hitchcock's silent films, this tale of a fairground boxer (Brisson) whose wife takes a shine to the far more socially sophisticated new champion (Hunter), sees the young director completely confident in his control of the medium. The title is ambivalent, referring not only to the boxing-ring (scene of Brisson's first humiliation), to the wedding-ring and to the bracelet Hunter secretly gives to his rival's wife, but also to the circular shape of the story, which stresses the philanderer's apathy when his adulterous affair comes to nothing. Impressive, too, is Hitchcock's keen eye for social detail, and his command of expressionist visual devices to suggest his characters' states of mind, perhaps most memorably a shot which 'melts' off the screen to evoke the cuckold's drunken slide into oblivion. GA

Ring of Bright Water
(Jack Couffer, 1969, GB) Bill Travers, Virginia McKenna, Peter Jeffrey, Roddy McMillan, Jean Taylor-Smith, Helena Gloag.
107 min.
Civil servant Travers and pet otter Mij forsake their cramped London flat for the wide-open spaces of the Scottish Highlands and the tender care of Dr McKenna in this much-loved everyday story of furry folk (from the book by Gavin Maxwell). Accomplished wildlife photography, and solid work from the cast, who are old hands at this sort of thing. The 'aahhh' factor is not insubstantial. TJ

Rio Bravo 100
(Howard Hawks, 1959, US) John Wayne, Dean Martin, Angie Dickinson, Walter Brennan, Ricky Nelson, Ward Bond, Claude Akins, John Russell, Bob Steele, Harry Carey Jr.
141 min.
Arguably Hawks' greatest film, a deceptively rambling chamber Western made in response to the liberal homilies of *High Noon*. Here the marshal in need of help is Wayne, desperately fending off a clan of villains determined to release the murderer he's holding in jail until the arrival of the state magistrate. Unlike Cooper, however, he rejects rather than courts offers of help, simply because his supporters are either too old (Brennan), too young (Nelson), female (Dickinson) or alcoholic (Martin). Thus the film becomes an examination of various forms of pride, prejudice and professionalism, as the various outcasts slowly cohere through mutual aid to form one of the director's beloved self-contained groups. Little of the film is shot outdoors, with a subsequent increase in claustrophobic tension, while Hawks peppers the generally relaxed and easy narrative – which even takes time out to include a couple of songs for Dino and Ricky – with superb set pieces: Dino's redemptory shooting of a fugitive villain, the explosive finale in which Duke realises he needs all the help he can get. Beautifully acted, wonderfully observed, and scripted with enormous wit and generosity, it's the sort of film, in David Thomson's words, which reveals that 'men are more expressive rolling a cigarette than saving the world'. GA

Rio Conchos
(Gordon Douglas, 1964, US) Richard Boone, Stuart Whitman, Anthony Franciosa, Edmond O'Brien, Wende Wagner, Jim Brown, Rodolfo Acosta, Timothy Carey.
107 min.

This borrows a star (Whitman), a screenwriter (Clair Huffaker) and the plot of another Fox Western, *The Comancheros* (1961). A stolen shipment of repeater rifles forces an unlikely – and severely tested – alliance between a Yankee Captain (Whitman), his black sergeant (Brown), an Indian-hating Rebel (Boone), and a Mexican killer (Franciosa). Their common foe: a megalomaniac Southern Colonel (O'Brien) who plans to revive the Civil War and strike back at the Union by arming the Apaches. While it shares the earlier film's taste for the picaresque, this version is in far darker register: Gordon Douglas directs with a blistering vehemence Michael Curtiz never dreamed of. It begins with the massacre of an Indian burial party, and ends with an extraordinarily baroque conflagration: a voyage from dust to ashes only one of the men will survive. TCh

Rio Grande

(John Ford, 1950, US) John Wayne, Maureen O'Hara, Ben Johnson, Harry Carey Jr, Claude Jarman Jr, Victor McLaglen, J Carrol Naish, Chill Wills.
105 min. b/w.
Wayne's Captain York from *Fort Apache* has become a Colonel by the time *Rio Grande* closes the Ford cavalry trilogy, but is still much exercised by troubled notions of authority in both the mirrored families of home life (O'Hara and estranged son Jarman) and command (hamstrung by the inconveniently close Mexican border while keeping down marauding Apaches). A bit wordy, a bit plot-heavy, and with an unfortunate tendency to saccharine musical excess (the Sons of the Pioneers), it's fairly minor but still resonant Ford. PT

Rio Lobo

(Howard Hawks, 1970, US) John Wayne, Jorge Rivero, Jennifer O'Neill, Jack Elam, Victor French, Chris Mitchum, Susana Dosamantes, Mike Henry, David Huddleston, Bill Williams, Sherry Lansing, Jim Davis.
114 min.
Though Hawks' last film moves away from the claustrophobic night-time interiors of *Rio Bravo* and the second half of *El Dorado*, the third Western in this loose trilogy scripted by Leigh Brackett retains many similarities with its predecessors. Wayne is the Union cavalry officer who, after the Civil War, joins forces with a couple of Confederates he once captured, in an effort to hunt down a treacherous bootlegger. Rambling, relaxed (though with several superbly staged set pieces), and often shot through with laconic humour, it's another of Hawks' fascinating portraits of disparate individuals brought together into a cohesive moral force by a mutual sense of respect, responsibility, and physical and emotional needs. If it lacks the formal perfection of *Rio Bravo* and the moving elegy for men grown old of *El Dorado*, it's still a marvellous film. GA

Riot in Cell Block 11

(Don Siegel, 1954, US) Neville Brand, Emile Meyer, Frank Faylen, Leo Gordon, Robert Osterloh, Paul Frees, Don Keefer, Dabbs Greer, Whit Bissell.
80 min. b/w.
A classic of the genre, almost documentary in approach – low budget, no stars, Folsom Prison locations, inmates as extras – and boiling up an explosive violence kept under perfect control. Not looking for cosy answers (in fact, final victory shades ironically into defeat), the script's prime concern is less to establish the need for reform than to demonstrate the fallibilities that militate against its accomplishment: Brand's riot leader and Meyer's warden are men of integrity in essential agreement as to what needs to be done, but each is attended by an evil genius – one psychopathic, the other corrupt – so that simple issues mutate into an entirely different ball game. A riveting movie. TM

Ripa Hits the Skids (Ripa Ruostuu)

(Christian Lindblad, 1993, Fin) Sam Huber, Mari Vainio, Merja Larivaara, Leena Votila.
80 min.
Another dour sub-Kaurismäki comedy-drama from Finland, with the slobby, drunken hero of the title, a none-too-promising would-be film-maker, getting up to his neck in trouble thanks

to his professional ambitions and easy-going promiscuity. With its vaguely Chandler-esque voice-over, it's clearly meant to be a *noir* parody – but mostly it's just tiresome. GA

Ripoux, Les
see Le Cop

Ripoux contre ripoux
see Le Cop 2

Ripples Across Stagnant Water (Sishui Wei Lan)

(Ling Zifeng, 1992, HK/China) Xu Qing, You Yong, Zhao Jun, Cheng Xi.
95 min.
Ten years ago, when he made *Rickshaw Boy*, veteran director Ling Zifeng began a shift from Communist propaganda cinema to much more personal film-making: idiosyncratic adaptations from his favourite literature of the '30s and '40s, centred on strong-willed, independent women, and formed by his interests in visual art, history and sexuality. Much of the present film is as vivid and youthful as anything by Léos Carax. A young woman stuck in a Sichuan backwater town at the turn of the last century marries a grocer but then openly takes a lover; can she hold her own when enemies in the community strike at her and the men in her life? The closing scenes seem choppy and over-compressed, but the film as a whole is clear-sighted, gripping and very beautiful. TR

Rise and Fall of a Little Film Company from a novel by James Hadley Chase (Grandeur et Décadence d'un Petit Commerce de Cinéma d'après un roman de J H Chase)

(Jean-Luc Godard, 1986, Fr) Jean-Pierre Léaud, Jean-Pierre Mocky, Marie Valéra, Jean-Luc Godard.
90 min.
Characteristically, Godard's contribution to the TV thriller series *Série Noire* retains only the most rudimentary trappings of the thriller (mysterious voice-overs, secretive assignations, random shootings). He focuses his attentions on the nuts-and-bolts process of TV production as a neurotic genius (Léaud) and his harassed producer (Mocky) swallow their auteur pride and get down to the business of casting for a James Hadley Chase flick. In one long sequence after another, director Léaud attempts to resurrect theories and images from the great days of the French cinema, torturing actors, chucking out references to everyone from Stanislavsky to Cocteau, until the appearance of Godard himself, a shuffling, nicotine-stained cynic whose pragmatism debunks the mystique of movie-making too much for all concerned. The movie ends with a dead producer, a starving director, and Godard shuffling off to retirement in Iceland, as a new generation of video darlings swamp their efforts in the high gloss pop-promo pouting and posturing. Any criticism that this is too much a movie about a movie about a movie is understandable, but *Rise and Fall* goes further into that territory than anyone (including Godard) has gone before. RS

Rise and Fall of Idi Amin
see Amin, the Rise and Fall

Rise and Fall of Legs Diamond, The

(Budd Boetticher, 1960, US) Ray Danton, Karen Steele, Warren Oates, Elaine Stewart, Jesse White, Simon Oakland.
101 min. b/w.
Quite the equal of Boetticher's classic B-Western series starring Randolph Scott, this ferocious gangster biopic indulges in none of the nostalgia for the Depression or glamorisation of its anti-heroes so prevalent in most such movies. As incarnated by Danton, Diamond is a bundle of pure, destructive energy, so ruthless in his sexual, social and financial ambitions that he'll do *anything* to increase or protect his criminal domain; even to the point of agreeing to his brother's death as insurance that the law doesn't reach him

through his inevitably softer sibling. With superb *noir* photography from Lucien Ballard, the tone is almost existential: wisely, Boetticher defines his protagonist not through psychology but through action. Indeed, the very form of the film mirrors the speed, intelligence, and amoral cunning of its hell-bent mobster. GA

Rise and Rise of Michael Rimmer, The

(Kevin Billington, 1970, GB) Peter Cook, Denholm Elliott, Ronald Fraser, Vanessa Howard, Arthur Lowe, George A Cooper, Harold Pinter, Roland Culver, Dennis Price, John Cleese, Ronnie Corbett, Graham Chapman.
94 min.
Billington once described this political satire as a kind of British *Z*, but after the subtlety of his first feature, *Interlude*, it seemed blunt and a bit pointless. Written and performed by a host of satirical talent, it chronicles the rise of a self-appointed business efficiency expert (Cook), who becomes an autocratic dictator by submitting every issue to national referendum. Somehow the jokes fall a bit thin, and the script can't make up its mind whether to go out for narrative or a string of weak sketches. Despite Cleese's script credit (along with Cook, Chapman and Billington), the writing is miles below *Monty Python* standard. DP

Rise to Power of Louis XIV, The
see Prise de Pouvoir par Louis XIV, La

Rising Damp

(Joe McGrath, 1980, GB) Leonard Rossiter, Frances de la Tour, Don Warrington, Christopher Strauli, Denholm Elliott, Carrie Jones, Glynn Edwards, John Cater.
98 min.
In which it is demonstrated that moderately droll TV boarding-house sitcoms ought not to be stretched to 98 minutes. Scriptwriter Eric Chappell (he also wrote the series) seems to have bundled together a few rejected TV scripts while in the grip of some sort of *Carry On* frenzy. At feature length, the characters – angular spinster, seedy landlord, young painter, smirking black medical student with public school accent – would have been better placed circa 1960. Their sentiments and prejudices (mostly about race and sex) are so overblown, archaic and unlikely that the sour, deft humour of the telly programmes has simply gone. JS

Rising Sun

(Philip Kaufman, 1993, US) Sean Connery, Wesley Snipes, Harvey Keitel, Cary-Hiroyuki Tagawa, Kevin Anderson, Steve Buscemi.
129 min.
Striving to downplay the more racist elements of Michael Crichton's novel, Kaufman's PC adaptation falls awkwardly between the conventions of the Hollywood conspiracy thriller and something intended as more artily significant. When a good-time girl is found dead at a party given by a Japanese conglomerate, various cops – boorish lieutenant Keitel, liaison officer Snipes, and Connery's semi-retired expert on all things Japanese – move in to investigate. Connery lectures at length on his favourite subject, which wouldn't be so dull if the suspense was more adroitly handled, but Kaufman, regrettably, gets the pacing all wrong. *Blow-Up*-style video detection scenes provide a modicum of interest. GA

Risky Business

(Paul Brickman, 1983, US) Tom Cruise, Rebecca De Mornay, Joe Pantoliano, Richard Masur, Bronson Pinchot, Curtis Armstrong, Nicholas Pryor, Janet Carroll.
99 min.
17-year-old Cruise suddenly finds himself in possession of the classic young man's dream: parents away for the weekend, empty house, his father's forbidden Porsche. He finds a girl, and she's a hooker, and they get on fine with all his friends ('Nice friends you have – clean, polite, quick'), and then the Porsche falls into Lake Michigan, and he gets pursued by Guido the Killer Pimp. So far, so glossy, a working comedy of embarrassment that hinges on the weird, and all as hip as a pair of Ray-Bans. What distin-

guishes it, however, is that it's hovering permanently on the brink of stark, staring disaster in a way that strangely recalls *The Graduate*. Good performances from Cruise and De Mornay. CPea

Rita Sue and Bob Too
(Alan Clarke, 1986, GB) Siobhan Finneran, Michelle Holmes, George Costigan, Lesley Sharp, Willie Ross, Patti Nicholls, Kulvinder Ghir.
93 min.
Trading as ribald comedy, this film reflects a cruel and widespread reality, yet maintains an unnerving distance from its own implications. Neighbours on the rough side of a run-down Bradford estate, Rita and Sue (Finneran and Holmes, grittily authentic) are best buddies nearing school-leaving age. They babysit for *nouveau riche* sleazeball Bob (Costigan) and his wife Michelle (Sharp), whose disaffection with sex becomes her husband's justification for getting it any which way he can – one way being on the reclining front seat of his flash car, taking Rita and Sue, incredibly, in quick succession. It's all fun and games until Michelle finds out: Rita becomes pregnant, moves in with Bob, and has a miscarriage; and Sue opts for a haphazard shack-up with a bully of an Asian boy. Thereafter director Clarke's keenly observed 'naff' character nuances, never a comfortable laugh, really begin to stick in the throat, and his persistent rib-tickling in the face of the girls' desperation provokes a moral dilemma which the ludicrous 'Carry On Coupling' finale simply aggravates. Humour in the worst possible taste. EP

Rite, The (Riten)
(Ingmar Bergman, 1969, Swe) Ingrid Thulin, Anders Ek, Gunnar Björnstrand, Erik Hell.
74 min. b/w.
All Bergman's films around this time centre on isolated social groups (often the partners of a marriage) and show them under attack from both inside and out: Laingian fissures and cracks open up between the characters, and their precarious security is challenged by irruptions from the outside world. Bergman preserves and extends his private mythologies (witness the way that images and names recur from film to film), but in a broader (less precious, more honest) context: *The Rite*, with a trio of actors under examination by a judge on charges of obscenity, tries to expose the bonds that tie an artist to his audience, and pushes towards a theory of non-communication. A bold step forward in Bergman's analysis of human isolation. TR

Ritratto di Borghesia in Nero
see Nest of Vipers

Ritz, The
(Richard Lester, 1976, GB) Jack Weston, Rita Moreno, Jerry Stiller, Kaye Ballard, F Murray Abraham, Paul B Price, Treat Williams, John Everson, Dave King, Bessie Love, George Coulouris.
91 min.
A camp farce, based with unrelenting obviousness on a Broadway play, this is one of those masochistic comedies that rely entirely on the (corpulent) vacillations of the leading man. Jack Weston proves that he is strictly a one-dimensional character actor, yet the action is constructed to provide as little relief from him as possible. It concerns his frenetic adventures as a straight forced to hide out in an all-gay New York bath-house of dream-like dimensions populated by cosmetic studs. After the single joke (Weston is nearly raped by a short, thin 'chubby-chaser', Lester devotes himself with single-minded malevolence to repeating the same routine with weak variations for the entire length of the film. Despite the plot's superficial claims to be breaking new sexual ground, the resulting stale comedy is likely to be as boring to the gay community as to every other. DP

River, The
(Jean Renoir, 1951, US/Ind) Patricia Walters, Radha, Adrienne Corri, Nora Swinburne, Esmond Knight, Thomas E Breen, Sahjan Singh, Arthur Shields, Richard Foster.
99 min.
Adapted from Rumer Godden's novel about an English family living in Bengal during the autumn years of the Raj, *The River* is cast as a nostalgic recollection of life as experienced by an adolescent girl undergoing the splendours and miseries of first love. Contemporary guru-worship may have overtaken Renoir's mystic view of India as an alien, unfathomable landscape which lends due proportion to the everyday sufferings and aspirations of humanity, but his tranquil vision of life as a river flowing on, barely disturbed by the ripples of being born, growing up, falling in love, and dying, remains enormously moving. The performances are sometimes amateurish, the exotic detail sometimes a little touristy (though captured in colour as exquisite as anything ever likely to grace the screen), but it hardly matters. The magisterial lyricism and the warmth of Renoir's humanity are the thing. TM

River, The
(Mark Rydell, 1984, US) Mel Gibson, Sissy Spacek, Shane Bailey, Becky Jo Lynch, Scott Glenn, Don Hood, Billy Green Bush, James Tolkan.
124 min.
Another in a long line of films dealing with the hardships of smallholdings in the sort of rural America usually depicted as containing nothing but corn silos and bigotry. This time, Gibson and Spacek battle against odds much the same as far as nature goes (floods from the river, rather than the conventional tornado), but different on the human front. The villain here is less the Government than the local land baron, who has expansionist schemes, a ploy which vitiates the film's point since the villain is no more than the hero writ larger. Moreover, the message of continuous hardship is somewhat at odds with the same impulse towards idyllic lyricism which Rydell brought to *On Golden Pond*. Vilmos Zsigmond contributes his usual handsome photography, but this is one river that seems unlikely to run. CPea

River, The (Heliu)
(Tsai Ming-Liang, 1997, Tai) Lee Kang-Sheng, Miao Tien, Lu Hsiao-Ling, Chen Chaorong, Chen Shiang-Chyi.
124 min.
A top prize-winner in Berlin, this takes the absurd/poignant observation of urban isolation and loneliness found in Tsai's two earlier features one step further. A father, mother and son live together-but-apart in a nondescript Taipei apartment, each trapped in a private circle of hell. The taciturn father visits the city's gay saunas for anonymous hand-jobs; the deeply unhappy mother is stuck with an apathetic lover; and the sullen and resentful son finds himself with an agonising (and seemingly incurable) neck pain after an unwise dunking in the polluted Tanshui River. The film's narrative drive has two motors: the quest to alleviate the son's pain and the father's berserk attempts to shore up the ceiling of his room against a leak from the apartment above. Tsai brilliantly conflates the two problems in a climax which is in equal parts real, surreal, melodramatic and inexplicably mysterious. Looks like a future classic. TR

River of Grass
(Kelly Reichardt, 1994, US) Lisa Bowman, Larry Fessenden, Dick Russel, Michael Buscemi.
75 min.
Born in the backwaters of Florida, the daughter of a homicide detective father and a narcotics agent mother, 31-year-old co-writer and director Reichardt clearly puts a lot of herself into this striking feature debut, which turns the roster of love-on-the-run B-picture clichés right on its head. An unprepossessing 30-year-old with a couple of children and an absent husband, Cozy (Bowman) lives out the dreariest of existences until one night she sneaks out of the house, hooks up with the extremely aimless Lee (Fessenden), and winds up on the lam after the pair think they've shot a local home-owner. With its cast of losers and never-weres, its catalogue of lives in apparent suspension, this down-home drama must be the slackest piece of slacker cinema yet to hit our screens, but the film's crisp framing and even crisper editing signals a sharp intelligence at work behind the camera. What emerges is a wry and telling account of the kind of folks that movies never reach. Watch out for a terrific climactic moment

that out-guns *Thelma & Louise*, listen out for a top soundtrack that makes superb use of the Beach Boys' lulling 'Disney Girls'. TJ

River of No Return
(Otto Preminger, 1954, US) Robert Mitchum, Marilyn Monroe, Rory Calhoun, Tommy Rettig, Murvyn Vye, Douglas Spencer.
91 min.
Saloon singer Monroe, two-fisted farmer Mitchum, and the young son he hardly knows, may be drifting down-river by raft from both immediate dangers and their immediate pasts, but the thrust of Preminger's only Western consistently forces them to attempt the 'impossible' return: to restart their variously broken lives and reconstitute the 'ideal' family. While Mitchum's performance is excellent, the film holds most interest as an early appraisal of the Monroe enigma: in revealing analogy to the posthumous cult, Mitchum's ability to see beyond her sex symbol/whore facade extends only as far as her fitness for the role of Mother. There really is no return. PT

River Rat, The
(Tom Rickman, 1984, US) Tommy Lee Jones, Nancy Lea Owen, Brian Dennehy, Martha Plimpton.
93 min.
Tom Rickman was screenwriter on C&W biopic *Coal Miner's Daughter* in which Tommy Lee Jones played Loretta Lynn's husband. Here, in Rickman's directorial debut, the ever-reliable Jones is first rate as an ex-con visiting his family after an absence of many years and trying to make up for lost time with awkward teenager Martha Plimpton. Regrettably, the film doesn't find a great deal to do with their burgeoning relationship. TJ

River Runs Through It, A
(Robert Redford, 1992, US) Craig Sheffer, Brad Pitt, Tom Skerritt, Brenda Blethyn, Emily Lloyd, Edie McClurg, Stephen Shellen, Nicole Burdette.
123 min.
Montana, 1910. Norman and his younger brother Paul grow up under the watchful eye of their father (the ever-wonderful Skerritt), a Presbyterian minister of Scots descent. Mornings are spent studying, afternoons devoted to fly-fishing in the nearby river, a quasi-mystical pastime which serves as the film's central metaphor: while they cast their lines and wait, the boys learn the importance of grace, harmony and patience. At home, however, the family's inability to express emotions hints at trouble to come; and so while nice-guy Norman (Sheffer) matures and dates good-girl Jessie (Lloyd), bad Paul (Pitt) turns to gambling and liquor. Redford (who reads passages from Norman Maclean's source novella in voice-over) explores the brothers' changing relationship with intelligence and restraint; however, because events are filtered through the author's fictional persona, certain sequences involving Paul lack his much-needed perspective. Humour brings things back to earth, and saves the film from becoming over-earnest. Leave your preconceptions about fishing at the door: you'll be caught hook, line and sinker. CM

River's Edge, The
(Allan Dwan, 1957, US) Ray Milland, Anthony Quinn, Debra Paget, Harry Carey Jr, Byron Foulger.
87 min.
Made for spare change like the rest of his flurry of late, worthwhile B-pictures, this is yet another example of Dwan's enterprise under pressure. He gets a scathing performance out of Milland, for instance, as the crook with a wad of hot money he needs to smuggle into Mexico, proves characteristically at home with the expanses of CinemaScope, and blithely proceeds with a storyline that oh-so-conveniently marries off the villain's old flame to border guide Quinn. TJ

River's Edge
(Tim Hunter, 1986, US) Crispin Glover, Keanu Reeves, Ione Skye Leitch, Daniel Roebuck, Dennis Hopper, Joshua Miller, Roxana Za
100 min.
Kicking off with an overweight and slobbish teenager (Roebuck) sitting dispassionately next to the naked corpse of the girl he's just murdered, this

raw picture of the lost generation tackles thorny issues of responsibility and loyalty: will the psycho killer's peers remain true to their (lack of) ideals, or turn fink and risk retribution? In Hunter's smalltown hell, the dilemma is not easily dealt with: on the one hand, Roebuck's barely motivated act of violence escalates beyond fun into nightmare territory; on the other, society is truly fucked – why bother saving it? – with the kids gripped by the baleful influence of the dope-dealin', gun-totin', mannequin doll-lovin' Feck (Hopper, excessively indulged). For all its uncompromising toughness, the film, like the kids, gets out of hand, its bleak portrait of alienated, antisocial behaviour increasingly wrecked by hysterical performances (Glover especially), a sentimental teen-romance subplot, and melodramatic contrivance. There are some good, frightening scenes of volatile lunacy, but the whole thing badly lacks a controlling distance and perspective; much inferior to Hunter's script for Jonathan Kaplan's superficially similar *Over the Edge*, it continually teeters on the verge of self-parody. GA

River Wild, The

(Curtis Hanson, 1994, US) Meryl Streep, Joseph Mazzello, David Strathairn, Kevin Bacon, John C Reilly, Elizabeth Hoffman, Victor H Galloway.
111 min.
This tense family-therapy thriller doesn't produce any surprises, but sometimes, perhaps, it's enough just to go along for the ride, knowing you'll arrive not too far from where you set off. Gail (Streep) whisks reluctant husband Tom (Strathairn) and troubled son Roarke (Mazzello) to Montana for a week's white-water rafting. The purpose of the trip is not only to commune with nature, but to heal the rift between husband and wife, father and son. Tom, though, is not unduly delighted to be at his wife's mercy, especially when the suspiciously charming Wade (Bacon) starts paddling in their wake, a line at the ready, a rod in his pocket. While it's true that the men rely on Streep's superior kayak skills and knowledge of the river, the movie is only interested in a kind of halfway feminism: much of it is concerned with young Roarke, and the contrasting father-figures of Wade and Tom. Bacon scores strongly, but it is Streep's beautifully natural, unshowy performance which keeps the film on course, even when the machinations of the plot become very rocky indeed. TCh

Road, The

see Strada, La

Road Flower

(Deran Sarafian, 1993, US) Christopher Lambert, Craig Sheffer, David Arquette, Adrienne Shelley, Noah Fleiss.
86 min.
A cautionary thriller which plays like a cross between *The Hitcher* and *Cape Fear*. It's the story of a middle-class family whose vacation turns into a nightmare when they get on the wrong side of a bunch of tearaways halfway across a Midwestern desert. Goaded into playing chicken with the youths, one adult ends up dead, and the others are taken prisoner while the mentally unstable leader (Sheffer) decides how to dispose of them. After a taut, provocative opening, the improbabilities soon mount up (a situation not helped by Sheffer's OTT performance). The film never really finds its feet, but settles down to a series of action clichés (note how Lambert's specs disappear once his gravitas has been established). It's ironic, given the emphasis on dysfunctional families of one kind or another, that the film is itself a family affair: written and produced by Tedi Sarafian, while sometime director Richard Sarafian appears in a cameo role. TCh

Roadgames

(Richard Franklin, 1981, Aust) Stacy Keach, Jamie Lee Curtis, Marion Edward, Grant Page, Thaddeus Smith, Stephen Millichamp.
100 min.
It's precisely its pretensions which make this a surprisingly agreeable cross of angst-ridden '70s road movie with Hitchcockian thriller. In homage to *Rear Window*, the windshield of poetry-quoting truck driver Keach's lorry stands in as the blank sheet upon which he sketches fantasies about what he observes on the road. A string of grisly murders which follow him across Australia, and a lift given to hitchhiker Jamie Lee Curtis, who later dis-

appears, fuel his already vivid imagination still further. Effective as a string of cinematic shocks, the movie manages a good number of coups, with its cargo of raw meat, use of Jamie Lee's association with endless knife-flicks, and the ever-so-slightly surreal placing of figures in a vast landscape, making for an endearing horror pic. RM

Road Home, The

(Jerzy Kaszubowski, 1987, GB/Pol) Rafal Synowka, Jerzy Binczycki, Marzena Trybala, Slawa Kwasniewska, Boguslaw Linda, Jerzy Kaszubowski.
95 min.
In 1945, the Red Cross take Jerzy (Synowka) from Germany, where he has spent the war, back home to his mother and his paternal grandparents who occupy a large house somewhere near the Black Forest, then under the jurisdiction of the Red Army. The boy's father, a Polish cavalryman, disappeared in 1939 and a flame is kept burning at night to guide him home. Written and directed by the English-born Jerzy Kaszubowski, this Anglo-Polish production focuses tight on its historical moment, on a section of Poland sandwiched between its past (Germany) and its future (the Soviet Union). It's heavily symbolic, with an eagle and a grey horse making several appearances (and the director himself playing the father's ghost). At the end Jerzy and his stepfather Edward, a government placeman, wander through a forest after their truck has been ambushed by partisans. Jerzy has often imagined killing the now terrified usurper. The opportunity presents itself, but he declines to take it. Cue the grey horse. JPy

Road Home, The

see Lost Angels

Road House

(Jean Negulesco, 1948, US) Ida Lupino, Cornel Wilde, Celeste Holm, Richard Widmark, OZ Whitehead, Robert Karnes.
95 min.b/w.
A bizarre, subdued weepie-cum-thriller, centered around Lupino's sultry presence as a nightclub chanteuse who inspires such feelings of love and hate in her blood-brother employers (Widmark and Wilde) that they turn on each other with a vengeance. Aided by strong performances, Negulesco smooths over the strange shifts in plot and characterisation, manages somehow to lend credibility to the melodramatic proceedings, and delivers one of the great drunkard scenes en route. Mad, perhaps, but memorable too. GA

Road House

(Rowdy Herrington, 1989, US) Patrick Swayze, Kelly Lynch, Sam Elliott, Ben Gazzara, Marshall Teague, Julie Michaels, Red West, Sunshine Parker, Kevin Tighe, Kathleen Wilhoite.
114 min.
Swayze gives up 'Dirty Dancing' for dirty fighting in this violent, spectacular and immensely enjoyable study of Zen and the art of Barroom Bouncing. A former philosophy student now majoring in martial arts, he is hired to clean up the Double Deuce, a beleaguered Missouri nightclub where the band plays behind wire and the staff 'sweep up the eyeballs after closing'. Like a modern Western hero, Swayze cleans out the sadists, till-skimmers, drug dealers and loafers, but he's also up against a ruthless businessman (Gazzara) whose heavies extort money for a 'town improvement' scheme. When Swayze's employer refuses to cross Gazzara's palm with silver, heads roll, bones crack, blood flows, buildings explode, and plausibility flies right out the window along with the bodies. Swayze's drippy romance with the local Doc, a leggy blonde (Lynch) who tends his wounds and more besides, slows things down; but when his ageing mentor (Elliott) comes to town, they kick serious ass, while director Herrington and stuntman Charlie Picerni pile on the senseless mayhem as the two factions perform their Dance of Death. Mindless entertainment of the highest order. NF

Roadie

(Alan Rudolph, 1980, US) Meatloaf, Kaki Hunter, Art Carney, Gailard Sartain, Don Cornelius, Rhonda Bates, Joe Spano, Richard Marion.
105 min.

Meatloaf plays a Texas lunk called Travis W Redfish whose ability to fix electronics with manure and bits of potatoes gets him caught up in a highly sanitised, if surreal, version of the rock business. Hank Williams Jr, Roy Orbison, Alice Cooper and Blondie all show up, but the film's best quality is its combination of trash-culture gags and redneck humour: 'I just love these National Geographic Specials' cries Redfish as he watches *The Giant Spider Invasion* on TV. The good ole boy gags are keen enough to make *Roadie* a late night staple, but you can see why UA had cold feet about a wider audience for the film. DP

Roadside Prophets

(Abbe Wool, 1992, US) John Doe, Adam Horovitz, John Cusack, Arlo Guthrie, David Carradine, Timothy Leary.
96 min.
Writer/director Wool has created a genuine weirdo with her part allegorical, part satirical road movie. Complete with cameos from Timothy Leary, Arlo Guthrie and David Carradine, it's a throwback to the vacuous philosophising and psychobabble of the late '60s. And maybe this is fitting. As Joe (Doe) quests for a contemporary El Dorado in Nevada – where he wants to bury a fellow biker who electrocuted himself on a video game – we're continually witness to the conflict between present-day values, as embodied by Sam (Horovitz), who may just be the dead man's ghost, and those of the Summer of Love, as represented by virtually everyone Sam and Joe meet. For deadhead druggies only. GA

Roads of Exile, The (Les Chemins de l'Exil)

(Claude Goretta, 1978, Fr/Switz/GB) François Simon, Dominique Labourier, Roland Bertin, Michel Berto, Gabriel Cattand, Martine Chevallier, Sylvain Clément, William Fox.
165 min.
Long, slow, and probably not to everybody's taste, but a fascinating study of the Swiss philosopher/novelist Jean-Jacques Rousseau, which attempts to elucidate certain aspects of his life and work left obscure in his supposedly completely honest *Confessions*. Covering the years from Rousseau's exile after the burning of *Emile* in 1762 to his death in 1778 (years marked by his progressive persecution mania), it also ranges back to privileged earlier moments as he attempts to alleviate his present misery by recapturing or exorcising his past. It's almost a pointilliste film, as quietly undemonstrative as *The Lacemaker*, alternating between gorgeously idyllic natural landscapes and stark, severe interiors that would not have shamed Vermeer. Rossellini was originally slated to direct, but Goretta has done the subject proud, very much in the master's manner. TM

Road to Corinth, The

see Route de Corinthe, La

Road to Frisco, The

see They Drive By Night

Road to Glory, The

(Howard Hawks, 1936, US) Fredric March, Warner Baxter, Lionel Barrymore, June Lang, Gregory Ratoff, Victor Kilian, Paul Stanton, John Qualen.
95 min. b/w.
Hawks brings *The Dawn Patrol* down into the trenches, with Baxter as the (French) CO coming to the end of his tether as the death toll mounts, and March as the junior officer who takes over. There's a conventional love interest (Lang as a nurse), a sticky subplot involving Barrymore (he's Baxter's father, and though considerably over-age, joins up to do his bit alongside his son), and some swivelling between anti-war and jingoistic moods. The climax, a heroic twin death scene (with Barrymore redeeming his former cowardice by suicidally guiding the blinded Baxter to a crucial observation post) is embarrassingly OTT. But elsewhere Hawksian understatement keeps the lachrymose tendencies at bay (though William Faulkner co-scripted, it appears that Nunnally Johnson did a rewrite job), turning the film into another of his finely-tuned studies of comradeship under stress; and there is some superb battle footage, in fact borrowed from a French film of 1932, Raymond Bernard's *Les Croix de Bois*. TM

Road to Morocco

(David Butler, 1942, US) Bing Crosby, Dorothy Lamour, Bob Hope, Dona Drake, Anthony Quinn, Vladimir Sokoloff, Monte Blue, Yvonne De Carlo.
83 min. b/w.
The third, and along with *Road to Utopia*, probably the best in a series which began in 1940 with *Road to Singapore*, continued with *Road to Zanzibar* (1941), *Road to Utopia* (1945), *Road to Rio* (1947), *Road to Bali* (1952), *The Road to Hong Kong* (1962). Like Webster's dictionary, Bob and Bing are Morocco bound and gagging as they vie, as ever, for Lamour's hand. The Hope persona is here at its most complete – the stud who baulks at the last fence, the sharp talker who always seems to be talking to himself, the complacent wit who depends on our recognition of references, situations, generalised feelings. At base, it's an unsympathetic character – asexual, craven, treacherous – but Hope's skill in timing, and his ability to work cold what is an extended cabaret act, carries him through. Frank Butler and Don Hartman, who also wrote the two earlier *Road* movies, know their man completely. Crosby is a pleasant foil, and croons 'Moonlight Becomes You' as his party piece. SG

Road to Nhill, The

(Sue Brooks, 1997, Aust) Bill Young, Bill Hunter, Patricia Kennedy, Vikki Blanche, Monica Maughan, Terry Norris.
85 min.
One day in the sleepy outback community of Nhill, four elderly members of the ladies' bowls team have a car accident and find themselves hanging upside down by their seat belts. The wait begins for the emergency services, and an extended comedy of errors gets under way – not out-and-out farce, but a kind of amiable, plausible fumbling. Alison Tilson's screenplay tells us again and again that Australian men are crap, but the womenfolk have to put up with them, while Sue Brooks' direction backs it up with a lot of portentous aerial shots. If droll detachment was intended, such over-emphasis breaks the spell. TJ

Road to Salina
(Sur la Route de Salina)

(Georges Lautner, 1969, Fr/It) Mimsy Farmer, Robert Walker, Rita Hayworth, Ed Begley, Bruce Pêcheur, Sophie Hardy, David Sachs.
103 min.
A complicated little epic, told in flashback, concerning a rather sinister case of mistaken identity being imposed by Rita Hayworth and her screen daughter (tubby, snub-nosed Farmer) on an itinerant stud (Walker). In explaining just why this should be, the film gets through incest, a very unconvincing murder or two, a few flashes of rather unattractive genitalia, and a fair bit of sexual grumbling and grunting. As an excuse for the odd flash of tit and prick, well, better skinflicks have been made for less than a sixth of what Joe Levine must have coughed up to produce this.

Road to the Racetrack
(Kyongmachang Kanungil)

(Jang Sun-Woo, 1991, SKor) Moon Sung-Kuen, Kang Soo-Yeon, Kim Bo-Yeon, Lee In-Ok.
138 min.
The film which shot Jang into the premier league nudges the sex-war into the 21st century. 'R' (Moon) comes back to Korea from several years of study in France, expecting to resume his affair with fellow student 'J' (Kang). But she is now a 'different' woman, adept at abandoning him in hotel rooms every time he tries to corner her and insistent that he should go back to his working-class wife and kids. Jang raises indirection to a fine art: he maintains the sense that the film could veer off in any direction at any time, and never fully explains the title metaphor. But anyone struggling through a screwed-up relationship will recognise this as the real thing. TR

Road to Utopia

(Hal Walker, 1945, US) Bing Crosby, Bob Hope, Dorothy Lamour, Hillary Brooke, Douglass Dumbrille, Jack LaRue.
90 min. b/w.
A typical *Road* movie (Utopia being Alaska), this has Lamour oscillating between Bob and Bing for possession of both halves of the map to her gold-mine. But kiss-kiss and moonlight serenading aside, it's always the quipping rivalry of the duo that rules (Bing: 'We've shared a couple of things that money can't buy' – Bob: 'Yeah, and I always got the ugly one'), where possession is the objective and *L'Amour* the object. But share they do, right down the middle. She loves Bing, marries Bob, but the offspring is a dead ringer for 'We adopted him' they chorus, to the tune of Family Entertainment, accompanied by a broad wink. FF

Road to Wellville, The

(Alan Parker, 1994, US) Anthony Hopkins, Bridget Fonda, Matthew Broderick, John Cusack, Dana Carvey, Michael Lerner, John Neville.
120 min.
If you're tickled by rectal complaints, this film of T Coraghessan Boyle's novel about Dr Kellogg and his turn-of-the-century sanitarium is the movie for you. It's an ensemble piece, but the real star is the re-creation of the Battle Creek Sanitarium, replete with sitz baths, a Fecal Analysis room, and enemas on the hour. Alan Parker has the true cartoonist's eye for the juxtapositioning of wobbly flesh and corrective machinery, and Hopkins' Kellogg does nothing to let him down. All bounce and buck teeth, this Cornflake King is a splendid comic creation, though his adopted son (Carvey) errs on the side of Fungus the Bogeyman. The stories are less interesting than the setting, with constipated Will (Broderick) and his sexually curious wife (Fonda) the victims of, respectively, colonic irrigation and a fraudulent clitoris expert. Battle Creek, Michigan, was like a gold-rush town in 1907, with rival cereal manufacturers battling to dominate the credulous market – clearly an appealing pathology to an old socialist like Parker, but sloppily rendered here. Still, an amusing farce. BC

Roald Dahl's Matilda

(Danny DeVito, 1996, US) Mara Wilson, Danny DeVito, Rhea Perlman, Embeth Davidtz, Pam Ferris, Brian Levinson.
98 min.
This adaptation is paradoxical, a film celebrating the fruits of book-reading that's not as good as the original novel. DeVito can't resist the Hollywood touch – special effects, suspect stereotypes, crushing music – especially in the latter stages. Still, mainly he's stuck to the book, and anyway, there's scope enough in Dahl's slipstream for something worthwhile. Our heroine (Mara Wilson) is a precocious, bright, spunky young thing somehow born to mindless, amoral, stupid neanderthals. Dad (DeVito) is a crooked car dealer, Mum (Perlman) a bingo junkie; they both ignore her. When she's finally sent to school, it's as part-receipt for a used car Dad's sold to the headmistress, Miss Trunchbull (Ferris). Alas, the teaching methods of this Olympic hammer-throwing harridan are open to question – her idea of a perfect school is one with no children. DeVito's snappy, kinetic visual style fits the cartoon feel of the material, and the cast is great. It's a modern-day pantomime about childhood solidarity and self-empowerment: the real joy here is the view of generational war, the children's assumption of zero tolerance for injustices inflicted by absurd adults, and the recognition that the big meanies should be punished, by fair means or foul. NB

Roar

(Noel Marshall, 1981, US) Noel Marshall, Tippi Hedren, John Marshall, Jerry Marshall, Melanie Griffith, Kyalo Mativo.
101 min
Being savaged by delinquent gulls in Hitchcock's *The Birds* must have given Tippi Hedren a masochistic approach to wildlife. In *Roar*, the brainchild of husband Marshall, the hapless woman is pursued around an African jungle holiday home by 150 assorted Big Cats and a couple of jumbos. The narrative is a farcical melange of pseudo David Attenborough and Disneyspeak, married to equally fickle camerawork. The bizarre contradictions insist that the film be evaluated as a curiosity. Its value is as an ingenuous documentary portrait of the Marshalls as mega-eccentrics and misguided animal lovers (they have more than 100 lions and tigers as pets at their LA pad). Who can deny the grisly charm of Noel explaining what wonderful human beings leos are as a pride member playfully gnaws his leg? BPa

Roaring Twenties, The

(Raoul Walsh, 1939, US) James Cagney, Priscilla Lane, Humphrey Bogart, Gladys George, Jeffrey Lynn, Frank McHugh, Paul Kelly, Joe Sawyer.
106 min. b/w.
Marvellously mixing semi-documentary aspects with traditional genre motifs, Walsh's archetypal gangster thriller follows the fates of three WWI doughboys who return to an America plagued with unemployment: while Lynn goes straight, Cagney's the good guy reluctantly drawn into bootlegging and killing by a ruthless Bogart, and forever pining for good girl Lane while ignoring the attentions of George's tart-with-a-heart. Most impressive for its frantic pace and its suggestion that in times of Depression almost everyone is corruptible, it's also a perverse elegy to a decade of upheaval: that sense of sadness and waste is perfectly encapsulated by George's final line, laconically pronounced over Cagney's corpse, 'He used to be a big shot'. GA

Robbery

(Peter Yates, 1967, GB) Stanley Baker, James Booth, Frank Finlay, Joanna Pettet, Barry Foster, William Marlowe, Clinton Greyn, George Sewell, Glynn Edwards.
114 min.
It was thanks to his brash handling of the chases in this thriller, loosely based on the Great Train Robbery, that Peter Yates was asked to go to America to make *Bullitt*. That said, there's more than a whiff of *The League of Gentlemen* about the script, but Yates makes efficient use of his locations, and the chase sequences are genuinely exciting. PH

Robbery Under Arms

(Ken Hannam/Donald Crombie, 1985, Aust) Sam Neill, Steven Vidler, Christopher Cummins, Liz Newman, Ed Devereaux.
141 min.
A would-be Australian Western, based on Rolf Boldrewood's novel (previously filmed, equally tediously, in 1957). Raffish pommy crook Captain Starlight and his faithful abo lead a couple of brothers on a sequence of japes that includes bushwhacking, rustling, jail-breaking and bank-robbing. There is also skinny-dipping, elephants and fireworks, but the interest of these supposedly rumbustious antipodean antics is never more than vague. Without a trace of irony or parody, the emotional response of the characters is either a fist in the face or a knee in some cobber's cobblers. With 148 'actors', 2,000 extras (mainly cattle) and 120 crew members, it claims to be 'the most ambitious and expensive film ever made in Australia': a shame it only really deserves the title 'Wankabout'. MS

Robe, The

(Henry Koster, 1953, US) Richard Burton, Jean Simmons, Victor Mature, Michael Rennie, Richard Boone, Jay Robinson, Dawn Addams, Dean Jagger, Betta St John.
135 min.
Much touted on release as the first film made in CinemaScope (though it was also shot in Academy ratio, which is how it is seen on TV), *The Robe* has now receded into that lost genre, the religious epic. An uncomfortable Burton plays a Roman centurion whose love of a slave girl leads him to a more sympathetic view of the man his forces are about to crucify. Turgid direction, probably not helped by a necessarily cautious approach to framing, is married to creaky dialogue and stiff performances to render this of purely historical interest. DT

Roberta

(William A Seiter, 1935, US) Irene Dunne, Fred Astaire, Ginger Rogers, Randolph Scott, Helen Westley, Claire Dodd, Victor Varconi, Luis Alberni.
105 min. b/w.
Fred'n'Ginge fans won't need a nudge, but the uninitiated should start with almost any of their other movies. The star role here belongs to Irene Dunne, hard to warm to as a musical performer. She gets the classiest Jerome Kern numbers, 'Lovely to Look At' and the indestructible 'Smoke Gets in Your Eyes', both accompanied by staggeringly unimaginative camerawork. Other pills are Randolph 'Gee, that's swell' Scott, the fashion parade (this is what was called 'a woman's pic-

ture' before women became people), and the
yukky plot revolving around Dunne's fluctuating
fortunes as a Parisian fashion designer. Still, Fred
– mind-bogglingly in a role Bob Hope played on
stage – and Ginger do 'I Won't Dance'. And
Ginger does her Polish accent. Remade in 1952 as
Lovely to Look At. SG

Robert A. Heinlein's
The Puppet Masters
see Puppet Masters, The

Robert Altman's Jazz '34:
Remembrances of Kansas
City Swing
(Robert Altman, 1996, US) Jesse David, David
'Fathead' Newman, Ron Carter, Christian
McBride, Tyrone Clarke, Don Byron, Russell
Malone, Mark Whitfield, Victor Lewis, Geri
Allen, Cyrus Chestnut.
72 min.
An off-shoot from *Kansas City*, this keeps the
focus entirely on KC's legendary all-night jam
sessions where the likes of Lester Young plied
their trade. The music is stonking, but the documentary aspects are disappointingly half-hearted (brief oral testimonies sound suspiciously
phony), and even the jam re-creations feel contrived. Handsomely shot and immaculately
recorded, so it should please the jazzers. TCh

Robert Ryland's
Last Journey
(Gracia Querejeta, 1996, Sp/GB) Ben Cross,
William Franklyn, Cathy Underwood, Gary
Piquer, Lalita Ahmed, Maurice Denham.
100 min.
'Freely' adapted from Javier Marias' acclaimed
novel, this mystery-cum-psychological drama,
about the return of a veteran non-conformist professor (Franklyn) to Oxford after a decade away,
and the effect of this on a don (Cross) and his sister (Underwood), is so stilted, clumsy and dramatically tedious as to be virtually unwatchable.
Celluloid Oxbridge at its very worst. GA

Robin and Marian
(Richard Lester, 1976, US) Sean Connery,
Audrey Hepburn, Robert Shaw, Richard
Harris, Nicol Williamson, Denholm Elliott,
Kenneth Haigh, Ronnie Barker, Ian Holm, Bill
Maynard, Esmond Knight.
107 min.
Maybe it was because audiences expected anoth-
er *Four Musketeers*-style romp that this flopped
on its first release. There are quite a few typical
Lester gags on the fringes of its tale of an elderly Robin returning to Sherwood from the
Crusades and finding that Marian has become
Abbess of a local priory; but the movie is conceived and executed in an elegiac key (not unlike
Siegel's *The Shootist*), and played with an unfashionable depth of feeling (especially by Connery
and Hepburn, both terrific). It's one of those rare
movies, like King Hu's *Touch of Zen*, that handles its historical imagery so cleanly, and contains its pretensions so solidly within sure
characterisation and plotting, that it is often sublimely expressive. TR

Robin and the 7 Hoods
(Gordon Douglas, 1964, US) Frank Sinatra,
Dean Martin, Bing Crosby, Sammy Davis Jr,
Edward G Robinson, Barbara Rush, Peter
Falk, Sig Ruman.
123 min.
The Rat Pack moves the 'robbing the rich...' rou-
tine from mouldy old Sherwood Forest to
Prohibition-era Windy City, else the plot motiva-
tion for Sinatra belting out 'My Kinda Town,
Chicago Is' might have seemed somewhat
opaque. Otherwise, it's exactly as you'd expect.
The gang do their stuff (for the last time on
screen), and Sammy Cahn and Jimmy Van
Heusen picked up an Oscar nomination for the
songs. TJ

Robin Hood
(Allan Dwan, 1922, US) Douglas Fairbanks,
Wallace Beery, Enid Bennett, Sam De Grasse,
Paul Dickey, William Lowery, Alan Hale,
Willard Louis.
10,680 ft. b/w.
Dwan's control of crowds and imaginative use of

the sets give an effect of epic pageant that's better than many a later blockbuster. The extras do
at least look as if they're in on the action, and not
just there to fill up the screen. However, the acting of the central characters disarms criticism.
Fairbanks possesses all the skill and enthusiasm
of an eleven-year-old in a school play, and
behaves like one too, usually backslapping and
tussling with the lads. His other characteristic
expression, exaggerated surprise, reminds you of
the Bisto Kids. In Sherwood, he skips everywhere, flapping his arms: merriness at all costs
in the face of the darkest the Dark Ages can offer.
The fact that Sam De Grasse turns in a very good
performance as Prince John hardly matters.

Robin Hood
(Wolfgang Reitherman, 1973, US) voices: Brian
Bedford, Peter Ustinov, Terry-Thomas, Roger
Miller, Phil Harris, Andy Devine, Monica
Evans.
83 min.
Er, basically, no one makes cultural appropria-
tion as much fun as Walt Disney. America is
what he does best, so he does it to Robin Hood.
Animated, Sherwood Forest becomes more like
Nashville, Tennessee, with a slob of a sheriff
humming 'Taxes are doo, doo de doo', and cute
suburban kid byplay among the bunnies. While
Prince John, 'a lion of diminished character',
sucks his thumb, the furry faces of the poor are
being relentlessly ground, the raccoons are on the
chain gang, and Allan-a-Dale sings a Johnny
Cash prison lament. Ustinov is the voice of the
lion, flattered by Terry-Thomas as Sir Hiss, a
courtly reptile: it is their domestic bickering and
not the foxy schmaltz of Little John, Robin and
Marian that jollies the film along. Good baddies,
good poignant bits, and an archery contest that
degenerates into all-action American football
make up for the familiar, repetitive plot and the
several lapses of taste and intelligence inevitable
in medieval Nashville. RP

Robin Hood
(John Irvin, 1990, GB) Patrick Bergin, Uma
Thurman, Jürgen Prochnow, Jeroen Krabbé,
Edward Fox, Jeff Nuttall.
104 min.
Judging by this swashbuckler, the genre has died
and been teleported to outer space. Robin's outlawry, escape, encounters with Little John and
Friar Tuck are routine, and the love story is limp.
Not much pledging troth and sighing like furnaces about this Robin and Marian; he's phoning
it in, she's truculent and dislikeable, and what
varlet would not see through her (big Uma
Thurman) disguise as a boy? Fatally, Bergin's
Robin Hood lacks the snap for action, scrambling
where bounding is required, good-eggish rather
than noble in resolve, and mistaking lounging for
blithe insouciance in the courtship. The main
interest lies in the trio of villains: a death's-head
Folcanet with extraordinary Norman consonants
(Prochnow), a perplexingly ambiguous Baron
Daguerre (Krabbé), and a brief, effective guest
spot for Prince John (Fox). BC

Robin Hood – Men in Tights
(Mel Brooks, 1993, US) Cary Elwes, Richard
Lewis, Roger Rees, Amy Yasbeck, Isaac
Hayes, Tracey Ullman, Patrick Stewart, Mel
Brooks, Clive Revill.
104 min.
What took the director so long to get around to
Robin Hood? A standard, camp, unapologetic Mel
Brooks parody, with digs at Kevin Costner's
Prince of Thieves and its multi-racial Merry Men,
and an arsenal of throw-away gags. An impres-
sive cast – Stewart, Hayes, Ullman – cannot
unfortunately save the day. NKe

Robin Hood of El Dorado, The
(William A Wellman, 1936, US) Warner
Baxter, Ann Loring, Bruce Cabot, Margo, J
Carrol Naish, Edgar Kennedy, Eric Linden.
86 min. b/w.
A Western of some reputation, largely undeserved. Based on the Walter Noble Burns biography of Joaquin Murrieta, set in California in
1848, it deals with the racial tensions in the
newly-ceded territory, exacerbated by the discovery of gold at Sutter's Mill. Baxter (uncomfortably cast) plays Murrieta, a Mexican farmer
who believes in peaceful co-existence until his
wife (Margo) is raped and killed by riff-raff

American prospectors; outlawed after exacting
revenge, he continues to wage a guerrilla war for
justice, realising too late that he has become little better than the villainous bandit Three-
Fingered Jack (Naish) with whom he joins forces.
Though fuelled by an admirable anger at racist
barbarities, the film is sunk by poor performances
(Naish excepted) and a below-par script which
indulges endless montage sequences (gold rush,
wanted posters, fiestas, etc) or sententious intertitles in the silent movie manner ('Where men and
women lived for the moment's happiness – with
danger and death ever the next day's promise').
Wellman and cameraman Chester Lyons at least
contrive a pleasant, soberly muted visual sheen.
TM

Robin Hood:
Prince of Thieves
(Kevin Reynolds, 1991, US) Kevin Costner,
Morgan Freeman, Mary Elizabeth
Mastrantonio, Christian Slater, Alan Rickman,
Sean Connery, Geraldine McEwan, Michael
McShane, Brian Blessed, Nick Brimble.
143 min.
After escaping his infidel captors with Indiana
Jones-style panache, Robin of Locksley (Costner)
returns from the Crusades with Moorish companion Azeem (Freeman), ready to avenge his
father's murder. Azeem cracks jokes about the
English weather while Robin gets to know
Marian (Mastrantonio), but it isn't until they
engage in open conflict with the Sheriff of
Nottingham (a gloriously hammy Rickman) that
the pace picks up and arrows start to fly. The mix
of comedy, '90s sensibility, and swashbuckling
action is more hit than miss, even if the overall
effect is rather slapdash. Spirited, irreverent stuff,
but not for those who like their myths kept
sacred. CM

Robinson Crusoe
(aka Adventures of
Robinson Crusoe)
(Luis Buñuel, 1952, Mex/US) Dan O'Herlihy,
Jaime Fernández, Felipe de Alba.
89 min.
A deceptively simple adaptation of Defoe's classic desert island novel. Few strikingly surrealist
flourishes here: brief dreams of guilt, sexual frustration, and cruel power. Rather, Defoe's caustic
analysis of mankind's foibles is translated into a
moving account of one man's moral rebirth. The
isolation and hardships that befall the bourgeois
Crusoe, previously so dependent on servants for
survival, leave him faithless, fearful for his sanity, and forced to become his own God, feeding
insects and despairing of salvation. But with
Friday's arrival, his ideas of religion and civilisation's hierarchy are really put to the test: trust,
equality, and mercy replace the master-servant
relationship as the necessary conditions of companionship and contentment. As in his other
films, irony and a refusal to indulge in sentimentality are the hallmarks of Buñuel's vision; but
the overwhelming impression here is one of surprising warmth, proof that, whatever humanity's
faults, he remained forever interested in his own
species and ultimately sympathetic to them. GA

Robinson Crusoe on Mars
(Byron Haskin, 1964, US) Paul Mantee, Vic
Lundin, Adam West.
109 min.
Intelligently imaginative sci-fi version of the
Defoe classic, in which an astronaut and his monkey are stranded on Mars, and later joined by the
humanoid slave of an alien race. Haskin and producer George Pal provide the same excellent camerawork and special effects that marked their
earlier *War of the Worlds* and *Naked Jungle* (the
hostility of the Martian landscape is spectacularly evoked in California's Death Valley); but
here, harnessed to a surprisingly faithful rendition of Defoe's conception, the result is an economical, subtle study both of Crusoe's will to
survive, and of the hesitant growing friendship
between the astronaut and his futuristic Friday.
Most remarkably, Haskin avoids sentimentality
even when dealing with the monkey, such is the
assured sensitivity of the film. GA

Robinson in Space
(Patrick Keiller, 1997, GB)
82 min.

In *London*, the anonymous, unseen narrator (Paul Scofield) accompanied the art lecturer Robinson on a series of eccentric, quizzical journeys in and around the capital. Here, he's again invited by his friend, now an impoverished teacher, to help with a project initiated by an ad agency and designed to investigate 'the problem of England'. As the pair embark on their seven voyages, ranging from the Thames to the Channel ports, the Midlands to the far North, Robinson meditates in his inimitable way on geography, history, architecture, economy, politics and culture. Like its predecessor this is an offbeat, verbose, witty mix of documentary, fiction and essay: are we really a poor, terribly provincial nation plagued by industrial decline, or are our hardships and low morale the outcome of choices made by self-serving politicians? As before, references abound: Defoe, Wilde, Austen; the Tolpuddle Martyrs, Engels, Michael Portillo, Greenpeace; the Stones; the Cerne Abbas Giant, architect Buckminster Fuller, Dracula. All this erudition is balanced by the writer/director/cameraman's admirably dry, deeply ironic sense of humour, and by his immaculately framed images, which manage to make the familiar look strangely strange yet oddly normal. And if the satirical political asides don't have quite the bite of those in the earlier movie, this is still provocative, determinedly left-field film-making: bright, adventurous, engrossing and...well, very English. GA

RoboCop

(Paul Verhoeven, 1987, US) Peter Weller, Nancy Allen, Daniel O'Herlihy, Ronny Cox, Kurtwood Smith, Miguel Ferrer.
102 min.
In a futuristic Old Detroit, the crime rates are soaring. Thirty-one cops have been wasted since Omni-Consumer Products took over responsibility for the police department; but, undaunted, Officer Murphy (Weller) and his cocky colleaguette Lewis (Allen) pursue a van-load of bank bandits into a derelict steel mill, where the sado-capitalists corner Murphy and use him for target practice. OCP's plans to construct Delta City can only go ahead if the designated area is safe enough for workers to go about their business unmolested. Their 'enforcement droid' ED 209, a galumphing giant cyborg, short-circuits at its unveiling, leaving the moribund Murphy, his insides wired into a computer-controlled titanium shell, to save the day. But RoboCop is not programmed to deal with corruption within the organisation.Verhoeven's blend of comic strip and snuff movie is vile, violent, and very funny. The pace is breakneck, and when the wit does run out, way-out weaponry and whole-scale destruction keep the appalled excitement burning. MS

RoboCop 2

(Irvin Kershner, 1990, US) Peter Weller, Nancy Allen, Belinda Bauer, Daniel O'Herlihy, Tom Noonan, Gabriel Damon, Willard Pugh, Felton Perry, Patricia Charbonneau.
118 min.
The title refers to both the sequel and the rival, a new megadeath killing machine built on the same lines as the original, but employing the spinal column and brain of the chief villain, demonic drug king-cum-seer Cain (Noonan). But while RoboCop 2, the model, is a mean mother with a positive state-of-the-art kitchen of murderous gadgets, *RoboCop 2* the movie is every bit as messy as a dog's breakfast. It still has all the old wit, the hellish vision of a Detroit plagued by everything from Little League robber gangs to bent or striking cops, and the dependable line-up of actors (Allen, O'Herlihy, Weller). What it doesn't have very much of is the original's energy, passion and remorseless narrative logic. Kershner's direction is never more than adequate, and the story seems full of unfulfilled promise and tangled threads. It's also deeply, disturbingly violent in a way which is more manipulative than gory; unlike the original, with its prophetic vision of the future, this sequel seems to spend too much time glorying in the very horrors it has outlined. SGr

RoboCop 3

(Fred Dekker, 1992, US) Robert Burke, Nancy Allen, Rip Torn, Remy Ryan, John Castle, Jill Hennessy, CCH Pounder, Mako.
104 min.
Dekker's third instalment also comes third in terms of merit. In tune with the times, the techno-violence here is tempered with appeal to 'fam-ily' values. Omni Consumer Product Corporation are now in uneasy alliance with the Japanese multi, Kanemitsu. Debts and permanent crisis have forced them into an ambitious city-building project, Delta, which requires the clearing of the remaining city-centre communities of Detroit. Meanwhile guerilla gangs make life hard for underground groups of determined hippie-like evictees. When RoboCop (Burke) finds himself in loco parentis to kid Nikko (Ryan), he also finds his loyalties and martial arts skills siding with the homeless. The familiarity of the high-armour shoot-outs and sfx-assisted set-pieces make most of this sequel feel surprisingly low-tech. Not bad entertainment, though. WH

Robot Monster

(Phil Tucker, 1953, US) George Barrows, Gregory Moffett, George Nader, Claudia Barrett, Selena Royle, John Mylong.
63 min. b/w.
'For the budget and for the time' said Tucker, 'I felt I had achieved greatness'. His 3-D cheapster in fact lifted all its special effects wholesale and without reconsideration from its 1940 predecessor, *One Million B.C.* Yet it's the winner of the Golden Turkey Award for Most Ridiculous Monster in Screen History (a plump, hirsute little robot). CR

Rob Roy

(Michael Caton-Jones, 1994, US) Liam Neeson, John Hurt, Tim Roth, Brian Cox, Jessica Lange, Eric Stoltz.
130 min.
The Scottish Highlands, 1713. Clan-leader Rob Roy MacGregor (Neeson) asks the Marquis of Montrose (Hurt) for a loan. The aloof Machiavellian hesitantly agrees; but Rob hasn't bargained for the laird's house-guest, the foppish wastrel Cunningham (Roth), who together with Montrose's scheming factor (Cox) steals the money, killing Rob's friend Alan (Stoltz) in the process. The scene is set for deadly enmity between Rob and Montrose. As scripted by Alan Sharp and directed by Caton-Jones, this stirring historical drama is less swashbuckler than transposed Western, with a feel for landscape, intrigue, romance and questions of honour reminiscent of Mann's *Last of the Mohicans*. Neeson makes a less dashing action hero than did Day-Lewis, but he brings enough gravitas to his role to endow his love for his wife Mary (Lange) and his conflict with Cunningham with real emotional punch. Still better are Lange, Hurt, Cox and, notably, Roth, whose final duel with Neeson is a tour de force. While the film's chief virtue is the mythic clarity, Sharp's script, which shifts easily between the fruity innuendo of the aristos and the more demotic colloquialisms of the clansmen, never soft-pedals the historical and political context. GA

Rocco and His Brothers (Rocco e i Suoi Fratelli)

(Luchino Visconti, 1960, It/Fr) Alain Delon, Renato Salvatori, Annie Girardot, Katina Paxinou, Roger Hanin, Paolo Stoppa, Suzy Delair, Claudia Cardinale, Spiros Focas.
180 min. b/w.
The last gasp of the neo-realist spirit in Visconti's work, *Rocco* chronicles at length the misfortunes that befall an Italian peasant family when they move to The Big City. There's a grey conviction about much of the scene-setting and the location shooting, but the film gathers interest as it escalates into melodrama; the tragic climax is pure opera. Delon is unconvincing as the saintly Rocco, but Renato Salvatori makes the thuggish elder brother who falls in with a gay boxing promoter his best part ever. TR

Rocinante

(Ann Guedes/Eduardo Guedes, 1986, GB) John Hurt, Maureen Douglass, Ian Dury, Carol Gillies, Jimmy Jewel, Gillian Heasman.
93 min.
At the start of this portrait of England as 'a garden of secrets, full of tradition and myth, violence and cover-up', Hurt hides away from reality in a derelict cinema (geddit?), until a conversation about narrative with the ex-projectionist (Jewel) forces him to take to the road aboard a truck named Rocinante. The allusion to Quixote's horse (and thus, presumably, to Cervantes' wittily wayward storytelling) is misleading: during the ide-ologically unconscious Hurt's aimless odyssey to Dartmoor, his main encounter is with Jess (Douglass), a political activist scarred by the '84 miners' strike and intent on industrial sabotage. Meanwhile, 'jester' Dury pops up to spout poetry and make ironic comment. Despite the film's good intentions, it is, quite simply, appalling. Such bourgeois conventions as plausible, pacy narrative, realist characterisation, and the potential for an audience's emotional involvement, are jettisoned in favour of stilted, 'significant' dialogue, banal parallels with myth, and clumsily contrived symbolism. The result is a mess: dry, humourless, half-baked obscurantism that insults the viewer. GA

Rock, The

(Michael Bay, 1996, US) Sean Connery, Nicolas Cage, Ed Harris, Michael Biehn, William Forsyth, David Morse, John Spencer, John C McGinley, Tony Todd, Bokeem Woodbine.
136 min.
The Rock, of course, is Alcatraz, prison-turned-tourist site, which is seized by disgruntled, decorated-to-hell General Harris with his elite corps (psycho captain, loyal colonel); they take 83 hostages and aim four VX-gas missiles at San Francisco; the rockets will be fired unless pensions are provided for the families of dead, 'deniable' Special Forces. The twist here is getting Navy SEALS *into* the rock to take the bastards *out*. Step forward as team-leaders reluctant heroes Cage, a Beatles-lovin' FBI boffin with chemical-weapons badges, and ex-SAS officer Sean Connery, the only man to escape from Alcatraz, and presently serving 30-odd years for obtaining US government secrets. Director Michael Bay (with only *Bad Boys* to his name) propels this brew of combat war-movie, *Die Hard*-style actioner and *Indiana Jones* adventure on enough octane to leave objections to the clichéd dialogue and implausible of the plot in the slipstream. Fake countdown and knowing reactionary tone, but the best SF car chase to date. WH

Rock-a-Bye Baby

(Frank Tashlin, 1958, US) Jerry Lewis, Marilyn Maxwell, Connie Stevens, Salvatore Baccaloni, Reginald Gardiner, James Gleason, Hans Conried, Isobel Elsom.
103 min.
An often forgotten Lewis/Tashlin production (loosely based on Preston Sturges' script for *The Miracle of Morgan's Creek*) that contains some very good stuff indeed – all in the first half, unfortunately. Lewis is the lifelong fan of a movie star (Maxwell) who gives him her triplets to look after while she's in Africa making a film. The supporting cast is particularly good (Gardiner, Conried, Connie Stevens), but the gear-change from manic slapstick (watch out for the berserk hosepipe) to cringing sentimentality about babies and nappies is hard to take. DMcG

Rock-a-Doodle

(Don Bluth, 1990, GB) voices: Phil Harris, Glen Campbell, Eddie Deezen, Christopher Plummer, Sandy Duncan, Sorrell Booke.
77 min.
With a gob-smacking opening zoom, Bluth grabs his audience and transports them from outer space to an earthbound farmyard. Here, Chanticleer the rocking rooster (voiced by velvet-larynxed Campbell) is humiliated in front of his animal chums when the sun rises one morning without his usual boisterous bidding. Dismissed as useless, Chanticleer trudges off to seek stardom in the big city, whence he is pursued by his erstwhile pals and by the evil emissaries of the fiendish Grand Duke Owl (Plummer), who now threatens to devour the rain-drenched farmyard. As with so much of Bluth's work, the narrative strengths necessary to support his fiesta of colourfully frenzied animated action are sadly absent. The film's dizzying pace leaves one longing for the plodding reliability of a sturdy Disney storyline. Bluth remains a rebellious visual talent to be reckoned with, but the overall effect is messy. MK

Rock All Night

(Roger Corman, 1957, US) Dick Miller, Russell Johnson, Jonathan Haze, Abby Dalton, The Platters, Robin Morse.
63 min. b/w.

Fugitive killers Johnson and Haze stumble into hot-spot Cloud Nine, where Miller's aptly nicknamed Shorty has just reached the point where he's truly fed up with taller guys pushing him around. Pretty flimsy, but it's cheering to see much-loved character stalwart Miller play the lead. Stand by for some perfunctory and completely unrelated footage of The Platters in action at the start of the movie. TJ

Rock Around the World
see Tommy Steele Story, The

Rockers
(Theodoros Bafaloukos, 1979, US/Jam) Leroy Wallace, Richard Hall, Monica Craig, Marjorie Norman, Jacob Miller, Gregory Isaacs.
99 min
A Trenchtown variant on *Robin Hood*, with dreadlocked drummer Horsemouth (Wallace) up against the local minor-league mafia. An excellent soundtrack (Peter Tosh, Burning Spear, Bunny Wailer, etc), and an endearingly witty script digresses through explanations of the Rasta faith and countless idiosyncratic solidarity rituals, make for a delightful piece of whimsy. Complete with subtitles transliterating the Rasta patois. FL

Rocketeer, The
(Joe Johnston, 1991, US) Bill Campbell, Jennifer Connelly, Alan Arkin, Timothy Dalton, Paul Sorvino, Terry O'Quinn, Ed Lauter, James Handy, Tiny Ron.
108 min.
In this comic book adaptation, chisel-faced pilot Cliff Secord (Campbell) discovers a rocket pack that enables him to zoom through the skies, only to find himself pursued by villains employed by film star Neville Sinclair (Dalton). Sinclair, a dastardly egomaniac, wants the rocket, but so do the Feds, since the Nazis are after it. Poor old Cliff can't tell the good guys from the bad. What's his actress girlfriend Jenny (Connelly) to do? Her man isn't earthbound long enough to finish a date. The late '30s are beautifully evoked, Hiro Narita's cinematography captures some lush images, and director Johnston has a freshness and lightness of touch. The rocket sequences are quite exhilarating, but the scenes in between are the problem; Cliff and Jenny make a bland couple, and the Fascist threat lacks real menace. Neat idea, peachy visuals, but there ain't much else to grip the imagination. CM

Rockets Galore (aka Mad Little Island)
(Michael Relph, 1958, GB) Jeannie Carson, Donald Sinden, Roland Culver, Gordon Jackson, Noel Purcell, Duncan Macrae, Ian Hunter, Jean Cadell, Catherine Lacey.
94 min.
Rank's belated riposte to the 1948 Ealing hit *Whisky Galore*, adapted from another Compton Mackenzie story by Monja Danischewsky who, from the position of associate producer, had fought Alexander Mackendrick over the first film's script. This time the Hebridean Todday islanders are up in arms over plans to site a missile base in their midst, and resort to such quaint defensive tactics as painting seagulls pink to mobilise the naturalist lobby. A rare attempt at whimsy by social drama stalwarts Relph and Dearden, it's amusing enough but somewhat faltering in tone. PT

Rock Hudson's Home Movies
(Mark Rappaport, 1993, US) Eric Farr.
63 min. Video.
This humorous video lecture replays and freeze-frames the movies of model-male beefcake and former truck driver Hudson until his gayness stares you in the face. It's also a passionate, albeit critical, tribute to the man, an analysis of the screen parts, and a warning. Hudson's AIDS diagnosis and subsequent death in 1985 rocked a few preconceptions. Here are clips from the early Universal days, through the '50s adventure pics, the Oscar-nominated role in *Giant*, his melodramatic grand hour with Douglas Sirk, the suggestive pyjama games with Doris Day, right up to the late comedies and soaps. Eric Farr, a weed in white singlet, impersonates the Rock and presents the well-argued case for the offence, taking the liberty of having Hudson discuss himself from beyond the grave, wringing his screen hypochondria to dubious premonitory effect. When Rock explains

his dislike of 'fish' to Paula Prentiss in *Man's Favorite Sport?*, Farr screams, 'What do you *think* they were talking about, dickhead?' Such hectoring palls, but all in all it's a healthy rant. WH

Rocking Horse Winner, The
(Anthony Pelissier, 1949, GB) John Howard Davies, Valerie Hobson, John Mills, Ronald Squire, Hugh Sinclair, Charles Goldner, Susan Richards.
90 min. b/w.
In introducing DH Lawrence to the screen, the Mills/Pelissier team made a strange choice with this brief, terse evocation of Oedipal love (a sensitive child, threatened by a rift between extravagant mother and jobless father, discovers an ability to predict racing winners while pretending to be a jockey, frenziedly astride his rocking horse). Though no one noticed at the time, the Lawrentian sexual undertones are clearly transposed to the film. The boy's masturbatory riding is given a frightening potency, and his attempt to win the love of his glitteringly powerful mother has little to do with filial affection. Pelissier's direction is occasionally overblown, but Mills (as the groom who feeds the boy's fantasies), obviously relishing the opportunity to use his native Suffolk accent, is admirably restrained, and a British film which explores the complex links between sex, money and power is rare indeed. RMy

Rock n'Roll Cop (Sheng-Gang Yihao Tongji Fan)
(Kirk Wong, 1994, HK) Anthony Wong, Carrie Ng, Wu Xingguo, Wu Wing-Kwong.
93 min.
The last of three Kirk Wong films drawn from the reminiscences of a real-life cop, this centres on an idiosyncratic Hong Kong detective (actually more a 'bring back vinyl' man than a rocker) who's sent across the border into China to help their police track down a vicious killer. It complicates matters that the villain's current squeeze was once seduced and abandoned by the China cop. The movie contrasts stolid Mainland procedures with laconic Hong Kong pragmatism (Anthony Wong contributes his usual 'Michel Piccoli plays Caliban' persona as the laid-back detective), but ends up bending over backwards to stress the joys of future co-operation. It sure delivers as an action thriller, though. TR

Rock'n'Roll High School
(Allan Arkush, 1979, US) PJ Soles, Vincent Van Patten, Clint Howard, Dey Young, Mary Woronov, Dick Miller, Paul Bartel, Don Steele, Grady Sutton, The Ramones.
93 min.
For all its throwaway humour, this is basically just a pleasant reworking of the kids versus adults rock'n'roll movie format of the '50s, with Paul Bartel in the traditional role of the adult kook who goes hip, and legendary DJ Don Steele as the radio commentator who brings the confrontation to the nation. Naturally the struggle between the generations gets a little further than before, with a high school burned to the ground and adults thrown out of windows, but it's basically kleenteen fun. If you're worried about the Ramones, rest assured; they make a very adequate chunka chunka chunka chunka sound. DP

Rock, Rock, Rock
(Will Price, 1956, US) Tuesday Weld, Teddy Randazzo, Alan Freed, Frankie Lymon and the Teenagers, The Moonglows, Chuck Berry, The Flamingos, Johnny Burnette Trio.
83 min.
Pioneering DJ/impresario Alan Freed (later harassed by payola probes and mythologised by *American Hot Wax*) chaperones a customarily incongruous bunch of early rockers through this prototype rocksploitation quickie, in which 13-year-old Tuesday Weld (playing 18, and lyrically dubbed by Connie Francis) pines for a strapless dress for the school prom, until perked up by such authentic novelties as Lymon's kitsch classic 'I'm Not a Juvenile Delinquent'. Wonderfully grotesque. PT

Rockshow
(Director not credited, 1979, US) Paul McCartney, Linda McCartney, Jimmy McCulloch, Joe English, Denny Laine.
103 min.

Not so much a movie as a scrapbook folly which captures Wings' last concert on their 1976 world tour. Held at the cavernous King Dome in Seattle, it's beer and skittles for affluent suburbia. Cheesy grins and dully-directed spectacle abound as the band zip through a selection of the greatest hits from the period – with an odd Beatle song thrown in to show who actually wrote it. Paul McCartney is the epitome of good-natured professionalism; Linda is gawky and excited; the late Jimmy McCulloch, pasty-faced and a mite nervous; Joe English, beefy and flailing; Denny Laine, laddish and competent. The show reinforces how erratic McCartney can be. While his voice, bass playing and songwriting can be genuinely adventurous ('Maybe I'm Amazed' is a rare high point), he still comes up with an inanity like 'Silly Love Songs' (surely a nadir in pop). And why does he persist in surrounding himself with musicians who flatter rather than provoke his talent? An interminable experience. IB

Rocky
(John G Avildsen, 1976, US) Sylvester Stallone, Talia Shire, Burt Young, Carl Weathers, Burgess Meredith, Thayer David, Joe Spinell.
119 min.
'I coulda been a contender, Charlie': Brando's classic lament in *On the Waterfront* finds a new and vigorous echo in this low-budget film whose huge success, against all odds, mirrors its own theme. *Rocky* is an old-fashioned fairytale brilliantly revamped to chime in with the depressed mood of the '70s. Although its plot – nonentity gets to fight the heavyweight champ – is basically fantasy, the film deftly manages to suspend disbelief by drawing back at its most implausible moments. Despite a few clumsy early scenes, the dialogue hits some bull's-eyes ('I'm really a ham-and-egger' mumbles Stallone in disbelief when he hears he'll get a crack at the champ), and Burgess Meredith gives his best performance in years as a slobbering, aged trainer. But without its climax, *Rocky* would add up to very little: the big fight is cathartic, manipulative Hollywood at its best. In a word: emotion. DP

Rocky II
(Sylvester Stallone, 1979, US) Sylvester Stallone, Talia Shire, Burt Young, Carl Weathers, Burgess Meredith, Tony Burton, Joe Spinell.
119 min.
An old-fashioned sequel which plumbs depths and hits heights, in which the lovable Rocky Balboa gets another crack at the world heavyweight championship. On the way, the script really sweats to get your heart pumping: with a risk of blindness and doe-eyed wife Talia Shire's postnatal coma, Rocky's virtuoso dumbness (unable to read the idiot-cards on TV) gets close to the bone. Stallone's performance as a Philadelphia saint in a B movie physique leaves you undecided whether to gag or sob, but the final fight sequences make up for it; a full-blooded Hollywood finale reaching giddy heights of cathartic glee. As a comic strip story stretched to 119 minutes, it has few rivals. DMacp

Rocky III
(Sylvester Stallone, 1982, US) Sylvester Stallone, Talia Shire, Burt Young, Carl Weathers, Burgess Meredith, Tony Burton, Mr T, Hulk Hogan.
99 min.
Learning, especially from Scorsese, in his approach to action and performance, writer/director/star Stallone has somehow contrived to make each of his movies into a more magnificent spectacle than the last, eliminating much of the coy sentimentality that tainted the first film, and pacing the boxing scenes with an increasing fury that makes them less like a sport than the epic symbolic struggle of Ray Harryhausen monsters. 'The worst thing happened to you that could happen to any fighter' someone tells Rocky here, 'You got civilised'. And *Rocky III* depicts the fighter's struggle to come to terms with success, in a progression from danger and defeat to triumph which – as in all the best genre movies – is incredibly simple. As audience movie watching in its purest form, the film is a delight, but it's also so obviously based on Stallone's own personal struggle with success that the mind boggles as to what Rocky can possibly do next. Make movies, perhaps? DP

Rocky IV

(Sylvester Stallone, 1985, US) Sylvester Stallone, Talia Shire, Burt Young, Carl Weathers, Brigitte Nielsen, Tony Burton, Michael Pataki, Dolph Lundgren, James Brown.
91 min.
Film reduced to the barest of three acts. Act I: Russian bionic mauler Drago (Lundgren) clubs Rocky's chum (Weathers) to extinction. Act II: Spaniel Features drives around in the dark night of his soul, compiling memories of *Rockys I/II/III* into a flashy rock vid. Act III: He goes to Russia, trains in the snow, and takes revenge. Never mind that all other characters are reduced to shadows, that the dialogue is witless, that the political message is a heart-warming call for detente. This, as Fuller said, is film as battleground, love, hate, violence, action, death – in a word: emotion. Pity it's about Rocky. CPea

Rocky V

(John G Avildsen, 1990, US) Sylvester Stallone, Talia Shire, Burt Young, Sage Stallone, Burgess Meredith, Tommy Morrison, Richard Gant.
104 min.
The 15-year soap opera of Rocky Balboa comes full circle. Bankrupted by a crooked accountant, suffering from brain damage which prevents him from fighting again, Rocky sells his mansion and returns to the Philadelphia back streets of his youth. He trains up a young boxer (Morrison), but as his protégé falls prey to the manipulations of an impresario (Gant), Rocky almost loses sight of the most important thing in his life: his son. This is yooman drama, with Rocky as New Man and the fights taking place outside the ring. The back-to-basics approach, with original director Avildsen back at the helm, is sensible, since nothing could have topped the bone-crunching climax of *Rocky IV*. But whereas the first and far superior *Rocky* had real heart, this tries and fails to have brains. Sentiment is substituted for sorrow, shouting for anger, mumbling for self-doubt. The scenes between Sly and his real-life son Sage have a certain poignancy, but there are more perceptive insights into parent-child relationships in an Oxo ad. And Sage acts his dad off the screen. DW

Rocky Horror Picture Show, The

(Jim Sharman, 1975, GB) Tim Curry, Susan Sarandon, Barry Bostwick, Richard O'Brien, Jonathan Adams, Nell Campbell, Peter Hinwood, Meatloaf, Patricia Quinn.
101 min.
Nowhere near as good as the original stage show, and lumbered with an overweight cameo from Meatloaf (miscast as Eddie the Hell's Angel); but still a mildly enjoyable mixture of spoof sci-fi and camp horror, laced with some terrific musical numbers written by O'Brien, who here reprises his stage role as Riff Raff the hunchbacked butler. Sarandon and Bostwick play Janet and Brad, the all-American couple who get stranded in an old dark house belonging to mad transvestite scientist Frank N Furter, and find their old-fashioned morals under threat of corruption from all manner of kinky Transylvanians. Tim Curry camps up a storm as the definitive Frank N Furter. Best watched on video, where you're less likely to be surrounded by Rocky Horror freaks singing along with all the lyrics. AB

Roger & Me

(Michael Moore, 1989, US) Michael Moore.
90 min. b/w & col.
Moore's hilarious, scathing film traces the decline of his home town of Flint, Michigan, after General Motors systematically closed down plants and laid off thousands of workers. The action spans three years as Moore (camera team in tow) tracks GM chairman Roger Smith in order to confront him with the human consequences of corporate policy. Interspersed are Moore's narrative, outlining the changes which beset the town, and on-camera interviews with assorted locals, celebrities and executives. Chronology has been jumbled, resulting in controversy over this 'documentary'. Moore terms it a 'docucomedy', a political sketch rather than a measured analysis, deploying humour and exaggeration to make its point. It's only right that Moore should be accountable to standards of journalistic 'truthfulness'; but ultimately, remaining constant at the heart of his film, is the way it tellingly and ruthlessly presents the cumulative effects of industrial ruthlessness. CM

Roger Corman: Hollywood's Wild Angel

(Christian Blackwood, 1978, US) Roger Corman, Allan Arkush, Paul Bartel, David Carradine, Joe Dante, Jonathan Demme, Peter Fonda, Ron Howard, Jonathan Kaplan, Martin Scorsese.
58 min.
It may have nothing particularly profound to say about its subject-hero, but this documentary is put together with the slam-bang panache of Corman's own movies as director. It also provides a welcome and entertaining update on Corman's own thoughts about his role at this time as head of his own immensely successful production company, New World Pictures. The mix of extracts, trailers, and anecdotal interviews with Corman and many of his protégés, past and present, makes it perfect late-night viewing. RM

Roger Corman's Frankenstein Unbound

(Roger Corman, 1990, US) John Hurt, Raúl Julia, Bridget Fonda, Jason Patric, Michael Hutchence, Nick Brimble, Catherine Rabett, Bruce McGuire, Catherine Corman.
85 min.
Despite a starry cast, the daft plot premise (loosely derived from Brian W Aldiss' novel *Frankenstein Unbound*) scuppers any hope of intelligent entertainment from the outset. Aided by cheapo effects, scientist Buchanan (Hurt) is catapulted back from the future to a Gothic-style past. Worse still, Corman's directing style is stuck in a '60s time warp. Vacillating between all-out gore and tongue-in-cheek humour, Corman manages occasional flashes of wit (such as a scene in which Buchanan presents Mary Shelley with a photocopy of her unfinished novel *Frankenstein*). Mostly, it's too ludicrous even to aspire to campness. No explanation is offered as to why Mary Shelley's *fictional* Monster comes to be roaming the shores of Lake Geneva in a rubber suit, while the antics of Byron (Patric) and his poet pal Shelley (Hutchence) are as redundant as they are fey. Meanwhile, the painfully under-used Hurt, Julia (Baron Frankenstein) and Fonda (Mary Shelley) wander the Villa Diodati in search of a plot that seems to have slipped through a hole in the time continuum. NF

Rogue Cop

(Roy Rowland, 1954, US) Robert Taylor, Janet Leigh, George Raft, Anne Francis, Steve Forrest, Vince Edwards.
92 min. b/w.
The year after writing *The Big Heat*, the story of an upright detective avenging his murdered wife, William McGivern published *Rogue Cop*, a more interesting variation, in which a corrupt detective avenges his murdered brother. Auteur principles being what they are, Fritz Lang's movie of the former is a classic, while Rowland's adaptation of the latter is little known, though dramatically it's tougher, more complex, more unpredictable. It also has Anne Francis playing, as it were, Gloria Grahame, which many will find an improvement, and an iconic, if dull Janet Leigh. The fashion for location filming having just ended, we are returned, unfortunately, to MGM's standing city-street set, though it's atmospherically shot by John Seitz. BBa

Roi de Coeur, Le

see King of Hearts

Roi des Aulnes, Le (The Erl King)

(Volker Schlöndorff, 1996, Fr/Ger/GB) John Malkovich, Marianne Sägebrecht, Armin Mueller-Stahl, Volker Spengler.
116 min.
Schlöndorff and Jean-Claude Carrière find in Michel Tournier's novel a companion piece to their earlier Günter Grass adaptation, *The Tin Drum*. The focus is again on a highly peculiar individual set on ignoring the onslaught of history, this time by remaining in a world of magical forests, loving animals, innocent children, despite accumulating evidence that life is providing something altogether opposite. Malkovich, wearing the creepiest pair of specs in movie history, is successively an unjustly convicted child molester, a PoW, a flunky at Goering's hunting lodge, and finally a hooded horseman combing the countryside for suitably Aryan youths to enroll in the SS academy: the catcher in the rye turned into the big bad wolf, or, from another viewpoint, Buñuel's Nazarin let loose in the Third Reich. As in *The Tin Drum*, the director shapes individual scenes so powerfully (cameraman Bruno De Keyser, composer Michael Nyman) that the abstractions we should presumably be inferring seem piffling alongside such muscularly rendered specifics: this snorting stag, that dead child. BBa

Roi et l'Oiseau, Le

see King and Mister Bird, The

Role, The (Bhumika)

(Shyam Benegal, 1977, Ind) Smita Patil, Anant Nag, Amrish Puri, Naseeruddin Shah, Swabha Deshpande.
142 min.
Based on a book by one of Bombay's movie queens from the '40s, this sometimes looks like one of those riproaring melodramas through which Joan Crawford used to suffer so splendiferously. But put together with deceptive skill, it draws remarkable riches from its interlocking of past and present as the movie star heroine – saddled with a workshy husband, breadwinner for her entire family, but not allowed even a chequebook of her own – simultaneously tries to break out of her sexist cage and to understand how she came to be locked into it. The result is a complex exploration of female emancipation, making striking use of the Hindi cinema (wonderful parodies of the traditional *Madras Curry*, with its stoic, self-sacrificing heroines) as setting, symbol and catalyst. TM

Roller and Violin

see Katok i Skrypka

Rollerball

(Norman Jewison, 1975, US) James Caan, John Houseman, Maud Adams, John Beck, Moses Gunn, Pamela Hensley, Barbara Trentham, Ralph Richardson, Shane Rimmer.
129 min.
Behind the vision of a future society, where the corporate world state controls the bloodlust of the populace through lethal games of rollerball, lies the familiar theme of individual struggle: Caan's champ takes on the grey eminence who wants to force his retirement. The script grapples with notions of freedom and privilege, but finally remains too oblique to throw much light either on our own society or on our possible future. Occasionally, though, insight triumphs, and Caan's struggle towards articulation remains one of the film's strong points. Otherwise, its main interest lies in the tensions generated by the gap between the script's intellectual aspirations and the gut reaction appeal of the games, which are highly physical and brutal. Hence, a group of drunken revellers deliberately and callously burning down some old fir trees makes more impression than all the destruction of human meat in the games. Ultimately, *Rollerball* gets by on its sheer monolithic quality – an abundance of quantity. Despite indifferent direction and dire humour, it is well mounted and photographed. CPe

Rollercoaster

(James Goldstone, 1977, US) George Segal, Richard Widmark, Timothy Bottoms, Henry Fonda, Harry Guardino, Susan Strasberg, Helen Hunt, Dorothy Tristan.
118 min.
In 1952, when Cinerama was born, its makers placed a camera on the front of a Coney Island rollercoaster to magnificent effect. Universal here came up with the ingenious idea of incorporating the rollercoaster gimmick into a mad bomber thriller, and adding Sensurround for good measure. The results should have been sensational, not just because of the added sound effects, but because American rollercoasters were far bigger, faster and more chilling than they ever were in 1952. *Rollercoaster* does deliver its share of thrills, but ultimately the film-makers botched the job. Many of the best runs are interrupted by close-ups, and the filler plot is dumb in the extreme. DP

Roller Derby

see Derby

Rollicking Adventures of Eliza Fraser, The (aka A Faithful Narrative of the Capture, Sufferings and Miraculous Escape of Eliza Fraser)

(Tim Burstall, 1976, Aust) Susannah York, Noel Ferrier, John Waters, Trevor Howard, John Castle.
115 min.
Beware rollicking heroines, especially from the perpetrator of *Stork* and *Alvin Purple*. The factual history of Eliza Fraser (shipwrecked and conscripted as a member of an aboriginal tribe) is thrown away in a lumberingly burlesque period romp about a lady with a roving eye, and a pompously straitlaced husband, who becomes involved in a farce of lusty humiliations before ending up peddling a spicy account of her adventures in carnivals. Moments of bizarrerie escape the general heavy-handedness, but the more serious purpose evident in David Williamson's script – of confronting sexual attitudes and hypocrisies – doesn't get a look in. TM

Rollover

(Alan J Pakula, 1981, US) Jane Fonda, Kris Kristofferson, Hume Cronyn, Josef Sommer, Bob Gunton, Macon McCalman.
115 min.
A generally underrated film, admittedly not always easy to follow in its voyage through the rarefied reaches of high finance and merchant banking, discovering conspiracy and murder along the way, with the fate of the entire Western economy hanging in the balance. Disconcerting in its kaleidoscopic shifts in tone, it's nevertheless too absorbing simply to dismiss. Matching gamesmanship with gamesmanship as his financiers elaborate on their abstruse gambits in incomprehensible computer-speak, what Pakula seems to be trying to demonstrate – with the final confrontation suggesting a standoff between two gunfighters, stalemated because the villain proves able to justify his villainy – is that the complex power plays of international finance constitute an entirely new genre with which the old ones arrayed here (film noir, romantic comedy, political exposé, Western) are ill-equipped to cope. It's a fascinating experiment, well worth seeing anyway as another of Pakula's marvellous evocations of urban paranoia. TM

Roma

see Fellini's Roma

Roma, Città Aperta (Open City/Rome, Open City)

(Roberto Rossellini, 1945, It) Anna Magnani, Aldo Fabrizi, Marcello Pagliero, Maria Michi, Harry Feist.
101 min. b/w.
Rossellini's film, one of the definitive works of the Italian neo-realist period, was shot under extremely difficult circumstances at the end of WWII. Its greatest achievement remains its study and placing of the Resistance movement – and on a wider level, the war itself – against a background of everyday events. The film evolved from a documentary about a priest serving in the Resistance, which perhaps accounts for its refusal to compromise or to entertain conventional notions of heroism. CPe

Romance

see Some Kinda Love

Romance and Rejection

(Kevin W Smith, 1997, GB) Reece Dinsdale, John Hannah, Victoria Smurfit, Clara Bellar, Frank Finlay, Rowena King, Susannah York, Maryam D'Abo.
92 min.
Very Nick Hornby, but some way short of the real thing. Mike – 36, single, and unhappy about it – hasn't had much luck with the fairer sex since his mother abandoned him and dad back in the dark ages. His congenital jealousy is the problem, though it should be said neither of his current hot and cold girlfriends wins marks for consistency.

Dinsdale lacks the charm to allow us to overlook Mike's failings, and the big emotional scenes with the parents are heavy handed. TCh

Romance of a Horse Thief

(Abraham Polonsky, 1971, Yugo/US) Yul Brynner, Eli Wallach, Jane Birkin, Oliver Tobias, Laine Kazin, David Opatoshu.
100 min.
Blacklisted director Polonsky (best known for 1949's John Garfield boxing classic *Force of Evil*) made a comeback in the early '70s with Robert Redford's liberal Western *Tell Them Willie Boy Is Here* and this now rarely seen Yugoslavian-shot offering. In turn-of-the-century Poland, Jewish horse traders try to best Cossack soldiers seeking to commandeer their animals for the Russo-Japanese war, a scenario (by David Opatoshu) to which Polonsky brings both humour and equine action. TJ

Romance of Book & Sword, The (Shujian Enchou Lu)

(Ann Hui, 1987, HK) Zhang Duofu, Da Shichang, Oyilore, Liu Gui.
(2 parts) 181 min.
A two-part historical epic, filmed all over China, centred on conflict between the Manchu Emperor Qianlong and a resistance group who are fighting to restore Chinese rule. (Echoes of contemporary debates about the future of Hong Kong under Chinese sovereignty are not entirely coincidental.) This is the nearest thing in present-day Chinese cinema to the spectacles that King Hu made in the 1960s: prodigious use of locations, rousing action climaxes, shameless exoticism, and set pieces that flaunt it because they've got it. Part II gets rather bogged down in folksy frippery about a Muslim tribe in Xinjiang, but the breathtaking act of treachery at the end erases any doubts about Hui's vision and seriousness of purpose. TR

Romance on the High Seas (aka It's Magic)

(Michael Curtiz, 1948, US) Jack Carson, Janis Paige, Don DeFore, Doris Day, Oscar Levant, SZ Sakall, Fortunio Bonanova, Franklin Pangborn, Eric Blore.
99 min.
A bland but amiable musical marking Doris Day's debut. With vague jealousies in the air, millionaire DeFore hires a private eye (Carson) to check up on his wife (Paige) while she is on a cruise to Rio. But Paige, with her own checking up in mind, hires an aspiring singer (Day) with a yen for luxurious travel to take her place. Carson and Day promptly fall in love during the cruise, and much confusion ensues when Carson guiltily confesses in his report to her supposed husband, while Day can't resist a career-enhancing chance to sing under her assumed name at a society charity do in Rio. Likeable performances (backed by a sterling supporting cast), plus good Jule Styne-Sammy Cahn songs, make it all pleasantly painless. TM

Romance with a Double Bass

(Robert Young, 1974, GB) Connie Booth, John Cleese, Graham Crowden, Freddie Jones, John Moffatt, Denis Ramsden, June Whitfield.
41 min.
An adaptation of a Chekhov short story, set in Russia, with Cleese as a doleful double-bass player booked to perform for the forced engagement of Princess Constanza (Booth). To pass time before rehearsals, he strips off for a quick dip in a nearby river, whereupon someone steals his clothes. Meanwhile, downstream, the same fate has befallen the Princess. This leads to a very funny, innocent and tastefully filmed nudist romp in which the two of them (without peeking) try to work their way back to the huge mansion, the Princess squeezed into his double-bass case. One classic moment has Cleese running back and forth across the picturesque countryside, dropping the case and having to sprint back to pick up his double-bass. DA

Romancing the Stone

(Robert Zemeckis, 1984, US) Michael Douglas, Kathleen Turner, Danny DeVito, Zack Norman, Alfonso Arau, Manuel Ojeda, Holland Taylor, Mary Ellen Trainor.
106 min.
Typical Tennessee Williams seediness (it's an

Treasure maps, crocodiles, romantic novelists and psychotic Latins, this slings them all together, along with a hefty slug of wish-fulfilment, to engaging effect. Stuck with her miniatures and cat called Romeo in New York, Turner pines for schmaltz to turn into life as she churns out Mills and Boonies. Then sister Elaine (Trainor) gets kidnapped by the splendid Zack Norman and his cackling sidekick down in Columbia, and it's eyes down for galloping caper thrills. The script is sharp and funny, the direction sure-footed on both the comedy and action fronts, and the whole thing adds up to rather more concerted fun than Indiana Jones' latest flab-ridden escapade in the Temple of Doom. There's also the added bonus of Ms Turner, at the sight of whom this dispassionate arbiter of public taste came perilously close to self-combustion.JP

Roman de Renard, Le (The Tale of the Fox)

(Wladyslaw Starewicz, 1930, Fr) voices: Claude Dauphin, Romain Bouquet, Sylvain Itkine.
65 min. b/w.
Adapted from Goethe's fable – about a fox whose carnivorous cunning, deplored and feared by the rest of the animal kingdom, brings him into legal conflict with the lion king – this vintage animated film impresses, first of all, by the sheer virtuosity of its stop-motion puppet work. Some sequences feature literally dozens of immaculate creatures on superbly detailed sets. Its creator, Wladyslaw Starewicz (1882–1965), was a Polish-Lithuanian who moved to France after the Soviet revolution, whose work today is known mostly by reputation. *The Tale of the Fox* is marked by a sardonic wit. Much of the frantic violence puts Tom and Jerry to shame, and much of the imagery – hares drunk on communion wine, tightrope walking mice, a castle filled with Heath Robinson battle contraptions – springs from a genuinely surreal imagination. GA

Roman Holiday

(William Wyler, 1953, US) Audrey Hepburn, Gregory Peck, Eddie Albert, Tullio Carminati, Harcourt Williams, Hartley Power.
119 min. b/w.
This has the hallmarks of a Billy Wilder picture – Americans abroad, masquerades leading to moral transformation – and Wilder would doubtless have turned it into a blazing masterpiece. Wyler's style was not particularly suited to comedy – the film is a little long, a little heavy at times, the spontaneity a little over-rehearsed – and he simply makes a wonderfully enjoyable movie. Hepburn is the Princess bored with protocol who goes AWOL in Rome; Peck (Holden would have been better, edgier) is the American journalist who has the scoop fall into his lap; and Albert (the best performance) is the photographer who has to snap all of Hepburn's un-royal escapades. This sort of thing was churned out by Lubitsch in the '30s, on the Paramount back-lot; Wyler went on location, and in 1953 that was a real eye-opener, Hollywood's answer to neo-realism. The movie remains a great tonic. ATu

Roman Scandals

(Frank Tuttle, 1933, US) Eddie Cantor, Ruth Etting, Edward Arnold, Gloria Stuart, David Manners, Verree Teasdale, Alan Mowbray.
92 min. b/w.
A pleasantly entertaining pot-pourri of humour, song, and dance, structured around the goggle-eyed gaucheries of Cantor as the small-town boy, run out by the authorities because of his troublesome social conscience, who dreams that he is a slave in Ancient Rome (graduating to the perilous post of food-taster for Arnold's Emperor). Though the wit has dated somewhat, it's still worth seeing for its typically lavish Goldwyn production values: Richard Day's impressive set designs, Gregg Toland's camerawork, and Busby Berkeley's usual excesses in a slave-market scene, populated by masses of all but naked Goldwyn girls. GA

Roman Spring of Mrs Stone, The

(José Quintero, 1961, US) Vivien Leigh, Warren Beatty, Lotte Lenya, Jill St John, Jeremy Spenser, Coral Browne, Ernest Thesiger.
104 min.
Typical Tennessee Williams seediness (it's an

adaptation of his first novel), with Vivien Leigh doing her faded beauty bit as a widowed actress lolling around in Rome and trying to find final romance with gigolo Beatty. Florid and sordid simultaneously, and forever verging on the nonsensical, but saved by a charismatic performance from Lotte Lenya as a bitchy procuress. GA

Romantic Agony, The (Vaarwel)

(Guido Pieters, 1973, Neth) Pieke Dassen, Nettie Blanken, Rik Bravenboer, José Ruyter, Wim Hoogendam.
85 min.
An excursion into an area of Tolkien-type fantasy, centering on a seemingly immortal old man's wanderings through time, taking in episodes historical and modern. Its obvious low budget is compensated by some pleasantly autumnal photography, and by Morricone's score. But its mythweaving trendiness at times becomes excessively cute, with embarrassing episodes (like a nocturnal rite around a phallic totem, detachedly observed by the old man) jarring against others handled with some delicacy (like those involving a ghost unable to frighten anyone any more, and a lady vampire now living on bottled plasma from the blood bank).

Romantic Englishwoman, The

(Joseph Losey, 1975, GB/Fr) Glenda Jackson, Michael Caine, Helmut Berger, Marcus Richardson, Kate Nelligan, Rene Kolldehoff, Michel Lonsdale, Béatrice Romand, Nathalie Delon.
116 min.
'Return to Losey Country' might be a more suitable title for The Romantic Englishwoman, in which Caine plays a prestigious novelist whose wife (Jackson) feeds his jealous fantasies by slipping off to Baden Baden for the weekend. The two play out their trapped games, prior to a highly romanticised intrusion from Helmut Berger, amid an opulence so mannered and preposterous that it verges on self-parody; in fact, the familiar icy excess of Richard MacDonald's set matches the pomposity of the characters. Most of the film is passably entertaining, and Tom Stoppard's dialogue has its moments, but the basic material contains less that is real or relevant about it than the flimsiest of romantic melodramas. DP

Romeo and Juliet

(Franco Zeffirelli, 1968, GB/It) Leonard Whiting, Olivia Hussey, Milo O'Shea, Michael York, John McEnery, Pat Heywood, Natasha Parry, Paul Hardwick, Robert Stephens.
152 min.
Zeffirelli's mod adaptation of Romeo and Juliet isn't one of the very slim handful of masterfully filmed Shakespeare plays, but it's nowhere near as mawkish as the simple-minded pantheism on display in the later Brother Sun, Sister Moon. It is successful in one very important respect, the handling of the hot-headed youth of the feuding Verona families, and the street brawling scenes are admirable. The rot sets in with Zeffirelli's treatment of the 'stern' parents, the sentimentality of his Irish friar (O'Shea) and Cockney nurse (Heywood), and the tragic denouement. Mostly it remains enjoyable for its colour and visual flair. Danilo Donati's costumes are, as usual, breathtaking. RM

Romeo & Juliet

see William Shakespeare's Romeo & Juliet

Romeo in Pyjamas

see Parlor, Bedroom and Bath

Romeo Is Bleeding

(Peter Medak, 1992, US) Gary Oldman, Lena Olin, Annabella Sciorra, Juliette Lewis, Roy Scheider, Will Patton.
109 min.
Jack Grimaldi (Oldman) is a New York cop on the take and then some. He sells out witnesses to the Mob and buries the pay-offs in his backyard. He's got a wife (Sciorra) and a girlfriend (Lewis). He's keeping it together, he thinks. Then he meets Mona Demarkov (Olin). A glamorous Russian gangster, she's in bed with the Feds and at the head of the Mafia's death list – but Jack just could be her trump card. Director Medak goes off the rails in high style with this dementedly doleful

exercise in pop noir. But the film plays out the battle of the sexes at such an unflinchingly amoral pitch it really isn't funny anymore. Like Oldman's deluded operator – playing both ends and getting caught in the middle – Hilary Henkin's script isn't as smart as it thinks it is, and only Olin's breathtakingly excessive femme fatale hits the right note of campy panache. TCh

Rome, Open City

see Roma, Città Aperta

Romero

(John Duigan, 1989, US) Raúl Julia, Richard Jordan, Ana Alicia, Eddie Vélez, Alejandro Bracho, Tony Plana, Harold Gould, Claudio Brook, Martin Lasalle.
105 min.
Financed in part by Catholic organisations in the States, this was apparently made under Church auspices, nearly ten years after the death of the Salvadorean archbishop it commemorates. One wonders, however, whether the Vatican is quite as fond of these turbulent priests when they're alive. Certainly the screenplay dramatises the intolerable position of a passionate priest in El Salvador: mistrusted as an agent of the state by the guerillas, menaced by the army for his championship of human rights, Romero (Julia), initially selected as a soft, safe candidate for archbishop, surprised everyone by speaking out against violence on both sides. Certain scenes seem almost too heroic, but overall this treatment has a ring of truth; horrendous events occur, but there's no lewd lingering over the details of death. Though the slightly ponderous script jars in the early scenes (leaden exposition of political verities, characterisation by numbers), the bulk of the film works up a considerable emotional charge, with doe-eyed Julia attaining a mythic simplicity. SFe

Rommel – Desert Fox

see Desert Fox, The

Romper Stomper

(Geoffrey Wright, 1992, NZ) Russell Crowe, Daniel Pollock, Jacqueline McKenzie, Alex Scott, Leigh Russell, Daniel Wyllie.
91 min.
If it's hard to fault Wright's stated anti-racist reasons for making this portrait of Melbourne's skinhead life, you can't help but doubt the wisdom of the stylistic choices he's made. A disaffected young girl, Gabe (McKenzie), who takes up with a gang led by neo-Nazi Hando (Crowe), is attracted by his brute sexuality, the power he wields over his less articulate minions, and the bloody violence they mete out to Vietnamese immigrants. But when the victims decide to fight back, the gang begins to fall apart, and Gabe's affections are transferred to Hando's right-hand man Davey (Pollock). The fact that Wright has opted for such a visceral style tends to vitiate what few insights he may provide into the racist mentality; the raw, semi-documentary narrative may make for plausibility, but the high-adrenaline, souped-up visuals ensure a lack of moral perspective. The cheap 'message' of the ending fails to salvage a film that at best is well-meant but misguided, at worst, flashy and garbled. GA

Romuald et Juliette (Romuald & Juliette)

(Coline Serreau, 1989, Fr) Daniel Auteuil, Firmine Richard, Pierre Vernier, Maxime Leroux, Gilles Privat, Muriel Combeau, Alain Fromager.
112 min.
Coline Serreau's last film inspired (if that is the word) Three Men and a Baby, and this one also looks a likely candidate for an American remake. Despite the title, there's little here Shakespeare would recognise, with the star-crossed romance a long time coming. Instead, Serreau builds up a complicated situation involving insider dealing at Romuald's yoghurt company. Ousted and cuckolded, Romuald (Auteil) finds himself with only one friend in the world, the company's black cleaning-woman Juliette (Richard, splendid). Together, they plot to put him back at the top; in the meantime, he hides out in Juliette's cramped, broken-down apartment with her five children. Cross-cutting between the life-styles of rich and poor (or of whites and blacks), Serreau makes her

points implicitly, but also fashions a surprisingly generous, romantic movie in which everyone has the right to follow his or her heart. Spirited performances and some fine blues on the soundtrack help to make this warm comedy a real pleasure. TCh

Romy and Michele's High School Reunion

(David Mirkin, 1997, US) Mira Sorvino, Lisa Kudrow, Alan Cumming, Julia Campbell, Janeane Garofalo, Vincent Ventresca.
91 min.
Longtime pals Sorvino and Kudrow have achieved, well, not very much since graduation day, but both film-makers and tuned-in performers contrive never to look down on their big hair, Valley Girl vowels and full set of vacant attitudes. The pair do comic-irrepressible to a tee, as gnawing curiosity draws them back to the old school, and old scores are just waiting to be settled. Flavourful character playing jazzes up the central riff on friendship surviving the scorn of the mainstream. Cumming has obliterated his Scots accent sufficiently to play the teenage übergeek in the flashbacks, but star of the show is undoubtedly Garofalo's hilariously abrasive turn as the adolescent outsider of yore, who's turned her chain-smoking habit to advantage by inventing a quick-drawing ciggie you can inhale with a single puff. She looks haggard, wears a lot of shit-brown, and, boy, do you miss her when she's off screen. First-time director Mirkin doesn't quite sustain the momentum, and the big 'Post-It' gag is laboriously over-extended, but by then Lisa and Mira have won you over. A chipper little comedy (exec producer Robin Schiff adapted her play The Ladies Room) with a hint of Simpsons bite. TJ

Ronde, La

(Max Ophüls, 1950, Fr) Anton Walbrook, Simone Signoret, Serge Reggiani, Simone Simon, Daniel Gélin, Danielle Darrieux, Fernand Gravey, Odette Joyeux, Jean-Louis Barrault, Isa Miranda, Gérard Philipe.
97 min. b/w.
Not one of the director's very greatest films on desire (see Letter from an Unknown Woman and Lola Montès for those), Ophüls' circular chain of love and seduction in 19th century Vienna is still irresistible. Embellishing Arthur Schnitzler's text with metaphors that are entirely his own (a carousel; an omniscient/omnipotent narrator/MC, with Walbrook at times actually seen splicing the celluloid stories together; and that perfect expression of the Ophülsian circle, the waltz), Ophüls almost manages to make you forget that the performances in the first half (Signoret, Reggiani, Simon, Gélin, Darrieux, Gravey) are much better than those in the second. And there are more than enough moments of cinematic magic to excuse the occasional longueurs of talkiness. RM

Rooftops

(Robert Wise, 1989, US) Jason Gedrick, Troy Beyer, Eddie Vélez, Tisha Campbell, Alexis Cruz, Allen Payne, Steve Love.
95 min.
With such a preposterously dewy-eyed premise, how could this have been anything but awful? Orphaned T (Gedrick) lives in an empty watertower atop a deserted Lower East Side tenement in New York. In fact there's an entire community of kids up there, who hang out by night in a vacant lot named 'The Garden of Eden', peaceably sorting out their differences through 'combat dance' (a stylised descendant of the Afro-Brazilian martial arts discipline Capoeira, which involves no physical contact). Enter serpent-like trouble in the form of neighbourhood pusher Lobo (Vélez), aided and abetted by nubile young Elena (Beyer), with whom our hero is besotted. Time for teen-love torn apart once more by divided loyalties. Nearly 30 years after West Side Story, Wise's return to the 'street-sussed musical' is painfully disappointing: a parade of frantic, vacuous gestures which, like combat dancing itself, simply never delivers the punch as lithesome muscles sweat aimlessly under clingy vests, accompanied by Dave (Eurythmics) Stewart's blusterous soundtrack. By the time Lobo's henchmen start blowing up water-towers and chucking kids off rooftops, you can't help but sympathise. MK

Rookery Nook

(Tom Walls/Byron Haskin, 1930, GB) Ralph
Lynn, Tom Walls, Winifred Shotter, Mary
Brough, Robertson Hare, Ethel Coleridge,
Margot Grahame.
76 min. b/w.
Though Hitchcock's *Blackmail* is remembered as
the first great British talkie, it was this filmed version of Ben Travers' Aldwych farce – distressed
damsel embarrasses newly-wed chinless wonder
in country cottage rest-cure setting – which
scored at the box-office. According to producer
Herbert Wilcox, it cost £14,000 to make and
grossed £150,000 in Britain alone. Recorded on
discs rather than film and directed by Walls with
an arrogant unconcern for anything cinematic,
the bizarre look and sound of the film give it the
quality of a fascinating historical relic. RMy

Rookie, The

(Clint Eastwood, 1990, US) Clint Eastwood,
Charlie Sheen, Raúl Julia, Sonia Braga, Tom
Skerritt, Lara Flynn Boyle, Pepe Serna.
121 min.
Having salved his artistic conscience with *White
Hunter, Black Heart*, Eastwood returned to the
action-adventure genre with this astonishingly
inadequate piece of piffle. Promoted to the Grand
Theft Auto Division of the LAPD, rookie cop
David Ackerman (Sheen) teams up with Nick
Pulovski (Eastwood), a cigar-smoking ex-racing
driver hell-bent on avenging his former partner's
murder. Naturally, Ackerman at first despises his
new colleague's working methods – beating people up, using his badge as an AMEX card, etc
–but when Pulovski is kidnapped by fiendish,
mustachioed hun Eric Strom (Julia), the nappie-
brained new boy realises it's time to get manly
forthwith. Directed by Eastwood with the same
stupefied lethargy that characterises his performance, this tedious rites of passage movie is full
of caricatured cops and robbers, and punctuated
with interminably dull car-chases. Only Sheen's
hysterically inept handling of the godawful dialogue relieves the boredom. MK

Rookie of the Year

(Daniel Stern, 1993, US) Thomas Ian Nicholas,
Gary Busey, Albert Hall, Amy Morton, Bruce
Altman, Eddie Bracken, Dan Hedaya, Daniel
Stern.
103 min.
It was a magic bat in *The Natural*, and a magic
park in *Field of Dreams*; now it's a magic arm.
The 100 mph pitch which propels 12-year old
Henry Rowengartner (Nicholas) into major league
baseball is not, however, manna from heaven, but
the surprising result of a fall. For this is not an
enchanting, mystical film, but an exhaustingly
physical one. Surrounded by such stock characters as the single mum and her slimy boyfriend,
the conniving pitcher and his has-been employer, Henry inspires the goodies, foils the baddies.
First-time director Stern – Macaulay Culkin's
punching bag in the *Home Alone* films – gives a
broad performance as the pitching coach who
knows nothing about baseball. Approach with
aspirin. AO

Room at the Top

(Jack Clayton, 1959, GB) Laurence Harvey,
Simone Signoret, Heather Sears, Donald
Wolfit, Donald Houston, Allan Cuthbertson,
Hermione Baddeley, Raymond Huntley.
117 min. b/w.
Acclaimed as the first British film to treat sex
seriously – ie. to show it as enjoyable rather than
sinful – and as one of the first to show the North
of England as it 'really was'. In retrospect, this
adaptation of John Braine's Bradford-set novel,
with its moral melodramatics as Laurence
Harvey cheats his way to success (a good marriage) via the death of his 'true love' and the bed
of his mistress (Signoret), may not stand the test
of time. But it remains intriguing as a sort of *Brief
Encounter*, '50s-style. PH

Roommates

(Alan Metzger, 1993, US) Randy Quaid, Eric
Stoltz, Elizabeth Peña, Charles Durning, Frank
Buxton, Jill Teed.
90 min.
An AIDS picture about an angry Irish-American
roughneck (Quaid) and a saintly piano-playing
WASP (Stoltz) thrown together in a Seattle apart-
ment house for the terminally ill, in which the

death of the latter teaches the former the virtues
of tolerance and acceptance. It's hard to write ill
of a film so obviously made from the heart, but
sentimentality is, regrettably, the dominant mood
of this sanitised and improbable story. JPy

Room Service

(William A Seiter, 1938, US) The Marx
Brothers, Frank Albertson, Ann Miller, Lucille
Ball, Donald MacBride.
78 min. b/w.
Under some sad whim, the Marx Brothers moved
to RKO to appear in this limp version of a popular Broadway comedy, slightly adapted to fit their
established characters. It's a loose fit indeed:
Groucho plays a penniless theatrical manager
trying to mount a socially-conscious play about
miners (oh yes); Chico is the play's director,
quotes Latin, and wears a check suit. Harpo at
least is still unbridled, and does nice things chasing a turkey and eating food like an automaton.
Apart from Harpo's bits, *Room Service* is to be
seen once, and then forgotten. GB

Room With a View, A

(James Ivory, 1985, GB) Maggie Smith, Helena
Bonham Carter, Denholm Elliott, Julian Sands,
Daniel Day Lewis, Simon Callow, Judi Dench.
117 min.
Hard on the heels of David Lean's grandiose,
touristic version of EM Forster's *A Passage to
India*, the Merchant/Ivory/Jhabvala team get the
scale of Forster's vision down to its right size. The
story of the awakening of young Lucy (Carter),
thanks to the liberating effect of the Tuscan countryside and the Latin temperament, is translated
with perfect judgment, with the only lapses occurring over Forster's wry sense of humour. His
satiric judgments can too often become arch: the
'grotesquely' illustrated intertitles here are a miscalculation of this order. None the less, in line
with Forster's dicta on 'fully rounded characters',
there is a fine gallery here; and the 'tea tabling'
effect of the Home Counties upon grand emotion,
from an era when dynastic families could topple
over a single kiss, is mapped out with perfect precision. Decent, honest, truthful and, dearest of all
to Forster, it connects. CPea

Rooster Cogburn

(Stuart Millar, 1975, US) John Wayne,
Katharine Hepburn, Anthony Zerbe, Richard
Jordan, John McIntire, Strother Martin.
108 min.
Obviously meant to cash in on the success of
True Grit – the Wayne vehicle that won him a
sentimental Oscar – this pairing of two
Hollywood veterans is forced to rely totally on
their performances and personalities, in the
absence of any other interesting features. Wayne
repeats his role as the ornery ol' crittur of a marshal, teaming up with the Bible-pounding spinster Hepburn in an attempt to bring her father's
killers to justice. Like *The African Queen* (to
which it bears a strong resemblance), and to a
lesser extent *On Golden Pond*, it's the sort of film
whose *raison d'être* consists in manipulating an
audience's familiar sympathies with its ageing
stars. In this case, however, it fails dismally. GA

Roosters

(Robert M Young, 1993, US) Edward J Olmos,
Sonia Braga, Maria Conchita Alonso, Danny
Nucci, Sarah Lassez.
110 min.
A broody melodrama, set on the US-Mexican border, with Olmos, the con released after eight years
in stir, returning to his family and occasioning
crisis. He's a cock-fighting man, a macho old-
schooler. He dismisses his son's bird-fighting
prowess as a Filipino-Mexican match looms. His
disturbed daughter (Lassez, looking like a
younger Julia Roberts) wears angel wings and
builds elaborate graveyards for dead pets, and
clearly misses paternal care. His sister,'the encyclopaedia of love' (Alonso), has sex coming out of
every pore. This plays like a melancholic
Tennessee Williams piece – its dialogue betrays
its theatrical roots – beautifully shot (by
Villalobos Reynaldo) from dirt level under clear
blue skies, accompanied by plaintive slide-guitar.
Atmospheric, well-acted (especially by Olmos),
but, as ever with middlebrow director Young, it
ends disappointingly: all showing and no meaning. WH

Roots Rock Reggae

(Jeremy Marre, 1977, GB) Bob Marley and the
Wailers, Jimmy Cliff, The Heptones, Junior
Murvin, The Gladiators, the Mighty
Diamonds.
55 min.
Marre's documentary is not just about a form of
music, but about its cultural source. Although it
deliberately makes political points, it sensibly
allows the people involved to explain themselves,
and it's here that it is most successful. No amount
of commentary could evoke the class barriers and
poverty as poignantly as shots of kids 'auditioning' in the hills for a big Kingston producer; nor
could commentary explain as effectively as film
of Bob Marley's lifestyle why the kids choose
music as their way out. But perhaps it all works
so well because it captures some of the spontaneity that lies at the heart of the music – a spontaneity undoubtedly assisted by the biggest
joints in the world, and by a sense of humour in
the face of desperation. SM

Rope

(Alfred Hitchcock, 1948, US) James Stewart,
John Dall, Farley Granger, Cedric Hardwicke,
Joan Chandler, Constance Collier, Douglas
Dick.
81 min.
One of Hitchcock's more experimental films, with
the tale of two young gays, keen to prove their
intellectual and spiritual superiority, killing a
friend and hiding his body in a trunk in order to
see whether dinner guests will suspect anything.
Constructed entirely from uncut ten-minute
takes, shot on a beautifully-constructed set, it's
certainly a virtuoso piece of technique, but the
lack of cutting inevitably slows things down,
entailing the camera swooping from one character   to
another during dialogues. On a thematic level,
however, the film is more successful: while the
arguments about Nietzschean philosophy
between the couple and their professor, Stewart
(whose ideas have inadvertently prompted the
murder), are hardly profound, what is interesting
is the way Hitchcock's sly amorality forces us,
through the suspense, to side with the killers.
Add to that the black wit and strong performances from Dall, Granger and Stewart, and you
have a perverse, provocative entertainment. GA

Rosalie Goes Shopping

(Percy Adlon, 1989, WGer) Marianne
Sägebrecht, Brad Davies, Judge Reinhold,
Erika Blumberger, Willy Harlander, John
Hawkes, Patricia Zehentmayr, Alex Winter.
94 min.
Rosalie (Sägebrecht) would seem to have it made:
her crop duster hubby (Davies) dotes on her, her
countless kids dote on her, even her priest
(Reinhold) is less than harsh in his condemnation
of her penchant for cheque and credit card fraud.
But Rosalie – a corpulent, ever-smiling *hausfrau*
who has landed up in Stuttgart, Arkansas – is so
infected by the material greed of the American
Way that she can never own enough. Adlon's
third film with Sägebrecht may have been conceived as an anarchic dig at Western capitalism,
but it is so smugly conspiratorial that any such
intentions have been transformed into a paean to
avaricious cunning. Ethics aside, the film also
suffers from having no plot to speak of; a good
hour is spent dwelling on the loveable wackiness
of Rosalie's brood, and the mix of sluggish sentiment and forced eccentricity is tiresomely reminiscent of Capra's oddball simple folk in *You
Can't Take It With You*. Adlon does his usual
stuff with bright-coloured decor, but the vaguely modernist veneer can't conceal the dearth of
genuine feeling at the film's manipulative core.
GA

Rosa Luxemburg

(Margarethe von Trotta, 1986, WGer) Barbara
Sukowa, Daniel Olbrychski, Otto Sander,
Adelheit Arndt, Jürgen Holtz, Doris Schade.
124 min.
Rosa Luxemburg has a lot going for her when it
comes to the myth factory: female, lame, Polish,
internationalist, pacifist, revolutionary, imprisoned on nine separate occasions, a leader of the
Spartacists in their brief revolutionary success in
postwar Germany, and cruelly murdered in 1919.
This film won awards at Cannes and Berlin, two
for Sukowa in the title role; and utterly splendid

she is too, conveying a delicate mixture of strength and vulnerability. But though the film avoids many of the pitfalls of the *Hello Mozart, Hello Salieri* school of biopic, it still falls badly between the two stools of personal chronicle and politico-historical analysis, despite the intriguing use of archive newsreel footage, and the sterling contributions of Sander (as Karl Liebknecht) and Olbrychski (Leo Jogiches). SGr

Rosary Murders, The
(Fred Walton, 1987, US) Donald Sutherland, Charles Durning, Josef Sommer, Belinda Bauer, James Murtaugh.
101 min.
Although director Walton worked with Elmore Leonard, no less, in adapting William X Kienzle's novel for the screen, somewhere along the line someone must have seen Hitchcock's *I Confess*, to which this suspense thriller bears a distinct resemblance. Here it's Father Sutherland who hears the confession of Detroit's most wanted man, the killer who's targeted the city's priests, but instead of breaking his vow of secrecy, this man of the cloth takes to the streets to track down the perpetrator himself. Oddly enough, the more derivative first half works better than the lame detective work in the second. TJ

Rose, The
(Mark Rydell, 1979, US) Bette Midler, Alan Bates, Frederic Forrest, Harry Dean Stanton, Barry Primus, David Keith, Sandra McCabe.
134 min.
The Rise to Fame; the Stab in the Back; the Tragic Demise...With its ageless conventions and stylish history, the musical biopic is Hollywood's haiku, and the last two years have seen two of its finest examples: *The Buddy Holly Story* and *Coal Miner's Daughter*. But *The Rose* mixes its models and pays the price, stumbling awkwardly between a historical portrait (of Janis Joplin and other shooting stars of '60s rock) and a concert movie showcase for Bette Midler. Even her fiery mix of raunch'n'tease, though, can't make up for a bubblegum plot and sentimentality on parade. Only Alan Bates, surprisingly well cast as the Rose's ruthless manager, and Harry Dean Stanton (confirming himself as the grittiest sourpuss actor in Hollywood) raise a frown or a smile. The rest of it will just have you yawning in the aisles. CA

Roseanna's Grave (aka For Roseanna)
(Paul Weiland, 1996, US/GB) Jean Réno, Mercedes Ruehl, Polly Walker, Mark Frankel, Luigi Diberti, Roberto Della Casa, Giovanni Pallavicino.
98 min.
Stereotypical Italian drama which hammers home the indomitable, colourful, roguish but romantic spirit of the simple rural life. Marcello (Réno) will do anything to ensure that his beloved, ailing wife Roseanna (Ruehl) gets one of the last three plots in the village cemetery. Trouble is, old age, illness and accidents throw up rivals for the remaining space. Meanwhile, Roseanna, worried that Marcello will be alone after her death, tries to fix him up with her younger sister Cecilia (Walker). She, however, already has an admirer in lawyer Antonio (Frankel), nephew of a wealthy local who refuses to sell the church the land it needs for burial purposes. While Saul Turteltaub's screenplay fleetingly suggests the film might turn into a mildly interesting black comedy, too often the broad acting, the sentimentality and the manipulation of our emotions give the impression that this is an inferior attempt to cash in on the success of *Il Postino*. GA

Roseaux Sauvages, Les (The Wild Reeds)
(André Téchiné, 1994, Fr) Elodie Bouchez, Gaël Morel, Stéphane Rideau, Frédéric Gorny, Michèle Moretti.
113 min.
An intelligent, bitter-sweet account of teenage life in south-west France in 1962. The Algerian War still rages, forging alliances and creating divisions between a group of schoolchildren already confused by issues of class and sexuality: François anguished over his passion for the briefly responsive Serge, peasant brother of a would-be army deserter; Maïté, daughter of the

boys' communist teacher, and François' best friend; and new-kid Henri, clever, stand-offish and, having been born in Algeria, virulently against the idea of independence. These four variously fall out, make up, and edge hesitantly towards adulthood. The film impresses for its authenticity, careful delineation of mood, and subtle balancing of the personal and political. Téchiné wins sterling support from his young cast, who give the kind of quiet, naturalistic performances the French are so good at. A delicacy to savour. GA

Rosebud
(Otto Preminger, 1974, US) Peter O'Toole, Richard Attenborough, Cliff Gorman, Claude Dauphin, John V Lindsay, Peter Lawford, Raf Vallone, Adrienne Corri, Amidou, Isabelle Huppert, Kim Cattrall, Françoise Brion.
126 min.
Preminger's wordy, sprawling, but mostly involving, movie exploits Middle East tensions with a plot about the search for five rich girls kidnapped by the Palestinian Liberation Army in an effort to bring the Arab cause to international attention. But in a world of irreconcilable differences of opinion, governments too prove capable of using terrorist tactics to their own ends. Preminger handles the dramatic exposition with a curious mixture of panache and risible heavy-handedness, making it look increasingly like a Frederick Forsyth thriller, an imbalance that O'Toole's 'star' performance does little to correct. With the English O'Toole tracking down a fellow countryman, the eccentric mastermind Sloat (Attenborough) – and the former's government agent ethics perhaps more dubious than the latter's – the film engagingly if irrelevantly suggests that Perfidious Albion is still capable of pulling a few strings in world power games. Doubtless, like most Preminger, it'll improve with age. CPe

Roseland
(James Ivory, 1977, US) Teresa Wright, Lou Jacobi, Geraldine Chaplin, Helen Gallagher, Joan Copeland, Christopher Walken, Lilia Skala, David Thomas.
104 min.
The far-flung projects of independent director/producer team Ivory and Merchant have resulted in films ranging from the staggeringly pretentious to the absorbingly informative. This trilogy of short stories set in the famed New York ballroom could easily have suffered from Ivory's most irritating characteristic as a director: an aloof condescension to the weaknesses of even his most sympathetic characters. Moreover, Ruth Prawer Jhabvala's script suffers from an obvious 'literariness', although its subtle, sharp and sympathetic qualities make the film surprisingly likeable. As do the patently sincere performances (which avoid mawkishness) and, most important, the themes rarely touched upon in commercial cinema: the loneliness, decay, and tenaciously-held illusions of impending old age. RM

Roselyne and the Lions (Roselyne et les lions)
(Jean-Jacques Beineix, 1989, Fr) Isabelle Pasco, Gérard Sandoz, Phillippe Clevenot, Gunter Meisner, Wolf Harnisch, Gabriel Monnet.
137 min.
Roselyne (Pasco), a teenage lion-tamer with a blonde mane of her own, befriends Thierry (Sandoz), who plays truant to hang around the Marseilles zoo where – under the demanding tutelage of a veteran (Monnet) – she cracks the whip to put the beasts through their paces. Fired by mutual passion, the pair fall in love both with the exhilaration of facing the big cats, and with each other. On the road with a circus, honing their skills, they graduate into professional artistes. Beineix says the film is a metaphor for the act of creation, 'the transformation of rough material into a piece of choreography, a moment of show, a performance'. However, like an underlying concern with the price of professionalism – as the pair become more skilled, innocence and love are lost – this theme remains implicit. Most viewers will remember only the dangerous exoticism of the caged beasts, and the lingering, sensuous shots of Roselyne's lithe, bespangled body. The dazzling finale, in which the elemental confrontation between female and feline aspires through baroque artifice to the level of myth, is a sensational moment. But two hours is a long time to wait for it. NF

Rosemary's Baby
(Roman Polanski, 1968, US) Mia Farrow, John Cassavetes, Ruth Gordon, Sidney Blackmer, Maurice Evans, Ralph Bellamy, Angela Dorian, Patsy Kelly, Elisha Cook, Charles Grodin.
137 min.
A supremely intelligent and convincing adaptation of Ira Levin's Satanist thriller. About a woman who believes herself impregnated by the Devil (in the guise of her husband), its main strength comes from Polanski's refusal to simplify matters: ambiguity is constant, in that we are never sure whether Farrow's paranoia about a witches' coven is grounded in reality or a figment of her frustrated imagination. Sexual politics, urban alienation, and a deeply pessimistic view of human interaction permeate the film, directed with a slow, careful build-up of pace and a precise sense of visual composition. Although it manages to be frightening, there is little gore or explicit violence; instead, what disturbs is the blurring of reality and nightmare, and the way Farrow is slowly transformed from a healthy, happily-married wife to a haunted, desperately confused shadow of her former self. Great performances, too, and a marvellously melancholy score by Krzysztof Komeda. GA

Rosemary's Killer
see Prowler, The

Rosencrantz and Guildenstern Are Dead
(Tom Stoppard, 1990, US) Gary Oldman, Tim Roth, Richard Dreyfuss, Joanna Roth, Iain Glen, Donald Sumpter, Joanna Miles, Ian Richardson.
118 min.
Stoppard's 1967 play was a delicious and profound theatrical conceit, a pastiche which turned Shakespeare's famous flunkies from *Hamlet* into pathetic, confused victims. It seems odd that we should be treated to a cinematic version of what is essentially a very theatrical experience, while other more obviously filmable Stoppard works remain unadapted. Stoppard opens up the narrative, turning the pair from passive clowns into a restless duo, a costumed Butch Cassidy and Sundance Kid, constantly turning up in the wrong place at the wrong time. Every piece of stage business, from pirate siege to coin toss to verbal banter in a tennis court, is aimed at needlessly fleshing out the original; while, as Ros and Guildy, both Oldman and Roth turn in flat and uninspiring performances. Only Sumpter as a youthful Claudius, and Richardson's splendid Polonius give life to the *Hamlet* scenes. Disappointing. SGr

Rose of Washington Square
(Gregory Ratoff, 1939, US) Tyrone Power, Alice Faye, Al Jolson, William Frawley, Hobart Cavanaugh, Horace McMahon, Moroni Olsen.
86 min. b/w.
A fictionalised biopic of Fanny Brice, later celebrated in *Funny Girl* but unacknowledged here, which led to a law suit (settled out of court). Faye sings (nicely and nostalgically), Power is the nogoodnik she loves, and Jolson the 'Mammy'-singing buddy who advises her to pour her heart into a rendition of 'My Man', thus making Power see the error of his ways. Stock stuff but enjoyably done, with excellent camerawork from Karl Freund, and notable chiefly for the number of Jolson standards crammed in for him to sing. TM

Rosie Dixon, Night Nurse
(Justin Cartwright, 1978, GB) Debbie Ash, Caroline Argyle, Beryl Reid, John Le Mesurier, Arthur Askey, Liz Fraser, Lance Percival, John Junkin, Bob Todd.
88 min.
Christopher Wood's screenplay is stamped with the Gold Seal of the Ancient Order of Most-Elementary British Scriptwriters. This string of charmless high-jinks is naturally set in a hospital: Bob Todd malingers without his dentures; John Le Mesurier, an absent-minded consultant, dithers over the racing pages; Arthur Askey pinches bums; a quartet of bibulous junior doctors attempt to tumble our vacuous heroine. Come back, James Robertson Justice. JPy

Rothschild's Violin (Le Violon de Rothschild/ Rothschildin Viulu)

(Edgardo Cozarinsky, 1996, Fr/Switz/Fin/Hun) Sergei Makovetsky, Dainius Kazlauskas, Miklós B Székely, Mari Törőcsik, Sándor Zsótér.

98 min.

Things are tense at the Leningrad Conservatoire in 1939. Shostakovich's *Lady Macbeth of the Mtensk District* has been berated in the press, and such criticism can have fatal results. In class, the discussion on Mussorgsky's *Boris Godunov* focuses on the character of the holy fool – but who now will speak the truth in music about today's Russia? This superb study of musical expression under totalitarian rule follows the efforts of Shostakovich's pupil Benjamin Fleischmann to answer this question. He was to die in the siege of Leningrad, but not before writing a one act opera, *Rothschild's Violin*, about the struggle for existence in a rural Jewish community. Here was a work drawing on traditional folk melodies and daring to suggest that all was not rosy in the Russian state. The authorities were not amused. Splicing footage of smiling Joe Stalin and May Day parades into a persuasive dramatic reconstruction, Cozarinsky also delivers where current TV arts documentaries usually fall down: he lets us hear a full performance of the opera (Gennady Rozhdestvensky conducting the Rotterdam orchestra). TJ

Rotten to the Core

(John Boulting, 1965, GB) Anton Rodgers, Eric Sykes, Ian Bannen, Dudley Sutton, Kenneth Griffith, James Beckett, Charlotte Rampling, Victor Maddern, Thorley Walters, Avis Bunnage, Raymond Huntley.

88 min. b/w.

Two people are credited with the 'idea' elaborated by four other writers into the script for this movie; all of which seems rather excessive, given that everything in it has seen long and tedious service in British comedy over the years. Newly out of jail, three moronic crooks (Griffith, Sutton and Beckett) attach themselves to a big army payroll robbery set up by a mastermind (Rodgers). The plan involves establishing a phony nature cure clinic as a cover (comic business about old ladies swigging spa waters liberally laced with gin), is attended by many funny disguises (Eric Sykes' private eye sporting Indian garb, Rodgers as a German general), and ends in farcical disaster with crooks, army and police meeting face to face. Some mildly funny moments, but most of the jokes are laboriously set up and loudly telegraphed (like the comic highlight in which the most moronic crook has his IQ tested, and the computer collapses in a fit of grumbling despair). TM

Rouge (Yanzhi Kou)

(Stanley Kwan, 1988, HK) Anita Mui, Leslie Cheung, Emily Chu, Man Tsz-leung.

93 min.

Tale of a courtesan who died for love in the 1930s, roaming present-day Hong Kong as a wraith because she has failed to meet her lover in the after-life. A sharp, mildly satirical portrait of Hong Kong life in the '80s is shot through with flashbacks to the '30s, suffused with a heady, opium-hazed decadence worthy of Huysmans, yielding an elegant and deeply felt movie about the transience of things – especially love. Stunning visuals and sophisticated performances add up to a terrific, stylish movie. TR

Rouge Baiser

(Véra Belmont, 1985, Fr/WGer) Charlotte Valandrey, Lambert Wilson, Marthe Keller, Günter Lamprecht, Laurent Terzieff, Laurent Arnal.

112 min.

Belmont's endearing if daft reminiscences of a '50s Parisian adolescence. In the jazz clubs of St Germain, Bechet-soundalikes occupy the stand, and black rollneck sweaters proliferate in the audience, but despite the title (the name of a hit lipstick of the period), the film is more interested in the evanescence of ideologies. 15-year-old Nadia (Valandrey) is an ardent Stalinist, tirelessly selling the party paper and demonstrating against American imperialism, which doesn't stop her longing to be Rita Hayworth in *Gilda*. She is rescued from a police beating by cool, non-

political Paris Match photographer Stéphane (Wilson), who soon erodes her beliefs and underwear. Her Polish-Jewish mother's old lover Moische (Terzieff) arrives in Paris from Siberia, and his revelations about the gulags compound the teenager's turnaround. The make-up department are over-enthusiastic on wounds and the pallors of pining, but the genuine memories of a rite of passage survive the shortcomings. BC

Rough Cut

(Donald Siegel, 1980, US) Burt Reynolds, Lesley-Anne Down, David Niven, Timothy West, Patrick Magee, Al Matthews, Susan Littler, Joss Ackland, Isobel Dean.

111 min.

There are a few extreme auteurists who claim that everything Siegel shoots is wonderful, but some of his more recent efforts have been frankly disappointing, few more so than this glossy, shallow comic heist movie. Down and Reynolds are rival jewel thieves, half prepared to help, half to betray each other, as Niven of the Yard tries to bag Reynolds by using the kleptomaniac Down as bait. The whole thing is incredibly anonymous, jokey without wit, and spattered with pointless movie references (to Hitchcock in particular). And to make matters worse, the Ellington tunes on the soundtrack have been turned into pure muzak by Nelson Riddle. GA

Rough Cut and Ready Dubbed

(Hasan Shah/Dom Shaw, 1982, GB) Patrik Fitzgerald, Colin Peacock, Jake Burns, Stiff Little Fingers, UK Subs, Cockney Rejects.

56 min.

A slick editing job (courtesy of a BFI grant) applied to street-level *vérité* footage produces a virtual *Disappearing World* on the tribal poses and fragmented rock culture of 1980, replete with mutual slag-offs from bands and fans about skins, mods, police, fascists, and 'selling out', a laughable subtext of pop-press punditry, and much middling gig coverage. Something of a wake for punk's decline, it's full of self-parodic shock values, and best communicates a sense of musical recession, mapping a territory rife for the subsequent easy ascendancy of back-tracking trends. John Peel contributes his customary good sense in small doses; almost everyone else dissipates enthusiasm in antagonism. Primarily one for the sociologists and amnesiac nostalgists. PT

Rough Diamonds

(Donald Crombie, 1994, Aust) Jason Donovan, Angie Milliken, Peter Phelps, Max Cullen, Hayley Toomey, Joceyln Gabriel.

88 min.

Deep in the outback, a girl and her mother are distancing themselves from the adulterous man of the family, when grizzled cattle-rancher Mike (a single father, as it happens) puts their car in the garage and offers them lodgings while it's fixed. You can see where this is headed: comedy of manners, attraction of opposites, slow-burning romance. Indeed, that's about the size of it. Mike is the sort of role Burt Reynolds or Clint Eastwood might have taken in their redneck days, but Jason Donovan is hardly the type. Mundane and mediocre. TCh

Rough Magic (Miss Shumway jette un sort)

(Clare Peploe, 1995, GB/Fr) Bridget Fonda, Russell Crowe, Jim Broadbent, DW Moffet, Paul Rodriguez, Euva Anderson.

105 min.

A cack-handed venture into *Romancing the Stone* territory, miscast, racist, old-fashioned, and all in all not much fun. Nice scenery, though. As a magician's assistant who takes off for Mexico to consult a shamen, Fonda lacks the charisma to hold this ramshackle lark together, while Peploe's duff special effects aren't exactly magical. The funniest sequence is also the most offensive: a comic-relief Mexican heavy is transformed into a fat sausage, and promptly eaten by a dog. Oh yes, and Bridget lays an egg. TCh

Rough Night in Jericho

(Arnold Laven, 1967, US) Dean Martin, George Peppard, Jean Simmons, John McIntire, Slim Pickens, Don Galloway, Brad Weston.

102 min.

It's a rough night anywhere with this dispiritingly routine Western. Dean Martin is the bad guy determined to become boss of his whole town, Simmons the victim of his evil machinations (she owns the stagecoach line), and Peppard the handsome stranger (ex-deputy marshal, now professional gambler) looking on. The only question is, how long will it take Peppard to make up his mind to intervene? The answer is, a long time. The characterisation is rudimentary, the direction sluggish, the action brutishly brutal. TM

Rough Shoot (aka Shoot First)

(Robert Parrish, 1952, GB) Joel McCrea, Evelyn Keyes, Herbert Lom, Marius Goring, Roland Culver, Karel Stepanek, Frank Lawton, Patricia Laffan, David Hurst, Megs Jenkins, Laurence Naismith.

87 min. b/w.

Scripted by Eric Ambler from Geoffrey Household's novel, this curiously pedestrian thriller, set during WWII, looks like a throwback to Hitchcock's British period on a very off day. An American army colonel (McCrea), having rented a cottage in Dorset for a spot of shooting on the moors, fires a deterrent charge of buckshot at an intruder he takes to be a poacher. Panicking when the man dies (though not at his hands), McCrea hides the body, and soon finds himself up to his neck in British secret service agents (led by Culver) and a Nazi spy ring (headed by Goring). With credibility already low as plot and characters bumble around like something out of a *Boy's Own Paper* serial, it sinks even lower as a German plane (landing on rough moorland at night!), brings in a specialist agent (Hurst) to collect information about atomic tests, his rendezvous with the traitor being scheduled (in a chase climax that goes off half-cocked) at Madame Tussaud's. Only Lom, as a perky Polish agent busily swashing an Errol Flynn buckle, brings any enlivening wit to the proceedings. TM

Rough Treatment (Bez Znieczulenia)

(Andrzej Wajda, 1978, Pol) Zbigniew Zapasiewicz, Ewa Dalkowska, Andrzej Seweryn, Krystyna Janda, Emilia Krakowska, Roman Wilhelmi.

114 min

Rough Treatment takes up where *Man of Marble* left off, with its exploration of the contemporary (1978) political situation in Poland and its pursuit of the relationship between the individual and society. The film follows the downfall of an urbane and well-known political correspondent (a phenomenal performance from Zapasiewicz), who steps out of line during a TV interview and simultaneously discovers that his wife is leaving him. The cold, grey society of which he's part is discovered in the grim attitudes of those around him; at the same time his own faults and inadequacies build with every scene. Working in the wake of the censorship problems which beset *Man of Marble*, Wajda had this to say on its release: 'I worked on this film in a blind rage...it has no flourishes. Its impact was to come solely from a logically constructed chain of events'. The end isn't entirely satisfactory, but that doesn't matter – the rest is fascinating, and he's already made his point. HM

Roujin Z (Rojin Z)

(Hiroyuki Kitakubo, 1991, Jap) voices: Allan Wenger, Toni Barry, Barbara Barnes.

84 min.

Not exactly a parody of Katsuhiro Otomo's *Akira*, this Japanese animated feature (shorn of six minutes in its English version) does have a lot of fun challenging and sometimes reversing the psychedelic-punk precepts of the earlier film. Otomo's storyline and machinery designs are as imaginative as ever, but the sci-fi elements are subordinated to a celebration of old-time Japanese working-class humour, sexuality and values. It's set in the real world, where women are strong and make all the running, and men are bombastic, cowardly or weak – none weaker than the elderly widower Takazawa, who must have his every want attended to by student nurse Haruko. Takazawa is selected as guinea-pig for trials of a computer-controlled bed, which offers all the services of a geriatric ward in one ultra-tech package. The plot hinges on the moment when the machine's core bio-chip is taken over by the spirit of Takazawa's wife, who wants to resume a mature sexual relationship with her husband. TR

Rounders, The

(Burt Kennedy, 1964, US) Henry Fonda, Glenn Ford, Sue Ane Langdon, Hope Holiday, Chill Wills, Edgar Buchanan, Kathleen Freeman, Denver Pyle, Barton MacLane.
85 min.
A pleasantly lackadaisical comedy Western, about a pair of itinerant cowboys who are forever talking about settling down, but instead find themselves once more moving on to the next job. Their running battle with a cussed horse that perennially refuses to be broken is delightful; their run-in with two zany chorus girls (Langdon and Holiday) might have been equally so but for Holiday's over-playing. Ford and Fonda are excellent, but the contrived sentimentality involving the horse gets a little hard to take, and the gently quirkish humour misses out rather too often for comfort. TM

'Round Midnight
(Autour de Minuit)

(Bertrand Tavernier, 1986, US/Fr) Dexter Gordon, François Cluzet, Gabrielle Haker, Sandra Reaves-Phillips, Lonette McKee, Christine Pascal, Herbie Hancock, Victoria Gabrielle Platt, John Berry, Martin Scorsese, Philippe Noiret.
131 min.
Tavernier's offbeat love letter to bebop gets the best jazz film award since Sven Klang's Combo. Night after night in the pouring rain, a young Frenchman (Cluzet) squats outside a Parisian jazz club, listening to the sublime saxophone of one 'Dale Turner'. Since Turner, a shambling bear of a man, is troubled by the jazzman's classic demons of drink and drugs, it is not long before the young man has befriended him, rescued him from cheap flophouses, and installed him in his own flat, where kindness and devotion achieve some kind of advance over the depredations of the jazz life. The film reeks of the authentic stuff of jazz, smoky with atmosphere and all as blue as a Gauloise packet. Dale Turner, as played by Dexter Gordon, seems to be an amalgam of Bud Powell and Lester Young, but the private, rueful dignity that he brings to bear is all his own. CPea

Round-Up, The
(Szegénylegények)

(Miklós Jancsó, 1965, Hun) János Görbe, Tibor Molnár, András Kozák, Gábor Agárdy, Zoltán Latinovits.
94 min. b/w.
A vast, burned-out plain; dwarfed in the middle of it two buildings, whitewashed walls blazing in the sun, against which black-cloaked figures flit to and fro; silence, except for occasional curt words of command, as a man running for the horizon is coolly shot down, others are taken away never to return. As one watches, fascinated but mystified, a pattern begins to emerge, and one realises that a terrifying cat-and-mouse game is being played. The setting is the years following the collapse of the 1848 revolution against Hapsburg rule; the authorities, to crush the last traces of rebellion, must eliminate the legendary Sándor Rózsa's guerilla bandits; and the plan deploys a Kafkaesque mix of fear and uncertainty to winnow, slowly but inexorably, the guerillas from the peasant populace which has been rounded up. Jancsó's formally choreographed camera movements later developed into a mannerism; but here the stylisation works perfectly in making an almost abstract statement of the relationship between oppressor and oppressed. There are effectively no characters, no heroes one can admire or villains to hate; simply the men who always win, those who always lose. TM

Route de Corinthe, La
(The Road to Corinth)

(Claude Chabrol, 1967, Fr/It/Greece) Jean Seberg, Maurice Ronet, Christian Marquand, Michel Bouquet, Saro Urzi, Antonio Passalia, Claude Chabrol.
90 min.
One of the most outrageous films from Chabrol's first 'commercial' period, before Les Biches renewed critical interest in the wayward New Wave instigator. Released here cut, dubbed and

lacking an essential prologue featuring a mad illusionist, lumbered with the title Who's Got the Black Box? in the States, it's a wonderfully maddening mix of clattering allusions (to Greek tragedy and Hitchcock), characteristic black humour, and stunning visual irrelevancies, all poured into the deliberately banal mould of the spy thriller. 'I do not ask you to believe it, but I suggest that you dream about it' runs the film's opening epigraph. 'The silliness was more important than the spying' runs Chabrol's own retrospective line. PT

Route One/USA

(Robert Kramer, 1989, US/Fr/GB/It) Paul McIsaac, Robert Kramer.
255 min.
On the road again, two uneasy riders: Doc (McIssac), back from ten years in Africa, and independent film maker Kramer, ageing liberals who decide to follow Route 1, from the Canadian border through New England to Miami. Much of what they find is depressing. Endemic paranoia, poverty and bigotry – be it religious or patriotic – induce a desperate, introspective mood. With Kramer behind the camera, Doc becomes the focal point of interest, conducting hesitant, respectful interviews, meeting old friends, missing others, and not finding much to reassure him en route. There are odd glimmers of light: the liberal tradition of Massachusetts, Thoreau and Whitman, and community care projects that battle on against the odds. Not for Doc or Kramer the cool irony of Errol Morris or the conscious wackiness of Michael Moore. Doc wants to 'do something useful in all this shit', and three-quarters into the movie he surprisingly drops out to do just that. The last 45 minutes or so become distinctly ramshackle, with shifting centres and over-lapping voices. The camerawork and cutting have a snapshot feel, and the overall effect is rather like a book of photographs, 'A day in the life of America', fascinating in its detail, overwhelming in its diversity. TCh

Roxanne

(Fred Schepisi, 1987, US) Steve Martin, Daryl Hannah, Rick Rossovich, Shelley Duvall, John Kapelos, Fred Willard, Max Alexander, Michael J Pollard.
107 min.
Rostand's Cyrano de Bergerac, thanks to Martin's adaptation which translates the big-nosed duellist-philosopher-poet into the Fire Chief of a small American town, provides the perfect vehicle for his comic intelligence. His Chief Bales is a complex creation, falling in love with astronomer Roxanne (Hannah), a romantic beauty who craves communion with a fine mind, but automatically taking a back seat because of his appearance. Chivalrously, he supports the courtship of Roxanne by Chris (Rossovich), the dimmest of his firemen, winning her for him with his words, dictating the love letters and even hilariously stage-managing the wooing via radiowaves until the duffer repeats police messages. Chris, and the inept firemen in general, seem to have been cast in Martin's old role as the jerk, leaving the star free to parade subtler gifts. As a result, Roxanne is far and away his richest film to date, lyrical, sweet-natured, touching, and very, very funny. BC

Roxie Hart

(William Wellman, 1942, US) Ginger Rogers, Adolphe Menjou, George Montgomery, Lynne Overman, Nigel Bruce, Phil Silvers, William Frawley, Spring Byington, Iris Adrian.
75 min. b/w.
Rogers is Roxie Hart, a brash, perpetual gumchewer, who admits to a murder that was obviously committed by her weak, rat-fink husband. Not, however, the story of a strong woman sacrificing herself on the altar of love and marital devotion, but that of a sly minx, banking on attracting invaluable publicity for her so far non-existent dancing career. This long shot in the name of ambition is based on the premise that 'a Chicago jury would never convict a pretty woman'; an over-riding vein of cynicism that filters down from the gaggle of fickle press scribblers, interested only in hot news, never the truth, to the posturing defence counsel, who never defend the innocent. The total lunacy culminates in a courtroom melodrama with a difference, where Roxie crosses and uncrosses her legs for the jury's benefit, faints, cries, but always manages a radiant smile for the courtroom photographers, and where justice ultimately depends on the wrinkling of a pert nose. Subversive, outrageous, but always very funny. FF

Royal Flash

(Richard Lester, 1975, GB) Malcolm McDowell, Alan Bates, Florinda Bolkan, Britt Ekland, Oliver Reed, Lionel Jeffries, Tom Bell, Christopher Cazenove, Joss Ackland, Alastair Sim, Michael Hordern, Roy Kinnear.
118 min.
Lester long cherished an ambition to make a film out of George MacDonald Fraser's Flashman books, but once the swashbuckling gets under way, it begins to seem far too much like The Four Musketeers Part III. The director's visual style is as strong and witty as ever, and he does score one bull's-eye with Oliver Reed's Bismarck. But after an opening which promises some kind of riotous comic strip of Victorian England, and a particularly good scene involving a boxing-match, the plot begins to parody itself too overtly and too loosely, finally overreaching itself completely with an endless and unimaginative duel between Bates and McDowell. The film might perhaps get by on its superb visuals and the occasional good gag, but the casting sinks it: whatever Lester's intentions, McDowell and Bolkan are no match for Michael York and Faye Dunaway at this kind of thing. DP

Royal Hunt of the Sun, The

(Irving Lerner, 1969, GB) Robert Shaw, Christopher Plummer, Nigel Davenport, Michael Craig, Leonard Whiting, Andrew Keir, James Donald, William Marlowe, Percy Herbert.
121 min.
Given that Peter Shaffer's play was ripe for screen adaptation, it's surprising that this is so resolutely stagey. Concentrating almost entirely on the intimate confrontation between the Spanish conquistador Pizarro and the Inca godking Atahualpa, which takes in issues of immortality, religious belief, and the worth of gold (Pizarro is searching for El Dorado), it unwisely ignores the material's potential for the combined spectacle of landscape and material wealth. That said, it's still quite watchable, thanks largely to the intelligence of Shaffer's original, and to strong if idiosyncratic performances from Shaw and Plummer. GA

Royal Scandal, A

(Otto Preminger, 1945, US) Tallulah Bankhead, Charles Coburn, Anne Baxter, William Eythe, Vincent Price, Sig Ruman, Mischa Auer.
94 min. b/w.
This should have been an Ernst Lubitsch film: it's a remake of his 1924 movie Forbidden Paradise, and he had just started it when he succumbed to his fifth heart attack. (He still gets nominal producer credit.) Preminger stepped in, fresh from the triumph of Laura, and obviously had little success in getting Tallulah Bankhead to tone down the fruitiness of her performance as Catherine the Great, torn, as usual, between lust and sentimentality. There are hints of what might have been in the performances of Coburn and Price. TR

Royal Wedding
(aka Wedding Bells)

(Stanley Donen, 1951, US) Fred Astaire, Jane Powell, Sarah Churchill, Peter Lawford, Keenan Wynn.
93 min.
Not, thankfully, a documentary about a couple with cotton wool in their mouths, but a lively Technicolor musical (produced by Arthur Freed), with Astaire and Powell as a brother-and-sister musical act who travel from America to London at the time of the Queen's wedding (then Princess Elizabeth, of course), and both find romance, he with a dancer, she with a lord. A pleasant enough score by Burton Lane and Alan Jay Lerner, helped out by Donen's stylish direction; best number is 'You're All the World to Me', with Astaire energetically dancing his way round the walls and ceiling of a hotel room. GA

Roy Cohn/Jack Smith

(Jill Godmilow, 1993, US) Ron Vawter.
90 min.
Roy Cohn was Senator Joe McCarthy's right-hand

attorney and a vociferous opponent of the loosening of gay rights; Jack Smith a wild performer and film-maker whose celebration of transvestite perversity, *Flaming Creatures*, became a notorious underground film of the '60s. Both men died of AIDS within a year or so of each other. As 'presented' by Jonathan Demme and filmed in New York, Vawter's one-man show places these two apparently dissimilar individuals side by side, focusing on the element of performance that seems to have enabled each to have survived in his particular stratum of society. Vawter is extraordinary in the way he switches roles: zeroing in on a toweringly homophobic speech Cohn gave to the American Society for the Preservation of the Family in 1978, then adorning himself in glitter for a distilled re-creation of one of Smith's languorous, fragmented monologues. Some jarring cross-cutting aside, the film's an absorbing, intelligent take on the compromises of gay identity and the masks people hide behind. It's also a testament to Vawter, who himself died of AIDS, shortly after this performance was recorded. TJ

Ruby

(Curtis Harrington 1977, US) Piper Laurie, Stuart Whitman, Roger Davis, Janit Baldwin, Crystin Sinclaire, Paul Kent.
85 min.
This starts rather well: it's 1951, and a drive-in projectionist is attacked and strangled by the film he is projecting. Unfortunately it's the high-point of the film, for as the unseen force which animated the celluloid is revealed to be the spirit of Piper Laurie's murdered lover, Harrington strolls the gamut of contemporary horror influences in search of the completely predictable. He finds it: Ruby's daughter (Baldwin) is possessed and thrashes on a levitating bed. The cluttered art direction and the nostalgic flashbacks to the gangster '30s are stillborn mementoes of Harrington's own *What's the Matter with Helen?*, and the drive-in location never has its possibilities fully developed. Given that the film is always watchable, if never exciting, the drive-in isn't so much a location as the film's probable market. SM

Ruby

(John MacKenzie, 1992, US) Danny Aiello, Sherilyn Fenn, David Duchovny, Arliss Howard, Marc Lawrence, Tobin Bell, Joe Cortese, Richard Sarafian, Joe Viterelli.
110 min.
Sadly, MacKenzie's film about Jack Ruby will probably be viewed as an appendix to Oliver Stone's *JFK*, though it has merits in its own right. Particularly well caught is the easy-going and long-standing venality between strip-joint owner Ruby and the Dallas police, the CIA and the Mafia. Ruby is a bafflingly multi-faceted character, and Aiello pulls out all the stops in portraying the whole ingratiating, generous, sentimental, homicidal, paranoid mess. Perhaps the most startling depiction of Ruby's volatility occurs in Cuba when, forced against his wishes to carry out a hit, he suddenly turns the gun on the hirer. His relationship with stripper Candy Cane (Fenn) seems oddly avuncular, but then he may have been a non-practising homosexual. Writer Stephen Davis drafts Candy into JFK's bed, and plasters her with blood from the President's assassination in Dealey Plaza – without straining credulity. Veteran Marc Lawrence, as Santos Alicante, makes a chillingly believable mobster. BC

Ruby Cairo

(Graeme Clifford, 1992, US) Andie MacDowell, Liam Neeson, Viggo Mortensen, Jack Thompson.
100 min.
'What on earth was Johnny going to do with all that ink? And what did it have to do with his airplane salvage business?' What, indeed? Talking like a character out of a '40s thriller, Bessie Faro (MacDowell) follows a trail of baseball cards left by her deceased husband to a fortune stashed in various exotic locations: Mexico, Berlin, Athens. Neeson pops up briefly in Vera Cruz as a humanitarian 'Feed the World' worker, before reappearing as a romantic lead in sunny Cairo. Cue travelogue footage of pyramids, deserts, bustling markets. The script is packed with lines like 'Dead men do not write cheques' and 'Ink is the life-blood of civilisation', while Bessie must vocalise her every thought: 'Hmmm, this must be a code,' she declares, fingering a card covered in

hieroglyphics that must, indeed, be a code. Add some unbelievably straggly plot ends, and you've got a good-looking package tour which can doubtless be written off against tax. MK

Ruby Gentry

(King Vidor, 1952, US) Jennifer Jones, Charlton Heston, Karl Malden, Josephine Hutchinson, Tom Tully, Bernard Phillips.
82 min. b/w.
With *Duel in the Sun*, the most primitive and hysterical of Vidor's films, *Ruby Gentry* is a Southern family drama set in motion by the love of a girl from the wrong side of the tracks (Jones) for a member of the local gentry (Heston). An explicitly sensual film – notably in the ride along the beach and in the final sequences – it draws much of its force from Vidor's consistent identification of the viewer with Ruby as she struggles to come to terms with each situation her high-powered emotions place her in. Not entirely successful, but well worth seeing. PH

Ruby in Paradise

(Victor Nuñez, 1993, US) Ashley Judd, Todd Field, Bentley Mitchum, Allison Dean, Dorothy Lyman.
114 min.
Ruby (Judd) is running from her mother's death and thankless chores in the family business in Tennessee. She arrives in Florida, the Sunshine State, at nightfall, seeking identity and love. Her first priority is work, however, and though it's off-season, perseverance pays off with a job in a tacky gift shop. She's warned not to mess with the owner's flashy son (Mitchum), but loneliness drives her to joyless sex. Then she meets Mike (Field), a sensitive intellectual, and it looks as though she might realise the 'dream of belonging'. You know there's truth in these drab small-town lives, but, regrettably, there's little drama or humour to sustain interest in Ruby's vague musings on her bleak search for paradise. CO'S

Rude Awakening

(Aaron Russo/David Greenwalt, 1989, US) Cheech Marin, Eric Roberts, Robert Carradine, Buck Henry, Louise Lasser, Cindy Williams, Andrea Martin, Cliff De Young, Julie Hagerty.
100 min.
After 20 years 'out to grass' in Central America, draft-dodgers Jesus (Marin) and Fred (Roberts) wake up to modern political reality when they find the body of a CIA agent whose suitcase contains secret plans for a full-scale American invasion of Managuador. Realising that when they dropped out they also copped out, they instantly resume radical politics and return to New York to spill the beans. To their horror, their far-out pals now pursue respectable careers while enjoying the consumerist benefits of post-Reagan capitalism. A string of unrelated skits masquerading as a plot, this is a feeble one-joke movie: idealistic hippies culture-shocked by yuppie lifestyles, nuclear power, the ozone layer, acid rain and, most heinous of all, the colorisation of black-and-white movies. Only Louise Lasser, as the vivacious owner of the Nouveau Woodstock vegetarian restaurant, gives any hint of what might have been achieved with a little imagination. NF

Rude Boy

(Jack Hazan/David Mingay, 1980, GB) Ray Gange, The Clash, Johnny Green, Barry Baker, Terry McQuade, Caroline Coon.
133 min.
Scoring highly, if only for its excellent Clash concert footage, this blunt portrait of post-Jubilee Britain actually does much more: showing both left and right as cynical manipulators, and a Clash fan following his leftish band even though himself a potential National Front recruit, it has its finger (if not brains) on the pulse. Marred by some simplistic editing, it's another nail hammered into the coffin of rock and roll. See it and find out why *The Daily Mail* was disgusted and The Clash disowned it. DMacp

Rudy

(David Anspaugh, 1993, US) Sean Astin, Ned Beatty, Charles S Dutton, Jason Miller, Robert Prosky, Lili Taylor, Christopher Reed.
116 min.
Rudy (Astin) is an all-American dreamer: he wants to play football for Notre Dame, but, as everyone keeps telling him, 'Notre Dame is not for everyone.'

The son of a steelworker, he has only a mediocre academic record, a slight build, and he's not a great natural athlete. At 22, after four years in the steel mill, the death of his best friend moves Rudy to re-evaluate his life. He goes East and enrolls in a junior college, determined to make the grade. Eventually, he does – but surely all the guts and determination in the world can't make him a varsity football star? Underdogs are the grist of sports movies; even so, it's unusual to find a hero so ill-equipped for the task at hand. Directed with composure, but no great fervour, the film's conspicuously uninterested in American football, and much concerned with testing the limits and the resilience of the American dream. TCh

Rudyard Kipling's The Jungle Book

see Jungle Book, The

Rue Cases Nègres

see Black Shack Alley

Rue Saint-Sulpice

see Favour, the Watch and the Very Big Fish, The

Ruggles of Red Gap

(Leo McCarey, 1935, US) Charles Laughton, Mary Boland, Charlie Ruggles, ZaSu Pitts, Roland Young, Leila Hyams.
91 min. b/w.
Ruggles is a British butler (don't you know), Red Gap is the American shack of a town he comes to work in, having been won in a poker game. After initial incomprehension, he recites Lincoln's Gettysburg address and becomes the country's greatest fan. Sounds awful? Not so; this is the archetypal film they don't make any more, partly because comedy has now grown too raucous to favour the quiet drollery of players like Charlie Ruggles and Mary Boland, partly because after the '30s even McCarey himself had problems in separating sentiment from sentimentality. Laughton, as always, enjoys himself enormously; we can only follow. GB

Rules of the Game, The

see Règle du Jeu, La

Ruling Class, The

(Peter Medak, 1971, GB) Peter O'Toole, Alastair Sim, Arthur Lowe, Harry Andrews, Coral Browne, Michael Bryant, Nigel Green, William Mervyn, James Villiers, Hugh Burden, Carolyn Seymour, Graham Crowden, Kay Walsh.
155 min.
Peter Barnes' adaptation of his own play takes as its targets British chauvinism, British institutions, the sadistic education system, and the sexual perversion and social misery it feeds off. Loosely the plot covers the death of the old Earl of Gurney (Andrews) during one of his masochistic evening rituals, and the accession to the title of his insane son (O'Toole), who believes he is God but eventually switches to Jack the Ripper. This is buried beneath a load of old jokes, song'n'dance routines, bad jokes, physical obsessions, random send-ups. A very long two and a half hours does throw up some good performances and a few memorable images; otherwise the latent and overt ideas are fleshed out all too obviously. VG

Rumba

(Marion Gering, 1935, US) George Raft, Carole Lombard, Lynne Overman, Margo, Gail Patrick, Akim Tamiroff, Iris Adrian.
71 min. b/w.
Criminal waste of the delectable Lombard, once more playing second fiddle to Raft at his most repellently lounge lizardish in this follow-up to their inexplicably successful *Bolero*. Even the dances (again performed mostly by doubles) are shoddy this time round, while the fatuous plot oozes sluggishly to a climax in which Raft defies a supposed death threat from gangsters to go on stage and perform a dreary rumba routine. TM

Rumble Fish

(Francis Coppola, 1983, US) Matt Dillon, Mickey Rourke, Diane Lane, Dennis Hopper, Diana Scarwid, Vincent Spano, Nicolas Cage, Christopher Penn, Larry Fishburne, Tom Waits, SE Hinton.
94 min. b/w & col.

Shot back-to-back with *The Outsiders*, similarly based on a novel by SE Hinton, and signalled by Coppola as 'Camus for kids', *Rumble Fish* does indeed have a hero figure (Rourke) who belongs to a former age of existential 'outsiders', coasting through the world in an insulated state of deafness and colour blindness from too many rumbles. His kid brother (Dillon) idolises him, but is too stupid to see the damage done to all concerned by the continuous gang-fights of frightful violence but no importance. All of which is all very well; but Coppola's recent viewing seems to have been German silent films of the '20s, so he has decided to coat the whole enterprise in a startling Expressionist style, which is very arresting but hardly appropriate to the matter in hand. As with *The Outsiders* it's very hard to picture the audience at which the film is aimed. CPea

Rumble in the Bronx (Hongfan Qu)

(Stanley Tong, 1995, HK) Jackie Chan, Anita Mui, Françoise Yip, Bill Tung, Marc Akerstream, Garvin Cross.
105 min.
Actually shot in Vancouver, this is the Jackie Chan movie which finally cracked the US market, grossing some $28m on first release. Chan plays a Hong Kong cop visiting NYC for an uncle's wedding; he tangles with a multi-ethnic street gang and then teams up with them to defeat ultra-vicious Mafia types bent on retrieving some stolen gems. Not the best of Chan's large-scale action comedies: the big set-pieces (the demolition of a city building, a hovercraft rampage through downtown streets) strain for effect. But Chan's insistence on his own fallibility and vulnerability, taken with virtuoso scenes like the fight involving 101 domestic appliances, shows why he means more to his countless fans than six US action stars put together. TR

Runaway

(Michael Crichton, 1984, US) Tom Selleck, Cynthia Rhodes, Gene Simmons, Kirstie Alley, Stan Shaw, GW Bailey, Joey Cramer, Chris Mulkey.
100 min.
This near-future tale, in which Selleck heads a police division tracking murderous machines, is technically quite as accomplished as Crichton's previous work, carrying a strong atmosphere of menace and some virtuoso effects (including a tracking shot behind a bullet that makes the Bond movies seem old-fashioned). But once it turns from the hardware and the action to people, you can hardly believe your eyes or your ears. 'That's no bullet, it's an exploding shell' Selleck announces to a colleague. 'God, you're right' the other replies, not even turning to look at it. With its villain straight out of *Batman*, Crichton is clearly intending to lighten the tone, but instead the thing congeals. DP

Runaway Train

(Andrei Konchalovsky, 1985, US) Jon Voight, Eric Roberts, Rebecca De Mornay, Kyle T Heffner, John P Ryan, TK Carter, Kenneth McMillan.
110 min.
So brutish a prisoner that the Warden (Ryan) had him welded into his cell for three years, Voight goes on the run through the Alaskan winter with only Eric Roberts to keep him warm. They sneak into the back of a four-engine work train, but the engineer has a heart attack, the brakes burn out, the track controller's computers can't cope, and the engineer's sleeping assistant turns out to be – a woman. So sit tight and watch four matt black shunters, looking like beasts from the pit of hell, go charging through the tundra, while Voight and Roberts slug it out over the girl, life, fate, and who's going to have to go outside. Then there is the problem of the Warden being winched down by chopper for one last showdown. The surprise is that Konchalovsky has taken such an obviously pat formula (from an original screenplay by Kurosawa) and made it work remarkably well. Somehow one leaves aside the blatant implausibilities, even Eric Roberts, and takes great pleasure in a breakneck ride to the end of the line. And Voight has finally found his niche, abandoning all those wet-eyed liberal roles and playing to the hilt a hideous, raving beast, with scars. Great ending, too. CPea

Run for Cover

(Nicholas Ray, 1955, US) James Cagney, John Derek, Viveca Lindfors, Jean Hersholt, Grant Withers, Ernest Borgnine.
93 min.
Made between *Johnny Guitar* and *Rebel Without a Cause*, Ray's second Western lacks the baroque, bizarre excesses of his first, and the intensely troubled romanticism of the Dean film. Despite its superficially conventional plot, however, its theme is again the gulf between generations: Cagney rides into town with Derek, whom he has only just met, only to be mistaken for train-robbers. Before the error is recognised, the boy is crippled by a bullet, provoking his bitter slide into delinquency while his surrogate father accepts a job as sheriff. The situations may be the stock ones of deception, betrayal and revenge, but the film is rare in Ray's work in that it focuses not on the youth but on Cagney, who attempts to curb his own anger at the injustices he has suffered. Despite the violence of certain scenes, it's a strangely gentle, even poignant Western, and Ray's sensitive handling of actors and his exact compositional sense are as much in evidence as ever. GA

Run for the Sun

(Roy Boulting, 1956, US) Richard Widmark, Jane Greer, Trevor Howard, Peter Van Eyck, Carlos Henning.
99 min.
An adaptation, by Boulting and Dudley Nichols, of Richard Connell's much filmed short story *The Most Dangerous Game*. Widmark is a novelist and Greer a journalist who crash-land in the jungle, are given hospitality by three Europeans who may be Nazis, and escape pursued by a pack of dogs. The film never really gets to grips with the grotesquerie of the original story, though Howard, as a dead ringer for Lord Haw-Haw, is excellent. It was filmed in SuperScope 235, one of the widest film processes available. ATu

Run for Your Money, A

(Charles Frend, 1949, GB) Donald Houston, Meredith Edwards, Moira Lister, Alec Guinness, Hugh Griffith, Julie Milton, Joyce Grenfell.
85 min.
Released in a vintage Ealing year (*Passport to Pimlico*, *Whisky Galore!*, *Kind Hearts and Coronets*), this comic effort, co-written by the novelist Richard Hughes, seems a bit winded. Edwards and Houston are the Welsh brothers who win a newspaper competition to see their countrymen take on the England rugby team at Twickenham; Guinness is the journo who tags along to do the story on them, and grows anxious as their misadventures take unexpected (but not that unexpected) turns. TJ

Runner, The (Dawandeh)

(Amir Naderi, 1984, Iran) Majid Nirumand, Musa Torkizadeh, A Gholamzadeh, Reza Ramezani.
94 min.
An astonishing piece of film-making in which Naderi's harsh account of modern poverty supports passages of extravagant but unsentimental lyricism. Amiro (Nirumand) is an illiterate ten-year-old orphan living in a rusting tanker hulk, beached in a Persian Gulf shantytown. Life is a struggle, and garbage-picking and peddling water just about pay for a watermelon diet. Bigger boys try to steal his empty bottles, a man snatches the block of ice he needs to cool the water he sells. Amiro learns to fight back. He's a runner, and he wants to run with the best of them. Young Nirumand gives a performance to make Rossellini weep, and the soundtrack is a joy. PHo

Runners

(Charles Sturridge, 1983, GB) Kate Hardie, James Fox, Jane Asher, Eileen O'Brien, Robert Lang, Ruti Simon, Shay Gorman, Bernard Hill.
106 min.
How does it feel when your teenage daughter goes missing? *Runners* poses the question that even a heartless tabloid hack might hesitate over, but looks forward two years after Rachel's disappearance, when sympathy has waned. Her father (a role well suited to Fox's seedily neurotic screen manner), alone in his conviction that she is alive, and encouraged by a self-help group where he meets Asher, a woman who has simi-

larly lost her son, goes to London to find her. The amazing thing is that he does – briefly – and what seems to be just a behind-the-headlines story of an obsessive odyssey becomes an impressively ambiguous thriller. The unfancy realism of Sturridge's direction emphasises that this is a small film; but unlike, say, a TV drama-doc, it doesn't just flesh out a contemporary social problem. Rather, *schadenfreude* gives way to shaggy dog as writer Stephen Poliakoff weaves a quirky tale out of the loose ends of the here and now. JS

Runner Stumbles, The

(Stanley Kramer, 1979, US) Dick Van Dyke, Kathleen Quinlan, Maureen Stapleton, Ray Bolger, Tammy Grimes, Beau Bridges.
110 min.
The appeal of Kramer's consistent line in numbing worthiness (*Judgment at Nuremberg*, *Ship of Fools*, *Guess Who's Coming to Dinner?*) has always been to those who like their popcorn heavily salted. A veteran auteur-for-all-issues, he now comes up with this irrelevantly monumental crisis-of-faith movie, in which Father Dick Van Dyke (as close to Hamlet as he'll ever get) finds himself on trial for the murder of young nun Kathleen Quinlan, over whom he's been getting increasingly hot under the dog-collar. Deadly earnestness over Van Dyke's tortured celibacy becomes risible long before the Perry Mason conclusion and a final scene of indescribable bathos. Now perhaps if Sidney Poitier had played the role... PT

Running Brave

(DS Everett ie. Donald Shebib, 1983, US) Robby Benson, Pat Hingle, Claudia Cron, August Schellenberg, Margo Kane, Jeff McCracken.
106 min.
This is the true story of soft-spoken Billy Mills, a Sioux who left the reservation on an athlete's scholarship to the University of Kansas. There he encounters a dictatorial coach, a selection of racist bigots, the WASP girl he eventually marries. The real story is Mills' internal struggles – grasping the 'killer' notion of winning, dealing with the attitude of whites, and with the contempt of the Sioux who think he's become white. The examination of Mills' motivation is sketchy, though Benson endows him with a thoroughgoing niceness (runs well, too), and the climax of Mills' athletic career – and of the film – concerns one of the great long distance finals (the 1964 Olympic 10,000 metres), ending in a final lap of unsurpassed drama. Sadly, the staged race does not recapture the excitement of the original. GB

Running Hot (aka Highway to Hell)

(Mark Griffiths, 1983, US) Monica Carrico, Eric Stoltz, Stuart Margolin, Richard Bradford, Joe George, Virgil Frye, Sorrells Pickard.
95 min.
Sentenced to death for the patricide actually committed by his sexually-abused sister, Stoltz escapes from his escort and reaches the fantasising romantic hooker (Carrico) who has been writing to him in prison. They take off on the run, with the humiliated and vengeful police escort (Margolin) on their heels. Griffiths (his debut as writer/director) knows how to use a camera and set up a scene, but he wrote this for Monica Carrico, and it shows. She's terrific, vibrant, sexy and compelling; but Stoltz, who has all the acting vices of the young Peter Fonda and then some, lacks the resources to overcome the inherent weaknesses of his role, and leaves a gaping hole in the heart of what is otherwise a rather good low-budget movie. An odd piece of miscasting, since everybody else, down to the smallest bits, is superb (especially Pickard as an ex-con). JCo

Running Man, The

(Carol Reed, 1963, GB) Laurence Harvey, Lee Remick, Alan Bates, Felix Aylmer, Eleanor Summerfield, Allan Cuthbertson, Fernando Rey, Fortunio Bonanova.
103 min.
Alas, this is no Panavision and colour version of *The Third Man*, despite the teaming of Reed and ace cameraman Robert Krasker. Scripted by John Mortimer (from a novel by Shelley Smith), it's an extremely routine thriller about an insurance swindle, with Harvey as the ne'er-do-well, Remick as his soon disenchanted wife, and Bates as the

man from the Pru who smells a rat while on holiday in travel brochure Spain. The scenery takes first place, and you almost expect the dire Anne Gregg to pop up to show Harvey how to buy an orange in the market. ATu

Running Man, The

(Paul Michael Glaser, 1987, US) Arnold Schwarzenegger, Maria Conchita Alonso, Yaphet Kotto, Jim Brown, Jesse Ventura, Erland Van Lidth, Marvin J McIntyre, Richard Dawson.
101 min.

Pretty warmed-over stuff, this future world of the terminal TV game shows, and director Glaser fails to muster much pace and punch. Lifer Schwarzenegger, framed for a massacre he didn't commit, hops the hutch with fellow con (Kotto), hooks up with love interest (Alonso), and briefly takes refuge with the underground revolutionaries before being betrayed and recaptured. Offered up to the bloodthirsty populace as a sacrificial contestant on TV's *Running Man* show, he is shot down a chute on to the wasteland killing floor to be hunted by big, grotesquely specialised assassins – Buzzsaw, Subzero, Dynamo, Fireball. None is unstoppable, and each is awarded the appropriate jokey payoff line. The film doesn't look good; it's as if the flat lighting and boring set of the TV show had infected everything else. And Big Arnie's quilted outfit makes him look like a duvet. BC

Running on Empty

(Sidney Lumet, 1988, US) Christine Lahti, River Phoenix, Judd Hirsch, Jonas Abry, Martha Plimpton, Ed Crowley, LM Kit Carson, Steven Hill, Augusta Dabney.
116 min.

Growing up is hard, but the difficulties are compounded for 17-year-old Danny Pope (Phoenix) by the fact that Mom and Dad (Lahti and Hirsch) are still on the run years after their engagement in terrorist action against America's napalm bombing raids on Vietnam. Danny merely wants to come to terms with school, girls, and his talent as a musician, but the Popes' record forces them into a nomadic life spent in rented rooms in various towns. This is a rites of passage movie with a difference, in that it's politically intelligent and never crass. Danny's relationships with family, girlfriend (Plimpton) and teachers are sensitively handled, while the film's attitude towards the value of radical commitment balanced against individual pain is gently probing. Both acting (particularly Phoenix) and characterisation are top-notch. A film about lives indelibly marked by the past, and by the lies we tell each other just to protect ourselves, it displays the narrative sophistication and ironic grasp of moral and emotional nuances characteristic of Lumet's best work. GA

Running Out of Time

see Dias Contados

Running Scared

(David Hemmings, 1972, GB) Robert Powell, Gayle Hunnicutt, Barry Morse, Stephanie Bidmead, Edward Underdown, Maxine Audley, Georgia Brown.
98 min.

Hemmings' debut as a director, an odd, Antonioni-ish mood piece, adapted from a novel by Gregory Mcdonald, about a student (Powell) who leaves Cambridge under a cloud because he sat and looked on while his best friend bled to death after slashing his wrists in their rooms. He had no right to interfere, he insists; and the rest of the film is a sort of *crise de conscience* in which, under an assumed name, he seeks self-justification and/or forgiveness in an oblique confrontation with the dead friend's sister (Hunnicutt). Beautifully acted throughout, attractively shot (much of the action takes place around canals and barges), it emerges as a curious mixture of razor-sharp incisiveness (the tentative inquiry into the suicide; a tongue-tied dinner party) and soulfully introspective tedium. TM

Running Scared

(Peter Hyams, 1986, US) Gregory Hines, Billy Crystal, Steven Bauer, Darlanne Fluegel, Joe Pantoliano, Dan Hedaya, Jonathan Gries, Tracy Reed, Jimmy Smits.
107 min.

Following in Eddie Murphy's footsteps, Billy

Crystal – another stand-up comedian from New York TV's *Saturday Night Live* – here patrols Chicago's mean streets in his first feature, teamed with Gregory Hines as a pair of streetwise cops who prefer firing wisecracks to bullets to get them through the day. With four weeks until retirement, all they have to do is stay alive. Unfortunately, evil dope pusher Julio Gonzales (Smits), along with what would appear to be Chicago's entire Hispanic community, is out to get them. With their sloppy slapstick and wet Menudo jokes, one only wonders why more people aren't out to kill them. But Crystal and Hines do flavour the film with genuine warmth, and despite some cheap gags, work well together to produce some truly funny moments. SGo

Run of the Arrow

(Samuel Fuller, 1957, US) Rod Steiger, Sarita Montiel, Brian Keith, Ralph Meeker, Jay C Flippen, Charles Bronson, Tim McCoy, Olive Carey.
85 min.

With an ostensibly similar narrative and theme to *Lawrence of Arabia*, Fuller's film exhibits all the genuine cinematic intelligence and forcefulness that Lean's so sadly lacks. Here Steiger is the 'victim' of a cultural identity crisis, turning his back on America after the Civil War and being accepted into a Sioux tribe, his sojourn equating in many ways with Lawrence's among the Arabs. A 'mere' genre movie, but its subject is the concept, the ideal and the imperfect reality of the United States; political and psychological reconciliation in the face of hate, prejudice and guilt, vigorously expressed. PT

Run of the Country, The

(Peter Yates, 1995, Ire) Albert Finney, Matt Keeslar, Victoria Smurfit, Anthony Brophy, David Kelly, Dearbhla Molloy.
109 min.

If Gillies MacKinnon's *The Playboys* came closer to Shane Connaughton's portrait of County Cavan village life, it did not supply the star part that Albert Finney simply inhabits in Peter Yates' film of the same writer's novel *The Run of the Country*. They're both small but touching movies, though here Finney's policeman father is so psychologically layered that his magnetic field at times suggests Lear, the Mayor of Casterbridge and Liam O'Flaherty's anguished protagonists. Teenage Danny (Keeslar) finds it impossible to reconcile himself to life with father (Finney) after his mother dies, and moves out to shack up with Prunty (Brophy), the local wide-boy. Danny falls in love with Annagh (Smurfit), gets her pregnant, and falls foul of the local lynch mob. There's a cautious reconciliation with his father, and a realisation that they both suffer similar character deficiencies. Finney's village policeman dreams of the windfall of a murder in place of missing tail-lights, and bitterly resents what Ireland has become after its republican idealism. But the root cause of his frustration is sexual, and this gives great momentum to the clashes with his randy son. BC

Run on Gold, A

see Midas Run

Rupture, La

(Claude Chabrol, 1970, Fr/It/Bel) Jean-Pierre Cassel, Stéphane Audran, Annie Cordy, Michel Bouquet, Michel Duchaussoy, Marguerite Cassan, Jean-Claude Drouot, Mario David, Catherine Rouvel, Dominique Zardi, Margo Lion.
125 min.

Another characteristic Chabrol onslaught on the bourgeois family, which falls chronologically between the warmth of *Le Boucher* and the aridity of *Ten Days' Wonder*, and comprises the usual scrupulous mix of elements chosen to shock with the kind of cinematic references critics feel happy about only in quality movies. The plot comes from a Charlotte Armstrong thriller (*The Balloon Man*), and is loaded with the true stuff of pulp. Sex and dope, for instance, meet in a scene where a subnormal girl is drugged and forced to watch porn movies; earlier, Audran's husband, escalating to schizophrenia with help from interfering in-laws, tries to murder wife and child; while countering these, along with references to Balzac, is a wonderful echo of Murnau's *Sunrise*. What does it all add up to? Essentially, the Chabrol pup-

pet threesome again, but in a different combination this time: a crazy construction that is magical and magnificent, although you may have to look twice to make sure it isn't just crazy.

Rush

(Lili Fini Zanuck, 1991, US) Jason Patric, Jennifer Jason Leigh, Sam Elliott, Max Perlich, Gregg Allman, Tony Frank, William Sadler, Special K McCray.
120 min.

Despite a gritty screenplay by Pete Dexter from Kim Wozencraft's factual book, Zanuck's debut feature fails to keep its dramatic sightlines clear. Perhaps it would take an ironist *à la* Kurt Vonnegut of *Mother Night* to give us some perspective on the two undercover narcotics cops (Patric and Leigh) who begin to use the stuff heavily as a cover, and blur into the sort of mess they're pledged to eradicate. Set in the unlovely '70s, there's no shortage of going downhill in loons. If the film doesn't cheat, it doesn't stir one to pity either, perhaps because neither lead is sympathetic – both cops pose and mumble – and their love affair on the physical level borders on rape. Leigh simply isn't police material, particularly for Texas. Eric Clapton's music and the presence of a villainous Gregg Allman will be flashcards to those who like that sort of thing. A downer. BC

Rush to Judgment

(Emile de Antonio, 1967, US)
110 min. b/w.

A documentary on the Kennedy assassination and the Warren Report. Mark Lane proffers the legal brief for the defence of Lee Harvey Oswald he could not give in court and was barred from presenting to the Warren Commission, and develops a compelling point-by-point refutation of the governmental and judicial conclusions on JFK's assassination. Meanwhile, de Antonio is simultaneously presenting a damning indictment of the media's role in shaping the public image of the events of November 1963. His insistence on underlining every cut or dissolve, and buffeting together network and amateur footage, belies the seamlessness of the 'authorised version', the hastily-erected TV consensus which soon had eyewitnesses disbelieving their own evidence, and which rapidly assumed the status of 'reality'. Lane may come to a worthy and credible conclusion, but de Antonio restores the dimension of healthy inconclusiveness; Lane fights selective facts, but more importantly in the long run, de Antonio exposes a selected myth. PT

Russia House, The

(Fred Schepisi, 1990, US) Sean Connery, Michelle Pfeiffer, Roy Scheider, James Fox, John Mahoney, Michael Kitchen, JT Walsh, Ken Russell, David Threlfall, Klaus Maria Brandauer.
123 min.

John Le Carré's far-from-best novel gets the big-bucks treatment: Connery and Pfeiffer in unlikely amorous conjunction; script by the much-employed Tom Stoppard; a strong supporting cast; and ravishing location work in Moscow and Leningrad. Pfeiffer can act, but her assumption of a role for which her pouty glamour is inappropriate – a Russian office-worker seen rubbing shoulders in the bus queues – is a jarring note in a film which brings from Connery, as bluff, incorrigible, jazz-loving publisher Barley Blair, his finest performance in ages. And almost as an antidote to Pfeiffer's restrained Hollywoodness, there is Brandauer, oozing rugged charm and earnestness as the dissident scientist who sets this spy-versus-spy thriller moving. Overtaken by East-West events, and with an over-optimistic ending which sets personal against political loyalty, it's still highly enjoyable, wittily written, and beautiful to behold in places, at others somehow too glossy for its own good. SGr

Russian Roulette

(Lou Lombardo, 1975, US) George Segal, Cristina Raines, Denholm Elliott, Gordon Jackson, Richard Romanus, Bo Brundin, Val Avery, Louise Fletcher, Nigel Stock, Peter Donat.
93 min.

With the producers, director, and a number of the cast associated with Robert Altman films, one might have expected something a little more idiosyncratic than this straightforward thriller. Set in Vancouver prior to a visit by Kosygin, the film follows the sudden upsurge of movement by the Russians, the CIA and the Canadian Secret Police around a suspected plot to assassinate the Russian premier. Lombardo handles it all quite comfortably, dealing best with the action set pieces, and getting solid performances from most of the cast, with Segal as reliable as ever as a reluctant recruit to the espionage game.

Russicum

(Pasquale Squitieri, 1987, It) F Murray Abraham, Treat Williams, Danny Aiello, Rita Rusic, Luigi Montini, Robert Balchus, Nigel Court, Leopoldo Mastelloni, Rosanno Brazzi.
112 min.
An incompetently directed, incredibly tedious espionage thriller set in Rome. Williams is an American embassy official, Abraham a Jesuit priest, and Aiello the US consul: good actors wasted by the execrable process of dubbing. Although in sync, the line readings are all wrong; heavy pauses in mid-sentence, emphasis misplaced, the voices flat and unnatural. Trying to unravel the incomprehensible plot could be dangerous (despite several lengthy explanatory speeches at the end), but it revolves around a planned visit by the Pope to Russia; an unlikely cue for covert shenanigans from glamorous KGB agents, rough CIA men, worldly carabinieri, and Jesuit computer buffs. It's not nearly so much fun as it sounds, although the Gregorian chants are pleasant. TCh

Rust Never Sleeps

(Bernard Shakey i.e. Neil Young, 1979, US) Neil Young and Crazy Horse.
108 min.
The film catches Neil Young and backing band Crazy Horse in fine form during the 1979 'Live Rust' tour, and showcases both sides of Young's music, lyrical and abrasive, very satisfyingly indeed for fans. It would be pointless to pretend it's of any interest to the unconverted, despite Young's attempt to inject some cinematic interest with stage props dwarfing the musicians and standing as part of Young's statement about his 'small' place in rock history. But those who consider that his place in the rock pantheon is well deserved will reject the false modesty on display here and simply enjoy. RM

Ruthless

(Edgar G Ulmer, 1948, US) Zachary Scott, Louis Hayward, Diana Lynn, Sydney Greenstreet, Lucile Bremer, Martha Vickers, Raymond Burr.
104 min. b/w.
Often described as Ulmer's *Citizen Kane*, this is, alongside *The Black Cat, Bluebeard* and *Detour*, one of the Poverty Row king's very finest films. Given a far better cast and a slightly larger budget than usual, he follows Welles in choosing to view the rise to power of Horace Woodruff Vendig (an admirably cast Scott) through flashbacks which both stress his destructive use of others and refuse to explain his ambitions through clear-cut motivations (although, as with Kane, lost love is hinted at as a subconscious driving force). Indeed, like so many of Ulmer's unsympathetic protagonists, Vendig seems to be a puppet of Fate, a motif perhaps reinforced by the harsh precision of the stark, even *noir*-like visuals. Whether the film is a subversive critique of the American Dream, or merely adheres to the populist sop that wealth necessarily entails loneliness and anxiety, is ambiguous; there is no doubting, however, the effectiveness of Ulmer's pulp poetry, especially in the final scenes when Vendig drowns, choked by Greenstreet's vengeful, ruined Southern tycoon. GA

Ruthless People

(Jim Abrahams/David Zucker/Jerry Zucker, 1986, US) Danny DeVito, Bette Midler, Judge Reinhold, Helen Slater, Anita Morris, Bill Pullman, William G Schilling.
94 min.
The *Airplane* team dusts off the old idea of kidnappers abducting someone so obnoxious that no one wants to know. Sleazy garment mogul DeVito is planning how to murder his wife Midler ('I had to live with that squealing, corpulent toad all these years'), when she is bundled away by two young innocents – Slater, designer of the Spandex miniskirt which DeVito stole, and Reinhold, a wimp who sells dodgy hi-fi. It is Midler who sets the tone of prurient sexual hatred, flaring her nostrils and threatening the couple with chainsaw enemas if they don't set her free. With everyone else also deep in sin and sexual blackmail, it's all going splendidly along its nasty route when, alas, the tone shifts three-quarters of the way in, and Midler acquires some of her captors' tedious niceness, conniving with them at the downfall of the baddies. A pity that the directors prove less ruthless than their own creations, but there is more than enough here for people who enjoy murder attempts on cute pet poodles. CPea

Ryaba My Chicken

see Riaba Ma Poule

Ryan's Daughter

(David Lean, 1970, GB) Sarah Miles, Robert Mitchum, Trevor Howard, Christopher Jones, John Mills, Leo McKern, Barry Foster.
206 min.
An awe-inspiringly tedious lump of soggy romanticism, set in Ireland amid the Troubles of 1916, but with much of the action centreing on clifftop and beach, where the characters tend to congregate either to have sex or to brood about not having it, and where the wind and waves have a pathetically fallacious time of it. Pert Rosy Ryan (Miles), as Trevor Howard's wise old Father Collins knows, isn't one to settle for just any old lad from the village. So she marries the kindly, prosaically middle-aged schoolteacher (Mitchum), but is soon prancing into the woods with a dashingly battle-scarred English officer (Jones), to dally while spiderwebs glisten, dandelion puffballs flutter away in the soughing winds, and so forth. Banal, utterly predictable, ludicrously overblown, it drags on interminably, with our heroine finally getting her comeuppance by being accused (falsely) of betraying the Nationalist cause and having her hair cut off by a flock of rhubarbing peasants. TM

S

Sons of the Desert

Saadia

(Albert Lewin, 1953, US) Cornel Wilde, Mel Ferrer, Rita Gam, Michel Simon, Cyril Cusack, Wanda Rotha, Marne Maitland, Peter Bull.
82 min.

Lewin's weakest film, which he adapted from a French novel (*Echec au destin* by Francis D'Autheville), is set in Morocco and deals with the efforts of a Parisian doctor (Ferrer), abetted by the progressive, French-educated Caid (Wilde), to stamp out witch-doctoring in the villages. He begins with a successful field operation on lovely young Saadia (Gam), popularly believed to be possessed by devils, for acute appendicitis; whereupon the evil Fatima (Rotha) sharpens up her spells to conjure vengeful demons. You can see why Lewin wanted to make it, since the doctor's sceptical stance allows Lewin to pursue his own scholarly preoccupation with the rational foundations of myth and superstition. But the plot is a fine old farrago, choppily strung together, and drained of all credibility by the pot-pourri cast: Michel Simon as a bandit chief, Cusack as a wise old *mullah*, Wilde and Gam as Hollywood hero and heroine, Ferrer about as expressive as a block of wood. Some fascinating details, and good camerawork (Christopher Challis) where crude colour processing permits. TM

Sabata
(Ehi, Amico ... C'è Sabata, hai chiuso!)

(Frank Kramer i.e. Gianfranco Parolini, 1969, It) Lee Van Cleef, William Berger, Franco Ressel, Linda Veras, Pedro Sanchez, Gianni Rizzi.
106 min.

This flamboyant spaghetti Western comes with acrobats, bearded knife-wielding drunks, a strolling minstrel with a banjo which doubles as a gun, pantomime villains and standard virtuoso gunplay. Van Cleef, all in black, looks mean and surly, but this doesn't stop him from standing up for the Texas small folk whose livelihoods are threatened by rapacious railroad tycoons. The sound editing is ludicrous, the costumes are absurdly gaudy, performances come close to caricature and the dubbing is always noticeable, but that doesn't lessen the entertainment value one jot. GM

Sabotage

(Alfred Hitchcock, 1936, GB) Oscar Homolka, Sylvia Sidney, John Loder, Desmond Tester, Joyce Barbour, Martita Hunt, Peter Bull, Torin Thatcher.
76 min. b/w.

One of the most playful of Hitchcock's British thrillers, this was adapted by Charles Bennett from Joseph Conrad's novel *The Secret Agent*, which in fact had been the title of Hitch's previous film. The foreign saboteur at large in London is cinema-owner Homolka, and in part at least, his profession allows Hitchcock to indulge in the sort of movie-movie self-consciousness of which he would become the object some 40 years on. The film proceeds from the point where the lights go out (Battersea power station is the first sabotage target), and even includes a telling screen-within-a-screen homage to Disney and the *Silly Symphonies*. The narrative's a bit perfunctory, but is neatly overbalanced by the joyously rule-breaking sequence of a boy, a bus and a time bomb. PT

Saboteur

(Alfred Hitchcock, 1942, US) Robert Cummings, Priscilla Lane, Norman Lloyd, Otto Kruger, Alan Baxter, Alma Kruger.
108 min. b/w.

A trial run for *North by Northwest*, though lacking the thematic resonances, with the innocent hero (Cummings) on the run after being framed as a saboteur in the munitions factory where he works, and trying to get the Nazi agents before the police get him. A little on the bland side in its two leads, though suave Kruger and sweaty Lloyd compensate with their vivid villainies. Lots of echoes of earlier British Hitchcock, plus the charmingly bizarre encounter with the caravan-load of circus freaks, the charity ball from which there appears to be no exit, and the classic climax atop the Statue of Liberty. TM

Sabrina

(Sydney Pollack, 1995, US) Harrison Ford, Julia Ormond, Greg Kinnear, Nancy Marchand, John Wood, Richard Crenna, Angie Dickinson, Fanny Ardant.
127 min.

There's the touch of a dead hand on this remake of Billy Wilder's romantic tale of a love between April bloom and late September, but it doesn't flatten it completely. Trouble is, disbelief is never suspended. In Pollack's film, one's always aware that Ford (workaholic mega-corporation boss Linus) is competing with Humphrey Bogart; and Ormond (his servant's gawky daughter Sabrina, moonstruck since her puppy days on his playboy brother David) has the inimitable Audrey Hepburn dogging her tracks. As a cure for her infatuation, Sabrina's despatched to Paris as an assistant on *Vogue* – a whirl through famous landmarks, berets and Piaf – and returns a damned Pretty Woman, sporting a makeover so complete that David doesn't recognise the chauffeur's daughter. When David, engaged to a rival billionaire's daughter, falls for this Cinderella, Linus must take action to secure the merger. Ormond's face is certainly not hard to gaze at, but she looks so often ill at ease that her 'confident' gay smiles suggest, inappropriately, some masked psychological distress. Likewise, Ford's hard, impassive demeanour takes an age to warm up, almost past the patience point. WH

Sabrina (aka Sabrina Fair)

(Billy Wilder, 1954, US) Humphrey Bogart, Audrey Hepburn, William Holden, John Williams, Walter Hampden, Martha Hyer, Marcel Dalio, Francis X Bushman.
114 min. b/w.

Bogart plays a cold-hearted tycoon whose sole companion in life is *The Wall Street Journal*. Holden is his wastrel brother, and Hepburn the chauffeur's daughter. Yes, you've guessed what happens. Holden fools around with her, she attempts suicide, is sent to France for a cookery course, returns to melt Bogart's heart, and Holden is left to chair the board. Getting to this characteristic Wilder reversal of roles is romantic, funny and astringent all at the same time. Bogart is the man of plastic – he doesn't burn, melt or scorch – and Wilder satirises him and his ideals ruthlessly. Bogart's age here is crucial: he looks like an undertaker who has sidestepped the youth which Hepburn will give him. The golden boy Holden is the other extreme and equally ridiculous, driving around in his snazzy cars, coerced into a marriage between corporations, and forced to sit on some champagne glasses, enabling Bogart to sort out the Hepburn problem. It's a Cinderella story that gets turned on its head, a satire about breaking down class and emotional barriers (neatly signified in the array of window and glass imagery), and a confrontation between New World callousness and Old World humanity. ATu

Sabrina Fair

see Sabrina

Sacrifice, The (Offret)

(Andrei Tarkovsky, 1986, Swe/Fr) Erland Josephson, Susan Fleetwood, Valérie Mairesse, Allan Edwall, Gudrún Gísladóttir.
149 min. b/w & col.

In a house on the south Swedish coast, a retired actor and critic (Josephson) holds court over an unfaithful wife (Fleetwood), a moody daughter, an unpleasant doctor (the wife's lover), and various other eccentrics. Midway through their peculiar meditations, the unthinkable happens — an announcement of doom from the TV, and the end of the world is nigh. The man then makes a pact with the Almighty that he will sacrifice himself, and all that he is, if only the world is restored to its former condition. In Tarkovsky's elliptical and visionary world, the outcome is indeterminate; but the opening condition of fear and the later weight of prayer are as palpable as a roll of distant thunder. No one else can approach his sense of the Apocalyptic. His death leaves a gaping hole in the cinema of spiritual quest. CPea

Sacrificed Youth
(Qingchun Ji)

(Zhang Nuanxin, 1985, China) Li Fengxu, Feng Yuanzheng, Song Tao, Guo Jianguo, Yu Da.
96 min.

A lyrical, elegiac tale about the generation of students banished to remote agricultural regions of China during the Cultural Revolution. 17-year-old Li Chun, a shy, even repressed Han girl from Beijing, is sent to work in a small village in the Dai countryside, down near Laos. At first disdainful of the natives' rural superstitions and poverty, only slowly does she overcome her outsider status and learn the value of the Dais' appreciation of beauty, nature and human warmth. An unsentimental celebration of tradition, exotic landscape and cultural independence, Zhang's film is both a loving portrait of Dai life and a sensitive, partly autobiographical study of one girl's hesitant awakening to sensuality. Infused with a discreet, gentle eroticism and a final, touching sense of loss, it charms through its narrative simplicity and visual elegance. GA

Saddle the Wind

(Robert Parrish, 1958, US) Robert Taylor, Julie London, John Cassavetes, Donald Crisp, Charles McGraw, Royal Dano, Richard Erdman, Ray Teal.
84 min.

As contemporary reviewers mockingly noted, Cassavetes brings an inescapable tang of Method juvenile delinquency to the old West, which doesn't prevent this Western (scripted by Rod Serling) from being way above par. He plays a youth brought up since childhood by a much older brother (Taylor), now a rancher but hero-worshipped in the boy's memory as a once-feared gunslinger; Taylor changed under the influence of his own father-figure, a puritanically upright cattle baron (Crisp); and Cassavetes conceives it as his role to protect the protector he now sees as grown old and weak. He hones himself as a fast draw, but in so doing unleashes a mad dog killer instinct in himself... Parrish handles both action and relationships with great fluency and flair, bringing off moments of genuine inspiration: as Cassavetes obsessively practises his gun-slinging, for instance, he impulsively fires at his own reflection in a pool, gazing awe-struck as the human image abruptly shatters. Julie London is striking in an underdeveloped role as a saloon singer, shyly picked by Cassavetes as a bride, then standing helplessly by as Jekyll turns into Hyde; and there are stand-out cameos from McGraw, Dano and Erdman. TM

Sadie Thompson

(Raoul Walsh, 1928, US) Gloria Swanson, Lionel Barrymore, Raoul Walsh, Blanche Frederici, James Marcus, Charles Lane.
97 min. b/w.

The first of three adaptations of Somerset Maugham's novella (the others were Lewis Milestone's *Rain* and Curtis Bernhardt's *Miss Sadie Thompson*), Walsh's late silent movie profited from the absence of dialogue to avoid some of the inevitable censorship problems. Sadie, a prostitute escaping prosecution in San Francisco, lands up on a South Pacific island where she finds a sympathetic sailor lover (played by Walsh himself), but is threatened with deportation by a reformer – a priest in the novella – whose feelings towards her are not entirely spiritual. Walsh's version is high on atmosphere and vitality, though sadly the final reel has been lost, and a restoration has had to resort to stills to reach the conclusion. DT

Sadistic City (Ma-o Gai)

(Ryuichi Hiroki, 1993, Jap) Tomoro Taguchi, Haku Ryu, Sakurako Akino, Rena Hirota, Rie Kondo.
88 min.

Another unheralded wonder from the bizarre sub-culture of Japanese sex movies. Kishi (Taguchi from the *Tetsuo* films) is a timid salaryman, married with one neglected daughter. His one-time classmate Daimon (Haku Ryu, looking more like Christopher Walken than ever) singles him out for what seems to be an experiment in psycho-sexual damage. Daimon transforms Kishi's life by offering kinky sexual encounters with his own girlfriend – but then wants disturbing reciprocal favours. Backed by a great John Zorn score, Hiroki's ultra-sheer visual style turns Tokyo into an elegant fantasy city, bursting with perversity and paranoia. Just the thing to erase unhappy memories of Polanski's *Bitter Moon*. TR

Safe

(Todd Haynes, 1995, US) Julianne Moore, Xander Berkeley, Dean Norris, Julie Burgess, Peter Friedman, Susan Norman, James LeGros, Jessica Harper.
118 min.

A superbly ditzy Julianne Moore plays Carol White, a San Fernando Valley housewife whose closeted middle-class existence results in multiple allergies, a nervous breakdown and her eventual absorption into a 'New Age' retreat for the socially dysfunctional. Haynes' earlier films include a life of Karen Carpenter featuring animated Bardie Dolls and the stylistically splintered *Poison*. Here, he again beats his own path in terms of genre and tone, but his stance is so coolly detached that one's left at the end in a state of deliberate uncertainty about whether Carol quits or finds a 'safe' life. The ironic handling of decor and characterisation builds an eerie portrait of the blissed-out West Coast bourgeoisie at their most brainwashed. DT

Safe Passage

(Robert Allan Ackerman, 1995, US) Susan Sarandon, Sam Shepard, Nick Stahl, Marcia Gay Harden, Robert Sean Leonard, Sean Astin, Matt Keeslar.
98 min.

Though she's seen all but one of her seven sons grow up and leave home, Mag Singer (Sarandon) still has sufficiently strong maternal impulses to get in a blind funk every time she has a dream she thinks is a premonition of danger; she'll even ring her reluctantly estranged husband (Shepard) about her anxieties. However, just as she and 14-year-old Simon are about to move out of the family home, one of Mag's 'signs' proves true: Percival, who'd become so tired of life at home that he'd joined the Marines, is feared dead after a terrorist bomb at his Sinai barracks. Cue for the rest of the family to gather to work over old resentments, rivalries, loyalties and memories. Despite sturdy performances (the sons include Leonard and Astin), this film, from a novel by Ellyn Bache, is a tepid, dispiriting effort. A tidy, small-town world is on display. Irritations are minor and all, ultimately, forgivable. Everyone, however outcast they may sometimes feel, has a place and function in the grand familial scheme of things. The metaphors – notably Shepard's incipient blindness – are flagged, and the whole thing's a string of clichés. GA

Safe Place, A

(Henry Jaglom, 1971, US) Tuesday Weld, Jack Nicholson, Orson Welles, Philip Proctor, Gwen Welles.
92 min.

Jaglom's first feature is a non-narrative fairy story of the emotional vulnerabilities of a young New York girl. Her yearning for past innocence reflects in her relations with a magician of uncertain powers, and in her interweaving fantasy around the two men who serve but can't fulfil her needs. Although a psychological reading is there for the taking, the film also offers a lament on the cinema's loss of magic. The nostalgic songs, the conspicuous presence of Orson Welles as the magician, show how much its roots lie in the past, while the film's experimental structure reveals the impossibility of trying to recapture that past. Despite the non-linear development, Jaglom's composition is sufficiently coherent, and Tuesday Weld's performance adds a real focus point. The result is sometimes indulgent, often fragile, and occasionally enchanting. With Welles as presiding spirit, it's also funnier than you might expect. CPe

Safety Last

(Fred Newmeyer/Sam Taylor, 1923, US) Harold Lloyd, Mildred Davis, Bill Strothers, Noah Young, Westcott B Clarke, Mickey Daniels.
77 min. b/w.

One of the best of Lloyd's thrill-comedies, developing the precarious perch-clinging scenes in earlier shorts like *High and Dizzy* and the stunning *Never Weaken*. If he steered clear of the cloying sentimentality that characterised Chaplin and Langdon, Lloyd nevertheless lacked the narrative and visual ambitions that made Keaton a truly great director/comedian. That said, the clock-hanging climax that caps this generally charming tale of a country boy out to make his fortune

in the big city – having suggested a high-rise climb as a publicity stunt for the store where he is employed, he finds himself forced to substitute when the real 'human fly' proves otherwise engaged – is a superb example of his ability to mix suspense and slapstick. GA

Saga of Anatahan, The (Anatahan)

(Josef von Sternberg, 1953, Jap) Akemi Negishi, Tadashi Suganuma, Kisaburo Sawamura, Shoji Nakayama, Jun Fujikawa.
90 min. b/w.

Sternberg's last film was made in a Japanese studio, and drawn from a factual incident: a dozen Japanese merchant seamen were shipwrecked on Anatahan in 1944, and found a man and woman living on the island; by the time they were persuaded that World War II was over, in 1951, five men had died in fights over the woman. If the material is fascinating, the treatment is just amazing. Sternberg respects what's known of the historical truth, but uses it as a point of entry to darker, more dangerous areas. Sequences of dream-like abstraction and images of staggering beauty are recognisably the work of the man who created the image of Marlene Dietrich, but here they go way beyond Hollywood evasions and compromises. The surface perfection seems a little remote at first sight, but the film works subversively by implicating its audience in the patterns of desire and violence, discipline and surrender. It's brilliant. When was the last time you felt stark naked after a movie? TR

Sahara

(Zoltan Korda, 1943, US) Humphrey Bogart, Bruce Bennett, Lloyd Bridges, Rex Ingram, Dan Duryea, J Carrol Naish, Kurt Kreuger.
97 min. b/w.

WWII actioner in which Bogart's tank corps sergeant, retreating from El Alamein, picks up a motley crew of stragglers and survivors of assorted creeds and colours, who band together to defend a desert well against 500 Germans. Watchable more for its strong cast than for its credibility or its pretensions: the script was adapted from a Russian movie called *The Thirteen* by John Howard Lawson (one of the Hollywood Ten), who saw the mixed ethnic group as an allegory of brotherhood. TM

Sahara

(Andrew V McLaglen, 1983, US) Brooke Shields, Lambert Wilson, Horst Buchholz, John Rhys-Davies, Ronald Lacey, Cliff Potts, Perry Lang, John Mills, Steve Forrest.
111 min.

This isn't as bad as one might expect. Brooke Shields as Dale Gordon, a leggy little rich girl attempting to fulfil her dead daddy's dream by winning a trans-Sahara car race, is bound to attract some cheap jokes. Yet although an ugly crier and an indifferent actress, Shields throws herself into the part with gusto, doing many of her own stunts and suggesting that, given the right script, she would work real hard to be more than just a pretty face. But this isn't the right script, and everyone is just a pretty face, including Lambert Wilson as the dashing sheik who takes her in his strong arms. McLaglen marshals his desert scenery well, and the plot almost manages to hold one's attention much of the time. It really isn't as bad as one might expect; but then expectations raised by this sand-strewn romantic adventure, inspired by the Prime Minister's son driving a fast car into the middle of Africa and getting lost, barely reached ankle height. FD

Saigon

see Off Limits

Sailor Beware (aka Panic in the Parlor)

(Gordon Parry, 1956, GB) Peggy Mount, Shirley Eaton, Ronald Lewis, Gordon Jackson, Cyril Smith, Thora Hird, Esma Cannon, Alfie Bass.
86 min. b/w.

Much-loved British character actress Peggy Mount got her film break when the stage farce (by Philip King and Falkland Cary) that she'd made a huge success transferred to the big screen. She dominates the proceedings as the sailor Lewis' mother-in-law from hell, who gives sailor Lewis

a major attack of cold feet when he realises just what he's getting into with his plans to marry fiancée Eaton. This being a '50s British movie though, it turns out she's not as bad as all that, just misunderstood. Hits you right there, doesn't it? TJ

Sailor from Gibraltar, The

(Tony Richardson, 1966, GB) Jeanne Moreau, Ian Bannen, Vanessa Redgrave, Orson Welles, Zia Mohyeddin, Hugh Griffith, Umberto Orsini.
91 min. b/w.

Highfalutin nonsense adapted (though not so you would notice) from a Marguerite Duras novel. Bannen plays an English registry office clerk on holiday in Italy, bored by his life and a mistress (Redgrave) who keeps shepherding him off to art museums. In search of he knows not what, he takes up with a mysterious Frenchwoman (Moreau) who sails the seas in her yacht searching for the lover – a sailor from Gibraltar – with whom she experienced perfect happiness until he disappeared. The sailor, it seems, is symbolic of something everyone needs but doesn't usually find; so when Moreau and Bannen decide they are madly in love after sailing about the world a bit, she stops worrying about the sailor. Encounters *en route* with assorted enigmatic characters bring more loony tunes, none more so than Orson Welles, grubbily impersonating one Louis from Mozambique, since you can't understand a word he says. The whole film, in fact, seems to be coming filtered through cotton-wool. In the circumstances, Raoul Coutard's camera-work isn't half bad. TM

Sailor's Return, The

(Jack Gold, 1978, GB) Tom Bell, Shope Shodeinde, Mick Ford, Paola Dionisotti, George Costigan, Clive Swift, Ray Smith, Ivor Roberts, Bernard Hill.
112 min.

Originally intended for cinema release, this independently-produced feature finally surfaced on TV. Every frame looks like a movie, with detail and composition in depth only possible with 35 mm. But that, Tom Bell's typically strong performance, and Mick Ford's exuberant support, are as much as there is to be enthusiastic about. As a tale from the mid-19th century, with an English master mariner bringing home a black princess as his wife, it's curiously devoid of any contemporary resonance. Scripted by James Saunders from David Garnett's 1924 novel, it seems confused and naive in its treatment of the racism the couple encounter in a sleepy Dorset village. Religion and an awareness of class are seen to form attitudes, but there's no real sense of a historical context. An awareness of the vital element of imperialism is entirely lacking, so the supposed plea for a multi-racial society seems, to be charitable, only muddle-headed. JW

Sailor Who Fell from Grace with the Sea, The

(Lewis John Carlino, 1976, GB) Sarah Miles, Kris Kristofferson, Jonathan Kahn, Margo Cunningham, Earl Rhodes, Paul Tropea.
105 min.

A farcically misconceived attempt to transplant Yukio Mishima's engagingly perverse novel to an English setting, and to make its peculiarly Japanese psychology and motivations work with a set of improbable Anglo-American characters. The two main strands of plot (genteel but sex-starved widow falls for sailor who's ready to quit the sea; teenage son gets hooked on the Dangerous Ideas of the school bully and his gang) remain obstinately unrelated, and both swing wildly between inept naturalism and half-assed melodrama; the whole thing is shot like a cross between a travelogue and a substandard '50s weepie. Writer-director Carlino first castrates the book by betraying both its tone and its meaning, but then tries to compensate by introducing bits of would-be nastiness (an exploding seagull!) and scenes of would-be daring (Miles and Kristofferson discreetly nude). The result is more depressing than amusing, an insult to any audience. TR

Saint, The

(Phillip Noyce, 1997, US) Val Kilmer, Elisabeth Shue, Rade Serbedzija, Valery Nikolaev, Henry Goodman.
116 min.

This glossy action picture bears little resemblance to the '60s British TV series on which it's based. Simon Templar, multi-faceted thief turned rescue-hero, is suffering an identity crisis: you can tell by the frequency with which he changes persona. Thankfully, a tough upbringing has prepared him for a world full of megalomaniacs like Ivan Tretiak (Serbedzija), a corporate boss with an eye on the presidency of the new Russian Empire. Ivan needs something to get the public vote: the fusion formula discovered by British scientist Dr Emma Russell (Shue). Emma takes Templar to her bosom, where, conveniently, she keeps the equations to her theory. Cue more improbablities than *Mission Impossible*. Kilmer has the Templar face, but not the charm. Eminently forgettable. DA

St Ann's

(Stephen Frears, 1969, GB)
47 min. b/w.
The St Ann's district of Nottingham has two cinematic associations. At the start of the century it was the birthplace of Alma Reville, future writer and wife of Alfred Hitchcock; and almost a lifetime later, after the place had become a sodden, peeling slum and its narrow Toytown streets were being demolished brick by brick, Stephen Frears, leading-British-director-to-be, then the merest tyro, showed up to record an anomaly, as it seems in retrospect – the poverty-stricken '30s still persisting alongside the swinging '60s. Frears' directorial tone (lucid, unsentimental, unassertive) is displayed here already fully formed, ensuring that the piece has hardly dated at all, except for the style of deprivation being recorded. BBa

St Elmo's Fire

(Joel Schumacher, 1985, US) Emilio Estevez, Rob Lowe, Andrew McCarthy, Demi Moore, Judd Nelson, Ally Sheedy, Mare Winningham, Martin Balsam, Joyce Van Patten.
108 min.
Yet another film for the Yuppy Generation, this follows (or rather dabbles in) the fortunes of seven disparate chums shortly after their graduation. The chums are so disparate that one wonders how they ever managed to pal up in the first place, but of course it gives the members of the Brat Pack an opportunity to prove their acting versatility by swapping their stereotypes around. There is much minor trauma and subsequent dawning of responsibility, all set to a soundtrack-album soundtrack, but the characters are too numerous and too perfunctorily sketched, and the whole thing looks like a feeble excuse for a lot of half-baked 'ensemble' acting. AB

Saint-Ex

(Anand Tucker, 1995, GB) Bruno Ganz, Miranda Richardson, Janet McTeer, Ken Scott, Katrin Cartlidge, Brid Brennan, Eleanor Bron.
86 mins.
A biographical reverie on the life of Antoine de Saint-Exupéry (1900-44) that makes a virtue of a limited budget. The flying shots are clearly studio jobs, but lit so that they convey the romance of the air that utterly seduced Saint-Ex from childhood on. Mixing interviews with family, friends and fellow writers with imaginative re-enactments of key moments in his life – the death of his boyhood friend (to become the spectral Little Prince), the postal delivery runs over the stormy Atlas Mountains, the crash in the Libyan Desert, the courtship of the Argentinian Consuela (Richardson) and their turbulent marriage – the essay concludes that the writer/aviator (Ganz) never really grew up. The best scene has the imperious Consuela ('I'm bored. Astonish me') persuaded to kiss Saint-Ex during an engineless free fall. BC

Saint in New York, The

(Ben Holmes, 1938, US) Louis Hayward, Kay Sutton, Sig Ruman, Jack Carson, Paul Guilfoyle, Jonathan Hale, Frederick Burton.
71 min. b/w.
A one-off for Louis Hayward, kicking off RKO's series featuring Leslie Charteris' latter-day Robin Hood, although he did in fact return to the role in 1953 for Hammer's attempt to revive the character, *The Saint's Return* (aka *The Saint's Girl Friday*). Rakishly raffish rather than dashingly debonair, Hayward was less bland than his successor George Sanders, and *The Saint in New York* is accordingly much darker than subsequent films in the series as the Saint sets out to dispose of six New York gangsters, disguises himself as a nun, falls in love (happily for the series, it runs into a dead end), and ends up uncovering a seventh villain known as The Big Fellow. The plus here is Joe August's fine camera-work. Sanders took over for five films, starting with *The Saint Strikes Back* (1939, admirably directed by John Farrow), and continuing to formula, enjoyably but unexceptionally, with *The Saint in London* (1939, a British quota quickie), *The Saint's Double Trouble* (1940), *The Saint Takes Over* (1940), *The Saint in Palm Springs* (1941). Following a dispute with Leslie Charteris, RKO simply metamorphosed the character into *The Falcon*; RKO British tried Hugh Sinclair in two films (*The Saint's Vacation* and *The Saint Meets the Tiger* both 1941); and the character found a happy home on TV during the '60s in the person of Roger Moore. TM

St Ives

(J Lee Thompson, 1976, US) Charles Bronson, John Houseman, Jacqueline Bisset, Maximilian Schell, Elisha Cook, Burr De Benning, Harry Guardino, Harris Yulin, Robert Englund, Jeff Goldblum.
94 min.
Neither Houseman's presence as the criminal mastermind, nor Lucien Ballard's crisp photography can rescue this routine thriller from the implausibilities of script (from a novel by Ross Thomas, writing as Oliver Bleeck) and heavy-handed direction. Bronson seems tired from the start as the ex-crime reporter turned would-be novelist who gets involved in a simple theft that escalates into murder and large-scale robbery. Though the script is larded with post-Watergate cynicism – the caper is the stealing of an American electronics firm's huge bribe to an Arab oil sheik, and all the cops but one are corrupt – the film consistently skirts the issues it raises, however obliquely, preferring instead such time honoured clichés as the cutaway to Bisset looking glamorous/mysterious or Bronson looking muscular/brooding for its resolutions. PH

Saint Jack

(Peter Bogdanovich, 1979, US) Ben Gazzara, Denholm Elliott, James Villiers, Joss Ackland, Rodney Bewes, Mark Kingston, Lisa Lu, Monika Subramaniam, Judy Lim, George Lazenby, Peter Bogdanovich.
115 min.
Gazzara simply plays himself, in this adaptation of Paul Theroux's novel, as a genial American pimp in Singapore who tangles first with the local Triads, and then with the CIA. Bogdanovich turns the character into a sentimental paragon of virtue, and softens the hard profile of America's Far Eastern imperialism, ending up with a movie that reeks of the hollow travelogue sincerity it purports to despise. The director's smugness effortlessly trumps Robby Müller's camera-work and the good performances (notably from Denholm Elliott). Hard to imagine how anyone could make less of such a promising subject.

Saint Joan

(Otto Preminger, 1957, GB) Jean Seberg, Richard Widmark, John Gielgud, Anton Walbrook, Richard Todd, Harry Andrews.
110 min. b/w.
Even hardcore Preminger fans number this stage adaptation among his lesser works. As usual ambiguity is the theme within the theme – no big surprise when a play by an agnostic (GB Shaw) is adapted by a Catholic (Graham Greene). The film inverts the Joan enigma, with a number of ironical insights. The very production seems equivocal: deliberately bare and skimped to enable us to concentrate on the text, and/or because Preminger was not about to splash out on such a dubious box office prospect. The subsequent troubled progress and self-murder of Jean Seberg adds a further layer of ambiguity, both as eerie distraction and poignant complement. BBa

St Louis Blues

(Allen Reisner, 1958, US) Nat King Cole, Eartha Kitt, Juano Hernandez, Pearl Bailey, Cab Calloway, Mahalia Jackson, Ruby Dee, Ella Fitzgerald.
93 min. b/w.
The usual liberties are taken in this so-called biopic of WC Handy, which ends with the usual embarrassingly patronising attempt to dignify jazz by showing its triumphant arrival in the concert hall. Otherwise, despite some heady melodramatics (Handy suffering psychosomatic blindness because of his preacher father's stern disapproval) which are defused by sympathetic handling and excellent performances from Nat King Cole and Juano Hernandez, this is a pleasing film with a distinct feel for jazz. Above all, Nelson Riddle's arrangements provide an excellent account of Handy's marvellous blues, and the cast assembled to play and sing them is well worth listening to (with only Eartha Kitt remaining obstinately out of period). TM

St Martin's Lane
(aka Sidewalks of London)

(Tim Whelan, 1938, GB) Charles Laughton, Vivien Leigh, Rex Harrison, Tyrone Guthrie, Larry Adler, Gus McNaughton.
85 min. b/w.
A ripe performance from Laughton as an ageing busker pouring heart and soul into stirring renditions of 'If...' and 'The Green Eye of the Little Yellow God' But despite location shooting among theatre queues and some convincingly shabby sets, verisimilitude is not high (not with Leigh's Cockney accent shading into Kensington), nor are the musical sequences particularly appealing. Though written by Clemence Dane for Laughton, the script as revised by producer Erich Pommer constantly seems to be edging into Emil Jannings territory, with much gloom and sentimentality as Laughton is seemingly spurned on the way to stardom by the waif he has helped. This was the second of three productions from the Pommer/Laughton partnership, sandwiched between *Vessel of Wrath* and *Jamaica Inn*. TM

Saint of Fort Washington, The

(Tim Hunter, 1993, US) Danny Glover, Matt Dillon, Rick Aviles, Nina Siemaszko, Ving Rhames, Joe Seneca.
103 min.
Matthew, a gentle homeless Brooklyn boy (Dillon), makes his way to the Fort Washington shelter, and is befriended and defended by the grouchy veteran Jerry (Glover). We learn, bit by bit, of his history of schizophrenia and abandonment. Jerry takes this holy fool under his wing, teaching him the lore of the road, the car-wash game, and introducing him to his homeless friends, the crack down at The Blarney Stone boozer, and big plans. Though something of a failure in its own terms, this social-conscience movie does produce a strong emotional tug, helped no end by the dignified performances of Dillon and Glover. Essentially, however, content and form work against each other. Fred Elmes' fine location camerawork imbues the movie with a warm but inappropriate air of nostalgia. Likewise, Lyle Kessler's honourable script and Hunter's leisurely direction drive for a sense of distance – which results, regrettably, in only a glaze of humanitarian compassion. WH

St Valentine's Day Massacre, The

(Roger Corman, 1967, US) Jason Robards, George Segal, Ralph Meeker, Jean Hale, Clint Ritchie, Frank Silvera, Joseph Campanella, Bruce Dern, David Canary, Kurt Kreuger, John Agar.
99 min.
One of Corman's best films, far superior to Richard Wilson's *Al Capone* as a study of Capone's Chicago. The film revels in the mythology of the genre, both paying homage to it and reinterpreting. It was one of the few films up to that time, for example, to stress the purely Sicilian nature of the Mafia and its relations with non-Sicilians like Capone. The elaborate intrigue of the gang warfare is treated in a hard, almost documentary style, with newsreel-type commentary. It also remains unmarred by spurious moralising: morality, in fact, is suspended in favour of mythology. DP

Salaam Bombay!

(Mira Nair, 1988, Ind/Fr/GB) Shafiq Syed, Raghubir Yadav, Aneeta Kanwar, Nana Patekar, Hansa Vithal.
114 min.
The streets of Bombay teem with children beg-

ging, dealing, sleeping rough, surviving. Working on a scale that would make Dickens envious, Nair draws together the seemingly disparate threads of life in a red-light district, centering around the experience of an 11-year-old boy who runs away from his village. At first frightened and alienated, he soon becomes part of a complex hierarchy of exploitation, abuse and affection as he befriends the prostitutes, drug-dealers and children of the streets. Far from being episodic or disjointed, the film brings the lives of all its characters into a common embrace, never pointing a finger of blame but constantly emphasising the difficulties and dangers that surround young and old alike. Shot entirely on location with its child actors recruited from the streets, *Salaam Bombay!* enters into its subjects' lives with rare authority and absolute compassion, the material generated largely from workshops that Nair and her team ran for a period of months prior to filming. A revelation for audiences of any background. RS

Saladin
(An-Nasr Salah ad-Din)
(Youssef Chahine, 1963, Egypt) Ahmed Mazhar, Nadia Loutfi, Salah Zulfikar, Leila Fawzi, Hussein Riad.
183 min.
After enduring years of Anthony Quinn playing Arabs, the Egyptian film industry finally wreaks its dreadful revenge. With a nomadic cast of zillions, *Saladin* sets out to boil your brains with three hours of unrelieved apology for hanging on to Jerusalem. Caught up in endless exposition, Richard I is no *Coeur de Lion* but, like all the Europeans, a red-wigged mongoloid given to lines like 'We can take Acre by lunchtime.' Saladin smoulders. Any visual magnificence (massed gatherings in the desert) is blown by tacky action sequences. CPea

Salaire de la Peur, Le
see Wages of Fear, The

Salamandre, La
(The Salamander)
(Alain Tanner, 1971, Switz) Bulle Ogier, Jean-Luc Bideau, Jacques Denis, Véronique Alain, Marblum Jéquier, Marcel Vidal
129 min. b/w.
A journalist recruits a novelist friend to help him rustle up a quick TV script based on a news item in a local paper about a man who accused his niece of shooting and wounding him. She claimed the gun went off while he was cleaning it; eventually dropped for lack of evidence, the case was never resolved. The novelist (Denis) sets out to create the script from imagination, while the journalist (Bideau) goes after the facts. But dedicated to a celebration of instinctive revolt, the film is less concerned with what happened than with the girl herself; and Bulle Ogier conveys volumes in the part as the film counterpoints her view of society with its varying view of her. There is, for instance, a scene where she has a job as sales-girl in a shoe shop, and without warning begins to caress the legs the customers present to her: it's a gesture that's at once funny, profoundly erotic, incongruous, and deeply shocking, and one that places both Rosemonde and the world she finds herself living in. A rare treat, infused with a rich and unforced vein of quiet humour. VG

Salem's Lot
(Tobe Hooper, 1979, US) David Soul, James Mason, Lance Kerwin, Bonnie Bedelia, Lew Ayres, Reggie Nalder, Ed Flanders, Elisha Cook, Marie Windsor, Kenneth McMillan.
112 min.
A surprisingly successful small screen adaptation of Stephen King's vampire novel. In the Maine town of Jerusalem's Lot, it slowly dawns on writer Soul that antique dealer Mason is a harbinger of blood-sucking evil. Edited down from the 190 minute, two-part TV movie, this cinema release version is slightly gorier and tighter than the original. Paring away the excessive plot exposition of Paul Monash's teleplay, it places the emphasis on Hooper's fluid camerawork, creepy atmospherics, and skilful handling of the gripping climax. NF

Sallah
(Ephraim Kishon, 1964, Isr) Haym Topol, Geula Noni, Gila Almogor, Arik Einstein, Shraga Friedman.
105 min. b/w.
An early Menahem Golan production, this is a sort of Yiddish Ealing comedy, with Topol as the eponymous hero, an Oriental Jew who arrives in Israel in 1948 with his wife and seven kids. He finds his family being housed in a ramshackle transit camp instead of the elegant flat they were led to expect; and the comedy, such as it is, revolves around the workshy patriarch's remorselessly cute and very repetitive efforts to avoid doing a hand's turn while battling bureaucracy and accumulating enough money for a flat. Strictly for fans of Topol's particular brand of folksy charm. TM

Sally of the Sawdust
(DW Griffith, 1925, US) Carol Dempster, WC Fields, Alfred Lunt, Effie Shannon, Erville Alderson, Glenn Anders.
9,500 ft. b/w.
A slightly heavy-handed, sentimental melodrama, from Griffith's years of decline when he lost full control of his projects. Its interest would be no more than historical were it not also the movie that launched WC Fields. His show-stopping performance as Eustace McGargle, conman and sideshow juggler, contains the seeds of all his later glories. Highlights are his 'find the lady' routines, and his struggles to get out of an overheating oven or to master a juggernaut Ford, the latter as it crosses a furrowed field. There's also Carol Dempster's best role in a Griffith film as the tomboy heroine; and Griffith himself clearly found some rapport with his own vaudeville childhood in the backstage circus scenes. TR

Salmonberries
(Percy Adlon, 1991, Ger) kd lang, Rosel Zech, Chuck Connors, Jane Lind, Oscar Kawagley, Wolfgang Steinberg.
95 min.
Adlon wrote this slight, quirky but often moving film for singer-songwriter kd lang. Shot in English, set partly in the icy wastes of Alaska, partly in the wintry former no man's land of a newly reunified Berlin, it casts her as an orphaned Eskimo who hides his/her gender beneath layers of baggy clothes, and his/her emotional emptiness behind the scowling face of a Wild Child. Zech plays an exiled and widowed German librarian who befriends her and comes to terms, through their edgy relationship, with her own familial past. The fragmented early scenes fail to gel, but once lang lures Zech out of the warm interior of her cabin into the magical, frozen landscape, lang's haunting theme song ('Barefoot') helps to establish a more consistent, engaging tone. During a subsequent visit to Berlin, their ambiguous relationship trembles on the edge of lesbian love, but is complicated by Zech's coyness and lang's longing for maternal affection. A minor return to form for Adlon after *Rosalie Goes Shopping;* but the real praise goes to the two stars for breathing so much human warmth into some chilly scenes of winter. NF

Salome
(Charles Bryant, 1923, US) Alla Nazimova, Mitchell Lewis, Nigel de Brulier.
7,200 ft. b/w.
1920's art, California style. Despite careful stylisation and exquisite photography, this adaptation of Oscar Wilde's play boasts a healthy streak of vulgarity of which Wilde, one suspects, would have secretly approved. Sets and costumes, designed by Valentino's wife Natacha Rambova, are fashioned after Beardsley's drawings, but the film's atmosphere comes less from the artist's effete preciousness than from the robust and strapping decadence of '20s Hollywood.

Salomé
(Claude d'Anna, 1985, Fr/It) Tomas Milian, Pamela Salem, Tim Woodward, Jo Champa, Fabrizio Bentivoglio, Jean-François Stévenin.
95 min.
This production, declaring itself to be 'freely adapted' from Wilde's play, replaces perverted passion with something resembling puppy love. Here the little slut ends up, after her climactic thrash, demanding the prophet's head as some

sort of well-meaning euthanasia in order to help him shuffle off to a holier plane; at which the Roman Empire Strikes Back and Herod's corrupt court is overrun by Darth Vader look-alikes. The acting and dialogue are disappointingly reasonable, while the decadent glimpses of shaved pussy and gleaming buttock are too rare to satisfy smut-seekers. It looks suspiciously like a stab at Great Art that doesn't come off. Not nearly Wilde enough. AB

Salome's Last Dance
(Ken Russell, 1987, GB) Glenda Jackson, Stratford Johns, Nickolas Grace, Douglas Hodge, Imogen Millais-Scott, Denis Ull, Russell Lee Nash, Ken Russell.
89 min.
Russell's worst film to date. Stagily constrained to a single set, it has Oscar Wilde (Grace) taking time off from enviable epigrams to suffer a private production of his banned play, put on by his friends, the staff and clients of a singularly decadent Victorian brothel. They're a motley crew: Johns made up like a pier-show performer as Herod, Jackson whining Mrs Cravatt-style as Herodias, and our Ken himself as a dementedly salacious photographer. The petulant nymph, as incarnated by Millais-Scott – seemingly a graduate of the Toyah Wilcox School of Over-Emphatic-Diction and-Hyperactive-Eyelids – is depressingly tiresome; as is Russell's spastic balancing act between reality and illusion, which tenuously ties the text to Wilde's tormented longings for handsome young Bosie (Hodge). The in-jokes are plain silly, Russell's customary irreverence a matter of flatulent, leering *Carry On*-style humour, the decor sub-Beardsley, the whole thing redolent of a retarded pornographer's revue. GA

Salon Kitty
(Tinto Brass, 1976, It/WGer/Fr) Helmut Berger, Ingrid Thulin, Teresa Ann Savoy, Bekim Fehmiu, John Steiner, Stefano Satta Flores, John Ireland, Tina Aumont, Maria Michi.
129 min.
Masquerading as an essay on decadence and Fascism, this predictably speculative slice of Nazi sex is aimed squarely at the box-office. Brass says his film is about 'denuding power', a thesis which he pursues with cretinous earnestness: mostly Nazis spend time stripping off in a brothel bugged by the SS. Helmut Berger stalks through this 'Cabaret' playing the Snow Queen, hiding his glacial passions beneath increasingly outrageous haute couture Nazi uniforms. A dreary love story gives the film a supposedly decent core, but the camera's gaze is firmly fixed elsewhere at the climax: Helmut's final piece of upstaging is to have himself gunned down in the shower, naked saved for Swastika wristbands. CPe

Salón México
(Emilio Fernández, 1948, Mex) Marga López, Miguel Inclán, Rodolfo Acosta, Roberto Cañedo.
95 min. b/w.
Inspired (like Aaron Copland's suite of the same name) by the eponymous Mexico City dance club, this engagingly exotic melodrama focuses on the trials and tribulations of a reluctant *cabaretera* (López), struggling to pay her sister's boarding school fees and determined to conceal her profession and her pimp lover. Tragedy will out, and not without a heap of escapist moralising (catch the sister's air force hero fiancé!); despite the hackneyed plotting, however, Gabriel Figueroa's *noir* photography and the splendidly glamorous seediness of the nightclub scenes make for passable entertainment. GA

Saló, o le Centoventi Giornate di Sodoma (Saló, or the 120 days of Sodom)
(Pier Paolo Pasolini, 1975, It/Fr) Paolo Bonicelli, Giorgio Cataldi, Umberto P Quintavalle.
117 min.
Pasolini's last movie before his being brutally murdered may now seem strangely prophetic of his death, but it is undeniably a thoroughly objectionable piece of work. Transporting De Sade's

novel to Mussolini's Fascist republic of 1944, Pasolini observes with unflinching gaze the systematic humiliation and torture of beautiful young boys and girls, herded into a palatial villa by various jaded, sadistic members of the wealthy upper classes. According to the director, the story was meant to be a metaphor for Fascism, but the revolting excesses shown on screen (shit-eating and sexual violence included), coupled with the fact that the victims seem complaisant in, rather than resistant to, their ordeals, suggest murkier motives in making the movie. It's *very* hard to sit through and offers no insights whatsoever into power, politics, history or sexuality. Nasty stuff. GA

Salsa

(Boaz Davidson, 1988, US) Robby Rosa, Rodney Harvey, Magali Alvarado, Miranda Garrison, Moon Orona, Angela Alvarado, Loyda Ramos.
99 min.
Rico (Rosa) plans to be this year's 'King of Salsa' if he can sort out the complications of the threadbare plot. With father dead, he works as a motor-mechanic to support mother and sister, and he doesn't get down in grease all day just so Sis (Magali Alvarado) can jeopardise her schooling by dating his best friend. What's more he has women problems: will girlfriend and dance partner Vicki (Angela Alvarado) forgive him for flirting with Lola (Orona)? Will he sacrifice love for a better chance of winning the big prize with ex-Salsa Queen Luna (Garrison)? Will anyone care? Not with the cast delivering lines as if they're reading off autocue, and Davidson treating the plot as a meddlesome device required to stretch out the dance sets. So it's up to salsa to save the movie, but there's nothing hot and spicy served up here. The finale has the feel of a junior *Come Dancing* EP

Salt & Pepper

(Richard Donner, 1968, GB) Sammy Davis Jr, Peter Lawford, Michael Bates, Ilona Rodgers, John Le Mesurier, Graham Stark, Robertson Hare.
101 min.
Salt (Davis) and Pepper (Lawford) are owners of a Soho (London) nightclub, where a Chinese girl is murdered and turns out to have been a British secret agent. Harried by suspicious police, hunted by murderous thugs, the pair eventually uncover and contrive to thwart a coup d'état by power-crazed Colonel Woodstock (Le Mesurier), who plans to hijack a Polaris submarine and threaten to destroy a major city unless the Government bows out. The action is threadbare sub-James Bond, the gags are invariably mistimed, and most of the jokes are repeated to make sure you got them the first time round. Jerry Lewis was roped in to direct a sequel, *One More Time*, but it was, if anything, even worse. TM

Salto al Vacio

see Jump into the Void

Salt of the Earth

(Herbert J Biberman, 1953, US) Rosaura Revueltas, Juan Chacon, Will Geer, Mervin Williams, Frank Talavera, Clinton Jencks, Virginia Jencks.
94 min. b/w.
Director Biberman, producer Paul Jarrico, writer Michael Wilson, composer Sol Kaplan and actor Will Geer were all blacklisted at the time, and this extraordinary film was a unique act of defiance. Production was subject to constant FBI harassment, the leading actress was repatriated to Mexico (shots of her final scenes were done surreptitiously), and projectionists refused to screen the finished film, which *still* looks incredibly modern. Financed by the American mineworkers union, it deals with a strike in the New Mexico community of Zinc Town, formerly San Marcos. While the Anglo workers enjoy reasonable living conditions, the Mexicans live without adequate sanitation in a form of apartheid. At pains not to feature traditional romantic leads (like *Matewan* or *The Milagro Beanfield War*), it focuses on two decidedly unglamorous people, a Mexican worker (Chacon) and his pregnant wife (Revueltas), who are victims of an economic trap, and whom America's post-war boom – symbolised by the gleaming

cars that drive through the picket line – has passed by. As the strike for better conditions progresses, the women play an increasing role, overcoming the traditional macho ethos by doing both picket duty and time in jail (while the men, fed up with washing dishes, go off hunting). The film's targets multiply – workers' rights, racism, feminism – and for 1953 this is pretty amazing. ATu

Salto nel Vuoto

see Leap into the Void

Salut Cousin! (Hey Cousin!)

(Merzak Allouache, 1996, Fr/Bel/Alg/Luxembourg) Gad Elmaleh, Mess Hattou, Magaly Berdy, Ann-Gisel Glass, Jean Benguigui, Xavier Maly.
102 min.
Alilo (Elmaleh) arrives in Paris from Algiers on an errand from his fashion wholesaler boss. He must collect a consignment of clothes, but he's lost the contact details. It's the weekend, so he's stranded on the streets until he remembers cousin Mok (Hattou). Mok seems to have it made, with his hipster clothes, his own flat and an upcoming gig as a rap artist. By his side, Alilo feels like a real country bumpkin, yet the more time he spends around this self-styled city slicker, the more he realises that the Parisian dream can easily turn hollow. This is no dogged social realist trudge through the immigrant nightmare. There's much sly comedy as we gradually see through Mok's motormouth bragging, a touch of tingly romance as Alilo starts making eye contact with Mok's West African neighbour Fatoumata (Berdy), and a sturdy narrative line that builds up tension the closer Alilo comes to delivery day. The performances never mistake insight for exaggeration, and the rich camera-work refuses to settle for off-hand grunge. Most memorable of all is the film's feeling for those Algerians who can never return to their ravaged homeland, but know they'll never truly be at home in France. TJ

Salute of the Jugger, The

(David Peoples, 1989, Aust) Rutger Hauer, Joan Chen, Anna Katarina, Vincent Philip D'Onofrio, Delroy Lindo, Gandhi McIntyre, Justin Monju.
91 min.
Or, Mad Max Beyond Rollerball. After the apocalypse, nomadic juggers roam the wastelands, challenging local teams to bouts of gladiatorial rugby. Seduced by this life of glamour, petite peasant Chen persuades rugged Hauer to sign her up. He resists, relents, and eventually sets up a showdown exhibition match with big subterranean city juggers. Scripted by Peoples himself, this thin, sloppy scenario hasn't an original idea to its name. Despite defiantly cool stars (Chen was Bertolucci's last empress and the *Twin Peaks* mill-owner; Hauer will always be Batty), there's little to look at and nothing worth hearing. Even the game itself is a drag. Footnote: Peoples shot the movie at Coober Pedy, in the Australian outback, because 'deserts in the US have been filmed a lot and have become well-known'. 'Coober Pedy' comes from the aboriginal words for 'white man's hole'. TCh

Salvador

(Oliver Stone, 1986, US) James Woods, James Belushi, Michael Murphy, John Savage, Elpidia Carrillo, Tony Plana, Colby Chester, Cindy Gibb.
122 min.
In 1980, Richard Boyle, an American journalist on the skids, drove down to Salvador, believing the place would provide both a story and all those things he remembered so fondly from the late 1960s – booze, drugs, sexual freedom. What he found was civil war, with his own government supporting the right wing incumbents and their death squads. Boyle, as portrayed by the excellent Woods, is naïve, manic, and dangerous. He suffers terror and humiliation, risks death, and re-discovers his professional integrity. Stone's film (co-written by Boyle with the director) is about North American ignorance, Central American tragedy, and how the two are related. The polemic may seem obvious and at times laboured, but the action sequences are brilliant, and the film does achieve a brutal, often very moving, power. RR

Salvation! Have You Said Your Prayers Today? (aka Salvation!)

(Beth B, 1987, US) Stephen McHattie, Dominique Davalos, Exene Cervenka, Viggo Mortensen, Rockets Redglare, Billy Bastiani.
85 min.
Quite what Beth B – known best, if at all, for her Super-8 and pop promo work – is trying to do with this uneasy blend of camp melodrama and straight satire is unclear. The film starts promisingly with barely-sane TV evangelist Reverend Randall (McHattie) ranting direct to camera about atheism in the Big Apple. But things immediately slide downward into some sort of strident 'alternative' comedy when a sacked factory worker and his sister (Mortensen and Davalos) break into Randall's Fort Knox-like mansion and hold him hostage. Heavy Metal gets an airing, there is much post-punk posturing, and the depiction of both Randall and his devotee-abductors as universally corruptible is stale and unfunny. GA

Salvation Hunters, The

(Josef von Sternberg, 1925, US) Georgia Hale, George K Arthur, Bruce Guerin, Otto Matiesen, Nellie Bly Baker, Olaf Hytten, Stuart Holmes.
7,650 ft. b/w.
It's hard now to appreciate the bomb-shell that Sternberg's first feature must have been in Hollywood at the time: its slow pace, its lyrical pessimism, and its strong emphasis on the psychological over the physical set it far apart from anything that the American cinema had produced. The angry-young-man plot (apathetic, cowardly boy loses girl to city slicker, who presses her into brothel service) verges on allegory, despite the wish-fulfilment ending, and looks more pretentious than committed at this remove. Yet there are lots of pointers towards Sternberg's future glories, and the sheer nagging intensity of mood is still extremely potent. TR

Salvatore Giuliano

(Francesco Rosi, 1961, It) Frank Wolff, Salvo Randone, Federico Zardi, Pietro Cammarata, Fernando Cicero.
125 min. b/w.
The film that first brought Rosi international recognition: a masterly semi-documentary about – or rather around – the notorious Sicilian bandit, told in a series of flashbacks taking off from scenes recreating the discovery of his bullet-riddled body in July 1950, his laying-out and burial, and the trial of his associates. If Giuliano himself remains an enigma as the centrepiece of the jigsaw – deliberately so, since Rosi refuses to guess at mysteries – the complex lessons offered by his life and death in terms of Sicilian society and Mafia politics are laid out with exemplary clarity. Stunningly shot in stark black-and-white by Gianni Di Venanzo. TM

Samba Traore

(Idrissa Ouedraogo, 1992, Burkina Faso) Bakary Sangare, Mariam Kaba, Abdoulaye Komboudri, Irene Tassembedo.
85 min.
On the face of it, Samba is a village boy who struck it rich in the city. He comes home, marries the single mother Saratou and opens a bar with his friend Salif. But then awkward questions start to arise about the source of his wealth. The hint of ethnography which hovered just off screen in Ouedraogo's *Yaaba* and *Tilai* is missing here. This tale of a criminal trying to go straight is almost generic, and could be set almost anywhere. Maybe this points the way out of African cinema's impasse? As usual the director picks a fine cast and directs them with great empathy. TR

Same Old Song (On connaît la chanson)

(Alain Resnais, 1997, Fr/Switz/GB) Pierre Arditi, Sabine Azéma, Jean-Pierre Bacri, André Dussollier, Lambert Wilson, Jane Birkin.
120 min.
Dedicated to Dennis Potter, this borrows his idea of having characters burst into lip synched song to express the feelings they cannot voice in ordinary conversation. This doesn't work quite the same way with French *chansons* as it did with Anglo-American

standards (although there is a delicious moment when Jane Birkin, doing a cameo, 'sings' a snatch of one of her own songs), but the real problem is that Resnais remains fixated on the toothless bourgeois satire which has dominated his work since *Mélo*. The characters here – an unhappy salesman who writes radio plays on the side, a tourist guide, a ruthless property developer – are simply too banal for their romantic longings and misunderstandings to matter to most viewers. And that fatally weakens Resnais' point that clichéd passions simmer beneath the blandest exteriors. TR

Same Time, Next Year

(Robert Mulligan, 1978, US) Ellen Burstyn, Alan Alda, Ivan Bonar, Bernie Kuby, Cosmo Sardo.
119 min.
A holiday romance begun in 1952 somehow stumbles over 25-plus years. Annually, the only-slightly odd couple desert their spouses and kids for a passionate weekend reunion. Every five years or so, we pick up on them and their inevitable changes, as the world spins in a montage of stills. OK, so with only two lead actors and a single location, the film wears its Broadway origins prominently on its chest, and sits somewhat anachronistically amid the movie-movie flow of New Hollywood. But for all that it's a surprisingly, refreshingly welcome throwback, with the sort of sparklingly literate dialogue it used to take an army of studio screenwriters to polish and which you rarely hear today; with two superbly versatile performances from Burstyn and Alda; and with direction from Mulligan that's the undemonstrative epitome of old-fashioned craftsmanship. And it is very funny. PT

Sammy and Rosie Get Laid

(Stephen Frears, 1987, GB) Shashi Kapoor, Frances Barber, Claire Bloom, Ayub Khan Dim, Roland Gift, Wendy Gazelle, Badi Uzzman.
101 min.
A genial, retired Indian political torturer (Kapoor) returns to England to visit son Sammy (Dim) and daughter-in-law Rosie (Barber) in war-torn Ladbroke Grove. Family explanations are conducted in the thick of riots, the first of many preposterous juxtapositions. Sammy accommodates his father because he wants his money; social worker (yawn) Rosie is less of a pushover, wanting political commitment and sexual freedom, ie. to have her cock and eat it. So does this film, tossed together from a Hanif Kureishi screenplay which labours so many right-on themes that none leave their mark. Black Danny (Gift) smiles enigmatically in a woman's hat ('Call me Victoria'), symbolising some seraphic quality or other; hectoring lesbians swap het-hating slogans; a peace commune beneath the Westway is bulldozed to the strains of patriotic music; and in one of the worst sequences in this oratorio of half-baked agitprop, the screen splits into three layers to show six people fucking at once, serenaded by close-harmony Rastas. Finally, in a last-ditch attempt at dramatic structure, the retired torturer, hounded by the grotty ghost of one of his victims, strings himself up. *My Beautiful Laundrette* it is not. MS

Sammy Going South
(aka A Boy Ten Feet Tall)

(Alexander Mackendrick, 1963, GB) Fergus McClelland, Edward G Robinson, Constance Cummings, Harry H Corbett.
128 min.
While widely regarded as an example of Mackendrick's decline after the masterpiece that was *Sweet Smell of Success*, this is certainly not the mere 'family fodder' that disappointed Leslie Halliwell. Indeed, like *A High Wind in Jamaica* and *Mandy*, it is another of the director's dark, somewhat sour studies in child psychology: as the young McClelland, suddenly orphaned during an air-raid on Port Said, makes his long and lonely journey down through Africa in search of his aunt in Durban, he encounters all kinds of danger and criminality with barely a blink of an eye. If the pace is oddly flaccid in places and the photography sometimes verges on travelogue territory, there is no denying the vitality of the performances, Robinson being particularly affecting as the diamond mining outlaw who takes Sammy

temporarily under his wing. Indeed, as in *High Wind*, it is the adults, rather than Sammy, who finally suffer the most, and the film stands alongside *The Man in the White Suit*, *Whisky Galore!* and *The Ladykillers* as a sceptical overturning of conventional ideas about innocence and experience. GA

Samourai, Le 100
(The Samurai)

(Jean-Pierre Melville, 1967, Fr/It) Alain Delon, Nathalie Delon, François Périer, Cathy Rosier, Jacques Leroy, Jean-Pierre Posier, Catherine Jourdan.
95 min.
Melville's hombres don't talk a lot, they just move in and out of the shadows, their trenchcoats lined with guilt and their hats hiding their eyes. This is a great movie, an austere masterpiece, with Delon as a cold, enigmatic contract killer who lives by a personal code of *bushido*. Essentially, the plot is about an alibi, yet Melville turns this into a mythical revenge story, with Cathy Rosier as Delon's black, piano-playing nemesis who might just as easily have stepped from the pages of Cocteau or Sophocles as *Vogue*. Similarly, if Delon is Death, Périer's cop is a date with Destiny. Melville's film had a major influence in Hollywood: Delon lying on his bed is echoed in *Taxi Driver*, and Paul Schrader might have remade *Le Samourai* as *American Gigolo*. Another remake is *The Driver*, despite Walter Hill's insistence that he'd never seen it: someone on that movie *had* to have seen it. ATu

Samson and Delilah

(Cecil B DeMille, 1949, US) Victor Mature, Hedy Lamarr, George Sanders, Angela Lansbury, Henry Wilcoxon, Olive Deering, Fay Holden, Russ Tamblyn.
128 min.
Wonderfully chintzy and hokey Bible epic once described as the only film in which the hero had bigger tits than the heroine. Mature looks as constipated as ever, and Lamarr is the Philistine's philistine, but great camp performances from Sanders and Lansbury, and glorious papier-maché sets. Fab.

Samurai, The

see Samourai, Le

Sam Whiskey

(Arnold Laven, 1969, US) Burt Reynolds, Clint Walker, Ossie Davis, Angie Dickinson, Rick Davis, William Schallert, Woodrow Parfrey.
97 min.
A dim script and flat direction counteract amiably lively performances in this comedy Western, which functions very much as a caper movie in reverse: Reynolds is the gambler leader of a trio of ne'er-do-wells employed by Dickinson to return a mass of gold to the Denver Mint, whence her now dead husband stole it. The plotting is laborious enough to ensure that the audience is always two steps ahead of the characters, but Reynolds – in his first serious attempt to be funny – just about keeps it watchable. GA

Sanctuary

(Tony Richardson, 1961, US) Lee Remick, Yves Montand, Bradford Dillman, Odetta, Reta Shaw, Howard St John, Strother Martin.
100 min. b/w.
Invited to Hollywood after *Look Back in Anger* and *The Entertainer*, Tony Richardson made only one film there before fleeing back to Britain. That film was *Sanctuary* a disastrous attempt to bring Faulkner to the screen: it forever fudges the issues, preferring the easy dramatics of a Tennessee Williams-like script to the mythic drama of the Faulkner novel. Richardson's diffidence in handling his story of rape and murder, eliciting nervous performances from Remick and Montand, points the way forward to the failure of nerve that characterises the majority of his subsequent films. PH

San Demetrio, London

(Charles Frend, 1943, GB) Walter Fitzgerald, Mervyn Johns, Ralph Michael, Robert Beatty, Charles Victor, Frederick Piper, Gordon Jackson.
105 min. b/w.
A prototype docudrama, still inspiring in its

fusion of entertainment and wartime propaganda, produced by Michael Balcon at Ealing Studios and co-directed by Robert Hamer after Frend fell ill. The San Demetrio is an oil tanker, critically damaged by German gunfire in mid-Atlantic and abandoned to the flames by its crew, then heroically salvaged and brought safely home by part of the same crew when they happen on it, still floating, after drifting for three days in a lifeboat. The ship, in fact, becomes a microcosm or a symbol of the war: the ship is Island Britain, almost sunk (Dunkirk), its salvage the Churchillian ethos in action, with all hands pulling together and without a pompous officer chappie ordering people around. There is even an American aboard (Beatty) to make it an Allied victory. A fascinating and rather neglected picture. ATu

Sandlot Kids, The

see Sandlot, The

Sandlot, The
(aka The Sandlot Kids)

(David Mickey Evans, 1993, US) Tom Guiry, Mike Vitar, Patrick Renna, Chauncey Leopardi, Marty York, Brandon Adams.
101 min.
Ever since *Stand by Me*, it seems that every Boy's Own yarn is deemed incomplete without a nostalgic, pseudo-ironic voice-over waxing lyrical about the mythology of short pants and acne. There was too much of this baloney in director Evans' spec script for *Radio Flyer*, but he obviously hasn't got it out of his system yet. His directorial debut is chock-a-block with cute reminiscence – which is a shame, because if it weren't so knowing, this would be quite a likeable little comedy about nothing in particular. A spotty crew of dead-end kids throw a baseball around. The new kid in town, Scotty Smalls (Guiry), is accepted simply as a gofer, but the gang's leader, Rodriguez (Vitar), takes him under his wing. The boys are quirkily characterised and spiky dialogue mercifully keeps the sporting ardour in check, but the pumped-up climax ('the biggest pickle any of us had ever seen,' we're assured three times) turns out to be the biggest botch. TCh

Sandman, The
(Der Sandmann)

(Nico Hofmann, 1995, Ger) Götz George, Karoline Eichhorn, Barbara Rudnik, Martin Armknecht, Jürgen Hentsch, Michael Brandner.
94 min.
An ambitious young TV researcher (Eichhorn) looks to boost her show's ratings by interviewing a controversial, arrogant author, Henry Kupfer, who killed a prostitute in his youth. As she gets to know Kupfer, she becomes convinced he's responsible for a number of brutal sex-murders committed in the locality and resolves to unmask him on air. Undecided as to whether it's a sinister (if fairly ingenious) thriller or a comment on media attitudes towards violence and morbid psychology, Hofmann's film is intriguing and frustrating in equal measure. George is charismatic as the suspected serial killer, but genre clichés, implausibilities, and a few gloating women-in-peril scenes make this less satisfying than it might have been. GA

Sand Pebbles, The

(Robert Wise, 1966, US) Steve McQueen, Richard Attenborough, Richard Crenna, Candice Bergen, Marayat Andriane, Mako, Larry Gates, Simon Oakland, Joseph Turkel.
193 min.
Splendid camera-work by Joseph MacDonald, otherwise a three-hour plod through a bestseller. Set in China in 1926, it deals with the trials and tribulations of an American gunboat crew who learn to love the natives while trying to save them from their own follies and the depredations of everybody else. Behind its timid criticism of imperialist attitudes, lies a much louder and heartfelt American cry – with China 1926 standing in for Vietnam 1966 – of 'Why doesn't everybody love us when we do our best for you?' To leaven the message, McQueen and Attenborough, as the two most humanitarian members of the crew of a ship run by coolie labour, both get romances: McQueen with Bergen's American mission teacher (hair in tight bun), Attenborough with Andriane's half-caste girl (highly cultured). There are also some well-staged battles. TM

Sandpiper, The

(Vincente Minnelli, 1965, US) Elizabeth Taylor, Richard Burton, Eva Marie Saint, Charles Bronson, Robert Webber.
116 min.
Despite the behind-the-camera credits – not only Minnelli, but writers Dalton Trumbo and Michael Wilson – a truly dire romantic melodrama. Taylor is the free-lovin' atheist beatnik artist who lives in a Big Sur beach shack; Burton's the married Episcopal minister who falls in love after coming into conflict with her over her bastard son's lack of proper schooling. Meanwhile, a repressed and angst-ridden Eva Marie Saint hovers in the wings as his wife, and Bronson makes for an extremely unlikely sculptor. The film is quite simply so much soap: Burton's guilt is unreal, Taylor's redemptive boho is an embarrassingly clichéd travesty of '60s idealism, and the dialogue is both risible and turgid. Only the shots of the Californian coastline are at all classy, and they are totally superfluous to everything. GA

Sandra

see Vaghe Stelle dell'Orsa

Sands of Iwo Jima

(Allan Dwan, 1949, US) John Wayne, John Agar, Adela Mara, Forrest Tucker, Arthur Franz, Julie Bishop, Richard Jaeckel.
110 min. b/w.
Hugely successful Republic flag-waver, recounting in heroic terms the World War II capture of a strategic Pacific island by US marines. Wayne is in his element as the tough sergeant sternly moulding a group of recruits, from training camp to beachhead, into an efficient fighting force. They hate him for it, but he only wants them to stay alive, as they eventually learn. Dwan's deft handling of the action counteracts the dramatic clichés of the conflict between Wayne and his rebellious substitute son, Agar. GA

San Francisco

(WS Van Dyke, 1936, US) Clark Gable, Spencer Tracy, Jeanette MacDonald, Jack Holt, Jessie Ralph, Ted Healy, Shirley Ross, Al Shean, Harold Huber.
115 min. b/w.
MGM's old war-horse just about scrapes by on starpower – Gable's cynical saloon keeper, MacDonald's showgirl, and Tracy's Irish priest battle for each other's souls – until San Francisco gets clobbered by the earthquake of 1906. Then it's another matter entirely, for this is one of the greatest action sequences in the history of cinema, rivalling the chariot race in both *Ben-Hurs* as well as the Odessa Steps in *Battleship Potemkin*. It's a symphony of editing and special effects that more than makes up for the first 90 minutes or so. ATu

Sang d'un Poète, Le
(The Blood of a Poet)

(Jean Cocteau, 1930, Fr) Lee Miller, Pauline Carton, Odette Thalazac, Enrique Rivero, Jean Desbordes, Fernand Dichamps.
53 min. b/w.
Cocteau described this first feature as the playing with one finger of a theme that he orchestrated in *Orphée* twenty years later. That puts it fairly enough: the movie has an avant-garde roughness and unpredictability in its construction and use of symbols, but it's fundamentally a very characteristic, neo-Romantic study of the joys and agonies of being an artist. It's in two distinct parts. The first presents the artist (Rivero) trapped by his own work, eventually opting for the rebirth of a romantic martyrdom; the second plunges back into autobiography (reworking the snowball fight from *Les Enfants Terribles*), and resolves itself into a 'cosmic' riddle. The honesty and robustness of the images prevents the movie from lapsing into pretension or preciousness; it remains extremely interesting as a source of Cocteau's later work. TR

Sanjuro (Tsubaki Sanjuro)

(Akira Kurosawa, 1962, Jap) Toshiro Mifune, Tatsuya Nakadai, Yuzo Kayama, Takashi Shimura, Takako Irie, Reiko Dan.
96 min. b/w.
Kurosawa was pressured by his producers into directing this sequel to *Yojimbo*, and rose to the occasion by making his funniest and least overtly didactic film. The plot has Sanjuro (Mifune)

running lazy rings around nine would-be samurai and two genteel ladies while cleaning up a spot of corruption in local government. Kurosawa plays most of it for laughs by expertly parodying the conventions of Japanese period action movies, but the tone switches to a magnificent vehemence in the heart-stopping finale. TR

Sankofa

(Haile Gerima, 1993, US/Ger/Ghana/Burkina Faso) Oyafunmike Ogunlano, Alexandra Duah, Kofi Ghanaba, Nick Medley, Mutabaruka.
125 min.
While Mona (Ogunlano), a black American fashion model, cavorts for a (white) photographer during a shoot at a fortress town on the Ghanaian coast, an old drummer, Sankofa (Ghanaba), warns that her actions are sacrilegious to the now-forgotten sufferings of what was once a slaving post, and orders her to return to the past. Miraculously, she is transported back through time to become Shola, house slave on an American sugar plantation, where she is repeatedly abused by her master and where she witnesses the different resistance strategies of her lover Shango and her African-born friend Nunu, who has a power verging on the magical. While there's no doubting the sincerity of writer/director Gerima's film, one can't help sensing more than a little déjà vu in his account of the manifest evils of slavery. GA

Sansho Dayu 100
(Sansho the Bailiff)

(Kenji Mizoguchi, 1954, Jap) Kinuyo Tanaka, Yoshiaki Hanayaki, Kyoko Kagawa, Eitaro Shindo, Akitake Kono, Masao Chimizu.
123 min. b/w.
A humane provincial governor in 11th century Japan is forced into exile by his political opponents, and the members of his family (wife, son and daughter) fall victim to all the cruelties of the period while on their way to join him. Mizoguchi views this deliberately simple story (in Japan it is known as a folk-tale) from two perspectives at once: from the inside, as an overwhelmingly moving account of a man (the son) facing up to his own capacity for barbarism; and from the outside, as an infinitely tender meditation on history and individual fate. The twin perspectives yield a film that is both impassioned and elegiac, dynamic in its sense of the social struggle and the moral options, and yet also achingly remote in its fragile beauty. The result is even more remarkable than it sounds. TR

Sans Pitié

see Sin Compasión

Sans Soleil (Sunless) 100

(Chris Marker, 1983, Fr)
100 min.
Imagine getting letters from a friend in Japan, letters full of images, sounds and ideas. Your friend is an inveterate globe-trotter, and his letters are full of memories of other trips. He has a wry and very engaging sense of humour, he's a movie fan, he used to be quite an activist (though he was never much into 'ideology'), and he's thoughtful and very well read. In his letters, he wants to share with you the faces that have caught his eye, the events that made him smile or weep, the places where he's felt at home. He wants to tell you stories, but he can't find a story big enough to deal with his sense of contrasts, his wish to grasp fleeting moments, his recurring obsessions. Above all he hopes to excite you, to share his secrets with you, to consolidate your friendship. Now stop imagining things and go to see *Sans Soleil*, in which Marker, the cinema's greatest essayist, sums up a lifetime's travels, speculations and passions. Among very many other things, his film is the most intimate portrait of Tokyo yet made: from neighbourhood festivals to robots, under the sign of the Owl and the Pussycat. TR

Sans Toit ni Loi

see Vagabonde

Santa Claus

(Jeannot Szwarc, 1985, GB) Dudley Moore, John Lithgow, David Huddleston, Burgess Meredith, Judy Cornwell, Jeffrey Kramer.
108 min.

Children are now facing the prospect of permanent brain-softening from 1985's *Superman* stand-in. High up in the glacial wastes, stunted people with names like Boog, Vout and Honka fight a losing battle to be noticed among a production line of toys in hideous primary colours. Moore is relieved of his elf duties, and so defects to sell trade secrets to the villainous toy manufacturer BZ (Lithgow). After the Christmas hostilities, when you are finally sick to death of the little beasts, get your revenge. Pack them off to this. CPea

Santa Claus
Conquers the Martians

(Nicholas Webster, 1964, US) John Call, Leonard Hicks, Vincent Back, Victor Stiles, Donna Conforth, Pia Zadora.
82 min.
Suitably tacky tale of how some depressed Martians kidnap Santa to brighten things up at home. A staple after-midnight cult movie, this hilariously bad stab at sci-fi naturally earned a high position in the book *The Fifty Worst Movies of All Time*. One of the Martian kids appropriately grew up to be Pia Zadora, the pouter pigeon of the equally awful *Butterfly* and *Lonely Lady*. CR

Santa Clause, The

(John Pasquin, 1994, US) Tim Allen, Judge Reinhold, Wendy Crewson, Eric Lloyd, David Krumholtz, Larry Brandenburg, Peter Boyle.
98 min.
A vehicle for Tim Allen, star of TV's *Home Improvements*, this turns out to be an unexpected treat. Divorced businessman Scott Calvin rediscovers the love of son Charlie when he dons Santa's red mantle after an unfortunate accident on his roof. The sleigh, the elves, and the magic all seem to indicate a dream, but when, ten months later, Scott can't stop himself putting on the pounds and growing a fluffy white beard, he realises that perhaps he should have read the small print before signing the Santa clause. Perennial bug-bears like the absence of chimneys and the size of Santa's sack are readily explained by contemporary morphing effects, while the sarcastic Allen makes an admirably grumpy Father Christmas. The movie steers a shrewd course between bracing cynicism and old-fashioned make-believe. TCh

Santa Fe Trail

(Michael Curtiz, 1940, US) Errol Flynn, Olivia de Havilland, Raymond Massey, Ronald Reagan, Alan Hale, Van Heflin, William Lundigan, Ward Bond, Guinn Williams.
110 min. b/w.
History is bunk, and politics pushed aside in favour of professionalism, as Flynn's Jeb Stuart – the future Rebel general – leads a bunch of West Point graduates against abolitionist John Brown, and finally gets involved in the battle at Harper's Ferry, thus beginning the Civil War. Far from liberal in attitude (Massey's John Brown is seen as a fanatic, ruthless and violent; the blacks are portrayed as barely willing to fight for their freedom), it's nevertheless fast and spectacular enough to warrant a look, if only to see Reagan playing Custer. Now that was inspired casting. GA

Santa Sangre

(Alejandro Jodorowsky, 1989, It) Axel Jodorowsky, Blanca Guerra, Guy Stockwell, Thelma Tixou, Sabrina Dennison.
123 min.
Like some Fellini-esque nightmare, this heady mix of circus freaks (a tattooed lady, an exotic midget, sad-faced clowns) and weird religious and hallucinatory imagery (an armless virgin saint, writhing snakes, zombie brides) is pregnant with disturbing psychological undercurrents. Traumatised at an early age by a violent argument between his knife-throwing father (Stockwell) and trapeze-artist mother (Guerra), former child magician Fenix (Axel Jodorowsky), now 20, escapes from an asylum into the outside world. Reunited with his jealous mother, Fenix becomes her 'arms' in a bizarre pantomime act, a role which spills dangerously over into real life. With a tapestry of cultural references that embraces the Venus de Milo, Marcel Marceau, Liberace and *Night of the Living Dead*, Jodorowsky's is a strange, violent, but ultimately liberating vision. NF

Santee

(Gary Nelson, 1972, US) Glenn Ford, Michael
Burns, Dana Wynter, Jay Silverheels, Harry
Townes, John Larch, Robert Wilke.
93 min.

Soft-centred Western. Ford, close to pensionable
age, plays a gnarled, misanthropic cowboy whose
values have been warped by the murder of his
son. All he wants out of life is to hunt down outlaws with high prices on their heads. After killing
a renegade, he adopts the man's homeless teenage
son. Gradually, his bitterness thaws and he forgets his grudge against the world. GM

Santiago
(aka The Gun Runner)

(Gordon Douglas, 1956, US) Alan Ladd,
Rossana Podesta, Lloyd Nolan, Chill Wills,
Paul Fix, LQ Jones.
93 min.

Formula adventure, with gun-running mercenary
Ladd discovering conscience, cause and com-
monsense when righteously 'politicised' by the
passion of Cuban patriot (1898 version) Rossana
Podesta. Martin Rackin produced and co-scripted to protect his own novel from too much imaginative input, while director Douglas – fresh from
the lunacies of the Liberace showcase *Sincerely
Yours* – treated the whole thing as a cakewalk.
PT

Santos Inocentes, Los

see Holy Innocents, The

São Paulo, SP

(Olivier Koning, 1990, Neth)
94 min.

'It's astonishing and frightening,' says an engineer, dwelling on statistics which reveal that
there's a building erected every hour in São Paulo,
Brazil. Koning's absorbing documentary selects
a cross-section of residents – from an architect to
a street-sweeper – and alternates interviews in
which they talk about their lives and ambitions.
Packed with fascinating insights and, as in the
case of a family who make their home under a
viaduct, an often moving depiction of resilience.
CM

Saphead, The

(Herbert Blaché, 1920, US) Buster Keaton,
William H Crane, Irving Cummings, Carol
Holloway, Beulah Booker.
7 reels. b/w.

Buster Keaton's first feature, though charming
and lightly amusing, is something of a disappointment. Having picked up on his talent after
the Fatty Arbuckle shorts, MGM clearly had no
idea what to do with it, and settled for an old
warhorse of a play (*The New Henrietta* by
Winchell Smith and Victor Mapes) which had
already served as a vehicle for Douglas
Fairbanks. Playing the dim, pampered son of *The
Wolf of Wall Street*, Keaton dumbfounds everyone by making an unexpected killing on the stock
market, thereby winning the girl of his dreams.
The character closely foreshadows Keaton's later
persona, but is wedged in throughout by acres of
creaky, conventional plotting, which only once
opens out – a splendid scene of upheaval on the
stock market floor – to allow him to do his own
acrobatic thing. TM

Sapphire

(Basil Dearden, 1959, GB) Nigel Patrick,
Michael Craig, Paul Massie, Yvonne Mitchell,
Bernard Miles, Earl Cameron, Gordon Heath,
Orlando Martins.
92 min.

Hot on the heels of the Notting Hill race riots came
Sapphire. Children playing ball on Hamp-stead
Heath stumble across a murdered girl. A nice,
respectable white girl in prim tweeds. But, horror of horrors, she's three months pregnant and
wearing scarlet taffeta undies! Poor Sapphire
only looks white and, as the film sagely informs
us, 'No matter what the colour of the skin, you
can always tell when the bongo-drums start beating'. Actually, in spite of Horace Big Cigar and a
host of no-good blacks, the real murderer is a
fanatical white racist. Dearden's analysis of
English prejudice is comprehensive and uncompromising, but the film's 'impartiality' leads it
perilously close to condoning what it sets out to
condemn. RMy

Saps at Sea

(Gordon Douglas, 1940, US) Stan Laurel,
Oliver Hardy, James Finlayson, Dick Cramer,
Ben Turpin.
57 min. b/w.

The last film Laurel and Hardy made for Hal
Roach, a scrappy but often very funny affair in
which Dr Finlayson prescribes a sea cruise after
Ollie goes crazy working in a honking horn factory (a sequence destructively elaborated from
Modern Times). Less inventive when, after Stan
has inadvertently destroyed their apartment,
they find themselves not only at sea (they
meant to stay safely tied up in harbour) but
slaving on behalf of an evil-tempered escaped
convict (Cramer): the highlight here – they prepare a revolting meal for Cramer, but are forced
to eat it themselves – is both drawn-out and
unfunny. A comedy of much charm, nevertheless. TM

Saraband for Dead Lovers

(Basil Dearden/Michael Relph, 1948, GB)
Stewart Granger, Joan Greenwood, Flora
Robson, Françoise Rosay, Peter Bull,
Frederick Valk, Anthony Quayle, Michael
Gough, Megs Jenkins.
96 min.

One of Ealing Studios' most lavish period pieces.
A sombre, romantic drama about the arranged
marriage between the young Sophie
(Greenwood) and the gross George Louis of
Hanover, later George I of Britain (Bull, superbly
repulsive), and the unhappy lady's dalliance
with the dashing Konigsmark (Granger).
Warner Brothers would have made it as a
swashbuckling epic, but the English approach
to these things was always different: the emphasis here is on power politics and doomed love,
with special weight given to an anarchic carnival presided over by the Lord of Misrule, and to
Flora Robson's role as an ageing lady of the
court. Relph's designs are magnificent;
Dearden's direction veers towards the pretentious (rain on stained glass makes a Madonna
'weep') but is for the most part functionally
emotional. TR

Sarafina!

(Darrell James Roodt, 1992, SAf) Leleti
Khumalo, Whoopi Goldberg, Miriam Makeba,
John Kani, Dumisani Diamini, Mbongeni
Ngema.
116 min.

A (Molotov) cocktail mixing scenes of appalling
violence with song and dance, Mbongeni
Ngema's 1987 Soweto-based musical makes an
uneasy transition to the screen. After some awkward opening sequences, the film's agenda
becomes more readily apparent. Reprising her
lead role as an embattled, star-struck schoolgirl,
Khumalo plays Sarafina, who dreams of staging a school musical about Nelson Mandela,
while at the same time teaming up with young
activists who seek mass action against
apartheid. Their energies are guided by teacher
Mary (Goldberg), who flouts the authorised syllabus in order to instil knowledge of people
power. A low-key Goldberg serves as catalyst
and the children's conscience, while the emotions are left to Khumalo in a striking, moving
depiction of defiance. Even her charismatic character, however, fails to give a proper consistency to the narrative, and the structure goes badly
adrift. CM

Saragossa Manuscript,
The (Rekopis Znaleziony
w Saragossie)

(Wojciech Has, 1964, Pol) Zbigniew Cybulski,
Kazimierz Opalinski, Iga Cembrzynska,
Joanna Jedryka, Franciszek Pieczka.
175 min. b/w.

Wojciech Has contrives a Chinese-box, Borgesian
teaser from his story of a Belgian officer
(Cybulski) who travels across Spain during the
Peninsular War and becomes involved in a chain
of narratives. But the film's real (and secret) subject is the Gothic imagery of the Tarot and
Cabbalistic traditions: multiple storyline, trains
of resemblance, mysterious icons of Fate and
Death. It remains sadly unclear, though, from the
British print (cut by a third of its length to 124
minutes) whether this elaborately literary film
fails because it is now too short...or because it was
always too long. CA

Saratoga Trunk

(Sam Wood, 1945, US) Gary Cooper, Ingrid
Bergman, Flora Robson, Jerry Austin, John
Warburton, Florence Bates, John Abbott, Ethel
Griffies.
135 min.

A thoroughly bad, seriously miscast costume
drama, with Bergman playing the illegitimate
Creole beauty who upsets New Orleans society in
the Gay Nineties when she sets out to avenge her
mother by trashing the well-heeled family of her
father. Cooper is a gambler called Clint Maroon
whom she takes up with, while Robson, smeared
with boot polish, plays Hattie McDaniel. Edna
Ferber's doorstop novel should have become a
delirious vehicle for Bette Davis or Tallulah
Bankhead. Bergman is all wrong – she has the
beauty but not the bravado – and Sam Wood has-
n't a clue. ATu

Sarraounia

(Med Hondo, 1986, Fr/Burkina Faso) Aï Keïta,
Jean-Roger Milo, Féodor Atkine, Didier
Sauvegrain, Roger Mirmont, Luc-Antoine
Diquero.
121 min.

Sarraounia is a young warrior queen of the Azna
tribe, whose mastery of the ancient 'magic' skills
of martial arts and pharmacology is first put to
the test when she defends her people from attack
by a neighbouring tribe. But the real trial of
strength comes when the French army marches
south to widen its colonial grip on the African
continent. The second half of the film centres on
the French, acidly but plausibly satirised as little
tyrants whose megalomania swells in proportion
with their failure to grasp the realities of the culture they are trying to crush. Everything here is
grounded in careful but never pedantic historical
research. The film is superbly crafted and expansive; the tone is celebratory, loud, assertive and
spirited; but Hondo doesn't allow the visual and
musical splendours to swamp his certainty that
Africans need to learn to value and develop the
identity that was theirs before the white man
came. TR

Satan Bug, The

(John Sturges, 1964, US) George Maharis,
Richard Basehart, Anne Francis, Dana
Andrews, Edward Asner, Frank Sutton, John
Larkin.
113 min.

One of umpteen Alistair MacLean paperback
thrillers (this one written under the pseudonym
of Ian Stuart) definitively pulped in their transition to celluloid, this is the would-be *Dr
Strangelove* of biological warfare, with rebel scientist Basehart legging it alone with a stolen vial
of deadly virus, threatening global annihilation.
Half-hearted and dull, despite the contributions
of heavyweight adaptors James Clavell and
Edward Anhalt, working at odds with an out-of-
his element Sturges. PT

Satanic Rites of Dracula, The
(aka Count Dracula and His
Vampire Bride)

(Alan Gibson, 1973, GB) Christopher Lee, Peter
Cushing, Michael Coles, William Franklyn,
Freddie Jones, Joanna Lumley, Richard
Vernon, Patrick Barr.
88 min.

The beguiling message underlying Hammer's
modern-dress Dracula movie is that the real vampires of modern London are property speculators.
The legendary Count (Lee in fine form) has built
a Centre Point-type construction on the site of his
old crypt, and comes on like a cross between
Howard Hughes and Harry Hyams as he plans to
lay waste the city. The idea is amazing (after all,
Dracula started as a subversive myth), but
inevitably it tends to get lost in the usual mundane complexities of espionage melodrama and
occult lore. A lot of weak action scenes and weaker lines, but still a vast improvement on *Dracula
A.D.1972*. DP

Satan Met a Lady

(William Dieterle, 1936, US) Warren William,
Bette Davis, Alison Skipworth, Arthur
Treacher, Marie Wilson, Winifred Shaw,
Porter Hall.
75 min. b/w.

The second version of Hammett's *The Maltese*

Falcon, somewhat disguised (doubtless because the novel had been filmed only five years earlier): the Fat Man becomes a dignified dowager, Joel Cairo is turned into a languid Englishman, and the falcon is replaced by Roland's fabled horn, stuffed with jewels by the Saracens to silence it after the hero's death. It doesn't bear comparison with the 1941 Huston version, mainly because Sam Spade (here 'Ted Shane', as played by Warren William with an eye to the success of *The Thin Man*, is a cavalier, wisecracking ladies' man-about-town; the darker overtones of the Huston film are therefore elided, and his final unmasking of Bette Davis goes for nothing by comparison with the two-way Bogart-Astor 'betrayal'. Thanks to Dieterle's stylishly witty direction and excellent performances, it's nevertheless enjoyably and quirkily funny, at least until just before the end, when a whole wedge of undigested plot exposition suddenly catches up with the action. TM

Satan Never Sleeps (aka The Devil Never Sleeps)

(Leo McCarey, 1962, US/GB) William Holden, Clifton Webb, France Nuyen, Weaver Lee, Athene Seyler, Martin Benson, Edith Sharpe.
126 min.
McCarey's last film is a dreadful, trashy yarn about two priests in China (Holden and Webb) sticking out for their beliefs against the onslaught of communism. The man had clearly gone feebleminded. The film is propaganda designed to equate Communism with Satan. China is the Evil Empire here (though it was in fact filmed in England and Wales). As *Variety* noted, more occurs in the final 15 minutes than in the whole of the rest of the picture. Satan may not sleep, but you will. TCh

Satan's Brew (Satansbraten)

(Rainer Werner Fassbinder, 1976, WGer) Kurt Raab, Margit Carstensen, Helen Vita, Volker Spengler, Ingrid Caven, Ulli Lommel, Armin Meier.
112 min.
The scurrilous movie that marked a turnaround in Fassbinder's film-making practice, following the disbandment of his 'stock company' of actors as a theatre troupe. The familiar faces are still around, this time distorted by pebble glasses, pustules or gross make-up, but there's a new sense of liberation from theatrical stylisation gusting through the proceedings. The plot is a benignly black celebration of the art of literary theft: Kurt Raab plays a clapped-out writer who regains his stride when he begins 'accidentally' reproducing the complete works of Stefan George. He is surrounded by freaks, perverts and grotesques, and so hardly anyone notices. It's no accident that this frolicsome tale reverses Fassbinder's standard 'victim' formula: it transpires that the tyrannical Raab is secretly a masochist, and one who actively enjoys being victimised. Bouncy. TR

Satan's Skin (aka Blood on Satan's Claw)

(Piers Haggard, 1970, GB) Patrick Wymark, Linda Hayden, Barry Andrews, Avice Landon, Simon Williams, Tamara Ustinov, Howard Goorney, James Hayter, Michele Dotrice.
93 min.
Not nearly so atmospheric as Michael Reeves' *The Witchfinder General*, but for the first hour Piers Haggard keeps his theme and the blood flowing nicely. It begins in style, with a farmer in 17th century England digging up a skull with one eye still working, and then there is a disembodied furry arm and claw on the rampage. The only thing the cast of Olde Worlde actors can think of is human sacrifice, and there are a lot of nubile actresses to choose from. Sadly, Haggard lets things slip, and the make-up man takes over. ATu

Satan's Slave

(Norman J Warren, 1976, GB) Michael Gough, Martin Potter, Candace Glendenning, Barbara Kellermann, Michael Craze, James Bree, David McGillivray.
86 min.
Another absolute stinker from the withered pen of David McGillivray, who this time permits himself a small but telling role – yes that's the author playing the priest who drags the naked witch to the tree ('filmed entirely on location in Surrey') in order to brand and then flog her. Elsewhere this home movie drags out the theme of possession, with the nutty-family-in-big-country-house striving to reincarnate the witch (imaginatively named Camilla) in Candace Glendenning's body. It also shows how bad experienced actors – Potter, Kellermann, Gough – can be when matched dialogue as matchless as 'It's at moments like this that I'm glad I'm a doctor'. AN

Satisfaction

(Joan Freeman, 1988, US) Justine Bateman, Liam Neeson, Trini Alvarado, Britta Phillips, Julia Roberts, Scott Coffey, Deborah Harry.
92 min.
A tacky rock'n'roll drama which regurgitates clichés without any sense of shame. The script might have been written twenty-five years ago – like the rock standards the band specialise in – but it is meant to be taken seriously. Bateman, the daughter from TV's *Family Ties*, can't sing. Nor does Julia Roberts play the drums too convincingly; and as for Liam Neeson, moping around as a songwriter who's lost the muse, he ought to be ashamed of himself. TCh

Saturday Night and Sunday Morning

(Karel Reisz, 1960, GB) Albert Finney, Rachel Roberts, Shirley Anne Field, Bryan Pringle, Hylda Baker, Norman Rossington, Colin Blakely.
89 min. b/w.
The big box-office success of the British New Wave in the early '60s, no doubt because its hero's defiant watchword of 'Don't let the bastards grind you down' struck a responsive chord before everybody started never having had it so good. Much of the freshness survives in Finney's abrasive performance as the young Nottingham factory worker lashing blindly out at the bleak working class horizons to which he has been bred by parents 'dead from the neck up'. Trying to grab what life can offer with both hands without regard for consequences or for anybody else, he ends up with nothing but the final gesture of defiance of hurling a stone at the housing estate where he is about to settle down and live unhappily for ever after. But it all seems terribly glib now, at worst sailing close to parody, at best suffused with the faintly patronising sincerity of the Angry Young Man/New Left era. TM

Saturday Night at the Baths

(David Buckley, 1974, US) Robert Aberdeen, Ellen Sheppard, Don Scotti, Steve Ostrow, Janie Olivor, Larry Smith.
90 min.
Unlike *Fox*, *Dog Day Afternoon* and *A Bigger Splash*, in which the central theme of homosexuality occurred within a larger framework, *Saturday Night at the Baths* approaches its subject on a more basic level. Against a semi-documentary background of New York's Continental Baths, the film traces a straight musician's progression from a heterosexual relationship to a homosexual one. It approaches the subject sympathetically and seriously, but finally becomes trapped by its own lack of resources: uneven acting and an indifferent script which does little more than put the characters through the motions. Good footage of the Baths, and the film's increasing confidence as it develops help it along. CPe

Saturday Night at the Palace

(Robert Davies, 1987, SAf) Paul Slabolepszy, Bill Flynn, John Kani, Marius Weyers.
90 min.
Slabolepszy's a foul-mouthed unemployed white racist, Kani the manager of a Johannesburg diner and the victim whom he singles out for abuse. Slabolepszy created the role in his own play, which he adapted for the screen with co-star Flynn, and though time and politics have moved on, the film version stands as a concerned reminder of South Africa's bitter divisions. TJ

Saturday Night Fever

(John Badham, 1977, US) John Travolta, Karen Lynn Gorney, Barry Miller, Joseph Cali, Paul Pape, Donna Pescow, Julie Bovasso.
119 min.
A disco movie for people who don't go to discos, this is really about Growing Up – which the movie interprets as Growing Out of a Disco Mentality and into Personal Relationships. The relationship between Tony (Travolta) and Stephanie (Gorney) is at least as angst-ridden as anything in *Annie Hall*, but like almost everything else in the movie, it's played dead straight. This, of course, makes it extremely funny, up to a point, though in the end the real killer is the movie's abject sincerity. Pity, really, since there's certainly room for at least one decent movie about the actual appeal and experience of discos. The only true drug culture of the '70s, they deserve better than to be represented as watering-holes for arrested adolescents. TR

Saturday's Children

(Vincent Sherman, 1940, US) John Garfield, Anne Shirley, Claude Rains, Lee Patrick, George Tobias, Roscoe Karns, Dennis Moore.
101 min. b/w.
This third version of Maxwell Anderson's play in less than 12 years indicates how much producers and audiences were willing to buy its smug middlebrow social conscience. Adapted by the *Casablanca* brothers Julius and Philip Epstein, it follows the struggling young couple Garfield and Shirley as they try to cope with poverty and unemployment in the tough urban arena of New York City. Rains steals the movie as her dear old dad, who's willing to commit suicide so they can cash in on the insurance, but it's po-faced stuff.

Saturday the 14th

(Howard R Cohen, 1981, US) Richard Benjamin, Paula Prentiss, Jeffrey Tambor, Severn Darden, Kari Michaelsen, Kevin Brando, Rosemary De Camp.
77 min.
Is there life after *Friday the 13th* Parts One, Two and Three? Well, as the Book of Evil says, it gets worse on Saturday the 14th. Actually, it gets better, as the all-American family moves into the old dark house and finds late Uncle Henry's warning note: 'Don't open the book'. Young Billy does just that, and all hell is let loose, in the shape of assorted bogeymen and a mysterious force which does the washing-up, while the TV refuses to play anything but *The Twilight Zone*. Every horror cliché in the bugabook goes through the New World Cormangle for a funny twist: a Rentokil man called Van Helsing, a Venus Fly-Trap which screeches 'Feed me!', the Creature from the Black Lagoon lurking in a bubble bath, and best of all, a climactic duel between exterminator and vampire which manages to subvert the entire mythology of the fang-film genre. The globs of gore and ultra-tacky effects are exploited with such demonic glee that the odd anaemic joke doesn't matter much. For connoisseurs of cheap humour in the jugular vein. AB

Saturn 3

(Stanley Donen, 1980, GB) Farrah Fawcett, Kirk Douglas, Harvey Keitel, Douglas Lambert, Ed Bishop.
87 min.
Some handy tips on how to enjoy *Saturn 3* One, you can play 'Spot the Rip-off', a game requiring only a cursory knowledge of successful sci-fi/horror movies. Watch for the *Star Wars* special effects, the claustrophobic chase scenes from *Alien*, the rampant robots of *Dark Star*. Or you can while away the credibility gaps by guessing how much Kirk Douglas got paid for not cracking up over lines like 'I guess I'm near abort-time', or how much Martin Amis got paid for writing them. Alternatively, try to figure out whether Harvey Keitel's baddie talks in such a clipped monotone because he's a baddie, or because he's gritting his teeth. And if all else fails, you can ponder the absurd central premise: could any biped – let alone the film's Meccano-built robot – be driven blood-lust crazy for Farrah Fawcett's fanny? Just another miserable muddle from the Lew Grade empire; there's more fun to be had cleaning out your cat litter tray. FL

Satyricon

see Fellini-Satyricon

Saut de l'Ange, Le

see Cobra

Sauvage, Le

(Jean-Paul Rappeneau, 1975, Fr/It) Yves Montand, Catherine Deneuve, Luigi Vannucchi, Dana Wynter, Bobo Lewis, Tony Roberts.
107 min.

A commonplace *toujours l'amour* tragi-farce whose only justification lies in the decorative presence of its two stars. The urbane Montand as a self-sufficient *sauvage* on the run from the unacceptable face of his wife's cosmetic empire, growing vegetables on an island retreat, is a strain on the imagination. But for credibility he has the edge on Deneuve. Her divine sang-froid hardly lends itself to a role that requires her to be part Doris Day, part Claudia Cardinale. The runaway pace is maintained by operatic slapstick, tempestuousness verging on insanity, hysterical dialogue that occasionally lurches into Spanish and American, and a dazzling range of locations (Venezuela, New York, Provence). JS

Sauve Qui Peut – la Vie (Every Man for Himself/Slow Motion)

(Jean-Luc Godard, 1980, Switz/Fr) Isabelle Huppert, Jacques Dutronc, Nathalie Baye, Roland Amstutz, Anna Baldaccini.
89 min.

Godard's return to celluloid after a decade of experiment in video is in one sense forced: the sources of finance for his projects were drying up, and he himself admits that the film was made as a passport back into the business. But in another, this is his most personal work in years, less important for its return to narrative (the story of two women and a man joined in almost arbitrary ways) than for its chilled sense of autobiography – Dutronc plays an egotistical, washed-out video film-maker called 'Godard'. In that light, the resurrection of earlier themes (especially prostitution) is no return at all, but a confessional fantasy about a generation of men now in middle age, alienated from their sexuality, dissatisfied with their 'commerce', and unwilling to cope with a new sexual/political order. It would be hard to imagine a more courageous project; harder still to find one executed with the kind of stylistic wit and haunting elegance that have made Godard leader of the pack for over twenty years. CA

Savage Bees, The

(Bruce Geller, 1976, US) Ben Johnson, Michael Parks, Gretchen Corbett, Paul Hecht, Horst Buchholz, Bruce French, James Best.
99 min.

'Somebody's poisoned mah dawg' wails Sheriff Ben Johnson, only to discover that the mutt's been stung to death by a swarm of killer bees up from South America (pause for lecture) for the New Orleans Mardi Gras. This made-for-TV movie, unwarrantedly exposed on the big screen, is so weakly plotted that efforts to generate suspense never appear more than mechanical. The bees look real enough, but attention wanders long before Horst Buchholz gets himself killed trying to capture the queen bee in a hot-dog stand. For the protracted finale, the bees obligingly settle on the heroine's VW, only to succumb without a murmur. CPe

Savage Capitalism

(Andre Kloetzel, 1993, Braz) Fernanda Torres, Jose Mayer, Marisa Orth.
86 min.

Investigating a mining company which is encroaching on Indian lands, journalist Elisa (Torres) discovers that the company's handsome, schizophrenic chairman (Mayer) is actually of native descent. They embark on a passionate affair, until the man's 'dead' wife comes back to life. This eccentric ecological romance was apparently inspired by the films of Pedro Almodóvar – but it's hard to believe the director has ever seen one. For all the weirdness on display (notably an office that transforms into a jungle), this is a fundamentally banal picture, with embarrassingly naive hippie-mystic sentiments ('You aren't the man I met behind a desk, you are the Lord of the Forest…' etc). And is the title ironic? It is not. TC

Savage Innocents, The

(Nicholas Ray, 1961, US/It) Anthony Quinn, Yoko Tani, Peter O'Toole, Carlo Giustini, Marie Yang, Andy Ho, Lee Montague.
110 min.

Though scuppered by problems worse than those usually associated with international coproductions, this is nonetheless rather more than just another engaging oddity from Ray. Further evidence of his ethnological interest in 'outsider' societies, it charts the hardships suffered by Quinn the Eskimo as he struggles to survive not only against the harsh conditions of life in the Artic, but – more lethally – against the invasion of Western 'civilisation', embodied by Christianity, capitalism and rock'n'roll. Much of the story is episodic and semidocumentary in tone, illustraing Eskimo hunting habits, marital rituals, and so forth, while the misguidedly 'poetic' dialogue is stilted and unconvincing. But, as ever, Ray's deployment of the 'Scope frame throws up images of an often startling, even surreal beauty: polar bears diving from the ice-flows become a rhapsody in blinding whites and br illiant blues, and the sound of a juke box screaming out over the empty, snowy wastes is a withering, wicked symbol of man's destructive influence on nature. GA

Savage Islands

(Ferdinand Fairfax, 1983, NZ) Tommy Lee Jones, Michael O'Keefe, Max Phipps, Jenny Seagrove, Grant Tilly, Peter Rowley.
99 min.

More in the vein of *Raiders of the Lost Ark* thrills and spills than Fairbanks swash and buckle, the story is told in flashback with good old-fashioned cut-and-thrust. In the South Pacific islands in the 1880s, Captain Bully Hayes (Jones) saves maidens in distress, performs impossible feats of agility, does battle with a German count (Tilly) intent on nasty military annexations with the aid of an ironclad warship, in a plot that is as credible as Hitler's diaries. Which makes not a lot of difference, for the film is to be enjoyed on a tongue-in-cheek level: lots of stunts and not too much mushy lovey-dovey stuff. Originality never raises its head, but it'll keep the kids from clammering for a glimpse of those video nasties. FL

Savage Man...Savage Beast (Ultime Gride della Savana)

(Antonio Climati/Mario Morra, 1975, It)
100 min.

A bloody, blatantly exploitative mess of a movie, cutting bewilderingly between North and South America, Australia, Europe and Africa, with flimsily related scenes of animals killing each other and men killing animals for survival, sport and profit. A woefully inadequate English commentary (the original was by Alberto Moravia) tries to make sense of all this slaughter. Finally, however, this patched-up documentary reveals its true colours: just another opportunity to gawp at raw scenes of sex and (more especially) violence. In the Burundi jungle, two soon-to-be-hanged brothers are seen squatting in the rain with the cannibalised remains of their father; a foolish tourist leaves his car and is eaten by lions; a van carrying a crew filming cheetahs overturns at sickening speed. Rock bottom is reached with the inclusion of 16 mm home movie footage of white mercenaries cheerfully mutilating and butchering Amazonian tribesmen. JPy

Savage Messiah

(Ken Russell, 1972, GB) Dorothy Tutin, Scott Antony, Helen Mirren, Lindsay Kemp, Michael Gough, John Justin, Aubrey Richards, Peter Vaughan.
103 min.

Vorticist sculptor Henri Gaudier-Brzeska (Antony) becomes Russell's archetypal angry young man, scorching his way through a stereotyped collection of Edwardian culture figures, dashing off sculptures by candlelight. Henri's interesting relationship with the ageing authoress Sophie Brzeska (they decided to unite in name) is lost in the director's overriding credo that both art and films are a matter of how much energy you exert.

Savage Nights (Les Nuits Fauves)

(Cyril Collard, 1992, Fr) Cyril Collard, Romane Bohringer, Carlos Lopez, Corine Blue, Claude Winter.
126 min.

Based on his partly autobiographical novel, the late Cyril Collard's film is an exception to most AIDS-issue movies. Returning from a trip to Morocco in 1986, Jean (Collard) finds he is HIV-positive. However, the 30-year-old bisexual filmmaker/musician continues to live to the full – cruising strangers, taking up with Samy (Lopez), embarking on a relationship with Laura (Bohringer), with whom Jean has unsafe sex, initially omitting to warn her. But that's not what upsets the teenager, who believes her love is stronger than death. Only when she fears losing him to Samy does she crack up. Besides the raw vitality of its visuals, what distinguishes Collard's film is its unrepentant honesty. If none of the main characters is especially admirable, or likeable, they are all credible. The film has a few longueurs, but its refusal to simplify or soften the plight facing Jean, Laura and Samy guarantees a powerful provocative and relevant account of lives on the emotional edge. GA

Savages

(James Ivory, 1972, US) Louis Stadlen, Anne Francine, Thayer David, Susan Blakely, Russ Thacker, Salome Jens, Kathleen Widdoes, Sam Waterston.
106 min. b/w & col.

Strip away our veneer of civilisation, cast a dispassionate eye on our frantic attempts to gratify ourselves, and what do you find? You guessed. Ivory's earlier made-in-India movies got by on their 'delicacy' and 'sensitivity'; but this half-assed fable – about a bunch of jungle primitives turning, when a croquet ball mysteriously intrudes on their human sacrifice, into '30s socialites and then reverting back again – exposed the pseud beneath the aesthete. No wit, no thought, no surrealist flair, just vacuous decoration. It plays like a Ken Russell movie worked over by a taxidermist. TR

Save the Tiger

(John G Avildsen, 1972, US) Jack Lemmon, Jack Gilford, Laurie Heineman, Norman Burton, Patricia Smith, Thayer David.
100 min.

Lemmon's nervy performance as the garment manufacturer harassed by financial problems and moral compromises is the best thing in this well-meaning but very wordy look at the failure of the American Dream. Middle-aged, disillusioned, and nearing a nervous breakdown, he bewails the passing of his youth when things were simpler, while resorting to insurance fraud to revive his ailing fortunes. Cynical, occasionally hollow stuff (scripted by Steve Shagan), but thanks to Lemmon, sometimes quite moving. GA

Saving Grace

(Robert M Young, 1985, US) Tom Conti, Fernando Rey, Erland Josephson, Giancarlo Giannini, Donald Hewlett, Edward James Olmos, Patricia Mauceri, Guido Alberti.
111 min.

A troubled man, hemmed in by the protocol of his position, Pope Leo XIV (Conti) impulsively opts for a working holiday. Moved by a little girl's story of her village – stricken by an earthquake and without a priest – the undercover Holy Father hitchhikes deep into the (picture postcard) Italian south, and proceeds to preach the protestant work ethic to people whose major source of income is government aid derived from the odd staged epidemic. Through his arduous efforts – 'he's a Pope who smiles, a Pope who cries, a Pope who loves, hates, and learns to love again' – Leo sets the villagers in motion once more. Despite a plot veiled in about as much mystery as an uncracked soft-boiled egg, *Saving Grace* does retain a certain Disneyesque charm as an innocent modern fable. SGo

Sawdust and Tinsel

see Gycklarnas Afton

Say a Little Prayer

(Richard Lowenstein, 1992, Aust) Sudi de Winter, Fiona Ruttelle, Lynn Murphy, Micky Camilleri, Rebecca Smart.
97 min.

Less audacious than Lowenstein's underrated *Dogs in Space*, this at first seems a rather tame tale of meeting-cute between a bored kid in his early teens – staying with a strict guardian for the summer holidays – and a spacy girl of around 20 who lives nearby. Gradually, however, it becomes noticeably tougher, as it fills in the reasons – without sermonising – for the girl's damaged innocence. But what finally impresses is the fluid elegance of the camera movements, the top-notch design, and the director's light touch with the boy's fantasy life, which even runs to a delicious interlude incorporating the Aretha Franklin classic of the title. Most engaging. GA

Say Anything

(Cameron Crowe, 1989, US) John Cusack, Ione Skye, John Mahoney, Joan Cusack, Lili Taylor, Amy Brooks, Pamela Segall, Eric Stoltz, Lois Chiles.
100 min.
This product of the factory of youth, written and directed by first-timer Crowe, sports the intelligence and humanity of producer James L Brooks (*Terms of Endearment, Broadcast News*) like a buttonhole on a blind date. It's a relief to find characters with dignity in this context: Mahoney, in particular, relishes the opportunity to play an adult with some depth to him. Essentially though, it is teen romance time. Skye is a (very) straight 'A' student, and Cusack an easygoing kid who thinks his future might be in kickboxing. They fall for each other. The love story is as old-fashioned as the jokes are old hat, but Crowe's amusing script and unforced direction allow the actors to develop reasonably authentic characters from stereotypical roles…and the Cusacks are something special. Joan, who in *Working Girl* and *Stars and Bars* wiped the floor with everyone in sight, gently underplays in a cameo to her brother John, whose quiet integrity and oddball personality tap the charm of a jive-talking Jimmy Stewart. We are always growing up with American teenagers at the movies; at least these two are coming of age. TCh

Sayonara

(Joshua Logan, 1957, US) Marlon Brando, Red Buttons, Miiko Taka, Miyoshi Umeki, James Garner, Patricia Owens, Ricardo Montalban.
147 min.
This operatic picture from James A Michener's novel has worn remarkably well. An ace fighter pilot (Brando) is unwillingly pulled from combat in the Korean War and sent to Japan so that romance can blossom with a general's daughter. The affair falters and the pilot slowly falls for the distant charms of a Japanese actress (Miiko Taka). The big theme is the injustice of the US policy of the day discouraging but not forbidding American servicemen from taking Japanese brides. The cruelty of this policy, demonstrated in a powerful subplot which ends in a double suicide, cuts through the film's overlay of exoticism and romantic sentimentality. Brando, more matinee idol than method actor, and none the worse for that, is contained and always watchable; but Red Buttons, in his first major role, as a chipper, angry young flier, with no family in America but the possibility of a life in Japan, gives perhaps the more heartfelt performance. JPy

Sbarco di Anzio, Lo (Anzio/The Battle for Anzio)

(Edward Dmytryk, 1968, It) Robert Mitchum, Peter Falk, Earl Holliman, Mark Damon, Reni Santoni, Arthur Kennedy, Patrick Magee, Robert Ryan.
117 min.
Timidity at the top is soundly but turgidly castigated in this otherwise run-of-the-mill account of World War II's Anzio landing, when the Allies might have marched straight on Rome, but instead dug in on the beaches and allowed the Germans to prepare emergency defences. Some superb camera-work by Giuseppe Rotunno, and nicely choreographed action sequences; but the whole thing is sunk by the pseudo-philosophical profundities spouted by a war correspondent (the hapless Mitchum). TM

Scalawag

(Kirk Douglas, 1973, US/It) Kirk Douglas, Mark Lester, Neville Brand, George Eastham, Don Stroud, Lesley Anne Down, Danny DeVito, Phil Brown.
93 min.
Well accustomed to losing bits of his anatomy for his art (an eye in *The Vikings*, an ear in *Lust for Life*, a finger in *The Big Sky*), Kirk Douglas quite naturally appears in his own directorial debut, a kids' treasure hunt yarn based on Robert Louis Stevenson, as a one-legged pirate. Having set up a potential stablemate to *A High Wind in Jamaica*, though, he blows it conclusively with an

increasingly treacly performance and erratic direction. The involvement of veteran 'Hollywood Ten' screenwriter Albert Maltz seems as incongruous as the decision to have Yugoslavian locations doubling for Mexico and California. PT

Scalphunters, The

(Sydney Pollack, 1968, US) Burt Lancaster, Ossie Davis, Telly Savalas, Shelley Winters, Armando Silvestre, Dan Vadis, Dabney Coleman, Nick Cravat.
103 min.
An amiable enough liberal comedy Western, with colour-coded cultural conflict worked through an ironic circular plot. Lancaster's trapper is forcibly traded an ex-slave (Davis) for his pelts by an Indian band, after which the pair set off in uneasy alliance and in pursuit as the pelts are in turn appropriated by a gang of scalphunters. William Norton's script glosses both the racial antagonism and interdependence with a thankfully light hand; Pollack gets in some backwoods practice for the later mythologisation of *Jeremiah Johnson*. PT

Scamp, The

(Wolf Rilla, 1957, GB) Richard Attenborough, Terence Morgan, Dorothy Alison, Jill Adams, Colin Petersen, Geoffrey Keen, Margaretta Scott.
89 min. b/w.
Attenborough gives a decent enough performance as a schoolmaster who befriends the winsome ten-year-old urchin of the title (Petersen), finds that he is being neglected by his drink-swilling father (Morgan), and contrives to take him home under his temporary care. Cue some soapy melodramatics, what with the father coming on like Bill Sikes, Attenborough's wife getting antsy (she's a career woman, so the boy seems to point a finger at their childless marriage), and Attenborough himself provoking the crisis when forced to thrash the boy for a minor theft by a snotty woman (Scott) who threatens otherwise to call in the police. In a lurid climax, the boy comes to believe he caused his father's death: 'All my life I'll know I killed my father,' he emotes woodenly (a scriptwriter's line, not a child's, if ever there was one), whereupon the wheels grind loudly into the happy ending. TM

Scandal

(Michael Caton-Jones, 1988, GB) John Hurt, Joanne Whalley-Kilmer, Bridget Fonda, Ian McKellen, Leslie Phillips, Britt Ekland, Daniel Massey, Roland Gift, Jean Alexander, Ronald Fraser, Jeroen Krabbé.
115 min.
Caton-Jones' first feature is a serious, almost low-key affair, strong on period detail and imbued with a sense of genuine outrage on behalf of both the ruined Stephen Ward (Hurt) and the deranged and derailed Christine Keeler (Whalley-Kilmer) which lifts it above the merely exploitative. Both main performances are strong at the core of a still compelling story (Hurt in particular, a riveting jumble of weakness, seediness, vanity and kindness). Less satisfying are McKellen's Profumo, who looks more like a samurai warrior than a war minister; Bridget Fonda's Mandy Rice-Davies, and Jean Alexander's Mrs Keeler, who seem to have succumbed to the cutting-room jitter machine. Others must decide on the propriety of this cinematic exhumation; for those who weren't around at the time of the scandal in the early '60s, and even for those who were, it certainly makes dismaying if illuminating viewing. SGr

Scandale, Le

see Champagne Murders, The

Scandalous

(Rob Cohen, 1983, GB) Robert Hays, John Gielgud, Pamela Stephenson, M Emmet Walsh, Nancy Wood, Conover Kennard, Jim Dale.
92 min.
Not so much a film, more of a mail-order catalogue. Potential customers will find it easy to overlook the story, about a dirt-digging TV reporter (Hays), who gets a taste of his own muckmongering when he encounters a duo of wacky blackmailers: Stephenson flaunting funny accents in a wide selection of base couture, and Gielgud as her Uncle Willie, taking his 1930 punk Hamlet to its logical conclusion in leather and

studs. It resembles softcore with all the smut taken out, but it's hard sell product: lashings of lingerie, wall-to-wall furnishing, and edible interiors for the tasteless consumer. AB

Scanners

(David Cronenberg, 1980, Can) Jennifer O'Neill, Stephen Lack, Patrick McGoohan, Lawrence Dane, Michael Ironside, Adam Ludwig, Robert Silverman.
103 min.
This looks less like Cronenberg's popular mid-'70s exploiters (*Rabid, Shivers*) than one of his early experimental films remade on a higher budget, with a small group of 'scanners' (warrior-telepaths) fighting off a sinister mind-war army that is backed, indirectly, by industry and the state. Part conspiracy thriller, part political tract, it is Cronenberg's most coherent movie to date, drawing a dark (but bland) world in which corporate executives engineer human conception to produce ever more powerful mental samurai. And he punctuates it with spectacular set piece confrontations which really do dramatise the abstract, ingenious premise. As always, there's a nagging feeling that the script is not quite perfectly realised on screen, but Patrick McGoohan's bizarre cameo performance, and the extraordinary moral and sexual ambiguity of the final scanning contest, more than make up for it. CA

Scanners II: The New Order

(Christian Duguay, 1991, Can) David Hewlett, Deborah Raffin, Yvan Ponton, Isabelle Mejias, Tom Butler, Raoul Trujillo, Vlasta Vrana.
105 min.
It is telling that this superfluous sequel to Cronenberg's mind-blowing 1980 movie opens, not with an exploding head, but with a psycho scanner using his telepathic powers to trash a video games arcade. The plot suggests a computer game called 'RoboCop meets the Scanners', while Duguay's visual style consists entirely of pop promo clichés. For years, Dr Morse (Butler) and ambitious police commander Forrester (Ponton) have been trying to harness the scanners' powers, frustrated by the addictive drugs needed to control their volatile guinea-pigs. Then they stumble upon 'clean' scanner David Kellum (Hewlett), a naive country boy whose latent powers they plan to use to fight crime and instigate a fascistic New Order. The cast is anonymous, the plot confused and sluggish; only Michael Smithson's cheap, inventive special effects warrant attention. NF

Scar, The

see Hollow Triumph

Scar, The (Blizna)

(Krzysztof Kieslowski, 1976, Pol) Franciszek Pieczka, Mariusz Domochowski, Jerzy Stuhr, Jan Scotnicki, Stanislaw Igar, Stanislaw Michalski, Michal Tarkowski, Halina Winiarska, Agnieszka Holland.
104 min.
Kieslowski's first theatrical feature is a rather dour slice of social realism. Adapted from a journalist's report, it's set in 1970 and examines the ramifications surrounding the construction of a huge chemical plant near a relatively backward rural community. Pieczka's project director suffers an ongoing crisis of conscience when the locals complain about the disruption. Meanwhile Stuhr's sinister Party manager tries to keep the lid on negative reporting by a roving film crew. There's understanding for points of view on all sides, but the absence of dramatic impetus reveals the film-maker's difficulty in adapting from the documentary work which had comprised the bulk of his previous output. That's bespectacled Agnieszka Holland as the factory secretary. TJ

Scar, The (Prae Kaow)

(Cherd Songsri, 1978, Thai) Sarapong Chatri, Nantana Ngaokrachang.
130 min.
Made for local distribution but by a partly Western-trained director, this – the first feature from Thailand to be seen in Britain – is based on a true Romeo and Juliet story set in the medieval Thai society of fifty years ago. Reflecting the conventions of Indian popular film, a couple of songs are crucial to the courtship; but otherwise the considerable technical expertise is at the service of a vivid narrative style. BP

Scaramouche

(George Sidney, 1952, US) Stewart Granger, Eleanor Parker, Janet Leigh, Mel Ferrer, Henry Wilcoxon, Lewis Stone, Nina Foch, Richard Anderson, Robert Coote.
118 min.

A near-classic swashbuckler, adapted from the Rafael Sabatini novel set in 18th century France, with Granger desperate to avenge his dead friend by killing Mel Ferrer. But since he's not quite deadly enough with the rapier, he has to get some tuition. While all this revenge stuff simmers away, he falls in love with Miss Leigh, who may be his sister; and so, drawing the line at incest, he goes moodily back to sharpening his blade, while the plot unravels everyone's ancestry. Granger shows he can swash a buckle with the best of them, but whereas Fairbanks and Flynn did it with a grin, Granger wields the dirk with a smirk. ATu

Scarecrow

(Jerry Schatzberg, 1973, US) Gene Hackman, Al Pacino, Dorothy Tristan, Ann Wedgeworth, Richard Lynch, Eileen Brennan.
115 min.

A tale with a moral about two drifters who meet on a deserted highway, and find antagonism gradually replaced by curiosity, need, trust and love. Lion (Pacino) clasps a present he is taking to the kid he deserted all those years ago; Max (Hackman) is an ex-con moving a step closer towards his dream of a self-owned carwash. Their relationship is charted like a love affair, full of petty jealousies, little tricks to forestall bad moods, recriminations, regrets. Then Schatzberg throws away the more interesting implications in order to make emotional hay. The pair land in prison, their relationship is tested by the grim realities they find there, and we are off into an embarrassing last section which ends with Max mourning over Lion's catatonic body. A pity – there could have been a movie in there. As it is, *Scarecrow* owes a lot to Vilmos Zsigmond's photography and little to Garry Michael White's over-insistent and finally rather silly script.

Scarecrow, The

(Sam Pillsbury, 1981, NZ) John Carradine, Tracy Mann, Jonathan Smith, Daniel McLaren, Denise O'Connell, Anne Flannery.
88 min.

Set in the Kiwi equivalent of Middle Wallop in the '50s (with an intrusive jazz soundtrack to date it), Pillsbury's adaptation of a local classic is a valiant but botched first effort. Related by a voice-over reminiscent of Clive James with dyspepsia, the story concerns Ned and Pru Poindexter's last summer of adolescence. Into their lives of chicken rustling, gangs, and skinny dips comes the embodiment of destructive sexual power in the guise of arthritic-fingered Carradine, looking more like Steptoe on a rough day than any crazed killer bogeyman. Better at evoking the grim horrors of small town life than the terrors of a murder mystery, the film suffers from a plot which takes a beard-growing age to get going, then hops, skips and jumps to the dénouement. Unsentimental character portrayals, the depiction of parochial decay, the sly humour, and the odd haunting, sinister image are in its favour, but add up to little more than wrapping around a dull present. FL

Scarecrows

(William Wesley, 1988, US) Ted Vernon, Michael Simms, Richard Vidan, Kristina Sanborn, Victoria Christian, David Campbell.
88 min.

Thieves who have hijacked a plane, its crew and the $3 million it was carrying, make a forced landing near a seemingly deserted farmhouse after a greedy member of the gang bails out with money. The cornfields around the house are dotted with scarecrows, whose spindly limbs and rag faces take on an eerie quality as the sun goes down. Tensions between captors and captives heighten as members of both groups mysteriously disappear, to turn up later as disembowelled corpses stuffed with straw...Although a little slow to get started, this better-than-average horror movie makes excellent use of its creepily-lit monsters, is reasonably well put together, and features some stomach-turning grisliness. NF

Scarface

(Howard Hawks, 1932, US) Paul Muni, Ann Dvorak, Karen Morley, Osgood Perkins, Boris Karloff, C Henry Gordon, George Raft, Vince Barnett.
90 min. b/w.

Its seminal importance in the early gangster movie cycle outweighed only by its still exhilarating brilliance, this Howard Hughes production was the one unflawed classic the tycoon was involved with. Hawks and head screenwriter Ben Hecht were after an equation between Capone and the Borgias: they provided so much contentious meat for the censors amid the violent crackle of Chicago gangland war that they managed to slip a subsidiary incest theme through unnoticed. Two years' haggling ended with the subtitle *Shame of a Nation* being appended, one cardboard denunciation scene being added, and a hanging finale being substituted for the shootout – happily restored – which closes proceedings with forceful poetry. Unmissable – if only as the first film in which George Raft flips a dime... PT

Scarface

(Brian De Palma, 1983, US) Al Pacino, Steven Bauer, Michelle Pfeiffer, Mary Elizabeth Mastrantonio, Robert Loggia, Miriam Colon, F Murray Abraham, Paul Shenar, Harris Yulin, Angel Salazar.
170 min.

The first motel shootout bodes well, a set piece handled with panache and the right note of clammy terror, but the rest of this lengthy modern morality tale (updating Hawks' film to 1980) is downhill all the way. When Castro last threw out all his scum, most of them fetched up in Florida, including Tony Montana (Pacino), a man with only 'balls of steel and my word, and I don't break either for anyone'. He attaches to the right sort of godfather, and rises and rises through a world of conspicuous consumption which would make the Borgias blanch. Filmed in the bright widescreen glare of a thousand white suits, the movie is still empty at its heart; where Coppola gave you a whole dynasty in *The Godfather*, with a world and all its moral confusions behind it, De Palma spends three hours sketching out another tetchy little fiend with no more than the ability to nosedive into mountains of cocaine and come up to razor a few more rivals. Pacino gives a monstrous performance as the Cuban heel, clearly aiming for role of the year, but the abiding memory is of just another Method boy chewing the scenery in his quiet way. CPea

Scarlet Blade, The (aka The Crimson Blade)

(John Gilling, 1963, GB) Lionel Jeffries, Oliver Reed, Jack Hedley, June Thorburn, Duncan Lamont, Suzan Farmer, Michael Ripper.
82 min.

A fairly presentable but sometimes tedious Hammer romp through Cromwell's England, with Hedley and Thorburn battling for the Royalist cause against Colonel Judd (Jeffries), while Reed hovers in between as a love-smitten, treacherous turncoat. Judd is prepared to use the torture chamber when it suits him, but – apart from the period – there is no analogy with *Witchfinder General*, since this film carried a 'U' certificate and lacks any real period atmosphere. Gilling went on to do much better things for Hammer like *The Reptile* and *Plague of the Zombies*. DP

Scarlet Buccaneer, The

see Swashbuckler

Scarlet Claw, The

(Roy William Neill, 1944, US) Basil Rathbone, Nigel Bruce, Gerald Hamer, Arthur Hohl, Miles Mander, Ian Wolfe, Paul Cavanagh, Kay Harding.
74 min. b/w.

One of a run of three films in the Rathbone/Bruce Sherlock Holmes series – it came sandwiched between *Sherlock Holmes and the Spider Woman* and *The Pearl of Death* – which made effective use of elements more properly belonging to the horror genre. Here Holmes and Watson travel to remoter Quebec (cue for some of the World War II propaganda uplift deemed essential at the time) to solve the mystery of the marsh monster of La

Morte Rouge. With the fog machine working overtime, Neill makes nicely atmospheric use of the old inn and the gloomy marshes where citizens are having their throats bloodily torn out and a revenge-crazed old actor lurks in assorted disguises. Highly enjoyable. TM

Scarlet Empress, The

(Josef von Sternberg, 1934, US) Marlene Dietrich, John Lodge, Louise Dresser, Sam Jaffe, C Aubrey Smith, Gavin Gordon.
109 min. b/w.

Sternberg's penultimate film with Dietrich was the visual apotheosis of their work together: a chronicle of the rise of Catherine of Russia, with elements of burlesque and pastiche, conceived principally as a delirious, extravagant spectacle. (It could almost be read as Sternberg's homage to silent cinema, with its strong alliance of music and visuals, and its narrative relegated to intertitles; but it's also a prefiguration of *Ivan the Terrible*.) Catherine begins as an ostensibly naive innocent, tucked up in bed to tales of the Tsars' atrocities, and winds up in male military drag, killing her halfwit husband, leading her cavalry into the palace, herself merging with icons of Christ. In other words, beneath the surface frivolities, it's tough stuff. The decor and costumes, and the *mise-en-scène* that deploys them, have never been equalled for expressionist intensity. TR

Scarlet Letter, The

(Roland Joffé, 1995, US) Demi Moore, Gary Oldman, Robert Duvall, Lisa Jolliff-Andoh, Edward Hardwicke, Robert Prosky, Joan Plowright, Roy Dotrice, Tim Woodward.
135 min.

New England, the 17th century, when everyone spake in 'thees' and 'thous'. Independent Hester Prynne (Moore) arrives from England to begin a new life in a puritanical community entrenched on the beautiful coastline. Her husband (Duvall) is to follow her. If only he knew what lay ahead. For less than seven seconds elapse before Hester learning of her husband's alleged death at the hands of Indians, and her jumping into the grain with the estimable Rev Dimmesdale (Oldman). The result's a baby girl, followed by imprisonment and ostracism for Hester, who's eventually forced by her elders to wear a scarlet 'A' and divulge the name of 'the fornicator'. Those acquainted with Hawthorne's novel, from which Joffé's long, cumbersome, at times unintentionally Python-esque, period saga was 'freely adapted', may think they know the outcome. They'd be wrong, because the word 'freely' in the opening credits should have read 'ever so freely'. Not only does the film bear little resemblance to the source novel, but it's cluttered with ridiculous symbolism (a Dayglo bird signposts Hester's way, Duvall dances around with a dead deer on his head) and filtered through a horrid chocolate-ad score. DA

Scarlet Letter, The

(Victor Sjöström, 1927, US) Lillian Gish, Lars Hanson, Karl Dane, Henry B Walthall, William H Tooker.
8,229 ft. b/w.

One of Gish's great performances as Hester Prynne, a woman branded an adulteress in 17th century Salem, and forced to wear a scarlet 'A' of shame. Necessarily truncated from Hawthorne's novel about the terrors of Puritan intolerance, the film itself stumbles over occasional loose ends and melodramatic coincidences, not least the inopportune reappearance of Hester's husband, presumed dead but brought in from the wilderness for ransom by Indians. More damagingly, the references to witchcraft have gone, and with them Hawthorne's implication that Hester's illegitimate child is something of a changeling, and that her seducer – the parson Dimmesdale (a fine performance from Hanson) – has become satanically tainted over the years by his guilt. Sjöström papers this over quite effectively by turning the errant husband into a sort of Wandering Jew, vengefully hounding the tormented parson into his eventual confession and expiation. But what holds the film together above all is Sjöström's extraordinary feeling for rural Americana (despite the theme, much of the action takes place in bright sunlight and idyllically pastoral settings), which was to achieve its fullest expression in *The Wind* the following year. TM

Scarlet Letter, The (Der scharlachrote Buchstabe)

(Wim Wenders, 1972, WGer/Sp) Senta Berger, Hans Christian Blech, Lou Castel, Yelena Samarina, Yella Rottländer, William Layton.
89 min.

Hawthorne's novel offers, however improbable a project, themes that connect with the main lines of Wenders' work: the central figure of the adulteress is an outsider in her own society, and the community of European immigrants are strangers in a strange land. But the movie is as uncharacteristic as you'd expect. Wenders made it (just after *The Goalkeeper's Fear of the Penalty*) as a kind of exercise in fiction, and it definitely lacks the emotional conviction that usually distinguishes his work. But Wenders' admirers will find a lot to interest them. The only major weakness is Jürgen Knieper's excessive score. TR

Scarlet Pimpernel, The

(Harold Young, 1934, GB) Leslie Howard, Merle Oberon, Raymond Massey, Joan Gardner, Nigel Bruce, Bramwell Fletcher, Anthony Bushell, Walter Rilla.
98 min. b/w.

Though it meant changing directors mid-stream (he initially took over himself when Rowland Brown was fired), Korda determinedly eschewed blood-and-thunder and structured the film around the dual personality of the Pimpernel. The low-key action scenes seem indeed to function as an alibi, assuring us that the outrageously effeminate Howard is a man's man really, cool and resourceful enough to defeat even the machinations of sneeringly sinister Chauvelin (Massey zestfully playing the villain). With an eye to the American market, Korda subtly caricatures the reactionary sentiments of Orczy's novel (America too had its revolution!); and with Oberon's opaque beauty making her an ideally iconic counterfoil to Howard's fey Pimpernel, the film seems to operate more as a meditation on heroism and romantic love than as a celebration of aristocratic ideals. RMy

Scarlet Street

(Fritz Lang, 1945, US) Edward G Robinson, Joan Bennett, Dan Duryea, Jess Barker, Margaret Lindsay, Rosalind Ivan, Samuel S Hinds, Vladimir Sokoloff.
103 min. b/w.

A remake of Renoir's *La Chienne* of 1931, and a key psychological *film noir*, one of Hollywood's most tortuous and bleak visions of the delusive power of the imagination. Edward G Robinson's meek, middle-aged, middle class cashier/Sunday painter suffers with 'problems with perspective' when driven into an obsessive infatuation with Joan Bennett's sensual, scheming prostitute/actress; and a potent combination of Fate, an unusually incisive script, Lang's claustrophobic visuals, and a haunting score are enough to shape him into the essential portrait of tragic vulnerability. The film, taking representation and perception as its dominant themes, practically begs for close textual analysis while rushing headlong towards its subversive climax – offering further proof that the tight framework of American narrative genres provided the ideal context for Lang to work in. PT

Scarlet Tunic, The

(Stuart St Paul, 1997, GB) Jean-Marc Barr, Emma Fielding, Simon Callow, Jack Shepherd, John Sessions, Lynda Bellingham.
92 min.

Former stuntman Stuart St Paul's first feature is an adaptation of Thomas Hardy's story *The Melancholy Hussar*. Though it cost only £350,000, it has none of the self-conscious flashiness of a 'calling card' movie. Never balking at the melodramatic elements of Hardy's vision, this tale of doomed love is told with clarity, passion and a keen eye for the beauty of Dorset. Barr smoulders as the German hussar, whose love for solicitor's daughter Fielding leaves her torn between duty and desire, while Sessions is slyly convincing, too, as the weasel-like suitor favoured by Fielding's loving but misguided father. Only the eye rolling Callow, as the martinet captain whose hounding of Barr betrays his own homosexual desire, misjudges the emotionally overwrought tone – one expects him to start twirling his impressive moustaches at any moment. Disappointingly, St Paul also over-eggs the pudding

with a conciliatory coda that softens the original tragic ending. A credit, however, to all those who lent their time and talent. NF

Scarred

(Rose-Marie Turko, 1983, US) Jennifer Mayo, Jackie Berryman, David Dean, Rico L Richardson, Debbie Dion.
85 min.

'You are what you eat, not what you fuck'. Just one of the erudite nuggets of wisdom to be gleaned from this sordid story of pimps and prozzies, set on Hollywood's sleazier sidewalks. 16-year-old Ruby (Mayo) is an unmarried mum who sets up as an 'independent' in order to pay the babysitter. But she finds she needs the support of other hookers, and the guidance of a pimp called Easy (Dean). The daily drudgery of a whore's life is depicted in depressing detail, occasionally enlivened by a certain wacky humour, as when Ruby wrecks the set of a pornopic *Star Wars* rip-off, or when old-maidish pimps with their hair in rollers gossip bitchily at the barber's. Cheapo stuff, but probably more realistic than *The Streetwalker* and its glossy offshoots, and pushed up a few notches by Mayo's performance. AB

Scars of Dracula, The

(Roy Ward Baker, 1970, GB) Christopher Lee, Dennis Waterman, Jenny Hanley, Christopher Matthews, Patrick Troughton, Michael Gwynn, Anoushka Hempel.
96 min.

This was Hammer's last 'period' Dracula before they plunged the Count disastrously into Swinging London. The plot follows the usual ploy of bringing a young couple (Waterman and Hanley) to the vampire's doom-laden castle, in this instance with the twist that they are bent on revenge. Despite attempts to restore some elements from Stoker previously omitted in the Hammer cycle (the Count is seen scaling the castle walls), and despite Lee's dogged efforts to give the Count a truly aristocratic bearing, the strained plot simply lurches from one gory set piece to another with (literally) extra lashings of sadism and sex. DT

Scavengers, The

see Recuperanti, I

Sceicco Bianco, Lo

see White Sheik, The

Scene at the Sea, A (Ano Natsu, Ichiban Shizukana Umi)

(Takeshi Kitano, 1991, Jap) Kuroko Maki, Hiroko Oshima.
101 min.

A U-turn in the blood-spattered career of actor-director Takeshi Kitano, still fondly remembered as the sentimental sadist Sergeant Hara in *Merry Christmas, Mr Lawrence*. This time he stays behind the camera and does without his usual recourse to violence. Working on a garbage truck in a seaside town (we realise only gradually that he and his girlfriend are profoundly deaf) finds a broken surf-board, tries to repair it, and teaches himself to surf. That's pretty much the whole plot, but it encompasses a truly rapturous love story, a lot of humour, and some piercing truths about human nature. It's also superbly acted, and has the best-judged editing since Bresson's last movie. TR

Scene of the Crime, The (Le Lieu du Crime)

(André Téchiné, 1986, Fr) Catherine Deneuve, Victor Lanoux, Danielle Darrieux, Wadeck Stanckzak, Nicolas Giraudi.
90 min.

The scene is the rustic vicinity of a small provincial town, the crime what happens to a small boy disaffected by his parents' divorce and by troubled loyalties when an escaped convict commits murder to save him from harm. His mother (Deneuve) promptly falls ass-over-tit for the convict (Stanckzak), his father (Lanoux) huffs around stockbroker-style, and his grandparents (including the imperishable Darrieux, alas) seem to have wandered in from a yokel movie. As vacuously pretentious as Téchiné's earlier *Rendez-vous*. TM

Scenes from a Mall

(Paul Mazursky, 1990, US) Woody Allen, Bette Midler, Bill Irwin, Paul Mazursky, Daren Firestone, Rebecca Nickels.
88 min.

In this irksome comedy, set mostly in the Beverly shopping mall in LA, Allen – his first dramatic outing since *The Front* – plays a neurotic, ponytailed sports lawyer, married 16 years (she says 17) to successful shrink and writer Midler. They pack off the kids, have their anniversary fuck, then proceed to discuss the secret of their success. The discussions go on all movie. We move down to the mall and all the lies come out – infidelity, hypocrisy, yawn, yawn, yawn, yawn. Ugly amounts of bucks were spent on rebuilding the mall so that cameras could swoop up and down every inch of it, ogling merchandise and fetishising every commodity as 2,000 extras pass by, trying not to gaze at the camera. Woody and Bette eat sushi, clothe themselves, waltz in the piano bar, followed around by a mime, a rap group, and a Victorian-style barber-shop quartet harmonising – it's Christmastime – 'Walking in a Winter Wonderland'. Allen's admittedly funny lines get lost in the mess, and Midler, in relatively restrained mode, fades away altogether. Thematically, the film comes over as a piss-take of Mazursky by Mazursky. WH

Scenes from a Marriage (Scener ur ett äktenskap)

(Ingmar Bergman, 1973, Swe) Liv Ullmann, Erland Josephson, Bibi Andersson, Jan Malmsjö, Anita Wall, Gunnel Lindblom.
168 min. (TV version: 300 min.)

Though edited down (under Bergman's supervision) from a six-part series originally made for TV, this remains an exhaustive study of the doubt, despair, confusion and loneliness experienced by a woman (Ullmann) when she learns that her fickle husband (Josephson) is having an affair. Bergman, as in *Face to Face*, is here at his most stylistically stark: very little actually happens (much of the film consists of conversations in rooms), so that it's left to the performers (all superb, and mostly framed by Sven Nykvist in revealing close-ups) to bring the litany of pain to life. And they do, with the result that the film is an uncompromisingly harrowing and honest account of male-female relationships. GA

Scenes from the Class Struggle in Beverly Hills

(Paul Bartel, 1989, US) Jacqueline Bisset, Ray Sharkey, Mary Woronov, Robert Beltran, Ed Begley Jr, Wallace Shawn, Arnetia Walker, Paul Bartel, Paul Mazursky, Edith Diaz.
103 min.

Less the poor versus the rich than the poor struggling to emulate the rich. 'Anyone who spends $3,000 on a bathrobe deserves to die' says one of the scheming manservants who form the pivot of this cheerful sex comedy, but Bartel takes pains to show both flunkeys lolling in said garment. The sexual oneupmanship (a mild satire on decadence) revolves around widowed ex-soap star Clare (Bisset), keeping house with resident 'thinologist' (a camp cameo by Bartel) and dishy Hispanic houseboy (Beltran). Next door lives neurotic Lisabeth (Woronov), who's having her mansion de-infested in an unconscious attempt to rid it of her ex-husband's noxious influence. As this involves pumping it full of poison gas, she and her withdrawn teenage son, her playwright brother, his new black bride, and the houseboy (Sharkey) all take refuge with Clare. The servants each vow to bed the other's employer, and the sumptuous stage is set for frantic upstairs-downstairs bed-swapping, performed with charm and gusto. SFe

Scenic Route, The

(Mark Rappaport, 1978, US) Randy Danson, Marilyn Jones, Kevin Wade, Grant Stewart, Arthur Ginsberg.
76 min.

Rappaport contrives a strikingly seductive fusion of wit with seriousness, a New York tale of two sisters – Estelle (Danson) and Lena (Jones) – both working through a sort of love for Paul (Wade): male, fake-macho, hilariously silent. Though its baroque 'landscape' of interiors and tableaux, opera and soap opera, is held together by an unerring sense of visual style and persistently wry humour, the film ultimately suffers from an overweening sense of ironical self-esteem. Estelle, neurotic fantasist, diarist, reader of the voice-over that comments the action, is constantly undercut by the stylish visual gags, and confessions like 'I must have made it happen' make her an object of laughter: woman under a yoke of Christian (or Freudian) guilt. Here women are tyrants or martyrs (or both), and the token male in the film is irrelevant because we're busy endorsing the male behind the film. Estelle finally burns her diaries: castration. It's a strange example of sophisticated chauvinism; how much you laugh will depend on just how witty, intelligent and cultured you feel. CA

Scent of a Woman
(Martin Brest, 1992, US) Al Pacino, Chris O'Donnell, James Rebhorn, Gabrielle Anwar, Philip S Hoffman, Richard Venture, Bradley Whitford.
156 min.
This takes its inspiration from an Italian film of 1974, *Profumo di donna*, and concerns the relationship between Frank Slade (Pacino), a blind and very bitter ex-Vietnam army officer, and a 17-year-old boy (O'Donnell) hired to look after him over a weekend. The film splices two plots together, more ambitiously than successfully: O'Donnell's Charlie Simms is a bright young scholarship kid whose academic hopes face the chop when he becomes embroiled in a schoolboy prank played by some well-off classmates. Charlie has the weekend to decide whether to tell or not; Slade plans to enjoy himself on a spree to New York before ending his life in a military-style suicide. The outcome is as predictable as it is wholesomely traditional, but Pacino pulls out all the stops as the blind warrior, dancing a mean impromptu tango, taking a car for a suicidal spin, barking orders, charming ladies with his super-hearing, and finally coming good on Charlie's behalf. Corny and heart-warming, with O'Donnell proving almost a match for the master. SGr

Scent of Green Papaya, The (L'Odeur de la Papaye Verte/ Mui Du Du Xanh)
(Tran Anh Hung, 1993, Fr) Yen-Khe Tran Nu, Man San Lu, Thi Loc Truong, Anh Hoa Nguyen, Hoa Hoi Vuong.
104 min.
The story of Mui, a peasant girl who comes to Saigon to serve in the house of a bourgeois family: grandmother, parents, three sons and a maid. It's 1951, the influence of the West is beginning to make itself felt, but already the old conventions are beginning to crack. Tran's first feature – shot, remarkably, in France – is sensuous, evocative and politically ambivalent. It focuses particularly on the servitude of women. We watch in close-up as Mui learns her duties: cleaning up after the youngsters, running errands, cooking rice and papaya for the family. At first these are mere chores, but later, as she grows into a woman, they take on a more fulfilling purpose. The movie's poetic-realist design meshes detailed, patient observation and delectable, poignant travelling shots; it grounds us in the quotidian duties of service and dissects contemporary Vietnamese social hierarchies, yet adds up to something much more subtle and enticing: a lyrical portrait of the human spirit in work and in love. Exquisitely controlled. TCh

Schaukel, Die
see Swing, The

Schiele in Prison
(Mick Gold, 1980, GB) Grant Cathro, David Suchet, Nicholas Selby.
48 min.
Sex, boredom and suicide in crumbling World War I Vienna. An Arts Council documentary by former rock photographer Gold on Egon Schiele (with readings from his prison diary): a paranoiac narcissist, jailbird, and friend of Klimt, his tortured, spindly self-portraits once heavily influenced David Bowie. Oddly dull, considering its subject, it errs on the side of politeness. DMacp

Schindler's List 100 (100)
(Steven Spielberg, 1993, US) Liam Neeson, Ben Kingsley, Ralph Fiennes, Caroline Goodall, Jonathan Sagalle, Embeth Davidtz.
195 min. b/w & col.

The film of Thomas Keneally's novel is Spielberg's finest since *Jaws*. The elastic editing and grainy camerawork lend an immediacy as surprising as the shockingly matter-of-fact depiction of violence and casual killing. And Spielberg can handle actors – Neeson as Schindler, the German profiteer whose use of cheap labour in his Cracow factory saved 1,100 Jews from death; Kingsley as Stern, the canny accountant; Fiennes as Goeth, bloodless commandant of Plaszow camp. Wisely, the director rarely seeks to simplify the mysterious complexity of Schindler, an opportunist whose deeds became giddily selfless. As in his earlier work, there's a sense of wonder at the inexplicable, but it's no longer childlike. At times the film becomes a scream of horror at the inhumanity it recalls and recreates, and the b/w images never become aesthetically sanitised. True, the Jews are huddled, victimised masses. True, too, that Spielberg finally relents and tries to 'explain' Schindler so that the last hour becomes steadily more simplistic and sentimental. Otherwise, however, it's a noble achievement, and essential viewing. GA

Schizo
(Pete Walker, 1976, GB) Lynne Frederick, John Leyton, Stephanie Beacham, John Fraser, Jack Watson, Queenie Watts, Trisha Mortimer, John McEnery.
109 min.
Walker and writer David McGillivray's most ambitious project to date attempts to shake off the low-budget horror/exploitation tag with a move into more up-market psychological suspense. If the formula is threadworn – a trail of victimisation, sexual paranoia, and murder in the wake of the heroine's wedding – at least some effort is made to locate it (rich middle class London). But things collapse disastrously in the second half. Caught between sending itself up and taking itself seriously, the film ends closer to the silliness of Francis Durbridge than to the menace of Alfred Hitchcock. CPe

Schizophrenia (aka Angst)
(Gerald Kargl, 1983, WGer) Erwin Leder, Silvia Rabenreither, Edith Rosset, Rudolf Götz, Renate Kastelik.
95 min.
Released after serving a prison sentence for the shooting of an old lady he had never met, a psychopath (Leder) breaks into a house, terrorising and ultimately murdering an old lady, her wheelchair-bound husband and their daughter. Savage, stylistically brilliant and at times virtually unwatchable, this film bears comparison with *Henry: Portrait of a Serial Killer*. But where *Henry* employed a cold objectivity, Kargl achieves a curious pull-push effect, the camerawork rubbing our noses in the as-it-happens atrocity while the director's disturbingly intimate voice-over gives a cool, dislocated account of events. Moments of black humour, as when the family dachshund picks up the old lady's false teeth, only serve to emphasise the quotidian nature of the horror. Stunning. NF

School (La Scuola)
(Daniele Luchetti, 1995, It) Silvio Orlando, Anna Galiena, Fabrizio Bentivoglio.
102 min.
A critical and commercial hit in Italy, this portrait of a hard-pressed Roman secondary school is a witty, well-observed exposé of the foibles of institutional life, while at the same time hinting at the moral funk and the economic strictures affecting the wider national psyche. Instead of the usual *Blackboard Jungle* melodramatics, the tone here is affectionate and faintly absurdist, and the focus is as much on the clashing personalities of the staff – fumbling likeable history teacher Orlando has the hots for Galiena's maths mistress, but she seems taken by Bentivoglio's disciplinarian deputy head – as it is on the ever-boisterous students. A hugely enjoyable movie which barely wastes a scene. TJ

School Daze
(Spike Lee, 1988, US) Larry Fishburne, Giancarlo Esposito, Tisha Campbell, Spike Lee, Kyme, Joe Seneca, Ossie Davis.
120 min.
Swiftian satires on popular taste can backfire badly, and Spike Lee's attempt at black consciousness-raising through the armature of

Animal House movies almost dies of the contusion it is trying to lance. One glance at Julian (Esposito) leading the Gamma Phi Gamma fraternity, who crawl along barking in unison in gladiatorial togas, is enough to topple satire into farce. Half-Pint (Lee) finally passes his initiation test and loses his virginity in the frat Bone Room. The football coach (Davis) delivers a locker-room pep talk straight out of Sanctified Church, and the Dean is in bed with the college's white benefactress. The musical numbers are uniformly uninventive. Here and there the sociology is clear, but much of the film may seem incomprehensible to English audiences. On the evidence of *She's Gotta Have It*, Lee has a small, intimate talent; here he goes for the big podium and blows it. BC

School for Scoundrels
(Robert Hamer, 1960, GB) Ian Carmichael, Alastair Sim, Terry-Thomas, Janette Scott, Dennis Price, Peter Jones, Edward Chapman, John Le Mesurier.
94 min. b/w.
Hamer's last film before losing out to alcohol is, ironically, about taking short cuts to success. Based around the sneeringly facile concept of 'one-upmanship' (how to tread on people and make them thank you for it), the film follows the fortunes of upper class twit Carmichael as he struggles for supremacy with waiters, women and Terry-Thomas. The first half, in particular a sequence where used-car salesmen Dudley and Dunstan Dorchester 'the Winsome Welshmen' (Price and Jones) perpetrate a con even Richard Nixon would have been proud of, has its moments of cruel humour; but when, with the benefit of a course in 'lifemanship', Carmichael is reborn as a winner, things become tediously silly. RMy

School for Vandals
(Colin Finbow, 1986, GB) Anne Dyson, Charles Kay, Tamara Hinchco, Peter Bayliss, Jeremy Coster, Samantha McMillan.
80 min.
A mixture of 'Famous Five' antics and kidnapping from the Children's Film Unit. The parents of youngsters Rupert and Tiger Lily (so named because of their mother's obsession with Rupert Bear) have invested a pools win in a run-down former reform school in Sussex, which they plan to reopen as a school. The winnings have dwindled, so chancing upon the elderly Miss Duff (Dyson) wandering around her former school, the kids and three friends plan her kidnapping with the intention of squeezing some money out of the locals. No such luck. However, they soon strike up a friendship with the old dear, who isn't quite what she seems...Cosier than some of the unit's earlier productions, and what we are seeing here is hopefully the future of the British film industry; and it's looking good. DA

Schramm
(Jörg Buttgereit, 1992, Ger) Florian Koerner von Gustorf, Monika M.
75 min.
This cinematic excuse for extremity – from the director of *Nekromantic* – is based on the true story of 'The Lipstick Killer', murderer and necrophile Lothar Schramm (von Gustorf), and his relationship with prostitute Marianne (Monika M). As well as his taste for having sex with the dead, Schramm's unusual style of DIY includes nailing his own penis to the table. NF

Schreckliche Mädchen, Das
see Nasty Girl, The

Schtonk!
(Helmut Dietl, 1992, Ger) Götz George, Uwe Ochsenknecht, Christiane Hörbiger, Rolf Hoppe, Dagmar Manzel, Veronica Ferres.
111 min.
This *could* have been funny – after all, the 1983 scandal of the forged Hitler diaries should be fertile ground for satire – but Dietl and producer Ulrich Limmer's script is so leadenly obvious that the film is almost wholly bereft of laughs. Focused on the swindling partnership of 'Professor' Fritz Knobel (Ochsenknecht) – a past master of forgery in the art and antiques field – and scoop-hungry hack Hermann Willié (George),

the story seems intended to highlight the hypocrisy, corruption, and enduring Nazi sympathies rampant in certain sectors of modern German society. Fair enough; but hysterical scenes of nostalgia for the Führer, witless innuendoes, and repeated readings of ludicrously banal diary entries about flatulence don't exactly make for a light touch. Indeed, the whole movie is woefully heavy-handed, with grotesquely OTT performances, most of it looks ugly, and it never gets beyond that one-joke premise about hypocrisy, corruption, etc. GA

Scissors

(Frank De Felitta, 1991, US) Sharon Stone, Steve Railsback, Ronny Cox, Michelle Phillips.
105 min.
An identikit psycho thriller sadly in need of a bit of sex, gore or something to liven up a plot that employs every predictable twist, cliché and red herring in the book. Stone is a woman haunted by a repressed childhood trauma involving – you guessed it – scissors. Cox is her sympathetic but sexually frustrated shrink, and Railsback her smitten neighbour. Railsback's embittered, wheelchair-bound brother and his spurned exlover (Phillips) are the obvious bad guys, which means that it's someone else trying to drive her mad. Pretty daft, but perversely enjoyable in a ludicrously overheated kind of way. NF

Scorchers

(David Beaird, 1991, US) Faye Dunaway, Denholm Elliott, James Earl Jones, Emily Lloyd, Jennifer Tilly, James Wilder, Anthony Geary, Leland Crooke.
82 min.
Beaird's adaptation of his own play begins with a folksy five-minute monologue exhorting us to believe what we feel, not what we are told. It is set in Bayou country, where accents are thick as molasses and the nights fair palpitate with desire. Lloyd is Splendid, a Louisiana belle terrified by the prospect of losing her virginity. It's her wedding night. As the groom reaches the end of his tether, it falls to Jumper (Crooke) to philosophise his daughter out from under the bed. Meanwhile, at the town bar, alcoholic has-been actor Howler (Elliott) debates sex and the classics with barkeep Bear (Jones) and prostitute Thais (Dunaway), until irate bridesmaid Talbot (Tilly) storms the joint with a bellyful of sexual resentment and a revolver. Saddled with a derivative script that apes Tennessee Williams none too successfully – a perilous mixture of ribald humour and highflown poeticism – the cast revert to type: Jones growls, Elliott snivels, Dunaway smokes, and Lloyd tries ever so hard, bless her. A hopelessly theatrical film from what must have been a poor play. TCh

Scorpio

(Michael Winner, 1972, US) Burt Lancaster, Alain Delon, Paul Scofield, John Colicos, Gayle Hunnicutt, JD Cannon, Joanne Linville, James B Sikking.
114 min.
Conventional and convoluted tale of betrayal and death among spies, with Lancaster's CIA agent coming under suspicion, being marked for extermination by the reluctant but seemingly persuadable freelance killer he trained (Delon), and turning in his disillusionment to his equally disillusioned Russian opposite number (Scofield) for aid. Winner directs with typically crass abandon, wasting a solid performance from Lancaster and a story that a director like Jean-Pierre Melville might have made something of. GA

Scorpion, The
(De Schorpioen)

(Ben Verbong, 1984, Neth) Peter Tuinman, Monique Van de Ven, Rima Melati, Senne Rouffaer, Walter Kous, Adrian Brine.
98 min.
When Lew Wolff (Tuinman), burdened with a criminal past and a bleak future, arrives in an out-of-season coastal resort on his way to a new life in America, he's hardly prepared for the danger and confusion that arise after he exchanges his own papers for a false passport: he reads reports of his death, is warned off, finds his room ransacked. For all the potential thrills thrown up by this premise, Verbong's film resembles his earlier The Girl with the Red Hair in emphasising theme, character and atmosphere rather than

suspense. Set in Holland in 1956, the film examines the mysterious legacy of that country's colonial involvement in Indonesia during the '40s; and in asking where Sukarno's rebels obtained their arms in order to repel the Dutch, proposes some pretty unconvincing answers in some pretty awkward flashbacks. The main body of the film, however, is sensitive and engaging, and in moments of noir-flecked seediness comes truly alive. GA

Scorpio Rising

see Anger Magick Lantern, Cycle

Scorta, La (The Escort)

(Ricky Tognazzi, 1993, It) Claudio Amendola, Enrico Lo Verso, Carlo Cecchi, Ricky Memphis, Leo Gullotta, Tony Sperandeo.
92 min.
An old man upsets his drink in panic at a loud explosion outside. Racing to investigate, his fears are confirmed...a judge has been assassinated, and the old man's son along with him. This is bold, emotional film-making, torn from the headlines, and from here on director Tognazzi never leaves the side of his four protagonists. La scorta – the escort – are the ordinary young policemen assigned to protect magistrates investigating the Mafia in Italy. The film focuses on the bodyguards of a particularly determined Sicilian judge. Andrea (Lo Verso) is the supervising officer. Married with kids, he's an obvious target for blackmail. Angelo (Amendola) is a tougher customer: a friend of the murdered escort, he's out to bring the killers to justice. Police work is just a job for Raffaele and Fabio (Sperandeo and Memphis), but they too become inspired by the integrity of their charge (Checchi) and the camaraderie of the group. An effective thriller, closer to Hollywood's muckrakers than any of Francesco Rosi's political gangster movies. Not subtle, exactly, but pointed. TCh

Scotch on the Rocks

see Laxdale Hall

Scott of the Antarctic

(Charles Frend, 1948, GB) John Mills, Derek Bond, James Robertson Justice, Kenneth More, John Gregson, Harold Warrender, Reginald Beckwith, Diana Churchill, Christopher Lee.
111 min.
Respectable account of Scott's doomed expedition to the South Pole. With so many frozen upper lips, the performances are rather buried behind balaclavas (at the end it's hard to tell who's who), and the studio colour backdrops are sometimes intrusive. However, Vaughan Williams' score effectively upstages the dialogue; and the early scenes, when Mills scratches around for financing and assembles his crew, are a fair evocation of Edwardian England, even if the failure of the mission, and the reverberations that failure had for Imperial Britain, are beyond the scope of the movie. The movie says, with characteristic aplomb, well done chaps, at least you tried. ATu

Scoumoune, La
(Hit Man/Scoundrel)

(José Giovanni, 1972, Fr/It) Jean-Paul Belmondo, Claudia Cardinale, Michel Constantin, Michel Pereylon, Aldo Bufi Landi.
105 min.
Giovanni, a Série Noire writer, here adapted and directed his own novel about the Marseille underworld, previously filmed in 1961 (also with Belmondo) by Jean Becker as Un Nommé la Rocca. Ineptitude in both departments makes a hash of the theme of underworld loyalties so beautifully handled in Melville's Le Deuxième Souffle (also based on a Giovanni novel). Even the original title (meaning 'the jinx') becomes pointless, because Belmondo's crude tough guy performance makes the persistent failure of his gallant efforts on behalf of a friend look more like bad scripting than the consequence of changing underworld ways. TM

Scoundrel

see Scoumoune, La

Scoundrel in White

see Docteur Popaul

Scream

(Wes Craven, 1996, US) Drew Barrymore, Neve Campbell, David Arquette, Courteney Cox, Rose McGowan, Skeet Ulrich.
111 min.
Wes Craven draws on a shared pop cultural heritage in horror flicks to fashion this bloody brand of post-modern comedy. 'So you like scary movies? Name the killer in Friday the 13th?' demands the anonymous caller of Barrymore's lone teen in the prologue. 'Hang up again and I'll gut you like a fish!' The killer describes his apparently irrational vendetta against the high school population of Woodsboro as a game, and in this he's surely speaking for screenwriter Kevin Williamson and director Craven, who kill off the clichés and all the wrong characters with panache. At times, it's too clever, but it's sure scary, with the jokes notching up the general level of hysteria. As a bonus, Craven throws in half a dozen of Hollywood's brightest hopefuls: Campbell in the central role of the teenager haunted by the murder of her mother; Arquette as a naive local deputy; Cox as a TV star; McGowan as the doomed best friend; and Ulrich as the evocatively named Billy Loomis. Intelligence, wit and sophistication – at last, a horror movie to shout about! TCh

Scream 2

(Wes Craven, 1997, US) Neve Campbell, Courteney Cox, David Arquette, Liev Schreiber, Sarah Michelle Gellar, Jamie Kennedy, Laura Metcalf, Elise Neal, Jerry O'Connell, Timothy Olyphant, Jada Pinkett, Wes Craven.
120 min.
This being the sequel, scriptwriter Kevin Williamson includes a scene in which film students discuss the fact that such movies never match the inventiveness of the original. Quite so. To be fair, by changing the location and concentrating on the haunted victims rather than the demonic killer(s), No 2 avoids a couple of obvious pitfalls. Two years after the Woodsboro murders, Sidney Prescott (Campbell) is a college student, piecing her life together with a new boyfriend, her old friend Randy (Kennedy) and a sympathetic roommate. But when a spectator is slashed to death during the local premiere of horror movie Stab – from a book on the Woodsboro incident by cynical TV reporter Gail Weathers (Cox) – the nightmare begins anew. Although returning characters such as ex-deputy Dewey (Arquette) have moved on, the film itself is stuck in a cycle of repetition, with slight variations. Compared to most contemporary horror fare, this is intelligent and frightening; compared to the original, it just doesn't cut it. NF

Scream and Scream Again

(Gordon Hessler, 1969, GB) Vincent Price, Christopher Lee, Peter Cushing, Alfred Marks, Anthony Newlands, Peter Sallis, Michael Gothard.
95 min.
An impressive if somewhat fragmented horror film in which mad scientist Price uses surgery and organ transplants to create a super race of emotionless creatures, one of which (Gothard) attracts the attentions of the police by going berserk and committing a number of grisly vampiric murders. The underlying narrative thread about the creatures taking over positions of authority is not sufficiently well developed to have any real impact, but individual scenes are conceived to gory and striking effect. NF

Screamers

(Christian Duguay, 1995, Can/US/Jap) Peter Weller, Andy Lauer, Jennifer Rubin, Roy Dupuis, James Powell, Ron White, Michael Caloz.
109 min.
Based on a Philip K Dick story, scripted by Dan O'Bannon and Miguel Tejada-Flores, and directed by the maker of Scanners II, this Canadian sci-fi movie lacks the intelligence to follow through its grim premise. That said, and a worrying resemblance to Charles Band's cheapo, quarry-bound sci-fi pics aside, it does offer many of the guilty pleasures of unachieving B-pictures. The mining planet of Sirius 6B, in 2078: a handful of Alliance soldiers led by Col Hendricksson (Weller) and including rookie hotshot Ace Jefferson (Lauer) resolves to negotiate peace with

their similarly depleted New Economic Block enemies. But the post-nuclear wasteland they must cross is guarded by self-replicating 'Screamers', anti-personnel devices with flying blades that slice and dice. The sporadic and increasingly sophisticated Screamer attacks lend suspense to an unexceptional plot, the least intriguing aspect of which is a telegraphed flip-over finale. Weller's fine and Lauer has a nice line in gung-ho naiveté, but Rubin's wasted as a permanently pissed-off black-marketeer. Despite limited resources, the design and effects teams have lent scale and impact to the futuristic locations and sets. If only Duguay's flashy, aimless direction had succeeded in filling these barren wastes and antiseptic interiors with something resembling human life. NF

Scream for Help
(Michael Winner, 1984, US) Rachael Kelly, David Brooks, Marie Masters, Rocco Sisto, Lolita Lorre, Corey Parker.
90 min.
A hybrid so mind-boggling that viewers may rush back to Winner's *Death Wish* to reassess a hitherto unsuspected comic talent. 16-year-old Christie confides to her diary her suspicions that her stepfather Paul is up to no good. First, the meter reader is electrocuted. Then Christie catches Paul *in flagrante* with a big-bazoomed tart called Brenda. Then her friend Janey announces she is pregnant, and has the whole of life ahead of her. She is immediately killed by a hit-and-run driver. Brenda's brother (who is really her husband) teams up with Brenda and Paul to push Christie and her mom down the cellar steps. But Christie is a resourceful heroine. She fights back by making blueberry pancakes. Played to po-faced perfection by its cast of TV soap graduates, and underscored by ex-Led Zep star John Paul Jones with a soundtrack so inappropriate as to be positively existential. AB

Scream from Silence, A
see Mourir à Tue-Tête

Screaming Mimi
(Gerd Oswald, 1958, US) Anita Ekberg, Phil Carey, Harry Townes, Gypsy Rose Lee, Romney Brent, Red Norvo.
79 min. b/w.
Curious cod Freudian potboiler from a novel by Fredric Brown with Ekberg playing a woman who topples into a nervous breakdown after being sexually assaulted, takes a job as a stripper, and ends up on the couch of a dubious shrink. If only Oswald had injected such a provocative scenario with the same eerie imagination that fuelled his version of *A Kiss Before Dying* then this might have been truly something to shout about. LF

Scream of Fear
see Taste of Fear

Screwballs
(Rafal Zielinski, 1983, Can) Peter Keleghan, Kent Deuters, Lynda Speciale, Alan Deveau, Linda Shayne.
80 min.
Few hopes of good cinema survive the title; none the opening scenes, where two big-breasted cheerleaders and an outsize sausage set the tawdry tone. What relentlessly follows concerns the students of Taft and Adams High School, remarkable only for their average age (around thirty) and their avid interest in tits. Now, however one rates the bosom as an erogenous zone, it takes the talents of a Russ Meyer to make it interesting for eighty minutes. Watching the unflagging, unfunny efforts of five callow youths to see the homecoming queen's breasts, one only wonders if ever in the field of endeavour so much has been done by so many for just two. FD

Screwballs II – Loose Screws
(Rafal Zielinski, 1985, Can) Bryan Genesse, Lance Van Der Kolk, Alan Deveau, Jason Warren, Annie McAuley, Karen Wood.
92 min.
Brad Lovett, Steve Hardman, Marvin Eatmore and Hugh G Rection are so brainless that they are transferred from Beaver High School to Coxwell Academy in Wadsworth. They promptly rub Principal Arsenal up the wrong way by posing as doctors and persuading the female students to strip down to their bras and panties. 'Some slots are smaller than others', says Arsenal to Mona Lott the French mistress, who replies, 'I get my share of mail'. Steve gives sports coaching ('The secret's all in the stroke'), Marvin falls through the ceiling of the girls' changing-room, Brad sneaks into the health club disguised as Hung-Lo the masseur. The fun-loving panty-jocks are peeved when Arsenal expels them for bawdy behaviour, so they contrive to humiliate both him and Mona Lott. There is also a song called 'I've Got a Rubber in My Wallet'. How strange that this film should have an '18' certificate when it is so obviously aimed at infants. AB

Scrooge
(Ronald Neame, 1970, GB) Albert Finney, Alec Guinness, Edith Evans, Kenneth More, Michael Medwin, Laurence Naismith, David Collings, Anton Rodgers, Suzanne Neve.
118 min.
A misbegotten musical adaptation of Dickens' much too perennial tale, featuring songs by Leslie Bricusse that are not only anaemic but piffling in their up-front relevance ('I Hate People', 'I Like Life', 'I'll Begin Again'). Even Dickens would surely have blenched when Tiny Tim, hugging a manifestly unnecessary crutch, hobbles up to simper blessings on us every one, and to brighten the Cratchit Christmas by singing of 'The Beautiful Day' he hopes is just around the corner. Finney, in a balding wig, mugs abominably as Scrooge; the dances are full of energy but not noticeably choreographed; and the colour (musty brownish for the Scrooge-and-poverty scenes, garishly tinselled for the Christmas fantasy visions) is variable to say the least. Some slight relief is afforded by cameos from Guinness (looking like a camp pixie as Marley's Ghost), Edith Evans (regally quavering in scarlet robe as the Ghost of Christmas Past), and Kenneth More (vastly bearded and militantly jolly as the Ghost of Christmas Present). TM

Scrooged
(Richard Donner, 1988, US) Bill Murray, Karen Allen, John Forsythe, John Glover, Bobcat Goldthwait, David Johansen, Carol Kane, Robert Mitchum, Michael J Pollard, Alfre Woodard, John Murray, Robert Goulet, John Houseman, Buddy Hackett, Lee Majors.
101 min.
An update on the Dickens classic, with Murray as a miserly TV network president who rejoins the human race following spectral visitations. The tone is set by a machine-gun assault on Santa's North Pole toy workshop and the timely arrival of the first of a series of guest star drop-ins. Miles Davis and David Sanborn busk in the wintry streets beside a needy musicians' sign, the usually elegant Forsythe turns up as a disintegrating ghoul, a golf ball embedded in his skull. *Scrooged* is not subtle stuff, and since Murray's comic persona is uniquely hands-off in terms of emotion, his final impassioned speech about the true meaning of Christmas is as embarrassing as Chaplin's at the end of *The Great Dictator*. Rowdy stuff for the light in head. BC

Scrubbers
(Mai Zetterling, 1982, GB) Amanda York, Chrissie Cotterill, Elizabeth Edmonds, Kate Ingram, Amanda Symonds.
93 min.
Part-written by Roy 'Scum' Minton, this follows the career of two Borstal girls: a lesbian orphan who busts herself back inside to rejoin her faithless lover, and a single mother who, separated from her child, puts an ever-increasing gap between them by her escalating violence. But blatant audience manipulation backfires: the more the mother bashes her way through the film, the less your sympathies are engaged. A script which bridles with a grim wit more akin to *Porridge* than *Scum*-in-a-skirt, and a filtered use of colour so dense it appears to be shot in black-and-white, are both points in favour. But no amount of effing and blinding, unconvincing slow-motion violence, scatological inventiveness, and buckets of flying excreta, can hide the fact that *Scrubbers* is a very noisy film that manages to say nothing novel. An entertaining washout. FL

Scum
(Alan Clarke, 1979, GB) Ray Winstone, Mick Ford, Julian Firth, John Blundell, Phil Daniels, John Fowler.
97 min.
Roy Minton's teleplay about Borstal life and its vicious circle of violence, remade as a movie after being banned by the BBC: a toughened docudrama (schools of BBC/old Warners/Corman) that carries the same force as the improvised weapons Ray Winstone uses to bludgeon his way through the Borstal power structure. A far-from-blunt instrument itself (and containing some necessary leavening humour), this is potentially knife-edge film-making: will audiences buy the reformist liberalism and stomach the violence, or in fact buy the violence and racism and miss the message? The careful calculations show, but you're still likely to leave at the end feeling righteously angry. PT

Scuola, La
see School

Sea Chase, The
(John Farrow, 1955, US) John Wayne, Lana Turner, David Farrar, Tab Hunter, Lyle Bettger, James Arness, Claude Akins, John Qualen.
117 min.
WWII yarn with The Duke as a German, though not of course a card-carrying Nazi. That's Lana Turner as a sultry spy who goes all gooey. The Duke is captain of a freighter leaving Sydney Harbour en route for the Mudderland as the war begins. If he makes it across the Pacific and the Atlantic, he'll be arrested for *not* card-carrying; and if he doesn't – then blame the British Navy, who have him in their gunsights. Lyle Bettger makes a strutting SS psycho, and Tab Hunter is a very Aryan-looking cadet. ATu

Seacoal
(Murray Martin, 1985, GB) Amber Styles, Ray Stubbs, Corrina Stubbs, Benny Graham, Tom Hadaway, Murray Martin.
82 min.
Mixing fiction with documentary, this looks at the lives of the sea-coal collectors working the beaches of the Northumberland coast, and at the economic and political realities permeating their hard, rude existence. Gritty Loach-style realism, leavened by lyrical camerawork and a strong – even romantic – sense of community, as seen through the eyes of a woman newly introduced to the unrelenting labour of hardship by her chauvinist lover. Intelligent and sensitive, but be warned: the dialect and accents are sometimes impenetrable. GA

Sea Gull, The
(Sidney Lumet, 1968, GB) James Mason, Vanessa Redgrave, Simone Signoret, David Warner, Harry Andrews, Ronald Radd, Eileen Herlie, Kathleen Widdoes, Denholm Elliott, Alfred Lynch.
141 min.
Basically an actors' film, for which Lumet has assembled a distinguished cast, found a marvellous lakeside location in Sweden, and vaselined the lens to give an air of autumn melancholy. That the result is sometimes dull and almost always unsatisfactory, despite excellent performances, is thanks partly to the traditional English-speaking failure to play Chekhov for comedy and let his tragedy take care of itself (hence the miscasting of Mason as a darkly brooding Trigorin, the over-intensity of Warner's Konstantin); and partly because the prerequisite of any Chekhov cast is a sense of familiarity bred of a lifetime together (so how come Signoret's Arkadina, with an accent you could cut with a knife, has the impeccably English Harry Andrews as a brother?). TM

Sea Gypsies, The
(aka Shipwreck!)
(Stewart Raffill, 1978, US)
Robert Logan, Mikki Jamison-Olsen, Heather Rattray, Cjon Damitri Patterson, Shannon Saylor.
101 min.
A fairly formulary kid's adventure out of the Wilderness-Family-Robinson mould, this makes a half-hearted attempt to break away from the

triteness of the Disney stereotype, before succumbing to a catalogue of the beauties and savageries of nature and the blissful benefits of family life. Peopled with such representatives of the 'New Consciousness' as a widowed father ready to sail his young daughters round the world to show them 'what kind of man' he is, an independent female photojournalist, and a 12-year old street-smart black stowaway, the film spends a short time promising interesting tensions between them, before dumping them on the Alaskan coastline to fend for themselves in exemplary Baden-Powell fashion (though the women do turn out to be the better providers) while awaiting rescue/attempting escape. *Déja vu* for all but the youngest viewer. PT

Sea Hawk, The

(Michael Curtiz, 1940, US) Errol Flynn, Flora Robson, Brenda Marshall, Claude Rains, Henry Daniell, Donald Crisp, Alan Hale, Gilbert Roland, Una O'Connor.
127 min. b/w.
A hugely enjoyable swashbuckler from the days when 'packaging' wasn't such a dirty word and Jack Warner was a master of the art. Flynn plays novelist Rafael Sabatini's privateer, royally encouraged into deeds of derring-do against the wicked Spanish, as an amalgam of *Captain Blood* (also Sabatini-based) and *Robin Hood*. Robson repeats her Good Queen Bess from *Fire Over England*. House action specialist Curtiz directs what is in total a remake of a 1924 Frank Lloyd silent. Practice, as they say, makes perfect. PT

Seance on a Wet Afternoon

(Bryan Forbes, 1964, GB) Kim Stanley, Richard Attenborough, Mark Eden, Nanette Newman, Judith Donner, Patrick Magee, Gerald Sim.
116 min. b/w.
Kim Stanley can hardly be known to most of today's cinema audiences: she appears in only four films, and her fame rests on her stage work (even that is pretty sparse). She plays degenerating women, yet her technique is not the Mad Medusa writ large, such as Swanson in *Sunset Boulevard* or Davis in *What Ever Happened to Baby Jane?* She's creepier than that, and more believable. In the movie, she is married to a meek and mild Attenborough – a childless marriage in a gloomy Victorian house. She concocts a scheme to kidnap a child, and then gain notoriety by discovering the child's whereabouts through psychomancy. Her performance is utterly superb, and so too is Attenborough's: with his leather crash helmet, goggles and clapped-out motorbike, he looks like a reject Hell's Angel from *Orphée*. ATu

Sea of Love

(Harold Becker, 1989, US) Al Pacino, Ellen Barkin, John Goodman, Michael Rooker, William Hickey, Richard Jenkins, Paul Calderon, Gene Canfield.
113 min.
Efficient enough as a thriller, but what makes this mandatory viewing is the return of Pacino. There are isolated scenes as good as anything he's done, and if the role is less demanding than Sonny in *Dog Day Afternoon* or Michael in *The Godfather*, his presence lifts the production in the way De Niro lifted *Midnight Run*. Lonely, middle-aged, divorced, Frank Keller (Pacino) breaks a major cop rule by falling for a suspect while investigating a series of Lonely Hearts murders. Someone has been answering ads in a singles' magazine and bumping off the guys; and Helen (Barkin), sexually predatory in spades, could be the one. Following a night of passion – the standard frisk for weapons takes on tropical dimensions here – Frank scratches her from the list. The conclusion is pretty guessable, and you wonder whether the trust theme wouldn't play outside the genre. Goodman brings warmth and wit to Keller's sidekick, and Barkin is just fine. BC

Sea of Sand

(Guy Green, 1958, GB) Richard Attenborough, John Gregson, Michael Craig, Vincent Ball, Barry Foster, Andrew Faulds, Ray McAnally.
97 min. b/w.
Just before the Battle of El Alamein, in 1943, the Eighth Army's Long Range Desert Group launches an attack on one of Rommel's key petrol dumps. Object: knock out the Afrika Korps. Standard heroics, partially redeemed by trenchant visuals, courtesy of former cameraman Green, and a typically sweaty performance by Attenborough. TJ

Search, The

(Fred Zinnemann, 1948, US) Montgomery Clift, Aline MacMahon, Wendell Corey, Ivan Jandl, Jarmila Novotna.
105 min. b/w.
As the first Hollywood movie to be shot in post-WWII Germany, the authenticity of Zinnemann's film cannot be faulted. Recounting the wartime experiences of a ten-year-old Czech boy (Jandl), separated from his mother and cared for by an American soldier (Clift), it seems snatched from the pages of a newspaper. Although there's a slight suspicion that (as in Rossellini's work from this period) the plight of children is being used as a sort of emotional shorthand, the integrity and moving effect of this piece is never really in doubt. TJ

Searchers, The 100 (100)

(John Ford, 1956, US) John Wayne, Jeffrey Hunter, Vera Miles, Ward Bond, Natalie Wood, Hank Worden, Henry Brandon, Harry Carey Jr, Olive Carey, John Qualen, Antonio Moreno.
119 min.
A marvellous Western which turns Monument Valley into an interior landscape as Wayne pursues his five-year odyssey, a grim quest – to kill both the Indian who abducted his niece and the tainted girl herself – which is miraculously purified of its racist furies in a final moment of epiphany. There is perhaps some discrepancy in the play between Wayne's heroic image and the pathological outsider he plays here (forever excluded from home, as the doorway shots at beginning and end suggest), but it hardly matters, given the film's visual splendour and muscular poetry in its celebration of the spirit that vanished with the taming of the American wilderness. TM

Searching for Bobby Fischer (aka Innocent Moves)

(Steven Zaillian, 1993, US) Max Pomeranc, Joe Mantegna, Joan Allen, Ben Kingsley, Laurence Fishburne, Michael Nirenberg.
110 min.
An absorbing, fact-based study – a first feature from the writer of *Schindler's List* – of the trials and triumphs of a young chess prodigy. Max Pomeranc (a top 100 player himself) is Josh Waitzkin, seven-year-old son of New York sports reporter Fred (Mantegna), a child whose fascination with chess is initially spurred on by park hustler Vinnie (Fishburne, remarkably convincing) before pushy dad signs him up with tutor Bruce Pandolfini (Kingsley). As Josh battles through increasingly daunting tournament matchplay, his progress reflects his mentors' unfulfilled aspirations as much as the his own developing strategic maturity. Ranking performances, and evocative camerawork from veteran Conrad Hall. True, James Horner's score seems to have strayed in from a fists-in-the-air crowd-pleaser, but it's the one weak link in an accomplished, unexpectedly winning movie. TJ

Searching Wind, The

(William Dieterle, 1946, US) Robert Young, Sylvia Sidney, Ann Richards, Dudley Digges, Albert Basserman, Norma Varden, Douglas Dick.
108 min. b/w.
A smooth and surprisingly sharp-tongued version of Lillian Hellman's play berating America for its persistently blinkered isolationism during the years preceding World War II. The weakness it never quite overcomes is the taint of soap opera apparent in the way every major political crisis, from Mussolini's March on Rome in 1922 to the Munich Pact by way of the Spanish Civil War, is trotted out as yet another stage in the diplomat hero's domestic troubles between wife (Richards, who keeps hobnobbing with well-placed Fascists) and Other Woman (Sidney, a journalist who tries to arouse his political awareness). Heady stuff, but given credibility by fine performances and excellent packaging. TM

Seashell and the Clergyman, The (La Coquille et le Clergyman)

(Germaine Dulac, 1928, Fr) Alex Allin, Lucien Bataille, Gênica Athanasiou.
44 min. b/w.
One of the most celebrated of French avant-garde movies of the '20s, partly because Antonin Artaud wrote the script, partly because the British censor of the time banned it with the legendary words 'If this film has a meaning, it is doubtless objectionable'. Artaud was reputedly unhappy with Dulac's realisation of his scenario, and it's true that the story's anti-clericalism (a priest develops a lustful passion that plunges him into bizarre fantasies) is somewhat undermined by the director's determined visual lyricism. But the fragmentation of the narrative and the innovative imagery remain provocative, and the film is of course fascinating testimony to the currents of its time. TR

Season Five (Fassloh Padjom/Cinquième saison)

(Rafi Pitts, 1997, Iran/Fr) Roya Nonahali, Ali Sarkhani, Parviz Poorhosseni, Ghorban Nadjafi, Golab Adineh.
80 min.
Based on an unfilmed screenplay by Bahram Beyzai (a thorn in the side of the Shah's censors during an earlier flowering of Iranian cinema), this is a first feature from an Anglo-Iranian director working out of France. On the day of his intended wedding to Mehrbanou, villager Kamarat deliberately rekindles the ancient feud between their clans, which the marriage was supposed to heal. He goes on to lease a dilapidated bus to provide the first mechanised transport to the nearest town. The jilted bride, implacably set on revenge, pushes her hapless brother into launching a rival service – and the internecine struggle soon starts to threaten lives. The vision of the village as a mullah-free zone tips you the wink that there are elements of social satire in play here, which will inevitably by-pass non-Iranians, but there is plenty to enjoy in the performances and the working out of the underlying morality play. TR

Season of Dreams (aka Stacking)

(Martin Rosen, 1987, US) Christine Lahti, Frederic Forrest, Megan Follows, Jason Gedrick, Ray Baker, Peter Coyote, James Gammon, Kaiulani Lee.
109 min.
Director Rosen made animated features in Britain (*Watership Down* and *The Plague Dogs*) before moving to the US for this unenlightening rites-of-passage tale set in 1954 Montana. Megan Follows is the teenager trying to hold off the romantic advances of older youth Gedrick while rebuilding her own relationship with hard-pressed waitress mum Lahti, left to cope on her own when her husband is hospitalised. A solid cast make it all easily watchable, but there's not quite enough in the material to make it really distinctive (the similar *Desert Bloom*, for instance, has an A-bomb angle that gives its story a significant lift). TJ

Season of the Witch

see Jack's Wife

Seawife

(Bob McNaught, 1957, GB) Richard Burton, Joan Collins, Basil Sydney, Cy Grant, Ronald Squire.
81 min.
Ludicrously portentous adaptation of JM Scott's novel (originally published as *Sea-Wyf and Biscuit*) elucidating the real-life mystery of the small ads in which one 'Biscuit' agonised after the whereabouts of a certain 'Seawife'. Flashback to World War II unfolds a hasty mash of romance, religion and racism, so silly that it's almost disarming, as four survivors from a ship torpedoed during the fall of Singapore make it by life raft to a desert island. There broody Burton falls for Collins, but gets no joy because she (though wearing no wimple) is actually a nun, and God seems to have answered her with a miracle to pull them through; meanwhile the token racist (Sydney) succumbs to devilish impulses to get rid of the token black (Grant), and starts suffering guilts... Rossellini was the original director but copped out, sensible fellow. TM

Sea Wolf, The

(Michael Curtiz, 1941, US) Edward G Robinson, John Garfield, Ida Lupino, Alexander Knox, Gene Lockhart, Barry Fitzgerald, Stanley Ridges, Howard da Silva.
90 min. b/w.

A superbly malevolent adaptation of Jack London's story about two fugitives (Garfield and Lupino) who come together on a ship, only to find themselves trapped as witnesses to a demonic battle of wits between Robinson's psychopathic captain (a Bligh in sadism, an Ahab in driven obsession) and an altruistic writer (Knox) attempting to assert intellectual dominion with no other weapon but his understanding. Given Robert Rossen's strikingly literate script, Sol Polito's wonderfully eerie camerawork, and Robinson's terrific performance – all pulling together to elaborate the Luciferian motto borrowed from Milton by which the captain lives, 'Better to reign in hell than to serve in heaven' – this is one of Curtiz's best movies. TM

Sea Wolves, The

(Andrew V McLaglen, 1980, GB/US/Switz) Gregory Peck, Roger Moore, David Niven, Trevor Howard, Barbara Kellerman, Patrick Macnee, Patrick Allen, Bernard Archard, Faith Brook, Kenneth Griffith, Donald Houston.
122 min.

The Sea Wolves answers the pressing problem of how to repay the debt we owe to all those superannuated English stiff-upper-lippers now that all the major war campaigns have been filmed. Solution: dredge up some creaking piece of now-it-can-be-told war marginalia about a retired Territorial regiment of polo-playing boozers (The Calcutta Light Horse!) who bid goodbye to the memsahib for a fortnight and blow up some Jerry ships in Goa harbour. McLaglen previously demonstrated a certain competence with physical action in The Wild Geese, but here it's a very pedestrian hour-and-three-quarters before the final crunch – a risible affair with geriatric schoolboys wheezing about, getting hernias. Peck and Niven shamble amiably through the dross as if it were a Navaronian old boys reunion (class of '44), and Roger Moore finds new ways of smirking in a dinner jacket. As a genre – the arterio-sclerotic war movie – it'll never catch on. CPea

Sebastian

(Svend Wam, 1995, Nor/Swe) Hampus Björck, Nicolai Cleve Broch, Ewa Fröling, Helge Jordal.
84 min.

Sixteen going on 17, Sebastian is in the back-bedroom casualty stage, spending hours cloistered away when he's not dawdling around his rural Norwegian home town with the pals he's known for years. Mum and dad sense there's something eating at him, but only in the course of this rudimentary youth drama does Sebby himself come to terms with what it is – he thinks he's gay, and he's sure he's in love with best mate Ulf. Plodding and obvious. TJ

Sebastiane

(Derek Jarman/Paul Humfress, 1976, GB) Leonardo Treviglio, Barney James, Neil Kennedy, Richard Warwick, Donald Dunham, Ken Hicks, Lindsay Kemp.
86 min.

Not exactly typical of the British independent cinema, this not only tackles an avowedly 'difficult' subject (the relationship between sex and power, and the destructive force of unrequited passion), but does so within two equally 'difficult' frameworks: that of exclusively male sexuality, and that of the Catholic legend of the martyred saint, set nearly 1,700 years ago. Writer/director Jarman sees Sebastian as a common Roman soldier, exiled to the back of beyond with a small platoon of bored colleagues, who gets selfishly absorbed in his own mysticism and then picked on by his emotionally crippled captain. It's filmed naturalistically, to the extent that the dialogue is in barracks-room Latin, and carries an extraordinary charge of conviction in the staging and acting; it falters only in the slightly awkward elements of parody and pastiche. One of a kind, it's compulsively interesting on many levels. TR

Seclusion Near a Forest
(Na samote u lesa)

(Jiri Menzel, 1975, Czech) Josef Kemr, Zdenek Sverák, Dana Kolárová, Ladislav Smoljak.
97 min.

Menzel was still treading very warily after five years in the political doghouse. Skilfully avoiding any sort of dangerous involvements or interpretations, this is a featherweight comedy about the rural hazards encountered by a city family when they rent a summer cottage with a view to permanence. Not least of their problems, especially since they want to start renovations in a hurry, is the obstinate presence of the ancient peasant owner, who has changed his mind about selling up and going to live with his family. There's not a lot to it, but with exquisite camerawork casting a shimmering summery haze over his characteristically delicate blend of tenderness and humour in observing human foibles, Menzel transforms the film into a magical invocation of a lost, simpler and more leisurely world. TM

Seconda Volta, La

see Second Time, The

Second Awakening of Christa Klages, The
(Das zweite Erwachen der Christa Klages)

(Margarethe von Trotta, 1977, WGer) Tina Engel, Sylvia Reize, Katharina Thalbach, Marius Müller-Westernhagen, Peter Schneider.
93 min.

Few film-makers wear their hearts as openly on their sleeves as Margarethe von Trotta, and her fascination with women (their relationships with each other and their definition – often redefinition – of themselves) is as apparent in this, her first solo feature, as it was in the later The German Sisters or Friends and Husbands. Christa Klages (Engel) is a young mother who turns terrorist and bank robber to prevent the closure of a crèche which she helps to run and her daughter attends. On the run with her friend and sometime lover, Christa is pursued by the police, and more mysteriously by a young woman (Thalbach) who was her hostage in the bank raid. What von Trotta has to say about her women is compelling, and she remains one of the few filmmakers to portray terrorists convincingly. But the enigma of the hostage runs through the film as elusively as a character in a dream – vitally important at any given moment, but irritatingly meaningless when taken as a whole – and undermines the conviction of this feminist thriller which is otherwise so gloriously rooted in West Germany's present. FD

Second Best

(Chris Menges, 1993, US) William Hurt, Chris Cleary Miles, Jane Horrocks, Keith Allen.
101 min.

William Hurt, who works in a sub-Post Office in rural Wales, is the son of self-absorbed parents. He decides to adopt a child and is finally allocated the disturbed son of Keith Allen's wild survivalist con. The movie starts in a threatening register with the boy being 'abducted' from school and taken to a woodland foxhole where he is forced to promise to love only his father, and then settles down to a 'Play for Today'-like examination of the difficult path towards trust and acceptance between boy and adopted father. Hurt excels in these buttoned-down roles and his performance here is something of an exemplar, full of intelligence and feeling. Allen's character and performance are misguided, but they don't scupper the film. WH

Second Breath

see Deuxième Souffle, Le

Second Chance

(Rudolph Maté, 1953, US) Robert Mitchum, Linda Darnell, Jack Palance, Reginald Sheffield, Roy Roberts.
82 min.

Originally made in 3-D, this unpretentious and very enjoyable RKO thriller has Mitchum as a prizefighter helping out ex-gangster's moll Darnell in Mexico, where she is being stalked by hired killer Palance. Far from noir, given the simplicity of the plot and the lack of romantic pessimism, it nevertheless works very well thanks to the assured performances (the luscious Darnell makes a lovely companion for the similarly statuesque Mitchum), and to a genuinely exciting climax aboard a broken-down cable car. GA

Second Chance
(Si c'était à refaire)

(Claude Lelouch, 1976, Fr) Catherine Deneuve, Anouk Aimée, Charles Denner, Francis Huster, Niels Arestrup, Colette Baudot, Jean-Pierre Kalfon.
99 min.

'The whole idea is mad!' screams lawyer Denner when the newly imprisoned heroine (Deneuve) suggests that they conceive a child in her cell to give her something to live for. But this is a film by Claude Lelouch, the master of eccentric kitsch, and everything is mad – not least the finale, when yet another man and another woman find total happiness on the heights of Mont Blanc. But for once the madness isn't full-blooded enough to be satisfying: instead of juggling four storylines in the air, Lelouch is content with one and a half. And time hangs increasingly heavy as the plot ambles along portentously, following the heroine's adjustment to the pangs of life and love after sixteen years in a swish prison. Not exactly a cruel disappointment, but a disappointment none the less. GB

Seconds

(John Frankenheimer, 1966, US) Rock Hudson, Salome Jens, John Randolph, Will Geer, Jeff Corey, Richard Anderson, Murray Hamilton, Karl Swenson, Khigh Diegh, Wesley Addy.
106 min. b/w.

Is your life getting you down? Do you think you could do things properly if you had another chance? Then, like middle-aged banker Arthur Hamilton (Randolph), you could go in for Seconds. Summoned by a mysterious corporation, Randolph undergoes drastic plastic surgery and psycho-adjustment, and emerges (after much doctorspeak) as handsome Rock Hudson, aka boho artist Tony Wilson. With a faked death taking care of his old persona, the re-model lives it up in a swanky Malibu Beach house. Actually, all we see of his groovy new life is a Bacchanalian grape-squishing orgy and a cocktail party – not much meaningful stuff there, and it's no wonder he thinks about going back for 'thirds'... In this grim parable, Wong Howe's discomforting, distortive photography evokes the claustrophobic nightmare of a man who finds that 'freedom' is a dodgy concept, a mind is not to be changed by place or time, there are always strings attached, and they're pulled by the guys who play at God. The ending is so downbeat that it's positively six feet under. AB

Second Time, The
(La Seconda Volta)

(Mimmo Calopresti, 1996, It/Fr) Nanni Moretti, Valeria Bruni Tedeschi, Valeria Milillo, Roberto de Francesco.
80 min.

Calopresti's feature debut is a modest but intriguing study of the psychological legacy of the terrorism that beset Italy in the '70s. Set in a hauntingly gloomy Turin, the film follows the actions and emotions of Moretti, a lecturer and ex-Fiat executive, after he recognises in the street a woman sentenced to 30 years in prison for having shot him in the head some 12 years earlier. As he sets about getting to know her – she, not having recognised him, thinks he's merely trying to chat her up, and pretends she's just a normal working woman – Calopresti leaves us in the dark as to Moretti's exact intentions, so that his cool, intelligent drama also achieves a welcome level of unsettling suspense. GA

Secret, The (Le Secret)

(Robert Enrico, 1974, Fr/It) Jean-Louis Trintignant, Marlène Jobert, Philippe Noiret, Jean-François Adam, Solange Pradel.
103 min.

Best known for his short film Incident at Owl Creek, Enrico here deals once more with a man at the end of his rope. Trintignant plays a fugitive from an institute who is befriended by an artistic couple (Noiret, Jobert), refugees from Paris now living a slightly dull life in the country. Suspense is generated somewhat needlessly through teasing the audience about Trintignant's sanity: is he a maniac on the loose, or as he claims, the victim of a government conspiracy? The film shamelessly litters red herrings along the way. More promisingly, it elsewhere displays (but does not explore) the philosophical anxieties that the French have so often found in American movies, leading to an increasing fatalism as events move towards a bleak conclusion. But too much remains withheld from the audience by the film's sleights of hand, although Trintignant's worried performance counters one's graver doubts. CPe

Secret, The (Fengjie)

(Ann Hui, 1979, HK) Sylvia Chang, Teresa Chiu, Tsui Siu-Keung, Alex Man, George Lam.
89 min.
Aside from fleeting glimpses of a hospital and a disco, Hui's first feature shows nothing of modern Hong Kong – which is fitting, since the theme is the hold of the past over the present and the focus is on the power of superstition in the characters' lives. Based on a then recent real-life murder mystery, the film takes an inconclusive autopsy, a supposedly dangerous madman and a suspected haunting in its stride as it moves to a truly hysterical climax. Gory, suspenseful, impressive. TR

Secret Admirer

(David Greenwalt, 1985, US) C Thomas Howell, Lori Laughlin, Kelly Preston, Dee Wallace Stone, Cliff De Young, Leigh Taylor-Young, Fred Ward.
98 min.
An unsigned billet doux slipped between the pages of 'The Pageant of World History' triggers an escalating comedy of errors as it passes round a group of college kids and their equally gullible parents, massaging each reader's *amour propre* with wild fantasies of a secret admirer. Here is the stuff of classic French farce – Marivaux rewritten Neil Simon-style – were it not that this game of love and chance offers no notable insights into the lust, delusion, and other deadly boring sins of Middle America. Howell, the young star of *The Outsiders* and *Red Dawn*, evinces a certain ingenuous comedic flair. For the rest, the characters are rather less memorable than the Pepsi cans, Fruit Loops and other brand name junk foods looming large in the foreground of almost every frame. And how could anyone endorse an ending where-in the girl-next-door gives up a world cruise to stay at home with the boy-next-door? SJo

Secret Adventures of Tom Thumb, The

(Dave Borthwick, 1993, GB) Nick Upton, Deborah Collard, Frank Passingham, John Schofield, Mike Gifford.
60 min.
This animated film from Bristol's bolexbrothers studio impresses for its interwoven techniques (mainly claymation and pixilated live action) and its nightmare vision. Born to a poor, boorish couple after an accident at an artificial insemination plant, little Tom is soon abducted by government heavies and subjected to torturous experiments. With the help of a mutant, he escapes from the lab into a cruel, filthy world where desperate little people wage an unending war of survival against the ordinary 'giants'. Borthwick, the writer, editor and director, has the knack of making everyday things seem peculiarly strange and sinister. GA

Secret Agent, The

(Alfred Hitchcock, 1936, GB) Madeleine Carroll, John Gielgud, Peter Lorre, Robert Young, Percy Marmont, Lilli Palmer, Charles Carson, Michael Redgrave.
85 min. b/w.
Based loosely on a couple of Somerset Maugham's *Ashenden* stories, this thriller may not be one of Hitchcock's best English films, but it is full of startling set pieces and quirky characterisation. About a British spy (Gielgud) who travels to Switzerland to kill an enemy agent, but murders the wrong man, it delights in the rivalry for Madeleine Carroll's affections between Gielgud, Lorre and Young, and in the numerous opportunities for unusual thriller ingredients that the (studio-concocted) Swiss settings afford: a chase through a chocolate factory, murder atop a mountain, death in a quaint church. And there is a more serious side, with Gielgud doubting his profession and patriotism after killing the wrong man. GA

Secret Agent, The (aka Joseph Conrad's The Secret Agent)

(Christopher Hampton, 1996, US/GB) Bob Hoskins, Patricia Arquette, Gérard Depardieu, Jim Broadbent, Christian Bale, Eddie Izzard, Elizabeth Spriggs, Peter Vaughan, Robin Williams.
95 min.
In 1936, Alfred Hitchcock took the bones of Joseph Conrad's 1907 novel and sculpted the contemporary thriller *Sabotage*, with Oscar Homolka as a cinema owner waging a terrorist campaign on London with the unwitting assistance of his wife and her brother. Hampton's version restores the tale to the 1880s, and is more respectful of Conrad's narrative, characters and tone, yet it's this new adaptation which travesties the novel. At least, the Hitchcock – minor, by his standards – catches an authentic whiff of terror. On the plus side, Hoskins is well cast as the 'corpulent anarchist', Verloc, who is in fact a double agent working for the Russian embassy and Scotland Yard. With his bowler hat, umbrella and squat rotund frame, Hoskins makes an appropriately sorry spy, but Hampton squanders the performance. After an atmospheric opening, he loses his grip on the material and shuffles awkwardly between a handful of variable cameos. Most disastrous is Arquette's phonetically precarious Mrs Verloc, Cockney by way of Timbuktu. TCh

Secret Agent Club, The

(John Murlowski, 1996, US) Hulk Hogan, Richard Moll, Lesley-Anne Down, Matthew McCurley, Edward Albert, Lyman Ward, Barry Bostwick.
90 min.
Raymond Chase (Hogan) seems to be a 'dweeb', a klutzy single-parent who can't catch a ball to save his life. In fact he's a member of the secret government agency, Shadow. Ray's pre-teen son Jeremy (McCurley) discovers this the hard way when father turns superhuman in a failed effort to elude the henchmen of terror-queen Eve (Down). Chase has Eve's billion-dollar laser gun, and she wants it back. An inane farce, dreadfully acted, with echoes of *Crocodile Dundee II* and several Bond films. DA

Secret Beyond the Door

(Fritz Lang, 1948, US) Joan Bennett, Michael Redgrave, Anne Revere, Barbara O'Neil, Natalie Schaefer, Paul Cavanagh.
98 min. b/w.
An example of Hollywood's mooncalf affair with Freud during the '40s, ending in an absurd instant cure for psychopathy. But the premise is fascinating, and fraught with Gothic overtones as Bennett's heroine ('This is not the time to think of danger', she murmurs at the outset, shaking off premonition, 'this is my wedding day') gradually realises that, married to an architect (Redgrave) who literally and obsessively 'collects' rooms in which murders have occurred, she must uncover the secret of the one room always kept locked. Lang himself didn't think much of the film, but nevertheless set it under his usual sign of destiny ('This is not the time to think of danger...') and invested it with roots in older myths of the magic power of love. His direction is masterly, imposing meanings and tensions through images that are spare, resonant and astonishingly beautiful. A remarkable film. TM

Secret Ceremony

(Joseph Losey, 1968, GB) Elizabeth Taylor, Mia Farrow, Robert Mitchum, Pamela Brown, Peggy Ashcroft.
109 min.
It's difficult to know why Mitchum, slouching through a few scenes in the ill-fitting disguise of an ageing, bearded academic with little girls on his mind, should have accepted this part. Taylor, however, is very fine as a tacky madonna: a devout prostitute who's offered a respite from the streets when a regressive child-woman called Cenci (Farrow in long wig and Pollyanna tights) adopts her as substitute mother and moves her into a mansion of art-déco splendour. No wonder then that Taylor/Laura should fervently pray 'Oh Lord, let no one snatch me from this heaven'; and as the strange 'secret ceremonies' begin, her treatment of Cenci displays the same mix of greed and generosity. Losey's mannered direction, somehow entirely appropriate, makes for a memorable film. JCl

Secret Cinema

(Paul Bartel, 1965, US) Amy Vane, Gordon Felio, Philip Carlson.
28 min.
An early film by Bartel, putty-faced schoolmaster (and comic) of the Roger Corman stable (he made *Death Race 2000*), which exudes an amiable naïveté. A mad secret society, of uncertain membership and dubious morality, runs a 'secret cinema' in which they screen *ciné-vérité* films of the characters in this film losing their marbles. Some of it is hilarious; all of it is fresh enough; but none of it is avant-garde: the camp sensibility of the New York underground now increasingly looks like irony updated. CA

Secret de Mayerling, Le

(Jean Delannoy, 1948, Fr) Jean Marais, Dominique Blanchar, Jean Debucourt, Silvia Monfort.
96 min. b/w.
Time was, circles were, you were liable to be treated like the scum of the earth for even *seeing* a Jean Delannoy movie, let alone finding things to admire in it. Yet this seizes the attention from the start: midnight, the Archduke in his carriage, his body propped up by boards, the head rolling back and forth, Marie Vetsera marched away between two strong shoulders, feet dragging in the snow, her shattered forehead glimpsed through reflected light. This is narrative cinema at its most vigorous, and the whole piece manifests an intelligence unfazed by a subject apparently squeezed dry already by Litvak and Ophuls. Marais' regal authority is to the fore, even as another Marais quality – he is sometimes referred to by the euphemism 'feline' – undermines his suitability for the role of a Habsburg stud. BBa

Secret Face, The (Gizli Yuz)

(Omer Kavur, 1991, Ger) Zuhal Olcay, Fikret Kushan, Utkay Aziz.
115 min.
This esoteric movie starts with a quote from Ferriduddin Attar and gets more obscure by the moment. A young man having defied his father by refusing to study, takes to photographing faces in late night Istanbul cafés. These he shows to a mysterious woman. She sends him off to locate one of the faces, a clockmaker in a provincial town. The woman subsequently disappears and he embarks on a year-long quest (through the City of the Sad and the City of the Hearts) to find her. The movie is hard to categorise. If the faces seen against the walls and the shots of strange lone trees remind one of Tarkovsky, the woman's Maria Casarès-like face receding into the shadows evokes the poetry of Cocteau; and the unexplained histories and motivations of the characters suggest Kafka. Director Omer Kavur is nevertheless determinedly his own man. It's a disconcerting, captivating, spiritual journey, perfectly accompanied by atmospheric oscillating, one-note music reminiscent of Popul Vuh. WH

Secret Friends

(Dennis Potter, 1991, GB) Alan Bates, Gina Bellman, Frances Barber, Tony Doyle, Joanna David, Colin Jeavons, Rowena Cooper, Ian McNeice, Davyd Harries.
97 min.
Beset by fantasies careering out of control, John (Bates) is driven towards madness and a total obliteration of self. As a child, he conjured up an imaginary 'secret friend' rebellious enough to withstand his father's Victorian discipline. Years later, the friend is still on hand, feeding the anger and guilt which find a compliant victim in John's wife Helen (Bellman). In this adaptation of his own novel *Ticket to Ride*, Potter's complex linking of sexual fantasy and destructive forces is unwieldy and embittered. Nothing is what it seems. John appears to have committed a murder, and as the film intercuts between past and present to reveal clues, he struggles with amnesia and impending insanity. Did he, will he kill his wife? Is she, was she a prostitute? Sex exacts penalties ('We all pay for it'), bleak humour recompenses ('Sex is funny, a bloody hoot'), and women, tiresomely, are by turns dependent and predatory. CM

Secret Game, The

see Jeux Interdits

Secret Garden, The

(Fred M Wilcox, 1949, US) Margaret O'Brien, Herbert Marshall, Dean Stockwell, Gladys Cooper, Brian Roper, Elsa Lanchester.
92 min. col & b/w.

The first screen version of the Frances Hodgson Burnett story has O'Brien (in her last film role before she retired, aged 12) as the orphan who transforms the lives of embittered uncle Marshall and his bed-ridden son Stockwell when she starts tending an off-limits garden in the grounds of their country mansion. All is gothic doom and gloom to begin with, Ray June's b/w camerawork streaking the imposing mansion sets with dark shadow, but more and more light intrudes, brightening with master Stockwell's psychological regeneration (disarmingly insightful from a child performer), and culminating in a climactic *coup de cinéma* when Technicolor proves the very essence of Life itself. MGM's production recalls *The Wizard of Oz*, but there's some stiffness here and Garland is not eclipsed. TJ

Secret Garden, The

(Agnieszka Holland, 1993, GB) Maggie Smith, John Lynch, Kate Maberly, Heydon Prowse, Andrew Knott, Laura Crossley.
100 min.

Frances Hodgson Burnett's much-loved children's novel could all too easily come across on screen as the last word in period fustian, but the unforced approach of Holland and scriptwriter Caroline Thompson pierces to the emotional core of a still potent tale. Shipped back from colonial India to the inhospitable Yorkshire manor of her reclusive hunchback uncle (Lynch), orphan Mary Lennox (newcomer Maberly) tangles petulantly with the no-nonsense housekeeper (Smith). Even so, the spoilt girl's rebelliousness soon distils into a recuperative influence over her bedridden cousin Colin (Prowse) when she begins to tend the long-neglected walled garden tucked away in the grounds. With well-judged performances played straight, and topical subtexts (Green consciousness, the dysfunctional family), this 'children's' film sets no age limit on its potential audience. TJ

Secret Honor

(Robert Altman, 1984, US) Philip Baker Hall.
90 min.

Alone in his study late at night, Richard Milhouse Nixon ponders the pardon he's been offered for the Watergate scandal, and contrasts his secret honour with his public shame. Cue for raving resentment galore and perceptive insights into the politics of power and money. Made with a student crew at the University of Michigan, Altman's one-man theatrical adaptation, for all its dense verbosity, is resolutely cinematic, employing a prowling camera to illuminate the dark areas of its melancholy, megalomaniac hero's soul. While Baker Hall, ranting with drunken fervour at presidential portraits and a bank of security videos, suggests nothing less than a sometimes lucid, sometimes lunatic incarnation of mediocrity, irredeemably tainted by fame and failure. Fascinating stuff. GA

Secret Invasion, The

(Roger Corman, 1964, US) Stewart Granger, Raf Vallone, Henry Silva, Mickey Rooney, Edd Byrnes, William Campbell, Mia Massini.
95 min.

This *Dirty Dozen* predates Aldrich's by three years, with Granger leading five convicts, against the promise of free pardons, in a suicidal World War II bid to kidnap an influential Italian general from a Nazi fortress in Dubrovnik. Corman delivers the action all right, making particularly suspenseful use of a device – lacking watches, each member of the team keeps time by rhythmically snapping his fingers so that stages of the kidnap plan can be coordinated – which springs several ingenious surprises on both Nazis and audience. But the real fascination of the film is the extent to which it is cloaked in characteristic Corman/Gothic motifs: Silva's role as the killer with 'dead eyes', inevitably fated to kill his own love; the disguise as hooded monks adopted for the final showdown; Granger's death in an idyllic forest glade after using his own blood to lead a pack of tracker dogs astray. Unexpectedly, the overall tone is strangely elegiac. TM

Secret Life of an American Wife, The

(George Axelrod, 1968, US) Walter Matthau, Anne Jackson, Patrick O'Neal, Edy Williams, Richard Bull, Paul Napier.
92 min.

Basically, as Axelrod has pointed out, the feminine angle on *The Seven Year Itch* (which he also scripted, from his own play): a charmingly immoral little morality play about a suburban housewife, apprehensive about her declining desirability, who nervously hires herself out for the afternoon as a callgirl in order to test the response. Jackson's excellent performance is matched by Matthau's as her client, an ageing Hollywood star sagging in all directions, and too riddled with hangover, sinus and self-pity to maintain his image as a sex symbol. The 25-minute bedroom sequence in which the pair gradually strip away their protective shells and pretences is funnier and more touching than anything Neil Simon ever dreamed up. Axelrod makes his mistakes here and there, but never resorts to the snide sniggers with which Wilder disfigured *The Seven Year Itch*. TM

Secret Life of Walter Mitty, The

(Norman Z McLeod, 1947, US) Danny Kaye, Virginia Mayo, Boris Karloff, Fay Bainter, Ann Rutherford, Florence Bates, Thurston Hall, Robert Altman.
105 min.

A buoyant adaptation from James Thurber (who in turn offered Sam Goldwyn $10,000 to leave the book well alone), following the vibrant fantasy life of a timid publishing worker whose escape into daydream makes up for a humdrum existence, until, that is, genuine adventure falls into his lap in the shape of distressed heiress Virginia Mayo. It degenerates into slapstick at the end, but Danny Kaye makes pathological shyness seem charismatic.

Secret Nation, The (La Nación clandestina)

(Jorge Sanjinés, 1989, Bol) Reynaldo Yujra, Delfina Mamani, Orlanda Huanca, Roque Salgado.
120 min.

Eight years in the making, with a cast of hundreds of Aymara Indians – assisted, the credits tell us, 'by the powerful didactic gods of the altiplano' – Sanjinés' film explores the multiplicity of nations composing his native Bolivia. The 'secret nation' is the indigenous culture that continues alongside the urban-based and westernised political structures. It is also the 'society within society' of a nation divided into soldiers and spies on the one hand, and those labelled and hunted down as 'subversives' on the other. The conflicts and contradictions are explored through the person of Don Sebastián, a coffin-maker living on the city outskirts, who returns to his native village to die in the dance of expiation and death that opens and closes the film. Wearing a mask of both angel and devil, his propitiation is to the extraordinary high and misty mountains, wild skies and haunting music that are the true 'gods' – or inspiration – of this powerful film. AH

Secret of Convict Lake, The

(Michael Gordon, 1951, US) Glenn Ford, Gene Tierney, Ethel Barrymore, Zachary Scott, Ann Dvorak, Barbara Bates, Cyril Cusack, Richard Hylton, Helen Westcott, Jeanette Nolan, Ruth Donnelly.
83 min. b/w.

Somewhat ponderous revenge-morality tale (allegedly true), set in the California mountains in 1871, about five escaped convicts who seek refuge in a hamlet where the women have been left to hold the fort while their menfolk are off prospecting. Ford, it turns out, is intent on killing Tierney's absent fiancé who in another life framed him for murder and vamoosed with some loot. Moves along quite nicely, with one of the convicts, a disturbed teenage rapist, pitchforked to death by the women, but as soon as Ford shaves off his wicked whiskers it becomes pretty obvious how things are going to turn out. JPy

Secret of My Success, The

(Herbert Ross, 1987, US) Michael J Fox, Helen Slater, Richard Jordan, Margaret Whitton, John Pankow, Christopher Murney, Fred Gwynne.
111 min.

In this, the ultimate yuppie wish-fulfilment movie, Fox plays an enterprising post-room boy who, simply by reading the mail which passes through his hands, devises a brilliant scheme for streamlining his rich uncle's multinational corporation. On his way up the ladder of success, Fox catches the eye of attractive fellow-executive Helen Slater, but also suffers the unwelcome amorous advances of his boss' wife – whose husband is in turn involved in a clandestine office affair with the capable Ms Slater. So far, so neat. But as the action shifts from boardroom to bedroom, the film degenerates into a silly bed-hopping farce, and the corporate back-stabbing gets filed away until the final reel, when the whole thing is resolved by a wave of the wicked wife's magic wand. The same old capitalist fairytale, in other words. NF

Secret of NIMH, The

(Don Bluth, 1982, US) voices: Derek Jacobi, Elizabeth Hartman, Arthur Malet, Dom DeLuise, Hermione Baddeley, John Carradine, Aldo Ray.
82 min.

Two years earlier, several Walt Disney animators (including Bluth) left the company to set up on their own, complaining that Disney was lowering its animation standards and heading for the dreadful cut-price techniques that are pumped out daily on children's television. This is their first animation feature, and visually they make their point well. It's a spectacular return to the shimmering, mesmerising deep-focus animation associated with Disney's classic period: a marvellous use of lighting to create atmosphere, dew-drops glisten from every tree, and the villains are as primally terrifying as cartoon villains should be. The choice of material (Robert O'Brien's novel *Mrs Frisby and the Rats of NIMH*) is less fortunate, since it lacks the wonder of early Disney, and the mouse heroine is far too insipid and twee. It's still a pretty effective family film, though. DP

Secret of Roan Inish, The

(John Sayles, 1993, US) Mick Lally, John Lynch, Jeni Courtney, Eileen Colgan, Richard Sheridan.
103 min.

This Irish fable, from a novel by Rosalie K Fry, may be pretty atypical of John Sayles' work, but it's still a lovely movie. Set in a remote Irish fishing community in the '40s, it charts the experiences of a young girl who comes to stay with her grandparents and is intrigued by the mysterious, seemingly fantastic stories of an infant relative's death. Tales within tales, a subtle sense of economic and social realities, fine landscape photography and strong performances make for an engrossing, unusual fantasy. GA

Secret of Santa Vittoria, The

(Stanley Kramer, 1969, US) Anthony Quinn, Anna Magnani, Virna Lisi, Hardy Krüger, Sergio Franchi, Renato Rascel, Giancarlo Giannini, Valentina Cortese, Eduardo Ciannelli.
140 min.

Lost without a message to sledgehammer home, Kramer turned to bombastic comedy with this World War II yarn of an Italian village's attempts to hide a million bottles of wine from the occupying Germans. Just to keep the irritation factor of his movies constant, though, he hand-picked a full-throttle cast more than adequate to the task of previewing the effect of Sensurround. PT

Secret of the Sword, The

(Ed Friedman/Lou Kachivas/Marsh Lamore/Bill Reed/Gwen Wetzler, 1985, US) voices: John Erwin, Melendy Britt, Alan Oppenheimer.
91 min.

It is a dark and stormy night in this animated feature. Prince Adam of Eternia (alias He-Man) is summoned to Castle Grayskull and magicked to Etheria to quest the meaning of the secret of the sword, a secret worthy of Dynasty. In the Whispering Woods, our Aryan hero teams up with swish Bo and villeins against the evil

Hordak, leader of the Horde, whose villains include Shadow Weaver and other Mattel characters from the TV series *He-Man and Masters of the Universe*. Magna-Beam Transporters are no defence against Good Manners. There is the usual gamut of silly voices and gang of goody-goody creatures, including a gluttonous green tiger, but the cuteness is kept to a minimum. The amalgam of fairytale, sci-fi and Greek mythology is exciting, the backgrounds dynamic, the music catchy, the pace furious: kids will love it. MS

Secretos del corazón
see Secrets of the Heart

Secret People
(Thorold Dickinson, 1951, GB) Valentina Cortese, Serge Reggiani, Audrey Hepburn, Charles Goldner, Irene Worth, Megs Jenkins, Reginald Tate, Athene Seyler, Michael Shepley.
96 min. b/w.
A striking thriller inspired by a newspaper item about a woman working for the IRA who suffered a change of heart, informed on her husband, and was forced to assume a new identity under police protection. Set in London in 1937, the film generalises the issue by turning the heroine into a refugee from the dictatorship that killed her father (Fascist Italy by any other name), and who is persuaded by her lover to join a terrorist plot to kill the dictator, which goes horribly wrong. Although slipping into convention here and there (stereotyping of minor characters, the facile melodrama of the final scene), the script manages to avoid offering easy answers to its questions as to whether violence corrupts and whether it can ever be justified, at least until the scene of the bomb outrage at a society reception, almost Hitchcockian in its suspense as the wrong people come and go and a waitress finally becomes the victim. Superbly staged by Dickinson (directing with fluid subtlety throughout), this sequence brings the film unequivocally out on the side of its motto borrowed from Auden: 'We must love one another or die'. But the complex abysses that lie between private feelings and political beliefs are nevertheless plumbed with remarkable thoroughness in the relationship between Cortese and Reggiani (both giving superb performances). TM

Secret Places
(Zelda Barron, 1984, GB) Marie-Thérèse Relin, Tara MacGowran, Claudine Auger, Jenny Agutter, Cassie Stuart, Ann-Marie Gwatkin, Pippa Hinchley, Adam Richardson.
98 min.
Zelda Barron's first feature as director is a sympathetically observed story of how a group of English schoolgirls react when an exotic German refugee arrives in their midst early in World War II. The film's main quality lies in a luminous performance from Tara MacGowran as Patience, who befriends the refugee and experiences with her the early rites of sexual passage. Its weakness is its lack of ambition: little is made of the wartime setting (handled to better effect elsewhere – *Imitation Game, Rainy Day Women, f Plenty*, and the central relationship is shut off just at the point when it becomes fascinating. As such, stifled by its own good manners, *Secret Places* cries out to be shown on the small rather than the large screen. RR

Secret Policeman's Ball, The
(Roger Graef, 1979, GB) John Cleese, Peter Cook, Clive James, Eleanor Bron, Pete Townshend, Rowan Atkinson, John Williams, Billy Connolly, Tom Robinson, Michael Palin.
94 min.
Second of the ragbag stage revues in which satirists and musicians did their thing on behalf of Amnesty International (the first was *Pleasure at Her Majesty's*). With Cleese and Cook sticking to their party pieces, much of the material seemed pretty *déjà vu* even at the time. But there were highlights like Rowan Atkinson's malevolent roll-call of a class of imaginary pupils, and Billy Connolly's ruminations on the mysteries of life ('How come, every time you're sick, there's always diced carrots in it?') in a disquisition on drunken Scotsmen. TM

Secret Policeman's Other Ball, The
(Julien Temple, 1982, GB) Rowan Atkinson, Alan Bennett, John Cleese, Billy Connolly, Sting, Bob Geldof, Phil Collins, John Fortune, Michael Palin, John Wells.
99 min.
Technically smoother than its predecessors, this is otherwise the mixture as before: comics and musicians, sometimes in unfamiliar permutations, doing their party pieces on behalf of Amnesty. The musical punctuations are often outstanding: Sting soaring on a contemplative 'Message in a Bottle', Jeff Beck and Eric Clapton reunited for a loose-limbed blues. Among the bright moments: a perfectly controlled dialogue for John Fortune and Alan Bennett, a Billy Connolly ramble, and John Wells in his Denis Thatcher role. JC

Secret Policeman's Third Ball, The
(Ken O'Neill, 1987, GB) Joan Armatrading, John Cleese, Robbie Coltrane, Phil Cool, Duran Duran, Stephen Fry, Hugh Laurie, Ben Elton, Lenny Henry, Lou Reed, Ruby Wax.
96 min.
Real music is provided by Joan Armatrading, Lou Reed, Mark Knopfler with Chet Atkins, and Peter Gabriel, whose Biko lament closes the film. There is also a tribute to Los Campañeros of El Salvador by Paul Brady, but otherwise – apart from a few swipes at Reagan and Thatcher courtesy of Spitting Image – politics are out. All the comedians are on top form: Fry & Laurie cocking up 'The Hedge Sketch' to perfection; Phil Cool impersonating the XR4i'd rep on the jammed M25; Lenny Henry as an ancient bluester; and Ben Elton on liberation sexuality (ie. DIY). O'Neill's direction makes for more than just a run-of-the-mill variety bill. MS

Secret Rapture, The
(Howard Davies, 1993, GB) Juliet Stevenson, Joanne Whalley-Kilmer, Penelope Wilton, Neil Pearson, Alan Howard, Robert Stephens, Milton McRae.
95 min.
Whiffle, whiffle, whiffle. There's a dead old man in the bed and Stevenson is balled on the floor, weeping, moisture pouring from every facial orifice. Enter Wilton, surreptitiously. Giving her father's corpse a scant glance, not even noticing her grieving sister, she rummages through the jewellery on the dressing table and purloins a ring. Caught out, she's shamed, then furious. It's a response Stevenson's Isobel Coleridge seems to provoke, an illustration of writer David Hare's central question: why do good people make everyone around them behave badly? Everyone wants to dump or defuse the alcoholic widow (Whalley-Kilmer). Long-suffering Isobel takes her on, only to discover too late she sucks up everything in her path. The film is something of an '80s morality play, with characters behaving like Lust, Greed and Ambition instead of real people, but thanks to first-time director Davies' luminous moods, accelerating menace and chiaroscuro images, it packs a considerable emotional punch – while holding the mirror implacably up to the audience. SFe

Secrets
(Frank Borzage, 1933, US) Mary Pickford, Leslie Howard, C Aubrey Smith, Blanche Frederici, Doris Lloyd, Ned Sparks.
85 min. b/w.
The last picture Mary Pickford acted in, a fairly nutty tale of pioneer homesteaders heading across America in covered wagons. Leslie Howard makes the most unlikely Westerner in movie history (but there must have been some wimps out West), and Pickford suffers all the privations of the journey and the Indian attacks just the way she always did – Victorian picturebook style. First time around, Little Mary wrote off $300,000 on the film in 1930. She started over in 1932, hiring sentimental story specialist Borzage (who had made the silent version with Norma Talmadge in 1924) to direct. It flopped, arguably because it didn't feel like a real Western. Today it's an engaging curiosity. MA

Secrets
(Philip Saville, 1971, GB) Jacqueline Bisset, Robert Powell, Per Oscarsson, Shirley Knight, Martin C Thurley.
107 min.
Drearily familiar stuff as a young married couple (Powell and Bisset), still in love but bored with each other, each enjoy a brief encounter (with Knight and Oscarsson, respectively), and then return – surprise, surprise – renewed and refreshed to their marriage. The acting is fair, but script and direction are dismayingly obvious. This was the first feature shot in Super-16mm, a process designed to reduce costs and (not that you would guess from this sample of pure predictability) 'liberate' film-makers from conventional pressures. TM

Secrets
(Michael Pattinson, 1992, Aust) Beth Champion, Malcolm Kennard, Dannii Minogue, Noah Taylor.
90 min.
On the day the Beatles arrive in Melbourne, the accompanying scrum at the hotel sees five teenagers accidentally locked in the basement, where confined surroundings force them to reveal the innermost longings behind their fandom, or indeed hatred of the Fab Four. This antipodean cross between 'I Wanna Hold Your Hand' and *The Breakfast Club* is intriguing for its opening archive footage, but screenwriter Jan Sardi (*Shine*) makes the characters and their revelations all too cut-and-dried. Taylor, though, is engaging as a self-proclaimed man of the world, complete with fake Scouse accent. TJ

Secrets & Lies (100)
(Mike Leigh, 1995, GB) Timothy Spall, Brenda Blethyn, Marianne Jean-Baptiste, Phyllis Logan, Claire Rushbrook, Elizabeth Berrington, Michele Austin, Lee Ross, L esley Manville.
141 min.
Her adoptive parents now dead, Hortense (Jean-Baptiste), a young middle-class optometrist, decides to find her natural mother. What she doesn't anticipate is that her search will lead to Cynthia (Blethyn), a sad, boozy woman saddled with an argumentative, determinedly morose road-sweeper daughter, Roxanne (Rushbrook), and lent spasmodic moral and financial support by her brother Maurice (Spall), a successful wedding-and-portrait photographer whose prissy suburban house is the obsessive delight of his wife Monica (Logan). When Hortense first phones Cynthia, she knows nothing of the family or the tensions that divide it – and is she really her daughter anyway? After all, she's black, and Cynthia's white. Even as Leigh derives gentle comedy from the plight, aspirations and often pathetic attempts at communication of Cynthia and her tribe, an immense, unforced sympathy is extended to all involved, a generosity of spirit thoroughly in keeping with the performances. Everyone's superb, Blethyn and Spall in particular. Yes, it's long, visually a little static, and rather narrowly concerned with the everyday experiences of one family, but that depth, focus and intensity of concentration result in a film of extraordinary emotional riches. Spellbinding. GA

Secrets of a Soul (Geheimnisse einer Seele)
(GW Pabst, 1926, Ger) Werner Krauss, Ruth Weyher, Jack Trevor, Pavel Pavlov, Ilka Grüning.
7,265 ft. b/w.
Fascinating as the first 'serious' attempt to deal with Freudian psychoanalysis on the screen, Pabst's film is also notable for bringing a solid intellectual perspective to the 'expressionist' idiom of contemporary German movies. It's essentially a bourgeois melodrama, about a chemistry professor whose frustrated desire to father a child meshes with his jealousy of his wife's childhood sweetheart. The professor's fantasies are, of course, generously illustrated in the remarkable dream sequences, awash with sexual symbols. The deciphering of these dreams as he consults a psychoanalyst is necessarily too pat, but Pabst's aims still look as bold and daring as they must have done in 1926. TR

Secrets of the Heart
(Secretos del corazón)
(Montxo Armendáriz, 1997, Sp) Andoni Erburu, Carmelo Gómez, Charo López, Vicky Peña, Silvia Munt, Alvaroo Nagore.
105 min.
A nine-year-old gradually discovers the skeletons in the family closet when he and his elder brother, who live with their aunts in Pamplona during the 1960s, pay a visit to their widowed mother in a Pyrenean village. The portrait of lives partly defined by repression and superstition is sensitive, the re-creation of the rituals of rural Basque life fascinating, and the characterisations mostly subtly detailed. Unlike such comparable films as The Spirit of the Beehive and Cria Cuervos, however, this one never really pulls away from the curious young protagonist to tell us much about the wider political realities of the period. GA

Secrets of the
Phantom Caverns
(Don Sharp, 1984, GB) Robert Powell, Lisa Blount, Richard Johnson, Timothy Bottoms, Anne Heywood, AC Weary.
90 min.
Lacklustre British adventure in which Powell's mission to install a radio transmitter in a Spanish mountainside is stymied by archeologists' shock discovery of a malign presence deep within the caverns. It's one of those occasions when you wait a long time for something to happen, only to sigh with disappointment when the great whatever-it-is is finally unveiled. TJ

Secret Wedding
(Boda secreta)
(Alejandro Agresti, 1989, Arg/Neth/Can) Tito Haas, Mirtha Busnelli, Sergio Poves Campos, Nathan Pinzon, Floria Bloise, Elio Marchi.
95 min.
A naked man emerges at dawn on the deserted streets of Buenos Aires. Arrested and questioned, he protests total ignorance of his identity or past; but files lead the police to assume he is one Fermin Garcia, a bus driver and political activist reported to have been executed 13 years before. He travels to a remote village to find his girlfriend; she, like the other villagers, doesn't recognise him...Agresti's third feature, part love story, part political drama, returns to a theme from his earlier Love Is a Fat Woman: the spectre of the desaparecidos, the thousands who 'vanished' in Argentina's unfunny dirty little war. Again he employs parable to investigate the hypocrisy at work in the 'new democratic' Argentina, his target the unholy trinity of church, business and state. This, a calmer, more mature and subtle film, has beautiful colour compositions which lend dignified repose to the rural landscape; the performances (Haas' Fermin is excellent) are restrained and expressive. Fired by a feeling of intense, hidden anger and disappointment, the film has all the persuasive force of a nightmare giving way to reality. WH

Sect, The (La Setta)
(Michele Soave, 1991, It) Kelly Leigh Curtis, Herbert Lom, Mariangela Giordano.
120 min.
This third film by Italian horror maestro Dario Argento's most gifted acolyte (Soave previously directed Stagefright and The Church) establishes him as a horror stylist in his own right. Relying more on suspense and scares than graphic gore, it's an atmospheric chiller about a young German schoolteacher (Curtis) who becomes involved with the Manson-like devil-worshipping sect headed by Lom. The Alice in Wonderland references, subterranean secrets, and general dreamlike ambience echo Argento's Inferno; but the stylish visuals and bravura set pieces achieve a subtle terror that is all Soave's own. NF

Section Spéciale
(Special Section)
(Costa-Gavras, 1975, Fr/It/WGer) Louis Seigner, Michel Lonsdale, Jacques Perrin, Ivo Garrani, Bruno Crémer, François Maistre, Roland Bertin, Henri Serre, Pierre Dux.
118 min.
One of Costa-Gavras' glossy political melodramas, set in Occupied France and dealing with one of the Vichy government's shabbier episodes: the drafting of retroactive anti-terrorist laws which allowed the French judiciary to re-sentence a number of pathetically harmless prisoners in order to appease the Germans. At first the glossy production provides a rather effective counterpoint to the political intrigue. But issues here become clear-cut – over-simplified, even – and the visual elegance looks increasingly hollow. The script becomes bogged down in wordy repetitions on the corruption of power and the power of corruption. The final third – the show trials – is pure playing to the gallery, in much the same way as Z. By way of compensation, some of the performances – Louis Seigner, especially, as the Minister of Justice – stand against the film's tendency towards caricature. CPe

Seduction of Joe Tynan, The
(Jerry Schatzberg, 1979, US) Alan Alda, Barbara Harris, Meryl Streep, Rip Torn, Melvyn Douglas, Charles Kimbrough, Carrie Nye.
107 min.
A film using familiar themes – the personal pressures of success, power as an aphrodisiac – to recount its Kennedy-style success story of the young, dynamic, but blandly selfish Senator Tynan (Alda), who jeopardises family and friends in pursuit of power, and succumbs with understandable swiftness to Meryl Streep. Though it shows political and personal distinctions blurred by ambition and by the inevitable erosion of honesty, the film still seems to want the system to work. Perhaps Schatzberg deferred too much to Alda, who stars and wrote the script; a pity, because he seems less sympathetic to Tynan than Alda is. Once again Schatzberg proves himself a strong director of actors, but keeps the film within the safe confines of semi-sophisticated Adult Entertainment. CPe

Seedling, The
see Ankur

See Here My Love
see Ecoute Voir...

See How They Fall
see Regarde les hommes tomber

Seems Like Old Times
(Jay Sandrich, 1980, US) Goldie Hawn, Chevy Chase, Charles Grodin, Robert Guillaume, Harold Gould, George Grizzard, Yvonne Wilder.
121 min.
After such hits as The Goodbye Girl, Murder by Death and California Suite, screenwriter/playwright Neil Simon has cornered the market in Broadway-inspired snappy comedies for, or about, the suave and sophisticated: all in all, 'the kind of movies they used to make'. In this madcap comic farce, the homage to '30s screwball is explicit in the title, unflagging pace, and plot: a liberal lawyer (Hawn), married to an uptight DA (Grodin), gets messed up by a rogue ex-husband (Chase), their ex-convict servants, and her six dogs. A little of Adam's Rib or The Philadelphia Story creeps in as you drift into wondering how Cary Grant or Katharine Hepburn would have mastered the roles of slightly cracked, snobbish professionals. But after an hour, you begin to realise the irony of Neil Simon winning awards for Outstanding Writing: it doesn't mean it's funny, just that it stands out like a sore thumb. Once you realise that, the whole exercise gets to be an expertly crafted drag. DMacp

See No Evil, Hear No Evil
(Arthur Hiller, 1989, US) Richard Pryor, Gene Wilder, Joan Severance, Kevin Spacey, Alan North, Anthony Zerbe, Louis Giambalvo, Kirsten Childs.
102 min.
Pryor is blind, Wilder is deaf. Together they witness a murder, become principal suspects, and are threatened by the real killers: you can probably work out the rest for yourself. Given it's a comedy, you might imagine a scene in which the blind man drives a car, and you'd be right. You might imagine a fight in which the blind man does the punching, following instructions from his sighted pal; right again. Pryor is his usual loudmouth self; Wilder is in shy, sensitive mode. There's a resolutely untouching scene in which the pair discuss their relative philosophies for dealing with disability, but otherwise it's a long, painfully unfunny series of things being smashed up and fallen over. Worst of all, the male villain has the most embarrassing 'English' accent heard in many a long year, old chap, don't you know. JMo

See You in Hell, Darling
see American Dream, An

See You in the Morning
(Alan J Pakula, 1988, US) Jeff Bridges, Alice Krige, Farrah Fawcett, Drew Barrymore, Lukas Haas, David Dukes, Frances Sternhagen, Linda Lavin, Theodore Bikel.
119 min.
This risible divorce drama opens strikingly. Successful psychiatrist Larry Livingston and wife Jo (Bridges and Fawcett) with a couple of cute infants gambolling in the countryside; cut to another happy couple (Krige and Dukes) with two kids moving into their New York dream home; cut to Bridges and Krige in flagrante. Turns out her concert pianist husband died, while his vapid wife left him to continue a modelling career. It's about starting over, with Krige's kids forced to come to terms with a (somewhat ingratiating) new dad. The story of their new life is reasonably told, but the Farrah Fawcett subplot is a major drawback as Bridges skips over to remonstrate with his ex-wife, visit his small children, and swap philosophies with a sickeningly spiritual mother-in-law (Sternhagen). There's a lengthy scene with Bridges (who rises engagingly above the tosh) reading a retch-inducing bedtime story about a dolphin called Caring, and spook-eyed, sinister Krige is less than ideally cast as a sweet young mother. SFe

Sehnsucht der
Veronika Voss, Die
see Veronika Voss

Seins de glace, Les
(Someone Is Bleeding)
(Georges Lautner, 1974, Fr) Alain Delon, Mireille Darc, Claude Brasseur, Nicoletta Machiavelli.
97 min.
Brasseur as a hack TV writer who meets the beautiful Darc on a beach, and finds that she is being kept more or less a prisoner by the mysterious Delon in a villa. What he doesn't know (yet) is that she is a psychopath... and Delon is pretty mixed up too. A routine but watchable, well-acted thriller adapted from Richard Matheson's first novel (Someone Is Bleeding), which it manages to screw up, not least by being altogether too glossy. TM

Seize the Day
(Fielder Cook, 1986, US) Robin Williams, Joseph Wiseman, Jerry Stiller, Glenne Headly, Tony Roberts, Richard Shull, Jo Van Fleet, Eileen Heckart.
93 min.
A Robin Williams film for people who don't really like Robin Williams, this edgy adaptation of Saul Bellow's novel sees the star for once submerging his overpowering comic persona inside the demands of the role – and the result is certainly the least mannered, arguably the most effective performance of his screen career to date. Williams is Tommy Wilhem, a failed actor hitting 40 and still scraping a buck selling children's furniture, who vainly looks to his successful doctor father (Wiseman) and a commodities broker pal (Stiller) to help him out of the mess his life's become. As a grim, compelling trudge through familiar Bellow neuroses, it makes for surprisingly uncompromising viewing. TJ

Sélect Hotel
(Laurent Bouhnik, 1996, Fr) Julie Gayet, Jean-Michel Fête, Serge Blumental, Marc Andreoni, Sabine Bail, Eric Aubrahn.
85 min.
Volatile, alienated but still hanging together, Tof (Fête) is loyal to his drugged out sister Nathalie (Gayet), but frustrated by her inability to dispense with the insistent services of her smarmy pimp (Andreoni). Their problems escalate as Tof

turns to robbery, and, carried away with contempt and a sudden sense of power, sexually humiliates a shopkeeper and his wife. Tragedy beckons. Set in and around a seedy hotel in Place Clichy, the movie (from a first time writer/director) clearly isn't out to paint a pretty picture. Though rough at the edges, it features fine photography and an impressive use of music. There may be misjudgments: using Blumental's wronged shopkeeper as a kind of audience identification figure, for example, or the misleading faux documentary opening; but overall the film has conviction, honesty and the smack of truth. WH

Self-Made Hero, A
see Héros très discret, Un

Sellout, The
(Peter Collinson, 1975, GB/It) Richard Widmark, Oliver Reed, Gayle Hunnicutt, Sam Wanamaker, Vladek Sheybal, Ori Levy, Assaf Dayan.
102 min.
Routine espionage thriller in which the CIA and KGB play silly buggers in Israel, much to the chagrin of the local secret service. Meanwhile a more personal triangle works itself out between former colleagues Reed and Widmark, and Hunnicutt, ex-lover of the former now living with the latter. But all this confusion adds up to very little. The script relates everything, with increasing tedium, to the games that people and nations play. Everything else about the film helps make it a journeyman's outing – from the boring references to old Bogart movies to the uncomfortable acting, tourist locations, and succession of unnecessary camera angles. CPe

Semaine de Vacances, Une (A Week's Holiday)
(Bertrand Tavernier, 1980, Fr) Nathalie Baye, Michel Galabru, Philippe Noiret, Flore Fitzgerald, Gérard Lanvin, Jean Dasté, Philippe Léotard.
103 min.
Twelve years on from 1968, and the children of Marx and Coca-Cola are hitting their first mid-life crises' – in this case forcing a Lyonnaise teacher (Baye) to take une semaine de vacances and reassess her life. Tavernier avoids the reactionary ploys of 'unmarried women' stories, and his combination of solidly-crafted European finesse and fluid transatlantic shooting style effectively staves off intimations of the film's middlebrow nature. At the same time, the tentative celebrations of life's minor felicities – food, friendship, a community of good, nameless people – provide genuine warmth, and the final mood of cautious optimism is justified surprisingly well. CPea

Semi-Tough
(Michael Ritchie, 1977, US) Burt Reynolds, Kris Kristofferson, Jill Clayburgh, Robert Preston, Bert Convy, Roger E Mosley, Lotte Lenya, Richard Masur, Carl Weathers, Brian Dennehy.
107 min.
Though not as sharp or as unusual as Ritchie's earlier Smile, this is still a delightful, gentle satire on the American ideal of winning, which also takes broad but often hilarious swipes at fashionable health fads. Concerning the cracks that appear in the strange ménage à trois between pro-footballers Reynolds and Kristofferson, and multi-divorcee Clayburgh, when the guru of a weird EST-style therapy cult finds a disciple in Kristofferson, the film succeeds because the comedy derives less from smart one-liners than from character. Although some of Ritchie's targets are a little obvious, what makes the film so appealing is the immense generosity extended toward the protagonists. Beautifully performed, subtly scripted, it accentuates the sadness of Ritchie's later descent into more conventional material. GA

Senator Was Indiscreet, The
(George S Kaufman, 1947, US) William Powell, Ella Raines, Peter Lind Hayes, Arleen Whelan, Hans Conried, Allen Jenkins, Myrna Loy.
74 min. b/w.
Playwright George S Kaufman had a somewhat arm's length relationship with Hollywood

(although he was famously well paid for his work on A Night at the Opera) and this jaunty political satire, scripted by Charles MacArthur, proved to be his only film as director. The lost diary of presidential candidate Powell, and the incriminating detail contained within it, provide the impetus for some mild, somewhat unfocused fun. Powell's Thin Man partner Myrna Loy pops up unbilled. TJ

Sender, The
(Roger Christian, 1982, GB) Kathryn Harrold, Zeljko Ivanek, Shirley Knight, Paul Freeman, Sean Hewitt, Marsha Hunt.
91 min.
Send what? Send where? Send you screaming up the walls, that's what. Picked up after a suicide attempt and plonked in the bonkers bin, Ivanek is soon inflicting unpleasant nightmares on the other inmates and nursing staff. Not on purpose, you understand, but it's nevertheless disturbing for the sensitive young Dr Gail Farmer (Harrold). A first feature by Roger Christian, whose short The Dollar Bottom won a 1980 Oscar, this is a bewildering blur of reality and hallucination which sacrifices many of its interesting psychodramatic angles to a lot of full-blooded Grand Guignol. AB

Send Me No Flowers
(Norman Jewison, 1964, US) Rock Hudson, Doris Day, Tony Randall, Paul Lynde, Edward Andrews, Clint Walker.
100 min.
Probably the best of the Doris Day/Rock Hudson vehicles, extracting a surprising amount of black (though sugar-coated) comedy out of the situation in which hypochondriac Rock, mistakenly believing he is dying, thoughtfully tries to arrange a remarriage for his widow-to-be with an old flame (Walker); whereupon she, sniffing out self-interest, suspects an attempt to cover up an affair of his own. Nicely set in a pastel-coloured suburban dreamworld, but the ineradicable blandness gets you down in the end. TM

S'en fout la mort (No Fear, No Die)
(Claire Denis, 1990, Fr) Isaach de Bankolé, Alex Descas, Jean-Claude Brialy, Solveig Dommartin.
91 min.
From the director of the acclaimed Chocolat, this is something else entirely: rough-edged almost to the point of being documentary, it's a look at the world of cockfighting in the Paris suburbs, with de Bankolé as an African lovingly guiding his feathered charges through a casual daily bloodletting. An extremely uncomfortable film to watch – although it was apparently filmed without violence to the birds – it has a seedy, claustrophobic power that says as much about human as about animal exploitation. Wenders protégée Dommartin lends a largely decorative presence, but New Wave veteran Brialy stands out as a slimeball entrepreneur. Abdullah Ibrahim again provides broody, pacy music. JRo

Seniors, The (aka The Senior)
(Rod Amateau, 1978, US) Jeffrey Byron, Gary Imhof, Dennis Quaid, Lou Richards, Priscilla Barnes.
87 min.
US college seniors open a bogus sex clinic for reasons that soon become obvious, yet unwittingly find themselves at the centre of a million-dollar business. A lot of foolish plotting is wrapped around not very much in the way of excitement – with a young, very geeky Dennis Quaid. A satire of sorts. TJ

Sensations
(Juan Esteban/Viviana Cordero, 1993, Ecuador) Juan Esteban, Viviana Cordero, Ricardo Contag, Luis Miguel Campos.
110 min.
A newly formed band, sequestered in the high Andes, get together musically and emotionally. Zac, the leader, is the arrogant one, recently returned from a successful few years in New York, who tries to discipline the disparate musicians: a gay schizo hedonist, Zac's footloose brother, a guy in touch with his Ecuadorian roots,

a sexy singer known as 'the fake'. Lines like, 'Let's make Inca blues!' and 'Art is flying, not making money!' sum up the philosophical debate. It's beautifully shot and contains extensive sequences of the group jamming, rehearsing and playing . The music is mostly composed by the film's writing/directing/producing team of Esteban and Cordero. WH

Sense and Sensibility
(Ang Lee, 1995, US) Emma Thompson, Hugh Grant, Kate Winslet, Alan Rickman, Greg Wise, Elizabeth Spriggs, Robert Hardy, Hugh Laurie, Harriet Walter, Imelda Staunton, Imogen Stubbs, Jemma Jones.
136 min.
Rendered homeless and relatively poor by the patrilineal laws that dictated their father's will, Elinor and Marianne Dashwood (Thompson and Winslet) are not exactly the most marriageable young women in a world where desirability is usually conferred by property and birth. Shy, kindly Edward Ferrars (Grant) – favoured by the pragmatic Elinor – is likely to be disinherited should he marry 'low', while solid Col Brandon (Rickman) is forgotten by the headstrong Marianne as soon as popular, dashing John Willoughby (Wise) appears on the scene. First impressions, however, aren't always reliable. While this is hardly adventurous or original cinema, it's most enjoyable. Thompson's screenplay stays true both to Austen's themes (the gulf between romanticism and materialism, the difference between hearsay, opinion and empirical knowledge) and to her delightfully ironic wit. Grant is just Grant (albeit with old togs and deeper stammer), and Rickman sometimes looks a little creepy, but Thompson and Winslet give fine performances ably supported by the rest of the ensemble. GA

Sense of Loss, A
(Marcel Ophüls, 1972, US/Switz) Ian Paisley, Bernadette Devlin, Michael Farrell, Rita O'Hare, Gerry O'Hare, Sam Dowling.
132 min.
Though the BBC's rejection of Ophüls' documentary in 1972 added fuel to the arguments of those who maintained that a conspiracy of silence operated regarding reportage of events in Northern Ireland, the fact is that his film is not particularly enlightening. Ophüls' partisanship is undisguised from very early on, but it's still difficult to forgive the way he loads the evidence (Bernadette Devlin interviewed on a deserted beach, Paisley fulminating from his pulpit); and the long funeral sequence at the end is shot and edited as all-stops-out melodrama. When left to speak for themselves, the spokesmen for the British presence and some of the more bigoted Protestants are sufficiently eloquent in condemning themselves without interference from Ophüls' self-satisfied liberal smugness. Still, in the absence of anything better... RM

Senso (The Wanton Countess)
(Luchino Visconti, 1954, It) Alida Valli, Farley Granger, Massimo Girotti, Heinz Moog, Rina Morelli, Marcella Mariani, Christian Marquand.
115 min.
Like other Visconti melodramas, sumptuous in its Technicolor expressionism, Senso sees heterosexual love through homosexual eyes: Farley Granger (in the Helmut Berger role) plays the young Austrian officer in the force occupying Venice in the 1860s, and Alida Valli (in the Burt Lancaster role) the older, married woman who falls insanely in love with him, betraying her husband, her principles, and finally Italy itself in the headlong folly of her passion. The man sadistically exploits his own beauty and willingly prostitutes himself; the woman submits to one humiliation after another, her masochism finally indistinguishable from madness. Fassbinder's version of this story was called The Bitter Tears of Petra von Kant. Visconti, using English dialogue by Tennessee Williams and Paul Bowles, generates emotions so violent that even his operatic vision can barely contain them. TR

Sensual Paradise
see Together

Sentimental Journey

(Walter Lang, 1946, US) Maureen O'Hara, John Payne, William Bendix, Cedric Hardwicke, Mischa Auer, Connie Marshall.
94 min. b/w.
A domestic drama in which a Broadway actress (O'Hara) succumbs to a heart complaint of which her doting producer husband (Payne) is miraculously unaware, yet in the meantime she's adopted orphan Connie Marshall and trained the child to care for the old boy after she's gone. The film is more or less the epitome of '40s slush. Depending on temperament, it's either vastly enjoyable as camp spectacle, or steadfastly resistible as cheesiest hokum. TJ

Sentinel, The
see Sentinelle, La

Sentinel, The

(Michael Winner, 1976, US) Chris Sarandon, Cristina Raines, Martin Balsam, John Carradine, José Ferrer, Ava Gardner, Arthur Kennedy, Burgess Meredith, Sylvia Miles, Deborah Raffin, Eli Wallach, Christopher Walken, Beverly D'Angelo, Tom Berenger, Jeff Goldblum.
92 min.
A film which plagiarises so brazenly – and so badly – that it seems like little more than a pile of out-takes from recent supernatural successes. Take a Catholic heroine and her treacherous lover in a spooky apartment block (*Rosemary's Baby*). Add the nutty priest and the ominous prophecy from *The Omen*, not to mention a touch of demonic masturbation from *The Exorcist*. And what do you have? In Winner's hands, just a mass of frequently incomprehensible footage, acted so badly that even the most blatant shocks go for little. Out of sheer desperation, given the thinnest basis imaginable for a horror movie (fashion model finds her apartment is over the gateway to hell), some genuinely deformed people are brought in for the climax. The only frightening thing about *The Sentinel* is its director's mind. DP

Sentinelle, La (The Sentinel)

(Arnaud Desplechin, 1992, Fr) Emmanuel Salinger, Thibault de Montalembert, Jean-Louis Richard, Valerie Dreville, Marianne Denicourt, Jean-Luc Boutte, Fabrice Desplechin.
145 min.
Uneven but fascinating movie in which a medical student from a diplomatic family suddenly finds himself the unexpected owner of a severed head, following which he's plunged into the dark confusing world of espionage. Too long for its own good, but packed with intriguing, beautifully observed details. GA

Senyora, La

(Jordi Cadena, 1987, Sp) Silvia Tortosa, Hermann Bonnin, Luis Merlo, Fernando Guillén-Cuervo.
103 min.
Lorca and the Buñuel of *El* contribute to the deep Catalan atmosphere of this study of stifled sexuality and its misshapen fruit. Teresa (Tortosa) is married off to old Nicolau (Bonnin), who wears gloves in bed, fears dirt on the Howard Hughes model, and in place of sexual congress offers her a golden thimble of semen. She masturbates with fans, she watches. He wants an heir, she rinses his thimbles down the sink, the marriage drags on until he dies, when she contemptuously makes free with his corpse. Teresa inherits everything, but the nephew she wishes to settle upon – in both senses – dies of shock diving into her pool to wash prior to consummating their passion. Hard cheese on Teresa, and she has to make do with her gardener (Merlo). Eventually the story comes full circle, with her terms as inhuman as Nicolau's. Pathological, indeed, but not remotely leering, the history certainly puts a damper on the hope centres. BC

Separate Lives

(David Madden, 1994, US) Linda Hamilton, James Belushi, Vera Miles.
98 min.
As a result of childhood trauma, an uptight psychotherapist splits personality at night to become a sexually rapacious club-goer. But is she also responsible for a spate of murders? You can see why Hamilton signed on for this one: a dual role is always a good showcase. But though she tries hard, as does Belushi as the ex-cop who falls for her (but which one of her?), neither can rise above the collection of clichés that passes for a script. DW

Separate Rooms
see Notre Histoire

Séparation, La

(Christian Vincent, 1994, Fr) Daniel Auteuil, Isabelle Huppert, Jérôme Deschamps, Karin Viard, Laurence Lerel, Louis Vincent.
88 min.
'We have to change our way of living.' So says Ingrid Bergman in the Rossellini film Pierre (Auteuil) and Anne (Huppert) go to see shortly before she feels moved to tell him she's fallen in love with another man. And Ingrid's right: Pierre and Anne may have been comfortable together for years – they're well-off, they have a smart apartment, a two-year-old son, supportive friends – but while Anne's admission seems at first barely to impinge on Pierre's consciousness, pretty soon he's suffering wild swings of emotion. Could they stay together? Will she leave? Should he throw her out? Whatever, the entire edifice of the relationship they've built up over the years looks set to crumble. Plotwise, that's about it in this study of a disintegrating partnership, but no matter: the film (a subtle, intelligent adaptation of Dan Franck's perceptive but rather indulgent novel) is about the minute shifts in power that occur as Anne tries to make up her mind about her future and Pierre attempts to keep up with or even forestall her changing behaviour. Happily, Vincent is beautifully served by the performers, with Huppert and Auteuil equally superb as the couple striving, against all odds, to emerge intact from a nightmare scenario. GA

September

(Woody Allen, 1987, US) Denholm Elliott, Dianne Wiest, Mia Farrow, Elaine Stritch, Sam Waterston, Jack Warden.
83 min.
Like *Interiors*, a Serious Drama: a Chekhovian chamber piece investigating the twisted bonds that tether a handful of lonely, arty, upper-crust Americans gathered, as fall approaches, at a Vermont country retreat. Unlike *Interiors*, however, this is no misguided tribute to Bergman: Allen's style is now so self-assured that the film simply looks like *Hannah and Her Sisters* without the laughs. Admittedly it's all rather familiar and schematic: disillusioned writer (Waterston) torn in his affections between Farrow and her best friend Wiest; Farrow's former film star mother (Stritch) turning up with latest lover (Warden), threatening to deprive Farrow of her home and to embarrass all with a volume of lurid memoirs; neighbour (Elliott) whose forlorn eyes betray unrequited love for Farrow. There are moments in Allen's script that smack of self-conscious contrivance, and Farrow's miserable victim is so wimpy as to be genuinely irritating. But the other performances – most notably those of Wiest and Warden – are superb, while Allen's direction shows admirable economy both in establishing and sustaining mood, and in clearly delineating the claustrophobic parameters of his characters' emotional lives. GA

September Songs: The Music of Kurt Weill

(Larry Weinstein, 1994, Can) Lou Reed, PJ Harvey, Elvis Costello, William S Burroughs, Betty Carter, Teresa Stratas.
89 min.
A career trajectory that includes collaboration with Bertolt Brecht, and takes in both the Hollywood screen and the Broadway stage makes Kurt Weill among the most fascinating 20th century composers, but this is a sketchy tribute. Serving chiefly as a showcase for sundry stars to deliver their own versions of Weill's tunes, it relegates the strictly biographical information to odd moments between the numbers. More frustrating is the lack of contextualising information around the performances, and the often wayward choice of artists (Lou Reed murders the normally swoonsome 'September Song'). Chief highlights are Elvis Costello and the Brodsky String Quartet with an impassioned 'Lost in the Stars' and PJ Harvey's superbly controlled 'Ballad of a Soldier's Wife'. A very mixed bag. TJ

SER
see Freedom Is Paradise

Sérail

(Eduardo de Gregorio, 1976, Fr) Leslie Caron, Bulle Ogier, Marie-France Pisier, Corin Redgrave, Marilyn Jones, Pierre Baudry.
87 min.
As a scriptwriter (mainly for Rivette and Bertolucci), de Gregorio repeatedly subverted narrative expectations, and here – his first feature as writer/director – he indulges in the perilous but pleasing game of developing the characters played by Ogier and Pisier in the film-within-the-film of *Céline and Julie*. An English novelist (Redgrave) is lured, with disconcerting and disorienting results, into purchasing a crumbling mansion by what he imagines are the deliberately 'literary' ploys of its housekeeper (Caron) and two mysterious, lurking women. Richly photographed, what starts as a slightly self-conscious exercise develops, after many deceptive twists, into an intriguing and gratifying sensual entertainment. JPy

Será Posible el Sur

(Stefan Paul, 1985, WGer) Mercedes Sosa.
75 min.
Paul's documentary about Argentinian singer Mercedes Sosa's return to her native country, after a three-year exile caused by the Junta's censorship of her politically oriented songs, is something of a fiasco. Sloppily put together, it substitutes banal propaganda and sycophantic hagiography for an analysis either of the political problems facing the Argentinian people, or of Sosa's own elevated position as a celebrated national heroine. GA

Serbian Girl, The (Das serbische Mädchen)

(Peter Sehr, 1990, Ger) Mirjana Jokovic, Ben Becker, Iva Bekjarew.
96 min.
A Yugoslav girl (Jokovic) sneaks across the border and sets off to meet her German boyfriend (Becker) in Hamburg. Her journey starts out promisingly enough, but evading the authorities proves easier than forging a relationship with her lover. Sehr's road movie (his debut feature) is consistently absorbing: it throws up all manner of hazards – from near-rape to robbery – yet remains ultimately optimistic, and Jokovic's performance is fresh and defiant. CM

Serena

(Peter Maxwell, 1962, GB) Patrick Holt, Emrys Jones, Honor Blackman, Bruce Beeby, John Horsley, Vi Stevens, Wally Patch.
62 min. b/w.
Stagy detective picture in which an artist (Jones) devises a switched-identity scam to get hold of an inheritance, by having his girlfriend (Blackman) call at a rose-covered cottage and blast his wife in the face with a shotgun (off screen, naturally). The sort of British B-picture in which artists wear cravats and oil paintings of nude women appear to have no nipples. Not a very taxing mystery, though Scotland Yard (Holt) is slow on the uptake. JPy

Sergeant Madden

(Josef von Sternberg, 1939, US) Wallace Beery, Tom Brown, Alan Curtis, Laraine Day, Fay Holden, Marc Lawrence, David Gorcey, Horace McMahon.
82 min. b/w.
A Sternberg rarity these days, but little cause for excitement since it's one of MGM's insufferably smug family entertainments. Beery (his usual mugging toned down somewhat) plays a roguish New York cop, much given to adopting strays on his beat, but let down when his natural son (Curtis) follows him into the force, gives way to his overweening ambition, and drifts into crime. Stoically, Beery sets out to take him in; but never mind, his ploddingly honest adopted son (Brown) is there to take over dad's mantle. Sternberg, abetted by John Seitz's fine camerawork, lends the film vestiges of his UFA look, but can do nothing about the gross mawkishness. TM

Sergeant Rutledge

(John Ford, 1960, US) Jeffrey Hunter, Woody Strode, Constance Towers, Billie Burke, Carleton Young, Juano Hernandez, Willis Bouchey, Mae Marsh.
118 min.

Though often pigeonholed as one of Ford's late trio of guiltily amends-making movies (to blacks here; to Indians in *Cheyenne Autumn*; to women in *Seven Women*), *Sergeant Rutledge* is both more complex and infinitely more confused than that simplistic formula would suggest. Possessing in broad outline an integrationist perspective (at a time when the Civil Rights movement was gaining strength), it's riddled with liberal compromises and evasions with its portrait of Strode's dignified black cavalry sergeant on trial for alleged miscegenatory rape. Ford can show us an innocent victim of American racism, and stress in courtroom flashbacks his heroic credentials in white man's uniform, but he can never make the leap to offering us a black who actually rejects the role of honorary white. He can make the cinepolitical connection back to *The Birth of a Nation* (by the bit-casting of Mae Marsh, the rape victim in Griffith's film) and consider his film compensatory, but he can't confront the cultural fear of miscegenation that mechanises both movies, only its distorted expression. PT.

Sergeant York

(Howard Hawks, 1941, US) Gary Cooper, Walter Brennan, Joan Leslie, George Tobias, Stanley Ridges, Margaret Wycherley, Ward Bond, Noah Beery Jr.
134 min. b/w.
Based on the true story of a deeply religious pacifist who became a much-decorated WWI hero, this is simultaneously Hawks' most 'respectable' and most artistically conventional major film. Oscar-winning Cooper is in engagingly relaxed form as the country boy who goes to war, in a fit of pique, after feeling cheated out of some farmland he wanted to buy, and Hawks manages to chart his transformation from pacifist to soldier with disarming ease. But, with serious issues and moral pieties at its heart, it lacks the subversive wit and depth of feeling for individuals that typifies his best work; too often it is picturesque (although the battle scenes, with the exception of the famous 'turkey-shoot' in which Germans are bumped off like birds, are shot with a strong feel for the pain and squalor of war) and poorly paced. GA

Serial Mom

(John Waters, 1994, US) Kathleen Turner, Sam Waterston, Ricki Lake, Matthew Lillard, Scott Wesley Morgan, Justin Whalin.
93 min.
Housewife Beverly Sutphin (Turner) seems to enjoy a life of domestic bliss. She has a loving husband (Waterston), two fine teenage kids, and a beautiful Baltimore home. Hell, she even gives the birds in her backyard Christian names. Admittedly, she's a little highly strung. A comedy, persuasively illustrating how suburban conformity hides its own latent psychopathic tendencies. When Beverly goes on the rampage with a knife, chasing a scruffy teenager through the streets in her Sunday best, it's in defence of all she holds most dear: family values, impeccable manners, road safety. Although this is John Waters' most approachable effort yet (a sign, perhaps, of how inextricably linked camp and mainstream cultures have become), the film loses focus in a poorly scripted courtroom anti-climax. A killer comedy all the same, with an uproariously funny, marvellously malicious performance from Turner. TCh

Serpent, The (Le Serpent)

(Henri Verneuil, 1973, Fr/It/WGer) Yul Brynner, Henry Fonda, Dirk Bogarde, Philippe Noiret, Michel Bouquet, Martin Held, Farley Granger, Virna Lisi, Marie Dubois, Robert Alda.
121 min.
A very traditional spy fable based on 'true events' in which a top-ranking KGB colonel (Brynner) defects and delivers a list of traitors who are in positions of great power in each major Western country. There is the usual glib characterisation, and the usual wall of disillusionment descending at the end. In fact, the only thing that sets this film apart is the totally consistent layer of impenetrable gloss with which Verneuil covers it, and his general directorial tricksiness, which runs the gamut from the irrelevant to the pretentious and back. He has a capable starry cast on hand; why he never uses it is a mystery. VG

Serpent and the Rainbow, The

(Wes Craven, 1987, US) Bill Pullman, Cathy Tyson, Zakes Mokae, Paul Winfield.
97 min.
Craven's tale of voodoo and revolution on the island of Haiti is like a bad Graham Greene adaptation seen under the influence of hallucinogenic substances. A Harvard anthropologist (Pullman), searching for the toxic drug used by voodoo priests to zombify their victims, spends a lot of time hanging around graveyards, checking out charlatan goat-revivers, and experiencing weird dreams. He is much taken with psychiatrist Cathy Tyson, less keen on the attentions of Baby Doc Duvalier's Ton Ton Macoute, especially when head honcho Winfield acquaints him with a blowtorch and threatens to drive a nail through his dick. Making effective use of snakes, tarantulas, scorpions and zombie brides, Craven piles on the nightmare sequences and nerve-jangling sounds. Unfortunately, the political parallel between the ideological repression of Baby Doc's regime and the stultifying effects of the zombifying fluid is only sketchily developed, leaving us with a series of striking but isolated set pieces. NF

Serpent's Egg, The (Das Schlangenei)

(Ingmar Bergman, 1977, WGer/US) Liv Ullmann, David Carradine, Gert Fröbe, Heinz Bennent, James Whitmore, Glynn Turman.
119 min.
Whether stimulated by his brush with the Swedish tax-man or his brief self-imposed exile in West Germany, Bergman's paranoia runs dementedly and tediously out of control in this Grand Guignol recreation of 1923 Berlin as studio set for close encounters of the most portentous kind. Carradine is improbably cast in the central role of a Jewish trapeze artist called Abel Rosenberg, wandering innocently through a night-town world of bottles, brothels, and (inevitably) cabarets, and trying to ignore the violence, depravity and anti-semitism screeching at him from every street corner. The torments he endures, with a sadly miscast Ullmann (who's further afflicted with throwaway lines like 'I can't stand the guilt'), have indeed been devised by a foresighted mad scientist straight out of *Dr Strangelove*. This last-reel revelation comes too late to restore audience disbelief to its proper state of suspension. JD

Serpent's Kiss, The

(Philippe Rousselot, 1997, GB) Ewan McGregor, Greta Scacchi, Pete Postlethwaite, Richard E Grant, Carmen Chaplin.
110 min.
A misbegotten attempt to ring changes on the British costume drama, former cameraman Rousselot's directorial debut tells of a landscape gardener (McGregor) tumbling into a snake's pit of deceit and deadly intrigue when he agrees to create a new estate for wealthy landowner Postlethwaite and his wife Scacchi. The film founders on stilted performances (Grant's death throes are spectacularly risible), conspicuously artificial set design, and dialogue – half 'literary', half colloquially contemporary (including inappropriate modern profanities) – that makes much of supposedly sophisticated metaphor but barely makes sense. And there's another problem: it's all too clearly derivative of *The Draughtsman's Contract*, comparison with which only makes Tim Rose Price's screenplay seem even worse. GA

Serpico

(Sidney Lumet, 1973, US) Al Pacino, John Randolph, Jack Kehoe, Biff McGuire, Barbara Eda-Young, Cornelia Sharpe, Tony Roberts.
130 min.
Like a practice run for Lumet's *Prince of the City*, this deals with police corruption in New York: Pacino's idealism and odd-style dress alienate him from his fellow cops, who take bribes left, right and centre. But whereas the later film built up an impressively complex series of narrative strands and psychological motivations, this is far more one-dimensional, and is so laxly structured that its rambling story seems to last longer than the (almost) three-hour *Prince of the City*. Another problem, these days, is Pacino's characterisation; he seems at times more like a misplaced hippy than a plainclothes cop. GA

Servant, The

(Joseph Losey, 1963, GB) Dirk Bogarde, James Fox, Wendy Craig, Sarah Miles, Catherine Lacey, Richard Vernon, Ann Firbank, Patrick Magee, Harold Pinter.
115 min. b/w.
Losey's first bid for success as a 'prestige' director now looks embarrassingly contrived: an allegory on class conflict (derived from Robin Maugham's novel) in which Bogarde's crafty manservant achieves a sinister, game-playing role-reversal in the home of his wealthy, decadent, upper class master (Fox). Neither Pinter's pregnant dialogue nor the generally svelte performances can disguise the fact that there's less here than meets the eye and ear. TR

Servante et Maîtresse

(Bruno Gantillon, 1976, Fr) Victor Lanoux, Andrea Ferreol, Evelyne Buyle, Gabriel Cattand, David Pontremoli, Jean Rougerie.
90 min.
Tediously artistic game-playing in a luxurious mansion. An old man dies, the maid (Ferreol) gets all the money and becomes mistress, forcing the expected beneficiary, a no-good nephew (Lanoux), to assume the servant's role. And so the film plods it's weary way, offering nothing that couldn't be said in half-an-hour. However, it would be far wearier with less accomplished performers. GB

Servicer, The (Cream – Schwabing-Report)

(Leon Capetanos, 1970, WGer/US) Sabi Dor, Astrid Bonin, Rolf Zacher, Hartmut Solinger, Ula Kopa.
85 min.
Age and disillusionment catch up with the speed generation of the '60s (Schwabing being Munich's Chelsea or Greenwich Village). Everyone succumbs: Franco, a gigolo suffering his share of ennui, marries the girl with her hair in plaits, who steals (a revolutionary and purifying act) but only in order to surround herself with the trappings of bourgeois comfort; his friend George wants to open a huge Disneyland for sex where you can make it with Mickey Mouse. Well-made and surprisingly ambitious for what is ostensibly a sex film, the result is a curious but not unlikeable mixture. The more pretentious overtones are deliberately spiked by the hack American commentary, which ends with 'the names, of course, have been changed to protect the innocent'. Such a confusion of styles emphasises the film's uncertainty about what it has to say, but the humour and general readiness to try something slightly different make it a cut above its type.

Se Sei Vivo, Spara

see Django Kill

Set It Off

(F Gary Gray, 1996, US) Jada Pinkett, Queen Latifah, Vivica A Fox, John C McGinley, Kimberly Elise, Blair Underwood.
122 min.
Frankie (Fox) has a bank job – until someone she knows from South Central LA holds her at gunpoint, the attempted robbery turns into a bloodbath, and the boss sends her packing. Life gets much harder. Her homegirls (Pinkett, Latifah, Elise) fix her up with the office-cleaning firm where they work nights, but it's not long before they hatch a plan to capitalise on Frankie's qualifications, in particular her inside knowledge of bank security procedures. In the wake of all those gun-toting white women and black men, black women are due their own loaded action adventure. This noir *Thelma and Louise* rekindles some of the subversive fire of Jonathan Demme's '70s exploitation flicks, although it's far too polished to have come from the Corman stable. The intense heist sequences show a command of thriller dynamics that's right up there with the best of them, but director Gray is equally convincing on the character front, eliciting funny, grounded performances from the four women (Latifah notably refuses to caricature her lesbian role). On the down side, Blair Underwood is too good to be true as the man who comes into Pinkett's life, while the police procedural stuff is strictly routine. Minor misdemeanours, though, given such an energising spree for the Girlz n the hood. TCh

Setta, La

see Sect, The

Set-Up, The

(Robert Wise, 1948, US) Robert Ryan, Audrey Totter, George Tobias, Alan Baxter, Wallace Ford, Percy Helton, Darryl Hickman, James Edwards.
72 min. b/w.
One for the Ten Best lists. This is the boxing movie to lick all others, with Ryan impeccable as the ageing fighter gearing up for a bout he's expected to lose; Audrey Totter leaving him because she can't stand the mental and physical battering of the fight business, wandering the streets amid snatches of ringside radio commentary; and an invading sense of desolation the result. Great blue moments in black-and-white from a director whose early work is still outstanding: the film burns with the humanity that *Raging Bull* never quite achieves, an expression of masochism mixed with futile pride that is the essence of boxing as a movie myth. CA

Set Up, The

(Strathford Hamilton, 1995, US) Billy Zane, James Coburn, Mia Sara, James Russo.
90 min
Not to be confused with the '40s boxing classic, this is a double-crossing latter-day caper, with security expert Zane working for banker Coburn, and in the process falling for his daughter Sara. His old buddy Russo then becomes the fly in the ointment, holding her hostage to force Zane into breaking into the bank for him. And there are further complications on the way, in a movie that's more plot than characterisation, and is already doomed from the moment they cast the synthetic male lead. Based on James Hadley Chase's *My Laugh Comes Last*. TJ

Seven

(Andy Sidaris, 1979, US) William Smith, Guich Koock, Barbara Leigh, Art Metrano, Martin Kove, Ed Parker, Richard LePore, Reggie Nalder.
101 min.
Called on to perform a 'no-news wipeout' on seven Hawaiian mafiosi, Drew Sevano (Smith) assembles his own charmless bunch of seven heavies, and then spends his time driving around brooding on new methods of homicide. It's the sort of film where you keep seeing the microphone boom; in other words a tawdry mess, unrelieved by acts of crazed eccentricity (skateboarding crossbowmen, a hang-gliding bomber), and epitomised by its grossly insulting attitude to women, their sole function being to climb in and out of bikinis. Strictly for the brain-damaged. CPea

Seven (aka Se7en) (100)

(David Fincher, 1995, US) Brad Pitt, Morgan Freeman, Gwyneth Paltrow, Richard Roundtree, R Lee Ermey, Kevin Spacey.
127 min.
Serial killers and mismatched cops overcoming antagonism are seldom fresh, fruitful subjects for movies, but this exceptionally (and impressively) nasty thriller blends genres to grim and gripping effect. Somerset (Freeman) and Mills (Pitt) are the detectives brought together when an obese corpse is discovered in a dismal apartment. Mills, who with his wife (Paltrow) has recently moved to the city from upstate, resents what he perceives as Somerset's patronising attitude; still, the older cop, about to retire and weary of crime and moral apathy, is unusually educated, as becomes clear when they find a second mutilated body and he insists his young partner start reading the likes of Milton, Chaucer and Dante. Somerset's theory? That a messianic murderer is perpetrating crimes to punish the Seven Deadly Sins – in which case there are five more to go. The film's world is so shadowy, decaying and intentionally dated that one often wonders whether anyone involved has heard of electricity; at the same time, however, Somerset and Mills' slow voyage from claustrophobic murk into blinding light makes for a vivid dramatic metaphor. Moreover, Fincher handles the violence with sensitivity, announcing its obscenity in spoken analyses and briefly glimpsed post mortem shots, but never showing the murderous acts themselves. GA

Seven Beauties (Pasqualino Settebellezze)

(Lina Wertmller, 1975, It) Giancarlo Giannini, Fernando Rey, Shirley Stoler, Elena Fiore, Piero Di Iorio.
115 min.
American art house success led to Wertmller being compared to Bergman and Fellini, but as *Seven Beauties* confirms, it is her taste for a vaguely intellectualised sado-masochism which aroused middle class American enthusiasm. The film recounts the picaresque adventures of a pop-eyed Italian shark (Giannini) who lives off women, is institutionalised for killing in defence of his honour, 'rehabilitated' by army service after committing rape in the asylum, and ends up facing the problem of survival in a Nazi concentration camp. Much of it is fifth-rate slapstick, decked out in gaudy sub-Ken Russell style with the occasional interpolation of gruesome or violent images, plus some nudgingly insistent music. There is a lingering climax in which he steels himself to seduce the pig-like woman Commandant of the concentration camp (awesomely played by Shirley Stoler of *The Honeymoon Killers*); his subsequent sexual debasement is memorable, but in such an uninspiring context it reeks of artifice. DP

Seven Brides for Seven Brothers

(Stanley Donen, 1954, US) Howard Keel, Jane Powell, Jeff Richards, Russ Tamblyn, Tommy Rall, Marc Platt, Matt Mattox, Jacques d'Amboise, Virginia Gibson, Julie Newmar.
103 min.
Circuitously derived from the tale of the rape of the Sabine women, this rather archly symmetrical movie musical is best seen as a dance-fest, with Michael Kidd's acrobatic, *pas d'action* choreography well complemented by ex-choreographer Donen's camera. Gene De Paul and Johnny Mercer's score is cosy ('Spring, Spring, Spring' and all that), and Keel, avoiding even the odd faked toe-step, is at his least expressive, but it's vigorous and colourful if you can watch the Anscocolor process which also marred *Brigadoon*. The bearded Matt Mattox went on to become something of a legend for his jazz classes at London's Dance Centre. SG

Seven Chances

(Buster Keaton, 1925, US) Buster Keaton, Ruth Dwyer, Ray Barnes, Snitz Edwards.
6,210 ft. b/w.
Less ambitious and less concerned with plastic values than the best of Keaton, this is nevertheless a dazzlingly balletic comedy in which Buster has a matter of hours to acquire the wife on which a seven million dollar inheritance depends. Having insulted his sweetheart by explaining the necessity of marriage, been turned down by seven possible candidates at the country club, and (in a series of innocently inept gags) found his path beset by uglies, blacks or female impersonators, he advertises – only to find a horde of applicants besieging the church. From this leisurely start, the film takes off into a fantastically elaborate, gloriously inventive chase sequence, in which Buster escapes the mob of pursuing harridans only to find an escalating avalanche of rocks taking over at his heels as he hurtles downhill. Added only after an initial preview, the rocks make for one of the great Keaton action gags. TM

Seven Days in May

(John Frankenheimer, 1964, US) Burt Lancaster, Kirk Douglas, Fredric March, Ava Gardner, Edmond O'Brien, Martin Balsam, George Macready, Whit Bissell, Hugh Marlowe, John Houseman.
118 min. b/w.
Political thriller in which the military Chiefs of Staff (led by Lancaster) plot to overthrow the US president (March) after he concludes what they consider to be a disastrous nuclear treaty with Russia. Conspiracy movies may have become more darkly complex in these post-Watergate days of Pakula and paranoia, but Frankenheimer's fascination with gadgetry (in his compositions, the ubiquitous helicopters, TV screens, hidden cameras and electronic devices literally edge the human characters into insignificance) is used to create a striking visual metaphor for control by the military machine. Highly enjoyable. TM

Seven Days to Noon

(John Boulting, 1950, GB) Barry Jones, Olive Sloane, Andre Morell, Joan Hickson, Sheila Manahan, Marie Ney.
94 min. b/w.
When an atomic scientist (Jones) entertains serious doubts about his work and promises to blow up London unless the government rids Britain of nuclear weapons, rumours of war spread, panic grows, and the suspense is killing. Still relevant and surprisingly powerful, *Seven Days to Noon* impresses by its ambiguity: while we sympathise with the ordinary Londoners menaced by the professor's drastic policy, and are told by politicians and boffins that he is mad from overwork, what we see is an intelligent, sane man of intense, apolitical commitment. London, both in the grip of evacuation and deserted, is beautifully evoked by the *noir*-ish camerawork, and John Addison's Herrmannesque score helps to keep the atmosphere nervy. Only the cosy Cockney cameos (all pluck and chatter) deflate the otherwise carefully sustained paranoia. GA

7 Faces of Dr Lao

(George Pal, 1963, US) Tony Randall, Barbara Eden, Arthur O'Connell, John Ericson, Kevin Tate, Lee Patrick, Argentina Brunetti, Noah Beery Jr, John Qualen.
100 min.
Randall gets to show off as the old, bald Chinese illusionist who arrives in a Western town and whose multifarious circus show soon begins to cast a spell over local events (newspaperman Ericson is leading a fight against expansionist magnate O'Connell). A pleasingly inventive diversion from top movie fantasist George Pal, here coming up with an original story (script by Charles Beaumont from Charles G Finney's novel *The Circus of Dr Lao*), rather than adapting a fairytale (*Tom Thumb*) or a myth (*Atlantis, The Lost Continent*). Make-up artist William Tuttle won an Oscar for his endeavours. TJ

Seven Men from Now

(Budd Boetticher, 1956, US) Randolph Scott, Gail Russell, Lee Marvin, Walter Reed, John Larch, Donald Barry.
78 min.
Neither as bleak nor as concise as the greatest collaborations between Scott and Boetticher (*The Tall T*, *Ride Lonesome*, *Comanche Station*), their first outing together nevertheless remains a terrific B Western. Scott is beautifully assured as Ben Stride, vengefully hunting down the men who killed his wife during a robbery, while Larch and (most especially) Marvin are memorable as the outlaws he encounters out in the desert, keen to get their hands on a gold shipment secretly being carried by a couple from back east. Burt Kennedy's script is characteristically terse and witty, William Clothier's camerawork sharp and direct, and Boetticher's direction a model of inventive economy. GA

Seven Minutes (Georg Elser)

(Klaus Maria Brandauer, 1989, US/WGer) Klaus Maria Brandauer, Rebecca Miller, Brian Dennehy, Nigel Le Vaillant.
90 min.
Brandauer, an arresting screen actor, notably in Szabo's *Mephisto* and *Colonel Redl*, turns plodding director for this functional fact-based thriller, adapted by Stephen Sheppard from his novel *The Artisan*. Brandauer stars as the Munich clockmaker Georg Elser who intends to assassinate Hitler when he visits a nearby beer hall. But the waitress Elser's in love with is scheduled to be on duty in the hall at the time set for the killing. Dennehy gets on with the job as the Gestapo security chief. TJ

Seven Minutes, The

(Russ Meyer, 1971, US) Wayne Maunder, Marianne McAndrew, Yvonne De Carlo, Philip Carey, Jay C Flippen, Edy Williams, Lyle Bettger, Ron Randell, John Carradine, Tom Selleck.
115 mins.
Based on Irving Wallace's novel about a pornography trial, with much ado around a politically-motivated attempt to link a murder to the supposedly corrupting influence of a book condemned as obscene on its publication thirty years earlier. This is Russ Meyer's dullest film, because it abandons his usually salacious tone to attempt

a 'serious' attack on the American version of the Mary Whitehouse brigade. Curious only for its unwitting fag-end-of-the-'60s proof that moralists and pornographers are equally appalled by the prospect of sexual liberation.

Seven Nights in Japan

(Lewis Gilbert, 1976, GB/Fr) Michael York, Hidemi Aoki, James Villiers, Peter Jones, Charles Gray, Lionel Murton, Yolande Donlan.
104 min.
A loose update of *Roman Holiday*, with Michael York in the Audrey Hepburn role and without Wyler's witty handling. It's the hoariest of escapist fantasies, mixing royalty (in disguise as a common chap, no less), romance and foreign parts in equal measure as our Prince – obviously Charles, though called George – absconds from convincingly boring duties to savour love on the loose with a Japanese tour guide. The first two nights slip by painlessly enough, but after that it's minutes one counts, not nights. There's an alarmingly silly assassination plot, and only very tentative gags (like the familiar voice on the telephone, backed by yelping corgis). VG

Seven-Per-Cent Solution, The

(Herbert Ross, 1976, US) Alan Arkin, Vanessa Redgrave, Robert Duvall, Nicol Williamson, Laurence Olivier, Joel Grey, Samantha Eggar, Jeremy Kemp, Charles Gray, Georgia Brown.
114 min.
Conan Doyle's description of Holmes' ultimate struggle with Moriarty, *The Final Problem*, was written with such a quasi-religious intensity that it was a sacred text of popular fiction until 1974, when Nicholas Meyer conceived that the story had been written to disguise both Holmes' cocaine dependency and his encounter with Freud in Vienna. As a book, *The Seven-Per-Cent Solution* was a pertinent pastiche. As a film, it is an almost unrelievedly insipid costume drama. Once the basic coup of teaming Holmes (Williamson) and Freud (Arkin) has been achieved, the 'mystery' simply degenerates into a spectacularly silly chase across Europe, blandly staged and staggeringly boring. The whole cast appear to be struggling, and ultimately it's camp whodunit. DP

Seven Samurai 100 (100) (Shichinin no Samurai)

(Akira Kurosawa, 1954, Jap) Takashi Shimura, Toshiro Mifune, Yoshio Inaba, Seiji Miyaguchi, Minoru Chiaki, Daisuke Kato, Ko Kimura.
200 min. b/w.
Kurosawa's masterpiece, testifying to his admiration for John Ford and translated effortlessly back into the form of a Western as *The Magnificent Seven*, has six masterless samurai – plus Mifune, the crazy farmer's boy not qualified to join the elect group, who nevertheless follows like a dog and fights like a lion – agreeing for no pay, just food and the joy of fulfilling their duty as fighters, to protect a helpless village against a ferocious gang of bandits. Despite the caricatured acting forms of Noh and Kabuki which Kurosawa adopted in his period films, the individual characterisations are precise and memorable, none more so than that by Takashi Shimura, one of the director's favourite actors, playing the sage, ageing, and oddly charismatic samurai leader. The epic action scenes involving cavalry and samurai are still without peer. RM

Seven Sinners

(Tay Garnett, 1940, US) Marlene Dietrich, John Wayne, Albert Dekker, Broderick Crawford, Anna Lee, Billy Gilbert, Mischa Auer, Oscar Homolka.
87 min. b/w.
A return to the territory (if not quite the spirit or the style) of Dietrich's great films with von Sternberg in the early '30s. Here she plays Bijou, another member of that 'foreign legion of women' introduced in *Morocco*: a singer who shuttles around the islands of South-East Asia on a string of deportation orders, a trail of wrecked nightclubs and local riots in her wake. This time, her hopeless affair is with Wayne's staunch US Navy lieutenant (fortunately they both love the navy as much as each other), but she winds up sharing a tipple with the alcoholic doctor of a tramp steamer. True to form, Garnett directs it with panache but without finesse. His lighting and his use of Dietrich as an icon both reflect a viewing of the

Sternberg films, but he doesn't seriously attempt the cruelty or the emotional pain of his models. Dietrich, as the woman 'not quite ready for the word derelict', is wonderful. TR

Seven Sinners (aka Doomed Cargo)

(Albert de Courville, 1936, GB) Edmund Lowe, Constance Cummings, Thomy Bourdelle, Henry Oscar, Felix Aylmer, Allan Jeayes, OB Clarence.
70 min. b/w.
Crisply scripted by Frank Launder and Sidney Gilliat, this set out as a remake of *The Wrecker*, a 1929 melodrama about sabotage on the railways, but – evidently under their influence – metamorphosed into something rather different: a fast-moving, serio-comic thriller which kicks off with an American detective (Lowe) investigating a murder when a corpse turns up in his hotel room in Nice, then mysteriously vanishes, only to reappear subsequently amid the debris of a wrecked train (the plot allows for several crashes, using spectacular footage from *The Wrecker*, as it moves back and forth across the Channel). Clearly intending to ape Hitchcock in both plot and manner, the film creaks here and there, but is brisk, occasionally gripping, and often amusing. Lowe (well backed up by Constance Cummings as a sidekick Nora to his Nick Charles) proves surprisingly adept at the throwaway touch and the nonchalant wisecracks. TM

1776

(Peter H Hunt, 1972, US) William Daniels, Howard da Silva, Ken Howard, Donald Madden, Blythe Danner, John Cullum, David Ford.
141 min.
Straightforward transfer of the Broadway musical by Sherman Edwards and Peter Stone about the conception and passing of the American Declaration of Independence. Suspense mounts as the nays change to yeas, and Benjamin Franklin and Thomas Jefferson do a one-two-three-kick routine. They also sing. Everybody sings. Amazingly plastic film-making. The mind boggled, gave up, and enjoyed it. They've even included the slavery cop-out. Very long at 141 minutes.

7th Cavalry

(Joseph H Lewis, 1956, US) Randolph Scott, Barbara Hale, Jay C Flippen, Jeanette Nolan, Frank Faylen, Leo Gordon, Harry Carey Jr, Denver Pyle.
75 min.
One of Lewis' two colour films, a weird and occasionally wonderful little Western focusing on the enmity between white and red man as Scott, accused of deserting Custer out of cowardice during the fiasco of Little Big Horn, sets out to discover the truth of the massacre. Beautifully shot and briskly paced, it's most interesting for a surprising anti-Custer stance, and for its surreal, almost supernatural finale, which sees Custer's horse appearing like a ghost from the wilderness to bring peace between enemies. GA

Seventh Cross, The

(Fred Zinnemann, 1944, US) Spencer Tracy, Signe Hasso, Hume Cronyn, Jessica Tandy, Agnes Moorehead, George Macready, Ray Collins, Felix Bressart, Steve Geray, George Zucco, Karen Verne.
110 min. b/w.
With Tracy heading the cast and a host of great character actors in support, it's hardly surprising that the performances are the most memorable aspect of Zinnemann's first major feature. Tracy pulls all the stops out as one of seven anti-Nazi Germans escaping from a concentration camp in 1936, and heading (with the Gestapo in pursuit) for Holland and freedom; en route, his bitterness dissipates and his faith in human nature is restored. Polished professionalism all round, in fact, with the odyssey tensely evoked in the studio by ace cameraman Karl Freund. GA

7th Dawn, The

(Lewis Gilbert, 1964, US/GB) William Holden, Susannah York, Capucine, Tetsuro Tamba, Michael Goodliffe, Allan Cuthbertson, Maurice Denham, Sidney Tafler.
123 min.

A very pale shadow of *The Ugly American*, attempting to sort out tangled loyalties during the terrorist troubles in Malaya but only succeeding in reducing them to a mess of pottage. Clichés blossom in the wilderness and love, of course, becomes a many-splendoured thing as the cardboard characters react to assorted atrocities and slog through endless jungle, with poor Holden as the planter trying to sort out his politics while getting into sentimental difficulties between an Eurasian (Capucine) and an English rose (York). TM

7th Heaven

(Frank Borzage, 1927, US) Janet Gaynor, Charles Farrell, Ben Bard, David Butler, Albert Gran, Marie Mosquini, Gladys Brockwell, Emile Chautard, George Stone.
8,500 ft. b/w.
Borzage's films – or at least the coherent collection made between the mid-twenties and World War II – are sublime demonstrations of a system of sensual spirituality; products of their director's uncompromising romanticism and fluent sense of cinemotion. *7th Heaven* tracks the transformational love of Farrell and Gaynor from the sewers to the stars, across time and space, and beyond death itself, affirming triumphantly that melodrama can mean much more than just an excuse for a good weep. PT

Seventh Heaven

(Henry King, 1937, US) Simone Simon, James Stewart, Jean Hersholt, Gregory Ratoff, Gale Sondergaard, J Edward Bromberg, John Qualen.
102 min. b/w.
Henry King's remake of Borzage's incandescent romance is a film of some sensitivity but little conviction. The setting is again a Paris slum, but Borzage's eternal anywhere becomes both too specific and too vague, tying the action to a time and place that is a never-never land of novelettish convention, while the dark shadow cast by World War I seems more a dramatic convenience than a haunting memory. But the real problem is James Stewart's ineradicably American persona: the ebullient optimism with which his Chico shows Simone's Diane the way to the stars, teaching her to shed her fear of life and to have faith in love, makes him sound like a gung ho boy scout. An affecting little tale, all the same. TM

Seventh Seal, The 100 (100) (Det Sjunde Inseglet)

(Ingmar Bergman, 1956, Swe) Max von Sydow, Gunnar Björnstrand, Bengt Ekerot, Nils Poppe, Bibi Andersson, Ake Fridell, Maud Hansson, Gunnel Lindblom.
95 min. b/w.
Bergman's portentous medieval allegory takes its title from the Book of Revelations – 'And when he (the Lamb) opened the seventh seal, there was a silence in heaven about the space of half an hour'. In the opening scene, a knight returning from the Crusades is challenged to a game of chess by the cloaked figure of Death (Ekerot), and from this point onwards an air of doom hangs over the action, like the hawk which hovers in the air above them. The time of Death and Judgement prophesied in the Bible has arrived, and a plague is sweeping the land. Bergman fills the screen with striking images: the knight and Death playing chess for the former's life, a band of flagellants swinging smoking censers, a young witch manacled to a stake. Probably the most parodied film of all time, this nevertheless contains some of the most extraordinary images ever committed to celluloid. Whether they are able to carry the metaphysical and allegorical weight with which they have been loaded is open to question. NF

Seventh Sign, The

(Carl Schultz, 1988, US) Demi Moore, Michael Biehn, Jürgen Prochnow, Peter Friedman, Manny Jacobs, John Taylor.
97 min.
An apocalyptic thriller which focuses on an intimate familial dilemma, this should find favour among those who prefer supernatural disquiet to visceral shocks. A young mother-to-be (Moore) suffers recurring nightmares. Disturbed by these fragmentary premonitions, she begins to imagine that the fate of her child is somehow bound up with a series of strange natural phenomena

which, some say, herald the end of the world: the sea around a Haitian island boils, an Israeli desert village freezes over, the sun is eclipsed, the moon glows red. Her nightmares also seem to be linked to a mysterious stranger (Prochnow), who moves into an adjoining apartment, and whose silent brooding and unnatural interest in the unborn child she interprets as a diabolical threat. Schultz's stylish visuals and sympathetic handling of the actors creates an unsettling atmosphere of understated menace; and the unfolding mystery (drawing upon both the Book of Revelations and ancient Jewish mythology) generates a tremendous cumulative tension, the climactic scene working all the better for being staged on a human scale. NF

Seventh Veil, The
(Compton Bennett, 1945, GB) James Mason, Ann Todd, Herbert Lom, Hugh McDermott, Albert Lieven.
94 min. b/w.
Ineffable tripe which mixes a heady stew of kitsch, culture and Freud as a concert pianist obsessed with the idea that she can never play again (people will keep rapping her over the knuckles) is cured by a psychiatrist (Lom) who guides her through her past in quest of the man she really loves. With Mason providing the catchpenny dream of (masochistic) romance – lame, dark and sardonically brooding, he's the guardian who relentlessly drives her towards success and away from frivolous affairs of the heart – you know that McDermott's cheery bandleader and Lieven's society portrait painter don't stand a chance. Enjoyable, sort of. TM

Seventh Victim, The
(Mark Robson, 1943, US) Tom Conway, Jean Brooks, Isabel Jewell, Kim Hunter, Evelyn Brent, Elizabeth Russell, Erford Gage, Ben Bard, Hugh Beaumont.
71 min. b/w.
What other movie opens with Satanism in Greenwich Village, twists into urban paranoia, and climaxes with a suicide? Val Lewton, Russian émigré workaholic, fantasist, was one of the mavericks of Forties' Hollywood, a man who produced (never directed) a group of intelligent and offbeat chillers for next-to-nothing at RKO. All bear his personal stamp: dime-store cinema transformed by 'literary' scripts, ingenious design, shadowy visuals, brooding melancholy, and a tight rein over the direction. The Seventh Victim is his masterpiece, a brooding melodrama built around a group of Satanists. The bizarre plot involves an orphan (Hunter) searching for her death-crazy sister (Brooks), but also carries a strong lesbian theme, and survives some uneven cameos; the whole thing is held together by a remarkably effective mix of menace and metaphysics – half noir, half Gothic. CA

Seventh Voyage of Sinbad, The
(Nathan Juran, 1958, US) Kerwin Mathews, Kathryn Grant, Richard Eyer, Torin Thatcher, Alec Mango, Danny Green.
87 min.
Ray Harryhausen's first Dynamation effort in Arabian Nights territory. His knockout special effects include a cyclops, dragon, and duelling skeleton (forerunner of the battling skeletons sequence in Jason and the Argonauts), all expertly and realistically manipulated, employing techniques learned and developed from his mentor, the late, great Willis H King Kong O'Brien. Torin Thatcher's evil magician (a part he repeated for the less enthralling Jack the Giant Killer, also for Juran, three years later) more than compensates for Kerwin Mathews' rather wet Sinbad, while Bernard Herrmann's typically effective score tops off the whole adventure. PM

71 Fragments of a Chronology of Chance (71 Fragmente einer Chronologie des Zufalls)
(Michael Haneke, 1994, Aus/Ger) G Cosmin Urdes, Lukas Miko, Otto Grühandl, Anne Rennent.
95 min.
As cool, cerebral and painstaking as Haneke's earlier Benny's Video, this fragmented account of numerous events leading up to or loosely linked

with a seemingly motiveless murder never really gets very far beyond images of alienation, anxiety and frustration, but thanks to its awareness of how time's very passing affects us, the film weaves a persuasively hypnotic spell. Oddly, the structure, which unexpectedly makes for considerable suspense, suggests not chance but destiny, while the final news collage is a corrosive statement on how even the most extraordinary events are packaged and trivialised by the media. GA

Seven-Ups, The
(Philip D'Antoni, 1973, US) Roy Scheider, Victor Arnold, Jerry Leon, Ken Kercheval, Tony Lo Bianco, Larry Haines, Richard Lynch, Bill Hickman.
103 min.
D'Antoni, who produced The French Connection, here turned director and came up with a flawed mirror image of the earlier film. Led by Scheider in the Gene Hackman-type role, the Seven-Ups, a crack squad of New York detectives, pit their wits against a gang of heavies whose hit-man is played by the film's stunt co-ordinator, Bill Hickman. Most of the excitement is well handled, usually as a result of Hickman's amazing skill at setting up car chases and spectacular bits of action. But even the best sequences can't redeem an unremarkable and rather confused script, or D'Antoni's unimpressive handling of actors. DP

Seven Women
(John Ford, 1965, US) Anne Bancroft, Margaret Leighton, Sue Lyon, Flora Robson, Mildred Dunnock, Betty Field, Anna Lee, Eddie Albert, Mike Mazurki, Woody Strode.
87 min.
Easy to disparage Ford's last feature, a bizarre transposition of a classic Western situation into war-torn China of the '30s, with a group of WASP women trapped at a mission besieged by brutal Mongols. The plot is almost formulaic, the fear of miscegenation outdated, a made-up Mazurki as the Mongol leader faintly ludicrous. But in many ways this does qualify as the director's mature masterpiece of his twilight years, partly because he is for once treating women as more than just (h)earth mothers, partly because his sympathies lie so completely with Bancroft, who manages to face a fate worse than death with admirable stoicism. The sense of menacing claustrophobia and sexual repression is beautifully conveyed by the studio setting; the shifting relationships between the women are handled with lucid economy; and the film is totally devoid of the sentimentality that mars so much of Ford's work. GA

Seven Women for Satan (Les Weekends Maléfiques du Comte Zaroff)
(Michel Lemoine, 1974, Fr) Michel Lemoine, Nathalie Zeiger, Joël Coeur, Martine Azencot, Howard Vernon.
80 min.
Essentially an offshoot from the fashion for sex and sadism that blanketed the nether reaches of the French cinema during the '70s, this spices its de Sadeian theme with tenuous horror connections (the excuse for the protagonist's strange sexual tastes being his descent from Count Zaroff). The trouble with the film is that Lemoine seems unwilling to relinquish either the bounds of bourgeois good taste or an undernourished, 'Vogue'-ish style of camera-work. The result, with sanitised sadism inserted among the blameless pleasures of the good life, is a dauntingly pretentious exercise. VG

Seven Year Itch, The
(Billy Wilder, 1955, US) Marilyn Monroe, Tom Ewell, Evelyn Keyes, Sonny Tufts, Victor Moore, Oscar Homolka, Carolyn Jones, Robert Strauss.
105 min.
Fondly remembered as the film in which Marilyn has problems with her skirt on a New York subway grating, this isn't quite the smasheroo that Some Like It Hot is: Monroe flaunts her attributes too blatantly, and seems less human because of it, while George Axelrod's play, fresh and risqué in the '50s, now appears a little obvious and over-plotted. Writer Tom Ewell's wife goes on a summer vacation, and the timid hubby becomes a flaming ball of sex, but – as with most Axelrod heroes (Roddy McDowall in Lord Love a Duck, Jack Lemmon in How to Murder Your Wife) – it's all in the mind. GB

Seven Years in Tibet
(Jean-Jacques Annaud, 1997, US/GB) Brad Pitt, David Thewlis, BD Wong, Mako, Danny Denzongpa, Victor Wong, Ingeborga Dapkunaite, Lhakpa Tsamchoe.
136 min.
Ace mountaineer Heinrich Harrer (Pitt, inert) leaves wife, unborn child and Austria to take a crack at the unconquered Himalayan peak of Nanga Parbat. The expedition ends prematurely in India, however, when Harrer and the nominal leader, Peter Aufshnaiter (Thewlis), are interned at the start of WWII. Escape to Tibet brings the men closer to the nub of the drama as Harrer is unexpectedly taken on by the country's youthful figurehead to provide a potted education in Western culture. Though French director Annaud's camerawork persuades us that Tibet is a special place, the dramatic structure seems to imply that it's all a mere backdrop to one man's path from self-absorbed arrogance to enlightened humanity. (Harrer neglected to mention his Nazi associations in the memoir on which the film is based.) TJ

Severed Arm , The
(Thomas S Alderman, 1973, US) Deborah Walley, Paul Carr, David G Cannon, Vincent Martorano, Roy Dennis, Marvin Kaplan.
92 min.
Dismal hokum about a group of geologists who find themselves trapped in a cave by a rockfall. One of them has the bright idea of surviving by eating one anothers' limbs. Of course, no sooner have they amputated the first limb than they are rescued. Years later, the guy goes on the rampage...or does he? The trouble is that the film is directed with a total lack of conviction that has to be seen to be believed, and the script is riddled with lines indicative of desperation ('Gee, he has to show himself soon', or 'What do we do now?'). Someone has evidently added a professionally-shot final sequence in an attempt to save the day. They needn't have bothered. VG

Sevillanas
(Carlos Saura, 1992, Sp) Paco De Lucia, Manolo Sanlúcar, Rocio Jurado, Lola Flores.
55 min.
Yet another Saura excursion into flamenco (though this time without a story), this simply works its way through various dance and musical forms, using solos, duets and ensemble pieces performed in stark rooms, to paint a picture of a popular culture that appeals to all ages and types. It's all elegantly shot, of course, and there's a certain fascination in seeing OAP's strutting their stuff; but after a while, the accent on variety actually becomes tedious, so that one finally feels exhausted by the endless parade of dancers proudly tossing their heads, waving their arms, twisting their wrists, and flashing their eyes. GA

Sex and the Single Girl
(Richard Quine, 1964, US) Natalie Wood, Tony Curtis, Lauren Bacall, Henry Fonda, Mel Ferrer, Fran Jeffries, Leslie Parrish, Edward Everett Horton, Otto Kruger, Howard St John, Stubby Kaye.
110 min.
A coyly leering comedy, with Wood as Helen Gurley Brown (real-life author of a bestseller on marital relations), and Curtis as the smut-magazine writer out to demonstrate her lack of personal experience in sexual matters. But...oh, you guessed? That's right, they fall in love. Graceless stuff, criminally wasting Bacall and Fonda as a couple with marital problems (they're in love, but constantly quarrelling), and with Quine's moderate flair for comedy nowhere in evidence. TM

Sex and the Vampire
see Frisson des Vampires, Le

Sex Crime of the Century
see Last House on the Left, The

Sex Is...
(Marc Huestis, 1992, US)
80 min.
Such candour! Years in the making, Huestis' documentary on hot sex in the time of HIV eclipses all those sensitive coming-out testimonies that were so important in the early years of Gay Lib. The opening dump on the noxious Jesse Helms

sets the tone for an extremely raunchy collage of memories, life stories, object lessons and fantasies that gets to grips with the challenge of keeping desire alive and in focus. TR

sex, lies and videotape

(Steven Soderbergh, 1989, US) James Spader, Andie MacDowell, Peter Gallagher, Laura San Giacomo, Ron Vawter, Steven Brill.
100 min.
Ann (MacDowell) is not happy: her husband John (Gallagher) is a lawyer who, unbeknownst to her, is having an affair with her virtually estranged sister (San Giacomo). The deception only comes to light with the arrival of John's old friend Graham (Spader), a shy, impotent eccentric who gets his kicks from watching interviews he has taped with women about their sexual experiences...Soderbergh's first feature is impressively mature, less concerned with actions *per se* than with the gulf between deed and motivation, between what we feel and what we say we feel. Despite the title, there is almost no explicit nudity or sexual activity; by avoiding sensationalism, Soderbergh leaves himself free to focus unblinkingly on moral and psychological complexities. No character is entirely without dishonesty or hang-ups; all initially shrink from taking full responsibility for their actions. The actors are superb; working from Soderbergh's funny, perceptive, immaculately wrought dialogue, they ensure that the film stimulates both intellectually and emotionally. GA

Sex Life in a Convent (Klosterschülerinnen)

(Eberhard Schroeder, 1971, WGer) Doris Arden, Ulrich Beiger, Astrid Bohner, Felix Francky, Ellen Frank.
92 min.
A confused semi-documentary effort in which a Voice of America-style commentator tries to wring some titillation from the much-repeated fact that the daughters of the nasty rich are abandoned in convents through lack of parental concern, and hence exposed to unnatural temptations (by which the film seems to mean lesbianism and the odd jaunt into town for a quickie with a local lad). One great scene in which the whole dorm leaps into bed, each girl clutching her own candle – but such moments are few. VG

Sex Mission, The (Seksmisja)

(Juliusz Machulski, 1984, Pol) Olgierd Lukaszewicz, Jerzy Stuhr, Bozena Stryjkwna, Boguslawa Pawelec, Beata Tyszkiewicz.
121 min.
Two men volunteer as guinea-pigs for an experiment in human hibernation, but instead of waking up in three years, they regain consciousness fifty years behind schedule in a totalitarian postnuclear world populated entirely by women. Machulski's comic strip fantasy may be intended as a withering satire on any form of authoritarianism, but quite frankly it fails, partly due to a stance that may easily be interpreted as extremely misogynistic (all that these futuristic femmes need is a good hetero fuck, etc), partly because it simply isn't funny. GA

Sexorcist, The (L'Ossessa)

(Mario Gariazzo, 1974, It) Stella Carnacina, Chris Avram, Lucretia Love, Luigi Pistilli, Gianrico Tondinelli, Umberto Raho, Ivan Rassimov.
87 min.
Blatant Italian rip-off which ages the possessed heroine of *The Exorcist* by a few years to get its sexploitation angle. What is intermittently interesting (but only just) is the director's preoccupation with the disintegration of the affluent Italian family, and with Ken Russell (he actually contrives to have the heroine transferred to a convent hospital to enable elaborate cross-cutting with the nuns during the exorcism scenes). But an excessively noisy soundtrack hardly compensates for the visual poverty of this quickie. RM

Sex Play (aka The Bunny Caper)

(Jack Arnold, 1974, GB) Christina Hart, Ed Bishop, Murray Kash, Eric Young, Steve Plytas, David Beale.
90 min.
Yes, Jack Arnold – the incredible shrinking sci-fi

film director, who since the early '60s has been providing various varieties of pap, mainly for TV. As sex movies go, this is particularly well crafted, and at one or two points even manages to be (intentionally) funny. The heroine is the daughter of a bigwig American who comes to London and causes havoc among visiting diplomats (including a crude caricature of Henry Kissinger). But it's not really interesting – Arnold fans would be better off dreaming of creatures from the black lagoon and incredible shrinking men. GB

Sex Shop

(Claude Berri, 1972, Fr/It/WGer) Juliet Berto, Claude Berri, Nathalie Delon, Jean-Pierre Marielle, Francesca Romana, Catherine Allégret, Batrice Romand, Claude Piéplu, Grégoire Aslan.
105 min.
To call this an adult comedy would be generous, it's really no more than smug titillation. Happily-married bookshop owner (Berri) can't make ends meet, so opens sex shop instead; makes ends meet, but isn't happy; returns to his loving wife (Berto), having learned the error of his ways and after failing to make Nathalie Delon. Conventional happy ending: all else wilts in the face of *L'Amour Vrai*. The husband's errant ways provide an excuse for the usual round of female torsos, plus the odd snatch of pubic hair as a concession to these liberal times, but it's all pretty synthetic. Limp voyeurism that provides a few laughs along the way, but not enough to justify anything. CPe

Sex Symbol, The

(David Lowell Rich, 1974, US) Connie Stevens, Shelley Winters, Jack Carter, William Castle, Don Murray, James Olson, Nehemiah Persoff, Madlyn Rhue.
110 min.
The biopic at its most seedy and vulgarly full-blown, scripted by 'Hollywood Ten' blacklist victim Alvah Bessie from his own novel *The Symbol*. Dripping with clichés, it's based, perhaps too closely for some, on the life of Marilyn Monroe. Connie Stevens acts as far as the title and the camera's preoccupation with her cleavage will allow, displaying at least a talent for tantrums. The film's value, if any under the leering censoriousness and tatty analysis, lies in its stripping of illusions to reveal the pathetic vulnerabilities underneath. A callous, if unintentional, exposé of a myth, and another instance of Hollywood's insensitivity towards itself. This version, prepared for cinema release, is half-an-hour longer than the original shown on American TV under threat of libel action.

Sexual Life of the Belgians 1950-1978, The (La Vie Sexuelle des Belges 1950-1978)

(Jan Bucquoy, 1995, Bel) Jean-Henri Compère, Sophie Schneider, Noé Franq, Isabelle Legros, Pascale Binneri, Michele Shor.
80 min.
Belgian writer/director Jan Bucquoy can hardly be accused of vanity in his choice for the central role in this autobiographical portrait of the artist as a young slob. Hair by Mazola, complexion by Blue Circle, Compère only puts away one bag of chips and mayo during the course of the film, but looks as though he subsists on nothing else. The first thing we see in his mouth, however, is his mother's breast; and it's her money-saving motto ('Life is so expensive') that dominates the first half of the film, and, like her equally stingy affection for her son, rings throughout his subsequent progress. From awkward, greasy small-town boy to awkward, greasy big-city near-man: such is the making of this would-be revolutionary, aspirant novelist and ever-hopeful lover, the anti-Gump with whom we spend the rest of the picture. Episodic and conversational, this is no lurid exposé of salacious goings-on in the realm of beer and mussels; instead, it's a shambling, rather disarming survey of the amorous mishaps and potentially numbing provincialism that make post-'68 model Jan ready to change the world, and downright desperate to get his leg over in the interim. Not that the point is pushed home too hard in a film that ambles along through a welter of endearing emphemera (from tacky caravan parks and errant homing pigeons, to jibes at Godard's 'political' period and a striking tribute

to *Johnny Guitar*), plays sleight-of-hand with fantasy and reality, and half by accident, half by design, ends up matching its abundant slow-burn humour with an unexpected degree of genuine poignancy. TJ

S.F.W.

(Jefery Levy, 1994, US) Stephen Dorff, Reese Witherspoon, Jake Busey, Joey Lauren Adams, Pamela Gidley, David Barry Gray, Jack Noseworthy.
96 min.
An aggressive satire on consumerism, violence and the media, this mind-numbingly profane film apes the shrill, in-your-face teenage disaffection which makes its protagonist, Cliff Spab (Dorff), a TV phenomenon and a colossal bore. Spab is one of the customers held hostage for weeks at a supermarket by what appears to be an armed group of radical documentary film-makers, who insist their acuality footage is broadcast to the nation – and that's just the first five minutes. Very alienating. TCh

Sgt Bilko

(Jonathan Lynn, 1996, US) Steve Martin, Dan Aykroyd, Glenne Headly, Phil Hartman, Daryl Mitchell, Max Casella, Eric Edwards, Austin Pendleton, Catherine Silvers.
94 min.
For anyone who loves the classic '50s TV army base sit-com, the notion of doing Bilko without Phil Silvers suggests a travesty. Bilko was the ultimate finagler, but Martin hasn't the required calculation, though he's proved capable of inspired lunacy in the past, and has an ironic cool that might have seen him through. Director Lynn did a good job with *My Cousin Vinny* (not forgetting his *Yes, Minister* days) and Silvers' daughter Catherine pops up in the supporting cast, along with Aykroyd (Col Hall) and Headly (Bilko's girl). You might be forgiven for hoping against hope that these people couldt produce the goods just this once. You'd be wrong. This is a travesty all right, but a travesty with perhaps four laughs, tops. There's a good sight gag involving a horse early on, and one chuckles indulgently when Martin updates one of Bilko's classic routines (mistaking the Colonel's wife for Sharon Stone), but it's apparent within minutes not only that this isn't going to work, but that no one much cares. This is shoddy hackwork, replaying classic scenarios (the honest new recruit, audits by Pentagon bigwigs and manoeuvres in Nevada) with such disregard for narrative structure the reels might be in the wrong order. TCh

Sgt. Pepper's Lonely Hearts Club Band

(Michael Schultz, 1978, US/WGer) Peter Frampton, The Bee Gees, Frankie Howerd, Paul Nicholas, Donald Pleasence, Sandy Farina, Steve Martin, Aerosmith, Alice Cooper, George Burns.
111 min.
The Stigwood Organisation did the '70s (*Saturday Night Fever*), the '50s (*Grease*), and here tackle a prolonged dramatisation of the Beatles' lyrics and images. The songs themselves were so archly attuned to the highs and lows of the '60s that any sustained literal appreciation (Strawberry Fields as the girl-next-door?) is risky. This crass moral pantomime is plain embarrassing. The story, an allegory of big business versus simple music and love is centred around 'Heartland', home town of the Lonely Hearts Club Band, which depressingly combines the ethics and appearances of Toytown and Peyton Place, picked out in nursery colours. The Bee Gees (who do all the numbers impeccably) and little Peter Frampton fight off evil, which materialises as punks, litter, and a sadly unfunny Frankie Howerd. But somehow Bee Gees Against Capitalism doesn't quite ring true. It's almost 'guaranteed to raise a smile'. JS

Shadey

(Philip Saville, 1985, GB) Antony Sher, Billie Whitelaw, Patrick Macnee, Katherine Helmond, Leslie Ash, Bernard Hepton.
106 min.
Preposterous piffle in which hopelessly miscast stage actor Sher makes a ludicrous plot worse by parading a veritable text-book of camp and wildly inappropriate theatrical gestures as the epony-

mous hero, a bankrupt garage owner who tries to cash in on his precognitive powers in order to raise funds for a sex-change operation. Desperate for cash, Shadey approaches an eminent businessman (Macnee), who sells him to a military research establishment, where his pacifist leanings conflict with their hawkish aspirations. Thrown in for bad measure is a voyeuristic subplot concerning Macnee's incestuous desire for his daughter (Ash). The only enjoyable moment is when Macnee's mad wife (Helmond) stabs Shadey in the balls with a fork, his exquisite agony matched by our gratifying sense of revenge. NF

Shadow, The
(Russell Mulcahy, 1994, US) Alec Baldwin, John Lone, Ian McKellen, Penelope Ann Miller, Peter Boyle, Tim Curry, Jonathan Winters, André Gregory.
107 min.
Can the original haunted superhero of the '30s and '40s connect with a modern audience? Probably not. Despite classy production values, Mulcahy's attempt to emulate the sombre appeal of Tim Burton's *Batman* movies is too episodic, sketchy and uneven. Hiding his true identity beneath a cloak of invisibility, the Shadow (Baldwin) is a self-appointed crime fighter haunted by a murky past as a drug-dealer in the East. Now redeemed, he uses his supernatural powers to thwart the plans of Oriental villain Shiwan Khan (Lone), who through mind-control has forced Professor Lane (McKellen) to create a pseudo-atomic bomb. The Shadow's suave alter ego, playboy Lamont Cranston, finds time to romance Lane's daughter Margot (Miller). Baldwin's low-key performance lacks charisma, Lone alternates between lip-smacking villainy and camp humour, and Miller is chiefly a clothes-horse for a series of slinky '30s frocks. NF

Shadow Conspiracy
(George P Cosmatos, 1996, US) Charlie Sheen, Donald Sutherland, Linda Hamilton, Stephen Lang, Ben Gazzara, Nicholas Turturro, Theodore Bikel, Sam Waterston, Gore Vidal.
103 min.
An action movie for the wannabe liberal '90s, this tracks the political awakening of slick but decent presidential aide Bobby Bishop (Sheen). Right-wing traitors are at work in the White House – when Bobby starts to investigate, all hell breaks loose. His only allies are an ex-girlfriend (Hamilton) and the paternal Chief of Staff (Sutherland), but can they be trusted? Shadows are a bit of a theme here, and Washington, DC, provides plenty. Unfortunately, the movie has no such murky depths. Instead of an atmosphere of corruption, we have repeated shots of a cinema showing *Touch of Evil*. Similarly, there's no deep dialogue, just lots of deep faces: Sutherland, with his bulging, psychotically innocent eyes; Hamilton, with her rawhide skin and generous, manly mouth. Meatiest of all is Vidal, who pops up as a Southern politician. Sadly, Sheen doesn't even look profound. Like a zombie who's spent too much time in the gym, he blunders heavily from one stunt to the next, his pursed lips conveying nothing more than pique. CO'Su

Shadowlands
(Richard Attenborough, 1993, GB) Anthony Hopkins, Debra Winger, Joseph Mazzello, Peter Firth, John Wood, Michael Denison.
131 min.
1952. Theologian and essayist, CS 'Jack' Lewis (Hopkins) conducts a life of faintly mildewed bachelorhood at Magdalen College, Oxford. If there's any hint of desperation in his quietude, it's not to be found in his philosophical discourse, but in his children's books about Narnia, the magical land that lies behind the wardrobe. These strange and wonderful tales bring American poet Joy Gresham (Winger) and her son Douglas (Mazzello) into Lewis's small circle, an unlikely meeting which is to affect them all. Biting down on his pipe, his shirt collar permanently askew, Hopkins assays another concerted study in English repression – a condition unexpectedly relieved by Winger's brash intelligence and brittle wit. Attenborough does a good job with the musty hallowed halls and condescending donnish banter without letting the mise-en-scène clog up the works. Taken from the play by William Nicholson, this is the director's least sanctimo-

nious, least verbose picture. It's just a shame that, given the emphasis on the primacy of emotional experience, it feels like such a self-contained, studious exercise. TCh

Shadow Makers
see Fat Man and Little Boy

Shadowman
see Street of Shadows

Shadowman
see Nuits Rouges

Shadow of a Doubt
(Alfred Hitchcock, 1943, US) Joseph Cotten, Teresa Wright, Macdonald Carey, Patricia Collinge, Henry Travers, Hume Cronyn, Wallace Ford.
108 min. b/w.
One of Hitchcock's finest films of the '40s, with Cotten as the infamous 'Merry Widow' murderer, who takes refuge with the small-town family of his sister (Collinge). Focusing on adoring niece Wright's dawning realisation that her kind, generous and handsome uncle is in fact a cold and cynical killer, the film is not only psychologically intriguing (both niece and uncle are called Charlie, and he arrives in town as if in answer to her prayers for excitement), but a sharp dissection of middle American life, in its own quiet way an ancestor of *Blue Velvet*. Is Uncle Charlie all these gentle folk deserve, when adolescent girls dream of the romantic life, and middle-aged men (papa Travers and neighbour Cronyn) endlessly discuss gruesome murder? Funny, gripping, and expertly shot by Joe Valentine, it's a small but memorable gem. GA

Shadow of Doubt, A
see Ombre du Doute, L'

Shadow of the Hawk
(George McCowan, 1976, Can) Jan-Michael Vincent, Marilyn Hassett, Chief Dan George, Pia Shandel, Marianne Jones, Jacques Hubert.
92 min.
A tired, TV-style chase movie, which has 200-year-old evil spirits hounding a young man of Red Indian descent over 300 miles of assault course: snakes, bears, evil winds and the like. The only points of interest are Chief Dan George as the hero's medicine-man grandfather, and McCowan, whose previous directorial credits include the excellent natural pest/exploitation movie, *Frogs*. RG

Shadows
(John Cassavetes, 1959, US) Lelia Goldoni, Ben Carruthers, Hugh Hurd, Anthony Ray, Rupert Crosse.
87 min. b/w.
Admirers of *Mean Streets* may have wondered how Scorsese came by his dizzy vision of nervy New York neurotics: Cassavetes' first film may well have been a strong influence. As in the later film, what matters is less the story – two brothers and a sister working out various tensions between themselves and other friends and lovers – than the electric atmosphere and edgy performances. The trio trudge through their seedy city lives (smoky nightclubs, pretentious parties, disastrous sexual encounters, brawls, and beery beatnik conversations) suffering from heady hypertension, although what is now so surprising about this milestone of improvisational cinema is that it is often very funny. The jumpy editing, free-focus camerawork, and naturalistic dialogue (made the same year as Godard's *Breathless*, it centres around many of the same impulses towards a new form of film-making) may no longer shock, but back in '59 must have been a revelation. With a blue and moody Mingus soundtrack and steel-grey photography, it's still a delight. GA

Shadows and Fog
(Woody Allen, 1992, US) Woody Allen, Kathy Bates, John Cusack, Mia Farrow, Jodie Foster, Fred Gwynne, Julie Kavner, Madonna, John Malkovich, Kenneth Mars, Kate Nelligan, Donald Pleasence, Lily Tomlin, Philip Bosco, Wallace Shawn, Josef Sommer, David Ogden Stiers.
86 min.
An inconclusive charade for celebrity guests, Allen's film – made before *Husbands and Wives* – will add to the general sifting through the *oeuvre* for relevances to his personal predicament, without registering as a work on its own. This is Woody as Bergman, Woody as Punchinello, both over-familiar. He plays Kleinman, a *nebbich*, hopelessly besotted with a sword-swallower from the circus (Farrow). She has run away from her husband (Malkovich), an egotistical womanising clown who is cheating with the trapeze artiste (Madonna). There's a desultory subplot about The Ripper, but most of the action features Woody and Mia wandering nighttown, he witteringly supportive, she kvetching. The shadows of German Expressionist cinema have been superbly revived, but to little purpose. BC

Shadows in the Night
(Eugene Forde, 1944, US) Warner Baxter, Nina Foch, George Zucco, Minor Watson, Edward Norris, Charles Halton.
67 min. b/w.
The third in the *Crime Doctor* series of whodunits (ten films, 1943-49), by which time the character's peculiarly unconvincing history had been safely got out of the way (a criminal suffering from amnesia, he studied psychiatry and turned to doctoring crime). Fairly tacky stuff, with Foch being driven mad in rehearsal for *My Name is Julia Ross*. But the Gothic elements, headed by Zucco as a suavely sinister uncle and a ghostly apparition dripping wet from the sea, are done with great relish, and even some flair until the wrap-up explanations come. TM

Shadows of Our Forgotten Ancestors (Teni Zabytykh Predkov)
(Sergo Paradjanov, 1964, USSR) Ivan Nikolaichuk, Larissa Kadochnikova, Tatiana Bestaeva, Spartak Bagashvili.
95 min.
Paradjanov was considered a safe director of Ukrainian 'quota' features until he seized a unique moment of freedom to make this Carpathian rhapsody, which spoke loud his own closet dissidence and ushered in a flood of nonconformist movies from the other regional Soviets, including Tarkovsky's *Andrei Rublev* and Abuladze's *The Wishing Tree*. The 'forgotten ancestors' are mid-19th century villagers, who frolic naked in their youth and grow up into adulterers, lovelorn misfits, and feuding murderers. Their 'shadows' are not exactly sombre either: Paradjanov stops at nothing in his quest for startling images. The athletic camerawork and the bizarre visual effects take their tone from the folk ballads that recur on the soundtrack, sometimes touching an authentically barbaric or tragic poetry. The film is as chaotic as *The Colour of Pomegranates* is formalised, but it confirms that Paradjanov was 'dangerous' because he was committed to artifice – and imagination. TR

Shaft
(Gordon Parks, 1971, US) Richard Roundtree, Moses Gunn, Charles Cioffi, Christopher St John, Gwenn Mitchell, Lawrence Pressman, Victor Arnold.
100 min.
Renowned for its Isaac Hayes score, and as the first mainstream, commercially successful film about a black private eye, Parks' film is a hip, cool, entertaining thriller that in fact never really says very much at all about the Black experience in America; rather, it merely takes the traditional crime-fighting hero, paints him black, and sets him down in a world populated by more Blacks than Hollywood movies were used to. Roundtree turns in a strong performance, investigating a racketeer's criminal activities, while at the same time trying to find the man's kidnapped daughter. GA

Shaft in Africa
(John Guillermin, 1973, US) Richard Roundtree, Frank Finlay, Vonetta McGee, Neda Arneric, Debebe Eshetu, Spiros Focas, Glynn Edwards, Cy Grant.
112 min.
Third of the *Shaft* films (followed by a TV series), this one spreading itself pretty thinly over three continents, with Shaft versus slave-trader Frank Finlay. The uptown private eye of the first film

makes it into the big league caper and goes international, probably at the demand of the producers. The wisecracks are still dutifully tripped out, and Shaft himself is obliged to fill the gaps between the action by furnishing the myth of black potency. It's surprising that Roundtree, like Connery in the Bond films (and the similarities between the two series don't end there, in spite of Shaft's protests that he's no James Bond), manages to conduct himself with some dignity through all the surrounding debris. CPe

Shaft's Big Score!

(Gordon Parks, 1972, US) Richard Roundtree, Moses Gunn, Drew Bundini Brown, Joseph Mascolo, Kathy Imrie, Wally Taylor, Julius W Harris, Joe Santos.
105 min.
Disappointing sequel to the likeable *Shaft*, with Roundtree's black private eye – here up against rival takeover bidders for an illegal numbers racket – now operating from a lavish love nest instead of his fly-blown office. The film, in other words, has developed an 007 complex, and instead of being Chandler in Harlem, threading its way through a maze of quirky characters and dark mysteries, it makes a dreary beeline for its prolonged climax: a duel between superman Shaft and a hovering helicopter. TM

Shag

(Zelda Barron, 1987, US) Phoebe Cates, Scott Coffey, Bridget Fonda, Annabeth Gish, Page Hannah, Robert Rusler, Tyrone Power Jr, Shirley Anne Field.
98 min.
Lest you snigger, the title refers to a dance indigenous to South Carolina. Set in 1963, this teen movie with a well-connected cast has Gish (no relation), Fonda (daughter of Peter), Hannah (sister of Daryl) and Cates set off on a pre-college romp to Myrtle Beach, 'where the boys are'. Their aim is to dissuade the morally self-righteous Cates from marrying deadly dull Tyrone Power Jr; she resists, but soon hunky Buzz (Rusler), an advocate of free love, is tapping her primal instincts. Meanwhile, the other three pursue their aim of 'getting engaged by 20'. Kenny Ortega (*Dirty Dancing*, *Salsa*) choreographs, but has little to do; the dance sets are minimalised, and too often shot inappropriately at shoulder height. The adolescent antics may be familiar, but Barron directs with affection both for her characters and for back-combing and boned underskirts; her young professionals turn in appropriately corny performances; and the soundtrack is a corker. EP

Shaggy D.A., The

(Robert Stevenson, 1976, US) Dean Jones, Tim Conway, Suzanne Pleshette, Jo Anne Worley, Vic Tayback, Dick Bakalyan, Keenan Wynn, Dick Van Patten, Warren Berlinger, Hans Conreid.
92 min.
Some of Stevenson's Disney entertainments have been very polished and respectable, but not this mess. The sieve-like script tries to mix together Dean Jones' would-be district attorney turning into a lolloping dog (not once but repeatedly), some satire of electioneering and crooked politics, a slap-up pie fight, jokes about Dean Martin and Sarah Bernhardt, satire of ladies' clubs and other small-town Americana, police cars skidding on ice-cream fillings, dogs who talk with Bogart and Cagney voices. Nothing jells at all – least of all the central conceit of the hero becoming shaggy (sometimes the dog's a dog, sometimes a man with fur). It's also not much fun seeing Jones, Pleshette and Wynn getting older and older, staler and staler, playing the parts they've been stuck with for years. GB

Shakedown
(aka Blue Jean Cop)

(James Glickenhaus, 1988, US) Peter Weller, Sam Elliott, Patricia Charbonneau, Antonio Fargas, Blanche Baker, Richard Brooks, Jude Ciccolella.
96 min.
'Hey, Boesky, you wanna condom?' No, but the heavy black mutha sharing his cage does; such is the humour going down in NY penitentiaries, according to the man who brought you *The Exterminator*. Glickenhaus' state-of-the-art thriller on cracked-up, seamy New York stars the

familiar unlikely duo as a legal attorney (Weller) and a renegade detective (Elliott) attempt to solve a fatal shooting between a drugs dealer and a corrupt cop. No celluloid cliché that could possibly fit into *Escape from New York* or *Dirty Harry* is left unstitched. Plenty of blood, tension, and complex stunt sequences leave precious little time to ruminate on the popcorn. This heady mix of sleaze and comic book heroes smacks of big box office bucks and a long life on the video shelf. There ain't many better accolades than that. JCh

Shaker Run

(Bruce Morrison, 1985, NZ) Cliff Robertson, Leif Garrett, Lisa Harrow, Shane Briant, Peter Hayden, Peter Rowell.
90 min.
Ex-racing ace Robertson and his mechanic sidekick (Garrett), a couple of down-on-their-luck Yanks touring New Zealand with a stunt team, are enlisted by a concerned scientist (Harrow) to race a deadly virus to a remote rendezvous, safe from unscrupulous clutches. Director Morrison straps a camera to their souped-up Trans Am, hurtling along the highways of South Island, pursued by a grisly assortment of baddies, CIA agents, and military. The whole thing is really an excuse for a series of finely executed daredevil stunts, but what holds it together is the tongue-in-cheek direction and humorous ensemble playing. No masterpiece, but we's only out for some fun, ain't we? WH

Shakespeare-Wallah

(James Ivory, 1965, Ind) Felicity Kendal, Shashi Kapoor, Geoffrey Kendal, Laura Liddell, Madhur Jaffrey, Utpal Dutt.
125 min. b/w.
The second film from the Merchant-Ivory-Jhabvala collaboration: despite occasional longueurs, a hauntingly funny, rather Chekhovian piece about a group of English-led travelling players stoutly striving to keep Shakespeare alive in India long after the Raj has gone. Loosely inspired by the experiences of the Kendal family, who here recreate parts of their Shakespearean repertory, it was shot by Ray's cameraman Subrata Mitra, has a fine score by Ray himself, and at its best has much of Ray's quizzical charm. Dialogue and performances, though, tend towards the stilted; and although Felicity Kendal and Shashi Kapoor aren't bad as the young lovers parted not so much by the racial divide as by character and circumstance, Madhur Jaffrey runs away with all prizes as an outrageously arrogant Indian movie queen further spurred by jealousy. TM

Shaking the Tree

(Duane Clark, 1990, US) Arye Gross, Gale Hansen, Doug Savant, Steven Wilde, Courteney Cox, Christina Haag.
107 min.
Four old high school buddies now face the '90s with mounting dread. The marital and extra-marital agonies, late adolescent angst attacks, flirtations with low life: Clark's film could almost be 'Diner: The Next Generation'. Michael (Savant) is wondering whether his wife will produce a baby before he produces his novel; nerdish power broker Barry (Gross) can't stop kvetching about his wife's sexual history; amiable ex-boxer Duke (Wilde) is having trouble Relating to Daddy; and Sully (Hansen), a rich kid, likes to live seedy. For the first half-hour, the film just about overcomes its limitations by fielding sound acting, promising characterisations, and a winning sense of place (this is a Chicago movie and proud of it). But having told their menfolk 'We need to talk' once too often, the women vanish into the background, while the guys embark on a dreary, mechanical round of griping, barroom buddying, and nick-of-time problem solving. JRo

Shalako

(Edward Dmytryk, 1968, GB) Sean Connery, Brigitte Bardot, Stephen Boyd, Jack Hawkins, Peter Van Eyck, Honor Blackman, Woody Strode, Eric Sykes, Alexander Knox.
113 min.
There's an engaging premise to this British Western shot in Spain, with a group of European aristocrats on safari in the wild west (complete with chilled wine and sterling silver), looking for big game but finding warlike Apaches. But its notions of humour (Eric Sykes as an imper-

turbable butler) don't go too well with Dmytryk's attempts to ape the spaghetti Western style, and it very quickly goes downhill. TM

Shallow Grave

(Danny Boyle, 1994, GB) Kerry Fox, Christopher Eccleston, Ewan McGregor, Ken Stott, Keith Allen, Colin McCredie.
92 min.
When their mysterious new flatmate suffers a fatal overdose, David, Alex and Juliet (Eccleston, McGregor and Fox) find a fortune in bank notes stashed in his room. They quickly resolve to keep the money, but nothing comes for free, and the price here involves not only dismemberment and burial, but the trio's trust, sanity and friendship. This impressively assured, highly accomplished British feature doesn't dwell on moral niceties, but goes straight for the gut. John Hodge's screenplay has the kind of unrelenting forward momentum and close-to-the bone sense of purpose which sees you safely through a good many logical minefields, even if nagging question marks occur in retrospect. Given that most of the action takes place in the flat, it's remarkable how agile and invigorating Boyle's direction is. As the friends fall out, the movie loses some of its black comic edge, perhaps, but only to gain in sheer, backstabbing, bloody-minded mayhem. TCh

Shall We Dance?

(Mark Sandrich, 1937, US) Fred Astaire, Ginger Rogers, Edward Everett Horton, Eric Blore, Jerome Cowan, Ketti Gallian, Harriet Hoctor.
116 min. b/w.
RKO temporarily parted Fred and Ginger after this musical, which didn't have the flow of earlier efforts. Taking off from an ocean-going romance, in which the outrageous assumption is made that Astaire has got Rogers pregnant, it stops adumbrating Leo McCarey's great *Love Affair* by getting into a silly will-they-won't-they round, saved only by the Gershwin numbers. These include 'Let's Call the Whole Thing Off', which has a rather strained and cumbersome roller-skating sequence with sticky moments on Ginger's part, and the outright winner, 'They Can't Take That Away from Me'. SG

Shall We Dance?

(Masayuki Suo, 1995, Jap) Koji Yakusho, Tamiyo Kusakari, Naoto Takenaka, Eriko Watanabe, Akira Emoto.
136 min.
This entertaining Japanese comedy opens with a dreamy shot of Blackpool's Tower Ballroom, but it's back in suburban Tokyo that Masayuki Suo's film really begins. A salaryman (Yakusho) is locked in routine until curiosity gets the better of him: each evening, from the train, he sees a beautiful woman gazing out of the window of a ballroom dancing class, and one night he plucks up the courage to go in. As lessons progress, his secret cannot remain hidden for long – dancing has entered his bloodstream and he'll never be the same again. All he needs now is the girl. While the film's balancing act, between the love interest in fragile beauty Tamiyo Kusakari and the call of the protagonist's domestic ties, is ultimately contrived, unlike Hollywood tosh, it never feels blatantly manipulative. The salaryman's reserve carries a significant charm, and although the overly careful pacing at times threatens to dull our involvement, director Suo still knows when to throw in the comic fizz. The real star of the show is Naoto Takenaka as the office colleague transformed into a rumba tornado. TJ

Shame

(Steve Jodrell, 1987, Aust) Deborra-Lee Furness, Tony Barry, Simone Buchanan, Gillian Jones, Peter Aanensen, Margaret Ford, David Franklin.
94 min.
From the shadow of the controversial *The Accused* comes Jodrell's first feature, also dealing with gang rape. Furness (excellent) plays Asta, a self-reliant barrister and biker who breaks down while travelling alone through the outback. The garage mechanic's daughter Lizzie (Buchanan) has been gang-raped by a group of local hoods, and is trapped in a 'she asked for it' conspiracy of silence. Asta takes on Lizzie's case, finding herself in a vicious battle with the sheriff and the rest of the male community. Furness handles her role

with calm strength and obvious skill; and where *The Accused* manipulated sensation, this avoids the gratuitous voyeurism of including the rape scene. Working by allusion, it succeeds in striking exactly the right note, responsibly, movingly, and yet rivetingly. IA

Shameless Old Lady, The

see Vieille Dame indigne, La

Shame, The (Skammen)

(Ingmar Bergman, 1968, Swe) Liv Ullmann, Max von Sydow, Gunnar Björnstrand, Sigge Fürst, Birgitta Valberg.
103 min. b/w.
Bergman's magisterial confrontation with war, set in a characteristically ambivalent decor, either a peaceful farm somewhere in Sweden or a landscape from Goya secreting intimations of disaster. Here live a man and wife, indifferent to the war until it arrives on their doorstep to strip their lives to the bone. Presenting war with shattering power as a blindly destructive force, Bergman uses it brilliantly as a background to the real pain: the way the couple are forced to look at each other, and to realise that the only honest feeling they have about their relationship is shame. It ends with one of the cinema's most awesomely apocalyptic visions: not the cheeriest of films, but a masterpiece. TM

Shampoo

(Hal Ashby, 1975, US) Warren Beatty, Julie Christie, Goldie Hawn, Lee Grant, Jack Warden, Tony Bill, Carrie Fisher, Jay Robinson, Luana Anders, Brad Dexter.
110 min.
Made with all the awareness of hindsight, *Shampoo* offers a sharp sexual satire and a mature statement on both America and Hollywood in 1968, *The Graduate* as it should have been, perhaps. Everyone is shown to act out of the same fatal expediency, as the country elects Nixon for President while Beatty's chic Hollywood hairdresser tries to sort out an increasingly dishevelled sex life, a campaign against the Establishment via its wives and mistresses that's subversive only by default. Ostensibly a farce about fucking for fun and its repercussions, but the laughs are tempered by bleakness and the film ends up saddened by its characters' waywardness. CPe

Shamus

(Buzz Kulik, 1972, US) Burt Reynolds, Dyan Cannon, John Ryan, Joe Santos, Giorgio Tozzi, Ron Weyland.
106 min.
No-nonsense title for a no-nonsense ex-pool player turned private eye. Hired by a shady rich man to find out who killed a diamond thief, Reynolds stumbles on something bigger: gun-running and the illicit sale of surplus US military equipment. He is also stumbled upon (metaphor intended) by Dyan Cannon, as the voluptuous sister of an ex-football star, who thinks her brother's somehow involved and enlists the shamus' professional help. It's a stereotyped, amoral tale; the film doesn't bother to tell us who is running guns, where and why. Kulik is more concerned with careful social and dramatic realism; the shamus is no Bond-fantasy hero, just a tough guy who hits first and asks questions later, and is frankly a stud. Little details (like the way he mouths 'Shit!', and when the window sticks), the unsentimental but real moments of male comradeship between him and a cop, him and his underworld contacts, the downbeat ending, make the film worth watching. MV

Shane

(George Stevens, 1953, US) Alan Ladd, Jean Arthur, Van Heflin, Jack Palance, Brandon de Wilde, Ben Johnson, Edgar Buchanan, Elisha Cook Jr, Emile Meyer, John Dierkes.
118 min.
Stevens' classic Western, with its inflated reputation, now looks as if it were self-consciously intended as a landmark film right from the start. Certainly its story, of a lone, laconic stranger riding out of the desert to lend aid to a pioneer farming family in their battle against a gang of dark-hearted villains, has been much imitated since (notably in Clint Eastwood's *Pale Rider*), while its deliberately epic landscape photography is now a *sine qua non* of the genre. But the

slow pace and persistent solemnity reduce tension, prefiguring the portentous nature of Stevens' later work. That said, the cast is splendid, and both the emotional tensions between Ladd and Arthur, and the final confrontation with Palance, are well handled. GA

Shanghai Blues (Shanghai zhi Ye)

(Tsui Hark, 1984, HK) Sylvia Chang, Sally Yip, Kenny Bee, Loretta Li.
108 min.
Shanghai before and after the Japanese occupation, but gleefully anachronistic in every way. The plot (boy meets girl; boy loses girl; boy and girl wind up as feuding neighbours without recognising each other) is collaged together from classic Shanghai movies like *Street Angel Crossroads* and *8000 Li Under the Clouds and Moon*. The cast is pretty, but it looks and sounds like a 90-minute commercial. It will certainly boost sales of paracetamol. TR

Shanghai Express

(Josef von Sternberg, 1932, US) Marlene Dietrich, Clive Brook, Warner Oland, Anna May Wong, Eugene Pallette, Lawrence Grant, Gustav von Seyffertitz, Louise Closser Hale.
80 min. b/w.
Von Sternberg, who was forever looking for new kinds of stylisation, said that he intended everything in *Shanghai Express* to have the rhythm of a train. He clearly meant it: the bizarre stop-go cadences of the dialogue delivery are the most blatantly non-naturalistic element, but the overall design and dramatic pacing are equally extraordinary. The plot concerns an evacuation from Peking to Shanghai, but it's in every sense a vehicle for something else: a parade of deceptive appearances and identities, centering on the *Boule de Suif* notion of a prostitute with more honour than those around her. Dietrich's Shanghai Lily hasn't aged a day, but Clive Brook's stiff-upper-lip British officer (her former lover) now looks like a virtual caricature of the type. None the less, the sincerity and emotional depth with which Sternberg invests their relationship is quite enough to transcend mere style or fashion. TR

Shanghai Gesture, The

(Josef von Sternberg, 1941, US) Gene Tierney, Walter Huston, Victor Mature, Ona Munson, Maria Ouspenskaya, Phyllis Brooks, Albert Basserman, Eric Blore, Mike Mazurki.
106 min. b/w.
Sternberg's last Hollywood masterpiece, a delirious melodrama of decadence and sexual guilt that uses its Oriental motifs as a cypher for all that is unknown or unknowable. The battle is waged between a Western hypocrite (Huston) and an Eastern pleasure queen (Munson); the erotic skirmishes occur between the self-willed but helpless heroine (Tierney) and the apathetic object of her passion (Mature, amazing, 'Doctor of nothing, poet of Shanghai...and Gomorrah'); the chief arena is a casino built like a circle of hell, where nothing is left to 'chance'. Subversive cinema at its most sublime. TR

Shanghai Lil (Hao Ke/aka The Champion)

(Zhuge Qingyun/Yang Jingchen, 1973, HK) Shih Szu, Chin Han, I Yuan, Lung Fei, Chang Feng.
91 min.
A fair example of mid-period Shaw Brothers martial arts film, enlivened by some fairly lethal-looking stunt work around a mine face, and an attractive performance from female martial artist Shih Szu. Chin Han's hero, released from prison after serving a term in place of his half-brother, returns to find the latter working the family mine in cahoots with the Russians. Inevitably, rejecting an underhand offer of Japanese aid, he goes on (with the aid of Shih Szu) to win the mine back – quite explicitly sidestepping a situation with revolutionary potential. The Chin Han character, while physically resembling the heroes of mainland Chinese films very closely, fails to carry the kind of populist charge so crucial to the martial arts hero, and without this he comes off decidedly palely compared to the trenchant Japanese contingent, despite the statutory Chinese triumph at the end. VG

Shanghai Surprise

(Jim Goddard, 1986, GB) Sean Penn, Madonna, Paul Freeman, Richard Griffiths, Philip Sayer, Clyde Kusatsu, Kay Tong Lim, Michael Aldridge.
97 min.
A water-coloured, watered-down romantic comedy set in Shanghai in 1937, with the helplessly miscast Madonna (would you buy a used Bible from this woman?) trading on her ironic stage name to play an American missionary. She, with the aid of Penn's gaudy tie salesman, is desperately seeking 'Faraday's Flowers', a hidden opium stockpile which will help relieve the suffering of soldiers wounded in the war with Japan. The action is simply an implausible chain of events sensationally strung together, a Saturday morning serial formula which worked for *Raiders of the Lost Ark*; here, the heavy-handed manipulation of genre ingredients simply results in vulgar, often embarrassing, kitsch. SGo

Shanghai Triad (Yao a Yao Yao dao Waipo Qiao)

(Zhang Yimou, 1995, HK/China/Fr) Gong Li, Wang Xiaoxiao, Li Baotian, Li Xuejian, Sun Chun, Fu Biao, Chen Shu, Liu Jiang.
108 min.
To '30s Shanghai comes 14-year-old yokel Shuisheng (Wang Xiaoxiao), whose uncle finds him work with the triad gang headed by ruthlessly manipulative Tang (Li Baotian). His job is to wait on fiery-tempered Bijou (Gong Li), the boss's mistress whose routines have made her 'Queen' of the Shanghai music halls. Dealing with her demands is difficult enough, but when Tang's rival Fat Yu seeks revenge for a murder by Tang and his right-hand man Song (who, it transpires, is Bijou's secret lover), Bijou and the boy flee to a remote island, Shuisheng little knows what treachery he will witness. Despite being related through the eyes of the naive Shuisheng, this sumptuous gangster drama centres on the experience of Bijou, a woman who initially believes she's able to exploit her position as the mistress of an ageing crime boss, but who comes, belatedly, to realise she's simply a pawn in a man's world and, thereby, to regain some of her lost innocence. Unfortunately, with its faintly uneven pacing and straggling structure, the film lacks depth or narrative economy. That said, Zhang's use of colour is as vivid as ever, his stylised depiction of violence is mostly effective, and Gong Li is gloriously watchable. GA

Shanks

(William Castle, 1974, US) Marcel Marceau, Tsilla Chelton, Philippe Clay, Cindy Eilbacher, Helena Kallianiotes, Larry Bishop.
93 min.
The old gimmick-master's last film, a genuine weirdie with the mime Marceau in a dual role (one speaking, one not) as a scientist working on the galvanic reanimation of dead animals, and as a downtrodden puppeteer brought in to assist with his experiments. When the old scientist dies, the puppeteer gleefully discovers that he can re-animate human corpses: some extraordinary stuff here, making macabre use of mimic talents (Clay and Chelton in addition to Marceau) to suggest the nightmarishly jerky, tortured movements of the living dead as the puppeteer deals with his immediate enemies. It gravitates into more routine territory – revenge against a gang of brutish Hell's Angels who rape and kill a sweet young girl (Eilbacher) who had become the puppeteer's only friend – but nevertheless remains a strikingly effective experiment. TM

Shape of Things to Come, The

(George McCowan, 1979, Can) Jack Palance, Carol Lynley, Barry Morse, John Ireland, Nicholas Campbell, Eddie Benton.
98 min.
Somewhere deep in hype-space, the crew of the spaceship Starstreak ponder over the fact that once they were almost stars, and continue the seemingly never-ending search for their script, lost in the black hole of the *Star Wars* boom. 'Man's future is limited only by his imagination', the scientist says; and films only by his greed, the audience sighs. HG Wells' novel was filmed in 1936 as *Things to Come*, with brilliant set designs by William Cameron Menzies and a script in part by Wells himself, full of (admittedly often half-

digested) ideas. Masquerading under the original title, but set 50 years later and providing its own risibly inept plot, this is the unacceptable face of exploitation. SM

Shark

(Samuel Fuller, 1969, US/Mex) Burt Reynolds, Barry Sullivan, Arthur Kennedy, Silvia Pinal, Enrique Lucero.
92 min.
Although Fuller disowns this because it was cut against his wishes, it still remains worth seeing for what's left. The search for sunken treasure by four totally amoral protagonists, all intent on double-crossing each other, is capably handled; but the lasting impression is of how well Fuller conveys the atmosphere of hot and dusty small towns in the middle of nowhere.

Shark Callers of Kontu, The

(Dennis O'Rourke, 1986, Aust)
52 min.
In Papua New Guinea, in the coastal village of Kontu, there are men who are able to kill sharks with their bare hands. First mentioned by Abel Tasman back in 1643, the fishermen attribute their power to catch the creatures – which they believe carry the spirits of their ancestors – to magic. But as 'civilisation' gains its hold upon the village, that magic is inevitably disappearing, together with the village's community spirit. Though superbly detailed in its observation of the rituals and daily rounds of Kontu life, O'Rourke's marvellous documentary is no mere anthropological record. Refusing to indulge in paternalistic notions of the noble savage, he offers a persuasive analysis of how and why this culture is being destroyed by the outside world. Closer to, say, Lévi-Strauss than to romantics like JG Frazer or Werner Herzog, O'Rourke's sympathies are deeply political, although *Shark Callers* is no dry manifesto. Rather, by allowing the villagers to speak for themselves and the camera simply to reveal the remarkable nature of the men's work, he relates the spiritual world of 'magic' to more comprehensible forces with admirable lucidity. GA

Sharks' Cave, The (Bermude: La Fossa Maledetta)

(Anthony Richmond ie. Teodoro Ricci, 1978, It/Sp) Andrés Garcia, Janet Agren, Arthur Kennedy, Pino Colizzi, Maximo Valverde.
90 min.
The pulse of any trash addict must pound over the idea behind this fin film (molto cheapo), where the mysteries of the Bermuda Triangle are explained in terms of killer sharks controlled by tiny Toltec aquanauts. Hapless, scantily-outfitted divers keep running across their underwater city (made out of fish-bowl decorations), Arthur Kennedy plays a threatening Mafioso much as Truman Capote might, and the planes and ships which founder in the Triangle are obviously toys. The powers of the Toltecs ('ultimately inexplicable', thanks to the low budget) are symbolised by orgasmic moans. There is one great totally unexplained scene, with a cruiser full of hippies, looking like a floating detoxification project, who commit mass suicide by jumping over the side. CR

Shark's Son (Le Fils du Requin)

(Agnès Merlet, 1993, Fr) Sandrine Blancke, Ludovic Van Den Daele, Erick Da Silva.
90 min.
Though apparently based on a real-life story, this study of two uncontrollable delinquent brothers – it comes on like *Les Valseuses* for ten-year-olds – often seems far-fetched. The children are convincing, but the narrative is not, alternating as it does between scenes of outrageous anti-social behaviour, implausible escapes from authority, and poetic interludes of dreamy meditation. Aren't these knowing boys *ever* just boys? Despite Merlet's admirably unsentimental handling of her amoral script, the two-note tone soon becomes wearisome. GA

Sharks' Treasure

(Cornel Wilde, 1974, US) Cornel Wilde, Yaphet Kotto, John Neilson, David Canary, Cliff Osmond, David Gilliam, Caesar Cordova.
95 min.

Always primitive, Wilde's films seem to operate increasingly in a strange limbo, with no points of reference outside their own simple view of the world. The astonishing naïveté of Wilde's script can scarcely cope with the different strands of the plot queueing up and waiting to be dealt with: fights against sharks (well handled), underwater searches for treasure (*Look at Life*-like), confrontations with desperadoes (risible). Rather more unified is Wilde's homespun philosophising: the perils of nicotine and drink, and the virtues of keeping fit, with the spry 60-year-old Wilde doing one-handed press-ups on deck. But most curious are the closeted emotions of the all-male group, which threaten to run riot without writer/producer/director/star Wilde in the least aware of them. A real oddity.

Sharky's Machine

(Burt Reynolds, 1981, US) Burt Reynolds, Vittorio Gassman, Brian Keith, Charles Durning, Earl Holliman, Bernie Casey, Henry Silva, Darryl Hickman, Rachel Ward, Joseph Mascolo.
120 min.
Demoted to the vice squad after a bungled drugs bust, Reynolds puts together a team of 'loser' cops to investigate links between high class hookers and possible political corruption. Unfortunately, Reynolds the director is as uncertain about the tone of the picture as Reynolds the star is about his screen *persona*. So while the action veers from lightweight action to extreme violence, Reynolds' character vacillates between macho tough guy and sensitive, vulnerable leading man. One minute he's busting heads and uttering expletives, the next he's talking to emotionally scarred tart-with-a-heart Ward about his passion for wood-carving. Still, William A Fraker's first-rate location photography invests the seedy locations with an authentic feel, while the relish with which the unhinged assassin (Silva) and Oriental torturers go about their business enliven the routine plot about a mysterious Mr Big. NF

Shattered (Les Passagers)

(Serge Leroy, 1976, Fr/It) Jean-Louis Trintignant, Mireille Darc, Bernard Fresson, Adolfo Celi, Richard Constantini.
103 min.
Trintignant escorts his 11-year-old stepson from school in Italy to their new home in Paris, where wife (Darc) awaits. They're pursued, *Duel* style, by a psychopathic killer (Fresson) who terrorises them with his Ford Panel van. Along the way, Leroy handles a host of proven topical elements capably enough – urban paranoia, misogynistic killer, precocious kid, bigoted cop (Celi); and the rip-off of the basic plot mechanism from Spielberg's movie (by way of Dean Koontz's novel *Shattered*, published under the pseudonym K.R. Dwyer) is effective enough. But casting and pay-off are both too predictable to make what emerges anything more than an efficient, glossy thriller delivered without any particular conviction. RM

Shattered

(Wolfgang Petersen, 1991, US) Tom Berenger, Bob Hoskins, Greta Scacchi, Joanne Whalley-Kilmer, Corbin Bernsen, Scott Getlin, Theodore Bikel.
98 min.
Based on Richard Neely's novel *The Plastic Nightmare*, Petersen's first American feature is a credible and gripping thriller, using ambiguous clues and a complex flashback structure to draw us into the dark heart of an amnesiac maze. Berenger plays a wealthy architect whose life is shattered when he and his wife (Scacchi) plunge over a cliff in their car. Emerging from a coma, he has his face reconstructed, but his memory of the crash has been erased. When he tries to reassemble his life with the help of his wife, who was thrown clear, some pieces of the jigsaw just won't fit. Photos of Scacchi with another man lead him to private eye Hoskins, whom he had hired before the accident to spy on her infidelities with a mystery lover. Meanwhile, his partner's wife (Whalley-Kilmer) is insisting that she and Berenger had been having a torrid affair. Knowing only what Berenger knows, we share his sense of disorientation and vulnerability, while Petersen's sure-footed script and controlled direction eschew self-conscious *hommage* for good old-fashioned adult entertainment. NF

Shattered Dreams: Picking Up the Pieces

(Victor Schonfeld, 1987, GB) narrator: Jack Klass.
173 min.
A documentary chronicle of what Schonfeld sees as the present-day betrayal of Israel's original democratic and cooperative ideals, this traces the contradictions within Zionism back to an unresolved conflict between religious and secular law, and to an ongoing critics of racial and national identity. He emphasises the wide range of responses to the so-called 'Holy War in Galilee' (the invasion of Lebanon), the expropriation of Palestinian land on the West bank, and the racist views of Rabbi Kahane. Contrasting the idealistic newsreels of the late '40s with contemporary footage and interviews, he suggests that such chauvinist notions are not endemic to Zionism but a corruption of it. The film's left-of-centre liberalism isn't always as clearly focused as it might be, but for the most part it eschews partisan rhetoric in favour of opening up new and vital areas of debate. NF

Shawshank Redemption, (100) The

(Frank Darabont, 1994, US) Tim Robbins, Morgan Freeman, Bob Gunton, William Sadler, Clancy Brown, Gil Bellows, Mark Rolston.
142 min.
In 1946 a young New England banker, Andy Dufresne (Robbins), is convicted of murdering his wife and her lover and sentenced to life at the Shawshank State Prison – twice over. Quiet and introspective, he gradually strikes up a friendship with the prison 'fixer', Red (Freeman), and over the next two decades wins the trust of the governor and guards, but in his heart, he still yearns for freedom. Darabont's adaptation of a Stephen King novella is a throwback to the kind of serious, literate drama Hollywood used to make (*Birdman of Alcatraz*, say) though the big spiritual resolution takes some swallowing – ditto the colour-blind relationships within the prison and the violent disavowal of any homosexual implications. Against this weighs the pleasure of discovering a first-time director with evident respect for the intelligence of his audience, brave enough to let character details accumulate without recourse to the fast-forward button. Darabont plays the long game and wins: this is an engrossing, superbly acted yarn, while the Shawshank itself is a truly formidable mausoleum. TCh

She

(Irving Pichel/Lansing C Holden, 1935, US) Helen Gahagan, Randolph Scott, Helen Mack, Nigel Bruce, Gustav von Seyffertitz, Noble Johnson.
95 min. b/w.
The first talkie version of Rider Haggard's much (and unsatisfactorily) filmed yarn. Though produced by Merian C Cooper, who was very much at home in the jungles of King Kong and Count Zaroff, the action was for some ineffable reason shifted in locale from Africa to the Arctic, so that the fantastic underground kingdom of She (who bathed in the mysterious Flame of Life centuries ago and tries to entice Scott away from his mortal love) nestles picturesquely among the snowscapes. Frequent recourse to backdrops rather undercuts the spectacular effect (though the furnishings and costumes prevailing in She's domain have a certain tacky splendour); the dialogue is routine Hollywood period adventurespeak; and it's difficult to decide, between Gahagan and Scott as the two leads, who gives the more inexpressive, uncharismatic performance. TM

She

(Robert Day, 1965, GB) Ursula Andress, John Richardson, Peter Cushing, Bernard Cribbins, Christopher Lee, Andre Morell, Rosenda Monteros.
165 min.
Rider Haggard's *She Who Must Be Obeyed* (now you know where Rumpole of the Bailey got his tag line from) emerges predictably in this low-rent exotica from Hammer as she who must be ogled, and the old hunt-for-the-lost-city formula doesn't even cut it as camp. At least the setting returned to warmer climes from the Arctic setting of the 1935 version, no doubt to explain Andress' undress. PT

Sheba Baby

(William Girdler, 1975, US) Pam Grier, Austin Stoker, D'Urville Martin, Rudy Challenger, Dick Merrifield.
89 min.

Private eye Sheba Shayne plays a lone hand against a gang of racketeers trying to take over her father's business. Any 'generic significance' claimed for Pam Grier's movies clearly dissipated long before this travesty, where jive-talkin', posturing blacks conform so closely to stereotype that they are not merely uninteresting but offensive. Not only do all the characters behave as the epitome of the urban 'street nigger', they have all assimilated the American Dream without question: a dream of patronising liberalism, non-confrontation and self-fulfilment, here clearly used to keep everyone in their places. Pap, made with contempt. SM

She Creature, The

(Edward L Cahn, 1956, US) Chester Morris, Tom Conway, Cathy Downs, Lance Fuller, Ron Randell, Marla English, Frieda Inescort.
77 min. b/w.

Cheerful grade-Z monster mayhem as the assistant of a carnival hypnotist is sent into a trance only to reveal her true self, swiftly transforming into a rampaging prehistoric sea beast. In time-honoured showbiz tradition, the mesmerist and his associates soon try to make a fast buck by 'predicting' the creature's killings. Quite a convincing monster. TJ

She Demons

(Richard E Cunha, 1958, US) Irish McCalla, Tod Griffin, Victor Sen Yung, Rudolph Anders, Leni Tana.
80 min. b/w.

If you're curious about the more baroque sensations usually untapped by the normal film-making brain, this is your tacky dream drama. A vicious hurricane shipwrecks our heroes on a suspicious island, where the beached debutante combs her peroxide locks and complains, 'Where's my powder blue cashmere shortie?' Attention is soon distracted by Native Drums, then by radio news that they're sitting on a Navy bomb target (promptly forgotten for the next hour by the cast), and the discovery of a bevy of jungle babes in bikinis engaged in a hoochie-coo hula around a fire. Festivities are interrupted by a whip-wielding Nazi who holds the franchise on this Iggy Pop School of Dance...and from there the action proceeds along paths explicable only in terms of heavy hallucinogenic use among the script team. CR

She-Devil

(Susan Seidelman, 1989, US) Meryl Streep, Roseanne Barr, Ed Begley Jr, Sylvia Miles, Linda Hunt, Elisebeth Peters, Bryan Larkin, A Martinez.
99 min.

Cinematic adaptations of novels are under no obligation to remain rigorously faithful to the original, but even with that in mind, this version of Fay Weldon's The Life and Loves of a She-Devil is misjudged. The story is relocated across the Atlantic, its tone altered to leave audiences on an upbeat note. Fat, frumpy housewife Ruth (Barr) is deserted by her husband (Begley), who goes to live with glamorous romantic novelist Mary Fisher (Streep) in her high tower by the sea. With demonic conviction, Ruth sets about depriving the lovers of their new-found happiness. She makes a list of her husband's assets – Home, Family, Career and Freedom – and destroys each in turn. Thus circumscribed, the film plods to its conclusion. Streep's tentative foray into comedy is deliberately mannered, but the breathy delivery and constant fluttering of hands are nevertheless excessive. And in her film debut, Barr just isn't imposing enough to inspire notions of devilish vengeance. The filmmakers have opted for frothy satire, but as comedies go this is lamentably short on laughs. CM

She Done Him Wrong

(Lowell Sherman, 1933, US) Mae West, Cary Grant, Owen Moore, Gilbert Roland, Noah Beery, Rochelle Hudson, Rafaela Ottiano, Louise Beavers.
66 min. b/w.

West's first starring vehicle, and one of her best (ie. least diluted) movies. Adapted from her stage success Diamond Lil, it features her as Diamond Lou (a change occasioned by the original's notoriety), mistress of a Naughty Nineties saloon, setting her sights on the righteous young man (Grant) investigating the place for signs of corruption. West, making her way through ditties like 'I Like a Man What Takes His Time' and 'Frankie and Johnny', keeps most of her double-meanings single. Marvellous stuff. GA

Sheena (aka Sheena – Queen of the Jungle)

(John Guillermin, 1984, US) Tanya Roberts, Ted Wass, Donovan Scott, Elizabeth of Toro, France Zobda, Trevor Thomas, Clifton Jones.
117 min.

African shaman Elizabeth of Toro adopts an orphaned 'golden-girl-child' and calls her Sheena. The tiny Tarzanette learns from her the art of summoning wild animals (by affecting a bad migraine), and fleshes out to become Tanya Roberts, clad in suede bikini and showing lots of loin. Being a true child of nature, she sometimes takes off her junglewear in public, which endears her to an American TV sports presenter (Wass), who tags after her into the undergrowth. She also swings from creepers, rides bareback on a horse painted with black and white stripes, and tosses flaming arrows at the evil Prince Otwani (Thomas), who is planning to muck about with the sacred Zambucca mountain. But despite all these amazing abilities, Sheena loses her heart to the first chap with a furry chest who comes along. 'You are my man', she tells the media hack proudly. Nobody's perfect. AB

Sheepman, The

(George Marshall, 1958, US) Glenn Ford, Shirley MacLaine, Leslie Nielsen, Mickey Shaughnessy, Edgar Buchanan, Pernell Roberts, Slim Pickens.
91 min.

A minor but irresistibly amiable semi-comic Western that looks both backwards to Marshall's own glorious Destry Rides Again and forwards to the Burt Kennedy films of the late '60s. The plot is archetypal – sheep farmer Ford arrives in town, only to incur the wrath of cattle baron Nielsen, whose girl MacLaine he eventually steals – and the comedy lies in the twists of characterisation. The tone is set as soon as Ford mildly asks for a cigar instead of setting up the usual whisky in the saloon: a symbol not of weakness (as the town bully reads it) but of his uncompromising independence (he immediately proceeds to beat up said thug). Sturdy performances all round, so that even the action sequences deliver a punch. GA

She Gods of Shark Reef

(Roger Corman, 1956, US) Don Durant, Bill Cord, Lisa Montell, Jeanne Gerson, Carol Lindsay.
63 min.

Strictly zero-budget exotica, less Corman's South Pacific than, one suspects, an excuse for the film unit to take a Hawaiian holiday. Despite the flimsiest of scripts and not much evidence of more than a long day's shooting, Corman at least honours the implications of the title and offers two chunky beefcake Tab Hunter/Pat Boone lookalikes, prowling around somewhat hilariously in loincloths, as brothers (one good, one bad) stranded on an island inhabited only by women. A film that invites running commentary from the stalls. CPe

She Lives to Ride

(Alice Stone, 1994, US)
76 min.

This debut documentary looks behind the lust'n'leather, 'Girl of a Motorcycle' clichés to portray the everyday women who decide that riding pillion is no longer enough. Constructed round a series of interviews, including one with the leader of the lesbian pack who form the vanguard of New York's Gay Pride marchers, and another with the redoubtable owner of a shocking pink Harley, still biking in her 82nd year, this entertaining and informative film reveals the camaraderie and sense of freedom these women gain from hitting the road together – without waiting for the man to decide where to stop for a pee. TJ

She'll Be Wearing Pink Pyjamas

(John Goldschmidt, 1984, GB) Julie Walters, Anthony Higgins, Jane Evers, Janet Henfrey, Paula Jacobs, Penelope Nice.
90 min.

A motley octet of women go on an outward bound course, rock-climbing, canoeing and orienteering around travelogue footage of the Lake District, and snivel on one another's shoulders about what a raw deal they've had from love, life and lovers. The tedious trudge (scripted by Eva Hardy) is dominated by Julie Walters' big-mouthed bore, whose hardboiled shell cracks open at the first sign of blistered soles. What we have here is an example of the female stereotype for the '80s: the neurotic individual who can talk about nothing but men. The sort of film that gives women a bad name. AB

Sheltering Sky, The

(Bernardo Bertolucci, 1990, GB/It) Debra Winger, John Malkovich, Campbell Scott, Jill Bennett, Timothy Spall, Eric Vu-An, Amina Annabi.
138 min.

Paul Bowles' novel presents the problem of interiorisation, and a presiding morbidity that would clear most movie-houses. Bertolucci has wisely elected to open things out and to humanise his characters, relenting a little in favour of romance. The American travellers in North Africa, Kit and Port Moresby, still go down the drain, but in this version you care. Remote husband Port (Malkovich) unwisely samples Arab prostitutes, neurotic Kit (Winger) has a fling with their travelling companion Tunner (Scott); but where the story really hooks in is their realisation, after an abortive attempt at sex, that reconciliation is impossible. Port contracts typhoid, and the couple's frantic search for help in increasingly primitive terrain makes for horrifyingly powerful cinema. After Port's death, Kit loses both identity and compass bearings, wanders into the desert, and enters into a sexual delirium with the Tuareg Belqassim (Vu-An). As you'd expect, it's a big, handsome film, rich and strange in psychological depths and eroticism. Malkovich and Winger play woundingly well. BC

Shelter of the Wings (Charachar)

(Buddhadeb Dasgupta, 1993, Ind) Rajit Kapoor, Laboni Sarkar, Sadhu Mehar, Shankar Chakraborty.
97 min.

Dull if well-meaning fable, written and directed by the Bengali poet Buddhadeb Dasgupta, about an impoverished bird-catcher whose preference for freeing birds causes trouble with his more practical, less poetically inclined wife. Slow, slight and (speaking as a die-hard ornithologist/conservationist) excessively sentimental. GA

She Must Be Seeing Things

(Sheila McLaughlin, 1987, US) Sheila Dabney, Lois Weaver, Kyle DeCamp, John Erdman, Ed Bowes, Uzi Parnes.
91 min.

Vivacious blonde Jo (Weaver) is making a film about Catalina, a 17th century woman forced to live her life as a man. Jo's lover Agatha (Dabney), suffering a crisis when she reads Jo's diary detailing previous affairs with men, takes to spying on Jo and imagining her in compromising situations with male members of the film crew. Meanwhile, Catalina's experiences in Jo's film mirror Agatha's inner turmoil. The vague cross-cutting between what Agatha sees and what she imagines becomes intriguing, as does Catalina's tragic story, but there's a disconcerting subtext. Agatha's insecurity manifests itself as penis envy – a too simplistic response to a complex situation which, coupled with McLaughlin's disruptive technique of having her characters speak to camera whenever they're alone, sets a slightly patronising tone. On the other hand, the sex scenes are refreshingly frank and often funny. EP

Sheriff, Le (Le Juge Fayard dit le Sheriff)

(Yves Boisset, 1976, Fr) Patrick Dewaere, Aurore Clément, Philippe Léotard, Michel Auclair, Jean Bouise, Jean-Marc Thibault, Daniel Ivernel, Jacques Spiesser.
112 min.

Judge Fayard (Dewaere) is a bright-eyed amalgam of Errol Flynn and Uomo Vogue, whose cowboy nickname is the result of his tendency to come on like *The Sweeney*. A petty crime leads him to uncover a major one, its multi-million franc haul partly ending up as a Gaullist candidate's campaign bankroll. Unfortunately the film skates to a familiar denouement, content to offer the occasional crumb of irony amid an odd blend of plodding realism and tough guy staples.

Sheriff of Fractured Jaw, The

(Raoul Walsh, 1958, GB) Kenneth More, Jayne Mansfield, Bruce Cabot, Henry Hull, William Campbell, Robert Morley, Ronald Squire. ·
110 min.
An oddball comic Western, shot by Walsh on Spanish locations (and British studio interiors), with Kenneth More as the unsuccessful English inventor, turned gun salesman in the American West, who is mistaken for a gunman and eventually tames the town with the aid of some amiable Indians. Chiefly memorable for the strange vision of buxom Jayne Mansfield and wimpish sheriff More grappling with the incompatibility of their bodies, providing an occasional hoot and many an exercise in single entendre. DMacp

Sherlock Holmes and the Spider Woman

(Roy William Neill, 1944, US) Basil Rathbone, Nigel Bruce, Gale Sondergaard, Denis Hoey, Vernon Downing, Alec Craig.
62 min. b/w.
With Gale Sondergaard providing a superbly malevolent adversary, this is one of the most striking entries in the Rathbone/Bruce Sherlock Holmes series. Making her social calls accompanied by an unnervingly unsmiling mute child who catches flies on the wing, she is secretly masterminding a devilish insurance racket, preying on the wealthiest men in London by using a dwarf to gain entrance to their homes and leave venomous spiders to do their bit. She also (hopefully) reserves a fiendish fate for Holmes at the carnival which serves as her HQ: Dr Watson proudly demonstrates his skill at the shooting gallery, unaware that behind the effigy of Hitler serving as his patriotic target, Holmes waits helplessly bound and gagged. Started by 20th Century-Fox (*The Hound of the Baskervilles* and The *Adventures of Sherlock Holmes*, both 1939), the series was revived by Universal with *Sherlock Holmes and the Voice of Terror* (1942), the new regime signalled by a switch to modern dress (neatly provided by having Holmes select, then discard, his deerstalker as inappropriately old-fashioned). Although saddled with a tag-line or two of World War II propaganda uplift, and sometimes direct confrontation with evil Nazi agents, the watchword was Holmesian business as usual; and thanks to a gift for sinister atmospherics displayed by Roy William Neill (who directed the last eleven films in a series of fourteen, ended with his death in 1946), a remarkably high standard was maintained throughout this B movie series. TM

Sherlock Junior

(Buster Keaton, 1924, US) Buster Keaton, Kathryn McGuire, Joe Keaton, Ward Crane, Jane Connelly.
4,065 ft. b/w.
Keaton's third feature under his own steam is an incredible technical accomplishment, but also an almost Pirandellian exploration of the nature of cinematic reality. Buster plays a cinema projectionist, framed for theft by a jealous rival for his girl's hand, who daydreams himself into life as a daring detective. In an unforgettable sequence, Buster (actually fallen asleep beside the projector) forces his way onto the screen and into the movie he is projecting, only to find himself beset by perils and predicaments as the action around him changes in rapid montage. The sequence is not just a gag, but an astonishingly acute perception of the interaction between movie reality and audience fantasy, and the role of editing in juggling both. The timing here is incredible (a technical marvel, in fact); even more so in the great chase sequence, an veritable cascade of unbelievably complex gags (like the moment when Buster, on the handlebars of a riderless, runaway motor-bike passing some ditch-digging roadworks, receives a spadeful of earth in the face from each oblivious navvy in turn). It leaves Chaplin standing. TM

Sherman's March

(Ross McElwee, 1985, US) narrator: Ross McElwee, (introduction) Richard Leacock.
160 min.
General Sherman's march through the South in the American Civil War was unrivalled up to that time for its ferocity towards a civilian population. McElwee's march through identical terrain was little more than a *cinema verité* girl hunt, though the alternative ethos is closer to the era of Richard Brautigan's *A Confederate General from Big Sur* than *The Confessions of a Window Cleaner*. It is extremely long, inconsequential and low-budget, but if you surrender to it, it is not devoid of delights and resources. Honours are divided between the director's sister, with her reluctant explanation of her 'fanny tuck', and the buxom and biting Charleen, who tries to bully him into falling for one of her stable of eligible girls. McElwee's voice-over commentary is another of the movie's little pleasures. BC

She's Been Away

(Peter Hall, 1989, GB) Peggy Ashcroft, Geraldine James, James Fox, Rachel Kempson.
103 min.
Scripted by Stephen Poliakoff, the first 35mm movie wholly financed by the BBC, this has the incomparable Ashcroft as an elderly woman, put into institutional care when still a young woman, released in her twilight years by the agency of her liberal nephew (Fox). Ashcroft's problem is not mental illness but a surfeit of stubborness and independence, the former communicated by her weapon of silence against repressiveness, the latter by flashbacks which show her as a young, vaguely libertarian and feminist black sheep. But the impetus of the film is the relationship between Ashcroft and Fox's contented but stifled wife (splendidly played by Geraldine James). The grudging but gradual bond between the two women leads, almost inevitably with Poliakoff, into a spot of picaresque delinquency in the family Daimler and the realisation that all is not well with this seemingly ideal marriage. Good stuff, slightly pat, but as with most of Poliakoff's writing, always engaging and often amusingly sly. SGr

She's Gotta Have It

(Spike Lee, 1986, US) Tracy Camila Johns, Tommy Redmond Hicks, John Canada Terrell, Spike Lee, Ray Dowell, Joie Lee.
85 min. b/w & col.
Lee's first feature focuses around the attempts of Nola Darling (Johns), aware but not ashamed of her reputation as a good-time girl, to sort out the three steady men in her life with a view (maybe) to marriage: the sincere and caring Jamie (Hicks), the self-obsessed model Greer (Terrell), and the outrageous bicycle messenger Mars (Lee). Each lover, convinced that he is the solution to Nola's problem, makes his prospective pitch (to the girl and audience alike) in a series of painfully funny character vignettes. The action centres on Nola's spacious Brooklyn studio, where the men take it in turns to assassinate each other's characters, before gathering round Nola's Thanksgiving table to do it face-to-face. Structurally, it could be compared to Kurosawa's *Rashomon* for its subjective cross-examination of Nola's loves; but this delightful low-budget comedy, with its all black cast and black humour, is 100% Lee. SGo

She's Having a Baby

(John Hughes, 1988, US) Kevin Bacon, Elizabeth McGovern, Alec Baldwin, Isabel Lorca, William Windom, Cathryn Damon, Dennis Dugan, Edie McClurg.
106 min.
Taking his erstwhile teen lovers into young adulthood, marriage and parenthood, John Hughes fashions a curiously disaffected portrait of the artist as a frustrated chauvinist. Bacon – an aspiring writer who lands a job in advertising, just as Hughes did – narrates the film. We are privy to his daydreams about freedom and his resentment towards his bride (McGovern in a terrible role), and then we watch his change of heart in a thoroughly unconvincing last reel. This is bitter-sweet compartmentalised, with the saccharine spooned on at the end. Even then it lacks flavour. TCh

She's Out of Control

(Stan Dragoti, 1989, US) Tony Danza, Catherine Hicks, Wallace Shawn, Dick O'Neill, Ami Dolenz, Laura Mooney, Derek McGrath, Dana Ashbrook.
95 min.
What Katie (Dolenz), daughter of single parent Doug (Danza), has out of control is her sexuality. She's sweet 15, never been kissed (teeth brace and glasses don't help), and Dad can't hear the prologue of 'The Rites of Spring' playing for her. Then he returns from a convention connected with his failing '60s-sounds radio station to find his ugly duckling descending the stairs (slo-mo, to Frankie Avalon's 'Venus') in swan-white mini, cascading hair and contacts. Suitors follow in numbers: every dope-head, biker and cast-eyed no-hoper in Southern California queues outside the door, while precocious little sister mans the telephone dating system. It's desperation time for dad, his only hope being loopy Middle-European child psychiatrist Dr Fishbinder (another Wallace Shawn caricature). Dragoti's dire, dishonest, seldom humorous social comedy has all the nauseating hallmarks of a big-budget sitcom. Can't wait for the John Waters remake. WH

She's So Lovely

(Nick Cassavetes, 1997, US) Sean Penn, Robin Wright Penn, John Travolta, Harry Dean Stanton, Debi Mazar, Gena Rowlands, James Gandolfini.
112 min.
Based on what looks like an unfinished script written by his late father, Nick Cassavetes' film – about the troubled, on-off relationship between lowlife boozers Eddie and Maureen (the two Penns), the latter taking up with a steadier type (Travolta) while Eddie serves time – merely shows the gulf between the sloppily 'naturalistic' mannerisms on view here and the kind of authentic psychological and emotional epiphanies John Cassavetes used to give us. Harry Dean Stanton provides some much needed humour, but the film's celebratory attitude towards a dangerously wild love that defies logic and convention lacks depth and genuine insights. GA

She's the One

(Edward Burns, 1996, US) Jennifer Aniston, Maxine Bahns, Edward Burns, Cameron Diaz, Mike McGlone, John Mahoney, Anita Gillette.
96 min.
Burns' follow-up to *The Brothers McMullen* is a disappointment. It's basically the same film, only longer, more expensive, and a whole lot more tiresome. This time, Burns plays Mickey, 'the only English-speaking white guy driving a cab in New York.' He's still hung up on Heather, a blonde dream who long ago turned into a nightmare. That is, until he picks up a fare, Hope (Bahns), and she picks up him. Meanwhile, McGlone (the religious McMullen) gets to be the philandering brother this time, Francis, an obnoxious yuppie who's cheating on wife Renee (Aniston) with – you guessed it – Heather. Confused? You won't be, as the film spells out every relationship in detail. The brothers Fitzpatrick lay the blame squarely on pop (Mahoney), but the writer/director is much too easy on them. His characters' blank incomprehension when it comes to the female of the species looks less like comic observation, more unalloyed chauvinism. This movie reeks of it like aftershave. Diaz's Heather is one of the most misogynistic femmes fatales this side of *film noir*. A bland, so-so romantic comedy without the charm to see it through. TCh

She Wore a Yellow Ribbon

(John Ford, 1949, US) John Wayne, Joanne Dru, John Agar, Ben Johnson, Harry Carey Jr, Victor McLaglen, Mildred Natwick, George O'Brien, Arthur Shields.
103 min.
he centrepiece of Ford's cavalry trilogy (flanked by *Fort Apache* and *Rio Grande*) and a film of both elegiac sentiment and occasionally overeloquent sentimentality, structured around a series of ritual incidents rather than narrative conflicts. Wayne's captain and McLaglen's sergeant face up to impending retirement from a force whose role and self-awareness is changing in the wake of Custer's defeat; America, however, still has to be willed into existence and

unity. Winton Hoch's Technicolor cinematography of Monument Valley (modelled at Ford's insistence on Remington pictorialism) won him an Oscar. PT

Shine

(Scott Hicks, 1996, Aust/GB) Armin Mueller-Stahl, Noah Taylor, Geoffrey Rush, Lynn Redgrave, John Gielgud, Googie Withers, Sonia Todd, Nicholas Bell.
106 min.
Teenage pianist David (Taylor) has all the usual problems and then some. His father, a Polish-Jewish immigrant in working-class Perth, Australia, places such a burden of hope on his son that he won't let him leave the family nest, and insists on his working towards 'The Rach 3' – Rachmaninov's bone-crunching 3rd Piano Concerto – whether he's ready for such a super-virtuoso piece or not. With a scholarship to London's Royal College of Music there for the taking, the future has some tough questions to ask, answered by a nervous collapse of cataclysmic proportions, years of psychological damage, and a painful recovery sprung from the most unlikely surroundings – requests for the popular classics in a Perth wine bar. Scott Hicks' film, where the rites-of-passage pic meets high-falutin' backstage melodrama, is based on the true story of the prodigy David Helfgott, whose flashing finger work we hear on the soundtrack. Stage actor Geoffrey Rush has total command of the mature artist's chattering eccentricities and with striking on-screen keyboard skills creates a characterisation so minutely observed you expect him to stride naked off the screen. Helfgott's turbulent personal history fits few preconceived patterns. Entirely attuned, Hicks's switchback time-scheme reserves a canny facility for surprise as it guides us round a fine supporting cast – Gielgud (ripe old piano tutor), Mueller-Stahl (a stage papa to reckon with), Lynn Redgrave (warmly supportive spouse) – while the music comes over as if life itself depended on it. Compassionate, deft, unsentimental, inspirational. TJ

Shin Heike Monogatari (New Tales of the Taira Clan)

(Kenji Mizoguchi, 1955, Jap) Raizo Ichikawa, Ichijiro Oya, Michiyo Kogure, Eijiro Yanagi, Tatsuya Ishiguro, Yoshiko Kuga.
107 min.
One of Mizoguchi's two late films in colour, this describes a conflict between three power groups in feudal Japan: the priests, the court, and a clan of samurai. The samurai embody ideals of individual integrity, just service, and male prowess; the court, ideals of rightful authority, but equally, the faults of ministerial corruption; the clerics, the degeneration of institutionalised religion into factional Fascism (gang-like violence in support of political ends). Characteristically, the tale of the conflict is hinged round a courtesan figure's relations with the three groups ('mother' for the samurai, 'mistress' for the court, 'whore' for the priests). Needless to say, the 'personal' virtues of the samurai win out, the hero becomes superman. Shot with all the sensitivity and stylish trappings to be expected from Mizoguchi; also, some sharp observation of social relations, and some acute insights into the vagaries of the power boys' shit-games. JDuC

Shining, The 100

(Stanley Kubrick, 1980, GB) Jack Nicholson, Shelley Duvall, Danny Lloyd, Scatman Crothers, Barry Nelson, Philip Stone, Joseph Turkel, Anne Jackson.
146 min.
If you go to this adaptation of Stephen King's novel expecting to see a horror movie, you'll be disappointed. From the start, Kubrick undercuts potential tension builders by a process of anti-climax; eerie aerial shots accompanied by ponderous music prove to be nothing more than that; the setting is promising enough – an empty, isolated hotel in dead-of-winter Colorado – but Kubrick makes it warm, well-lit and devoid of threat. Granted, John Alcott's cinematography is impressive, and occasionally produces a 'look behind you' panic; but to hang the movie's psychological tension on the leers and grimaces of Nicholson's face (suited though it is to demoniacal expressions), while refusing to develop any sense of the man, is asking for trouble. Similarly,

the narrative is too often disregarded in favour of crude and confusing visual shocks. Kubrick's unbalanced approach (over-emphasis on production values) results in soulless cardboard cutouts who can do little to generate audience empathy. FF

Shining Hour, The

(Frank Borzage, 1938, US) Joan Crawford, Margaret Sullavan, Robert Young, Melvyn Douglas, Fay Bainter, Allyn Joslyn, Hattie McDaniel, Frank Albertson.
80 min. b/w.
Produced by Joseph L Mankiewicz, this is a stylish soap with Crawford as a night-club dancer, of some notoriety but yearning for respectability, who lets herself be persuaded to marry a gentleman farmer from Wisconsin (Douglas). But at the home farm – a stately mansion – she is met with implacable hostility from the groom's matriarchal older sister (Bainter), and similar hostility that turns to desire from his younger brother (Young); only Young's devoted wife (Sullavan) welcomes her unreservedly. Uneasily aware that she is tempted by Young, Crawford begs Douglas to take her away, only to be stymied by Sullavan's willingness to sacrifice herself if her husband can find happiness in his new love. So far, so good, with a sharpish script (Ogden Nash contributed) that makes good use of the casting (Crawford's disillusioned cynicism versus Sullavan's naive romanticism) to make incisive points about the many-splendoured aspects of love. Latterly, alas, the film nosedives into silly melodrama, with Bainter running mad to commit arson, Crawford saving the self-immolating Sullavan, and all the problems coming out Persil-white in the wash. Recognisable, with all faults, as a Borzage film. TM

Shining Through

(David Seltzer, 1992, US) Michael Douglas, Melanie Griffith, Liam Neeson, Joely Richardson, John Gielgud, Francis Guinan, Sheila Allen, Sylvia Syms, Mathieu Carrière.
132 min.
A lavish, ludicrous WWII melodrama in which Griffith plays a plucky, half-Jewish secretary from New York who, through her job with lawyer and secret spymaster Douglas, becomes involved in romance, mystery and adventure. Hired for her German-speaking skills, Griffith is on hand when a key Berlin spy is murdered, and volunteers to replace him. Taken on as a cook by a prominent Nazi, she plans to microfilm documents and pass them on to US Intelligence. In no other respect does intelligence, or plausibility, come into it. As Griffith tries to save the Free World from prototype 'doodlebug' rockets, the contrived plot and manufactured suspense spiral into absurdity ('Mein Gott, you've got guts'). Griffith provides an earthy counterpoint to Douglas' stern father-figure, but everyone else is just plain embarrassing. NF

Shining Victory

(Irving Rapper, 1941, US) James Stephenson, Geraldine Fitzgerald, Donald Crisp, Barbara O'Neil, Montagu Love, Sig Ruman.
80 min. b/w.
Perfunctory medical drama, adapted from an AJ Cronin play (Jupiter Laughs), in which Stephenson is a gifted scientist who takes a posting at a private Scottish mental hospital after his earlier reasearch results have been commandeered by an unscrupulous Budapest department head. In the new environment, he at first fails to register nurse Fitzgerald's affection for him, but the jealousy of co-worker O'Neil soon snaps the plot into predictable shape. TJ

Shinjuku Triad Society (Shinjuku Kuro Shakai: China Mafia Senso)

(Takashi Miike, 1995, Jap) Kippei Shina, Takeshi Caesar, Sabu, Tomoro Taguchi, Eri Yu, Shinsuke Izutsu.
102 min.
Even viewers hardened to the perversities which tend to crop up in Japanese exploitation genres may find themselves rubbing their eyes at some of the images and incidents in Miike's extremist thriller about a Taiwanese triad gang muscling in on traditional yakuza territory in Tokyo. A near-psychotic 'lone wolf' from Shinjuku police station sets out to bust the Dragon's Claw gang

for its involvement in drugs, body-parts trading, extortion racketeering and male prostitution; one obstacle is that his own (sexually ambivalent) younger brother is a legal adviser to the gang, which is fronted by a deranged gay sadist (Taguchi, from the Tetsuo films). Just when you think that a scene of sodomy – used as an aid to police interrogation – can't be topped, along comes an eye-gouging or another coke-fuelled blow job to keep things moving. Miike's stylish, gleeful direction establishes him as the most distinctive new 'voice' in the genre since Rokuro Mochizuki. TR

Ship of Fools

(Stanley Kramer, 1965, US) Simone Signoret, Oskar Werner, Vivien Leigh, José Ferrer, Lee Marvin, Michael Dunn, Heinz Rühmann, George Segal, Elizabeth Ashley, José Greco, Lilia Skala, Charles Korvin.
149 min. b/w.
Don't look now, but as you might expect with message-mad Kramer at the helm of this adaptation of Katherine Anne Porter's novel, there's a heavy allegory aboard: it's 1933, the ship is German, and there's a Jew among the mixed bag of passengers. Yards and yards of liberal cliché are relentlessly unfolded, but the superb cast – struggling valiantly with the sort of problems more at home in disaster movies – make it almost watchable. Among them are Signoret as a drug-addicted countess mournfully loving the ship's doctor (Werner), Vivien Leigh as a divorcee looking for a last fling before middle-age sets in, and Michael Dunn as a marvellously sharp-tongued dwarf who finds himself in a minority group of two with the Jew (Rhümann). TM

Ship That Died of Shame, The (aka PT Raiders)

(Basil Dearden, 1955, GB) Richard Attenborough, George Baker, Bill Owen, Virginia McKenna, Roland Culver, Bernard Lee.
95 min. b/w.
A valuable record of bewildered British masculinity in the post-war years. Some old mates discover their trusty former gunboat decommissioned and languishing in the knacker's yard. They vow to make her seaworthy again, but betray the faithful sloop by using her for smuggling. Take away the absurd nautical anthropomorphism and the tortuous stuff about how hard it is for WWII veterans to adapt to civvy street, and you're left with a pretty threadbare thriller (from a Nicholas Monsarrat novel). The story is told in such a brisk, understated fashion that it's easy to overlook quite how odd it is. Memorable finale seemingly filmed in the producer's bath. GM

Ship Was Loaded, The

see Carry On Admiral

Shipwreck!

see Sea Gypsies, The

Shipwrecked

see Naufragos, Los

Shipyard Sally

(Monty Banks, 1939, GB) Gracie Fields, Sydney Howard, Morton Selten, Norma Varden, Tucker McGuire, Oliver Wakefield, Monty Banks.
80 min. b/w.
Shoddily mounted populist pap, with our Gracie as a singing barmaid taking the plight of the Clydeside shipyard workers to heart, masquerading farcically as an American star to bulldoze her way to the Minister concerned, and making such an impassioned plea that their jobs are saved. Her last British film before her departure for America, it ends glutinously with her rendition of 'Land of Hope and Glory' as royalty launches a new liner. TM

Shirin's Wedding (Shirins Hochzeit)

(Helma Sanders-Brahms, 1976, WGer) Ayten Erten, Aras Oren, Jürgen Prochnow, Peter Franke.
116 min. b/w.
What John Berger's book A Seventh Man did for

the male migrant worker, this unrelenting and delicate film attempts for his female counterpart. Shirin, a peasant girl from Anatolia, follows her betrothed Mahmud to Cologne, taking her handmade trousseau. Inevitably she is drawn into the downward spiral of female immigrant labour, and even the support and affection of other women cannot mitigate the tragic ironies of the circumstances in which she finally meets Mahmud. Sanders-Brahms' understanding of the unorganised impotence of both migrant and German workers is enacted not only through the storyline, as Shirin is made into a Western woman, but through a projective narration which both conveys information and – by suggesting indictment rather than despair – hints at the possibility of a solidarity more political than that shown in the film itself. Very moving. MV

Shirley Valentine

(Lewis Gilbert, 1989, US) Pauline Collins, Tom Conti, Julia McKenzie, Alison Steadman, Joanna Lumley, Sylvia Syms, Bernard Hill, George Costigan.
108 min.
Willy Russell transforms his one-hander into a superior kitchenette adventure which roams from Liverpool to Mykonos, finding room for all the characters who in the more satisfying theatre version were figments of Shirl's imagination. 42-year-old Shirley (Collins) is so raddled by life that she talks to the wall of her strip-pine kitchen, and wonders 'Why, if they give us so much life, aren't we allowed to make use of it?' Hence an improbable plot device by which her feminist friend wins a holiday for two in Greece, and Shirley, after much guilt, doubt and abuse from her plankish husband (Hill), decides to go. But the virtue of Russell's writing is that, for all the cracks, occasional duff lines, and tendency to simplify and stereotype, few can match his ability to make us laugh, cry and ultimately care. Loneliness creeps with Shirley to the Med, and only after a brief dalliance with a Greek local (Conti) does she start to live for real: self-respect and self-reliance beat sex on a boat anyday. Collins is magnificent, and though the film's sexual politics may not be to all tastes, it deserves to be seen for its glowing belief in the worth of personal rediscovery. SGr

Shivers

see Parasite Murders, The

Shoah

(Claude Lanzmann, 1985, Fr)
566 min.
Lanzmann's 9 hour documentary meditation on the Holocaust is a distillation of 350 hours of interviews with living 'witnesses' to what happened at the extermination camps of Treblinka, Auschwitz, Sobibor, Chelmno and Belzec. Feeling that the familiar newsreel images have lost their power to shock, Lanzmann concentrates instead on the testimony of those survivors who are 'not reliving' but 'still living' what happened, and on 'the bureaucracy of death'. One of the two Jews to survive the murder of 400,000 men, women and children at the Chelmno death camp describes his feelings on revisiting Poland for the first time. A train driver who ferried victims to the concentration camps is seen making that same journey to 'the end of the line' again and again; a retired Polish barber who cut the hair of those about to enter the gas chambers describes his former work; an SS officer talks about the 'processing' of those on their way to the concentration camps; a railway official discusses the difficulties associated with transporting so many Jews to their deaths. The same questions are repeated like an insistent refrain, the effect is relentless and cumulative. One word of caution as you watch the witnesses giving testimony; bear in mind Schiller's observation that 'individual testimony has a specific place in history but doesn't, alone, add up to it'. NF

Shock Corridor

(Samuel Fuller, 1963, US) Peter Breck, Constance Towers, Gene Evans, James Best, Hari Rhodes, Larry Tucker, James Zuckert, Philip Ahn.
101 min. b/w & col.
You may have to swallow a morsel of disbelief over the wonderfully Fullerian premise that a reputable newspaper editor and a psychiatrist would connive at the crazy scheme whereby the reporter

hero (Breck) has himself committed to an asylum so that he can win the Pulitzer Prize by solving the murder of an inmate. Once done, you're in for a gripping ride. The journalist's latent paranoia is beautifully observed in his relationship with his stripper girlfriend (Towers), as well as in the relish with which he notes the success of his simulation of madness; and the gradual descent into real madness, as he frustratedly waits and watches for flashes of lucidity in the three inmates who witnessed the murder, is riveting story-telling. The camera-work (Stanley Cortez), tracking and constantly adumbrating the descent into darkness, is amazing. TM

Shocker

(Wes Craven, 1989, US) Mitch Pileggi, Peter Berg, Michael Murphy, Cami Cooper, John Tesh, Heather Langenkamp, Jessica Craven.
110 min.
Wholesome college boy Jonathan (Berg) is beset by nightmares, visions of mayhem which are subsequently enacted in real life by serial killer Horace Pinker (Pileggi). When his foster family and girlfriend come under the knife, the teenager uses his 'psychic bond' to facilitate Pinker's arrest and electrocution. The massive shock turns Pinker into a vengeful entity who can travel through bodies, televisions and household wiring with ease...After the uncertain cross-generic wanderings of The Serpent and the Rainbow, this finds Craven returning to his low budget origins, delivering straightforward kinetic horror with unapologetic brashness, his usual preoccupations to the fore: psychic dream states, parental guilt revisited upon children, the intrusion of a chaotic, alternative world into comfy suburbia. Problems arise from an uncharacteristically loose structure, which frequently brings the movie to the brink of narrative collapse; Craven's visual flair and enthusiastic pacing nevertheless deliver ample (if sometimes frustrating) rewards. MK

Shockproof

(Douglas Sirk, 1949, US) Cornel Wilde, Patricia Knight, John Baragrey, Esther Minciotti, Howard St John.
79 min. b/w.
Written by none other than the great Sam Fuller, this superior blend of love-on-the-run thriller and social comment, filtered through film noir, follows the fraught, doomed relationship between a parole officer and the female ex-con with whom he falls in love. The depiction of the ways in which society refuses to forgive criminals for their past misdemeanours is none too sophisticated, but Fuller's punchy, tabloid-like script, Sirk's stylishly economical direction, and the unsentimental characterisations lend it power. A pity about the contrived ending, imposed on Sirk by Columbia, but the film still looked good enough for Richard Hamilton to base a series of paintings on its shots of Knight. NF

Shock to the System, A

(Jan Egleson, 1990, US) Michael Caine, Elizabeth McGovern, Peter Riegert, Swoosie Kurtz, Will Patton, Jenny Wright, John McMartin, Barbara Baxley, Philip Moon.
88 min.
Alec Guinness played almost all the parts in the homicidal black comedy Kind Hearts and Coronets. Michael Caine, with a smaller repertoire, once pointed out that he could play both Woody Allen and Clint Eastwood, and in the not dissimilar A Shock to the System, proves it. Ageing advertising executive Graham Marshall (Caine) starts out as schlemiel, henpecked at home and passed over for promotion at work. The worm's turning point occurs on the subway, when Marshall shoves a panhandler under a train and gets away with it, after which murder becomes a shot in his locker. He hooks up his wife (Kurtz) to the National Grid, and consoles his bereavement with Stella at work (McGovern). Interestingly, murder puts lead in his pencil, confirming Mailer's thesis in The American Dream. The corporate world's dedication to ruthless efficiency meets its apotheosis in Marshall, and his obnoxious new boss (Riegert) wins the battles but loses the war. Seldom have Caine's cobra eyes been used to better effect; it's a chilling tale, cleanly directed. BC

Shock Treatment

see Traitement de Choc

Shock Treatment

(Jim Sharman, 1981, GB) Cliff De Young, Jessica Harper, Patricia Quinn, Richard O'Brien, Charles Gray, Nell Campbell, Ruby Wax, Barry Humphries, Rik Mayall.
94 min.
The Rocky Horror Picture Show again, thinly disguised. The same writers (Richard O'Brien and Richard Hartley), the same director, virtually the same songs. As an exercise in nostalgia, it might work, but who wants to remember the '70s? Harper proves she can sing, O'Brien proves he can't act, and Sharman films inventively, but fringe theatre material does not a big screen musical make. Rocky Horror succeeded in its spot-on sense of style, but here the style, like the whole concept of rock musicals, seems a decade out of date, bypassed by films like Quadrophenia which integrate music and story in a different way. MB

Shoemaker

(Colleen Murphy, 1996, Can) Randy Hughson, Alberta Watson, Hardee T Lineham, Carl Marotte, Ellen Ray Hennessy.
82 min.
The Mr Happy Face shoe repair shop becomes an unexpected hotbed of romantic intrigue in this gentle, though ultimately unsatisfying Canadian independent. Hughson is the shy unprepossessing cobbler who strikes up a hesitant relationship with travel agent Alberta Watson (of Spanking the Monkey fame), despite the alternating concern and scorn he meets from his embittered boss. While Watson makes believable her character's need for a sincere and uncalculating partner, Hughson's contribution overplays the ungainliness and naivety of a role that never really lifts off the printed page. TJ

Shoes of the Fisherman, The

(Michael Anderson, 1968, US) Anthony Quinn, Oskar Werner, Laurence Olivier, David Janssen, Barbara Jefford, Leo McKern, Vittorio De Sica, John Gielgud, Clive Revill, Paul Rogers, Niall MacGinnis, Frank Finlay.
157 min.
A dour and thoroughly unconvincing film of Morris West's novel about a Russian bishop who survives twenty years in Siberia to become Pope Zorba, and who undertakes to spend the Church's wealth to stave off nuclear war. At which point you might expect the Vatican to have him quietly bumped off, but there's no such realism here, just weighty performances, rich settings, and David Janssen as a US journalist with domestic troubles. TCh

Shogun

(Jerry London, 1980, US) Richard Chamberlain, Toshiro Mifune, Yoko Shimada, Frankie Sakai, Alan Badel, Michael Hordern, Damien Thomas.
151 min.
Startled blue eyes above silky beard, Richard Chamberlain in a kimono looks more like an actor on his way to the bathroom than a grizzled English seafarer, cast ashore in 17th century Japan, where he turns samurai and becomes romantically and actively involved in a virulent political intrigue. Based on James Clavell's huge novel, Shogun was originally a 10-hour TV miniseries. Shamefully hacked down to 151 minutes (still a yawning long haul), the plot has been rendered action-packed but utterly incomprehensible. Though production credits and cast point to a lively synthesis of oriental/occidental interests, the end result reduces the complex moral codes of feudal Japan to an inexplicable death wish. The threat of harakiri follows Chamberlain's illicit hanky-panky with the Lady Mariko (Shimada) as surely as day follows night, and yet again that rising sun blobs onto the screen like a pulpy tangerine. JS

Shogun Assassin

(Kenji Misumi/(US version/Robert Houston, 1980, Jap/US) Tomisaburo Wakayama, Masahiro Tomikawa, Kayo Matsuo.
86 min.
This started screen life in Japan in 1972 as a Kenji Misumi samurai sword actioner with the wonderful export title of Baby Cart at the River Styx; it was then thoroughly overhauled by Roger Corman's New World (gaining a credit for 'psycho-acoustics', and the dubbed voice of Lamont Johnson for the hero) as a quickie cash-

in on the popular TV mini-series *Shogun*. Any sense of *déja vu* is down to the fact that the simultaneously-shot sequel to *Baby Cart*, featuring the same pram-pushing avenger and son, has been doing the rounds here for years as *Lightning Swords of Death*. Clear as mud, innit? The exotic cheap thrills are, anyway, with the self-parodying laughs and gory comic-strip savagery making it a snappy little mongrel all round. PT

Shonen
see Boy

Shooter, The
(Ted Kotcheff, 1994, US) Dolph Lundgren, Maruschka Detmers, John Ashton, Assumpta Serna, Gavan O'Herlihy, Simon Andreu.
104 min.
While Jean-Claude Van Damme, his erstwhile rival in the Euro Action Hero stakes, ploughs on in A-picture productions, Dolph Lundgren, who showed greater acting range when they were paired in *Universal Soldier*, gets stuck in dreck like this. In a nod to thawing East-West relations, this action adventure is set in Prague on the dawn of a US-Cuban summit, where feelings are running high after the murder of Castro's ambassador to New York. Enter Lundgren's Czech-born CIA man, teamed with his former agency mentor (Ashton) and given the task of tracking down the alleged assassin, Detmers' Gallic femme fatale. Very dull. TJ

Shoot First
see Rough Shoot

Shooting, The
(Monte Hellman, 1966, US) Warren Oates, Will Hutchins, Millie Perkins, Jack Nicholson, BJ Merholz, Guy El Tsosie, Charles Eastman.
81 min.
Probably the first Western which really deserves to be called existential. Bounty hunter Gashade (Oates) and his young sidekick Coley (Hutchins) are persuaded by an unknown woman (Perkins) to lead her into the desert. On the skyline appears a spectral figure who later turns out to be Billy Spear (Nicholson), a sadistic gunman whose relationship to the woman remains obscure. The prevailing atmosphere of fear and despair intensifies as Gashade and Coley realise they are involved in the hunting of an unidentified man, and as strange suggestions about the nature of the hunt multiply. On the way they encounter a dying man, and Coley, in an absurdist gesture typical of the film, offers him coloured candy. There is talk of 'a little person, maybe a child', who was killed back in the town they left, but this is never clarified; instead Hellman builds remorselessly on the atmosphere and implications of the 'quest' until it assumes a terrifying importance in itself. 'It's just a feeling I've got to see through' says the bounty hunter, and Gregory Sandor's excellent photography manages to create the feeling visually, with dialogue kept to a bare minimum. What Hellman does here is to take the basic tools of the Western, and use them, without in anyway diluting or destroying their power, as the basis for a Kafkaesque drama. DP

Shooting Fish
(Stefan Schwartz, 1997, GB) Dan Futterman, Stuart Townsend, Kate Beckinsale, Nickolas Grace, Claire Cox, Peter Capaldi, Annette Crosbie, Jane Lapotaire, Phyllis Logan.
112 min.
The slang title refers to the ease with which mugs are found for scams. Dylan (Futterman) is a brash American tethered by friendship and history to Jez (Townsend), a gifted but unsophisticated inventor. The film begins with an attempt at the big time – a con involving voice-recognition computers and City investors – before introducing us to Jez and Dylan's home, an Aladdin's cave, incredibly, inside a large gasometer in the London suburbs. Cash-strapped trainee doctor Georgie (Beckinsale) is lured to work for the boys. Though she soon susses their game, she stays on board for a complicated mixture of motives involving an Down's Syndrome brother and her growing affection for the lads. The straggly plot – they're saving to buy a country house – has an Ealing-esque energy, but the portrayal of Englishness seems ersatz and overly accommo-

dating to the international audience. A succession of cameos provides light relief, and the film's saved by the amiable performances of Futterman, Beckinsale and, especially, Townsend. WH

Shooting Party, The
(Alan Bridges, 1984, GB) James Mason, Edward Fox, Dorothy Tutin, John Gielgud, Gordon Jackson, Cheryl Campbell, Robert Hardy, Aharon Ipal, Rebecca Saire, Sarah Badel, Rupert Frazer, Judi Bowker.
96 min.
Infidelity, class exploitation, and mindless male competitiveness pepper this adaptation of Isabel Colegate's novel, set just before the First World War, when an assortment of toffs gather for pheasant shooting and post-prandial charades. The producer obviously spent a small fortune acquiring the excellent cast, and the film evokes the period admirably, especially through a series of cut-ins anticipating the coming European carnage. But the attack on the values of the time is ultimately far too glossy and toothless. CS

Shooting Stars
(Le Ciel est à nous)
(Graham Guit, 1996, Fr) Romane Bohringer, Melvil Poupaud, Elodie Bouchez, Jean-Philippe Ecoffey, Jean-Claude Flamand, Patrick Lizana.
87 min.
This very flash, very knowing, vastly entertaining French thriller is so ironic it almost ends back at innocence. Poupaud is a naive small time con artist who gets in way over his head when he puts together a drugs deal with the reptilian Ecoffey and his independent-minded protégée, Bohringer. Graham Guit, director and co-writer, has fun and games with a Tarantino-esque chronology, a joyous kitsch soundtrack, and a novice's delight in the mechanics of the genre: he tears it apart, reassembles it, then hides the spare parts behind a ready wit. Bright stuff. TCh

Shootist, The
(Don Siegel, 1976, US) John Wayne, Lauren Bacall, Ron Howard, James Stewart, Richard Boone, Hugh O'Brian, Bill McKinney, Harry Morgan, John Carradine, Sheree North, Scatman Crothers.
100 min.
From the opening montage of clips from Wayne's earlier films to the final superb shootout in a cavernous saloon, Siegel's film is a subtle, touching valedictory tribute to both Wayne and the Western in general. With none of the indulgence that permeated *True Grit*, Wayne is perfect as the dying gunfighter attempting to live out his last days in peace and obscurity, but prevented from doing so by various younger gunmen out for revenge or to prove their worth against him. The performances are uniformly excellent, Bruce Surtees' photography is infused with an appropriately wintry feel, and Siegel handles both pace and tone beautifully; the admitted sentimentality is thoroughly in keeping with the elegiac tale of old-timers reconsidering their lives. If you're one of those who still feel that Wayne couldn't act, watch this and change your mind. GA

Shoot the Moon
(Alan Parker, 1981, US) Albert Finney, Diane Keaton, Karen Allen, Peter Weller, Dana Hill, Viveka Davis, Tracey Gold, Tina Yothers, Leora Dana.
123 min.
There is a sentimental optimism in both Parker's films and Bo Goldman's scripts. So it's no surprise that together they made this Californian coming-to-terms-with-a-relationship movie. Finney plays a successful writer who first picks up a literary award, and then throws up his marriage (to Keaton), four believable daughters, and a large country house. It's a superior film of its kind, for much as one may kick against Finney and Keaton's much-exploited mannerisms (rage and winsomeness respectively), they, like the script, have impressive moments, balancing hilarity and tragedy. But even Parker's direction, with its unerring sense of pace, cannot disguise an awkwardly episodic narrative which just cannot find a sense of an ending. JS

Shoot the Pianist
see Tirez sur le Pianiste

Shoot to Kill
see Disparen a Matar

Shoot to Kill
(aka Deadly Pursuit)
(Roger Spottiswoode, 1988, US) Sidney Poitier, Tom Berenger, Kirstie Alley, Clancy Brown, Richard Masur, Andrew Robinson.
110 min.
Nice to see Poitier back and full of pep, albeit in a routine thriller. It begins promisingly with the owner of a jewellery store helping himself to the gems, getting busted, and breaking down to explain that he needs them because his wife is being held hostage by a homicidal maniac. Presiding FBI agent Stantin (Poitier) is outsmarted at every turn, and the hostage is killed. Vengefully, Poitier follows the trail up into the remote mountains on the Canadian border, a city cop comically out of water. The killer hijacks a fishing party, and makes off with the good scout girlfriend (Alley) of the trail guide Knox (Berenger). Knox and Stantin reluctantly team up, and earn each other's respect over daunting terrain in the usual way. All the clichés clock in, characterisation is cardboard, and the locations are stunning. BC

Shop Around the Corner, The
(Ernst Lubitsch, 1940, US) James Stewart, Margaret Sullavan, Frank Morgan, Joseph Schildkraut, Felix Bressart, Sara Haden, William Tracy.
97 min. b/w.
Teaming Stewart, Sullavan and Morgan, just as in Borzage's *The Mortal Storm* (made the same year), this also deals with troubled romance in Central Europe, though here the threat is not Nazism but pride and the interference of others, as Stewart and Sullavan, shop staff at loggerheads in Morgan's gossip-ridden emporium in Budapest, only slowly realise that they have been carrying on an anonymous romance by letter. It's a marvellously delicate romantic comedy, finally very moving, with the twisted intrigues among the staff also carrying narrative weight, Morgan's cuckolded proprietor being especially affecting. Thoroughly different from *To Be or Not To Be* but just as exhilarating, it's one of the few films truly justifying Lubitsch's reputation for a 'touch'. It was later turned into a musical as *In the Good Old Summertime*. GA

Shopping
(Paul Anderson, 1993, GB) Sadie Frost, Jude Law, Sean Pertwee, Fraser James, Sean Bean, Marianne Faithfull, Jonathan Pryce, Danny Newman.
107 min.
Poised precariously between raw, 'realist' social comment and neon-lit, American-influenced genre-riffing, Anderson's directorial debut is praiseworthy for its high-octane, unsentimental look at the contemporary phenomena of joyriding and ram-raiding. Billy (Law, photogenic but expressively limited) is a 19-year-old nihilist who finally cares only for the speedy glee of stealing a car – usually in company with Jo (Frost), a feisty but marginally more cautious Irish girl in her early 20s – racing down empty streets with cops in pursuit, and crashing through any suitable shopfront that presents itself. The film is impressively energetic and for the most part appropriately amoral, although motivation rarely rises above 'There must be more than this' or 'I want to be somebody' variety. GA

Short Circuit
(John Badham, 1986, US) Ally Sheedy, Steve Guttenberg, Fisher Stevens, Austin Pendleton, GW Bailey, Brian McNamara.
98 min.
A message film to please all ages. Goofy Guttenberg plays a brilliant but totally reclusive inventor who has constructed robots with the power to nuke whole cities. At a military demonstration, the fifth of the series is struck by lightning, and receives the intelligence that it is alive. Eager to escape those who wish to terminate it, Number Five – a multi-purpose kitchen implement on wheels – takes refuge with fanatical animal lover Sheedy, and the chase is on. Cuteness is never far off, though Badham has enough sense of pace, and the robotics are sufficiently inventive, to keep the laughs coming. Only Guttenberg's tongue-twisted Asian sidekick (Stevens) is off-key. DT

S

Short Circuit 2

(Kenneth Johnson, 1988, US) Fisher Stevens, Michael McKean, Cynthia Gibb, Jack Weston, Dee McCafferty, David Hemblen.
110 min.

If the original *Short Circuit* brought us a mechanised version of *E.T*, this sequel is more a chromium *Crocodile Dundee*. Number Five, a military robot which received the spark of life, turned peacenik, and renamed himself Johnny Five, answers a distress call from his co-creator (Stevens) to join him in the Big City. His naive candour and sociological observations provide simple humour (of punks: 'Whoah! Human porcupines!'), as does his unwitting involvement in a bank robbery; and a terrific set piece is his attempt to prompt love-struck Stevens from afar by way of the '50s manual *Dating Dos and Don'ts for Modern Teens*. Though the direction by TV veteran Johnson is a little sparing of the big screen, and though the saccharine monitor keeps lurching dangerously into the red, this is that rare thing – a moderately intelligent kids' film, and a sequel that is better than the original. But why, when the theme is the prejudice encountered in Johnny Five's quest for acceptance among humans, is his Indian friend an absurd stereotype played by a blacked-up white actor? DW

Short Cuts

(Robert Altman, 1993, US) Tim Robbins, Lily Tomlin, Tom Waits, Matthew Modine, Frances McDormand, Andie MacDowell, Annie Ross, Jack Lemmon.
188 min.

From the exhilarating opening, you know Altman's epic 'adaptation' of eight stories and a poem by Raymond Carver is going to be special. Like *Nashville*, it's a tragicomic kaleidoscope of numerous barely interlinked stories (plus a similarly portentous ending). Here, the focus is on couples whose relationships are, at one point or another, subjected to small, seismic shudders of doubt, disappointment or, in a few cases, disaster. A surgeon suspects his wife's fidelity; a poolcleaner worries over his partner's phone-sex job; a waitress is racked by guilt after running down a child; a baker makes sinister phone calls to the injured boy's parents; the discovery of a corpse threatens a fishing-trip...and a marriage. The marvellous performances bear witness to Altman's iconoclastic good sense, with Tomlin, Waits, Modine, Robbins, MacDowell and the rest lending the film's mostly white, middle-class milieu an authenticity seldom found in American cinema. But the real star is Altman, whose fluid, clean camera style, free-and-easy editing, and effortless organisation of a complex narrative are quite simply the mark of a master. GA

Shortcut to Paradise

see Desvio al Paraíso

Short Film About Killing, A (Krótki Film o Zabijaniu)

(Krzysztof Kieslowski, 1987, Pol) Miroslaw Baka, Krzysztof Globisz, Jan Tesarz.
85 min.

Kieslowski's title is accurate: a hideous murder is directly followed by a hideous execution; both illegal and legal acts are detailed and protracted. The film does not set out to explain the punkish young killer's motivation, but restricts the viewer to his tunnel vision from the start, with the edges of the picture sludged over and a lowering yellow light at the centre. The depiction of violence is far removed from the usual camera choreography, and is, in consequence, truly appalling. The killing of the taxi driver is achieved in amateurish instalments, and takes even longer than the famous killing in Hitchcock's *Torn Curtain*. Not for the squeamish. See also the original TV version *Dekalog 5: 'Thou shalt not kill'*. BC

Short Film About Love, A (Krótki film o milosci)

(Krzysztof Kieslowski, 1988, Pol) Grazyna Szapolowska, Olaf Lubaszenko, Stefania Iwinska, Piotr Machalica.
87 min.

Like *A Short Film About Killing*, this is a movie spin-off from Kieslowski's ten-part TV series *The Decalogue*, each segment of which sardonically re-examines one of the Ten Commandments. It's about a 19-year-old postal clerk who covets the

slightly older woman in the flat opposite, to the extent that he keeps his astronomical telescope fixed on her windows and spends his every free minute glued to its sys-piece. Without fathoming the depths of his passion, the woman learns of his obsession and starts responding to his surveillance – with potentially disastrous results. Well aware that Hitchcock and Michael Powell have been down these streets before him, Kieslowski turns in an absolutely masterly movie that yields equal parts of humour and wry emotional truth. As an account of love in the late 20th century, it's in a league of its own. See also *Dekalog 6: 'Thou shalt not commit adultery'*. TR

Short Time

(Gregg Champion, 1987, US) Dabney Coleman, Matt Frewer, Teri Garr, Barry Corbin, Joe Pantoliano, Xander Berkeley, Rob Roy.
102 min.

Dabney Coleman has a problem. He's a cop just eight days short of retirement, but his doctors also give him only two weeks to live. With admirable pragmatism, he resolves to die in the line of duty, thereby bequeathing a fortune in insurance money to pay his ten-year-old son's Harvard fees. Naturally, dying turns out to be a pain in the neck, and he becomes an inadvertent supercop. Directed by former second unit man Gregg Champion, *Short Time* boasts some well-staged action sequences; in particular a hilarious car chase with Coleman in kamikaze pursuit of Uzi-toting hoods, yelling his war cry, 'This one's for you, little guy'. Matters get bogged down when the film-makers feel the need to redress the hero's death wish with schmaltzy life-affirming sentiments. Still, when did you last see a movie where the hero dived *towards* an exploding grenade? TCh

Shot Down

(Andrew Worsdale, 1987, SAf) Robert Colman, Megan Kruskal, Mavuso, Irene Stephano.
90 min.

Made by the Johannesburg group Weekend Theatre, this follows the moral and political confusion of one Paul Gilliat, hired by the State Bureau to investigate a subversive township performance group and track down its leader, enigmatic Black artist Rasechaba. He hitches up with a bunch of white bohemians who perform satirical cabaret, and sees for himself the systematic intimidation by security forces and assorted right wing bully-boys. Turning his back on his employers, he wanders off into the wilderness to find himself, and ends up battered and bewildered, despised by Rasechaba and his cabaret friends. The film is at its strongest when it relies on the performance skills of the actors: the cabaret scenes are heady and dangerous, garishly lit and with a real sense of illegality enhanced by some (deliberately?) shaky camerawork. Sadly, too much time is spent following Gilliat on his interior journey, and interest flags after one too many moral crises. As a slice of South African cultural resistance, however, *Shot Down* is extraordinary, full of self-mocking humour, and – in bursts – exhilarating. RS

Shot in the Dark, A

(Blake Edwards, 1964, GB) Peter Sellers, Elke Sommer, George Sanders, Herbert Lom, Tracy Reed, Graham Stark, Burt Kwouk.
101 min.

First of the *Pink Panther* sequels, establishing Sellers' incompetent Inspector Clouseau as a viable series character, and prompting Blake Edwards into an unchallenging downhill coast for far too long. Sellers, smitten by Elke Sommer's pretty parlourmaid and determined to prove her innocent of the charge of shooting her lover, is given plenty of opportunity for knockabout. PT

Shout

(Jeffrey Hornaday, 1991, US) John Travolta, James Walters, Heather Graham, Richard Jordan, Linda Fiorentino, Scott Coffey, Glenn Quinn.
89 min.

Rural Texas in the '50s finds rebellious teen Walters landed high and dry at the Benedict Home for Boys, until new teacher Travolta arrives and starts getting the kids hip to the sounds of rock'n'roll. You'll count the clichés in this affectionate but unpersuasive romp. From Travolta's pre-Tarantino doldrum days. TJ

Shout, The

(Jerzy Skolimowski, 1978, GB) Alan Bates, Susannah York, John Hurt, Robert Stephens, Tim Curry, Julian Hough.
86 min.

'Every word I'm telling you is true' adds Crossley (Bates), beginning his terrible story which makes up the substance of *The Shout*: a means of whiling away time at the village *versus* asylum cricket match where he and Robert Graves (author of the source story, played by Curry) are designated scorers. And fascinatingly, it is the boundaries between truth and falsehood that merge, rather than those between madness and insanity. For Crossley is undoubtedly mad, mendacious and cunning, viciously manipulating his chosen victims – a musician (Hurt) and his wife (York) – appealing sometimes across omniscient peaks of rationality and sometimes by scornful superiority. But what seems like his biggest whopper – his claim to kill with his shout – is proven. Skolimowski's second feature made in Britain is something of a triumph for independent production, with an impressively streamlined screenplay and faultless performances. JS

Shout at the Devil

(Peter Hunt, 1976, GB) Lee Marvin, Roger Moore, Barbara Parkins, Ian Holm, Rene Kolldehoff, Gernot Endemann, Karl Michael Vogler, Jean Kent, George Coulouris, Murray Melvin.
147 min.

Set in East Africa in 1913 in the days of German and English brinkmanship, this ostentatiously displays its large budget, but makes a mostly unsuccessful return to the world of colonial intrigues. Combining a slim plot about ivory poaching with some *African Queen* malarkey (involving blowing up a battleship), the film offers a comedy adventure that Ford or Hawks could have directed standing on their heads. But Peter Hunt seems incapable of controlling his leading men. Marvin behaves increasingly like a caricature of himself, turning to leer at the camera at the end of each take, while Moore, displaying officer qualities with all the conviction of Biggles, shows little aptitude for comedy. Barbara Parkins provides the only emotional complexity on display. Otherwise it's a Big Man's Adventure – Big locations, Big hearted, full of Manly Sentiments. CPe

Show Boat

(James Whale, 1936, US) Irene Dunne, Allan Jones, Helen Morgan, Paul Robeson, Charles Winninger, Hattie McDaniel, Donald Cook.
112 min. b/w.

No one ever made more than a singing dummy of Allan Jones, and no one could possibly carry off the last-minute flurry of plot preparing for a ludicrously mushy happy ending (made even worse by a risibly 'aged' Jones). Otherwise Whale does superbly by this much-loved Kern-Hammerstein musical, abetted by modestly handsome sets and lustrous camerawork from John Mescall. Dunne and Jones may look and act a little pallid, but they do well by Jerome Kern's lovely melodies, while Paul Robeson (in magnificent voice for 'Ol' Man River' and 'I Still Suits Me') and Helen Morgan ('Can't Help Lovin' That Man' and 'Bill') are as near perfection as makes no odds. Morgan, through her phrasing of the heart-rending 'Bill', almost makes a tragic figure out of the tragic Julie – no mean achievement. TM

Show Boat

(George Sidney, 1951, US) Kathryn Grayson, Ava Gardner, Howard Keel, Joe E Brown, Marge and Gower Champion, Agnes Moorehead, William Warfield, Robert Sterling.
108 min.

Not surprisingly, Arthur Freed's production values put this ahead of Whale's 1936 version as sheer spectacle, but the earlier version had two big plusses in Robeson (Warfield here is secure, but lacks the mystique), and Helen Morgan (here Ava Gardner's voice is dubbed, and try as she might she can't shake off the big star bit). Keel and Grayson are as colourless as ever, but no less so than Jones and Dunne were in 1936. As a film musical it survives on sheer class and some of Jerome Kern's richest melodies. As an anti-racist tract, though, it must have looked a lot less ingenuous when it first opened than it does now. Instead, enjoy the unashamed sentiment of the tale, and the spirited hoofing of Marge and Gower Champion. SG

Showgirls

(Paul Verhoeven, 1995, US) Elizabeth Berkley, Kyle MacLachlan, Gina Gershon, Glenn Plummer, Robert Davi, Alan Rachins, Gina Ravera, Lin Tucci.
131 min.
Joe Eszterhas' by-numbers script recycles the baggy, Faustian 'ingénue comes to the big bad city' tale and stuffs it into a skimpy, lamé-bedecked version of the 'let's put on a show' musical. Plus topless. Alarm bells sound in the gauche opening sequence where hot-panted Nomi (Berkley) hitches her way into Las Vegas in the car of a predatory 'slick'. Thereafter, it's red lights all the way. You couldn't call the film misogynist; director Verhoeven's targets are too wide-ranging for it to be anything less than purely misanthropic. WH

Show of Force, A

(Bruno Barreto, 1990, US) Amy Irving, Robert Duvall, Andy Garcia, Lou Diamond Phillips, Kevin Spacey, Joe Campanella.
93 min.
Amid turbulent events in Puerto Rico, in 1978, TV reporter Irving uncovers the hand of the FBI in killings intended to influence the local elections. There might be a sound documentary to be made from this material, but between the fact and the drama Barreto's film falls oddly flat. Watch out for Phillips cast against type as an eccentric heavy, but blink a couple of times and you'll miss Duvall and Garcia – strongly billed, barely featured. TJ

Show People

(King Vidor, 1928, US) Marion Davies, William Haines, Dell Henderson, Paul Ralli, Polly Moran, Albert Conti.
83 min. b/w.
Although perhaps not the hilarious comic masterpiece of repute, nevertheless a delightful look at silent Hollywood, in which Marion Davies (the mistress of William Randolph Hearst and thus the model for Susan Alexander in Citizen Kane) reveals her talents as a likeable parodist, playing a young hopeful who graduates from custard-pie target in slapstick comedies to Gloria Swanson-style grande dame. All twitchy lips and histrionic gestures, she manages to make credible the character's rise to fame, despite minimal talent, through her combination of glamour, seduction and acute ambition. A fine example of Hollywood gently satirising itself, with cameo appearances from many luminaries (including Fairbanks, Chaplin, William S Hart, John Gilbert and Elinor Glyn), plus Vidor himself during the final romantic reunion with her long-forgotten fiancé GA

Shtetl

(Marian Marzynski, 1996, US)
180 min.
Narrated by the Polish-born film-maker, Marzynski, this engrossing, sober, deeply moving documentary reconstructs, through visits, photographs and memories the Shtetl of Bransk, a town 160 km east of Warsaw with a Jewish population of 2,500 in 1939, now with none. Most perished in the Holocaust, the rest scattered throughout the world. Marzynski, who survived the Holocaust by hiding with Christians, acts as translator for, first, a 70-year-old Chicago Jew, Nathan Kaplan, whom he takes to Bransk to visit the home of his family, and later another American, Jack Ruby, a concentration camp survivor who revisits his childhood home. In the middle section, Marzynski takes a Gentile historian of Bransk Jewish history, Zbyszek Romaniuk, to America to meet Kaplan, thus raising questions of Romaniuk's objectivity and the Polish people's responsibility for the fate of the Jews. Marzynski is an intent interviewer, but he adopts a leisurely, slightly meandering approach to structure, which nevertheless pays off in moments of extraordinary passion. WH

Shuroo

(Savi Gabizon, 1990, Isr) Moshe Ivgi, Sharon Hacoen, Sinai Peter.
83 min.
This comedy about life among Tel Aviv's 30-

something bourgeoisie is nothing if not proof that self-absorbed, would-be hipsters are the same the world over. The central character is Asher, an unbecoming depressive amd all-round schlemiel who publishes a book on 'How to Be an Idiot', and finds himself becoming the guru of a self-help circle. A liberal sprinkling of sight gags and non-sequiturs – and even a slight flavour of Almodóvar in the sexual absurdities – keeps things lively. But unless a lot has got lost in the subtitling, the all-pervading psychobabble is nothing like as funny as it's clearly meant to be. JRo

Shut Down

(Curtis Clark, 1978, GB) Brian Godber, Lydia Lisle, Tim Cook.
41 min.
A glossy companion-piece to Clark's earlier essay on the same subject, Cruisin' – all chrome, custom-jobs and bubblegum rock – this focuses on British drag racers and street rodders, in another celebration of adopted US culture. Information for non-initiates is in short supply, restricted to the Santa Pod Raceway tannoy commentary and a few mechanics' rhubarbs, while the whole enterprise is cripplingly sabotaged by the intrusion of a cliché scripted encounter between two would-be James Deans. Very much the colour supplement movie, complete with compilation soundtrack album. PT

Shvitz, The

(Jonathan Berman, 1993, US)
47 min.
An enjoyable look at New York's vanishing steambath culture, which provides warm, wet gathering places for Jews of every profession, class and moral hue (including gangsters). The rub-downs, massages and hose-downs are only part of the appeal. Here, senior citizens meet to escape the family, swap intimate secrets and gags, play cards and indulge in a nostalgia taken up by this sweet, funny film. An engaging slice of oral history. GA

Shy People

(Andrei Konchalovsky, 1987, US) Jill Clayburgh, Barbara Hershey, Martha Plimpton, Merritt Butrick, John Philbin, Don Swayze, Pruitt Taylor Vince.
119 min.
Worried by the precocious habits of her teenage daughter Grace (Plimpton), Cosmo journo Diana (Clayburgh) visits distant relations living a spartan existence down in the Louisiana bayou. At first, Konchalovsky's depiction of the culture clash is merely clichéd: while Diana and Grace worry about things like make-up, matriarch Ruth (Hershey) still sets a place at table for her long-lost outlaw husband and exercises an iron will over her own cretinous brood. Pretty soon, however, it's a case of loony tunes with a vengeance: an attack on her son by poachers provokes Ruth to take a rare trip to town, gun in hand; Grace's druggy seduction of a cousin under lock and key results in violence and panicky flight; Diana's excursion into the misty swamps in search of the girl courts alligators and ghosts. Proceeding from hackneyed Cold Comfort Farm territory to a grotesque Gothic nightmare, Konchalovsky's fatuous fable misfires on all counts: it remains melodramatic hokum, pure and simple-minded, the luminous photography and Hershey's sterling performance notwithstanding. GA

Siao Yu (Shaonü Xiao Yu)

(Sylvia Chang, 1995, Tai) Joyin Liu, Daniel J Travanti, Tou Chung-Hua, Marj Dusay.
104 min.
Why are Chinese women directors so drawn to illegal immigrant/Green Card movies set in New York? After Mabel Cheung and Clara Law comes Sylvia Chang with this modest adaptation of a novel by Geling Yan, reciting the familar litany of dead-end jobs and marriages of convenience. Siao Yu (newcomer Liu, promising) has to cohabit with her paid-for Italian-American husband (Travanti, impressive) to convince the Immigration Department that the marriage isn't phoney. The predictable complications include her growing to like him, her long-term boyfriend Jiang getting ratty and the husband having a guilty secret in his closet. Sensitive, decent, fatally dull. TR

Siberian Lady Macbeth (Sibirska Ledi Magbet)

(Andrzej Wajda, 1961, Yugo) Olivera Markovic, Ljuba Tadic, Kapitalina Eric, Bojan Stupica, Mile Lazarevic.
95 min. b/w.
Shakespeare at substantially more than a mere geographical remove: Wajda's Yugoslav production is based on Russian novelist Nikolai Leskov's imaginative transposition of the tragedy, while the catalogue of crimes passionnels at its heart suggests nothing so much as Eastern bloc Cain: 'The Swineherd Always Rings Twice' perhaps. Katerina, brooding mistress of the village mill, coolly despatches father-in-law and long-absent husband to instal hired hand Sergei at her side; shading motivation and psychology away from femme fatale typing, only to be betrayed by her own emotional investment. Wajda, carefully composing in 'Scope, tops his functional naturalism with a bleakly symbolic retributive coda, in the first of several 'exile' parentheses in his more fruitful interaction with postwar Polish history. PT

Sibling Rivalry

(Carl Reiner, 1990, US) Kirstie Alley, Bill Pullman, Carrie Fisher, Jami Gertz, Scott Bacula, Frances Sternhagen, John Randolph, Sam Elliott, Ed O'Neill.
88 min.
From the moment Alley – a doctor's frustrated wife urged by her sister to indulge an affair – screws charming, grey-haired stranger Sam Elliott to death, you know this is going to be a stiff. Pullman mugs his way through the part of a bungling window-blind salesman who agrees to help Alley make it look like suicide. Gertz is the randy sister who falls for the investigating cop (O'Neill), while Fisher makes Alley's medically-obsessed in-laws. The sitcom contrivance of Martha Goldhirsh's script is exacerbated by farcically overwrought performances. Chief among these is from Alley herself, all 'big hair', neurotic snivelling and shrieking hysteria. And the scene where she has to remove a condom from the corpse's rigor mortised dick... Laugh? I almost changed my method of contraception. NF

Si c'était à refaire

see Second Chance

Sicilian, The

(Michael Cimino, 1987, US) Christopher Lambert, Terence Stamp, Joss Ackland, John Turturro, Richard Bauer, Barbara Sukowa, Giulia Boschi, Ray McAnally, Barry Miller, Aldo Ray.
146 min.
In adapting Mario Puzo's novel, eschewing the political complexity of Francesco Rosi's classic Salvatore Giuliano, Cimino opts for silly and mendacious mythologising. Here the Sicilian bandit Giuliano (Lambert) becomes a heroic Christ figure, his acts of theft and murder prompted by sympathy for the peasantry, his death the result of a Judas-like betrayal manipulated by sinister and dishonorable figures of State, Church and Underworld; incredibly, he is even exonerated from responsibility for the notorious massacre of innocent Communists. Bathos abounds: American Duchess Sukowa falls head over heels for the noble savage; even Mafia capo Ackland sheds a tear for the brave son he never had. The dialogue is ponderously poetic, stilted and over-emphatic, characters are convenient cyphers, and both cutting and photography tend towards the bombastic. Folly, then, but gloriously inept and overblown. GA

Sicilian Clan, The (Le Clan des Siciliens)

(Henri Verneuil, 1968, Fr) Jean Gabin, Alain Delon, Lino Ventura, Irina Demick, Amedeo Nazzari, Sydney Chaplin, Karen Blanguernon.
120 min.
Cast as the patriarch of a spaghetti-eating Sicilian family who are crooks to a man, the once formidable Gabin – stout, white-haired and now a bit past it – mostly sits back and glowers while the younger members of the cast squabble, lust and plot a caper involving the hijack of a plane-load of jewels. He finally rouses himself from his lethargy to defend his honour by executing Delon, a Corsican who had the temerity to play

S

around with his daughter-in-law. Verneuil, not for the first time, tries to direct like Jean-Pierre Melville and fails to make it, though the action scenes are passable, and Henri Deca's moody photography is rather more than that. TM

Sicilian Cross (Gli Esecutori)
(Maurizio Lucidi, 1976, It) Roger Moore, Stacy Keach, Ivo Garrani, Fausto Tozzi, Ennio Balbo, Ettore Manni, Rosemarie Lindt.
102 min.
A run-of-the-mill Mafia potboiler which leaps between San Francisco and Sicily in a tediously bloody search for a stolen heroin consignment, and asks us to accept Roger Moore as an Italo-American lawyer. A committee of six came up with the derivative mess of a script, surprisingly including *Grease* director Randall Kleiser and *Shaft* author/*French Connection* scriptwriter Ernest Tidyman. Surprises, however, stop there. PT

Sick: The Life & Death of Bob Flanagan, Supermasochist
(Kirby Dick, 1997, US) Bob Flanagan, Sheree Rose, Cathy Flanagan, Bob Flanagan Sr, Tim Flanagan, Sara Douchette.
90 min.
Bob Flanagan was a sick man. Born with cystic fibrosis in 1952, the doctors gave him a life expectancy of six or seven years – but rather than conform, he survived to 1995, hammering nails into his penis, and the like, and turning the results into art. This documentary, shocking and enlightening, succeeds in contextualising, and thus humanising, misunderstood sexual 'deviancy'. You get some insight into Bob's troubled relationship with his body, watching him create a clear plastic, self-modelled 'Invisible Man' that produces a flow of brown, white and green goo from three orifices. He met his perfect dominatrix partner in Sheree Rose, and married her in 1982, while she hung him upside down from the ceiling. Documenting Bob's domestic life, masochism, art, illness and more masochism for good measure, it's a tough watch – certain scenes especially – but warm and witty, too. And the moral? 'You always hurt the one you love.' NB

Sid and Nancy
(Alex Cox, 1986, GB) Gary Oldman, Chloe Webb, David Hayman, Debby Bishop, Andrew Schofield, Xander Berkeley, Perry Benson.
114 min.
As Cox has been at pains to point out, this is not the story of the Sex Pistols but a love story pure and simple. And since love is never simple and rarely pure, Cox follows his emetic pair, Sid Vicious and Nancy Spungen, on their long downhill slide. From the coarse idiocies of the punk movement, through the permanent scrabble for any mind-frying drug, through the screeching knock-down rows to the final abandonment far from home in the Chelsea Hotel, New York, it's a long hard ride down a tunnel filthy with every kind of degradation. Why then should anyone of sane disposition wish to see the film? Because it is still a love story, and a very touching one at that; whether waiting for her in the rain, or ripping her stockings so he can suck on her toes, or simply kissing in an alley with garbage falling all around them, there never seems to be any doubt that Sid loves Nancy OK. Quite why is hard to explain; but the movie (like Sid, as portrayed by Oldman, not without a sense of humour) is shot through with an oblique feeling for the blacker absurdities of life. Not the least of which is that, nowadays, love is not stronger than death. CPea

Siddhartha
(Conrad Rooks, 1972, US) Shashi Kapoor, Simi Garewal, Romesh Sharma, Pincho Kapoor, Zul Vellani.
94 min.
A glossy feature-length ad whose genesis is Hesse's slight novel about a beautiful Brahmin who hits the road in search of truth. Accompanied by his baby-faced friend, he freaks out with the Sadhus in the wild, listens to Buddha in the grove (exit friend as monk), fucks in silhouette with a rich courtesan, and makes a lot of money as a merchant. He drops out again to find ultimate and absolute contentment ferrying folks across a river. The familiar Hesse dialectic between profligacy and asceticism is followed faithfully

enough, and there's small chance of anyone leaving without receiving the message that there is no path to truth, that to search is not to find, and that 'everything returns' on the wheel of life. Unfortunately the film is made with such lack of imagination that it's impossible to get the true feel of the states of mind our Bombay ad-star goes through. Everything becomes a soft, vaguely symbolic spectacle, a love story in a chocolate-box landscape. JDuC

Side by Side
(Bruce Beresford, 1975, GB) Terry-Thomas, Barry Humphries, Stephanie De Sykes, Billy Boyle, Frank Thornton, Dave Mount.
84 min.
This unbelievably dreadful piece of '70s kitsch has rival club owners Boyle and Terry-Thomas battling to evade closure by searching out new pop talent, with the latter's right-hand man Humphries and his recording agency contact De Sykes off to a head start. The acts include Mud, the Rubettes and Second Generation, the big finale has the wall between the two establishments falling down to make one big party, and, yes, the director is *that* Bruce Beresford – the one who made *Tender Mercies* and *Driving Miss Daisy*. TJ

Sidewalks of London
see St Martin's Lane

Sidewalk Stories
(Charles Lane, 1989, US) Charles Lane, Nicole Alysia, Sandye Wilson, Darnell Williams, Trula Hoosier.
97 min. b/w.
An ambitious but sadly misguided attempt to make a contemporary silent comedy which opts for simplistic plotting, sentimentality and mime as it tells of a homeless, black New York street artist's attempts to trace the mother of a baby girl whose father's murder he has witnessed. The black-and-white photography is of some appeal, but Lane's own central performance is so winsome that the plot's (unintentional?) borrowings from Chaplin's maudlin *The Kid* become irritating in the extreme. Only the last minute is memorable, but it comes far too late to endow the film with anything but novelty value. GA

Sidney Sheldon's Bloodline
see Bloodline

Siege
(Paul Donovan/Maura O'Connell, 1982, Can) Doug Lennox, Tom Nardini, Brenda Bazinet, Darel Haeny, Terry-David Despres, Jack Blum.
81 min.
Such a blatant low-budget steal of the *Assault on Precinct 13* idea that one could almost praise it for bare-faced cheek. On the first night of an official police strike, a gay club is invaded by some vile recruits of the 'New Order', a local variant on the National Front, who sport a nasty line in queer-bashing (shooting them in the back of the head). One gay runs free, takes refuge in a large house peopled by resourceful outdoor types of that particularly Canadian sort, and the siege begins. Many scenes are badly in need of tightening, but there is some pleasure to be had from the ingenuity of the besieged in contriving makeshift weaponry (a drainpipe bazooka, the old James Bond flaming aerosol trick). There's the Hawksian standby of the last cigarette, and there's even the dead-villain-who-won't-lie-down. Not quite there, but not a bad try. CPea

Siegfried
see Nibelungen, Die

Sierra
(Alfred E Green, 1950, US) Audie Murphy, Wanda Hendrix, Dean Jagger, Burl Ives, Elliott Reid, Tony Curtis, Sara Allgood.
83 min.
It's safe to say that Audie Murphy was the only film star to have killed 240 men, and here we catch him just a few years after his wartime tribulations, trying his luck in Hollywood. He marches into the frame like a good soldier and duly recites his lines; but he's nowhere near an actor and, despite the baby faced looks, a slightly disturbing presence. This is a characteristic example of the sort of juvenile-oriented Western in

which he made his name. Burl Ives, as Lonesome the Hermit, sings 'The Ballad of Suzie the Whale' and such, while Tony Curtis, being groomed for stardom, looks cool in a black hat. The location scouts have assembled a choice assortment of geography for Russell Metty's camera to celebrate. BBa

Siesta
(Mary Lambert, 1987, US) Ellen Barkin, Jodie Foster, Gabriel Byrne, Martin Sheen, Julian Sands, Isabella Rossellini, Alexei Sayle, Grace Jones.
97 min.
Barkin, coming to on an airfield, dress around her ears and blood all over the place, utters the first of many crass expositions: 'This isn't my blood, so it must be somebody else's!' In a crazed panic, she sets off to solve the mystery, along the way falling into the clutches of a lecherous taxi-driver and a group of young ingrates (Sands and Foster among them) emulating Fellini party scenes. Flashbacks reveal that Barkin is Claire, a brassy American stunt-woman, whose fear of dying in a dare has driven her away from her railroading husband (Sheen) for one last night of spunky passion in Spain with her former lover and trapeze instructor (Byrne), whose new wife (Rossellini) stalks them with a knife. Lambert's debut fields farcical menace, wildly theatrical performances, a confusing plot and a corny resolution, while the script is a hilariously overblown gem. Miles Davis' soundtrack is the sole subtlety. EP

Sigmund Freud's Dora
(Anthony McCall/Claire Pajaczkowska/ Andrew Tyndall/Jane Weinstock, 1979, US) Suzanne Fletcher, Joel Kovel, Silvia Kolbowski, Anne Hegira.
35 min.
Feminine desire, displacement, obsessive housewifery, the image of the Madonna, smoke... fire. No wonder Freud's fragmented analysis of his rebellious teenage patient has become a feminist touchstone. This witty and ambitious film bends the rules of classic couch cinema, while inserts of telly ads and porno films interrogate woman's status as the object of desire. MM

Signal Left, Turn Right (Da Zuo Deng, Xiang You Zhuan)
(Huang Jianxin, 1996, China/HK) Niu Zhenhua, Ding Jiali, Ju Hao, Qi Qiao, Wang Gang.
110 min.
As its title makes plain, the final part of Huang's 'urban attitude' trilogy is about a driving school. Any connection with larger questions about China's current direction is, of course, purely coincidental. Driving schools are run on military lines. The film focuses on one group of three adult pupils (there should be four, but one has married a foreigner and emigrated) and dissects their dubious reasons for wanting to learn to drive. Niu, the trilogy's chubby mascot, plays a wily photo-journalist with a yen for prestige; he is the first to cotton on to the various scams operated by their instructor. Less a plot-driven film than a series of vignettes and gags, it's often riotously funny and certainly says a lot about Chi...er, Chinese driving schools in the 1990s. TR

Signal 7
(Bob Nilsson, 1983, US) Bill Ackridge, Dan Leegant, Bob Eldross, Herb Mills, Hagit Farber, John Tidwell.
92 min.
Shot over six nights on videotape and partially funded by the film-maker's own credit cards, this portrait of life amid the San Francisco cabbing community unfolds in semi-improvised fashion, focusing on failed actors Ackridge and Leegant, who can't quite leave their former aspirations behind. Nothing new really, but the performers look comfortable with the rambling dialogue, and the dedication to John Cassavetes is not entirely unwarranted. TJ

Signed: Lino Brocka
(Christian Blackwood, 1987, US) Lino Brocka, JayIlagan.
83 min.
Documentaries about film-makers are generally a major snooze, but Lino Brocka (arch-foe of Imelda Marcos, best known for his *Manila: In the Claws of Darkness*) tells tales that could cure deaf-

Time Out Film Guide **821**

ness. Blackwood has the good sense to simply let him rip, and he ranges freely over his extraordinary life story, his attachment to the city's slum-dwellers, his struggle to make movies of adult interest, and his troubles with successive Filipino governments. Most movingly, Brocka comes out as gay, presents clips from his first gay-themed film (the long-lost *Gold-Plated*), and shows rehearsals for his upcoming film about a rent boy, *Macho Dancer*. The combustible mixture of sex, radicalism and soap generates more heat than many a fiction film. TR

Signe du Lion, Le
(The Sign of Leo)

(Eric Rohmer, 1959, Fr) Jess Hahn, Van Doude, Michle Girardon, Jean Le Poulain, Stéphane Audran, Franoise Prévost, Jean-Luc Godard.
90 min. b/w.
Rohmer's first feature, not so much a moral tale as a cautionary anecdote (loosely modelled on Murnau's *The Last Laugh*) in which an impoverished American musician living in Paris (Hahn) runs himself into debt on the strength of an inheritance he doesn't inherit. Very much of its *nouvelle vague* day in its amused anatomy of the Latin Quarter fauna as the hero desperately does the rounds in quest of a loan, having no luck because it is summer and everyone's on holiday, and gradually slipping without realising it into becoming a *clochard*. But also a precise, poetic documentary on Paris, with the city turning into a stone prison that gradually crushes resistance until the musician suffers total moral and physical disintegration. TM

Sign of the Cross, The

(Cecil B DeMille, 1932, US) Fredric March, Elissa Landi, Charles Laughton, Claudette Colbert, Ian Keith, Vivian Tobin, Nat Pendleton.
124 min. b/w.
A prologue tacked on in 1944 ludicrously attempts to link the Allies' advance over Italy to the dreadful happenings in Nero's time. But history was always a plaything to DeMille, useful only as a surefire way of offering up sex, violence and visual spectacle under the guise of cultural and moral enlightenment. And this slice of 'history' has it all: Laughton's implicitly gay Nero fiddling away while an impressive miniature set burns, Colbert bathing up to her nipples in asses' milk, Christians and other unfortunates thrown to a fearsome menagerie, much suggestive slinking about in Mitchell Leisen's costumes, much general debauchery teetering between the sadistic and the erotic. Not for people with scruples. GB

Sign of the Gladiator
(Nel segno di Roma)

(Guido Brignone, 1958, It/Fr/WGer) Anita Ekberg, Georges Marchal, Jacques Sernas, Folco Lulli, Lorella De Luca, Gino Cervi, Chelo Alonso.
100 min.
Syrian queen Zenobia (Ekberg) takes time out from rebellion against the Roman Empire to fall for enslaved general Marco Valerio (Marchal). He remains faithful to Rome, however, and in the climactic battle receives a javelin in the chest from Zenobia. The general recovers from his wound in time to plead successfully for Zenobia – who's by now up before the Senate in an off-the-shoulder evening dress. Lavishly mounted and splendidly preposterous. Sergio Leone – then Roberti Sergio Leone – was one of the five scriptwriters. Cut by 15 minutes on its first British release. TJ

Sign of the Pagan

(Douglas Sirk, 1954, US) Jeff Chandler, Jack Palance, Ludmilla Tcherina, Rita Gam, Jeff Morrow, George Dolenz, Eduard Franz, Alexander Scourby.
92 min.
An immensely interesting though finally unsuccessful film. Sirk's hopes of transforming the project into a version of Marlowe's *Tamburlaine the Great* were thwarted by Universal. However, the film's historical dimension – Attila the Hun's attempt to destroy the Roman Empire, with Palance as Attila, and Chandler as Rome's would-be Christian defender – together with Sirk's unusually hysterical conception of the central character, throw a suggestive light on the seemingly slight reverberations of his better-known domestic melodramas. PH

Signora di Tutti, La

(Max Ophuls, 1934, It) Isa Miranda, Memo Benassi, Tatiana Pavlova, Nelly Corradi, Federico Benfer, Franco Coop.
97 min. b/w.
Ophuls' only Italian film, in which once again his subject is female sexuality – as a 'danger' or threat, as a source of beauty, as a marketable commodity. The film star Gaby Doriot (Miranda) attempts suicide, and under anaesthetic she recalls the events that shaped her life. Commerce, industry and high finance are viewed with sharp irony throughout, but the melodrama centres on a seductive ambiguity: is Gaby a victim of those around her, or their willing accomplice? As ever, Ophuls' highly mobile camera shows rather than tells, emotionally sensitising all it lights upon. TR

Signora senza camelie, La
(Camille without Camellias/
The Lady without Camellias)

(Michelangelo Antonioni, 1953, It) Lucia Bosè, Andrea Cecchi, Gino Cervi, Ivan Desny, Alain Cuny.
105 min. b/w.
An early Antonioni drama that looks at the sad fate of a manipulated woman, as well as taking a satirical swipe at the commercial end of the Italian film industry. Bosè plays a shopgirl, recently elevated to movie stardom, whose idolising producer husband (Cecchi) puts her into a disastrous production of *Joan of Arc* and sends her career into a downward spiral. Characteristically, Antonioni is less concerned with plot than with creating fluid set pieces and eloquent framings of his beautiful actress and the surrounding decor. The resulting cocktail is slight on psychology, but invariably stunning to behold. DT

Signs of Life
(Lebenszeichen)

(Werner Herzog, 1968, WGer) Peter Brogle, Wolfgang Reichmann, Julio Pinheiro, Athina Zacharopoulou, Wolfgang von Ungern-Sternberg.
90 min. b/w.
Herzog's first feature is his most conventional: three bored German soldiers spend the last months of the World War II occupation 'guarding' a useless munitions dump on the Greek island of Cos, killing time as best they can until one of them – inevitably – flips out. It's the one occasion that Herzog has tried to draw characters in any psychological depth, and (predictably) the going is sometimes heavy, but the film is still loaded with idiosyncratic, remarkable details...like the devastating moment that sparks the soldier's madness. TR

Si Jolie Petite Plage, Une
(Such a Pretty Little Beach)

(Yves Allégret, 1948, Fr) Gérard Philipe, Madeleine Robinson, Jane Marken, Jean Servais, Julien Carette.
90 min. b/w.
A late bloom for the Carné-Prévert brand of poetic realism, set in a wintry beach resort in Normandy where a young man (Philipe), returns to the scene of his childhood after involvement in a crime of passion in Paris (he has just killed the singer he was seduced by and ran away with to escape his orphanage background). Undergoing much soul-searching torment, focused by the presence of a sinister stranger (Servais) as well as by speculation and gossip about the crime centering on the nosy hotel proprietress (Marken), he finds some temporary warmth in the love of the bedraggled chambermaid (Robinson). An exercise in unrelieved gloom, much admired at the time, it now looks much too studied; despite sound performances and Henri Alekan's impressively moody evocation of the deserted, permanently rain-swept landscape, it emerges as rather a bore. TM

Silas Marner

(Giles Foster, 1985, GB) Ben Kingsley, Jenny Agutter, Patrick Ryecart, Freddie Jones, Rosemary Martin, Patsy Kensit, Jim Broadbent, Frederick Treves, Angela Pleasence.
92 min.
For sheer prettiness, this is the apotheosis of BBC

tea-time classicism. Real locations (carefully muddied roads, immaculately authentic masonry) look more artificial than any studio mock-up. Foster's ambling treatment of George Eliot's novel – embittered outcast rediscovering humanity – generates the urgency of a waxworks show in its picturesque rollcall of accomplished players, Kingsley's self-consciously actorish miser included. MHoy

Silence, The (Tystnaden)

(Ingmar Bergman, 1963, Swe) Ingrid Thulin, Gunnel Lindblom, Jörgen Lindström, Hakan Jahnberg, Birger Malmsten.
96 min. b/w.
The final part of Bergman's trilogy (after *Through a Glass Darkly* and *Winter Light*) is a bleak and disturbing study of loneliness, love and obsessive desire. Sisters Ester (Thulin) and Anna (Lindblom), together with the latter's young son, book into a vast but virtually empty hotel – the only other guests are a troupe of dwarf entertainers – in a country seemingly occupied or threatened by war. Once again exploring the conflicts between physicality and spirituality, Bergman candidly portrays Ester's latent lesbian desire for her sister, as well as Anna's own compulsive sexuality (she picks up a waiter and brings him back to the hotel). Despite the overt eroticism, the sisters' craving for emotional warmth is filmed in a cold, objective style; in this way, Bergman's severe symbolism emphasises both the seeming impossibility of, and the absolute necessity for, human tenderness in a Godless world. NF

Silence and Cry
(Csend és Káiltás)

(Miklós Jancsó, 1967, Hun) András Kozák, Zoltán Latinovits, József Madaras, Mari Törocsik, Andrea Drahota.
79 min. b/w.
The Round-Up and *The Red and the White* both dealt with key moments in the Hungarian suppression of Communism, and introduced Jancsó's method as an ultra-stylised manipulation of politically symbolic figures in harsh, unyielding landscapes. *Silence and Cry* resumes the discussion at a newly intimate, domestic level, and introduces the psychological questions that dominate some of Jancsó's later movies. It centres on a refugee from the 'Red' army, hiding out from the police in the farmhouse of some politically dubious peasants, and focuses on his horror at his hosts' bland acceptance of their situation, which eventually provokes a 'meaningless' tragedy. Jancsó's characteristic sequence-shots turn the chamber drama into a political thriller pregnant with wider connotations, including veiled comments on the contemporary state of Hungary. TR

Silence de la mer, Le

(Jean-Pierre Melville, 1947, Fr) Howard Vernon, Nicole Stéphane, Jean-Marie Robain, Ami Aroe, Denis Sadier.
86 min. b/w.
Melville's extraordinary first feature, an adaptation of Vercors' classic novella about the French Resistance, is in effect a triangular drama in which two people don't speak. A German officer (Vernon), convalescing from a wound, is billeted on an elderly Frenchman (Robain) and his niece (Stéphane). Respecting their obstinate refusal to address the hated invader, he meets their silence with a series of monologues, apparently ignored, in which he recalls his life before the war and all the things he values; but what he reveals about himself causes the girl to fall in love, without being able to declare her feelings. Filmed in the most daring way imaginable, using a new cinematic language of transient expressions and glances, the film was a root influence on Bresson and the whole French New Wave. CPea

Silence est d'Or, Le
(Man About Town)

(René Clair, 1947, Fr) Maurice Chevalier, François Périer, Marcelle Derrien, Dany Robin, Robert Pizani, Raymond Cordy, Paul Olivier, Gaston Modot.
100 min. b/w.
Even in 1947, Clair's belated Valentine to the silent period, one of his few memorable postwar films, was so deliciously *passé* in style as almost to pass for an example of the work to which it pays wistful tribute. With Chevalier (whose heav-

ily accented delivery sounds decidedly odd in French) as an ageing boulevardier, Périer as his youthful nemesis, and Dany Robin as the *midinette* who comes between them, the plot is pure convention, but the gentle humour and wealth of period detail (from both the turn of the century and the '40s) have an enduring charm. GAd

Silence of the Hams, The
(Il silenzio dei prosciutti)
(Ezio Greggio, 1993, It/US) Billy Zane, Ezio Greggio, Dom DeLuise, Charlene Tilton, Joanna Pacula, Martin Balsam, Phyllis Diller, Shelley Winters.
81 min.
The US debut of Italy's favourite television comedian, Ezio Greggio, in which trainee FBI agent Jo Dee Fostar (Zane) encounters characters called Sharon Bone, Dr Animal Cannibal Pizza (an incarcerated psychiatrist who ate his patients in a pizzeria after closing time), and Inspector Putrid, is a wholly redundant exercise. The vogue for this flimflam is to forget pointed satire and instead recycle old plots in knowingly cack-handed fashion, along with some blunt physical comedy. NB

Silence of the Lambs, The
(Jonathan Demme, 1990, US) Jodie Foster, Anthony Hopkins, Scott Glenn, Ted Levine, Anthony Heald, Diane Baker, Brooke Smith, Kasi Lemmons, Tracey Walter, Roger Corman.
118 min.
In its own old-fashioned way, this is as satisfying as that other, more modernist Thomas Harris adaptation, *Manhunter*. When FBI trainee Clarice Starling (Foster) is sent to conduct an interview with serial killer shrink Dr Hannibal Lecter (Hopkins) in his high-security cell, she little knows what she is in for. The Feds want Lecter to help them in their search for homicidal maniac 'Buffalo Bill'; but in exchange for clues about Bill's behaviour, Lecter demands that Clarice answer questions about herself, so that he can penetrate the darkest recesses of her mind. It's in their confrontations that both film and heroine come electrically alive. Although Demme does reveal the results of the killer's violence, he for the most part refrains from showing the acts themselves; the film could never be accused of pandering to voyeuristic impulses. Understandably, much has been made of Hopkins' hypnotic Lecter, but the laurels must go to Levine's killer, admirably devoid of camp overstatement, and to Foster, who evokes a vulnerable but pragmatic intelligence bent on achieving independence through sheer strength of will. GA

Silences of the Palace, The
(Saimt el Qusur/Les Silences du Palais)
(Moufida Tlatli, 1994, Fr/Tun) Ahmel Hedhili, Hend Sabri, Najia Ouerghi, Ghalia Lacroix, Sami Bouajila, Kamel Fazaa.
127 min.
Moufida Tlatli's remarkable debut describes the days of slavery in her native Tunisia. At 25, Alia, a singer and lute-player, who is pregnant by her boyfriend, learns of the death of Prince Sidi Ali. This prompts a visit to his palace, giving rise to memories of her own and her mother's days of service there years ago. The film captures the texture of life in the palace – its gardens, its fading opulence, the kitchens, corridors and ante-rooms, all lit crystal clear. There are scenes of group activity (dyeing, washing, dancing, singing), but the dominating mood is of the monotony and soul-threatening burden of servitude. The prince exercised his *droit du seigneur*: an indignity which would drive Alia's mother to near-frenzy – had not her life been so focused on the interests of her 15-year-old daughter. A most memorable account of the complex relationship between mothers and daughters suffering the distortions of injustice. WH

Silencieux, Le (The Man Who Died Twice/The Silent One)
(Claude Pinoteau, 1973, Fr/It) Lino Ventura, Leo Genn, Robert Hardy, Lea Massari, Suzanne Flon, Bernard Dhéran, Pierre Zimmer.
118 min.
Lino Ventura, like Robert Mitchum, has held together more than one movie by his presence

alone, and almost does so here. He plays a French nuclear scientist, kidnapped by the Russians some 16 years earlier, forced to defect back by the British, who offer him 'freedom' in exchange for names. With the KGB after his blood, the film develops into a watchable chase thriller, best when reminiscent of Hitchcock: escapes from hotels, a killing on a train, and a climax involving a Russian orchestral conductor, the key to Ventura's real freedom. A bit too glossy, and the English dubbed version is appalling.

Silent Cry, The
(Stephen Dwoskin, 1977, GB/WGer/Fr) Ernst Brightmore, Bobby Gill, Harry Waistnage, Mary Rose, Beatrice Cordua.
98 min. b/w & col.
The title recalls Münch, but the film could almost be a radicalised Resnais project. Dwoskin traces the history of a woman dominated from childhood by male definition of her 'place'. She's trapped within a series of reflections of her image, which the film explores in an obsessive forward-and-backward movement that ranges over memory, fantasy, and 'the presentation of self in everyday life'. Although highly fragmented, this constructs a fuller narrative than any of Dwoskin's earlier features; but the narrative line is constantly disorganised by the disturbance of childhood memory and speech. An impressive renewal of the concerns that had been preoccupying Dwoskin for nearly a decade. IC

Silent Fall
(Bruce Beresford, 1994, US) Richard Dreyfuss, Linda Hamilton, JT Walsh, John Lithgow, Ben Faulkner, Liv Tyler, Zahn McClarnon.
101 min.
When their parents are brutally murdered, Sylvie (Tyler) names her autistic younger brother Tim (Faulkner), aged 9, as the culprit. However, sheriff Mitch Rivers (Walsh) has his doubts, and calls in reluctant, haunted shrink Jake Rainer (Dreyfuss) to break down the boy's wall of silence. Although this device is a variation on that old thriller stand-by, 'selective amnesia', interest in the unravelling mystery is sustained not by a need to discover the killer's identity (obvious early on), but by involvement with the damaged characters and the need to establish a motive. Initially avoiding clever plot-twists in favour of intense character study, Beresford draws the best from a fine cast. Only when he tries to up the thrill quotient near the end are the contrivances of Åkiva Goldsman's debut script revealed, like cracks in the smooth surface of a frozen lake. NF

Silent Flute, The
(aka Circle of Iron)
(Richard Moore, 1978, US) David Carradine, Jeff Cooper, Roddy McDowall, Eli Wallach, Christopher Lee, Erica Creer, Earl Maynard.
102 min.
Made in Israel with predominantly Israeli money and technicians, this is a berserk attempt at a martial arts fantasy, somewhat in the vein of *Conan the Barbarian*. Cooper plays the monosyllabic Cord, who wins a martial arts contest by what are considered foul means, and is disqualified from participating in a quest for a book of knowledge. He goes anyway, and meets a variety of bizarre challenges on the road, as well as a variety of foes, all played by David Carradine except for the man who is dissolving his penis in a barrel of oil, who is played by Eli Wallach. Eventually, having learned that man cannot live by brawn alone, he reaches the cloistered isle where a cowled Christopher Lee guards the book...It may sound, well, different, but Richard Moore's cumbersome direction reduces everything to the pedestrian or the banal. The storyline is credited to Bruce Lee and James Coburn (it was actually no more than the ghost of an idea dreamed up during Lee's days as a martial arts instructor in Los Angeles), but it's more significant that the script is credited to Stirling Silliphant, the 'versatile' writer lately responsible for the script of *The Swarm*. TR

Silent Movie
(Mel Brooks, 1976, US) Mel Brooks, Marty Feldman, Dom DeLuise, Bernadette Peters, Sid Caesar, Harold Gould, Ron Carey, Fritz Feld.
87 min.
Right from the opening seconds, when the single word 'Hello' appears on the screen, we all know

that *Silent Movie* is going to be very silly indeed, even for Mel Brooks. And so it is – a silent movie about the attempts of Mel Funn (Brooks), a has-been director dragged down by drink, to film a contemporary all-star silent movie, complete with raucous musical effects and explanatory titles. The trouble is, it's the kind of silliness that's too strained and self-indulgent to be enjoyable. James Caan, Liza Minnelli, Burt Reynolds and others contribute grating guest appearances. Only Brooks himself combines frenzy with grace, and there are occasional moments of barmy splendour. GB

Silent One, The
see Silencieux, Le

Silent Partner, The
(Daryl Duke, 1978, Can) Elliott Gould, Christopher Plummer, Susannah York, Celine Lomez, Michael Kirby, Sean Sullivan, John Candy.
105 min.
Tarting up a flagging project has rarely been taken quite so literally as here, with the climactic revelation that the misogynistic, sadistic villain (Plummer) has a predilection for drag. If it weren't for the gimmicks (and the sadism is so gratuitous it could be nothing else), then the film could easily pass for a minor caper thriller of the '60s, all convoluted plot and calculated kookiness. But cyphers (both female leads) and question-marks (who'll get the money, who'll survive – who cares?) dominate the script as every labyrinthine twist becomes more plodding. SM

Silent Rage
(Michael Miller, 1982, US) Chuck Norris, Ron Silver, Steven Keats, Toni Kalem, William Finley, Brian Libby, Stephen Furst.
105 min.
The idea of pitting karate champion Norris against a virtually indestructible psychopath is intriguing, but the resulting confusion of clichés proves disappointingly incompetent. Itching to try out his new drug, one of a trio of Frankenstein doctors fastens upon a mad axeman who has been shot to pieces (Libby), and revives him with startling effectiveness. Norris, as a small-town sheriff lumbered with a comic teddy-bear of a deputy and a posse of suspiciously well-scrubbed Hell's Angels, has to take time off to deal with the problem. The doctors bumble through their moral dilemmas, the biologically reinforced monster expresses his silent rage, and a bemused Norris wanders through the *Halloween*-ish landscape unsure whether he's playing Clint Eastwood or Hopalong Cassidy. Still, his *jodan mawashi geri* (a swivelling kick to the head) is a joy to behold. RMy

Silent Running
(Douglas Trumbull, 1971, US) Bruce Dern, Cliff Potts, Ron Rifkin, Jesse Vint.
89 min.
A wonderful film. The message of *2001: A Space Odyssey* (for which Trumbull did the special effects) was that man needed guidance from beyond; the message of *Silent Running*, symbolically set in the year 2001, is that man (and his creations: the film's robots) must, even at the risk of madness, be his own saviour. Adrift in space in a literal Garden of Eden that was intended to refurbish an Earth devastated by nuclear war, Bruce Dern refuses to destroy his private world when ordered to. Instead, with the help of his drones (robots), he tends his garden, and then sends it out into deep space to seed a possible second chance for mankind. Full of stunning visuals, the ideas in the film more than compensate for the awkward scene-setting of the beginning. PH

Silent Scream
(David Hayman, 1989, GB) Iain Glen, Paul Samson, Anne Kristen, Alexander Morton, Andrew Barr, John Murtagh.
85 min.
After shooting a barman in a Soho pub in 1963, Larry Winters was sentenced to life imprisonment. In 1973, a violent prisoner addicted to the drugs prescribed to control his depressions, he became one of the first inmates at the Barlinnie Special Unit, a liberal community, where he wrote poetry and the prose piece that gives Hayman's powerful film its title, and there in 1977 he died

of a drugs overdose, aged 34. The film unfolds – a complex series of flashbacks – as Winters wrestles with his demons for the last time, recollecting incidents from his childhood in Glasgow and Carbisdale, his time in the Parachute Regiment, and his single taste of freedom in the last 13 years, a visit home. Hayman adopts a bold, subjective style for his directing debut. The elliptical editing owes something to Roeg, but Hayman goes further, evoking a hallucinatory mood in which guitars wail like banshees, ghosts torment the murderer, and even Winters' poems come to life. The film comes close to pretentiousness, and Bill Beach's screenplay is a mite wordy. Full of ambition and conviction, though; and Glen, as Winters, gives a ravenous, intensely physical performance. TCh

Silent Thrush, The (Shisheng Huamei)

(Cheng Sheng-Fu, 1991, Tai) Li Yu-Shan, Lu Yi-Ch'An, Chang Ying-Chen, Yuan Chia-P'ei.
100 min.
Essentially a backstage soap opera, a peek behind the scenes at a touring troupe. Ah Yun joined the group voluntarily, because of her love for traditional Taiwanese opera, but the reality in the 1980s is that the customers prefer striptease, and the company is barely solvent. The film's *raison d'être* appears to be social, but the political analysis is skin deep. We're left with a banal, heavy-handed, neo-Victorian melodrama, hackneyed characters, and a specious lesbian relationship ambiguous enough to be embraced by the politically correct crowd. TCh

Silent Tongue

(Sam Shepard, 1993, US) Richard Harris, Sheila Tousey, Alan Bates, River Phoenix, Dermot Mulroney, Jeri Arredondo.
101 min.
Prescott Roe (Harris) kidnaps the half-Indian daughter of drunken showman McCree (Bates). He needs the girl, Velada (Arredondo), to appease his son Talbot (Phoenix), deranged by the death of his wife – Velada's sister. McCree gives chase. Although the late River Phoenix figures large in the movie's advertising, he's actually relegated to a virtually speechless supporting role. Then again, there's a mournful, hallucinatory quality to his scenes, keening for ghosts beside his lover's body. For the rest, writer/director Sam Shepard's Western is a curious throwback to the grubby eccentricities of '70s 'revisionist' oaters, laced with brooding mysticism and the playwright's familiar emotional violence. The film is shot in 'Scope, and there's an awful lot of space here. The landscape is so expansive it seems to have driven its few inhabitants over the edge, into drink or despair. Bates, especially, looks the worse for wear and out of his natural habitat. Harris, however, turns in a fine, dignified performance of an old man's grief. Intriguing, then, but defiantly slow and awkward. TCh

Silent Touch, The

(Krzysztof Zanussi, 1992, GB/Pol/Den) Max von Sydow, Lothaire Bluteau, Sarah Miles, Sofie Grabol, Aleksander Bardini, Peter Hesse Overgaard.
96 min.
Zanussi's original story starts intriguingly, but needs all the gifts of its star to reach the finishing line. Polish music student Stefan (Bluteau) is troubled by a recurring dream that long inactive composer Henry Kesdi (von Sydow) needs the tune that is running just out of reach through his head in order to start writing again, and hitches off to Denmark to help him. Ill, alcoholic, reclusive, Kesdi first attacks him with a knife, but when Stefan proves to have extraordinary gifts of healing, invites him to move in and starts work again. Their relationship deteriorates as Kesdi reveals the depths of selfishness and manipulation he is capable of, but the work gets finished, and the issue of art versus life gets an airing. Bluteau does his familiar saintly abstemiousness; Miles endures as Kesdi's wife; but the dynamo that drives the production is von Sydow. Violent, coarse, lecherous, cunning, arrogant, his Kesdi is a monster and utterly convincing; without him it would be a chamber work. BC

Silent Voice

see Amazing Grace and Chuck

Silent Witness, The

(David W Rolfe, 1978, GB) Richard Hamer, Sarah Twist, Angela Ellis, Daphne Odin-Pearse.
55 min.
The opening shots of a bleeding body might indicate a Pete Walker extravaganza. Not so: this is the film trade's nod to Easter, a serious investigation into the Holy Shroud of Turin, which contains a clear image of Christ's body and has been the subject of much study since it was found that the picture was a photographic negative (the effect of radiation? transfiguration?). The director unfortunately seems stylistically at sixes and sevens, including a bit of dramatic reconstruction here, a gaggle of talking heads there, a chunk of location scene-setting here, there and everywhere, and blending nothing together with ease. Compared to this, most TV documentaries resemble Bresson. Subsequent research has overtaken it anyway, which should put it out of its misery. GB

Silent World, The

see Monde du Silence, Le

Silken Skin

see Peau Douce, La

Silk Stockings

(Rouben Mamoulian, 1957, US) Fred Astaire, Cyd Charisse, Janis Paige, Peter Lorre, Jules Munshin, George Tobias, Joseph Buloff.
117 min.
The last completed film of one of the cinema's great stylists and camera choreographers. Sniffily treated at the time (and since) by critics nursing over-fond memories of Garbo and Lubitsch, this is in fact a dazzling musical version of *Ninotchka*, with Charisse and Astaire at the top of their dancing form as the Soviet commissar and the decadent American who reconciles her to capitalism in a string of superb Cole Porter numbers. Memorabilia include 'Stereophonic Sound' (a witty dig at widescreen movies), 'The Ritz Roll'n' Rock' (a terrific top hat, white tie and cane solo for Astaire), and 'Silk Stockings' itself, a dance for Charisse reminiscent of the bedroom-stroking scene in *Queen Christina*. Irresistible. TM

Silkwood

(Mike Nichols, 1983, US) Meryl Streep, Kurt Russell, Cher, Craig T Nelson, Diana Scarwid, Fred Ward, Ron Silver, Charles Hallahan, Josef Sommer, M Emmet Walsh.
131 min.
A 'people' movie rather than an 'issue' movie, setting nuclear martyr Karen Silkwood's battle with an uncaring nuclear industry against a backdrop of a troubled love affair, unwanted lesbian affection, child custody, and the eternal favourite of One Woman Against It All. But this is precisely where the film's fault lies. Silkwood's 'ordinariness' protects her from being labelled a wild-eyed Trot, but that should not be allowed to obscure her courage or the whitewash ladled onto her story after her death. Tiptoeing up to the final seconds of her life, swerving around any contentious points during it, and trying to have it both ways in the contradictory final reel, *Silkwood* runs a mile from hazarding its own opinion, and instead treats us to countless back-porch heart-to-hearts and lots of lovely countryside. Streep, Cher and Russell all turn in fine performances, and to the innocent or the uninformed the story may still come as a shock. But ultimately it's rather akin to making a film about Joan of Arc and concentrating on her period pains. JG

Silverado

(Lawrence Kasdan, 1985, US) Kevin Kline, Scott Glenn, Kevin Costner, Danny Glover, Brian Dennehy, Linda Hunt, Jeff Goldblum, Rosanna Arquette, John Cleese.
132 min.
This takes as its subject the Western itself; but what could have been a bankrupt exercise is saved by exuberance, goodwill, and sheer excitement. Here is every Western scene you ever loved: from the cattle stampede, the shoot-outs, the fist fights, the laconic one-liners, to the saloon bar queen, the slick gambler, the attractive villain, and a Magnificent Four who ride together in search of their destiny at the fateful Silverado. New elements include a black cowboy and a very English sheriff (Cleese), both of which are at the

least historically accurate. If you never bother with Westerns, pilgrim, this here Peacemaker has six good reasons why you should. CPea

Silver Bears

(Ivan Passer, 1977, GB) Michael Caine, Cybill Shepherd, Louis Jourdan, Stéphane Audran, David Warner, Tom Smothers, Martin Balsam, Charles Gray, Joss Ackland, Moustache.
113 min.
Paul Erdman's *The Silver Bears*, an amusing novel about high finance and high-level chicanery, becomes a film about lowest common denominators and low-level buffoonery. Passer brings to the subject all the subtle wit of *Pravda*, and scriptwriter Peter Stone fumbles it by being both confusing and condescending. But the really insuperable burden is the feeble pack of turns from the cast (they can't be called performances): Caine as the financial wizard, Audran as a woman who wears lots of different clothes, and Jourdan doing his professional European act. Worst is Cybill Shepherd as a kind of giggling California wholefood cereal, wearing layers of woollens and layers of spectacles. If your idea of a good laugh is watching Caine spill his breakfast onto his lap – twice in a row – this is your movie. SM

Silver Bullet

(Daniel Attias, 1985, US) Gary Busey, Everett McGill, Corey Haim, Megan Follows, Robin Groves, Leon Russom, Terry O'Quinn.
95 min.
An adaptation of Stephen King's dreary *Cycle of the Werewolf*, which sounds like werewolves on wheels but is actually an account of the usual Smallsville USA being terrorised by a lycanthrope whose identity any seasoned horror-watcher can spot a mile off. Ranged against the teeth'n'claws are a crippled boy (Haim), his sister (Follows), and their alcoholic uncle (Busey). There is a simpering female voice-over, and a supporting cast full of rednecked pot-bellies and grown-ups. The juveniles do daft things like sneaking out in the woods after dark to let off fireworks, and the parents do even dafter things like going off for a dirty weekend and leaving the kids with the alcoholic uncle when there's a werewolf on the loose. They all deserve to die. It is very *déja vu*, including the hair-sprouting transformation sequences, and might have been aimed at an audience of ten-year-olds were it not for a few bits of graphic decapitation and fake torso-gouging. AB

Silver City

(Sophia Turkiewicz, 1984, Aust) Gosia Dobrowolska, Ivar Kants, Anna Jemison, Steve Bisley, Debra Lawrance, Ewa Brok.
110 min.
Set in postwar years, when Australia rather ungraciously 'welcomed' an influx of 'new Australians' from Southern and Eastern Europe. The depiction of arrival in the Promised Land, whether in the hostile customs shed, where the attitude of the officers belies the razzmatazz of the official welcome, or in the inevitable small town, is both sensitive and beautifully realised. Unfortunately, the love story between Nina (Dobrowolska) and a fellow Polish immigrant who happens to be married, soon begins to replace this as the central interest, and the focus is lost in some soupy romanticism and a few loose ends. NR

Silver Dream Racer

(David Wickes, 1980, GB) David Essex, Beau Bridges, Cristina Raines, Clarke Peters, Harry H Corbett, Diane Keen, Lee Montague, Sheila White.
111 min.
A catatonic David Essex hauls himself up, Sheene-style, to higher sponsorship on the motorcycle racing circuit. Beau Bridges, every inch of his torso already adorned with paying customers, does all he can to stop him. There is an Elton John song that repeats endlessly 'Life Isn't Ev-ery-thi-ing' on the death of a young motorcyclist. This film is the logical extension of that deeply superficial statement.

Silver Lode

(Allan Dwan, 1954, US) John Payne, Lizabeth Scott, Dan Duryea, Dolores Moran, Emile Meyer, Robert Warwick, Harry Carey Jr, Alan Hale Jr, Stuart Whitman.
81 min.

Made as a quickie for producer Benedict Bogeaus, *Silver Lode* is one of Allan Dwan's unqualified masterpieces. From a simple story of revenge – Payne is wrongfully accused of murder on his wedding day, and becomes the object of a man-hunt led by Dan Duryea as he tries to clear his name – Dwan produced both the most succinct anti-McCarthy tract ever made in Hollywood, and a delirious film about the function of memory – visualised in repeated images in different contexts. PH

Silver Streak

(Arthur Hiller, 1976, US) Gene Wilder, Jill Clayburgh, Richard Pryor, Patrick McGoohan, Ned Beatty, Clifton James, Ray Walston, Scatman Crothers, Richard Kiel.
113 min.
Silver Streak, the train which travels from LA to Chicago and houses a murder, dawdles rather than streaks. Characters and plot ramble at will, and no matter how high Colin Higgins' script flies, Arthur Hiller's direction remains with feet and hands firmly on the ground. Wilder, who witnesses the foul deed, keys his performance to the right pitch of muted madness ('You like my new shoes?' he asks, stretched out on the heroine's bed). Clayburgh is a real sweetie, and Pryor isn't too far behind as a black dude thief. On the debit side, the fooling occasionally gets too boisterous for its own good; but it's rare enough to find a film designed to provide fun on a spectacular scale that succeeds even part of the time. GB

Simba

(Brian Desmond Hurst, 1955, GB) Dirk Bogarde, Virginia McKenna, Donald Sinden, Earl Cameron, Basil Sydney, Marie Ney.
99 min.
Rank's attempt to wring drama from Kenya's Mau Mau rising is not surprisingly riddled with colonial assumptions (the source novel was by Anthony Perry), but as Bogarde joins McKenna and policeman Sinden on the family farm in the district where violence has been most extreme, some attempt at least is made to explain the rebels' point of view. The problem, however, is plausibility. The stars never left Pinewood and it shows. TJ

Simon

(Marshall Brickman, 1980, US) Alan Arkin, Madeline Kahn, Austin Pendleton, Judy Graubert, William Finley, Wallace Shawn, Fred Gwynne.
97 min.
The satirical and neurotic scope of the initial premise is immense: Simon (Arkin), a Columbia professor brainwashed by a mischievous government research unit into believing his mother was a spaceship, sets out to right America's evils. He starts by cutting out Hawaiian music in elevators. Unfortunately, Arkin's hysterical performance screws up the hilariously clever script of one-liners and set pieces by Brickman, Woody Allen's collaborator here making his debut as a director. The result is a rough ride indeed, and you may well be better off seeing *Sleeper* again in terms of laughs-per-minute. Clever, but not clever enough. DMacp

Simon and Laura

(Muriel Box, 1955, GB) Peter Finch, Kay Kendall, Muriel Pavlow, Hubert Gregg, Maurice Denham, Ian Carmichael, Richard Wattis, Thora Hird, Joan Hickson, Charles Hawtrey, Gilbert Harding.
91 min. b/w.
Throughout most of the '50s, British cinema regarded its pushy new rival, television, with a mix of alarm and disdain. While Hollywood tried to combat the small screen with CinemaScope and 3-D, the Brits mocked the medium in a series of gentle satires. Here, Simon and Laura (Finch and Kendall) are the Richard and Judy of their day, a married couple who feign domestic bliss for the sake of the small screen, but bicker constantly as soon as they're off-air. Just as in Finch's later, more savage TV satire, *Network*, they soon learn that acting angry for the cameras does wonders for the ratings. GM

Simon of the Desert
(Simón del Desierto)

(Luis Buñuel, 1965, Mex) Claudio Brook, Silvia Piñal, Hortensia Santovana, Jesús Fernández.
45 min. b/w.

Short, sharp and astounding, this film provides a teasing bridge between the Old Testament Buñuel of *Nazarin* and *Viridiana*, and the new – *Belle de Jour* and *Discreet Charm of the Bourgeoisie*. Simon Stylites, literally perched on a pedestal, is assailed by a cynical dwarf and a series of temptations (including Silvia Piñal and some vintage surrealist images) before being swept, like King Kong, from timelessness to the cacophony of modern New York. Not a very reassuring vision, but worth 45 minutes of any sceptic's time. SG

Simple Men

(Hal Hartley, 1992, GB/US) Robert Burke, William Sage, Karen Sillas, Elina Löwensohn, Martin Donovan, Mark Chandler Bailey, Joe Stevens, Marietta Marich, John Alexander MacKay.
105 min.
It begins, startlingly, in mid-robbery. Within minutes, Bill McCabe (Burke) has been deserted by his partners in crime, learned that his imprisoned father – sporting hero or political terrorist? – has vanished, and set off for Long Island with his bookish brother (Sage) in search of dad. So starts a series of speedy adventures in which the brothers come to understand not only each other, but – after a mysterious, maybe perilous encounter with Sillas, Löwensohn and Donovan – themselves too. There's so much to enjoy in Hartley's quizzical account of the ups-and-downs of being young, serious and footloose in upstate New York. It looks great, with saturated colours and sharp medium shots complementing the laconically stylised axioms and ironies of Hartley's droll dialogue. The story contains more than enough twists and digressions to fuel a film twice its length; the actors are admirably in tune with the director's quirky sense of characterisation; and he himself never yields to the temptation of weirdness for weirdness' sake. Most impressive, perhaps, is that the formal audacity and inventiveness are topped off with such sparkling wit. GA

Simple Twist of Fate, A

(Gillies MacKinnon, 1994, US) Steve Martin, Gabriel Byrne, Stephen Baldwin, Laura Linney, Byron Jennings, Michael des Barres.
106 min.
Inspired by George Eliot's *Silas Marner*, Martin wrote this ambitious contemporary drama of parents and parenthood, and assigned himself the demanding role of cabinet-maker Michael McCann, a reclusive, miser offered a chance to rebuild his life by a chance encounter on a winter's evening. As her mother lies dying in the snow, a toddler wanders into McCann's isolated homestead, a little girl whom he adopts only to discover, a decade later, that her real father is local politico John Newland (Byrne). Power now allows Newland to admit his claims on the child. By the time the legal contest begins to define the true nature of 'family' ties, the film has already generated a fair head of sympathy in the viewer. The early exposition is crisply handled by Scottish director MacKinnon, while the scenes between Martin and his adopted daughter deftly blend light comedy and an emotional bond that carries through to the rest of the film. The stumbling point, really, is the contrived narrative line, which throws on coincidence with the abandon of a Victorian potboiler, while the tension between the two 'fathers' would seem even more pat were not Martin and Byrne's performances so humanely drawn. TJ

Simple Wish, A

(Michael Ritchie, 1997, US) Martin Short, Kathleen Turner, Mara Wilson, Robert Pastorelli, Amanda Plummer, Francis Capra, Ruby Dee, Teri Garr.
89 min.
Little Anabel (Wilson) loves New York, but her careworn dad (a widower) threatens to drag her off to Nebraska if he doesn't get the lead in a Broadway musical. Enter Murray (Short), the first male fairy godmother, and hopeless to boot. Anabel's confused about her wishes, and with the appearance of megalomaniac Claudia (Turner) – a good godmother turned bad – it seems like curtains. Murray looks interesting (think Emo Phillips impaled on Maurice Gibb's teeth), but is he a super-modern wit or the traditional lovable clown? It might've been nice if he'd become emotionally connected to Anabel or, indeed, to any of

the other characters. His antics, however, are uninvolving, and Claudia, though a similarly lazy construct, steals the show. Like Frankenstein, director Ritchie has begged and borrowed from too many sources. CO'Su

Sinai Field Mission

(Frederick Wiseman, 1978, US)
127 min. b/w.
A group of Texans, cut off like some latter-day defenders of the Alamo in the waste land of the Sinai, re-enact the rituals of home while overseeing the Egyptian-Israeli standoff agreement. The enervating boredom of their task (and particularly the official praise they receive for it) is neatly captured by Wiseman's sympathetic, humorous camera. A goldmine for anthropologists, and a good deal more watchable than Wiseman's previous documentary, the enervatingly boring *Canal Zone*. JPy

Sinbad and the
Eye of the Tiger

(Sam Wanamaker, 1977, GB) Patrick Wayne, Taryn Power, Jane Seymour, Margaret Whiting, Patrick Troughton, Kurt Christian.
113 min.
The regular Charles Schneer/Ray Harryhausen adventure formula, but slightly more moth-eaten, with children of the famous (John and Tyrone) menaced or rescued in turn by various metamorphosing creatures of the *fantastique* as Sinbad and Princess Farah seek to undo the spell on her brother, transformed into a baboon by their wicked stepmother (Whiting). It's difficult at times to tell which of the monsters or humans are being artificially animated. PT

Since You Went Away

(John Cromwell, 1944, US) Claudette Colbert, Joseph Cotten, Jennifer Jones, Shirley Temple, Agnes Moorehead, Monty Woolley, Lionel Barrymore, Guy Madison, Robert Walker, Hattie McDaniel, Craig Stevens, Keenan Wynn, Albert Basserman, Nazimova.
172 min. b/w.
Scripted by producer David O. Selznick from Margaret Buell Wilder's book, this is a Midwestern *Mrs Miniver*, 'the story of an unconquerable fortress, the American home, 1943', as an introductory title has it. Claudette Colbert is the valiant wife praying for the return of her man, Jones and Temple are her daughters, Joseph Cotten an old flame, and Hattie McDaniel is the maid, naturally. At nearly three hours, this manages to be banal without being tedious, utterly phony and quite revealing, if only because it reflects how America liked to picture America. There's a definition of Hollywood for you. TCh

Sin Compasión
(Sans Pitié)

(Francisco J Lombardi, 1994, Peru/Mex/Fr) Diego Bertie, Jorge Chiarella, Adriana Davila, Marcello Rivera, Ricardo Fernandez, Carlos Onetto, Hernán Romero.
120 min.
The second film by leading Peruvian director Francisco J Lombardi to find distribution in Britain is a typically committed adaptation of *Crime and Punishment*, which relocates the action to the streets of modern Lima. Here Raskolnikov is Ramón (Bertie), a gifted but arrogant philosophy student whose written work, declaiming the ability of a certain moral elect to discern a 'natural' justice that may defy conventional behaviour, understandably goes down badly with his lecturer; it does, however, supply an ethical framework for his decision, driven by the severest financial straits, to kill his landlady for her stash of rent money. With Ramón left to come to terms with the brutal axe murder, and police officer Portillo (Chiarella, terrific) swiftly on the trail of suspicion, the rest of the film portrays a society riddled with poverty and injustice. Lombardi's sometimes over-earnest drama wrestles with the big questions, but does so in a way that seems genuinely to germinate from a particular set of personal and social circumstances. The result is a dogged, but keenly felt and cumulatively thought-provoking piece. For all its flaws, the film burns with a humanity that firmly contradicts its title. TJ

Sinful Davey

(John Huston, 1968, GB) John Hurt, Pamela
Franklin, Nigel Davenport, Ronald Fraser,
Robert Morley, Maxine Audley, Fionnuala
Flanagan, Noel Purcell, Donal McCann, Niall
MacGinnis.
95 min.
An inconsequential but likeable romp, set in early
19th century Scotland and retailing the roguish
adventures (allegedly based on fact) of Davey
Haggart, who deserts from the army to follow his
father's more romantic calling as a not very efficient highwayman, finally laid low by a hard-hit
golf-ball. Huston shot it in his beloved Ireland,
most of the cast boast Irish brogues, and although
this hardly helps credibility, the fact that the director's tongue is firmly in cheek is definitively signalled when a proud Highlander (played by that
archetypal screen Paddy, Noel Purcell) coins 'Curse
me for an Irishman!' as a particularly relishable
oath. A sort of ramshackle *Tom Jones*, occasionally tiresome but shorn of Tony Richardson's artistic pretensions, it looks attractive, is played with
infectious good humour by the entire cast, and
boasts an engaging performance from John Hurt
as the artful dodger of the title. TM

Sing

(Richard Baskin, 1989, US) Lorraine Bracco,
Peter Dobson, Jessica Steen, Louise Lasser,
George DiCenzo, Patti LaBelle, Susan Peretz.
98 min.
In Brooklyn, a 'sing' is a school revue, a traditional end of term show-down between juniors
and seniors. So when their local high school is
threatened with closure and the sing is cancelled,
kids and teachers unite to save ...the sing. For all
its noisy inner-city colour, this is just another
variation on *Romeo and Juliet* and that old 'Let's
put on a show' cliché. There is not a shot you have
not seen, a line you have not heard, or a thought
you have not rejected. *Sing* also fails to deliver
where it really counts; the music isn't up to
scratch, and the dancing doesn't cut it. The finale,
all *Rocky* sentimentality and Lloyd Webber spectacle, is designed to raise a tear and a cheer, but
Sing is nothing to shout about. TCh

Singapore Sling

(Nicos Nicolaidis, 1990, Greece) Meredyth
Herold, Micele Valley, Panos Thanassoulis.
115 min. b/w.
Shot in contrasty black-and-white, this is *film
noir à la grecque:* the tale of a displaced shamus
caught up in a bizarre sexual charade ritualisti-
cally enacted by a mother and daughter, both evidently deranged. It is not a pretty sight. With
galling pretentiousness, writer-director Nicolaidis
pays homage to various movies, most notably
Otto Preminger's *Laura*, from which he 'borrows'
not only the missing heroine, but also snatches
of David Raksin's score and even lines of dialogue. But the real story here is Nicolaidis' obsession with sex and violence, or more specifically,
violent sex and sexual violence. No taboo is left
unbroken as the film contorts itself into an explicit orgiastic nightmare of role-playing, degradation and fetishism. The director claims he meant
it as a black comedy, but the acridly misogynous
tone isn't funny, just boring. TCh

Singer Not the Song, The

(Roy Baker, 1961, GB) Dirk Bogarde, John
Mills, Mylene Demongeot, Laurence Naismith,
Eric Pohlmann.
129 min.
A bit of a jaw-dropper this one: Bogarde is a
Mexican gunslinger – but, of course! – a man in
black who seems to have an obsessive love-hate
thing with the local Irish priest (Mills). Beneath
the surface you have the vague feeling that
there's something deeply perverted and fetishistic going on, so relentless is the tone and handling
(script by Nigel Balchin) – but then you think better of it. See it and disbelieve. TJ

Singin' in the Rain 100 (100)

(Stanley Donen/Gene Kelly, 1952, US) Gene
Kelly, Donald O'Connor, Debbie Reynolds,
Jean Hagen, Cyd Charisse, Millard Mitchell,
Douglas Fowley.
102 min.
Is there a film clip more often shown than the title
number of this most astoundingly popular musical? The rest of the movie is great too. It shouldn't
be. There never was a masterpiece created from

such a mishmash of elements: Arthur Freed's
favourites among his own songs from back in the
'20s and '30s, along with a new number, 'Make 'Em
Laugh', which is a straight rip-off from Cole
Porter's 'Be A Clown'; the barely blooded Debbie
Reynolds pitched into the deep end with tyrannical perfectionist Kelly; choreography very nearly
improvised because of pressures of time; and Kelly
filming his greatest number with a heavy cold.
Somehow it all comes together. The 'Broadway
Melody' ballet is Kelly's least pretentious, Jean
Hagen and Donald O'Connor are very funny, and
the Comden/Green script is a loving-care job. If
you've never seen it and don't, you're bonkers. SG

Singing Ringing Tree, The (Das singende klingende Baumchen)

(Francesco Stefani, 1958, EGer) Christel
Bodelstein, Charles-Hans Vogt, Eckart Dux,
Richard Kruger.
73 min.
Haughty Princess Thousandbeauty (Bodelstein)
learns kindness and humility when her scornful
treatment of a princely suitor (Dux) renders him
victim to a cruel spell and transforms her into an
ugly hag. Only the legendary singing ringing tree
has the power to assess her passage into maturity, and will mark the event with a tune. The story
is conveyed with an appealing simplicity; deep,
rich hues in clothing and production design overcome budgetary limitations, and effects are kept
to a minimum. Betrayal, deceit, jealousy, forgiveness and love – what more do you expect out
of a 73-minute children's fairytale? CM

Singles

(Cameron Crowe, 1992, US) Bridget Fonda,
Campbell Scott, Kyra Sedgwick, Sheila Kelley,
Jim True, Matt Dillon, Bill Pullman, James Le
Gros, Tom Skerritt, Eric Stoltz, Peter Horton.
99 min.
Grunge rock may provide the backdrop, but anyone expecting extended footage of Soundgarden
in concert will be disappointed. But there's rich
compensation to be found amid the aspirations
of six love-hungry hopefuls as they explore
Seattle's singles scene. Steve (Scott) falls for
Linda (Sedgwick), who's been burnt by a smooth-
talking Spaniard. Janet (Fonda, terrific) is sufficiently besotted by grunge rocker Cliff (a
wonderfully self-mocking Dillon) to flirt with the
idea of breast implants. Meanwhile, Debbie
(Kelley) searches for a husband, and Bailey (True)
finds his calling as agony uncle. Writer-director
Crowe suffuses the film with tender humour and
affection as the characters, most of them living
in the same apartment block, swap stories, ponder sexual come-ons where none exist, and
remain resolute in the face of emotional horrors.
Pearl Jam, Mudhoney and Soundgarden contribute to the soundtrack, and the film's tone
couldn't be sweeter. CM

Single Spark, A (Jeon Tae-Il)

(Park Kwang-Su, 1995, SKor) Moon Sung-
Kuen, Hong Kyoung-In, Kim Sun-Jae, Lee Joo-
Shil, Myung Kae-Nam, Kim Yong-Man.
100 min. col & b/w.
Largely financed by public subscription (the closing credits acknowledge nearly 5,000 names),
Park's film sets out to exorcise South Korea's
dark years under military dictators while paying
dues to the heroes who dared to dissent. Jeon Tae-
Il was a labour activist in the 1960s who committed suicide as a gesture of protest against the
authorities' failure to honour workers' rights
already enshrined in law. Park offers not a standard bio-pic about Jeon but a meditation on the
boy's self-sacrifice through the eyes of a '70s radical who researches and writes an idealised biography while trying to stay one step ahead of the
police. Very far from the tone and style of agit-
prop, it turns into an elegiac movie about the
points where life and art meet and diverge. TR

Singleton's Pluck

see Laughterhouse

Single White Female

(Barbet Schroeder, 1992, US) Bridget Fonda,
Jennifer Jason Leigh, Steven Weber, Peter
Friedman, Stephen Tobolowsky, Frances Bay,
Michele Farr.
108 min.

When career girl Allie (Fonda) learns that her
lover Sam (Weber) has slept with his ex, she turfs
him out and advertises for a flatmate. Successful
applicant Hedy (Leigh) may not seem particularly mature, but who would expect her to start
dressing up in Allie's clothes, moving in on Sam,
and generally making life hell for the landlady she
professes to adore? Actually, anyone who's seen
a few movies would expect Hedy to do precisely
those things, especially given the heavy-handed
way Schroeder signposts the imminent homicidal
carnage right from the start (stay out of that laundry room!). If his two leads are adequate to the
slick mechanisms of a formulaic thriller, neither
they nor Don Roos' script (based on the novel by
John Lutz) offer any original insights into insatiable emotional dependence. GA

Sin of Father Mouret, The

see Faute de l'Abbé Mouret, La

Sin of Harold Diddlebock, The (aka Mad Wednesday)

(Preston Sturges, 1946, US) Harold Lloyd,
Frances Ramsden, Jimmy Conlin, Raymond
Walburn, Edgar Kennedy, Arline Judge,
Franklin Pangborn, Lionel Stander, Rudy
Vallee.
91 min. b/w.
Lloyd's last film – by no means the total disaster
of reputation – kicks off with the final reel of *The
Freshman*, then goes on to show Harold the go-getter of 1925, fired after 22 years stuck in the same
dead-end job, breaking out in a wild *Mad
Wednesday* spree which results in him drunkenly
sowing the seeds of future success. Admittedly the
quirkily sophisticated Sturges characters ('Sir, you
bring out the artist in me' beams the bartender presented with the challenge of mixing Harold's very
first drink) co-exist a trifle uneasily with Lloyd's
cliffhanger exploits (which here include a rather
tired rehash of the skyscraper antics from *Safety
Last*). But the film is studded with gems, many of
them contributed verbally by the Sturges stock
company. It was re-released in 1950, cut to 78 minutes and retitled *Mad Wednesday*. TM

Sin Remitente

see No Return Address

Sins of Rachel Cade, The

(Gordon Douglas, 1960, US) Angie Dickinson,
Peter Finch, Roger Moore, Rafer Johnson,
Woody Strode, Scatman Crothers.
124 min.
The sins are mainly those of negligible credibility. Moore's an American volunteer in the RAF,
whose plane just happens to land in the Belgian
Congo where nurse Dickinson is plying her trade.
An illegitimate child ensues. No wonder love-
struck doc Finch looks slightly miffed throughout this enjoyably trashy colonial soapfest. TJ

Sirène du Mississippi, La (Mississippi Mermaid)

(François Truffaut, 1969, Fr/It) Jean-Paul
Belmondo, Catherine Deneuve, Michel
Bouquet, Nelly Borgeaud, Marcel Berbert,
Roland Thénot.
123 min.
Belmondo, owner of a cigarette factory on the
African island of Réunion, advertises for a wife,
gets Deneuve (who isn't what she seems), falls in
love, and finds himself embroiled in a succession
of crises and suspicions. Derived from Cornell
Woolrich's novel *Waltz into Darkness* (a title that
effectively matches at least one aspect of the film),
this belongs to the group of Truffaut films that
includes *The Bride Wore Black* and *A Gorgeous
Bird Like Me*; it's an elaborate, low-key thriller-fan-
tasy that strains and modifies, comments on and
fondly sends up pulp fiction, while taking pulp fiction's more mythic elements as its base. Gags multiply. And at the film's centre, remaining firmly in
the mind, is Belmondo's Louis, ensnared, almost
ensnaring himself and loving it, the victim of recurring nightmares in the Clinique Heurtebise. VG

Sirens

(John Duigan, 1994, Aust/GB) Hugh Grant,
Tara Fitzgerald, Sam Neill, Elle MacPherson,
Portia De Rossi, Kate Fischer, Pamela Rabe,
John Duigan.
95 min.

Having discovered sex in his sensitive autobiographical films *The Year My Voice Broke* and *Flirting*, Australian director Duigan is at it again with another foray into nonsense and sensuality. Grant is Anthony Campion, a progressive Anglican priest taking up a parish Down Under with his young wife Estella (Fitzgerald). His first duty is to visit the provocative libertarian artist Norman Lindsay (Neill) to dissuade him from exhibiting an erotic religious painting. However, over the course of a languorous weekend in the presence of the painter's uninhibited wife and models, it's prudish Estella who experiences a spiritual and physical conversion. Headily atmospheric, Duigan's film takes place in an outback of 'perpetual tumescence'. It's all very DH Lawrence, and consequently a mite predictable. The picture's strongest suit is Duigan's deft, witty touch, and the confident, classy playing (Grant's familiar stuttering Englishman notwithstanding). Duigan seems to lose his sense of irony entirely, however, when it comes to celebrating the standard soft-core coupling. TCh

Sir Henry at Rawlinson's End
(Steve Roberts, 1980, GB) Trevor Howard, Patrick Magee, JG Devlin, Sheila Reid, Denise Coffey, Harry Fowler, Vivian Stanshall.
71 min. b/w.
Sir Henry's disgusting ancestral home has spawned an industry: a Radio 4 sketch, Peel-show episodes, Bonzo track, complete album, stage readings. His motto is '*Omnes Blotto*'; his home is Knebworth outside, and a dusty heap of rotten food, excrement, and empty bottles within. Vivian Stanshall has pieced together a shambolic poem, stuffed with extraordinary one-liners, with the sad, manic skeleton necessary to all great comedy; a satire tempered with nostalgia. Fixing this down visually is ultimately as self-defeating as filming a *Goon Show*: Steve Roberts has opted for a grainy monochrome, and has fortunately resisted the temptation to 'explain'. With the surprising exception of Denise Coffey, the actors quite correctly play the farrago dead straight: Trevor Howard, in particular, relishes the role of Sir Henry as if shooting for an Oscar. Too many favourite album lines are missing to prevent a little disappointment, and the edifice gets close to collapse on occasions, but this is one film it would have been impossible to get irrefutably 'right'. JC

Sister Act
(Emile Ardolino, 1992, US) Whoopi Goldberg, Maggie Smith, Harvey Keitel, Bill Nunn, Kathy Najimy, Wendy Makkens, Mary Wickes, Robert Miranda, Richard Portnow.
100 min.
A nun's life is hell – or so thinks nightclub singer Deloris (Goldberg) when she takes sanctuary in a convent after witnessing a gangland murder. To make matters worse, Mother Superior (Smith) coerces her into joining the tone-deaf choir. But Deloris is a can-do kind of gal, and in no time the motley crew are belting out '60s tunes. Church attendance is revitalised, confidence abounds, but the convent's new-found fame stretches as far as Mob headquarters. A bizarre mix of actors goes some way towards bolstering this flyweight caper; but the last third degenerates into farce, with nuns and thugs playing cat-and-mouse in a Reno casino. A one-note movie. CM

Sister Act 2: Back in the Habit
(Bill Duke, 1993, US) Whoopi Goldberg, Kathy Najimy, Barnard Hughes, Mary Wickes, Maggie Smith, James Coburn.
107 min.
'Nun sings soul music' summarised *Sister Act*. In Part 2, her Whoopiness, responding to the desperate pleas of Mother Superior Maggie Smith, is tempted from the cushioned lifestyle of the Los Angeles stage. Re-installed as the bogus Sister Mary Clarence, she takes on a musical challenge in San Francisco's toughest high school. The school is set to become a parking lot unless the wimpled wonder can transform her class of crazy teenage miscreants into a harmonious ensemble fit to win the all-state choral competition. Bouncy musical numbers and plenty of social concern, but the star, regrettably, is on autopilot. TJ

Sister My Sister
(Nancy Meckler, 1994, GB) Julie Walters, Joely Richardson, Jodhi May, Sophie Thursfield.
89 min.

A blood-spattered staircase, the glimpse of a corpse's foot: thus we are enticed into the true story of a murder which occurred in Le Mans in 1933. Two sisters (Richardson and May) become maids in the bourgeois household of Mme Danzard (Walters) and her daughter Isabelle (Thursfield). Immaculately groomed, discreet and conscientious, at first they seem ideal servants. But upstairs in the sisters' attic bedroom a heated incestuous relationship is developing. The film, backed by Channel 4, is enveloped by the claustrophobia of the house, where Madame dominates her lumpen daughter and obsessively checks for dust with white gloves. The tensions within unhealthy relationships are convincingly explored, but never quite justify the final eruption of appalling violence. JBa

Sisters
see Some Girls

Sisters (aka Blood Sisters)
(Brian De Palma, 1972, US) Margot Kidder, Jennifer Salt, Charles Durning, William Finley, Lisle Wilson, Barnard Hughes.
92 min.
A hideous lump of scar tissue on Kidder's thigh testifies to some kind of Siamese twin separation. The half of sister that 'disappeared' was, of course, off her head and a potential murderer. But has she really disappeared? This slick horror was greeted at the time as, among other superlatives, 'absolutely superb' and 'brimful of ideas' by TO. In retrospect, it does indeed appear as a highly efficient gut-ripper, with far more suggestion than De Palma's later work of the loose-end flux of real life going on in the background. There is, however, much early evidence of his rampant misogyny, his increasingly blatant stealings from Hitchcock, and most unforgivable of all, his clear distaste for the people he creates. De Palma's father was a surgeon, which may explain such greedy sadism. CPea

Sisters, The
(Anatole Litvak, 1938, US) Errol Flynn, Bette Davis, Anita Louise, Ian Hunter, Donald Crisp, Jane Bryan, Lee Patrick, Beulah Bondi, Patric Knowles, Alan Hale.
98 min. b/w.
Turn-of-the-century melo about three sisters (Davis, Louise, Bryan) and their romantic problems, most pressing of which is Davis' fling with dipso-journalist Errol Flynn. Not content with this, the picture has an intriguing political background, and abruptly tosses in the San Francisco earthquake, from which Davis takes refuge in a brothel, where tarts with heart nurse her back to health. Beginning with Roosevelt's election and ending with Taft's, the film may actually be about the emancipation of women, a concept that would have shaken the foundations of Jack Warner's office, since he, more than any other mogul, kept stars like Davis on a tight, legally-binding leash. ATu

Sisters or the Balance of Happiness (Schwestern oder die Balance des Glücks)
(Margarethe von Trotta, 1979, WGer) Jutta Lampe, Gudrun Gabriel, Jessica Früh, Konstantin Wecker, Heinz Bennent, Rainer Delventhal.
95 min.
A Grimm tale of two little girls lost in the big black forest sets the mood for this disturbing adult fairystory which shows the sisters grown up, apparently successful – one a graduate student, one a brisk executive secretary – but each still frightened and helpless inside. Anna (Gabriel) seems dependent, emotionally and economically, on Maria (Lampe), but successive inward turns of the screw reveal them, Siamese twin-like, in bondage one to the other, so that eventually it's uncertain as to who exploits and dominates whom. The theme of destructive sibling rivalry prefigures von Trotta's following film *The German Sisters*, though it's less explicitly political, opting for depth rather than breadth. A probe into psychic extremes, it's both tender and violent, delicate and melodramatic. SJo

Si tous les gars du monde... (Race for Life/If All the Guys in the World...)
(Christian-Jaque, 1955, Fr) André Valmy, Jean Gaven, Jean-Louis Trintignant, Hélène Perdrière, Georges Poujouly.
111 min. b/w.
The crew of a trawler in the North Atlantic is stricken with botulism and radios for help. A succession of short-wave amateurs from Togoland to Paris to East and West Berlin and finally Denmark rise above their personal problems, obtain the necessary serum and, just in time, get it parachuted down to the fishermen. At no point does anyone suggest contacting any official organisation – was there really none? The film skids along efficiently enough from one crisis to the next, and its theme of international co-operation at street level is a Cold War antidote. But it's superficial stuff, of interest today for the involvement of the usually more cynical H-G Clouzot (he co-scripted), for marking the debut of Trintignant and – for British audiences – providing the genesis of Tony Hancock's TV classic 'The Radio Ham'. Pierre Fresnay narrates. BBa

Sitting Ducks
(Henry Jaglom, 1978, US) Michael Emil, Zack Norman, Patrice Townsend, Irene Forrest, Richard Romanus, Henry Jaglom.
90 min.
A comedy road movie built around the clashing of charismas rather than the crashing of cars, this is an instantly likeable triumph of optimism over opportunism which reserves a wide conspiratorial wink for its five sunny-side crazies – all packed into a getaway limo after a nervous heist; all busily airing their various obsessions over health, wealth and the great American orgasm. Jaglom hooks you early with his 'old-fashioned' little-guy duo, then steps up the surprises and widens the sparring ring for an improvised unisex tag-match. The result's the sort of movie you'll find yourself humming along to. PT

Sitting in Limbo
(John N Smith, 1986, Can) Pat Dillon, Fabian Gibbs, Sylvie Clarke, Debbie Grant, Compton McLean.
95 min.
This likeable low-budget offering from the National Film Board of Canada fields a fairly unfamiliar slice of life: West Indian immigrants in French-speaking Montreal. Using a non-professional teenage cast and a script evolved out of interviews and improvisation, with a lot of hand-held camera and natural lighting, the director nevertheless mines a little charm from the documentary approach. Flat-sharing with two unmarried mothers on relief, Pat (Dillon) is naturally jaded on the subject of men, but finds herself involved with feckless Fabian (Gibbs). A high school dropout, Fabian doesn't stand much chance on the market, and his warehouse job lasts just long enough to launch him and Pat on the road to disaster. Reggae and the unemphatic coolth of the principals prevents doom from gathering around the economics. BC

Sitting Pretty
(Walter Lang, 1948, US) Clifton Webb, Robert Young, Maureen O'Hara, Richard Haydn, Louise Allbritton, Ed Begley.
84 min. b/w.
Hummingbird Hill in deepest suburbia, and stressed-out parents Young and O'Hara have seen their three brats run a succession of domestics out of the house. Their pleas for help are, however, met by the unlikeliest saviour, self-confessed genius and all-round efficiency expert Webb, who takes no nonsense whatever from the little devils and soon has a semblance of harmony restored, until the real reason for his presence in the household is revealed. Webb, the caustic Waldo Lydecker in Preminger's classic *Laura*, showed the sharpness of his comic touch in this occasionally acid, genuinely funny portrait of manners and mores in the middle-American home, and proved so popular with audiences that Fox brought back his Lynn Belvedere character for a couple of sequels, *Mr Belvedere Goes to College* and *Mr Belvedere Rings the Bell*. TJ

Six Degrees of Separation

(Fred Schepisi, 1994, US) Will Smith, Donald Sutherland, Stockard Channing, Ian McKellen, Mary Beth Hurt, Bruce Davison, Richard Masur, Kitty Carlisle Hart, Osgood Perkins.
111 min.

John Guare's adaptation of his stage hit has Smith's young pretender talking his way into the Central Park household of 'liberal' art dealer Sutherland. In preppy clothes and purportedly a friend of his host's student son, Smith assuages the suspicions of Sutherland and wife Channing, and also of their prospective client, millionaire South African McKellen, to such an extent that he's soon cooking them a gourmet meal and letting on that he's the son of actor Sidney Poitier. Too safe to work as satire, Schepisi's film comes over more as bourgeois farce, beginning at a frenetic pitch as Ian Baker's camera darts madly around the apartment when a painting is discovered to be missing, and flashing back repeatedly to the ruse. Smith's fine as the impostor, but scenes of his Travis Bickle-style preparations stretch credulity (this guy's clearly too gifted an actor not to find work), and although he manages to retain the requisite mystery as to his identity, it's hard to accept him as a mirror to hypocrisy or as a catalyst to responsibility. In the end only Channing, reprising her award-winning stage role, manages to inject some authentic feeling into this somewhat mechanical enterprise. WH

6.5 Special
(aka Calling All Cats)

(Alfred Shaugnessy, 1958, GB) Avril Leslie, Diane Todd, Pete Murray, Jo Douglas, Finlay Currie, Josephine Douglas, Lonnie Donnegan, Dickie Valentine, Jim Dale, Petula Clark, Russ Hamilton, Joan Regan, Johnny Dankworth, Cleo Laine, Mike and Bernie Winters.
85 min. b/w.

BBC TV's hit pop series of the '50s transferred to the cinema with the minimum of plot and the maximum of music: showbiz wannabes Leslie and Todd hop on the 6.05 Glasgow to London train; a host of stars, not surprisingly, are rehearsing on board. The line-up includes Petula Clark, Dankworth and Laine, Jim Dale (and youthful comic duo Mike and Bernie Winters), but when we finally reach the studio, it's Lonnie Donegan who closes the show. TJ

Six in Paris

see Paris vu par...

Sixteen Candles

(John Hughes, 1984, US) Molly Ringwald, Anthony Michael Hall, Michael Schoeffling, Paul Dooley, Gedde Watanabe, John Cusack, Joan Cusack.
93 min.

In which writer/director Hughes reinvented the teen movie by introducing real emotions and anxieties behind the usual run of dating decisions, wild parties and adolescent pranks. Ringwald's star-making turn plunges her into the trauma of turning 16, when her crush on the class hunk fails to work out and she finds unlikely solace in the shape of Hall's Ted the Geek. Sly humour and an appreciative ear for the demotic improv of teenage chat completes an attractive package. TCh

Sixth Happiness, The

(Waris Hussein, 1997, GB/Ind) Firdaus Kanga, Souad Faress, Khodus Wadia, Nina Wadia, Ahsen Bhatti.
97 min.

Firdaus Kanga, born in Bombay, was different three times over: gay, disabled and a Parsee. His fictionalised autobiography, *Trying to Grow*, was a hilarious account of a kid with bones as brittle as clay pots, but a spirit stronger than steel. This adaptation conveys the book's joie de vivre and most particularly its gloriously non-PC take on the subject. Kanga wrote the screenplay, plays the lead and also does pieces to camera commenting on the action. Astonishingly, he pulls off all three with aplomb, assisted by a strong cast – notably Souad Faress as his mother. Waris Hussein's direction uses some interesting tricks without being tricksy. A witty film: perspicacious and generous in its gaze. AJ

'68

(Steven Kovacs, 1988, US) Eric Larson, Robert Locke, Sandor Tecsi, Anna Dukasz, Mirlan Kwun, Terra Vandergaw, Neil Young.
98 min.

Kovacs' episodic attempt to evoke the trippy, dippy and momentous days of '68 centres on San Francisco, where Hungarian exile Zoltan Szabo (Tecsi) and family are putting the final touches to their newly acquired ethnic restaurant. Throughout, radio bulletins, television broadcasts and posters conveniently announce that this is the year of the Tet offensive, the Chicago Convention, etc, but that's as deep as it goes. Zoltan puts his faith in his two sons, but law student Peter (Larson) is soon dropping out, turning on, wising up and getting laid, and his brother (Locke) comes out as gay to beat the draft. Shot like a pastiche of '60s soap opera, it finally peters out in a bathetic happy resolution of sorts. WH

67 Days
(Uziska Republika)

(Zika Mitrovic, 1974, Yugo) Boris Buzancic, Bozidarka Frajt, Neda Arneric, Rade Serbedzija.
175 min.

Given that the socialist-realism school of Eastern European film-making – 'the aesthetic of the short-sighted camera' – tends to concentrate on historical reconstructions for home-market consumption/inspiration, it is surprising to find this turning up in London (even cut to 118 minutes). It's perhaps not so surprising that the film itself is a truly dire partisan epic, of minor interest only as a didactic lesson on the 'Uzice Republic', which survived as a springboard for Yugoslav communist resistance for a couple of months in 1941, in the face of a combined assault by the Germans and royalist Chetniks. A predictable script outlines the fate of a workers' battalion led by a Tito surrogate (while the great man himself is portrayed in mock actuality footage), and runs its tedious course through a series of logistically-confusing battle scenes and a few sentimental vignettes. PT

Six Weeks

(Tony Bill, 1982, US) Dudley Moore, Mary Tyler Moore, Shannon Wilcox, Bill Calvert, John Harkins, Joe Regalbuto, Katherine Healy.
108 min.

Signs of desperation here: like the aptly titled *Lovesick* (made later, though shown in Britain first), this Dudley Moore vehicle uses every trick in the Hollywood book to tug at the heartstrings – not to mention the pursestrings – of whatever bankable generation lapped up the lachrymose *Love Story* a decade ago. *Six Weeks* might have worked in 1932, but looks decidedly dodgy in the tense present. Who'd believe a congressional candidate would take time off to enrich the last weeks of the fatherless, leukemia-doomed child of a perfume heiress? And if that heiress happens to be the still glam Mary Tyler Moore (her throat's not what it was, but then neither is Dud's), who'd believe the relationship would remain platonic? The Moral Majority will lap up every tear-jerking minute; if you're lucky, you may just be able to keep your lunch. GD

Sizzlers

see Delinquent School Girls

Skateboard

(George Gage, 1977, US) Allen Garfield, Kathleen Lloyd, Leif Garrett, Richard Van Der Wyk, Tony Alva, Anthony Carbone.
97 min.

This would seem to promise a rip-off *Bad News Bears* on wheels, and visions of yet another exploitative US sub-culture package hardly whet the appetite. Yet anticipations of doom are happily dashed: the familiar ingredients of cynical but loveable coach (Garfield), bronzed, blond-curled Southern Californian kids, the absurdist razzmatazz of American competitive sport, and a rock soundtrack, here actually mesh into a rather endearing entertainment. The film neatly explores the psychology (and the economics) of hype and 'pressure', and its many skateboard action sequences are well shot and edited. A good, lightweight, upbeat family film. PT

Ski Bum, The

(Bruce Clark, 1971, US) Zalman King, Charlotte Rampling, Joseph Mell, Dimitra Arliss, Tedd King, Anna Karen.
136 min.

This adaptation of Romain Gary's novel emerges as a nebulous something about a naïve young man caught up with a moneyed bunch of schemers who are after his body, not only to seduce but to run errands and to stumble after on the slopes. Clark doesn't make things easy by having the characters babble, sometimes all at once; if, despite this ploy, you manage to catch what's going on, you're faced with characters so utterly unbelievable that you begin to doubt what little you thought you knew. How can one believe the hero to be the darling of the jet set when he has a nose capable of casting half the skiable piste into shadow? As for the jet setters, they simply haven't got the Right Stuff. If you're just greedy for a glimpse of any skiing, don't bother; you'd see more icy action staring at your refrigerator. FD

Skin & Bone

(Everett Lewis, 1995, US) b Wyatt, Alan Boyce, Garret Scullin, Nicole Dillenberg, Chad Kula, Susannah Melvoin.
110 min. b/w & col.

A couple of cops pull over a car and beat up its occupant, an army general. Turns out he's paying for their services. An episodic portrait of hustlers making ends meet by acting out sexual fantasies for the '12 Noon' male escort agency, this low-budget indie reveals just how demeaning it is to be an out-of-work actor in LA – or even an in-work actor, if you're reduced to crud like this. Are there no restaurant jobs anymore? The movie's pretensions (flash-frame editing, b/w and colour visuals) are particularly galling given the lame dialogue and hackneyed dramatics, not to mention a cast with across the board learning difficulties (the soundtrack is so appalling it merits special mention; it's not aided by Lewis's inexplicable propensity for staging scenes beside the LA freeway). Presumably this is getting a UK release on the strength of its (bi-sexual) prurience quota, which is really nothing to get excited about. TCh

Skin Deep

(Blake Edwards, 1989, US) John Ritter, Vincent Gardenia, Alyson Reed, Joel Brooks, Julianne Phillips, Chelsea Field, Peter Donat, Don Gordon, Nina Foch, Michael Kidd.
101 min.

It's voyage around my fodder time again in another of Blake Edwards' cautionary comedies. All the staples clock in, with Ritter going through the motions as alcoholic, blocked Pulitzer Prizewinner and compulsive womaniser Zach, who we see dumped in scene three by pissed-off wife Alex (Reed), and watch crawl his pathetic way to forgiveness by the end credits. Be impressed by the ritzy Pacific Palisades locations; enjoy the kitschy decor and designer threads of the rich and famous; be instructed, between tears of laughter, by the serious undertow about self-delusion and the possibility of discovery. The film's difficulty is the total obnoxiousness of the central character. Set pieces include a funny nighttime encounter involving fluorescent penises, and Zach being attacked by a strangely out-of-time Brit-punk musician. After much maudlin mooning over the piano in Barney's Bar, Zach has a midnight revelation on the beach: 'God's a gag writer!' Must be. WH

Skinflicker

(Tony Bicat, 1972, GB) Hilary Charlton, Will Knightley, Henry Woolf, William Hoyland, Brendan Barry, Elizabeth Choice.
41 min. b/w & col.

Skinflicker is about the kidnapping and assassination of a government minister (Barry), intended as a symbolic revolutionary act by three dissidents. The entire event is filmed by the kidnappers themselves on 8mm colour stock, and (by arrangement with them, to secure a more objective record) by a blue movie cameraman on 16mm black-and-white sound stock; and the whole is presented as part of a secret government training film. Howard Brenton's script is thus masterly in deploying the low-budget at his disposal, with the silent colour footage used to underline the extremity of the violence, and the dialogue in the black-

and-white footage revealing the near-insane elation of the protagonists (brilliantly edgy, unnerving performances from Knightley and Woolf). Bicat's sure direction fails only in the rather heavy-handed opening sequence, and in the capture of the minister (it's too cleanly shot amid the confusion, and you sometimes wonder who is supposed to be holding the camera, which erodes the documentary reality). A fascinating experiment nevertheless, even if what it's trying to say remains obscure. JF

Skinless Night
(Rokuro Mochizuki, 1991, Jap) Kin Ishikawa, Yasuko Yagami, Aya Katsuragi.
105 min.
Kayama, pushing middle-age, makes video porn for a living. His average day might include a shopping trip to a rubberware boutique, a childminding stint at the office, and an evening shoot spent struggling with the special effects for a 'golden shower' scene. One day he gets it into his head that he needs to make a 'serious' feature film, and meets steadfast opposition from his financier, his staff and his wife. Skinless Night (the title is swiped from Japan's best-selling brand of condoms) offers a wry portrait of Kayama as a man belatedly in search of 'integrity', and an authentic and riotously funny account of the sex industry. It takes on added piquancy when you know that its obviously talented director Mochizuki is a prolific maker of porno tapes. TR

Ski Patrol
(Richard Correll, 1989, US) Roger Rose, Yvette Nipar, TK Carter, Leslie Jordan, Ray Walston, Martin Mull, Corby Timbrook.
92 min.
'The idea', explains executive producer Paul Police Academy Maslansky, 'is to make the first mainstream ski film in about six years, which will appeal to skiing enthusiasts, and to put it in comedic form with gorgeous actresses and interesting, panoramic scenic backgrounds, and then combine it with high action skiing and a hot music track'. First-time director Correll faithfully relays his boss' vision of a world populated entirely by haircuts with legs, playmates, second-rate clowns, and the Machiavellian rich. The plot, obviously not a high priority, has baddies scheming to oust nice old Pop by ensuring that his ski lodge fails a safety inspection; but wait…our wacky heroes in the Ski Patrol get wise to the saboteurs in the nick of time. 'I think you're an immature, wisecracking ski bum,' gorgeous Ellen tells hunky Jerry, 'actually I think you're pretty irresistible'. Actually, she was right the first time. Why do these 'zany' comedies fall back on the corniest situations and the most predictable stereotypes? TCh

Skip Tracer
(Zale R Dalen, 1977, Can) David Peterson, John Lazarus, Rudy Szabo, Mike Grigg, A Rose, Sue Astley.
94 min.
Operating at the extremer edges of capitalism's unacceptable face, a skip tracer is a man who pulls your legs off if you don't repay his company's loan. What might have been another action flic of routine Sweeneyish nastiness is lent a worthwhile extra dimension by the psychological tensions that the job clearly entails – all that externalised aggro is seen as just another sign of internal fear and loathing. David Peterson carries the film single-handed, playing the tracer as mean as a wired ferret, until the pressure tells and he hits the slide. Some scenes and most of the supporting cast are best excused by Vancouver's general lack of a glorious cinematic heritage; but there's still enough low-budget energy and lurking menace to mark it up as a genuine curio. CPea

Skull, The
(Freddie Francis, 1965, GB) Peter Cushing, Patrick Wymark, Christopher Lee, Jill Bennett, Nigel Green, Michael Gough, George Coulouris, Patrick Magee.
83 min.
Originally The Skull of the Marquis de Sade, but the title had to be changed when De Sade's descendants in France complained. It's about a collector of occult objects (Cushing) who is offered the skull of the 'divine Marquis', and the vicious murders that subsequently take place. The script from Robert Bloch's short story hasn't been worked out very well, but there is one extraordinary dream sequence, and the whole film is directed by Freddie Francis with much technical panache. DP

Skullduggery
(Gordon Douglas, 1969, US) Burt Reynolds, Susan Clark, Roger C Carmel, Paul Hubschmid, Chips Rafferty, Alexander Knox, Edward Fox, Wilfrid Hyde-White.
105 min.
An engagingly ramshackle adventure that gradually takes on a burden of messages as Reynolds and Carmel latch on to Susan Clark's archaeological expedition, which has permission to explore the New Guinea interior. The pair are secretly prospecting for phosphorus (highly profitable since the advent of colour TV), but instead find a tribe of ape-like, intelligent creatures (played by diminutive University of Djakarta students in gingery, hairy suits) who may be 'the missing link'. Dropouts one and all, they certainly believe in flower-power, which turns Reynolds all radical when the Establishment – in the shape of the archaeological expedition's financial backer – proposes to breed them like animals for cheap labour. Cue for a rousingly melodramatic courtroom finale, engineered in desperation by Reynolds, in which the definition of 'humanity' comes under hot debate from all sides (Black Panthers, apartheid apologists, et al). Naïve, uncertain in tone, but despite all faults, an appealing curiosity. TM

Skyjacked
(John Guillermin, 1972, US) Charlton Heston, Yvette Mimieux, James Brolin, Claude Akins, Jeanne Crain, Roosevelt Grier, Walter Pidgeon, Leslie Uggams, Mariette Hartley, Mike Henry.
101 min.
A routine Airport-style thriller, with Heston as the pilot whose nerves are battered when the 707 he's flying from LA to Minneapolis is discovered to have a bomb on board, ready to explode unless he agrees to head for Moscow. The skyjacker is a disgruntled Vietnam veteran (Brolin), but the film is much too busy with its disaster movie routine (pregnant lady giving birth, and so forth) to make anything of this. Only a highly professional cast alleviates the general predictability and tedium. GA

Skyline (La Linea del Cielo)
(Fernando Colomo, 1983, Sp) Antonio Resines, Beatriz Pérez-Porro, Patricia Cisarano, Jaime Nos, Roy Hoffman, Irene Stillman, Whit Stillman.
86 min.
This charming Spanish feature, about a photographer (Resines) who travels to New York with the intention of finding work and learning English, is based on the director's own experiences while trying to set up a film. Shot on a low budget, it gently pokes fun at various Big Apple pretensions and rituals – the dinner party, how to handle a telephone call – while making a few serious observations en route about innocents and foreigners abroad. GA

Sky Pirates
(Colin Eggleston, 1985, Aust) John Hargreaves, Meredith Phillips, Max Phipps, Bill Hunter, Simon Chilvers, Alex Scott.
86 min.
Third-rate cash-in on Raiders of the Lost Ark: Dakota pilot Bomber Harris (bet they thought hard on that one) meets up with a scatty brunette, and both go off in search of some ancient stone tablet that is supposed to provide amazing power to whoever possesses it. 'Bomber' is played by Hargreaves, a hammy sort of bloke who tries ever so hard to be the macho Indiana Jones, but fails dismally. In fact, nearly everything about this movie is pretty awful, and that includes the most appalling editing you're ever likely to see. DA

Sky Riders
(Douglas Hickox, 1976, US) James Coburn, Susannah York, Robert Culp, Charles Aznavour, Werner Pochath, Zou Zou, Kenneth Griffith, Harry Andrews, JohnBeck.
93 min.
Pure slop. 'Hang-Gliders versus Left Wing Political Extremists' sounds like a bad kung-fu film, and it has about the same depth of characterisation. Laconic Coburn rescues ex-wife (bra-less Susannah) and brood from clutches of 'World Activists Revolutionary Army' (sic), who pack even bazookas in their mountain retreat somewhere in Greece. How to get at them, there's the prob. Hey! A nearby group of hang-gliding freaks! Sure enough, the Pepsi generation outwit the former Paris rioters. Hickox directs in his usual cold-blooded style, and the last twenty minutes is sheer violence and destruction (like the end of a Godzilla picture, only more mindless). AN

Sky's the Limit, The
(Edward H Griffith, 1943, US) Fred Astaire, Joan Leslie, Robert Benchley, Robert Ryan, Elizabeth Patterson.
89 min. b/w.
Astaire returned to RKO with the chance to dance to his own choreography, and amid some primitive airman-on-leave musical plotting, took it with both feet in one memorable nocturnal solo ('One for My Baby') in a deserted bar. Leslie is a magazine snapper who unwittingly scoops the incognito war hero; Benchley contributes a characteristically cockeyed oration; and the score is by Harold Arlen and Johnny Mercer. PT

Slacker
(Richard Linklater, 1991, US) Richard Linklater, Rudy Basquez, Jean Caffeine, Jan Hockey, Stephen Hockey, Mark James, Bob Boyd.
97 min.
A little like David Byrne's True Stories, minus the music and plot, this is a freewheeling, documentary-style celebration of the bizarrely normal, charmingly oddball, and terminally hip residents of Austin, Texas. It starts with a guy boring a taxi driver to death with talk about parallel realities, shifts gear when the backseat philosopher sees a woman hit by a car, then swerves into comic absurdity when the victim's son is arrested for her murder. And that's just the first five minutes. After this, one character from each scene provides the link to the next, as we encounter a string of bar-room philosophers, New Agers, old anarchists, and other weirdly entertaining specimens – one of whom is hawking what she claims is Madonna's cervical smear. At times, it's like watching someone else's home movies, but there's something oddly compelling about such studied eccentricity. NF

Slade in Flame
see Flame

Slam Dance
(Wayne Wang, 1987, US) Tom Hulce, Mary Elizabeth Mastrantonio, Don Opper, Harry Dean Stanton, Adam Ant, Robert Beltran, Virginia Madsen, Millie Perkins.
101 min.
Cynical cartoonist CC Drood (Hulce) has problems: his wife (Mastrantonio) has left him, his landlady opens his mail, and a mysterious girl he had a brief affair with (Madsen) has been found dead. Suspected of murder by Detective Smiley (Stanton), he is also the victim of brutal interrogations carried out by a hood named Buddy (Opper). Combining state-of-the-art stylishness with comedy and suspense, Wang turns an otherwise straightforward conspiracy thriller into a pacy, racy fable with distinctly oddball dimensions. The deft, dark humour (notably a supremely funny scene set in a police station seemingly populated by psychos) reinforces the shock value of its sudden incursions of crunching violence; while Drood's descent into danger involves a drastic reassessment of his shallow, self-regarding attitudes. Tautly scripted by Don 'Android' Opper, who also turns in a bizarrely touching performance as Buddy), stunningly shot and designed, the movie may not display the emotional honesty and complexity of Wang's earlier Dim Sum, but as polished adult entertainment it sparkles. GA

Slanted Vision
(Ming-Yuen S Ma, 1995, US)
50 min.
An ambitious, perceptive but finally rather chaotic exploration (taped on video) of attitudes towards the sexuality of Asian (gay) men. Part one examines their representation in porn and martial arts cinema; part two their responses to AIDS and safe sex; part three is a not very funny, sexually oriented parody of a TV cooking show. GA

Slap Shot

(George Roy Hill, 1977, US) Paul Newman, Michael Ontkean, Lindsay Crouse, Jennifer Warren, Jerry Houser, Strother Martin, Andrew Duncan, Melinda Dillon.
124 min.

While Newman's ice hockey manager struggles to revive his ailing team's fortunes with a trio of recruits who specialise most successfully in foul tactics, the movie tries, sadly, to have its cake and eat it: ostensibly deploring the commercialisation and violence that has increasingly taken over the arena, it simultaneously revels in the bone-crunching dirty play on display. Similarly, it's really just an old-fashioned piece of wish fulfilment, rather duplicitously dressed up in foul language and sexual references in a cynical attempt to look modern. That said, there are still some nice touches of absurdist satirical wit hanging out along the sidelines, given extra bite by Dede Allen's superbly pacy editing. GA

Slasher, The

see Cosh Boy

Slate, Wyn & Me

(Don McLennan, 1987, Aust) Sigrid Thornton, Simon Burke, Martin Sacks, Tommy Lewis, Lesley Baker, Harold Baigent.
91 min.

Recipe for Road Movie Rehash, Australian-style. Take basic stock of bungled bank robbery, panic shooting of cop, and flight of two Chevy-driving teenage delinquents with young female hostage. Throw in leftovers from Bonnie and Clyde, Badlands, Thieves Like Us or The Grissom Gang. Add slices of indigenous wild life and a pinch of James Dean posturing, then spice with three-way sexual power games. A smidgen of rock'n'roll and the vaguest hint of early '60s iconography will impart the requisite period flavour. Half-bake under a hot sun for approximately 90 minutes, checking from time to time for signs of originality. Garnish generously with widescreen sunsets and shots of attractive young men and women in figure-hugging jeans. This is a useful recipe for making something out of nothing; it is reasonably filling, and if presented properly can make an impression on the eye. Consume immediately, as the contents tend to evaporate rapidly. NF

Slaughter

(Jack Starrett, 1972, US) Jim Brown, Stella Stevens, Rip Torn, Don Gordon, Cameron Mitchell, Marlene Clark.
92 min.

Opening with Billy Preston singing about 'bold, beautiful and black...', this is the familiar mixture of mafia machismo (laced with a little camp) and black avenger theme, as Jim Brown's Slaughter, Vietnam vet, takes out after the syndicate responsible for the death of his parents. Best things about the film are its outrageous set-ups (for once, visual distortion is used to genuinely amazing effect), and Rip Torn's mean-arsed slob of a mafioso. Otherwise it tends to the mechanical: a broad beaten up here, a car chase there...Not in the Superfly class.

Slaughter's Big Rip-Off

(Gordon Douglas, 1973, US) Jim Brown, Ed McMahon, Brock Peters, Don Stroud, Gloria Hendry, Art Metrano.
93 min.

If nothing else, Gordon Douglas keeps the action moving in this sequel to Slaughter. Jim Brown's eponymous hero (the rest is equally subtle) tracks down the organisation that's after him for what he did to them in the earlier film. As he moves through the coke-sniffing city jungle, he encounters the usual police/syndicate tie-ups and the list in a safe that names names. Apart from some scenes and casting of total miscalculation, there are things to enjoy: a miserable hit-man who has missed his target is introduced to his own assassin at a poolside party; a man sniggers while trying to pick a safe and listen to the love-making couple in the next room. And for collectors of punko dialogue there are such gems as 'I should have known you ten years ago. We'd have ripped off the whole world in a week.' CPe

Slaughterhouse-Five

(George Roy Hill, 1972, US) Michael Sacks, Ron Leibman, Eugene Roche, Sharon Gans, Valerie Perrine, Roberts Blossom, Sorrell Booke, John Dehner, Perry King, Friedrich Ledebur.
103 min.

A curiosity, really. A slight and conservative adaptation of Kurt Vonnegut's tale about a man whose time sense is dislocated: his wartime past, which includes being bombed in Dresden, his American bourgeois present as an optometrist, and his sci-fi fantasy future on the planet Tralfamadore, develop as three concurrent narratives. Occasionally Hill comes up with some nice touches of the unexpected: a few moments of black humour, the suggestion of a deliberate pastiche here and there, but on the whole he's too resolutely fashionable a director to really get behind Vonnegut's idea of time-tripping. It ends up the wrong side of unadventurous. CPe

Slave of Love, A (Raba Lubvi)

(Nikita Mikhalkov, 1976, USSR) Elena Solovei, Rodion Nakhapetov, Alexander Kalyagin, Oleg Basilashvili.
94 min.

Crimea, 1917: a film crew shooting a silent melodrama while away a long summer in sub-Chekhovian languor. Gradually, intimations of distant revolution become intrusive. In true social-realist style, the idyll gives way to grainy realism, but the film is fatally undecided on whether to celebrate the glamour of a world with which it is more than half in love yet feels obliged to condemn. CPea

Slave of the Cannibal God

see Montagna del Dio Cannibale, La

Slavers

(Jürgen Goslar, 1977, WGer) Trevor Howard, Ron Ely, Britt Ekland, Jürgen Goslar, Ray Milland, Ken Gampu, Cameron Mitchell.
102 min.

Darkest Africa, 1884: cynical, grizzled trader (Howard), beautiful white woman (Ekland), self-aggrandising husband (Goslar), illicit lover (Ely), plus an endless supply of disposable natives and evil, foul-mouthed whites. The incoherent narrative sometimes tries to rectify itself with lumpen expository dialogue, and – no doubt in the name of historical accuracy – it's nasty to watch, unless you relish brandings, rape, cruelty to animals, spurting arteries, vultures working over dead natives, baby trampling, assorted deaths, and repeated shots of ankles chafed to the bone by iron anklets during the great slave trek. Black exploitation at its worst. JS

Slaves

see Blacksnake

Slaves of New York

(James Ivory, 1989, US) Bernadette Peters, Madeleine Potter, Adam Coleman Howard, Nick Corri, Charles McCaughan, Jonas Abry, Steve Buscemi, Betty Comden, Tammy Grimes, Mary Beth Hurt, Mercedes Ruehl, Chris Sarandon, Tama Janowitz.
125 min.

Tama Janowitz' collection of stories – some of which she adapted for this film – focuses on the middlebrow, middle class thirty-somethings who colonised Manhattan's East Village. Dizzy hat-designer Eleanor (perfectly played by Peters) lives with a shit called Stash (Howard) who paints cans of spinach. The decline of their doomed relationship is the pretext for a saunter through an airless world of galleries, parties and clubs, where everyone is on the make and no one except Eleanor has redeeming features. This doesn't matter so much, given that New York itself is the leading character; it's in the short scenes capturing the atmosphere of the city – skyscrapers at sunrise, sidewalks at sunset, rain reflected neon, a raccoon truffling through trash, gleaming limos parked beside burnt-out wrecks – that Ivory is at his best. He works hard to find a visual equivalent of Janowitz's jaunty prose, but the result, despite an eclectic rock score, bold colours, and nifty optical tricks, is more cooked-up than fizzy. Relentlessly good-looking, the movie is all surface; the few moments of wit and comic tenderness hint at what might have been. MS

Slayground

(Terry Bedford, 1983, GB) Peter Coyote, Mel Smith, Billie Whitelaw, Philip Sayer, Bill Luhrs, Marie Masters.
89 min.

An adaptation of a Richard Stark novel which, like Point Blank pits a small-time crook against an implacable, all-powerful enemy. When their driver falls victim to a marauding sex kitten, nice guy hold-up man Coyote and his chicken-farmer buddy (Luhrs) recruit a crazy punk car thief to help out, with disastrous consequences: a rich and unscrupulous promoter's little daughter is accidentally killed, and nemesis in the form of the sadistic Shadowman stalks Coyote (his partner already gunned down in his chicken house) from New York to London and a sinister finale in a Southport funfair. Unfortunately, in making the transition from cameraman to director, Terry Bedford seems to have neglected to learn about old-fashioned virtues like pace and plausibility, suspense and characterisation. Despite some eerily atmospheric photography, it's about as exciting as a rainy night in Rotherham. RMy

Sleeper

(Woody Allen, 1973, US) Woody Allen, Diane Keaton, John Beck, Mary Gregory, Don Keefer, Don McLiam.
88 min.

She: 'You haven't had sex in 200 years!?!?' He: '204, if you count my marriage'. Woody Allen's Rip Van Winkle movie, in which his Greenwich Village jazz musician/health food faddist awakes from an accidental cryogenic immersion to find that he's in 2174, cast reluctantly in the role of Little Man against the Fascist State. Plenty of one-liners, and it has the best banana-skin joke in film history. TR

Sleepers

see Little Nikita

Sleepers

(Barry Levinson, 1996, US) Robert De Niro, Dustin Hoffman, Brad Pitt, Kevin Bacon, Jason Patric, Vittorio Gassman, Billy Crudup, Ron Eldard.
147 min.

According to Lorenzo Carcaterra's best-seller, in the summer of 1967, four friends from New York were sent to reform school after a fatal, misjudged prank. There, they were mentally and physically abused by the guards. In 1981, two of the boys – now gangsters – came face to face with one of their old tormentors, and murdered him. The district attorney who volunteered to prosecute the case was, in fact, another of the original four friends, and he secretly conspired with the defence to ensure a not-guilty verdict, while finally exposing the heinous activities of the guards. And this is a true story? The novel is badly written but queasily compelling – indeed the clumsy prose is one of the more authentic aspects of an illogical, highly improbable revenge fantasy. In his flat-footed, exorbitant adaptation, writer/-director Levinson has done nothing to sift the half-truths from the melodrama, and the baroque handling of the reform school sequence even undermines the material's strongest claim on our attention, the revelation of child abuse. In the first half – with De Niro as a basketball-playing priest – Levinson never distills whatever it is that makes these kids stick together, while the second is strictly sub-Lumet courtroom histrionics. It's indicative of the all-round lack of focus that Hoffman (as an alcoholic lawyer) and Bacon (as the terrifying chief guard) are able to steal the movie with extravagant supporting turns, while the ostensible leads – Patric as the narrator Lorenzo, Pitt as the DA, Billy Crudup and Ron Eldard as the defendants – make such meagre impressions. TCh

Sleeping Beauty

(Clyde Geronimi, 1959, US) voices: Mary Costa, Bill Shirley, Eleanor Audley.
75 min.

Although this rarely achieves the heights of classics like Snow White and Dumbo, it still has its moments. Typical Disney elements abound: polished if sometimes stodgy animation; sugary soundtrack based on Tchaikovsky; a delicate, vapid princess, square-jawed prince, and cutesy creatures of the forest. The early scenes of domestic bliss with the matronly good fairies, interspersed with interludes of romance and regal pomp, are frequently overlong and uninspired. But in the final thundering confrontation with the wicked witch, set in the decaying Gothic splendours of the Forbidden Mountain, the magic works once more. An epic brilliance conjures up impossible monumental castles, shadows and monstrosities, with exciting action marvellously orchestrated across the CinemaScope frame. GA

Sleeping Car Murder, The (Compartiment Tueurs)

(Costa-Gavras, 1965, Fr) Yves Montand, Simone Signoret, Pierre Mondy, Catherine Allégret, Jacques Perrin, Jean-Louis Trintignant, Michel Piccoli, Claude Mann, Charles Denner.
95 min. b/w.
Straightforward detective thriller (adapted from a whodunit by Sébastien Japrisot), made by Costa-Gavras – his first film – before he climbed on his political bandwagon. The plot is pure Agatha Christie as the witnesses to a murder on a train are picked off one by one, but at least the characters inhabit the 20th century and are beautifully played (especially Signoret as the obligatory ageing actress, and Piccoli as a furtive lecher). The ending is one of those ingenious absurdities that haunt the genre, but the lively pace and attention to detail make up for the implausibility. TM

Sleeping Dogs

(Roger Donaldson, 1977, NZ) Sam Neill, Warren Oates, Bernard Kearns, Nevan Rowe, Ian Mune.
101 min.
Noteworthy mainly for its rarity (at the time) as a New Zealand feature, and for a brief cameo as a US military 'adviser' by Warren Oates, this formulary political action-thriller rests on a less than intriguing paradox: to emphasise the realism and spectacle of his tale of a totalitarian government beefing up its power through anti-terrorist legislation (and devoting most of its energies to hunting a back-to-nature innocent), Donaldson enlists and prominently displays the cooperation of no less than the NZ Air Force. Subversive, eh? PT

Sleeping Man (Nemuru Otoko)

(Kohei Oguri, 1995, Jap) Sung-Ki Ahn, Christine Hakim, Koji Yakusho, Masao Imafuku, Akiko Nomura, Masako Yagi.
103 min.
Gunma Prefecture in rural Japan conceived an unusual way to celebrate its population passing the two million mark, commissioning Kohei Oguri to take this reflective look at life in the region. Injured in a climbing accident, a young man lies in a coma, much to the consternation of family and friends, but the film's focus is more on the community as a whole, and life must go on. It's an ensemble piece which seems to pick up and drop plot strands and incident as it goes along, reflecting on both the influence of immigration and the call of escape. Oguri's determination to leave things tantalisingly unresolved may frustrate the viewer's expectations, but his pacing and composition have an other-worldly resonance. TJ

Sleeping Tiger, The

(Joseph Losey, 1954, GB) Dirk Bogarde, Alexis Smith, Alexander Knox, Hugh Griffith, Patricia McCarron, Maxine Audley, Glyn Houston, Harry Towb.
89 min. b/w.
Forget the plot, which errs on the wild side as a psychoanalyst (Knox) experimentally instals a handsome young gunman (Bogarde) in his home, only to discover – to no one's surprise but his own – that the sleeping tiger of his wife's id easily outbids his patient's. Enjoy the high-wire tension of Losey's direction, the lurking paranoia that charges his images with electricity. Losey's first British feature, made under a pseudonym in the shadow of the blacklist, it sheds the classic modulations of The Prowler. Instead, you see the birth pangs of what came to be known as Losey baroque, erupting grandiosely in the closing sequence, with the lovers' car crashing through a hoarding to founder beneath the rampant paws of the Esso tiger. TM

Sleeping with the Enemy

(Joseph Ruben, 1990, US) Julia Roberts, Patrick Bergin, Kevin Anderson, Elizabeth Lawrence, Kyle Secor, Claudette Nevins.
99 min.
This is in the 'never trust appearances' mould popularised by Fatal Attraction and Pacific Heights. Julia Roberts is Laura, whose particularly smooth but psychotic hubby (Bergin) demands gourmet dinners and sex on tap, and is prone to duffing her up if she fails to hang towels in the prescribed manner. Roberts is so driven by such mistreatment that she fakes her own death, reappearing as a free-at-last nobody, and is courted by a yukkily wholesome drama teacher (Anderson) in the film's risible middle section. Cue return of Bergin's unreconstituted psycho, madder and nastier than ever, for the usual climactic punch-out and final, audience-cheering pay-off. A tacky footnote to the battered wife issue. SGr

Sleepless in Seattle

(Nora Ephron, 1993, US) Tom Hanks, Meg Ryan, Ross Malinger, Rita Wilson, Rosie O'Donnell, Rob Reiner, Bill Pullman.
105 min.
A comedy for the AIDS era, Ephron's movie puts a continent between the lovebirds. Sex doesn't come much safer than this. Mourning his beloved wife, widower Sam Baldwin (Hanks) moves to Seattle with his young son. When the boy arranges for dad to discuss his pain on air with a radio shrink, journalist Annie Reed (Ryan) is just one of thousands of women to fall in love at first sob with 'Sleepless in Seattle'. Unfortunately, she's 3,000 miles away and otherwise engaged to dull, dependable Walter (Pullman). This variation of the 'him and hers' schtick Ephron first tapped in her screenplay for When Harry Met Sally comes complete with another of Ryan's ditzy romantics and a fine cameo from Harry director Rob Reiner. The picture is both old fashioned and very knowing, and occasionally tart. As Annie's friend Becky (O'Donnell) recognises, it's about 'movie love' – the love that will not be denied. The schmaltzy soundtrack is overdone, but cameraman Sven Nykvist wraps it all up in an appropriately warm glow. TCh

Sleep, My Love

(Douglas Sirk, 1948, US) Claudette Colbert, Robert Cummings, Don Ameche, Rita Johnson, George Coulouris, Hazel Brooks, Queenie Smith, Keye Luke, Raymond Burr, Ralph Morgan.
97 min. b/w.
Though dismissed by Sirk himself, and far from equal to his superb work of the mid to late '50s, this is a fine thriller in the Gaslight mould, with Colbert's demise being planned by her apparently loving husband Ameche. From the opening moments aboard a train rushing through the night, the tension is kept up by taut pacing and Joseph Valentine's expressionist photography, giving rise to a suitably nightmarish evocation of insanity and shifting appearances; while the acting is strong throughout, nowhere more so than in a sinister Coulouris as a bogus psychiatrist. GA

Sleepwalkers

(Mick Garris, 1992, US) Brian Krause, Madchen Amick, Alice Krige, Jim Haynie, Cindy Pickett, Ron Perlman, Lyman Ward, Dan Martin, John Landis, Joe Dante, Stephen King, Clive Barker, Tobe Hooper.
91 min.
Teen hunk Krause and his incestuous mother Krige are the last of a line of creatures who feed on the virtue and suffering of small-town virgins like Amick. So when Amick takes Krause to a graveyard to make out, he transforms into the date-rapist from Hell. The creature and transformation effects are impressive, but undermined by wild swings of tone: here, for example, explicit physical horror gives way to misjudged jokey taunts, until ended by the truly laughable intervention of a fearsome kitty cat. The slide into implausibility gathers pace as the scratched and wounded Krause is nursed by his fading mother in a house surrounded by a growing horde of vengeful pussies. It's never explained why they're afraid of domestic cats, why they're the last of their line, or why they're called Sleepwalkers.

Garris is left by Stephen King's typically threadbare script to extract what few frights he can with tricksy camerawork, shock effects, and flesh-ripping gore. NF

Sleep With Me

(Rory Kelly, 1994, US) Eric Stoltz, Meg Tilly, Craig Sheffer, Todd Field, Susan Traylor, Dean Cameron, Thomas Gibson, Quentin Tarantino.
94 min.
Dreamed up over drinks by Eric Stoltz, Rory Kelly and their writing buddies, this contemporary relationships comedy might be described as a kind of Californian Four Weddings and a Funeral – just forget any religious aspect! Instead we have half a dozen party scenes (each by a different screenwriter), spanning the period between Stoltz's wedding to Tilly and the near breakdown of their relationship a few months later. The twenty-something central drama is not desperately engaging, but the ensemble scenes around it are well observed and often acutely funny, with each party plumbing new depths of social embarrassment. TCh

Sleuth

(Joseph L Mankiewicz, 1972, GB) Laurence Olivier, Michael Caine.
139 min.
Although a previous TO reviewer's claim that this is closer to Borges than Agatha Christie is perhaps overstating the case, it must be said that Mankiewicz films Anthony Shaffer's two-hander play – about a thriller writer's attempts to play lethal games with his wife's lover – with admirable style and intelligence. Less a whodunit than a howdunit, Shaffer's plot is labyrinthine enough to grip from start to finish, and the performances are superb; and while he never tries to open the action out, Mankiewicz explores his set with an amazing attention to detail and atmosphere, emphasising the twists and turns of the perverse power play at work. Thoroughly entertaining. GA

Sliding Doors

(Peter Howitt, 1997, US/GB) Gwyneth Paltrow, John Hannah, John Lynch, Jeanne Tripplehorn, Zara Turner, Douglas McFerran, Virginia McKenna.
99 min.
Helen (Paltrow) loses her high-powered PR job and returns unexpectedly to her London flat to find boyfriend Gerry (Lynch) in bed with his ex Lydia (Tripplehorn). Or she doesn't. In one alternate reality, Helen is delayed, arrives home a few minutes after Lydia has left, and remains in the dark about the affair. Meanwhile, the other Helen – the one who walked out – finds a new life and a new admirer, a real charmer, James (Hannah). While touching on such perennials as the nature of destiny, fate and self-determination, this is essentially a romantic comedy with a nifty gimmick. As such, it's entertaining and smart. Although writer/director Howitt botches the dramatic fulcrum – the point where Helen's twin fates diverge – he pulls off the more difficult task of keeping both scenarios in the air with ease. The actors are crucial, none more so than the wonderful Paltrow, whose impeccable English accent is so precise it's disconcerting. Howitt might have pushed her harder to distinguish between the two Helens (she lets her hairdo do the work), but then this isn't meant to change your life – that's just a happy side effect. TCh

Slight Case of Murder, A

(Lloyd Bacon, 1938, US) Edward G Robinson, Jane Bryan, Allen Jenkins, Willard Parker, Ruth Donnelly, John Litel, Edward Brophy, Harold Huber, Bobby Jordan.
85 min. b/w.
This broad, acidic black comedy allows Edward G Robinson the opportunity to spoof his tough guy persona, as a beer baron who goes straight when Prohibition ends, only to find his fortune rapidly dwindling because his ale is unpalatable. Both accomplices and rivals naturally take a dim view of things, especially when his daughter (Bryan) starts dating a state trooper (Parker); and dastardly schemes are hatched to frame or fix him for good (notably by way of a stash of dead bodies, which have to be carefully redistributed, then re-collected when they prove to have a reward on their heads). The pace rises with the

body count in this amusing version of a Damon Runyon/Howard Lindsay farce. Remade with Broderick Crawford in 1952 as *Stop, You're Killing Me*. TCh

Slightly Pregnant Man, The (L'Evénement le plus Important depuis que l'Homme a Marché sur la Lune)

(Jacques Demy, 1973, Fr/It) Catherine Deneuve, Marcello Mastroianni, Micheline Presle, Marisa Pavan, Claude Melki, Michéle Moretti, Mireille Mathieu.
95 min.
Demy's usually feather-light touch deserts him with this clodhopping farce that hectically proceeds nowhere from a motive idea/image that only someone like Marco Ferreri should really have had: a pregnant Mastroianni, getting over morning sickness and into modelling 'paternity' clothes, before an inevitable anticlimax. A few limp forays into a philosophy of societal imbalance are belied by the overall stultifying air of comic convention. PT

Slightly Scarlet

(Allan Dwan, 1956, US) John Payne, Rhonda Fleming, Arlene Dahl, Kent Taylor, Ted de Corsia, Lance Fuller.
99 min.
Based on a novel by James M Cain, this big-city corruption chronicle is a smart example of Dwan's '50s output, a *film noir* that just happens to be in colour and SuperScope. Gang leader Payne meeting his comeuppance when he tangles with sisters Fleming and Dahl, the former the mayor's innocent secretary, the latter a dangerous kleptomaniac. (Martin Scorsese, incidentally, has tipped his cap to Dwan and acknowledged him as an influence.) TJ

Sling Blade

(Billy Bob Thornton, 1996, US) Billy Bob Thornton, Dwight Yoakum, JT Walsh, John Ritter, Lucas Black, Natalie Canerday, Robert Duvall, James Hampton, Jim Jarmusch.
126 min.
Thornton made his mark as writer and actor in *One False Move*, and his directorial debut (from his own Oscar-winning script) is similarly impressive. He gives a magnificent, hugely credible performance as a retarded man who returns to his hometown in the Deep South after spending years in a psychiatric hospital for having murdered his mother as a child. When he befriends a young boy, his life takes a dramatic new turn. Tender but rarely sentimental, beautifully acted, and shot through with dark humour, this sensitive, insightful drama avoids the usual stereotypes to powerful effect. (And catch the lovely Jim Jarmusch cameo.) GA

Slingshot, The (Kådisbellan)

(Åke Sandgren, 1993, Swe) Jesper Salén, Stellan Skarsgård, Basia Frydman, Niclas Olund, Ernst-Hugo Järegård.
102 min.
It doesn't take long to realise that Jesper Salén's 12-year-old Roland is going to have a hard time in '20s Stockholm: daddy's a rampant socialist with a dodgy back; mum's an expatriate Russian (and Jewish); his schoolmaster is stern and handy with the cane. With suffering duly dispatched, it's time for the dash of eccentricity – to the lad's rescue comes a handy box of prophylactics, banned by the authorities but actively distributed by the welfare-conscious Red underground. A condom catapult earns Roland social acceptability – but also, eventually, a place in reform school. Given assured performances and a convincing, unshowy production job, these events proceed convincingly enough. It's just that the director plods through it all with the flattening style of a TV movie. TJ

Slipper and the Rose, The

(Bryan Forbes, 1976, GB) Richard Chamberlain, Gemma Craven, Annette Crosbie, Edith Evans, Christopher Gable, Michael Hordern, Margaret Lockwood, Kenneth More, Julian Orchard.
146 min.
A musical version of *Cinderella* that looked redundant before even leaving the starting-blocks. Despite all the critical plaudits (a misplaced patriotism?), it's top heavy, over-lavishly mounted, full of unmemorable songs in the Disney vein by Richard and Robert Sherman, and moves at a snail's pace. In a coasting cast, only Annette Crosbie as the harassed Fairy Godmother manages to alleviate the gloom.

Slipstream

(Steven M Lisberger, 1989, GB) Mark Hamill, Bob Peck, Bill Paxton, Kitty Aldridge, Eleanor David, Ben Kingsley, F Murray Abraham, Robbie Coltrane.
102 min.
Much of the exceptional aerial footage for this futuristic fantasy was shot, appropriately, in Turkey. The incomprehensible storyline concerns a purifying wind which swept the polluted planet clean, leaving a detritus of nomadic pilots and wind-worshippers. Star warrior Hamill is surprisingly hard-edged as the lawman trying to bring renegade robot Peck to justice. Perhaps hoping to compensate for the atrocious dialogue, Paxton overacts wildly as a bounty hunter with an eye on the reward. For some reason, they all end up in an isolated community of wind-worshipping hippies, whose watchword seems to be 'Go fly a kite', by which time you'll wish you had. Religious leader Kingsley dies under a millstone, and F Murray Abraham pops up as the leader of a bunch of decadent aristos holed up in an abandoned museum. Sentiment runs rampant near the end, when Peck's android falls for the film's only credible character (David). NF

Slither

(Howard Zieff, 1973, US) James Caan, Peter Boyle, Sally Kellerman, Louise Lasser, Allen Garfield, Richard B Shull, Alex Rocco.
96 min.
The movie that virtually defines the term 'offbeat', in the very best sense of the word. Part thriller, part road movie, part heist caper, and part parody (most notably of *Duel*) Zieff's first and (along with *Hollywood Cowboy*) best film sees ex-con car thief Caan joining up with *recvee* (recreation vehicle, ie. caravan) fanatic Boyle and his wife Lasser in a search for an embezzled fortune, and getting into pretty nasty trouble en route. What makes the film so disarmingly enjoyable is its cool, dry sense of absurdity, and its unsentimental affection for the eccentric but definitely not wacky characters. It's a tale of ordinary people with extraordinary dreams and delusions, the sort of film that can conjure magical mayhem out of a caravan park bingo tournament. GA

Sliver

(Phillip Noyce, 1993, US) Sharon Stone, William Baldwin, Tom Berenger, Polly Walker, Colleen Camp, Martin Landau, CCH Pounder.
108 min.
Stone looks distinctly ordinary in this glossy, glassy sex-thriller. She's an uptight book editor who moves into a fancy Manhattan high-rise (the sliver of the title). Neighbours include blocked crime novelist Berenger and smirking Baldwin. Both pursue her, but which is the blonde-fixated serial killer? If *Basic Instinct* played off *Vertigo*, Noyce's film would like to be a sort of sexed-up *Rear Window*. Here, however, voyeurism is not so much subtext as designer-look apparel trimmed with chic post-feminist accessories. Though based on an Ira Levin novel, the movie is essentially just another variation on Joe Eszterhas's rudimentary 'psychotic fuck' scenarios. TCh

Slow Attack (Endstation Freiheit)

(Reinhard Hauff, 1980, WGer) Burkhard Driest, Rolf Zacher, Katja Rupé, Carla Egerer, Kurt Raab.
112 min.
In which art (violent criminal fresh out of jail writes a book about a kidnapping) mirrors crime (his doomed partner carries out the job for real). The irony inherent in the plot's development is horribly overstated in the climax, but more disturbing is the lack of distance established by Hauff from the protagonist's macho problems. Gays and women versus leather jacket and cratered face results in a thriller with possibly 'limited appeal'. SJ

Slow Dancing in the Big City

(John G Avildsen, 1978, US) Paul Sorvino, Anne Ditchburn, Nicolas Coster, Anita Dangler, Hector Jaime Mercado.
110 min.
'New York is a people place...and ultimately, *Slow Dancing in the Big City* is a people movie'. The mawkishness of this snippet from the movie's PR belies a curiously offbeat film, in which sentimentality for once seems more deliberate than accidental, with Sorvino playing a chubby New York news columnist who, while simultaneously trying to rescue an 8-year-old Puerto Rican drug addict, falls in lurv with divine (but actually rather wooden) ballet dancer Anne Ditchburn, who is struggling against a physical affliction that will eventually put an end to her dancing. Avildsen's career has a certain wavering integrity to it (from *Save the Tiger* to *Rocky*) which mixes gently left-of-Hollywood-centre politics with an unfortunate degree of righteousness. Which is why this one is, in the end, a failure, with its socially conscientious plot too episodic, and its kids (as always) too cute by half. Audiences will simply go to town on the finale: the journalist's street waif hits a heroin overdose, and his beloved collapses, crippled for life, after a triumphant final performance. CA

Slow Motion

see Sauve Qui Peut – la Vie

Slow Moves

(Jon Jost, 1983, US) Roxanne Rogers, Marshall Gaddis, Debbie Krant, Barbara Hammes, Geoffrey Rotwein.
93 min.
Jost has supplied his audience with plenty of reasons for avoiding this film. He freely admits that its characters make a pair of Mike Leigh marrieds look like *Fun with Dick and Jane*, and that the usual narrative trappings – backgrounds, personalities, events, causality – are obscured, that the film parts with its secrets only grudgingly. But with that established, it becomes a fascinating, oddly gripping, and often visually stunning film. It's not unlike a Peter Greenaway mystery translated to the dry, dusty heartland of Malick's *Badlands*, although here the emphasis is on spiritual paralysis rather than Greenaway's elegant intellectual conceits. It does have a similar wit – sly games with camera angles, image, dialogue and cliché – but unravelling them yourself is half what the movie is about. Jost's story of two charmless no-hopers, drifting through life without reason or direction, might sound like pure valium, but the gradual seepage of narrative turns it into all manner of movies. JG

Slumber Party '57

(William A Levey, 1976, US) Janet Wood, Debra Winger, Rainbeaux Smith, Noelle North, Bridget Holloman, Mary Ann Appleseth, Rafael Campos, Will Hutchins.
88 min.
A film for those for whom the spoken bits of Shangri-La's tracks strike a special chord. Six high school girls decide to have a slumber party, and clad in baby-doll shorty pyjamas they swap stories about their romances ('Did you really go all the way?'). The characters of the girls are nicely contrasted, and signs of the times are inserted into the dialogue like neon billboards ('Hey, give me back my hula hoop!'). As an exercise in nostalgia it never attempts the solidity of *American Graffiti*, but its lack of pretension and soundtrack backing of key tracks from the period (Paul and Paula, Big Bopper, Jerry Lee Lewis) make it rather winning entertainment. VG

Slumber Party Massacre, The

(Amy Jones, 1982, US) Michele Michaels, Robin Stille, Michael Villela, Debra DeLiso, Andree Honore, Gina Mari.
84 min.
With Aaron Lipstadt (director of the marvellous *Android*) as co-producer and Rita Mae Brown (author of *Rubyfruit Jungle*) as writer, you might expect this to be a superior send-up of the schlock shocker. All the more disappointing, then, that the result is just another escaped driller killer with a yen for carving up high school girls. There are a few token sops to feminism, but otherwise it's the sort of nauseous characterisation that has you groping for the nearest power-driven tool. Only in the last 15 minutes does the action come

fast and funny enough to banish the overwhelming sense of *déjà vu*. Until then, it's just an illustration of how to enliven dubious Californian taste in home furnishing with the addition of a few strategically-placed blood-spattered corpses. AB

Small Back Room, The

(Michael Powell/Emeric Pressburger, 1948, GB) David Farrar, Kathleen Byron, Jack Hawkins, Leslie Banks, Michael Gough, Cyril Cusack, Milton Rosmer, Walter Fitzgerald, Renée Asherson, Robert Morley.
108 min. b/w.
Powell made *The Small Back Room* just after *The Red Shoes*, and was clearly looking for a 'homely', manageable subject after the lavish ambitions of the earlier film. He found it in Nigel Balchin's novel about a military bomb-disposal wizard, and turned in a thriller that would look like a masterpiece in the filmographies of most British directors. But it rests on a not-very-interesting dramatic idea: a man whose private life is in ruins (he's lost a foot in a bomb blast, is having trouble with his girlfriend, and is becoming alcoholic) gets new drive from the challenge of mastering a new kind of German bomb. And Powell's characteristic desire to ornament leads to the inclusion of some bizarre fantasy footage (when the hero suffers DTs) which simply doesn't belong in this context. It remains extremely tense in a workmanlike way, and full of good visual and syntactic ideas...but it's a fair way short of Powell's best. TR

Small Change

see Argent de Poche, L'

Smallest Show on Earth, The

(Basil Dearden, 1957, GB) Bill Travers, Virginia McKenna, Peter Sellers, Margaret Rutherford, Bernard Miles, Leslie Phillips, Sidney James.
81 min. b/w.
A delightfully eccentric comedy, with Travers and McKenna inheriting a fleapit cinema called The Bijou, and fighting a takeover by the owners of The Grand, which 'conveniently' burns down. An Ealing-style allegory of English resolve, scripted by William Rose and John Eldridge, it's memorable chiefly for Sellers' drunken old projectionist, clinging to his machines whenever a train goes by, and Rutherford's belligerent cashier. ATu

Small Faces

(Gillies MacKinnon, 1995, GB) Ian Robertson, JS Duffy, Joseph McFadden, Clare Higgins, Laura Fraser, Kevin McKidd, Mark McConnochie.
108 min.
Glasgow, 1968: time for the Maclean brothers to decide where their loyalties and ambitions lie. The eldest, Bobby (Duffy), misses his dead dad, suffers nightmares, and hangs out with a local gang; Alan (McFadden) devotes his time to painting and Joanne (Fraser), an uncommonly self-assured lass, known to have attracted the jealous attentions of various neighborhood hardnuts; while Lex (Robertson), a feisty 13-year-old, is not only torn between the lifestyles of his brothers, but is facing pressure from the hoodlum tribes who engage in battle in and around the estates. Small wonder the boys' mother (Higgins) is often at her wits' end. It's hard to pin down exactly why Gilles MacKinnon's quasi-autobiographical rites-of-passage movie, co-written with his producer brother Billy, is so satisfying. As ever there's an unflashy visual intelligence at work, and again MacKinnon proves an expert director of actors. But what perhaps best distinguishes the film is its unsentimental honesty: everything – from the bloody rumbles between rival gangs to the mysteries of courtship, from anxieties over the precise intentions of a visiting uncle to Alan's anti-Americanism and Lex's first alcoholic binge – seems somehow absolutely right. A gem. GA

Smalltime

(Shane Meadows, 1996, GB) Mat Hand, Dena Smiles, Shane Meadows, Gena Kawecka, Jimmy Hynd.
61 min.
Sneinton, a suburb of Nottingham: Should Malc (Hand) carry on a dual life of petty crime with his boozing pals, or clean up his act, as his wife Kate

(Smiles) insists? It's a tough choice, influenced not only by questions of cash and camaraderie, but by the fact that Jumbo (writer/director Meadows in memorably terrible wig) seems bent on wrecking any relationship Malc tries to establish outside their gang. Shot on video for a pittance, *Smalltime* may be rough and ready, but the title belies its big heart and acute perceptions. Though often very funny, this proudly parochial fable never opts for knowing caricature: the authenticity of these lives, defined by a shell-suited, Lambrusco-glugging lack of sophistication and unthinking laddishness, still allows for unsentimental affection and the odd serious insight. GA

Small Time

(Norman Loftis, 1990, US) Richard Barbozo, Carolyn Kinebrew, Scott Ferguson.
90 min.
An impressive low-budgeter, dealing with the hard life and times of Vince, an ineffectual young New York hood, Loftis' film uses a mix of dramatic vignettes, location vérité, and staged voxpop 'witness' interviews to create a picture of a two-time loser dwarfed by circumstances he can't begin to comprehend. Occasionally, the film reveals a street theatre staginess, letting its dramatic flow get swamped under a slightly antiseptic, at times teacherly, tone. But as a sympathetic portrait of a thoroughly unsympathetic protagonist, *Small Time* is impressively tough, capturing the pulse of the small-time life, without for a minute glamorising it. JRo

Small Wonders

(Allan Miller, 1995, US) Roberta Guaspari-Tzavaras, Itzhak Perlman, Isaac Stern, Midori, Arnold Steinhardt, Mark O'Connor.
77 min.
The East Harlem Violin Program and its moving force, tutor Roberta Guaspari-Tzavaras, are the subject of this rousing musical documentary which shows the forging of perspiration and inspiration in her multi-ethnic primary school charges. The junior violinists make their way from the elementary exercises to the annual parents' night – and a Carnegie Hall all-star fundraiser. TJ

Smash Palace

(Roger Donaldson, 1981, NZ) Bruno Lawrence, Anna Jemison, Keith Aberdein, Greer Robson, Desmond Kelly, Lynne Robson.
108 min.
This turkey treads similar ground to Mike Newell's *Bad Blood* (middle-aged New Zealander cracks up and is forced into the role of outlaw). But while Newell constructed a web of social, communal and familial tensions, Donaldson wallows in male menopausal *angst* via dumbly overstated symbols. Thus the hero runs a wrecked car dump (his marriage is failing), but is building a racing car (he clings to a relationship with his daughter, whom he eventually kidnaps). Get the connections? Instantly forgettable. SJ

Smash-Up, The Story of a Woman

(Stuart Heisler, 1946, US) Susan Hayward, Lee Bowman, Eddie Albert, Marsha Hunt, Carl Esmond.
103 min. b/w.
Hayward hits the skids with a flourish in the kind of showy role Bette Davis or Joan Crawford might have made even more of. As husband Bowman's crooning career hits the big time, her liquor bill makes it big too, before a burning orphanage takes a bow in the finale and schematic redemption is the order of the day. It makes you smile to think that the alcoholic misanthrope Dorothy Parker had a hand in the script. TJ

Smile

(Michael Ritchie, 1974, US) Bruce Dern, Barbara Feldon, Michael Kidd, Geoffrey Lewis, Nicholas Pryor, Colleen Camp, Annette O'Toole, Melanie Griffith.
113 min.
A gentle, sometimes sharp look at small-town American life via the build-up to Santa Rosa's *Young American Miss* competition, a meat market underlining the community's obsession with appearances, its self-deception and complacency. At its centre, the film is concerned with the lack of intercourse, both social and private, between

men and women, and how institutions like the *Young American Miss* reinforce the sexes' suspicions of each other. Perhaps a more caustic picture was intended, but the film grows to like its characters, and the final result is amusingly indulgent and generous in a way few current American films are: one has to look to East Europe (especially the work of Milos Forman) for a similar quality of ironic compassion. CPe

Smile Orange

(Trevor D Rhone, 1974, Jam) Carl Bradshaw, Glen Morrison, Vaughan Crosskill, Robin Sweeney, Stanley Irons.
88 min.
Where Trevor Rhone's script for *The Harder They Come* relocated Hollywood B movie conventions in a specifically Jamaican context, his first film as director does much the same with the stock material of British comedy. From this he's crafted a genuinely hilarious politicised farce; a satire on tourism that centres on hotel waiter Ringo Smith's efforts to exploit the exploiters. One long, two-handed scene exemplifies the balance Rhone achieves, when Ringo (Bradshaw) takes a raw busboy in hand, informs him that 'any black man that can't play a part's gonna starve to death', and proceeds first to teach him waiting etiquette, then how to screw white tourists, literally and figuratively. The Mocho Beach Hotel, main locale of this anarchic entertainment, has inevitably been characterised as a Jamaican *Fawlty Towers*, but it's hard to imagine even Basil rigging a crab race! Black joy indeed, from which a few technical rough ends detract nothing. PT

Smiles of a Summer Night (Sommarnattens Leende)

(Ingmar Bergman, 1955, Swe) Eva Dahlbeck, Ulla Jacobsson, Harriet Andersson, Margit Carlqvist, Gunnar Björnstrand, Jarl Kulle, Ake Fridell, Björn Bjelvenstam, Naima Wifstrand, Bibi Andersson.
110 min. b/w.
Bergman's first major success, inspiration for both Stephen Sondheim's *A Little Night Music* and Woody Allen's *A Midsummer Night's Sex Comedy*, this enchanting comedy of manners assembles a team of couples, ex-couples and would-be couples, and puts them through their paces in a game of love at a country house party during one heady midsummer weekend in 1900. Ruthless towards its characters' amorous pretensions, but extending a kind of ironic tenderness when they get hoist with their own petards, it is a wonderfully funny, genuinely erotic, and quite superbly acted *rondo* of love. Dig too deeply and it disintegrates, but its facade – decked out in elegant turn-of-the-century settings and costumes – has a magical, shimmering beauty. TM

Smiling Ghost, The

(Lewis Seiler, 1941, US) Wayne Morris, Brenda Marshall, Alexis Smith, Alan Hale, Lee Patrick, David Bruce, Willie Best, Richard Ainley.
71 min. b/w.
Very much the *Cat and the Canary* formula, set in an old dark house with the wisecracks flying and the secret panels flapping, while Willie Best provides his usual study in knock-kneed terror. Cheaply made but moderately amusing/exciting, thanks largely to the accomplished cast, with Smith as the heiress whose three previous fiancés have come to grisly grief, Morris as the young man hired for bait, Hale as the bumbling detective, and Marshall as the intrepid girl reporter determined to fathom the mystery. TM

Smiling Madame Beudet, The

see Souriante Madame Beudet, La

Smilla's Feeling for Snow (Fräulein Smillas Gespür für Schnee/aka Smilla's Sense of Snow)

(Bille August, 1996, Ger/Den/Swe) Julia Ormond, Gabriel Byrne, Richard Harris, Robert Loggia, Mario Adorf, Bob Peck, Jim Broadbent, Tom Wilkinson, Vanessa Redgrave.
122 min.
This intellectual thriller, adapted from Peter

Høeg's best-seller, is dominated by Ormond's frosty heroine, half-American, half-Greenlander, who tries tenaciously to unravel the mysterious death of six-year-old Isaiah, son of an alcoholic Greenlander neighbour. Helped only by another neighbour, the enigmatic Engineer (Byrne), Smilla pursues cryptic clues and interrogates frightened witnesses. Could there be a link between Isaiah's rooftop fall and the death of the boy's father some years earlier in a hushed-up mining accident? The ensuing quest takes Smilla from Copenhagen to Greenland, where her Inuit skills come into their own. The strength of the novel lay chiefly in the Copenhagen scenes, where an interplay of skilfully drawn characters established a narrative enigma and an authentic sense of pinched, alienated lives. The same is true of the film, by Høeg's Danish compatriot Bille August: the first half benefits from the foursquare contributions of Redgrave, Broadbent and Wilkinson, but thereafter it ploughs like an ice-breaker on a suicide mission. Our involvement, however, melts once Smilla and the others board the rusting Russian ship 'Kronos' and set sail for the preposterous anti-climax. NF

Smithereens
(Susan Seidelman, 1982, US) Susan Berman, Brad Rinn, Richard Hell, Nada Despotovich, Roger Jett, Kitty Summerall.
93 min
Wren (Berman) is a working class girl from the wrong side of the Hudson River, come to Manhattan to take her peck at the big, bad apple. Equipped with little more than a talent for self-promotion, she plays the peacock in her bright punk plumage, chasing a dream of rock'n'roll fame and fortune amid the lotus eaters of the Lower East Side. This debut feature from Seidelman (ex-New York Film School) may be small and unambitious, but its old tale of the little girl lost in the city is told with energy and verve. Seidelman's sure feeling for the squalor and glamour of urban decay, and her speedy, stylish editing, combine with a pulsating soundtrack from The Feelies to create a febrile sense of Lower Manhattan street life: fast living on a permanent adrenalin high. SJo

Smoke
(Wayne Wang, 1995, US) Harvey Keitel, William Hurt, Forest Whitaker, Stockard Channing, Harold Perrineau, Clarice Taylor, Jared Harris.
108 min.
Wang's full atonement for the melodramatic excesses of *The Joy Luck Club* is a collaboration with the novelist Paul Auster, who contributes his first original screenplay. Five main characters, each with his or her own quirk or problem, find their criss-crossing over a few days in 1990 in and around Brooklyn, in ways that leave all of them changed for the better. Keitel's tobacco-store manager, serving as the neighbourhood sage and grieving over a stash of Cuban cigars ruined in a plumbing accident, is the most colourful; Whitaker's failed father and husband, presiding over a run-down garage, the most touching. The precision of the plotting and execution sometimes seems a shade over-calculated, but the sheer warmth of the performances (and the spirit behind them) carries the film through to its extremely cheering finale. TR

Smokey and the Bandit
(Hal Needham, 1977, US) Burt Reynolds, Sally Field, Jerry Reed, Jackie Gleason, Mike Henry, Pat McCormick, Paul Williams.
97 min.
The first of the 'Citizens Band' movies to reach Britain. Despite a thin premise for an action-comedy road chase, the film's enthusiasm makes up for its lack of ideas. Reynolds and Reed accept a bet to ship an illegal lorry-load of beer back to Georgia, getting involved with Field (a chorine running from marriage to the sheriff's dim son) along the way. The direction, by a former stuntman, concentrates on the action and happily leaves everyone to their own devices, with almost nothing much to do. Field shows what natural acting is all about, and Reynolds' send-ups of himself are, despite repetition, becoming more likeable. Here his kidding around is exactly in tune with this fast-moving but essentially lazy vehicle. As Reynolds confides to Field, he just does what he does best: show off. CPe

Smokey and the Bandit II
(aka Smokey and the Bandit Ride Again)
(Hal Needham, 1980, US) Burt Reynolds, Jackie Gleason, Jerry Reed, Dom DeLuise, Sally Field, Paul Williams, Pat McCormick, David Huddleston, Mike Henry.
104 min.
Three years after *Smokey and the Bandit* took the hard-drinking, fast-driving, trickster ethos of the American redneck into the big box-office league, Reynolds has proved he 'just does what he does best: show off'. This reunites the hit team round Reynolds as the self-mocking, loveable sonofabitch who, this time, goes on the road with a cargo of an elephant, hotly pursued by overweight cop Gleason and his dumb son. Alternating exquisitely timed gags with stunts, and going for broke with a massive demolition derby, means there's little to grouse about. From the start, when Reynolds surfaces from behind a mountain of empty beer cans, you know what's in store – a lightweight caper that Reynolds must truly be sick of by now, but which he has elevated into something impossible to dislike. DMacp

Smoking/No Smoking
(Alain Resnais, 1993, Fr) Sabine Azéma, Pierre Arditi.
146 min (Smoking). 147 min (No Smoking).
Resnais' double-barrelled screen version of Alan Ayckbourn's expansive stage cycle *Intimate Exchanges* immediately hits the stumbling block of language. Here are the emotionally stunted denizens of the English middle class; yet what we hear is the vernacular French of Azéma and Arditi grandstanding in five roles apiece. In short, if you're expecting a BBC-style adaptation, almost everything about these films will seem fake – which is precisely what makes them so captivating. Once you get used to dialogue in translation and the cartoonish view of Little England, what's on offer is a disarming, impish delight in storytelling. Each piece proceeds to travesty dysfunctional marriages and illusory dreams of escape before fanning out in a series of alternative destinies for its variably articulate protagonists. When the films are seen singly, the overriding concept is clear enough. Viewed in tandem, their criss-crossing content provides all sorts of contextual pay-offs. There are miscalculations in some of the broader comedy, and *No Smoking* is probably the more entertaining of the two, but this is Ayckbourn gone Cubist, and that you have to see. TJ

Smoky
(Louis King, 1946, US) Fred MacMurray, Anne Baxter, Burl Ives, Bruce Cabot, Esther Dale, Roy Roberts.
87 min.
Technicolor Fox Western from a novel by Will James: MacMurray's the cowboy, Baxter the Nebraska ranch owner he works for, but the real star's Smoky, one of those Western wonder horses who seems considerably more intelligent than any of its riders. GM

Smooth Talk
(Joyce Chopra, 1985, US) Treat Williams, Laura Dern, Mary Kay Place, Margaret Welch, Sarah Inglis, Levon Helm.
91 min.
Chopra's sympathetically observed study of a teenage girl trembling on the brink of womanhood is adapted from a short story by Joyce Carol Oates, and sometimes it shows. It begins, deceptively, like a standard 'coming of age' picture, with Laura Dern's gawky girlishness and tough relationship with her perplexed parents deftly sketched in. But Dern is left alone in the house, and the older, enigmatic Treat Williams drives up in his flashy convertible, his powerful physicality and cajoling seductiveness conjuring a more dangerously appealing sexuality. This central confrontation is a mesmerising set piece, but the allegorical subtleties (is this episode real, or merely a product of Dern's wishful imagining?) work better in a literary context. Here, as elsewhere, one senses that the images are being asked to carry rather more metaphorical weight than they are able to bear. NF

Smugglers
see Kung-Fu Gangbusters

Snake Eyes
(aka Dangerous Game)
(Abel Ferrara, 1993, US) Harvey Keitel, Madonna, James Russo, Nancy Ferrara.
107 min.
When he's in the mood no one digs deeper into the emotional gut than Abel Ferrara – like *Bad Lieutenant*, this is a gruelling experience. Many will find it alienating. Keitel is a director (his wife is Nancy Ferrara) making a movie about a couple breaking up – Madonna and Russo are the stars. There's inevitable confusion between reality and illusion, but the real subject here is the battle (or rather massacre) of the sexes. TCh

Snake Fang (Dandane Mar)
(Masud Kimiai, 1990, Iran) Faramarz Sedighi, Ahmad Najafi, Golchehreh Sajjadieh.
105 min.
Since Khomeini's death, Iranian cinema has regained a lot of its former energy and unpredictability, producing movies like this bizarre mixture of frontier western and neo-realist drama. A middle-aged intellectual, poleaxed by the deaths of his mother and brother (the latter in the Iran-Iraq war), takes up residence in a seedy hotel room that he shares with a swaggering black marketeer, and gets a crash course in low-life realities. The mood of post-war anomie and desolation is caught strongly, and the director (who has twelve other features to his credit) has a keen eye for the details of crime and violence. The climactic plot twists made very little sense to me, but maybe you had to be there to understand. TR

Snake Pit, The
(Anatole Litvak, 1948, US) Olivia de Havilland, Mark Stevens, Leo Genn, Celeste Holm, Leif Erickson, Glenn Langan, Beulah Bondi, Lee Patrick, Isabel Jewell, Ruth Donnelly, Betsy Blair.
108 min. b/w.
Overrated at the time as a piece of mature and realistic cinema with a strong social conscience, this now works best as lurid melodrama. De Havilland pulls out the stops as the woman committed to a mental hospital; pronounced fit to leave before her consultant thinks she's ready, she soon returns in an even worse state, and enters the ward for the very seriously disturbed. The plea for better treatment might now seem rather muddled, given the film's advocacy of shock treatment; and the documentary-style footage inside the asylum merges poorly with the strong narrative. But it's entertaining enough in a hysterical sort of way, even if it never matches up to the excesses of Fuller's later *Shock Corridor*. GA

Snakes and Ladders
see Jeu de l'oie, Le

Snapper, The
(Stephen Frears, 1993, GB) Tina Kellegher, Colm Meaney, Ruth McCabe, Eanna MacLiam, Peter Rowen, Joanne Gerrard.
90 min.
This adaptation of Roddy Doyle's novel may not display the glitz and relentless energy of *The Commitments*, but it has wit, feeling and authenticity. The story is tougher and potentially more downbeat – a Dublin family, the Curleys, face a crisis when 20-year-old Sharon (Kellegher) finds herself pregnant but refuses to name the father – nevertheless, there's still enough laconic humour to lift it above dour urban realism. In particular, Colm Meaney shines as the warm, well-meaning dad torn by shame, anger, guilt and pride. Indeed, that tangle of emotions indicates the film's unpretentious complexity as Doyle's script charts the subtle changes in the relationships between family, friends and neighbours. While the film is less obviously feel-good than *The Commitments*, its final resolution is more thoroughly earned – and, as a result, deeply affecting. GA

Snares
see Pièges

Snatched
(aka Little Girl...Big Tease)
(Roberto Mitrotti, 1975, US) Jody Ray, Rebecca Brooks, Robert Furey, Phil Bendone, Joey Mancini, Joey Adinaro.
83 min.

'You've been fucked, and you've been fucked good, by one of the best' says kidnapper to kidnapped in this depressing piece of gym-slip rubbish. Heiress naturally falls in love with captors – the woman among them being her domestic science teacher – and proceeds to have it away with all three. That's about it, apart from mild stabs at a fetish or two, and the usual business of blowjob and rapes being performed with the trousers firmly fastened. Guarantees a high walk-out rate even on a wet afternoon. AN

Sneakers

(Phil Alden Robinson, 1992, US) Robert Redford, Dan Aykroyd, Ben Kingsley, Mary McDonnell, River Phoenix, Sidney Poitier, David Strathairn, James Earl Jones, Timothy Busfield, George Hearn, Stephen Tobolowsky.
125 min.
This is a bizarre hybrid, a hi-tech caper movie with lo-tech charm; an action pic with incongruously mellow Californian pacing; a post-Cold War thriller with sassy wit. Redford heads a team of 'sneakers' – freelance tech-heads who execute computer heists to test corporate security systems. It's basically an old folks' operation, with crusty CIA vet Poitier, wild card conspiracy nut Aykroyd, blind genius Strathairn, and McDonnell as a mature femme fatale; only Phoenix guarantees the teen market. When Redford's radical past catches up with him, so do the intelligence goons, who want him to procure a black box, the ultimate hackers' McGuffin. The plot gets twistier than a Mandelbrot curve, leading to Kingsley as a slimy master criminal. A '60s-radical alternative to the 'flying glass' action pic prevalent in Hollywood, the film is sustained by a personable ensemble who generously trade off each other rather than grandstand. Right up to an ending designed to crack the sternest critical poker-face, this is gourmet popcorn of the highest order. JRo

Sniper

(Luis Llosa, 1992, US) Tom Berenger, Billy Zane, Aden Young, Ken Radley, JT Walsh, Reinaldo Arenas.
97 min.
As action films go, Llosa's debut is more mindful than mindless. Berenger is Marine sniper Tom Beckett, a military hit-man with 74 kills under his belt and a troubled conscience squirming in his head. In partnership with greenhorn government agent Richard Miller (Zane), a training school grad with top brass plans but no field experience, his latest mission is to penetrate the jungles of post-Noriega Panama and take out a would-be right wing dictator. The smooth running of the operation is swiftly jeopardised by growing personal tensions... A virtual two-hander, the narrative proceeds by contrasting Berenger's edgy pragmatism with Zane's unwilling induction to the art of murder, though the director's inventive bullets' eye-view shots still fail to dispel the suspicion that the film has little new to say. TJ

Sniper, The

(Edward Dmytryk, 1952, US) Adolphe Menjou, Arthur Franz, Gerald Mohr, Richard Kiley, Marie Windsor, Mabel Paige.
87 min. b/w.
After a couple of years under the Hollywood blacklist cloud, Dmytryk returned to the fray with this low-budget offering for producer Stanley Kramer, shot on location in the self-consciously realist *Naked City* style then making waves. Franz doesn't quite convince as the psycho obsessively drawn to taking fatal potshots at passing brunettes, but Menjou, one of the movies' great professionals, registers his involvement as the cop on his tail. Good use of the streets of San Francisco, and you can see the film's influence on Peter Bogdanovich's rather artsier 1967 offering *Targets*. TJ

Snobs

(Jean-Pierre Mocky, 1961, Fr/Switz) Gérard Hoffmann, Véronique Nordey, Francis Blanche, Michel Lonsdale, Claude Mansard, Henri Poirier, Elina Labourdette, Noël Roquevert, Jacques Dufilho.
90 min. b/w.
An outrageous satire on the in-fighting which ensues among four possible successors when the chairman of a milk cooperative disappears down the drain of a vat. Undeniably funny, intermit-

tently at least, as it flails wildly at every conceivable target from church and army to sex and snobbery, in the hope of offending everybody. With all the characters despicable in one way or another, the aim is evidently Swiftian. But since much of the direction is dismayingly crude ('Your life...' one character starts to say – sound of family squabble starting up – 'is filled with love'), and since most of the cast tart up their caricatures with grotesquely unfunny accents, the effect as often as not is of a Gallic *Carry On*. TM

Snow Queen, The (Snezhnaya Koroleva)

(Gennadi Kazanski, 1966, USSR) Natalya Klimova, V Nikitieako, L Proklova, S Tsiupa, E Melzhnikova.
83 min.
The Snow Queen (Klimova) withers the red roses given to Kay and his sister Gerda by their teacher. She then freezes the boy's heart and abducts him to her palace in the north. Gerda to the rescue. In the original, peculiarly eerie Hans Andersen story, childish innocence and Christian love overcome evil; in this less fanciful Lenfilm adaptation (part live action, part animation), human love and an adult capacity to overcome fear do the job. Nothing is made of Andersen's significant anthropomorphism, and some tiresome knockabout dilutes the powerful storyline. JPy

Snows of Kilimanjaro, The

(Henry King, 1952, US) Gregory Peck, Susan Hayward, Ava Gardner, Hildegard Knef, Leo G Carroll, Torin Thatcher, Marcel Dalio.
117 min.
Hemingway's portrait of the artist as a romantic hero provides Twentieth Century-Fox with ample scope to meander from Africa to Paris, Spain and back again, sampling the attractions of Hayward, Gardner and Knef *en route*. Although Henry King shows some sympathy for these suppliant females, veteran screenwriter Casey Robinson's intelligent, talky adaption finally endorses the great white writer's bullish philosophy: 'Real writing is like a hunt...a life-long safari; and the prey is truth'. Framed as a deathbed reminiscence, the film does tend to ramble, and seems particularly uneven in its mixture of back-projected wildlife footage, studio and location work, while Peck's weighty Harry Street remains resolutely aloof, to the point where he will not deign to expire. TCh

Snow Was Black, The

see Neige était sale, La

Snow White and the Seven Dwarfs

(Walt Disney 1937, US)
83 min.
Disney's first animated feature takes the Grimms' fairy-tale and turns it into a generally cute fantasy for American kids: Snow White herself might be felt to be almost unbearably winsome, and the anthropomorphic characterisation of the forest creatures soon becomes tiresome. But the animation itself is top-notch, and in a number of darker sequences (Snow White's terrified entry into the forest, for example), Disney's adoption of Expressionist visual devices makes for genuinely powerful drama. Ideologically, however, what remains most intersting, as one writer has noted, is the way Walt's obvious desire to promote the American Way (off to work we go, indeed!) is married – presumably unthinkingly – to a virtual celebration of polygamy in which, moreover, it is a woman, not a man, who lives with seven members of the opposite sex! GA

Snow White: A Tale of Terror

(Michael Cohn, 1996, GB/US) Sigourney Weaver, Sam Neill, Gil Bellows, Taryn Davis, David Conrad, Brian Glover, Monica Keena, Bryan Pringle.
100 min.
Stripped of Grand Guignol theatricality and the usual sentimentality, Weaver's 'straight' wicked stepmother and Neill's caring, if ineffectual father stress the sheer unattractiveness of the roles in this adult fairytale. Putting the Grimm back in the story is not necessarily a bad thing, but here the makers provide insufficient atmosphere or developed characterisation to satisfy grown-ups. The film plays like light Hammer horror with

inappropriate period finery and design. The script goes the cod Freudian route, with Weaver's actions explained by postnatal depression and grief (accompanied by lots of menstrual imagery), her narcissistic fear of ageing, her unhealthy relationship with her mute brother, and the baggage she brings with her, notably the armoire with its gigantic looking glass. Monica Keena's Lilli/Snow White is a problem. A lightweight, pretty actress, she seems too insignificant to raise her stepmother's vengeful jealousy, and you couldn't care less about her rites of passage. WH

Soapdish

(Michael Hoffman, 1991, US) Sally Field, Kevin Kline, Robert Downey Jr, Whoopi Goldberg, Carrie Fisher, Cathy Moriarty, Teri Hatcher, Paul Johansson, Elizabeth Shue, Garry Marshall.
97 min.
Celeste (Field) is getting all the awards for her performance in a tacky daytime soap, 'The Sun Also Sets', and the rest of the cast naturally despise her. Meanwhile, co-star Montana (Moriarty) teases the producer (Downey) with seductive talk; and in a bid to sabotage Celeste's character in the soap, these two scheme to bring back Celeste's real-life ex-lover (Kline), last seen in the series minus his head. His arrival leaves the star teetering between rage and insanity; and when his charm snares Celeste's actress niece (Shue), the trio start to enact genuine dramas live on the air. Nothing succeeds like excess, this comedy would have us believe. But the thwarted egos, rampant libidos, and starry cast – while wonderful at first – begin to look frayed around halfway through. CM

S.O.B.

(Blake Edwards, 1981, US) Julie Andrews, William Holden, Richard Mulligan, Robert Vaughn, Robert Webber, Robert Preston, Larry Hagman, Shelley Winters, Marisa Berenson, Loretta Swit, Stuart Margolin, Rosanna Arquette, Craig Stevens, Robert Loggia, Larry Storch.
121 min.
Though, like many of Edwards' films, it lurches uncertainly from slapstick farce to mordant humour in an extremely hit-or-miss fashion, this surprisingly bitter satire on Tinseltown – in which a producer (Mulligan) beefs up his latest turkey of a movie by introducing some pornographic sex scenes and having his wife/star (Andrews) bare her breasts on screen – does hit the mark once or twice. That said, it seems more like an expectorant for Edwards' bile than an entertainment aimed at an audience. NF

Society

(Brian Yuzna, 1989, US) Bill Warlock, Devin DeVasquez, Evan Richards, Ben Meyerson, Charles Lucia, Connie Danese, Patrice Jennings, Heidi Kozak, Ben Slack, Tim Bartell.
99 min.
A bizarre fable that starts like a TV soap but soon darkens into a disturbing thriller about an idyllic Beverly Hills community where something is subtly skewed. Handsome teenager Bill (Warlock) feels uncomfortable with his affluent peers. But the usual teen insecurities take on a more sinister aspect when his sister's ex-boyfriend Blanchard plays him a clandestine recording of her 'coming out' party which suggests perverse, incestuous sexual initiation; but when Bill's shrink later plays the tape back to him, he hears only innocuous conversation. How does this connect with rich kid Ted's exclusive teen clique, or Blanchard's death in a road accident? Is there a dark conspiracy, or is Bill losing his marbles? First-time director Yuzna is happier with the sly humour and clever plot shifts than with the appropriately iconic but sometimes dramatically unconvincing cast. He nevertheless generates a compelling sense of paranoid unease, and shifts into F/X overdrive for an unforgettable horror finale. Suffice it to say that the 'surrealistic make-up designs' by Screaming Mad George (who did the cockroach sequence in *Nightmare on Elm Street 4*) will stretch even the most inelastic mind. NF

So Dark the Night

(Joseph H Lewis, 1946, US) Steven Geray, Micheline Cheirel, Eugene Borden, Ann Codee, Egon Brecher, Helen Freeman.
70 min. b/w.

This is what Joseph H Lewis is all about. The script is a perfunctory and frequently silly murder mystery, with an ending that's equal parts cod-Freud and O.Henry. Furthermore, it is set in a ludicrous evocation of France, most embarrassing in the opening scenes in Paris, but still irritating when the plot takes the police inspector hero (Geray) into the country to romance with an innkeeper's daughter (Cheirel) who yearns for the Big City. However, none of this matters. The film is directed like a million bucks. Visually, it compares with *The Big Combo* as one of Lewis' purest *noir* achievements; beyond that, it has more cinematic ideas and effects per square foot of screen than any number of contemporary A features. In other words, it's a 'typical' Lewis movie: low on things, but with enough style to send lovers of cinema reeling. TR

Sodom and Gomorrah (Sodoma e Gomorra)

(Robert Aldrich, 1962, It/Fr) Stewart Granger, Anouk Aimée, Stanley Baker, Pier Angeli, Rossana Podesta, Claudia Mori, Daniele Vargas, Rik Battaglia.
153 min.
A low point in Aldrich's erratic career, this tale of Lot's dealings with the treacherous inhabitants of the twin cities of evil never lives up to its first line of dialogue, in which a beautiful spy is warned to 'Beware of the Sodomites', who come up and capture her from behind. Sin is suggested by languid groups of people, nattily dressed in '60s evening gowns, lolling around on the floor, while the virtuous Hebrews look more like a bunch of self-sufficient drongos droning on about making the land fertile. Granger's Lot wields a mighty staff, Anouk is as charmingly beautiful as ever as the evil Queen of Sodom, and Baker gets by on leering at every woman who comes near. Watchable for Ken Adam's sets, though God's final destruction of the cities is very tacky. They don't make 'em like this any more. GA

So Evil My Love

(Lewis Allen, 1948, GB) Ray Milland, Ann Todd, Geraldine Fitzgerald, Raymond Huntley, Martita Hunt, Leo G Carroll, Raymond Lovell, Moira Lister, Finlay Currie, Hugh Griffith.
109 min. b/w.
A not uninteresting offshoot from the *noir* cycle, made by Paramount in Britain and derived from a factually-based novel by Joseph Shearing, who specialised in Victorian Gothic (*Moss Rose, Blanche Fury*). Lots of loving period frills as Milland, a caddish charmer taking over the *femme fatale* role, lures a missionary's staid widow into (literally) letting her hair down, then wantonly sets her on the path to blackmail and murder. Allen's bleakly measured direction (he made the wonderfully atmospheric *The Uninvited*) is unfortunately tipped towards dullness by somewhat bland characterisations from Todd and Milland. TM

Sofie

(Liv Ullmann, 1992, Den) Karen-Lise Mynster, Ghita Norby, Erland Josephson.
146 min.
Denmark, 1886. 29-year-old Sofie lives with her affluent, extended Jewish family, but her happiness is marred by parental fears that she will become a spinster. Despite her love for a gentile painter, she is manoeuvred into marriage with a respectable Jewish cousin... Ullmann's directorial debut is marked by an attention to fussy period detail and rigorous, symmetrical framing, which convey a sense of repression; but combined with a running-time of nearly two-and-a-half hours, this leaves the film somewhat airless. Most impressive are the sensitive performances she elicits from her cast, especially Mynster (as Sofie) and Josephson (as her father). CM

So Fine

(Andrew Bergman, 1981, US) Ryan O'Neal, Jack Warden, Mariangela Melato, Richard Kiel, Fred Gwynne.
91 min.
On the long list of comedy ideas screenwriters should never have had, this film must rank high. O'Neal reprises his performance from *What's Up, Doc?*, here cast as a *klutz* of a college professor co-opted to revive his father's ailing rag-trade business when he accidentally hits upon a craze in

denims. The gimmick is jeans with see-through derrière, and most of the humour on display in this would-be screwball comedy has an inanity which follows suit with this central conceit. Directing his own script, Bergman executes his knowing movie references – O'Neal as Cary Grant, embarrassed in improvised drag; a nod toward the lustful satire of Tashlin's *The Girl Can't Help It*; a Marx Brothers-inspired night at the opera finale – with a kind of vulgar energy that does little to decorate his otherwise threadbare sitcom material. RM

Soft Beds, Hard Battles

(Roy Boulting, 1973, GB) Peter Sellers, Lila Kedrova, Curd Jürgens, Béatrice Romand, Jenny Hanley, Françoise Pascal, Gabriella Licudi, Rula Lenska, Timothy West, Thorley Walters.
107 min.
A wretchedly titled offering in the Boulting Brothers' compulsively satirical vein, largely set in a brothel in occupied Paris, with Kedrova and Jürgens typecast as the sentimental madame and a friendly German officer, and the gorgeous Béatrice Romand wasted as Madame's innocent niece. But its *raison d'être* is Peter Sellers, back in brilliant form as six variations on blinkered authority, including Hitler and a De Gaulle-ish French general, but particularly as the Gestapo chief Schroeder, limping-cum-strutting from disaster to disaster, an extraordinary amalgam of Dr Strangelove and Fred Kite. Worth a visit for Sellers and one classic joke about a PoW. SG

Soft on the Inside

(Katy Radford, 1990, GB) Andy Sheppard.
46 min.
A nicely done concert film featuring the 15-piece band British saxophonist Andy Sheppard put together for a short tour of France and Britain. The band, composed of soloists from all over the world (nutter drummer Hans Bennink, Gary Valente's superb trombone, the inspired Peruvian guitarist Manc Ventura among them), perform four songs for Sheppard's eponymous new album. Intercut is the usual on-the-road commentary, of the 'So-and-so's a wild and crazy guy and I've always wanted to play with him' kind, here done with a minimum of pretentiousness. Sheppard says he prefers 'inside' players. He certainly gets them cooking. WH

Soft Skin, The

see Peau Douce, La

Soft Top, Hard Shoulder

(Stefan Schwartz, 1992, GB) Peter Capaldi, Elaine Collins, Richard Wilson, Frances Barber, Phyllis Logan, Simon Callow, Catherine Russell, Jeremy Northam.
95 min.
Having failed to make it in London as a comic-book artist, Gavin Bellini (Capaldi) – an Italian-Glaswegian from an ice-cream dynasty – reluctantly yields to his uncle's demands that he return home for his dad's sixtieth birthday party; if he makes it, the uncle (Wilson) may give him a share of the family fortune. But as he heads north in his worn-out Triumph convertible, Gavin meets countless obstacles. When the car breaks down, hitcher Yvonne (Collins) helps to get it going, but Gavin soon tires of her company. Worse, he loses his wallet, and their progress becomes ever slower. Will Gavin reach the party on time? Can he and his feisty passenger put aside their differences? The echoes of *It Happened One Night* and Bill Forsyth's comedies are rather too strong, but Capaldi's script has its fair share of engagingly offbeat one-liners, and the characters are deftly sketched. The ending doesn't convince, and Schwartz's direction is erratic, but overall this is a modestly enjoyable comedy. GA

Soigne ta Droite

(Jean-Luc Godard, 1986, Fr/Switz) Jean-Luc Godard, Jacques Villeret, François Périer, Jane Birkin, Dominique Lavanant, Michel Galabru, Rufus, Eva Darlan, Isabelle Sadoyan, Les Rita Mitsouko.
81 min.
The relationship between Godard and his audience has for ages been that of teacher and pupil, with Godard the invariably foul-tempered prof, and his audience the recalcitrant C stream, regarded as bringing nothing to the encounter

except their own shortcomings. This is modified in those films where Godard is an on-screen participant: teacher starring in the school play. Here his role is a film director, referred to as 'The Idiot', who'll make any rubbish assigned him, and who Godard renders via a rather good imitation of Harry Langdon (or possibly Pee-Wee Herman). The film comprises a series of charades (as opposed to 'scenes') which never achieve a middle ground between the over-obvious and the over-obscure. (Air travel as a metaphor for – what? Life?) As in *One Plus One* much time is spent with a bunch of musicians trying to get their sound right. But the hail of allusions, quotes and gnomic declarations seldom coalesce into more than a groan of schoolmasterly dissatisfaction over things in general. BBa

So I Married an Axe Murderer

(Thomas Schlamme, 1993, US) Mike Myers, Nancy Travis, Anthony LaPaglia, Brenda Fricker, Charles Grodin, Alan Arkin.
92 min.
Myers (half of the *Wayne's World* duo) takes a giant step for nerdkind in this less than subtle Hitchcock spoof, which aims a blunderbuss at serial killers, multi-lingual lounge singers, and the Queen Mother. While buying haggis for his bizarre Scottish family, Myers meets butcher's assistant Travis. Despite an aversion to long-term relationships, he falls for her hook, line and sinker – until he begins to suspect that she may be a deadly serial marrier who has already claimed three victims. The crass Scots jokes are irresistible; Alan Arkin's cameo as a mild-mannered police chief is sheer perfection; and the cultish references to Beat poetry should please slumming hipsters. Like an exploding haggis, funny but extremely messy. NF

Solarbabies (aka Solarwarriors)

(Alan Johnson, 1986, US) Richard Jordan, Jami Gertz, Jason Patric, Lukas Haas, Charles Durning.
94 min.
All-purpose sci-fi rip-off, set on a planet where evil Jordan lords it over a cadre of roller-skating minor brat-packers who call on ancient mystical force – 'Bodhi' – to escape his sway. A misbegotten Brooksfilm which sank without trace in the US. Director Johnson remains best known for staging the 'Springtime for Hitler' routine in *The Producers*.

Solaris

(Andrei Tarkovsky, 1972, USSR) Donatas Banionis, Natalya Bondarchuk, Yuri Jarvet, Anatoli Solonitsin, Vladislav Dvorjetzki.
165 min.
Apparently conceived as a socialist response to *2001: A Space Odyssey*, Tarkovsky's film in fact offers only the flabbiest kind of sentimental humanism by way of a riposte to Kubrick. It starts out promising both poetry (of the Dovzhenko Ukrainian school) and dialectics (of the Marxist school?), and proceeds to squander both on kindergarten psychology and inane melodrama. Its hero journeys into space only as a metaphor for a journey inward; after 2 hours, he's got no further than the lap of his father, which he rejected ten years earlier. Watching Tarkovsky render the sci-fi mechanics of his own movie redundant as he goes along is a genuinely brain-freezing experience. TR

Solarwarriors

see Solarbabies

Sol del Membrillo, El

see Quince Tree Sun, The

Soldier, The (aka Codename: The Soldier)

(James Glickenhaus, 1983, US) Ken Wahl, Alberta Watson, Klaus Kinski, William Prince, Jeremiah Sullivan.
96 min.
The credits signal 'world politics' to Tangerine Dream, the opening carnage disposes of a KGB hit squad by judicious use of the posed square jaw and helicopters. The Soldier is a secret, extra-legal square jaw, with what the Russians (the bald ones chewing toothpicks) term an 'unusual-

ly broad charter'. Glickenhaus' *The Exterminator* at least gave us a witty and reluctant killer with an understandable grudge and modest ambitions. Here nothing less than global salvation will do: kidnapped nuclear stuff, oilfields threatened, Middle East crisis, Mossad sex interest, Moscow implicated – the kind of nonsense best left to real puppets in *Thunderbirds*. RP

Soldier and the Lady, The

see Adventures of Michael Strogoff, The

Soldier Blue

(Ralph Nelson, 1970, US) Candice Bergen, Peter Strauss, Donald Pleasence, Bob Carraway, Jorge Rivero, Dana Elcar, John Anderson.
114 min.
A grimly embarrassing anti-racist Western about the US Cavalry's notorious Sand Creek Indian massacre in 1864. In the interests of propaganda, one might just about stomach the way the massacre itself is turned into a gleefully exploitative gore-fest of blood and amputated limbs; but not when it's associated with a desert romance that's shot like an ad-man's wet dream, all soft focus and sweet nothings. To complete the rout, the script has an unerring instinct for cliché. 'Why, why, why?' yells the appalled hero. Box-office, is the curt answer. TM

Soldier Girls

(Nicholas Broomfield/Joan Churchill, 1980, US) 87 min.
For their second American documentary, British film-makers Broomfield and Churchill took on the US Army, following three women recruits through induction and basic training. They learn the marching chant 'Kill, maim, rape, pillage', how to bite the head off a chicken, and how to accept/subvert the repressive machine of the military that still believes it was cheated of victory in Vietnam and is guaranteed to win the next war. An object lesson in the mechanisms of patriarchal power-play that is by turns appalling, amusing and amazing. MA

Soldier's Story, A

(Norman Jewison, 1984, US) Howard E Rollins Jr, Adolph Caesar, Art Evans, David Alan Grier, David Harris, Dennis Lipscomb, Denzel Washington.
101 min.
From the man who brought you *In the Heat of the Night*, another spotlessly liberal look at racial problems, again in the Deep South. This time it's a question of murder as, back in 1944, Rollins' Poitier-style army captain is called in to investigate the killing of a black sergeant (Caesar) on a military base. Here the subject is less racial hatred between whites and blacks than problems with racial identity: what it means to be black in a white man's world. Nothing very original, to be sure, and the film's theatrical origins are clear from both the wordy script and the intense performances. But Rollins' charisma works wonders, and Jewison reveals enough solid professionalism in the deft handling of flashbacks to make it gripping entertainment. GA

Sole anche di notte, Il

see Night Sun

Soleil des Hyénes

see Hyenas' Sun

Soleil trompeur

see Burnt by the Sun

Solid Gold Cadillac, The

(Richard Quine, 1956, US) Judy Holliday, Paul Douglas, Fred Clark, John Williams, Arthur O'Connell, Neva Patterson, Ray Collins.
99 min. b/w.
Several classic Hollywood notions combine here: that capitalism is tickety-boo as long as businessmen aren't corrupt, that one dumb broad can defeat the wiliest crooks in the business, that a male and a female goody will inevitably fall in love. With the rallying cry of 'Somebody's got to keep an eye on these big businesses', Judy Holliday, in a variation on the part that made her in *Born Yesterday*, takes on the wicked businessmen and rallies Middle America behind her. It's pernicious, but fun. SG

Solitaire for 2

(Gary Sinyor, 1994, GB) Mark Frankel, Amanda Pays, Roshan Seth, Jason Isaacs, Maryam D'Abo, Helen Lederer, Annette Crosbie.
106 min.
Daniel Becker (Frankel) knows all the right moves. A management consultant on body language and behavioural science, and the author of a self-help manual, he's a dab hand at manipulating people. Especially women. Then he meets beautiful palaeontologist Katie Burrill (Pays), and suddenly he can't put a foot right. She sees through his every ploy, beats him to every punchline, almost as if she can read his mind. In fact, that's exactly what she's doing. The question is: can Daniel make it up? It's a fantastic idea for a screwball comedy, but writer/director Sinyor's first solo effort after the *Leon the Pig Farmer* collaboration doesn't entirely come off. The fault is less with the script – which is packed with sharp observations and promising comic set-ups – than with the hit-or-miss direction. Some subtle scenes prove unduly tentative, while more physical sequences veer towards the inflated buffoonery of sit-com land. For all that, it's a convivial entertainment, with enough wit and imagination to bode well for Sinyor's future. TCh

Soliti Ignoti, I (Big Deal on Madonna Street/Persons Unknown)

(Mario Monicelli, 1958, It) Vittorio Gassman, Renato Salvatori, Marcello Mastroianni, Toto, Memmo Carotenuto, Claudia Cardinale.
105 min. b/w.
A charming comedy, perhaps a little *déjà vu* after countless imitations and variations culminating in Louis Malle's distinctly iffy 1983 remake as *Crackers*. Countering the famous sequence in *Rififi* which observed in meticulous detail the perfect execution of a robbery, Monicelli offers a robbery equally meticulously planned (by a sad sack mix of desperate unemployed and washed-up pros) in which everything goes hilariously wrong. It may not sound much, but Monicelli's timing (giving the series of disasters an almost malevolent inevitability) is brilliant, the ensemble playing couldn't be bettered, and the deliberate cartoon-style stereotyping of the characters is neatly offset by a neo-realist emphasis on real locations in the dank slums of Rome. TM

So Little Time

(Compton Bennett, 1952, GB) Maria Schell, Marius Goring Gabrielle Dorziat, Barbara Mullen, John Bailey, Lucie Mannheim Harold Lang.
88 min. b/w.
A World War II movie set in Occupied Belgium which has a marginally unusual plot. It's about a good German officer, Colonel von Hohensee (Goring), who is appointed military governor of Brussels, and falls in love with a Belgian girl, Nicole (Schell). After a time, Nicole is approached by the gangster-type Resistance movement and told to steal some documents, but she finds Hohensee considerably more sympathetic...There were protests when the movie first came out, and it's certainly refreshing to find this kind of inversion (Nazi humanitarian versus cruel 'freedom fighters') in a British film, even though it remains on a naïve level. DP

Solomon and Sheba

(King Vidor, 1959, US) Yul Brynner, Gina Lollobrigida, George Sanders, Marisa Pavan, David Farrar, John Crawford, Laurence Naismith, Alejandro Rey, Harry Andrews.
142 min.
The Bible's sultriest couple, bar Samson and Delilah, deserve better than this empty Super Technirama epic. There's so much visual padding (feathers, armour, redundant crowd scenes) it's hard to focus on the romance. Lollobrigida does her pouting best, but she's no Gloria Swanson. Tyrone Power, the original Solomon, died halfway through production; Brynner, his replacement, is decidedly ill at ease. More fun to tuck up with the Old Testament. GM

So Long at the Fair

(Terence Fisher/Anthony Darnborough, 1950, GB) Jean Simmons, Dirk Bogarde, David Tomlinson, Honor Blackman, Cathleen Nesbitt, Felix Aylmer, Marcel Poncin, Eugene Deckers, Austin Trevor.
86 min. b/w.
A visitor to the Paris World Fair of 1889 vanishes overnight, along with his hotel room and all traces of his existence. An appropriate training ground for Fisher's later ventures into horror, but his opportunities for exploring the macabre are restricted here by the demands of an insipid romance between Simmons, as the disappearing man's distraught sister, and Bogarde as the English artist who believes her story. Simmons is too sweet and self-assured to inspire more than mild concern for her predicament, and Bogarde's potential for debonair caddishness remains sadly unfulfilled in the face of his partner's redoubtable innocence. Enthusiasm has to be reserved for the period trappings, a clever Offenbach-ish score, and the fine support playing of Nesbitt, Blackman and Poncin. RMy

Somebody Killed Her Husband

(Lamont Johnson, 1978, US) Farrah Fawcett-Majors, Jeff Bridges, John Wood, Tammy Grimes, John Glover, Patricia Elliott.
97 min.
Good comic acting might have pumped some life into this leaden comedy-thriller scripted by Reginald Rose, a tale of cutesy lovers secreting hubby's corpse in the fridge while tracking the killer who's framed them. But Jeff Bridges is given a nigh-impossible brief (he responds by breathing heavily to convey panic), while Farrah Fawcett-Majors, in her big screen debut, proves predictably inadequate to the task of impersonating Goldie Hawn (let alone Myrna Loy), and simply flashes her teeth at regular intervals. Charmless and dispiriting, the film incidentally elevates word (Bridges sidelines as a writer) over image (cinemas are places to go to annoy other patrons) to confirm its own redundancy. PT

Somebody to Love

(Alexandre Rockwell, 1994, US) Rosie Perez, Harvey Keitel, Anthony Quinn, Michael DeLorenzo, Steve Buscemi, Stanley Tucci, Sam Fuller, Quentin Tarantino.
102 min
Rockwell's shambolic follow-up to *In the Soup* fails to confirm whatever promise the earlier film suggested. Mercedes, an LA taxi dancer, steps on a few toes in her determination to make it big in pictures. She has a thing going with a one-time bit-part actor (Keitel), but can't entirely resist the innocent courtship of a Mexican immigrant labourer (DeLorenzo). When it falls to a benevolent old gangster (Quinn) to play cupid, it's pretty clear we're back 'In the Soup'. Rockwell favours long takes and authentic locations, but his movie stumbles from one actory moment to the next: Keitel in a gorilla suit, Buscemi in drag. At times the film feels like a throwback to the '60s New Wave, with its Sam Fuller cameo and nods to Fellini, at others it resembles one long Rosie Perez audition tape (she sings! she dances! she does improv!). It's a credit to Perez that the story holds together at all (she can practise elocution brushing her teeth with a book on her head, and make it seem natural), but the film's occasional virtues don't survive a prevailing sense of self-indulgence. TCh

Somebody Up There Likes Me

(Robert Wise, 1956, US) Paul Newman, Pier Angeli, Everett Sloane, Sal Mineo, Eileen Heckart, Robert Loggia, Harold J Stone, Steve McQueen.
113 min. b/w.
A disappointing biopic of Rocky Graziano, East Side delinquent turned World Middleweight Champion. The trouble is that Wise forsakes the terse economy and unpretentious naturalism of *The Set-Up* for a rather straggling narrative which spends far too long throwing up mildly socially-conscious observations about poverty, and trying to turn the whole thing into a movie with a message about hope and determination. It's still not that bad a film, however. Newman's performance, though inflected by Method mannerisms, is powerful, and Joseph Ruttenberg's photography keeps the atmosphere sleazy and strong. Perhaps the main problem is the fact that it is a biopic, thus demanding an uplifting ending which seems to go against the grain of the romantic pessimism that governs the boxing genre. GA

Some Call It Loving

(James B Harris, 1973, US) Zalman King, Carol White, Tisa Farrow, Richard Pryor, Veronica Anderson, Logan Ramsey.
103 min.

Wonderfully bizarre fantasy, based on a John Collier short story, about a world-weary jazz musician (King) obsessed with the dream of innocence incarnated by a carnival sleeping beauty (Farrow) whom he buys, takes back to his baroque Californian mansion (already inhabited by two ambivalently voluptuous women), and awakens for a haunting game of death and love betrayed. Conceived by Harris after working with Kubrick on the script of *Lolita*, it works as a kind of free jazz improvisation (there is a marvellous score by Richard Hazard), and might be described as a further exploration of what Nabokov's Humbert Humbert called his 'petrified paroxysm of desire'. Unmissable for anyone with an open mind and a sense of cinematic adventure. TM

Some Came Running

(Vincente Minnelli, 1958, US) Frank Sinatra, Dean Martin, Shirley MacLaine, Martha Hyer, Arthur Kennedy, Nancy Gates, Leora Dana.
136 min.

A marvellous, garish drama about a writer (Sinatra) returning from the war to the small town he grew up in, *Some Came Running* is probably best remembered for the reference in Godard's *Le Mépris*. Like Godard's, it's a contrived film, populated by types rather than characters: Martha Hyer = conformity, Shirley MacLaine = freedom, Dean Martin = conformity. Minnelli's great achievement is the superbly orchestrated intensity of feelings the central characters generate in their various clashes. As a result, the dramatic curve of Sinatra's agonising voyage of self-discovery through the cheap neon-lit bars and cold houses, which ends in the clam of self-acceptance, is given an intensified realism which precisely reflects the neurotic 'writerly' view of life that he must overcome before he can write again. PH

Some Girls (aka Sisters)

(Michael Hoffman, 1988, US) Patrick Dempsey, Jennifer Connelly, Sheila Kelley, Lance Edwards, Lila Kedrova, Florinda Bolkan, André Gregory, Ashley Greenfield.
93 min.

Michael (Dempsey) arrives in Quebec to spend Christmas with his girlfriend (Connelly), but no sooner has he stepped through the imposing door of the family mansion than she tells him she no longer loves him. Thus a chain of peculiar incidents is set in motion, with Michael an innocent among eccentrics. Dad (Gregory) is an intellectual who wanders the house naked, Mum (Bolkan) is a strict Catholic, Granny (Kedrova) mistakes Michael for her dead husband, and the sisters (Kelly, Greenfield) share a strange bond which translates into a common desire for their confused visitor. A number of interesting ideas are thrown up but never fully developed. Instead, we get teen comedy laden with plenty of Adult Atmosphere. To its credit, the film is well cast and boasts imaginative production design, but is neither particularly funny nor emotionally credible. CM

Some Kinda Love (Romance)

(Shunichi Nagasaki, 1995, Jap) Koji Tamaki, LaSalle Ishii, Kaori Mizushima, Shinya Tsukamoto, Takeshi Naito, Chikako Aoyama.
94 min.

Two former classmates (one a town hall planner, the other a less than high minded property developer) have their lives turned upside down by close encounters with Kiriko (Mizushima), a charming flake whose obsession with UFOs somehow matches her inability to stay in one place for long. Probably too light to be a real *Jules et Jim* for the 1990s; it needs more of the darker colourings Nagasaki brings to most of his films. But it has many pleasures, including cameos from *Tetsuo* director Shinya Tsukamoto as a corruptible bureaucrat and Nagasaki veteran Takeshi Naito as Kiriko's hapless husband, a forlorn but stoic dentist. TR

Some Kind of Hero

(Michael Pressman, 1981, US) Richard Pryor, Margot Kidder, Ray Sharkey, Ronny Cox, Lynne Moody, Olivia Cole, Paul Benjamin.
97 min.

A minor but infinitely more appealing comedy vehicle for Pryor than the earlier *Stir Crazy*. He plays a hapless PoW returning from Vietnam to find he can't draw his army pay, his wife has fallen for someone else, his business is bankrupt, and a stroke has left his mother with only one word in her vocabulary: 'Shit!' What follows could easily have been mawkish drivel, but Pryor is one of the great exponents of comic masochism, and is able to make even such ancient set pieces as the timid bank robber passably funny. Kidder pitches into the comparatively feeble role of a high-class hooker with her usual exuberance, and the result is an amiable but hardly memorable two-against-the-world farce that can't quite persuade you Pryor's talents are being properly used. DP

Some Kind of Love

see Some Kinda Love

Some Kind of Life

(Julian Jarrold, 1995, GB) Jane Horrocks, Ray Stevenson, Gwen Taylor, Andrew Tiernan.
102 min.

A low-key tale, funded by Granada TV, of a woman's struggle to rebuild her life after husband Steve, a mechanic, is brain-damaged in a motorcycle accident. Alison (Horrocks) has to fight for compensation and fend off over-protective parents, but she also has to stop Steve (Stevenson) initiating food fights with the young son whose mental age he now shares. Before long, she's considering what she wants. Not without clichés, but the performances are unfussy and a Kay Mellor's screenplay avoids 'issue drama' dreariness. JO'C

Some Kind of Wonderful

(Howard Deutch, 1987, US) Eric Stoltz, Mary Stuart Masterson, Lea Thompson, Craig Sheffer, John Ashton, Elias Koteas, Molly Hagan.
93 min.

Who said John Hughes doesn't have artistic integrity? When preview audiences threw out his misfit romance in favour of preppie love at the end of *Pretty in Pink* (which Deutch also directed), Hughes sat right down and wrote the story again – this time with Stoltz in the Molly Ringwald role, Masterson as Jon Cryer, and Thompson as Andrew McCarthy. And this time it ends with the underdogs together. Oddly enough, it's this conclusion that feels phony, seeing as Stoltz has spent the last 80 minutes arranging his dream date with Lea. Watch the opening title sequence for a handy summation of the teen movie's staple ingredients: class, sex, music. TCh

Some Like It Hot [100] (100)

(Billy Wilder, 1959, US) Tony Curtis, Jack Lemmon, Marilyn Monroe, Joe E Brown, George Raft, Pat O'Brien, Nehemiah Persoff, Joan Shawlee.
121 min. b/w.

Still one of Wilder's funniest satires, its pace flagging only once for a short time. Curtis and Lemmon play jazz musicians on the run after witnessing the St Valentine's Day massacre, masquerading in drag as members of an all-girl band (with resulting gender confusions involving Marilyn) to escape the clutches of Chicago mobster George Raft (bespatted and dime-flipping, of course). Deliberately shot in black-and-white to avoid the pitfalls of camp or transvestism, though the best sequences are the gangland ones anyhow. Highlights include Curtis's playboy parody of Cary Grant, and what is surely one of the great curtain lines of all time: Joe E Brown's bland 'Nobody's perfect' when his fiancée (Lemmon) finally confesses that she's a he. RM

Some Mother's Son

(Terry George, 1996, Ire/US) Helen Mirren, Fionnula Flanagan, Aidan Gillen, John Lynch, David O'Hara, Tom Hollander, Tim Woodward, Ciaran Hinds, Gerard McSorley.
111 min.

As the title suggests, this film about the 1981 Republican Hunger Strikes, by Belfast-born writer/director Terry George, is more interested in human emotions than political manoeuvring. Ten men starved themselves to death when the IRA prisoners' strategic request for 'political' status came up against the Thatcher administration's determined 'criminalisation' of the terrorists. Into that grinding head-to-head, we follow two very different mothers whose boys are part of the protest. Mirren's Kathleen Quigley is a quiet middle-class widow, shocked by the conviction of her eldest son Gerard (Gillen) for murdering a British soldier, while Flanagan's Annie Higgins, from staunch Republican stock, takes pride in her son Frank (O'Hara), when he's arrested after the same incident. Detailing their contrasting responses to a traumatic situation allows the film to tap unpartisan sympathy while keeping its own counsel on the terminal machinations of the ideologues on both sides. Performances scar the screen, while George shows keen organisational instinct and delivers the urgent immediacy of news footage throughout. IRA propaganda it is not. Instead, it's a plea for simple humanity over ideological point-scoring, an urgent message even yet, no matter that the film seems to expose old wounds. Of all the films to have come out of the Troubles, this one offers the most complex analysis and cuts the deepest. TJ

Someone at the Door

(Herbert Brenon, 1936, GB) Billy Milton, Aileen Marson, Noah Beery, Edward Chapman, John Irwin, Hermione Gingold.
74 min. b/w.

Brenon was a leading Hollywood director in the '20s, working with the likes of Theda Bara and Ronald Colman. But his career fizzled with the coming of sound. He couldn't see it lasting. By the time he pulled his head out of the sand, there was no work left, so he returned to his native England and made a series of lively but forgettable comedies. This is a prime example of British Brenon, a creaky but well-crafted comic thriller (from a play by Dorothy and Campbell Christie) about a mischievous journalist who fabricates a murder mystery to further his career. GM

Someone Else's America
(L'Amérique des autres)

(Goran Paskaljevic, 1996, Fr/GB/Ger) Tom Conti, Miki Manojlovic, Maria Casarès, Zorka Manojlovic, Sergej Trifunovic.
96 min.

This Euro pudding film, made by a Belgrade-born director, finds a corner of low-rent New York that is forever the Old Country. In the backyard of Brooklyn's Paradiso bar, the blind mother of the Spanish owner, Alonso, draws water each morning from a well and milks the goat. When the family of Montenegran odd-job man Bayo eventually gains illegal entry to the US, his mum isn't so immediately at home, but ne'er-do-well eldest boy Luka gets right into the enterprise spirit and starts creating a future everyone can build on. This sentimental, deeply unpersuasive look at the immigrant's lot, dies virtually the minute Conti ambles on as Alonso, reprising his caricature Greek fisherman from *Shirley Valentine*. Almost as bad is the Brooklyn backdrop rigged up in a Hamburg studio, which resembles nothing so much as a set for *Sesame Street*. TJ

Someone Is Bleeding

see Seins de glace, Les

Someone to Love

(Henry Jaglom, 1987, US) Orson Welles, Henry Jaglom, Andrea Marcovicci, Michael Emil, Sally Kellerman, Oja Kodar, Stephen Bishop, Dave Frishberg.
105 min.

Having re-lived, in *Always*, the dissolution of his own marriage, Jaglom here confronts the dilemma of post-marital solitude: try again, or opt for autonomy? Film-maker Danny (Jaglom) wants to settle down, but girlfriend Helen (Marcovicci, Jaglom's real-life girlfriend) is reluctant to surrender her independence. Curious why so many of his peers live alone, Danny hosts a party in an abandoned theatre, and invites his guests to open up for the camera. Only Jaglom/Danny's friend and mentor Orson Welles – his last performance – injects some objectivity into the proceedings. Orson's observations on film, feminism ('the great revolution of our times'), marriage etc. are as wittily perceptive as one might expect; but our Henry lacks any proper perspective on his own reactionary mores, and seems as ill-equipped as Danny to divorce life from the movies. As an exercise in creative editing and a sociological document, the film is occasionally fascinating; but its endless romantic confessions and airhead philosophising make you want to scream. GA

Someone to Watch Over Me

(Ridley Scott, 1987, US) Tom Berenger, Mimi Rogers, Lorraine Bracco, Jerry Orbach, John Rubinstein, Andreas Katsulas.
106 min.

Most of New York, indoors and out, looks about as good as the Chrysler Building in Scott's gleaming fusion of eternal triangle and killer-on-the-loose. Happily married cop Berenger is assigned to protect a key witness to a murder, wealthy Upper East Side socialite Rogers, and they fall in love. She has class, he has none. Would a slob and a snob go for each other? Well, possibly, since his professionally protective side is involved, and her poise is replaced by fear for her life. It is beautifully played, and the restaurant scene in which the honest cop finds himself unable to lie to his wife (Bracco) shudders with shame, dread, pain and helplessness. You feel for all three of them. There are splendid economies, too: Rogers' mirrored dressing-room registers first as a social humiliation for the cop, who can't find the exit, but later his intimacy with her surroundings gives him an edge over a killer. There's little waste, though the thriller element could have been tuned up a bit. BC

Somersault in a Coffin
(Tabutta Rövasata)

(Dervis Zaim, 1996, Tur) Ahmet Ugurlu, Tuncel Kurtiz, Aysen Aydemir, Serif Erol, Fuat Onan.
76 min.

This no-budget first feature from a Cyprus-born director is very likely the best Turkish movie of the 1990s. Mahsun (Ugurlu, a distinguished stage actor) is an alcoholic and a street sleeper, known to the Istanbul cops as an expert car thief. Essentially a picaresque account of this human wreck's exploits, which include a turbulent relationship with a junkie prostitute and the theft of a peacock from a national park, the film uses Mahsun as an index of the currents of fear and loathing which it sees permeating life in 'modern' Turkey. Zaim says the character is based on a real-life prototype, but the film has none of the limitations of docu-drama: vigorous hand-held camerawork complements a sophisticated grasp of pacing and structure. TR

Something Big

(Andrew V McLaglen, 1971, US) Dean Martin, Brian Keith, Honor Blackman, Carol White, Ben Johnson, Albert Salmi, Paul Fix, Denver Pyle, Harry Carey Jr.
108 min.

One gruesome symptom of the Death of the Western was the 'comedy Western', a messy, confused genre that flourished briefly in the late '60s and early '70s. Occasionally, the genre produced the odd bizarre gem – notably Cat Ballou and There Was a Crooked Man – but this was one of the less honourable efforts. Martin plays a baddie in town to give his retiring adversary, cavalry colonel Keith, a last, leadenly parodic run for his money. Typically for the genre, a few Brits are around to add incongruity – here, Blackman and then-trendy starlet White. TCh

Something for Everyone (aka Black Flowers for the Bride)

(Harold Prince, 1970, US) Angela Lansbury, Michael York, Anthony Corlan, Heidelinde Weis, Eva-Marie Meineke, John Gill.
113 min.

Black comedy from stage director Prince, based on Harry Kressing's novel The Cook, fatally flawed by the casting of York as the mastermind behind various 'disappearances' and so forth as he schemes his way to ownership of Ornstein Castle. Shot on location in Bavaria, and full of downhill-going nobility with shrinking purses and growing pretensions. If you can take stray eyefuls of Sound of Music, you'll be rewarded by a beautiful performance from Angela Lansbury.

Something of Value

(Richard Brooks, 1957, US) Rock Hudson, Sidney Poitier, Dana Wynter, Wendy Hiller, Robert Beatty, Michael Pate.
113 min. b/w.

The best-seller status of Robert Ruark's novel, and Brooks' affinity with liberal issues generally, explains why MGM rather improbably found itself tackling the ramifications of the Mau Mau campaign against white settlers of the early 1950s. With Kenya represented by the leafier bits of the studio backlot plus sore-thumb location inserts, with the blacks speaking in variously Puerto Rican and Jamaican accents, and with Hudson and Hiller supposed to be brother and sister, this never really stood a chance. Brooks' chief insight – good and bad on both sides, tolerance the answer – hardly seizes the imagination, and the contentious climax, with Hudson carrying a wounded Poitier on his back, has every indication of being intended symbolically A brief prologue written and spoken on-camera by Winston Churchill was deleted pre-release, having bored a preview audience. BBa

Something to Believe In

(John Hough, 1997, GB/Ger) William McNamara, Maria Pitillo, Tom Conti, Maria Schneider, Ian Bannen, Robert Wagner, Jill St John, Roddy McDowall.
113 min.

A jaw-dropping amalgam of syrupy romance, terminal illness, divine intervention and classical music. McNamara plays an American pianist whose improvisatory flair shocks the Paris Conservatoire, but who may still secure a concert career if he wins the Barbarina competition in Naples. Pitillo is a Las Vegas croupier forced to quit her job after diagnosis of fatal disease. Her sole hope lies in travelling to an Italian village church where a weeping Madonna has prompted talk of miracle cures. Guess who she bumps into? This sets up a finale that works in the redemptive power of love over mortality, Lalo Schifrin's Piano Concerto performed on live TV watched by the entire world, and the hand of the Almighty Himself. TJ

Something to Hide

(Alastair Reid, 1971, GB) Peter Finch, Shelley Winters, Colin Blakely, John Stride, Linda Hayden, Harold Goldblatt.
99 min.

Winters and Finch, sparring out a last drunken evening together, make a sufficiently unlikely married couple for one to regret her exit after ten minutes. What might have happened between them is a more interesting conjecture than what actually develops in this adaptation of Nicholas Monsarrat's novel, with Finch acting reluctant midwife to an unmarried teenage hitchhiker (Hayden) under very implausible circumstances. He goes through his alcoholic male menopause looking as if he wished Burton had got the part. What really sinks the thing is the impossible mixture of symbolism – striving for universal significance and stopping little short of lionesses whelping in the streets – and heavy-handed observation, where (for example) mental crack-up is primarily indicated by wearing odd-coloured socks. Melodrama runs amok on the Isle of Wight, and the nodding references to Chabrol make it all the more uncomfortable. CPe

Something to Talk About

(Lasse Hallström, 1995, US) Julia Roberts, Dennis Quaid, Robert Duvall, Gena Rowlands, Kyra Sedgwick, Brett Cullen, Haley Aull.
105 min.

After a couple of false starts, Lasse Hallström appears to have found a niche for himself in Hollywood as a purveyor of eccentric character pieces; mellow-dramas with class. Working here from a choice script by Callie Khouri (Thelma & Louise), he's fashioned a gently caustic soap about adultery, parenthood and independence. Roberts is Grace Bichon, wife, mother, daughter and manager at the family's award-winning stables – not necessarily in that order. Grace has allowed herself to drift into the absent-minded inertia expected of a respectable Southern woman. She's shocked to find out that husband Eddie (Quaid) has been fooling around, but disappointed when the folks (Duvall and Rowlands) try to talk her back into the fold. Only her sister (Sedgwick, very plausible) understands, planting her knee firmly in Eddie's groin. Although the film-makers ill-advisedly saddle themselves with a brattish kid with a speech impediment and a corny-as-Kelloggs show jumping finale, for the most part this is a pleasing, polished affair, honest enough to steer a compassionate middle course without succumbing to caricature or conservative sentimentality. TCh

Something Wicked This Way Comes

(Jack Clayton, 1982, US) Jason Robards, Jonathan Pryce, Diane Ladd, Pam Grier, Royal Dano, Vidal Peterson, Shawn Carson, James Stacy.
95 min.

No wonder Disney executives went wild when they saw what Clayton had done to Ray Bradbury's novel, turning the tone several shades blacker and dampening down the sentimentality. With the arrival of Dark's Pandemonium Carnival in a small midwestern town, all hell breaks loose. Soon the locals are queueing up outside the Temple of Temptation where, for a quick moral sacrifice, everything your heart desires pops up in glorious array; children start to despise their parents, who in turn hanker after their children's youth. Clayton takes a distinctly unwholesome relish in stirring up this puritan nightmare, piling a heap of torments on the heads of his two boy heroes, and finally restoring cosy order with thoroughly forced conviction. Ultimately, though, it's an uneasy blend of horror and whimsy, with the allegory being hammered a little too hard for comfort. It's also marred by some dreadfully tacky special effects and set designs. JP

Something Wild

(Jonathan Demme, 1986, US) Jeff Daniels, Melanie Griffith, Ray Liotta, Margaret Colin, Tracey Walter, Dana Preu, Jack Gilpin, John Waters, John Sayles.
114 min.

When squeaky-clean Big Apple businessman Charlie Driggs (Daniels) walks away from a diner without paying the bill, his brief excursion into crime attracts the attention of Louise Brooks lookalike Lulu (Griffith). This distinctly downmarket femme fatale hijacks the lad with the offer of a lift that soon develops into a lunatic weekend of stealing booze and bondage sex. More alarmingly, Charlie's confusion at the woman's wobbly, protean personality is soon aggravated by the arrival of her ex-con ex (Liotta), who abducts the odd couple for his own violently vengeful purposes. A truly original cocktail, mixing Bringing Up Baby-style comedy with the lethal paranoia of film noir, Demme's gem distinguishes itself from other 'yuppie nightmare' movies (Blue Velvet, After Hours) by its very real sympathy for its oddball characters. Demme observes the human eccentricity that underlies the corner-store banalities of Middle America with warmth and loving detail; while a magnificent rock soundtrack and faultless performances from Daniels, Griffith and Liotta ensure pleasures galore. GA

Sometimes a Great Notion (aka Never Give an Inch)

(Paul Newman, 1971, US) Paul Newman, Henry Fonda, Lee Remick, Michael Sarrazin, Richard Jaeckel, Linda Lawson, Cliff Potts.
114 min.

Taken on by Newman half way through (the film was started by Richard A Colla), the surprising thing about this adaptation of Ken Kesey's novel is that it holds together at all: a drama about a family of independent lumberjacks, ruled over by Henry Fonda's biblical father, whose unity is shattered by the arrival of a wayward son (Sarrazin) in the midst of a dispute with other (striking) loggers. If the struggle within the family too quickly degenerates into hand-me-down Tennessee Williams dramatics, Newman's handling of the outdoor scenes, especially those involving work, is – like his own acting – restrained but powerfully evocative. PH

Sometimes I Look at My Life (A Veces Miro Mi Vida)

(Orlando Rojas, 1982, Cuba) Harry Belafonte, Letta Mbulu, Falumi Prince.
79 min.

It's rare to see any movie which manages to get everything so conclusively wrong as this does. From its random use of film clips (often in the wrong format, and in black-and-white from colour films) to its central uninspired interview with Belafonte, this 'Cuban view of an American entertainer' (who visited Cuba for a concert in 1980) takes a potentially interesting subject and squanders it. If you like Belafonte, you'd be better off with an album; if you don't, then rest assured that this would do nothing to kindle your enthusiasm. SM

Sometime, Somewhere (Oridathu)

(G Aravindan, 1987, Ind) Nedumudi Venu, Sreenivasan, Thilakan, Vineeth, MS Trippunithura.
112 min.
Aravindan's incandescent film is a dream come true: a perfectly plotless movie that is paradoxically crammed with incident, much of it at least notionally dramatic. It offers a richly detailed picture of life in a Kerala village in the 1950s, at the moment of transition prompted by the arrival of electricity. The tyranny of a storyline is kept at bay by spreading the focus around a huge cast; what binds it all together is the unique poetry of the film language, full of unorthodox editing patterns and compositions. Aravindan looks more and more like India's answer to Ozu, but his poetry is less rigorous, more intuitive, and possibly even more beautiful. TR

Somewhere in the Night

(Joseph L Mankiewicz, 1946, US) John Hodiak, Nancy Guild, Lloyd Nolan, Richard Conte, Josephine Hutchinson, Fritz Kortner, Margo Woode, Sheldon Leonard, John Russell, Houseley Stevenson.
110 min. b/w.
Hodiak as a marine blown up at Okinawa who returns to Los Angeles armed only with a name that means nothing to him and a letter from a girl, now dead, who hated him. Out of this familiar premise, Mankiewicz has fashioned a classic *film noir* account of the amnesiac who suspects he isn't going to like rediscovering the man he once was. His odyssey in quest of himself leads through a long dark night with murder and a missing $2 million dollars at the end of it, peopled along the way by the lost and the lonely, the suave and the sinister (wonderful supporting performances) and taking in a series of suitably clammy settings (waterfront fortune-telling parlour, mission hall, sanatorium for the insane). Mankiewicz's superb control of a complex plot (as both writer and director) takes him into at least one outstanding set piece: an elaborate nightclub sequence in which Hodiak questions a bartender, the latter casually tips off two hoods, a bowl of pretzels is slipped down the bar to identify the target, and just as something is about to explode, the lights dim as the band strikes up a new number...TM

Somewhere in Time

(Jeannot Szwarc, 1980, US) Christopher Reeve, Christopher Plummer, Jane Seymour, Teresa Wright, Bill Erwin, George Voskovec.
104 min.
Adapting his own novel *Bid Time Return*, and with characteristic indifference to current film taste, Richard Matheson has here provided one of the most idiosyncratic scripts of 1980, about a writer who wills himself back in time to the early 1900s in order to fall in love with a distinguished actress. In its unashamed romanticism, this is the kind of thing David O Selznick was producing in the 1940s; but scripts cannot make themselves, and *Somewhere in Time* is cursed with truly atrocious staging, plus Christopher Reeve looking awkwardly man-of-steelish as the hero. A few emotional echoes remain, and one climactic coup in which the hero is dragged forward in time; otherwise this must go down as a missed opportunity. DP

Sommaren med Monika (Monika/Summer with Monika)

(Ingmar Bergman, 1952, Swe) Harriet Andersson, Lars Ekborg, John Harryson, Georg Skarstedt, Dagmar Ebbeson, Ake Fridell.
97 min. b/w.
A tender yet unsentimental account of a love affair that turns sour. Harriet Andersson gives a precociously assured performance as a wild, feckless girl from Stockholm's poorer quarter who falls in love with a 19-year-old youth. During an idyllic motor-boat holiday among the islands of the Stockholm archipelago, the girl becomes pregnant and the couple, forced to marry, set up home

in a tiny, cramped flat. Very soon, love gives way to distrust and hostility, and they agree to part. Bergman's sympathetic eye and Gunnar Fischer's atmospheric photography invest the locations with a poetic significance, the light and open spaces of the holiday islands contrasted tellingly with the dark claustrophobia of the city, where the flame of the couple's love is slowly extinguished by the lack of air. NF

Sommarlek (Illicit Interlude/ Summer Interlude)

(Ingmar Bergman, 1950, Swe) Maj-Britt Nilsson, Birger Malmsten, Alf Kjellin, Georg Funkquist, Renée Björling, Mimi Pollak.
96 min. b/w.
Told in flashback as the memories of a ballerina approaching the end of her career, this sensitively observed story traces a teenage love affair which took place one idyllic summer on the archipelago near Stockholm. Bergman's preoccupation with the transition from youthful innocence to adult experience is already clearly marked here, as is the double movement of a journey backward into one's own past which nevertheless marks a spiritual progression. For it is through her re-living of her past that the heroine comes to embrace the tentative possibilities for her future. The translation of the title, incidentally, is incorrect and misleading. *Sommarlek* means *Summer Games*, and Bergman's concern is with the transience of playful youth. NF

Sommersby

(Jon Amiel, 1993, US/Fr) Richard Gere, Jodie Foster, Bill Pullman, James Earl Jones, Lanny Flaherty, William Windom.
113 min.
Seven years after leaving to fight in the Civil War, Jack Sommersby (Gere) returns to his wife (Foster), son and Tennessee home a changed man. Formerly a brute and none-too-successful plantation owner, he credits his much-improved personality to what he learned from a fellow PoW, now dead. But is he Jack? The doubt, strongest in his wife's mind but also entertained by the community, is swept aside, thanks to the happiness and prosperity he brings. But accusations of murder are less easily ignored... This sumptuous Hollywood remake of *The Return of Martin Guerre* is better than one might expect (though Jack comes over as far too much the modern New Man: sensitive hubby, visionary businessman, committed to racial equality, etc). The solid script makes the most of the dilemmas and paradoxes of the couple's predicament; Philippe Rousselot's photography manages to be lyrical without becoming too cloyingly picturesque; and surprisingly (the *only* surprise in this craftsmanlike but unremarkable movie), it doesn't cop out at the end. GA

Sonatine

(Takeshi Kitano, 1993, Jap) Takeshi Kitano, Aya Kokumai, Tetsu Watanabe, Masanobu Katsumura, Susumu Terashima.
94 min.
The terrific thing about *Sonatine* is its freshness, its ability to surprise. Basically, it's a slightly offbeat variation on the traditional yakuza thriller, with Kitano as Murakawa, the taciturn, influential hit-man who, pushed by his boss to involve himself in an Okinawa gang war, comes to realise that he wants out. But what's truly arresting is the star/director's attitude towards the film's formal qualities. Structurally, the movie – like a sonata – is tripartite. It starts fortissimo with tempestuous scenes of gangland machinations and warfare. Then when Murakawa and his men take refuge in a coastal hideaway, their surreal, jokey seaside antics have all the light playfulness of a scherzo. While the final lyrical focus on death is virtually an adagio of moody introspection. Challenging, witty, adventurous and utterly singular. GA

Song for Beko, A (Ein Lied für Beko/ Klamek ji bo Beko)

(Nizamettin Ariç, 1992, Ger/Arm) Nizamettin Ariç, Bêzara Arsen, Lusika Hesen, Cemalê Jora.
99 min.
This elegy for the persecuted Kurdish peoples of Turkey, Iraq and Iran is simple, unforced, and

extremely moving. It may lack the epic grandeur of *Yol*, but it has the same telling eye for figures in a harsh landscape, and is infused with the same heartfelt compassion. After his brother Cemal flees the village to avoid conscription into the Turkish army, Beko is arrested in his place, but soon escapes. Peshmerga freedom fighters take him to the mountain hideout in the Iraqi highlands where their wives, and orphans from a nearby village, have taken refuge. While waiting for news of his brother, Beko befriends the children, including the painfully withdrawn Ziné. A more obvious film would have focused on Cemal's brave flight; Beko, we learn, served his two-year military service without complaint. The exiled Ariç's vision, though, is a broader one, dealing with how an ordinary man, the strong women and the orphaned children cling to their tenuous Kurdish identity. The first film to be made in the suppressed Kurdish language, this gives eloquent voice to the plight of a displaced people. NF

Song for Tibet

(Anne Henderson, 1991, Can)
57 min.
A moving documentary which conveys rare sympathy for a family exiled to Canada in the aftermath of the Chinese invasion of Tibet, as they affirm their determination to stay in touch with Tibetan people and tradition, and their unshakeable faith in the future. The sober account of Chinese atrocities, and the evident dignity and compassion of the Dalai Lama (who was ignored by the government when he visited Ottawa), paint a shameful picture of western foreign policy and China's restored Most Favoured Nation trading status. TCh

Song Is Born, A

(Howard Hawks, 1948, US) Danny Kaye, Virginia Mayo, Steve Cochran, Hugh Herbert, Felix Bressart, J Edward Bromberg, Ludwig Stossel.
113 min.
A curiously lifeless musical remake of Hawks' own comedy classic *Ball of Fire*, with Kaye taking the Gary Cooper role and transformed into a shy musicologist, whose quiet existence is disturbed by the arrival of Mayo's nightclub singer, who not only brings the attention of the Mob down on Kaye and his elderly colleagues, but also teaches them the joy of jazz. Mainly wrecked by the performances, although there are some fine musical spots for the likes of Louis Armstrong, Benny Goodman, Lionel Hampton and Tommy Dorsey. GA

Song of Bernadette, The

(Henry King, 1943, US) Jennifer Jones, William Eythe, Charles Bickford, Vincent Price, Lee J Cobb, Gladys Cooper, Anne Revere, Roman Bohnen, Patricia Morison, Linda Darnell.
156 min. b/w.
A two-and-a-half hour wallow, adapted by George Seaton from the Franz Werfel novel, with Jennifer Jones becoming a star as the peasant girl who had a vision of the Virgin Mary (that's Linda Darnell, uncredited) and thereby gave birth to the tourist industry at Lourdes. Some of the political and religious shenanigans momentarily conceal the mush at the heart of the picture, which begins with a glorious prologue that says if you believe it you're okay, and if not, shove off. ATu

Song of Ceylon

(Basil Wright, 1934, GB) narrator: Lionel Wendt.
40 min. b/w.
Stigmatised by leftist critics as a hymn to imperialism, Wright's complex documentary essay is much, much more ambiguous. The lyrical, evocative imagery is pushed and prodded into functional service by a subtle multi-layered soundtrack. Overt criticism was hardly possible in a film sponsored by the Ceylon Tea Board, but Wright radically declines either to romanticise Ceylon's pre-colonial past or to celebrate the 'progress' brought by British imperialism. RMy

Song of Chao-Phrya, The (Nong Mia)

(Chatri-Chalerm Yukol, 1990, Thai) Chatchai Plengpanich, Passorn Boonyakiat, Pattamawan Khaomoonkhadee, Komsom Pongsutham.
100 min.

Named after the river which flows through Bangkok, Prince Chatri's film is an updated remake of another written and shot by his father, Prince Anusorn Mongkalkarn. It plays like a tropical variation on *L'Atalante*. A family (husband, wife, baby, sister-in-law) scrapes a living ferrying goods up and down the river; the wife runs away in search of urban glamour and excitement, and her husband has to comb the city's brothels and girlie bars to look for her. It's not shy of the odd glimpse of cruelty and violence, but too stylish to get trapped in grimy social realism. One of its many pleasures is a cameo by film director Komson Pongsutham as a taxi driver who gets plastered at the husband's expense. TR

Song of Norway

(Andrew L Stone, 1970, US) Toralv Maurstad, Florence Henderson, Christina Schollin, Frank Poretta, Harry Secombe, Robert Morley, Edward G Robinson, Oscar Homolka.
141 min.
A saccharine fantasy biopic of Grieg, with 45 musical numbers, 25 songs, international uvulas, and production line fjords. Grieg lived a life of exemplary dullness, and Stone has tried to ginger it up with white-knuckle cliff-hangers like whether the composer will be able to create an indigenous national music for Norway or not. Edvard, hold the phone. Edward G Robinson plays a piano salesman, Harry Secombe does not play Neddy Seagoon, Little Eyolf fails to show. *Life* magazine raved: 'Godawful'. *The New Yorker* wondered whether it had been made by trolls. The Medved Brothers dubbed Florence Henderson, who plays Grieg's wife, 'the female Peter Frampton for the Geritol generation'. BC

Song of Scheherazade

(Walter Reisch, 1947, US) Yvonne De Carlo, Jean-Pierre Aumont, Brian Donlevy, Eve Arden, Philip Reed, Charles Kullman, John Qualen.
106 min.
Colourful campery with Donlevy baring his manly torso as a martinet Russian naval captain striking terror into his fledgling crew. Among the musical comedy sailors is Rimsky-Korsakov (Aumont), soon to unearth his muse (De Carlo) dancing in a Moroccan dive, transport her (disguised as a cadet) to the St Petersburg opera, and write his immortal melodies for her. Typical Hollywood tripe, presumably tongue-in-cheek but done with more verve than wit. TM

Song of Songs

(Rouben Mamoulian, 1933, US) Marlene Dietrich, Brian Aherne, Lionel Atwill, Alison Skipworth, Hardie Albright.
89 min. b/w.
A delightful mix of Sternbergian splendour and Mamoulian send-up, this hits exactly the right note of knowingness as Dietrich puts in her first appearance, an innocent peasant maid complete with demure braids and Bible (her favourite reading being the erotic ecstasies of the *Song of Solomon*). She quickly finds 'him whom my soul loveth' in a sculptor (Aherne) whom she inspires to his masterwork; but financial stringencies being what they are, she is passed on to the eagerly lecherous baron (Atwill) who had commissioned the sculpture; and it only remains for her to achieve a woman's revenge, then find her natural habitat as a sultry chanteuse in a nightclub (where she embarks on the sexy 'Johnny' with all she's got: 'I need a kiss or two, or maybe more...'). Needless to say, Dietrich positively glows with demure innocence or malice aforethought as the need arises – posing shyly in the nude for the handsome sculptuor, or swooping into the arms of an abashed but responsive riding-master – and the whole thing has a glitteringly opulent beauty, sparked with an irresistible sense of the absurd. TM

Song of the Exile
(Ketu Qiu Hen)

(Ann Hui, 1989, Tai) Chang Shwu-Fen, Maggie Cheung.
98 min.
Ann Hui's semi-autobiographical film about a troubled mother-daughter relationship opens shakily with scenes set in the London of the late 1960s, but finds its feet as soon as it reaches Hong Kong and sets off for other points East. Hui uses an intricate web of flashbacks to explore the roots of the problem between the two women: the mother turns out to be Japanese, and she had a very hard time when she married into a Chinese family just after the war; the daughter has always considered herself wholly Chinese, and was taught by her grandparents to despise her mother. The complications are explored (and ultimately exorcised) in moving and intelligent scenes that throw light on areas long dark. Very well acted, too, especially by Maggie Cheung as the daughter. TR

Song of the Shirt, The

(Susan Clayton/Jonathan Curling, 1979, GB) Martha Gibson, Geraldine Pilgrim, Anna McNiff, Liz Myers, Jill Greenhalgh.
135 min. b/w.
A remarkably ambitious, multi-faceted project that uses the condition of the sweated seamstresses of 19th century London as a starting point from which to examine such varied subjects as the establishment of a sexual division of labour under capitalism, the nature of the Welfare State as a prop of male dominance, History as a disparate series of representations, and film itself. What should be stressed is the pleasure afforded by its strategic variation of image quality (video, etchings, stills) and by a witty score (by members of the Feminist Improvisation Group) which challenges the conventions of film music. MM

Song of the Siren, The
(Shirat Ha'Sirena)

(Eytan Fox, 1995, Isr) Dalit Kahn, Boaz Gur-Lavi, Yair Lapid, Avital Diker, Orly Zilberschatz-Banai, Yaffa Yarkoni.
91 min.
This slightly sour, not particularly funny romantic comedy, set in Tel Aviv at the outbreak of the Gulf War, centres on Talila, a young advertising executive who vacillates between the lover who ditched her for a 22-year-old, her boss, and a seemingly sweet hick named Noah with whom, against her own expectations, she falls in love. The precautions widely adopted against Saddam's SCUDs and the marital problems of the heroine's sister contextualise and counterpoint Talila's own reckless rush towards marriage, though she's too moody, possessive and self-obsessed, even selfish, to elicit wholehearted sympathy. GA

Song of the South

(Wilfred Jackson/Harve Foster, 1946, US) Ruth Warrick, James Baskett, Bobby Driscoll, Luana Patten, Hattie McDaniel.
94 min.
A plantation in the Old South: young Bobby Driscoll learns of life through the stories of former slave Uncle Remus (James Baskett). This rather mushy combination of animation and live-action remains one of Disney's most controversial efforts. It contains magical graphic work – notably the standout 'Zip-a-Dee-Do-Dah' number – but racial stereotyping drew furious protests from the National Association for the Advancement of Colored People. Hollywood's response? An honorary Oscar for Baskett. TJ

Song Remains the Same, The

(Peter Clifton/Joe Massot, 1976, GB) John Bonham, John Paul Jones, Jimmy Page, Robert Plant, Peter Grant.
136 min.
This could trouble even the devout in the Led Zeppelin coven. Essentially a chord by chord documentation of their '73 Madison Square concert, the heavy metal onslaught is intercut with lavish psychedelic effects, New York by night, seedy backstage wrangles, and five fantasy sequences. Here the band and manager Peter Grant indulge in some awesomely heavy-handed wish fulfilment. It ranges from the laboured (Grant as overblown Chicago gangster) to the dire (vocalist Robert Plant interprets his Viking saga like a TV ad for hairspray) and neurotic (guitarist Jimmy Page supernaturally experiences the seven ages of man). It's gruellingly long, the four-track stereo relentless, and the music a mechanical recreation of Zeppelin standards (eg. 'Whole Lotta Love', 'Stairway to Heaven). IB

Song to Remember, A

(Charles Vidor, 1945, US) Cornel Wilde, Paul Muni, Merle Oberon, Stephen Bekassy, Nina Foch, George Coulouris, Sig Arno, George Macready.
113 min.
The film that contained the deathless line (Georges Sand to Chopin), 'Discontinue that so-called Polonaise jumble you've been playing for days'. Hilariously inept even by Hollywood biopic standards, this preposterous farrago has Wilde's Chopin, a Polish freedom fighter against the Czarist oppressor, forgetting his patriotic principles in the heady wine of Paris, success and Georges Sand's possessive arms, but coming to himself in time to cough out his life's blood on a grand concert tour for the cause. Amazingly stilted kitsch, packed with unspeakable dialogue. TM

Song Without End

(Charles Vidor, 1960, US) Dirk Bogarde, Capucine, Genevieve Page, Patricia Morison, Martita Hunt, Ivan Desny, Lyndon Brook, Alex Davion, Lou Jacobi.
142 min.
Outstandingly silly biopic of Liszt, and a return to the floridly romantic style of Vidor's earlier film about Chopin, *A Song to Remember*. History is bunk, and the conception of creative genius as half-baked as, say, a Ken Russell film, in that it's purely love that makes the music flow. But at least James Wong Howe's photography of the elegant sets is suitably impressive. Cukor finished the film after Vidor's death – but it doesn't show. GA

Songwriter

(Alan Rudolph, 1984, US) Kris Kristofferson, Willie Nelson, Melinda Dillon, Rip Torn, Lesley Ann Warren, Richard C Sarafian.
94 min.
Unexpectedly, at three days' notice, Rudolph was asked by producer Sydney Pollack to take the helm on this carefree comedy set in the world of Country & Western music. The result was Rudolph's fastest paced and most uninhibited film to date: a quirky, rambling tale of two star performers on the road. Incorporating songs specially written by Nelson and Kristofferson, the film indulges their male-bonding, hard-drinking, womanising life style, as well as giving Lesley Ann Warren her own shot at performing (not bad). A likeable shaggy dog of a movie, assuming the music's to your taste. DT

Sonic Outlaws

(Craig Baldwin, 1995, US)
88 min.
The subject matter of this film/video documentary – copyright infringement and (some of) the consequences – is interesting enough. What isn't so interesting is the manner in which director Baldwin and cameraman/editor Bill Daniel have presented it. It runs like an early '80s 'scratch' video: masses of found footage (most of it unrelated to the accompanying sound-bites) is cut, tossed, turned and generally fiddled with to produce either a slant on the original or a different interpretation. And it's fine when taken in small doses. At the film's centre is a group of American 'Media Hackers' called Negativland who incurred the wrath of Irish rockers U2 for infringement of copyright. Questions are asked, few are answered (the interviews create the impression of an empty bread bin). Indeed, it's a relief when we get introduced to some of the other forms of artistic plagiarism (or parody, as some hackers call it) including billboard 'vandalism' (some of it amusing) and a hilarious item on the work of the 'Barbie Liberation Organisation'. DA

Son in Law

(Steve Rash, 1993, US) Pauly Shore, Carla Gugino, Lane Smith, Cindy Pickett, Mason Adams, Patrick Renna.
95 min.
This teen comedy is the second vehicle for Pauly Shore, a purveyor of spacey West Coast dialtalk. His character is a reprise of his post-adolescent wisecracker in *California Man*. He plays a geek called Crawl, a student advisor at a California co-ed college. When print-frocked Rebecca (Gugino) finds the crazy partying at Halloween all too much, Crawl steps in and persuades her into a Valley-girl make-over and butterfly tattoo. Within days she's down on the beach, eyeing up 'the guys with the big stones'. By Thanksgiving they're firm enough friends for her to invite him home to South Dakota to meet the folks. When Crawl poses as Rebecca's fiancé, to save her from her old beau, and declares an interest in their farmin' ways he's subject to a

series of humiliations. But you know he's a-startin' to win their hearts. Mind-boggling stuff of moronic banality, but most appealing. Anybody cool or sane should think twice. WH

Son of Blob
see Beware! the Blob

Son of Dracula
(Robert Siodmak, 1943, US) Lon Chaney Jr, J Edward Bromberg, Robert Paige, Louise Albritton, Evelyn Ankers, Frank Craven.
79 min. b/w.
A characteristically stylish piece from Siodmak, who nevertheless looks somewhat constrained by budget and genre. Chaney is fine as the Count (not, note, his son, despite the title), masquerading as one Alucard when he turns up in American Deep South society, and woos Louise Albritton over to the vampiric cause. But the script is far from wonderful, and offers Siodmak little to get his teeth into, notwithstanding a beautifully atmospheric first entry for the Count (Chaney and coffin rising from the misty depths of a lake) and an effective finale. GA

Son of Frankenstein
(Rowland V Lee, 1939, US) Basil Rathbone, Boris Karloff, Bela Lugosi, Lionel Atwill, Josephine Hutchinson, Edgar Norton, Donnie Dunagan.
99 min. b/w.
Predictably, with four of the horror genre's most sinister presences in the cast, this is highly entertaining; but Rowland Lee (who made the wonderful *Zoo in Budapest*) creates a sumptuous, atmospheric tale worthy of following Whale's originals. The set, shot in a style reminiscent of the German Expressionist classics, is superb – a labyrinthine castle of gloomy shadows – and there are enough strong moments, as when the monster (Karloff, far less sympathetic than in his previous incarnations) tears off policeman Atwill's artificial arm, to make the film memorable in its own right. GA

Son of Godzilla (Gojira no Musuko)
(Jun Fukuda, 1967, Jap) Tadao Takashima, Akira Kubo, Beverly Maeda, Akihiko Hirata, Yoshio Tsuchiya.
86 min.
A scientific experiment on a Pacific atoll goes wrong, causing flowers to grow into triffids and mangoes to swell like footballs. Praying mantises become mechanical diggers, and an unearthed egg hatches out the son of you know who. Big Daddy is snorkelling out on the reef, but soon runs back for a bit of the usual murder and mayhem (though a giant spider is the real anti-mankind villain). The energy level is high, the technology ridiculous, and the subtext bang up to date. This one's about global warming. ATu

Son of Paleface
(Frank Tashlin, 1952, US) Bob Hope, Jane Russell, Roy Rogers, Douglass Dumbrille, Bill Williams, Lloyd Corrigan, Harry Von Zell.
95 min.
A superior sequel to the original Hope/Russell vehicle, *The Paleface*, which Tashlin co-wrote. Again it's the tale of a timid braggart who falls in with a far more able woman (here an outlaw on the run from Rogers' federal marshal), and it's tailor-made for Hope's cowardly bluster and Russell's sassy sensuality. What's more, the verbal gags are nicely complemented by Tashlin's brashly wacky visual slapstick, which – like his later work – takes great pleasure in spoofing/deconstructing the genre to which the film subscribes. GA

Sons
(Alexandre Rockwell, 1989, US) William Forsythe, DB Sweeney, Robert Miranda, Samuel Fuller, Jennifer Beals.
90 min.
Erratic talent Alexandre Rockwell, perpetrator of one of the *Four Rooms*, made his breakthrough with the Steve Buscemi movie-movie *In the Soup*. This is one of three earlier efforts, a comedy drama that played the festival circuit before vanishing without trace. Forsythe, Sweeney and Miranda are the trio of stepbroth-

ers accompanying paralysed father Fuller on a jaunt to Normandy, where the old boy saw combat and romantic action during the war. (Jennifer Beals, a regular in husband Rockwell's movies, plays a transvestite.) TJ

Sons (Erzi)
(Zhang Yuan, 1996, China) Li Maojie, Fu Rongde, Li Ji, Li Wei.
95 min.
A shatteringly intense docu-drama chronicling episodes in the breakdown of the Li family in present-day Beijing. The central problem is the father, Li Maojie, a former dancer who's declined into alcoholism and violence since stiffening joints forced him to retire. Both his sons hate him, partly because they're afraid they'll take after him; they're slackers, on the fringes of the city's underground rock scene. Seeing something universal in their problems – especially the mutual withholding of love – Zhang has the family re-enact its own domestic strife for the camera. Made with palpable warmth and affection for its characters, the film provides the most credible account of street-level realities in China's cities yet seen. TR

Sons and Lovers
(Jack Cardiff, 1960, GB) Dean Stockwell, Trevor Howard, Wendy Hiller, Mary Ure, Heather Sears, Donald Pleasence, Ernest Thesiger.
103 min. b/w.
A slack and superficial adaptation of Lawrence's novel. Laudably avoiding the temptation to sensationalise Paul Morel's amorous adventures, the film finds little else to stress, since these affairs take up an awful lot of screen time, while the character's inner conflicts (with his background, his mother etc) are left ill-defined and inconclusive. Great care has been taken with the period atmosphere (splendid camerawork by Freddie Francis), but the rather stiffly literary dialogue makes it all look like a series of animated Edwardian tableaux. TM

Sons of the Desert (aka Fraternally Yours)
(William A Seiter, 1933, US) Stan Laurel, Oliver Hardy, Charley Chase, Mae Busch, Dorothy Christie, Lucien Littlefield.
69 min. b/w.
One of the very finest Laurel and Hardy features, and certainly the most typical in terms of plot and characterisation, this sees the pair as henpecked husbands who manage to fulfil their dream of attending an absurdly infantile, riotous convention (held by the eponymous fraternity) only by lying to their wives; the trouble inevitably is that the girls discover their deceit, thus turning L & H's return into a nightmare of flattery, feigned innocence, and farcical intrigue. Despite Ollie's inimitable slow burn whenever confronted by Stanley's whimpering idiocy, the film is far faster than most of their features, while the duo's essentially childish amiability is beautifully contrasted both with the down-to-earth if somewhat aggressive maturity of their spouses, and with the ghastly mischief wrought by Chase's ever-effervescent convention regular. GA

Sophie's Choice
(Alan J Pakula, 1982, US) Meryl Streep, Kevin Kline, Peter MacNicol, Rita Karin, Stephen D Newman, Greta Turken, Josh Mostel.
158 min.
A summer in Brooklyn in 1947, and an infatuated boy (MacNicol) tries to learn the dreadful secret of Sophie's awful Choice. It's Pakula's first film as his own screenwriter, and his scrupulous adherence to the dense details of William Styron's novel seems to have slowed down the deft visual sense so marked in *Klute*. A more serious problem occurs in long flashback scenes as Sophie describes her ordeal in Auschwitz. The information (for on one level, this is a tantalising Gothic romance) comes thrillingly, in fits and starts, with revelations following on the heels of half-truths. But one watches uneasily as the obscenity of the Holocaust is served up for our entertainment yet again, and another actress with perfect cheekbones and a crew cut loses a few pounds to lend credibility to a death camp scene. By the end, the accumulated weight and lethargy of the production fails to invest Sophie's fate with the significance Styron achieves. JS

Sopyonje (Seo-Pyon-Jae)
(Im Kwon-Taek, 1993, SKor) Kim Myung-Gon, Oh Jung-Hae, Kim Kyu-Chul.
112 min.
This heart-rending and accessible melodrama concerns the relationship between two children and their adoptive 'father'/master, a travelling – necessarily poor – *pansori* musician. The *pansori*, a traditional music of aching love laments or upbeat festive songs, performed to the accompaniment of a lone drum, gives the movie its elegiac tone. Flashing back to the early '50s, it follows the three on their journeys through the loving photographed by Korean landscapes, in all seasons, as they fight for a living, while their music is literally drowned out by the emerging fashion for Western sounds. It's a film of looks, rhythms, intimations and feelings, expressed in pure cinematic terms, and it's almost impossible not to be moved by it. The *sopyonje* is a song described as sorrowful and tender – there are few films more tender, if not more sorrowful than this. Unmissable. WH

Sorcerer (aka Wages of Fear)
(William Friedkin, 1977, US) Roy Scheider, Bruno Crémer, Francisco Rabal, Amidou, Ramon Bieri, Peter Capell.
121 min.
Friedkin's remake of Clouzot's 1953 thriller, *The Wages of Fear*, at a cost of more than twenty million dollars, bombed spectacularly in the States. Even cut by almost thirty minutes for British release, the film's narrative of four desperate men trucking nitroglycerin through 300 miles of South American jungle advances at far too slow a pace to aspire to the suspense value of the original. Friedkin hints at political themes, but the film suffers most from condescendingly over-emphatic direction, and a generally tedious, relentless grimy realism in the opening half hour. One simply wonders what, say, Peckinpah might have made of it. RM

Sorcerers, The
(Michael Reeves, 1967, GB) Boris Karloff, Catherine Lacey, Ian Ogilvy, Elizabeth Ercy, Susan George, Victor Henry.
104 min.
Perhaps the much-touted multiplex generation of movie-brat directors who purport to care so much about British genre cinema should take a look at this picture some time. Reeves directed his first feature when he was only 23, already displaying the virtuosity which would make its most astonishing manifestation in *Witchfinder General*. The story, adapted from John Burke's novel, follows an ageing couple, the Monserrats (Karloff and Lacey), who have devised a contraption that allows them to control the minds of others and vicariously experience the world through others. This has a particular kick when they find young prey in the form of Ogilvy to experiment on. As the Monserrats play audience to their victims' living scenarios, which the couple write to their own perverse specifications, this psychedelic horror film deals with the apparatus of cinema, and it still puts the mind in a spin. LF

Sorority Girl
(Roger Corman, 1957, US) Susan Cabot, Dick Miller, Barboura O'Neill, Barbara Crane, Fay Barker, June Kenney.
61 min. b/w.
A delightfully over-the-top campus drama, which Corman has said he originally intended as a microcosmic portrait of the ills of modern society, but which actually works best as a gleeful comic celebration of emotional sadism. Cabot is utterly entrancing as the twisted bad girl who has no truck with notions of sisterhood, preferring to get her kicks from blackmailing fellow students into abject submission and exposing unwanted pregnancies. She gets her comeuppance, naturally, but it's clear where Corman's sympathies lie. Deliriously cheap and nasty. GA

Sorry, Wrong Number
(Anatole Litvak, 1948, US) Barbara Stanwyck, Burt Lancaster, Ann Richards, Wendell Corey, Ed Begley, William Conrad, Leif Erickson.
89 min. b/w.
Stanwyck in one of her most famous roles, as an invalid who overhears a telephone conversation

between conspiring murderers, and slowly realises that she is their intended victim. Based on Lucille Fletcher's celebrated 22-minute radio play, the film is none the less well sustained. Litvak's camera paces the confines of Stanwyck's lacy bedroom like an accused man in his cell; and although she is for the most part restricted to acting from the head up, Stanwyck's metamorphosis from indolence to hysteria is brilliantly executed. TCh

S.O.S. Titanic

(William Hale, 1979, GB) David Janssen, Cloris Leachman, Susan Saint James, David Warner, Ian Holm, Helen Mirren, Harry Andrews, John Moffatt.
105 min.
Historical and disaster should be a lucrative combination: this succeeds elegantly with its plush settings, but it hams the spectacle dreadfully. 'The Titanic' never seems more than a model, especially when the unsinkable happens in mid-Atlantic, and director Hale seems a little confused about the weather conditions, which change from shot to shot. The film drops all too soon and too snugly into the standard disaster formula, though there are a couple of good observations; the rich ladies adjusting their life jackets in front of the mirror, for instance, and the illuminating depiction of the ship's rigid three-tier class system (first class: first saved). MPl

So That You Can Live

(Cinema Action, 1981, GB) Shirley Butts, Roy Butts, Royston Butts, Diane Butts.
83 min.
This is a spiky and uncompromising non-fiction feature: part-biography, part-documentary, part-history, and part elegy to a dying landscape. It's structured around five years in the life of Shirley Butts, a union convener who, as the film opens, loses first her job, and consequently her union card. The effect that this has on her life is then used as an opportunity to study the political and social history of the Cardiff working class area where she lives. Made by the independent Cinema Action collective, So That You Can Live avoids nudging its audience towards any facile political conclusion, however. Instead, the technical presentation of the film is used to destroy the illusion that this is a 'story' with a 'message', and to force the audience to make up its own mind. RR

So there, (Alors voilà,)

(Michel Piccoli, 1997, Fr) Maurice Garrel, Dominique Blanc, Arno, Roland Amstutz, Bernard Bloch.
93 min.
A wretched first feature from the 72-year-old Piccoli, which aims for the space between Raoul Ruiz and Mike Leigh, but winds up stewing in its own misanthropy, misogyny and latent sadism. A grizzled patriarch with gangster connections (Garrel) presides over his three sons and their families, who live in identical apartments in the same block. One son is suicidal, and spends more time in hospital than out; another runs a trucking company but goes into sudden psychotic rages. Presumably intended as grunge surrealism, the view of dysfunctional working class families is actually redolent of the most patronising middle class attitudes. Less a French answer to Nil by Mouth than an hysterically brutalised soap, as tedious in its way as Neighbours. TR

Souffle au Coeur, Le (Dearest Love/Murmur of the Heart)

(Louis Malle, 1971, Fr/It/WGer) Lea Massari, Daniel Gélin, Benoît Ferreux, Michel Lonsdale, Fabien Ferreux, Marc Winocourt.
118 min.
Although it stirred up a double vein of controversy – from those outraged, and those disappointed – Malle's film is less about incest and its implications than about the frustrations of bourgeois convention. The year is 1954, and the period is effortlessly caught in the opening sequence as two schoolboys swing down a street in Dijon, rattling collecting-boxes for the wounded of Dien-Bien-Phu in the intervals of rhapsodising over Charlie Parker, whose latest record they airily steal while making the shop-owner fork out a donation, 'pour la France, Monsieur'. More than anything else, the film reminds one

of Truffaut and the joyous spontaneity of Les Quatre Cents Coups as 14-year-old Laurent (a stunningly natural performance by Benoît Ferreux) agonises over the problem of how to lose his virginity in the face of a tight family circle which cramps his style while ignoring his needs. He finally makes it when convalescing at a spa from a heart murmur brought on by scarlet fever, and his mother – who has hitherto treated him as a baby, while seeking escape from her own unhappiness in an extra-marital affair – obliges (after a quaintly old-fashioned courtship) in a moment of pure, liberating joy. Tender and funny rather than daring or provocative, it's a film as gracefully and elegantly teasing as the best of Eric Rohmer. TM

Soufrière, La

(Werner Herzog, 1977, W Ger)
30 min.
As 75,000 people were being evacuated from the island of Guadeloupe in 1976, Herzog characteristically flew in to film the predicted eruption of 'La Soufrière' volcano and find the one peasant reported to have remained behind. Manic adventure had its reward. The holocaust didn't occur, the one peasant turned out to be a handful of calmly resigned natives; and the film metamorphosed into an essay on a deserted civilisation, like a surreal fourth chapter to Fata Morgana, or a sci-fi documentary on a city of starving dogs and blinking traffic lights. PT

Soul Food

(George Tillman Jr, 1997, US) Vanessa L Williams, Vivica A Fox, Nia Long, Michael Beach, Mekhi Phifer, Jeffrey D Sams, Irma P Hall, Gina Ravera, Brandon Hammond.
115 min.
Sunday lunches are the gist of the movie: communal nourishment prepared the traditional way, back home under the aegis of Mother Joe (Hall). We're in modern-day Chicago, among Mother Joe's three daughters, their spouses and offspring. The eldest, Teri (Williams), a professional success, but hard and embittered, rubs against her sisters and even her husband Miles (Beach); Maxine (Fox) lives more easily with Kenny (Sams) and their two young children; and newly-wed Bird (Long) finds life with Lem (Phifer) is loving but uncertain. It's Maxine's eldest, Ahmad (Hammond), who assumes Mother Joe's burden when she's hospitalised, and narrates the story which, as he says, is about the things that brought the family together and the things that tried to pull it apart. This is the limit of the film's ambitions, but if there are no surprises, it nevertheless makes sense: the dilemmas have emotional grounding, thanks to sure, steady direction and, especially, the ensemble cast. A hearty, old fashioned meal of a film. NB

Soul Investigator, The

(Kal Ng, 1994, Can) Patrick Cho, Edwin Cheung, Alice Ng, Edmond Chu, Kal Ng.
82 min.
At last: an émigré Chinese movie which goes beyond the templates Wayne Wang designed all those years ago in Chan Is Missing and Dim Sum. Kal Ng's dark psychodrama, shot mostly in steely, psychedelic shades of grey but with spasms of luscious colour, sends a downcast man on a spiritual quest to discover why he has a perpetually bleeding wound which no one else can see. Guidance comes from the title character Chide the Wind (played by Ng himself), who tells him three anti-Confucian parables designed to help him out of his personal prison. Wonderfully idiosyncratic, it plays rather like Doctor Strange stories directed by Bresson. TR

Soul Man

(Steve Miner, 1986, US) C Thomas Howell, Arye Gross, Rae Dawn Chong, James Earl Jones, Melora Hardin, Leslie Nielsen, James B Sikking.
105 min.
The plot of Soul Man – white middle class boy takes an overdose of suntan pills to enable him to qualify fraudulently for a black law students' scholarship – is sufficient to leave the meekest ideologue screeching with rage. But it's hard to be angry with a film which at least is an honest attempt to make a responsible (if lightweight) comedy encompassing aspects of racism in America. It's often extremely funny, but the prob-

lem is that Miner undermines his good intentions by allowing too many jokes about racial stereotypes. Soul Man is at its most incisive when questioning everyday racist assumptions, and is helped to that end by fine performances from Howell (as the fraud), Chong and Jones. In the end, however, it's let down by one easy laugh too many. DPe

Soultaker

(Michael Rissi, 1990, US) Vivian Schilling, Gregg Thomsen, David Shark, Joe Estevez, Jean Reiner, David Fawcett, Chuck Williams, Robert Z'Dar.
94 min.
This micro-budget variation on Ghost starts with a 'fatal' car crash, following which Natalia (Schilling), her old flame Zach (Thomsen), and bad boy Brad (Shark) are caught in limbo between life and death. Invisible to others and unable to influence events around them, they are pursued by 'Soultaker' (Estevez), racing against time to reunite their displaced souls with their barely living bodies. Rissi's uneven direction and cheapo special effects are no match for actor/writer Vivian Schilling's neatly turned script, but the film as a whole pays off nicely. NF

Soul to Soul

(Denis Sanders, 1971, US) Wilson Pickett, Ike and Tina Turner, Santana, Willie Bobo, Roberta Flack, Les McCann, Eddie Harris.
96 min.
The Soul to Soul Festival was staged in Ghana to mark the 14th anniversary of the country's independence. It was basically a 'roots' idea: getting black American musicians and singers to perform alongside native artists. It doesn't look as if it worked, and the film certainly doesn't have any tricks up its sleeves to make it work. Some of the performances are great (notably Flack and Pickett), but the filming is hopelessly dull; and the spliced-in travelogue interludes don't help at all. TR

Sound Barrier, The (aka Breaking the Sound Barrier)

(David Lean, 1952, GB) Ralph Richardson, Ann Todd, Nigel Patrick, Denholm Elliott, Dinah Sheridan, John Justin, Joseph Tomelty.
118 min. b/w.
In his third and final film with his erstwhile wife Ann Todd, Lean strove to chart the human cost of scientific progress; unfortunately, Terence Rattigan's script, while solidly structured, never probes beyond the basic conceit that an obsession which works towards the glory of mankind in general may wreak havoc on private lives. Certainly Richardson impresses as the De Havilland-like aircraft manufacturer whose passion brings suffering, even death, to his own family, while Nigel Patrick, as his test pilot son-in-law, is solid. But Todd herself typifies the awfully upper-crust restraint of the whole movie, and for all the intimate drama on view, it is the stirring aerial footage, accompanied by Malcolm Arnold's score, that remains most firmly fixed in the memory. GA

Sounder

(Martin Ritt, 1972, US) Cicely Tyson, Paul Winfield, Kevin Hooks, Carmen Mathews, Taj Mahal, James Best, Yvonne Jarrell.
105 min.
Conscientiously made, with a script by a well-known black playwright and small parts filled in by locals, this attempts to go some way beyond the merely nostalgic in its recreation of the life of a black sharecropper's family during the Depression. Beneath the apparent resignation of the characters, there lurks a determination to beat the life they've been forced into. It even points, through the boys' discovery of an all-black school which teaches black history and black pride, to a militant future. But if you compare Ritt's film to Third World movies about oppressed people living in startlingly similar conditions, you notice what's missing: the feeling of bone-edge existence and incipient anger. These films serve an immediate function, to change the lives of the people they're made about and for; Ritt's film must respond to the needs of an entertainment industry, and in its desire to be uplifting, leaves its characters one-dimensional without ensuring that the one dimension is heroic. VG

Sound of Fury, The (aka Try and Get Me)

(Cyril Endfield, 1951, US) Frank Lovejoy, Lloyd Bridges, Richard Carlson, Kathleen Ryan, Katherine Locke, Adele Jergens, Irene Vernon, Art Smith, Renzo Cesana.
92 min. b/w.

A flawed but strikingly dark thriller about a World War II veteran (Lovejoy), unable to provide for his family, who drifts into petty crime, is inveigled by an unbalanced acquaintance (Bridges) into a kidnapping that goes wrong, and ends on the wrong side of a lynch mob. Although based on a factual case from the '30s, it is designed as an anti-McCarthyist plea (Endfield was blacklisted soon after), and its weakness lies in the elements of message: the journalist who whips up mob hysteria against the criminals, and the Italian professor who provides a civilised commentary deploring what is going on. But the background is sharply observed, the first half is rivetingly done, and the tension reasserts itself for the lynching finale. TM

Sound of Music, The (100)

(Robert Wise, 1965, US) Julie Andrews, Christopher Plummer, Eleanor Parker, Richard Haydn, Peggy Wood, Charmian Carr, Heather Menzies.
174 min.

Call me a drongo, but this really is quite watchable (yes, I've seen it more than once). Of course it's reactionary shit, about how a woman's true vocation is to look after kids (even if they're not her own), turn curtains into clothes, and stand by her man. But the threat of Nazism is better evoked than in *Cabaret*, it's remarkably well edited, and it's cleverly scripted by Ernest Lehman (of *North by Northwest* and *Sweet Smell of Success* fame). Get smashed first, and you'll be singing along with the inescapably memorable tunes. GA

Sound of Trumpets, The

see Posto, Il

Soupirant, Le (The Suitor)

(Pierre Etaix, 1962, Fr) Pierre Etaix, Laurence Lignères, France Arnell, Claude Massot.
85 min. b/w.

Etaix's first feature after serving as assistant to Jacques Tati. Though his penchant for obtrusive sound effects (mostly creaks and squeaks) at the expense of dialogue makes this uncomfortably reminiscent of a silent classic revamped by Robert Youngson, and though his approach to humour can on occasion be as laboured as his protagonist's endeavours to acquire a wife, the comic temperament is real enough, and the gags are often brilliant. GAd

Souriante Madame Beudet, La (The Smiling Madame Beudet)

(Germaine Dulac, 1922, Fr) Germaine Dermoz, Alexandre C Arquillière, Madeleine Guitty, Jean d'Yd.
32 min. b/w.

Now celebrated as the first explicitly feminist film, *Madame Beudet* is a rare and outstanding example of Dulac's pioneering work (hard to categorise, the director is best known as a theorist and a leading member of the avant-garde). It marked a major advance towards psychological development in film, with its symbolism and experimental use of camera, lighting, superimposition and slow motion techniques to evoke the shifting mental and emotional state of an unsmiling woman (Germaine Dermoz) crushed by an oppressive marriage and finding momentary liberation in fantasy. LH

Soursweet

(Mike Newell, 1988, GB) Sylvia Chang, Danny An-Ning Dun, Jodi Long, Speedy Choo, Han Tan, Soon-Teck Oh, William Chow.
111 min.

Timothy Mo's novel, via Ian McEwan and Mike Newell, reaches the screen as something of a mess: so many narrative points fail to register, so many scenes are misjudged, that the viewer is left dangling, and the ending doesn't help. Chen (Dun, rotten) marries Lily (Chang) in Hong Kong, and the pair start a new life in London. He works as

a waiter until he falls foul of the Soho Triad societies through a gambling debt. Rather than be roped in as a drug runner, Chen hightails it for the wastelands of the East End and opens a takeaway. A family idyll ensues, with instant examples of culture shock for each generation. Meanwhile rival Chinatown gangs work through some old-style feuding (bloody stuff with cleavers and shotguns) but they haven't given up the search for Chen. Chinese ways are shown as being chipmunk cute, and the symbolism is thumpingly obvious. The biggest mistake is to raise expectations of Lily's lethal fists as the daughter of a martial arts expert, and then give her nothing to do when push comes to shove. BC

Sous le Soleil de Satan (Under Satan's Sun)

(Maurice Pialat, 1987, Fr) Gérard Depardieu, Sandrine Bonnaire, Maurice Pialat, Alain Artur, Yann Dedet, Brigitte Legendre, Jean-Claude Bourlat, Jean-Christophe Bouvet.
103 min.

Adapted from Georges Bernanos' novel, Pialat's ascetic meditation on faith, sainthood, and the nature of evil is a film of shattering intensity. Depardieu plays troubled Father Donissan, whose chance meeting with an insinuating horse-dealer (the Devil?) and confrontation with pregnant teenage murderess Mouchette (Bonnaire) convince him that human actions are governed not by God but by a manipulative Satan. The worries of Donissan's concerned superior (Pialat) about the priest's excessive physical and psychological self-flagellation are tempered by intimations of an unorthodox saintliness. Is Donissan motivated by a divine calling or merely by mortal pride? Through the coldly-lit images and restrained flesh-and-blood performances, self-confessed atheist Pialat insists on the absolute reality of events, an approach which allows something intangible (spiritual?) to seep in at the edges of the frame. Despite the confusing cutting from scene to scene, the narrative's rigorous logic, the performances, and the stark visual beauty yield profound pleasures. NF

Sous les Toits de Paris

(René Clair, 1930, Fr) Albert Préjean, Pola Illéry, Gaston Modot, Edmond Gréville, Paul Olivier.
92 min. b/w.

From its graceful opening pan across the (studio recreated) rooftops of the title to the multiple variations on its naggingly memorable theme song, the enchantment of Clair's first talkie has remained intact. Even the slight awkwardness of the semi-synchronised soundtrack, as scratchy as if played on a wind-up phonograph, complements its nostalgic, almost anachronistic visuals. That, plus Lazare Meerson's elegantly spare sets, George van Parys' jingly score, and the naïve if still affecting performances, make for a miniaturist masterpiece. GAd

South, The (El Sur)

(Victor Erice, 1983, Sp/Fr) Omero Antonutti, Lola Cardona, Sonsoles Aranguren, Iciar Bollàn, Rafaela Aparicio, Germaine Montero, Aurore Clément.
94 min.

The sublime *Spirit of the Beehive* was a daunting act to follow, but ten years on Erice produced a film to equal that earlier masterpiece. The setting is northern Spain in the late '50s. We look again through the eyes of a child, ever watchful and all-seeing, winkling out the secrets of this world apart, where there is neither Good nor Evil; no heroes, no escape; and life is lived in spluttering bursts of poetic intensity. Erice creates his film as a canvas, conjuring painterly images of slow dissolves and shafts of light that match Caravaggio in their power to animate a scene of stillness, or freeze one of mad movement. The dramatic impact of gorgeous image and tantalising message is enormous. FD

South Africa Belongs to Us

(Chris Austen, 1980, WGer/SAf)
55 min.

Shot covertly and smuggled out of South Africa, this portrait of five ordinary black women experiments with a non-conceptual form of documentary – minimal voice-over, direct address to camera, narrative-style establishing shots. This

creates a powerful, almost textural feel for the day-to-day existences of women kept permanently separated from their families by the oppressive economy of apartheid and its system of migrant workers, tribal trustlands, and single-sex hostels. But it's also a tribute to the resilience and growing militancy, a source of great strength for the women activists who broke banning orders to participate in the film. MPo

South Central

(Steve Anderson, 1992, US) Glenn Plummer, Carl Lumbly, Byron Keith Minns, LaRita Shelby, Christian Coleman.
99 min.

Writer/director Anderson's debut feature is a parable – punching its message home – about the enormous effort required from within the poor black community to break the cycle of violence in South Central Los Angeles. When Bobby (Plummer) is released from jail, he finds things have changed in the 'hood: friend Ray (Minns) has turned their gang into a drug ring, while his 'bitch' Carole (Shelby) is neglecting the baby born while he was inside. Torn between paternal instinct and peer pressure, Bobby is cajoled into murder; back behind bars, he undergoes a miraculous conversion. Low on directorial inspiration, but more relevant and resonant than much of the big-budget white trash churned out by Hollywood. CO'S

Southern Comfort

(Walter Hill, 1981, US) Keith Carradine, Powers Boothe, Fred Ward, Franklyn Seales, TK Carter, Lewis Smith, Peter Coyote, Les Lannom.
106 min.

Transposing *The Warriors* from Brooklyn to the bayous of Louisiana, this reactivates the old genre of the platoon movie, echoes to the distant trumpets of Vietnam, unconcernedly risks pigeonholing as *Deliverance II*, and generally sets up more reverberations from its pared-down premise than do any number of scatter-shot epics. Nine part-time National Guardsmen embark on weekend training manoeuvres in the southern swamplands, expecting only a long, wet walk towards a whorehouse – until the gun-play abruptly stops being kids' stuff, and eight virgin soldiers suddenly face long odds on survival, lost and leaderless in a guerrilla war of attrition against the native Cajuns. Hill's characters exercise their own deadly group dynamics in the firing line, while Ry Cooder's score, an eerily-shot alien landscape, and a lifestyle familiar mainly from Les Blank documentaries point up the internal cultural divide. Straight-line conflicts, low-light visuals: the film's basics, its strengths, and its critical Achilles' heel are all those of the classic American male action movie. PT

Southern Cross (aka The Highest Honor – A True Story)

(Peter Maxwell, 1982, Aust) John Howard, Atsuo Nakamura, Stuart Wilson, Steve Bisley, Michael Aitkins, George Mallaby.
143 min.

Adding the subtitle *A True Story* for British release doesn't make this any the more convincing. Even though the World War II friendship it resurrects between an earnest young Australian captain, survivor of an abortive raid on Singapore, and one of his Japanese captors, comes to an improbable head by Western standards, it's the inadequate, *Boy's Own* serial treatment that wrecks the film's credibility. A rambling first half tries to map out the two main characters, but they're swathed in loose ends. While the characters sweat and frown, all efforts to underline the inherent pathos end up as mawkish melodrama, and the film's ironies – the parallels between Eastern and Western notions of heroism and honour – get only a nod in passing. HH

Southerner, The

(Jean Renoir, 1945, US) Zachary Scott, Betty Field, J Carrol Naish, Beulah Bondi, Percy Kilbride, Blanche Yurka, Charles Kemper, Norman Lloyd.
91 min. b/w.

A harsh yet human antidote to traditional Hollywood attitudes about 'real people', this is (with *Diary of a Chambermaid*) Renoir's most successful American film, loose, free-flowing, honest. A year-in-the-life of Zachary Scott, Betty Field and family, poor sharecroppers turned self-employed, both romantic and realistic in its investigation of courage and freedom, both accurate and impressionistic in its view of 'nature', so that you can smell the river and the dead rain after the flood that almost ends their struggle. CW

Southern Yankee, A
(Edward Sedgwick, 1948, US) Red Skelton, Brian Donlevy, Arlene Dahl, George Coulouris, John Ireland.
90 min. b/w.
A Yankee ninny causes comic turmoil during the Civil War in this poor reworking of Keaton's *The General*. Skelton is no match for Buster in any department and the script is clearly beyond salvation, even after Keaton himself had been hired for the gag sequences and his old director Sedgwick dragged from retirement to supervise the proceedings.

South of St Louis
(Ray Enright, 1948, US) Joel McCrea, Alexis Smith, Zachary Scott, Dorothy Malone, Douglas Kennedy, Alan Hale, Victor Jory, Bob Steele, Art Smith.
88 min.
McCrea, Scott and Kennedy are partners in a Texan ranch burned out by 'Cottrell's Raiders' (a snarling Jory standing in for Quantrill) during the Civil War. Kennedy joins the Confederate army, while McCrea and Scott – balking at army discipline – are recruited by a saloon girl (Smith) for a profitable venture running munitions from Mexico through the Union blockades. Disillusioned by Scott's increasingly murderous lust for money, McCrea opts out and turns to drink after his girl (Malone) falls for Kennedy. When the war ends, Scott decides to consolidate his position by eliminating Kennedy, now a Texas Ranger; and McCrea is persuaded by Smith, who loves him, to retrieve his self-respect by helping Kennedy. Plenty of action, plus personable performances (McCrea especially); but the characters are so thin, the situations so contrived, and the dialogue so unfocused that one couldn't care less who does what to whom. TM

South Pacific
(Joshua Logan, 1958, US) Rossano Brazzi, Mitzi Gaynor, John Kerr, Ray Walston, Juanita Hall, France Nuyen.
170 min.
Plodding screen version of Rodgers and Hammerstein's stage musical in which an American Navy nurse on a South Pacific island falls in love with a middle-aged French planter, who later becomes a war hero. The lush visuals make the most of the exotic locations, but Logan's excessive use of colour filters is more distracting than effective. Some of the songs, at least, survived the transition: 'There Is Nothing Like a Dame', 'I'm Gonna Wash That Man Right Outa My Hair', and, of course, 'Bali Ha'i'. NF

South Riding
(Victor Saville, 1937, GB) Ralph Richardson, Edna Best, Ann Todd, John Clements, Edmund Gwenn, Marie Lohr, Glynis Johns, Milton Rosmer, Edward Lexy.
91 min. b/w.
'Take a look at the baby, Liz' a slum-dweller tells his big, tough, poetry-spouting daughter, 'he's frothing like a bottle of beer'. And not surprising, too, born into this hot-bed of passion and corruption. Saville carries Winifred Holtby's tart, witty exposé of Yorkshire power politics to the screen with breathtaking, and totally unexpected, panache. A film which makes a hero of the local squire (Richardson) and a dupe of the idealistic socialist councillor (Clements) must be ideologically suspect; but as rivalries are resolved in midnight calfing sessions and school cloakroom brawls, all reservations are swept aside. The sort of consensus politics which saw the gentry converting stately homes into schools and building council houses in the grounds is, after all, irresistible. RMy

Southwest to Sonora
see Appaloosa, The

Souvenir
(Geoffrey Reeve, 1987, GB) Christopher Plummer, Catherine Hicks, Michel Lonsdale, Christopher Cazenove, Lisa Daniely, Jean Badin, Patrick Bailey, Amelia Pick.
93 min.
Based on David Hughes' novel *The Pork Butcher*, this is the tale of ageing German expatriate Kestner (Plummer), who heads for France to see daughter Tina (Hicks), rescues her from a loveless marriage, and whisks her off to the small town of Lascaud where, as a Nazi soldier in the Occupation, he had a torrid affair with a French girl. Befriended by a British journalist (Cazenove), they discover that Lascaud was the scene of a Nazi massacre in 1944, and that Kestner's erstwhile girlfriend was among the victims. The bulk of the film concentrates on questioning the extent of Kestner's guilt, interspersed with flashbacks of the young lovers romping in haylofts. Sadly, a potentially absorbing moral conundrum is rendered pedestrian by a banal script, and superficial performances from Hicks and Cazenove. Plummer is convincing, and the recreation of occupied Lascaud reasonably schmaltz-free, but complexities of character, ethics and politics are too often reduced to lowest-common-denominator thrillerama. RS

Soylent Green
(Richard Fleischer, 1973, US) Charlton Heston, Leigh Taylor-Young, Edward G Robinson, Chuck Connors, Joseph Cotten, Brock Peters, Paula Kelly, Mike Henry, Whit Bissell.
97 min.
A depressingly plausible vision of the future, based on Harry Harrison's novel *Make Room! Make Room!*, which depicts New York in the year 2022 as a run-down ghetto teeming with hungry people. Heston, as an embittered cop, pokes his nose into the true and nefarious nature of the synthetic foodstuff (known as Soylent Green) with which the authorities have been feeding the populace. Edward G, in his last role, plays the elderly friend due for euthanasia who can still remember the halcyon days of the 20th century. An early example of mainstream sci-fi film, and consequently weighing in with the meaningful messages. AB

Spaceballs
(Mel Brooks, 1987, US) Mel Brooks, John Candy, Rick Moranis, Bill Pullman, Daphne Zuniga, Dick Van Patten, George Wyner, John Hurt.
96 min.
Brooks' *Star Wars* spoof employs the familiar scattergun approach, featuring gags old and new, something borrowed and something blue. Typically, the best conceits end in pratfalls, and non-Brooks fans may find that the gravitational pull towards the thumpingly obvious outweighs the wit. The story is a chip off the old Lucas block, with Darth Vader translated into the pipsqueak Dark Helmet (Moranis), The Force into The Schwartz, and Luke Skywalker becomes the slobbish space bum Lone Starr (Pullman), accompanied by his trusty dog Barf (Candy). The director's 2000-year-old man turns up, as well as a Druish princess (Zuniga) threatened with the return of her old nose. A flying Winnebago, a giant vacuum cleaner, and controls marked Light Speed and Ludicrous Speed get plenty of play, and there's a protracted rib-nudge as Brooks lets us in on the mystery of filming before proceeding to advertise Spaceball merchandise. In short, it is all exactly as you would imagine. BC

SpaceCamp
(Harry Winer, 1986, US) Kate Capshaw, Lea Thompson, Kelly Preston, Larry B Scott, Leaf Phoenix, Tate Donovan, Tom Skerritt, Barry Primus.
108 min.
'We're going to train you just like real astronauts', says SpaceCamp instructor Capshaw, 'We're here to provide you with hands-on hardware'. In real life, SpaceCamp is like a NASA-sponsored playgroup, a cross between summer camp and Colditz, where teenagers who believe in the American space dream can learn how it feels to be an astronaut. In the movie, it's more of a device to explore the usual hang-ups and foibles of the five teenage participants, none of whom carry much conviction. The action starts to heat up as the young astros get a chance to put what they've

learned into practice. Up until then, *Space Camp* plods along like any other half-baked teenage flick; but once in space, it gathers momentum for a gripping hands-on hardware climax. CB

Spaced Invaders
(Patrick Read Johnson, 1989, US) Douglas Barr, Royal Dano, Ariana Richards, JJ Anderson, Gregg Berger, Fred Applegate, Patrika Darbo, Tonya Lee Williams.
102 min.
A half-hearted, plagiaristic kids' sci-fi comedy, featuring one amusing idea which woefully fails to sustain an entire movie. After receiving a pasting from the neighbouring Arcturians, a disoriented Martian warship mistakenly intercepts a Halloween-night radio broadcast of *War of the Worlds* from Earth. Believing their comrades to be industriously trashing the humans, Captain Bipto and his crew – little green men with antennae – proceed swiftly to Earth to join the invading forces, only to be met with derision by the locals who, mistaking them for children in fancy dress, enlist them for a trick-or-treat party. Despite the neat comic inversion of its central premise (this time it's the spacemen who are taken in by Welles' classic hoax), the film soon comes a cropper as the chaotic script descends into a mêlée of limp and disjointed knockabout gags. MK

Space Firebird
(Osamu Tezuka, 1983, Jap)
116 min.
Tesuka's animated vision of Earth in the future: babies are born in test tubes, evaluated at an early age, and raised by robots to be trained in requisite skills. There is a stringent social hierarchy, with dissenters sent to labour camps, and the planet is slowly being destroyed as its mineral resources are consumed. Not exactly the stuff of light-hearted children's science fantasy, yet that's what it's meant to be. There are some conventional kiddies' bits, like the odd nauseating musical interlude, and a Jiminy Cricket-like whingeing dice-bird (or something), but these are the weakest points in the film. The animation is uniformly excellent, with some very effective sequences, especially in outer space, where the occasional quite violent moment is assisted by a glorious splash of colour. The whole thing is a very odd mix of cataclysmic religious hysteria, the worst imaginable Orwellian vision, and a Weetabix commercial. Loopy. And interesting. But awful for kids. DPe

Spacehunter: Adventures in the Forbidden Zone
(Lamont Johnson, 1983, US) Peter Strauss, Molly Ringwald, Ernie Hudson, Andrea Marcovicci, Michael Ironside, Beeson Carroll.
90 min.
True Grit gets mugged by *Mad Max 2* along an outer-space backstreet in this 3-D extravaganza for kids. Galactic adventurer Strauss matches the resoluteness of the late Duke Wayne with Mel Gibson's leather-glam, and teaming up with a teenage waif (Ringwald), boldly goes into the plague-infested technological wasteland of the Forbidden Zone. Their mission is to rescue three stranded Earth girls captured by the wonderfully villainous tyrant Overdog (Ironside), whose mechanical appendages make the dark side of The Force look positively pedestrian. Thankfully, Johnson uses the 3-D with restraint and doesn't bombard the audience with unnecessary projectiles, the copious action sequences being all the more effective as a result. The film suffers, however, from having to keep to a PG certificate: some fantastically eerie moments (brushes with barracuda women in the indoor swamp, and with humanoid blobs that appear out of nowhere) are not exploited to their full potential. What could have been a sci-fi horror classic is instead just a better-than-average children's adventure story. DPe

Space Jam
(Joe Pytka, 1996, US) Michael Jordan, Wayne Knight, Theresa Randle, Manner 'Mooky' Washington, Larry Bird, Bill Murray, Charles Barkley.
87 min.
As a cynical exercise in franchise exploitation this live-action/animated feature takes some beating; as a film, its target audience appears to be child

fans of the cartoon characters' live-action co-star, basketball player Michael Jordan. Realising he doesn't get a penny from the spin-off toys owned by Jordan's kids, Bugs Bunny considers getting a better agent. To revive his ailing Moron Mountain theme park, Swackhammer dispatches his minions, the Nerdlucks, to Looney Tunes Land, to kidnap Bugs, Daffy Duck, Wile E Coyote, et al. To save their skins, the Looney Tunes challenge their would-be abductors to a game of basketball, whereupon the Nerdlucks transform themselves into their fearsome alter egos, the Monstars, before siphoning off the ball-playing skills from a bunch of NBA stars. To even up the odds, Bugs and Co kidnap Jordan and beg him to lick them into shape for the big game. The set plays are transparently simple, the execution sloppy and the ending signposted days in advance. Visually, it's a mess: the attempts to blend 2- and 3-D animation with live-action and computer-generated images produce scenes that are fuzzier than the storyline. NF

Spaceman and King Arthur, The

see Unidentified Flying Oddball, The

Space Truckers

(Stuart Gordon, 1996, US/Ire) Dennis Hopper, Stephen Dorff, Debi Mazar, George Wendt, Vernon Wells, Barbara Crampton, Shane Rimmer, Charles Dance.
96 min.
Stuck in a dead-end job trucking square pigs across the galaxy for Interpork, John Canyon (Hopper) is happy enough to agree to ferry a one-off cargo of 'sex dolls' to Earth for a black market contractor. For one thing, it'll mean he can give his girlfriend Cindy (Mazar) a lift back to the home planet in time for her mum's operation; for another, if he can meet his delivery deadline, he's promised five times his standard wages – not bad, given that the company doesn't pay him anyway. But Canyon doesn't realise that he'll actually be ferrying a cargo of new-fangled killer Bio-Mechanical Warriors to kick-start corporate head EJ Saggs' plans for universal conquest. Director Gordon's sci-fi comedy, a dystopian spoof, comes across as a toytown *Alien*-cum-*Total Recall* pastiche. Bright, brash and occasionally almost amusing, perhaps, but also a waste of space. NB

Spaceways

(Terence Fisher, 1953, GB) Howard Duff, Eva Bartok, Andrew Osborn, Michael Medwin, Alan Wheatley, Philip Leaver, Cecile Chevreau.
76 min. b/w.
Before *Dracula* and *Curse of Frankenstein* made his name and put Hammer Films on the map, Fisher turned out this U-certificate adaptation of a radio play by Charles Eric Maine for the studio. Howard Duff is the US scientist accused of stashing his wife's corpse in a rocket, but the budget didn't stretch to much in the way of effects work. A decided oddity. TJ

Spanish Fly

(Bob Kellett, 1975, GB) Leslie Phillips, Terry-Thomas, Graham Armitage, Nadiuska, Frank Thornton, Ramiro Oliveros, Sue Lloyd.
86 min.
Dire comedy which doubles as a series of plugs for an underwear company. It's clearly intended as entertainment for the businessman – all the jokes are about impotence and gins-and-tonics – and it's shot mainly in close-up, like a TV show. Here's the plot: desperate for some dough to preserve his lavish life-style in sun-kissed Minorca, Sir Percy de Courcy (Terry-Thomas) buys up all the local plonk, having discovered that mixing it with ground-up flies produces a powerful aphrodisiac. So when fashion photographer Mike Scott (Phillips) descends on the island with a bevy of beautiful models, the fun comes fast and furious. But what's this? An unpleasant side-effect whereby everyone drinking the wine starts barking like a dog. Whoops... AN

Spanish Gardener, The

(Philip Leacock, 1956, GB) Dirk Bogarde, Jon Whiteley, Michael Hordern, Cyril Cusack, Maureen Swanson, Bernard Lee, Rosalie Crutchley, Geoffrey Keen.
97 min.

Minor diplomat Hordern, separated from his wife and repeatedly passed over for promotion, becomes jealous of the developing friendship between his small son Whiteley and Bogarde's locally hired gardener. Based on AJ Cronin's novel, this is the kind of small scale, low-key character study that British film-makers can sometimes do rather well, and one of the earliest suggestions that then matinee idol Bogarde might be turning into a fine screen actor. At this stage, though, he can't compete with Hordern, who's growing sense of desperation is affecting ly detailed. TJ

Spanish Main, The

(Frank Borzage, 1945, US) Paul Henreid, Maureen O'Hara, Walter Slezak, Binnie Barnes, John Emery, Barton MacLane, JM Kerrigan, Nancy Gates, Fritz Leiber.
101 min.
No scope for Borzage's gorgeously swooning, religiose romanticism in this swashbuckler, one of his most conventional movies. But it's also very enjoyable, most notably for Slezak, revelling as the villainous Spanish viceroy whose intended (O'Hara in fine fiery mood) is abducted by honest pirate Henreid, and for George Barnes' lavish Technicolor photography, which makes the most of the glorious sets, costumes and locations. If the script (co-written by Herman J Mankiewicz and George Worthing Yates) is hackneyed, Borzage films it with just the right amount of tongue in cheek. Wittier than Polanski's *Pirates* by a long way. GA

Spanking the Monkey

(David O Russell, 1994, US) Jeremy Davies, Alberta Watson, Benjamin Hendrickson, Carla Gallo.
100 min.
A nicely matter-of-fact, sensitively performed US indie debut about a white middle-class pre-medical student lumbered by his dad, a travelling video salesman, with the task of caring for his attractive invalid mum during the summer holidays. Much confusion and anxiety result, mainly because the boy suddenly begins to feel longings for his mother. Russell's script and direction hit just the right note: the film being at once wittily satirical and poignant, erotic and uncomfortable, as it refuses either to romanticise or to make a mountain out of an admittedly troubling molehill. Watson and Davies, as mother and son, are especially watchable. GA

Sparrow (Storia di una Capinera)

(Franco Zeffirelli, 1993, It) Angela Bettis, Jonathan Schaech, Sara-Jane Alexander, John Castle, Valentina Cortese, Sinead Cusack, Frank Finlay, Dennis Quilley, Vanessa Redgrave.
106 min.
It's 1854, and Maria (Bettis), soon to become a nun, is evacuated from plague-ridden Catania in Sicily to the opulent villa near Mt Etna shared by her loving father (Castle) and manipulative stepmother (Cusack). Here Maria meets Nino (Schaech), a family friend whose passionate love prompts a conflict between her instincts and her vocation. Finlay plays a nasty priest, and Redgrave a crazed nun. A full-blown very unpersuasive Zeffirelli melodrama, lamentably performed, with so many poorly framed wide-angles and zooms that no two shots seem capable of being edited together smoothly. AO

Sparrow of Pigalle, The

see Piaf

Sparrows Can't Sing

(Joan Littlewood, 1962, GB) James Booth, Barbara Windsor, Roy Kinnear, Avis Bunnage, Brian Murphy, George Sewell, Barbara Ferris, Murray Melvin.
94 min. b/w.
Pity Joan Littlewood left no filmed record of her major Theatre Workshop productions, which shook semi-moribund classics such as *Arden of Faversham* and *Edward II* into dazzling life, and bore witness to the most excitingly inventive imagination in the British theatre of the '50s. This one was distinctly minor, a Cockney chortle about a merchant seaman (Booth) who comes back to his native Stepney to find his wife (Windsor) living with another man. Much bouncy good humour, but no real pace or incisiveness, as he tangles with perky local characters in trying to persuade her to come back, while the real locations simply point up the sitcom phoniness. TM

Spartacus

(Stanley Kubrick, 1960, US) Kirk Douglas, Laurence Olivier, Jean Simmons, Tony Curtis, Charles Laughton, Peter Ustinov, John Gavin, Nina Foch, Woody Strode, John Ireland, John Dall, Herbert Lom, Charles McGraw.
196 min.
Although not a Kubrick project (he took over direction from Anthony Mann, and had no hand in Dalton Trumbo's script), this epic account of the abortive slave revolt in Ancient Rome emerges as a surprisingly apt companion piece to *Paths of Glory* in its consideration of the mechanisms of power. The first half, up to the superbly staged revolt and escape, is brilliant as it details the purchase and selection of slaves, the harsh discipline and routine of the gladiators' school, the new comradeship balked by the realisation that a gladiator must kill or be killed, the point of no return when the black slave (Strode) unexpectedly refuses to break the bond of brotherhood by killing Spartacus (Douglas). Thereafter some excellent performances come into play (Laughton, Olivier, Ustinov) as vested interests spark an involved struggle for power in the senate, but tension is simultaneously dissipated by the protracted battle sequences, and by a fulsome account of joyous fraternisation amid the slave army (sing-songs, swimming in the nude, having babies, etc). The sentimentality, rampant in the finale (Spartacus dying on the cross, his wife holding up his baby son before they walk free into the sunset) seems alien to Kubrick. TM

Spawn

(Mark AZ Dippé, 1997, US) John Leguizamo, Michael Jai White, Martin Sheen, Theresa Randle, Melinda Clarke, Miko Huges, Nicol Williamson, DB Sweeney.
96 min.
Live-action cartoon about a cape. It's a big cape, smooth, crimson and graceful, and it belongs to Spawn (White) who, having died, has unwittingly sold his soul to the Devil, who reckons the ex-assassin will lead his army to the Gates of Heaven. In return, Spawn gets a metallic body armour-cum-armoury, with matching cape. Now he can fly, form an impenetrable cocoon or disappear. He can even provide fancy cuts between scenes. Admittedly, that's a simplified analysis: you could argue the subject's a hunchbacked clown (Leguizamo), Satan's henchman, who, having tired of spewing out grim jokes, morphs into a monstrous dog-beast. In future, Dippé, an old SFX hand, needs to think about how to tell a story, rather than merely throw together elements of *Batman, Blade Runner, Star Wars* and James Bond. NB

Speaking Parts

(Atom Egoyan, 1989, Can) Michael McManus, Arsinée Khanjian, Gabrielle Rose, Tony Nardi, David Hemblen, Patricia Collins, Gerard Parkes.
92 min.
Pursuing the obsession with sex, death and videotape evident in *Family Viewing*, Egoyan here addresses the dangers of 'living in a situation in which everything depends upon one's attachment to, or rejection of, certain images'. For Clara (Rose), the danger lies in her desire to turn her dead brother's life into a TV movie, a project from which she is progressively erased. For shy hotel chambermaid Lisa (Khanjian), who watches videos of the man she loves as an extra in movies, it's her naive ignorance of the medium's potential for manipulation. Handsome gigolo Lance (McManus) has a role in both their lives; as the object of Lisa's unrequited, strangely ritualised love; as Clara's lover and the actor playing her brother in the film. In striking contrast to the flat, degraded video images of *Family Viewing*, the visuals here are lush and beautifully designed; still, a sensation of unreality persists. Machines like the video telephone link used by Lance and Clara as a sex aid seem to hinder rather than aid communication. Nevertheless, far from condemning recording media out of hand, Egoyan scrutinises our ambiguous relationship with them; and as the characters grope towards less alienated (self) images, the film achieves a remarkable synthesis of intellectual analysis and deeply felt emotion. NF

Special Day, A
(Una Giornata Particolare)

(Ettore Scola, 1977, It/Can) Sophia Loren, Marcello Mastroianni, John Vernon, Françoise Berd, Nicole Magny, Patrizia Basso.
105 min.
If American audiences could buy the films of Lina Wertmüller wholesale, it's hardly surprising that *A Special Day*, a more restrained but equally spurious piece of Italo-attitudinising on sex and politics, pulled two Oscar nominations. It looks 'serious': newsreels set the scene as the day of Hitler's visit to Rome in May 1938; the colour is bleached to an approximation of sepia; Loren eschews make-up. It sounds 'meaningful': Mastroianni mouths philosophy down the phone; the radio blares Fascist agit-prop. It boils down, however, to the worst kind of sentimental tosh, as Loren's dowdy housewife sets aside her dreams of the *Duce* for a day and embarks on a brief encounter with Mastroianni's hounded homosexual from across the courtyard. And its supposed 'achievement' is to present this unlikely coupling as a revolt against their mutual oppression, itself 'explained' by Fascism. QED: rubbish. PT

Special Effects

(Larry Cohen, 1984, US) Zoe Tamerlis, Eric Bogosian, Brad Rijn, Kevin O'Connor, Bill Oland, Richard Greene.
103 min.
One of Cohen's lurid chunks of low-budget lunacy, this starts off in total sleaze territory, with a tacky blonde tartlet (Tamerlis) resisting the attempts of her earnest hicksville husband (Rijn) to take her away from Manhattan and back into the bosom of her family. She takes up, briefly, with a crazed film director (Bogosian) who is still reeling from the effects of his latest multi-million dollar flop. Just when it looks set to develop into a skinflick, the film shoots off into new and unexpected directions – murder, manipulation, and identity crisis, capped with a dizzy thriller climax. There are a couple of expository hiccups, but Cohen gleefully takes the piss out of his own profession, and Tamerlis (the mute *Ms. 45* Angel of Vengeance), plays her (speaking) part to the hilt. A diverting and demented peek through the eye of a very warped lens. AB

Specialist, The

(Luis Llosa, 1994, US) Sylvester Stallone, Sharon Stone, James Woods, Rod Steiger, Eric Roberts, Mario Ernesto Sanchez.
110 min.
Stallone is Ray Quick, a bomb-disposal expert with a difference: it's people he disposes of. Not indiscriminately, mind you. He can 'control his explosions, shape his charges' – which must be why May Munro (Stone) decides he's just the man to execute her revenge on half a dozen Cuban sleazeballs (played by the likes of Roberts and Steiger). Cast as a security expert hired by the sleazeballs, Woods clearly knows trash when he's in it: conjuring up a spellbinding sequence out of a gram of Semtex and a ballpoint pen, or hilariously scandalising a funeral congregation, he has a bite and gusto at odds with the vacuity of almost everything else going on around him. TCh

Special Section

see Section Spéciale

Special Treatment
(Poseban Tretman)

(Goran Paskaljevic, 1980, Yugo) Ljuba Tadic, Dusica Zegarac, Milena Dravic, Danilo Stojkovic, Petar Kralj.
93 min.
Special Treatment is what the inmates of an alcoholic ward receive from their doctor/director – a dour regimen of psychodrama, physical jerks and Nietzschean will-to-power, dished out with the usual righteous sadism. A 'therapeutic' trip to a beer factory confronts authoritarianism with the more human desire for a little happy excess: the old joke of a piss-up in a brewery is crossed with some high-key political power-plays. If Paskaljevic's relentless focus on the nature of Fascism is a shade extended, it's tempered by some great moments of outrageous hilarity, playful echoes of Pirandellian illusion, an electric enactment of sexual politics from the wonderful Milena Dravic (the sex-warrior in *W.R.–*

Mysteries of the Organism), and a conclusion of joyous anarchy. If Fassbinder's persistent cruelty gets you down, then see a film just as tough on the vanity of totalitarianism, but which genuinely likes people. CPea

Species

(Roger Donaldson, 1995, US) Ben Kingsley, Michael Madsen, Alfred Molina, Forest Whitaker, Natasha Henstridge, Marg Helgenberger.
108 min.
A hybrid created from human and alien DNA escapes from the top-secret laboratory of Dr Xavier Fitch (Kingsley); with her accelerated growth and insatiable desire to procreate, Sil (Henstridge, 'conceived and designed' by HR Giger) is a primed mobile sex-bomb. Fitch assembles a team of experts and weirdos to track down and destroy the broody alien babe. Madsen's heartless killing machine, Helgenburger's token female scientist, and Molina's dorky anthropologist join the hunt. But Whitaker's wigged-out 'empath' feels more deeply, and alone can tell the wood from the trees: standing in a wrecked train carriage, he looks down at a dead guard on the floor, then at the slime-oozing cocoon clinging to the wall, before declaring in a hushed voice, 'Something bad happened here.' Like some state-of-the-art remake of *Lifeforce*, this is every bit as bad as Tobe Hooper's film, but nothing like as enjoyable. Worst is the transition in the final scenes from snatched glimpses of a woman in a rubber suit to some oddly alienating motion-control effects. Floating like the ghosting on a poorly tuned TV, these are far too clean and artificial to be believable or remotely scary. Deserves extinction. NF

Species II

(Peter Medak, 1998, US) Michael Madsen, Natasha Henstridge, Marg Helgenberger, George Dzundza, James Cromwell, Austin Lazard, Peter Boyle.
93 min.
The one group likely to find this amusing are, in theory, too young to be allowed near it. Moving briskly from one Grand Guignol number to the next, Medak hardly pretends to tell a story, let alone a plausible one. Again, sex and horror are associated in scenes where copulating bodies are rent asunder and turned into an arrangement of what look like pulsating worms and turds, plus spurting blood and sticky stuff generally. The routine obscenities in the dialogue are interrupted only by some deliberately dumb one-liners, to provoke the audience. BBa

Specter of the Rose

(Ben Hecht, 1946, US) Judith Anderson, Michael Chekhov, Ivan Kirov, Viola Essen, Lionel Stander.
90 min. b/w.
A ballet melodrama with a score by George Antheil, this is one of eight pictures directed by the legendary screenwriter Ben Hecht, one of Hollywood's most grizzled cynics. The storyline centres on a schizophrenic male ballet star (an American with a 'continental' pseudonym) who starts murdering his partners during performances of the title ballet. Hecht's plotting fulfils every hope it may conjure up, but the real delight is his dialogue, which is among the most ineffably pretentious ever heard on screen. 'Press yourself against me so hard that you're tattooed on to me' whispers our hero (Kirov) as he chats up his ballerina wife-to-be (Essen) in a seedy hotel foyer. It has a curious and quite moving integrity at heart...but it's also the *Beyond the Valley of the Dolls* of its day. TR

Spectre of
Edgar Allan Poe, The

(Mohy Quandour, 1972, US) Robert Walker, Mary Grover, Cesar Romero, Tom Drake, Carol Ohmart.
86 min.
A rather endearing slice of hokum in which Edgar Allan Poe becomes a horror film hero battling to save his cataleptic love Lenore (Grover) from the clutches of an old-fashioned mad scientist (Romero), whose private asylum comes complete with basement snake-pit and furtive man-beast experiments. Robert Walker looks right for Poe, but the overall tone of the production is finally no more interesting than the average TV series. DP

Speechless

(Ron Underwood, 1995, US) Michael Keaton, Geena Davis, Christopher Reeve, Bonnie Bedelia, Ernie Hudson, Charles Martin Smith, Gailard Sartain, Mitchell Ryan.
98 min.
The premise is promising – a couple 'meet cute', each unaware that the other is a speechwriter for opposing candidates in an Arizona senate race – but the treatment sinks it. Unlike say, *Dave*, which wove a well-chosen cast into a nicely topical scenario to produce a Capra-esque comedy of populist ideology, this relegates the fertile ground of American politics to mere backdrop for a misconceived *Adam's Rib*-style screwball romance. Mugging to an unfunny script, Keaton and Davis are no Tracy and Hepburn, and the funereal pace doesn't help. AO

Speed

(Jan De Bont, 1994, US) Keanu Reeves, Dennis Hopper, Sandra Bullock, Joe Morton, Jeff Daniels, Alan Ruck.
116 min.
Reeves is a Los Angeles SWAT cop, Hopper the regulation bomber-with-a-grudge who wires first a lift, then a public bus. If the bus's speed drops below 50 mph, boom! Keanu hops on board to map-read, and, when the driver retires hurt, feisty passenger Bullock takes the wheel – and effectively steals the movie. It's mindless, but ingenious. Graham Yost's script dispenses with excess baggage: a handful of characters face certain – well, near-certain – death. First-time director De Bont (cameraman of *Die Hard* and *Basic Instinct*) makes good use of a hand-held camera and conveys a real sense of volition: you'll believe a bus can fly! He seems to identify so thoroughly with the characters that the pace never flags. Eventually, inevitably, he goes too far, too fast, and ends up off the rails. TCh

Speed 2: Cruise Control

(Jan De Bont, 1997, US) Sandra Bullock, Jason Patric, Willem Dafoe, Temuera Morrison, Brian McCardie, Christine Firkins, Lois Chiles.
125 min.
Further evidence, after the computer-generated vapidity of *Twister*, that De Bont's directorial career has expended the promise of his debut *Speed*. Making the sequel without Keanu Reeves was a desperate move, and this proceeds to throw overboard every other component of the first film's success: familiar settings, fleet pacing, a witty plot and irreverent characterisation. Here the characters are cut-outs, the settings alien (who outside Hollywood can picture themselves trapped on a luxury cruiser?), and the action interminable. 'Relationships based on extreme circumstances never work out,' Bullock's character repeats incessantly to explain (and remind us of) Keanu's absence. She thinks her new beau's a beach guard – only to discover he's actually another daredevil cop. To make up, they take a Caribbean holiday, alongside Dafoe, recently sacked, feeling under-appreciated and planning revenge. Dafoe's take on Dennis Hopper's Hopper impersonation is plain pointless; Bullock too is wasted in a ditzy half-role; and Patric is unsmiling and resolutely uncharismatic. NB

Speedtrap

(Earl Bellamy, 1977, US) Joe Don Baker, Tyne Daly, Richard Jaeckel, Robert Loggia, Morgan Woodward, Dianne Marchal, Timothy Carey.
101 min.
'The only trouble with this business is that it's one wild goose chase after another', says pudgy 'all-American-saint' Joe Don Baker of his assignment to catch the notorious Roadrunner, purloiner of flash fast cars. That's an accurate summation of *Speedtrap*, a tedious little number which trades heavily on burning rubber, squealing tires, and a police force hell-bent on crashing into each other at every available opportunity. FF

Speedy

(Ted Wilde, 1928, US) Harold Lloyd, Ann Christy, Bert Woodruff, Brooks Benedict, George Herman Ruth.
86 min. b/w.
Lloyd's last silent picture is a lazy affair, of interest chiefly, now at the end of the century, for its affectionate and detailed portrait of New York City in the 1920s. The story concerns an old timer who drives the city's last horse drawn tram along

a certain route which he won't give up to satisfy some ruffianly railroad developers. Harold 'Speedy' Swift (Lloyd), who works as a soda jerk and is baseball mad (cue Babe Ruth cameo), is in love with the old man's daughter, and shows her a good time (interminably) on Coney Island. There are one or two elegant sight gags (a dollar bill attached to a piece of cotton obtains the love birds a seat on a trolley), but the climactic rescue of the clanky hijacked tram lacks the adrenalin rush of an authentic Lloyd chase sequence. JPy

Spell, The (Telesm)

(Dariush Farhang, 1988, Iran) Jamshid Mashayekhi, Soosan Tasslimi, Parviz Poorhosseini, Attila Pessyani.
90 min.
A stirring mish-mash of cultural allusion, sledge-hammer symbolism, and something approaching camp humour, if such a thing exists in modern Iran. It's an Old Dark House movie, in which a newly-wed peasant couple take shelter from the storm in a sinister palace. The young bride finds herself imprisoned with the master's wife, a pallid ghost who plots revenge on her tormentor, the hollow-cheeked servant who engineered her disappearance. The protracted agonies of revenge and reconciliation look exactly like late Strindberg; the high seriousness invites and allows laughs aplenty. Altogether surprising, and unexpectedly moving. RS

Spellbound

(Alfred Hitchcock, 1945, US) Ingrid Bergman, Gregory Peck, Leo G Carroll, John Emery, Michael Chekhov, Wallace Ford, Rhonda Fleming.
111 min. b/w.
In 1945, Freud & Co were beginning to have a profound influence on American thinking, so armed with a script by Ben Hecht and the services of a consultant, Hitchcock decided to 'turn out the first picture on psychoanalysis'. The story is simple enough: Bergman is a psychoanalyst who falls in love with her new boss Peck, and when it's discovered that he has a Problem (an amnesiac, he may also be a killer), goes to work on his memory. The characterisation is also straightforward, with a maternal Bergman fascinated by father figures (a delightful cameo from Michael Chekhov) and young boys (Peck, suitably artless). But *Spellbound* is also a tale of suspense, and Hitchcock embellishes it with characteristically brilliant twists, like the infinite variety of parallel lines which etch their way through Peck's mind. The imagery is sometimes overblown (doors open magically down a corridor when Peck and Bergman kiss), and the dream sequences designed by Dali are exactly what you'd expect; but there are moments, especially towards the end, when the images and ideas really work together. HM

Speriamo che sia Femmina

see Let's Hope It's a Girl

Spetters

(Paul Verhoeven, 1980, Neth) Hans Van Tongeren, Renee Soutendijk, Toon Agterberg, Maarten Spanjer, Marianne Boyer, Rutger Hauer, Jeroen Krabbé.
115 min.
Rutger Hauer returns to his native Holland to make a cameo appearance playing world motor-cross champion. The main action centres on three 'ordinary' young men, two of them aspirants to the motorcross crown, and on a scheming minx who serves suggestive sausages from a fast-food-mobile. She manages to work her way through most of the male cast, via a lot of Kingsize Biking innuendo, before exchanging her picaresque lifestyle and lovely leather jacket for the most bourgeois of the boys and a ghastly fur coat. The filming, alternately gorgeous and goreously trite, adds to the hilarity as Verhoeven piles on the melodrama: slickly choreographed sexploitation and adolescent humour escalate into queer-bashing, with a suicide and gay gang-bang to complement the nice locations. Admirers of Fassbinder and *Soap* should find much to amuse them. AB

Sphere

(Barry Levinson, 1998, US) Dustin Hoffman, Sharon Stone, Samuel L Jackson, Peter Coyote, Queen Latifa, Liev Schreiber.
134 min.

Author Michael Crichton is to science fiction what Stephen King is to horror: although his work lacks originality, his ability to write page turning pulp novels allows him to pass off recycled ideas as something apparently more profound. For *Sphere*, he lifted the premise of Tarkovsky's *Solaris*, in which a physical object – here a mysterious shimmering sphere discovered in a sub-merged spaceship at the bottom of the ocean – causes those who enter it to give physical form to their inner thoughts. Drawn to the sci-fi genre by a scenario that relied less on hardware than the relationships between a group of investigating scientists trapped inside a claustrophobic submarine pod, director Levinson has made a *Solaris*-meets-*The Abyss* with dramatic knobs on. Hoffman's idealistic psychologist, Stone's emotionally unstable biochemist and Jackson's sceptical mathematician all apply specialist knowledge to the conundrum, watched over by enigmatic team leader Coyote. Three major stars being involved, it all wraps up happily but implausibly. NF

Sphinx

(Franklin J Schaffner, 1980, US) Lesley-Anne Down, Frank Langella, Maurice Ronet, John Gielgud, Vic Tablian, Martin Benson, John Rhys-Davies.
118 min.
Scripted by John Byrum from a Robin Cook novel, this is basically *Coma*-goes-to-Egypt, with smuggling statuettes replacing smuggling live organs. Striking use of locations, but lousy script, uneasy heroine, and weak material. A clear case of a lame project that only a 'best selling' (ie. heavily pre-sold) novel could have financed. Avoid. MA

Spice World

(Bob Spiers, 1997, GB) The Spice Girls, Richard E Grant, Barry Humphries, Alan Cumming, Claire Rushbrook, Naoki Mori, Meatloaf. Stephen Fry, Elvis Costello, Richard Briers, Roger Moore, Bob Geldhof, Bob Hoskins, Bill Paterson, Jennifer Saunders.
93 min.
The Spice Girls (not quite the Beatles) try to make their Albert Hall gig in the face of mounting pressure from the press, their manager (Grant) and, in a literal sense, their best friend Nicola (Mori). Spiers' pseudo-documentary bubble-and-squeak allows the girls to dress up, dress down, change identities, ride around in a Union Jack bus, rub shoulders with a large cameo cast, and indulge in vacuous banter. Help! DA

Spicy Rice (Drachenfutter)

(Jan Schütte, 1987, WGer/Switz) Bhasker, Ric Young, Buddy Uzzaman, Wolf-Dieter Sprenger.
72 min. b/w.
Shot in high-contrast black-and-white, documentarist Schütte's first fiction feature is a disarmingly low-key look at the lives of immigrant workers in Hamburg. One such is Shezad, a Pakistani seeking political asylum from the less-than-sympathetic West German authorities; another is Xiao, waiter at the Chinese eatery where Shezad works, who dreams of opening his own restaurant. With wry humour and an admirable lack of sentimentality, Schütte charts the hesitant progress of the pair's friendship. While the realist tone and understated performances sustain interest in themselves, still more affecting is the assured control of mood, with a lovingly shot, wintry Hamburg constituting a major character. A modest, deceptively simple film, its brevity is a distinct bonus. You're left wishing it had continued for another 30 minutes. GA

Spider, The

see Earth vs the Spider

Spider and Rose

(Bill Bennett, 1994, Aust) Ruth Cracknell, Simon Bosell, Max Cullen.
94 min.
Writer/director Bennett's road comedy pits an irresponsible young ambulance driver (on his last day at work) against a grouchy old widow, still reeling from her husband's death in a car accident a year earlier. During a long, eventful journey together, the pair predictably come to terms with each other, but thanks to an occasionally tart script and Ruth Cracknell's unsentimental, convincingly vigorous performance, the movie man-

ages to avoid the worst pitfalls of the genre. Minor but – at least after a hesitant start – surprisingly engaging. GA

Spider and the Fly, The

(Robert Hamer, 1949, GB) Eric Portman, Guy Rolfe, Nadia Gray, Edward Chapman, Harold Lang, George Cole, Maurice Denham, Sebastian Cabot, Jeremy Spenser, Arthur Lowe.
95 min. b/w.
Undervalued at the time, more mood piece than thriller, this is a fascinating attempt to express the uncertain moral climate of a period of change (eve of WWI) through a cat-and-mouse game between a gentleman cracksman (Rolfe) and a Parisian police inspector (Portman) who knows very well who the thief is, but is unable to discover how he covers his tracks. A sort of friendship springs up between them, foundering only on ethical and legal barriers; but their curious kinship is further defined by the lovely provincial innocent (Gray) used as a decoy by Rolfe, then abandoned to her fate when she is arrested by Portman in an attempt to force a gentlemanly confession. Struck by their dignity and integrity under duress, both men begin to fall in love with her... Instead of fully exploring the moral and psychological implications, the script opts for a lightly ironic (but still pleasingly apt) coda in which both men find themselves hoist by their own prejudices and petards. But the look of the film, bleak and penumbral, with sets, camerawork and beautifully chosen locations conspiring to recapture the poetic quality of Feuillade's Paris, makes it rank with Hamer's best work. TM

Spider-Man

(EW Swackhamer, 1977, US) Nicholas Hammond, Lisa Eilbacher, Michael Pataki, David White, Thayer David, Ivor Francis, Jeff Donnell.
94 min.
In translating comic strips to the screen (in this case, as pilot for a TV series), film-makers generally seem either to remove all the guts, or to adopt such a derisive tone that they come out looking a whole lot dumber than their source. Some attempt is made to avoid these traps here: Stan Lee worked on the script, and most of Marvel Comics' larger-than-life characters are retained, while the plot just about takes itself seriously enough to generate a certain momentum. But the film falls down largely because its lack of resources necessitates so much repetition. The video special effects of Spider-Man crawling up walls work a whole lot better than the way it was done on *Batman*; but as *Star Wars* so decisively showed, comic strips demand budgets as lavish as their conception. DP

Spider-Man Strikes Back

(Ron Satlof, 1978, US) Nicholas Hammond, Robert F Simon, Michael Pataki, Chip Fields, JoAnna Cameron, Robert Alda, Randy Powell.
93 min.
The insubstantiality of this low-rent product is pleasantly refreshing – we learn that Spider-Man is a lot smaller than most of the villains, sensitive to slurs about his 'little blue tights', and chronically short of cash. For a change, the script is riddled with trashy jokes, silly set-ups, and a lack of excessive special effects. CR

Spider Man – The Dragon's Challenge

(Don McDougall, 1979, US) Nicholas Hammond, Robert F Simon, Ellen Bry, Chip Fields, Myron Healey, Rosalind Chao, Richard Erdman, Benson Fong, Ted Danson.
96 min.
Min Lo Chan (Fong), Minister for Industry and Development in the People's Republic of China, visits New York editor Jonah Jameson (Simon) for help in clearing himself of the charge that he sold secrets about Mao's advancing army to US Marines during World War II. And Jameson enlists Peter Parker (Hammond), in reality superhero Spider-Man. Kung-fu and an acupuncture cure (when Spider-Man gets wounded) are both mooted, but when the moment arrives to deliver, the camera weasels out. And sad to say, there's a complete lack of the slight but delightful political savvy that redeemed *Spider-Man Strikes Back*. CR

Spiders, The

see Spinnen, Die

Spider's Stratagem, The (La Strategia del Ragno)

(Bernardo Bertolucci, 1970, It) Giulio Brogi, Alida Valli, Tino Scotti, Pippo Campanini, Franco Giovanelli, Allen Midgett.
97 min.
Bertolucci's precipitous decline into political and aesthetic misjudgments (signalled by parts of *Last Tango* and confirmed by long stretches of *1900*) shouldn't make anyone forget that his intelligence, erotic sensibility, and wit once made him the only Italian director comparable to Pasolini. Made after *The Conformist* and showing Bertolucci at the height of his powers, *The Spider's Stratagem* transposes a Borges short story to the Po Valley in Italy, introduces a dazzling density of cultural references, and remains thrilling and extraordinary. Athos Magnani (Brogi) returns to his home town, where the defacement of the memorial to his father (a hero of '36) sets him on the trail of the truth about his parent; the world he explores is full of mysteries, omens, ambiguities, and signs of incipient madness, and it resolves itself into a riddle that is the cinema's richest homage to all that's remarkable in Borges. TR

Spiegel, Der

see Mirror, The

Spies

see Spione

Spies Like Us

(John Landis, 1985, US) Dan Aykroyd, Chevy Chase, Steve Forrest, Charles McKeown, Donna Dixon, Derek Meddings, Bruce Davison, William Prince, Bernie Casey.
109 min.
A double act with Chase and Aykroyd playing US State Department misfits whose gross bad behaviour during an informal exam leads them into hurried training for a deadly mission in Soviet-controlled Pakistan and Afghanistan. Sadly, the script is so patchy that most of the genuine laughs are squeezed into the first half; the rest is a rather tacky and confused extended joke about the nuclear arms race, which is tasteless only because it fails to be funny. There are token guest slots for the likes of Bob Hope, BB King, and a whole string of film-makers from Ray Harryhausen and Larry Cohen to Costa-Gavras and Michael Apted. SGr

Spikes Gang, The

(Richard Fleischer, 1974, US) Lee Marvin, Gary Grimes, Ron Howard, Charlie Martin Smith, Arthur Hunnicutt, Noah Beery.
96 min.
An engaging Western, based on Giles Tippette's novel *The Bank Robber* but designed more or less as a sequel to Robert Benton's *Bad Company*, with Marvin as a wounded gunman helped by three boys, and later (after they run away from home in search of the excitement and easy living conjured by his reminiscences) tutoring them on the downward path. Familiar territory (ageing outlaw hemmed in by shrinking frontiers and cruel options), but beautifully acted, sharply scripted, and often very funny en route to the bitter final lessons in disillusionment. One of Fleischer's best movies from the '70s. TM

Spin

(Brian Springer, 1994/5, US) George Bush, Bill Clinton, Ross Perot, Larry King, Pat Robertson.
76 min. Video.
Satellite interviews are part of the furniture of news and current affairs programmes. If you've ever felt concern about the degree of collusion between the politicos and the media, this documentary will set your jaw dropping. In a brief intro, Springer describes how he used an ordinary satellite tuner to record some 100 hours of TV satellite link time, capturing the studio-to-interviewee feeds in their entirety, rather than just the familiar on-air Q&A routines we see every day. What follows, distilled to 76 minutes, is a catalogue of off-hand revelations, unwitting gaffes,

blind prejudice and unalloyed hucksterism: the off-guard moments of Bush, Clinton and Perot during 1992's presidential election campaign. Some of this stuff is amazing. CNN talk-show host Larry King boasts how he's changed the world, between talking about sleeping pills with Bush; Perot mentions the time he took Michael Jackson out on his speed boat; moral majority hatemonger Pat Robertson is a smiling mound of brazen homophobia. Springer avoids authorial comment. He doesn't need it: most of these guys have just hanged themselves thrice over before our very eyes. Unreservedly recommended. TJ

Spinnen, Die (The Spiders)

(Fritz Lang, 1919/20, Ger) Carl de Vogt, Ressel Orla, Lil Dagover, Paul Morgan, Georg John, Bruno Lettinger.
6,240 ft (Part I)/7,281 ft (Part II). b/w.
Lang's third venture as a director, which he also scripted. Often reminiscent of Feuillade in its delirious invention and tongue-in-cheek humour, it's a wild and woolly serial about a secret society of arch-criminals who plan (of course) to dominate the world, and make a start by initiating a quest for the fabulous lost treasure of the Incas. Fiendish cruelties, fluttering heroines, and Oriental villains are all welded together in some wonderfully exotic settings by Lang's superb architectural sense. Two projected further instalments were never filmed, although Lang had already prepared the scripts. TM

Spione (Spies/The Spy)

(Fritz Lang, 1928, Ger) Rudolf Klein-Rogge, Gerda Maurus, Willy Fritsch, Lupu Pick, Fritz Rasp, Lien Deyers, Craighall Sherry.
14,318 ft. b/w.
In its very idiosyncratic way, *Spione* beats Lang's three Mabuse pictures as his definitive vision of a criminal mastermind. The reason is probably that this film entirely lacks the socio-political overtones of the Mabuse trilogy: the exploits of the evil genius Haghi (Klein-Rogge) here represent criminality almost in the abstract, and plunge the movie into a delirium of disguises, deaths, double-motives, and labyrinthine tricks. The tone is somewhere between true pulp fiction and pure expressionism, and the result remains wholly thrilling. TR

Spiral Staircase, The

(Robert Siodmak, 1946, US) Dorothy McGuire, George Brent, Ethel Barrymore, Kent Smith, Rhonda Fleming, Elsa Lanchester, Gordon Oliver, Rhys Williams.
83 min. b/w.
Superb thriller about a manic killer dedicating himself to beauty by ridding the world of maimed or disfigured women. Hitchcock couldn't have bettered the casual mastery with which the opening defines not just time and place (small town, turn of the century) but the themes of voyeurism and entrapment as a carriage draws up outside a hotel, the townsfolk assemble inside for a silent picture show, and the camera lifts to a room above where a crippled girl is being watched by a malevolently glaring hidden eye as she undresses. This first murder, discreetly executed as the girl pulls her dress over her head and we see her arms convulsively cross in agony, introduces a note of expressionism which Siodmak uses sparingly but with unfailing elegance throughout as the shadows close in on McGuire's mute, terrified heroine. It's one of the undoubted masterpieces of the Gothic mode, even if the happy ending comes more than a shade too pat. TM

Spiral Staircase, The

(Peter Collinson, 1975, GB) Jacqueline Bisset, Christopher Plummer, Sam Wanamaker, Mildred Dunnock, Gayle Hunnicutt, Sheila Brennan, Elaine Stritch, John Ronane, Ronald Radd, John Phillip Law.
89 min.
Who has been killing off young girls with physical defects, and obviously has an eye on Jacqueline Bisset, rendered speechless by a shock (doubtless on finding herself in a movie like this)?. There's a lush in the kitchen, a bedridden grandmother, a secretary on the make, an ex-Vietnam vet, a kindly uncle, an even more kindly doctor, a trigger-happy cop, and a storm outside. Any interest soon gets lost in the rambling rooms of the huge house that serves as the base for the plot. The moral of the tale would seem to be that if you

want your voice back, have someone try to strangle you. Whatever happened to the chilling Gothic tale made by Robert Siodmak in 1946? CPe

Spirit of the Beehive, The 🔲100🔲 (El Espíritu de la Colmena)

(Victor Erice, 1973, Sp) Fernando Fernán Gómez, Teresa Gimpera, Ana Torrent, Isabel Telleria, Laly Soldevilla, José Villasante.
98 min.
Erice's remarkable one-off (he has made only one film since, the generally less well regarded *El Sur*) sees rural Spain soon after Franco's victory as a wasteland of inactivity, thrown into relief by the doomed industriousness of bees in their hives. The single, fragile spark of 'liberation' exists in the mind of little Ana, who dreams of meeting the gentle monster from James Whale's *Frankenstein*, and befriends a fugitive soldier just before he is caught and shot. A haunting mood-piece that dispenses with plot and works its spells through intricate patterns of sound and image. TR

Spirit of the Eagle

(Boon Collins, 1991, US) Dan Haggerty, William Smith, Trevor Yarrish.
90 min.
Fans of the *National Geographic* will enjoy this lumbering saga about an anguished father (Haggerty) roaming mountains, forests and prairies in search of his son, who's been sold to the Indians. The script borrows from *The Searchers*, but the landscapes are what really matter. GM

Spirit of the Wild

see Adventures of Frontier Fremont, The

Spirits of the Dead

see Histoires Extraordinaires

Spite Marriage

(Edward Sedgwick, 1929, US) Buster Keaton, Dorothy Sebastian, Edward Earle, Leila Hyams, Will Bechtel, Hank Mann.
9 reels. b/w.
Keaton's last silent feature takes the classic Keaton form: an incompetent discovers a growing sense of confidence and physical ingenuity, overcomes the villains, and wins the girl. Part of the plot harks back to *The Navigator*, but three of the sequences (a play ruined by Buster's gaucheness, getting a drunk bride to bed, and an extraordinary shipboard fight) put the film up in Division One, crowning a decade of unparalleled creativity which was then stifled by studio inflexibility. JC

Spitfire

see The First of the Few

Spitfire

(John Cromwell, 1934, US) Katharine Hepburn, Robert Young, Ralph Bellamy, Martha Sleeper, Sara Haden, Sidney Toler.
88 min. b/w.
Cromwell, who played the doddery priest in Altman's *A Wedding*, had a lengthy career as a director particularly adept with women leads; and certainly the entirely wonderful Katharine Hepburn constitutes the main interest in this otherwise plain sentimental comedy of backwoods superstition confronting civilisation in the form of a dam construction company. Not remotely dismayed by the role of hillbilly, nor by having to mouth down-home Christian cracker mottoes, she cuts an acidic path through the general coyness, and runs counter to the formulary script by suggesting that finally she remains a shrew. CPea

Spitfire Grill, The (aka Care of the Spitfire Grill)

(Lee David Zlotoff, 1996, US) Alison Elliott, Ellen Burstyn, Marcia Gay Harden, Will Patton, Louise De Cormier, Ida Griesemer.
116 min.
Elliott's released from prison into a waitressing job at Burstyn's cafe, under the watchful eyes of the entire town. This would-be inspirational, Capra-esque melodrama wears its heart on its sleeve. It's not a bad heart, just very soft. James Horner supplies a bathetic scorer, the Maine locations (actually Vermont) are made much of, and the wistful vision of small town America is too

cute for words. On the plus side, newcomer Elliott stands up to heavily accented performances from Burstyn and Harden. TCh

Splash

(Ron Howard, 1984, US) Tom Hanks, Daryl Hannah, Eugene Levy, John Candy, Dody Goodman, Shecky Greene, Richard B Shull, Bobby DiCicco.
110 min.
The beauty here is that the love is purely innocent. Not quite sexually innocent, although the carnal problems of falling for a mermaid are handled very well by the movie, which simply ignores them; rather, it is a love which has nothing to do with getting to know him, or his friends, or whether you like his apartment, or his job. It is love without conditions, much as in *E.T.*, except that here, one half of the match (Hanks) is adult, and the other half (Hannah) considerably more attractive than the waddling mud pie. Howard demonstrates exactly the correct soft touch, skirting the myriad problems of taste; and Hannah, who was the punkish replicant in *Blade Runner*, is somehow, very much, right there. CPea

Splendor

(Ettore Scola, 1988, It/Fr) Marcello Mastroianni, Massimo Troisi. Marina Vlady, Paolo Panelli, Pamela Villoresi, Giacomo Piperno.
99 min. b/w & col.
To the priest in a small Italian town, the Splendor cinema (now sold for redevelopment) is a 'dark grotto of sin'; to owner Jordan (Mastroianni), it's a shrine. But writer/director Scola is more concerned with the grey areas between such views: the patrons who desert cinema in droves when TV offers cheap, undemanding entertainment. Using flashback and clips, he conveys something of the medium's superiority over the box, at the same time beautifully unravelling a tale of life-long devotion and hard graft from Jordan, his long-term lover/usherette (Vlady), and the projectionist (Troisi). Their temperamental relationships over two decades are conveyed with great affection by the accomplished cast; and the film is full of wonderful moments – such as the homage to Capra at the climax – which manage to be both magical *and* unsentimental. CM

Splendor in the Grass

(Elia Kazan, 1961, US) Natalie Wood, Warren Beatty, Pat Hingle, Barbara Loden, Sandy Dennis, Audrey Christie, Gary Lockwood, Zohra Lampert, Phyllis Diller.
124 min.
With Beatty (his debut) and Wood star-crossed by parental opposition to their adolescent romance, William Inge's script is a sort of *Romeo and Juliet* translated to Depression Kansas. Attacked by many as being a hysterical account of sexual neurosis, praised by others for the acting (especially of Wood, as the daughter who goes mad) and for its occasional moments of great beauty, this is probably Kazan's most fought-over movie. A complicated film that never really successfully yokes together the themes of money-making and sexuality, it reveals both Kazan's operatic sensibility and his inability to follow an argument rigorously through. PH

Split, The

(Gordon Flemyng, 1968,US) Jim Brown, Diahann Carroll, Julie Harris, Gene Hackman, Ernest Borgnine, Warren Oates, Donald Sutherland, James Whitmore, Jack Klugman.
91 mins.
Based (like *Point Blank* and *The Outfit*) on a novel by Richard Stark (Donald E Westlake), this often impressively bleak caper-thriller benefits enormously from its strong cast. Brown is the gang-leader who recruits a number of criminal experts to rob the LA Coliseum after a sold-out football game; Hackman is the cop who hunts him down after the chance murder of Brown's wife links him with the immaculately executed heist. Flemyng's direction is efficient if lacking in real flair, but Burnett Guffey's crisp camera-work, the taut plotting, and the generally high standard of the performances make for a pleasing, if undemanding modern *noir* thriller in the tradition of *The Killing* and *The Asphalt Jungle*. GA.

Split Second

(Tony Maylam, 1991, GB) Rutger Hauer, Kim Cattrall, Neil Duncan, Michael J Pollard, Alun Armstrong, Pete Postlethwaite, Ian Dury, Roberta Eaton, Tony Steedman.
90 min.
Set in the flooded and polluted London of 2008, this low-budget sci-fi movie has renegade cop Harley Stone (Hauer) and his rookie partner Durkin (Duncan) on the trail of a monstrous serial killer who rips out its victims' hearts. Splashing about the waterlogged city, Stone senses some telepathic connection with the killer, who leaves cryptic occult messages written in blood. Neither the instinctive Stone nor his eccentric boffin partner can figure it out, so they do what all good macho cops do when confronted with an evil force they don't understand: they strap on some major firepower and blast everything in sight. This derivative eco-horror movie recycles dozens of disposable plots, flinging together all-purpose action man Hauer, a futuristic setting, and a reptilian alien. Hauer could do this stuff in his sleep, and the film looks as though Maylam did. NF

Splitting Heirs

(Robert Young, 1993, GB) Eric Idle, Rick Moranis, Barbara Hershey, Catherine Zeta Jones, John Cleese, Sadie Frost, Stratford Johns, Brenda Bruce, Eric Sykes.
87 min.
Eric Idle's script may pack in any amount of would-be comedic standbys – big bosoms, naked men hiding in wardrobes, national and ethnic stereotypes, bungled murder attempts, more big bosoms – but its cynical contrivance and lumbering execution fail to raise a laugh from beginning to end. The basic plot is *Kind Hearts and Coronets* rewritten for the mall-rat generation. Tommy Patel (Idle), a humble city broker, discovers that he's the lost Duke of Bournemouth, heir to a fortune currently hogged by American imposter Henry Maitland (Moranis). With the sinister complicity of legal vulture Shadgrind (Cleese, self-parodic), our aspirant aristo decides to bump off the Yank pretender; but before he can claim the title, there's a near-incestuous entanglement with the man-hungry widowed Duchess (Hershey) to be negotiated. Hershey's embarrassed presence, and the flailing efforts of the former Pythons, make this tedious cavalcade of thumping obviousness even more cringe-worthy than it already is. TJ

Split William to Chrysis: Portrait of a Drag Queen

(Andrew Weeks/Ellen Fisher Turk, 1992, US)
58 min.
Told through a combination of interviews, archive and home movie footage, this story of a boy who wanted to be more than just William has the makings of a modern parable. Rejected by his family, driven to accentuating his natural assets with dangerously high doses of hormones, the poor boy from Brooklyn created Chrysis, the woman he grew up to be. In her relatively short life, Chrysis turned herself from a downtown hooker into an international attraction, wowing audiences, winning the affections of Warhol (among others) and becoming muse to Salvador Dali, before finally succumbing to the cancer which started in her artifical breasts. Interviewed shortly before and after her death, friends testify to her courage, generosity, and ability to make the best of any situation. But the only proof we need is Chrysis herself. Already in advanced stages of illness by the time filming started, she's a performer to the end, refuting suggestions that she's taken the tough route with the dismissive 'Somebody's got to do it'. It's a dizzying story, and a moving one. PBur

Spoiled Children

see Des Enfants Gâtés

Spooky Bunch, The (Zhuang Dao Zheng)

(Ann Hui, 1980, HK) Josephine Siao, Kenny Bee, Kwan Chung, Tina Lau, Lau Hark-Sun.
97 min.
Quick and quirky, this follow-up to Ann Hui's debut feature, *The Secret*, juggles broad farce with guignol in an oddball yarn about a second-rate Cantonese Opera troupe bedevilled by an army of revenge-seeking ghosts. Exotic theatricals and their backstage rivalries, eccentric char-

acterisations (which include a playfully vengeful spirit named 'Cat Shit'), and an energetic camera style jostle for attention a little too clamorously at times, but the deceptive aura of greasepaint tackiness and the slapstick horror are all of a uniquely entertaining piece. PT

Spoor (aka Guns Across the Veldt)

(Howard Rennie, 1975, SAf) Giles Ridley, George Jackson, Ivor Kissin, Victor Melleney, Ian Yule.
81 min.
A monumentally hamfisted movie set in 1901 South Africa, when the British under Kitchener were fighting the insurgent Boers. A neurotic, Sandhurst-starched captain (Ridley) obsessively tries to hunt down an elusive guerilla general. With him go a brooding Afrikaaner scout, the *Observer* correspondent who shudders at the notion of 'participation', and two gin-swilling, recalcitrant privates. In addition to their hysterically wooden performances, an insulting script, misuse of location, and extremely laborious pace make this a must to avoid. IB

Spoorloos

see Vanishing, The

Spot

see Dogpound Shuffle

Spotswood

(Mark Joffe, 1991, Aust) Anthony Hopkins, Ben Mendelsohn, Toni Collette, Alwyn Kurts, Dan Wyllie, Bruno Lawrence, Rebecca Rigg, Russell Crowe.
95 min.
Errol Wallace (Hopkins) is all that one could ask of a time-and-motion expert. But when he moves from recommending redundancies at a Melbourne car factory to figuring out the financial problems of Ball's Moccasin Factory – a small family affair in the backwater suburb of Spotswood – he slowly realises that he lacks one essential virtue: the warming, common touch of humanity. Joffe's gentle comedy-drama, set in the mid-'60s, is as old-fashioned as the Ealing-esque community that is its main setting; a faintly hackneyed romantic subplot and the quietly sentimental tone of moral uplift only underline the film's overall caution. That said, it is genuinely funny, thanks to deft characterisations, a wry eye for the absurdities of working life, and a nice line in throwaway visual gags and verbal non-sequiturs. Hopkins' taciturn performance, meanwhile, injects a welcome, credible note of pain into the light-hearted proceedings. Small, slight, but surprisingly affecting. GA

Spring and Port Wine

(Peter Hammond, 1969, GB) James Mason, Diana Coupland, Susan George, Rodney Bewes, Hannah Gordon, Adrienne Posta, Arthur Lowe, Frank Windsor, Bernard Bresslaw.
101 min.
Obdurate Rafe Crompton (Mason), an engineer at a Bolton, Lancashire, cotton mill, finds his authority challenged when Hilda (George), the younger of his two daughters, refuses to eat a plate of herring, which he then serves up to her day after day, forcing the battle of wills to breaking point. Bill Naughton's play may have worked on stage, but on screen (in the playwright's own adaptation) it's as inconsequential as an expanded sitcom, and Mason's much too big a star for the material. TJ

Spring in a Small Town (Xiao Cheng zhi Chun)

(Fei Mu, 1948, China) Wei Wei, Shi Yu, Li Wei, Zhang Hongmei, Cui Chaoming.
85 min.
The crowning achievement of one of China's finest directors, this unique film both reflects and dissects the mood of helpless impotence which afflicted many Chinese in the years after the war. After a 10-year absence, a doctor visits a married couple living in a bomb-scarred country town. The husband is a broken man, close to suicide; the wife was once his lover and they start to drift back into an affair under the nose of her husband. The sense of frustration and enervation is palpable, underlined by

Fei's brilliant idea to use dissolves within scenes, but the counter-current of renascent desire (sparked by Wei Wei's phenomenal performance as the wife) makes this also a very sensual movie. TR

Spring in My Hometown (Areumdaun Sijeol)

(Lee Kwang-Mo, 1998, SKor) Ahn Sung-Ki, Bae Yoo-Jung, Song Ok-Sook, Yoo Seon-Hoi, Lee In.
110 min.
Lee, a UCLA graduate who is now Korea's leading art-film distributor, excavates two histories (one domestic, one national) from the time of the Korean War. The story unfolds in discrete episodes, shot in wide angle, each prefaced with a caption counterpointing events in one village with off-screen affairs of state. Sung-Min's father (Ahn, excellent as ever) is the first villager to find lucrative work at a nearby US Army base, because his daughter Young-Sook is the first local to date a GI. But Sung-Min and his best friend Chang-Hee discover that dad's services to the Americans include pimping for local women – including Chang-Hee's mother. The parallels between the ensuing tragedies and the fate of South Korea in the early 1950s remain tantalisingly elusive, but Lee directs both kids and adults with real insight and captures the flavour of distant childhood memories with some precision. TR

Spring into Summer (Pleure Pas la Bouche Pleine)

(Pascal Thomas, 1973, Fr) Annie Colé, Frédéric Duru, Jean Carmet, Christiane Chamaret, Bernard Menez.
117 min.
The sap rises, the blood flows, lush verdant hues and a robust fecundity abounds: little girls have their first periods, while the heroine and elder sister loses her virginity, not to the bumbling boy she'll perhaps marry but to some oaf who's been around and drives a white sports car. Get the picture? Pascal Thomas' loving picture of the cycle of life in a French village has both humour and an obvious charm; at its best when dealing with the heroine's relationship seen through the eyes of her elders and youngers, or with the banality of her seduction (it's he who undresses behind the screen). But with every shot set up with the same loving care, from the old venerables in the café to our heroine painting her nails, the final impression, for all the warm-heartedness and sensitivity, is of Thomas slowly loving his film to death.

Spring Shower

see Tavaszi Zápor

Spring Symphony (Frühlingssinfonie)

(Peter Schamoni, 1983, WGer) Nastassja Kinski, Herbert Grünemeyer, Rolf Hoppe, André Heller, Bernhard Wicki.
103 min.
A serious, if ponderous, biopic that traces a tumultuous ten years in the life of composer Robert Schumann. Schumann's life lurches queasily between the prosaic and the paradisaical (as he turns from the piano to drink, and from his engagement to the titled Ernestine to sex with a serving wench), driven by a dual passion for Clara Wieck (the daughter of his tutor) and music, which seems to be no more than a by-product of a monumental and masochistic selfishness. Schamoni's film is impeccably cast, with Hoppe as Wieck, his damp eyes suggesting incest here as chillingly as they did evil in his portrayal of Goering in *Mephisto*; Grünemeyer pale and intense as the boy-genius; and Kinski irritatingly placid as Clara. And the director captures perfectly the spirit of a Germany founded equally upon the tenets of stuffy burghers and high-minded student drinking associations, while cinematically echoing the Romantic style of Schumann's music. FD

Spy, The

see Spione

Spy Hard

(Rick Friedberg, 1996, US) Leslie Nielsen, Nicollette Sheridan, Andy Griffith, Charles Durning, Marcia Gay Harden, Barry Bostwick, John Ales, Stephanie Romanov.
81 min.

Nielsen is the Agency's star operatve Dick Steele (codename: WD-40). Intrepid, debonair, yet surprisingly accident-prone, Steele leaves a trail of destruction in his wake. When his beloved fellow agent Victoria Dahl falls to her death from a cliff as Steele puts paid to the ambitions of his nemesis General Rancor (Griffith), WD-40 feels it's time to hang up his badge. Fifteen years on, and Rancor's back, unarmed limb-wise, though he does have a very large rocket and he's threatening to use it unless he gets the final microchip that'll bring him world domination. Bond may be the main target, but *Spy Hard* is hardly frugal with its references. After the *Naked Guns*, and *Wayne's Worlds*, this Hollywood spoofery is becoming almost a genre in itself. Like *Hot Shots!* there's the same mistaken belief that simply tagging other films will be intrinsically funny: Nielsen running into a convent dressed as a nun and conducting the sisters through 'Raindrops Keep Falling on My Head' does not a great *Sister Act* parody make. NB

Spy in Black, The

(Michael Powell, 1939, GB) Conrad Veidt, Valerie Hobson, Sebastian Shaw, Marius Goring, June Duprez, Athole Stewart.
82 min. b/w.
Darkness, foreboding and regret, rather than any sense of propaganda, dominate this extraordinarily atmospheric World War I spy story made on the eve of World War II. It signals the end of a peacetime era even more clearly than *The Lady Vanishes*. Daringly, the audience is asked to sympathise with the 'enemy' as the magnificent, shadowy Veidt moves through remarkable Scottish sets on a mission to Scapa Flow to destroy the British fleet. Intrigue, uncertainty and confused loyalties build to a bitter, ironic climax, and along the way Powell effortlessly produces more memorable shots and scenes than can be found in a dozen contemporary films. CPe

S*P*Y*S

(Irvin Kershner, 1974, GB) Donald Sutherland, Elliott Gould, Zouzou, Joss Ackland, Kenneth Griffith, Vladek Sheybal, Kenneth J Warren.
100 min.
Finely written espionage spoofery, with the finesse of a classic Hollywood comedy. Very classy, very assured, with exactly the right degree of underlying blackness: international relations come down to an openly acknowledged credo of a corpse for a corpse, a Russian defects for the promise of a Thunderbird, CIA torturers take time out to join in a chorus of 'America, America' with the tortured. *S*P*Y*S* takes post-Watergate disillusionment as read, and goes on to outdo *M*A*S*H*, the humour moving with ease from the verbal to the visual to the situational and back. Sutherland and Gould counterpoint each other superbly (Sutherland in particular performing excellently, like a zanier Cary Grant). Kershner directs with utter skill, enabling even the most notoriously cameo-ridden actor to rise to unexpected heights. VG

Spy Story

(Lindsay Shonteff, 1976, GB) Michael Petrovitch, Philip Latham, Don Fellows, Michael Gwynne, Nicholas Parsons, Tessa Wyatt, Derren Nesbitt.
102 min.
Len Deighton's cold and vivid view of cynical power-mongering, his existential anti-heroes coopted forcibly into a labyrinthine and rigid power structure, translated an American idiom into a specifically British context. It is an acerbic distillation that should have fuelled a far richer strand of cinema than it has. Shonteff's film catches Deighton's nuances of power and corruption, but sequences that do for starters hardly work as a continuing ploy; and soon characters are locked in limp confrontation, exchanging increasingly cryptic chunks of information while the plot works towards total incomprehensibility. VG

Spy Who Came In From the Cold, The

(Martin Ritt, 1965, GB) Richard Burton, Claire Bloom, Oskar Werner, Peter Van Eyck, Sam Wanamaker, George Voskovec, Rupert Davies, Cyril Cusack, Michael Hordern, Robert Hardy, Bernard Lee, Beatrix Lehmann, Esmond Knight.
112 min. b/w.

Without his customary good liberal message to hang on to, Ritt is forced to rely on pure professionalism, and as a result turns out one of his better films. John Le Carré's novel about betrayal and disillusionment in the world of East/West espionage is treated with intelligence and a disarming lack of sentimentality or moralising, while Burton gives one of his best screen performances as the spy out to get even with an East German counterpart. What finally impresses, however, is the sheer seediness of so much of the film, with characters, buildings, and landscapes lent convincingly grubby life by Oswald Morris' excellent monochrome camera-work. GA

Spy Who Loved Me, The

(Lewis Gilbert, 1977, GB) Roger Moore, Barbara Bach, Curd Jürgens, Richard Kiel, Caroline Munro, Walter Gotell, Geoffrey Keen, Bernard Lee, George Baker.
125 min.
Bond for Britain: 007's spectacular ski jump is aided by an ostentatious Union Jack parachute; caught in bed by his superiors, Bond smirks that he's keeping the British end up. Something of a straggler from the campy late '60s, this one mainly pushes the myth of British technological wizardry. Patriotic schoolboy flagwaving is accompanied by pre-pubescent sexuality and puerile innuendoes. Britain, Russia, and Martini-style locations conspire to thwart Curd Jürgens from destroying the world. The film has its moments – Kiel's indestructible heavy racks up a good score – but the rest is desperately weak. Interesting that a film which seems so often on the verge of impotence should boast so many phallic substitutes. CPe

Square, The (Guangchang)

(Zhang Yuan/Duan Jinchuan, 1994, China)
100 min.
Zhang Yuan's defiant response to finding his name on a government blacklist was to shoot this 'illegal' documentary in and about Tiananmen Square – not only the most public space in Beijing, but also the symbolic heart of Communist China. Observing without comment, the film sees the activities in the square as a microcosm of the state. It builds up a convincing analysis of China's political and social economy simply by watching the way the square is policed, patrolled and used by both the authorities and the public; it also poses some trenchant questions about China's future by showing the 'Little Emperors' who are the product of the country's single-child policy. No politics, of course, but the absence of references to 1989 speaks loudly enough. TR

Square Circle, The (Daayraa)

(Amol Palekar, 1996, Ind) Nirmal Pandey, Sonali Kulkarni, Faiyyaz, Rekha Sahay.
98 min.
An unnamed woman (Kulkarni) is kidnapped into prostitution by a madam and her henchmen, then gang raped by a three louts when she's plucky enough to escape. Salvation is at hand, however, in Pandey, a wandering entertainer. Having found his own identity through dressing as a woman, he puts the girl in men's clothes so they can pass as a 'straight' couple and travel in relative safety back to her home village. The direction is restrained for Bollywood (the dance number has been cut for the UK print), but pretty rough and ready to Western eyes, though once you adjust, it's easy to get swept up in the way every emotion is played to the hilt. The film's thematic daring is exceptional: the exploration of the tension between sexual identity and social circumstance in a staunchly traditional society. TJ

Square Dance

(Daniel Petrie, 1986, US) Jason Robards, Jane Alexander, Winona Ryder, Rob Lowe, Deborah Richter, Guich Koock, Elbert Lewis.
112 min.
Petrie's handling of this odd, faintly moralistic tale is at best sickly, at worst sick. Teenage Bible-basher Gemma (Ryder) abandons her crotchety grandfather (Robards) to join her loose-living mother (Alexander). Horrified to discover that Mom likes to get poked by the local cowpokes, Gemma strikes up a loving, innocent bond with hunky, mentally deficient Rory (Lowe), until an enthusiastic floozie introduces him to more stimulating games and Gemma catches them in the act. Rory, in vague remorse, viciously attacks his

offending member (yeuch!), while Gemma high-tails it back to Dullsville. Alexander and Ryder's intelligent performances are upstaged by Lowe, who comes across like rampant beefcake on valium. Ultimately, though, Petrie's twee vision of Midwest life kills the film – it's so cotton-pickin' clichéd. *The Waltons* with willies. EP

Squeaker, The

(William K Howard, 1937, GB) Edmund Lowe, Ann Todd, Sebastian Shaw, Alastair Sim, Tamara Desni, Robert Newton, Stewart Rome.
77 min. b/w.
Clumsy casting and sloppy direction from the once-promising alcoholic Howard drain the vitality from Edgar Wallace's story of the unmasking of a master criminal who holds the underworld in thrall and uses Scotland Yard for his own advantage. Vincent Korda's elegant sets and Georges Périnal's subtle, inventive lighting are memorable, but the attempt to substitute atmosphere for suspense fails, despite a flamboyantly melodramatic climax. Fading American star Lowe seems out of his element in English crime, and Tamara Desni struggles in vain to bring exoticism to the British cinema. Fortunately there is compensation in young Alastair Sim, and in Robert Newton's passionate jewel thief, desperately trying to 'give up crime and live like a human being'. RMy

Squeeze, The

(Michael Apted, 1977, GB) Stacy Keach, David Hemmings, Edward Fox, Stephen Boyd, Carol White, Freddie Starr, Hilary Gasson.
107 min.
Booze-sodden ex-cop (Keach) has to dry out when ex-wife and daughter are kidnapped. For the most part, this flashy, hard-edged film sells itself to a TV audience by providing more nudity, sexual innuendo, strong language, and thumping violence than the small screen. Under the surface brashness, Apted's direction does attempt to think the film through, although his handling of certain episodes suggests too much sensitivity for the job in hand. Good performances. CPe

Squeeze, The

(Roger Young, 1987, US) Michael Keaton, Rae Dawn Chong, Joe Pantoliano, Danny Aiello III, Leslie Bevis, Lou Criscuolo, Meatloaf.
102 min.
Keaton is a snake on the make who cheats at cards and whose life's ambition is to win the great American lotto. He spends most of his time building a room-size neon-lit lizard, and generally fooling around like he never left high school. Then into his life steps the alluring Chong, a private dick carrying a court summons from Keaton's ex-wife over non-payment of alimony. The couple haven't seen each other for three years, but she turns up wanting a favour: can he pick up a black box from her apartment? It sounds simple enough, but the box is also wanted by a couple of hoods working for a French dealer in shrunken heads, who has hired the unwitting Chong to track it down. This attempt at comedy is a disaster, laboriously plotted and inanely scripted; the enthusiasm of the cast can do nothing to redeem its sheer lack of wit and invention. CB

Squibs

(Henry Edwards, 1935, GB) Betty Balfour, Gordon Harker, Stanley Holloway, Margaret Yarde, Morris Harvey, Michael Shepley, Ronald Shiner.
77 min. b/w.
A Cockney flower girl (Balfour) falls in love with a policeman (Holloway) after he saves her from an oncoming car. But her inveterate gambler of a dad (Harker) is in trouble with the law. A cheerful enough British comedy with surprisingly high production values, this none the less seems like a film out of time. Its star is reprising a role she first performed in 1921 in a play by Clifford Seyler and George Pearson. Inevitably, the years tell. Judging by all the singalongs, the film-makers are trying to pass her off as London's answer to Gracie Fields. Unfortunately Britain's one time 'Queen of Happiness' has long since passed her sell by date. GM

Squirm

(Jeff Lieberman, 1976, US) John Scardino, Patricia Pearcy, RA Dow, Jean Sullivan, Peter MacLean, Fran Higgins.
92 min.
Far better and more interesting than the obvious schlock appeal its plot would suggest: a small town is terrorised by a plague of lethal worms. In his debut, Lieberman reveals a genuine talent and ambitiousness (subsequently confirmed by *Blue Sunshine*), turning the film into a variation on the sexual paranoia theme, distinguished by his tendency to present his characters – especially the mother of the two wittily-observed girls who are central to the story – as keyed-up to an unexplained pitch of barely-controlled hysteria. The whole thing resembles a black Famous Five adventure. The atmosphere of the Georgia swampland locations is convincing, and the excellent special effects deliver the requisite shocks. Slyly entertaining stuff. VG

Sssssss (aka Sssssnake)

(Bernard L Kowalski, 1973, US) Strother Martin, Dirk Benedict, Heather Menzies, Richard B Shull, Tim O'Connor, Jack Ging.
99 min.
Often so bad that you have to laugh. Reckoning that snakes will be among the creatures to survive the imminent ecological holocaust, Dr Carl Stoner attempts to turn his unsuspecting assistant David into a King Cobra. Complications arise when the boy falls for Stoner's daughter, but by the time she's twigged that the snake man in a circus sideshow is a former assistant to her father, David's no more than a cobra being chewed up by a mongoose. A complete mess, with biblical references (for some reason the central love story parallels the Fall), hallucinatory sequences, laboured borrowings, and moronic direction, yet quite enjoyable in its rubbishy way. Nice performance from Strother Martin as the doctor, plus some good special effects. CPe

S.T.A.B. (aka Thong)

(Chalong Pakdivijt, 1975, Thai) Greg Morris, Sombat Metanee, Krung Srivilai, Tham Thuy Hang.
91 min.
An oriental potboiler, of tangential interest as a rabid anti-Communist tract, with bounty hunter Morris mowing down Vietcong hordes during a behind-the-lines operation to recover skyjacked gold earmarked for an opium deal. Early on, one of his help-mates, a large girl in hotpants, strips down in a jungle monsoon to divert two enemy guards, and the film is littered with similar scenes of classic improbability. No one, incidentally, makes any reference to the Strategic Tactical Airborne Brigade of the opportunistic title. JPy

Stacking

see Season of Dreams

Stacy's Knights

(Jim Wilson, 1983, US) Andra Millian, Kevin Costner, Eve Lilith, Mike Reynolds, Garth Howard, Ed Semenza.
95 min.
Costner met up with writer Michael Blake and director Wilson, the team with whom he'd later make *Dances with Wolves*, on this early effort, the first time he'd played a leading part on film. The central role in this pretty duff thriller though goes to Millian as a shy young woman whose gambling fever leads her to get together a gang of card-sharps to take on the blackjack tables at a Mafia-owned casino. TJ

Stagecoach

(John Ford, 1939, US) John Wayne, Claire Trevor, Thomas Mitchell, George Bancroft, John Carradine, Andy Devine, Louise Platt, Donald Meek, Berton Churchill, Tim Holt.
96 min. b/w.
Impossible to overstate the influence of Ford's magnificent film, generally considered to be the first modern Western. Shot in the Monument Valley which Ford was later to make his own, it also initiated Wayne's extraordinarily fertile partnership with the director, and established in embryo much of the mythology explored and developed in Ford's subsequent Westerns. Wayne plays the Ringo Kid, an outlaw seeking revenge for the murder of his father and brother, first seen 'holding up' the stagecoach containing banished prostitute Trevor, dipso doctor Mitchell, cynical gambler Carradine, timid salesman Meek, and a pair of ostensibly respectable characters: pregnant 'lady' Platt, and crooked banker Churchill. The contrast between the innocence of the wilderness and the ambiguous 'blessings of civilisation' are brilliantly stitched into a smoothly developed narrative, which climaxes with the famous Indian attack on the stagecoach. NF

Stagecoach

(Gordon Douglas, 1966, US) Alex Cord, Van Heflin, Bing Crosby, Red Buttons, Ann-Margret, Michael Connors, Robert Cummings, Stefanie Powers, Slim Pickens, Keenan Wynn.
114 min.
Look again at the credits before you're tempted: this is the witless remake of Ford's classic, with neither colour nor Cord anything like adequate recompense for Bert Glennon's dusty monochrome or Wayne's early strut as the Ringo Kid. PT

Stage Door

(Gregory La Cava, 1937, US) Katharine Hepburn, Ginger Rogers, Adolphe Menjou, Andrea Leeds, Gail Patrick, Constance Collier, Lucille Ball, Eve Arden, Ann Miller, Franklin Pangborn, Jack Carson.
92 min. b/w.
Alongside *The Women* and *Dance, Girl, Dance*, one of the great sassy-women comedy-dramas of the '30s. Taken from the stage success by Kaufman and Ferber, it's a bitchy, pacy slice of sociology that throws together a bunch of aspiring actresses in a theatrical boarding house, and watches them interact with lecherous producers (Menjou, marvellous), boyfriends, and most of all each other. The casting is perfect: Hepburn as the Bryn Mawr upper crust type determinedly slumming it, Rogers (in her first bid as a serious actress) as the no-nonsense girl-next-door, and Leeds as the frail, hypersensitive thesp with real talent who introduces a touch of melodrama into the proceedings. Individuals and darker moments apart, however, it's the crackling ensemble pieces that remain in the memory, expertly timed by La Cava's civilised, generous direction, and located in lovingly authentic sets beautifully shot by Robert de Grasse. GA

Stage Door

see Hu-Du-Men

Stage Fright

(Alfred Hitchcock, 1950, GB) Marlene Dietrich, Jane Wyman, Michael Wilding, Richard Todd, Alastair Sim, Sybil Thorndike, Kay Walsh, Joyce Grenfell.
110 min. b/w.
A fairly routine thriller, noted chiefly for its cheating flashback, though with much more to enjoy than its detractors – including Hitchcock – make out. The plot involves a young RADA student (Wyman) trying to clear a boyfriend (Todd), who claims he's been framed for the murder of his mistress' husband. Along the way, the heroine disguises herself as a maid, falls in love with the investigating detective (Wilding), and discovers that her friend is actually guilty. The proceedings are enlivened mainly by two good comic performances, from Dietrich at her most blatantly vulgar as the musical comedy star/mistress, and Sim as the heroine's droll father. There are also some good set pieces towards the climax, notably the garden party and the theatrical dénouement in a theatre. RM

Staggered

(Martin Clunes, 1993, GB) Martin Clunes, Michael Praed, John Forgeham, Anna Chancellor, Sylvia Syms, Griff Rhys Jones, David Kossoff, Virginia McKenna.
95 min.
Toy-demonstrator Neil (Clunes) wakes up in the all-together, stranded on the empty beach of a remote Scottish island hundreds of miles from the previous night's stag party. It seems his best man Gary (Praed) has pulled off quite a prank – but perhaps it's not so funny: the wedding's fast approaching, and Gary's using the groom's absence to put the moves on his intended. This low-budget farce has a frustrating tendency to set up promising situations only to squander them. The script is both too devious for its own good and insufficiently thought through, while Clunes' debut as a director is decidedly hit or miss. Amusing and eventful, none the less. TCh

Stain, The (Laka)
(Aleko Tsabadze, 1987, USSR) Kishward
Glunchadze, Rusudan Kvlividze, Z
Begalishvili, O Bazgadze.
90 min.
Made in Georgia on the sly with filmstock earmarked for another production, Tsabadze's first
feature, a grungy yet darkly comic portrait of the
bohemian underworld, was greeted with dismay
by the Soviet authorities, who were nevertheless
chuffed when it came away with a prize at the
1987 Locarno TV Festival. The story of a free-
wheeling student who bets a million cigars on the
toss of a coin and subsequently finds himself on
the run from the local Mafia, it's often rough at
the edges technically, but presents a compelling
picture of a society in the midst of falling apart.
The Soviet broadcasting chief condemned the
film for looking at 'a certain stratum of society
with a cold pernicious, venomous atmosphere
which cannot but provoke disgust, resentment
and disapprobation.' Bloody students, eh? TJ

Stain on the Snow, The
see Neige était sale, La

Staircase
(Stanley Donen, 1969, US) Richard Burton, Rex
Harrison, Cathleen Nesbitt, Beatrix Lehmann,
Stephen Lewis.
101 min.
A drab, sincere homosexual drama, essentially a
stage two-hander stupidly glossied up and
opened out, but still emerging as dreadfully verbose. Burton and Harrison – the latter in the Liz
Taylor part – do their best as two Brixton hairdressers whose 30-year relationship is beginning
to fray, further taxed by worries about Burton's
ailing mum (Nesbitt) and Harrison's impending
court appearance on a charge of transvestism. On
this evidence, they've already lasted better than
Charles Dyer's play. Dudley Moore wrote the
musical score, and if you don't recognise Brixton,
that's because it was filmed in Paris. TCh

Stairway to Heaven
see Matter of Life and Death, A

Stakeout
(John Badham, 1987, US) Richard Dreyfuss,
Emilio Estevez, Madeleine Stowe, Aidan
Quinn, Dan Lauria, Forest Whitaker.
117 min.
Quinn is surprisingly thrilling in the role of a
crazed murderer, and the bone-crushing brutality of the opening sequence (he pummels a
prison doctor's head to pulp with a truncheon)
gives this bad guy an unpredictable edge. It's a
deceptive ploy on Badham's part, as the film
soon pitches into familiar car chase territory,
where a couple of cops are establishing a prickly love/hate relationship. Dreyfuss is cuddly,
cheeky and caring (when is he not?) as Chris
Lecce, an experienced detective who should
know better than to fall in love with the girlfriend of an escaped convict while staking out
her apartment. Young Bill Reimers (Estevez,
poor) is keen and conscientious, and resents covering for his partner's philandering. Between
Lecce's illicit courtship and Reimers' consternation, there are some hearty laughs of a juvenile
nature. Meanwhile, the raging Quinn approaches...It's all tied up in a slick, empty package by
Badham's direction. EP

Stalag 17
(Billy Wilder, 1953, US) William Holden, Don
Taylor, Robert Strauss, Harvey Lembeck,
Neville Brand, Richard Erdman, Otto
Preminger, Peter Graves, Sig Ruman.
120 min. b/w.
Wilder's PoW movie is a mass of contradictions,
perhaps explained by the fact that it was based
on a successful Broadway play which partly
resisted his characteristic attempt to have his
black squalor and eat his airy comedy. On the one
hand, uproariously and buffoonishly funny, it can
be seen simply as the natural sire of such TV sitcoms as Hogan's Heroes and Sergeant Bilko. On
the other, anticipating King Rat through the character of the cynical PoW capitalist played by
Holden, it satirically notes that the free enterprise
ethic, extended into PoW circumstances, can no
longer command Horatio Alger approval; and
goes on from there to ask what price democracy

when a traitor is suspected, and the PoWs gang
up like Fascists to assign arbitrary blame and
punishment. The problem is that the two moods
aren't properly cross-fertilised, with the resolute
bleakness of the settings and Wilder's direction
positing a reality that is constantly undercut by
the comic opera crew of Germans headed by
Preminger. A fascinating film, nevertheless. TM

Stalingrad
(Joseph Vilsmaier, 1992, Ger) Dominique
Horwitz, Thomas Kretschmann, Jochen Nickel,
Sebastian Rudolph, Dana Vavrova, Martin
Benrath.
138 min.
Director/cinematographer Vilsmaier's WWII
chronicle is a convincingly hard-edged movie,
contextualising subtitles to the fore, detailing
the most fateful hours of the European conflict.
But, impressive as a monument of reconstruction, the film lacks the extra emotive dimension
which would fulfil its humanist aspirations.
Instead, surrounded by production values which
suggest the Russian city has been demolished
anew, the sentiments are very much of the war-
is-hell and all-officers-are-bastards school, as a
group of German soldiers is whittled away one
by one during the ill-fated 1942 Siege of
Stalingrad. With efficient performances that
leave the big statements to the action set-pieces
and a screenplay which merely hints at exorcising Nazi culpability in a single evasive
exchange, the film's enveloping veracity is its
most striking aspect. You'll certainly feel you've
been to the Russian front – a fact which, ironically perhaps, may endear the film more to genre
buffs and Sven Hassel readers than the youthful generation for whom the monolithic display
of carnage is obviously intended as a bitter
warning. TJ

Stalker
(Andrei Tarkovsky, 1979, USSR) Aleksandr
Kaidanovsky, Anatoly Solonitsin, Nikolai
Grinko, Alisa Freindlikh.
161 min. b/w & col.
Against the fractured density of Mirror, Stalker
sets a form of absolute linear simplicity. The
Stalker leads two men, the Writer and the
Professor, across the Zone – a forbidden territory deep inside a police state – towards the Room,
which can lay bare the devices and desires of
your heart. However, let no one persuade you that
this is sci-fi or common allegory. The ragged,
shaven-headed men are familiar from
Solzhenitsyn, and the Zone may be a sentient
landscape of hallucinatory power, but its deadly
litter of industrial detritus is all too recognisable.
The wettest, grimiest trek ever seen on film leads
to nihilistic impasse – huddled in dirt, the discovery of faith seems impossible; and without
faith, life outside the Zone is impossible. But hang
on in to the ending, where a plain declaration of
love and a vision of pure magic at least point the
way to redemption. As always, Tarkovsky conjures images like you've never seen before; and
as a journey to the heart of darkness, it's a good
deal more persuasive than Coppola's. CPea

Stamboul Quest
(Sam Wood, 1934, US) Myrna Loy, George
Brent, Lionel Atwill, C Henry Gordon, Douglas
Dumbrille, Mischa Auer.
88 min. b/w.
Good credits for this hokey slice of MGM exoti-
ca. Written by Herman J Mankiewicz (Citizen
Kane), photographed by James Wong Howe, and
directed by the reliable Sam Wood, the only thing
wrong is that it's nothing special. Loy's a top
German agent during WWI, Brent's the
American student vacationing in Turkey, the rest
(romance, espionage, the studio backlot) you can
probably figure out for yourself. TJ

Stammheim
(Reinhard Hauff, 1985, WGer) Ulrich Pleitgen,
Ulrich Tukur, Therese Affolter, Sabine
Wegner, Hans Kremer.
107 min.
Hauff's reconstruction of the Baader-Meinhof
trial is the most honourable shot at tackling the
terrorism conundrum since Fassbinder's The
Third Generation. Cast with lookalikes and
using the trial transcripts as the basis for its
script, it ploughs through the issues with almost
hysterical intensity, comparing the fanaticism

of the defendants with the unthinking brutality
of the court. More controversially, it also imagines ideological arguments between Baader,
Meinhof, Ensslin and Raspe in the 'privacy' of
their cells, citing 'letters and prison reports' as
its sources. The film ultimately fails, because its
scrupulously liberal stance prevents it from
developing any coherent point of view of its
own. But as a microcosm of West German society tearing itself apart at the seams, it's one hell
of a lot tougher than the kind of earnest socio-
political dramas that the BBC and C4 tend to
produce. ATu

Stamping Ground
(aka Love and Music)
(Hansjürgen Pohland, 1971, WGer) Jefferson
Airplane, Santana, Country Joe MacDonald,
Pink Floyd, Dr John, Family, Soft Machine.
101 min.
Was the 1970 Rotterdam Pop Festival as dull as
this? It probably was, but that's no excuse for the
scrappiness of the filming and editing, or for the
sheer incompetence of the linking interviews
(conducted in English). TR

Stan and George's New Life
(Brian McKenzie, 1990, Aust) Paul Chubb,
John Bluthal, Julie Forsyth, Margaret Ford.
102 min.
Stan is a shy, none too quick-witted 40-year-old
who abandons the tedium of the family barber's
shop for the relative excitement of a clerical job
in a backwater meteorological office; George –
perhaps the only sane person to work there – is
the dumpy but determined girl of his dreams.
McKenzie's oddball romantic comedy has a tendency towards lethargic pacing, but Chubb and
Forsyth are credible and engaging as the misfit
lovers; and if you ignore the contrived conspiracy subplot, the quirky account of office politics
offers some sharp insights. Though not nearly as
good as Jane Campion's work, its similar eye for
absurdity is far from negligible. GA

Stand and Deliver
(Ramon Menendez, 1988, US) Edward James
Olmos, Lou Diamond Phillips, Rosana De Soto,
Andy Garcia, Virginia Paris, Carmen
Argenziano.
103 min.
Jaime Escalante (Olmos) gives up a lucrative job
in electronics to teach math at an East LA barrio
school notorious for drugs and gang-related violence. Many students have difficulty writing their
own names, but Escalante, oozing oddball charm,
transmogrifies his 18 airheads into an educational élite, making them sign a contract promising they will do no less than 30 hours homework
a week, attend pre-school classes, and extra
lessons on Saturdays and holidays. Sums hardly
come into it; emotional blackmail ensures there
are no failures, and everybody receives a college
credit. However, the Educational Testing Service,
amazed at the results, cries 'Foul!', and the celebrating swots are compelled to stand and deliver, ie resit the exam. It's hard to believe this really
happened, but Escalante is apparently still performing the same miracle. The ensemble acting
is excellent. Remember, kids, it all comes down
to Self Respect. MS

Stand by Me
(Rob Reiner, 1986, US) Wil Wheaton, River
Phoenix, Corey Feldman, Jerry O'Connell,
Kiefer Sutherland, Casey Siemaszko, Richard
Dreyfuss.
89 min.
It's a summer weekend, and four schoolboy
friends are trekking cross-country to see a body
lying dead by the railroad track. In this gently
observed study of the passage from childhood
into maturity, the story is narrated by the
grown-up Wheaton (Dreyfuss), remembering it
as the watershed when he stopped telling tall
tales and decided to take his writing seriously,
egged on by his best buddy (Phoenix). Reiner
directs with the sensitive touch he displayed in
The Sure Thing, and the four juvenile leads are
so good they make the Brat Pack look redundant. Even if your childhood memories are catalogues of humiliation, embarrassment, and
being toughed up, many a mental chord will be
struck by such vexing questions as: 'Mickey's a
mouse, Donald's a duck...so what's Goofy?' A
real low-key treat. AB

Stand-In

(Tay Garnett, 1937, US) Leslie Howard, Joan Blondell, Humphrey Bogart, Alan Mowbray, Marla Shelton, C Henry Gordon, Jack Carson.
90 min. b/w.
With a few scabrous exceptions (*The Big Knife, The Bad and the Beautiful, The Last Command*, possibly *Sunset Boulevard*), Hollywood movies on Hollywood tend to end up endorsing the body politic of the studio system after indulging in gentle satirical sideswipes at the warts along the way. *Stand-In* is an example of this peculiar form of incest. Howard plays a mathematical whizzkid (very reminiscent of Cary Grant's professor in the later *Bringing Up Baby*) sent West to save an ailing independent studio almost crippled by its temperamental female superstar and its last-gasp epic, *Sex and Satan*. Howard displays few of the lapses into sanctimonious drivel he was later party to, while Blondell (as down-at-heel stand-in) and Bogart (dipsomaniac producer) lend admirable support. But what's most interesting is the Capra-style populism which informs the script's cockeyed notion of grassroots capitalism, and lifts the film well above the level of lightweight screwball comedy. RM

Stand Up, Don't Grovel! (Zhanzhiluo, Bie Paxia!)

(Huang Jianxin, 1993, China) Niu Zhenhua, Feng Gong, Da Shichang, Zhang Lu, Fu Lili, Liu Xiaohua, Ma Shuanqing.
115 min.
Looking for peace, quiet and privacy, a writer (Feng) and his wife move into a new apartment, only to find themselves sandwiched between conservative communist-party cadre Liu (Da) on one side and bolshie entrepreneur Zhang (Niu) on the other. Simmering tensions erupt when Zhang turns his apartment into a fish farm and strange moulds start appearing on the walls. Huang's delicious comedy (inaugurating his 'urban attitude' trilogy) is also a pitiless satire. It gets as much mileage out of the rise of get-rich-quick freelancers and the endemic spinelessness of China's intellectuals as it does out of the communists' waning sense of their own correctness and authority. TR

Stand Up Virgin Soldiers

(Norman Cohen, 1977, GB) Robin Askwith, Nigel Davenport, George Layton, John Le Mesurier, Warren Mitchell, Robin Nedwell, Edward Woodward, Irene Handl, Pamela Stephenson.
90 min.
Though the original *Virgin Soldiers* was no masterpiece, it certainly never deserved the retrospective slur of association with this appalling sequel, upping the nudge-nudge quotient with Leslie Thomas' apparent complicity, and all too easily characterised as *Confessions of a National Serviceman*. One for old Singapore sweats and lovers of jokes about parading privates. PT

Stanley & Iris

(Martin Ritt, 1989, US) Jane Fonda, Robert De Niro, Swoosie Kurtz, Martha Plimpton, Feodor Chaliapin, Zohra Lampert.
105 min.
Written by Harriet Frank Jr and Irving Ravetch, this free adaptation of Pat Barker's *Union Street* is relocated from Teeside to the industrial landscape of New England and turned into a worthy vehicle for two mature stars. All that remains from Barker's original seems to be the survival instinct of the average home-maker. Iris King is a cake factory veteran, recently widowed, who takes on the task of teaching illiterate Stanley to read when she inadvertently causes his dismissal from said confectionery establishment. We're talking quality here, Ritt being the man who directed *Hud, Sounder* and *Norma Rae*, the leads being De Niro and fellow double Oscar winner Jane Fonda, and the overriding theme of literal word blindness being handled with charm and dignity. The problem is that, given Fonda and De Niro's established images, one can't help thinking what is their *problem*; and the ending, despite good intentions, is American cinema at its tackiest and most hollow. SGr

Stanno tutti bene

see Everybody's Fine

Star!

(Robert Wise, 1968, US) Julie Andrews, Richard Crenna, Michael Craig, Daniel Massey, Robert Reed, Bruce Forsyth, Beryl Reid, Jenny Agutter.
174 min.
Julie Andrews has been compared to everything from a mechanically charming air hostess to a knitted coverlet for a toilet roll, but one comparison she has escaped – especially since *Star!* – is to Gertrude Lawrence. Nevertheless, Wise's biopic hardly deserved the rough treatment it received from most critics and audiences, who had been led by the studio's advertising to expect another *Sound of Music*. This was a far more ambitious project; it backfired, but it backfired with a certain amount of honour. Daniel Massey's mincing portrayal of his godfather Noël Coward wins hands down over all the other impersonations. GB

Star, The

(Stuart Heisler, 1952, US) Bette Davis, Sterling Hayden, Natalie Wood, Warner Anderson, Minor Watson, June Travis.
89 min. b/w.
A couple of years on from *All About Eve*, Bette Davis plays an Oscar-winning actress coming to the realisation that her fading career is at an end. Hayden's the ordinary Joe who tries to get her a new start outside the movie industry in this intriguing, though small-scale drama dominated by a ripe star presence. Davis sometimes overdoes the drink-fuelled self-pity, but at least she got another Oscar nomination out of it. TJ

Star Chamber, The

(Peter Hyams, 1983, US) Michael Douglas, Hal Holbrook, Yaphet Kotto, Sharon Gless, James B Sikking, Joe Regalbuto, Don Calfa.
109 min.
Where is the justice, High Court Judge Hardin (Douglas) wonders, when the innocent suffer and the clearly guilty go free on a technicality. In books? In the judicial system he has sworn to uphold? Or is he the law? Reluctantly, he joins The Star Chamber, a clandestine society of judges who retry and pass sentence on certain 'messy' cases. From the opening sequence – a pell-mell chase through a confusion of colour, movement and sound – Hyams constructs a tense and absorbing thriller; but as in previous filmic efforts to confront this elusive moral issue (*...And Justice for All*, for example), the subtleties escape faster than the criminals. Just as Douglas discovers that he can go only so far along the extra-judicial path, so the film's line of reasoning twists part-way, falters, then ties itself into tangled and inconclusive knots. FD

Starchaser: The Legend of Orin

(Steven Hahn, 1985, US) voices: Joe Colligan, Carmen Argenziano, Noelle North, Anthony Delongis, Les Tremayne.
100 min.
In this animated feature, the obsession with technology only serves to hurtle the kids' space-fantasy genre along the cosmic cul-de-sac it has already entered. The plot is the usual hotch-potch of quasi-heroics and mock-mythical exploits, transposed to a futuristic world realised with all the eclectic visual imagery (embellished with 3-D) one has come to expect. Orin, our svelte young hero, takes the predictable step from oppressed toiler in megabaddie Zygon's mines to nascent superhero with ne'er a doubting moment. Teaming up with cigar-chewing crystal smuggler Dagg, and armed with the obligatory magic sword, he sets out to foil Zygon's plans to subjugate the universe. Along the way, we are treated to some pretty spectacular landscapes and a whole range of repulsively animalistic robots. The otherwise fine vocal characterisations are spoiled by over-emphasis on sexual innuendo, and the length will probably have kids screaming for ice-creams long before the finish. WH

Starcrash

(Lewis Coates ie. Luigi Cozzi, 1979, US) Marjoe Gortner, Caroline Munro, Christopher Plummer, David Hasselhoff, Robert Tessier, Joe Spinell.
91 min.
A trash-addict sci-fi spectacular from AIP in which Stella Star (Munro) and sundry buddies leap millions of light years around the universe, with enviable nonchalance and a distinct lack of consideration for the laws of nature. Their mission: to save Imperialism from Something Far Worse, and along the way to provide for Stella's future by convincing Plummer's heir apparent that, despite her bizarre style of dress, she'd make a neat Empress one day. FF

Stardust

(Michael Apted, 1974, GB) David Essex, Adam Faith, Larry Hagman, Ines Des Longchamps, Rosalind Ayres, Marty Wilde, Ed Byrnes, Keith Moon.
111 min.
Enjoyable attempt at the impossible task of reflecting the whole sprawl of '60s British pop through the rise and fall of one rock star. Ray Connolly's script for this sequel to *That'll Be the Day* functions on numerous levels: as a piece of nostalgia for over 25s; as wish fulfilment for Essex's teenage fans, in which he becomes greatest rock'n'roll singer in the world; and, God help us, as a would-be art movie, with its central relationship between Essex's singer and roadie Adam Faith more than reminiscent of *The Servant*. The script is at its best when knocking the stuffing out of the music industry and its myths, less successful when asking us to believe in the fictional achievements of its central character (3,000,000 fans and a *Time* magazine cover). Best are Adam Faith, Keith Moon's anarchic performance, and Dave Edmunds' music. CPe

Stardust Memories

(Woody Allen, 1980, US) Woody Allen, Charlotte Rampling, Jessica Harper, Marie-Christine Barrault, Tony Roberts, Helen Hanft, John Rothman.
88 min. b/w.
The schlemiel strikes back: at critics, at sycophants, at pigeons ('rats with wings'), and at a universe that can contain both Charlotte Rampling's face and human-skin lampshades. Tactically adopting his most autobiographical persona yet, Allen finally lets his anger loose, and it dumps on everything with unaccustomed savagery. Crossed with the strain of vengeance are his own attempts to make a film (which looks like Art), and also his snagged-up relations with three different ladies. A movie of great moments rather than the coherence of *Manhattan*, as if acknowledging that Memory works best in fragments. But, having stolen Fellini's 8 1/2 structure, Allen stands in danger of likewise painting himself into a corner of solipsism. His 'early, funny' films, that everyone complains he no longer makes, were good exactly because they contained sufficient sadness and pain to make the comic triumph well-earned. One long cry of anguish about the price of fame comes perilously close to self-pity. And self-abuse. CPea

Star 80

(Bob Fosse, 1983, US) Mariel Hemingway, Eric Roberts, Cliff Robertson, Carroll Baker, Roger Rees, David Clennon, Josh Mostel, Lisa Gordon.
103 min.
The all singin'n'dancin' Fosse turns his hand to straight tragedy with the true story of Dorothy Stratten's pathetically short career as *Playboy* pin-up and film starlet (her only starring role was in Peter Bogdanovich's *They All Laughed*), before being cruelly, senselessly murdered by her jealous husband. Hemingway has reinforced not only her breasts but her promise of becoming a sensitive and accomplished actress in her portrayal of the ill-fated Dorothy. The rest, however, is a disappointingly shallow display of images cut together in an apparently haphazard fashion; flashes back and forward are liberally sprinkled with meaningless vistas of naked flesh. This superficial view extends to the characters; in particular, Dorothy's ambitious, hustling husband (Roberts), and her quiet film director/lover (Rees), never really step outside their cardboard cut-outs, making the whole thing feel more like a naughty snapshot than any artistic achievement. HR

Starflight: The Plane That Couldn't Land (aka Starflight One)

(Jerry Jameson, 1982, US) Lee Majors, Hal Linden, Lauren Hutton, Ray Milland, Gail Strickland, Tess Harper, Michael Sacks, Robert Webber.
155 min.

Like a souped-up *Airport* episode, made for TV and cut by 40 minutes for cinema release, this populates the world's first hypersonic jet on its maiden flight with the usual selection of stereotypes, and – thanks to the dastardly designs of several greedy opportunists – plunges them out of the atmosphere into orbit. Then the problems really begin as the cast struggle hopelessly with trite script and flaccid direction. Through a totally unconvincing series of manoeuvres – like an advert for NASA – most of these cardboard characters make it back to Earth; that an audience might survive unscathed is far less likely. GA

Stargate

(Roland Emmerich, 1994, US) Kurt Russell, James Spader, Jaye Davidson, Viveca Lindfors, Alexis Cruz, Mili Avital, Leon Rippy.
121 min.
Approached with a generous spirit and a vacant mind, this bombastic sci-fi epic is hugely enjoyable. Having deciphered the symbols on an ancient stone, eccentric Egyptologist Dr Jackson (Spader), accompanied by hardass Colonel O'Neil (Russell) and a crack marine patrol, walks through the stone portal to an alternate world where a raggle-taggle band of desert-dwellers are ruled by despotic King Ra (Davidson). O'Neil has secretly brought with him an atomic device, his suicide mission to close the Stargate for ever. The unwitting Jackson, however, has eyes only for the lovely Skaara (Cruz), whose downtrodden people rise up against their oppressors. At this point, it's best to surrender to the bombardment of glossy images and spectacular fx, a (manu)script from which many pages appear to be missing, and a stirring score that drives all before it. Futuristic tosh, certainly, but fun all the same. NF

Star Is Born, A

(William Wellman, 1937, US) Fredric March, Janet Gaynor, Adolphe Menjou, May Robson, Andy Devine, Lionel Stander, Franklin Pangborn.
111 min.
Despite the tragic ending, Cukor's remake of *A Star Is Born* is primarily a glowingly nostalgic evocation of Hollywood knowhow and razzmatazz, with Garland's musical numbers blending effortlessly with the gala premieres, Oscar ceremonies, and privileged moments on set. Wellman's non-musical version (attractively shot in the early Technicolor process), though starting more sentimentally with Gaynor as a wide-eyed innocent dreaming every girl's dream of stardom in her small-town home, develops a much more caustic edge, maintaining a bitterly critical distance from the dream factory. This is no doubt because in 1937 the real-life tragedies that fuelled the script were so much closer in time (Esther Blodgett and Norman Maine were inspired by the story of Colleen Moore and her husband/producer John McCormick, though March's Maine, here an actor, draws variously on the fates of John Gilbert, John Barrymore and John Bowers). The two films make fascinating comparison. TM

Star Is Born, A

(George Cukor, 1954, US) Judy Garland, James Mason, Jack Carson, Charles Bickford, Tommy Noonan, Lucy Marlow.
175 min.
Of all Hollywood's heartbreakers, this must be one of the saddest. Made at a time when Garland was fast approaching final crack-up, the story of the rise of a young singing star at the expense of the actor she loves and yearns to keep intact (Mason) seemed to touch exactly the right raw nerves in its performers to make it a major discomfort to watch. Garland's tremulous emotionalism, which so often left her unwatchable, is here decently harnessed to a story which makes good sense of it and to a man worth yearning for. But the acting honours belong to Mason: whether idly cruising the LA dance-halls for a new woman, sliding into alcoholism, or embarrassing everyone at an Oscar ceremony, he gives a performance which is as good as any actor is ever allowed. Previewed at 182 minutes, the film was promptly trimmed by Warners and released at 152 minutes. The version reissued in 1983 features much of the excised footage, rediscovered in archives. Many scenes admirably fill gaps in the original, a few are redundant, but it's a major work of movie archaeology, and a very good wallow. CPea

Star Is Born, A

(Frank Pierson, 1976, US) Barbra Streisand, Kris Kristofferson, Paul Mazursky, Gary Busey, Oliver Clark, Marta Heflin.
140 min.
70mm screens have been filled with some vacuous stuff in their time, but this monstrous remake takes the biscuit. It's set in the rock world, but the kind of rock these people peddle is the softest thing next to jelly. And the embarrassment when Streisand gets to shake her loins in rhythm...Kristofferson is much better as the fading drunkard who promotes and marries the rising star. Apart from the flash new environment, this version vaunts its modernity by vulgarising everything in sight, making the characters mouthpieces for foul language and equally foul sentimentality. Maybe Brian De Palma with his *Phantom of the Paradise* days could have wrested a film from all this, but Pierson (replacing Jerry Schatzberg, Streisand's hairdresser Jon Peters, and probably a million others) just lets it hang out, uncoordinated and ridiculous. GB

Starke Ferdinand, Der (Strong-Man Ferdinand)

(Alexander Kluge, 1976, WGer) Heinz Schubert, Verena Rudolph, Joachim Hackethal, Heinz Schimmelpfennig, Gert Günther Hoffmann.
97 min.
Kluge's marvellously deadpan parable about society and its official guardians is irresistible. Ferdinand the Strong (Schubert) is an ex-policeman turned factory security expert who carries out his duties with surrealistic fervour, finally becoming so obsessed with possible security leaks that he turns terrorist to prove his own case. Unlike some of Kluge's more cerebral works, a highly accessible film, bitingly funny in its satire of the perils of power syndromes. TM

Star Kid

(Manny Coto, 1997, US) Joseph Mazello, Ashlee Levitch, Joey Simmrin, Lauren Eckstrom, Corinne Bohrer.
101 min.
The peaceable Trelkins are defending their planet against the Broodwarriors. Closer to home, young Spencer (Mazello) is also down on his luck: dad lives for work, big sis (Levitch) calls him 'fungus', school bully Turbo Bruntley (Simmrin) has singled him out. Worse yet, classmate Michelle (Eckstrom) is too good to be true – she's pretty, she likes the 'Midnight Warrior' comics behind which Spencer hides. She's even tried speaking to him. His nice teacher (Bohrer) explains how running away from scary things just makes it worse. At this point a Phase One Cyber Assault Suit lands behind his house, requiring a biotic host to test its combat enhancement abilities. Climbing inside, Spencer finds himself piloting an intelligent eight-foot robot, with bionic powers and very friendly to boot. Writer/director Coto's film may be taken tongue in cheek, but it's immensely enjoyable both as straightforward kids' entertainment and, perhaps, as a subtle, fanciful induction in matters pubescent. NB

Starlight Hotel

(Sam Pillsbury, 1987, NZ) Greer Robson, Peter Phelps, Marshall Napier, Ian Brackenbury Channell, Alice Fraser.
94 min.
This tale of a 12-year-old girl's cross-country trek to find her father seems like a New Zealand version of *The Journey of Natty Gann*, lacking the winsome dog and mercifully much else in the winsome vine. During the Depression, Kate (Robson) is parked with relatives so that her father can seek work in the big city. Unhappy, she runs away, hooking up with a young war veteran (Phelps), himself on the run. They ride the rails, pilfer from farms, queue up at soup kitchens, and sleep under the stars. He doesn't notice a substantial young bosom under her boy's disguise until he throws her into a creek – 'Christ! A bloody sheila!' – a myopia which perhaps explains the lack of compass bearing in his life. It's a thin, underwritten film, with muffled emotional climaxes, and with neither of the main players equipped to bring much to their parts. A walk on the mild side. BC

Starmaker, The

see *Uomo delle stelle, L'*

Starman

(John Carpenter, 1984, US) Jeff Bridges, Karen Allen, Charles Martin Smith, Richard Jaeckel, Robert Phalen, Tony Edwards.
115 min.
Carpenter forsakes action and horror, and delivers a rather lame sci-fi love story. Alien Bridges journeys to Earth on what he imagines will be a straightforward mission of friendship. He imagines wrong, of course, as all the pesky earthlings prove to be nasty, brutish and violent. All, that is, except for widowed, childless Karen Allen, who is first kidnapped by Bridges, then falls in love, and finally has to save him. This lacks the drive, energy and surprise which one associates with Carpenter. The best special effects are in the first five minutes. Thereafter, it's all rather predictable. The normally excellent Bridges shuffles his way through a robotic performance as though he's just been unplugged, and the film's (very) basic gag – his naïve response to what he experiences – wears thin pretty quick. RR

Stars and Bars

(Pat O'Connor, 1988, US) Daniel Day Lewis, Harry Dean Stanton, Kent Broadhurst, Maury Chaykin, Matthew Cowles, Joan Cusack, Keith David, Glenne Headly, Laurie Metcalf.
94 min.
William Boyd's novel may be set in the States, but it isn't a million miles away from the comical crew of *Cold Comfort Farm*. O'Connor's version is fortunate in its cast. Day Lewis in particular, as silly ass Henderson Dores, a diffident Britisher who relocates in New York, doodles a hilarious bumbler, one of nature's natural de-bagees. Despatched by art auctioneers to acquire a legendary Renoir in an unlikely Georgia Dogpatch household, he is promptly overwhelmed by grotesques. Patriarch Stanton is willing to sell, but his eldest son (Elvis-look-alike Chaykin) has sold it already on the sly, and threatens death. One brother believes himself to be a damaged Vietvet, but is just damaged, and another is a time-warp hippy. A horny fundamentalist preacher is added to the mix, along with a pregnant alcoholic runaway, no phones, no car, and no trousers. No trousers befalls our empty-handed hero again back in New York, placing the proceedings unashamedly in the farce bag. I laughed a lot. BC

Starship Troopers

(Paul Verhoeven, 1997, US) Casper Van Dien, Dina Meyer, Denise Richards, Jake Busey, Neil Patrick Harris, Clancy Brown, Michael Ironside.
129 min.
High school graduates Johnny Rico, Dizzy, Carmen and Carl enlist in the armed forces of the Federation. Training takes its toll, and Johnny is on the point of throwing in the towel when space insects wipe out his home town Buenos Aires. The infantry are despatched to the outer limits of the galaxy to give 'em what for, but...you guessed it. An adaptation of a Robert A Heinlein novel, this replays World War II as sci-fi spectacular – and this time we're rooting for the fascists. Presumably director Verhoeven meant it as a sour, ironic joke. If so, he's kept an admirably straight face. His totalitarian utopia looks like a daytime soap: bright, clean, empty. And his lead players might be caricatures of Aryan perfection. It falls to Ironside's motivational teacher/commander, Rasczak, to whip them into shape ('If you don't do your job, I shoot you!'). It says a lot about the director that the movie only kicks into life when the carnage starts. The bugs make up in numbers what they lack in charm, the scale of the battle scenes takes the breath away, and the violence is unremittingly gruesome. On the surface, this is grotesque, reactionary trash, yet by the end, when Verhoeven turns a giant brain-sucking maggot into an object of pity, it's hard not to be impressed by the sheer perversity of the enterprise. TCh

Stars Look Down, The

(Carol Reed, 1939, GB) Michael Redgrave, Margaret Lockwood, Emlyn Williams, Edward Rigby, Nancy Price, Allan Jeayes, Cecil Parker, Linden Travers.
110 min. b/w.
Some two decades before the Kitchen Sink cinema of the British New Wave, Carol Reed made this serious, committed film about life in a north-

ern mining community, co-scripted by AJ Cronin from his own novel. The central romance, though by no means all roses, dates the picture (Redgrave, an idealistic miner's son, goes to university, and temporarily forgets his political resolve when he marries Margaret Lockwood); but the mining sequences have a degree of authenticity (above-ground sequences were shot at Workington, in Northumberland), and the film ends with a rousing call for nationalisation of the industry, to 'purge the old greeds'. TCh

Starstruck

(Gillian Armstrong, 1982, Aust) Jo Kennedy, Ross O'Donovan, Margo Lee, Max Cullen, Pat Evison.
102 min.
An unlikely follow-up to *My Brilliant Career*, this comic rock opera in which two weirdo kids from downtown Sydney stare hungrily across the bay to where the talons of the Opera House beckon, promising fame and fortune in a talent contest. Jackie (Kennedy) can sing but no one will listen, until her cousin Angus (O'Donovan), a dwarfish Svengali, persuades her to don a bird costume and tightrope walk high above a busy street. From that angle her star quality, like her false plastic tits, sticks out a mile (opportune knockers, as the TV show almost had it). Although at times a little ragged around the edges, the whole is so persistently bizarre, and the two leads so consistently excellent, that the plusses (her voice, his legs, their spit-and-sawdust family) quickly outweigh the minuses (some dire set pieces and some ugly, ugly people). Alternately cudgelled and cajoled, one cannot help but have a good time. FD

Starting Over

(Alan J Pakula, 1979, US) Burt Reynolds, Jill Clayburgh, Candice Bergen, Charles Durning, Frances Sternhagen, Austin Pendleton, Mary Kay Place.
106 min.
What to do if you are male, American, no spring chicken, and abandoned by your wife on the ground that you get in the way of her career? One answer is to wedge the tongue firmly in cheek, join a Divorced Men's Workshop, get yourself a new girl, and regard your ex-wife with the careful patience usually reserved for the demented. The irrepressible ebullience of Burt Reynolds, which has been known to buoy up less fragile craft than this, is here in danger of swamping not only Jill Clayburgh's rather mousy rendition of Marilyn-the-nursery-school-teacher, but the movie as a whole. Moments of little-boy-lost helplessness, thrown in to indicate his 'earnestness', merely make you wonder if he's schizoid or just a complete philanderer. It's as if Pakula had got on a fairground horse that has gone out of control, and is undecided whether to go with it or try to stop it. FD

Star Trek – The Motion Picture

(Robert Wise, 1979, US) William Shatner, Leonard Nimoy, DeForest Kelley, James Doohan, George Takei, Majel Barrett, Walter Koenig, Nichelle Nichols, Stephen Collins.
132 min.
Before embarking on *Star Trek II*, Paramount engaged in market research to see whether fans would tolerate the demise of Mr Spock. In the event he was indeed killed off (though not permanently). Here the Vulcan is very much alive, aiding his buddies from the old starship Enterprise in their sluggish fight against a malignant force field headed Earthwards. For non-addicts, the smart plot and effects go some way towards compensating for the plastic characters and costumes. DP

Star Trek II: The Wrath of Khan

(Nicholas Meyer, 1982, US) William Shatner, Leonard Nimoy, DeForest Kelley, James Doohan, Walter Koenig, George Takei, Nichelle Nichols, Ricardo Montalban, Paul Winfield, Kirstie Alley.
114 min.
Not only a movie sequel, but a follow-up to the 1967 TV series episode *Space Seed*, in which Captain (now Admiral) Kirk exiled cosmic renegade Khan to the outer limits, where he's been hatching revenge ever since. Foregoing the special effects bonanza of its predecessor, it settles for low camp humanoid melodrama. The ageing

Shatner and his equally self-amused Enterprise cohorts now 'boldly go' wreathed in soft focus, smiling down on a shipful of apprentice Trekkies until summoned to urgent comic strip action when Khan threatens to reverse creation with a destructively-wielded Genesis device. The net effect, between embarrassed guffaws, is incredulity: a movie at once post-TV and pre-DW Griffith. PT

Star Trek III: The Search for Spock

(Leonard Nimoy, 1984, US) William Shatner, Leonard Nimoy, DeForest Kelley, James Doohan, Walter Koenig, George Takei, Nichelle Nichols, Judith Anderson, James B Sikking, Christopher Lloyd, Robert Hooks.
105 min.
An all-time low for the Enterprise and her crew, with Spock dead, the ship condemned, and everyone else looking about 104. But hold! Why is Bones behaving so oddly? Could it be that he contains part of Spock's essence? A sluggish start gives way to quite a fun romp, as the crew's valiant efforts to find Spock are impeded by a bunch of malign Klingons (all with a distinct resemblance to Lemmy of Motorhead), and reaching one surprising anti-climax when the lilywhite Kirk actually starts spluttering and swearing! Decent SFX, but a little more action wouldn't have gone amiss. GD

Star Trek IV

see Voyage Home: Star Trek IV, The

Star Trek V: The Final Frontier

(William Shatner, 1989, US) William Shatner, Leonard Nimoy, DeForest Kelley, James Doohan, Walter Koenig, Nichelle Nichols, George Takei, David Warner, Laurence Luckinbill, Charles Cooper.
107 min.
A portentous *Dune*-like prologue is followed by an aerial shot of an awesome cliff-face; the camera swirls, picks out a fearless lone climber, zooms in, then cuts to a close up of…you guessed it, ageing paunch-features Kirk himself. Thereafter the plot, about a quest for the Ultimate Answer, resembles something Douglas Adams would have thrown in the bin, complete with triple-breasted whores decorating the journey to God's front door. 'Nobody ever went *through the barrier!*' scream the cast. One sub-*2001* light show later, Kirk is boldly splitting infinitives in heaven itself, unscarred and (naturally) unimpressed by God, who after all isn't any good with girls. Polarities are duly reversed while Uhura does the dance of the seven veils and smooches with Scotty (warped factor 5!), whose dilithium crystals clearly canna take it any more. Beam me up this instant. MK

Star Trek VI: The Undiscovered Country

(Nicholas Meyer, 1991, US) William Shatner, Leonard Nimoy, DeForest Kelley, James Doohan, Walter Koenig, Nichelle Nichols, George Takei, Kim Cattrall, Christopher Plummer, David Warner, Mark Lenard, Grace Lee Whitney, Brock Peters, John Schuck, Kurtwood Smith, Iman, Christian Slater.
110 min.
A quarter of a century after the Enterprise first went where no TV programme had gone before, it's zimmer frames ho! as the crew finally shuffle off to the Dunbeamin' Twilight Home for Bewildered Space Travellers. The film is full of in-jokes about their age, but with a serious point: in a none-too-subtle parallel with the fall of the Soviet Union, the ailing Klingon Empire is on the verge of making peace with the Federation, and Kirk feels too old to adjust. When he is charged with the assassination of the Klingon ambassador, and exiled to a grim prison planet with only Bones and an alien shape-changer (supermodel Iman) for company, he has time to reflect on the evils of prejudice. Though patchy, this is a lot more fun than the disastrous *Star Trek V*. DW

Star Trek: Generations

(David Carson, 1994, US) Patrick Stewart, Malcolm McDowell, William Shatner, Walter Koenig, Levar Burton, Michael Dorn, Gates McFadden, Marina Sirtis, Whoopi Goldberg.
118 min.

Kirk, Scottie and Chekov join the inaugural voyage of a newly commissioned Starship, but when Kirk (Shatner) is 'killed' while facing evil immortality-seeker Dr Soran (McDowell), he gets lost in the mists of time, while the plot jumps forward 78 years and goes on without him. Then, the Next Generation commanded by Picard (Stewart) takes over, confronting the ageless Soran and his Klingon cohorts as Soran tries to re-enter the Utopian time continuum of the Nexus, where past, present and future are one. The series' dullest instalment. NF

Star Trek: First Contact

(Jonathan Frakes, 1996, US) Patrick Stewart, Jonathan Frakes, Alice Krige, Brent Spiner, LeVar Burton, Michael Dorn, Gates McFadden, Marina Sirtis, Alfre Woodard.
111 min.
This makes little concession to non-initiates. The Borg, a species of cyborg linked in a hive-consciousness and dedicated to the 'absorption' of all other life-forms, build on their reputation as the TV series' best baddies to invade the Federation: only Picard (Stewart) stands between them and conquest of the Earth. But just when we think we're in for 'Independence Day 2', the routed Borg go back in time to win the war before it began, and we're hurled along with the Enterprise into much darker territory. The Borg's infiltration of the starship recalls some of the tension of *Alien*, while the attempts of the Borg Queen (Krige) to convert the android Data (Spiner) to the pleasures of the New Flesh are positively transgressive. Certainly Spiner convinces you that androids do dream of electric sheep, and electric ladylands; while Stewart, confronting his conscience, draws a sci-fi blockbuster audience into the intimacy of a fringe play. DW

Star Wars (100)

(George Lucas, 1977, US) Mark Hamill, Harrison Ford, Carrie Fisher, Peter Cushing, Alec Guinness, Peter Mayhew, David Prowse.
121 min.
Hollywood began in an amusement arcade, so it's appropriate that its most profitable film should be as formally enchanting and psychologically sterile as a Gottlieb pinball machine. *Star Wars* is at least 40 years out of date as science fiction, but objections pale beside the film's major achievement: nearly 50 years after it was conceived, pulp space fiction is here for the first time presented as a truly viable movie genre. Discounting *2001*, which isn't a genre movie, it's like watching the first Western to use real exteriors. And audiences rightly feel that this is something they've been owed for some time. *Star Wars* itself has distinct limitations, but the current return to a cinema of spectacle and wonder is wholly encouraging. Or would you prefer *The Sound of Music*? DP

Star Wars, Episode IV, A New Hope

(George Lucas, 1977/1997, US) Mark Hamill, Harrison Ford, Carrie Fisher, Peter Cushing, Alec Guinness, Peter Mayhew, David Prowse.
125 min.
Don't expect radical revisions in this 20th anniversary reissue of George Lucas's spellbinding space opera. The sfx may now be unimpeachable, but none of the much heralded extra sequences fashioned from out-takes – the confrontation between Han Solo and Jabba the Hutt; Luke and his childhood friend, Biggs, bantering about the good old days – actually contributes anything meaningful in narrative terms. It's the minor tweaks which most impress. The computer-generated beasties scurrying around Mos Eisley's spaceport are triumphs of animation, and the dogfight scenes benefit immensely from more convincingly nuclear-looking explosions and the removal of unsightly matte lines. For the most part, you'd never guess the film was 20 years old. Only the innocence of its universe testifies to the sea change in film-making it provoked. The jaw-dropping wetness of Mark Hamill's Luke continues to astound, while Harrison Ford's amphetamine enema of a turn, which shifts the film into top gear after its rather too leisurely first act, merely confirms what we've always known: stars will out. JO'C

State Fair (aka It Happened One Summer)

(Walter Lang, 1945, US) Charles Winninger, Jeanne Crain, Dana Andrews, Vivian Blaine, Dick Haymes, Fay Bainter, Frank McHugh, Percy Kilbride, Donald Meek.
100 min.

Odious Rodgers and Hammerstein musical, as fey and insipid as they come, too obviously modelled on *Meet Me in St Louis* (1944). The story's about the (non-) adventures of the Frake family at the Iowa State Fair. If you're a fan of the music, you may be able to overlook the general mawkishness, but it'll take an effort. Songs include 'Isn't It Kinda Fun' and the Oscar-winning 'It Might As Well Be Spring'. Henry King made an earlier version with Will Rogers and Janet Gaynor in 1933. GM

State of Grace

(Phil Joanou, 1990, US) Sean Penn, Ed Harris, Gary Oldman, Robin Wright, John Turturro, John C Reilly, RD Call, Joe Vitorelli, Burgess Meredith.
134 min.

While not in the same class as *GoodFellas*, this saga about Irish-American hoods in Hell's Kitchen during the 1970s is out of the same stable; and though sometimes monstrously violent, it's a hugely impressive piece of work for a young director previously known for his documentary *U2 Rattle and Hum*. The plot is familiar: youthful loyalty compromised, betrayal, kinship, ethnic rivalry, protection of territory, return to roots, revenge. More important is the visual impact of the film, which begins in a blur of motion and ends with a bloody St Patrick's Day shoot-out. But most impactful are the performances: the much underrated Penn as a prodigal returnee, Wright as the ghetto woman who moved up and away, Harris as the bossman, and – most astonishingly – Oldman showing the ferocity of a Joe Pesci, the aimlessness of a *Mean Streets* De Niro, and the sex-appeal of a pre-fight Mickey Rourke. SGr

State of Siege (Etat de Siège)

(Costa-Gavras, 1973, Fr/It/WGer) Yves Montand, Renato Salvatori, OE Hasse, Jacques Weber, Jean-Luc Bideau, Evangeline Peterson, Maurice Teynac.
120 min.

How easily should one dismiss political potboilers? *Z* caused a lot of stir, with its topical subject and excellent performance from Trintignant; its audience was large, its message clear. *State of Siege* betrays its later date in the laboured difficulty of its subject: Tupamaro guerillas vs the CIA. It's the more courageous film, but far less 'successful', simply unable to contain the subject of terrorism within a basically thriller format. Both films sacrifice analysis and integrity in favour of popular polemic and an exploitative format, but then both films told the truth before it became 'true'; well worth seeing, if only to wonder what similar films could be made on Ulster or any of the other 'forgotten' aspects of British democracy in action. CA

State of the Union (aka The World and His Wife)

(Frank Capra, 1948, US) Spencer Tracy, Katharine Hepburn, Van Johnson, Angela Lansbury, Adolphe Menjou, Lewis Stone, Raymond Walburn, Charles Dingle.
124 min. b/w.

An over-long and over-emphatic political satire, in which Tracy's presidential candidate enlists the help of his estranged wife (Hepburn) in order to present a happy, respectable front to the voters (as always with Capra, seen as gullible little people, here in danger of being duped by corrupt industrialists). It's the usual Capra recipe of homespun sentiment and mindless optimism, enlivened a little by the performances (though one can only dream of what Cukor might have done with Hepburn and Tracy), but turned unusually bitter by Cold War cracks. Horribly dated, too. GA

State of Things, The

(Wim Wenders, 1982, US/Port) Patrick Bauchau, Allen Garfield, Isabelle Weingarten, Samuel Fuller, Roger Corman, Geoffrey Carey.
121 min. b/w.

Shooting a remake of an old Hollywood sci-fi film on the furthest westerly point in Portugal, the cast and crew suddenly find themselves high and dry on the beach, looking across the water to the US where the producer has vanished with the money. The motley crew begin killing time, relaxing into those day-to-day 'things' which somehow become privileged under Wenders' gaze; the need for narrative vanishes along with the old Hollywood pressures. When the director finally pursues the producer to LA and finds him fleeing the Mob, he encounters a different kind of killing time. Literally made on the run, during a hiatus in the troubled shooting of *Hammett*, the film is far more than Wenders' slap in the face to Hollywood. Supremely assured of itself and its method, it becomes a grave and beautiful meditation on the state of the art: the creative impasse of European film, the narcotic temptations of the last resort, the impossibility of telling stories any more, death. Wenders calls it the last of the B movies, but it may be cinema at its very limits. CPea

State Secret (aka The Great Manhunt)

(Sidney Gilliat, 1950, GB) Douglas Fairbanks Jr, Jack Hawkins, Glynis Johns, Herbert Lom, Walter Rilla, Karel Stepanek, Carl Jaffe, Anton Diffring.
104 min. b/w.

Launder (co-producer) and Gilliat (writer/co-producer/director) drew on the lessons they'd learned when working for Hitchcock in the '30s to turn out this nifty little thriller (from a novel by Roy Huggins) with a welcome sprinkling of humour. Fairbanks is the American surgeon called into the authoritarian Mittel-European state of Vosnia to receive honours from the country's medical fraternity, but he's embroiled in the local political turmoil when asked to operate on the ailing military premier, becoming one of the privileged few who know the secret of the general's fading health. TJ

Static

(Mark Romanek, 1985, US) Keith Gordon, Amanda Plummer, Bob Gunton, Lily Knight, Barton Heyman.
93 min.

Ernie Blick (Gordon) whiles away his time in a crucifix factory collecting the assembly line cockups. His mind, however, is far away, on the invention he is perfecting in his motel room, which he hopes will give people a vision of heaven. All very weird and amiable in a Capraesque way, until frustration sets in, and Ernie hijacks a bus and demands local air-time in order to publicise his invention. If the film is about the different ways in which people seek to believe, then it is not held down by any preaching or heavyweight message; it's all far too open-ended, optimistic and humorous for that. Its very unclassifiability is its strength. CPea

Stationmaster's Wife, The

see Bolwieser

Station Six – Sahara

(Seth Holt, 1962, GB/WGer) Carroll Baker, Peter Van Eyck, Ian Bannen, Denholm Elliott, Jörg Felmy, Mario Adorf, Biff McGuire.
101 min. b/w.

On an isolated oil pipeline station in the desert, five men bicker and squabble in the appalling heat and boredom. Then the incredible happens: a large American car crashes in their midst, one of its two occupants a beautiful blonde siren (Baker). Her presence drives the men crazy with lust for her, and with increasing antagonism towards each other. From a script by Bryan Forbes and Brian Clemens, the underrated Holt directs with a tight grip, and clearly delights in such moments as the frisson created by Baker's bra-strap falling casually from her shoulder. It's an unexpected black sheep of British cinema, not least for its unrepressed sense of anger and strident eroticism. DT

Stavisky...

(Alain Resnais, 1974, Fr/It) Jean-Paul Belmondo, François Périer, Anny Duperey, Michel Lonsdale, Robert Bisacco, Claude Rich, Charles Boyer, Jacques Spiesser, Gérard Depardieu.
117 min.

Resnais' film about political destiny in France in the '30s is always thoroughly chilling, never merely elegant. The chill stems not simply from the cold precision of the images, but from the unshakeable implications of what he allows us to witness. On the one hand, and occupying centre stage, is Stavisky (Belmondo), swindler and entrepreneur; on the other, in the wings, is Trotsky, arriving in France, working, and finally exiled. Around them, *sotto voce* political machinations in which gradually and unmistakeably a grand design becomes visible – the breaking of the Left and the drift to Fascism. Stavisky's fall reveals him to be a pawn in a swindle of vaster dimensions than even he dreamed of, the fall itself a screen behind which other forces operate. Resnais conveys the atmosphere of moral degeneracy with a tact which makes it all the more insidious, through a film that is superbly paced. VG

Stay Hungry

(Bob Rafelson, 1976, US) Jeff Bridges, Sally Field, Arnold Schwarzenegger, RG Armstrong, Robert Englund, Helena Kallianiotes, Roger E Mosley, Woodrow Parfrey, Scatman Crothers.
102 min.

After the sombre melancholy of *Five Easy Pieces* and *The King of Marvin Gardens*, Rafelson pursued his interest in social dropouts and marginal life-styles with this offbeat comedy drama. Bridges oozes carefree charm as a young Alabama heir caught up in a property speculation involving a gym, but instead investing his interest in Arnie and his muscle-building pals. His relationship with gutsy working gal Field helps fill out the picture, although the preponderance of loose narrative threads tends to leave one with an impression of individual scenes rather than any sense of coherent plot. The scene in which Bridges slips though a hole in the social hedge to join a bunch of fiddle players in a country hoedown epitomises the gentle, quirky feel of the film. Based on a Charles Gaines novel about the rootlessness of the so-called 'New South', it has its slack spells, but Rafelson's sure feel for the inexpressible subtleties of emotional relationships is evident throughout. NF

Staying Alive

(Sylvester Stallone, 1983, US) John Travolta, Cynthia Rhodes, Finola Hughes, Steve Inwood, Julie Bovasso, Charles Ward.
96 min.

Six years on from *Saturday Night Fever*, Travolta's Tony Manero is very much the same: one dimensional, bovine, manipulating, self-obsessed, as he fights his way from dancing obscurity to a starring role in some God-awful Broadway parody of a multi-million-pound Zanussi ad. On the way, he falls in and out with the ice-cool English star (Hughes), before opting for faithful old stablemate Jackie (Rhodes). The dance sequences seem poor beer when set against the vibrant amateurism of *Saturday Night Fever*, mostly rudimentary Martha Graham, with lots of close-ups to hide Travolta's obvious failings in that department. All could be forgiven if it weren't for the soulless overall slickness. SGr

Staying Together

(Lee Grant, 1989, US) Sean Astin, Stockard Channing, Melinda Dillon, Jim Haynie, Levon Helm, Dinah Manoff, Dermot Mulroney, Tim Quill, Keith Szarabajka, Daphne Zuniga.
91 min.

This genial family drama is formulaic without being entirely predictable. There's a symmetry to the story of three sons going through that troublesome teen phase: the smooth flow of their emotional lives is disturbed as each in turn has problems relating to Mom and Pop, and to the opposite sex. Gradually they come to realise – aaah! – that their greatest strength is each other. Everyone gets a Big Problem to wrestle with. How's Brian (Quill) ever gonna get reconciled with Pop? He's breaking his Mom's heart. How's Kit (Mulroney) gonna rescue his girl, due to be married to the town rich creep? How's Duncan (Astin) ever gonna lose his irksome virginity? When will any of them twig that Mom (Dillon) is more than just a service unit? There's an admirable lack of wish-fulfilment plotting, plus a casual, bollocks-scratching realism in the depiction of the teenage boys. The three leads all strain a bit after sensitivity, but overall it's amiable enough. SFe

Stay Tuned

(Peter Hyams, 1992, US) John Ritter, Pam
Dawber, Jeffrey Jones, David Tom, Heather
McComb, Bob Dishy, Joyce Gordon.
88 min.
A pointless 'satire' which attempts to ridicule
American television by revelling in the conventions of game shows, commercials and mini-
series. Roy (Ritter) is your average TV junkie: he
watches over seven hours a day and is blind to
the needs of his wife (Dawber) and two children
(Tom and McComb). Enter devilish Spike (Jones),
the supremo of an other-worldly entertainment
channel who sells Roy a 600-channel satellite system, thereby luring him into a Faustian pact that
will test his devotion to the box. The question is:
does this human sponge possess a soul? The film
boasts the emotional depth of a 30-second soap
commercial, and Hyams' direction fails to sustain
humour or tension. A dismal affair which goes
down the tube. CM

Stazione Termini

see Terminal Station

Steal, The

(John Hay, 1994, GB) Heathcote Williams,
Alfred Molina, Helen Slater, Patricia Hayes,
Stephen Fry, Jack Dee, Peter Bowles, Dinsdale
Landen, Bryan Pringle, Patricia Hayes.
91 min.
Williams is the mysterious lawyer who acts as
commissioning officer for a PC scam to liberate
funds from an evil merchant bank whose investment portfolios have devastated the Asian demi-
paradise of Golanda. To this end, he enlists brash
computer hacker Slater and old pal Molina, a
reserved council traffic-planner. Pretty much a
non-starter as a Brit caper-comedy, writer/direc-
tor Hay's barely adequate picture is nevertheless
sweet in the way it fails. It's like the kind of keen,
bad school essay which shows all the heartbreaking evidence of a pupil having heard, but
not learned, from teacher's advice. In their efforts
to make an economic modern Ealing comedy the
producers have thrown everything into the pudding: American star, impersonations, car chases,
rural interludes – all executed in delightfully mid-
scale, lightweight, familiar and mildly diverting
style. The rest is spot the TV actor.
Undemanding, old-fashioned and old hat. WH

Steal Big, Steal Little

(Andrew Davis, 1995, US) Andy Garcia, Alan
Arkin, Rachel Ticotin, Joe Pantoliano, Holland
Taylor, Ally Walker, David Ogden Stiers,
Kevin McCarthy.
134 min.
Double trouble, take two. Garcia is Reuben, who
runs an organic farm as a collective for South
American immigrants; and Garcia is Robert,
who's trying to steal the land out from under their
feet, to convert it into a holiday ranch for businessmen. Reuben wears natty collarless shirts
and a Boho leather waistcoat, while Robert sports
garish cowboy suits and a ten-gallon hat. Director
Davis paid his dues making disreputable action
films with Steven Seagal and Chuck Norris,
before graduating to reputable action films with
Harrison Ford. But while this reveals a hitherto
latent Marxist tendency, it lacks any of the distinctive qualities the director brought to his genre
work: the powerhouse narrative drive, unsentimental intelligence and brusque humour.
Sincerely philanthropic, predictably dismal. TCh

Stealing Beauty (Io ballo da sola/Beauté Volée)

(Bernardo Bertolucci, 1995, It/GB/Fr) Sinead
Cusack, Jeremy Irons, Jean Marais, Liv Tyler,
Donal McCann, Carlo Cecchi, DW Moffett,
Rachel Weisz, Steffania Sandrelli, Joseph
Fiennes, Jason Flemyng.
118 min.
When Lucy (Tyler), a 19-year-old American,
whose poet mother has recently died, visits friends
in a Tuscan villa, her plans involve more than a
simple holiday. For one thing, she cherishes memories of a first kiss, four years earlier, from young
Niccolò to whom she'd now like to lose her virginity; for another, she's puzzled by a note in her
mother's diary hinting that the man she's considered her father isn't her real parent. At the same
time, she soon becomes the focus of interest for
the villa's inhabitants, notably the jaded menfolk

who are revitalised by her innocence and burgeoning womanhood. The self-obsessed complacency of the arty, Chiantishire expats tries the
patience, and the camera's relentless ogling
of Tyler's limbs opens the film to charges of
voyeurism. And yet, after the deliberate, overblown portentousness of his recent epics, the
looseness, leisurely pacing and the intimacy of
mood are a welcome reminder of Bertolucci's
directorial assurance. He brings a light touch to
small details: the expats' isolation from the 'real
world' being revealed through deft short scenes
depicting, say, their reaction to the building of a
nearby television mast or their encounter with an
army officer. But there's also a real sensuousness,
less in the emphasis on Tyler herself than in the
evocation of the colours, aromas, temperatures
and sounds of a particular time and place. GA

Stealing Heaven

(Clive Donner, 1988, GB/Yugo) Derek de Lint,
Kim Thomson, Denholm Elliott, Bernard
Hepton, Kenneth Cranham, Rachel Kempson,
Angela Pleasence, Patsy Byrne, Cassie Stuart,
Philip Locke.
115 min.
Abelard and Heloise retold with more than a
touch of *Emmanuelle*, and no sense of the
medieval anywhere. All in all, the tale comes
across like a Mills & Boon bodice-ripper. Theirs
is a forbidden passion since his vocation as a
teacher enjoins chastity, but boarding in her
uncle's house and giving her private tuition saps
his resolve. Tolerant Bishop Martin (Hepton)
would probably have let him off lightly, but Uncle
Fulbert (Elliott), a vain, power-hungry prelate
who sells bogus holy relics on the side, sends a
gang to castrate him. After that, Abelard and
Heloise take holy orders, but bump into each
other a bit around the cloisters and get to play
house as the century wears on. Fairly feeble
except for Denholm Elliott, who tops up his role
with such a convincing character study that you
regret every minute he's off screen. BC

Stealing Home

(Steven Kampmann/Will Aldiss, 1988, US)
Mark Harmon, Jodie Foster, Blair Brown,
William McNamara, Harold Ramis, Jonathan
Silverman, Richard Jenkins, John Shea.
98 min.
Down-at-heel baseball pro Harmon returns home
when he learns that his childhood sweetheart
Foster has killed herself. It's up to him to dispose
of her ashes. Lame melodrama, pitched firmly at
the emotions, which comes complete with syrupy
music and excruciating flashback sequences. The
baseball references are hardly an integral part of
the story, but seem to have been tagged on to
ensure a punchy title. Foster's intense, heartfelt,
and entirely humourless performance as the
young rebel with the death wish just about takes
the movie to first base. GM

Steamboat Bill, Jr

(Buster Keaton/Charles F Reisner, 1928, US)
Buster Keaton, Ernest Torrence, Marion
Byron, Tom McGuire, Tom Lewis, Joe Keaton.
6,400 ft. b/w.
A marvellous comedy set in a lazy riverside town
in the Deep South, with Buster as the foppish,
city-educated boy who returns home to prove a
grave disappointment to his father, a burly
steamboat captain looking for stout filial support,
and reluctantly joins him in his efforts to fight off
a wealthy rival threatening to take over the river.
Hilarious, of course, with both delicately
observed jokes and energetically athletic stuntwork coursing through the movie. But what really delights is the detailed depiction of small town
life, plus Keaton's comic awareness of his own
persona; a sequence in which he and his father
are buying a hat to replace his wimpy beret is a
model of film comedy, played, remarkably, direct
to camera. And the final masterstroke is the
cyclone sequence, in which the entire town is
destroyed but Buster remains miraculously
untouched. GA

Steaming

(Joseph Losey, 1984, GB) Vanessa Redgrave,
Sarah Miles, Diana Dors, Patti Love, Brenda
Bruce, Felicity Dean, Sally Sagoe, Anna
Tzelniker.
95 min.
The screen version of Nell Dunn's play, which

posits an all-female cast of stereotypes in a
Turkish Bath where they mix, mouth off, and
mellow, is the swansong of both Losey and Dors,
who plays the earth-mother caretaker, watching
benignly over her chicks as they let off steam and
unite, despite their differences, to save their baths
from demolition. Losey refrains from opening out
the action, preserving the speechy theatricality
of the piece. Verbose group therapy, performed
by very proficient actresses in various stages of
undress. AB

Steamroller and the Violin, The

see Katok i Skrypka

Steel

(Steve Carver, 1979, US) Lee Majors, Jennifer
O'Neill, Art Carney, George Kennedy, Harris
Yulin, Redmond Gleason, Terry Kiser, Richard
Lynch, Roger Mosley, Albert Salmi, RG
Armstrong.
101 min.
Uninspired piece of high-rise melodrama. O'Neill
is the svelte daughter of a hard-hat steel construction boss (Kennedy) who steps into daddy's
shoes when he falls to a tragic death. The jokes
and the sexual sparring are predictable, sexist,
and too lame to redeem themselves with even a
minimum of irony. And the cracks at trade union
safety regulations look particularly ugly when
you think that one of the stuntmen on the crew
really did fall to his death during shooting. CA

Steel Bayonet, The

(Michael Carreras, 1957, GB) Leo Genn, Kieron
Moore, Michael Medwin, Robert Brown,
Michael Ripper.
85 min. b/w.
No-budget British war movie (avoid confusion
with Sam Fuller's *The Steel Helmet* or *Fixed
Bayonets*) directed by Michael Carreras, a
Hammer studios' mainstay. Salisbury Plain
stands in for Tunis, 1943, as a group of infantrymen hold a farmhouse dangerously close to
enemy lines. Despite an honourable effort in the
direction of psychological grittiness, the picture
never really exerts much grip. TJ

Steel Helmet, The

(Samuel Fuller, 1950, US) Gene Evans, Robert
Hutton, Richard Loo, Steve Brodie, James
Edwards, Sid Melton, Richard Monahan.
84 min. b/w.
A characteristically hard-hitting war movie from
Fuller, charting the fortunes of Gene Evans'
Sergeant Zack, sole survivor of a PoW massacre
in Korea. Saved by a Korean orphan and joining
up with other GIs cut off from their units, Evans'
cynical veteran embodies the writer-director's
abiding thesis that, to survive the madness of
war, a ruthless individualism is necessary. Fuller
glamorises neither his loner protagonist nor the
war itself: if he clearly supports the US presence
in Korea, battle is still a chaotic, deadly affair, and
nobody has much idea of why they fight. The
action scenes are terrific, belying the movie's very
low budget. GA

Steel Magnolias

(Herbert Ross, 1989, US) Sally Field, Dolly
Parton, Shirley MacLaine, Daryl Hannah,
Olympia Dukakis, Julia Roberts, Tom Skerritt,
Sam Shepard, Kevin J O'Connor.
117 min.
The loves, lives and losses of six Southern women
of different ages, fortunes and temperaments, united by a feisty self-confidence, irrepressible humour,
and steely fortitude in the face of life's setbacks. It
takes place over several years – much of it set in
the beauty parlour run by Dolly Parton – from the
wedding of beautiful Shelby Eatenton (Roberts),
through the birth of her first child and her untimely death. The plot's main thrust deals with diabetic Shelby's determination, against the wishes of her
mom (Field), to have a child despite the risks.
Thanks to Field's no-nonsense performance, this
potentially maudlin scenario is briskly handled. Set
against flower-like Shelby (a strong, sensitive characterisation by Roberts) are two raddled fairy god-
mothers: MacLaine and Dukakis, revelling in some
wonderful one-liners. With all the male characters
kept strictly functional, it makes a shameless bid
for your heart, aiming to have you smiling one
moment, sniffling the next. SFe

Steelyard Blues

(Alan Myerson, 1972, US) Jane Fonda, Donald Sutherland, Peter Boyle, Garry Goodrow, Howard Hesseman, John Savage.
93 min.
Perhaps the best American comedy since *The President's Analyst*, mainly because its humour is never imposed, but allowed to develop from the situations in which the characters find themselves. Demolition derby fanatic Sutherland teams up with a gang of junkyard misfits, including Boyle as a nut who dresses up and takes off movie actors, plus Fonda as the inevitable hooker, and they set about resurrecting an old seaplane with the idea of flying away from it all. Humour and paranoia go hand in hand, before the film spirals off into fantasy. There's enough to suggest that it considers itself an allegory on dark America, but this remains sufficiently deadpan to take or leave. Otherwise it's just very funny, full of moments of irrelevant humour. Good soundtrack too, from Nick Gravenites and Paul Butterfield. An impressive first film. CPe

Stella

(John Erman, 1990, US) Bette Midler, John Goodman, Trini Alvarado, Stephen Collins, Marsha Mason, Eileen Brennan, Linda Hart, Ben Stiller, William McNamara.
109 min.
This second remake of *Stella Dallas* updates the story, with Stella (Midler) a single parent struggling through the '70s who still makes the ultimate sacrifice, giving up her daughter in the interest of the latter's social advancement. Handsome doctor Stephen Dallas (Collins) first notices bartender Stella when she leaps on the bar to do a mock striptease routine. Becoming pregnant, she fiercely rejects his offers of marriage or financial support. Years later, their teenage daughter Jenny (Alvarado) grows weary of mother's bad dress sense, and the ultimate humiliation comes when Stella is arrested outside a local bar. Off she goes to Dad and prospective stepmother (Mason) for blueberry pancakes and cocktails. Whatever challenge existed in rendering the class conflict credible has been missed: Robert Getchell's script milks the story for maximum tears, but wrestles unsuccessfully with the inherent absurdity of Stella's predicament, delivering clichéd situations and dialogue. And Midler's larger-than-life performance is daunting against the subtler approaches of Alvarado and Mason. CM

Stella Dallas

(King Vidor, 1937, US) Barbara Stanwyck, John Boles, Anne Shirley, Alan Hale, Barbara O'Neil, Tim Holt, Marjorie Main.
105 min. b/w.
A pretty millworker with her mind on upward mobility via a suet-faced, sexless millionaire's son (Boles), Stella (Stanwyck, wonderful) turns from radiant grisette into a restless wife who sublimates frustration into maternal martyrdom and ever more outrageous dress. Meanwhile husband Stephen flees to a wealthy and conveniently widowed old flame who epitomises pedigree breeding and impeccable (but mean-spirited) good taste. The film stays tantalisingly undecided whether Stella's vulgarity and wild narcissism are a fatal flaw or a snook knowingly cocked at country-club dullness and decorum; and Stanwyck's extraordinary performance keeps open the cleft between weepy pathos and mocking defiance to the very end when, alone outside in the rain, she spies on her daughter's high society wedding through a window, then turns from the puppet-show, striding, smiling enigmatically, towards the camera. SJo

Stella Does Tricks

(Coky Giedroyc, 1996, GB) Kelly Macdonald, Hans Matheson, James Bolam, Ewan Stewart, Lindsay Henderson, Andy Serkis.
99 min.
It may not be explicit on the physical front, but this kitchen-sink study of teenage prostitution is dubious: yes, we should know that such exploitation exists, but what's this first feature actually saying? Kelly Macdonald (from *Trainspotting*) is impressive in the lead, oppressed by deceptively helpful pimp Bolam and prepared to make a new start with junkie Mathieson, but she's not helped by AL Kennedy's obvious script, clumsy flashbacks, and, despite the project's liberal stance, an overall prurience (a gang-rape scene is particularly nasty). GA

Stepfather (Beau-père)

(Bertrand Blier, 1981, Fr) Patrick Dewaere, Ariel Besse, Maurice Ronet, Nicole Garcia, Nathalie Baye, Maurice Risch.
120 min.
What is a man to do when the accidental death of his wife leaves him alone with a 14-year-old stepdaughter who keeps crawling into his bed with the dewy-eyed persistence of Humbert Humbert's Lolita? The answer, wrapped up in yards of dreary solemnity before ultimately blowing up into absurdity, provides some polite porn designed for bourgeois coffee tables. Not one of Blier's more successful provocations. TM

Stepfather, The

(Joseph Ruben, 1986, US) Terry O'Quinn, Jill Schoelen, Shelley Hack, Charles Lanyer, Stephen Shellen, Stephen E Miller.
98 min.
This above-average domestic slasher derives a modicum of interest from the script's discreet, if unoriginal, reworking of Hitchcockian motifs and situations. Teenage Stephanie happily shares her Seattle home with her young widowed mother until Jerry Blake (O'Quinn) appears out of the blue to court and marry mom. Steph's natural jealousy soon turns into outright suspicion when she is led to believe that he is in fact a psychokiller with a history of changed identities and previous slaughtered families who had failed him somehow. An over-emphatic score, heavy symbolism, and the inevitable Steadicam stuff are thankfully countered by an admirable lack of gore. But while O'Quinn is effectively scary, one is left longing for Hitchcock's dark, daring wit and disturbingly amoral insights. GA

Stepfather II, The

(Jeff Burr, 1989, US) Terry O'Quinn, Meg Foster, Jonathan Brandis, Caroline Williams, Mitchell Laurance, Henry Brown, Renata Scott.
86 min.
A welcome return for O'Quinn's sinister psycho. Picking up where the previous slasher left off, this has him in a psychiatric hospital for the criminally insane, where a caring shrink ponders the question as to what drove a seemingly charming gentleman to move in with a series of fatherless families, assuming happy paternal roles, only to leave them gurgling on their own claret. Explaining in simple terms before driving home his primitive blade, the psycho then strolls out of the hospital, throws on a new, somewhat inadequate-looking disguise, and ventures forth in search of his next kill. Forget the supporting cast (most of them are dispensed with anyway): this is essentially O'Quinn's film, his glassy-eyed killer moving from relaxed father-figure to enraged psychotic in less time than it takes for one's heart to skip a beat, while his effective delivery of such murderous connotations as 'You go ahead while I just crack open this bottle' adds a spattering of humour to the grisly proceedings. DA

Stepfather III

(Guy Magar, 1992, US) Rob Wightman, Priscilla Barnes, David Tom, John Ingle, Season Hubley.
105 min.
This second sequel is far better than one might expect from the end of *Stepfather II*, when the titular psycho was being butchered and battered by various members of his latest family. Miraculously surviving, he opens proceedings here in a particularly gruesome bout of plastic surgery, without anaesthetic and performed by a drunken surgeon. He then fixes himself up with another widow and child in no time, and is on his beastly traditional-values way again. The reason for the plastic surgery, of course, is that the excellent Terry O'Quinn has been replaced. Wightman, with that prissy, scary, whiny voice makes a good fist of it, and seems more barmy than ever. The violence is genuinely gory, and climaxes with a death in a garden threshing-machine that surely defies all efforts at restorative surgery. SGr

Stepford Wives, The

(Bryan Forbes, 1974, US) Katharine Ross, Paula Prentiss, Peter Masterson, Nanette Newman, Patrick O'Neal, Tina Louise, Carol Rossen, William Prince.
115 min.
William Goldman's leisurely script and Forbes' dull direction never quite capture the subtleties of Ira Levin's novel about an idyllic Connecticut commuter village where the housewives are a bunch of domesticated dummies. Ross and Prentiss play a pair of newly-arrived wives who are puzzled by the excessive clubbishness of the men and the unquestioning docility of their wives. The final revelation is marred by a melodramatic, sub-Hitchcockian showdown that dispels the more subtly unnerving atmosphere of polite menace. That said, the final supermarket scene does at least have the courage to see the original premise through to its logical conclusion. NF

Stephen King's Thinner

(Tom Holland, 1996, US) Robert John Burke, Joe Mantegna, Lucinda Jenney, Michael Constantine, Kari Wuhrer, Joy Lenz, Stephen King.
92 min.
Billy Halleck (Burke, unrecognisable as the Hal Hartley actor) is a well connected attorney in Fairview, Maine, whose body is ballooning as his arrogance grows. His attention distracted while driving (by a congratulatory blow-job from his wife), Billy knocks down an ageing gypsy woman. His cronies cover up the crime, but gypsy elder Tadzu Lempke (Constantine) utters a curse which sets Greg Cannom's make-up effects department into reverse, with Halleck wasting away into a cadaverous skeleton. Even as the psychological tension is wound up – as the ghost-cheeked attorney suffers tormented nightmares, fantasises infidelities, and falls deeper into the compromising grip of mobster Ginelli (Mantegna) – second league horror director Holland seems unable to invest the film with anything resembling conviction. Having reached the crossroads signposted 'Spoof' and 'Delirious Nightmare', he sits down and goes nowhere. Light fun can be had either from watching ethnic minorities and women take their revenge (albeit, intriguingly, through the agency of supernatural spells), or from idly scrutinising Burke's wobbling bodysuits. But this is basically best left as fodder for a media studies thesis entitled 'Anxiety in American Cinema in the age of PC'. WH

Stepkids

see Big Girls Don't Cry... They Get Even

Stepmother, The

(Hikmet Avedis, 1972, US) Alejandro Rey, John Anderson, Katherine Justice, Larry Linville, Marlene Schmidt, Duncan MacLeod, Rudy Herrera Jr, John D Garfield.
94 min.
A building contractor (Rey) strangles his wife Margo's lover and while burying the body sees a man beating up a Mexican girl who's later murdered. A cop (Anderson) fits the jigsaw together. Producer/director Avedis (who later answered to the first name Howard) scripted this overheated Southern California thriller: punctuated by ugly freeze shots, the plot trudges in a straight line, while striving to give the impression of twisting in the Chandler manner, and comes to a blood-stained conclusion when Margo (Justice) is discovered in bed (in almost forgotten justification of the come-on title) with her college stepson. JPy

Steppenwolf

(Fred Haines, 1974, US) Max von Sydow, Dominique Sanda, Pierre Clémenti, Carla Romanelli, Roy Bosier, Alfred Baillou.
106 min.
Faced with Hesse's intensely introspective text about the intellectual and emotional crisis of a middle-aged man, Haines opts for a '60s-ish semi-psychedelic approach, with some fetching animated interpolations, an amusing appearance by Clémenti, and a marginal, simplistic 'let's all get stoned' moral. The latter aspect now looks distinctly corny, and some might regard it as a gross misreading of the original. But even the staunchest Hesse devotee will find compensations in Sydow's characterisation and the comparative fidelity of the film's first half. DP

Stepping Out

(Lewis Gilbert, 1991, US) Liza Minnelli, Shelley Winters, Robyn Stevan, Jane Krakowski, Bill Irwin, Ellen Greene, Sheila McCarthy, Andrea Martin, Julie Walters, Carol Woods, Luke Reilly, Nora Dunn.
110 min.

Schlepping out, more like. Another feel-good movie to follow *Shirley Valentine*, this is set in a New York dance class run by feisty coulda-been Mavis (Minnelli), who had her week of glory understudying on Broadway. Now, her career hampered by her boyfriend's ego, fulfilment lies in teaching a lovable bunch of stereotypes and social inadequates under the steely eye of cantankerous pianist Winters. Asked to stage a routine for a charity show, Mavis has to whip these no-hopers into a crack *corps de tap*. This isn't a Willy Russell job, but the rules are the same: plain folk overcome problems in one life-affirming moment, braving the disapproval of society and/or him at home. There's little room for a strong cast to manoeuvre. Minnelli plies her gamine act likeably, although when it comes to her big 'what-good-is-it-sitting-alone-in-your-room' closer, tacked on as a cynical box-office sop, she's the same old Liza with a Zzzz. Gilbert opens up Richard Harris's church-hall bound stage play with all the visual flair of a sitcom episode. JRo

Stepping Razor – Red X

(Nicholas Campbell, 1992, Can) Peter Tosh, Lloyd 'Rocky' Allen, Edward 'Bigs' Allen, Andrea Davis, Rab Leon, Ron Headley.
104 min.
'I learned to multiply zero with zero and get one,' mutters the recorded voice of reggae star Peter Tosh in this thunderous documentary of his life and times, at once defying logic and hitting the spot, as was his wont throughout an iconoclastic career as Wailer, ex-Wailer, political agitator and spiritual rhetorician. Tosh was murdered in ambiguous circumstances in 1987 and this long, dense film rumbles across the infernal landscape of his world with the dispassion of an apocalyptic war report. A harsh, angry, frightened description of a harsh, angry, frightened life. NC

Sterile Cuckoo, The (aka Pookie)

(Alan J Pakula, 1969, US) Liza Minnelli, Wendell Burton, Tim McIntire, Elizabeth Harrower, Austin Green.
107 min.
Pakula's debut as a director, two years before making *Klute*, is one of those rare American films which manage to be gently observational without succumbing to the Europeanism of Mazursky or Cassavetes. Liza Minnelli, improbably, is the kook of the title, a college girl who tumbles through an autumn romance with a bashful student (Burton). Not a lot happens: the camera watches, winter comes, the kids split up, Pookie drops out...but the sympathy of the direction for once makes romantic realism likeable. CA

Stevie

(Robert Enders, 1978, US/GB) Glenda Jackson, Mona Washbourne, Alec McCowen, Trevor Howard, Emma Louise Fox.
102 min.
This at least captures two fine performances, both from the original stage production of Hugh Whitemore's play about the late poet Stevie Smith, the Emily Dickinson of Palmers Green: Glenda Jackson as Stevie, Mona Washbourne as her maiden aunt. But the screen adaptation is fairly calamitous. Instead of sucking us into Stevie Smith's claustrophobic world, it jolts us about with sepia flashbacks, mood shots of trains entering tunnels and of Highgate Ponds in winter. Perhaps such tricks were needed, though, to obscure the play's lack of direct action: it's almost entirely reminiscences and confidences. GB

Stick

(Burt Reynolds, 1985, US) Burt Reynolds, Candice Bergen, George Segal, Charles Durning, José Perez, Richard Lawson, Alex Rocco.
109 min.
Poor old Elmore Leonard, always getting dud movies made of his books. In this case, he's partly responsible, since he co-wrote the script, which sees Reynolds as an ex-con bent on avenging the death of a buddy and getting involved with the drug-dealing low-lifers of Miami. It's deeply flawed by Reynolds' less than lustrous but screen-hogging performance, by a tortuous but dull plot, and by leaden direction. One for completists only. NF

Stick, The

(Darrell Roodt, 1988, SAf) Nicky Rebelo, James Whyle, Frank Opperman, Winston Nishana, Sean Taylor.
90 min.
A 'stick' is a small infantry detachment, and this one is used to browbeat the audience into realising that war is futile. No marks for originality of thought, then, nor for that matter for the director, who seems to be paying homage to *Platoon*. A bunch of Boer brutes (including, of course, a drug-crazed maniac) is sent on a search-and-destroy mission 'across the border'. When they encounter a zebra's head in a tree, their black tracker goes all funny, and when a witch doctor is shot all hell breaks loose. The naive voice-over is corny, but the veldt is stunningly photographed, and the action is full of nasty moments. Crude but effective. MS

Sticky Fingers

(Catlin Adams, 1988, US) Helen Slater, Melanie Mayron, Eileen Brennan, Loretta Devine, Christopher Guest, Carol Kane, Stephen McHattie, Danitra Vance, Shirley Stoller, Gwen Welles.
97 min.
Red-haired Lolly (Mayron, who co-wrote with Adams) and bleached-blonde Hattie (Slater) dress loudly and needle each other's neuroses. They busk for rent money, but squander it on hash delivered by streetwise dudette Diane (Devine), who leaves a mysterious green bag containing $1 million in their Manhattan pad. Threatened with eviction and then burgled, they're soon dipping into the stashed cash – and for less pressing purposes, like therapeutic shopping. Trouble starts when Diane returns, ruthless hoods on her heels. For the most part, Adams' debut is a lot of fun; she directs with a feel for the state of suspended adolescence induced by flat-sharing, and with an irreverent but affectionate eye for bohemian Manhattan that's supported by some intriguingly eccentric peripheral characters, notably the sublime Brennan's brassy landlady. EP

Stiff Upper Lips

(Gary Sinyor, 1997, GB) Peter Ustinov, Prunella Scales, Georgina Cates, Samuel West, Sean Pertwee, Brian Glover, Frank Finlay, Kate Harper.
90 min.
Sinyor revels in the snooty aristos, the wrinkled retainers, the corseted beauties, the bons mots and buttoned-up passions of BritLit cinema at its most risibly predictable. The story, set in 1908 and divided into 'chapters' introduced by curlicued intertitles, is a nonsensical romance that follows the sentimental education ('I want my sexual awakening and I want it now!') of young Emily (Cates), torn between Lawrentian, well-hung scum-of-the-earth George (Pertwee) and the upper crust suitors favoured by her aunt Agnes (Scales) and halfwit brother Edward (West). As the characters leave Ivory Hall for a rather less than Grand Tour of Tuscany and India, the heat and lust, linens and (portable) lawns, fillies and facial hair take their toll. Frequently silly, consistently spot on, and beautifully acted, this may be obvious, but it's a delight. While the gags, visual and verbal, are precise enough to lampoon the excesses of individual movies, the tone remains affectionate, from the opening salvo against *Chariots of Fire* bombast to Glover's ludicrously servile underling and Ustinov's dotty colonial plantation owner. Spiffing! GA

Still Love You After All (Nian Ni Hao Xi)

(Stanley Kwan, 1997, HK/Tai)
43 min.
A personal memoir on the state of Hong Kong made during the last months of British rule. While Ann Hui's companion piece (*As Time Goes By*) puts together half a dozen friends around a table, Kwan takes a more idiosyncratic approach, dwelling on his sense of place as an openly gay director, his relationship with his mother, and a recent theatre work (*Journey to the East*). TCh

Still of the Night

(Robert Benton, 1982, US) Roy Scheider, Meryl Streep, Jessica Tandy, Joe Grifasi, Sara Botsford, Josef Sommer, Rikki Borge.
91 min.

A welcome attempt to redevelop the Hitchcock-style thriller form minus violence or supernatural bogeymen. Scheider plays a psychiatrist who falls in love with a woman (Streep) who may have brutally murdered one of his patients. The film is classy enough to be enjoyable, with a few set pieces deliberately resembling such classics as *North by Northwest*, Tourneur's *Cat People*, and others. But Benton's movie is eventually suffocated, perhaps by the gloss of the Manhattan auction world in which it is set. The plotting becomes rushed and implausible, while Streep falls into the breathless clichés of screen neuroses. Worst of all, a narrative which might have broken new ground by adding a feminine dimension, reverts to that most familiar of B feature formats: the psychological sleuth. Indeed, the hero's faith in dream interpretation would have seemed touching even in the '40s. DP

Sting, The

(George Roy Hill, 1973, US) Paul Newman, Robert Redford, Robert Shaw, Charles Durning, Ray Walston, Eileen Brennan, Harold Gould, John Heffernan, Dana Elcar.
129 min.
Hill's follow-up to *Butch Cassidy and the Sundance Kid*, teaming Newman and Redford again, sticks to the same proven box-office formula. The story takes place in 1936 Chicago this time, but the two protagonists remain the same, outlaws who ply their trade as conmen. The film ends up relying on different chapter headings to explain what's going on, but it's all very professional, with fine attention to period detail. All a bit soulless, but at least there's no equivalent of the 'Raindrops Keep Falling on My Head' sequence. All those who liked the earlier film should enjoy this as much. CPe

Sting II, The

(Jeremy Paul Kagan, 1983, US) Jackie Gleason, Mac Davis, Teri Garr, Karl Malden, Oliver Reed, Bert Remsen.
102 min.
Laborious sequel set in 1940 New York, with the victim of the original elaborate con (Robert Shaw, now played by Reed), out for revenge against Paul Newman and Robert Redford (now played by Gleason and Davis), but getting taken all over again. First time round, if you got bored with the endlessly twisting convolutions of the scam, there were compensations in the fancifully nostalgic settings and the host of quirky minor characters. This time you stay bored. TM

Sting of Death, The (Shi no Toge)

(Kohei Oguri, 1990, Jap) Keiki Matsuzaka, Ittoku Kishibe, Takenori Matsumura.
115 min.
This lugubrious auteur-piece won a top prize at Cannes (from the same jury that gave its Grand Prix to *Wild at Heart*) – a decision not greeted with universal enthusiasm. It's a weird adaptation of an 'I-novel' by Toshio Shimao about the near break-up of a marriage in the 1950s. Oguri's answer to the problem of dramatising the novel's committed subjectivity is to adopt an oppressive degree of stylisation: lingering static compositions and performances that come from some deeply sedated fog of the mind. Some Japanese critics took it as black comedy, but Oguri's earlier movies (*Muddy River*, *For Kayako*) don't suggest a very developed sense of humour. TR

Stir

(Stephen Wallace, 1980, Aust) Bryan Brown, Max Phipps, Dennis Miller, Michael Gow, Phil Motherwell, Gary Waddell.
100 min.
The title has it: indicating just what Wallace has done (rather well) with the choicest ingredients of prison-pic precursors from *Riot in Cell Block 11* to *Scum*. Within the common angry blend of casual sadism and communal solidarity, though, the individualised confrontation of reluctant opponents neatly re-emphasises the mutually brutalising effect of a repressive penal system. PT

Stir Crazy

(Sidney Poitier, 1980, US) Gene Wilder, Richard Pryor, Georg Stanford Brown, JoBeth Williams, Miguel Angel Suarez, Craig T Nelson.
111 min.
Repeating the teaming first aired in *Silver Streak*, Pryor plays a street-sussed cynic, the perfect foil

to Wilder's (by now tedious) ingenuous naif. In the first and funniest half, these no-hopers, disenchanted with the Broadway melody, head for Hollywood in seach of...well, it doesn't matter. Halfway there, they get framed for a bank robbery and end up in clink serving a 125-year sentence, where the golden moment occurs (Pryor doing a chicken impersonation in an attempt to 'look ba-a-a-a-d, look mean'). Maybe the disruption caused by Pryor's accident taxed their imaginations, or maybe the slapstick's just too wild; mildly amusing, at best. FL

Stockade

see Count a Lonely Cadence

Stolen Children, The (Il Ladro di bambini)

(Gianni Amelio, 1992, It) Enrico Lo Verso, Valentina Scalici, Giuseppe Iaercitano.
110 min.
What is it about Italian neo-realists, even in this day and age, which drives them to film their view of the corruptions of society through the eyes of a child? Sentimentality, perhaps. Amelio's film, at any rate, soon falls foul of maudlin worthiness as it recounts the tale of two kids – the 11-year old girl (Scalici) a prostitute – taken away from their mother and entrusted to a cop (Lo Verso). As he escorts them from Milan to Sicily after an orphanage in Rome refuses to accept the girl, the pair gradually come to love and be loved by their reluctant guardian. Decently acted, but alarmingly bereft of originality or analytical insights, it's a well-meaning dirge of a movie. GA

Stolen Hearts

see Two if by Sea

Stolen Kisses

see Baisers Volés

Stolen Life, A

(Curtis Bernhardt, 1946, US) Bette Davis, Glenn Ford, Dane Clark, Walter Brennan, Charles Ruggles, Bruce Bennett.
107 min. b/w.
Bette Davis' first film as producer for Warners, a remake of a 1938 British vehicle for Elisabeth Bergner, also offered her the first chance to play the double role of identical twins she was to repeat in 1964 in Paul Henreid's *Dead Ringer*. Here her split-screen performance lasts only until good sister Kate falls victim to bad sister Pat's murderous jealousy over Glenn Ford, but Bernhardt encourages her to glorious melodramatic excess as she subsequently plays wolf in sheep's clothing, stealing Kate's identity. The cod psychology of doubling and splitting had by now infiltrated the Hollywood public domain with a vengeance: Bernhardt's next film saw him directing Joan Crawford as a schizophrenic in *Possessed*. PT

Stone

(Sandy Harbutt, 1974, Aust) Ken Shorter, Sandy Harbutt, Helen Morse, Hugh Keays-Byrne, Vincent Gil, Bindi Williams.
103 min.
Eight years after its Australian debut, *Stone* was wheeled onto the British circuits by distributors clearly chasing the audience that made the *Mad Max* cycle so successful. But any comparison with those films – or its true American ancestor *Wild Angels* – reveals that this is strictly a moped of a movie. To be fair, L plates are on display: it's a first feature for director Harbutt, who also produced, co-stars, and co-scripted. Stone himself (Shorter) is an undercover cop who infiltrates a gang of bikers known as The Undertakers (they bury their dead standing up 'so they won't have to take anything lying down'). His cover eloquently blown – 'This cat's a pig, man' – Stone ingratiates himself by riding a mean machine. Much footage of bikers abusing less than picturesque locals – cadging ciggies, stealing sauce-bottles, and so on – follows until suddenly it's all over. Like its hero's 'Levi originals', *Stone* badly needs the piss taken out of it. PK

Stone Boy, The

(Christopher Cain, 1984, US) Robert Duvall, Jason Presson, Glenn Close, Frederic Forrest, Wilford Brimley, Cindy Fisher.
93 min.

Another quietly good film from Robert Duvall, sharing a similar emotional appeal to *Tender Mercies*. A young boy is killed in a shooting accident, and his nine-year-old brother is traumatised by the feeling of guilt and lack of emotional response from his family, who are cracking up all around him. The sense of stoicism from these Midwestern farm people is very well conveyed; as are some magic scenes between the boy and his grandfather, played by Wilford Brimley. CPea

Stone Cold

(Craig R Baxley, 1991, US) Brian Bosworth, Lance Henriksen, William Forsythe, Arabella Holzbog, Sam McMurray, Richard Gant, David Tress.
92 min.
Way down in Mississippi, a group of outlaw bikers is all revved up, performing William Tell acts with cans of beer while one bald, mean daredevil blasts priests from their pulpits. Uncovering the Brotherhood's plans to join forces with the Mafia, the FBI recruits suspended cop Joe Huff (ex-American football star Bosworth in his debut); a maverick with anti-social tendencies and a sterling record in 'biker-related arrests', he goes undercover to infiltrate the Brotherhood. The first ten minutes offer rampaging bikers and Bosworth laying waste to armed thugs, with the remaining running-time spent on variations of the same. Stuntman turned director Baxley piles on the corpses, punch-ups and exploding cars with the passion of a pro in this formulaic action fodder. Henriksen, as the maniacal lead biker, steals the movie from under Bosworth's nose. CM

Stone Killer, The

(Michael Winner, 1973, US) Charles Bronson, Martin Balsam, Ralph Waite, David Sheiner, Norman Fell, Eddie Firestone, Paul Koslo.
96 min.
Do we need yet another lone cop movie? This time it's Bronson uncovering an underworld plot to take over part of the Mafia. Winner manages to make Bronson look dull even by his standards (which is some feat), and resorts to formula car chases (which he handles with more flair than he does actors). There's a picture of America that occasionally phases into near fantasy, and one or two nice moments: like the ex-Vietnam soldiers brought in to execute the coup, and the ending where the Mafia leader, with a lot of blood on his hands, confesses a string of venial sins to his priest. A serviceable thriller, but a few weeks later you won't be able to remember a thing about it.

Stoner (Tiejin Gang Da Po Zi Yang Guan)

(Huang Feng, 1974, HK) George Lazenby, Angela Mao, Betty Ting Pei, Wong In-Sik, Joji Takagi.
105 min.
Dreadful martial arts potboiler in which an Australian cop goes after a Hong Kong drugs ring when his girlfriend dies from an overdose in Sydney. Charming policewoman Angela Mao does her best to make one forget the inanities of this cobbled-together revenge plot by pounding the opposition in her best athletic form. George ('Deadlier than Bond') Lazenby is the poker-faced Aussie cop who gets driven sex-mad by a new drug being pushed by the ring. JPy

Stonewall

(Nigel Finch, 1995, GB) Guillermo Diaz, Frederick Weller, Brendan Corbalis, Duane Boutté, Bruce MacVittie, Peter Ratray, Dwight Ewell.
99 min.
Director Nigel Finch of BBC TV's 'Arena' series (who died of AIDS during editing) and New York independent producer Christine Vachon (*Swoon*, *Go Fish*) only partly succeeded in constructing a dramatic narrative around a legendary moment in the history of gay liberation, the 1969 riot outside the Stonewall Inn, Greenwich Village. The intersecting lives of drag queen LaMiranda, peachy-keen new boy Matty Dean, cross-dressing bartender Bostonia, and repressed bar-owner Skinny Vinnie were intended to cohere into an emotionally compelling whole. That this never quite happens is partly down to the ensemble (only MacVittie's Vinnie really makes us feel for him), partly a by-product of a tight budget and zero access to key locations (notably the Stonewall Inn itself). More significant, however,

is the unresolved tension between the flashy, trashy side of the movie, which flaunts its all-conquering drag artistes to effect, and the documentary side which turns up all manner of uncomfortable details about the conditions gay men and women had to endure not that long ago. TJ

Stoolie, The

(John G Avildsen, 1972, US) Jackie Mason, Marcia Jean Kurtz, Dan Frazer, Richard Carballo, Lee Steele, William McCutcheon, Anne Marie.
88 min.
Financed by nightclub comedian Mason, completed by George Silano (it was shot in sequence) when Avildsen left to start *Save the Tiger*, this wry look at society's margins and its realities is quite a charmer in its modest way. Mason plays a small-time drug-pusher and police informer who absconds to Miami with police funds after coming face-to-face with the bleak future that awaits him. Frazer is the police officer blamed for the loss, who hounds him but (a little predictably) comes to view life from the other side of the fence, and Kurtz the lonely secretary who brings a fumbling hint of romance to his life. A touch of *Marty* here (although the film is really more like *Midnight Cowboy* without the pretensions), but whenever sentimentality threatens to raise its head, it is kept firmly at bay by the quirkish characters, the marvellously offbeat locations, and the gently mocking humour that reigns throughout. TM

Stop Making Sense

(Jonathan Demme, 1984, US) Talking Heads.
88 min.
A documentary record of Talking Heads in concert, using material from three shows in Hollywood, December '83. Apart from what artifice the Heads themselves allow on stage, Demme restricts himself to a cool, almost classic style, with the camera subservient to the action. Building from David Byrne performing a solo acoustic 'Psycho Killer', to the full nine-piece leaping through 'Take Me to the Water', its distinction is more what it omits than what it includes. Tacky rock theatre razzle is stripped down to humorously 'minimal' conceits of staging, lighting and presentation. Apart from a few moments of incongruous boogieing, the allegedly over-intellectual Heads are revealed to be human, warm-hearted, and possessed of a sizeable humour. A quietly large achievement. JG

Stop! or My Mom Will Shoot

(Roger Spottiswoode, 1992, US) Sylvester Stallone, Estelle Getty, JoBeth Williams, Roger Rees, Martin Ferrero, Gailard Sartain, Dennis Burkley, John Wesley.
95 min.
Stallone plays LA cop Joe Bomowski, confirmed slob, who finds his life disrupted when his bossy mom Tutti (Getty) comes to visit: she regales strangers with baby stories, does housework at 3am, and interferes in his romance (with JoBeth Williams). After witnessing a murder, Tutti becomes embroiled in the subsequent investigation, dispensing wisecracks and threatening the villain (Rees) with a good spanking. Most of the blame for this unimaginative effort can be attributed to the script, but Spottiswoode's flat direction doesn't help. He seems to have given up on his actors: Stallone merely goes through the motions, while Getty suffers when deprived of the ensemble playing and sharper writing offered on TV's *The Golden Girls*. CM

Storia di una Capinera

see Sparrow

Stories from a Flying Trunk

(Christine Edzard, 1979, GB) Murray Melvin, Ann Firbank, Tasneem Maqsood, John Tordoff, John Dalby, Johanna Sonnex.
88 min.
Why does the idea persist that Hans Andersen's stories should still be enjoyed by children? These three tales are preciously middlebrow in appeal: a combination of choreography, live-action and stop-frame animation, contemporary in setting but frankly Victorian in spirit. A fey and sinister Andersen (Melvin) introduces sickly little episodes in which death and gloom are never far away. For example, in the middle episode, a poor

Asian girl from Dickensian East End slums meets a crazed tramp who sends her up West, where she dies after imagining that she has seen the Queen (!). CPe

Stories of the Kronen (Historias del Kronen)

(Montxo Armendariz, 1995, Sp) Juan Diego Botto, Jordi Molla, Nuria Prims, Aitor Merino.
95 min.
The Kronen being the club where 21-year-old Carlos (Botto) and his cronies go, night after night, to dance, get blasted, find a partner and generally do what bored, hedonistic middle-class kids do. Only Carlos is a little more hedonistic, bored, selfish, vain and irresponsible than the rest, so – this being a movie – a comeuppance is in the offing. Hackneyed, obvious and strangely dated, Armendariz' hyper-agitated film tells us nothing about flaming youth that we haven't heard many times before, and does so in such a relentless, repetitive way that its characters soon become irritating rather than figures we'd like to try and understand. Charmless stuff. GA

Stork

(Tim Burstall, 1971, Aust) Bruce Spence, Graham Blundell, Sean McEuan, Helmut Bakaitis, Jacki Weaver, Peter Green.
90 min.
Stork is the nickname of a 6 foot 7 inch Walter Mitty with revolutionary leanings, who quits his secure job with General Motors to opt out in a flat full of frowning, culturally-aspiring colleagues. At the heart of Stork's freak behaviour, sick practical jokes, and constant fantasising, a vast timidity with women unfortunately lies. Stork is in fact more Adventures of Barry McKenzie; and if you were able to wheeze and giggle your way through that, you'll probably do the same with this totally appalling mess of dismal Aussie gags about beer and chundering.

Storm Center

(Daniel Taradash, 1956, US) Bette Davis, Brian Keith, Kim Hunter, Paul Kelly, Joe Mantell.
85 min. b/w.
The first explicitly anti-McCarthyite Hollywood movie, Storm Center took five years to reach the screen. Davis plays a small-town librarian who refuses, on principle, to remove a book called 'The Communist Dream' from the shelves when the local council deems it subversive. Her stand is undermined by a political opportunist (Keith) who plays on the citizens' intrinsic suspicion of intellectuals and anything remotely pinko. The only film directed by Taradash (who scripted From Here to Eternity and Rancho Notorious), it is, sadly, a didactic, laborious piece, making far too much play with a confused small boy driven from an eager exploration of books into angry arson on the library. Played with some conviction by Davis, though. TCh

Storm Within, The

see Parents Terribles, Les

Stormy Monday

(Mike Figgis, 1987, GB) Melanie Griffith, Tommy Lee Jones, Sting, Sean Bean, James Cosmo, Mark Long, Brian Lewis.
93 min.
Mix American gangsters, molls and majorettes with Polish avant-garde jazz musicians against a Newcastle background – and what you've got is a curious homage to B movie Hollywood and the rain-washed neon of the pulps. The plot stammers a bit trying to sustain these exotic transplants in Geordieland – it's America week – and generally sacrifices believability for the flourish, but it's an endearingly personal enterprise. At its oddest, the Cracow Jazz Ensemble plays a whinnyingly discordant 'Star Spangled Banner' to Newcastle councillors; at its most violent, enforcers descend upon jazz club owner Sting with a blowtorch, but find they've bitten off more than they can chew. Night-town drifter (Bean) falls in love with American waitress (Griffith), who is struggling to ditch her old life as a hostess in the employ of a vicious businessman (Jones) with plans to muscle in on the city. All these strands are brought together in a fireball conclusion that owes everything to life learned from the screen, tilts at tragedy, but racks up merely moody bad luck. On the credit side, Roger

Deakins' camerawork is ravishing, Don Weller takes a solo, and Sting shows he hasn't forgotten his old accent or instrument. BC

Stormy Weather

(Andrew L Stone, 1943, US) Lena Horne, Bill Bojangles Robinson, Cab Calloway, Fats Waller, Dooley Wilson, Ada Brown, Katherine Dunham.
77 min. b/w.
Fox's all-black musical answer to MGM's Cabin in the Sky. No Minnelli this time, so no contest, especially as the wispy plot – one of those up-down romances that span 25 years – serves chiefly to string together a revue collection of items matching the various periods. With those stars let loose on classic songs, and the Nicholas Brothers providing a stunning tap dancing finale, who's complaining? Often quite imaginatively staged, the numbers are strikingly well shot by Leon Shamroy. TM

Story of Adèle H., The (L'Histoire d'Adèle H.)

(François Truffaut, 1975, Fr) Isabelle Adjani, Bruce Robinson, Sylvia Marriott, Joseph Blatchley, Reubin Dorey, François Truffaut.
98 min.
Truffaut's film follows the course of Adèle Hugo (Adjani), the daughter of Victor Hugo, as she travels from Guernsey to Nova Scotia, and finally to Barbados, in search of a man who clearly doesn't love her. The film is a disaster because, in place of the self-conscious reflection of her predicament conveyed by Adèle's journal (on which the film is based), Truffaut opts for the Hollywood formula of hapless unrequited love. The result is a movie that centres on a woman's weakness, rather than on the strength necessary to put into practice her considered decisions. PH

Story of GI Joe, The

(William Wellman, 1945, US) Burgess Meredith, Robert Mitchum, Freddie Steele, Wally Cassell, Jimmy Lloyd, Jack Reilly.
109 min. b/w.
Not so very different in mood from The Big Red One, Wellman's film about the WWII Italian campaign not surprisingly won Sam Fuller's nod of approval for 'its feeling of death and mass murder'. Based on the front-line dispatches of war correspondent Ernie Pyle, this is not a film about flag-waving or heroism. Shot almost documentary style, with deliberately sketchy characterisation of individual soldiers (though Mitchum makes a powerful impression), it presents what is very much an infantryman's view of war as a meaningless vista of mud, muddle and fatigue, ending very probably in a wooden cross. Its masterstroke is to use Pyle himself (beautifully played by Meredith) as the omnipresent eyes and ears of the film, stuggling to fathom the mystery of the ordinary soldier ('This was their baptism of fire; it was chaos... each boy facing the worst moment of his life, alone') and to find the words to explain it to the folks back home. His homely dispatches may fringe sentimentality at times, but Wellman's images magnificently capture their compassion for the GI 'who lives so miserably, dies so miserably'. TM

Story of Gilbert and Sullivan, The (aka The Great Gilbert and Sullivan)

(Sidney Gilliat, 1953, GB) Robert Morley, Maurice Evans, Peter Finch, Eileen Herlie, Martyn Green, Dinah Sheridan, Isabel Dean, Wilfrid Hyde-White.
109 min.
Despite the importance of Gilbert and Sullivan as an English institution, the lives of two such solidly respectable Victorians offer little in the way of dramatic excitement. Fortunately Launder and Gilliat are able to burrow deep into their scriptwriting past, coming up with a whole galaxy of tricks and devices to fill out the flimsy narrative and overcome the obstacle of obligatory slabs of operetta, producing a chocolate-box extravaganza where less hardy professionals would have made a celebratory mess. They're helped by some splendid performances, particularly from Morley, amazingly effective as Gilbert once he's able to channel his exuberant eccentricity into pathos rather than caricature. RMy

Story of Qiu Ju, The (Qiu Ju da Guansi)

(Zhang Yimou, 1992, China/HK) Gong Li, Lei Laosheng, Ge Zhijun, Liu Peiqi, Yang Liuchun.
100 min.
Zhang and his constant muse Gong Li reinvent themselves (and Chinese social-realist cinema in the process) with this docu-drama about a peasant woman's dogged fight for what she thinks is justice. Qiu Ju is furious when the chief of her village refuses to apologise for kicking her husband in the balls during a fight, and takes the matter to court to demand compensation; the film charts her stubborn climb up the legal hierarchy. The plot seems expressly designed to placate the bureaucrats who banned Zhang's two previous films in China, but the quasi-documentary approach (involving scores of non-professional actors, hidden cameras and radio mikes) is brilliantly finessed. TR

Story of Sin, The (Dzieje Grzechu)

(Walerian Borowczyk, 1975, Pol) Grazyna Dlugolecka, Jerzy Zelnik, Olgierd Lukaszewicz, Roman Wilhelmi.
128 min.
Like Borowczyk's earlier Blanche, this traces the misfortunes that befall an erotic innocent when she tries for love in a world dedicated to repressing or exploiting it. The source here is a turn-of-the-century Polish novel, and Borowczyk films it (with absolute period fidelity) as a full-blooded melodrama, carrying his audience off on swings of emotion, alternately rapturous and harrowing. At the same time, though, he invests it with countless reminders of his own background as the most idiosyncratic of contemporary surrealists: by bringing décor and design to the same prominence throughout as the physical action (incidentally 'eroticising' many of the objects that appear), and by framing the story of Eva's amour fou with precise descriptions of the religious, moral and economic factors that conspire to thwart it. His control of everything from his attractive cast to his speed-of-thought editing is unassailable. The result is passionately intense, and extremely entertaining. TR

Story of the Late Chrysanthemums, The (Zangiku Monogatari)

(Kenji Mizoguchi, 1939, Jap) Shotaro Hanayagi, Kakuko Mori, Kokichi Takada, Gonjuro Kawarazaki, Yoko Umemura.
143 min. b/w.
Bristling with passion, Mizoguchi's film is a true find: a heartbreaker to end them all. Tokyo, 1885: a Kabuki actor of little self-awareness offends his famous father and transgresses tradition by insisting on his love for his brother's nurse. Trapped by the father's refusal to countenance the affair, dragged together into ignominy, she realises that only through her self-sacrifice can her love reclaim his familial glory. As the plot twists inexorably round their doomed affair, it says much more by showing less: an eloquently long tracking shot can follow remarkably understated scenes of intense emotion so that tears flow as if by magic. Unashamed sentimentality and anger controlled by extreme formal precision justify its reputation as the peak of Mizoguchi's film-making. DMacp

Story of Vernon and Irene Castle, The

(HC Potter, 1939, US) Fred Astaire, Ginger Rogers, Edna May Oliver, Walter Brennan, Lew Fields, Etienne Girardot, Donald MacBride.
90 min. b/w.
Fred and Ginger's last partnership (until their reunion in 1949 with The Barkleys of Broadway) was a nostalgic biopic about a famous ballroom couple from World War I days whose career was cut short by an air accident. Ably welding dance numbers and plot, courtesy of light comedy director Potter, it overcomes its lack of '30s snap and crackle with lavish doses of elegance and charm to a tango or foxtrot rhythm. DMacp

Story of Women, A (San ge Nüren)

(Peng Xiaolian, 1988, China) Zhang Wen Rong, Zhang Min, Shong Ru Hui.
90 min.

A road movie from one of the few women directors of China's 'Fifth Generation' (Peng's subsequent film was halted in mid-production, and she moved to New York). Three peasant women from a village near the Great Wall decide to earn some money by taking their spun and dyed yarn to the free markets in the cities; they travel first to Beijing, and then much further south to Chongqing. Their journey embodies a panorama of women's lives in present-day China, taking in everything from the weight of patriarchal traditions to the issue of enforced abortions. Peng achieves a convincing level of naturalism and keeps melodrama at bay. TR

Story of Woo Viet, The (Hu Yue de Gushi)

(Ann Hui, 1981, HK) Chow Yun-Fat, Cora Miao, Cherie Chung, Lo Lieh.
92 min.
Rooted in Hui's research into real-life 'boat people' refugees from Vietnam, her third feature is essentially a doomed *noir* romance which incorporates – as Hong Kong movies do – everything from action thriller shoot-outs to a transvestite hooker and a dwarf cabaret troupe. The charismatic Chow Yun-Fat plays a Vietnamese-Chinese refugee who's trying to smuggle himself from Hong Kong to the US when he gets stuck in Manila and enmeshed in its vice; Lo Lieh (fondly remembered as the hero of kung-fu movies like *King Boxer*) is memorable as an ageing Chinese roué who's been marooned there for years. TR

Storyville

(Mark Frost, 1992, US) James Spader, Joanne Whalley-Kilmer, Jason Robards, Charlotte Lewis, Woody Strode, Piper Laurie.
113 min.
Mark Frost's ambitious directorial debut is an oedipal thriller – Greek tragedy by way of *Chinatown* – in which the sins of the father have political, social and environmental ramifications. Even so, this flat transposition of an Australian novel (*Juryman* by Frank Galbally and Robert Macklin) will disappoint admirers of Frost's scripts for *Twin Peaks* and *Hill Street Blues*. Cray Fowler (Spader), scion of a Louisiana dynasty, is expected to assume the family seat in Congress. Unaware that one should never dally with cocktail waitresses during an election campaign, he lays himself open to blackmail and a murder charge, at which point the skeletons start to emerge from the family closet. Whalley-Kilmer wraps a Cajun accent around lines of numbing banality. TCh

Stowaway Girl

see Manuela

Strada, La (The Road)

(Federico Fellini, 1954, It) Giulietta Masina, Anthony Quinn, Richard Basehart, Aldo Silvani, Marcella Rovena.
104 min. b/w.
For all its sentimentality, this overshadows virtually everything Fellini has made since *La Dolce Vita*. As ever for *il maestro*, life is both cyclic odyssey and circus, a teeming, tragicomic arena of pain, cruelty and solitude. Masina plays Gelsomina, a naïve waif whose simpleton innocence provides a direct line to life's eternal mysteries; when she is sold into virtual slavery to play clown to itinerant strongman Zampano (Quinn), the boorish brute simply exploits his new assistant's desire for affection at every opportunity. It's basically a road movie: she vainly tries to escape, they join a circus, and her friendship with the tightrope-walking Fool (Basehart) brings its own problems. Despite the pessimism of much of the story, memorably embodied in the grey, desolate towns the pair visit, Fellini has already m o v e d far from his roots in neo-realism; symbols, metaphors, and larger-than-life performances hold sway, and moments of bizarre if inconsequential charm abound. GA

Straight Out of Brooklyn

(Matty Rich, 1991, US) George T Odom, Ann D Sanders, Lawrence Gilliard Jr, Barbara Sanon, Reana E Drummond, Matty Rich, Mark Malone.
91 min.
From its powerhouse opening, in which young,

gifted and black New Yorker Dennis (Gilliard) is woken by his father's ferocious attack on his mother, it's immediately evident that Rich's low-budget debut as writer-director will be a no-holds-barred affair. Dennis has had it with his dad's drunkenly despairing rages, even though they're fired by poverty and racism; so, despite his plans to go to college and his girlfriend's vows that she'll leave him if he does anything illegal, his desire to make fast money for his family impels him to coax a couple of friends into joining him in armed robbery. If this harrowing melodrama is raw and occasionally a mite predictable in terms of plot, its emotional maturity, honesty and assurance are suggestive of a talent far older than the film-maker's 19 years. GA

Straight Talk

(Barnet Kellman, 1992, US) Dolly Parton, James Woods, Griffin Dunne, Michael Madsen, Deirdre O'Connell, John Sayles, Teri Hatcher, Spalding Gray, Jerry Orbach, Philip Bosco.
91 min.
Scuzzy Chicago news-hound Jack Russell (Woods) is ordered to sniff out the truth about radio agony aunt Doctor Shirlee Kenyon (Parton). Shirlee isn't really a doctor, merely a simple country girl with a blouse full of straight-talkin', home-spun advice. Russell's editor wants Shirlee nailed, and soon Russell's penis shares a similar goal. Sharply written by Craig Bolotin and Patricia Resnick, this sassy comedy has musical aspirations, with diphthong-clanging Dolly numbers offering a running (if unnecessary) commentary. But the film's success rests squarely upon the efficacy of the Woods-Parton double act, an amiable partnership of mismatched, seasoned troupers. Only in the third act, with its 'on-air confession' denouement, do things take a gushing, sentimental nosedive. Otherwise it's a tongue-in-cheek romp with far less hog-washing than you'd expect. MK

Straight Time

(Ulu Grosbard, 1977, US) Dustin Hoffman, Theresa Russell, Gary Busey, Harry Dean Stanton, M Emmet Walsh, Rita Taggart.
114 min.
Hoffman, spivvy and moustached for maximum seediness, is an ex-con on parole who can't go straight, adrift like a midnight bellboy in lowlife LA. One yearns for a routine cops and robbers story, but Grosbard lingers with illusory impartiality over the technical details of the parole system, the problems of finding accommodation and work, and the nastiness of the backyard pool-and-barbecue life-style of *riche* America. Not for a moment are you allowed to suspect that hoodlums might be smart or attractive, or that crime pays. It's such a relief when Hoffman finally drives off into his bleak future, and this fiction of fact reaches its non-conclusion. JS

Straight to Hell

(Alex Cox, 1986, GB) Dick Rude, Sy Richardson, Joe Strummer, Courtney Love, Biff Yeager, Shane MacGowan, Spider Stacy, Frank Murray.
86 min.
Cox's Spanish quickie comes on like a snorter's rag revue and resembles the result of roadies bouncing ideas off each other after the gig. With the exception of Richardson, the cast are every bit as tall in the saddle as Arthur Askey in *Ramsbottom Rides Again*. As a parody of the spaghetti Western, it's as witless and one-note as The Young Ones' *A Fistful of Travellers Cheques*, and longer, by Christ. Students of end-of-tether desperation will find a sexpot in hot pants shampooing the exhaust pipe of a motorbike, a Spanish fly which settles on various noses, and no shortage of bandidos with Lancashire accents and tartan thermos flasks. The trio of gringos wear Warren Oates grifter suits, and there are many pans around Mexicans laughing. The penultimate line in this yawping indulgence says it all: 'Who's paying for all this?' BC

Strait-Jacket

(William Castle, 1963, US) Joan Crawford, Diane Baker, Leif Erickson, Howard St John, John Anthony Hayes, Rochelle Hudson, George Kennedy.
93 min. b/w.
Robert Bloch (*Psycho*) scripted this *What Ever Happened to Baby Jane?* rip-off which unleashes

Crawford for another bout of unrestrained self-parody. She's an axemurderer, who's released after 20 years in an asylum and returns to daughter Baker, whereupon the old girl's hallucinations recur and (surprise!) the slayings begin again. Basically terrible, and there's another mask-ripping scene at the end, but Joan's fans will not be disappointed. No patented gimmicks from director William Castle this time though, because cinema managers had gotten sick of his cheap tricks. TJ

Strange Affair, The

(David Greene, 1968, GB) Michael York, Jeremy Kemp, Susan George, Jack Watson, George A Cooper, Artro Morris, Barry Fantoni, Nigel Davenport, Madge Ryan.
106 min.
York plays a solemn young constable new to the Metropolitan Police who is convinced that right is right, but gradually discovers that life just isn't like that; caught in a squeeze, he takes one hapless step after another, until the bitterly cynical ending has him languishing in jail while the particularly vicious gang of crooks go free. Essentially it's a well-written anecdote about police manners and methods, straight out of some TV cop series, but as viewed by Greene's wilfully wayward camera, it becomes a bizarre, quirkishly funny thriller which laces its documentary surface with a fine grain of fantasy. Much of Greene's later work disappointed, but here he displays a visual flair (gang violence in an echoing warehouse, murder among the wrecked cars in a scrapheap, seduction in a fantastically opulent boudoir) that would not entirely have shamed Welles in his *Lady from Shanghai* mood. TM

Strange Affair of Uncle Harry, The (Uncle Harry)

(Robert Siodmak, 1945, US) George Sanders, Geraldine Fitzgerald, Ella Raines, Sara Allgood, Moyna McGill, Samuel S Hinds.
80 min. b/w.
Though less deliriously *noir* than Siodmak's best work (*Phantom Lady, The Killers, Cry of the City*) this rather Hitchcockian smalltown thriller, produced by the Englishman's former associate Joan Harrison, is a typically impressive psychological study in various forms of obsession. Sanders is both superb and unusually touching as the shy, naive designer who falls for Raines, newly arrived from the city; Allgood and Fitzgerald are the sisters he lives with, the latter a scheming hypochondriac so possessive of her brother that she'll do anything to wreck his budding romance. A relatively conventional story is lent depth and originality by Siodmak's sense of detail and mood; Raines literally introduces colour into Sanders' life by daubing paint on his pedantically minaturist floral illustrations, while his repressed romanticism is evoked through his obsession with astrology. Sadly, Siodmak was saddled with an ending that undercuts the dark emotions preceeding it, but the overall effect is still gripping, intelligent, and oddly critical of staid petit bourgeois aspirations. GA

Strange Brew

(Dave Thomas/Rick Moranis, 1983, US) Dave Thomas, Rick Moranis, Max Von Sydow, Paul Dooley, Lynne Griffin, Angus MacInnes, Tom Harvey, Douglas Campbell.
90 min.
Stars, directors and co-writers Dave Thomas and Rick Moranis originated Bob and Doug McKenzie, their beer-making, beer-swilling sibling act in a series of TV sketches. Here Von Sydow's a rival beer manufacturer hoping to take over the world by drugging his brew, but the plotline (derived from *Hamlet*) soon goes flat. TJ

Strange Cargo

(Frank Borzage, 1940, US) Clark Gable, Joan Crawford, Ian Hunter, Peter Lorre, Paul Lukas, Albert Dekker, Eduardo Ciannelli.
113 min. b/w.
Ace melodramatist Borzage always injected his tales of romance and hardship with more than a touch of spiritual redemption, and this is one of his most explicit statements about the uplifting power of love. Gable is one of a group of convicts who escapes from the prison on Devil's Island; through his relationship with Crawford, which develops from basic sexual attraction to intense emotional commitment, and through his hard-

ships as they trek through the jungle, he finds not only physical but also spiritual liberation. Most remarkable, however, is the Ian Hunter character, who helps lead them to salvation: omniscient and at one with nature, he becomes almost a Christ-figure endowed with strange powers and the gift of mercy. Borzage lends the tale quite extraordinary conviction. GA

Strange Case of Dr Rx, The
(William Nigh, 1942, US) Patric Knowles, Lionel Atwill, Anne Gwynne, Samuel S Hinds, Mona Barrie, Paul Cavanagh, Ray Corrigan, Mantan Moreland, Shemp Howard.
66 min. b/w.
A routine but fast-moving whodunit with horror-comedy overtones as private eye Knowles, pursuing a masked killer, is threatened with a gorilla brain transplant. This is merely bluff, alas, designed to scare him out of his wits while the killer pursues his purpose: eliminating a series of shady businessmen whom justice has failed to deal with. Atwill is great fun in a red herring role as the sinister, aptly-named Dr Fish, and the underrated Woody Bredell contributes some nicely creepy camerawork. TM

Strange Days
(Kathryn Bigelow, 1995, US) Ralph Fiennes, Angela Bassett, Juliette Lewis, Tom Sizemore, Michael Wincott, Vincent D'Onofrio, Glenn Plummer, Josef Sommer.
145 min.
LA, Year Zero: 30 December 1999. Riot police are on the streets. The angry, poor, disenfranchised – the blacks – are ready to tear down the walls of the city. Yet Lenny Nero fiddles while LA burns. A sleazeball in an Armani suit, Lenny's dealing illicit 'playback clips', raw human experience recorded direct from the cerebral cortex. Bigelow's spectacular millennial maelstrom has divided critics, and apparently repelled audiences. Written by James Cameron and Jay Cocks, this is tech-noir, action movie and love story rolled into one. It also pursues a sophisticated treatise on the nature of voyeurism, the psychic dangers of vicarious entertainment and cinema itself. A sequence in which Nero watches a snuff clip of rape and murder has excited accusations of exploitation and hypocrisy. It's certainly hard to stomach, but then shouldn't it be? The impeccable moral centre is to be found in Bassett's karate-chopping single mother 'Mace', who rescues Lenny from his own faithless stupor. Nero isn't irredeemable, either: Fiennes makes him a persuasively seedy knight errant. In fact, despite its own barely suppressed despair, the film exhibits markedly progressive leanings. Flawed, but often brilliant, provocative film-making. TCh

Strange Door, The
(Joseph Pevney, 1951, US) Charles Laughton, Boris Karloff, Sally Forrest, Richard Stapley, Michael Pate, Alan Napier.
81 min. b/w.
Very much a B movie, luridly adapted from Stevenson's story The Sire de Malétroit's Door, but solidly implanted in the old Frankenstein sets and looking like a rough prototype for Corman's Poe series. Laughton goes enjoyably over the top as a love-crazed madman prowling a Gothic castle where the rightful owner (his elder brother) lies rotting in a dungeon and a room with clashing walls awaits the unwary intruder. Karloff balances him beautifully as the baleful but sympathetic servant who bides his time, eventually contriving a rather splendid comeuppance involving a remorselessly grinding water-wheel. It's surprisingly imaginatively put together in its thick-ear way. TM

Strange Incident
see Ox-Bow Incident, The

Strange Invaders
(Michael Laughlin, 1983, US) Paul LeMat, Nancy Allen, Diana Scarwid, Michael Lerner, Louise Fletcher, Wallace Shawn, Fiona Lewis, Kenneth Tobey, June Lockhart.
93 min.
'I've got you, under mah skeeen-ah!'. Loss of face gets a whole new twist in this unexpectedly well-developed pastiche: a welcome surprise, as it initially looks like a Disneyish soft-pedal over the familiar territory of Invasion of the Body Snatchers. The twist is that when the aliens

colonised a small town in the '50s – doing the usual trick of covering their own unsightly physogs with plastic replicas of several hundred decent Americans – it all happened with full governmental approval. Hassled hero LeMat has to confront opposition from both the official and the alien fronts before getting to the bottom of the mystery. The necessarily upbeat ending is all but made up for by some brilliant SFX and stabs of humour in the midnight vein of the great Gahan (National Lampoon, Playboy etc) Wilson. Hugely entertaining and refreshingly gore-free. GD

Strange Love of Martha Ivers, The
(Lewis Milestone, 1946, US) Barbara Stanwyck, Van Heflin, Kirk Douglas, Lisabeth Scott, Judith Anderson, Roman Bohnen, Frank Orth.
117 min. b/w.
Superb performance by Stanwyck (as coldly calculating as she was in Double Indemnity) as the apex of a traumatic triangle comprising the two men who (maybe) saw her club her wealthy aunt to death when they were children. Now a tycoon in her own right, bonded to one of the witnesses (Douglas) in a guilt-ridden marriage, she finds the other (Heflin) resurfacing in her life as both promise of escape and threat to security – and the stagnant waters begin to stir again with murderous crosscurrents of fear and desire. A gripping film noir, all the more effective for being staged by Milestone as a steamy romantic melodrama. TM

Strange One, The
(aka End as a Man)
(Jack Garfein 1957, US) Ben Gazzara, George Peppard, Pat Hingle, Mark Richman, Geoffrey Horne, James Olson.
100 min. b/w.
Advertised as 'the first picture filmed entirely by a cast and technicians from The Actors' Studio, New York': in 1957, this was quite a selling point, because the screen was under invasion by young, brilliant Method actors, and Elia Kazan, co-founder of the Studio, was the prestigious movie and play director. Calder Willingham's novel (End As a Man), about a sadistic cadet in a Southern military academy, certainly went against the Hollywood grain. Most movie versions of military life – Ford's The Long Gray Line is a fair example – endorsed the system, but Willingham, who had suffered under a similar regime, dissented: discipline and honour were dehumanising, and bred only bullying. Garfein, Kazan's assistant, wasn't much of a director, and some of the actors appear almost incapacitated with mannerisms. Gazzara, however, is sensational, playing the malevolent Jocko De Paris with a subtlety honed by Studio stage performances. Reptilian, glowering with banked-down hatred – even his outfit of military cap, Hawaiian shirt, shorts and sock suspenders, cigarette holder and swagger stick, communicates a sardonic androgyny that couldn't have done much for the military peace of mind. He is, in short, Iago. Fellow cadets Peppard and Hingle don't stand a chance against his cunning. BC

Strange Ones, The
see Enfants Terribles, Les

Strange Place to Meet, A
(Drôle d'Endroit pour une rencontre)
(François Dupeyron, 1988, Fr) Catherine Deneuve, Gérard Depardieu, André Wilms, Nathalie Cardone, Jean-Pierre Sentier, Alain Rimoux.
98 min.
Talk about minimal: Dupeyron's feature debut is a road movie where they only travel 10 kilometres. Deneuve, booted out of her husband's car after a row, ends up in a lay-by with Depardieu, who's mending his motor (metaphor for mending his life). They get a lift to the service station, and spend the next two days alternately chasing and repulsing each other. Deneuve's in the throes of a very heavy, possibly masochistic relationship with the man who dumped her; Depardieu is a lonely, romantic doctor who's doggedly hopeless with the opposite sex. Nothing is entirely resolved, tempting hints about the characters' lives aren't

elaborated upon (is she married, mad, or a high class hooker?), and the film retains the haunting inconsequentiality of a chance encounter. The romantic protestations, set against the grim background of a plastic café, are poignant and dreamlike, the characters are drifters seeking refuge or escape, and the whole film is comic and bittersweet. SFe

Stranger, The
(Orson Welles, 1946, US) Orson Welles, Loretta Young, Edward G Robinson, Richard Long, Konstantin Shayne, Philip Merivale, Billy House.
95 min. b/w.
Welles' third film, often described as his worst, but still a hugely enjoyable thriller as Robinson's man from the Allied War Crimes Commission patiently stalks Welles' former top Nazi, now ensconced as a prep school teacher in a small Connecticut town and newly married to the innocent Young. Admittedly some wobbles develop (not least in Orson's own overpitched performance), and the script has its naïve moments (as when the Nazi gives himself away in a dinner-table gambit: 'Marx wasn't a German, he was a Jew'). But it is studded with great scenes like the stranger's furtive flight through the dockyards at the beginning, the murder in the woods with boys streaming by on a paperchase, or the Nazi's death high on the clock tower, impaled by the sword wielded by a mechanical figure as the hour begins to strike. Terrific camerawork from Russell Metty throughout. TM

Stranger, The
see Intruder, The

Stranger, The (Agantuk)
(Satyajit Ray, 1991, Ind/Fr) Deepankar Dey, Mamata Shankar, Bikram Bhattacharya, Utpal Dutt, Dhritiman Chatterjee.
105 min.
Out of the blue, Anila receives a letter from her uncle Manmohan. After 35 years abroad, he wants to stay a few days with his only living relative. While Anila prepares for his arrival, her husband Sudhindra remains suspicious: what is the nature of this man who invites himself to their home? How can they even know he is who he claims to be? Manmohan's arrival hardly clarifies matters. Cultured and intellectually superior to his perplexed hosts and their friends, he is prepared to play devil's advocate when they quiz him about his past and his motives. Like much of his late work, Ray's final film has a rigidly functional visual style and a rather old-fashioned trust in dialogue ('It's a Bengali invention, discussion,' says Manmohan). For all that, it's a pleasingly graceful last testament, both engrossing and emotionally revealing. Manmohan is clearly Ray himself – a traditionalist yet a stranger in his own land, an anthropologist 'with Shakespeare, Tagore, Marx and Freud in my bloodstream'. The film, which is beautifully played, reflects Ray's ambivalence about the nature of civilisation. It works as a mystery, and as a satire on bourgeois mores – the perpetual struggle between faith and good form. It ends on a subtle, touching, grace note. TCh

Stranger
(Yoru no Stranger – Kyofu!)
(Shunichi Nagasaki, 1991, Jap) Yuko Natori, Kentaro Shimizu, Takeshi Naito.
90 min.
A model for all directors given the chance to make a low-budget genre quickie, Stranger offers Nagasaki's most charged vision of fear and loathing on the streets of Tokyo. Kiriko was a bank teller until she went to jail for fraud. Now she works as a taxi driver, lives alone and does her best to be 'one of the guys'. Her problems begin the night a passenger gives her a big note and leaves without waiting for change. Next time he gets in her cab, he tries to kill her – in what turns out to be the start of a sustained assault on her life at work and at home. Like the truck in Duel, this stranger just keeps on coming and Kiriko has no choice but to gear herself up to fight back. Powerhouse stuff. TR

Stranger and the Gunfighter, The
see Blood Money

Stranger on the Third Floor, The

(Boris Ingster, 1940, US) Peter Lorre, John McGuire, Margaret Tallichet, Charles Waldron, Elisha Cook Jr.
64 min. b/w.
A weird expressionist investigation of personal guilt that takes its jaunty, banal hero (McGuire) from the bright lights of a cafeteria into a strange interior odyssey. The plot revolves around the reporter hero's unwitting conviction, through his evidence, of an innocent man (Cook) at a murder trial. He returns to his apartment to rest, and the brittle, unremarkable surface of the film begins to break up in a kind of guilt-whirlpool of humiliation and sexual repression. The court, jury and whole legal system are exposed in the hero's dreams as little more than vampiric; and when he wakes up, even reality begins to take on the dimensions of nightmare (with a special spot reserved for Lorre, terrific). Finally the film returns its audience to the banal starting-point of its investigation, but the happy ending just can't look the same in the light of everything that has preceded it. A remarkable movie. DP

Strangers

see Viaggio in Italia

Strangers

(Danny Cannon, 1991, GB) Michael Ceveris, Al Sapienza, Michele Palermo.
67 min.
Two brothers are reunited under terrifying circumstances in this impressive offering from the British National Film and Television School. John Reece (Ceveris) has made a precarious living by selling cocaine to actors and bands, but now he owes his violent associates in the Los Angeles underworld $30,000 – and they don't care how they get it. His upstanding brother (Sapienza) tries to rescue him, in turn exposing his wife and young son to danger. Polished direction, an intelligent use of music, and atmospheric visuals from cinematographer Gavin Finney combine to make this a menacing, highly accomplished thriller. CM

Strangers in Love

see In Love

Strangers Kiss

(Matthew Chapman, 1983, US) Peter Coyote, Victoria Tennant, Blaine Novak, Dan Shor, Richard Romanus, Carlos Palomino, Linda Kerridge.
94 min. b/w & col.
Fascinating film structured a little like a series of Chinese boxes. First comes the fiction of a young director in Hollywood (Coyote) trying to set up an independent B movie about a young boxer's *noir*-ish efforts to save a taxi dancer from her villainous protector. This, given the date 1955 and a marked resemblance between the two plots, merges into a speculative 'history' of the circumstances surrounding the making of Kubrick's *Killer's Kiss*. Then life begins to imitate art as the villainous realtor backing Coyote's movie, in which his girl is playing the lead, realises that she is falling for the actor playing the boxer; and art begins to give life a stage direction or two as Coyote encourages this perilous triangle in the hope of lending emotional conviction to his film. Marvellously shot and finely acted, it grips simultaneously as a critical extension of Kubrick's film, as a comment on movie-making mania, and as a dark thriller in its own right. TM

Strangers on a Train

(Alfred Hitchcock, 1951, US) Farley Granger, Robert Walker, Ruth Roman, Leo G Carroll, Patricia Hitchcock, Laura Elliott, Marion Lorne, Howard St John.
101 min. b/w.
Adapted from Patricia Highsmith's novel, *Strangers on a Train* takes as its central proposition the meeting and ensuing guilty association of two complete strangers, Granger and Walker. Walker buttonholes Granger, a star tennis player anxious to remarry but with a clinging wife, and initiates a hypnotic discussion of exchange murders. Walker then does 'his' murder (the wife), and threatens to incriminate Granger if he doesn't fulfil his half of the 'bargain' (Walker's father). Significantly, Hitchcock didn't use much of Raymond Chandler's original script, because

Chandler was too concerned with the characters' motivation. In place of that, Hitchcock erects a web of guilt around Granger, who 'agreed' to his wife's murder, a murder that suits him very well, and structures his film around a series of set pieces, ending with a paroxysm of violence on a circus carousel, when the circle Granger is trapped within is literally blown to pieces, leaving Walker dead beneath it and Granger a free man again. PH

Strangers When We Meet

(Richard Quine, 1960, US) Kirk Douglas, Kim Novak, Ernie Kovacs, Barbara Rush, Walter Matthau, Virginia Bruce.
117 min.
Evan Hunter adapted his novel of suburban infidelities for this glossy but unsatisfying and very dated 'Scope melodrama, in which unhappily wed architect Douglas carries on with restless housewife Novak, until neighbour Matthau happens on one of their trysts and makes a play for Novak himself. Ends tamely with Douglas and wife Rush reconciled and setting off for a new life in Hawaii. TJ

Stranger Than Paradise

(Jim Jarmusch, 1984, US/WGer) John Lurie, Eszter Balint, Richard Edson, Cecillia Stark, Danny Rosen.
89 min. b/w.
A beautiful little independent film that paved the way for the more accessible (but perhaps less exhilarating) delights of *Down by Law*, this three-part road-movie-with-a-difference is shot in long, static black-and-white takes, and features an excellent score that straddles both Screaming Jay Hawkins and Bartok. The story is slight: cool, laconic New Yorker Lurie (of Lounge Lizards fame) reluctantly plays host when his young female cousin arrives on a visit from Hungary. When the girl finally disappears to Ohio to stay with an eccentric old aunt, Lurie suddenly finds himself feeling lonely, and he and his buddy Edson slope off westwards in search of...whatever. It's an ironic fable about exile, peopled by carefully, economically observed kooks who, at least after the first half-hour, are drawn with considerable warmth and generosity. Not a lot to it, certainly, but the acting and performances combine to produce an obliquely effective study of the effect of landscape upon emotion, and the wry, dry humour is often quite delicious. GA

Strangler, The

(Burt Topper, 1964, US) Victor Buono, David McLean, Ellen Corby, Jeanne Bates, Wally Campo, James Sikking.
89 min. b/w.
Having played a chubby mother's boy in Robert Aldrich's *What Ever Happened to Baby Jane?*, Victor Buono brought a certain class to this compelling tawdry exploiter as an obese mother-fixated lab technician who murders nurses. Pre-dating *The Boston Strangler* by a few years, this is a very different take from that offered by Tony Curtis in Richard Fleischer's 1968 movie. NF

Stranglers of Bombay, The

(Terence Fisher, 1959, GB) Guy Rolfe, Allan Cuthbertson, Andrew Cruickshank, George Pastell, Marne Maitland, Marie Devereux.
80 min. b/w.
One of Hammer and Terence Fisher's most notorious and Sadean horror movies, about the thuggee atrocities in India in the 1820s. Guy Rolfe battles against a fatal sect of Kali worshippers whose mascot is a sexy teenager called Karim (Devereux). As men have their tongues pulled out or are castrated, Karim drools and wriggles so much that the film became a cult sensation on the continent and was cut in England. Actually, it isn't at all bad, even on a straight adventure level, and the Karim figure remains one of the purest incarnations of evil in all of Fisher's work. Be prepared for a few laughs, though, as rural Bucks is substituted for the sweltering plains of India. DP

Strapless

(David Hare, 1988, GB) Blair Brown, Bruno Ganz, Bridget Fonda, Alan Howard, Michael Gough, Hugh Laurie, Suzanna Burden.
100 min.
Romance is explored here with logical exactitude; an uneasy, not altogether satisfying combination

of impulses. Lillian (Brown) is an overworked American doctor, single and approaching 40. Against the life-and-death extremities of her work, she has established a controlled routine. But she is disturbed by two influences: the attentions of mysterious millionaire Raymond (Ganz), and the freewheeling lifestyle of her pregnant, husbandless sister Amy (Fonda). Will Lillian scurry back into her corner, or mellow and adopt a more spontaneous approach to her professional and private lives? 'They shouldn't stay up but they do', murmurs Fonda in reference to her strapless gowns, by implication a testament to female independence. A forced comparison, it's a mite condescending. Ganz's catalytic character embodies an ideal, but is so exaggerated in depiction that the relationship with Lillian fails to ring true. An interesting conception has suffered in execution. CM

Strapped

(Forest Whitaker, 1993, US) Bokeem Woodbine, Kia Joy Goodwin, Fredro, Michael Biehn.
102 min.
This first feature strains a little hard (it's another in-your-face Scorsese), but the handling becomes more assured and the final result is impressive. Set on the streets of New York, it's the tale of Diquan, a youth who turns to selling guns *and* information as a way of raising his pregnant girlfriend's bail. A burning indictment of the inner-city circle of strife. TCh

Strasse, Die (The Street)

(Karl Grune, 1923, Ger) Eugen Klöpfer, Aud Egede-Nissen, Lucie Höflich, Max Schreck.
75 min. b/w.
Rebellious middle-aged bourgeois ventures out from his parlour to sample the fleshpots of *The Street*, only – inevitably – to skulk home chastened to the cosy security of spouse and soup tureen. Variations on this artless moral fable formed the basis for a whole cycle of 1920s 'street films', of which Murnau's first American movie, *Sunrise*, was perhaps the most memorable. Ex-theatre director and Max Reinhardt disciple, Grune tells the story with minimal intertitles and some visual panache in suggesting the iridescent but deadly seductiveness of the street. This is his most famous film, but it doesn't rank with the very best of German silent cinema: poor characterisation (Klöpfer contrives to be both dull and dislikeable as the ill-fated philistine, though Egede-Nissen, the dancer in *Dr Mabuse the Gambler*, is more lively as the vamp), flaccid sentimentality, and an often flagging pace make it seem more like a deserving revival than an exciting rediscovery. SJo

Strategia del Ragno, La

see Spider's Stratagem, The

Strategy of the Snail, The (La Estratagia del Caracol)

(Sergio Cabrera, 1993, Col) Frank Ramirez, Humberto Dorado, Florina Lemaitre, Gustavo Angarito, Vicky Hernandez.
116 min.
An oddly likeable movie about the tenants of an old tenement ('the Casa Uribe') in central Bogotá who decide to resist eviction. The story proceeds a bit like an Ealing comedy. The fight for the right strategy is between the legal delaying tactics of Dr Romero ('The Fox') and the more inventive ideas of an old Spanish Civil War veteran. Politically a little sentimental, but made with gusto and a fine feel for eccentricity. WH

Strawberry and Chocolate (Fresa y Chocolate)

(Tomás Gutiérrez Alea/Juan Carlos Tabío, 1993, Cuba) Jorge Perugorría, Vladimir Cruz, Mirta Ibarra, Francisco Gattorno.
111 min.
The core problem with Cuba's first gay-themed movie is that it's so...Cuban. It's about everybody's favourite party topics, but it's so busy worrying about machismo and homophobia that it forgets to let its hair down. In Cuban terms, it must seem tremendously daring to put acid social criticisms into the mouth of a raging queen. To the rest of us, the result feels more like Stanley Kramer than Lily Savage. The film replays the central gestalt of *Kiss of the Spiderwoman* (stol-

id communist meets and is subverted by florid queen) with a simple twist: here the queen is the smart one. Sociology student David, a true child of Castro's revolution and an inner minefield of misogyny and prejudice, runs into long-suffering queer Diego, whose cluttered apartment is a cross between a library, a dodgy art gallery and a junk shop. The encounter changes both of them. Dull, obvious and bafflingly timid. TR

Straw Dogs

(Sam Peckinpah, 1971, GB) Dustin Hoffman, Susan George, David Warner, Peter Vaughan, TP McKenna, Del Henney, Sally Thomsett, Colin Welland, Peter Arne.
118 min.
Taking elements of both the Western and the British horror film, Peckinpah's masterstroke was to shoot *Straw Dogs* absolutely straight, without the reassuring signposts of either type of film. Hoffman's American mathematician settles with his wife in the village where she grew up, encountering first hostility, then violence from the remote, backward (inbred?) Cornish community. 'Civilised' man's confrontation with irrational violence is handled with impeccable logic. Indeed, looking back, it's hard to see what the charges of gratuitous violence were all about. More intriguing and questionable is Peckinpah's total annihilation of Hoffman's marriage. The violence that befalls it can be interpreted partly as an externalisation of the couple's latent incompatibility (stressed again and again). But the ensuing mixture of fantasy wish fulfilment and pure terror seems more informed by a general misogyny than specific doubts about that particular relationship. CPe

Stray Dog (Nora Inu)

(Akira Kurosawa, 1949, Jap) Toshiro Mifune, Takashi Shimura, Ko Kimura, Keiko Awaji, Reisaburo Yamamoto.
122 min. b/w.
An early encounter between Kurosawa and two of his favourite actors, Mifune and Shimura, both playing detectives in Japan's uneasy postwar period under US imperialism. When Mifune's pistol is stolen, he is overwhelmed by a feeling of dishonour rather than failure, and sets out on a descent into the lower depths of Tokyo's underworld, which gradually reveals Dostoievskian parallels between himself and his quarry. A sweltering summer is at its height, and Kurosawa's strenuous location shooting transforms the city into a sensuous collage of fluttering fans and delicate, sweating limbs. A fine blend of US thriller material with Japanese conventions, it's a small classic. CPea

Streamers

(Robert Altman, 1983, US) Matthew Modine, Michael Wright, Mitchell Lichtenstein, David Alan Grier, Guy Boyd, George Dzundza, Albert Macklin.
118 min.
Another of Altman's gripping demonstrations of how to transform theatre by means of composition and close-up. As in *Come Back to the Five and Dime*, he restricts his material to a single set, this time an army barracks dormitory, where a group of young US recruits live, laugh and lay into each other while waiting to be sent off to action in Vietnam. Sex, class, race and war are the main topics under discussion, brought to boiling point by the arrival of the ranting Carlyle (Wright), an argumentative black whose abrupt changes in articulacy and temper reveal a madman's insights into reality. Confusion and confinement are the keynotes here: freedom of thought and action has been removed from these boys, with the result that finally they turn with inexorable anguish upon one another. Altman's direction keeps the atmosphere admirably taut and claustrophobic, while allowing the cast plenty of opportunity to excel with spontaneous, vivid performances, subtly explored by a hesitantly prowling camera. GA

Street, The

see Strasse, Die

Street Angel

(Frank Borzage, 1928, US) Janet Gaynor, Charles Farrell, Alberto Rabagliati, Gino Conti, Guido Trento, Henry Armetta.
9,221 ft. b/w.

'Everywhere...in every town...in every street...we pass, unknowing, souls made great by adversity'. Not, perhaps, the most modish sentiment for the '80s, but nevertheless the cornerstone of a wholly modern movie: one in the coherent collection made between the mid-'20s and World War II, sublime demonstrations of a system of sensual spirituality, the products of their director's uncompromising romanticism and fluent sense of cinemotion. Testing the same screen lovers almost as stringently as he had in *Seventh Heaven*, Borzage here damns 'morality' and opts for the pure passion of a sacred *amour fou*. Both films affirm, triumphantly, that melodrama can mean much more than just an excuse for a good weep. Both just have to be seen to be believed. PT

Street Angel (Malu Tianshi)

(Yuan Muzhi, 1937, China) Zhao Dan, Wei Heling, Qian Qianli, Zhou Xuan.
100 min. b/w.
This glimpse of the Chinese left wing cinema of the '30s is a true revelation. Maturely assimilating various lessons from Hollywood, it sketches the street life of the poorest quarter of Shanghai just before the city's fall to the Japanese; the main characters are a street musician, a hooker, a newsvendor, and a 'sing-song' girl. Its conclusions are inevitably pessimistic, but both script and performances are warmly humorous; and the attitude to issues like prostitution makes Western cinema of the '60s seem antiquated by comparison. TR

Streetcar Named Desire, A

(Elia Kazan, 1951, US) Vivien Leigh, Marlon Brando, Kim Hunter, Karl Malden, Randy Bond.
122 min. b/w.
The film in which the Marlon mumble and scratch gave the Method a bad name and Tennessee Williams a yellow paper reputation as the playwright of steamy sex. Actually pretty mild (Stanley's 'liberating' rape of Blanche is coyly elided while we watch a hose washing away garbage with portentous symbolism), it remains impressive largely because of Brando's superbly detailed performance (which rather wipes the floor with Leigh's showy but superficial bundle of mannerisms). Directing with his camera sticking as close to the characters as if they were grouped on a stage, Kazan achieves a sort of theatrical intensity in which the sweaty realism sometimes clashes awkwardly with the stylisation that heightens the dialogue into a kind of poetry. What the film lacks, in fact, is some sort of perspective – and perhaps a dash of the dark humour that made *Baby Doll* with Kazan's best film and the screen's best Williams adaptation. TM

Street Fighter

(Steven E de Souza, 1994, US) Jean-Claude Van Damme, Raul Julia, Ming-Na Wen, Damian Chapa, Kylie Minogue, Simon Callow, Roshan Seth, Wes Studi.
102 min.
As a scriptwriter, Steven E de Souza made his name with *Die Hard* and its sequel; on the strength of this directorial debut, the day-job option would seem the better bet. Like many before him, director de Souza falls foul of transferring a necessarily repetitive computer game to the big screen: instead of a fluid narrative, we have a stop-start plot with too many heroes, multiple plot threads, and virtually no suspense or excitement. Having taken 63 hostages, renegade warlord General M Bison (Julia) demands a hefty ransom. Colonel Guile (Van Damme) and more than a dozen multi-ethnic heroes then try to penetrate the defences of Bison's impregnable hi-tech fortress. Julia (in his final role) hams it up shamelessly as the camp commandant, but not even his suave presence and throwaway quips can save this noisy, brainless mess. NF

Streetfighter, The

see Hard Times

Street Fleet

see D.C.Cab

Street Girls

(Michael Miller, 1974, US) Carol Case, Paul Pompian, Art Burke, Chris Souder, Jimmy Smith, Michael Albert Weber.
84 min.

Hardly a gem, but at least a genuine piece of grit. Filmed on low-rent locations in Oregon, it boasts a sharp screenplay co-written by Miller and Barry Levinson, a nice bit of Muddy Waters on the soundtrack, and an oddball assortment of pimps, dealers and hippies. The story, with a father rooting round among the dregs in search of his daughter, is *Hardcore* without the refinements. He meets a burnt-out hophead who burbles on about interesting buildings and transcendental Dante, and whose search for self involves dressing up in drag. She, meanwhile, gets smacked out and turns her first trick – a gas-jock with a taste for the Golden Shower. Crude, rude, with enough go-go stuff to keep the raincoats happy, but a real bit of rough for the curio buff. AB

Streetlife

(Karl Francis, 1995, GB) Helen McCrory, Rhys Ifans, Christine Tuckett, Donna Edwards.
98 min.
Tough, uncompromising and very bleak story of a woman on a Caerphilly housing estate, so unlucky in life and love that she ends up killing her baby, born in secret and alone in her mother's caravan, and then sending it down a rural stream like Moses in his basket. This is a telling indictment of the '90s 'dustbin' society in which dysfunctional people seem abandoned and prey to council worker and drug dealer alike. Clumsy in parts and laid on a mite too thick, the film is nevertheless a cry of anguish that Ken Loach would have recognised. McCrory gives a vibrant performance in her first big film role. SGr

Street Music

(Jenny Bowen, 1981, US) Elizabeth Daily, Larry Breeding, Ned Glass, Marjorie Eaton, WF Walker.
93 min.
In the Tenderloin district of San Francisco, an old residential hotel (ironically named 'The Victory') is scheduled for demolition. Will the residents (most of them elderly) accept their fate or become politicised in the struggle to defend their collective home? You guessed it. If only Bowen, writer/director of this independent feature (her first), had risked making the old folk the protagonists, instead of focusing on a dumb street singer and her boorish bus driver boyfriend, she might have overcome the cuteness that undercuts the movie's humanist pleading. MA

Street of Shadows
(aka Shadowman)

(Richard Vernon, 1953, GB) Cesar Romero, Kay Kendall, Edward Underdown, Victor Maddern, Simone Silva, Bill Travers.
84 min.
Part matron, part vamp, Kendall manages to combine the dowdy appeal of a '50s housewife who's just bought her first washing machine with Hollywood-style glamour. Romero is Luigi, the Soho nightclub owner who falls for her, Bogart to her Bacall. An excellent harmonica-based score and a half sympathetic villain in Maddern's scorned, deformed Limpy make for a dark atmospheric frame-up thriller, more Graham Greene than Edgar Wallace. GM

Street of Shame
(Akasen Chitai)

(Kenji Mizoguchi, 1956, Jap) Machiko Kyo, Ayako Wakao, Aiko Mimasu, Michiyo Kogure.
96 min. b/w.
Mizoguchi's final film is a grim but profoundly moving study of a group of prostitutes in Tokyo's red light district. While they go about their daily business, there are constant references to the anti-prostitution legislation which Parliament is debating. As is made clear, merely passing a law won't save the women. For whatever reasons they became prostitutes (money-related in every case), they can never escape the judgment passed on them by the repressive, patriarchal society which shunned them in the first place. The settings are a far removed from the medieval landscapes of *Ugetsu* or *The Life of Oharu*, but Mizoguchi's focus on the plight of his women characters is as intent and heart-rending as ever. GM

Streets of Fire

(Walter Hill, 1984, US) Michael Paré, Diane Lane, Rick Moranis, Amy Madigan, Willem

Dafoe, Deborah van Valkenburgh, Richard Lawson, Rick Rossovich, Elizabeth Daily, Marine Jahan.
94 min.
Continuing his love affair with movies that go bang in the night, Hill here gives us a futuristic rock fantasy which is, at heart, a Western. An itinerant soldier (Paré) returns to his home to discover that his former girlfriend, the local girl who's made it big in the rockbiz (Lane), has been kidnapped by a villainous street-gang. Cue for fisticuffs and fireworks as Paré, aided by a tough-talking female sidekick (Madigan), hikes over to the bad part of town and unlocks Ms Lane from the bed to which she's been handcuffed. Result? Showdown. *Streets of Fire* is fast and loud, with music from Ry Cooder and, perhaps misguidedly, Jim Steinman; it is also violent, though its violence lies not in the depiction of blood and entrails, but in the sheer energy and speed with which the dark and brooding images rush after one another. The message is that there is no message; if this isn't action cinema in its purest form, then it's pretty close. RR

Streets of Gold
(Joe Roth, 1986, US) Klaus Maria Brandauer, Adrian Pasdar, Wesley Snipes, Angela Molina, Elya Baskin, Rainbow Harvest, Daniel O'Shea, John Mahoney.
94 min.
Brandauer plays an exiled Soviet boxing champ, now a self-pitying drunk and washer-up in a New York Russian restaurant. Banned from fighting in the Soviet Union for using his anti-Semitic coach as a punch-bag, he takes on a couple of local prospects, training them up for a grudge match against a visiting Soviet team. You can guess the rest, right down to the *Rocky*-style finale. Director Roth never uses a short jab when he can take a wild swing, usually at the cold inhumanity of Soviet society. NF

Streetwalker, The
see Marge, La

Streetwalkin'
(Joan Freeman, 1984, US) Melissa Leo, Randall Batinkoff, Dale Midkiff, Deborah Offner, Julie Newmar, Julie Cohen, Greg Germann, Kirk Taylor, Antonio Fargas.
85 min.
In flight from a wretched family life, naive Cookie (Leo) arrives in New York with only her tears, pocket money, and dumb younger brother (Batinkoff) for company. Quick to comfort her is charming, handsome Duke (Midkiff); trouble is, he's a psychopathically violent pimp, and soon she's selling her body on the seedy streets. Blinded by love, it's only after he's transformed her room-mate's face into steak tartare that she turns to another pimp for protection, and Duke sets out in search of his errant breadwinner, murder on his mind. Given that, like Penelope Spheeris and Amy Jones, Joan Freeman made this, her first feature, under the aegis of producer Roger Corman, high hopes seemed in order. No such luck. Starting off as lurid, documentary-style melodrama before it settles into an over-extended and often risible cat-and-mouse chase, this witless pile of prurient sleaze is poorly paced and saddled with a predictable script, stereotype characterisations, and distastefully voyeuristic direction. GA

Streetwise
(Martin Bell, 1984, US)
91 min.
A grimly fascinating *cinéma-vérité* documentary about a bunch of kids (aged between 13 and 19) living rough on Pike Street, Seattle. Unable or unwilling to live with their parents, the kids hustle a living by begging, diving into garbage dumpsters for thrown-out pizzas, and selling their bodies. Seen through the unblinking eye of Bell's sharply focused camera, the kids flirt with, fight, support and sometimes exploit one another. Police, social workers and parents drift in and out, but their concern for the kids' long-term future seems irrelevant in the face of their immediate struggle to survive until the next meal or meal-ticket. Saddest of all, given the raw deal they've had from the system, is the kids' unquestioning conservatism. All they want from life is a nice house, a colour TV, and a life-style that conforms to their soap opera ideals. The inevitable reservations aside (56 hours of footage reduced to 91

minutes; the occasionally voyeuristic camera-work), this is an impressive achievement. Bell and his team clearly gained the confidence of their subjects, and despite their depressing lives, the kids reveal themselves in all their naive vitality. NF

Street with No Name, The
(William Keighley, 1948, US) Mark Stevens, Richard Widmark, Lloyd Nolan, Barbara Lawrence, Ed Begley, Donald Buka, Joseph Pevney, John McIntire.
91 min. b/w.
Fresh from giggling his sadistic way through *Kiss of Death*, Widmark steals a march on this follow-up to the documentary approach of *House on 92nd Street* with his brilliantly quirky characterisation of a gangster in the throes of hypochondria (terrified of germs and draughts, he draws his nasal inhaler more often than his gun) and misogyny (in between bouts of wife-beating, he flirts coyly with Stevens, the young FBI agent who has infiltrated his gang). Inspired by the FBI's concern over the re-emergence of organised crime, and saddled with a narrator boasting what a great job the Bureau is doing, the film slips quietly into the *noir* genre with its shadowy camerawork, its ambiguous relationships, and its subversive delight in the personable Widmark's city of corruption. It was later reworked by Fuller as *House of Bamboo*. TM

Strictly Ballroom
(Baz Luhrmann, 1992, Aust) Paul Mercurio, Tara Morice, Bill Hunter, Pat Thomson, Gia Carides, Peter Whitford, Barry Otto, John Hannan, Sonia Kruger, Antonio Vargas.
94 min.
Right from the glorious opening, it's obvious that Baz Luhrmann knows *exactly* what he's doing. The story recounts the struggles of talented dancer Scott (Mercurio) to make it to the Pan-Pacific Grand Prix, despite setbacks resulting from his refusal to stick to the steps approved by his team: his dance-tutor mum (Thomson) has screaming fits, the Dance Federation director (Hunter) threatens disbarment, and the only club member prepared to partner him is shy, clumsy novice Fran (Morice). Partly a hilarious satire of the bizarre rituals of the ballroom world, partly a contemporary fairy-tale romance, Luhrmann's exhilarating debut transcends its shamelessly familiar plot through endlessly inventive details, through an expertly balanced blend of stylish cinematic technique and camp theatricality, and through the care and affection it devotes to the characters, dancing and music. Crucially, the film's enormous charm is never rammed down the throat, but acknowledged for the calculating ploy it is, with a winning, ironic wink. GA

Strictly Confidential
see Broadway Bill

Strike (Stachka)
(Sergei Eisenstein, 1924, USSR) Maxim Straukh, Grigori Alexandrov, Mikhail Gomorov, I Ivanov, I Klukvin.
6,460 ft. b/w.
Eisenstein's first feature also remains his most watchable; if his theories of montage and typage were already much in evidence, at least they had not yet turned into the over-emphatic academic tropes that marred so much of his later work. The story itself is simple: workers clash violently with employers and police during a drawn-out factory strike provoked by the sacking and subsequent suicide of one of their number. But Eisenstein's methods are both complex and extraordinary: his decision to make the masses rather than any single individual his hero lends the film a truly epic sweep; the vicious caricatures of the bourgeois capitalists make for wit and effectively powerful emotional manipulation; and the editing, rapid, fluid and razor-sharp, provides not only pace but a myriad of metaphorical meanings that extend way beyond mere propaganda. The harshly beautiful imagery – most memorably, shots of a slaughterhouse intercut with the massacre of the strikers – roots the movie effortlessly in down-to-earth reality, but its relentless energy and invention transform the whole thing into a raucous, rousing hymn to human dignity and courage. GA

Strikebound
(Richard Lowenstein, 1983, Aust) Chris Haywood, Carol Burns, Hugh Keays-Byrne, Rob Steele, Nik Forster, David Kendall.
100 min.
Appalling conditions at Australia's Sunbeam Colliery in the '30s led to a miners' strike, and Agnes Doig, a dour Salvation Army schoolmistress, to a lifelong commitment to the labour movement. Although filmed with visual flair and authenticity, this reconstruction never works up steam. Perhaps the fact that Agnes and her miner husband Wattie appear in person, recalling the strike and affirming their continuing pride in being of the working-class, explains the rather deferential handling. In the flashback sequences, Haywood's Wattie has a puckish charm, and Burns works hard to establish Agnes' compassion and grit, but they rarely engage the emotions. The events of the strike likewise unfold with a terse cheeriness that rarely gains a truly threatening accent or a compelling momentum; and before you know it, the action has petered out. HH

Strike Up the Band
(Busby Berkeley, 1940, US) Mickey Rooney, Judy Garland, Paul Whiteman, June Preisser, William Tracy, Larry Nunn.
120 min. b/w.
Don't be misled by the Berkeley credit – this is no girlie extravaganza. Rather, it's the second of those musical concoctions designed for the strident, irrepressible Rooney to dominate with Garland tagging along. Whiteman is once again offered as everybody's favourite uncle. High school big band theme, with Rooney determinedly whipping the school orchestra into a sensational swing band, and a rather sticky plot about raising funds for an operation. But the Roger Edens-Arthur Freed songs are just so-so, and Berkeley keeps a low profile except in the dizzily shot 'Do The La Conga' number. Title song is Gershwin. SG

Striking Distance
(Rowdy Herrington, 1993, US) Bruce Willis, Dennis Farina, Sarah Jessica Parker, Tom Sizemore, Brion James.
101 min.
After the shooting of his police-captain father, Pittsburgh cop Tom Hardy (Willis) accuses the force of hushing up the murder and finds himself demoted to the river patrol. Two years later, with his uncle Nick (Farina) in charge and an unlikely assailant convicted of the crime, Hardy is sure that a new spate of killings is the work of the same hand. His unauthorised investigation, with partner Jo Christman (Parker), is a routine affair, the film's familial and professional tensions sunk by a script that's all development and no pay-off. The supporting cast supplies some basic viewer-comfort, but this and the stock video ingredients are hardly enough to captivate the audience. TCh

Stripes
(Ivan Reitman, 1981, US) Bill Murray, Harold Ramis, Warren Oates, PJ Soles, John Larroquette, Sean Young, John Diehl, Lance LeGault, John Candy.
106 min.
Purposeless slob Murray loses car (repossessed), apartment and girlfriend (thrown out) all in the same day, and on a whim joins the US Army; a decision he spends most of the film regretting. Though the overall tone is as unquestioning of the virtues of the military life – discipline, duty, honour, etc. – as was *Private Benjamin*, at least at its centre Murray is a genuine couldn't-give-a-shit character meant for the early '80s. Reitman, who also originated *Animal House* and *Meatballs*, manages a reasonable success rate at pulling off the numerous verbal and sight gags with which the script is peppered. RM

Strip Jack Naked: Nighthawks II
(Ron Peck, 1991, GB) John Brown, John Diamon, Nick Bolton.
91 min. b/w & col.
When *Nighthawks* was released, its sincere but self-pitying study of a gay London teacher searching for Mr Right while struggling to emerge from the closet already looked dated. A dozen years on, Peck attempts to put his feelings

at that time into some sort of context, mixing personal and political histories with a selection of out-takes from the original movie. Though it doesn't really work – the dreamy connecting shots of naked men fiddling with an editing machine are far too self-consciously arty – there are moments which, due to Peck's readiness to reveal his own discomfort, achieve a genuine if somewhat naive poignancy. His story begins with an unrequited schoolboy crush, proceeds through years of guilt and repression, and ends on a note of hope, with Peck arguing that the gay community's reaction to AIDS has made it both more conspicuous and more united. As autobiographical documentary, the film is ambitious, earnest, heartfelt; as a history of the British gay experience, it suffers from excessive subjectivity. GA

Striptease
(Andrew Bergman, 1995, US) Demi Moore, Burt Reynolds, Rumer Willis, Ving Rhames, Armand Assante, Robert Patrick, Paul Guilfoyle.
117 min.
The first of Carl Hiaasen's hilarious thrillers to reach the screen, this faithfully reproduces the novel's anti-Republicanism. Reynolds plays right-wing Congressman David Dilbeck as a bewigged buffoon with a penchant for vaseline, and a fatal obsession with stripper Erin Grant (Moore). Writer/director Bergman contrasts Dilbeck's hypocritical advocacy of traditional family values with the sustaining alternative-family group at the Eager Beaver club – in which single mom Erin brings up her daughter (Rumer Willis) – comprising a bunch of strippers and bouncer Shad (Rhames). Unfortunately, the movie's so dire you wonder if it isn't an elaborate double-bluff designed to reveal the ineptitude of liberals. The kind of comedy thriller which cancels itself out, this is pitched too close to caricature to engender suspense, but lacks the crisp, acerbic wit which distinguishes Hiaasen's prose. There's a no-nonsense approach to nudity in general, but everything gets very self-conscious whenever Demi is called on to strut her stuff – which is often. TCh

Striptease Lady
see Lady of Burlesque

Stromboli, Terra di Dio (Stromboli)
(Roberto Rossellini, 1949, It) Ingrid Bergman, Mario Vitale, Renzo Cesana, Mario Sponza.
107 min. b/w.
In Rossellini's first film with Bergman, the overpowering symbol of the volcanic island almost overwhelms its delicate story: a World War II refugee (Bergman) marries a young fisherman to escape from an internment camp. Brutalised by war, but coming to loathe the terrifying savagery of the island, her drama is a conflict between self-pity and acceptance of Something Greater. Praised as an example of cinema devoid of the excesses of formal artifice, a 'lesson in humility', its achievement is less modest: a sequence of tunny-fishing remains one of the most amazing ever filmed. DMacP

Stronger Than Fear
see Edge of Doom

Strong Man, The
(Frank Capra, 1926, US) Harry Langdon, Priscilla Bonner, Gertrude Astor, William V Mong, Robert McKim, Arthur Thalassa.
6,882 ft. b/w.
Second of the three features on the strength of which Langdon was briefly hailed as another Chaplin, here playing a Belgian soldier happily resorting to his catapult instead of a machine-gun in the World War I trenches, then heading for America after the armistice (as assistant to a brutish strong man) in quest of the pen pal he has fallen for, unaware that she is blind. Pathos aside, there are some really very funny gags, and – if you can stand Langdon's somewhat obscene persona as an overgrown, pudding-faced baby – a beautifully constructed sequence in which he is subjected to ferociously close pursuit by a vamp, hungering not for his body as he assumes but for the loot hidden in his pocket. Capra's first feature, incidentally. TM

Strong-Man Ferdinand
see Starke Ferdinand, Der

Stroszek
(Werner Herzog, 1977, WGer) Bruno S, Eva Mattes, Clemens Scheitz, Burkhard Driest, Pitt Bedewitz, Wilhelm von Homburg.
108 min.
Herzog seems to have run for cover after *Heart of Glass*, a supposedly 'difficult' film beneath whose seemingly impenetrable surface lay a simple reconstruction of key elements from horror films. And *Stroszek* has been labelled unfairly as a travelogue comedy featuring Bruno S from *The Enigma of Kaspar Hauser*. Bruno (S for Superstar? He struts like some remedial cousin of Jack Nicholson) and oddball entourage – including the excellent Eva Mattes as prostitute girlfriend – leave modern Berlin for the golden opportunities of America; in reality, the despair of Railroad Flats, Wisconsin. Although relatively indulgent for Herzog, the film's comedy works well enough, because Herzog's idiosyncratic imagination finds an ideal counterpoint in the bleak flatlands of poor white America. His view of that country is the most askance since the films of Monte Hellman. For all the supposed lightness, it is the film's core of despair which in the end devours everything. CPe

Struggle, The
(DW Griffith, 1931, US) Hal Skelly, Zita Johann, Charlotte Wynters, Jackson Halliday, Evelyn Baldwin, Edna Hagan.
87 min. b/w.
Griffith's last movie looks like a naturalistic 'human' story struggling to emerge from a stern moral tract on the evils of demon alcohol, a tension that's fascinating at this remove. Despite a robust DTs nightmare climax, it gets nowhere near the intended attack on Prohibition and the perils of 'bad' liquor; but it does have a good eye for the vulnerability of its miserable hero (Skelly, excellent), and a surprisingly sharp way with its pre-Depression satire (catch the Jewish insurance salesman with a sideline in home-made wine). No question, much of the humour springs from Anita Loos' swing-time script ('Get hot, Bozos!'), but it incidentally proves that Griffith mastered the innovations of talkies better than any of his contemporaries believed. TR

Stuart Saves His Family
(Harold Ramis, 1995, US) Al Franken, Laura San Giacomo, Vincent D'Onofrio, Shirley Knight, Harris Yulin, Lesley Boone, John Link Graney.
95 min.
Stuart Smalley's beloved self-help Chicago cable show is cancelled, whereupon he discovers that, what with depression, alcoholism, unemployment and obesity, his dysfunctional family back in Minnesota is far worse off than he is. Writer/performer Al Franken created Smalley for TV's *Saturday Night Live*, but his catchphrase – 'I'm good enough, I'm smart enough, and doggone it, people like me' – here in an expanded context proves somewhat wide of the mark. Franken squeezes a few chuckles out of the moon-faced, cardigan-wearing, therapy-dependent Stuart, and those familiar with Alcoholics Anonymous' 12-step recovery programme may bond in sympathy. The sentimentality, however, doesn't play. AO

Stubby (Fimpen)
(Bo Widerberg, 1974, Swe) Johan Bergman, Magnus Hörenstan, Inger Bergman, Arne Bergman.
89 min.
Six-year-old kid gets to play for the local league team, moves on to the Swedish side one game later, and scores a string of Roy of the Rovers goals in the World Cup qualifying games, usually after the opposition has gone ahead, culminating in the defeat of the USSR at Dynamo Stadium. But he gives it all up to learn how to read and write. As a fantasy, *Stubby* is reasonably engaging, if somewhat unimaginative; but as a satire on fame and exploitation, it's barely even sketchy. Writer/director Widerberg doesn't develop his ideas much beyond the comic strip stage. The film was shot on the fringes of the World Cup, and offers the novelty of various national sides taking on a six-year-old, except that it looks like action replay, because they have to slow down to make him look fast. CPe

Stud, The
(Quentin Masters, 1978, GB) Joan Collins, Oliver Tobias, Sue Lloyd, Mark Burns, Doug Fisher, Walter Gotell.
90 min.
Like Dickens, Joan and Jackie Collins (the former starring in this adaptation of the latter's novel) offer a panoramic exposition of contemporary urban life, tracing the decline of stud Tony Blake (Tobias), from promising young disco manager and darling of lonely, beautiful women who treat him as a sex object, back to his East End origins, where he suddenly displays a three-day growth of beard and a new moral awareness. Joking and comparisons apart, this is a dreadful film. The dreary, awkward narrative seems largely dependent on the locations they could get – disco, swimming pool, lift. The script (by Jackie herself), permeated with an appalling and deep-rooted snobbery, contrives to be completely inaccurate and therefore offensive to every facet of the social structure, in a London that swings like a corpse at the end of a rope. JS

Student Days (Xuesheng zhi Ai)
(Lin Ch'ing-chieh, 1981, Tai) Li Mu-ch'en, Lin Nan-shih, Ch'in Ch'ang-ming, Wang Hsing.
85 min.
Director Lin, himself an ex-teacher, has made four low-budget independent features about the lives of high school kids in provincial Taiwan, with more or less the same cast each time. This one is the most polished, although not the most imaginative. By Taiwanese standards, it has a likeable taste of reality in its character sketches, and depiction of delinquency and emotional problems. However, it also suffers from both major vices of Taiwanese cinema: careless photography and scenes of outrageously excessive sentiment. TR

Student Teachers, The
(Jonathan Kaplan, 1973, US) Susan Damante, Brooke Mills, Bob Harris, John Cramer, Dick Miller, Don Steele, Robert Phillips.
79 min.
Foremost among Kaplan's virtues as a film-maker are economic characterisation and a fast, taut sense of pacing, learned no doubt during his apprenticeship with the Roger Corman exploitation factory. Demonstrating that he always showed promise, this movie from those cheapo, cheerful days takes the typical tale of its heroines' extra-curricular activities and turns it against all expectations. While paying lip-duty to traditional audience titillation techniques by frequently baring the upper regions of the nubile educationalists, Kaplan prefers to concentrate on issues of sexual politics, crime and racism, at the same time revelling in an often hilarious sense of absurd parody (Sandra Dee as a source of syphilis in a sex-education film). No great movie, but great fun. GA

Study in Terror, A
(James Hill, 1965, GB) John Neville, Donald Houston, John Fraser, Anthony Quayle, Barbara Windsor, Adrienne Corri, Frank Finlay, Judi Dench, Peter Carsten, Robert Morley, Cecil Parker, Georgia Brown, Barry Jones, Kay Walsh.
95 min.
A careful but curiously ineffective piece of Sherlockiana in which Holmes (Neville) and Watson (Houston) tangle with Jack the Ripper in circumstances much less ingenious than those imagined for *Murder by Decree*. Donald and Derek Ford's script goes for the Conan Doyle flavour, but gets caught between the devil and the deep blue sea, since the producers (Compton, raised above their station, willy-nilly, by Polanski and *Repulsion*) were exploitation merchants at heart. All the pedantically pastiched dialogue, reverently played straight by a distinguished cast, therefore sits very uncomfortably with the crudely and gleefully shock-cut murders. The colour is nice, so are Alex Vetchinsky's sets, which include a delightfully smoky Whitechapel pub for Georgia Brown to belt out a couple of period numbers in. TM

Stuff, The
(Larry Cohen, 1985, US) Michael Moriarty, Andrea Marcovicci, Garrett Morris, Paul Sorvino, Scott Bloom, Danny Aiello, Patrick O'Neal, Alexander Scourby, Brooke Adams, Tammy Grimes.
87 min.

Larry Cohen's demons have never been your average little devils: Q the Winged Serpent lived atop the Chrysler Building, his anti-Christ lived in a Brooklyn basement, and J Edgar Hoover wasn't exactly human. This one is a white glop which comes bubbling out of the ground, tastes nice, and is immediately mined and marketed by a fast food chain under the logo 'Enough is never enough'. In other words, the monster doesn't come after you, you have to go out and consume it. Once eaten, it does strange things to people. Leading the anti-Stuff campaign for the forces of good is Michael Moriarty, in his customary persona as the laid back bozo who isn't as stupid as he looks ('Nobody is as stupid as I look'). As usual, Cohen's humour is chaotic (importing a right wing private army for the finale), surreal, and very, very subversive. If the drive-in crowd took its message to heart, they'd never eat again. *Invasion of the Body Snatchers* for our time. CPea

Stunt Man, The

(Richard Rush, 1979, US) Peter O'Toole, Barbara Hershey, Steve Railsback, Sharon Farrell, John Garwood, Allen Garfield, Alex Rocco, Adam Roarke, Chuck Bail.
130 min.
Lacking the innocence of Rush's previous work, this is also short on the really sardonic wit that its storyline (based on Paul Brodeur's novel) demands. A young Vietvet on the run (Railsback) tumbles onto the location of an all-action World War I epic, and falls into uneasy partnership with the movie's imperious, soliloquising director, O'Toole. That piece of casting is driven home with a sledgehammer insistence, while Railsback's engagingly twitchy performance – as the new stuntman filling in for a dead predecessor – is passed over in favour of more 'serious' themes. The result is a movie filled with gags and excellent stunts which remains curiously humourless at heart. Stunted, not stunning.

Stunts

(Mark L Lester, 1977, US) Robert Forster, Fiona Lewis, Joanna Cassidy, Darrell Fetty, Bruce Glover, James Luisi, Richard Lynch, Candice Rialson.
89 min.
From the director of *Truck Stop Women* comes a respectful showcase for the stunt trade with a cool regard for the fast buck. Lester twins the investigations by an outsider woman journalist (Lewis) and insider stunt hero (Forster) into the 'accidental' deaths of stunt people on the location for some clapped-out all-action pic. The result is a rehash of Hollywood's pathetic dedication to the cult of the gambler, which sacrifices visual opportunism in order to sit awestruck at the risks it boasts as 'truth' ('You can't bullshit a stunt – it either works or it doesn't'). Without the courage to trust fully in the action set pieces or the suspense plot, it still gives a sense of the stupefying, routine greed of movie production...and almost makes us believe that this highly-paid freedom to smash things is the last hope of mankind. Less than cunning. RP

Stuntwoman, The

see Ah Kam

Stupids, The

(John Landis, 1995, US) Tom Arnold, Jessica Lundy, Bug Hall, Alex McKenna, Mark Metcalf, Matt Keeslar, Christopher Lee, David Cronenberg, Costa-Gavras, Gillo Pontecorvo.
94 min.
The Stupids are a weird family, but entirely lacking the intriguingly dysfunctional nature of, say, the Simpsons (which Tom Arnold used to write). Ex-mailman Stanley (Arnold), Joan (Lundy), and kids Buster (Hall) and sweet Petunia (McKenna) inhabit a '50s world of candy-stripe colours, gingham bows, puff skirts and alien-movie speech patterns. Their true provenance, however, is American children's television and its dim never-never land of permutational studio sitcoms. The dumb surreal – Stanley taking the goldfish for a walk, the expostulations on the weekly theft of their garbage – one can accept. But the rambling, episodic narrative, laden with naff sight gags, dissipates attention in minutes. WH

Subject Was Roses, The

(Ulu Grosbard, 1968, US) Patricia Neal, Jack Albertson, Martin Sheen, Don Saxon, Elaine Williams, Grant Gordon.
107 min.

Having done Frank D Gilroy's Pulitzer Prize-winner on Broadway, Albertson and Sheen reprised their roles for this respectable film version, stage director Grosbard made his feature debut, and Neal came back from a serious stroke to complete the team. Sheen's the WWII veteran whose return to a less-than-happy home ignites long-standing animosities between mom and pop (Neal and Albertson), a set-up which may have had some residual resonance during the Vietnam era, but which is mainly a platform for three detailed, honest performances. TJ

Subjective Factor, The (Der subjektive Faktor)

(Helke Sander, 1981, WGer) Angelika Rommel, Nikolaus Dutsch, Lutz Weidlich, Dominik Bender, Johanna Sophia.
144 min.
Anni, the 'heroine' and thinly fictionalised director-surrogate, is a single mother who joins a Berlin commune, gets turned on to the utopian militancy of '68, then quickly converted to a figurehead of the emergent Women's Movement by the discovery that her male comrades are chauvinistic *Schweine* who affect macho trenchcoats and keep their socks on during sex. As the title implies, it's a defiantly and meanderingly personal film that often drags, then ends up by jumping abruptly from the first stirrings of feminism to 1980s sell-out (erstwhile anti-Nam demonstrators dining out at a chic Vietnamese eatery). Sander's modish theme is a suppressed woman's history, but with the heady radicalism under consideration now evaporated into the mists of history, the film emerges (presumably unintentionally) almost as a piece of period nostalgia. SJo

Submarine Patrol

(John Ford, 1938, US) Richard Greene, Nancy Kelly, Preston Foster, George Bancroft, Slim Summerville, John Carradine, J Farrell McDonald, Elisha Cook Jr, Maxie Rosenbloom, Jack Pennick, Ward Bond, George E Stone.
95 min. b/w.
A claustrophobic and mannered flagwaver (adapted by several hands from Ray Milholland's novel *The Splinter Fleet of the Otranto Barrage*) in which an arrogant playboy, Perry Townsend III (Greene), signs up with the US Navy in WWI and is put aboard a rickety old boat to chase submarines. A strict but decent disciplinarian shapes up an unruly crew. Greene has the conceit knocked out of him and wins the affections of all-American girl Nancy Kelly. Ford keeps the narrative and action buzzing, but this is a pale example of the Master's work. The following year he made *Stagecoach* and *Young Mr Lincoln*. GM

Submarine X-1

(William Graham, 1967, GB) James Caan, Norman Bowler, David Sumner, Brian Grellis, William Dysart.
90 min.
Standard WWII drama in which Lt Commander Caan and his three midget subs mount a revenge attack on the German battleship 'Lidendorf' in a Norwegian fjord. Writer/producer John Champion churned out another very similar picture, Paul Wendkos' *Attack on the Iron Coast*, in 1967, also for the Mirisch company. Caan's career had not quite turned the corner, and he found little to get his teeth into in this attenuated story. TJ

Substitute, The

(Robert Mandel, 1996, US) Tom Berenger, Ernie Hudson, Diane Venora, Glenn Plummer, Marc Anthony, Cliff De Young, Richard Brooks, Rodney A Grant.
114 min.
Most pupils at George Washington High, the Miami hellhole where Jane Hetzko (Venora) struggles to stay alive, let alone teach, may be marginally younger than the seeming thirty-somethings in *The Lords of Flatbush*, but they're far more heavily armed. Typical is the sneering class nasty, Juan (Anthony), who has Hetzko's legs baseball-batted for a slight. At hand, luckily, kicking his heels after a covert operation in Miami, is a facially scarred, wish-fulfilling avenger, Hetzko's Special Forces boyfriend Shale (Berenger), who takes over the class, posing as a Harvard man named 'Mr Smith'. It's not long before he discovers a drug ring, implicating the politically aspirant head Mr Rollé (Hudson),

but first, to wage successful war, the class's respect has to be won. In director Mandel's unsophisticated hands, this all comes over like an amusingly preposterous mix of *Kindergarten Cop* and *Dangerous Minds*. But the script, by at least three writers, doesn't have the dialogue, characterisations, plotting, or plain interest to sustain a school-based drama. You can sense Mandel's sigh of relief when he's finally able to launch into an Uzi-blazing actioner, second grade. WH

Subterraneans, The

(Ranald MacDougall, 1960, US) George Peppard, Leslie Caron, Janice Rule, Roddy McDowall, Anne Seymour, Jim Hutton, Scott Marlowe, Art Pepper, Art Farmer, Gerry Mulligan, Carmen McRae.
89 min.
Jack Kerouac's Beat odyssey is well and truly beaten to a pulp in this sanitised Hollywood claptrap. Groovester Peppard falls not for the black girl featured in the original novel but for decidedly French waif Caron. Jazz musos passing through on their way to their connection include saxman Art Pepper and flugelhorn virtuoso Art Farmer. McDowall's words of youthful wisdom: 'Hey, life is a party and everyone else is a party-crasher!' Like profoundsville, daddy-o, and in 'Scope to boot. Hypnotically abominable. TJ

Suburban Commando

(Burt Kennedy, 1991, US) Hulk Hogan, Christopher Lloyd, Shelley Duvall, William Ball, Laura Mooney, Michael Faustino, Larry Miller, Tony Longo, JoAnn Dearing, Roy Dotrice, Dennis Burkley, Jack Elam.
90 min.
In this likeable kids' action-adventure, Hulk Hogan, the blond-maned, 6'7" World Wrestling Federation superstar, plays an intergalactic warrior, first seen traversing the universe in silver-plastic armour (the production design is self-consciously tacky), single-handedly saving planets from arch-villain Suitor (Ball). Dropped into 'stressed-out' suburban California when the crystals on his space-pod need recharging, he finds board and lodging – posing as a Frenchman – with a downtrodden wimp (Lloyd), his loopy wife (Duvall) and their kids. Most of the laughs come from watching the gentle giant learning to skateboard with the kids, taking video games 'for real', and the like. His intergalactic bounty-hunting enemies arrive, and Lloyd, his help enlisted, turns from wimp to hero. Directed with glee, from a fine tongue-in-cheek script, it should amuse boys and child psychologists of all ages. WH

Suburbia

see Wild Side, The

SubUrbia

(Richard Linklater, 1996, US) Jayce Bartok, Amie Carey, Nicky Katt, Ajay Naidu, Parker Posey, Giovanni Ribisi, Samia Shoaib, Steve Zahn.
121 min.
Linklater's film covers much the same territory as *Slackers* and *Dazed and Confused*. It charts one long momentous night in the lives of a group of suburban 20-year-olds, for whom entertainment consists mainly of booze, banter and arguments with the Pakistani proprietors of the convenience store where they habitually hang out, and examines the friends' reactions to the visit of a former schoolmate-turned-rock star. Allegiances shift, animosities erupt, violence rears its head, tragedy looms. While it's true that playwright Eric Bogosian's screenplay fails to avoid the kind of tidy twists and contrivances favoured by theatre, and that the reluctance to leave the street corner setting makes for a certain staginess, Linklater keeps matters engrossing, partly through the strong performances he elicits, partly through his firm grasp of the rhythms, colours and moods of suburban existence. Crucially, no character is quite as he or she first appears, nor is the film's attitude towards the kids simplistically sympathetic or condemnatory. GA

Subway

(Luc Besson, 1985, Fr) Isabelle Adjani, Christopher Lambert, Richard Bohringer, Michel Galabru, Jean-Hugues Anglade, Jean-Pierre Bacri.
102 min.

Safecracker Lambert hides in the Parisian Métro from a wealthy businessman's wife (Adjani), with whom he has fallen in love; from her husband's thugs; and from the Métro police. He becomes part of a strange netherworld of eccentric social misfits, all living outside the law. Setting the movie in this unfamiliar but realistic world is intriguing enough, and Besson handles the action with consummate mastery. But the punk-chic style only accentuates the film's emptiness. That said, Adjani once again proves herself not only one of the most versatile actresses in European cinema, but also the most beautiful. GA

Subway Riders
(Amos Poe, 1981, US) Robbie Coltrane, Charlene Kaleina, Cookie Mueller, John Lurie, Amos Poe, Susan Tyrrell, Bill Rice.
118 min.
Not so much subway riders as underground poseurs, Poe's Manhattan melodramatists – psychotic saxophonist, sweaty cop, junkie *femme fatale*, assorted night people – do little more than stand still for Johanna Heer's stylishly *noir*-conscious camera. Every shot might come ready to be framed, but it's a frustratingly long walk through the post-Pop gallery when Poe shows no inclination to cut, and even less to encourage his cast to get on with the off-handedly minimal 'plot'. Irksome narcissism. PT

Success
see American Success Company, The

Success Is the Best Revenge
(Jerzy Skolimowski, 1984, GB/Fr) Michael York, Joanna Szczerbic, Michael Lyndon, Jerry Skol, Michel Piccoli, Anouk Aimée, John Hurt, Jane Asher.
91 min.
Like *Moonlighting*, this was shot very quickly, using the director's Kensington home as a major location. Once again the Polish crisis is central: Alex Rodak (York) is a theatrical director exiled with his family (actually the Skolimowskis) and planning an ambitious theatrical 'happening' to establish himself. While his self-preoccupation leads everyone to despair, his 15-year-old son Adam mulls over his own comparative lack of identity and plans to fly to Warsaw. Adam is played by Skolimowski's son (credited as Michael Lyndon); the film's basic idea was his, and clearly a lot of subsequent dabbling with the script is to blame for the way the various strands shoot off in all directions. The result is very disjointed and discursive (with time for a hilarious Thatcherite bank manager cameo from Jane Asher); but reservations aside, Skolimowski creates something which is genuinely cinematic. Spritely, humorous, dazzlingly filmed, the intense energy easily compensates for the often bewildered acting. DT

Succubus (Necronomicon – Geträumte Sünden)
(Jesús Franco, 1967, WGer) Janine Reynaud, Jack Taylor, Howard Vernon, Nathalie Nort, Michel Lemoine, Adrian Hoven.
82 min.
Franco, the prolific Spanish director, decks out a glossy Freudian sex movie with a mass of undigested cultural reference, and an endless series of studiously sub-surrealist dream sequences. But despite a promisingly erotic opening, he can't hide the grinding banality of the plot, which has absolutely nothing to do with the title or even 'bizarre sexual rites' (as the ads claimed). In fact, it's a standard 'girl commits murder in a trance' situation which will have you sunk in boredom within a very few minutes. DP

Such a Gorgeous Kid Like Me
see Belle Fille comme moi, Une

Such a Pretty Little Beach
see Si Jolie Petite Plage, Une

Such Good Friends
(Otto Preminger, 1971, US) Dyan Cannon, James Coco, Jennifer O'Neill, Ken Howard, Nina Foch, Lawrence Luckinbill, Louise Lasser, Burgess Meredith, Sam Levene, Rita Gam, Nancy Guild.
102 min.

Made in the same year as *The Hospital*, but the script by Esther Dale (Elaine May) is less of a medical exposé than Chayevsky's for the Arthur Hiller film, more of a brittle comedy about the rich at play while one of their number (Luckinbill) slowly dies in hospital after a simple operation – to remove a mole on his neck – goes disastrously wrong. Sadly, Preminger seems unsure whether to take May's characters at face value or to 'feel' for them. As a result, the cardboard emotions of Cannon (the wife seeking revenge for her dying husband's newly-discovered infidelities) and Coco (the family doctor who is losing his patient) are too often taken for real, and the script's brilliantly witty cameos are shunted too quickly out of sight. PH

Sudden Death
(Peter Hyams, 1995, US) Jean-Claude Van Damme, Powers Boothe, Raymond J Barry, Whittni Wright, Ross Malinger, Dorian Harewood.
110 min.
Reuniting Hyams and Van Damme, director and star of *Timecop*, this spectacular nail-biter exploits their combined, if limited, abilities to the full. As 17,000 fans cheer on their ice hockey teams in Pittsburgh's magnificent Civic Arena, ruthless smoothie Joshua Foss (Boothe) and *his* team infiltrate the owner's box and kidnap the US Vice President. Foss's demands include the electronic transfer of frozen foreign-government funds, allowing hi-tech thief Boothe to siphon off a cool $500 million. Unless these fiscal transactions are completed before the game ends, bombs planted all over the stadium will explode. Foss however, has not reckoned with Darren McCord (Van Damme), a haunted ex-fireman turned security guard whose young son and daughter are in the crowd. Fortunately, McCord has seen *Die Hard* and *Under Siege*, so he's able to use his hand-me-down Bruce Willis-like quips and Steven Seagal-style booby traps to frustrate Foss's plans. As always, Van Damme's at his best when cracking heads; his overplaying of the caring, sensitive father role, on the other hand, is irksome in the extreme. NF

Sudden Fear
(David Miller, 1952, US) Joan Crawford, Jack Palance, Gloria Grahame, Bruce Bennett, Virginia Huston, Mike Connors.
110 min. b/w.
Definitely a walk on the wild side, this has Crawford as a well-heeled playwright sacking hatchet-faced Palance from her latest production as lacking the right romantic personality, then falling for him in a whirlwind courtship when they 'happen' to meet on a train. Cue for a deadly cat-and-mouse game as Palance, aided by sulky Grahame, sets out to kill Crawford for her money and she uses her playwright's wiles to devise a counterplot. With suspense screwed way beyond the sticking point, superb camerawork from Charles Lang, and Crawford in nerve-janglingly extravagant form, it's hugely enjoyable. TM

Sudden Fortune of the Good People of Kombach, The (Der plötzliche Reichtum der armen Leute von Kombach)
(Volker Schlöndorff, 1970, WGer) Georg Lehn, Reinhard Hauff, Karl-Josef Kramer.
102 min.
In 1819, a desperate band of Hessian peasants hold up a tax-wagon, only to find their sudden wealth even more dangerous than the threat of starvation that provoked them; they have brought the full legal, intellectual and moral weight of the ruling class down upon themselves, and they have no defences. Schlöndorff chronicles the situation rather than the individual characters, and uses elements like an anachronistic score to undercut a merely emotional involvement. His analysis of the events as a chapter in an ongoing class struggle tends to the obvious; the movie functions best as a kick in the teeth to the romantic notion of jolly rustics. Bonus for collectors: Fassbinder appears in a tiny bit part. TR

Sudden Impact
(Clint Eastwood, 1983, US) Clint Eastwood, Sondra Locke, Pat Hingle, Bradford Dillman, Paul Drake, Audrie J Neenan, Jack Thibeau.
117 min.

It's the man again; back with a flatulent dog and his brand new .44 Magnum Automatic, investigating the trail of a corpse with 'a .38 calibre vasectomy' and a woman on a rape revenge crusade. This, the fourth of the *Dirty Harry* cycle, finds Clint as the usual pillar of troubled infuriation, his brows creased even more deeply by the usual dilemmas of inadmissible evidence and consequent vigilante justice; the villains are the standard Hollywood collection of unshaven lowlife, lesbians and giggling psychos bent upon the familiar course of distressing the more gentle citizenry ('One false move and the retard's brains get spread across the wall'). It seems rather pointless to cry Fascist once more in the looming face of Inspector Harry Callahan. The real problem here is technical; Eastwood the director is far less sure-footed than he was with the likes of *Play Misty for Me* or *The Outlaw Josey Wales*. Eastwood the star needed a hit to bolster his flagging ratings; now that he's got it, maybe Harry will be put out to stud, with his Magnum. CPea

Suddenly
(Lewis Allen, 1954, US) Frank Sinatra, Sterling Hayden, James Gleason, Nancy Gates, Willis Bouchey, Kim Charney, Paul Frees.
77 min. b/w.
The title refers to a small town in California, upon which a trio of assassins descends, taking over a house with a fine parallax view of the railroad station, and making prisoners of the occupants, an upstanding suburban family (Gleason and Gates). The movie is lifted from the routine – it was made as a four-week quickie – by Sinatra's performance. When he was interested he could be terrific (*Some Came Running*, *Pal Joey*, *The Detective*). As John Baron, the nobody who became a somebody when WWII put a rifle in his hands and taught him to be a sniper, he's a strutting, sneering psycho. Even better he wears his hat indoors. He won a Silver Star for wiping out Germans. Now he's hauling down $500,000 to hit the President and nobody's gonna get in his way, including town sheriff Sterling Hayden. BC

Suddenly Last Summer
(Joseph L Mankiewicz, 1959, US) Elizabeth Taylor, Katharine Hepburn, Montgomery Clift, Mercedes McCambridge, Albert Dekker, Gary Raymond.
114 min. b/w.
From a Tennessee Williams play, an outrageous, melodramatic shocker touching on madness, homosexual prostitution, incest, disease and cannibalism, replete with enough imagery to sustain an American Lit seminar for months. On film, with Taylor as the woman who saw something nasty and Clift as the psychiatrist trying to probe her trauma, the one-act material is stretched perilously thin; but it works for Hepburn as the incarnation of civilised depravity, the matriarch trying to keep the lid on things by persuading Clift to lobotomise her niece (Taylor, whose performance suggests that surgery has already taken place). JS

Suez
(Allan Dwan, 1938, US) Tyrone Power, Loretta Young, Annabella, Henry Stephenson, Joseph Schildkraut, J Edward Bromberg, George Zucco, Nigel Bruce, Sig Ruman.
104 min. b/w.
The story of the building of the Suez canal, this highlights both Dwan's virtues and his flaws. The action/catastrophe sequences are marvellously assured without ever going over the top, as is the handling of the human drama. However, in contrast to directors like Walsh, Vidor and Anthony Mann, who use dramatic action to exteriorise the inner tensions of their characters, Dwan – who is concerned with the modest virtues of honesty and fairness – is unable, indeed unwilling, to so combine both strands of his story. Accordingly, *Suez* is a series of incidents unconnected by dramatic urgency; Dwan, quite simply, is unconcerned with the building of the canal. PH

Sugarbaby (Zuckerbaby)
(Percy Adlon, 1985, WGer) Marianne Sägebrecht, Eisi Gulp, Toni Berger, Manuela Denz, Will Spindler.
86 min.
A sweet romantic comedy, with chubby Sägebrecht playing a lonely undertaker's assistant who falls for a young knight on a shiny yel-

low subway train and stalks him in, one initially supposes, forlorn pursuit – the punchline being that her U-Bahn inamorato (Gulp) is married to a black-clad harpy and highly susceptible to a little old-fashioned seduction. Adlon paints working class Munich like Pabst on speed, in acid-drop colour and expressionistic camera angles – a kaleidoscopic visual gloss on the characters' repressed and unspoken emotions. He ponders on the feminist and fatness and the folly of cultural stereotypes in the most diverting and persuasive of ways, providing food for thought as well as a feast for the eye. SJo

Sugar Hill

(Leon Ichaso, 1993, US) Wesley Snipes, Michael Wright, Theresa Randle, Clarence Williams III, Abe Vigoda, Larry Joshua.
123 min.
Roemello and Raynathan Skuggs may be partners in drug-dealing, but temperamentally they're so different that only their mutual love holds them together. Roe (Snipes) wants out of the dangerous game they play with the Family men who resent and challenge their control of the streets, while Ray can't bear the thought of little brother leaving him to fend for himself. Something's gotta give – especially after Roe meets Melissa (Randle), a nice middle-class girl who abhors the life he's always promising to abandon. There's much to commend in Ichaso's not unambitious movie. The generally strong performances do justice to scriptwriter Barry Michael Cooper's evident desire to avoid the New Jack stereotyping of many contemporary black crime movies; the fluid camera and lush jazz score ensure that it looks and sounds classy; and much of the time the director's understatement and attention to detail are a distinct advantage. However, matters are not helped by an actorly tone, some plot-stopping big speeches, and an often sluggish pace. GA

Sugarland Express, The

(Steven Spielberg, 1974, US) Goldie Hawn, Ben Johnson, Michael Sacks, William Atherton, Gregory Walcott, Steve Kanaly, Louise Latham.
110 min.
Fugitive couple (Hawn, Atherton) plus kidnapped cop (Sacks) and patrol car take on police chief Ben Johnson in an ever-growing caravan of assorted cars, newsmen, sightseers and wide-boys out for a shoot-up in an across-Texas chase caper that has its protagonists overtaken by events beyond their control and comprehension. Despite the obvious similarity to the Roadrunner cartoon that appears at one point – both as a comedy and in the casually destructive violence employed – Spielberg's first feature for the big screen also touches on many aspects of American life and cinema: the role of the media, the matriarchal society, consumer possession, the decline of the American hero, and the increasing depersonalisation of everything. A beautifully put together, assured film. CPe

Sugartime

(John N Smith, US, 1995) John Turturro, Mary-Louise Parker, Maury Chakin, Elias Koteas, Louis Del Grande, Deborah Duchene.
110 min.
Passable if routine biopic (for TV) about one-time Chicago Mafia king, Sam Giancana, the original Teflon Don, against whom nothing would stick. But this is less a gangster film than a love story about Giancana's long-time affair with minister's daughter and singing sister Phyllis McGuire (Parker). It's hard to make someone like Giancana loveable, especially when his lavish courting technique is intercut with images of associates being clubbed to death with baseball bats. Giancana's more fascinating links through lust with the Kennedys are hardly explored, and while Turturro is always watchable as the Worm Giancana, one is hardly moved at the conclusion, which posits that the Mob had him killed because he wouldn't give up the excessively popular entertainer. SGr

Suite 16

(Dominique Deruddere, 1995, GB/Bel) Pete Postlethwaite, Antonie Kamerling, Geraldine Pailhas, Tom Jansen, Bart Slegers, Suzanne Colin.
110 min.
A young hustler, Chris, hides from the police in

a hotel room. He threatens the resident, a rich invalid called Glover (Postlethwaite): he has killed once, he says, and will do so again. Glover is entirely accommodating; in fact, he persuades Chris (Kamerling) to stay on after the storm has passed. He will provide for the youth's every need in return for the vicarious pleasure this will afford him. At first, Chris can't believe his luck… but soon Glover's jaundiced palette demands more violent stimulation. Deruddere's third film is a sleazy, degenerate and thoroughly compelling yarn, a wayward thriller which calls equally on the extremes of continental exploitation and art movies. Despite a colourless performance from Kamerling, Deruddere mines the maximum impact from the psychological power games, and the film kicks into a higher gear with the introduction of the talented Pailhas as Helen, the third side of a climactic SM triangle. It runs hot and cold – like blood. TCh

Suitor, The

see Soupirant, Le

Sukiyaki

(Junichi Suzuki, 1995, Jap) Rica Sekiya, Yuka Sekiya, Sachiko Hidari, Tamio Kawachi, Kai Shishido.
94 min.
The average Godzilla pic is closer to believable human values than this fatuous blend of soap and sitcom, which plays like the omnibus edition of a daytime TV series. The inept cook running the Boston Grill in Yokohama has twin daughters, both with romance problems: one is epileptic and sure no man will marry her, the other unsure of her love for her fiancé. A couple of oddball merchant-marine cooks come along to take over the kitchen and set the girls' hearts aflutter. Even worse than it sounds. TR

Sullivan's Travels

(Preston Sturges, 1941, US) Joel McCrea, Veronica Lake, Robert Warwick, William Demarest, Franklin Pangborn, Porter Hall, Robert Greig, Eric Blore.
91 min. b/w.
Irresistible tale of a Hollywood director, tired of making comedies and bent on branching out with an arthouse epic called *Brother, Where Art Thou?*, who sets out to research the meaning of poverty. Suitably costumed as a hobo and starting down the road, discreetly dogged by a studio caravan ready to record the great man's thoughts and serve his needs, he angrily sends this absurd prop packing; only to realise much later, while sweating out a sentence on a chaingang, that severing the lifeline has left him to all intents and purposes a stateless person. He emerges a wiser and more sober man, having seen his fellow-convicts forget their misery in watching a Disney cartoon. The film has sometimes been read as a defence of Hollywood escapism, but what Sturges is really doing is putting down the awful liberal solemnities of problem pictures and movies with a message. Whatever, *Sullivan's Travels* is a gem, an almost serious comedy not taken entirely seriously, with wonderful dialogue, eccentric characterisations, and superlative performances throughout. TM

Summer Affair, A

see Moment d'Egarement, Un

Summer and Smoke

(Peter Glenville, 1961, US) Geraldine Page, Laurence Harvey, Una Merkel, John McIntire, Pamela Tiffin, Rita Moreno, Thomas Gomez.
118 min.
Faltering, prissy adaptation of Tennessee Williams play set in 1916. Geraldine Page (Oscar-nominated) an ageing small-town Mississippi spinster gets the hots for medical student Harvey, who in turn is more interested in Hispanic firebrand Moreno. Much overwrought dialogue, but the whole thing's treated like bone china by British theatre type Glenville, and even Page is curiously studied. One for students of the thick-stirred Southern accent. TJ

Summer at Grandpa's, A (Dongdong de Jiaqi)

(Hou Xiaoxian, 1984, Tai) Wang Qiguang, Gu Jun, Mei Fang. Lin Xiuling.
98 min.

Young Tung-Tung and his little sister spend the vacation with their grandparents while mother lies sick in hospital. It's an eventful stay, but Hou never opts for melodrama, and at first his quietly amused observation of events seems to border on the inconsequential. Not so, however. What makes the film so affecting is its unflinching honesty. As boy and girl take time off from playing games to become barely comprehending witnesses to the adult world, the film examines, with precision and wit, both the innocence and the unthinking cruelty of childhood. But life among the grown-ups is no better, and the children are confronted with violence, crime, sexual passion, and the presence of death. It's a clear-eyed movie, never sentimental, always intelligent and revealing. GA

Summerfield

(Ken Hannam, 1977, Aust) Nick Tate, Elizabeth Alexander, John Waters, Michelle Jarman, Geraldine Turner, Charles Tingwell.
93 min.
Hannam remains best known here for *Sunday Too Far Away*, an intelligent outback variant on Howard Hawks's poignant Hollywood classics of male camaraderie and competitive professionalism. This follow-up also invokes an honoured movie heritage, but only insofar as it toys inventively with audience expectations of the genre patterns of the mystery-thriller. A new schoolteacher arrives in a small coastal community, to be immediately assailed by portents of unease: off-centre welcomes from adults and children alike, casual news that his predecessor has inexplicably disappeared, a violently accidental introduction to the enigmatic family at isolated Summerfield. 'You've come the wrong way' is the first line in the film, and all the subsequent atmospherics revolve around the teacher's inevitable attempt to make things add up: only to find the equation both more tragically complex and infinitely simpler than suspected. Neither as accomplished nor as affecting as Hannam's debut, but a neatly manipulative entertainment. PT

Summer Holiday

(Peter Yates, 1962, GB) Cliff Richard, Lauri Peters, Melvyn Hayes, Una Stubbs, Ron Moody, David Kossoff.
107 min.
As guys'n'gals commandeer a red London bus and head Europe-wards for sun, it's easy to mock the put-on jollity of it all, yet somehow the high spirits are infectious. And doesn't Cliff have a much lighter touch on the screen than the dread Elvis? TJ

Summer Interlude

see Sommarlek

Summer in La Goulette, A (Un été à La Goulette)

(Férid Boughédir, 1996, Fr/Tun) Gamil Ratib, Mustapha Adouani, Gay Nataf, Ivo Salerno, Claudia Cardinale.
100 min.
Tunis, 1967: Three teenage girlfriends, neighbours in a cheap apartment building, seem to embody hope for the future: one is Jewish, another Muslim, and the third Catholic. When they make a pact to lose their virginity, however, their fathers' friendship breaks down, as each blames the others for instilling loose morals in the children. Shot in a warm, amber light, this is a modest but quietly affecting re-creation of a moment of optimism in Mid-East relations. TCh

Summer in the City

(Wim Wenders, 1970, WGer) Hanns Zischler, Edda Köchl, Libgart Schwartz, Marie Bardischewski, Gerd Stein, Helmut Farber, Wim Wenders.
125 min. b/w.
Titled in English, made on a shoestring provided by the Munich film school, Wenders' first feature – 'My longest short', as he wryly put it – has a plot about an ex-jailbird drifting through Germany until he escapes, not to the America of his dreams but to Holland. Essentially, though, it's a documentary about the time and the place, and as such it's a fascinating source book for Wenders' later work. The aimless odyssey with ubiquitous rock songs; the endless shots (by Robby Müller) of landscapes and nocturnal

streets seen speeding by from the windows of cars and trains; the tangential encounters with strange friends or friendly strangers; the laments for lost movie palaces; above all, the celebration of obsessive enthusiasms, including a delightfully tangled attempt by someone never seen again to articulate the solemnity of John Wayne's association with the Three Wise Men in Ford's *Three Godfathers*. TM

Summer Lovers

(Randal Kleiser, 1982, US) Peter Gallagher, Daryl Hannah, Valerie Quennessen, Barbara Rush, Carole Cook.
98 min.
Improbably bland sweethearts Michael and Cathy (Gallagher, Hannah) rent a holiday villa on a Greek island teeming with wanton youths sporting colourful nylon rucksacks and all-over tans. The couple's fragile happiness is shattered when Michael has an affair with another woman (Quennessen), then restored when she moves into their villa and bed. For us to believe in these liberated living arrangements, Kleiser brings the women into unusually sharp relief (for this type of film), knocking Michael from the film's and *ménage*'s centre. However, by so revealing the two women, Kleiser makes us wonder why they would turn to the resoundingly dull Michael for anything. But the film plays safe, presumably a concession (like the pounding disco soundtrack) to the conservative taste of the American public, which was polled throughout the making of the film. But all this cannot entirely remove the piquant sensuality that will titillate more subtle palates. FD

Summer Madness

see Summertime

Summer Magic

(James Neilson, 1962, US) Hayley Mills, Burl Ives, Dorothy McGuire, Deborah Walley, Una Merkel, Michael J Pollard.
104 min.
Widow McGuire does up a dilapidated house in Maine as a home for her three kids. Hayley Mills, Disney's top live-action draw of the time, spreads sweetness, light and a queasy feeling in the pit of the stomach in this adaptation of Kate Douglas' novel *Mother Carey's Chickens*, but it's singing postman Osh Popham (Ives) who delivers the most memorable moment, the hit song 'The Ugly Bug Ball', in 1938. TJ

Summer of Aviya, The (Hakayitz shel Aviya)

(Eli Cohen, 1988, Isr) Gila Almagor, Kaipo Cohen, Eli Cohen, Marina Rossetti, Avital Dicker, Dina Avrech.
95 min.
A beautifully modulated, affecting film (based on an autobiographical book by Gila Almagor) dealing with the aftermath of the Holocaust. Set in a small settlement in the harsh early years of the Israeli state (1951), it depicts the summer 'holidays' unexpectedly spent by nine-year-old Aviya (Kaipo Cohen) with her mother Henya (Almagor), an institutionalised survivor of the camps who turns up on graduation day at Aviya's boarding-school. The delineation of the mother-daughter relationship is accomplished with remarkable sensitivity and restraint. That the bonding may not be easy is shown when Henya, convinced that Aviya has lice, ruthlessly shaves her hair until she resembles a camp inmate; but equally well conveyed are their tentative moves toward an expression of mutual love, despite the mother's severe emotional lurches and outbursts. Cohen never indulges in the pain and suffering of his characters, but anchors the film in significant detail, gently recalling the pressures and realities of their situation. Rich, insightful, and healing. WH

Summer of '42

(Robert Mulligan, 1971, US) Jennifer O'Neill, Gary Grimes, Jerry Houser, Oliver Conant, Lou Frizell, Christopher Norris, Katherine Allentuck.
104 min.
Zeroing in (with much of Mulligan's usual quiet sympathy) on adolescence and the moment of sexual awakening with the added weight of *The*

Way We Were type of nostalgia, this is a mess of contradictions. A surprising commercial success with its tale of the teenager and the unhappy war widow – as a sort of cry tough version of *Love Story*? – it forever misses, unlike *American Graffiti*, the heady sexual climate of adolescence to concentrate on the circumstances of the sex act itself. PH

Summer Paradise (Paradistorg)

(Gunnel Lindblom, 1976, Swe) Birgitta Valberg, Sif Ruud, Margaretha Byström, Agneta Ekmanner, Solveig Ternström, Holger Löwenadler.
113 min.
Produced by Bergman and dealing with tensions between a family and friends gathered in the country to celebrate midsummer's eve, Gunnel Lindblom's debut as a director seemed all too likely to fall foul of terminal Swedish gloom. But she is clearly too talented and sensitive to be heavy-handed about her ideas, and the film carries an affecting sense of its characters' continuing existence outside the film's time/space. From reactionary father and middle-aged doctor daughter to disturbed adolescent, Lindblom displays a serious commitment to portraying complex human behaviour and emotions. There are no facile answers here; there is as fine a depiction of family life, friendship, and especially middle-age, as one is likely to see on film. Any occasional unsureness of tone is easily overcome by superb central performances from Valberg and Ruud. SM

Summer School

(Carl Reiner, 1987, US) Mark Harmon, Kirstie Alley, Robin Thomas, Dean Cameron, Gary Riley, Shawnee Smith, Courtney Thorne-Smith, Carl Reiner.
98 min.
Genial teen comedy about a high school teacher (Harmon) on vacation in Hawaii who's inveigled into looking after an anarchic class of delinquents at a remedial school. A bit bland compared to Reiner's Steve Martin comedies, but engagingly played. GM

Summer Snow (Nüren Sishi)

(Ann Hui, 1994, HK) Josephine Siao, Roy Chiao, Law Kar Ying, Allen Ting.
100 min.
This is Hui's most wholly satisfying movie since *The Spooky Bunch* (1981) – which also, perhaps not coincidentally, starred HK cinema's greatest comedienne, Josephine Siao. Her role here isn't written as comedy (she plays a woman beset with problems at work and at home who finds herself stuck looking after her senile father-in-law, a man she's always hated), but her expertly judged playing is irresistibly comic: deadpan reaction shots, little surges of pride and self-esteem to help her through her worst moments, strategic eruptions of exasperation. TR

Summer Soldiers

(Hiroshi Teshigahara, 1971, Jap) Keith Sykes, Lee Reisen, Kazuo Kitamura, Toshiro Kobayashi, Barry Cotton.
103 min.
Using mostly non-professional actors, Teshigahara's movie deals with the plight of US Forces deserters from Vietnam on the run in Japan, centering on the culture clash between various fugitives and the Japanese who try to help them. Its weaknesses are slightly misplaced emphases in the English dialogue scenes, and a certain over-schematisation in John Nathan's script, which flanks the uncommitted central character with a racist slob on one side and a firebrand radical on the other. Its strengths, which are considerable, include a rigorous honesty about the psychology of desertion, a complete absence of sentimentality, and a meticulous naturalism in the settings and incidental details. TR

Summer Stock (aka If You Feel Like Singing)

(Charles Walters, 1950, US) Judy Garland, Gene Kelly, Eddie Bracken, Gloria De Haven, Phil Silvers, Marjorie Main, Carleton Carpenter.
109 min.
The British release title was a cruel irony, since

Judy Garland did not feel like singing. Indeed, after the six months of shooting were completed, she was fired by MGM and slashed her own throat with a broken glass. The picture added to her depression: it's just a rehash of all those juvenile Garland-Rooney affairs, with farm girl Judy outraged that her barn has been loaned to a theatre troupe to put on a show, falling in love with Kelly, and becoming a star. The undisputed highlight is Garland's great number 'Get Happy', filmed three months after principal photography and when she had lost a considerable amount of excess weight. ATu

Summer Storm

(Douglas Sirk, 1944, US) George Sanders, Linda Darnell, Edward Everett Horton, Anna Lee, Sig Ruman, Hugo Haas, Frank Orth.
106 min. b/w.
Not even Sirk's intelligence and stylish visuals can save this adaptation of Chekhov's short story *The Shooting Party* from collapsing into compromised mainstream ordinariness. The action takes place in Russia in 1912, and Darnell turns in an excellent performance as the peasant girl whose passionate affair with a provincial judge (Sanders) escalates into tragedy. The black-and-white photography by Archie Stout lends an eye-pleasing gloss to the proceedings, and the flashback device reinforces the sense of the inexorability of the characters' fates. Ultimately, though, the mismatch between European culture and Hollywood screen romanticism is just too incongruous. NF

Summer's Tale, A

see Conte d'été

Summer Story, A

(Piers Haggard, 1987, GB) Imogen Stubbs, James Wilby, Ken Colley, Sophie Ward, Susannah York, Jerome Flynn.
96 min.
Frank Ashton (Wilby), a sensitive, poetic type of chappie, and Balliol man to boot, espies rosy-lipped-and-cheeked Megan (Stubbs) a-gathering flowers on the blooming Dartmoor heather. She's a poor orphan. He's twisted his ankle. He lodges at the humble 19-roomed cottage lovingly polished by Megan's adopted aunt Mrs Narracombe (York), and love blooms, much to the dismay of Mrs Narracombe and son Joe (he of the cloth cap). Piers Haggard adapts John Galsworthy's Edwardian Wessex-set novella in suitably tasteful scenes: a dappled shot of Megan hanging out washing, frame in leaves; much wistful glancing out of windows; a lamp-lit scene of merry country dancing with the yokel peasants, where they first touch; a warm and glowing love-tryst in a cow-shed loft. Sadly, Frank is called away, but promises to return and marry, for be damned their class differences. The film is framed as a remembrance, in *Go-Between* fashion, of an older, sadder, and wiser Frank. Old-fashioned and avoidable. WH

Summertime (aka Summer Madness)

(David Lean, 1955, US) Katharine Hepburn, Rossano Brazzi, Isa Miranda, Darren McGavin, Mari Aldon, Andre Morell.
99 min.
Hepburn is a spinster from Ohio making a lone trip to Venice, desperately in search of a 'miracle'. She gets more than she bargained for, though, when she falls for the distinctly continental charms of antique dealer Rossano Brazzi. *Shirley Valentine* later shamelessly milked all the exotic romance clichés, but this (based on Arthur Laurents' play *The Time of the Cuckoo*) is an infinitely more subtle, poignant piece, with a lovely performance from Hepburn at its centre. David Lean may well have identified with this 'fancy secretary', her ciné camera always primed, for the film marks a turning point in his career: this was his first movie shot on location abroad, an experience he obviously enjoyed. ATu

Summer Vacation 1999 (Sen-Kyuhayaku-Kyuju-Kyu-Nen no Natsu Yasumi)

(Shusuke Kaneko, 1988, Jap) Eri Miyajima, Tomoko Otakara, Miyuki Nakano, Rie Mizuhara.
90 min.

This is every imagined childhood summer, and it focuses on those fleeting months when you had a crush on your most beautiful and unapproachable classmate. Three boys are whiling away their vacation in a deserted boarding school; a fourth has just killed himself because one of the others rejected his love. Then a newcomer arrives early for next term, and turns out to be a dead ringer for the boy who died. Is he a ghost? Or has the boy feigned his death and come back to work things out differently? Laying siege to the heart of the beautiful loner, the newcomer finally gets him to admit that he doesn't know how to accept affection; but this step forward unleashes jealous passions in the other two boys…Brilliantly original, Kaneko's sci-fi approach uses a lush visual style to evoke pre-pubescent feelings with great poignancy, but it also uses a precise, coiled-spring structure to snap everything into place. The result plays like a secret, stoned collaboration between Oscar Wilde and Alain Robbe-Grillet. But what makes the film truly remarkable is the casting: the boys are played by teenage girls. TR

Summer Wishes, Winter Dreams

(Gilbert Cates, 1973, US) Joanne Woodward, Martin Balsam, Sylvia Sidney, Dori Brenner, Win Forman, Tresa Hughes.
93 min.
Sensitive study of an ordinary, well-off woman's fast-cracking facade, or just a superior piece of schmaltz about a selfish woman with two ungrateful grown-up kids, a difficult mother, and a boring husband? The best thing is Joanne Woodward in a not particularly sympathetic role, constantly finding fault in others while her own weaknesses are suppressed to the level of hallucinations and dreams. But she too often gets lost in the development of the plot, which pulls out quite a few stops on the way to its ray-of-hope ending, and unwisely strays from America to Tourist London and the Continent. For those who can get over that, plus that it tries too hard to be an 'art' movie with its references to Bergman, there should be enough to appreciate. CPe

Summer with Monika

see Sommaren med Monika

Sun Also Rises, The

(Henry King, 1957, US) Tyrone Power, Ava Gardner, Errol Flynn, Mel Ferrer, Juliet Greco, Marcel Dalio, Henry Daniell.
129 min.
Lavish but lifeless adaptation of Hemingway's novel about the 'lost generation' of expatriates who hung out in Paris after WWI. King's plodding direction and the miscasting of Power as the impotent, thrill-seeking hero are major handicaps. Singer/actress Greco's sympathetic prostitute is a scene-stealer, Gardner is stunning as the lubricious aristo whom Power falls for, and Flynn – in his penultimate screen role – is delightfully self-mocking. Even so, only the occasional sequence, such as the running of the bulls at Pamplona, achieves any real excitement. NF

Sun and Rain (Taiyang Yu/ aka Sunshine and Showers)

(Zhang Zeming, 1988, China) Yan Xiaopin, Sun Chun, Yi Xinxin.
90 min.
This second movie from the director of 'Swan Song' gives the most eye-opening picture yet of modern Chinese city life. A quiet young woman drifts away from her brash boyfriend and, despite her inhibitions, develops a crush on a blowsy teenage girl. Elegantly shot and persuasively acted, it is set in the libraries, boutiques and high-rise apartments of Shenzhen, just across the border from Hong Kong... but it could equally well be Paris or Notting Hill. TR

Sunburn

(Richard C Sarafian, 1979, GB/US) Farrah Fawcett-Majors, Charles Grodin, Art Carney, Joan Collins, William Daniels, John Hillerman, Eleanor Parker, Keenan Wynn.
98 min.
Lumpy-but-loveable Charles Grodin is the insurance investigator, sniffing out a swindle among Acapulco's lotus-eaters; Fawcett-Majors (comely but coy) is posing as his wife, while emphasising that a quick bunk-up is out of the question.

Together they're in a routine comedy-thriller, which looks good but is neither funny nor thrilling, and carelessly wastes its supporting cast, with Art Carney reduced to caricature and Joan Collins on automatic pilot in a hilarious replay of her rich-bitch nympho persona. AC

Sunchaser, The

(Michael Cimino, 1996, US) Woody Harrelson, Jon Seda, Anne Bancroft, Alexandra Tydings, Matt Mulhern, Talisa Soto, Richard Bauer, Harry Carey Jr.
122 min.
When high-flying but psychically unsatisfied doctor Michael Roberts (Harrelson), on the verge of a major promotion, examines Blue (Seda), a dangerous half-Navajo prisoner, his diagnosis – Blue's sarcoma means he has weeks to live – is overheard by his patient. Roberts agrees with senior staff to transfer Blue to a neighbouring hospital, but en route Blue overpowers him and a police officer, and forces Roberts to drive him to a sacred Navajo mountain site in Colorado. As the long journey progresses – with attempted escapes, fights with redneck bikers, near-death rattles, etc – a relationship painfully develops, so that WASP achiever and ghetto no-hoper slowly come to recognise their common humanity and spiritual connectedness. But with death beckoning, where to place one's faith? In the mountain's magic or your fellow man? Cimino's film takes him back to the bonding movies that started his career, but is shot with the technical overkill and dramatic over-emphasis of his post-*Heaven's Gate* action pictures. Doug Milsome's often superb landscape photography, the generally languid pace, the pseudo-Western themes and soundtrack may give a hint of the film's would-be epic ambition, but the kindergarten psychology of Charles Leavitt's script, the implausible dramatic development and contrived emotions render it hollow. WH

Sunday

(Jonathan Nossiter, 1997, US) David Suchet, Lisa Harrow, Jared Harris, Larry Pine, Joe Grifasi, Arnold Barkus.
92 min.
A man leaves a flophouse in Queens, New York. He's greeted by an actress who recognises him as one of her old directors. He's monosyllabic, bewildered, and quite possibly not who she says he is. She takes him home. He tells her a story, about being mistaken for a film director by a woman on the street. They make love. The masquerade continues (if it is a masquerade). This beguiling first feature won the grand prize at the 1997 Sundance festival, gathered great reviews, then disappeared in the States. It's a small picture, little more than an anecdote on the surface, but immensely tantalising. TCh

Sunday, Bloody Sunday

(John Schlesinger, 1971, GB) Glenda Jackson, Peter Finch, Murray Head, Peggy Ashcroft, Maurice Denham, Vivian Pickles, Frank Windsor, Thomas Baptiste, Tony Britton.
110 min.
In effect, if not intention, a reworking of *Brief Encounter* given a gloss of modernism. In its plot (Murray Head is the detached lover of both Peter Finch and Glenda Jackson), acting (threshing limbs and facial twitching), and direction (stridency alternating with 'cool' observation), *Sunday, Bloody Sunday* is a classic example of a film running out of control at every moment, while its creators, director Schlesinger and screenwriter Penelope Gilliatt, strive for 'meaning' with little regard for the simple matters of shot-by-shot consistency, let alone formal unity. Finch tries hard as the Jewish homosexual doctor, but Jackson (like Julie Christie in *Darling*) is given little opportunity to be anything other than a cypher by Schlesinger's exploitative camera. PH

Sunday Daughters (Vasárnapi Szlüok)

(János Rózsa, 1979, Hun) Julianna Nyakó, Julianna Balogh, Andrea Blizik, Melinda Szakács, Erszi Pásztor.
100 min.
Rózsa's reputation in Hungary is founded on a series of Ken Loach-like problem pictures of which *Sunday Daughters*, a story of delinquent girls in a remand home who are fostered out on

Sundays to long-suffering guardians, is easily the strongest. Performances are passionate, and while Rózsa's direction is at times over-dramatic, there's a keen sense of social criticism on show here, which will surprise those who subscribe to the view that movies in Eastern Europe can only attack the system through allusion or allegorical comedy. MA

Sunday in Hell, A (En Foråsdag i Helvede)

(Jørgen Leth, 1977, Den) Eddie Merckx, Roger de Vlaeminck, Freddy Maertens, Francesco Moser.
105 min. col & b/w.
Although not quite as prominent a cycle race as the Tour de France, the Paris-Roubaix is, nevertheless, no less gruelling. The final stage is especially arduous: a narrow, cobbled roadway more suited to mountain bikes than highly tuned racers. Not for nothing has this section been dubbed 'L'Enfer du Nord' (Hell of the North). This documentary on the 1976 event is especially fascinating as it focuses on the tussle between three of the greatest road racers of the period: Eddie Merckx, the Miguel Indurain of his day; his chief rival and three-times winner, Roger de Vlaeminck; and Freddy Maertens, the predominant rider at that time. There's no comfort zone here: in the wet, it's muddy and miserable; in the dry, as in this particularly drought-ridden year, the bikes and support vehicles kick up huge clouds of lung-filling dust. Despite a few lagging moments, the film is most notable for its honest, home-movie structure and its informative, old-fashioned commentary. DA

Sunday in the Country

(John Trent, 1974, Can) Ernest Borgnine, Michael J Pollard, Hollis McLaren, Louis Zorich, Cec Linder, Vladimir Valenta.
92 min.
Three killer hoodlums on the run get more than they bargained for when they come up against churchgoing country farmer Borgnine, a man with his own brand of rough justice. A film that revolves around little more than a clash between the acting styles of Pollard and Borgnine. The flyweight against the heavyweight in a battle to define the meaning of psychopath: the one snivelling, giggling and spastic, the other granite-like and pop-eyed. Elsewhere it's messy and violent, but quite competently handled. CPe

Sunday in the Country (Un Dimanche à la Campagne)

(Bertrand Tavernier, 1984, Fr) Louis Ducreux, Sabine Azéma, Michel Aumont, Geneviève Mnich, Monique Chaumette, Claude Winter.
94 min.
1910, a French country house in high summer. A well-honoured painter is at the end of his working life. As usual, he invites his son, son's family, and his single daughter to visit him, and in the span of one hot day, Tavernier encompasses not only the happiness and sorrows of family life, but also subtler side-comments on life, art and the relation of one to the other. For the painter has lived through the Impressionist revolution, but preferred to hoe his own quiet furrow, away from what he admired but could not connect with. The statement is brave, for it aligns with Tavernier's own position as the leader of the mainstream in France. A mention of Renoir is no accident: the film once more returns to the solid decency and the hedonism of both Renoir *père* (painter) and *fils* (film-maker). Tavernier still shoots in a fluid transatlantic/classic style, but his forte is those fleeting moments that are happy until destroyed by reflection. CPea

Sunday Too Far Away

(Ken Hannam, 1974, Aust) Jack Thompson, Phyllis Ophel, Reg Lyle, John Charman, Gregory Apps, Max Cullen.
95 min.
Easily one of the best of the 'new' Australian films: an outback variant on the Hawksian Hollywood formula of male camaraderie and competitive professionalism, set on an isolated sheep station where the shearing sheds become both a personal and a political testing ground for notions of individualism and collectivism. Marked by an unemphatic but affecting poignancy that owes nothing to nostalgia (though it's set in 1955) or spurious romanticism, the film trades

of a resonant matter-of-fact engagement with character against any temptation to strain the material towards 'epic' statement or national myth. PT

Sundown

(Anthony Hickox, 1989, US) David Carradine, Bruce Campbell, Jim Metzler, John Ireland, Morgan Brittany, Maxwell Caulfield, M Emmet Walsh.
90 min.
An engaging modern-day Vampire Western, about a community of bloodsuckers that has settled down in the remote desert town of Purgatory, where – with the help of a visiting scientist (Metzler) – they are trying to perfect an artificial blood-making machine that will free them from their anti-social appetites. But the rebellious Ireland and his degenerate cohorts hanker for the delicious pleasures of the Old Ways. Despite the tacky bat effects and an over-busy plot, Hickox makes good use of existing vampire lore, while introducing some new twists: sun-block cream (factor 200) and wooden bullets instead of stakes. Carradine is excellent as the vampires' imposing leader, Count Mardulak, and there are good cameos by Campbell (as vampire-hunter Van Helsing's grandson) and Walsh (as an old-timer with a taste for the red stuff). The ending, too, is bold and surprising, which after 70 years of vampire movies is no small achievement. NF

Sundowners, The

(Fred Zinnemann, 1960, GB) Deborah Kerr, Robert Mitchum, Peter Ustinov, Glynis Johns, Chips Rafferty, Dina Merrill, John Meillon, Ronald Fraser, Mervyn Johns.
124 min.
Sprawling family saga set in the Australian wilderness of the '20s finds Kerr, Mitchum and his old shipmate Ustinov hoping to make a new life for themselves from the proceeds of a lengthy cross-country sheep-drive. Zinnemann's customary care for detail pays occasional dividends, but the film goes on rather too long. Sturdy performances and location work. Isobel Lennart wrote the script from a novel by Jon Cleary. TJ

Sunflower (I Girasoli)

(Vittorio De Sica, 1969, It/Fr) Sophia Loren, Marcello Mastroianni, Ludmila Savelyeva, Galina Andreeva, Germano Longo.
107 min.
Excruciating tosh in which Loren plays a bereft Italian spouse wandering over what feels like the whole of Russia looking for hubby Mastroianni, who never returned after serving on the Russian front in World War II. Much picturesque scenery and soul-searching later, she finds him with a Russian wife, a child, and amnesia. Off she slogs back to Italy to forget, marry, have a child. At which point guess who turns up, having remembered? It's much worse than it sounds. TM

Sunless

see Sans Soleil

Sunless Days
(Meiyou Taiyang de Rizi)

(Shu Kei, 1990, HK/Jap) Duo Duo, Hou Xioxian, Cheung Kin-Ting.
90 min.
Shu Kei's documentary takes as its starting point the fact of the Tiananmen Square massacre; then, just when you expect the film to start the usual trawl through personal testimonies and political protests, it takes off in a different direction entirely. The director's first person narration (spoken in English) explains: Shu Kei wanted to express his feelings of outrage and helplessness, but didn't want to make another journalistic documentary like the ones shown on TV every night that summer. so he turned to his family and friends for their thoughts, embarking on a journey that took him to Australia and Canada, London and Venice, tracing the ways in which the Beijing crackdown affected all who think of themselves as Chinese. It's a Chinese tradition to keep intimate family matters to yourself; when Shu Kei discusses his brother's decision to emigrate and his own quandary over the future of his mother, his words have the force of a full-scale transgression. The willingness to confront personal feelings with great honesty makes the film exceptionally moving, and takes it into the area previously associated with mavericks like Chris Marker, far above the grind of mere reportage. TR

Sunlight on Cold Water

see Peu de Soleil dans l'Eau Froide, Un

Sun Ra: A Joyful Noise

(Robert Mugge, 1980, US) Sun Ra and his Arkestra, John Gilmore, Marshall Allen, June Tyson, James Jacson.
60 min.
A wholly apt description of this film on the eccentric visionary Sun Ra. His noise spans and includes styles from post-bop big band jazz to the outer limits of contemporary improvisation. The joy is the totally natural, celebratory, and always danceable way Ra and Arkestra play that noise. Open ears will wallow in his amniotic funk – even those discerning solos – and rock fans will cower at his invention. There's a sly irony about his cosmic/Egyptian theories, and the interviews with his band, their involvement in Philadelphia's black community, and final, blessedly noisy live proof will leave you wondering – what if he's right? JG

Sunrise 100

(FW Murnau, 1927, US) George O'Brien, Janet Gaynor, Margaret Livingston, Bodil Rosing, J Farrell MacDonald.
8,729 ft. b/w.
Apart from its sheer poignancy, the main achievement of Murnau's classic silent weepie is how it puts pep into pap. Its folksy fable is distinctly unusual: a love triangle dissolving into an attempted murder is only the start; two thirds of the movie is actually about a couple making up. The tension is allowed to drop in a glorious jazz-age city sequence, and then twisted into breaking-point as a journey of murderous rage is repeated. But its dreamlike realism is also to be enjoyed: when lovers appear to walk across a crowded city street, into (superimposed) fields, and back to kiss in a traffic jam, you have an example of True Love styled to cinema perfection. Simple, and intense images of unequalled beauty. DMacp

Sunset

(Blake Edwards, 1988, US) Bruce Willis, James Garner, Malcolm McDowell, Mariel Hemingway, Kathleen Quinlan, Jennifer Edwards, Patricia Hodge, Richard Bradford, M Emmet Walsh, Joe Dallesandro.
107 min.
Willis gets to wear the rhinestone suits and the made-to-measure role of self-regarding actor Tom Mix, legendary big-hat cowboy of silent screen oaters. It's 1929, and Mix is saddled with living-legend gunslinging marshal Wyatt Earp (Garner, a delight throughout), who is drafted in as Technical Advisor by the sadistic, manipulative studio boss (McDowell) to help Mix cope with the threat of the new talkies. From here on in, we're into a Tinseltown detective romp involving the murdered proprietress of the famous Candy Store, an array of vintage cars, in-jokes, and arcane and Kenneth Anger-ry allusions to the Golden Days of Hollywood. All complete nonsense, of course, with Willis grinning, prancing and tango-dancing himself into ridiculousness, while Garner upstages him with wit, mastery, drapes and ribbon tie. For a comedy, it rarely raises a laugh and soon runs out of steam; but for an hour, it's great entertainment. WH

Sunset Boulevard 100

(Billy Wilder, 1950, US) Gloria Swanson, William Holden, Erich von Stroheim, Nancy Olsen, Fred Clark, Jack Webb, Cecil B DeMille, Buster Keaton, Hedda Hopper.
111 min. b/w.
One of Wilder's finest, and certainly the blackest of all Hollywood's scab-scratching accounts of itself, this establishes its relentless acidity in the opening scene by having the story related by a corpse floating face-down in a Hollywood swimming-pool. What follows in flashback is a tale of humiliation, exploitation, and dashed dreams, as a feckless, bankrupt screenwriter (Holden) pulls into a crumbling mansion in search of refuge from his creditors, and becomes inextricably entangled in the possessive web woven by a faded star of the silents (Swanson), who is high on hopes of a comeback and heading for outright insanity. The performances are suitably sordid, the direction precise, the camerawork appropriately *noir*, and the memorably sour script sounds bitter-sweet echoes of the Golden Age of Tinseltown (with has-beens Keaton, HB Warner and Anna Q Nilsson appearing in a brief card-game scene). It's all deliriously dark and nightmarish, its only shortcoming being its cynical lack of faith in humanity: only von Stroheim, superb as Swanson's devotedly watchful butler Max, manages to make us feel the tragedy on view. GA

Sunsets

(Michael Idemoto/Eric Nakamura, 1997, US) Josh Brand, Nicholas Constant, Michael Idemoto.
98 min. b/w.
Co-directed by the editor of *Giant Robot* magazine, this account of three young men growing up bored and drunk in Watsonville, California, fits into the long line of male rite-of-passage movies which stretches back to Fellini's *I Vitelloni*. The three friends have varied racial origins: Gary is white trash, constantly in and out of jail on assault charges; Dave is Hispanic, damaged by a bad love affair and stuck working in a comic-book store; and Mark is Japanese-American, the brainy one who'll leave for college in San Francisco after the summer. Shot in extended takes (16mm, b/w) which throw a lot of weight on the actors, the film's stylistic purity makes it unexpectedly compelling. And as a sketch of the mediocrity of the California backwoods, it's smarter and more credible than anything Gregg Araki has come up with. TR

Sunshine

(Joseph Sargent, 1973, US) Cristina Raines, Cliff De Young, Meg Foster, Brenda Vaccaro, Billy Mumy, Corey Fischer.
103 min.
Based on a true story and originally made for TV (where it ran 130 minutes), this contains some redeeming features behind its blandness. At worst it's the *Love Story* of the Woodstock generation, with its couple and their alternative society patronisingly depicted for a mass audience (John Denver's songs being entirely consistent with this vision). Its plot – young, beautiful mother, dying from a malignant tumour – for the most part places the film firmly in the realms of Hollywood's Terminal Casebook. However, Carol Sobieski's script manages to hint at deeper things. Kate, the heroine (Raines), appears sympathetic and misguided in turns, and the tensions that her illness cause are treated with some integrity. Equally, the sustained and irritating zaniness of her husband (De Young) in the face of something he can't and doesn't want to comprehend is absolutely right. She is left recording her thoughts into a tape recorder while he has an affair with the neighbour. That she dies a human being, rather than in the angelic limbo usually reserved for such occasions, remains some sort of achievement. But the valid confusions of the script become dissipated by the direction. Thus, in the context of Sargent's pedestrian direction, Kate's 'Life was just so incredibly beautiful' takes on an unintended irony. CPe

Sunshine Part II
(aka My Sweet Lady)

(Daniel Haller/John Badham/Leon Benson/Robert Day/Joseph Sargent, 1973/75, US) Cliff De Young, Elizabeth Cheshire, Bill Mumy, Meg Foster, Corey Fischer, Cristina Raines.
94 min.
After Kate's death, husband Sam (De Young) struggles without success to bring up his step-daughter Jill; they decamp to a dilapidated houseboat somewhere in the Canadian West; the boat breaks its moorings and Sam contracts pneumonia swimming ashore; girlfriend Nora (Foster), a free spirit, repeatedly turns down Sam's offers of marriage; at the close, Jill tells her dad she doesn't need a new mother – like him, she's sustained by the memory of Kate. A mawkish compilation of flashbacks to Part I and clips from the TV soap which sprang from it: Jill will doubtless grow into an '80s high-achiever, while the witless Sam will probably continue to strum his guitar into old age and beyond. JPy

Sunshine and Showers

see Sun and Rain

Sunshine Boys, The

(Herbert Ross, 1975, US) Walter Matthau,
George Burns, Richard Benjamin, Carol
Arthur, Lee Meredith, F Murray Abraham,
Howard Hesseman, Fritz Feld.
111 min.
Relatively young actors playing old men is usually an excuse for some indulgent theatricals,
and Matthau's 70-year-old is unfortunately no
exception. George Burns was tempted out of
retirement (when Jack Benny died) to appear
alongside him in this Neil Simon comedy about
two old boys reviving their vaudeville act –
despite a mutual loathing – for the sake of posterity and a TV spectacular; a winning enough
formula for a hit and a couple of Oscar nominations, but the film still disappoints. The ponderous direction is a good deal less spritely than the
80-year-old Burns, and though it correctly
ignores the script's fumbling attempts to confront old age, it places far too much emphasis on
the performances. Matthau overplays his
grouchiness dreadfully. At least Burns is an old
man, but more than that, his glint-eyed, deadpan
performance is the only natural element in an
otherwise contrived and over-theatrical picture.
CPe

Sun Shines Bright, The

(John Ford, 1953, US) Charles Winninger,
Arleen Whelan, John Russell, Stepin Fetchit,
Jane Darwell, Grant Withers, Russell Simpson.
92 min.
Usually cited as Ford's personal favourite
among his own films, this picks up the story of
Judge Priest, his 1934 Will Rogers vehicle, and
follows the picaresque experiences of the old
judge of Fairfield, Kentucky, some 15 years on,
as the twentieth century exerts a pull forward
equal to the retrograde magnetism of the Civil
War. Winninger's judge casts benevolent paternalism over an American community idealised
almost to the extent of the Irish village in *The
Quiet Man*, but still riven with vestiges of
racism, religious prudery, and the scars of the
North/South divide, and now facing an electoral
tussle between the Old and the New. A mosaic
of Americana both sentimental and self-consciously critical, with the emphatic past tense its
safety valve. PT

Sun Valley (Riguang Xiagu)

(He Ping, 1996, China/HK) Yang Kuei-Mei,
Zhang Fengyi, Wang Xueqi, Ku Feng, Chan
Yuen.
100 min.
He Ping invented the 'Chinese Western' in *The
Swordsman in Double-Flag Town*, and the
Freudian psycho-drama with Chinese characteristics in *Red Firecracker, Green Firecracker*. This
sets out to combine the two in the self-consciously
mythic tale of a widow, her lover and the taciturn
hitman who turns up to kill the lover. If the result
is less than terrific, it's because He has to strain
so hard to avoid repeating himself; only the extraordinary PoV shots in which all colours except
red are bleached to monochrome (expressing the
killer's pathological fear of blood) are genuine
visual and dramatic coups. But the actors are fine
and the Gansu locations help, anchoring the psycho-sexual problems in credible physical details:
scorching days, cold nights, hot baths, encrusta-
tions of mud. TR

Sun Valley Serenade

(H Bruce Humberstone, 1941, US) Sonja Henie,
John Payne, Glenn Miller, Milton Berle, Lynn
Bari, Joan Davis, Dorothy Dandridge, Nicholas
Brothers.
86 min. b/w.
Forget the slim storyline which has Payne, on
tour as band manager with the Glenn Miller
Orchestra, signing up as a publicity stunt to
adopt a war orphan. What he gets is the sickeningly cute Sonja Henie, irrepressibly throwing herself at his head until she wins him away
(an unlikely story) from Lynn Bari. Tune in
instead for the band playing 'Chattanooga
Choo-Choo' (beautifully danced to by the
Nicholas Brothers), 'In the Mood' and other
evergreens, and a marvellous bit of Hermes Pan
choreography performed by skater Henie on
black ice. GA

Suor omicidio

see Killer Nun

Superargo (Superargo e i Giganti Senza Volto)

(Paul Maxwell i.e. Paolo Bianchini, 1968, It/Sp)
Guy Madison, Ken Wood ie.Giovanni
Cianfriglia, Luisa Baratto, Diana Loris, Aldo
Sambrell.
95 min.
A diabolically soporific effort, too dull to be
funny, and so lacking in imagination as to be
utterly unable to wring any mileage from its
promisingly ridiculous plot about a Batman-like
ex-wrestler (Cianfriglia) called in by the Secret
Service to track down the man behind the disappearance of hordes of athletes. Madison makes a
singularly colourless villain, and it becomes hard
to tell the automata our hero confronts apart from
the equally robot-like characters who make up
the rest of the cast. VG

Superbeast

(George Schenck, 1972, US) Antoinette Bower,
Craig Littler, Harry Lauter, Vic Diaz, Jos
Romulo, John Garwood.
93 min.
Shot back-to-back in the Philippines with the
dreadful *Daughters of Satan*, this is a surprisingly imaginative and topical revamping of *The
Hounds of Zaroff*. In this version, the Zaroff character becomes a well-intentioned medical
researcher (Littler), who is forced to use a big
game hunter (Lauter) in order to track and kill the
human animals that result from his experiments
on incurable psychopaths. The direction is stylish and ambitious, and Schenck doesn't altogether skate over the issues raised by the plot. In
particular, he reserves a memorable coup for the
climax, in which the scientist/hero mistakenly
swallows his own serum, is transformed into an
apeman, and then abandoned by the heroine to
roam through the jungle in solitary splendour. DP

Super Citizen Ko (Chaoji Da Guomin)

(Wan Jen, 1995, Tai) Lin Yang, Su Ming-ming,
Ke Yizheng.
104 min.
This is what the Germans call a *Trauerarbeit*: a
labour born of unassuageable sadness. Ko (Lin
Yang) was one of many victims of the fanatical
anti-communist White Terror of the 1950s;
imprisoned for his membership of a political
study group, he was wrecked physically by
prison tortures and destroyed mentally by a mixture of guilt, fear and incomprehension. In old age
he stumbles through a Taipei he no longer recognises, trying to make sense of the past and to
patch things up with his near-estranged daughter. The story is in essence a political melodrama,
but Wan turns it into a dignified elegy for dead
ideals and hushed-up crimes against the heart
and mind. TR

Super Cops, The

(Gordon Parks Jr, 1973, US) Ron Leibman,
David Selby, Sheila E Frazier, Pat Hingle, Dan
Frazer, Joseph Sirola.
94 min.
After tributes to real-life cops Popeye Doyle (*The
French Connection*) and Frank Serpico, comes
this rather directionless homage to two New York
rookie cops who spent their off-duty time busting the Bedford-Stuyvesant drug trade. Instead
of analysing the motives of the duo, the film opts
for investing them with a semi-mythical standing (constant comparisons with Batman and
Robin) that avoids the need to probe why they do
what they do (perhaps wisely, given the implausibility of the very similar *Serpico*). As such, a
comedy adventure that occasionally cranks into
life, especially in its amusing look at the totally
baffling and conflicting investigations made by
various departments (The Knapp Commission,
the Police Department's Division, the CLU, the
DA's office, etc.) into corruption within the force.
As for the two cops, one looks like Phil Everly,
the other like something from a Cheech and
Chong album come to life. CPe

Superdad

(Vincent McEveety, 1974, US) Bob Crane,
Barbara Rush, Kurt Russell, Joe Flynn,
Kathleen Cody, Dick Van Patten.
95 min.
Disney film devoted to that timeless source of
gags and nervous breakdowns, the relationship
between father (Crane) and teenage daughter
(Cody) just out of bobbysox into 36C cups. With
its all-American storyline and cast, it recalls happier times when Eisenhower was in the White
House and Hollywood had been given the Joe
McCarthy seal of approval. There are signs, however, that subversion is reaching even such
havens of security. Part of the plot turns around
a strike, and one scene is actually shot on a picket line. NJ

Super Dick

see Cry Uncle

Super 8½

(Bruce LaBruce, 1994, Can/Ger) Bruce
LaBruce, Liza Lamonica, Christeen Martin.
100 min.
Circumstantially low-down and committedly
dirty, LaBruce is a white-collar faggot's nightmare: an unrepentant queer who amuses himself
by fictionalising episodes from his own sordid life
and bringing them to the screen in the name of
art. *No Skin Off My Ass* was bad enough, but
Super 8½ is much worse. For one thing, it's made
with four times the technical skill and ten times
the wit of the earlier movie, which makes it, to
say the least, dangerously provocative. For
another, as the indefensible title suggests, this
time he casts himself as a major cine-auteur and
gives himself the full Fellini 'blocked artist' treatment. To be specific, LaBruce appears as a burnt-
out porno star, an alcoholic wreck supported by
his ex-boyfriend (that punk skinhead again), who
works as a hustler. Our man gets new hope for
his career when avant-dyke film-maker Googie
proposes to shoot a portrait-documentary of him,
little suspecting that she's using her Canadian
Film Board grant to finance her own pet project
Submit to My Finger. In short, it's closer to scumbags like George Kuchar, John Waters and Andy
Warhol than Fellini. Still, it's sexier than *Forrest
Gump* and funnier than *Priest*. Me, I gurgled like
a drain. TR

Superfly

(Gordon Parks Jr, 1972, US) Ron O'Neal, Carl
Lee, Sheila Frazier, Julius W Harris, Charles
McGregor, Nate Adams, Polly Niles.
98 min.
One of the most successful of the early '70s blaxploitation cycle. Coke-dealing Priest (O'Neal), so-
called because he carries his samples in a crucifix,
sinks his capital into purchase of thirty keys of
the stuff – the final deal that will get him out of
'the life', so the legend goes. Dancing along from
tacky prologue to no-shit ending, it strips the old
dream down to its last threads and then sends it
up. Notable as having been picketed by blacks on
the grounds of its 'glorification of drug-pushers'.
VG

Supergirl

(Jeannot Szwarc, 1984, GB) Faye Dunaway,
Helen Slater, Peter O'Toole, Mia Farrow,
Brenda Vaccaro, Peter Cook, Simon Ward,
Mart McClure, Hart Bochner.
124 min.
From Argo City, a chip off the old Planet Krypton,
Supergirl (Slater) zooms Earthwards in pursuit of
a stray Omegahedron (a revolving paperweight
with fabulous powers) which has fallen into the
perfectly manicured paws of the megalomaniac
Selena (Dunaway). Supergirl, alias Clark Kent's kid
cousin Linda Lee, is soppy, given to gazing wonderingly at sunsets and rabbits and going gooey-
eyed over the first chunky chap she rescues. It
might have been fun to watch the forces of super-
dom battling against black magic; but Dunaway
damps down her wickedness with a wet blanket
of campy dumbcracks, and Cook, as a maths master who dabbles in demonology, seems hopelessly
out of place. And it's impossible to feel concern for
a superperson when the worst fate that can befall
her is to get sucked into some shockingly blatant
back-projection, or trapped in the Phantom Zone
with Peter O'Toole. On second thoughts, perhaps
that is a fate worse than death. AB

Supergrass, The

(Peter Richardson, 1985, GB) Adrian
Edmondson, Jennifer Saunders, Peter
Richardson, Dawn French, Keith Allen, Nigel
Planer, Robbie Coltrane, Alexei Sayle, Michael
Elphick.
107 min.

Pretending to be a drugs-smuggler in order to impress a girlfriend, naive and boorish young Dennis (Edmondson) finds himself in a pickle when eavesdropping cops refuse to believe in his innocence. Agreeing to inform on non-existent villains, he is carted off to the West Country by surly sergeant (Richardson) and WPC (Saunders), themselves troubled lovers in a state of perpetual jealousy. This first feature by the talented Comic Strip team shows much the same vein as their TV work, gently parodying genre while revelling in absurdly petty characters indulging daft dreams of self-importance. The thriller context barely thrills, and at times the material seems stretched perilously thin, but there are some wonderful characters and glorious moments. GA

Superman

(Richard Donner, 1978, GB) Christopher Reeve, Margot Kidder, Gene Hackman, Marlon Brando, Valerie Perrine, Ned Beatty, Jackie Cooper, Marc McClure, Glenn Ford, Phyllis Thaxter, Trevor Howard, Susannah York, Jeff East, Harry Andrews, Maria Schell, Terence Stamp, Larry Hagman.
143 min.
Given the publicity hoop-la, it is easy to overlook how effectively Richard Donner visualised this revamping of the Depression-born defender of the weak and righter of wrongs. Without really plumping for any particular interpretation of the myth (or any one visual style for that matter), Donner and his screenwriters Mario Puzo, Robert Benton and David Newman (plus Leslie Newman) flip through various genre possibilities, and allow that we might see Superman as either a Big Joke or the Son of God. By keeping the spectacular possibilities open, through the opening scenes of the destruction of Krypton, and the subsequent growth to manhood of the planet's only son on the plains of the Midwest, the film allows naiveté and knowingness to coexist. Only when it goes all out for cold Batmanesque villainy in the second half does it narrow its focus and lose its way. MA

Superman II

(Richard Lester, 1980, GB) Christopher Reeve, Margot Kidder, Gene Hackman, Ned Beatty, Jackie Cooper, Valerie Perrine, Susannah York, Clifton James, EG Marshall, Marc McClure, Terence Stamp, Sarah Douglas, Jean-Pierre Cassel, Jack O'Halloran.
127 min.
This is movie-making on a less grandiose scale than before, but the combination of Richard Donner's superb original casting and visual attack with Lester's wit and his ear for sound proves a pretty formidable alliance. The basic plot (Supervillains enslave Earth) is potentially far more interesting than before, and though you occasionally miss the essential seriousness Donner brought to the subject, Lester generally replaces it with an intelligent satirical edge and some good gags. Purists may find certain things hard to take, but audiences have little cause for complaint. DP

Superman III

(Richard Lester, 1983, GB) Christopher Reeve, Richard Pryor, Jackie Cooper, Marc McClure, Annette O'Toole, Annie Ross, Pamela Stephenson, Robert Vaughn, Margot Kidder.
125 min.
A splendid opening during the credits, with Lester displaying his dazzling skills in perfectly timed slapstick, sets the tone for the most satirical of the series so far. Here our superhero undergoes a psychotic reversal and turns into a real sleazo as he comes up against a megalomaniac tycoon (Vaughn in fine form) who is using computer wizard Pryor as an accomplice in his attempts to take over the world and destroy Superman. Unfortunately the pacy humour of the first half soon dwindles to a weak climax, and Pryor hams shamelessly, yet again proving that he's best in serious parts or as a stand-up man. Enjoyable, nevertheless. GA

Superman IV:
The Quest for Peace

(Sidney J Furie, 1987, US) Christopher Reeve, Gene Hackman, Jackie Cooper, Marc McClure, Jon Cryer, Sam Wanamaker, Mariel Hemingway, Margot Kidder, Mark Pillow.
93 min.

About as dreary as a summit conference in Belgium. Moved by a schoolboy's letter requesting him to intervene in the nuclear arms race, Superman whizzes about the ionosphere bagging up missiles unilaterally. Once again Lex Luthor (Hackman) is his implacable enemy, and clones Nuclear Man (Pillow) from a single strand of the Caped Crusader's hair, stolen from a museum. Unfortunately, since both titans are subject to energy crises, the clash in outer space resembles a push-fight between sea cucumbers. The flight sequences seem more shuddery around the edges than usual, and special effects in general are half-hearted. Worst of all, the story lacks momentum to a degree. There's a weedy subplot in which Warfield's daughter (Hemingway) falls for Clark to beef up the flagging yearnings of Lois Lane (Kidder) for Superman, but the comic possibilities of a double date soon ground in tiresome quick costume changes. BC

Super Mario Bros.

(Rocky Morton/Annabel Jankel, 1993, US) Bob Hoskins, John Leguizamo, Dennis Hopper, Samantha Mathis, Fiona Shaw, Fisher Stevens.
104 min.
The Mario industry is the biggest outpouring of the computer age – and all from the ramblings of two Brooklyn plumbers of Italian extraction, who spend their time leaping and bouncing, dodging turtles and dinosaurs. What do punters reap for 48 million bucks? Hoskins mugging in a romper-suit; Hopper mugging as a Lizard King villain; Shaw ditching her cred as villainess Lena; and a garbled storyline about Dinohattan, where a parallel reptilian world exists some 65 million years after a meteorite supposedly wiped out all the big lizards. Yes, designer David L Snyder has done wonders with the set; yes, there's decent photography and effects; yes, the giant Goombas are splendid. But the whole is not a dinosaur, it's a dog. It will baffle kids, bore adolescents, and depress adults. SGr

Supernatural

(Victor Halperin, 1933, US) Carole Lombard, Randolph Scott, Vivienne Osborne, HB Warner, Beryl Mercer, William Farnum.
60 min. b/w.
A rip-along Paramount weirdie that gaily yokes primitive psychobabble with spiritualist charlatanism, yet concedes to the afterlife all the important plot interventions. Supernatural was the only big studio outing for the unsung Halperin brothers (Victor Hugo directing, Edward producing), whose low-budget toils had paid off the previous year with the poetic horror classic White Zombie. Here a mourning Lombard falls prey to a fake medium, while her doctor's dabblings lead to her possession by the evil soul of an executed murderess – seeking, wouldn't you know it, revenge on the same medium. Looney stuff, of course, but enlivened by a superb opening montage sequence (school of Vorkapich); by Halperin's toying comparisons of the trickster's art with his own accomplished illusionism; and by Lombard's half-incredulous presence in such surroundings. PT

Supersonic Man

(Juan Piquer, 1979, Sp) Michael Coby, Cameron Mitchell, Diana Polakow, Richard Yesteran, José Maria Caffarel.
88 min.
This Superman spin-off doesn't just fall flat; it's right down there with the most incoherent movies ever made. It features cod science, cod dialogue, Supersonic Man's codpiece, and an understandable air of resignation which permeates every scene. Just as Biblical B-holder lets you know that Our Redeemer shaved his armpits, so this tortuous D-flick surprises you with the information that 'Shakespeare said death can be expensive, painful and ugly'. Bombastic Cameron Mitchell plays the heavy, endlessly misquoting history's megalomaniacs so you'll know that he's one too, and Supersonic Man looks like Ted Kennedy in tights. Send back the cornflakes; this one isn't even fit for Saturday morning TV. CR

Superstar: The Karen
Carpenter Story

(Todd Haynes, 1987, US)
43 min.
Haynes examines the Carpenter phenomenon without succumbing to the sensationalism which

surrounded Karen's death at the age of 32. But in using Barbie dolls and minatures, his film pays less heed to the individual and more to the singer's status as a symbol for wholesome America. On the more intimate level, it links impossibly overbearing parents to Karen's anorexia nervosa, cutting between family rows, images of food, and on-screen text to outline the psychological basis and physical symptoms of the illness. But our emotional grasp on the subject is somewhat compromised by Haynes' methods. The use of dolls is inventive, and successfully conveys the idiocy of objectifying women's bodies, but it's also unintentionally funny to see them bobbing around on screen with voice-overs spouting deliberately clichéd dialogue. The effect is curiously distancing, and one is left with an uncomfortable sense that a real-life death is being trivialised. CM

Superstition (aka The Witch)

(James W Roberson, 1982, US) James Houghton, Albert Salmi, Larry Pennell, Lynn Carlin, Maylo McCaslin.
85 min.
A sorceress, dunked and roasted to death in 1692, returns to wreak bloody vengeance on the mortals who have the temerity to move into an empty house near her unresting place. The victims are an assortment of obnoxious teens, detectives, and men of the cloth. Their various fates range from bisection by sash window and compression by printing-press, to decapitation and subsequent auto-explosion of head in microwave oven. A competent roller-coaster ride of revoltingness, but little else... AB

Supervixens

(Russ Meyer, 1975, US) Shari Eubank, Charles Pitts, Charles Napier, Uschi Digard, Henry Rowland, Christy Hartburg, Sharon Kelly.
105 min.
Not Chapter 2 of Beyond the Valley of the Dolls, but it does find that old sexist reprobate Russ Meyer in agreeably rumbustious form. It returns to the format of Meyer's early independent successes, following its long-suffering hero as he flees across country from a trumped-up charge of murdering his wife, trying to keep his trousers and his hands clean. Things begin spectacularly with some racy cross-cutting, then get bogged down in repetitions, but eventually rally with a hilarious race-against-time finale that outdoes a dozen vintage serials. Meyer's ideas are consistently good, and the dexterity of his editing makes contemporary mainstream Hollywood look all but geriatric; applied to more substantial material, his talents could obviously have produced something really remarkable. But his gift for caricature still makes him a wittier comedy director than, say, Mel Brooks. TR

Support Your Local Sheriff

(Burt Kennedy, 1968, US) James Garner, Joan Hackett, Walter Brennan, Harry Morgan, Jack Elam, Bruce Dern, Henry Jones, Walter Burke, Gene Evans.
93 min.
Kennedy's best film, an irresistibly irreverent Western parody which starts with a streak of yellow (actual, not metaphorical) spotted in the late sheriff's newly-dug grave and starting a wild gold rush. Soon after, stranger Garner rides into the badass town, proves himself the fastest draw by shooting a hole through a rubber washer ('The bullet went through the centre'), and gets himself the sheriff's job. Beautifully played by Garner with deadpan wit, he tames the town less by his gunfighting than by his Lewis Carroll logic. A sequence in which, not at all put out by the fact that the brand-new jail has no bars yet, he brainteases the villainous Dern into mesmerised captivity – with some chalk, a little red paint, and the limitless power of suggestion – is high comedy of the first order. One by one, all the Western clichés are turned upside down and reinvented, with William Bowers' fine script proliferating enough invention and wonderful gags to make one forgive the occasional sag. TM

Support Your
Local Gunfighter

(Burt Kennedy, 1971, US) James Garner, Suzanne Pleshette, Jack Elam, Joan Blondell, Harry Morgan, Marie Windsor, Henry Jones, John Dehner, Chuck Connors, Dub Taylor.
92 min.

An amiable but rather disappointing sort-of-sequel to *Support Your Local Sheriff*, sharing the same director but different scriptwriters (here it's James Edward Grant). Conman Garner is the link, though not the same character, alighting from a train in the town of Purgatory to be mistaken for an infamous gunslinger. Unabashed, Garner adopts bumbling oaf Elam as his sidekick, with the latter delightedly playing up until the missing gunfighter he's impersonating turns up bent on settling scores ('I'm slow,' Garner assures the uneasy Elam, 'but you're slower'), and Garner meanwhile playing both ends against the middle in order to profit from a local mining dispute. Garner's laid-back charm helps to fill the gaps between funny scenes. GA

Sur

(Fernando E Solanas, 1988, Arg/Fr) Miguel Angel Sola, Susu Pecoraro, Phillippe Léotard, Lito Cruz, Ulises Dumont, Roberto Goyeneche.
127 min.
The exiled Solanas marked his return to post-dictatorship Argentina with this melancholy and enthrallingly cinematic love letter – to home, liberty and love itself. It takes the form of a long night's wandering through a city by political prisoner Floreal (Sola); freed after five years in jail, he finds he needs time for reflection before returning to wife Rosi (Pecoraro). It begins and ends with a tango, whose impassioned, poetic impact it shares: the main set is a sad café, suffused in misty greys and blues through which flashes a red neon sign ('Sur' – 'South'). An old musician sings as figures from Floreal's past pass by: the dead, the disappeared, stopping to share memories and stories, bringing Floreal up to date. He discovers Rosi has taken up with his best friend Roberto the Corsican (Léotard), and flashbacks show how these two lonely people came painfully together. How can Floreal reunite with his wife, with his life? Solanas excitingly fuses theatrical forms, song, poetry, operatic choreography, the personal and the political. The chronology may be broken, but the emotional flow is sustained, making it almost unbearably moving when morning comes and the long-separated husband and wife prepare to come together. WH

Sur, El

see South, The

Sure Fire

(Jon Jost, 1990, US) Tom Blair, Kristi Hager, Robert Ernst, Kate Dezina.
83 min.
Wes (Blair) is a boomer. 'Boom,' he'll say. 'There are two sides to every coin: win and lose.' And 'Boom!' again, to ram home the point. These verbal eruptions echo the explosion of gunpowder – Wes's only true rapport is with his rifle. Wes lords it over family and 'friends' in Circleville, Utah – the Mormon Dixie. A successful entrepreneur and a driven man, he'll pay off a neighbour's bank loan without so much as a by-your-leave, but can't accept rejection from any quarter, least of all from his teenage son during their annual hunting trip. Blair plays Wes as if he had walked off the pages of a Jim Thompson novel, but for the rest the pickings are relatively slim. There are persuasive performances, three long (baffling) Mormon texts and a leisurely sense of pace, but Jost's curious, avant-garde naturalism doesn't find much purchase on this terrain. TCh

Sure Thing, The

(Rob Reiner, 1985, US) John Cusack, Daphne Zuniga, Anthony Edwards, Boyd Gaines, Tim Robbins, Lisa Jane Persky, Viveca Lindfors.
94 min.
This eschews bratpack bleating and gross-out antics in favour of a return to the romantic comedy of manners. Cusack and Zuniga get stuck with each other en route to California. He's on his way to get laid by the lithe itemette of the film's title; she's on her way to join her straight-assed lawyer boyfriend. The ensuing relationship is entirely credible: they bicker, blow their tops, and form a fragile alliance. Funny, touching, and rather sweet. AB

Surf Nazis Must Die

(Peter George, 1986, US) Barry Brenner, Gail Neely, Dawn Wildsmith, Michael Sonya, Joel Hile, Dawne Ellison, Bobbie Bresee.
83 min.

Nadir of the 'great title, shame about the movie' genre. Abysmally uninteresting scenes of rival youth gangs hanging around on a pseudo-post-apocalyptic beach, intercut with apparently unconnected (and uninteresting) surfing footage, and occasional soft-core fumblings. Neither the 'female vengeance' nor the racial tension motifs succeed in raising even a glimmer of interest. Utter horse-shit. MK

Sur la Route de Salina

see Road to Salina

Surrender

(Jerry Belson, 1987, US) Sally Field, Michael Caine, Steve Guttenberg, Peter Boyle, Jackie Cooper, Iman, Julie Kavner, Louise Lasser.
95 min.
In his Beverly Hills dream home, successful pulp novelist Sean Stein (Caine) broods over the wrong done him by women in the alimony courts. Elsewhere in LA, dreamy painter Daisy (Field) works in a commercial art studio and wonders when she will meet the man she wants to have babies with. Then a strange quirk of fate finds them face-to-face, victims of a stick-up, naked and in bondage, at which point Stein appears to fall in love...What could so easily have turned into a sickly parable of the unimportance of money compared to Real Human Virtues in fact comes over as an exhilaratingly cynical comic view of the love market, completely undermining the banalities that usually come with the territory. Misogynistic, misanthropic, nasty-minded, *Surrender* is great comedy. RS

Surrogate Mother (Sibaji)

(Im Kwon-Taek, 1987, SKor) Kang Soo-Yeon, Lee Goo-Soon, Han Eun-Jin, Bang Hee, Yoon Yang-Ha.
85 min.
Im's first international prize-winner (best actress for Kang at Venice) is a more-in-sorrow-than-in-anger attack on the principles of male lineage and ancestor worship in the traditional Korean family. It's set in the late Yi Dynasty (late 19th century) to stress how deep rooted these things are, but its resonances are squarely contemporary. The well-born Shin and his wife are happy but lack an heir; behind his back, the family conspires with his wife to bring in a surrogate to bear him a son. Their choice is Ok-Nyo (Kang), a free-spirited girl who endures various physiological and sexual indignities (intended to ensure that she produces a boy) because she comes to like Shin and enjoy the relatively pampered life – forgetting she is there only as a servant. The emphasis on female suffering has come in for some critical stick, but Im's analysis of Confucian blockages in the Korean psyche seems all too cogent. And his mastery of image, tone and rhythm is unassailable. TR

Surveillance (Maifu)

(Huang Jianxin, 1997, China) Feng Gong, Jiang Shan, Niu Zhenhua, Teng Rujun, Zhang Xiaotong, Shi Xiaohong.
105 min.
This is a sort-of thriller, but as in Huang's 'urban attitude' trilogy the emphasis is on humour, human foibles and the fallibility of 'the system'. Ye is a hard-working security guard who has a good sexual relationship with his girlfriend. At just the moment that he's assigned to a round-the-clock stake-out, a rival for the girl's affections turns up in the shape of her handsome former boyfriend. There's plenty of incident (Ye nearly starves to death before we find out whether or not he'll get the girl), but Huang sensibly leaves some mysteries unsolved. The best thing here is seeing what he makes of a 'mystical' relationship born from a misdialled phone number. TR

Survive! (Supervivientes de los Andes)

(René Cardona Sr, 1976, Mex) Hugo Stiglitz, Norma Lazareno, Luz Maria Aguilar, Fernando Larranga, Lorenzo De Rodas.
86 min.
Based on the air disaster of 1972, when a plane taking a Uruguayan college rugby team across the Andes crashed into the mountains, and the revelations of cannibalism that followed the rescue, *Survive!* has all the ingredients for the ulti-

mate in disaster movies. More's the pity, then, that it is relentlessly cheapskate, woodenly performed, and appallingly dubbed. VG

Surviving Desire

(Hal Hartley, 1991, US) Martin Donovan, Mary Ward, Merritt Nelson, Matt Malloy.
53 min.
Seen by Hartley partly as a workshop experiment providing an opportunity to tell an unresolved story, film a rock band, and choreograph a dance number, this made-for-TV featurette nevertheless bears a strong resemblance to his feature work proper. About a lecturer in literature (Donovan) whose obsession with Dostoievsky is replaced by an infatuation with one of his students (Ward), it's packed with literary allusions, ironic wit, sparkling non-naturalistic banter, and moments of playful formal experimentation (most notably a deliciously absurd street dance performed without music). The cast of Hartley regulars makes the most of the droll, discursive dialogue, the saturated primary colours are a joy to behold, and there's the usual concentration on themes relating to trust, ambition, and the solaces and dangers of living too cerebrally. Great fun. GA

Surviving Picasso

(James Ivory, 1996, US/GB) Anthony Hopkins, Natascha McElhone, Jane Lapotaire, Julianne Moore, Susannah Harker, Peter Eyre, Joss Ackland, Joseph Maher, Bob Peck, Joan Plowright, Vernon Dobtcheff.
125 min.
For Merchant Ivory to choose the man who is arguably the 20th century's greatest artist for a film portrait might suggest a departure from their recent studies of (usually English) repression. Nobody could accuse Pablo of being a wallflower, and his at times arrogant, selfish and sexually voracious zest gives Anthony Hopkins a field day, enabling him to avoid the restraint, for instance, of his portrayal of the buttoned-up Stevens in *The Remains of the Day*. This film, loosely adapted from Arianna Stassinopoulos' tome *Picasso Creator and Destroyer*, focuses on the years 1943 to 1953, tracing the ups and downs in the stormy relationship he struck up with an artist almost 40 years his junior, Françoise Gilot (McElhone, a serene, Sphinx-like presence). For all the (episodic) scenes of furious artistic and domestic activity, the movie turns out to be about suffering, fortitude and dignity at a price – the price of living with or near this Spanish force of nature. Merchant Ivory's ability to make a still-life from a tempest doesn't fail them here. There's much to admire, not least sterling support from an accomplished cast (Lapotaire, Moore and Harker's trio of mistresses, Eyre superb as the agent Sabartes, Ackland's keenly judged Matisse), Tony Pierce-Roberts' diverting cinematography of the Paris cafés and the aquamarine skies of the South of France, and the reconstructions of the studios by Luciana Arrighi. But as the movie progresses, its lack of dramatic heart becomes more apparent; this is spectacle without a committed moral view. Watching Hopkins' Picasso is like watching a beautiful animal: a magnificent bull left to head-butt and impale with impunity the sensibilities and psyches of all who venture into his arena. WH

Surviving the Game

(Ernest Dickerson, 1994, US) Rutger Hauer, Ice-T, Gary Busey, F Murray Abraham, Charles S Dutton, John C McGinley, Jeff Corey.
96 min.
A mysterious businessman (Hauer) takes a tough, homeless man (Ice-T) from the city to the wilderness to act as prey in a deadly manhunt for a group of wealthy thrill-seekers – among them Abraham's powerful Wall Street exec and Busey's unstable CIA psychiatrist. Technically adept and capably performed, this is above average for its type (you've seen it before in *The Most Dangerous Game*), and though the downside is some excessive cruelty without much governing morality, that's a given in action pictures these days. AO

Survivors, The

(Michael Ritchie, 1983, US) Walter Matthau, Robin Williams, Jerry Reed, James Wainwright, Kristen Vigard, Annie McEnroe.
102 min.

When executive Robin Williams is fired by a parrot because his boss cannot cope with confrontations, one has high hopes. And even when Matthau's garage blows up, the movie is still amusing. But shortly afterwards, when the two stars meet on the dole queue, witness a hold-up and become targets for a hit-man, the ideas evaporate. Matthau and Williams look good on the marquees, but actually they fail to play well together, mainly because the script has not been tailor-made to their requirements. Produced by Ray Stark, it's a bland piece of merchandise. ATu

Survivors, The Blues Today
(Robert Schwartz/Cork Marcheschi, 1984, US) John Lee Hooker, Dr John, Gravenites-Cipollina Band, Willie Murphy & the Bees, Minnesota Barking Ducks, Lady Bianca.
87 min.
A 'celebration' of contemporary American blues of various hues shot at a weekend festival in St Paul, Minnesota. Live performances are interspersed with chats with some of the dozen or so featured artists. Sadly, those one would expect to excel in this context – notably Dr John and John Lee Hooker – merely go through the motions. The film leans heavily on white boys playing de blooz, such as the Nick Gravenites/John Cipollina Band, who approach their music with the subtlety of Status Quo. Others of the bar band ilk – Willie Murphy & the Bees, the Minnesota Barking Ducks – are defter, while Lady Bianca, a merry black woman, injects the ribaldry which is the life blood of fifty percent of blues. As to the interviews, several of the performers are less than responsive (some of them clearly not on this planet at the time). The most effusive speaker, Gravenites, tells how a few young men (he in particular, one infers) 're-invented' blues in Chicago at the end of the '60s. His claim to be a saviour is not reflected in the cumbersome playing of his plodding bar band. GBr

Susan Slept Here
(Frank Tashlin,1954, US) Dick Powell, Debbie Reynolds, Anne Francis, Glenda Farrell, Alvy Moore, Red Skelton.
98 min.
Powell plays a Hollywood writer (author of 'The Gob and the Geisha'), Reynolds a 17-year-old reform school girl who's supposed to be 'research' for his script on juvenile delinquency. Talk about meeting cute. This started life as a Broadway comedy and remains very theatrical, despite Tashlin's efforts to goose it into life, notably with Susan's dream sequence, a pink and blue affair featuring a sexy spider, a birdcage and a big gold key. Leading *noir* cameraman Nicholas Musuraca unobtrusively colour codes the characters, the set of Powell's apartment is a cornucopia of early-'50s chic; and Debbie is adept at delivering such lines as her hopeful 'Great additional dialogue, huh?' as she checks out one of her intended's early credits. Incidentally at least 20 seconds go by before Tashlin ventures the first breast joke, something involving an actress with an Oscar clutched to her cleavage. BBa

Suspect
(Peter Yates, 1987, US) Cher, Dennis Quaid, Liam Neeson, John Mahoney, Joe Mantegna, Philip Bosco.
121 min.
Morality seems to be the issue in Yates' courtroom thriller, but issues remain at the level of character traits, and there is no serious investigation of the alliances necessary to achieve simple justice. *Suspect* remains a routine *Jagged Edge* follow-up. Tired but tireless public defender (Cher) is stuck with a violent deaf-and-dumb derelict defendant (Neeson) in a murder trial. Prosecution (Mantegna) is nasty, the judge (Mahoney) partial, and the case apparently unwinnable, when on to the jury is drafted Sanger (Quaid), a Washington lobbyist. Used to greasing the wheels and bending the rules, Sanger starts sleuthing on his own, and progresses from being an embarrassment to being indispensable. Far from the open-and-shut case of a vagrant killing for a few bucks, the trail leads dangerously upwards, and there are close shaves among the filing cabinets after hours, and a red herring. Cher is workmanlike, Quaid excellent before he settles for loveable, Neeson unexpected, and the killer wildly improbable. BC

Suspect, The
(Robert Siodmak, 1944, US) Charles Laughton, Ella Raines, Henry Daniell, Rosalind Ivan, Stanley Ridges, Dean Harens.
85 min. b/w.
Oppression, guilt, blackmail and murder in turn-of-the-century London's quiet Laburnum Terrace – the plot specifics of *The Suspect* inevitably evoke Hitchcock's world, even if the studio choice of *noir* specialist Siodmak as director suggests a more darkly labyrinthine atmosphere. As it turns out, the generic common denominator of psychological suspense proves stronger than the auteurist imprint, and if any individual has a right to 'sign' the film, it is Laughton in one of his most engaged and engaging roles, as a sympathetic wife-killer and victim of blackmail, whose fatal flaw is eventually revealed to be his sense of simple decency. Between the characters of Laughton, his shrewish wife (Ivan), innocent *femme fatale* (Raines), a suspicious detective (Ridges), and a wife-beating good-for-nothing neighbour (Daniell), are etched some intricate moral shadings; and some teasing reflections on manipulation emerge from within the narrative, echoing the virtuoso audience manipulation. PT

Suspicion
(Alfred Hitchcock, 1941, US) Cary Grant, Joan Fontaine, Nigel Bruce, Cedric Hardwicke, May Whitty, Leo G Carroll, Isabel Jeans, Heather Angel.
99 min. b/w.
Despite a silly cop-out ending (imposed by RKO), a gripping domestic thriller with Fontaine suitably nervy as the prim young woman who marries Grant, only to come increasingly to suspect that he intends to murder her. Marred by a blatantly artificial English countryside and by a somewhat clichéd story, it's nevertheless a supreme example of Grant's ability to be simultaneously charming and sinister, and of the director's skill with neat expressionistic touches (most notably, the glass of milk). GA

Suspiria
(Dario Argento, 1976, It) Jessica Harper, Stefania Casini, Flavio Bucci, Miguel Bosé, Udo Kier, Rudolf Schöndler, Alida Valli, Joan Bennett.
97 min.
From his stylish, atmosphere-laden opening – young American ballet student arriving in Europe during a storm – Argento relentlessly assaults his audience: his own rock score (all dissonance and heavy-breathing) blasts out in stereo, while Jessica Harper gets threatened by location, cast, weather and camera. Thunderstorms and extraordinarily grotesque murders pile up as Argento happily abandons plot mechanics to provide a bravura display of his technical skill. With his sharp eye for the bizarre and for vulgar over-decoration, it's always fascinating to watch; the thrills and spills are so classy and fast that the movie becomes in effect what horror movies seemed like when you were too young to get in to see them. Don't think, just panic. SM

Suture
(Scott McGehee/David Siegel, 1993, US) Dennis Haysbert, Mel Harris, Sab Shimono, Dina Merrill, Michael Harris, David Graf, Fran Ryan.
96 min. b/w.
Vincent (Michael Harris), a wealthy sophisticate, and Clay (Haysbert), a construction worker, have met only once, at their father's funeral. So when Vincent asks his half-brother to visit him in Phoenix, Arizona, then disappears on a business trip, Clay is perplexed. But that's only the start of his worries. After dropping Vincent at the airport, the car Clay is driving explodes, leaving him burnt beyond recognition and with amnesia. Then, when psychoanalyst Shinoda (Shimono) and plastic surgeon Renée Descartes (Mel Harris) start piecing his mind and body together, as if they were (the now missing) Vincent's, Clay's enjoyment of his newly acquired riches is tempered by the fact that, as Vincent, he's suspected of murder. This first feature is a witty, imaginative *noir* thriller exploring questions of identity, memory, and the duality of mind and body. In this last respect, the seemingly perverse decision to have Vincent and Clay played, respectively, by a white and a black actor makes perfect sense,

complementing the balanced ironies and structural antitheses of the narrative. Most impressive. GA

Suzaku (Moe no Shuzaku)
(Naomi Kawase, 1997, Jap) Jun Kunimura, Machiko Ono, Sachiko Izumi, Kotaro Shibata, Yasuyo Kamimura.
95 min.
Impressionistic portrait of a dying family in a dying mountain village in Nara Prefecture: a 'nothing happens' film which rather ly cleverly camouflages its own lack of grip and focus by hinting at hidden themes (incest, ghosts) and using people from the real-life village as actors. It opens in 1971: recession is already thinning the population but Kozo Tahara (Kunimura, the only professional actor) believes that a rail link will bring new prosperity and eagerly helps dig the tunnel through the mountain. Fifteen years later the railroad is a forgotten dream, the tunnel seems haunted and the Taharas are fading fast. According to Kawase, the obscure title refers to a local bird deity; she wants to see the Tahara family as if through this creature's eyes. Somebody must buy this stuff, because the film won the 1997 *Caméra d'Or* at Cannes. TR

Suzanne's Profession
see Carrière de Suzanne, La

Sven Klang's Combo (Sven Klangs Kvintett)
(Stellan Olsson, 1976, Swe) Anders Granström, Henric Holmberg, Eva Remaeus, Jan Liddell, Christer Boustedt.
100 min. b/w.
Thought by many to be one of the best ever films about the jazz environment, this follows the travails of the members of an amateur dance band that for a moment becomes a jazz group when a real jazzman, saxophonist Lars Nilsson (Boustedt) joins them, bringing with him (the year is 1958) the tang of Charlie Parker. Slowly, however, the group retreats from the inspiring but fearful world Lars has introduced them to – here, for once, the clichéd association of drugs and jazz works well – leaving Lars listening to the music in his head but stumbling through life. Ultimately, the film holds to the romantic view of creativity, but its virtues lie in director Olsson's careful (often very funny) observation of its characters and their worlds. PH

Swallows and Amazons
(Claude Whatham, 1974, GB) Virginia McKenna, Ronald Fraser, Simon West, Sophie Neville, Zanna Hamilton, Stephen Grendon.
92 min.
Claude Whatham continues his love affair with the past, moving back from working class youth of the '50s in *That'll Be the Day* to middle class children of the '20s in this adaptation of Arthur Ransome's story, which used to be required reading for all well brought up kids. Dealing with the adventures of six children one suitably idyllic summer holiday spent messing about in boats in the Lake District, it comes over as a labour of love rather than a commercial proposition. Period detail is strong, and the children gain in confidence as the story develops, but it's probably too slight to hold the attention of either children or accompanying adults, though individual scenes work, like the meeting with the charcoal-burners, and Sophie Neville is very good as one of the kids. It's pleasant/innocuous, depending on your frame of mind. CPe

Swallowtail Butterfly
(Shunji Iwai, 1996, Jap)
149 min.
Is this meant to be self-parody? If so, it backfires; if not, it's horribly shallow and pretentious. A vaguely futuristic 'fairytale', at times reminiscent of Kurosawa's *Dodes'ka-den*, about a bunch of outsiders trying to make a go of it in 'Yentown' (i.e. Tokyo), the film opts for an alarming plethora of clichés, including the old warhorse of puttin' on a show (here a punk nightclub – cue naff musical numbers) against the wishes of gangsters and establishment alike. GA

Swamp Bait
see 'Gator Bait

Swamp Thing

(Wes Craven, 1982, US) Louis Jourdan, Adrienne Barbeau, Ray Wise, Davis Hess, Nicholas Worth, Dick Durock.
91 min.

A research scientist (Wise), contaminated while working on a government project in Louisiana bayou country, mutates into the peaceable and amorous 'swamp thing' (played by Durock). Craven tries to do this 'veggie-man' horror in a suitable DC Comics style; and with Louis Jourdan as arch-villain 'Arcane', not to mention Adrienne Barbeau (Mrs John Carpenter) as the Thing's object of desire, he's definitely on the right track. At other times, the picture is right off its trolley. The budget limitations are pretty obvious, though the money did stretch to oodles of gunk and goo. TCh

Swamp Water

(Jean Renoir, 1941, US) Dana Andrews, Walter Brennan, Anne Baxter, Walter Huston, Virginia Gilmore, John Carradine, Ward Bond, Guinn Williams, Eugene Pallette.
92 min. b/w.

Renoir's first job in America for Fox: a rather sullen affair set in a Georgia swamp which harbours snakes, alligators, mud, and Walter Brennan, a fugitive criminal with whom the hero (Andrews) becomes strangely and melodramatically involved. As Raymond Durgnat points out in his Renoir book, it's a film with strong John Ford overtones in the casting, the regional subject-matter (post Tobacco Road and Grapes of Wrath), its music, and its script by the worthy but wordy Dudley Nichols. But Ford would undoubtedly have punched the story out with more action, more obvious emotion; Renoir is content to let the scenes lie there moodily, looking a bit drab and unbelievable for all the location shooting (quite a rare occurrence for this kind of Hollywood product at the time). GB

Swamy

(Shankar Nag, 1987, Ind) Manjunath, Rohit, Raghuram, Girish Karnad, Vaishali Kasaravalli.
100 min.

Less than enticing tale of childhood in a small Indian town at the time of coming independence, taken from the Malgudi (town) tales of RK Narayan. It focuses on a 9-year-old boy, Swami, son of a Hindi lawyer, who finds his Eurocentric school lessons (Lisbon is the capital of Spain, he's told) and the sadistic religious-affairs teacher to his distaste. New pal Rajam, son of the local police superintendent, sparks arguments in the playground with assertive Mani, but all is partly resolved over a game of cricket. Episodic and poorly paced, the film is rumoured to have been compiled from a kiddies' TV series, and the politics look like street theatre. Best scenes are of the kids chucking stones by the riverside. WH

Swann

(Anna Benson Gyles, 1996, Can/GB) Miranda Richardson, Brenda Fricker, Michael Ontkean, David Cubitt, Sean Hewitt, John Neville.
96 min.

Low-key drama set in rural Ontario, from a novel by Carol Shields, with Fricker as the spinster librarian guarding the memorabilia and reputation of a local 'primitive' poet murdered by her husband. When celebrity author Richardson turns up to research a book on the dead woman, desperate to beat the ruthless academics who want a monopoly on the subject, Fricker finds her hitherto tranquil lifestyle threatened. Thanks to a firm grasp of detail and the sturdy lead performances, the film works rather better as a character study than a feminist drama about the varieties of violence inflicted on women by men. GA

Swann in Love
(Un Amour de Swann)

(Volker Schlöndorff, 1983, Fr) Jeremy Irons, Ornella Muti, Alain Delon, Fanny Ardant, Marie-Christine Barrault, Anne Bennent, Nathalie Juvet.
111 min.

The filming of Proust's massif central had been looming on the horizon for eighteen years, surely the longest gestation period of any movie ever. Proustians had been hiding under the bed ever since this latest stab was announced, directed by

a German, part-scripted by an Englishman (Peter Brook), starring an Englishman as Swann (Irons), and with an Italian (Muti) as Odette. In spite of the multi-national packaging, however, it is pulled off with a good grace and considerable emphasis on the humour and sexiness of the original – two factors that people seem to forget. Schlndorff shows an uncharacteristic visual organisation; and the clever notion of collapsing the thing into just one day in the life of Swann is vindicated by an elegiac coda which casts a suitable Proustian net over the whole enterprise. Piquant; if only for the fact that the subject matter – consuming jealousy – is rare in modern cinema. CPea

Swan Princess, The

(Richard Rich, 1994, US) voices: John Cleese, Jack Palance, Steven Wright, Michelle Nicastro, Sandy Duncan.
89 min.

This likeable animated fairytale takes the story of Swan Lake and ruffles up its feathers for '90s PC audiences. Prince Derek is about to marry his childhood sweetheart Princess Odette when he goes and spoils it all by making a chauvinistic remark regarding his bride-to-be's gorgeous looks. Miffed, Odette sulks back to her own kingdom only to be abducted by Rothbart (voice by Palance), a morphing megalomaniac desperate for her hand in marriage so that he may become ruler of her father's kingdom. When she proves unwilling, Rothbart seethes, then rages, then turns her into a swan for the hours from dawn to dusk. Derek, in the meantime, enlists the help of the cute forest creatures – a frog called Jean-Bob, a turtle called Speed, and a puffin called Puffin – to investigate her disappearance. Youngsters will find much to enjoy in the jokey dialogue, lush landscapes and comical action sequences, though not, one suspects, in the naff theatrical songs. DA

Swan Song (Juexiang)

(Zhang Zeming, 1985, China) Kong Xianzhu, Chen Rui, Mo Shaoying, Liang Yujin, Lui Qianyi.
100 min.

Zhang Zeming's beautiful debut feature opens in the early 1960s, just before the nightmare of the Cultural Revolution, and focuses on a Cantonese composer unable to get his music published or performed. His troubles with the authorities are lifelong; he entered 'New China' with an opium habit, a black mark that cost him his job, broke up his marriage, and pushed him into the shadows, where the only people who will play his stuff are a street orchestra of blind musicians. All his hopes are invested in his son, a promising musician, who runs off as a 'Red Guard' and returns ten years later a street-smart delinquent. Tracing an elaborate pattern of betrayals and disappointments, the films avoids all taint of miserabilism. The spirit running through it is that of the music itself: haunting and elegiac, but also strong and proudly rooted in traditional Cantonese culture. TR

Swarm, The

(Irwin Allen, 1978, US) Michael Caine, Katharine Ross, Richard Widmark, Richard Chamberlain, Olivia de Havilland, Henry Fonda, Ben Johnson, Lee Grant, José Ferrer, Patty Duke Astin, Slim Pickens, Bradford Dillman, Fred MacMurray, Cameron Mitchell.
116 min.

Swarms of African killer bees infiltrate a Texan Air Force base, stinging a number of missile button-pushers to death. But relax; in their wake strolls Caine, an able entomologist who has in his wallet the phone number of leading immunologist Dr Krim (Fonda). He also has the ear of a presidential advisor, and was passing through with a truckload of miracle sting-relief called Cardio-pep. 'Cardio-pep?' breathes the doctor (Ross), strangely excited. Their eyes meet. Meanwhile, the bees have brought down a couple of helicopters, sharply curtailed a family picnic, and...At this point a number of journalists, rolling in the aisles with laughter, were ejected from the press screening. All they missed was the slow death of a risibly inadequate disaster movie. JS

Swarm in May, A

(Colin Finbow, 1983, GB) Oliver Hicks, Milo Twomey, Frank Middlemass, Jack May, Charles Lewsen, Hugh Hastings, Douglas Storm, Petra Davies.
82 min.

The Children's Film Unit's third feature, this is surprisingly adult in its nostalgia for childhood (pre 'Grange Hill', prime Billy Bunter). Returning to Cathedral Choral School from his broken home, an unpopular 'wet' (Hicks) learns to his greater misery that he is to be 'bee-keeper', a symbolic role merely requiring plenty of singing. Mix the occasional melodious 'Nunc Dimittis' with some investigation into the mystery of the first bee-keeper's secrets, and you come up with a moral that tradition is a Good Thing when you know what it's all about. Finbow avoids the amateur raucousness of the earlier Captain Stirrick; and his youthful production team has evoked a fine sense of the close-up familiarity of boys (strictly no girls), summer warmth, and the lingering flow of time. LU

Swashbuckler
(The Scarlet Buccaneer)

(James Goldstone, 1976, US) Robert Shaw, James Earl Jones, Peter Boyle, Genevieve Bujold, Beau Bridges, Avery Schreiber, Geoffrey Holder, Anjelica Huston, Dorothy Tristan.
101 min.

The success of Jaws sent Hollywood scurrying for movie adventure styles to refurbish; hence this multi-million dollar pirate swashbuckler. Although Jeffrey Bloom's arch and relatively uninspired script lacks the more evocative components of a Robert Louis Stevenson story, it still manages to combine all the staples of the genre with a certain gusto: treasure, duelling, knife-throwing, ambushes, dungeon escapes, sea fights, disguise, and hints of exotic sado-masochism are all here in grandiose style, plus the usual sexual hostility between hero (Shaw) and heroine (Bujold). Shaw and Boyle (the villain) camp it up too much, but at least the pirate ship and tropical sea beaches are spectacularly real, not the tanks and crude sets that the genre has almost invariably suffered in the past. DP

Swastika

(Philippe Mora, 1973, GB)
113 min. b/w & col.

Philippe Mora's study of Nazism (using documentary material, including 16mm colour footage shot by Eva Braun) works best as a testament to the lost hopes of a duped generation, charting the slow slide from apparent peaceful prosperity to the takeover of more sinister elements; by which time the process of seduction was well under way. You realise what an insidiously high standard of propaganda the Nazis developed. The portrait of Hitler, mainly through Eva Braun's home movies, although fascinating, is less successful. It attempts to give the man a human face, but the strange washed-out colours, the repetition of footage to a point where it assumes a hallucinatory quality, and the credit sequence of a huge gold swastika revolving in space, do little to make the myth more accessible. Rather, they reinforce it. A fascinating document, none the less, that spares us a commentary, letting the material speak for itself. CPe

Swedish Massage Parlour
(Blutjunge Masseusen)

(Manfred Gregor i.e. Erwin C Dietrich, 1972, Switz) Rena Bergen, Nadine de Rangot, Chitta Coray, Claudia Fielers, Antje Schlärf.
82 min.

Purported sex comedy which raises not a single snigger and from which all traces of the sex act have been censor-trimmed. A world tour of massage parlour brothels via Copenhagen, Bangkok, Zurich, Paris, Granada and Rome, it contrives to set all its interiors in the same orange-and-blue painted office block. Producer/director Dietrich hides behind a pseudonym but will be laughing all the way to the bank: he must have had change from a fiver on his production budget. PT

Sweeney!

(David Wickes, 1976, GB) John Thaw, Dennis Waterman, Barry Foster, Ian Bannen, Colin Welland, Diane Keen, Michael Coles, Joe Melia, Brian Glover.
89 min.

For a piece of shitty incompetence, this spin-off from the seventies' TV cop series would be hard to outdo. Shot with a contemptuous disregard for focus, colour and composition, it tells a ridiculous tale of oil sheiks, callgirls and Big Deals, dressed up in everyone's favourite London locations. Ranald Graham's script is mainly to blame – how come one of the regular TV writers didn't get to do it? – with the Regan/Carter (Thaw/Waterman) relationship consisting of 'You sod!', 'You bastard!' etc.; the fictitious names – 'Media Ltd', 'The Dunchester Club', 'New Democrat' magazine – give further clues as to what the whole is like. The Bad-Acting honours are shared by Barry Foster (American) and Ian Bannen (pissed). AN

Sweeney 2
(Tom Clegg, 1978, GB) John Thaw, Dennis Waterman, Denholm Elliott, Barry Stanton, John Flanagan, Georgina Hale.
108 min.
On TV, *The Sweeney* usually got its story under way with minimum fuss, and allowed Regan and Carter to carry the show. But here Regan (Thaw) is at his most avuncular and long-suffering as he tackles a bunch of violent bank robbers, a would-be League of Gentlemen operating out of Malta. Unfortunately the film-makers (many of the TV team) can bring little pictorial or thematic depth to the big screen, opting for easy laughs, slick action, and large filler sections which develop neither plot nor character. CPe

Sweet Bird of Youth
(Richard Brooks, 1961, US) Paul Newman, Geraldine Page, Ed Begley, Rip Torn, Shirley Knight, Mildred Dunnock, Madeleine Sherwood.
120 min.
Brooks' second involvement with Tennessee Williams has Newman repeating his Broadway role as the no longer quite pristine gigolo who returns to his home town with fading movie queen (Page) in tow, scheming to establish himself as someone in the eyes of the corrupt political boss (Begley) who once ran him out of town for aspiring to marry his daughter (Knight). Like *Cat on a Hot Tin Roof*, the play gets the glossy clean-up treatment, so that Newman's comeuppance (what he hadn't realised in leaving town was that he also left Knight pregnant) no longer comes through castration, but simply by having his pretty face messed up a bit. It might still have worked, except that Brooks' direction seems a little too stolid for all the sleazy, flaming passions. These are, however, given full measure by an excellent cast. Geraldine Page, in particular (like Newman, repeating her Broadway role) is stunningly and wittily outsized in her rendition of the ageing movie queen seeking refuge in a haze of drink, drugs and sex. TM

Sweet Bird of Youth
(Nicolas Roeg, 1989, US) Elizabeth Taylor, Mark Harmon, Rip Torn, Valerie Perrine, Ruta Lee, Kevin Geer.
100 min.
Liz Taylor takes the role Genevieve Page made her own, on stage and in Richard Brooks' 1961 movie version, as the fading Hollywood idol seeking solace in booze, pills, and the arms of masseur Harmon. Retreating to his small home town, she exploits his dreams of glamour, but the threatening ghosts of his past aren't far away. For all the cast's earnest efforts, passion fails to rise, and the stature of the Tennessee Williams source material seems diminished this time round (for TV), even if modern frankness allows more of the playwright's savage vision to come through than three decades previously. TJ

Sweet Charity
(Bob Fosse, 1968, US) Shirley MacLaine, Sammy Davis Jr, Ricardo Montalban, John McMartin, Chita Rivera, Paula Kelly, Stubby Kaye, Barbara Bouchet.
149 min.
Making his debut as a director on this adaptation of the Broadway musical derived from Fellini's *Notte di Cabiria*, Fosse starts on the wrong foot by showing off with an irritating flurry of zooms, dissolves and jump-cuts. Luckily his own choreography intervenes, settling the film down and offering at least two classic anthology pieces: the superbly weary, sleazy erotica of 'Hey, Big Spender', in which a row of disillusioned taxi-dancers laconically display their wares, and the trio of bizarre fantasies ('The Rich Man's Frug') performed by a vampiric night-club dancer. For the rest, the film belongs to Shirley MacLaine, splendidly funny as the 'extremely open, honest

and stupid broad' who earns a dubious living as a taxi-dancer at the Fandango Ballroom, meanwhile overflowing with innocent love for everybody and everything and being left short of the altar by a succession of men. No masterpiece, but a generally underrated musical all the same. TM

Sweet Degeneration
(Fang Lang)
(Lin Cheng-Sheng, 1997, Tai/Jap) Lee Kang-Sheng, Chen Xiangqi, Chen Shihuang, Zhang Penyu, Lin Zhilong.
118 min.
A plaintive sax solo blows through Lin's third feature, evoking both the romantic fecklessness of Chuen-Sheng (Lee), a young man fresh out of military service with dreams of making it as a musician, and the forlorn longing of his sister Ah Fen, unhappily married, who nurses a secret incestuous passion for him. While Chuen-Sheng steals money from his father and squanders it on roach-infested hotel rooms and cheap hookers, Ah Fen decides she can't face her life any more and runs away. In other words, there's no plot: just scenes from unfulfilled lives, acutely framed and sharply observed, which work to dissect all the ways that people can fool themselves emotionally. Lin has said that Chuen-Sheng is essentially a candid self-portrait, based on the years when he was a petty criminal and jailbird; maybe that, as much as Lee's excellent performance, explains why it all rings so true. TR

Sweet Dreams
(Karel Reisz, 1985, US) Jessica Lange, Ed Harris, Ann Wedgeworth, David Clennon, James Staley, Gary Basaraba, John Goodman, PJ Soles.
115 min.
Reisz's film concentrates almost exclusively on the ups and downs of Patsy Cline's painful marriage to the aptly named Charlie Dick (Harris). In outline, this is the stuff of soap opera – rags to celebrity plane crash via grievous bodily harm – but of a superior kind. The two main performances are excellent: Lange plays the singer without a hint of condescension to her dreams of 'a big house with yellow roses', while Harris is persuasively menacing, with an inventively foul mouth. And Reisz studiously avoids any of those crashingly neat life/lyric juxtapositions until the very end, by which time even the most hardened palenecks should be sobbing into their beer. KJ

Sweet Emma, Dear Böbe
(Edes Emma, Drága Böbe)
(István Szabó, 1992, Hun) Johanna Ter Steege, Enikö Börcsök, Péter Andoral, Eva Kerekes, Erszi Gaal, Zoltan Mucsi.
81 min.
Szabó's return to Hungary after *Meeting Venus* resulted in this almost heart-breaking account of a country in transition; an intimate portrait which may lack the production values of lavish period dramas like *Mephisto* and *Colonel Redl*, but which exerts a subtle pressure and exposes raw wounds. The story revolves around two women, Budapest-based teachers of Russian who find their skills useless in a post-Communist society and adopt English as their speciality, practising consonants and staying only one step ahead of their students. Emma (Ter Steege in a striking performance) is unhappy about her married, vacillating lover, while Böbe picks up rich foreign men. As they share a room in a hostel, their friendship withstands disturbing revelations and differences which remain unfathomable. Portraying a society where anger and exploitation have replaced mediocrity, Szabó's sensitive handling of the material culminates in a meditative passage in which Emma stands in church, musing on the 'passion for love' which masks lack of purpose. 'Collective sin' may be dead, according to Böbe, but this movingly delineates the private pain of atonement. CM

Sweet Grass (Huang Sha, Qing Cao, Hong Taiyang)
(Zhou Youchao, 1995, China) Zheng Tianwei, Sun Haiying, Wang Gang.
87 min.
Another Chinese 'Western', set on the grasslands of Gansu in the 1920s, scripted by the writer of *The Swordsman in Double-Flag Town* and directed by a former assistant of Zhang Yimou.

Nothing startlingly new in the plot (young widow has to choose between two surrogate fathers for her son – one a feckless gambler and knife-thrower, the other a klutzy itinerant pedlar – and she makes the mistake of choosing the sexy one), but plenty of pleasure in the performances, the score, the widescreen cinematography, and in baroque details like a game of mahjong played with tiles the size of tombstones. TR

Sweethearts
(Aleks Horvat, 1996, US) Janeane Garofalo, Mitch Rouse, Bobcat Goldthwait, Margaret Cho, Van Quattro.
83 min.
Janeane Garofalo may have no more than a cult following here, but it's growing fast. She's the best reason to check out this near-miss, a black sex war comedy about a blind date which proves that love isn't (blind, that is). Waiting for his dream girl to walk in, Arliss (Rouse) is buttonholed by the unfashionably forthright Jasmine (Garofalo). He's looking for slender and attractive; she's up for stimulating conversation – as long as he's doing the listening. This rather static piece, written, directed and produced by Aleks Horvat, is pretty funny for a while, but loses credibility when it tries for something wilder. It's refreshing to see a woman on screen who can string whole paragraphs together; a pity she has to be a bipolar manic depressive. TCh

Sweet Hearts Dance
(Robert Greenwald, 1988, US) Don Johnson, Susan Sarandon, Jeff Daniels, Elizabeth Perkins, Kate Reid, Justin Henry.
101 min.
After 15 years together, Wiley and Sandy Boon (Johnson and Sarandon) seem to have lost their desire for each other; Wiley moves out, prompting good buddy and neighbour Sam (Daniels) – himself struggling to establish an on-going romance with fellow teacher Adie (Perkins) – to try and get the family together again. After a meandering start, the scene is set for an ensemble piece which strives to show that staying in love is a question of continuous hard work. The acting (especially Sarandon) is fine, the Vermont small-town setting picturesquely photographed, and much of the dialogue successfully suggests the awkwardness of people unable to speak openly about their emotions. Yet potentially riveting rows are abbreviated before they get properly under way, continually deflecting the pain and confusion of separation into scenes of near inconsequentiality, worsened by a dire revamped rock-'n'roll soundtrack, and rounded off with the usual mawkish ending. Not so much bad as frustrating. GA

Sweet Hereafter, The
(Atom Egoyan, 1997, Can) Ian Holm, Sarah Polley, Bruce Greenwood, Tom McCamus, Arsinée Khanjian, Alberta Watson.
110 min.
Adapted from the Russell Banks novel, this is Egoyan's warmest and, despite the sophisticated time structure of the fragmented narrative, his most conventional film to date. Holm is the big-city lawyer – with family problems of his own – who starts investigations into a tragic school bus accident that has robbed a remote rural community of all but one of its children, in the hope of persuading the parents to sue for compensation; inevitably, they react in different ways to his solicitude. Beautifully performed, edited and shot (the crash itself is extraordinarily effective), the film is certainly sensitive in its treatment of grief, guilt and anger, and strong on atmosphere. Whether it finally offers any fresh insights into how a community is changed by such a tragedy is less certain. GA

Sweet Hunters
(Ruy Guerra, 1969, Pan) Sterling Hayden, Maureen McNally, Susan Strasberg, Stuart Whitman, Andrew Hayden.
100 min.
An ornithologist (Hayden) goes on a field trip to a deserted island near the mainland with his wife (McNally) and small son, and is joined by the wife's sister (Strasberg), who is getting over an abortion; later, an escaped convict (Whitman) is discovered. A situation which may seem naturalistic enough, but the form never is: incidents are isolated, cross-relations are oblique, emotions

are unexplained. And as the narrative gradually coheres, Guerra daringly undercuts it with a series of disturbing emphases. As haunting and ambiguous as anything of Herzog's. TR

Sweetie
(Jane Campion, 1989, Aust) Genevieve Lemon, Karen Colston, Tom Lycos, Jon Darling, Dorothy Barry, Michael Lake.
100 min.
Kay (Colston) fears darkness and the secret, stifling power of plants; her teenage sister Dawn (Lemon) is crazy, throwing tantrums at all and sundry, and dreaming, unrealistically, of stardom. When the latter and her bombed-out boyfriend (Lake) arrive unannounced at the suburban home Kay shares with her equally loopy lover Lou (Lycos), all hell breaks loose. Tragedy looms. And all the aforementioned is played, partly, as comedy. Campion's first theatrical feature is a remarkable, risky exploration of the weird and wonderfully surreal undercurrents that can lie just beneath the surface of everyday suburban life, ordinary folk harbour dark, unfathomable obsessions, phobias and desires, and a familiar world is unsettlingly distorted by grotesque close-ups, harsh overhead angles and narrative ellipses. Amazingly, as she veers without warning from black comedy to bleak melodrama and back again, she manages to make us laugh at *and* like her confused, barely articulate characters, so that her *dénouement* is simultaneously ludicrous and deeply affecting. *Sweetie* confirms Campion as a highly original movie talent. GA

Sweet Kill
(aka The Arousers)
(Curtis Hanson, 1971, US) Tab Hunter, Cherie Latimer, Nadyne Turney, Isabel Jewell, Linda Leider, Roberta Collins, Kate McKeown.
87 min.
Something smells very peculiar here, and it's not just the body of his first victim which Tab Hunter has hidden in the pigeon loft. The aged beach boy, interestingly enough, plays an impotent PE instructor surrounded by predatory women. He picks them off one by one, and is gradually revealed as a pantie-collector, foot fetishist, and the type who wanks by the bedside of a callgirl dressed up as his dead mom. With his stark titles and moodily shot interiors, writer/director Hanson no doubt wanted it all to add up to a classy case history; but there's too much that's hackneyed and explicit, and too little clarification of Tab's psychosis. AN

Sweet Liberty
(Alan Alda, 1985, US) Alan Alda, Michael Caine, Michelle Pfeiffer, Bob Hoskins, Lise Hilboldt, Lillian Gish, Saul Rubinek, Lois Chiles, Linda Thorson.
107 min.
Alda casts himself as a liberal college professor whose 'Reader's Digest'-style book on the War of Independence is being made into a gross-out movie by the manic film crew who take over his somnolent home town for the summer. His struggles to drag the production back to the path of middlebrow virtue are impeded by the film's pathologically vulgar screenwriter (Hoskins), by his dotty old mother (Gish), and by his growing fascination with the leading lady (Pfeiffer). Surprisingly, all this is nearly as dull as it sounds, intermittently enlivened only by Hoskins and Caine, the latter effortlessly amusing as the production's leading man. KJ

Sweet Movie
(Dusan Makavejev, 1974, Fr/Can/WGer) Carole Laure, Pierre Clémenti, Anna Prucnal, Sami Frey, Jane Mallet, Marpessa Dawn, Roy Callender, John Vernon.
99 min.
Potentially one of the most scandalous films ever made – except that it has been little seen outside France and has not aged well. Seemingly completely episodic, the 'plot' follows the adventures of a beauty queen (Laure), a certified virgin who escapes a disastrous honeymoon with the richest man in the world to join a group of carefree sensualists. The latter are the once-notorious Otto Muehl troupe, who delight in pissing and shitting as a public spectacle. This is cross-cut with the journey of the good ship SS Survival (which sports Karl Marx for a masthead) on the Seine. Laure herself sought legal suppression of certain

shots which, in their blanked out form, ironically suggest even more sexual activity on her part. Sadly, this highly idiosyncratic melange of sex and politics, for all its liberating pretensions, only served to put Makavejev's career back a good few steps. DT

Sweet November
(Robert Ellis Miller, 1968, US) Sandy Dennis, Anthony Newley, Theodore Bikel, Burr DeBenning, Sandy Baron, Marj Dusay.
113 min.
Not written by Neil Simon, though you might be forgiven for so guessing, this is a comedy with heart. Sandy Dennis, positively twitching with charm, plays a kooky girl – beloved by everybody in a neighbourhood seemingly peopled exclusively by oddballs – who shares her apartment with a new man every month (she favours the insecure, sending them on their way with new confidence). After she and November's patient (Newley) fall madly in love, it transpires that she is suffering, Marguerite Gautier style, from an incurable disease. It all ends in a flood of insufferably gooey tears. TM

Sweet Revenge
see Dandy, the All-American Girl

Sweet Smell of Success [100]
(Alexander Mackendrick, 1957, US) Burt Lancaster, Tony Curtis, Susan Harrison, Martin Milner, Sam Levene, Barbara Nichols, Emile Meyer.
96 min. b/w.
A *film noir* from the Ealing funny man? But Mackendrick's involvement with cosy British humour was always less innocent than it looked: remember the anti-social wit of *The Man in the White Suit*, or the cruel cynicism of *The Ladykillers*? *Sweet Smell of Success* was Mackendrick's American debut, a rat trap of a film in which a vicious NY gossip hustler (Curtis) grovels for his 'Mr Big' (Lancaster), a monster newspaper columnist who is incestuously obsessed with destroying his kid sister's romance...and a figure as evil and memorable as Orson Welles in *The Third Man* or Mitchum in *The Night of the Hunter*. The dark streets gleam with the sweat of fear; Elmer Bernstein's limpid jazz score (courtesy of Chico Hamilton) whispers corruption in the Big City. The screen was rarely so dark or cruel. CA

Sweet Sweetback's
Baadasssss Song
(Melvin Van Peebles, 1971, US) Melvin Van Peebles, Rhetta Hughes, John Amos, Simon Chuckster.
97 min.
Arguably the most important black American film of its age, yet it's remained virtually unseen in Britain. In part that's because it *is* truly independent, shot on a shoestring and determinedly flouting Hollywood conventions of self-censorship. A 'Yeah Production', 'starring The Black Community', and dedicated to 'all the Brothers and Sisters who had enough of the Man', it's not what you'd call 'bourgeois art'. The story, such as it is, concerns a stud, Sweetback (Van Peebles), who's moved to fight back when two white cops casually beat up a political activist in front of him. He's on the run for the rest of the movie, with occasional stops for sex and/or further police brutality. Totally uncompromising and grindingly repetitive, the film nevertheless accumulates a kind of hallucinatory groove, with unexpected shafts of bizarre humour and vigorous, experimental new wave direction (psychedelic negative images, split screen and so forth). Written, composed, produced, directed and edited by Van Peebles, it remains one of a kind. TCh

Sweet William
(Claude Whatham, 1979, GB) Sam Waterston, Jenny Agutter, Anna Massey, Daphne Oxenford, Geraldine James, Arthur Lowe, Peter Dean.
90 min.
Taken from a Beryl Bainbridge novel, this is basically the education of the English Rose by an American *Sweet William*. She wears bras, uses the term 'queers', and screws on the floors of taxis; he uses lines like 'This is an idyll...They're

episodic'. Basically he (Waterston) is supposed to be a loveable, irresistible shit; unfortunately he comes across as neither of the first two, only 100% the last, and herein lies the collapse of the movie. For instead of feeling any sense of identification with the lovers in this 'contemporary romance', the sheer implausibility of their relationship leads to an intense sense of frustration and confusion as to which of the two – him, for being such a self-obsessed bastard, or her (Agutter), for being such a self-destructive ninny – one would most like to strangle. FF

Swept Away...by an Unusual Destiny in the Blue Sea of August (Travolti da un Insolito Destino nell'Azzurro Mare d'Agosto)
(Lina Wertmüller, 1975, It) Giancarlo Giannini, Mariangela Melato, Riccardo Salvino, Aldo Puglisi.
120 min.
The film that started the Wertmüller vogue in the States. Beautiful, blonde Raffaella of the jet-set loses her yacht while with beautiful, dark Gennarino of the working class. Their dinghy founders on a sun-soaked island. A banal political polarisation, fostered by North-South Italian antagonism, keeps them at each other's throats for a while; but it's no surprise when proximity resolves itself in a blissful, sadomasochistic orgy. Raffaella's shrill invective turns to self-abasing adoration; Gennarino gets his freshly caught fish cooked, and flower arrangements in his pudenda. Though seemingly a prettily made, pretty erotic exploitation movie, one suspects that there is value in Wertmüller's observation of the potency of sexual chauvinism. The film fails, however, through the absence of credibility and objectivity, and its refusal to move into the realms of fantasy, allegory, or even irony. JS

Swept from the Sea – The Story of Amy Foster
see Amy Foster

Swimmer, The
(Frank Perry, 1968, US) Burt Lancaster, Janet Landgard, Janice Rule, Tony Bickley, Marge Champion, Nancy Cushman, Bill Fiore, Kim Hunter.
95 min.
A largely loony but oddly compulsive allegory, taken from a John Cheever story, in which Lancaster, clad only in swimming trunks, makes his slow way home by swimming through various people's pools. Partly an abusive satire on the idle rich, partly an eccentric commentary on disillusionment and dreams, it is almost – but, importantly, not quite – nonsense. That said, it is totally engrossing, thanks to its very strangeness, and to the superb performances and the vivid location photography. GA

Swimming Prohibited (Yuei Kinshi)
(Hiroyuki Oki, 1989, Jap) Hiroyuki Oki.
89 min.
The first major film from Oki, the pioneer of Japanese queer cinema, is an extraordinary experiment in first-person film-making, related to the Japanese tradition of the *shi-sosetsu* ('I-novel'). The off-screen protagonist (played, of course, by Oki himself) journeys from the mountain resort Tsumeta, where he has a job in a youth hostel, to the Osaka suburb Suita and on to the sea. He's present visually only when his hands, feet or penis enter the frame, but editorially all the time, since his moods affect what he looks at and his tastes dictate where he goes and what he does. His behaviour is sometimes frisky, as when he approaches schoolboys in the street and asks them whether or not they masturbate yet. But his voiced thoughts are often dark, despite the hints that he's a Buddhist. A movie unique in form, tone and content. TR

Swimming to Cambodia
(Jonathan Demme, 1978, US) Spalding Gray.
85 min.
In filming Spalding Gray's mesmerising monologue 'about' his experiences acting in Roland Joffé's *The Killing Fields*, Demme simply shoots

the raconteur seated behind a table and lets him rant. Equipped only with a glass of water, two maps, and a pointing-stick, Gray takes us on a meandering magical mystery tour that encompasses poetry, humour, political education and the confessional. Linking it all is a lucid personal history of US military aggression and Cambodia Year Zero. And it is here that Gray is most powerful: tossing out outrageous analogies, images, conceits and connections for our quick consideration, he paints a portrait of genocide as perceptive as it is original, as scary as it is scathingly funny. Remarkably, Demme does the man justice, utilising only lighting, Laurie Anderson's sound images, and eminently sensible editing to bring the love, pain and the whole damn thing gloriously to life. GA

Swimming with Sharks
(George Huang, 1994, US) Kevin Spacey, Frank Whaley, Michelle Forbes, Benicio del Toro, TE Russell, Roy Dotrice, Matthew Flynt.
93 min.
Nobody hates Hollywood like the people who live and work there. Most movie-movies concentrate on the creative talent: ego-maniacal stars, hard-pressed directors, and abused screenwriters. Unusually, this film sticks to business. Buddy Ackerman (Spacey) is senior VP in charge of production at Keystone Pictures. When he says 'Jump', the ground shakes. His new assistant Guy (Whaley) is the latest in a prestigious line of dogsbodies: as Guy discovers, a year with Buddy and you're ready for anything. Even murder. Given that first-time writer/director Huang spent six years in menial jobs at Lucasfilm and Columbia, this is not so much a calling card as a poison-pen letter to the system. Ackerman is the boss from hell, a megalomaniac who wields his authority like a machete. It's biting stuff, but despite fashionably tricky flashbacks and a sour punchline, it feels a little flimsy, even naive. It's hard to believe Buddy would go for a project called 'Real Life' by one Foster Kane. Still, the picture's raison d'être has to be Spacey's 'loud and nasty' performance: he's the sort of actor who grabs you by the throat and beats you about the head without ever lifting his feet from the desk. And when he's off screen, you miss him. TCh

Swimming with Tears (Afureru Atsui Namida)
(Hirotaka Tashiro, 1992, Jap) Ruby Moleno, Shiro Sano, Jun Togawa.
104 min.
Tashiro's debut feature is a weird mix of breast-beating, social concern, museum-piece melodramatics and coolly detached style. It's one of the many contemporary movies to focus on Asian immigrants to Japan: in this case, a Filipina mail-order bride who gives up on her Japanese peasant husband and flees to Tokyo in search of her Japanese father. There are a couple of interesting plot strands (the best concerns a kindly but odd Japanese couple with a guilty secret in their closet), but the film founders on the sheer sentimentality of its view of Asians in Japan. Pity: if it had an ounce of cynicism to it, comparisons with Fassbinder might have been in order. TR

Swindlers, The
see Bidone, Il

Swing, The (Die Schaukel)
(Percy Adlon, 1983, WGer) Anja Jaenicke, Lena Stolze, Joachim Bernhard, Susanne Herlet, Rolf Illig, Christine Kaufmann.
133 min.
This could hardly be more different from Adlon's earlier Celeste, where that sombre duologue crept at a stately (not to say sluggish) pace, The Swing fairly races along as it traces the changing fortunes of a French/German family in Munich towards the end of the 19th century. It's not merely the colourful sequence of events – parties, theatre visits, hesitant romantic trysts, country outings – that hold the interest, but also the generally playful tone and the energetic, even eccentric direction, which manages to invest the most mundane of domestic occurrences with a bright, breathless vitality. The film effortlessly avoids the dull conventions of TV costume drama by means of its breezy way with narrative and its eye-catching style. GA

Swingers
(Doug Liman, 1996, US) Jon Favreau, Vince Vaughn, Ron Livingston, Patrick Van Horn, Alex Desert, Heather Graham, Deena Martin.
96 min.
This first feature follows Mike (Favreau) as he gets back into the dating game after the abrupt and unwelcome termination of a six-year relationship. An out-of-work New York actor looking for a break in LA, he's dragged out of his mope by pals Rob (Livingston), Charles (Desert), Sue (Van Horn) and, especially, the irrepressible Trent (Vaughn), who insists they chase down some honeys in Vegas. Wiser, and poorer, they return to trawl the Angelino hotspots. Love it and loathe it, this film wants it both ways. We're supposed to be appalled at the callous chauvinism of the predatory male, but also to get off on his jive, sharp suits and cool car. We do, too. It's a bit smug, a bit smarmy, but you should still see this movie, and here are ten reasons why: (i) Vince Vaughn – a louche, lanky ego salesman, he's the definitive '90s lounge lizard. (ii) Jon Favreau – a subtler actor than Vaughn, he spends the entire picture sulking, and still has you pulling for him. Plus, he wrote the script, and (iii) this is the most quotable movie since Clueless. (iv) It boasts the best answerphone gag in the history of the movies. Bar none. (v–x) Ninety minutes spent learning how not to pick up girls. This is what the movies were made for, isn't it? TCh

Swingin' Summer, A
(Robert Sparr, 1965, US) William Wellman Jr, Quinn O'Hara, James Stacy, Martin West, Raquel Welch, Mary Mitchell, Allan Jones.
80 min.
By the '60s, we'd evidently got past the syndrome of 'putting on a show right here'; but promoting one was a different matter. So the rocky road to getting the Righteous Brothers, the Rip Chords, and Gary & the Playboys on stage at Lake Arrowhead is duly traversed in this early dim-witted script from the prosaic pen of Leigh Chapman (Steel, Boardwalk etc.). On the way a certain morbid fascination hinges on the wait for Raquel Welch to shed glasses, head-band and psycho-jargon in order to swing, but you've also got to put up with a chicken-run on water-skis, and the obligatory appearance of the crooked killjoys. Given the director's obsession with bikini bottoms, this really is the arse-end of the beach movie cycle. PT

Swing Kids
(Thomas Carter, 1993, US) Robert Sean Leonard, Christian Bale, Frank Whaley, Barbara Hershey, Kenneth Branagh, Martin Clunes, Tushka Bergen.
114 min.
Germany in the '30s: Peter (Leonard) and Thomas (Bale) are devoted to Swing, record collecting and wild dancing. They aren't oblivious to the activities of the Hitler Jugend, though it takes time for the pfennig to drop. The dice are fatally loaded when it comes to fellow swingster Erwin. Bespectacled, wise, humane and crippled, he takes an inevitable early bath, leaving the two friends to choose between conformity or an increasingly risky rebellion. The dance-hall scenes have a wonderful febrility, as have the counterpointed HJ rituals. This appears to be a youth movie, but even the dumbest teen will gather there was more to Nazism than sending kids with long hair into the army. The use of token Jews turns the stomach, and it's hard not to conclude that the Swing Kids' idealisation of America is the real message. SFe

Swing Shift
(Jonathan Demme, 1984, US) Goldie Hawn, Kurt Russell, Christine Lahti, Ed Harris, Fred Ward, Sudie Bond, Holly Hunter, Roger Corman.
100 min.
A gentle romantic comedy set during World War II, which sees housewife Hawn finding her feet when hubby Ed Harris goes off to fight. First, against his wishes, she takes a job in an aircraft factory, then – after a lengthy courtship – she takes a lover in the form of hunky, helpful, hot trumpeter Kurt Russell. Hawn, atypically cast and supported by all-round excellent performances, proves that she can act. But still this bit-

ter-sweet concoction is very much Demme's: not only in the warming celebration of friendship and community values (the unsentimental generosity extended towards the characters positively glows), but also in the assured handling of period, place, music and mood. GA

Swing Time
(George Stevens, 1936, US) Fred Astaire, Ginger Rogers, Victor Moore, Helen Broderick, Eric Blore, George Metaxa, Betty Furness.
103 min. b/w.
The slow burn of misunderstanding brings Fred and Ginger together at last in the second of Stevens' three musicals for RKO, long before he got into the serious business of Shane and Giant and The Diary of Anne Frank. 'No one could teach you to dance in a million years' is typical of the irony's light touch. However, if plot, script and supporters are below par, the score by Jerome Kern and Dorothy Fields is peerless – 'A Fine Romance', 'The Way You Look Tonight', 'Pick Yourself Up', and Fred's turn with Berkeley-esque trimmings, 'Bojangles of Harlem'. And nothing Fred and Ginger did together surpasses their lengthy, climactic duet, taking off from 'Never Gonna Dance', which reminds you that dance is the most perfect sexual metaphor of them all. SG

Swiss Conspiracy, The
(Jack Arnold, 1975, US/WGer) David Janssen, Senta Berger, John Ireland, John Saxon, Ray Milland, Anton Diffring, Elke Sommer, Arthur Brauss.
89 min.
A monotonous, glossily vacuous co-production thriller that sends Janssen skidding through the scenic snow in the midst of an incomprehensible blackmail-and-murder plot involving five shadowy Zurich account-holders. Such farragos, along with stabs at softcore comedy and blaxploitation, were the dispiriting lot of veteran sci-fi/mutant movie auteur Arnold after the studio system fell apart. From the German side of the package, incidentally, comes Arthur Brauss, Wenders' hang-dog 'Goalkeeper', as a heavy. PT

Swissmakers, The (Die Schweizermacher)
(Rolf Lyssy, 1978, Switz) Walo Löönd, Emil Steinberger, Beatrice Kessler, Wolfgang Stendar, Hilde Ziegler.
108 min.
Lyssy's essentially fond, humane parody of cuckoo-clock Switzerland, in which an amiable young bureaucrat has to snoop on immigrants to see if they are 'suitable' for Swiss citizenship. British political parallels immediately spring to mind, but the humour here is more slapstick than documentary, so Love and Liberalism carry the day with little difficulty. Not exactly sophisticated (and the camerawork leaves something to be desired), but infinitely preferable to the forced, jangling misanthropy of the Italian Bread and Chocolate in dealing with the same subject. CA

Switch
(Blake Edwards, 1991, US) Ellen Barkin, Jimmy Smits, JoBeth Williams, Lorraine Bracco, Tony Roberts, Perry King, Bruce Martyn Payne, Lysette Anthony, Victoria Mahoney.
114 min.
Blake Edwards playing with questions of sexual identity again. King and Barkin share the role of a man who has his sex switched in a pact between God and the Devil. Steve Brooks (King), a sexist pig, is murdered by three of the women he has mistreated. Instead of going straight to hell, Brooks' soul ends up in purgatory; God decides that Brooks must return to earth and find one woman who actually likes him before he can pass through the pearly gates. To spice things up, the Devil insists that he must perform this feat while inhabiting a woman's body. Much simple comedy ensues as Brooks, waking up as Barkin, has to cope with breasts, heels and long hair, then returns to his/her career in advertising to face discrimination. There are some funny moments, and though she hams it up at times, Barkin is very good in her first comic role. But Edwards milks the comedy, keeps the sexual comment to a minimum, and brings the film to a silly, cop-out resolution. CO'S

Switchboard Operator, The (Ljubavni Slucaj)

(Dusan Makavejev, 1967, Yugo) Eva Ras, Slobodan Aligrudic, Ruzica Sokic, Dr Aleksander Kostic, Dr Zivojin Aleksic.
69 min. b/w.

Given that four of Makavejev's first five features are essentially the same film, it seems increasingly unlikely that he'll ever improve on this, his second movie, the most interesting and concentrated treatment of his recurrent themes. A tragi-comic love affair between a switchboard operator and a corporation rat-catcher starts out idyllic, but turns sour under external pressures; Makavejev breaks up the time sequence of his story with constant flashes forward, and brings in a lot of apparently extraneous material, from lectures on sex in art to a poem about rats. The disjunctions and contradictions yield a lot of ideas about personal freedom and oppression (especially within a 'socialist' state), and the profusion of images is well enough organised to make the movie continuously provocative and suggestive. The use of historical newsreels is finally as glib as in *W.R.*, but the emphasis on the banalities of day-to-day living is trenchant, and more than compensates. TR

Switching Channels

(Ted Kotcheff, 1987, US) Kathleen Turner, Burt Reynolds, Christopher Reeve, Ned Beatty, Henry Gibson, George Newbern, Al Waxman.
105 min.

This fourth cinema version of Hecht and MacArthur's *The Front Page* warrants only a brief mention in the obituary column. Kotcheff's workmanlike update shifts the action to the newsroom of a satellite TV station, where Reynolds' workaholic newshound is trying to lure ex-wife and fellow hotshot journo Turner away from tanned tycoon Reeve with talk of a once-in-a-lifetime scoop. The human interest angle is Gibson, a doomed convict who killed the man who supplied his son with the drugs on which he OD'd. But the supplier happened to be an undercover policeman, hence the tabloid moniker 'Cop Killer Dad' and the imminent appointment with the electric chair. Ned Beatty gets the best comic lines as the slimy DA who's also trying to manipulate the situation to his best advantage. Neither Jonathan Reynolds' enervated script nor the lacklustre performances do anything to dispel the feeling of *déjà vu*. NF

Swoon

(Tom Kalin, 1991, US) Daniel Schlachet, Craig Chester, Ron Vawter, Michael Kirby, Michael Stumm, Valda Z Drabla, Robert Read.
94 min. b/w.

The story of Leopold and Loeb – two young intellectual aesthetes, from wealthy Jewish families, who murdered a 14-year-old boy for kicks in Chicago in 1924 – has been filmed twice before. *Rope* located the roots of fascism in Nietzschean discourse. *Compulsion* was a more muddled 'true crime' saga. Kalin's film is the least naturalistic and most factual. It is also the first to expand on Clarence Darrow's argument for the defence, that the pair's homosexuality was a sign of pathological deviance; *ergo* they were not accountable for their actions. The film's second half sticks to court transcripts, to diagnose a repressive, racist, homophobic pathology on a wider social scale, endemic to patriarchy itself. Sketched in deft, sharp strokes, this is no more than a postscript to the earlier exploration of the lovers' sado-masochistic relationship: how Loeb bartered crime for sex, and how their transgressive games escalated to the point of no return. With its sinuous monochrome finish, *Swoon* is decadent and economical, subjective and detached, fascinating and appalling – conjunctions Sacher Masoch himself might have recognised. TCh

Sword and the Flute, The

(James Ivory, 1959, US)
24 min.

A documentary composed entirely of shots of Indian miniature paintings illustrating the history of the Mogul and Rajput schools. James Ivory, who became his own photographer when his original cameraman was conscripted, was later to return directly to the subject in *Hullabaloo Over Georgie and Bonnie's Pictures*, and indirectly in a number of his theatrical feature films, in which the appreciation of fine art is regarded, in a sense, as an index of civilisation (and also of greed and vanity). JPy

Sword and the Sorcerer, The

(Albert Pyun, 1982, US) Lee Horsley, Kathleen Beller, Simon MacCorkindale, George Maharis, Richard Lynch, Richard Moll, Barry Chase, Nina Van Pallandt, Jeff Corey.
99 min.

Having raised (and disposed of) an ancient sorcerer to capture a kingdom, medieval tyrant Cromwell (Lynch) naturally finds himself plagued by revolts. Director Pyun apparently trained under Kurosawa, and one might have expected some of the Master's empathy with myth and legend to have rubbed off; but there's only a clumsy amalgam of sci-fi special effects and old-style blood and thunder, with a mind-numbing thickie of a hero and a scrawny underage heroine. There are compensations, though: the real baddie, born-again sorcerer Xusia (Moll), makes a splendidly bad-tempered villain, and there are nice cameos from a bald-headed torturer, a Rastafarian pirate, and a sex-mad python; and editor Marshall Harvey stitches the messy pieces together with considerable panache. RMy

Sword in the Stone, The

(Wolfgang Reitherman, 1963, US) voices: Ricky Sorenson, Sebastian Cabot, Karl Swenson, Junius Matthews.
80 min.

A beautifully animated Disney feature, adapted from TH White's tale of the young (soon to be King) Arthur and his mad adventures with Merlin the Magician. Together with snooty sidekick Archimedes the owl, Merlin educates the boy in some of the basic facts of life. With his magic wand, he can change both himself and his pupil into anything he wishes, which results in one of the best episodes: a duel between Merlin and the evil witch Madam Mim, where they both try to gain the upper hand by transforming themselves into some of the nastiest creatures possible. It was produced by Walt himself, with tuneful music supplied by the Sherman brothers. DA

Sword of the Valiant – The Legend of Gawain and the Green Knight, The

(Stephen Weeks, 1983, GB) Miles O'Keefe, Trevor Howard, Sean Connery, Peter Cushing, Ronald Lacey, Cyrielle Claire, Emma Sutton, Douglas Wilmer, Lila Kedrova.
102 min.

Weeks' second attempt to film this subject, on a considerably larger budget than *Gawain and the Green Knight* (1973). Sir Gawain (O'Keefe), a complete drip with a Linda Evans hairdo, is the only person at King Arthur's court fool enough to accept the challenge of the Green Knight, played by Connery in a glittery wig. After the Green Knight's head is severed, it mysteriously reattaches itself to its body, and grants Sir G one year to answer a bit of psychobabble it calls a riddle. Sir Gawain then experiences Life in the form of dolly birds and battles in Tourist Board castle locations, reacting to it all with lighthearted comments like 'How the hell do I relieve myself in this tin suit?'. It is a galumphing tale of idiot chivalry – fewer laughs than *Excalibur* and less poetic intensity than *Monty Python and the Holy Grail*. AB

Swordsman (Xiao'ao Jianghu)

(King Hu/Tsui Hark/Ching Siu-Tung, 1990, HK) Samuel Hui, Jacky Cheung, Cecilia Yip, Fennie Yuen, Cheung Mun.
120 min.

Rather tendentiously credited to the veteran King Hu (it was supposed to be a 'comeback' film for the director of *A Touch of Zen*, but he left the production very early on and none of his footage remains), this actually plays like a vulgar and resolutely modern-spirited pastiche of the kind of movie he used to make. As such, it's a lot of fun: a roller-coaster ride through memories of the great Chinese swordplay movies of the '60s. It plays out the joke about an explosion in a dye-factory, and then romps through a series of gravity-defying fight scenes in which the antagonists not only clash in mid-air and slice each other in half, but also unleash darts, poisons and swarms of deadly insects at each other. TR

Swordsman II (Xiao'ao Jianghu zhi Dongfang Bu Bai)

(Ching Siu-Tung, 1991, HK) Jet Li, Lin Ching Hsia, Rosamund Kwan, Fannie Yuen, Michelle Li.
111 min.

A further collaboration between the director of *A Chinese Ghost Story* and producer Tsui Hark, *Swordsman II* resembles a super-hero comic book brought to life. Set in a mythical past at a time of internecine power struggles within competing clans and sects, the film finds Ling and his siblings taking a stand against the ruthless 'Master Asia', who has sacrificed his manhood to attain magical powers, and who anonymously flirts with Ling as a woman. A playful attitude to sexuality permeates the movie; more to the point, however, are countless spectacularly realised supernatural confrontations which would have Albert Einstein's head spinning. Camp it may be, and messy, but mundane it ain't. TCh

Swordsman in Double-Flag Town, The (Shuang Qi Zhen Dao Ke)

(He Ping, 1991, China) Giao Wei, Zhao Ma Lin, Chang Jiang, Sun Hai Ying.
95 min.

Parched with thirst and jumpy from encounters on the trail, young Hai Ge rides into town (actually a walled village in the desert) to find and marry the girl he was engaged to in the cradle. He finds the place cowering with fear of two bandit brothers and their gang, and more by accident than design, kills one of the brothers. Facing up to swordplay skills he never knew he had, he waits nervously for the inevitable showdown with the dead man's vengeful brother... Whether you take He Ping's film as a sardonic commentary on American Westerns or as a new approach (in the vein of *Red Sorghum*) to Chinese folk-myth, it's a show-stopper. Leone himself would have cheered. TR

Sybil

(Daniel Petrie, 1977, US) Joanne Woodward, Sally Field, Brad Davis, Martine Bartlett, Jane Hoffman, Charles Lane, William Prince.
132 min.

This began life as a two-part TV movie (here edited down from 198 minutes) based on the true story of the eleven-year treatment by psychiatrist Cornelia Wilbur of Sybil Dorsett and her sixteen warring personalities. As Dr Wilbur, Joanne Woodward (who had herself essayed a schizophrenic role in *The Three Faces of Eve* back in 1957) is fascinating, because she employs a theatrical stillness around which all Sally Field's agonised personalities flutter like trapped birds. Field herself resists the temptation to let go and ham. The result is essentially a classic two-hander: moving despite the surrounding schlock. DSi

Sylvia

(Michael Firth, 1984, NZ) Eleanor David, Nigel Terry, Tom Wilkinson, Mary Regan, Martyn Sanderson, Terence Cooper.
98 min.

Sylvia Ashton-Warner develops her own teaching methods based on the emotional, personal life of the children in her classroom. She achieves wondrous results but is more than just a teacher, and in a remarkably sensitive portrayal, Eleanor David depicts her artistry, nervousness, gift for friendship, cultural isolation, and courage. Unfortunately, Firth concentrates on her passing romance with a sympathetic schools' inspector (Terry). With tantalising glimpses of the uneasy coexistence of white man and Maori, but with little individualisation of the children or understanding of their background, this is a sympathetic biopic when it could have been something altogether more inspirational and fascinating. JE

Sylvia Scarlett

(George Cukor, 1936, US) Katharine Hepburn, Cary Grant, Edmund Gwenn, Brian Aherne, Dennie Moore, Natalie Paley.
90 min. b/w.

A small and intriguingly bizarre gem, its picaresque story once again revealing Cukor's abiding interest in the joys and pains, deceptions and truths associated with the art of acting. The performer here is young Sylvia (Hepburn), forced to dress as a boy when her embezzler father (Gwenn) returns to England from France in dire straits. The pair fall in with troublesome landladies, a touring theatrical company, a roguish con-man (Grant), and a romantic painter (Aherne); and the film comes to centre on the way Hepburn's life of pretence affects not only her own emotional development but those around her. Just as the sexual nuances of her various encounters remain ambiguous, so the film seems unable to decide whether to opt for comedy, romantic adventure, or tragedy; Gwenn, for example, gradually loses his sanity, a darkening backdrop to the scenes of light, breezy banter between the leads. Odd, then, but entirely civilised and engaging, and Hepburn was rarely more radiant or moving. GA

Sympathy for the Devil
see One Plus One

Symphonie Pastorale, La
(Jean Delannoy, 1946, Fr) Michèle Morgan, Pierre Blanchar, Line Noro, Louvigny, Jean Desailly, Andrée Clément.
105 min. b/w.
A French Protestant pastor (Blanchar) falls in love with his blind ward (Morgan, the '40s Faye Dunaway). Delannoy's version of Gide's then still scandalous novel is correct, melancholy, icy. That's his auteurial tone. André Bazin admired the movie, and speculated that its emphasis on snow was a true filmic equivalent of Gide's use of tenses. It oddly mixes hot drama, cold style, and an accusatory stance; and the weathering of age may have sharpened its Sirkian effect. RD

Symptoms
(aka The Blood Virgin)
(Joseph Larraz, 1974, GB) Angela Pleasence, Peter Vaughan, Lorna Heilbron, Nancy Nevinson, Ronald O'Neil, Marie-Paul Mailleux.
91 min.
Made by a Spanish director working for an English company, with Angela Pleasence running mad in an old dark house and giving murderous vent to her sexist grievances, this is the finest British horror movie from a foreigner since Polanski's Repulsion. The comparison is inevitable, because thematically the films have a good deal in common, charting the gradual mental dissolution of their spectral heroines. Symptoms imitates, but also improves on its original in a multiplicity of ways. The muted love affair between Pleasence and Lorna Heilbron is etched with enormous suggestiveness, and Larraz's eye for visual detail is mesmerising.

Titanic

t

t

Täällä Pohjantähden alla (Here Beneath the North Star/Akseli and Elina)

(Edvin Laine, 1968/70, Fin) Aarno Sulkanen, Risto Taulo, Titta Karakorpi, Ulla Eklund, Anja Pohjola.
279 min.
If the action seems a trifle hectic early on, it's probably because an hour was trimmed for British release. But only a masochist would demand the full version of this lumbering Finnish family chronicle derived from a famous trilogy by Väinö Linna, detailing the break-up of feudal society early in the century and the farmers' fight for socialism. This dinosaur of a film played in Finland as a television serial, as well as being carved up into two features for cinema release; and the television influence shows in the relentless artificial lighting, the cramped compositions which hinder Laine's attempt to achieve an epic sweep. Occasional scenes are pretty in a picture postcard way (workers marching through snow shouting the national anthem), but it's all laboriously unreal and unimaginative. GB

Table for Five

(Robert Lieberman, 1983, US) Jon Voight, Richard Crenna, Marie-Christine Barrault, Millie Perkins, Roxana Zal, Robby Kiger, Son Hoang Bui, Kevin Costner.
124 min.
Prodigal parent Voight comes to reclaim his kids from their mother and her new husband, and scoops them off on a plush Mediterranean cruise. Yes, it's another of New Hollywood's hymns to the Joys of Fatherhood, though this time potential custody tussles are forestalled by conveniently dispatching the wife in a car crash. Voight's shipboard romance is kept safely marginal too, and the final happy family – three kids, two fathers – looks decidedly bizarre. Lieberman pads out thin material with a welter of reaction shots and sequences of Voight mooning around looking very, very sad. What's worse, he seems to have scant confidence in the potency of his characters' emotions, attempting to make them into something monumental by having Voight's life crumble amid the more spectacular ruins of Western civilisation. This is essentially soap opera with fancy production values and grandiose pretensions: the result is the purest kitsch. SJo

Tabu

(FW Murnau, 1931, US) Anna Chevalier, Matahi, Hitu, Kong Ah.
90 min. b/w.
Murnau's last film (after three years of mixed fortunes in Hollywood) was begun as a collaboration with the documentarist Robert Flaherty, but resolved itself into Murnau's purest and least inhibited celebration of physical sensuality and love. Its plot is a simple Pacific islands folk tale: a young man and woman fall in love, thereby violating a local taboo, and their romance ends in inevitable tragedy. The film is a rhapsody of textures and an exceptionally sensuous play of light, rhythm and composition. Its narrative pretext is (necessarily) heterosexual, but Murnau's homosexual sensibility was never clearer: the central image (and texture) of the film is the flesh of its young hero, and it is his virility that sets the tragedy in motion. Fetishistic to a degree, the film is none the less never patronising to its subject or its actors. It plays as a pre-colonial anachronism, rather like one of Melville's South Seas novels. It's extremely beautiful. TR

Tacones lejanos
see High Heels

Tadpole and the Whale

(Jean-Claude Lord, 1988, Can) Fanny Lauzier, Denis Forest, Marina Orsini, Félix-Antoine Leroux, Jean Lajeunesse.
92 min.
Winsome, winning adventure tale from producer Rock Demers, about a young girl, gifted with exceptional hearing, who forms a close relationship with a dolphin named Elvar. The film has a strong educational element: lots of footage of hump-backed whales spouting off the East Canadian coast (and elsewhere), and a marine biologist at hand to explain the science. The adventure seems to consist of characters rushing about everywhere and much falling out of speedboats, followed by lots of affirmative hugging and smiles. An eco-sound kids' movie, with a liberal pinch of sea-salt. WH

Taebaek Mountains, The (Taebaek Sanmaek)

(Im Kwon-Taek, 1994, SKor) Ahn Song-Gi, Kim Gap-Soo, Kim Myung-Kon, Oh Jung-Hae, Shin Hyun-Joon.
168 min.
Im's masterly epic opens up the shadowiest period in Korea's modern history: the months in 1948/9 when a region in the deep south went communist and the state fought dirty to bring it back under control in what was effectively a dress rehearsal for the coming Korean War. The core issues are ideological, of course, but Im carefully relates them to family rivalries and other down-to-earth factors: the fascistic leader of the anti-communist guerillas, for instance, is the brother of the idealist who tries to promote communist values. The whole thing is seen through the neutral eyes of a local schoolteacher (Ahn, working with Im for the first time in ten years), who finally seeks solace in the rituals of a shaman. Kim Soo-Chul contributes a truly memorable score. TR

Taffin

(Francis Megahy, 1987, GB/US) Pierce Brosnan, Ray McAnally, Alison Doody, Jeremy Child, Dearbhla Molloy, Jim Bartley, Alan Stanford.
96 min.
A confused and unexciting thriller set in a small Irish coastal town, where the hero Taffin (Brosnan) earns his keep as a debt collector who's handier with his fists than with the legal paperwork. When it is revealed that a newly built access road will serve a proposed chemical plant, Taffin at first refuses to help the action committee set up by his former teacher (McAnally). But when the crooked businessmen behind the scheme, who have the local councillors in their pockets, start roughing up OAPs, he agrees to act as the protesters' paid heavy. The character of Taffin is too complex for Brosnan's limited acting talents, though he's good in the action scenes and displays his coarse good looks to some advantage. Also unconvincing are Taffin's passionate affair with an independent and worldly-wise barmaid (Doody), and his father-son conflict with former mentor McAnally. Struggling hard against the script's stock elements, Megahy delivers some effective bursts of action without ever generating any real tension or involvement. NF

Tagebuch einer Verlorenen, Das
see Diary of a Lost Girl

TAG, The Assassination Game

(Nick Castle, 1982, US) Robert Carradine, Linda Hamilton, Kristine DeBell, Perry Lang, Frazer Smith, John Mengatti, Bruce Abbott.
92 min.
This first film by ex-John Carpenter collaborator Castle may wear its references too visibly on its sleeve, but is prepared to run a disparate group, ranging from Ida Lupino to *The Man from UNCLE*. Its unusual amalgam of comedy (a battery of amusing supporting characters and absurd situations) and thrills (De Niro lookalike Abbott as a killer who aspires to stylish assassination) blends with a sexy '40s-style romance to produce a pleasingly human thriller. Particularly strong performances make it a perfect entertainment for late-night viewing. SM

Taipei Story (Qingmei Zhuma)

(Edward Yang, 1984, Tai/China) Ts'ai Ch'in, Hou Hsiao-hsien, Wu Nien-chen, Lin Hsiu-ling.
115 min.
The film that introduced Yang's prodigious talent to the West is a quietly stunning drama which sees the various problems facing a rapidly modernised city reflected in the lives of a dozen or so subtly observed characters. At the centre are a troubled upper middle-class couple: a failed businessman lost in dreams of the past (Hou), and a budding executive whose reaction to redundancy is more in tune with the future. Though there's little in the way of story, Yang's insights and honesty about emotions ensure interest throughout; and it looks absolutely superb. TCh

Take, The

(Robert Hartford-Davis, 1974, US) Billy Dee Williams, Eddie Albert, Frankie Avalon, Vic Morrow, Sorrell Booke, Tracy Reed, Albert Salmi.
92 min.
Super-tough, super-cynical product of the Nixon era in which it is futile to worry overmuch about such hair-splitters as whether our hero is a bent cop playing good or vice versa. Hartford-Davis' direction is all flash, laced with a couple of this'll knock 'em dead-type shock cuts and an introductory countdown to the shootout that threatens to be never-ending. Lovers of bizarre relics from the great age of pop will relish Frankie Avalon in a small part as a punk gangster screaming 'Don't hurt me! Don't hurt me!' to our hero in a police cell. As the cop, Billy Dee Williams, who may be remembered for a soulful performance in *Lady Sings the Blues*, is plainly misused. VG

Take a Hard Ride

(Anthony M Dawson ie.Antonio Margheriti, 1975, US/It) Jim Brown, Lee Van Cleef, Fred Williamson, Catherine Spaak, Jim Kelly, Barry Sullivan, Harry Carey Jr, Dana Andrews.
109 min.
A rather crude attempt to expand the Italian Western, cashing in on the blaxploitation and kung-fu markets. Two black dudes (Brown, Williamson), in uneasy alliance and carrying a heap of money, pick up a couple of waifs and strays, including a kung-fu fighting Indian, while a vast army of bounty hunters headed by Lee Van Cleef chase after the loot. All an excuse for some undemanding thrills, listlessly put together. The film only rouses itself to kill people off: they don't just die, they fall from heights, slam into railings, and throw themselves into puddles just in front of the camera. Ironic that it's only in their dying seconds that most of the cast come alive. CPe

Take Care of Your Scarf, Tatjana (Pida Huivista Kinni, Tatjana)

(Aki Kaurismäki, 1994, Fin) Kati Outinen, Matti Pellonpaa, Kirsi Tykkylainen, Mato Valtonen.
65 min.
A gem from the variable Kaurismäki, this beautifully economic anti-romantic road comedy is both hilarious and strangely touching. The slim story charts the encounter between two morose Finns (one devoted to vodka, the other to coffee) and two Russian women who hitch a lift on their way back to Estonia. The men suffer much discomfiture at the proximity of two talkative members of the opposite sex. Marvellously observed and understated, the film exudes a delicious sense of the absurd. This is deadpan as good as it gets. GA

Take It Easy

(Albert Magnoli, 1986, US) Mitch Gaylord, Janet Jones, Michelle Phillips, John Aprea, Michael Pataki, Stacy Maloney.
101 min.
Steve's father is a little upset that his son, one time high school football and gymnast star, is going to seed; Steve (Gaylord) is a little miffed that father doesn't seem to care any more – 'We were a team!' – and runs from the house into the arms of new girl in town Julie (Jones). She's a gymnast too, and he joins her in training under the stern gaze of Coach Soranhoff (Pataki), who is busy drumming discipline into his class before they take a crack at getting into the national team. The film offers a full schedule of gratuitous muscle-stretching, in which the fact that Jones and ex-Olympic champ Gaylord do their own flip-flops would have been more impressive had it also come up with anything resembling a proper plot. The boy-from-the-wrong-side-of-the-tracks-makes-good theme, already used in Magnoli's awful *Purple Rain*, simply doesn't wash, while the tedious disco soundtrack serves only to thud home the pointlessness of it all. CB

Take It Like a Man, Ma'am (Ta' det som en Mand, Frue!)

(Elisabeth Rygård/Mette Knudsen/Li Vilstrup, 1975, Den) Tove Maës, Alf Lassen, Berthe Quistgård, Hans Kragh Jacobsen.
96 min.

An entertaining commercial feature arising from certain preoccupations within the women's movement, this represents a reasonably successful attempt to popularise aspects of feminist theory and film-making practice: respectively, the potential relationship between the movement and the older woman, and the realisation of an all-female production. The film traces the gradual coming-to-consciousness of a 50-year-old housewife, diagnosed as menopausal and prescribed tranquillisers and a little dog to look after. But the basis of its broad appeal is a long dream sequence which is a devastatingly accurate and hilarious depiction of role reversal. It's the seemingly simple strategy of this section which proves to be the film's real strength. PT

Take It or Leave It
(Dave Robinson, 1981, GB) Graham McPherson, Mark Bedford, Lee Thompson, Carl Smith, Dan Woodgate, Christopher Foreman, Mike Barson, John Hasler.
87 min. b/w & col.
This purports to be the 'true story' of the formative years of the north London bluebeat-inspired band Madness. By conveniently ending just before the onset of the band's unbroken spell of singles charts successes, the film sidesteps the usual rock movie concerns: the pressures of the music biz, the personal toll of overnight success, etc. Instead, it delivers an enjoyable enough picture of what it's like to be young, broke, working class, and trying to put a band together. The problems, according to Madness, are personnel changes, in-fighting, sheer idleness and selfishness, and – not least – lack of musical competence. But given the band's succession of fine hit singles, this last claim, and the fact that it fudges the issue of Madness' relationship with its early skinhead following, are the two things it's most difficult to swallow about the film. Otherwise, it's an adequately mythologising promo job. RM

Take Me Out to the Ball Game (aka Everybody's Cheering)
(Busby Berkeley, 1949, US) Gene Kelly, Frank Sinatra, Esther Williams, Jules Munshin, Betty Garrett, Edward Arnold.
93 min.
More like a Donen/Kelly musical than a Busby Berkeley (not a chorine in sight), which is hardly surprising since they staged and filmed the numbers, while Berkeley left after doing the dialogue scenes. With Kelly, Sinatra and Munshin teaming up for the brilliant vaudeville-baseball routine of a number like 'O'Brien to Ryan to Goldberg', it often looks like a run-in for On the Town. Less 'integrated', perhaps, but enormously enjoyable. The plot is an airy something with a non-swimming Esther Williams becoming the new owner of a turn-of-the-century baseball team, and charming the boys out of their chauvinist scowls. But what matters is the stylish ebullience, and the excellent score by Roger Edens, Adolph Green and Betty Comden. TM

Take Me to Town
(Douglas Sirk, 1952, US) Ann Sheridan, Sterling Hayden, Philip Reed, Lee Patrick, Phyllis Stanley, Lane Chandler.
81 min.
A charming slice of backwoods Americana (with music) about three boys who decide that saloon gal Sheridan, no better than she ought to be and keeping a wary eye out for the law, is just the thing to make a wife for their widowed preacher father (Hayden), in preference to the more 'suitable' widow lady (Stanley) he has in mind. All the traditional stops are pulled out as Sheridan proves herself a born housewife, at the end even graduating to conducting a Bible class. But glowingly shot by Sirk without any of the subversive malice that marked his view of bourgeois America, it has real tenderness and warmth. Lovely performances from Sheridan and Hayden, too. TM

Take the Money and Run
(Woody Allen, 1969, US) Woody Allen, Janet Margolin, Marcel Hillaire, Jacquelyn Hyde, Lonny Chapman, Jan Merlin.
85 min.
Discounting the abortive What's Up, Tiger Lily?, this was Woody Allen's debut as his own director, and it marked the beginnings of his idiosyn-

cratic 'one shot – one gag' technique. Its tale of the eagerly criminal career of Virgil Starkwell is as unpredictably structured as Annie Hall, if not yet anything like as sustained in tone and mood. But it has plenty of hilarious jokes and concepts, like the ventriloquists' dummies at prison visiting time, and the return home from a chaingang break with five shackled cons in tow. TR

Taking Care of Business (aka Filofax)
(Arthur Hiller, 1990, US) James Belushi, Charles Grodin, Anne DeSalvo, Veronica Hamel, Mako, Hector Elizondo.
108 min.
Take a con and a yuppy: the con (Belushi) is a good-natured slob, popular with the guys, into baseball and chicks; the yuppy (Grodin) is wound a little tight, basically okay, but ambitious and a tad prissy. Now give the con a break, teach the yuppy a lesson. Put them in neutral territory – the no man's land of LA – and give Belushi Grodin's credit cards, ID and contacts. Give him his filofax. And Grodin gets zilch. There's a good comic idea somewhere here, and it's called Trading Places. Through crass over-emphasis and sloppy continuity errors, Hiller fumbles most of the jokes away. The roles fit Belushi/Grodin like rubber, but the rest is second-rate. TCh

Taking Off
(Milos Forman, 1971, US) Lynn Carlin, Buck Henry, Linnea Heacock, Georgia Engel, Tony Harvey, Audra Lindley, Allen Garfield.
92 min.
A delightfully touching comedy, Forman's first in America and far better than his later One Flew Over the Cuckoo's Nest or Ragtime, this deals with the attempts of a middle-aged, middle class American couple to trace and lure back their run-away daughter. Scenes of their search are intercut with sequences at a musical audition for disillusioned youth, and Forman's wry but sympathetic humour derives largely from the incongruities he observes in both situations: deserted parents, concerned and conservative, getting stoned in an effort to understand why kids smoke dope; a rosy, virginal young girl singing a quiet folk song in praise of fucking. Never taking sides, but allowing both factions engaged in the generation gap war plenty of space and generosity, its gentle wit has aged far more gracefully than the hectoring sermons of most youth movies churned out in the late '60s and early '70s. GA

Taking of Pelham One Two Three, The
(Joseph Sargent, 1974, US) Walter Matthau, Robert Shaw, Martin Balsam, Hector Elizondo, Earl Hindman, James Broderick, Dick O'Neill, Lee Wallace, Tom Pedi, Kenneth McMillan.
104 min.
Four hijackers, got up like Groucho Marx and led by Robert Shaw with the voice of a Dalek, kidnap a New York subway train and hold the city to ransom. Saviour of the system is Transit Authority Inspector Matthau, harking back to his early acting days as a grim heavy, and with a Bronx accent as thick and fancy as a piece of angel cake. It's a slice of Urban Crisis life, you see, and to prove it the occupants of the train 'represent a cross-section of New York: a pimp, a Puerto Rican pregnant girl, a hippie, a hooker, a WASP, a wino and a homosexual'. This movie's so up-to-date even the mayor's a laughing-stock. Yet, despite the caricature, the facile screenplay by Peter Stone, and the desperate direction from Sargent ('who has directed some of television's finest hours'), the film retains a fascination – the way Juggernaut did; and needless to say, it's been a monster hit in cities with an underground system. AN

Tale of a Vampire
(Shimako Sato, 1992, GB) Julian Sands, Kenneth Cranham, Suzanna Hamilton, Marian Diamond, Michael Kenton.
102 min.
Shot on inventive locations around London, this modern-day vampire pic takes its thematic inspiration from Edgar Allan Poe's sombre poem 'Annabel Lee'. Sands plays Alex, an ageless bloodsucker haunted by the loss of his true love, Virginia. Trailing Alex is a mysterious stranger (Cranham) hell-bent on revenge; and when Alex becomes obsessed with Virginia-lookalike Anne

(Hamilton, gratingly winsome), the stranger uses her to lure his prey. Although director Sato is Japanese, her visual style owes more to Tony Scott than to any oriental tradition; smoke swathes the screen and light blasts elegantly through half-drawn blinds at every opportunity. For such a low-budget film, it looks terrific, and comparison with The Hunger does it an injustice, in that understated dialogue is used here to evoke a genuine sense of loss entirely lacking from most mainstream fodder. Although Sato's script unravels far too slowly, strong performances by Cranham and Sands keep the life-blood flowing in this flawed but impressive debut. MK

Tale of Springtime, A (Conte de Printemps)
(Eric Rohmer, 1989, Fr) Anne Teyssèdre, Hugues Quester, Florence Darel, Eloise Bennett, Sophie Robin.
112 min.
Inaugurating a new Rohmer series (Tales of the Four Seasons), this begins with an atypically wordless sequence which effectively introduces the mood of mystery and ambiguity that will recur throughout. Caught between apartments, philosophy graduate Jeanne (Teyssèdre) attends a party, where a young girl, Natasha (Darel), invites her to stay at the flat she shares with her father Igor (Quester). So far so innocent, but presently Jeanne finds herself witness to, then participating in, recriminatory scenes between daughter, father and his youthful lover Eve (Bennett): jealous Natasha detests Eve, accusing her of theft, while Igor – encouraged by Natasha? – seems more than willing to be left alone with Jeanne. As ever, Rohmer examines their hidden motives and analyses the consequences of their actions with great lucidity, repeatedly delving beneath words to uncover, through gesture and intonation, their real meaning; nobody is wholly innocent, no one completely blameless, in the web of intrigue spun between Jeanne and her hosts. Rohmer may not be breaking new ground, but who else could explore his familiar territory so fruitfully? GA

Tale of the Fox, The
see Roman de Renard, Le

Tale of the Three Jewels (Conte des trois diamants)
(Michel Khleifi, 1995, Bel/GB/Palestine) Makram Khouri, Bushra Qaraman, Mohammad Bakri, Hana Ne'meh.
112 min.
A frontline portrait of Palestinian life on the Gaza Strip (in a period between the Hebron events and the withdrawal and new peace initiatives), told from the viewpoint of a 12-year-old boy who becomes involved with a 'gypsy' girl. The raids by Israeli special forces are powerfully filmed and cleanly integrated into the narrative – as unexceptional to the boy as the activities of the young Palestinian fighters. Michel Khleifi (writer, director, producer) adds an elevating metaphysical/religious dimension that embraces elements of orthodox Middle Eastern mysticism, the boy's dream-founded intuition and the girl's nature-oriented world view. WH

Tales from a Hard City
(Kim Flitcroft, 1994, GB)
80 min.
Lively documentary about a handful of dreamers in Sheffield: a petty thief into dope, karaoke, awful mates and sponging off his mum; a boxer turned would-be actor hustling for sponsored advertising gigs; a single mum hoping to become a pop star; and a well-off nightclub owner with massive entrepreneurial ambitions. All are naive and fuelled by a need for a sense of self-importance (though none approaches the vacuity and arrogance of the self-appointed 'image consultant' working on the boxer). A saddening film, leavened by humour and flashes of hope. GA

Tales from the Crypt Presents Demon Knight
(Ernest Dickerson, 1995, US) John Kassir, Billy Zane, William Sadler, Jada Pinkett, Brenda Bakke, CCH Pounder, Thomas Hayden Church, John Schuck, Dick Miller.
92 min.
Dickerson, who shot most of Spike Lee's films

t

before directing the feature *Juice*, knows his way round a horror picture, but in the end this spin-off from the HBO cable TV series (derived from the 1950s EC comic books of William Gaines) feels pedestrian and moribund. Mysterious fugitive Brayker (Sadler) takes refuge from demonic, stetson-hatted smoothie the Collector (Zane) in a small-town flophouse that's immediately besieged by flesh-eating, green-eyed demons. Matters get bogged down as Brayker seals the building's doors with holy blood in order to protect the stereotyped characters trapped within. Not to be thwarted, the Collector uses telepathy to exploit their vulnerabilities, offering mock affection to love-starved tart Cordelia (Bakke), super-model stardom to delinquent Jeryline (Pinkett) and a topless bar awash with hooch to pickled old-timer Uncle Willy (Miller). The action is set-bound, the gory sfx no more than adequate, and the fright quotient far too low. Nor is any depth lent to the proceedings by repeated flashbacks to an MTV video of the Crucifixion. The first in a series, but standards will need to impove if it's to survive. NF

Tales from the Darkside: The Movie
(John Harrison, 1991, US) Deborah Harry, Matthew Lawrence, Christian Slater, Robert Sedgwick, Steve Buscemi, Julianne Moore, David Johansen, William Hickey, James Remar, Rae Dawn Chong, Robert Klein.
93 min.
An anthology featuring stories adapted by George Romero and Michael McDowell. McDowell also wrote the neat 'wraparound story', in which a housewife (Harry) is distracted from roasting and eating a young boy (Lawrence) by his reading of stories from a favourite anthology. In the '40s-style 'Lot 249', a boffin (Buscemi) tricked out of a scholarship revives a 3,000-year-old mummy to exact his revenge. Hickey takes the honours for 'Cat from Hell' – in which cat's eye view shots add suspense – as a mad millionaire who hires a killer (Johansen) to rid him of a homicidal puss. Though it relies on the same flip irony and black humour, 'Lover's Vow' comes closest to succeeding in its own right. After seeing a winged monster tear off a man's head, a struggling New York artist (Remar) is spared on condition that he never reveals the creature's hideous appearance. Fame, fortune and romance (with Chong) ensue, but can he keep a secret forever? Definitely an improvement on the lamentable *Creepshow* or *Cat's Eye*, but Harrison never quite transcends the inherently limited format. NF

Tales from the Gimli Hospital
(Guy Maddin, 1988, Can) Kyle McCulloch, Michael Gottli, Angela Heck, Margaret-Anne MacLeod.
77 min. b/w.
There's a thin line between weird and strange, and Maddin's debut falls just the wrong side. For all that, it's hugely enjoyable, a shaggy-dog story set in Manitoba in a bygone age of bucolic gambolling, innocent erotic idylls, and dark, dark shadows. Lonely Einar succumbs to an epidemic that leaves cracks across its victims' faces, and ends up in the local hospital, where he whiles away the hours carving bark fishes and envying the narrative skills of his voluminous neighbour. The two spin tales of love, loss and necrophilia, and mortal combat ensues, to the sound of ghostly bagpipes. A nearly wordless '20s pastiche, the film obeys no logic except the impulse to fling in as many campy, incongruous images as possible. There are moments of jaw-dropping inspiration, and many that are just impenetrably odd. But this is immensely winning for the rawness alone. JRo

Tales from the Vienna Woods (Geschichten aus dem Wiener Wald)
(Maximilian Schell, 1979, WGer/Aus) Birgit Doll, Hanno Pöschl, Helmut Qualtinger, Jane Tilden, Adrienne Gessner, Lil Dagover.
96 min.
You'd never guess it from this film version, but Odin von Horvath's play, premiered in Germany in 1931 and successfully staged by Schell at the National Theatre in 1977, has been held up for favourable comparison with Brecht. Set in the Vienna of Hitler's day but ironically drenched in Strauss waltzes, it chronicles the tragi-comic

tribulations of an honest middle class shopkeeper whose rebellious daughter runs away from an approved marriage, gets herself pregnant, and ends up face-to-face with daddy in the nightclub to which she has sinfully gravitated. The film is so lumpishly stagebound that its satire of the bourgeoisie and conventional values emerges as painfully crude caricature. TM

Tales of Beatrix Potter (aka Peter Rabbit and Tales of Beatrix Potter)
(Reginald Mills, 1971, GB) Dancers from the Royal Ballet company.
90 min.
Largely unimaginative interpretation of a number of Beatrix Potter's stories, which accumulates a lot of top-line dancers and totally obscures them from view under piles of rigid costumes (Michael Coleman's Jeremy Fisher is a rare exception). There was, perhaps, a virtue in the ballet being set in a natural (as opposed to theatrical) landscape, and the muted photography evokes the original Potter drawings. Inserts show Potter as a young girl drawing animals in the nursery of a forbidding Victorian household, taking her solitary joy in the Lakeland countryside. Otherwise, perhaps the chief interest lies in choreographer Frederick Ashton's performance as Mrs Tiggy-Winkle, and in the fact that the film was co-written and designed by one Christine Edzard, who went on to direct *Little Dorrit*, *The Fool*, etc. WH

Tales of Hoffman, The
(Michael Powell/Emeric Pressburger, 1951, GB). Moira Shearer, Robert Helpmann, Leonid Massine, Ludmilla Tcherina, Pamela Brown, Frederick Ashton.
127 min.
Made at the instigation of Sir Thomas Beecham – who conducts the Offenbach operetta – Powell and Pressburger's follow-up to *The Red Shoes* lacks the earlier film's coherence and emotional pull, but is equally lavish in its attempts to combine dance, music and film. Basically a trio of stories (plus prologue and epilogue) in which unrequited love figures strongly, the movie is inevitably uneven, and some have pointed to a rather kitschy element in its equation of Cinema and Great Art. But Powell's eye – aided by Hein heckroth's designs and Chris Challis's camera – is as sharp and distinctive as ever, revelling in rich colours, fantastic compositions, and swooning movements (most notably in the lavish episode featuring a Venetian courtesan). Sumptuous spectacle. GA.

Tales of Mystery
see Histoires Extraordinaires

Tales of Ordinary Madness (Storie di Ordinaria Follia)
(Marco Ferreri, 1981, It/Fr) Ben Gazzara, Ornella Muti, Susan Tyrrell, Tanya Lopert, Roy Brocksmith, Katia Berger.
108 min.
'When Hemingway put his brains on the wall, that was style...' drones the gutbucket poet (Gazzara) to a dozing audience in New York, before retreating home to LA among the 'defeated, demented and damned' to stagger through his quotidian tales of ordinary madness. A groan from the lower depths, this is adapted from the autobiography of leftover-beat poet Charles Bukowski. The problem is that Ferreri's grip on the English language seems too infirm to inject the necessary irony into a phrase like the one above. Gazzara is fine as the grizzled soak of a poet, his snake eyes forever gloating on some distant private joke, but his portentous pronouncements would look better in subtitles. And among the various madonna/whores that people his circle of purgatory is a sloe-eyed seraph (Muti) given to such acts as closing up her vagina with a safety-pin (presumably the corollary to Depardieu carving off his own prick in The Last Woman). For all that, there is a final scene on a beach which proves that Ferreri is the equal of Antonioni when it comes to spatial beauty. CPea

Tales of Terror
(Roger Corman, 1961, US) Vincent Price, Peter Lorre, Basil Rathbone, Debra Paget, Joyce Jameson.
90 min.

For the fourth of his Poe films, Corman adopted a portmanteau front and introduced, into the second of his three stories, a vein of grisly black comedy that would reappear more successfully in the later *The Raven*. The first tale, *Morella*, has Price as a typically necrophile introvert mourning the death in childbirth of his mummified wife until his long banished daughter returns to the fold; in *The Black Cat*, Lorre dominates as the drunkard who reacts to Price's adulterous liaison with his wife by walling the couple up in his wine cellar; and in *The Case of M Valdemar*, a dead Price exacts revenge on the hypnotist who sent his soul to eternal limbo with a view to stealing his wife. Stylish and fun, but the short story format denies Corman the stately, melancholy pace that distinguished his best work in the cycle. GA.

Talking History
(HO Nazareth, 1983, GB) CLR James, EP Thompson.
60 min.
The two most famous radical historians of our day – EP Thompson and CLR James – talk to each other about Paris 1968, Nelson Mandela, Solidarity, 'Atlanticism in crisis', and the nature and purpose of their kind of history. The predominant image is of two grey-haired, one-time *enfants terribles* slipping easily into the roles of charismatic prophets. They share a devotion to history, not as a frozen catalogue of isolated events, but as signposts to future developments – what Thompson calls 'history as process'. They both discern the coming end of political parties – in the East and the West – and the growth of large 'people's movements'. The film-makers have sought to enliven the proceedings with headlines and film clips that illustrate the topics of conversation; but despite the assiduousness of their picture research, the end effect is simply distracting. James and Thompson talking are excitement enough for the attentive viewer. MH

Talk of the Town, The
(George Stevens, 1942, US) Cary Grant, Jean Arthur, Ronald Colman, Edgar Buchanan, Glenda Farrell, Charles Dingle, Rex Ingram, Lloyd Bridges.
118 min. b/w.
An attractive serio-comic tale of civic corruption, with Grant as a factory worker on the run from a trumped-up charge of arson and murder, Arthur as the childhood friend with whom he seeks shelter, and Colman as the stuffy professor already ensconced as her lodger (and whose presence requires that Grant be passed off as the gardener when he tires of seclusion in the attic). The comedy of social proprieties as the inevitable triangle raises its head is nicely played against discussions in which the two men bring each other to a new understanding of the law and its application. Beautifully written by Irwin Shaw and Sidney Buchman, it's equally well directed and acted, even if the situations (including a lynch mob that comes complete with laughs) are not a little contrived. TM

Talk Radio
(Oliver Stone, 1988, US) Eric Bogosian, Alec Baldwin, Ellen Greene, Leslie Hope, John C McGinley, John Pankow, Michael Wincott.
109 min.
Bogosian co-scripts and stars in this adaptation of his play about 'shock broadcasting' (the provocation of extremist attitudes), here expanded to incorporate details from Stephen Singular's book *Talked to Death: The Life and Murder of Alan Berg*. Barry Champlain (Bogosian) is a late-night radio host based in Dallas. He indulges in a perversely abusive relationship with callers. It's a formula that works, and Champlain is offered a chance for national syndication. But his telephone tactics bring self-destruction gets into full swing, and he brings his ex-wife (Greene) to Dallas for what amounts to a distressing, seemingly pointless stroll down memory lane. Much too long, these flashbacks are decidedly less effective than the studio-bound sequences which focus on Champlain's mania and rapid-fire exchange with his lonely, lunatic fans, one of whom finally gets out of hand. At these moments, Champlain's distorted perspective is compelling, despite Stone's sometimes flashy direction as he attempts to wrest cinematic qualities out of the essentially stagey material. CM

Tall Guy, The

(Mel Smith, 1989, GB) Jeff Goldblum, Emma Thompson, Rowan Atkinson, Geraldine James, Emil Wolk, Kim Thomson, Harold Innocent, Anna Massey.
92 min.

This tall tale concerns Dexter (the excellent Goldblum), an actor unlucky in love, life, hay fever, and job as fall guy to obnoxious, egocentric comedian Ron Anderson (Atkinson). Falling for nurse Kate Lemon (Thompson), he subjects himself to a course of injections, ostensibly to cure his sneezing. Close encounters with the needle pay off in an unbridled close encounter with Kate, but also get him the push for missing a show. Richard (*Blackadder*) Curtis's script then leads Dexter through a series of failed auditions (including a fine Berkoff take-off) before he lands the title role in the musical of *The Elephant Man* (which features the memorable lyrics of 'I'm Packing My Trunk') and settles accounts with Ron. Mel Smith's directorial debut is uninhibited by finesse, but it has its laughs. JGl

Tall Men, The

(Raoul Walsh, 1955, US) Clark Gable, Jane Russell, Robert Ryan, Cameron Mitchell, Juan Garcia, Harry Shannon, Emile Meyer.
122 min.

An unpretentious but masterly trail-drive epic, one of the purest and simplest examples of the effortless professionalism of Walsh and his collaborators (including co-writer Frank Nugent, John Ford's son-in-law and writer-in-chief), and almost incidentally a sustained exploration of the Western landscape and the place of the stock characters within it. Gable pushes the herd and his own horizons westward through disaster and peril; though the film is probably best remembered by some for Jane Russell's bath scene, frontier-style. PT

Tall T, The

(Budd Boetticher, 1957, US) Randolph Scott, Richard Boone, Maureen O'Sullivan, Skip Homeier, Henry Silva, John Hubbard, Arthur Hunnicutt.
77 min.

Admirably scripted by Burt Kennedy from a story by Elmore Leonard, this is the best and bleakest of the Boetticher/Scott Westerns. A marvellous mechanism is set in motion by the stagecoach hold-up at the beginning where a solid citizen cravenly bargains for his life by suggesting that his wife be held for ransom. Boone's bluffly amiable villain promptly guns him down in contempt, but fulfils his elective role by taking up the suggestion. Thereafter, conceptions of justice and social justification are slyly questioned as Boone is hounded by Scott, bodies pile up, and the two men, gradually emerging as opposite sides of the same coin, face the inevitable showdown that neither of them wants but which society demands. Wonderful, with a full roster of fine performances. TM

Tall Target, The

(Anthony Mann, 1951, US) Dick Powell, Paula Raymond, Adolphe Menjou, Marshall Thompson, Ruby Dee, Richard Rober, Leif Erickson, Will Geer, Florence Bates.
77 min. b/w.

A cheapo gem of a thriller: a *noir*-influenced costume drama set largely aboard a train carrying Abe Lincoln (the date is 1861) to Baltimore to make a pre-inauguration speech. Hitching a ride is Powell, a New York cop who has wind of an assassination attempt, has resigned from the force because of the scepticism of his superiors, and finds that playing a lone wolf hand with no official backing has its hazards as he does everything in his power to avert disaster. Ingeniously and inventively plotted, taut and unpretentious, the film dashes along at a furious pace, with a strong period feel and nicely understated performances, well served by Mann's straightforward direction. GA

Talmage Farlow

(Lorenzo DeStefano, 1981, US) Talmage Farlow, Tommy Flanagan, Red Mitchell, George Benson, Lenny Breau, Red Norvo.
58 min.

A gentle and intimate portrait of the lauded jazz guitarist Tal Farlow. The dinner-plate-handed virtuoso was discovered by pianist Jimmy Lyons, but 'disappeared' in the late '50s, cloistering himself in the New England port of Sea Brake, fishing and resuming his first job of sign-painting. His preference for this quiet idyll away from the numbing club round is obvious, and enviable, but as vibist Red Norvo and other friends point out in the film, the gentle giant is far from retired. DeStefano's film proves as much with a sensitivity that never slips into sycophancy. JG

Tamarind Seed, The

(Blake Edwards, 1974, GB) Julie Andrews, Omar Sharif, Anthony Quayle, Dan O'Herlihy, Sylvia Syms, Oscar Homolka, Bryan Marshall.
125 min.

Blake Edwards sometimes has an amazing way with plastic people and plastic situations, but he can't do much with the weighty, wordy romance that blooms as Julie Andrews and Omar Sharif spar leadenly, and at length, and fend off the final clinch until an appropriate *Sound of Music*-style landscape descends around their ears. Nor can he do much with the spy story that develops out of this holiday affair in Barbados, because she happens to be a Home Office secretary, and he a KGB official. Much more satisfying is the round of Embassy parties captured in all their ritualistic bitchness of acrid marriages and double-faced relationships. As usual, too, Edwards invests the film with a great spatial feeling, but the good things remain strictly marginal. VG

Tampopo

(Juzo Itami, 1986, Jap) Tsutomu Yamazaki, Nobuko Miyamoto, Koji Yakusho, Ken Watanabe, Rikiya Yasuoka.
114 min.

Into Tampopo's ramen-bar trundles trucker Goro who, Shane-like, offers to make her the finest noodle-chef in Tokyo. This involves a *Seven Samurai*-style gathering of talents, military regimentation, and industrial espionage. On to this loose structure, Itami grafts a plethora of comic vignettes whose sole link is their focus on food: a Zen lesson in the proper way to contemplate, caress, and devour pork noodles; how to enhance your love life with salt, lemon and cream; how to let dreams of yam sausages ease the onset of death. Itami's episodic satire bulges with invention, ranging from a continuing concern with Japanese concepts of correct behaviour to numerous quirky movie parodies (from Western, gangster and sex films to *The Seven Samurai* and *Death in Venice*). It is often very amusing, although the ragged, free-wheeling structure tends to blunt Itami's somewhat obvious thesis, that eating is more closely connected to sex than we would normally admit. Spasmodically effective rather than bitingly funny. GA

Tango

(Patrice Leconte, 1993, Fr) Philippe Noiret, Richard Bohringer, Thierry Lhermitte, Carole Bouquet, Jean Rochefort, Miou-Miou.
90 min.

This comic-strip caper sees Leconte taking a truculent detour from his previous wacky explorations of sexual obsession, *Monsieur Hire* and *The Hairdresser's Husband*. For this road movie, he bonds together a trio of despicable males: the judge (Noiret), a self-satisfied epicurean; the aviator, Vincent (Bohringer), grounded by guilt for the unpunished murder of his unfaithful wife and her lover; and the pathetic cuckold Paul (Lhermitte), who wishes to kill his wife ('So I can forget her!'). The judge, having fixed Vincent's trial, now blackmails him into killing Paul's wife. They set off south to Valence to do the deed. An absurd Gallic leg-pull, the movie takes sly swipes at psycho-sexual politics – though unlike Buñuel and Blier, Leconte tries less to *épate le bourgeoisie* than simultaneously to flabbergast and titillate the politically correct. Shot in 'Scope and primary colours, the film delights in attention-grabbing wide-angles, isolating long shots, airplane swoops and car chases. The melancholic undertow is echoed by Leconte's ever idiosyncratic choice of music: here 'sensuous and fateful' tango-rock. WH

Tango & Cash

(Andrei Konchalovsky, 1989, US) Sylvester Stallone, Kurt Russell, Jack Palance, Teri Hatcher, Michael J Pollard, Brion James, Geoffrey Lewis.
102 min.

'I heard you were the second best cop in LA', quips sartorially sleek Tango (Stallone). 'That's funny', retorts T-shirted slob Cash (Russell), 'I heard the same thing about you', The buddy-buddy banter is a set-up; so is the doped and 'wired' stiff they find on their first 'joint' operation. Result: a one-way ticket to the slammer on a trumped-up charge, leaving big-shot gun-runner Jack Palance free to take delivery of his biggest-ever shipment. All that remains is for our mis-matched duo to go through the motions. So, after taking the obligatory beating from their fellow prisoners, they escape, tool up, and set about clearing their names while plotting Palance's comeuppance. Koncha-lovsky handles the slam-bang action with robust efficiency, but what makes this shoot-'em-up nonsense surprisingly watchable is Randy Feldman's rapid-fire dialogue, which constantly undercuts the macho posturings while parodying Stallone's screen image…even though the spectacularly empty finale eschews character-based comedy in favour of Bond-style megabuck explosions and gadgetry. NF

Tango Lesson, The

(Sally Potter, 1997, GB/Fr/Arg/Jap/Ger) Sally Potter, Pablo Verón, Gustavo Naveira, Fabian Salas, David Toole, Peter Eyre, Heathcote Williams.
102 min. b/w & col.

While working on a thriller, British film-maker Sally Potter attends a Parisian dance recital by Pablo Verón, and is so entranced that she asks him to give her tango lessons. As time passes, her obsession with the music, the dance and her teacher becomes all consuming. She abandons her script to improve her skills as a dancer, and to prepare a movie about tango featuring herself and Verón. On one level, it's simply a terrific dance movie. On another, it offers a canny analysis of male-female relationships, with tango functioning as a model for the interrogation of power, passion, independence and cultural difference. And, inspired by writer/director Potter's real life experiences, Potter, Verón and most of the cast play 'versions' of themselves, allowing the movie to explore the fertile no man's land between reality and fiction. Though some may find Potter's cinematic presence a little 'cool' in terms of charisma and dramatic range, there's no denying that her partnering of Verón and others on the dance floor is both skilful and exhilarating. GA

Tank

(Marvin Chomsky, 1984, US) James Garner, Shirley Jones, C Thomas Howell, Mark Herrier, Jenilee Harrison, GD Spradlin.
113 min.

An Army sergeant due for retirement, Zack Carey (Garner) is the proud owner of a World War II Sherman tank, which he has been patiently restoring; and which he uses to flatten a small-town Georgia jail when the redneck local sheriff (Spradlin), irritated by Zack's intervention in a matter involving police brutality, trumps up a drug charge against his teenage son (Howell). The tank then carries the pair, plus Harrison as the cheery tart who was being slapped around when Zack intervened, across the state line (with the aid of some good guy Hell's Angels) and into folk-hero status (in imitation of *The Sugarland Express*). Part vigilante movie, part sitcom, part tearjerker, part cracker melodrama, it's redeemed by yet another of Garner's graceful, effortless performances.

Tank Girl

(Rachel Talalay, 1995, US) Lori Petty, Malcolm McDowell, Naomi Watts, Ice T, Don Harvey, Jeff Kober, Reg E Cathey, Iggy Pop.
104 min.

Generous souls may try to blame this travesty of the Deadline comic-strip on the studio execs who forced director Talalay to tone down and re-edit her cut. But what remains of Petty's anodyne sexless heroine and the dull, episodic live-action sequences suggests we may have been spared something worse even than this movie. At least the dynamic, vibrantly coloured (and clearly inserted) animation sequences allow us to imagine a tougher, ballsier film. In 2033, our post-apocalyptic planet is a desert where water is jealously guarded by megalomaniac Kesslee (McDowell). Fighting a rearguard action is Tank Girl – here pathetically renamed Rebecca – a crop-headed punkette who guzzles beer, sucks on ciggies, tries to swear properly and, yes, drives a tank. Providing back-up are the fearsome Rippers, a gang of rubber-faced, mutant kangaroos led by an embarrassed-looking Ice T. The damage-control editing aside, the most chaotic element is a soundtrack that throws together Richard Hell's punk anthem 'Blank Generation', the theme from *Shaft*, Hole's 'Drown Soda', and a jaw-dropping song-and-dance number based on Cole Porter's 'Let's Do It'. NF

Tank Malling

(James Marcus, 1988, GB) Ray Winstone, Jason Connery, Amanda Donohoe, Glen Murphy, Marsha Hunt, Peter Wyngarde, John Conteh, Terry Marsh.
109 min. b/w & col.
'I wonder if he's still wearing his rubber under-pants', ponders high-class prostitute Helen (Donohoe). She knows the Met's Assistant Commisioner of old, but now she's in hiding with investigative reporter Tank Malling (Winstone), spilling the beans on high-level involvement with prostitutes and drug abuse. Police, judiciary, politicians – none averse to a spot of S&M – are manipulated by Sir Robert Knights (Wyngarde), who oversees the depravity under the auspices of the Moral Revival Campaign. The last time Tank took on Sir Robert and his shady lawyer (Connery), he ended up framed for perjury; but this time the dogged newshound intends to write the definitive exposé. *Tank Malling* doesn't believe in subtlety where a sledgehammer will do. Characters don't talk, they shout; scenes don't merely evolve, they're telegraphed. The actors do their best (Donohoe in particular), but they're left struggling with impossible stereotypes and hack-neyed dialogue. CM

Tant qu'on a la Santé (As Long as You're Healthy)

(Pierre Etaix, 1965, Fr) Pierre Etaix, Denise Peronne, Simone Fonder, Sabine Sun, Véra Valmont.
78 min. b/w.
Etaix's last worthwhile feature in a relatively short career shows him emulating his master Jacques Tati (Etaix was assistant on the exe-crable *Mon Oncle*) as a young man at odds with his modern urban environment, especially build-ing sites. There's nothing here you haven't seen in Buster Keaton or in Chaplin's *Modern Times*. Watching Etaix and Tati in action suggests that the French must be profoundly worried by the apparatus or trappings of the modern world if they find this sort of caper funny. MA

Tap

(Nick Castle, 1988, US) Gregory Hines, Suzzanne Douglas, Sammy Davis Jr, Savion Glover, Joe Morton, Dick Anthony Williams, Sandman Sims, Bunny Briggs.
111 min.
An undemanding backstage romantic melodra-ma set in contemporary New York, *Tap* is also a homage to the great black dancers who liberated tap with their exuberant, inventive and personal interpretations pre rock'n'roll. The plot concerns Max (Hines) and his redemption from Ye Traditional Life of Crime through his paternal heritage as a tapper. The twists and turns are entirely predictable, but at least it's better plot-ted and acted than *Dirty Dancing*, doesn't attempt to rewrite black cultural history like *The Cotton Club*, and isn't cluttered with too many subplots as was *Fame*. Most enjoyment comes from the dance set pieces, notably a 'challenge' in which old-timers like Bunny Briggs, Sammy Davis Jr and the wonderfully grouchy Sandman Sims trade licks with each other and with Max, newly freed from Sing Sing. GBr

Tapdancin'

(Christian Blackwood, 1980, US) John Bubbles, Nicholas Brothers, Chuck Green, Tommy Tune, Jerry Ames, Honi Coles, Jazz Tap Percussion Ensemble.
75 min.
Blackwood (director of the slick and snappy *Roger Corman: Hollywood's Wild Angel*) has rather irritatingly tailored his fascinating docu-mentary on the dying art of tap dancing for sale to American television. Again and again, his (unlabeled) clips of tap veterans in action are cut short. But the film at least displays an intriguing sense of cultural ironies: the skill's black origins and its appropriation by whiteys. RM

Tapeheads

(Bill Fishman, 1988, US) John Cusack, Tim Robbins, Katy Boyer, Mary Crosby, Clu Gulager, Doug McClure, Connie Stevens, Lyle Alzado, Jessica Walter, Susan Tyrell, Junior Walker, Sam Moore.
97 min.
Cusack and Robbins are a couple of bored secu-rity guards who get their kicks by playing around with the closed circuit television. This leads them first to unemployment, then to a new career as music promo auteurs. It's all good fun: likeable performances, unpretentious, larky direction, and a haphazard story encompassing political shenanigans, an ageing hip soul duo called The Swanky Modes (Walker and Moore), deep fried chicken, and Jello Biaffra of the Dead Kennedys as an FBI agent! If *Repo Man* bounced politics off a B movie sensibility, this does the same with MTV. TCh

Taps

(Harold Becker, 1981, US) George C Scott, Timothy Hutton, Ronny Cox, Sean Penn, Tom Cruise, Brendan Ward.
126 min.
About a group of American cadets who take over their military college by force when they learn it is to be sold as real estate, this proved to be a freak success in America. Written off from scratch by industry insiders, including 'Variety', with even Fox itself evidently holding out no hopes, it nevertheless became a top box-office grosser, offering an intriguing reflection of America's military anxieties at the time. Hutton is highly effective as the senior boy who is so inspired by his school's head (Scott doing a *Patton* replay) that he mounts a full-scale mili-tary operation to repel the police; ultimately, though, a fascinating first hour is drowned in the clichés of siege cinema. DP

Tarantula

(Jack Arnold, 1955, US) John Agar, Mara Corday, Leo G Carroll, Nestor Paiva, Ross Elliott, Edward Eddie Parker, Ed Rand, Clint Eastwood.
80 min. b/w.
An uneven but largely effective merging of mad scientist and mutant monster movie from one of the best sci-fi directors of the '50s. Though it's far more routine than, say, *Creature from the Black Lagoon*, not to mention *The Incredible Shrinking Man*, there is a pulp poetry to the desert scenes through which the giant arachnid, created by Carroll's careless experiments, stalks murdering all and sundry. The cast is as wooden as ever, though sharp eyes might catch a glimpse of a young Clint Eastwood in a minute role as a fighter pilot during the climactic napalming of the creature. GA

Tarea, La

see Homework

Target

(Sandip Ray, 1995, Ind) Om Puri, Mohan Agashe, Anjan Srivastava.
104 min.
Hired as the *shikari* (huntsman) for an overbear-ing landowner, untouchable Rambharosa (Puri) can't believe his luck. He's housed, fed and clothed – but on the day of the hunt, he learns that there is something more important than money: respect. Directed by Sandip Ray from a script by his late father Satyajit Ray, *Target* takes aim at the entire caste system, but proves such a melo-dramatic blunderbuss one half expects the hero-ine to be tied to the rail tracks for the climax. TCh

Target

(Arthur Penn, 1985, US) Gene Hackman, Matt Dillon, Gayle Hunnicutt, Victoria Fyodorova, Ilona Grubel, Herbert Berghof, Josef Sommer.
118 min.
The Lloyds are a typical middle class American family, beset by dullness and young Chris' feel-ings that his Dad is a staid, materialist cop-out. Typical, that is, until Mom (Hunnicutt) suddenly disappears during a trip to Paris: when father (Hackman) and son (Dillon) follow in search and are welcomed by hails of bullets, all kinds of mys-teries erupt, not the least of which concerns Dad's secret past as a CIA agent. Penn's film might seem an altogether ordinary foray into the world of international espionage were it not for his teas-ing examination of various concepts of 'family', a word much abused throughout to denote not only the Lloyds, but also the several murderous organisations out to destroy them. An uneven film, to be sure, but far more ambitious and intel-ligent than most spy thrillers. GA

Targets

(Peter Bogdanovich, 1967, US) Boris Karloff, Tim O'Kelly, Nancy Hsueh, James Brown, Sandy Baron, Arthur Peterson, Peter Bogdanovich.
90 min.
Karloff in effect plays himself as Byron Orlok, a horror star on the point of retiring, who sudden-ly confronts the reality of contemporary American horror in the form of a psychopathic sniper (O'Kelly) picking off anyone he can see with a vast artillery of weapons. Bogdanovich was given the money to make the film by Roger Corman, who also allowed him to use extensive footage from Corman's Poe movie *The Terror* in the sequences at the drive-in cinema where the confrontation takes place. The result is a fasci-natingly complex commentary on American mythology, exploring the relationship between the inner world of the imagination and the outer world of violence and paranoia, both of which were relevant to contemporary American trau-mas. It was Bogdanovich's first film, and despite his subsequent success, he has yet to come up with anything half as remarkable. DP

Tarka the Otter

(David Cobham, 1978, GB) Peter Bennett, Edward Underdown, Brenda Cavendish, John Leeson.
91 min.
This episodic adaptation of Henry Williamson's novel seems determined to include stock shots of all British flora and fauna, whether relevant or not. It's a tale of love, tears, adventure, and close shaves, in which the animal stars act well; but only at the end, in the final confrontation between Tarka and his nemesis, Deadlock the otter-hound, does the film really jell. The rest suffers, as does the book, from a mixture of feyness and anthro-pomorphism, perhaps endearing in the 1920s but emerging as weakness in this more cynical age. SP

Tarnished Angels, The

(Douglas Sirk, 1957, US) Rock Hudson, Robert Stack, Dorothy Malone, Jack Carson, Robert Middleton, Troy Donahue.
91 min. b/w.
Arguably Sirk's bleakest film – perhaps because it was shot in greyish monochrome rather than luridly stylised colour – and one of his finest, this adaptation of Faulkner's *Pylon* reassembles the three principles from *Written on the Wind* for a probing but sympathetic study in failure and despair. In the South during the Depression, Hudson's down-at-heel reporter becomes fascinat-ed by a group of stunt fliers, led by Stack's disillusioned WWI veteran pilot and Malone's parachute jumper. In terms of plot very little real-ly happens; characters deceive each other and themselves, try in vain to communicate more fully, and repeatedly sell themselves short. Inevitably, it all culminates in death, which ironically provides some sort of half-hearted liberation, but Sirl's som-bre, tender awareness of the illusions that fuel his no-hopers' lives allows no respite. A film totally at odds with the bland optimism of postwar America, it might be depressing were it not for the consum-mate artistry on view. And Hudson, Stack, Malone and Carson were never better. GA

Tartuffe

(Gérard Depardieu, 1984, Fr) Gérard Depardieu, François Périer, Elisabeth Depardieu, Hélène Laptower.
138 min.
Depardieu's directorial debut is difficult to assess, since it is little more than a long, sombre and state-ly record of the Molière play. The sets are minimal, and since the camera doesn't move much, the film exists for the performances. Happily, these are excellent. As the grasping, lecherous cleric who takes over a gullible man's household, Depardieu is arrestingly different from the comically robust reading embodied in Anthony Sher's stage per-formance. This false devout is a loathsome cre-ation, his cunning as bloodless as his white face make-up. His evil is beyond explanation, like some-thing vampirical from German Expressionist cin-

ema; and the closing shot of him lying powerless on the floor, staring into the camera, is deeply unsettling. The hapless householder Orgon (Périer) is persuaded to surrender his daughter – a stunning moment from Laptower as she screams soundlessly – and his property to the intruder, and only comes to his senses when his wife (Elisabeth Depardieu) exposes Tartuffe as a lecher. One either surrenders to the slow drip of Molière's mesmerism or one doesn't. BC

Tarzan, the Ape Man

(John Derek, 1981, US) Bo Derek, Richard Harris, John Phillip Law, Miles O'Keeffe, Akushula Selaya, Steven Strong.
112 min.
Judging by the amount of time everybody spends swimming, the African jungle resembles Hornsey Baths filled with oversized pot plants. When not actually in the water, Bo Derek is having water poured over her, giving her mammary glands the Playboy Wet Look. Asked to act, the Wet Look invades her face and she whimpers, giggles, and sticks a finger in her mouth while reciting such blatant lies as 'I'm still a virgin'. Harris, as dad, takes the opposite approach and shouts all his lines at the top of his lungs. But O'Keeffe, as Tarzan, has the best part: he never says a word, unless you count 'Aaa-awaa-awaa'. His visual presence is striking enough: Bjorn Borg's head bolted on to Arnold Schwarzenegger's body. The plot, such as it is, climaxes when Bo is kidnapped by a bunch of sex-mad darkies, ruthlessly washed, and then painted white. A classic closing credits sequence finds Bo, Tarzan and an orang-utan – all officially still virgins – struggling to invent the Missionary Position. MB

Task Force (Rexue Zuiqiang)

(Patrick Leung, 1997, HK) Leo Ku, Charlie Young, Eric Tsang, Karen Mok, Waise Lee, Orlando To, John Woo.
100 min.
Vaulting over the wreckage of a film industry in deep recession, Patrick Leung's witty policier does nothing very new but still registers as one of the best Hong Kong movies of its year. Virginal cop Rod Lin (Ku, cute) first meets hooker Fanny Chan (Young, terrific) during an operation to entrap illegal immigrants working in the sex trade. She becomes the bane of his life, alternately a tormentor and a flirt; but she's really in love with a jailed boyfriend who has promised to take her to Paris for the World Cup. Their non-affair (which comes with quizzical voice-overs in the *Chungking Express* vein) is interspersed with non-stop subplots, digressions and flashbacks, not to mention homages to various Chinese and Japanese action classics. But as Danny Wong's unusual piano score suggests, it's finally less a thriller than a study of emotional reckonings: how to cope with a dying parent, how to handle an uncommitted lover. John Woo and other directors put in cameo appearances. TR

Taste of Cherry, A (Ta'ame-Gilas)

(Abbas Kiarostami, 1997, Iran) Homayoon Irshadi, Abdol Hossain Bagheri, Afshin Khorshid Bakhtiari, Safar Ali Moradi.
99 min.
A man drives around villages and the desert hills offering a series of carefully selected men a lift and unusually well paid work; he's not looking for a pick-up but, as we discover after a while, someone to help in his planned suicide. Characteristically, Kiarostami's *Palme d'Or* winner is low on narrative drive, slowly but steadily revealing more and more information, visual and verbal, until we are totally caught up in his protagonist's psychological and ethical dilemma. (Suicide is forbidden to Muslims.) As ever, the subtle, deceptively simple *mise-en-scène* speaks volumes, notably a nightmare of noisy industrialism in the desert, and the remarkable penultimate scene, which goes even further in its minimalist ambiguity than the final shots of the last two movies of Kiarostami's trilogy. GA

Taste of Fear (aka Scream of Fear)

(Seth Holt, 1960, GB) Susan Strasberg, Ann Todd, Ronald Lewis, Christopher Lee, Leonard Sachs.
81 min. b/w.
An above-par Hammer thriller, scripted by

Jimmy Sangster and brazenly plagiarising Clouzot's *Les Diaboliques* as wheelchair-bound Strasberg arrives to visit her father on the Riviera, believes she sees his corpse (more than once), but is told that he's away on a trip. The plotting is very contrived indeed, but thanks partly to Douglas Slocombe's camerawork and to taut, shock-cut editing, Holt manages a *tour de force* of brooding, genuinely unsettling atmosphere. GA

Taste of Honey, A

(Tony Richardson, 1961, GB) Rita Tushingham, Dora Bryan, Robert Stephens, Murray Melvin, Paul Danquah.
100 min. b/w.
A perfect example of how the 'New British Cinema' of the late '50s and early '60s has dated and become almost unwatchable. Richardson's version of Shelagh Delaney's play about a Salford girl getting pregnant after leaving home highlights the style's many faults: kitchen sink realism, when pursued as an end in itself, can be as tedious and unrevealing as an uninspired episode of *Coronation Street*. It's all very well dwelling on grimy streets, factory chimneys, sluttish individuals, and so on, but with no real attempt to place characters in an explicit social or political context, the story becomes reduced to a drab, voyeuristic celebration of ordinariness and poverty. There's no anger, no joy, and ultimately no insight in this film; its shallow reliance on clichés reeks of complacency. GA

Taste of the Black Earth, The (Sól Ziemi Czarnej)

(Kazimierz Kutz, 1969, Pol) Olgierd Lukaszewicz, Jerzy Binczycki, Jerzy Cnota, Wieslaw Dymny.
103 min.
A film about the 1920 Silesian uprising, when bands of insurgents rebelled against the German occupation troops. The story is told through the eyes of a 16-year-old boy, youngest of a family of seven sons who join the uprising; and in approach the film owes more to Hollywood than to a Communist propaganda tradition, though without the simplification of issues or the false heroics of the Western attitude to immediate history. Visually it's a small masterpiece, stunningly shot in the beautiful browns and greens of the 'land' for which the men are fighting.

Taste the Blood of Dracula

(Peter Sasdy, 1969, GB) Christopher Lee, Geoffrey Keen, Gwen Watford, Linda Hayden, Peter Sallis, Ralph Bates, John Carson, Anthony Corlan, Isla Blair, Roy Kinnear.
95 min.
Depraved Lord Courtley (Bates) involves three other rich Victorian thrill-seekers in the resurrection of the blood-sucking Count (Lee), by means of an elaborate ritual performed in a derelict church. Imaginatively realised and shot with flamboyant style, the ritual ends with Courtley's death and the flight of the three others, setting the scene for a lurid tale in which Dracula wreaks revenge on the fugitives by seducing and corrupting their daughters. Though the film never quite lives up to its brilliantly staged opening scenes, its variation on the idea of the decadent, aristocratic Dracula's threat to the sanctity of the Victorian middle class family highlights an intriguing aspect of Hammer's vampire mythology. NF

Tatie Danielle

(Etienne Chatiliez, 1990, Fr) Tsilla Chelton, Catherine Jacob, Isabelle Nanty, Neige Dolsky, Eric Prat, Laurence Février.
112 min.
After *Life Is a Long Quiet River*, Chatiliez' second film is again a black comedy, a scabrous assault on middle class mores. Tatie Danielle (Chelton) is an ailing, respectable widow – or so she appears. As her relatives the Billards soon discover, behind her feeble demeanour lurks an indomitable will and a malicious mind. If only for sheer bloody-mindedness, the movie earns a few chuckles in the beginning, but once Tatie's true nature is established, it goes nowhere fast. Chatiliez seems to share Tatie's contempt for this stereotyped middle class family; but on the evidence presented, it is hard not to conclude that the bourgeoisie are in pretty good shape, their restraint and kindness lasting well beyond the

call of duty. After this satiric backfire, there's the inevitable back-down as the old lady meets her match in the shape of a no-shit young house-sitter (Nanty). For an encore, Chatiliez stages an ending that is at once anticlimactic, predictable and illogical: an apt conclusion for a clumsy, tiresome, unendearing film. TCh

Tattoo

(Bob Brooks, 1980, US) Bruce Dern, Maud Adams, Leonard Frey, Rikke Borge, John Getz, Peter Iachangelo.
103 min.
Made by a British-based commercials and TV director, working from a script by Buñuel's daughter-in-law, this emerges as a reworking of John Fowles' *The Collector*. Only the kinks have been changed to excite the prurient. Loner tattooist (played by Hollywood's favourite nutter, Dern) stalks, abducts, and tattoos his beautiful model (Adams) before he fucks her. Despite vague attempts to give tattoos global significance, the result is a peepshow of psychopathology, devoid of insight or even context. See the mad artist kidnap the hysterical girl! See him make her masturbate while he watches through a hole in the door! Roll over Sigmund Freud and tell Bill Reich the bad news. MB

Tattooed Tears

(Nick Broomfield/Joan Churchill, 1978, US)
85 min.
Broomfield and Churchill's 'sequel' to their controversial *Juvenile Liaison* raises urgent structural and institutional problems for the investigative form. The workings of a purportedly liberal Youth Training School for delinquents in California are examined, and condemned through an intensely dramatic concentration on four of its victims, ostensibly there for rehabilitation, but actually undergoing repetitive and vindictive punishment. In the process, the film raises the spectre of individual suffering exploited: one inmate dramatising his resistance specifically for the camera receives humiliating treatment which the camera duly observes but cannot forestall. Though the film's purpose may be agitational in the immediate US context, the result as received here tends, unfortunately, to the disturbingly voyeuristic. PT

Tausend Augen des Dr Mabuse, Die

see 1000 Eyes of Dr Mabuse, The

Tavaszi Zápor (Marie – a Hungarian Legend/Marie, légende hongroise/Spring Shower)

(Paul Fejos ie. Pál Fejös, 1932, Hun/Fr) Annabella, István Gyergyai, Ilona Dajbukát, Karola Zala, Germaine Aussey.
68 min. b/w.
The 'legend' itself is sanctimonious drivel: Marie (Annabella), dismissed from her job as a maid for getting pregnant, wanders lonely and rejected, weeping for her namesake the Blessed Virgin, until she's taken in by the fallen women of a brothel; her soul fetches up in a heavenly replica of the kitchen where she started out, safeguarding the virtue of her illegitimate daughter back on earth. Censorship of the time gave her an 'invisible' pregnancy, and left the depiction of the brothel and its dykey madame bafflingly opaque. The large redeeming features are Fejös' visual style, and László Angyal's more or less continuous score. TR

Tawny Pipit

(Bernard Miles/Charles Saunders, 1944, GB) Bernard Miles, Rosamund John, Niall MacGinnis, Jean Gillie, George Carney, Christopher Steele, Joan Sterndale Bennett, Katie Johnson.
85 min.
English whimsy at its mildest follows the fuss and consternation when convalescent airman MacGinnis and his nurse John discover a pair of tawny pipits nesting in the meadow near their Cotswold village. It's a rare event, since the birds have only once been sighted in England before, so the whole local community ends up guarding the spot day and night to ward off prospective egg-snatchers. Scripted by the directors and printed in sepia. TJ

t

Taxandria
(Raoul Servais, 1995, Fr/Bel/Ger) Armin
Mueller-Stahl, Daniel Emilfork.
80 min.
This technically innovative blending of actors
with, for much of the movie, animated settings is
a surreal, allegorical fantasy about a young
prince who, with the help of a lighthouse-keeper,
witnesses a strange world where progress, clocks,
modern machinery and sexual equality have been
banned. Alain Robbe-Grillet had a hand in the
screenplay, but it's still something of a dog's dinner, initially intriguing but delivering a tale far
too unfocused to be anything more than a visual
curiosity. GA

Taxi
(Carlos Saura, 1996, Sp) Ingrid Rubio, Carlos
Fuentes, Agata Lys, Angel de Andres Lopez,
Eusebio Lazaro.
113 min.
Saura's first film scripted by another hand is a
crude, uneven exposé of vigilante taxi drivers
who spend their nights ridding Madrid of undesirables – blacks, gays and drug addicts. While
it concentrates on the middle-aged cabbies' murderous conspiracy, the flesh-and-blood performances by Lys and Lopez fuse with Vittorio
Storraro's crisp, almost futuristic cinematography, drawing us into their nocturnal world.
However, once Santiago Tabernero's script shifts
to the drippy teen romance between idealistic
teenager Paz (Rubio) and her reluctantly
racist/homophobic boyfriend Dani, matters go
fuzzy at the edges. Only the instinctive power of
19-year-old newcomer Ingrid Rubio relieves the
tedium of watching liberal sentiments fall into
place. NF

Taxi!
(Roy Del Ruth, 1931, US) James Cagney,
Loretta Young, David Landau, Guy Kibbee,
George E Stone, Leila Bennett, Matt McHugh.
68 min. b/w.
Cagney gets to bawl a lot, talk to a customer in
Yiddish and even enter a dance competition in
this busy little entertainment set in New York's
cab community. He's an independent taxi company boss who defends his drivers against the
tactics of organised syndicate head honcho
Landau, who wants all the best spots for his men.
The action spirals into violence and revenge, but
it's much less of a hard-hitting exposé than the
general run of '30s Warners crime pictures, and
pleasingly compact with it. TJ

Taxi Blues
(Pavel Lounguine, 1990, USSR/Fr) Piotr
Mamonov, Piotr Zaitchenko, Vladimir
Kachpour.
110 min.
There's something basically phony about
Lounguine's flashy debut feature, which is forever congratulating itself on being so 'daring' in
showing the wrong side of Moscow's tracks. It
centres on an 'odd couple' relationship between a
stolid, seen-it-all cab driver (Zaitchenko) and a
wayward, alcoholic Jewish jazz musician
(Mamonov), thrown together by one's demand
that the other meet his debts (after the musician
skips out on paying his cab fare). The director
apparently sees this as a paradigm of worker-
intellectual relations, but he's too interested in
exposing scuzzy life-styles, and wallowing in
vodka, crime and sex, to get too tied up in politics. Trouble is, he has no idea at all how to end
it. Skip the last 15 minutes, and you might come
out with a wry smile. TR

Taxi Driver 100 (100)
(Martin Scorsese, 1976, US) Robert De Niro,
Cybill Shepherd, Jodie Foster, Harvey Keitel,
Peter Boyle, Leonard Harris, Martin Scorsese,
Steven Prince, Diahnne Abbot, Albert Brooks.
114 min.
Taxi Driver makes you realise just how many
directors, from Schlesinger to Friedkin and
Winner, have paddled around on the surface of
New York in their films. Utilising, especially,
Bernard Herrmann's most menacing score since
Psycho, Scorsese has set about recreating the
landscape of the city in a way that constitutes a
truly original and terrifying Gothic canvas. But,
much more than that: Taxi Driver is also, thanks
partly to De Niro's extreme implosive performance, the first film since Alphaville to set about

a really intelligent appraisal of the fundamental
ingredients of contemporary insanity. Its final
upsurge of violence doesn't seem to be cathartic
in the now predictable fashion of the 'new'
American movie, but lavatorial; the nauseating
effluence of the giant flesh emporium that the film
has so single-mindedly depicted. DP

Taxi Mauve, Le
see Purple Taxi, The

Taxing Woman, A
(Marusa no Onna)
(Juzo Itami, 1987, Jap) Nobuko Miyamoto,
Tsutomu Yamazaki, Masahiko Tsugawa,
Yasuo Daichi, Eitaro Ozawa.
127 min.
In this, his third helter-skelter satire on modern
Japanese mores, Itami turns his witty attention
to the subject of Money, with tighter construction
and deeper characterisation making it his most
entertaining yet. Miyamoto plays divorcée
Ryoko, an Inspector for the Japanese National
Tax Agency whose considerable energies are
channelled into the collaring of tax evaders. Her
tenacious, seemingly heartless exposure of the
scams, perks and false expenses of small-time
gambling arcade proprietors, corner-shop owners and the like, trades beautifully on the guilty
pleasures to be had in seeing the other guy get
his deserts. But success gives her the chance to
go for the big fish: Rachmanesque hoodlum and
'entertainment' hotel boss Gondo (Yamazaki). As
the movie gears up for the final bust, Itami
exploits and inverts every known cliché of the
detective thriller with a breathless style, and a
sexual excitement in criminal minutiae reminiscent of Bresson's Pickpocket. WH

Taxi zum Klo
(Frank Ripploh, 1980, WGer) Frank Ripploh,
Bernd Broaderup, Orpha Termin, Peter
Fahrni, Dieter Gidde.
94 min.
Ill-matched gay lovers: Bernd prefers to stay at
home cooking supper and scrubbing pans, while
Frank (engagingly played by director Ripploh)
scours Berlin's Klos (public lavatories) and
leather-bars for cheap thrills and one-night
stands. With an impressive sureness of touch, the
schoolteacher/cruiser double life-style is shown
in explicit though never exploitative detail, as
undoubtedly 'different' yet in no way perverse
(contrast the sexpol prudery of Nighthawks or
Looking for Mr Goodbar). Shot on a very thin
shoestring (û25,000; no State grant) and, like
many good – and not so good – first films, openly autobiographical, it succeeds on the strength
of a surprising irony and wit, and a tacky exuberance (the title says it all) that can't fail to disarm, entertain, and maybe even dispel a few
myths along the way. SJo

T. Dan Smith
(Amber Films, 1987, GB) T Dan Smith, Jack
Johnston, Ken Sketheway, Dennis Skinner,
George Vickers.
86 min.
Resembling Evelyn Waugh facially and perhaps
Huey 'Kingfish' Long historically, T Dan Smith
proves a mesmerising speaker in this documentary by the Amber Films collective. Was he the
fall-guy for the Establishment in the Poulson
Affair, imprisoned to save Home Secretary
Reginald Maudling's neck, or was he a Trot idealist who dreamed of transforming Newcastle
into the Milan of the North, infiltrated the system,
but surrendered his soul in the process? That face
doesn't give much clue, and the linking investi-
gatory journalists confess themselves no wiser
by the end. A compilation of newsreel, interview
and dramatic reconstruction, the film is sometimes clumsy, but the facts are strong enough to
tether the viewer. Unfair immunity at the top
seems to be the commercial. BC

Tea and Sympathy
(Vincente Minnelli, 1956, US) Deborah Kerr,
John Kerr, Leif Erickson, Edward Andrews,
Darryl Hickman, Dean Jones, Norma Crane.
122 min.
Filming The Servant with Harold Pinter, Losey
could treat the homosexual relationship between
master and manservant with both visual élan and
verbal acuity. Minnelli was less lucky. Robert

Anderson's sensitive if fancifully written play,
about a housemaster's wife coaxing a pupil out
of latent tendencies, was weakened to such a
degree through the combined forces of censorship
and CinemaScope that the tendencies threatened
to disappear completely. Which can hardly be
said for the students' garish shirts and pullovers,
the phony exterior sets, or the gleaming '50s automobiles – all on constant parade. Yet the film's
details – indeed, its very timidity – still ensure
fascinating viewing. GB

Teachers
(Arthur Hiller, 1984, US) Nick Nolte, JoBeth
Williams, Judd Hirsch, Ralph Macchio, Allen
Garfield, Lee Grant, Richard Mulligan, Royal
Dano, William Schallert, Art Metrano, Laura
Dern, Zohra Lampert.
106 min.
This is about wastage in the field of education.
But the film manages to waste: Nolte, playing a
disillusioned teacher with all the fire of a tranquillised tiger; fine character actors like Royal
Dano and Allen Garfield; and, finally, a potentially dynamic subject. Hiller's sledgehammer
direction turns the problems common in education into an endless parade of clichés, feebly
propped up by wacky humour, inarticulacy, ham
and corn. Avoid. GA

Teahouse of the
August Moon, The
(Daniel Mann, 1956, US) Marlon Brando, Glenn
Ford, Eddie Albert, Machiko Kyo, Paul Ford,
Henry Morgan.
123 min.
A likeable, if overlong and distinctly verbose
adaptation of John Patrick's Broadway play,
which wrings some mild amusement out of a
clash between cultural stereotypes (American
efficiency gives way to Oriental lethargy as the
occupying force on Okinawa is beguiled into
building a teahouse rather than a schoolhouse).
The very stuff that sitcoms are made of, it's kept
alive by genial contributions from Glenn Ford,
Eddie Albert, and especially Paul Ford as the
mulishly obtuse Colonel (who later resurfaced as
a fixture in TV's Sergeant Bilko series). As all too
often in Brando movies, his performance as the
crafty Okinawan interpreter is streets ahead of
the dialogue and direction he gets. TM

Teckman Mystery, The
(Wendy Toye, 1954, GB) Margaret Leighton,
John Justin, Michael Medwin, Roland Culver,
George Colouris, Raymond Huntley.
90 min. b/w.
Commissioned to write the biography of a dead
test pilot, John Justin walks into more than a tight
deadline. He's knocked unconscious, his flat's
turned upside down and he's offered lots of dosh
by a very shady character. A mindlessly diverting British thriller, neatly adapted from a Francis
Durbridge TV serial, but essentially unremarkable. TJ

Teenage Caveman
(Roger Corman, 1958, US) Robert Vaughn,
Leslie Bradley, Darrah Marshall, Frank De
Kova.
66 min. b/w.
You'll chuckle the first time you see fresh-faced
Vaughn in his off-the-shoulder loincloth, but
Corman's no-budget prehistoric epic is endearing
in the way it refuses to cheapen an admittedly
fairly tacky sub-genre. In fact, as the youthful
protagonist ignores the warnings of his tribe and
crosses the river to face the much-feared monster
that lives on the other side, the picture gathers
imaginative momentum and conjures up at least
one satisfying plot reversal. No wonder the star
called it 'one of the best-worst films of all time'.
TJ

Teenage Mutant Ninja Turtles
(Steve Barron, 1990, US) Judith Hoag, Elias
Koteas, Josh Pais, Michelan Sisti, Leif Tilden,
David Forman.
93 min.
This live action feature pits the crime-fighting,
man-sized turtles against Shredder, their arch
enemy, who is recruiting hordes of teens to his
evil ways. Reporter April O'Neil (Hoag) has been
investigating a sudden increase in New York
crime, and becomes embroiled in their mission

after the pizza freaks save her from a mugging. Jim Henson's Creature Shop has created splendid animatronic characters (including a four-foot talking rat), though extra distinguishing marks between the turtles would be appreciated. Between the dubbed dialogue and the dark visuals, the cumulative effect is curiously dislocating. The big plus for fans, of course, is the boisterous interplay between the four heroes and some engaging slapstick humour; both redeem more functional elements like the love-hate relationship between April and martial arts enthusiast Casey (Koteas). CM

Teenage Mutant Ninja Turtles II: The Secret of the Ooze

(Michael Pressman, 1991, US) Paige Turco, David Warner, Michelan Sisti, Leif Tilden, Ernie Reyes Jr, Kenn Troum, Mark Caso, Kevin Clash.
87 min.
The first 'Turtles' film aroused a ridiculous controversy over how, because they ate pizza and grew big and strong from radioactive ooze, the Turtles were not healthy role-models. Perhaps in response, this sequel's 'plot' centres on saving the city from that self-same ooze. The original fell between two age groups: the late teens and gonzo students at whom the 1984 comic book was aimed, and the tiny tots who enjoyed the subsequent TV cartoons. The sequel drags the target audience back towards the latter, with toned-down violence, a terrifically funny cameo from two retarded mutant Muppets, and a terrifically crass cameo from the similarly retarded Vanilla Ice. It does, however, retain the essential elements that first turned the world Turtle – the affectionate squabbling between the four, the pantomime villains, the cracking one-liners – and the bigger budget is a blessing. DW

Teenage Mutant Ninja Turtles III

(Stuart Gillard, 1992, US) Elias Koteas, Paige Turco, Stuart Wilson, Sab Shimono, Vivian Wu, Mark Caso.
96 min.
The first Teenage Mutant Ninja Turtles was, for all its faults, a minor miracle. Here, for small children, were heroes who were streetwise, anti-authority, and loved to fight. It couldn't last. In their third film, which is shorn of nearly all the elements which made the Ninjas popular, one turtle pontificates: 'Fighting's for grown-ups, and only if they've got no other choice.' One of the most enjoyable things about the Turtles was their interaction with a modern city. Here, however, writer/director Gillard misguidedly sends them back to medieval Japan. The wisecracks have been cut back, and where once the Ninjas' dude-speak was original (influencing, for example, Wayne's World) it's now merely imitative. DW

Teen Agent

(William Dear, 1991, US) Richard Grieco, Linda Hunt, Roger Rees, Robin Bartlett, Gabrielle Anwar, Geraldine James, Michael Siberry, Carole Davis, Roger Daltrey.
88 min.
This marriage made in TV heaven boasts a script by Beverly Hills 90210 writer Darren Star, while the nice teeth and hair are modelled by 21 Jump Street star Grieco, playing Michael Corben, a high school dunce who must get a pass grade in French in order to graduate. While travelling to Paris with his teacher and classmates, he is mistaken for a secret agent and briefed by British Intelligence. Off he zooms in his specially-equipped sportscar, ready to rid the world of whip-wielding Ilsa Grunt (Hunt) and maniacal Augustus Steranko (Rees). Aside from Michael's curious penchant for dark eyeliner, it's hard to find anything of interest in this mediocre offering. Even the hi-tech gadgetry is boring. CM

Teenagers from Outer Space (aka The Gargon Terror)

(Tom Graeff, 1959, US) David Love, Dawn Anderson, Harvey B Dunn, Bryan Grant, Tom Lockyear.
87 min. b/w.
An epic attempting to cash in on the teenpic boom with its tale of two alien teens sent to Earth. One is 'good', and falls in love with a local high school honey; one is 'bad', and rampages with a ray gun.

A major period feature is the theme of teen martyrdom: the 'good' alien commits suicide in a bid to save Earth from an army of spaceships (never seen on the screen) and the giant lobster (watch for the hand holding what you can see of it) which has accompanied them. CR

Teen Kanya (Two Daughters)

(Satyajit Ray, 1961, Ind) Soumitra Chatterjee, Aparna Das Gupta, Anil Chatterjee, Chandana Banerjee, Kanika Mazumdar.
171 (114) min. b/w.
The title should translate as Three Daughters, since the film originally comprised a trio of Tagore stories, all touching on the problems of emancipation through women of contrasting classes. In the export version, one episode was cut for reasons of length: a ghost story about a woman obsessed by her jewellery, this is comparatively weak (though extremely striking visually). But the other two are Ray at his best, particularly the tale of a young university graduate who rejects the bride his mother has selected for him, but offers to marry the village tomboy (who has caught his eye but piqued his pride by her mockery of his pretensions). A marriage is duly arranged, despite the tomboy's furious protests, and what follows is a variation on The Taming of the Shrew, wonderfully funny and tender, and played to perfection by Soumitra Chatterjee and Aparna Das Gupta. But a bitterly ironic undertone lingers despite the happy end (love prevails): too emancipated to agree to a marriage with a girl he does not love, the hero never for a moment realises that he is denying the same privilege to the girl of his choice. TM

Teen Wolf

(Rod Daniel, 1985, US) Michael J Fox, James Hampton, Susan Ursitti, Jerry Levine, Matt Adler, Lorie Griffin.
92 min.
High school student Scott Howard (Fox in a personable performance) bemoans his ordinariness, but soon discovers that he comes from a long line of werewolves, and that, in wolfish guise, he gets all the things he ever wanted: popularity, ace basketballing skills, and Pamela, the local blonde venus (Griffin). Far from being saturated with horrific special effects, the film is planted firmly in lighthearted sitcom territory. There's too much basketball and mucking about on car roofs (to music), the moral is thumpingly obvious, and Fox's make-up makes him look more simian than lupine. AB

Teen Wolf Too

(Christopher Leitch, 1987, US) Jason Bateman, Kim Darby, John Astin, Paul Sand, James Hampton, Mark Holton, Estee Chandler.
94 min.
While Teen Wolf didn't exactly provoke howls of laughter, its innocuous humour did benefit greatly from the light comic touch of its diminutive star, Michael J Fox. This tedious sequel casts the producer's uncharismatic son (Bateman) as Fox's similarly afflicted cousin Todd, but offers only a faint echo of its predecessor. Having come to terms with his lupine lineage, and ditched studious virgin Nicki (Chandler) in favour of fast times in a Porsche with a pair of big-breasted bimbettes, Todd suffers the same crisis of identity. Do his fickle fans love him or the wolf? Parents forced to suffer alongside their kids may salvage some amusement from the antics of Todd's gluttonous chum Chubby (Holton), who steals the show throughout. NF

Telefon

(Don Siegel, 1977, US) Charles Bronson, Lee Remick, Donald Pleasence, Tyne Daly, Alan Badel, Patrick Magee, Sheree North, John Mitchum.
103 min.
At least the Cold War fired Hollywood's imagination, which is more than can be said for the first East-West détente picture (from the producer of Dr Strangelove). Russian agents planted as ordinary US citizens years earlier are suddenly activated via Telefon by a crazy unreconstructed Stalinist (Pleasence), and perform sundry kamikaze sabotage missions. Moscow is embarrassed, and sends in Bronson to team up with Remick, in fact a double agent. Not unlike the 'sleeper' agents, Bronson gives a strong impres-

sion of deep-hypnosis throughout, thereby suggesting possible plot twists infinitely more interesting than those provided in the dull script by Peter Hyams and Stirling Silliphant. Most disappointing is Siegel's contribution: he, of all directors, should have been able to inject some life into the proceedings, but this is his most nondescript outing in years. CPe

Telephone Book, The

(Nelson Lyon, 1971, US) Sarah Kennedy, Norman Rose, James Harder, Jill Clayburgh, Ondine, Barry Morse, Ultra Violet, Roger C Carmel.
88 min.
Any humour in the original idea – an obscene phone-caller of such seductive skill that his victims long for aural molestation – is soon sabotaged by the director's blind intent on demonstrating that, although it may be a comedy, he sure knows how to make a film, and an arty one at that. The brief presence of three ex-Warhol personalities merely emphasises that, where the Warhol movies were funny and interesting (and boring) because the people in them were recognisable human beings, the characters teetering through this tired script are actors pretending to be kooky people. Having misunderstood the connection between sex and '60s avant-garde, Lyon – in a desperate bid to save a failed project – tarts things up at the end with a bit of explicit animation. SM

Tell England

(Anthony Asquith/Geoffrey Barkas, 1931, GB) Fay Compton, Tony Bruce, Carl Harbord, Dennis Hoey, CM Hallard, Wally Patch.
88 min. b/w.
Few enough films deal with the traumatic experience of the First World War, and Asquith deserves some credit for tackling the disastrous Gallipoli campaign. His gilded youth protagonists now look unbearably priggish: 'Just fetch my bath-water in the morning and brush my clothes and see that my buttons are clean and polish my boots and my belt', an 18-year-old officer tells the middle-aged soldier detailed to look after him. And the action sequences, handled by veteran director Barkas, endorse the public-school heroism. Asquith, with his staunch liberal insistence on the futility of war, puts up a brave fight, but overwhelmed by the 8,000 extras and the flotillas of troop-carriers, he ends up celebrating patriotism rather than pacifism. RMy

Telling Lies in America

(Guy Ferland, 1997, US) Kevin Bacon, Brad Renfro, Maximilian Schell, Calista Flockhart, Paul Dooley, Jonathan Rhys Meyers.
101 min.
It's 1960 and Renfro's Hungarian immigrant teen determines to get into the pants of winsome co-worker Flockhart by having his name mentioned on the 'High School Hall of Fame' by Cleveland's top DJ, Billy Magic (Bacon). Whizz kid Billy is so impressed by Renfro's denial that he sent in several hundred nomination cards himself that he makes the lad his assistant. These are the days of payola, but young Master Sheltered Life is unaware of the significance of the envelopes he passes to his boss from sundry shady types. And since he and his dad (Schell) are applying for US citizenship, trouble with the police is the last thing he wants. Bacon revels in the greased back hair, flip on-air patter and ersatz R&B stylings on the soundtrack, but it's absolutely no surprise that his icon of cool turns out to be a dud. Director Ferland can only move the elements of the hackneyed plot (by Joe Eszterhas) into place and hope we like Bacon enough not to notice. TJ

Telling Tales

(Richard Woolley, 1978, GB) Bridget Ashburn, Stephen Trafford, Patricia Donovan, James Woolley, Ian Masters.
93 min.
Woolley's reference points here are British TV soap serials like Coronation Street and Crossroads, contemporary British politics of class, and the school of 'deconstructed' narrative film-making in which Woolley has situated himself. Dealing with the life of two typical households, one middle and the other working class, Telling Tales attempts a breakdown of the inventory of clichés of which much of filmic language

894 Time Out Film Guide

consists. It's often very funny and revealing, as in the use of sound effects early on in the film, and in the use of deliberately banal dialogue foregrounded by Woolley's deadpan use of actors moving in and out of the camera frame. Sometimes it's less effective: where the actors are required to be more emotional, for instance. But there is no escaping the film's value as an implicit criticism of the humourlessness of most current work in this area. RM

Tell Me a Riddle

(Lee Grant, 1981, US) Melvyn Douglas, Lila Kedrova, Brooke Adams, Lili Valenty, Dolores Dorn, Ron Harris, Zalman King.
90 min.
An elderly Midwestern couple take off across America for a last visit to their children (and aghast confrontation with dropout San Francisco). They are Russian-Jewish, which naturally means that every other image conjures a pogrom-haunted memory. And just to open the taps on the already gushing sentimentality, she (Kedrova at her most winsome) is dying of cancer. Douglas, thank God, is at least agreeably tart. TM

Tell Me That You Love Me, Junie Moon

(Otto Preminger, 1969, US) Liza Minnelli, Ken Howard, Robert Moore, James Coco, Kay Thompson, Fred Williamson, Ben Piazza, Leonard Frey, Anne Revere.
113 min.
Another in the great series of disasters with which Preminger seemed intent on finishing his career, this is the tale of three mentally and physically handicapped social outcasts (facially disfigured girl, homosexual paraplegic, introverted epileptic) who set up home together. For all its SAS-like attacks on its audience's desire for charmingly handicapped people – Preminger refuses to favour the 'good' profile of Liza Minnelli's scarred Junie Moon – the script is little but a series of Smart Aleck exchanges/platitudes. PH

Tell Them Willie Boy Is Here

(Abraham Polonsky, 1969, US) Robert Redford, Katharine Ross, Robert Blake, Susan Clark, Barry Sullivan, Charles McGraw, John Vernon, Shelly Novack.
98 min.
Polonsky's return to direction after 21 blacklist years since Force of Evil, with a contemporary Western about a manhunt for a Piute Indian (Blake, excellent) presumed guilty of a crime defined by circumstance rather than by fact. The allegory about witch-hunting is there for the asking, taken a stage further than usual in the bitter irony whereby the hitherto Americanised Willie, accused in effect of being an Indian, gradually reverts to being an Indian in the archetypally savage sense. A powerful film, even though the script wears its liberal conscience on its sleeve (and further hedges its bets by casting nice Robert Redford as the sheriff), directed with austere authority in desert landcapes marvellously shot by Conrad Hall. TM

Tempest

(Paul Mazursky, 1982, US) John Cassavetes, Gena Rowlands, Susan Sarandon, Vittorio Gassman, Raúl Julia, Molly Ringwald, Sam Robards, Paul Stewart.
142 min.
Just what we need, another Mazursky film where bright women wear the whitest of knickers, and where New Yorkers hide insecurities of seismic scale beneath that wonderfully direct way they have of talking at each other. Shakespeare's story is just another Manhattan mid-life crisis, and frankly, who cares? Mr Success (Cassavetes) ditches everything for a simple life in remotest Greece with his daughter Miranda. Yet Cassavetes, sporting the fanciest haircut since Frederic Forrest in Hammett, performs with such crusty conviction that one does start to care about what happens. That old Shakespearean magic survives even this loosest of adaptations, and by the end one is wallowing in the length and indulgence of it all (thinking as much about a summer holiday as about the film). Only later does one realise with the greatest relief what has been missing all along from the picture: Woody Allen. CPe

Tempest, The

(Derek Jarman, 1979, GB) Heathcote Williams, Karl Johnson, Toyah Wilcox, Peter Bull, Richard Warwick, Elizabeth Welch, Jack Birkett.
95 min.
Jarman's rendering of the Bard's last act is his best picture to date, superbly shot in crumbling abbeys and mansions that look like Piranesi's Gothic drawings of fallen Rome, and turning the triteness of camp into absurdist comedy. The ending is pure Python and a major mistake – a cabaret with Elizabeth Welch singing 'Stormy Weather'– but until then Jarman's gleeful re-imagining of the play and his serious debate with it works wondrously well. Ages and influences crash together – Caliban as an Edwardian butler, Ariel a sight for gay eyes, Prospero a character out of Blake – but it's all of a piece, directed like a magic show. ATu

Temptation (Pokuszenie)

(Barbara Sass, 1995, Pol) Magdalena Cielecka, Olgierd Lukaszewicz, Krzysztof Pieczynski, Maria Ciunelis, Edward Zentara.
101 min.
Post-war Poland in the tightening grip of the Communist authorities is the setting for this sombre drama of faith from a contemporary of Agnieszka Holland. Cielecka is the young nun moved to a rural detention centre, where she re-encounters an interned cardinal for whom she's long had a secretive burning passion. As their military overseers try to play both sides off against each other, the notion of confession takes on both spiritual and political meanings as personal, theological and ideological imperatives vie for supremacy. Although the performances milk every nuance from Sass's careful screenplay, the avoidance of overt melodramatics and the predominant tones of grey are a constant reminder of the worthiness of the material. TJ

Temptation Harbour

(Lance Comfort, 1947, GB) Robert Newton, Simone Simon, William Hartnell, Margaret Barton, Marcel Dalio, Edward Rigby, Charles Victor.
104 min. b/w.
Reviewers contrasted this unfavourably with Renoir's La Bête Humaine, but Simenon's story, with the fates leading a well-intentioned hero to his destruction in the docks of Dieppe (here Newhaven), now looks like an interesting bridge between the gloomy French melodramas of the '30s and American film noir. Newton is the harbour signalman who retrieves a suitcase full of money after witnessing a murder, fails to report it to the police, and finds himself the object of murderous and mercenary interest. He gives a wonderfully tension-ridden performance, fleetingly caressing Simone Simon's slip, erupting into exasperated anger with the nervy Hartnell, but never allowing full expression to the lust and violence clearly visible beneath the kindly surface. The ending may appear disappointingly conformist, and Simone's bored femme fatale fails to fulfil her potential (despite having 'enough atomic energy in the lobes of her ears to flatten London'); but this is the price one has to pay for Comfort's dogged refusal to simplify, to sacrifice realism to melodrama, which is in itself interesting. RMy

Tempter, The (Il Sorriso del Grande Tentatore)

(Damiano Damiani, 1973, It/GB) Glenda Jackson, Claudio Casinelli, Lisa Harrow, Adolfo Celi, Arnoldo Foà, Francisco Rabal.
106 min.
A diabolical piece of work which pointlessly indulges the Italian obsession with convents, nuns, and – ever so discreetly – mortification of the flesh. Just who tempts whom and why remains a mystery: possibly the clues were lost in translation. It is never really sorted out why the film's medley of tormented characters – an incestuously-inclined minor prince; a woman remorseful after betraying her secret police torturer husband to her revolutionary lover; a worker priest who has been provoking strikes; a radical Bishop – remain within the decidedly photogenic but otherwise uninteresting confines of this particular convent hostelry. Nor is it at all obvious who the devil in the woodpile is – Glenda Jackson's Mother Superior or Claudio Casinelli's

intruder. As Damiani protractedly works and reworks his material, the whole thing – especially with our heroine offering herself to the most ghoulish TV repairman ever to have graced the screen – looks more and more like a reworking of Theorem on a more pedestrian level. VG

Tempter, The

see Anticristo, L'

Temptress Moon (Fengyue)

(Chen Kaige, 1996, HK/China) Leslie Cheung, Gong Li, Kevin Lin, He Saifei, David Wu.
132 min.
Opium addiction, incestuous desire, thwarted dreams, blackmail, secrets and lies: Chen's lavish, tortuous film has all this and more. Set mainly in the '20s, it concerns the wealthy but dysfunctional Pang family and the unrequited passions afflicting gigolo Cheung, clan head Gong Li and her poor but devoted cousin Lin. After a confusing start, it's an enthralling melodrama, sumptuously and imaginatively shot by Chris Doyle, which deals tangentially with the clash between the new and the old China, and shows, for probably the first time in Chen's work, a very real interest in sexual passion. GA

'10'

(Blake Edwards, 1979, US) Dudley Moore, Julie Andrews, Bo Derek, Robert Webber, Dee Wallace, Sam Jones, Brian Dennehy, Max Showalter.
122 min.
Before 10 was released in America, its producers were so certain it was a clinker that they tore up contracts for two other Blake Edwards pictures. The miscalculation was understandable. Much of the film comes on like a Jill Clayburgh picture someone rewrote for Bob Hope, with Moore playing an ageing Unmarried Man who pursues lubricious women (rating them out of an ideal ten) to stave off menopause. Technically it's atrocious, trading on absurd coincidence, lame slapstick, and some peculiarly ugly photography. But the studio failed to see that Edwards had hit on a subject (male sexual insecurity) which was bound to strike a chord with the post-Clayburgh audience. The climactic love scene – in which Moore proves utterly unable to perform when he gets his emancipated dream woman (Derek) to bed – is very funny and represents a real catharsis in the history of Hollywood romance: Dudley Moore became the first actor to turn screen impotence into superstardom. DP

Tenant, The (Le Locataire)

(Roman Polanski, 1976, Fr) Roman Polanski, Isabelle Adjani, Shelley Winters, Melvyn Douglas, Jo Van Fleet, Bernard Fresson, Lila Kedrova, Claude Dauphin, Claude Piéplu.
126 min.
With Polanski becoming a naturalised Frenchman, it was logical that he should start tackling specifically French subjects, and this small-scale return to the territory of Repulsion seemed a promising beginning. But it's precisely because Polanski and urban paranoia were made for each other that The Tenant is so disappointing. The tenant (Polanski himself) takes over the lease of a gloomy Parisian apartment from a suicide victim, and soon finds himself at the centre of a real or imagined conspiracy that pushes him into assuming the identity of his predecessor. The twist is that the last tenant was a girl, and our nervous, virginal hero's exploration of his latent bisexuality hits the one new note in an otherwise formulary catalogue of bizarre coincidences, inexplicable appearances, and hints of the supernatural. Everything except the dubbing of the French supporting cast is a model of craftsmanship, but as the plot escalates into increasingly arbitrary excesses of fantasy and heads for the predictable pay-off, the movie looks more and more like a potboiler. TR

Ten Commandments, The

(Cecil B DeMille, 1956, US) Charlton Heston, Yul Brynner, Anne Baxter, Edward G Robinson, John Derek, Yvonne De Carlo, Vincent Price, Cedric Hardwicke, Debra Paget, HB Warner, Nina Foch, Martha Scott, Judith Anderson, Henry Wilcoxon, John Carradine.
220 min.
According to Jesse L Lasky Jr, he and his fellow-writers 'felt so inoculated with significance that

we hardly dared write at all, certainly not with such profane tools as pencils and typewriters'. *The Ten Commandments* sure isn't remembered as literature – the script is a sort of prose doggerel Biblespeak of unerring shallowness; or for its acting, with only Edward G Robinson and Hardwicke emerging as more than pawns in DeMille's vast game. Rather it's the gigantic vulgarity, the obsessive righteousness of the director himself, which keeps the show on the road and suffuses the movie with its daft power. There are two wondrous scenes. The exodus itself, gigantic aerial shots of the DeMillions underpinned by meticulous detail, is a genuine mover. The other goodie, surprisingly, is a dialogue scene in which Hardwicke, confronted by an enchained Heston, hands the succession (and Anne Baxter as a smouldering bonus) to Brynner. Most of the rest is arid nonsense a mile high. But you have to admire DeMille's seriousness of purpose. He took three weeks on the orgy scene alone. SG

Ten Days That Shook the World
see Oktyabr

Ten Days' Wonder (La Décade Prodigieuse)
(Claude Chabrol, 1971, Fr) Orson Welles, Marlène Jobert, Anthony Perkins, Michel Piccoli, Guido Alberti, Tsilla Chelton.
108 min.
Here Chabrol inaugurates a new genre, the theological thriller. Charles (Perkins at his most charismatically unstable) wakes from a dream of Creation to find himself with blood on his hands. He turns for help to his erstwhile professor of philosophy (Piccoli), and persuades him back to the Van Horn country estate to use his 'Logic of Science' in sorting out the family mess. The estate is a 1925 dream engineered by Charles' adoptive father Theo Van Horn (Welles), who is worshipped by his child-bride (Jobert), and sculpted as Jupiter by the awed Charles. Chabrol's movies, echoing Fritz Lang's, have long been edging towards a confrontation with the theme of Fate. This is it. Theo Van Horn chooses to play God, creating his own world, dictating the behaviour of those he places in it, taking care to add flaws to his creation to keep it breathing. But God hasn't reckoned with his own capacity for imperfection, for such shining qualities as jealousy, hatred, revenge; so he comes to his own grief, faced with the lonely fact that his creation is a nine-day wonder...Chabrol's movies grow less and less like anyone else's; this is one worth seeing again and again. TR

Tender Comrade
(Edward Dmytryk, 1943, US) Ginger Rogers, Robert Ryan, Ruth Hussey, Patricia Collinge, Mady Christians, Kim Hunter, Jane Darwell.
102 min. b/w.
A remarkable curiosity, if nothing else, this sentimental tale of World War II has Rogers, 'widowed' while her husband is away fighting, turning first to work as a welder in an aircraft factory, and then to a communal household arrangement with other women in the same circumstances. It was later denounced during the HUAC witch-hunts as Commie propaganda. Hard to see how the domestic economies practised by working girls (even phrased as 'Share and share alike, that's democracy') could cause so much trouble for Dmytryk and writer Dalton Trumbo (two of the 'Hollywood Ten'); especially when there is so much American patriotism on view, not least the glutinously stirring speech Rogers makes to her baby when she finally gets word that her husband has been killed. GA

Tender Hours (Dulces Horas)
(Carlos Saura, 1981, Sp) Assumpta Serna, Iñaki Aierra, Alvaro de Luna.
103 min.
A playwright rehearses his latest work, a melodrama that delves into his own childhood incest fantasies and his adult obsession with understanding his mother's character and suicide. As in *Cria Cuervos*, Saura has his actors take double, even triple roles, and moves deftly between past and present, dream, fiction and memory, putting on a bravura display of technique which dazzles by its skill, but which – despite the title (surely ironic) – has an emotional chilliness that is ultimately faintly unpleasant. SJo

Tender Mercies
(Bruce Beresford, 1982, US) Robert Duvall, Tess Harper, Betty Buckley, Wilford Brimley, Ellen Barkin, Allan Hubbard.
92 min.
A real gem. It tells of Duvall's drunken, down-on-his-luck country singer's slow road to redemption by way of an unromantic marriage to a Texan widow, Beresford's film (scripted by the admirable Horton Foote) offers an attractive if unassuming alternative to the Hollywood mainstream. Refusing to get into heavy plotting – the story's most dramatic event occurs off-screen – it relies on mood, gesture and observation to offer the unfashionable thesis that life, however hard or disappointing, is always worth living. Stunningly shot and performed (not least by Duvall, singing his own songs with conviction, as well as producing), it bears more resemblance to, say, the films of Wenders (or even, at a stretch, Ozu) than to commercial Hollywood, though it grips from start to finish. Beautiful. GA

Tenderness of the Wolves (Zärtlichkeit der Wölfe)
(Ulli Lommel, 1973, WGer) Kurt Raab, Jeff Roden, Margit Carstensen, Hannelore Tiefenbrunner, Wolfgang Schenck, Rainer Hauer, Rainer Werner Fassbinder, Brigitte Mira, Ingrid Caven, Jürgen Prochnow.
83 min.
Fritz Haarmann, con-man, black marketeer and police informer, got through the depression years in Germany in an enterprising way: he picked up runaway boys, seduced them, vampirised them, and then sold their remains as meat. His crimes inspired Fritz Lang's *M*, made six years after his execution. In Lommel's remarkable film, the character gets the Fassbinder treatment: he's the resourceful but ultimately helpless loser at the centre of a black social comedy of manners. Lommel and his writer/star Kurt Raab (both veterans of numerous Fassbinder movies) tell Haarmann's story through a patchwork of broadly comic vignettes – from nosy neighbours and complicit cops to lovers' tiffs and expert contricks – and finally draw their plot threads together in a pastiche of the Hollywood crime thriller. The comedy doesn't blunt the horror of Haarmann's murders, but it does enable Lommel to implicate the 'tender wolves' – the society that makes such crimes possible – without resorting to didacticism or moralising. TR

Tendres Cousines
see Cousins in Love

Tendresse Ordinaire (Ordinary Tenderness)
(Jacques Leduc, 1973, Can) Esther Auger, Jocelyn Bérubé, Luce Guilbeault, Jean-René Ouellet.
82 min.
The sort of plotless film (about a young Quebec couple, she waiting for him to return home on the train) which gives the word 'charm' a bad name. The tedium of waiting is almost perfectly transferred to the spectator. You'd be much better off visiting a friend and catching him/her peel vegetables. RM

Tenebrae (Sotto gli Occhi dell'Assassino)
(Dario Argento, 1982, It) Anthony Franciosa, John Saxon, Giuliano Gemma, Daria Nicolodi, Christian Borromeo, John Steiner.
110 min.
A hybrid horror, both thriller and slasher, not to mention chopper and shocker, this confirms what *Suspiria* and *Inferno* led one to suspect. When it comes to plotting, Argento is one hell of a basket weaver: with holes in his story big enough to sink credibility, he cheats and double-crosses like mad to conceal the killer's identity. Successful crime writer (Franciosa) arrives in Rome to promote his new book 'Tenebrae', an event which triggers off a trail of bloody murders in the manner described in his book. By the end, the entire cast save one has undergone savage cutting, something which would have benefited the film itself, which is unpleasant even by contemporary horror standards. It does confirm Argento's dedication to the technicalities of constructing images – Grand Guignol for L'Uomo Vogue, perhaps – but you'll still end up feeling you've left some vital digestive organs back in the seat. FL

Ten Fingers of Steel (Tangren Biao Ke)
(Jian Long, 1973, Tia) Wang Yu, Chang Chin Chin, Kan Tai, Tze Lan.
96 min.
Poverty row kung-fu entertainment. With one clue, a perfume sachet, Tai Yuang (an interestingly unheroic, almost diffident performance from Wang Yu) comes to Japan to seek the villain who murdered his family. It isn't giving anything away to say he gets his man, with the help of a female pickpocket who turns out to be a Chinese martial arts champion. The film is so fragmented, so concerned to ring the changes on the fights (on a moving train and in a river) that any suspense involved in the tale is dissipated. The fact that nothing of interest is made of some promising scenes – a fight on a beach with a background of towering waves, the appearance of a character playing a flute and wearing a basket on his head – suggest that the film may have been tampered with. VG

Ten Little Indians
see And Then There Were None

Ten Little Indians
(George Pollock, 1965, GB) Hugh O'Brian, Shirley Eaton, Fabian, Leo Genn, Stanley Holloway, Wilfrid Hyde-White, Daliah Lavi, Dennis Price.
91 min. b/w.
Excruciatingly boring version of the Agatha Christie play filmed as *And Then There Were None* in 1945 and 1974. This time the setting is a remote house in the Austrian Alps, with cardboard characters hovering around mouthing chunks of exposition while waiting to get murdered. Tedium is not helped by a 'whodunnit break' (for audiences to play detective) attended by instant replays of the murders. TM

Ten Little Niggers
see And Then There Were None

Tennessee's Partner
(Allan Dwan, 1955, US) John Payne, Ronald Reagan, Rhonda Fleming, Coleen Gray, Angie Dickinson, Leo Gordon, Morris Ankrum.
87 min.
While nowhere near as strong as *Silver Lode*, this is still an impressive little Western, adapted from a story by Bret Harte: a complex tale of loyalty, deceit and betrayal, with Payne as the smooth gambler in a mining township, Reagan as the cowpoke who saves his life, Fleming as the former's saloon-owner girlfriend, and Gray as the girl who becomes an object of contention. Like most of the Westerns Dwan made for producer Benedict Bogeaus, the film features typically impressive colour camerawork by John Alton (the red-headed Fleming seldom seemed riper!) and typically muscular, no-nonsense direction. GA

10 Rillington Place
(Richard Fleischer, 1970, GB) Richard Attenborough, Judy Geeson, John Hurt, Pat Heywood, Isobel Black, Phyllis MacMahon, Geoffrey Chater, Robert Hardy, Andre Morell.
111 min.
For a director whose work reveals a fascination with the reconstruction of actual events, especially famous murder cases (*The Girl in the Red Velvet Swing*, *Compulsion*, *The Boston Strangler*), Fleischer seems oddly at sea with the Christie/Evans cause célèbre. Although all the '40s period details are (presumably correct – Clive Exton's script is based on Ludovic Kennedy's book – none of the ambience of post-war Britain is caught on the screen. Also, by concentrating closely on Christie (Attenborough) and the hysterical Evans (Hurt), Fleischer leaves himself open to the excesses of British character acting. The result is a melodrama rather than an examination of criminal pathology. PH

Ten Seconds to Hell
(Robert Aldrich, 1958, GB/US) Jack Palance, Jeff Chandler, Martine Carol, Robert Cornthwaite, Dave Willock, Richard Wattis.
94 min. b/w.
Fair to middling Aldrich, which would pack more punch if the characterisation had a little more oomph. The storyline certainly grabs at the nerve

ends: six German bomb disposal experts return from a British PoW camp to post-war Berlin, where they agree to pool their monthly pay packets in a kitty to be offered to the last survivor from their number. Palance and Chandler are left to sweat it out over unexploded devices and the similarly potent presence of love interest Carol. Ernest Laszlo's crisp monochrome camerawork makes the German capital look grim indeed. TJ

Tension at Table Rock

(Charles Marquis Warren, 1956, US) Richard Egan, Dorothy Malone, Cameron Mitchell, Billy Chapin, Angie Dickinson, DeForest Kelley.
93 min.
Agreeably taut minor Western has outlaw Egan riding into town and saving nervy lawman Mitchell's bacon by seeing off a gang of gung-ho desperadoes. The down side is that he falls for sheriff's wife Malone. An above-average RKO programmer that works well within its own rather derivative limits, it's buoyed by lots of familiar faces in the supporting cast. Look out, in particular, for young DeForest Kelley, a good decade before he picked up his galactic telescope as *Star Trek*'s Bones.

Tentacles (Tentacoli)

(Oliver Hellman ie. Sonia Assonitis, 1976, It) John Huston, Shelley Winters, Bo Hopkins, Henry Fonda, Delia Boccardo, Cesare Danova, Claude Akins.
102 min.
Having ripped off *The Exorcist* with *Devil Within Her*, Oliver Hellman here does a follow-up Italian job on *Jaws*. Taking *Tentacles* to the lab for analysis would reveal many similarities to its finny predecessor, with the following exceptions: wit, imagination, storytelling skill. Huston is grotesque as the type of grizzled investigative journalist who wears his nightdress on the porch. Winters is worse in yet another of her fat flustered parts, and Fonda must have needed the few days' work as 'Mr Whitehead', whose drilling company sends the octopus mad with its vibrations. One scene *Jaws* doesn't have, thankfully, is ichthyologist Bo Hopkins addressing his killer whales as though they were long-lost buddies from 'the streets' whence he came. They duly dispatch the monster, which incidentally seems of quite normal size, as in *Grizzly*. AN

10:30 P.M. Summer

(Jules Dassin, 1966, US/Spain) Melina Mercouri, Romy Schneider, Peter Finch, Julián Mateos, Beatriz Savón.
85 min.
Nobody had a good word to say for this adaptation of Marguerite Duras' novel which, though a potentially good script (by Duras and Dassin), is treated so heavily that it becomes risible. Finch and Schneider play a couple deciding whether to or not, while Finch's alcoholic wife (Mercouri) goes bananas to the point of being obsessed by a local *crime passionel*. Much of the blame can be attributed directly to Mercouri's barnstorming performance, though the inappropriately tarted-up Spanish postcard settings don't help either. Strange that a director like Dassin, who spearheaded the neo-realist movement in Hollywood after World War II, should look so completely out of touch with any level of reality in later years. CPe

10 to Midnight

(J Lee Thompson, 1983, US) Charles Bronson, Lisa Eilbacher, Andrew Stevens, Gene Davis, Geoffrey Lewis, Robert Lyons, Wilford Brimley.
102 min.
'I remember when legal meant lawful' mutters cop Bronson, 'Now it means some kind of loophole'. Bronson's had a case thrown out of court after he's forced to admit that he planted evidence on a psychopathic murderer (Davis) too smart to leave any of his own. The psycho's release puts Bronson back in his *Death Wish* shoes. The producers have made it clear that the movie isn't intended to be a mere vigilante thriller, but rather a film that questions the law as regards insanity pleas. Smokescreen. For all its emotional blackmail, it's nothing more than a brutal reiteration of the most basic macho values, and one that leaves a nasty aftertaste. GD

Tenue de Soirée (Evening Dress)

(Bertrand Blier, 1986, Fr) Gérard Depardieu, Michel Blanc, Miou-Miou, Michel Creton, Jean-François Stévenin, Mylène Demongeot, Bruno Crémer.
85 min.
Blier's scabrous comedy is, for most of its length, achingly funny. The opening is misanthropically arresting. At a dance, Monique (Miou-Miou) tears into her meekly devoted spouse Antoine (Blanc), itemising his shortcomings while ever closer looms the enormous, eavesdropping Bob (Depardieu). With shocking suddenness, Bob knocks her to the floor and contemptuously pelts her with banknotes – 'Here's a grand – now shut up!' – before outlining his blueprint for solvency and spiritual emancipation, and sweeping the stunned pair along on a night of burglary. Noise doesn't seem to be a consideration: wealthy awakened householders are so bored that they happily collaborate with the intruders. A *ménage-à-trois* develops, but with a twist: Big Bob is desperately smitten with mousy Antoine, and, egged on by the pimping Monique, who doesn't want to lose the meal ticket, pursues the scuttling hetero around the breakfast bar. The physical casting is preposterously inspired; if the coda is less than satisfying, blame Blier's anarchistic spirit and reluctance to finish a film. BC

Teorema

see Theorem

Tequila Sunrise

(Robert Towne, 1988, US) Mel Gibson, Michelle Pfeiffer, Kurt Russell, Raúl Julia, JT Walsh, Arliss Howard, Budd Boetticher.
115 min.
A romantic thriller which confirms Towne's outstanding talent as a screenwriter, but like *Personal Best*, leaves doubts about his skill as a director. Gibson is an ex-drugs dealer looking for a way out, Russell is the relentless cop who's out to nail his old high school pal, and Pfeiffer is a beautiful restaurant owner suspected of fronting for Gibson's drugs business. Gibson is in the clear until another old friend, dealer Julia, calls in one last favour involving several million dollars worth of drug money. The set-up has the precision of fine needlepoint, picking out the plot outline before embroidering it with a complex pattern of interwoven relationships. Pfeiffer is perfect as the immaculately dressed and icily controlled restaurateur caught between Gibson's honest (ex-)criminal and Russell's ambiguously motivated cop. For while Gibson is totally up-front about both his shady past and his emotions, Russell's romantic advances are overlaid by professional interest in his rival's criminal activities. Sadly, when Julia finally shows up, this fascinating exploration of the limits of friendship, loyalty and trust gives way to explosive action and empty pyrotechnics. NF

Terence Davies Trilogy, The

(Terence Davies, 1974-83, GB) Phillip Maudesley, Terry O'Sullivan, Wilfrid Brambell, Sheila Raynor. (Three parts: 'Children', 1974, 'Madonna and Child', 1980, 'Death and Transfiguration', 1983)
85 min.
Not so much an 'I-had-it-tough' catalogue of economic and physical hardships as a strangely stirring account of human dignity triumphing over emotional and spiritual confusion. And indeed, the form reflects this, transforming Liverpudlian Robert Tucker's development – from victimised schoolboy, through a Catholic closet-gay middle-age, to death in a hospital – into a rich, resonant tapestry of impressionistic detail. There is plenty to enjoy: a bleak, wry wit and an imaginative use of music undercutting the grim but beautiful imagery; flashes of surrealism; and superb performances throughout (none more so than Brambell as the 80-year-old Tucker, wordlessly struggling the last few steps to meet his Maker). But what really elevates the films into their own timeless realm is the luminous attention to faces in close-up: a stylish strategy that turns an otherwise chastening look at a lonely man's life into an uplifting experience. GA

Terminal Man, The

(Mike Hodges, 1974, US) George Segal, Joan Hackett, Richard A Dysart, Jill Clayburgh, Donald Moffat, Matt Clark, James B Sikking.
107 min.
A thoughtful and unusually pessimistic sci-fi pic based on Michael Crichton's novel about a psychotic (Segal) who has a tiny computer planted in his brain to control his violent impulses. Unfortunately, the plan backfires: Segal enjoys the sensation of being calmed down so much that he goes on a murder spree in order to enjoy further mental restraint. Opening with a brilliant sequence in which Segal is reborn on the operating table, and building towards a finale in which the scientists realise that they can do nothing to control this hi-tech monster of their own making, the film's bleak futuristic vision also benefits greatly from some extraordinary sets, and from writer/producer/director Hodges' confident direction. NF

Terminal Station (Stazione Termini/Indiscretion of an American Wife)

(Vittorio De Sica, 1952, It/US) Jennifer Jones, Montgomery Clift, Gino Cervi, Richard Beymer.
87 min. b/w.
De Sica started out wanting to film a small scale love story, but the casting of Jennifer Jones brought with it the attentions of her producer husband David Selznick. He insisted on shooting in Rome's grand new central railway station and drafted in Truman Capote to polish up Zavattini's screenplay about an ill-fated romance between a visiting American and an Italian with an American mother (Clift, who gives a tender performance). In the end, though, Selznick reckoned the finished picture too arty and cut it to 63 minutes for US distribution (as *Indiscretion of an American Wife*). TJ

Terminal Velocity

(Deran Sarafian, 1994, US) Charlie Sheen, Nastassja Kinski, James Gandolfini, Christopher McDonald, Gary Bullock, Melvin Van Peebles, Hans R Howes.
102 min.
Sheen is a dumb, daredevil sky-diving instructor mixed up with the Russian Mafia and $600m of stolen Soviet gold. Things get off to an attention-grabbing start when, soon after her flatmate is murdered by Russkie thugs, blonde babe Chris (Kinski) persuades 'Ditch' Brodie (Sheen) to take her up for her first jump. She then redefines the meaning of drop-dead beautiful – she jumps, she drops, she's dead. Or is she? Is that unidentifiable body really hers? To cut a long story short, Ditch stumbles about looking for clues to Chris's nose-dive, which lead him to members of the KG-used-to-B, who plan to fund an anti-democratic coup with the stolen gold. While Kinski unwisely takes the whole thing seriously, Sheen simply grins inanely and makes flip remarks. If you can wait long enough, the extended airborne finale is one of the most extraordinary stunts you're ever likely to see; but like the soundtrack, it's too big for the picture. Most people will have bailed out long before then. NF

Terminator, The

(James Cameron, 1984, US) Arnold Schwarzenegger, Michael Biehn, Linda Hamilton, Paul Winfield, Lance Henriksen, Rick Rossovich, Bess Motta, Earl Boen, Dick Miller.
107 min.
Back from the future in which the machines rule comes a rippling robot (Schwarzenegger) who terminates opponents with extreme prejudice (like ripping their hearts out). His goal is to kill a woman (Hamilton) destined to bear the child who will become the great freedom fighter of the future. Fortunately she has a champion in the shape of another time traveller, Arnold's all-too-human opponent (Biehn). The gladiatorial arena is set, with vulnerable flesh and cunning versus a leviathan who totes around massive weapons like so many chic accessories and can rebuild his organs as they get shot away. The pacing and the action are terrific, revelling in the feral relentlessness which characterised *Assault on Precinct 13* and *Mad Max 2*; even the future visions of a wasted LA are well mounted. More than enough violence to make it a profoundly moral film; and Arnold's a whizz. CPea

Terminator 2: Judgment Day

(James Cameron, 1991, US) Arnold Schwarzenegger, Linda Hamilton, Edward Furlong, Robert Patrick, Earl Boen, Joe Morton, S Epatha Merkerson, Xander Berkeley, Jenette Goldstein.
135 min.

Having failed, in Cameron's impressive original, to prevent the birth of future resistance leader John Connor, the machines running the world in 2029 again send a cyborg to our era to kill him off as an unruly LA teenager (Furlong). Again, too, the resistance responds by sending the boy a protector: a T800 cyborg (Schwarzenegger) physically identical to the one which formerly laid siege to John's mom Sarah (Hamilton). That Arnie is now a good guy is one twist; the other is that he's the underdog, since the T1000 (Patrick) despatched by the machines is far more sophisticated, constructed from liquid steel so that it can adopt the appearance of anyone or anything it chooses. The film is much the same as its predecessor, except that the effects are more spectacular, there's a lumbering anti-nuke subtext, and the script's good-natured wit is undercut by the sentimentality of Arnie's becoming a caring cyborg. Structured as a simple chase, the story sags midway, but the first hour and last 30 minutes display an enjoyably relentless bravura. GA

Terminus

(Pierre-William Glenn, 1986, Fr/WGer) Johnny Hallyday, Karen Allen, Jürgen Prochnow, Gabriel Damon, Julie Glenn, Dieter Schidor.
110 min.

It had to happen: the film of the video game. The plot, with 27 minutes cut in this dubbed release print, is utterly incomprehensible. The Monster, a hi-tech camper-van driven by gutsy heroine Gus (Allen), is trying to reach the Terminus, evading Government Forces and an evil Doctor's camouflaged pursuit vehicle en route. A little later Max Max clone Stump (Hallyday) takes over The Monster. The game seems to have something to do with the stowaway Princess he finds on board, and some experiments in genetic mutation being conducted by the evil Doctor. It's hard to tell, but only a masochist would wish this snail-paced kiddies sci-fi pic – with its second-hand images, appalling dialogue, and cardboard sets – to last a moment longer. Terminal boredom sets in long before the end of the journey, its purpose still obscure. NF

Term of Trial

(Peter Glenville, 1962, GB) Laurence Olivier, Simone Signoret, Sarah Miles, Hugh Griffith, Terence Stamp, Roland Culver, Thora Hird, Frank Pettingell, Dudley Foster.
130 min. b/w.

Olivier as a boozing schoolteacher, trapped in a fearful marriage to Signoret, and trapped also by nympho student Sarah Miles, who has a crush on him and, crikey, offers herself during a school outing to Paris. Instead of laying her or giving her a good slippering, he simply tells her to go home and do her homework. So she accuses him of rape, which leads to some real acting, especially when Olivier, after being cleared of misconduct by the enquiry, has to lie to his wife to earn her respect as a man with a spine. Terence Stamp as the school bully deservedly gets a good thrashing for non-acting, and this trip through the blackboard jungle is about as convincing as the jungle in Kew Gardens. ATu

Terms of Endearment

(James L Brooks, 1983, US) Shirley MacLaine, Debra Winger, Jack Nicholson, John Lithgow, Danny DeVito, Jeff Daniels, Lisa Hart Carroll.
132 min.

Until Debra Winger finds she has The Illness, this ambles along quite amusingly but unremarkably as a sharp-eyed family comedy: Winger leaves her neurotic mother (MacLaine) for an unfaithful husband, while MacLaine consoles herself with astronaut-next-door Nicholson. It is Nicholson who dominates this section, attacking the role and usefully distracting attention from the blatant unreality and sentimentality of the MacLaine character. Then The Illness strikes, and the film changes gear completely, pulling out all the stops and almost incidentally delivering one of the best-acted, most moving death-bed scenes in recent memory. The emotional wipe-out is impressive, confirming Winger as one of the major stars of

the '80s. But it also unbalances the film, and makes you wonder if director Brooks is as good at construction as he obviously is at emotion. DP

Terra-Cotta Warrior, A (Qin Yong)

(Ching Siu-Tung, 1990, HK/Can) Zhang Yimou, Gong Li, Yu Yung Kang.
120 min.

A misfired attempt at a sweeping adventure-comedy in the Indiana Jones style. Back in the Qin Dynasty, an imperial guardsman is turned into a terra-cotta soldier as punishment for seducing a virgin – but she passes him a Pill of Immortality when she gives him One Last Kiss. Two thousand-odd years later, in the 1930s, he wakes to defend the Qin Emperor's tomb from robbers, and finds his long-lost love reincarnated as a pin-brained Shanghai starlet filming on location in Xi'an. Slack scripting and pacing conspire with the overall shortage of laughs and thrills to make this less than exhilarating, despite the plethora of talents on both sides of the camera. TR

Terror, The

(Roger Corman, 1963, US) Boris Karloff, Jack Nicholson, Sandra Knight, Dick Miller, Jonathon Haze.
81 min.

Notable mainly for being the film that was screened at the drive-in in Bogdanovich's Targets, this is the real dud of Corman's Poe cycle, largely because he said, 'I had the weekend off before the last week of shooting The Raven; I was going to play tennis and it rained'. Not wanting to waste the set he'd had built, he embarked upon an almost incomprehensible tale of an officer in Napoleon's army (Nicholson) who falls for a woman who keeps disappearing; it turns out she's the long dead wife of Mad Baron Karloff. The film, despite its elements of necrophilia, has nothing whatsoever to do with Poe, and the fact that it was directed by about five different people (including Coppola, Monte Hellman and Nicholson himself) hardly makes for coherence. There are, however, a few strikingly moody images that make effective use of the California coastline, and the general air of chaotic improvisation is not altogether without its own special charm. GA.

Terror

(Norman J Warren, 1978, GB) John Nolan, Carolyn Courage, James Aubrey, Sarah Keller, Tricia Walsh, Glynis Barber.
87 min.

Atmospheric camerawork and some bright dialogue provide momentary relief in what is otherwise stock schlock about a film-maker (Nolan) who inadvertently conjured a malevolent ancestral witch while making a movie about his own family history. Nasty things start happening when he previews it at a party; but echoes of The Exorcist tend to hang increasingly heavy over the proceedings, while Warren's direction administers the coup de grâce by persistently cutting to lip-licking close-ups of slashed or garrotted throats. TM

Terror at the Opera

see Opera

Terror by Night

(Roy William Neill, 1946, US) Basil Rathbone, Nigel Bruce, Alan Mowbray, Dennis Hoey, Renee Godfrey, Mary Forbes, Billy Bevan.
60 min. b/w.

Holmes, Watson, a suspiciously eccentric passenger list, and the Star of Rhodesia diamond are all aboard the London to Edinburgh express (which, if the wonderfully inconsistent exterior stock footage is to be believed, changes engines several times en route), and the ensuing mayhem ranges from a corpse in a carriage to a false-bottomed coffin in the guard's van. Despite the train-movie format, there are distinct signs that Universal's Rathbone-Bruce series was running out of steam (only one more film was to come, in fact). An early screenplay from Frank Gruber, who merrily titled his autobiography The Pulp Jungle. PT

Terror House

see Night Has Eyes, The

Terror in a Texas Town

(Joseph H Lewis, 1958, US) Sterling Hayden, Sebastian Cabot, Carol Kelly, Ned Young, Eugene Martin, Victor Millan.
80 min. b/w.

Take a hired gun with a steel fist and an almost tragic awareness of his failing nerve (Young). Pit against him a stolid Scandinavian armed only with a whaling harpoon (Hayden), and the film does at least achieve the kind of bizarre climax appropriate to its low-budget format. The rest is a triumph of expression over economy: Lewis makes a virtue of the frame's emptiness (the budget, it seems, didn't run to extras), and disguises the excessive talk with unobtrusive camera movements that show a craftsmanship and pureness lacking in many more expensive films. Something of an exemplar of its type. CPe

Terror in the Aisles

(Andrew J Kuehn, 1984, US) Donald Pleasence, Nancy Allen.
85 min. b/w & col.

'The name of the game is suspense' announces Allen, stuck with her co-presenter Pleasence in a 'typical' cinema audience and, like us, being subjected to a barrage of slammings, slashings, and defenestrations, a sort of That's Entertainment! for sicko types. But suspense is precisely what is lacking in this compilation. Without any of the nail-nibbling build-up, there is little fun to be had in seeing a shark attack from Jaws, an exploding head from Scanners, or the shower murder from Psycho. Such snippets are either frustrating (you wish you were watching the whole of Halloween) or dreary (you make a mental note never to go near Vice Squad or Nighthawks). Hardcore horror hounds may derive limited satisfaction from totting up the number of extracts they can identify, and watching the tooth torture sequence from Marathon Man saves you from being bored to death through the rest of its running time; but dopey Donald Pleasentries, such as 'Maybe, deep down, we have a need to be scared', fail dismally to throw meaningful light on the psychology of fear and the reasons why some of us enjoy watching horrible teenagers being chopped up into little pieces with lots of blood. AB

Terroriser, The (Kongbufenzi)

(Edward Yang, 1986, Tai/HK) Cora Miao, Li Liqun, Jin Shijie, Gu Baoming, Wang An.
109 min.

Yang's masterly film keeps numerous plot strands going in parallel, finds a high level of interest and suspense in all of them, and dovetails them together into a composite picture plausible enough to make you cry and shocking enough to leave you gasping. The characters span the full urban spectrum: a research scientist jockeying for promotion, a bike-gang hoodlum on the run from the cops, a woman novelist looking for a painless way to end her marriage. Yang sees each of them clearly and will consummate honesty, and notes how their taste in clothes and decor serve to underline their personalities and betray their histories. Neither sociological essay nor soap opera, it's an intensely cinematic movie, finding mystery, pity and fear in every life it scans. The title character is a girl delinquent whose prank phone calls spark off crises in the lives of other characters. But the film suggests that we all have our ways of 'terrorising' each other, and that we'd all like our lives to be as coherent and resolved as fiction. Yang reaches high, and his aim is true. TR

Terror of Dr Chaney, The

see Mansion of the Doomed

Terror Train

(Roger Spottiswoode, 1979, Can) Ben Johnson, Jamie Lee Curtis, Hart Bochner, David Copperfield, Derek MacKinnon, Sandee Currie, Timothy Webber.
97 min.

This effectively exploits all the inherent violence and abandon of a riotous student party aboard a hired steam train. The horror elements are accounted for 'naturally': party masks provide grotesque images and a disguise for the killer; darkness alternating with the mottled lights of a disco give an uneasy visual feel, heightened by the swaying of the train; and the feats of a performing magician arouse expectations of a supernatural dimension. Instead, there is a psychological angle:

the students, the killer's victims, are fairly callous themselves, given to gruesome medical school 'pranks' and fundamentally self-centred. Jamie Lee Curtis plays the only one of the gang with a conscience – and the only one to survive. But although the film's terror mileage is fuelled by her outwitting the killer, being a woman she must – as usual – finally be saved by the fatherly guard. Still, better than most of its kind. JWi

Terror 2000

(Christophe Schlingensief, 1992, Ger) Margit Carstensen, Peter Kern, Susanne Bredehöft, Alfred Edel, Udo Kier.
80 min.
A shrill, chaotic and confused exposé of the racism allegedly inherent in German culture, in which ex-gangster Edel and sidekick Kern open a furniture store in a small town, and then set about harassing immigrant families and campaigning against a local home for them. The last part of the trilogy that began with *100 Years of Adolf Hitler* and continued with *The German Chainsaw Massacre*. NF

TerrorVision

(Ted Nicolaou, 1986, US) Diane Franklin, Mary Woronov, Gerrit Graham, Chad Allen, Jonathan Gries, Bert Remsen, Alejandro Rey, Randi Brooks.
85 min.
The aesthetics of trash sink to new depths of delirium in this kooky sitcom variation on *Poltergeist*. Its TV-fixated family is every bit as wacked-out as the mutant monster which is inadvertently beamed into their trendy new satellite dish by the sanitation department of the planet Pluton. There's a survivalist grandpa (Remsen) who eats lizard tail, and most satisfyingly, Woronov and Graham doing an outrageous double act as the parents, enticing like-minded swingers back for sex in the jacuzzi. AB

Terry Fox Story, The

(Ralph L Thomas, 1983, Can) Robert Duvall, Eric Fryer, Christopher Makepeace, Rosalind Chao, Michael Zelniker.
97 min.
Terry Fox (Fryer) is living...sorry, dead proof that you can lose your leg to a malignant tumour and still run...sorry, hop across continents. This film of his life (made for TV, where it should have stayed) wisely avoids the pitfall of sentimentality by making Terry out to be an obnoxious and egocentric prat, and embraces realism by having a plucky half-Badered boy acting as the one-legged one, stumbling across the vast, never-ending Canadian landscape on his Marathon of Hope. Lest cancer sufferers get above themselves and start thinking that a dose of chemotherapy will aid their sporting and sexual prowess (Terry gets his girl), we are gently reminded that True Stories do not always end happily: you may lick the Big C in your knee, but unless you rest it'll spread to your chest. AB

Terry on the Fence

(Frank Godwin, 1985, GB) Jack McNicholl, Neville Watson, Tracey Ann Morris, Jeff Ward, Matthew Barker.
70 min.
Though distinctly tame and old-fashioned compared with, say, *Grange Hill*, this low-budget Children's Film Foundation feature does succeed in its stated intention of 'getting away from the black and white of goodies and baddies'. Innocent victim Terry is forced by skinhead Les and his gang to join them in a raid on his own school, from which they steal a cassette radio each. When the police arrive at his school the next day, Terry confesses, but insists that he was coerced. However, crucial evidence given by the caretaker tends to undermine Terry's position, as does his continuing refusal to implicate Les. In addition to the relationship between victimiser and victim, the film's clear narrative delves into the fuzzy area between right and wrong. NF

Tesis

see Thesis

Tess

(Roman Polanski, 1979, Fr/GB) Nastassja Kinski, Leigh Lawson, Peter Firth, John Collin, Richard Pearson, John Bett.
180 min.
Having all the strengths and excesses of a middlebrow film (visual beauty, lush soundtrack, arty direction), this adaptation's appeal to the senses leaves them cloyed. Although true enough to Thomas Hardy's novel to become a useful aid to 'O' and 'A' levels, Polanski omits small but vital details (such as the initial cause of Tess' guilt, which does much to explain her ensuing acquiescence), and misuses those he includes (the landscape, in Hardy both a part of and a mirror to the protagonists, is relegated to a pastoral backcloth, and was furthermore filmed in Brittany and Normandy instead of Dorset), thus removing substance from this hollow film. Finally, *Tess* tells one rather more about its director's much publicised preoccupations than about Hardy's themes. FD

Tess of the Storm Country

(Paul Guilfoyle, 1960, US) Diane Baker, Jack Ging, Lee Philips, Wallace Ford, Robert F Simon, Bert Remsen, Archie Duncan, Nancy Valentine.
84 min.
This umpteenth version of Grace White's overwrought novel, scripted by Charles Lang, follows Scots lass Tess MacLean (Baker) who comes to Pennsylvania only to find that her fiancé has been fatally poisoned by the pollution from a chemical plant. Before matters are sorted out, Tess's new love, a young Mennonite named Peter (Ging), whose family sold the polluters their land, is wrongfully imprisoned for burning down the despised plant. Highly contrived; CinemaScope photography by James Wong Howe. JPy

Testament

(Lynne Littman, 1983, US) Jane Alexander, William Devane, Ross Harris, Roxana Zal, Lukas Haas, Philip Anglim, Lilia Skala, Leon Ames, Lurene Tuttle, Kevin Costner.
90 min.
In a momentary flash, an American suburb (carefully established) is pitched into nightmare: clearly the end has come, but apart from a power failure, the town's position in a mountain bowl has saved it from the worst effects of nuclear blast. With Dad (Devane) missing, Mother (Alexander) and her three kids have to struggle on as radioactive dust appears on their cereal bowls, friends and neighbours begin to succumb to radiation sickness, everything begins to fall apart, and finally the first of the family has to be sewn into a shroud for burial in the garden. The subject of a family and community falling victim to a silent, invisible massacre is hardly usual cinema fare, but Littman keeps sentimentality at bay, refuses to court sensationalism, and coaxes some superb performances from her cast. A gentle, loving, noble, angry and heartrending film. JG

Testament

(John Akomfrah, 1988, GB) Tania Rogers, Evans Hunter, Emma Francis Wilson, Frank Parkes, Errol Shaker.
80 min.
A subtitle, 'The War Zone of Memories', gives a better indication of this film's fragmentary, poetic style, in which a plot about a television journalist's quest for an interview is interspersed with recurrent images of conflict and renewed faith. The setting is Ghana, and Abena (Rogers) has returned to her native land from Britain in order to interview Werner Herzog on location with *Cobra Verde*. But Herzog proves elusive, leaving Abena with time to ponder her hasty departure from Ghana following the collapse of the Nkrumah regime and her subsequent arrest by the military. Akomfrah and the Black Audio Film Collective offer the complex ethical and emotional issues in telling flashes and seemingly inconclusive discussions. Abena's dilemma and her political past are revealed only gradually, and the process of exposition, while sometimes bewildering, is always fascinating. Ambitious and visually inventive, this acutely personal tale of discovery is marred only by Rogers' rather lifeless performance. CM

Testament d'Orphée, Le (Testament of Orpheus)

(Jean Cocteau, 1959, Fr) Jean Cocteau, Edouard Dermithe, Henri Crémieux, Jean-Pierre Léaud, Maria Casarès, François Périer, Jean Marais, Yul Brynner.
83 min. b/w.
Cocteau's last film is as personal and private as its title suggests, and it makes little sense for viewers unfamiliar with his other work. It's a wry, self-conscious re-examination of a lifetime's obsessions, with Cocteau playing himself at the centre of the mythology that he created in countless books, plays, films and paintings. This mythology yields a torrent of familiar characters, situations, effects and images, all of them quoted in a spirit of bewilderment and growing disillusionment: Cocteau finally disappears into his fictional world, leaving the real world to a noisy new generation. Nothing about the film is in the least seductive except for its fundamental openness; the tone veers between gentle irony and low-key pessimism. Cocteau admirers will probably find it very moving. TR

Testament of Dr Mabuse, The (Das Testament des Dr Mabuse)

(Fritz Lang, 1933, Ger) Rudolf Klein-Rogge, Otto Wernicke, Oscar Beregi, Gustav Diessl, Vera Liessem, Karl Meixner.
122 min. b/w.
In 1922, Fritz Lang conceived Mabuse as a cypher for Weimar Germany's corruption and decadence: the two-part *Dr Mabuse, the Gambler/Inferno* shows him as a criminal mastermind, casinos and stock exchange equally in hand, enmeshed in a web of dope, killing, fake seances and madness. By 1932, the character had become rather more than just king villain of the serials: *Testament* finds him mouthing undisguised Nazi slogans from his asylum prison, and using hypnotism to maintain control over his criminal empire outside; he's opposed by the same cop who hunted Peter Lorre in Lang's *M* the year before. Goebbels banned the movie but offered leadership of the German film industry to Lang, who left the country overnight. TR

Testimony

(Tony Palmer, 1987, GB) Ben Kingsley, Terence Rigby, Ronald Pickup, Sherry Baines, Magdalen Asquith, John Shrapnel, Robert Stephens.
157 min. b/w & col.
Palmer's epic biopic of the Soviet composer Dmitri Shostakovich (Kingsley), adapted from memoirs he 'related' shortly before his death in 1975, concentrates primarily on the period (early '30s to '50s) of his deeply ambivalent relationship with Stalin (Rigby). Long, daringly shot in 'Scope and glorious black-and-white, it's a fascinating, ambitious work, but finally overwrought and unrevealing. Despite some stunning individual scenes, featuring expressionist imagery, montage techniques, and historical reconstructions, (and inventive use of our dour Victorian industrial landscape to suggest the Leningrad and Moscow locations), the cumulative effect is bewildering and lacking in intellectual rigour; the array of 'hello Meyerhold, goodbye Khachaturyan' cameos distract (Pickup's betrayed Marshal Tukha-chevsky excepted), and Kingsley, scribbling away, is left as little more than a pile of soulless period clothing. The music (the Violin Concerto No 1, the late symphonies, the Michelangelo sonnet) is magnificent. WH

Test Tube Babies (aka The Pill)

(Merle Connell, 1953, US) John Maitland, Monica Davis.
70 min. b/w.
George and Kathy talk about babies, but get distracted by protracted peekaboo necking parties, California early '50s-style, which lead to anything but consummation. More talk about babies before it's discovered that George is 'sterel'. A very odd doctor performs the necessary op upon Kathy (after a long lecture on the benefits of artificial insemination) wearing *leather* gloves, a detail typical of the effortless surrealism this film unintentionally achieves. Classical stuff in that everyone acts like statues. Is there life on Mars? CPe

Teta y la luna, La

see Tit and the Moon, The

Tête contre les Murs, La (The Keepers)

(Georges Franju, 1958, Fr) Jean-Pierre Mocky, Pierre Brasseur, Paul Meurisse, Anouk Aimée, Charles Aznavour, Jean Galland, Edith Scob.
98 min. b/w.
Franju's first feature (after a notably idiosyncratic career as a director of shorts) confirmed his stature as a poet of the darker regions of the human

psyche, and his vision as that of one of the cinema's least blinkered social moralists. It deals with an upper middle class dropout (played by Mocky, who scripts and intended to direct it himself) who finds himself in an insane asylum after committing 'irrational' acts of vandalism aimed against his father; he breaks out with an epileptic friend (Aznavour, in his first screen role), and lands in deeper water than ever...It's part psychological thriller, part subversive bourgeois drama, and all *film noir* of the most devastating sort. TR

Tête de Normande St-Onge, La

(Gilles Carle, 1975, Can) Carole Laure, Raymond Cloutier, Renée Girard, Reynald Bouchard, Carmen Giroux.
116 min.
Quite where the lady's head is at, as they used to say, is a question better left to clinical enquiry than the speculations of one unconvinced by the film's anti-psychiatric contortions. It's the sort of film where fantasies (erotic and otherwise) proliferate, and the lines between sanity and madness are purposefully blurred; as, in passing, are the lines between exploitation, voyeurism, and (?) art. The erratic Normande (an outsider like the heroine of Carle's *The True Nature of Bernadette*) she 'rescues' her mother from a mental home to set up a counter-culture family) is framed and reflected in a compatibly fragmented, flashy style, so it's all of a piece. Either you buy it or you don't – in which case it's intensely irritating. PT

Tetsuo (Tetsuo: The Iron Man)

(Shinya Tsukamoto, 1989, Jap) Tomoroh Taguchi, Kei Fujiwara, Nobu Kanaoku, Shinya Tsukamoto.
67 min. b/w.
This is a movie that springs from all the fantasy entertainment Japanese kids grow up with: Godzilla movies, sci-fi animation, manga comic strips and 'hardcore' rock music. In Tsukamoto's hands, these childhood influences mature into fantasies with a more adult shading: dark sexual fantasies, fantasies of brutal violence, fantasies of molecular mutation, apocalyptic fantasies. Not for nothing have Tokyo critics referred to Tsukamoto as 'Japan's answer to Sam Raimi, David Cronenberg *and* David Lynch'. TR

Tetsuo II: Bodyhammer

(Shinya Tsukamoto, 1991, Jap) Tomoroh Taguchi, Nobu Kanaoka, Shinya Tsukamoto, Keinosuke Tomioka, Sujin Kim.
83 min.
Significantly more accessible than Tsukamoto's first, black-and-white, 16mm foray into new-flesh-horror (*Tetsuo: The Iron Man*), this colour, hi-tech reworking of the original is a relentlessly inventive sci-fi cinepoem, whose story – again about a man suffering strange and deadly anatomical changes, which this time result partly from the rage he feels at his son being abducted – is largely an excuse for a series of virtuoso sequences based around the motif of physical/psychological mutation. *Manga* merges with Cronenbergian grotesquerie in a violent, frantic, technically audacious epic full of images that are alternately homoerotic and heartstopping in their cruel brilliance. GA

Texas, Addio (aka The Avenger)

(Ferdinando Baldi, 1966, It/Sp) Franco Nero, Cole Kitosch, José Suarez, Elisa Montes, Livio Lorenzon, José Guardiola.
92 min.
Ultrascope spaghetti Western in which Texas sheriff Burt Sullivan (Nero, standard issue laconic) crosses the border with kid brother Jim (Kitosch) to square matters with Cisco Delgado (Suarez), the outlaw who murdered their father. The twist? Jim turns out to be Cisco's abandoned son. Workmanlike and unpretentious, but not a patch on Leone or even the Django series. TJ

Texas Chain Saw Massacre, The

(Tobe Hooper, 1974, US) Marilyn Burns, Gunnar Hansen, Allen Danziger, Edwin Neal, Paul A Partain, William Vail.
83 min.

A band of charmless youngsters ignore all the warnings and stumble across a psychopathic family (closer to Charles Addams than *Psycho*) in remote farmland. This abattoir of a movie boasts sledgehammers, meathooks and chainsaws, and the result, though not especially visceral, is noisy, relentless, and about as subtle as having your leg sawed off without anaesthetic. It's notable only for taking woman-in-jeopardy about as far as she can go. The three men are despatched unceremoniously, and the women (bra-less and hotpants respectively), their screams rising into orgasms of fear, are toyed with endlessly while the camera often assumes a pointedly aggressive stance. Pernicious stuff and not even true, like the ads suggested – the Ed Gein case, on which this is supposedly based, bears little relation. CPe

Texas Chainsaw Massacre 2, The

(Tobe Hooper, 1986, US) Dennis Hopper, Caroline Williams, Bill Johnson, Jim Siedow, Bill Moseley.
95 min.
After the claustrophobic horrors of the original, Hooper's messy stab at outré black humour comes as something of a relief. Deep in the bowels of Texas, the mutant family display their annoyance at a local DJ's blatherings in typically visceral style. Hopper hams it up massively as a psychotic ex-Texan Ranger, hell-bent upon bringing the cannibals to justice, while Williams provides a feisty female lead who (once again) gives the in-bred mental cases a run for their money. Despite the BBFC's perfunctory refusal to certificate the movie for public showing in Britain, it contains little to offend anyone with the slightest sense of irony. Gaudy highlights include: a driver having his head chainsawed in half to lively effect; Hopper picking out the biggest bastard chainsawer in a hardware store; Williams taunting Leatherface about his inability to 'get it up' as he impotently waggles an unstartable chainsaw between her legs. The only truly yucky moment comes when Williams is forced to don facial skin freshly peeled from a corpse's face, but in these post-*Silence of the Lambs* days even that seems a tad tame. Not a patch on the original (or indeed Jeff Burr's Part III), but amusing enough none the less. Isn't it about time the censors developed a sense of humour? MK

Texas Chainsaw Massacre III

see Leatherface: The Texas Chainsaw Massacre III

Texas Rangers, The

(King Vidor, 1936, US) Fred MacMurray, Jack Oakie, Jean Parker, Lloyd Nolan, Edward Ellis, George Hayes.
97 min. b/w.
Riding silently in column, past towering cliffs and beneath ornate cloudscapes, the Rangers proceed on their implacable way, to showdowns featuring such declarations as 'Ain't no more room for your kind of Texan' and would-be amusing dialogue equating dead Indians with rotten apples. Redskin beware! Outlaw beware! (Though the latter merits the post-mortem valediction, 'Hope you'll let him in up there. He just got on the wrong trail, that's all.') The dilemma arising from this movie is whether to emphasise the correspondences between it and contemporary Nazi cinema or whether to focus on the distinctions. Vidor was himself a Texan and unembarrassed, it seems, by the concept of Texas as (after the elimination of undesirable elements) a paradise situated in the south of Utopia. It's mildly amusing, therefore, that the archetypal scenery framing all those stereotypical characters should actually be situated near Gallup, New Mexico. Nothing else is amusing though. BBa

Texasville

(Peter Bogdanovich, 1990, US) Jeff Bridges, Cybill Shepherd, Annie Potts, Cloris Leachman, Timothy Bottoms, Eileen Brennan, Randy Quaid.
125 min.
Bogdanovich's sequel to *The Last Picture Show*, set in 1984, finds the small Texan town of Anarene afflicted by moral, economic and social breakdown. Duane Jackson (Bridges), now an oil mogul, faces bankruptcy, his kids are virtually delinquent, and his marriage to Karla (Potts) is

on the rocks. Duane's old flame, homecoming B movie queen Jacy (Shepherd) looks set to seduce his family away from him; and the mayor, Duane's lifelong buddy Sonny (Bottoms), with whom he is organising Anarene's centennial pageant, is mentally and emotionally unstable. In other words, life is a mess. So is the film's narrative, adapted by Bogdanovich himself from Larry McMurtry's sprawling novel. The first half comes over as deliriously cynical satire, suggesting nothing less than a Paul Bartel pastiche of *Dallas*. Then sentimentality intrudes as Bogdanovich, determined to introduce a hymn to the healing power of friendship, loses the courage of his comic convictions. It all looks good, though, and the actors – especially Bridges and Potts – are clearly having a ball. GA

Thank God It's Friday

(Robert Klane, 1978, US) Valerie Landsburg, Terri Nunn, Chick Vennera, Donna Summer, Ray Vitte, Jeff Goldblum, Debra Winger, The Commodores.
89 min.
Like several other movies that have trodden in the wake of *American Graffiti*, this evening-in-the-life-of-a-disco uses a largely unknown cast and keeps eight or nine lines of narrative going at once. It also crams in countless plugs for its sponsors, Motown and Casablanca. It's at least as formulary and dumb as it sounds – but it's also very, very funny. The jokes are strictly mainstream, of course, but the fact that most of them are anti-sexist and anti-racist distinctly helps, as does the freshness of the cast. Most commendable of all is the fact that no one feels the need to moralise or get serious in the closing scenes: the running gags keep right on running, and they're strong enough to send you out with a fixed grin. TR

Thank You, Aunt

see Grazie Zia

Thank You, Jeeves!

(Arthur Greville Collins, 1936, US) Arthur Treacher, Virginia Field, David Niven, Lester Matthews, Colin Tapley.
57 min. b/w.
Niven was a support player for Sam Goldwyn when Fox borrowed him for third-billing in this charming B-picture scripted by Joseph Hoffman and Stephen Gross from the novel by PG Wodehouse. Bertie Wooster gets entirely the wrong idea when mystery woman Field asks for help in fending off pursuing gangsters. Treacher steals the show as Jeeves, but Niven makes a very passable Bertie. Relatively minor, but, unlike a lot of bigger movies, it knows not to demand too much of your time. TJ

Thank You, Life

see Merci la vie

Thank Your Lucky Stars

(David Butler, 1943, US) Eddie Cantor, Dennis Morgan, Joan Leslie, Bette Davis, Humphrey Bogart, Errol Flynn, John Garfield, Ida Lupino, Olivia de Havilland.
127 min.
During WWII, Hollywood came up with the notion that all-star revues would be just the thing to revive the audience's flagging spirits, and soon these extravaganzas started rolling out of the backlot like dreadnoughts down a slipway. Paramount turned out *Star Spangled Rhythm*, followed a year later by this Warners offering, which gave the studio's contract players a rare opportunity to strut their stuff in a musical context. The plot's the usual puttin'-on-a-show concoction, but the excessive length is worth it for Bette Davis' showstopping 'They're Either Too Young or Too Old' and Errol Flynn (that's right, all-singing all-dancing) offering the worst Cockernee accent this side of Dick Van Dyke in his party piece, 'That's What You Jolly Well Get'. TJ

That Championship Season

(Jason Miller, 1982, US) Bruce Dern, Stacy Keach, Robert Mitchum, Martin Sheen, Paul Sorvino.
109 min.
Backslapping, whooping, and blubbering abound when four college buddies foregather to relive the

moment twenty years earlier when coach (Mitchum) led them to glory in the state basketball league. Jollity soon gives way to maudlin nostalgia, and as the liquor flows, the inner men begin to peek through in a depressingly familiar succession of outbursts, breakdowns, and confessions of inadequacy. Locker-room camaraderie is held up as the US apotheosis of brotherly love, and the old 'winning is everything' ethic gets trotted out with suspiciously few ironic sideswipes. Excellent performances, but writer/director Miller obviously couldn't bear to discard one finely crafted chestnut of his Pulitzer prizewinning play, and makes his distinguished cast wade through one of the most torrential masses of verbiage ever to hit the screen. JP

That Cold Day in the Park

(Robert Altman, 1969, Can) Sandy Dennis, Michael Burns, Susanne Benton, Luana Anders, Michael Murphy, John Garfield Jr. 112 min
Made immediately before *M*A*S*H*, this has Sandy Dennis, in her characteristic role as a frustrated spinster, picking up a dropout (Burns) on a Vancouver park bench and inviting him home for food, care and shelter. The results are distressingly predictable (though, to be fair to Altman, this area of modern Gothic hadn't been quite so overworked in 1969). With signs of the visual daring evident in Altman's later work, however, there is sufficient interest in his treatment of yet another woman character going bananas to repay committed admirers. RM

That Darn Cat

(Robert Stevenson, 1965, US) Hayley Mills, Dean Jones, Dorothy Provine, Roddy McDowall, Neville Brand, Elsa Lanchester, William Demarest, Ed Wynn. 116 min.
This typical – not unentertaining – mid-'60s Disney live-actioner has Hayley's Siamese following a trail of juicy salmon and unwittingly uncovering a kidnap plot. Federal agent Jones and neighbour McDowall are in personable form, but the two legged cast play second string to the marvellous moggie. TJ

That Eye, the Sky

(John Ruane, 1994, Aust) Lisa Harrow, Peter Coyote, Jamie Croft, Amanda Dogue, Mark Fairall. 105 min.
Australian writer/director Ruane followed his first film, the sparkling black comedy *Death in Brunswick*, with this very different, mystical rites-of-passage chronicle. When his father is returned home in a coma after a car accident, 12-year-old Ort (Croft) places his faith in a charismatic stranger (Coyote) to effect a cure. But what role in the healing process has the weird light which the boy spots in the sky above the house? The emotional knots of a problem family are played against an unfussily supernatural background affecting all their lives. Hard to categorise, but definitely haunting. TJ

That Gang of Mine

(Joseph H Lewis, 1940, US) Bobby Jordan, Leo Gorcey, Clarence Muse, Dave O'Brien, Joyce Bryant, David Gorcey. 62 min. b/w.
A salutary reminder of the poverty row milieu in which Lewis had to toil for years before producing the belatedly recognised masterpieces of his maturity, made on budgets only marginally more luxurious. A Monogram series movie featuring the East Side Kids in an absurd horse race comedy that induces as many groans (not least for racist stereotyping) as laughs, it's none the less distinguished (and lifted) by the energetic visual style and wit which Lewis invests it. PT

That Hamilton Woman
(aka Lady Hamilton)

(Alexander Korda, 1941, US) Vivien Leigh, Laurence Olivier, Alan Mowbray, Gladys Cooper, Sara Allgood, Henry Wilcoxon, Heather Angel. 128 min. b/w.
Being Churchill's favourite film may not be much of a recommendation, but it's easy to see why he welcomed this wartime offering from the English community in Hollywood. Olivier may be outra-

geously hammy, but his Lord Nelson is an icon of eccentric English heroism. Patriotism is only half the story, though. Olivier and the splendidly coquettish Leigh distil the essence of their stormy off-screen romance so effectively that the Americans insisted on a ridiculously prurient prologue showing its unfortunate consequences for the lady. RMy

That'll Be the Day

(Claude Whatham, 1973, GB) David Essex, Ringo Starr, Rosemary Leach, James Booth, Billy Fury, Keith Moon, Rosalind Ayres, Robert Lindsay, Brenda Bruce. 91 min.
Hugely overrated dip into the rock'n'roll nostalgia bucket, which says more about the '70s, when it was made, than about the '50s, whose teen themes it plagiarised. The one-dimensional Essex plays Jim MacLaine, a working class lad who throws over his wife and kiddy and hangs around fairgrounds, hoping to make a name for himself as a pop star. (He gets his just deserts in the follow-up, *Stardust*). Ringo turns in a thoroughly cringeworthy performance as a teddy boy, and writer Ray Connolly uses a trowel to pile on the banal social significance. Youth culture my eye: they're all at least a decade too old. But good tunes, and worth catching for Billy Fury's gold lamé act. AB

That Lady

(Terence Young, 1955, GB) Olivia de Havilland, Gilbert Roland, Paul Scofield, Françoise Rosay, Dennis Price, Anthony Dawson, Christopher Lee. 100 min.
Soporific yarn from a novel by Kate O'Brien set in 16th century Madrid. Olivia de Havilland is Ana de Medoza, a widow with a Moshe Dayan eyepatch, who stirs up unholy feelings at court. Scofield's King Philip II has a crush on her and is furious when she starts an affair with one of his ministers. The film falls victim to spectacularly fussy production design and Robert Krasker's 'Scope photography. Everybody's decked out in best medieval finery and we're treated to endless picture postcard shots of historic Spain, but there isn't a hint of any sexual tension between de Havilland and Scofield. GM

That Lucky Touch

(Christopher Miles, 1975, GB) Roger Moore, Susannah York, Shelley Winters, Lee J Cobb, Jean-Pierre Cassel, Raf Vallone, Sydne Rome, Donald Sinden. 93 min.
After the success of *Gold*, Moore and York team again, smoothiechops as an arms merchant to her independent journalist with principles, a divorce, and a young son. Out to scupper Moore's weapons deal with NATO, while trying not to fall in love with him, York's real nature is revealed through a remark her son and the scriptwriter let slip: 'Mother makes news happen where she wants to be'. The film itself is just as calculating – a romantic comedy bogged down by some desperately protracted humour, tourist Brussels locations, and the manner in which British, American, and Continental sales are all glaringly kept in mind. The result is, as one character says apropos of something else, like getting a troop of horses to piss at the same time. CPe

That Man Bolt

(Henry Levin/David Lowell Rich, 1973, US) Fred Williamson, Byron Webster, Miko Mayama, Teresa Graves, Satoshi Nakamura, Jack Ging, Paul Mantee. 105 min.
Packaged consumer product, with a black hero (albeit somewhat like Uncle Tom's answer to Desperate Dan – all chin and about as subtle), and a plot that escalates from straightforward thriller (he's an international 'courier') into a fantasy of Bond-like proportions, which ends with Bolt coming on like a one-man army. It's given something of a lift by the now almost obligatory kung-fu influence: Bolt lands up in Hong Kong, taking on the local syndicate villain and a score of oriental pugilists, the highlight being a fight in a firework factory (preceded by a bit of torture by acupuncture) which ends with a large firework display. CPe

That Man from Rio

see Homme de Rio, L'

That Man George

see Homme de Marrakesh, L'

That Night

(Craig Bolotin, 1992, US) C Thomas Howell, Juliette Lewis, Helen Shaver, Eliza Dushku, John Dossett, J Smith-Cameron. 89 min.
Although whisked out with no great fanfare, this familiar tale of growing up in the early '60s is actually pretty good. It's 1961, Sputnik is circling the skies, and JFK's in the White House. Kicked around by her slightly older friends and largely ignored by her father, Alice (Dushku) becomes besotted with 17-year-old Sheryl (Lewis) across the street. She's everything Alice wants to be: confident, attractive and a little wild. The two become firm friends when the youngster paves the way for Sheryl's liaison with Brooklyn bad boy Rick (Howell). Writer/director Bolotin's sensitive, nuanced adaptation of Alice McDermott's novel surpasses expectations by keeping nostalgia at arm's length, adopting a comparatively restrained voice-over narration, and adhering closely to the ten-year-old's perspective. Lewis acts her bobby sox off as the teenager in heat, but she's hardly the princess Alice describes, while Howell is an unprepossessing object for her affections. Thankfully, young Dushku is very good, and Bruce Surtees' photography lifts the film to an altogether higher plane. TCh

That Night in Rio

(Irving Cummings, 1941, US) Don Ameche, Alice Faye, Carmen Miranda, SZ Sakall, J Carrol Naish, Curt Bois, Leonid Kinsky, Maria Montez. 90 min.
Rudolph Lothar and Hans Adler's play *The Red Cat* was first adapted for the cinema as *Folies Bergère de Paris* (Roy Del Ruth, 1935), with Maurice Chevalier, and later metamorphosed into *On the Riviera* (Walter Lang, 1951), with Danny Kaye. Between times it served in this Fox frolic. Dapper count Ameche lands in bother when spouse Faye unwittingly hires a showbiz entertainer (his own secret sideline) to impersonate him as part of a business deal, a situation that requires nifty footwork when, as the nightclub impressionist rather than the married aristo, he falls for Faye all over again. Miranda strutts her stuff to a little ditty titled, 'Chica, Chica Boom Chic'. TJ

That Night in Varennes
(La Nuit de Varennes)

(Ettore Scola, 1982, Fr/It) Jean-Louis Barrault, Marcello Mastroianni, Hanna Schygulla, Harvey Keitel, Jean-Claude Brialy, Daniel Gélin, Andrea Ferreol, Michel Vitold, Laura Betti, Jean-Louis Trintignant. 165 min.
Featuring such notables as Tom Paine (Keitel), the ageing Casanova (Mastroianni), the randy writer Restif de la Bretonne (Barrault), and an Austrian countess (Schygulla), this is a picaresque story of the coach and party that followed hard on the one which tried to transport Louis XVI and Marie Antoinette to safety in 1791. Thus is history viewed not through the eyes of its main participants, but through the appetites, passions and prejudices of its commentators and bit players. The result is like *Tom Jones* crossed with *Stagecoach*, with the addition of Sergio Amidei and Scola's wise and witty dialogue, some sumptuous painterly landscapes, and a subtle feeling for the period far removed from the clichés of British imagining. There's a real sense both of history in the making and of life in the living: a warm, bravura work of lasting majesty. SGr

That Obscure Object of
Desire (Cet Obscur Objet
du Désir)

(Luis Buñuel, 1977, Fr/Sp) Fernando Rey, Carole Bouquet, Angela Molina, Julien Bertheau, André Weber, Piéral, Milena Vukotic. 103 min.
Buñuel's last film, adapted from the Pierre Louys novel (about a woman who drives a man to distractions of frustrated desire) which also served as a basis for Sternberg's *The Devil Is a Woman*. Full of echoes from Buñuel's earlier work, it

might almost be seen as a summation of his pre-occupation with the connection between sex and violence, first annotated in *L'Age d'or*. His great coup here is to have the object of the hero's lusts played by two different actresses, with the alternation of svelte coolness and steamy voluptuousness lending teasing credibility to the way in which his ardour is cruelly cooled and heated by turns. These sexual games are brilliantly and tantalisingly funny, but the film is meanwhile secretly pursuing another obscure object of desire: the terrorism which surfaces in various forms (moral, social, cultural, economic, psychological, and even political), ranging from the bomb outrages that accompany the hero in his sexual odyssey down to the financial pressures he exerts in order to have his way. And just as *L'Age d'or* ended with an equation between the sexual and revolutionary acts, so does *That Obscure Object of Desire*, though in a deliberately coded, mystificatory form. TM

That Old Feeling

(Carl Reiner, 1997, US) Bette Midler, Dennis Farina, Paula Marshall, Gail O'Grady, David Rasche, Jamie Denton, Danny Nucci.
105 min.
Movie star Lilly (Midler) and journalist Dan (Farina) have always bickered like Punch and Judy. Now, as ex-partners, they're about to be flung together for their daughter Molly's prim-and-proper wedding. Though both have new mates, their genitals engage in a fit of nostalgia. Let the chaos begin. As ever, Midler – a queasy cross between Dolly Parton and Anna Magnani – is a sight to behold, the cruel lighting transforming her skin into a substance worthy of *Star Trek*. Farina, too, has rarely looked worse. Both, however, have enough pure showbiz talent, flinty and vulgar, to hook you. Grim, nevertheless. CO'Su

That Riviera Touch

(Cliff Owen, 1966, GB) Eric Morecambe, Ernie Wise, Suzanne Lloyd, Paul Stassino, Armand Mestral, Peter Jeffrey.
98 min.
When British TV comics become firmly established as household favourites, some klutz will always suggest that they make a feature film (even Cannon and Ball made one,*The Boys in Blue*). This was Morecambe and Wise's second cinema job (after *The Intelligence Men*): a routine caper with jewel thieves, gangsters, and speedboats – and plenty of padding shots of the Côte d'Azur. It was unworthy of their talents then; it looks even worse now. MA

That's Carry On

(Gerald Thomas, 1977, GB) Barbara Windsor, Kenneth Williams.
95 min. b/w & col.
Kenneth Williams and Barbara Windsor are trapped in a projection box with cans containing prints of the 28 *Carry On* films: they enthusiastically reminisce in that inimitable fashion which has become part of our national heritage, and with the help of clips lead us in a rather desultory way through the history of the series. Strictly for addicts, who will doubtless chortle, as they have done for twenty years, at the changeless sexual innuendoes. JPy

That's Dancing!

(Jack Haley Jr, 1985, US) narrators: Gene Kelly, Sammy Davis Jr, Mikhail Baryshnikov, Ray Bolger, Liza Minnelli.
104 min. b/w & col.
This is the way to see Hollywood dance sequences: no flimsy plot or vacuous dialogue, just the dancers doing their stuff. The only problem is that the pleasure of seeing the clips themselves is compromised by the sycophantic narration (Liza Minnelli's contribution in particular) and the random chronology of the arbitrary selection. So, while we may be mesmerised by the extraordinary silent Charleston sequence from *So This Is Paris* or the kaleidoscopic patterns of Busby Berkeley's *42nd Street*, the compilation itself is a formless mess. An extraneous ballet sequence featuring Mikhail Baryshnikov sticks out like a sore toe amid the furious tap dancing of the Nicholas Brothers, the sinuous sexiness of Cyd Charisse, and a charming ad-lib routine featuring Shirley Temple and 'Mr Bojangles'. And when the suave smoothness of Fred and Ginger

in *Swing Time* gives way to the tight-trousered posturing of John Travolta and the gymnastic gracelessness of flashdancer Marine Jahan, the nostalgia bubble bursts. NF

That's Entertainment!

(Jack Haley Jr, 1974, US) narrators: Fred Astaire, Bing Crosby, Gene Kelly, Peter Lawford, Liza Minnelli, Donald O'Connor, Debbie Reynolds, Mickey Rooney, Frank Sinatra, James Stewart, Elizabeth Taylor.
137 min. b/w & col.
On with the motley. Hollywood begins to package its feasts, and *That's Entertainment!* has all the flavour of the Vesta dehydrated line. The wondrous progeny of producers Arthur Freed and – to a lesser extent – Jack Cummings made MGM the home of the film musical. Jack Haley Jr selected his fave raves, chopped them into skimpy segments, and thrown them together with little rhyme and less reason. Ageing superstars stroll on to recite his deliberately agog script. Little info, no view, no shape, no explanations emerge. The rarity of some items makes a trip worthwhile, but to seek out showings of *The Broadway Melody of 1938, Babes in Arms, Meet Me in St Louis, On the Town, The Band Wagon* and *Gigi* would be to learn much more about how Metro and Freed together developed the genre. SG

That's Entertainment Part II

(Gene Kelly, 1976, US) narrators: Fred Astaire, Gene Kelly.
126 min. b/w & col.
With the most obvious plums already picked and the less obvious plums still ignored, this concoction is boosted with some non-musical items. It would be a hard-hearted person who couldn't find odd morsels of pleasure, but the compilation still enshrines the mediocre: Gene Kelly's ungainly stabs at Art, Doris Day, and scenes from thudders like *Till the Clouds Roll By*. The juxtaposition of clips is mindless; and between the indigestible chunks come newly-filmed scenes with Kelly and Astaire, which manage to be even worse than some of the clips. And their asinine commentary damagingly intrudes into the numbers. Who wants to hear Kelly reminisce when Garland's singing the sublime 'Have Yourself a Merry Little Christmas'? That's not entertainment. GB

That's Entertainment! III

(Bud Friedgen/Michael J Sheridan, 1994, US) narrators: June Allyson, Cyd Charisse, Lena Horne, Howard Keel, Gene Kelly, Ann Miller, Debbie Reynolds, Mickey Rooney, Esther Williams.
113 min. b/w & col.
An MGM 70th anniversary 'docutainment' directed by the editors of the two previous clipfests. Since many of the famous sequences have been bagged already, this trawl through the archives is padded with out-takes, screen tests and off-screen footage. The period covered is bookended by *Hollywood Revue of 1929* and *Gigi* (1958). Some stuff we can do without, and did: Joan Crawford dancing like a donkey as she mimes 'Two Faced Woman' for *Torch Song*. On the other hand, Ava Gardner's 'Can't Help Loving Dat Man', unused in *Showboat*, is sweet indeed. Prints have been restored and soundtracks digitally enhanced, though there's some rough editing and aspect ratios are not always respected. Minor buff's stuff, but fun. WH

That Sinking Feeling

(Bill Forsyth, 1979, GB) Robert Buchanan, John Hughes, Janette Rankin, Derek Millar, Danny Benson, Eddie Burt.
92 min.
The image of the Scots in British films had largely been confined in the past to the wayward eccentrics of *Whisky Galore* or to Glaswegian thugs. Refreshingly, in his first feature (independently produced on a risibly small budget), Bill Forsyth successfully captured the subversively ironic optimism of the Glasgow streets and somehow managed to combine it with the good-humoured charm of the best Ealing comedies. It's a street-smart fairytale about a group of unemployed teenagers embarking, enthusiastically but incompetently, on a big heist, and is played with such relish by members of the Glasgow Youth Theatre that it's guaranteed to win any audience over to its side within minutes: the British dispossessed's version of *Rockers*. SM

'That's Life'

(Blake Edwards, 1986, US) Jack Lemmon, Julie Andrews, Sally Kellerman, Robert Loggia, Jennifer Edwards, Rob Knepper, Chris Lemmon, Felicia Farr.
102 min.
A none-too-edifying examination of middle-life crisis, much in the autobiographical vein of *S.O.B* and set in Edwards' own home in Malibu, where he has gathered around him a veritable plethora of real-life friends and family. Lemmon plays a hypochondriacal architect, panicked at the thought of his impending 60th birthday, who is too obsessed with his fear of failing sexual and creative powers to notice the real anxieties of his family. While his singer wife (Andrews) busies herself organising a family get-together in his honour (while awaiting, unbeknownst to him, the results of a biopsy for suspected throat cancer), he is off indulging himself in a little extra-marital shenanigan with a seductive client, dabbling with a return to the church, or finding solace with a sexy fortune-teller's therapeutic line in massage. Lemmon, though presented with funny lines and set pieces, is irritating rather than sympathetic, and allowed to coast in a hackneyed retread of the neurotic he has been playing for too many years. The rest is a thinly veiled tribute to Edwards' wife Andrews, which shows him at his most embarrassing. WH

That Summer!

(Harley Cokliss, 1979, GB) Ray Winstone, Tony London, Emily Moore, Julie Shipley, Jon Morrison, Andrew Byatt, Ewan Stewart, John Junkin.
93 min.
Unfairly treated in the rock press, because the excellent soundtrack album led everyone into believing they were getting a hard-nosed film about the summer of punk. In fact this is a polished, if rather traditional, summerfuntime feature about a group of kids hanging out in Torquay. The storyline is necessarily slim, and to win an 'AA' certificate the film had to go easy on sex, drugs and rock'n'roll, but within its limited format Cokliss has performed small wonders: the acting is good (notably Byatt as a stomping Glasgow heavy), the script is funny, and the photography has some of the shimmering surface energy of *American Graffiti*. The pity is that the superb music has largely been thrown away, and the ending degenerates into Boy's Own Paper twaddle. DP

That Summer of White Roses

(Rajko Grlic, 1989, GB/Yugo) Tom Conti, Susan George, Rod Steiger, Nitzan Sharron, Alun Armstrong, John Gill, John Sharp, Geoffrey Whitehead, Miljenko Brlecic, Vanja Drach.
103 min.
Although the riverside bathing beach proves popular with the Nazis (this being Yugoslavia in 1945), the token lifeguard – simple-minded Andrija (Conti) – hardly has his work cut out, and can therefore spend his days gazing at the water and mummering on about the 'river demon'. Considering the proximity to the Nazi base, it seems perverse that fugitive Ana (George) should pick this spot as a hideout; even stranger that she thinks a rush marriage to the village idiot will deflect suspicion. The gentle rhythms of life continue until Andrija dramatically saves a fat old gent from drowning. Is he partisan or Nazi? Whatever, good-hearted Andrija seems fated to attract unwelcome attention…Conti invests the character with cheerful dignity, but remains some way short of the noble and tragic dimensions hopefully indicated. The elegiac riverside scenes, set against crashing portrayals of Nazi swinishness, work rather better than the romantic or action stuff. SFe

That Thing You Do!

(Tom Hanks, 1996, US) Tom Hanks, Tom Everett Scott, Liv Tyler, Johnathon Schaech, Steve Zahn, Ethan Embry, Rita Wilson.
108 min.
The year's 1964, and young Guy (Hanks-looka-like Scott) is drafted in to play drums with a rock'n'roll high school band. One catchy tune transforms the One-ders into local heroes, and brings them to the attention of first regional, then national talent scouts, until 'The Wonders' find themselves with a Top Ten hit and a record con-

tract. Their progress is uncomplicated, if not exactly quick. Hanks is such a nice guy, he can't bring himself to imagine anyone who isn't, which tends to preclude anything so base as dramatic conflict. Episodes of *Happy Days* have more narrative tension. The nearest we get to a bad guy is Schaech as the group's career-driven singer-songwriter: the artist. Love-interest Tyler gets to mouth lyrics in the wings; when things hot up, she catches a cold. As writer/director, Hanks recreates the period with nostalgic affection, in pastel shades and design straight from a retro catalogue, but his film shows no interest in the musical process, and the title track is reprised ad nauseam (eight times!). Sweet nothing, then, but what would you expect of a rock movie devoted to the drummer? TCh

That Was Then, This Is Now
(Christopher Cain, 1985, US) Emilio Estevez, Craig Sheffer, Kim Delaney, Jill Schoelen, Barbara Babcock, Morgan Freeman, Frank Howard.
101 min.
If that was then and this is now, now certainly bears one uncanny resemblance to then: the joyrides, the high school dance, the midnight parking-lot punch-ups which send cowardly punks running as that venomous taunt of taunts hangs in the still night air – 'Get a haircut!'. Get a haircut? The fact is that SE Hinton's novel, published in 1971 and set in the late '60s, has been updated, complete with contemporary rock score, for the '80s. The story is classic – a pair of childhood friends go their separate ways as adolescence gives way to manhood – the treatment pure Hollywood. Mark (Estevez) and Bryon (Sheffer) are the dynamic duo of suburban St Paul, Minnesota, laying down the law in whatever batmobile they can get their hands on. There's a girl who comes between them, and a death that brings an understanding of their own mortalities. Estevez is the rebel without a cause, newcomer Sheffer is cast as the romantic lead, and both are heading at breakneck pace towards an inescapable loss of innocence. SGo

That Woman, That Man
(Ke Yeoja, Ke Namja)
(Kim Ui-Seok, 1993, SKor) Kang Soo-Yeon, Lee Kyung-Young, Ha Yu-Mi, Kim Sung-Su, Cho Sun-Mook.
109 min.
Kim's follow-up to *Marriage Story* redefines everything that can go wrong in 1990s relationships. Eun (Kang) and Chang (Lee) are neighbours in Peace Apartments; both are on the rebound from failed affairs. She's a maternity nurse who hates babies; he's a TV journalist who compiles obit material for the not-yet-dead. They hate each other on sight, and the stormy non-romance which develops between them is as much scary as funny, not least because it's so frank about the sex. Kim has the wit to frame this front-line bulletin from the sex war as an oblique homage to the late Audrey Hepburn. TR

Theatre Girls
(Kim Longinotto/Claire Pollak, 1978, GB)
82 min. b/w.
Down in Soho's Greek Street is the Theatre Girls Club, a dilapidated hostel for homeless single women. This stark documentary picture of some of its occupants by National Film School students allows the women (many were in the theatre, and are delightfully, painfully extroverted) to tell their own story; humour and self-deprecating irony are punctuated by moments of aggression, tenderness, and sheer, terrifying isolation. There's not enough analysis: of the reasons the women are there; of why their 'open door' refuge is so pitifully under-subsidised; or, ultimately, of the film's own motives. But it does present a shocking vision of largely middle-aged, frustrated losers, their minds often addled by drink or drugs, their fantasies injected with the harshest self-knowledge. Not a film recommended if you're already depressed, but one which ought to make you think. HM

Theatre of Blood
(Douglas Hickox, 1973, GB) Vincent Price, Diana Rigg, Ian Hendry, Harry Andrews, Coral Browne, Robert Coote, Jack Hawkins, Michael Hordern, Arthur Lowe, Robert Morley, Dennis Price, Diana Dors.
102 min.
Comedy horror that really does give Vincent Price a chance to do his stuff, with deliciously absurd results. He plays a vilified classical actor driven to mount a series of elaborate Shakespearean charades in which eight drama critics will die: one is decapitated in his bed, another is forced to give a pound of flesh, yet another is drowned in a barrel of wine, and all are subjected beforehand to the manic posturing and rambling of the mad actor romping through a succession of tragic characters with grotesque brilliance. Price's Richard III is enough on its own to make the film worthwhile (as he snakes his way through a cobwebbed corridor in full royal gear, hissing 'Now is the Winter of our discontent...'); but unfortunately the overlong script eventually runs out of steam, and the ending is feeble. DP

Theft Under the Sun
(Haoqing Gai Tian)
(Cha Chuen-Yee, 1997, HK) Michael Fitzgerald Wong, Cheung Chi-Lam, Gigi Lai, Francis Ng, So Chi-Wai, Timmy Ho.
110 min.
Act One of Cha's workmanlike thriller centres on a large scale robbery foiled by the involvement of Ka-Ho (Cheung), an undercover cop who has spent three years posing as a triad footsoldier; the standard shoot outs and explosions are executed with some panache. But Act Two never really catches fire as Ka-Ho tags along with American-Chinese mercenary Dan Peterson (Wong) on a trip to Mongolia to buy black market missiles and then drive them back to Hong Kong in a truck; the edgy progress of their relationship is cross cut with extended debates about Ka-Ho's trustworthiness between a no nonsense officer and a bullshitting psychologist back in police HQ. Act Three, in which the truck reaches Hong Kong and all hell breaks loose in a docklands warehouse, is fairly spiffy. But it looks as if Cha is one of those directors who is most interesting when he's stuck with tight schedules and limited budgets. TR

Thelma & Louise
(Ridley Scott, 1991, US) Susan Sarandon, Geena Davis, Harvey Keitel, Michael Madsen, Christopher McDonald, Stephen Tobolowsky, Brad Pitt.
129 min.
Leaving her husband a meal in the microwave, Thelma (Davis) sets off with her friend Louise (Sarandon) for a weekend holiday. But at their first stop, Thelma is nearly raped outside a bar; Louise shoots and kills the man. Gone is the care-free mood, and their destination is now Mexico. Along the way, the pistol-packing fugitives become ever bolder, robbing a convenience store, shooting up a leering driver's truck, and locking a cop in his car boot. Directing with blistering energy, Scott delivers the goods, while Sarandon and Davis, together with sympathetic cop Keitel, are acutely convincing throughout the deepening chaos. Callie Khouri's script is nevertheless simplistic in the way it reduces many of the men to stereotypes, while the women gain strength less through self-knowledge than through the American gun laws. Ultimately, this road movie calls on too many knee-jerk reactions: its shocking and funny scenes rely squarely on role reversals within a traditionally male genre. CM

Thelonious Monk:
Straight No Chaser
(Charlotte Zwerin, 1988, US) Thelonious Monk, Nelly Monk, Johnny Griffin, Thelonious Monk Jr.
90 min. b/w & col.
The image that sticks is Monk rotating slowly like a great black top, impregnable, unknowable, and sadly knowing. Produced for Clint Eastwood's Malpaso company, this is a jazz film in the old sense, which means that it is dignified and museumly. It comprises documentary footage from 1967 of the great pianist in transit, in the studio and playing live, intercut with interviews with relevant dudes; a downbeat, often dull, but unfailingly honest imprint of a singular mystique. Yes, the guy was weird; no, you can't see the stitching; certainly, we shall never see his like again. He wrote ugly-beautiful tunes, and improvised on them in entropic frenzy. In bamboo spectaculars and halibut hat, he addressed the keyboard like a man pats an alligator. Ultimately, this is a portrait of a man who dared,
which means, by cosmic law, that the picture sells the subject way short. There is nothing here that really adds to what we know. We might be moved by Monk's childlike dependency on his wife, baffled by his esoteric humour, honoured simply by his presence, but all we really need now are the records. NC

Them!
(Gordon Douglas, 1954, US) James Whitmore, Edmund Gwenn, Joan Weldon, James Arness, Onslow Stevens, Chris Drake, Leonard Nimoy, Dub Taylor, Fess Parker.
94 min. b/w.
By far the best of the '50s cycle of 'creature features', *Them!* and its story of a nest of giant radioactive ants (the result of an atomic test in the New Mexico desert) retains a good part of its power today. All the prime ingredients of the total mobilisation movie are here: massed darkened troops move through the eerie storm drains of Los Angeles, biblical prophecy is intermixed with gloomy speculation about the effect of radioactivity. Almost semi-documentary in approach, the formula is handled with more subtlety than usual, and the special effects are frequently superb. DP

Theme, The (Tema)
(Gleb Panfilov, 1979, USSR) Inna Churkova, Stanislav Lubshin, Natalya Seleznyova, Mikhail Oulianov, Evguenia Netchaieva.
100 min.
A key movie in *glasnost* cinema, Panfilov's film was refused a release by the Soviet authorities until 1987, when it promptly won the Golden Bear at Berlin. Oulianov is a mediocre writer who makes a good living toeing the Party line, but he knows he's a fake and that his success has little to do with genuine talent. By siding with the real artists rejected by the system, Panfilov makes a courageous statement against the conformity suffocating cultural life under the Brezhnev regime. A dour, very Russian piece, but a substantial one. TJ

Themroc
(Claude Faraldo, 1972, Fr) Michel Piccoli, Béatrice Romand, Marilú Tolo, Francesca R Coluzzi, Coluche.
110 min.
A quirky, anarchic satire that sees factory worker Piccoli cracking up, turning his bedroom into an urban cave, enjoying incest with his sister, and preying on cops for dinner. Some hilarious moments depicting the absurdity of routine life, but the predictable, episodic plot, and the gimmick of using grunts rather than dialogue, wear too thin to sustain more than one viewing. Joyfully tasteless, nevertheless. GA

Theodora Goes Wild
(Richard Boleslawski, 1936, US) Irene Dunne, Melvyn Douglas, Thomas Mitchell, Thurston Hall, Spring Byington, Rosalind Keith.
94 min. b/w.
A forerunner of much '30s craziness: literary editor Douglas discovers that the author of several racy best-sellers is, in fact, small-town girl Irene Dunne, who nobody would suspect of such a thing. Regrettably, the movie dips in the second half, when attention shifts from Douglas's attempts to persuade Dunne to go public, to her efforts to make him stand up to his corrupt politician father. TJ

Theorem (Teorema)
(Pier Paolo Pasolini, 1968, It) Terence Stamp, Silvana Mangano, Massimo Girotti, Anne Wiazemsky, Laura Betti, Andrés José Cruz, Ninetto Davoli.
98 min.
In *Theorem*, Pasolini achieved his most perfect fusion of Marxism and religion with a film that is both political allegory and mystical fable. Terence Stamp plays the mysterious Christ or Devil figure who stays briefly with a wealthy Italian family, seducing them one by one. He then goes as quickly as he had come, leaving their whole life-pattern in ruins. What would be pretentious and strained in the hands of most directors, with Pasolini takes on an intense air of magical revelation. In fact, the superficially improbable plot retains all the logic and certainty of a detective story. With bizarre appropriateness, it was one of the last films made by Stamp before he virtually disappeared from the international film scene for some years. DP

There's a Girl in My Soup

(Roy Boulting, 1970, GB) Peter Sellers, Goldie Hawn, Tony Britton, Nicky Henson, John Comer, Diana Dors, Gabrielle Drake.
96 min.
In this adaptation of Terence Frisby's stage play – a traditional romantic comedy, despite its cynical trappings – Peter Sellers is badly miscast as the suave TV personality and professional wolf who meets his match in an innocently depraved girl. Looking more like a moonlighting comedian than a ladykiller (he plays with a fixed smirk evidently meant to suggest irresistible charm), Sellers makes it a very long haul to the point where he finally makes up his mind, too late, that marriage might be preferable to a life of one-night stands. Goldie Hawn is delightful as the fey charmer who, for reasons of her own, disconcertingly counters his seduction techniques by jumping the gun. But even she cannot turn suet pudding into soufflé. TM

There's Always Tomorrow

(Douglas Sirk, 1956, US) Barbara Stanwyck, Fred MacMurray, Joan Bennett, Pat Crowley, William Reynolds, Jane Darwell.
84 min. b/w.
Sirk's second ostensible triangle drama with Stanwyck is, like the earlier *All I Desire*, a brilliant example of his mastery of lacerating irony. In demolishing the social fantasy of the 'happy home', the embodiment of the complacent surface values of '50s America, Sirk simultaneously exposes its tragic pervasiveness. Toy manufacturer MacMurray's alienation and isolation from his savagely conformist household is marked immediately by his blatant identification with his invention, Rex the Walkie-Talkie Robot. Yet when Stanwyck returns from his past, conventionally cast as the 'designing woman' (and at one point wearing a triangle-patterned dress!), it eventually transpires that all she has to offer him is a twenty-year-old romantic fantasy of (re-)establishing that same conformist model. Her generically-correct fairytale 'sacrifice' of self to the sanctity of the family, and the sanctioned role of the independent woman, merely intensifies the romantic agony of both dreamer-victims. Tomorrow never comes. PT

Thérèse

(Alain Cavalier, 1986, Fr) Catherine Mouchet, Aurore Prieto, Sylvie Habault, Hélène Alexandridis, Jean Pelegri, Clémence Massart.
91 min.
Thérèse Martin achieved sainthood by doing very little. Along with her three sisters, she entered the Carmel convent in Lisieux at the end of the 19th century, and after contending with the appalling privations of the order, the death of her father, and a bout of tuberculosis for which she was allowed no medical attention, she died in her early twenties. Goodness which is not active does not sound like the most promising of cinematic subjects, but in the scrupulous hands of Alain Cavalier, one is virtually forced to reassess just what is meant by cinematic. Filmed against the barest of grey walls, convent life is mapped out in a series of tableaux in which drama resides in the minute shifts of the human face and the odd telling gesture. Catherine Mouchet as Thérèse achieves that most difficult task of embodying goodness without being dull; her face glows with the innocent beauty of a medieval icon. Bresson is always a dangerous name to invoke for comparison; but while *Thérèse* lacks the master's taste for complexity and the paradoxes of the Catholic faith, the film's purity and simplicity nevertheless qualify it as another great enquiry into the operation of divine grace in our daily lives. CPea

There's No Business Like Show Business

(Walter Lang, 1954, US) Ethel Merman, Dan Dailey, Donald O'Connor, Marilyn Monroe, Johnnie Ray, Mitzi Gaynor, Hugh O'Brian, Frank McHugh.
117 min.
In this archetypal Fox musical, such details as plot, cast, and character development are swept aside by the mindless but fairly irresistible anthem to razzmatazz embodied in its title. For the record (and with a dozen Irving Berlin standards enshrined in decors of surpassing garishness, one might be better off buying it), the plot involves two generations of a vaudevillian family; the cast includes Merman at her loudest, Dailey at his crassest, and Monroe, thank heaven, at her 20th Century Foxiest; while character development is mostly confined to crooner Johnnie Ray's anguished decision to enter the priesthood (in scenes that are not merely mawkish but downright mawk). GAd

There's No Sex Like Snow Sex (Beim jodeln juckt die Lederhose)

(Alois Brummer, 1974, WGer) Judith Fritsch, Franz Muxeneder, Rosl Mayr, Peter Wacker.
85 min.
The English title says it all: an ineffable example of the writer/director Alois Brummer's broad Bavarian humour. A bouncing couple swish down a snowy mountain on top of a mobile hayrick observed by two impassive oldsters in leather breeches. Brummer churned out a string of similar films in the '70s. They found an audience in West Germany, but somehow failed to catch on in Britain. JPy

There Was a Crooked Man

(Joseph L Mankiewicz, 1970, US) Kirk Douglas, Henry Fonda, Hume Cronyn, Warren Oates, Burgess Meredith, John Randolph, Arthur O'Connell, Martin Gabel, Lee Grant.
126 min.
A sharply and literately witty Western comedy of manners, scripted by Benton and Newman (of *Bonnie and Clyde*) and set largely in an Arizona prison, 1883 vintage, peopled by a wonderful collection of rogues including a homicidal Chinaman, a dimwitted gunslinger (Oates), a pair of old-maidish conmen (Cronyn, Randolph), and – most memorably – the Missouri Kid (Meredith), once a great train robber but now a rheumy-eyed old man dreaming of the past and of the idyllic little farm he will never own. King of this community is new arrival Douglas, a cold-blooded outlaw smiling amiably behind steel-rimmed glasses, biding his time (he has lost stashed outside) but seen as a potential leader of men by the new warden (Fonda), a staunch believer in the milk of human kindness who enlists his aid in turning the place into a model prison. The resolution, cynically demonstrating the relativity of good and evil, comes a little too pat; but the performances, the set pieces, and the overall tone are irresistible. TM

These Foolish Things (Daddy Nostalgie)

(Bertrand Tavernier, 1990, Fr) Dirk Bogarde, Jane Birkin, Odette Laure, Emmanuelle Bataille.
95 min.
Tetchy, selfish, plagued by the pains of old age, retired Brit Tony (Bogarde) lives on the Côte d'Azur with his distant, taciturn French wife (Laure). He's never been very close, either, to their screenwriter daughter (Birkin), who arrives from Paris when he's suddenly taken into intensive care. A virtual three-hander, largely set in and around a small villa, Tavernier's film – about the problems of communication that often infect family life – might seem a most unappealing concoction were it not for the talent involved both before and behind the camera. With Bogarde (lent strong support by Birkin and Laure) giving one of his best performances ever, and Tavernier demonstrating his usual quietly assured professionalism, it impresses in the way it avoids all the usual pitfalls (with a welcome absence of maudlin, moralising sentiment). But what finally lifts this touching, consistently intelligent chamber piece is Tavernier's absolute control of mood, with Denis Lenoir's exquisite 'scope compositions and stealthy camera movements illuminating every nook and cranny of the trio's troubled relationships. GA

These Three

(William Wyler, 1936, US) Miriam Hopkins, Merle Oberon, Joel McCrea, Bonita Granville, Marcia Mae Jones, Catherine Doucet, Alma Kruger, Margaret Hamilton, Walter Brennan.
93 min. b/w.
The original talking point about Wyler's film was that Lillian Hellman's play *The Children's Hour* had been shamefully bowdlerised, with the lesbian theme masked behind a plot which has the two teachers victimised because gossip says one has slept with the other's fiancé. The film tries to hint at the original theme, not very satisfactorily, by shooting certain scenes so that it remains momentarily ambiguous as to who loves who. Paradoxically, though, as Wyler's more outspoken 1962 remake *The Loudest Whisper* demonstrated, this expurgation proves to be the film's strength. No longer having to worry about attitudes to lesbianism, and no longer adrift in areas of special pleading, it can simply expose the social mechanism whereby (as in the McCarthy witch hunts) idle malice can wreck innocent lives. It's still a stagey piece, but its closed world of lies and hysteria suits Wyler's rat-trap style to perfection, and the performances couldn't be bettered. TM

Thesis (Tesis)

(Alejandro Amenábar, 1995, Sp) Ana Torrent, Rafael Martínez, Eduardo Noriega, Nieves Herranz, Rosa Campillo.
125 min.
Torrent, a student researching violence in audio-visual media, gets more than she bargained for after asking a porno/gorefest freak to show her some of his heaviest videos. It's not his sick fascination that's so disturbing as the fact that her professor dies after watching what turns out to be a snuff movie, perhaps shot by someone in the university. A slick thriller muddled by its attempt to give its basic woman-in-peril theme a serious spin: it condemns our morbid interest in producing and watching violent images, then proceeds to satisfy it. Dubious and derivative, but delivered with some élan. GA

They All Laughed

(Peter Bogdanovich, 1981, US) Ben Gazzara, Audrey Hepburn, John Ritter, Colleen Camp, Patti Hansen, Dorothy Stratten, Blaine Novak.
121 min.
The temptation to respond 'No, they didn't' is overwhelming, and unfortunately it's also accurate. Bogdanovich's romantic comedy (involving three operatives from a detective agency and the women they have been assigned to watch) crucially lacks wit, and gauche clumsiness proves no substitute. Ritter's totally graceless performance punctures more laughs than it raises, and Gazzara is still in his expressionless period. There are occasional glimmers of what might have been in the fresh performances of the actresses. But it plods where it should sparkle, like a celebration where the champagne's gone flat. SM

They Call Him Marcado (Los Marcados)

(Alberto Mariscal, 1972, Mex) Antonio Aguilar, Flor Silvestre, Eric Del Castillo, Javier Ruan, José Carlos Ruiz.
82 min.
In spite of looking a mess (as though it had been subjected to some sort of butchery), this remains a weirdie of the first order: a perverse religious allegory in the form of a Western. The Kid (Ruan) is a vicious psychopath given to laughing a lot, an actor manqué (anyone who doesn't like his 'performance' is shot) who leads a gang of looters and rapists, and is incestuous with his father (Del Castillo) to boot. The town's resident Mater Dolorosa (Silvestre), madam of the brothel, hires her lover Marcado (meaning scarred: 'We all have scars, and the ones inside never heal'), a tight-lipped killer in the Eastwood mould (Aguilar), to kill the Kid, who is of course her son. The characters are all Western stereotypes, but given a strained and exaggerated twist – as, for example, when the Kid is given a snake tattoo, while the tattooist ridicules him for the softness of his skin and the design begins to run with blood. Unsurprisingly, the shadow of Nicholas Ray never seems all that far away. VG

They Call Me Bruce

(Elliott Hong, 1982, US) Johnny Yune, Ralph Mauro, Pam Huntington, Margaux Hemingway, John Louie, Bill Capizzi.
88 min.
The Bruce in question is Bruce Lee, idol of a klutzy Chinese chef, layed by 'popular American comic' Yune (record-holder for number of appearances on the Johnny Carson Show). Yune slings pasta for a family of Sicilian types, who decide that he's their man for conveying cocaine past the FBI. But Yune's cross-country jaunt soon peters

t

out into a series of messy skits, tempered by a certain cross-cultural confusion: Yune has a penchant for sushi, and at one point even speaks in Japanese. Despite the promising vision of a Mafia don growling 'I'm gonna make sashimi out of you' as he bites the head off his pet goldfish, the jokes are nowhere near gross enough to rank with the *Porky's* canon, and Yune is no Jackie Chan, let alone Brucie. A foo-foo film. AB

They Call Me MISTER Tibbs!

(Gordon Douglas, 1970, US) Sidney Poitier, Martin Landau, Barbara McNair, Anthony Zerbe, Jeff Corey, David Sheiner, Juano Hernandez, Edward Asner.
108 min.
Further adventures of Lieutenant Virgil Tibbs, the black cop who took on an entire Southern town in *In the Heat of the Night*. Poitier plays the role again, but this time his beat is San Francisco, the script studiously avoids racial issues, and the film goes the way of most sequels. Poitier duly solves his murder mystery and survives some domestic problems, but neither he nor director Gordon Douglas can turn this into anything more than a routine thriller. TM

They Call Me Trinity
(Lo Chiamavano Trinità)

(EB Clucher ie. Enzo Barboni, 1970, It) Terence Hill ie. Mario Girotti, Bud Spencer ie. Carlo Pedersoli, Farley Granger, Steffen Zacharias, Dan Sturkie, Gisela Hahn.
100 min.
The first and best in the 'Trinity' series of spaghetti Westerns, rare in that it is successful in combining laughter and some degree of interest in the action. It's carried off with considerable panache, thanks largely to the inspired Laurel & Hardy teaming of 'Hill', the sloppiest fast draw in the West, with the large, laconic 'Spencer' as his straight-man brother. Here they find themselves in conflict with an insane band of Mexicans manipulated by Farley Granger as the effete Major Harriman, who is bent on driving a settlement of Mormons from their fertile land. As usual it's horribly dubbed into English, but the nonchalant and expertly calculated ham that decorates the easy, breezy action makes you drop any reservations you might have in that direction.

They Call That an Accident
(Ils Appellent ça un Accident)

(Nathalie Delon, 1981, Fr) Nathalie Delon, Patrick Norbert, Gilles Ségal, Jean-Pierre Bagot, Robert Benoît.
90 min.
A woman's only son is killed through the negligence of his doctor. Her husband, in practice at the same clinic, colludes in the cover-up. *They Call That an Accident* has interesting credentials: it's the first directorial effort of its star, Nathalie Delon (who also scripted); it was produced by Island, and features music by their artists Steve Winwood and Marianne Faithfull, including her splendidly sour song 'Guilt'; and it's a revenge thriller, a sort of *Death Wish* with a female protagonist. A clue to the film's main problem is in fact in the title of that Faithfull song: the tightrope between self-destructiveness and revenge proves a difficult one to negotiate generically in a way that leaves the heroine with her – and our – convictions intact. Obsession is on occasion frittered away into mere whimsy, or even modishness, despite some unfailtably bleak locations. VG

They Came from Within
see Parasite Murders, The

They Came to Rob Las Vegas
(Las Vegas 500 Millones)

(Antonio Isasi, 1968, Sp/Fr/WGer/It) Gary Lockwood, Elke Sommer, Lee J Cobb, Jack Palance, Georges Géret, Jean Servais, Roger Hanin.
129 min.
An EEC production and an audacious thriller, mainly due to the consistency of Isasi's direction (overriding the usual hybrid problems) and to the casting of Cobb and Palance. The opening is tremendous: Jean Servais breaks out of jail, fails to persuade brother Lockwood to help out on a robbery of Cobb's security business, and is

gunned down. Then Lockwood goes out for revenge, insinuating his way inside Cobb's mistress (Sommer) and his IBM systems. Palance is the T-Man who smells a rat. Shot mainly in Almeria, it's a thriller equivalent to Leone's Westerns, reworking old formulas and paying tribute to them at the same time. But the parallel with Leone goes only so far: Isasi, rather than swirl his camera about, adopts the static, Zen-like posture of Ozu. Not flawless by any means, but well worth a look. ATu

They Died With
Their Boots On

(Raoul Walsh, 1941, US) Errol Flynn, Olivia de Havilland, Arthur Kennedy, Gene Lockhart, Sydney Greenstreet, Anthony Quinn, Charley Grapewin, Stanley Ridges.
140 min. b/w.
Never did Walsh's reputation as an action director and master of period flavour fit more comfortably. Cheerfully agreeing that history is bunk and printing the legend, he turns what is essentially a biopic of George Armstrong Custer (Flynn at his most dashing) from West Point to Little Big Horn into a glorious Western. Few facts here, but what matter when the fiction of Custer as tempestuous cavalier and Indian sympathiser, chivalrously dying to save his army colleagues and simultaneously acknowledge the validity of Crazy Horse's cause, has the breathless sweep and dash of the last romantic gesture. Absolutely irresistible. TM

They Drive By Night

(Arthur Woods, 1938, GB) Emlyn Williams, Ernest Thesiger, Allan Jeayes, Anna Konstam, Ronald Shiner.
84 min. b/w.
Warner Brothers churned out hundreds of 'quota quickies' from their small British studio in Teddington, most of which are no doubt best left in the dustbin of history. Occasionally, though, the fusion of quirky British realism and slick Hollywood melodramas produced a real gem. Here the revelation of '30s British society as a world of spivs and cardsharps, lecherous lorry drivers and sybaritic sex maniacs, is worth discovering in itself. But director Woods, soon to die in the war, takes the workmanlike story of a petty criminal (Williams) hunted for a murder he didn't do, and invests it with an atmosphere of unrelenting wind, rain and gloom which makes the average American *film noir* look bright and breezy by comparison. RMy

They Drive By Night
(aka The Road to Frisco)

(Raoul Walsh, 1940, US) George Raft, Ann Sheridan, Ida Lupino, Humphrey Bogart, Alan Hale, Gale Page, Roscoe Karns.
93 min. b/w.
A good example of Warner Brothers' social 'realism', adapted from AI Bezzerides' novel *Long Haul*. Raft and Bogart as truck-driving brothers trying to set up their own business, directed in typically gutsy style by Walsh. It degenerates into a courtroom murder melodrama about halfway through, with Ida Lupino (bored wife of their boss, trying to involve Raft in a title *Postman Always Rings Twice* malarkey) losing her marbles in the witness box in what Hollywood likes to think of as an acting *tour de force*. Still, the first half has pace, and the wisecracking wit is often laid on thick and fast by Jerry Wald and Richard Macaulay's script, particularly in a scene with Ann Sheridan as a roadside café waitress. All the performances are good. RM

They Knew What
They Wanted

(Garson Kanin, 1940, US) Charles Laughton, Carole Lombard, William Gargan, Harry Carey, Frank Fay, Karl Malden.
96 min. b/w.
More concerned with selfless charity than the title might suggest, this astringent social comedy (the third screen adaptation of Sidney Howard's play) sets an Italian grape-farmer to woo his San Franciscan mail-order bride, and embodies its implicit racial tensions in the opposed acting styles of the central characters: ugly Laughton, unabashedly running the gamut of racial stereotypes (virility-conscious, volatile, forgiving),

against the effortless acting of WASP pin-up Carole Lombard. His tolerance eventually conquers her more venal qualities, but the ending is left peculiarly open – presumably by a studio wary of the star system and anxious about the implications of miscegenation. CPea

They Live

(John Carpenter, 1988, US) Roddy Piper, Keith David, Meg Foster, George 'Buck' Flower, Peter Jason, Raymond St Jacques, Jason Robards III.
94 min. b/w & col.
John Nada (Piper)is grouchy because ever since he arrived in Los Angeles from Colorado, there's been nothing but trouble. People are rude, he lives on a campsite, and then the place is demolished by the cops. Things get worse when he happens across a hidden stash of special sunglasses. Donning a pair, his vision is literally reduced to black-and-white, revealing a terrible plot being perpetrated on the underclass. Skeletal aliens have invaded earth, taking on human guise, hogging the best jobs, and placing subliminal messages on hoardings and magazines which instruct the man on the street to 'Obey', 'Submit', 'Marry and Reproduce'. It's sunglasses for all as Nada and his pal Frank (David) attempt to infiltrate the media and expose the conspiracy. The black-and-white visuals disturb for only so long, and while themes of indoctrination and conspiracy prove initially intriguing, the film quickly descends into fistfights and gunfire. Still, there's little about the comic strip action to suggest that we should be taking this too seriously. CM

They Live By Night

(Nicholas Ray, 1948, US) Farley Granger, Cathy O'Donnell, Howard da Silva, Jay C Flippen, Helen Craig, Will Wright.
95 min. b/w.
Where Altman's later adaptation of Edward Anderson's novel (as *Thieves Like Us*) opted for the detachment of hindsight, Ray offers us the poetry of doomed romanticism, introducing his outcast lovers with the caption, 'This boy and this girl were never properly introduced to the world we live in'. Though Ray never shirks from action and violence (indeed, Howard da Silva's crushing of Christmas baubles as he warns Granger against going straight is extremely menacing), he turns the film to focus upon his misfit innocents, continually contrasting their basically honourable ideals with the corrupt compromises of 'respectable society'. Passionate, lyrical, and imaginative, it's a remarkably assured debut, from the astonishing opening helicopter shot that follows the escaped convicts' car to freedom, to the final, inexorably tragic climax. GA

They Might Be Giants

(Anthony Harvey, 1971, US) Joanne Woodward, George C Scott, Jack Gilford, Lester Rawlins, Rue McClanahan, Ron Weyand, Kitty Winn, Sudie Bond, M Emmet Walsh, F Murray Abraham.
98 min.
A delightfully quirky movie about a New York lawyer (Scott) who imagines he is Sherlock Holmes, adopting the deerstalking garb and savouring four-pipe problems. The pressures of modern life and the death of his wife have, of course, turned him into a textbook case of paranoid delusion. His somewhat sinister brother sends him to a shrink, Dr Mildred Watson (Woodward), whose Freudian analysis of him is rather overshadowed by his Holmesian analysis of her. Watson's other case is a man who refuses to speak – he thinks he's silent screen star Valentino. Meanwhile, Scott refuses to get better; indeed, he lures everyone into his fantasy, gathering a bunch of Bleeker Street Irregulars who go into snowbound Central Park for a final showdown with the Napoleon of crime, Moriarty. Produced by Paul Newman, it was a box-office disaster (shorn of ten minutes on its original release) that now seems years ahead of its time. ATu

They Passed This Way
(aka Four Faces West)

(Alfred E Green, 1948, US) Joel McCrea, Frances Dee, Charles Bickford, Joseph Calleia.
90 min. b/w.
Excellent minor Western, beautifully shot by Russell Harlan (*Red River*). Joel McCrea is the

reluctant outlaw who robs the bank when it won't lend him the money he needs to help his father – and to show he's no ordinary thief he leaves an IOU. Charles Bickford, always a commanding screen presence, is the town's new marshal, Pat Garrett, who pursues him across the desert. GM

They're a Weird Mob

(Michael Powell, 1966, Aust/GB) Walter Chiari, Claire Dunne, Chips Rafferty, Alida Chelli, Ed Devereaux, John Meillon
112min
The first of Michael Powell's Australian ventures, a very bizarre comedy about the prejudicial problems that face a young Italian who emigrates to Sydney. There are many delightful moments of almost Hitchcockian humour centred around social embarrassment (how to eat a meringue without making a mess), and pleasing parodies of movie styles (epic Eisensteinian expressionism at a building site). Hardly a great film, but an exhilarating and playful demolition of nationalist stereotypes. GA

They're Playing with Fire

(Howard Avedis, 1984, US) Sybil Danning, Andrew Prine, Eric Brown, Paul Clemens, KT Stevens.
96 min.
Sleazy slasher pic with the statuesque Danning cast as a greedy English professor (?!) who seduces a young male student, then embroils him in the murder of her mother. Meanwhile, a psycho killer in a ski-mask is bumping off all and sundry with an axe. Punctuated by gruesome slayings and shots of the ex-'Playboy' pin-up's naked body. NF

They Shoot Horses, Don't They?

(Sydney Pollack, 1969, US) Jane Fonda, Michael Sarrazin, Susannah York, Gig Young, Red Buttons, Bonnie Bedelia, Michael Conrad, Bruce Dern, Severn Darden, Allyn Ann McLerie.
129 min.
Pollack's adaptation of Horace McCoy's novel about the competitive dance marathons of the Depression years was enthusiastically received when first released, and had a string of Academy Award nominations, several of them for its performances. The acting is strident and overblown, the narrative technique gimmicky and obvious, and the implication that the competitors' situation is a microcosm of a wider-reaching American malaise (though safely distanced by the period and the flash-back-and-forth narrative technique) rather pretentious.

They Were Expendable

(John Ford, 1945, US) Robert Montgomery, John Wayne, Donna Reed, Ward Bond, Jack Holt, Marshall Thompson, Louis Jean Heydt, Russell Simpson, Leon Ames, Cameron Mitchell, Robert Barrat.
135 min. b/w.
Ford and Montgomery were both under Navy orders when returning from active service to MGM to make this tribute to World War II hero John Bulkeley (Brickley in the film) and his squadron of motor torpedo boats which had covered the Pacific retreat of US forces in the wake of Pearl Harbor. The tugs of docudrama, emotionalism and sheer timing produced a major work of surprisingly downbeat romanticism. Commitments to cause and career are raised as genuine conflicts as Wayne's second-in-command questions notions of teamwork and sacrifice; and even at the end, when Ford has ennobled his warriors in a succession of classic images, the narrative has to acknowledge that the ranking pair's heroism consists in knowingly leaving their men to a near-certain doom. A curious movie, whose premises Ford would obsessively rework in his subsequent cavalry pictures, with the luxury of historical distance. PT

They Were Not Divided

(Terence Young, 1950, GB) Edward Underdown, Michael Brennan, Ralph Clanton, Helen Cherry, Stella Andrews.
102 min. b/w.
Writer/director Young went on to helm the first James Bond offering *Dr No*, but in this wartime slice-of-life he's on somewhat different terrain.

Englisher Underdown, Welshman Brennan and Yank Clanton all join the Welsh Guards during WWII, and the narrative charts their experiences as it swings between propaganda and quasi-documentary and back again. In its day a sound success at the home box office. TJ

They Won't Believe Me

(Irving Pichel, 1947, US) Robert Young, Susan Hayward, Jane Greer, Rita Johnson, Tom Powers, George Tyne, Don Beddoe, Frank Ferguson.
95 min. b/w.
A man (Young) comes round after a car accident, and realises that a perfect crime is now possible: any movie with this scene can't fail. From this halfway point, the anxious mood of this rare *noir* thriller thickens fast, with specialities in its whiff of a James M Cain world in which women literally explode: 'She was a special kind of dynamite neatly wrapped in nylon and silk...But I was powder shy' says Robert Young. Jane Greer and Susan Hayward in turn tempt Young (a spineless louse) from his rich wife (Johnson). We know he's wretched, but is he guilty of murder? No prizes for guessing the pulpy symbolism of a palomino stallion 'with a weakness for sugar'. DMacp

They Won't Forget

(Mervyn LeRoy, 1937, US) Claude Rains, Gloria Dickson, Otto Kruger, Allyn Joslyn, Elisha Cook Jr, Edward Norris, Clinton Rosemond, Lana Turner.
95 min. b/w.
Certainly the bleakest of Hollywood's social conscience cycle of the '30s. At its most impressive in the elaborate opening sequence which rhymes the Memorial Day parade in a Southern town (Civil War veterans waxing nostalgic about the heroic past as they watch) with the murder of a white girl in the school-house (a tightly sweatered Lana Turner making her debut). The subsequent machinations seem a little contrived now as the ambitious DA deliberately selects the most inflammatory of three suspects (not the black janitor but a Northern teacher), planning to railroad him to the death cell and himself to the governor's chair on a wave of Southern pride. And although the script (by Robert Rossen and Aben Kandel) steamrollers through the resulting lynching without having to worry about a happy ending like *Fury*, Lang's remains the better film because he is more honestly involved with the characters than with the logistics of the plot. One of LeRoy's best films, even so, and the performances (especially Rains as the DA and Joslyn as a greedy journalist) are terrific. TM

Thief, The

(Russell Rouse, 1952, US) Ray Milland, Martin Gabel, Rita Gam, Harry Bronson, Rita Vale, Rex O'Malley.
85 min. b/w
A phone shrills, two bursts of three rings; the man on the bed (Milland) leaves his room; out in the night a waiting man (Gabel) lights a cigarette, throws down the empty packet, and vanishes. Milland picks up the packet, reads the message in his room, resignedly gets out a micro-camera; a shot of an award for his services to nuclear physics; and Rouse's movie is embarked on its challenge to tell the story of a spy without dialogue. There's an element of gimmickry here (even passers-by never say a word), but it's far outweighed by the tangible sense of a man isolated by his sense of fear (you never learn his motives), by the anonymity of his associates (all contact is by prearranged signal and at second remove), by the caution which edges into paranoia as things suddenly go wrong. Rouse's dispassionate, evenly-paced direction, abetted by Sam Leavitt's superb noir camerawork, strands Milland in a shadowy world of fellow-humans, any one of whom might spell disaster. The moment at the end, as Milland waits despairingly for word of his escape, and the teasingly sexy girl across the hall (Gam) closes her door in his face as she realises he is watching her, is one Bresson might have been proud of. TM

Thief (aka Violent Streets)

(Michael Mann, 1981, US) James Caan, Tuesday Weld, Willie Nelson, James Belushi, Robert Prosky, Tom Signorelli,
123 min.
A silently professional night-time jewel robbery, reduced to near-abstract essentials and paced by a Tangerine Dream score, sets the electric tone

for Mann's fine follow-up to *The Jericho Mile*: a philosophical thriller filled with modernist cool. Caan's the thief, contradictorily building and risking a future mapped out as meticulously as any of his lucrative hi-tech jobs; testing his emotional and criminal independence to the limits; eventually recognising that he's either exercising or exorcising a death wish. PT

Thief of Bagdad, The

(Raoul Walsh, 1924, US) Douglas Fairbanks, Julanne Johnston, Anna May Wong, Snitz Edwards, Charles Belcher, Brandon Hurst, Sojin.
11,812 ft. b/w.
Fairbanks' Arabian Nights spectacle presents American silent cinema at its most flamboyant. The collection of sets were said to extend over six-and-a-half acres; the designs, partly by William Cameron Menzies, are a dizzy conglomeration of Manhattan chic, Art Deco, and rampant Chinoiserie, guaranteed to amaze the eyes. Fairbanks leaps and grins through them all, the personification of American 'pep'. Korda's version of 1940 has the quirks and the luscious colour, but this one has the electric energy. GB

Thief of Bagdad, The

(Michael Powell/Ludwig Berger/Tim Whelan/Zoltan Korda, 1940, GB) Conrad Veidt, Sabu, June Duprez, Rex Ingram, John Justin, Miles Malleson, Mary Morris, Morton Selten.
106 min.
A delightful hocus-pocus of colour, dashing adventure, and special effects, this Korda-produced epic for grown-up kids is basically *Star Wars* meets *The Arabian Nights* with its plot of an all-seeing eye stolen from a Tibetan temple. The highlight has to be the genie (Ingram) who escapes from the bottle, though Sabu the elephant boy lends just that dash of imperialist sentiment to lift it into camp. Magical, classically entertaining, and now revalued by Hollywood moguls Lucas and Coppola, it was made fitfully in Britain during the World War II Blitz (but completed in Hollywood) by a team of directors spearheaded by the remarkable Powell. DMacp

Thief of Baghdad, The

(Clive Donner, 1978, GB/Fr) Roddy McDowall, Peter Ustinov, Terence Stamp, Kabir Bedi, Frank Finlay, Marina Vlady, Pavla Ustinov, Daniel Emilfork, Ian Holm.
102 min.
It's a faltering hand stoking the high camp fire here. Behind the ornate theatricality and sumptuous effects of this remake there lurks a total lack of conviction. Hyperactive McDowall (the thief) is upstaged by old pro Ustinov as the Caliph; Kabir Bedi, once India's 'highest paid male model', is a joke as the prince, meant to symbolise the alliance of magic and muscle; and Terence Stamp, as a lethargic representative of Supreme Evil, simply waits around for henchmen or flying carpets to do the dirty work. CR

Thieves' Highway

(Jules Dassin, 1949, US) Richard Conte, Valentina Cortese, Lee J Cobb, Barbara Lawrence, Jack Oakie, Millard Mitchell, Joseph Pevney, Morris Carnovsky.
94 min. b/w.
Jules Dassin's trendy reputation (and an awful lot of money) was made with *Rififi*, *Never on Sunday* and *Topkapi* – triumphant European success for a blacklisted Hollywood talent. But cultists groaned, for the 'real' Dassin was surely to be found in the baroque and electrifying *Brute Force*, the grotesquely Dickensian *Night and the City*, and – a personal favourite – *Thieves' Highway*. Al Bezzerides' script (from his own novel *Thieves' Market*) and the performances of Conte, Cobb, and Cortese (in her American debut) help restrain Dassin's feverish artistic ambitions in this tale of racketeering in the California fruit markets. The result slots sleazy eroticism and rigorous action seamless-ly together into a high-grade trucking melo. Nothing more, but nothing less, which in the '40s was the most triumphant kind of American success. CW

Thieves Like Us

(Robert Altman, 1973, US) Keith Carradine, Shelley Duvall, John Schuck, Bert Remsen, Louise Fletcher, Ann Latham, Tom Skerritt.
123 min.

Perhaps Altman's most persistently charming film, a remake of Nicholas Ray's *They Live By Night* (or rather, second adaptation of Edward Anderson's novel), in which a trio of semi-competent bank robbers attempt to emulate the bigtime gangsters publicised by the media, comics, and radio serials, and finally get their comeuppance after a brief respite from prison and poverty. Altman adheres to Ray's conception of the youngest criminal (Carradine) and his plain-Jane lover (Duvall) as innocents all at sea in an uncaring world, although the tone here is one of bitter-sweet irony rather than romantic pessimism. And while casting a critical eye on Depression America, with a New Deal being promised that would keep democracy safe, there is none of the cynicism that has occasionally flawed some of Altman's fascinating genre parodies/tributes. Never portentous, never a mere spoof, this is a touching, intelligent, and – in its own small way – rather wonderful movie. GA

Thin Air
see Body Stealers, The

Thin Blue Line, The
(Errol Morris, 1988, US) Randall Adams, David Harris, Edith James, Dennis White, Don Metcalfe.
101 min.
Documentarist-extraordinary Morris' original and delightfully bizarre slice of investigative film-journalism attempts, successfully, to set the record straight about one Randall Adams, imprisoned in 1976 for the murder of a Dallas cop. It is also a philosophical thesis on problems of knowledge and truth, which uses highly stylised dramatic reconstructions of the crime to offer a multitude of perspectives on what really happened, and a darkly comic, nightmarish study in self-delusion and deception. The legal figures and witnesses Morris interviews are transparently weird, shifty, obsessive and unreliable. Indeed, the movie – immaculately structured, beautifully shot, sensitively scored by Philip Glass – is a poignant and hilarious essay on oddball America. Morris' skill in suggesting that Adams' original trial involved at best a miscarriage of justice, at worst corruption, ensures that the audience becomes a surrogate jury. The film provokes sadness, anger, relief, admiration, and wonder; enjoy it, and worry. GA

Thing, The
(John Carpenter, 1982, US) Kurt Russell, Wilford Brimley, TK Carter, David Clennon, Richard Dysart, Richard Masur, Donald Moffat.
109 min.
In re-adapting the John W Campbell story (*Who Goes There?*) already filmed so superbly in 1951 as *The Thing from Another World*, Carpenter provides a punchy enough action thriller as the men of a lonely Antarctic research team are menaced by a shape-changing alien from outer space. But there comes a time when spectacular special effects – even by the estimable Rob Bottin – are just not enough. Carpenter avoids the subtle suspense of the earlier version – all the guessing and paranoia and wonder – in favour of a mindlessly macho monster mash which looks and feels just like an ineptly plotted remake of *Alien*, right down to the chest-bursting scene. Russell's sub-Eastwood heroics hardly compensate for the absence of all characterisation, while Bill Lancaster's script boasts the most illogical climax any monster movie ever had. It's only fair to add that, had this been made by anybody else, one might be recommending it for its special effects; but that's the price Carpenter pays for having made so much better movies. DP

Thing Called Love, The
(Peter Bogdanovich, 1993, US) River Phoenix, Samantha Mathis, Dermot Mulroney, Sandra Bullock, KT Oslin.
116 min.
Would-be country singer Miranda Presley (Mathis) arrives in Music City – Nashville, Tennessee – and is soon waitressing, failing auditions and watching other people get the breaks. Her friends include like-minded young hopefuls: Phoenix (in his last completed film), the talented, driven one; Mulroney, sensitive and sweet; and Bullock, nervous and lost. Not a lot happens. But

a thoughtful script (by Carol Heikkinen) reminds us that there's more to growing up than fast cars and Tom Cruise: that experience brings sacrifice as well as rewards. Bogdanovich's modest staging is occasionally awkward – his kids still watch John Wayne movies at the drive-in – but there's a convincing sense of what Nashville's like and how country music works. As for the stars, Phoenix is fine in an odd, transitional role, but Mathis (who looks more like his sister than his girlfriend) really steals the show with a bright, sassy performance. TCh

Thing from Another World, The (100)
(Christian Nyby, 1951, US) Kenneth Tobey, Margaret Sheridan, Robert Cornthwaite, James Arness, Douglas Spencer, Dewey Martin.
87 min. b/w.
One of the great sci-fi classics, a Hawks film in all but director credit (he produced, planned the film, supervised the shooting). The gradual build-up of tension, as a lonely group of scientists in the Antarctic discover a flying saucer and its deadly occupant, is quite superb; while The Thing itself (played by Arness) is shown sufficiently little to create real menace. As in most of Hawks's work, the emphasis is on professionalism in a tiny, isolated community, on a love relationship evolving semi-flippant fashion into something important, and on group solidarity. Also characteristic is the contrast with a film like Robert Wise's *The Day the Earth Stood Still* (made the same year), which took a liberal stand in exposing the stupidity of men when confronted with an alien. Hawks rejects out of hand the idea that the alien might be worth trying to understand or communicate with; in fact, the scientist who tries to do this is made to seem feeble and even inhuman, so that the overall message of *The Thing* emerges as distinctly hawkish. Reactionary or not, though, it's still a masterpiece. DP

Things Change
(David Mamet, 1988, US) Don Ameche, Joe Mantegna, Robert Prosky, JJ Johnston, Ricky Jay, Mike Nussbaum, Jack Wallace.
100 min.
Mamet's second film is not intellectually fast, nasty, and dazzling like *House of Games*, but more like a leisurely variant on *The Last Detail* (and indeed, some Preston Sturges and Capra capers). It chronicles a masquerade whereby an insignificant shoeshine man, Gino (Ameche), is paid to become a fall guy for the Mob. His boastful minder Jerry (Mantegna), assigned to keep Gino on ice until his reluctant court confession, takes pity on him and resolves to give him an outing at the Lake Tahoe gambling resort. 'They always like you when you're someone else' is Jerry's one observation in life, and he is soon hoist by it, floundering in the wake of the folk-wisdom-spouting oldster as he finds himself at the high table with the Dons. It's a film of enormous charm and beguiling sentimentality, and it's played to the hilt by Ameche and Mantegna, the veteran blithely dignified, his captor sweatily alive to every danger, and right to fear the worst. Together, they cast quite a spell. BC

Things I Never Told You
(Isabel Coixet, 1995, Sp/US) Lili Taylor, Andrew McCarthy, Alexis Arquette, Richard Edson, Debi Mazar, Leslie Mann, Seymour Cassel.
93 min.
Engagingly offbeat take on the meeting-cute movie in which camera shop assistant Taylor, grieving over the boyfriend who left her, encounters McCarthy, a despairing real-estate salesman who comforts the lonely and depressed over a Samaritan-style phone line. Strong performances, quirky characterisations, and a seemingly wayward narrative with a capacity to surprise. GA

Things of Life, The
see Choses de la Vie, Les

Things To Come
(William Cameron Menzies, 1936, GB) Raymond Massey, Ralph Richardson, Edward Chapman, Margaretta Scott, Cedric Hardwicke, Sophie Stewart, Ann Todd, Derrick de Marney.
113 min. b/w.

HG Wells thought *Metropolis* to be 'quite the silliest film', but a decade later Alexander Korda gave him enormous creative freedom to write a movie version of *The Shape of Things to Come*, which turned out to be just as silly. However, like *Metropolis*, it isn't just silly. It is a spectacular production wherein Wells takes his 'science versus art' preoccupations into the future (as seen from the '30s); and to make it work, only lacks the kind of pure cinematic form which a Powell/Pressburger would have given it, for its scale and love of 'ideas' pre-figure their films and make it just as unique in British cinema history. In the realm of 'prophetic science fiction', it is a genre landmark. CW

Things to Do in Denver When You're Dead
(Gary Fleder, 1995, US) Andy Garcia, Christopher Walken, Gabrielle Anwar, William Forsythe, Treat Williams, Christopher Lloyd, Bill Nunn, Jack Warden, Steve Buscemi.
115 min.
Former gangster Jimmy the Saint (Garcia) has got himself a legit business (video-recording advice from the dying to their families), so he's reluctant to do one more job for the Man (Walken), who wants the frighteners put on the creep dating his slow-witted son's dream girl. Besides, after meeting Dagney (Anwar), Jimmy's in love himself. Still, the Man wants no real violence done, and lets Jimmy pick his own team: Franchise (Forsythe), Pieces (Lloyd), Easy (Nunn), and Critical Bill (Williams), a deranged morgue attendant and boxer who works out by using corpses as punchbags. Thanks, however, to Bill's volatile temper, the job goes horribly wrong, with the result that the Man deems Jimmy's crew 'buck-wheats', human prey for hitman Mr Shhh (Buscemi) to kill in the most painful way possible. Much of the fun to be had from Fleder's stylish, engrossing first feature derives from Scott Rosenberg's lively, literate and engagingly offbeat script. The witty dialogue, its slangy, profane poetry is even more delightful than the plot's tight twists and turns, while the colourful characterisations, sufficiently rock solid to have attracted and inspired a marvellous cast, simultaneously play fast and loose with the conventions of crime fiction. GA

Thing with Two Heads, The
(Lee Frost, 1972, US) Ray Milland, Roosevelt Grier, Don Marshall, Roger Perry, Chelsea Brown.
93 min.
One of AIP's carefully cultivated jokes-in-bad-taste, in which the head of a terminally ill, racist brain surgeon (Milland) is grafted onto the body of a death row black (Grier) intent on clearing his name. This outrageous notion is milked for all it's worth as the two heads wisecrack away, tussle for control of 'the body', and charge around pursued by some inept cops. Special effects are in keeping with the general tone of the film (the difference between Milland's florid face in close-up and the ashen colour of the wax model used for long shot is hilariously obvious), and there are sufficient laughs along the way to sustain interest. Don't expect too much, though. CPe

Thin Ice
(Fiona Cunningham Reid, 1994, GB) Charlotte Avery, Clare Higgins, Sabra Williams, James Dreyfus, Cathryn Harrison, Gwyneth Strong, Suzanne Bertish, Guy Williams, Ian McKellen.
92 min.
Black lesbian Steffi needs a partner for the skating pairs in the Gay Games, and the only gal good enough in the time available is shy Natalie (Avery). Straight, white, middle-class, she's Steffi's polar opposite (though Steffi's strangely free from family, or indeed black culture). Natalie's own family suffers from a strange premature-ageing disease. Mum looks like her gran, her sister (Higgins, camping it) seems old enough to be her mum, and Nat herself will clearly never see 21 again. The predictable playing out of the plot (will Nat fall for Steffi and her schemes?) is underlined by naff dialogue. It's not all disaster, though. Williams' Steffi and Dreyfus as her gay photographer friend find an emotional balance that anchors the film, and it would take a harder heart than mine not to be charmed by the women's blithe performance in the Gay Games. SFe

Thin Ice
(aka Lovely to Look at)

(Sidney Lanfield, 1937, US) Sonja Henie, Tyrone Power, Arthur Treacher, Raymond Walburn, Joan Davis, Sig Rumann, Alan Hale.
78 min. b/w.

A three-power Ruritanian summit convenes at an Alpine hotel and Prince Rudolph (Power) falls for skating instructor Lilly Heiser (Henie). Joan Davis, a daffy, slip-sliding orchestra singer ('My Swiss Hilly Billy', 'Olga from the Volga'), and Arthur Treacher, the Prince's camp butler Nottingham, take one's mind off the romantic cottonwool, while Sonja Henie still skates with the captivating elegance which made her a star at Fox for a brief period before the war. JPy

Thin Line Between Love and Hate, A

(Martin Lawrence, 1995, US) Martin Lawrence, Lynn Whitfield, Della Reese, Regina King, Bobby Brown, Malinda Williams.
120 min.

This *faux* thriller kicks off with a nod to Sunset Boulevard: smooth womaniser and club manager Darnell Wright (star TV comedian Lawrence) face down in a Beverly Hills pool with blood pouring from his head. Flash back to Chocolate City, Darnell's night-spot, where Brandi (Whitfield), a classy 'honey', is passing by outside – or so she thinks. This fatal attraction takes a lot of chatting up, but Darnell's soon in the back of her stretch limo, having rejected the advice of his wiseacre Ma (Reese, excellent) and the evidently more suitable attractions of childhood pal Mia (King), who's newly returned to the neighbourhood. When Darnell begins to dither, Brandi unleashes the psychosis of the woman scorned. This self-consciously upbeat enterprise trades on Lawrence's pooky persona and a soundtrack of modern hip R&B. There are some fun 'hangin'' scenes, with the boys in the back chewing the cud and cracking jokes, and Lawrence's ejaculations prove him an able physical comedian. But the script lacks wit and depth, while Lawrence's direction is meandering and undramatic, full of showy, over-elaborate camera movements. WH

Thin Man, The

(WS Van Dyke, 1934, US) William Powell, Myrna Loy, Maureen O'Sullivan, Nat Pendleton, Minna Gombell, Cesar Romero, Edward Brophy.
93 min. b/w.

Dashiell Hammett's fifth and last novel was something of a departure in that it was less a hardboiled thriller than a spray of sophisticated banter in which nobody – least of all detective Nick Charles and his delightful Nora – took the tough guy ethos very seriously. With Powell and Loy fitting the roles to perfection, the film draws happy doodles around the mystery of the missing scientist (lingering, for instance, over an irresistibly irrelevant sequence in which Nick, given an airgun as a present by the understanding Nora, spends a contented hour potting baubles on the Christmas tree). What enchants, really, is the relationship between Nick and Nora as they live an eternal cocktail hour, bewailing hangovers that only another little drink will cure, in a marvellous blend of marital familiarity and constant courtship, pixillated fantasy and childlike wonder. None of the five sequels that followed (1936-47) recaptured quite the same flavour. TM

Thinner

see Stephen King's Thinner

Third Generation, The
(Die Dritte Generation)

(Rainer Werner Fassbinder, 1979, WGer) Volker Spengler, Bulle Ogier, Hanna Schygulla, Harry Baer, Vitus Zeplichal, Udo Kier, Margit Carstensen, Eddie Constantine.
111 min.

Just what we always wanted: the every-day angsts of a terrorist cell as *Life with the Lyons*. Fassbinder's basic proposition is simple: the West German state is already so repressive that it might well have invented its terrorists as scapegoats for its own growing totalitarianism. Hence this 'comedy in six acts, just like the fairy stories we tell our children, to make their short lives more bearable'. It's a return to the grotesquely overplayed melodrama of *Satan's Brew*, acted by the

entire RWF stock company, plus Bulle Ogier and Eddie Constantine, with a gaggle of haute couture 'subversives' going through the *film noir* motions of paranoia and anti-capitalist rhetoric. And it's formulated as an affront to all conceivable audiences: if the concept doesn't make you ill, then the interpolations of lavatory graffiti and the constant barrage of background noise from TV and radio will certainly give you headaches. Essential viewing. TR

Third Key, The

see Long Arm, The

Third Man, The 100 (100)

(Carol Reed, 1949, GB) Joseph Cotten, Orson Welles, Alida Valli, Trevor Howard, Bernard Lee, Paul Hörbiger, Ernst Deutsch, Wilfrid Hyde-White.
104 min. b/w.

Justly celebrated British *noir*, charting post-war dis-ease in Vienna as Cotten's naïve American pulp writer chases the shadows of Welles' quintessential underground man Harry Lime, an old friend now involved in black market drug-dealing and hiding out in the foreign sector of the rubble-strewn city. Robert Krasker's camerawork matches the baroque conception of Graham Greene's characters, Welles' contributions (script rewrites included) add intriguing internal tension, and even the 'gimmick' of Anton Karas' solo zither score works perfectly. A tender/tough classic. PT

Third Part of the Night, The
(Trzecia Czesc Nocy)

(Andrzej Zulawski, 1971, Pol) Malgorzata Braunek, Leszek Teleszynski, Jerzy Golinski, Jan Nowicki.
106 min.

World War II Poland: a man gets a second chance. Michal's wife and child are killed by German soldiers, but in a nearby town he discovers and stays with a woman in labour who looks just like his dead wife. A complex and surreal work, the film is obsessed with the distinctions between love as self-preservation and self-sacrifice. But it's just as much the hallucinations of a dying man. Images of death are everywhere: endless corridors, figures framed in doorways (and later in coffins), a couple gunned down in bed. Not an easy film to come to terms with because of its cerebral nature and its self-consciousness; a haunting first feature, all the same.

39 Steps, The

(Alfred Hitchcock, 1935, GB) Robert Donat, Madeleine Carroll, Godfrey Tearle, Lucie Mannheim, Peggy Ashcroft, John Laurie, Wylie Watson, Helen Haye.
86 min. b/w.

Other English Hitchcocks' may be more provocative, but few offer such a ripping good yarn. Donat's smooth and upright Richard Hannay flees from London in pursuit of a spy ring, responsible for leaving a murdered woman in his flat; the police inevitably take him for the murderer, and the spies are after him too. His itinerary includes an overnight stop in John Laurie's crofter's cottage, a political meeting where he improvises a speech without knowing who or what he's supporting, and a period when he's handcuffed to the resentful heroine. It ends, suitably, in a music hall. The inspiration came from John Buchan's novel, though Hitchcock followed it at some distance, concocting with scriptwriter Charles Bennett what really amounts to a little anthology of Hitchcock stories and motifs. Great fun. GB

39 Steps, The

(Ralph Thomas, 1959, GB) Kenneth More, Taina Elg, Barry Jones, Brenda de Banzie, Faith Brook, James Hayter, Michael Goodliffe, Sidney James.
93 min.

More an attempt to copy Hitchcock than to re-film Buchan, and it suffers by the comparison. The few changes are not for the better (Peggy Ashcroft's wistfully frustrated crofter's wife, for instance, becomes a man-hungry spiritualist, played by Brenda de Banzie), since they broaden the characterisations into caricature. For the rest, the tension is dismally slack, the comedy overdone, and the Scottish scenery ladled out in travelogue dollops.

Thirty-Nine Steps, The

(Don Sharp, 1978, GB) Robert Powell, David Warner, Eric Porter, Karen Dotrice, John Mills, George Baker, Ronald Pickup, Timothy West.
102 min.

Though boasting a greater period fidelity to John Buchan's novel than either the Hitchcock entertainment or its dire Ralph Thomas remake, and blessed with the resonant image of Powell hanging from the face of Big Ben in an attempt to make time stand still, this blows its coherence as a thriller by a ramshackle construction of gimmicky set pieces and a nostalgic sheen of BBC costume drama proportions. Strangely enough, archetypal British hero Richard Hannay had been better served, placed and analysed on TV in Mark Shivas' almost contemporaneous adaptation of *The Three Hostages*: here he merely rushes from pillar to post to avert the inevitable outbreak of World War I (and the 20th century) by a matter of days. PT

36 Chowringhee Lane

(Aparna Sen, 1981, Ind) Jennifer Kendal, Dhritiman Chatterjee, Debashree Roy, Geoffrey Kendal, Soni Razdan.
122 min.

Being the tatty Calcutta apartment where a sixty-ish Anglo-Indian schoolteacher stagnates in austere spinsterhood. The companionship temporarily promised by a young couple who use her flat as a secret trysting-place tempts her out of self-imposed purdah, but her disillusionment is swift and terrible. In fact her life is portrayed as a succession of downbeat events – from the early loss of a sweetheart, fallen in the war, to her brother's death and the final indignity of demotion – and the material doesn't mesh with debut director Aparna Sen's predilection for extravagant effects (arty editing, a surreal dream sequence, clumsily signalled climaxes). However, the film is miraculously rescued from shallow melancholia by Jennifer Kendal's performance, which invests the 'repressed old maid' stereotype with surprising subtlety and tenderness. SJo

36 Hours

(George Seaton, 1964, US) James Garner, Eva Marie Saint, Rod Taylor, Werner Peters, John Banner, Russell Thorson, Celia Lovsky, Alan Napier, Martin Kosleck.
115 min. b/w.

A spiffing WWII adventure in which a US intelligence officer (Garner) is kidnapped by Nazis, and subjected to an elaborate plot to make him think that D-Day happened five years ago, so that he will give away vital invasion secrets. It might have been even more spiffing had the audience been kept hoodwinked for as long as Garner. But Seaton's inventive script keeps it going beautifully as a sort of cat-and-mouse game in which Garner tells the Nazis (Taylor and Peters) all they need to know, is horrified to discover the deception (through an ingenious, carefully planted detail), but realises that they don't quite believe him...Highly enjoyable. TM

36th Chamber of Shaolin, The
(Shaolin Sanshiliu Fang)

(Lau Kar-Leung aka Liu Jialiang, 1978, HK) Gordon Liu, Lo Lieh, Qiang Han, Lau Kar-Wing, Tsui Siu-Keung.
105 min.

The first half hour is standard Shaw Bros melodrama: vignettes from the Manchu army's subjugation of Canton in the early Qing Dynasty, following the usual script, staged on the usual sets with all the usual 'guest stars' and extras. But once the wounded hero (Liu) reaches the Shaolin Temple and – one year of sweeping floors later – starts learning the monks' secret knowledge of martial arts, the movie becomes extraordinary. The temple has 35 training rooms, each one dedicated to the perfection of a physical skill, a mental reflex or a spiritual insight. Once our boy graduates *cum laude* the abbot pragmatically expels him for insubordination, freeing him to rally anti-Manchu resistance in the province and turn the whole of Guangdong into a 36th 'chamber' of Shaolin. Fine myth making, anchored in a heroic central performance. The UK video release is panned-and-scanned, dubbed and cut: a travesty. TR

'36 to '77

(Mark Karlin/Jon Sanders/James Scott/Humphrey Trevelyan, 1978, GB) Myrtle Wardally, Alan Nielson.
97 min.

This curious movie began life as *Nightcleaners 2* by the Berwick Street Collective, and ended up as a kind of portrait of a Grenadan woman called Myrtle Wardally (born in 1936 – hence the title), credited to four members of the former Collective. Ms Wardally was a leader of the Cleaners' Action Group strike in Fulham in 1972, and she here reminisces about the limited success of that campaign, but also describes her childhood in Grenada and speaks about her present life. There is rigorous separation of sound and image throughout, to the extent that the film is less about social politics than about the politics of film-form. There are visual recollections from *Nightcleaners*, but most of the image-track comprises shots of Ms Wardally's face, frames frozen and then slowly animated, out of synch with her words. Curious. TR

Thirty Two Short Films About Glenn Gould

(François Girard, 1993, Can) Colm Feore, Derek Keurvorst, Katya Ladan, Devon Anderson, Joshua Greenblatt, Sean Ryan.
93 min.

Some films are so good that they remind us of cinema's capabilities, by, in a sense, reinventing the medium's customary form. This is one of those films. It's true that director Girard and his co-writer Don McKellar started out with an extraordinary subject – the great, eccentric Canadian pianist Glenn Gould (who died, aged 50, in 1982) – but Girard's masterstroke was to take his cue from Gould's most famous piece, his interpretation(s) of Bach's Goldberg Variations, and to structure the film as 32 fragments, each revealing a different perspective. This approach pays off handsomely. We see Gould at various junctures, but while they're loosely in chronological order, these sequences are not really biographical, but tasters of a strangely distant, always compelling personality. Beyond this, Girard gives us interviews with those who knew Gould, excerpts from radio broadcasts, brief excursions into abstraction, even a segment of Norman McLaren's animation *Spheres*. Despite such formal dexterity, however, what's most impressive is the simplicity and clarity of the enterprise – and, of course, the music. TCh

This Above All

(Anatole Litvak, 1942, US) Tyrone Power, Joan Fontaine, Thomas Mitchell, Nigel Bruce, Alexander Knox, Henry Stephenson, Gladys Cooper, Melville Cooper.
110 min. b/w.

Companion piece to *Mrs Miniver* which contrives to take all the edge off Eric Knight's novel (a surprising bestseller for 1941) about a working class soldier who deserts because he feels the ruling classes are conspiring to preserve the status quo. Played by Power (as much like a Yorkshire tyke as a Borzoi), carefully established as heroic before he deserts, he suffers more of a spiritual crisis than a political revelation. Not that it matters, since he meets a WAAF (Fontaine) who is true blue (and proves it with one of the stickiest speeches of uplift to grace the World War II movie scene), is swept up into fulsome romance, and realises what he should be fighting for. Lushly directed crap. TM

This Boy's Life

(Michael Caton-Jones, 1993, US) Robert De Niro, Leonardo DiCaprio, Ellen Barkin, Jonah Blechman, Eliza Dushku.
115 min.

Michael Caton-Jones's second US outing is an able adaptation of Tobias Wolff's autobiographical novel about growing up in backwoods Washington state. It's a rites-of-passage drama with the kind of period small-town setting that the director is making his own. Teenage Toby (DiCaprio, fine throughout) and mom (Barkin) leave dad and big bro' back East and motor West with high hopes of a new life. First stop Utah offers evidence of mom's unerring eye for male suitors, which is confirmed when they hightail to Washington, where she accepts some old-fashioned courting from Dwight (De Niro). She marries only to discover, too late for escape, that

Dwight is a tyrant. De Niro unfolds Dwight's character by stages, and resists toppling into *Cape Fear*-style psychosis, but he's clearly driving in cruise gear. WH

This Boy's Story

(John Roberts, 1992, GB) Simon Adams, Steven Arnold, Kevin Arnold, Jennifer Calvert, Thomas Craig, Daryl Fishwick, Carl Chase, Arturo Venegas, George Best.
50 min.

Writer/director Roberts, who went on to make the children's film *War of the Buttons* for producer David Puttnam, shot this affecting, well-acted '60s slice-of-life as his graduation project from the National Film and TV School. Navy man Adams recalls his childhood and the time he and his young bother (the Arnold siblings) set out from a broken home in search of their soccer idol, the great George Best. Catching the train to Liverpool with money stolen from ma's purse, they hope to make it to Anfield where Manchester United are the visitors, but fate places more than a few obstacles between them and their hero. TJ

This Day and Age

(Cecil B DeMille, 1933, US) Charles Bickford, Judith Allen, Richard Cromwell, Harry Green, Eddie Nugent, Ben Alexander.
85 min. b/w.

A crude but efficient vigilante melodrama from the early sound days, and quite unlike the epics that came to be associated with DeMille, except in its reactionary nature. Bickford gives a powerful performance as a wealthy gangster who kills an old shopkeeper the local kids looked on as a friend; corrupt city officials do nothing, so a group of high school boys torture him into a confession (they hold him over a pit full of rats). Dismayingly fascistic, all the more so in that the action takes place during 'youth week', when the school kids temporarily assume positions of civic authority in the interests of learning how government works, and as such subject the gangster to 'trial'. TCh

This Gun for Hire

(Frank Tuttle, 1942, US) Alan Ladd, Veronica Lake, Robert Preston, Laird Cregar, Tully Marshall, Marc Lawrence, Mikhail Rasumny.
80 min. b/w.

A definitive opening: Alan Ladd's hired gun wakes in a seedy hotel, then, with the distracted air of a schizophrenic, pays visit to his victims, first gunning down the man, then the woman as she tries to hide behind the door. Ladd's unsmiling performance – the prototype of the killer as angel of death – employs a repertory of classic gestures: no wonder Melville and Delon lifted so much of this film for *Le Samourai*. The film's amorphous conspiracy plot (this in 1942) lacks the conviction of the terse introduction, but director Tuttle wisely concentrates on the set pieces and performances rather than the script's loose adaptation of Graham Greene's novel. The dialogue, however, remains admirably laconic – 'How do you feel when you're doing it?' 'I feel fine' – faltering only at the end with Freudian motivation. Laird Cregar's urbane heavy and Veronica Lake's slinky undercover agent offer fine support. Ladd smiles in the end. He shouldn't have. CPe

This Happy Breed

(David Lean, 1944, GB) Robert Newton, Celia Johnson, John Mills, Kay Walsh, Stanley Holloway, John Blythe, Amy Veness, Alison Leggatt.
114 min.

One of a number of British films in the '40s attempting to depict the lives of 'ordinary people', adapted by Noël Coward from his own play. Coward's homage to his roots daringly spans the whole of the inter-war period through the lives of Frank Gibbons (Newton) and his bickering, feuding, lower middle class family. Ronald Neame's camera rarely strays outside the family home of the decidedly unfunky Gibbonses, but there is a constant in-rush of public events – from wars to Wembley festivals – to leaven the domestic squabbling, and the evocation of the recent past proved enormously successful in war-torn Britain. Though Lean and Coward are less happy here than in the brittle, refined atmosphere of *Brief Encounter*, their adventurous excursion into suburban Clapham remains endlessly fascinating. RMy

This Is Elvis

(Malcolm Leo/Andrew Solt, 1981, US) David Scott, Paul Boensch, Johnny Harra, Lawrence Koller.
101 min. b/w. & col.

Documentary footage intercut with dramatic reconstructions. Easy to overlook the risible 'dramatised' inserts: a substantial proportion of the footage is for real, and it includes numerous gems. Shadow kinescopes of early TV appearances point an almost obscene contrast with the close-up coverage of Presley at the end, mumbling through the ironies of 'My Way'; while in between, such socialising agents as Sullivan, Sinatra, the US Army, and MGM are seen contributing to the taming of a legend. PT

This Island Earth

(Joseph Newman, 1955, US) Jeff Morrow, Faith Domergue, Rex Reason, Lance Fuller, Russell Johnson, Douglas Spencer.
86 min.

Let down by variable acting and less evocative in theme than *Forbidden Planet* (the plot has aliens shanghai-ing two human scientists – male and female by happy coincidence – to help save their doomed planet), but still done with a grandiose solemnity that makes it worthy of the name of space opera. The settings, in particular, are brilliantly imaginative, with superb use of colour in conjuring the almost surrealistic landscape of Metaluna, a cratered wasteland concealing the labyrinthine underground city soon to be overrun by a hideous race of insect-like mutants with exposed brains and dead eyes, originally bred by the Metalunians for menial work. TM

This Is My Affair (aka His Affair)

(William A Seiter, 1936, US) Robert Taylor, Barbara Stanwyck, Victor McLaglen, Brian Donlevy, Sidney Blackmer, John Carradine, Alan Dinehart.
101 min. b/w.

In 1901, a young naval lieutenant (Taylor) is entrusted by President McKinlay with a mission to infiltrate a gang responsible for a string of bank robberies; since crucial information is evidently being leaked to the gang from high places, no one else is to be privy to the assignment. This promising premise is rather let down when the gang turns out to be the usual B movie unit: smooth-talking Donlevy, McLaglen as his brutish henchman, Stanwyck as the reluctant moll who falls for the handsome lieutenant. Routine shenanigans end with mission accomplished. But the President has been assassinated, so unless Taylor can prove it *was* a mission, he faces the electric chair. Sterling lead performances (plus a delightful cameo from Blackmer as Teddy Roosevelt), and elegant camerawork from Robert Planck; but it never quite makes the grade on credibility. TM

This Is My Life

(Nora Ephron, 1992, US) Julie Kavner, Samantha Mathis, Gaby Hoffmann, Carrie Fisher, Dan Aykroyd, Bob Nelson, Marita Geraghty.
105 min.

As her script for *When Harry Met Sally* proved, Nora Ephron is a gifted, extremely funny writer; on the evidence of her directorial debut, however, she should not give up her day job. Despite the formidable comic presence of Kavner, as a single mother from Queens who gives up selling cosmetics to become a full-time stand-up comedienne, the film suffers from too much syrup and not enough schtick. When she gets her first club date, her daughters (Mathis and Hoffmann) are thrilled to bits; but when she graduates to big-time Vegas shows, they begin to resent her maternal neglect. They also resent her tendency to incorporate these familial tensions into her act. Most disappointingly, it is the script more than the images that lacks focus; by dividing the voice-over narration between mother and daughters, Ephron and her sister/co-writer Delia multiply the points of view and introduce unnecessary confusion. Like her character, Kavner struggles valiantly to reconcile the demands of comedy and domestic drama, but ultimately succumbs to a surfeit of schmaltz and Carly Simon songs. NF

This Is Spinal Tap

(Rob Reiner, 1983, US) Christopher Guest, Michael McKean, Harry Shearer, RJ Parnell, David Kaff, Rob Reiner, June Chadwick, Ed Begley Jr.
82 min.

Since the antics of so many heavy metal bands already teeter on the edge of self-parody, it would have been no surprise if this spoof 'rockumentary' about a comeback tour by a has-been English rock group had turned out to be a one-joke movie. In the event, Reiner's brilliantly inventive script and smart visuals avoid all the obvious pitfalls, making this one of the funniest ever films about the music business. Filmed in *cinéma vérité* style, it follows the group from venue to venue, observing the trials and tribulations of life on the road, personal tensions within the group, and problems with expanding egos. Interviews with the group fill in the details of their chequered musical career: they have trouble keeping their drummers, one of whom choked on vomit (somebody else's), while another spontaneously combusted on stage. Most importantly of all, the musical numbers acutely mimic the crashing drums, thudding bass lines, whining lead guitar solos, and juvenile, sexist lyrics of heavy rock. NF

This Is the Sea

(Mary McGuckian, 1996, Ire/US/GB) Richard Harris, Gabriel Byrne, John Lynch, Dearbhla Molloy, Samantha Morton, Ross McDade, Stella McCusker.
104 min.

Northern Ireland during the IRA ceasefire of 1995: a Romeo and Juliet story of two youngsters (McDade and Morton) trying to make a go of it despite distrust and enmity between Catholics and Plymouth Brethren. The film's heart is in the right place, but dramatically it alternates between clumsy, contrived and predictable, while the performances are generally disappointing, given the impressive cast. Waterboys fans might enjoy the soundtrack, but this, like *Resurrection Man*, offers further evidence that there's only so much cinematic mileage in returning to the Troubles for inspiration. GA

This Land Is Mine

(Jean Renoir, 1943, US) Charles Laughton, Maureen O'Hara, George Sanders, Walter Slezak, Kent Smith, Una O'Connor, Philip Merivale, George Coulouris.
103 min.

Renoir's second American film, made in the same brutal year as Stalingrad and El Alamein, is one of his quietest and least startling, featuring Laughton as a timid village schoolteacher 'somewhere in occupied Europe' who muddles his way to martyrdom. Both Laughton – happier in this role than many – and O'Hara are fine, but the film's main attractions remain the elegant Renoir set-ups (some recalling *La Bête Humaine*) and the script's unusual ethical stance: not that Nazism was wrong because it denied free enterprise, but that it was wrong because it stood against the possibility of Socialism, human dignity, and political emancipation. CA

This Love of Mine (Wo de Ai)

(Chang Yi, 1986, Tai) Yang Hui-shan, Wang Hsia-chun, Ch'en Yen-yen, Yang Li-ching.
107 min.

An impressive study of a wealthy Taipei woman – already neurotically obsessed with hygiene and health – driven to total distraction by the discovery that her husband is having an affair with another, younger woman. Hardly innovatory, the film nevertheless benefits from strong, understated performances (none more so than Yang Hui-shan as the wife), and brilliant, precisely framed images reminiscent of Bergman's more claustrophobic work. GA

This Other Eden

(Muriel Box, 1959, GB) Audrey Dalton, Leslie Phillips, Niall MacGinnis, Geoffrey Golden, Norman Rodway, Milo O'Shea, Harry Brogan.
80 min. b/w.

Lame comedy, from a play by Louis d'Alton, in which Phillips plays a hothead who reacts explosively to the news that his dad was an IRA boss. Of interest to feminist film students, as a Muriel Box film, and to anyone composing a thesis on Ireland and the British cinema. GM

This Property Is Condemned

(Sydney Pollack, 1966, US) Natalie Wood, Robert Redford, Mary Badham, Kate Reid, Charles Bronson, Jon Provost, Alan Baxter, Robert Blake.
112 min.

Considering the wealth of talent that participated in this Tennessee Williams adaptation, the results are disappointing in the extreme. It was co-scripted by Francis Coppola, produced by John Houseman, photographed by James Wong Howe, and features a more than acceptable cast. But despite the array of talent, it's a very banal reworking of Williams' one-act play about a tragic Southern belle longing for a handsome gentleman caller to whisk her away from the family boarding-house to glamorous New Orleans, but who dies disillusioned of a lung complaint. Originally a two-hander, the play told her tawdry story entirely through the eyes of her younger sister, magically transformed through romantic adolescent reminiscence. On screen, inevitably and disastrously opened out, it is constructed as a series of long, unmemorable flashbacks. DP

This Sporting Life

(Lindsay Anderson, 1963, GB) Richard Harris, Rachel Roberts, Alan Badel, William Hartnell, Colin Blakely, Vanda Godsell, Arthur Lowe.
134 min. b/w.

A reminder that something really was stirring in those days of the British New Wave before it frittered itself away. There's a touch of the cloth-cap poseur about the way this adaptation of David Storey's novel flaunts pubs, tenements and North Country accents, but also real intelligence in its use of rugby league football as a sidelong metaphor for the rat race, and real passion behind its tormented affair between Harris' inarticulately demanding miner/footballer and his dowdily uncomprehending landlady (Roberts), which ultimately acquires the authentic ring of *amour fou*. Anderson films here with a rare power, compared to which most of his later work is mere petulance. TM

This Sweet Sickness (Dites-lui que Je l'aime)

(Claude Miller, 1977, Fr) Gérard Depardieu, Miou-Miou, Claude Piéplu, Dominique Laffin, Jacques Denis, Christian Clavier.
106 min.

Miller's second film, an adaptation of Patricia Highsmith's novel about a young man (Depardieu) who secretly builds a house for his childhood sweetheart (Laffin), then busily sets about getting her to live there with him, oblivious not only to the fact that she is already married and can't stand him anyway, but to the other girl (Miou-Miou, terrific) meanwhile pursuing him with a love just as hopeless. Often a little self-conscious in its nods to Hitchcock and one rather forced echo of Cocteau, it perhaps errs in departing from Highsmith's original (to favour the psychology over the *policier*), but is often dazzlingly effective. Particularly striking is the dreamy, semi-subjective camera work (it's beautifully shot by Pierre Lhomme throughout) which turns the snowbound roadways leading to the house of fantasy into a mental landscape. TM

This Window Is Yours (Kono Mado wa Kimi no Mono)

(Tomoyuki Furumaya, 1993, Jap) Yukako Shimizu, Hideo Sakai, Toshio Kamiaki, Yoshiyuki Kubota, Hiromi Kurose, Ayako Noma.
95 min.

The long summer holiday begins in a rural town, and Yoko (Shimizu) is taking reluctant leave of her friends while her family finalise plans to move to Hokkaido. It's clear she'd rather stay with her friend Taro (Sakai), who's laid up with a broken leg. A delicately observed, warm, languorous rear-window romance, strong on mood, group dynamics and the hesitations of teenage relationships. A highly accomplished first feature.

This World, Then the Fireworks

(Michael Oblowitz, 1996, US) Billy Zane, Gina Gershon, Sheryl Lee, Rue McClanahan, Seymour Cassel, William Hootkins, Will Patton.
100 min

The most perverse and most powerful of pulp *noir* writers, Jim Thompson worked on the scripts of Kubrick's *The Killing* and *Paths of Glory*, but it wasn't until censorship broke down in the 1970s that his novels started reaching the screen: *The Getaway* and *The Kill-Off*, among others. It's a pity that his belated popularity with film-makers coincides with the fashion for retro-*noir* chic and all things ironic. That said, this Thompson adaptation begins with a bang: Fourth of July fireworks, adultery, murder and incest, all in the first two minutes. It doesn't leave the film anywhere to go. Twins Marty and Carol grow up despising everyone but each other. She's a hooker, he's a con-man. Such harmless diversions turn nasty as their incestuous love gets out of hand. Director Oblowitz tries to keep faith with the material with a distorting wide-angle lens, lurid, theatrical lighting and a chopped, staccato rhythm. The movie is the spit of a '50s dime store paperback cover, not brought to life, but preserved in amber. Even the actors resemble old B-movie icons. Throw screenwriter Larry Gross's voice-over into the mix, simmer with cod-blues sax and banjo, and the stylisation is complete. Too bad they forgot to put over the story. TCh

Thomas Crown Affair, The

(Norman Jewison, 1968, US) Steve McQueen, Faye Dunaway, Paul Burke, Jack Weston, Yaphet Kotto, Todd Martin, Biff McGuire.
102 min.

Slick, silly romantic thriller, with Dunaway as an insurance investigator falling for McQueen, the property developer led to commit a bank robbery through boredom. Much obvious 'significance' (the pair playing chess; symbolic, see?), much glossy imagery (courtesy of Haskell Wexler) fashionably fragmented into interminable split-screen nonsense, and little of any real interest. The whole thing is as irritatingly meaningless as its Oscar-winning song, 'Windmills Of My Mind'; a sad product of its times. GA

Thomas l'Imposteur (Thomas the Imposter)

(Georges Franju, 1964, Fr) Emmanuèle Riva, Fabrice Rouleau, Jean Servais, Sophie Darès, Michel Vitold, Rosy Varte, Edith Scob, André Méliès.
93 min. b/w.

On the face of it, it's hard to imagine two artists with less in common than Jean Cocteau and Georges Franju, but Cocteau himself chose Franju to film his early novel. Cocteau's *Thomas* is a magically charming innocent who poses as the nephew of a general in order to serve in a civil (aristocratic!) ambulance corps during World War I; the war is the circus of his dreams, and his fantasies connect with fact only at the moment of his death. Tougher, more materialistic in his view of fantasy, and with a broader sense of philosophical and social contexts, Franju reformulates the book with surprising fidelity, but disengages his audience from Thomas' subjective experience. The war is seen as an 'absurd' unreal backdrop, a network of extraordinary images and moods, but Franju has made a film about fantasy, not a fantasy film. It is compulsive, and utterly absorbing. TR

Thong

see S.T.A.B.

Thoroughly Modern Millie

(George Roy Hill, 1967, US) Julie Andrews, Mary Tyler Moore, Beatrice Lillie, James Fox, John Gavin, Carol Channing, Jack Soo, Philip Ahn.
138 min.

Patchy but lively musical following in the wake of Sandy Wilson's *The Boy Friend* (though more movie-oriented in its terms of reference) and gently guying the era of the flapper, the Charleston, and the raccoon coat as Julie Andrews sallies forth from Kansas to the Big Apple in search of spouse, success and sophistication *à la mode*. Nicely acted by a reliable cast (Bea Lillie's white-slave-trading landlady is a delight), while the selection of standards and new songs is listenable enough, but the film is far too long for its own good. GA

Those Glory, Glory Days

(Philip Saville, 1983, GB) Zoe Nathenson, Sara Sugarman, Cathy Murphy, Liz Campion, Julia

McKenzie, Bryan Pringle, Danny
Blanchflower.
90 min.
Julie Welch, football writer on *The Observer*, has
written a charming – perhaps too charming – tale
of schoolgirl enthusiasm based on her own youthful adulation of Tottenham Hotspur's '60s captain Danny Blanchflower. Only flashes of the
acerbic wit and gift for satirical characterisation
that graced her teleplay *Singles* are evident in this
drawn-out and cloying contribution to David
Puttnam's *First Love* series for C4 (unwisely
given a cinema release after being seen on TV).
14-year-old Zoe Nathenson acts her heart out as
the football-mad Julia, but the film itself, though
likeable enough, never catches fire. MH

Those Who Love Me Will Take the Train (Ceux qui m'aiment prendront le train)
(Patrice Chéreau, 1998, Fr) Pascal Greggory,
Valéria Bruni-Tedeschi, Charles Berling, Jean-
Louis Trintignant, Vincent Perez, Roschdy
Zem.
120 min.
A group of family, friends, hangers-on and assorted others travel by train from Paris to Limoges
for the funeral of a seemingly misanthropic,
promiscuous painter; on arrival, they encounter
the artist's nearest (but not, necessarily, his dearest), and a host of revelations and resentments.
There's not much substance to this drama of all
round dysfunctionality, but the well chosen cast
are excellent, the script is intriguingly naturalistic (and at times inconsequential), and the direction often virtuoso: not merely in the use of music
and the skilled exploration of the characters on
the confined train, but in a stunning final shot
swooping over a huge cemetery. GA

Those Wonderful Movie Cranks (Bájecni Muzi s Klikou)
(Jiri Menzel, 1978, Czech) Rudolf Hrusinsky,
Vlasta Fabiánová, Blazena Holisová, Vladimir
Mensik, Jiri Menzel.
88 min.
The cranks in question are pioneers of the Czech
silent cinema – an opportunist travelling showman and his female entourage, a dopey documentarist, and a faded stage actress – vacillating
over whether or not posterity deserves a record
of the latter's histrionics. They are not wonderful. And the film, in its *faux-naïf* flatness, is not
'charming': it's leaden, slushy and slapdash, and
ill serves the memory of silent cinema. Saddening,
tedious, and intermittently annoying. PT

Thousand Acres, A
(Jocelyn Moorhouse, 1997, US) Michelle
Pfeiffer, Jessica Lange, Jennifer Jason Leigh,
Colin Firth, Keith Carradine, Kevin Anderson,
Pat Hingle, Jason Robards.
105 min.
A patriarch (Robards) announces that he means
to divide his land between his three daughters,
but when one of them, the most beloved (Leigh),
tries to dissuade him, he sends her packing. Jane
Smiley's novel earned points for chutzpah, but
Jocelyn Moorhouse's adaptation makes heavy
weather of this latter-day *King Lear*. Despite the
leisurely *Waltons*-style voice-over, Larry Cook
and his kin don't convince as a Midwestern
farming dynasty, while the film itself has only
a picturesque sense of the land. It makes for
rocky terrain on which to base the ensuing melodramatics. Breast cancer, infertility, adultery,
wife beating – it seems as if someone's ticking
off a list of female 'issues'. If only Laura Jones'
screenplay had allowed the characters more
respite, a time to draw breath between calamities, the fine performances from Pfeiffer and
Lange (as the older daughters) might just have
made it stick. Robards' senile paterfamilias is,
regrettably, a grave embarrassment. TCh

1000 Eyes of Dr Mabuse, The (Die Tausend Augen des Dr Mabuse)
(Fritz Lang, 1960, WGer/It/Fr) Dawn Addams,
Peter Van Eyck, Gert Fröbe, Wolfgang Preiss,
Werner Peters, Andrea Checchi, Reinhard
Kolldehoff, Howard Vernon.
103 min. b/w.

Lang's last film. Resisting the producer's
requests for a remake, sequel or *Son of...*, Lang
instead updated the setting to postwar
Germany, and invented a new Mabuse-type
character (Preiss). Set in a large hotel where the
characters' every move is monitored by the mastermind's TV screens, *1000 Eyes* is none the less
distinctly and wilfully old-fashioned in a way
that is all Lang's own. Lines like 'Don't leave
town', exploding telephones, blind prophets,
gadgets more quaint than modern, and a
supremely elaborate thriller plot where no one
and nothing are what they seem, give it an anti-
realist ambience more reminiscent of the
Hollywood serial than of contemporary film-
making. And, of course, Lang's anti-Fascist sentiments are unmistakably as up-to-date as they
were in the '20s. Great stuff. RM

Thousand Pieces of Gold, A
(Nancy Kelly, 1990, US) Rosalind Chao, Dennis
Dunn, Michael Paul Chan, Chris Cooper.
105 min.
The misadventures and sufferings of a mail-
order Chinese bride in the 19th century California
gold-rush, based on fact. Given that her
Manchurian father sells her off to a 'marriage
broker' without telling her what he's doing, Lalu
has an understandably deep distrust of men in
general; but the proto-feminist dimension of her
struggle seems imposed from a modern perspective, not something that grows from the
material. Still, it's decently written and directed,
and features very assured performances from
Chao as the heroine and Dunn (a regular in John
Carpenter movies) as the kindly man she ought
to have trusted. TR

Three Ages
(Buster Keaton/Eddie Cline, 1923, US) Buster
Keaton, Wallace Beery, Margaret Leahy, Joe
Roberts, Lillian Lawrence.
6 reels. b/w.
Keaton's first feature – a parody, to some extent,
of films like Griffith's *Intolerance* – revels in the
same anachronistic view of history as did his earlier short *The Frozen North*: the basic story common to all three intercut episodes, charting Buster
and Beery's rivalry over their beloved Leahy,
allows him to construct a delicious series of gags
spoofing the clichés of film through their very
absurdity and incongruity. In the Stone Age,
Buster arrives to court Leahy sitting astride a
dinosaur, and plays golf with real clubs; in
ancient Rome, black slaves start up a crap game
upon seeing a soothsayer's dice, and Buster,
forced into a chariot race (neatly guying *Ben Hur*)
during a blizzard, enters the arena on a sled-cum-
chariot drawn by huskies. The modern-day story
is least successful, though even here his eye for
sheer idiocy of many contemporary fashions is
admirably sharp. Widely underrated, the film
may lack the sheer brilliance of, say *Our
Hospitality* and *The General*, but its sense of detail
and pace, its originality and invention remain
undimmed. GA

Three Amigos!
(John Landis, 1986, US) Chevy Chase, Steve
Martin, Martin Short, Alfonso Arau, Tony
Plana, Patrice Martinez, Joe Mantegna.
104 min.
Already Hollywood has-beens by 1916, a trio of
Western serial stars (Martin, Chase and Short)
receive a cable offering them muchos pesos to
strut their stuff in a Mexican village. Little do
they know that they are expected to take on the
forces of a vicious bandit (Arau) terrorising the
village. Western spoofs are never notable for original plots, and this is no exception. Nevertheless,
it revels in the cornball clichés of the low-budget
oater, and benefits from amiably innocent performances. The characterisation is paper thin,
and Landis' timing as sloppy as ever; but if you
enjoy brainless slapstick that allows space for
irrelevant absurdities like a singing bush and an
invisible swordsman, it's entertaining enough.
GA

Three Brothers (Tre Fratelli)
(Francesco Rosi, 1980, It/Fr) Philippe Noiret,
Charles Vanel, Michele Placido, Vittorio
Mezzogiorno, Andrea Ferreol, Maddalena
Crippa.
111 min.
For too much of its length, Rosi's film threatens to

disappear into the mist of its quest for Big Themes.
Its story of three men – a Rome magistrate, a reform
school teacher, and a trade union activist – summoned by their aged father to assemble in the
southern Italian village of their upbringing for their
mother's funeral, provides Rosi with the dynamic
for investigations into various Burning Questions
affecting Italy today – the issue of terrorism and
political justification of terrorist violence; the division of the country into two distinct economic
regions, one privileged, the other deprived, and
what to do about it. So far, so relevant.
Unfortunately, Rosi also sees fit to grapple with
such eternal themes of the human condition as the
symbolic contrasts offered between Life and Death,
Youth and Age, Innocence and Experience, often
leaving you wishing for the simpler but much more
compelling attractions of investigative gangster
and thriller genre pieces like *Lucky Luciano* and
The Mattei Affair. It's only in the realisation of the
various characters' dreams, reveries and memories
that this really ever becomes seductive. RM

Three Bullets for a Long Gun
(Peter Henkel, 1970, SAf) Beau Brummell,
Keith Van der Wat, Patrick Mynhardt, Tulio
Moneta, Brian Kiley.
84 min.
Jokey, South African-financed spaghetti Western,
concocted by its star Beau Brummell, in which
the nameless 'Major' (who drops not a manly
cigar stub but a faintly ludicrous peanut husk)
makes common cause with a fast-talking bandit,
Lucky, to find the hidden gold of Lucky's murdered father. Okay gunfights, but very ragged
subplot. JPy

Three Came Home
(Jean Negulesco, 1950, US) Claudette Colbert,
Patric Knowles, Sessue Hayakawa, Florence
Desmond, Sylvia Andrew.
106 min. b/w.
Taken prisoner with husband Patric Knowles and
their young son during the 1941 invasion of North
Borneo, Claudette Colbert suffers courageously in
a Japanese internment camp, in Nunnally
Johnson's adaptation of the true-life testimony of
writer Agnes Newton Keith. Hayakawa's impressive, too, as the humane commanding officer, thus
holding xenophobia somewhat at bay. TJ

Three Coins in the Fountain
(Jean Negulesco, 1954, US) Clifton Webb,
Dorothy McGuire, Jean Peters, Louis Jourdan,
Maggie McNamara, Rossano Brazzi, Howard
St John, Cathleen Nesbitt.
102 min.
This touristy romance was an unexpected hit in
its day, but you'd hardly think it to look at it now.
Three American gals in Rome chuck their cur-
rency into the Trevi fountain to see if dreams real-
ly do come true – and guess what? McGuire ends
up with Clifton Webb's charmer of a boss, while
Peters and McNamara go for something a little
more European (Jourdan, Brazzi). Meanwhile,
Sinatra croons the title choon, and CinemaScope
cameraman Milton Krasner made The Eternal
City look so scrummy he got an Oscar for it.
Remade by Negulesco in 1964 as *The Pleasure
Seekers*, with Madrid taking over from Rome. TJ

Three Colours: Blue (100) (Trois Couleurs: Bleu)
(Krzysztof Kieslowski, 1993, Fr) Juliette
Binoche, Benoît Régent, Hélène Vincent,
Florence Pernel, Emmanuelle Riva.
98 min.
Failing to find the courage to commit suicide after
her husband and infant daughter die in a car
crash, Julie (Binoche) decides to build a new,
anonymous and wholly independent life. Leaving
her country mansion for a Paris apartment, she
soon finds that freedom is not as easy to achieve
as she hoped. Neighbours seek help and friendship, and doubts about her husband's fidelity
inflame jealousy. Most troubling there's the
music: Julia can't escape the sounds in her head.
Kieslowski's film – the first of three inspired by
the ideals of the French Revolution – is an arresting study of notions of individual freedom in the
modern world. There's no facile moralising, simply a lucid examination of a woman's state of
mind. Binoche responds with her best work to
date: quiet, strong, stubborn, and deeply aware
that the heart holds mysteries neither we nor
those close to us will ever understand. GA

Three Colours: Red (Trois Couleurs: Rouge) 100 (100)

(Krzysztof Kieslowski, 1994, Fr/Switz/Pol)
Irène Jacob, Jean-Louis Trintignant,
Frédérique Feder, Jean-Pierre Lorit, Samuel
Lebihan, Juliette Binoche, Julie Delpy, Benoît
Régent, Zbigniew Zamachowski.
99 min.
The conclusion to the 'Three Colours' trilogy is set
in Geneva and focuses on Valentine (Jacob), a young
model with an absent but possessive boyfriend.
After running over a dog, Valentine tracks down its
owner, a reclusive, retired judge (Trintignant) who
eavesdrops on phone calls, including those between
a law student and his lover, a weather reporter.
While Kieslowski dips into various interconnecting
lives, the central drama is the electrifying encounter
between Valentine – caring, troubled – and the
judge, whose tendency to play God fails to match,
initially, the girl's compassion. It's a film about destiny and chance, solitude and communication, cynicism and faith, doubt and desire; about lives
affected by forces beyond rationalisation. The
assured direction avoids woolly mysticism by using
material resources – actors, colour, movement, composition, sound – to illuminate abstract concepts.
Stunningly beautiful, powerfully scored and immaculately performed, the film is virtually flawless, and
one of the very greatest cinematic achievements of
the last few decades. A masterpiece. GA

Three Colours: White (Trois Couleurs: Blanc)

(Krzysztof Kieslowski, 1993, Fr/Pol) Zbigniew
Zamachowski, Julie Delpy, Janusz Gajos, Jerzy
Stuhr, Juliette Binoche.
92 min.
After the visual sheen and spiritual uplift of *Blue*,
part two of Kieslowski's trilogy may at first seem
raw, even slight. The story, hung loosely round
notions of political and personal equality, concerns
the despair and desire for revenge felt by Polish
hairdresser Karol (Zamachowski) when his French
wife Dominique (Delpy) divorces him after six
months of unconsummated marriage in Paris.
Initially, having lost everything, he has no idea
what to do with his life. But, after a macabre transaction with fellow expatriate Mikolaj (Gajos)
enables him to return to Poland, Karol starts afresh
and directs his newly developed cunning to re-
igniting Dominique's love. A droll black comedy
that takes a scalpel to the impoverished ethics of
the new money-obsessed Poland, and to the selfish impulses tied up with our desires for a balanced
sexual relationship, *White* is at times reminiscent
of the satire of the last episode of the *Dekalog*. It's
often cruel, of course, and cool as an ice-pick, but
it's still endowed with enough unsentimental
humanity to end with a touching, lyrical admission of the power of love. Essential viewing. GA

Three Comrades

(Frank Borzage, 1938, US) Robert Taylor,
Margaret Sullavan, Franchot Tone, Robert
Young, Lionel Atwill, Guy Kibbee, Monty
Woolley, Henry Hull.
98 min. b/w.
Notable as the only film on which Scott Fitzgerald
received a script credit, although his conception was
softened by some pussyfooting around the crucial
Atwill character. So what begins as a 'lost generation' tale as the three comrades (Taylor, Tone and
Young) return home to Germany after the 1918
armistice, flaunting the familiar mixture of cynicism
and idealism as they pursue fun and fast cars while
trying to set about the task of rebuilding their lives,
soon becomes sidetracked as Fitzgerald's pessimism runs into Borzage's romanticism. No question here that Sullavan's ethereal heroine, though
penniless, jobless, and suffering from malnutrition
which turns into terminal TB, will have any seriously sordid truck with the proto-Nazi sugar-daddy
played by Atwill. Instead, the film exercises a little
sleight-of-hand and, still trailing wisps of
Fitzgerald's conception, takes off with Sullavan and
Taylor into one of those incandescent Borzage
romances where time is simply non-existent: impossibly pure, absurdly naïve, yet magically tender. TM

Three Crowns of the Sailor (Les Trois Couronnes du Matelot)

(Raúl Ruiz, 1983, Fr) Jean-Bernard Guillard,
Philippe Deplanche, Nadége Clair, Lisa Lyon,

Jean Badin, Claude Dereppe.
122 min. b/w & col.
Students commit mad and meaningless acts, sailors
tell the tallest stories. When one of the former, having murdered his tutor, meets one of the latter at
the start of Ruiz's film, the images are in muddy
green sepia; but as the sailor begins his extraordinary life story – listening is his price for granting
the youth safe passage on a departing ship – the
movie becomes literally and figuratively more
colourful. Story piles upon story, scenes grow vivid
and dissolve, characters come and go as in a dream.
No one speaks or behaves as they would in 'real
life', for that is neither the territory nor the objective of Ruiz's cinema; his is a hypothetical world,
governed by the reversal of narrative expectations.
The sailor's tale begins in Valparaiso, and revisits
in flashback the various ports of call in a lifetime's
voyaging, each of which yields its own strange
story. The elements of the sailor's yarn are timeless
and universal: family ties, journeying away from
home, sex, violence, and death. Ruiz conjures them
into a poetic parable on the theme of debts long
unpaid and finally called in...A vigorous imagination is at work here in the tradition of Cocteau,
Fellini, Tarkovsky; open your eyes and your mind
to it. A dream of a picture, in every sense. MA

Three Days of the Condor

(Sydney Pollack, 1975, US) Robert Redford,
Faye Dunaway, Cliff Robertson, Max von
Sydow, John Houseman, Addison Powell.
118 min.
Set in the world of CIA power games and scientific hardware, but dominated by an intriguing
Borges-like riddle: why should a mystery thriller
that didn't sell be translated into obscure languages? And why should the American Literary
Historical Society in New York be massacred
while one of their readers (Redford) is out getting
lunch? With the telephone his only method of
contact with Olympian and untrustworthy superiors, Redford becomes lost, unpredictable, even
sentimental. He holes up in Dunaway's apartment and starts making mistakes. Thanks to an
intelligent script, partly by Lorenzo Semple Jr
(*Pretty Poison, The Parallax View*), the action
rarely falters, and at its best the film offers an
intriguing slice of neo-Hitchcock. A certain gloss
irritates, but enough scenes compensate for the
chic portrayal of the Redford/Dunaway relationship: Redford's sudden intrusion into civilisation when he visits a dead man's apartment,
and finds the wife preparing her husband's dinner; the postman whose pen won't work; Redford
in the strange, darkened house of his quarry, taking the initiative by blaring soul music from the
hi-fi. CPe

Three Faces of Eve, The

(Nunnally Johnson, 1957, US) Joanne
Woodward, David Wayne, Lee J Cobb, Nancy
Kulp, Edwin Jerome, Vince Edwards.
91 min. b/w.
Based on a true case history of a schizophrenic –
here a woman with three personalities: a slatternly housewife, a seductive flirt, and a smart,
articulate woman – this is worthy but somewhat
turgid and facile, a typically Hollywoodian
account of mental illness. Despite fine monochrome camerawork by Stanley Cortez, Johnson's
direction remains remarkably mundane in visual terms (one need only compare it to, say, *Psycho*
or *Lilith* to realise its shortcomings), so that it's
left to the cast to bring the film to life. And that
Woodward certainly does, responding with what
can only be described as a *tour de force*, for which
she won the Best Actress Oscar. GA

Three for All

(Martin Campbell, 1974, GB) Adrienne Posta,
Lesley North, Cheryl Hall, Graham Bonnet,
Robert Lindsay, Paul Nicholas, Christopher
Neil, Richard Beckinsale, Diana Dors.
90 min.
Clap hands, another British movie. This one
emanates from the Tudor Gates 9-5
Scriptwriting Factory (which brought you vam-
pire horrors such as *Carmilla, Mircalla,
Caramello* etc). Now the Great Pen has turned out
a musical, built for TV stars and aimed at the C-
D Benidorm market. *Billy Beethoven*, a group
managed by Richard Beckinsale, tour Spain and
are pursued by their three girlfriends (the fourth
member has a fixation for Diana Dors, his mum).
In order of appearance, the girls bump into
Arthur Mullard, David Kossoff, Hattie Jacques,

John Le Mesurier, Ian Lavender...What makes
the film less than terrible is the professionalism
of the players, who could all have used a much
better story and dialogue. Adrienne Posta is
great as usual; Graham Bonnet acts well and his
songs are okay. AN

Three for the Road

(Bill WL Norton, 1987, US) Charlie Sheen,
Kerri Green, Alan Ruck, Sally Kellerman,
Blaire Tefkin, Raymond J Barry.
88 min.
Wannabe political aide Sheen and college pal
Ruck ferry misbehavin' senator's daughter Kerri
Green to boarding school in this redundant
youth-oriented road movie. TJ

Three Friends (Sechinku)

(Yim Soon-Rye, 1996, SKor) Kim Hyun-Sung,
Lee Jang-Won, Jung Hee-Suk.
92 min.
This terrific first feature by one of Korea's very
few women directors is focused entirely on young
men: three kids from screwed-up families, failures at school and with no real social prospects,
looking ahead with dismay at two years of compulsory military service. Yim's story (parts of
which are a deliberate challenge to Korean censorship) faithfully reflects social realities at the
bottom of the economic scale, but her approach
to character and situation is far from grungy
social realism. She never forgets that real people
laugh, even when there's not much to laugh
about, and she roots her underlying anger in her
wry awareness that people tend to blame society
when they've fucked up their own lives. TR

Three Fugitives

(Francis Veber, 1989, US) Nick Nolte, Martin
Short, Sarah Rowland, Doroff, James Earl
Jones, Alan Ruck, Kenneth McMillan, Bruce
McGill.
96 min.
Adapted by Veber from his own French movie
(*Les Fugitifs*, 1986), this robust, often very funny
farce casts Nolte and Short as chalk-and-cheese
bank robbers thrown together by ludicrous coincidence. Released after five years in the slammer
for armed robbery, Nolte is greeted by the cop
(Jones) who put him away, and who promises to
do so again. Caught up in an inept hold-up
attempt by Short, Nolte is taken hostage, then
mistakenly presumed to be the perpetrator of the
crime. Forced to assume that role in order to
escape, hard man Nolte reveals a softer side when
he learns that Short only pulled the job in order
to pay for special schooling for his mute six-year-
old daughter (Doroff). Some sentimentality creeps
in around the angelic child; but making excellent
use of Nolte's controlled toughness and Short's
hysterical freneticism, Veber plays the comic
action hard and fast, grounding the humour in
believable reality that has spiralled out of control
(one hilarious scene sees Nolte having a gunshot
wound treated by a senile veterinarian who
thinks he's a dog). NF

Three Godfathers

(John Ford, 1948, US) John Wayne, Pedro
Armendariz, Harry Carey Jr, Ward Bond, Mae
Marsh, Jane Darwell, Ben Johnson, Mildred
Natwick.
105 min.
Dedicated to the memory of Harry Carey Sr
('Bright star of the early western sky'), who had
starred in Ford's first version of this much-filmed
story (*Marked Men*, 1919), *Three Godfathers* is
much better than is usually allowed. The bulk of
the film, loosely paralleling the story of the Magi
as three bank robbers on the run reluctantly give
up their freedom to save a baby found in the
desert, and are faced with a parched and desperate journey during which two of them die, is
filmed with harsh and hallucinating splendour in
Death Valley. Alas, with Wayne's arrival in
New Jerusalem, to lay the baby on the saloon bar
on what just happens to be Christmas Day ('Set
'em up, Mister, milk for the infant and a cold beer
for me...'), the distressing Ford penchant for symbols of religiosity which had marred *The
Fugitive* does the same disservice here. The last
reel, with Wayne explicitly identified as the
Prodigal Son and a general collapse into mawkishness, might almost have strayed in from
another movie. TM

Three Hours to Kill

(Alfred L Werker, 1954, US) Dana Andrews, Donna Reed, Dianne Foster, Stephen Elliott, Richard Coogan, Lawrence Hugo.
77 min.

A superior B-picture from the last years of Werker's 30-plus years in the business, a catalogue of routine assignments broken by highlights including *The Adventures of Sherlock Holmes* (1939), *He Walked by Night* (1949), the prototype serial-killer *film noir*, and a string of interesting minor Westerns from the '50s. Andrews plays a gunslinger accused of murdering his fiancée's brother and all but pulled to pieces by a small town lynch mob including many of his so-called friends. He's back in town now and wants to track down the real killer. The film neatly slots together the dual time frames and generates a strong sense of bitterness at the speed with which Andrews feels himself betrayed. TJ

301–302

(Park Chul-Soo, 1995, SKor) Bang Eun-Jin, Hwang Sin-Hye, Kim Chu-Ryun, Park Chul-Ho.
100 min.

In this splendidly lurid thriller a detective checks out the disappearance of a single woman in Room 302 of the New Hope Apartments, Seoul, a haven for the upwardly mobile. His chief informant (and soon his prime suspect) is the woman's pushy neighbour in 301, another single woman in many ways the exact opposite of the absentee. What unfolds is a hair-raising history of marital discord, sexual abuse, anorexia and bulimia…and the truth about the Korean penchant for dog-meat. TR

Three Into Two Won't Go

(Peter Hall, 1969, GB) Rod Steiger, Claire Bloom, Judy Geeson, Peggy Ashcroft, Paul Rogers, Lynn Farleigh, Elizabeth Spriggs, Sheila Allen.
94 min.

Irredeemably awful permissive melodrama from the Swinging Sixties, scripted by Edna O'Brien from Andrea Newman's novel about a middle-aged businessman's adulterous flirtations with a young hitchhiker, leading to the breakdown of his marriage. Overheated codswallop, given a ludicrous veneer of respectability by the distinguished cast, it already looked dated when it was made. And it has a score by Francis Lai. GA

Three Lives and Only One Death

see Trois Vies et une Seule Mort

Three Men and a Baby

(Leonard Nimoy, 1987, US) Tom Selleck, Steve Guttenberg, Ted Danson, Nancy Travis, Margaret Colin, Celeste Holm, Philip Bosco, Paul Guilfoyle.
102 min.

The American remake of *3 Men and a Cradle* is sleeker, costlier than the French original: the three swinging bachelors are still all thumbs around the infant which unexpectedly turns up on their doorstep, but shout less than the Frenchmen, and in the main eschew the klutzy walks. Inconvenient wee wees, poo poos, and nocturnal crying remain the same. As much of the action is confined to the bachelor pad, Nimoy was smart to fork out on the design. Even smarter, he pixillates little moments of life with Baby Mary, since it is much of a muchness. Guttenberg plays in the register hysterical, wearing a snorkel to entertain the six-month-old tot, Selleck features a roving dimple, and Danson changes from self-regarding sybarite to responsible parent, or nearest offer. It is shamelessly sentimental, and could well send the hard-boiled home to kick the cat. BC

3 Men and a Cradle (3 Hommes et un Couffin)

(Coline Serreau, 1985, Fr) Roland Giraud, Michel Boujenah, André Dussollier, Philippe Leroy Beaulieu, Dominique Lavanant, Marthe Villalonga.
106 min.

In this comedy, three Parisian swingers find their bachelor pad invaded by the fruit of a night of forgotten passion. Horizons narrow to three-hourly feeds and nappy changes, during which the gesticulation rate rises into the paint cards. The father (Dussollier) gets off light, being on vacation in the Orient, but the other two not only learn to cope with parenthood, but also have to contend with a subplot dealing with drugs, drug-dealers and the police, in which the nappy features as a stash. When the mother reclaims the baby, the trio discover that their old ways no longer appeal, and begin to question the meaning of life itself. Only itchy-koo will do. Noisy, and not short of unison waddling walks. BC

Three Men and a Little Lady

(Emile Ardolino, 1990, US) Tom Selleck, Steve Guttenberg, Ted Danson, Nancy Travis, Robin Weisman, Christopher Cazenove, Sheila Hancock, Fiona Shaw, Jonathan Lynn.
104 min.

In this good-natured sequel to *Three Men and a Baby*, English actress Sylvia (Travis) and her daughter Mary have been living with our bachelor heroes for five years, but now Sylvia is hankering after a husband. Forget Michael (Guttenberg) and Jack (Danson), the obvious choice is upright architect Peter (Selleck). But both parties are scared to declare their feelings, so she accepts a proposal of marriage from smoothie English director Edward (Cazenove). Once it's understood that there's nothing even vaguely credible about the storyline, there's some harmless fun to be had as Michael and Peter go to England in pursuit, with their rescue mission taking on the proportions of a jailbreak when they discover that Mary is being primed for boarding school. Highlights stem chiefly from the performances: Fiona Shaw is funny as a frustrated headmistress, while Danson's variation on his *Cheers* persona keeps the mood light. CM

Three Men in a Boat

(Ken Annakin, 1956, GB) David Tomlinson, Jimmy Edwards, Laurence Harvey, Shirley Eaton, Jill Ireland, Martita Hunt, Lisa Gastoni, Robertson Hare, Miles Malleson.
94 min.

When they weren't making such prestigious Anglo-American affairs as *The African Queen* and *Moulin Rouge*, producers John and James Woolf often turned their hand to small-scale British comedy. This mannered, eccentric adaptation of Jerome K Jerome's equally mannered, eccentric novel, wasn't one of their great successes. Shooting was dogged by bad weather. Then, when the film was complete, it all but sank at the box office. (For some reason, it did extremely well in Paris, even as it failed elsewhere.) Still, it's entertaining stuff, enlivened by rum performances from Tomlinson, Edwards and Harvey as the three Edwardian duffers cruising down the Thames. GM

Three Musketeers, The

(Stephen Herek, 1993, US) Kiefer Sutherland, Charlie Sheen, Chris O'Donnell, Rebecca De Mornay, Tim Curry, Oliver Platt, Gabrielle Anwar, Julie Delpy.
106 min.

The disbanded musketeers re-muster when they discover Richelieu's plans to assassinate boy-king Louis, who is showing foolish signs of wishing to grasp the reins of state power. The ageing brat-packers – Sutherland (Athos), Sheen (Aramis) – are under orders to play straight, which they do. Satisfying, old-fashioned family romp, but hardly a modern classic. WH.

Three Musketeers: The Queen's Diamonds, The

(Richard Lester, 1973, Pan) Michael York, Oliver Reed, Raquel Welch, Richard Chamberlain, Frank Finlay, Charlton Heston, Faye Dunaway, Christopher Lee, Geraldine Chaplin, Jean-Pierre Cassel, Spike Milligan, Roy Kinnear, Sybil Danning.
107 min.

Lester romps through Dumas' novel, coming up with an indulgent and enjoyable excuse to revive and send up the swashbuckling film. The plot is perfunctory, and centres round Cardinal Richelieu's attempts to embarrass the Queen of France, and the efforts of the loyal D'Artagnan and the Three Musketeers to retrieve her diamonds which, of course, the King insists she must wear to the ball. No expense has been spared, and Lester obliges with a visually extravagant piece, a cross between the low-life realism of Pasolini and the lavishness of Zeffirelli. The cast is good (though it remains very much Lester's film), the fights appropriately energetic, and it all moves along at a fair pace, sprinkled with a number of good gags. The second half of the story was issued separately as *The Four Musketeers*. CPe

3 Ninjas (aka 3 Ninja Kids)

(Jon Turteltaub, 1992, US) Victor Wong, Michael Treanor, Max Elliott Slade, Chad Power, Rand Kingsley.
87 min.

Wise old Japanese granddad (Wong) instructs three boys in the deadly ninja arts. Their dad, an FBI agent on the trail of gun-runner Kingsley, is dead against their training – at least until the latter kidnaps them to get the Feds off his back. Can the trio use their ninja secrets to escape? Will granddad defeat the gun-runner in hand-to-hand combat? If you can't guess the answers to these questions you are under 11 and will absolutely love this film, with its amazing fight scenes, bungling *Home Alone* kidnappers and thoroughly nasty bad guys. Send mum and dad shopping. NKe

Three O'Clock High

(Phil Joanou, 1987, US) Casey Siemaszko, Anne Ryan, Richard Tyson, Jeffrey Tambor, Philip Baker Hall, John P Ryan, Stacey Glick, Jonathan Wise.
101 min.

High-school shenanigans as Siemaszko is asked by Wise, editor of the student newspaper, to write a profile of the new kid in class without actually knowing that the subject is the meanest badass ever to stalk a lunch-hour corridor. Joanou, later to find greater exposure with the concert picture *U2 Rattle and Hum* and the Oldman/Penn crime movie *State of Grace*, directs with a lot of energy, but the material just isn't there. TJ

Three of Hearts

(Yurek Bogayevicz, 1992, US) William Baldwin, Kelly Lynch, Sherilyn Fenn, Joe Pantoliano, Gail Strickland.
110 min.

Shallow and virtually compromised out of existence, this film claims to examine the complex dynamics of a hetero-lesbian triangle, but does nothing of the kind. Jilted lesbian Connie (Lynch) hires outwardly macho, inwardly sensitive male escort Joe (Baldwin) to seduce her ex-lover Ellen (Fenn), break her heart and send her running back. The film settles for the obvious: half-hearted lesbian Ellen falls for Joe. Everything here is disingenuous, starting with the fact that the only lesbian relationship depicted is over before the film begins. Ironically, the one friendship which persuades is Joe and Connie's. NF

Three of Us, The

see Noi tre

Three Palm Trees

see Três Palmeiras

Threepenny Opera, The

see Dreigroschenoper, Die

3pm Paradise

see Oksutan

Three Resurrected Drunkards (Kaettekita Yopparai)

(Nagisa Oshima, 1968, Jap) Kazuhiko Kato, Osamu Kitayama, Norihiko Hashida, Kei Sato, Fumio Watanabe, Mako Midori.
80 min.

Oshima took to the spirit of '68 like a needle to a vein. This riotous comedy (in colour and Scope) is a cocktail of dumb cops, desperate Koreans, and Japanese students who don't know what's hit them. It starts with the students taking a swim, and finding their clothes stolen from the beach; the thieves are illegal immigrants from Korea, who soon want the identities that went with the clothes. It proceeds through a series of chases, misunderstandings, and riddles, which in turn evolve into conceptual games with the structure of the film itself. If anyone imagines that Oshima broke new ground when he cast Bowie and Sakamoto in *Merry Christmas, Mr Lawrence*, they should note that the lead here is Kazuhiko Kato, founder/leader of the Sadistic Mika Band, who also contributes an impeccable pop theme song. TR

3 Ring Circus

(Joseph Pevney, 1954, US) Dean Martin, Jerry
Lewis, Joanna Dru, Zsa Zsa Gabor, Wallace
Ford, Sig Ruman, Elsa Lanchester.
103 min.
Discharged soldiers Lewis and Martin run away
and join the circus. Not one of the duo's most
inspired vehicles, but there's a certain pleasure to
be had watching Lewis pull faces at the lions.
While the buck-toothed comedian gets up to his
usual histrionics, Martin, the most laid-back actor
since the late Robert Mitchum, tries in his own
desultory way to fend off the advances of the
equally predatory Zsa Zsa Gabor. GM

Three Sisters

(Laurence Olivier, 1970, GB) Jeanne Watts,
Joan Plowright, Louise Purnell, Derek Jacobi,
Alan Bates, Kenneth Mackintosh, Sheila Reid,
Laurence Olivier, Ronald Pickup, Frank Wylie.
165 min.
Olivier's painfully stagebound record of the
1967 National Theatre production of Chekhov's
play, in which he himself took a comparative
back seat as Chebutikin. Two fantasy sequences
are added as a sop to cinema (one of them a
redundant visualisation of Irina's wish-fulfilment dream of Moscow as a paradise of glittering ballrooms and theatres). Moments of passion
survive from Joan Plowright's Masha; otherwise
it's a catalogue of pregnant pauses from which
all Chekhovian intent has long since ebbed
away. TM

Three Sisters
(Paura e amore)

(Margarethe von Trotta, 1990, It/Fr/Ger)
Fanny Ardant, Greta Scacchi, Valeria Golino,
Peter Simonischek, Sergio Castellito, Agnès
Soral, Paolo Hendel.
112 min.
Von Trotta uses Chekhov's sorority tale as a
springboard, transposing the scene from Russia
to a chilly and autumnal Italy. It opens with a
funeral party following the death of the sisters'
adored father. A guest, oleaginous lecturer
Massimo (Simonischek) is the catalyst in their
lives. The eldest, Velia (Ardant), also an academic, embarks on a shrewd and, she thinks, open-
eyed affair; Massimo swiftly passes on to
younger, sillier Maria (Scacchi). The thinly
sketched youngest, Sandra (Golino), is bent on a
medical career. It's a Euro production: multi-lingual cast puréed in a blender and poured out like
glop. Every landscape is swathed in mist, buildings are clad in crumbling stucco, interiors dusty-
creamy, and the actresses wear wool. There's a
creditable ease and willingness just to let the
women's story unroll, to let their beautiful, char-
acterful faces tell the tale as negative gently turns
to positive. Whiffs of testosterone, in the form of
Simonischek and Castellito (hauntingly desperate as cuckolded brother Roberto), however loath-
some/interesting, are seen strictly through female
eyes. A muffled subplot concerns nuclear fears
and student unrest, but you'd hardly notice. SFe

Threesome

(Andrew Fleming, 1994, US) Lara Flynn Boyle,
Stephen Baldwin, Josh Charles, Alexis
Arquette, Martha Gehman, Mark Arnold,
Michele Matheson.
93 min.
When Alex (Boyle) turns up at college, she's dismayed to find herself in adjoining rooms with
two males: studious, uptight Eddy (Charles)
and obnoxious, neanderthal Stuart (Baldwin).
Stuart puts the moves on her, but it's intellectual Eddy she hankers after. Eddy, unfortunately, is more interested in Stuart. They
become inseparable. Fleming's risqué comedy
has a rather supercilious, hipper-than-thou attitude which makes it difficult to warm to, while
sequences in which the threesome freeze out
interlopers leave a somewhat sour aftertaste.
And then, of course, in opening up this particular can of worms, the film courts suspicion
from all sides of the sexual divide. (For my
money, though, it doesn't have the courage to
see through its bisexual convictions. The film
is, however, notably more relaxed about the
shifting sands of sexual identity than most, and
at the very least it does dare to eroticise a male
friendship.) Simply as a comedy, it's witty and
assured enough to mark Fleming out as someone to watch. TCh

3.10 to Yuma

(Delmer Daves, 1957, US) Glenn Ford, Van
Heflin, Felicia Farr, Leora Dana, Henry Jones,
Richard Jaeckel, Robert Emhardt.
92 min. b/w.
A classic Western scenario, adapted from a short
story by Elmore Leonard. For $200, the sum he
desperately needs to save his land from drought,
a small-time farmer (Heflin) agrees to escort a
notorious outlaw (Ford) to the state penitentiary
in Yuma; holed up in a hotel to await the train,
with the outlaw's gang gathering in force outside, the escort finds himself in effect the prisoner; nevertheless, although the financial
inducement evaporates (he's offered more to let
matters slide by both the outlaw and the town's
alarmed mayor), he insists on fulfilling his contract. It's of necessity a talkative film, with Ford
working on Heflin's nerves in a stream of
Machiavellian banter, but one held in perfect balance by Daves, who keeps the tension strung
taut (especially in the gauntlet-running final
walk to the station) while at the same time elaborating a subtle psychological conflict. The
nerve centre is exposed in an early scene where
Heflin, the dour family man careworn by responsibilities, watches as his wife and sons come
under the spell of Ford's carefree charm: the conflict, ultimately, stems from each man's envy of
what the other has. TM

Three the Hard Way

(Gordon Parks Jr, 1974, US) Jim Brown, Fred
Williamson, Jim Kelly, Sheila Frazier, Jay
Robinson, Charles McGregor, Howard Platt,
Alex Rocco.
92 min.
This is the way the cycle ends, as in the days of
the monster rallies. A Fascist millionaire
(Robinson) is assuring his place in history
through subsidy of a mad doctor's serum, a Tizer-
ish liquid which, when dumped into the reservoir,
will kill off all the black folks within hours (it
doesn't work on whites). Why settle for one blaxploitation star? Not good enough. Why not make
that three reservoirs, then we can have three of
Shaft's grandchildren, three times the action, and
turn a Man from UNCLE rewrite into a movie!
Dully predictable, thoroughly gratuitous after the
first few minutes as the possibilities for genuine
suspense are forsaken in favour of a three-figure
body count and several automobile demolition
clichés. GD

3 Women

(Robert Altman, 1977, US) Shelley Duvall,
Sissy Spacek, Janice Rule, Robert Fortier, Ruth
Nelson, John Cromwell.
124 min.
One of Altman's most enigmatic and personal
films, this study of three women who exchange
personalities (based on a dream of Altman's) combines comedy, suspense, social comment, and
Bergmanesque reverie to weird but often wonderful effect. What really holds the film together
is Shelley Duvall's breathtaking performance as
the vacuous, gossipy therapist who becomes
mentor to the naïve Spacek after the latter moves
in as her flatmate. The third woman is a mute
painter (Rule), fashioning her fears and fantasies
into mythic murals of male aggression and
female victimisation. Although any feminist content is undercut by the advent of insanity halfway
through, and the plot construction is not entirely
cohesive, the film succeeds through its perky,
acute portrait of ordinary people living stunted
lives against a backdrop of consumer-orientated
glamour fuelled by films and advertising. Often
very funny, always stylish, it's a fascinating film
for all its faults. GA

3 Women in Love
(Der Philosoph)

(Rudolf Thome, 1988, WGer) Johannes
Herrschmann, Adriana Altaras, Friederike
Tiefenbacher, Claudia Matschulla.
83 min.
A young, cropped-haired and other-worldly
philosopher (Herrschmann) celebrates the publication of his book – on a snippet of the work of
Heraclitus – by visiting an up-market clothes
shop for a new suit, and there attracts the attention of three shop girls. One of the girls,
Franziska (Altaras) seduces him, then persuades
him to go and live in the apartment which the
three girls share…Thome's film is an amusing

comedy of sexual manners, not so much Rohmer-
esque as fitting with that new breed of German
satire (from such directors as Doris Dörrie and
Percy Adlon) which employs a faux naif stance
the better to probe gently into people's motives,
inhibitions and aspirations. Not for the hard-
boiled. WH

Three Wishes

(Martha Coolidge, 1995, US) Patrick Swayze,
Mary Elizabeth Mastrantonio, Joseph
Mazzello, Seth Mumy, David Marshall Grant,
Jay O Sanders.
120 min.
In this torpid fantasy, proto-hippie Jack (Swayze)
and his mangy mutt are taken in by Korean War
widow Jeanne Holman (Mastrantonio) and her
two sons, a decision that affects all their lives.
This, after all, is America in the '50s, where an
unattached woman taking a single man into her
home is tantamount to shagging him on the front
porch. Mastrantonio is admirably down-to-earth
as a resourceful single parent struggling to raise
troubled 11-year-old Tom (Mazzello) and five-
year-old Gunny (Mumy) on her own; the elder is
worried about not fitting in with his pals on the
Little League baseball team, the younger terrified
of everything from dogs to imaginary closet monsters. As the visionary vagabond, Swayze is even
more metaphysical here than in Point Break, but
going one better is his cosmic canine Betty Jane,
who causes Gunny's irrational fears to manifest
themselves as computer-generated special effects.
Reasonably diverting family drama about kids
coming of age in Edendale, California, in an era
of stifling conformity, but too often spilling over
into cod-Zen nonsense. NF

Three Worlds of Gulliver, The

(Jack Sher, 1959, GB) Kerwin Mathews, Jo
Morrow, June Thorburn, Lee Patterson, Basil
Sydney, Grégoire Aslan.
97 min.
This all-action – if bland – kids' version of
Gulliver's Travels marks an early collaboration
between producer Charles Schneer and special
effects wizard Ray Harryhausen. By the standards of present-day technical expertise, it's pretty creaky, and Swift admirers are not advised to
seek it out; but otherwise it is old-style adventure
of a reasonable kind, with the distinct advantage
of a Bernard Herrmann score. DP

Thrill of It All, The

(Norman Jewison, 1963, US) Doris Day, James
Garner, Arlene Francis, Edward Andrews,
Reginald Owen, ZaSu Pitts, Elliott Reid.
108 min.
Frothy romantic comedy with Garner taking over
from Rock Hudson as Day's foil. The script, by
Carl Reiner, takes a mildly satiric look at the
world of TV advertising. Day is a squeaky clean
housewife who's snapped up to appear in soap-
powder commercials. This enrages her husband
who thinks she should stay at home and do the
dishes.

Throne of Blood
(Kumonosu-jo)

(Akira Kurosawa, 1957, Jap) Toshiro Mifune,
Isuzu Yamada, Minoru Chiaki, Akira Kubo,
Takamaru Sasaki, Takashi Shimura.
110 min. b/w.
Kurosawa's adaptation of Macbeth is reckoned
by many, Peter Brook among them, to be one of
the very few successful efforts at filming
Shakespeare. Translating the familiar story to
medieval Japan, with Macbeth as the samurai
Washizu (Mifune), the adaptation deletes most of
the minor characters, transforms the witches'
scenes into a magical encounter with an old
woman spinning in a forest glade, perches
'Cobweb Castle' high in the hilly moorland where
the clouds roll by like ground-fog, and conceives
a stunningly graphic fate for the usurper, clinging stubbornly to his promise of glory even as he
is being turned into a human pin-cushion by vol-
leys of arrows. It's visually ravishing, as you
would expect, employing compositional tableaux
from the Noh drama, high contrast photography,
and extraordinary images of rain, galloping horses, the birds fleeing from the forest; all of which
contribute to the expression of a doom-laden universe whose only way out for its tragic hero is
auto-destruction. RM

Through a Glass Darkly (Sasom i en Spegel)

(Ingmar Bergman, 1961, Swe) Harriet Andersson, Gunnar Björnstrand, Max von Sydow, Lars Passgard.
91 min. b/w.
Preserving a strict unity of time and place, this stark tale of a young woman's decline into insanity is set in a summer home on a holiday island. It is the first part of the trilogy that comprises *Winter Light* and *The Silence*, films which are generally seen as addressing Bergman's increasing disillusionment with the emotional coldness of his inherited Lutheran religion. In particular here, Bergman focuses on the absence of familial love which might perhaps have pulled Karin (Andersson) back from the brink; while Karin's mental disintegration manifests itself in the belief that God is a spider. As she slips inexorably into madness, she is observed with terrifying objectivity by her emotionally paralysed father (Björnstrand) and seemingly helpless husband (von Sydow). NF

Through the Looking Glass

(Jonas Middleton, 1976, US) Catharine Burgess, Douglas Wood, Jamie Gillis, Laura Nicholson, Marie Taylor.
91 min.
All we get on both sides of this particular looking glass, situated in the dark room at the top of the stairs, is a repetitive series of masturbatory fantasies as a poor man's Catherine Deneuve (Burgess) is beckoned into the hereafter, or at least the elsewhere, by her dead father. The film tricks some interest out of its echoes of countless Gothic woman-in-jeopardy pics, but abandons all in an absolutely risible flame-out pastiche at the end. Full of half-thought-out elements like a pair of incestuous servants, pubertal traumas, and a dose of good old Oedipus, this shallow movie hardly rates the 's' in sexploitation. PT

Through the Olive Trees (Zir-e darakhtan-e zeyton/ aka Under the Olive Trees)

(Abbas Kiarostami, 1994, Iran) Mohammad Ali Keshavarz, Farhad Kheradmand, Hossein Rezai, Zarifeh Shiva,Tahereh Ladanian.
103 min.
In *And Life Goes On…* (1992), the 'director' of Kiarostami's earlier *Where Is My Friend's House?* (played by the actor Farhad Kheradmand) returned to the mountain village of Koker. He wished to discover if the locals who'd acted in *Where Is My Friend's House?* had survived a devastating earthquake. In this third instalment, we see the (fictionalised) behind-the-scenes events that occurred during the shooting of *And Life Goes On…* If this Chinese Boxes format sounds confusing, fear not, for the storyline is simplicity itself; virtually all that happens is that the director of *Life…* (played by Mohammad Ali Keshavarz) wishes to use survivors about their lives, deals with non-professionals unable to remember their lines, and witnesses the romantic complications that arise when Hossein, an extra, decides to use his one and only scene to pursue his troubled courtship of Tahereh, the girl he loves in real life. Get used to the long takes and what at first appears to be an inconsequential narrative, and pretty soon the many levels of intellectual and emotional meaning will work their magic: it's a witty, poignant, illuminating film about the problems that affect movie-makers faced with intractable reality, about cinema's potential as a unifying force, and about the determination and the ability of people to survive tragedy, poverty, injustice and the vicissitudes of love. Sheer brilliance. GA

Throw Away Your Books, Let's Go into the Streets (Sho o Suteyo, Machi e Deyo)

(Shuji Terayama, 1971, Jap) Hideaki Sasaki, Masaharu Saito, Yukiko Kobayashi, Fudeko Tanaka, Sei Hiraizumi.
159 min.
Japanese independent Terayama has a handful of recurrent obsessions, like monstrously tyrannical mothers, flying (as an image of freedom), and the difficulty of losing one's virginity.

They're at the heart of this, his first feature, which tells the happy/sad story of an unemployed working class kid struggling towards adulthood. Terayama's extensive experience in Tokyo fringe theatre has led him to distrust 'realism': the movie is framed as a riotous collage of fantasies, digressions, and surrealist shocks, laced with moments of extraordinary pathos and outbursts of quite desirable rock. It's as entertaining and provocative as Ken Russell was in his BBC days. TR

Throwing Down

(Lawrence O'Neil, 1995, US) Colleen Werthmann, Kevin Pinassi, Jeffrey Donovan, Timothy Wheeler, Scott Shepherd.
90 min.
A quirky genre piece, from a first-time director, about a couple of New York hoods – Scorsese exiles – bickering their way through a drugs scam which takes them to a West Virginia rat-shack. The handheld, improvisational feel inspires loose, funny performances from Pinassi and Donovan, but the crummy soundtrack, lazy violence and inconsistent tone are major drawbacks, and it wasn't a great idea to pin the climax on a (late) mail delivery. TCh

Throw Momma from the Train

(Danny DeVito, 1987, US) Danny DeVito, Billy Crystal, Kim Greist, Anne Ramsey, Kate Mulgrew, Branford Marsalis, Rob Reiner, Bruce Kirby, Annie Ross, Oprah Winfrey.
88 min.
When creative-writing teacher Larry (Crystal) suggests that Owen (DeVito), dimmest of many dim students, see a Hitchcock movie to learn about motivation and alibi in murder thrillers, he little realises what he's letting himself in for. Owen, whose interpretation of *Strangers on a Train* leads him to believe that Larry would like him to kill his wife in return for the prof's disposal of Owen's obscenely senile, tyrannical mother, turns Larry's life (already a mess: ever since his wife stole his first novel, he's suffered from writer's block) into an absolute nightmare. A lively black comedy, surprisingly stylishly directed by DeVito (his début), it thankfully soft-pedals on the hysteria front to concentrate on verbal non-sequiturs and quirky characterisation. If it all gets a little soft-centred towards the end, there's more than enough vitality and invention to be going on with. GA

Thumbelina

(Don Bluth/Gary Goldman, 1994, US/Ire) voices: Jodi Benson, Gino Conforti, Barbara Cook, Will Ryan, Joe Lynch, Carol Channing, John Hurt.
87 min.
An animated version of Hans Christian Andersen's story about a tot who wants to pick on someone her own size. The doe-eyed dame is whisked away from her dream prince, and suffers the predations of villainous low-life offering marriage and more: ugly Berkeley Beetle, an immature runt toad, an entirely unsuitable bachelor mole. Twittering in and out as Thumbelina's helpmeet is an annoying cartoon Frenchie, Jacquimo, whose rendition of Barry Manilow's 'Follow Your Heart' keeps her pure and true. Broad-line animation with little facial expression and poor lip-synching. For girls under 12 only. WH

Thunder Alley

(JS Cardone, 1984, US) Roger Wilson, Jill Schoelen, Scott McGinnis, Cynthia Eilbacher, Clancy Brown, Leif Garrett.
111 min.
Another glob of teen-scene fantasy from the Cannon duo of Golan and Globus. Hunks, chicks and rock'n'roll combine in a modern morality tale about a band who hit the little big time in Tucson, Arizona. The torrential expletives cannot disguise the naivety of the script nor the prudish attitude to sex – sadly, most of the meat on show is ham. MS

Thunder and Lightning

(Corey Allen, 1977, US) David Carradine, Kate Jackson, Roger C Carmel, Sterling Holloway, Ed Barth, Ron Feinberg, George Murdock.
93 min.
Basically a 90mph sleepwalk for David Carradine, the Corman factory's answer to Burt

Reynolds, this formulary automotive action-comedy features an engaging line in absurd Southern-folksy dialogue and a frenzied attempt to ring the changes on the staples of the hot-car genre. A hovercraft duel across the Florida Everglades nevertheless soon gives way to the usual protracted car chase, interesting only for its blatant copying of stunts from numerous precursors, including the Bond movies. The script is a lame excuse for the invariably non-fatal, cartoon-style pyrotechnics, with moonshiner Carradine distinguished from Mob-backed gutrot-runner Carmel only by his stated independence (perhaps as close as you'll get to a policy statement on producer Corman's relationship to the Hollywood majors). PT

Thunderball

(Terence Young, 1965, GB) Sean Connery, Claudine Auger, Adolfo Celi, Luciana Paluzzi, Rik Van Nutter, Bernard Lee, Martine Beswick, Roland Culver.
130 min.
The fourth Bond, marking the point at which spectacular hardware began to dominate the series. Sleek and quite fun all the same, with SPECTRE holding the world to ransom after stealing a couple of nuclear bombs, Bond almost getting his in the villain's shark-infested swimming pool, and a cleverly choreographed underwater battle to provide the icing on the mix.

Thunderbolt

(Josef Von Sternberg, 1929, US) George Bancroft, Richard Arlen, Fay Wray, Tully Marshall, Eugenie Besserer.
95 min. b/w.
Very much an inferior gangster picture designed to trade on the success of his earlier *Underworld*. Sternberg's first talkie suffers from painfully slow pacing, poor performances, and gobbets of excruciating sentimentality. It starts efficiently enough with Bancroft's eponymous hoodlum making plans to murder honest Arlen, old flame of his fur-loving mistress Wray, but after both men end up facing each other on Death Row (Arlen framed, of course, by Bancroft's mob), it grinds to a virtual standstill: endless threats, broken only by uneasy moments of misplaced comedy and much maudlin ado with a mutt (the chink in Bancrofts armour, natch). A museum piece, then, for Sternberg completists only. GA

Thunderbolt and Lightfoot

(Michael Cimino, 1974, US) Clint Eastwood, Jeff Bridges, George Kennedy, Geoffrey Lewis, Catherine Bach, Gary Busey, Jack Dodson, Vic Tayback, Dub Taylor.
115 min.
This was Cimino's only preparation as director for the epic undertakings of *The Deer Hunter* and *Heaven's Gate*, and is separated from them both in time (four years until *The Deer Hunter*) and in subject (a buddy love/honour among thieves caper). The male bonding of *The Deer Hunter* is one connection, but *Thunderbolt and Lightfoot* still more or less merges with its production circumstances. Having written the script, Cimino was given his first chance to direct by Eastwood (for whom he had previously collaborated with John Milius on *Magnum Force*). The likeable result, made for and with the personnel of Eastwood's Malpaso Company, looks like a throwaway Eastwood vehicle, through which he drifts as the 'older' partner, allowing Jeff Bridges to strike most of the sparks and steal the movie as his good-natured sidekick. MA

Thundercloud

see Colt .45

Thundercrack!

(Curt McDowell, 1975, US) Marion Eaton, George Kuchar, Melinda McDowell, Mookie Blodgett, Moira Benson, Rick Johnson.
158 min. b/w & col.
The cult classic of weirdo hardcore, an irresistibly infuriating bad taste whip of raunch and skewed melodrama, like a very horny *Soap*, that quite literally leaves you unsure of whether you're coming or going. Often seen cut, but in the full-length version there's more of George Kuchar's parodically overripe dialogue, tracking the convergence of storm-tossed travellers (a gorilla included) on

cackling Gertie's Old Dark masturbatorium, and
giving a slower fuse to the series of casual libidinous explosions there. But there's also more of
Kuchar's truly brilliant trash-*noir* lighting
through which to peer at the pickles, the puke,
and the polymorphs. PT

Thunderhead, Son of Flicka

(Louis King, 1945, US) Roddy McDowall,
Preston Foster, Rita Johnson, James Bell,
Diana Hale, Carleton Young.
78 min.
Young master McDowall enters his new young
colt Thunderhead in the county handicap and
helps pop Foster to track down the wild albino
stallion that's been tempting the rancher's mares
away. Equine entertainment by numbers. TJ

Thunderheart

(Michael Apted, 1992, US) Val Kilmer, Sam
Shepard, Graham Greene, Fred Ward, Fred
Dalton Thompson, Sheila Tousey, Chief Ted
Thin Elk, John Trudell.
119 min.
Ray Levoi (Kilmer), an FBI agent of Indian blood,
is sent to a South Dakota reservation when an
Oglala Sioux is found face down in the dust. While
his cynical superior (Shepard) leads the hunt for
the killer, Levoi – complete with gum, gun and
shades – clings to power and the trappings of
white privilege. Predictably enough, professional
conflicts lead to personal growth and cultural
reawakening: as Levoi uncovers evidence of conspiracy and environmental abuse, his sense of
betrayal reflects on larger outrages perpetrated
against Native Americans. Apted and cinematographer Roger Deakins focus unblinkingly
on the poverty endemic to the reservation. This
directness, however, contrasts with an over-complicated script by John Fusco, who sets the action
in the aftermath of the 1975 battle at Wounded
Knee and the controversial arrest of American
Indian Movement leader Leonard Peltier, accused
of killing two FBI agents. But while appreciation
may be enhanced by previous knowledge of these
events, the story boasts integrity and serves as a
forceful indictment of on-going injustice. CM

Thunder Road

(Arthur Ripley, 1958, US) Robert Mitchum,
Gene Barry, Jacques Aubuchon, Keely Smith,
Trevor Bardette, Sandra Knight, Jim Mitchum.
92 min. b/w.
Very much a personal project for Mitchum – he produced, took the lead (his son also appears, as his
younger brother), wrote the story, even composed
the theme song – with a subject very dear to his
heart, since it depicts the activities of an
Appalachian community of moonshiners up
against the feds (and more organised rivals) as they
race the highways with tanks full of illegally-
brewed whisky. Cheaply made, disreputable, and
blatantly anti-authority, it's a winner all the way,
what with a stunningly laconic performance from
Mitchum, white-hot night-time road scenes, and an
affectionate but unsentimental vision of backwoods
America rarely seen in cinema to this day. GA

Thunder Rock

(Roy Boulting, 1942, GB) Michael Redgrave,
Barbara Mullen, James Mason, Lilli Palmer,
Finlay Currie, Frederick Valk.
112 min. b/w.
Best known for their limp late '50s comedies, the
Boulting Brothers are often far more interesting
for their more serious earlier work, like this propagandist drama adapted from Robert Ardrey's
anti-isolationist play. Redgrave plays the surly,
cynical keeper of the eponymous Lake Michigan
lighthouse; a former British war correspondent
disillusioned by his compatriots' complacency
towards the rise of Fascism in Europe, he now
peoples his ivory tower with the ghosts of immigrants drowned in a shipwreck almost a century
before. As his conscience – in the form of the
boat's dead captain – forces him to rethink his
romantic ideas about the simplicity and optimism
of times past, and thus to regain his sense of political commitment, the film effortlessly transcends
its theatrical origins, merging dream and reality,
past and present, propaganda and psychological
insight, to complex and intelligent effect.
Beautifully performed, closer in tone and style to
Powell and Pressburger than to the British mainstream, it's weird and unusually gripping. GA

THX 1138

(George Lucas, 1970, US) Robert Duvall,
Donald Pleasence, Don Pedro Colley, Maggie
McOmie, Ian Wolfe, Marshall Efron.
95 min.
Lucas' first film, a reworking of *1984* set in a computer-controlled future world where THX 1138
(Duvall) becomes an outlaw hounded by android
police after rediscovering love, long banned in this
drug-soothed Garden of Eden where children are
created by test-tube. Overall the film is a little hazy,
and inclined to fall back on familiar messages
about humanity and inhumanity after what one
presumes was the nuclear fall. But visually it is
often extraordinary, with Lucas playing on perspectives and dislocations throughout, nowhere
more brilliantly than in the 'prison' represented by
a limbo of whiteness that seems to stretch as far
as the eye can see. White-clad against this whiteness, human figures disappear except for their
hands and faces, others mysteriously appear out
of the blinding glare of nothingness, and one can
readily believe in this infinity through which THX
1138 must journey endlessly if he is to escape.
Some nice touches of humour, too. TM

Tiara Tahiti

(William T Kotcheff, 1962, GB) James Mason,
John Mills, Rosenda Monteros, Herbert Lom,
Claude Dauphin, Madge Ryan, Peter
Barkworth, Roy Kinnear.
100 min.
Wartime tensions between working class Lt-Col
Mills and aristocratic Capt Mason rumble on into
peacetime and the South Seas, bringing further
clashes between go-getting upstart and dissolute
old money in this uneven mix of character study
and situation comedy. Good roles for both the stars
(Mills gets the tougher assignment, Mason the
usual), but even co-writer Geoffrey Cotterell
seemed at a loss in transferring the flavour of his
original novel to the big screen. Lots of effort, but
it doesn't really come off. First feature (for Rank)
of the Canadian-born TV director Ted Kotcheff. TJ

Tibet: A Buddhist Trilogy

(Graham Coleman, 1978, GB)
Three parts: 54/125/52 min.
This three-part 'documentary on Tibetan Buddhist
culture and politics' was four years in the making,
and contains some footage of rituals and daily life
rarely seen by outsiders (it was shot in Southern
India, where the Dalai Lama and his followers fled
in 1959 after the Maoist Revolution). But its framework is a sluggish mixture of *National Geographic*
photography and liberal reverence; the voice-over
is so awe-filled it sounds completely somnolent.
Particularly amusing are some of the more bizarre
juxtapositions ('His Holiness the Dalai Lama is
looked upon by his people as the supreme embodiment of insight and compassion' intones the voice-
over, as a title reading 'The Carpet Co-operative'
pops up on the screen). There is much debate about
'the form and formlessness of the illumined mind',
which sounds pretty woolly. But the narrator
assures us that 'These contemplative gestures are
very deep'. Deeply Tibetan, certainly. CR

Tibetan New Year, A

(Jon Jerstad, 1986, GB)
43 min.
A beautifully shot and fascinating documentary
about the Tibetan New Year celebrations carried
out by the monks at the Bonpo monastery, founded high in the mountains of Northern India in 1966,
a few years after the Bonpos had fled the Chinese
Red Army. Wisely, Jerstad never attempts to probe
the complexities of the Bonpos' religious beliefs,
although the significance of the monks' ritualised
actions is briefly explained at every turn. What
most impresses is the way Jerstad allows the
music, dance, chants, costumes and masks to
speak for themselves, using landscape, movement,
colour and sound to convey a feeling of liberation
and rejuvenation. And the Bonpos' Abbot – articulate, open, and evidently a man of great compassion ('Not all the monks have to take the ceremony
that seriously') – is great. GA

Ticket

(Im Kwon-Taek, 1986, SKor) Kim Ji-Mi, Jun Se-
Young, Lee Hye-Young, Myoung Hee, Park
Kun-Hyoung.
100 min.
Comparable with Mizoguchi's *Street of Shame*,
this account of four prostitutes working from a

snack bar in an unnamed port generated huge
controversy in Korea on first release. The 'ticket' is a bar fine which the women must pay to
their employer whenever they go out to 'deliver
an order'. Madam Min (veteran star Kim at her
career best) tries to run her 'teahouse' with an
iron fist, but she's as doomed to disappointment
as any of her girls: she discovers that the man
she's waiting for (a political prisoner) has left jail
and married someone more respectable. Each of
the women suffers abuse or emotional setbacks
in the course of her work, but Im's stance is
notably matter of fact and unsentimental. Seen
now, the film works less as an exposé than as an
intimate and poignant portrait of a group of
women. TR

Tickets for the Zoo

(Brian Crumlish, 1991, GB) Alice Bree, Tom
Smith, Micky MacPherson.
90 min.
On this evidence, Cormorant Films should have
stuck to documentaries. Dramatising teenage
homelessness in Edinburgh, Crumlish shoots for
Little Nell. Orphan siblings Carol and George
think positive, but lose their flat when she refuses to do a little bondage on the side for the landlord – clearly no man to mess with, since we later
see his heavies hurling an old lady's Zimmer
frame out the door. *Pixote* underdone. BC

Ticket to Heaven

(Ralph L Thomas, 1981, Can) Nick Mancuso,
Saul Rubinek, Meg Foster, Kim Cattrall, RH
Thomson, Jennifer Dale.
108 min.
Unremarkable but fairly solid story of a young
man, thrown into despair by the departure of his
girlfriend, who joins up with the Heavenly
Children, a Moonie-like group. When he comes
increasingly to reject the outside world, his family is driven to kidnap and 'deprogramme' him
back to some sense of normality. All fairly predictable stuff, but delivered without too much
sensationalism, strong on showing how the
apparently harmless cult insidiously undermines
the man's confidence and independence. Notable
for performances of unusual conviction. GA

Ticket to Tomahawk, A

(Richard Sale, 1950, US) Dan Dailey, Anne
Baxter, Rory Calhoun, Walter Brennan,
Charles Kemper, Connie Gilchrist, Arthur
Hunnicutt, Chief Yowlachie, Victor Sen Yung,
Marilyn Monroe.
90 min.
Jolly comedy Western along *Paleface* lines. Dan
Dailey's the greenhorn travelling salesman on an
eventful train journey across the wilderness to
the Colorado Rockies. The rival stagecoach com-
pany is determined to stop the train arriving on
time and places all sorts of obstacles in its path.
Dailey encounters trigger-happy gunslingers and
a doe-eyed chorus girl (Marilyn Monroe). TJ

Tickle in the Heart, A

(Stefan Schwietert, 1996, Ger) Max Epstein,
Willie Epstein, Julie Epstein.
87 min. b/w.
Max, Willie and Julie Epstein could have jumped
from the pages of a Carl Hiaasen novel: three
elderly Brooklyn brothers who've settled in the
spick-and-span, horribly neat and conservative
retirement community that is Florida. They're
suitably colourful characters, too, whether reminiscing about their lives or achieving unexpected success performing on stage at home and
abroad. For what makes them special is the
Yiddish Klezmer music they play on clarinet,
trumpet and drums, surprisingly coming back
into fashion. And while this solid, amiable documentary is, cinematically speaking, nothing
remarkable, the trio's music is for the most part
terrific. GA

Ticks

(Tony Randel, 1993, US) Rosalind Allen, Ami
Dolenz, Seth Green, Virginia Keehne.
82 min.
An ecologically sound update of the classic '50s
bug movie, efficiently directed by Tony (*Hellbound*) Randel and featuring 'the vampires of the
insect world'. Two social workers take a party of
misfit city kids to the woods for some therapeutic communing with nature. Instead, they're
attacked by ticks affected by the steroid fertilis-

ers sprayed on a secret marijuana crop. Cue scenes of scuttling blood-suckers burrowing into their victims and, in one case, growing giant-sized inside a body-builder's steroid-saturated body. Unusually for a low-budget horror film, Randel takes the trouble to establish his characters before the ticks start bugging them, which means we care a little more when they're confronted with pulsing egg sacs and fearsome claws. The suspenseful, crowd-pleasing 'bug hunt' finale rounds things off nicely. NF

Tidikawa and Friends
(Jef Doring/Su Doring, 1972, Aust)
83 min.
A documentary about the Bedamini people in Papua, New Guinea. Aggressive and cannibalistic by reputation, they've led a comparatively secluded existence, farming in the jungle. With little commentary, the film-makers present the principal daily activities of the village, plus more unusual events like a child's funeral and the initiation ceremony of seven young males. The life appears friendly and unhurried, with no signs of the usual boss-slave structures. The photography is lush and uninspired, perhaps something to do with trying not to aggress on the subjects; the result is often a discreetness which can make concentration difficult. It remains interesting, though, for its presentation of such an obviously non-authoritarian society. JDuC

Tie Me Up! Tie Me Down! (Atame!)
(Pedro Almodóvar, 1989, Sp) Victoria Abril, Antonio Banderas, Loles Leon, Francisco Rabal, Julieta Serrano.
102 min.
After the kitschy melodrama of Women on the Verge of a Nervous Breakdown, Almodóvar returns to the darker terrain of Law of Desire, concentrating on the relationship between softporn actress Marina (Abril) and the two men who try to control her. The more benign is her director in the movie-within-the-movie (Rabal), a genial, wheelchair-bound obsessive who leaves romantic messages on her answering machine and beguiles his lonely hours watching her masturbate on video. Less kindly are the attentions of Ricky (Banderas), recently released from a psychiatric hostel and determined to father Marina's children. He kidnaps her in her apartment, beats her up, and ties her to the bed while he goes out to score drugs for her. Almodóvar turns a standard hostage thriller into a grim examination of the power games implicit in marriage; Marina, addictive in all things, soon becomes a willing accomplice in Ricky's fantasy. Almodóvar withholds all comment, and many will hate his refusal to moralise; others will relish the opportunity to think for themselves. A very black comedy in the vein of Buñuel's Belle de Jour, and worthy of the comparison. RS

Tierische Liebe (Animal Love)
(Ulrich Seidl, 1995, Aus)
110 min.
Voyeuristic documentary about people using pets as substitute love (sex) objects. Various sad loners nuzzle, jerk off, frolic and sleep with their animals. Why does nobody here have a normal owner-pet relationship? Why are so very many of the human subjects grotesque low-lifes? Just how much of this is staged for the benefit of the camera, and why? Any film in which the most sympathetic character is a ferret has got to be doing something wrong. Horrible. GA

Tierra (Earth) 100
(Julio Medem, 1995, Sp) Carmelo Gómez, Emma Suárez, Silke Klein, Karra Elejalde, Nancho Novo.
125 min.
Gómez is Angel, a bug fumigator with schizophrenic tendencies, called in to clear up the woodlice infecting a wine-growing district. The first thing he sees is an electrified sheep smouldering by the roadside after being struck by lightning. This is the kind of movie where lightning always strikes twice, a metaphysical melodrama which mixes everything up: absurdism, symbolism, romanticism, surrealism, and any other -ism you can think of. An acquired taste, perhaps, but distinctive. TCh

Tieta of Agreste (Tieta do Agreste)
(Carlos Diegues, 1996, Braz/GB) Sonia Braga, Marilia Pera, Esteves Chico Anisio, Cláudia Abreu, Zezé Motta.
120 min.
Adapted from a popular Brazilian novel, Homônimo by Jorge Amado, that also spawned a TV soap opera, this shambolic, incident-packed melodrama, from the veteran director Diegues, is held together by a powerhouse performance from Braga. Her earthy, big-hearted and filthy rich Tieta returns in triumph from São Paolo to the village from which she was banished as a teenager. Although the source of her fortune's a mystery, she makes peace with her greedy family, wins the people's hearts, and stirs the loins of every man in town. But the spectre of pollution from a planned titanium processing plant threatens her idyllic homecoming. Unforgivably baggy, but so full of life it almost succeeds despite itself. NF

Tie That Binds, The
(Wesley Strick, 1995, US) Daryl Hannah, Keith Carradine, Vincent Spano, Julia Devin, Moira Kelly, Ray Reinhardt, Barbara Tarbuck.
98 min.
Six-year-old Janie (Devin) is abandoned by criminal couple Leann (Hannah) and John (Carradine), and later adopted by perfectly adjusted Russell (Spano) and Dana (Kelly). This second pair, who chose not to have a child of their own, deal with the traumatised Janie with love and care. Until, that is, Leann and John decide to reclaim their child. Domestic horror movies like this (technically efficient, emotionally exploitative) drive a pile into the heart. The odds are stacked in the yuppies' favour. The Pavlovian use of 'pure cinema' works – the rhythm and dart of the camera movements, Graeme Revell's score, Marcia Hinds-Johnson's production design – and the audience waits for sweet closure. Performances are secondary: Carradine, for instance, looking so bored you expect him to yawn, has only to incarnate threat; Hannah models perverted motherhood; Kelly and Spano enact the semblance of a functional couple, caught by the camera in poses of heartening 'normality'. The climax is a would-be tour de force in a half-built new house, reminiscent of the church in Witness. First-time director Strick, to be fair, does more than justice to Michael Auerbach's hyperbolic script. WH

Tiffany Jones
(Peter Walker, 1973, GB) Anouska Hempel, Ray Brooks, Susan Sheers, Damien Thomas, Eric Pohlmann, Richard Marner.
90 min.
Based on the Daily Mail comic strip, a British comedy of the worst type, full of banalities so trite that they don't even masquerade as clichés. Fascist president (Pohlmann) falls for reluctant dolly English model (a performance of laboured effervescence from Hempel), so providing an apology for a plot involving Marxist revolutionaries (all buffoons), denim-clad prince, and a score of nudes. Even Anouska Hempel's Health and Efficiency nudity palls after a while, and terminal boredom sets in long before the bread for the big pay-off turns up as several vanloads of Wonderloaf. CPe

Tiger of Eschnapur, The (Der Tiger von Eschnapur) [Part I]/The Indian Tomb (Das Indische Grabmal) [Part II]
(Fritz Lang, 1958, WGer/It/Fr) Debra Paget, Walter Reyer, Paul Hubschmid, Claus Holm, Sabine Bethmann, Valery Inkijinoff, Victor Francen, Luciana Paluzzi.
101 min (Part I)/95 min (Part II).
A two-part escapist adventure in exotic locations: a despot, a European architect who becomes involved with a temple dancer...It would be easy to fall into the trap that many did over Lang's American films, saying the subjects were unworthy of the director. But here the spectacle permits one of Lang's most formal achievements. Above all, here are two films to be looked at. In this respect, it's not surprising that the project started as a silent movie, which Lang co-scripted in 1920 with Thea von Harbou, and was preparing to direct until Joe May decided to

make it himself. Nor is it coincidence that a central character is an architect: these two movies are like cathedrals of cinema. Eroticism, another perennial theme in Lang's work, is given its most tangible form in Debra Paget's temple dancer. Some may find the films irritating, but there's no denying their formal achievement. CPe

Tiger Bay
(J Lee Thompson, 1959, GB) Hayley Mills, John Mills, Horst Buchholz, Megs Jenkins, Anthony Dawson, Yvonne Mitchell, Kenneth Griffith.
105 min. b/w.
Young Hayley Mills made her screen bow as the Cardiff dockland stray, Gillie, who spots Polish sailor Buchholz killing his faithless girlfriend, then protects him from the law, in the mackintoshed person of Mills père. The storyline may be synthetic (co-scripted by producer John Hawkesworth from Noel Calef's novel Rodolphe et le Revolver), but the players are strong and affecting, and director Thompson makes the most of the grungy locale. TJ

Tiger by the Tail (aka Crossup)
(John Gilling, 1955, GB) Larry Parks, Constance Smith, Lisa Daniely, Cyril Chamberlain, Donald Stewart, Thora Hird.
85 min.
It was once a sure sign that a career was in decline when a Hollywood actor was reduced to accepting a part in a British movie. That was the fate that befell Larry Parks, who'd so memorably played Al Jolson a few years before. As a former communist, he was hounded by the House Un-American Activities Committee. It would be nice to think that the Brits found him a vehicle worthy of his talents, but this soporific thriller adapted from John Mair's novel Never Come Back is nothing of the sort. He plays an American journalist kidnapped by a gang of hoodlums when he gets wind of their plans. GM

Tigers Don't Cry
(Peter Collinson, 1976, SAf) Anthony Quinn, John Phillip Law, Simon Sabela, Marius Weyers, Sandra Prinsloo, Joe Stewardson, Ken Gampu.
102 min.
Quinn, a beat-up ex-sailor suffering from a terminal illness, conceives a plan to kidnap the President of an emergent African nation who has flown to South Africa, would you believe, to undergo medical tests. Quinn becomes fast friends with the President (Sabela), and finally redeems himself by stopping an assassin's bullet intended for the latter. Collinson screws up the pace of this singularly distasteful cut-price thriller in a vain attempt to disguise the script's efforts to ignore, trivialise and misrepresent the realities of social and political life in South Africa. JPy

Tiger Shark
(Howard Hawks, 1932, US) Edward G Robinson, Zita Johann, J Carrol Naish, Richard Arlen, Leila Bennett, Vince Barnett.
80 min. b/w.
A minor but highly enjoyable Hawks adventure, with Robinson in expansive form as the Portuguese tuna fisherman who marries a friend's daughter, only to find that she has lost her heart to his younger buddy. Warners revamped the love-triangle story countless times, and Hawks himself reworked it for Barbary Coast; but the film's virtues lie less in its plot (which, with its protagonist mutilated by a shark, occasionally drifts rather waywardly into Moby Dick territory) than in its jaunty mood and in the evocative tuna-fishing sequences, shot on location on the Monterey coast. GA

Tiger's Tale, A
(Peter Douglas, 1987, US) Ann-Margret, C Thomas Howell, Charles Durning, Kelly Preston, Ann Wedgeworth, William Zabka, Tim Thomerson.
97 min.
Between wrestling his pet tiger and pumping gas, Texas high school senior Bubber (Howell) finds time to seduce middle-aged lush Rose Butts (Ann-Margret). Her daughter Shirley – Bubber's ex-

girlfriend – is real pissed off, and when the pair decide to live together for the summer, she joins her estranged father and his girlfriend. But not before getting her own back on the little prick by making a little prick of her own, in her mother's diaphragm. Before long, a kid is on the way, and the couple's idyll turns sour. Will Rose keep the baby? Will she and Bubber separate at the end of the summer as agreed? Will Bubber release the film's only sympathetic character, the pet tiger who steals the whole show by snaffling a customer's Pekinese? Will they ever stop making this sort of coy sex comedy? NF

Tiger Walks, A

(Norman Tokar, 1963, US) Brian Keith, Vera Miles, Pamela Franklin, Sabu, Kevin Corcoran, Edward Andrews, Una Merkel, Arthur Hunnicutt.
91 min.
Formulary Disney yarn about a tiger which escapes from a circus and prowls around a terrified community, hunted by all and sundry until the children start a nationwide Save the Tiger campaign. Ninety minutes seems an unnecessarily long time to take to prove that a tiger is an American citizen like anybody else. It doesn't even get to eat one of the little beasts. TM

Tiger Warsaw

(Amin Q Chaudhri, 1987, US) Patrick Swayze, Piper Laurie, Lee Richardson, Mary McDonnell, Barbara Williams, Bobby DiCicco.
93 min.
Chuck 'Tiger' Warsaw (Swayze), a reformed drug addict with hangover paranoia, returns to his home town 15 years after a violent family row that involved a shooting and left his father (Richardson) mentally unhinged. The cause of the fight is never made clear: was Tiger having an incestuous affair with sister Paula (McDonnell), or was he just peeking when she was undressing? Was he ransacking the house for drugs money? Only Tiger's mum (Laurie) and ex-girlfriend (Williams) are prepared to give him a second chance. It's a fraught movie that lurches between trauma and tearjerker towards a predictable conclusion, carrying the dubious message that matrimonial bliss and domestic harmony is the ultimate aspiration. Swayze gives the part knitted-brow intensity; he almost succeeds in shrugging off his heart-throb image by looking more pathetic than sympathetic. EP

Tight Little Island

see Whisky Galore

Tightrope

(Richard Tuggle, 1984, US) Clint Eastwood, Genevieve Bujold, Dan Hedaya, Alison Eastwood, Jennifer Beck, Marco St John.
114 min.
This features as nasty a piece of wacko-scum-on-the-loose as Clint has ever faced. Unlike the last three Dirty Harry thrillers, however, in which Eastwood's pillar of the law has been unequivocal, his new creation, New Orleans detective Wes Block, is more steeped in the mire than any major US star has ever dared play. His quarry is only one step ahead of Wes himself in frequenting the jacuzzis, massage parlours, and S/M dives of the red light district; and while the cop/killer doppelgänger game is nothing new, Wes' taste for using the handcuffs in bed as well as out would have choked Philip Marlowe. A film about desire and its control is hardly what one might expect, but then Eastwood has always been Hollywood's most experimental star. And he's still one of the best. CPea

Tigrero – A Film That Was Never Made

(Mika Kaurismaki, 1994, Fin) Sam Fuller, Jim Jarmusch.
75 min.
Grizzled, cigar-chomping director Fuller returns to an Indian village in the Amazon forest – accompanied by Jarmusch, who watches over and interviews his pal and mentor – where 40 years previously he shot 16mm footage (seen briefly in Shock Corridor) in preparation for a Fox adventure drama that fell foul of insurance problems. A somewhat lackadaisical blend of anthropology, movie archaeology and character profile, held together by Jarmusch's laconic good sense

and Fuller charismatic (and mercifully none too gaga) sense of fun and wonder. GA

Tilaï

(Idrissa Ouedraogo, 1990, Burkina Faso/Switz/Fr) Rasmane Ouedraogo, Ina Cissé, Roukietou Barry, Assane Ouedraogo, Mariam Ouedraogo.
81 min.
Saga (Rasmane Ouedraogo), the wayfarer returned, learns that in his absence his beloved Nogma (Cissé), the girl he has waited so long to marry, has been taken to wife by his father. When a rendezvous is arranged between Saga and Nogma, they realise at once that their destinies are sealed. Committing incest, they know that according to traditional law ('tilaï') Saga's life will be called for. Explosive problems are unleashed. Who will be asked to kill Saga? Will he and Nogma be able to flee and avoid tragedy? Emphatically African, despite Ouedraogo's clear intention to universalise his themes, the story is mythic and simple. What is the role of law in society? To what does one owe one's greatest loyalty? If there are rules in social and moral conduct, are they fixed? The film is shot – with an emphasis on landscape – with a rare beauty, using a spare, ritualised style, aided by a bare and expressive score by Abdullah Ibrahim. Unflinching, almost to the degree of cynicism, Ouedraogo presents a fascinating, brave look at the contradictions at work in his impoverished homeland. WH

Till Death Us Do Part

(Norman Cohen, 1969, GB) Warren Mitchell, Dandy Nichols, Anthony Booth, Una Stubbs, Liam Redmond, Bill Maynard, Brian Blessed, Sam Kydd, Frank Thornton, Cleo Sylvestre.
100 min.
This big screen spin-off from the then current TV series (both written by Johnny Speight) traces the Garnett family saga right back to 1939 to figure out just how Alf (Mitchell) became such an opinionated old so-and-so in the first place. In its favour, it preserves the original characterisations at something like full strength and doesn't attempt to stitch three weekly episodes together and pass it off as a feature. TJ

Till Sex Us Do Part (Troll)

(Vilgot Sjöman, 1972, Swe) Solveig Ternström, Birje Ahlstedt, Margaretha Byström, Frej Lindqvist, Jan-Olof Strandberg.
99 min.
Vilgot (I Am Curious) Sjöman here ventures into the awkward territory of parodying the sex film. Though happily married for five years, a young couple believe (and almost make you believe) that if they consummate their marriage they'll die. Ninety unsuccessful minutes later they decide on a suicide pact, taking the predictable way out. It's often leaden (he's particularly oafish), sometimes funny (an operatic sequence at an orgy), and occasionally touching; but the constant flashes of knickers do tend to obscure the film's basic point, which argues that there's more to sex than meets the eye.

Till There Was You

(John Seale, 1990, Aust) Mark Harmon, Deborah Unger, Jeroen Krabbe, Shane Briant, Ivan Kesa.
95 min.
New Yorker Frank Flynn (Harmon) packs his saxophone and travels to the South Pacific island of Vanuatu, adopted home of his brother Charlie. On arrival, he learns of Charlie's murder, and encounters sultry blonde Anna (Unger). Regretting her marriage to raving villain Big Viv (Krabbe), she joins Frank in his investigation, which leads to the jungle where the Bunlap tribe reside. Seale (cameraman on Dead Poets Society, Gorillas in the Mist) makes an unremarkable debut as director on this laboured hokum, which involves sunken treasure and an uneasy mix of violence and humour. One notably silly scene has Frank execute a bungy jump, a sacred Bunlap ceremony rounded off when – complete with funny sound effects – tribal members line up to squeeze his balls. CM

Till We Meet Again

(Frank Borzage, 1944, US) Ray Milland, Barbara Britton, Walter Slezak, Lucile Watson, Mona Freeman, Vladimir Sokoloff.
88 min. b/w.

Borzage's admirers – and who'll not claim at least associate membership of that circle? – will find this movie to be in a familiar case. The writing suggests melodrama at its most mechanical and life cheapening, yet the director infuses individual scenes with such warmth and spontaneity as to ensure that the affections are celebrated even as they're being betrayed. This time the love affair is explicitly non-sexual, since the plot is to do with shot down flyer Milland and virginal nun Britton pretending to be husband and wife while on the run in occupied France – a situation requiring fancy footwork from all concerned to keep the censors at bay. It's salutary to watch the usually tight-lipped Milland transformed into a model Borzage hero, enthusiastic and brimming with tenderness. BBa

Tilt

(Rudy Durand, 1978, US) Brooke Shields, Ken Marshall, Charles Durning, Harvey Lewis, Robert Brian Berger, John Crawford, Geoffrey Lewis, Gregory Walcott.
111 min.
Tilt (Shields) is a pinball wizard. She is also a precocious little squirt whose 14-year-old heart is touched by an aspiring singer (Marshall) who can't take the bad breaks, but can and does take her for a ride as they hustle pinball games from Santa Cruz to Texas. She thinks she's using her talent for 'art' (funding a demo record for him), but all he wants is easy money for more Elvis outfits. Don't be fooled, this is not about pinball, though there's much incidental footage of flashing lights, ricocheting balls, scores clicking over, and the gyrations of the players' hips. It is in fact a thoroughly objectionable movie which subscribes to the theory that behind every weak male is a strong woman – be she only fourteen – and then connives at her exploitation. Outrage subsides into apathy, however, with the wearisome smart-ass attitude and lack of appeal of the two leads; you feel they deserve all they get. FF

Tim

(Michael Pate, 1979, Aust) Piper Laurie, Mel Gibson, Alwyn Kurts, Pat Evison, Deborah Kennedy, Peter Gwynne.
108 min.
An older woman (Laurie) falls in love with her handsome, slightly retarded gardener (Gibson). A downer? Not really, it's triumph over adversity/love conquers all, and not a dry eye in the house at the fadeout. Gibson acquits himself well in this tricky early role, but Pate's adaptation of Colleen McCullough's first novel doesn't break any ground. TCh

Tim Burton's The Nightmare Before Christmas

see Nightmare Before Christmas, The

Time After Time

(Nicholas Meyer, 1979, US) Malcolm McDowell, David Warner, Mary Steenburgen, Charles Cioffi, Kent Williams, Patti D'Arbanville.
112 min.
An idealistic HG Wells (McDowell) chases the villainous Jack the Ripper (Warner) when he escapes into the 20th century – specifically, San Francisco in 1979 – by courtesy of the Time Machine. Once there, they respectively try to protect and destroy a cutesy women's libber (Steenburgen), discovering en route that violence is more at home in our times than gentleness. It's a bookish joke which comes unstuck: after nearly two hours the tension has evaporated, and all that's left is a curdle of jokes and brutality.

Time and Judgement

(Menelik Shabazz, 1988, GB) Doris Harper-Wills, Thomas Pinnock, Anita Breveld, Prince Albert Morgan.
80 min.
Shabazz's first feature since his 1981 debut with Burning an Illusion eschews narrative for the more direct, didactic methods of narrated documentary. A rich collage of archive footage presents a picture of riots, assassinations, wars, famines and invasions, in Africa, the Caribbean, the US and Britain, the saddening year-by-year analysis punctuated by secondary gains like the sporting success of Carl Lewis or the election of black MPs in Britain. Although its anger and urgency may well offend liberal sensibilities, it is

undoubtedly one of the most fascinating and substantial documents to come out of the independent black film-making community in recent years. A cogent, if non-consensual, political/religious agenda presented from the militant 'African' or Rastafarian standpoint, it is also something of a celebration of the range and creative abilities of British black poets (Zephaniah, Iyapo, Williams), painters and musicians. WH

Time Bandits

(Terry Gilliam, 1981, GB) John Cleese, Sean Connery, Shelley Duvall, Katherine Helmond, Ian Holm, Michael Palin, Ralph Richardson, Peter Vaughan, David Warner, David Rappaport, Craig Warnock.
113 min.
An extraordinarily inventive fantasy in which schoolboy Warnock is rescued from a dull suburban existence by a band of renegade dwarfs, who emerge from his wardrobe and whisk him off on an incredible journey through time and space. Guided by a 'Time Hole Map of the Universe', Warnock and his diminutive pals gatecrash history, meeting up with Robin Hood and Napoleon, and turning up uninvited in Ancient Rome and on the deck of the ill-fated Titanic. Sometime *Monty Python* animator Gilliam fills the screen with bizarre images, and directs with a breathless ingenuity. NF

Timecop

(Peter Hyams, 1994, US) Jean-Claude Van Damme, Mia Sara, Ron Silver, Bruce McGill, Gloria Reuben, Scott Bellis.
98 min.
Van Damme returns to the sci-fi genre as a human future-cop charged with policing Time itself. In the year 2004, the dream of time travel has become a nightmarish reality, with criminals and corrupt businessmen trying to alter the course of history. Together with his ballsy black partner Agent Fielding (Reuben), Timecop Max Walker (Van Damme) zips back to 1994 to unravel the mystery surrounding the meteoric rise of Senator McComb (Silver). Walker also has a private agenda of his own. Haunted by the death of his wife Melissa (Sara), he wants to discover the truth about her murder. Hyams is no stranger to large-scale sci-fi, so his management of the massive sets and slightly mechanical fx is more than adequate. His handling of the time-shift narrative and emotional undertow, on the other hand, is thoroughly pedestrian. NF

Time for Dying, A

(Budd Boetticher, 1969, US) Richard Lapp, Anne Randall, Bob Randon, Victor Jory, Audie Murphy.
90 min.
Boetticher's last Western (after a long gap filled with his work on a bullfighting project) is a sad affair, far removed from the precision and resonance of the Randolph Scott films. Produced by Audie Murphy, who takes a bit part as Jesse James, the film looks at the life of an aspiring gunfighter (Lapp), who meets his end through foolish bravado. Not much bravado is visible on-screen, however, as the production values are strictly TV (flat lighting, crummy sets), and the actors fail to give their characters any credibility. DT

Time for Loving

(Christopher Miles, 1971, GB) Joanna Shimkus, Mel Ferrer, Britt Ekland, Philippe Noiret, Susan Hampshire, Mark Burns, Lila Kedrova, Robert Dhéry, Michel Legrand.
104 min.
With the possible exception of Grémillon's *Pattes Blanches*, Anouilh's work as a scriptwriter has always proved dispiritingly leaden by comparison with his plays, nowhere more so than in his rewrite of Arthur Schnitzler for Vadim's horrible remake of *La Ronde*. Displaying much the same sort of predictable playfulness, this trilogy of bitter-sweet romantic anecdotes (the last with a touch of farce), set in Paris between 1937 and 1945, is not helped by direction which drenches it in an ooh-la-la atmosphere of Eiffel Tower, accordion music and toujours l'amour. TM

Time Is on Our Side

see Let's Spend the Night Together

Timeless Bottomless Bad Movie (Napun Younghwa)

(Jang Sun-Woo, 1997, SKor)
144 min.
This dizzying collage of scenes from the lives of street kids and elderly winos in Seoul is in many ways the movie Larry Clark tried to make in *Kids*: a kaleidoscope of broken hopes, blow jobs, dope, petty crime, video games, liquor and rapes. Jang does everything possible to abdicate from the director's conventional role and responsibilities, using *ciné-vérité* to shoot the winos and turning over the scripting of the rest to the street kids themselves. He also shot everything with three cameras simultaneously (one 35mm, one 16mm, one digital 8) and cuts freely between the resulting rushes to minimise any sense of an orderly *mise en scène*. His own moral perspective on the characters is never stated but continuously implied by the juxtaposition of the two generations. Many of the episodes are shocking or disturbing; the film was released in Korea minus 30 minutes of sex and anti-social behaviour, but it can be seen uncut abroad. TR

Time Machine, The

(George Pal, 1960, US) Rod Taylor, Alan Young, Yvette Mimieux, Sebastian Cabot, Tom Helmore, Whit Bissell, Doris Lloyd.
103 min.
Retaining the period setting but stripping away the attack on the British class system, George Pal (who made a much better job of *War of the Worlds*) reduces HG Wells' sci-fi novel to its bare bones. Taylor is the scientist flung forward in time to the year 802,701, where he encourages the peace-loving Elois to rise up against their subterranean enemies, the Morlocks. The quaint time machine and Oscar-winning special effects hold one's interest initially, but the overall effect is one of glossy emptiness. NF

Time of Destiny, A

(Gregory Nava, 1988, US) William Hurt, Timothy Hutton, Melissa Leo, Francisco Rabal, Concha Hidalgo, Stockard Channing, Megan Follows.
118 min.
Sadly, though this sweeping WorldWar II melodrama reunites Gregory Nava and producer/co-writer Anna Thomas from *El Norte*, the emotions here are not so much exquisitely overwrought as wildly over-pitched. Prevented from marrying her soldier lover (Hutton) by her domineering father (Rabal), Melissa Leo elopes on the eve of his departure. Her father pursues her, the car runs off the road into a river, and he drowns. Enter Hurt, black sheep of the Californian immigrant Basque family, who swears revenge for his father's death. Since Hutton has never met him, he transfers to Hutton's frontline regiment in Italy, scheming to kill him under cover of battle. From this point on, implausibility begins to stretch suspension of disbelief to breaking point. After each in turn saves the other's life, they become best pals, and the scene is set for confrontation when the war ends. The showdown turns out to be a reworking of the climax of Hitchcock's *Vertigo*. NF

Time of the Gypsies (Dom za Vesanje)

(Emir Kusturica, 1989, Yugo) Davor Dujmovic, Bora Todorovic, Ljubica Adzovic, Husnija Hasmovic.
142 min.
This remarkable tragic-comic drama, set in a Yugoslavian gypsy community, is hard to take seriously at first. Perhan, the bastard boy hero, seems a clichéd victim figure – patched spectacles, gormless face – wandering the noisy shantytown like a holy fool. His grandmother has healing powers; Perhan is telekinetic, and spends his time moving spoons up walls. Too poor to marry his beloved Azra, Perhan is taken to Italy by the 'Sheik', ostensibly to obtain a leg operation for his crippled sister, but in fact as part of the child-selling Sheik's business, to learn 'traditional' skills – pimping, begging, stealing – on the streets of Milan. His sad getting-of-wisdom is a long haul, but executed at breakneck pace, trilling with music, drama, tears and wry humour. The film has an eclectic look: an off-the-hip semi-documentary style, punctuated with Paradjanov-style miraculous imagery. Anchoring it to reality are the stunning performances by a cast of most-

ly illiterate Romany non-professionals, its precise observation of gypsy life, and its immense humanity. Astonishing and deeply moving. WH

Timescape

(David N Twohy, 1991, US) Jeff Daniels, Adriana Richards, Emilia Crow, George Murdock.
90 min.
Small-town widower Ben Wilson (Daniels) is trying to function after the death of his wife and his ostracism by her socially powerful family. His life, shared with a small daughter in a large, run-down house, is suddenly overturned by the arrival of visitors who are suspiciously keen to rent his spare rooms. At first he thinks they're just eccentric out-of-towners, but when he sees one having difficulty tying his shoelaces – indeed, acting as if he's never worn shoes before – it becomes clear that the truth is stranger than that. They don't seem to belong to this century, shun overtures of friendship, are eagerly waiting for something to happen... To avert the doom facing the town, Ben, with the help of a lovely alien, has to tamper with the fabric of time itself. It's an intriguing premise, well teased out, and with enough mind-boggling twists to keep going. SFe

Timeslip (aka The Atomic Man)

(Ken Hughes, 1955, GB) Gene Nelson, Faith Domergue, Peter Arne, Joseph Tomelty, Donald Gray.
93 min. b/w.
A typically tacky thriller from Merton Park Studios, latter-day home of the British B movie. But the script by sci-fi novelist Charles Eric Maine (later published as *The Isotope Man*) is quite ingenious, hingeing on a nuclear physicist (Arne) working on a secret project who suffers seven seconds of clinical death when attacked by saboteurs, and thereafter lives seven vital seconds ahead of the plot. Briskly competent direction helps it along nicely, even though the time-slip notion gets rather muffled by routine spy larks involving the inevitable impersonation by a double. TM

Times of Harvey Milk, The

(Robert Epstein, 1984, US) narrator: Harvey Fierstein.
86 min.
Harvey Milk, a gay activist elected to San Francisco's Board of Supervisors (or city council) in 1977, was assassinated in 1978 alongside mayor George Moscone by fellow-supervisor Dan White, who had recently lost his appointment and had targeted on the pinko left for his revenge. The murders inspired a 45,000-strong candlelit vigil, and the scandalously lenient sentence given White caused riots the like of which the city had never seen. Epstein and producer Richard Schmiechen expanded a projected film on anti-gay legislation into a feature-length documentary about America's first 'out' gay politician. Charismatic and outspoken, Milk was headed for the job of mayor, and deserves a place in the pantheon of specifically American radicalism. This documentary about his career and the repercussions of his assassination deservedly won an Oscar. JG

Times Square

(Allan Moyle, 1980, US) Tim Curry, Trini Alvarado, Robin Johnson, Peter Coffield, Herbert Berghof, David Margulies.
113 min.
Nail your TV to the floor and lock up your daughters: the message here – run away from home, live in a derelict warehouse, and you too can become a cult heroine – is an appealingly romantic one, and there's a fair sprinkling of magic dust to help the fairytale along. Streetwise Nicky (Johnson), elder of two runaways, metamorphoses from scruffy, disturbed urchin to punk-chic Jagger clone, venting her anger as lead singer of the Blondells. Sheltered Pamela (Alvarado), rich and introverted, breaks out and forces an overbearing parent to see her as she is, not as he wants her to be. It's a world where a black plastic bag is a fashion garment, where a TV-smashing campaign is a serious social statement, where teenage runaways in New York do not fall prey to pushers and pimps, where a jaded disc jockey (Curry) promotes their cause. Socially irresponsible and refreshingly optimistic: a *Wizard of Oz* for the '80s. FF

Time Stands Still
(Megáll az Idó)

(Péter Gothár, 1981, Hun) Istvàn Znamenàk, Henrik Pauer, Sàndor Söth, Péter Gàlfy, Anikó Iván.
99 min.
An impressive period film which portrays the life of college kids in late '50s Hungary. Dubbed by some *Hungarian Graffiti*, this is always much more than a movie about students getting high on Coke (the capitalist drink) and screwing around. Gothár uses historical footage, even patches of pathos and bathos and snatches of rock'n'roll, to probe the painful memories of a generation (his own) that grew up under the shadow of the 1956 'National Tragedy'. Awkward and elusive in parts, it's still a rewarding experience from a director to watch out for. MA

Time to Die
(Tiempo de Morir)

(Jorge Alí Triana, 1985, Col/Cuba) Gustavo Angarita, Sebastiàn Ospina, Jorge Emilio Salazar, Maria Eugenia Davila, Lina Botero.
98 min.
After 18 years in jail, Juan Sáyago returns to his small Colombian home town. The proud sons of the man he had killed thirst for his blood, but Juan won't run, nor will he take up the gun again. Gabriel García Marquez's first original screenplay, though set in contemporary Colombia, is first and foremost a Western. Besides the many pleasures to be had from the reworking of the genre's classical conventions, Márquez and Triana also construct a bleak, caustic critique of machismo and its absurd codes of honour. Vengeance is vain, bloodlust psychosis; amid superstition and self-sacrificing ritual, every man of violence is a loser. While occasionally brutal and prone to overstatement, the film retains a raw, unsentimental power, at once formally elegant and intelligent, thanks partly to Angarita's Juan, a morose Donald Sutherland lookalike exuding taciturn dignity. Simple, but oddly effective and very watchable. GA

Time to Kill

(Herbert I Leeds, 1942, US) Lloyd Nolan, Heather Angel, Doris Merrick, Ralph Byrd, Richard Lane, Sheila Bromley, Morris Ankrum, Ethel Griffies.
61 min. b/w.
The seventh in Fox's B series starring Lloyd Nolan as Brett Halliday's private eye Mike Shayne. Tough, wisecracking and down-at-heel (the opening shot displays large holes in his shoes as he answers the phone with his feet on the desk), Shayne is hired by a venomous old battleaxe (Griffies) to retrieve a stolen doubloon (and a matching shot shows he's collected his advance: the shoes have been soled). Three murders later, the plot has become distinctly *déjà vu;* that's because it's borrowed intact from Chandler's *The Brasher Doubloon*. Cheap and cheerful, this lacks the fine Gothic atmospherics John Brahm brought to his version four years later, but it does have pace, wit, and an excellent performance from Nolan (he'd have made a fine Philip Marlowe). TM

Time to Kill, A

(Joel Schumacher, 1996, US) Matthew McConaughey, Samuel L Jackson, Sandra Bullock, Donald Sutherland, Oliver Platt, Kevin Spacey, Brenda Fricker, Charles Dutton, Kiefer Sutherland, Patrick McGoohan.
149 min.
Justice may be blind, but rarely have courtroom dramas presumed quite so heavily on cultural myopia as this heinous version of John Grisham's first novel. An apologia for vigilantism masquerading as a liberal race-movie, it has McConaughey as small town Southern lawyer Jake Brigance, defending Jackson's Carl Lee after he shoots down the white trash who raped his daughter. The defendant's black, the crime was committed on the courthouse steps, and the judge is called Noose. No wonder Jake's reduced to tears – an unusual legal manoeuvre, but on this evidence, effective. An insulting travesty of Faulkner and Harper Lee, riven with such politically correct confusion that it implicitly equates the KKK with the NAACP, this would be more insidious if it weren't altogether botched. Jake's allies are idealistic student Bullock, boozy old mentor Donald Sutherland and sleazy divorce special-

ist Platt; that they have nothing to contribute to the plot but phoney histrionics is indicative of the fact that they don't have a case, legally speaking – everything is designed to disguise that void. TCh

Time to Love and
a Time to Die, A

(Douglas Sirk, 1957, US) John Gavin, Lilo Pulver, Jock Mahoney, Don DeFore, Keenan Wynn, Erich Maria Remarque, Dieter Borsche, Barbara Rutting, Thayer David, Dorothea Wieck, Klaus Kinski.
133 min.
Under the opening credits of Sirk's penultimate masterpiece, set during World War II and filmed on location in Germany, the camera rests on the branches of a tree, its blossom forced early by the heat of a nearby bomb blast. It is the perfect symbol for the love between John Gavin's German soldier on leave and a barely remembered childhood friend, Lilo Pulver: a love forced by the everyday facts of war. This superb adaptation of Erich Maria Remarque's novel rests on a painful symmetry between the scenes at the Russian front and the central section in the half-ruined home town, and on a typically tough-minded acknowledgment of the irony that the doomed romance exists not in spite of the war, but because of it. PT

Time to Live and
a Time to Die, A

see Feu Follet, Le

Time to Live and the Time to
Die, The (Tongnian Wangshi)

(Hou Hsiao-hsien ie. Hou Xiaoxian, 1985, Tai) You Anshun, Tian Feng, Mei Fang, Tang Ruyun, Xiao Ai.
137 min.
A subtle, deeply moving picture of Taiwanese history seen through the eyes of a boy whose family has recently emigrated from the Mainland. As a child in the '50s, Ah Xiao's life seems one long summer of playing marbles, chasing friends, and listening to grandma's plans to return home. But family illness provides his first taste of death, and years later he has grown into a loutish teenager, torn between filial duty and the need to prove himself on the streets. Hou's autobiographically-based film is as beautifully performed, shot and scored as his earlier *Summer at Grandpa's*, but there is a distinct progress in the depiction of the wider dynamics of society. It is the unflinching, unsentimental honesty that supplies the elegiac intelligence: Hou's quiet style bursts forth, here and there, into sudden, superlative scenes of untrammelled emotional power. It's a brilliantly simple but multi-faceted portrait of loss and the complacency of childhood: quite literally, we can't go home again. GA

Time Travellers, The

(Ib Melchior, 1964, US) Preston Foster, Philip Carey, Merry Anders, John Hoyt, Steve Franken.
84 min.
In spite of some feeble romantic comedy (notably in the android factory sequence) and an occasionally trite musical score, this is an accomplished and enjoyable sci-fi film which contains more ideas than many movies made on far higher budgets. It's about a team of scientists who construct a mirror to the future. The mirror becomes a door, and they get stranded on the wrong side. The middle part has some relatively standard sub-Wellsian plot material involving two future civilisations; but the ending, in which they get caught in a time-trap, is utterly amazing and completely original; it even compares favourably to the trip sequence in *2001: A Space Odyssey*. The cameraman, incidentally, was Vilmos Zsigmond. DP

Time Will Tell

(Declan Lowney, 1991, GB)
89 min. b/w & col.
'We don't have education, we have inspiration. If I was educated, I'd be a damn fool.' Just one thought-provoking statement from reggae superstar Bob Marley, and this documentary offers many more. It's a cut-and-paste montage of interviews, live and in-rehearsal footage, which follows Marley's life from the Trenchtown ghetto to superstardom, capturing simply and succinctly his spiritual and political beliefs, and the bril-

liance of his music. On-stage footage of the earnest, dreadlocked singer predominates, and there's many a passionate rendering of hits, as well as acoustic versions of less well-known numbers. Marley is the film's only narrator, and in heavy *patois* he expounds on Rastafarianism, human rights and the Herb, with forthright candour. It's a moving portrait, and the coverage of Marley's death is especially poignant. This will certainly make those who never saw him live wish they had. LC

Time Without Pity

(Joseph Losey, 1957, GB) Michael Redgrave, Ann Todd, Leo McKern, Peter Cushing, Alec McCowen, Renee Houston, Paul Daneman, Lois Maxwell, Richard Wordsworth, George Devine, Joan Plowright.
88 min. b/w.
An adaptation of Emlyn Williams' potboiling play *Someone Waiting*, about a young man wrongly convicted of murder (McCowen), and the last-minute hunt for the real killer by his dipsomaniac father (Redgrave). This was the first time Losey had filmed under his own name since the trauma of the blacklist, and it shows in the overstatement: the persistent play with clocks, for instance, indicating not just that Redgrave is racing against a 24-hour deadline to uncover the truth, but that his alcoholism was a way of making time stand still by shutting out his responsibilities (to his son, to society). By shifting the emphasis from thriller to anti-capital punishment pleading, Losey also strains the structure almost to breaking point. An undeniably powerful film, all the same, superbly shot by Freddie Francis and conceived with a raw-edged brilliance, right from the brutal opening murder, that accommodates even the symbolism of a Goya bull, with the real killer (McKern) finally cornered and goaded into a murderous/suicidal charge. TM

Tina: What's Love Got to Do
With It (aka What's Love Got
to Do With It)

(Brian Gibson, 1993, US) Angela Bassett, Laurence Fishburne, Vanessa Bell Calloway, Phyllis Yvonne Stickney, Khandi Alexander.
118 min.
Tina Turner's story is like the song: river deep, mountain high – a tale of ambition, talent, desire; drugs, violence and despair. In other words, it's the usual showbiz tattle. This is very much the authorised biopic. It's based on the autobiography, *I, Tina*, and the singer was on hand throughout the production. Not surprising, then, that along with the usual streamlining of history, we get a good deal of first-hand emotion and little critical perspective. It's hard not to feel a twinge of cynicism, for example, when Tina turns her life round with a spot of Buddhist chanting. On the other hand, the movie is surprisingly hard-edged: it doesn't go easy on husband Ike's brutality, while Tina's resilience, her strutting sex appeal and performing heat all come through loud and clear. Angela Bassett shakes her tail feather with aplomb and pins down the singer's gestures with amazing precision. Top honours, however, belong to Fishburne's swaggering, savage portrayal of Ike. TCh

Tin Cup

(Ron Shelton, 1996, US) Kevin Costner, Rene Russo, Cheech Marin, Don Johnson, Linda Hart, Dennis Burkley, Rex Linn.
135 min.
Roy 'Tin Cup' McAvoy (Costner) is a natural born swinger. Such a natural, in fact, that his golf sense by-passes his brain altogether. That's why he's marooned in Salome, West Texas, living out of a trailer, picking up chump change teaching follow-through to golf virgins like psychologist Molly Griswold (Russo). Molly makes Roy want to get his act together, especially when he sees she's with PGA star David Simms (Johnson). Thus, Tin Cup embarks on a quixotic tilt at the American Open and a belated date with destiny. After the perceived failure of the ambitious *Cobb*, Ron Shelton has come up with a light, relaxed return to the popular romanticism of his *Bull Durham*. The sexual sparring is a bit lop-sided, Molly is too much of an onlooker, especially during the prolonged final tournament, but Shelton never indulges Roy's own delusions of tragic grandeur: there's a kind of poetry in his bullshit. This is a

t

wish-fulfilment movie about failure, and Roy's triumph is bitter-sweet indeed. Costner hasn't been this charming and spontaneous for years. TCh

Tin Drum, The (Die Blechtrommel)

(Volker Schlöndorff, 1979,W Ger) David Bennent, Mario Adorf, Angela Winkler, Daniel Olbrychski, Charles Aznavour, Heinz Bennent, Andrea Ferréol.
142 min.
Sumptuously shot and designed, Schlöndorff's respectful film of Günter Grass's epic novel is nevertheless inevitably inferior to the original. The problem perhaps is that it is all too literal an adaptation of the book, which looked at the realities of German history from the fantastic, subjective viewpoint of a child who, by sheer will-power, refuses ever to grow up; the result is that, as the kid witnesses the rise of the Nazis, what we see is rarely convincing in itself, while the complexities of Grass's book are largely sacrificed for eye-catching scenes of the grotesque and the bizarre. Still, the performances are strong and the film just about works as middlebrow entertainment for those put off by the length of the novel. GA.

Tingler, The

(William Castle, 1959, US) Vincent Price, Judith Evelyn, Darryl Hickman, Philip Coolidge, Patricia Cutts.
82 min. b/w & col.
A cultish chiller that acquired some fame on its original US release when Castle wired up the cinema seats with electrical buzzers to give his audiences a little extra shock value. The plot is ingeniously ludicrous: a doctor (Price) discovers that fear breeds a centipede-like organism in the base of the spine. The organism can kill if its grip is not released, and only a scream can do that. So the good doctor experiments on a deaf-mute, the wife of a cinema-owner who only shows silent movies. Castle was a real Hollywood showman, a downmarket Hitchcock whose work shows considerable flair. The scenes in the movie theatre are very striking, and the way the doctor torments his victim – by providing her with visual shocks (a kind of acid trip) and by causing running water from a tap to turn into blood (black-and-white gave way to colour here) – is clearly the work of a sick mind. Castle recalled, 'I was asked by somebody at Yale whether *The Tingler* was my statement against the establishment and whether it was my plea against war and poverty. I said, Who knows?' ATu

Tin Men

(Barry Levinson, 1987, US) Richard Dreyfuss, Danny DeVito, Barbara Hershey, John Mahoney, Jackie Gayle, Stanley Brock, Seymour Cassel, Bruno Kirby.
112 min.
Levinson's Tin Men are aluminium siding salesmen not averse to posing as *Life* magazine photographers to get the foot in the door to offload their wares on the unwary householder. Among themselves, their vision is Jonsonian, and their respect is reserved for the fittest alone. A feud develops between two of them, BB (Dreyfuss) and Tilley (De Vito), over a bumped Cadillac fender, and escalates beyond knock-for-knock reprisals to the cruel seduction of Tilley's wife (Hershey) by BB as revenge. But BB finds himself hoist by his own petard when he falls in love, a depleting experience which has not previously figured in his game plan. Happily, the film does not turn squashy, and allows its salesmen to preserve their duplicity. It's a confident return to form and to Baltimore for the *Diner* man. A terrific cast grabs the naturalistic speech patterns, and Hershey manages movingly to register her reality as the sole bearer of human values. BC

Tin Star, The

(Anthony Mann, 1957, US) Henry Fonda, Anthony Perkins, Betsy Palmer, Neville Brand, John McIntire, Lee Van Cleef, Michel Ray.
93 min. b/w.
Scripted by Dudley Nichols, a Western in the traditional mould, much more predictable than Mann's marvellous series with James Stewart, and a little too overtly didactic in detailing the relationship between a disillusioned sheriff turned bounty-hunter (Fonda) and the young

greenhorn (Perkins) to whom he becomes a father-figure, teaching him the hard facts of a lawman's life and regaining his self-respect in the process. But Mann directs with an impressive classical elegance, and the performances are fine, even if (as David Thomson remarked) 'Fonda and Perkins look like business executives dressed up in cowboy togs'. TM

Tintorera

(René Cardona Jr, 1977, GB/Mex) Susan George, Hugo Stiglitz, Andres Garciá, Fiona Lewis, Jennifer Ashley, Robert Guzman.
91 min.
La Dolce Vita on an exclusive island resort off Mexico is disrupted by a heavy-breathing shark. The standard of this *Jaws* rip-off is lamentable, as the press handout lets slip: 'The crazed shark attacks the hunter furiously – in a scene that is among the most appalling ever filmed'. Everyone and everything competes for last prize in this no-no: Susan George beds down with two shark-hunting dilettantes for one of the most listless three-way relationships ever; the script flounders even more than the shark. 'I am worried about how this is going to read' confides one character in a moment of rare candour. 'But I know it must end one of these days' he concludes hopefully – an act of faith beyond the grasp of the languishing audience. CPe

Tiré à Part

(Bernard Rapp, 1997, Fr) Terence Stamp, Daniel Mesguich.
90 min.
When Edward (Stamp), an established London publisher, receives a manuscript from Nicholas (Mesguich), a French friend and trashy novelist, he's shocked to discover that inspiration for this Tunisian romance came from events surrounding the suicide of his past beloved – in which, he believes, Nicholas was inextricably involved. Once the book is published to acclaim, and Nicholas is enjoying the trimmings of success, Edward seeks revenge by orchestrating a scam to accuse his friend of plagiarism. Despite Mesguich's convincing performance and stunning photography (London has rarely looked so stylish), Rapp's theatrical directing and limp script turns this into an insipid exercise, devoid of suspense and emotional tension. Most torturous is Stamp's rendition of the repressed English 'gentleman'. Stilted and corpse-stiff, you get a niggling suspicion he may just be playing it for laughs. HK

Tirez sur le Pianiste (Shoot the Pianist/Shoot the Piano Player)

(François Truffaut, 1960, Fr) Charles Aznavour, Marie Dubois, Nicole Berger, Albert Rémy, Claude Mansard, Daniel Boulanger, Michèle Mercier, Richard Kanayan.
80 min. b/w.
Truffaut's second feature is now recognised as one of the key films of the French *nouvelle vague*. Based (not too loosely, except in mood) on David Goodis' novel *Down There*, it's a strange pastiche of gangster movie, love story, and cabaret film, with a totally and calculatedly unpredictable plot about a lonely pianist with a past. The story is by turns comic and pathetic, often flashing midstream from one mood to the other, and Aznavour's performance as the wounded hero is a masterstroke of casting. In many ways fantastic, the film is paradoxically much more realistic than most in the way it uses both character and environment. Which is, after all, what the New Wave was about. RM

'Tis Pity She's a Whore (Addio, Fratello Crudele)

(Giuseppe Patroni Griffi, 1971, It) Charlotte Rampling, Oliver Tobias, Fabio Testi, Antonio Falsi, Rik Battaglia.
109 min.
What Patroni Griffi has done here is simply to lift the doom-laden incest theme out of the centre of Ford's Jacobean tragedy, carefully re-tailoring it into a loweringly measured mood piece exactly matching his own extraordinary first film *Il Mare*. A setting of brooding, obsessive melancholy: three characters locked in a personal hell of no exit (brother, sister, the importunate husband to whom she is hurriedly married when incest bears fruit); and a carnivorous battle escalating, not as in *Il Mare* into the despair of soli-

tude, but into a fine bout of Jacobean blood-letting. Directing with breathtaking control over his images (the camera-work is by the remarkable Vittorio Storaro), Patroni Griffi has in effect turned the play into sonorous opera. The voices, given that this is an Italian film 'shot in English', admittedly leave something to be desired, but it hardly matters. TM

Tit and the Moon, The (La teta y la luna/La teta i la lluna/La Lune et le téton)

(Bigas Luna, 1994, Sp/Fr) Mathilda May, Gérard Darmon, Miguel Poveda, Biel Duran, Abel Folk, Genis Sanchez.
91 min.
After the satiric machismo of *Jamón, Jamón* and *Golden Balls*, Bigas Luna here adopts a more reflective approach. Nine-year-old Tete (Duran) has a problem any older brother can relate to, for the family's new arrival has replaced him at his mother's breast. He must invoke the moon for a new tit to call his own – which is where the imposing May comes in as Gallic cabaret performer Estrellita. However, adolescent Miquel (Poveda) already has his eyes on Estrellita, while the lady herself seems sweet on her *pétomane* stage partner, Maurice (Darmon), never mind his impotence. The director sets up symbolic oppositions between the relative youth and sexual experience of the various males, and even the French, Spanish and Catalan speaking participants in the drama – the whole affair being unified by the image of the breast suckling one and all. A paean to a Mediterranean culture, perhaps? That's as may be, but the movie's fundamental problem is its failure to generate the sort of narrative drive that would forge its metaphorical patterns into compelling drama. It's a gentler, more likeable piece than its immediate predecessors, however, and Darmon's anguished romantic is genuinely touching, but somehow it's the shock value of dream-sequence lactation that still succours the strongest impression. TJ

Titan Find, The (aka Creature)

(William Malone, 1984, US) Stan Ivar, Wendy Schaal, Lyman Ward, Robert Jaffe, Diane Salinger, Annette McCarthy, Klaus Kinski.
97 min.
Alien-type goings-on (and rippings-apart) on one of Saturn's moons, with the usual gormless crew investigating the non-return of a previous expedition. The characters do all those things that you or I would never dream of doing – splitting up, walking around in dark rooms, and turning their backs on things. Klaus Kinski (killed off all too soon) and a couple of zombies momentarily pep things up. AB

Titanic

(Jean Negulesco, 1953, US) Clifton Webb, Barbara Stanwyck, Robert Wagner, Thelma Ritter, Richard Basehart, Brian Aherne.
98 min. b/w.
An Oscar-winning screenplay by Charles Brackett and Walter Reisch grounds domestic drama for most of the ill-fated Atlantic crossing, yet proves that there's nothing like a major disaster to bring the most fractious family back together again. Webb and Stanwyck are the husband and wife not getting on, but both are outflanked by the model work in the final reel. Overall, not quite as sobering as the British take on the same events, 1958's *A Night to Remember*. TJ

Titanic

(James Cameron, 1997, US) Leonardo DiCaprio, Kate Winslet, Billy Zane, Kathy Bates, Frances Fisher, Jonathan Hyde, Danny Nucci, David Warner, Bill Paxton.
195 min.
Cost: well over $200m. Disregarding the ethics of such expenditure on a film, this unprecedented extravagance has not resulted in sophisticated or even very satisfying storytelling (11 Oscars notwithstanding). The main problem concerns characterisation and structure. A framing device in which contemporary fortune hunters question a now ancient survivor, followed by a romance between upper-crust but frustrated Rose (Winslet) and a poor but plucky artist (DiCaprio), entails not only a needlessly protracted build-up to the colli-

sion, but primitive plotting and performances. Moreover, the sudden, skimpy, soggy love story leads to a conclusion that's perversely uplifting: if your love's strong, you never really lose each other. (Piffle!) That said, the effects mostly ensure pretty gripping spectacle once the boat begins breaking up. Even then, however, most of the best scenes – excepting a memorably macabre floating necropolis – are so reminiscent of Rank's superior 1958 movie *A Night to Remember* that Eric Ambler's name would not look amiss on the new film's credits. (Bizarrely, however, Cameron neglects the poignant fact that a nearby ship failed to respond to the *Titanic*'s SOS, thus upping the body count considerably.) Unlike its namesake, this glossy, bombastic juggernaut will not sink. Everyone will see it anyway, and so they should, if only to ponder the future of mainstream cinema. GA

Titfield Thunderbolt, The

(Charles Crichton, 1952, GB) Stanley Holloway, John Gregson, George Relph, Naunton Wayne, Godfrey Tearle, Gabrielle Brune, Hugh Griffith, Sidney James.
84 min.
The film that marked the beginning of Ealing's decline into whimsy and toothless eccentricity. A confederation of local clergy and gentry band together to save their local branch-line from British Rail cuts by taking it over themselves (with an engine resurrected from the local museum). An unfunny hymn to British parochial values, bathed in a cosy, romantic glow by Douglas Slocombe's photography. TR

T-Men

(Anthony Mann, 1947, US) Dennis O'Keefe, Alfred Ryder, Mary Meade, Wallace Ford, June Lockhart, Charles McGraw, Jane Randolph, Art Smith.
96 min. b/w.
The best of early Mann. A cracking little thriller about a pair of Treasury agents (O'Keefe and Ryder) required to infiltrate a Detroit counterfeiting gang, it effortlessly transcends its semi-documentary brief (with blandly 'official' commentary) to land deep in *noir* territory, concerned less with the heroic exploits of its T-Men than with personality perversities involved in undercover work (the wrenching imperative to deny friends, wives, feelings, even to the point of standing by while a partner is cold-bloodedly executed). John Alton's superlative camerawork counterpoints tensions and perspectives with almost geometrical precision. TM

To an Unknown God (A un Dios Desconocido)

(Jaime Chavarri, 1977, Sp) Héctor Alterio, Angela Molina, Maria Rosa Salgado.
100 min.
A loose chain of affectionate encounters between a gay magician and his family, acquaintances, and lover, held together by the magnetic central presence of Alterio. Praised for its 'political' treatment and theme, it's actually less a crusading attack on sexual repression than an oblique meditation, inlaid with Lorca's lyrical if equally enigmatic verse, on (homo)eroticism, growing old, 'trying not to be afraid', relinquishing lost illusions and childhood dreams; and a muted but sympathetic portrait of the ageing prestidigitator, as gently elegiac as his own final words: 'Sleep well, for nothing abides'. SJo

Toast of New Orleans, The

(Norman Taurog, 1950, US) Kathryn Grayson, Mario Lanza, David Niven, J Carrol Naish, Rita Moreno.
97 min.
Mario Lanza belts out 'Be My Love' and that's almost all you need to know about this rudimentary vehicle, retaining the romantic partnership from the previous year's star-making extravaganza *That Midnight Kiss*. This time Lanza's a humble Louisiana fisherman who becomes the tenor at the turn-of-the-century New Orleans opera house, where he quickly sets his sights on Grayson, the diva in *Madam Butterfly*. Niven, the show's director, looks as though he'd rather be elsewhere. TJ

Tobacco Road

(John Ford, 1941, US) Charley Grapewin, Marjorie Rambeau, Gene Tierney, William Tracy, Elizabeth Patterson, Dana Andrews,

Ward Bond, Zeffie Tilbury, Russell Simpson.
84 min. b/w.
Ford's next film but one after *The Grapes of Wrath*, obviously intended by Fox as a follow-up in the Oscar-winning social conscience stakes, was generally castigated as a crude, stagy mockery, derived at one or two censorship removes from the play based on Erskine Caldwell's bawdily earthy novel. In retrospect, however, it emerges as a fascinatingly subversive piece, undermining the starry-eyed humanism of the earlier film's 'We are the people' view. Instead of Steinbeck's Joads of Oklahoma, stubbornly maintaining their faith in the American Dream even in the depths of misery, we get the Lesters of Georgia, poor white trash perfectly content to wallow flecklessly in their mire of animal sexuality (when young) or tranquil sloth (when old age takes over). Beautifully realised by Ford, not unlike Kazan's *Baby Doll* in its blackly comic blend of dark sexuality and overheated melodrama, *Tobacco Road* is often very funny, sometimes deeply moving, and always provocative in its acknowledgment of an alternative to 'the American way of life'. TM

To Begin Again (Volver a Empezar)

(José Luis Garcia 1981, Sp) Antonio Ferràndis, Encarna Paso, José Bódalo, Agustín González, Pablo Hoyos.
92 min.
A slow miniature about an expatriate author who, after collecting a Nobel Prize, returns to his home town and rekindles an old romance, this is nothing if not international in its theme of 'one only gets old when one doesn't love' (the film won an Oscar for Best Foreign Language film). Some deft performances do not really compensate for a painless academicism in the direction, and a truly numbing over-use of that baroque pop, Pachelbel's 'Canon', on the soundtrack. And the revelation that the author is suffering from a terminal disease only adds to the sentimental obviousness of the message. DT

To Be or Not To Be

(Ernst Lubitsch, 1942, US) Jack Benny, Carole Lombard, Robert Stack, Felix Bressart, Lionel Atwill, Stanley Ridges, Sig Ruman, Tom Dugan.
99 min. b/w.
Like *Ninotchka*, Lubitsch's comedy was developed from an idea by Melchior Lengyel: an anti-Nazi satire set in World War II occupied Warsaw, centering on the resistance of a Polish theatre company and the ham antics of its narcissistic husband-and-wife stars (Benny and Lombard). It was criticised at the time for its alleged bad taste, but Benny, Lombard and script are all hilarious; while Lubitsch gets much mileage from the idea of role-playing, and his particular directorial tic of timing every conceivable gag around entrances and exits through doorways. It's certainly one of the finest comedies ever to come out of Paramount, the allegations of dubious taste missing the point of Lubitsch's satire – not so much the general nastiness of the Nazis as their unforgiveable bad manners. RM

To Be or Not To Be

(Alan Johnson, 1983, US) Mel Brooks, Anne Bancroft, Tim Matheson, Charles Durning, José Ferrer, George Gaynes, Christopher Lloyd, George Wyner.
107 min.
From the opening moment when Brooks and Bancroft belt out an impassioned and apparently faultless version of 'Sweet Georgia Brown' in Polish, it's clear that this is going to be nothing if not slick. In the event, Johnson has thankfully refrained from monkeying about with either the plot or the tone of the original, and opted for a reverent but nevertheless sprightly remake. For Lubitsch's film is, after all, one of the most perfectly structured and audacious of screen comedies as a troupe of Polish actors try to outwit the occupying Nazi forces in World War II Warsaw; the wit is constantly underlaced with danger, the absurd expedients prompted by mounting desperation. Johnson may not quite have Lubitsch's lightness of touch, but he puts an excellent cast through their paces with great verve, and the charm is as potent as ever. The only weak link is Durning as the Nazi commander, who hams it up rotten and thus dampens down the essential menace, without which the film is in danger of basking in the glow of its own good nature. JP

To Catch a Spy

see Catch Me a Spy

To Catch a Thief

(Alfred Hitchcock, 1955, US) Cary Grant, Grace Kelly, Charles Vanel, Jessie Royce Landis, John Williams, Brigitte Auber.
107 min.
One of the most lightweight (and not even particularly deceptively so) of Hitchcock's comedy-thrillers; a retreat from the implications of *Rear Window* into the realm of private jokes and sunny innuendo, with a Côte d'Azur romance that hinges on Kelly's testing of retired high-line thief Grant, to find whether 'The Cat' has indeed been neutered or is still able to prowl the Riviera rooftops. Even determined analysts Rohmer and Chabrol had to take comfort in celebrating Hitch's 'flowers of rhetoric': the famous image of the cigarette stubbed out in an egg, and the cheeky cliché of cross-cutting foreplay and fireworks. PT

Today It's Me...Tomorrow You! (Oggi a me...domani a te!)

(Tonino Cervi, 1968, It) Brett Halsey, Bud Spencer, William Berger, Tatsuya Nakadai, Wayde Preston, Stanley Gordon, Diana Madigan.
95 min.
Kurosawa regular Tatsuya Nakadai is the ruthless villain who murders the Indian wife of Bill Kiowa (Halsey) then ensures that the grieving widower is framed for the killing. A five-man revenge posse is soon on the agenda in this worthwhile Italian Western. Some deft touches in a script co-written by horror specialist Dario Argento. The well-sustained climax takes place against a memorable autumnal landscape. TJ

Todd Killings, The

(Barry Shear, 1970, US) Robert F Lyons, Richard Thomas, Belinda Montgomery, Barbara Bel Geddes, Sherry Miles, Joyce Ames, Holly Near, James Broderick, Gloria Grahame, Fay Spain, Edward Asner, Michael Conrad.
93 min.
The Todd Killings establishes a microcosm of American matriarchal society, and then tosses in a suitably bourgeois Manson figure to stir it up. Good-looking dropout Skipper Todd (Lyons) hates old age (though the pensioners in his mother's hostel indirectly provide his allowance), hates girls (and screws them to prove what trash they are), and hates his father-substitute teacher (whose liberal homilies are very wide of the mark). Bored with dope of all kinds, he starts to live more dangerously: falling in love with a butch lad (Thomas) just out of remand home, and destroying the girls in a series of thrill-killings. Shear's astounding film goes beyond the alienation, bikini beaches, and campus revolt of earlier 'youth pics' to a hardcore nihilism, and it spells out the message underlying the long Hollywood heritage of misogynistic, latent homosexual heroes. Mounted like true tabloid journalism, as sensational as anything of Sam Fuller's, it's a genuinely provocative account of the souring of the American Dream. TR

To Die For

(Gus Van Sant, 1995, US) Nicole Kidman, Matt Dillon, Joaquin Phoenix, Casey Affleck, Illeana Douglas, Alison Folland, Dan Hedaya, Buck Henry, David Cronenberg.
107 min.
For New Hampshire girl Suzanne Stone (Kidman), you're nobody in America unless you're on TV; indeed, she'd die to achieve small-screen celebrity. Fortunately for her, she's both determined and attractive enough to work her seductive wiles on the local cable-station boss, who appoints her weather presenter – and then allows her to work on a documentary about and about high school kids. Against all odds, she befriends three awesomely inarticulate no-hopers – but there's method to her madness: her husband Larry (Dillon) wants to have kids, so she exerts her influence over the trio to defend her endangered career. If you've hitherto failed to respond to the laid-back oddball appeal of Van Sant's movies, fear not: this is a sharp, consistently funny blend of black comedy and satire on the deleterious effects of television. GA

To Die For

(Peter Mackenzie Litten, 1994, GB) Thomas Arklie, Ian Williams, Tony Slattery, Dilly Keane, Jean Boht, John Altman, Caroline Munro, Ian McKellen.
101 min.
When drag queen Mark (Williams) died of AIDS, hunky, HIV-negative boyfriend Simon (Arklie) throws his belongings into the back of the closet and goes on the prowl. You can't keep a good drag queen down, however, and it isn't long before Mark comes back to haunt his faithless' lover. The film doesn't live up to its billing as 'the first British gay mainstream movie'. But it is the first to handle the subject of AIDS with a comic touch. The script is patchy, making for more laughs than were intended, but the director draws impressive performances from newcomers Williams and Arklie. PBur

Tödliche Maria, Die (Deadly Maria)

(Tom Tykwer, 1994, Ger) Nina Petri, Josef Bierbichler, Peter Franke, Joachim Krol.
80 min.
Young German director Tykwer embraces a panoply of cinematic possibilities. In this story of a wife and daughter's drudgery-filled existence, he finds much light and shade, for, as Petri's put-upon heroine sacrifices her own liberty to the demands of her husband and father, you'll find a Fassbinder-like vision of domestic dystopia, Hitchcockian suspense, the tenderness of a Truffaut, and a whole lot more besides. A compassionate, sometimes shocking, very substantial achievement – with one truly gobsmacking sequence (you'll know when you get there). TJ

Todos Somos Estrellas (We're All Stars)

(Luis Felipe Degregori, 1994, Peru) Milena Alva, Mariella Balbi, Elida Brere, Katia Condos.
86 min.
The Huanbachano family from Lima's tenements all watch the popular TV show We're All Stars ; aspiring actress Rita is, however, the one who submits the forms applying for an appearance. A mix-up at the TV office sends two-faced presenter Mery and her cameraman along to the house, but student Tabo blows the show when he reveals that his absent real father is to be covertly replaced by his mum's naff suitor Nicolas. Degregori's engaging if facile satire has a sit-com plot and surface texture, but its moments of pathos are genuinely felt. The awesome music (dramatic moments signalled by bassoon fares, etc) shows how seriously the director stays true to the story's TV-saturated milieu. It's a surprisingly non-patronising film, which simultaneously exposes and dignifies the family's aspirations and conflicts, ending in a spirit of gentle celebration of their collective indviduality. WH

To Find a Man

(Buzz Kulik, 1971, US) Pamela Martin, Darren O'Connor, Lloyd Bridges, Phyllis Newman, Tom Ewell, Tom Bosley, Miles Chapin.
93 min.
The man in question is not what you might think: he's a doctor, needed to perform an abortion on a spoiled, rich, sex-obsessed New York schoolgirl who gets pregnant after being seduced by the gigolo who lives with the mother of one of her spoiled, rich, sex-obsessed schoolfriends. The film chronicles the attempt of an intellectual schoolboy admirer to solve 'her' problem for her: a lesson in life for the children of the idle rich. It's fairly trivial, but what is interesting about it – in spite of the often corny camerawork and post Simon and Garfunkel music – is the way, without hysteria or moralising – we become inextricably involved with the quest, even going through the abortion with the girl in the surgery. It's a rare thing for most people to have to spend 90 minutes contemplating abortion. MV

To Forget Venice

see Dimenticare Venezia

Together (aka Sensual Paradise)

(Sean S Cunningham, 1971, US) Marilyn Chambers, Maureen Cousins, Sally Cross, Jade Hagen, Vic Mohica.
72 min.

The usual homage to permissiveness (what's left of it after the removal of 11 minutes by the British censor), wrapped up in the usual semi-sociological interviews with sexual pundits and some vox pop. The message urges the reciprocity of sexual response, the importance of doing away with competitiveness, and the reawakening of a genuine enjoyment of sensual experience. Not without its own brand of wish fulfilment, the film lets us watch the young and lean and privileged disport themselves at Dr Curry's sexual health farm, hear them comment gee whiz style on their new insights, and regale ourselves with a sequence of naked doings involving porno queen Marilyn Chambers. VG

To Have and Have Not

(Howard Hawks, 1945, US) Humphrey Bogart, Lauren Bacall, Walter Brennan, Hoagy Carmichael, Dan Seymour, Marcel Dalio, Walter Molnar, Dolores Moran.
100 min. b/w.
An unassuming masterpiece, nominally based on Hemingway's novel and set in Martinique during World War II, this is Hawks' toughest statement of the necessity of accepting responsibility for others or forfeiting one's self-respect – the sum total of morality for Hawks – and the perfect-bridge from the free and open world of Only Angels Have Wings to the claustrophobic one of Rio Bravo. Bogart is the doubting fishing-boat privateer who finally throws in his hand with the Free French because he loves a girl (Bacall, electric in one of filmdom's most startling debuts), and Walter 'stung by a dead bee' Brennan is his partner. Bogie and Bacall fell in love while making the film, and their scenes reflect this, giving To Have and Have Not a degree of emotional presence that is unusual in the 'bite on the bullet' world of Hawks. PH

To Kill a Mockingbird

(Robert Mulligan, 1962, US) Gregory Peck, Mary Badham, Philip Alford, John Megna, Frank Overton, Rosemary Murphy, Brock Peters, Robert Duvall.
129 min. b/w.
Tackling Harper Lee's novel, Stanley Kramer would have hit us over the head with a hammer, so perhaps we can be grateful that Mulligan merely suffocates with righteousness. The film sits somewhere between the bogus virtue of Kramer's The Defiant Ones and the poetry of Laughton's Night of the Hunter, combining racial intolerance with the nightmares of childhood, born out of Kennedy's stand on civil rights and Martin Luther King's marching. In Alabama in the early '30s, Peck is a Lincoln-like lawyer who defends a black (Peters) against a charge of rape, while loony-tune Duvall scares the shit out of Peck's kids. It looks like a storybook of the Old South, with dappled sunlight and woodwormy porches, and Peck is everyone's favourite uncle. But screenwriter Horton Foote does less well by Harper Lee's novel than Lillian Hellman did by Foote's The Chase for Arthur Penn. That movie really was a pressure-cooker; this one is always just off the boil. ATu

To Kill a Priest

(Agnieszka Holland, 1988, US/Fr) Christopher Lambert, Ed Harris, Joss Ackland, Tim Roth, Timothy Spall, Peter Postlethwaite, Cherie Lunghi, Joanne Whalley, David Suchet.
117 min.
Solidarity seen through a Cold War lens, ie. plucky nationalist Catholics vs the club-wielding forces of darkness. The Solidarnosc we get here is against Communism (or, as translated here, Socialism), for religion, and barely aware of trade unionism. Instead, Father Alek (Lambert), a fictionalised version of the cleric Jerzy Popieluszko, enjoys a frustrated flirtation with Whalley while making the odd speech about the aspirations of the Poles. Alek then runs into a whole heap of trouble with gritty local Militia chief Harris, who bludgeons the priest and dumps him in the river before being dumped on himself by his superiors. The script (an international co-production number) sounds like a Lada service manual; Poland looks like the North Peckham Estate; The Zomo (secret police) behave like Keystone Cops; and the attempts to turn Father Al symbolically into JC himself offended even this card-carrying atheist. JMo

Tokyo Drifter (Tokyo Nagaremono)

(Seijun Suzuki, 1966, Jap) Tetsuya Watari, Chieko Matsubara, Hideaki Natani, Ryuji Kita.
83 min.
Deliriously playful yakuza pic, in which Suzuki lets logic hang. Basically just another tale of gang warfare, it's kitted out with plot ellipses, bizarre sets and colour effects, inappropriate songs, absurd irrelevancies (nice hair-drier gags!), action scenes that verge on the abstract, and some visual jokes tottering precariously between slapstick and surrealism. Somehow, it still just about works as a thriller, with (very, very faint) echoes of Melville and Leone. Inspired lunacy. GA

Tokyo Fist

(Shinya Tsukamoto, 1995, Jap) Shinya Tsukamoto, Koji Tsukamoto, Kaori Fujii, Naoto Takenaka, Naomasa Musaka, Koichi Wajima.
87 min.
Tsukamoto's follow-up to the Tetsuo diptych punches (and I do mean punches) into a new combat zone, beyond mere body horror. The director himself plays an insurance salesman whose life with his fiancée is turned upside down by an encounter with a former classmate, now a pro boxer with problems. A love triangle of the '90s: the 'new man' gets body conscious, the macho meathead gets nightmares, and the hip young woman flexes her options and gets her nipples pierced. Psycho-kinetic film-making in the patented Tsukamoto manner: bloody, convulsive, tender and blackly comic. TR

Tokyo-Ga

(Wim Wenders, 1985, WGer/US) Chishu Ryu, Yuharu Atsuta, Werner Herzog.
92 min. b/w & col.
In this 'diary', Wenders tried to relate his impressions of Tokyo to those he had gleaned from the work of the late, great Yasujiro Ozu. No mere travelogue, the film is like a less complex version of Chris Marker's Sans Soleil, with Wenders' ideas fewer and less fruitful than his images. His eye for the bizarre, as sharp as it is selective, revels in long, engrossing sequences shot at a pachinko arcade, a golf stadium, a wax-food factory, and a rockabilly gathering; though his narration never admits to finding them absurd, he is clearly fascinated by the obsessive nature of his subjects' recreational activities. More rewarding (if less funny) are interviews with Chishu Ryu (lead actor in countless Ozu films) and cameraman Yuharu Atsuta, who worked almost exclusively with Ozu for decades. Both are modest, intelligent and very likeable, but Atsuta steals the show, shedding valuable light on Ozu's unique, contemplative camera style, and offering a profoundly moving personal valediction to the man himself. GA

Tokyo Kyodai

(Jun Ichikawa, 1994, Jap) Naoto Ogata, Urara Awata, Toru Tezuka.
92 min.
The Ozu-esque title (it means 'Tokyo Siblings') is supposed to alert you to the fact that this picture is about the end of a brother-sister relationship is yet another 'homage' to the old master. What it lacks, of course, is the least hint of Ozu's wry and playful humour, along with anything to match his formal skills and worldly wisdom. The characters are young people who have lost their parents. Yoko waits hand and foot on her older brother Kenichi, who sells second-hand books, the deeply repressed erotic bond between them is shattered when Yoko finds a man she wants to marry. Most viewers will want to give the selfish and complacent Kenichi a good kicking long before this lugubrious movie grinds to its close. TR

Tokyo Olympiad 1964

(Kon Ichikawa, 1965, Jap)
130 min.
The director of Fires on the Plain and An Actor's Revenge didn't seem the obvious choice to mastermind a record of the 1964 Olympics, and in the event Ichikawa's film didn't please all the people all the time. Most riled were probably the bona fide sports fans, because Ichikawa's attitude to the games and participants seems quizzical rather than committed, sensual rather than gutsy. Least riled were probably Ichikawa fans, because

the unpredictable humour, the 'bold delicacy' of the visuals, and the occasional real intensity, are all quite consistent with his fiction films. The only sustained 'performance' is Abebe Bikila's triumph in the marathon, but the rest is funny, sexy, beautiful, or atmospheric enough to give a lot of pleasure to the open-eyed. TR

Tokyo Pop

(Fran Rubel Kazui, 1988, US) Carrie Hamilton, Yutaka Tadokoro, Taiji Tonoyama, Tetsuro Tamba, Daisuke Oyama, Hiroshi Kabayashi, Hiroshi Sugita.
99 min.
Rock'n'roll proves an international language in this amiable but naff musical travelogue. Hamilton's an aspiring artiste whose career's going nowhere in New York, so she accepts a friend's invite to join her in the Japanese capital, where local muso Tadokoro reckons she's the perfect frontwoman for his new beat combo. Tokyo itself comes over rather better than the songs devised by this cross-cultural supergroup. TJ

Tokyo Story (Tokyo Monogatari) 100 (100)

(Yasujiro Ozu, 1953, Jap) Chishu Ryu, Chiyeko Higashiyama, Setsuko Hara, So Yamamura, Kyoko Kagawa.
139 min. b/w.
Ozu's best known (because most widely distributed) movie is a very characteristic study of the emotional strains within a middle class Japanese family that has come to Tokyo from the country and dispersed itself. All that happens in dramatic terms is that the family grandparents arrive in Tokyo to visit their various offspring, and grow painfully aware of the chasms that exist between them and their children; only their daughter-in-law, widowed in the war, is pleased to see them. Ozu's vision, almost entirely un-inflected by tics and tropes of 'style' by this stage in his career, is emotionally overwhelming, and arguably profound for any engaged viewer; it is also formally unmatched in Western popular cinema. TR

To Live

see Ikiru

To Live (Huozhe)

(Zhang Yimou, 1994, HK) Ge You, Gong Li, Niu Ben, Guo Tao, Jiang Wu, Ni Dahong, Liu Tianchi, Zhang Lu.
125 min.
China in the mid-'40s: relatively well off until his gambling results in the loss of the family house, Xu Fugui (Ge You) is temporarily abandoned by his pregnant wife Jiazhen (Gong Li) and their deaf-mute daughter Fengxia. Poverty, however, brings him to his senses, and when, working as a travelling shadow-puppeteer, he finds himself embroiled in the Civil War. But as Mao's regime tightens its grip with ever sterner strictures, it becomes harder and harder merely to survive. A straight synopsis may make Zhang Yimou's film sound similar to The Blue Kite, or even, perhaps, Farewell My Concubine. Certainly it shares with these films both a mix of the personal and the political, and a panoramic view of Chinese life. There, however, the similarities stop. For Zhang's purpose is less to show the oppressive iniquities of Mao's era than to evoke the optimistic spirit that allowed people to survive it. Accordingly, the film is lighter in tone, less provocative, complex and tough, even leavening scenes of misfortune with surprising incursions of black comedy. GA

To Live and Die in L.A.

(William Friedkin, 1985, US) William L Petersen, Willem Dafoe, John Pankow, Debra Feuer, John Turturro, Darlanne Fluegel, Dean Stockwell, Steve James, Robert Downey.
116 min.
Dafoe is an LA supercrook, forging dollar bills for a city whose sole form of social intercourse resides in the getting, counting, and spending of large sums of money. This is a city (photographed by Robby Müller with the same luminosity he brought to Paris, Texas) where everyone is on the take, and that includes the two FBI agents (Petersen and Pankow) who are out to break Dafoe by any means. It all goes horribly wrong when they decide to pull their own heist

in order to secure the necessary funds to stay in hot pursuit. Friedkin plays it as brutal and cynical as he ever did with The French Connection; and this time the car chase takes place on a six-lane freeway at the height of the rush hour, going against the traffic. Today, the play-dirty antics of Popeye Doyle probably look rather dated; God knows what state we will have to get into before all this looks tame. CPea

To Live in Freedom

(Simon Louvish, 1974, GB)
54 min.
A progressive rather than militant film on the Israel-Palestine problem. It does not claim to know the solution, nor does it take a dogmatic stance in presenting the issues. It sees Israel as a permanent State, but calls into question the values that maintain the State under the present conditions. The film-makers argue for a real class-oriented revolution, a revolution which must necessarily involve both Israelis and Palestinians. Where Golda Meir and her generation naturally have to justify their presence in Israel, these young film-makers go much further by questioning and analysing the very quality of life, as well as the official line the establishment clings to. The myth of Israel is exploded. JPi

Tom and Jerry: The Movie

(Phil Roman, 1992, US) voices: Richard Kind, Dana Hill, Anndi McAfee, Henry Gibson.
84 min.
A severely dull animated feature. After a brief reprise of the duo's antics, they talk...then become chums! The cutie-pie script has them leave the white-frame house to unite orphan Robyn Starling with her long-lost dad. Spot the sources: Robyn's aunt has traces of Cruella de Ville and Snow White's stepmum; lawyer Lickboot could be a George Sanders pastiche; Dr Applecheek behaves uncannily like the doctor from Altman's The Long Goodbye (and, surprise, the voice is Henry Gibson's). Very poor. WH

Tom & Viv

(Brian Gilbert, 1994, GB) Willem Dafoe, Miranda Richardson, Rosemary Harris, Tim Dutton, Nickolas Grace, Geoffrey Bayldon, Clare Holman, Philip Locke, John Savident,Joanna McCallum.
125 min.
Having eloped with eccentric aristo Vivienne Haigh-Wood, TS Eliot soon discovers that not only is his wife mentally unstable, but that she's afflicted with a hormonal imbalance causing her to menstruate almost continuously. This is tough on the shy, painfully repressed poet, but so, too, is Viv's increasingly bizarre behaviour, which culminates in a knife attack on the novelist Virginia Woolf. This is hardly the most flattering portrait of the author of 'The Waste Land', yet the emphasis on Viv's extreme behaviour often feels like special pleading, and Tom's precise role in her committal is fudged. Expanded from Michael Hastings' play, the film is too spacially and emotionally constricted to achieve its ends, a problem compounded by flat direction and stilted dialogue. Dafoe concentrates on reproducing Eliot's absurd diction, while the usually faultless Richardson overacts, making Viv's antics appear ridiculous rather than pitiable. NF

Tombes du Ciel (Lost in Transit)

(Philippe Lioret, 1993, Fr) Jean Rochefort, Michel Ganz, Marisa Paredes, Ticky Holgado, Laura del Sol.
91 min.
A socially concerned comedy tailor-made for the hangdog persona of Jean Rochefort. A well-to-do iconographer (Rochefort) is trapped in the transit zone of Charles de Gaulle airport, Paris, where he meets and gets to like a wacky band of displaced persons. Making their households in the corridors, engine rooms and back exits of the airport are a kid from Guinea, an ex-mercenary, an Ethiopian who speaks only an ancient lost language, a political refugee, and more. First-time director Lioret tackles the clichés head on, and thanks to fine performances creates a likeable if lightweight romantic drama. WH

Tomb of Ligeia, The

(Roger Corman, 1964, GB) Vincent Price, Elizabeth Shepherd, John Westbrook, Oliver Johnston, Derek Francis, Richard Vernon, Ronald Adam.
81 min.
After his long sequence of Poe movies filmed in various studio interiors, Corman decided that The Tomb of Ligeia demanded a change of style and emphasis. Consequently he shot it on a number of highly effective English locations, having commissioned Robert Towne (who subsequently wrote Chinatown) to script it. The result is one of the best in the whole series, an ambiguous, open-ended film which features one of Vincent Price's most decisive performances. There is a long early sequence involving a long monologue by Verden Fell (Price), juxtaposed against Rowena (Shepherd) climbing a gothic tower, which has a syntactic originality that has rarely been equalled in horror movies. But even more importantly, Corman – like Michael Reeves in Witchfinder General – utilised the English landscape in a way that Hammer had often neglected. DP

Tom Brown's Schooldays

(Gordon Parry, 1951, GB) John Howard Davies, Robert Newton, Diana Wynyard, Hermione Baddeley, Kathleen Byron, James Hayter, John Forrest, John Charlesworth, Michael Hordern, Max Bygraves, Rachel Gurney.
96 min. b/w.
Master Howard Davies (later a successful BBC producer who worked on the early Monty Python series) may be a precursor of the Mark Lester school of terribly English moppetry, but he doesn't detract too much from this solidly carpentered third screen version of Thomas Hughes' famous Rugby story – atmospherically shot on location in the old school itself. Newton restrains himself admirably as the ultimately good-hearted headmaster, but it's Forrest's show as the caddish bully Flashman, dispensing ignominy with a curl of the lip and a dash of hauteur before his eventual and not unexpected comeuppance. TJ

Tombstone

(George P Cosmatos, 1993, US) Kurt Russell, Val Kilmer, Sam Elliott, Bill Paxton, Powers Boothe, Michael Biehn, Joanna Pacula.
129 min.
The old story of how Wyatt Earp and Doc Holliday took on the Clanton mob and brought law and order to the town of Tombstone. This version fields an impressive supporting cast (in addition to the above, Michael Rooker, Stephen Lang, Charlton Heston, Harry Carey Jr, Billy Zane and Jason Priestley), a screenplay by Kevin Jarre which is at least on speaking terms with history, and decidedly no-frills direction by George (Rambo) Cosmatos. Kilmer makes a surprisingly effective and effete Holliday, but Russell lacks the stature for Earp – Sam Elliott as his older brother Virgil suggests a better movie. There's a misguided romantic subplot and the ending rather sprawls, but mostly this is rootin', tootin' entertainment with lots of authentic facial hair. TCh

Tom Horn

(William Wiard, 1980, US) Steve McQueen, Linda Evans, Richard Farnsworth, Billy Green Bush, Slim Pickens, Peter Canon, Elisha Cook, Geoffrey Lewis.
97 min.
A severely beautiful Western based on the life of a semi-legendary cowboy who served as a cavalry scout, was then hired to wage secret war on Wyoming rustlers, and was eventually hanged by a society which had outgrown his maverick values. McQueen's performance is all the more affecting (his penultimate film) now that we know he was suffering from an incurable cancer. But the film's glaring production problems – rewrites to Thomas McGuane's script, change of director (it was started by James William Guercio), extensive re-editing – ruin what might otherwise have been an extraordinarily eloquent political fable. CPe

Tom Jones

(Tony Richardson, 1963, GB) Albert Finney, Susannah York, Hugh Griffith, Edith Evans, Joan Greenwood, Diane Cilento, George Devine, Joyce Redman, David Warner, David Tomlinson, John Moffatt, Wilfrid Lawson, Freda Jackson.
128 min.

Too risky for penny-pinching British financiers, *Tom Jones* was rescued by United Artists, and its massive success released a flood of American money into the British film industry. Richardson's England is full of 18th century atmospherics, but its big attraction was the bawdy licence it allowed '60s permissiveness. Osborne's courageous hatchet job on Fielding's 1,000 page classic novel and Finney's gutsy performance add up to produce an enjoyable piece of irreverent entertainment. RMy

Tommy

(Ken Russell, 1975, GB) Ann-Margret, Oliver Reed, Roger Daltrey, Elton John, Eric Clapton, Keith Moon, Jack Nicholson, Robert Powell, Tina Turner.
108 min.
Although in criticising Russell's lack of discipline people tend to forget that he was virtually the first film-maker to escape the strictures of realism and telestyle that have dogged British cinema since the heyday of Powell and Pressburger, it must nevertheless be admitted that watching his more excessive movies tends to be a wearisome experience. The Who's ludicrous rock opera was in fact tailor-made for the baroque, overblown images and simplistic symbolism of Russell's style, which only means that this is both the movie in which he is most faithful to the ideas and tone of his material, and one of his very worst films. GA

Tommy Boy

(Peter Segal, 1995, US) Chris Farley, David Spade, Bo Derek, Dan Aykroyd, Brian Dennehy, Julie Warner, Sean McCann.
97 min.
When auto magnate Tommy Snr (Dennehy) dies in the arms of his scheming new bride (Derek), she persuades the board to put the factory up for sale – jeopardising the livelihood of the entire town. Only Tommy Boy (Farley) can save them, if he and Richard (Spade) can drum up enough business on a last desperate road trip. But Tommy takes to sales like a duck to soup, and the town looks to be dead in the water. This cinematic folly from the *Saturday Night Live* stable is enough to make you yearn for the golden days of John Belushi and Dan Aykroyd. Farley is the physical pratfaller, a clumsy oaf with the brawn of a bison and a brain to match; Spade the slimline sidekick with a long line in snide. It's some indication of the wit involved that Farley is reduced to cracking fat jokes at his own expense. TCh

Tommy Steele Story, The (aka Rock Around the World)

(Gerard Bryant, 1957, GB) Tommy Steele, Lisa Daniely, Patrick Westwood, Hilda Fenemore, Dennis Price.
82 min. b/w.
This is one of the few biographical movies in which the subject has the gall to play himself. From humble beginnings in Bermondsey, young Thomas discovers his seemingly limitless talent, joins the Merchant Navy (his only sensible move), then finds fame and fortune in the coffee bars of Soho. All complete hokum, of course, but often unintentionally hilarious. Steele is so cute and wholesome you can't help fantasising that something horrible and sordid was going on behind the scenes. Worth seeing for purely kitsch reasons. RS

Tommy Tricker and the Stamp Traveller

(Michael Rubbo, 1988, Can) Lucas Evans, Anthony Rogers, Jill Stanley, Andrew Whitehead.
105 min.
Rubbo's made-for-kids philatelic tale starts with young sting-merchant Tommy Tricker smooth-talking his wimpish pal Ralph out of his father's most treasured stamp. In the doghouse, Ralph and his sister Nancy spot the rarity in the local stamp shop. No chance, $600 price tag, but the dealer offers the pair a dusty old album as solace. Lo and behold, out pops a hand-written letter dated 1928, stating the whereabouts and means of recovering several old and extremely valuable stamps. Ralph is reduced to pinhead size (by way of some fairly clever animation), planted firmly on a current 1st class stamp, and popped in a letter-box. En route to his final destination, the film

gets bogged down in various worldwide locations: the whole thing could quite easily be condensed into a 45-minute TV short. DA

Tomorrow Never Comes

(Peter Collinson, 1977, Can/GB) Oliver Reed, Susan George, Raymond Burr, John Ireland, Stephen McHattie, Donald Pleasence, Paul Koslo, John Osborne.
109 min.
Young Frank (McHattie) returns from out-of-town to learn that his girl Janie (George) has given herself to a local big-shot (Osborne) in return for a teak-veneered cabana in the grounds of his luxury hotel. A nasty blow on the head in a bar fight has the effect of a lobotomy, and mild-mannered Frank is transformed into a twitchy psychopath. He holds Janie hostage in the cabana, and demands that her white-suited seducer make an appearance. Ollie Reed lumbers into the picture as a cheerless policeman who looks for the non-violent solution in the face of small-town political corruption. A drab, lightweight film with an extremely overweight cast from whom Collinson has extracted embarrassingly eccentric performances, notably Raymond Burr as a police chief who plays with clockwork toys. But what else can you do with such a crass script? JS

Tomorrow Never Dies

(Roger Spottiswoode, 1997, GB/US) Pierce Brosnan, Jonathan Pryce, Michelle Yeoh, Teri Hatcher, Joe Don Baker, Desmond Llewelyn, Geoffrey Palmer, Judi Dench, Samantha Bond, Terence Rigby.
119 min.
Brosnan's second outing as agent 007. Media mogul Elliot Carver wants to start a war to ensure exclusive broadcast rights. He must be stopped (that's about it, for plot). The first half builds promisingly, adding depth to Bond's character, along with the usual mix of violence, humour and gadgetry, but after the amazing carpark car-chase, things start to go awry, as 007 resorts to standard tactics, waving weaponry about without bothering to dodge the bullets. All very entertaining, but not really Bond. This is a pity, because by then girl A (Hatcher, lacklustre) has been replaced by girl B, Wai Lin (Yeoh, who's such a great foil for the hero that she's worth a franchise of her own). Sadly, if her role is badly underwritten, the script problems are most evident in Pryce's Carver, who peaks too early and doesn't get nasty enough lines to elicit boos and hisses. Luckily, Brosnan, whose Bond is easily the best since Connery's, is more than strong enough to paper over the cracks. Flawed, but fantastic fun all the same. NK

Tomorrow's Warrior (Avrianos Polemistis)

(Michael Papas, 1981, Cyp) Christos Zannides, Aristodemos Fessas, Dimitri Andreas, Jenny Lipman, Joanna Shafkali.
95 min.
Set in Cyprus at the time of the 1974 Turkish invasion, this forms an impassioned and unashamedly partisan sequel to Michael Papas' previous saga of that country's troubled history, *The Private Right*. But 'tomorrow's warrior' unfortunately turns out to be a tousle-haired, insufferably winsome Greek Cypriot boy who imposes a confused, child's-eye perspective on events, not helped by hectic cutting and interminable reaction shots of his innocent, bewildered little face. What's worse, Papas opts for easy emotionalism in the future hero's heart-tugging devotion to his old grandpa, naïve painter of peasant lore, who exudes quiet dignity and will, of course, be killed off by wicked Turks. Sticky-sweet as a slice of baklava, this is highly resistible fare. SJo

Tom Sawyer

(Don Taylor, 1973, US) Johnny Whitaker, Celeste Holm, Warren Oates, Jeff East, Jodie Foster, Henry Jones, Dub Taylor.
103 min.
A *Reader's Digest* production, with songs by the Sherman brothers of Disney fame, and surprisingly enjoyable. Highly professional old-style movie-making which has the wit to ditch its set piece white-picket-fenced Southern town, its inhabitants, and even Tom himself, to fill the screen with dazzling helicopter shots of the Mississippi River (complete with Howard Keel-

style ballads) whenever it can. Of course there are the statutory moments of schmaltz, the Indian bogeyman, and a marked absence of blacks (in a Southern town?). Nice, if over-detailed, performance from Warren Oates as Muff Potter.

Tom Thumb

(George Pal, 1958, US) Russ Tamblyn, June Thorburn, Peter Sellers, Terry-Thomas, Alan Young, Jessie Matthews, Bernard Miles, Ian Wallace.
98 min.
A lively predecessor to *Honey, I Shrunk the Kids*, loosely based on the Brothers Grimm tale, but bearing a remarkable resemblance to *Pinocchio*. Tamblyn is the five-inch child bestowed on a peasant couple (Miles and Matthews) by the Forest Queen. All too soon, Tom falls in with bad company: Terry-Thomas and Sellers, relishing their own villainy. Pal, an architecture student whose first films were self-styled 'Puppetoons', put his training to good use here, cleverly meshing miniatures, giant props and animation techniques to create an impression of the world as Tom sees it. With a good deal of unforced humour, acrobatic dancing, and some likeable songs (a couple sung by Peggy Lee), it makes for pleasant entertainment. TCh

Tongpan

(Euthana Mukdasanit/Surachai Janthimathorn, 1977, Thai)
65 min. b/w.
The first serious movie from Thailand is a dramatised reconstruction of events in 1973-74, the one time when Thai peasants had been invited to participate in discussions about planning issues affecting them. It's a low-key, sombre film, spelling out the inadequacies of the consultation mechanisms as clearly as it reveals the staggering poverty of the peasants themselves. The film was completed outside Thailand after the military coup of 1976, and it stands as a chastening primer on the disgraceful state of Thai politics. TR

Tongues Untied

(Marlon T Riggs, 1989, US) Kerrigan Black, Blackberri, Bernard Brannier, Gerald Davis.
55 min.
A polemical, avowedly personal video documentary on the American black gay experience. It's a bit of an ordeal: a barrage of images, newsreel, stories narrated to camera, poetry readings, 'Vogue' dance performance, voices and rap, which examines, with savage but poetic candour, those questions of identity, culture, history and self-expression that are most pertinent to black gays and lesbians. Are they gay first, or black first? Why have they little or no voice in the American gay movement? Riggs takes great risks: he challenges and threatens to offend all sensibilities here, gay or straight, black or white, but does so with remarkable composure, humour and positive attitude. At heart, it's a celebratory film which buzzes with intelligence, unashamed emotion, adrenalin, and that strange tenderness forged in suffering. As a character says in the film: 'If in America a black is the lowest of the low, what is a gay black?' Riggs says to black gays: stand up, speak out, tell your story; to others: listen. WH

Toni

(Jean Renoir, 1934, Fr) Charles Blavette, Célia Montalvan, Jenny Hélia, Max Dalban, Edouard Delmont, Andrex.
95 min. b/w.
A melodrama about love and sex, jealousy and murder – the sort of staples that have kept the cinema going for ninety years or so – but Renoir invests it with a sense of character and place that gives it an unusually blunt and sensual impact. Neither romanticising his workers nor turning them into rallying-points, he accepts them as they are and follows them where they go. The plot is based on a real crime that occurred during the '20s in Martigues, a small town in the South of France where the film was shot. Jacques Mortier, an old friend of Renoir's who was the local police chief, assembled the facts, and Renoir wrote the script with another friend, art critic Carl Einstein. The results are both stark and gentle, as well as sexy: Toni sucking wasp poison from Josefa's lissome neck is a particularly fine moment. JR

Tonight Let's All Make Love in London

see Tonite Let's All Make Love in London

Tonight's the Night

see Happy Ever After

Tonite Let's All Make Love in London

(Peter Whitehead, 1967, GB) Mike Jagger, Andrew Oldham, Julie Christie, Michael Caine, David Hockney.
70 min.
Whitehead's focus-pulling, dolly-bird-at-Biba documentary on Swinging London scores low on technique but fields fascinating interviews with the trend-setters of the era – Jagger (thick), Oldham (crunching), Christie (shy), Caine and Hockney (funny). BC

Tony Rome

(Gordon Douglas, 1967, US) Frank Sinatra, Jill St John, Richard Conte, Gena Rowlands, Simon Oakland, Jeffrey Lynn, Lloyd Bochner, Joan Shawlee, Sue Lyon, Rocky Graziano.
110 min.
Rather slow-moving, but otherwise a witty and thoroughly enjoyable attempt to revive the cynical, corpse-laden, bafflingly plotted Chandler thrillers of the '40s. Here the quest for a diamond pin lost by a rich but unhappy girl (Lyon) leads through some exotic Miami locations and a fine assortment of blackmailers and sleazy undesirables, including a striptease dancer and her lesbian protectress, a venal doctor and his moronically muscle-bound son, a raffish dope peddler, and a drink-sodden mamma kept shut away in a derelict house. Most of them come to a bad end while Sinatra, standing in ably for Bogart as the tough private eye, times his deadpan cracks perfectly, takes his beatings like a man, and batters his way to some sort of solution. TM

Too Beautiful for You

see Trop belle pour toi!

Too Hot to Handle

(Jack Conway, 1938, US) Clark Gable, Myrna Loy, Walter Pidgeon, Walter Connolly, Leo Carrillo, Johnny Hines, Virginia Weidler.
105 min. b/w.
An action-packed drama, with news cameramen Gable and Pidgeon fighting for footage and the girl, a famous aviatrix, in locations as diverse as China and the Amazon jungle. Taken at face value, the picture seems dated and even objectionable, but there's a lively black comic edge to it that suggests appearances may be deceptive. The first sequence might have come from TV's Drop the Dead Donkey, with Gable unscrupulously shooting at Japanese planes to provoke an air raid on-camera. TCh

Too Hot to Handle

see Marrying Man, The

Too Late (Trop Tard)

(Lucian Pintilié, 1996, Fr/Romania) Razvan Vasilescu, Cécilia Barbora, Victor Rebengiuc, Dorel Visan.
104 min.
A distinct disappointment after Pintilié's earlier An Unforgettable Summer, this clumsy blend of conspiracy thriller, comedy and political allegory centres on a public prosecutor sent to investigate a series of suspicious deaths in a mining town in contemporary Romania. Inevitably, there seems to be a cover-up, mainly on the part of the mine's management, who fear political unrest among their employees; equally inevitably, Pintilié implies (heavy-handedly) that old Commie habits die hard. The film's various mismatched components are held together only by the thesis that no one, save the investigator, wants to reveal or know the truth, while the 'romance' that develops between the hero and a surveyor seems sexist, hopelessly dated, and somewhat gratuitous. In short, a mess. GA

Too Late Blues

(John Cassavetes, 1961, US) Bobby Darin, Stella Stevens, Everett Chambers, Rupert Crosse, Vince Edwards, Seymour Cassel.
103 min. b/w.

Though regarded almost universally (and that includes Cassavetes) as a failure, this attempt to recapture the spontaneous energy and 'realism' of his much-acclaimed, independently-made Shadows in a rather more plot-bound film for Paramount remains one of the more impressive Hollywood movies set in the hip, flip jazz world. Admittedly, Darin and Stevens (as an uncompromising pianist wary of selling out, and the neurotically scarred would-be singer he loves but cannot trust) seem uncomfortable with Cassavetes' semi-improvisational methods, and at times the emotional scab-picking threatens to bring what story there is to a halt. But the music, scored by David Raksin and played by the likes of Benny Carter, Red Mitchell and Shelley Manne, is mostly terrific, and the mood convincingly edgy in the scenes of conflict between Darin and the band he finally abandons for the more lucrative cocktail circuit. GA

Too Late the Hero

(Robert Aldrich, 1969, US) Michael Caine, Cliff Robertson, Ian Bannen, Harry Andrews, Denholm Elliott, Ronald Fraser, Lance Percival, Ken Takakura, Henry Fonda.
144 min.
Aldrich tries the Dirty Dozen formula again. This time the setting is the Pacific sector in World War II, and the premise has a band of reluctant heroes required to get from one end of a Jap-infested island to the other in order to transmit a decoy message (hopefully to distract attention from the US fleet). Along with some wry reflections on class and officer-like qualities, fairly predictable anti-war sentiments are aired by Caine and Robertson as the two main protagonists, rubbing national hostilities off each other and chiefly concerned with saving their own skins. The usual collection of cowards, bullies and wimps go along for the trip, but there are some excellent character sketches (Denholm Elliott and Ian Bannen, in particular), the action has its moments (with the patrol's paranoia fed by taunting messages from Japanese loudspeakers hidden in the jungle), and the bantering dialogue is often very funny. TM

Toolbox Murders, The

(Dennis Donnelly, 1977, US) Cameron Mitchell, Pamelyn Ferdin, Wesley Eure, Nicolas Beauvy, Tim Donnelly.
95 min.
The gory, censor-hacked murders (all of women) and the revelation of the nut's identity (he's gone on to kidnap a virgin as substitute for his dead daughter) are all out of the way inside half-an-hour, leaving a lot of dead time to establish this awful movie's single original gimmick: the novelty encounter of two psychos, who end up at each other's throats. Orson Welles' cameraman Gary Graver (The Other Side of the Wind) makes it all look better than it deserves. PT

Too Many Chefs

see Who Is Killing the Great Chefs of Europe?

Too Much Happiness

see Trop de Bonheur

Tootsie

(Sydney Pollack, 1982, US) Dustin Hoffman, Jessica Lange, Teri Garr, Dabney Coleman, Charles Durning, Bill Murray, Sydney Pollack, George Gaynes.
116 min.
Hoffman plays an actor, quite as temperamental and impossible as Hoffman himself evidently is in real life, who pretends to be a woman just to get a part in a daytime TV soap opera. Numerous writers came and went in production conditions that were apparently agonising, but for once little of this is apparent on the screen. The tone is quick-witted and appealing, with some of the smartest dialogue this side of Billy Wilder, and a wonderfully sure-footed performance from Jessica Lange (as her/his girlfriend). But the film never comes within a thousand miles of confronting its own implications: Hoffman's female impersonation is strictly on the level of Dame Edna Everage, and the script's assumption that 'she' would wow female audiences is at best ridiculous, at worst crassly insulting to women. Provided you ignore this central idiocy, Tootsie is certainly one of the most polished situation comedies in recent years. But then the field has hardly been over-crowded. DP

To Our Loves (A Nos Amours)

(Maurice Pialat, 1983, Fr) Sandrine Bonnaire, Dominique Besnehard, Maurice Pialat, Evelyne Ker, Anne-Sophie Maillé, Christophe Odent, Cyr Boitard.
102 min.
15-year-old Suzanne (Bonnaire) seems unable to progress beyond a rather doleful promiscuity in her relations with boys. Alone of her family, her father (played by Pialat himself) understands her, but when he leaves home for another woman, family life erupts into a round of appalling, casual violence, until Suzanne escapes into a fast marriage, and finally to America. Pialat's methods of close, intimate filming may place him close in many ways to our own Ken Loach, but his interests are rooted in a very cinematic approach to personal inner life, rather than any schematic political theory. The message may be that happiness is as rare as a sunny day, and sorrow is forever, but a counterbalancing warmth is provided by Pialat's enormous care for his creations. The rapport between father and daughter is especially moving. Pialat once acted in a Chabrol film, and one French critic's verdict on his film: 'Massive, abrupt, and incredibly gentle'. CPea

Topaz

(Alfred Hitchcock, 1969, US) Frederick Stafford, Dany Robin, John Vernon, Karin Dor, Michel Piccoli, Philippe Noiret, John Forsythe, Roscoe Lee Browne, Claude Jade, Michel Subor.
125 min.
Despite the odd critical effort to salvage the film's reputation, it has to be said that Hitchcock's lumbering adaptation of Leon Uris' novel, about international espionage at the time of the Cuban missile crisis, has not aged well. The near-incomprehensible plot (something about French and American parties trying to find out more about a Russian undercover group, directly involved with Cuba and working within the French security network) might appeal to devotees of Le Carré et al, but it certainly doesn't make for dramatically exciting cinema, especially given Hitchcock's flat, seemingly uninterested direction. The bland performances don't help much, either. GA

Top Dog (Wodzirej)

(Feliks Falk, 1978, Pol) Jerzy Stuhr, Slawa Kwasniewska, Wiktor Sadecki, Michael Tarkowski.
115 min.
This enshrines a brilliantly loathsome characterisation by Stuhr as the provincial entertainer driven by the sweet smell of success as he wheels and deals to achieve his pathetic goal of becoming MC for a gala inaugurating a new hotel. The political parable is neat enough as his power plays are scrutinised in vivid detail, but also pretty facile. Satires digging at the state through representations in microcosm became a dime a dozen in Eastern European films around this time. TM

Top Gun

(Tony Scott, 1986, US) Tom Cruise, Kelly McGillis, Val Kilmer, Anthony Edwards, Tom Skerritt, Michael Ironside, Rick Rossovich.
110 min.
The story is risible, the direction routine, the underlying ethic highly questionable; but the flying stirs the blood like speed. This concerns the exploits of one 'Maverick' (Cruise), who aspires to be top gun at the Top Gun, the US Navy Fighter Weapons School at San Diego. In what looks suspiciously like a retread of the An Officer and a Gentleman storyline, Maverick, an arrogant piece of Officer Material, climbs the ladder of fly-boy success, falls in love with his aeronautics instructor (an unlikely McGillis), and has his best friend and navigator (Edwards) fall off the ladder and into a concrete cloud. However, the traditional mainstays of love and death are here supplied by lengthy and highly realistic dog-fight sequences, in which the pupils and instructors tail-chase each other all over the desert sky, and then do it for real with an unnamed enemy over the Indian Ocean. A great ride to hell and back; kick the tyres, light the fires, and you're away. CPea

Top Hat (100)

(Mark Sandrich, 1935, US) Fred Astaire, Ginger Rogers, Edward Everett Horton, Helen Broderick, Erik Rhodes, Eric Blore.
101 min. b/w.

The third Astaire-Rogers movie (not counting *Flying Down to Rio*) and one of the best, with a superlative Irving Berlin score (it includes 'No Strings', 'Isn't This a Lovely Day?', 'Top Hat, White Tie and Tails' and 'Cheek to Cheek'), and equally superlative Hermes Pan routines which spark a distinct sexual electricity between the pair. Oddly enough, the film is almost slavishly patterned on *The Gay Divorcee*, with the scene again shifting from London to a resort (Venice in this case), the plot again turning on mistaken identity, and the comedy again reliant on Horton, Blore and Rhodes. The reason you don't really notice this – with *Top Hat* readily springing to mind as the archetypal Fred'n'Ginger movie – is the booster given by Van Nest Polglase's stunning white *Art Deco* designs, which were to set the tone for the series. TM

Topkapi

(Jules Dassin, 1964, US) Melina Mercouri, Peter Ustinov, Maximilian Schell, Robert Morley, Akim Tamiroff, Gilles Segal, Jess Hahn.
120 min.
An attempt by Dassin to top his own hit *Rififi*: a glossy international heist movie, using a hammy multi-cultural cast and a screenplay by ex-Ealing stalwart Monja Danischewsky (based on Eric Ambler's novel *The Light of Day*) to chart a hit on an Istanbul museum. As a caper, its convolutions of comedy and suspense are par for the course, and at least it's free of the pretensions that usually scuttle Dassin's efforts in Europe (especially in tandem with his wife Mercouri); but it's a far cry from his classic American thrillers or his brilliant British *noir*, *Night and the City*. PT

Topless Women Talk About Their Lives

(Harry Sinclair, 1997, NZ) Danielle Cormack, Joel Tobeck, Ian Hughes, Willa O'Neill, Andrew Binns, Shimpal Lelisi.
89 min.
This low budget first feature is somewhat in the vein of Emma-Kate Croghan's *Love and Other Catastrophes* (catchy title, freewheeling tone, and the romantic entanglements of a circle of pre-professional 20-year-olds). The title's a bit of a cheat: it's the name of the film-within-the-film, whose director proceeds to a nervous breakdown after discovering his friends think the film's crap. Meanwhile, currently between boyfriends, Liz (Cormack) is pregnant after missing an abortion appointment. While the characters are more credibly real and messy than Croghan's cute packages, most of them lose out to the writer/director's rambling storytelling. Cormack, however, just about holds the picture together; and Sinclair does throw in a handful of memorably eccentric scenes – like have you ever seen a rabbit swimming lengths. NB

Topo, El (The Mole)

(Alexandro Jodorowsky, 1971, Mex) Alexandro Jodorowsky, Brontis Jodorowsky, Mara Lorenzio, David Silva, Paula Romo.
124 min.
A religious allegory in the framework of a Western, lavish, violent, and wildly eclectic, including Fellini and farce among its influences, with the first half following a leather-clad gunman (Jodorowsky) through a desert scattered with biblical references in a highly ritualised search for fulfilment through feats of physical prowess. Death, rebirth and the New Testament follow his failure, with Jodorowsky now cropped and clownish, playing Servant of Man to a bunch of cripples and freaks, while the film opens out into an indictment of Western society. For all the film's aspirations, the juxtapositions made often appear obvious, lacking the repercussions of true surrealism, while the symbolism is so oblique that it never rises above its own security. With style constantly contradicting content, and the prevailing mood redolent of egotism and misogyny, it leaves one the feeling of having waded through a full-blown fantasy where even the self-degradation emerges as just another form of narcissism. CPe

Top of the World

(Lewis R Foster, 1955, US) Dale Robertson, Evelyn Keyes, Frank Lovejoy, Nancy Gates, Paul Fix.
90 min. b/w.
The off-the-mark geography of the title is symptomatic of a military love story too tepid to melt the Alaskan snow: a routine set of meaningful glances between grounded USAF Major Robertson, his ex-wife (Keyes) and her latest ranking inamorato (Lovejoy). The unambitious Foster had just turned freelance after an eleven-film stint with Paramount's B units, only to follow his Reagan/Fleming/Payne vehicles with more of the same. PT

Topper

(Norman Z McLeod, 1937, US) Constance Bennett, Cary Grant, Roland Young, Billie Burke, Alan Mowbray, Eugene Pallette, Hedda Hopper.
97 min. b/w.
Thorne Smith's novel about a dull banker (Young) haunted by dashing ghosts (Bennett and Grant) proved popular enough as a film to spawn two sequels and a TV series. Now it seems an archetypal piece of cinematic fluff from the '30s – too gentle and leisurely to survive as a solid classic, though there's pleasure to be found in the cast's graceful way with comedy and their smooth ensemble playing. GB

Top Secret!

(Jim Abrahams/David Zucker/Jerry Zucker, 1984, US) Val Kilmer, Lucy Gutteridge, Peter Cushing, Christopher Villiers, Jeremy Kemp, Warren Clarke, Michael Gough, Omar Sharif.
90 min.
Having spoofed one genre with considerable success, the *Airplane* team cast their net wider to send up a host of venerable movie chestnuts. Set in a peculiar national and temporal limbo, it has US teen rock idol Nick Rivers (Kilmer) travelling to Nazified East Germany to entertain culturally deprived Iron Curtain bobby-soxers. The gags come thick, fast and arbitrary – surfing gags, Pakman gags, Steve McQueen *Great Escape* gags – all aimed at the belly or lower, with a variable strike rate. The first half chugs along quite happily, but whereas in *Airplane* the jokes could simply be strung on a hand-me-down storyline, here the demands of the plot start to play havoc with the levity. Signs of desperation have begun to creep in some time before the end. JP

Tora no O o Fumu Otokotachi (The Men Who Tread on the Tiger's Tail/Walkers on the Tiger's Tail)

(Akira Kurosawa, 1945, Jap) Denjiro Okochi, Susumu Fujita, Masayuki Mori, Takashi Shimura, Aritake Kono.
58 min. b/w.
Very early Kurosawa (although it wasn't released in Japan until 1952 because of the US censor's sensitivity about 'feudal' subjects) and in no sense a major work. Based on a traditional story that exists in both Noh and Kabuki stage versions, and Kurosawa makes use of elements from both. A young nobleman has to cross a checkpoint in his flight from a vengeful brother, and impersonates a porter to do so; one of his juniors has to beat him to make the deception more convincing, but thereby violates one of the prime tenets of the feudal code...Kurosawa's chief contribution to the project was to add a second, comic porter to the plot. TR

Tora! Tora! Tora!

(Richard Fleischer, 1970, US/Jap) Martin Balsam, Soh Yamamura, Jason Robards, Joseph Cotten, Tatsuya Mihashi, EG Marshall, James Whitmore, Neville Brand, George Macready.
144 min.
A prototype disaster movie, reconstructing the attack on Pearl Harbor, which cost somewhere in the region of 25 million dollars, making it one of the most expensive American films to date. A distinguished cast gets a bit lost in the welter of special effects; and with the sequences giving the Japanese viewpoint directed by Japanese filmmakers (Toshio Masuda and Kinji Fukasaku), there's something of a soft shoe shuffle to avoid treading on national sensibilities. But the climax, in particular, manages to be more than just a shootout, with Fleischer's intelligent direction generating a real feeling of chaos and apocalypse. DP

Torchlight

(Tom Wright, 1984, US) Pamela Sue Martin, Steve Railsback, Ian McShane, Al Corley, Rita Taggart.
90 min.
Horrendously inept romance-cum-problem pic, with Ms Martin – reputed to be rampantly anti-drugs – falling for a loutish construction engineer (Railsback, who once played Charlie Manson) in the first five minutes, and then, in between dabbling in a little bit of painting, watching in horror as hubby gets hooked on assorted evil substances. The root of all evil is McShane, a hammy hustler who signals his debauched ways by wearing dressing-gowns, sporting a tacky tan, and grinning a lot. Ultra-conservative in tone, directed with little care for continuity or conviction, it might just send you into hysterics with its unintentional hilarity; or it could easily turn you into a valium addict. GA

Torch Song

(Charles Walters, 1953, US) Joan Crawford, Michael Wilding, Marjorie Rambeau, Gig Young, Henry Morgan, Dorothy Patrick.
90 min.
All-singing, all-dancing Joan is a Broadway musical star whose tantrums cause her accompanist to walk out, only to be replaced by blind pianist Wilding, whose criticism of her professional standards tempers her growing romantic attachment to him. All's resolved, however, in a plot development of such gob-smacking trashiness that it needs Crawford at full tilt to put it over. With MGM welcoming the star back with full honours after a 10-year absence, this toweringly nutty melodrama should prove irresistible to fans of the bigger-than-life star. TJ

Torch Song Trilogy

(Paul Bogart, 1988, US) Harvey Fierstein, Anne Bancroft, Matthew Broderick, Brian Kerwin, Karen Young, Eddie Castrodad, Ken Page.
119 min.
It's New York in 1971. Virginia Hamm wants a child, but the odds are stacked against her. She's single, given to emotionally masochistic relationships with immature men...and she's a Jewish professional female impersonator named Arnold Beckoff. But forget the drag, this is not another *La Cage aux Folles*; it's a straightforward, very funny love story which glows with fulfilment and promise. Beckoff (Fierstein) picks up Ed, a bi who's not happy about being so (Kerwin), and they embark on some sort of affair. It falls apart. Alan (Broderick), the big romantic interest, pursues the reluctant and disbelieving dragster, they set up home, they fight, they come through it and get ready to adopt. The second half of the movie – featuring a manic performance from Bancroft as Arnold's Ma, the epitome of Jewish Mommishness – is a rollercoaster of politics, parenthood (Arnold's and Ma's), death, independence, reconciliation, and more romance. It's a solid, old-fashioned, soppy movie – Arnold has been described as 'Doris Day with a dick' – and a great retro-romance. TC

Torment

see Enfer, L'

Torment

see Hets

Torn Between Two Lovers

(Delbert Mann, 1979, US) Lee Remick, Joseph Bologna, George Peppard, Giorgio Tozzi, Murphy Cross, Jess Osuna.
100 min.
We must have done something awful bad to deserve first the song and now the film. Wherever possible, stereotypes are substituted for three-dimensional characters, and clichés for dialogue. It's the story of a middle-aged woman married to an Italian-American family (a macho 'all I gave up when I got married was my motorbike' husband, a father-in-law who gives out pieces of advice as if they were sweeties, and a mother-in-law who makes you feel guilty by cooking). She falls in love with an architect who has only caviar and yoghurt in his fridge. The blossoming of their illicit love (indicated by blazing log fires being superimposed when they kiss) and her inability to choose between her

lovers threatens to destroy her marriage. Made for TV, the film's elevation to the big screen only heightens its inadequacies. It's not that it's bad, merely insipid, like a Martini on the rocks. FD

Torn Curtain

(Alfred Hitchcock, 1966, US) Paul Newman, Julie Andrews, Lila Kedrova, Hansjïrg Felmy, Tamara Toumanova, Wolfgang Kieling, Ludwig Donath.
128 min.
Spy thriller in which Newman's defecting scientist is followed to East Berlin by his troubled fiancée/assistant (Andrews), unaware that he is playing a double agent game. Hitchcock, seemingly too dour or too uninterested to turn in the title's promise of a Cold War ripping yarn, settles instead for a dissection of the limits of domestic trust, as Andrews' doubts about Newman's fidelity (to her, to the American Way) blunt his undercover mission in pursuit of an Eastern bloc MacGuffin. An above-average quota of glaringly shaky process work; but at least one classic sequence of protracted violence in a farmhouse kitchen. PT

Torpedo Run

(Joseph Pevney, 1958, US) Glenn Ford, Ernest Borgnine, Diane Brewster, Dean Jones.
98 min.
Submarine commander Glenn Ford pursues the ship that led the attack on Pearl Harbor back to Tokyo, where he plans to sink the bastard. But there's a freighter in the way, and gee whiz, on board are his wife and children, who are prisoners of the Japs and whom we have grown to love in flashbacks. To hell with it, he thinks, his country comes first, and he blows the freighter out of the water. That's heroism for you. ATu

Torre de los Siete Jorobados, La

see Tower of the Seven Hunchbacks, The

Torrents of Spring (Acque di primavera)

(Jerzy Skolimowski, 1989, It/Fr) Timothy Hutton, Nastassja Kinski, Valeria Golino, William Forsythe, Urbano Barberini, Christopher Janczar, Jerzy Skolimowski
101 min.
Russian landowner (Hutton) falls in love with German shopkeeper's daughter (Golino), is seduced by formidable aristocrat (Kinski), and loses both of them. So much for story. Even so, motives and desires remain confusingly ambiguous in Skolimowski's lightweight adaptation of Turgenev's novel. This aspires to be a prestigious international production, which means the ill-assembled cast speak in thick, dubbed accents, the photography is ravishing, the sun is always setting, and even the peasant extras are beautifully turned out. If chocolate boxes could move, this is how they'd look. Odd touches of bizarre humour apart, nothing spells the signature of the director of The Shout and Moonlighting, and when the man himself appears at the bewilderingly abrupt finale, ascribing to Hutton 'a life empty of all meaning', one wonders if that wasn't the problem all along. TCh

Torrid Zone

(William Keighley, 1940, US) James Cagney, Pat O'Brien, Ann Sheridan, Andy Devine, Helen Vinson, Jerome Cowan, George Tobias.
88 min. b/w
Rip-roaring Warners melodrama set in a South American banana plantation but with the same larger-than-life performances and coruscating dialogue found in the studio's best gangster movies. Cagney is the plantation foreman. He's sick of the job and wants to up sticks and head home to the States. But wily owner Pat O'Brien is determined to keep him where he is. Nightclub singer Ann Sheridan ('The Oomph Girl') is an added distraction. GM

Torso Murder Mystery, The

see Traitor Spy

Tortue sur le Dos, La

see Turtle on Its Back

Torture Garden

(Freddie Francis, 1967, GB) Jack Palance, Burgess Meredith, Beverly Adams, Michael Bryant, John Standing, Peter Cushing, Maurice Denham, Robert Hutton.
93 min.
The second Amicus horror omnibus and one of the best, with a clever framing device involving Burgess Meredith as a Mephistophelean fairground charlatan who offers clients grisly glimpses of the future, in four Robert Bloch stories which get progressively better until the splendid climax of The Man Who Collected Poe. Terrific performances from Palance as the manic Poe collector who achieves apotheosis by turning himself into a character straight out of one of Poe's more apocalyptic stories, and from Standing as a concert pianist saddled with a murderously possessive grand piano. TM

To Sir, With Love

(James Clavell, 1966, GB) Sidney Poitier, Christian Roberts, Judy Geeson, Suzy Kendall, Lulu, Faith Brook, Geoffrey Bayldon.
105 min.
A British Blackboard Jungle that bears no resemblance to school life as we know it. The kids try hard, but apart from Lulu (an impressive feature debut) are very unconvincing, and the hoodlums' miraculous reformation a week before the end of term (thanks to teacher Sidney Poitier) is laughable. Incessant Cockney street market vignettes and shots of London buses seem to suggest that it was all primarily intended for American consumption anyway. DP

To Sleep, So As to Dream

(Kaizo Hayashi, 1986, Jap) Kamura Moe, Sano Shiro, Otake Koji, Oizumi Akira.
81 min. b/w
A red herring-strewn mystery, shot in black-and-white and almost silent, Hayashi's debut is something like a Japanese Tintin adventure made by Alain Resnais. It concerns a silent swashbuckler film that combusts before its finale, a trio of magicians, and the venerable Madame Cherry-Blossom, whose daughter has been abducted by the shady consortium 'M Pathé and Co'. To Sleep, So As to Dream prospects the borders between film and reality, dream and wakefulness, but it's also a larky pastiche of the '20s sleuth genre, with detective heroes Uotsuka (Shiro) and Kobayashi (Koji) as intrepid stout-hearts in the Sexton Blake and Tinker tradition. Hayashi lays on surreal humour with flair, but the movie is above all a disquisition on film conventions, Japanese and Western, antique and modern. Most audaciously, Hayashi punctures the silence with ringing phones and the spoken interventions of a benshi, the traditional commentator of silent cinema. Although it doesn't quite approach the magic of Circus Boys, it's a wonderfully inventive, genuinely eerie narrative experiment. JRo

To Sleep with Anger

(Charles Burnett, 1990, US) Danny Glover, Paul Butler, Mary Alice, Carl Lumbly, Vonetta McGee, Richard Brooks, Sheryl Lee Ralph.
102 min.
Burnett's ambitious blend of folklore and family feuding opens startlingly: Gideon, an elderly black paterfamilias, sits unflinching as a conflagration slowly engulfs first his feet, then his body, to the soulful gospel strains of 'Precious Memories'. The scene, at once baffling, poignant and absurd, is a fine indication of the hybrid vision that follows. Emerging from his hallucination to a waking nightmare, Gideon (Butler) finds his family threatened with destruction. Catalysing the domestic turmoil is Harry Mention (Glover), a brooding, malevolent charmer whose mystique stems from a professed allegiance to the ancient forces of darkness, and whose arrival sows dissent between Gideon's sons, threatening his patriarchal role and even, perhaps, his life. Poised between mystical fantasy and humdrum melodrama, the film muses on the complex relationship between present and past, while remaining firmly grounded in a linear (yet ghostly) narrative. Despite uncertain pacing, Burnett's evocation of a thriving cultural milieu that embraces both superstition and mysterious wisdom is almost flawless. Laughs, too, are frequent and full-blooded. For those who fall under the film's spell, the rewards are magical. MK

To Speak the Unspeakable: The Message of Elie Wiesel (Mondani a mondhatatlant: Elie Wiesel uzenete)

(Judit Elek, 1996, Hun/Fr) Elie Wiesel.
105 min. b/w & col.
Framed between Wiesel's address at the American Holocaust Museum and his acceptance of the Nobel Peace Prize in 1986, this assembly of archive material recalls what appears to have been the lost pre-war paradise of schtetl, family and shul in the Carpathians. The b/w footage has the beauty of Roman Vishniac's work, and William Hurt's unassertive narration is deceptively powerful: 'If I explain, it's not so you'll understand, it's so you'll never understand.' Wiesel's journey back to find his roots is blocked by the discovery that there are no Jews in his part of Romania any more, and their houses have gone, giving rise to an urge to warn the world that there are people hungry for blood. 'We were naive. We didn't expect that our neighbours were mad dogs.' He revisits Auschwitz and Buchenwald where he lost his family – 'If we are separated, we'll meet back at the house after the war,' were his mother's parting words – and views again the 'unspeakable' set against the roar of the furnaces. BC

Total Balalaika Show

(Aki Kaurismäki, 1994, Fin) The Leningrad Cowboys Band, The Alexandrov Red Army Chorus and Dance Ensemble.
55 min.
From 'Finlandia' through 'Volga Boatman' to 'Knockin' on Heaven's Door' and 'Those Were the Days', this is a delightful record of a huge Helsinki concert bringing together the Leningrad Cowboys, the band that used to pride itself on being the worst in the world (they've improved no end) and the massed voices of the Red Army Chorus. The combination of outrageously long quiffs and winkle-pickers, with medals strewn across middle-aged military chests makes for a pleasing absurdity, especially when the Cowboys start Cossack dancing to 'Kalinka' – and it's clear that all but a few of the soldiers were having a ball too. Highlight: a magical version of the Turtles' 'Happy Together'. One helluva noise, and you won't stop smiling. GA

Total Eclipse

(Agnieszka Holland, 1995, Fr/GB/Bel) Leonardo DiCaprio, David Thewlis, Romane Bohringer, Dominique Blanc, Felicie Pasotti Carbarbaye, Nita Klein, Christopher Hampton.
111 min.
September, 1871: Arthur Rimbaud arrives in post-revolutionary Paris from Charleville at the invitation of Paul Verlaine. Verlaine, an accomplished poet with a growing reputation and a pregnant young trophy wife to match, is as instantly entranced by the precocious, anarchic, contemptuous 16-year-old as by the unprecedented talent evinced in the boy's poetry. Drinking their way through the city's literary salons, the pair strike out on a passionate, illicit affair. But it's a woefully imbalanced relationship, with Rimbaud compulsively abusing his elder, and the weak-willed Verlaine resorting ever more to the bottle. Christopher Hampton's screenplay presents a thoroughly researched reading whose historical authenticity only skims the surface of any emotional truths. Whether you take to this at all probably depends on your reaction to the affair on show. It's abusive, sordid, violent – but then this was hardly a coupling made in heaven. DiCaprio (Rimbaud) and Thewlis (Verlaine) provide dynamic if mismatched performances, though there's no excusing Hampton's own laughable cameo, nor the protracted coda with DiCaprio doing a Peter O'Toole in the desert. NB

Totally F***ed Up

(Gregg Araki, 1993, US) James Duval, Roko Belic, Susan Behshid, Jenee Gill, Gilbert Luna, Lance May, Alan Boyce.
80 min.
Turning aside from the in-your-face sloganeering of The Living End, Gregg Araki returns here to the slangy, intimate, domestic domain of his earlier work. Crashing ennui and tortured love-lives are again the keynote, as an assortment of young gay Angelinos laze around each other's apart-

ments, get bored with cruising the local scene, mess up their relationships and major in teenage angst. Between times, Araki – who directed, co-produced, wrote, photographed and edited the picture – weighs in with an intermittent flutter of suicide statistics, found footage and pointed intertitles. It's all very self-consciously cool, of course, but from this side of the Atlantic, you can forgive the film's endless posturing and tune in to its honest, sympathetic portrayal of late adolescence. Araki covers any number of bases, revolving around two-timing would-be movie-maker Steven (Luna) and melancholy existential hipster Andy (Duval, a real find). Indeed, for all its rather obvious attitude, the film's conventional at heart: a soap for the slack generation, that'll strike a chord way outside the confines of the New Queer Cinema. TJ

Total Recall

(Paul Verhoeven, 1990, US) Arnold Schwarzenegger, Rachel Ticotin, Sharon Stone, Ronny Cox, Michael Ironside, Marshall Bell.
113 min.
Picking up from where he left off in *RoboCop*, Verhoeven pictures a lean, mean future controlled by conglomerates via a hands-on designer technology. Doug Quaid (Schwarzenegger) is a working stiff who dreams of living on Mars. What quicker, cheaper, safer way of making his dreams come true than purchasing memory implants: a two-week trip to Mars, first class, with a personal ego-trip as an optional extra. But something goes wrong (or does it?). Quaid has already been to Mars (or has he?), and his memories have been erased (hence those dreams?). Now They want him dead. 'The best mind-fuck yet!' says Quaid, as the plot takes another Z-bend at warp factor ten. Inevitably there are contrivances, but Verhoeven's gusto, ingenuity and guts know no bounds...especially the guts: the comic-edged violence is shockingly brutal. The inspiration, as with *Blade Runner*, comes from Philip K Dick (his short story *We Can Remember It For You Wholesale)*, and many of his themes recur: identity, self-determination, perception, and yes, we're talking about memories here, alongside a revolutionary parable, two great female characters, and some colossal effects. The future doesn't come any better. TCh

To the Devil a Daughter

(Peter Sykes, 1976, GB/WGer) Richard Widmark, Christopher Lee, Honor Blackman, Denholm Elliott, Michael Goodliffe, Nastassja Kinski, Anthony Valentine.
93 min.
Hammer's second attempt at a Dennis Wheatley black magic thriller bears little comparison with the earlier *The Devil Rides Out*. It is very much a contemporary post-*Exorcist* movie, full of rampaging foetuses, obscene pregnancy rituals, and stray sexual suggestions as Christopher Lee's excommunicated priest and his satanist followers hound young Nastassja Kinski with malevolent intent. The film's unlikely trump card is Richard Widmark as a credibly sceptical supernatural investigator, who romps through the proceedings with a disarming stoicism, but regrettably faces his devilish opponent Lee only in the closing sequence. It's a good deal more interesting than the rest of the possession cycle, but still a disappointment. DP

To the Heart (Al Corazón)

(Mario Sábato, 1995, Arg) Sergio Renán, Adriana Varela, Ernesto Sábato, Enrique Cadicamo, Mónica Cadicamo and Trio, Sexteto Mayor, Cárlos Gardel.
92 min.
If you like tango – the music, the dance, the sensibility – you'll love this, since it trawls through a host of clips from the Argentinian cinema's golden age, featuring numerous greats including the legendary Cárlos Gardel. The explanatory interruptions from Enrique Cadicamo and Ernesto Sábato (seen wandering around rooms, streets and staircases) are regrettably rather a drag. GA

To the Last Drop
(Até a Ultima Gota)

(Sergio Rezende, 1980, Braz) José Dumont.
52 min.
In Latin America there are ten thousand com-

mercial blood banks, where the forty million who are unable to sell their labour sell their blood, often in such large quantities that they die of anaemia. The blood and its by-products are resold at enormous profit, mostly to wealthier countries, via multi-national corporations. This blood traffic is both the documentary subject of the film, and a metaphor for the bleeding dry of Third World countries by the West, of the poor by the rich: a metaphor worked through in the commentary, with a passion often lacking from 'committed' documentaries. The wider resonances of the commentary are anchored by precise, pointed images; the uninhibited use of camera and editing to draw attention to things is refreshing rather than heavy-handed, and looks positively subtle by comparison with the crude and exploitative view of the world which sanctions profiteering in human blood. JWi

To the Starry Island
(Gesom e Kako Shipta)

(Park Kwang-Su, 1993, SKor) Ahn Song-Gi, Moon Sung-Kuen, Shim Hae-Jin.
102 min.
Like Park's earlier films, this provides an intimate close-up vision of a handful of characters, then pulls back to expose the political framework in which they are forced to exist. Unlike the other films, this takes place in a rural peasant community, and involves the supernatural as well as lengthy flashbacks to the Korean War of the 1950s. It's about the ramifications of that war on a lonely off-shore island – how a traditional people were swept up by events they barely understood, and how the bitterness of the experience still persists. A fascinating movie, with a bold, shocking climax. TCh

To the Victor
see Owd Bob

Toto the Hero (Toto le héros)

(Jaco Van Dormael, 1991, Bel/Fr/Ger) Michel Bouquet, Jo De Backer, Gisela Uhlen, Mireille Perrier, Sandrine Blancke, Peter Böhlke, Didier Ferney.
91 min.
This deliciously offbeat film tells of the now elderly Thomas (Bouquet), who has harboured dreams of murderous revenge ever since it first occurred to him that, as a baby during a maternity ward fire, he was exchanged with Alfred, the kid next door. As Thomas sifts through his memories, revelling in his jealous hatred of Alfred, and wistfully recalling his love for his sister Alice and her adult lookalike Evelyne (Perrier), Van Dormael takes us on a twisting trip through his melancholy protagonist's mind: a trip jam-packed with the simple, surprising joys of existence. That Thomas' life, as we see it, is the product of his imagination is made clear not only by the presence of his comic-strip *alter ego* (the avenging detective of the title), but by the dreamily surreal story and visuals. But if the film's outlandish elements allow Van Dormael (in his feature debut) to exercise an engagingly witty eye for the absurd, he has rooted it in *emotional* reality, so that Thomas' life, loves, desires and anxieties take on great poignancy. An immensely vibrant, inventive, compassionate movie. GA

Totschweigen
(A Wall of Silence)

(Margareta Heinrich/Eduarde Erne, 1990, Aus)
88 min.
'The Jews have their Wailing Wall and we have our wall of silence.' So says one of the occupants of Totschweigen Reichnitz, a village on the Austro-Hungarian border where, in 1945, 180 Jews were shot by the retreating Nazis and buried in a still unlocated mass grave. The locals' stonewalling frustrates all efforts to give them a proper burial. It's a compelling subject, and some pertinent links are made to wider issues. A pity, then, that the film's construction ties it down so: after the first half hour of exposition, there's nowhere to go, and it ends up tracing its footsteps as unproductively as the search it observes. NB

Touch, The

(Ingmar Bergman, 1970, US/Swe) Elliott Gould, Bibi Andersson, Max von Sydow, Sheila Reid, Barbro Hiort af Ornäs.
113 min.

Bergman's first English language movie looks more accessible than most of his work at this period, a 'love story' (as he has called it) telling how middle class Swedish housewife Anna (Andersson) meets Anglo-Jewish archaeologist David (Gould), has an intermittent and rocky affair with him, and ends up losing both lover and husband, the penalty of compromise. 'It is possible to live two lives' says Anna hopefully to David, 'and slowly combine them in one good, wise life'. But the film demonstrates conclusively that it isn't: not only does the double life involve deceit, but it is always threatened by the incalculable factors in human nature. David's love for Anna alternates with spells of motiveless violence and morose indifference; Anna's seemingly kindly and myopic husband (von Sydow) does discover the affair and does give Anna an ultimatum. Anna thus keeps finding, to her dismay, that she cannot predict how either man will act next. Conversely, David's violence and the husband's growing coldness are their reactions to Anna's unpredictability. Bergman may have temporarily shelved his metaphysical concerns – no religious questionings, no fantasy, no artist-in-society debate – but his analysis of human relationships is as complex as ever. NAn

Touch and Go

(Robert Mandel, 1986, US) Michael Keaton, Maria Conchita Alonso, Ajay Naidou, Maria Tucci, Max Wright, Jere Burns, Lara Jill Miller.
101 min.
An enjoyable, undemanding comedy-drama, with Michael Keaton as famous Chicago ice hockey player Bobby Barbato, a man with humour as dry as his ice and a constant look of hilarious vacancy. One evening Bobby is mugged by an incompetent gang of schoolkids, fronted by obnoxious 11-year-old Louis (Naidou). Grabbing the little toerag by the collar, he drags him home to confront his fiery Latin mum Denise (Alonso). They don't exactly hit it off at first, but soon the odd couple find their lives unavoidably interwoven when Denise is beaten up while Bobby is puck-whacking for the championship. Although a little more ice action wouldn't have gone amiss, the pace rarely slackens and Keaton is in fine form. DA

Touched by Love

(Gus Trikonis, 1980, US) Deborah Raffin, Diane Lane, Michael Learned, John Amos, Cristina Raines, Mary Wickes, Clu Gulager.
94 min.
Dreadful pap about a young nurse (Raffin) starting work at a home for handicapped children, finally managing to break the communication barrier with a girl obsessed by Elvis Presley (a penpal letter from Elvis figures in the therapy) and dying from cerebral palsy. Based on a true story, but sanitised throughout; only Raines, as Raffin's cynical room-mate, adds a touch of reality. GA

Touchez pas au Grisbi
(Grisbi/Honour Among Thieves)

(Jacques Becker, 1953, Fr/It) Jean Gabin, René Dary, Paul Frankeur, Paul Oettly, Lino Ventura, Jeanne Moreau, Dora Doll, Daniel Cauchy.
94 min. b/w.
This model French gangster picture set the rules for the great sequence of underworld movies from Jean-Pierre Melville that followed. An ageing and weary Gabin attempts to retire after one last robbery. Instead he finds himself in a world of moody double-crosses. Becker's film, full of neat angles and delightful little bits of business, is laconic and admirably methodical. If its code of honour and its world of safe houses (and the absence of any police) make it seem like a wartime resistance film, it does also show what other gangster movies often ignore: that the reason for earning money dishonestly is to be able to live in style. And this film takes as much pleasure in watching Gabin open a bottle of wine as it does observing him in action. A fine supporting cast includes a young Lino Ventura and an even younger Jeanne Moreau. CPe

Touch of Class, A

(Melvin Frank, 1972, GB) George Segal, Glenda Jackson, Paul Sorvino, Hildegard Neil, Cec Linder, K Callan, Mary Barclay.
106 min.

For the most part, this romantic comedy (married American businessman *versus* divorcee English designer) successfully fights off the implications of its title and appalling theme song, thanks to some sharp dialogue and an excellent performance from Segal at his edgy, harassed best. Melvin Frank has put in his share of years as a comedy scriptwriter, which probably accounts for the distinctly old-fashioned air. Sharp at the edges but soft in the centre, the film starts well with Segal's middle class stud fantasies being ripped to shreds by Glenda Jackson in full flight. Barbs fly, but too soon she degenerates into devoted clock-watching mistress, and the film into routine formula. Often enjoyable, though, if mainly for Segal holding the seeping sentimentality at bay. CPe

Touch of Evil [100] (100)

(Orson Welles, 1958, US) Charlton Heston, Janet Leigh, Orson Welles, Joseph Calleia, Akim Tamiroff, Marlene Dietrich, Dennis Weaver, Ray Collins, Mercedes McCambridge, Lalo Rios, Zsa Zsa Gabor, Keenan Wynn, Joseph Cotten.
108 min. b/w.
A wonderfully offhand genesis (Welles adopting and adapting a shelved Paul Monash script for B-king Albert Zugsmith without ever reading the novel by Whit Masterson it was based on) marked this brief and unexpected return to Hollywood film-making for Welles. And the result more than justified the arrogance of the gesture. A sweaty thriller conundrum on character and corruption, justice and the law, worship and betrayal, it plays havoc with moral ambiguities as self-righteous Mexican cop Heston goes up against Welles' monumental Hank Quinlan, the old-time detective of vast and wearied experience who goes by instinct, gets it right, but fabricates evidence to make his case. Set in the backwater border hell-hole of Los Robles, inhabited almost solely by patented Wellesian grotesques, it's shot to resemble a nightscape from Kafka. PT

Touch of the Sun
see No Secrets!

Touch of Zen, A (Xia Nü)

(King Hu, 1969, Tai) Shih Chun, Hsu Feng, Pai Ying, Tian Feng, Roy Chiao, Han Yingjie.
175 min.
King Hu's remarkable Ming Dynasty epic deliberately makes itself impossible to define, beginning as a ghost story, then turning into a political thriller, and finally becoming a metaphysical battle as the role of the monk Hui-Yuan (Chiao) comes to the fore. Structured like a set of Chinese boxes, twice forcing you to expand your frame of reference and reassess the meaning of what you've seen, it begins with a realistic portrait of life in a sleepy town outside Peking, and ends with extended fantasies of Zen Buddhism in action – and in between has a core of action scenes that transform Peking Opera stagecraft into sheer flights of imagination. Delights include a heroine who holds her own with men without being 'masculine', and transcendent moments like the stabbing of the monk, who bleeds gold...And the visual style will set your eyes on fire. TR

Tough Guy
see Kung Fu – The Headcrusher

Tough Guys

(Jeff Kanew, 1986, US) Burt Lancaster, Kirk Douglas, Charles Durning, Alexis Smith, Dana Carvey, Darlanne Fluegel, Eli Wallach, Monty Ash, Billy Barty.
103 min.
This excessively nostalgic caper comedy has Lancaster and Douglas as ex-cons of pensionable age attempting to fit in with the modern world following a 30-year jail stretch for a train robbery. Douglas, pushy and petulant, flexes his physique with aerobics teacher Fluegel, while Lancaster, more dignified and regretful of time lost, is relegated, jobless, to an old folks home. The observation that 'old is a dirty word' is swiftly shoved aside as the pair strut their stuff, fend off muggers, and indulge in amiably rebellious antics before making one last bid for fame and freedom by hijacking, once again, the Gold Coast Flier. So self-consciously elegiac

that its too-good-to-be-true heroes are imprisoned in a slim storyline of implausible fantasy, the movie would have been more effective had Burt and Kirk simply been allowed to be themselves. Of course, it's fun to watch old pros, and Wallach, as a mad, myopic hit-man, is genuinely funny; but one can't help feeling that a rare gathering of Golden Age talent has been criminally wasted. GA

Tough Guys Don't Dance

(Norman Mailer, 1987, US) Ryan O'Neal, Isabella Rossellini, Debra Sandlund, Wings Hauser, John Bedford Lloyd, Lawrence Tierney, Penn Jillette.
109 min.
Deserted husband and ex-drug dealer Tim Madden (O'Neal) wakes from a hangover to find gore all over his car, a new tattoo on his arm, and a severed head in his drug stash. The only person he can turn to is his old dad (Tierney), who has his work cut out deep-sixing heads and corpses in the ocean. Police Chief Regency (Hauser), involved with Madden's chippie wife and married to Madden's old flame (Rossellini), is out to fit him up for the murders, but has an epileptic fit in his Green Beret uniform instead. Norman Mailer's novel, *Tough Guys Don't Dance*, wasn't so hot, but his potboiler on screen is a disgrace. No scene generates a complex reaction, and his attempts at turning his Manichean material and existential dread into a chortle-fest is as unsuccessful as is the high camp, for the film forfeits sympathy from the start. Neither thrilling nor horrific, the camera, plotting, dialogue and atmosphere are uniformly unconvincing: a conservatoire of false notes. BC

Tough Life
see Monde sans pitié, Un

Tournoi, Le (The Tournament)

(Jean Renoir, 1928, Fr) Aldo Nadi, Jackie Monnier, Enrique Rivero, Blanche Bernis, Manuel Raabi.
6,562 ft. b/w.
This epic medieval drama, detailing the conflict between Catholics and Protestants in Carcassonne, would have little in common with Renoir's later, more personal and mature work, were it not for the decidedly human perspective from which he views the story. Not only is this a question of his clearly having felt rather more at home with the intimate scenes than with the action-packed spectacle; it's also a matter of his characters being far more recognisably prone to ordinary human shortcomings than are the larger-than-life heroes of more stilted epics. Indeed, his eye for telling detail was already sharp, while both the sparsely decorated interiors and the naturalistic performances lend his vision of the past a rare feeling of lived-in authenticity. GA

Tous les matins du monde

(Alain Corneau, 1992, Fr) Jean-Pierre Marielle, Gérard Depardieu, Anne Brochet, Guillaume Depardieu, Caroline Sihol, Carole Richert, Michel Bouquet.
115 min.
For all his success as court composer at Versailles, the aged Marin Marais (Gérard Depardieu) acknowledges the spiritual emptiness of his music. Lost in memories, he recalls another master of the *viola da gamba*, Monsieur de Sainte Colombe (Marielle), whose magnificent, melancholy compositions and hermetic life style, away from the tempting glamours of Paris, were inspired by undying love for his late wife. Not a warm man, Sainte Colombe had consented to tutor Marin Marais in his prodigious youth (Guillaume Depardieu), a favour which the pupil repaid by seducing one of Sainte Colombe's daughters (Brochet). Only years later had he taken to heart the real lesson his master had to offer... From its lengthy, opening close-up of Depardieu's face, it's clear that Corneau's 17th century fable will be no ordinary costume drama. The story is slow, stately, and told with minimal dialogue, with Corneau trusting to Yves Angelo's painterly camerawork – and even more importantly, to the lovely baroque music – to give his admirably restrained tale of passion, betrayal and creativity its emotional power. The cast, too, play beautifully. GA

Toute une Nuit (All Night Long)

(Chantal Akerman, 1982, Fr/Bel) Aurore Clément, Jan Decorte, Angelo Abazoglou, Frank Aendenboom.
89 min.
Akerman, the mistress of minimalism, has made her own midsummer night's sex comedy, with a superabundance of stories and a cast of (almost) thousands. The film shows an endless series of brief encounters that take place in Brussels in the course of one delirious, torrid June night, with the twist that each relationship is condensed into a single moment of high melodrama – the *coup de foudre*, the climax of passion, the end of an affair – with the spectator left to fill in the fictional spaces between scenes. Each couple compulsively plays through the same gestures, each mating rite is a variation on the same theme: repetitions which Akerman uses both as a rich source of comedy and as a device to show erotic desire as a pattern of codes and conventions. Marrying the pleasure of narrative to the purism of the avant-garde, this is her most accessible film to date. SJ

Toute une Vie
see And Now My Love

Tout Va Bien

(Jean-Luc Godard/Jean-Pierre Gorin, 1972, Fr/It) Yves Montand, Jane Fonda, Vittorio Caprioli, Jean Pagnol, Pierre Oudry, Anne Wiazemsky.
95 min.
Godard's return to mainstream film-making after his self-imposed four-year Marxist-nihilist exile is a sort of auto-critique, craftily type-casting Fonda and Montand as media intellectuals (she an American journalist, he a former New Wave film-maker now working in commercials) who eagerly committed themselves to the revolutionary struggle in 1968, but are now led to revise that commitment (and their personal relationship) through their involvement in a factory strike in 1972. A little simplistic at times but acidly funny, with Godard's genius for the arresting image once more well to the fore. TM

Tovarich

(Anatole Litvak, 1937, US) Claudette Colbert, Charles Boyer, Basil Rathbone, Anita Louise, Isabel Jeans, Morris Carnovsky, Melville Cooper.
98 min. b/w.
Boyer, one of Hollywood's most exotic male leads, specialised in playing suave, displaced European aristocrats. He's at his most irrepressibly smooth here as a White Russian refugee who's reduced to working as a butler for a French banker. (His equally haughty wife Colbert is taken on as the maid.) There is no hiding the snobbery behind this upstairs/downstairs comedy. You never doubt for a moment that class will out and that the two unlikely domestics will be restored to their previous, lofty social positions. Director Litvak, himself a Russian émigré in Hollywood, acquits himself well enough, but this is a film which surely would have been better suited to the talents of Lubitsch. GM

Toward the Unknown (aka Brink of Hell)

(Mervyn LeRoy, 1956, US) William Holden, Lloyd Nolan, Virginia Leith, Charles McGraw, Murray Hamilton, LQ Jones, James Garner, Paul Fix, Karen Steele.
115 min.
In this routine commingling of both mental and metal fatigue, Holden is a Korean veteran pilot (he broke under brainwashing) who's expected to grin and bear a desk jockey posting to Edwards Air Base, but itches to test the new X-2 rocket plane (which will retrieve his self-respect and his girl). Stolidly directed by former Warners contractee LeRoy in his men-in-uniform period, between the naval comedy *Mr Roberts* and the army farce *No Time for Sergeants*, and before the plainclothes hymn *The FBI Story*. James Garner makes his screen debut here, only a year before the first *Maverick*. PT

Towering Inferno, The

(John Guillermin, 1974, US) Steve McQueen, Paul Newman, William Holden, Faye Dunaway, Fred Astaire, Susan Blakely,

Richard Chamberlain, Jennifer Jones, OJ Simpson, Robert Vaughn, Robert Wagner.
165 min.
Although producer Irwin Allen's *The Poseidon Adventure* actually led the way a couple of years before, this is the disaster film which set the style for the genre in the decade to come (the trailer for *The Towering Inferno* declared such skyscraper conflagrations to be nothing less than 'the new art form of the twentieth century'). A starry cast share out roles that are less like characters than places in a lifeboat, either as victims (Chamberlain, Wagner, Jones) or firefighters (McQueen and Newman). Director Guillermin deserved to be made an honorary fire chief, though he is driven to some desperate measures to cap each mounting disaster with ever more outlandish rescues. MA

Tower of the Seven Hunchbacks, The (La Torre de los Siete Jorobados)
(Edgar Neville, 1944, Sp) Antonio Casal, Isabel de Pomés, Julia Lajos, Manolita Moran, Julia Pachelo, Guillermo Marin.
90 min. b/w.
A real oddity: young Basilio is visited by the ghost of a dead, one-eyed archaeologist, who asks him to protect his niece from imminent danger. After introducing himself to the lovely girl, our intrepid hero discovers that the threat emanates from a huge underground city populated entirely by hunchbacks...Neville's film is not exactly *good*, but it certainly is fascinating. In many ways it's like a rather corny Universal horror movie of the '30s (featuring a few performances that would show even Lugosi in an impressive light); but no Hollywood film-maker – with the possible exception of Whale or Browning – would pepper a plot with such delightful nonsense (the ghost of Napoleon turns up at one point) and grotesquerie. The Spanish taste for the fantastic, the bizarre and the surreal is much in evidence, and one is left breathless by the sheer audacity of the ludicrous plot. It can, of course, be seen as an allegory on the state of the nation after the Civil War, but is best viewed as weird but wonderful wackiness. GA

Town Bloody Hall
(DA Pennebaker/Chris Hegedus, 1979, US) Jacqueline Ceballos, Germaine Greer, Jill Johnston, Norman Mailer, Diana Trilling, Susan Sontag.
85 min.
A hilarious documentary record of Norman Mailer chairing a debate on 'the feminist question' in New York's City Hall on April 30, 1971. Great cinema, with chauvinist Mailer shaking his fist at feminist hecklers and being ripped apart by Greer and Sontag: the camera patiently hears out one of its 'stars', then flashes across the crowd to catch a face in full flight of uncontrolled expression. The battle of ideas in the debate is fascinating, the effects of the gap between 1971 and 1979 bizarre (so little has changed). But above all this is a demonstration of how the apparent one-dimensionality of film can become intensely dramatic: sounds disproportionate to images, voices erupting off-screen, dreams and convictions at their purest because caught in the moment of conflict. CA

Town Called Bastard, A
(Robert Parrish, 1971, GB/Sp) Robert Shaw, Stella Stevens, Martin Landau, Telly Savalas, Michael Craig, Fernando Rey, Dudley Sutton, Al Lettieri.
97 min.
Shot in Spain with a motley cast and crew, starting with the striking image of Stella Stevens, beatifically asleep in a coffin and being driven in a hearse across the desert by a deaf-mute gunman (Sutton) to the little Mexican village where she intends to claim a corpse after killing the man who murdered her husband, this suffers from the worst excesses of the spaghetti Western. On the other hand, behind the leering violence and allied crudities, both a purpose and a director are clearly evident. Involving a whisky priest (Shaw), a sadistic bandit (Savalas), a puckish traitor to the Revolution (Craig), and a military catalyst (Landau), the complex plot hinges on illusion, arguing obliquely and hauntingly that there is no comfort in loyalty, friendship, heroism, or even in doing the right thing. Scripted by Richard

Aubrey, it's a strange, disturbing film, despite being plain bloody awful for much of the time. TM

Town Like Alice, A (aka The Rape of Malaya)
(Jack Lee, 1956, GB) Virginia McKenna, Peter Finch, Takagi, Marie Lohr, Maureen Swanson, Jean Anderson, Renee Houston, Nora Nicholson, Geoffrey Keen.
117 min. b/w.
This adaptation of Nevil Shute's best-seller looks dated now that the cinema is rather less reticent in depicting wartime brutalities. Needless to say, it's stiff upper-lips and Japanese stereotypes all round as a group of female PoWs suffer at the hands of their captors. The US release title, *The Rape of Malaya*, was more explicit than the movie itself, and the bogus sets don't help much either. BBC TV's long-running series *Tenko* capitalised on the same formula. TJ

Town of Love and Hope, A (Ai to Kibo no Machi)
(Nagisa Oshima, 1959, Jap) Hiroshi Fujikawa, Yoko Mochizuki, Fumio Watanabe, Kakuko Chino, Yuki Tominaga.
63 min. b/w.
Early Oshima is forever being compared with early Godard, but this debut feature (exactly contemporary with *Breathless*) shows that Oshima's political acumen was a great deal stronger than Godard's at this time. A schoolboy lives in a slum with his widowed mother and infant sister; his sole income derives from selling (and reselling) his sister's pigeons, which invariably escape from their buyers and fly home. This 'fraud' is eventually discovered, and the boy angrily accepts society's verdict that he is a 'criminal'. Oshima defines poverty in explicit terms of class oppression, and celebrates the boy's anger and pride. Along the way, he demolishes various liberal stances, and gives Japan's ruling class several short, sharp shocks. The film is rather schematic, not much flesh on its bones, but none the less powerful for that. TR

To Wong Foo, Thanks For Everything! Julie Newmar
(Beeban Kidron, 1995, US) Patrick Swayze, Wesley Snipes, John Leguizamo, Chris Penn, Stockard Channing, Blythe Danner, Melinda Dillon.
108 min.
Three drag queens on a cross-country journey get bogged down in a one-horse town. Sounds familiar? Though the journey is from New York to LA, and the mode of transport a 1967 Cadillac convertible, this is a rip-off of *Priscilla, Queen of the Desert*. Made for Spielberg's Amblin Entertainment, it's low camp for narrow-minded Middle Americans who can't cope with the idea of a cock in a frock. Leguizamo's Chi Chi is the only one who looks anything like a drag queen, let alone a woman; yet we are asked to believe that it's Swayze's breathy Vida and Snipes' squealing Noxeema who've got their stocking seams straight. The queens' gayness is simply never addressed. These are not rope-suckers, these here are big, blowsy women with attitude. And for all their hip-wiggling, hand-flapping and eye-rolling, they still manage to liberate the town's battered wives, closet gays and lovestruck teenagers, while dealing in a more manly way with its shit-kicking good ol' boys and beer-swillin' wife-beaters. The script is as subversive as *Are You Being Served?*, and the cross-dressing on a par with *Mrs Doubtfire*. NF

Toxic Avenger, The
(Michael Herz/Samuel Weil, 1984, US) Andree Maranda, Mitchell Cohen, Jennifer Baptist, Cindy Manion, Robert Prichard, Gary Schneider, Mark Torgi.
100 min.
This has no redeeming features whatsoever, unless you happen to respond to its perversely beguiling mix of eco-splatter and rock-bottom humour. The small town of Tromaville (as in the same team's later *Class of Nuke 'Em High*) is the destination for noxious chemical waste in the form of open vats of bubbling green gunge. Into one of these plunges Melvin (Torgi), nerdish mop-boy at the local aerobics club. He emerges as a do-gooding monster (Cohen) with a penchant for dunking hoodlums into sizzling chip fat or mash-

ing drug-dealers' heads in the Nautilus equipment. Love interest is provided by a blind girl who lovingly prepares scrambled eggshells and Drano sandwiches for her hero. Sicko interest is served up by the psycho-slut who masturbates over polaroids of mangled hit-and-run victims. Yuck and yuck again. AB

Toxic Avenger Part II, The
(Michael Herz/Lloyd Kaufman, 1988, US) Ron Fazio, John Altamura, Phoebe Legere, Rick Collins, Rikiya Yasuoka, Tsutomo Sekine, Lisa Gaye.
96 min.
Having rid Tromaville of all evil, Toxie hangs out at the blind home with his visually-impaired bimbo girlfriend Claire – until the vengeful chairman of Apocalypse Inc, purveyors of toxic waste, trashes the home and lures our hero to Japan, to be reunited with his long-lost 'father'. Discovering that dad is a loathsome drug dealer, Toxie suffers an Oedipal crisis. Meanwhile, the toxic revengers terrorise the Tromavillians and turn their town back into a radioactive dump. An unimaginative re-run of Part I, minus the high school nerd comedy and chronic bad taste, plus some irrelevant Japanese footage. Puerile garbage with a memory half-life of about ten seconds. NF

Toy, The
(Richard Donner, 1982, US) Richard Pryor, Jackie Gleason, Ned Beatty, Scott Schwartz, Teresa Ganzel, Wilfrid Hyde-White.
102 min.
In this far from fair world, the larger a man's native talent, the higher the standard we set him, and so one's disappointment with successive Richard Pryor comedies has dragged the emotions from dismay to anger, forgiveness to apathy. While it's hard to be angered by this particular vehicle, *The Toy* (based on a 1976 French film, *Le Jouet*) is undeniably another wasted opportunity. The plot is fairly implausible: unemployed man (Pryor) is hired as a bauble for billionaire store-owner Gleason's nine-year-old son (welcome again to the New Depression). After virtually every imaginable stock comic situation, Pryor humanises both spoiled son and money/power fixated pop in a moral, weepy ending. Played straight, this could make some quite serious points about the predicament of the unemployed (Pryor as prostitute), but the film finds it easier to opt for cheap laughs. GB

To You, From Me (Neo-ege Narul Bonenda)
(Jang Sun-Woo, 1994, SKor) Moon Sueng-Kuen, Chung Sun-Kyung, Yeo Kyun-Dong.
107 min.
One of the most gleefully offensive films ever made anywhere, Jang's excoriation of trash culture is directed specifically at Korean society in the go-getting '90s, but there's nothing parochial about its satire. Three main characters (a blocked writer/plagiarist, an impotent bank clerk with a thing about *Bonnie and Clyde*, and a factory girl/ex-jailbird) wrestle with each other and with weighty issues like pornography, fraud, drug use, civic corruption, prostitution, phoney activism, gay fascism – you name it. Relentlessly vulgar and committedly sexy, the film shows up American trash-culture celebrants like John Waters for the kindergarten figures they are. TR

Toys
(Barry Levinson, 1992, US) Robin Williams, Michael Gambon, Joan Cusack, Robin Wright, LL Cool J, Donald O'Connor, Arthur Malet, Jack Warden.
121 min.
Levinson's film not only establishes a daunting benchmark for the year's worst, its dire whimsicality will impel many viewers to rush home and kick the hamster. Following the death of toy manufacturer Zevo (O'Connor) whose beanie has ceased to spin, Zevo Toys is inherited by villainous Uncle Leland (Gambon), who plans to pervert the innocent business into the production of lethal military weapons. For most of the film, nephew Leslie (Williams) is too wimpish to oppose him, and his sister Alsatia (Cusack) is clearly one step ahead of the butterfly nets. It's all finally resolved by a war between the toys, with teddy bears dropping like ninepins before the computerised tanks. Some marks for Scarfiotti's sets, but the concept

– 'Open the doors to your imagination' goes the injunction – is so sub-Tim Burton that those doors fly shut. The script is haphazard, and our Gambon gets a scene to explain why, as an American general, he sounds so English. Williams has been playing nauseatingly cute for ages, but achieves a new squashiness here as a chatterbox Andy Pandy. Unbelievably rotten. BC

Toy Soldiers
(Daniel Petrie Jr, 1991, US) Sean Astin, Wil Wheaton, Keith Coogan, Andrew Divoff, Denholm Elliott, Louis Gossett Jr, R Lee Ermey, Mason Adams.
112 min.
When a notorious Colombian drug dealer is extradited to the US for trial, his son (Divoff) invades a school for problem students with his crack terrorist squad, planning to kidnap the judge's son. The boy has been removed, but there are enough errant offspring of famous fathers to provide the necessary leverage. As police and army surround the booby-trapped school, five tough young under-achievers (led by Astin) and two wimps play their part in keeping America safe for democracy. The kids' attainment of self-respect and adulthood through sabotage and risky business is achieved at considerable cost, with Petrie pulling no punches in his depiction of violence. The exciting action set pieces, likewise, are staged with a verve and skill above and beyond the call of duty. NF

Toy Story
(John Lasseter, 1995, US) voices of Tom Hanks, Tim Allen, Don Rickles, Jim Varney, Wallace Shawn, John Ratzenberger, R Lee Ermey.
80 min.
Thanks to Lasseter's sure sense of characterisation (and his technical wizardry), the first wholly computer-generated animation feature is a gem. From a familiar premise (toys come alive whenever humans leave the room) the ingenious, witty script proceeds to work marvels. Hitherto, the likes of Mr Potato Head, Slinky the dog, Rex the dinosaur, Bo Peep and Hamm the piggy bank have accepted as their benevolent lawgiver Woody, a pullstring cowboy and Andy's favourite toy. Come the kid's birthday, however, their world is thrown into disarray by new arrival Buzz Lightyear, a Powers Boothe lookalike in hi-tech spacesuit who not only usurps Woody's place in Andy's affections, but doesn't know he's a toy. While kids will get off on the bewitching colours, the slapstick and the action-packed (and expertly paced) story, the film will probably be more fully appreciated by adults, who'll love the snappy, knowing verbal gags, the vivid, deftly defined characters, and the overall conceptual sophistication. After all, Randy Newman songs, mutant toys reminiscent of Bosch or Svankmajer, and a surprisingly affecting foray into existential crisis are hardly conventional Disney fare. GA

Traces of Red
(Andy Wolk, 1992, US) James Belushi, Lorraine Bracco, Tony Goldwyn, William Russ, Faye Grant, Michelle Joyner, Joe Lisi.
105 min.
Billed as 'an erotic thriller', but devoid of thrills or frills. As Belushi and his clean-cut partner (Goldwyn) trail a serial killer, the womanising Palm Beach detective narrates the events in flashback while lying face-down in a swimming pool, à la Sunset Boulevard. The murderer sends Belushi cryptic, taunting letters, written on a conveniently damaged daisy-wheel typewriter, à la Jagged Edge. The partner suspects Belushi's jealous lover (Bracco), who gets the Kathleen Turner Body Heat role of ex-stewardess turned gold-digger. But there's no shortage of suspects, and soon everyone's dirty linen is being washed in public. The problem is, you don't really care what any of them has to hide; and when you do find out, it's so laughable that you wish you hadn't. The upbeat, double-twist ending makes no sense, the visuals are tawdry rather than glossy, and the tepid sex scenes involving Bracco's body double are more ludicrous than lubricious. NF

Trackdown
(Richard T Heffron, 1976, US) Jim Mitchum, Karen Lamm, Anne Archer, Erik Estrada, Cathy Lee Crosby, Vince Cannon.
98 min.

After vaguely promising a low-grade version of Coogan's Bluff ('straight' Montana cowboy goes to 'hip' LA in pursuit of runaway sister, who has drifted into prostitution), this settles into a run-of-the-mill vigilante movie. As the film-makers run out of ideas, they resort to mayhem as the solution to all their problems, and Jim Mitchum obliges by becoming increasingly bull-like. He tries hard to emulate the deadpan acting of his father Robert, for whom he could almost double, but – somewhat hilariously – gets it all wrong.

Track of the Cat
(William A Wellman, 1954, US) Robert Mitchum, Teresa Wright, Diana Lynn, Tab Hunter, Beulah Bondi, Philip Tonge, William Hopper, Carl 'Alfalfa' Switzer.
102 min.
A magnificently dark, brooding Western – Wellman's second adaptation of a Walter Van Tilburg Clark novel (he also wrote The Ox-Bow Incident) – set during the 1880s on a small, isolated ranch in the Californian mountains, where the depredations of a mountain lion bring simmering family resentments to a head. The god-fearing puritanism of the matriarch (Bondi) has turned sour in her favourite son (Mitchum), brought up to ignore feelings and simply grab what he wants; another son (Hopper), a gentle soul, is mystically in tune with nature; the rest of the family have retreated into a variety of repressions and resentments. Scorning the idea that the marauding beast might be the 'black painter' of legend (spirit of the agelessly old, dispossessed Indian kept about the place as a handyman, Hopper suggests), Mitchum sets out to hunt and kill it. A little perfunctory compared to the novel, where the hunt turns into a dark night of the soul as the hunter gradually realises he has become the hunted, these scenes nevertheless have an extraordinary charge (and weird beauty, with the snowy landscapes shot by William H Clothier in black-and-white on colour stock), reinforcing the subtextual theme that the virgin land is at last exacting revenge on the pioneer who raped it. TM

Tracks
(Henry Jaglom, 1976, US) Dennis Hopper, Taryn Power, Dean Stockwell, Topo Swope, Michael Emil, Zack Norman, James Frawley.
92 min.
'He doesn't seem like he's connected' says a girl of Dennis Hopper's distraught Vietnam veteran. Connected? The man's a virtual zombie! In Tracks, as in Taxi Driver, the neuroses of the war come home to roost. In contrast to the latter's muddle of Catholic and Calvinist sensibilities, Jaglom opts for a more explicitly Freudian approach. Set on a train, with Hopper escorting the coffin of a dead buddy and encountering sundry American archetypes, the film becomes an increasingly specific psychological journey. But the deeper it delves into symbolism, the more incoherent and hallucinatory it becomes, fragmenting faster even than Hopper. Nevertheless, Hopper's sweaty paranoia, a sustained and terminal piece of Method acting, keeps the film on the rails. Perhaps Jaglom would be more incisive if he tried less hard to make 'art'. CPe

Track 29
(Nicolas Roeg, 1987, GB) Theresa Russell, Gary Oldman, Christopher Lloyd, Colleen Camp, Sandra Bernhard, Seymour Cassel, Leon Rippy.
90 min.
So obsessed with his model train set is North Carolina geriatrician Lloyd that he neglects the complaints of wife Russell about their sexless, childless union. Her suicide is averted only by the sudden arrival of English oddball Oldman, who claims to be her long-absent illegitimate son. Cue fiery rows and frantic role-playing. Roeg and screenplay-writer Dennis Potter's brash, over-emphatic psychodrama tosses out enough tricky ambiguities (is Oldman merely a child of Russell's frustrated imagination?), musical and cinematic references, and verbal and visual puns, to suggest that there's far more here than meets the eye. Finally, however, it's merely an inflated Oedipal riddle, and an exploration of guilt, desire and impotence that ends up as a curiously unilluminating and predictable vision of the world as funny-farm. Lloyd performs with a certain verve, but Russell and Oldman seem to have confused range with wobbly histrionics. GA

Trading Places
(John Landis, 1983, US) Dan Aykroyd, Eddie Murphy, Ralph Bellamy, Don Ameche, Denholm Elliott, Jamie Lee Curtis, Kristin Holby, James Belushi.
116 min.
When two bastardly billionaire brothers, Duke and Duke of Duke & Duke Commodities Brokers (Bellamy, Ameche), have a one dollar wager about the respective merits of breeding or environment on a man's character, they engineer the 'trading places' of one of their young financial wizards (Aykroyd, in fine smug form) with a black low-life hustler (Murphy), and sit back to watch Murphy rise and Aykroyd fall. This absurdly wayward premise may be a re-run of the Prince and the Pauper theme, but its snowy Christmas setting in Philadelphia provides the film with more than a hint of Christmas Carol fairytale warmth; it's also a great vehicle for the talents of Murphy, who fulfils with outrageous confidence all that he promised in 48 HRS. As a satire on the internecine savagery of fiscal doings under late Reaganite capitalism, the movie is not as biting as it thinks it is; but it's still the best hoot since Arthur. CPea

Traffic (Trafic)
(Jacques Tati, 1970, Fr/It) Jacques Tati, Maria Kimberly, Marcel Fraval, Honoré Bostel, Tony Kneppers.
96 min.
Admirers of Playtime won't be too disappointed, but for the Tati heretic it's a long, slow haul between the occasional brilliant gag. With all the wonder of someone just back from Crusoe's island, Tati here discovers the joys of traffic problems. Jammed drivers, not just one but several, pick their noses as they wait, so that Tati can milk all the behavioural possibilities out of furtiveness, relish, pretending I'm doing something else, and so forth. Then there's the crash, a ballet of yawning boots and bonnets as cars pile up from nowhere and detached parts take on a life of their own as they spin off on unpredictable joyrides. Or there's the rainy bit, with windscreen wipers sweeping rhythmically, chattily, pompously or excitedly, depending on the personality of the owner. All very clever, but done with the sort of calculated precision that has one chalking up points rather than laughing. TM

Tragedy of a Ridiculous Man, The (La Tragedia di un Uomo Ridicolo)
(Bernardo Bertolucci, 1981, It) Ugo Tognazzi, Anouk Aimée, Laura Morante, Victor Cavallo, Olympia Carlisi, Riccardo Tognazzi, Vittorio Caprioli, Renato Salvatori.
116 min.
Tognazzi plays a rich Parma dairy farmer forced to sell up his greatest love – his material possessions – to meet the ransom demanded by a gang of terrorists who have kidnapped his son. In an attempt to fathom the siege mentality induced in an Italian society which had by then accepted terrorist violence as a commonplace, Bertolucci inverts the son-in-search-of-the-father theme of his most widely admired film, The Spider's Stratagem, and his small ensemble of lead characters begin to spin webs of deception – on each other, on us. The result is a mordantly witty tragicomedy which matches the sombre tones of Carlo Di Palma's cinematography, but the style is no less flamboyant and seductive than that of Bertolucci's earlier films. RM

Tragedy of Carmen, The (La Tragédie de Carmen)
(Peter Brook, 1983, Fr) Hélène Delavault, Howard Hensel, Agnès Host, Jake Gardner, Jean-Paul Denizon, Alain Maratrat.
85 min.
Brook's interpretation of the evergreen myth (luminously photographed by Sven Nykvist) cuts incisively through the lush romanticism of Bizet's opera (although retaining all his best tunes) to the tighter fantasy of Mérimée's original story, leaving only a sinewy passion to bind together this tale of a gypsy, a soldier, and their love. Delavault is inspired as Carmen, displaying a malignity that is as motiveless as that of Shakespeare's Iago, but as resigned to the inexorable workings of fate as Lear. The rest of the excellent cast work at a fever

pitch, keeping events within Brook's earthy arena at a rolling boil, while Brook's choice of title leaves no room to doubt that it will, as ever, end in tears. FD

Trail of the Pink Panther

(Blake Edwards, 1982, GB) Peter Sellers, David Niven, Herbert Lom, Richard Mulligan, Joanna Lumley, Capucine, Robert Loggia, Harvey Korman, Burt Kwouk.
96 min.
The presence of Blake Edwards and most of the original *Pink Panther* team shouldn't fool you into thinking that this is an entirely new adventure. Instead, there are some out-takes of Sellers from the previous movies, tacked together with an anorexic plotline. After that, we suffer Lumley's French aksonted TV reporter, whose task is to track down 'the essential Clouseau', linking a lot of 'flashback' clips, interviews with the 'Panther' stars in character, and some embarrassingly unfunny reconstructions of the detective's early life. Made two years after Sellers' death, possibly motivated as a tribute, this garbled piece of incestuous myth-massaging forfeits any sympathy through its shamefully mismanaged construction. FL

Train, The

(John Frankenheimer, 1964, US/Fr/It) Burt Lancaster, Paul Scofield, Jeanne Moreau, Michel Simon, Suzanne Flon, Charles Millot, Albert Rémy, Wolfgang Preiss, Howard Vernon.
140 min. b/w.
Discount some self-conscious talk about Art as a national heritage, as well as clumsy dubbing of the supporting cast, and you have a rattling good thriller about a World War II German general (Scofield) determined to flee Paris just before the liberation with a trainload of Impressionist paintings. One obsession runs headlong into another as a French railway inspector (Lancaster), once unwillingly started out in opposition, finds he cannot stop, and must go on finding new ways and means of delaying the train for an hour here, a day there. In Frankenheimer's hands, the whole paraphernalia of trains, tracks and shunting yards acquires an almost hypnotic fascination as the screen becomes a giant chessboard on which huge metallic pawns are manoeuvred, probing for some fatal weakness but seemingly engaged in some deadly primeval struggle. TM

Train of Events

(Basil Dearden/Charles Crichton/Sidney Cole, 1949, GB) Valerie Hobson, John Clements, Jack Warner, Gladys Henson, Susan Shaw, Joan Dowling, Laurence Payne, Peter Finch.
88 min. b/w.
Trying to repeat the formula of *Dead of Night*, Ealing came a horrible cropper with this portmanteau telling, in flashback from a train crash, the stories which brought three groups of people aboard the Euston-Liverpool express. Shorn of the talents of Cavalcanti and Hamer, the direction is flat. The trilogy of shoddy yarns (melodramatic, comic, tragic) sprout clichés by the yard, and arbitrarily resort to the crash as a resolution. Worst of all is the linking device involving scenes from the life of a Cockney engine-driver and his wife, soon – as played by Jack Warner and Gladys Henson – to achieve cosy apotheosis as Mr and Mrs Dixon of Dock Green in *The Blue Lamp*. TM

Train of Shadows (Tren de Sombras)

(José Luis Guerin, 1996, Sp) Juliette Gaultier, Ivon Orvain, Anne Céline Auché, Céline Laurent, Simone Mercier, Carlos Romagosa.
80 min.
Though slow, determinedly poetic, and in places rather abstract, this casts a spell. It begins with home movies shot at the family chateau in the '30s by Parisian lawyer Gérard Fleury, who disappeared mysteriously while off looking for a special quality of light. The film then visits the now empty Normandy chateau, the images suggesting the presence of ghosts. Finally, the archive footage is returned to, though this time treated, reversed and repeated, and new suggestions of relationships between the people begin to emerge. It's a strange exercise, haunting, even at times erotic (writer/director Guerin seems – quite understandably – obsessed by Fleury's stunningly beautiful daughter). GA

Train Robbers, The

(Burt Kennedy, 1973, US) John Wayne, Ann-Margret, Rod Taylor, Ben Johnson, Bobby Vinton, Christopher George, Ricardo Montalban, Jerry Gatlin.
92 min.
Inoffensive Western with Wayne, rheumy-eyed and overweight, called upon to reminisce about old times with Ben Johnson at every available moment, leading a gang that rides like a U Certificate version of Peckinpah's *Wild Bunch*. Wayne, as self-appointed guardian of the law, injects his boys (including Bobby Vinton, singer from the early '60s) with his particular brand of benevolent fascism. In return for every fist-whipping, they learn to respect him all the more and to call him 'Sir'. The band ride after half a million's worth of stolen gold so they can turn it in for the 50,000 dollars reward; it's that sort of film. Loads of male camaraderie and big country theme music, plus Ann-Margret riding along as a box-office concession and to get the rest of the cast horny in a U Certificate sort of way.

Trainspotting

(Danny Boyle, 1995, GB) Ewan McGregor, Jonny Lee Miller, Ewen Bremner, Robert Carlyle, Kevin McKidd, Kelly Macdonald, Pauline Lynch, Irvine Welsh.
93 min.
A shocking, painfully subjective trawl through the Edinburgh heroin culture of the 1980s, Irvine Welsh's cult novel is hardly an obvious choice for the team who made *Shallow Grave*. Yet the film's a triumph. Audaciously punching up the pitch-black comedy, juggling parallel character strands and juxtaposing image, music and voice-over with a virtuosity worthy of Scorsese on peak form, *Trainspotting* the movie captures precisely Welsh's insolent, amoral intelligence. Amoral, but not unthinking, and certainly not unfeeling. Nihilism runs deep in this movie, emotion cannot be countenanced, only blocked off by another hit, another gag, but the anarchic, exhilarating rush of the highs can't drown out the subsequent, devastating lows – these are two sides of the same desperation. Danny Boyle's intuitive, vital, empathetic direction pushes so far, the movie flies on sheer momentum – that and bravura performances from Bremner's gormless Spud, Carlyle's terrifying Begbie and, especially, McGregor's Renton, who supplies a low-key, charismatic centre. This may not have the weight of 'Great Art', but it crystalises youthful disaffection with the verve of the best and brightest pop culture. A sensation. TCh

Traitement de Choc (The Doctor in the Nude/ Shock Treatment)

(Alain Jessua, 1972, Fr/It) Alain Delon, Annie Girardot, Michel Duchaussoy, Robert Hirsch, Jean-François Calvé, Guy Saint-Jean.
91 min.
Jessua's first two films, *Life Upside Down* and *Comic Strip Hero*, attracted little more than good notices over here, so his third was distributed as an exploitation picture retitled in honour of Delon's cock-flashing sequence. Don't be misled, since the film is actually a political allegory fashioned as a horror story. Girardot, visiting Dr Devilers' clifftop clinic for rejuvenation treatment, discovers behind the futuristic settings a nightmare world of primeval instincts and ruthless logic that holds no place for the weak. Jessua handles his mixture of suspense and satire with assurance, drawing fine performances from Girardot, confused and finally uncertain of her sanity, and Delon as the diabolic yet half-sympathetic doctor in whose arms she finds herself. A neat cautionary tale on human vanity cum fable about hypocrisy.

Traitor Spy (aka The Torso Murder Mystery)

(Walter Summers, 1939, GB) Bruce Cabot, Marta Labarr, Tamara Desni, Romilly Lunge, Percy Walsh, Edward Lexy, Frederick Valk.
75 min. b/w.
If transposing Marie Stopes' *Married Love* to the screen didn't win undying fame for Summers, this – his last picture for an ungrateful world – surely should have done. Cabot plays a British armaments worker and freelance spy who is forced to go on the run after killing (and dismembering) a disgruntled German agent who makes an attempt

on his life. As the film moves from toy-town Devon to a very seedy London, it rapidly takes off from the cardboard conventions of the British thriller. In its creation of authentic atmosphere – an Italian dentist/tattooist's parlour in the Waterloo Road, a sleazy night-club populated by spivs, whores and multi-national gangsters – the film offers a fascinating glimpse into the under-world of the '30s, and presages the realism of the following decade. Summers skilfully exploits the paranoia of the phony war to create satisfyingly red-blooded villains, and the melodramatic conflagration of an ending is remarkably, and effectively, uncompromising. RMy

Tramp, Tramp, Tramp

(Harry Edwards/Frank Capra, 1926, US) Harry Langdon, Joan Crawford, Edwards Davis, Carlton Griffin, Alec B Francis.
5,625 ft. b/w.
Langdon's first venture into features has echoes of Harold Lloyd (when our hero is dangling helplessly over the edge of a cliff), and concludes with a raging typhoon reminiscent of Keaton's natural disasters, but the bulk of the gags are wholly individual. Langdon enters a cross-continent walk to boost the local brand of footwear; Joan Crawford is the girl he can hug only if he crosses the finishing line first. After many strange convolutions, he does so. GB

Trancers (aka Future Cop)

(Charles Band, 1984, US) Tim Thomerson, Helen Hunt, Michael Stefani, Art Le Fleur, Telma Hopkins, Richard Erdman.
85 min.
Three hundred years hence, trooper Jack Deth (Thomerson) is busy wiping out zombified humans ('trancers') under the evil influence of megabaddie Martin Whistler (Stefani). But Whistler hotfoots it back into 1985 to inhabit the body of his ancestor – LA's chief of police – and proceeds to pick off predecessors of the all-important Counsellors. Deth, assigned to protect the survivors, fetches up in the body of one of his own forebears, and links up with a resourceful heroine (Hunt), who manages more than once to save his bacon. An engaging rip-off of *The Terminator* with bits of *Blade Runner* thrown in, complete with cheap and cheerful thrills and queasy continuity, held together by a pleasantly self-deprecating hero. AB

Trances (El Hal)

(Ahmed El Maanouni, 1981, Mor/Fr) Nass El Ghiwane, Taieb Seddiki.
87 min.
A documentary on the music group Nass El Ghiwane. We eavesdrop on the group, whose troubadour style has won them a large and rapturous following in their home country of Morocco. The debt owed to the musical traditions of their faith and land is freely acknowledged, and vividly brought to mind by the trance-like state their compelling, percussive music induces in their fans. Amid nostalgic and folkloric anecdotes, they bicker over recording contracts. Nothing new here, but interesting. FD

Transatlantic Tunnel

see Tunnel, The

Trans-Europ-Express

(Alain Robbe-Grillet, 1966, Fr) Jean-Louis Trintignant, Marie-France Pisier, Nadine Verdier, Christian Barbier, Charles Millot, Daniel Emilfork, Alain Robbe-Grillet.
90 min. b/w.
Written and directed by the high priest of the French *nouveau roman*, this now looks considerably more literary than cinematic. Robbe-Grillet himself plays the focal character, the author-within-the-film, dreaming up a surreal melodrama involving a man (Trintignant) who boards the same train, during a journey through Europe: dope-pushing, gangsterism, bondage fantasies. Trintignant's cool is as unshakeable as ever, but the vague 'modernism' of the project can't conceal an underlying pomposity. CA

Transformers – The Movie, The

(Nelson Shin, 1986, US) voices: Eric Idle, Judd Nelson, Leonard Nimoy, Robert Stack, Lionel Stander, Orson Welles.
85 min.

Following on the bad scent of feature-length commercials for *The Care Bears* and *My Little Pony*, comes this animated sci-fi tinbot battle between the forces of good and evil. The good guys are a bunch of heavy metallurgists called Autobots who, involved in an age-old conflict, are once again waging war on the equally powerful Decepticons, led by the mega-nasty Megatron. You'd be amazed at what these characcers, collectively known as *Transformers*, are capable of. With the flick of a hinge...Is it a bird? Is it a plane? No, it's...In fact, they all look rather similar, all talk with synthesised voices, and all race around the Galaxy to the thump of a diabolical but appropriate heavy metal score. Still, the animation is extremely well done, with plenty of action in the fight sequences as the heroic Autobots, with the help of the Matrix of Leaders (a sort of all-powerful crystal ball), restore peace to the Universe. Hopefully, for the last time. DA

Trapped in Paradise

(George Gallo, 1994, US) Nicolas Cage, Richard B Shull, Jon Lovitz, Mädchen Amick, Dana Carvey, Jack Heller, Vic Manni.
111 min.
This gormless Christmas comedy drama has a New York restaurant manager Bill Firpo (Cage), and his two con brothers, Dave (Lovitz) and Alvin (Carvey), plying their dumb klutz criminal ways. Alvin is the klepto who steals the toys from cereal packets; Dave the conniving one, masquerading as a Catskill comic; and Bill, the sensible one of these three latter-day Stooges, is suffering and exasperated. They go to Paradise, Pennsylvania, to succour the daughter of hard con Vic Mazzucci (Manni), but find the bank where she works irresistible to rob. It's an odd plot-potty, frenetic movie, shot at some snow-blown Canadian location with irrelevant panache. Cage looks cold most of the time, and has retractable stubble. The rest of the cast look like they're waiting for summer. WH

Trash

(Paul Morrissey, 1970, US) Joe Dallesandro, Holly Woodlawn, Jane Forth, Michael Sklar, Geri Miller, Andrea Feldman.
103 min.
A companion piece to *Flesh*, with Dallesandro as a down-and-out junkie living on New York's Lower East Side whose heroin addiction has rendered him impotent; just as Joe's desirable virility formed the (nominal) subject of *Flesh*, so his undesirable impotence is at the centre of *Trash*. The surprise value of Morrissey's films (the 'liberating nudity', the frankness about sexuality, the playful reversals of sex-roles) camouflaged a number of crucial failings. *Flesh* and *Trash* are both eulogies to Dallesandro's body, but are also both moralistic to the point of being puritan about sex in general, and the female sex in particular. TR

Traveller

(Joe Comerford, 1981, GB) Judy Donovan, Davy Spillane, Alan Devlin, Johnny Choil Mhaidhc, Paddy Donovan, Joe Pilkington.
80 min.
Scripted by Neil Jordan, this has something of the same bizarre thriller quality as *Angel*, with a young couple – reluctantly submitting to an arranged marriage, and sent on a smuggling mission from Limerick to Strabane – running from a mysterious encounter into robbery and murder while crossing the border from Southern Ireland. Instead of the strange wonderland of *Angel*, a strikingly desolate picture of rural poverty, but the film never quite manages to clinch its supposedly thematic connection between politics and violence. TM

Traveller

(Jack Green, 1997, US) Bill Paxton, Mark Wahlberg, Julianna Marguilies, James Gammon, Luke Askew, Nikki Deloach.
100 min.
Intriguing set-up: gypsy initiation drama plus grifter thriller. The Travellers are an insular gypsy group with Oirish roots and smart suits, who congregate in the backwoods of the Deep South for a spot of traditional dancing before hiving off in their 4x4s to hoodwink local gullibles. Bokky (Paxton) likes selling them stitched-up trailers and water-based 'sealant' for their drive-ways. Enter Pat O'Hara (Wahlberg) who wants into the Family. He has the blood (and 'the blood don't lie'), but not the breeding – his father was cast out when he married a gentile. Could it be Bokky's turn to fall for one of his victims (Marguilies)? Though competently directed by Clint Eastwood's cameraman Jack Green, matters unravel when the film ratchets up the tension and become entirely implausible at the close. NB

Travelling Executioner, The

(Jack Smight, 1970, US) Stacy Keach, Marianna Hill, Bud Cort, Graham Jarvis, James J Sloyan, M Emmet Walsh, John Bottoms, Ford Rainey.
94 min.
More a grotesque theatrical farce than a black comedy: Jonas Candide (Keach) travels the American South of 1918, hiring out his electric chair at 100 bucks a throw, but loses his omnipotence when he falls for his first lady 'victim' (Hill), and starts conniving to save her. It works best as – and is worth seeing for – an extravagant, outsize performance from Keach, a mixture of trash rhetoric, sinister dedication, and fairground showmanship. But what it desperately needs is a director capable of anchoring the fantasy in recognisable human realities. TR

Travelling Light: a Portrait of Lindsay Kemp

(Theo Eshetu, 1991, It)
57 min.
Style over content has always been a hallmark of Lindsay Kemp, but in this case, Kemp's own outrageously marvellous sense of theatre is subverted by Eshetu's self-serving, self-congratulatory camera techniques. He leaves viewers with the impression that Kemp's visions, awash with a tacky, extravagant glamour all their own, need electronic manipulation. Eshetu's approach is jagged and uneven. Yes, there are clips from many of Kemp's most important works, but they leave you feeling dissatisfied and deprived of anything more substantial than soundbites. The clips, including some early footage of David Bowie, are interwoven with interviews, both backstage and at home. It all adds up to a frustrating hour-long trailer. AR

Travelling North

(Carl Schultz, 1986, Aust) Leo McKern, Julia Blake, Graham Kennedy, Henri Szeps, Michele Fawdon, Diane Craig.
97 min.
David Williamson's filmed play is a bit like an Australian *On Golden Pond*. Frank (McKern) retires to his Queensland dream home overlooking a lake with his middle-aged girlfriend Frances (Blake), but heart trouble erodes the idyll. A bossy old bully, Frank soon offends their boring but helpful neighbour Freddie (Kennedy), overrides the local doctor (Szeps) in the matter of prognosis and prescription, and drives even patient Frances back to her daughters in Melbourne with his increasing cantankerousness. This slight, unsensational history depends almost entirely upon our sympathy for the central character, a shoo-in thanks to the McKern outline in shorts, eye-patch and paunch. The actor would serve as a definition of the word curmudgeon. 'The autumn of our days?' he mocks the registrar, having asked Frances to return and marry him, 'Get on with it before we slide into winter'. BC

Travelling Players, The (O Thiassos)

(Theodor Angelopoulos, 1975, Greece) Eva Kotamanidou, Aliki Georgoulis, Statos Pachis, Maris Vassiliou, Petros Zarkadis.
230 min.
Made, incredibly, under the noses of the military police during the Colonels' regime, Angelopoulos' film examines, with a passionate radicalism, the labyrinth of Greek politics around that country's agonising civil war. This is done through the eyes of a troupe of actors, whose pastoral folk drama *Golfo the Shepherdess* is continually interrupted as they become unwitting spectators of the political events that ultimately polarise them. This slow, complex, four-hour film will obviously provide problems for people raised on machine-gun cutting techniques. Editing is very restrained, and some takes last up to five minutes, but the stately pace of the film soon becomes compulsive; and the shabby provincial Greece of rusting rail-way tracks and flaking facades which the slow camera examines is visually beguiling. The closing passage, when one of the actors is buried after being executed, and his colleagues spontaneously raise their hands above their heads to applaud not a performance but a life, is an incredibly moving moment. DPer

Traviata, La

(Franco Zeffirelli, 1982, Neth) Teresa Stratas, Placido Domingo, Cornell MacNeil, Allan Monk, Axell Gall.
109 min.
Zeffirelli's talents are well-matched to *La Traviata*. Based on Dumas' novel *The Lady of the Camellias*, with an original soundtrack by Verdi, this is grand opera at its most pathetic, in which Romantic heroines suffer and expire amid the fluttering demi-monde of 19th century Paris. Teresa Stratas, as that most famous of TB cases, has a suitably angelic face, though her voice is a touch less seraphic in the higher registers; the masterful Placido Domingo brings an ingenuous charm to the role of Alfredo; Zeffirelli directs as he has always done, in a style high on gloss and bravura, with occasional nods to film realism via exteriors and voice-overs. The sumptuousness comes close to overkill, but fine musical moments help some magic to survive. LU

Treasure Island (Ostrov Sokrovishch)

(Eugen Fridman, 1971, USSR) Boris Andreiev, Aare Laanemets, L Noreika, A Massulis, L Urmonavichus, L Chagolova, A Pikialis, P Klass.
87 min.
This Gorky Studio production of Stevenson's romance is played chiefly for derring-do, and judging from the battle in the Admiral Benbow director/co-writer Fridman has seen a few spaghetti Westerns. Creditable re-creation of 18th century English life, plus plausible West Country dubbing for the British release print; but the attractive voyage out is too long for a pirate tale, and Jim's account of how none of his companions gained lasting happiness from his doubloons makes for a flat finish (as well as leaving us in no doubt about where the movie came from). JPy

Treasure Island

(Fraser C Heston, 1990, US) Charlton Heston, Christian Bale, Richard Johnson, Julian Glover, Clive Wood, Oliver Reed, Christopher Lee.
132 min.
Ah-aaarh, Jim lad! Where would we be without Robert Louis Stevenson? With Heston *père et fils* attempting some kind of comeback for the great old piratical fable, this has coral-blue location cinematography somewhere off the Spanish Main, one of those solid True Brit casts, and Charlton Heston, plus parrot, making what is not even a really interestingly bad job of old Long John himself. An over-familiar (and over-*familial*) version of Stevenson's novel, made for TV, it has a few fine moments, an excellent eccentric Squire Trelawny from Richard Johnson, and some sweet seaside shots of late Georgian Bristol. Apart from that, it's even longer than Ben Gunn's whiskers, and deeply tedious, shiver me aching timbers. SGr

Treasure Island

see *Ile au trésor, L'*

Treasure of Matecumbe

(Vincent McEveety, 1976, US) Robert Foxworth, Joan Hackett, Peter Ustinov, Vic Morrow, Johnny Doran, Billy Attmore, Jane Wyatt.
117 min.
Not a great deal more than a standard Disney yarn, to be sure: a chase down the Mississippi; two fearlessly resourceful schoolboys; man-eating mosquitoes, a spectacular hurricane; no sex, no serious injuries, and only one fatality. McEveety, having the measure of his duties, delivers the action with the minimum of fuss; and the plot, drawn from a novel by Pulitzer prizewinner Robert Lewis Taylor, bashes along at a cracking pace. Hackett, radiant and wet-lipped, offers an energetic character study of a sturdy Southern belle fleeing from a devilish Yankee suitor (the action takes place just after the Civil War); show-

stealing honours, however, go to Ustinov as a loquacious quack pedlar whose foul medicine doubles, when the need arises, as the ingredients for Molotov cocktails. First-rate escapist nonsense. JPy

Treasure of the Four Crowns
(Ferdinando Baldi, 1982, US/Sp) Tony Anthony, Ana Obregón, Gene Quintano, Jerry Lazarus, Francisco Rabal.
100 min.
A marked improvement on *Comin' at Ya!*, the previous miserable effort from the team of Tony Anthony, Gene Quintano and Baldi. Which isn't to say much for this nonsense about ancient prophecies and modern mettle, bloated with the cruder possibilities of 3-D, plus sound effects and scenes shamelessly stolen from other films. One sorry borrowing, where the hero is chased by a flaming ball of fire, doesn't even compare to the similarly plagiarised TV chocolate commercial, let alone their source in *Raiders of the Lost Ark*. Burning balls are the least of the hero's problems: when you're up to your neck in Visigoth legends, pitted against a multi-million dollar messianic sect with only a few unlikely friends for help, and a cheap rally jacket for cool-customer credibility, such physical imperfections hardly seem important. FD

Treasure of the Sierra Madre, The 100
(John Huston, 1948, US) Humphrey Bogart, Walter Huston, Tim Holt, Bruce Bennett, Barton MacLane, Alfonso Bedoya, John Huston.
126 min. b/w.
For once, Bogart plays a really vicious bastard, Fred C Dobbs, in this, the first of two movies he made in 1948 with Huston. It's a sort of lifeboat drama for three, with Holt the young innocent and director's dad Walter as the wise old buzzard, flanking Bogart's bravura paranoia. Director Huston tries to yank the basic elements – gold lust in a Mexican wilderness – into the spare eloquence of a fable, and tends to look pretentious rather than profound. In any case, outrageously Oscar-seeking performances like actor Huston's, coupled with director Huston's comparative conviction with action sequences, work against any yearning for significance. There's a quite enjoyable yarn buried under the hollow laughter. SG

Tree of Hands
(Giles Foster, 1988, GB) Helen Shaver, Lauren Bacall, Malcolm Stoddard, Peter Firth, Paul McGann, Kate Hardie, Tony Haygarth, Phyllida Law.
89 min.
This unimaginative adaptation of Ruth Rendell's dark-edged psychological thriller, set in and around London, straightens out most of her subtle twists and kinks, dissipating tension and interest apace. Bacall, loony mom of Shaver (an American writer resident in Hampstead), steals a council estate kid to replace the divorced Shaver's recently deceased child. Shaver, initially horrified, is soon on the horns of a dilemma as the catatonic boy (his back a railway map of weals and lacerations) reawakens her maternal instincts. The abduction is soon broadcast news; a crazy chauffeur (Firth) and enamoured doctor friend (Stoddard) pitch in with their respective versions of sweet-and-sour emotional blackmail. The result is on the whole pleasureless, uninvolving, and visually dull; it reflects little of Rendell's delicious and implicating sense of (a)moral relativism and distaste. Paul McGann, as the stolen child's contemptuous working class father, makes a stab at a performance, but is hauled away into implausibility and gun-toting mania. WH

Tree of Wooden Clogs, The (L'Albero degli Zoccoli)
(Ermanno Olmi, 1978, It) Luigi Ornaghi, Francesca Moriggi, Omar Brignoli, Antonio Ferrari.
186 min.
Olmi's uncompromising reconstruction of peasant life in turn-of-the-century Lombardy marks a return to his origins in neo-realism and non-professional casts. Choreographed as an ensemble work that admits no star performers, his film takes its unhurried pace from the lives of the dirt

farmers it observes – lives of repetitive drudgery punctuated by cautious moments of felicity. Its gently muted colour camerawork succeeds in covering the exquisite landscape with a thin patina of mud, while for two of its three hours the changing of the seasons is the closest the film comes to a dramatic event. By showing peasant exploitation as neither triumphant Calvary nor action-packed drama, Olmi refutes both *1900* and *Padre Padrone*, and creates a near-perfect hermetic universe, punctured only in those rare moments when, as tautologous as the film's English title, he dots the 'i's on the amply demonstrated Marxist message. Still, a near faultless and major film. JD

Trees Lounge
(Steve Buscemi, 1996, US) Steve Buscemi, Chloe Sevigny, Anthony LaPaglia, Elizabeth Bracco, Daniel Baldwin, Mark Boone Jr, Seymour Cassel, Carol Kane, Debi Mazar, Brooke Smith, Michael Imperioli, Mimi Rogers.
95 min.
Tommy Basilio (Buscemi), a no-hoper living in suburban Long Island, is not exactly happy. He's been sacked for 'borrowing' money from the garage owned by his buddy Rob (LaPaglia), with whom Tommy's girl Theresa (Bracco) has now taken up. His family tend to regard him as a black sheep, while Jerry (Baldwin), Theresa's volatile brother-in-law, is anxious about Tommy hanging around his teenage daughter Debbie (Sevigny). Small wonder Tommy takes to getting legless with troubled family man Mike (Boone), trying to pick up anyone in a skirt, and generally making a nuisance of himself in the unprepossessing Trees Lounge bar. Buscemi's semi-autobiographical first feature as writer/director is a beautifully low-key, disarmingly perceptive blue- collar character-study, reminiscent of vintage Cassavetes in its sociological and emotional authenticity. If nothing here is quite as risky or inspirational as the late indie king's nerviest masterpieces, there's still much to savour: a cherishably naturalistic, extremely witty script packed with tasty trivialities and non sequiturs; top-notch performances from a superb cast; a smattering of subtle sight-gags; and sufficient drama to ensure that the overall understatement never outstays its welcome. Crucially, despite the loose narrative structure and amiable air of inconsequentiality, it's all held together, and lent poignancy, by Buscemi's Tommy: irresponsible, selfish even, but endowed with enough scrawny charm to allow us to care about his need, and capacity, for some kind of redemption. GA

Tre Fratelli
see Three Brothers

Tregua, La
see Truce, The

Tremors
(Ron Underwood, 1989, US) Kevin Bacon, Fred Ward, Finn Carter, Michael Gross, Reba McEntire.
96 mins.
'The phones are dead, the roads are out…we're on our own!' All is not well in Perfection, Nevada, a remote desert town. Itinerant cowpokes Val (Bacon) and Earl (Ward) are all set to up sticks when they happen across a corpse perched incongruously atop a telegraph pole…and then another, apparently swallowed up by the earth. Huge, carnivorous, worm-like creatures, capable of tunnelling at incredible speeds in response to seismic vibrations, are literally undermining Perfection. With a tip of the hat towards its '50s forefathers, this canny genre entry exploits its novel subterranean threat to the max, the ingenious situations being orchestrated with considerable skill by first-time director Underwood. Bacon and Ward project a wonderful low-key rapport, based initially on jokey ignorance before giving way to terse apprehension. It's great to hear authentic B movie talk again, especially when the cast takes it upon itself to name the monsters, only to come up with 'graboids' by default, and to debate their probable origin: 'One thing's for sure…them ain't local boys'. This is what a monster movie is supposed to be like, and it's terrific. TCh

Trenchcoat
(Michael Tuchner, 1983, US) Margot Kidder, Robert Hays, Daniel Faraldo, David Suchet, Ronald Lacey.
91 min.
It's a Maltese teaser for would-be thriller author Kidder when she finds herself involved in genuine murder and intrigue during a Mediterranean holiday. *Airplane!* pilot Hays is on hand to explain the plot. A very minor offering from the Disney company at a time when it was tentatively trying to alter its image. TJ

Tren de Sombras
see Train of Shadows

37°2 le Matin
see Betty Blue

36 Fillette
see Virgin

Três Palmeiras (Three Palm Trees)
(João Botelho, 1994, Port) Teresa Roby, Pedro Hestnes, Isabel de Castro, Rita Lopes Alves.
68 min.
Botelho's typically exquisite feature is a bizarre compendium of seemingly unrelated stories, told (mostly) by a man to his heavily pregnant wife, and taking place in Lisbon over a period of eight hours. Some of it is very sombre, though there are lovely irruptions of comedy and surreal fantasy. Tying it all together is the writer/director's assured control of mood, sensitive use of music, and the superbly elegant images. It's too experimental a narrative exercise to be to everyone's taste, but recommended to fans of *Hard Times* and *A Portuguese Goodbye*. GA

Trespass
(Walter Hill, 1992, US) Bill Paxton, Ice T, William Sadler, Ice Cube, Art Evans, De'Voreaux White, Bruce A Young.
101 min.
Starting from an implausible conceit – Arkansas firemen Paxton and Sadler lay their mitts on a map to stolen gold possibly hidden in a derelict East St Louis factory – this concerns the greedy pair's attempts to escape, alive and much the richer, from a black drugs gang who use the building for making deals and dumping corpses. Cue stereotyped characters, lashings of violence, fallings-out in the rival camps (with crack-king Ice T facing challenges from would-be usurper Ice Cube), and a tortuous plot that spirals inexorably from the ingenious to the ludicrously overblown. Everything subscribes to the modish: the moral cynicism, the superfluous use of video, the rap soundtrack, the flip aftermath to the fiery carnage of the finale. Perhaps that's the result of an uneasy meeting of disparate talents: scriptwriters Bob Gale and Robert Zemeckis are known for frantic action and slick twists, Hill (at least in his early, better films) for laconic, mythic heroes, pared-down plotting and sudden bursts of violence. For the undemanding, it may seem a fair stand-off; but compared to Hill's best work, it's merely a jerk-off. GA

Tre Volti della Paura, I
see Black Sabbath

Trial, The
(David Jones, 1992, GB) Kyle MacLachlan, Anthony Hopkins, Jason Robards, Juliet Stevenson, Polly Walker, Alfred Molina, David Thewlis, Tony Haygarth.
120 min.
The effect of nightmare is muted in this Pinter-scripted version of Kafka's classic. MacLachlan would seem appropriately cast as the much put-upon minor bank official, but as soon as he's arrested problems arise. His variable English accent and declamatory style militate against audience identification essential to this dystopian chronicle, creating a hollowness at the film's core from which it never really recovers. A cavalcade of top British thesps do, however, come up with the goods (Hopkins' oppressive priest, Stevenson as K's enigmatic neighbour). The film pits an incredulous, almost self-righteous individual against the

absurdist machinations of an institutionalised (in)justice system gone mad, and grounds events in authentic Prague locations and 1912 period detail, yet the result boxes in the parameters of Kafka's imagination. Unlike Welles' dizzying city of the imagination, Jones' faithful run-through doesn't quite conjure up the keynote of pervasive unease. TJ

Trial, The (Le Procès)

(Orson Welles, 1962, Fr/It/WGer) Anthony Perkins, Orson Welles, Jeanne Moreau, Elsa Martinelli, Romy Schneider, Akim Tamiroff, Suzanne Flon, Madeleine Robinson, Arnoldo Foà, Fernand Ledoux, Michel Lonsdale.
120 min. b/w.
The blackest of Welles' comedies, an apocalyptic version of Kafka that renders the grisly farce of K's labyrinthine entrapment in the mechanisms of guilt and responsibility as the most fragmented of expressionist *films noirs*. Perkins' twitchy 'defendant' shifts haplessly through the discrete dark spaces of Welles' ad hoc locations (Zagreb and Paris, including the deserted Gare d'Orsay), taking no comfort from Welles' fable-spinning Advocate, before contriving the most damning of all responses to the chaos around him. The remarkable prologue was commissioned from pioneer pinscreen animators Alexandre Alexeieff and Claire Parker. PT

Trial and Error

(Jonathan Lynn, 1997, US) Michael Richards, Jeff Daniels, Charlize Theron, Jessica Steen, Austin Pendleton, Alexandra Wentworth, Rip Torn.
98 min.
Charles Tuttle (Daniels) is living in the fast track. Newly promoted to partnership in his LA law firm, he's also about to marry the boss's pampered daughter. But privilege entails corporate responsibility, and when he's despatched to a desert town to request a continuance on a fraud case, it looks like there'll be no stag party. That's reckoning without the perseverance of chronically accident-prone best man Richard Rietti (Richards), an out-of-work fringe actor who springs a surprise in Charles' hotel room; come the next morning, Charles is seeing Indians. Whoops! To help out, Rick dons a suit, goes to court and screws up the request. Double whoops! It's trial time, and the judge has Rick pegged as Counsellor Tuttle, to Charles' mounting horror. 'The Second Most Outrageous Trial of the Century,' this bills itself. That's a little harsh. Sure, I'd rather not have had to sit through the film – it's flaccid and substantially unfunny – but there's little to offend. The one highlight is Torn's preposterously blithe, perky defendant. NB

Trial by Combat (aka A Choice of Weapons/ Dirty Knight's Work)

(Kevin Connor, 1976, GB) John Mills, Donald Pleasence, Barbara Hershey, David Birney, Margaret Leighton, Peter Cushing, Brian Glover.
90 min.
An awkward line-up of stars adds little lustre to this tediously derivative, vaguely black comedy. The plot, cobbled together by several writers who seem to have been set to produce an *Avengers* spin-off, revolves creakingly around the attempts of an eccentric, unflappable ex-policeman (Mills) to link a series of underworld killings to an upper-crust fancy-dress society of knights (led by Pleasence), originally dedicated to the ideals of medieval chivalry. The action sequences – on which all attention is presumably meant to focus in compensation for the numbing silliness of the rest of the movie – consist of knights on horseback, brandishing lances, chasing a car across country in hopes of impaling an East End villain (Glover), plus interminable clanking sword fights, the last of which ends with Pleasence impaled on his own portcullis. JPy

Trial by Jury

(Heywood Gould, 1994, US) Joanne Whalley-Kilmer, Armand Assante, Gabriel Byrne, William Hurt, Kathleen Quinlan, Ed Lauter.
107 min.
This New York courtroom drama crowds its narrative to such a degree that the small matter of characterisation doesn't really stand a chance. Valerie Aston (Whalley-Kilmer) is a single mother and proprietor of an antique clothes shop who finds herself under heavy pressure from mob boss Rusty

Pirone (Assante) to stick with a 'not guilty' verdict when the said low-life faces a major murder trial. Prosecutor Graham (Byrne) is hoping to nail his man but unaware of the blackmail going on behind the scenes, while ex-cop Tommy Vesey (Hurt) is the mob gofer trying to ease the young woman into the shakedown, and falling in love in the process. Writer/director Gould never quite finds a way of grounding these people's dilemmas in convincing emotions. Not terrible, just ordinary. TJ

Trial of Joan of Arc

see Procès de Jeanne d'Arc

Trial on the Road (Proverka na Dorogakh)

(Alexei Gherman, 1971, USSR) Rolan Bykov, Anatoly Solonitsin, Vladimir Zamansky, Oleg Borisov, Fyodor Odinokov.
98 min. b/w.
Controversy hovered around Gherman's first film (shelved for fifteen years), largely because the main character is a Red Army officer who defected to the Nazis in the early stages of World War II. The film centres on his attempt to redeem himself after being captured by a Russian platoon, which is plotting to derail a German supply train. The ex-turncoat becomes a focus of conflict between two of the platoon's officers, a gruff, trusting lieutenant and an immature, over-zealous major, and his professed contriteness is put to the test in a series of skirmishes in the snows of Karnaukhovo. There are plentiful signs here of the Gherman films to come: seemingly oblique and offhand plotting, a strong preference for mobile camerawork, and an emphasis on human values at the expense of the usual ideological pedantry. It adds up to the most interesting debut film in Soviet cinema since Tarkovsky's *Ivan's Childhood*, which it sometimes resembles in its glittering black-and-white cinematography, its moments of stasis punctuated by violence, and its sense of larger, off-screen perspectives. TR

Trial Run

(Melanie Read, 1984, NZ) Annie Whittle, Judith Gibson, Christopher Broun, Philippa Mayne, Stephen Tozer, Martyn Sanderson.
89 min.
Rosemary (Whittle) is a family woman, an enthusiastic jogger, and a keen photographer. When commissioned to study the extremely rare yellow-eyed penguin, she leaves the family and instals herself in an isolated beach house. But 'Stranger things have happened at that cottage than Women's Lib' intones her neighbour ominously, and pretty soon Rosemary is also a Woman-in-Peril, being menaced by her neighbour's dog, a lot of subjective camerawork, and things that go squeaky-scrabble in the night. Seasoned thriller-watchers will spot the culprit a mile off, and any intimations of feminist self-sufficiency are rapidly undercut by the woman's unbelievably stupid insistence on sticking it out in the face of escalating threat. AB

Trials of Alger Hiss, The

(John Lowenthal, 1979, US) Alger Hiss, John Lowenthal, Gussie Feinstein, Robert E Stripling, Richard M Nixon, Whittaker Chambers.
166 min. b/w & col.
Hiss was a Roosevelt aide who served on the US delegation at the Yalta Conference; he was charged with being a Communist in 1949 by Whittaker Chambers, a former spy and guilty homosexual who had found religion and become a senior editor of *Time*. Lowenthal's long, intricate study of the case, using archive footage and interviews with many of the principals, clarifies the national hysteria of the early Cold War years and the opportunism of prosecutor Richard Nixon. It rationally argues the case for a re-examination of Hiss' conviction, proving that film and investigative journalism were made for each other. TR

Trials of Oscar Wilde, The (aka The Man With the Green Carnation)

(Ken Hughes, 1960, GB) Peter Finch, Yvonne Mitchell, James Mason, Nigel Patrick, Lionel Jeffries, John Fraser.
123 min.
One of two Oscar Wilde biopics produced in 1960, Ken Hughes' widescreen offering had the advantage of a charismatic and finally moving central performance by Finch as the great ill-fated writer,

delivering the epigrammatic dialogue as the judicial noose tightens. A pity that Mason is so uncharacteristically bland in the final-reel courtroom conflict. TJ

Tribulation 99: Alien Anomalies Under America

(Craig Baldwin, 1991, US)
50 min.
A scattershot onslaught of montaged found-footage, Baldwin's film starts off in strident '50s sci-fi fashion as an apocalyptic 'TRUE STORY!!'. Crazed energy-sucking vampires from the planet Quetzalcoatl arrive on Earth, mutant zombies stalk America, and Godzilla looms in all his rubbery glory over Manhattan. As the pace hots up, subliminal snippets of political information flash up on screen, and incongruous elements emerge from the sprawling paranoid narrative. JFK, UFOs, the Bay of Pigs and the Bermuda Triangle all take their place in a relentlessly incoherent babble about the alien menace that conspires to eat away at the very fabric of reality – reality Pentagon-style, that is. Using the language of '50s Cold War paranoia to account for the United States' murky intervention in world events, this brilliantly ironic ideological deconstruction invites us to imagine a world-view in which Third World politicians are fiends from hell, and in which Kissinger, Pinochet, Klaus Barbie and Contra goons are fearless vampire-fighters. This is dazzling, audacious political graffiti, like an unimaginable collaboration between Noam Chomsky and Edward D Wood Jr. JRo

Tribute

(Bob Clark, 1980, Can/US) Jack Lemmon, Robby Benson, Lee Remick, Colleen Dewhurst, John Marley, Kim Cattrall, Gale Garnett.
125 min.
In a role designed to flatter his talents, Lemmon (who had starred in Bernard Slade's play on Broadway) is unwisely allowed to let rip as a wisecracking, rascally Broadway press agent who discovers – on the eve of his ex-wife (Remick) and grown son (Benson) arriving in New York for the summer vacation – that he has a critical illness. By a series of pitiful gags, he tries to win back the affection of his son, who only hates him the more. Shamelessly geared to theatrical applause, the movie is a truly grotesque mix: part soppy father/son love story, part new morality of how vulnerable men can be through Fear of Failure and Meaningful Relationships. Addicts of filmed theatre and knighthood-aspiring performances will revel in it; all others are advised to carry smelling salts. DMacp

Tribute to a Bad Man

(Robert Wise, 1956, US) James Cagney, Irene Papas, Vic Morrow, Don Dubbins, Stephen McNally, Royal Dano, Lee Van Cleef.
95 min.
Cagney dominates the Wyoming range in this absorbing Western. Jack Schaefer's story focuses on a cattle baron's ruthless hold on his vast territory and the tension that arises when his Greek mistress Papas attracts the wrong kind of attention from farmhand Dubbins. Good stuff, with a worthwhile concentration on the way the West actually worked for a living, and Cagney making an impressive replacement for Spencer Tracy, who walked off the picture after quarrelling with director Wise. 'Scope photography by Robert Surtees; music by Miklos Rozsa. TJ

Trick or Treat

(Charles Martin Smith, 1986, US) Marc Price, Tony Fields, Lisa Orgolini, Doug Savant, Elaine Joyce, Gene Simmons, Ozzy Osbourne.
97 min.
A high school romp pitched somewhere between *Carrie* and *Animal House*. Eddie (Price), a fanatical heavy metal fan desolated by the death in a fire of his idol, the hideous Sammi 'Ragman' Gurr (Fields), is somewhat consoled when a DJ friend gives him the only copy of Ragman's last album, having first taped it to broadcast (as per Ragman's instructions) at midnight on Hallowe'en. Victimised by the school jocks, Eddie swears revenge, and receives unexpected occult help – via the album – when the deceased Ragman materialises. Soon Eddie's tormentors get their nasty deserts. But Ragman's destructiveness gets out of hand, and realising what it will mean if the record is played on Hallowe'en, Eddie turns hero

to stop the wave of terror. All utter rubbish but fun, benefiting greatly from outrageous SFX à la *Videodrome*, and from two neat cameos by real life HM stars Ozzy Osbourne and Gene Simmons. DPe

Trigger Happy
see Mad Dog Time

Trikal: Past Present and Future (Trikal)
(Shyam Benegal, 1985, Ind) Naseeruddin Shah, Kulbhushan Kharbanda, Leela Naidu, Neena Gupta, Anita Kanwar, Soni Razdan, Dalip Tahil.
137 min.
A potentially intriguing return for Shyam Benegal to the last days of colonialism in India, this time involving not the Raj but the Portuguese colony of Goa. Politically critical but elegiacally cast as a sort of latter-day *Cherry Orchard* (the setting is a fading mansion with the Indian army lurking at the off-screen gates), it is disappointingly pedestrian, with few of the subtle reverberations and sharp perceptions that marked Benegal's earlier *Junoon*. TM

Trio
(Ken Annakin/Harold French, 1950, GB) James Hayter, Kathleen Harrison, Michael Hordern, Nigel Patrick, Anne Crawford, Jean Simmons, Michael Rennie.
91 min. b/w.
One story less, otherwise much the same Somerset Maugham portmanteau mixture as *Quartet*, similarly introduced by Maugham himself, and with the cast similarly making up for indifferent staging. The first and last stories (*The Verger* and *The Sanatorium*) are diffuse, facile, and pretty predictable; but *Mr Knowall* – with a clever performance from Nigel Patrick as th e insufferable bore whose veneer of crashing insensitivity, inflicted on his fellow passengers on a cruise ship, momentarily cracks to reveal a surprising delicacy – is a neatly judged anecdote. TM

Trio Infernal, Le
see Infernal Trio, The

Trip, The
(Roger Corman, 1967, US) Peter Fonda, Susan Strasberg, Bruce Dern, Dennis Hopper, Salli Sachse, Katherine Walsh, Barboura Morris, Dick Miller, Luana Anders.
85 min.
An earlier Corman picture, *The Man with the X-Ray Eyes*, had uncannily predicted the rise and fall of a Timothy Leary-type hero, whose desire to see beyond human limits was punished by humiliation as a sideshow freak and by self-inflicted blindness. *The Trip*, a definitive commercial for acid scripted by Jack Nicholson, is in contrast boundlessly optimistic. Its advertising director hero, Fonda, takes a trip with no retribution at all: no death, no disillusionment, but much bikinied girls on sea shores, swirling psychedelia, and mumbling of 'Wow!' by the obligatory Dennis Hopper in the land of a thousand visual clichés. Despite the hedonistic panache, its lack of a comeuppance means it now lacks credence (as it once lacked a censor's certificate). Rich pickings for the pathologist of '60s lifestyles, but it took Coppola to work out that the best movies were about bad trips, not good ones. DMacp

Triple Bogey on a Par Five Hole
(Amos Poe, 1991, US) Eric Mitchell, Daisy Hall, Angela Goethals, Jesse McBride, Alba Clemente, Robbie Coltrane, Olga Bagnasco.
88 min. b/w & col.
The Levys, a glamorous couple, used to make their living robbing golfers, until they met their fatal handicap. Years later, scriptwriter Remy Gravelle (Mitchell), investigating their death, decides to observe the Levy progeny as they sail endlessly round Manhattan in their luxury yacht. It's a hothouse atmosphere, brat-generation neurosis taken to its limits: Satch (McBride) is a macho punk; dreadlocked kid sister (Goethals) is precociously insightful; and ice queen Amanda (Hall) walks like Madonna and talks like Truman

Capote. Remy isn't likely to get the answers from them, their lawyer (Coltrane), or his niece (Clemente). Here is a Manhattan you won't have seen before, viewed strictly from the outside in sweeping vistas shot in glacial black-and-white, and starkly contrasting with the claustrophobic stillness below deck, as the Levys' cat-and-mouse dialogues with Remy are interspersed with Poe's own home-movie footage of family memories. A detective story with no real mystery and no solution, this is a stimulating, occasionally magical exercise in stylistic and intellectual tail-chasing, and that rare thing these days – a film that dares to go nowhere. JRo

Triple Echo, The
(Michael Apted, 1972, GB) Glenda Jackson, Oliver Reed, Brian Deacon, Anthony May, Gavin Richards.
94 min.
An adaptation of an HE Bates story, set in an isolated Wiltshire farm in 1942. With her husband a prisoner-of-war, lonely wife (Jackson) strikes up an intimate relationship with a young soldier (Deacon), a farmer's boy who hates the army. When he impulsively deserts, she hides him, disguised in drag as her sister. The inevitable tensions of their life are increased when two soldiers from the nearby camp discover 'the girls', and the lecherous sergeant (Reed) takes a fancy to the one in drag. The relationship between the wife and the deserter is built carefully and convincingly, but in going for laughs as the bullish sergeant, Oliver Reed lets some of the potential tension slip away. As with many of Bates' stories, the plot is in any case resolved suddenly and melodramatically. JC

Trip to Bountiful, The
(Peter Masterson, 1985, US) Geraldine Page, John Heard, Carlin Glynn, Richard Bradford, Rebecca De Mornay, Kevin Cooney.
107 min.
Jessie Mae (Glynn) refuses her mother-in-law (Page) her one pleasure in life: singing hymns. The doughty old lady lights out for a sentimental journey to her birthplace and her past, meeting all kinds of decent friendly folks along the way. Scripted by Horton Foote from his own play, this is a fragile blend of moods and memories with one solid showcase role for a skilled actress. Geraldine Page seizes her chance, though she is too generous to swamp the supporting players. Masterson's images of small-town America are imbued with a luminous and melancholy nostalgia, but otherwise the film is not mounted with any special imagination, and its fusty, old-fashioned (not to say reactionary) lauding of homespun values sticks in the craw. SJo

Tristana
(Luis Buñuel, 1970, Sp/It/Fr) Catherine Deneuve, Fernando Rey, Franco Nero, Lola Gaos, Antonio Casas, Jesús Fernández.
105 min.
This is late Buñuel, mockingly sensible black comedy, set in Toledo in the early 1930s, in which an old guardian (Rey) seduces/rapes his young ward Tristana (Deneuve) but is unable to possess her, betrayed by Surrealist lurches in time and reality, and by Tristana's changing 'nature' (the amputation of a tumorous leg). Fernando Rey is brilliant as the mephistophelean, anti-clerical Socialist, dandy and outmoded master of social graces: father, lover and husband all in one. His passion ruins and softens him, but (caught as she is in the chauvinist paradox of woman as cause and eternal object of male aggression) it hardens Tristana from innocent virginity to icy revenge. CA

Triumph of the Spirit
(Robert M Young, 1989, US) Willem Dafoe, Edward James Olmos, Robert Loggia, Wendy Gazelle, Kelly Wolf, Costas Mandylor, Kario Salem.
120 min.
There's no doubting the sense of commitment which touches every aspect of this grimly detailed Holocaust drama. But the impulse to provide an authentic reconstruction of conditions in Auschwitz finds distractions (most glaringly from an intrusive score and Young's gimmicky direction) which swamp the stark brutalities. The plot is based on the real-life

experience of Greek boxer Salamo Arouch (Dafoe), who survived the camp only after fighting endless bouts for the entertainment of his captors. The defeated, too weak to work, were sent to their deaths, while Arouch was awarded extra rations which he divided among his family. Arouch's fiancée and her sister are similarly incarcarated, and a sub-plot traces the back-breaking labour and physical indignities they suffer. Dafoe gives a charged, compelling performance, while Olmos provides convincingly understated support; but the attempt to convey the terrible magnitude of the atrocities has overwhelmed the film-makers and left them resorting to over-familiar tactics. CM

Triumph of the Will (Triumph des Willens)
(Leni Riefenstahl, 1935, Ger)
120 min. b/w.
Riefenstahl's record of the sixth Nazi congress at Nuremberg in 1934, a massive documentary tribute to the German concept of the Aryan superrace. Technically brilliant, and still one of the most disturbing pieces of propaganda around. Interesting to note that at the same time the British were also indulging in mass demonstrations of physical prowess – women were putting on large PT displays in Wembley Stadium. CPe

Triumphs of a Man Called Horse (El Triunfo de un Hombre Llamado Caballo)
(John Hough, 1982, Sp) Richard Harris, Michael Beck, Ana De Sade, Vaughn Armstrong, Buck Taylor, Sebastian Ligarde, Anne Seymour.
89 min.
The Triumphs of a Man Called Horse are few in this second sequel, and those right puny. The man himself, who you will recall was an English aristo who obeyed the call of the wild and enlisted in the Sioux, returns only briefly in the now battered shape of Harris. He has only the barest time available for a quick flashback to his finest hour, when he was strung up by his pectorals, before being despatched by greedy prospectors looking for the gold on his land. The gauntlet is taken up for the rest of the film by his son, the aptly named Koda (Beck), who – in company with his faithful Crow girlfriend – rides like the wind, dynamites prospectors, and runs rings around the cavalry. What *Variety* used to call 'a routine oater'. CPea

Trois Couleurs: Blanc
see Three Colours: White

Trois Couleurs: Bleu
see Three Colours: Blue

Trois Couleurs: Rouge
see Three Colours: Red

Trois Couronnes du Matelot, Les
see Three Crowns of the Sailor

3 Hommes et un Couffin
see 3 Men and a Cradle

Trois Vies et une Seule Mort (Three Lives and Only One Death)
(Raul Ruiz, 1996, Fr) Marcello Mastroianni, Anna Galiena, Marisa Paredes, Melvil Poupard, Chiara Mastroianni, Arielle Dombasle, Féodor Atkine.
123 min.
Shock horror! Raul Ruiz makes an accessible, intelligible, entertaining film! An intriguing comedy in which Mastroianni plays four roles – a travelling salesman, an anthropologist-turned-tramp involved with a somewhat unusual hooker, a strangely laconic butler, and a wealthy industrialist – in (in)consequential stories which finally begin to overlap. What it all adds up to is a mystery (though the title may provide a hint), but the playfulness, the first-rate cast, the charm of Mastroianni's performance, and the discreet elegance of the whole make for very civilised entertainment. GA

Trojan Eddie

(Gillies MacKinnon, 1995, GB/Ire) Richard Harris, Stephen Rea, Brendan Gleeson, Sean McGinley, Angeline Ball, Brid Brennan.
105 min.

A predominantly downbeat tale of the relationship between Rea's down-at-heel chancer – a real loser despite his gab – and his boss (Harris, in convincingly nasty form), the big man of the local underworld, who puts Rea in a perilous middleman position when he takes a shine to a young gypsy girl. Despite plenty of wit and pleasing twists in the story, this is essentially an unusually sombre character study, played to perfection by a strong cast and enormously assured in its vivid but decidedly untouristy depiction of Irish landscape and society. GA

Troll

(John Carl Buechler, 1985, US) Michael Moriarty, Shelley Hack, Noah Hathaway, Jenny Beck, Sonny Bono, Phil Fondacaro, Brad Hall, June Lockhart.
86 min.

An amiable and humorous fantasy-cum-Faery tale in the *Gremlins* mould. When the Potter family – Mom, Dad, little Wendy Ann and Harry Jr – move into their new apartment house, they have more than their kooky neighbours to contend with. Wendy is the first to go, possessed by the gruesome little meanies, and then it's cue special effects sequences as, flat by flat, the trolls transform the house into a burgeoning forest of ferns and all manner of repulsive creations. The whole thing is jogged along nicely by the cast (especially the excellent Moriarty, jigging around manically to his '60s records), and has exactly the right balance between child-like wonder and gentle self-parody. WH

Troma's War

see War

Tromeo & Juliet

(Lloyd Kaufman, 1996, US) Jane Jensen, Will Keenan, Valentine Miele, Maximillian Shaun, Steve Gibbons, Sean Gunn, Lemmy.
107 min.

Motorhead's Lemmy is the narrator and stumbles through the verse in this schlock Shakespeare rewrite as lumpenly as the other cast members. Between times, sundry inadequates serve up a menu of body-piercing, decapitation, dismemberment, mutilation, soft-core nudity and lots of coloured goo. Strange that a film with so much carnage should prove so tedious, but that's the magic of Troma (*Toxic Avenger*) productions. TJ

Tron

(Steven Lisberger, 1982, US) Jeff Bridges, Bruce Boxleitner, David Warner, Cindy Morgan, Barnard Hughes, Dan Shor.
96 min.

Disney's twenty million dollar bid to break into the booming fantasy market is a sympathetic but slightly clumsy rewrite of *The Wizard of Oz*, with a whizkid programmer (Bridges) trapped inside a computer world. The film boasts some impressive computer-animation, but for all its inventiveness, *Tron* never reaches a level of excitement commensurate with its effects budget. Indeed, in what might have proved to be a dire precedent for the cinema, *Tron* the video game is probably better than *Tron* the movie. DP

Troopship

see Farewell Again

Trop belle pour toi!
(Too Beautiful for You)

(Bertrand Blier, 1989, Fr) Gérard Depardieu, Josiane Balasko, Carole Bouquet, Roland Blanche, François Cluzet.
91 min.

Bernard (Depardieu) is a wealthy businessman, happily married to beautiful, elegant Florence (Bouquet). Much to his astonishment, he falls in love with his comparatively dowdy secretary, Colette (Balasko). It's no office fling but the real thing, and – to Bernard – completely incomprehensible. Once again charting the outrageous repercussions of an obsessive love, Blier proceeds to explore the situation from every conceivable angle, merrily constructing and deconstructing alternative stories for all he's worth. Although the film fails to sustain itself over 90 minutes, much of the first half is very funny and occasionally sharp; Buñuelian motifs are mischievously resurrected, and Blier's parodies and fantasy sequences are brilliantly dovetailed in a series of waltzing, switchback camera movements that are a joy to behold. Blier is a classy, amusing film maker, but one suspects he is too fundamentally bourgeois to truly shock or surprise; and this movie ends dispiritingly with the most banal of all its potential options. TCh

Trop de Bonheur
(Too Much Happiness)

(Cedric Kahn, 1994, Fr) Estelle Perron, Caroline Trousselard, Malek Bechar, Didier Borga.
85 min.

An excellent feature, from a series in which various French directors treated a theme from their adolescence, set in a none-too-picturesque town in the Midi. It simply charts the shifts in relationships, over a day or so, between a bunch of kids around school-leaving age. Most of the last hour takes place at an impromptu drunken 'party', where the director's imaginative use of gesture, glances, dance and group composition to portray attraction and repulsion, lust and jealousy really comes into its own. Superbly evocative of teenage desire (with a few substantial asides on racial tension thrown in), this beautifully acted film takes an everyday situation and, thanks to acute observation, makes it both horribly familiar and totally compulsive. GA

Tropical Fish

(Chris Rodley, 1994, GB) Michael Harris, O-Lan Jones.
27 min.

This adaptation of Raymond Carver's story *Neighbors* is an exemplary short. While the neighbours are on vacation, a vaguely bored suburban couple agree to tend their fishtank, and find their lives subtly transformed by their insights into and impressions of other people's private lives. Stylishly shot, wittily scripted and beautifully performed. GA

Tropical Fish
(Redai Yu)

(Chen Yu-Hsun, 1995, Tai) Wen Yin, Lien Pi-Dong, Lin Cheng-Sheng, Shi Ching-Luen, Lin Chia-Hong.
107 min.

Quirky character-based comedy about a kidnapping which goes wrong when the prime mover is killed in a car crash; two kidnapped boys wind up being held for ransom by a none-too-smart peasant family in a fishing village. For one of the boys, an inveterate dreamer, this is a wonderful excuse not to swot for exams. Serious themes hover in the background (ecological disaster, the dumbing of the media, exam hell), but the film is more sweet than sour. The first-time director (an unreconstructed rock guitarist) makes it a paean to daydreaming. TR

Tropic of Cancer

(Joseph Strick, 1969, US) Rip Torn, James Callahan, Ellen Burstyn, David Bauer, Laurence Lignères, Phil Brown, Dominique Delpierre.
88 min.

An incredibly tedious adaptation of Henry Miller's incredibly tedious novel. With the action transposed to contemporary Paris, America's famous lost generation of the '30s are stranded like fish out of water, scrabbling ludicrously for sexual satisfaction from prostitutes when all they need to do is ask any nice, permissive girl passing by. Bereft of its context, Miller's overheated prose – intoned, voice-off, by Rip Torn as Miller in the intervals between his breathless sexual encounters – is revealed as a mixture of bad poetry and bad travelogue. Four-letter words and female pubic hair have themselves a field day. TM

Trop Tard

see Too Late

Trou, Le
(The Hole/The Night Watch)

(Jacques Becker, 1959, Fr/It) Philippe Leroy, Marc Michel, Jean Kéraudy, Raymond Meunier, Michel Constantin, André Bervil.
140 min. b/w.

A secular response to Bresson's *A Man Escaped*. No question of grace here, simply of grind and grime as four prisoners – joined and eventually betrayed by a fifth – laboriously tunnel their way to a derisory glimpse of freedom. Telling a true story, Becker maintains a low-key approach, courting reality, avoiding music in favour of natural sound, constantly stressing the sheer physicality (warders' hands laconically slicing foodstuffs in search of hidden files, prisoners' hands feverishly hacking at the unrelenting stone). Yet there is more than a touch of Bresson (even more, however, of Becker's mentor Renoir) to the close-ups which punctuate the evolving relationship between the escapees and their final discovery of a sort of forgiveness for their betrayer. Classical in its intense simplicity, this is certainly Becker's most perfectly crafted film. TM

Trouble in Mind

(Alan Rudolph, 1985, US) Kris Kristofferson, Keith Carradine, Lori Singer, Genevieve Bujold, Joe Morton, Divine, George Kirby, John Considine.
112 min.

After the witty, emotional roundelay of *Choose Me*, Rudolph here plunges even further into his own imaginative world, and the result is wonderful. Located in a mythic, dangerous 'Rain City', his tenderly observed characters pick their way through the battlefield of love, all in search of their peculiar fulfilment. Former cop Hawk (Kristofferson) completes his prison sentence for killing a mobster and returns to his favourite haunt, a café run by old flame Wanda (Bujold). There he falls for a blonde princess (Singer), while she loses touch with her recklessly ambitious hubby (ebulliently played by Carradine, sporting increasingly wacky hairdos as he falls deeper into criminal ways). Forever in the background lurks mean fat cat Hilly, a local Sydney Greenstreet (unexpectedly incarnated by a poised Divine). Rudolph's script is both playful and precise, his images fantastic yet real, the music elegiac but ecstatically sung by an impassioned Marianne Faithfull. Part thriller, part comic fantasy, part love story, *Trouble in Mind* even offers an ambiguous, high-flown ending that suggests this really is the stuff that dreams are made of. DT

Trouble in Paradise

(Ernst Lubitsch, 1932, US) Herbert Marshall, Miriam Hopkins, Kay Francis, Edward Everett Horton, Charles Ruggles, C Aubrey Smith, Robert Greig.
83 min. b/w.

Right from its opening joke – a Venetian romantically serenading a gondola full of garbage – *Trouble in Paradise* spins a wonderful, sophisticated tale in praise of immorality, money and sex, with two aristocratic impostors (Marshall and Hopkins) battling over their plans to rob a rich widow (the languorous Kay Francis). Lubitsch's regular script collaborator Samson Raphaelson never bettered the lethal irony of his dialogue here, as the thieves pass insinuations to and fro with the same lightning grace they give to pickpocketing. And the director's famed 'touch', which can on occasion seem like a thump, remains featherweight and incisive throughout, matching the performances of his charmingly bogus lead players. If ever a film slipped down a treat, this one does. GB

Trouble in Store

(John Paddy Carstairs, 1953, GB) Norman Wisdom, Margaret Rutherford, Lana Morris, Moira Lister, Derek Bond, Jerry Desmonde, Joan Sims, Megs Jenkins.
85 min. b/w.

First of the Norman Wisdom comedies that provided Rank with a once-a-year commercial lifeline well into the 1960s, and established Wisdom as the natural heir to George Formby. His persona – shy, ever eager, haplessly uncoordinated, inevitably both misunderstood and prone to embarrassing accidents – not only transcended the context of a given film, but usually ended up demolishing it as well, as here where his window-dressing ambitions bring chaos to a department store run by eternal stooge Jerry Desmonde and plagued by shoplifters of Margaret Rutherford's class. PT

Troubles We've Seen, The
see Veillées d'Armes

Trouble with Harry, The
(Alfred Hitchcock, 1955, US) Edmund Gwenn, John Forsythe, Shirley MacLaine, Mildred Natwick, Mildred Dunnock, Jerry Mathers, Royal Dano.
99 min.
The trouble with Harry is that he's dead, won't stay buried, and won't give the inhabitants of a small Vermont village any peace: an elderly sea captain, an old maid, an artist, and the deceased's young widow get involved in the problem of disposing of him, because they all feel guilty about his demise. But Hitchcock loved the project's potential for macabre understatement, so he has the group reacting with cool, callous detachment toward death. There are delights to savour here: Robert Burks' location photography, all russet reds and golds, underlining the theme of death; Bernard Herrmann's spritely score, ironically counterpointing the dark deeds on screen; finely modulated performances from Natwick and (making her film debut) MacLaine. But Hitchcock is reluctant to follow the subversive premises of the story through to their outrageous logical conclusion; the dialogue's sexual innuendoes now seem coy and awkward; the male leads are wooden; the ending too complacent; and the discreet style stranded by that dreaded British restraint so dear to the director. Now, if Buñuel had made it...GA

Trou Normand, Le (Crazy for Love)
(Jean Boyer, 1952, Fr) Bourvil, Brigitte Bardot, Jane Marken, Nadine Basile, Noël Roquevert, Pierre Larquey, Jacques Deray.
98 min. b/w.
This featherweight farce would have been long forgotten if it didn't mark Bardot's debut (introducing her posed in front of a mirror, buttoning her dress). Seventeen years old, not yet made-over by Vadim, with puppy fat still clinging to her cheeks, she's evidently captivating. Her co-heroine (Basile) takes one look and rushes off to sob into her pillow ('Papa, am I ugly?'), not appreciating that BB's aphrodisiac presence might have made Aphrodite herself feel inadequate. The film is a vehicle for Bourvil's good-natured simpleton character, a slightly less innocent George Formby (he even gets to sing a novelty number). The plot is similarly Formby-like: before he can inherit Le Trou Normand inn, our hero must return to the classroom and pass his school certificate. The humour, however, derives more from behaviour than gags, and is utterly conventional BBa

Truce, The (La Tregua)
(Francesco Rosi, 1997, It/Fr/Ger) John Turturro, Massimo Ghini, Rade Serbedziha, Stefano Dionisi.
115 min.
While there's no denying the integrity and general accuracy of Rosi's adaptation of Primo Levi's book about his post-war odyssey back to Italy from Auschwitz, heartfelt concern for the plight of the future author and other survivors of the Nazi camps doesn't guarantee a dramatically compelling movie. To be sure, the film is sensitive enough to the psychological dilemmas and doubts facing the liberated prisoners, and never underplays the obstacles strewn along the route to spiritual rebirth; the problem, rather, stems from the fact that Turturro's Levi is essentially a loner and an observer, and therefore too passive to function as the 'hero' proposed and required by the all too conventional narrative. As a result, the film never really comes alive emotionally, and remains a rather staidly cerebral, worthy exercise. GA

Truck Stop Women
(Mark L Lester, 1974, US) Lieux Dressler, Claudia Jennings, Gene Drew, Dolores Dorn, Dennis Fimple, Jennifer Burton, Paul Carr.
87 min.
A cult movie – about the Organisation's efforts to move in on the truck hijacking operation run by Anna and her girls – that drew lavish praise

as Greek tragedy transposed to New Mexico and the funniest film since Lubitsch's *To Be or Not To Be*. How this relates to a juicy pulp movie with its (to quote the ad) 'double-clutchin'...gear-jammin' mamas who like a lot of hijackin' by day...a lot of heavy truckin' by night', you'll have to work out for yourself. The manic glee that Lester elicits from his performers, and his eye for incongruities, make for a true eccentricity. And the sight of his matriarchy consistently undermining male morale should shake staider patrons by the scruff of the neck. Complete with sub-Johnny Cash soundtrack and virtually incomprehensible plot. VG

True Believer (aka Fighting Justice)
(Joseph Ruben, 1988, US) James Woods, Robert Downey Jr, Yuji Okumoto, Margaret Colin, Kurtwood Smith, Tom Bower, Charles Hallahan.
103 min.
A riveting legal drama which casts James Woods as a jaded, ex-radical lawyer, once dubbed 'The bastard son of Mother Teresa' but now reduced to defending scumbag drug dealers. His '60s idealism rekindled by a new, wide-eyed assistant (Downey), he takes on the case of a young Korean serving '25 to life' for murdering a Chinatown gang leader. Things get nasty when the DA starts pressuring Woods to drop the case; but convinced of his client's innocence and determined to salvage his self-respect, he presses on with a desperate, almost evangelical zeal. Ruben's smart direction keeps one guessing throughout, with an investigation that takes in a paranoid Vietnam veteran, white racist vigilantes, a retired detective with a guilty secret, and plumbing supplies. A taut, intelligent and engrossing thriller, featuring yet another manic performance by Woods, the undisputed King of Misdirected Energy. NF

True Blue
(Ferdinand Fairfax, 1996, GB) Johan Leysen, Dominic West, Dylan Baker, Geraldine Somerville, Josh Lucas, Brian McGovern, Ryan Bollman.
117 min.
Would-be *Chariots of Fire*-style sports movie centred on the preparations for the celebrated 1987 Oxford vs Cambridge Boat Race. Many news stories focused on controversy about imported American pros up against traditionally trained Brit oarsmen, prompting Oxford coach Daniel Topolski to unravel the serpentine rivalries, machinations and mutinies that preceded the race in a successful book co-authored with Patrick Robinson. Rupert Walters' script straightens out the book's episodic ins and outs, but it still retains a dozen or so main oarsmen, resulting in a loss of focus and the niggling problem that the movie's half-over before the viewer can identify who's who. Thematically muffled and boring. WH

True Confession
(Wesley Ruggles, 1937, US) Carole Lombard, Fred MacMurray, John Barrymore, Una Merkel, Porter Hall, Edgar Kennedy, Lynne Overman, Fritz Feld.
85 min. b/w.
Delightful screwball comedy, with the delectable Lombard as a compulsive liar who causes hubby MacMurray no end of embarrassment with her inventions (a lawyer with boy scout principles, he doesn't take kindly to being described to neighbours as insane, dead or a drug addict). Duly contrite, she confesses to a murder in the hope of furthering his career, on the blithe assumption that with hubby on hand to defend her – only he proves not so hot as a criminal lawyer – she is sure to get off. Invention flags latterly, with a particularly weak ending, but the performances are wonderful, not least Barrymore as the ghoulishly bizarre killer. TM

True Confessions
(Ulu Grosbard, 1981, US) Robert De Niro, Robert Duvall, Charles Durning, Kenneth McMillan, Ed Flanders, Cyril Cusack, Burgess Meredith, Rose Gregorio, Dan Hedaya.
108 min.
This adaptation of John Gregory Dunne's novel uses its plot base – who cut Lois Fazenda in two? – to explore and draw together the worlds of Tom Spellacy, cynical homicide cop, and his brother

Des, priest on the make in the upper reaches of Los Angeles Catholicism in the '40s. Unfortunately, Grosbard's direction is full of overstated cross-cutting and nudging, empty 'references' (to *Kiss Me Deadly*, *Chinatown*, *The Godfather* among others), but never satisfactorily summons up the moral demons haunting his characters. In fact, scriptwriter Dunne (adapting his own novel with wife Joan Didion) is equally guilty, with a tragically schematic reduction of his own excellent novel. Numerous vital characters are dropped and the case-solving stripped of its complexity, with the resulting film over-linear and one-dimensional. The two Roberts (Duvall as cop, De Niro as priest) turn in potentially great performances, but are given precious little to work with. SJ

True Glory, The
(Carol Reed/Garson Kanin, 1945, GB/US)
85 min. b/w.
This expertly assembled WWII documentary, about the last year of the war in Europe, was financed by the American Office of War Information and the British MOI. It occupies a middle ground between the conventional propaganda films churned out in their hundreds and the poetic realism of Humphrey Jennings. Some of the footage is astonishing (unfortunately, William Alwyn's music is an often redundant dramatic enhancement), and parts of the commentary have a macabre humour. A British tommy, for instance, tells of his encounter in a bombed-out German village with a woman complaining that if the British had given up in 1940 she would still have a home to live in. ATu

True Grit
(Henry Hathaway, 1969, US) John Wayne, Glen Campbell, Kim Darby, Jeremy Slate, Jeff Corey, Robert Duvall, Dennis Hopper, Strother Martin.
128 min.
It was in *El Dorado* that Wayne ruefully admitted his reflexes weren't quite what they were. Here, amiably sending up his own image, he plays a way-worn, one-eyed, drink-hardened marshal who would rather stay at home with his cat and the aged Chinaman who looks after him and lets him cheat at cards, but who is shamed out on to the trail by a teenage girl bent on avenging her murdered father, even if she has to do it herself. He gets his man in the end, of course, but only at the expense of a series of humiliations climaxed when, instead of hurling herself into his arms as a grateful heroine should, the tenderfoot girl (beautifully played by Kim Darby) sweetly tells him that when he dies she will make sure he is buried alongside her own dear father. Lazily directed by Hathaway, it's pleasant enough, if rather too self-consciously coy. Peckinpah did it so much better in *Ride the High Country*. TM

True Identity
(Charles Lane, 1991, US) Lenny Henry, Frank Langella, Charles Lane, JT Walsh, Anne-Marie Johnson, Andreas Katsulas, Michael McKean, James Earl Jones, Melvin Van Peebles.
93 min.
Struggling black actor Miles Pope (Henry) is fed up with being offered parts in movies like 'Uptown Harlem Pimps on Crack'. Instead, he longs for the lead in *Othello*, but the closest he can get to stardom is as an understudy. Life is about to get worse: during the flight to an acting job, he learns that a fellow passenger is one-time mob boss Frank Luchino (Langella). Miles is now a marked man whose survival rests on the skills of special effects artist Duane (Lane). What better disguise, reasons Duane, than to change his pal into a white man? There are only so many jokes to be milked out of this scenario, and this frantic comedy milks them all. The transformation in Henry's appearance is truly amazing, but once the novelty has passed, the film proceeds to lumber from one signposted comic blunder to another. Henry's skills are tested by the poor script, but he does a spectacular job with a variety of American accents and guises. CM

True Lies
(James Cameron, 1994, US) Arnold Schwarzenegger, Jamie Lee Curtis, Tom Arnold, Bill Paxton, Tia Carrere, Art Malik, Eliza Dushku.
141 min.

t

Half the time, this hi-tech action movie delivers, in a mindless kind of way: it's fast, crude and has enough explosions and cartoon-style violence to satisfy our baser instincts. Harry Tasker (Schwarzenegger) is a special agent up against a terrorist group (led by wild-eyed Malik) out to show the world it means business by stealing a nuclear warhead. So far, so traditional. But what's meant to give the film its emotional edge is that Harry hasn't told his wife Helen (Curtis) what he does. The crunch comes when a predatory used-car salesman (Paxton) looks like worming his way into her pants by pretending to be an international spy. When Harry finds out, colleagues and agency gizmos are all pressed into service. The film's entire middle section is devoted to this marital 'crisis' which, thanks to Curtis' enthusiastic if barely plausible turn, is quite amusing, despite the offensive take on male-female relationships. Happily, the last 40 minutes pick up with a feast of neck-breaking, torso-blasting violence. GA

True Love

(Nancy Savoca, 1989, US) Annabella Sciorra, Ron Eldard, Aida Turturro, Roger Rignack, Star Jasper, Michael J Wolfe, Kelly Cinnante.
104 min.
A bad-tempered, foul-mouthed, hilarious Bronx love story, this tells of Michael (Eldard) and Donna (Sciorra), young Italian-Americans about to get hitched. Savoca guides them twixt the Scylla and Charybdis of their respective families' expectations, only to have them founder on the rocks of their own selfishness. Michael and Donna have had lessons to learn, and major humble pie to eat before they can even make it to the altar; and their strident battles are fought out against a backdrop of colourful, crude characters. Wise moms, sassy girlfriends and boozing mates, all chip in with advice on the debate: what do men and women seek from marriage, and can they ever be compatible? It's told in a belligerent, noisy, da-fucksa-matter-wit-you urban growl; a sour belch in the face of marriage, and very funny, too. SFe

True Nature of Bernadette, The (La Vraie Nature de Bernadette)

(Gilles Carle, 1971, Can) Micheline Lanctôt, Donald Pilon, Reynald Bouchard, Maurice Beaupré, Ernest Guimond.
97 min.
A subversively light-hearted movie in which Bernadette, a Montreal housewife, leaves her lawyer husband to practice vegetarianism and free love on a dilapidated Quebec farm, while her disapproving and less romantic neighbour, Thomas, gets on with the harder task of actually earning a living from the land, and trying to form an agricultural union to combat the indifference of the federal government. Carle's script finally brings his heroine (an engaging debut performance from Lanctôt) down on Thomas' side; but the real interest of this quirky movie lies less in the director's avowedly political moral than in his eclectic and often ironic method. Religion, factory farming, the sexual liberation of a group of old men, the disposal problem of a removal van full of 'possessions', all become loosely but satisfyingly involved, with Bernadette – revolutionary mother, saintly whore – radiating an infectious optimism and a joyful, open-hearted sexuality. JPy

True Romance

(Tony Scott, 1993, US) Christian Slater, Patricia Arquette, Christopher Walken, Dennis Hopper, Val Kilmer, Gary Oldman.
119 min.
When Detroit comic-store assistant Clarence (Slater) and novice whore Alabama (Arquette) meet, not only do they immediately fall in love, but the tone of her voice-over lets us know that we're in for a *Badlands*-style rerun. Having killed her monstrous pimp (Oldman, OTT) and accidentally stolen his coke haul, the pair head for Hollywood, pausing only to bid farewell to his drunkard dad Clifford (Hopper). But the couple's get-rich-quick plans go awry when suave mob boss Coccotti (Walken) tries to 'persuade' Clifford to divulge his son's whereabouts. If the romance seldom seems 'true', the spiralling violence (script, Quentin Tarantino) does succeed, in a brutish, cod-Jacobean kind of way. GA

True Stories

(David Byrne, 1986, US) David Byrne, John Goodman, Annie McEnroe, Jo Harvey Allen, Spalding Gray, Alix Elias, Swoosie Kurtz.
89 min.
Byrne gleaned the inhabitants for his hypothetical small town (Virgil, Texas) from mad American tabloids like the *Weekly World News*, which trades in stories about Mexicans who can read your nose, illegal immigrants from outer space, and suchlike. As the film's on-screen narrator, he wanders through the streets, homes and shopping malls of Virgil during its sesquicentennial 'celebration of specialness' with an air of quizzical, bemused wonder, and meets as rich and strange a bunch of characters as we've seen since Altman's *Nashville*. Like Altman's film, *True Stories* has a handful of brilliant musical set pieces, each in a different musical idiom, from gospel to C & W. It's also heir to *Nashville* in its multiple, interweaving plots and its plethora of vivid performances, notably from Jo Harvey Allen as the Lying Woman, and (best of all) John Goodman as Louis Fyne, the lonely bachelor with a consistent panda bear shape. And that's not the half of it. *True Stories* is an unprecedented crossbreed: a rock film with a brain, an 'art' movie with belly laughs, a state of the nation address without boredom. KJ

True Story of Eskimo Nell, The (aka Dick Down Under)

(Richard Franklin, 1975, Aust) Max Gillies, Serge Lazareff, Paul Vachon, Abigail, Kris McQuade, Elli Maclure.
104 min.
Entertainment from every orifice in this visceral demonstration of just what Australia stands for in the world today: boozing, screwing, pissing, spewing, farting, swearing, etc. It purports to be a version of the ballad in which legendary Eskimo Nell is sought by Deadeye Dick and Mexico Pete – now owner of 'the most famous prick in the southern hemisphere'. Ninety percent of the film is atrocious; but there are enough striking moments in the remainder – overtones of impotence and voyeurism, the odd sunset and bit of music, sepia tinting – to give it the occasional balladic feel and look. These moments are a long time coming, though, and as everything else is in such a different gear the overall effect is a pretty shithouse...or is that a strine compliment? AN

True Story of Jesse James, The (aka The James Brothers)

(Nicholas Ray, 1957, US) Robert Wagner, Jeffrey Hunter, Hope Lange, Agnes Moorehead, Alan Hale, John Carradine, Alan Baxter, Frank Gorshin.
92 min.
Nick Ray takes the Jesse James legend and turns it around his own feelings of disenchantment. Freely adapting the original (1939) Nunnally Johnson script (which initiated the long line of motifs still recognisable in *The Long Riders*), he transmutes Jesse into one of his familiar outsiders ('the spokesman for everyone whose life is quietly desperate'): an adolescent who turns to outlawry from a disaffection with adult values, rather than Civil War rivalries. This outlaw, like James Dean in *Rebel Without a Cause*, entertains dreams of the good life (along the lines of teen-dream romance), but it's never more than a gesture of hope in a surrounding gone rotten. A fine Western, the only regret being Robert Wagner. Imagining Dean in the central role makes it one of the great might-have-beens. CPea

Truly, Madly, Deeply

(Anthony Minghella, 1990, GB) Juliet Stevenson, Alan Rickman, Bill Paterson, Michael Maloney, Jenny Howe, Carolyn Choa, Christopher Rozycki, Keith Bartlett, Stella Maris.
106 min.
The BBC's sweet, feminine answer to *Ghost* concentrates on the emotions (and the ratty flat) of Juliet Stevenson, so desperately unhappy after her lover's death that he comes back from the grave to be with her. As a metaphor for the experience of bereavement, the conceit is over-extended, though Stevenson almost makes it work. Minghella has an irritating sub-Forsythian tendency to cloy, most nauseatingly over Michael

Maloney's New Man, who gradually comes to fill the gap in Stevenson's life. Much more fun is Alan Rickman's chauvinistic apparition, inviting his deathly mates round to watch Woody Allen videos at all hours of the night. TCh

Truman Show, The

(Peter Weir, 1998, US) Jim Carrey, Ed Harris, Laura Linney, Noah Emmerich, Natascha McElhone.
102 min.
Truman Burbank is beginning to wise up. People seem to listen to him, but they never really connect; he feels trapped in a job he doesn't care about, a marriage he doesn't believe in, and a small island community he's never been able to leave. It's as if his life has been pre-programmed from the start: as indeed it has, for Truman is the unwitting subject of television's most audacious experiment, a real-life soap following one man from birth to death. When Truman (Carrey) appeals to a higher power, he's actually addressing the show's omniscient creator/director, Christof (Harris). The best comedy since *Groundhog Day* – better, even, than that – this is more than just a savvy and ingenious satire on media saturation, it's a moving metaphysical fable. One movie you can pronounce a modern classic with absolute confidence. TCh

Trust

(Hal Hartley, 1990, GB/US) Adrienne Shelly, Martin Donovan, Merritt Nelson, John MacKay, Edie Falco, Gary Sauer, Matt Malloy, Suzanne Costellos.
106 min.
To some extent, Hartley's second feature may be seen as a reprise of the small-town situations of *The Unbelievable Truth*. Again it stars Shelly as a disillusioned teenage brat, the slatternly Maria, whose admission that she is pregnant by her football jock boyfriend drives dad to keel over with a cardiac. Again she takes up with a serious young man with a history of violence: the volatile Martin (Donovan), whose endless rows with his father and with his computer-manufacturer bosses induce ideas of suicide. Again, too, the couple's attempts to forge a trusting relationship, in the face of hostility, rumour and absurd notions of bourgeois respectability, are played out as dead-pan farce. This is funnier and more stylish than its predecessor; and for all the bright, brash hues of Michael Spiller's sleek camerawork, it's also darker, slyly combining social comment and satire as it embraces issues like abortion, child abduction, sexual harassment and parental cruelty. GA

Trust Me

(Bobby Houston, 1989, US) Adam Ant, David Packer, Talia Balsam, William DeAcutis, Joyce Van Patten.
104 min.
Adam Ant's cash-strapped art dealer will stop at nothing to increase the value of talent-free Packer's latest canvases, even if it means killing him, in this patchy satire on the skewed values of the art market. Not that many laughs though, given such an easy target, mainly because of an uncertain cast and half-finished script. Genuine works by Andy Warhol and Keith Haring contextualise the pastiche offerings Packer knocks out. TJ

Truth About Cats & Dogs, The

(Michael Lehmann, 1996, US) Uma Thurman, Janeane Garofalo, Ben Chaplin, Jamie Foxx, James McCaffrey, Richard Coca, Stanley DeSantis.
97 min.
Your fish is depressed, your tortoise won't look you in the eye, and the dog's careering about on roller-skates. Who you gonna call? Abby Barnes, that's who. Abby (Garofalo) is a radio pet-therapist, dispensing sound practical advice to distressed animals and owners alike. Abby is warm, funny and intelligent, but she's made for radio; men never give her a second glance. When a caller, Brian (Chaplin), asks her for a date, Abby panics, and sends her beautiful, dizzy neighbour Noelle (Thurman) in her stead. Heavy petting ensues. A pleasingly old-fashioned romantic comedy, this plays a mildly feminist variation on *Cyrano de Bergerac*, with Abby dishing out amorous advice and promptly regretting it, as Brian falls head over heels with

the wrong woman – or rather, with her brains and Noelle's body. Granted, this misunderstanding is pretty silly, but it's a tribute to the cast that we don't lose patience with them. Garofalo, especially, is the cat's meow; in part, it's such an appealing performance because Abby is clearly her own worst enemy. It's a relief to come across a Hollywood comedy which doesn't talk down to the audience. Bravo to screenwriter Audrey Wells for her sophisticated script, and to director Lehmann, who gives the material a light, airy feel. TCh

Truth or Dare
(aka In Bed with Madonna)
(Alek Keshishian, 1991, US)
119 min. b/w & col.
'This movie has been worth five years of psychoanalysis,' Madonna has said. Indeed, Keshishian's record of the 'Blonde Ambition' tour is memorable not so much for the live footage (electrifying, but brief), nor for the few risqué moments contrived to provide hype, but for its study of the loneliness of stardom and the ties of family. Madonna's shrink would be interested to meet her father: their love-hate relationship, combined with a Catholic upbringing, might explain the mild SM fetish that surfaces in 'Hanky Panky' and 'Justify My Love'. There's also the classic guilt complex over her mother's death. Madonna comes across as warm, generous, impulsive, casting herself as mother to her dancers. She also comes across as spoilt, bitchy, witty, incapable of sitting still. Her shrink may agree that this is the most intriguing rockumentary since Don't Look Back, but he won't advise her to cancel her appointments yet. DW

Try and Get Me
see Sound of Fury, The

Tucker:
The Man and His Dream
(Francis Coppola, 1988, US) Jeff Bridges, Joan Allen, Martin Landau, Frederic Forrest, Mako, Elias Koteas, Christian Slater, Lloyd Bridges, Dean Stockwell.
111 min.
It's tempting to view Coppola's version of the destruction of a self-promoting American original by the big corporations as a personal metaphor: Preston Tucker's visionary 1948 automobile went the way of Zoetrope Studios. Whatever, Tucker is a visually dazzling piece of cinema, though about as psychologically profound a portrait of post-war American optimism as a Saturday Evening Post cover. Emphatically, this is not the reverent Paul Muni-Warner Brothers treatment, though it does fling period biopic devices at the screen in exhilarating handfuls. Coppola's dreamer is determinedly loveable, surrounded by moiling dogs and family. Tucker (Bridges) also imbues his crew with fierce loyalty, most movingly embodied by cringing Abe Karatz (Landau), who confesses that he got too close and caught his dreams. Even Howard Hughes (Stockwell), recognising a kindred spirit, offers valuable advice under the wings of his chimerical Spruce Goose. The Motown monopoly works through corrupt Senator Ferguson (Lloyd Bridges), and drags Tucker to court, but not before 50 beautiful cars of the future roll off the production line, causing even the partial judge to smile. The cinematic sleight-of-hand parallels the bombast of its hero, but you never get a glimpse of either visionary. BC

Tuff Turf
(Fritz Kiersch, 1984, US) James Spader, Kim Richards, Paul Mones, Matt Clark, Claudette Nevins, Olivia Barash, Robert Downey.
111 min.
Morgan Hiller, new boy in town (LA), incurs the enmity of gangleader Nick (Mones) by canoodling with his girlfriend Frankie (Richards). Morgan (Spader) does a lot of tuff-boy brooding, and gets pep talks from his pop – 'Life isn't a problem to be solved, it's a mystery to be lived!' – and the tuffer-uppers end up slugging it out in a ludicrously protracted and bloody bout of fisticuffs. The soundtrack, featuring Marianne Faithfull and Lene Lovich, is a mite more sussed than usual, but the whole caboodle has a curiously dated feel, with Grease-style high school interludes and 'punk' dancers coming on like extras

from West Side Story. And Nick, in a fit of total tufflessness, sinks so low as to actually propose marriage to Frankie, before regaining his sociopathic credentials by tuffing up her dad. Semi-tuff stuff. AB

Tugboat Annie
(Mervyn LeRoy, 1933, US) Marie Dressler, Wallace Beery, Robert Young, Maureen O'Sullivan, Willard Robertson, Frankie Darro.
87 min. b/w.
Amiable and amusing comedy-drama, uniting for the second time (after Min and Bill) MGM's older and uglier alternatives to the likes of Garbo and Gilbert: the admirably cynical, world-worn Dressler and the rumbustious but surprisingly subtle Beery. Most delightful are their scenes of brawling and quarrelling as the husband-and-wife skippers of a tugboat, although Dressler also manages to inject a more sentimental touch into her scenes with upwardly mobile son Young. For sheer uncomplicated professionalism of performance, the old-timers can't be beat. GA

Tumult (Gir-Gir)
(Yemane I Demisse, 1996, Ethiopia/US) Jima Assefa, Seble Tekle, Eskinder Berhanu, Tabi Gebre-Hiwot, Samson K Guma.
117 min. b/w & col.
Seven years in the making, this is a landmark in Ethiopian film-making. It's set during the period of political upheaval pre-dating the dismissal of Haile Selassie in 1974, and personalises the conflicting pulls on the younger members of Ethiopia's middle (and upper) class elite in the story of Yoseph, who joins anti-government rebels following his return from studies in America. Yemane I Demisse (director, producer, writer, editor and production designer) adopts a desultory tone that echoes the feeling of malaise and defeat that met the rebels when the country failed to ignite in opposition. Following the young man on the run, the film observes people and events afresh, albeit now from a hunted perspective. An impressive, sophisticated work, with a controlled handling of mood, actors, and location, but the resonances produced by the use of religious music, ethnic song and poetry may be lost on many non-Ethiopians. WH

Tunde's Film
(Maggie Pinhorn/Tunde Ikoli, 1973, GB) Harry Curran, Lesley Easteale, Colin Hennessy, Tunde Ikoli.
43 min.
Written and co-directed by 18-year-old Tunde Ikoli, this was made, he said, 'to show people what we have to put up with'; and its immediacy in dealing with the repressive influences on teenagers living in the East End of London often compensates for its lack of technical gloss. Particularly effective are a pointless search by goon-like policemen, and a café conversation between Tunde's friends, both of which do more to 'explain' delinquency than all of your glib sociological theorising. Like all neo-realism, Tunde's Film has the authority of performers re-enacting lived experience rather than acting. RM

Tune in Tomorrow
(aka Aunt Julia and
the Scriptwriter)
(Jon Amiel, 1990, US) Barbara Hershey, Keanu Reeves, Peter Falk, Bill McCutcheon, Patricia Clarkson, Richard Portnow, Jerome Dempsey, Richard B Shull, Henry Gibson, Buck Henry, Hope Lange, John Larroquette, Elizabeth McGovern.
104 min.
Transposed in William Boyd's adaptation from Peru to New Orleans in 1951, Mario Vargas Llosa's novel has lost much of its flavour, but enough of its Chinese-box trickery remains. Aunt Julia (Hershey) is the woman with a past who casts a spell over her puppyish nephew Martin (Reeves). The Scriptwriter is the mercurial and possibly dangerous Pedro Carmichael (Falk), dramaturge of the nail-biting radio schlock-opera 'Kings of the Garden District'. With the mad, moustache-curling genius at the helm, the ratings soar – but why the sniping obsession with Albanians, more virulent with each episode? The film ends up rather uneven in its attempt to balance the demands of the love interest (lukewarm) and the

spiralling lunacy of the soap. But it has a lot going for it in its playfulness and performances (including a number of guest cameos in the serial). Amiel may not get to ring the reality-fantasy changes as ingeniously as he did in The Singing Detective, but a good time was clearly had by all. JRo

Tunes of Glory
(Ronald Neame, 1960, GB) Alec Guinness, John Mills, Susannah York, Kay Walsh, Dennis Price, John Fraser, Duncan Macrae, Gordon Jackson, Allan Cuthbertson, Peter McEnery.
107 min.
The British cinema is littered with movies (from Bridge on the River Kwai to Tiara Tahiti) purporting to explore the military mind and caste ethics, but withdrawing into compromise before getting anywhere much. Here (an adaptation by James Kennaway of his own novel), as the English martinet taking over a Highland regiment in its bleak Scottish quarters, Mills comes across with rather more conviction than Guinness as his raffishly pawky predecessor, 'Jock' Sinclair. The clash of native temperaments and military customs between the two, leading both to mental crack-ups, has the stuff of real drama to it, but is gradually frittered away into silly sentimental melodramatics. TM

Tunisian Victory
(Hugh Stewart/Roy Boulting/Frank Capra, 1944, GB)
105 min. b/w.
The sequel to Boulting's Desert Victory, in which the British 8th Army's advance is seen as part of an Allied masterplan to drive the Germans out of Africa. Two huge convoys – one British, the other American – meet at a predetermined point in mid-Atlantic; a lengthy flashback takes us back to the previous summer, when the masterplan was conceived, and the remainder of the film follows the course of the North African campaign chronologically. Apart from two sequences – the British attack on Wadi Zig Zaou and the American assault on Hill 609, staged in England and Arizona respectively – the movie is all combat footage. MA

Tunnel, The
(aka Transatlantic Tunnel)
(Maurice Elvey, 1935, GB) Richard Dix, Leslie Banks, Madge Evans, C Aubrey Smith, George Arliss, Helen Vinson, Jimmy Hanley, Walter Huston, Basil Sydney.
94 min. b/w.
League of Nations pacifism bred some strange fruits, but none stranger than this extravagant hymn to peaceful coexistence. In a vaguely futuristic era beyond 1940, the building of a Transatlantic tunnel is suggested as the solution to the world's problems. As the suspiciously Disraeli-like Prime Minister declares, the tunnel will be 'an artery through which will course the life-blood of our two nations, flowing into the hearts of Anglo-American relations'. In a slow-moving but complex melodrama, Dix and Banks, with their radium drills, televisors, and tough, no-nonsense technology, battle their way through tunnel sickness and high finance treachery, subterranean volcanos and feminine intrigue, to reach at last the light at the end of their 2,000 mile tunnel. RMy

Tupamaros
(Jan Lindqvist, 1972, Swe/Uru)
50 min.
Essentially, the film behind Costa-Gavras' State of Siege. Edited by Jan Lindqvist from clandestine footage shot by a whole series of different people, all unaware of the final purpose of the film, it combines polemic and information into a persuasive piece of committed radical film-making. Interviews with Geoffrey Jackson, Dan Mitrione, and others in the Peoples' Prison; interviews with the parents of a Tupamaro who find their house bombed out nightly; interviews with people in the street, alternating with shots of the landed oligarchy enjoying their wealth; information about the domination of foreign companies; information about the history and desperation of the struggle. And that is what comes across most forcefully – the desperation behind the seemingly impudent tactic of what the film calls 'the faceless power' in the Uruguayan situation.

Turbulence

(Robert Butler, 1997, US) Ray Liotta, Lauren Holly, Brendan Gleeson, Ben Cross, Rachel Ticotin, Jeffrey DeMunn, John Finn, Hector Elizondo.
100 min.
The NYPD choose a deserted 747 flight on Christmas Eve to transport two criminals – a bank robber and a serial killer – across country. Lonely stewardess – excuse me, flight attendant – Teri (Holly) takes quite a shine to the psycho, Ryan (Liotta), who may have been framed and has a way with women. Even when both pilots are dead, the passengers have disappeared and there's a hole in the side of the plane, Ryan can coax Teri out of the cockpit with his soft-spoken schizo charm. Guess Teri picked the wrong week to give up glue sniffing. The ads for *Turbulence* promise 'over-the-top action', but this is surely a misprint; over-the-top acting is the main attraction here. It's hard to tell with Holly, who sheds her dignity and her uniform with stoic resignation, but Liotta seems well aware just how appalling this movie is, flashing his chops with an alacrity to rival the Big Bad Wolf, pitching his performance several thousand feet above ground level, and refusing to come down. TCh

Turkey Shoot

(Brian Trenchard-Smith, 1981, Aust) Steve Railsback, Olivia Hussey, Michael Craig, Carmen Duncan, Noel Ferrier, Lynda Stoner, Roger Ward.
93 min.
Turkey shite, more like, a tuppeny ha'penny rehash of *The Most Dangerous Game*. It's 1995, world peace at last, although it takes global totalitarianism to enforce. Dissidents are sent to what looks like *Camp on Blood Island*, only cheaper. As well as being beaten by bullies with whips, they have to wear canary jumpsuits. New arrivals Railsback and Hussey are among those chosen for the sport of C.O. Thatcher (Craig) and his decadent chums. Five unarmed kids, one jungle, half-a-dozen armed pursuers with transport. So who wins? The film had some 'shock horror' press over its violence. But ghouls won't be satisfied with scenes like one where a nasty gets his hands lopped and advances on the audience with bloody stumps that are the same cuff-over-the-knuckles trick most of us learned before junior school. If it was that funny even a quarter of the time, it wouldn't be so bad. Despite a heap of 'action', the pic's about as lively as a snail full of downers. GD

Turkish Bath – Hamam,The (Il Bagno Turco – Hamam)

(Ferzan Ozpetek, 1997, Sp/It/Tur) Alessandro Gassman, Francesca d'Aloja, Carlo Cecchi, Halil Ergun, Serif Sezer, Mehmet Gunsur.
94 min.
Interior designer Francesco (Gassman) leaves Rome and his fading marriage and travels to Istanbul to assess the inheritance left to him by his aunt: an old-fashioned Turkish bath ('hamam') on a quiet backstreet. Lodging with the establishment's kindly retainers, he falls under the spell of the alien city, and strikes up a relationship with the son of the family which promises a freedom he may not have enjoyed at home. This first feature conveys the relaxed rhythm of life in Istanbul with assurance, while the warmth of Francesco's welcome, the story's sexual undercurrent and the film's ethnic influenced score complete a persuasive (if somewhat dramatically unfocused) package. TJ

Turkish Delight (Turks Fruit)

(Paul Verhoeven, 1973, Neth) Monique van de Ven, Rutger Hauer, Tonny Huurdeman, Wim van den Brink, Dolf de Vries.
106 min.
An expensive excuse for a love/sex/death porno exercise. Sculptor falls in love with a spoiled rich young thing who is too young and full of sexy life to live, so a brain tumour happens along. Young sexy girls grow up to lose their bloom, and the only way the media mythology can deal with its own limitations is to kill them off while they're still young and beautiful, and use them as an excuse to make a pseudo-philosophical statement about love, life and decay. MV

Turk 182!

(Bob Clark, 1985, US) Timothy Hutton, Robert Urich, Kim Cattrall, Robert Culp, Darren McGavin, Steven Keats, Peter Boyle, James Tolkan, Dick O'Neill, Maury Chaykin.
98 min.
Adamantly sincere but utterly redundant populism from Bob *Porky's* Clark, a boy scout's stab at *Bonfire of the Vanities* starring Timothy Hutton's noble adam's apple (gulp!), which he thrusts this way and that for all the world like an ostrich with a social conscience. Hutton's a kind of contemporary James Stewart, a graffiti guerrilla taking on City Hall. And for what? To get some support for his brother, a fireman injured in the line of duty. You can't help wondering why he didn't just find a good lawyer. TCh

Turnabout

(Hal Roach, 1940, US) John Hubbard, Carole Landis, Adolphe Menjou, William Gargan, Mary Astor, Verree Teasdale, Donald Meek, Franklin Pangborn.
83 min. b/w.
Adapted from Thorne Smith's fantasy about sexual role reversal, this probably seemed daring once, but hasn't worn well. An Indian sculpture with magical powers, tired of endless quarrels between a married couple (Hubbard and Landis) as to who has the best of the marriage contract, grants their wish to change roles. So while she (Hubbard, dubbed with Landis' voice and indulging excruciatingly stereotyped camp mannerisms) goes to work as an advertising executive, he (Landis, dubbed with Hubbard's voice and striding out a bit) tries to cope with the housewife's lot. Causing endless havoc and confusion, both are relieved when their wish to return to normal – prompted by Hubbard's fearful discovery that he/she is pregnant – is granted. The marital status quo is never questioned for a moment, of course; and the revelation that the statue made a mistake in rectifying matters – the husband is now pregnant – is chickenheartedly thrown away as a curtain line. The best bits come from the supporting cast, especially Pangborn and Meek, archetypal Preston Sturges characters without the Sturges dialogue to bring them fully to life. TM

Turner & Hooch

(Roger Spottiswoode, 1989, US) Tom Hanks, Mare Winningham, Craig T Nelson, Reginald VelJohnson, Scott Paulin, JC Quinn, John McIntire.
99 min.
Why does Tom Hanks so often work with unworthy material? Why has Roger Spottiswoode never fulfilled the promise of *Under Fire*? Small-town cop Turner (Hanks) reluctantly adopts an ugly, scene-stealing, monster dog when its ancient owner (McIntire) is murdered. Keen (for no clear reason) to prevent the beast from being put down, and convinced it will prove a key witness in his investigation of the mystery (if such it can be called), Turner lets Hooch demolish his home, imperil his blossoming romance with a local vet, and turn Rin Tin Tin. A couple of vaguely amusing monologues apart, this lame, tame variation on the buddy-buddy comic cop thriller is flaccid, predictable, and as sickeningly anthropomorphic as one might fear. From the moment when Hooch first appears to the strains of Strauss' 'Also sprach Zarathustra', the gags can be smelt a mile off, and the thriller elements are as hackneyed as an episode of *Murder She Wrote*. GA

Turning Point, The

(Herbert Ross, 1977, US) Anne Bancroft, Shirley MacLaine, Mikhail Baryshnikov, Leslie Browne, Tom Skerritt, Martha Scott, Antoinette Sibley, Alexandra Danilova.
119 min.
A film about classical ballet which is also about friendship, usually the cinematic prerogative of men. From a deceptively simple script – renewed acquaintance between an ageing ballerina (Bancroft) and a former colleague (MacLaine) who is now a housewife with a daughter just starting out as a dancer – emerge jealousies and resentments about lost chances, maternity-vs-career, comfort-vs-austere dedication; conflicts all purged in Bancroft and MacLaine's magnificent fishwife scene. There's some beautiful dancing and a wealth of detail about the world of classical ballet. Interesting and entertaining. JS

Turtle Beach

(Stephen Wallace, 1992, Aust) Greta Scacchi, Joan Chen, Jack Thompson, Art Malik, Norman Kaye, Victoria Langley, Martin Jacobs.
88 min.
Australian journalist Judith Wilkes (Scacchi) leaves her estranged husband and children and takes off for Malaysia, where Vietnamese boat people are being slaughtered or moved into makeshift holding camps. Once there, her main contact is Vietnamese ex-prostitute Minou (Chen), now married to the Australian High Commissioner, who seeks to be reunited with the three children she left behind in Saigon. In the process of researching her story, Judith abandons professional objectivity and becomes emotionally involved, both with Minou and with black marketeer Kanan (Malik). Ann Turner's stilted script is burdened by a metaphorical link between the life-cycle of giant sea turtles and that of boat people who land on the same spot. Even worse is the clumsy editing and flat direction, with Wallace indulging in innumerable close-ups in a misjudged attempt to emphasise emotional tension. CM

Turtle Diary

(John Irvin, 1985, GB) Glenda Jackson, Ben Kingsley, Richard Johnson, Michael Gambon, Rosemary Leach, Eleanor Bron, Harriet Walter, Jeroen Krabbé, Nigel Hawthorne.
96 min.
Jackson plays an unmarried lady who writes children's books under the pseudonym of Delia Swallow, and Kingsley a sales clerk living in limbo between a Bloomsbury bookshop and Fulham bedsitland: two lonely people drawn out of their shells by an elaborate heist to liberate the turtles from London Zoo. Absent, however, is the American-born Russell Hoban's quizzical perspective on his uptight Brits in his novel. What's left is not quite Delia Swallow for grown-ups; but the bland world this film inhabits is almost as quaint, complacent and parochial. SJo

Turtle on Its Back (La Tortue sur le Dos)

(Luc Béraud, 1978, Fr) Jean-François Stévenin, Bernadette Lafont, Claude Miller, Virginie Thévenet, Véronique Silver.
109 min.
A splendid, unsettling first feature from writer Béraud, about a bad case of writer's block. Béraud's achievement lies in finding a visual and visceral language to describe the process of writing as work (more perspiration than inspiration, and more neurosis than either). After sketching the tense domestic relations between financially supportive girlfriend (Lafont) and impotent writer (Stévenin), the film follows the writer off the rails, sliding into a delirious nightmarish journey through a night-town whose torments and triumphs, though vividly real, may also represent the creative process itself. JD

Tva Killar och en Tjej (Happy We/Two Lovers and Their Lass/Two Guys and a Gal)

(Lasse Hallström, 1982, Swe) Brasse Brannstrom, Ivan Oljelund, Magnus Harenstam, Pia Green, Lars Amble.
111 min.
Three university friends meet '20 years on'. They're Nordic thesps who all love performing, and are only too keen to relive moments from their old stage successes. Between times, they swap notes on their marriages, divorces and general swings in fortune. Hallström keeps matters light, avoiding a Bergman-like probe into tortured souls. GM

TV Dante: Cantos I–VIII, A

(Peter Greenaway/Tom Phillips, 1989, GB) John Gielgud, Bob Peck, Joanne Whalley-Kilmer, David Rudkin, David Attenborough.
88 min. b/w & col.
It's easy to see what attracted Greenaway to Dante. *Inferno*, the first of the three books of *The Divine Comedy* – still the world's most complex account of the male menopause – teems with symbols, allusions, lists and numbers. Pre-empting the Renaissance, it is an *omnium gatherum* of history, science, animal behaviourism, cos-

mology and medicine. Collaborating with artist Phillips, Greenaway exploits state-of-the-art video techniques to lay image after image on top of each other, thus creating a picture that corresponds in depth of meaning, colour and excitement to that of the written text. Monologue, mud-wrestling and Muybridge animation are all part of the ordered mêlée. Peck is Dante, Gielgud is Virgil, and Whalley-Kilmer is Beatrice. Each of the eight cantos completed lasts 11 minutes, which is roughly equal to reading time, and is by turns horrifying, beautiful, creepy and fascinating. This is TV designed to be viewed over and over again: 'a pop person's think-video'. MS

Twelfth Night
(Trevor Nunn, 1996, GB) Imogen Stubbs, Helena Bonham Carter, Nigel Hawthorne, Ben Kingsley, Richard E Grant, Mel Smith, Imelda Staunton, Toby Stephens, Stephen MacKintosh.
133 min.
Set in a Hardy-esque English countryside, circa 1890, this starts boldly with a shipwreck and scene-setting voice-over from Kingsley's Feste, whose journeyman troubadour and hedgerow philosopher bestrides the piece like a rustic colossus. Shakespeare's greatest comedy is bittersweet, involving parted siblings, a fair amount of sexual confusion, which, thankfully, director/adaptor Nunn doesn't turn into a tediously modish essay on cross-dressing and sexuality, and the come-uppance of Hawthorne's churlish Malvolio, which deliberately waters down the heady wine of the joyous ending. Filming the play brings an obvious problem: the point of much of both the comedy and the transcendence relies on the audience wearing the fact that Viola, disguised as a bloke, is the spitting image of her brother Sebastian. An impressive Stubbs does everything in her and the make-up department's power to look like Stephen MacKintosh's young blade, but the attempt still falls short. It's not a terminal problem, however: the direction is assured, and the cast is masterly. SGr

12 Angry Men
(Sidney Lumet, 1957, US) Henry Fonda, Lee J Cobb, Ed Begley, EG Marshall, Jack Klugman, Jack Warden, Martin Balsam, John Fiedler, George Voskovec, Robert Webber, Edward Binns, Joseph Sweeney.
95 min. b/w.
Lumet's origins as a director of teledrama may well be obvious here in his first film, but there is no denying the suitability of his style – sweaty close-ups, gritty monochrome 'realism', one-set claustrophobia – to his subject. Scripted by Reginald Rose from his own teleplay, the story is pretty contrived – during a murder trial, one man's doubts about the accused's guilt gradually overcome the rather less-than-democratic prejudices of the other eleven members of the jury – but the treatment is tense, lucid, and admirably economical. Fonda, though typecast as the bastion of liberalism, gives a nicely underplayed performance, while Cobb, Marshall and Begley in particular are highly effective in support. But what really transforms the piece from a rather talky demonstration that a man is innocent until proven guilty, is the consistently taut, sweltering atmosphere, created largely by Boris Kaufman's excellent camerawork. The result, however devoid of action, is a strangely realistic thriller. GA

Twelve Chairs, The
(Mel Brooks, 1970, US) Ron Moody, Frank Langella, Dom DeLuise, Bridget Brice, Robert Bernal, David Lander, Mel Brooks.
93 min.
Gambolling about the Balkans is the theme of Mel Brooks' second feature, with comic Moody and personable Langella chasing the one chair out of a set which is stuffed with pre-Russian Revolutionary booty. They run into Dom DeLuise, playing a Zero Mostel-in-*The Producers* role, and Brooks himself as a loony lackey. It's all very fairytale, delightful to watch, and certainly not as self-indulgent as the major Brooks works it slips in between (*The Producers* and *Blazing Saddles*). What's more pleasant about it is the direction; both of the performers and of the action within scenes: the excellent timing can now be seen as preparation for the sort of classical control that made a lot of *Young Frankenstein* so good. AN

12 Monkeys
(Terry Gilliam, 1995, US) Bruce Willis, Madeleine Stowe, Brad Pitt, Christopher Plummer, Joseph Melito, Jon Seda.
129 min.
In 1996, a virus kills five billion people. 'This already happened,' James Cole (Willis) explains to Dr Railly (Stowe) in 1990. He knows because he's been there. Six years and a matter of minutes after he vanishes from a padded cell, Cole is back in his psychiatrist's life. He must trace the contagion, but he needs Railly's help to track down former patient Goines (Pitt), whose environmental action group, the Army of the 12 Monkeys, may be behind the disaster. With its shifts in tone and style signposted by Pitt's buggy loony-toon and Willis's movingly bewildered introvert, Terry Gilliam's apocalyptic fantasy is even weirder than it sounds. Less a *Terminator*-type action pic than a spectacularly disorienting *inaction* movie, with Cole as a helpless Cassandra hooked on an image from his own past, hoping against hope that he may in fact be crazy…the film's a terrible mess, but a terribly beautiful, tender mess. The screenplay by Janet and David Peoples (*Blade Runner*, *Unforgiven*) takes off from Chris Marker's 1962 short, *La Jetée*, but soon spirals into more pressing millennial obsessions (insanity, chaos and ecological catastrophe), before a vertiginous Hitchcockian make-over in the last reel. Gilliam gives the material a lunatic poetry of his own, but remains impervious to the requirements of narrative pacing. TCh

Twelve O'Clock High
(Henry King, 1949, US) Gregory Peck, Hugh Marlowe, Gary Merrill, Millard Mitchell, Dean Jagger, Paul Stewart.
132 min. b/w.
Along with *The Gunfighter* (also directed by the erratic but undervalued King), one of Peck's best performances as the martinet required to take over an exhausted World War II American bomber group in England because High Command feels that the present CO (Merrill) is too emotionally involved with his men: appalled by the casualty rates, Merrill is reluctant to turn the screw, and their deteriorating performance is casting doubts in high places about the value of daylight precision bombing, still in its experimental stages. A superb first half dissects the sense of demoralisation, with the group, already bowed under its reputation as a hard-luck outfit, initially wilting even further as Peck applies kill or cure remedies (like segregating the worst misfits and malingerers as a crew known as 'The Leper Colony'). Latterly, with Peck beginning to crack under the emotional strain and go the same way as Merrill, the film sails close to becoming a (less romantic) remake of *The Dawn Patrol*. But King's control, the electric tension, and the performances all hold firm. TM

12 Storeys (Shi-er Lou)
(Eric Khoo, 1997, Singapore) Jack Neo, Chuan Yi-Fong, Koh Boon-Pin, Lucilla Teoh, Lum May-Yee, Ritz Lim.
107 min.
The benign spirit of Kieslowski hovers over Khoo's second feature, which picks up where *Mee Pok Man* left off with more funny/sad accounts of screwed-up lives in a typical Singaporean government-housing block. Khoo focuses on the inhabitants of three apartments: an overweight single woman who can't get her late mother's cruel nagging out of her head, a working-class slob put through the mill by his brought-from-China wife, and a very uptight guy who crashes into the discovery that his younger sister has a sex life. As a social satire of Lee Kuan-Yew's nanny state, this is witty and sophisticated stuff. As an anthology of lives blighted by self-delusion and peer-group pressure, it's so truthful it hurts. TR

Twelve Tasks of Asterix, The (Les 12 Travaux d'Astérix)
(René Goscinny/Albert Uderzo, 1975, Fr) voices (English version): George Baker, Sean Barrett, John Ringham, Barbara Mitchell.
82 min.
In this product of the Idéfix studio, established by Goscinny, creator of the stocky Gallic hero Asterix, French humour strikes a common note with the British in the struggle of the plucky, apolitical bourgeois against bureaucratic authority.

Although the film achieves nothing startling in its use of animation techniques, the narrative moves along at a fair pace as Astérix and Obélix tackle the twelve Herculean labours imposed by Julius Caesar, relying on the virtues of audacity, tenacity, fortitude, sheer ignorance, and the magic potion scored off Getafix the Druid. The most appealing task is a sortie into the Madhouse of Bureaucracy to obtain a permit for their next move. Our heroes find that the only way to combat the insane system is to create further confusion. JS

Twelve Views of Kensal House
(Peter Wyeth, 1984, GB) Maxwell Fry, Stephen Bayley, Lady Newall, Margaret Wilson, Eva Wilson.
55 min.
Wyeth's documentary investigates Maxwell Fry's ideas when he designed one of Britain's first modern flat complexes in London's Ladbroke Grove. Fry's views were basically well-founded, if a little blinkered and paternalistic, determined to create a better environment for working-class tenants. But what in the late '30s was something of an idyllic community project, has become an archetypal North Ken wasteland, semi-derelict, under-funded, and devoid of any sense of purpose or friendship. It's not so much the fault of Fry and the Gas Board, who constructed the block as a publicity stunt, as of the increasing poverty – both economic and social – of Britain at large. Nor are the tenants entirely blameless. Several of those interviewed sadly and characteristically lay the blame for the death of their community on the influx of immigrants (commonly referred to as 'bad' or 'rough' types). A fascinating look at the aims and effects of social architecture which is warmly human and sharply analytical, and which offers insights, by implication, on the changes in postwar British society. GA

Twentieth Century
(Howard Hawks, 1934, US) John Barrymore, Carole Lombard, Walter Connolly, Roscoe Karns, Etienne Girardot, Ralph Forbes, Edgar Kennedy.
91 min. b/w.
Hecht and MacArthur never wrote a better film script (or play) than this madcap tale of a theatrical producer chasing after his absconding star. Barrymore was an actor (and a drinker) after their own hearts, particularly since his grandiloquent gestures and delivery were then edging towards self-parody – exactly what the part of Oscar Jaffe, Broadway producer extraordinary, demands. And Lombard's mercurial beauty, Lily Garland, is a perfect match. Thanks to Hawks, the film not only takes place on an express train, it moves like one too. GB

Twenty Days Without War (Dvadtsat Dnei bez Voini)
(Alexei Gherman, 1976, USSR) Yuri Nikulin, Liudmila Gurchenko, R Sadykov, A Petrenko, A Stepanova.
100 min. b/w.
Banned for a decade, Gherman's anti-war film avoids all butchery to make its case through a subtly layered interplay between fact, fiction, and the evidence of the landscape and the human face. Lopatin (Nikulin), a writer and war correspondent, is on leave from the front during World War II. Travelling home by train, he listens impassively to a soldier's marital problems, and watches a young woman in tears; most of the incidents appear at a tangent to the theme, yet evoke the feel of an emotional destitution. Lopatin's responses are at their least dislocated in his reaction to the filming of one of his books, which processes his reality into inspirational propaganda. His brief affair with the woman who cried on the train is the sole positive in this portrait of an unremittingly anguished era. IC

25 Years
(Peter Morley, 1977, GB)
77 min.
Anyone staying awake through this compilation celebrating the Queen's Silver Jubilee deserves a medal. What it is, is 'a highly personal selection picked from an infinite variety of home and world events, all jostling for inclusion', designed to show that 'through good times and bad, and there have been many of both, through tumultuous

changes for better and for worse, the monarchy in the person of Queen Elizabeth II has provided continuity and stability'. It starts off seductively enough with the Royal Yacht steaming serenely into Boston while the Yanks go ape trying to get ready in time. But then we're into the Pathé News footage, a barrage of Danvers-Walker, making you shut your eyes and stuff up your ears. The Queen looks and sounds fed up throughout, as well she might; horses, investitures, state visits, all are presented as being dull as hell. AN

20 Million Miles to Earth
(Nathan Juran, 1957, US) William Hopper, Joan Taylor, Frank Puglia, Thomas Browne Henry, John Zaremba, Tito Vuolo.
82 min. b/w.
There is nothing that master animator Ray Harryhausen likes more than going on a wrecking spree. Over the years, his monsters, painstakingly galvanised frame by frame, have laid Washington to waste, devastated New York, and wrapped their clammy tentacles round the Golden Gate Bridge. Here, a blubbery-looking beastie from Venus ends up careering through Rome. The showdown in the Colosseum is a treat. Don't worry about the dotty script or cardboard performances – just sit back and watch this gelatinous blob in action. GM

Twenty-One
(Don Boyd, 1991, GB) Patsy Kensit, Jack Shepherd, Patrick Ryecart, Maynard Eziashi, Rufus Sewell, Sophie Thompson, Susan Wooldridge.
101 min.
There's plenty of frank sex talk when director/co-writer Boyd takes his Steadicam through doors normally marked private. No sooner have the credits rolled than we're in with Katie (Kensit) in the bathroom of her New York apartment, where she scrubs her feet in the bidet and delivers her first direct-to-camera monologue about sex and friendship. Cue a series of flashbacks to her life in London: Dad (Shepherd) endures a failed marriage, her lovers (Sewell and Ryecart) are respectively on drugs and married, and her confidante (Thompson) is a compulsive eater. The discursive approach is strangely alienating, and too often the relationships smack of contrivance. Kensit brings the right buoyancy to some of her monologues, but there's not enough introspection for the more demanding emotional exchanges. CM

TwentyFourSeven
(Shane Meadows, 1997, GB) Bob Hoskins, Danny Nussbaum, Bruce Jones, Frank Harper, Annette Badland.
96 min. b/w.
Those who have seen Shane Meadows' camcorder gem Smalltime will already know the young writer/director is one of Britain's most promising talents. This, his first full length feature, lives up to expectations splendidly. Though it's never quite as funny as the earlier movie, and the bigger (£1.5m) budget has resulted in more conventional characterisation and plotting, the extra polish comes with no significant drop in energy, flair or invention. Darcy (Hoskins) decides to inject a sense of community and purpose into the disaffected youth of a Nottingham suburb by reopening a club. While determination and a canny ability to win over most people he meets results in camaraderie and a modicum of sporting success, resentment, cynicism and even violence are so deeply ingrained in certain locals that the club is never entirely without enemies. What lifts the film beyond the constraints of this potentially corny story is Meadows' engagingly blend of authentic naturalism, robust rapscallion humour, jaunty editing and off-the-cuff lyricism. GA

20,000 Leagues Under the Sea
(Richard Fleischer, 1954, US) Kirk Douglas, James Mason, Paul Lukas, Peter Lorre, Robert J Wilke, Carleton Young.
126 min.
Still one of Disney's most ambitious live action adaptations, only marginally vulgarising Jules Verne's original and notable for some staggering designs, including the beautiful 'Nautilus' submarine itself, with its lush Victorian interior. It was the first Disney film to use very big stars,

with Mason contributing a thoroughly sympathetic performance as the anguished Captain Nemo, and Lorre as one of his foils. Time hasn't been quite so kind to Kirk Douglas' role as a lusty harpooner, who looks as though he was inserted to reassure American audiences in the face of what might seem to be a sternly anti-colonial plot. Otherwise this is one of the great movie adventures, fully deserving its canonisation in Disney World, where an elaborate underwater ride attempts – with mixed success – to duplicate some of the film's major thrills. DP

20,000 Years in Sing Sing
(Michael Curtiz, 1932, US) Spencer Tracy, Bette Davis, Arthur Byron, Lyle Talbot, Warren Hymer, Louis Calhern, Grant Mitchell, Sheila Terry, Edward J McNamara.
78 min. b/w.
Cagney was Warners' first choice for Tommy Connors, the 'tough bird' who eventually goes to the electric chair with a touch of cool resignation. Tracy, however, is suitably gritty in this taut but somewhat implausible moral drama which puts its protagonist through riots, solitary confinement and an escape before he realises that the warden (Byron) is a 'swell guy' deserving his trust. Connors' girl Bette Davis rather overdoes the acid tongue, but the quasi-documentary scenes of prison life are compelling. Based on a book by Sing Sing's liberal warden Lewis E Lawes who believed in rewarding good behaviour and facilitated location shooting inside the walls of the New York prison. TJ

23:58 (23h58)
(Pierre-William Glenn, 1995, Fr) Jean-François Stévenin, Jean-Pierre Malo, Gérald Garnier, Yan Epstein, Kader Boukanef, Sophie Tellier.
85 min.
While cinematographer Glenn (best known for his work with Truffaut and Tavernier) has come up with a diverting update of Kubrick's race-track-heist thriller The Killing, it's easy to accuse him of indulgence. For one thing, there's rather too much stock footage of the Le Mans 24-hour motorcycle race, setting for the daring robbery planned by former track stars Bernard (Stévenin), Thierry (Garnier) and their team of assorted little criminals and low-lifes. For another, making Morin (Malo), the top cop on the case, not only a bike connoisseur but a movie-buff, tends to tip the whole thing into anorak territory. Finally, a framing story, in which a couple of kids (one the offspring of a dead biker champ) read a letter from Bernard while playing on the beach, never manages to convince that it's anything more than poetic whimsy. That said, it's an amiably brief spin, fair on atmosphere (though the promise of the opening Melville-like shots of an empty grey northern coastline is never fulfilled), and strong on occasional quirky detail. Minor, for sure, but sufficiently different to pass the time. GA

Twice in a Lifetime
(Bud Yorkin, 1985, US) Gene Hackman, Ann-Margret, Ellen Burstyn, Amy Madigan, Ally Sheedy, Brian Dennehy, Stephen Lang, Darrell Larson.
117 min.
Yorkin sets up a family drama with Hackman as paterfamilias, Burstyn devoted wife, Dennehy drinking chum, Madigan married daughter, Sheedy unmarried daughter. Having given us the satiric Divorce American Style two decades ago, he now serves up 'Divorce Serious Style', with Hackman falling for barmaid Ann-Margret. But while there is an admirable depiction of 'real' people at work or settling down for the big match with a six-pack, the material is still no more than the great middle class drama of adultery, worked out with its very familiar rows and guilts. The acting, however, is a fascinating primer in just who can handle the medium. Burstyn and Madigan come out as if born to the art. CPea

Twilight
(Robert Benton, 1998, US) Paul Newman, Gene Hackman, Susan Sarandon, James Garner, Stockard Channing, M Emmet Walsh.
95 min.
'Prostate acting up yet?' enquires Garner of Newman, thereby identifying this as the private eye equivalent of Hawks's autumnal Western El Dorado. The pervading air of melancholy suggested by the title – the ruefulness, the regrets,

the wrong moves, the lost loves – is offset by the bantering dialogue and by the casually authoritative performances from players with about 200 years of stardom between them. The main problem is that, like Benton's other genre exercises, it's the work of a fan rather than a real practitioner, and as a mood piece, let alone as a mystery story, most audiences will always be several moves ahead of the game. BBa

Twilight City
(Reece Auguiste, 1989, GB) Homi Bhaba, Andy Coupland, Paul Gilroy, Gail Lewis, Savriti Hensman, Femi Otitoju, George Shire, Rosina Visram, David Yallop.
52 min.
In his novel The Moviegoer, Walker Percy writes about how seeing your everyday surroundings up on a cinema screen somehow authenticates them, conferring a reality they never had before. This is partly what the Black Audio Film Collective's work achieves, for London is the Twilight City now. As in Handsworth Songs and Testament, the BAFC adopts an evocative, poetic free form, comprised of powerful documentary and archival footage, narrative devices, and symbolic imagery. Liberating documentary from its didactic conventions, they synthesise the emotional and the political; the effect is urgent and memorable. 'Sacrifice a piece of the past for the whole of the future': the slogan reverberates through the film like a bell, a nightmarish Orwellian alarm and an elegiac knell. Other voices speak of other Londons: remembered, imagined, dreaded…cities of the mind. Immigrant experience, Section 28, architecture, Big Bang, the Docklands development, down-and-outs – there is too much here for the 52-minute running time, but Trevor Mathison's cacophonous score pulls it together in a cinematic stream of consciousness. TCh

Twilight of the Ice Nymphs, The
(Guy Maddin, 1997, Can) Pascale Bussières, Shelley Duvall, Frank Gorshin, Alice Krige, RH Thomson.
91 min.
An acquired taste they may have been, but from the mock early sound-era Nordic saga Tales from the Gimli Hospital to the deconstructed, de-Nazified mountain film Careful, the camp pastiche melodramas of Canadian experimentalist Maddin had a compelling (if confounding) hallucinatory logic of their own: surreally funny, but halo'd by a haze of 'lost age' romantic nostalgia. Forsaking at last the creaky conventions of '20s cinema, Maddin takes his inspiration here from the equally kitsch but more ethereal magical reaches of such '30s movies as the Reinhardt/ Dieterle A Midsummer Night's Dream. Sadly, it collapses dizzily amid a baroque shower of bejewelled costumes, Kenneth Anger style colour overload, mock fairytale purple prose, and pixillated anti-naturalistic performances: mournful ugly sister Amelia (Duvall); mesmerist Dr Solti (Thomson), the object of her affection; widowed Zephyr (Krige), a returned convict, and a dog called Aesop among them. Finally pretty tedious. WH

Twilight's Last Gleaming
(Robert Aldrich, 1977, US/WGer) Burt Lancaster, Richard Widmark, Charles Durning, Melvyn Douglas, Paul Winfield, Burt Young, Joseph Cotten, Roscoe Lee Browne, Gerald S O'Loughlin, Richard Jaeckel.
146 min.
Nuclear missiles raise their warheads, but this time the paranoia is inward, and it's American vs American as Lancaster's renegade Air Force General captures a Montana missile base in order to 'blackmail' the President into revealing the shameful secrets of former administrations. The plea for 'open' government makes this in many ways the first film of the Carter administration. On reflection, the script is often contrived and the acting less than dynamic. But praise to Aldrich for his no-nonsense direction, which fashions the material into a fairly riveting computer hardware thriller. His handling of the countdown – 'It stopped at 8. Next time they go!' – is sufficiently convincing for one to think that the film and everything else might end prematurely. Aldrich turns in a neat, professional job, and even his use of split-screen is unusually uncluttered. CPe

Twilight Zone – The Movie

(John Landis/Steven Spielberg/Joe Dante/George Miller, 1983, US) Dan Aykroyd, Albert Brooks, Vic Morrow, Scatman Crothers, Bill Quinn, Kathleen Quinlan, Jeremy Licht, Kevin McCarthy, John Lithgow.
101 min.

These revamped episodes from the old supernatural TV series begin splendidly with Aykroyd and Brooks driving down a dark road at night, singing along to Creedence Clearwater and trying to guess TV theme songs. Four episodes follow, and it's ironic that producer Spielberg's geriatric remake of *Peter Pan* set in an Old People's home is easily the weakest of the lot, exhibiting all the churning sentimentality of a great film-maker going OTT. The others have a comic strip zeal which makes them intensely watchable, but ultimately it's left to *Mad Max* wizard Miller to steal the show with an extraordinary remake of Richard Matheson's story about an airline passenger who spies a demon noshing the starboard engine. DP

Twinkle, Twinkle, Killer Kane

see Ninth Configuration, The

Twin Pawns
(aka The Curse of Greed)

(Léonce Perret, 1920, US) Mae Murray, Warner Oland.
74 min. b/w.

Perret first worked with Feuillade as an actor, and obviously picked up a flair for poetic hokum which is displayed to great effect in this fast-paced melodrama (made during a four-year spell in America). The 'twin pawns' are identical sisters whose fortunes are manipulated by a greedy bookmaker suitably called Bent. The story (from Wilkie Collins) may be nothing special, but the treatment certainly is, for Perret shows astonishing mastery of all the elements of cinema. The lighting, sets, compositions (impeccable use of doors, windows, and mirrors), editing, use of close-ups, even the design of the linking titles – all are pertinently stylish, full of the kind of visual texture usually associated with Sternberg, Sirk or Welles. GB

Twin Peaks

(David Lynch, 1989, US) Kyle MacLachlan, Michael Ontkean, Peggy Lipton, Jack Nance, Russ Tamblyn, Joan Chen, Piper Laurie, Troy Evans.
112 min.

Although financed by television, this – the pilot for an eight-part serial – was shot on film, allowing Lynch free rein to work in the partly surreal, partly expressionist style that has suffused his work to date. Set in the eponymous small lumber town in the Pacific Northwest, it begins with the discovery of a girl's corpse on a lakeside beach. Her parents are devastated, and when another girl is found wandering into town, dazed and speechless after having suffered unthinkably horrific torture, the local sheriff (Ontkean) calls in the FBI to help investigate the case. Already the spiritual unease and corruption of the community has begun, but when agent Dale Cooper (MacLachlan) drives into town, entranced by the Douglas firs, conversing endlessly with a cassette recorder, and grinning like a madman, the inimitable Lynch vision begins to grip like a strangler. Nightmare merges with comedy, and normality flies out the window. The result, like a soap reimagined by a Bosch or Magritte, is more genuinely cinematic than many a big screen thriller. See it, and shudder. GA

Twin Peaks:
Fire Walk with Me

(David Lynch, 1992, US) Kyle MacLachlan, Sheryl Lee, Harry Dean Stanton, Kiefer Sutherland, Moira Kelly, David Bowie, Chris Isaak, Ray Wise, James Marshall, Pamela Gidley, Grace Zabriskie, Jürgen Prochnow, David Lynch.
134 min.

'Goddamn, these people are peculiar!' opines Harry Dean Stanton's trailer-park manager in Lynch's big screen prequel to his cult TV series. He's right: not only are his fellow-characters weird, but the film's makers must be pretty odd too. For one thing, they evidently never felt that the tortuous narrative need make sense to audiences; for another, they appear to have made no attempt to conceal the cynicism that presumably motivated their desire to cash in on their TV suc-

cess. It begins a year before Laura Palmer's death, with FBI agent Desmond (Isaak) investigating the murder of one Teresa Banks (Gidley); meanwhile, Dale Cooper (MacLachlan) has his usual premonitory dreams. The whole thing looks like off-cuts from the series that were eliminated because they were either too nasty or too inept. Moreover, the cast consists largely of the series' weakest performers (Lee, particularly, as Laura Palmer, proves she can't carry a movie). Self-parody would seem too generous an assessment of Lynch's aims and achievement. GA

Twins

(Ivan Reitman, 1988, US) Arnold Schwarzenegger, Danny DeVito, Kelly Preston, Chloe Webb, Bonnie Bartlett, Marshall Bell, Trey Wilson.
107 min.

Tailor-made for Schwarzenegger and DeVito, this slick comedy about a pair of genetically-engineered twins is too tight for comfort, and works best when the odd couple parody their familiar personae and play off one another. The result of a scientific experiment, in which their mother was impregnated with a 'sperm milk-shake' derived from six male geniuses, the twins were separated at birth. Arnie is now a naive, super-intelligent virgin, DeVito a small-time hustler. So when Arnie finally tracks down his long-lost brother, it's hardly fraternal love at first sight. The subplots about DeVito's problems with loan sharks, exposing his residual avarice, help to flesh out what is essentially a one-joke scenario; but more emotionally revealing are DeVito's selfish, venal desire for Chloe Webb, and Arnie's innocent affection for her long-limbed sister (Preston). DeVito displays his remarkable ability to shift from fast-talking cynicism to affecting sentiment, while Arnie reveals a reasonable talent for light comedy. NF

Twins of Evil

(John Hough, 1971, GB) Madeleine and Mary Collinson, Peter Cushing, Kathleen Byron, Dennis Price, Harvey Hall, Isobel Black, Damien Thomas, David Warbeck, Katya Keith.
87 min.

Hammer climaxed scriptwriter Tudor Gates's Sheridan Le Fanu trilogy (*The Vampire Lovers* and *Lust for a Vampire*) with this little number: Puritan witch-hunting and rum goings-on at Castle Karnstein in Pinewood Austria. The centrefold Collinson twins are a sabre-toothed fiend (Madeleine) and a damsel in distress (Mary), effectively marking out the tension between virginal repression and unchecked licentiousness lying at the core of the genre. Some moments of Gothic atmosphere though, don't quite dispel the feeling that much of the plot is devoted to developing situations where its leading ladies might be disrobed for the camera. TJ

Twin Town

(Kevin Allen, 1997, GB) Llyr Evans, Rhys Ifans, Dorien Thomas, Dougray Scott, Biddug Williams.
99 min.

Port Talbot, and school dropout twins Julian and Jeremy are revelling in daily joyriding, solvent abuse and petty vandalism. Meanwhile, over in the chintzier reaches of twin town Swansea, coppers Terry and Greyo, mates of bent building contractor Cartwright, argue about the appropriate scale of their drug deals. Their fates intertwine when the kids' father Fatty, pegged on a job for Cartwright, is hospitalised but refused compensation, triggering tit-for-tat threats, humiliations, slaughtered dogs and finally arson and multiple murder. This urban black comedy is a plain misfire. Strangely, for all its pulse-taking pretensions, it most resembles some old-fashioned criminal caper movie, albeit psyched-up and overdone for the '90s: the moral perspective has merely been flipped from the majority's to that of the confused offender, keeping the facile narrative and quaint social caricature intact. Llyr Evans (Julian) and Rhys Ifans (Jeremy), on the other hand, display a louche robe-boy energy that betokens fine things for the future. WH

Twister

(Michael Almereyda, 1990, US) Harry Dean Stanton, Suzy Amis, Crispin Glover, Dylan McDermott, William Burroughs.
93 min.

An engagingly slapdash tale of an everyday American family: soda pop billionaire Dad (Stanton), *fin de siècle* fop son (Glover), teenage single-parent daughter (Amis), and her moppet progeny who drags around her pet plastic lizard in a jar. When Amis' lovelorn suitor and Dad's evangelist fiancée come a-calling, all hell doesn't *quite* break out, but there's some entertainingly freaky dialogue – and even freakier acting – to liven things up along the way. With verbal, visual and narrative non-sequiturs at every turn – the freak weather conditions of the title, a mysterious helicopter, and a wildly incongruous William Burroughs cameo – *Twister* is clearly lost without a map from the first frame. Languorous pace and uneasy self-consciousness notwithstanding, it's in a similar bracket to the work of Hal Hartley and Atom Egoyan; it has a spaced-out charm of its own. And Glover's ludicrous wardrobe and whip-dancing skills make this a must for completists of Crazy Crispin. JRo

Twister

(Jan De Bont, 1996, US) Helen Hunt, Bill Paxton, Jami Gertz, Cary Elwes, Lois Smith, Philip Seymour Hoffman, Alan Ruck, Sean Whalen.
113 min.

Effects apart, this is dire: predictable, clichéd, sloppily written, pitifully performed and surprisingly short of real shocks and suspense. The story can be described in two ways: as a rip-off of *Only Angels Have Wings*, in which Paxton's implausibly intuitive tornado expert is torn between two women, his ex (Hunt) and his fiancée (Gertz), and two lives, a safe weatherman job, or a risky return to the group of crazily devoted storm-chasers trying to get a gizmo up inside a twister's 'suck-zone'; or as a repetitive spectacle where all that happens is that the objects hurled around in the air simply get bigger. Forget the many redundant references to *The Wizard of Oz*, this hasn't a fraction of that movie's logic, imagination or ambitions. Seriously depressing. GA

Two Daughters

see Teen Kanya

2 Days in the Valley

(John Herzfeld, 1996, US) James Spader, Danny Aiello, Teri Hatcher, Paul Mazursky, Jeff Daniels, Eric Stoltz, Greg Cruttwell, Marsha Mason, Robert Carradine, Louise Fletcher.
107 min.

Hatcher hires Spader to kill her ratbag of a husband. That's the stone tossed into the pool: the ripples take in Mazursky's suicidal film director, Daniels' and Stoltz's variously troubled cops, Cruttwell's travails with a kidney stone, and more. The result is not so much complexity as a mildly entertaining collection of rather superficial short stories; or perhaps it's best described as an elementary elaboration of a greater number of subsidiary characters than usual, inside a piece of pulp fiction. Smoothly constructed, for such a busy piece of work, and Hatcher's ascent to stardom continues. BBa

Two Deaths

(Nicolas Roeg, 1994, GB) Michael Gambon, Sonia Braga, Patrick Malahide, Ion Caramitru, Sevilla Delofski, Nickolas Grace.
103 min.

Secrets and lies in Bucharest. Dr Daniel Pavenic (Gambon) hosts the annual evening get-together of four old friends. Outside, civil war rages. Inside, everything's perfect: delicious food and self-effacing service by the beautiful housekeeper Ana (Braga). Pressed by his companions, Pavenic tells Ana's story – a tale that turns into a sordid confession. Gradually the war outside seeps through the walls of these well-appointed male bourgeois lives, and long-established convictions and relationships crumble to dust. Although Roeg and screenwriter Allan Scott have transposed Stephen Dobyns' novel *The Two Deaths of Señora Puccini* from the original Chile to Romania, the budget seems not to have stretched much further east than a soundstage at Pinewood – giving this dinner party conversation piece a dourly theatrical air. This impression is exacerbated by ungainly chunks of speechifying and pontificating, some uneven performances, choppy editing and hand-held camerawork. Visually, this must be the least distinguished of Roeg's films. There's enough sting in the tale to keep you watching, but *Two Deaths* marks no career resurrection – indeed it only rarely comes to life at all. TCh

2 Duo
(Nobuhiro Suwa, 1996, Jap) Eri Yu, Hidetoshi Nishijima, Makiko Watanabe.
90 min.
A low-budget first feature with an exemplary grasp of what it's doing (and why it was worth doing in the first place), this account of a young couple falling apart together has real bite. The guy is an aspiring actor, the girl works in a smart boutique; her sense that things are going really really wrong starts when he turns a trivial apology into a proposal of marriage. Suwa began with a full script but told his actors to forget it and invent their own actions, reactions and dialogue. He shoots the results in long takes from fixed angles, and compounds the quasi-documentary feel by adding sequences in which the characters respond to questions about themselves from an off-screen interviewer. The resulting feeling of truthfulness makes it all remarkably moving. TR

Two English Girls
see Deux Anglaises et le Continent, Les

Two-Faced Woman
(George Cukor, 1941, US) Greta Garbo, Melvyn Douglas, Constance Bennett, Roland Young, Ruth Gordon, Robert Sterling.
94 min. b/w.
Garbo's last film, graced by some charming scenes and directed with Cukor's usual flair, but hardly sending her off in a blaze of glory. A sophisticated comedy, it has Garbo vamping it up as her imaginary twin sister in order to reseduce the wandering attention of her husband (Douglas). The Garbo persona is really too dreamy for this sort of flightiness, and although she amiably parodies her own image, she tends to be upstaged by Constance Bennett as the other woman. The script, in any case, is something of a disaster area, not least because the film was denounced by the Legion of Decency, hurriedly withdrawn, and partially redubbed into a blandness that sometimes becomes meaningless. TM

Two Faces of Dr Jekyll, The (aka House of Fright)
(Terence Fisher, 1960, GB) Paul Massie, Dawn Addams, Christopher Lee, David Kossoff, Francis De Wolff.
88 min.
Robert Louis Stevenson in the mincer again, courtesy of Sir James Carreras' K-Tel strategy and the appropriately named Wolf Mankowitz at the typewriter. Jekyll is a whiskery and sinister scientist, and Hyde a debonair charmer wenching through those familiar London stews where Hammer's wardrobe department always kept their wenches' dumplings on the boil. This is Explicit City sex-wise, with a snake-dancing floor show. Oliver Reed appears in a bijou part. The mantis-like Christopher Lee displays his usual grip as Hyde's friend, despite inner discontent at keeping decomposing company. Mediocre, but all right for late-night viewing. BC

Two for the Road
(Stanley Donen, 1966, GB) Audrey Hepburn, Albert Finney, Eleanor Bron, William Daniels, Claude Dauphin, Nadia Gray, Jacqueline Bisset.
111 min.
Old-fashioned romantic comedy tricked out with some new-fangled ideas. Donen does some tricksy time-jumping between past and present as a couple (Hepburn and Finney) look back over their twelve years of marriage, while Frederic Raphael's script provides some crisply disillusioned dialogue for their quarrels. The trouble is that smart direction and smart dialogue slide off the glossily idealised couple like water off a duck's back. Arid, crowd-pleasing stuff, in which the soul-searchings take place very conveniently on annual holidays in France and in a variety of luxuriously furnished interiors. TM

Two Friends
(Jane Campion, 1986, Aust) Emma Coles, Kris Bidenko, Kris McQuade, Stephen Leeder, Peter Hehir, Tony Barry.
76 min.

The first feature-length film from Jane Campion; made for TV, like *An Angel at My Table*, and still a little unpolished, it is nevertheless a remarkable picture. It's the story of two inseparable schoolmates, Kelly and Louise (Bidenko and Coles), and how over the course of ten months they become, in fact, separated. Campion's films are acutely personal and absolutely distinctive. They combine an oblique, detached point of view with startling human insight. She has the knack of invading private space by standing back; a sort of estranged intimacy. Here, she tells this very simple story (written by Helen Garner) in reverse. It begins in July, cuts back to February, to January, December, and finally October. The effect is puzzling at first, but stimulating, and it ends appropriately on a note of unforeseen poignancy. TCh

Two Guys and a Gal
see Tva Killar och en Tjej

200 Motels
(Frank Zappa/Tony Palmer, 1971, GB) Frank Zappa, Mothers of Invention, Ringo Starr, Theodore Bikel, Keith Moon.
98 min.
A real dinosaur, this purports to give a warts 'n' all snapshot of life in Zappa's touring rock circus. Along the way Frank indulges in time-locked psychedelic frippery, and there's a certain amount of dodgy cavorting with the groupies. Mocked-up at Pinewood, shot on video. TJ

Two if by Sea (aka Stolen Hearts)
(Bill Bennett, 1996, US) Denis Leary, Sandra Bullock, Stephen Dillane, Yaphet Kotto, Mike Starr, Jonathan Tucker, Wayne Robson, Michael Badalucco.
96 min.
Co-written by spitball comedian Leary, whose previous, far superior vehicle *Hostile Hostages*, met with similar lack of attention by its distributors both in Britain and the US, this is a romantic comedy from the wrong side of the tracks. Leary's a small-time, small-thinking Boston thief and decorator, who takes along girlfriend Bullock when he steals a 'Henry Matis' painting so they can enjoy a weekend away from it all in Rhode Island, where he's to make the sale. Kotto reprises his *Midnight Run* role as the FBI man on their (very exposed) tail, and Dillane is the wealthy sophisticate who romances Bullock right in front of her blue-collar beau. It begins smartly, and occasionally serves up the kind of venomous, vulgar put-down at which Leary excels, but the invention fades and Bullock is really just along for the ride. TCh

Two Jakes, The
(Jack Nicholson, 1990, US) Jack Nicholson, Harvey Keitel, Meg Tilly, Madeleine Stowe, Eli Wallach, Ruben Blades, Frederic Forrest, David Keith, Richard Farnsworth, Tracey Walter, Perry Lopez, Joe Mantell, Tom Waits.
138 min.
Neither the glittering sequel to *Chinatown* nor the expected mess that its distribution troubles and production history would suggest, this is often pretty good and never less than intriguing. The problem is the plot, which is dense indeed – a Robert Towne hallmark – and a recent viewing of the Polanski might come in handy. Jake Gittes (Nicholson) is still the loyal gumshoe, and eleven years on, remains in thrall to his tragic past. 'You might think you know what's going on, but you don't,' the bent real estate developer Jake Berman (Keitel) tells him, after which the gumshoe lights a cigarette and is blown sky high, confirming the statement. *Chinatown* was conspiratorial about water, the sequel concerns oil. Both women in the case (Tilly and Stowe) move in mysterious ways. LA earth tremors interrupt the action at random, bringing a surreal air to social interchange. It's beautifully acted with a fine '40s feel to it, and lingers in the mind long after you've left the cinema. BC

Two-Lane Blacktop
(Monte Hellman, 1971, US) James Taylor, Warren Oates, Laurie Bird, Dennis Wilson, David Drake, Rudolph Wurlitzer.
101 min.
Hellman, as his later inactivity testifies, seems to have turned himself into box-office anathema by

toying once too often with his beloved *actes gratuites*, so open-ended that they would delight even the most demanding existentialist. Here two young hot-rodders (Taylor, Wilson), making their way across America by picking up racing bets on the side, challenge (or are challenged by) the boastful middle-aged owner of a gleaming new Pontiac (Oates). As their mesmeric duel unfolds within a landscape that narrows down to a claustrophobic tunnel of highways, filling stations and roadside cafés, it soon becomes apparent that Hellman is less interested in allegory (class and generation conflicts as in *Easy Rider*) or in the race itself (which simply fizzles out), than in the mysterious process whereby a challenge is subtly metamorphosed into an obsession. Self-enclosed, self-absorbed, and self-destructive (as the last shot of the film catching in the projector and burning suggests), it's absolutely riveting. TM

Two Lovers and Their Lass
see Tva Killar och en Tjej

Two-Minute Warning
(Larry Peerce, 1976, US) Charlton Heston, John Cassavetes, Martin Balsam, Beau Bridges, Marilyn Hassett, David Janssen, Jack Klugman, Gena Rowlands, Walter Pidgeon, Brock Peters.
115 min.
More unsettling in its implications than in execution, this places a faceless gunman in a tower overlooking a Los Angeles football stadium filled to capacity. The persistent high-angle shots, use of long lenses (equivalent to the rifle's telescopic sight), and subjective camerawork inevitably distance the 'human' vignettes being enacted on the terraces below. Coldly and unemotionally, the film portrays the crowd individually as losers, collectively as innocent bystanders in a struggle between two sinister psychopathic forces, the assassin and the cops. The paranoid, edgy movie (best represented by Cassavetes' SWAT sergeant) finally erupts when the crowd turns almost effortlessly and devours itself in a climax of panic. Efficient enough as formula suspense, but it fails to confront the implications of its subject, preferring instead evasiveness and fast cynicism to pull it through. CPe

Two Moon Junction
(Zalman King, 1989, US) Sherilyn Fenn, Richard Tyson, Louise Fletcher, Burl Ives, Kristy McNichol, Martin Hewitt, Juanita Moore, Millie Perkins, Don Galloway, Herve Villechaise, Screamin' Jay Hawkins.
105 min.
Fenn plays pampered April Delongpre, irritatingly dubbed Princess, Baby, Sugar and Darlin' (but then she *is* a Southern belle) and engaged to be married to the finest beau in the state. Perry (Tyson) is the fairground worker who teases, pursues, menaces and finally beds her. April is without doubt a corker; the same cannot be said for the wholly unappetising Perry, all rippling ringlets and pug features. What tiny tension the plot affords rests in April's choice between privilege and passion, and typically it's fudged: she gets to keep her swanky marriage *and* her bit of rough. Sex sequences are diappointingly non-specific: blurred nipples and vaguely flickering tongues, set to That Disco Beat and invariably followed by post-coital blubbing. Louise Fletcher is sinister as April's deeply creepy gran, and Kristy McNichol puts in a likeable performance as chirpy drifter Patti Jean, despite the ill-advised flirtation with lesbianism. 'Times like this ah know why men like women so much' she chirrups at April's uncorseted bosom. Sick-making. SFe

Two Much (Loco de amor)
(Fernando Trueba, 1996, Sp/US) Antonio Banderas, Melanie Griffith, Daryl Hannah, Danny Aiello, Joan Cusack, Eli Wallach, Austin Pendleton.
118 min.
Banderas is Art Dodge, a Miami art dealer, and Griffith is Betty Kerner, a fabulously wealthy divorcee. She thinks he'll make a virile third husband; he thinks she's the answer to his financial problems – and we think she's far too old for him. No surprise, then, when he falls for her younger sister Liz (Hannah). He dons wire-rimmed specs,

wears his hair down, and – hey presto! – meet Art's twin Bart. Cue bed-hopping, wardrobe changes and contrivance. A big hit in Spain, and a considerable flop in the US, the film was adapted from a Donald Westlake novel and goes through the motions of classic screwball farce. Everything, however, feels stilted and second-hand. TCh

Two Mules for Sister Sara
(Don Siegel, 1969, US) Shirley MacLaine, Clint Eastwood, Manolo Fabregas, Alberto Morin, Armando Silvestre.
116 min.
A witty and slightly whimsical Western, which teams MacLaine – as a whore playing at being a nun – with the ever-chivalrous Eastwood as the man who steps in and prevents a three-way desert rape by drunken bandits. They go on to become involved with the Mexican revolutionary movement, with Eastwood's respect for her chastity becoming increasingly strained and her true profession coming in handy for infiltrating an enemy fort. Siegel devotees will find much to enjoy in the languid but not unexciting story by Budd Boetticher (who was originally to direct himself). VG

Two of a Kind
(John Herzfeld, 1983, US) John Travolta, Olivia Newton-John, Charles Durning, Oliver Reed, Beatrice Straight, Scatman Crothers, Richard Bright, Vincent Bufano.
87 min.
God, returning to heaven after a brief holiday, decides to wipe out the errant human race. The archangels, earning a stay of execution provided two randomly selected specimens prove to be Good, rest their case upon Zack (Travolta) and Debbie (Newton-John): he immediately holds up a bank, and she walks off with the loot. What follows is a rather complicated orchestration, with musical interludes, of this simple story in which Good and Evil battle it out with Zack and Debbie in between, as oblivious to all these earth-stopping machinations as the teenagers flocking to see Hollywood's best-brushed teeth will be to superior antecedents like A Matter of Life and Death. There are worse ways to spend an afternoon. FD

Two of Them, The (Ök Ketten)
(Márta Mészáros, 1977, Hun) Marina Vlady, Lili Monori, Jan Nowicki, Miklós Tolnay.
95 min.
Mészáros is one of the world's most prolific women directors. Here she treats the relationship between two women with a delicate feminist sensibility which never degenerates into heavy-handed polemicism. Vlady plays the happily married, perfectly organised superintendent of a women's hostel. She meets Monori, whose husband is an alcoholic, and is gradually drawn into the life and problems of this woman whose cluttered personality and background are so different from her own. All the characters, including that of the dipso husband, are sketched with a sympathetic warmth which makes one occasionally yearn for a spot of old-fashioned Hollywood bitchiness. AB

Two of Us, The
see Vieil Homme et l'Enfant, Le

Two or Three Things I Know About Her
see Deux ou Trois Choses que Je Sais d'Elle

Two Rode Together
(John Ford, 1961, US) James Stewart, Richard Widmark, Shirley Jones, Linda Cristal, Andy Devine, John McIntire, Mae Marsh, Anna Lee.
109 min.
Dismissed by Ford as a casual favour to Columbia's boss Harry Cohn, this neglected Western repays careful attention. Stewart is the cynical marshal hired to repatriate pioneer children captured by the Comanche, and Widmark the cavalry officer who accompanies him. Gone is the clean frontier as would-be garden of The Searchers and earlier; instead, Ford offers us a nightmare vision, the frontier overrun by hysteria and (Eastern/Yankee) hypocrisy, with even the Indians seen as primitive entrepreneurs. PH

Two Stage Sisters (Wutai Jiemei)
(Xie Jin, 1964, China) Xie Fang, Cao Yindi, Feng Ji, Gao Yuansheng, Shen Fengjuan.
114 min.
A real delight, attractive on many levels. The story concerns two women who start out working for a travelling musical theatre company. As they become more famous, their friendship weakens and they take radically different paths; one becomes increasingly politically committed, the other is attracted to the trappings of urban success. Made before the Cultural Revolution by a man, the film manages to embrace feminist issues, political ideologies, thriller and musical motifs, and a surprisingly Hollywood-style sense of 'weepie' melodrama. The performances are terrific, but what really distinguishes this amazing hybrid (in Western terms, that is) is the director's fluid and elegant style. Colour, composition, pace, and above all, camera movement, create an exhilarating spectacle that is never thematically shallow. Imagine Sirk's colours and emotional sense, Scorsese or Minnelli's craning camera shots, allied to a politically perceptive treatment, and you're half way to imagining this film. GA

2001: A Space Odyssey

(Stanley Kubrick, 1968, GB) Keir Dullea, Gary Lockwood, William Sylvester, Daniel Richter, Leonard Rossiter, Margaret Tyzack, Robert Beatty.
141 min.
A characteristically pessimistic account of human aspiration from Kubrick, this tripartite sci-fi look at civilisation's progress from prehistoric times (the apes learning to kill) to a visionary future (astronauts on a mission to Jupiter encountering superior life and rebirth in some sort of embryonic divine form) is beautiful, infuriatingly slow, and pretty half-baked. Quite how the general theme fits in with the central drama of the astronauts' battle with the arrogant computer HAL, who tries to take over their mission, is unclear; while the final farrago of light-show psychedelia is simply so much pap. Nevertheless, for all the essential coldness of Kubrick's vision, it demands attention as superior sci-fi, simply because it's more concerned with ideas than with Boy's Own-style pyrotechnics. GA

2010
(Peter Hyams, 1984, US) Roy Scheider, John Lithgow, Helen Mirren, Bob Balaban, Keir Dullea, Madolyn Smith, Dana Elcar, Taliesin Jaffe.
116 min.
Hyams' sequel to Kubrick's big daddy of sci-fi movies may not have the novelty of 2001: A Space Odyssey, but it is still a better film than anyone could have dared to expect. Scheider plays the American space agency boss trying to find out what happened to the ill-fated 'Discovery' spacecraft and its surviving crewmember. He joins a Russian space mission to Jupiter captained by the formidable Mirren, but things get pretty sticky when news comes through that back on Earth the super-powers are on the point of war. Hyams has not come up with a climax to match Kubrick's rush through the star-gate; but this is still space fiction of a superior kind, making the Star Trek movies look puny by comparison. DP

Two Thousand Women
(Frank Launder, 1944, GB) Phyllis Calvert, Patricia Roc, Jean Kent, Flora Robson, Reginald Purdell, Renee Houston, Thora Hird, Dulcie Gray, Carl Jaffe.
97 min. b/w.
Typically lively wartime offering from Launder and Gilliat, made under the Gainsborough banner and set in a women's prison in Nazi-occupied France. The prisoners attempts to conceal three daring RAF chaps from the authorities. On the one hand, it stands as a progenitor of Launder and Gilliat's later, equally zestful St Trinian's movies, coming complete with lashings of knockabout humour and a chaotic fight which would have done the Fifth Form proud. On the other, however, in its own Tenko-like way, it's also surprisingly touching. GM

2 x 50 Years of French Cinema
(Anne-Marie Miéville/Jean-Luc Godard, 1995, GB/Fr) Michel Piccoli.
52 min.
You might have guessed that Miéville/Godard's contribution to the BFI's 'Century of Cinema' would be a demolition job on the series' premises. Godard invites Michel Piccoli (in his capacity as chairman of the official Centenary Committee) to a hotel lake and asks him what there is to celebrate. Isn't the cinema dead? Isn't French cinema forgotten? Disturbed by his host's harangue, Piccoli spends the rest of the movie asking hotel staff what they know of French cinema and discovering Godard was right. His hilariously hang-dog field research is overlaid with stills and lines of dialogue from everyone's best-loved French movies, and the whole is rounded off with Godard and Miéville's elegy for the great tradition which has died. More of a wake than a funeral, and wickedly funny. TR

Two-Way Stretch
(Robert Day, 1960, GB) Peter Sellers, Wilfrid Hyde-White, Maurice Denham, Irene Handl, David Lodge, Lionel Jeffries, Liz Fraser, Bernard Cribbins, Thorley Walters, Beryl Reid.
87 min. b/w.
Convicts Sellers, Cribbins and Lodge treat prison like a holiday camp and hatch a plan with bogus clergyman Hyde-White to escape from the joint, deprive a maharaja of his jewels, then break back in again to ensure a watertight alibi. Unfortunately, new warden Jeffries is determined to initiate a tougher regime, which puts the gang's plans in jeopardy. With a tight narrative and a raft of top British character actors, this ebullient comedy could hardly go wrong – and it didn't. Reliably amusing stuff.

Two Weeks in Another Town
(Vincente Minnelli, 1962, US) Kirk Douglas, Edward G Robinson, Daliah Lavi, George Hamilton, Claire Trevor, Rosanna Schiaffino, Cyd Charisse, James Gregory, George Macready.
107 min.
Having dealt superbly with Hollywood ten years earlier in The Bad and the Beautiful, Minnelli returned to the topic of movie-making, this time changing the location to Rome's Cinecittà, and using Douglas not as a ruthless producer but as a washed-up actor reduced largely to dubbing international movies. While the plot nominally deals cynically and sensationally with corruption and intrigue within the movie world's jet set as it follows Douglas' attempts to persuade producer Robinson to help him make a comeback, it really concerns itself more with failure, compromise, and disillusionment. Superb performances throughout, although it's Minnelli's remarkable direction that really lifts the movie up among the classics. Described by some as gaudy or overheated, it is in fact imbued with a thoroughly appropriate expressionism. GA

Two Weeks with Love
(Roy Rowland, 1950, US) Jane Powell, Ricardo Montalban, Louis Calhern, Ann Harding, Debbie Reynolds, Phyllis Kirk, Carleton Carpenter, Clinton Sundberg.
92 min.
Nostalgic, turn-of-the-century musical set in the Catskills, and dealing with the romantic adventures of sisters Powell and Reynolds while on holiday with their parents. Busby Berkeley supervised the dance routines, but it's the lively Reynolds who steals the show, singing 'Aba Daba Honeymoon' with her gangling boyfriend Carpenter. There's a weird Freudian dream sequence, too, with Reynolds' underdeveloped sister (Powell) longing to be fitted with a corset, as well as swept off her feet by the handsome Montalban. NF

Two Women (Iki Kadin)
(Yavuz Ozkan, 1992, Tur) Zuhal Olcay, Serap Aksoy, Haluk Bilginer.
124 min.
When a high-class prostitute taunts a cop client about his sexual drive, he rapes her and has her thrown on the street. She decides to prosecute. The woman, who has a blind daughter, later becomes best friends with the culprit's wife. A bit of a haul. GA

Two Years Before the Mast

(John Farrow, 1946, US) Alan Ladd, Brian Donlevy, William Bendix, Esther Fernandez, Howard da Silva, Barry Fitzgerald, Albert Dekker, Darryl Hickman.
98 min. b/w.
Well-to-do, Harvard-educated Richard Henry Dana went to sea for his health, and his experiences as a common sailor determined him to 'redress the grievances and sufferings of that class of beings with whom my lot had so long been cast'. This he attempted to do in *Two Years Before the Mast*, published way back in 1840. Farrow, an authentic sea-dog himself, directs this adaptation (with Donlevy as Dana) as a labour of love. Despite its *Mutiny on the Bounty* overtones, and the latent sensationalism of flogging scenes, the film is most impressive for its sobriety, and the way Farrow gets an ensemble-type feel from a cast as disparate as he has here. There are no star turns or glamorous set pieces, no sea battles and very little 'action' as such, but it's an engrossing mix of formula/genre/humanism. CW

Typewriter, the Rifle & the Movie Camera, The

(Adam Simon, 1996, GB) Sam Fuller, Tim Robbins, Quentin Tarantino, Jim Jarmusch, Martin Scorsese.
55 min.
This documentary covers all the main facets of Sam Fuller's life and career: his years as a copyboy and crime reporter for the Hearst press; his experiences during World War II; his first time behind a camera, at a concentration camp liberated by the US army; and the two decades as a bona fide Hollywood *auteur*. The format is fun: Tim Robbins interviewing the inimitably brash old codger in Paris; Robbins and Tarantino gleefully checking out the memorabilia in Sam's LA garage; Jim Jarmusch commenting on how Fuller films were preoccupied with the 'American Lie' and how the man himself is not exactly rational; Scorsese on his camera style, the films' emotional authenticity and the ferocious primal force of Fuller's characters; Sam babbling on about Balzac and the art of storytelling, and finally revealing the identity of 'Griff', a moniker that turns up in just about every movie he ever made. Mouth-watering clips. GA

u

Uccellacci e Uccellini (Hawks and Sparrows)

(Pier Paolo Pasolini, 1966, It) Totò, Ninetto Davoli, Femi Benussi, Rossana Di Rocco, Lena Lin Solaro.
88 min. b/w.
Given Italy's shameful record of allowing the wholesale slaughter of just about everything with wings, it's ironic that the only movie (outside of Disney) with a talking crow as one of its leads should have been made by Pasolini. Unsurprisingly, it's a mess. Its human leads, comedian Totò and Ninetto Davoli, take double roles: as a father and son discussing politics and philosophy as they wander a bleakly absurd landscape, and – in a parable told them by a wise Marxist crow they meet – as two hapless disciples of St Francis, sent forth to convert the hawks and their feathered prey to the Christian ideal of universal love. Intended as a darkly comic allegory on class conflict and the injustice of the world, the film looks and sounds good (the music, including sung opening credits, is by Morricone), but suffers throughout from obscure whimsicality. The crow's performance is the best thing in it. GA

Uccello dalle Piume di Cristallo, L' (The Bird with the Crystal Plumage/The Gallery Murders)

(Dario Argento, 1969, It/Ger) Tony Musante, Suzy Kendall, Eva Renzi, Umberto Raho, Enrico Maria Salerno, Mario Adorf.
98 min
Now king of the spaghetti slasher, Argento made his directorial debut with this tightly constructed thriller in which an American writer is witness to an attempted knife attack, and then finds himself obsessed with tracking down a serial killer whose next victims could be himself and his lover.. There are some extravagant false leads, but tension is well sustained with the aid of Vittorio Storaro's stylish 'Scope photography and a Morricone score. Particularly effective are the opening attack, viewed through a maze of locked windows, and a scene with the victim caught on a stairway suddenly plunged into darkness. Certain elements seem to have been an influence on Dressed to Kill and The Shining, but Argento himself zoomed into more and more abstract shock effects, neglecting the Hitchcockian principles observed here. DT

Ugetsu Monogatari [100]

(Kenji Mizoguchi, 1953, Jap) Masayuki Mori, Machiko Kyo, Sakae Ozawa, Mitsuko Mito, Kinuyo Tanaka.
96 min. b/w.
Mizoguchi's best-known work, based on two stories by the 18th century writer Akinari Ueda (often described as the Japanese Maupassant), was one of a handful of Japanese films to sweep up numerous awards at European festivals in the early '50s. Its reputation as one of Mizoguchi's finest works and a landmark of the Japanese 'art' cinema has remained undented ever since. Mizoguchi's unique establishment of atmosphere by means of long shot, long takes, sublimely graceful and unobtrusive camera movement, is everywhere evident in his treatment of the legend of a potter who leaves his family to market his wares during the ravages of a civil war, and is taken in and seduced by a ghost princess. A ravishingly composed, evocatively beautiful film. RM

Ugly, The

(Scott Reynolds, 1996, NZ) Paolo Rotondo, Rebecca Hobbs, Roy Ward, Jennifer Ward-Lealand, Darien Takle.
91 min.
Invited by multiple murderer Rotondo to say whether he's sane enough to stand trial, publicity-seeking shrink Rebecca Hobbs is determined to control the assessment interviews. Instead, she's drawn into the killer's world, where past and present are fluid, logic's skewed, and figures called The Visitors haunt his disturbed mind. Writer/director Reynolds knows his horror movies, but this is no fanboy knock-off – having absorbed his influences, he's able to take bold formal risks. Although there's a nagging doubt that this is just a low concept horror pic, tricked out with clever stylistic flourishes and a complex narrative structure, it's an auspicious debut that refuses to resolve the psychological ambiguities or tie up the worrying loose ends. NF

Ugly, Dirt and Mean

see Brutti, sporchi e cattivi

Ugly, Dirty and Bad

see Brutti, sporchi e cattivi

UHF

(Jay Levey, 1989, US) 'Weird Al' Yankovic, Victoria Jackson, Kevin McCarthy, Michael Richards, David Bowie, Emo Philips.
97 min.
Installed as the chief exec of a local TV station that his uncle's just won in a poker game, the self-proclaimed strange one's wacky ideas on programme development – like turning janitor Richards into the operation's biggest on-screen asset – soon prove surprisingly powerful in the ratings battle. Moments of off-centre humour, but an hour and a half of parodist Weird Al is a severe test. TJ

Ulee's Gold

(Victor Nunez, 1997, US) Peter Fonda, Patricia Richardson, Jessica Biel, J Kenneth Campbell, Tom Wood, Christine Dunford.
113 min.
Vietnam vet Ulysses (Ulee) Jackson (Fonda) lives in the swampy backwoods of the Florida panhandle, patiently farming Tupelo honey. On the one hand, since his wife Penelope died, Ulee has been content to withdraw into gruff self-dependence. On the other, blood will out, and the combination of Ulee's remoteness and the younger generation's hotheaded reaction have rent the Jackson family. While Ulee tends his two grand-daughters, his son Jimmy (Wood) sits out a sentence for a robbery. Jimmy's wife Helen (Dunford), who has disappeared, surfaces in Orlando with a heroin habit and in the custody of her husband's two ex-partners in crime. She lets slip that Jimmy had secretly hidden bank money on Ulee's land, and the hoods are calling it in. Part vehicle for Fonda's seasoned presence, part depiction of the honey harvest, this low-key drama is played slow and sage. NB

Ultima Donna, L'

see Last Woman, The

Ultimas Imágenes del naufragio

See Last Images of the Shipwreck

Ultimate Solution of Grace Quigley, The

see Grace Quigley

Ultrà (Ultras: Some Lose, Some Die...Some Win)

(Ricky Tognazzi, 1990, It) Claudio Amendola, Ricky Memphis, Gianmarco Tognazzi.
86 min.
This second feature by Ugo Tognazzi's son offers a thoroughly joyless hour and a half in the company of football hooligans, much of it spent on the train from Rome to Turin. The moral core of the piece is the struggle of one guy to get married, go straight, and get a job – ambitions tragically thwarted when he decides to take the rap for a murder accidentally committed by his best friend. The emphasis on mindless adolescent violence and vulgarity is convincing enough, but the drama, alternately muffled and overstated, has neither grip nor punch. The climactic football match, by the way, occurs off-screen. TR

Ulysses

(Joseph Strick, 1967, GB) Milo O'Shea, Barbara Jefford, Maurice Roëves, TP McKenna, Anna Manahan, Maureen Potter, Martin Dempsey.
132 min. b/w.
A completely foolish venture, which only looks promising when put beside the even worse adaptation of Portrait of an Artist Strick went on to make a decade later. Naturally the naughty bits of James Joyce's great and revolutionary novel caused quite a rumpus in their screen transposition, but while certain sections work well as naturalistic comedy, Strick's embarrassingly literal interpretation of the more fantastical passages sink the film completely. Barbara Jefford's rapturous reading of Molly Bloom's final monologue deserves commendation, however. DT

Ulysses' Gaze (To Vlemma Tou Odyssea/ aka The Gaze of Ulysses)

(Theo Angelopoulos, 1995, Greece/It/Fr) Harvey Keitel, Erland Josephson, Maia Morgenstern.
180 min.
When film-maker A... (Keitel) returns, after 35 years in the US, to his hometown in Greece for a retrospective of his work, he takes the opportunity to pursue an obsession: to track down the missing three reels of the first film footage ever shot (by the Manakia brothers) in the Balkans. His odyssey, from Ptolemais through Albania, Macedonia, Bulgaria and Romania, to Belgrade and Sarajevo, allows for a meditation on changing borders, national identity, and the relationship of film to historical and political reality. Angelopoulos' stately epic is hugely ambitious, and despite some art movie clichés – A's encounters with various women, each played by the same actress – and some clumsiness in the English dialogue, by and large it succeeds. Constructed from long elegant takes, and moving fluidly between naturalism and tableaux-like theatricality, it's a mesmerising work of arresting beauty and impressive emotional power. GA

Ulzana's Raid

(Robert Aldrich, 1972, US) Burt Lancaster, Bruce Davison, Jorge Luke, Richard Jaeckel, Joaquin Martinez, Lloyd Bochner, Karl Swenson.
103 min.
Even though Aldrich himself proclaimed a certain amount of dissatisfaction with the way this Western turned out, it's still one of his very finest films. A bleak and complex account of a platoon's hunt for a small group of Apaches who have escaped from their wretched reservation and committed acts of rape, murder, and mutilation, it never strays into the pitfall of portraying the Indians either as noble savages or as evil barbarians. Rather, Alan Sharp's marvellous script elucidates the issues and psychological causes of racial warfare, with Lancaster's weary army scout as the mouthpiece for unusually honest perceptions about both the Indians and the whites who have simply failed to comprehend them. It's brutally but never gratuitously violent, laden with images of death and destruction (beautifully caught by Joseph Biroc's camerawork), and far more than just an extraordinarily intelligent horse opera: the parallels with America's involvement in Vietnam should be easy to see. GA

Umberto D.

(Vittorio De Sica, 1952, It) Carlo Battisti, Maria Pia Casilio, Lina Gennari, Memmo Carotenuto, Alberto Albani Barbieri.
89 min. b/w.
Judging by his demeanour, the D stands for Deep Depression. But the old man at the centre of De Sica's famous film from the heyday of Italian neorealism hasn't got much to be happy about, stripped bare as he is of all money and all friends except a little fox terrier. There's no denying the director's compassion, nor the dignity and strength of Carlo Battisti's performance, but there's nothing so wilting as doom and gloom couched in sweetly sentimental terms. GB

Umbrellas of Cherbourg, The

see Parapluies de Cherbourg, Les

Umbrella Woman, The (aka The Good Wife)

(Ken Cameron, 1986, Aust) Rachel Ward, Bryan Brown, Steven Vidler, Sam Neill, Jennifer Claire, Bruce Barry.
97 min.
Hot thighs under the cold tap, blood-kin and wife-sharing in the shack – no, not Erskine Caldwell, but New South Wales in the late '30s. Marge (Ward) tries hard to be a pillar of the community, to live down her infamous mother's horizontal career, and marries the dependable Sonny (Brown). Her life seems humdrum, however, and when Sonny's weak younger brother Sugar

(Vidler) proposes sex, she lets her husband decide with the comment that one man is much like another. Sugar proves even less exciting than Sonny, and boasts of his conquest in town, which sets tongues wagging. Becoming obsessed with the new bartender at the hotel (Neill), an unscrupulous womaniser, Marge lays embarrassing siege to him...This could easily have been one of those old devil-in-the-flesh absurdities, but the plot is full of surprises, with Marge's hunger for a grand passion resulting in humiliation all round and a sadly chastening ending. Within its small compass, a moving experience. BC

Unbearable Lightness of Being, The
(Philip Kaufman, 1987, US) Daniel Day Lewis, Juliette Binoche, Lena Olin, Derek de Lint, Erland Josephson, Pavel Landovsky, Donald Moffat, Daniel Olbrychski, Laszlo Szabo.
172 min.
Prague, 1968: womanising doctor Tomas (Day Lewis) and his lover Sabina (Olin) are giddy with the social and sexual liberation of Czech communism. But when Tomas meets shy, sensitive Teresa (Binoche), he is forced to re-think his self-protective irresponsibility towards others, just as Prague suffers traumatic changes when the Russian tanks arrive. Kaufman's intelligent, faithful version of Milan Kundera's novel wisely jettisons the woolly philosophising, focusing on characters, relationships, and the many facets of loyalty and betrayal. It's a rich, ambitious film, repetitive and voyeuristic in its eroticism, but exhilarating in its blend of documentary and fictional recreation to depict the Soviet invasion. The narrative, now linear (unlike the book), is leisurely, the camerawork evocative; the progress from cynical irony to something more heartfelt rarely falters. Binoche and Olin avoid being reduced to symbols of Tomas' polarised soul, and Day Lewis seems increasingly one of the most versatile actors of his generation. GA

Unbelievable Truth, The
(Hal Hartley, 1989, US) Adrienne Shelly, Robert Burke, Christopher Cooke, Julia McNeal, Mark Bailey, Gary Sauer, Katherine Mayfield.
90 min.
Undecided whether to go to college, burdened by anxieties about nuclear apocalypse, forever at loggerheads with her Mom and Dad, teenager Audry (Shelly) finds life in her small Long Island hometown impossibly tedious. But when tall, dark, handsome Josh (Burke) arrives on the scene cloaked in mystery, her mundane world is transformed, not only by the erotic attraction she feels for the silent stranger, but by the rumours concerning his past: is he a priest, a mechanic, or – as most townsfolk would have it – a mass murderer? Like Mystery Train and Metropolitan, Hartley's independent first feature partly concerns problems of knowledge and truth: how do hearsay and personal bias relate to reality? He adopts an engagingly low-key form of farce to make his point, and to paint an affectionate, accurate satire on the shortcomings of small-town life. The director's delicately turned script is well served by colourful but credible performances, and by Michael Spiller's stark but stylish camerawork. GA

Uncanny, The
(Denis Héroux, 1977, Can/GB) Peter Cushing, Ray Milland, Susan Penhaligon, Joan Greenwood, Simon Williams, Roland Culver, Alexandra Stewart, Chloe Franks, Donald Pleasence, Samantha Eggar, John Vernon.
85 min.
Truly terrible trio of tales, all based on the (false) premise that, since a shot of an ordinary domestic cat is already fairly scary, then shots of several hundred cats must be very frightening indeed. Yet the animals come out of it better than the poor actors, forced to do their best with such dusty Amicus anthology-type plots as the bedridden aunt with the cats and the changed will; the child with the cat and the occult power (using the girl from The House That Dripped Blood, but here dubbed by what sounds like a middle-aged Canadian); and the self-parodying horror film star and starlet (Pleasence and Eggar, making you wish you were watching Dr Crippen instead) who own a cat. The stories are linked by cat-crazy Cushing and purring Milland – as sad a pair of back tax-payers as you could wish to see. AN

Uncle Buck
(John Hughes, 1989, US) John Candy, Jean Louisa Kelly, Gaby Hoffman, Macauley Culkin, Amy Madigan, Elaine Bromka, Garrett M Brown, Laurie Metcalf, Jay Underwood.
100 min.
Tia (Kelly) is an unlovely specimen, her face fixed in a scowl of post-pubescent parent-hating, generated by mom's inattentiveness. When granny has a heart attack, mom and dad rush to her bedside, leaving the kids in the care of the family's black sheep, Uncle Buck (Candy). While the younger brats soon take to the slobby, loveable newcomer, Buck and Tia swiftly settle down to a war of attrition (he demobilises her dating power by fending off suitors with axes and power-drills, she throws a spanner in his affair with Amy Madigan). It's clear from the outset that by the time the parents return all will be reconciled; what is unclear is quite why this formulaic film fails to click, providing only interludes of satisfying Candy comicry amid the peculiarly meandering plot expositions. Set piece scenes arrive without warning and depart without conclusion, notably a painfully unfunny interview with a pimpled school principal in which crass 'don't-mention-the-melonoma' jokes fly thick and fast. Candy still raises laughs simply by playing himself, but the film is a heavy weight for even his imposing form to carry. MK

Uncle Tom (Zio Tom)
(Gualtiero Jacopetti/Franco Prosperi, 1971, It)
130 min.
A documentary on American slavery by the makers of Mondo Cane. Using reconstructions of how black slaves were transported, sold, bred like cows, chained, raped, abused, the film purports to be a testament to the barbarism of our ancestors. In fact, with its wheeling camera movements over slave markets, its concentration on eccentric slave owners (massaging the breasts of their 'prize bitches'), its jaunty music, its obsession with black sensuality, it turns out as nasty sensationalism. Ironically, it was made in Haiti before Papa Doc died, but never for a moment conveys the idea that slavery, in a 20th century form, still exists. CAub

Uncommon Senses
(Jon Jost, 1987, US) Jon Jost.
117 min.
Jost's documentary about how America constructs and consumes its own mythology begins as an oblique attack on its subject, but in an odd way ends up as American as the Constitution it criticises. Divided into ten parts, each looking at different aspects of the USA – its centre, its coasts, its roads, people, money, military power and so on – the film amounts to a lengthy and eloquent broadside on the 'entrepreneurial' ethic in America, and ends with a controversial straight-to-camera speech from the director that might be described as a contemporary and cinematic version of Thoreau's On Civil Disobedience. Funny, sinister and engrossingly watchable, a riveting vision of a country and the forces that shape it, it's a surprising and accessible success for a director notorious for his low-budget minimalism. JG

Uncommon Valor
(Ted Kotcheff, 1983, US) Gene Hackman, Robert Stack, Fred Ward, Reb Brown, Randall 'Tex' Cobb, Patrick Swayze, Harold Sylvester, Tim Thomerson.
105 min.
Kotcheff's film may look like a none too subtle piece of wish fulfilment, but is in fact grounded in one of the many painful emotional outcomes of the Vietnam war. Hackman is haunted by his son's fate – MIA (missing in action) – and so assembles a team of the usual veterans: the jock, the pilot, the war-junkie, the Tai Chi freak, and the one who can't sleep at nights. They then undergo the classic 'mission movie' format: first they train in a model camp, then they do it for real, where nothing goes as planned and acts of uncommon valour are called for. After North Dallas Forty and First Blood, Kotcheff seems to be moving into the action picture arena, and he acquits himself admirably with the more strenuous details of firefighting. CPea

Unconquered
(Cecil B DeMille, 1947, US) Gary Cooper, Paulette Goddard, Howard da Silva, Boris Karloff, Cecil Kellaway, Ward Bond, Katherine DeMille, C Aubrey Smith, Henry Wilcoxon.
147 min.

Paulette Goddard runs a typically lusty DeMille gamut from torture by Indians to saucy bath scene as an English wench deported to America for theft in the 1760s (she's innocent, of course), and finding a champion in Gary Cooper's Virginia militiaman. Nicely shot in colour, but overlong and curiously listless despite all the bustling adventures (and hilariously ludicrous dialogue). It isn't exactly improved by the lumbering right wing allegory which has Howard da Silva being un-American in subverting the Indians while Coop upholds the anti-Red American way of life. TM

Un©ut
(John Greyson, 1997, Can) Michael Achtman, Matthew Ferguson, Damon D'Oliveira, Maria Redstra.
92 min.
'Learn your alphabet,' this genre bending exercise in cut-and-paste film polemic exhorts us. 'C' is for copyright, censorship and circumcision, which are central, and to some extent connected, themes at play here. There are three principals – Peter (Achtman), Peter (Ferguson) and Peter (Damon) – whose various projects and passions provide an index to the film's own: Peter is writing a thesis on 'The psychosexual meanings of circumcision and the foreskin'; Peter has a crush on Pierre Trudeau, manifested in pastel cartoons of doubtful taste and authenticity; and Peter is compiling a scrapbook home video barrage of whatever material comes to hand, set to a rewrite of the Jackson 5's 'ABC'. How else to describe it? The film perhaps does for the docu-drama what Mark Rappaport's ciné-essays (From the Journals of Jean Seberg, etc) do for the film course lecture: it's a witty, imaginative and frequently subversive reappraisal of cinematic form, technique and focus, although it lacks Rappaport's discipline and depth. NB

...und der Himmel steht still
see Innocent, The

Undead, The
(Roger Corman, 1956, US) Pamela Duncan, Richard Garland, Allison Hayes, Val Dufour, Mel Welles, Billy Barty, Bruno VeSota, Richard Devon.
75 min. b/w.
An early low-budget Corman effort which begins in the realms of modern science – troubled call-girl (Duncan) consults psychiatrist (Garland) – before shamelessly leaping back centuries to a tale of witches, virgins and knights, which thinly covers the movie's selling point, sexual temptation. The results are pretty nutty, especially the energetic cod Shakespearean dialogue provided by Charles Griffith and Mark Hanna. Good moments include the heroine in a coffin with a corpse, and a reasonable pay-off. CPe

Undeclared War, The
see Guerre sans nom, La

Undefeated, The
(Andrew V McLaglen, 1969, US) John Wayne, Rock Hudson, Tony Aguilar, Roman Gabriel, Bruce Cabot, Lee Meriwether, Ben Johnson, Harry Carey Jr, Paul Fix, Jan-Michael Vincent, Royal Dano, Richard Mulligan, John Agar.
118 min.
A characteristically folksy Western, sprawling around in the post-Civil War rivalries between Union (Wayne) and Confederacy (Hudson, remarkably good). Wayne, discovering that the Union army intends to cheat him on a horse-trading deal, decides instead to drive his herd down to Mexico to sell to the Emperor Maximilian; Hudson, meanwhile, is leading a wagon train of disgruntled Southerners to settle in Mexico at the Emperor's invitation. Their odysseys converge, and when their arrival in Mexico coincides with the Juarez revolt, they decide that the good old USA is better than these pesky foreigners after all. It's all stirringly traditional stuff, with a lively supporting cast, and made very easy on the eye by William Clothier's camerawork. TM

UndeRage
(Kim Longinotto/Lizzie Lemon, 1982, GB)
57 min.
This documentary on no-hope teenagers in Coventry naturally had sections of the press crying scandal. But simply applauding the film's

'honest realism' in its depiction of a daily round of glue-sniffing, aggressive racism, and sexism isn't adequate defence. The problem is that the self-effacing method blocks any attempt by the film-makers to analyse/account for the disturbing discourses which speak through their subjects. Instead, the latter are simply given screen space to perform – see them weep, throw up, abuse blacks, and threaten violence. Realism or voyeuristic exploitation? Predictably, the only hint of contradiction comes from the teenagers themselves, some of whom display an ironic self-awareness at odds with the project's low-key miserabilism. Towards the end, a freeze-frame unites black and white at a Specials concert: a revealingly artificial gesture, which in this context seems desperately and pathetically romantic. SJ

Under Capricorn

(Alfred Hitchcock, 1949, GB) Ingrid Bergman, Joseph Cotten, Michael Wilding, Margaret Leighton, Cecil Parker, Jack Watling.
117 min.
A strangely unexciting but emotionally intriguing Hitchcock costume drama with echoes of *Rebecca* and *Suspicion*. Set in the 1830s, it details the aristocratic Bergman's disastrous marriage to rakish stable-hand Cotten, who is deported to Australia convicted of murder. When the Governor's nephew (Wilding) visits them, he finds her an alcoholic wreck, and suspects she is being poisoned. Slow, a mite predictable, and rather verbose, the film nevertheless has an elegance (thanks to long, sweeping takes) and a poignant romanticism that looks forward to Hitchcock's more pessimistic account of human relationships in *Vertigo*. GA

Undercover Blues

(Herbert Ross, 1993, US) Kathleen Turner, Dennis Quaid, Fiona Shaw, Stanley Tucci, Larry Miller, Obba Babatunde, Tom Arnold.
90 min.
Jeff and Jane Blue (Quaid and Turner) are vacationing in New Orleans with their baby. But the plans of these amorous FBI agents are spoiled when arch-enemy Novacek (Shaw) turns out to be the mastermind of an arms-smuggling ring. One can understand how this project might have appealed to the leads: the sassy by-play and brassy derring do is reminiscent of *Romancing the Stone*, while Quaid is back in *Big Easy* territory. Herbert Ross, however, appears to think he's directing a spin-off from *Police Academy*. Disappointingly infantile. TCh

Undercover Man

(Joseph H Lewis, 1949, US) Glenn Ford, Nina Foch, James Whitmore, Barry Kelley, Howard St John, David Wolfe, Leo Penn, Anthony Caruso.
89 min. b/w.
A superior crime thriller in the semi-documentary style beloved by Hollywood in the late '40s. With the Big Fellow clearly inspired by Capone (he's prosecuted for tax evasion when normal policing methods fail to nail him), and Glenn Ford's Federal Treasury agent wading through piles of paperwork (as well as resorting to the customary action-packed physical pursuit), it achieves an authenticity rare in the genre. Perhaps even more impressive is the acknowledgement that mob crime affects not only cops and criminals, but innocents too: witnesses are silenced, bystanders injured. And Lewis – one of the B movie greats – directs in admirably forthright, muscular fashion, making superb use of Burnett Guffey's gritty monochrome camerawork. GA

Undercurrent

(Vincente Minnelli, 1946, US) Katharine Hepburn, Robert Taylor, Robert Mitchum, Edmund Gwenn, Marjorie Main, Jayne Meadows.
116 min. b/w.
Although best known for his marvellous MGM musicals, Minnelli also directed several superbly stylish melodramas (*The Bad and the Beautiful, Some Came Running*). This early example is a sombre, faintly *noir*-ish romantic thriller, with Hepburn marrying the handsome, wealthy, but cruel Taylor, and finding help when she needs it from his mysterious brother (Mitchum). Echoes of *Rebecca, Gaslight*, etc, but in its quiet understatement it becomes less of a full-blown weepie, more a haunting and subtle study of malevolence

and gullibility. Surprisingly, it finally impresses by the very absence of those memorably hysterical, stylistically baroque touches that make Minnelli's musicals and later dramas so wonderful. GA

Under Fire

(Roger Spottiswoode, 1983, US) Nick Nolte, Gene Hackman, Joanna Cassidy, Jean-Louis Trintignant, Ed Harris, Richard Masur, Hamilton Camp, Alma Martinez, Holly Palance, René Enriquez, Martin Lasalle.
127 min.
Riding to another Central American firefight come three journalists: reporter Hackman, tired of Third World wars; Nolte, Hackman's colleague and obsessive lensman; Cassidy, a radio reporter shifting her affections from Hackman to Nolte. Spottiswoode constructs a true portrait of these people, with no part of their lives, personal, moral, or political, which is not deeply informed by journalism; everything they do is subsumed in the great quest for the major scoop. Cassidy gives us a generous, no-nonsense Hawksian woman; Nolte is superb, American cinema's nearest thing to a tiger and a true heir to Robert Mitchum. As an immediate picture of what it feels like to be under fire, the black fear of being shot for nothing in a rubble-strewn street, the movie is way ahead of earlier examples like *Missing*; indeed, it takes an honourable place alongside classic war-torn romance pictures like *Casablanca* and *To Have and Have Not*; and there are ways in which it exceeds them. A thrilling film, with a head, a heart, and muscle. CPea

Underground

(Anthony Asquith, 1928, GB) Elissa Landi, Brian Aherne, Cyril McLaglen, Norah Baring.
81 min. b/w.
Asquith's first solo feature is set in the strangely surreal world of the Northern Line in the 1920s, with shopgirls and porters, dressmakers and power station workers tangling and untangling their love lives between Leicester Square and Stockwell. Asquith virtually dispenses with titles, and relies on some splendid acting – particularly from lynx-eyed Landi and weaselly cloth-capped womaniser McLaglen – and on Karl Fischer's sensitively expressionistic lighting to carry his trite but well-constructed story from light romance to brooding melodrama, with an emotional triangle leading to murder and a chase through the Battersea Power Station. RMy

Underground

(Emile de Antonio, 1976, US) Billy Ayers, Kathy Boudin, Bernadine Dohrn, Jeff Jones, Cathy Wilkerson.
88 min.
With a somewhat greater reputation as a 'cause' than as a film (FBI subpoenas on de Antonio, Haskell Wexler and Mary Lampson to surrender all footage brought an outcry from left-liberal Hollywood, before being withdrawn), this clandestinely-shot interview with five leading members of the Weather Underground marks both de Antonio's weakness and his strength as a radical film-maker. Soft-pedalling the analysis of the Weather-people's position on revolutionary armed struggle in the States (the questioning suggests reverence for 'the outlaw' rather than rigorous enquiry), and accordingly obtaining a number of rather woolly theoretical self-justifications, he none the less firmly situates the group in a recent US political history constructed largely from his own previous films and those of his followers, constantly relating his almost anonymous (obliquely shot) fugitive subjects to the events and conditions that radicalised them and sent them underground. PT

Underground

(Emir Kusturica, 1995, Fr/Ger/Hun) Miki Manojlovic, Lazar Ristovski, Mirjana Jokovic, Slavko Stimac.
192 min.
There's no denying Kusturica's technical virtuosity as he mounts one hectic, large-scale setpiece after another, but in the end it's hard to fathom the exact purpose of this epic allegory. Starting in 1941 with the German bombing of Belgrade, and moving through the post-war Tito years to the present, it follows the antics of two irrepressible con-men who become, in different ways, national heroes. One, having hidden his

friend, along with many others, in a cellar to save them from the Gestapo, neglects to tell them of the war's end, profiting from their arms-making industry, until they finally break free to discover that some things never change (even though countries may disappear). Played as broad, noisy black farce, the film is about the deception of politics and heroism, dog-eat-dog morals and the propensity for violence, but one can't help thinking that behind the sometimes sensational apocalyptic imagery, there's less here than meets the eye. GA

Underground U.S.A.

(Eric Mitchell, 1980, US) Patti Astor, Eric Mitchell, Rene Ricard, Tom Wright, Jackie Curtis, Cookie Mueller, Taylor Mead, Duncan Smith.
85 min.
The *Sunset Boulevard* of underground cinema, and a suitably ambivalent retrospect on the stargame casualties of New York's upper depths, with Patti Astor statuesquely hysterical as a 20-year-old Norma Desmond, made up to recall Edie Sedgwick and surrounded by Warhol's lost children. We've been here before, but without the hindsight: a camera cruise along a hustler's meat-rack, kitchen-talk over cold canned spaghetti, Taylor Mead grimacing in a spastic dance, the silent stud a sullenly passive observer. Mitchell's ear for campy native wit and eye for figures in a loft-scape happily keep at bay the otherwise contagious NY ennui. PT

Under Milk Wood

(Andrew Sinclair, 1971, GB) Richard Burton, Elizabeth Taylor, Peter O'Toole, Glynis Johns, Vivien Merchant, Sian Phillips, Victor Spinetti, Angharad Rees.
88 min.
An appallingly pedestrian adaptation of Dylan Thomas' radio play, reverently rendered as a cultural exercise, simply waiting for the script to drop a particularly fulsome poetic image and then illustrating it with stultifying literalness. Burton wanders zomboidally through the night as the Narrator (sonorous but peculiarly toneless), while O'Toole hams it up no end as Captain Cat (energetic but peculiarly un-Welsh). TM

Underneath, The

(Steven Soderbergh, 1995, US) Peter Gallagher, Alison Elliott, William Fichtner, Paul Dooley, Joe Don Baker, Shelley Duvall, Elisabeth Shue, Adam Trese.
99 min.
Michael Chambers (Gallagher), a reformed gambler, follows his losing streak back home to Austin, Texas. Moving in with mom and her new husband Ed (Dooley), Michael finds work driving an armoured car, but he runs straight into trouble when he looks up his ex-wife Rachel (Elliott), now the jealously guarded property of local hood Tommy Dundee (Fichtner). Rachel needs an escape route, and Michael wants her back, but the odds are stacked against a happy ending. Michael is 'not very present tense', we're told, and nor is Soderbergh, who uses colour-coded overlapping time-frames to tease us into the story and filter our responses. A remake of Siodmak's *Criss Cross*, the film is like a sci-fi *noir*, emotionally inhibited, sparse and strange in oppressive blues, reds and greens. It could use more humour, and some of the supporting roles are sketchy, but it's a slow-burner and never less than intelligent and engrossing. Gallagher is particularly good as the cocksure anti-hero who can barely see past his own nose, and take note of Fichtner's scary turn in the old Dan Duryea role. A rather remote film on the surface, but eventually it gets right under your skin. TCh

Underneath the Arches

(Redd Davis, 1937, GB) Bud Flanagan, Chesney Allen, Lyn Harding, Stella Moya, Enid Stamp-Taylor, Aubrey Mather.
72 min. b/w.
Routine, seedy vehicle for Flanagan and Allen as stowaways in a silly spy plot, with less songs and more daftness than needed. Some gems: a suicide pact with a policeman in a London fog, a drunk Scotsman, a rigged boxing match. But overall, 'orrible. This was the film that set the pattern for the series of Crazy Gang comedies that followed. DMacp

Under Satan's Sun

see Sous le Soleil de Satan

Under Siege

(Andrew Davis, 1992, US) Steven Seagal, Tommy Lee Jones, Gary Busey, Erika Eleniak, Patrick O'Neal, Damian Chapa, Troy Evans, David McKnight.
102 min.
Action-man Seagal plays Casey, whose position as cook aboard the USS Missouri hides a past as a Navy SEAL and top-level combat operative in Vietnam and Panama. Right from the beginning, it's clear that he hates Commander Krill (Busey, wonderfully demented), who spits in his bouill-abaisse before holing him up in the meat locker. But worse is to come. Krill and the even loonier William Strannix (Jones) hijack the ship, planning to steal its nuclear arsenal. So Casey has to bust out of the freezer, organise a rescue team, and kick ass to save the world from nuclear war. Davis handles the pacy action sequences confidently, with dark, claustrophobic interiors enhancing the suspense; so it's all the more disappointing when corny dialogue and barely-sketched characters let things down. CM

Under Siege 2

(Geoff Murphy, 1995, US) Steven Seagal, Katherine Heigl, Eric Bogosian, Everett McGill, Morris Chestnut, Brenda Bakke, Nick Mancuso, Andy Romano.
99 min.
A superior train-board Seagal adventure featuring bug-eyed bastard Bogosian, backed up by mean-as-a-Doberman henchman McGill. Whenever the star threatens to get sincere or sentimental, Kiwi director Murphy cuts to bone-crunching violence or cliff-hanging suspense. Shortly after his estranged brother's death in an air crash, Casey Ryback (Seagal) and his orphaned 17-year-old niece Sarah (Heigl) board the Grand Continental train from Denver to LA. Uncomfortable in his new surrogate father role, Ryback is relieved when the train is hijacked by megalomaniac scientist Travis Dane (Bogosian) and his terrorist gang. Using state-of-the-art technology, Dane seizes control of a military satellite he designed before being sacked, then demonstrates its awesome power by wiping out China (yes, all of it). Next up is the Pentagon and the entire Eastern seaboard – unless Uncle Sam stumps up $1bn. The one duff element is young black porter Bobby (Chestnut), a reluctant backup man whose underwritten role is a cynical sop to the non-white segment of Seagal's fan base. That aside, this is Seagal's best movie since *Out for Justice*. NF

Under Suspicion

(Simon Moore, 1991, GB) Liam Neeson, Kenneth Cranham, Laura San Giacomo, Maggie O'Neill, Alan Talbot, Malcolm Storry, Stephen Moore, Alphonsia Emmanuel.
100 min.
Tony Aaron (Neeson) is a private investigator with a seedy line in divorce work and dogged charm fraying with desperation. Then the bottom drops out of his low-rent world: his wife and a wealthy client are slaughtered in a bloody double murder, and naturally Aaron is the prime suspect. Cannily set in downtown Brighton on the very brink of the '60s, *Under Suspicion* is the sort of polished British crime melodrama that might have been made in the '50s with Richard Todd and some circumspection. Modern audiences may have doubts about the enterprise: the denouement hinges on a series of shameless contrivances and a last gasp race against the gallows. More damagingly, perhaps, Aaron's relationship with an American *femme fatale* (San Giacomo) smacks less of *amour fou* than an affair of convenience. Nevertheless, it's an engrossing mystery, snappily written and smartly directed by Moore in a promising debut. TCh

Under the Cherry Moon

(Prince, 1986, US) Prince, Jerome Benton, Kristin Scott-Thomas, Steven Berkoff, Emmanuelle Sallet, Alexandra Stewart, Francesca Annis, Victor Spinetti.
100 min. b/w.
Prince portrays a pianist/gigolo, on the make on the French Riviera until true love puts an end to his philandering and, ultimately, to his life. A moral tale indeed. Wiry and perched on high heels, he makes an unlikely gigolo, which any amount of coy pouting and flashing eye contact cannot disguise. He is, of course, lampooning himself wildly (isn't he?). His buddy (Benton, currently one of his backing singers) is a far more believable character, in what is rather a wasted supporting cast. Shot in black-and-white in an attempt to evoke the sophisticated burr of '40s films, its intent is hamstrung by over-familiar gags, though the script comes more to life when Prince and Benton lapse into black street talk during their pursuit of moneyed women. GBr

Under the Clock

see Clock, The

Under the Doctor

(Gerry Poulson, 1976, GB) Barry Evans, Liz Fraser, Hilary Pritchard, Penny Spencer, Jonathan Cecil, Elizabeth Counsell.
86 min.
Amused by 'confessional sex comedies' like Tudor Gates' *Intimate Games*? Then here's your chance to guffaw at another remarkably similar bit of British rubbish. Harley Street psychiatrist listens to the stupefying fantasies of three women patients, and is at last – not surprisingly – driven bonkers by his work. Liz Fraser, a veteran of this sort of nonsense, is allowed to keep her bra on; the other women strip with the usual offhand indifference. No male genitalia, but a superabundance of wilting puns. JPy

Under the Gun

(Ted Tetzlaff, 1950, US) Richard Conte, Audrey Totter, Sam Jaffe, John McIntire, Royal Dano, Shepperd Strudwick.
83 min. b/w.
No forgotten masterpiece, but a neat little crime thriller, ingeniously plotted by George Zuckerman (who also provided source material for *Border Incident* and *99 River Street*) around the teasing legal anomaly that a prison trusty who kills an escaping convict can earn himself a pardon. Worth watching for the admirable Conte, the Florida locations, and fitful direction by Tetzlaff, a fine cameraman (*My Man Godfrey*, *Notorious*) who never quite hit his director's stride again after the excellent *The Window* in 1949. TM

Under the Red Robe

(Victor Sjöström, 1937, GB) Conrad Veidt, Raymond Massey, Romney Brent, Annabella, Sophie Stewart, Wyndham Goldie, Lawrence Grant.
82 min. b/w.
As one might expect from a director famous for his ability to concretise interior struggles on celluloid, this adaptation of Stanley Weyman's costume romance of 17th century France (dealing with Cardinal Richelieu's hounding of the Huguenots) is a swashbuckler more concerned with character than action. Set in a deliciously stylised Sternbergian world – a contrast to the realistic tone of most of Sjöström's films – it follows Conrad Veidt's attempts to square his role as a mercenary with his conscience and his eventual salvation in love. Massey is equally sombre as Richelieu, and the photography by Georges Périnal and James Wong Howe is stunning. PH

Under the Olive Trees

see Through the Olive Trees

Under the Skin

(Carine Adler, 1997, GB) Samantha Morton, Claire Rushbrook, Rita Tushingham, Christine Tremarco, Stuart Townsend, Matthew Delamere, Mark Womack.
83 min.
Iris (Morton) has always been jealous of sister Rose (Rushbrook), but when their mother (Tushingham) dies, she's thrown into numb, furious confusion. Rejecting her old life (Rose and boyfriend Gary) Iris turns instead to the discomfort of strangers. At first glance, writer/director Adler's film seems extremely thin. Morton has charisma in spades and wears oddball clothes well. Such blasted poise proves irresistible to Adler, whose frenetic camera feasts on Morton as if she were a piece of meat. We never believe Iris is part of a community; she's more a wandering Lolita, slumming it among ignorant, treacherous low life. And though the sexual commentary is clearly intended to be cold, it's also tiresome. Are the sex scenes exploitative? Who can say. In the last third, however, Adler's strategy becomes clear: she's been playing a waiting game. Rose acquires an integrity that goes beyond mere respectable virtue, and when Iris's grief thaws, her helpless, animal-like pain is overwhelming. More surprisingly, our sense of the will-o'-the-wisp mother gathers force, the 'story' of her complex mothering told through the daughters' pinches, pokes and eventual tender fumblings towards each other. In its own twisty way, then, the film avoids both sentimentality and art-school cool, and with the help of superlative performances from Morton and Rushbrook, digs deep into the psyche. CO'Su

Under the Volcano

(John Huston, 1984, US) Albert Finney, Jacqueline Bisset, Anthony Andrews, Ignazio Lopez Tarzo, Katy Jurado, James Villiers.
111 min.
Everyone will be doing Huston's film a favour if they try hard not to compare it with the now classic Malcolm Lowry novel. In fact it captures the doomed spirit of the original, while – rightly – in no way apeing its dense, poetic style. Huston opts for straightforward narrative, telling the story of Geoffrey Firmin, an alcoholic English ex-diplomat who embraces his own destruction in Mexico shortly before the outbreak of World War II. As the limp-wristed observers of this manic process, Andrews and Bisset are at best merely decorative, at worst an embarrassment, and the film's success rests largely on an (often literally) staggering performance from Finney as the dipso diplo. Slurring sentences, sweating like a pig, wobbling on his pins, he conveys a character who is still, somehow, holding on to his sense of love and dignity. Not for the purists, maybe, but the last half-hour, as Firmin plunges ever deeper into his self-created hell, leaves one shell-shocked. RR

Underworld

(Josef von Sternberg, 1927, US) George Bancroft, Evelyn Brent, Clive Brook, Larry Semon, Fred Kohler, Helen Lynch, Jerry Manda.
7,643 ft. b/w.
Ex-reporter Ben Hecht drafted the script for *Underworld*, and clearly saw the project as a reflection of his experiences on the crime beat. Sternberg had no interest in Chicago realities, but it took him a while to muster the confidence to abandon Hecht's outline. Hence the clumsiness of the opening scenes, which introduce the central triangle (bank-robber Bancroft, his girl Brent, and alcoholic lawyer Brook) and establish the deadly rivalry between Bancroft and gangster Buck Mulligan (Kohler), whose front is a flower-shop that specialises in wreaths. Sternberg comes into his own with the scene of the gangsters' ball, where emotional and physical violence erupt amid a storm of confetti and streamers. Thereafter, the film radiates total confidence in its own means and methods, and the themes are wholly Sternberg's: a woman breaks free of the codes that imprison her, a macho thug discovers the depths of his own feelings, and sexual love proves stronger than handguns, prison bars, and the entire police force. Hecht wanted his name taken off the film, but that didn't stop him from accepting an Oscar for it the following year. TR

Underworld U.S.A.

(Samuel Fuller, 1960, US) Cliff Robertson, Beatrice Kay, Larry Gates, Robert Rust, Dolores Dorn, Robert Emhardt, Paul Dubov.
99 min. b/w.
In typical fashion, Fuller transforms the 'organised crime on the move' plot into that of a war film, with the FBI and the Syndicate each housed in their own skyscrapers overlooking the battlefield of America on which their troops are locked in conflict. The film's opening sees the Syndicate and the FBI at war, but it is the behind-the-scenes skirmishings and double-dealings of Tolly Devlin (Robertson), fighting his own no-holds-barred war of revenge (the Syndicate killed his father), which finally win the day for the FBI. For Fuller, the State is maintained not by its own machinery, but by the personal efforts of its citizens. PH

Un Deux Trois Soleil (1, 2, 3, Sun)

(Bertrand Blier, 1993, Fr) Anouk Grinberg, Marcello Mastroianni, Olivier Martinez, Myriam Boyer.
105 min.
An absurdist comedy about a poor family living in an ugly housing project in the South of France. Anouk Grinberg (from *Merci la Vie*) plays 15 or so years beneath her actual age as the six-year-old daughter of alcoholic Mastroianni and the unstable Boyer. Sufficiently provocative to put it beyond the pale as far as the BBFC goes, but Blier's ruminations are becoming tediously circular (and even sentimental). TCh

Undying Monster, The

(John Brahm, 1942, US) James Ellison, Heather Angel, John Howard, Bramwell Fletcher.
60 min. b/w.
A curse hangs over the ancestral home of the Hammonds. These English toffs are all destined to die at the claws of the hairiest monster the make-up department can cobble together. Fox made a foray into Universal territory with this admirably eerie werewolf pic. Lucien Ballard, one of Sternberg's protégés, provided the gloomy chiaroscuro photography. The story's a howler, but direction and performances have plenty of bite. GM

Une Chante, l'Autre Pas, L'

see One Sings, the Other Doesn't

Unfaithfully Yours

(Preston Sturges, 1948, US) Rex Harrison, Linda Darnell, Kurt Kreuger, Barbara Lawrence, Rudy Vallee, Robert Greig, Lionel Stander, Edgar Kennedy.
105 min. b/w.
The Sturges film with the odd flavour. As nutty as usual in its treatment of character and language, it adds a strong dash of poison to its tale of a famous conductor (Sir Thomas Beecham wickedly parodied) who comes to suspect his wife's fidelity. His imagination, fed by Rossini, Wagner and Tchaikovsky, conceives scenes of delirious revenge, reconciliation, and renunciation, only to find reality letting it down with a humiliating bang on each occasion. A bitter black comedy, some of it (like Harrison's struggles with a recalcitrant recording machine in preparing the perfect murder) is incredibly funny, but the rest is shot through with a painful tang of despair. Not much liked at the time, but a small masterpiece just the same in its skilful blending of moods, genuinely moving and quite beautifully played by Harrison and Darnell. TM

Unfaithfully Yours

(Howard Zieff, 1983, US) Dudley Moore, Nastassja Kinski, Armand Assante, Albert Brooks, Cassie Yates, Richard Libertini, Richard B Shull.
96 min.
This would seem to have the odds stacked against it. First, and most damningly, there's the memory of the 1948 Preston Sturges original. Then there's Moore bringing his irritatingly familiar little tics and obligatory drunk scene to the role of the symphony conductor who suspects his wife of fiddling around with his handsome violinist friend. Then there's Kinski doing her irritatingly familiar pouting sex kitten act as the wife. Whereas Sturges had his protagonist plotting revenge in three different ways appropriate to the three classical pieces he was conducting, Zieff reduces this to one Tchaikovsky concerto, and Moore's bumbling attempts to put his plan into practice aren't nearly as bumbling or as hilarious as they should have been. Despite all this, it ticks over happily enough in a mildly amusing way. AB

Unfaithful, The

(Vincent Sherman, 1947, US) Ann Sheridan, Lew Ayres, Zachary Scott, Eve Arden, Steve Geray, Jerome Cowan, John Hoyt.
109 min. b/w.
A fine melodrama loosely updating Somerset Maugham's *The Letter* to take in the problem of lonely wartime wives. The magnificent Sheridan gives one of her best performances as the woman who falls from grace, and is then forced to kill her importunate lover (alleging that he is an intrud-

er) to prevent the husband she loves from finding out. A little florid as her trial builds to an impassioned plea for understanding (though Scott as the husband, and Ayres as the sympathetic defence counsel, both give good support); but the rest, co-scripted by David Goodis and including a blackmailer among its tortuous thriller-style ramifications, is beautifully handled. TM

Unfaithful Wife

see Femme Infidèle, La

Unfinished Piece for Mechanical Piano (Neokonchennaya Pyesa dlya Mekhanicheskogo Pianin)

(Nikita Mikhalkov, 1976, USSR) Alexander Kalyagin, Elena Solovei, Eugenia Glushenko, Antonina Shuranova, Yuri Bogatyrev, Nikita Mikhalkov.
100 min.
Mikhalkov's version of Chekhov's first play, *Platonov*, has a lyrical naturalism that Chekhov would have loved. Beautifully paced, the film knows when to draw back from its lethargic liberals, impotent idealists, and hedonists in hock. Stolidly unlikely to inflame even provincial female hearts, Alexander Kalyagin's once promising schoolmaster rings uncomfortably true as he rouses a sleeping household with the tragic self-realisation of the non-achiever down the ages. 'I'm thirty-five!' he shrieks, yesterday's radical now a blubbering clown. The household clucks, consoles, squabbles, goes back to sleep as dawn breaks. Chilly for some. MHoy

Unfish, The (Der Unfisch)

(Robert Dornhelm, 1997, Aus) Maria Schrader.
98 min.
Dornhelm returns to home turf for this offbeat, so-called fairytale about the fortunes of a picturesque Austrian village, following the arrival of a giant model whale and its owner Sophie (Schrader) – who finds she has the powers of a benign sorceress. She invites the males of the village one by one to have sex with her and their wishes fulfilled (they include a priest, a 'capitalist' who rapes her and – pushing it over the edge – a dog), with chaotic and communally destructive results. The narration annoyingly parades the story's absurdity. The elements of French frivolity, Germanic folkloredom and leaden Central European comedy make for a discombobulating concoction. WH

Unforgettable

(John Dahl, 1996, US) Ray Liotta, Linda Fiorentino, Peter Coyotte, Christopher McDonald, Kim Cattrall, Kim Coates.
117 min.
The Last Seduction looked like a career maker for director Dahl and star Fiorentino, but four long years on, this dire effort suggests it could have been a flash in the pan. Liotta is Dr David Krane, a forensic scientist in the coroner's department. An ex-alcoholic, he's still suspected of his wife's murder, a night he can't remember but will never forget. Then he meets neuro-biologist Martha Briggs (Fiorentino), who claims to have identified a serum which enables her to transfer the memory of lab rats, and the movie takes a terminal credibility dive. Inspired by the rats, and undeterred by potentially lethal side effects, Krane volunteers as a human guinea pig, sampling memory cells taken from his wife's autopsy and sundry victims of a serial killer. Bill Geddie's script is a lame whodunit with a lunatic gimmick and a bad dose of the flashbacks. Fiorentino does her best, but her hands are tied. TCh

Unforgettable Summer, An (Un Eté inoubliable)

(Lucian Pintilié, 1994, Fr/Romania) Kristin Scott-Thomas, Claudiu Bleont, Olga Tudorache, Marcel Iureş.
82 min.
1925, in Dobroudja, an area of Romania on the Bulgarian border, populated by a variety of nationalities: to an isolated army garrison come captain Bleont and his wife Scott-Thomas. To avenge the massacre of frontier guards by Macedonian bandits, Bleont takes Bulgarian villagers hostage; but when he's ordered to shoot

them, encouraged by his wife's humane sympathy for their captives, he refuses. Firmly rooted in history, this is far more than just another costume drama; the insane savagery of the conflict depicted inevitably recalls more recent Balkan hostilities and 'ethnic cleansing'. It's a tough, unsentimental film, fuelled by a hatred of nationalistic delirium and tribal aggression, its anguish wonderfully incarnated by Scott-Thomas's characteristically fine (albeit dubbed) performance. GA

Unforgiven

(Clint Eastwood, 1992, US) Clint Eastwood, Gene Hackman, Morgan Freeman, Richard Harris, Jaimz Woolvett, Saul Rubinek, Frances Fisher, Anna Thomson, David Mucci, Anthony James.
131 min.
A magnificent movie that transcends its familiar tale of a reformed gunman forced by circumstance to resume his violent ways. When a cowhand cuts up a prostitute and a bounty is placed on his head, killer-turned-farmer Will Munny (Eastwood) joins his old partner (Freeman) and a bluff youngster (Woolvett) in the hunt. But in Big Whiskey, they must face the rough justice of Sheriff Daggett (Hackman)... While Eastwood's muscular direction shows he's fully aware of genre traditions, he and writer David Webb Peoples have created something fresh, profound, complex. It's not only a question of the excellent characterisations, but of situations given a new spin: the prostitutes and the spirit of Munny's dead wife introduce a feminist angle; there are insights into the thin line dividing law from justice; and the accent on ageing, fear and death establishes a dark tone perfectly complemented by Jack Green's sombre images. All of which links with the way this very violent film shows the cost of violence, painting a persuasive portrait of people increasingly given to emotions they have no control over. Refuting conventional cowboy heroics, Eastwood presents an alternative myth whereby a man, goaded by Furies to yield to a past that still haunts him, despatches himself to a living Hell. In this dark, timeless terrain, the film achieves a magnificent intensity. GA

Unforgiven, The

(John Huston, 1959, US) Burt Lancaster, Audrey Hepburn, Audie Murphy, Charles Bickford, Lillian Gish, John Saxon.
125 min.
Though neglected, and not entirely convincing in its treatment of racial identity, prejudice and tension, Huston's Western is one of his more intriguing films. Hepburn is an Indian girl adopted by Gish after her family was killed by whites. Raised as a white, she becomes the centre of a maelstrom of hatred, bigotry and violence when her true history is discovered: the Indians want her back, while local whites turn against her and her adoptive family. Notable chiefly for Franz Planer's fine photography and for a brace of sturdy performances (with Gish admirably evoking the pioneer spirit), the film is sadly flawed by its stereotyped depiction of the Indians, strangely at odds with its anti-racist impulses. It is, however, mercifully lacking in the sort of dry, clumsy solemnity that mars many of Huston's more self-consciously 'serious' movies, and remains unusually affecting. GA

Unheimliche Geschichten

see Living Dead, The

Unholy, The

(Camilo Vilo, 1987, US) Ben Cross, Ned Beatty, William Russ, Jill Carroll, Hal Holbrook, Trevor Howard, Peter Frechette, Claudia Robinson.
102 min.
A tediously solemn horror pic which abandons an intriguing conflict between repressed sexuality and disruptive desire in favour of the usual battle between Christian good and Satanic evil. Having survived a fall from a 17th floor window, young New Orleans priest Cross is made the pastor of a church whose last two incumbents have been murdered. Unsettled by a series of strange omens, he heeds the advice of cop Beatty and tracks down a frightened girl (Carroll), who used to help out at the church but now dances at a nightclub run by a sleazoid reptile (Russ) who

uses chic Devil worship as an erotic floorshow. This sort of daft dabbling Cross can cope with; more disturbing are the warnings of blind Father Howard, who says that he must face a terrifying demon called 'The Unholy'. Sadly, for all the emphasis on diabolism and kinky sex, the toothy, red-eyed rubber monster simply preys on the devout and innocent. Unlikely to generate any fervour, religious or otherwise. NF

Unholy Garden, The

(George Fitzmaurice, 1931, US) Ronald Colman, Fay Wray, Estelle Taylor, Tully Marshall, Mischa Auer, Warren Hymer.
74 min. b/w.
Ever urbane Colman is the gentleman thief in this picturesque Sam Goldwyn trifle. Hiding out in a desert hotel that's a refuge for a coterie of international criminals, he joins the plot to rob blind innkeeper Marshall and ward Wray of their hardearned nest egg, but romance is on the menu. Colman apparently didn't think much of the piece, though screenwriters Ben Hecht and Charles MacArthur found it hard to turn in a completely duff assignment. TJ

Unholy Three, The

(Tod Browning, 1925, US) Lon Chaney, Mae Busch, Victor McLaglen, Harry Earles, Matt Moore, Matthew Betz.
86 min. b/w.
Although they had worked together twice before, this is the first in the remarkable series of Browning/Chaney collaborations which served as a source for all that is best in the horror movie. Based like *Freaks* on a story by Tod Robbins, it is curiously muted compared to the macabre fancies dreamed up later in the series. But there is many a pleasing frisson to be had from the weird family circle formed by three carnival refugees – ventriloquist in drag as granny (Chaney), malevolent midget as baby (Earles), strong man in moronic attendance (McLaglen) – to further their criminal activities with the reluctant aid of Mae Busch's heroine, using a thriving pet shop as their HQ. Slightly tongue-in-cheek (baby sporting a huge cigar as he checks his bonnet and bootees; a murderous ape thrown in for the finale), it also displays considerable subtlety in depicting the perverse passions that tear the trio apart. TM

Unholy Three, The

(Jack Conway, 1930, US) Lon Chaney, Lila Lee, Elliott Nugent, Harry Earles, Ivan Linow, John Miljan.
72 min. b/w.
Chaney's final film (and his only talkie) is far from wonderful but it's certainly weird, with its tale of crimes committed by a gang comprising a ventriloquist disguised as a bird-shop proprietress, a strong man, and a midget who dresses and babbles like a baby when the occasion warrants. As if these weren't enough, there's also a romantic hero (played by chipper Elliott Nugent, pal of James Thurber and later a movie director) and a very bad-tempered gorilla. With that cast list, coherence is the last thing you should expect, and you certainly never get it. Much more slackly directed than Browning's original (which it often cribs from), it's still fun of a creaky historical kind. GB

Unhook the Stars (Décroches les étoiles)

(Nick Cassavetes, 1996, Fr) Gena Rowlands, Marisa Tomei, Gérard Depardieu, Jake Lloyd, David Sherrill, David Thornton, Moira Kelly.
105 min.
Though her husband died leaving her financially secure, life isn't exactly great for Mildred (Rowlands). Her teenage daughter Ann Mary Margaret (Kelly) is an argumentative ungrateful sort who only visits when she wants something; her beloved son Ethan (Thornton) is supportive and solicitous, but he's keen to take her with his family to San Francisco and install her in a granny flat, and Mildred's not sure she wants to move. Mildred's a little bored and lonely – not that she'd complain – so when a new neighbour, foul-mouthed, frequently drunk Monica (Tomei), asks her to babysit for six-year-old JJ (Lloyd), Mildred's happy to oblige. Little does she know the encounter will change her life. Nick Cassavetes' debut as writer/director is a sensitive, honest, touching study of the seemingly limited options faced by a woman whose age belies her energy, enthusiasm and ability to enjoy herself whenever the opportunity presents itself. If it lacks the raw intensity and brilliant insights of his father John's work, Cassavetes Jr still provides enough subtly observed moments to suggest he's a talent to watch. The film features a clutch of terrific performances, headed by the director's mother – sweet, strong, vulnerable and iron-willed, Rowlands is entirely credible and affecting throughout. The film's only misjudgment is the inclusion of Depardieu in a minor but important role: while there's nothing wrong with his performance, we're just too aware of who he really is to be properly convinced that he's a French-Canadian trucker. GA

Unidentified Flying Oddball, The (aka The Spaceman and King Arthur)

(Russ Mayberry, 1979, US) Dennis Dugan, Jim Dale, Ron Moody, Kenneth More, John Le Mesurier, Rodney Bewes, Sheila White, Robert Beatty.
93 min.
An intelligent film with a cohesive plot and an amusing script, this is one of the better Disney attempts to hop on the sci-fi bandwagon. Based on Mark Twain's *A Connecticut Yankee in King Arthur's Court*, it has a strong cast of British character actors who keep things ticking over nicely, and sweeten the rather depressingly obvious opening at NASA, where a freak accident sends Dugan and his lookalike robot back in time. Arthur (More) and Gawain (Le Mesurier) are rather touchingly portrayed as friends who have grown old together and, no longer really capable of holding the reins, are being jostled for power by evil Sir Mordred (Dale), abetted by the wicked Merlin (Moody). The final 'big battle' is fought with imaginative special effects, no blood is shed, good triumphs, love is requited, and peace once more reigns in good King Arthur's green and pleasant land. FF

Uninvited, The

(Lewis Allen, 1944, US) Ray Milland, Gail Russell, Ruth Hussey, Donald Crisp, Cornelia Otis Skinner, Barbara Everest, Alan Napier.
98 min. b/w.
Set in a distinctly Hollywoodian but nevertheless persuasive Cornwall, this is an impressive supernatural thriller, not unlike *Rebecca* in its use of an eerily atmospheric house and a sense of morbid brooding about the troubled past. Milland and Hussey are the siblings who buy the old house, only to find it haunted and exerting a sinister influence over the previous owner's granddaughter (Russell). Allen's direction tightens the screws of tension to genuinely frightening effect, aided by an intense performance from Russell as the girl who believes herself haunted by the malevolent ghost of her mother, and by beautiful camerawork in the *noir* style from Charles Lang. The real strength of the film, though, is its atypical stance part way between psychology and the supernatural, achieving a disturbingly serious effect. GA

Union City

(Mark Reichert, 1979, US) Dennis Lipscomb, Deborah Harry, Irina Maleeva, Everett McGill, Sam McMurray, Taylor Mead.
87 min.
A film of relentless tediousness. Based loosely on a Cornell Woolrich story, it's about a placid accountant, with a bored, frustrated wife, who gets so worked up by someone stealing his milk delivery every day that he eventually turns to murder. Admittedly Edward Lachman's gaudy camerawork is very accomplished, and the attention to period detail (New Jersey, '53) is admirable, if superfluous; but the monotonous acting, total lack of suspense, and endless punk chic makes it less a tribute than an insult to classic *film noir*. GA

Union Maids

(Julia Reichert/James Klein/Miles Mogeluscu, 1976, US)
50 min. b/w & col.
A clear-eyed documentary look at the rise of the Union movements in Chicago during the '30s, combining archive material and contemporary interviews with three women union organisers. The women, two white, one black, talk separately with clarity and conviction about working conditions during the Depression and the need to organise into unions. In the ensuing battle between big businesses and an increasingly militant labour force, the police were frequently called upon to intervene brutally: 'To us it was class warfare' says one of the women. The film uses its hindsight well, resisting over-simplification. Problems of racial prejudice, problems of women organisers working alongside men, the decline of the unions into conservatism, current difficulties between the middle class women's movement and its working class counterpart – all are discussed or touched upon. CPe

Union Station

(Rudolph Maté, 1950, US) William Holden, Nancy Olson, Barry Fitzgerald, Lyle Bettger, Jan Sterling, Allene Roberts.
80 min. b/w.
Despite implausibilities in its police procedural aspects, a sharp, brilliantly staged thriller about the kidnapping of a blind girl (Roberts), and the massive surveillance operation set up at Chicago's Union Station, the contact point established with the girl's father. Luck aiding, the kidnapper's plan starts to unravel almost immediately, with one associate trampled to death by cattle after being pursued into the stockyards; another spilling all he knows when cops threaten to throw him under a train; and a third (Sterling) left dying in the gutter when the hideout has to be abandoned. Undeterred, the dementedly vindictive kidnapper (Bettger) stashes the blind girl alone in a tunnel under the station strewn with naked high tension wires, then proceeds to try to collect the ransom... Agreeably ruthless on both sides of the law, the whole thing is considerably boosted by being shot on location (though not actual locations). Good performances down the line too, from Holden as the caring cop, Fitzgerald as the cynical one, and Olsen (secretary to the girl's father) as the bystander whose sharp eyes help crack the case. TM

Universal Soldier

(Roland Emmerich, 1992, US) Jean-Claude Van Damme, Dolph Lundgren, Ally Walker, Ed O'Ross, Jerry Orbach, Leon Rippy.
103 min.
Martial arts hero Van Damme finally joins the major league Action Men with this futuristic picture, originally developed as a Sylvester Stallone vehicle. He and Lundgren are UniSols – Vietnam vets brought back from the dead and transformed into state-of-the-art cyborg soldiers. Their memories have been wiped, but during an SAS-style action, Van Damme flashes back to a My Lai-type incident in 'Nam... Mostly this is an amalgam of ideas, images and whole scenes lifted from other movies. Emmerich, director of the low-budget stiff *Moon 44*, moves things along at a cracking pace, staging the fights and senseless destruction with savage efficiency. No prizes for originality, then, but full marks for giving Van Damme ample opportunity to display his limited talents to maximum advantage. NF

Unknown, The

(Tod Browning, 1927, US) Lon Chaney, Joan Crawford, Norman Kerry, Nick de Ruiz, John George.
65 min. b/w.
As with Browning's *Freaks*, one wonders how MGM ever got conned into making this resplendent study in morbid psychology. As much a casebook as a horror movie, it tells the truly marvellous tale of Alonzo the Armless Wonder (Chaney, of course), who uses his feet to perform a circus knife-throwing act. Only masquerading as armless (wanted by the police for a strangling, he's concealing the telltale evidence of a hand with two thumbs), he falls for pretty Estrellita (Crawford), the bareback rider. But she has a trauma about being touched by men, so he besottedly decides to have his arms amputated, only to find a handsome strong man emerging as a successful rival for her heart...cue for a fiendishly vengeful Grand Guignol finale staged during the strong man's act. One of the great silent movies, astonishing in its intensity, this is by far the best of the remarkable series of Browning/Chaney collaborations. TM

Unlawful Entry

(Jonathan Kaplan, 1992, US) Kurt Russell, Ray Liotta, Madeleine Stowe, Roger E Mosley, Ken Lerner, Deborah Offner, Carmen Argenziano, Andy Romano, Dick Miller.
111 min.

When a knife-wielding intruder invades the spacious LA home of Michael and Karen Carr (Russell and Stowe), along comes friendly neighbourhood policeman Pete Davis (Liotta), whose concern leads the trio towards an unlikely friendship. But that's before the cop turns out to be a psycho who gets Michael caught up in a spiralling nightmare and starts making moves on Karen. Kaplan is in his element in the first half, neatly stressing social differences; but the contrivances which alienate the couple become more glaring as we approach the OTT climax demanded of the genre. It's all designed to keep you on the edge of your seat (none too excusably in an over-extended prelude preying on fundamental fears of rape). Solid performances lend weight to the flakier elements, with Liotta turning crazed excess into something wild. CM

Unmarried Woman, An
(Paul Mazursky, 1977, US) Jill Clayburgh, Alan Bates, Michael Murphy, Cliff Gorman, Pat Quinn, Kelly Bishop, Lisa Lucas.
124 min.
Very much the product of its New York setting, in the well-established tradition of Annie Hall or a novel like Fear of Flying. The heroine is a woman suddenly deserted by her husband. Though enviably rich, smart and healthy, she suffers. She moves towards a kind of feminism, motivated by her touchiness concerning the men who step blithely into her life offering help, homes, approval, sex, or just a friendly drink. They're all the young middle-aged. They jog, take pills, vacations, analysis, and laugh at themselves. They're absurd and at the same time perfectly believable. JS

Unnatural Causes: The Agent Orange Story
(Lamont Johnson, 1986, US) John Ritter, Alfre Woodard, Patti LaBelle, John Sayles, Sean McCann, John Vargas, Gwen E Davis.
100 min.
John Sayles scripted (and appears in) this true-life telemovie about Vietnam vet Ritter (atoning for the Problem Child) trying to prove that his chronic ill health can be directly traced to the ill effects of the US military's use of the defoliant Agent Orange. Woodard's tremendous as the counsellor who takes on her superiors to battle it out for him. Impassioned and involving, it's far, far superior to the usual run of small-screen fare from the US networks, a credit to all concerned – including experienced director Johnson, who made his name on series like The Twilight Zone some two decades earlier. TJ

Un Nos Ola Leuad
see One Full Moon

Unseen, The
(Lewis Allen, 1945, US) Joel McCrea, Gail Russell, Herbert Marshall, Phyllis Brooks, Isobel Elsom, Norman Lloyd, Richard Lyon, Nona Griffith.
82 min. b/w.
Taken from Ethel Lina White's Midnight House – she also wrote the excellent The Wheel Spins, which became The Lady Vanishes – and co-scripted by Raymond Chandler, this follow-up to The Uninvited is labyrinthine, New England atmospheric, and delivers what the New York Herald Tribune called 'bona fide creeps'. Maybe some of it was down to the creaking of unidexter Herbert Marshall, the doctor from over the road. 'The last one was pretty, too' says a retainer to new governess Gail Russell, with heavy foreboding. One of her charges (the more mutinously sinister one) was played by the very junior Richard Lyon, son of Ben and Bebe, paying his dues for the subsequent radio hit, Life with the Lyons. Bad-tempered Chandler had one contretemps with producer John Houseman. 'Look, John, I'm the fucking writer'. BC

Uns et les Autres, Les (Bolero/The Ins and the Outs)
(Claude Lelouch, 1981, Fr) Robert Hossein, Nicole Garcia, Geraldine Chaplin, James Caan, Daniel Olbrychski, Evelyne Bouix.
173 min.
To cinema's cognoscenti, Lelouch's name is mud, yet this three-hour folly makes the mud seem not so much unjustified as inappropriate. True, Lelouch rarely finds images to match the ambitions of his story (there are four multi-national musical families, journeying through the 20th century); and for all the inspiration in authentic histories, the lives of his dancers, bandleaders, Auschwitz survivors, conductors, pop stars, waifs and strays, are still gilded clichés. But there is a point when the director's fatuity becomes sublime. The growling spectator is swept along by plot absurdities, camera pirouettes, and the unfashionable drift towards happiness; by the time the finale is reached, with Ravel's 'Bolero' played, danced and sung in front of the Eiffel Tower (in Dolby stereo), one's scruples lie in smithereens. At one point the narrator berates history for lacking imagination; history, as revealed here, certainly lacks taste, and its imagination could be toned up, but there's no shortage of silly entertainment. SJo

Unsinkable Molly Brown, The
(Charles Walters, 1964, US) Debbie Reynolds, Harve Presnell, Ed Begley, Jack Kruschen, Hermione Baddeley, Martita Hunt, Audrey Christie, Harvey Lembeck.
127 min.
A minor but likeable musical, partly based on fact, with Debbie Reynolds as the innocent backwoods orphan who, thanks to a combination of push, shove and money from her placid husband's lucky silver strike, makes good her burning ambition to gate-crash turn-of-the-century Denver society, finally conquering the snobs and achieving her finest hour during the 'Titanic' disaster. As ebulliently energetic as ever, Reynolds makes the brash social climbing both funny and touching, but the film itself gets trapped in two minds between satire and sentimentality. The score, by Meredith Willson of The Music Man, though pleasant, is rather thinly spread; but the sets are a delight in the best traditions of the MGM musical, and Walters does a wonderfully graceful job of direction. TM

Unstable Elements – Atomic Stories 1939-85
(Paul Morrison/Andy Metcalf, 1985, GB) Donald Sumpter, Caroline Hutchison, Susanna Kleeman, Sam Kolpe, David Henry.
90 min.
Two-thirds documentary, one-third dramatic moral exemplar, this traces a new history of the bomb and its domestic spin-offs: the World War II race between the Allies and the Axis to get there first, the complicity of politicians and scientists, the international bullying antics of America (riding to world domination on the back of the bomb), and the fallacy of the 'Atoms for Peace' campaign, portrayed here as a whitewash over a deliberate policy of using nuclear power stations to produce plutonium for the bomb. Using documentary footage, interviews with Manhattan Project scientists and their UK counterparts, excellent montages from Peter Kennard, and interviews with the relatives of dead nuke industry workers, it's a powerful indictment. But the final part – a mystifyingly oblique drama about the human, emotional effect of the nuke industry, based around Sizewell B – presents such an abrupt change as to almost scupper what went before. JG

Unstrung Heroes
(Diane Keaton, 1995, US) Andie MacDowell, John Turturro, Nathan Watt, Michael Richards, Maury Chaykin, Kendra Krull, Joey Andrews.
93 min.
Twelve-year-old Steven Lidz (Watt) lives a pleasant if unexceptional sort of life in early '60s suburban LA. Dad (Turturro) is a boffin, whose family input consists largely of unusual labour-saving inventions; mom (MacDowell) takes care of home and isn't averse to the occasional ciggie. Cancer duly strikes, dad can't cope with both a dying wife and the demands of his kids, and Steven runs away to live with his uncles Danny and Arthur in the city. Under their diligent tutelage, he's soon changed his name to Franz, trawls the city sewers for collectable objects, and has caught religion. Cue worried parents. Keaton's first feature is a highly enjoyable, predictably wacky family drama. The zestful direction captures the kid's-eye-view wonderfully, and the performances are exemplary. If the film succeeds, though, it's primarily thanks to the strength of Richard LaGravenese's script (from a novel by Franz Lidz); some of the most endearing moments recall the Gothic abandon of his earlier The Fisher King. A film to be enjoyed for its numerous surface charms – above all, the gloriously paranoiac Danny's broadside against Steven's odious rival for class president. NB

Unsuitable Job for a Woman, An
(Christopher Petit, 1981, GB) Billie Whitelaw, Pippa Guard, Paul Freeman, Dominic Guard, Elizabeth Spriggs, David Horovitch.
94 min.
Toss a girl down a disused well, and watch her struggle to get out: a scene which deserves a corner in cinema history. Based on the novel by PD James, this is a stinging film noir played out in the long, russet shadows of an English summer: the story of a young woman (Guard) who, after the quiet suicide of her partner, takes control of the private detective agency he has bequeathed to her, and is asked (by Whitelaw) to investigate another suicide – the son of a prominent businessman – found hanged in a rented cottage. The plot is spare, bitter, and buried in the past. All the more credit to director and co-writer Petit (in his second film) for not resorting to the easy recourse of flashback; it's a restraint that contributes to the film's special, uneasy quality of the here-and-now. JS

Unsuspected, The
(Michael Curtiz, 1947, US) Claude Rains, Joan Caulfield, Audrey Totter, Constance Bennett, Hurd Hatfield, Michael North, Fred Clark, Jack Lambert.
103 min. b/w.
A gilt-edged performance from Rains, revelling in sinister ambiguities as a radio personality/criminologist who, while regaling his fans with titillating tales of true crime and learned speculations as to the tortuous ways of the criminal mind, secretly commits a murder of his own. Based on a marvellous novel by Charlotte Armstrong, the film is considerably weakened by the fact that her intricate plot is partly discarded. But this hardly matters, since Curtiz wraps the rest up in a pyrotechnic display of expressionistic effects, including one shot in which a girl dying of poison is coolly watched through the bubbles in a champagne glass, and another in which a reluctant killer broods in his sleazy hotel room while Rains (who is blackmailing him into killing again) can be heard droning away on the radio and part of a neon sign seen flashing on and off outside urges 'kill...kill...kill'. The use Curtiz makes of the weirdly opulent mansion in which most of the action takes place is almost as psychologically acute as in Losey's The Prowler. TM

Untamed
(Henry King, 1955, US) Tyrone Power, Susan Hayward, Richard Egan, Agnes Moorehead, Rita Moreno, John Justin.
111 min.
Expensive, long and dreary attempt at a South African Western with the Zulus as makeshift Indians. Power is the rugged trekking Boer, Susan Hayward the love interest, a fiery Irishwoman who emigrated in the wake of the potato famine. Shot in 'Scope, with matte shots and back projection masking the fact that none of the principals ventured to Africa. GM

Untamed Heart
(Tony Bill, 1993, US) Marisa Tomei, Christian Slater, Rosie Perez, Kyle Secor, Willie Garson.
102 min.
Tony Bill's Minneapolis melodrama begins with washed-out, anaemic shots of an orphanage and a fey bedtime story passed from a nun to a young invalid about a boy with a baboon heart. It's a shock how suddenly the film is back on course after such a sickly sentimental prologue, kick started by a happening actress firing on all cylinders. Tomei's after-hours waitress, Caroline, is vulnerable, funny and wholly unaffected. Her banter with friend Rosie Perez is like verbal pinball. Slater's busboy Adam is an angelic wild child, so shyly distant his work mates assume he'd retarded. When he saves Caroline from two rapists, she becomes curious...and falls in love.

Slater's greasy-haired 'Beast' is not for the hard-boiled, but see the film for Tomei's sensitive, doe-eyed 'Beauty', and for Bill's sure feel for an authentic downtown milieu. TCh

Until Death
see Hasta Morir

Until the End of the World (Bis ans Ende der Welt)
(Wim Wenders, 1991, Ger/Fr/Aust) Solveig Dommartin, William Hurt, Sam Neill, Jeanne Moreau, Max von Sydow, Chick Ortega, Eddy Mitchell, Adelia Lutz, Ernie Dingo, Rüdiger Vogler, Chishu Ryu, Allen Garfield, Lois Chiles, David Gulpilil.
158 min.
Wenders' stab at making the ultimate road movie is a severe disappointment. Co-scripted by Wenders and novelist Peter Carey, it's set somewhat portentously during the last weeks of 1999. The Indian nuclear satellite is out of control, but Claire (Dommartin) is too busy with her own chaotic existence to get caught up in apocalyptic panic. Carrying a stash of dodgy money to Paris for two hoods, she meets an American (Hurt) also involved in a mysterious mission. As her odyssey continues via Berlin, Lisbon, Moscow, Beijing, Tokyo and San Francisco to the Australian outback, others join the chase: notably her novelist ex (Neill), a missing persons investigator (Vogler), and Hurt himself, whose plans to help his blind mother (Moreau) see again, with a camera his dad (von Sydow) has devised, set the limits for the film's geographically static last hour or so. If all this sounds needlessly complicated, it is. The first half is simply an over-plotted caper, devoid of suspense, comedy or anything else. The second gets heavily philosophical, and muses none too illuminatingly on dreams, images, obsessions, love, the mystery of life, etc. Despite a few felicitous moments, the film is turgid, pretentious, and dramatically lifeless. GA

Untouchables, The
(Brian De Palma, 1987, US) Kevin Costner, Sean Connery, Charles Martin Smith, Andy Garcia, Robert De Niro, Richard Bradford, Jack Kehoe, Brad Sullivan, Billy Drago.
120 min.
Time-honoured mayhem in the Windy City, and if there are few set-ups you haven't seen in previous Prohibition movies, it's perhaps because De Palma and scriptwriter David Mamet have settled for the bankability of enduring myth. And boy, it works like the 12-bar blues. The director's pyrotechnical urge is held in check and trusts the tale; the script doesn't dally overmuch on deep psychology; the acting is a treat. Connery's world-weary and pragmatic cop, Malone, steals the show because he's the only point of human identification between the monstrously evil Al Capone (De Niro) and the unloveably upright Eliot Ness (Costner), and when he dies the film has a rocky time recovering. Costner looks like the kid who got a briefcase for Xmas and was pleased, but painfully learns under Malone's tutelage how to fight dirty. De Niro establishes his corner courtesy of a bloody finger in close-up, and unleashes uncontrollable rage to electrifying effect, most notably at the blood-boltered baseball-bat board meeting. The Odessa Steps set piece at the railway station could maybe do with one more angle to shuffle, and the battle at the border bridge diminishes the claustrophobic grip of the corrupt city, but the narrative thunders to its conclusion like a locomotive. BC

Unzipped
(Douglas Keeve, 1994, US) Isaac Mizrahi, Kate Moss, Linda Evangelista, Cindy Crawford, Naomi Campbell, Christy Turlington, Ertha Kitt, Sandra Bernhardt.
73 min. b/w & col.
'It's about women not wanting to look like cows, I guess…' So says fashion designer *extraordinaire* Isaac Mizrahi in this witty, insightful 'fly on the changing-room wall' documentary by his then lover, photographer Douglas Keeve. The film begins with Mizrahi reading the reviews for his latest show, and charts the progress of his next (New York, 1994) – '50s cheesecake meets eskimo fake fur' – bursting into colour for the fabulously decadent climax. Not only does the film establish the credentials of the art of fashion, it's also a whole lot funnier than Altman's *Prêt-à-Porter*. TCh

Uomo avvisato mezzo ammazzato…parola di Spirito Santo
see Blazing Guns

Uomo delle stelle, L' (The Starmaker)
(Giuseppe Tornatore, 1994, It) Sergio Castellitto, Tiziana Lodato, Leopoldo Trieste, Nicola Di Pinto, Franco Scaldati, Tony Sperandeo, Jane Alexander.
107 min.
Back in his native Sicily, where he scored his greatest triumph with *Cinema Paradiso*, director Tornatore confronts the magic of celluloid with distinctly less happy results in this story of a man with a movie camera. It's 1953, television hasn't yet reached Italy's poverty-stricken South, and Joe Morelli has little difficulty in persuading the locals to part with their hard-earned lire for the price of a screen test. Here's their big chance at movie stardom, since the footage is sent back to the studios in Rome and the right face might just be plucked from obscurity for a glittering new career. That's how the theory goes, but even the hustling, bustling Joe can't fail to notice the burden of dreams he carries around with him, particularly when the teenage orphan Beata pins all her hopes on his battered van and its travels across the Sicilian landscape. As the unprepossessing Joe, Castellitto tries hard to veil the ugly truth behind his character's money-making scheme, but the effort is so obvious it's hard to care about him either way, especially when his treatment of newcomer Tiziana Lodato's striking Beata veers on the neolithic side of macho. Much more palatable is the notion that the villagers' open-hearted confessions to Morelli's camera prove more touching and true than anything in the Italian movies of the time. Disappointing. TJ

Up Close & Personal
(Jon Avnet, 1996, US) Robert Redford, Michelle Pfeiffer, Stockard Channing, Joe Mantegna, Kate Nelligan, Glenn Plummer, James Rebhorn, DeDee Pfeiffer.
124 min.
A soppy May-December romance masquerading as a deadly earnest issues movie (script by Joan Didion and John Gregory Dunne, 'suggested' by the book *Golden Girl* by Alanna Nash). Pfeiffer is Tally Atwater, a perky klutz who dreams of being a TV news anchor. She's picked up by respected old pro Warren Justice (Redford). If Nicole Kidman had had a Warren, she'd have had no reason *To Die For*. Warren thinks Tally 'eats the lens'. She's 'hungry', so he gives her a 'live feed'. With a little mood music from Celine Dion, they do the do, but Tally's career takes off, while the obstinately sanctimonious Warren is deemed too political for TV (think *Broadcast News* without the wit, *A Star Is Born* without the alcohol). Somehow the film-makers spin this dramatic vacuum out for another hour or so, putting Ms Pfeiffer in a new hairdo every few minutes to relieve the tedium, until finally they come up with the TV-reporter-in-a-prison-riot routine. Blow-dried, bleached blonde-on-bland entertainment. TCh

Up in Arms
(Elliott Nugent, 1944, US) Danny Kaye, Dinah Shore, Dana Andrews, Constance Dowling, Louis Calhern, Elisha Cook Jr, Walter Catlett.
106 min.
Kaye's very scrappy first starring vehicle, in which he plays a hypochondriac drafted in World War II and packed off to the Pacific sector along with the Goldwyn Girls (handy for filling in when inspiration flags). The tiresome patter song with which he had already wowed Broadway ('Malady in 4-F'), and which set the pattern for his frenzied double-talk speciality, is much in evidence. So, as Parker Tyler noted, is the shameless fixation on the camera which made him rather unprepossessing for all his obvious talents. Still, there are moments of genuine splendour in his bizarre satire on screen musicals ('Manic-Depressive Presents'). TM

Up in Smoke
(Lou Adler, 1978, US) Cheech Marin, Tommy Chong, Strother Martin, Edie Adams, Stacy Keach, Tom Skerritt.
86 min.
Cheech and Chong's first movie is the epitome of the serious doper's heaven and hell. Heaven: they drive around in a van made entirely from 100% 'Fibreweed'. Hell: they don't know it. Heaven: they find a whole plateful of coke in the aftermath of a party. Hell: they also find a lady with a nose like the Blackwall tunnel and sniffing power equal to any Jet-vac. Covering the gamut of a laid-back, laid-out LA dope bum's world – dumb cops, 'Nam, being busted, the eternal search for a 'lid' – the movie eventually gets too out of it, and tails off into easy visual gags rather than maintaining the spaced-out repartee that made Cheech and Chong so memorable. As the most fun comes not from watching the movie but from recalling great lines later, it would seem that the audio success of C & C has not translated too well into visuals. FF

Up 'n' Under
(John Godber, 1997, GB) Gary Olsen, Richard Ridings, Samantha Janus, Ralph Brown, Neil Morrissey, Tony Slattery, Griff Rhys-Jones, Brian Glover.
90 min.
Based on characters from a play by director John Godber, this patronising feel-good comedy is set in the world of Yorkshire pub seven-a-side rugby. Ex-pro Olsen bets flash git entrepreneur Slattery his house that the Wheatsheaf team of lifelong losers will beat the seemingly invincible Cobblers Arms squad of brick shithouses. Olsen is ordinary and vulnerable enough to be convincing. Samatha Janus, too, as the gym owner who helps whip the team into shape, is sufficiently feisty and natural in the 'strong woman' role to mask the script's contrivance. However, the 'money shot' of her in the nude – 'You've had a look, now piss off!' – is typical of the film's casual sexual-political hypocrisy. Too concerned with courting sympathy, thin on laughs – and the rugby's a joke. WH

Up on the Roof
(Simon Moore, 1997, GB) Billy Carter, Adrian Lester, Clare Cathcart, Amy Robbins, Daniel Ryan.
101 min.
Adapted by Simon Moore and Jane Prowse from their successful stage musical, this concerns five friends from the university of Hull, class of '79. Golden couple Bryony and Scott (Robbins and Lester), tubby geek Angela (Cathcart), cheery hanger-on Tim (Carter) and scaly Keith (Ryan) all belong to an a cappella group. On the last day of term, they vow to meet again in 1989. First problem: as a group, they fail to convince. As for the singing, Prowse and Moore are obviously going for heartfelt sweetness, but only Lester has a really fine voice, while the arrangements are literally soul-destroying. Would the sight of the singing, grinning five, high on a building, overwhelm a whole campus of laidback dudes? A far more likely response would be a unanimous 'Jump!' CO'Su

Upper Hand, The
see Rififi à Paname

Uproar in Heaven (Danao Tiangong)
(Wan Lai-Ming, 1961–64, China)
110 min.
Wan Lai-Ming and his brothers were China's pioneers in animation, but their work was suppressed after the Cultural Revolution of 1966. This ambitious animated feature is adapted from the first seven chapters of the 16th century novel *Journey to the West* (best known here in Arthur Waley's translation as *Monkey*), and it celebrates the mischievous Monkey King's challenge to the celestial autocracy. Wan makes no real effort to produce 'charming' or sympathetic characters, and so his main appeal is to those familiar with the book – which means everyone in China. His figure animation is like simplified Disney without the sentimentality, but his backgrounds derive rather beautifully from traditional Chinese painting. TR

Upstairs and Downstairs
(Ralph Thomas, 1959, GB) Michael Craig, Anne Heywood, Mylène Demongeot, James Robertson Justice, Claudia Cardinale, Sidney James, Joan Hickson, Joan Sims, Daniel Massey.
101 min.

Oh, the problems of nice upper-class couples in British comedies of the '50s. Newly-weds Craig and Heywood simply can't find the right domestic and they've got to do lots of entertaining for her wealthy father's business clients. After trying and failing with the likes of Claudia Cardinale (her first English-speaking role) and Joan Hickson, they hit pay-dirt with Sid James. Very genteel. Began life as a novel by Ronald Scott Thorne. TJ

Up the Down Staircase

(Robert Mulligan, 1967, US) Sandy Dennis, Patrick Bedford, Eileen Heckart, Ruth White, Jean Stapleton, Sorrell Booke, Roy Poole, Ellen O'Mara.
123 min.
Documentary-style drama dealing with the problems that face an idealistic young schoolteacher when she is assigned to a rough school in a slum area. Some of the characters are very accurately drawn (by Sandy Dennis as the teacher, Ellen O'Mara as a lovesick schoolgirl); others are stereotypes. Some of the situations work (the plot is little more than a catalogue of events); others don't. It comes to precious few conclusions, but does at least provide a talking-point of sorts in its portrayal of a frighteningly unenlightened American educational system. DMcG

Up the Junction

(Peter Collinson, 1967, GB) Suzy Kendall, Dennis Waterman, Adrienne Posta, Maureen Lipman, Michael Gothard, Liz Fraser, Hylda Baker, Alfie Bass, Susan George.
119 min.
Hard to see what all the fuss was about (at least from this movie cash-in on Kenneth Loach's teleplay version of Nell Dunn's novel). The idea that the decision of middle class Polly (Kendall) to forsake Chelsea and move to Battersea should provide enough substance for either a book or a film now seems ludicrous. Nevertheless here it all is. In the shadow of the power station, she helps working class Rube (Posta) cope with abortion and death: part of the short-lived and generally muffed attempt by the film industry to make a foray of sorts into the realities of working class life in Britain. VG

Up the Sandbox

(Irvin Kershner, 1972, US) Barbra Streisand, David Selby, Jane Hoffman, Jacobo Morales, John C Becher, Paul Benedict, Paul Dooley.
98 min.
Good old Hollywood doing its bit to keep the giggles going about Women's Lib. The wife of a radical prof at Columbia, Streisand feels somewhat dissatisfied with life. Egged on by the more forthright comments of housewife/mother friends, and hormonally motivated by the fact that she is pregnant for the third time, she enacts the problems of her marriage through a series of fantasies: a confrontation with a South American revolutionary who turns out to be a woman, a hair-tearing session with her possessive Jewish mother, a cathartic attack on her devoted husband, and one about abortion where she drifts through a children's playground in a white gown on the operating-table. In spite of a number of funny lines, it all ends up as though happy-ever-after had only just been invented. Well, we always knew that women – especially stars – were really content just to be wives and mothers. MV

Uptown Saturday Night

(Sidney Poitier, 1974, US) Sidney Poitier, Bill Cosby, Harry Belafonte, Flip Wilson, Richard Pryor, Rosalind Cash, Roscoe Lee Browne, Paula Kelly, Calvin Lockhart.
104 min.
An efficient enough comedy in which Poitier directs himself as straight man to Cosby's slightly demented taxi driver. The film takes off from the first night of their vacation, when a winning lottery ticket is stolen and their attempts to retrieve it involve them in a movie fantasy world of gangsters. Radiating professionalism rather more than inspiration, it boils down to the sum of its star turns, and with the exception of a fairly nauseous opening sequence sketching in Poitier's 'happy marriage', emerges not unlikeably. Calvin Lockhart etches a neat thumb-nail sketch of a ghetto gangster; Belafonte takes off Brando's Godfather; Roscoe Lee Browne adds a touch of acid to his portrayal of a black con-

gressman. But it's Richard Pryor's fleeting yet totally three-dimensional Sharp Eye Washington, a perspiring and achingly nervous phony private eye, who really walks away with the honours. VG

Upworld

see Gnome Named Gnorm, A

Up Your Alley

(Bob Logan, 1988, US) Linda Blair, Murray Langston, Bob Zany, Kevin Benton, Ruth Buzzi, Glen Vincent, Jack Hanrahan, Melissa Shear.
88 min.
Here we have Linda Blair in her 'comedy debut' as a yuppy junior reporter dressing up as a bag lady in order to write a tear-jerking piece about 'street people'. In no time at all she's falling in lurve with the cutest derelict in town (Langston), giving her smarmy editor the thumbs-down for the hot-tub option, and helping to solve a murder. And all without the aid of make-up! Unusually, she manages to make it through the entire movie without getting imprisoned, raped, abused, possessed or murdered. The whole thing is fittingly low budget: it looks like it was filmed in about four days. MK

Uranus

(Claude Berri, 1990, Fr) Philippe Noiret, Gérard Depardieu, Jean-Pierre Marielle, Michel Blanc, Michel Galabru, Gérard Desarthe, Fabrice Luchini, Daniel Prévost, Florence Darel.
99 min.
The troubled mood of guilt, recrimination and persecution that plagued France at the end of WWII has rarely been even hinted at by that country's cinema, and one would like to be able to commend Berri's adaptation of Marcel Aymé's novel for bravery, if nothing else. But while this account of vicious, hypocritical intrigue in a small, recently liberated town certainly admits to the existence of both collaborators and communist fanatics, the histrionic performances, excessively eventful narrative, and two-dimensional characterisations make for ludicrous melodrama. The sense of quiet drama that made *Jean de Florette* so popular is conspicuously absent, and *everyone* overacts. It may aspire to tragedy, but the overblown script and emphatically drab period dressing reduce it to little more than an indulgent wallow in petty corruption. GA

Urban Cowboy

(James Bridges, 1980, US) John Travolta, Debra Winger, Scott Glenn, Madolyn Smith, Barry Corbin, Brooke Alderson, Cooper Huckabee.
135 min.
In Hollywood parlance, *Urban Cowboy* is just like *Saturday Night Fever* but completely different. It began life as a factual article in *Esquire* about the weekend cowboys of Houston, who live a split existence between their factories and the fantasy world of the honky-tonk bars. Bridges builds this material into a well acted, eye-catching romance about the aspirations and romances of a new kid in town (Travolta). But the stream of incidents and pick-ups around the mechanical rodeo bull in the ballroom cannot disguise the fact that the film badly lacks a central narrative hook. It is too obviously a starring vehicle, and – unlike *Saturday Night Fever*, which did present some insights into a subculture – its major events are crudely imposed on the setting. In fact, the film's virtues derive not from Travolta at all, but from Bridges' obvious enjoyment of the country milieu, and the fine performances he wins from Travolta's co-stars. Debra Winger, as his wife, lends her part far more spirit and sympathy than the writing deserves; but the trump card is Scott Glenn as the villain, looking uncannily like a new Eastwood. DP

Urga

(Nikita Mikhalkov, 1990, Fr/USSR) Badema, Bayaertu, Vladimir Gostukhin, Babushka, Larissa Kuznetsova, Jon Bochinski.
118 min.
Best known for his Chekhov adaptations, Mikhalkov here came up with a film full of narrative surprises. Set for the most part in the vast, empty steppes of Chinese Mongolia, it's partly a docudrama detailing the day-to-day existence of a herdsman's family, partly a fable about the material and spiritual threats facing a robust but

largely forgotten culture (the *urga* is a herdsman's lasso, but also a symbol of traditions in harmony with nature). Into this strange, remote world comes a Russian ex-soldier, working on a road-building project. Nothing here is quite as it seems, and as Mikhalkov guides us on a voyage into a fascinating but unfamiliar landscape, he deploys dreamy images, rapturous music, and bizarre incongruities to undermine our assumptions about 'primitive' Mongolian life. Admittedly, towards the end the narrative gets a little out of control, but much of it is very funny, and the engagingly naturalistic performances, the ravishing camerawork, and the mostly subtle use of natural symbols sustain interest throughout. GA

Urinal

(John Greyson, 1988, Can) Pauline Carey, Paul Bettis, George Spelvin.
100 min.
This overly ambitious film, part documentary and part fantasy, is centered around a research project on the policing of cottaging (or 'washroom sex', as Canadians term it) in Ontario. The most interesting parts of the film (revealing the lengths that the Canadian police go to, including the use of *agents provocateurs* and video surveillance, in order to make easy arrests and bump up prosecution figures) are the interviews with men who have been charged with 'gross indecency', with gay activists, with a lawyer working on behalf of prosecuted gay men, and with Svend Robinson, Canada's first 'out' gay MP. Unfortunately, you also have to wade through a nonsensical framework involving the ghosts of famous lesbian, gay and bisexual figures (including Eisenstein, Frida Kahlo, Mishima and Langston Hughes), who are summoned to the garden of two dead Toronto sculptors to talk about the history of lavatories and debate the question of police entrapment. Aiming for imagination, it just becomes weird… and boring. MG

Ursula and Glenys

(John Davies, 1985, GB) Brid Brennan, Gaylie Runciman, Ric Morgan, Joe Davies, Kieran Davies.
54 min.
This is a spiky film with a certain trenchant humour contributed by the Glenys character (Runciman), a Soho hooker. This is played off against the slightly soured strength of Ursula (Brennan). They are respectively the 'bad' and 'good' half-sisters who provide the focus for this rather disengaged exploration of fragmented families, incest, and moral disenchantment. Perhaps appropriately for a stagnant Britain (that image of parked car, doors open against a flat landscape, 'Islands in the Stream' on the radio), the only form of communication is confession. Hallmark of the '80s? The film has surprising charm, and the locations are well used. VG

U.S. Marshals

(Stuart Baird, 1998, US) Tommy Lee Jones, Wesley Snipes, Robert Downey Jr, Joe Pantoliano, Irène Jacob, Kate Nelligan, Patrick Malahide, Tom Wood.
131 min.
A sequel to *The Fugitive* starring Jones' hardass marshal is not a bad idea; but this lazy follow-up is simply a carbon of the original, with a few token changes. This time, it's Snipes, not Harrison Ford, on the run. The wrongfully imprisoned Snipes escapes after a crash involving a plane not a train; and the jaw-dropping stunt is a Tarzan swing from a high rise not a swan dive from a dam. When Jones utters the words, 'We have a fugitive,' we know we're in *Die Hard 2* territory. The cosmetic changes, though, alter the balance of the story significantly. We must divide our sympathies between Snipes, set up as a fall guy by his former government employers, and Jones' no nonsense lawman, who always gets his man; but Snipes plays second fiddle to Jones' pursuing hero. Director Baird stages the buttock clenching plane crash with skill, and despite letting the chase drag on too long keeps things moving brisk, if sometimes fitful pace. NF

Used Cars

(Robert Zemeckis, 1980, US) Kurt Russell, Jack Warden, Gerrit Graham, Frank McRae, Deborah Harmon, Joseph P Flaherty, Michael McKean, David L Lander, Wendie Jo Sperber.
111 min.

With their unerring eye for potential, the distributors didn't release this hilarious black comedy to cinemas in Britain. Zemeckis subsequently went on to make *Romancing the Stone, Back to the Future, Who Framed Roger Rabbit* and loadsa money. Infinitely more caustic than these blockbusters, *Used Cars* runs on a contemporary screwball motor with a slapstick chassis. Centred on the outrageous rivalry of two car dealerships (both owned by Jack Warden, as twins), it's an amoral celebration of the all-American wheeler-dealer – like *Tin Men* on speed. Even Jimmy Carter lends his support! TCh

Used People

(Beeban Kidron, 1992, US) Shirley MacLaine, Marcello Mastroianni, Bob Dishy, Kathy Bates, Jessica Tandy, Marcia Gay Harden, Sylvia Sidney.
116 min.
Kidron's beguiling American debut sprinkles moments of everyday oddity and genuine pain into the usual Hollywood syrup of think-positive platitudes. Queens in 1969 bustles with Jewish familial ructions when middle-aged mum Pearl Berman (MacLaine) gets picked up at her husband's funeral by spiv-suited Italian Joe Meledandri (Mastroianni), a long-time secret admirer. Initially awkward, eventually rejuvenating, this romantic late late show puts Pearl's toiling years of marriage into proper perspective and throws the rest of the household's problems into sharper relief... MacLaine bristles to touching effect as a woman at last grasping some time for herself; Mastroianni's Casanova codger is a hangdog charmer of a Hollywood debut. Elsewhere, myriad minor characters and switchback shifts from tears to whimsy jostle for attention in Todd Graff's densely populated script. More lunatic than *Moonstruck*, sweeter than *Sweetie*, the film's breezy domesticity is the acceptable face of sentimental guff. TJ

Usual Suspects, The ⟨100⟩

(Bryan Singer, 1995, US) Gabriel Byrne, Kevin Spacey, Stephen Baldwin, Chazz Palminteri, Pete Postlethwaite, Giancarlo Esposito.
108 min.
This labyrinthine, very well played thriller – a huge improvement on the Bryan Singer's intriguing but awkward debut, *Public Access* – never lets up. It begins with the explosion of a docked ship, before one of the two survivors goes on to detail, to the cops and the audience, the events of the previous six weeks that led him to the vessel. It's a yarn involving five criminals unwittingly brought together in a police cell due to one thing they have in common: the master criminal Keyser Soze, who may or may not exist... Working from Christopher McQuarrie's marvellously tortuous, colourful script, Singer creates a classy, thought-provoking mystery that is pleasingly old-fashioned (the settings, characters and sassy mood recall Hammett and Chandler) and absolutely modern in the sly, slightly self-conscious play it makes with myth and methods of storytelling. GA

Utamaro o Meguru Go-nin no Onna

see Five Women Around Utamaro

Utu

(Geoff Murphy, 1983, NZ) Anzac Wallace, Bruno Lawrence, Tim Elliott, Kelly Johnson, Wi Kuki Kaa, Tania Bristowe.
104 min.
This does for the 19th century Land Wars in New Zealand what *Ulzana's Raid* did for the contemporary Apache campaign in the USA, making it clear that the white man's destiny to conquer new and fertile corners of the earth was totally irreconcilable with the interests and culture of the previous inhabitants. The story of a series of revenge raids by Maori rebel Te Wheke is violent in every sense: in the action of many scenes; in the abrupt changes of tone, from the horror of the opening massacre, through spaghetti Western-style confrontations, to the almost mystical ending; and in the violence it does to the idea of liberal democratic understanding as a universal panacea. There are rough passages and uncertain performances, but both Lawrence as a sort of serio-comic Eastwood figure, and Wallace as the brooding, mercurial Te Wheke, are excellent. A film both fascinating and disconcerting, all but bringing off the gamble of combining a serious look at history with a thrills'n'spills action movie. NR

U Turn

(Oliver Stone, 1997, US/Fr) Sean Penn, Jennifer Lopez, Nick Nolte, Powers Boothe, Claire Danes, Joaquin Phoenix, Billy Bob Thornton, Jon Voight.
125 min.
When his Mustang breaks down in Superior, Arizona, gambler Bobby Cooper (Penn) has no idea how low his luck has sunk. He picks up the lusty Grace (Lopez), or she picks up him – either way, her husband Jake (Nolte) isn't happy. In fact, he has his own proposition for the stranger. He wants his wife dead and reckons Bobby's the man for the job. He might be, too, if Grace can't make a better offer. John Ridley's script (from his book *Stray Dogs*) affects the tortuous contrivances of a malign and witty fate, in the manner of James M Cain, Jim Thompson, or more recently *Red Rock West*. But it's this affectation which kills the film. Stone directs with the same inebriated three-second attention span he adopted for *Natural Born Killers*, experimenting with different film gauges, stocks and speeds every other shot. To be fair, going by Ennio Morricone's spaghetti-and-meatballs score, Stone is fishing for laughs much of the time. Penn turns in a crisp, unfussy comic performance, Lopez vamps like a scorpion in heat, Nolte sustains a pretty good John Huston impression, and Thornton is mighty peculiar as the mechanic from hell. TCh

U2 Rattle and Hum

(Phil Joanou, 1988, US) Bono, The Edge, Adam Clayton, Larry Mullen, BB King.
99 min.
Joanou perpetuates the image of U2 as Eastwood-style Men with No Name: dressed like extras from a spaghetti Western, in interview they fumble over answers with brows furrowed as if words can't express their depth of feeling. The implication is that U2's music speaks for them. A shame, then, that they don't get down to it earlier. U2's place as rock regents is emphasised by a visit to Graceland, with drummer Larry Mullen contemplating Elvis's grave, and by a wonderful moment in which singer Bono shows BB King how to play a U2 song. A gospel version of 'I Still Haven't Found What I'm Looking For' provides a rare glimpse of the band's feeling for their craft, but for the most part the documentary footage is unsatisfactory, saying nothing new about the men behind the myth. The live footage, shot at one of the later American 'Joshua Tree' concerts, is another matter. Seamlessly edited, the camera entirely unobtrusive, and the sound impeccably produced by Jimmy Iovine, this gives you a front row seat at a textbook stadium show. Bono's visionary poetic preaching, which takes in a little Irish/American history and a brave tirade against the IRA's Enniskillen massacre before launching into the utterly inspired 'Sunday Bloody Sunday', is something you can stomach or not, but it won't leave you unmoved. EP

V

Voyager

Vacances de M. Hulot, Les (Monsieur Hulot's Holiday/ Mr Hulot's Holiday)

(Jacques Tati, 1952, Fr) Jacques Tati, Nathalie Pascaud, Michèle Rolla, Louis Perrault, André Dubois, Valentine Camax.
91 min. b/w.
Tati's most consistently enjoyable comedy, a gentle portrait of the clumsy, well-meaning Hulot on vacation in a provincial seaside resort. The quiet, delicately observed slapstick here works with far more hits than misses, although in comparison with, say, Keaton, Tati's cold detachment from his characters seems to result in a decided lack of insight into human behaviour. But at least in contrast to later works like *Playtime* and *Traffic*, there's enough dramatic structure to make it more than simply a series of one-off gags. GA

Vacas (Cows)

(Julio Medem, 1992, Sp) Emma Suárez, Carmelo Gómez, Ana Torrent, Karra Elejalde.
96 min.
The second Carlist war, 1875. Panicking under fire, Basque woodcutter Irigibel drops to the earth and smears himself with blood gushing hot from the neck of his mortally wounded neighbour, Mendiluze. The battle over, he crawls out from a cart-load of the dead, naked but unremarked, except by a curious, solitary cow. Medem's trenchant, daring directorial debut cuts through the decades like an axe. 1905: the neighbours' sons feud and Irigibel embarks on a clandestine affair with his counterpart's sister. 1915: her bastard son Peru grows up alongside his half-sister, while the boy's parents elope to America and take him with them. 1936: Peru returns to photograph the Spanish Civil War. Medem is unexpectedly impatient with that old standby of Spanish cinema, the epic historical melodrama. His movie is swift and urgent – it's closer to Jane Campion than Carlos Saura – and he has a sharp eye for *la vida loca*. Captured at moments of crisis and decision, his characters are forced to confront the precariousness of their rural existence and the great black hole of their own mortality. Imperviously, implacably bovine – it's somehow typical of this startlingly original picture that cows should carry the bulk of the symbolism. TCh

Vacation from Marriage

see Perfect Strangers

Vagabonde (Sans Toit ni Loi)

(Agnés Varda, 1985, Fr) Sandrine Bonnaire, Macha Méril, Yolande Moreau, Stéphane Freiss, Marthe Jarnias, Joël Fosse.
106 min.
Varda's lyrical requiem to Mona, a teenage tramp discovered dead from exposure, shows (in flashback) her last few months and her effect on people she met briefly and variously: a smart middle class professor (Méril) mesmerised and repelled by the fierce young woman, peasant drudges in whom she inspires romantic dreams of freedom, a dour ageing *soixante-huitard*, now the most conventional of them all. Varda boldly explains nothing about Mona, who simply holds up an unflattering mirror to others' follies, prejudices, and fears. Spare, poetic images of the mid-winter Midi are offset by the warmth and vigour of the well-chosen, largely non-professional cast, with a formidable central performance from Sandrine Bonnaire. SJo

Vaghe Stelle dell'Orsa (Of a Thousand Delights/Sandra)

(Luchino Visconti, 1965, It) Claudia Cardinale, Jean Sorel, Michael Craig, Marie Bell, Renzo Ricci.
100 min. b/w.
Visconti's retelling of the Electra story starts with Sandra/Electra (Cardinale) returning to her ancestral home in Italy – and reviving an intimate involvement with her brother (Sorel) which troubles her naive American husband (Craig) – on the eve of an official ceremony commemorating the death of her Jewish father in a Nazi concentration camp. As ever with Visconti, he is ambivalently drawn to the decadent society he is ostensibly criticising; and Armando Nannuzzi's camera lovingly caresses the creaking old mansion, set in a landscape of crumbling ruins, where the incestuous siblings determine to wreak revenge on the mother (Bell) and stepfather (Ricci) who suppos-

edly denounced their father. Something like a Verdi opera without the music, the result may not quite achieve tragedy, but it *looks* marvellous. The title, culled from a poem by Leopardi, has been better rendered as 'Twinkling Stars of the Bear'. TM

Valdez Horses, The

see Valdez il Mezzosangue

Valdez il Mezzosangue (Chino/The Valdez Horses/ Valdez the Halfbreed)

(John Sturges, 1973, It/Sp/Fr) Charles Bronson, Jill Ireland, Vincent Van Patten, Marcel Bozzuffi, Melissa Chimenti, Fausto Tozzi, Ettore Manni.
97 min.
Bronson suffers from galloping symbolism as Valdez, a wild horse-taming Mexican halfbreed representing different things to different people. Overall, he is the mustang, caught in a wild West which is being tamed and fenced in by white settlers. To Jamie, a young white boy, he is manhood, tough and tender. To the white English lady (Ireland), he is mustang again. And to her brother, he is contaminating dirty devilry. The wild and the tame correlate with the old and the new, against the backdrop of a magnificent herd of wild horses, led by a superb stud. Despite a few dodgy moments when one really fears for Valdez' co-optability by Ireland's well-kept fragility, the film maintains its contradictory stance right through to a bitter-sweet ending. Valdez leaves, sans wife, sans house, but on his own terms, and after ensuring that if he can't tame the wild horses no one else will. MV

Valdez Is Coming

(Edwin Sherin, 1970, US) Burt Lancaster, Susan Clark, Jon Cypher, Barton Heyman, Richard Jordan, Frank Silvera, Hector Elizondo, Phil Brown.
90 min.
A fairly impressive Western adapted from Elmore Leonard's novel, with Lancaster as the Mexican Valdez, working part-time as a shotgun guard for a powerful rancher (Cypher) in the South West, who is forced to kill a negro in self-defence while on the rancher's business. Mindful of his status as a local constable, he demands compensation for the dead man's widow; and when this is refused, aware that Cypher was up to no good in the first place, he declares a private war. It's a little cramped, but Sherin's background as a Broadway director (this was his first movie) serves him well in his lucid delineation of the characters, while Lancaster brings a subtle ambiguity to his central role as the outsider-idealist fighting against unfeeling prejudice and materialism. GA

Valdez the Halfbreed

see Valdez il Mezzosangue

Vale Abraão

see Abraham Valley

Valentino

(Ken Russell, 1977, GB) Rudolf Nureyev, Leslie Caron, Michelle Phillips, Carol Kane, Felicity Kendal, Seymour Cassel, Peter Vaughan, Huntz Hall, Alfred Marks, Anton Diffring.
127 min.
Structured as a series of flashbacks from Valentino's funeral to his early years in America, the first hour or so of this biopic is Russell's sanest and most controlled work in several years, despite its hollow cynicism. About halfway through, though, the movie degenerates into a series of typical Russell hyperboles. There is also a shift in tone from comedy to pathos, resulting in a dismal drop in entertainment value. Nureyev (in his debut) dances agreeably often, but his acting is hopelessly under-directed. TR

Valerie and Her Week of Wonders (Valerie a Tyden Divu)

(Jaromil Jireš, 1970, Czech) Jaroslava Schallerová, Helena Anýzková, Petr Kopriva, Jiri Prymek, Jan Kluzák.
77 min.

Shot in the lyrical *Elvira Madigan* mode, this celebrates the 'first stirrings of adolescence' of a beautiful young girl in a vaguely-defined Transylvanian townscape sometime in the last century. A student of folklore and mythology could perhaps detect a logical thread in the continuous sequence of vampires, devils, black magic, ritual and dance that the film presents, but for most people it will be a simpler and undemanding pleasure to sit back and be agreeably surprised as the images unfold. There is no clearly-defined story; the film's logic is that of the subconscious, its images those of the Gothic fairytale and the psychiatrist's couch, and its overall effect is stunning. JC

Valiant Ones, The (Zhonglie Tu)

(King Hu, 1974, HK) Roy Chiao, Pai Ying, Hsu Feng, Zhao Lei, Tu Guangqi, Liu Jiang.
106 min.
No surprise that a movie which reunites the director/writer and three stars of *A Touch of Zen* should offer hitherto untasted pleasures. *The Valiant Ones* delivers as an exemplary piece of Ming Dynasty Chinese historiography, and at the same time as a daringly innovative action adventure, quite different in tone and visual style from the pyrotechnics of *A Touch of Zen*. An enfeebled emperor appoints a loyal official to tackle the problem of Sino-Japanese pirate bands who are pillaging the south coast of China; the official assembles a team of peasants and intellectuals, and plans a war of strategies, not confrontations. Plot developments, however, occur between scenes rather than in them. The film dreams a series of martial set pieces, with increasingly abstract action once again derived from the Peking Opera tradition. The glittering images include a chess game that suddenly becomes a battle plan, a silent woman with heightened sight and hearing, and a rumbustious zen archer. TR

Vallée, La (The Valley)

(Barbet Schroeder, 1972, Fr) Jean-Pierre Kalfon, Bulle Ogier, Michael Gothard, Valérie Lagrange, Jérôme Beauvarlet, Monique Giraudy.
114 min.
Journey to the Centre of a Cliché. Assorted Anglo-French hippies set off in search of a 'lost' valley in uncharted New Guinea, accompanied by the spaciest Pink Floyd music, and expose assorted bourgeois neuroses en route. Nestor Almendros' landscape photography is succulent. TR

Valley, The (Volgy)

(Tamás Rényi, 1969, Hun) Gábor Koncz, István Avar, Tibor Molnár, György Bardi, János Koltai.
76 min. b/w.
An arresting, ambitious anti-war drama, shot in widescreen and stunning black-and-white, about a group of army deserters (from an unspecified conflict) who seek refuge in a remote village populated entirely by women and girls (their menfolk are presumably in war service). The women are persuaded to let them stay, an act that carries a severe penalty... The film is as interested in sexual politics and the survival of traditional (and repressive) social forms as it is in its overall pacifist thrust, and sets up a series of remarkable tableaux (the envious, hardened faces of the black-clad elders) and formal, almost ritualist, set pieces (a sexually frenzied dance between one of the deserters and the virgin white-dressed girls, for instance). There is a pained, poetic quality to the film and its imagery that produces a strong pull on the imagination, but the (deliberate) omission of specific references (what is the film-maker saying, if anything, about the Hungary of 1969?) leads to a slightly disconcerting obscurity. WH

Valley of Gwangi, The

(James O'Connolly, 1968, US) James Franciscus, Gila Golan, Richard Carlson, Laurence Naismith, Freda Jackson, Gustavo Rojo.
95 min.
A Charles Schneer/Ray Harryhausen fantasy for Dynamation special effects fans only: a reworking of the *King Kong* structure that has turn-of-the-century Wild West show boss Franciscus venturing into Mexico's Forbidden Valley in search of prehistoric specimens. A formula writing credit for William Bast, one of the very few

screenwriters to have been characterised on screen: by Michael Brandon in the telemovie *James Dean*, which tracked the friendship between the actor and Bast from UCLA to Dean's death. PT

Valley of Song
(aka Men Are Children Twice)
(Gilbert Gunn, 1953, GB) Mervyn Johns, Clifford Evans, Maureen Swanson, John Fraser, Rachel Thomas, Rachel Roberts, Kenneth Williams, Alun Owen.
74 min. b/w.
Who will sing the contralto role in *The Messiah*? Two families, the Davies and the Lloyds, fall to feuding in this small-town Welsh comedy based on Cliff Gordon's successful radio play *Choir Practice*. Sub-Ealing whimsy memorable for Rachel Roberts' debut as gossip Bessie the Milk. GM

Valley of the Dolls
(Mark Robson, 1967, US) Barbara Parkins, Patty Duke, Paul Burke, Sharon Tate, Susan Hayward, Tony Scotti, Martin Milner, Charles Drake, Alex Davion, Lee Grant.
123 min.
Jacqueline Susann's 'exposé' of Hollywood gets the cliché-ridden treatment it deserves from Robson. Parkins, Tate, Duke and Hayward are the actresses whose career vicissitudes take us on the round tour of drink, drugs, sex, disillusion, infidelity, and clawing up to the top or sliding down to the bottom. That said, the film is regarded in some quarters as a marvellous piece of camp. The songs, curiously, are by André and Dory Previn. CPe

Valmont
(Milos Forman, 1989, Fr/GB) Colin Firth, Annette Bening, Meg Tilly, Fairuza Balk, Sian Phillips, Jeffrey Jones, Henry Thomas, Fabia Drake, TP McKenna, Ian McNeice.
137 min.
Comparisons may be odious, but here they are unavoidable. *Valmont* and Stephen Frears' *Dangerous Liaisons* were both based on the same 18th century French novel, and shot at the same time; but the latter's phenomenal success quite eclipsed Forman's more lavish effort, and its British release was held back. The basic story is the same: the Marquise de Merteuil and the Vicomte de Valmont spin an intricate web of deception, using sex as a weapon and destroying lives for fun. But the claustrophobic interiors of *Dangerous Liaisons* are here replaced with horseback rides and landscaped gardens, beautifully shot by Miroslav Ondricek; and where the acid cynicism of Glenn Close and John Malkovich provided a clash of titans, *Valmont* gives us, in the youthful enthusiasm of Bening (too naive) and Firth (too nice), little more than a childish spat. It's a warm, energetic, humorous film, with some excellent ensemble playing; but the cruelty and psychological complexity are lost, and the ensuing tragedy has little resonance. DW

Valseuses, Les
(Going Places/Making It)
(Bertrand Blier, 1974, Fr) Gérard Depardieu, Patrick Dewaere, Miou-Miou, Jeanne Moreau, Jacques Chailleux, Michel Peurelon, Brigitte Fossey, Isabelle Huppert.
118 min.
A huge hit in France, about two youths waving a finger at society. Their pursuits include car theft, robbery, three-way sex, and general impulsive offensiveness, while their development is limited to the degree of selectivity they start showing towards their compulsive fucking. Forsaking a girl who can't have an orgasm, they cultivate an older woman just out of prison, on the assumption that she must be dying for it (which she is, literally). With a couple of deaths sending them on the run, their rambling delinquency takes on rather more romantic fugitive connotations. The physical robustness and frankness prevails (the film deliberately evokes the sounds and smells of sex), but as the characters develop into something approaching human beings, much of the bite is lost. It ends relatively tame: an unfocused comedy whose sense of the outlandish extends little further than screwing on the back seat of a Rolls. A lot of good points, though. CPe

Value for Money
(Ken Annakin, 1955, GB) John Gregson, Diana Dors, Susan Stephen, Derek Farr, Ernest Thesiger, Joan Hickson, Donald Pleasence, Leslie Phillips.
93 min.
Despite inheriting his old man's millions, rag magnate Gregson still counts every penny, so much so that fiancée Stephen turns down his marriage proposal, unable to face a life of drudgery as his replacement housekeeper. Rejection leaves the moneybags skinflint to drag his sorrows down to London, where Cup Final night throws him together with gold-digging chorus gal Ruthine West (Dors) who knows a good thing when she sees it. Cliché piles on cliché in this moderate '50s comedy spun out from a novel by Derrick Boothroyd. TJ

Vamos a Matar, Compañeros!
see *Compañeros*

Vamp
(Richard Wenk, 1986, US) Chris Makepeace, Sandy Baron, Robert Rusler, Dedee Pfeiffer, Gedde Watanabe, Grace Jones, Billy Drago.
94 min.
Today's vampires are afflicted with ingrowing toenails and a terrible skin complaint. That's life after death for you. That's also Grace Jones, astutely cast as an exotic dancer whose dialogue is confined to snarling through curled canines. Grace struts her stuff in a seedy dive called 'After Dark', where three freshmen fetch up when they go in search of a stripper for the frat party. The ladies of the night turn out to be unexpectedly toothsome, and the moral of the tale is clear: nice young juvenile leads should not go slumming on the nasty side of town, particularly when it is infested with albino punk gangs, murderous hotel elevators, gruesome garbage, and dead people. AB

Vampira (aka Old Dracula)
(Clive Donner, 1974, GB) David Niven, Teresa Graves, Peter Bayliss, Jennie Linden, Nicky Henson, Linda Hayden, Bernard Bresslaw.
88 min.
Clive Donner had been living in limbo since the famous disaster of *Alfred the Great*, but making a movie like *Vampira* is no way to set any man's career to rights. It's a horror spoof with no sense of style and no sense of humour, for which Jeremy Lloyd's infantile script is as much to blame as Donner's slap-happy direction. Count Dracula's beloved Vampira is mistakenly brought back to life black rather than white, and Dracula (Niven) runs amok in a still-swinging London trying to find an antidote – a plotline which provides sufficient excuse for jokes and wheezes that one thought had gone out with *The Munsters*. One consolation is that the movie wasn't called 'Fangs Ain't Wot They Used To Be'. GB

Vampire at Midnight
(Gregory McClatchy, 1987, US) Jason Williams, Gustav Vintas, Lesley Milne, Jeanie Moore, Esther Alise, Ted Hamaguchi, Robert Random.
93 min.
Count Drac (Vintas) is unalive and well and living in Beverly Hills. He is a hypnotherapist. As might be expected, there's a lot of necking of one form or another. The barely existent plot is padded out with a sequence of dirty dancing and several pairs of naked breasts. Also, the dumb detective (Williams) gets handcuffed to his bed and raped by a lustful colleague. It's OK, she's a woman. Scares don't come into it, and the general corn-flakiness of the whole enterprise just goes to show that old Terror Teeth was one of the very first cereal killers. MS

Vampire Bat, The
(Frank R Strayer, 1933, US) Lionel Atwill, Melvyn Douglas, Fay Wray, Dwight Frye, Maude Eburne, George E Stone.
71 min. b/w.
As creaky as an old church door, but with some of the same antique charm, this is a B horror picture shot on the village sets of Universal's *Frankenstein* (1931), and using the interiors from *The Old Dark House* (1932). Bat-loving village idiot Frye is suspected of a series of vampyric murders, but when obsessive doctor Atwill's

soon-to-be-married assistant (Wray) stumbles on the truth, she's menaced by the real culprit. New wine in old bottles, but hardly vintage. NF

Vampire Beast
Craves Blood, The
see Blood Beast Terror, The

Vampire Circus, The
(Robert Young, 1971, GB) Adrienne Corri, Laurence Payne, Thorley Walters, John Moulder Brown, Lynne Frederick, Elizabeth Seal.
87 min.
The circus of the title is an evocative 19th century troupe which weaves magic spells around a naive woodland village in Serbia. For a while, Young (here making his first feature) manages to use this basic premise to establish a delicate fairy-tale atmosphere, with a genuine sense of strangeness as the circus people gradually take over the imaginative life of the community (isolated from the rest of the world by plague), changing back and forth into animals nightly before their eyes; and he is greatly aided by some unusually restrained performances (from the girls in particular). But sadly the whole fragile effect eventually gives way to formula, and as clichés mount, the fashionably explicit sexuality of the vampires jars badly against the rest of the film. Lines like 'One lust feeds another' can't disguise the awkwardness of the transition from vampirism to sex. DP

Vampire in Brooklyn
(Wes Craven, 1995, US) Eddie Murphy, Angela Bassett, Allen Payne, Kadeem Hardison, John Witherspoon, Zakes Mokae, Joanna Cassidy.
102 min.
Introducing classy production values and comedy to the blackvampire cycle that surfaced in the '70s, Murphy plays a modern debonair Nosferatu (as well as adding some unnecessary icing to the cake by impersonating an alcoholic preacher and an Italian hood). Caribbean-born Maximillian sails to New York in search of his unwitting blood sister, troubled cop Rita (Bassett). With the help of reluctant ghoul Julius (Hardison), he tries to seduce her with promises of eternal life and untold riches. Things get complicated when Maximillian falls for his blood relative, and she in turn rejects her shy, sensitive police partner (Payne) in favour of the suave vamp. Murphy's choice of director was shrewd: making good use of his biggest budget to date, Craven brings his knowledge of the genre to bear, allowing time for humour while ensuring that the requisite shocks arrive on cue. Bassett brings a little extra to her role as a woman torn between the calling of her blood and fear for her eternal soul. There's some scary fun to be had here. NF

Vampire Lovers, The
(Roy Ward Baker, 1970, GB) Ingrid Pitt, Pippa Steele, Madeleine Smith, Peter Cushing, George Cole, Dawn Addams, Douglas Wilmer, Jon Finch, Kate O'Mara, Ferdy Mayne.
91 min.
The film which made Ingrid Pitt a major horror movie cult figure (she plays a voracious lesbian vampire). Based on Sheridan Le Fanu's *Carmilla*, it is well mounted and enjoyable, with solid performances: the pre-credits sequence, in particular, has a dreamy beauty. But some of the action is a bit flat; and overall it marks the point at which vampirism in British movies became so overtly erotic that the films virtually ceased to be about anything except sex. Later examples of the strain were to become terribly monotonous. DP

Vampires, Les
(Louis Feuillade, 1915, Fr) Musidora, Edouard Mathe, Marcel Levesque, Jean Aymé, Louis Leubas.
440 min. (approx). b/w.
1915: Slaughter at Gallipoli; first use of gas on the Western Front; *Lusitania* sunk. And as diversion, this serial saga (in 10 episodes) of a band of robbers whose principals include Satanas, who keeps a howitzer behind the fireplace and a bomb under his top hat, and Irma Vep, the notorious anagram, to whom Olivier Assayas rendered homage 80 years later. There's a hero (a resolute reporter), but all the interest goes to Irma and Co – their heists, their feuds with a rival gang and with the

agents of law and order, all conducted by means of slaughter, gassing and sinking, on a scale and insouciance appropriate to the time. There's a comic strip aspect ('Episode 1: The Severed Head'), a roundelay of disguises, kidnappings, secret codes and acrobatic getaways. And simultaneously there's the poetry of the grey deserted Paris streets, our consciousness that the trenches are only a bus ride away; and the idea of a separate world of mischief and anarchy, situated just beyond the everyday. It's possible to overstate the extent to which all this is a bunch of fun: if shown, as it often is, in one great unnatural marathon, it can be sheer torture. Best viewed on tape. BBa

Vampires in Venice (Nosferatu a Venezia)

(Augusto Caminito, 1988, It) Klaus Kinski, Christopher Plummer, Barbara De Rossi, Yorgo Voyagis, Donald Pleasence, Anne Knecht, Elvire Audray.
90 min.
Nosferatu vanished, we're told, from plague-stricken Venice during the Carnival of 1786. Called back to the city by a present-day Transylvanian princess, he compels an old lady to impale herself on a railing, ravishes a young woman in a church and causes a vampire hunter (Plummer) to jump despairingly into a canal. Kinski's Nosferatu longs wearily for death, but this will come only when a virgin surrenders to him willingly. The princess obliges. Unpersuasive. JPy

Vampire's Kiss

(Robert Bierman, 1988, US) Nicolas Cage, Maria Conchita Alonso, Jennifer Beals, Elizabeth Ashley, Kasi Lemmons, Bob Lujan, Jessica Lundy.
103 min.
Cage gives a manically mannered performance as Peter Loew, a literary agent whose obsession with a missing contract pushes him over the edge. Increasingly alienated, he alternates between harassing his timid secretary (Alonso), clubbing all night, and visiting his shrink (Ashley). One night, in a moment of orgasmic pleasure, the mysterious Rachel (Beals) bites his neck. Obsessed with the idea that he is a vampire's victim, he starts pulling down shades, hunches over in a grotesque parody of Max Schreck's Nosferatu, and – sporting plastic fangs – stalks the dark streets and pulsing discos in search of necks to bite. Cage's excessive acting style has been called neo-expressionist, a term that might also be applied to the moody, burnished colours of Stefan Czapsky's photography, which transforms New York into the Gothic city of Loew's distorted imagination. A viciously funny study of yuppie alienation, scripted by Joseph Minion (who wrote *After Hours*), Bierman's striking first feature leaves one trembling between corrosive laughter, edgy terror, and a residual sadness at Loew's pitiful plight. NF

Vampire Thrills

see Frisson des Vampires, Le

Vampyr

(Carl Theodor Dreyer, 1932, Ger) Julian West i.e. Nicolas de Gunzburg, Henriette Gérard, Jan Hieronimko, Maurice Schutz, Sybille Schmitz, Rena Mandel.
83 min. b/w.
Based on Sheridan Le Fanu's story *Carmilla* and shot in France using real locations, *Vampyr* is one of the first psychological horror films. Helped by a dream-like logic, the film takes its main character on a voyage through light and darkness to a point where he can imagine his own burial (disturbingly shot from a subjective point of view). With the help of Rudolph Maté's luminous photography, Dreyer creates a film of great beauty. Often the close-ups are particularly haunting, but the main achievement is the correctness of each shot, and their relationship to each other; notably, in the climactic juxtapositions of the trapped doctor being buried alive in the mill, and of the young couple in a boat, inching their way to safety through the fog. CPe

Van, The

(Stephen Frears, 1996, Ire/GB) Colm Meaney, Donal O'Kelly, Ger Ryan, Caroline Rothwell, Neili Conroy, Ruaidhri Conroy, Jack Lynch.
100 min.

In the winter of '89, Bimbo (O'Kelly), a baker from Dublin's Barrytown, is made redundant, but the last thing he wants is to loaf all day in a pub like his jobless mates. The mobile chip-and-burger business beckons. By the spring he and Larry (Meaney) have gone into partnership, buying a filthy run-down van in the hope of cashing in on the euphoria igniting Ireland during the 1990 World Cup. It's tough work, but both men's families chip in. Indeed, Larry's so keen to keep his own brood in work that Bimbo sometimes feels the need to remind him who's boss. The final film adaptation of Roddy Doyle's Barrytown trilogy is a jauntily enjoyable comedy about unemployment. Occasionally the direction is too determinedly feel-good, but as the film proceeds and the men's partnership becomes increasingly strained, the jokes are underpinned by something more substantial: it gradually becomes clear that Larry's larky ways are partly symptomatic of irresponsibility, partly a defence against despondency; and that friendship depends on some sort of equality. Fun, on the whole. GA

Vanessa

(Hubert Frank, 1976, WGer) Olivia Pascal, Anton Diffring, Günter Clemens, Uschi Zech, Eva Eden.
91 min.
The virginal Vanessa – 'sexual plaything of lewd lechers', as the expensive bilingual publicity handout cheerfully announces – is in fact a putty-faced actress (an animated centrefold) whisked to Hong Kong for the usual wearisome round of soft-core shenanigans. The fun includes a bout of love-making in a barn beneath a cascade of grain, and in conclusion, the devilish Diffring flaying our heroine with an understandably half-hearted lack of conviction. JPy

Van Gogh

(Maurice Pialat, 1991, Fr) Jacques Dutronc, Alexandra London, Bernard Le Coq, Gérard Sety, Corinne Bourdon, Elsa Zylberstein, Leslie Azoulai, Jacques Vidal.
159 min.
This stunningly photographed and skilfully acted film uses an accretion of naturalistic detail to present an emotionally restrained but utterly compelling account of the last three months of Van Gogh's life. Living in Auvers-sur-Oise with his sensitive and knowledgeable patron Gachet (Sety), Van Gogh (Dutronc) works quietly and steadily, meanwhile flirting with Gachet's precocious daughter Marguerite (London). However, his ill health, a brief return to the debauchery of brothels and drink, and his irrational resentment of his brother Theo's failure to sell his work, provoke erratic swings from brooding introspection to frustrated anger. Since Pialat has no desire to canonise the artist, there is no attempt to trace the origins and development of his 'creative genius'; nor, avoiding the hazards of biopic cliché, does he seek to illuminate these dark corners of his subject's troubled soul. In the leading role, Dutronc has exactly the right quality of physical frailty and stooped sadness to complement Pialat's beautiful, poignant images. NF

Vanishing, The

(George Sluizer, 1993, US) Jeff Bridges, Kiefer Sutherland, Nancy Travis, Sandra Bullock, Lisa Eichhorn, Park Overall.
110 min.
In directing this misjudged, compromised Hollywood remake of his Dutch-French thriller, Sluizer has held down his waywardly inspired child with studio and scriptwriter Todd Graff have lobotomised it with a sharp, cruel scalpel. Worse, by replacing cerebral dread with knee-jerk reaction, this depressing travesty taints forever our memory of the devastating original. Shifting emphasis from Sutherland's impotent obsession with his missing girlfriend to abductor Bridges' coldly calculating psychopathology, the film-makers pander to the lowest common denominator – beefing up Bridges' misconceived role as the villain and transforming Sutherland into an active, albeit perversely motivated hero. NF

Vanishing, The (Spoorloos)

(George Sluizer, 1988, Neth/Fr) Bernard-Pierre Donnadieu, Gene Bervoets, Johanna Ter Stegge, Gwen Eckhaus, Bernadette Le Saché.
106 min.

An unforgettably chilling psychodrama which twists the slenderest of plots into a hellish exploration of human potential. On a driving holiday in France, a young Dutch couple, Saskia and Rex (Ter Steege and Bervoets), stop at a service station to refuel; as Rex waits, Saskia walks to a nearby toilet, and vanishes without trace. Three years later, an embittered Rex finds himself drawn into a nightmarish relationship with Saskia's awesomely mundane abductor, Raymond Lemorne (Donnadieu), who via taunting postcards promises to reveal the fate of his lost love. Consumed by his desire for knowledge, Rex resolves to confront his nemesis and end the Nietzschean conflict of wills in which he is embroiled...Adapted from Tim Krabbé's novel *The Golden Egg*, this is a beautifully understated study of obsession that investigates the edges of rationality and the destructive capacity of idealistic devotion. at the heart of its icy spell is Donnadieu's utterly plausible evocation of everyday madness, a resolutely banal picture of evil. Sluizer's direction is seamless throughout, effortlessly juggling domesticity and damnation as it ploughs inexorably towards an appaling *dénouement*. MK

Vanishing Corporal, The

see Caporal Epinglé, Le

Vanishing Point

(Richard Sarafian, 1971, GB) Barry Newman, Cleavon Little, Dean Jagger, Victoria Medlin, Paul Koslo, Bob Donner, Karl Swenson, Severn Darden.
107 min.
Having just driven 1,500 miles non-stop from California to Colorado, Sarafian's sullenly uncommunicative anti-hero pauses long enough to grab a supply of bennies, accept a bet that he won't make it back in 15 hours, and zooms off again. It's a marvellous idea: a strange, obsessive odyssey by a man driven like the lemmings by an inexplicable need to keep on going. Then the script starts explaining in embarrassing memory flashes, the echoes of *Easy Rider* multiply, bits of mysticism and a blind black DJ called Super-Soul are injected, and the woodenness of both direction and Newman's performance becomes increasingly apparent. Marvellously shot on location by John A Alonzo, though. TM

Vanya on 42nd Street

(Louis Malle, 1994, US) Wallace Shawn, Julianne Moore, André Gregory, George Gaynes, Brooke Smith, Larry Pine, Phoebe Brand, Lynn Cohen, Jerry Mayer, Madhur Jaffrey.
120 min.
A select audience gathers for André Gregory's workshop production of *Uncle Vanya* in Broadway's crumbling New Amsterdam theatre. The staging is sparse – a table, a few chairs – and Malle's direction is as discreetly self-effacing as Gregory's, shifting from *cinéma vérité* in the establishing sequence to a more intimate style as the drama casts its spell (intervals are respected with the minimum of fuss). Thus we can concentrate on David Mamet's fluent, sensitive adaptation and some (unexpectedly) enthralling performances: Shawn as the wretched, resentful Vanya; Gaynes – a long way from the 'Police Academy' – as the Professor; and Julianne Moore as his lovely, long-suffering wife Yelena. Moore is simply outstanding, composed and modulated, shouldering her companions' pain with a compassion and forbearance that's also a kind of defeat. Chekhov's astonishingly modern *fin de siècle* concerns are expressed with a rare and vivid clarity: ennui, environment, old age, the difficulty of change, and the disappointments of love. There's more power here than in all the multi-million dollar fireworks of Hollywood. TCh

Varieté (Variety/Vaudeville)

(EA Dupont, 1925, Ger) Emil Jannings, Lya de Putti, Warwick Ward, Mady Delschaft, Georg John, Kurt Gerron.
9,331 ft. b/w.
Dupont's most celebrated film (it was one of the most famous films in the world in 1925) unfolds in a long series of flashbacks from a prison straight out of a Van Gogh painting: prisoner No 28 (Jannings) with his back to the camera more often than not) is granted remission, and in return tells the story of his crime to the governor. The story itself is a banal triangle melodrama: a

trapeze duo in the Berlin music-hall becomes a trio, and the lady switches gentlemen, driving the cuckold to murder his rival. The treatment, though, is something else again. Impressionistic lighting, lingering expressionist imagery, and giddily mobile camerawork are all pushed to unprecedented extremes, like Murnau on speed. Hard to take it too seriously, but the bravura style and Lya de Putti's coquettish performance remain as impressive as ever. TR

Variety

(Bette Gordon, 1983, US) Sandy McLeod, Luis Guzman, Will Patton, Nan Goldin, Richard Davidson.
100 min.
Written by blood-and-guts flavour of the month Kathy Acker, and directed by New York feminist film-maker Gordon, this boldly goes into feminine response to pornography – and the results are by no means predictable. Christine (McLeod) takes a job as a ticket vendor at a porn cinema; she finds herself slowly drawn towards both the ambience depicted on the screen and to one of the older clients, Louis (Davidson), a suave shark with apparent Mafia connections. She follows him around, eavesdropping on his world of very masculine power and money, while simultaneously indulging her curiosity in the equally voyeuristic roles played out in sex shops and movie houses. The elision of the two worlds is a good device, and well handled, for is not every sexual adventure also a form of detection? The film is not prescriptive in its designs, nor is it remotely prurient. A brave foray across a minefield. CPea

Variety Lights

see Luci del Varietà

Vassa

(Gleb Panfilov, 1983, USSR) Inna Churikova, Vadim Medvedev, Nikolai Skorobogatov, Valentina Yakunina, Olga Mashnaya, Yana Poplavskaya.
136 min.
For the wondrously sour-mouthed Vassa Zheleznova (Churikova), troubles come not in threes but in great swinging clusters. Her husband is accused of child-molesting, her brother is a lush who has got the maid pregnant, one of her daughters is 'wrong in the head', while the other is scampering through puberty towards nymphean alcoholism. Add murder, suicide and hefty dollops of greed, and you have Maxim Gorky's version of Dynasty on the Volga, with the ripples extending out to embrace imminent revolution. Set in 1913, this presents a portrait of a society fit for rupture, viewed with sad disgust. Panfilov wisely never forces the pace, letting the richness of the piece come through in a host of finely tailored performances. An unexpected delight. JP

Vaudeville

see Varieté

Vault of Horror

(Roy Ward Baker, 1973, GB) Daniel Massey, Anna Massey, Terry-Thomas, Glynis Johns, Curt Jürgens, Dawn Addams, Michael Craig, Edward Judd, Tom Baker, Denholm Elliott.
86 min.
Amicus' sixth portmanteau film. Following up Tales from the Crypt with another selection from the William Gaines horror comics, it simply slaps down its Grand Guignol climaxes after hopefully buttressing them with dreary slabs of plot and chatter. The result is paralysingly pedestrian, despite the fact that each of the stories harbours an ingeniously ghoulish conceit (like the suburban wife driven to murder, and an impeccably tidy disposal of the corpse, by her house-proud husband's constant nagging about her housekeeping). As tedious as anything is the framing device whereby the five heroes (Massey, Terry-Thomas, Jürgens, Craig and Baker) confide their recurring nightmares in turn after delivery by lift to a no-exit room in the basement of a skyscraper. TM

Veillées d'Armes
(The Troubles We've Seen)

(Marcel Ophuls, 1994, Fr) Marcel Ophuls, John Burns, John Simpson, Martha Gellhorn, Philippe Noiret.
74 min (First journey). 135 min (Second journey).
The title is significant: Ophuls' Sarajevo docu-

mentary is concerned less with the Serbo-Croatian war than with our perception of the conflict, the way journalists filter their experience of the front-line, and how our inaction in the West translates as moral complicity – as Philippe Noiret points out at the beginning of the film, people used to say that if they'd known about the Nazi atrocities, things would have been different; today, we know what's going on in the former Yugoslavia, and it makes no difference. This is a personal, rogue (and often roguish) vision. Ophuls shows us clips from his father's film De Mayerling à Sarajevo, about the start of WWI, which was shooting just as WWII broke out. He counterpoints news footage with sequences from Annie Hall and Henry V, and he reveals elements in the manufacture of 'the truth' no other film-maker would consider – more than anything, this is a film about self-censorship, a condition which is often unconscious and, perhaps, inevitable. Startling, candid, intelligent – and essential viewing. TCh

Velvet Goldmine

(Todd Haynes, 1998, GB) Jonathan Rhys Meyers, Ewan McGregor, Toni Collette, Christian Bale, Eddie Izzard.
120 min.
This witty, evocative re-creation of the heady days of glam rock is loosely structured on the lines of a Citizen Kane-style flashback narrative, with a journalist (Bale) sent back from New York to Britain to investigate, ten years on, the disappearance of Bowie-like star Brian Slade (Meyers) after an on-stage assassination is revealed to have been a publicity stunt. Partly a film à clef which retranslates real-life events and personalities into a dazzling fiction, partly an unsentimental celebration of an era of (potential) pan-sexual liberation (complete with unexpected but fitting tribute to Oscar Wilde), and partly a typically Haynesian study of transgression, identity and the gulf between private and public image, it's superbly shot, edited and performed, and exhilaratingly inventive throughout. GA

Velvet Vampire, The
(aka Cemetery Girls/
The Waking Hour)

(Stephanie Rothman, 1971, US) Sherry Miles, Michael Blodgett, Celeste Yarnall, Paul Prokop, Gene Shane, Jerry Daniels.
80 min.
Like Daughters of Darkness, this is a toothsome (but fang-free) reworking of the female vampire theme, with the emphasis on kinky sex and floating red chiffon. After casually sticking her stiletto into a potential rapist, Yarnall's Diane Le Fanu (or should we call her Carmilla?) slinks into the Stoker Art Gallery and invites a young married couple (Blodgett, Miles) for the weekend to her isolated desert home, where the sun-drenched surroundings turn out to be more sinister than you would at first suppose. The acting is totally breadbasket in the typical New World house style, but the locations are exploited to unsettling effect. And Diane, riding around in her dune buggy or scoffing raw liver while clad in chic marabou, is a femme fatale and a half. AB

Vendetta

(Mel Ferrer, 1950, US) Faith Domergue, George Dolenz, Hillary Brooke, Nigel Bruce, Joseph Calleia, Hugo Haas, Donald Buka.
84 min. b/w.
A typical Howard Hughes folly, begun in 1946, in which his aim of making Faith Domergue as mean, moody and magnificent as Jane Russell ran him through an intriguing palette of directors (Max Ophüls, Preston Sturges, Stuart Heisler, Hughes himself) before Ferrer made whatever grade he was after. It also led to a betrayal of Prosper Mérimée's source novella Colomba, a coolly ironic account of a Corsican blood feud which here becomes imbued with heavy-breathing romanticism. Overblown and somewhat turgid, the film is quite striking visually, with Franz Planer's moody camerawork making the most of the rocks, gaunt trees and desolate moorlands that stand in for the Corsican exteriors. TM

Vengeance
(Joko, Invoca Dio...e Muori)

(Anthony Dawson, 1968, It/WGer) Richard Harrison, Claudio Camaso, Werner Pochat, Paolo Gozlino.
100 min.

This spaghetti Western stars Richard Harrison, a more-than-competent cowboy actor who refused the lead in A Fistful of Dollars, and, in fact, suggested that Sergio Leone check out the young guy who played Rowdy Yates in Rawhide... We have, however, Anthony Dawson's film to judge what might have been. Harrison is Joko, a half-breed with a lethal grudge against the bandits who betrayed his sidekick (brother? – lover?). The English title says it all. Crude sensibilities are the price of brute force. There's a sterling score by Carlo Savina, a juicy climax in a sulphur mine, and a remarkable opening shot – a God's-eye view of a man scrabbling in the dirt with a noose round each limb and four banditos on horseback straining to be off. You don't see that in many John Ford flicks. TCh

Vengeance, the Demon

see Pumpkinhead

Venial Sin (Peccato Veniale)

(Salvatore Samperi, 1973, It) Laura Antonelli, Alessandro Momo, Orazio Orlando, Lilla Brignone, Tino Carraro.
97 min.
The sin is venial but the film is barely excusable: yet another saga of a boy's sentimental education, softcore in format and with a nasty puritanism beneath a wafer-thin fashionable permissiveness (we are supposed to laugh when father thanks the Lord that his boy is not gay after all). Basically, on a family vacation by the seaside, kid brother (Momo) works out his adolescent pangs through a crush, eventually consummated, on his big sister-in-law (Antonelli). The generally lame and/or slushy performances are not even relieved by the bursts of humour, which are on a par with tenth rate graffiti; the camerawork is ploddingly intimate, with – of course – the climactic misty lens; and the score is spectacularly awful pasta muzak. IB

Venice:
Theme and Variations

(James Ivory, 1957, US)
28 min.
Ivory's first, slightly intoxicated film (part of his MA thesis for the University of Southern California) is a documentary on the history of Venice as revealed through the work of some of the artists who made its architecture and citizens (from Gentile Bellini to Saul Steinberg). In The Europeans, Ivory cast himself as an austere silent collector eyeing an objet d'art; in A Room with a View, Cecil Vyse mounts a chair to take a closer look at a portrait; in Hullabaloo Over Georgie and Bonnie's Pictures, Saeed Jaffrey flicks back a sheet of tissue to reveal an erotic Indian miniature for the delectation of Peggy Ashcroft; Slaves of New York finds keen young artists frantically painting in New York lofts; and in Savages, one of the Mudpeople goes so far as to lick an oil painting to discover, perhaps, if it is real. Thesis writers start here. JPy

Venom

(Peter Sykes, 1971, GB) Simon Brent, Neda Arneric, Derek Newark, Sheila Allen, Gerard Heinz, Gertan Klauber.
91 min.
Shelved for nearly five years after completion (reputedly for tax reasons), this was Sykes' feature debut: not – contrary to appearances in an opening sequence involving nude bathing and a mysterious nymph – sexploitation but a spirited horror/adventure movie. The script, about mysterious goings-on in a Bavarian forest (with the hero tangling with a supposed spider goddess, murderous villagers, and evilly-experimenting Nazis) is full of holes; but the action remains tautly visual, and the direction is imaginative enough to gloss over the worst narrative clichés. DP

Venom

(Piers Haggard, 1981, GB) Sterling Hayden, Klaus Kinski, Sarah Miles, Oliver Reed, Cornelia Sharpe, Nicol Williamson, Susan George.
92 min.
Woefully archaic in its British B-pic reliance on very cheap thrills and very worn dramatic clichés, and without any self-parodic saving grace, Venom spells box-office poison. A kidnapped kid, a killer snake loose in the house, sibi-

lant Teuton Kinski and sneering Bulldog Reed hamming villainy against each other, and Nicol Williamson the sorely tried bobby out in the sealed-off London street. Get the picture? There is more (by way of disgressive star turns, that is), but never enough to raise a glimmer of interest or tension in the static rituals of siege cinema. PT

Vent d'Est (Wind from the East)

(Jean-Luc Godard, 1970, It/Fr/WGer) Gian Maria Volonté, Anne Wiazemsky, Glauber Rocha, Jean-Luc Godard, George Götz.
95 min.

Godard's target is representational cinema (Nixon-Paramount/Brezhnev-Mosfilm), and this film is one step in his struggle to create images and sounds that lie outside all ruling hegemonies. It's formulated as a barrage of angry sounds and a trickle of dramatically minimal images, returning constantly to a set of very basic questions: how can you represent oppression without being oppressive? Can you articulate revolutionary ideas without forging a new language to express them? Is any representation of a reactionary society bound to be politically wrong? TR

Venus in Furs (Venus im Pelz)

(Massimo Dallamano, 1968, WGer) Laura Antonelli, Renate Kasche, Ewing Loren, Peter Heeg, Mady Rahl, Werner Pochath.
87 min.

Not to be confused with the Jess Franco version released the following year, this is an updated, softcore adaptation of Leopold Sacher-Masoch's novel about voyeurism, the fetishistic thrill of fur, and the desire to be sexually dominated. Through fantasy, role-playing and sexual experiment, bland hunk Severin (Kasche) and his blonde lover Wanda (Antonelli) explore the power dynamics of their relationship: 'Each day Wanda seems more beautiful to me,' reflects Severin, 'but what is a woman's beauty compared with her cruelty?' Much of the coupling and lashing is coyly filmed from behind strategically placed foreground objects, but those with a tolerance for repeated zoom shots, atrocious dubbing and irritating '60s muzak may find this titillating. More problematic is an extended scene, filmed subjectively through the manacled Severin's mask, which depicts the rape of a maid by an animalistic man. Surely it is the maid and not Severin who is being humiliated here, a misogynist slide that is compounded by the suggestion that she eventually begins to enjoy it. Sleazy this may be, subversive it ain't. NF

Venus Peter

(Ian Sellar, 1989, GB) Ray McAnally, David Hayman, Sinead Cusack, Gordon R Strachan, Sam Hayman, Caroline Paterson, Alex McAvoy, Emma Dingwall, Robin McCaffrey.
94 min.

Growing up in the Orkneys in the late '40s, young Peter leads a strange and magical life. Christened with sea water, he sometimes fancies he is a boat; his wise-old-fisherman grandfather (McAnally) rails against human greed and burbles on about whales and eternity; his ancient aunt extols the virtues of poetry; and his teacher (Cusack) is heavily into the appreciation of beauty. Not surprisingly, Peter spends much of his time in dreams, usually about his father, who is either dead or (sensibly) a fugitive from this inbred island community, where harsh prejudice, acts of cruelty towards beached whales, and vacuous, whimsical mysticism are the norm. Sellar's first feature looks nice enough, in a picture-postcard sort of way, but its script is so much nonsense: the film dishes up a series of loosely connected, impressionist vignettes that appear to have no narrative rhyme or reason. Someone, somewhere along the line, should have put the brake on the indulgently fanciful poeticism and insisted on rather more plot logic. GA

Vera Cruz

(Robert Aldrich, 1954, US) Burt Lancaster, Gary Cooper, Denise Darcel, Cesar Romero, Sarita Montiel, George Macready, Ernest Borgnine, Jack Elam, Jack Lambert, Charles Bronson.
94 min.

A brash, lively, and totally appealing Western about a couple of American adventurers – Cooper, a decent but cynical Southern gentleman, and Lancaster, a supremely conniving crook – getting involved with Maximilian's imperial court and the Juarez revolutionaries in 1860s Mexico. Basically, the film is played as a game of bluff and betrayal, with the pair continually voicing their distrust of each other as they transport a countess and her crock of gold to Vera Cruz, allowing Aldrich to alternate with ease between earthy comedy and taut suspense. Beautifully shot by Ernest Laszlo, it conjures up a Mexico that in some ways looks forward to Peckinpah's *The Wild Bunch*, a country at once romantic and treacherous, wild and lovely, an outpost of freedom for exiles yet oppressed by a corrupt government. And the performances, as you might expect, are highly professional. GA

Verboten!

(Samuel Fuller, 1958, US) James Best, Susan Cummings, Tom Pittman, Paul Dubov, Steven Geray.
94 min. b/w.

The great Fuller at his punchy, unsubtle best, beginning with a long tracking shot of an American GI clambering through the grim rubble of war-torn Berlin (the rifle shotd of snipers intercut with the opening chords of Beethoven's 5th), and ending with an image of raging flames. In between, the film, set mostly in the immediate postwar period, charts the troubled relationship of the American, working for the occupying Allied Forces, with a German woman who saved his life and whi is surrounded by compatriots – including her younger brother – determined to revive the power of the Nazi movement. It's a tale of betrayal, violence, confusion and stark ironies, and takes in bravura action sequences, scenes of argumentative discourse, and documentary footage of the Nazi atrocities shown at the Nuremberg War Criminals Tribunal. Fuller's methods may not be sophisticated, but they are complex; as such, his own inimitably brash brand of didacticism makes for riveting and powerful cinema. GA

Verbrechen am Seelenleben eines Menschen

see Kaspar Hauser

Verdict (The Verdict)

(André Cayatte, 1974, Fr/It) Sophia Loren, Jean Gabin, Henri Garcin, Julien Bertheau, Muriel Catala.
97 min.

Cayatte is the Frenchman's Stanley Kramer, with an unswerving penchant for expounding knotty points of law and morals in a narrative framework, giving audiences a lot of fun and education all at once. Here, Sophia Loren's worthless son is up for trial under clauses 296, 297, 302, 304 and 332 of the French penal code. Despite this daunting array of transgressions, the judge (Gabin) urges his jurors to acquit the wretch, for Loren has his diabetic wife locked up, and his conscience goes to pot as a result. Acting and direction are uniformly sober, and you don't learn a thing. GB

Verdict, The

(Don Siegel, 1946, US) Sydney Greenstreet, Peter Lorre, Joan Lorring, George Coulouris, Rosalind Ivan, Paul Cavanagh, Morton Lowry.
86 min. b/w.

Siegel's first film, an ingenious locked room mystery set in London in 1890, adapted from a novel by Israel Zangwill (often described as the father of the genre). Greenstreet plays a genial Scotland Yard inspector who, dismissed after thirty years of distinguished service when an oversight results in the hanging of an innocent man, deviously stages a second case; this not only sees justice done (the victim is himself a killer), but puts Greenstreet's baffled successor (Coulouris, the ambitious underling who shopped him in the first place) on the road to perpetrating a similar miscarriage of justice in solving it. Fascinatingly, though, Siegel deliberately plays on ambivalences throughout, leaving motivations not quite explained and opening up dark, speculative avenues of paranoia and perversity, not least through Greenstreet's teasing, subtly suggestive intimacy with Lorre as an amiably decadent, inimitably sinister artist friend. The result, impeccably performed and beautifully shot by Ernest Haller, emerges as splendid cross between Gothic melodrama and *film noir*. TM

Verdict, The

(Sidney Lumet, 1982, US) Paul Newman, Charlotte Rampling, Jack Warden, James Mason, Milo O'Shea, Julie Bovasso, Roxanne Hart, Wesley Addy.
128 min.

Newman as a washed-up lawyer, given one last chance to prove himself with a rather squalid medical malpractice suit. David Mamet has delivered a fast-paced, eloquent, and suspenseful screenplay which, like all the best genre movies, plunges its hero so far into the abyss that it seems impossible for him to climb out. And for once Lumet makes story rather than performance his first priority, with the paradoxical result – so familiar in American movies – that the acting sometimes reaches a near-invisible perfection. Admittedly this is a legal *Rocky*, convincing rather than realistic, witty rather than analytical, but it amounts to a far more effective indictment of the US legal system than ...*and Justice for All*, and is the first courtroom drama in years to recapture the brilliance of the form. DP

Verdugo, El (The Executioner/ Not On Your Life)

(Luis Berlanga, 1963, Sp/It) Nino Manfredi, Emma Penella, José Isbert, José Luis López Vázquez, Angel Alvarez.
110 min. b/w.

Regularly voted by its country's critics as the best Spanish film of all time, Berlanga's brilliantly dark comedy on the peculiar horror of the garotte has not lost its power over the years. Manfredi plays an undertaker's hapless assistant who marries the executioner's daughter, then discovers that they can keep their precious apartment only if he agrees to become his father-in-law's successor. Full of sharp and disturbing insights into the corrupt world engendered by the Francoist mentality, the film's build-up to its terrifying conclusion – when Manfredi, as the new executioner, is dragged literally kicking and screaming to perform his duty – is inexorable. DT

Vérité, La (The Truth)

(Henri-Georges Clouzot, 1960, Fr/It) Brigitte Bardot, Charles Vanel, Marie-Josée Nat, Paul Meurisse, Louis Seigner, Sami Frey.
130 min. b/w.

A dissection of life and amorality among the young and disaffected in the late '50s, with Bardot giving her finest ever performance as the girl whose headlong rush from her stiff bourgeois home into a series of frustrating affairs with Parisian intellectuals leads to her trial for murder. Clouzot, the man who made the wonderful but terribly cynical *Le Corbeau, The Wages of Fear* and *Les Diaboliques*, is as cold and savage as ever in his observation of French manners, although the courtroom scenes that frame the flashbacks to Bardot's past tend to decrease the tension inherent in the subject. Far from his finest work, but still compelling viewing: compared to Clouzot, even Fassbinder seemed a romantic. GA

Verlorene, Der (The Lost One)

(Peter Lorre, 1951, WGer) Peter Lorre, Karl John, Helmut Rudolph, Renate Mannhardt, Johanna Hofer, Lotte Rausch.
98 min. b/w.

Der Verlorene would have been remarkable in virtually any context; as a product of the depressed German film industry of the post-war years, it's absolutely phenomenal. It was Lorre's only film as writer/director, and it clearly represents a personal comment on the side of Germany that forced him into exile in 1933, just as his own performance in the lead is a rethinking of the psychopath roles that he played in *M* and many Hollywood movies. The plot, developed entirely in flashbacks, shows how research doctor Rothe (Lorre) is forced into political complicity with the Nazis by their shrewd, cold-blooded exploitation of his emotional and psychological weaknesses; everything about it (including the spasms of expressionism in the imagery) is haunted by a sense of the German past, until the powerhouse melodrama of the ending rockets the film into the even bleaker present. TR

Verlorene Ehre der Katharina Blum, Die

see Lost Honour of Katharina Blum, The

Vernon, Florida

(Errol Morris, 1980, US) Claude Register, Albert Bitterling, Henry Shipes, Snake Reynolds, Roscoe Collins.
60 min.
Anyone who saw *Gates of Heaven* will need no inducement to try Errol Morris' second idiosyncratic foray into documentary. While less sharply focused than the pet cemetery film, this is equally delightful in its loving – but detached – portrait of the more eccentric inhabitants of small-town America, in this case the backwater community of the title. The subjects discussed include turkey hunting, sand-growth (a couple have a jarful from Los Alamos, New Mexico, which they insist is growing apace), and people with multiple brains. Morris, thankfully, never patronises his subjects' loony views. Touching and funny, the film is a real-life predecessor to David Byrne's fictional *True Stories*. GA

Verónico Cruz (La Deuda Interna)

(Miguel Pereira, 1987, Arg/GB) Juan José Camero, Gonzalo Morales, René Olaguivel, Guillermo Delgado.
96 min.
Despite its very evident sincerity, Pereira's feature debut offers a sometimes muddled, wanly liberal response to the human waste incurred during the Falklands War. In a tiny, remote village high in the Argentinian mountains, the uneducated population is barely aware of events in the outside world; only a teacher from the city – whose growing friendship with shepherd boy Veronico forms the core of the film's narrative – seems conscious of the implications of 1976's military coup. True, life in the village changes; but any real political criticism would seem to lie in the character of Veronico's father, whose absentee status may serve to tug the heartstrings in regard to our perception of his son's predicament, but does little to clarify either the mechanisms of Argentine fascism or the war itself. Finally, both strengths and weaknesses are rooted in the film's decidedly poetic humanism; only the most bigoted Brits could find such a well-meaning anti-war movie offensive. GA

Veronika Voss (Die Sehnsucht der Veronika Voss)

(Rainer Werner Fassbinder, 1982, WGer) Rosel Zech, Hilmar Thate, Annemarie Düringer, Doris Schade, Cornelia Froboess, Erik Schumann.
104 min. b/w.
Intended as just another chapter in the continuing indictment of the post-war German economic recovery, but Fassbinder's death means that this will have to take its place as a loose third panel of the *Maria Braun/Lola* triptych. Unlike those heroines, however, Veronika (Zech) doesn't even pretend to any kind of upward social mobility. When 'discovered' by a crusading journalist (Thate), she is already on the skids, a washed-up Third Reich film star. His infatuation and subsequent investigation reveals her dependency on a snow white clinic, and her sado-masochistic relationship with the female doctor who feeds her morphine habit; and that's just the beginning of the downward slide. If Sirk's colourful melodramas were once Fassbinder's models, this is closer to Wilder's monochrome *Sunset Boulevard*, not just in theme, but in the reductive cynicism that views all human motivation as grounded on folly and greed; a world in which love is just a power struggle, dirty 'habits' are murderous, and happiness is simply the art of being well deceived. CPea

Versailles rive gauche (A Night in Versailles)

(Bruno Podalydès, 1991, Fr) Isabelle Candelier, Denis Podalydès, Philippe Linchan, Michel Vuiuermoz.
47 min.
A beautifully elaborated, extended gag about a bumbling intellectual and Tintin fan (Podalydès) who invites his dream date (Candelier) for an inti-

mate evening in, but gets hopelessly entangled in his own fastidious embarrassment. Nothing could be simpler than this deliciously excruciating comedy of errors (it's as if a bunch of Rohmer characters had accidentally stumbled into a Feydeau farce), but Podalydès (who also co-scripted and plays the lead) carries it off with perfect timing. JRo

Verso sera

see By Nightfall

Versprechen, Das

see Promise, The

Vertiges

(Christine Laurent, 1985, Fr/GB) Magali Noël, Krystyna Janda, Paulo Autran, Hélène Lapiower, Henri Serre, Thierry Bosc.
107 min.
A moonstruck enterprise, from the maverick independent international producer Paulo Branco, in which, on the first night of a fraught production of *The Marriage of Figaro*, Serre, playing the count, shoots dead Bosc, playing Figaro, with the latter's own pearl-handled pistol. This is no more than the lippy servant deserves since throughout rehearsals he's tormented the conductor with hints of some old injustice. The conductor, meanwhile, has grown increasingly obsessed with the memory of his former mistress, La Gravida, and her perfect voice. One of the singers (Janda) loses her voice. 'You have to be a *real* diva to lose your voice,' the conductor's current mistress says, comfortingly. News arrives of La Gravida's retirement. The conductor swoons and expires. The Countess swears vengeance, and the Count, in the event, acts the gentleman. Vertigo, indeed. JPy

Vertigo 100 (100)

(Alfred Hitchcock, 1958, US) James Stewart, Kim Novak, Barbara Bel Geddes, Tom Helmore, Henry Jones, Ellen Corby, Lee Patrick.
128 min.
Brilliant but despicably cynical view of human obsession and the tendency of those in love to try to manipulate each other. Stewart is excellent as the neurotic detective employed by an old pal to trail his wandering wife, only to fall for her himself and then crack up when she commits suicide. Then one day he sees a woman in the street who reminds him of the woman who haunts him...Hitchcock gives the game away about halfway through the movie, and focuses on Stewart's strained psychological stability; the result inevitably involves a lessening of suspense, but allows for an altogether deeper investigation of guilt, exploitation, and obsession. The bleakness is perhaps a little hard to swallow, but there's no denying that this is the director at the very peak of his powers, while Novak is a revelation. Slow but totally compelling. GA

Verweigerung, Die

see Refusal, The

Very Curious Girl, A

see Fiancée du Pirate, La

Very Important Person

(Ken Annakin, 1961, GB) James Robertson Justice, Leslie Phillips, Stanley Baxter, Eric Sykes, Richard Wattis, John Le Mesurier.
98 min. b/w.
Dated British comedy poking fun at *Wooden Horse* and *Colditz*-style PoW movies. Bellowing beard James Robertson Justice, always good value, plays a distinguished radar scientist who takes very badly to life in a Nazi camp. When his fellow prisoners realise he's vital to Britain's war efforts, they reluctantly agree to help him escape. All sorts of radio and TV comedians pop up in the supporting cast, but if some of the jokes fall a little flat, it's hardly a surprise – Norman Wisdom's regular screenwriter, Jack Davies, helped provide the script. GM

Very Moral Night, A (Egy Erkölcsös Ejszaka)

(Károly Makk, 1977, Hun) Margit Makay, Irén Psota, Carla Romanelli, Györgyi Tarján, György Cserhalmi.
99 min.

Makk's film suffers by comparison with his later, more serious *Another Way*; a certain turn-of-the-century light-weightedness is not quite the same thing as buoyancy. A small town's brothel takes a medical student as a lodger, much to the all round delight of the girls, student, and madame. When his mother arrives to visit unexpectedly, the girls rally round with a charade to keep up appearances. The mask slips occasionally, but the old lady is beyond corruption, and to the pure all things are pure. Indeed, the film's main delight rests on Margit Makay's performance as the mother, a strong portrait of kindness and innocence preserved into old age. CPea

Vessel of Wrath (aka The Beachcomber)

(Erich Pommer, 1938, GB) Charles Laughton, Elsa Lanchester, Tyrone Guthrie, Robert Newton, Dolly Mollinger, Eliot Makeham.
93 min. b/w.
Laughton's venture into independent production, of which this was the first fruit, afforded him a welcome opportunity to escape typecasting as a monster. Set in the Dutch East Indies, the Somerset Maugham story – gradual defrosting of a frigid spinster by a drunken reprobate ('I suppose I'm jealous of the reckless way he squanders the precious treasure of life') – may be clichéd, but Laughton's performance adds an extra dimension. Burdened and embarrassed by his homosexual inclinations, he obviously entered with gusto into this portrayal of a man with problems in every area of his life apart from sex. Playing opposite his real life wife, he carefully combines conventions of masculinity with the self-doubt and inadequacy of his own persona to create an almost Falstaffian screen character. RMy

Viaggio in Italia (Journey to Italy/The Lonely Woman/ Strangers/Voyage to Italy)

(Roberto Rossellini, 1953, It) Ingrid Bergman, George Sanders, Maria Mauban, Paul Muller, Leslie Daniels, Natalia Ray, Anna Proclemer.
100 min. b/w.
Some films have to be seen to be believed: the secret of this most beautiful and magical of films is 'nothing happens'. From the slight tale of a bored English couple holidaying in Italy, Rossellini builds a magnificently passionate story of cruelty and cynicism swirling into a renewal of love: life is so short, we must make the most of it...Rarely has screen chemistry worked so indefinably well; Sanders' suave, caddish businessman superbly complements Bergman's Garbo-like presence and the sensuous locations in which they feel so ill at ease. And though critics may have always praised it as 'one of the most beautiful films ever made', its genuinely romantic tenderness (it ends in 'I love you') mark it as never so unfashionable, never so moving. DMacp

Viaje, El

see Voyage, The

Vices in the Family (Vizio di Famiglia)

(Mariano Laurenti, 1975, It) Edwige Fenech, Renzo Montagnani, Juliette Mayniel, Susan Scott, Gigi Ballista, Roberto Cenci.
94 min.
An incomprehensible black comedy (any charm it may have had has gone in the dubbing and cutting of the version released in Britain), this concerns the cack-handed efforts of a group of scheming ladies to relieve a dying Count of his fortune. It borrows shamelessly from Polanski's *What?*, and throws in a few nods towards Pasolini, but basically attempts no more than a bit of absent-minded titillation. Laurenti directs as though he were being paid by the minute, and the result is a crashing bore. VG

Vice Squad

(Gary A Sherman, 1981, US) Season Hubley, Gary Swanson, Wings Hauser, Pepe Serna, Beverly Todd.
98 min.
Sadistic pimp (Hauser) beats LA prostitute to death; her friend (Hubley) collaborates with police to trap him; he escapes and seeks murderous revenge. Apart from a marginally more lurid

approach to sex and violence, this could be any old episode from any old TV cop series, right down to the appalling sub-disco score. There's also a pretty insulting opening which reveals that (gasp) prostitutes have feelings too. DP

Vice Versa
(Peter Ustinov, 1947, GB) Roger Livesey, Kay Walsh, Petula Clark, David Hutcheson, Anthony Newley, James Robertson Justice.
111 min. b/w.
Ustinov was in his mid-20s when he wrote and directed this sparkling comedy about a Victorian businessman (Livesey) who ends up trapped in his young son's body after meddling with a magical Indian gem. (The son, a very cheeky Anthony Newley, takes over his father's body.) A sort of cross between the Arabian Nights and a Whitehall farce, it's every bit as funny as Penny Marshall's *Big*, made from a similar premise 40 years later. GM

Vice Versa
(Brian Gilbert, 1988, US) Judge Reinhold, Fred Savage, Corinne Bohrer, Swoosie Kurtz, Jane Kaczmarek, David Proval, William Prince.
98 min.
Divorced workaholic department store executive (Reinhold) and his 11-year-old son (Savage) both wish they could lead each other's lives: a magical skull, mysteriously come into Dad's possession during a trip to Thailand, makes the wish come true. After a tedious prologue, Dick Clement and Ian La Frenais' role-reversal script settles for bland farce, with son (in Dad's body) forced to negotiate the executive boardroom, while Dad (in son's body) takes on school bullies. Moments of rather tasteless complexity arise with Dad's girlfriend (Bohrer), but mostly the hoary gags give rise to less tantalising ideas. Reinhold does his darnedest, but both script and direction are instilled with a numbing predictability. GA

Victim
(Basil Dearden, 1961, GB) Dirk Bogarde, Sylvia Syms, John Barrie, Peter McEnery, Anthony Nicholls, Dennis Price, Norman Bird, Charles Lloyd Pack, Nigel Stock, Derren Nesbitt, Hilton Edwards.
100 min. b/w.
A fascinating slice of social history. Bogarde plays a homosexual barrister being blackmailed by a young man who commits suicide when arrested. Bogarde can either shut up or 'come out', and opts for the latter, putting a strain on his marriage and his reputation. Bogarde, the Rank matinee idol, risked almost everything by playing the role, and he gives an open and sincere performance, with Sylvia Syms also good as his appalled but supportive wife. By today's standards the film is of course compromised, and in 1961 it could be nothing else (Dearden apparently insisted that homosexuals should be called 'inverts'). It flirts with the subject, as did the same team's exposé of racism in the earlier *Sapphire*; but although treated as a thriller, it does seek to normalise (rather than glamourise) homosexuality by finding it in every side street, every Rolls Royce, and every club in town. ATu

Victoire en Chantant, La
see Black and White in Colour

Victors, The
(Carl Foreman, 1963, GB) George Hamilton, George Peppard, Eli Wallach, Vincent Edwards, Rosanna Schiaffino, James Mitchum, Maurice Ronet, Jeanne Moreau, Romy Schneider, Michael Callan, Peter Fonda, Melina Mercouri, Mervyn Johns, Albert Lieven, Senta Berger, Elke Sommer, Albert Finney.
175 min. b/w.
A World War II picture with a weightiness all its own that follows an American infantry unit from Sicily, up through Europe, to the fall of Berlin and after. Foreman adds nothing to William Wellman's portrait of an ordinary GI unit in *Battleground* (1949). Instead of the emotional complexity of the earlier film, Foreman offers a rather cheap and shallow sense of irony, sometimes effective, more often ponderous. Interludes between campaigns are beefed up with the presence of various sexy European actresses;

Hamilton, Peppard, Wallach and Fonda play some of the soldiers who get theirs at various stages of the long slog towards the death of the last one at the hands of a drunken Russian soldier (Finney) in a knife fight in Occupied Berlin. CPe

Victor/Victoria
(Blake Edwards, 1982, GB) Julie Andrews, James Garner, Robert Preston, Lesley Ann Warren, Alex Karras, John Rhys-Davies, Graham Stark, Peter Arne.
134 min.
There is so much to like and admire in Edwards' intricate comedy about sexual identity which is neither vulgar nor preachy, combining a Clouseau-esque bedroom farce – and the prospect of characters coming out of the closet in all possible ways – with a convincing love story and just enough show-stopping musical numbers. It gives Andrews her best role ever as the beanpole English soprano peddling 'Cherry Ripe' to unimpressed cabaret managers in a wonderfully fake 'Paris 1934'. Befriended by Toddy (Preston), a very together 'gay' (much of the excellent dialogue's zip comes from the conscious use of anachronisms), Victoria is easily persuaded to pass herself off as a Bowie-elegant young man, and develops a scintillating drag act which delights Paris, confuses devout hetero King Marchan (Garner), and broadens the implications of the film, forcing the audience to ponder its own response to our sweet, safe and usually unsexy Julie suddenly coming on so attractive as a fella in a dress. Well, as the song says, climb every mountain. Don't miss this one. It sends sparks. JS

Victory
(John Cromwell, 1940, US) Fredric March, Betty Field, Cedric Hardwicke, Jerome Cowan, Sig Ruman, Rafaela Ottiano.
77 min. b/w.
A curious adaptation of Joseph Conrad's novel, with March as the tender-hearted misanthrope whose ivory tower on an island in the Dutch East Indies is simultaneously invaded by a downtrodden girl (Field) he rescues from a lecherous hotel-keeper, and by an unscrupulous gentleman adventurer (Hardwicke) – attended by his male 'secretary' and a brutish thug – who is after the mythical treasure supposedly hidden there. No prizes for guessing that subtleties go by the board, with Hollywood romance winning the day as a tropical storm orchestrates the passions. But the characterisations are vivid, the relationships (Hardwicke's sadistic sexual domination of Cowan, for example) surprisingly explicit, and the camerawork (Leo Tover) lushly atmospheric. TM

Victory
(aka Escape to Victory)
(John Huston, 1981, US) Sylvester Stallone, Michael Caine, Max von Sydow, Amidou, Daniel Massey, Pele, Bobby Moore, Osvaldo Ardiles.
117 min.
Unsatisfactory both for fans of star-studded prison escape dramas and for football fans hoping to see cunningly devised tactics from Pele and his squad of internationals (half the Ipswich team in addition to Moore and Ardiles). If one buys the barely plausible notion of a squad of PoW soccer stars escaping from a Paris stadium, one is still constantly reminded by the rip-off music score just how inferior this is to *The Great Escape*. Stallone comes off best among the familiar gallery of Nazi and prisoner stereotypes. RM

Victory at Entebbe
(Marvin J Chomsky, 1976, US) Helmut Berger, Linda Blair, Kirk Douglas, Richard Dreyfuss, Julius Harris, Helen Hayes, Anthony Hopkins, Burt Lancaster, Christian Marquand, Elizabeth Taylor, Jessica Walter, Harris Yulin.
119 min.
Six months after the event came the first of the action replays of the Entebbe hijack. Flatly directed and poorly shot on video (the TV version ran 150 minutes), it offers a sorry approximation to a sub-standard disaster movie rather than any semblance of truth. That Mrs Bloch has become the uncommonly wise Mrs Wise (Helen Hayes, angelically wistful) is fair example of the confection on offer. Rather than examine the hijacking in context, the film instead revives the spectre of Nazi Jewish oppression. Amin (atrociously portrayed by Harris)

is 'the builder of a memorial to Hitler', the hijackers relentless Teutonic fanatics, which causes the Jewish hijacked to indulge in much emoting and dredging of their collective consciousness. Of all the stars paraded to no effect, the wooden Helmut Berger gives the most flexible performance. CPe

Vida Criminal de Archibaldo de la Cruz, La
see Criminal Life of Archibaldo de la Cruz, The

Vida en Sombras
see Life in Shadows

Vidas Secas
see Barren Lives

Videodrome
(David Cronenberg, 1982, Can) James Woods, Sonja Smits, Deborah Harry, Peter Dvorsky, Les Carlson, Jack Creley, Lynne Gorman.
89 min.
Cronenberg has always crossed the line between taste and distaste with his combinations of vile glop-horror and social criticism, and this is no exception. A cable TV programmer (Woods) becomes increasingly intrigued by the hardcore S/M movies he is beaming down from satellite, and so does his girlfriend (Harry), a dead-eyed sensation-seeker with cigarette brands on her breast to prove it. The plotline becomes too contorted to go into here, and far, far too weird; sufficient to note that Cronenberg's most interesting trick is to eradicate the difference between hardware and software by giving his hero a pulsing vagina-like slot in his stomach through which he can be programmed by ..it gets much worse. There are distinct signs of strain in the plot convolutions, not least in the spectator's loss of faith over indiscriminate and cheating use of hallucination; what certainly survives is Cronenberg's wholesale disgust with the world in general. CPea

Vie à l'Envers, La
(Life Upside-Down)
(Alain Jessua, 1964, Fr) Charles Denner, Anna Gaylor, Guy Saint-Jean, Nicole Gueden, Jean Yanne, Yvonne Clech.
92 min. b/w.
This first feature from Jessua, who made the wonderful *Jeu de Massacre*, coolly and wittily watches its central character, a serious but unexceptional estate agent, withdraw from things into a world of his own. First he lets go his job, and then his wife of only two weeks. The strength of the film, which begins with a calculated mundaneness, is its lack of either explanation or interpretation of the man's behaviour. Whether he is retreating into a life of inner contemplation, as some have claimed, or whether he is cracking up, is left deliberately unclear. As a piece of observation and as a description of human behaviour, particularly domestic, it's rather fine and consistently droll. CPe

Vie de Bohème, La
(Bohemian Life)
(Aki Kaurismäki, 1991, Fin) Matti Pellonpää, Evelyne Didi, André Wilms, Kari Väänänen, Jean-Pierre Léaud, Samuel Fuller, Louis Malle.
100min. b/w.
British audiences have thus far shown stoic indifference to the work of Finnish fashion victim Kaurismäki, and this straight-faced adaptation of Henri Murger's melodramatic novel (1851) is unlikely to quicken their pulses. A polyglot cast (most of them long-haired Finns) enact the depressed lives of failed artists and their consumptive muse Mimi in fractured French, spurred on by names from the director's address-book and a dog named Baudelaire. The one-note joke palls fast, and Kaurismäki's endless quest for emotional truth at the heart of miserabilist clichés winds up in its usual cul-de-sac. TR

Vie devant Soi, La
see Madame Rosa

Vie de Jésus, La
(The Life of Jesus)
(Bruno Dumont, 1996, Fr) David Douche, Marjorie Cottreel, Geneviève Cottreel, Kader Chaatouf, Sébastien Delbaere.
96 min.

Making use of locals instead of professional actors lends authenticity to this impressive look at a group of otherwise innocuous teenage lads in a boring northern French town (Bailleul in Flanders), driven to violence by a mixture of boredom, jealousy, macho pride and ingrained racism. Essentially it's a work of low key 'realism' in the Bressonian tradition (albeit less obviously 'spiritual'), though it includes odd touches, such as the local marching band's unexpectedly dissonant music, and a couple of brief sequences (involving body doubles) so sexually frank they look like out-takes from *Ai No Corrida*. Perhaps strangest of all is that the protagonist's girlfriend seems for most of the film to be the only young female in town, but that's a very minor criticism when compared to writer/director Dumont's tough, confident handling of mood, milieu, pace, performance and theme. GA

Vie en rose, La (Changmi Bit Insaeng)

(Kim Hong-Joon, 1994, SKor) Choi Myung-Gil, Choi Jae-Sung, Cha Kwang-Su, Lee Ji-Hyung, Hwang Mi-Sun.
95 min.
Remarkably original and recklessly emotive, this debut feature by a former assistant to Im Kwon-Taek takes elements from gangster thrillers, melodramas, martial arts movies and *film noir* to colour an hallucinatory descent into Seoul's 'lower depths'. The setting is a rough part of town in the months just before the 1988 Olympics, a time when the military dictatorship slackened its grip in the hope of presenting a more liberal face to the visiting world. A young woman runs a basement flop-house, renting out comic books and screening soft-porn videos on the side; her life gets turned upside down by a taciturn macho man with enough trouble on his back to fill several flashbacks. TR

Vie est à nous, La (The People of France)

(Jean Renoir, 1936, Fr) Jean Dasté, Jacques Brunius, Simone Guisin, Teddy Michaux, Pierre Unik, Max Dalban, Madeleine Sologne, Charles Blavette, Jean Renoir, Roger Blin, Gaston Modot, Jacques Becker.
66 min. b/w.
Described in its original credits simply as 'a film made collectively by a group of technicians, artists and workers' with no names appearing, *La Vie est à nous* was made with the assistance of Jacques Becker and Henri Cartier-Bresson, among others, and produced by the Communist Party. Basically a collection of documentary footage and vignettes satirising bourgeois society, offering up plenty of Communist-inspired optimism; but what marks it out from most propagandist tracts is the familiar Renoir theme of community ideals transcending social classes, expressed so eloquently in his previous feature, *Le Crime de Monsieur Lange*. A film of its time, conceived in the shadow of Hitler, it still communicates its message with an irrepressible joy and swagger. DT

Vie est belle, La

(Benoit Lamy/Ngangura Mweze, 1987, Bel/Fr/Zaire) Papa Wemna, Bibi Krubwa, Landu Nzunzimbu Matshia, Kanku Kasongo, Lokinda Menji Feza.
72 min.
Papa Wemba, one of Zaire's most exuberant and enterprising musicians, plays Kouru, a traditional musician whose popularity dwindles when local villagerslatch on to the more exciting possibilities of electric instruments. Kouru decides to travel to the city to pursue his dream of becoming a superstar. In his eventful, funny journey to success, he lands a job as a houseboy and falls in love. Only problem is, he and his boss fall for the same woman…Set against the bustling backdrop of the town of Kinshasa, the film paints a more honest and vivid picture of African life than any blockbuster with sunset safari scenes ever could. And Wemba is given plenty of scope to perform, leading to a joyous all's well that ends well musical finale, 'La Vie est belle'. IA

Vie est un long fleuve tranquille, La

see Life is a Long Quiet River

Vie est un Roman, La (Life Is a Bed of Roses)

(Alain Resnais, 1983, Fr) Vittorio Gassman, Ruggero Raimondi, Geraldine Chaplin, Fanny Ardant, Pierre Arditi, Sabine Azéma, Robert Manuel, André Dussollier.
111 min.
Resnais speculates on the utopian dream that life is infinitely perfectable, that human chaos, despair and horror can be spirited or educated out of existence. There are two stories, to correspond to each of these possibilities. In the first, set in 1914, Count Forbek (Raimondi), aristocrat, aesthete and visionary, erects a Temple of Happiness in which a select few will be drugged into a state of original innocence. In the second, set in the present, a gaggle of theorists (Gassman, Chaplin) have taken over Forbek's castle to conduct a seminar on the 'education of the imaginative'. Both enterprises come to grief, though in the process Resnais does realise his own utopia, a realm of vast imaginative possibility. A third story, a simple but charming fairytale on similar themes, is offered as 'objective' proof. RC

Vie et rien d'autre, La

see Life and Nothing But

Vieil Homme et l'Enfant, Le (The Two of Us)

(Claude Berri, 1966, Fr) Michel Simon, Alain Cohen, Luce Fabiole, Roger Carel, Paul Préboist, Charles Denner.
90 min. b/w.
Berri's fictionalised memoir – the Jewish child, Claude, billeted on a curmudgeonly old anti-Semite, was the director himself in the final months of the World War II Occupation – wears its heart stitched on to its sleeve like a Star of David. But, though compromised by the facility with which its glib antitheses (old age/childhood, country/city, Gentile/Jew) are reconciled by the (un)likely friendship of the ill-matched pair, the film's good humour and discretion, plus Simon's virtuoso performance, make it never less than watchable. GAd

Vieille Dame indigne, La (The Shameless Old Lady)

(René Allio, 1965) Sylvie, Malka Ribovska, Etienne Bierry, Victor Lanoux, Jean Bouise, François Maistre.
94 min. b/w.
81-year-old Sylvie is magnificent in this adaptation of Brecht's fable about an old woman who suddenly starts a new life of delightful irresponsibility after the death of her husband, wonderfully wry and funny as she breaks out of a lifetime of devoted household drudgery to enjoy a round of whipped cream sundaes, movies and fast cars. Equally (or more) importantly, Allio never loses sight of Brecht. For the first time in her life, in her new friendship with the local whore (Ribovska) and an anarchist shoemaker (Bouise), the old lady begins to respond to people on their own terms instead of out of duty. Meanwhile her family, outraged at her irresponsibility, are seen to be irresponsibly frittering away their lives, toiling at jobs which serve only to build prisons for their souls. Witty, wise and gently funny, it is also, in its quiet way, a genuinely subversive film. TM

Vieille qui Marchait dans la Mer, La

see The Old Lady Who Walked in the Sea

Vie Rêvée, La

see Dream Life

Vie Rêvée des Anges, La (The Dream Life of Angels)

(Erick Zonca, 1998, Fr) Elodie Bouchez, Natacha Régnier, Grégoire Colin, Jo Prestia, Patrick Mercado.
113 min.
This first feature starts out looking as if it's simply going to be a well-observed female buddy movie about two 20-year-olds: drifter Isa (Bouchez) and seamstress Marie (Régnier) meet when the former turns up virtually penniless in Lille. As the film progresses, however, with Marie falling, against both her own and her friend's bet-

ter instincts, for a callous but wealthy young womaniser (Colin), it enters darker, more troubling territory. It's a beautifully insightful movie which views its characters (the type of 'marginal' folk rarely shown in the cinema) sympathetically but unsentimentally, and after the scene setting of the first half-hour, it grips like a vice as it proceeds to a shocking and profoundly moving conclusion. GA

Vie Sexuelle des Belges 1950-1978, La

see Sexual Life of the Belgians 1950-1978, The

Vietnam Journey

(Christine Burrill/Bill Yahrhaus/Jane Fonda/Tom Hayden/Haskell Wexler, 1974, US)
64 min.
A deceivingly quiet and relaxed film, almost a home movie of Jane Fonda's travels within North Vietnam with her husband Tom Hayden (including a visit to Hanoi film studios, where she interviews actress Tra Giang). Certainly no political tract, it is, in fact, the tour as covered by Fonda in *Rolling Stone*. While the film perhaps doesn't solve the central problem of coping with Fonda's status as a personality, its openness, warmth, and occasional gaucheness lend it notably radical dimensions by comparison with the relentlessly single-note coverage of the war and its bizarre aftermath on TV and in the press. VG

View to a Kill, A

(John Glen, 1985, GB) Roger Moore, Christopher Walken, Tanya Roberts, Grace Jones, Patrick Macnee, Patrick Bauchau, David Yip, Fiona Fullerton.
131 min.
Bond struck camp long ago, so it would seem pointless to complain about the dilution of Fleming's cruel stud into a smirking dinner-jacket with a crude line in double entendres. But the problem here is that the elements which act as consolation in late Bondage are missing. Chiefest of these is a strong villain: Walken, far from being able to flood Silicon Valley by imploding the San Andreas faultline, looks more like an effete gigolo, just waiting to scratch Roger's eyes out. Grace Jones is badly wasted. The digital countdown to Armageddon trick has been worn smooth with overuse. The operatic sets of yore have shrunk, and something has gone very wrong when the climax belongs to something as serene and harmless as an airship. Even the tottering finale, high up on the Golden Gate Bridge supports, left this vertigo sufferer in a deep state of lacquered composure. Once 007 was licensed to kill; now he not only eats quiche, he cooks it himself. CPea

Vigil

(Vincent Ward, 1984, NZ) Bill Kerr, Fiona Kay, Gordon Shields, Penelope Stewart, Frank Whitten.
90 min.
Though often in danger of sinking into a heavy mythical mud of its own making, Ward's would-be visionary account of life on a remote New Zealand sheep farm does achieve occasional moments of striking visual beauty. Following the death of farmer Justin Peers, his wife Liz (Stewart) and daughter Lisa (Kay) labour on with the help of senile grandfather (Kerr) and Ethan (Whitten), an itinerant hunter who hires on as help. Ward creates a powerful sense of the struggle between the farmers, their machines, and the elemental forces of nature, while the sexual tension between Liz and Ethan, and Lisa's strange dreams, suggest deeper mysteries. Ultimately, though, the images and rather portentous soundtrack tend to hint at more than they actually deliver. NF

Vigilante Force

(George Armitage, 1975, US) Kris Kristofferson, Jan-Michael Vincent, Victoria Principal, Bernadette Peters, Brad Dexter, Judson Pratt.
89 min.
Californian small town becomes lawless boom town after the re-working of dormant oil deposits. To restore order, the helpless legal guardians draft Vietnam hero Kristofferson, the town's erstwhile rebel. What emerges is an awkward combination of cheapo war and cowboy comics: gold replaced by black gold; a near-parody of saloon

rowdiness; a brooding anti-hero; urban guerilla warfare that explodes into open hostilities. Kristofferson (long-haired) shuffles through quite convincingly, especially as his inability to adapt to a peacetime situation becomes more apparent. His Abel-like brother Jan-Michael Vincent (short-haired) does more driving than acting, and Victoria Principal is almost totally self-effacing as his girlfriend, but Bernadette Peters plays an ill-treated, down-at-heel, after-hours singer with real style. The dialogue veers towards the self-consciously smart-ass (enraged drinker attacks jukebox playing '70s rock: 'There must be a Buddy Holly record here somewhere!'), and the direction has irritatingly jagged, grisly violence alternating with manly introspection. IB

Vikings, The

(Richard Fleischer, 1958, US) Kirk Douglas, Tony Curtis, Ernest Borgnine, Janet Leigh, Alexander Knox, Frank Thring, James Donald, Maxine Audley.
114 min.
Viking half-brothers Douglas and Curtis fight it out for the throne of Northumbria. Plenty of pillaging, axe-throwing, hearty quaffing of ale, storming of castles, heroic jumping into wolf pits, and manly talk about the glories of entering Valhalla with sword in hand. Handsomely shot by Jack Cardiff, and directed with muscle and verve by Fleischer, this thoroughly entertaining historical epic stands up to umpteen viewings. NF

Viking Women and Their Voyage to the Waters of the Great Sea Serpent, The

(Roger Corman, 1957, US) Abby Dalton, Susan Cabot, Brad Jackson, Richard Devon.
66 min. b/w.
As sundry Nordic lasses set off to rescue their menfolk from the Monster of the Vortex, little do they suspect the brief glimpses of laughable effects work that lie in store for them. TJ

Village Has No Walls, The (Bangarwadi)

(Amol Palekar, 1995, India) Chandrakant Madray, Adhishree Athray, Chandrakant Kulkarni.
130 min.
Into the 1940s Maharashtra village comes a fledgling teacher on a mission from the Raja to provide the local children with an education. It takes time for him to win the elders' confidence; to persuade the shepherd villagers to spare their children for lessons; to allay fears that he's after their women; to overcome the jealous threats of one inhospitable local; to come to terms with traditional disciplines and superstitions – until eventually he finds himself an indispensible part of the community. This leisurely, well-populated film has ethnological and historical interest, but as drama it rather saps one's patience. (Adapted by Vynakatesh Madgulkar from his own famous 1953 Marathi novel.) NB

Village in the Mist (Angemaeul)

(Lim Kwon-Taek, 1983, SKor) Ahn Song-Ki, Chong Yun-Hee, Lee Yea-Min, Kim Ji-Yung, Choi Dong-Jun, Jin Bong-Jin.
90 min.
A startling Korean variation on Straw Dogs. A young woman schoolteacher is posted to a remote village for a year, and senses something odd about it as soon as she gets off the bus; by the time she's been raped (with total impunity) by the mysterious village tramp, she's on the way to uncovering its strange and guilty secret. Hard to judge the film's contribution to Korean sexual politics, but it's certainly expert film-making by a world-class director. TR

Village of Dreams (E No Naka no Boku no Mura)

(Yoichi Higashi, 1996, Jap) Keigo Matsuyama, Shogo Matsuyama, Mieko Harada, Kyozo Nagatsuka.
112 min.
Co-scripted by Takehiro Nakajima, the director of Okoge, this magic-realist evocation of a rural childhood is chiefly interesting for its undercurrent of homosexual panic: twin boys are warned

that the thunder god will steal their penises if they go naked and imagine being smothered by their gruff landlord's animated fundoshi loincloth. Elsewhere, the film rehearses the standard Freudian reading of the approach to puberty: ground already well-covered by Hou Xiaoxian in A Summer at Grandpa's. Amusing and skilfully executed, but nothing new. TR

Village of the Damned

(Wolf Rilla, 1960, GB) George Sanders, Barbara Shelley, Martin Stephens, Michael Gwynne, Laurence Naismith, Richard Vernon, John Phillips.
78 min. b/w.
A modest but intelligent and extremely effective adaptation of John Wyndham's novel The Midwich Cuckoos, about a small English village which mysteriously and inexplicably succumbs to a 24-hour trance-like sleep, after which the womenfolk all discover that they are pregnant. The alien children, strangely alike in appearance, prove to be endowed with telepathic and kinetic powers...You don't get much explanation, and the overall plot may not withstand detailed analysis. But the atmosphere and pace are superbly handled, and the performances of the sinister, inhumanly intelligent 'children' never falter. The allegorical possibilities (generation gap?) are there, but they don't get in the way. DP

Villain

(Michael Tuchner, 1971, GB) Richard Burton, Ian McShane, Nigel Davenport, Donald Sinden, Fiona Lewis, TP McKenna, Joss Ackland, Cathleen Nesbitt.
98 min.
An underworld saga scripted by Dick Clement and Ian La Frenais, who look as though they were disgorging a semi-masticated lesson culled from Nic Roeg, Donald Cammell and Performance. A ludicrous exposé of the lower depths of London crime, it tarts up the hoariest old gangster clichés with a bit of homosexuality and a lot of thuggery, and manages to be both brutish and maudlin. Burton gives a performance of ripe grotesquerie as the gay gang boss who is the spirit of devotion to his mother and a leering Marquis de Sade to his victims. TM

Villain, The (aka Cactus Jack)

(Hal Needham, 1979, US) Kirk Douglas, Ann-Margret, Arnold Schwarzenegger, Paul Lynde, Foster Brooks, Ruth Buzzi, Jack Elam, Strother Martin.
89 min.
Having flopped in the States as The Villain, this abysmally unfunny comedy Western would need a lot more changed than just its title to even begin to fulfil its implicit promise as a live-action Roadrunner cartoon. Douglas mugs his way through a tedious routine of graceless, mistimed slapstick as his incompetent outlaw repeatedly fails to waylay the miscast Schwarzenegger and Ann-Margret, while director Needham – apparently lost without Burt Reynolds – resorts to hackneyed camera trickery, and only stops the rot with a truly offensive resolution. PT

Villa Rides!

(Buzz Kulik, 1968, US) Yul Brynner, Robert Mitchum, Grazia Buccella, Charles Bronson, Robert Viharo, Frank Wolff, Herbert Lom, Alexander Knox, Fernando Rey, John Ireland, Jill Ireland.
124 min.
The Mexican revolution according to Hollywood. Scripted by Robert Towne and Sam Peckinpah, it makes some gestures towards indicating the political and personal complexities behind the career of Pancho Villa (played by Brynner with hair for once). Unfortunately, these are rather nullified by the need to centre the whole thing on an American identification figure – Mitchum as a freebooting pilot – who can serve as a focus for the statutory clichés about simple peasant loyalties and not killing people when you don't hate them. Bronson steals the picture as Villa's brutal lieutenant, who likes to shoot prisoners personally, then have his trigger-finger gently massaged by a pretty wench. Filmed in Panavision in Spain. TM

Ville des Pirates

see City of Pirates

Villeggiatura

see Black Holiday, La

Vincent & Theo (Vincent et Theo)

(Robert Altman, 1990, Fr/GB) Tim Roth, Paul Rhys, Johanna Ter Steege, Wladimir Yordanoff, Jip Wijngaarden, Jean-Pierre Cassel, Hans Kesting.
140 min.
Scripted by Julian Mitchell, this covers much the same period (from Van Gogh's decision to paint full-time to the death of his art-dealer brother) as Minelli's Lust for Life. Indeed, the films are not so very different. True, the focus on the brothers' close but troubled relationship not only mirrors the uneasn symbiosis between art and finance, but offers through their parallel experiences a quasi-mystical dimension entirely in keeping with Vincent's art. But the film goes further than Minelli's in its palpable – sordid, even – physicality and readiness to depict vincent's less endearing qualities. Tim Roth, superb as Vincent, veers convincingly between morose introspection and fervered intensity, while Paul Rhys' twitchy Theo lends depth to a traditionally shadowy figure. Best of all is Altman's simple, uncluttered direction, which makes sensitive use of a strong cast, Jean Lepine's evocative location photography, and Gabriel Yared's compulsive music. Nowhere does Altman sermonise about the artist's greatness; his achievement is allowed to speak for itself. If only more film-makers had such confidence and integrity. GA

Vincent: The Life and Death of Vincent Van Gogh

(Paul Cox, 1987, Aust) John Hurt (narrator), Gabi Trsek, Marika Rivera.
99 min.
Cox's version of the life and work of Van Gogh will surprise those unfamiliar with the painter's correspondence with his brother Theo, where what emerges is a far cry from the fevered illiterate loony of popular mythology. Read by Hurt, the letters, besides being intensely moving, reveal an artist both mystical and intellectual, and a practical man taking steps to defend himself from the well-known enemy of madness within. The words are wonderful, and of course the paintings too. Each time the screen commemorates that perfectly poised tug between the precision of the draughtsmanship and the expressionist writhings of the brushwork, you can guess at the strength of mind necessary to produce such art. Cox's film presents a more complex man than the Kirk Douglas of Minnelli's gorgeous Lust for Life. There isn't much on the turbulent relationship with Gauguin at Arles, and the self-mutilation, like the suicide, favours reeling subjective camera. At times the filmed landscape is flooded with the subject's psychology – fields of flowers whoosh past into an exaltation of abstract colour, the windmills of Van Gogh's native land revolve like the windmills of the mind. Like most of Cox's work, unclassifiable and considered. BC

Violated Angels (Okasareta Byakui)

(Koji Wakamatsu, 1967, Jap) Juro Kara, Reiko Koyonagi, Miki Hayashi, Shoko Kidowaki, Makiko Saegusa, Kyoko Yayoi.
56 min. b/w & col.
Based on the factual case of a young man who broke into a nurses' home in Chicago, mutilating and killing several of the inmates, Wakamatsu's film mercifully has nothing to do with casebook killings. What emerges from the film's rigorous beauty, sense of ceremony, and unsparingly attentive gaze, is a precise, sad delineation of a particular aspect of masculine sexual consciousness. The finale, in which the arrest of the murderer merges with police suppression of student protest, underlines its political relevance. VG

Violation of Justine, The (Justine de Sade)

(Claude Pierson, 1974, Fr/It/Can) Alice Arno, France Verdier, Yves Arcanel, Georges Beauvillier, Dominique Santarelli.
110 min.
Exceedingly dull porno version of de Sade's Justine, which half-heartedly strives for respectability. To prove that they're performing

a classic, no one says one word when ten will do, and the film kicks off with a mini-documentary on de Sade's life and times, concluding with the cheeky suggestion that the whole is designed as a stiff warning against 'unbridled perversity'. But there's nothing unbridled about the perversity on display: as the pure-in-heart heroine, the strapping Alice Arno receives the most routine chastisements before being charmingly struck down by a lightning flash obviously borrowed from one of Corman's Poe adaptations. GB

Violator, The

see Act of Vengeance

Viol du Vampire, Le

(Jean Rollin, 1967, Fr) Bernard Letrou, Solange Pradel, Ursule Pauly.
90 min. b/w.
Two wan French babes think they're vampires and sit around their gloomy mansion fretting about the night 60 years ago when peasants burst in and blinded one and raped the other. A group of youngsters turn up and free the girls from their obsession. It's incomprehensible, unscary, but prettily shot in b/w, and everyone looks like Juliet Greco. SFe

Violence at Noon (Hakuchu no Torima)

(Nagisa Oshima, 1966, Jap) Saeda Kawaguchi, Akiko Koyama, Kei Sato, Matsuhiro Toura, Fumio Watanabe.
99 min. b/w.
As in almost every other films, Oshima takes the story of a real-life criminal (here, a rapist and murderer) and uses it as the key to a sweeping analysis of the ills of post-war Japanese society. Very little time is wasted on the nuts-and-bolts of the police manhunt; the focus is on two women who know the criminal, and – through them – on the history of the village in Shinshu where the wretched man was born and raised. Oshima reveals his real subject gradually, piecing it together like a mosaic. It is an account of the decay of post-war idealism, the collapse of brave ventures like a collectively run farm, the inexorable restoration of old inequalities and injustices. The visual approach, too, is like a mosaic: there are incessant changes of camera angle, as if to stress that no one point of view is 'true'. TR

Violent Cop, The (Sono Otoko Kyobo ni Tsuki)

(Takeshi Kitano, 1989, Jap) Takeshi Kitano, Haku Ryu.
103 min.
From its updated Erik Satie score to its shockingly sadistic gay villain, this 'rogue cop' thriller has very obvious debts to western precedents: it tells a not-very-surprising story about a lone detective who takes on both a yakuza gang and his own corrupt superiors, and generates considerable mayhem in the process. But this formulary material makes for electrifying entertainment in the hands of Takeshi Kitano (remember him as Sergeant Hara in Merry Christmas, Mr Lawrence?), who stars and directs. The whole movie is imbued with his personality, a mix of stubborn pig-headedness, blatant prejudices, committed violence, and hard, self-deprecatory humour. It's also superbly paced. TR

Violent Professionals, The (Milano Trema: La Polizia Vuole Giustizia)

(Sergio Martino, 1973, It) Luc Merenda, Silvano Tranquilli, Richard Conte, Martine Brochard, Carlo Alighiero.
100 min.
A direct crib from Siegel's Dirty Harry (in fact almost every scene can be matched from one or other of Siegel's films), given a pernicious Red Scare overlay, and with clean-cut Prince Valiant-cum-Captain Marvel (referred to as such in the script) Luc Merenda as Caneparo, 'The Man', whose methods get him suspended from the police force. He vows to go it alone after the death of a colleague, and infiltrates an underworld composed entirely of drugged-out hippies and anarchists trying to force the birth of a new order by robbing banks. A text-book example of smear-type propaganda of the simplest sort, plus a quota of the formula shocks,

dispensed at the press of a button, that seem to be Martino's forte. Luc Merenda's expression of non-comprehending idiocy has to be seen to be believed. VG

Violent Saturday

(Richard Fleischer, 1955, US) Victor Mature, Richard Egan, Stephen McNally, Lee Marvin, Sylvia Sidney, Ernest Borgnine, Tommy Noonan, J Carrol Naish.
91 min.
A competent bank job movie that takes place in the widescreen DeLuxe Color burning light of the Midwest noonday sun, without a shadow in sight. Any movie which features Mature, Borgnine and Marvin has to be some kind of primer in slobdom; but in fact Borgnine plays a religious fundamentalist farmer, and hero Mature soon becomes marginal when up against Marvin's minimal performance as a loose-lipped killer with a permanent head cold. Growling that women and children 'make me nervous', he can make his continual inhalation of benzedrine look like deep degeneracy. When a boy knocks the nasal spray out of his hand, he treads all over the kid's fingers. Sadly, Fleischer takes attention away from the action and into a moral battleground back at the farm, but Borgnine finally gets his pitchfork into Marvin's back. The devil you know...CPea

Violent Streets

see Thief

Violent Tradition

(John Woo, 1996, US/Can) Sandrine Holt, Ivan Sergei, Nicholas Lea, Michael Wong, Jennifer Dale.
96 min.
The title and the packaging are misleading. This isn't the ultra-violent action bonanza they would have us believe, but a kinder, gentler John Woo flick, a made-as-a-cable pilot introducing an eccentric crime-fighting trio: two refugees from the Hong Kong triads, Li Ann (Holt), and Mac (Sergei), who is in love with her, and an ex-cop (Lea) who is her fiancé. Li Ann's admirers don't stop there: there's also Michael (Wong), heir to a powerful crime family. Inspired by Woo's 1991 HK comedy Once a Thief, this conceit harks back further to classy crime capers like Topaz or Gambit. Very minor, but quite watchable. TCh

Violette et François

(Jacques Rouffio, 1977, Fr) Isabelle Adjani, Jacques Dutronc, Serge Reggiani, Lea Massari, Sophie Daumier, Françoise Arnoul.
98 min.
Cashing in on the powerful combination of crime, passion and conjugal bliss, Rouffio has his young couple (Adjani and Dutronc) resort to shoplifting, a practice which keeps them in bohemian comfort and stunning clothes. Typically European, it's superiority they're after, not just shekels. Accordingly they display an in-bred aristocratic anarchism, have madcap adventures, and do cutesy things. All this is silly enough and not unfunny, but François' growing angst and his (sadly) unfulfilled suicidal urges destroy the last vestiges of irresponsible charm. JS

Violette Nozière

(Claude Chabrol, 1977, Fr/Can) Isabelle Huppert, Jean Carmet, Stéphane Audran, Mario David, Bernadette Lafont, Lisa Langlois, Jean-François Garreaud.
122 min.
The Chabrol film for people who don't really like Chabrol films. Based, like the infinitely superior but much maligned Les Noces Rouges, on a real-life murder case – the 18-year-old Violette poisoned her parents in 1933 – it begins brilliantly with a characteristic demolition job on the dreary, furtive squalors of petit bourgeois life that drive Violette to murder. But the political and social implications thus raised are never really confronted. Instead, leaving all sorts of questions unanswered and avenues unexplored, Chabrol ('I fell in love with Violette Nozière he roundly declared) settles down latterly to canonise her for no very apparent reason as a patient and saintly Grizelda. The period evocation is gorgeous, but ultimately it's an empty slice of sleight-of-hand. TM

Violon de Rothschild, Le

see Rothschild's Violin

Violons du Bal, Les

(Michel Drach, 1974, Fr) Michel Drach, Jean-Louis Trintignant, David Drach, Christian Rist, Nathalie Roussel, Marie-Josée Nat, Guido Alberti.
108 min. b/w & col.
More personal memories of France under the German Occupation in World War II: the director Michel Drach (charmingly played by his son David) was, however, no Lucien Lacombe, ready to accommodate the conqueror, but a wide-eyed Jewish boy who, despite a spell in hiding with the family of a canny, treacherous peasant, was blessed with a handsome, wealthy mother and survived the war with his trusting nature still intact. Les Violons du Bal comprises episodes in Michel's escape to Switzerland, intercut with semi-humorous scenes of the still-trusting Drach (played as an adult by Trintignant) attempting to finance the film ('When are you shooting the sex scenes?' a fat, pin-headed producer enquires). Drach's earnest confusion about the sort of film he is making does not ultimately diminish these deeply-felt, nostalgic, and often affecting memories. JPy

V.I.P.s, The

(Anthony Asquith, 1963, GB) Elizabeth Taylor, Richard Burton, Louis Jourdan, Elsa Martinelli, Margaret Rutherford, Maggie Smith, Rod Taylor, Orson Welles, Linda Christian, Dennis Price.
119 min.
Asquith, once a card-carrying member of the Communist Party and a determinedly radical filmmaker, subsided in the '50s and '60s into lavish productions which were in some cases entertaining and glossy, but politically middle-of-the-road conservative. This one concerns the various problems and predicaments of a group of wealthy people stranded at London Airport by fog. The level of the Terence Rattigan script is typified by the episode in which 'devoted secretary' Maggie Smith persuades millionaire Richard Burton to write a cheque for a vast sum of money in order to save her boss (Rod Taylor) from ruin. The performances are all reasonably enjoyable, but it's the sort of film the British cinema could well do without. DP

Virgin (36 Fillette)

(Catherine Breillat, 1988, Fr) Delphine Zentout, Etienne Chicot, Olivier Parnière, Jean-Pierre Léaud, Jean-François Stévenin.
88 min.
Yet another film that catches the thrills and fears of a young girl's sexual awakening. Unromantic and shot in long, unflinching takes, Breillat's film sees 14-year-old Lili (Zentout), on a family camping holiday, accept a lift in a flash car from balding smoothie Maurice (Chicot). They meet later at a nightclub, and a mating ritual based on his lust and her paralysed desire begins. Things get complex. In the course of alternately teasing Maurice to distraction and insulting him cruelly – in his hotel room, on the beach, in his ex-girl-friend's bed – Lili reveals a fragility that arouses affection and protectiveness in her playboy seducer. He falls in love, and when he does, Lili senses that her use for him is over. In Lili, Breillat has created a new kind of sex symbol: a voluptuous ingénue who is sharp-tongued, quick-witted, and independent of spirit to the bitter end. But will that appeal to men? Probably not. EP

Virgin (Virgina)

(Srdjan Karanovic, 1991, Yugo/Fr) Marta Keler, Miodrag Kreivokapic.
118 min.
Until recently, in certain areas of Yugoslavia, families without male children were regarded as cursed; accordingly, they would select a daughter to live as a son. In exploring the fate of one such family, this fascinating drama has hapless young 'Stephen' struggling with the deception, though defying both her father and repressive religious orthodoxy to find illicit joy in femininity. Karanovic's framing sets characters against the harsh, stark landscape to convey a sense of lives completely integrated with nature, while domestic scenes capture back-breaking hardship. Forceful and tender by turns, this boasts sequences of haunting intensity. CM

Virgin and the Gypsy, The

(Christopher Miles, 1970, GB) Joanna Shimkus, Franco Nero, Honor Blackman, Mark Burns, Maurice Denham, Fay Compton, Kay Walsh.
95 min.

If casting were everything, this sensitive adaptation of DH Lawrence's novella would rate very high indeed: Joanna Shimkus is painfully convincing as the clergyman's virginal daughter trembling on the brink of womanhood when she falls for the smouldering sexual magnetism of gypsy Franco Nero. Despite Alan Plater's faithful screenplay, however, Miles' direction tends too much towards the pictorial, lacking the visual brio that brought Ken Russell's *Women in Love* so much closer to the dark, physical essence of Lawrence's writing. Miles later directed the turgid Lawrence biopic, *Priest of Love*. NF

Virgin and the Soldier, The
see Petit Matin, Le

Virgin for Saint Tropez, A (Une Vierge pour St Tropez)
(Gregory Freed, 1975, Fr/It) Marianne Remont, Jean-Pierre Delamour, Georges Alexandre, Favre Bertin, Gilda Arrancio.
85 min.
Had the ingredients of this mishmash been more expertly blended, one might have credited the writer/director with the intention of sending us out of the theatre ruminating on the wisdom of unmarried girls defending their virginity. In the event – having endured this wholly implausible tale of a devout Spanish girl and a mercenary Frenchman who finally deflowers her for the entertainment of some ageing swingers – one is left merely yawning. Set in the '60s Côte d'Azur; zero for titillation, in case you wondered. JPy

Virgin Machine (Die Jungfrauenmaschine)
(Monika Treut, 1988, WGer) Ina Blum, Marcello Uriona, Dominique Gaspar, Peter Kern.
85 min.
Journalist Dorothee (doe-eyed Blum) pedals around Hamburg in print dresses and heavy eye make-up. She's writing a book about romantic love, fuel for which are two doomed relationships. She visits the zoo and a hormone specialist, but it isn't until she hears an American feminist speak about reclaiming porn that she decides to head for California in pursuit of her runaway mother and her undiscovered libido. The San Francisco conjured up by director Treut is charged with sexuality, from the purring sex-line ads on TV to the SM shenanigans of Dorothee's plump neighbour. Soon Dorothee is belting around SF on her bike, in flat cap and britches, but still with the eye-make-up, and though her quest for love continues she has at least made some very special friends, and has gained an entry into the fabulous dyke scene. SFe

Virgins and Vampires
see Requiem pour un Vampire

Virgins of the Seven Seas
see Enter the 7 Virgins

Virgin Spring, The (Jungfrukällan)
(Ingmar Bergman, 1959, Swe) Max von Sydow, Birgitta Valberg, Gunnel Lindblom, Birgitta Pettersson, Axel Düberg, Tor Isedal, Allan Edwall.
88 min. b/w.
Bergman won his first Oscar for this cruel but unsensational medieval allegory, a tale of superstition, religious faith, rape and revenge set in a 14th century Sweden where the populace is vacillating between Christianity and paganism. On her way to church, the 15-year-old virgin daughter (Pettersson) of peasant parents (von Sydow and Valberg) is raped by two goatherds. Later, in a bizarre twist of fate, the culprits ask for food and shelter at the house of the dead girl's parents. Discovering the truth when the goatherds offer to sell them their dead daughter's bloodstained clothes, the parents exact a brutal revenge. The formal simplicity and overt symbolism (light and dark, fire and water) undercut the potentially sensationalist elements of the material, Sven Nykvist's luminous black-and-white photography conspiring with the austerity of Bergman's imagery to create an extraordinary metaphysical charge. NF

Viridiana
(Luis Buñuel, 1961, Sp/Mex) Silvia Pinal, Francisco Rabal, Fernando Rey, Margarita Lozano, Victoria Zinny, Teresa Rabal.
91 min. b/w.
After years in Mexican exile, Buñuel returned to his native Spain to make this dark account of corruption, which was immediately banned. A young nun, full of charity, kindness, and idealistic illusions about humanity, visits her uncle and tries to help some local peasants and beggars. But her altruism is greeted with ridicule and cruelty. Pinal gives a superb performance in the title role, and Buñuel's clear-eyed wit is relentless in its depiction of human selfishness, ingratitude, and cynicism. The final beggars' orgy – a black parody of the Last Supper, performed to the ethereal strains of Handel's 'Messiah' – is one of the director's most memorably disturbing, funny, and brutal scenes. A masterpiece. GA

Virus (Fukkatsu no Hi)
(Kinji Fukasaku, 1980, Jap/Can) Sonny Chiba, Chuck Connors, Glenn Ford, Olivia Hussey, George Kennedy, Cec Linder, Bo Svenson, Henry Silva, Robert Vaughn, Stephanie Faulkner, Masao Kusakari, Edward James Olmos.
155 min.
A rip-roaring apocalypse thriller about a germ warfare virus that escapes and devastates the world. Bearing strong echoes of Stephen King's book *The Stand* and Romero's *The Crazies*, plus more than a hint of *On the Beach*, the film has as many locations and characters as a fat paperback, but is saved from the anonymity that sometimes afflicts such ventures by its wonderfully fatalistic tone: in this English-speaking co-production, Kinji Fukasaku allows his Japanese masochism full rein ('How can the entire Japanese population have died in three months?' someone pleads) and dispatches an all-star American cast with happy abandon. Admittedly his film contains some slightly repellent notions about the submission of sexuality to reason, which are as hard to swallow as Chuck Connors playing a British Naval Captain, but you can forgive a lot to a film-maker audacious enough to destroy the world twice over in one movie. DP

Vision Quest (aka Crazy for You)
(Harold Becker, 1985, US) Matthew Modine, Linda Fiorentino, Michael Schoeffling, Ronny Cox, Harold Sylvester, Roberts Blossom, Madonna.
105 min.
Retitled for British video release to cash in on several milliseconds of Madonna strutting her stuff in a nightclub (singing 'Crazy for You'). Actually, neither handle bears much relation to the plot of this growing-pains movie, which has Matthew 'Birdy' Modine aiming to lose those extra pounds so he can take on a rival college's wrestling champ. Lots of shots of scantily-clad boys rolling around on the floor with their arms round each other. AB

Visions of Eight
(Juri Ozerov/Mai Zetterling/Arthur Penn/Michael Pfleghar/Kon Ichikawa/Claude Lelouch/Milos Forman/John Schlesinger, 1973, US).
110 min.
The 1972 Munich Olympics as seen by eight directors; eight sequences devoted entirely to sport, with only passing reference to the intrusion of politics. About half of them work. Perhaps Lelouch on the losers is the most surprising, given his indifferent films; his study of private humiliation in a public place succeeds almost to the point of intrusion. Penn's sequence on the pole vault, shot almost entirely in slow motion and silence by Walter Lassally, is the most beautiful to look at. Penn lets the event speak for itself, unlike Ichikawa, who tries to show the 100 metres as representative of modern human existence, takes 34 cameras, shoots 20,000 feet of film, and still fails. Schlesinger's treatment of the marathon emerges as the most individual piece, but with its straining after hallucinatory and atmospheric effects, ends up overdone. Mai Zetterling's study of weightlifters deserves mention, while the other three are forgettable. The final impression that remains is of a public relations campaign – what makes the Games transcend the physical into the

spiritual, as the press handout said – for an event that is becoming increasingly complex and out-of-hand; a pity that no one explored those implications. CPe

Visions of Light
(Arnold Glassman/Todd McCarthy/Stuart Samuels, 1992, US/Jap) Nestor Almendros, Bill Butler, Michael Chapman, Allen Daviau, Caleb Deschanel, James Wong Howe, Sven Nykvist, Haskell Wexler, Gordon Willis, Vilmos Zsigmond.
92 min.
Subtitled 'The Art of Cinematography', this American Film Institute documentary turns the camera back on the people (mostly men) behind the lens: the directors of photography. As this intelligently structured interview-based film implicitly recognises, the history of cinematography is also an alternative history of cinema itself. Hence, we start with the silent era and the innovations of Billy Bitzer, DW Griffith's cameraman, and move on to the glamorous monochrome photography of the '30s, Gregg Toland's contribution to *Citizen Kane* and the 'primal imagery' of *film noir*. The documentary really comes into its own, however, when the interviewees – Allen Daviau (*ET*), Gordon Willis (*The Godfather*), Nestor Almendros (*Days of Heaven*), Michael Chapman (*Raging Bull*) and many others – reminisce about their own experience: the switch from the 'more abstract' b/w to colour, the anamorphic space, and, most intriguingly, the way in which new technology subtly redefines the texture of the movies. TCh

Visiteurs, Les
(Jean-Marc Poiré, 1993, Fr) Christian Clavier, Jean Reno, Valérie Lemercier, Marie-Anne Chazel, Christian Bujeau.
107 min.
This quixotic time-travel movie comes on like a lunatic blend of *Time Bandits*, Tati and Benny Hill. Tall 12th century knight Godefroy de Montmirail (Reno) and his short-arse servant Jacquouille (Clavier) return to France from foreign wars. Under a witch's curse, Godefroy mistakes his intended father-in-law for a bear and shoots him with an arrow. A potion from wizard Eusebius intended to take him back in time instead hurtles him and his servant into contemporary France, where he finds their castle is now an upmarket chateau-restaurant run by Godefroy's distant relative, the effete Béatrice (Lemercier). Shot in the verdant hills of Languedoc, this puerile caper is likely to appeal more to fans of Will Hay and Mr Bean than those of Monty Python. Exquisite period detail and sophisticated effects. WH

Visiteurs du Soir, Les (The Devil's Envoys)
(Marcel Carné, 1942, Fr) Arletty, Alain Cuny, Jules Berry, Marie Déa, Marcel Herrand, Fernand Ledoux, Gabriel Gabrio, Roger Blin.
110 min. b/w.
Forced to retreat into the past during the German Occupation, the poetic realism of Carné and Prévert degenerated into fey surrealism in this lazy medieval ballad about the Devil's malicious meddling in affairs of the heart. The opening sequences, with two mysterious strangers riding out of the desert and beginning to work their magic in the magnificent white castle created by Trauner, have a true fairytale touch. But as the hearts get tangled, with the devil's emissary falling despairingly in love with the beautiful princess, the dialogue gets increasingly lachrymose, and the slow pace begins to take its toll. Wonderful performances, though, and graced with an undeniable visual splendour. TM

Visiting Hours
(Jean-Claude Lord, 1981, Can) Michael Ironside, Lee Grant, Linda Purl, William Shatner, Lenore Zann, Harvey Atkin.
105 min.
A fatuous attempt to amalgamate the maniac-with-the-knife format of *Halloween* with the street realism of *Taxi Driver*. As any horror fan knows, *Halloween* worked so well precisely because it was not set in any gritty urban context but in a dream-like adolescent world. In contrast, this film concerns a fascist sicko (Ironside) who terrorises a liberal woman TV reporter (Grant) just seen making an outspoken contribution to a discus-

sion on battered wives, continuing after she has been hospitalised: a thuddingly literal theme that not only shatters any spooky atmosphere the film might have, but makes its lingeringly voyeuristic style all the more reprehensible. Not content with flashbacks to the villain's childhood, the sexist script also takes time out to congratulate the heroine on being worth killing: 'He's after you because you're a strong woman' says Grant's boss Shatner, conveniently ignoring about eight other victims. The fact that the film is not tacky in appearance, and is energetically acted, only makes it more depressing. If you want horror in a hospital, try *Halloween II*. DP

Visitor, The (Cugini Carnali)

(Sergio Martino, 1974, It) Riccardo Cucciolla, Alfredo Pea, Claudio Nicastro, Susan Player, Hugh Griffith, Fiorella Masselli.
99 min.
One of those Italian sex'n'satire movies, this deliberates for most of its ponderous 99 minutes over the problems leading up to that magical first fuck. The boy's skinny, keeps his head in his Latin text and his mind elsewhere; the girl's more beautiful than one can reasonably expect of a cousin; and there's a muscle-bound friend to kick sand around and complicate the plot. Meanwhile the clergy, fat mothers, and constipated fathers are lampooned in a heavy-handed sort of way, while maids stand around and scratch their legs. An hour and a half leading up to something that probably only lasted thirty seconds (there's a discreet fadeout), and you have an idea of what a huge waste of time it all is. Worth noting in passing that it was exactly this type of film that Polanski took apart so effectively in *What?*. The fact that Carlo Ponti produced both is also fairly revealing. CPe

Vita è Bella, La

see Life Is Beautiful

Vitelloni, I

(Federico Fellini, 1953, It) Franco Interlenghi, Alberto Sordi, Franco Fabrizi, Leopoldo Trieste, Riccardo Fellini, Leonora Ruffo, Achille Majeroni.
109 min. b/w.
The best of Fellini went into this bleakly funny study of five young men adrift in the wasteland of their provincial home town. Middle class layabouts living by cadging off their families, aimlessly spending their days in pursuit of amusement and girls while nursing vague ambitions never likely to be more than pipe-dreams, they are trapped as much by their own moral bankruptcy as by the futureless society in which they have never quite grown up. Beautifully shot and performed, and governed by an inextricable mixture of affectionate sympathy and acid satire, it clearly (and beneficially) trails the neo-realist roots which Fellini later shook off. TM

Vivacious Lady

(George Stevens, 1938, US) James Stewart, Ginger Rogers, James Ellison, Charles Coburn, Beulah Bondi, Frances Mercer, Grady Sutton, Franklin Pangborn, Jack Carson.
90 min. b/w.
Mostly a light-hearted fable in which nightclub dancer Rogers meets, falls for, and marries Professor James Stewart. Much humour is derived from the couple's inability to consummate their wedding owing to family and social pressures, but there are also traces of a critique of the institution of marriage itself: it is always the women who have to adapt and make sacrifices for the sake of monogamy. Rogers is the accomplished centrepiece of the film, slightly atypical as the soft-focus romantic heroine, but with welcome eruptions of her tough and shrewd persona throughout. JCl

Viva Erotica! (Seqing Nan Nü)

(Derek Yee/Lo Chi-Leung, 1996, HK) Leslie Cheung, Karen Mok, Shu Qi, Tsui Kam-Kong, Law Kar-Ying, Lau Ching-Wan.
97 min.
One of the first mainstream movies tailored for 'Category III' (adults only) release in Hong Kong, this opens with a wildly orgasmic sex scene between Leslie Cheung and Karen Mok and ends with the cheering sight of an entire film crew

working in the nude. In between the two it's a not-very-sharp satire of the Hong Kong film industry, centred on an art movie director with two flops to his name (Cheung) who wrestles with his conscience as he shoots a porno movie for the money. The mix of parodies, sentimentality, melodrama and earnest pretensions never really gels, but the overall anti-moralist thrust is decent enough. TR

Viva Knievel!

(Gordon Douglas, 1977, US) Evel Knievel, Gene Kelly, Lauren Hutton, Leslie Nielsen, Red Buttons, Cameron Mitchell, Albert Salmi, Marjoe Gortner.
106 min.
A mountain of self-love, revealing stunt biker Knievel as a saintly combination of Batman and Billy Graham. Anyone who saw the Ray Charles vehicle *Ballad in Blue* knows the format: sole object is to show the star (playing Himself) in the best light, preferably with some orphans or cripples around to be nice to. Knievel comes out of it badly, since he also has thespian cripple Hutton to cope with, plus Gene Kelly – 'an embittered ex-champ whose wife died in childbirth on the day of his big accident ten years before' – who, with his croaking voice and shambling appearance, is in line for a 'Most Pitiful Come-down' Oscar. Gordon Douglas, handling the action sequences adequately and gritting his teeth at the rest of the drug-busting plot nonsense, deserves sympathy as well. AN

Viva la Muerte

(Fernando Arrabal, 1970, Fr/Tun) Mahdi Chaouch, Nuria Espert, Anouk Ferjac, Ivan Henriques, Jazia Klibi.
90 min.
Arrabal's first feature as director generalises out from a series of autobiographical memories, in time-honoured surrealist fashion; personal Oedipal anguish is meshed with strands of social and political criticism, until the two become indistinguishable. Various 'psychedelic' colour effects serve to blur the drama's focus even more. Bourgeois 'outrage' is generated quite mechanically, by showing shit, carcasses, maggots, and so on; when hints of authentic feeling peep through, they turn out to be outrageous only in their sentimentality – as in the fantasy images of Lorca's funeral, thronged with naked street-boys. TR

Viva Las Vegas (aka Love in Las Vegas)

(George Sidney, 1963, US) Elvis Presley, Ann-Margret, Cesare Danova, William Demarest, Nicky Blair, Jack Carter.
86 min.
Thin even by Presley standards, this has him as a racing driver yearning to win the Las Vegas Grand Prix, and filling in as a singing waiter while Ann-Margret revs her chassis at him. Directed with lethargic brashness, it matches the gaudy vulgarity of Las Vegas pretty well. There's a generous quota of songs, pretty unimaginatively staged apart from an impromptu rendering of 'The Yellow Rose of Texas'. TM

Viva la Vie

(Claude Lelouch, 1984, Fr) Michel Piccoli, Charlotte Rampling, Jean-Louis Trintignant, Evelyne Bouix, Charles Aznavour, Anouk Aimée.
110 min.
This sci-fi is a decidedly un-Lelouchian Lelouch. At a time of international tension, a businessman and an actress vanish at precisely the same time and in similar circumstances. A few days later they reappear, apparently traumatised and with a message of peace and tolerance from some all powerful Beyond. Reality, hoax, or feature length dream sequence? All of the above. Bags of swank, of course (Lelouch hasn't changed that much), plus an impression of slightly more substance than usual. But be advised Trintignant keeps performing a chant of such insidious, brainwashing monotony that it's impossible to flush out of your system. BBa

Viva Maria!

(Louis Malle, 1965, Fr/It) Jeanne Moreau, Brigitte Bardot, George Hamilton, Gregor Von Rezzori, Paulette Dubost, Claudio Brook, Carlos López Moctezuma.
120 min.

Bardot and Moreau in irresistibly carefree mood as a pair of chorines who invent the striptease and become twin inspirations for a Latin American revolution, 1907 vintage. Like *Zazie dans le Métro*, this is Malle in his freewheeling guise, casually tossing out gags like so many fireworks, and shortly afterwards he embarked for India as a spiritual refresher course in countering the hollowness of commercial film-making. *Viva Maria* is certainly empty, but fun. A fair percentage of its gags may fall by the wayside (especially if you happen on the English dubbed version), but nothing can dim the pyrotechnics of Henri Decaë's camerawork, which has all the colour and charm of a carnival. And the songs Georges Delerue provides for the two stars in their act are delightful. TM

Viva Max!

(Jerry Paris, 1969, US) Peter Ustinov, Pamela Tiffin, Jonathan Winters, John Astin, Keenan Wynn, Harry Morgan, Alice Ghostley, Kenneth Mars.
92 min.
A sort of Ealing comedy transplant, with Ustinov in his element as a bumbling Mexican generalissimo who leads an army of 87 men into Texas to recapture the Alamo, huffed because his lady friend scoffed that his troops wouldn't follow him even into a whorehouse. He gets there just before closing time – the Alamo now being a museum – and raises the Mexican flag before realising he has forgotten to issue any ammunition. But that's all right, since the American National Guardsmen haven't any either. In the ensuing stand-off, gentle satirical swipes are taken at bureaucracy, nationalism, militarism and anti-Commie hysteria. It is amusing enough, if whimsical and distinctly patchy, but is given a lift by some fine supporting performances (Keenan Wynn and Harry Morgan, especially) and by location shooting in the streets of San Antonio. The scenes in the Alamo, however, were staged at Cinecittà in Rome: the Daughters of the Republic of America were not amused by the threat of desecration to their national souvenir shop. TM

Viva Portugal

(Christiane Gerhards/Malte Rauch/Samuel Schirmbeck/Serge July/Peer Oliphant, 1975, WGer/Fr)
99 min.
Made by a group of French and West German journalists (the English version was assembled by Cinema Action), this traces the first year of the Portuguese revolution. Besides documenting the political changes, from the overthrow of Caetano's dictatorship to the failure of a right wing coup in March 1975 (largely because soldiers questioned their officers' orders), the film deals with the effect of the revolution on the people. Factory and village committees, independent trade unions, are shown being set up; the plight of the farmworkers and the power of the anti-Communist Church are dealt with. It culminates with the occupation of an empty manor house, which is converted into a people's hospital. CPe

Viva Villa!

(Jack Conway, 1934, US) Wallace Beery, Leo Carrillo, Fay Wray, Donald Cook, Stuart Erwin, George E Stone, Katherine DeMille.
115 min. b/w.
An uncredited Howard Hawks directed some of the material in this rumbustious traversal of the Mexican revolutionary leader's rise and fall, with Beery leading from the front as future president Pancho, part moral crusader, part crazy bandito. The big MGM production typically plays fast and loose with the facts so it's as much an action spectacular as a genuine historical chronicle, but there's much good humour and a terrifically hammy death scene where one unfortunate villain is coated in honey and left under the sun for the ants. TJ

Viva Zapata!

(Elia Kazan, 1952, US) Marlon Brando, Jean Peters, Anthony Quinn, Joseph Wiseman, Margo, Frank Silvera, Mildred Dunnock, Henry Silva.
113 min. b/w.
Covered in an unconvincing mess of Mexican make-up, Brando adds a touch of fire to this otherwise frequently dull tale of the outlaw who became a revolutionary hero in the struggle

against the tyrannical President Diaz. An actorly film, of course – what else would one expect from Kazan? – but the direction and John Steinbeck's script seem stranded in a no man's land between straightforward adventure and a pessimistic allegory about the corrupting nature of power. GA

Vive l'Amour (Aiqing Wansui)
(Tsai Ming-liang, 1994, Tai) Yang Kuei-mei, Chen Chao-jung, Lee Kang-sheng.
118 min.
A lot of city life flows through Tsai's masterly follow-up to *Rebels of the Neon God*, but our attention is focused on just three people. Mei, a woman pushing middle age, lives alone, sells real estate and longs to be loved. Hsiao Kang has left home and sells burial lockers in a new designer cemetery; possibly gay, he longs to love someone. And the cocky Ah Jung sometimes sells clothes at the night market; he neither loves anyone, nor feels any need to be loved. Watching Tsai manoeuvre these people into proximity with each other so that their lives may be changed is a large part of the film's pleasure, but it doesn't eclipse the sheer joy of discovering gradually where the film's own heart lies. Funny and heartbreakingly sad. TR

Vivement Dimanche! (Confidentially Yours/ Finally, Sunday!)
(François Truffaut, 1983, Fr) Fanny Ardant, Jean-Louis Trintignant, Philippe Laudenbach, Caroline Sihol, Philippe Morier-Genoud, Jean-Pierre Kalfon, Jean-Louis Richard.
111 min. b/w.
Based on an American novel (Charles Williams' *The Long Saturday Night*, but set in small-town South of France, the plot introduces Trintignant as the owner of an estate agency and Ardant as his long-suffering secretary. Trintignant is first implicated in one murder. Then his wife is killed. While he is on the run, it falls to Ardant to solve the crimes, with the neat role reversal allowing Truffaut both to cover familiar genre ground in unfamiliar manner, and to reflect on the fragility of the male ego. Thoughtfully composed, elegantly performed, and shot atmospherically in black-and-white, it could so easily have become a brittle exercise in form. But the sentimentality is constantly undercut, and almost every scene is infused with deft, sometimes dark humour, even as the corpses pile high on the sidewalks of those not particularly mean French streets. RR

Vivre pour Vivre (Live for Life)
(Claude Lelouch, 1967, Fr/It) Yves Montand, Candice Bergen, Annie Girardot, Irène Tunc, Anouk Ferjac.
130 min.
Whatever else, Lelouch must have acquired a super tan making this successor to *Un Homme et une Femme*, so generously does he allow the sun to dazzle his camera lens. An unsalvageably meretricious melodrama (Montand's TV reporter torn between patient wife Girardot and fashion model Bergen) played out against the glamorous backdrops of downtown Manhattan and up-country Vietnam, it is rendered even more preposterous by the pretentious dialogue, inept performances, cross-eyed cross-cutting, and a score by Francis Lai more suited to a hotel lounge than a film. GAd

Vivre sa Vie (It's My Life/ My Life to Live)
(Jean-Luc Godard, 1962, Fr) Anna Karina, Sady Rebbot, André S Labarthe, Guylaine Schlumberger, Brice Parain, Peter Kassowitz.
85 min. b/w.
Twelve Brechtian tableaux chronicle the life and death of a whore, starting out as a documentary on prostitution, ending as a Monogram B movie. In retrospect, Godard expressed doubts about the cheap gangster pyrotechnics as being merely a nod to cinephilia. But like the highly stylised prostitution scenes, they are in fact a distantiating device forcing a more direct confrontation with the film's true subject: the enigmatic beauty and troubling presence of Karina, and the mystery of Godard's own passionate involvement with her. This film, as Godard has noted, was the first stage in the inevitable dissolution of their marriage, as described in *Pierrot le Fou*; and

every scene in the film obliquely pinpoints that crisis as originating in the awareness that, as director to star actress, he found himself rapturously but humiliatingly playing client to her prostitute. TM

V I Warshawski
(Jeff Kanew, 1991, US) Kathleen Turner, Jay O Sanders, Charles Durning, Angela Goethals, Nancy Paul, Frederick Coffin, Charles McCaughan, Stephen Meadows, Wayne Knight.
89 min.
Even stripped of her liberal politics and souped up to Emma Peel levels of retaliation, thrillerwriter Sara Paretsky's private eye V I Warshawski (Turner) should have been a plausible alternative to the screen's male peepers. Kanew's vehicle, however, proves a wheelclamped affair. Hired by foul-mouthed but vulnerable 13-year-old Kat (Goethals) to find out who killed her dad, V I digs into the case, which turns out to be a disappointing piece of all-purpose fluff about an inheritance. Since she's out there on her own, V I has a pit-stop team comprising on-off lover Murray (Sanders) and a caring cop who knew her way back when (Durning); and some of the interchanges between them recall, in a debased form, the old Howard Hawks routines for bantering buddies. The hook is Warshawski's feminism, delivered, and the relationship with the kid, vastly borrowed from Cassavetes' wonderful *Gloria*. Not good. BC

Vixen
(Russ Meyer, 1968, US) Erica Gavin, Harrison Page, Garth Pillsbury, Michael Donovan O'Donnell, Vincene Wallace.
71 min.
Voracious Erica Gavin indulges a little choreographed foreplay with a wet fish; a black draft-dodging biker discovers during a mid-air hijack that even Cuba-bound IRA commies hate niggers. Just two cherishably iconic moments from *Vixen*, the film that showed Meyer to have the most dynamic editing style in American cinema, and took him from nudie king to national monument via the most outrageous exploitation of bosom buddydom ever. PT

Vizi Privati, Pubbliche Virtú
see Private Vices & Public Virtues

Vladimir et Rosa (Vladimir and Rosa)
(Jean-Luc Godard/Jean-Pierre Gorin, 1970, Fr/WGer/US) Anne Wiazemsky, Jean-Pierre Gorin, Juliette Berto, Ernest Menzer, Jean-Luc Godard, Yves Afonso.
103 min.
Wind from the East and the other Dziga-Vertov Group films put themselves forward as positive steps. *Vladimir and Rosa* does the same, but it's dominated by an angry sense of defeat. It centres on a grotesque parody/reconstruction of the Chicago Conspiracy Trial, but the actors playing the defendants are also seen in a few domestic scenes (dominated by discussions of feminism), while Godard and Gorin themselves continually interrupt the proceedings to mull over the film's implications and reassess their strategies. The black humour and the new emphasis on the material processes of film-making give the film a distinctive place in the Group's researches, even if its discussion is a rather defeatist rehash of arguments rehearsed more cogently elsewhere. TR

Voce della luna, La
see Voice of the Moon, The

Voice of Kurdistan, The
(Georges Drion/Jacqueline Bottagisio, 1980, GB/Aust)
109 min. b/w.
National liberation movements rarely have any tradition in cinema, for obvious reasons: celluloid is not a major priority in guerrilla warfare. When films do emerge from or about such struggles, the makers often understandably try to make up for lost time by cramming a whole complex history and current context into one giant macro-statement. But are such ambitious, all-embracing projects tactically the best vehicles for eliciting solidarity in the West? Certainly the first part of this film about the struggle of the Middle East's

18 million Kurds is somewhat intimidating, with its barrage of names, groups, uprisings, and incomprehensible archive footage (rarely labelled). But once the broad outlines have been established, the later material (from 1961 to 1978) is fascinating, particularly on the role of the Shah, and the realignment and move to the left of the Kurdish movement since the defeat by the Ba'ath regime in 1975. As 'one of the largest nations to have been denied a state', Kurdistan, divided among four Middle East dictatorships, certainly deserved to have its revolution popularised. CG

Voice of the Moon, The (La Voce della luna)
(Federico Fellini, 1989, It) Roberto Benigni, Paolo Villaggio.
115 min.
A noisome, sprawling slab of pretentious nonsense, charting the odyssey of a dreamy simpleton-cum-poet (Benigni) through an Emilian landscape populated by the usual Fellini collection of grotesque eccentrics, and clearly intended to evoke the various ills of the modern world. Profoundly reactionary, almost without narrative structure, and embarrassingly self-indulgent, it is virtually unwatchable. GA

Voice Over
(Chris Monger, 1981, GB) Ian McNeice, Bish Nethercote, John Cassady, Sarah Martin, David Pearce.
105 min.
When shown at the Edinburgh Festival, this caused a minor furore over its supposed misogyny; and indeed its story of radio personality Fats Bannerman (McNeice), writer and presenter of a bland romantic costume serial, far outdoes John Fowles' *The Collector* as an instance of ultimate male possessiveness of the female object. When Fats is accused in an interview of escapism, the programme begins to darken; and when he comes across and takes in a catatonic rape victim (Nethercote), it gets farther and farther out (Gothic vampires, improvised sax doodlings), as does his mental state, finally erupting in (predictably phallic) violence. Accompanying Fats' decline is some increasingly obvious visual and aural symbolism: attempts to strangle himself with his own tape recordings, regression to a childhood stammer. Sick and disturbing. RM

Voices
(Kevin Billington, 1973, GB) David Hemmings, Gayle Hunnicutt, Lynn Farleigh, Russell Lewis, Eva Griffiths, Adam Bridge.
91 min.
Hemmings and Hunnicutt arrive at their auntie's dilapidated mansion; she (brooding over the death of their son) hears ghostly voices, he (brooding over his failure as a writer) doesn't. That's about all there is to it. There's a surprise twist ending, but its impact is somewhat reduced by the one-and-a-half hours of circuitous chit-chat that's gone before. Based on a play by Richard Lortz, it's staggeringly boring (and blatantly illogical into the bargain).

Voices from the Front
(Sandra Elgear/Robyn Hutt/David Meieran, 1990, US)
90 min.
A combative documentary from the New York AIDS activist group Testing the Limits, its point being that people with AIDS are on a war footing. It takes an unapologetically polemical line, diametrically opposed to the 'neutral' reportage found in the mainstream media, and begins by looking at the media's subtly prejudicial rhetoric of 'victims' and ghettoisation, before focusing on the work of the American 'empowerment movements' and direct-action groups like ACT-UP and People With AIDS Coalition. What's at stake in this battle, the film argues, is a genuinely insurrectionary groundswell that not only proposes a radical challenge to institutionalised exclusions – of women, racial minorities and gay men – but also calls for a direct confrontation of the power structures of the US Government and the drugs multinationals. The film's technique – collaging interviews, demo footage and TV excerpts – makes for a punchy broadsheet approach, punctuated with info-crammed flashes of text, and (unfortunately) a rousing anthem in the 'We are the World' school. Potent stuff, although at times it wears its pamphleteering a little heavily. JRo

Voie Lactée, La (The Milky Way)

(Luis Buñuel, 1968, Fr/It) Laurent Terzieff, Paul Frankeur, Delphine Seyrig, Edith Scob, Bernard Verley, Georges Marchal, Jean-Claude Carrière, Pierre Clémenti, Marcel Pérès, Michel Piccoli, Alain Cuny, Claudio Brook.
102 min.

One of the least accessible (and successful) of Buñuel's later films, it is mainly of interest for its pre-*Discreet Charm of the Bourgeoisie* narrative structure: as it follows a couple of tramps on their pilgrimage from Paris to a shrine in Spain, they encounter various characters and slip through time-warps, space-warps, and numerous narrative digressions en route. It is of course beautifully put together, and there are frequently very amusing interludes. But much of the humour is either too obvious in its general anti-clerical stance, or conversely, too obscure in its examination of the niceties of different Catholic doctrines. One for the Buñuel collectors, or for those knowledgeable about religious dogma. GA

Volcano

(Donald Brittain, 1976, Can) narrator: Donald Brittain.
99 min.

Malcolm Lowry, author of the highly charged, semi-autobiographical *Under the Volcano*, seems to have had more problems than hot dinners, and this film portrait produced by the National Film Board of Canada puts them all on to the screen with enough clarity to wipe the grin off anyone's face. There are alcoholic bouts, homosexual traumas, practical catastrophes (a late draft of his painfully written novel went up in smoke), everything culminating in the numbing loss of creativity in 1947, and death through whisky and pills in a Sussex village ten years later. It's a survey which digs deeper and longer than most such jobs, and presents its findings in a complex manner, with strong bursts of visual symbolism (derived from location footage of Lowry landscapes) constantly peppering the conventional interview material (with Lowry's widow, college chums, and knights of the bottle). Topping off the heady brew, passages from Lowry's writings are read by Richard Burton. GB

Volcano

(Mick Jackson, 1997, US) Tommy Lee Jones, Anne Heche, Gaby Hoffmann, Don Cheadle, Jacqueline Kim, Keith David, John Corbett.
104 min.

Only emergency chief Jones and spunky seismologist Heche stand between Los Angeles and meltdown. The most striking aspect of this fun, old-fashioned disaster movie is the novelty of seeing the most familiar of backdrops used as a creative resource in its own right. Throwing in-jokes and tourist landmarks on to the fire with a pyromaniac's passion, Mick Jackson turns the city into a kind of postmodern theme park. Such is the lightness of touch, it's possible even to interpret the pat sermonising which mars the later sequences as a subtle joke – what would this kind of film be without moral closure? Jones and Heche work hard to dig up an emotional rapport from next to nothing, while the slow but inexorable progress of the lava makes for more suspense than the usual slam bang firework display. TCh

Volere, Volare

(Maurizio Nichetti/Guido Manuli, 1991, It) Angela Finocchiaro, Maurizio Nichetti, Mariella Valentini, Patrizio Roversi, Remo Remotti.
96 min.

Maurizio (Nichetti) is a shy sound effects man who wanders around the city in search of the perfect honk, creak or squeak for whatever cartoon he is dubbing. Martina (Finocchiaro) likes to describe herself as a social worker, but is in fact a callgirl catering to a kinky clientèle. Of course these two lonely romantics meet, and Maurizio begins to feel strange stirrings. Little does he realise, he is turning into a cartoon! Like Nichetti's *Icicle Thief* (Manuli is responsible for the animation), this harks back to a golden cinematic era from a bold, post-modernist perspective. Nichetti evokes comparison with the great slapstick comedians; indeed, he is referred to occasionally as 'Little Moustache', surely a nod to Chaplin's 'little fellow'. But Chaplin the on-screen moralist would probably have had a heart attack if he'd

seen the outrageous climax contrived here: a sex scene to titillate the most jaded palate, with the fully-animated Maurizio hilariously credible. The film takes a good half-hour to find its feet, and Nichetti himself is sometimes a rather graceless clown, but there are brilliantly inventive gags even in the slack passages. TCh

Voleurs, Les

(André Téchiné, 1996, Fr) Daniel Auteuil, Catherine Deneuve, Laurence Côte, Benoît Magimel, Fabienne Babe, Ivan Desny.
116 min.

Kicking off with a scene in which a young boy, woken by his mother's scream, discovers that for some reason his father has been killed, Téchiné's ambitious attempt to deconstruct (and put a less generic, more humanist slant on) the crime thriller continues by telling the story through a variety of 'voices', including Auteuil as the dead man's detective brother, Deneuve as a philosophy professor, and Côte as the tortured young woman involved, at one time or another, with all three. Ambitious, yes; successful, no. Though script and direction have their moments, as a whole the film is simply too diffuse to add up to very much, either intellectually or emotionally; notwithstanding the strong performances, it all seems rather academic and, well, pointless. GA

Volunteers

(Nicholas Meyer, 1985, US) Tom Hanks, John Candy, Rita Wilson, Tim Thomerson, Gedde Watanabe, George Plimpton, Allan Arbus.
107 min.

Compulsive gambler Lawrence Bourne III (Hanks) joins the Peace Corps to evade a pack of creditors. In Thailand (oh yeah? And this is Patagonia) he encounters a manic blancmange (Candy), defeats the local black marketeer, an army of gooks and CIA, and gets his girl (Wilson). From titles to credits, this is a cynical exploitation of every film in the book – *The Bridge on the River Kwai*, *Apocalypse Now*, *Indiana Jones and the Temple of Doom*, even *Casablanca* – but is by no means as good as this might suggest. A blasé Hanks redeems this string of sexist, racist, comic clichés with winning charm. It's funny. MS

Von Richthofen and Brown (aka The Red Baron)

(Roger Corman, 1971, US) John Phillip Law, Don Stroud, Barry Primus, Karen Huston, Corin Redgrave, Hurd Hatfield, Peter Masterson, Stephen McHattie.
97 min.

Corman's Poe-derived motifs are transposed exuberantly to the skies as WWI biplanes fight it out with romantic heroism. Law's Baron von Richthofen, an airborne Teutonic knight, carries the seed of inevitable disaster within him: his mistake being that he removes the goggles from the first pilot he shoots down (the eye fixation again) and looks into the dead man's eyes; his perversion, that he needs to remember each kill. The Baron is firmly identified with the past, and his plebeian Canadian counterpart Brown (Stroud), representative of the new generation, ends up not with grudging respect for a gentlemanly enemy, but with the growing realisation that both of them are instruments of a destructive force. Good fights evil as in the regulation war movie, only here good and evil are neither separable nor where you'd expect to find them. Corman may have risen through the ranks, but his production economies are still blatant. Period reconstruction is abandoned, and each plane, one would swear, crashes to the same whizzbang soundtrack. Originally the German segments were shot in natural Yankee, now they are dubbed into German-accented English: 'Effry moment I am in ze air viz zees schpandaus in my hands – zat iss forever!' Schterling schtuff.

Von Ryan's Express

(Mark Robson, 1965, US) Frank Sinatra, Trevor Howard, Raffaella Carra, Sergio Fantoni, Brad Dexter, John Leyton, Wolfgang Preiss, James Brolin, Adolfo Celi.
117 min.

Set in a World War II PoW camp in Italy, this starts with what looks like becoming solemn *Bridge on the River Kwai* stiff-upper-lippery, but soon turns into a ripping adventure. Directed with amused panache by Robson, and helped no end by a fine cast, it's action all the way as Sinatra

contrives a mass escape which culminates in the theft of a train and a wild dash through German-occupied Italy to Switzerland and liberty. There's the masquerade in German uniforms to obtain the papers which will permit them to proceed; a sinister encounter with a Gestapo agent who turns out to be more interested in black marketeering; an attack on the main railway control tower at Milan; a superb final battle with the train perched precariously on a slender viaduct high in the Alps while the prisoners struggle to free a blocked tunnel, ward off attacking aircraft, and halt their pursuers. As much fun as an old-time serial. TM

Voodoo Man

(William Beaudine, 1944, US) Bela Lugosi, John Carradine, George Zucco, Michael Ames, Henry Hall, Wanda McKay.
62 min. b/w.

White voodoo in American suburbia, '40s style! A pleasantly tacky Monogram B movie, with paper-thin action and Bela Lugosi hamming wildly from start to finish as the mad doctor who tries to bring his wife back to life by kidnapping young women for use in psycho-surgery. Two retarded henchmen and a tongue-in-cheek finale save the day. CA

Voodoo Woman

(Edward L Cahn, 1956, US) Tom Conway, Maria English, Michael Connors, Lance Fuller.
77 min. b/w.

No budget nonsense in which mad scientist Conway turns jungle adventuress Maria English into a psychopathic monster. See if you can work out what's going on – and why. TJ

Vortex

(Scott B/Beth B, 1982, US) James Russo, Lydia Lunch, Bill Rice, Ann Magnuson, Brent Collins, Bill Corsair, Tom Webber, Scott B.
87 min.

The very accomplished (and self-consciously wry) first 16mm feature by the NY new wave underground film-makers Scott and Beth B finds private eye Angel Powers (poet, singer and playwright Lydia Lunch) – hard boozing, foul mouthed, clad in black leather, and her mind not always on the job – set to solve the mystery of a Congressman's assassination, against a background of serpentine paranoia and 'Star Wars' gadgetry. Bill Rice plays a Howard Hughes-like recluse (in the cadaverous manner of Klaus Kinski) who commissioned the hit to ensure that a defence contract went to a rival. Made on a tiny budget, with striking chiaroscuro visual effects, the movie pulses with a punk sensibility. It meanders and is sometimes chaotically makeshift, but it's all of a part: tough and buzzing with New York zip. JPy

Vortex, The

(Adrian Brunel, 1928, GB) Ivor Novello, Frances Doble, Willete Kershaw, Simeon Stewart.
6,281 ft. b/w.

A tale of fraught emotional intrigues set among the wealthy and sophisticated: a prig, pianist and wimp Nicky has a hard time with journalist Bunty, who's still attracted to old flame and cad Tom, who is Nicky's age – concealing mother's paramour. First staged in 1924, Nöel Coward's *succès de scandale* about incest, promiscuity, and morphine addiction was not surprisingly toned down for the screen; and now the hoohah about adultery on the tennis court, pill popping in the studio, and other such beastly japes, seems stale and dated. Novello as Nicky is irritatingly wet, while the succession of hounders, rotters, and chic shams looks like the creation of a posturing moraliser with a puritannically reactionary message. A dreadfully stagey curio. GA

Vous Intéressez-vous à la Chose?

see First Time with Feeling

Voyage

(John MacKenzie, 1993, It/GB/Malta) Rutger Hauer, Eric Roberts, Karen Allen, Connie Nielsen.
58 min.

A somewhat pale shadow of *Dead Calm*. Before going on a Mediterranean sailing trip to help their ailing marriage, Morgan (Hauer) and Kit Norvell (Allen) meet Gil Freeland (Roberts) at their Class of '72 college reunion. Gil, now a dentist, and wife Ronnie (Nielsen) invite themselves on board and proceed in the nasty, psychotic behaviour we just knew lay behind those sweet smiles. In the end, Hauer works out the murderous plot, and, clutching Roberts' dental bag, exclaims, 'These teeth were meant for us!' Heavy signposting, insistent Carl Davis score; not bad performances. FM

Voyage, The (El Viaje)
(Fernando E Solanas, 1991, Arg/Fr) Walter Quiroz, Soledad Alfaro, Ricardo Bartis, Cristina Becerra, Marc Berman.
150 min.
Solanas's cinematic trip – ramble, rather – from tip to toe of South America comes as a disappointment after the melancholic pleasures of *Sur*. This is a voyage round my fatherland: part magic-realist travelogue, part politico-satirical parable. It follows the journey taken by 17-year-old Martin – by bicycle! – from his snow-frozen school in Tierra del Fuego in search of his 'real' father, a cartoonist turned anthropologist believed to be in the Amazon. On his way north – visiting his grandmother in a drowned valley outside Buenos Aires, then on through the Andes to Nicaragua, the gold mines of Peru and Mexico – he meets various 'characters' from his father's work, a mysterious girl, a blind Jamaican, a drummer. Where *Sur* was suffused with fragile optimism, reflecting the hope that came with the return of democracy, *The Voyage* presents a more diffuse, enervated vision, expressive of an anomie of political failure and neglect. As a sad state-of-the-nations address to the younger generation it has pertinence, but its length and aimlessness often prove tedious. WH

Voyage Home: Star Trek IV, The
(Leonard Nimoy, 1986, US) William Shatner, Leonard Nimoy, DeForest Kelley, James Doohan, George Takei, Walter Koenig, Nichelle Nichols, Jane Wyatt, Catherine Hicks, John Schuck, Brock Peters.
119 min.
Kirk & Co return to present-day San Francisco to save the whales in the most enjoyable film of the series so far, also returning to the simplistic morality-play format that gave the original TV series its strength. The crew embark on a chase through contemporary California: Spock gets to put the Vulcan pinch on a punk, Kirk gets lost on a downtown bus, and Chekov hits the street to find a nuclear 'wessel' (in order to get enough juice for the ship, whales and water to make the jump through time). Nimoy's irreverent tone makes it more digestible than it sounds: a myth whose heart lies 20 years in the past, and whose eyes look 2,000 years into the future. SGo

Voyage of the Damned
(Stuart Rosenberg, 1976, GB) Faye Dunaway, Max von Sydow, Oskar Werner, Malcolm McDowell, James Mason, Orson Welles, Katharine Ross, Ben Gazzara, Lee Grant, Sam Wanamaker, Lynne Frederick, Julie Harris, Helmut Griem, Luther Adler, Wendy Hiller, Maria Schell, Fernando Rey, José Ferrer, Denholm Elliott.
155 min.
In May 1939, to define the Jewish 'problem' to the world, Goebbels had 937 German Jews shipped to the apparent safety of Cuba. Refused entry into Havana, the luxury liner was forced back towards Hamburg and the camps. Rosenberg here confuses seriousness with tedious solemnity, and with the star glut has produced a compacted TV series. Too many dramas vie for attention on board. The political doings in Havana are confusing; and the prelude to each Cuban scene – maracas, rumbas, cut-price Carmen Mirandas – irritates. Very idiosyncratic performances from the big shots: Welles' wryly charitable Cuban magnate; Captain von Sydow, humane and anguished; steward McDowell hitting new heights in public school deference; Dunaway in jackboots and monocle. The best moments, such as they are, come in the big passenger scenes; though awkwardly filmed, they generate hysteria, a sense of despair. JS

Voyager
(Volker Schlöndorff, 1991, Ger/Fr) Sam Shepard, Julie Delpy, Barbara Sukowa, Dieter Kirchlechner, Traci Lind, Deborah Lee-Furness, August Zirner.
117 min.

The fifty-year-old man revitalised by a love affair with a twenty-year-old girl is one of life's clichés, but Schlöndorff's film, adapted from Max Frisch's novel *Homo Faber* (and filmed in English), also examines the price. Faber, laconically played by Shepard, is the rational man who has no time for emotion, and his relationships are cursory. Dodging an intimate dinner-for-two in his New York apartment, he makes his excuses, impulsively hops on a liner bound for France – and falls in love with fellow-passenger Delpy, of the Pre-Raphaelite looks. By the time they dock, they can't bear to say goodbye, and he hires a car to take her to Greece, where a tragic irony from the past awaits him. Unfortunately, audiences will see this coming a mile off, and may also resent the symbolic signposts. At least Schlöndorff isn't afraid of ideas, even if they derive from literary sources. BC

Voyage-Surprise
(Pierre Prévert, 1947, Fr) Maurice Baquet, Martine Carol, Etienne Decroux, Pierre Piéral, Annette Poivre, Marcel Pérès, Max Revol, Sinoël.
85 min. b/w.
Dazzlingly masterminded by Jacques and Pierre Prévert, first generation Surrealists both, this is not only the movie that Buñuel wanted *Discreet Charm of the Bourgeoisie* to be, but also one of the most laceratingly funny provocations ever launched in France. A guileless old tour proprietor trumps his new-fangled rival by offering a genuine mystery trip; the takers are a crowd of eccentrics and dropouts from all backgrounds and classes, who find themselves experiencing all their wildest dreams and fears as they follow their truly arbitrary itinerary. Jacques Prévert's effortlessly brilliant dialogue points up the fact that the comedy is founded on benign-but-tough assumptions about eroticism, social attitudes, and revolution. It's an ecstatic experience. TR

Voyage to Cythera (Taxidi sta Kithira)
(Theo Angelopoulos, 1984, Greece/WGer/It/GB) Julio Brogi, Manos Katrakis, Mary Chronopoulou, Dionyssis Papayannopoulos, Dora Volanaki.
136 min.
A film-maker, Alexandros (Brogi), auditions a succession of old men who speak the line, 'It's me, it's me.' Tiring of the task, he goes to a café and sees his perfect actor, a lavender-seller. Alexandros follows the man to Piraeus where, it transpires, the film-maker is to meet his father, a resistance fighter (Katrakis) returning to Greece after 32 years in the USSR. The father descends from a huge anonymous vessel to an empty quay. 'It's me,' he says. Not knowing what to do, Alexandros reaches to take the old man's violin case. 'Aren't you going to kiss me?' his father asks. Angelopoulos once again plays a variation on the theme of what it means to be a modern Greek artist living in the shadow of the civil war. The first half of the film, which is told naturalistically, with the father visiting his native village and resolving not to sell his barren ancestral land (now required for a winter sports centre), is suffused with that peculiar melancholy which Angelopoulos has made entirely his own. One begins to lose the thread in the second half, however, when the old man and his wife are cast adrift on a symbolic voyage to Cythera, birthplace of Aphrodite, the goddess of love and regeneration. JPy

Voyage to Italy
see Viaggio in Italia

Vraie Nature de Bernadette, La
see True Nature of Bernadette, The

Vredens Dag
see Day of Wrath

Vroom
(Beeban Kidron, 1988, GB).Clive Owen, Diana Quick, David Thewlis.
89 min.
Down those cobbled streets a man must go in Beeban Kidron's feature debut, about two Lancashire lads – Owen the smooth guy all the

girls want to kiss, Thewlis a spiky-haired loon – who decide to kick it all in and joyride off to nowhere. The brightly promising first half has Owen conducting a passionate affair with sultry divorcée Quick, and the direction has zip and sensuality to spare, with especially atmospheric photography. However, Jim Cartwright's script is thin on the ground and detours into road movie clichédom, losing the film its early exuberance and eventually flying off into unconvincing whimsy. But then that's probably the message – that pure fantasy is the only way out of the mortgage repayments. DT

W

White Heat

Wackiest Ship in the Army, The

(Richard Murphy, 1960, US) Jack Lemmon,
Ricky Nelson, John Lund, Chips Rafferty, Tom
Tully, Joby Baker, Patricia Driscoll.
100 min.
Lemmon flaps amiably enough as the lieutenant
in charge of scrap-bound gunship 'The Echo', surprisingly charged with providing an escort
through Japanese-controlled waters in the South
Pacific in 1943, yet the vessel's real role is to provide an erratic decoy that'll suitably bamboozle
enemy strategists. Passable blend of laughter and
heroics, thankfully never quite as 'zany' as the
title suggests. TJ

Wages of Fear

see Sorcerer

Wages of Fear, The (Le Salaire de la Peur)

(Henri-Georges Clouzot, 1953, Fr/It) Yves
Montand, Charles Vanel, Peter Van Eyck,
Folco Lulli, Véra Clouzot, Dario Moreno,
William Tubbs.
144 min. b/w.
Buried at the time of William Friedkin's shabby
remake (Sorcerer) but now blessedly with us
again, this confirms the view of Clouzot as one of
the sourest of modern film-makers. A slow first
hour establishes a world of sweating, poor expatriates hanging out in the feverish bars in French
colonial Latin America, which inevitably brings
to mind such far-flung adventurer films as Only
Angels Have Wings. But Hawks's classic depends
upon the fraternal bonds forged among his existential heroes by flying in the face of death. When
Clouzot's foursome decide to drive a load of nitroglycerine through the jungle in order to raise
some cash, the motive is greed and the results are
as black a vision of human infidelity as any since
Othello. The cliff-edge tension wracks the nerves,
of course, but never obscures the fact that men in
contest with each other will crack up and die; one
truck blows away without reason; the other only
arrives by running over its co-driver, in an oil-
pool that looks like the pit of hell. A reeking bandana movie, with all the expected thrills, but a
vision of men as scurrying insects with no
redeeming features. CPea

Wagner

(Tony Palmer, 1983, GB/Hun/Aust) Richard
Burton, Vanessa Redgrave, Gemma Craven,
László Gálffi, John Gielgud, Ralph Richardson,
Laurence Olivier, Ronald Pickup, Joan
Plowright, Arthur Lowe, Franco Nero.
300 min.
Palmer's 5-hour biopic of Wagner (nine hours in
the TV version) is a long haul for anyone: sumptuous, overblown, lumbering, and riddled with
narrative non sequiturs. The strangest aspect is
that the music often seems peripheral rather than
central, relegated to being film music as though
we might as well be watching a biopic about
Ennio Morricone. The visuals are splendid and
you can play spot the cast, but somehow it's all
a bit sub-Ken Russell, without the redeeming vulgarity and with a lot less cinematic energy. SM

Wagon Master

(John Ford, 1950, US) Ben Johnson, Joanne
Dru, Harry Carey Jr, Ward Bond, Alan
Mowbray, Jane Darwell, Charles Kemper,
Russell Simpson, James Arness.
86 min. b/w.
Another Fordian epic positing the American community as the sum of its bands of outsiders, with
a Mormon wagon train bound for the westward
Promised Land in alliance with a pair of rootless
horse-traders, a trio of theatricals, and a tribe of
nomadic Navajos, tested by the landscape and the
threat of their perverse familial mirror image, the
villainous Uncle Shiloh Clegg and his boys. A
moral fable, but with a refreshing lack of rhetoric
to its poetry. Athlete/actor Jim Thorpe, here playing the Navajo leader, was himself portrayed by
Burt Lancaster the following year in the biopic
Jim Thorpe – All-American. PT

Wagons East!

(Peter Markle, 1994, US) John Candy, Joe Bays,
Abe Benrubi, Jill Boyd, Ellen Greene, Robert
Picardo, Ed Lauter, Rodney A Grant.
107 min.
John Candy takes his place at the head of a wagon
train leading a handful of disenchanted pioneers
back to the home comforts of the East. Alarmed
that the quitters may set a trend, a railway baron
hires assorted gunslingers and even the US
Cavalry to stop them, while by the same token,
formerly hostile Indians are only too happy to
provide safe passage. The humour is sufficiently scattershot to hit the mark once or twice, but
basically a no-brains comedy. TCh

Wag the Dog

(Barry Levinson, 1997, US) Dustin Hoffman,
Robert De Niro, Anne Heche, Denis Leary,
Willie Nelson, Andrea Martin, Kirsten Dunst,
William H Macy, Woody Harrelson.
95 min.
A sex scandal is about to break around the
President, threatening to derail his re-election
bandwagon less than two weeks before polling
day. Veteran Conrad Brean (De Niro) quickly
formulates a rescue policy: to deflect public
attention, the US will go to war. Not in real life,
but where it matters, on America's TV screens.
He co-opts veteran Hollywood producer Stanley
Motss (Hoffman) and they thrash out the
details: the rumours and denials of military
mobilisation, the video footage of terrified
refugees, the rousing patriotic anthem. And the
venue? How about Albania. Adapted from
Larry Beinhart's novel American Hero by
Hilary Henkin and David Mamet, this is intended as an airy semi-political comedy. Lazily
assembled by director Levinson, it slides into a
series of soft, extended skits on engineering a
media war, not helped by several badly handled
leaps in the story. In short, a telling symptom
of the malaise of mainstream American cinema
– once capable of producing such taut political
thrillers as The Candidate and The Parallax
View. NB

Waiting

(Jackie McKimmie, 1990, US) Noni Hazlehurst,
Deborah Lee-Furness, Frank Whitten, Helen
Jones, Denis Moore, Fiona Press, Ray Barrett.
94 min.
When Clare (Hazlehurst) agrees to become a surrogate mother for her friend Sandy (Jones), the
pregnancy proves less worrying than the behaviour of old friends. With the big day approaching, the friends converge on Clare's rambling
farmhouse outside Sydney to help, hinder, bicker and worry. Sandy is accompanied by her
right-on husband (Whitten) and adopted children; feminist film-maker Terry (Press) brings
her daughter and throws herself into making a
documentary; and glamorous fashion editor
Diane (Lee-Furness) comes with wealthy
boyfriend (Moore) in tow. Writer-director
McKimmie creates an almost casual rhythm,
concentrating on character and incidental
details in the build-up to a series of confrontations and revelations. Some longueurs strain
patience, and compounding our detachment is
the way certain characters observe and analyse
others' behaviour. Still, sympathetic performances and a fair amount of humour deflate
pomposity. CM

Waiting for the Light

(Christopher Monger, 1989, US) Teri Garr,
Shirley MacLaine, Colin Baumgartner, Hillary
Wolf, Clancy Brown, Vincent Schiavelli, John
Bedford Lloyd, Jeff McCracken.
94 min.
Monger's engaging comedy is set against the
unlikely backdrop of the Cuban missile crisis. The
political turmoil provides the springboard for an
exploration of superstition and religion, which are
treated with equal doses of scepticism and wonderment. When Kay (Garr) inherits a diner in the
Pacific Northwest, she and her two young children uproot from Chicago in order to transform
the ramshackle eatery. An attempt by their amateur magician Aunt Zena (MacLaine) to scare
reclusive neighbour Mullins (Schiavelli) backfires
– he mistakes her ghostly apparition for an angel
– and the community starts buzzing with the
news that Mullins' orchard is a hot-spot for divine
visitations. This somewhat incredible plot is
embellished with curious details and carried along
by the sheer professionalism of Garr and
MacLaine, who make entirely convincing relatives. If the characters are fairly two-dimensional, Monger compensates with odd observation and
dry humour. CM

Waiting to Exhale

(Forest Whitaker, 1995, US) Whitney Houston,
Angela Bassett, Loretta Devine, Lela Rochon,
Gregory Hines, Dennis Haysbert, Mykelti
Williamson, Michael Beach.
123 min.
As Hollywood genres go, the black women's film
is a non-entity, so any effort should be welcomed.
It's New Year's Eve in Phoenix, Arizona, and
Savannah (Houston) arrives in town on the look
out for a good man. Fat chance: simultaneously,
Bernardine (Bassett) is dumped by her husband
for his white secretary; Gloria (Devine) discovers the reason she can't persuade her ex-husband
back into the sack is that he's gay; and Robin
(Rochon) is finding her rotund lover's sexual
technique spectacularly uninvolving. The odd
honky temptress apart, race isn't an issue here.
Trysts with married men, widowers, widowers-
to-be and crackheads are interspersed with the
four friends getting together for some quality
bitching therapy about the men in their lives.
This is about girls-together solidarity, as the
audience I was in loudly demonstrated. For every
crowd-pleasing set-piece, there's the shambolic
structure, uncomfortable shifts of tone, over-
glossed visuals, and the music: rightly not trusting his scenes to stand alone, Whitaker
wallpapers his film with unconscionably bland
slush-pop. Shallow, semi-coherent, overlong, but
a likely hit. NB

Wait Till the Sun Shines, Nellie

(Henry King, 1952, US) David Wayne, Jean
Peters, Hugh Marlowe, Albert Dekker, Alan
Hale Jr, Warren Stevens, Helene Stanley.
108 min.
Diverting slice of turn-of-the-century nostalgia
has Wayne as the small-town barber left to raise
two children when spouse Peters skips off for the
delights of city living. Trial and tribulation follow, including a fire and the influence of bad company on the younger son. Adapted by Allan Scott
from the novel by Ferdinand Reyher, and very
capably put together. TJ

Wait Until Dark

(Terence Young, 1967, US) Audrey Hepburn,
Alan Arkin, Richard Crenna, Efrem Zimbalist
Jr, Jack Weston, Samantha Jones.
108 min.
An effective shocker which has the blind
Hepburn alone in the house when psychotic villain Arkin and his hoodlum pals (Crenna and
Weston) arrive to retrieve a doll containing heroin which her husband (Zimbalist) unwittingly
brought through customs for them. The nail-biting climax, during which Hepburn turns the
tables by smashing the light-bulbs and leaving
the place in darkness, is a classic. Though based
on a stage play (by Frederick Knott), the skilful
use of interiors for once transcends the visual limitations. NF

Wake Up, Love (Despabílate Amor)

(Eliseo Subiela, 1996, Arg) Darío Grandinetti,
Juan Leyrado, Soledad Silveyra, Marilyn
Solaya, Gustavo Garzón.
90 min.
This romantic drama follows the efforts of one
Ricardo (Leyrado) – nicknamed 'Elvis' for his all
too evident belief in rock'n'roll as a way of keeping young at heart – to reassemble the old college crowd of 30 years back. During
preparations for the reunion, his wife Ana
(Silveyra) rekindles her torch for Ernesto 'The
King of Insomnia' (Grandinetti), a senior journalist of Hamlet-like melancholy, who in turn
breaks his carnal fast with attractive cellist
Silvia. Its nostalgic bent is expressed in a character's complaint that compared to the '60s,
these days 'people's hearts are dry – it's ages
since it rained dreams!' Using amusing kitschy
flashbacks to old trysts, and Paul Anka-domi-
nated parties (this is Argentina, don't forget), it's
full of genuine feeling, nice comic touches (Ana
pulling on her old jeans with the aid of coat
hanger hook), all poetically swooned in sad but
defiant music (Bach's Cello Suites 1–6) and poetry (Mario Beneddetti's). WH

Waking Hour, The

see Velvet Vampire, The

Walkabout

(Nicolas Roeg, 1970, Aust) Jenny Agutter, Lucien John, David Gumpilil, John Meillon.
100 min.

Roeg's second film (made after the massively delayed *Performance*) is at first sight uncharacteristic: the story of two posh English kids abandoned in the Australian outback and left to fend for themselves when their father commits suicide. In fact, the shimmering light and colour, the conflict of cultures, and the emergence of semi-mystic sexual forces in the desert landscape make this as Roeg-ian a film as *The Man Who Fell to Earth* or *Bad Timing*. Only the rather cute casting of Jenny Agutter as an English Rose and some implausibly romantic moments detract. CA

Walk East on Beacon

(Alfred Werker, 1952, US) George Murphy, Finlay Currie, Virginia Gilmore, Karel Stepanek, George Roy Hill, Louisa Horton.
98 min. b/w.

Documentary-style Cold War spy picture, shot on location in Boston and produced by Louis de Rochemont, best known for the *March of Time* newsreel. A celebration of the FBI, it makes frightening and/or funny viewing today. Says one apologetic Commie, finding you have a Party card is like 'finding yourself married to a woman you hate'. Made of sterner stuff is Red George Roy Hill: resisting arrest with the original 'You can't pin anything on me!', he went on to direct subversive classics like *Butch Cassidy and the Sundance Kid* and *The Sting*. More surprisingly, journalist Nora Sayre learned that the CIA was leasing some ten prints a year from Columbia, including a number dubbed into foreign languages, as late as 1977. TCh

Walker

(Alex Cox, 1987, US) Ed Harris, Richard Masur, René Auberjonois, Keith Szarabajka, Sy Richardson, Xander Berkeley, John Diehl, Peter Boyle, Marlee Matlin.
94 min.

Funded by grasping capitalist Cornelius Vanderbilt (Boyle), 19th century American adventurer Walker (Harris) and his band of mercenaries invade Nicaragua and join forces with the liberals against the country's corrupt ruler. Despite his disastrous military campaigns and political naïveté Walker eventually falls into the president's chair (a historical figure, he was self-proclaimed president of Nicaragua from 1855-57). He even makes the cover of *Newsweek*, because to drive home the obvious contemporary parallels, Cox litters the screen with historical anomalies: Zippo lighters, a Mercedes limo, journos with tape recorders. He presents this fascinating episode, which would have had far more potential as a straight political allegory, as a shambolic, Pythonesque satire. Only Ed Harris seems to have grasped this point: his controlled and credible performance is curiously at odds with a chaotic plot that shoots off in all directions without once finding its target. NF

Walkers on the Tiger's Tail

see Tora no O o Fumu Otokotachi

Walking and Talking

(Nicole Holofcener, 1996, GB/US) Catherine Keener, Anne Heche, Todd Field, Liev Schreiber, Kevin Corrigan, Randall Batinkoff, Joseph Siravo.
85 min.

Amelia (Keener) and Laura (Heche) have been best friends since childhood, but when Laura agrees to marry live-in lover Frank (Field), Amelia begins to feel abandoned. True, she decides to try giving up therapy once and for all, but her support system – an adored but ailing cat, an ex (Schreiber) now addicted to phone sex with a woman in California – isn't all it might be, while an ill-starred date with a weirdo video-store assistant (Corrigan) doesn't do much for her confidence either. Still, at least she has some idea of what she wants, whereas Laura, once engaged, starts finding fault with everything Frank does and says, and fantasising (irony of ironies – she's a trainee shrink) about her clients. Writer/director Nicole Holofcener's deliciously witty first feature is a perceptive comedy-drama which, despite its New York setting and its fascination with neuroses, anxieties, desire and relationships, is far fresher and more rewarding than the 'female

Woody Allen' tag invoked by some critics. The sassy, snappy dialogue is less a matter of one-liners than a wryly amusing exploration of personality; story and gags alike are at the service of characterisation, so that we're never allowed to forget the very real pain, confusion, guilt and affection that underpins the movie. Great cast, immense fun. GA

Walking a Tightrope

see Equilibristes, Les

Walking Dead, The

(Michael Curtiz, 1936, US) Boris Karloff, Edmund Gwenn, Ricardo Cortez, Marguerite Churchill, Barton MacLane.
66 min. b/w.

No great shakes in terms of plot – Karloff's wronged innocent, executed for murder, returns from the dead to wreak vengeance on his persecutors – but Curtiz' fondness for the heavy shadows of Gothic expressionism, and Karloff's characteristically committed performance, lend this moody chiller a welcome touch of class. *Mystery of the Wax Museum* it ain't, but for all the creaky clichés of the story, it still generates the odd frisson. GA

Walking Stick, The

(Eric Till, 1970, GB) David Hemmings, Samantha Eggar, Emlyn Williams, Phyllis Calvert, Ferdy Mayne, Francesca Annis, Dudley Sutton.
101 min.

A romantico-psychological thriller, with fine, persuasively detailed performances from Eggar as a crippled girl with a sexual chip on her shoulder, and Hemmings as the enigmatic artist who melts it, gradually persuading her to abandon the walking-stick on which she has leaned since a childhood bout with polio, but also leading her to a dark brink of crime and betrayal. Rather too stolidly directed by Till, with meticulous fidelity to Winston Graham's novel, it is reminiscent enough of *Marnie* (also from a novel by Graham) – here, rather than the colour red, the heroine's problem is a claustrophobic aftermath of her time in an iron lung – to make one wonder whether Hitchcock could have screwed excitement out of the situation as well as sympathetic character studies. TM

Walking Tall

(Phil Karlson, 1973, US) Joe Don Baker, Elizabeth Hartman, Gene Evans, Noah Beery, Rosemary Murphy, Brenda Benet, John Brascia, Bruce Glover, Arch Johnson.
125 min.

Based on the real life experiences of Sheriff Buford Pusser's lone fight against gambling, moonshining, and prostitution in an effort to make Tennessee's McNairy County the sort of place decent folks could live. He cudgels his opposition into submission with the huge stick he carries wherever he goes, and suffers a few hundred stitches, a couple of shootings, and a dead wife in return. But he comes through walking tall, leaving a trail of cardboard villains splattered in his wake. As much as anything, the film is about Nixon's silent majority. They emerge at the end once the enemy are scattered or dead, to tear down and burn the local gambling saloon-cum-cathouse. Even more depressing is that American readers of *Photoplay* voted the film their 'Favorite Motion Picture of the Year'. It's an interesting example of how a stock Western plot can assume some fairly explicit political ramifications once it is transposed to a modern setting (not that that is any recommendation). CPe

Walk in the Clouds, A

(Alfonso Arau, 1995, US) Keanu Reeves, Aitana Sanchez-Gijon, Anthony Quinn, Giancarlo Giannini, Angelica Aragon, Evangelina Elizondo, Freddy Rodriguez.
102 min.

Watching Arau's follow-up to *Like Water for Chocolate* is like finding yourself in Shangri-La, a lost valley where time has stood still for decades, and movies still end with 'The End'. Reeves is Paul Sutton, a GI recently returned from WWII. He has a wife who doesn't love him, nightmares from the front (dream sequences by Alejandro Jodorowsky), a two-bit job as a travelling chocolate salesman, and no prospects. A chance encounter with Victoria Aragon (Sanchez-

Gijon) changes all that. She's on her way home to face the music: pregnant, alone, and terrified of her father (Giannini), who oversees the family vineyard in Southern California. Paul agrees to play her husband and then disappear into the night, but he's waylaid by what he finds there, and the kindly efforts of the elderly Don Pedro (Quinn). This is shameless stuff: happy, barefoot peasants sing that traditional Latin *cancion*, 'Crush the grapes, crush the grapes,' the moonlight is so strong you could get burned, and the metaphors are writ large as tabloid headlines; it's all about putting down roots. See it, if you must, for Keanu's pure puppy-love, and for a peerless drunken duet with Quinn. Tch

Walk in the Spring Rain, A

(Guy Green, 1969, US) Anthony Quinn, Ingrid Bergman, Fritz Weaver, Katherine Crawford, Tom Fielding.
98 min.

A dish of tripe that has to be seen to be believed. Quinn does his nature boy act yet again as a Tennessee backwoodsman who always knows where to find the first darling buds of spring and can lay fires in the hearth so that the smoke isn't twisted. Whatever that means, it makes him irresistible enough to ensnare poor Ingrid Bergman ('You're full of love, ain't you?'), a college professor's wife down in the menopausal dumps and seemingly bent on becoming a dropout grandmother. Since both have family ties and problems, the course of their true love doesn't run smooth, but Quinn is philosophical to the last: 'You know what I found out? The clouds just keep on moving'. Stirling Silliphant scripted, if you can call it that. TM

Walk in the Sun, A

(Lewis Milestone, 1945, US) Dana Andrews, John Ireland, Richard Conte, Sterling Holloway, Norman Lloyd, Lloyd Bridges, George Tyne, Herbert Rudley, Huntz Hall.
117 min. b/w.

One of the best movies to have come out of World War II literately scripted by Robert Rossen from Harry Brown's fine novel, and making marvellous use of the repetitive rhythms of GI banter (with the cheery Conte's Nobody dies!, for instance, gradually assuming the quality of an ironic incantation). Discreet, dispassionate, and subtly poetic, it traces the experiences, through one brief action, of an infantry platoon which 'came across the sea to sunny Italy and took a little walk in the sun'. Characterisation is sharp and simple, the focus kept strictly to the immediate realities of fear and boredom, so that there is none of the special pleading of Milestone's earlier *All Quiet on the Western Front*. Here messages are left to take care of themselves, although the introspective Ireland's habit of composing letters to his sister in his head is used more than once to subversive effect. 'We just blew a bridge and took a farmhouse' he begins after the action in which a lot of his platoon died, 'It was easy...so terribly easy': a rare acknowledgement at that time of every soldier's innocently selfish joy that he didn't die. TM

Walk Like a Man

(Melvin Frank, 1987, US) Howie Mandel, Christopher Lloyd, Cloris Leachman, Colleen Camp, Amy Steel, George DiCenzo.
86 min.

Scraggy slapstick comedy which attempts to give the Kaspar Hauser myth a new twist. Bobo Shand, son of a wealthy family, is lost in the woods as a kid and raised by wolves. Twenty-eight years pass before he's found by an animal behaviourist and reintroduced into human society. Needless to say, his grasping, wheedling family is considerably less civilised than his old feral friends. Neither Leachman's class nor Lloyd's clowning can put meat on this very dry bone. GM

Walk on the Wild Side

(Edward Dmytryk, 1962, US) Laurence Harvey, Capucine, Jane Fonda, Barbara Stanwyck, Anne Baxter, Richard Rust, Karl Swenson.
114 min. b/w.

A prowling black cat taking a 'walk on the wild side' creates the brilliant promise of Saul Bass' famous credit sequence. The rest just doesn't match it, despite the tale of passion: Laurence Harvey seeking his former love (Capucine), now a high-class 'harlot' for 'Madame' Barbara Stanwyck, who is also in love with her; meanwhile a full-blooded Anne Baxter and a raunchy Jane Fonda succumb to Harvey's moralising Texan. If Dmytryk had only concentrated more on the women instead of the dull central male, this might have been a superb dark work, not just a fairly steamy melodrama. Still, it certainly has its moments. HM

Walk Through H, A
(Peter Greenaway, 1978, GB) Jean Williams; narrator: Colin Cantlie.
41 min.
Greenaway's unique short feature is one of the best British movies of the decade. It defeats efforts at description. You could call it a cross between a vintage Borges 'fiction' and a Disney True Life Adventure, but that wouldn't get close to its humour or the compulsiveness of Michael Nyman's romantic score. It's nominally a narrative about an ornithologist following a trail blazed by the legendary Tulse Luper, but it's a narrative without characters...See it at all costs. TR

Walk with Love and Death, A
(John Huston, 1969, US) Anjelica Huston, Assaf Dayan, Anthony Corlan, John Hallam, Eileen Murphy, Anthony Nicholls, Robert Lang, Michael Gough, John Huston.
90 min.
A Huston curiosity, deliberately contemporary in preoccupation despite its medieval setting: two young lovers rove through strife-torn France making love not war, seeking involvement only with each other. In emphasising youthful passion and integrity, questioning accepted values, and setting the film in a period of social and civil unrest, it becomes a self-evident reflection of the moods of the late '60s; but a mere reflection, and unsatisfyingly inconclusive, because Huston is far too sceptical and knowing to believe in his subject. As the lovers become more committed, the film grows less certain: the essential simplicity of their relationship eludes Huston, who is far more interested in the deviant characters who take up the rest of the film. Further dislocation is caused by the inexperienced leading couple; most of the film's coherence comes from the lustrous photography, and a brief appearance from Huston as a wily old fox. CPe

Wall, The (Le Mur)
(Yilmaz Güney, 1983, Fr) Tuncel Kurtiz, Ahmet Ziyrek, Emel Mesci, Isabelle Tissandier, Ali Berktay.
116 min.
There has never been a prison movie like this, but then it's doubtful that any major film-maker ever spent as long behind bars as Güney. It's not a bleeding chunk of autobiography, but an imaginative reconstruction of the events that led up to the revolt in the children's dormitory in Ankara Prison in March 1976. Yol saw all of Turkey as a kind of prison; The Wall reverses the metaphor, seeing the prison as a microcosm of the country, crippled both spiritually and physically under its fascistic government. Güney has no need of melodrama or extremes of violence or horror. He simply demonstrates the mechanisms of tyranny: the way that mindless and arbitrary routines stunt jailers and prisoners alike, creating a desperate conspiracy of ignorance and defeat. A deeply provocative vision of what happens when idealism runs out, it's not easy to watch or think about, but Güney sees it and shows it as unflinchingly as Buñuel would have done in his prime. TR

Wall of Silence, A
see Totschweigen

Walls of Glass
(Scott Goldstein, 1985, US) Philip Bosco, Geraldine Page, Linda Thorson, Olympia Dukakis, Brian Bloom, Steven Weber, Louis Zorich.
86 min.
Taxi driver Flanagan (Bosco) dreams of the stage, but with middle age setting in, feels time is running out. Imprisoned by his work, he sees no escape. Down on his luck, all Flanagan has left is the comfort of the printed word (Shakespeare), and the love of an ageing mother (Page). Granted flashbacks to whisky-swigging immigrant fathers quoting sonnets are tough to swallow, but

if you can get past the mechanics, you're in for some warm moments. Top marks to Goldsteinn, in his first feature, for tasting the flavour of New York's outer boroughs. His contemporary taxi trip, despite the affected after-taste, grasps the traditional essence: all the world's a stage, even the back seat of Flanagan's cab. SGo

Wall Street
(Oliver Stone, 1987, US) Michael Douglas, Charlie Sheen, Daryl Hannah, Martin Sheen, Terence Stamp, Hal Holbrook, Sean Young, Sylvia Miles, Richard Dysart, Annie McEnroe, Millie Perkins.
126 min.
Remove the restless camera pyrotechnics and incomprehensible jargon, and you have a corny old melo: broker Charlie Sheen (green) perpetrates illegal practices to please surrogate poppa/company-trader Douglas (tough), a mega-villain mastermind who spits out absurdities like 'Lunch is for wimps' and longs to destroy his rival Stamp (lost). Soon Charlie's climbing the ladder in search of a fast buck and a flash fuck: Hannah (vacuous). Inevitably, he descends into a mire of insider-dealing, Faustian intrigue, and personal betrayal, culminating in his responsibility for Douglas' near-liquidation of the company where Sheen Sr (natch) is an Incorruptible Working Class Hero union rep. Charlie's cured, of course, by the most clichéd comeuppance of 'em all – family illness – which he should have foreseen, given the homespun homilies about abysses and doom repeatedly offered by full-time office soothsayer Holbrook (solemn). Dramatically inept, the film also muddles its naïve moralising: though condemnatory of avarice and dishonesty, Stone seems seduced by the financiers' luxurious lives and frantic energy, and even expects us to sympathise with the ghastly Charlie's final regret and redemption. GA

Walter (aka Loving Walter)
(Stephen Frears, 1982, GB) Ian McKellen, Barbara Jefford, Arthur Whybrow, Tony Melody, Jim Broadbent, Nabil Shaban.
65 min.
This short feature film, set in straitened postwar England about the fate of a mentally handicapped young man institutionalised after the death of his parents, was adapted from a novel by David Cook and memorably inaugurated Channel 4's 'Film on Four' series in November 1982. It's a copybook exercise in bleak unvarnished realism, punctuated by moments of operatic violence and emotion, but what makes it special is its unsentimental tone of melancholy inevitability, and, above all, McKellen's perfectly pitched performance. (The film was amalgamated with its somewhat histrionic sequel, Walter & June, and retitled Loving Walter for its US release.) JPy

Wanda
(Barbara Loden, 1970, US) Barbara Loden, Michael Higgins, Charles Dosinan, Frank Jourdano.
100 min.
A remarkable one-off from Elia Kazan's wife. Shot in 16mm and blown up to 35, it's a subtly picaresque movie about the wanderings of a semi-destitute American woman. Directing herself, Barbara Loden manages to make the character at once completely convincing in her soggy and directionless amorality, yet gradually sympathetic and even heroic. After a desultory involvement with a bank robber, to whom she becomes attached despite his unpredictable temper, Wanda botches everything – having agreed to drive a getaway car for him – by getting lost in a traffic jam; and our last glimpse of her is back on the road, being picked up in a bar. The film is all the more impressive for its refusal to get embroiled in half-baked political attitudinising; it's good enough to make one regret that the director/star produced nothing else before her untimely death from cancer. DP

Wanda Nevada
(Peter Fonda, 1979, US) Peter Fonda, Brooke Shields, Fiona Lewis, Luke Askew, Ted Markland, Severn Darden, Paul Fix, Henry Fonda.
105 min.
The easy rider exchanges motorbike for horse, but the tempo rarely rises above a trot in this clod-hopping Western. Fonda is a gambler. When he wins cowgirl Brooke Shields in a poker game,

he's obliged to take her along in his search for gold. Perhaps bent on some oedipal revenge trip, the director/star casts his more illustrious father in a thankless bit-part as a bearded old loon of a prospector – it was the only time these two Fondas worked together.

Wanderer, The (Le Grand Meaulnes)
(Jean-Gabriel Albicocco, 1967, Fr) Brigitte Fossey, Jean Blaise, Alain Libolt, Alain Noury, Juliette Villard, Christian de Tilière.
103 min.
A film made with vaseline and railway tracks, which takes some adjusting to; but you soon forget to read the subtitles, because you can understand all you need without them. It's based on the book Le Grand Meaulnes by Alain-Fournier, and explores a strange adolescence in provincial France at the end of the last century. In the film, Roger Corman meets Proust, Elvira Madigan rides again, and Renoir takes acid. JC

Wanderers, The
(Philip Kaufman, 1979, US/Neth) Ken Wahl, John Friedrich, Karen Allen, Toni Kalem, Alan Rosenberg, Jim Youngs, Tony Ganios, Linda Manz, Val Avery.
117 min.
The Bronx, 1963. Gangland. Rumbles, racism, and rock'n'roll; but the times they are a-changin'. Kennedy's dead and the Marines are calling. This adaptation of Richard Price's episodic novel plays like the urban flip-side of American Graffiti: a macho mini-community grows up and apart in the cultural gulf between Dion and Dylan. The comic indulgence is streaked with hindsight analysis and irony, but thankfully avoids moral schematics as the wonderfully-cast characters confront a world beyond their tenement horizons and, well...wander. The film survives cuts to deliver some great, gross, comic book capers. And rock history gets its most intelligent illustration since Mean Streets. PT

Wanted Dead or Alive
(Gary Sherman, 1987, US) Rutger Hauer, Gene Simmons, Robert Guillaume, Mel Harris, William Russ, Susan McDonald, Jerry Hardin.
106 min.
A fast, high-powered political thriller, with Hauer as ex-CIA agent turned bounty hunter, renowned for hauling in hardened criminals – dead or alive. He has his work cut out when a group of Middle Eastern terrorists start a bombing campaign in leafy LA. Led by Malak Al Rahim (played by Simmons like an evil comic book character), the group has already killed scores in a cinema bombing, and now plan to blow up a chemical plant containing lethal cyanide. Hauer is unwittingly being used as bait by CIA schemers, and following the loss of his girlfriend and best pal in a mistaken identity mishap, he's provoked into seeking personal revenge...The film is enjoyably tense, explicitly violent, yet at times quite humorous; and Hauer, having collared the psycho market, here makes a similarly irresistible claim in the hard-man-with-heart stakes. DA

Wanton, The
see Manèges

Wanton Countess, The
see Senso

War (aka Troma's War)
(Michael Herz/Samuel Weil, 1988, US) Carolyn Beauchamp, Sean Bowen, Michael Ryder, Patrick Weathers, Jessica Dublin, Steven Crossley.
99 min.
After their airliner crashes on a deserted island, a group of survivors stumble upon a terrorist training camp, from which the Commies plan to infiltrate and take over the United States. Can the gutsy blonde heroine, the hunky hero, the psycho Vietvet, and other assorted Airplane! types frustrate their fiendish plans and save democracy? The budget, slightly higher than usual by Troma standards, is mostly eaten up by endless gunfire, feeble explosions and monotonously repeated stunts, while the one-dimensional villains speak in funny accents, and the good guys (and gals) do what they gotta do. Come back, Chuck norris, all is forgiven. NF

War, The

(Jon Avnet, 1994, US) Kevin Costner, Elijah Wood, Mare Winningham, Lexi Randall, LeToya Chisholm, Christopher Fenell, Donald Sellers.
125 min.

Oozing sincerity and restraint, this coming-of-age tale submerges under the weight of its own worthiness. If you go with the flow, the languorous atmosphere and fine acting may draw you in, but a lack of dramatic focus frequently leads to a blurring of the edges. For young Stu Simmons (Wood) and his sister Lidia (Randall), growing up in small-town Mississippi in the early '70s is tough. Their father, Vietnam vet Costner, is unemployed and withdrawn due to post-traumatic stress, their mother struggles to make ends meet, and their clashes with the bullying Lipnicki boys repeatedly threaten to escalate into violence. The siblings' sole refuge is a tree-house they're building out of scrap metal; but unbeknown to Stu, his sister and her two black friends have been taking time out from their dance routines to steal these materials from the Lipnickis' scrapyard. With their feral, shaven-headed enemies now hellbent on revenge, Stu and Lidia must either fight for what's theirs or embrace the pacifism espoused by their repentant father. Once the film spills over into blatant anti-war allegory, everything starts to unravel. Already over-written to within an inch of its life, it lurches from one climax to the next, tugging at the heart-strings until they snap. NF

War and Peace

(King Vidor, 1956, US/It) Audrey Hepburn, Henry Fonda, Mel Ferrer, Vittorio Gassman, John Mills, Herbert Lom, Anita Ekberg, Barry Jones, Oscar Homolka, Jeremy Brett, Helmut Dantine.
208 min.

Hepburn apart, a miscast and largely misconceived – but not unenjoyable – epic. The fact that six writers collaborated on the screenplay tells its own story of a lavish, respectful, essentially hollow reduction-by-committee of Tolstoy's novel. The first couple of hours, rambling episodically on, seems less a panoramic view of the social scene than a gaggle of characterisations with nowhere much to go. But after Borodino, Vidor and the film seem to be pulling together for the first time in the flurry of magnificently staged battle scenes (the retreat from Moscow, the crossing of the Beresina). As Vidor has commented, 'My favourite subject is the search for truth. This is also the essential theme of Tolstoy's book. It is Pierre who forces himself to discover what is at the heart of man. All that we see, he sees. I wanted to show his point of view'. Although this point of view is never really anchored in the film, it does lend a belated sense of purpose. TM

War and Peace (Voina i Mir)

(Sergei Bondarchuk, 1967, USSR) Ludmila Savelyeva, Sergei Bondarchuk, Vyacheslav Tikhonov, Anastasia Vertinskaya, Vasily Lanovoi.
357 min.

Compared to this 70mm monster (five years in the making, and running 507 minutes in its original Russian version), most other epics have the visual dimensions of an Edgar Wallace potboiler. Battles, duels, ballroom scenes, and even trips in a troika are staged with unsparing picturesqueness; at the battle of Borodino, a staggering twenty thousand extras mill around the cannons, smoke, and horses. But spectacle apart, Bondarchuk's version of Tolstoy falls into the category of respectable mediocrity, and matters aren't helped by the loud American voices with which everyone speaks in this much-edited and dubbed version. As a movie excursion into Russian literature, *Love and Death* still wins hands down. GB

War Games

(John Badham, 1983, US) Matthew Broderick, Dabney Coleman, John Wood, Ally Sheedy, Barry Corbin, Juanin Clay, Dennis Lipscomb.
113 min.

As teenage David (Broderick) makes use of his pet computer for personal entertainment, little does he know that 'Global Thermonuclear War' is not just another variation on Space Invaders; it's part of the Defense Department's early-warning system, and his gleeful decision to nuke Las Vegas precipitates a full-scale countdown to

Armageddon. It's a pity that the film relaxes its grip by abandoning the hardware arena of combat for some routine leg-action and teen romance; but it finally and utterly blows its own fuse by resorting to such simplistic pro-humanitarian clichés that even the most uni of lateralists are likely to squirm with embarrassment, while hard-nosed hawks will merely shrug with contempt. Worth seeing, though, for the droll first half. AB

War Gods of the Deep

see City Under the Sea

War Is Over, The

see Guerre est finie, La

Warlock

(Edward Dmytryk, 1959, US) Richard Widmark, Henry Fonda, Anthony Quinn, Dorothy Malone, Dolores Michaels, Wallace Ford, Tom Drake, Richard Arlen.
122 min.

An incredibly overwrought Freudian Western, with Fonda as the notorious killer hired by the cowardly citizens of Warlock to defend them from a vicious gang. Fonda brings with him his lifelong partner (and possible lover), the blond, neurotic, club-footed Anthony Quinn. After a few rousing shoot-outs, one of the opposition (Widmark) joins them, and he is appointed sheriff. Enter Dorothy Malone, whose fiancé has been murdered by Quinn, and she falls in love with Widmark, whom she hopes will avenge her. It all ends with a Viking-style funeral, and with Fonda starting to think beyond his guns. Dmytryk (after the blacklist days, at least) was usually one of Hollywood's dullest directors, but not here. The movie is overlong yet dynamic, juxtaposing moments of repose, when the script shuffles relationships like a stacked deck, and bursts of action which have something of the operatic stylisation of Sergio Leone. ATu

Warlock

(Steve Miner, 1988, US) Richard E Grant, Julian Sands, Lori Singer, Kevin O'Brien, Mary Woronov, Richard Kuss, Juli Burkhart.
102 min.

This updated witch-finder movie eschews hardcore horror in favour of supernatural action adventure, with enjoyable results. Its masterstroke is the inspired casting of blond-haired wimp Sands as the suavely malevolent warlock, and raven-haired Grant as the witch-hunter. None too keen on being hanged and then burned over a basket of live cats, Sands uses his magic powers to escape across time, from 17th century Massachusetts to modern day Los Angeles, where waitress Singer is a little put out when she finds a cool-looking guy with a weird accent in her apartment, then really pissed off when Grant turns up in pursuit. But when Sands casts a spell which causes her to age 20 years every day, she teams up with Grant. Marred only by some silly dialogue and naff flying effects, the ensuing cross-country chase is confidently handled; and with the help of Sands' subtly evil performance, Miner tones down the violence while hinting at some really nasty stuff. NF

War Lord, The

(Franklin Schaffner, 1965, US) Charlton Heston, Richard Boone, Rosemary Forsyth, Maurice Evans, Guy Stockwell, Niall MacGinnis, Henry Wilcoxon, James Farentino, Michael Conrad.
122 min.

An interesting attempt to break away from stereotype epic. Heston plays the war lord in 11th century Normandy who finds that the land he controls is steeped in primitive tradition. The rituals of pagan mythology are well observed – cabalistic idols, sacrifices – as in Heston's disintegration in the face of a mental force that he can't understand. Well put together by Schaffner (it's one of his best films, along with *Planet of the Apes* and *Patton*), and strongly photographed by Russell Metty. CPe

Warlords of Atlantis

(Kevin Connor, 1978, GB) Doug McClure, Peter Gilmore, Shane Rimmer, Lea Brodie, Michael Gothard, Hal Galili, John Ratzenberger, Robert Brown, Cyd Charisse, Daniel Massey.
96 min.

Although the title promises something new, this is a rehash of exactly the same old fantasy formula used by Connor and producer John Dark in *The Land That Time Forgot*, *At the Earth's Core* and *The People That Time Forgot*: the discovery of a lost community, the imprisonment of one of the party, a rescue attempt, and final escape from the lost world as it's about to be destroyed. The structure has so little to commend it that it's amazing they pursue it with such dogged persistence. As always, Connor's approach is commendably stolid, but this production lacks almost all the more pleasing elements of the earlier movies, and is sickeningly vulgar in its portrayal of Atlantis, right down to the leering emphasis on Cyd Charisse's legs. DP

Warm December, A

(Sidney Poitier, 1972, GB/US) Sidney Poitier, Esther Anderson, Yvette Curtis, George Baker, Johnny Sekka, Earl Cameron, Hilary Crane.
101 min.

Black radical chic with a tragic twist. Poitier, a widowed doctor, runs a ghetto clinic in Washington DC, races motor-bikes on the side, and has enough money to live in style. While in London on holiday with his 10-year-old daughter, he meets and falls in love with Catherine (Anderson), daughter of an ambassador from a new African state. Punctuated by unnecessary mystery music and mysterious-looking foreigners in raincoats, the secret emerges that Catherine is dying of sickle cell disease. The love is short-lived. She is beautiful, bright, and brave. We all leave in tears. MV

Warning Shot

(Buzz Kulik, 1966, US) David Janssen, Ed Begley, Keenan Wynn, Sam Wanamaker, Lillian Gish, Stefanie Powers, Eleanor Parker, George Grizzard, George Sanders, Steve Allen, Carroll O'Connor, Joan Collins, Walter Pidgeon, John Garfield Jr.
100 min.

Staking out an apartment block on the watch for a psycho killer, Detective Sergeant Valens of the LA police (Janssen) is forced to shoot a man who keeps on coming with a gun when challenged. The dead man turns out to be a highly respected doctor, and there is no trace of the gun. Suspended with the threat of a manslaughter charge hanging over him, Valens goes rogue to clear his name. Neatly scripted from Whit Masterson's novel *711 – Officer Needs Help*, the film is very enjoyable in the time-honoured private eye manner, even though the parade of vivid 'guest cameos' uncovered during Janssen's dogged trek through the spiralling mystery smacks less of *noir* tradition than of TV practice (Kulik had only recently graduated to movies). TM

Warnung vor einer heiligen Nutte

see Beware of a Holy Whore

War of the Buttons, The

see Guerre des Boutons, La

War of the Buttons

(John Roberts, 1993, GB/Fr) Gregg Fitzgerald, John Coffey, Paul Batt, Gerard Kearney, Eveanna Ryan, Frank Grimes, Declan Mulholland.
94 min.

Slim pickings from David Puttnam, reunited with *Chariots of Fire* screenwriter Colin Welland: this mildly diverting entertainment is a remake of Yves Robert's *La Guerre des Boutons* (1962). Transposed to County Cork, the film charts the feud between the pupils of neighbouring village schools, the Carricks and the Ballys. While the dispute's origins remain hazy, it soon escalates via public humiliation and private recrimination to 'all-out war', sticks and stones – and buttons – at the ready. Relatively unsentimental. TCh

War of the Colossal Beast

(Bert I Gordon, 1958, US) Sally Fraser, Roger Pace, Dean Parkin, Russ Bender, Charles Stewart.
68 min. b/w & col.

Sci-fi schlock merchant Gordon followed *The Amazing Colossal Man* with this reprise of the same 'tall actor knocks over miniature sets' formula. Eschewing the Cold War paranoia of the previous offering, this one has Roger Pace as a 60ft giant with the mind of a wild beast, and a handy loincloth, who goes on the rampage when the powers that be whisk him from the wilds of Mexico to LA captivity. Watch out for the climactic burst of colour. TJ

War of the Monsters (Gojira Tai Gaigan)

(Jun Fukuda, 1972, Jap) Hiroshi Ishikawa, Yuriko Hishimi, Tomoko Umeda, Minoru Takashima.
89 min.

Although Godzilla doesn't really cut it in the special effects department, he does have a certain lumbering charm. So does the script: Godzilla fights off monsters from outer space to save Tokyo from colonisation by a group of intelligent cockroaches with imperialist tendencies (the only species to have survived pollution on their planet). The monster battle is overlong, though the one with a rotary saw in his chest (a Texan?) is a novelty, and like the others, all too obviously a man in a moth-eaten suit. They bump into each other to see how often they can fall down, and Godzilla takes some time to find his pace. As he's floored again and again but comes back fighting, his performance more and more resembles Stallone in *Rocky*, even to the mumbling. If you're in the right silly mood, kind of fun. SM

War of the Roses, The

(Danny DeVito, 1989, US) Michael Douglas, Kathleen Turner, Danny DeVito, Marianne Sägebrecht, GD Spradlin, Peter Donat.
116 min.

Adapted from Warren Adler's novel, this portrait of a disintegrating marriage is a riotous mix of of wicked and wince-inducing humour. After seventeen years of marital bliss, Barbara Rose (Turner) asks her lawyer husband (Douglas) for a divorce. The reason? 'Because when I watch you sleeping, when I see you eating, when I look at you now, I just want to smash you face in'. From then on, their showcase home – complete with two kids, dog and cat – becomes a battlefield. She smashes his collection of porcelain figures, he saws the heels off all her shoes; he disrupts her gourmet evening by pissing on the fish dish, she trashes his Morgan sports car. This dark comic tone, though, is lightened into a cautionary fairytale by the pro-marriage moralising of a framing device in which divorce lawyer De Vito relates the events to a prospective client. There is also a sneaking suspicion that what the couple are tearing to shreds is not so much the emotional fabric of their relationship as the soft furnishings of their home. Still, De Vito's quirky camera angles and Kathleen Turner's steely-eyed spite inject a sadistic comic-strip madness into a film that for once has the nerve to see its nastiness through. NF

War of the Satellites

(Roger Corman, 1958, US) Susan Cabot, Dick Miller, Richard Devon, Robert Shayne, Jerry Barclay, Eric Sinclair.
66 min. b/w.

In which Dick Miller hushes the United Nations, saves the world, and wins Ms Cabot in mid-space. In which alien-controlled scientist Devon walks off in two directions at once. In which Corman himself is glimpsed auteuristically knob-twiddling at Mission Control. Compared to which even *The Outer Limits* looks opulent. Which is no surprise for a flick started the day after Sputnik was launched, and on-screen only eight weeks later. Cheap, but very cheerful. PT

War of the Worlds

(Byron Haskin, 1953, US) Gene Barry, Ann Robinson, Les Tremayne, Henry Brandon, Robert Cornthwaite, Jack Kruschen.
85 min.

Updated from London 1890 to contemporary California, George Pal's version of the HG Wells novel still works pretty well, thanks to its attractive special effects. You can on occasion see the wires manipulating the Martian ships, but their graceful sting-ray design (replacing Wells' tripod conception) is sleekly sinister; the wholesale destruction of (miniature) cities is surprisingly convincing; and the one-eyed humanoid/octopoid alien with the sucker fingers is an engaging creation. Too bad about the wooden cast, the tacki-

ly conventional romance, and a draggy religious message; but at least, given the time it was made, it isn't imbued with Cold War hysteria. TM

War Party

(Franc Roddam, 1989, US) Billy Wirth, Kevin Dillon, Tim Sampson, Jimmie Ray Weeks, M Emmet Walsh, Kevyn Major Howard, Jerry Hardin, Tantoo Cardinal, Bill McKinney.
97 min.

Sonny (Wirth) leads a mundane life on a Montana reservation, and only reluctantly agrees to participate in a local re-enactment of the battle which killed his Indian ancestors. The gala occasion brings out Cavalry uniforms and racial prejudice; there are real-life killings on both sides, prompting Sonny, his best friend (Dillon) and a couple of pals to take to the hills. What starts out promisingly enough as a firmly deglamorised depiction of reservation life declines into a routine chase thriller. Roddam shifts fluently between depictions of the original conflict and modern-day tensions, but there's a stagy atmosphere to the historic sequences which weakens their dramatic impact. The film's political will is more forcefully evident in exchanges between the tribal council leader and his wife as they discuss the circumstances leading to Sonny's defiant gesture. Their opportunity to air long-standing grievances is all too brief; but at least the film commendably refuses to offer an easy, upbeat resolution. CM

Warren Oates: Across the Border

(Tom Thurman, 1992, US) Peter Fonda, Ned Beatty, Stacy Keach, Harry Dean Stanton, Thomas McGuane, David Thomson, Monte Hellman, Sam Peckinpah.
54 min.

'Nobody loses all the time,' mused Warren Oates in his greatest role, Benny, in *Bring Me the Head of Alfredo Garcia*. But if anyone was born to play losers it was Oates. As Ned Beatty recalls, 'You could smell whisky and bad breath on him; he was toothy and small, with eyes that have seen too much solitary confinement – but for some of us, he was the only human being in motion pictures.' Although he never made it as a star, you only have to look at the friends and collaborators Thurman has assembled here to know the ragged glory of the man: novelist Thomas McGuane; directors Hellman and Peckinpah; Harry Dean Stanton and Peter Fonda. He was a 'constitutional anarchist', says Harry Dean, and the movies bear him out. TCh

War Requiem

(Derek Jarman, 1988, GB) Nathaniel Parker, Tilda Swinton, Laurence Olivier, Patricia Hayes, Rohan McCullough, Nigel Terry, Owen Teale.
93 min. b/w & col.

Jarman's finest work to date takes as its soundtrack/score Benjamin Britten's masterly religious/poetic choral work. A work of unrelieved mourning – an unfashionable sentiment – it mingles Wilfred Owen's World War One poems (written in the trenches) with the text of the Latin mass. The score is complex, long, non-narrative, and uninterrupted, which demands much of Jarman; and he delivers. His script subtly intertwines the poems' slight strains of a story – guns, dying, death, hell, loss, and reconciliation – with imagined scenes around the poet at war, along with cruelly honest, uncensored found footage of wars distant and current. He also wrings remarkable silent performances from Swinton, who embodies the awful roles traditionally allotted the female principle in war; from Parker as the poet; and Teale as an unknown soldier transmuted by war. TC

War Room, The

(DA Pennebaker/Chris Hegedus, 1993, US) James Carville, George Stephanopolis.
96 min.

'The most expensive single act of masturbation in history' – James Carville on Ross Perot's 1992 campaign for the US presidency. If this documentary record of the Clinton team's own campaign doesn't quite warrant such abusive language, it nevertheless comes across as an indulgent piece of self-preening. The film follows campaign manager Carville (see him in *The People vs. Larry Flynt*) and George Stephanopolis, director of communications, from a pre-Primary

February breakfast with Clinton to the night of the November election results. The two 'stars', Carville, a 'ragin' Cajun' with fiercely intelligent Simian features and a forthright approach to the press corps, and Stephanopolis, telegenic Harvard boy, twinkle-eyed and soft-spoken, make a great double-act, though Carville is the stand-out. But the focus is way too far over on the side of personalities. There's scant political revelation: it's less behind-the-scenes than the scenes from a different perspective. NB

Warriors, The

see Dark Avenger, The

Warriors, The

(Walter Hill, 1979, US) Michael Beck, James Remar, Thomas Waites, Dorsey Wright, Brian Tyler, David Harris, Deborah Van Valkenburgh.
94 min.

From its powerhouse opening, in which all the gangs of New York gather in tribal splendour in Riverside Drive Park, to the last ditch stand in dilapidated Coney Island, Hill has elevated his story of a novice gang on the run into a heroic epic of Arthurian dimensions, with sex as sorcery and the flick-knife as sword. Anyone expecting gritty realism will be disappointed, because Hill is offering something better: shooting entirely on NY locations at night, he has transformed the city into a phantasmagoric labyrinth of weird tribes in fantastic dress and make-up who move over (and under) the streets as untouched as troglodytes by the civilisation sleeping around them. The novice gang from Coney accidentally encounters some middle class swingers on the subway, and the two groups stare at each other like aliens from different galaxies (while the gang's new female recruit has to be gently restrained from instinctively putting a hand up to straighten her hair). Mixing ironic humour, good music, and beautifully photographed suspense, it's one of the best of 1979. DP

Warriors of Virtue

(Ronny Yu, 1996, US/HK) Angus MacFadyen, Mario Yedidia, Marley Shelton, Jack Tate, Doug Jones, Don W Lewis, J Todd Adams.
103 min.

Stuntmen in kangaroo suits knock the stuffing out of one another. Yedidia's the kid with a gammy leg who disappears down a whirlpool when he's bullied by schoolmates, only to wake in the magical kingdom of Tao – a land whose harmony is threatened by the rampant ham of MacFadyen's warlord Komodo. Only the reunion of the five Warriors of Virtue, super-marsupials using the power of the elements to defeat their enemies without killing them, can save the day. Hong Kong director Yu's flashy combat sequences and the fairytale production design by Eugenio Zanetti unfortunately count for little when the exposition holding it all together is both cluttered and hamfisted. TJ

Warsaw Ghetto Uprising, The

(Jolanta Dylewska, 1993, Pol) Marek Edelman.
70 min. b/w & col.

This moving documentary, subtitled 'Chronicle According to Marek Edelman', begins with 15 minutes of archive footage, presumably taken by the Nazis, of the Warsaw Ghetto between 1940 and 1943, to the accompanying music of Jan Kanty Pawluskiewicz. This is the background to the testimony of Edelman, a young leader of the Jewish Battle Organisation during the 53 days of the Warsaw Ghetto Uprising. Edelman recalls in perfect detail the suffering and courage of the Jews. WH

Warshots

(Heiner Stadler, 1996, Ger) Herbert Knaup, Peter Franke, Özay Fecht, Hassan Farhat, David Kehoe, Jamal Hamdan.
93 min.

February 1995: Having witnessed the shooting of an Irish rebel by British soldiers in Belfast, German conflict-photographer Jan Loy (Knaup) ventures into a Somalia-like civil war constituted by warlords, journalists and UN troops. With his experience in Ireland still hanging over him – despite a press award for his shots of the incident, fellow reporter (Franke) blames him for the Irishman's death – Loy meets a local sniper and is struck by the similarities between their trades, furthering his doubts about the ethics of his profession. It could be promising, but, with director and co-writer Stadler's elliptical, disjointed style and low word count, the effect is ponderous and unrevealing. NB

War Wagon, The

(Burt Kennedy, 1967, US) John Wayne, Kirk Douglas, Howard Keel, Robert Walker, Keenan Wynn, Bruce Cabot, Valora Noland, Gene Evans, Bruce Dern.
101 min.
Kennedy is very nearly at his tongue-in-cheek best in this Western which affably carries on the mood and manner of Hawks' *El Dorado*. Wayne and Douglas play the old friends from way back, one hired to kill the other but joining forces – along with a pleasingly motley band of helpers – to turn the tables on the villainous Cabot with a handsome profit on the side. 'Mine hit the ground first' Douglas boasts as they simultaneously outdraw two opponents. 'Mine was taller' says Wayne laconically. No masterpiece, but very engaging. TM

War Zone

(Nathaniel Gutman, 1986, WGer) Christopher Walken, Marita Marschall, Hywel Bennett, Arnon Zadock, Amos Lavie, Etti Ankri.
99 min.
The approach employed here is so unimaginative, the format so tired, that electro-cardiac shock couldn't save this melodrama (filmed in English) from its own dubiously oversimplified politics. Don Stevens (Walken), jaded war correspondent, finds himself in the Lebanon, a disengaged hack who wanders somnolently through the gunfire, until an exclusive (which turns out to be a set-up) plunges him into the middle of the battle. Another chapter of recent history reduced to an amalgam of censored memory, romance, and imagination. SGo

Washington Square

(Agnieszka Holland, 1997, US) Jennifer Jason Leigh, Albert Finney, Ben Chaplin, Maggie Smith, Judith Ivey, Betsy Brantley.
116 min.
When Wyler made *The Heiress*, he was, of course, filming a Broadway adaptation of Henry James's novel. This version goes back to the original book, jettisoning the stage-related business, and retrieving details and scenes lost in the translation from page to stage. Other 'corrections' include a greater teasing of the audience concerning the affections of the heroine's suitor: is anything stirring there besides opportunism? And Wyler's ending – a melodramatically decisive balancing of the moral books – here becomes a faithful transcription of the low key but equally deadly last interview described by James. But one does miss the severe monochrome of 1949, amid all this colour, all this brightness. BBa

Wasp Woman, The

(Roger Corman, 1959, US) Susan Cabot, Fred Eisley, Barboura Morris, Michael Marks, William Roerick, Frank Gerstle.
73 min. b/w.
A film that highlights Corman's ability to ring interesting changes on proven formulas. The she-creature and the havoc she wreaks are both predictable enough, but it's a novel touch that she's a beautician, and that her metamorphosis is caused by experiments with new cosmetics ingredients. Susan Cabot (always Corman's favourite female sadist-figure) anchors the sexual mayhem in a very credible characterisation. TR

Watcher in the Woods, The

(John Hough, 1982, US) Bette Davis, Carroll Baker, David McCallum, Lynn-Holly Johnson, Kyle Richards, Ian Bannen, Richard Pasco, Frances Cuka, Eleanor Summerfield, Georgina Hale.
100 min.
The horror movie, Disney-style. After an American couple and their two daughters move into an English country house, one of the girls (Johnson) imagines she is being watched by a creature that lurks in the woods. Her experiences seem to be linked to the disappearance, thirty years before, of another young girl, creepy old crone Davis' daughter. When it became obvious that the film's mix of cutesy sentiment and vague scariness wasn't working, the company ordered whole sequences to be rewritten, re-shot or re-edited, then imposed a stupid ending that explains precisely nothing. NF

Watchers

(John Hess, 1988, Can) Michael Ironside, Lala, Corey Haim, Dale Wilson, Blu Mankuma.
91 min.
A secret government laboratory, which has been genetically engineering animals for combat, unaccountably explodes, allowing two creatures to escape: a super-intelligent golden retriever that only wants to be loved, and a super-nasty hairy beastie. The dog befriends a kid called Travis, who's basically a good sort; but because the beastie has been trained to kill, Travis is soon surrounded by dead people with missing eyeballs. The obligatory mad scientists run around attempting to catch their creations, and don't care who they walk over in the process, so pretty soon it's 'young boy and wonder dog against the world' time. Produced under the guiding influence of Roger Corman, this low budget adaptation of Dean R Koontz's novel is a Boy's Own adventure all the way, a cross between *Lassie Come Home* and *Predator*, with a terrifically evil performance from Ironside. The script is enjoyably laughable, and the special effects are reassuringly tacky. Good cheap nonsense. MK

Watch It

(Tom Flynn, 1993, US) Peter Gallagher, Suzy Amis, John C McGinley, Jon Tenney, Cynthia Stevenson, Lily Taylor, Tom Sizemore, Jordana Capra.
102 min.
John (Gallagher) moves in with Rick, Danny and Michael – all aimless twenty-somethings – and finds himself caught up in a life of parties, pranks and perfidy. But if their laid-back ways at first seem innocent, they mask a reluctance to grow up, and a fear of responsibility that sours their view of the world and hurts those who come close to them. So when John falls for one of Michael's cast-offs (Amis), it provokes a spate of jealousy and one-upmanship among the four – and a reassessment of their various relationships. NB

Watchmaker of Saint-Paul, The

see Horloger de St Paul, L'

Watch Out, We're Mad (Altrimenti ci Arrabbiamo)

(Marcello Fondato, 1974, It/Sp) Bud Spencer ie. Carlo Pedersoli, Terence Hill ie. Mario Girotti, Donald Pleasence, John Sharp, Deogratias Huerta.
102 min.
The double act from the 'Trinity' Westerns lend themselves rather absent-mindedly to this fairly resistible comedy geared to the great Italian fetish for gadgetry on wheels. The plot revolves around a highly-prized dune buggy, and is decorated with herds of trail-bikes, which at one point are involved in a joust-style contest. It is as bright and relentless as can be, with some of the side characters admittedly carrying a certain bite; but Fondato is a great one for never using a nuance if he can belabour the audience with a signpost. VG

Watch Your Stern

(Gerald Thomas, 1960, GB) Kenneth Connor, Leslie Phillips, Eric Barker, Joan Sims, Noel Purcell, Hattie Jacques, Sidney James, Eric Sykes, Spike Milligan, Victor Maddern.
88 min. b/w.
The 'Carry On' crew edge out of port under a flag of convenience as able seaman Connor dons a variety of disguises to stop the Admiralty top brass discovering he's accidentally destroyed a set of hush-hush torpedo plans. Milligan and Sykes steal the picture as a couple of chatty electricians, otherwise the awful puns and dodgy double entendres are all shipshape and Bristol-fashion. TJ

Water

(Dick Clement, 1985, GB) Michael Caine, Valerie Perrine, Brenda Vaccaro, Leonard Rossiter, Billy Connolly, Dennis Duggan, Fulton Mackay, Dick Shawn, Fred Gwynne.
97 min.
This movie has the conviction of a farce negligently translated from an obscure foreign dialect. The action takes place on the fictional island of Cascara, which becomes the subject of international dispute when a long-neglected oil well is reopened and strikes...Perrier. American oilmen, Brit paratroopers, film crews, assorted mercenaries and revolutionaries move in as the plot trickles towards a conclusion in which a gang comprising executive producer George Harrison's old mates (Starr, Clapton, et al) gives an exquisitely embarrassing rock performance. Fine actors such as Vaccaro, Connolly and Rossiter, recognising a lame horse when they see one, camp it up for all they're worth, and it is left to Caine, giving yet another understated and perfectly timed performance as Cascara's beleaguered governor, to push *Water* limping across the finishing line. Eau-ful. RR

Water and Power

(Pat O'Neill, 1993, US)
58 min.
Though the title of Pat O'Neill's ciné-poem evokes Los Angeles and southern California – ostensibly its subject – it might more fittingly be called 'Movements of the Sun' or 'Ghosts in the Machine'. For while this visually striking, technologically remarkable movie acknowledges water as the life force that enables LA to prosper in what would otherwise be a virtual desert, most of O'Neill's time-lapse camerawork, multi-layered superimpositions and dynamic optical effects are concerned with changes in light, whether they be shadows shifting over baking sands or concrete canyons, or the Bacon-esque contortions of wraithlike figures in surreal cloud-walled rooms. Whatever, rather like *Koyaanisqatsi* with even less narrative but far more imaginative sense, this immaculately edited, kaleidoscopic collage of densely textured images and sounds paints a persuasive picture of LA and its environs as a feverishly dreamlike state of mind. GA

Water Babies, The

(Lionel Jeffries, 1978, GB/Pol) James Mason, Billie Whitelaw, Bernard Cribbins, Joan Greenwood, David Tomlinson, Paul Luty, Tommy Pender, Samantha Gates.
92 min.
Charles Kingsley ended his amazing Victorian tale of chimney-sweep Tom's underwater odyssey with the earnest wish that his child readers learn their lessons and wash themselves in cold water 'like a true Englishman'. Times have obviously changed, and any modern adaptation has to softpedal the pious author's whimsical allegories of spiritual and social improvement. Jeffries' film achieves this by plunging into tepid animation when Tom (Pender) plunges into water. But with the allegories submerged, the string of animated adventures involving the smiling band of pure, fearless babies and the gallery of talking (and singing) fish seem just idle amusement, lacking all the driving force of the live-action framework. There's no cute buffoonery in those scenes, which are replete with solid Yorkshire atmosphere, narrative tension, and excellent acting (even from David Tomlinson). It's really two films in one. GB

Waterdance, The

(Neal Jimenez/Michael Steinberg, 1991, US) Eric Stoltz, Wesley Snipes, William Forsythe, Helen Hunt, Elizabeth Peña, William Allen Young.
107 min.
In 1985, Neal Jimenez, a successful young screenwriter, was left paralysed for life after breaking his neck. The same fate befalls novelist Joel Garcia (Stoltz) in Jimenez's first film as director, a moving drama set in a rehabilitation ward for paraplegics. At first Garcia maintains a degree of equanimity – he can still write, after all – but his latent frustration becomes more apparent in contact with his married girlfriend (Hunt) and the other patients in his ward, Raymond (Snipes) and Bloss (Forsythe). In essence another 'triumph-over-adversity' picture, its ensemble nature is both its strongest asset and its weakness. Neither lonely, black Raymond nor redneck biker Bloss has Joel's mental escape route: his talent. If this helps to ground things in a less sanguine vision than is usual, the movie cannot quite bring itself to resist the balm of male bonding, so that at worst it comes perilously close to something like a buddy movie on wheels. When it does, script, direction and performances are all right on the nose. It's frank and funny with it. TCh

Waterland

(Stephen Gyllenhaal, 1992, GB) Jeremy Irons, Sinead Cusack, Ethan Hawke, Grant Warnock, Lena Headey, David Morrissey, John Heard, Callum Dixon, Pete Postlethwaite.
95 min.

Graham Swift's Fenland novel paid homage to a part of Britain that's been ignored by film, unless you count *Dakota Road*. Gyllenhaal rises to the challenge of Swift's prose, capturing a flat land bogged down in its past, and creating an extravagant historical picture that avoids the traps of the Hovis-ad picturesque. The crazy-paving narrative and musings on the nature of history have inevitably been reduced in Peter Prince's script, but the essentials are there: memory, madness, incest, eels and real ale. History teacher Tom Crick (Irons), about to be axed by headmaster Heard, interrupts his classes to deliver a rambling memoir about his youth in the Fens, delving back to WWI and beyond to explain the multiple reasons behind the crack-up of his wife Mary (Cusack). There are obvious concessions to the US market; and as in his previous film, *Paris Trout*, Gyllenhaal bites off more narrative than he can chew, so that, for example, Cusack's character gets lost somewhere en route. Still, it's a brave endeavour, held together by Robert Elswit's poetic photography, and by Irons' authoritative impression of the crumbling desperation behind the chalk-dusted facade of a pensive history man. JRo

Waterloo

(Sergei Bondarchuk, 1970, It/USSR) Rod Steiger, Christopher Plummer, Orson Welles, Jack Hawkins, Virginia McKenna, Dan O'Herlihy, Rupert Davies, Philippe Forquet, Michael Wilding.
132 min.

Visually impressive, but a rather silly attempt to explain Napoleon, tracing his career from exile in Elba, through resurgence to power, to his defeat by Wellington at Waterloo. The main problem seems to lie in Bondarchuk's reliance on eye-catching gimmickry, and in his indecision as to whether to make a spectacular epic about nations at war, or an intimate portrayal of Bonaparte as a person. The early scenes, with less action, suffer most from this fault, although the whole thing is also blighted by Steiger's eccentrically mannered performance. GA

Waterloo Road

(Sidney Gilliat, 1944, GB) John Mills, Stewart Granger, Alastair Sim, Joy Shelton, Alison Leggatt, Beatrice Varley, George Carney, Jean Kent, Wylie Watson.
76 min. b/w.

Set in the mean streets around Waterloo Station in 1941, Gilliat's second feature is, like *Millions Like Us*, a populist drama commendably unpatronising in its view of the way the war left 'folks battling with themselves' at home. The simple narrative thread concerns Shelton as a young newly-wed left alone when her husband (Mills) is whisked away by the army. Unhappy, parked with in-laws, longing for the baby it didn't seem the right time to contemplate, she is fair game for a smooth spiv (Granger) proud of having bought himself medical exemption from the forces (which, ironically, it turns out he could have earned for free). But the meat of the film lies in the sleazy odyssey through the local pleasure domes (dance hall, pub, amusement arcade, hairdressing parlour, tattooist's shop) as the frantic Mills gets wind of the affair and goes AWOL to look for his wife. The hunt ends in happy reconciliation after a cleansing fist-fight between Mills and Granger (none too subtly waged to the sound of noises off from the blitz). No masterpiece, certainly, but it's often funny, sometimes touching, and always wonderfully evocative of the period. TM

Watermelon Man

(Melvin Van Peebles, 1970, US) Godfrey Cambridge, Estelle Parsons, Howard Caine, D'Urville Martin, Mantan Moreland, Kay Kimberly.
100 min.

Cambridge plays (admirably) a high-powered all-American insurance salesman, bursting with health, dirty jokes, and bigotry, who wakes up one morning to find that his skin has turned black. His frenzied attempts to explain the meta-

morphosis as an excess of tan and/or soya sauce won't wash any more than his skin will, so he finds himself forced to adjust. Often very funny in its topsy-turvy comments on racism, the script unfortunately has to battle against a director determined to use every gaudy trick in the book. The real pity, though, is that it fails to follow through on the logic of its premise whereby the hero is so heartily extrovert that everybody (wife and kids included) dislikes him. When he turns black, he also turns sympathetic, so nobody's reflex responses are really tested. TM

Watermelon Woman, The

(Cheryl Dunye, 1997, US) Cheryl Dunye, Guinevere Turner, Valerie Walker, Lisa Marie Bronson, Irene Dunye, Camille Paglia.
80 min.

A witty exploration of black American culture, past and present. Shooting in breezy, boppy fashion, Dunye soon has two narratives on the go: her quest for the 'truth' behind 'the Watermelon Woman', a beautiful, undocumented '30s film actress forever cast as a 'black mammy', and her own life working in a video store, bickering with her pal Tamara (Walker) and finding a girlfriend. Both these criss-crossing Philadelphia stories work in their own right. Dunye is fiercely charismatic, and while Tamara may seem like the stereotypically hardline, 'narrow' best friend, she also gets some great lines. It's the search for the Watermelon Woman, though, that really engrosses, throwing up a host of *Looking for Langston*-style images, as well as marvellous clips of Dunye's camera-shy mother suddenly denying all knowledge of the subject at hand. (Camille Paglia is a hoot, delivering patronising pearls of wisdom with irritable gusto.) CO'Su

Watership Down

(Martin Rosen, 1978, GB) voices: John Hurt, Richard Briers, Ralph Richardson, Roy Kinnear, Denholm Elliott, Zero Mostel, Harry Andrews, Michael Hordern.
92 min.

All one can say about this animated feature is thank God for myxomatosis. The book is another matter: once you've got past fey footnotes explaining that rabbits can count up to five, Richard Adams presents a good solid story, ingeniously and effectively told from the rabbit's minuscule perspective. Had the original director John Hubley been allowed to persevere, maybe some of the virtues would have remained; but as rejigged by producer Martin Rosen, there is nothing. The 'camera' takes a conventionally objective viewpoint, perpetually rolling over rolling countryside, which effectively robs the plot of all its terror and tension. And the bunnies are a crudely drawn, charmless bunch, with the final nail provided by the soundtrack's famous voices, who help turn the film into a radio play. GB

Water, Wind, Dust (Ab, Bad, Khak)

(Amir Naderi, 1989, Iran) Majid Niromand.
74 min.

Naderi made this for Iranian TV right after *The Runner*, and it plays like an expressionist twin to the earlier film. A boy searches for his missing parents in a huge, parched desert while the last inhabitants of the region flee as refugees and the sandstorms rise. There's no plot to speak of, but the boy faces a crisis of conscience when he finds himself responsible for an abandoned baby. There's hardly any dialogue either, just harsh, elemental imagery and a grim vision of life at the point of extinction. The slightly misjudged ending (which involves a burst of Beethoven on the soundtrack) confirms that allegorical interpretations are there for the asking. TR

Waterworld

(Kevin Reynolds, 1995, US) Kevin Costner, Jeanne Tripplehorn, Dennis Hopper, Tina Majorino, Zakes Mokae.
134 mins.

Water, water everywhere, and recycled urine to drink. The ice-caps have melted, and humans have split into three groups: eco-communities living together on deep-anchored, heavily guarded atolls; piratical 'Smokers' monopolising the scant reserves of oil; and lone mariners sailing in search of trade. Led by the Deacon (Hopper), the Smokers burn out an atoll looking for Enola (Majorino), a girl with a map to the mythical

'Dryland' tattooed on her back – but she escapes with the aid of her guardian Helen (Tripplehorn) and a mutant mariner with webbed feet and gills (Costner). After all the expense and negative speculation, the first thing to say about *Waterworld* is that it works – up to a point. The film inhabits its own brave new world and it's a real eyeful: witness the rusted techno-junk design of the atoll, the Smokers' kamikaze jet-ski attacks, and the Mariner's surprisingly nifty trimaran. Costner's acrobatic, taciturn hero is a charismatic figure, and his terse, uncomfortable relationship with the two female stowaways is the movie's dramatic strong point, but things drift when the Mariner softens, and the last half-hour is an inert retread of the familiar kidnap-rescue formula of contemporary action movies. A *Mad Max* rip-off at heart, but a blockbuster none the less. TCh

Wattstax

(Mel Stuart, 1973, US) Richard Pryor, Isaac Hayes, The Staple Singers, Luther Ingram, Johnnie Taylor, Rufus Thomas, Carla Thomas, The Emotions.
102 min.

A record of an all-day concert put on by Stax as part of the Watts Summer Festival to celebrate the riots. There isn't enough music, but Stax have at least had the wit to hire Richard Pryor to deliver one of his characteristic monologues (the rest of the time is filled out by chats with the denizens of Watts). Much good music all the same, from Carla Thomas and others, with an anti-climactic appearance from Isaac Hayes. See it for Rufus Thomas doing 'Funky Chicken', and for the genuinely stirring 'I am Somebody', the National Black Litany led, incredibly, by Jesse Jackson with the 100,000 auditorium joining in – a strong experience. VG

Wavelength

(Michael Snow, 1967, Can) Hollis Frampton.
45 min.

Snow is the uncontested master of the structural movement. *Wavelength*, his first major work, is a relentless 45-minute voyage across a loft that perpetually transforms, questions and illuminates everything in its path. Proposing and requiring a radically different form of perception of what a film experience entails, it repels passive attention as much as it rewards participation. As Snow describes it: 'The space starts at the camera's (spectator's) eye, is in the air, then is on the screen, then is within the screen (the mind)'. JR

Wax, or The Discovery of Television Among the Bees

(David Blair, 1991, US) David Blair, William Burroughs.
85 min. Video.

A curious pot-pourri of found footage, fantasy narrative and electronic visual trickery, this is proof that stylistic innovation and a taste for the bizarre don't always add up to galvanising effect. The narrative concerns a post-WWI English beekeeper, James 'Hive' Maker (William Burroughs in his most fleeting film cameo to date), with a miraculous swarm of Mesopotamian bees, and his descendant Jacob, who works in a military computer graphics unit in New Mexico. Starting off with a stack of antique documentary footage, Blair builds up an intrigue narrative that aspires to the po-faced absurdity of Peter Greenaway's early pseudo-documentaries. But it loses momentum when Blair himself takes centre stage as the protection-suited Jacob.

Waxwork

(Anthony Hickox, 1988, US) Zack Galligan, Deborah Foreman, Michelle Johnson, Dana Ashbrook, David Warner, Patrick MacNee.
97 min.

The portmanteau horror movie makes a hesitant comeback with this jokey teen splatter pic. Invited to a midnight show by the owner (Warner) of a mysterious waxwork exhibit, six teenagers are spooked by lifelike tableaux depicting the 18 most evil men who ever lived. Drawn into the victimless displays, they catapult back through time, and find themselves on the business end of the Wolfman's claws, Dracula's fangs, or the Marquis de Sade's riding whip. The clunking inconsistencies which litter the episodic plot mar enjoyment of the striking set designs and outrageous (censored) gore. The final showdown degenerates into a cross between a Western saloon brawl and a custard pie fight. In short, this cannot hold a candle to its AIP and Amicus predecessors, and mostly just gets on one's wick. NF

Waxworks
(Das Wachsfigurenkabinett)
(Paul Leni, 1924, Ger) Conrad Veidt, Emil Jannings, Werner Krauss, Wilhelm Dieterle, John Gottowt, Olga Belajeff.
7,028 ft. b/w.
Leni, a former designer for Reinhardt, seems to have conceived *Waxworks* as an inventory of expressionistic effects, using a different style, motif, and mood for each of its three episodes. The first is erotic and very funny, with Jannings as a wicked Caliph whose rotundity is echoed by the Bagdad sets, all bulbous walls and secret orifices. The second is a sadistic fantasia, with Veidt as Ivan the Terrible, eventually driven mad by his own tortures. The last is a phantasmagoria of Jack the Ripper (Krauss), pursuing young lovers through a nightmare London of cobblestones and fog. The result is consistently enthralling, years ahead of its time. The poet seen dreaming up the stories, incidentally, was to become the Hollywood director William Dieterle. TR

Way Ahead, The
(Carol Reed, 1944, GB) David Niven, Stanley Holloway, Raymond Huntley, William Hartnell, James Donald, John Laurie, Leslie Dwyer, Hugh Burden, Jimmy Hanley, Renee Asherson.
115 min. b/w.
Scripted by Eric Ambler and Peter Ustinov, this is more complex than Dick Lester's scornful '60s parody of it in *How I Won the War* suggests. Reed achieves his transformation of a bunch of lazy, quarrelsome civilians into a proficient fighting force with a minimum of machismo and glory. Unlike today's sinister professional force, this is a people's army. Niven's officer is a car mechanic up from the ranks, and Hartnell's thin-lipped sergeant scourges out class differences with a rigorous application of army discipline. Despite a framework which stresses regimental traditions and military valour, the film's celebration of the ordinary man as soldier leaves a residue of radicalism. RMy

Way Down East
(DW Griffith, 1920, US) Lillian Gish, Richard Barthelmess, Lowell Sherman, Burr McIntosh, Edgar Nelson.
9,000 ft. b/w.
Griffith's Victorian perspective on illegitimacy (plus his view of maternity as 'woman's Gethsemane', etc) threatens for a while to make *Way Down East* the tract on monogamy that it announces itself as. It has two virtues out of that morass: one is Lillian Gish, whose virtuoso performance makes the heroine's growth from gullible innocence to bitter experience credible; the other is Griffith's old standby, the reliable mechanism of suspense melodrama, here escalating busily and inventively right up to the famous ice-floe climax. The result is a good deal more interesting than camp, but Russ Meyer fans won't have any problem perceiving this as a rural prototype for *Beyond the Valley of the Dolls*, with its classical simplicity, its comic relief yokels, its villainous squire, and its matchless moral. TR

Wayne's World
(Penelope Spheeris, 1992, US) Mike Myers, Dana Carvey, Rob Lowe, Tia Carrere, Brian Doyle-Murray, Lara Flynn Boyle, Michael DeLuise, Meat Loaf, Ed O'Neill.
95 min.
Bill & Ted never quite got beyond cult status, while this low-budget imitator became the US box-office phenomenon of the year. Why? Wayne & Garth don't have the charisma and telepathic rapport that made B & T such a terrific comic duo, and the only significant addition to the B & T lexicon is a new range of sexist epithets and the all-conquering 'NOT!'. And, bizarrely, Wayne (Myers) still lives in his parents' house, though he's clearly well into his thirties. They are the acceptable mascots of Metal; boys you could take home to your parents. Much of the credit for the film's success lies with Spheeris, whose confident if rough-edged direction keeps it on track and cooking. The jokes come thick and fast, mostly deconstructing TV: 'Wayne's World' is a public access TV show hosted by Wayne and his dweebish best friend Garth (Carvey). They play games with film, too: Wayne and Garth's to-cam-

era monologues always hit the spot, and there's a signposted 'gratuitous sex scene'. Lowe is suitably slimy as the TV mogul who offers them fame and wealth without obligation (not!), and the whole thing chunters along nicely to the climax(es). DW

Wayne's World 2
(Stephen Surjik, 1993, US) Mike Myers, Dana Carvey, Tia Carrere, Christopher Walken, Ralph Brown, Kim Basinger, James Hong.
95 min.
A year has passed, Wayne and Garth (Myers and Carvey) are a little older, a little wiser, and 'starting to grow hair in really weird places'. While Cassandra (Carrere) pursues her rock career under the auspices of shady producer Bobby Cahn (Walken) and Garth falls into the welcoming arms of Honey Hornée (Basinger), Wayne is visited in his dreams by Jim Morrison and promises to put on a huge concert: Waynestock! Despite typically hip disclaimers, *WW2* is in many respects a standard sequel, careful to rerun not only the (very sketchy) form of the original, but often the content as well. Odd, then, that this should be much funnier than the first film. A headbanger with brains, Wayne is a teen hero for ex-teens, and while the film isn't exactly 'mature', it must be baffling to anyone who doesn't remember the '70s with at least a modicum of embarrassed amusement. TCh

Way of a Gaucho
(Jacques Tourneur, 1952, US) Rory Calhoun, Gene Tierney, Hugh Marlowe, Richard Boone, Everett Sloane, Enrique Chaico, Lidia Campos.
91 min.
Calhoun certainly makes an authentic cowboy. An ex-lumberjack, ranch hand and forester, he was given an unlikely break in movies after a chance meeting with Alan Ladd. He stars as the gaucho, a renegade from the Argentine pampas who bitterly resents the way that 'civilisation' is transforming his backyard. Despite the South American settings, this unfolds like a very conventional Western, and doesn't bear comparison with Tourneur's masterly *Out of the Past*, or his cult horror films *Cat People* and *I Walked with a Zombie*. GM

Way of the Dragon, The
(Meng Long Guo Jiang/aka Return of the Dragon)
(Bruce Lee, 1972, HK) Bruce Lee, Nora Miao, Chuck Norris, Wei Ping Ao, Robert Wall, Wang Ing Sik.
99 min.
The only film written, produced, and directed by Bruce Lee was to have been the first of a series in which he cast himself as Tan Lung, out-of-town strong-arm, here hired by the Chinese owner of a restaurant in Rome to sort out their problems with the local syndicate. The film has the roughness you might expect in a first dirctorial effort, and also a perhaps unexpected leaning towards comedy. Lee makes great play on his character as the country boy without weapons confronting the denizens of the technologically-powerful West and winning hands down. Fight fest addicts will relish confrontations with Chuck Norris, Robert Wall, and Wang Ing Sik, professionals all. VG

Way Out West
(James W Horne, 1937, US) Stan Laurel, Oliver Hardy, Sharon Lynn, James Finlayson, Rosina Lawrence, Stanley Fields.
65 min. b/w.
Arguably the most assured of Stan and Ollie's features, with the sparkling duo sent to Brushwood Gulch to deliver the deed for a gold mine to the daughter (Lawrence) of a deceased prospector. Looking for a quick buck, saloon-keeper Finlayson directs them to his own brassy girlfriend (Lynn)...Some classic moments, such as the pair's soft-shoe shuffle outside the saloon, and their vocal duet at the bar on 'The Blue Ridge Mountains of Virginia', as well as a razor-sharp satire of B Western conventions. ATu

Way to the Stars, The
(Anthony Asquith, 1945, GB) Michael Redgrave, John Mills, Rosamund John, Douglass Montgomery, Renee Asherson, Stanley Holloway, Trevor Howard, Basil Radford, Bonar Colleano, David Tomlinson, Jean Simmons.
109 min. b/w.

Good performances distinguish this evocation of a World War Two bomber base in Britain, studiously anti-heroic in its concentration on human relationships rather than stirring combat (as one might expect with a script by Terence Rattigan). But it has dated badly in its genteelly romantic view of the hazards and heartbreaks, and in its cosy cementing of Anglo-American relationships. The best things in it are moments of pure atmosphere, like the opening shot in which the camera prowls through the deserted post-war airfield, picking up forlorn tokens of the past – a torn photograph, a scribbled signature – whose history is recounted in flashback. TM

Way Upstream
(Terry Johnson, 1986, GB) Barrie Rutter, Marion Bailey, Nick Dunning, Joanne Pearce, Stuart Wilson, Lizzie McInnerny, Veronica Clifford.
102 min.
More point in filming this Alan Ayckbourn comedy than most, perhaps, since the floating motor launch on stage frequently got stuck. In Johnson's hands, everything but the launch gets stuck in an interminable tale of bickering couples on a Thames holiday cruise. The playwright is revered by actors for his plotting, but things go badly adrift here, with horror-film dream sequences and a bloodthirsty fight. Way offbeam. BC

Way West, The
(Andrew V McLaglen, 1967, US) Kirk Douglas, Robert Mitchum, Richard Widmark, Lola Albright, Michael Witney, Sally Field, Stubby Kaye, Jack Elam, Harry Carey Jr, William Lundigan.
122 min.
A mishandled version of AB Guthrie Jr's award-winning novel about a wagon train of pioneers charting the Oregon trail in 1843. The cast – Douglas as a frantically visionary senator, Mitchum as the veteran trail scout, Widmark as the leader of the settlers – is fine, and William Clothier's location photography impressive. But the script meanders badly, even taking time off for a bit of teenage romance involving nymphet Sally Field in her film debut, while McLaglen's direction is simply lacklustre. GA

Way We Were, The
(Sydney Pollack, 1973, US) Barbra Streisand, Robert Redford, Bradford Dillman, Lois Chiles, Patrick O'Neal, Viveca Lindfors, Allyn Ann McLerie, Murray Hamilton, Herb Edelman.
118 min.
A *Love Story* with Redford and Streisand making an undeniably attractive pair. Though doomed from the start (by class, ethnic background, commitment), they get in their share of mileage, from college days of '37 to the break-up of their marriage in '50s Hollywood, where he's a compromised writer. Like their relationship, the film works best when they are alone. But with the script glossing whole areas of confrontation (from the communist '30s to the McCarthy witch-hunts), it often passes into the haze of a nostalgic fashion parade. Although Streisand's liberated Jewish lady is implausible, and emphasises the period setting as just so much dressing, Redford's Fitzgerald-type character, whose easy success carries the seeds of his possible destruction, is an intriguing trailer for his later *Great Gatsby*. It's a performance that brings more weight to the film than it deserves, often hinting at depths that are finally skated over.

W.C. Fields and Me
(Arthur Hiller, 1976, US) Rod Steiger, Valerie Perrine, John Marley, Jack Cassidy, Bernadette Peters, Dana Elcar, Paul Stewart, Billy Barty.
112 min.
Based on the ghost-written memoirs of the comedian's 'last mistress' Carlotta Monti (played here by Perrine), this witless biopic leaps through pseudo-history with cretinous inaccuracy. Sloppily slung together, hell-bent on wringing hearts with the drama of the last, lonely, drink-sodden years, it can't get even the simplest facts straight, and doesn't do much of a job on the tear-jerking either. Nose heavily reinforced and voice caressing insults in the approved manner, Steiger makes a brave stab at the part, but the reality and genius of Fields never get a look in. TM

We Are Not Alone
(Edmund Goulding, 1939, US) Paul Muni, Jane Bryan, Flora Robson, Raymond Severn, Una O'Connor, Henry Daniell, Cecil Kellaway, Montagu Love.
112 min. b/w.
A modest James Hilton tale (mild mannered husband, domineering wife, sweet other woman) is subtly invested with more potent themes and a darker than expected edge in the excellent hands of Edmund Goulding. Muni, the De Niro of his day, gives a superb, meticulous performance as an unexceptional Englishman under exceptional duress: in love with the governess (Bryan), he finds himself accused of murdering his wife (Robson). It was his favourite film role, and you can see why. The film is set in a sufficiently credible backlot England, immediately prior to the First World War. Its sympathetic portrait of an Austrian abroad (the Bryan character) was thought to have put paid to its box-office chances just before WWII, though in any case Jack Warner considered it too long 'for this kind of suffering picture'. He was mistaken; a thoughtful and engrossing melodrama, it's no masterpiece but it was underrated. TCh

Weak and The Wicked, The
(J Lee Thompson, 1953, GB) Glynis Johns, John Gregson, Diana Dors, Sidney James, AE Matthews, Athlene Seyler, Sybil Thorndike, Rachel Roberts.
88 min. b/w.
Gambling debts land Glynis Johns in stir, where she's befriended by streetwise Diana Dors in this homegrown tilt at women-in-prison melodrama (from Joan Henry's novel *Who Lie in Gaol*). The focus is as much on the events that put the girls behind bars as on the inmates' daily grind, and if it doesn't exactly look hard-hitting these days, the performances (Dors especially) are game enough to avoid crassness. TJ

Weapons of Mass Distraction
(Stephen Surjik, 1997, US) Gabriel Byrne, Ben Kingsley, Mimi Rogers, Illeana Douglas, Chris Mulkey, Kathy Baker, Paul Mazursky.
92 min
Stephen Surjik directed the superior *Wayne's World* sequel, but the key credit here belongs to screenwriter Larry Gelbart – best known for *Tootsie* and the TV *MASH*. A fictional companion piece to his award winning 1993 cable movie *Barbarians at the Gate* (a satire about the corporate buy out of RJR Nabisco), it features Kingsley and Byrne as feuding multimedia tycoons whose one-upmanship escalates to the point of mutual destruction. This is cruder than *Barbarians* and lacks the same true-story sting, but it's even more savage in its portrait of capitalism run rampant. (Look out for Paul Mazursky in a cameo as a penis transplant specialist.) TCh

Weavers: Wasn't That a Time, The
(James B Brown, 1981, US) Pete Seeger, Lee Hays, Ronnie Gilbert, Fred Hellerman, Studs Terkel, Don McLean, Arlo Guthrie.
73 min.
An enormous influence upon the US folk boom of the late '50s and early '60s, the Weavers also brought a breath of fresh air to the charts when the quartet's version of Leadbelly's 'Goodnight Irene' became a No. 1 hit single. Formed in the late '40s when mainstream popular music was big band slickness and moon-in-June love songs, the group began by singing in such uncommercial venues as trade halls. When the group's resident wit, double-amputee Lee Hays, decided that it was time for a last reunion before he died, he invited documentarist Jim Brown to film the picnic performance. The result is a fascinating and very moving mix of concert film and historical reminiscence (Hays: 'If it weren't for the honour, I'd just as soon not been blacklisted'). RM

Weber, Die
(Friedrich Zelnik, 1927, Ger) Paul Wegener, Dagny Servaes, Wilhelm Dieterle, Theodor Loos, Hans von Twardowski.
8727 ft. b/w.
Proletarian kitsch from a director who subsequently proved himself more at home in the field of Viennese operetta. The film was quite ambitious for its time (the sets and costumes are lav-ish period reconstructions), but its main claim to cultural legitimacy was its derivation from a Gerhart Hauptmann play; this attracted a starrier cast than was usual, including Paul *Golem* Wegener and director-to-be Dieterle. The result was the most picturesque presentation of poverty and squalor until Hollywood discovered the visual possibilities of the Depression. Its main interest now is that it serves as a reminder of the fact that German cinema of the late '20s turned to 'left wing' subjects as much for reasons of fashion as from political commitment. TR

Web of Passion
see A Double Tour

We Can't Go Home Again
(Nicholas Ray, 1973, US) Nicholas Ray, students of Harpur College, New York State University.
90 min.
Subtitled 'A Film By Us', this began life as a practical exercise in film-making in which Ray and his students sought to redefine/reinvent cinema (much as Godard, years earlier, had predicted he might) through on-going experimentation. A disjointed narrative (assembled from an often bewildering plethora of simultaneously projected images, shot on 35, 16, 8mm and video) attempts to explore the sexual, social and political unrest in America in the late '60s. Certainly it's something of a mess, but there's no denying either Ray's unsentimental sympathy for the plight of the young, or the raw emotional power of scenes in which students act out their own real-life psychodramas. (NB: Ray continued working on the film right up to his death, and his widow Susan has long planned to release a re-edited version in accordance with his later ideas). GA

Wedding, A
(Robert Altman, 1978, US) Carol Burnett, Paul Dooley, Amy Stryker, Mia Farrow, Geraldine Chaplin, Vittorio Gassman, Lillian Gish, Nina Van Pallandt, Viveca Lindfors, John Cromwell, Pat McCormick, Desi Arnaz Jr, Lauren Hutton, Howard Duff, Dina Merrill, Peggy Ann Garner.
125 min.
Altman's attempt to repeat the magic formula of *Nashville*, by concentrating on the interweaving relationships between a large number of guests at a wealthy society wedding, is flawed by an often sadly unimaginative script, which lampoons obvious targets as it clears the skeletons out of the two families' closets. The staging of the action is as exhilarating as ever, and there are glorious moments in the twisted, kaleidoscopic narrative; finally, however, the effect seems curiously contrived and complacent. Entertaining, though, thanks to the top-notch ensemble acting. GA

Wedding, The (Wesele)
(Andrzej Wajda, 1972, Pol) Ewa Zietek, Daniel Olbrychski, Andrzej Lapicki, Wojciech Pszoniak, Maja Komorowska.
110 min.
In Poland, Stanislaw Wyspianski's verse play *The Wedding* carries huge historical resonance. First performed in 1901, it deals with the provincial wedding of a peasant girl to an urban poet, at which the guests encounter dramatic figures from Poland's tortured past – a wise court jester, the Black Knight, a ghostly peasant who led a revolt against the gentry in 1848, and so on. Particular significance is attached to a golden horn – a symbol of national mission – that goes missing in the increasingly frenzied proceedings. Wajda goes for all of this with full romantic abandon. The camera swings wildly like a drunken wedding guest, the actors cast caution (and verse speaking) to the winds, and there is a great deal of blood and smoke. Whether you find this bewildering or exhilarating depends on your sympathies for such an extreme approach to a nation's artistic sensibility. DT

Wedding Banquet, The (Xiyan)
(Ang Lee, 1993, Tai/US) Winston Chao, May Chin, Mitchell Lichtenstein, Sihung Lung, Ah-Leh Gua.
108 min.
Wai-Tung's life seems near perfect: a Taiwanese in New York, he's a natural at real estate, and shares an apartment with his long-time lover Simon (Lichtenstein). There's just one problem: he hasn't come out to his folks who still write from Taiwan of their desire for grandchildren. To forestall an arranged marriage, Wai-Tung persuades his tenant Wei-Wei (May Chin), a Shanghai woman in need of a Green Card, to join in a marriage of mutual convenience. His parents then announce they're coming for the wedding. Never patronising his characters, Ang Lee combines comedy, both subtle and raucous, with acute social asides. There's genuine pain and confusion amid the jokes, so that the bitter-sweet, tentatively positive coda packs real punch. Winston Chow's Wai-Tung is initially rather stilted, but the rest of the cast performs excellently, and the script is admirably matter-of-fact in its treatment of the threatened gay relationship. GA

Wedding Bells
see Royal Wedding

Wedding in Blood
see Noces Rouges, Les

Wedding in Galilee (Noce en Galilée)
(Michel Khleifi, 1987, Bel/Fr) Ali M El-Akili, Bushra Karaman, Makram Khouri, Anna Achdian, Sonia Amar.
116 min.
An excellent first feature from the Palestinian Khleifi, in which the mayor of an Israeli-controlled Palestinian village insists that his son be married in traditional Arabic style. But the village is divided when the Israeli governor, fearing a political demonstration, agrees to suspend martial law for the occasion only on condition that he himself be allowed to attend. Performed mainly by local people, shot in Galilee and the occupied West Bank, the film is intelligent, surprisingly sensuous, and a moving plea for liberty and understanding. GA

Wedding March, The
(Erich von Stroheim, 1927, US) Erich von Stroheim, Fay Wray, George Fawcett, Maude George, Cesare Gravina, Dale Fuller, Matthew Betz, ZaSu Pitts.
10,170 ft. b/w & col.
Like *Foolish Wives*, *Greed* and *Queen Kelly*, *The Wedding March* (originally made in two parts, of which only the first is extant) survives as a mutilated masterpiece, even this first part having been cut from 14 reels to 11. Charting the ill-starred romance between a Viennese prince (Stroheim in an unusually sympathetic role) and a lowly commoner (Wray), the film would perhaps appear to be its cynical creator's most romantic work, were it not for the marvellously detailed portrait of the corruption of society in general, rich and poor. Nevertheless, it is the love scenes, played beneath shimmering apple blossoms in lyrical soft focus, that stick in the memory, ironically turning what is now the film's ending – the frustration of that love – into one of the director's most bitterly pessimistic scenes. GA

Wedding Night, The
(King Vidor, 1935, US) Gary Cooper, Anna Sten, Ralph Bellamy, Walter Brennan, Helen Vinson, Sig Ruman.
83 min. b/w.
Basically a weepie about the star-crossed love between an unhappily married man and an immigrant girl being forced into an arranged marriage. Discreetly lavish (it was the last, following *Nana* and *We Live Again*, of Sam Goldwyn's three attempts to promote Sten as a major star) and beautifully shot by Gregg Toland, it is handled with sensitivity by Vidor. But Cooper is rather miscast as a writer escaping the New York socialite round to get back to the soil; the ethnic customs of the Polish tobacco-growing community are too sketchy as well as too picturesque (especially in the wedding sequence); and in determinedly avoiding the statutory happy ending, the film achieves melodrama rather than the tragedy it is aiming for. TM

Wedding Rehearsal
(Alexander Korda, 1932, GB) Merle Oberon, Roland Young, George Grossmith, John Loder, Maurice Evans, Lady Tree, Wendy Barrie.
84 min. b/w.

Escapism par excellence, with high society weddings, country house romances on warm summer nights, and the working class strange 'men in green baize aprons with long hairs on their arms'. Korda has an acute mid-European appreciation of English foibles, and is able to poke fun at, yet still celebrate, traditional concern with dogs, cats and debutantes. A witty, if structurally inconsequential script, superb performances from Grossmith and delicately twittering old Lady Tree, Korda's enthusiasm, and the presence (it's little more) of breathtakingly beautiful Oberon, sweep one into a hypnotic if sickly world of Gerties and Berties, where problems revolve around whether Rose-Marie should marry Bimbo and Mary-Rose should marry Tootles. RMy

Wedding Singer, The

(Frank Coraci, 1998, US) Adam Sandler, Drew Barrymore, Christine Taylor, Allen Covert, Angela Featherstone, Alexis Arquette, Jon Lovitz, Steve Buscemi.
97 min.
Sandler, a cult comedian here submerging himself in the mainstream, plays Robbie Hart, a wannabe rock star stuck on the wedding band circuit. He's happy enough, until his own bride leaves him standing at the altar – which prompts the film's funniest scene, a bitter breakdown in professional decorum at his next gig, when he turns into the wedding singer from hell. Luckily for Robbie, the delicious Julia (Drew Barrymore) is waitressing in the wings. Her fiancé Glenn is bad news, so it can only be a matter of time before Robbie and Julia figure out they're made for each other. The movie is set in 1985 and won't let you forget it for a second. Culture Club, Huey Lewis, Nena, Billy Idol, Hall & Oates, The Cars, Kajagoogoo, Wham! it's frightening how innocent all this stuff sounds now. Sandler himself sings in a personably reedy register, and sports an authentic, dopily romantic David Essex wig which somehow doesn't preclude our sympathy. As for Barrymore, playing a good girl at last, she deserves nothing less – you can't help pulling for the kids. Anyway, it's hard to be cynical about a film which finds time to let Alexis Arquette do Boy George and Buscemi tear up Spandau Ballet's 'True'. TCh

We Don't Want to Talk About It (De eso no se habla)

(Maria Luisa Bemberg, 1993, Arg/It) Marcello Mastroianni, Luisina Brando, Alejandra Podestá, Betiana Blum, Roberto Carnaghi, Alberto Segado, Jorge Luz.
105 min.
The title of Bemberg's subtle, touching film refers to the determination expressed by the proud widow Leonor (Brando) regarding the condition of her daughter Charlotte (Podestá). Quite simply, Leonor will not accept the fact that the girl is a dwarf. Instead, she showers her beloved progeny with kindness and encourages her interest in the arts – an interest which forms the basis of a friendship between the teenager and Don Ludovico D'Andrea (Mastroianni), an elderly bachelor of mysterious origins who falls profoundly in love with the girl. Set in a small Argentinian town in the '40s, Bemberg's poignant fable succeeds largely through understatement and the principals' superb performances. Mercifully, while there are a few faintly surreal touches, the magic here derives from the cool, unsentimental, down-to-earth appraisal of the trio's tangled emotions. It's a tender movie, but never needlessly romanticised, and not without its quiet cruelties. GA

Wee Geordie

see Geordie

Weekend (Week-end)

(Jean-Luc Godard, 1967, Fr/It) Mireille Darc, Jean Yanne, Jean-Pierre Kalfon, Yves Beneyton, Jean-Pierre Léaud, Juliet Berto, Anne Wiazemsky.
103 min.
Godard's vision of bourgeois cataclysm, after which he began the retreat from commercial cinema to contemplate his ideological navel. A savage Swiftian satire, it traces a new Gulliver's travels through the collapsing consumer society as a married couple set out for a weekend jaunt, passing through a nightmare landscape of highways strewn with burning cars and bloody corpses (a stunning ten-minute take) before emerging into a brave new world peopled by Maoist revolutionaries who like redskins in the woods off murder, pillage and rape. What takes the film one stage further into inimitable Godard territory is the note of despairing romanticism he first mined in Pierrot le Fou. Here too, his hero and heroine emerge as oddly tragic figures, modern Robinson Crusoes wandering helplessly in limbo because, even if they could find a desert island free of abandoned cars, they are incapable of surviving without consumer goods. TM

Weekend at Bernie's

(Ted Kotcheff, 1989, US) Andrew McCarthy, Jonathan Silverman, Catherine Mary Stewart, Terry Kiser, Don Calfa, Catherine Parks, Louis Giambalvo, Ted Kotcheff.
99 min.
A one-joke movie which moves puerile party humour from the Animal House to the yuppie world of work. Pals Larry (McCarthy) and Dick (Silverman) – one a smooth-talking sloppy-Joe, the other a tongue-tied whizz-kid-in-waiting – share desks and frustration on the trading floor at Trans Allied Insurance. When Dick finds a million-dollar discrepancy in payouts, they force their way into an audience with jet-setter boss Bernie (Kiser), who invites them, with Bela Lugosi smile, for a weekend at his Hamptons beach-house. Death is in the offing, but it's Bernie who gets stiffed (by his Mafia associates), not the boys. Question is, how long can they party, party, party with the bathing-suited bimbos and cool-cat coke-sniffers before anybody notices that Bernie's a corpse? Kotcheff aims straight for the juvenile and spends most of his effort, successfully, on getting the timing right for the endless gags with Bernie's adaver propped up on the sofa, falling downstairs, etc. But it's strictly kids'stuff and quickly palls. WH

Week's Holiday, A

see Semaine de Vacances, Une

Weird Science

(John Hughes, 1985, US) Anthony Michael Hall, Kelly LeBrock, Ilan Mitchell-Smith, Bill Paxton, Suzanne Snyder, Judie Aronson, Robert Downey.
94 min.
Two high school nerds hitch their computer up to a Barbie doll and create curvaceous womanhood incarnate (LeBrock). Not only does this sexpot cook breakfast and tidy the house, she also transforms their lives with her magical powers. But the boundaries of these powers are never delineated, so that as the plot drifts into the wild party territory of Risky Business, wacky special effect piles on top of wacky special effect, ultimately to very little effect. It is as though a load of schoolboys had been let loose with a film crew; even so-called anarchic humour needs to have its anarchy defined. There is also a distasteful subtext which implies that so long as boys are men enough to point guns at party-poopers, it doesn't matter if they're revolting little oiks – girls will still go to bed with them. AB

Welcome Home

(Franklin J Schaffer, 1989, US) Kris Kristofferson, JoBeth Williams, Sam Waterston, Trey Wilson, Ken Pogue, Brian Keith, Thomas Wilson Brown.
92 min.
Seventeen years after being declared missing in action in Cambodia, pilot Jake Robbins (Kristofferson) turns up in his American home town, where he is reunited with his wife Sarah (now happily remarried) and teenage son. Jake, it appears, has a new wife and kids in Cambodia, where he would have stayed had he not been wounded, hospitalised, and duly identified by the military. His reappearance causes Sarah (Williams) to reassess her marriage to Woody (Waterston), and shatters son Tyler's glorified image of his heroic father. Yes, it's big family crisis time, with little to commend it other than Waterston, who anchors the film in some form of credible behaviour while all around is mushy, tear-jerking melodrama. As the last drop of emotional manipulation is squeezed from the turmoil (accompanied throughout by Willie Nelson's nasal whining), the movie attempts to transform itself into a thriller about government secrecy and gung-ho rescue operations, but by then who cares? MK

Welcome Home, Roxy Carmichael

(Jim Abrahams, 1991, US) Winona Ryder, Jeff Daniels, Laila Robins, Thomas Wilson Brown, Joan McMurtrey, Graham Beckel, Frances Fisher, Robby Kiger, Dinah Manoff, Stephen Tobolowsky, Ava Fabian.
98 min.
Local bad girl Roxy (Fabian) left her small-town Ohio home in search of fame and fortune. Fifteen years later, as the burghers of Clyde prepare to pay awestruck homage to her homecoming, adopted teen misfit Dinky (Ryder) is also obsessed with the living legend, for her own neurotic reasons. From a script by Karen Leigh Hopkins, Abrahams has concocted an initially intriguing mishmash: part high school angst opera, part suburban schlocker (Daniels, always dependable as the dentist-next-door type, is surpassingly dull here), part 'search for origins' family romance. There are a few piquant ironies at work, but the selling point is Ryder, again doing her coming-of-age turn for the camera, with a performance that wavers between gangling fragility and a tough-girl Matt Dillonism. Otherwise, the movie falls flat, because of its leaden pacing, and because deep down it believes in the moral imperative of having perfect hair and teeth. JRo

Welcome to Blood City

(Peter Sasdy, 1977, Can/GB) Jack Palance, Keir Dullea, Samantha Eggar, Barry Morse, Hollis McLaren, Chris Wiggins.
96 min.
An utterly spineless sci-fi Western. The plot premise has possibilities: Dullea is hauled out of some unspecified urban crisis and into an equally unspecified laboratory, where a 'Western drama' is computer-programmed into his brain to test his ruthlessness quotient. The main dramatic problem is the feebleness of the Western (which occupies most of the running time); even Jack Palance as an urbane, unbeatable sheriff can't lend it more credibility than a playground version of Gunfight at the OK Corral. But what finally sinks the film is Sasdy and his writer Stephen Schneck's refusal to commit themselves to any social or political meaning; the way they trot out some newsreel atrocity footage to fuel a supposedly common paranoia about the Horrors of the Modern World is both facile and deeply offensive. TR

Welcome to Britain

(Ben Lewin, 1976, GB)
70 min.
Lewin's documentary concerns the appalling treatment meted out to immigrants and Commonwealth visitors on arrival in Britain rather than the question of whether immigration controls should exist. He chose the colourful and unorthodox entrepreneur Reuben 'Mr Fixit' Davis to illustrate his point about the system: that a man who (according to the Home Office) was able to earn thousands from helping his clients enter the country, was actually preferable to the insular bureaucracy of the official advisory service, let alone the immigration officers themselves. Well-made documentary that it is, it insists on taking sides, but without ever entering the realms of dogma: the scenes at Harmondsworth Detention Centre, peopled by the 'suspect' friends and relatives of those whom 'we don't need' any more, say it all. HM

Welcome to Hard Times (aka Killer on a Horse)

(Burt Kennedy, 1966, US) Henry Fonda, Janice Rule, Keenan Wynn, Janis Paige, John Anderson, Warren Oates, Fay Spain, Edgar Buchanan, Aldo Ray, Denver Pyle, Lon Chaney, Royal Dano, Elisha Cook.
105 min.
Adapted from EL Doctorow's novel, Kennedy's film casts a cold eye on the career of a one-horse frontier town, from its initial destruction by an itinerant hellraiser (Ray), through its redevelopment (initiated by a travelling whorehouse) and final near-extinction by the returning villain. Intriguing for its use of Fonda, whose personal cowardice is responsible for the town's internal death wish, and whose peace-making liberal intentions bring about the nihilistic ending: three-quarters of the population lying dead among the smoking ruins. There's also an immaculate cast of standard Western supporting actors. CPea

W

Welcome to L.A.

(Alan Rudolph, 1976, US) Keith Carradine, Sally Kellerman, Geraldine Chaplin, Harvey Keitel, Lauren Hutton, Viveca Lindfors, Sissy Spacek, Denver Pyle, John Considine, Richard Baskin
106 min.
In retrospect, more an intriguing taste of things to come than a throwback to the free-form, large-scale interactions of *Nashville* (on which Rudolph served time as Altman's assistant). Here, in his debut, the precise *La Ronde*-style choreography of its nine principal characters – assorted inhabitants of LA, all connected somehow or another with self-centred rock-writer Carradine's sexual one-night stands – tends to prefigure *Choose Me* in its elegance, dry wit, and flawless visual sense. Sadly, however, it lacks both the inspirational spontaneity of his producer and mentor Altman's best work, and the warmth of his own later films, since many of the characters are so bloody unsympathetic. That said, it's finely performed and well worth seeing. GA

Welcome to Sarajevo

(Michael Winterbottom, 1997, GB) Stephen Dillane, Woody Harrelson, Kerry Fox, James Nesbitt, Goran Visnjic, Emira Nusevic, Marisa Tomei, Emily Lloyd.
102 min.
The first Western feature to pick over the bones of the Bosnian conflict, this applies the trusty 'foreign correspondent finds his conscience' ploy to some effect. Dillane is Michael Henderson – based on ITN reporter Michael Nicholson – a hardened pro who none the less becomes obsessed with the plight of a Sarajevo orphanage during the 1992 siege, and promises refuge to one young girl. A crisp, rigorously unsentimental director, Winterbottom was a good choice for this project. Mixing film, video and a good deal of news footage, he captures a powerful sense of the jogging, jagged rhythms of life and death under siege, takes an unapologetically polemical line against Europe's hands-off policy, and consequently earns the emotional dividends. TCh

Welcome to the Dollhouse

(Todd Solondz, 1995, US) Heather Matarazzo, Victoria Davis, Christina Brucato, Christina Vidal, Siri Howard, Brendan Sexton Jr, Telly Pontidis.
88 min.
Whether at school or at home in the New Jersey suburbs, 11-year-old Dawn Wiener has a miserable time of it. Ostracised and vilified by classmates as a 'lesbo', the 'Wienerdog' comes a cropper sticking up for herself against rough tough Brandon (Sexton): he responds by promising to rape her when school's out. Meanwhile, Mom makes it all too obvious she prefers her youngest, Missy, while Dawn's snooty brother Mark is reluctant to let her anywhere near his guitarist friend Steve, whose looks, musical skills and unthinking displays of kindness ensure she develops a crush on him. But would the high school hunk ever go out with a seventh-grader, or even join the exclusive 'Special Persons' club Dawn has founded with her only friend, poor little Ralphy next door? Admirably unsentimental exploration of the bewildering, cruel nightmare that is early adolescence: astutely perceptive, darkly comic and often profoundly and provocatively unsettling. If the film veers a little too closely to melodramatic parody towards the end, for the most part script and direction are spot-on, with writer/director Solondz carefully balancing insight and irony, humour and real tenderness. Sterling acting, particularly from Heather Matarazzo, whose remarkable blend of vulnerability and determination, dignity and vivacity effortlessly enrols our sympathies. Talents to watch. GA

Welcome II the Terrordome

(Ngozi Onwurah, 1994, GB) Suzette Llewellyn, Saffron Burrows, Brian Bovell, Felix Joseph, Valentine Nonyela, Ben Wynter.
94 min.
This feature debut is an angry uncompromising take on race relations, guaranteed to put liberals on edge. Set ten or 15 years on in a claustrophobic black ghetto, it's the story of Spike (Nonyela) and his girlfriend Jodie (Burrows). Tensions are already running high – Jodie's pregnant and white – when a black kid is killed in a police raid and his mother goes on a vengeful killing spree.

Onwurah's dystopia isn't a comfortable place to be and the film isn't easy to watch. The makers have done wonders with a minuscule budget, creating a stylised but still credible environment hemmed in by metal cages, pierced by strobing searchlights and a bombardment of urgent rap. This is a world which doesn't breathe so much as pant. The acting, however, is variable, and the movie is sometimes both naive and repetitive. Imperfect, then, but also provocative: it never lies down on you. TCh

Welfare

(Frederick Wiseman, 1975, US)
167 min. b/w.
Wiseman's unsparing *vérité* camera takes us to a New York Welfare Center, where America's victims (all races, ages, and emotional conditions) parade their misery to receive enough money to survive. The film has a sharp eye for the exhausted, melancholy, and angry faces of social workers and clients, both groups ensnared in a vicious, heartless system – where who is responsible becomes the prime question, fatalism the reigning philosophy, and the general atmosphere one of claustrophobic bedlam. Wiseman avoids facile stereotypes: his case-workers are not callous heavies, nor are the clients members of a heroic, politically conscious mass. Some of the Center's staff attempt to ease the bureaucracy's dehumanising red tape, but given the hopelessness of the institution, their gestures are almost quixotic. The film never editorialises, sentimentalises, or attempts to be dramatic, but its cumulative effect is to make one enraged enough to cry out for the dismantling of the whole welfare (or is it the capitalist?) system. LQ

We Live Again

(Rouben Mamoulian, 1934, US) Anna Sten, Fredric March, Jane Baxter, C Aubrey Smith, Ethel Griffies, Gwendolyn Logan, Sam Jaffe, Dale Fuller, Leonid Kinsky.
84 min. b/w.
Conceived as a vehicle for Goldwyn's protégée Anna Sten, this adaptation of Tolstoy's novel *Resurrection* was turned into something more by Mamoulian's superb direction. He opens with an airy Dovzhenko pastiche to introduce the light-hearted farmyard flirtation between Prince Dmitri (March) and serving maid Katusha (Sten). Then, clearly drawing on his own background, he stages a stunning evocation of the Russian Orthodox Easter Mass, carrying the richly sensuous mood over into the seduction scene that immediately follows. The inescapable parallel between worship by the soul and by the senses intimates that Dimitri is motivated as much by love as by lust; and this lends conviction to his 'resurrection' when, seven years later, he realises his culpability in the girl's physical (though not spiritual) degradation, and follows her into Siberia. The second half of the film rather loses its momentum in a flurry of explanatory plot and scratchily staged scenes, but is sustained by the performances. Gregg Toland's camerawork is superlative throughout. TM

Well, The

(Leo Popkin/Russell Rouse, 1951, US) Richard Rober, Henry Morgan, Barry Kelley, Christine Larson, Maidie Norman, Ernest Anderson.
85 min. b/w.
Rouse's first film as director (co-written with Clarence Greene, with whom he had scripted *DOA* the previous year). The first half is a vividly etched portrait of small-town unease as a black child is reported missing, the suspicions deepening a racial divide that threatens to escalate into racial violence on both sides as circumstances suggest that a white transient (Morgan) had something to do with her disappearance. The discovery that the little girl, scarcely more than a baby, has in fact fallen down an abandoned well, opens a safety valve; and the rest of the film is devoted to the rescue operation. It still grips, but in a more overtly crowd-pleasing way, what with even the most bigoted coming round to the side of the angels, and the hazards of the rescue milked for all they are worth. An impressive piece, all the same, brilliantly shot by Ernest Laszlo. TM

Well, The

(Samantha Lang, 1997, Aust) Pamela Rabe, Miranda Otto, Paul Chubb.
102 min.

Out on a remote farm, Rabe takes on as home-help young Miranda Otto, an emotionally unstable waif who soon responds gratefully to Rabe's various kindnesses; but their blossoming relationship hits trouble when a car accident forces them to dump a body down the farm's well. Lang's portentous, hysterical psycho-drama about desire, guilt and repressed emotions wears its metaphors and symbols all too conspicuously on its sleeve. Undecided as to whether it's a horror pic or an art movie, and unconcerned with plot logic (why don't the women just tell the cops about their accident?), it resorts increasingly to contrived shop-worn melodrama. As a bonus, it includes one of the most risible dream sequences in years. GA

Wendy Cracked a Walnut

(Michael Pattinson, 1990, Aust) Rosanna Arquette, Bruce Spence, Hugo Weaving, Kerry Walker.
90 min.
The Australian cinema has built up a reputation for quirky, low-budget gems, but this comedy-romance succeeds only on the first two counts. Arquette tries hard, but is hopelessly miscast as a dowdy housewife (even with spectacles, you can't believe it) who is whisked off her feet by the man of her dreams (Spence). There's a bit of a twist at the end, and some good intentions, but you'd be better off staying home and reading Mills & Boon. DW

Went the Day Well?

(Alberto Cavalcanti, 1942, GB) Leslie Banks, Elizabeth Allan, Frank Lawton, Basil Sydney, Valerie Taylor, Mervyn Johns, Marie Lohr, Edward Rigby, David Farrar, Thora Hird, Harry Fowler, John Slater.
92 min. b/w.
An extremely effective wartime thriller which transcends its propagandist impulse (about the need to look out for fifth columnists or Germans in disguise), thanks to a tremendous story base by Graham Greene and to Cavalcanti's firm direction. As a small, remote village is taken over and cut off by a platoon of undercover German paratroopers, tensions and suspicions mount, and confusion reigns as to how to deal with the problem. What really distinguishes the film is not so much the impressive exploration of the way the invasion threatens the accepted hierarchy within the village, but Cavalcanti's cool, brutal depiction of suddenly erupting violence and death; not only are British 'heroes' often despatched with shocking realism, but quiet, cosy housewives find themselves killing the enemy with almost hysterical relish. And any film that includes Thora Hird as a flighty seductress has to be worth watching. GA

We of the Never Never

(Igor Auzins, 1982, Aust) Angela Punch McGregor, Arthur Dignam, Tony Barry, Tommy Lewis, Lewis Fitz-Gerald, Martin Vaughan.
134 min.
Down under, *We of the Never Never* is a well-loved turn-of-the-century classic by an Aeneas Gunn, who as a genteel Melbourne bride was expected to add a woman's touch to her husband's isolated cattle station. Phlegmatic British audiences, not much in touch with the pioneer spirit, will find in this adaptation an unashamedly old-fashioned celebration of corseted pluck as Jeannie Gunn rolls up her lacey sleeves and wins the grudging respect of the hitherto misogynistic stockmen. It's a pleasurably predictable formula, kept afloat by plangent orchestration, glorious cinematography, and a continuous supply of death-beds and simple outback funerals. The film's real difficulty lies in Jeannie's treatment of the Aborigines. She's nice to them but patronising (makes the gardener wear trousers). Is Auzins inviting us to make up our own minds about her naive colonialism, or just dodging what could have been the film's central issue? JS

We're Alive

(Women's Film Workshop, UCLA/Video Workshop, California Institution for Women, 1974, US)
48 min. b/w & col.
Made jointly by the Women's Film Workshop and some of the inmates of the California Institution for Women, this is a moving analysis

of why the women are in prison, what's happening to them, what's to become of them. It begins and ends with film taken outside the walls, while the rest is videotape transferred to film of the prisoners talking about race, sex and religion, class, economics and drugs. Occasionally statistics are inserted, but generally the women show such a degree of articulacy and radical thought that what they have to say is explanation enough. A remarkably undated combination of political anger and collective tenderness. HM

We're All Stars
see Todos Somos Estrellas

We're No Angels
(Michael Curtiz, 1955, US) Humphrey Bogart, Peter Ustinov, Aldo Ray, Joan Bennett, Basil Rathbone, Leo G Carroll.
106 min.
The ill-assorted trio of Bogart, Ray and Ustinov play escapees from Devil's Island who take refuge with a French shopkeeper's family, and demonstrate that beneath their rascally exteriors lie hearts of 40 carats. The lowest point comes when they all line up to croak Christmas carols. Based on a French play (La Cuisine des Anges by Albert Husson), it's static and laden with leaden talk, with nothing to interest the eye as recompense. Curtiz was going to the dogs at the time, but it's doubtful whether anyone could have worked wonders with such material. Bogart looks particularly ill-at-ease and silly. GB

We're No Angels
(Neil Jordan, 1989, US) Robert De Niro, Sean Penn, Demi Moore, Hoyt Axton, Bruno Kirby, Ray McAnally, James Russo, Wallace Shawn.
102 min.
Those who wrote off Neil Jordan as a director of comedy after High Spirits will have to think again. His first American film, scripted by David Mamet, is a nicely paced comedy of errors in which two escaped convicts, Ned (De Niro) and Jim (Penn) are mistaken for priests. The prison opening – a souped-up pastiche of old Warner Bros big-house movies, with the late Ray McAnally as the slavering, sadistic warden – is such a nightmare setting that you have to laugh. On the run, baying hounds on their trail, Ned and Jim take refuge in a monastery. Their only chance of getting across the border into Canada lies with the annual procession of monks bearing their miracle-working shrine across the bridge. Ned falls for sluttish Molly (Moore), mother of a deaf-and-dumb child, Jim for religion. De Niro's gift for pantomime, glimpsed in his plumber for Brazil, is a non-stop bombardment of mugging on the silent screen scale. There isn't much left for Penn, which is okay by me. Very entertaining. BC

Werewolf of London
(Stuart Walker, 1935, US) Henry Hull, Warner Oland, Lester Matthews, Valerie Hobson, Spring Byington, JM Kerrigan, Zeffie Tilbury, Ethel Griffies.
75 min. b/w.
Guy Endore created the definitive werewolf myth in his superb novel The Werewolf of Paris, published in 1933. Since Endore was snapped up under contract by MGM, Universal – determined to get in first with werewolves – had to go with a feeble myth about a rare Tibetan flower which is the only known control for lycanthropy. In Walker's patchy but mostly ineffective film, this flower becomes a bone of contention between an Oriental werewolf (Oland) and a distinguished London botanist (Hull). Oland is impeccably sinister and contributes most of the best moments, while Hull, dull as the botanist, becomes even duller in transformation after he is bitten. His make-up, designed by Jack Pierce to leave his face as nakedly expressive as Karloff's in Frankenstein, merely makes him look like a toothily hairy cretin in a rotten temper. TM

Werewolf of Washington, The
(Milton Moses Ginsberg, 1973, US) Dean Stockwell, Biff McGuire, Clifton James, Beeson Carroll, Jane House, Michael Dunn.
90 min.
A hit-or-miss comedy which blends political satire and lycanthropic laughs, but lacks bite. Stockwell plays a White House aide who is bitten by a werewolf while in Hungary, then returns to Washington

to wreak havoc in the corridors of power. The President (McGuire) and his pragmatic psychiatrist effect a cover-up (cf. Watergate), fearing the press will use Stockwell's senatorial snacks to discredit the presidency. A poorly integrated subplot involving a mad-dwarf scientist (Dunn) is good for a few laughs, but like the half-hearted pastiche of Universal's The Wolf Man, it goes nowhere. NF

Wes Craven's New Nightmare
(Wes Craven, 1994, US) Robert Englund, Heather Lagenkamp, Miko Hughes, John Saxon, Robert Shaye, Wes Craven.
112 min.
In this post-modern take on the enervated Elm Street series, the director of the original uses a complex film-within-a-film structure to reassess and revitalise the moribund Freddy Krueger mythology. Craven's conceptual coup is to cast himself; the man behind the Freddy mask (Englund), the heroine of the original (Lagenkamp), and even the supremo of New World Pictures (Bob Shaye) as both themselves and their fictional counterparts. Thus, he explicitly confronts the previous sequels' cynical softening of Freddy's once horrifying persona. During preparations for yet another sequel, Freddy is born again, spilling over from the pages of Craven's script-in-progress to threaten those involved with its making. Skilfully blending fairy-tale clarity with the skewed logic of nightmares, Craven also blurs the boundary between reality and fiction. There is creepy subversive stuff going on here, not to mention sly sideswipes at the censors. The climactic punch-up fails to match the power of the first film's true ending, but in deconstructing his own bastardised creation, Craven redeems both the series and his own tarnished reputation. NF

Western
(Manuel Poirier, 1997, Fr) Sergi Lopez, Sacha Bourdo, Elisabeth Vitali, Marie Matheron, Basile Siekoua.
134 min.
This amiable road movie follows two misfits – Catalan shoe salesman Paco and vertically challenged Russian-Italian Nino who meet under inauspicious circumstances – as they travel with no particular purpose through Brittany, the former giving himself and his new love a little space to consider their future, the latter in search of his own inamorata. Nothing extraordinary happens, the highlights of their journey being a drunken dinner with a barmaid and her cousin, and a survey conducted about the ideal man, but it's often funny and touching, mainly because the focus is on the credible, charming but never sentimentalised characters. Modest, but immensely engaging. GA

Western Approaches
(Pat Jackson, 1944, GB)
83 min.
This highly respected documentary tells the story of a group of British merchant seamen adrift in the Atlantic after their ship has been torpedoed by a German U-Boat. In essence it's a fictionalised account (using men on active naval service rather than actors) of a typical World War Two disaster, whereby merchant ships returning to Britain with vital supplies of food and goods from America ran the gamut of the Nazi subs in their attempt to beat the blockade. As a tribute to heroism, it's easier to take than many from the same period, and the outstanding colour camerawork by Jack Cardiff is all the more remarkable when you consider that it was shot under dangerous conditions similar to those portrayed in the film. MA

Western Union
(Fritz Lang, 1941, US) Robert Young, Randolph Scott, Dean Jagger, Virginia Gilmore, John Carradine, Slim Summerville, Chill Wills, Barton MacLane.
93 min.
Perhaps the most memorable moment in this fine and feisty Western comes with the superb 180-degree pan which starts at a cut telegraph line, moves slowly over to a coil of wire with an arrow through it, and then suddenly discovers a band of hostile Indians, fearsome and beautiful in startlingly brilliant warpaint and feathered headdresses. Lang was the first director really to exploit the possibilities of colour in the Western, and his marvellous sense of composition lifts an otherwise conventional story – the laying of the

first trans-continental telegraph wire in 1861, with the inevitable conflict between brothers backing opposing interests – clear out of the rut. TM

Westfront 1918
(GW Pabst, 1930, Ger) Gustav Diessl, Fritz Kampers, Claus Clausen, Hans Joachim Moebis, Gustav Püttjer, Jackie Monnier.
97 min. b/w.
Pabst's first talkie offered a grim, humanitarian perspective on trench warfare, not unlike that in the almost contemporary All Quiet on the Western Front. Hardly any film since has given such an unremittingly horrific picture of warfare-in-action, from the agonising lulls to the surprise attacks, from harsh resilience to the release of madness or a death wish. The point is ultimately a simple pacifism, with all the political limitations that implies. But Pabst's brilliant tracking shots along the trenches, through ruins, and across no man's land, remain more haunting than anything in 'expressionist' cinema. TR

Westler: East of the Wall
(Wieland Speck, 1985, WGer)
Sigurd Rachman, Rainer Strecker, Andy Lucas, Sala Kogo.
A refreshing, direct, and effective gay love story that displays the irrelevance of big budgets where honesty, imagination, and something to say takes their place. West Berliner Felix meets out-of-work waiter Thomas in Alexanderplatz while taking his Amerikanischer Freund for a day trip to East Berlin; they fall in love, but political, border, and visiting restrictions conspire to pull them apart. This low-budget first feature, composed partly of illegal video footage shot in the East, is full of fascinating semi-documentary-style detail and unforced insights into the lives of its protagonists, and provides a quietly uplifting, totally unpretentious attack on the absurdity and inhumanity of repression, whatever its form. WH

West Side Story [100]
(Robert Wise/Jerome Robbins, 1961, US) Natalie Wood, Richard Beymer, George Chakiris, Rita Moreno, Russ Tamblyn, Tucker Smith, Simon Oakland.
151 min.
Jerome Robbins, who choreographed and directed the Broadway production, was originally hired to direct this lavish film version. He got about three weeks into rehearsal before his painstaking perfectionism looked like doubling the budget, and in a state of panic, United Artists brought in Robert Wise to direct the non-musical sequences. More intrigue followed, and finally Robbins was sacked altogether. But before leaving the set, he had completed four song sequences which remain the unchallenged highlights of the film: the whole of the opening sequence ('The Jet Song'), 'America', 'Cool', and 'I Feel Pretty'. If only he had been allowed to do it all… DP

Westworld
(Michael Crichton, 1973, US) Yul Brynner, Richard Benjamin, James Brolin, Norman Bartold, Alan Oppenheimer, Victoria Shaw.
89 min.
Despite faults (chiefly a dispersal of its energies), a wonderfully enjoyable fantasy about a futuristic holiday resort offering robot worlds of exotic sex, romance or violence amid the licence of ancient Rome, the gallantries of a medieval chateau, or the gunslinging frontier town. Best and most fully realised of these worlds is the Western, with Brynner (brilliant) as the robot gunman required to die, bloodily, every time a greenhorn tourist challenges him to the draw. Until, that is, the robots begin to malfunction – or rebel: only the computers that designed them know exactly how they work – and the Brynner machine sets out, now part mad killer and part Frankenstein monster, in quest of revenge. Great stuff. TM

We the Living (Noi vivi)
(Goffredo Alessandrini, 1942, It) Fosco Giachetti, Alida Valli, Rossano Brazzi, Giovanni Grasso, Emilio Cigoli, Annibale Betrone.
174 min. b/w.
Based (unauthorised) on Ayn Rand's first, partly autobiographical novel, this was banned by the Fascist authorities, who disapproved of its anti-totalitarian stance. It was originally prepared for release in two parts, running 270 minutes in all; the

present version was re-edited in 1986 under the supervision of Rand's attorneys. The setting is post-revolutionary Russia, where 18-year-old Kira (Valli) and her family oppose the new order. Her ambitions for further education and a career as an engineer are disrupted – and the seeds for disaster sown – when two very different men fall in love with her: a former aristocrat on the run from the secret police (Brazzi), and a Party official committed to Communist ideals (Giachetti). Giuseppe Caracciolo's exquisite cinematography sets up a brooding, melodramatic atmosphere, and as Valli's and Brazzi's eyes sparkle into the lens, it's hard not to feel soppily sympathetic toward their cause. This is intended, of course. The romantic triangle defines the political debate (as it did in *Senso*, but with far more passion). Still, there is a luminous quality to the lead performances which lifts some of the weightier passages. CM

Wetherby

(David Hare, 1985, GB) Vanessa Redgrave, Ian Holm, Judi Dench, Stuart Wilson, Joely Richardson, Robert Hines, Tim McInnerny, Suzanna Hamilton.
102 min.
An uninvited guest (McInnerny) comes to the Yorkshire town of the title and blows his brains out in front of middle-aged schoolteacher Redgrave. Flashing back to the dinner party where she first met him, flashing even further back into her youthful romance with an airman, the film delves into the reasons for his suicide and her seemingly innocent involvement, and explores the way in which that 'disfiguring central blankness' within some of us acts as a magnet for the obsessions and desires of emotional retards. David Hare, making his film début directing his own screenplay, piles layers of wilful obfuscation on to the story. This gives it a gripping appeal and an appearance of emotional density; but despite excellent performances, the film suffers from the same 'disfiguring central blankness' as its subject. AB

We Think the World of You

(Colin Gregg, 1988, GB) Alan Bates, Gary Oldman, Frances Barber, Liz Smith, Max Wall.
91 min.
JR Ackerley's wonderfully moving novel wouldn't work without the central relationship between an ageing lonely gay and his Alsatian. Colin Gregg hasn't solved that one – how can you on screen? – and concentrates elsewhere, losing the point in a plethora of Brit caricatures, Liz Smith prominent among them. Bates does his over-familiar mannered queen in melancholy circs, effectively shafting any chance of sympathy, and only Oldman as his unreliable lover gives any sense of layered life, earning a pang as the trap snaps shut upon his prospects. BC

We Three

see Noi tre

We Were One Man (Nous Etions un Seul Homme)

(Philippe Vallois, 1978, Fr) Serge Avédikian, Piotr Stanislas, Catherine Albin.
90 min.
A low-budget but highly acclaimed study of love doubly forbidden by sexual and (because of its World War II setting) national taboos. Valois makes good use of his lonely Landes landscapes and the interestingly contrasted characters: an erratic, mercurial Frenchman; his blond German lover, reserved, slower, almost stolid; and the female figure in the triangle, treated – despite the film's title – with surprising generosity. It's not without its longueurs, nor certain of the clichés (love across the barricades; love among the trees) that often attend this particular mode of the Historical-Pastoral. But there's still a freshness and lyricism in the showing of shared activities (fishing, fighting, felling trees), and a delicacy in indicating how these small epiphanies, moments of elation familiar from many films of 'straight' mateships, can shade imperceptibly into a more overtly erotic passion. SJo

Whales of August, The

(Lindsay Anderson, 1987, US) Bette Davis, Lillian Gish, Vincent Price, Ann Sothern, Harry Carey Jr, Margaret Ladd, Tisha Sterling, Mary Steenburgen.
91 min.

Anderson's version of David Berry's play opens with a sepia-tinted Steenburgen joyfully watching the spouters of the title, before fast-forwarding into the future. Sixty years later, Libby (Davis) and Sarah (Gish) are still on the island where they spent the summers with their husbands who, like the leviathans themselves, have long since gone. Libby, who is blind, treats her sister with disdain, but allows her to brush her long ivory hair. When Sarah invites the exiled Russian charmer Mr Maranov (Price) to dinner, Libby expresses her disapproval by refusing to permit Joshua (Carey) to install a picture window. Sarah's patience begins to run out...Nothing much happens in this curious chamber piece – the pair of crumblies chinwag with their blowsy friend Tisha (Sothern); Mr Maranov catches a fish; Sarah pegs out the washing – but the dragonish Ms Davis is in fine form, and Ms Gish is as captivating as ever. A gentle interlacing of memory, comedy and pathos, this is a golden opportunity to enjoy, if not whale music, then the probable swansong of two giants of cinema. MS

What? (Che?)

(Roman Polanski, 1972, It/Fr/WGer) Sydne Rome, Marcello Mastroianni, Hugh Griffith, Romolo Valli, Guido Alberti, Roman Polanski.
113 min.
Polanski takes American innocence (Sydne Rome) abroad to Italy, and places her in the middle of a droll and inconsequential sex (or perversion) comedy. What lifts the film out of its one-joke level is Polanski's civilised handling of his material. Avoiding obvious laughs, he opts for a mixture of satire and comedy of embarrassment (as our heroine finds herself more and more preyed and pryed upon), with everyone playing games where only you don't know the rules. All suitably throwaway, it's held together by our own curiosity and Polanski's obvious delight in observing such strange goings-on in rich summer villas. CPe

What About Bob?

(Frank Oz, 1991, US) Bill Murray, Richard Dreyfuss, Julie Hagerty, Charlie Korsmo, Kathryn Erbe, Tom Aldredge, Susan Willis, Roger Bowen, Fran Brill.
99 min.
With Dreyfuss and Murray on top form, not even the familiar plotline – uptight rich person meets free-wheeling poor person and learns about life – can prevent this lunatic comedy from being funny. Ideally cast and perfectly matched as an anal-retentive shrink and his multi-phobic patient, the stars generate laughs a-plenty. As the author of a bestselling self-help manual, Dr Leo Marvin (Dreyfuss) should have no trouble coping with a deeply dependent patient who follows him to his lakeside holiday home. But Bob (Murray) fails to heed Leo's professional advice and wreaks havoc in Leo's messed-up family, liberating them from their neuroses. Leo's reaction is neither grateful nor rational... Occasionally, something dark and disturbing threatens to rise to the surface, but this being a formulaic comedy, the ripples caused by Bob's anarchic antics soon give way to the flat calm of normality. NF

What About Me?

(Rachel Amodeo, 1993, US) Rachel Amodeo, Richard Edson, Judy Carne, Richard Hell, Rockets Redglare.
87 min.
In Los Angeles, they say, everyone has a script. In New York, though, everybody goes ahead and actually makes their movie – usually in b/w and preferably with a rock guitar soundtrack, in this case by Johnny Thunders. Written, produced, directed and starring Rachel Amodeo, this is a late example of that old new wave scene which crested in the early '80s. Amodeo (formerly a drummer with Vacuum Bag and Das Furlines, apparently) is Lisa, lonely, unemployed and sharing her aunt's low-rent apartment. She buys a coffee cup from a bag lady (Carne) and spends her last dollar on a palm reading. Returning home, the landlord (Rockets Redglare) says her aunt is dead. Then he rapes her. Then he evicts her. Lisa becomes a bag lady. She is struck by a motorbike. She witnesses a mob hit. The victim dies in her arms. The film ends with her death on a bench beneath the Statute of Liberty. TCh

What About Me?

(Benjamin Allanoff, 1996, US) Benjamin Allanoff, Nicole Holofcener.
34 min.
Men! Do you feel lonely, abandoned, jealous and resentful when the woman you love achieves something in her working life that you're also proud of? If so, you'll identify with this often hilarious documentary about the way director, writer, cameraman and co-producer Ben Allanoff felt when his romantic and professional partner Nicole Holofcener got to make her feature debut, *Walking and Talking*. Men! Aren't we impossible? (Or is it the women?) GA

What a Carve Up!

(Pat Jackson, 1961, GB) Sidney James, Kenneth Connor, Shirley Eaton, Dennis Price, Donald Pleasence, Esma Cannon, Michael Gough, Adam Faith.
88 min. b/w.
Frank King and Leonard Hines' story *The Ghoul* has twice served as a straight shocker (once with Boris Karloff in 1933), but here it's treated as a spoof (co-written by Ray Cooney) with pals James and Connor knee-deep in horror-flick clichés (thunderstorms, mad relatives, Donald Pleasence) as they get caught in a a series of slayings at ye olde dark house, Blackshaw Towers on the Yorkshire moors. Fluff and nonsense, of course, but competently acted and directed. With appeal for fans of *Carry On Screaming*. TJ

What a Man!

see Never Give a Sucker an Even Break

What Are You Doing After the Orgy? (Rötmanad)

(Jan Halldorf, 1970, Swe) Carl Gustav Lindstedt, Ulla Sjöblom, Ernst Günther, Ulf Palme, Christina Lindberg, Eddie Axberg.
104 min.
Despite the come-on of the English title, not a sex pic but a long, lugubrious, and finally quite engaging black comedy in which a woman believed dead these two years (Sjöblom) suddenly descends on her bored but relatively peaceful holidaying family. Now a hooker by trade, she organises herself a procession of paying customers, and for her daughter a financially beneficial line in 'amateur photographers', while downtrodden dad mends the roof and gets the drinks. Her plots founder on young love, but there's a suitably murky ending. Slow and sometimes predictable, the film often commits virtual acts of aggression on its characters and actors in an attempt to exact humour or pathos; nevertheless Halldorf does manage to take it towards a bleakly amusing analysis of family relationships.

What Changed Charley Farthing?

(Sidney Hayers, 1974, GB) Doug McClure, Lionel Jeffries, Hayley Mills, Warren Mitchell, Dilys Hamlett, Alberto De Mendoza.
101 min.
This very inevitable adventure comedy, involving the attempts of a group of expatriates to escape from a revolutionary island, shows off with an excess of loveable rascals: McClure as the fun-loving sailor who falls for Hayley's incomprehensible accent; Jeffries as her stepfather, the wily, scheming last outpost of the Empire; and Mitchell as a blaspheming Scot. The only notable points are that the numerous brawls serve as very obvious time-fillers, and that all three men prove fairly game at showing off their buttocks – indeed, McClure can scarcely be induced to keep his trousers on. Wild horses shouldn't drag you to this film, but if they do, you might find Jeffries' desperate mugging sufficient to stave off utter despondency. CPe

What Did You Do in the War, Daddy?

(Blake Edwards, 1966, US) James Coburn, Dick Shawn, Sergio Fantoni, Giovanna Ralli, Aldo Ray, Harry Morgan, Carroll O'Connor, Leon Askin, Kurt Kreuger.
119 min.
An engaging comedy, scripted by William Peter Blatty, with Shawn as a keen young company

commander eager to prove his valour in the Italian campaign of 1943. Disconcerted to discover that the Italian unit he is supposed to attack asks nothing better than to surrender, but insists that the village first be allowed to hold its annual wine festival, he is persuaded to agree by his more worldly-wise lieutenant (Coburn); and both armies duly get so drunk that, to save face, they decide to stage a mock battle. This, alas, is observed and taken seriously by both German and American troops, who prepare to intervene, and complications pile up until the whole thing gets wildly out of hand. Some of it is very funny, like the mock battle, with attempts at choreographed strategy ruined by tired combatants sneaking away for refreshment. Some of it (especially the volubly excitable Italian bits) are tiresome. But it is held together by terrific performances, Philip Lathrop's exquisite, pastel-shaded photography, and Blake Edwards' instinct for composition and design, let loose in some pleasantly fantastical images. TM

What Ever Happened to Aunt Alice?

(Lee H Katzin, 1969, US) Geraldine Page, Ruth Gordon, Rosemary Forsyth, Robert Fuller, Mildred Dunnock.
101 min.
Reasonably enjoyable suspenser in the post-Aldrich manner. Geraldine Page – almost two decades before her Oscar for *The Trip to Bountiful* – is the impoverished Arizona widow who's gotten through a succession of housekeepers by nobbling them for their savings. But she meets her match in Ruth Gordon, the post's latest incumbent, a lady of natural curiosity and great strength of character. The oldsters clearly relish their roles, even if you can see the plot coming from miles off. TJ

What Ever Happened to Baby Jane?

(Robert Aldrich, 1962, US) Bette Davis, Joan Crawford, Victor Buono, Anna Lee, Maidie Norman, Marjorie Bennett.
133 min. b/w.
Faded child star of the '20s (Davis) terrorises faded matinee star of the '30s (Crawford) in a decaying Hollywood mansion, after a mysterious accident has confined the latter to a wheelchair. Aldrich didn't have the courage to break with mystery-thriller conventions, and so the whole thing turns out to hinge on the true responsibility for the accident, but the film's real centre of interest is its *Sunset Boulevard*-type acerbity about Hollywood. Clips from authentic old Crawford movies are used to represent her past, to teasingly 'biographical' effect, and much hinges on Bette Davis' real-life reputation for bitchery. The Grand Guignol elements themselves are relatively forced and unconvincing. TR

What Happened to Kerouac?

(Richard Lerner/Lewis MacAdams, 1986, US) Gregory Corso, Jan Kerouac, William Buckley, Allen Ginsberg, Edie Parker Kerouac, William Burroughs, Gary Snyder, Neal Cassady, Ann Charters, Steve Allen.
97 min.
A lovingly assembled mosaic of testimonials to the late lamented Daddy-O of the Beats. What did happen? Gregory Corso's guess is as good as any: 'The American media is a fucker'. The reclusive small-town boy simply shrivelled under the glare of publicity, and vowed that he'd drink himself to death since suicide was off-limits to Catholics. The dispiriting process is illustrated by footage of Kerouac reading his work on TV's Steve Allen Show in 1959, but reduced to impersonations of bleary bigotry a few years later on Buckley's 'Firing Line'. The Snyder and Burroughs interviews reveal sealed systems leaking no emotion, but Ginsberg gushes like a man in need of a washer. Biographer Ann Charters is reliable, but Corso, sounding like Mel Blanc reading from Slim Gaillard's *Dictionary of Vouteroonie*, is easily the best turn. Those who cling to the image of the handsome young writer toting 40 pounds of on-the-hoof manuscript in a doctor's bag will be pierced by the last twilight photos of the knock-nutty Marciano face. BC

What Have I Done to Deserve This? (¿Qué he hecho YO para merecer esto?)

(Pedro Almodóvar, 1984, Sp) Carmen Maura, Luis Hostalot, Angel De Andres-López, Gonzalo Suarez, Verónica Forque.
101 min.
Gloria is a typical Spanish housewife – or is she? Her small apartment would seem enough to keep her occupied, housing as it does her indifferent taxi-driver husband, two sons who have discovered the fringe benefits of drug-dealing, and a self-reliant mother-in-law with a pet lizard. But Gloria craves a better life, or at least, for starters, sex with a potent man. In Almodóvar's early feature, the mad inversions and absurdities familiar from *Law of Desire* and *Women on the Verge of a Nervous Breakdown* are delivered without the fuss of incorporating the imperatives of, respectively, melodrama and farce. The result is undiluted scabrous humour, with short, sharp scenes and a crazy string of plots involving the forging of Hitler's diaries, murder by hambone, and keeping a neighbour company during her bonking hour. Almodóvar directs throughout with splendid zip; all in all, the film's piquant look at high-rise life is far more cutting *and* funnier than his later box-office hits. DT

What I Have Written

(John Hughes, 1996, Aust) Angie Milliken, Jacek Koman.
102 min.
When a poet suffers a near fatal stroke, his wife receives the manuscript of an erotic novella he'd written (unbeknown to her) from a lecturer friend; suspecting it contains autobiographical elements about an intense, liberating affair, she begins to investigate and finds her ideas about her marriage, masculinity, sex and truthfulness overturned. This low-budget feature, while a tad predictable, is an intriguing, intelligent study in erotic obsession; if the narrative, with its flashbacks constructed largely from stills, is occasionally clumsy and over-arty, this is still a sporadically rewarding foray into territory previously charted by the likes of Resnais, Roeg and Kieslowski. GA

What Is Democracy? (¿Qué es la Democracia?)

(Carlos Alvarez, 1971, Col)
42 min. b/w.
A critique of party political democracy in Colombia. Using cartoon, old newsreel, and a barrage of photo-material, it exposes the way in which clerical, military and business interests colluded with the American government against the peasantry and workers. Alvarez demonstrates the futility of voting for a series of figurehead personalities, none of whom, liberal or conservative, are prepared to instigate the enormous changes necessary in the Colombian social system. While the Colombian people continue to believe in the party machine, while they continue to vote, while they continue not supporting the revolutionary vanguard, they will remain oppressed. Alvarez' points were brought home by subsequent events in Colombia. He himself was imprisoned without trial in 1972, on charges of 'conspiracy' against the state.

What Lola Wants

see Damn Yankees

What Maisie Knew

(Babette Mangolte, 1975, US) Epp Kotkas, Kate Manhein, Saskia Noordhoek-Hegt, Linda Patton, Yvonne Rainer, Philip Glass.
55 min.
It takes a certain audacity to adapt one's first film from a novel that has been described as 'one of the most remarkable technical achievements in fiction'. But Henry James' vision of venery seen through innocent eyes proves the perfect vehicle for Mangolte's own fascination with the peculiar ambivalence of the filmic, its ability to render perceptions that can be at the same time subjective and impersonal. Here her evocative sensual imagery traces out fragments of memories, glimpses of gestures from a remote, mysterious adult world of erotic desires, all observed with a detached curiosity which approaches the Jamesian ideal of allowing each scene 'to emerge and prevail – vivid, special and wrought hard to the hardness of the unforgettable'. SJo

What Makes David Run? (Qu'est-ce qui fait courir David?)

(Elie Chouraqui, 1982, Fr) Francis Huster, Nicole Garcia, Charles Aznavour, Magali Noël, Michel Jonasz, Nathalie Nell, Anouk Aimée, André Dussollier.
99 min.
David (Huster) – a frantic scriptwriter from an upwardly mobile Jewish family – struggles at both his relationship with his adoring but independent girlfriend, and with his latest movie project, a semi-comic, semi-autobiographical account of family life, the main scenes of which are shown as he dreams them up. The film's strengths and faults are similar to those in Fellini, to whose *8* and *Amarcord* there are clear resemblances. Family rituals are remembered with grotesque emphasis on their larger-than-life absurdity; history pokes its nervous nose in now and again; nostalgia is allowed free rein. Problems arise from the fact that the central character is such a self-obsessed, approval-seeking little shit that we never really care about his situation, even when the too-neatly muted moments of pain occur. Still, never taking itself too seriously, it is lively and amusing enough. GA

What Next?

(Peter Smith, 1974, GB) Peter Robinson, Perry Benson, Lynne White, James Cossins, Laurence Carter, Jerold Wells, Derek Deadman.
56 min.
Presumably it was the plot of this Children's Film Foundation adventure that led one American critic to call it the teenies' *Chinatown*: blustering right-wing property developer of eminent respectability (Cossins) is uncovered by three kids as the man behind the Great Plane Robbery. Rather, we're back in the world of the *Dandy* and *Beano*, where a hit on the head means a sudden acquisition of prophetic powers, where kids become super-sleuths moving through a world of half-disguised names (Pentonmarsh Prison, Whittlewoods Pools) and get their picture on the front page of the local paper. What's more, the kids actually look as though they were thought up by a DC Thompson artist. The film develops a refreshingly conspiratorial attitude to grown-ups, and a healthy irreverence towards figures of authority. Just the right amount of laughs and a scary sequence in the Ghost Train for kids. Excellent use of London locations, natural performances, and enough wit for attendant adults.

What Price Hollywood?

(George Cukor, 1932, US) Constance Bennett, Lowell Sherman, Neil Hamilton, Gregory Ratoff, Brooks Benedict, Louise Beavers.
88 min. b/w.
Terrific performances, a sharp story by Adela Rogers St John, and characteristically elegant, subtle direction from Cukor make this largely affectionate but sometimes biting satire on Hollywood and its star system a perennial delight. Its story – waitress-turned-actress Bennett's star rises while that of her mentor/director, the cynically self-loathing alcoholic Sherman, fades – served as a run-through for the more famous *A Star Is Born* (also produced by Selznick), and the steady shift from light, bubbly comedy to the genuine darkness of the scenes leading to Sherman's suicide is effortlessly made. Funny, moving, and unusually honest. GA

What's Eating Gilbert Grape

(Lasse Hallström, 1993, US) Johnny Depp, Juliette Lewis, Mary Steenburgen, Leonardo DiCaprio, John C Reilly, Darlene Cates.
118 min.
Hallström's finally struck a chord with the Americans, though it's much the same cocktail of whimsy and worry, the eccentric and the banal, that he's been mixing all along. The frustrated Gilbert (Depp) lives at home in Endora, Iowa, with his two younger sisters, his mentally disabled brother Arnie (DiCaprio), and his sofa-crushing 600lb mother (Cates). Deep in a Midwestern rut, Gilbert holds down a job at the local store, maintains a bored affair with housewife Betty Carver (Steenburgen), and tries to keep Arnie out of trouble, but his patience is running out – it's only when he meets teen traveller Becky (Lewis) that he can really take stock. Cute adolescent poetry with a sentimental kick. TCh

What's Love Got to Do With It

see Tina: What's Love Got to Do With It

What's New Pussycat?

(Clive Donner, 1965, US/Fr) Peter Sellers, Peter O'Toole, Romy Schneider, Capucine, Paula Prentiss, Woody Allen, Ursula Andress, Edra Gale, Michel Subor, Annette Poivre.
108 min.
At the time, Richard Williams' credit titles were thought to be better than the film they introduced. In retrospect, it is clear that while Woody Allen, who wrote the script and appears as the hero's friend, saw it as a satire on womanising – the O'Toole character is based on Warren Beatty – Clive Donner saw it as a morality tale in the form of a farce. The mixed results are entertaining, if flawed. O'Toole is the promiscuous hero, with Schneider, Andress, Prentiss and Capucine as some of his women, and Sellers the decidedly camp psychoanalyst he goes to for help. PH

What's the Matter with Helen?

(Curtis Harrington, 1971, US) Debbie Reynolds, Shelley Winters, Dennis Weaver, Agnes Moorehead, Michael MacLiammoir, Timothy Carey, Harry Dean Stanton.
101 min.
With a script by Henry Farrell (author of the source novel on which *What Ever Happened to Baby Jane?* was based), Baby Jane in effect slays again...except that this time she's directed by Curtis Harrington, erstwhile buddy of Kenneth Anger (he acts in *Inauguration of the Pleasure Dome*), who knows what's camp and what's not, and the difference between melodrama and expressionism. He films this as Sternberg might have, with a great emphasis on masks and facades, underpinned with gorgeous fairytale motifs. Plus he stages the best tango since *The Conformist*. TR

What's Up, Doc?

(Peter Bogdanovich, 1972, US) Barbra Streisand, Ryan O'Neal, Kenneth Mars, Austin Pendleton, Sorrell Booke, Stefan Gierasch, Mabel Albertson, Michael Murphy, Madeline Kahn, John Hillerman, Randy Quaid, M Emmet Walsh.
94 min.
A homage to Hollywood screwball comedy that by and large gets its pace and cartoon/slapstick timings right, this began life with a call from Bogdanovich (hot from the Hawksian *Last Picture Show*) to screenwriting team Robert Benton and David Newman (even hotter from *Bonnie and Clyde*): 'I've got a deal with Streisand and O'Neal, and no script. I want to do a remake of *Bringing Up Baby*, and we can do it just like that'. A remake it's not, but the spirit of Hawks (and of Preston Sturges and Frank Tashlin) survived two rapid drafts from Benton & Newman and a polish from Buck Henry, to infuse the misalliance of absent-minded musicologist O'Neal and all-purpose kook Streisand with about the right amount of madcap frenzy. PT

What's Up Tiger Lily?

(Senkichi Taniguchi/Woody Allen, 1966, US/Jap) Tatsuya Mihashi, Miyi Hana, Eiko Wakabayashi, Tadao Nakamaru, Woody Allen, The Lovin' Spoonful, China Lee.
79 min.
Sweet revenge for anyone who has sat through a foreign film suffering from a torrent of bad dubbing. For his first *auteur*-credit (!), Woody Allen got hold of a 1964 Japanese exploitation thriller and exploited it for his own ends, dubbing it delightfully with gags and Hollywood clichés. Invention flags, and the then hip interjections from The Lovin' Spoonful now seem quaint, but there are enough one-liners to leave you with happy memories. A jolly oddity. AN

Wheels & Deals

(Michael Hammon, 1991, Ger) Sello Ke Maake-Ncube, Kimberley Stark, Dominic Tyawa, Archie Mogorosi.
96 min. b/w.
Do we really need a 'politically correct' footnote to *Mapantsula*, directed by another young, white South African keen to establish Sowetan street-cred? Laid off during a strike at the metal foundry, the stolidly principled BT comes under pressure from the members of his late brother's gang to get into the car-theft business. No big problem, until he presents a stolen car to the woman he has a crush on – getting her and her right-on activist friends into trouble, and bringing BT himself under the thumb of a ruthless Mr Big. The real trouble is that this is written as a pessimistic lefty tract, rather amateurishly acted, and shot without flair. The old label fits: worthy but dull. TR

Wheels on Meals (Kuai-can Che)

(Samo Hung, 1984, HK) Jackie Chan, Yuen Biao, Samo Hung, Richard Ng.
102 min.
Jackie Chan is more than the sum of his stunts: it's his knack for comedy, as much as his martial arts virtuosity that makes him Asia's top star. This delirious comedy, set in Barcelona, is one of his better efforts. He and Yuen Biao are fast-food operators who somehow become entangled in a plot involving a prostitute, a lunatic and a missing heiress. The sheer haphazardness of the happenings recalls Hollywood's golden slapstick comedies. GM

When a Man Loves a Woman

(Luis Mandoki, 1994, US) Andy Garcia, Meg Ryan, Ellen Burstyn, Tina Majorino, Mae Whitman, Lauren Tom, Gail Strickland.
125 min.
Ryan excels as Alice Green, teacher and mother of two young children, whose apparently idyllic marriage cracks open to reveal a dependence on drink. The emphasis here, though, is neither on Alice's drinking and (self-)deception, nor on the gruelling drying-out period, but on the guilt, confusion and disruption provoked by her return to the dysfunctional family unit that caused her breakdown and which must now adjust to accommodate a wife/mother who is not only sober but irrevocably changed. Having spent much of her marriage rummaging in the laundry cupboard for vodka, Alice now starts to delve into her past for the missing pieces of an unfulfilled life. Ryan, with her trademark sobbing to the fore, gives a showier performance than Garcia, who nevertheless impresses as the husband unable to cope with Alice's growing self-confidence. Mandoki transforms what might have been a familiar story of personal redemption into a coruscating dissection of a marriage built on shifting sand. NF

When a Stranger Calls

(Fred Walton, 1979, US) Charles Durning, Carol Kane, Colleen Dewhurst, Tony Beckley, Rachel Roberts, Ron O'Neal.
97 min.
An anonymous phonecaller urges the babysitter to check the children...Two competently handled sequences of protracted suspense, featuring the killer at large in a darkened house, bracket a less effectively realised murder hunt through the city streets. However, this stab at the soft underbelly of American middle class paranoia looks increasingly contrived once the film loses direction in the daylight outside, and a realism intrudes that the film-makers just don't know how to handle. Not as atmospherically eerie as *Halloween* nor as mechanically effective as *Black Christmas*, but there's one great moment when the husband in bed turns into a stranger. Kane is the babysitter (later wife and mother), Beckley the killer, and Durning the cop. CPe

When Dinosaurs Ruled the Earth

(Val Guest, 1969, GB) Victoria Vetri, Robin Hawdon, Patrick Allen, Drewe Henley, Sean Caffrey, Magda Konopka, Imogen Hassall, Patrick Holt.
100 min.
Rousing tribal squabbles among scantily clothed men and women clambering amid the rocks, jungle foliage, and lumbering monsters of Shepperton Studios. The script is couched entirely in prehistoric syllables – a testament to Guest's valiant attempt at creating science-fact rather than fiction. Alas, the budget was too small for the facts to convince, but the film still includes a few of the strangest shots in British cinema. GB

When Eight Bells Toll

(Etienne Périer, 1971, GB) Anthony Hopkins, Robert Morley, Nathalie Delon, Jack Hawkins, Corin Redgrave, Ferdy Mayne.
94 min.
Adapted by Alistair MacLean from his own novel, this has young Hopkins as a secret service agent investigating the disappearance of gold bullion from vessels in the Irish Sea, with shipping magnate Hawkins apparently up to no good. It's a decent production job if you can work up any interest in this sort of espionage thriller. Great Panavision location photography by Arthur Ibbetson. TJ

When Father Was Away on Business (Otac na Sluzbenom Putu)

(Emir Kusturica, 1985, Yugo) Moreno de Bartoli, Miki Manojlovic, Mirjana Karanovic, Mustafa Nadarevic.
136 min.
In the wake of the Tito/Kremlin split in the early '50s, little Malik's dad is despatched 'on business' to a labour camp for his Stalinist leanings (and philandering habits). His son stolidly observes the hardship this brings upon the family, takes to sleepwalking, and experiences first love. A few smiles, a few tears, all most unexceptionable: the very stuff, in short, of a festival laureate. Meticulously crafted and full of delightful touches, but there is little to lift this Cannes prize-winner above the ordinary. SJo

When Harry Met Sally...

(Rob Reiner, 1989, US) Billy Crystal, Meg Ryan, Carrie Fisher, Bruno Kirby, Steven Ford, Lisa Jane Persky, Michella Nicastro.
95 min.
1977: cynical womaniser Harry (Crystal) and clean-living would-be journo Sally (Ryan) are thrown together on an 18-hour trip to New York. They don't exactly hit it off, but ten years later, having suffered the traumas of break-up and divorce, they meet again and find they can offer mutual support. Will their friendship move from platonic to romantic? It seems likely, but there's a problem: Harry is reluctant to commit himself, while Sally won't countenance one-night stands. Reiner's Woody Allen-ish comedy is, for all its up-front discussion of matters sexual, disarmingly old-fashioned. A mite too pat, it never really probes or challenges Harry and Sally's attitiudes; but Nora Ephron's extended, slightly sentimental, and none-too-original meeting cute scenario includes enough funny one-liners to hold the attention of all but the most jaded viewer. As ever, Reiner clearly likes his characters, and elicits sturdy performances from a proficient cast (Kirby and Fisher are especially fine as friends and confidants to the pair). GA

When I Fall In Love

see Everybody's All-American

When Joseph Returns (Ha Megjön József)

(Zsolt Kézdi Kovács, 1975, Hun) György Pogány, Lili Monori, Eva Ruttkai, Gábor Koncz.
88 min.
In the East European tradition of low-key, observational cinema, blending naturalistic acting styles into workaday urban backgrounds. Middle-aged woman shares small city apartment with new daughter-in-law while merchant seaman son is at sea. They soon find themselves on an emotional collision course: the older woman's furtive liaisons, and the girl's more open if bewildered drift into promiscuity, nurture mutual accusations of hypocrisy. The film's harmonious resolution rather belies what has gone before (the intense antagonism and misunderstanding that grows between generations); but writer/director Kovács displays a special feeling for everyday lives forever skirting boredom, and draws well-pitched performances from Monori (the daughter-in-law) and Ruttkai (the mother). CPe

When Ladies Meet

(Robert Z Leonard, 1941, US) Joan Crawford, Robert Taylor, Greer Garson, Herbert Marshall, Spring Byington.
108 min. b/w.

W

Adapted from Rachel Crothers' play, previously filmed in 1933 with Ann Harding and Myrna Loy. When the ladies in question are the supremely vulgar Joan Crawford and the svelte-but-deadly Greer Garson, quite a lot happens. Both in love with Herbert Marshall, the ladies have a lot of girl-talk before fighting it out. The screenplay, by Anita Loos (*Gentlemen Prefer Blondes*), ensures maximum bitch-factor. Crawford, playing a sophisticated (and ridiculously well-dressed) novelist, loses Marshall but gets Robert Taylor as a kind of consolation prize. No fool, our Joan; she trades romance for looks, in which department Taylor could beat any contender in Tinseltown. Hovering over the whole proceedings is the motherly form of Spring Byington. ATu

When Mother Comes Home for Christmas (Otan Erhtli Mama Gia ta Christougenna)
(Nilita Vachani, 1995, Greece)
109 min.
One in six Sri Lankan women work abroad, often as home-helps and nannies, sending money back to their families. This documentary, by a US-trained Indian film-maker based in Athens, focuses on Josephine, a nanny who hasn't seen her own kids in 8 years. They're having trouble with school and their love lives. Josephine gets on well with her charge and is more of a mother to the infant girl than the vain and horrendously selfish middle-class woman for whom she works. Chastening but over-extended. GA

When Night Is Falling
(Patricia Rozema, 1995, Can) Pascale Bussières, Rachael Crawford, Henry Czerny, David Fox, Don McKellar, Tracy Wright, Clare Coulter.
94 min.
Grief takes Protestant academic Camille to the laundrette, where circus performer Petra supplies tissues, sympathy and a sly switcheroo on the holdalls containing their respective smalls. The meeting-cute hurdle negotiated, the story proceeds to run a relatively fresh spin on ye old eternal threesome. The man in Camille's life is Martin, fellow lecturer at the College of New Faith, but how can the call of duty compete with this new woman winkling out the new woman in her. After all, tweed jackets and keynote speeches can't compete with tight black leather, arrows of desire fired through your window, and an epochal hang-gliding trip. No, it's not much of a contest, but Rozema provides ample pleasures to compensate for the lack of surprise, not the least of which is a warm sensuality that never feels exploitative, plus the good heart to make Czerny's boyfriend a decent stick and even to have the stern college principal question his own homophobia. While the surrounding Sirkus of Sorts frippery is endearing without being pushy, and Lesley Barber's terrific score provides emotional thrust, the key to the film's mercurial charm is the performances of the two leads: Bussières ranging engagingly from prim to perky, and Crawford a bewitching presence as the impish seductress. Cynics may demur, but the result is quite delicious. TJ

When Saturday Comes
(Maria Giese, 1995, GB) Sean Bean, Emily Lloyd, Pete Postlethwaite, Craig Kelly.
98 min.
Roy of the Rovers meets *Emmerdale* in this tale of soccer-mad Jimmy Muir (Bean) and his fight to make it as a professional footballer for local team Sheffield United. From the kick off, the omens aren't good. Jimmy has always shone in amateur teams, but suffers from a temperament problem. Yet when sprightly Irish lass Annie Doherty (Lloyd) starts at the brewery where he works, his luck begins to improve. First there's the snogging, then there's the fact that her uncle (Postlethwaite) runs a highly regarded local football team. It's difficult to convey how thoroughly dreadful this film is. It's like watching the football episode of Michael Palin's *Ripping Yarns*, but without the jokes. En route to its tedious, inevitable conclusion, every cliché about life oop north gets a good airing. The script is leaden and the direction has that unmistakable 'made for TV' look about it. Bean, Lloyd and Postlethwaite struggle dutifully with the material. NKe

When Strangers Marry (aka Betrayed)
(William Castle, 1944, US) Robert Mitchum, Kim Hunter, Dean Jagger, Neil Hamilton, Lou Lubin, Milton Kibbee.
67 min. b/w.
The Monogram B-picture that gave Mitchum his first starring role. Hunter's the innocent one, turning to former boyfriend Mitchum, when husband Jagger disappears after a couple of months of marriage. A trip to the cops reveals that the latter may not be quite the man she thought and thus the plot thickens. Future horror showman Castle keeps it simple, leaving the cast and the cracking dialogue to make the running. Mitchum shows promise. TJ

When the Cat's Away... (Chacun cherche son chat)
(Cédric Klapisch, 1996, Fr) Garance Clavel, Renée Lecalm, Zinedine Soualem, Olivier Py.
90 min.
When make-up artist Chloé (Clavel) takes a week's holiday, the only person who'll look after her beloved cat Gris-Gris is Mme Renée (Lecalm), an eccentric old biddy who promptly loses the animal during the girl's absence. In addition to Chloé and her gay flat-mate Michel (Py), the search party which Mme Renée helps to mobilise includes numerous elderly matrons and Djamel (Soualem), a kindly if somewhat naive Arab who develops a crush on Chloé. She, however, finds herself taking an unexpected shine to a local young drummer. The third feature from writer/director Klapisch is a beautifully observed comedy vaguely in the Rohmer tradition: light, spontaneous, seemingly inconsequential, but packed with deft, delicate insights into loneliness, love, the comforts of community and the changing nature of Paris. Crucial to the film's emotional pull is an unsentimental generosity extended to each character. The naturalistic performances help no end in this respect, while the affection stretches even to Gris-Gris, filmed, inspirationally, to the strains of Al Green's 'So Tired of Being Alone'. Witty, touching, refreshingly nonchalant, and very French. GA

When the Legends Die
(Stuart Millar, 1972, US) Richard Widmark, Frederic Forrest, Luana Anders, Vito Scotti, Herbert Nelson, John War Eagle.
105 min.
A fine contemporary Western, about a young Indian (Forrest) whose strange affinity for horses attracts the attention of an ageing rodeo rider (Widmark), who buys his freedom from the reservation by becoming his guardian, teaches him the trade, and builds him into a minor star. Simultaneously exploited by Widmark, who drinks away their winnings and tries to double them by rigging bets, Forrest determines to break away, convinced he can make the grade honestly. He finally manages his escape (although Widmark 'owns' him until he is 21), only to find himself still imprisoned, this time by the American dream of success. Elegiacally framed as an allegory (noble savage vs ignoble civilisation), the film is saved from pretension by the fact that its real flesh is the superbly detailed world of grubby towns and back street bars, of endless days and nights on the road or in faceless hotels, which forms a laconic background to the rough, tumbling, touchingly funny relationship in which Widmark simultaneously tears Forrest to pieces and becomes his only friend. Widmark's performance is absolutely magnificent. TM

When the Mountains Tremble
(Pamela Yates/Thomas Sigel, 1983, US) Shawn Elliot, Eddie Jones, Linda Segura, Shelly Desai, Ron Ryan.
83 min.
A documentary with a dramatic framework, made by a team which provides CBS News coverage of Guatemala, this tells the story of 30 years of US-initiated and backed military dictatorships in that country, through the family saga of Rigoberta Menchú, the Indian peasant woman narrator, whose father and brother were both burned alive by security forces. Made with the cooperation of both government and guerrillas, it is perhaps strongest in presenting attitudes: from the brutal, no-nonsense frankness of the military, through the even more repulsive blinkered stupidity of Americans, to the desperation of the poor and the optimism of the guerillas. With *El Salvador: Another Vietnam* and John Pilger's Nicaragua documentary, this helps to complete the picture of a region to which America, not Russia, is exporting revolution. JCo

When the North Wind Blows
(Stewart Raffill, 1974, US) Henry Brandon, Herbert Nelson, Dan Haggerty, Henry Olek, Sander Johnson.
113 min.
There is a distant place in north Alaska, far from where the caribou roam. Here a man is judged by his strength, not by how many books he has read. A man like Avacum (Brandon), who accidentally shoots the son of his best friend, Boris the storekeeper. Fleeing to the wilds, Avacum makes a new friend – the tigress who has been terrorising the village. They protect each other, she has a pair of cubs, he adopts them when mother is gunned down by anti-conservationists. Avacum survives a year of hardship, finally turning his back on so-called civilisation. The question remains: who got the tigress pregnant? In other words, an over-bearingly solemn slice of life-in-the-raw, whose often beautiful photography is let down by the Woody Allen-ish character of the peasantry involved. Some interest is kept going by the spectacle of large tigers on the attack and at play. It's a long winter, though. AN

When the Whales Came
(Clive Rees, 1989, GB) Helen Mirren, Paul Scofield, David Suchet, Barbara Jefford, David Threlfall, Barbara Ewing, Jeremy Kemp, Max Rennie, Helen Pearce.
100 min.
A rather simple-minded tale of magic, friendship and conflict, scripted by Michael Morpurgo from his own children's novel set on one of the Scilly Isles at the start of WWI, with soaring strings, sweeping landscapes, and a no-sex, no violence, uplifting storyline about redemption through being kind to animals and befriending lonely oldsters. Mirren perfectsher beautiful, battered but unbowed act; Scofield is magesterial as the Birdman, a kindly hermit; while the two children central to the action are played with delightful spontaneity by Max Rennie and lithping Helen Pearce. The endangered animal is an authentically mournful beached narwhal. A climactic, cinematically beautiful sequence has torch-wielding villagers wading into a twilt sea to ward off more of the beasts, but mostly Rees just points his camera at the wonders of nature. Don't even try to swallow the preposterously happy, mythic ending. SFe

When the Wind Blows
(Jimmy T Murakami, 1986, GB) voices: Peggy Ashcroft, John Mills, Robin Houston.
84 min.
There have been enough post-holocaust nuclear winter films nearly to constitute a genre, but there has never been anything quite like veteran animator Murakami's version of Raymond Briggs' cartoon book. Jim and Hilda Bloggs are living out an unexceptional retirement, when the unthinkable happens. Happily prattling about their World War II adventures in the blitz, they duly follow the government brochure advice and build a shelter with doors and cushions, then go about their business as their hair falls out and the dust rains down. The animation is at its best – and the film most effective – during sequences of their reminiscences, when the daily round of their past lives is seen as a delight in the ordinary and in a history which is not just forgotten but literally obliterated. But their slow degradation is almost unbearably moving. The only note of hope is that it might just get through to some people who have a say in such matters. Jim and Hilda are worth preserving. CPea

When Time Ran Out
(James Goldstone, 1980, US) Paul Newman, Jacqueline Bisset, William Holden, Red Buttons, Valentina Cortese, Burgess Meredith, Ernest Borgnine, James Franciscus, Veronica Hamel, Barbara Carrera, Edward Albert.
121 min.
Well, there's this island in the Pacific where maverick oil-driller Newman hits the black stuff, much to the delight of Franciscus, screwy scion

of the island's ruling family. A wooden effigy of Holden jets in with Bisset, summoned by Franciscus to locate one of his luxury hotels there. Bisset was mean to Newman, so he glowers at her. Franciscus' daddy was mean to him, so he glowers at daddy's portrait. Holden suspects Franciscus of telling whoppers about the future intentions of the island's volcano, so he glowers. (The subsidiary characters glower a lot too). Amid all the tension, the volcano blows its stack. 'Is anything wrong?' someone asks. 'No, nothing's wrong' says someone else. Something is very wrong. There's a tidal wave and an earthquake, flaming balls of fire and a menacing lava flow, and Newman decides to get the hell out with the major stars. A real movie disaster, scripted by Carl Foreman and Stirling Silliphant. DSi

When We Were Kings
(Leon Gast, 1996, US) Muhammad Ali, George Foreman, Don King, James Brown, BB King, Norman Mailer, George Plimpton, Spike Lee, Thomas Hauser, Miriam Makeba.
87 min. col & b/w.
Leon Gast's time-capsule of a film transports us to Zaire in 1974 (when most of the material was shot), and the heavyweight encounter between Muhammad Ali and George Foreman – the famous 'rumble in the jungle'. Gast was on hand to record the three-day music festival which preceded the bout, but stayed when the fight was delayed after Foreman was cut in a training session. Press conferences, gym sessions, and all the cultural paradox which accompanied two African-American superstars stranded with the world's media in Kinshasa for six weeks. Apparently Taylor Hackford, who has a producer credit, came up with the idea of using commentaries from Norman Mailer, George Plimpton and Spike Lee to structure the material, and though Lee (who wasn't there) has little to say, Plimpton and Mailer (who were) make enthralling guides. Mailer, especially, acknowledges the ironies congruent on this gladiatorial showpiece for black pride being staged by the Mobutu dictatorship and the Don King machine, and produces a penetrating emotional analysis of the boxing which is nothing short of inspired. TCh

When We Were Young
(Kak Molody My Byli)
(Mikhail Belikov, 1985, USSR) Taras Denisenko, Elena Shkurpelo, N Sharolapova, A Pashutin, A Sviridovsky.
92 min.
Set in the '50s, this follows the teenage hero, a trainee sanitary engineer, as he undergoes rites of passage of various kinds before marrying his mortally ill childhood sweetheart. The tone moves between mawkish comedy and melodrama, with the shadows of still fresh war memories falling exceedingly lengthily and darkly. Not brilliant, but very desperate, and offering a window on Russia during the high years of the Cold War. It also implies criticism of the high price of space technology. VG

When Willie Comes
Marching Home
(John Ford, 1950, US) Dan Dailey, Corinne Calvet, Colleen Townsend, William Demarest, James Lydon, Lloyd Corrigan, Evelyn Varden.
82 min. b/w.
One of Ford's most underrated films, this isn't as beady-eyed as Sturges' Hail the Conquering Hero in its take on patriotic fervour, but is still immensely engaging. Dailey plays small-town boy Bill Kluggs, son of a flag-waving American Legion stalwart (Demarest), who earns a civic send-off as the first to enlist after Pearl Harbor. After training, unfortunately, he is posted back home as an instructor. Repeated requests for combat duty are turned down; and cordiality turns to contempt among the townsfolk as other local boys meanwhile win glory. His chance finally comes as last-minute replacement on a bomber heading for London, leading to an inadvertent adventure in Occupied France, and an escape, engineered by the Resistance, with vital information concerning the new German rocket. He's back home within four days; and with the matter classified, everybody thinks he's lying or crazy until news comes of a pending decoration. Ford, steering a more naturalistic path than Sturges through the quirkish characters and semi-slapstick action, makes the

central irony ring loud and clear: while doing his despised duty as an aerial gunnery instructor, Bill Kluggs demonstrates considerable heroism; while earning his decoration at the hands of a grateful President, he is either asleep or dead drunk the entire time. TM

When Worlds Collide
(Rudolph Maté, 1951, US) Richard Derr, Barbara Rush, Peter Hanson, Larry Keating, John Hoyt, Judith Ames.
83 min.
Exciting science fantasy movie about the end of the world, no less. A dying star is on a crash course with the earth. Flyer Dave Randall (Derr) and astronomer Doc Hendron (Keating) put their heads together and organise the construction of a space ark to transport forty lucky workers to the nearest hospitable planet and save the human race. Based on a novel by Philip Wylie and Edwin Balmer once envisaged as a Cecil B DeMille project back in 1934, George Pal's production is better remembered for its apocalyptic special effects than for the perfunctory dialogue, but the gripping story keeps you watching. TCh

Where Angels Fear to Tread
(Charles Sturridge, 1991, GB) Helena Bonham Carter, Judy Davis, Rupert Graves, Giovanni Guidelli, Barbara Jefford, Helen Mirren, Thomas Wheatley.
112 min.
The fostering of Forster in a rash of movies since the mid-'80s continues with this adaptation of the novel in which Lilia Herriton (Mirren), a widow of a certain age, shocks her strait-laced in-laws by wedding the son of an Italian tooth-puller (played by Guidelli with dewy eyes and pouts). When this frightful news reaches Sawston, Mrs Herriton (Jefford) dispatches her son Philip (Graves) to Monteriano to rescue her. He fails. After Lilia dies in childbirth, he returns with his sister Harriet (Davis) to retrieve the bambino, only to fail again – but not before he's fallen for Lilia's former companion Caroline Abbott (Bonham Carter). Stiff upper lips prove no protection against the ancient charms of tourist Tuscany. The performances and scenery cannot be faulted. Mirren, defiantly vulnerable as ever, dominates the movie while she's in it. Thereafter, Davis steals the show as a hilariously hysterical spinster. Graves, too, proves he's not just a pretty face. But though things connect much better than they did in Sturridge's A Handful of Dust, the screenplay degenerates into a static succession of talking heads. Sturridge's work still seems to be TV masquerading as cinema. MS

Where Danger Lives
(John Farrow, 1950, US) Robert Mitchum, Faith Domergue, Claude Rains, Maureen O'Sullivan, Charles Kemper, Ralph Dumke, Billy House, Jack Kelly.
84 min. b/w.
Odd casting for Mitchum as a solid citizen, first cousin to Dr Kildare, who finds himself on the run after succumbing to the siren songs of a psychotic patient (Domergue, who asphyxiates her husband Rains, letting Mitchum think he killed him in a fight). Nick Musuraca's superb camerawork stresses the noir that is synonymous with the Mitchum persona; Charles Bennett's script seems to be hankering after all those innocent thrillers he wrote for Hitchcock in the '30s. The result is an impasse of cross-purposes which lends the film a sort of bleak abstraction, curious and rather compelling. TM

Where Eagles Dare
(Brian G Hutton, 1968, GB) Richard Burton, Clint Eastwood, Mary Ure, Patrick Wymark, Michael Hordern, Donald Houston, Peter Barkworth, Robert Beatty, William Squire, Derren Nesbitt, Anton Diffring.
155 min.
A conscientiously large World War II adventure, drawn from the novel by Alastair MacLean, about a 7-man team parachuted into the Bavarian Alps to rescue a high-ranking Allied officer held prisoner by the Germans in an impregnable mountain Schloss. It may be devoid of significance of any sort, but it is nevertheless passably entertaining, and certainly better viewing than most MacLean adaptations. Its ability to sustain interest depends on fine cinematography (Arthur Ibbetson), and a handful of genuinely exciting action sequences,

notably two extended scenes involving death-defying feats on a cable car slung between two snow-covered peaks. The climax simply involves blowing up everything in sight. VG

Where Is My Friend's House?
(Khaneh-Je Doost Kojast)
(Abbas Kiarostami, 1987, Iran) Babek Ahmed Poor, Ahmed Ahmed Poor, Kheda Barech Defai, Iran Outari, Aît Ansari.
85 min.
Familiar in Britain only to those who've caught his work at festivals or noted his name as writer of The White Balloon, Iran's Abbas Kiarostami has been acclaimed a key film-maker of the '90s. Judging by this (and by And Life Goes On…), he's a major talent – his work an enthralling blend of low-key realism and a more thought-provoking, sometimes playful formalism. Here young Ahmed tries to return a schoolmate's notebook he's unwittingly taken home. (Its loss might get its owner expelled.) Obstacles abound, chiefly in the shape of unhelpful, domineering adults, but also because, while Ahmed knows his pal lives in the next village, he's no idea of the address. While the film is often funny, it's also very moving. The repetitive structure of the boy's quest, and the poetic evocation of the landscape he moves through, highlight his vulnerability, frustration and, finally, his sterling determination. GA

Where No Vultures Fly
(aka Ivory Hunter)
(Harry Watt, 1951, GB) Anthony Steel, Dinah Sheridan, Harold Warrender, Meredith Edwards.
107 min.
Ealing moved from their modest studios to the wide open spaces of Kenya for this time-locked colonial adventure. Steel is square-jawed as the warden of Mt Kilimanjaro Game Reserve, seeing off ivory hunter Warrender and the local tribesmen he's stirred into helping him. Former documentarist Watt slightly makes up for the shortcomings in the plotting with some evocative wildlife footage. TJ

Where's Jack?
(James Clavell, 1968, GB) Tommy Steele, Stanley Baker, Fiona Lewis, Alan Badel, Dudley Foster, Sue Lloyd.
119 min.
Years before the Shogun millions rolled in, Clavell was the writer and director of some distinguished movies, like this one. Eighteenth century England is recreated with care as government agent Baker (who also produced) shakes down notorious highwayman Jack Sheppard, but the film never gets over the fact that some bright spark cast Tommy Steele in the lead. TJ

Where's Poppa?
(Carl Reiner, 1970, US) George Segal, Ruth Gordon, Trish Van Devere, Ron Leibman, Rae Allen, Vincent Gardenia, Barnard Hughes, Rob Reiner.
82 min.
Scripted by Robert Klane from his own novel, this is the ultimate in Jewish Momma jokes, with a despairing Segal dressing up in a King Kong suit in hopes of scaring his obstructively senile parent to death, while she, indestructibly played by Ruth Gordon at her battiest, serenely continues turning his sex life into an everlasting coitus interruptus while herself bearing a charmed life. Meanwhile the plot is assaulted by a riot of topsy-turvy New York neuroses: a brother-in-law who insists on walking home through Central Park because he has a cosy arrangement with the muggers waiting there to attack him every night; a General who gets so carried away while being cross-examined about military codes of conduct that he launches into a Molly Bloom monologue about the orgiastic delights of killing goons; a cop who refuses to press charges after being raped while disguised as a policewoman, instead sending a bouquet of roses to his assailant. An irresistible black comedy, it's probably Reiner's best film, not least because it shows such affection for all its crazies. TM

Where the Boys Are
(Hy Averback, 1984, US) Lisa Hartman, Lorna Luft, Wendy Schaal, Lynn-Holly Johnson, Russell Todd, Howard McGillin.
94 min.

The flesh-packed beaches of Florida's Fort Lauderdale beckon once again to thrill-seeking American youth, with four girl students setting out to spend their spring break mixing their drinks and dropping their drawers, although they assuredly didn't have lines like 'All you need is a bikini and a diaphragm' in the 1960 version of Glendon Swarthout's novel, starring Connie Francis. The accent is on fun: discos full of drunken people and exuberant beach-boys, parties full of exuberant drunks, all set to a crashingly tedious rock score. The heroines dally desperately with a muscled barbarian, a bronzed hitch-hiker, and a life-size inflatable buddy doll (with integral swimming-trunks), but the spectacle of girls going ape and getting their socks off is ultimately no more uplifting than that of the usual pimply youths doing the same thing. AB

Where the Buffalo Roam
(Art Linson, 1980, US) Peter Boyle, Bill Murray, Bruno Kirby, René Auberjonois, RG Armstrong, Danny Goldman, Rafael Campos, Leonard Frey.
99 min.
The Drury Lane stage version of Hunter S Thompson's imaginary biog stank, but Linson's movie lists closer to the vicarious thrill of the loathsome baby's fictitious experiences. Bill Murray passes well as Thompson, although Peter Boyle's occasional appearances as his 600lb Samoan attorney can't help but upstage him. It's all here: the copious drink, the superhuman drug intake, and the wind-ups shot at whatever symbol of authority Thompson considers as fair game; but, as with his writing, the attacks always fall short of delivering the final payload. Laughs aplenty for people who use drugs as a pose, but most will be left wondering if half a pint of Bass doesn't qualify as a revolutionary action. JG

Where the Green Ants Dream (Wo die grünen Ameisen träumen)
(Werner Herzog, 1984, WGer) Bruce Spence, Wandjuk Marika, Roy Marika, Ray Barrett, Norman Kaye, Colleen Clifford.
100 min.
A bunch of inscrutable Aboriginals occupy a patch of Australian desert, sitting down in the path of oil prospectors. Why these surly Abos? Why these belligerent Diggers? It's all because the land is a sacred burial site for mythical green ants – except that no such creatures figure in Aboriginal mythology, they're just bugs in Herzog's brain. That doesn't matter. We follow the protesting Aboriginals through a court case (the most laughable scene in this badly acted, sloppily directed movie), and back to their sit-down strike, still uncertain whether this is meant to be an adventure in anthropology, an exercise in environmental agit-prop, or just an excuse for Herzog to spend someone else's fortune laying classical music over shots of empty desert. MA

Where the Heart Is
(John Boorman, 1990. US) Dabney Coleman, Uma Thurman, Joanna Cassidy, Crispin Glover, Suzy Amis, Christopher Plummer, David Hewlett, Maury Chaykin.
107 min.
Boorman's ambitious and clearly allegorical black comedy explores (and exorcises?) a variety of problems facing modern youth: family tension, unemployment, ecology. To his wife's dismay, and in the hope that hardship fosters maturity, self-made demolition-tycoon Stewart McBain (Coleman) dumps their three spoiled, dreamy progeny – body-painter Chloe (Amis), computer fanatic Jimmy (Hewlett), and flaky no-hoper Daphne (Thurman) – in a derelict Brooklyn house. Inevitably, with a little help from their motley assortment of friends, the kids begin to make good, even as Dad's rugged individualism comes a cropper. While never less than a lively tribute to communal life, the script (by Boorman and his daughter Telsche) is sadly short of real focus and bite, and it's left to the director's keen visual sense, and fluent choreography of the ensemble scenes, to hold the interest. Moments of surrealism abound, but the actors are indulged, and the allusions to rain forests, conservation etc, are squeezed awkwardly into a farcical narrative, so that real issues are softened and sentimentalised. GA

Where the Red Fern Grows
(Norman Tokar, 1974, US) James Whitmore, Beverly Garland, Jack Ging, Lonny Chapman, Stewart Peterson.
97 min.
Depression? What Depression? It may be 1930s Oklahoma, but a 12-year-old boy (Peterson) can still hoard $50 to buy himself a pair of raccoon hounds and start adventuring towards manhood. A syrupy kids' yarn from former Disney animal-movie specialist Tokar, backed by appropriate soundtrack odes from the Osmonds and Andy Williams. PT

Where There's a Will
see Good Morning, Boys!

Where the River Bends
see Bend of the River

Where Were You When the Lights Went Out?
(Hy Averback, 1968, US) Doris Day, Robert Morse, Patrick O'Neal, Terry-Thomas, Lola Albright, Steve Allen, Jim Backus, Ben Blue, Robert Emhardt.
94 min.
A sprightly comedy, set during the great American East Coast power failure of 1965, which mercifully doesn't get all sniggery about the aftermath of the unexpected blackout (an unprecedented rise in the birthdate nine months later). Instead, it has Doris Day, gently satirising her own image, playing an actress tired of being known as 'The Constant Virgin', especially after catching her husband (O'Neal) almost in the act with a voluptuous journalist (Albright) sent to interview her. She runs off to sulk, a young business executive (Morse) runs off with his company's funds, the lights go out, and a perfectly logical series of circumstances finds the pair in bed together, happily unaware of each other's existence, when O'Neal arrives on the scene. A brilliantly funny sequence ensues as the enraged O'Neal threatens to run riot with a gun, but all the dazed 'guilty couple' want (since both are heavily sedated) is to be allowed to go back to bed. Not all of the film is as good, but the performances are superb (Morse, O'Neal and Albright, especially), and Averback's comic timing is spot on. TM

Which Way to the Front? (aka Ja, Ja, Mein General! But Which Way to the Front?)
(Jerry Lewis, 1970, US) Jerry Lewis, Jan Murray, Willie Davis, John Wood, Kaye Ballard, Steve Franken, Dack Rambo, Robert Middleton.
96 min.
Perhaps not classic Lewis (his directorial invention flagging a bit, even if his gibbering performance genius remains intact), but audaciously anachronistic enough in its retread of the Nazi impersonation schtick to bring tears to the eyes. A World War II draft reject, Lewis' millionaire sets up his own private army to help out the Allies in Italy, producing an outrageous inversion of The Dirty Dozen. PT

Whiffs (aka C.A.S.H.)
(Ted Post, 1975, US) Elliott Gould, Eddie Albert, Harry Guardino, Godfrey Cambridge, Jennifer O'Neill.
92 min.
Gould is discharged from the US Army on grounds of medical disability after years of being a guinea pig for the Medical Corps. Embittered, he takes revenge by putting the gases he knows and loves so well to use in a series of robberies. 'C.A.S.H.' (Chemical Air-Spray Holdup) is a perfect example of a film constructed around an idea that must have seemed funny to someone once.

While Parents Sleep
(Adrian Brunel, 1935, GB) Jean Gillie, Enid Stamp-Taylor, Mackenzie Ward, Romilly Lunge, Athole Stewart, Davy Burnaby.
72 min. b/w.
Brunel was the great might-have-been of British cinema. Tactless, radical, idiosyncratic, he was allowed frustratingly few outlets for his talents. His most prolific period was the mid '30s, when his sheer efficiency ensured him regular work making ultra-cheap 'quota quickies'. Thematic consistency is hardly likely where the sole consideration is cost, but Brunel's effectiveness as a stylist is remarkable. Here, with a stage play script, a couple of tatty sets, and a bunch of unknown actors, he produces a witty, sharply paced, economical essay on class and manners in inter-war Britain. It's ironic that while Brunel was energetically devoting his talents to programme fillers, the moguls of film production were bent on importing American and continental directors for their disastrously expensive 'prestige' productions. RMy

While the City Sleeps
(Fritz Lang, 1956, US) Dana Andrews, Ida Lupino, Rhonda Fleming, George Sanders, Howard Duff, Thomas Mitchell, Vincent Price, Sally Forrest, John Barrymore Jr, James Craig, Robert Warwick.
100 min. b/w.
A group of newsmen hunt for a sex murderer. Their motive is greed; the prize is control of a newspaper. 'Noble' Dana Andrews initially refuses to participate, but finally offers his fiancée (Forrest) as bait for the killer (Barrymore) who, naturally, is the film's most sympathetic character. Lang has inspired use of glass-walled offices, where all is seen and nothing revealed, and traces explicit parallels between Andrews and the murderer. Lang's most underrated movie. SJ

While You Were Sleeping
(Jim Turteltaub, 1995, US) Sandra Bullock, Bill Pullman, Peter Gallagher, Peter Boyle, Jack Warden, Glynis Johns, Micole Mercurio, Jason Bernard.
103 min.
Disney's fairytale romance is as cute and cuddly a bedtime story as anyone could wish for. Bullock stars as Lucy Moderatz, who sells tickets for the Chicago el-train. Lonesome Lucy has the hots for Peter (Gallagher): tall, dark, handsome – and he doesn't even know she's alive. Then, one day before Christmas, Peter collapses in a coma and Lucy pulls him from the tracks. After a mix-up at the hospital, she's introduced as Peter's fiancée and embraced to the bosom of his eccentric family (father Boyle, mother Johns, godfather Warden). Only brother Jack (Pullman) harbours any doubts – doubts Lucy is too ashamed to confirm. If Sleepless in Seattle was designer romance, While You Were Sleeping is comfortable fit: loose-knit sweaters, lumberjack shirts, blue jeans and Timberland boots. It's the difference between uptown Manhattan and blue-collar Chicago. There are no hip riffs on 'movie love' here, it's all the real McCoy. If there's a problem with the film, it's that this emphasis on authenticity is essentially just another style option, one that sits oddly with such an outrageously unlikely scenario. It's a mark of Bullock's radiant star quality that we're rooting for Lucy from the start. The movie coasts home on her charm. TCh

Whip Hand, The
(William Cameron Menzies, 1951, US) Elliott Reid, Carla Balenda, Raymond Burr, Edgar Barrier, Lurene Tuttle.
82 min. b/w.
Cut from Kremlin top brass scrutinising a wall-map of America to a holidaying reporter stumbling across an unfriendly US small town where all the fish have died and Raymond Burr eavesdrops on all outgoing phone calls. The Whip Hand progresses into such clinically clear-cut Cold War paranoia that it can hardly get through its multiple process shots quickly enough to warn that the resident Red scientists and fellow-travellers are all (gasp!) ex-Nazis; and inevitably about to destroy civilisation as we know it, unless...The delicious, delirious whirlwind of a plot affords sufficient uniquely '50s black'n'white fun to make recognition of the auteurist hand of William Cameron Menzies a decided bonus. Here Hollywood's most versatile art director/production designer (and inadequately-credited mastermind behind Gone With the Wind) manages (as director) a Hitchcockian playfulness with back-projection and wooden actors, even with the budget tying one hand behind his back. The tacky essence of B+. PT

Whirlpool
(Otto Preminger, 1949, US) Gene Tierney, Richard Conte, José Ferrer, Charles Bickford, Barbara O'Neil, Eduard Franz, Fortunio Bonanova, Constance Collier.
97 min. b/w.

The same themes and the same cool style as in *Laura* and *Angel Face* are at work in this portrait of the wealthy and sophisticated cracking apart at the seams, under pressure from psychological hang-ups, repressed passion, and innocent gullibility. When rich kleptomaniac Tierney turns for help not to her psychoanalyst husband (Conte) but to a hard-hearted hypnotherapist (Ferrer), she finds herself bereft of memory and implicated in a murder. Preminger translates the rather daft story (scripted by a pseudonymous Ben Hecht, loosely adapting Guy Endore's novel *Methinks the Lady*) into a typically unhysterical and lucid examination of people under stress: as the crime is investigated, currents of distrust, fear, and falsehood disturb the smooth waters of an apparently happy marriage. Content to observe rather than moralise, he creates a world of sympathetically flawed characters, the magnificent exception being the swindling quack, a manipulating charmer whose underplaying by Ferrer suggests credible evil. With its *noir* themes played out in cold, bright interiors, it's a fine example of the way Preminger, on occasion, managed to deflect routine melodrama into something more personal and profound. GA

Whisky Galore!
(aka Tight Little Island)
(Alexander Mackendrick, 1949, GB) Basil Radford, Joan Greenwood, Jean Cadell, Gordon Jackson, James Robertson Justice, Wylie Watson, John Gregson, Duncan Macrae, Catherine Lacey.
82 min. b/w.
Classic Ealing comedy about the no-holds-barred battle waged by a Hebridean island community, parched by wartime shortages, determined to put a shipwrecked cargo of whisky to proper use before officialdom can lay claim to it. Reminiscent of *Passport to Pimlico* in its amiable puncturing of bureaucracy, but a good deal sharper as a parable of colonialism, with the Scots contriving a humiliating double-edged comeuppance for their English laird and master (Radford). Delightful characterisations, lovely locations on the island of Barra. TM

Whisperers, The
(Bryan Forbes, 1966, GB) Edith Evans, Eric Portman, Avis Bunnage, Nanette Newman, Gerald Sim, Ronald Fraser, Leonard Rossiter, Kenneth Griffith.
106 min. b/w.
Forbes' ambitious but finally unsuccessful adaptation of Robert Nicolson's novel about an old working class woman, abandoned in her impoverished flat, who retreats into paranoid delusions of faded grandeur. Dame Edith Evans gives a spirited performance in the central role, but Forbes' direction is typically over-emphatic and obvious, underlining the social conscience of the film ad nauseam, and even putting its message into the mouth of a social worker (who asks a psychiatrist if the old lady wasn't happier with her illusions than with society's attempts to cure them). Forbes' daughter Sarah appears as the old lady when she was a child. DP

Whistle Blower, The
(Simon Langton, 1986, GB) Michael Caine, James Fox, Nigel Havers, John Gielgud, Felicity Dean, Barry Foster, Gordon Jackson.
104 min.
We've been here before. Bob Jones (Havers) is a translator in the Russian section at GCHQ. Following the trial of an employee, convicted of spying for the Eastern bloc, all personnel are requested to report any inconsistencies in the behaviour of their colleagues, and Bob becomes convinced that British intelligence is no better than the KGB. Meanwhile the CIA, worried about the apparent lack of security in England, begins to act with extreme prejudice. When Bob is bumped off, his father enters the fray to see that justice is done. In this role, Caine glides imperiously along, allowing none of the surrounding dross to tarnish his image. The rest of the cast do not come out of it so well. There are a couple of surprises, and the cynicism prevents the film from becoming overtly old-fashioned, but in general it is dreadful. The locations – Gloucester Cathedral, tourist Cheltenham, the Remembrance Day service at the Cenotaph – are stagy, the pace is slack, and the script pretentious. MS

Whistle Down the Wind
(Bryan Forbes, 1961, GB) Hayley Mills, Alan Bates, Bernard Lee, Norman Bird, Elsie Wagstaffe, Alan Barnes.
99 min. b/w.
Forbes' first film, a reef-ridden whimsy about three Lancashire farm kids who find a fugitive murderer (Bates) hiding in the barn and think he is Jesus. Done with a kind of grubby lyricism borrowed from *Jeux Interdits*, the early scenes are quite effective as the children matter-of-factly wonder how to react (should they curtsey, steal the family bottle of port?). But as the parable (and the parallels) extend towards a scene in which the killer is apprehended and adopts the posture of crucifixion as he is searched, it all becomes more than faintly embarrassing. TM

White Angel
(Chris Jones, 1993, GB) Harriet Robinson, Peter Firth, Don Henderson, Anne Catherine Arton, Harry Miller, Joe Collins.
96 min.
A 'thriller' which purports to examine the psychology of the banal 'blend-into-the-crowd' type that supposedly characterises the British serial killer. Leslie (Firth), a dentist transvestite and slayer of women-in-white, is, however, a signposted oddball: note his string singlets and see-through polyester shirts. He answers an ad placed by American crime writer Ellen (Robinson) and takes a room in her north London house. Ellen's no angel herself. Leslie seems to have twigged that she has, in fact, murdered her missing husband and presumes a bond of complicity between them – but the net is closing. This plays like a kitchen-sink horror movie, much of the action confined to the semi, all cramped camera angles and ill-lit close-ups, and more sofa fabric than a furniture ad. Hard to take seriously. WH

White Balloon, The
(Badkonak-E Sefid)
(Jafar Panahi, 1995, Iran) Aïda Mohammadkhani, Mohsen Kafili, Fereshteh Sadr Orfani, Anna Bourkowska, Mohammad Shahani.
84 min.
This extraordinary debut feature, about a 7-year-old's first journey alone into the streets of Tehran, is a movie of audacious subtlety and simplicity, and a deserving Cannes prize-winner. It takes place in 'real time', the 84 minutes leading to New Year (March 21), as little Razieh (Aïda Mohammadkhani) goes off to purchase, with her mother's last 500 *toman*, the 'chubby' gold-fish that has taken her fancy. Along the way, she encounters snake-charmers, irate shopkeepers, a country-born soldier, a young Afghan boy with a white balloon – a whole world hitherto 'forbidden'. Scripted in collaboration with leading Iranian director Abbas Kiarostami, this is a film of small incident, minute, telling observations, and enormous heart and intelligence. Tethering the movie to the child's point of view (both literal and metaphorical), Panahi absorbs us so entirely into his heroine's delicate, enquiring world, that the loss of her money and her separation from her brother create an atmosphere of suspense as gripping as that of any Hitchcock thriller. Moreover, suggestive intimations of the troubled adult world – the mother's anxiety in the bazaar, the lonely 'outsiders' – combine to produce a feeling of almost metaphysical tension. WH

White Buffalo, The
(J Lee Thompson, 1977, US) Charles Bronson, Jack Warden, Will Sampson, Kim Novak, Clint Walker, Stuart Whitman, Slim Pickens, John Carradine, Ed Lauter.
97 min.
Bronson plays Wild Bill Hickok, whose nemesis is the giant white buffalo of the title which haunts his nightmares. But the major struggle in the film is over whether it is a 'big' or 'small' picture. Biggest are: the buffalo, another Dino (*King Kong*) De Laurentiis presentation; the cast of mainly fading stars featured in cameo roles; and the self-consciously epic character names like Hickok, Crazy Horse and Custer. All of which suggests a thunderously empty yarn mounted around yet another mechanical gimmick. Yet Richard Sale's adaptation of his own novel hints at something more intimate. His Hickok is haunt-

ed, ageing, and diseased, trapped and uncertain in his own myth. Because of this, the movie occasionally takes an interesting turn, but less often than it should, because J Lee Thompson's direction clings to the increasing number of action set pieces with all the relief of a drowning man clutching a life raft. CPe

White Bus, The
(Lindsay Anderson, 1967, GB) Patricia Healey, Arthur Lowe, John Sharp, Julie Perry, Anthony Hopkins, Fanny Carby, Stephen Moore.
41 min. b/w & col.
Originally designed to be part of a feature called *Red, White and Blue*, a planned reunion of three 'Free Cinema' directors. When Karel Reisz' *Morgan, A Suitable Case for Treatment* turned into a feature, Lindsay Anderson and Tony Richardson were joined by Peter Brook, but their three contributions were never released together, and only Anderson's has stood the test of time. Shelagh Delaney's script takes an impassive young girl (Healey) out of her suicidal London office back to her Northern home town, which she views as part of a bizarre bus tour. The film looks forward to Anderson's blurring of the fantastic and the naturalistic in *If...*, and benefits from the poetic eye of the same Czech cameraman, Miroslav Ondricek. Fitting no conventional genre, the offbeat humour often hits the mark as a non-specific satire on British moribundity. DT

White Dawn, The
(Philip Kaufman, 1974, US) Warren Oates, Timothy Bottoms, Lou Gossett, Simonie Kopapik, Joanasie Salomonie, Pilitak.
110 min.
A surprisingly hypnotic B feature based on a true story that took place in the Canadian Arctic around 1900. Three sailors (Oates, Bottoms and Gossett), marooned on the ice cap, are taken in by a tribe of nomadic Eskimos. At a lyrically measured pace, the film unfolds how the three cultural aliens, ironically mistaken as 'dog children' by their protectors, variously adapt to and influence their new way of life. Bottoms, with misty-eyed reverence, drinks it up like a fish (the occasional moments of cloying sentiment are carefully structured around his character), while Gossett enjoys himself from the sidelines. A splendidly cantankerous Oates grudgingly accepts the help, and as his sole contribution to cultural exchange, initiates the Eskimos into alcohol. Most successful, however, is the presentation of the natural rhythms of the Eskimo life cycle, from religious rituals to hunting practices and recreation pursuits. The Baffin Island location, resonantly photographed, is in constant evidence, underlining its key position in the overall pattern. Even Henry 'Moon River' Mancini has come up trumps with a delicately pitched score. A treat. IB

White Dog
(Samuel Fuller, 1981, US) Kristy McNichol, Paul Winfield, Burl Ives, Jameson Parker, Lynne Moody, Marshall Thompson, Christa Lang, Samuel Fuller, Paul Bartel, Dick Miller.
90 min.
From the opening shot of a white flashlight piercing a black screen, Fuller's film is a model of intelligent simplicity. McNichol runs over a beautiful white Alsatian, takes it home to care for it, and discovers that the beast has been conditioned as a 'white dog' which attacks any black that it encounters. Rather than destroy it, she takes it to a black animal trainer (Winfield) to try to de-condition it...Just one of the many remarkable things about Fuller's impeccable treatment of racism is that it investigates that vile trait without showing a racist character; the dog is a perfect symbol for the confused and vicious conditioning that runs riot throughout the human world. Fuller has never heeded the false optimism of liberal creeds, and is well aware that there are no easy solutions to the problem; as the film's ending possibly suggests, you might just eradicate racism, but you'll never be rid of hatred. With Bruce Surtees' uncluttered camerawork, a superb score from Ennio Morricone, and fine acting throughout, this is one film of Fuller's which is most complex in its emotional sway: compassionate towards both animal and humans in the error of their ways, but fuelled by a seething anger. There is certainly no finer film on its subject. GA/CPea

White Fang (Zanna Bianca)

(Lucio Fulci, 1974, It/Sp/Fr) Franco Nero, Virna Lisi, Fernando Rey, Missaele, John Steiner.
101 min.

An unambitious, comic strip adaptation of Jack London's superb novel that nevertheless manages to capture something of the essence of London's world – the purity of the struggle with (not against) nature in the icy wastes, the corruption of the money-grabbing mining towns. One gets only glimpses of the original's intrepid reporter in Nero's performance, although Fernando Rey carries some resonance as the drink-sodden priest. The Indian child is suitably unwinsome, and the hound most mercifully un-Lassie-like. The overall feeling of the romance of the wilds survives the picture-book interpretation, making the film one any kid with an ounce of imagination should enjoy. VG

White Fang

(Randal Kleiser, 1990, US) Klaus Maria Brandauer, Ethan Hawke, Seymour Cassel, Susan Hogan, James Remar, Bill Moseley.
109 min.

This Disney version of Jack London's tale is run-of-the-mill stuff, offering spectacular icy locations set to a soapy orchestral score. Young Jack Conroy (Hawke) arrives in Alaska during the turn-of-the-century gold rush, determined to find his recently deceased father's claim. He enlists the aid of prospectors Alex (Brandauer) and Skunker (Cassel), and along the way develops a bond with White Fang, half-wolf and half-dog. The film charts their relationship, with White Fang at one point languishing in the hands of money-grubbing villain Beauty Smith (Remar) before Jack can stage a dramatic rescue. Despite moments of bravura and shameless tugs at the heart-strings, the film simply meanders towards a resolution. What's Brandauer doing here? CM

White Feather

(Robert Webb, 1955, US) Robert Wagner, John Lund, Debra Paget, Jeffrey Hunter, Noah Beery Jr, Hugh O'Brian, Eduard Franz.
102 min.

Can it be possible? Co-scripted by Delmer Daves five years after his *Broken Arrow*, another white man (Wagner) strives for peace with Jeffrey Hunter and the Indians, and falls in love with a squaw (Paget again). If you can withstand the feelings of *déjà vu* from the descendants of *Broken Arrow*, this is, in all fairness, a cut above its relatives. It looks convincing (it's based on fact – the defeat of the last of the Cheyenne warriors in 1877), the Indians are portrayed as human beings and not pantomime characters, and an exciting climax is well handled. DMcG

White Heat

(Raoul Walsh, 1949, US) James Cagney, Virginia Mayo, Edmond O'Brien, Margaret Wycherly, Steve Cochran, John Archer, Paul Guilfoyle, Fred Clark.
114 min. b/w.

White Heat = Scarface + Psycho. Cagney sits in his mother's lap as they plan their heists together with plans provided by classical mythology. In the prison canteen, they tell him she's dead, and he lurches, whimpers, and punches everybody in his way. Finally cornered by the cops on top of an oil refinery, he yells 'Made it Ma, to the top of the world, Ma!' and empties his gun into the gas tank to join her in gangster heaven. Despite chronology (deranged by the censor's influence on the studios), this is really the fitting climax of the '30s gangster movie. PH

White Hunter, Black Heart

(Clint Eastwood, 1990, US) Clint Eastwood, Jeff Fahey, George Dzundza, Alun Armstrong, Mel Martin, Marisa Berenson, Charlotte Cornwell, Timothy Spall, Boy Mathias Chuma.
112 min.

In this adaptation by Peter Viertel from his thinly fictionalised account of John Huston's arrogant antics immediately prior to filming *The African Queen*, Eastwood – directing himself as Huston/'Wilson' – proffers a supremely intelligent study of a man of monstrous selfishness and often irresistible charm, whose overwhelming passion for hunting drives him inexorably toward what even he acknowledges as an irredeemable sin: killing an elephant. Friendship, the

film, and ordinary ethics are sacrificed on the altar of his ego. Wisely, however, Eastwood doesn't preach or condemn, but simply reveals the man's magnetism while admitting to the terrible consequences of his ambition. After a comparatively stodgy opening in London, the film shifts to Africa, and at once settles into a tone of semi-comic high adventure which never allows the serious themes – wanton ecological destruction, colonial racism, and the necessity of remaining true to oneself – to lapse into portentousness. Ably aided by a fine cast and Jack Green's no-nonsense photography, Eastwood constructs a marvellously pacy, suspenseful movie which is deceptively easy on both eye and ear. GA

White Lies (Mentiras piadosas)

(Arturo Ripstein, 1988, Mex) Alonso Echanove, Delia Casanova, Ernesto Yanez, Luisa Hertas, Fernando Palavicini.
100 min.

Virtually from the opening shots, when the stallholder Israel's magical music-box plays 'Love is a Many Splendoured Thing', we know that this is a film more about love than lies. And, since love means dreams, Israel's fantasies take off in the direction of his Phenomenal Museum, north of the Mexican border, which is intended to house a mechanical light-and-music show that Israel has built with his gay friend Matilde. The stars of the show are a collection of fine porcelain dolls, which are forsaken as Israel finds himself falling for Clara, the municipal inspector who threatens to close his market stall. To her he shows a side of life he dare not show his wife: his love of astrology, necromancy and clairvoyance. In so doing, he puts the knowledge of her fate into Clara's hands…Alongside the sadness and inadequacies of the ordinary lives it describes, this is a rich and witty film that prises open the little secrets of the human condition. AH

White Lightning

(Joseph Sargent, 1973, US) Burt Reynolds, Jennifer Billingsley, Ned Beatty, Bo Hopkins, Matt Clark, Louise Latham, Diane Ladd, RG Armstrong.
101 min.

An example of what can go wrong with a movie. Ned Beatty as the corrupt Southern sheriff who drowns two long-hairs in a backwater; the down-home photography; the minor characters who bootleg whisky – they all make it look as if the film has something to say. But with Burt Reynolds, playing it light though all out for revenge as the brother of one of the dead boys, everything becomes one long car chase, and in the end it's just a matter of the fat bald bully getting his comeuppance at the hands of the not-so-fat toupeed hero. Reynolds returned to the character in *Gator* three years later. CPe

White Line Fever

(Jonathan Kaplan, 1975, US) Jan-Michael Vincent, Kay Lenz, Slim Pickens, LQ Jones, Leigh French, Don Porter, Sam Laws, RG Armstrong, Dick Miller.
92 min.

'You're a very charismatic man, Mr Hummer' says the smooth, evil corporation magnate (thereby pointing out something that hadn't hitherto been in evidence) to the young truck-driver who has taken a single-handed stand in refusing to carry stolen goods in his rig. Indeed, Jan-Michael Vincent looks decidedly puny trying to fill a part that would have given Eastwood trouble. This 'youth' movie, in which the lithe Vincent takes on the ageing, paunchy and corrupt – and wins, despite some heavy muscle from the organisation – gives evidence of little more than the recurring need to re-adapt various fantasies from Westerns. But as Vincent takes his stand and cleans up town, he joins a long line of American heroes whose capacity for punishment borders on masochism. There's also some particularly gratuitous agonising over the question of abortion, which is promptly resolved by having the mother-to-be beaten up and losing the child. CPe

White Man's Burden

(Desmond Nakano, 1995, US/Fr) John Travolta, Harry Belafonte, Kelly Lynch, Margaret Avery, Tom Bower, Andrew Lawrence, Bumper Robinson.
89 min.

An off-the-peg crime thriller with a reversible lining, screenwriter Nakano's first film as an indie hyphenate relies for effect on a crude racial twist meant to 'jar viewers out of their polarised complacency'. Sadly, his portrait of a contemporary American society in which the polarities of race and power are merely turned around – rich black boss, put-upon white worker – is so obvious and reductive as to be pointless. Given this, it's hard to imagine how his facile 'What if?' scenario could have lured elder statesman Belafonte out of retirement and attracted the attention of Travolta. Sacked from his job over a simple misunderstanding, Louis Pinnock (loyal working stiff) seeks justice from Thomas (suave, complacent factory owner), but never gets past the security gates of his suburban mansion; later, when he and his family are evicted from their home, Pinnock abducts Thomas at gun-point, and goes on the run. Since it's clear where the film's headed, the fitful plot is forced to tread a fine line between fatalistic inevitability and tedious predictability. NF

White Men Can't Jump

(Ron Shelton, 1992, US) Wesley Snipes, Woody Harrelson, Rosie Perez, Tyra Ferrell, Cylk Cozart, Kadeem Hardison, Ernest Harden Jr.
114 min.

America's homeboy comedy of the year is about basketball only in the sense that writer-director Shelton's *Bull Durham* was about baseball. It's a truly terrific piece of entertainment propelled by the magic and dynamism of its stars. Sidney Deane (Snipes) meets Billy Hoyle (Harrelson) on a public court where the game is played as a mix of macho combat, stand-up comedy and con-artistry. The jokes and banter are wonderful. But this is also a most unlikely buddy movie, where the black/white pair team up as hustlers floating around the rougher areas of Los Angeles, turn on each other, and finally bury the hatchet to get Billy out of hock to some surprisingly obliging hoods. Sadly, in doing so, the duo alienate Billy's long-suffering Hispanic girlfriend (Perez), who dreams of the straight life and spends her time memorising trivia in hopes of a TV game show break. Snipes and Harrelson bounce off the screen like Michael Jordan, while Shelton and cinematographer Russell Boyd perfectly capture the agile thrills of the game itself. A double-whammy slam-dunker of a movie. SGr

White Mischief

(Michael Radford, 1987, GB) Charles Dance, Greta Scacchi, Joss Ackland, Sarah Miles, John Hurt, Geraldine Chaplin, Ray McAnally, Trevor Howard, Susan Fleetwood, Alan Dobie, Jacqueline Pearce.
107 min.

Just in case you miss the point that one's betters are scum, Radford's version of the James Fox book opens on the decadent rich drinking champers in a London underground shelter during an air-raid. They took the party to Kenya, where one adultery too many led to the shooting of Josslyn Hay, twenty-second Earl of Erroll. Since we are never in much doubt that murder is inevitable, know the murderer's identity, and have no sympathy for any of the Happy Valley set, all that's on offer are hopefully scandalous tableaux of rude goings-on. Diana (Scacchi) hooks rich old Sir Jock (Ackland), but falls for the rogering Earl (Dance). Sir Jock bumps him off, gets acquitted, but tops himself anyway. So much for the story. On the sociological side, there's wife-swapping, Trevor Howard peering through a peephole at Scacchi in the bath, lots of drugs and drink, transvestite parties, Sarah Miles smearing her vaginal secretions on the lips of her dead lover in the morgue, and roomy shorts. Irising out on a cocktail party in a cemetery, we say farewell or too-dle-pip to the most stunningly boring crew this side of the Ralph Reader show. BC

White Nights (Le Notti Bianche)

(Luchino Visconti, 1957, It/Fr) Maria Schell, Marcello Mastroianni, Jean Marais, Clara Calamai.
107 min. b/w.

Visconti's version of the Dostoievsky story – about the chance encounter of a couple as she is waiting in vain for her lover, and the obsessive, panic-stricken relationship which then develops between them – later filmed by Bresson as *Four*

Nights of a Dreamer. Visconti traps his characters (three excellent performances) within a claustrophobic canal-side set, and the film is a series of brief walks, chases, attempted escapes, always frustrated. Shot as neo-realist high tragedy, the film offers its characters only one strange moment of escape from their night-time obsessions – a raucous, sexual, subversive scene in a dance-hall. Then the snow comes down, and with it a chilly desperation about the extent of human self-delusion. CA

White Nights

(Taylor Hackford, 1985, US) Mikhail Baryshnikov, Gregory Hines, Jerzy Skolimowski, Helen Mirren, Geraldine Page, Isabella Rossellini, John Glover.
135 min.

After the romance of *An Officer and a Gentleman* and the frequent excitement of *Against All Odds*, one would never have guessed that Taylor Hackford would prove just plain boring. Indeed, the premise of *White Nights* is good: the plane on which a Russian ballet dancer (Baryshnikov) is travelling makes a forced landing in Russia, the land from which he defected to the US ten years previously. But the grinding ins and outs of just what the KGB will use him for are constantly held up for long sequences in which he dances in partnership with Gregory Hines, a black American tap dancer who went to Moscow in protest over Vietnam; nor are these sequences filmed with the formal rigour that dance requires. The virulence of the film's anti-Russian stance makes *Rambo* looks distinctly spineless; and the happy ending is risible. Sole point of interest: Skolimowski as a KGB officer with a smile like liquid nitrogen. CPea

White of the Eye

(Donald Cammell, 1986, GB) David Keith, Cathy Moriarty, Alan Rosenberg, Art Evans, Michael Greene, Danko Gurovich, David Chow, China Cammell.
111 min.

Cammell transforms a stalk'n'slash thriller into a complex, cubist kaleidoscope of themes and images. Paul and Joan White (Keith and Moriarty) lead a happy enough life in a quiet Arizona mining town, until Paul suddenly finds himself chief suspect in a police investigation of a series of violently misogynistic murders. Matters are complicated by the reappearance of Joan's gun-crazy ex-husband (Rosenberg). A determinedly offbeat murder mystery, delving into dotty Indian mysticism and throwing up symbols, red herrings, and Steadicam flourishes for the asking, this nevertheless remains oddly effective. Imbued with a brooding, oppressive atmosphere and coloured by vivid performances, though often murkily motivated, it is genuinely nightmarish in its portrait of relationships where love is blinding and the past casts an intolerably heavy spell. GA

White Palace

(Luis Mandoki, 1990, US) Susan Sarandon, James Spader, Jason Alexander, Kathy Bates, Eileen Brennan, Spiros Focas, Gina Gershon, Steven Hill.
103 min.

In the years following his wife's death, Max (Spader) leads a carefully controlled life: a sense of purpose is found through work, and passion confined to a love of classical music. Then he meets no-nonsense Nora (Sarandon), for whom culture consists of Marilyn Monroe, and whose apartment boasts the Just-Ransacked look. He's 27, Jewish, and an affluent copy-writer; she's 44, Catholic, and a fast-food waitress. Will their affair survive differences in background, the age gap, and Thanksgiving dinner with Max's over-solicitous friends? Glenn Savan's novel offered a stronger exploration of Reaganism and consumerism, but overall he's served well by this intelligent, involving adaptation. There's an unmistakable charge between the two leads, and an acute sense of their mutual confusion. Acting honours go to Sarandon, who brings off a complex depiction of vulgarity, defiance and vulnerability. CM

White Rock

(Tony Maylam, 1976, GB) narrator: James Coburn.
76 min.

The official film of the 1976 Winter Olympics held at Innsbruck isn't even satisfactory as a documentary record of the major events. The trouble is that writer (Maylam) and narrator (Coburn) reduce virtually all the events – ski-jumping, ice hockey, the biathlon, bobsled, slalom, downhill racing – to the rock-bottom level of beefy American locker-room speed, thrills and spills, neglecting to pay any attention to the individual athletes, or (as in Herzog's *The Great Ecstasy of Woodcarver Steiner*) the inherent spiritual attraction of the sports on view. Coburn's running commentary seems more interested in recording his own participation in death-defying stunts (taking front position on a two-man bobsleigh, for instance) than in interviewing any of the athletes; while Rick Wakeman's 'bubble and squeak' synthesiser soundtrack and much flashy editing do little to gloss over the poverty of this tedious film. RM

White Room

(Patricia Rozema, 1990, Can/GB) Kate Nelligan, Maurice Godin, Margot Kidder, Sheila McCarthy, Barbara Gordon.
90 min.

A distinct change of tack for writer-director Rozema after the quirky *I've Heard the Mermaids Singing*, this strange, arty film follows a weedy voyeur (Godin) who witnesses a pop star's murder and meets a reclusive mystery woman who has the dead singer's voice. Although Sheila McCarthy provides a little light relief as the voyeur's wacky sidekick, and Kate Nelligan makes a strong impression as the recluse, the film virtually falls into abstraction. Imagine a Brian De Palma script directed by Jane Campion – or, better yet, watch it for yourself. TCh

White Sands

(Roger Donaldson, 1992, US) Willem Dafoe, Mary Elizabeth Mastrantonio, Mickey Rourke, Sam Jackson, M Emmet Walsh, Mimi Rogers, James Rebhorn, Maura Tierney.
101 min.

Deputy sheriff Ray Dolezal (Dafoe, in an assured performance) is an upstanding citizen, complete with wife (Rogers), son and white stetson. But life in his backwater New Mexico town is thrown into turmoil after the discovery of an apparent suicide victim, together with a case containing $500,000. Assuming the corpse's identity to investigate the mystery, Ray encounters villains who relieve him of the loot and the clothes off his back; but worse is to come in a meeting with FBI agent Meeker (Jackson), who reveals that the money belonged to the Bureau. It's all down to the do-good deputy to get it back, which means making friends with both shady-lady Lane Bodine (Mastrantonio) and Gorman Lennox (Rourke), who has the money earmarked for a weapons deal. In the absence of real substance, Donaldson's stylish direction borders on the self-conscious, though cinematographer Peter Menzies Jr captures images of startling richness and clarity. CM

White Sheik, The
(Lo Sceicco Bianco)

(Federico Fellini, 1951, It) Alberto Sordi, Brunella Bovo, Leopoldo Trieste, Giulietta Masina, Lilia Landi.
88 min. b/w.

Fellini's first solo feature, a delightful satirical comedy about a young honeymoon couple (Bovo and Trieste) who arrive in Rome with the wife yearning after her romantic ideal, *The White Sheik*, star of one of the *fumetti* (the photographic comic strips so popular in Italy). While she dashes off for a glimpse of her hero (Sordi), incarnated by a bedraggled hack actor who vainly tries to preen himself to meet her expectations, the disconsolate husband spends a lonely night wandering the streets until he meets a friendly prostitute. Agreeably abrasive in its attitude to illusions and the self-delusions that fuel them, vitriolically funny in evoking the world of the fumetti, Fellini lapses only briefly into his later mystico-sentimentality in the character of the prostitute (played, of course, by Masina). TM

White Squall

(Ridley Scott, 1996, US) Jeff Bridges, Caroline Goodall, Scott Wolf, John Savage, Jeremy Sisto, Ryan Phillippe, David Lascher, Balthazar Getty.
129 min.

Based on a real-life memoir, this nautical rites-of-passage story set in 1960 sees a crew of teenage boys on a school ship maturing rapidly under the hard-but-fair tutelage of 'Skipper' Sheldon (Bridges). They gain valuable lessons in character, responsibility and individual integrity as the 'Albatross' sails from the Caribbean into a ferocious hurricane that will fatefully test the mettle of all on board. Although the early sequences win no prizes for originality, Scott bathes his handsome young charges in plenty of tropical sun and draws a convincing partnership between brooding old hand Sheldon and his ship's doctor spouse (an impressively natural Goodall), which gives the material an emotional core later to prove deceptively potent. It is, however, the 'white squall' sequence that stands way above anything else in the movie, detailing with you-are-there intensity the vessel's helpless plight as she's buffeted by a series of enormous waves and the Skipper battles to keep her upright. This particular landlubber felt like jelly for the rest of the day, notwithstanding the hokey courtroom showdown that closes the picture. TJ

White Tower, The

(Ted Tetzlaff, 1950, US) Glenn Ford, Claude Rains, Alida Valli, Oscar Homolka, Cedric Hardwicke, Lloyd Bridges.
98 min.

Against a daunting Swiss mountain, pit an ill-assorted bunch of climbers: gruff guide (Homolka), diffident Yank (Ford), ex-Hitler Youth member (Bridges), alcoholic writer (Rains), English no-hoper (Hardwicke), and a woman trying to live up to her father's reputation (Valli). Then watch the mountain polarise their characters; the uncommitted find true grit, the weak go to the wall, and blond Teutons who rely on the 'Will to Power' tend to flake off and die. Even the heroine forsakes the summit for true love on the south col, and Glenn Ford becomes as obsessed as he was in *Gilda*, except that here it's a rock pile rather than Rita Hayworth. Can you take a Freudian *Eiger Sanction*? Come to that, has there ever been a great mountain movie? CPea

White Wall, The
(Den Vita Väggen)

(Stig Björkman, 1974, Swe) Harriet Andersson, Lena Nyman, Sven Wollter, Tomas Pontén, Rolf Larsson.
79 min.

Given that its central performance by Harriet Andersson is technically perfect, this study of female frustration displays hardly any other redeeming features. Settling for a one-track, frankly boring delineation of the tribulations of a newly-separated woman of 35, it progresses (infinitely slowly) by means of a line of clichéd encounters with representative boorish males and sympathetic girlfriend towards a cop-out fadeout that is the ultimate in arty pretentiousness. Throughout, the film treats Andersson's character as a 'specimen' under glass, even going so far as to parallel her situation with that of her son's goldfish. A sign of Björkman's inability to think his subject through is that he has to despatch the young son from the narrative halfway through; while his oblique references to Bergman merely highlight the emptiness of his own concept. PT

White Zombie

(Victor Halperin, 1932, US) Bela Lugosi, Madge Bellamy, Robert Frazer, Brandon Hurst, John Harron, Joseph Cawthorn.
73 min. b/w.

A dream-like encounter between Gothic romance and 'primitive' mythology, with an American innocent (Bellamy) plucked from her wedding feast and consigned to walk with the Haitian living dead by voodoo master Lugosi. Halperin shoots this poetic melodrama as trance; insinuating ideas and images of possession, defloration, and necrophilia into a perfectly stylised design, with the atmospherics conjuring echoes of countless resonant fairytales. The unique result constitutes a virtual bridge between classic Universal horror and the later Val Lewton productions. PT

Who?

(Jack Gold, 1974, GB) Elliott Gould, Trevor Howard, Joseph Bova, Ed Grover, James Noble, John Lehne.
93 min.

Looking rather better on TV than on the big screen, where its rough edges show up more, this is a very passable adaptation of a fine sci-fi/espionage novel by Algis Budrys. The basic premise is vividly laid out as an American scientist (Bova), injured in a car crash on the Russian border, is returned to the West after advanced medical treatment which has him looking like a Martian invader with a prosthetic metal head. Thereafter the script develops cold feet, and obscures its detective theme – is this the same man, and can he be safely returned to his secret research? – by making tiresome concessions to action adventure (routine car chase and so forth). MA

Who Am I This Time?
(Jonathan Demme, 1982, US) Susan Sarandon, Christopher Walken, Robert Ridgeley, Dorothy Paterson.
60 min.
Made for television, Demme's adaptation of a Kurt Vonnegut story is totally delightful. Sarandon is the new girl in town who joins an amateur dramatics group and falls for local star Walken. The only trouble is that, offstage, he is terminally shy. Finally, of course, she gets her man, but not before Demme has fleshed out the slim plot with vivid, likeable characters (both leads are superb), and a great deal of charm and wit. One of his very best. GA

Who Are You Polly Maggoo? (Qui êtes-vous Polly Maggoo?)
(William Klein, 1966, Fr) Dorothy McGowan, Jean Rochefort, Sami Frey, Philippe Noiret, Grayson Hall, Delphine Seyrig, Joanna Shimkus.
102 min. b/w.
First feature for Klein, the American expatriate king of visual razzmatazz and strident satire, drawing on his own early background in fashion photography. Polly Maggoo (McGowan) is a suddenly famous model whose true personality is probed by a multitude of people, including a TV interviewer (Noiret) and a lovelorn Ruritanian prince (Frey) who dispatches two secret agents to grab her for his own. Klein's satiric targets may be nothing more than clay pigeons (we all know about media madness), but it's churlish to complain when he shoots at them in such an agreeably nutty way. GB

Who Dares Wins
(Ian Sharp, 1982, GB) Lewis Collins, Judy Davis, Richard Widmark, Edward Woodward, Robert Webber, Tony Doyle, John Duttine, Kenneth Griffith, Rosalind Lloyd, Ingrid Pitt, Norman Rodway, Patrick Allen.
125 min.
Inspired by the Iranian Embassy siege, a kiddie-comic yarn about hardcore terrorists who subvert the 'Peace Lobby' and mount an armed attack on the American ambassador's London residence, holding the assembled VIP company to ransom. The terrorists are, of course, a ham-fisted bunch led by a sexy American bourgeoise (Davis), and they haven't reckoned with the superhuman skills and no-nonsense brutality of the SAS. Beneath the gung-ho action, the ideology of the movie stinks. Peace lobbyists are portrayed as spineless liberals, women are epitomised as the power-crazed rich bitch or the faithful wife-and-mother, and the SAS (following their 'heroic' image in the popular press) is depicted as an élite of supermen. A film to make the uncommitted want to join the next anti-nuclear demonstration from sheer outrage. MA

Whoever Says the Truth Will Die
(Philo Bregstein, 1981, Neth) Laura Betti, Bernardo Bertolucci, Alberto Moravia, Antonietta Macciochi.
59 min.
Even for someone disillusioned by the fall-off in originality of Pasolini's later films, this neat little documentary exerts considerable interest. Hardly surprising, given that the director led a pretty colourful life, making his name first as a poet and novelist, hanging out with the denizens of Rome's poorest suburbs, and repeatedly coming into conflict with the authorities (tried and acquitted 33 times) for his homosexuality and political views. Bregstein's film attempts to understand the man

himself and his place in Italian art and politics, while also questioning the verdict that had Pasolini killed by a single 17-year-old boy in 'self-defence after sexual threats'. From various pieces of evidence, it does indeed seem that no one person could have carried out such a brutal mutilation, nor would have wanted to. Whatever one feels about the answer posited here, however, it's a fascinating and provocative look at a complex and disturbing man. GA

Who Framed Roger Rabbit
(Robert Zemeckis, 1988, US) Bob Hoskins, Christopher Lloyd, Joanna Cassidy, Stubby Kaye, Alan Tilvern.
104 min.
Ever since his brother's death, seedy gumshoe Eddie Valiant (Hoskins) has hated Toons – the animated inhabitants of the '40s LA suburb of Toontown, most of whom make a living appearing in Hollywood cartoons. But when studio head Marvin Acme asks him to check up on the extra-marital activities of Jessica Rabbit, the humanoid, torch-singing, Toon spouse of our eponymous stunt-Toon hero, Eddie finds himself up to his fedora in murder, blackmail, and conspiracy. Zemeckis and Richard Williams' comedy-thriller blends live action, Warners-style animation, and a typically tortuous film noir plot to delirious effect. Virtually faultless on the technological front, it also excels in terms of a breathless, wise-cracking script, deft characterisation (both human and Toon), and rousing action. At its best, the humour is as cruel, violent, and surreal as vintage Chuck Jones. Supremely entertaining – especially for adults. BC

Who Is Harry Kellerman and Why Is He Saying Those Terrible Things About Me?
(Ulu Grosbard, 1971, US) Dustin Hoffman, Barbara Harris, Jack Warden, David Burns, Dom DeLuise, Betty Walker, Gabriel Dell, Regina Baff.
108 min.
Hoffman (oddly cast but excellent) as a fabulously successful rock musician driven to a head-shrinker by problems of ageing, loneliness, and the mysterious caller who is alienating his harem of women by casting libellous aspersions on his character. Waywardly whimsical in its satire of material success and the analyst's couch, the film suffered a critical clobbering. But it is also strangely moving, peopled by marvellously vivid characters dredged out of the hero's past and lending undertones of real pain and longing to the otherwise formulary comedy as he becomes a minor league Citizen Kane, beleaguered by sad ghosts in his lonely Xanadu (a New York penthouse lined with golden discs and Time magazine covers). Barbara Harris is outstanding as the would-be singer who belatedly shows him what-might-have-been. TM

Who Is Killing the Great Chefs of Europe? (aka Too Many Chefs)
(Ted Kotcheff, 1978, US/WGer) George Segal, Jacqueline Bisset, Robert Morley, Jean-Pierre Cassel, Philippe Noiret, Jean Rochefort, Madge Ryan.
112 min.
With exotic food providing the ground-bass imagery, it is only fitting that the film's one funny line should be delivered by walk-on Mr Chow, restaurateur to the rich and famous. The rest is a heavy plough through all the familiar routes along which comedy-thrillers frequently get lost: travelogue backdrops of Venice, Paris and London, gourmet Robert Morley doing battle with super-Wildean courage against unspeakable lines, a plot involving the methodical extinction of European chefs in various nasty ways (Noiret in a duck-press), and a level of joking which never exceeds puns on Bombe Surprise. Saddest of all is Segal's vulgarity, unleavened by his usually strong sense of irony. The only funny thing about all this is why Robert Aldrich was at one time interested in directing it. CPea

Who Killed Vincent Chin?
(Christine Choy/Renee Tajima, 1988, US)
87 min.
In June 1982, Vincent Chin, a Chinese American

draftsman, was beaten to death by two baseball-bat-wielding thugs outside a McDonald's in Detroit. Despite protests from the local Asian community, the murderers received three years' probation for manslaughter and a fine of $3,750: neither spent more than one night in jail. This documentary charts the growth of an emotive civil rights protest, the murderers' subsequent retrial, and the personal confusion of all involved. Through extensive interviews with killer Ronald Ebens, a honey-tongued redneck, and Lily Chin, Vincent's mother, an icon of inarticulate grief, the film builds to an outraged climax as the case continues to evade the much-vaunted American way of justice. Detailed, terse, and politically compelling. RS

Whole Town's Talking, The (aka Passport to Fame)
(John Ford, 1935, US) Edward G Robinson, Jean Arthur, Wallace Ford, Arthur Hohl, Edward Brophy, Arthur Byron, Donald Meek.
95 min. b/w.
A brisk, snappy comedy with Robinson in a double role: as the timid, dependable clerk Jones, and the notorious gangster, Killer Mannion. An accountant with a cat he calls Abelard and a canary named Heloise, Jones dreams of exotic places and his spunky colleague Miss Clark (Arthur). It is only after he has been mistaken for his doppelgänger (who then 'borrows' the special ID card issued to the clerk by the police to avoid similar errors in the future) that Jones finds the courage of his convictions. Adapted from a WR Burnett story by Frank Capra's regular collaborators Robert Riskin and Jo Swerling, this low budget comedy sneaked past the Hays Office ban on gangster movies, but proved so popular that the genre was immediately revived. Ford may parody the conventions of the crime film, but his picture is as subversive as any Little Caesar: when the worm turns, it might as well be on his boss or on the police as on the hoods who have kidnapped his precious Miss Clark. TCh

Who'll Stop the Rain? (aka Dog Soldiers)
(Karel Reisz, 1978, US) Nick Nolte, Tuesday Weld, Michael Moriarty, Anthony Zerbe, Richard Masur, Ray Sharkey, Gail Strickland, Charles Haid, David Opatoshu.
126 min.
A traumatised Vietnam war correspondent can draw 'no more cheap morals' from the bloody absurdity around him. 'In a world where elephants are pursued by flying men, everyone's gonna want to get high' he reasons, as he blindly steps into the heroin business and joins the 'Dog Soldiers' of Robert Stone's novel and Reisz's excellent adaptation. Involving old buddy Nolte and his own wife Weld in his doomed dope deal, he precipitates a compelling chase through the corrupt moral wasteland of counter-culture/CIA-culture America. On the way, Washington powerplay is mirrored in the casual sadism of the pursuers, and the conventional 'MacGuffin' role of the 2kg bag takes on a metaphorical charge. Reisz nimbly avoids the Big Theme style, finds the pace of his material early, and sustains it brilliantly, emerging with a contemporary classic of hard-edged adventure and three superb character studies. PT

Wholly Moses!
(Gary Weis, 1980, US) Dudley Moore, Laraine Newman, James Coco, Paul Sand, Jack Gilford, Dom DeLuise, John Houseman, Madeline Kahn, David L Lander, Richard Pryor, John Ritter.
109 min.
An opportunistic attempt to cash in on the diminutive Moore's post 10 stardom by shamelessly ripping off the premise of The Life of Brian. Here we have, instead of the Gospels, a Funny Thing Happened on the Way to the Promised Land, with Moore cast as the character denied his rightful place in Biblical history by some upstart called Moses. The director of Saturday Night Live opts for a comic style which falls uneasily between the New American anarchic comic farce and that pioneered by the 'Python' team. A string of promising cameos – DeLuise, Kahn, Pryor – none of which come off, and an underwritten script leave one very unsatisfied. Cecil B DeMille was cubits more comical than anything on show here. RM

Who Needs a Heart

(John Akomfrah, 1991, GB) Caroline Burghard, Treva Ettiene, Ruth Gemmell.
80 min. b/w & col.
Another very lively experimental film from the Black Audio Film Collective in the wake of *Handsworth Songs*, this is akin to a sophisticated home-movie history, a record of life on the fringes in London between 1965 and 1975. Inspired by the black political figurehead and/or criminal Michael X, the film nevertheless holds him at a distance, tracing his career through contemporary TV and radio bulletins which counterpoint and parallel the lives of a group of (racially mixed) friends and lovers involved in the Black Power movement. Dialogue is strictly a subsidiary element in Trevor Mathison's allusive, inventive sound design; narrative emerges in snatches, as Akomfrah flashes back from 1972 to the early '60s, and then forwards, recalling the properties of the times in music, fashion and art. It's an outside-in approach to cinema, and to politics, but there's more humour than pretension here. An intriguing, rewarding film. TCh

Whooping Cough (Szamárköhögés)

(Péter Gárdos, 1987, Hun) Marcell Tóth, Eszter Kárász, Deszõ Garas, Judit Hernádi, Mari Törõcsik, Anna Fehér.
87 min.
The Hungarian cinema tackles the October 1956 uprising again, this time seen through the eyes of two mischievous children in a family of confused and desperate adults. For the most part, the film is attractive and well staged, but the grinning brats are allowed to hog the camera too much, and the climactic intrusion of reality on their playground is badly fudged. DT

Whoops Apocalypse

(Tom Bussmann, 1986, GB) Loretta Swit, Peter Cook, Michael Richards, Rik Mayall, Ian Richardson, Alexei Sayle, Herbert Lom, Joanne Pearce.
91 min.
Charting the course of international misunderstanding, writers Andrew Marshall and David Renwick – of the original TV series – return with this feature length comedy lampooning events of the 'near future'. The film centres on a South American invasion by the 'Maguadorans' of British 'Santa Maya', and a British PM determined to give the public what it demands – a nuclear strike in retaliation. Despite the potential, the film sticks meekly to a conventional framework, with gags that never manage to sink their teeth into the tenuous absurdity of international affairs as *Dr Strangelove* did. The mechanical antics, though at times amusing, amount to a timid distraction – kind of like riding the underground in the rush hour. SGo

Whore

(Ken Russell, 1991, US) Theresa Russell, Benjamin Mouton, Antonio Fargas, Sanjay, Elizabeth Morehead, Michael Crabtree, John Diehl, Jack Nance, Frank Smith.
92 min.
Released in a version cut by 7 minutes, one part downbeat docudrama and two parts Russell rant, this adaptation of David Hines' play *Bondage* lacks the visual imagination and cutting edge of the director's earlier *Crimes of Passion*. He seems constrained by the seedy naturalism as low-rent hooker Liz (Theresa Russell) walks the streets, keeping one eye out for the vicious pimp she fled earlier. Delivering most of her lines direct to camera, the foul-mouthed Liz lectures the audience on the routine abuse and humiliations she suffers in her line of work. Bullied, beaten and branded by her sadistic pimp (Mouton), Liz has a sneaking affection for some of her older clients, but knows that most of them 'don't want sex, they want revenge'. Flashbacks to a broken marriage and a son taken into care bespeak an equally unhappy past, but there are occasional, fleeting moments of human tenderness. What is most depressing, given the hectoring tone of Liz's monologues, is the way the film comes alive when her hateful pimp usurps the voice-over to brag about his entrepreneurial skills. NF

Whores, The (Le Buttane)

(Aurelio Grimaldi, 1994, It) Ida di Benedetto, Guia Jelo, Lucia Sardo, Sandra Sindoni.
85 min. b/w.
An engagingly ramshackle, mostly light-hearted look at the lives of a group of prostitutes (one of them male), shot in b/w with a simplicity at times faintly reminiscent of Pasolini. Without moralising, Grimaldi proffers (largely inconsequential) vignettes revelling in the details of everyday life: the bitching, the camaraderie, the dealings with pimps and clients, the lack of business on Christmas Day. The overall matter-of-fact tone creates, for the most part, a surprising aura of sweet innocence, though odd moments involving violence and racism (a number of the women's johns are Turks and Moroccans) acknowledge the potential dangers of prostitution. Minor, then, but funny, perceptive and, now and then, touching. GA

Who's Afraid of Virginia Woolf?

(Mike Nichols, 1966, US) Elizabeth Taylor, Richard Burton, George Segal, Sandy Dennis.
132 min. b/w.
Edward Albee's vitriolic stage portrayal of domestic blisslessness translated grainily and effectively to the screen. Taylor gives what is probably her finest performance as the blowsy harridan Martha, while Burton is not quite so hammy as usual as her angst-ridden college professor husband. The verbal fireworks that occur when they invite a young couple to dinner are surprisingly convincing. In an interview much later, Sandy Dennis said that, amazingly, Taylor and Burton were in fact very happy together at the time. It doesn't show on screen. The film's one problem, however, is that it's played so relentlessly for realism, when in fact the subject is at least half fantasy. A very loud film. GA

Whose Life Is It Anyway?

(John Badham, 1981, US) Richard Dreyfuss, John Cassavetes, Christine Lahti, Bob Balaban, Kenneth McMillan, Kaki Hunter, Janet Eilber.
118 min.
To be fair, this is a livelier film than you'd expect, considering that its subject is a paralysed patient's struggle for the right to die. Badham has done his best to see that this adaptation of Brian Clark's play is filled with humour and emotion, and he's helped by a verbally energetic performance from Dreyfuss. But popular cinema is ultimately not about talk, and for all its verbal pyrotechnics, the film has the unmistakable narrative thinness of the filmed play. One of the results is that our sympathy for the eternally wisecracking Dreyfuss is stretched to the limit. 'So far as I am concerned' says Dreyfuss at one point, 'I am dead already'. Yet, despite some moving scenes, this is precisely what the film never conveys. DP

Who's Harry Crumb?

(Paul Flaherty, 1989, US) John Candy, Jeffrey Jones, Annie Potts, Tim Thowerson, Barry Corbin, Shawnee Smith.
90 min.
Candy makes the transition from sidekick to stardom as Harry Crumb, bumbling private eye. The plot is a lightweight concotion for a heavyweight hero, concerning the kidnapped daughter of multi-millionaire PJ Downing (Corbin). The incompetent sleuth has been given the assignment because the corrupt head of the investigation agency (Jones) is involved in the kidnapping and has every confidence that Crumb will fail. But, as always in such cases, stupidity triumphs over cynicism. Things plod to their inevitable conclusion, helped along by the script's assortment of stereotypical underdogs and manipulators, and with Candy hamming up the oppourtunity to get into lots of tight spots while wearing funny disguises. At their silliest, such moments actually provide light relief from an otherwise unremarkable comedy caper. CM

Who's That Girl

(James Foley, 1987, US) Madonna, Griffin Dunne, Haviland Morris, John McMartin, Bibi Besch, John Mills, Robert Swan, Drew Pillsbury.
94 min.
Would-be madcap comedy wallowing in the wake of *Bringing Up Baby*. Inoffensive Dunne, who wouldn't even park next to a fire hydrant, is sent to collect Madonna from jail and put her on a bus out of town, and to collect a species of cougar from the docks. The girl and the cat are kindred spirits, of course, and demonstrate their emancipation from dreary old straight life at every opportunity, to the mortification of their keeper. She's out to clear her name, the bad guys are out to stop her, but in the nick of time Dunne resurrects his skill with a rapier. Sir John Mills appears, briefly and embarrassingly, as a life-affirming zoo owner, and the billing and cooing in his menagerie finally activates our hero's libido. Tiring stuff. BC

Who's That Knocking at My Door? (aka I Call First)

(Martin Scorsese, 1968, US) Harvey Keitel, Zina Bethune, Lennard Kuras, Ann Collette, Michael Scala, Catherine Scorsese.
90 min. b/w.
Scorsese's first feature. Set in New York's Little Italy, and what amounts to a dress rehearsal for *Mean Streets*, this displays all the excesses of a first effort. Although technically under the spell of European cinema (Godard et al), the film is just as much a tribute to Hollywood (Ford, Hawks) and more experimental Americans, particularly Anger and Cassavetes. But behind this melange there's no doubting the talent. In the aggressive self-confidence, the use of rock music, and the perceptive observation, Scorsese reveals an anthropological feel for street life and the attitudes of male adolescence, particularly how introversion and weakness are reserved for moments with the opposite sex, kept carefully apart from the mainstream of life. CPe

Who's the Man?

(Ted Demme, 1993, US) Richard Bright, Dr Dré, Ed Lover, Denis Leary, Badja Djola, Cheryl 'Salt' James, Jim Moody, Ice T, Andre B Blake.
85 min.
A celebration of the hold that hip-hop's extended family of megastar rappers and DJs has on America, Demme's second film has rounded up a roster of stars. It's ostensibly about the threat posed to the community when evil property developer Demetrius (Bright) unveils his plans for Harlem. The only building in the way of his scheme is a barber shop, owned by pillar of the community, Nick. With the plot established, the film turns into a platform for rap stars Dr Dré and Ed Lover. Styled as a sort of black Abbott and Costello for the '90s, the pair exercise their appalling hairdressing skills in Nick's shop, until they become too much of a liability. Their natural timing goes a long way towards making the movie an effortless 85 minutes, but the 'raucous comedy' billing is justified only occasionally once they join the NYPD. Some diverting cameos. PP

Who Shot Patakango? (aka Who Shot Pat?)

(Robert Brooks, 1990, US) David Knight, Sandra Bullock, Kevin Otto, Aaron Ingram, Brad Randall.
102 min.
This slice of teen nostalgia (featuring an early appearance by Sandra Bullock) captures the life and times of a Brooklyn high school in 1957, during the moment of transition when a wave of migrant blacks arrived from the South and populated what had till then been a predominantly white down-home territory. Matters are enlivened somewhat by a plethora of vintage hits. TJ

Why? (Detenuto in Attesa di Giudizio)

(Nanni Loy, 1971, It) Alberto Sordi, Elga Andersen, Lino Banfi, Giuseppe Anatrelli, Tano Cimarosa.
102 min.
A film that attracted a certain amount of attention as an indictment of the hopelessly corrupt and inhuman Italian penal system. Sordi plays an expatriate engineer returning to Italy on holiday with his Swedish wife and kids. He is promptly arrested for no apparent reason, shipped from jail to jail, jumps through absurd legal hoops, and worries himself into an asylum for the criminally insane before even getting near a trial. The film suffers from looking like an American light comedy, and Sordi's performance diverts events away from an excursion into Kafka territory. It occasionally manages to rise above itself: a homosexual near-rape; a sharp portrayal of a prison governor; the boredom and dis-

comfort of long train journeys; the indignity of being watched while trying to shit. But for the most part it plays safe. CPe

Why Bother to Knock

see Don't Bother to Knock

Why Did Bohdi-Dharma Leave for the Orient? (Dharmaga tongjoguro kan kkadalgun?)

(Bae Yong-Kyun, 1989, SKor) Yi Pan-Yong, Sin Won-Sop, Huang Hae-Jin, Ko Su-Myong.
135 min.
Made completely utside the Korean film industry, this was a four-year labour of love for Bae, a 38-year-old teacher of painting. The title (an unanswerable zen riddle) gives a fair indication of his purpose and methods, which have nothing to do with drama but everything to do with Frommian notions of self-realisation and spiritual fulfillment. A zen master on the verge of physical death has two disciples, a young monk and an orphaned boy novice; the film shows their ascetic lives in a mountain retreat, and traces a cycle of death and rebirth that seems to guide the two disciples towards enlightenment. Of course, hardly anything happens in action terms. But the photography (worthy of Ansel Adams) and the imagery cast a potent spell, and the film comes as close as any other movie of the '80s to expressing the inexpressible. TR

Why Me?

(Gene Quintano, 1989, US) Christopher Lambert, Kim Greist, Christopher Lloyd, JT Walsh, Gregory Millar, Wendel Meldrum, Michael J Pollard, John Plana.
87 min.
A lacklustre action comedy that woefully fails to exploit the talents of its stars. When bungling safe-cracker Gus Cardinal (Lambert, miscast) and his eccentric accomplice Bruno (Lloyd) accidentally steal a cursed Turkish ruby known as the Byzantine Fire, much contrived capery ensues. The hapless pair are pursued by Turks, the CIA, the LAPD, and a bunch of deranged Armenians obsessed with preventing the rise of the Ottoman Empire. Based (very loosely) on a novel by Donald Westlake, this bears all the hallmarks of a straight-to-video production: functional script, limp direction, workaday performances and perfunctory stunt sequences, all played out amid the drab, tedious surroundings of Los Angeles. Lloyd attempts half-heartedly to enliven the proceedings with his characteristic blend of deadpan daftness, but it's a losing battle. Kim Greist is entirely wasted as the obligatory love interest. Less a case of why me than what for? MK

Why Shoot the Teacher

(Silvio Narizzano, 1976, Can) Bud Cort, Samantha Eggar, Chris Wiggins, Gary Reineke, John Friesen, Michael J Reynolds, Kenneth Griffith.
99 min.
Earnest amiability is both the keynote and the principal weakness of this movie, in which Cort stars as an adolescent Montreal teacher who takes up a post in the wilds of Depression Saskatchewan, where he learns about Life, Love, and Manhood the hard way. Impeccably good intentions are betrayed by occasional lapses of probability, and the project suffers from predictable faults: no reason is offered for the hardship of the people's lives other than the harsh climate; the 'realism' of it all breeds lush landscape photography. But as a hesitant testimony to a historical period (the growth of a Dominion into a nation), it manages its clichés with considerable grace. CA

Why Worry?

(Fred Newmeyer/Sam Taylor, 1923, US) Harold Lloyd, Jobyna Ralston, John Aasen, Leon White, Wallace Howe.
6 reels. b/w.
Not so much one of Harold Lloyd's thrill comedies, more a gag-packed celebration of/satire on the American go-getter determination that was an essential part of his persona. Here he's a wealthy hypochondriac advised to take the sun, and landing up in a strife-torn banana republic where, with the help of a giant he befriends in jail after pulling his sore tooth, he quells a revolution... simply to ensure peace and quiet for himself. There's no denying the technical expertise

behind the endless gags, but the remorseless optimism, coupled with the general blandness of Lloyd's character (there's no development here), makes the film somewhat wearying. GA

Why Would I Lie?

(Larry Peerce, 1980, US) Treat Williams, Lisa Eichhorn, Gabriel Swann, Susan Heldfond, Anne Byrne, Valerie Curtin, Jocelyn Brando.
105 min.
Comedy-romance with Williams as an habitual liar who's set to pick up a family inheritance if he can demonstrate he's doing something worthwhile with his life. Enter seven-year-old orphan Swann and love interest Eichhorn to try to prove his case. Heldfond makes for a feminist caricature villainess, and to tell the truth the overall point remains somewhat opaque. TJ

Wichita

(Jacques Tourneur, 1955, US) Joel McCrea, Vera Miles, Wallace Ford, Edgar Buchanan, Lloyd Bridges, Peter Graves, Robert Wilke, Jack Elam, Mae Clarke.
81 min.
'Everything Goes in Wichita' boast the signposts. The railroad has put the town on the map, but those businessmen set to become rich off the influx of hungry, thirsty, rowdy cattlemen are also concerned that their property should be protected against the cowboys' worst excesses. They persuade the reluctant Wyatt Earp (McCrea) to accept the marshal's badge, but have second thoughts when his civic law and order policies contradict their commercial instincts. This smooth, unassuming Western fits in neatly between the idealism of Ford's *My Darling Clementine* (1946) and the cynicism of Dmytryk's *Warlock* (1959). It ends optimistically enough, with Earp and his new bride leaving for a date with destiny in Dodge City, but not before the loss of at least two innocents, and many more gunmen. TCh

Wicked City, The (Yaoshou Dushi)

(Mai Tai Kit, 1992, HK) Jackie Cheung, Leon Lai, Michelle Li, Yuen Wo Ping.
90 min.
Special-effects hi-jinks from Tsui Hark's Film Workshop framed as a cross between Blade Runner and Japanese manga. Pop stars Jackie Cheung and Leon Lai, special-unit cops of the future, are assigned to hunt down and rub out shape-shifting monsters masquerading as humans. They are let down by dodgy visual effects (the climax, involving a 747 and IM Pei's Bank of China Tower, is particularly weak) and by the sheer monotony of the pacing. TR

Wicked Lady, The

(Leslie Arliss, 1945, GB) Margaret Lockwood, James Mason, Patricia Roc, Griffith Jones, Michael Rennie, Enid Stamp-Taylor, Felix Aylmer, Martita Hunt, Jean Kent.
104 min. b/w.
Post-war uplift becomes almost exclusively a matter of Ms Lockwood's cleavage in this period melodrama from Gainsborough that caused a censorious and highly profitable controversy in a teacup for its quaint bawdiness. Lockwood is the amoral aristo thrill-seeker who takes to highway robbery alongside Mason; former critic and screenwriter Arliss the unfortunate director having to contend with the recalcitrant mechanics of Lime Grove studio ruralism. PT

Wicked Lady, The

(Michael Winner, 1983, GB) Faye Dunaway, Alan Bates, John Gielgud, Denholm Elliott, Prunella Scales, Oliver Tobias, Glynis Barber, Joan Hickson.
99 min.
'Bawdy', 'full-blooded', 'boisterous romp' – jaded adjectives hover over this particular filmic carcass, and popular British cinema gets another Carry On Up the Restoration. Charles II is squeezing Nell's oranges ho ho, and the very wonderful Dunaway becomes a roaring girl by night, cantering out from secret back passages and getting their money or their lives from rentacrowd in full-bottomed wigs. No village green without a rollicking maypole, no keyhole without a rutting doxy behind it; Tyburn's in there somewhere, and so is that whip-fight which almost constituted a case for censorship. CPea

Wicked Reporter, The (Gokudo Kisha)

(Rokuro Mochizuki, 1993, Jap) Eiji Okuda, Haku Ryu, Maiko Kawakami, Keiko Suzuki, Makoto Kakeda.
100 min.
More than his indie debut *Skinless Night*, this was the film that launched Mochizuki on his distinctive trajectory through the crime and yakuza genres. Matsuzaki is a racing tipster for a sports paper, a lowlife who spends half his time drunk, hangs out with yakuza and other riff-raff and complicates his sex life by succumbing to advances from his girlfriend's sister. As played by Okuda, he's also a figure of considerable hangdog charm. Less a plot-based movie than a guide to the several forms of high stakes gambling in Japan, this centres on his attempt to help a friend swindled in a bent mahjong game. Korean-Japanese actor Haku Ryu appears (memorably) as an inscrutable yakuza in a black leather jacket. The film's success led to two sequels. TR

Wicked Stepmother

(Larry Cohen, 1988, US) Bette Davis, Lionel Stander, Colleen Camp, David Rasche, Barbara Carrera, Richard Moll, Seymour Cassel, Evelyn Keyes, Tom Bosley.
92 min.
A vegetarian Los Angeles couple return from vacation to find that her father, a widower (Stander), has married a chain-smoking carnivorous weirdo (Davis) and undergone a worrying personality change. The crack-voiced stepmother has a familiar, a cigarette-smoking cat, and a seductive daughter (Carrera), who from time to time appears to take over her body. A ramshackle supernatural spoof, beset with production difficulties, in which Bette Davis made her last, best forgotten screen appearance. JPy

Wicked, Wicked

(Richard L Bare, 1973, US) David Bailey, Tiffany Bolling, Randolph Roberts, Scott Brady, Edd Byrnes, Diane McBain.
95 min.
A silly, wretchedly derivative psycho movie in which a hotel handyman (Roberts), sexually humiliated as a child by his foster mother, goes around in a fright mask dismembering blondes. Bailey is the house dick doing most of the investigating, and Bolling is his ex-wife, conveniently hired by the hotel as resident singer and sporting a blonde wig while performing so that she's up for grabs as the climactic victim. As a gimmick, the film offers 'Duo-vision', which is simply a split screen offering the killer on one side, his victim (or his traumatic memories) on the other. TM

Wicker Man, The

(Robin Hardy, 1973, GB) Edward Woodward, Britt Ekland, Diane Cilento, Ingrid Pitt, Christopher Lee, Lesley Mackie, Walter Carr, Lindsay Kemp.
102 min.
A bona fide British eccentric near-classic: devoutly virginal protestant cop Edward Woodward is lured to a Scottish island to investigate a schoolgirl disappearance, and finds himself embroiled in a pottage of erotic paganism. Expertly scripted by Anthony Shaffer, and cast to get Christopher Lee into drag and Britt Ekland to play Lindsay Kemp's daughter, the movie is let down only by ham-fisted direction. A cult favourite in the US. TR

Wide Sargasso Sea

(John Duigan, 1992, Aust) Karina Lombard, Nathaniel Parker, Rachel Ward, Michael York, Martine Beswicke, Claudia Robinson.
98 min.
Jean Rhys' last novel unlocked the secret behind the door: who was the mysterious madwoman in Rochester's attic in *Jane Eyre*? Rhys imagined her as a Creole Jamaican plantation-owner's daughter and voodoo-child who becomes a victim of clashing cultural loyalties, degenerate family inheritance and disappointed love. Duigan's version retains much of the period detail, but wisely avoids getting swamped by diffuse political allegory, and settles instead as a full blown bodice-ripper. Presumably Karina Lombard was cast as the daughter to embody sensuality and suggest mixed-blood inheritance, but her limitations as an actress forbid audience

identification. Likewise, Parker's Rochester, shipped from Albion for the fateful arranged marriage, is merely a dashing cad. There's little sense of any of the proceedings, but the movie has a fascinating charged quality: Geoff Burton films the Jamaican locations in an intoxicating profusion of colour, and the colonialist soirées and the plantation-house fire are superbly mounted. A strange, dark, muddled dream of a movie, occasionally risible but rarely boring. WH

Widows Peaks

(John Irvin, 1993, GB) Mia Farrow, Joan Plowright, Natasha Richardson, Adrian Dunbar, Jim Broadbent, Gerard McSorley, Tina Kellegher.
101 min.
A peculiar concept, this hill where only single women and widows are permitted to live, but such a place forms the setting for director Irvin's first foray into comedy. Set in 1920s Ireland, it tells of a community of widows, spearheaded by Plowright, which is disrupted by the arrival of spirited war widow Edwina (Richardson, with American accent). Farrow plays the downtrodden Miss O'Hare who immediately takes a violent dislike to Edwina. Both seem to have a difficult past they want hidden, the unravelling of which forms a strong whodunit narrative and, ultimately, a clever plot twist. The robust characterisation of the trio is the film's main strength. JBa

Wifemistress (Mogliamante)

(Marco Vicario, 1977, It) Laura Antonelli, Marcello Mastroianni, Leonard Mann, William Berger, Olga Karlatos.
106 min.
A sickly Antonelli emerges from a moribund marriage to become a New Woman in the course of this classic comedy of concealment, deception, and revelation, played out in Northern Italy in the early 1900s. Vicario, through velvety, sensual camerawork, captures an era of intense intellectual and physical restlessness, when Italy dusted off the *Belle Epoque* and feverishly embraced anarchism, atheism, science, social reform, egalitarianism, and when political and sexual excitement might have seemed interchangeable. The film's shimmering eroticism is delicious. Bertolucci might have made this, if he wasn't such a prig. JS

Wilby Conspiracy, The

(Ralph Nelson, 1974, GB) Sidney Poitier, Michael Caine, Nicol Williamson, Prunella Gee, Persis Khambatta, Saeed Jaffrey, Rutger Hauer, Patrick Allen.
105 min.
Handcuffed together, white Caine and black Poitier pursue smuggled diamonds across the veld, and are themselves chased by the Jo'burg fuzz. Mix in some interracial screwing and violence, and Ralph Nelson's got himself a South African *Soldier Blue*, a sort of tin *Gold*. Assets there are: Caine is served with some nice deadpan lines by Rod Amateau, and John Coquillon's photography is characteristically cool. But this is an unpleasant and invidious film, like *Soldier Blue* creaming the surface off profound racial issues to ease the killing along. Its basic attitude is as leering as Nicol Williamson's security cop. AN

Wild Angels, The

(Roger Corman, 1966, US) Peter Fonda, Nancy Sinatra, Bruce Dern, Lou Procopio, Coby Denton, Marc Cavell, Michael J Pollard, Diane Ladd, Joan Shawlee, Gayle Hunnicutt.
93 min.
First shot: a kid on a trike pedals furiously away from his mother, to be stopped abruptly by a chopper's front wheel. Final shot: Peter Fonda shovels dirt over fellow-Angel Bruce Dern's grave, as police sirens wail closer. Moral: none. Roger Corman's notorious classic remains perhaps the most explicitly nihilistic movie ever made; revealed in retrospect to be less a rebellious youth picture than the extremist culmination of his horror movie cycle. Organised around Dern's death and protracted funeral rites, the film focuses a dispassionate scrutiny on the limits of inarticulate anarchy, with the Hell's Angels characterised with suitably satanic literalness as they 'fall' in the no-choice gulf between the cross

and the swastika. Paradise Lost, indeed, as *non serviam* leads inexorably, and very sourly, to 'nothing to say'...'nowhere to go'. Discomfiting, but timely. PT

Wild at Heart

(David Lynch, 1990, US) Nicolas Cage, Laura Dern, Diane Ladd, Willem Dafoe, Isabella Rossellini, Harry Dean Stanton, Crispin Glover, Grace Zabriskie, JE Freeman, W Morgan Shepherd.
124 min.
As petty criminal Sailor (Cage) and his lover Lula (Dern) go on the run through a murderous Deep South, fleeing but meeting sleazy oddballs hired by Lula's mom (Ladd) to end their relationship, Lynch evokes a surreal, sinister world a mite too reminiscent of his earlier work: bloody murder, violent sexual passion, kooky kitsch, freaky characters immersed in private fantasies, digressive metaphors, symbols and cultish references, and bizarre humour to lighten the nightmare. This *déjà vu* weakens the film; sometimes the weirdness seems so forced that Lynch appears merely to be giving fans what they expect. But it's churlish to focus on flaws when so much is exhilaratingly unsettling. Even more than a virtuoso shoot-out, two scenes – Stanton tortured by a gang of grotesques, a truly nasty car crash – exemplify Lynch's ability to disturb through carefully contrived atmosphere; while the performances lend a consistency of tone lacking in the narrative (but ever-present in Fred Elmes' fine camerawork). The film, finally, is funny, scary and brilliantly cinematic. GA

Wild Bill

(Walter Hill, 1995, US) Jeff Bridges, James Remar, David Arquette, Ellen Barkin, John Hurt.
97 min. b/w & col.
Hill's portrait of Wild Bill Hickok – trapper, gambler, sometime marshal, showman and drifter – is a touch disappointing. It's not the lead performance that's at fault: Bridges is as natural and easy as ever and gives Hickok a complexity and depth barely hinted at by Hill's script which, despite switching deftly between time frames, never really gets beyond the conceit that the legendary hard-livin' shootist cherished surprisingly tender, opium-induced memories of an old flame. In other words, we're more or less in *Judge Roy Bean* territory, with echoes of Leone, Ford and others thrown in for good measure. As various glory hunters turn up in 1870s Deadrock hoping to dispatch the West's fastest draw, and while Hickok himself loses his sight, his desire for Calamity Jane (Barkin) and, perhaps, his lust for life, Hill and cameraman Lloyd Ahern litter the plot proper with attractively bleached b/w flashbacks to 'explain' his reputation and state of mind. The uneven tone shifts between mythic elegy, heroic action and broad, ironic comedy, while the narrative's rapid pace reduces certain characters to mere cameos and, worse, undermines the film's aspirations to epic drama. Both as a modern Western and as a Hill movie, this is efficient but middling – which still, finally, means that it's worth catching. GA

Wild Bill: A Hollywood Maverick

(Todd Robinson, 1995, US) William Wellman, Clint Eastwood, Robert Redford, Sidney Poitier, Gregory Peck, Charles Buddy Rogers, Nancy Reagan, Robert Mitchum, Martin Scorsese.
95 min. b/w & col.
William Augustus Wellman ('My father gave me that name so I'd learn how to fight') came back from the Great War with a new nickname, a steel plate in his head, and enough experience to fuel 76 tough and tender movies, 'films you have to reach for', as Tab Hunter puts it. A handful are classics – the original *A Star Is Born*, *The Public Enemy*, *Nothing Sacred* – but somehow the oeuvre has escaped the critical attention it deserves. At the very least, this thorough, impressive documentary will have you desperate to catch up with half a dozen lesser known titles, but it also serves as a probing biography of a fascinating life. Unusually astute anecdotes and insights come from an all-star line-up: Eastwood, Redford, Peck, Poitier,

Mitchum, Scorsese, even Nancy Reagan, marred only slightly by the Alec Baldwin's purple narration ('directing a motion picture might be akin to helming a ship called Genesis'). TCh

Wild Bunch, The ▓100▓ (100)

(Sam Peckinpah, 1969, US) William Holden, Ernest Borgnine, Robert Ryan, Edmond O'Brien, Warren Oates, Jaime Sanchez, Ben Johnson, Emilio Fernandez, Strother Martin, LQ Jones, Albert Dekker, Bo Hopkins.
145 min.
From the opening sequence, in which a circle of laughing children poke at a scorpion writhing in a sea of ants, to the infamous blood-spurting finale, Peckinpah completely rewrites John Ford's Western mythology – by looking at the passing of the Old West from the point of view of the marginalised outlaws rather than the law-abiding settlers. Though he spares us none of the callousness and brutality of Holden and his gang, Peckinpah nevertheless presents their macho code of loyalty as a positive value in a world increasingly dominated by corrupt railroad magnates and their mercenary killers (Holden's old buddy Ryan). The flight into Mexico, where they virtually embrace their death at the hands of double-crossing general Fernandez and his rabble army, is a nihilistic acknowledgment of the men's anachronistic status. In purely cinematic terms, the film is a savagely beautiful spectacle, Lucien Ballard's superb cinematography complementing Peckinpah's darkly elegiac vision. NF

Wildcats

(Michael Ritchie, 1986, US) Goldie Hawn, Swoosie Kurtz, Robyn Lively, Brandy Gold, James Keach, Jan Hooks, Bruce McGill, Nipsey Russell, Wesley Snipes, Woody Harrelson, M Emmet Walsh, Ann Doran, Gloria Stuart.
107 min.
Football-crazy Goldie Hawn gets her wish to coach a high school team, but there's a catch. It's the roughest, toughest school in the city: Dobermans patrol the halls. Greeted with universal derision by a team of no-hopers, Goldie's got her work cut out for her; but sticking to her credo that 'you can be anything you want to be', she's soon kicking ass. Goldie's inspirational shot at playing Sly Stallone *and* Burgess Meredith is undone by the trite, inner-city Hollywood context she always favours. Instead of 'believe in yourself', the message becomes simply 'make believe'. TCh

Wildcats of St Trinian's, The

(Frank Launder, 1980, GB) Sheila Hancock, Michael Hordern, Joe Melia, Thorley Walters, Rodney Bewes, Deborah Norton, Maureen Lipman, Julia McKenzie.
91 min.
Launder and Gilliat's series about the dreadful girls' boarding school, inspired by Ronald Searle's cartoons, revived after a 14-year absence from the screen. Too late. The '60s versions were already failing in their attempt to find contemporary material on which to hang the myth (for that's what it had become – weekend wet dreams for suburbia). This one should never have been made: the old stock actors (Grenfell, Sim, et al) have died; the storyline is feebly offensive (the girls kidnap the daughter of a rich Arab to press their demand for Trade Union recognition of their strike); and the repressed anarchic energy of the '50s originals (Amazons for Chaos) has just dribbled away into more page three cheesecake. CA

Wild Child, The

see Enfant Sauvage, L'

Wilde

(Brian Gilbert, 1997, GB/US/Jap/Ger) Stephen Fry, Jude Law, Vanessa Redgrave, Jennifer Ehle, Gemma Jones, Judy Parfitt, Michael Sheen, Zoë Wannamaker, Tom Wilkinson, Peter Barkworth.
117 min.
If anybody was born to play Oscar Wilde, it must have been Stephen Fry: not only does he look like the Green Carnation Man, but he himself is often portrayed as being too clever, too complex for his own good. Gilbert's film, with an intelligent screenplay by Julian Mitchell based on Richard Ellmann's biography, looks curiously old-fashioned. More lavish than Merchant Ivory, it's a '60s-style Technicolor affair with a grown-up '90s

feel. Unlike its predecessors, it's able to be frank about the sexual encounters: with devoted friend Robbie Ross; with rent boys to whom Wilde was indulgently generous; and, fatefully, with the love of his life, the beautiful, wilful, spoilt brat Lord Alfred ('Bosie') Douglas, who didn't fancy Wilde, but saw him as the alternative father to his brutal, bullying pater, the Marquess of Queensberry. As Wilde, descending from would-be-doting husband and father to follower of his own 'nature', and finally ruined and disgraced martyr on the tree of English hypocrisy, Fry is utterly convincing. He speaks the witty lines as if he invented them and manages to square Wilde's weakness and arrogance with his immense generosity of spirit, while his prison cell reunion with dying wife Constance (Ehle) would make a traffic warden cry. The cast oozes real class: Redgrave is superb as Wilde's tigerish Irish mother; Wilkinson suitably revolting as Queensberry; Sheen perfect as Ross; and Law explosively arresting as the capricious, finally destructive Douglas. SGr

Wild Flowers
(Les Fleurs Sauvages)
(Jean-Pierre Lefebvre, 1982, Can) Marthe Nadeau, Michèle Magny, Pierre Curzi, Claudia Aubin, Eric Beauséjour.
153 min. b/w & col.
Anyone who has spent Christmas in the company of an ageing relative, and by Boxing Day felt a strangling fit coming on, will be on familiar territory here, with an elderly woman (Nadeau), tight-lipped and fussy, coming to stay for a week in the country with her daughter and grandchildren. Perhaps at 2+ hours of fairly slow-moving action you feel the tedium of the old lady's visit almost as much as her daughter (Magny) – a potter trying to reject a stereotyped role of wife and mother – but the film also raises many interesting questions about the importance of families and the nature of relationships within them. Its main purpose, though, working through this clash between generations, is a plea for tolerance, most effectively expressed in the portions of the film which lapse into black-and-white to indicate what the characters really feel about each other. CS

Wild Flowers
(Robert Smith, 1989, GB) Beatie Edney, Sheila Keith, Colette O'Neil, Stevan Rimkus, Amanda Walker, Kay Gallie.
69 min.
Robert Smith's film is set in a tight Scottish coastal community. Annie (O'Neil), a woman who loves women, is daggers drawn with her mother Marguerite (Keith, a superb performance of implacable bottled-up fury). Annie is a child of her mother's middle age, and Marguerite has laid out the corpses of all four of her brothers. At the centre of this intense, unexpected film, scripted by Sharman Macdonald and handsomely photographed by Witold Stok, is Annie's son Angus (Rimkus), who has returned home from Edinburgh with his friend Sadie (Edney). The trouble is that Angus lacks mettle. He adores nothing so much as the sweet sound of his own singing voice. And Annie finds herself compelled to save Sadie, a fellow free spirit, from this fastidious young man. JPy

Wild for Kicks
see Beat Girl

Wild Game (Wildwechsel)
(Rainer Werner Fassbinder, 1972, WGer) Eva Mattes, Harry Baer, Jörg von Liebenfels, Ruth Drexel, Rudolf Waldemar, Hanna Schygulla, Kurt Raab.
102 min.
Fassbinder made this (for TV) right after The Bitter Tears of Petra von Kant, in the year that Godard made Tout va Bien. Like Godard's film, Fassbinder's is about a male-female relationship in a 'political' context, but here the boy is 19 and the girl only 14, so that their mutual love outrages more than one lower middle class taboo. Despite a final flourish of misogyny (the girl betrays the boy after he's laid his life on the line for her), Fassbinder's stance is very sympathetically unsentimental; and his mixture of caricature (her parents), materialism (the depiction of a factory production line), carefully stylised realism (the central relationship), and a bold physical frank-

ness, is more than usually adroit. The movie created a censorship furore in Germany, not least because the author of the original play (Franz Kroetz) denounced Fassbinder's 'obscene' depiction of his characters. TR

Wild Geese, The
(Andrew V McLaglen, 1977, GB) Richard Burton, Roger Moore, Richard Harris, Hardy Krüger, Stewart Granger, Jack Watson, Winston Ntshona, John Kani, Frank Finlay, Kenneth Griffith, Barry Foster, Jeff Corey.
134 min.
Dried-out 'hellraisers' Burton and Harris totter together for this mercenary outing which transfers the fundamental plotline of The Professionals to Africa: sinister businessman Granger hires Burton as head of a private army to rescue imprisoned black liberal leader. Harris' gooey relationship with his son sets him up for the chop from the start; racist Krüger, to whom niggers are the white man's burden, ends up carrying black leader cross country and undergoes a last-minute change of heart; 'camp' doctor Kenneth Griffith gets ripped apart by lithe black men, much to his delight. The natives are more primitive than they were in Zulu. It's also the kind of film that would be deeply misogynist...if there were any women in it. CPe

Wild Geese II
(Peter Hunt, 1985, GB) Scott Glenn, Barbara Carrera, Edward Fox, Laurence Olivier, Robert Webber, Robert Freitag, Kenneth Haigh, Stratford Johns, Ingrid Pitt.
125 min.
What is a wild goose, exactly? 'A professional mercenary soldier' Scott Glenn explains to Rudolf Hess (Olivier), just busted out of Spandau disguised as a drunken football fan so he can appear on TV (top executive has scoop in mind). With heroes propelled by their allegiance to Mammon, it's tricky trying to identify the villains. The Russkies come in for some minor stick, but the film's truly international appeal stems from its casual swipes at evil Irish and Palestinians. A right load of proper gander. AB

Wild in the Country
(Philip Dunne, 1961, US) Elvis Presley, Hope Lange, Tuesday Weld, Millie Perkins, John Ireland, Gary Lockwood.
114 min.
'I'm carrying a cupful of anger and trying not to spill it' says Elvis, backwoods literary genius, to Hope Lange's psychiatrist in this extraordinary film. Actually, he's carrying scriptwriter Clifford Odets' cupful, much diluted since the '30s when he was hailed as the white hope of leftist drama. Odets' characteristic cascades of metaphors sit strangely on almost everyone in the cast. Only Tuesday Weld's small town gal dreaming of the big time convinces as a character, not a mouthpiece. There are just a few songs, and the whole's as wild as a glass of milk, but its curio quotient is enormous. GB

Wild in the Streets
(Barry Shear, 1968, US) Shelley Winters, Christopher Jones, Diane Varsi, Ed Begley, Hal Holbrook, Millie Perkins, Richard Pryor, Bert Freed, Michael Margotta.
96 min.
A wild, uneven frolic about a teenage takeover, directed with great verve by Shear from a witty script by Robert Thom. It's a nightmare fantasy about a millionaire pop star (Jones) who enters politics, gets the voting age lowered to 15, and is swept to the White House. Soon everyone over 35 is being herded off to 'Paradise Camps' to be force-fed LSD. But there's a small problem left for the new dictator: a small child crossly observes how old he is at 24... Despite its rough edges and airy trimmings, the film has a chilling nub of possibility to it, neatly underlined in a scene where the hero's mother (Winters) is dragged out of hiding by youthful guards deaf to her plea that she is a teenager. As she is dragged away, her despairing cry floats back: 'But I'm aryan...I mean, I'm young, I'm young'. TM

Wild Man Blues
(Barbara Kopple, 1997, US) Woody Allen, Soon-Yi Previn, Letty Aronson, Jean Doumanian, Nettie Konigsberg, Eddy Davis.
105 min.
After Deconstructing Harry comes this record of

clarinetist Woody Allen's 1996 European tour with his New Orleans jazz band (18 concerts, seven countries). The film was commissioned by Allen's producer Jean Doumanian, and the director apparently secured editorial freedom and 'access all areas'. This is a standard rockumentary: concert footage plus backstage eavesdropping, played out against the highs and lows of a sell-out tour. True to type, Allen gets seasick gliding round Venice in a gondola, and insists on twin suites everywhere he and companion Soon-Yi Previn stay – he needs his own personal shower. It's hardly a revelation, but Allen emerges as genuinely neurotic. He's also funny (especially on the discrepancy between the adulation of the crowds and his films' meagre takings) and not particularly likeable (there's no interplay with the band off-stage, for example). The horrors of Stardust Memories are very real to him. The only person who seems to break through this self-protective bubble is the singularly no nonsense, thoroughly unfazed and self-assured Soon-Yi. TCh

Wild One, The
(Laslo Benedek, 1953, US) Marlon Brando, Mary Murphy, Robert Keith, Lee Marvin, Jay C Flippen, Peggy Maley, Ray Teal.
79 min. b/w.
Effectively banned in Britain until 1968, Brando's biker seems disarmingly tame by comparison with the wild angels he spawned. Yet the film isn't half bad as it sets up characters and situation with neat economy, tracing the seeds of explosion when the Black Rebels ride into town, are detained by a minor accident, and hang around trading insults with a rival gang. A distinct bonus is the echt '50s insolence with which Brando handles bits like his famous response to the girl in the drugstore who asks what he's rebelling against: a pause, a quirk of the eyebrow, a drawled 'Whaddya got?'. But all too soon one is reminded that Stanley Kramer produced. Dissolving into a flurry of melodrama, it emits no more than a faint liberal yap about the misunderstood youth saved by an understanding girl. TM

Wild Orchid
(Zalman King, 1989, US) Mickey Rourke, Jacqueline Bisset, Carré Otis, Assumpta Serna, Bruce Greenwood.
111 min.
You are now entering soft-porn country. Your guides – Zalman King, co-scriptwriter Patricia Louisianna Knop, masterful stud Rourke – brought you $9^{1/2}$ Weeks, so you know what you're getting. Three acts: set-up, foreplay, bonk. Kansas boondocks ingénue Emily Reed (Otis, ex-model, no actress), a lawyer, gets a corporation job in sensuous, throbbing Rio de Janeiro, handling the papers for a complex hotel buy-out. The savage, passionate fucking she witnesses in an abandoned warehouse begins to distract her from work, as does interested party James Wheeler (Rourke), with his 16 inches of applied suntan, gitano bandana and Harley Davidson. He wines and dines Emily, asking challenging questions like 'Have you ever felt that primal, insatiable hunger?' How long can she resist? Even within its own terms the film is a disaster: all the acting is pathetic, the pacing poor, and the pay-off copulation scene merely mechanical. WH

Wild Party, The
(Dorothy Arzner, 1929, US) Clara Bow, Fredric March, Shirley O'Hara, Marceline Day, Joyce Compton, Jack Oakie, Phillips Holmes.
77 min. b/w.
A mischievous film featuring Clara Bow as Stella, a flighty girl with hair of fluff and heart (!) of gold. In a transatlantic tale of the Angela Brazil genre, Stella's good-time girl stereotype is challenged a) by another student for whom studying is a serious thing, and b) by a heroic professor whose savage heart beats beneath a pocket of tweed and a respect for learning. Despite the dashing moral ending, it's a very enjoyable film, and Arzner handles the exposition of and challenge to the stereotype very astutely, especially in a scene of sexually violent response by some men in a bar to a deliberately provocative bevy of girls. MV

Wild Party, The
(James Ivory, 1974, US) James Coco, Raquel Welch, Perry King, Tiffany Bolling, Royal Dano, David Dukes, Dena Dietrich, Jennifer Lee.
100 min.

Based on the bizarre narrative poem by Joseph Moncure March which celebrates the decadence of the Roaring Twenties in cheerful Kiplingesque doggerel, this tells of a chubby silent comedian who throws a Hollywood shindig that ends in murder. No doubt to emphasise the titillating (but misleading) echoes of the Fatty Arbuckle scandal, the film was originally released in Britain in a version cut and 'rearranged' by American International. Coming on like a sexploiter but failing to deliver, this naturally died the death. Ivory's original cut is a delightful tour de force, choreographed entirely around the serpentine party which represents the fading comedian's last desperate bid for success and happiness, but which ends by swallowing its own wild tail. An acid-tinted elegy for the Dream factory, it features some fine musical numbers and wonderfully baroque settings, but also takes a look at the skull beneath the skin just as the extravagance, the glamour, and the licence were beginning to wear thin under pressure from the coming of sound and of Hays Code censorship. TM

Wild Reeds, The

see Roseaux Sauvages, Les

Wild River

(Elia Kazan, 1960, US) Montgomery Clift, Lee Remick, Jo Van Fleet, Jay C Flippen, Albert Salmi, Barbara Loden, James Westerfield, Bruce Dern.
109 min.
Maybe it's the location shooting, maybe it's the performances, but Kazan's lyrical, liberal account of a Tennessee Valley Authority agent (Clift) struggling to persuade an obstinate old woman (Fleet) to abandon her home before it is flooded by a new project, is one of his least theatrical and most affecting films. Partly that's because the battle lines – between city and country, old and new, expediency and commitment – are effectively blurred, making the conflict more dramatically complex than one might expect; but Kazan's evident nostalgia for the '30s (New Deal) setting also lends the film greater depth and scope than is usually to be found in his work. GA

Wild Rovers

(Blake Edwards, 1971, US) William Holden, Ryan O'Neal, Karl Malden, Lynn Carlin, Tom Skerritt, Joe Don Baker, James Olson, Leora Dana, Moses Gunn, Rachel Roberts, Charles Gray.
132 min.
Arguably one of Blake Edwards' best films, this is a faintly derivative but highly enjoyable Western in the nostalgic, anti-heroic mould. Holden and O'Neal are the innocents tired of their unremarkable lives who team up for a bank robbery, and head off on a picaresque odyssey to Mexico with dreams of amounting to something as cattle barons. If most of the film is gently comic and lyrical, the harshness of the West is never played down, so that the duo's cruel destiny is foreshadowed throughout. Marvellous performances and elegiac photography (by Philip Lathrop) are well complemented by Edwards' unusually light touch. GA

Wild Side, The
(aka Suburbia)

(Penelope Spheeris, 1983, US) Chris Pederson, Bill Coyne, Jennifer Clay, Timothy O'Brien, Grant Miner, Andrew Pece, Don Allen.
96 min.
Far from the mad pretensions of Coppola's Camus-for-kids, far from the puerile pranks of Porky's, this combines intelligent social comment with the conventions of the teens-in-revolt exploiter to gripping effect. The group of nihilist punks who scandalise one of LA's seedier neighbourhoods are never glamorised, but shown warts and all. Eventually, however, they gain our sympathy, partly because Spheeris reveals why they have become so anti-social, partly because the irate locals who persecute them as scapegoats for every crime imaginable are even less attractive. A justifiably angry film, fast and full of violent action, though there's plenty of humour too; and the lack of originality is amply compensated for by its manifest sincerity. GA

Wild Strawberries
(Smultronstället)

(Ingmar Bergman, 1957, Swe) Victor Sjöström, Bibi Andersson, Ingrid Thulin, Gunnar Björnstrand, Naima Wifstrand, Björn Bjelvenstam, Max von Sydow.
94 min. b/w.
One of Bergman's warmest, and therefore finest films, this concerns an elderly academic – grouchy, introverted, dried up emotionally – who makes a journey to collect a university award, and en route relives his past by means of dreams, imagination, and encounters with others. It's an occasionally over-symbolic work (most notably in the opening nightmare sequence), but it's filled with richly observed characters and a real feeling for the joys of nature and youth. And Sjöström – himself a celebrated director, best known for his silent work (which included the Hollywood masterpiece The Wind) – gives an astonishingly moving performance as the aged professor. As Bergman himself wrote of his performance in the closing moments: 'His face shone with secretive light, as if reflected from another reality...It was like a miracle'. GA

Wild Style

(Charlie Ahearn, 1982, US) 'Lee' George Quinones, Sandra 'Pink' Fabara, Frederick Brathwaite, Patti Astor, Zephyr, Busy Bee
82 min.
As teenage lovers, Raymond and Rose are as gauche and uninteresting as other people's holiday snaps, but Ahearn fleshes out the bare bones of their story with characters and action that exercise an alien charm: saluting the rappin', breakin', and graffiti people of New York's rundown South Bronx, his film features many key figures from the city's street culture. Quinones, infamous wall and subway train-sprayer, plays the mild-mannered Raymond, who at night becomes the enigmatic Zoro, always painting one step ahead of the law; 'Pink' Fabara, whose 'writings' hang in New York art galleries, plays his 'Lady Bug' Rose, leader of the media-conscious Graffiti Union. Yet despite the sharp pace and Chris Stein's slick soundtrack, the movie doesn't quite succeed in presenting the essentially repetitious rappin' and breakin' without itself becoming repetitive. FD

Wild Target

see Cible émouvante

Wild Things

(John McNaughton, 1998, US) Kevin Bacon, Matt Dillon, Neve Campbell, Theresa Russell, Denise Richards, Carrie Snodgress, Bill Murray.
108 min.
Lombardo (Dillon) is 'Educator of the Year' at Florida's Blue Bay high school, a popular teacher with a taste for the good life. When Kelly (Richards), one of his students, accuses him of rape, the police don't give much credence to a rich bitch on heat. But when punky low class Suzie (Campbell) echoes her claims, Lombardo only has two-bit lawyer Ken Bowden (Murray) standing between him and jail. For about an hour, this shapes up promisingly: it's so blatant, you know it's got to be a tease. The director zooms in on wet T-shirts in slo-mo and maps out the social and sexual hierarchies with glee: think John Waters crossed with John Hughes. When the film-makers pull the rug out from under us, it's a doozy of a twist. Too bad there's still an hour to go, because then all bets are off. McNaughton double and triple-crosses the audience with such reckless abandon, it's impossible to care any more. This is one of those puzzle movies that's quite intriguing while it's feigning superficiality – and truly funny when Bill Murray is around – but really dumb once it thinks it's being smart. TCh

Wildwechsel

see Wild Game

Wild West

(David Attwood, 1992, GB) Naveen Andrews, Sarita Choudhury, Ravi Kapoor, Ronny Jhutti, Ameet Chana.
85 min.
Spurred cowboys are stalking down Southall Broadway, and stetsons bob up and down suburban streets in this engaging film about Country & Western-obsessed British Asian kids who form themselves into a band, the 'Honky Tonk Cowboys'. Likely to be referred to as an Asian version of The Commitments, this cuts much deeper than Alan Parker's Irish ensemble piece. Harwant Bains' script makes pertinent points about culture and identity, but without pushing them in your face. Naveen Andrews (wasted in London Kills Me) gets a chance to show what he can do, and Sarita Choudhury (from Mississippi Masala) gives a nice performance as the female lead. Attwood's direction is a touch undisciplined, but there are some nice allusions to classic Westerns. AJ

Wild Women of Wongo

(James L Wolcott, 1958, US) Jean Hawkshaw, Johnny Walsh, Mary Ann Webb, Ed Fury, Adrienne Bourbeau.
70 min.
Only the most dedicated follower of camp, the most ardent devotee of '50s hair lacquer and leopard-skin kitsch, will be kept genuinely amused throughout this High School Beach Party movie, thinly disguised as true tribal romance between the determined teenage virgins of Wongo (it's not their ethnic roots that are showing) and the dumb Caucasian hunks from the neighbouring Goona tribe – selected in preference to the neanderthal Wongo males. It's like a John Waters film without any disgusting bits, and as a conscious comedy one might argue that it lacks the innocent solemnity of the truly great bad movie. Needless to say, its prevailing ideology will prove deeply offensive to women, ugly people, and stuffed alligators everywhere.

William Christie et Les Arts Florissants ou la Passion du Baroque

(Andrea Kirsch, 1994, Fr) William Christie.
70 min.
Whether you're already a devotee of the astringent melodious sound of the French baroque, or you enjoyed the music of Tous les Matins du Monde and want to hear more, this portrait of conductor William Christie and his gifted group of players Les Arts Florissants should please and inform in almost equal measure. An American who has reawakened in the French a delight in their own musical heritage, notably through his performances of Charpentier and Rameau, Christie is seen here in rehearsal, in concert and at home, and is revealed as an aesthete, disciplinarian and enthusiast. TJ

William Shakespeare's Romeo & Juliet

(Baz Luhrmann, 1996, US) Leonardo DiCaprio, Claire Danes, Harold Perrineau, Pete Postlethwaite, Miriam Margolyes, Brian Dennehy, John Leguizanmo, Paul Sorvino.
120 min.
Leone-style face-off between gun-toting gangs at a gas station: outright street-warfare is evidently imminent, which presents something of a problem for young Montague when, at an absurdly extravagant costume ball thrown at the Capulets' mansion, he falls head over heels for Juliet. So starts WS's Romeo & Juliet. Baz Luhrmann's gleefully cinematic version of the play is so relentlessly inventive and innovative, it takes 20 minutes to get a grasp on how appropriate is his approach to the material. Bravely (but sensibly) sticking with the original dialogue, Luhrmann makes the central element of his audacious adaptation visual: as the camera races wildly around, or rests on luminous close-ups and ornate tableaux, the striking sets, costumes, characters, the colours and compositions serve perfectly to evoke the forces of wealth and poverty, love and hate, power and pride, prejudice and superstition that infest the chaotically sprawling post-punk, post-industrial, multi-ethnic world of millennial Verona (Mexico City and Vera Cruz, heavily made over). Fine as the rest of the cast is, it's DiCaprio and Danes – vulnerable, innocent, impassioned and beautiful, both of them – who steal the honours. GA

Willie & Phil

(Paul Mazursky, 1980, US) Michael Ontkean, Margot Kidder, Ray Sharkey, Jan Miner, Tom Brennan, Julie Bovasso, Natalie Wood.
116 min.

For sheer consistency in chronicling a decade's evolution of chic American manners, mores, and ménages, Mazursky has few rivals. But as Bob & Carol & Ted & Alice have been supplemented in his trend-spotter's log-book by the likes of Alex & Blume & Harry & Tonto (and the strangely anonymous *Unmarried Woman*), his satirical edge has become blunted to a dull indulgence. Accordingly, *Willie & Phil* – optimistically and improbably rhymed with Truffaut's *Jules and Jim* – are let off much too lightly as they pussyfoot around Margot Kidder (as the quicksilver Jeannette) while the '70s trickle away in the background. Undecided whether he's shooting an up-market buddy-love saga or simply shuffling a modish three-card deck, Mazursky piles on the nostalgic Age-of-Aquarius ephemera and shies away from the sexual grit, while Ontkean and the likeable Sharkey wrestle in awe with roles once earmarked for Pacino and Woody Allen. Wry, but on the rocks. PT

Will It Snow for Christmas? (Y'aura t'il de la neige à Noël?)

(Sandrine Veysset, 1996, Fr) Dominique Reymond, Daniel Duval, Jessica Martinez, Alexandre Roger, Xavier Colonna.
91 min.
A remarkable debut from writer/director Veysset, this depiction of farm life in the south of France mercilessly explodes the sentimentality and picturesqueness of, say, Claude Berri's films. Autobiographically inspired, it focuses on the hard frugal life of a mother (Reymond) and her seven children. Cinematographer Hélène Louvart keeps the camera close to the family's field of vision, making the viewer a kind of house guest, witness to the intimate rituals of family life – it takes time to become familiar with the children's names and their relationships with their older, emotionally distant stepbrothers, and to realise that their tyrannical father is keeping another 'legitimate' family some miles away. No music guides our attitude, merely 'natural' sound and the evidence of our eyes. The period and time are deliberately vague. Veysset concentrates instead on incident and detail, and nurtures an array of naturalistic performances. Her cinematic maturity and clarity of vision allow her to express passionate feelings with impressive restraint, while her feminism is one of acute understanding, avoiding both censure of the Reymond character, for continuing to love a man who makes her suffer to the point of suicide, and demonisation of the father. A movie of majestic non-judgmental authenticity. WH

Will My Mother Go Back to Berlin?

(Micha Peled, 1992, Ger/US)
53 min.
Micha Peled's mother left her native German for Palestine in 1937, never to return. As her 80th birthday approaches, Peled cooks up a plan with his producer. He will visit her armed with a personal invitation from the mayor of Berlin and an air ticket. The woman turns out to be a stern, rigorous thinker, and still an activist (she's seen Shoah twice, she says: 'Like a whip on my back…pointless of course'). It's clear to us, if not to Peled, that this plan is a mistake. In seeking some personal/political reconciliation, he only throws into relief the chasm between the generations. Worse, he brings a film crew along with him. At the end of this absorbing, ambivalent documentary, mother and son can only talk about the weather. TCh

Will o' the Wisp

see Feu Follet, Le

Willow

(Ron Howard, 1988, US) Val Kilmer, Joanne Whalley, Warwick Davis, Jean Marsh, Patricia Hayes, Billy Barty, Pat Roach.
126 min.
It is a dark and stormy night. In the bowels of evil Queen Bavmorda's fortress, a child is born with a birthmark. According to the prophecy, this innocent child signifies the end of Bavmorda's rule, and must die. However, a floating tussock carries her to safety in the land of the Nelwyns, a race of friendly munchkins. The chase is on...George Lucas may just be producing *Star*

Wars in furs, but it's still a great Christmas movie. The bulk of it concerns the attempts of Willow Ufgood (Davis) to take the child Elora Danan to the good witch Raziel (Hayes). On the quest he falls in with Madmartigan (Kilmer), a plausible rogue who develops the screaming thigh sweats for Sorsha (Whalley), daughter of bad Bavmorda (Marsh). Along the way they encounter Death Dogs, Brownies, Faeries, Trolls, and a two-headed, fire-breathing monster. The pace is breakneck, the plot so thin that it threatens to fragment into so many pieces, the SFX out of this world. MS

Will Penny

(Tom Gries, 1967, US) Charlton Heston, Joan Hackett, Donald Pleasence, Lee Majors, Anthony Zerbe, Jon Francis, Bruce Dern, Ben Johnson, Slim Pickens, Clifton James.
108 min.
This mean, moody and magnificent Western still remains Tom Gries' sole claim to fame: before it he directed mid-'50s piffle about the Korean War and lumberjacks; afterwards he went on till the mid-'70s directing piffle about absolutely anything, mostly for TV. It's a downbeat tale of hardships and loneliness out on the cattle trail, with Heston as the ageing, illiterate cowpuncher brought face to face with his own hopeless, dead end existence in an encounter with a good but unattainable woman (Hackett), while simultaneously tangling with a psycho preacher (Pleasence) and his three murderous sons. It's blessed with crystal-clear photography by Lucien Ballard, understated performances (Pleasence naturally excepted), and a neatly idiomatic script by Gries himself. GB

Will Success Spoil Rock Hunter? (aka Oh! For a Man)

(Frank Tashlin, 1957, US) Jayne Meadows, Tony Randall, Betsy Drake, Joan Blondell, John Williams, Henry Jones, Mickey Hargitay.
94 min.
A frantic, scattershot satire on '50s morals, advertising, sex and television. The not inconsiderable charms of Jayne Mansfield are much to the fore, but it's Randall's performance as timid advertising executive Rockwell Hunter that holds the whole thing together. While trying to persuade Mansfield to employ her oh-so-kissable lips in a commercial for Stay-Put lipstick, Randall finds himself inadvertently promoted as the world's hottest lover – much to the chagrin of his fiancée (Drake). Not in the same league as the wonderful *Girl Can't Help It*, but possessed of the same comic strip vitality and frenzied humour. NF

Willy Wonka and the Chocolate Factory

(Mel Stuart, 1971, US) Gene Wilder, Jack Albertson, Peter Ostrum, Michael Bollner, Roy Kinnear, Aubrey Woods.
100 min.
Despite indifferent Leslie Bricusse/Anthony Newley songs, an adaptation of Roald Dahl's charmingly eccentric novella (a Grimm-style moral tale) which has the true magic touch of fantasy. Slow to start, but once the youthful hero and four greedy companions arrive for their prize tour of the mysterious chocolate factory – hitherto operating behind locked gates, as hostile as Kane's Xanadu – the film really takes off. Whole landscapes of candy-striped trees, rivers of chocolate negotiable by gondola, sinister caverns manned by orange-faced dwarfs into which the greedier children disappear to suffer torments of their own devising. Great fun, with Wilder for once giving an impeccably controlled performance as the factory's bizarre owner. TM

Wilson

(Henry King, 1944, US) Alexander Knox, Charles Coburn, Geraldine Fitzgerald, Cedric Hardwicke, Thomas Mitchell, Vincent Price, Mary Anderson, Eddie Foy Jr, Francis X Bushman.
154 min.
This three-hour biopic was well reviewed in its day and nominated for a raft of Oscars, but the box-office tills did not ring. Knox, more a character actor than a leading man, made an excellent Woodrow Wilson, the President who founded the League of Nations in 1920, only for Congress to vote against US participation in it. Producer Darryl

Zanuck, fresh from his experiences of WWII, was keen to make a movie which addressed the problems of the age. The result'shandsome, worthy and solemn. GM

Wilt

(Michael Tuchner, 1989, GB) Griff Rhys Jones, Mel Smith, Alison Steadman, Diana Quick, Jeremy Clyde, Roger Allam, David Ryall.
93 min.
Griff Rhys Jones may not be everybody's idea of the hero of Tom Sharpe's delightfully black-humoured novel, but despite pedestrian direction, he does pull off the difficult task of sustaining interest and creulity throughout the accelerating absurdity (intentional and otherwise) of this bleak tale of misunderstandings. Wilt is a Liberal Studies lecturer at a Cambridge 'tec whose day-release students – leather-clad butcher's apprentices and the like – spend their time disputing the negligibility of his penis and fucking- rate. Wilt has no drive, but his socially aspirant, ball-breaking wife Eva (Steadman) has. Of the many incompetents around, Detective Inspector Flint (Smith, wasted) takes the wooden spoon. After various country house shenanigans involving predatory moves made towards Eva by over-attentice 'friend' Sally (Quick), which end in a prolonged scene with Wilt humiliatingly strapped to a life-size female doll, he and Flint finally clash. Wilt has disposed of the doll in concrete, his wife has disappeared, and Flint can add two and two and get the wrong answer. It all adds up to little more than a poorly paced, sporadically amusing farce which never finds a visual equivalent for Sharpe's wickedly acute social observations. WH

Winchester Conspiracy, The

(Ken Cameron, 1990, Aust) Gerald Kennedy, Terry Gill.
90 min.
Fact-based Australian police thriller detailing the controversial Operation Seville, in which the Federal and NSW forces collaborated with organised crime to cultivate and sell marijuana: the prize was a number of convictions, the price an influx of soft drugs on the streets of Melbourne and Sydney. Compelling material, efficiently handled. Raises tough questions about the motivation behind such doubtful methods of investigation. TJ

Winchester '73

(Anthony Mann, 1950, US) James Stewart, Shelley Winters, Dan Duryea, Stephen McNally, Charles Drake, Millard Mitchell, John McIntire, Jay C Flippen, Will Geer, Rock Hudson, Tony Curtis.
92 min. b/w.
Mann's first film with James Stewart, with whom he was to make a series of classic Westerns, this offers the clearest example of Mann's use of the revenge plot. Hero (Stewart) and villain (McNally) are brothers who have been taught to shoot by their father. After McNally murders the father, Stewart sets out to seek revenge and so prove himself worthy of his father's name, symbolised by the perfect Winchester Stewart wins in a shooting contest and McNally steals from him. So begins the long chase to one of the most neurotic shootouts in the history of the Western. PH

Wind

(Carroll Ballard, 1992, US) Matthew Modine, Jennifer Grey, Cliff Robertson, Jack Thompson, Stellan Skarsgard, Rebecca Miller, Ned Vaughn, James Rebhorn.
126 min.
On the surface, Ballard's effervescent celebration of the joys of competitive yachting seems little more than a formulaic gung-ho sports movie. With its risibly romantic plot (boy deserts girl to pursue ambitions, screws up big-time, realises he cannot win trophies without winning back girl's love), its surging musical score and multiple orgasm-style climaxes, this could easily be the sort of film Ron Howard knocks out in an afternoon. But dive beneath the shimmering surface, and some mysterious treasures can be found. While cinematographer John Toll's daredevil camerawork assaults the eyes, swooping impressively in and out of the crashing waves, it is the relentless undercurrent of Alan Splet's creaking, crunching sound effects accompanying the images that holds the key to the film's power, perfectly enhancing the exhilaration of Ballard's tale.

Solid performances by Modine and Grey lend a much-needed air of credibility to the proceedings, but Robertson delightfully scuppers their understated efforts by playing cantankerous old Captain Morgan Weld (Modine's Nemesis) as a camp pastiche of Robert Shaw's Quint in *Jaws*. MK

Wind, The
(Victor Sjöström, 1928, US) Lillian Gish, Lars Hanson, Montagu Love, Dorothy Cumming, Edward Earle, William Orlamond.
6,824 ft. b/w.
One of cinema's great masterpieces. The lovely Lillian Gish gives her finest performance ever as the young Virginian innocent who travels West to stay with relatives on the Texan prairie, only to be pushed into a harsh, unwanted marriage, and to find herself immersed in a maelstrom of rape, murder and madness. Swedish emigré Sjöström directs with immaculate attention to psychological detail, while making perfectly credible the film's transition from low-key, naturalistic comedy of manners to full-blown hysterical melodrama. Filmed under extremely difficult conditions on location in the Mojave desert, its climactic sandstorm sequence has to be seen to be believed, although the entire film – erotic, beautiful, astonishing – demonstrates such imagination and assurance that it remains, sixty years after it was made, completely modern. GA

Wind, The
see Finyé

Wind, The
(aka The Edge of Terror)
(Nico Mastorakis, 1986, US) Meg Foster, Wings Hauser, David McCallum, Steve Railsback, Robert Morley.
92 min.
Stultifyingly boring woman-in-periller about a lady writer (Foster) who cloisters herself in an isolated Greek village in order to churn out her latest pulp. The only other occupant of the village is a scythe-wielding Hauser. He chases her around before getting blown off a cliff by an extra strong gust of wind. There now: I've told you the ending, so you won't have to watch it. AB

Wind Across the Everglades
(Nicholas Ray, 1958, US) Burl Ives, Christopher Plummer, Gypsy Rose Lee, George Voskovec, Emmett Kelly, Mackinlay Kantor, Tony Galento, Peter Falk.
93 min.
One of Ray's most beautifully bizarre projects (though he never fitted easily into the restrictions of genre), merging Western conventions with ecological and philosophical concerns as, in turn-of-the-century Florida, teacher-turned-game warden Plummer takes on a gang of unruly, primitive poachers led by the awesomely charismatic Burl Ives, who are killing off the local rare birds for their fashionable, valuable plumage. With an often poetic script by Budd Schulberg and Joseph Brun's glistening location photography (in ravishing Technicolor), it effortlessly combines artifice with realism, and besides offering a strong argument in favour of conservation, also develops into an oblique meditation on the relativity of good and evil. Ives may spit in the face of God to win his hard-earned money through killing and commerce, but Ray makes no bones about his being closer to nature than Plummer. GA

Wind and the Lion, The
(John Milius, 1975, US) Sean Connery, Candice Bergen, Brian Keith, John Huston, Geoffrey Lewis, Steve Kanaly, Roy Jenson, Vladek Sheybal.
119 min.
Based very loosely on a historical incident which took place in 1904, involving president Teddy Roosevelt in vote-catching reprisals for the kidnapping of an American citizen (here transformed into Candice Bergen and her two children) by a group of Arab 'bandits' in Morocco, Milius' film revives the desert epic with wit, style and a compelling brilliance in his handling of the Panavision format. Milius once more reveals that his overriding concern is with the formation of myth rather than realism, as he balances the fates of his two legendary figures – Brian Keith's Roosevelt and Sean Connery's kidnapper Raisuli

– to dynamic effect. The result compares interestingly with the Paul Schrader-scripted *The Yakuza*, also much bound up with 'proving' an identity between two apparently alien codes. Towards the end, Milius does allow his film to become a distinctly naïve fanfare on behalf of American interventionist policies, but then it is a film that thrives on a species of *naïveté*. VG

Windbag the Sailor
(William Beaudine, 1936, GB) Will Hay, Moore Marriott, Norma Varden, Graham Moffatt, Dennis Wyndham.
85 min. b/w.
British comedy from a bygone age, produced by Michael Balcon at Gainsborough studios. Pub bore Hay, veteran of many a fabricated maritime tall story, gets his comeuppance when the local Sea Scouts trick him into captaining a dodgy old tub whose mutinous crew land them on an island populated by cannibals. Rudimentary. TJ

Wind Cannot Read, The
(Ralph Thomas, 1958, GB) Dirk Bogarde, Yoko Tani, John Fraser, Ronald Lewis, Anthony Bushell, Michael Medwin.
114 min.
Grisly romantic twaddle set during WWII, with Bogarde's chipper air force chappie arriving in Delhi for a language course, falling for and then marrying a Japanese dish (Tani), getting sent to Burma, enduring torture in a PoW camp, and escaping when he hears that his wife has a brain tumour. Love scenes are played against the Taj Mahal, and dear Dirk looks as if he wishes he hadn't read the script, which is all wind. ATu

Wind Echoing in My Being
(Nae-an e Unn Param)
(Jeon Soo Il, 1997, SKor) Cho Jae Hyun.
40 min.
A film about time: a writer, unable to finish his book, loses himself in memories, dreams, fantasies. Though elegantly shot in an oneiric, measured, not to say ploddingly slow style vaguely reminiscent of Tarkovsky, Angelopoulos and Antonioni, this very 'Zen' study in alienation looks more like a student exercise than the work of a 38-year-old professor of cinema. Beneath the emphatically artsy veneer there lies little but empty clichés. [The director later expanded the film into a 113 minute feature.] GA

Wind from the East
see Vent d'Est

Wind in the Willows, The
(Terry Jones, 1996, GB) Terry Jones, Steve Coogan, Eric Idle, Antony Sher, Nicol Williamson, John Cleese, Stephen Fry, Bernard Hill, Michael Palin, Nigel Planer, Julia Sawalha, Victoria Wood.
87 min.
Terry Jones' version of Kenneth Grahame's classic echoes Alan Bennett's successful stage play, but on the whole it's a dire miscalculation. Things start unpromisingly when Mole (Coogan, serviceably velveteen) quits his burrow, not to avoid spring cleaning, but to get away from the developer's bulldozer. Apart from turning up the impact on Toad's multiple car crashes and adding a big explosive ending, Jones introduces a nightmarish Dog Food Factory which, with its cogs and sprockets and steel-edged mincers, drags the gentle animals into its maw. It's showtime too, with a parade of stars bunged in to do tiny turns. The suitably threatening weasel dance in the woods is one of the film's few inventive moments. BC

Windjammer, The
(John Orton, 1930, GB) Michael Hogan, Tony Bruce, Hal Gordon, Charles Levey, Gordon Craig.
58 min. b/w.
This account of the five month voyage of the 'Grace Harwar' from Wallaroo in Australia to London in 1929 is an extraordinary combination of documentary and low-life drama. Working class hero Bert is as bloody-minded as Arthur Seaton in *Saturday Night and Sunday Morning*, and leads a chorus of eccentrically seedy sailors in grousing about the patched and battered old sailing ship. AP Herbert's phlegmatically salty dialogue, and the stunning photography of angry

seas and men swinging through the rigging like gibbons (which the young cameraman paid for with his life), give the film an almost hallucinatory resonance. An authentic glimpse into a lost world. RMy

Windom's Way
(Ronald Neame, 1957, GB) Peter Finch, Mary Ure, Natasha Parry, Michael Hordern, Robert Flemyng, Marne Maitland.
108 min.
Colonial drama in which a caring medic, Alec Windom (Finch), is sent to Malaya where he intervenes in local affairs and encourages the villagers to resist the Communist takeover of the newly independent territory. Decent performances and a genuine sense of concern throughout; scripted by Jill Craigie (Mrs Michael Foot) from a novel by James Ramsay Ullman. TJ

Window, The
(Ted Tetzlaff, 1949, US) Bobby Driscoll, Barbara Hale, Arthur Kennedy, Paul Stewart, Ruth Roman.
73 min. b/w.
A superior RKO B thriller variant on the boy who cried wolf fable, adapted from a short story by Cornell Woolrich. Driscoll is the kid who, from the fire escape one hot night, witnesses the couple in the apartment above killing a drunken seaman, only to have no one believe his story since they're all so used to his lying ways. Thrills begin when the culprits (Stewart and Roman) realise he knows the truth, and decide to ensure his silence. Pleasingly performed and shot, the film benefits from its evocative creation of the grimy New York tenements as a claustrophobic haven of crime and paranoia. Taut and gripping. GA

Window to the Sky, A
see Other Side of the Mountain, The

Windprints
(David Wicht, 1989, GB) John Hurt, Sean Bean, Lesley Fong, Marius Weyers.
100 min.
Wicht, a white South African, here tells a factually-based story of the hunting down of Nhadiep (Fong), a mute Namibian outlaw and killer legendary for his elusiveness. It's set in pre-independence Namibia in 1982, SWAPO is engaged in bloody war against South Africa, and there's increasing local unrest between Afrikaaner farmers and native Nama workers. Liberal Johannesburg cameraman Anton van Heerden (Bean) is despatched to work on Nhadiep's story with an out-of-touch English journo (Hurt) given to hanging out with 'colonial relics'. Why has Nhadiep killed only members of his own people? Is he in the pay of racist Afrikaaner Henning (Weyers), who is cynically buying up abandoned farmsteads? Wicht's use of van Heerden to examine contradictions within the white liberal consciousness (including his own?) – the cameraman's objectivity as reporter of events, his status as an Afrikaaner, the significance of his personal involvement in tracking the killer – is, despite its conventionality, brave and honest if not entirely successful. Despite the usual adumbration of roles for blacks, Wicht has the guts to admit the complexity of varying points of view without resorting to simplistic messages. WH

Winged Serpent, The
(aka Q – The Winged Serpent)
(Larry Cohen, 1982, US) Michael Moriarty, Candy Clark, David Carradine, Richard Roundtree, James Dixon, Malachy McCourt, John Capodice.
93 min.
A plumed serpent ('Whaddya mean? That fuckin' bird?') is nesting in the top of the Chrysler Building, from where it swoops and gobbles up hapless New Yorkers. Cop Carradine and robber Moriarty form an uneasy alliance to flush out the beast. This is the kind of movie that used to be indispensable to the market: an imaginative, popular, low-budget picture that makes the most and more of its limited resources, and in which people get on with the job instead of standing around talking about it. Cohen knows there isn't the time or money to question the logic of anything, so he keeps his assembly so fast and deft that we're prepared to swallow whatever he tells us; and his

script has much droll fun with a plot that keeps losing things ('Maybe his head just got loose and fell off'). He also gets great performances from Carradine as the cop who treats it all as part of a day's work, and (especially) Moriarty as the jittery criminal whose 15 minutes of fame ('I'm just asking for a Nixon-like pardon') leave him wondering if on some days it's better just to stay home in bed. We have no hesitation in awarding Oscars all round. CPe

Wings

(William A Wellman, 1927, US) Clara Bow, Charles 'Buddy' Rogers, Richard Arlen, Jobyna Ralston, Gary Cooper, Arlette Marchal, El Brendel.
12,240 ft. b/w.
Long touted as a classic by cinema historians, and justifying almost every adjectival extravagance. A spectacular tribute to the American flyers of World War One, born of Wellman's and screenwriter John Monk Saunders' own experiences with the Lafayette Flying Corps, it's distinguished by matchless aerial photography, logistically-detailed battle scenes and dogfights, a unique blend of 'European' directorial touches with Hollywood pace, and solid performances holding the straightforward love/duty/camaraderie plotline together. Clara Bow leaves 'It' behind to work as a volunteer ambulance driver, while the boy-next-door she loves (Buddy Rogers) performs airborne heroics with his friend and rival-in-love Arlen, and Gary Cooper makes a brief but telling early appearance. PT

Wings of Desire (100) (Der Himmel über Berlin)

(Wim Wenders, 1987, WGer/Fr) Bruno Ganz, Solveig Dommartin, Otto Sander, Curt Bois, Peter Falk.
128 min. b/w & col.
Part romance, part comedy, part meditation on matters political and philosophical, Wenders' remarkable movie posits a world haunted by invisible angels listening in to our thoughts. Such plot as there is concerns two kindly spirits (Ganz and Sander), posted to contemporary Berlin, who encounter a myriad of mortals, including an ageing writer blighted by memories of a devastated Germany; actor Peter Falk, on location shooting a film about the Nazi era; and a lonely trapeze artist, with whom Ganz falls in love, thus prompting his desire to become mortal at last. A film about the Fall and the Wall, it's full of astonishingly hypnotic images (courtesy veteran Henri Alékan), and manages effortlessly to turn Wenders' and Peter Handke's poetic, literary script into pure cinematic expression. Masterpiece? Maybe not, but few films are so rich, so intriguing, or so ambitious. GA

Wings of Eagles, The

(John Ford, 1957, US) John Wayne, Maureen O'Hara, Dan Dailey, Ward Bond, Ken Curtis, Edmund Lowe, Kenneth Tobey, Sig Ruman.
110 min.
Almost wholly incestuous, but about as impenetrable as a marshmallow for all that. Ford's biopic tribute to naval air ace Frank 'Spig' Wead is simultaneously a tip of the hat to the screenwriter of his earlier films Air Mail and They Were Expendable (Wead turned to cinema after an accident paralysed him), and it also includes Ward Bond's muted parody of Ford himself. There's a strange imbalance between knockabout comedy and reverential drama, but enough cherishable moments – like a post-operative Wayne going through actorly agonies to wiggle his toes again. PT

Wings of Fame

(Otakar Votocek, 1990, Neth) Peter O'Toole, Colin Firth, Marie Trintignant, Ellen Umlauf, Andrea Ferreol, Maria Becker, Gottfried John, Robert Stephens.
109 min.
Outside a festival première of his latest movie, celebrated '60s actor Cesar Valentin (O'Toole) is shot by agitated fan Brian Smith (Firth), who is in turn killed by a falling spotlight. Transported across a Styx-like river to a purgatorial hotel, they join a variety of celebrities whose continuing occupancy (and quality of accommodation) depends on how well their mortal fame is holding up. Einstein plays violin while Lassie sniffs around, and Hemingway rubs shoulders with such lesser immortals as Horace T Merrick (Stephens), famous for refusing the Nobel Prize for literature. So while O'Toole probes his assassin's obscure motives, Firth sustains his fit of pique and concentrates on pursuing the beautiful, amnesiac Bianca (Trintignant). Although the pacing is a shade too measured, the striking hotel setting and deft plot twists hold the attention throughout, especially in the weirdly funny finale, a game show lottery in which contestants are given the chance to return to the real world. Classily shot by veteran British cinematographer Alex Thomson, filmed in English by Czech director Votocek, this gentle allegory is slyly funny and quietly satisfying. NF

Wings of Honneamise, The (Oneamisu No Tsubasa)

(Hiroyuki Yamaga, 1994, Jap) voices: Robert Matthews, Melody Lee, Lee Stone, Alfred Thev.
121 min.
An animated manga feature set in an alternative reality where the north and south hemispheres of the world are locked in eternal combat and the hero is a member of the Royal Space Force. The sci-fi elements, however, are played down, and the journey into space is presented as a moral fable, the stars being 'a place where all mankind can find a new freedom'. Whether or not you swallow this, let alone the subplot of specifically Christian redemption, depends on whether tears spring to your eyes when you listen to 'Imagine'. First-rate score by Ryuichi Sakamoto, lighting effects that would shame Ridley Scott, lushly detailed background and a great eye for composition. A weak story, however, is required to go a long way. DW

Wings of the Apache

see Firebirds

Wings of the Dove, The

(Iain Softley, 1997, US/GB) Helena Bonham Carter, Linus Roache, Alison Elliott, Elizabeth McGovern, Michael Gambon, Alex Jennings, Charlotte Rampling.
102 min.
Kate Croy (Bonham Carter) loves Merton (Roache), a comparatively impoverished, 'progressive' journalist, but the aunt on whom she depends (Rampling) prefers a wealthier suitor and forbids them to meet. Reluctant to lose either her lover or her allowance, Kate takes advantage of her blossoming friendship with visiting American heiress Milly (Elliott), travelling with her to Venice and, unknown to her aunt, inviting her 'friend' Merton to join them. But things get still more complicated when it looks like Milly is starting to fall for Merton herself. For the early London scenes, Hossein Amini's adaptation of Henry James's novel (updated to 1910) seems merely an imaginatively designed Edwardian costumer about frustrated love. In Venice, however, it soon becomes noticeably more interesting, with Kate's motives and methods turning increasingly murky as she appears to drive Merton into Milly's arms. The familiar Jamesian conflict of American innocence and Old World intrigue emerges, darker and crueller than a conventional romantic triangle, and a palpable sense of anguish, guilt and confusion takes hold. The performances are sensitive and sturdy, most impressively so in a beautifully judged sex scene (between Merton and Kate) that is authentically despairing. GA

Wings of the Morning

(Harold Schuster, 1937, GB) Henry Fonda, Annabella, Stewart Rome, John McCormack, Leslie Banks, Irene Vanbrugh, Harry Tate, Edward Underdown, Helen Haye.
89 min.
So few British colour films survive from the '30s that one is inclined to be indulgent toward this misconceived cross between a screwball comedy and a gypsy melodrama. Fonda overacts even more than the stage Oirish and wooden gypsies, but really the characters and plot are of secondary importance. This was Britain's first Technicolor movie, and the green/blue/grey of the Killarney landscapes, and the bright rainbow colours of Epsom on Derby Day, must have had an overwhelming effect on contemporary audiences. What impresses most now, though, are the scenes shot within the baronial interior of Denham studios. They have that shimmering, iridescent quality only possible with (now fast-decaying) nitrate film. RMy

Winner, The

(Alex Cox, 1996, US/Aust) Rebecca DeMornay, Vincent D'Onofrio, Richard Edson, Saverio Guerra, Delroy Lindo, Michael Madsen, Billy Bob Thornton, Frank Whaley.
89 min.
At one point, casino boss Delroy Lindo says, 'Nobody likes anybody who goes too far.' Well, maybe Cox is desperate to be liked, for his story of Phillip (D'Onofrio), the holy fool who keeps hitting the jackpot in Las Vegas, stays way too close to home. The visuals are nice enough – Wizard of Oz colours beslimed by brutish '80s tack – but the characters are painfully predictable (all shysters or whores), and as if to make up for the duff gags and fortune cookie lines, a host of 'cult' faces (Whaley, Madsen) chew up the scenery. CO'Su

Winstanley

(Kevin Brownlow/Andrew Mollo, 1975, GB) Miles Halliwell, Jerome Willis, Terry Higgins, Phil Oliver, David Bramley, Alison Halliwell.
96 min. b/w.
In this adaptation of David Caute's novel Comrade Jacob, the story of England's first commune – the settlement formed by the Diggers, under the leadership of General Winstanley, on St George's Hill in Surrey in 1649 – is decorated with unromantic details of Cromwell's era, and edited with the emphasis one expects from Brownlow. But that's about all there is to it: overriding solemnity crushes the sympathy that is clearly demanded for the story's characters, almost inviting a shrug. The old problem of portraying misery without being miserable yourself hasn't been solved. AN

Winter Guest, The

(Alan Rickman, 1997, US/GB) Phyllida Law, Emma Thompson, Sheila Reid, Sandra Voe, Arlene Cockburn, Gary Hollywood, Douglas Murphy, Sean Biggerstaff.
104 min.
This confident directorial debut is unashamed of its theatrical origins. Alan Rickman, who helped create (and directed) Sharman Macdonald's play in Leeds and London, wrote the script with the playwright, and retains Phyllida Law as the meddling Elspeth who tries to rekindle a relationship with her grieving daughter Frances (Emma Thompson, Law's real daughter). Set against the snow, wind and ice-blasted landscape of a Fife fishing village, it follows and contrasts the diffident, often quarrelsome relationships of four pairs of characters – two teenage boys playing hooky; two ageing 'funeral' junkies; Frances' son and an independent young woman; and the mother and daughter. The distraction of the Pinteresque pauses and use of language notwithstanding, it's well acted (with child actors Murphy and Biggerstaff especially winning), sensitively directed and expressively shot (by Seamus McGarvey), but finally a shade too dramatically sealed up. WH

Winter Kills

(William Richert, 1979, US) Jeff Bridges, John Huston, Anthony Perkins, Sterling Hayden, Eli Wallach, Dorothy Malone, Ralph Meeker, Belinda Bauer, Richard Boone, Elizabeth Taylor, Brad Dexter.
96 min.
An excellent conspiracy thriller of unusual blackness and wit, from a novel by Richard Condon, author of The Manchurian Candidate and Prizzi's Honour. A dazzling cast is assembled for its helter-skelter narrative about the brother (Bridges) of a murdered US President, searching for the real assassin and stumbling across the bloodstained pieces of a jigsaw that refuses to be completed. For once the tag of 'any similarity' hardly stands up, since the family patriarch – richly played by Huston, even in red underwear – owns most of America, and the name begins with K. Richert's direction negotiates the plot's many pleasurably sharp bends with such skill that one emerges a little dazed, more than a little amused, and nagged by a worrying sense that it could just all be true. DT

Winter Light

see Nattvardsgästerna

Winter of Our Dreams

(John Duigan, 1981, Aust) Judy Davis, Bryan Brown, Cathy Downes, Baz Luhrmann, Peter Mochrie, Mervyn Drake.
90 min.
Contemporary urban life in the lucky country found wanting. Alas, this offering from the New Australian Cinema wears its heart and its didacticism on a rather tired old sleeve. The storyline bulges with stereotypes. The suicide of a folksy idealist turned hooker brings about the meeting of two people from two different realms of her past: her agitprop, Richard Neville-clone former lover, Rob (Brown), now owner of an arty Sydney bookshop; and fellow pro and junkie, Lou (Davis). Armed with her loser's uniform of peroxide crew-cut, kitsch togs, and aggressive vulnerability, Lou sets out to win Rob from his cosy refuge of bland materialism...Against a tritely sentimental screenplay and an eerily inert performance from Brown, Davis fights an uphill battle to provide convincing emotional light and shade. BPa

Winter People

(Ted Kotcheff, 1988, US) Kurt Russell, Kelly McGillis, Lloyd Bridges, Mitchell Ryan, Amelia Burnette, Eileen Ryan, Lanny Flaherty, Jeffrey Meek.
111 min.
Men proving their manhood, women feisty and maternal by turns: Appalacian sexual politics during the depression are certainly basic in these backwoods where Collie (McGillis) rears an illegitimate child after being spurned by her clean-cut kinfolk. Into her life wanders gentle, clock-making widower Wayland (Russell) and his daughter. Does Collie choose Wayland or her brutish ex-lover (Meek), who hails from an uncouth rival family? Will the two clans ever agree on matters of personal hygiene? No prizes for guessing the outcome. Adapted from John Ehle's novel, this is highly predictable romantic melodrama, of the kind you find in fat paperbacks. We're meant to draw some significant parallels between the title, the harsh landscape, and emotional isolation, but the contrived connections lack substance. Even a murder mystery is introduced, too late to kick life into events, such is the certainty that wholesomeness will triumph over the eye-for-an-eye crudity of the villans. CM

Winter's Tale, A (Conte d'hiver)

(Eric Rohmer, 1992, Fr) Charlotte Véry, Frédéric Van Den Driessche, Michel Voletti, Hervé Furic, Ava Loraschi, Christiane Desbois.
114 min.
Summer in Brittany: tearfully parting after an idyllic holiday romance with Charles (Van Den Driessche), hairdresser Félicie accidentally gives him an incorrect home address. Four years on, it's Christmas and he still hasn't contacted her; but such is her undying love for him – and the daughter he sired – that she finds it impossible to choose between two adoring suitors: her stolid boss Maxence (Voletti) and intellectual librarian Loïc (Furic). Reluctant to compromise her memories and dreams of true passion, she is hoping against hope for a miracle. In focusing on an often irritatingly indecisive heroine devoted to a barely reasonable romantic ideal, the second of Rohmer's 'Tales of the Four Seasons' is reminiscent of The Green Ray, while its wintry study of the varieties of love, faith and religious belief recalls the similarly sublime My Night with Maud. This is Rohmer at his very best, effortlessly and unsentimentally charting the absurd complexities of human psychology, while creating a compelling contemporary fairytale firmly rooted in the banality of everyday existence. It has, as ever, enormous compassion, wit and insight, and its ending is exquisitely affecting. GA

Winter's Tale, The

(Frank Dunlop, 1966, GB) Laurence Harvey, Jane Asher, Diana Churchill, Moira Redmond, Jim Dale, Esmond Knight, Richard Gale.
151 min.
A ludicrously stagebound record by Frank Dunlop of his own 'Pop Theatre' production of Shakespeare's play for the Edinburgh Festival in 1966. Shot on the original stage set, with lumbering cameras and inadequate lighting, it's a fair old shambles in which the colour varies from shot to shot and the use of close-ups is almost invari-

ably disruptive. With no attempt made to scale the acting from stage to screen, the performances – obviously no great shakes to start with – are something posterity is unlikely to be grateful to find preserved for its benefit. TM

Winter Tan, A

(Jackie Burroughs/Louise Clark/John Frizzell/John Walker/Aerlyn Weissman, 1987, Can) Jackie Burroughs, Erando González, Javier Torres Zarragoza, Anita Olanick, Diane d'Aquila.
91 min.
Strange movie, impossible to classify. It's based on letters by American feminist Maryse Holder, sent to girlfriends back home while she was abandoning herself to lust in Mexico, published (after her death at the hands of a Mexican stud) under the title Give Sorrow Words. The movie is framed as a sexual monologue: we see much more of the author (played by co-director Burroughs in a performance of awesome spiritual nakedness) than we do of the Mexican cocks she craves. The result is a bit like a female rewrite of Genet, a meditation in strictly physical terms on sex, desire, and frustration. Whatever else you think about it, it's certainly the only film of its kind. TR

Wired

(Larry Peerce, 1989, US) Michael Chiklis, Patti D'Arbanville, JT Walsh, Lucinda Jenney, Gary Groomes, Ray Sharkey, Alex Rocco, Jerre Burnes.
109 min.
It isn't easy to leave aside the Hollywood conspiracy against this John Belushi biopic, since threats of litigation have left such raw gaps in the action. One's sympathy for the underdog – producer Ed Feldman – is counterbalanced by one's boredom about Belushi and all his works, plus the high stultifying factor in Bob Woodward's biography. Perhaps the worst thing about Wired is that it is totally unfunny. Michael Chiklis works hard to bring the fat comic to life, but none of the routines work, and the samurai baseball-player sketch is embarrassing. This Dan Aykroyd (Groomes), perhaps haunted by the actual Aykroyd's curse, scarcely registers; Woodward (Walsh) is suitably beady as the investigator, but his function in the screenplay is clearly that of connective tissue. God knows why they decided to resurrect the dead Belushi from his slab in the morgue and take him on a tour of his life under the ageis of a guardian angel (Sharkey). Probably desperation. BC

Wisdom

(Emilio Estevez, 1986, US) Emilio Estevez, Demi Moore, Tom Skerritt, Veronica Cartwright, William Allen Young, Richard Minchenberg.
109 min.
A bathtub wallow in teenage narcissism. John Wisdom (Estevez), convicted of drunk driving at eighteen, finds it tough getting a decent job. Five years later, he's still living with Mom and Pop, and spending a great deal of time in front of the mirror (but it's OK folks, he's got a girl). Fired from Cityburger for lying, he opts for a career in felony. A TV programme on the social effects of bank foreclosure shows him what to do. Armed with home-made bombs, our suburban guerilla holds up banks, not for megabucks but to destroy all traces of mortgage agreements. With his chick (Moore) as chauffeuse, he travels the road pursued by the FBI. The cute couple become public heroes. It all ends in tears. As Wisdom (the name represents the single feeble attempt at irony), Estevez demonstrates an undeniable charisma, but in the roles of writer and director he is less successful. What initiative there is in this retread gets swamped by silliness, slackness and sentiment. MS

Wise Blood

(John Huston, 1979, US/WGer) Brad Dourif, Ned Beatty, Harry Dean Stanton, Daniel Shor, Amy Wright, Mary Nell Santacroce, John Huston.
108 min.
A comedy? A tragedy? Philosophical farce, rather...in which a young fanatic (Dourif) returns from the army to his home town in the Bible-belt South, and stages a doomed private rebellion against the evangelism and repression of his upbringing. The enemy is neither tangible, nor simply a feature of his lived memory, but per-

meates the whole town: Jesus is celebrated in neon, on the street, in the language of everyday chatter. The young heretic's 'Church of Truth Without Jesus Christ' finally founders under the weight of human deception, driving its twisted creator into a real-life imitation of the martyrdom of Christ. Tragically, desperately funny: this adaptation of Flannery O'Connor's novel is John Huston's best film for many years. CA

Wise Guys

(Brian De Palma, 1986, US) Danny DeVito, Joe Piscopo, Harvey Keitel, Ray Sharkey, Dan Hedaya, Julie Bovasso, Patti LuPone.
91 min.
Made in between Scarface and The Untouchables, De Palma's third gangster movie of the '80s is something completely different: a light-hearted and extremely wacky caper in which DeVito and Piscopo play small-time errand-runners for a local mobster. Failing in their efforts to essay a little double-crossing, each finds himself faced with a contract to kill the other. Instead they go on the run, and end up on a spending spree using the mob's credit card. Some great laughs, but it isn't hard to see why the film was never released theatrically in Britain: at times it just gets bogged down with over-the-top performances. The ending is great, though. DA

Wishing Tree, The (Drevo Zhelanya)

(Tenghiz Abuladze, 1976, USSR) Lika Kavzharadze, Soso Dzhachvliani, Zaza Kolelishvili, Kote Daushvili.
107 min.
Abuladze's film is a magically sustained fantasia about life in a Georgian village on the eve of the revolution, poetry rather than narrative thrust carrying it from one incident to another. The characters are eccentric, and their dreams and longings are gently indulged, from the simpleton who searches for the tree that will fulfil his wishes, to the dishevelled lady fortune-teller who promises herself the return of a long-lost lover. The central focus is a tragic love story (sweethearts denied marriage by the village elders), and this, more than any overtly political points, serves to intimate the social changes to come. Best seen in the original Georgian version (rather than the Russian-dubbed one), with its delicate aural lyricism matching the pictorial splendours. TR

Wishmaster

(Robert Kurtzman, 1997, US) Tammy Lauren, Andrew Divoff, Kane Hodder, Tony Todd, Robert Englund, Chris Lemmon.
90 min.
A psycho genie turns every wish put to him into an atrocity, until at long last Lauren tricks his nasty ass back into the lamp for good (unless, of course, he's required for a sequel). Englund goes all Peter Cushing, donning dressing gown and cravat to explain the plot, a simple-minded affair, structured around an explosion of body parts and giblets roughly every eight minutes. Wes Craven executive produced, a man without shame. BBa

Wish You Were Here

(David Leland, 1987, GB) Emily Lloyd, Clare Clifford, Barbara Durkin, Geoffrey Hutchings, Charlotte Barker, Tom Bell, Pat Heywood, Neville Smith.
92 min.
With mother dead and father emotionally ditto, 16-year-old Linda (Lloyd) hungers for love with a foul-mouthed exhibitionism that horrifies the strait-laced elders of her '50s South Coast home town. More scandalously, after an initiation into the disappointments of sex with a silly young bus clippie, she takes to sleeping with the local fleapit's limp projectionist (Bell), one of her dad's masonic mates. For his writer/director debut, Leland filches a few incidents from the early life of Cynthia Payne to create a teenage rebel whose frustrations lead her to kick against the pricks of repressively status-conscious, middle class Britain, double standards and all. The trouble is that Lloyd's loud, brattish performance makes Linda less a socially purgative Free Spirit than a pain in the neck. More a well-meaning romp than a credible analysis of the state of the nation, now or then. GA

Witch, The

see Superstition

Witchcraft Through the Ages (Häxan)

(Benjamin Christensen, 1921, Swe) Maren Pedersen, Clara Pontoppidan, Tora Teje, Benjamin Christensen, Oscar Stribolt.
6,840 ft. b/w.

A weird and rather wonderful brew of fiction, documentary and animation based on 15th and 16th century witchcraft trials, Christensen's film has a remarkable visual flair that takes in Bosch, Breughel and Goya (no wonder it was a particular favourite of the Surrealists). The director himself plays Satan, seducing a woman while she is in bed with her husband; another episode follows an accused witch through the tortures of the Inquisition. The film is now most commonly seen in a sound version, running 76 minutes, made in 1967 with a commentary by William Burroughs; a later restoration with tinted sequences is far preferable. DT

Witches, The

(Nicolas Roeg, 1989, US) Anjelica Huston, Mai Zetterling, Jasen Fisher, Charlie Potter, Bill Paterson, Brenda Blethyn, Rowan Atkinson.
91 min.

A gutsy version of Roald Dahl's story, reasonably faithful despite the changed ending. Luke (Fisher) and his Norwegian grandmother (Zetterling), both clued up on witch-lore, end up sharing a seaside hotel with a coven. Led by the Grand High Witch (Huston), the witches plan to turn all of England's children into mice. Distictive casting has paid off, (Huston splendidly glam, camp and evil; Zetterling the voice of maternal moderation; Rowan Atkinson an obsessive hotel manager), and the adaptation recreates the sense of foreboding that gives way to gruesome reality. Customary Roeg concerns are evident, but issues of identity are given darkly humourous expression, while directorial extravagance is held in check by an outrageous plot about supernatural transformation, and there are some wonderful special effects from Jim henson's crew. Strange and scary enough to fascinate parents and offspring alike. CM

Witches of Eastwick, The

(George Miller, 1987, US) Jack Nicholson, Cher, Susan Sarandon, Michelle Pfeiffer, Veronica Cartwright, Richard Jenkins, Keith Jochim, Carel Struycken.
118 min.

Very loosely based around the John Updike novel. Three women, bored by life in a small, sleepy New England town, find that they can make bizarre things happen. Cher, Pfeiffer and Sarandon are fine as the trio who conjure up their perfect man (Nicholson in the most manic part of his career to date). The four set up home together, but after a succession of mishaps, the girls realise that the decadent idyll has to come to an end. For three-quarters of the film, Miller triumphantly welds a strong comic element on to a taut, truly menacing atmosphere, but the last 20 minutes dive straight to the bottom of the proverbial barrel with a final crass orgy of special effects. Such a shame. DPe

Witchfinder General

(Michael Reeves, 1968, GB) Vincent Price, Ian Ogilvy, Hilary Dwyer, Rupert Davies, Robert Russell, Patrick Wymark, Wilfrid Brambell.
87 min.

Filmed on location in the countryside of Norfolk and Suffolk on a modest budget, this portrait of backwoods violence – set in 1645, it deals with the infamous witchhunter Matthew Hopkins, and the barbarities he practised during the turmoils of the Civil War – remains one of the most personal and mature statements in the history of British cinema. In the hands of the late Michael Reeves (this was his last film, made at the age of 23), a fairly ordinary but interestingly researched novel by Ronald Bassett, with a lot of phony Freudian motivation, is transformed into a highly ornate, evocative, and poetic study of violence, where the political disorganisation and confusion of the war is mirrored by the chaos and superstition in men's minds. The performances are generally excellent, and no film before or since has used the British countryside in quite the same way. DP

With a Song in My Heart

(Walter Lang, 1952, US) Susan Hayward, Rory Calhoun, David Wayne, Thelma Ritter, Una Merkel, Robert Wagner.
117 min.

The story of star radio singer and entertainer Jane Froman is the sort of stuff Hollywood would have gladly made up had not reality beaten them to it. Hayward was Froman's choice for the lead (although the singer dubbed her own songs) in this rags-to-riches story, capped by a near-fatal aircrash during WWII, a tough fightback from illness, and a big finale that has Froman out entertaining the troops again. Hideously schmaltzy and Hayward's not exactly anyone's idea of musical sparkle. But what songs! 'Blue Moon', 'Give My Regards to Broadway', 'Embraceable You', 'Get Happy'. Alfred Newman won an Oscar for musical direction. TJ

With Babies and Banners

(Lorraine Gray, 1976, US) Genora Dollinger, Babe Gelles, Lillian Hatcher, Mary Handa, Helen Hauer.
45 min. b/w & col.

A group of American grannies pore over old scrapbooks, pointing freckled fingers at tattered cuttings: not the obvious starting point for the stirring political documentary which this unashamedly is. They're not the Daughters of the Revolution, more like the instigators; women who joined the successful 1937 sit-down strike at the vast General Motors plant in Flint, Michigan, called to force GM into union recognition. Like *Salt of the Earth* and *Harlan County USA*, the film makes admirably clear that the women fought on two fronts: against management/politicians, and against male workers who took them to be 'on the make'. During the strike, the men occupied the plant, while the women (who left rather than provide the press with an opportunity to comment on sexual shenanigans within) formed an effective auxiliary and foil to police lines embarrassed about clubbing women or shooting them in the back. JS

With Honors

(Alek Keshishian, 1994, US) Joe Pesci, Brendan Fraser, Moira Kelly, Josh Hamilton, Gore Vidal, Deborah Fortson.
193 min.

Monty, a Harvard politics student (Fraser), is struggling to finish his thesis when the only copy falls into the hands of Simon, a wily bum (Pesci). Attempting to retrieve it, Monty realises he has much to learn and Simon that he has much to teach. As an entertaining demonstration, Simon delivers an impromptu lecture on the role of the common man in the US Constitution, hence the presence of Gore Vidal as a supercilious tutor who hopes that the repetition of his cynical ideals will allow Monty to graduate 'With Honors'. A slight film, reiterating the simpler aspects of its theme (making your way in the world), but one with brains and heart. Attractive performances, handsome photography by Sven Nykvist, and charming music by Patrick Leonard, go some way to offset the clichés and sentimentality. AO

Withnail & I (100)

(Bruce Robinson, 1986, GB) Richard E Grant, Paul McGann, Richard Griffiths, Ralph Brown, Michael Elphick, Daragh O'Malley.
107 min.

That rare thing: an intelligent, beautifully acted, and gloriously funny British comedy. At the buttend of the '60s, two 'resting' young thesps – Withnail (Grant, a revelation), a cadaverous upper middle class burning-out case with an acid wit and soleless shoes, and the seemingly innocent unnamed 'I' (McGann) – live on a diet of booze, pills, and fags in their cancerous Camden flat, until a cold comfort Lakeland cottage is offered for their use. For all its '60s arcana, this is no mere semi-autobiographical nostalgia trip, but an affecting and open-eyed rites-of-passage movie. Robinson's debut as writer/director (he scripted *The Killing Fields*) exhibits the value of the old virtues: characterisation, detail, and engagement. His characters are oddball, degenerate even, but rounded – none more so than the elephantine figure of Griffiths as Withnail's gay uncle Monty. Beautifully scripted, indecent, honest, and truthful, it's a true original. WH

Without a Clue

(Thom Eberhardt, 1988, GB) Michael Caine, Ben Kingsley, Jeffrey Jones, Lysette Anthony, Paul Freeman, Nigel Davenport, Pat Keen, Peter Cook.
107 min.

You'd think it would make your toes curl: a period buddy movie set in Victorian England, top names in top hats, carriages clattering on cobbles, puffer trains puffing through the Lake District. *Without a Clue* has all this, but the buddies are Sherlock Holmes and Dr Watson, and the usual set-up has been reversed: Watson (Kingsley) is the clever one, Holmes (Caine) is really Reginald Kincaid, an out-of-work actor hired to maintain Watson's credibility. When the boozy Kincaid begins to revel in his role, Watson becomes jealous and gives him the boot, but soon discovers that he can't do without him. Thanks to inspired casting, the result is superior schlock. The plot concerns the theft of the Treasury's £5 note plates; Moriarty (Freeman) is of course the culprit, and Inspector Lestrade of the Yard (Jones) is of course a dimwit. Although a bit long, it's full of incidental pleasures, and the climax in an empty gaslit theatre is slapstick at its silliest and best. MS

Without a Trace

(Stanley R Jaffe, 1983, US) Kate Nelligan, Judd Hirsch, David Dukes, Stockard Channing, Jacqueline Brookes, Keith McDermott, Kathleen Widdoes.
120 min.

If Jaffe's previous production credits aren't sufficient warning that this is one for Sensitive Drama suckers, the opening shot's a giveaway. The camera may be prowling Kate Nelligan's bedroom as if setting up a creepshow, but it's focused on a line of framed group photos on the mantelpiece. Nelligan's going to cry a lot, but she's not going to be conventionally imperilled. For this is another saga of the Ordinary Kramers, and it's the nuclear family itself that's once more in jeopardy. Hubby's already walked out, but ten minutes into the movie it's the pre-teen kid who goes missing. Kidnapped? Killed? Mum goes through the tearjerk agonies as her son's disappearance becomes a case, an issue, and as time drags on, (almost) a statistic. The sickies, the psychics, and the media swoop briefly and indistinguishably, though Judd Hirsch is on hand as the concerned cop with a family of his own. One interlude of gay-baiting apart, everything else from here on in is designed to be drowned in sobs. PT

Without Memory (Kioku-ga Ushinawareta-toki)

(Hirokazu Koreeda, 1996, Jap) Hiroshi Sekine and his family.
84 min.

Begun before *Maborosi*, this documentary records nearly two years in the life of a family faced with an exceptional difficulty. Severe Thiamin deficiency can cause Wernicke's Encephalopathy, a brain disorder which results in total loss of short term memory. Hiroshi Sekine was hospitalised in 1992 for a stomach operation; for five weeks he was fed on a glucose drip which starved his body of vitamins. He emerged with WE and (along with his wife and two sons) has been trying to cope with it ever since. It took the family three years to get a disability pension out of the authorities, and even longer for the government to admit that health service cuts have cost at least 41 lives and damaged many others. In part, Koreeda's film is a protest against medical malpractice and bureaucratic inertia. But it also offers a vision stranger than anything William Gibson might dream up of what it means to start each day with no memory more recent than 1992. TR

Without *You* I'm Nothing

(John Boskovich, 1990, US) Sandra Bernhard, John Doe, Steve Antin, Lu Leonard, Ken Foree, Cynthia Bailey.
94 min.

More of a pop video than a movie, this is the film version of outrageous comedienne Sandra Bernhard's off-Broadway show. Her pastiche of the Hollywood dream is a hilarious hit parade of tormented lesbian lullabies, awesomely bad '70s go-go girl costumes, and 'in your face' sexual politics. Bernhard, the original wide-mouthed frog, shimmies her way through a star-spangled show: an anorexic, Madonna-style strippergram one minute and a bad-assed impression of a 'sexpert' in the mould of Dr Ruth the next. She turns the old soul classic 'Me and Mrs Jones' into a sexually ambiguous anthem, and she kidnaps Prince's 'Little Red Corvette', transforming it into a bump-and-grind strip show. She also sends up her own life, from growing up in Michigan to revealing a hidden yearning to be a Gentile on Christmas Day. This is sure to catapult Bernhard (best known previously as the crazed groupie in *King of Comedy*) into the mainstream as a performer; whether the mainstream is ready for her is another matter. ACh

Witman Boys, The (Witman Fiúk)

(János Szász, 1997, Hun) Alpár Fogarasi, Szaboles Gergely, Maia Morgenstein, Dominika Ostalowska, Péter Andorai.
93 min.
A stylish, slightly pretentious but finally effective little movie, set in 1913, about two brothers who react to their disciplinarian father's death by retreating into a shared secret world of rituals involving sex, cruelty and death. When they also become involved with a prostitute, their distaste for their mother begins to verge on pure hatred. Though the measured pace and overall glumness make the movie sometimes feel a little strained, Producer/director Szász elicits superb performances from his young leads, while the vibrant, near expressionistic photography lends the proceedings the feel of a feverish dream. It's a dark tale of pain, confusion and misplaced desire, helped considerably by sensitive borrowings from the likes of Schubert and Richard Strauss on the soundtrack. GA

Witness, The (A Tanu)

(Pèter Bacsó, 1968, Hun) Ferenc Kállai, Lajos Oze, Zoltán Fábri, Béla Both, Lili Monori.
108 min.
Bureaucratically blocked in its homeland for a decade, Bacsó's anti-Stalinist comedy confronts the historical trauma of the post-war purges and show trials with the iconoclastic wit of true absurdism – tracking the farcical travails of a good, simple communist dyke-keeper as he's unwittingly targeted to become a key prosecution witness in the rigged case against a former comrade. The treacherous currents of party-line politics prove beyond the poor man's comprehension – he knows only those of the Danube – as he is buffeted, under sinisterly ludicrous secret police supervision, through a bewildering switchback of imprisonment and (invariably inappropriate) rehabilitation. As agit-prop clichés become running gags, the horrific ironies emerge from a series of classic comic set pieces: the well-meaning creation of a Socialist Ghost Train in the people's amusement park; the ceremonial passing off of a lemon as the first 'Hungarian orange'; the eventual unscripted débâcle of the trial. Exorcism through echoing laughter: brilliant. PT

Witness

(Peter Weir, 1985, US) Harrison Ford, Kelly McGillis, Josef Sommer, Lukas Haas, Jan Rubes, Alexander Godunov, Danny Glover.
112 min.
Weir's first film set in America explores a theme familiar from his earlier work: the discovery of an all but forgotten culture in modern society: in this case the Amish, a puritanical sect whose life in Pennsylvania has remained unchanged since the 18th century. Threat explodes into this community when an Amish boy witnesses a murder; cop Ford investigates the case and, finding his own life endangered, is forced to hot-foot it back to the Amish ranch with the bad guys in pursuit. The film also allows Ford to fall in love with the boy's mother (McGillis), and comments on the distance between the messy world Ford leaves behind and the cloistered one in which he takes refuge. Powerful, assured, full of beautiful imagery and thankfully devoid of easy moralising, it also offers a performance of surprising skill and sensitivity from Ford. RR

Witness for the Prosecution

(Billy Wilder, 1957, US) Marlene Dietrich, Tyrone Power, Charles Laughton, Elsa Lanchester, John Williams, Henry Daniell, Norma Varden, Una O'Connor.
114 min. b/w.
The undisputed star of this courtroom drama is Alexander Trauner's magnificent recreation of the Old Bailey, which is just as well, since the presence of Charles Laughton as the defence counsel, and the film's origins as an Agatha Christie novel and play, combine to give the movie a heavy – almost stolid – theatrical flavour. Tyrone Power is surprisingly good as the man accused of murdering his mistress, but the swift twists and turns of Ms Christie's plot soon drain Dietrich and Laughton's roles of any dramatic credibility. PH

Wits to Wits

see Conman and the Kung Fu Kid

Wittgenstein

(Derek Jarman, 1993, GB) Karl Johnson, Michael Gough, Tilda Swinton, John Quentin, Kevin Collins, Clancy Chassay, Jill Balcon, Sally Dexter, Nabil Shaban.
75 min.
Jarman's biopic brings to life the *seriously* eccentric philosopher Ludwig Wittgenstein: Viennese millionaire's son, schoolteacher, WWI infantry officer, hospital porter, gardener, naturalised Briton and homosexual. Initiated as a small-budget educational TV programme, then produced for the BFI by one-time Trot Tariq Ali from a script by Marxist professor Terry Eagleton, it hardly sounds enticing. But thanks to genuinely engaging performances by Johnson and Chassay (as Ludwig, man and boy), as well as a witty script and economical direction, this turns treatise into treat. It's shot on the simplest of sets against black backgrounds, with all the money spent on costumes, actors and lights, and framed like dark Enlightenment paintings. If it ranges wide rather than deep – the philosophy is either dropped into conversation or presented like a blackboard primer – Jarman still manages to capture the spirit and complexity of his fascinating subject. Of the entertaining cameos, Quentin's epicene John Maynard Keynes (in a delightful series of pastel shirts) and Gough's miffed Bertrand Russell are the most telling. WH

Wittstock, Wittstock

(Volker Koepp, 1997, Ger/Aus)
119 min. b/w.
A feature culled from one of those '7-Up' style documentaries in which the film-makers revisit a handful of characters every so often for updates. Here, the subjects are three women in a textile plant, in Wittstock, East Germany, and the period ranges from 1964 to 1996. The women are personable enough, but the film covers too much time to go into a lot of detail, and there's an inordinate amount of footage devoted to the comely Elsbeth smirking into the camera (her aspirations are tragically funny: a trip to Bulgaria and a Trabant – no, it's not funny, really). Boredom is averted by dismantling the Berlin Wall, with sorry results. TCh

Wives (Hustruer)

(Anja Breien, 1975, Nor) Anne-Marie Ottersen, Froydis Armand, Katja Medboe, Noste Schwab, Helge Jordal.
84 min.
'We want fun – we can screw at home!' This manifesto voiced by one of the three wives, part way through a spree begun in the wake of a school reunion, gives a small clue as to the direction taken by Breien's film. It is of course a reply to Cassavetes' *Husbands*, and a cheerful, relaxed, and good-humoured one, with some of the conspiratorial overtones of a school adventure story, and with some deliciously peppery gags. The script, with its astute contributions to script as well as performance from Breien's lead actresses, is quite a landmark in feminist cinema. VG

Wives: Ten Years After (Hustruer ti ar etter)

(Anja Breien, 1985, Nor) Froydis Armand, Katja Medboe, Anne-Marie Ottersen, Brasse Brännström, Henrik Scheele.
88 min.
A decade after their reckless spree together, the three friends from *Wives* meet up again at a pre-Christmas fancy dress party. However, when they try to relive the past, the changes wrought in them by age and the failure of their relationships with men generate unsettling tensions.
Even when they hole up together in a deserted Malmö hotel, where they were waited on hand and foot by the manager, they find little comfort in one another's company. A painfully honest film which benefits greatly from the reuniting of the original cast, all of whom again collaborated with Breien on the scenario. NF

Wives III (Hustruer III)

(Anja Breien, 1996, Nor) Froydis Armand, Katja Medboe, Anne-Marie Öttersen, Noste Schwab, Hedda Sandvig, Mathias Armand.
80 min.
Ten years after *Wives: Ten Years After*, and the three friends reconvene aboard a tram touring the late-night streets of Oslo: a surprise birthday-party for Kaja (Medboe), who's reached the 50 mark. She, Heidrun (Armand) and Mie (Ottersen) spend the next two days together, recounting, recollecting, reflecting, revaluating, bemoaning and celebrating life as 'wrinkled and weathered, wonderful women', with the city's Independence Day celebrations in the background, and a stolen bust of Norway's national poet somewhere in between. Breien again collaborated with her three leads on the writing, to similarly naturalistic effect. If formally slight, this well-seasoned and eccentric blend of wry comedy and candour provides a rare perspective on a constituency sorely under-represented in cinema. NB

Wiz, The

(Sidney Lumet, 1978, US) Diana Ross, Michael Jackson, Nipsey Russell, Ted Ross, Mabel King, Theresa Merritt, Lena Horne, Richard Pryor.
134 min.
Dorothy and her entourage of malfunctioning under-achievers move on from rural Kansas to face the contemporary perils of cocaine-sniffing, disco-chic New York in this all black, or rather Motown, version of Frank Baum's *The Wonderful Wizard of Oz*, adapted from the Broadway hit musical (with Charlie Smalls' original score augmented by Quincy Jones). Lumet adopts a bravely vacillating tone, alternating between tear-jerking schmaltz and smart-ass humour; both work, though you may well giggle when Lena Horne (as Glinda the Good) is seen, hanging in the sky in sequined shower-cap, urging you to 'Believe in Yourself'. On the plus side are vast, brilliant sets by Tony Walton, a couple of well-staged show-stoppers ('Everybody Rejoice' in the Wicked Witch's sweat-shop, and 'Emerald City Ballet'), Michael Jackson (the Scarecrow), Richard Pryor (The Wiz) and Diana Ross who, as Dorothy, is just gorgeous. JS

Wizard of Darkness

(Eko Eko Azaraku)(Shimako Sato, 1995, Jap) Kimika Yoshino, Miho Kanno, Shu-ma, Naozumi Takahoshi.
81 min.
The most striking element of Shimako (*Tale of a Vampire*) Sato's subtly erotic horror film about a Japanese high school at the centre of a satanic pentagram of evil is once again the juxtaposition of charged stillness with eruptions of blood-bolted violence. New student Missa impresses some but scares others with her apparently magical powers. Later, kept behind with 12 other pupils, she's trapped and hunted by an unseen assailant. Fluid direction; accomplished sfx. NF

Wizard of Oz, The (100)

(Victor Fleming, 1939, US) Judy Garland, Ray Bolger, Bert Lahr, Jack Haley, Frank Morgan, Billie Burke, Margaret Hamilton.
101 min. b/w & col.
The niece of Kansas homesteaders dreams of a magical land, over the rainbow. She and her dog Toto meet the Munchkins – the little people – who tell her to follow the yellow brick road, which will bring her to the Wizard. She joins up with a scarecrow who hasn't a brain, a tin man who hasn't a heart, and a lion who's cowardly. A good witch protects them from a wicked witch. But the Wizard is not what he seems...It's hard to imagine now the impact this classic fantasy must have had on a world sliding into war. Garland became a legend at 16. Bolger, Haley and Lahr were immortalised as her three blighted pals. It's still a potent dreamworld. The dubbing and some of the visual effects may creak a bit, but the songs, make-up, costumes and sets are magical. Infinitely preferable to Boorman's nightmare gloss for the '70s, *Zardoz*. SG

Wizard of Speed and Time, The

(Mike Jittlov, 1988, US) Mike Jittlov, Richard Kaye, Paige Moore, David Conrad, Steve Brodie, John Massari, Gary Schwartz.
98 min.

This bizarre and wacky conglomeration of SFX and fantasy slapstick is based around a fable-like tale mirroring Jittlov's own experiences: eccentric effects wiz (Jittlov) spends months touting his work around the big studios before he is finally offered a particle of air time on a high-rating TV show. The most amusing moments occur in the first quarter, as Jittlov attempts to secure the US equivalent of the Equity card. For the rest, the film labours through repeated scenes of the crew shooting in adverse conditions, lengthy car chases involving camera dollies, hired punks, and unscrupulous moguls hell-bent on disrupting the production. The effects themselves (brilliantly created through stop-motion and literally making a film studio come to life) unfortunately appear in their entirety only during the last 10 minutes. DA

Wizard of Waukesha, The

(Catherine Orentreich/Susan Brockman, 1980, US) Les Paul.
59 min.

A straightforward documentary, enlivened by the charisma of its puckish subject, the guitarist Les Paul. It follows the life story of the one-time Broadway entertainer ('We died'), inventor of the electric guitar, and granddaddy of rock recording. Likeable Les will retain even the uncommitted viewer's attention, although the deadbeat rockers wheeled on to give an expert's opinion may have the opposite effect. Full of lovely pop media kitsch, and a genuine rags-to-riches story. JG

Wizards

(Ralph Bakshi, 1977, US) voices: Bob Holt, Jesse Wells, Richard Romanus, David Proval.
81 min.

Bakshi, maker of Fritz the Cat and Heavy Traffic, is still waving a tattered flag for Underground Culture in this sentimental animated satire on the future ways of the world. Two brother wizards battle for supremacy. One's good, with a vast ginger beard and a George Burns voice, and is supported by a host of elf and fairy helpers (fairies are the true ancestors of man, we're told). The other's evil, all bones and no flesh; he fuels the hatred of his subjects with Nazi propaganda films found along with a movie projector in the rubble of the 20th century. Provided one can stomach the combination of elves and Nazis (and it's a big proviso), then there's moderate fun here and there. But the film shows all the signs of an economic freeze: it has quite lavish backgrounds, but bare, unimaginative character movement, and frequent use of still drawings to fill in portions of the narrative. GB

Wobblies, The

(Stewart Bird/Deborah Shaffer, 1979, US) narrator: Roger Baldwin.
89 min. b/w & col.

'Trust in the Lord and sleep in the streets': just one of the iconoclastic maxims coined by the Industrial Workers of the World ('The Wobblies') in song and agitation, and given new voice in this documentary. In the currently depressing US political situation, any recovery of that continent's militant, socialist tradition is welcome; especially the first two decades of this century, when the Wobblies tried to organise the whole booming, unskilled working class into one industrial union. Guided by the memories of several old World War I activists on film, this is a fascinating and often moving compilation of newsreel, photographs, and those amazing songs. But given its classic US documentary strategy, based primarily on 'personal testament', there are weaknesses. In particular, the film is unable to transcend the naive syndicalist politics of the IWW itself. As a film it has no critical distance on its chosen subject, so the movement is presented in celluloid aspic, with no past and, more importantly, no legacy. And the shooting style, characterised by the endemic docu-makers' disease of zoomitis, only serves to park the film more firmly in the labour movement museum. Despite this, one still emerges stunned and angry, admiring and amused. The World War I failed, the film half-fails, but both are still more than worthy of our attention. CG

Wolf

(Mike Nichols, 1994, US) Jack Nicholson, Michelle Pfeiffer, James Spader, Kate Nelligan, Richard Jenkins, Christopher Plummer, Eileen Atkins, Om Puri, Prunella Scales, Madhur Jaffrey.
125 min.

Quite frankly, it's hard to fathom why exactly anyone would have wanted to make this slick, glossy, but utterly redundant werewolf movie. Okay, maybe Nicholson sympathised with his Will Randall, a middle-aged New York book editor anxious about his job and his marriage, who finds his powers and senses not only restored but greatly sharpened when he's bitten by a wolf he ran into with his car. And maybe Spader, as Randall's smarmy, back-stabbing colleague Swinton, reckoned here was a juicy, villainous part to sink his teeth into. But for Pfeiffer – as Randall's love interest Laura – there's little of substance, while Nichols makes it clear that directing a horror movie was the last thing on his mind. Even make-up wiz Rick Baker is stymied by the air of restraint. Overall, this is needlessly polished nonsense: not awful; just toothless, gutless and bloodless. GA

Wolfen

(Michael Wadleigh, 1981, US) Albert Finney, Diane Venora, Edward James Olmos, Gregory Hines, Tom Noonan, Dick O'Neill.
115 min.

School-leavers whose ambitions lean towards criminal pathology will pick up useful tips on wielding the scalpel and the white sheet in this foray into the bleakly explicit world of the contemporary shocker: a werewolf movie for an ecology-conscious age. The last-reel process whereby the lurking terror breaks cover and is transformed into a 'sympathetic' but unconquerable force is smoothly convincing: we are a long way here from simply feeling a bit sorry for King Kong. The setting is two New Yorks: that of the multinational, politically-amoral corporations, and that of the slum wastelands, both with the same landlords. The camera's vision is a fresh one, and though the wolf's eye view sequences threaten at first to become a nuisance, they are soon justified as a dramatic device, and ultimately as essential to the plot. JC

Wolf Man, The

(George Waggner, 1941, US) Lon Chaney Jr, Evelyn Ankers, Claude Rains, Maria Ouspenskaya, Ralph Bellamy, Patric Knowles, Warren William, Bela Lugosi, Fay Helm.
70 min. b/w.

'It's only in your mind' says Claude Rains to his screen son Lon Chaney Jr, as he straps the suspected werewolf to a chair in Universal's second try at the Wolf Man saga. But he's three corpses too late, and we've already seen the transformation as Chaney stomps through a never-never land of foggy glades outside English villages set in Alpine scenery. Suspension of disbelief aside, this is interesting for its relatively modern equation between Chaney's wolfish desires and his unhappy fate, for its concern over the victims, and for the fact that – despite all odds – there's undeniable magic within the staid format. DMacp

Wolfshead: The Legend of Robin Hood

(Johnny Hough, 1969, GB) David Warbeck, Kathleen Byron, Dan Meaden, Ciaran Madden, Kenneth Gilbert, Joe Cook.
56 min.

How Robert of Locksley became an outlaw ('wolfshead') and took the name Robin Hood. A rather grave and pedantic account, short on zip and long on hammering the points. It's actually a TV pilot that never made it to your living room. Come back Richard Greene, nearly all is forgiven.

Wolves Cry Under the Moon (Guo Dao Feng Bi)

(Ho Ping, 1997, Tai) Chang Shih, Annie Shizuka Inoh, To Tzong-hua, Gu Bao-ming.
121 min.

Touching, funny and quirkily inventive, this interweaves the stories of four groups of characters during one long night when Taiwan's main north-south highway is closed to traffic. Taking to the side roads are a wacky punkette who conducts a mobile phone conversation with the stranger whose car she's just stolen; a chauffeur so stressed by doubts about his wife's fidelity that he begins to crack up; a hitman who hijacks a bus to take him to his next assignment and builds an unexpected relationship with the driver; and a trio of puppeteers who never seem to get anywhere. Clearly a reflection on contemporary Taiwanese life (generational and family problems; confusion about crime, jobs and relationships; everyone going round in circles), the film is at times reminiscent of Altman but still works admirably in terms of its individual characters. GA

Wolves of Willoughby Chase, The

(Stuart Orme, 1988, GB) Stephanie Beacham, Mel Smith, Geraldine James, Richard O'Brien, Emily Hudson, Aleks Darowska, Jane Horrocks, Eleanor David, Jonathon Coy, Lynton Dearden.
93 min.

Any fidelity to Joan Aiken's classic for kids is captured in the opening sequences, with their snowbound landscapes, helpless orphan traveller, and treacherous forests. Thereafter, bogged down in Victorian gloom, some of the book's more glorious passages are neglected, while there seems no dramatic point in beefing up the relationship between evil governess Slighcarp and her henchman Grimshaw, only to pit the two young heroines Bonnie and Sylvia against each other. They squabble over Sylvia's lack of courage, while Bonnie rebounds of life's knocks with distictly unappealing, gormless innocence. Eventually the pair are carted off from a life of splendour to a grim orphanage, while the greedy oppressors work in the wings. Budgetary restraints presumably worked against a more imaginative, broad-ranging use of locations, but this doesn't explain the casting of Stephanie Beacham as Slighcarp (playing on her soap opera associations) and of Emily Hudson as the dreadful Bonnie. Better are Geraldine James, Mel Smith, and Aleks Darowska (as Sylvia), who have just the right degree of moderation. A big disappointment. CM

Woman for Joe, The

(George More O'Ferrall, 1956, GB) George Baker, Diane Cilento, David Kossoff, Jimmy Kairoubh, Sydney Tafler, Miriam Karlin.
91 min.

Very minor homegrown drama in dubious taste has fairground hawker Baker finding a new top attraction in midget Kairoubh – 'The World's Smallest Man' – and then having to sort out some female company to keep him happy, hiring Cilento to sing in the lion's den. TJ

Woman in a Dressing Gown

(J Lee Thompson, 1957, GB) Yvonne Mitchell, Anthony Quayle, Sylvia Syms, Andrew Ray, Carole Lesley, Olga Lindo.
93 min. b/w.

Proof that the kitchen sink wasn't invented in the 1960s. Ted Willis' domestic drama was originally produced on television, then filmed (from his own script) to some contemporary acclaim. Yvonne Mitchell gives it the works in the juicy role of a drudge who fights to rekindle the affection of her husband (Quayle) when he asks for a divorce. There's a great bit when a rainstorm ruins her new hairdo, but it's heavy weather throughout; a depressing reminder of prevailing British sexual attitudes. TCh

Woman in a Twilight Garden

see Femme entre Chien et Loup, Une

Woman in Flames, A (Die flambierte Frau)

(Robert van Ackeren, 1983, WGer) Gudrun Landgrebe, Mathieu Carrière, Hanns Zischler, Gabriele Lafari, Matthias Fuchs.
105 min.

In the middle of a stuffy dinner party, Eva (Landgrebe) walks out of her marriage and into the world of high-class prostitution. She finds customers, a lover (Chris, a male prostitute), and that the thin veneer of chic separating her life from the ordinary world can be pierced by the new emotional strains. Van Ackeren casts a cold eye upon the German middle classes, for whom post-war prosperity has brought expectations of comfort, culture and sterile sex. The subject is not prostitution. Quite what it is, is hard to fathom, for the sexual politics and psychology are complex, and the shifts in tone – from carnal comedy to tragedy – dramatic. But for Eva it is about emotional and economic freedom, bought with sexual favours and too precious to surrender, even to the benign imperialism of Chris' love. Landgrebe spikes Eva's stubborn docility with an icy poise, in a performance which is mesmerising and the key that unlocks the strange pleasures of this film. FD

Woman in Love
see Enamorada

Woman in Red, The
(Gene Wilder, 1984, US) Gene Wilder, Charles Grodin, Joseph Bologna, Judith Ivey, Michael Huddleston, Kelly LeBrock, Gilda Radner.
86 min.
A long-legged lovely (LeBrock) is first glimpsed doing a Monroe-style cha-cha over a hot-air grating. Wilder, playing a happily married chap with children, flips his lid over this vision, and thereafter suffers from seagull noises and loud bursts of Stevie Wonder whenever he sees her. With the help of chums, he stumbles towards getting her into the sack for a good squelch, only to be thwarted at every turn of the hoped-for screw. This may sound familiar to fans of French frippery: it's a remake of *Pardon Mon Affaire*, which wasn't startlingly original in the first place, and Wilder is no substitute for lugubrious Jean Rochefort. AB

Woman in the Moon
(Frau im Mond)
(Fritz Lang, 1929, Ger) Gerda Maurus, Willy Fritsch, Fritz Rasp, Gustav von Wangenheim, Klaus Pohl.
14,292 ft. b/w.
Lang's last silent movie was planned as another giant sci-fi film in the vein of *Metropolis*. It didn't work out like that, partly because the design and trick-work are cramped and unimaginative, partly because Thea von Harbou's script centres on the exceedingly banal character conflicts on board the first rocket to the moon. As a result, it looks considerably more dated than other Lang silents: it's badly acted melodrama, and the sci-fi trimmings remain entirely secondary. One scene is distinguished by Lang's magnificent sense of spatial drama: the actual launching of the rocket. Otherwise, it's chiefly notable for being one of the rare Lang movies with a deliriously happy ending. TR

Woman in the Window, The
(Fritz Lang, 1944, US) Edward G Robinson, Joan Bennett, Dan Duryea, Raymond Massey, Edmund Breon.
99 min. b/w.
A classic *noir* thriller with Robinson in top form as the likeable professor of criminal psychology who finds his most vivid fantasies and fears fulfilled when his wife and kids take a vacation and leave him alone to cope with the evils of the big city. Meeting up (innocently, it seems) with the woman of his dreams – the subject of a painting in a gallery window he passes regularly – he becomes involved first in the violent killing of a man, then in blackmail. Meanwhile his DA pal (Massey) keeps him in touch with the police's search for the killer. With Bennett and Duryea superb as the eponymous heroine and the blackmailer, and atmospheric camerawork by Milton Krasner, it's not merely a dazzling piece of suspense, but also a characteristically stark demonstration of Lang's belief in the inevitability of fate: Robinson, basically a good man, makes one small slip in a moment of relaxation, and he's doomed. GA

Woman Is a Woman, A
see Femme est une Femme, Une

Woman Next Door, The
(La Femme d'à côté)
(François Truffaut, 1981, Fr) Gérard Depardieu, Fanny Ardant, Henri Garcin, Michèle Baumgartner, Véronique Silver.
106 min.
For all the period charm of his historical pieces –

from *Jules and Jim* to *The Last Métro* – Truffaut increasingly looks more comfortable with contemporary domestic dramas drawn from the bourgeois milieu so successfully explored by Chabrol in the early '70s. In this context, *The Woman Next Door* recounts its tale of *amour fou* in a provincial town – Depardieu (plus wife and kid) moves in next door to a newly-married woman (Ardant) with whom he had an obsessional affair eight years earlier – with absolute narrative confidence. But as Truffaut steers his audience towards the tragic dénouement, the effect is a curiously passive experience, as if, like passengers on a bus tour, we are offered a scenic excursion without ever being driven to the precipice from which his protagonists will fall. A long way from Hitchcock (and Chabrol), but a consistently watchable sub-thriller none the less. MA

Woman Obsessed
(Henry Hathaway, 1959, US) Susan Hayward, Stephen Boyd, Barbara Nichols, Dennis Holmes, Theodore Bikel, Ken Scott.
102 min.
Susan Hayward is a widow attempting to run a farm on the rugged plains of Canada. Boyd is the handsome hobo she falls in love with and eventually marries. Conditions are pretty bad – cyclones, blizzards, forest fires – and their relationship is on the stormy side too. It's up to Hayward to rid her new husband of his wife-beating, child-abusing tendencies, and to remould him as a decent cowboy. Hathaway made some fine Westerns, but this 'Scope epic wasn't one of them. GM

Woman of Paris, A
(Charles Chaplin, 1923, US) Edna Purviance, Adolphe Menjou, Carl Miller, Lydia Knott, Charles French, Henry Bergman, Charles Chaplin.
8,395 ft. b/w.
Emerging after being placed on the shelf by Chaplin for almost fifty years, with a reputation as the film that made all directors fall on their knees, *A Woman of Paris* had a lot to live up to. It's easy enough to appreciate the deftness with which Chaplin propels the narrative in this 'first serious drama written and directed by myself' (to quote the opening preamble); in particular, his use of objects (a pipe on the floor, a collar falling from a chest-of-drawers) to relay facts about events and relationships. Easy enough also to enjoy the insouciant charm of Menjou's lecher, who languishes in pyjamas, and tootles on a tiny saxophone while his mistress (Purviance) grows more and more bored at the frenzy of Parisian high society. Yet despite its wealth of detail and sharp observations about morality, the film remains curiously insubstantial with its refined dabbling in the elements of satire, sentiment and melodrama exploited with such panache in Chaplin's starring comedies. The final verdict has to be: fascinating, but...GB

Woman of Straw
(Basil Dearden, 1964, GB) Gina Lollobrigida, Sean Connery, Ralph Richardson, Johnny Sekka, Laurence Hardy, Alexander Knox.
117 min.
Richardson is the wheelchair-bound scourge of his family, hated by his nephew Connery, and nursed by Lollobrigida. Connery hatches a scheme to inherit the old man's money by marrying him off to La Lollo, but of course it goes rather awry, with Richardson getting bumped off earlier than expected. Despite good performances from the three stars, and a plot whose convolutions keep you awake, Dearden treats it rather timidly, afraid to go for the dramatic jugular. ATu

Woman of the Dunes
(Suna no Onna)
(Hiroshi Teshigahara, 1964, Jap) Eiji Okada, Kyoko Kishida.
127 min. b/w.
An entomologist finds himself trapped by mysteriously trilling villagers, and forced to cohabit with a desirable but inarticulate woman in an escape-proof sandpit. Leaving aside all the teasing questions of allegorical meaning, Teshigahara's film is a tour de force of visual style, and a knockout as an unusually cruel thriller. It builds on its blatantly contrived

premise (taken from Kobo Abé's novel) with absolute fidelity and conviction, which leaves the manifest pretensions looking both credible and interesting, and centres its effects on the erotic attraction between the man and woman, filmed with a palpable physicality that remains extraordinary. TR

Woman of the Year
(George Stevens, 1942, US) Spencer Tracy, Katharine Hepburn, Fay Bainter, Reginald Owen, William Bendix, Roscoe Karns, Dan Tobin.
112 min. b/w.
Tracy and Hepburn were a great team, and this, their first outing together, set the seal on the pattern to follow into the next decade. He's a sports journalist, she's an influential political columnist, and after they marry he wants her to be a woman as well. The comic byplay between opposites – everyday guy Spence and haughty Kate – is a consistent pleasure, even if its sexual politics are ambiguous: Spence scores many more points than Kate, and the whole film is geared toward the climax when she cooks him breakfast like a good little housewife. Produced by Joseph L Mankiewicz, the film has that MGM glitter and literary sparkle. ATu

Woman on Her Own, A
(Kobieta samotna)
(Agnieszka Holland, 1981, Pol) Maria Chwalibog, Boguslaw Linda, Pawel Witczak.
110 min.
One of the 'missing ten' films which ran into censorship trouble in Poland, not so much a cry from the heart as a hectoring scream of miserabilism. Agnieszka Holland traces the life, and love affair with an epileptic, club-footed no-hoper, of a prematurely-aged postwoman struggling to bring up her son. She lives in a rented cesspit of a one-bed flat by the railway tracks (the recurrent metaphorical image is of trains passing her by), sans TV set but replete with banging pans, totally unsympathetic landlord, and a chip the size of the Polish national debt. She faints from overwork in scene three, is made homeless in scene 17, then things start getting *really* bad. The three lead actors show considerable ability, but collapse, like the audience, under the farcial catalogue of woe they are required to endure. WH

Woman on Pier 13, The
see I Married a Communist

Woman on the Beach, The
(Jean Renoir, 1946, US) Joan Bennett, Robert Ryan, Charles Bickford, Nan Leslie, Walter Sande, Irene Ryan.
71 min. b/w.
The last film from Renoir's wartime exile in America, considered too obscure, too erotic, and cut by nearly a third of its running time by RKO after a preview. What might have been is anybody's guess (not least because it freely rewrites the emphases of its source novel, Mitchell Wilson's *None So Blind*), but what's left is great Renoir: a tormented triangle involving a blind painter (Bickford), his passionate wife (Bennett), and a shell-shocked sailor (Ryan), all three of them outcasts in different ways. A *film noir* in mood, with terrific performances, wonderful use made of the dead-end settings (the lonely clifftop house, the beach strewn with dead hulks), and darkly elemental overtones to the emotional battle (Ryan's recurring nightmare of drowning; Bickford's cleansing by fire of his past). Fragments, maybe, but remarkable all the same. TM

Woman or Two, A
(Une Femme ou Deux)
(Daniel Vigne, 1985, Fr) Gérard Depardieu, Sigourney Weaver, Ruth Westheimer, Michel Aumont, Zabou, Jean-Pierre Bisson, Yann Babilée.
97 min.
Depardieu is an archaeologist who stumbles across the bones of the first French woman, a two million-year-old number called (in his sculptured model of her) Laura. Alas, he is taken for a ride by a scheming American advertising executive (Weaver), who wants to use his eternal woman in a campaign to sell perfume, and deceives him into thinking she is the director of a foundation which

will give money for his digs. Then the real director (Westheimer) turns up...and the perfume woman gets kidnapped...and it all gets very silly. Depardieu coasts through it with his customary felicitousness and charm; Weaver's vaunted ambitions to do comedy are less well realised. There is more to it than crossing your eyes and sticking your tongue out. CPea

Woman Rebels, A

(Mark Sandrich, 1936, US) Katharine Hepburn, Herbert Marshall, Van Heflin, Elizabeth Allan, Donald Crisp, David Manners, Doris Dudley.
88 min. b/w.
Interesting proto-feminist movie, adapted from Netta Syrett's novel *Portrait of a Rebel*. Hepburn is the Victorian miss saddled with a stern father (Crisp), despite which she manages to get herself pregnant in a headily romantic affair with Van Heflin. A visit to a married sister in Italy enables her to pass the child off as her niece; after which, determined to stand on her own feet, she rejects an offer of marriage from an understanding diplomat (Marshall) and goes to work. Twenty years later, through journalism, she has become a leading campaigner for women's rights. The gradual growth of her militancy, fuelled by her own experience, is effectively detailed; but Hollywood crassness has to get its word in by way of one of those fatuous coincidences (the threat of incest rears its head when her daughter falls for a young man who happens to be her half-brother), and the inevitable happy ending (Marshall, still patient, faithful, and infinitely understanding, gets Hepburn in the end). With all faults, it's nevertheless held together by Hepburn's superb performance. TM

Woman's Face, A

(George Cukor, 1941, US) Joan Crawford, Melvyn Douglas, Conrad Veidt, Osa Massen, Reginald Owen, Albert Basserman, Marjorie Main.
105 min. b/w.
An absurdly melodramatic story, about a nurse-maid with a hideously scarred face, who beats a gradual retreat from her embittered life of blackmail and murder-plotting into a world of love and righteousness when she undergoes plastic surgery. Despite some rather silly dialogue (Veidt: 'Do you like music? Symphonies? Concertos?' – Crawford: 'Some symphonies, most concertos'), scripted by the usually reliable Donald Ogden Stewart from a French play, Cukor's civilised handling of the actors and his often expressionist visuals lend credence to the tale, with atmosphere thick and juicy enough to cut with a knife. Crawford herself was acclaimed for her courage in spending half the film with her distinctive beauty disfigured, but in fact it is Veidt who steals the show, satanic and sinister, as a decadent connoisseur of evil. For Cukor fans, it's also of interest as a peculiarly explicit example of his abiding obsession with the relationship between inner reality and external appearances. GA

Woman's Secret, A

(Nicholas Ray, 1949, US) Maureen O'Hara, Melvyn Douglas, Gloria Grahame, Bill Williams, Victor Jory, Mary Philips, Jay C Flippen.
85 min. b/w.
Something of an RKO chore for Ray, to be sure. But a nicely structured script by Herman J Mankiewicz – repeating the investigative flashback structure of *Citizen Kane* as it examines the events leading up to the death of ex-singer O'Hara's devious and ungrateful protégée (beautifully incarnated by Grahame) – is well served by the civilised direction, which not only turns the Vicki Baum melodrama into a *noir*-ish mystery, but also stresses, as so often in Ray, the importance of interior space and the way it reflects/influences action. Entertaining, and less routine than it sounds. GA

Woman's Tale, A

(Paul Cox, 1991, Aust) Sheila Florance, Chris Haywood, Gosia Dobrowolska, Norman Kaye, Ernest Gray, Myrtle Woods.
94 min.
Australia's art house maestro deals here with the life of an eccentric 80-year-old woman suffering from terminal cancer. Martha is not one to be daunted by the failure of the flesh. Her spirit is alive and well, and she gives to her friend, district nurse Anna (Dobrowolska), as good as she gets: love and support. Martha's son (Haywood) doesn't understand her fierce independence (or much else, to her chagrin) and tries to place her in a home – over her dead body! She's happier with her budgie Jesus, her books and painting, her confused and bedridden ex-RAF officer neighbour, and the prostitutes in the local park. It's an affirmative film, and a restrained one for Cox, who uses Florance to explicate his askance view on life: one that has little sympathy for landlords, closed minds, or people who refuse to take responsibility for (and joy in) their own lives. WH

Woman's World

(Jean Negulesco, 1954, US) Clifton Webb, June Allyson, Van Heflin, Arlene Dahl, Lauren Bacall, Fred MacMurray, Cornel Wilde.
94 min.
A well-cast rehash by 20th Century-Fox of MGM's *Executive Suite* (made the same year) that reads like a Neil Simon comedy, with Webb playing an automobile tycoon trying to choose a deputy. He summons the three top candidates and their wives to New York: Cornel Wilde and Allyson are homespun and want to remain in Kansas; MacMurray and Bacall are ambitious and divorcing; Heflin is a wimp, but his wife Arlene Dahl sets out to seduce Webb on her husband's behalf. The result is a victory for feminism and sexism, and it's fun getting there. The tendency to have characters on the edges of the frame, and the frequent travelogue shots of Manhattan, are there to advertise CinemaScope. ATu

Woman to Woman

(Donna Deitch, 1975, US)
48 min.
This documentary, in which women speak to each other about themselves, leaves one with a residual and positive sense of shared problems and collective strength. By involving women from as many social levels as possible, Deitch manages to avoid the aura of elitism and in-group morale-boosting that tends to haunt much of West Coast independent film-making. Opening with a montage of clips illustrating the history of women at work, *Woman to Woman* becomes even more assured once Deitch begins to talk to specific groups of women face-to-face. Perhaps her greatest asset, an infinitely valuable one, is the ability to convey, unfiltered, an immediate impression of the individual women and their particular experience. One comes out feeling stimulated by their company, rather than thinking they have been marshalled into the film as specimens illustrating a predetermined argument. VG

Woman Under the Influence, A

(John Cassavetes, 1974, US) Peter Falk, Gena Rowlands, Katherine Cassavetes, Lady Rowlands, Fred Draper, OG Dunn.
155 min.
One of Cassavetes' best films, with a suitably ambiguous title for a plot that manages to be political in its social implications without succumbing to any crass statements. Rowlands and Falk play a lower middle class couple with three kids, whose combined temperaments produce a potentially explosive emotional energy. He can let off steam in his work; she tries to do it at home, but ends up by turning her household into a cross between an encounter group and an adventure playground, to the fury of neighbours and mother-in-law. The brilliance of the film lies in its sympathetic and humorous exposure of social structure. Rowlands unfortunately overdoes the manic psychosis at times, and lapses into a melodramatic style which is unconvincing and unsympathetic; but Falk is persuasively insane as the husband; and the result is an astonishing, compulsive film, directed with a crackling energy. DP

Wombling Free

(Lionel Jeffries, 1977, GB) David Tomlinson, Frances de la Tour, Bonnie Langford, Bernard Spear, Yasuko Nagazumi, John Junkin, Reg Lye.
96 min.
A bit late for TV's Womble-mania gravy train, this feature spin-off does itself no favours by leading its 4ft, fat, and furry heroes into close encounters with a (purportedly) human family to press home the simple ecological message, or by relegating Mike Batt's inventive lyrics and music to backing for a few variable set pieces. There's a certain perverse joy in watching the shaggy creatures in a pastiche of the Hollywood musical, but there's little more than sheer perversity involved in the casting of Bernard Spear as a Japanese car salesman whose genuinely Oriental wife never speaks a word of English. Frances de la Tour is great, and is given great lines, but they belong to a different movie; the rest of her family belong to Disneyland. Lionel Jeffries' previous kids' films promised much, but this unfortunately doesn't begin to deliver. Shame, 'cos Wombles definitely rule Muppets, OK? PT

Women, The

(George Cukor, 1939, US) Joan Crawford, Norma Shearer, Rosalind Russell, Mary Boland, Paulette Goddard, Joan Fontaine, Lucile Watson, Phyllis Povah, Ruth Hussey, Virginia Weidler, Margaret Dumont, Marjorie Main.
132 min. b/w & col.
A real treat, and an unusual one in that it not only has an all-female cast, but it was scripted by Anita Loos and Jane Murfin from a play by Clare Boothe. Men are present, however, not just in the form of Cukor (rightly acclaimed as one of Hollywood's most sympathetic directors of women), but also in that the group of middle class socialites who make up the cast spend virtually the entire film discussing the men they love, hate, desire, or have just left. The bitchiness comes to the boil when go-getter shopgirl Crawford makes a play for, and wins, one of the group's men, resulting in divided loyalties, devious scheming, and delightfully sharp dialogue all round. Hardly a subversive proto-feminist manifesto, given that Shearer goes back to her faithless hubby with gooey eyes; but enough points are made *en route* about male pride and foibles, and enough laughs are had by all, to leave the abiding impression of a joyous, unsentimental celebration of womanhood. And the performances are wonderful. GA

Women in Love

(Ken Russell, 1969, GB) Glenda Jackson, Oliver Reed, Alan Bates, Jennie Linden, Eleanor Bron, Michael Gough, Alan Webb.
130 min.
Despite a growing portentousness towards the end, and moments of silliness (memorably, the fireside nude wrestling scene between Bates and Reed) scattered throughout, a surprisingly restrained, even respectful adaptation of DH Lawrence's novel. Much of the credit lies with the cast, camerawork (by Billy Williams), the art direction and Georges Delerue's score, though it must be said that Russell, if seemingly unconcerned with the novel's political thrust, is in fruitful sympathy with Lawrence's sexual politics. Far from good, but better than one might fear or expect. GA

Women in Revolt

(Paul Morrissey, 1971, US) Jackie Curtis, Candy Darling, Holly Woodlawn, Jonathan Kramer, Johnny Minute, Michael Sklar.
98 min.
Three transvestites play at being women playing at being Women. Candy tries for a job as an actress, but has a hard time avoiding the casting couch. Holly plays a spaced-out model who ends up on the Bowery. Jackie ends up looking after the kids. Some find the film anti-women in its parody of the notion of a women's movement...but after all, who better equipped to depict those male fantasies about women than transvestites? VG

Women in Tropical Places

(Penny Woodcock, 1900, GB) Alison Doody, Scarlett O'Hara, Huffty Reah, Alan Igbon.
90 min.
'I just have affairs with strangers who make things up' confesses elegant Argentinian Celia (Doody). Arriving in Newcastle to meet businessman George, she is dumped by one of his henchmen in a hotel suite, shared by bizarre cabaret artistes Scarlet (O'Hara) and her bald daughter Charmaine (Reah), plus assorted wacky visitors. George is nowhere in sight, but to the horror of Celia, an active member of the International Revolutionary League, a local hate campaign has

been launched against his proposal to redevelop the town using non-union labour... Penny Woodcock's first feature is full of half-realised ideas, but quickly loses all sense of pace and direction. The combination of cabaret turns, social commentary and frustrated libidos, while potentially intriguing, is ultimately too incohesive. Where is George? Why is he buying an ice-cream in one of Celia's fantasies? Why so many flashbacks of Celia's half-hearted ministrations to cheerfully posed peasants? Is she bored, patronising, or just well-dressed? You give up wondering. CM

Women on the Roof, The (Kvinnorna på taket)

(Carl-Gustaf Nykvist, 1989, Swe) Amanda Ooms, Helena Bergström, Stellan Skarsgård, Percy Brandt.
90 min.
'The light...See how it comes in. Licht, light, lumière. But Nordic light is the most beautiful in Europe'. If this sounds like Woody Allen satirising Bergman, it isn't, but you're close. In fact this is a first feature by the son of great Swedish cameraman (and Bergman-Allen collaborator) Sven Nykvist. We are in Stockholm, 1914. Anna (Bergström) is a sophisticated, tempestuous photographer with a mysterious history; innocent, timid Linnea (Ooms) gradually falls under her spell, and into her bed, before Anna's past interrupts their idyll. This falls into most of the pitfalls associated with the continental art movie, flirting as it does with pornography and proving strictly a tease on the intellectual front. The pensive piano score and pretty photography are par for the course, but the film, like the vapid Linnea, only threatens to come to life when events take a macabre turn towards the end; even then, the effect is chilly and rather too pat to convince. TCh

Women on the Verge of a Nervous Breakdown (Mujeres al Borde de un Ataque de Nervios)

(Pedro Almodóvar, 1988, Sp) Carmen Maura, Antonio Banderas, Julieta Serrano, Maria Barranco, Rossy de Palma.
89 min.
To attempt a synopsis of this extravagantly stylish farce would be daft and forgettable: suffice it to say that a lot happens in the absence of anything actually happening. What lingers in the memory is a sustained desperation, and scenes of Wilder-like sophistication dotted with improbable props, actions, inflated campery, and most of Almodóvar's usual repertory-style company. Somehow a deranged and oddly distanced plot is contrived from elements including infidelity, tranquiliser-spiked gazpacho, interior decor, bad fashion, beds on fire, caged animals, demented telephone answering machines, Shi-ite terrorists, motorbikes, sentimentalism, property rental, and madness. Don't expect the delirious, hilarious eroticism of Almodóvar's previous Law of Desire, although the two films share a taste for the thriller elements of high comedy. This is an altogether stranger film – looser, more dream-like, as if directed in the state to which the title refers. TC

Wonderful Life

(Sidney J Furie, 1964, GB) Cliff Richard, Walter Slezak, Susan Hampshire, Melvyn Hayes, Richard O'Sullivan, Una Stubbs, The Shadows.
113 min.
Frustrated by shooting a movie with a stuffy veteran director (Slezak) who's not hip to the scene, Cliff and the Shadows conspire to make their own musical version. Lively but contrived star vehicle, chiefly notable for the 'We Love Movies' sequence in which Cliff gets to dress up as Valentino, Jolson and Groucho Marx. NF

Wonder Man

(H Bruce Humberstone, 1945, US) Danny Kaye, Virginia Mayo, Vera-Ellen, Donald Woods, SZ Sakall, Allen Jenkins, Ed Brophy, Otto Kruger.
98 min.
Kaye is notably adept in a dual role: as a song-and-dance man murdered after witnessing a mob killing, and as the entertainer's timid intellectual twin. Since the shy half of the family is unwilling to get involved in the case, the dead brother's restless spirit comes back to share his body while exacting his revenge, causing romantic compli-

cations for the two respective girlfriends who now find themselves in love with the same man. John P Fulton's effects work won a deserved Oscar.

Wooden Crosses
see Croix de Bois, Les

Wooden Horse, The

(Jack Lee, 1950, GB) Leo Genn, David Tomlinson, David Greene, Anthony Steel, Bryan Forbes, Peter Finch.
101 min. b/w.
Solid retelling of one of WWII's most audacious and enduring escape stories as Genn, Tomlinson and Steel tunnel under a vaulting horse to escape Nazi captivity in Stalag Luft III and head for neutral Sweden courtesy of fake passports. Detailed handling gives a good idea of the men's ingenuity and courage in this dignified, reasonably tense Britflick. TJ

Wooden Man's Bride, The (Yan Shen)

(Huang Jianxin, 1993, Tai) Chang Shih, Wang Lan.
114 min.
From the director of The Black Cannon Incident, this is a piece of raunchy myth-making in the vein of Red Sorghum and The Swordsman in Double-Flag Town. A peasant bride is hijacked by bandits on the way to her wedding. Her intended husband meanwhile meets an untimely accident and bites the dust. Undaunted the groom's family presses ahead with the wedding ceremony, marrying the rescued girl to a wooden effigy of the dead man. The melodramatics and sexual exotica are routine for the genre, but the film looks good and plays well. Its most intriguing element is the gay subplot involving the bandit chief, a cross-dressing aesthete who gets a crush on the strapping hero. TR

Woodlanders, The

(Phil Agland, 1997, GB) Rufus Sewell, Jodhi May, Polly Walker, Tony Haygarth, Cal MacAninch, Emily Woof, Walter Sparrow, Sheila Burrell.
98 min.
Best known for spending a year in a remote Chinese village for his documentary series Beyond the Clouds, Agland comes down to earth with this, his first fiction film (scripted by David Rudkin). On the edge of the New Forest, the daughter of a sawmill owner (Woof), whose father has hopes for her betterment, loves a woodsman (Sewell), but is edged into marriage to a doctor (MacAninch). Result, tragedy. Underplaying the extreme melodramatics of Thomas Hardy's novel (a self-defeating exercise, perhaps) while hammering home the class theme, the movie feels tired and draggy even at ninety-odd minutes – and the blame rests squarely with Agland, whose direction is flat and uninspired. The scenes simply don't breathe, though the women in particular perform heroic acts of hopeless resuscitation. TCh

Woodstock

(Michael Wadleigh, 1970, US) Joan Baez, Joe Cocker, Country Joe and the Fish, Crosby Stills & Nash, Arlo Guthrie, Richie Havens, Jimi Hendrix, The Who.
184 min.
As the roaches moulder in the gutters of Haight Ashbury, and the Love generation consider their bank statements, we're left with this legendary piece of trend-setting opportunism to reflect on. The screen shatters into fragments of middle class kids in rags, of super-lays offering their love to millions, of nipples al fresco. Of course there's Hendrix coming orgasmically alive, Richie Havens shot from below and carved from granite, Joe Cocker timelessly manic, Crosby Stills & Nash in some peace-sodden heaven. A time capsule, yes, and a hallowed memory, perhaps. But gimme shelter. SG

Woodstock: The Director's Cut

(Michael Wadleigh, 1994, US) Jimi Hendrix, The Who, Janis Joplin, Crosby Stills & Nash, Sly & the Family Stone, Country Joe & the Fish, Canned Heat, Jefferson Airplane.
224 min.
The 'director's cut' has digitally improved sound

and imagery and about 40 minutes of extra footage, including previously unseen performances by Jefferson Airplane, Janis Joplin and Canned Heat. Pride of place goes to Jimi Hendrix, looking saintly for what was to be a last screen appearance. Remember a time when sex didn't carry the death penalty and records didn't come from commercials on the telly? SGr

Woo Woo Kid, The

(Phil Alden Robinson, 1987, US) Patrick Dempsey, Talia Balsam, Beverly D'Angelo, Michael Constantine, Betty Jinnette, Kathleen Freeman, Peter Hobbs.
98 min.
The beguiling true-life case of Sonny Wisecarver – who, aged 14, married two married women in their twenties in the dog days of World War II, and shared tabloid covers with Hitler and D-Day – was a moment's monument, and a perfect vehicle for the likes of Jonathan Demme. In Robinson's hands, it is sometimes crude, sometimes wonderfully small-print human, bailed out by the gravitational pull of documentary truth, and generally worth a look. The soundtrack alone is sharp enough to sell the movie to blind swing band fans. For Sonny (Dempsey) it was always true love, though the ladies suffer the strictures of the law for corrupting a minor. Sonny is played adenoidally open-mouthed and innocently good-hearted, and both wives (Balsam, D'Angelo) are experienced but achingly vulnerable. The film, validly, doesn't take a stance, but plays a cheeky catch-as-catch-can between tethered fact and sometimes surreal guesswork. Nice little film. BC

Word, The
see Ordet

Word Is Out

(Mariposa Film Group, 1977, US)
135 min.
A documentary by the San Francisco-based Mariposa Film Group, comprising interviews with 26 gay American men and women of varied classes and ethnic origins. It is neither militant (although it does contain some footage of civil rights demos) nor analytic (although the careful selection of interviewees bespeaks one level of analysis), and is an important film for those very reasons. It doesn't intimidate or alienate any potential viewer, but uses techniques of simple reasoning, and elements of mild surprise, to catch attention and hold it. If two hours of talking heads sounds like a long time, then it's a measure of the film-makers' success that the result is as gripping and persuasive as the most accomplished fiction. TR

Working Girl

(Mike Nichols, 1988, US) Harrison Ford, Sigourney Weaver, Melanie Griffith, Alec Baldwin, Joan Cusack, Philip Bosco, Nora Dunn.
113 min.
A New York romantic comedy which exhibits a touch, timing and inventiveness that puts the much acclaimed Moonstruck in its place, and the interaction between the female leads is so funny that you don't care if the leading man never turns up – the film's only problem. Tess McGill (Griffith) aches to graduate from the secretarial pool to executive level in the brokerage industry, but her male colleagues promise breaks and pass her round. The deal is no fairer under a female boss, Katharine Parker (Weaver), who never makes the coffee and steals Tess' best idea. When the boss breaks her leg skiing, Tess takes over her office, and meets investment broker Jack Trainer (Ford), with whom she works well until her boss returns breathing fire. Kevin Wade's screenplay is so sharply witty in all directions on class differences that the man in the middle appears neutral and all-purpose. All the women steal his scenes, including the wonderfully funny Joan Cusack as a back-combed secretary. A treat. BC

Working Girls

(Lizzie Borden, 1986, US) Louise Smith, Deborah Banks, Liz Caldwell, Marusia Zach, Amanda Goodwin, Boomer Tibbs, Ellen McElduff.
91 min.
Lizzie Borden takes an axe to the Hollywood image of the prostitute. Focusing on Molly

(Smith), a college girl who's trying to make some cash, prostitution is viewed as an economic alternative, another business in the world's financial capital. The overriding unsung leitmotif is that of a procession (of clients, rituals, preparations); the cold reality of Borden's vision is reminiscent of Frederick Wiseman's examinations of American institutions. But where Wiseman's seemingly neutral recording of a nightmare works, Borden's calculated dramatic reconstruction falters as one set of stereotypes is substituted for another. Wooden lines stand in lieu of dialogue, caricatures in place of characters. SGo

Work Is a Four Letter Word
(Peter Hall, 1967, GB) David Warner, Cilla Black, Elizabeth Spriggs, Zia Mohyeddin, Joe Gladwin, Julie May, Alan Howard.
93 min.
A disastrous reworking of Henry Livings' play *Eh?*, recognisable only in that the hero still grows aphrodisiac mushrooms in the boiler-room of the automated factory where he works and is currently honeymooning with his new bride. Livings' wonderful mental slapstick (with not so much his characters' bottoms as their minds exposed in long woolly underwear as their spiritual trousers fall down) has been reduced to a pitifully trite satire on automation. A few amusing bits survive the gaudily trendy direction. TM

World According to Garp, The
(George Roy Hill, 1982, US) Robin Williams, Mary Beth Hurt, Glenn Close, John Lithgow, Hume Cronyn, Jessica Tandy, Swoosie Kurtz.
136 min.
John Irving's bestselling book – one of those huge, baggy, scattergun novels that Americans imagine contain all human life – is noticeably shortened and not improved by Steve Tesich's script, which loses Irving's perceptions of Garp's life existing within a much larger flow of experience. All we are left with are some of those telling symbolic nuggets from another cradle-to-the-grave saga of a New England writer and his proto-feminist Mom. Williams is cuddly enough as the man whose talents for nurturing a family are constantly undermined by a malign fate, and there is a performance of some dignity from Lithgow as a six-and-a-half-foot ex-pro footballer transsexual. But it's the kind of movie which is brave – or stupid – enough to ask the meaning of life without having enough arse in its breeches to warrant a reply. CPea

World and His Wife, The
see State of the Union

World Apart, A
(Chris Menges, 1987, GB) Jodhi May, Jeroen Krabbé, Barbara Hershey, Nadine Chalmers, Maria Pilar, Kate Fitzpatrick, Tim Roth.
113 min.
What lifts cinematographer Menges' directorial debut above the worthiness of most anti-apartheid movies is the child's viewpoint. Like Maisie in *What Maisie Knew*, 13-year-old Molly (May) is walled off from much of the high passion of the adult world, but a casualty of the fallout. With her communist father (Krabbé) on the run, and her liberal journalist mother Diane (Hershey) totally preoccupied with the struggle against apartheid, Molly is resentful about her loveless and lonely upbringing. When Diane – whose involvement with the banned ANC brings down the brutality of the South African police on their comfortable white Johannesburg suburb – is imprisoned under the 90 Day Detention Act, Molly's schoolfriends ostracise her; meanwhile, subjected to intense psychological pressure driving at her maternal guilts, released and immediately imprisoned again, Diane attempts suicide. Few cause-movies point out how uncomfortable martyrs are to live with, and few stars are prepared to play them that way, but Hershey does. Intelligent, unsensational, and painful, it's a film to applaud. BC

World Apartment Horror
(Katsuhiro Otomo, 1991, Jap) Hiroki Tanaka, Yuji Nakamura, Weng Huarong, Kimiko Nakagawa.
97 min.
The global success of *Akira* earned Otomo the freedom to make this live-action feature, which launched a cycle of films about the situation of

Asian immigrants in Japan, most of them earnestly sociological. Otomo's film, though, is a yakuza horror comedy. The Black Dragon gang has its eye on a tumbledown apartment building rented to poor students and workers from Taiwan, China, Pakistan, the Philippines and Bangladesh. The first heavy sent to force the tenants out goes crazy. The second is Itta (Tanaka, now better known as a director under the name Sabu), who rushes in ego-first and finds himself facing not only uncowed Asians but also some very strong voodoo. TR

World for Ransom
(Robert Aldrich, 1954, US) Dan Duryea, Gene Lockhart, Patric Knowles, Reginald Denny, Nigel Bruce, Marian Carr, Arthur Shields, Douglas Dumbrille.
82 min. b/w.
A Monogram cheapie derived from the NBC TV series *China Smith*, this is a seminal Aldrich movie with Duryea, as private eye Mike Callahan, the first in a long line of compromised idealists who recur throughout the director's work. The plot concerns a kidnapped nuclear scientist – we're in Cold War country here – and the story's set in a Poverty Row Singapore. 'It was a parody on the usual exotic espionage adventure films' Aldrich remarked in an interview. He thought it 'interesting', indeed 'pretty good', but was sore about the excision of a scene which portrayed the girl Duryea loves as a lesbian (after Dietrich in *Morocco*). The whole point, he explained, was that Duryea could forgive her past life with men, but couldn't handle her love for women. Nor could the censors, it seems. Boys' Own material on the surface, maybe, but on the level of characterisation a compelling exploration of partnerships, brotherly bonds, and the fallibility of trust. MA

World Is Full of Married Men, The
(Robert Young, 1979, GB) Anthony Franciosa, Carroll Baker, Sherrie Cronn, Paul Nicholas, Gareth Hunt, Georgina Hale, Anthony Steel.
106 min.
Dreadful moral tale-cum-sex comedy, with Franciosa as an adulterous director of TV commercials, living a hypocritical double life with wife (Baker) and model (Cronn), until wife throws him out in favour of a rock star (Nicholas). Scripted by Jackie Collins from her own novel, it's a repeat of the formula of *The Stud*, with the same mixture of softcore jollies and 'comedy' scenes of humiliation/embarrassment. Ludicrous. RM

World of Gilbert & George, The
(Gilbert & George, 1981, GB) Gilbert & George.
69 min.
Art world dabblings with the fringe culture of the New Right bear all the slightly risible hallmarks of a hermetically-sealed conceptual con(troversy), though there are apparently some who claim the status of key political text for this Arts Council-funded effort. A first film by the 'living sculpture' pose-artists, the Morecambe and Wise of sober-suited, straight-faced pretension, it's a cumulatively noxious set of discreet statements, visual and musical quotes, and appropriated testimonies representing a claimed triumph of the artistic will over national decay and the inarticulate dead end. A manifesto for a troublesome, truthless Beauty, it's a thoughtfully cinematic provocation that inventively formalises the clichés of agit-prop and turns them around, but probably further marginalises itself in the process. Odd, though, that 'Jerusalem' makes as much sense ending this as it did *Chariots of Fire*. PT

World of Suzie Wong, The
(Richard Quine, 1960, GB) William Holden, Nancy Kwan, Sylvia Syms, Michael Wilding, Laurence Naismith, Jackie Chan.
129 min.
Holden plays the aspiring young artist in Hong Kong who falls for a Chinese prostitute (Kwan), and despite major difficulties – like his loathing of her way of life, a poor script, and the restrictions that taste demanded of films in those days – their relationship flourishes for a while. But denied the chance of being honest about its subject, it soon degenerates into euphemistic soap

opera, with vague gestures towards bohemianism and lukewarm titillation. Wisely, Quine seems to have devoted most of his attention to the Hong Kong locations. CPe

World's Greatest Lover, The
(Gene Wilder, 1977, US) Gene Wilder, Carol Kane, Dom DeLuise, Fritz Feld, Carl Ballantine, Matt Collins.
89 min.
Heading for Tinsel Town to compete for stardom as the World's Greatest Lover in an ailing studio's last ditch attempt at finding its own Valentino, Wilder's newly-wed small town baker is undaunted by the vast competition or by an embarrassing nervous disorder, and ignorant of the hunger harboured by his new wife (Kane) for the Divine Rudy. Wilder's second feature as writer/director hovers uneasily between homage and pastiche, and on occasion his specialised hysteria stretches too thin for comfort, particularly with several supporting characters being cut from the selfsame cloth. He also succumbs to the same kind of icky True Romance sentimentality that all but poleaxed Woody Allen's early features, thereby wasting much of Carol Kane's potential. For all that, there are enough laughs – DeLuise and Feld sparkle beautifully – to justify the price of a ticket. GD

World Without Pity, A
see Monde sans pitié, Un

Worm Eaters, The
(Herb Robins, 1977, US) Herb Robins, Lindsay Armstrong Black, Robert Garrison, Joseph Sackett, Mike Garrison, Muriel Cooper.
94 min.
A truly disgusting film. The director himself appears in the pivotal role of Ungar, a clubfooted weirdo who breeds worms in his shack up near the Melnick lake. The corrupt local mayor and his mad, bad cronies want Ungar out of the way so they can build condominiums on the site. When the efforts of the valley conservationists fail, Ungar spikes everyone's food with worms. There are lots and lots of big close-ups of mouths openly masticating spaghetti'n'worms, hot dogs'n'-worms, ice cream'n'worms, and tobacco'n'worms. Real live wriggling worms. The characters then turn into 'worm-people', which means that they crawl around with their lower limbs encased in slimy sleeping-bags. All this is played for laughs. The 'humour' is not exactly of the most sophisticated kind, but there are certainly gags galore. AB

Wot! No Art
(Christopher Mason, 1978, GB) narrator: Tom Kempinski.
55 min.
An entertaining if undeniably muddled retrospective on the social context of the arts in the period 1945-51, the years of the first post-war Labour government and the birth of the Arts Council: days of hope (and austerity) when public patronage for 'public art' was intended to promote a cultural renaissance to complement that in education, health and housing. The film is sound in tracing the dissipation of the dream (making good use of representative newsreels, with their uniquely patronising commentaries), but falters in drawing parallels with today's situation, and is insufficiently rigorous or coherent in its polemical assertion of the status of art as a social priority. Provocative, none the less. PT

Would You Kill a Child?
see ¿Quién Puede Matar a un Niño?

Woyzeck
(Werner Herzog, 1978, WGer) Klaus Kinski, Eva Mattes, Wolfgang Reichmann, Willy Semmelrogge, Josef Bierbichler.
81 min.
An anarchist's morality play; the tale of an army private tormented in private by visions of apocalypse, in public by the unbearable weight of social and sexual oppression; he flips. Herzog's harsh vision of human suffering beyond despair, adapted from the Georg Büchner play, casts Woyzeck as a proletarian King Lear (Kinski, extraordinary once again), but there are echoes, too, of Beckett and Brecht. A sharp parable on social oppression and dormant rebellion, made with a dispassionate, deliberate formality that some may find hard to take. CA

Woyzeck

(János Szász, 1994, Hun) Lajos Kovács,
Diana Vâcaru, Alexandr Porohovschikov,
Péter Haumann.
93 min. b/w.
Visually extraordinary version of Büchner's oft-
adapted play, with a sturdy performance from
Kovács as the hapless, humiliated Woyzeck, here
a railway signalman, who finally cracks when
he discovers his wife's infidelity. The combination of high-contrast b/w and some telling,
unusual angles makes for a strikingly poetic version that verges on the abstract, but it is slow, a
little too studied and far less poignant than
Herzog's more romantic account. GA

Wraith, The

(Mike Marvin, 1986, US) Charlie Sheen, Nick
Cassavetes, Sherilyn Fenn, Randy Quaid,
Griffin O'Neal, Matthew Barry.
92 min.
Sheen Jr is the mysterious new boy in town, possibly also a reincarnation of the good guy who
has been offed by the bad guys before the start
of the story. The bad guys are led by the resident psycho, Cassavetes Jr, with O'Neal Jr as
one of his henchmen. The ghost of the good
(RIP) guy drives a customised Chrysler
Interceptor and forces O'Neal Jr off the road,
because the good (RIP) guy is a sort of High
Lanes Drifter, out to avenge himself. This
becomes apparent very early on. Our motoring
correspondent asks: could this film be about the
death of the motor car as we know it? Bleeagh.
AB

Wrestling Ernest Hemingway

(Randa Haines, 1994, US) Robert Duvall,
Richard Harris, Shirley MacLaine, Sandra
Bullock, Nicole Mercurio, Piper Laurie.
123 min.
Frank (Harris) is an Irish sea-salt marooned in a
quiet Florida backwater. Lonely and forgotten,
he strikes up a friendship with a retiring old man
in the park, Walt (Duvall), a hairdresser from
Chicago. Frank is loud and full of blarney; Walt
is dapper, shy and in love with the sunny young
waitress (Bullock) at the local diner. They become
inseparable. The relationship between two
grumpy old codgers is not what you'd immediately expect from director Haines (Children of a
Lesser God), or from a 21-year-old screenwriter
(Steve Conrad), but then this is a film of discreet
pleasures and minor miracles. There aren't really any surprises, but it's a delight to see a movie
which idles away without anything more pressing on its mind than people. As good a way as
any of watching the world go by. TCh

Writing in the Sand, The

(Amber Films, 1991, GB)
45 min. b/w.
A cinepoem from the Amber Collective evoking
a day at the seaside, through a collage of recorded snippets of conversation and Sirkka Lüsa-
Konttinen's superb photographs of
holidaymakers at play. Atmospheric and frequently funny, it is imbued with an unsentimental nostalgia for simpler summertimes, but the
coda about environmental pollution seems rather
tagged on, and therefore less forceful than it
might have been. GA

Writing on the Wall, The
(Nous Etions Tous des
Noms d'Arbres)

(Armand Gatti, 1982, Fr/Bel) John Deehan,
Brendan 'Archie' Deeney, Paddy Doherty,
Nigel Haggan, John Keegan, Neil McCaul.
114 min.
A youth workshop in Derry is mounting various
projects, including a dramatised enquiry into the
death of a soldier. But when a squaddy is shot
on the doorstep, then real life intrudes in the
shape of the police and security forces. Gatti's
brave and honourable film forcefully engages
with a subject with which we on the 'mainland'
are often too ignorant – the images of violence
are plainly visible day after day, but the means
to interpret them is absent. By a diligent inclusion of the background cultural elements to the
drama, Gatti builds a penetrating account of the
Irish 'question' that does justice to the complexities of its condition. The film's confusions might
be said to mirror those of its subject, but it

demonstrates better than any other film to date
the passion that lies behind a whole community's grievances. CPea

Written Face, The
(Das Geschriebene Gesicht)

(Daniel Schmid, 1995, Switz/Jap) Tamasaburo
Bando, Han Takehara, Karuko Sugimura,
Kazuo Ohno, Yajuro Bando, Kai Shishido.
93 min.
This portrait of kabuki artist Tamasaburo Bando
explores the art of the Onnagata, the male performer who specialises in female parts. Alongside
lengthy stage excerpts, where music, movement
and dazzling costume changes trace the refined
expression of loss and longing, the man himself
attests that he's 'never seen the world with the
eyes of a woman', while several actresses who've
inspired him attest to the longevity of their own
careers – Tsutakiyomatsu Asaji, for instance, still
singing at 101. Schmid's approach is reverent, if
slightly functional, but he comes a cropper when
attempting a kabuki-style celluloid drama of his
own, and the use of Madame Butterfly is surely
a misjudgment. Occasionally captivating none
the less. TJ

Written on the Wind

(Douglas Sirk, 1956, US) Lauren Bacall, Robert
Stack, Dorothy Malone, Rock Hudson, Robert
Keith, Grant Williams.
99 min.
How many movies evoke the period in which they
were made and yet still look both fresh and modern as well? This seems like one of the quintessential films of the '50s: a high-powered Texas
oil-family drama, detailing the mis-matches
between the spoiled and variously bent children of
the family and the relatively 'normal' outsiders.
Sirk plays it as a conspicuously fierce critique of a
particular sector of American society, the disintegrating middle class, but one in which all the sympathy goes to the 'lost' children rather than to the
straights. The acting is dynamite, the melodrama
is compulsive, the photography, lighting, and
design share a bold disregard for realism. It's not
an old movie; it's a film for the future. TR

W.R. – Mysteries of
the Organism
(W.R. – Misterije Organizma)

(Dusan Makavejev, 1971, Yugo/WGer) Milena
Dravic, Jagoda Kaloper, Zoran Radmilovic,
Tuli Kupferberg, Jackie Curtis, Betty Dodson,
Jim Buckley, Nancy Godfrey.
86 min.
Although it seemed like some kind of breakthrough
at the time, Makavejev's film isn't improving with
age. Its comedy rests flimsily on cross-cutting
between two distinct sets of material: the American
footage starts with the life and ideas of Wilhelm
Reich, and goes on to explore some of the more
bizarre fringes of 'permissive' America; the
Yugoslav footage comprises a risible hymn to
Stalin from the archives, plus a satirical account of
an affair between a liberated Yugoslav woman and
a repressed Russian skating star. The Reichian
notion that everybody needs better orgasms has a
certain credibility; but neither Tuli Kupferberg
prowling New York as a 'hippie guerilla', nor the
juxtaposition of Stalin with Jim Buckley's erect
cock, says anything interesting about sex, power
politics, or the relation between them. TR

Wrong Arm of the Law, The

(Cliff Owen, 1962, GB) Peter Sellers, Lionel
Jeffries, Bernard Cribbins, Davy Kaye, Nanette
Newman, Bill Kerr, John Le Mesurier.
94 min. b/w.
On the face of it, a TV-style comedy inspired by
Ealing Studios, most notably The Lavender Hill
Mob. But somehow Owen, the cast, and a large
team of writers turn it into a very superior piece
of work, with both an eye and an ear for dialogue
and the absurd situation. Sellers, a smooth Bond
Street couturier, is also the rough-diamond leader
of a bunch of inept criminals. He keeps them
happy with luncheon vouchers, home movies,
and paid holidays in Spain. But their welfare state
criminality is undermined by the arrival of a gang
of Australians, forcing Scotland Yard to get its
act together. Not only is it genuinely funny, it's
also a sly portrait of Britain slowly emerging
from the Never Had It So Good days into the
Wilson era. ATu

Wrong Is Right (aka The Man
With the Deadly Lens)

(Richard Brooks, 1982, US) Sean Connery,
George Grizzard, Robert Conrad, Katharine
Ross, GD Spradlin, John Saxon, Henry Silva,
Leslie Nielsen, Robert Webber, Rosalind Cash,
Hardy Krüger, Dean Stockwell.
118 min.
Perhaps the oddest major Hollywood feature of
1982. Veering wildly between a quite well-written satire on the contemporary American political scene and a very ham-fisted nuclear
blackmail thriller, its sheer eccentricity is quite
engaging. Connery is excellent as a superstar TV
reporter, but he deserves a better plot; and the
adulation his character receives from Arab leaders seems as ridiculous as his network's apparently effortless ability to transmit live anywhere,
any time. Writer/director Brooks is on stronger
ground when tilting at the extraordinary contradictions in America's political morality, but
his one major coup is to demonstrate just how
good a TV performer Connery could indeed be.
DP

Wrong Man, The

(Alfred Hitchcock, 1956, US) Henry Fonda,
Vera Miles, Anthony Quayle, Harold J Stone,
Nehemiah Persoff, Charles Cooper,
Richard Robbins.
105 min. b/w.
Hitchcock's long-standing fear of the police is
what originally attracted him to a newspaper
account of a family man wrongly identified as
an armed robber. The Wrong Man pays scrupulous attention to such things as the details of
police procedure and the eventual apprehension
of the real culprit – before the conviction of the
wrongly accused man (Fonda), but after the
stress has driven his wife (Miles) to mental
breakdown. The result is Hitchcock's most sombre film, unrelieved by his usual macabre
humour; the black-and-white photography and
the persecuted Fonda's sharply chiselled features lend an impressive documentary feel. It's
not generally rated among the master's best
works, largely because of the intractability of
the source material (or Hitchcock's unwillingness to dramatise the events). But there's still
plenty here for Hitchcockophiles: a Jesuitical
strain (the man happened to be a devout
Catholic), a complicity of guilt (as the wife irrationally comes to blame herself); and it's pure
noir. RM

Wrong Man, The

(Jim McBride, 1992, US) Kevin Anderson,
Rosanna Arquette, John Lithgow, Robert
Harper, Jorge Cervera Jr, Ernesto LaGuardia.
110 min.
An exotic modern-day film noir from the director
of The Big Easy with a promising cast and a
soundtrack by Los Lobos. Drifting through
Mexico, Anderson finds himself wanted for mur-
der. He hitches a fast ride to town with two fel-
low Americans, bickering couple Lithgow and
Arquette, but his troubles are only just beginning.
Scrappy, obnoxious, shrill and tiresome, though
Rosanna Arquette fans may disagree. TCh

Wrong Movement
(Falsche Bewegung)

(Wim Wenders, 1975, WGer) Rüdiger Vogler,
Hanna Schygulla, Ivan Desny, Marianne
Hoppe, Hans Christian Blech, Nastassja
Kinski, Peter Kern.
103 min.
Made between Alice in the Cities and Kings of the
Road, this is an odd and rather uncharacteristic
work for Wenders. Basically, the problem arises
from Peter Handke's script ('inspired' by Goethe's
Wilhelm Meister), which tends towards a symbolism and explicitness Wenders usually steers
clear of. The film follows the attempts of the central character (Vogler) to get a grip on an embryonic vocation as a writer, at the same time coming
to some kind of working arrangement with the
spectres of Germany's past. But Wenders'
strengths are also tantalisingly in evidence: the
highly-charged road sequences, the meditative
use of landscape, and the tensions beneath apparently desultory encounters. VG

Wrony

see Crows

WUSA

(Stuart Rosenberg, 1970, US) Paul Newman, Joanne Woodward, Anthony Perkins, Laurence Harvey, Pat Hingle, Cloris Leachman, Don Gordon, Moses Gunn, Bruce Cabot.
117 min.
Adapted from Robert Stone's novel *A Hall of Mirrors*, this is a sophisticated political satire set in New Orleans, with Newman as a DJ on a right wing station (it's being used to propagandise a neo-Fascist movement) whose tough cynicism finally shatters his relationship with a timid girl he picks up (Woodward). The film is intelligent and well directed, but what makes it exceptional is Anthony Perkins' extraordinary performance as the neurotic liberal Rainey, which builds – after a few rather shaky scenes – into an agonisingly real force in the narrative. Someone had the astonishingly appropriate idea of taking Norman Bates out of *Psycho* and turning him into a torn and anguished liberal/revolutionary: it's less a character study than a kind of visible expression of the raw liberal conscience, a twitching, convulsive mass of uncertainty and pain. Newman's visual, verbal and structural dialogue with Perkins throughout the film is so impressive that it makes this one of the more important political statements to have come out of Hollywood in the early '70s. DP

Wuthering Heights

(William Wyler, 1939, US) Merle Oberon, Laurence Olivier, David Niven, Flora Robson, Donald Crisp, Geraldine Fitzgerald, Hugh Williams, Leo G Carroll, Cecil Kellaway.
103 min. b/w.
From the (prolific) output of a largely unfashionable director, Wyler's *Wuthering Heights* has a distinctive look that elevates it above the blandness Goldwyn productions are so often charged with. Handsomely designed by James Basevi and shot by Gregg Toland, the much-filmed tale of Cathy's passion for Heathcliff succeeds as fulsome melodrama; and while it has little to do with Emily Bronte's sense of environment and pre-Victorian society, it's nevertheless strong on performances – especially Olivier, seen here at the peak of his romantic lead period. MA

Wuthering Heights

see Abismos de pasión

Wuthering Heights

(Peter Kosminsky, 1992, GB) Juliette Binoche, Ralph Fiennes, Janet McTeer, Sophie Ward, Simon Shepherd, Jeremy Northam, Simon Ward, John Woodvine.
106 min.
Restoring the dangerous passion and morbid obsession crucial to Emily Bronte's novel, Kosminsky's debut feature eschews melodrama in favour of Gothic romance, with Anne Devlin's skilful screenplay delving deep into the swirling currents of Cathy's forbidden love for the gypsy foundling Heathcliff, whom she later abandons for sensitive, refined Mr Linton. Where the film falls down is in confining itself too much to gloomy rooms, thus failing to point up the contrast between imprisoning social conventions and the pagan pleasures of the moors. Similarly, while Fiennes' flowing black locks and piercing blue eyes make Heathcliff, striding the moors swathed in animal skins, a powerful, darkly attractive figure, Binoche's Cathy lacks the wild sensuality that should underpin her wilfulness. There are problems, too, with the French actress' wavering accent. Nevertheless, this is superior to the 1939 Hollywood version in one other respect: instead of ending with the romantic tragedy of Cathy's death, it continues into the next generation, when the spurned Heathcliff returns to claim Wuthering Heights and to take a cruel revenge. A brave stab, but it doesn't always pierce the heart. NF

W.W. and the Dixie Dancekings

(John G Avildsen, 1975, US) Burt Reynolds, Art Carney, Conny Van Dyke, Jerry Reed, Ned Beatty, Richard D Hurst, Don Williams, Furry Lewis.
94 min.
Reynolds at his best as a hillbilly conman (he robs gas stations with a water-pistol in hopefully swashbuckling imitation of his idol Errol Flynn) who finds himself steering a minor-league bunch of musicians to stardom in a Nashville considerably sleazier than Altman's. Quirky Deep South locations, fine '50s atmosphere (back street bars full of young hopefuls imitating Elvis), a wonderful interlude in which Furry Lewis sings 'Dirty Car Blues'. With all faults (chiefly Art Carney as a tiresome lawman-cum-hellfire preacher), a refreshingly irrepressible movie. TM

Wyatt Earp

(Lawrence Kasdan, 1994, US) Kevin Costner, Gene Hackman, Dennis Quaid, Michael Madsen, Bill Pullman, Jeff Fahey, Isabella Rossellini, Tom Sizemore, JoBeth Williams, James Gammon.
190 min.
Costner's Earp is a 'deliberate' man, and Kasdan's big-budget over-long epic is deliberate to a fault. Depicting Wyatt's youth, his first, tragic marriage, and especially the stern injunctions of paterfamilias Hackman, this prologue is ponderous and predictable. Where Kasdan/Costner insist on going back and crossing every 't', Eastwood might have conveyed the same information in the blinking of an eye. Costner creates a complex individual, but he's in virtually every scene, and one yearns for a less monotonous presence. There's a tremendous lift when Quaid's emaciated, debauched, wise-cracking Doc Holliday appears. Despite its longueurs, however, this is not a negligible movie. When Earp pins a badge on his pathology the picture begins to add up (the famous feud with the Clantons is tense and brutal); and when the Earp family falls apart, it's clear the mess is largely of Wyatt's making. Breathtakingly photographed by Owen Roizman, this serious picture slowly reveals the festering wounds at the at the heart of a key Western myth. TCh

xyz

Zulu

Xala

(Ousmane Sembene, 1974, Sen) Thierno Leye, Seune Samb, Miriam Niang, Younouss Seye, Dieynaba Niang.
123 min.

An invigorating film which tells, in leisurely fashion, of a middle-aged Dakar businessman whose social standing begins to slip when he takes a third wife and finds that he's lost his touch in bed ('xala' means impotence). There's no sniggering humour, though; instead, Sembene aims satirical thrusts at the Senegalese bourgeoisie, who impotently ape the worst aspects of their former colonial masters, particularly their corruption and extravagance (our hero, for instance, uses imported mineral water to wash his car). The jokes and details are delightful, yet there's real anger behind them, and it bursts spectacularly into view in the concluding frames. GB

Xanadu

(Robert Greenwald, 1980, US) Olivia Newton-John, Gene Kelly, Michael Beck, James Sloyan, Dimitra Arliss, Katie Hanley, Sandahl Bergman.
96 min.

An experience so vacuous it's almost frightening. Built around a threadbare Hollywood fairytale which has Newton-John (on roller-skates) playing a muse despatched by Zeus to help mortals realise their fantasies, it turns out in fact to be an unashamed show-case for Livvy's multifarious 'talents'. Alas, as the film grinds from one epic production routine to another, it becomes painfully clear that she can't deliver a line (the script, full of gnomic punchlines, is admittedly abysmal), hold a note (the Jeff Lynne/John Farrar songs are lowest common denominator), or step a pas de deux (despite the helping hand of Gene Kelly, who can still cut it on the dance floor). Not even Michael Beck, fresh out of The Warriors, can salvage the disaster. IB

Xenolith

(YN Wong-Ho, 1994, US) Tsui Wing-Chi, Tsui Wing-Sing, Pak Yiu-Charn, Chan Fung-Ping.
96 min.

Shot entirely in Hong Kong and nearly eight years in post-production, this no-budget indie feature looks like any number of HK social-realist TV films but dares to do without a storyline or any hint of hyped-up drama. A working-class man struggles to bring up his two school-age sons; his wife has divorced him and emigrated, but remains a significant absence in the minds of the boys. That's more or less it as far as the content goes. Wong-Ho centres her interest on the minutiae of the kids' lives in the cramped apartment, implicitly challenging the orthodox Confucian view that father-son relations are the core of Chinese society. Unmomentous, but modestly impressive. TR

Xiao Wu

(Jia Zhangke, 1997, China) Wang Hongwei, Hao Hongjian, Zu Baitao.
108 min.

Xiao Wu is a likeable but scummy petty criminal, lifting wallets from visitors to the provincial dirt town he calls home. Times are getting hard. His oldest friend, now a respected citizen, doesn't want to know him any more; the leggy girl from the karaoke hostess bar is stringing him along; and the cops are mounting an anti-crime campaign. This wonderful debut feature (like most decent Chinese films of the 1990s, it was made outside what remains of the studio system) takes an almost Bressonian path to the core of one man's psyche, stripping away layer after layer of his loser's armour until he's left as 'naked' as a person can be. Acted with absolute conviction by a cast of non-professionals and resourcefully shot by HK indie film-maker Yu Lik-Wai, this is an engrossing and moving achievement. TR

X – the Man with X-Ray Eyes (aka The Man with the X-Ray Eyes)

(Roger Corman, 1963, US) Ray Milland, Diana Van Der Vlis, Harold J Stone, John Hoyt, Don Rickles, John Dierkes, Lorie Summers, Vicki Lee.
80 min.

Corman's intelligent sci-fi movie has a powerful performance from Milland as Dr Xavier, whose experiments with X-Ray eye-drops allow him to cheat at cards, diagnose patients' internal complaints, and see through women's clothing (fortunately for them, they're all standing with their naughty bits shielded by inexplicably opaque plants and pieces of furniture). As the treatment continues, however, Milland becomes terrified as he starts to see beyond the material world into the heart of the universe. The rudimentary special effects and cheapo production notwithstanding, this is an undoubted cult classic. ATu

X the Unknown

(Leslie Norman, 1956, GB) Dean Jagger, Edward Chapman, Leo McKern, William Lucas, Peter Hammond, Anthony Newley, Kenneth Cope.
81 min. b/w.

1956 – the year of the Suez crisis, a sharp increase in the crime rate, and uneasy preparation for WWIII – spawned a whole series of gloomy thrillers (both in Britain and in America) in which the weight of the military is mobilised against various alien organisms from the bowels of the earth or outer space. This Hammer entry is photographed in shadowy monochrome by Gerald Gibbs, with a sense of muted hysteria and despair underlying the stalwart attempts to defeat a radioactive thing which erupts in the Scottish highlands. Trash to people who don't like sci-fi or horror movies, but in a lot of ways it communicates the atmosphere of Britain in the late '50s more effectively than the most earnest social document. As one example, note the film's obsession with radioactivity (the monster feeds on it), which even becomes the background to an assignation between a doctor and a nurse in a nearby hospital. DP

Xtro

(Harry Bromley Davenport, 1982, GB) Bernice Stegers, Philip Sayer, Danny Brainin, Simon Nash, Maryam D'Abo.
86 min.

A British horror picture incompetent enough to be prime drive-in fodder, if only we had such a thing, this throws together in random fashion a mish-mash of all the half-remembered elements from recent hungry alien films. Telekinesis, melting telephones, randy au pair girls getting sliced in the shower, pumas in the living-room, and – nastiest scene of the month – a woman giving birth to a fully-grown man, who then bites off his own placenta. The Xtro creature is a warty lizard which snatches family men off to its space craft for three years at a stretch; but its greatest service to mankind seems to be a taste for eating the drivers of Volvo estate cars, which is very heartening. CPea

X, Y and Zee

see Zee & Co.

Yaaba

(Idrissa Ouedraogo, 1989, Burkina Faso/Fr/Switz) Fatima Sanga, Noufou Ouedraogo, Barry Roukietou, Adama Ouedraogo, Amade Toure.
90 min.

In the Mooré language of Burkina Faso, 'yaaba' means grandmother, in the sense of respect towards an elder touched with wisdom and grace. And 'yaaba' is the name given by a young village boy to an old woman ostracised by the community and forced to live alone outside their walls. Ouedraogo's beautifully controlled film gently illustrates how the villagers' prejudice towards the old woman reveals to the boy an adult world of folly and generosity that he's about to join himself. Amid the palpable heat and dust, characters are confidently drawn in the great cinema tradition of the rural poor, wit more than an occasional nod to Satyajit Ray's Pather Panchali. Oudraogo's direction of actors is superb, and as in Cissé's Yeelen, an input of European money and talent gives the film a polished surface. Unlike Yeelen, though, this seeks not to create a magical universe, but to tell a direct, affecting story of superstition and love that marks Ouedraogo as a talent to watch. DT

Yaacov Ben Dov: Father of the Hebrew Film

(Yaacov Gross, 1989, Isr)
31 min.

Ukrainian Yaacov Ben Dov began as a still photographer before becoming Palestine's first documentary-maker. His footage of the emerging state of Israel is full of optimism – children plant groves of trees, schools rise, harvests are reaped. Palestine, Kafka wrote in his diary after seeing Ben Dov's work, needs earth, not lawyers. There's no shortage of Brits in pith helmets – General Allenby in 1917; Churchill and Balfour; High Commissioner Sir Herbert Samuel watching a camel race. BC

Yakuza, The

(Sydney Pollack, 1974, US) Robert Mitchum, Ken Takakura, Brian Keith, Keiko Kishi, Eiji Okada, James Shigeta, Herb Edelman, Richard Jordan.
112 min.

Writer Paul Schrader's homage to the Japanese gangster movie, with the standard plot opened out to accommodate Mitchum and American support, who share the screen with Ken Takakura (the No 1 star of such pictures) and some attractive Japanese locations. Behind an excessively wordy script, obligatory twists and double-crosses, and the celibate stance of the two leads, there emerges the familiar and increasingly explicit nostalgic celebration of the chivalric male relationships of countless American Westerns. The exposition is often laughably inscrutable, and obligations to both Japanese and American audiences frequently land in the mid-Pacific, but the film succeeds in casting its own slow spell. Takakura's terse, spring-coiled performance nicely complements Mitchum's somnolent bulk, and despite falterings in build-up, the formalised violence is rivetingly choreographed. The final show-down is one not to be missed. CPe

Yang ± Yin: Gender in Chinese Cinema (Nansheng Nüxiang)

(Stanley Kwan, 1996, HK) Leslie Cheung, John Woo, Edward Yang, Chen Kaige, Tsui Hark, Hou Hsiao-Hsien, Tsai Ming-Liang, Ang Lee, Stanley Kwan.
77 min.

Made for the BFI's 'Century of Cinema' series, this remarkable film combines ultra-candid autobiography (Kwan not only comes out as gay but also discusses his sexuality with his mother) with a highly original investigation of the ways that Chinese cinema has constructed images of masculinity and dealt with sexual ambivalence. Many directors chip in comments on the roles of fathers in Chinese families, male bonding and the sexual lure of elder-brother figures. Stand-out sequences include a celebration of drag king Yam Kin-Fai, a survey of Brigitte Lin's many androgynous roles, and an interview with veteran martial arts director Chang Cheh about the Freudian symbolism in his all male extravaganzas – which Kwan illustrates with a hair-raising clip of a half-naked man being impaled by the arse on a huge metal spike. TR

Yang Kwei Fei

see Empress Yang Kwei Fei, The

Yangtse Incident (aka Battle Hell/Escape of The Amethyst)

(Michael Anderson, 1957, GB) Richard Todd, William Hartnell, Akim Tamiroff, Donald Houston, Keye Luke, Robert Urquhart, Barry Foster, Sam Kydd.
113 min. b/w.

This well-worn '50s actioner of the stiff-upper-lip school has Richard Todd as the Lt Commander of HMS 'Amethyst', a crippled British cruiser caught on the Yangtse in 1949 and narrowly escaping capture by the Chinese communist forces. Screenwriter Eric Ambler marshals the facts into the usual account of true-Brit resolve, and the production looks the part. TJ

Yankee Doodle Dandy

(Michael Curtiz, 1942, US) James Cagney, Joan Leslie, Walter Huston, Irene Manning, Rosemary De Camp, Richard Whorf, Jeanne Cagney, SZ Sakall, Walter Catlett, Frances Langford, George Barbier.
126 min. b/w.

Who but theatre historians now bother with

George M Cohan, author of songs like 'Mary's a Grand Old Name' and shows like '45 Minutes from Broadway'? No one. But everyone remembers Cagney's impersonation, pitched as it is at fever level, even higher up the thermometer than Curtiz' direction or Ray Heindorf's musical arrangements. This was just the film to bombard American theatres with after Pearl Harbor: full of rousing sentiments and songs ('You're a Grand Old Flag', 'Over There' – Cohan's chief contribution to WWI), all designed to steel the morale of every patriot. Now it seems raucous, vulgar, over long; but if you like slick jobs, this is certainly one of the slickest. GB

Yankee in King Arthur's Court, A

see Connecticut Yankee in King Arthur's Court, A

Yank in the RAF, A

(Henry King, 1941, US) Tyrone Power, Betty Grable, John Sutton, Reginald Gardiner, Donald Stuart, Morton Lowry.
98 min. b/w.
Producer Darryl Zanuck provided the outline for this tiresome WWII yarn about lending a hand 'over there'. Power plays an experienced civil pilot who, because the pay is good, agrees to ferry a bomber to England. In London, he bumps into old flame Grable, a showgirl doing volunteer ambulance work on the side; and determined to stick around to win her back (she tired of his other women), he cynically joins the RAF. Cockily convinced that the war effort needs his knowhow, he meanwhile leads Grable an unhappy dance by his unreliability and busy skirt-chasing. Redeeming himself through a heroic deed or two, he originally died in action; preview audiences refused to buy this; so now he ends apparently reunited with Grable, but still, in his own wry but apt term, 'a worm'. As perfunctory in its action sequences as in its personal relationships – with a couple of song-and-dance routines for Grable thrown in to crowd-please – it is unpersuasive, to say the least. TM

Yanks

(John Schlesinger, 1979, GB) Vanessa Redgrave, Richard Gere, William Devane, Lisa Eichhorn, Chick Vennera, Rachel Roberts, Tony Melody, Wendy Morgan.
141 min.
From the arrival of a platoon of GIs in Northern England to their departure for D-Day, this chronicles three wartime romances, supposedly illuminating the fears and tensions that riddled the Anglo-American alliance. Good cast, scrupulous period reconstruction, and sentimentality; but it doesn't do much to redeem Schlesinger from the 'less-than-meets-the-eye' category.

Year My Voice Broke, The

(John Duigan, 1987, Aust) Noah Taylor, Loene Carmen, Ben Mendelsohn, Graeme Blundell, Lynette Curran, Malcolm Robertson, Bruce Spence.
105 min.
A film to restore one's faith in films about the transition from adolescence to adulthood. It's 1962 in the Australian backwater town where callow teenager Danny (Taylor) has grown up with the slightly older Freya (Carmen), an orphan child with a murky past who feels like an outsider. The Man Who Shot Liberty Valance is showing at the Astor, The Shadows strum 'Apache' on the radio, and car-stealing delinquent Trevor (Mendelsohn) fancies himself as the local rebel without a cause. Using telepathy, 'force fields', and hypnosis, Danny tries to win Freya's love, but the bad boy hunk aims lower and scores...So sure is writer/director Duigan's feel for the characters, the period, and the prevailing moral climate, that the faintly supernatural elements are effortlessly integrated: as the mystery surrounding the local 'haunted house' unfolds, there is an uncanny sense of a scandalous episode in the community's history repeating itself. A lovingly crafted and deeply affecting film, this might be likened, in terms of both quality and perception, to Rob Reiner's excellent Stand By Me. NF

Y'aura t'il de la neige à Noël?

see Will It Snow for Christmas?

Year of Living Dangerously, The

(Peter Weir, 1982, Aust) Mel Gibson, Sigourney Weaver, Linda Hunt, Bembol Roco, Domingo Landicho, Hermino de Guzman, Michael Murphy, Bill Kerr, Noel Ferrier.
115 min.
Bedeviled by much-publicised script wrangles (between Weir and source novelist Christopher Koch) and production difficulties (death threats to the crew on location in the Philippines), this bears too many signs of compromise betokening a wholly US-financed project. Gibson is adequate as the Aussie news journalist on assignment in the turbulent Indonesia of late 1965, teamed up romantically with the assistant to the British military attaché (Weaver), and professionally with a dwarf Chinese-Australian camera-man (actress Hunt, extraordinary as the movie's Tolstoy-quoting social conscience). Weir's steamy atmospherics often have the camera standing in for the unwelcome, uncomprehending Westerner in South East Asia to impressive effect; but the delineation of the political forces at work in the last days of Sukarno's regime is often less than clear. The result is a curiously languid affair, rather than the breathless Costa-Gavras-style thriller which was the least one might have expected from this kind of material. RM

Year of My Japanese Cousin, The

(Maria Gargiulo, 1995, US) Selene Vigil, Janis Tanaka, Jasper Streak.
70 min.
Un film de Gargiulo (she wrote, directed and edited), this slight tale concerns Stevie (Vigil), a rock guitar wannabe in trendy downtown Seattle, who's well and truly (and rather predictably) upstaged by cousin Yukari (Tanaka). It's hip, flashily edited and features lots and lots of grunge complaint rock, so much, in fact, that it resembles an audio-visual demo tape. Fans of Silly Rabbit, Deflowers and The Smugglers won't want to miss it, but Elvis movies have more substance. TCh

Year of the Beaver

(Steve Sprung/Sylvia Stevens/Dave Fox, 1985, GB) narrators: Anne Lamont, Steve Sprung.
77 min.
Transport and General Workers Union boss Jack Jones dubbed 1977 'Year of the Beaver', a time to encourage productivity and smoother union-management relations. It was also the year of the strike at the Grunwick photo processing plant. This documentary investigation into the 'staged media event' surrounding that strike, compiled from a mass of material (TV and independent interviews, news, radio and newspaper reports), builds up to a powerful indictment of the vacillation, compromise, and eventual betrayal by the official labour movement leadership, faced with the defence of the largely immigrant and female staff of George Ward's 'little photographic works' in West London. All the familiar spectacle of recent years is there: massed police ranks, hysterical reporting, Thatcher's dulcet tones urging the destruction of union power...Essential viewing for anyone interested in the mechanics of the evolving media show of industrial relations in our 'civilised state'. WH

Year of the Dragon

(Michael Cimino, 1985, US) Mickey Rourke, John Lone, Ariane, Leonard Termo, Ray Barry, Caroline Kava, Eddie Jones, Joey Chin, Victor Wong.
134 min.
Cimino's heroes have always been insufferably self-righteous, and Captain Stanley White (Rourke) is no exception. Standing alone, in the teeth of public opinion and police distrust, he conducts a clean-up campaign on New York's Chinatown which amounts to declared warfare (appropriate, since he is NYPD's most decorated veteran). His feud is conducted with such savage relentlessness and disregard for procedural nicety that he finds himself fighting his own police force, his wife, and his girlfriend as much as the local tong. Once again Cimino's ability to handle furious action set pieces is well to the fore: a shootout in a Chinese restaurant and a battle with two pistol-packing Chinese punkettes put him in the Peckinpah class. The connecting material, however, is by turns muddled, crass and dull,

amounting mostly to Stanley's interminable self-justification. His anger directed at any yellow skin, and his inability to distinguish between Asiatic races, mark him down as a racist. Whether this applies, by extension, to Cimino and the film as a whole, is a moot point. CPea

Year of the Gun

(John Frankenheimer, 1991, US) Andrew McCarthy, Sharon Stone, Valeria Golino, John Pankow, George Murcell, Mattia Sbragia, Roberto Posse.
111 min.
Frankenheimer's affinity for political subjects involving assassination, conspiracy and terrorism was proved by The Manchurian Candidate, Seven Days in May and Black Sunday, so what went so horribly wrong with this movie about Italy's Red Brigades? Rather than a viable script, it seems to be chunks from Michael Mewshaw's source novel, several of them leading nowhere, while the complicated political background is left to a university professor to pass off as conversation. The casting is dreadful, particularly smug McCarthy as the investigating American journalist, and Stone as a veteran war photographer, coiffured like one of Charlie's Angels. The Red Brigades are strictly pantomime: you expect them to carry round black fizzing bombs. Is our hero compiling a report on the revolutionaries or is he writing a novel about them? Much seems to depend upon this, though the outcome is far from clear. In short, Frankenheimer kneecaps himself. BC

Year of the Horse

(Jim Jarmusch, 1997, US) Neil Young and Crazy Horse.
107 min. b/w & col.
Since indie maestro Jarmusch made imaginative use of Young's soundtrack for Dead Man, it's fitting that he should have shot this documentary of the veteran band in concert on their 1996 tour, interspersed with interviews (some stoned, some illuminating) and footage from tours in the '70s and '80s. In contrast with the Young/Shakey-directed Rust Never Sleeps, Jarmusch uses film and video, colour and b/w to emphasise the music's rawness and immediacy, and by shooting mostly in medium and long shot, he catches the feel of actually being at a gig. Incidentally, the director also provides the film's funniest moment as he enlightens Young about God's mysterious ways. GA

Year of the Quiet Sun, A (Rok Spokojnego Slonca)

(Krzysztof Zanussi, 1984, Pol/US/WGer) Maja Komorowska, Scott Wilson, Hanna Skarzanka, Ewa Dalkowska, Vadim Glowna.
108 min.
1946, and amid the wreckage of a devastated town in West Poland, love grows between a Polish war widow and a shy American soldier too shattered by his experience of suffering to return home. As the troubled couple, barely able to communicate in words, try tentatively to find happiness together in a bleak landscape of doubt, suspicion, and hardship, Zanussi effortlessly avoids all the usual pitfalls, directing with exemplary restraint and an assured sense of period and place. With excellent performances from Wilson and the truly wonderful Komorowska, the film transcends its status as a sombre, sensitive love story, and becomes a moving meditation on the dignity and indomitability of the human spirit when beset by pain, cruelty, despair and death. Deeply human, with acute observation, wry humour, and a startling finale, it is as powerful and uplifting as Zanussi's earlier The Contract. GA

Years Without Days

see Castle on the Hudson

Yeelen (Brightness/The Light)

(Souleymane Cissé, 1987, Mali) Issiaka Kané, Aoua Sangaré, Niamanto Sanogo, Balla Moussa Keita.
105 min.
This luminous and beautiful film is set, at an indeterminate period, among the Bambara peoples of Cissé's Mali homeland, in Central North-West Africa. At its core is a spiritual battle waged

to the death between a father and son (Kané); the son coming to full maturity and potency, physically through his joining with one of a local chief's wives, and spiritually through his self-driven initiation into the ancient knowledge of the Bambara, encoded in the Komo. This is no ethnographic tract, despite being uniquely informed and filled with the fetishes, rituals and codes of this threatened culture. It is a film of complete integrity: the landscape stunning, the performances (non-professional) remarkable; full of light and fire, quiet passion and profundity, pure and simple. WH

Yellow Balloon, The

(J Lee Thompson, 1952, GB) Andrew Ray, Kathleen Ryan, Kenneth More, William Sylvester, Bernard Lee, Veronica Hurst, Sidney James.
80 min. b/w.
Britain's second 'X' certificate picture. Young master Ray loses papa More's sixpence and snatches a yellow balloon from another boy, who appears to fall to his death in the ensuing chase. Bad egg Sylvester, however, is the only other witness to the dreadful event, and blackmails the kid into taking part in a planned robbery. Tense direction from a promising newcomer and a strong central performance contribute to a '50s Britflick (from a story by Anne Burnaby) with a touch more bite than usual. (The balloon's colour must be taken on trust.) TJ

Yellowbeard

(Mel Damski, 1983, US) Graham Chapman, Peter Boyle, Richard 'Cheech' Marin, Tommy Chong, Marty Feldman, Peter Cook, Martin Hewitt, Michael Hordern, Eric Idle, Madeline Kahn, James Mason, John Cleese, Spike Milligan, Nigel Planer, Susannah York, Beryl Reid, David Bowie.
101 min.
Rollicking is the word the publicity people grab for when trying to sell a tedious piece of period-comic trash like this pirate spoof. Here it signifies the embarrassing sight of three generations of British comedy – Fringe to Python to Comic Strip – gritting their teeth through a series of gags in the meekest of bad taste, about sheep-shagging, cowflop, and big tits (Madeline Kahn in the Barbara Windsor parts), accompanied by token Americans to make it more acceptable to people in Idaho wondering why the accents are so weird. The script, for which Chapman and Cook must bear some responsibility, is a three-minute Python skit bloated out to feature length, involving buried treasure, revenge, and machinations close to the throne. Depressing stuff. KJ

Yellow Canary, The

(Herbert Wilcox, 1943, GB) Anna Neagle, Richard Greene, Albert Lieven, Margaret Rutherford, Nova Pilbeam, Valentine Dyall, Cyril Fletcher.
98 min. b/w.
Anna Neagle in bed with Adolf Hitler? Hardly likely, yet that's the set-up in this wartime spy drama, a sprightly collaboration between the husband-and-wife team of Neagle and Wilcox, which also boasts a curious meeting of minds in the screenplay department: Hollywood pro DeWitt Bodeen, and mild-mannered English actor and playwright Miles Malleson.

Yellow Dog

(Terence Donovan, 1973, GB) Jiro Tamiya, Robert Hardy, Carolyn Seymour, Joseph O'Conor, Hilary Tindall.
101 min.
The script credits list Kurosawa's writer Shinobu Hashimoto, Professor Alan Turney, and John Bird – which just about sums it up. This is a highly eccentric spy fable about a 'yellow dog' (Japanese private eye) who comes to London on a mission, only to find himself working in rather strained tandem with MI5. Kimura is given to making rice balls, moving into his superior's garden shed, and running round (literally) in small circles. The film is directed with much amiable if incoherent humour by Donovan, image maker of the '60s, who apparently gave in to his passion for things Japanese and even financed it himself; but somewhere along the line the original thread of Hashimoto's story seems to have got lost. Which doesn't help anyone follow the plot, but does make for a strange experience. CPe

Yellow Earth (Huang Tudi)

(Chen Kaige, 1984, China) Xue Bai, Wang Xueqi, Tan Tuo, Liu Qiang.
89 min.
The first 'modern' film to emerge from China, and one of the most thrilling debut features of the '80s. Its storyline couldn't be simpler. A Communist soldier visits a backward village in 1939, and is billeted with a taciturn widower and his teenage daughter and son. The soldier's mission is to collect folk songs, and it's through the exchange of songs that he gradually wins the trust and affection of his hosts. But the girl is to be sold into marriage with a much older man, and all the soldier's talk of breaking with feudal tradition fills her with unrealistic hopes of escaping her fate. The soldier returns to his base, leaving her to take her future in her own hands...There are political undercurrents here that got the film into trouble in China: the encounter between the CP and China's peasants is shown not as an instant meeting of minds, but as the uneasy, frustrating, and ultimately unresolved process that it actually was. But what really stirred things up in old Beijing was the film's insistence on going its own way. Chen Kaige and his cinematographer Zhang Yimou have invented a new language of colours, shadows, glances, spaces, and unspoken thoughts and implications; and they've made their new language sing. TR

Yellow Sky

(William A Wellman, 1948, US) Gregory Peck, Anne Baxter, Richard Widmark, Robert Arthur, John Russell, Henry Morgan, James Barton, Charles Kemper.
98 min. b/w.
A fine Western, harshly shot by Joe MacDonald in Death Valley locations, inevitably conjuring comparisons with Greed and The Treasure of the Sierra Madre as six bankrobbers on the run all but die in the desert salt flats before stumbling on a ghost town where a lone prospector (Barton) guards twin secrets: his rich gold strike and his fiercely tomboyish granddaughter (Baxter). Like a pack of wolves, the strangers are soon snarling lustfully after gold and/or the girl, with their leader (Peck) gradually detaching himself as his presence causes the girl to discover her femininity, and hers revives in him something of the man he was before Quantrill's Raiders descended on his home. Intriguingly, Lamar Trotti's screenplay develops WR Burnett's source story with The Tempest in mind, the subtler analogies serving to provide resonances. The situation again harks back to fraternal conflict (the year is 1867, in the aftermath of the Civil War); Yellow Sky also has its malign spirits, a band of renegade Apaches under the uneasy control of the prospector; and the conflict similarly resolves strangely, at its violent climax, into a sense of conciliation. Beautifully cast and characterised, this is one of Wellman's best films. TM

Yellow Smile, The (Sari Tebessum)

(Secklin Yasar, 1992, Tur) Sahika Tekland, Mahir Gunsiray, Leventn Ozdilek.
120 min.
Passions flair among the Turkish glitterati when art gallery owner Eda (Tekland), frustrated by her poet husband's alcohol-induced impotence, wanders from the straight and narrow and gets involved with artist friend Erdal (Gunsiray). The film adds little to the myriad other variations on the eternal triangle, but leading lady Tekland goes through the motions with a modicum of physical commitment. Be prepared for the odd splash of unintentional hilarity in this would-be sophisticated milieu (earnest discussions of Leonard Cohen's poetry and music rub shoulders with some of the most embarrassing disco scenes since Basic Instinct). TJ

Yellow Submarine

(George Dunning, 1968, GB) voices: John Clive, Geoffrey Hughes, Paul Angelus, Dick Emery, Lance Percival.
87 min.
Inspired by Beatlemania, this was the first feature-length animated movie made in Britain for 14 years, and it seemed determined to give a break to all those valiant animators who had been sweating to produce under-budgeted shorts throughout the '60s. Which is doubtless why there's such a wide disparity of graphic styles from sequence to sequence. Some of them, though, still look terrific: director George

Dunning's own contribution is the 'Lucy in the Sky with Diamonds' fantasia, with swirling, colour-washed couples counterpointing the song in a totally unexpected way. Speculation: maybe the banality of the over-long 'Love Conquers All' finale has less to do with John Lennon than with Erich ('Love Story') Segal, who had a hand in the script. TR

Yentl

(Barbra Streisand, 1983, GB) Barbra Streisand, Mandy Patinkin, Amy Irving, Nehemiah Persoff, Steven Hill, Allan Corduner.
133 min.
Despite Streisand's apparently hypnotic hold over a large portion of the earth's population, it's still almost impossible to equate the critical plaudits already bestowed on Yentl with the movie itself. This lumbering, overwrought, and wildly self-indulgent adaptation of Isaac Bashevis Singer's frail short story is clearly cranked up with the full quotient of sincerity and conviction. But it is this very earnestness of tone that topples a pretty dubious premise – Streisand dresses up as a boy in order to learn the Talmud – into galloping bathos. The end result looks like nothing so much as the raw material for every Woody Allen Jewish joke ever coined. JP

Yes, Giorgio

(Franklin J Schaffner, 1982, US) Luciano Pavarotti, Kathryn Harrold, Eddie Albert, Paolo Borboni, James Hong.
110 min.
An MGM extravaganza in which Pavarotti, not a natural film actor, plays an Italian opera star who falls for doctor Harrold after she helps him regain his voice which one day fails him completely in rehearsal. Best quietly to close the curtain on this one.

Yessongs

(Peter Neal, 1973, GB) Jon Anderson, Steve Howe, Chris Squire, Alan White, Rick Wakeman.
75 min.
Yes-freaks might use this footage of the group's 1972 Rainbow concert to plumb the topographic oceans of their consciousness; otherwise it's tedium in extremis. Jon Anderson's lyrics, given the extended arrangements in concert (long and indulgent solos, disjunctive and arbitrary time changes), are exposed as even slighter than on record. His vocals are reminiscent of a lone refugee from the Hollies (okay, if only he had some singles of that standard to trot out). Rick Wakeman and Steve Howe, with their respective instrumental prowess, should know better. Wakeman provides the film's only moment of humour, wrenching an atrocious 'Hallelujah Chorus' from his vast synthesiser bank. Howe slips into ragtime (for which he doesn't have the necessary sense of syncopation or off-rhythm) or flashy fingerboard runs at every opportunity. Apart from some Roger Dean graphics and opticals, the visuals are exceedingly murky, flattened by the stage lighting. Sound separation behind the vocals or lead guitar is equally muddy. RM

Yesterday Girl (Abschied von Gestern)

(Alexander Kluge, 1966, WGer) Alexandra Kluge, Günther Mack, Eva Maria Meinecke, Hans Korte, Edith Kuntze-Pellogio.
90 min. b/w.
Kluge's first feature traces the misadventures of Anita G. (played by his sister Alexandra), a young refugee from East Germany, as she wanders through the Economic Miracle but fails to find a place in it. Always penniless and often involved in petty crime, she meets a string of people who try to 'improve' and/or seduce her, but never gets to the root of her problems. Kluge makes it clear that she's a product of Germany's past, and his basic point is the simple one that Germany is trying to sweep its history under the carpet. But his Godardian wit and informality give the argument countless resonances, and keep the movie surprisingly fresh. TR

Yesterday's Hero

(Neil Leifer, 1979, GB) Ian McShane, Suzanne Somers, Adam Faith, Paul Nicholas, Sam Kydd, Glynis Barber.
95 min.

Not content with getting Leicester City relegated during his brief foray into management, 'football adviser' Frank McLintock compounds the sin by having Ian McShane's decadent Roy of the Rovers make his cup final comeback with two winning goals against the insultingly dubbed 'Leicester Forest'. Jackie Collins' script is a paste job of scandal-sheet sports page headlines (boozing striker, hard-line manager, rock star chairman), while US sports photographer Leifer works backwards from footage of the Southampton/Nottingham Forest League Cup Final to give a hilarious sense of skewed felicity to the comic strip giant-killing progress of The Saints and their repentant super-sub sinner. John Motson commentates. Irresistibly bad. PT

Yeux sans Visage, Les (Eyes Without a Face/The Horror Chamber of Dr Faustus)

(Georges Franju, 1959, Fr) Pierre Brasseur, Alida Valli, Edith Scob, Juliette Mayniel, François Guérin, Béatrice Altariba.
90 min. b/w.
An incredible amalgam of horror and fairytale in which scalpels thud into quivering flesh and the tremulous heroine (Scob) remains a prisoner of solitude in a waxen mask of eerie, frozen beauty. Having crashed the car which destroyed her face, her doctor father (Brasseur) feverishly experiments with skin grafts, each failure requiring his devoted assistant (Valli) to prowl the Latin Quarter in search of another suitable 'donor'. Finally, despair breeds madness and rebellion, erupting in an extraordinary sequence where the victim looses the dogs from the doctor's vivisection chambers to turn on their common torturer. Illuminated throughout by Franju's unique sense of poetry – nowhere more evident than in the final shot of Scob wandering free through the night, her mask discarded but her face seen only by the dogs at her feet and the dove on her shoulder – it's a marvellous movie in the fullest sense. TM

Yiddle with His Fiddle (Judel gra na Skrzypkach)

(Joseph Green/Jan Nowina Przybylski, 1936, Pol) Molly Picon.
92 min. b/w.
This lively musical comedy was a big hit in its day. It stars the vaudevillian Picon, an infectious mugger of strange bird-like mien who was then probably the biggest stage and film star in the Yiddish firmament. The tale – the prototype for Streisand's Yentl – has Picon as the optimistic street violinist who, disguised as a boy, leaves her shtetl with her bassist father in search of fame and fortune. It turns into an entertaining, if cheaper, version of a Hollywood staple, but especially in the early rural scenes, before the big-city success and the ocean-liner trip to America, Green injects a deeply lyrical atmosphere, with dream interludes and rhapsodic Renoir-esque shots of swaying trees and the countryside. Even more poignant, given how close this was to the coming Holocaust, is the incorporation of location work and the use of non-professionals: the shots of the old Polish shtetl courtyards and the villagers' faces which were shortly to vanish forever. WH

Yield to the Night

(J Lee Thompson, 1956, GB) Diana Dors, Yvonne Mitchell, Michael Craig, Geoffrey Keen, Olga Lindo, Mary Mackenzie, Joan Miller, Marie Ney.
99 min. b/w.
Loosely based, like Dance with a Stranger, on the Ruth Ellis case, this oddly austere thriller has Dors as the unrepentant murderess waiting in prison, thinking back over the events that made her kill, and agonising over whether she'll be given the death sentence or not. Decidedly anti-capital punishment, the film never actually excites, but thanks to the downbeat mood and the surprisingly effective performances, it does grip the attention. It never, however, attempts to explore in any depth the relationship between the legal practice of hanging and society's attitudes to crime. GA

Yojimbo

(Akira Kurosawa, 1961, Jap) Toshiro Mifune, Eijiro Tono, Kamatari Fujiwara, Takashi Shimura, Seizaburo Kawazu, Isuzu Yamada, Tatsuya Nakadai.
110 min. b/w.

Far from being just another vehicle for Mifune, this belongs in that select group of films noirs which are also comedies. It's not as uproarious as its sequel Sanjuro, but the story of a mercenary samurai selling his services to two rival factions in a small town, and then sitting back to watch the enemies destroy each other, certainly marks a departure from the predominantly sentimental moralising of earlier Kurosawa movies. Ultra-pragmatic, unheroic Sanjuro is the centre-piece: his laziness matches the sleepiness of the town, his quirky mannerisms echo the town's gallery of grotesques, and his spasms of violence reflect the society's fundamental cruelty. If the plot sounds familiar, it's probably because Leone stole it for A Fistful of Dollars. TR

Yol

(Serif Gören, 1982, Switz) Tarik Akan, Halil Ergün, Necmettin Cobanoglu, Serif Sezer.
114 min.
In Yilmaz Güney's extraordinary Turkish odyssey (filmed by Gören from his script and detailed instructions while he was in jail), five prisoners are allowed a week's parole to journey home. In many ways it's a story about the tragedy of distances: the geographical and historical ones that still separate Turkey, and the distances imposed upon people by a military state and by a heritage that still expects husbands to punish by death wives taken in adultery. A kind of distance, too, makes this a film of the highest order. Its homesickness, for freedom above all, is very particular. Güney can't go home, and completed the film in exile. This perspective gives great clarity to his picture of the state of the nation, a state in suspense where something has to change, which gathers complexity and shifts effortlessly into universal allegory. The film's poetry, its combination of sound and image especially, has an unconscious innocence no longer available to most European and American narratives, and it is inspired by an enormous compassion for the suffering people endure at each other's hands in a world where the strong pick upon the weak, the weak upon the weaker. CPe

Yo, la peor de todas

see I, the Worst of All

You and Me

(Fritz Lang, 1938, US) Sylvia Sidney, George Raft, Robert Cummings, Barton MacLane, Roscoe Karns, Harry Carey, Warren Hymer.
90 min. b/w.
In most interviews, Lang dismisses You and Me – within Hollywood categories, his only attempt at straight comedy – as a failure; but even if it were much more of a failure than it actually is, it would remain an utterly fascinating film. Raft and Sidney play a pair of ex-cons employed by a benign liberal (Carey) in his large department store. Sidney knows about Raft's past, but he is ignorant of hers; they marry secretly, breaking the terms of their parole, and the marriage is threatened when he accidentally discovers the truth. Lang's intention was a Brechtian Lehrstück (lesson-play); Kurt Weill worked on some of the songs, including the brilliant opening number; and for ideas about the criminal underworld, Lang borrowed as much from The Threepenny Opera as from his own M. It perhaps lacks stylistic unity, but still has many fine scenes. RM

You Are My Only Love

(Dimitri Astrakhan, 1993, Rus) Aleksander Zbruev, Marina Neelova, Svetlana Riabova.
92 min.
A girl tells her uncle Evgeny that 'I'll love you all my life', as she leaves Leningrad for New York, only to return years later, now an important sales executive, to work on a Russo-American project, involving the engineering company where hard-pressed Evgeny is now employed. Astrakhan's sour comedy uses this relationship as a springboard for analysing the post-communist malaise, with everyone jumping to the Yankee dollar. The flashback sequences to the Beatles-dominated '70s will please retro fans who like three-quarter length plastic macs, but they may be less impressed by the movie's enervated old-fashioned neo-realist feel. Here's an instance of a director finding a subject before he's found a style. WH

You Can't Cheat an Honest Man

(George Marshall, 1939, US) WC Fields, Edgar Bergen, Constance Moore, James Bush, Mary Forbes, Edward Brophy, Eddie 'Rochester' Anderson.
76 min. b/w.
'It is overloaded with two-reel comedy and no story, no pathos, no believable characters': the perceptive critic is Fields himself, who helplessly watched Universal mishandle his heartwarming story of a roguish circus owner. Most of the comedy is put into the sticky hands of Edgar Bergen, known now as the father of Candice, known then as a ventriloquist and the manipulator of dummy Charlie McCarthy, whose radio feud with Fields had all America doubled up. But their antics now seem far more historical than hysterical, and Fields' character emerges sadly belittled and coarsened. Still, good moments survive here and there. GB

You Can't Sleep Here

see I Was a Male War Bride

You Can't Take It With You

(Frank Capra, 1938, US) Jean Arthur, James Stewart, Lionel Barrymore, Edward Arnold, Mischa Auer, Ann Miller, Spring Byington, Eddie 'Rochester' Anderson.
127 min. b/w.
How true that is. And how revealing. Capra is at his most sentimental here, with James Stewart, the son of a munitions tycoon, falling for dizzy Jean Arthur, who comes from a poor but happy family of eccentrics. There are fireworks when the two fathers meet, but mostly the picture is a damp squib, trite, preachy, and desperately sincere. If the poor were a vocal minority, this would be denounced as the equivalent of Uncle Tomism. The cast is appealing, particularly Stewart and Arthur, but it's not enough. Polly Wolly Doodle indeed. BC

You Light Up My Life

(Joseph Brooks, 1977, US) Didi Conn, Joseph Silver, Michael Zaslow, Stephen Nathan, Melanie Mayron.
91 min.
With the American singles charts in their worst state since the days of Frankie Laine and Johnnie Ray, it was only a matter of time before some joker set about transposing the world of 'hip easy listening' to the screen. Joseph Brooks did just that with a vengeance. Not content with producing, writing, and directing, he also penned the title tune which drove US radio to new heights of palsied schmaltz. But what is unbearable on record can be hypnotically funny on screen. With breathtaking assurance, Light Up My Life follows a young soft-rock Angeleno hopeful (in moments of great emotion, she looks like an asphyxiated Pinocchio) in encounters with a beautiful movie producer who also happens to produce beautiful records, but who finally gives her a beautiful nervous breakdown on TV. Connoisseurs of LA sentiment will love it. DP

You'll Find Out

(David Butler, 1940, US) Kay Kyser, Peter Lorre, Boris Karloff, Bela Lugosi, Helen Parrish, Ginny Simms, Ish Kabibble.
97 min. b/w.
Considering the cast, this is disappointing fare. Fake swami Lugosi, family medic Karloff and mad scientist Lorre are actually a trio of crooks out to bump off heiress Parrish and claim her dosh, but the most horrifying thing about the movie is that someone in the front office thought it was just the place to dump five numbers by crazy bandleader Kay Kyser and his College of Musical Knowledge. TJ

You'll Like My Mother

(Lamont Johnson, 1972, US) Patty Duke, Richard Thomas, Rosemary Murphy, Sian Barbara Allen, Dennis Rucker.
93 min.
The tale of a pregnant girl (Duke), widow of a soldier killed in action, who undertakes a long journey to visit the mother-in-law (Murphy) she has never met. She finds herself snowbound in a sinister house on the edge of town inhabited by a subnormal girl (Allen), a shadowy figure (much is made of facial distortion through stained glass), and the mother-in-law, whose strident manner and skill as a nurse speak volumes. Johnson's direction tends to lay on

the spooks a bit heavily, while the over-familiar situation (with echoes of *Rosemary's Baby*) is a further strait-jacket. That said, though, several risky scenes are brought off with some aplomb.

You'll Never Get Rich

(Sidney Lanfield, 1941, US) Fred Astaire, Rita Hayworth, John Hubbard, Robert Benchley, Osa Massen, Frieda Inescort, Guinn Williams, Donald MacBride, Cliff Nazarro.
88 min. b/w.
Fred and Rita were a dream partnership, even better than Fred and Ginger, but with a stumbling script and so-so Cole Porter score, this musical never really gets off the ground. Astaire and Hayworth, he a star Broadway dancer, she in the chorus, are involved in one of those irritating on-off romances, courtesy of misunderstandings generated by their producer Benchley's penchant for pursuing chorines and then putting the blame on Astaire to pacify his wife. Astaire is drafted, and the misunderstandings then come wrapped up in acres of leaden boot camp comedy (much of it involving Nazarro, a dire double-talk comedian). Astaire has a joyous two-part solo while languishing in the guardhouse, and shares a fine, romantic Robert Alton routine with Hayworth to Porter's 'So Near and Yet So Far'. Otherwise, the pickings are thin. TM

You, Me, Jerusalem

(George Khleifi/Micha Peled, 1995, US)
54 min.
Directed by a Palestinian and an Israeli, this modest documentary sounds a note of muted optimism. Focusing on the Muslim/Jewish paramedic service, and their families on either side of the divide, the film-makers find a nostalgia among the elders for peaceful coexistence – but also, of course, the ancient current of recrimination. TCh

Young Americans, The

(Danny Cannon, 1993, GB) Harvey Keitel, Iain Glen, John Wood, Craig Kelly, Viggo Mortensen, Terence Rigby.
103 min.
Visually assured but unevenly paced, Cannon's ambitious first feature recalls such gritty British pictures as *Get Carter* and *The Long Good Friday*. Promising newcomer Kelly exudes vulnerability and confusion as Chris, a young club barman who is sucked into a maelstrom of greed and violence, after two criminals are gunned down by a posse of young wannabe gangsters, and a subsequent trial uncovers an international drugs operation. Keitel is the American cop, drafted in to 'advise' the drug squad, who cynically exploits Chris to settle an old score with dealer Mortensen. A sleek, violent, designer crime movie for style-conscious twenty-somethings. NF

Young and Dangerous (Guhuozai zhi Ren zai Jianghu)

(Andrew Lau, 1995, HK) Ekin Cheng, Jordan Chan, Gigi Lai, Francis Ng, Simon Yam, Ng Chi-Hung, Michael Tse, Jerry Lamb, Jason Chu.
99 min.
Based on a popular graphic novel (itself a thinly fictionalised commentary on real-life power struggles in the Hong Kong-Macau triad underworld), this low-budget firecracker is the kind of movie that gives immorality a good name. Shot (mostly hand-held) by its director and scripted by its producer Manfred Wong, it's founded on a clash between 'good' triads and 'bad' triads. The five adorable heroes are foot soldiers in the Hung Hing gang, laddish as they come but dedicated to ideals of loyalty, righteousness and 'brotherhood'. The bad guy is Hung Hing branch leader Kwan (Francis Ng), who usurps leadership of the gang but then overdoes the power thing. A huge – and largely deserved – hit in Hong Kong, it rocketed all its young leads to stardom. TR

Young and Dangerous 2 (Guhuozai 2 zhi Menglong Guo Jiang)

(Andrew Lau, 1996, HK) Ekin Cheng, Jordan Chan, Chingmy Yau, Gigi Lai, Anthony Wong, Simon Yam, Jerry Lamb, Michael Tse, Jason Chu.
98 min.

Already in production before the first film went ballistic, this is a direct sequel which fills in gaps in the story-so-far (a long flashback reveals how the Jordan Chan character Chicken got ahead during a period of exile in Taiwan) and goes on to chronicle a large-scale clash between the Hung Hing gang and Taiwan's San Luen gang over control of a new Macau casino. The main hero Ho Nam (singer Ekin Cheng) rises to the rank of branch leader in this episode, but much of the focus is on the high-baroque supporting roles, notably the femme fatale villain (Chingmy Yau). The incidental exposé of the links between triads and politicians in Taiwan is daringly forthright. TR

Young and Dangerous 3 (Guhuozai 3 zhi Zhishou Zhetian)

(Andrew Lau, 1996, HK) Ekin Cheng, Jordan Chan, Gigi Lai, Karen Mok, Roy Cheung, Ng Chi-Hung, Simon Yam, Jerry Lamb.
98 min.
Best to date in this on-going series, even if the emphasis on 'family' and the constant references back to the other episodes evoke soap opera. Hung Hing's dominance of Causeway Bay comes under threat from the rival Tung Sing gang, whose officers Crow and Tiger have forged secret links with drug lords in Amsterdam. Murders, double-crosses and entrapments ensue, some of them on location in Holland, although Ho Nam and Chicken incidentally get to spend more time than usual with girlfriends. Structure and pacing are very strong, and Roy Cheung's psychopathic Crow is the series' scariest villain yet. TR

Young and Innocent

(Alfred Hitchcock, 1937, GB) Nova Pilbeam, Derrick de Marney, Percy Marmont, Edward Rigby, George Curzon, Mary Clare, John Longden, Basil Radford.
82 min. b/w.
Not top-notch Hitchcock, but engrossing enough. At the centre is another of his odd couples: an innocent man accused of murder and on the run (de Marney), and the young daughter of a policeman (18-year-old Pilbeam) who finds herself helping him along the way. Both leads are very mannered: de Marney has a most odd whine of a voice, and Pilbeam is too gawky, too jolly-hockey-sticks (though she's fine in other films). So their parts, and their relationship, aren't as believable as they might be, with the result that most of the film is a bit loose. But there are at least two splendid sequences, with menace and suspense hovering, in typical Hitchcock fashion, over innocent amusements: first a children's party, and finally a hotel thé-dansant, where everything finally jells. GB

Young and the Damned, The

see Olvidados, Los

Young at Heart

(Gordon Douglas, 1954, US) Doris Day, Frank Sinatra, Robert Keith, Dorothy Malone, Ethel Barrymore.
117 min.
Fascinating attempt to bring together a number of disparate elements – whimsical comedy, songs, death – plus big city slum rat Sinatra and wholesome Day in the same frame. Sinatra's character has to pay a terrible price for daring to encroach on Andy Hardy-world, a reminder perhaps that the Fannie Hurst story ('Sister Act'), from which this derives, dates back to 1924, and that consequently there's a collision of eras going on here, as well as one of genres. As usual with Gordon Douglas movies, it's very mixed: Sinatra's rendition of the title song and 'One for My Baby' are certainly classics, even if the film itself scarcely qualifies as a musical. BBa

Young Bess

(George Sidney, 1953, US) Jean Simmons, Stewart Granger, Charles Laughton, Deborah Kerr, Kay Walsh, Kathleen Byron, Guy Rolfe, Cecil Kellaway, Leo G Carroll.
112 min.
MGM's contribution to the coronation of Elizabeth II was this piece of Tudor tosh about the early years of Elizabeth I. Simmons suppresses giggles, Granger makes Thomas Seymour a pompous ass, Laughton catches up on his Henry VIII, and Kerr plays well below Parr. All it lacks is a commentary by Richard Dimbleby. ATu

Youngblood

(Peter Markle, 1986, US) Rob Lowe, Cynthia Gibb, Patrick Swayze, Ed Lauter, Jim Youngs, Eric Nesterenko, George Finn.
110 min.
The kind of film you'd sooner forget, an ice-hockey romance aimed squarely at a sub-teenage audience. Teen heart-throb Lowe plays Dean Youngblood, the young hick from the sticks who wants to try his luck as an ice-hockey pro, and who joins up with a Canadian Junior League team, Hamilton Mustangs. There he is confronted both by the realities of his chosen sport, in the shape of a bully (Finn) who wants to grind his face into the ice, and by the traumas of puppy love as he falls for the nubile daughter (Gibb) of the team's macho coach (Lauter). Everything is predictable, except perhaps for the searching close-ups of the star's behind. In other respects, Lowe's performance is quite decent, and he cannot be blamed for the puerile humour of a director who considers putting false teeth into someone's beer to be a good joke. TRi

Young Cassidy

(Jack Cardiff, 1964, GB) Rod Taylor, Flora Robson, Maggie Smith, Julie Christie, Edith Evans, Michael Redgrave, Jack MacGowran, Sian Phillips, TP McKenna.
110 min.
Started by John Ford, who retired because of illness, this is an intelligent, powerfully cast, if slightly too pretty-pretty looking biography of Sean O'Casey. Taylor is excellent in the title role, digging ditches to support his mother (Robson) and sickly sister (Phillips), screwing his way through Julie Christie's chorus girl and Maggie Smith's demure librarian, dropping in on Michael Redgrave's WB Yeats and Edith Evans' literary sponsor, and still finding time to pen a line or two and support revolutionary causes. Ending with the first night of *The Plough and the Stars*, which Ford filmed in 1936, this undervalued picture deserves a look. ATu

Young Couples (Yuanyang lou)

(Zheng Dongtian, 1987, China) Ji Ling, Tian Shaojun, Song Xiaoying, Xiao Xiong.
125 min.
Zheng's film comprises six episodes, each featuring a young married couple and aiming to sketch a particular economic, moral or psychological problem; the cumbersome link is that they all live in the same high-rise in the Beijing suburbs. This was actually made to launch the careers of twelve new graduates from the Beijing Film Academy's acting classes, and it never manages to look anything but contrived. The script is weak, the performances are flat, and it all feels like TV drama. TR

Young Dillinger

(Terry Morse, 1965, US) Nick Adams, Mary Ann Mobley, Robert Conrad, John Ashley, Victor Buono, John Hoyt, Reed Hadley.
102 min. b/w.
Hoping to marry Mobley, yet desperately short of money, Adams' Dillinger attempts to rob her father's grain store. He's sent to prison where his association with Conrad's Pretty Boy Floyd and Ashley's Baby Face Nelson later sparks a crime spree that's to make him the Most Wanted Man in America. Unexceptional crime biopic, lacking the kind of compelling '30s detail seen two years later in *Bonnie and Clyde*. The brassy score is by jazzer Shorty Rogers. TJ

Young Doctors in Love

(Garry Marshall, 1982, US) Michael McKean, Sean Young, Harry Dean Stanton, Patrick Macnee, Hector Elizondo, Dabney Coleman, Pamela Reed, Taylor Negron, Saul Rubinek.
96 min.
A top US TV comedy director used to a mere half-hour slot isn't going to hang around for punchlines when he goes feature-length. No surprise, then, that Marshall directs this parody of TV hospital dramas at a maniacal pace. Meet the brilliant, callous young doctor with the secret fear, and the secret love for lovely Dr Brody, who has mysterious pain spasms; meet the overworked and oversexed intern turned speed freak, etc. And should the general idea and intermittently sharp dialogue fail to please, there are endless childish

visual jokes and pieces of slapstick (fortunately the blithe egomania of the medics is matched only by the indestructibility of the patients) which come and go faster than the nurse on roller-skates. The effect is crass, crowded, and pretty funny, as though the characters from half-a-dozen episodes of *General Hospital* had strayed onto a big screen and decided to misbehave. JS

Young Einstein

(Yahoo Serious, 1988, Aust) Yahoo Serious, Odile le Clezio, John Howard, Peewee Wilson, Su Cruickshank.
91 min.

Hyped with much the same spirit of vigorous nationalism as Paul Hogan and Castlemaine XXXX, this proves decidedly less successful. As writer/director/co-producer, Yahoo Serious (born Greg Pead) cats himself as turn-of-the-century entreprenuer Albert Einstein, who creates the theory of atomic energy in order to put bubbles into beer. Setting off from his parents' Tasmanian apple farm, he heads for Sydney to patent his idea. A human dynamo, he falls in love with scientist Marie Curie (studying at Sydney University), dreams up the Theory of Relativity, invents the surfboard, and devises rock'n'roll. The episodic structure and slapstick humour keep the pace superficially bubbling along, but, given a flimsy intellectual base, form and content are at odds with one another. Ultimately, a delirious sense of unwavering optimism lacks the perspective of decent comedy. CM

Young Emmanuelle, A

see Néa

Younger and Younger

(Percy Adlon, 1993, Ger) Donald Sutherland, Lolita Davidovich, Brendan Fraser, Julie Delpy, Sally Kellerman.
93 min.

The title refers to the Glendale depository business run by anglophile fantasist Sutherland – or rather prematurely-aged wife Davidovich, until her premature death during one of her husband's many bouts of sexual infidelity. Wandering in and out of the warehouse concourses are a variety of odd-ball characters – ex-star ZigZag Lillian (Kellerman) and daughter Melody (Delpy) among them – who are regularly entertained by Younger Snr's 'encouragements' and his turns on the upstairs Wurlitzer. Adlon's film sees him paddling headlong down the wish-fulfilling pseudo-feminist day-glo painted creek he has made his home since moving from Germany to America with *Bagdad Café*. It ends in a kitsch dance duet sequence, sprinkled with broken glass stardust, that would make fans of Fellini stare at their toes with embarrassment. WH

Young Frankenstein

(Mel Brooks, 1974, US) Gene Wilder, Peter Boyle, Marty Feldman, Madeline Kahn, Cloris Leachman, Teri Garr, Kenneth Mars, Gene Hackman, Richard Haydn.
108 min. b/w.

By and large, a rather pitiful parody of the Universal 'Frankenstein' movies, taking typically Brooksian liberties with characters and plot, resorting to juvenile mugging, and relying to a great extent on fairly authentic sets and photography for its better moments. A few gags work (notably when Brooks extends the spirit of the original, or comments on it, as in the Monster's scenes with the little girl and with the blind hermit). But for a really delightful parody, James Whale's own *Bride of Frankenstein* is far better value. GA

Young Giants

(Terrell Tannen, 1983, US) John Huston, Pelé, Peter Fox, Lisa Wills, F William Parker, Severn Darden.
97 min.

Pelé (pronounced alternately 'pale ale' and 'play') comes to the aid of his childhood mentor, a dying priest (Huston) whose orphanage is under threat from corporate baddies, who want to kick the kids' football team out onto the streets. 'Who are those men?' – 'I don't know' (cut to close-up on features hardening), 'but I'm sure gonna find out'. Yes, it's the Lone Ranger meets Tinkerbell. In the end, under Pale Ale's coaching, the kids win a fund-raising/feud match against the local rich kids' school. Well, they could hardly lose with God and Play on their side. PBu

Young Girls of Rochefort, The

see Demoiselles de Rochefort, Les

Young Guns

(Christopher Cain, 1988, US) Emilio Estevez, Kiefer Sutherland, Lou Diamond Phillips, Charlie Sheen, Dermot Mulroney, Casey Siemaszko, Terence Stamp, Jack Palance, Patrick Wayne, Sharon Thomas, Brian Keith, Alice Carter.
107 min.

Cain doesn't so much tip his hat to the Western as thumb his nose affectionately. The plot is a pastiche of the Doc Holliday and Billy the Kid legends, with a smattering of *The Magnificent Seven*, all wrapped up in the silliness of *Bonanza*. Stamp plays John Tunstall, an educated English gent with a dubious fondness for the youthful tearaways he hires as 'regulators' to guard his ranch, where new recruit Estevez is introduced to a life of cattle lassoing by day and poetry reading by night. If Stamp's namby-pamby ways endear him to his young charges, they don't go down too well with the wild and woolly townsfolk (led by Palance), who eventually shoot him down. What follows, as Estevez (Billy) and Sutherland (Doc Scurlock) lead the gang (including Sheen and Phillips) in a vengeful chase that culminates in a classic shootout, is a mixed homage to the craggy Arizona landscape and the pert boyishness of the bratpack cast. Little more than a flawed romp, but energetic and enjoyable, with sterling performances from Sutherland and Estevez. EP

Young Guns II

(Geoff Murphy, 1990, US) Emilio Estevez, Kiefer Sutherland, Lou Diamond Phillips, Christian Slater, William Petersen, Alan Ruck, RD Call, James Coburn, Balthazar Getty, Viggo Mortensen, Scott Wilson, Jack Kehoe.
104 min.

Those 'regulators' left standing at the end of *Young Guns* reassemble for another romp around a landscape shot in homage to John Ford. Phillips and Sutherland are back, while Charlie Sheen has been more than adequately replaced by Getty. Billy the Kid (Estevez, frantically scene-stealing) still leads the gang, and as the film opens with him stumbling out of the desert at (seemingly) the age of 120 to tell his story, he'll no doubt ride the teen-Western for some time. The plot is all pot-shots and posses, with a bit of Indian hocus-pocus thrown in for comic relief. In other words, more of the same. The Kid is dismayed to discover that, to save his own hide, his buddy Pat Garrett (Petersen, wasted) is hot on his trail. A tentative subtext plays with the psychology behind being the fastest gun, and with a little imagination you could make something of the group dynamics – but this is not the point. The point is that the soundtrack includes Jon Bon Jovi, and that the stars play to the audience with a nod and a wink that says, 'Well, no one takes Westerns seriously any more, do they?' EP

Young Ladies of Wilko, The (Panny z Wilka)

(Andrzej Wajda, 1979, Pol/Fr) Daniel Olbrychski, Anna Seniuk, Christine Pascal, Maja Komorowska, Stanislawa Celinska, Krystyna Zachwatowicz.
116 min.

'You've sort of wilted since then...' one of five sisters tells the brooding Viktor (Olbrychski), revisiting the family with whom he spent an idyllic summer as an adolescent. 'Then' was the eve of the Great War, 'now' is late 1920s Poland, and for Viktor it's the autumn of his life. Essentially a piece about lost romance, missed chances, and the doomed attempts of the youngest sister (Pascal) to revive Viktor's passion with the breath of summer, and thereby ensure that she doesn't become an 'old maid' like her sisters. This is minor key Wajda (made before *Man of Iron* and *Danton*), wistful, elegiac, seductive. MA

Young Lions, The

(Edward Dmytryk, 1958, US) Marlon Brando, Montgomery Clift, Dean Martin, Hope Lange, Barbara Rush, Maximilian Schell, Mai Britt, Lee Van Cleef.
167 min. b/w.

This version of Irwin Shaw's lengthy WWII novel, adapted by Edward Anhalt, is three movies for the price of one. We follow idealistic German Brando, American soldier Clift and crooner Martin from the time of enlistment until their paths eventually cross outside a concentration camp towards the end of the war. Clift, who accused Brando of turning the character of Diestl into a 'fucking Nazi pacifist', blocked his fellow Method actor from dying with his arms out-stretched as if on the Cross; and director Dmytryk dissuaded Brando from delivering an improvised speech about the plight of American blacks. Clift gave his deliberately unattractive Jewish GI, Noah Ackerman, a shuddering intensity. Perhaps wisely, Clift and Brando, shared no scenes together. Motivation, Dean Martin observed, is a lot of crap. 'Hell, I just played myself. A likeable coward.' BC

Young Man With a Horn (aka Young Man of Music)

(Michael Curtiz, 1950, US) Kirk Douglas, Lauren Bacall, Doris Day, Hoagy Carmichael, Juano Hernandez, Jerome Cowan, Mary Beth Hughes, Dan Seymour.
112 min. b/w.

Originally released in Britain as *Young Man of Music*, lest anyone got the wrong idea about Kirk Douglas' instrumentation, this Warner Bros biopic plays typically fast and loose with the life of its inspiration, legendary jazzer Bix Beiderbecke. Douglas' devotion to his (Harry James dubbed) trumpet drags him onto a stock melodramatic switchback, embracing booze and Bacall before submitting to a redemptive realliance with sweet-singing Doris Day. Hoagy Carmichael tells the tale from his time-honoured ringside seat, the piano stool; while the soundtrack bops along nicely with jazz-tinged standards. PT

Young Mr Lincoln

(John Ford, 1939, US) Henry Fonda, Alice Brady, Marjorie Weaver, Arleen Whelan, Richard Cromwell, Ward Bond, Donald Meek, Eddie Quillan, Milburn Stone, Francis Ford.
101 min. b/w.

This first product of the Ford-Fonda partnership – reputedly a favourite not only of Ford but of Eisenstein too – today commands classic status. Composed of serio-comic scenes from small town life, heavy with a future perfect sense of Myth-in-the-making, it's riven by tensions between insignificance and monumentality (Fonda: 'For me it was like playing Jesus Christ') that explode in the historionic splendour and 'excess' of the celebrated final sequence: Abe Lincoln setting out to scale unseen heights against the portentous gloom of a gathering storm. SJo

Young Mr Pitt, The

(Carol Reed, 1942, GB) Robert Donat, Robert Morley, Phyllis Calvert, John Mills, Max Adrian, Felix Aylmer, Raymond Lovell, Stephen Haggard, Herbert Lom.
118 min. b/w.

This sturdy biopic, written by Frank Launder and Sidney Gilliat, demonstrates Prime Minister Pitt's steadfast conduct during the Napoleonic era and did its bit as a WWII morale-booster. The roll call includes Donat as the handsome Pitt, Morley as his rival, the hissable Fox, Mills as William Wilberforce, Adrian as the playwright Sheridan, Haggard as Nelson, Aylmer as Lord North...and the 25-year-old Lom as Napoleon, a role he'd later reprise to even greater effect in the Vidor's *War and Peace*. TJ

Young One, The (La Joven)

(Luis Buñuel, 1960, Mex/US) Zachary Scott, Bernie Hamilton, Kay Meersman, Crahan Denton, Claudio Brook.
95 min. b/w.

Not one of Buñuel's more celebrated films, *The Young One* may be relatively crude in its production values and acting, but it is nevertheless thematically complex. A black jazz musician (Hamilton), escaping a wrongful rape charge, lands up on an island inhabited only by a gamekeeper (Scott) and his teenage ward (Meersman), an unspoilt nymphet. The gamekeeper's racial prejudice bursts forth, though it is he who eventually deflowers the consenting innocent. Buñuel has made of his potentially exploitative material an amoral parable, outlining the ways 'civilisation' can prove as harmful or as beneficial as untamed nature. DT

Young Poisoner's Handbook, The

(Benjamin Ross, 1994, GB/Ger) Hugh O'Conor, Antony Sher, Ruth Sheen, Roger Lloyd Pack, Charlotte Coleman, Paul Stacey, Samantha Edmonds.
105 min.
Teenage toxicologist Graham Young (O'Conor) is a budding genius with a predilection for ketchup and difficulties at home and school. Girls are turned off by his fascination with decapitation, and his family resent the chemical residue which clings to the kitchen utensils after his experiments. Undaunted, Graham resolves to solve his social problems once and for all, and make a name for himself in the process. He will be Neasden's most famous poisoner. Recounted by the arch-criminal himself, Graham's exploits have an unsettling rationality about them. O'Conor plays him unblinking and wide-eyed. Like a downwardly mobile *Kind Hearts and Coronets*, the film is at its sharpest satirising the suburban domestic kitsch of the '60s and '70s, the trendy psychological theories prison psychiatrist Dr Zeigler (Sher) uses to 'cure' Graham, and the doleful social camaraderie at the photographics laboratory where he's placed for rehabilitation. Director Ross has the confidence to pitch his malicious wit very close to the bone, so that at times you don't know whether to laugh or cry (or both). TCh

Young Sherlock Holmes (Young Sherlock Holmes and the Pyramid of Fear)

(Barry Levinson, 1985, US) Nicholas Rowe, Alan Cox, Sophie Ward, Anthony Higgins, Susan Fleetwood, Freddie Jones, Nigel Stock.
109 min.
Levinson (with a script by Chris Columbus of *Gremlins* and *The Goonies*) uses an apocryphal version of the early life of Holmes as the peg for an adventure which romps with the schoolboy Holmes and Watson through a London predictably shrouded in fog. Less predictably, it is populated by shrieking Egyptian fanatics who use a hallucinatory drug to kill their victims. This plot device is the cue for a series of virtuoso special effects sequences: hat-stands come malevolently to life, a roast pheasant bites back, and the youthful, portly Watson undergoes torture by patisserie. It's all a long way from Conan Doyle. But while lacking the clarity and breathtaking speed which Spielberg brings to this type of material, it's agreeable enough entertainment. RR

Young Soul Rebels

(Isaac Julien, 1991, GB) Valentine Nonyela, Mo Sesay, Dorian Healy, Frances Barber, Sophie Okonedo, Jason Durr, Gary McDonald, Debra Gillet, Eamon Walker.
105 min.
1977: Queen's Silver Jubilee year. Two London soul-boys want their pirate radio station to reach a wider public; but Chris (Nonyela) is distracted both by the big-time lure of the mainstream 'Metro' station and by Tracy (Okonedo), while Caz (Sesay) reacts to what he sees as his old friend's betrayal by taking up with gay socialist-worker punk Billibud (Durr). Worse, the cops suspect Chris of murdering one of Caz's gay friends in the park. Julien's brave, ambitious first feature makes all the right noises in terms of its sensitive treatment of thorny problems like racism and homophobia, and is largely successful in recreating various alternative cultural realities to the jingoistic claptrap which stands as the 'official' history of Britain during the summer of '77. Sadly, despite a strong soul soundtrack and fine camerawork, the film suffers from weak performances and an undernourished script that never frames its ideas within a gripping narrative. GA

Young Stranger, The

(John Frankenheimer, 1957, US) James MacArthur, James Daly, Kim Hunter, James Gregory, Jeff Silver, Marian Seldes, Whit Bissell.
84 min. b/w.
Frankenheimer had already directed MacArthur in the original play (*Deal a Blow*) for television, and his movie debut still smacks somewhat of small-screen ambitions in its emphasis on low-key 'realism' and dramatic intimacy. Nevertheless, it's one of the better generation gap

dramas of the '50s, since at least its tale of a movie executive's neglected and embittered son, who gets into trouble with the law after he assaults a cinema manager, is for the most past psychologically acute and sensitively acted. There's the usual explanatory pleading about lack of parental love, and the film lacks the force, dramatic unity and stylistic flair of *Rebel Without a Cause*. Still, Frankenheimer manages to avoid the pitfalls of most Hollywood portrayals of flaming youth, with MacArthur providing a performance of impressive depth and understatement. GA

Young Törless (Der junge Törless)

(Volker Schlöndorff, 1966, WGer/Fr) Mathieu Carrière, Bernd Tischer, Marian Seidowsky, Alfred Dietz, Barbara Steele.
87 min. b/w.
An adaptation of Robert Musil's novel (written in 1906) about schoolboy sadism in turn-of-the-century Germany, notable for its stylish period evocation. As young Törless arrives at school, a new senior pupil shepherded by a fond mamma, he looks a likely candidate for persecution. As it turns out, another boy (Seidowsky) – a Jew, as it happens – becomes the victim after being caught stealing; and Törless watches with clinical interest as the hapless boy is driven to despair by fiendish tortures and humiliations. Only an accidental encounter during the holidays makes Törless realise that this is, after all, happening to a human being; he duly brings it to the attention of the school authorities as a matter of moral obligation, but remains chiefly concerned with justifying his position as an intellectual observer. Beautifully acted, this bitter little anecdote is all the better in that Schlöndorff, sticking to the disturbing rites and mercurial friendships of the boarding-school world, resists the temptation to dress up its prophetic intimations of Nazism. TM

Young Warriors

(Lawrence D Foldes, 1983, US) Ernest Borgnine, Richard Roundtree, Lynda Day George, James Van Patten, Anne Lockhart, Tom Reilly, Mike Norris, Dick Shawn.
103 min.
Taking its inspiration from *Death Wish*, *National Lampoon's Animal House*, and Enid Blyton's *Famous Five*, this opens in the wacky world of college fraternity funsters, and descends by way of the rape and murder of hero Kevin's sister into a social, psychological, and cinematic sewer of destruction and revenge, taking in the usual dialogue clichés and softcore teen-exploitation hooks on the way. Young Kev (Van Patten), an intense young man whose decline into violent paranoia is symbolised by the animated movies he makes ('Kevin, that was so meaningful – where do you get your ideas?'), brushes aside his cop father Borgnine's advice and, accompanied by a guerilla-garbed white pet poodle (no kidding), leads four college chums into a bloodbath of vigilante vengeance. In the final scene the camera focuses on an ad on the wall: 'Schlitz' it says, 'makes everything great'. A high-tack classic. SPr

Young Werther

see Jeune Werther, Le

Young Winston

(Richard Attenborough, 1972, GB) Simon Ward, Robert Shaw, Anne Bancroft, Jack Hawkins, John Mills, Ian Holm, Anthony Hopkins, Patrick Magee, Edward Woodward.
157 min.
A frightfully Boering biopic chronicling the adventures of Second Lieutenant Winston Churchill, and ending with his election to the House of Commons. It comes across rather like an episode of the *Antiques Road Show* on location at Blenheim. Well, here we have a very fine example of John Mills that has been handed down over the generations, in perfect nick, about £10 at auction. Simon Ward, as the British bulldog pup, fetches rather less than Jeffrey Hunter as Jesus. ATu

You Only Live Once

(Fritz Lang, 1937, US) Sylvia Sidney, Henry Fonda, Barton MacLane, Jean Dixon, William Gargan, Warren Hymer, Margaret Hamilton, Jerome Cowan, Ward Bond.
86 min. b/w.

Looking back to the boldly-stated fatalism of his German films, and – in the on-the-run figures of Sidney and Fonda – forward to the likes of *Bonnie and Clyde* and *Pierrot le Fou*, Lang's superb *film noir* constantly breaks the boundaries of the 'social consciousness' movie category within which it was originally pigeonholed. Determinism is here at the crux of a social, psychological, and generic network, as three-time-loser Fonda finds his guilt or innocence merely the stuff of ready-set alternative newspaper headlines; and Lang constantly queries the narrative thrust with visuals that pose their own ambiguous riddles. Even the title is challenged by the movie's final shot: less a sentimental copout than the rigorous working through of a schema that incorporates three essential levels of perception: Fonda's own, society's, and the audience's. PT

You Only Live Twice

(Lewis Gilbert, 1967, GB) Sean Connery, Akiko Wakabayashi, Tetsuro Tamba, Mie Hama, Teru Shimada, Karin Dor, Donald Pleasence, Tsai Chin, Alexander Knox, Robert Hutton.
116 min.
Agent 007 travels to Japan, where he fakes his own death, gets married (?!), and thwarts a plan by cat-loving SPECTRE mastermind Blofeld (Pleasence) to use hijacked US and Soviet space capsules to blackmail the world super-powers. Roald Dahl's implausible script is padded out with the usual exotic locations, stunts, and trickery. Connery left the series after this one, but was lured back for *Diamonds Are Forever* four years later. NF

Your Beating Heart

see Coeur qui bat, Un

You're a Big Boy Now

(Francis Ford Coppola, 1966, US) Peter Kastner, Elizabeth Hartman, Geraldine Page, Julie Harris, Rip Torn, Karen Black, Tony Bill, Michael Dunn, Dolph Sweet.
97 min.
Coppola's second feature, a free-wheeling comedy about a young man (Kastner) and his frenzied efforts to rid himself of sexual and other inhibitions inculcated by smugly protective/possessive parents (Torn and Page). Though boarded out with a neurotically strait-laced landlady (Harris) whose brief is to keep him pure, he nevertheless contrives to be pursued by a nice girl who loves him (Black), while he perversely lusts after an all-too available actress (Hartman), only to be let down by his rebellious member. Very much of its time (i.e influenced by Godard, Dick Lester and the whole dropout thing), it now looks archly dated rather than spontaneous. But Coppola's style had healthy roots in the screwball comedies of the Thirties, and the glorious performances litter the film with moments to treasure (like Julie Harris' anguished cry when locked into a library vault with the innocent Torn: 'Trapped in the pornography collection of a fiend!'). TM

You're in the Army Now

see O.H.M.S.

You're Lying (Ni Ljuger)

(Vilgot Sjöman, 1969, Swe) Stig Engström, Börje Ahlstedt, Sif Ruud, Anita Ekström.
107 min. b/w.
This indictment of the comparatively liberal Swedish penal system argues that a prison system is still a prison system. Caught between pleading a cause and producing a drama, the film never entirely reconciles the two elements. Filmed as social realism in an almost *cinéma-vérité* style, it tells of a talented but highly-strung young artist whose instability is partly of his own making – through his compulsive exploitation of others, and of himself through drink – partly because of an overworked and uncaring prison system. The film is at its best in dealing with prison days, particularly when contrasting behaviour in isolation and in groups. Towards the end of two hours, things look increasingly unsteady as Sjöman concentrates on the destruction of the artist's individual creative impulse, but Stig Engström's strong, starry performance always remains a focal point. CPe

Your Past is Showing!
see Naked Truth, The

Your Three Minutes Are Up
(Douglas N Schwartz, 1973, US) Beau Bridges, Ron Liebman, Janet Margolin, Kathleen Freeman, David Ketchum, Stu Nisbet, Read Morgan.
92 min.
A modest buddy picture about straight Bridges and scam-artist pal Liebman, who doesn't mind bending the rules to get ahead, which adds up to a witty, well-observed tale of skewed American values. TJ

Yours, Mine and Ours
(Melville Shavelson, 1968, US) Lucille Ball, Henry Fonda, Van Johnson, Jennifer Leak, Tom Bosley, Tim Matheson.
110 min.
A horrendously cute premise: Navy widower with ten children meets and marries Navy widow with eight. There's worse to come, since all eighteen kids resent the new arrangement, and a nineteenth is shortly on the way. It's saved by the sheer professionalism of Lucille Ball and Henry Fonda, who share several very funny scenes, the best of which is a meeting in a crowded pub where he struggles with recalcitrant drinks and she with a descending undergarment as they try to make mutual confession as to the enormity of the contribution each is going to make to their marriage. TM

You Talkin' to Me?
(Charles Winkler, 1987, US) Jim Youngs, James Noble, Faith Ford, Mykel T Williamson.
90 min.
Obsessed by Robert De Niro's Travis Bickle character from *Taxi Driver*, unemployed actor Youngs arrives in Hollywood to be seduced by a white supremacist TV producer before coming to his senses and doing what Travis might have done in the same circumstances. A 'comedy' which insults its proclaimed inspiration. TJ

You Were Meant for Me
(Lloyd Bacon, 1948, US) Jeanne Crain, Dan Dailey, Oscar Levant, Barbara Lawrence, Selena Royle, Percy Kilbride.
92 min. b/w.
A virtual remake of 1942's *Orchestra Wives*, this Fox musical has small-town high school student Crain swept off her feet by bandleader Dailey and only to discover at length the difficulties of Depression life on the road and the ups-and-downs of the record industry. A half-decent script means you're not twiddling your thumbs between the production numbers (a raft of jazz standards), but Levant steals it entirely as the band's cynical manager and even puts in a storming, if abbreviated performance at the keyboard for Gershwin's Piano Concerto in F. TJ

You Were Never Lovelier
(William A Seiter, 1942, US) Fred Astaire, Rita Hayworth, Adolphe Menjou, Leslie Brooks, Adele Mara, Xavier Cugat, Larry Parks, Gus Schilling.
97 min. b/w.
Columbia's second teaming of Astaire and Hayworth is a vast improvement on *You'll Never Get Rich*, even though the script is merely adequate, and it keeps threatening to let Xavier Cugat and his Latin rhythms run riot (it doesn't). Astaire plays a Broadway hoofer stranded in Buenos Aires after a bad day at the races. His efforts to secure an engagement at the plushy Hotel Acuna (his insolently playful audition piece is a delight) founder on the temperamental preoccupation of the millionaire proprietor (Menjou), but he subsequently finds himself involved in the latter's devious plot to stoke fires in his supposedly cold-fish daughter (Hayworth). Naturally, both Astaire and Hayworth get caught up in more than mere masquerade; and with love blooming to dreamily romantic Jerome Kern standards (the title song, 'I'm Old-Fashioned', 'Dearly Beloved'), the musical sequences are marvellous, especially an ecstatic dance that whisks all over a moonlit garden. TM

Yoyo
(Pierre Etaix, 1965, Fr) Pierre Etaix, Luce Klein, Philippe Dionnet, Claudine Auger.
97 min. b/w.

The second and possibly the best of Etaix's features, which starts out by dogging Buster Keaton's footsteps as he plays a bored millionaire waited on hand and foot in his château. This first half-hour, set during the last days of the silents, is shot without dialogue (though not without sound effects) and at slightly accelerated speed. Come 1929, the film shifts into a Chaplin mood when, ruined by the Wall Street crash, the millionaire joins a circus to rediscover his first love (who became an equestrienne after bearing him a son). Etaix has just enough astringency to keep sentimentality at bay, and his mastery of the sight gag amply justifies Jerry Lewis' enthusiasm for the film, which is singularly beautifully shot by Jean Boffety. TM

Yukinojo Henge
see Actor's Revenge, An

Yumeji
(Seijun Suzuki, 1991, Jap) Kenji Sawada, Tomoko Mariya, Yoshio Harada.
128 min.
The final segment of Suzuki's Taisho trilogy suffers somewhat seen in isolation, without the earlier films *Zigeunerweisen* and *Heat-Haze Theatre*. Nevertheless, it's a spirited showing for a veteran director: a sensual, absurdist ghost story spun around the character and work of real-life painter and poet Yumeji Takehisa (1884-1934), seen as a chronic philanderer and dreamer. Kenji Sawada, the effete pop star featured as a glamorous masochist in Paul Schrader's *Mishima*, does his utmost to give the hero some substance, but Suzuki's saturated colours, delirious imagery, and narrative ellipses swamp all attempts at characterisation. The film goes nowhere, slowly, but the mood along the way is seductive enough. TR

Z
(Costa-Gavras, 1968, Fr/Alg) Yves Montand, Jean-Louis Trintignant, Jacques Perrin, François Périer, Irene Papas, Georges Géret, Charles Denner.
125 min.
Costa-Gavras' crowd-pleasing left wing thriller was based on the 1965 Lambrakis affair, in which investigation of the accidental death of a medical professor uncovered a network of police and government corruption. As Greece was under the Generals at the time, the film was shot in Algeria, with a script by Spaniard Jorge Semprun and music by Theodorakis. The recreation of the murder and the subsequent investigation uses the techniques of an American thriller to gripping effect, though conspiracies are so commonplace nowadays that it's hard to imagine the impact it made at the time. DT

Zabriskie Point
(Michelangelo Antonioni, 1969, US) Mark Frechette, Daria Halprin, Rod Taylor, Paul Fix, GD Spradlin, Kathleen Cleaver.
110 min.
Antonioni's sorrowing, stranger's-eye view of modern America is sadly flawed by the way his 'story' (a rambling, jumbled and mumbling mess scripted by a variety of writers including Sam Shepard, Tonio Guerra and Claire Peploe) is bogged down in the mood of student revolt dogging the nation in the late '60s. Frechette, suspected of shooting a cop during a campus riot, steals a plane, meets Halprin, and makes love with her in Death Valley before returning to give himself up; she meanwhile goes off to meet prospective employer and capitalist pig Taylor. It's clear that the director's interest in America was less political than visual: the painted slogans and billboards seem important less for their content than for their appearance, just as the repeated metaphor of the desert is picturesque rather than telling. That said, the final explosion of a house and its contents in slow-motion is a dazzling, almost celebratory symbol of youthful dreams of ending consumerism. GA

Zandalee
(Sam Pillsbury, 1990, US) Nicolas Cage, Judge Reinhold, Erika Anderson, Joe Pantoliano, Viveca Lindfors, Aaron Neville, Steve Buscemi.
104 min.
Every few years, a film redefines the boundaries of screen sexuality: *Last Tango in Paris* or *Ai no Corrida*, for example. On the other hand, there is

trite soft-porn rubbish like *9½ Weeks* or *Full Moon Junction*. This flaccid effort from Kiwi director Pillsbury wants to be 'Last Tango in New Orleans', but feels like nine-and-a-half weeks in Full Moon Junction. 'I wanna shake you naked and eat you alive, Zandalee' pants passionate artist Nicolas Cage. Amazingly, his best friend's wife (Anderson) falls for this line, immediately consenting to torrid sex. Zandalee's journey through the empire of the senses (from wanton knee-trembler to forced anal sex in a confessional) plumbs the usual depths of female masochism. Meanwhile, husband Judge Reinhold ponders the loss of his poetic muse, then cracks up completely. The plot is daft, the dialogue worse. Asked about working with naked female models, Cage admits: 'When that big red snatch is comin' at yer like a freight train, it's pretty hard to paint, I'll tell yer'. NF

Zandy's Bride
(aka For Better, For Worse)
(Jan Troell, 1974, US) Gene Hackman, Liv Ullmann, Eileen Heckart, Harry Dean Stanton, Susan Tyrrell, Joe Santos, Sam Bottoms, Frank Cady.
116 min.
Swedish director Troell, having won an international reputation with his sweeping historical saga *The Emigrants* and *The New Land*, headed off to America himself, where his career soon ground to a halt after this picturesque but rather vacant tale from the Old West. Hackman's the gruff rancher who's initially antagonistic when he sends off for a mail-order bride and gets Ullmann back, but her fighting spirit is soon to win him over. The performances strike sparks occasionally, but Jordan (*Alien*) Cronenweth's rural cinematography steals all the attention. TJ

Zardoz
(John Boorman, 1973, GB) Sean Connery, Charlotte Rampling, Sara Kestelman, Sally Anne Newton, John Alderton, Niall Buggy.
105 min.
A bizarre futurist fantasy which seems to have substituted itself when Boorman's plans to film Tolkien's *Lord of the Rings* fell through. Zardoz (joke ref: Wizard of Oz) is a vast, Blakean bust of a bearded Zeus which roams the air spewing arms and ammunition to its Exterminators on earth so that they may enforce the law: 'The gun is good, the penis is evil'. Liberated by the memory of a rape committed in the course of his liberties, one of these Exterminators (Connery) enters the godhead, kills the magician manipulating it, and finds he has penetrated the Vortex, a world of sterilised stasis established to preserve the sum of man's knowledge. At which point, poised to take off from its make love not war springboard, perhaps to explore the dichotomy between physical and spiritual forces, the script gradually falls apart into a mess of philosophical pottage under the whimsically pretentious Tolkien influence. But visually the film remains a sparkling display of fireworks, brilliantly shot and directed. TM

Zaza
(George Cukor, 1939, US) Claudette Colbert, Herbert Marshall, Bert Lahr, Constance Collier, Helen Westley, Genevieve Tobin, Walter Catlett, Monty Woolley.
83 min. b/w.
Minor but typically elegant and enjoyable Cukor, taken from a French stage success, in which Colbert's vivacious can-can dancer falls (somewhat implausibly) for Marshall, only to find that he's married. Hardly a blazingly original story, but Cukor makes the most of the turn-of-the-century theatrical milieu, rhyming Zaza's on-stage performances (with Colbert herself singing) with the various deceptions that define Marshall's treatment both of her and of his own family. It's a fine example of Colbert at her very engaging best. GA

Zazie
(Go Riju, 1989, Jap) Yoshito Nakamura, Masumi Miyazaki, Rikaco, Tetta Sugimoto, Yuki Matsushita.
95 min.
Zazie – a name given him by his many Tokyo waterfront buddies, ex-girlfriends, and ex-members of his successful punk-rock band 'Junk' – is trying to simplify his life. He resists flattery

('You're a legend, man'), and also invitations to join the re-formed band or get back together with his girl. He takes to wandering the waterfront and mooching about his large, dilapidated house, filming and talking philosophy to his new acquisition, a state of the art video camera. A waitress at his favourite café gently mocks his attempts at honesty ('It's a form of selfishness'); Buddha is invoked in hyperbolic comparison ('He had no responsibilities'); Zazie starts finding it easier to communicate with people by sending them videos. Riju's film wears its heart delightfully on its sleeve: exploratory, noisy, energetic, stylistically experimental and very moving though it may be, it avoids self-consciousness by a special brand of wry humour and its mood of knowing introspection. What surprises is Riju's control and vitality; his camera finds interest everywhere it shoots, and beauty too, not least in the bright industrial Tokyo landscapes. WH

Zazie dans le Métro

(Louis Malle, 1960, Fr) Catherine Demongeot, Philippe Noiret, Vittorio Caprioli, Yvonne Clech, Hubert Deschamps, Antoine Roblot, Annie Fratellini, Jacques Dufilho.
88 min.
Malle's third feature plunges us straight back into the world of New Wave jiggery-pokery, with jump-cuts, lavish in-jokes, and a whirlwind narrative (taken from Raymond Queneau's delightful novel) centred around a precocious brat (Demongeot) lewd enough to give a few tips to the Jodie Foster of *Taxi Driver*. It has survived the years much better than other indulgent frolics, mainly because Malle really does seem motivated by gleeful malice and anarchy – he's not just toying with a fashionable mood. This spirit captured even underground guru Jonas Mekas, who commented on the original US release, 'The fact that the film is a failure means nothing. Didn't God create a failure too?' GB

Zed & Two Noughts, A

(Peter Greenaway, 1985, GB/Neth) Andrea Ferreol, Brian Deacon, Eric Deacon, Frances Barber, Joss Ackland, Jim Davidson.
115 min.
A car accident caused by a swan outside Rotterdam Zoo leaves ex-Siamese twin brothers (Brian and Eric Deacon, the two noughts) widowers, so they take up with the driver, Alba Bewick (Ferreol), who had one leg amputated and is considering the other. Grief also propels them into investigations at the Zoo into death and decay. Then there is Van Meegeren, surgeon brother to the Vermeer forger, with designs on Alba's legs...As usual with Greenaway, the ideas are large, endless and perverse; and they are teased out with the exquisite formal perfection of a court minuet. Moreover he frames, colours, and shoots with a top dollar perfection (the camerawork is by Sacha Vierny). A film with all the cool, intellectual thrill of the Kasparov-Karpov game. CPea

Zee & Co (X, Y and Zee)

(Brian G Hutton, 1971, GB) Elizabeth Taylor, Michael Caine, Susannah York, Margaret Leighton, John Standing, Mary Larkin.
109 min.
One of those follies that everyone involved (especially writer Edna O'Brien) must look back on with cringing embarrassment. Arch-bitch Zee (Taylor, wearing an incredibly unflattering Beatrice Dawson wardrobe) fights tooth and manicured nail to retrieve her philandering husband (Caine) from his sensitive mistress (York), only to end up in the sack with the woman herself. The real highpoint is the sight of Margaret Leighton in a see-thru blouse with a pet faggot in tow. TR

Zelig

(Woody Allen, 1983, US) Woody Allen, Mia Farrow, Garrett Brown, Stephanie Farrow, Mary Louise Wilson, Sol Lomita, John Rothman.
79 min. b/w & col.
One of Allen's miniaturist exercises in style, *Zelig* is a one-joke movie about a man so self-effacing that he takes on the physical appearance of the person he is with. In addition to the chameleon-like ability for personal metamorphosis, Zelig manifests an equally unique capacity for materialising at important social gatherings and sig-

nificant historical events – at a garden party given by novelist Scott Fitzgerald, on the balcony of the Vatican during a Papal address, behind a ranting Adolf Hitler at a Nazi rally. Employing skilfully doctored black-and-white photographs and newsreel footage, Allen has created a painstaking and mildly amusing fictional documentary about a non-person who never lived. NF

Zéro de Conduite (Zero for Conduct)

(Jean Vigo, 1933, Fr) Louis Lefèvre, Gilbert Pluchon, Gérard de Bédarieux, Constantin Goldstein-Kehler, Jean Dasté, Robert Le Flon.
44 min. b/w.
Vigo's anarchic, disorienting vision of life in a French boarding school, banned until 1945 when Vigo had been dead for eleven years. Outwardly it appears to be an accurate picture; and yet nothing is real. The teachers, their idiosyncrasies appropriately magnified, are seen through the eyes of their pupils. The boys' revolt against mindless discipline culminates in a surreal battle in the playground on speech day. Thirty years later, Lindsay Anderson re-used the same symbols in his own attack on the Establishment, *If....* DMcG

Zero Patience

(John Greyson, 1993, Can) John Robinson, Normand Fauteux, Dianne Heatherington, Richardo Keens-Douglas, Bernard Behrens.
100 min.
A witty riposte to *And the Band Played On*, this is Canadian AIDS activist Greyson's personal take on 'official' AIDS history. Picking up where Randy Shilts left off, he introduces us to 'Patient Zero', the Air Canada flight attendant alleged to have brought AIDS to America. But scapegoating couldn't be further from the picture. Slyly inverting popular wisdom, the movie offers a sassy commentary on the epidemic of blame. The plot follows the fortunes of notorious Victorian explorer and sexologist Sir Richard Burton as he works to assemble a multi-media museum display on the origin of AIDS. His plans are thwarted when he runs into Zero, back from the dead and determined to clear his name. The film offers a timely reminder that AIDS movies needn't be all Kodak moments and earnest posturing. Matching a flagrant disregard for sentimental pieties with a passion for undermining generic conventions, Greyson has produced a film which engages your mind as much as your heart, and leaves you laughing. PBur

Ziegfeld Follies

(Vincente Minnelli, 1946, US) William Powell, Fred Astaire, Judy Garland, Lucille Ball, Lena Horne, Gene Kelly, Lucille Bremer, Esther Williams, Red Skelton, Fanny Brice, Edward Arnold, Victor Moore.
110 min.
Only partly directed by Minnelli, who took over from George Sidney (responsible for the opening girlie number with Lucille Ball) and suffered various meddlings. From his plushy celestial penthouse, Ziegfeld (Powell) dreams up a posthumous revue which proves predictably lavish and surprisingly garish. No plot, just thirteen items which drag in most of MGM's stars, include some horrendously unfunny sketches (Red Skelton's drunk act is the worst; Fanny Brice's famous 'Baby Snooks' sketch must be an acquired taste), and intermittently display the Minnelli touch (notably an operatic scene brilliantly conceived in black and white except for the diva's crimson dress). As so often, the honours are taken by Astaire's three numbers (including his only duet with Kelly, 'The Babbitt and the Bromide'), best of which is the gorgeous 'Limehouse Blues', danced with Lucille Bremer and partly shot on a foggy street set held over from *The Picture of Dorian Gray*. TM

Ziegfeld Girl

(Robert Z Leonard, 1941, US) James Stewart, Lana Turner, Judy Garland, Hedy Lamarr, Tony Martin, Jackie Cooper, Dan Dailey, Philip Dorn, Ian Hunter, Charles Winninger, Eve Arden, Edward Everett Horton, Al Shean.
131 min. b/w.
Classic MGM musical with Busby Berkeley pulling all stops out to retell the story of legendary showman Ziegfeld by way of the mixed

fortunes of three of his girls, with Turner as the one who hits the skids, Lamarr as the one who settles for marriage, and Garland as the one who makes the grade. An oddly intriguing mix of production numbers and melodrama, with Dailey outstanding as a sadistic prizefighter who gives Turner a hard time, and Garland at the height of her powers. Favourite numbers include: 'You Stepped Out of a Dream' and 'I'm Always Chasing Rainbows'. MA

Ziggy Stardust and the Spiders from Mars

(DA Pennebaker, 1982, GB/US) David Bowie, Mick Ronson, Trevor Bolder, Mick Woodmansy.
90 min.
The whole flashy, rockist affair is based on a wobbly premise of sentimentality. It's a record of the Ziggy character's farewell dates at the Hammersmith Odeon in 1973, and while the likes of 'Oh You Pretty Things' and 'All the Young Dudes' still raise a smile, the presiding image is of those flesh-crawling glam-rock costumes and stage antics. Go for the music, or not at all. JG

Zina

(Ken McMullen, 1985, GB) Domiziana Giordano, Ian McKellen, Philip Madoc, Paul Geoffrey, Tusse Silberg, Maureen O'Brien.
94 min.
This revisits the twin 20th century traumas of Revolution and Reich, as witnessed by the self-styled 'good-for-nothing daughter of the most important man of our time', namely Leon Trotsky. 1932 finds him in Turkey rallying forces against Stalin and Hitler, while she, both victim and visionary, lies on a couch in Berlin, where McKellen's neo-Freudian shrink sees her morbid insanity as mirroring a Germany in thrall to Thanatos. Is there more than a coincidental (anagrammatic?) link between Zina's and the Nazis' different madnesses? McMullen isn't entirely convincing, but his elegantly prowling camera, careful compositions, and astute use of locations ranging from Berlin and Blackpool to Lanzarote, create a powerful, onerous mood with much more assurance than the otherwise similar '1919'; and the wild and woolly Giordano, emotions scudding across her face like clouds, is simply magnificent as the volatile Zina. SJo

Zombie Flesh-Eaters (Zombi 2)

(Lucio Fulci, 1979, It) Tisa Farrow, Ian McCulloch, Richard Johnson, Al Cliver, Auretta Gay, Olga Karlatos.
91 min.
A slight but very gory pulp zombie tale in true spaghetti style: on a lurid voodoo isle (complete with white doctor), fading stars and clones slug it out with the living dead. A massacre. One twist: the cannibal-zombies eventually take over New York ('They're breaking through the door...aaargh!'), where they no longer look out of place. But the lack of suspense amid the Technicolor carnage disappoints. Subtle it ain't, but the title alone should keep art lovers away. DMacp

Zombies

see Dawn of the Dead

Zone Troopers

(Danny Bilson, 1985, US) Tim Thomerson, Timothy Van Patten, Art La Fleur, Biff Manard, William Paulson, Alviero Martin.
86 min.
The playful, plagiaristic Poverty Row spirit of early Roger Corman is not dead. Starting off as a conventional war film (Italy 1944), with a bunch of American GIs stranded behind enemy lines, it soon escalates/degenerates into an absurd semi-sci-fi thriller when an enormous rocket is discovered smouldering in the forest: it's a Martian spaceship, and a benign, burbling alien survivor is on the loose. Not as good as its producer Charles Band's own *Trancers*, and it would be unfair to recommend too highly any film featuring a distinctly un-Hitlerish Führer (Martin) and a daring escape ludicrously accompanied by the sounds of big band swing. But as inventive nonsense scarcely tainted by plot logic, it's more rewarding viewing than any Hugh Hudson film. GA

Zoo in Budapest

(Rowland V Lee, 1933, US) Gene Raymond, Loretta Young, OP Heggie, Paul Fix, Wally Albright.
85 min. b/w.

A strange, ecstatically beautiful little fantasy, set almost entirely within a quaint Douanier Rousseau zoo, all trailing palm fronds and swirling mists, where three innocents – a pair of lovers and a runaway child – seek refuge one night from the cruelties of the world outside. At first a hostile jungle, the zoo mysteriously mutates by night into a Garden of Eden, a transformation subtly painted in light by Lee Garmes' incredible camerawork, which draws delicate analogies in captivity between humans and animals, and culminates with the fantastic sequence of the revolt of the caged beasts, which points the way to freedom. Only marginally let down by the final scene – a brief coda showing the couple happily settled into their own little cottage 'just like anybody else' – the whole film reverberates like one of Blake's 'Songs of Innocence'. TM

Zoo la Nuit, Un

see Night Zoo

Zorba the Greek

(Michael Cacoyannis, 1965, Greece/US) Anthony Quinn, Alan Bates, Irene Papas, Lila Kedrova, George Foundas.
146 min. b/w.

The dreadful movie that launched a million package tours: timid writer Bates falls spellbound to the outsize folkloric 'charm' of Quinn's philosophically boisterous Cretan Character, a role he's revamped with minor cultural compensations in almost every one of his films since. PT

Zorro the Gay Blade

(Peter Medak, 1981, US) George Hamilton, Lauren Hutton, Brenda Vaccaro, Rob Leibman, Donovan Scott, James Booth, Clive Revill.
93 min.

This 'affectionate parody' of the swashbuckling Zorro myth is so determinedly amiable that one feels distinctly caddish for regretting that the laughs are not even more frequent. It fails only in that Leibman's villain shouts too much, and that the set pieces, the skeleton of most film comedy, are under-considered. The simple idea, for example, of every male guest at a masked ball turning up disguised as Zorro, making the villain's task of identifying the real one trickier than he expected, is almost hysterically thrown away: the scene is just good enough to make it doubly frustrating. This said, Hamilton's hamming is a delight rather than an annoyance, the sets and stuntwork well achieved. JC

Zouzou

(Marc Allégret, 1934, Fr) Josephine Baker, Jean Gabin, Pierre Larquey, Yvette Lebon, Madeleine Guitry, Palau.
100 min. b/w.

Basically a vehicle for Josephine Baker, who bubbles effervescently through some Busby Berkeley-ish production numbers, and also gets to sing her classic 'Pour moi, y'a qu'un homme à Paris', with a tearful eye on her adored but roving-eyed foster brother. It is Gabin who really catches the eye in this part, with his persona already almost fully developed. Impassive as ever, he is first glimpsed as a soldier in an oriental dive, reigning benignly over the pretty girls but still a stranger in a strange land. Then the fatal encounter with his dream during a *bal musette* waltz which he hoarsely croons in her ear; and finally the misunderstanding, the accusations of murder. Happy ending apart, you can already see the romantically doomed gangster of *Pépé le Moko*, stubbornly proletariat, eternally yearning for the purity denied by the world in which he is mired. TM

Zulu

(Cy Endfield, 1963, GB) Stanley Baker, Jack Hawkins, Michael Caine, Ulla Jacobsson, James Booth, Nigel Green, Ivor Emmanuel, Paul Daneman, Glynn Edwards.
135 min.

A film which comes with two heavy strikes against it: it was made during the '60s boom for epic adventures in exotic climes (which now look like a breed of cinematic dinosaur), and it recounts one of those heroic tales of the thin red line holding out against hordes of fuzzy-wuzzies that endlessly fuelled 'Boy's Own'. In fact, *Zulu* is a fairly tough-minded and interesting account of a company of Welsh soldiers doing their bit for somebody else's Queen and Country in an alien land (the script was co-written by the chronicler of the Highland Troubles, John Prebble), and is a more honest account of imperialism than the belated follow-up, *Zulu Dawn*, supposedly telling the Zulus' side of things. In his first starring role, Cockney wide boy Caine actually assumes an upper crust, but is finally one-upped by Baker's officer of Engineers. MA

Zulu Dawn

(Douglas Hickox, 1979, US/Neth) Burt Lancaster, Peter O'Toole, Simon Ward, John Mills, Nigel Davenport, Michael Jayston, Ronald Lacey, Denholm Elliott, Freddie Jones, Christopher Cazenove.
117 min.

A motion picture epic of (and about) timeless stupidity. Belonging to the 'overwhelming odds' school of cinematic dross, this recounts the massacre at Isandhlwana in 1879, the worst defeat ever suffered by British forces at the hands of natives, with the big-name colonials battling against well-oiled and statuesque blacks. Embarrassed by the fundamental attraction of this ripping yarn, the film abandons *Zulu*-style Celtic punk and sells itself instead on spectacle, in a wrap-around package of documentation and social insight (meaning shots of rows of native boobs vs elaborate Brit table manners). You can't fail to be staggered by the discrepancy between the film's wet-nosed anxiety to please, to affect, and its wide-screen parade of nervy little cosmetic clichés. RP

Zu: Warriors from the Magic Mountain (Shu Shan: Xin Shushan Jianxia)

(Tsui Hark, 1983, HK) Brigitte Lin, Samo Hung, Yuen Biao, Meng Hai, Adam Cheng, Judy Ong, Feng Ke'an, Tsui Hark.
97 min.

Reverend Long-brows (Hung) holds a ravening blood monster at bay for 49 days while four fallible humans comb the universe for the two celestial swords which can save the world. Tsui brought in technicians from *Star Wars*, *Star Trek* and *Tron* to help him make 'the ultimate Chinese mythological spectacular', inspired by a newspaper serial of the late 1920s by Li Shoumin. Thanks to Hollywood know-how (and William Chang's designs), it does look pretty good, and the starry cast just about holds its own amid all the special visual effects. But where was the script? So much effort has gone into the set-pieces that pacing, coherence and even dramatic impact all go hang. TR

Zweite Erwachen der Christa Klages, Das

see Second Awakening of Christa Klages, The

Film Categories

As a quick reference guide for readers hiring videos, there follows lists of films under 15 different category headings. The categorising of any film is a risky business – many films fall into several possible categories – so we have used headings similar to those of most video libraries, as well as some commonly recognised genres. The Appendices that follow do not include every film in the Guide, as many are simply beyond categorisation, but all the titles in them will be found in the main text. Also, Appendices 16 to 21 (*pages* 1059–1068) list films from the producer countries, other than the USA and Britain, most represented in the Guide.

The category headings we have adopted are:

Appendix 1
Action/Adventure

Accidental Legend
Adventures of Captain Marvel, The
African Queen, The
Africa – Texas Style
Air Force One
Airport
Airport 1975
Airport '77
Airport '80
Alien Thunder
Amazing Captain Nemo, The
Ambassador, The
American Ninja
Another Stakeout
Appât, L'
Appointment in Honduras
Around the World in 80 Days
Assassination
Assault on a Queen
Assault on Precinct 13
Atlantic Adventure
Avalanche
A.W.O.L.

Backdraft
Back from Eternity
Badge 373

Bamboo Gods and Iron Men
Bandido!
Bandit, The
Band of the Hand
Bard Wire
Barquero
Beach of the War Gods
Bear, The
Bear Island
Beau Geste
Beneath the 12-Mile Reef
Bengazi
Best of the Best
Best of the Best 2
Better Tomorrow, A
Better Tomorrow II, A
Beyond the Poseidon
   Adventure
Big Bad Mama
Big Boss, The
Big Brawl, The
Big Trouble in Little China
Big Zapper
Billy Jack
Bird People in China, The
Black Belt Jones
Black Eagle
Blind Fury

Blood of the Dragon
Blood on the Sun
Bloodsport
Bloody Fists, The
Blue Fin
Bodo
Bootleggers
Born Losers, The
Botany Bay
Boxcar Bertha
Breakout
Brigand of Kandahar, The
Broken Arrow
Bronx Warriors
Bucktown
Bulletproof
Bullfighter and the Lady, The
Burning Paradise

Cannonball
Caper of the Golden Bulls, The
Cape Town Affair, The
Captains Courageous
Caravans
Caravan to Vaccares
Cast a Giant Shadow
Catchfire
Ceiling Zero
Challenge
Chase, The
Cherry 2000
China Seas
Chinese Connection, The
City Beneath the Sea
City on Fire
Clan of the Cave Bear, The
Cleopatra Jones
Cleopatra Jones and
    the Casino of Gold
Cliffhanger
Cobra
Cockfighter
Codename: The Soldier
Code of Silence
Coffy
Commando
Comrade X
Con Air
Condorman
Congo
Congo Crossing
Conman and the Kung Fu Kid,
    The
Convoy
Countdown
Countryman
Crash
Crimson Tide
Crocodile Dundee
Crocodile Dundee II
Cuba
CutThroat Island

Dandy, the All-American Girl
Danger: Diabolik
Dante's Peak
Dark Journey
Daylight
Days of Thunder
Death in the Sun
Death Kick
Death Race 2000
Death Wish
Death Wish II
Death Wish 3
Death Wish 4
Deep, The
Deep, Impact
Defiance
Deliverance
Delta Force, The
Demolition Man
Desperate Search
Devil at 4 O'Clock, The
Devil's Island (Clemens)
Diamond Mercenaries
Diamonds
Diamonds are Forever
Dirigible
Dirty Ho
Dirty Mary, Crazy Larry

Dixie Dynamite
Dr No
Dogs of War, The
Donovan's Reef
Double Impact
Double Team
Dove, The
Downhill Racer
Dragon Dies Hard, The
Drive-In
Drop Zone
Drum, The
Dynasty

Eagle Has Landed, The
Earthquake
East of Sumatra
Eat My Dust!
Edge, The
Eiger Sanction, The
8 Million Ways to Die
8-Wheel Beast, The
Elephant Boy
Emerald Forest, The
Emperor of the North Pole, The
Enter the Ninja
Enter the 7 Virgins
Escape from New York
Escape from Zahrain
Escape to Burma
Evel Knievel
Evil That Men Do, The
Exterminator 2
Extreme Prejudice
Eye for an Eye, An
Eye of the Needle

Face/Off
Far Off Place, A
Fast Charlie,
    the Moonbeam Rider
Fast Company
Fate of Lee Khan, The
Fathom
Ferry to Hong Kong
Fighting Back
Fighting Mad
Figures in a Landscape
Finders Keepers
Fine Mess, A
Fire
Firebirds
Firefox
First Blood
First Great Train Robbery
First Strike
F.I.S.T.
Fist of Fury
Fist of Fury Part II
Fist of the North Star
Five Came Back
Fled
Flight from Ashiya
Flight of the Doves
Flight of the Phoenix, The
Force: Five
Force of One, A
Fort Apache, the Bronx
For Your Eyes Only
Four Feathers, The (Korda)
Four Feathers, The (Sharp)
Four Men and a Prayer
Fourth Protocol, The
Freebie and the Bean
Freedom Road
From Russia With Love
Fugitive, The

Game for Vultures
G.I. Jane
Giù la Testa
Gladiator
Glimmer Man, The
Glory Stompers, The
Gods Must Be Crazy, The
Gods Must Be Crazy II, The
Gold
Golden Child, The
GoldenEye
Golden Lady, The
Golden Needles

Golden Rendezvous
Goldfinger
Gone in 60 Seconds
Good Guys Wear Black
Good to Go
Goodbye Pork Pie
Gordon's War
Grand Jeu, Le
Grand Prix
Grand Theft Auto
Gray Lady Down
Great Texas Dynamite Chase,
    The
Great Waldo Pepper, The
Green Fire
Greystoke – The Legend of
    Tarzan of the Apes
Grizzly
Gunga Din
Gulag
Gunmen
Guns and the Fury, The
Guns for San Sebastian
Guns of Darkness
Gymkata
Gypsy Moths, The

Hap-Ki-Do
Hard Times
Harley Davidson and the
    Marlboro Man
Hatari!
Heartbreak Ridge
Helicopter Spies, The
Hellhounds of Alaska, The
Hell's Angels on Wheels
Hell Up In Harlem
Heroes, The
High Risk
High Road to China
Hit!
Homme de Rio, L'
House on Garibaldi Street, The
How to Destroy the Reputation
    of the Greatest Secret Agent
Hudson Hawk
Hunter, The
Hurricane
Hurricane, The

Iceman Cometh, The
Ice Palace
Ice Station Zebra
I Escaped from Devil's Island
Impasse
Indiana Jones and the
    Last Crusade
Indiana Jones and the
    Temple of Doom
Inferno
In Like Flint
Inside Out
Into the Night
Invasion U.S.A.
Iron Eagle
Iron Eagle II
Island, The

Jackal, The
Jaguar Lives
Jaws
Jaws 2
Jaws 3-D
Jaws – The Revenge
Jet Pilot
Jet Storm
Jewel of the Nile, The
Joan of Arc of Mongolia
John Carpenter's
    Escape from L.A.
Jungle 2 Jungle

Karate Kid, The
Karate Kid: Part II, The
Karate Kid: Part III, The
Karate Killers, The
Kawashima Yoshiko
Kickboxer
Killer, The (Chu Yuan)
Killer Elite, The
Killer Fish

Killpoint
Kim
King of Kung Fu
Kings of the Sun
King Solomon's Mines
    (Stevenson)
King Solomon's Mines
    (Thompson)
King Solomon's Treasure
Krakatoa – East of Java
K2
Kung Fu Fighting
Kung-Fu Gangbusters
Kung Fu Girl, The
Kung Fu - Girl Fighter
Kung Fu Street Fighter
Kung Fu – The Headcrusher

Lassiter
Last Dinosaur, The
Last Dragon, The
Last Hard Men, The
Last Hurrah for Chivalry
Last Voyage, The
Legend of Bruce Lee
Legend of the Lost
Le Mans
Licence to Kill
Live and Let Die
Living Daylights, The
Lock Up
Long Ride, The
Long Voyage Home, The
Lost World, The
Love and Bullets
Low Down Dirty Shame, A
Lustful Amazon, The
Lone Wolf McQuade
Longest Yard, The
Long Kiss Goodnight, The

Macao
Mackenna's Gold
Mackintosh Man, The
Macon County Line
Madame Sin
Mad Bomber, The
Mad Dog Morgan
Magnum Force
Mama's Dirty Girls
Man from Hong Kong, The
Man from Snowy River, The
Man With the
    Golden Gun, The
Marked for Death
Maximum Risk
Medicine Man
Mercenaries, The
Mighty Morphin Power
    Ranger: The Movie
Missing in Action
Mission Impossible
Mr Forbush and the Penguins
Mr Majestyk
Moby Dick
Mogambo
Molly Maguires, The
Montagna del Dio
    Cannibale, La
Moonraker
Moonrunners
Moonshine War, The
Morning Departure
Morocco
Mort en ce Jardin, La

Naked Jungle, The
Navy Seals
Ned Kelly
Neptune Factor, The
Never Cry Wolf
Never Say Never Again
New One-Armed
    Swordsman, The
Nickel Queen
Ninja III – The Domination
No Highway
No Retreat, No Surrender
North Sea Hijack
North to Alaska
North West Frontier

Octopussy
Odessa File, The
Oklahoma Crude
Old Man and the Sea
Once a Jolly Swagman
One Armed Boxer
On Her Majesty's Secret
    Service
Only Angels Have Wings
Open Season
Operation Thunderbolt
Orca
Osterman Weekend, The
Outcast of the Islands
Out for Justice
Overlanders, The
Over the Top

Papillon
Passage, The
Peacemaker, The
Penitentiary
People That Time Forgot, The
Perfect Weapon, The
Police Story (Chan)
Poseidon Adventure, The
Postman, The
Predator
Predator 2
Prisoner of Rio
Prisoner of Shark Island, The
Professionals, The
Project A
Punisher, The

Queimada!
Quest, The
Quigley Down Under

Race for the Yankee Zephyr
Raiders of the Lost Ark
Raid on Entebbe
Raise the Titanic!
Rambo: First Blood, Part II
Rambo III
Rampage
Rapid Fire
Raw Deal
Red Corner
Red Dawn
Red Dust
Red Line 7000
Remo Williams:
    The Adventure Begins
Return of the Dragon
Riddle of the Sands, The
Right Stuff, The
Road House
Robbery Under Arms
Robinson Crusoe
Rock, The
Rocky
Rocky II
Rocky III
Rocky IV
Rocky V
Rollerball
Romancing the Stone
Rookie, The
Rosebud
Rumble in the Bronx
Runaway Train
Run for the Sun
Running Man, The (Glaser)

Saadia
Sahara (McLaglen)
Sammy Going South
Sand Pebbles, The
Santiago
Satan Bug, The
Satan Never Sleeps
Savage Innocents, The
Scott of the Antarctic
Secret Invasion, The
Seven (Sidaris)
Seven-Ups, The
Shadow Conspiracy
Shaft
Shaft in Africa
Shaft's Big Score!

Shaker Run
Shanghai Lil
Sharks' Cave, The
Sharks' Treasure
She
She Demons
Sheena
She Gods of Shark Reef
Shogun Assassin
Shooter, The
Shout at the Devil
Siege
Silent Rage
Skullduggery
Sky Pirates
Sky Riders
Sniper
Soldier, The
Sorcerer
S.O.S. Titanic
Southern Comfort
SpaceCamp
Spoor
S.T.A.B.
Starflight: The Plane That
    Couldn't Land
Station Six – Sahara
Stick, The
Stone Cold
Stoner
Strange Days
Steet Fighter
Streets of Fire
Streets of Gold
Stunts
Sudden Death
Surf Nazis Must Die

Tank Girl
Tarzan, The Ape Man
Ten Fingers of Steel
Terminal Velocity
Terra-Cotta Warrior, A
That Lucky Touch
That Man Bolt
Thunder and Lightning
Thunderball
Thunderbolt and Lightfoot
Tigers Don't Cry
Tiger Shark
Till There Was You
Time After Time
Tintorera
Tomorrow Never Dies
Too Hot to Handle
Top Gun
Top of the World
Toward the Unknown
Towering Inferno, The
Toy Soldiers
Treasure of the Four Crowns
Treasure of the Sierra
    Madre, The
True Lies
Tunnel, The
Turbulence
Turkey Shoot
Twister (Du Bont)
Two Lane Blacktop
Two Years Before the Mast

Uncommon Valor
Under Fire
Under Siege
Under Siege II
Universal Soldier
U.S. Marshals

Vendetta
Victory
Victory at Entebbe
View to a Kill, A
Vigilante Force
Villa Rides!
Viva Knievel!
Viva Maria!
Vixen
Volcano

Wages of Fear, The
Walkabout

War
Warriors, The
War Zone
Way of the Dragon, The
What Changed Charley
    Farthing
When the North
    Wind Blows
When Time Ran Out...
Where No Vultures Fly
White Dawn, The
White Fang (Fulci)
White Fang (Kleiser)
White Squall
White Tower, The

Who Dares Wins
Wilby Conspiracy, The
Wild Angels, The
Wild Geese, The
Wild Geese II
Wind
Wind Across the Everglades
Wind and the Lion, The
Windjammer, The

Young Warriors
You Only Live Twice

Zulu
Zulu Dawn

Appendix 2

Children's Films

Adventures of Frontier
    Fremont, The
Adventures of Huck Finn, The
Adventures of Mark
    Twain, The
Adventures of Milo and
    Otis, The
Adventures of Pinocchio, The
Adventures of Tom
    Sawyer, The
Aladdin
All Creatures Great and Small
All Dogs Go to Heaven
All I Want for Christmas
Amazing Mr. Blunden, The
American Tail, An
American Tail: Fievel Goes
    West, An
Anastasia
Andre
Anne of Green Gables
Aristocats, The
Asterix and the Big Fight
Asterix Conquers America
Asterix in Britain

Babar: The Movie
Babe
Baby – Secret of the
    Lost Legend
Bambi
Beauty and the Beast
    (Trousdale/Wise)
Belstone Fox, The
Benji
Best of Walt Disney's True
    Life Adventures, The
Biggles
Big Mouth, The
Big Wheels and Sailor
Black Beauty
Black Cauldron, The
Black Stallion, The
Black Stallion Returns, The
BMX Bandits
Borrowers, The
Boy Named Charlie Brown, A
Boy Who Could Fly, The
Brave Litte Toaster, The
Bugsy Malone

Captain Stirrick
Care Bears Adventure in
    Wonderland, The
Care Bears Movie, The
Casper
Cat From Outer Space, The
Charlotte's Web
Cheetah
Chitty Chitty Bang Bang
Cinderella
Clarence, the Cross-Eyed Lion
Courage Mountain

Daemon
Danny the Champion
    of the World
Darby O'Gill and the
    Little People
Dark Enemy

Digby – The Biggest Dog in
    the World
Dimples
Dougal and the Blue Cat
Dumbo
Dunston Checks In

Escape from the Dark
Escape to Witch Mountain
Ewok Adventure, The

FairyTale – A True Story
Far from Home: The
    Adventures of
    Yellow Dog
Father, The
Feast at Midnight
Felix the Cat: The Movie
FernGully: The Last Rainforest
Flintstones, The
Flipper
Fly Away Home
Fox and the Hound, The
Freddie as F.R.O.7.
Free Willy
Free Willy II
Free Willy 3: The Rescue
Frog Dreaming

George of the Jungle
Gift, The
Girl with Brains in
    Her Feet, The
Glitterball, The
GoBots: Battle of the Rocklords
Golden Seal, The
Goonies, The
Great Mouse Detective, The
Gulliver's Travels

Hambone and Hillie
Hard Road
Harriet the Spy
Harry and the Hendersons
Heidi's Song
Herbie Goes Bananas
Herbie Goes to Monte Carlo
Herbie Rides Again
Hercules
Huckleberry Finn
Hugo the Hippo

Incredible Journey, The
Indian in the Cupboard, The
International Velvet
It Shouldn't Happen to a Vet

James and the Giant Peach
Jetsons: The Movie
Jingle All the Way
Journey of Natty Gann, The
Jungle Book, The (Reitherman)
Jungle Book, The (Sommers)
Just Ask for Diamond

King of the Wind

Lady and the Tramp
Land Before Time, The
Last Flight of Noah's Ark, The

Appendix 3

Comedy

Cannonball Run II
Can She Bake a Cherry Pie?
Can't Buy Me Love
Can You Keep It Up for a Week?
Caporal Epinglé, Le
Caprice
Captain Ron
Captain's Paradise, The
Captain's Table, The
Carbon Copy
Card, The
Carry On Admiral
Carry On Columbus
Carry On Sergeant
Car Trouble
Car Wash
Casanova's Big Night
Casino Royale
Castle, The
Casual Sex?
Cat and the Canary, The (Leni)
Cat and the Canary, The (Metzger)
Cat Ballou
Catch Me a Spy
Cat's-Paw, The
Chain, The
Champagne Charlie
Chance of a Lifetime
Chapter Two
Charles and Lucie
Cheap Detective, The
Cheaper by the Dozen
Checking Out
Cheech & Chong's Next Movie
Cheer, Boys, Cheer
Chicken and Duck Talk
Chiltern Hundreds, The
Chorus of Disapproval, A
Christmas in July
Christmas Story, A
Chump at Oxford, A
Cinderfella
Circus, The
Citizens Band
City Lights
City Slickers
City Slickers II: The Legend of Curly's Gold
Class
Class of Nuke 'Em High
Claudine
Clerks
Clinic, The
Clockwise
Closely Observed Trains
Club de Femmes
Cluny Brown
Coca Cola Kid, The
Cocoanuts, The
Cocoon
Cocoon: The Return
Cold Comfort Farm
Cold Dog Soup
Cold Feet
Cold Turkey
College
Come Blow Your Horn
Comedy of Terrors, The
Come on George
Come Play with Me
Comfort and Joy
Comic Magazine
Coming to America
Coming Up Roses
Confessions from a Holiday Camp
Confessions of a Bigamist
Confessions of a Driving Instructor
Confessions of a Pop Performer
Confessions of a Window Cleaner
Confucian Confusion, A
Consul, The
Consuming Passions
Cookie
Cool Runnings
Cop & ½
Couch Trip, The

Country Dance
Coupe de Ville
Courage, Fuyons
Court Jester, The
Cracksman, The
Crazy Family
Crazy Mama
Crazy People
Creator
Cremator, The
Crime Busters
Crossing Delancey
Crooks' Tour
Cry-Baby
Curdled
Curly Sue
Curse of the Pink Panther
Cutting it Short
Cyclone, The

Daddy's Dyin' – Who's Got the Will?
Dad's Army
Daisies
Dance, Girl, Dance
Dark Habits
Darling Lili
Dave
David Holzman's Diary
Day at the Races, A
Daydream Believer
Day for Night
Day the Fish Came Out, The
D.C. Cab
Dead Men Don't Wear Plaid
Death Becomes Her
Death in Brunswick
Decline and Fall...of a Birdwatcher!
Deconstructing Harry
Deep End
Defending Your Life
Delicate Delinquent, The
Delirious
Dennis the Menace
Dentist in the Chair
Dernier Milliardaire, Le
Desert Mice
Design for Living
Designing Woman
Desire
Desk Set
Desperate Living
Desperately Seeking Susan
Devil and Max Devlin, The
Devil and Miss Jones, The
Diary of a Mad Housewife
Didn't You Kill My Brother?
Different Story, A
Dinner at Eight
Dirty Rotten Scoundrels
Disorderly Orderly, The
Distinguished Gentleman, The
Disturbed
Divorce American Style
Doc Hollywood
Docteur Popaul
Doctor in the House
Dr Jekyll and Ms Hyde
Dr Strangelove: or, How I Learned to Stop Worrying and Love the Bomb
Dogpound Shuffle
Doña Flor and Her Two Husbands
Doña Herlinda and Her Son
Don Juan DeMarco
Do Not Disturb
Don't Just Lie There, Say Something!
Don't Make Waves
Don't Take it To Heart
Don't Tell Her It's Me
Don't Tell Mom the Babysitter's Dead
Do the Right Thing
Double Agent 73
Down Among the Z Men
Down and out in Beverly Hills
Down by Law
Down Memory Lane

Down Periscope
Dracula: Dead and Loving It
Dragnet
Dramma della Gelosia
Dream Team, The
Drop Dead Fred
Dry Rot
Duck Soup
Dudes
Dumb & Dumber
Dunston Checks In
During the Summer
Dutch
Dynamite Chicken

Early Bird, The
Easy Living
Easy Money
Eating Raoul
Eat the Rich
Eddie
Eddie Murphy Raw
Educating Rita
8 Heads in a Duffel Bag
18 Again!
Electric Moon
Eléna et les Hommes
Emmerdeur,L'
Encino Man
End, The
End of the Road
End Play
Entertaining Mr Sloane
Equinox
Ernest Saves Christmas
Every Little Crook and Nanny
Everything You Always Wanted to Know About Sex But Were Afraid to Ask
Every Which Way But Loose
Experts, The

Face in the Crowd, A
Falling For You
Family Business (Lumet)
Family Game
Family Jewels, The
Fandango
Fantome du Moulin Rouge, Le
Farmer's Wife, The
Fast Lady, The
Fast Talking
Fast Times at Ridgemont High
Fatal Beauty
Father Brown
Father Goose
Father of the Bride (Minnelli)
Father of the Bride (Shyer)
Father of the Bride Part II
Fathers' Day
Favourites of the Moon
Favour, the Watch and the Very Big Fish, The
Fear of a Black Hat
Feds
Feet First
Female Trouble
Femme du Boulanger, La
Ferris Bueller's Day Off
Fiancée du Pirate, La
Fiddlers Three
Fierce Creatures
Fifth Avenue Girl
Filofax
Fine Madness, A
Firemen's Ball, The
First Effort
Fish Called Wanda, A
Flamingo Kid, The
Flap
Fletch
Fletch Lives
Flim-Flam Man, The
Flubber
Folies Bergère
Folks!
Follow a Star
Folly to be Wise
Footman, The
Foreign Affair, A
For Keeps

For Love or Money
For Pete's Sake
Fortune, The
Fortune Cookie, The
Foul Play
Four Weddings and a Funeral
Fracture du myocarde, La
Francis
Freaked
Freaky Friday
French Mistress, A
French Mustard
French Without Tears
Freshman, The
Friday
Front Page
Front Page, The (Milestone)
Front Page, The (Wilder)
Front Page Woman
Full Monty, The
Full Moon in Blue Water
Full of Life
Funeral Rites
Funny About Love
Fun With Dick and Jane

Gabriel Over the White House
Gasbags
Gas-s-s-s, or it became necessary to destroy the world in order to save it
'Gator
Gazebo, The
Gazon maudit
Geisha Boy, The
General, The
Genevieve
Gentlemen Prefer Blondes
German Chainsaw Massacre, The
George and Mildred
Georgy Girl
Gert and Daisy's Weekend
Getting Any
Getting It Right
Getting Straight
Ghost and Mrs Muir, The
Ghost Breakers, The
Ghostbusters
Ghostbusters II
Ghost Catchers
Ghost Chase, The
Ghost Goes West, The
Ghost of St Michael's, The
Ginger & Fred
Girl from Maxim's, The
Girl in Every Port, A
Girl in the Picture, The
Girl Shy
Global Affair, A
Go for a Take
Going in Style
Going Steady
Golden Coach, The
Gold Rush, The
Good Burger
Goodbye, Columbus
Goodbye Girl, The
Good Morning, Boys!
Good Morning Vietnam
Goofy Movie, A
Go West (Keaton)
Go West (Buzzell)
Grace Quigley
Graduate, The
Grand Amour, Le
Grazie Zia
Greased Lightning
Great Dictator, The
Great McGinty, The
Great McGonagall, The
Great Man Votes, The
Great White Hype, The
Green Card
Green Ice Greetings
Greenkeeping
Green Man, The
Gregory's Girl
Groundhog Day
Groove Tube, The
Grosse Point Blank

Guerre des boutons, La
Guide for the Married Man, A
Gumball Rally, The
Gumshoe

Hail the Conquering Hero
Hairspray
Hallelujah the Hills
Hamlet Goes Business
Hands Across the Table
Hanky Panky
Happening, The
Happiest Days of Your
    Life, The
Happiness
Happy Birthday Wanda June
Happy Gilmore
Happy Hooker, The
Hardbodies
Hard Day's Night, A
Hard to Handle
Hard Way, The
Harlem Nights
Harold and Maude
Harry and Tonto
Harry and Walter Go to
    New York
Harvey
Harvey Middleman, Fireman
Has Anybody Seen My Gal?
Haunted Honeymoon
Having It All
Hawks
Head
Head over Heels
Health
Hear My Song
Heartbreakers
Heartbreak Kid, The
Heart Condition
Heathers
Heaven Can Wait (Lubitsch)
Heaven Can Wait
    (Beatty/Henry)
Heaven Help Us
Heavenly Pursuits
Heavens Above
Hello Again
Hellzapoppin'
Help!
Her Alibi
Hercules Returns
Here We Go Round the
    Mulberry Bush
Her Majesty, Love
Hero at Large
Héros très discret, Un
High Anxiety
High Hopes
High School High
High Spirits
Hi, Mom!
Hi, Nellie!
His Girl Friday
Histoire inventée, Une
History of the World Part One
Hobson's Choice
Hocus Pocus
Hog Wild
Hold Me, Thrill Me, Kiss Me
Hole in the Head, A
Holiday
Hollywood or Bust
Hollywood Shuffle
Home Alone
Home Alone 2: Lost in
    New York
Home Alone 3
Homebodies
Home for the Holidays
Homework
Homme de Marrakesh, L'
Honey, I Blew Up the Kid
Honey, I Shrunk the Kids
Honeymoon in Vegas
Honey Pot, The
Honky Tonk Freeway
Hooper
Hoots Mon!
Hopscotch
Horse Feathers

Hospital, The
Hôtel de la Plage, L'
Hôtel de Love
Hotel Sahara
Hot Enough for June
Hot Rock, The
Hot Shots!
Hot Shots! Part DeuxHot Stuff
Hot Times
House Calls
House on Trubnaya, The
House Party
Housesitter
How I Won the War
How to Be Very, Very Popular
How to Commit Marriage
How to Get Ahead in
    Advertising
How to Marry a Millionaire
Husbands and Wives

Iceland
Icicle Thief
Idle on Parade
If I Had a Million
I Hired a Contract Killer
I Love Trouble
I Love You Again
I Love You, Alice B Toklas
I Love You to Death
I'm All Right, Jack
I'm Gonna Git You Sucka
I Married a Witch
Importance of Being Earnest,
    The
Incredible Shrinking Woman,
    The
Indiscreet
In-Laws, The
Innocents in Paris
International House
In the Spirit
Intimate Games
Invitation, The
I Ought to Be in Pictures
Irma la Douce
Ishtar
Is there Sex After Marriage?
It Came from Hollywood
It Happened One Night
It's a Gift
It's a Mad, Mad, Mad, Mad
    World
It's a 2'6" Above the Ground
    World
It's Great to Be Young
It Should Happen to You
It's Love I'm After
It's Only Money
It Started in Naples
It Started With Eve
It's the Old Army Game
It Takes Two
I Wanna Hold Your Hand
I Want to Go Home
I Was a Male War Bride
I Was Born, But
I Was on Mars
I Will...I Will...for Now

Jabberwocky
Jack
Jake Speed
Jane and the Lost City
Jerk, The
Jerry Maguire
Jimmy the Kid
Jit
Jitterbugs
Johnny Suede
Jolly Bad Fellow, A
Jour de Fete
Julia Has Two Lovers
Jumping for Joy
Jumpin' Jack Flash
Junior
Just Like a Woman

Keep It Up, Jack!
Kentucky Fried Movie, The
Kermesse Héroique, La

Kicked in the Head
Kid, The
Kid Brother, The
Kids in the Hall: Brain Candy
Kids Return
Killer Klowns from
    Outer Space
Killing Dad
Kindergarten Cop
Kind Hearts and Coronets
Kingdom, The
Kingdom II, The
King in New York, A
King of Hearts
Kingpin
King Ralph
King Ubu
Kiss Me Goodbye
Kiss Me, Stupid
Kleiner Liebt Mich
Klondike Annie
Knack...and how to get it, The
Knave of Hearts
Knickers Ahoy
K-9
Knock on Wood

Labyrinth of Passion
Ladies' Man, The
Lady Eve, The
Lady Godiva Rides Again
Lady Killer
Ladykillers, The
Landlord, The
Larger Than Life
Lásky Jedné Plavovlásky
    (A Blonde in Love)
Last Boy Scout, The
Last Holiday
Last Italian Tango, The
Last Married Couple in
    America, The
Last of the Red Hot Lovers
LA Story
Late for Dinner
Laughter in Paradise
Lavender Hill Mob, The
Law and Disorder
Laxdale Hall
League of Gentlemen, The
Le Cop
Le Cop 2
Left, Right and Centre
Leon the Pig Farmer
Leningrad Cowboys
    Go America
Lenny Bruce Performance
    Film, The
Lenny Bruce Without Tears
Lenny Live and Unleashed
Let It Ride
Let's Do It Again
Let's Get Laid!
Let's Hope It's A Girl
Let the People Sing
Lewis & Clark & George
Liar Liar
Life Is a Long Quiet River
Life Is Cheap...But Toilet Paper
    Is Expensive
Life Is Sweet
Life Less Ordinary, A
Life Stinks
Like Father, Like Son
Likely Lads, The
Lily Tomlin
Limit Up
Lincoln County Incident
Linguini Incident, The
Little Hut, The
Little Shop of Horrors, The
    (Corman)
Littlest Rebel, The
Lonely in America
Long Live the Lady!
Long Shot
Look Who's Talking
Look Who's Talking Now
Look Who's Talking Too
Loose Cannons
Lord Love a Duck

Loser
Losin' It
Lost in America
Lost Paradise, The
Love and Death
Love and Other Catastrophes
Love at First Bite
Love Crazy
Loved One, The
Love Happy
Love in the Afternoon (Wilder)
Love on the Run
Loverboy
Lovers!, The
Lovesick
Love Test, The
Loving
Lock Up Your Daughters!
Lonely Hearts
Luna e l'Altra
Lunatic, The

Macunaima
Mad Adventures of 'Rabbi'
    Jacob, The
Made in America
Madhouse
Mad Miss Manton, The
Magnificent Seven Deadly
    Sins, The
Magnificent Two, The
Main Event, The
Major and the Minor, The
Major League
Major League II
Make Mine a Million
Making Mr Right
Malcolm
Malizia
Man Alive
Man, a Woman and a Bank, A
Man Friday
Man from Africa and Girl
    from India
Manhattan
Man of the House
Manifesto
Man in the White Suit, The
Man Is Not a Bird
Mannequin
Mannequin 2: On the Move
Man of the Moment
Man on the Flying Trapeze,
    The
Man's Favourite Sport?
Man Trouble
Man Who Came to Dinner, The
Man With Two Brains, The
Married to the Mob
Marrying Kind, The
Marrying Man, The
Mars Attacks!
Masala
Matinee
Matinee Idol, The
Matter of Honour, A
Mazel Tov ou le mariage
Meet the Applegates
Memoirs of an Invisible Man
Men at Work
Mermaids
Métisse
Metropolitan
Micki + Maude
Midnight
Midsummer Night's Sex
    Comedy, A
Mighty Aphrodiet
Million, Le
Millionairess, The
Million Pound Note, The
Milou en mai
Miracle of Morgan's Creek, The
Miracles
Missionary, The
Miss Robin Hood
Mr and Mrs Smith
Mr Billion
Mr Blandings Builds His
    Dream House
Mister Cory

Mr Deeds Goes to Town
Mr Drake's Duck
Mr Hobbs Takes a Vacation
Mr Jolly Lives Next Door
Mr Mom
Mr Nanny
Mr Peabody and the Mermaid
Mr Saturday Night
Mr Smith Goes to Washington
Mistress
Mrs Pollifax – Spy
Mixed Company
Mixed Nuts
Modern Times
Modesty Blaise
Moment d'Egarement, Un
Mo' Money
Mondo Trasho
Money Pit, The
Monkey Business (McLeod)
Monkey Business (Hawks)
Mon Oncle
Mon Père, ce héros
Monsieur Verdoux
Monty Python and the
    Holy Grail
Monty Python's Life of Brian
Monty Python's Meaning
    of Life
Moon is Blue, The
Moon Over Parador
Moonstruck
More American Graffiti
More Bad News
More the Merrier, The
Morgan, a Suitable Case for
    Treatment
Morons from Outer Space
Moscow on the Hudson
Mother, Jugs & Speed
MouseHunt
Mouse on the Moon, The
Mouse that Roared, The
Movie Crazy
Movie Movie
Moving
Mozart in Love
Multiplicity
Murder By Death
Murder, He Says
Mutiny on the Buses
My Best Friend's Girl
My Best Friend's Wedding
My Blue Heaven
My Cousin Vinny
My Father Is Coming
My Favourite Blonde
My Favourite Brunette
My Favourite Wife
My Favourite Year
My Girl
My Girl II
My Learned Friend
My Little Chickadee
My Man Godfrey (La Cava)
My Man Godfrey (Koster)
My New Gun
Myra Breckinridge
My Stepmother Is an Alien
Mystery Date
My Young Auntie

Nadine
Naked Gun, The
Naked Gun 2½: The Smell of
    Fear, The
Naked Gun 33⅓
Naked Truth, The
Nasty Habits
National Lampoon
    Goes to the Movies
National Lampoon's
    Animal House
National Lampoon's
    Class Reunion
National Lampoon's
    Loaded Weapon 1
National Lampoon's Vacation
Navigator, The
Necessary Roughness
Neighbors

Never Give a Sucker an
    Even Break
Never Say Die
New Leaf, A
Next Stop, Greenwich Village
Nick Carter in Prague
Nickelodeon
Night After Night
Night at the Opera, A
Night in Casablanca, A
Night Shift
Nine Lives of Fritz the Cat, The
1988: The Remake
1941
Nine to Five
Ninotchka
Nobody's Fool
No Deposit, No Return
Noises Off
Norman...Is That You?
Norman Loves Rose
Northerners, The
No Surrender
Not for Publication
Nothing in Common
Nothing to Lose
Nothing Sacred
Not Now, Comrade
Notre Histoire
No Way to Treat a Lady
Nude Bomb, The
Nuns on the Run
Nutty Professor, The (Lewis)
Nutty Professor, The (Shadyac)

O.C. & Stiggs
Ocean's 11
Odd Couple, The
Odd Job, The
Off and Running
Off Beat
Oh, God!
Oh, Men! Oh, Women!
Oh, Mr Porter
O-Kay for Sound
Old-Fashioned Way, The
Old Flames
Old Lady Who Walked in the
    Sea, The
On Approval
Once Upon a Honeymoon
Once Upon a Time
One and Only, The
One Flew Over the Cuckoo's
    Nest
One Hamlet Less
One More Time
One, Two, Three
Only Game in Town, The
Only the Lonely
Only Two Can Play
Only When I Laugh
On purge Bébé
On the Beat
On the Buses
Ooh...You Are Awful
Operation Petticoat
Orders are Orders
Oscar
Other People's Money
Otley
Our Hospitality
Our Man in Havana
Our Relations
Our Town
Outlaw Blues
Out of Order
Out-of-Towners, The
Outrageous!
Outrageous Fortune
Overboard
Over Her Dead Body
Over the Brooklyn Bridge
Owl and the Pussycat, The
Oxford Blues

Pack Up Your Troubles
Paleface, The
Palm Beach Story, The
Palookaville
Papa, les Petits Bateaux ...

Paper, The
Parade
Pardners
Pardon Mon Affair, Too
Pardon Us
Parenthood
Parents
Paris qui Dort
Parlor, Bedroom and Bath
Party, The
Party Party
Passport to Pimlico
Pat and Mike
Paternity
Patsy, The
Paws
Peeper
Pee-Wee's Big Adventure
Pelvis
People Will Talk
Percy
Percy's Progress
Perfect Couple, A
Perfectly Normal
Permis de Conduire, Le
Personal Services
Pete 'n' Tillie
Peter's Friends
Petomane, Il
Petticoat Pirates
Philadelphia Story, The
Philosopher's Stone, The
Pigs
Pillow Talk
Pink Panther, The
Pink Panther Strikes Again,
    The
Pirates
Plaff! or Too Afraid of Life
Planes, Trains and
    Automobiles
Platinum Blonde
Player, The
Play It Again, Sam
Playtime
Please Don't Eat the Daisies
Pleasure Principle, The
Plot Against Harry, The
Plunder
Police Academy
Police Academy 2:
    Their First Assignment
Police Academy 3:
    Back in Training
Police Academy 4:
    Citizens on Patrol
Police Academy 5:
    Assignment Miami Beach
Police Academy 6:
    City Under Siege
Police Academy 7:
    Mission to Moscow
Polyester
Pope Must Die, The
Porky's
Porky's II: The Next Day
Porky's Revenge
Porridge
Posto, Il
Pot Luck
Préparez Vos Mouchoirs
President's Analyst, The
Press for Time
Pretty Woman
Primrose Path, The
Prince and the Showgirl, The
Prisoner of Second
    Avenue, The
Prisoner of Zenda, The (Quine)
Private Benjamin
Private Club
Private Function, A
Private Parts
Privates on Parade
Private's Progress
Producers, The
Promise Her Anything
Protocol
Pulp
Punchline
Punch Me in the Stomach

Pure Hell of St Trinian's, The
Pure Luck
Purple Rose of Cairo, The
Pushing Hands
Putney Swope
Pyrates

Queen of Hearts
Quick Change
Quiet Man, The

Radio Days
Rain or Shine
Raising Arizona
Raising the Wind
Rake's Progress, The
Rally 'round the Flag, Boys!
Ratboy
Raven, The (Corman)
Real Genius
Real Life
Real Blonde, The
Rebel, The
Remember Last Night?
Remember Me?
Remember the Night
Rentadick
Repo Man
Repossessed
Restless Natives
Return of Captain Invincible,
    The
Return of the Pink Panther,
    The
Reuben, Reuben
Revenge of the Nerds
Revenge of the Pink Panther
Rhubarb
Richard Pryor...Here & Now
Richard Pryor Live in Concert
Richard Pryor Live on the
    Sunset Strip
Riff-Raff
Rigolboche
Rise and Rise of Michael
    Rimmer, The
Rising Damp
Risky Business
Rita, Sue and Bob Too
Ritz, The
Roadie
Road to Morocco
Road to Utopia
Robin Hood – Men in Tights
Rock-a-Bye Baby
Rockets Galore
Rock'n'Roll High School
Roger Corman's Frankenstein
    Unbound
Romance with a Double Bass
Roman Holiday
Romuald et Juliette
Romy and Michelle's High
    School Reunion
Rookery Nook
Room Service
Rosalie Goes Shopping
Rosie Dixon, Night Nurse
Rotten to the Core
Roxanne
Roxie Hart
Rude Awakening
Ruggles of Red Gap
Ruling Class, The
Run for Your Money, A
Ruthless People

Sabrina
Safety Last
Sailor Beware
Sallah
Salt & Pepper
Salvation! Have You Said Your
    Prayers Today?
Same Time, Next Year
Santa Clause, The
Saphead, The
Saps at Sea
Saturday the 14th
Sauvage, Le
Scenes from a Mall

Scenes from the Class Struggle in Beverly Hills
School Daze
School for Scoundrels
Schtonk!
Screwballs
Screwballs II – Loose Screws
Scrooges
Seclusion Near a Forest
Secret Admirer
Secret Agent Club, The
Secret Life of an American Wife, The
Secret of Santa Vittoria, The
Secret Policeman's Ball, The
Secret Policeman's Other Ball, The
Secret Policeman's Third Ball, The
Seems Like Old Times
See No Evil, Hear No Evil
Semi-Tough
Senator Was Indiscreet, The
Send Me No Flowers
Seniors, The
Sgt Bilko
Serial Mom
Seven Chances
Seven Year Itch, The
Sex and the Single Girl
Sex Shop
Shadows and Fog
Shaggy D.A., The
Shall We Dance?
Shanghai Surprise
She-Devil
She Done Him Wrong
Sherlock Junior
She's Gotta Have It
She's Having a Baby
She's Out of Control
Shirley Valentine
Short Time
Shot in the Dark, A
Sibling Rivalry
Sidewalk Stories
Silence of the Hams, The
Silent Movie
Silver Bears
Silver Streak
Simon
Singles
Sin of Harold Diddlebock, The
Sir Henry at Rawlinson's End
Sister Act
Sister Act II: Back in the Habit
Sitting Ducks
Skin Deep
Skinless Night
Ski Patrol
Skyline
Slacker
Sleeper
Sleepless in Seattle
Sleep With Me
Sliding Doors
Slight Case of Murder, A
Slightly Pregnant Man, The
Smallest Show on Earth, The
Smiles of a Summer Night
Smiling Ghost, The
Smokey and the Bandit
Smokey and the Bandit II
Snobs
Soapdish
S.O.B.
So Fine
Soft Top, Hard Shoulder
So I Married an Axe Murderer
Solarwarriors
Solid Gold Cadillac, The
Solitaire for 2
Soliti Ignoti, I
Somebody Killed Her Husband
Some Girls
Some Kind of Hero
Some Like It Hot
Something Big
Son in Law
Son of Paleface
Sons of the Desert

Soul Man
Soupirant, Le
Southern Yankee, A
Spaceballs
Spanish Fly
Special Treatment
Speedy
Spies Like Us
Spite Marriage
Spitfire
Splash
Splitting Heirs
Spotswood
Spy Hard
S*P*Y*S
Squeeze, The
Squibs
Stan and George's New Life
Stand-In
Stand Up, Don't Grovel!
Stand Up Virgin Soldiers
Stardust Memories
Stars and Bars
State of the Union
Static
Stay Hungry
Stay Tuned
Steamboat Bill Jr
Steelyard Blues
Stiff Upper Lips
Stir Crazy
Stop! or My Mom Will Shoot
Stork
Straight Talk
Straight to Hell
Strange Brew
Strictly Ballroom
Stripes
Strong Man, The
Stroszek
Stuart Saves His Family
Student Teachers, The
Stuff, The
Stunt Man, The
Stupids, The
Such Good Friends
Sugarbaby
Sugarland Express, The
Survivors, The
Sullivan's Travels
Summer School
Sweethearts
Sweetie
Sweet November
Switch
Sylvia Scarlett

Take the Money and Run
Taking Off
Tall Guy
Tampopo
Tango
Tank
Tant qu'on a la Santé
Tapeheads
Tatie Danielle
Taxing Woman, A
Teahouse of the August Moon, The
Teen Wolf
Teen Wolf Too
Telephone Book, The
'10'
Tenue de Soirée
That Gang of Mine
That Riviera Touch
That's Carry On
That Sinking Feeling
'That's Life'
That Summer!
Theodora Goes Wild
There's a Girl in My Soup
They All Laughed
They Call Me Bruce
They Knew What They Wanted
They Might Be Giants
They're a Weird Mob
Things Change
30 Is a Dangerous Age, Cynthia
This Is My Life

This Is Spinal Tap
Those Wonderful Movie Cranks
Three Ages, The
Three Amigos!
Three Fugitives
Three Men and a Baby
3 Men and a Cradle
Three Men and a Little Lady
Three Men in a Boat
3 Ring Circus
3 Women in Love
Throw Momma from theTrain
Tiger's Tale, A
Till Death Us Do Part
Till Sex Do Us Part
Tin Men
Titfield Thunderbolt, The
To Be or Not To Be (Lubitsch)
To Be or Not To Be (Johnson)
Tommy Boy
Tootsie
Topper
Top Secret!
Touch and Go
Touch of Class, A
Tough Guys
Toy, The
Toys
Trading Places
Traffic
Trail of the Pink Panther
Tramp, Tramp, Tramp
Transformers – The Movie, The
Trapped in Paradise
Travelling Executioner, The
Treasure of Matecumbe
Trial By Combat
Trois Vies et une Seule Mort
Tropical Fish
Trouble in Paradise
Trouble in Store
Trou Normand, Le
Truck Stop Women
True Confession
True Identity
True Love
True Nature of Bernadette, The
True Nature of Eskimo Nell, The
Tugboat Annie
Tune in Tomorrow
Turnabout
Turner & Hooch
Twelve Chairs, The
Twentieth Century
Twins
Twister
Two-Faced Woman
Two for the Road
Two if by Sea
Two-Way Stretch

UHF
Uncle Buck
Undercover Blues
Underneath the Arches
Under the Doctor
Un Deux Trois Soleil
Unfaithfully Yours (Sturges)
Unfaithfully Yours (Zieff)
Up in Smoke
Uptown Saturday Night
Up Your Alley
Used Cars
Used People

Vacances de M. Hulot, Les
Valley of Song
Valseuses, Les
Value for Money
Van, The
Verdugo, El
Versailles rive gauche
Vices in the Family
Vice Versa (Gilbert)
Vice Versa (Ustinov)
Victor/Victoria
Vieille Dame Indigne, La
Violette et François
Visitor, The

Viva Max!
Vivacious Lady
Volere, Volare
Volunteers
Voyage-Surprise

Wackiest Ship in the Army, The
Wagons East!
Wag the Dog
Waiting for the Light
Walking and Talking
Walk Like a Man
Wanderers, The
War of the Roses, The
Watch Out, We're Mad
Watch Your Stern
Water
Watermelon Man
Wayne's World
Wayne's World II
Way Out West
Way Upstream
Wedding, A
Weekend at Bernie's
Wendy Cracked a Walnut
We're No Angels
Werewolf of Washington, The
What?
What About Bob?
What a Carve Up!
What Are You Doing After the Orgy?
What Did You Do in the War, Daddy?
What Have I Done to Deserve This?
What Makes David Run?
What Price Hollywood?
What's New Pussycat?
What's Up Doc?
What's Up Tiger Lily?
Wheels on Meals
When Harry Met Sally...
Where's Poppa?
Where the Boys Are
Where the Heart Is
Where Were You When the Lights Went Out?
Which Way to the Front?
Whiffs
While Parents Sleep
While You Were Sleeeing
Whisky Galore!
White Men Can't Jump
White Sheik, The
Who Am I This Time?
Who Are You Polly Maggoo?
Who Framed Roger Rabbit?
Who Is Harry Kellerman andWhy Is He Saying ThoseTerrible Things About Me?
Who Is Killing the Great Chefs of Europe?
Whole Town's Talking, The
Wholly Moses!
Whoops Apocalypse
Who's Harry Crumb?
Who's the Man
Who's That Girl?
Why Me?
Why Worry?
Wildcats
Wildcats of St Trinian's, The
Wild Party, The
Wild in the Streets
Wild West
Wild Women of Wongo
Will Success Spoil Rock Hunter?
Wilt
Windbag the Sailor
Wise Guys
Wish You Were Here
Witches of Eastwick, The
Withnail & I
Without a Clue
Witness, The
Wizard of Speed and Time, The

Woman in Red, The
Woman of the Year
Woman or Two, A
Woman's World
Women on the Verge of a
  Nervous Breakdown
Working Girl
Work is a Four Letter Word
World is Full of Married
  Men, The
World's Greatest Lover, The
Wrong Arm of the Law, The
W.W. and the Dixie Dancekings
Yellowbeard

You and Me
You Can't Cheat an
  Honest Man
Young Doctors in Love
Young Einstein
Young Frankenstein
You're a Big Boy Now
Yours, Mine and Ours
Yoyo

Zelig
Zero de Conduite
Zorba the Greek
Zorro the Gay Blade

Appendix 4

Documentaries

Abba, The Movie
Above Us the Earth
Adventures of a Brown Man in
  Search of Civilization
Africa Addio
African Elephant, The
Ah-Ying
A.K.
All Visitors Must Be Announced
Alternative Miss World, The
Always for Pleasure
Amazonia: Voices from the
  Rainforest
America – from Hitler to M-X
American Boy
American Pictures
...and the pursuit of
  happiness
Angst
Animals Film, The
Anou Banou or the Daughters
  of Utopia
Army of Lovers or Revolt of
  the Perverts
Art Pepper: Notes from
  aJazz Survivor
Atomic Café, The
At Sundance
Attica
Attila '74

Ballet Black
Bantsuma: The Life and Times
  of Tsumasaburo
Bando
Bari-Zogon
Basic Training
Battle of Chile, The
Battle of the Ten Million, The
Beautiful People
Because of That War
Before Hindsight
Before Stonewall
Before the Nickelodeon: The
  Early Cinema of Edwin S
  Porter
Behind the Rent Strike
Best Boy
Best Hotel on Skid Row
Big Bang, The (Toback)
Big Time
Bird Now
Bit of Scarlet, A
Bitter Cane
Bix
Black Diamond Rush
Black Fox
Blacks Britannica
Black Wax
Blind Alley
Blue Notes and Exiled Voices
Blue Water, White Death
Boatman
Bombay Our City
Bongo Man
Born to Boogie
Bosna!
Bring On the Night
British Sounds
Broken Arrow 29
Broken Noses

Brother, Can You Spare a Dime?
Burden of Dreams
Burra Sahib
...But Then, She's Betty Carter
Bye-Bye Babushka

Cane Toads – an Unnatural
  History
Carmen Miranda: Bananas Is
  My Business
Carry Greenham Home
Celluloid Closet, The
Chantons sous l'Occupation
Chariots of the Gods
Charlie Mingus: The Triumph
  of the Underdog
Children of Theatre Street, The
Citizen Langlois
Chronique d'un Eté
Ciao! Manhattan
Cinema Cinema
Circle of Gold
Clowns, The
Color of Honor, The
Comic Book Confidential
Common Threads:
  Stories from the Quilt
Completely Pogued
Confessions of a Suburban Girl
Confessions of Winifred
  Wagner, The
Conversations with
  Willard Van Dyke
Coraje del Pueblo, El
Correction Please, or How We
  Got Into Pictures
Cortazar
Courtesans of Bombay, The
Cousin Bobby
Cross and Passion
Crumb

Dance Craze
Dark Circle
Day After Trinity, The
Dealers Among Dealers
Dear America: Letters Home
  From Vietnam
Decline of the Western
  Civilization, The
Decline of the Western
  Civilization Part II, The
  Metal Years
Demon Lover Diary
Derby
Desert Victory
Deus, Patria e Autoridade
¡Devils Don't Dream! Research
  on Jacobo Arbenz Guzmán
Diaries
Directed by Andrei Tarkovsky
Directed by William Wyler
Divine Madness
Donald Cammell: The Ultimate
  Performance
Don't Look Back
Double Headed Eagle, The
Driving Me Crazy

Eadweard Muybridge,
  Zoopraxographer

Eight-Tray Gangster: The
  Making of a Crip
80 Blocks from Tiffany's
El Salvador: Another Vietnam
El Salvador – Decision to Win
El Salvador – Portrait of a
  Liberated Zone
El Salvador – The People
  Will Win
Elvis on Tour
Elvis – That's the Way It Is
Emperor's Naked Army
  Marches On, The
Enfants de Lumière, Les
Eric Clapton and His
  Rolling Hotel
Escape Route to Marseilles
Europe After the Rain
Everest
Every Little Thing
Execution Protocol, The
Exodus – Bob Marley Live

Fall of the Romanov
  Dynasty, The
Family Business
Far From Vietnam
Farrebique
Fast Trip, Long Drop
Fatal Reaction: Singapore
Fetishes
F for Fake
Fillmore
Film from the Clyde
Fires Were Started
Fly a Flag for Poplar
For All Mankind
Forest of Bliss
For Love or Money
Fortini/Cani
Fountain, The
François Truffaut,
  Portraits Volés
Frank Capra's American Dream
Frantz Fanon: Black Skin,
  White Mask
From Mao to Mozart: Issac
  Stern in China
From Pole to Equator
From Russia with Rock
From the Cloud to the
  Resistance
From the Journals of
  Jean Seberg
F.T.A.

Galahad of Everest
Garlic Is as Good as
  Ten Mothers
Gates of Heaven
General Amin
Germany in Autumn
Get Back
Gilsodom
Gimme Shelter
Glastonbury: The Movie
God's Alcatraz
Good Fight, The
Good People of Portugal, The
Good Wife of Tokyo, The
Good Woman of Bangkok, The
G'Ole!
Grass
Great Day in Harlem, A
Great Ecstasy of Woodcarver
  Steiner, The
Grey Gardens
Gringo in Mañanaland, A
Guerre sans nom, La

Hail! Hail! Rock 'n' Roll
Half Life
Hamster Factor and Other tales
  of Twelve Monkeys, The
Handsworth Songs
Happiness in Twenty Years
Harlan County, U.S.A.
Heartland Reggae
Hearts and Minds
Hearts of Darkness: A
  Filmmaker's Apocalypse

Heaven
Heaven, Man, Earth
Heaven-6-Box
Heavy Petting
Heidi Fleiss –
  Hollywood Madam
Helter Skelter
Hero
Hitler – A Career
Hollywood on Trial
Hoop Dreams
Hotel Terminus: The Life and
  Times of Klaus Barbie
How Does It Feel

I Am a Dancer
I Am Anna Magnani
I Am a Sex Addict
I Am My Own Woman
I.F. Stone's Weekly
Imagine
Imago – Meret Oppenheim
Improper Conduct
Indian Story, An
In Georgia
In Ismail's Custody
In Search of Famine
In the Name of the People
Invocation Maya Deren
Ireland Behind the Wire
Italianamerican
It's All True
It's Trad, Dad!
I Was, I Am, I Shall Be

Jabula – A Band in Exile
James Baldwin: The Price
  of the Ticket
James Dean Story, The
James Dean – The First
  American Teenager
Jane
Janis
Jazz in Exile
Jazz on a Summer's Day
Jimi Hendrix
Joe Albany...A Jazz Life
Joe Louis – For All Time
John Heartfield: Photomonteur
Joli mai, Le
Joseph Cornell:
  Worlds in a Box
Journey to Beijing
Juvenile Court
Juvenile Liaison
Juvenile Liaison 2

Kamikaze Hearts
Kanehsatake (Oka) –
  270 Years of Resistance
Kashima Paradise
Kerouac
Kids Are Alright, The
Kids of Survival: The Art and
  Life of Tim Rollins & K.O.S.
Koyaanisqatsi
Krzysztof Kieslowski: I'm So So

Ladies and Gentlemen, The
  Rolling Stones
Land of Silence and Darkness
Last Date
Last Grave at Dimbaza
Last of the Blue Devils, The
Last Waltz, The
Law and Order
Lebanon...Why?
Lessons in Darkness
Let It Be
Let's Get Lost
Letter to Jane
Let the Good Times Roll
Life and Times of Allen
  Ginsberg, The
Life and Times of Rosie the
  Riveter, The
Listen Up: The Lives of
  Quincy Jones
Litany for Survival: The Life
  and Work of Audre Lord
Little People

Live a Life
Lodz Ghetto
London Rock and Roll
 Show, The
Looking for Richard
Lord of the Dance
Loving the Dead
Luck, Trust & Ketchup: Robert
 Altman in Carver Country

Mad Dogs and Englishmen
Mandela
Man of Africa
Man of Aran
Man of the Year
Manson
Manufacturing Consent: Noam
 Chomsky and the Media
Man With A Movie Camera
Martha & Ethel
Me & My Matchmaker
Mexico: The Frozen Revolution
Microcosmos
Milestones
Militia Battlefield
Millhouse, a White Comedy
Minamata
Miners' Film, The
Miniskirted Dynamo
Mirror Phase
Model
Monde du Silence, Le
Monster in a Box
Montand
Monterey Pop
Moon and the
 Sledgehammer, The
Moonwalker
More About the Language
 of Love
Motel
Motion and Emotion: the Films
 of Wim Wenders
Mueda – Memory and
 Massacre
Musicals Great Musicals: The
 Arthur Freed Unit at MGM
Music for the Movies:
 Bernard Herrmann
Music for the Movies:
 Toru Takemitsu
Mustang...The House that
 Joe Built
My Crasy Life
My New Friends
My Private War
Mystère Picasso, Le

Nela
Nicaragua – No Pasarán
Nico Icon
Nightcleaners
Night in Havana: Dizzy
 Gillespie in Cuba, A
Niños Abandonados, Los
No Maps on My Taps
No Nukes
Not a Love Story
Notebook on Cities and Clothes

O Amor Natural
Occupied Palestine
Occupy!
Of Great Events and
 Ordinary People
Olympische Spiele 1936
On Any Sunday
On Boys, Girls and the Veil
On Company Business
Ondeko-za on Sado, The
One by One
100 Years of Polish Cinema
One Man's War
One PM
One Way or Another
On Our Land
On the Bridge
On the Game
Ornette: Made in America
Osaka Story
Other One, The

Our Wall
Over Our Dead Bodies

Package Tour, The
Painted Boats
Painters Painting
Paolozzi Story, The
Paperback Vigilante
Paris Is Burning
Paris 1900
Paris Was a Woman
Passion of Remembrance, The
Pasternaks, The
Patriot Game, The
Patu!
Peasants of the Second
 Fortress, The
Pink Floyd Live at Pompeii
Platz, Der
Plutonium Circus, The
Point Is to Change it, The
Point of Order
Pop Gear
Portrait of a 60% 'Perfect' Man:
 Billy Wilder
Portrait of Jason
Portrait of Teresa
Poto and Cabengo
Powaqqatsi
Primate
Prince – Sign o' the Times
Promised Lands
Proud to be British
Public Enemy Number One
Pumping Iron
Pumping Iron II: the Women
Punk in London
Punk Rock Movie, The

Queen, The
Queens of the Big Time
Quince Tree Sun, The

Race, the Spirit of Franco
Raga
Rate It X
Refusal, The
Reggae
Reggae Sunsplash II
Reminiscences of a Journey
 to Lithuania
Repubblica Nostra
Requiem for Dominic
Return Engagement
Right Out of History: the
 Making of Judy Chicago's
 Dinner Party
Roar
Robert Altman's Jazz '34:
 Remembrances of Kansas
 City Swing
Rockshow
Roger & Me
Roger Corman: Hollywood's
 Wild Angel
Roots Rock Reggae
Rough Cut and Ready Dubbed
Route One/USA
Rush to Judgement
Rust Never Sleeps

St Ann's
São Paulo, SP
Savage Man...Savage Beast
Schiele in Prison
Seacoal
Sense of Loss, A
Será Posible el Sur
Sex Is...
Shark Callers of Kontu, The
Shattered Dreams: Picking Up
 the Pieces
She Lives to Ride
Shtetl
Shvitz, The
Sick: The Life & Death of Bob
 Flanagan, Supermasochist
Signed: Lino Brocka
Silent Witness, The
Slanted Vision
Small Wonder

Soft on the Inside
Soldier Girls
Sometimes I Look at My Life
Song for Tibet
Song of Ceylon
Sonic Outlaws
So That You Can Live
Soufrière, La
Soul to Soul
South Africa Belongs to Us
Spin
Split William to Chrysis:
 Portrait of a Drag Queen
Square, The
Stepping Razor – Red X
Stop Making Sense
Streetwise
Strip Jack Naked:
 Nighthawks II
Silent Witness, The
Summer in the City
Sunless Days
Superstar: the Karen
 Carpenter Story
Sword and the Flute, The

Tales from a Hard City
Talking History
Talmage Farlow
Tapdancin'
Tattooed Tears
T. Dan Smith
Theatre Girls
Thelonious Monk: Straight
 No Chaser
Thin Blue Line, The
'36 to '77
This is Elvis
Tibet: A Buddhist Trilogy
Tibetan New Year, A
Tickle in the Heart, A
Tidikawa and Friends
Tierische Liebe
Tigrero – A Film That Was
 Never Made
Time and Judgement
Times of Harvey Milk, The
Time Will Tell
Tokyo-Ga
Tokyo Olympiad 1964
To Live in Freedom
Tongues Untied
Tonite Let's All Make
 Love in London
To Speak the Unspeakable:
 The Message of Elie Wiesel
To the Heart
To the Last Drop
Totschweigen
Town Bloody Hall
Trances
Travelling Light: a Portrait of
 Lindsay Kemp
Trials of Alger Hiss, The
Tribulation 99: Alien
 Anomalies Under America
Triumph of the Will
True Glory, The
Truth or Dare
Tunisian Victory
Tupamaros
Twelve Views of Kensal House
25 Years
Twilight City
Typewriter, the Rifle & the

Movie Camera, The
Uncle Tom
Uncommon Senses
UndeRage
Underground
Union Maids
Unstable Elements –
 Atomic Stories
Unzipped
Urinal
U2 Rattle and Hum

Veillées d'Armes
Vernon, Florida
Vietnam Journey
Vincent: the Life and Death of
 Vincent Van Gogh
Visions of Eight
Visions of Light
Viva Portugal
Voice of Kurdistan, The
Voices from the Front
Volcano

Warren Oates: Across
 the Border
War Room, The
Warsaw Ghetto Uprising, The
Wattstax
Weavers, The: Wasn't
 That a Time?
Welcome to Britain
Welfare
We're Alive
Western Approaches
What About Me?
What Happened to Kerouac?
What Is Democracy?
When Mother Comes Home
 for Christmas
When the Mountains Tremble
When We Were Kings
White Rock
Whoever Says the Truth
 Will Die
Who Killed Vincent Chin?
Wild Bill:
 A Hollywood Maverick
Wild Man Blues
William Christie et Les Arts
 Florissants
Will My Mother Go Back
 to Berlin?
Witchcraft Through the Ages
With Babies and Banners
Without Memory
Without You I'm Nothing
Wittstock, Wittstock
Wizard of Waukesha, The
Wobblies, The
Woman to Woman
Woodstock
Word Is Out
Wot! No Art
Writing in the Sand, The

Yaacov Ben Dov: Father of the
 Hebrew Film
Year of the Beaver
Year of the Horse
Yessongs
You, Me, Jerusalem

Ziggy Stardust and the Spiders
 from Mars

Appendix 5

Epics

Al-Risalah
Alexander Nevsky
Alexander the Great
Andrei Rublev
Apollo 13

Barabbas
Ben-Hur (Niblo)
Ben-Hur (Wyler)
Bible...In the Beginning, The

Birth of a Nation, The

Cleopatra (DeMille)
Cleopatra (Mankiewicz)
Conqueror, The

Deluge, The
Demetrius and the Gladiators
Doctor Zhivago
Don Quichotte

El Cid
Emperor's Shadow
Ercole alla conquista
  di Atlantide

Fall of the Roman Empire, The
55 Days in Peking
Flametop

Gandhi
Goliath and the Barbarians
Gone With the Wind
Good Earth, The
Greatest Show on Earth, The
Greatest Story Ever Told, The

Hero (Platts-Mills)
Horsemen, The
Hwa-om-Kyong

Jason and the Argonauts

King David
King of Kings

Land of the Pharaohs
Last Days of Pompeii, The
Last Emperor, The
Lawrence of Arabia
Les Misérables (Boleslawski)
Les Miserables (Milestone)
Lion of the Desert
Little Buddha
Lord Jim

Misérables, Les (Le Chanois)
Misérables, Les (Lelouch)
Moses

Mountains of the Moon

Napoléon
Nicholas and Alexandra
Noah's Ark

Pathfinder
Pride and the Passion, The

Quo Vadis?

Regeneration
Robe, The
Romance of Book & Sword, The

Saladin
Samson and Delilah
Sign of the Cross, The
Sign of the Gladiator
Sign of the Pagan
Sodom and Gomorrah
Solomon and Sheba
Spartacus

Taebaek Mountains, The
Ten Commandments,The
Titanic (Cameron)
Touch of Zen, A

Ulysses' Gaze

Valiant Ones, The
Vikings, The

War and Peace (Vidor)
War and Peace (Bondarchuk)
Waterloo
Waterworld

Hawk the Slayer
Highlander
Highlander II –
  The Quickening
Highlander III –The Sorcerer
Hole, The
Hook
Hungarian Fairy Tale, A

Inhumaine, L'
Invincible Barbarian

Joe Versus the Volcano
Jumanji
Jurassic Park

Knightriders
Krull

Last Action Hero
Last Valley, The
Lord of Illusions
Lost World: Jurassic Park, The

Maciste Contro i Mostri
Mahabharata, Le
Man Who Could Work
  Meteor Man, The
Michael
Miracles, The
Moon Warriors
Mortal Kombat
Mortal Kombat 2: Annihilation

Navigator: A Medieval
  Odyssey, The
Nez au Vent, Le
Nibelungen, Die
No Escape
Nothing Lasts Forever
Nuit fantastique, La
Nutcracker –
  the Motion Picture

One Million Years B.C.
Orlando

Parking
Peau d'Ane
Phantom, The
Preacher's Wife, The
Prince Valiant

Rainbow
Raining in the Mountain
Red Sonja
Return to Oz
Rocketeer, The
Romantic Agony, The

Santa Sangre
Secret Life of Walter
  Mitty, The
Seventh Voyage of Sinbad, The
Shadow, The

Silent Flute, The
Sinbad and the Eye of the Tiger
Slipstream
Snow White: A Tale of Terror
Soultaker
Spawn
Spider-Man
Spider-Man Strikes Back
Spider-Man – the Dragon's
  Challenge
Super Mario Bros.
Swordsman
Swordsman II
Swordsman in Double-Flag
  Town, The

Teenage Caveman
Thief of Bagdad, The (Walsh)
Thief of Bagdad, The
  (Powell/Berger/
  Whelan/Korda)
Thief of Baghdad, The
  (Donner)
Three Worlds of Gulliver, The
Tiger of Eschnapur, The/The
  Indian Tomb
Time Bandits
Topo, El
Tromeo and Juliet
Troll
Truman Show, The
12 Monkeys
20,000 Leagues Under the Sea
Twilight of the Ice
  Nymphs, The
Twilight Zone – the Movie

Unidentified Flying
  Oddball, The
Uproar in Heaven
Unsuspected, The

Valley of Gwangi, The
Viking Women and Their
  Voyage to the Waters of the
  Great Sea Serpent
Visiteurs, Les
Visiteurs du Soir, Les

Warlords of Atlantis
War of the Colossal Beast
When Dinosaurs Ruled
  the Earth
Willow
Witches, The
Wizard of Oz, The
Wizards

Younger and Younger
Yumeji

Zardoz
Zoo in Budapest
Zu: Warriors from the
  Magic Mountain

Appendix 6

Fantasy

Adventures of Baron
  Munchausen, The (Gilliam)
Adventures of Baron
  Munchhausen, The
  (von Baky)
Adventures of Buckaroo Banzai
  Across the 8th
  Dimension, The
Adventures of Goopy and
  Bagha, The
Alice
Alice in Wonderland
  (McLeod)
Alice in Wonderland
  (Bower/Bunin)
Alice's Adventures in
  Wonderland
Angel Who Pawned Her
  Harp, The
Anger Magick Lantern
  Cycle, The
Animal Farm
Arabian Adventure
Arabian Nights
Ashik Kerib
Attack of the 50ft Woman
At the Earth's Core
Aurora Encounter, The

Barb Wire
Batman (Martinson)
Batman (Burton)
Batman Forever
Batman Returns
Batman & Robin
Bearskin
Being Human
Belles de nuit, Les
Blood Brothers, The
Blue Bird, The
Brazil
Butterfly Murders, The

Captain Kronos –
  Vampire Hunter
Captain Nemo and the
  Underwater City

Chinese Ghost Story, A
Chinese Ghost Story II, A
Cinderella – Italian-style
Cité des enfants perdus, La
City of Angels
City of Pirates
City Under the Sea
Clash of the Titans
Company of Wolves, The
Conan the Barbarian
Conan the Destroyer
Conquest
Conspirators of Pleasure
Craft, The
Creatures the World Forgot
Cremaster 5
Crow, The

Dark Crystal, The
Deaf and Mute Heroine, The
Delicatessen
Désert des Tartares, Le
Destiny
Dinosaurus!
DragonHeart
Dragonslayer
Dreamchild
Dybbuk, The

Edward Scissorhands
Eraserhead
Erik the Viking

Fantasia
Faust
Fire and Ice
Fisher King, The
5000 Fingers of Dr T, The
From Hell It Came

Game, The
Gnome Named Gnorm, A
Godzilla
Goto, l'île d'amour
Gremlins
Gremlins 2: the New Batch
Gunhed

Appendix 7

Film Noir

A Bout de Souffle
Across the Pacific
After Dark, My Sweet
American Friend, The
American Gigolo
Among the Living
Angel Dust
Asphalt Jungle, The
Au Nom de la Loi

Beyond Reasonable
  Doubt (Laing)
Big Clock, The
Big Sleep, The (Hawks)
Big Steal, The (Siegel)
Black Angel
Blood Simple
Body and Soul
Blue Dahlia, The
Body Heat

Border Incident
Born to Kill
Brasher Doubloon, The
Breathless
Brute Force

Call Northside 777
Captive City, The
Caught
Cause for Alarm!
Chinatown
Christmas Holiday
Clash by Night
Clay Pigeon, The
Conflict
Criss Cross (Siodmak)
Criss Cross
  (Soderbergh)
Cry Danger
Cutter's Way

Dangerous Mission
Dark City
Dark Corner, The
Dark Mirror, The
Dark Passage
Deadline at Dawn
Dead Reckoning
Dernier Tournant
Desperate
Desperate Hours, The
Detective Story
Detour
D.O.A (Maté)
Double Indemnity
Doulos, Le

Edge of Doom
Enforcer, The
Everybody Wins

Farewell, My Lovely (Dmytryk)
Farewell, My Lovely (Richards)
Fear in the Night
File on Thelma Jordon, The
Force of Evil

Garment Jungle, The
Gilda
Great Gatsby, The (Nugent)
Grifters, The
Gun Crazy

Hammett
Hangmen Also Die!
Hard Eight
He Died With His Eyes Open
He Walked By Night
High Sierra
His Kind of Woman
Hitch-hiker, The
Hot Spot, The
House of Strangers
Hustle

In a Lonely Place

Johnny O'Clock

Key Largo
Killers, The
Killing, The
Kiss Me Deadly
Kiss of Death

Lady from the Shanghai Cinema, The
Lawless, The
Light Sleeper

Maltese Falcon, The (Huston)
Man Hunt
Man I Love, The
Moonrise
Murder by Contract
Mystery Street

Naked City, The
Narrow Margin, The
Night and the City (Dassin)
Night and the City (Winkler)
Nightfall
Night Has a Thousand Eyes
Nightmare
Nightmare Alley
No Man of Her Own

On Dangerous Ground
Out of the Fog
Out of the Past

Panic in the Streets
Pitfall
Public Eye, The

Quai des Brumes, Le
Quai des Orfèvres

Raw Deal (Mann)
Reckless Moment, The
Reservoir Dogs
Road House
Ruthless

Samourai, Le
Scarlet Street
Shockproof
Singapore Sling
Slightly Scarlet
So Dark the Night
So Evil My Love
Somewhere in the Night
Sorry, Wrong Number
Strange Affair of Uncle Harry, The
Strange Love of Martha Ivers, The

They Live by Night
They Won't Believe Me
Thief, The
Thieves' Highway
This Gun For Hire
This World, Then the Fireworks
T-Men
Touch of Evil
Twin Peaks

Union Station
Unsuspected, The

Where Danger Lives
While the City Sleeps
Whirlpool
Window, The
Woman in the Window, The
Woman on the Beach, The
Woman's Secret, A
Wrong Man, The (Hitchcock)
Wrong Man, The (McBride)

You Only Live Once

Cat Girl
Cathy's Curse
Cat People (Tourneur)
Cat People (Schrader)
Cat's Eye
Cellar, The
Chamber of Horrors
Changeling, The
Chat, Le
Children of the Corn
Child's Play
Child's Play 2
Chi Sei?
Christine
Circus of Fear
Circus of Horrors
Colossus of New York, The
Come Back, The
Communion (Sole)
Corridors of Blood
Count Dracula
Countess Dracula
Count Yorga, Vampire
Craze
Crazies, The
Creature from the Black
    Lagoon
Creature Walks Among
    Us, The
Creepers
Creeping Flesh, The
Creepshow
Creepshow 2
Crimes of the Future
Critters
Critters 2: The Main Course
Cronos
Crucible of Terror
Cry of the Banshee
Cujo
Curse of Frankenstein, The
Curse of the Cat People, The
Curse of the Crimson Altar
Curse of the Mummy's
    Tomb, The
Curse of the Werewolf, The

Damien – Omen II
Dance of the Vampires
Dark Eyes of London
Dark Half, The
Darklands
Darkman
Daughters of Darkness
Daughters of Satan
Dawn of the Dead
Day of the Animals
Day of the Beast
Day of the Dead
Dead and Buried
Dead Can't Lie, The
Deadly Blessing
Deadly Friend
Dead Men Don't Die
Dead of Night
    (Hamer/Dearden/Crichton/
    Cavalcanti)
Dead of Night (Clark)
Dead Ringers
Dead Zone, The
Death Line
Death Trap
Death Valley
Death Weekend
DEF by Temptation
Dementia 13
Demons
Demons 2
Demons of the Mind
Deranged
Destroy All Monsters
Devil Commands, The
Devil-Doll, The
Devil Rides Out, The
Devil's Rain, The
Disciple of Death
Docteur Jekyll et les Femmes
Doctor Blood's Coffin
Doctor Death: Seeker of Souls
Dr Jekyll and Mr Hyde
    (Robertson)

Dr Jekyll and Mr Hyde
    (Fleming)
Doctor Jekyll and Sister Hyde
Dr Phibes Rises Again
Dr Terror's House of Horrors
Doctor X
Dogs
Dominique
Donovan's Brain
Don't Answer the Phone!
Doppelganger: The Evil Within
Dracula (Browning)
Dracula (Fisher)
Dracula (Curtis)
Dracula (Badham)
Dracula (Coppola)
Dracula A.D. 1972
Dracula Has Risen from
    the Grave
Dracula, Prince of Darkness
Dracula's Daughter
Driller Killer, The

Ebirah – Terror of the Deep
Edge of Sanity
Elvira, Mistress of the Dark
Empire of the Ants
Entity, The
Evictors, The
Evil Dead, The
Evil Dead II
Exorcist, The
Exorcist II: The Heretic
Exorcist III, The
Eye of the Cat

Face Behind the Mask
Face of Darkness, The
Feverhouse
Fiend Without a Face
Final Conflict, The
Final Terror, The
Flesh & Blood
Flesh and the Fiends, The
Flesh for Frankenstein
Fly, The (Cronenberg)
Fly, The (Neumann)
Fly II, The
Fog, The
Food of the Gods, The
Frankenhooker
Frankenstein
Frankenstein and the
    Monster from Hell
Frankenstein Created Woman
Frankenstein Meets the
    Wolf Man
Frankenstein Must Be
    Destroyed
Frankenstein: The True Story
Freaks
Freddy's Dead: The
    Final Nightmare
Friday the 13th
Friday the 13th Part Two
Friday the 13th Part VIII: Jason
    Takes Manhattan
Frightmare
Frighteners, The
Fright Night
Fright Night Part 2
Frisson des Vampires, Les
Frogs
From Beyond
From Beyond the Grave
Full Circle
Funhouse, The
Funny Games
Funny Man
Fury, The

Galaxy of Terror
Gate, The
Ghost of Frankenstein, The
Ghost Ship, The
Ghost Story
Ghoul, The (Hunter)
Ghoul, The (Francis)
Ghoulies
Giant Spider Invasion, The
Godsend, The

God Told Me To
Godzilla 1985
Godzilla vs the Smog Monster
Golem, The
Gorgo
Gorgon, The
Graveyard Shift
Grim Prairie Tales
Guardian, The

Halloween
Halloween II
Halloween III
Halloween 4: The Return of
    Michael Myers
Halloween: The Curse of
    Michael Myers
Hand, The
Hands of Orlac, The
Hands of the Ripper
Harlequin
Haunted Place
Haunting, The
Headhunter
Hellbound: Hellraiser II
Hell Night
Hellraiser
Hellraiser III: Hell on Earth
Hellstrom Chronicle, The
Hex
Hills Have Eyes, The
Histoires Extraordinaires
Hitcher, The
Holocaust 2000
Homicidal
Horror Express
Horror Hospital
Horrors of the Black Museum
House
House II
House by the Cemetery
House in Nightmare Park, The
House of Dracula
House of Exorcism, The
House of Fear, The
House of Frankenstein
House of Mortal Sin
House of the Long
    Shadows, The
House of Usher, The
House of Wax
House of Whipcord
House on Sorority Row, The
House that Dripped Blood, The
Howling, The
Hunter's Blood
Hush...Hush, Sweet Charlotte

I Bought a Vampire Motorcycle
I Don't Want to Be Born
I Know What You Did
    Last Summer
I, Monster
Impulse
Incense for the Damned
Incredible Melting Man
Incredibly Strange Creatures
    Who Stopped Living and
    Became Mixed-Up
    Zombies, The
Incubus
Inferno
Innocents, The
In the Mouth of Madness
Invisible Ray, The
Island of Dr Moreau, The
    (Taylor)
Island of Dr Moreau, The
    (Frankenheimer)
Island of Lost Souls
Island of Mutations
Isle of the Dead
It Lives Again
It's Alive
I Walked With a Zombie
I Was a Teenage Werewolf

Jacob's Ladder

Keep, The
Killer Nun

Killer Tongue
Kindred, The
Kingdom of the Spiders
King Kong (Cooper/
    Shoedsack)
King Kong (Guillermin)
Kiss, The
Kiss of the Vampire
Kitami
Konga
Kuroneko
Kwaidan

Ladies in Retirement
Lair of the White Worm, The
Last House on the Left, The
Leatherface: The Texas
    Chainsaw Massacre III
Legacy, The
Legend of Hell House, The
Legend of the Mountain
Legend of the Werewolf
Leopard Man, The
Leviathan
Lift, The
Link
Living Dead, The
Living Dead at the
    Manchester Morgue, The
Lost Boys, The
Lost Continent, The
Lovecraft

Macabre
Mad Doctor of Market
    Street, The
Mad Genius, The
Madhouse
Mad Love
Mad Magician, The
Mad Room, The
Magic
Magician, The
Mangler, The
Maniac Cop
Maniac Cop 2
Manitou, The
Man-Made Monster
Mansion of the Doomed
Man Who Changed His
    Mind, The
Mary Reilly
Maximum Overdrive
Mighty Joe Young
Mindwarp
Monkey Shines
Monolith Monsters, The
Monster and the Girl, The
Monster Club, The
Monster from Green Hell
Monster of Terror
Monster on the Campus
Monster Squad, The
Most Dangerous Game, The
Mummy, The (Freund)
Mummy, The (Fisher)
Mummy's Hand, The
Mummy's Shroud, The
Murders in the Rue Morgue,
    The (Florey)
Murders in the Rue Morgue,
    The (Hessler)
Murders in the Zoo
Mutant
Mutations, The
Mystery of the Wax Museum

Near Dark
Necronomicon
Nightbreed
Nightmare on Elm Street, A
Nightmare on Elm Street
    Part 2:
    Freddy's Revenge, A
Nightmare on Elm Street 3:
    Dream Warriors, A
Nightmare on Elm Street 4:
    The Dream Master, A
Nightmare on Elm Street 5:
    The Dream Child, A
Nightmares

Night of the Comet
Night of the Creeps
Night of the Demons
Night of the Eagle
Night of the Ghouls
Night of the Lepus
Night of the Living Dead (Romero)
Night of the Living Dead (Savini)
Nightwing
976-Evil
Nocturna
Nosferatu – eine Symphonie des Grauens
Nosferatu the Vampyre
Nothing But the Night

Oblong Box, The
Old Dark House, The
Omen, The
Omen IV: The Awakening
Organ
Out of the Dark

Pack, The
Paperhouse
Parasite Murders, The
Parts: The Clonus Horror
Patrick
Paura nella Città dei Morti Viventi
People Under the Stairs, The
Pet Sematary
Phantom of the Opera, The (Julian)
Phantom of the Opera (Lubin)
Phantom of the Opera, The (Fisher)
Phantom of the Opera (Little)
Piranha
Piranha II: Flying Killers
Pit and the Pendulum, The (Corman)
Pit and the Pendulum, The (Gordon)
Place of One's Own, A
Plague of the Zombies, The
Poltergeist
Poltergeist II: The Other Side
Poltergeist III
Possession
Possession of Joel Delaney, The
Premature Burial
Prince of Darkness
Prison
Prom Night
Prophecy
Prowler, The
Psychic Killer
Psycho
Psycho II
Psycho III
Pumpkinhead

¿Quién Puede Matar a un Niño?

Rabid
Rabid Grannies
Race with the Devil
Rats, The
Raven, The (Friedlander)
Razorback
Re-Animator
Re-Animator 2
Refrigerator, The
Relic, The
Reptile, The
Repulsion
Retribution
Return of Count Yorga, The
Return of Doctor X, The
Return of Dracula, The
Return of the Fly
Return of the Living Dead
Return of the Living Dead Part II
Return of the Living Dead III
Return of the Swamp Thing, The
Return of the Vampire, The

Revenge of Frankenstein, The
Revenge of the Creature
Revenge of the Dead
Roadgames
Rosemary's Baby
Ruby (Harrington)

Salem's Lot
Satanic Rites of Dracula, The
Satan's Skin
Satan's Slave
Savage Bees, The
Scarecrows
Scars of Dracula, The
Schizophrenia
Scream
Scream 2
Scream and Scream Again
Sect, The
Sender, The
Sentinel, The
Seven Women for Satan
Severed Arm, The
Shadow of the Hawk
Shanks
Shining, The
Shocker
Silver Bullet
Sisters
Skull, The
Sleepwalkers
Slumber Party Massacre, The
Society
Son of Dracula
Son of Frankenstein
Son of Godzilla
Sorcerers, The
Spiral Staircase, The (Siodmak)
Spiral Staircase, The (Collinson)
Squirm
Sssssss
Stepfather, The
Stepfather II, The
Stepfather III
Stephen King's Thinner
Strait-Jacket
Strange Door, The
Straw Dogs
Succubus
Sundown
Superstition
Swamp Thing

Tale of a Vampire
Tales from the Crypt Presents Demon Knight
Tales from the Darkside: The Movie
Tales of Terror
Tarantula
Taste the Blood of Dracula
Tenebrae
Tentacles
Terror (Warren)
Terror, The (Corman)
Terror in the Aisles
Texas Chain Saw Massacre, The
Texas Chainsaw Massacre 2, The
Theatre of Blood
Ticks
Thing with Two Heads, The
Tingler, The
Tomb of Ligeia, The
Torture Garden
To the Devil a Daughter
Tower of the Seven Hunchbacks, The
Toxic Avenger, The
Toxic Avenger Part II, The
Traitement de Choc
Trick or Treat
Twins of Evil
Two Faces of Dr Jekyll, The

Ugly, The
Uncanny, The
Undead, The
Undying Monster, The
Unholy, The

Unholy Three, The (Browning)
Unholy Three, The (Conway)
Uninvited, The
Unknown, The
Unseen, The

Vamp
Vampira
Vampire at Midnight
Vampire Bat, The
Vampire Circus, The
Vampire Lovers, The
Vampires in Venice
Vampire's Kiss
Vampyr
Vault of Horror
Velvet Vampire, The
Vendetta, The
Venom
Videodrome
Visiting Hours
Voice Over
Voodoo Man

Walking Dead, The
Wasp Woman, The
Watcher in the Woods, The
Waxwork
Waxworks
Werewolf of London
Wes Craven's New Nightmare
White Zombie
Wishmaster
Witchfinder General
Wizard of Darkness
Wolf
Wolfen
Wolf Man, The
Wraith, The

Xtro

Yeux sans visage, Les
You'll Like My Mother

Zombie Flesh Eaters

Musicals

Absolute Beginners
All This and World War 2
American in Paris, An
Anchors Aweigh
Annie
Annie Get Your Gun
Auntie Mame

Bal, Le
Balalaika
Babes in Arms
Babes on Broadway
Band Wagon, The
Barkleys of Broadway, The
Bawdy Adventures of Tom Jones, The
Beggar's Opera, The
Belle of New York, The
Bells are Ringing
Bert Rigby, You're a Fool
Best Foot Forward
Best Little Whorehouse in Texas, The
Best Things in Life Are Free, The
Billy Rose's Jumbo
Bloodhounds of Broadway
Blood Wedding
Blossom Time
Bluebeard's Castle
Blue Hawaii
Blue Skies
Blues Brothers, The
Blues Broithers 2000
Blues Under the Skin
Body Rock
Bohème, La
Bolero (Ruggles)
Born to Dance
Bowery to Broadway
Boy Friend, The
Breakin'
Breaking Glass
Brigadoon
Broadway Melody of 1936
Buddy Holly Story, The
Bundle of Joy
Butterfly Ball, The
Bye Bye Birdie
By the Light of the Silvery Moon

Can-Can
Can't Help Singing
Can't Stop the Music
Captain January
Carefree
Carmen (DeMille)
Carmen (Saura)
Carmen (Rosi)
Carmen Jones
Carousel

Catch My Soul
Centennial Summer
Chocolate Soldier, The
Chorus Line, A
Commitments, The
Congress Dances
Connecticut Yankee in King Arthur's Court, A
Cotton Club, The
Cover Girl
Crossover Dreams
Cry-Baby

Daddy Long Legs
Dames
Damn Yankees
Damsel in Distress, A
Dancers
Dangerous When Wet
Daughter of Rosie O'Grady, The
Days in London
Demoiselles de Rochefort, Les
Dick Deadeye, or Duty Done
Dirty Dancing
Dr Rhythm
Don't Knock the Rock
Double Trouble
Dreigroschenoper, Die
DuBarry Was a Lady

Earth Girls Are Easy
Easter Parade
Ek Baar Phir
Elstree Calling
Elvis
Emperor Waltz, The
Evergreen
Everyone Says I Love You
Expresso Bongo

Fame
Fast Forward
Ferry Cross the Mersey
Fiddler on the Roof
Finian's Rainbow
First a Girl
Five Heartbeats, The
Flame
Flashdance
Flying Down to Rio
Follow That Dream
Follow the Fleet
Footlight Parade
Footloose
Forget-Me-Not
For Me and My Gal
42nd Street
French Cancan
French Line, The
Funny Face
Funny Girl

Funny Lady
Funny Thing Happened on the
 Way to the Forum, A

Gang's All Here, The
Gay Divorcee, the
GI Blues
Gigi
Girl Can't Help It, The
Girl Most Likely, The
Girls! Girls! Girls!
Girls Just Want to Have Fun
Give My Regards to
 Broad Street
Glenn Miller Story, The
Go, Johnny, Go!
Gold Diggers of 1933
Gold Diggers of 1935
Gold Diggers of 1937
Golden Eighties
Good Companions, The
Goodnight Vienna
Grease
Grease 2
Great Waltz, The (Duvivier)
Great Waltz, The (Stone)
Green Pastures, The
Greenwich Village
Guys and Dolls
Gypsy (LeRoy)
Gypsy (Ardolino)

Hair
Half a Sixpence
Hans Christian Andersen
Happiest Millionaire, The
Harvey Girls, The
Heaven Tonight
Hello Dolly!
Hello, Frisco, Hello!
Here Come the Waves
High Society
Holiday Inn
Hound Dog Man
How to Succeed in Business
 Without Really Trying

I Love Melvin
Inside Daisy Clover
It Happened in Brooklyn
It's All Happening

Jailhouse Rock
Jesus Christ Superstar
Joy of Living
Jupiter's Darling

Kazablan
Kid from Spain, The
Kid Galahad
King and I, The
King Creole
King of Jazz, The
King Steps Out, The
Kismet
Kissin' Cousins
Kiss Me Kate

Lady in the Dark
Lambada
Les Girls
Let's Make Love
Li'l Abner
Lili
Little Nellie Kelly
Little Night Music, A
Little Prince, The
Little Shop of Horrors (Oz)
Lost in the Stars
Love Bewitched, A
Love Me or Leave Me
Love Me Tonight
Lullaby of Broadway

Madame Butterfly
Magic Flute, The
Mambo Kings, The
Mame
Meet Me at the Fair
Meet Me in St Louis

Meet the Feebles
Message of Love: The Isle of
 Wight Festival
Mikado, The
Mr Music
Mister Quilp
Mo' Better Blues
Mother Wore Tights
Music Machine, The
Music Man, The
My Fair Lady
My Sister Eileen

Nashville
Naughty but Nice
Naughty Marietta
Never Too Young to Rock
New Moon
Newsies
New York, New York
Night and Day
Nijinsky

Oh Rosalinda!
Oh! What a Lovely War
Oh, You Beautiful Doll
Oklahoma!
Oliver!
On a Clear Day You Can
 See Forever
One From the Heart
One Heavenly Night
One Hour With You
One Hundred Men
 and a Girl
One in a Million
One Touch of Venus
On Moonlight Bay
On the Town
Opera do Malandro
Opposite Sex, The
Orchestra Wives
Otello

Pagliacci
Paint Your Wagon
Pajama Game, The
Pakeezah
Pal Joey
Paradise – Hawaiian Style
Parapluies de Cherbourg, Les
Pin Up Girl
Pirate, The
Pirates of Penzance, The
Play It Cool
Popeye

Raise the Roof
Rappin'
Red Detachment of Women
Red Shoes, The
Rhapsody in Blue
Rigoletto
Roberta
Rock, Rock, Rock
Rocky Horror
 Picture Show, The
Romance on the High Seas
Roman Scandals
Rooftops
Rose, The
Rose of Washington Square
Royal Wedding

Sarafina!
Scrooge
Sgt Pepper's Lonely Hearts
 Club Band
Sevillanas
Seven Brides for
 Seven Brothers
1776
Shall We Dance?
Shock Treatment
Show Boat (Whale)
Show Boat (Sidney)
Silk Stockings
Sing
Singin' in the Rain
Sky's the Limit
Slipper and the Rose, The

Song Is Born, A
Song of Norway
Song of Scheherazade
Sound of Music, The
South Pacific
Stardust
Star Is Born, A (Cukor)
Star Is Born, A (Pierson)
Starstruck
State Fair
Staying Alive
Stepping Out
Stormy Weather
Strike Up the Band
Summer Stock

Take Me Out to the Ball Game
Tales of Beatrix Potter
Tales of Hoffman, The
Tap
Thank God It's Friday
That'll Be the Day
That's Dancing
That's Entertainment!
That's Entertainment! Part II
That's Entertainment! III
That Thing You Do
There's No Business Like
 Show Business
Thoroughly Modern Millie
Three For All
Times Square
Tommy

Tommy Steele Story, The
Top Hat
Torch Song
Traviata, La
Two of a Kind
Two Weeks With Love

Under the Cherry Moon
Unsinkable Molly Brown, The
Up in Arms
Up on the Roof

Vie est Belle, La
Viva Las Vegas

West Side Story
Wild in the Country
Wild Style
Wiz, The

Xanadu

Yankee Doodle Dandy
Yiddle with His Fiddle
You'll Never Get Rich
Young Man With a Horn
You Were Meant for Me
You Were Never Lovelier

Zaza
Ziegfeld Follies
Ziegfeld Girl
Zouzou

Appendix 11

Period/Swashbucklers

Adventures of Don Juan
Adventures of Michael
 Strogoff, The
Adventures of
 Robin Hood, The
Affaire du Courrier de Lyon, L'
Affairs of Cellini, The
Age of Innocence, The
Agony and the Ecstasy, The
Allonsanfan
All This and Heaven Too
Amistad
Anastasia
Anna Karenina (Brown)
Anna Karenina (Duvivier)
Anna Karenina (Rose)
Anne of the Indies
Anne of the Thousand Days
Anthony Adverse
Arena, The
Assassin of the Tsar

Bandit of Sherwood
 Forest, The
Barretts of Wimpole Street, The
Barry Lyndon
Baron Fantôme, Le
Beaumarchais
Becky Sharp
Billy Budd
Blackbeard the Pirate
Black Jack
Black Pirate, The
Black Swan, The
Blanche
Blanche Fury
Blood Brothers, The
Boogie Nights
Bostonians, The
Boule de Suif
Bounty, The
Bowery, The
Braveheart
Bride of Vengeance
Buccaneer, The

Camille Claudel
Canterbury Tales, The
Capitaine Fracassé, Le
Captain Blood
Captain Boycott
Carlota Joaquina, Princess

of Brazil
Catherine the Great
Charge of the Light Brigade,
 The (Curtiz)
Charge of the Light Brigade,
 The (Richardson)
Chartreuse de Parme, La
Charulata
Chess Players, The
Christopher Columbus
Christopher Columbus:
 The Discovery
Colonel Chabert, Le (Le Hénaff)
Colonel Chabert, Le (Angelo)
Colossus of Rhodes, The
Count of Monte-Cristo, The
Crimson Pirate, The
Cromwell
Crucible, The
Curse of the Wraydons, The
Cyrano de Bergerac

Dangerous Liaisons
Dark Avenger, The
Decameron, The
Deceivers, The
Destiny (Chahine)
Devils, The
Devil's Eye, The
Dialogue des Carmelites
Dog of Flanders, A
Doll, The
Don Quixote
Draughtman's Contract, The
Drum
Duellists, The

Ed Wood
Effi Briest
8-Diagram Pole Fighter, The
Eijanaika
El Dorado (Saura)
Elective Affinities
Elephant Man, The
Elusive Pimpernel, The
Emigrants, The
Emma
Empress Yang Kwei Fei, The
Enchanted April
Enfant Sauvage, L'
Enfants du Paradis, Les
English Patient, The

Ethan Frome
Evita
Excalibur
Executioners from Shaolin
Execution in Autumn
Exile, The

Fanny Hill
Far and Away
Farinelli Il Castrato
Feast of July
Femme Française, Une
Fencing Master, The
Fille de D'Artagnan, La
Fire Over England
First Knight
Five Women Around Utamaro
Fixer, The
Flame and the Arrow, The
Flowers of Shanghai
Forever Amber
Four Musketeers: The Revenge
   of Milady, The
1492: Conquest of Paradise
Francesco, giullare di Dio
French Lieutenant's
   Woman, The
Frenchman's Creek
Fury

Galileo (Cavani)
Galileo (Losey)
Gambler, The
Gawain and the Green Knight
Gentleman Jim
Ghost and the Darkness, The
Giant of Marathon, The
Goat Horn, The
Golden Swallow
Gonza the Spearman
Gorgeous Hussy, The
Great Expectations (Lean)
Great Expectations (Hardy)
Great Expectations (Cuarón)
Great Garrick, The
Great Sinner, The
Gypsy and the Gentleman, The

Hamlet (Plumb)
Hamlet (Olivier)
Hamlet (Kozintsev)
Hamlet (Richardson)
Hamlet (Coronado)
Hamlet (Zeffirelli)
Haunted Summer
Hellfire Club, The
Henry VIII and His Six Wives
Henry V (Olivier)
Henry V (Branagh)
Heritage, The
Hidden Fortress, The
HMS Defiant
House of Rothschild, The
Howards End
Hungry Hill
Hussard sur le toit, Le

Impromptu
Inheritance, The
In Love and War
Intolerance
I, the Worst of All
Ivanhoe
Ivan the Terrible

Jamaica Inn
Jane Eyre (Stevenson)
Jane Eyre (Mann)
Jane Eyre (Zeffirelli)
Jefferson in Paris
Journey to the Western Xia
Juarez
Jude
Julius Caesar
Justine

Kagemusha
Kama Sutra: A Tale of Love
Karakter
Keep the Aspidistra Flying

Kidnapped
King Lear (Brook)
King Lear (Kozintsev)
Kundun

Lady Caroline Lamb
Lady Jane
Lady L
Lancelot du Lac
Last Emperor, The
Last Supper, The
Les Miserables (Milestone)
Les Misérables (Boleslawski)
Liaisons Dangereuses 1960, Les
Life of Emile Zola, The
Life of Oharu, The
Light at the Edge of the
   World, The
Lion in Winter, The
Long Ships, The
Little Women (Cukor)
Little Women (Armstrong)
Lucie Aubrac
Ludwig

Macbeth (Welles)
Macbeth (Polanski)
Madame Curie
Madness of King George, The
Magnificent Doll
Mandingo
Man for All Seasons, A
Man in Grey, The
Man in the Iron Mask, The
   (Whale)
Man in the Iron Mask, The
   (Wallace)
Man Who Would Be King, The
Masada
Mask, The (Infascelli)
Mayerling
Michael Collins
Michael Kohlhaas
Middleton's Changeling
Misérables, Les (Le Chanois)
Misérables, Les (Lelouch)
Mission, The (Joffe)
Mrs Brown
Mrs Dalloway
Mistress Pamela
Moll Flanders
Month by the Lake, A
Moonfleet
Music Teacher, The
Mutiny on the Bounty (Lloyd)
Mutiny on the Bounty
   (Milestone)

Name of the Rose, The
Nana
Nell Gwyn
Nest of Gentlefolk, A
1900
Nicholas Nickleby
Night Sun
Noi Tre
Norseman, The
Northwest Passage
Nostradamus
November 1828
Nun and the Devil, The

Oblomov
Old Curiosity Shop, The
Oliver Twist (Lean)
Oliver Twist (Donner)
Once Upon a Time in China
Once Upon a Time in China II
Once Upon a Time…
   We Were Colored
Onibaba
Orphans of the Storm
Oscar and Lucinda

Passion de Jeanne d'Arc, La
Passione d'Amore
Peg of Old Drury
Peking Opera Blues
Père Goriot, Le
Photographing Fairies
Plaisir, Le

Pope Joan
Portrait of a Lady, The
Pride and Prejudice
Prince of Foxes
Prince of Homburg, The
Prince of Jutland
Princess Caraboo
Prise de Pouvoir par
   Lous XIV, La
Prisoner of Zenda, The
   (Cromwell)
Prisoner of Zenda, The
   (Thorpe)
Private Affairs of Bel Ami, The
Private Life of Henry VIII, The
Private Lives of Elizabeth
   and Essex, The
Procès de Jeanne d'Arc

Queen Christina
Queen Kelly
Queen of Spades. The
Que la Fête Commence
Quiz Show

Rachel's Man
Raintree County
Ran
Rashomon
Rasputin and the Empress
Rebecca's Daughters
Rebellion
Rebel Nun, The
Red Beard
Reign of Terror
Reine Margot, La
Rembrandt
Remains of the Day, The
Retour de Martin Guerre, Le
Return of the Three
   Musketeers, The
Revolution
Richard III (Olivier)
Richard III (Loncraine)
Ridicule
Road to Wellville, The
Robin and Marian
Robin Hood (Dwan)
Robin Hood (Irvin)
Robin Hood: Prince of Thieves
Rob Roy
Rollicking Adventures of
   Eliza Fraser, The
Ronde, La
Room With a View, A
Rosa Luxemburg
Royal Flash
Royal Hunt of the Sun, The
Royal Scandal, A

Sailor's Return, The
Saint-Ex
Sansho Dayu
Saraband for Dead Lovers
Saratoga Trunk
Savage Islands
Scaramouche
Scarlet Blade, The
Scarlet Empress, The
Scarlet Letter, The
Scarlet Pimpernel, The
Scarlet Tunic, The
Scent of Green Papaya, The

Sea Hawk, The
Secret Agent, The
Secret de Mayerling, Le
Serpent's Kiss, The
Seven Years in Tibet
Shadowlands
Shawshank Redemption, The
Shin Heike Monogatari
Shogun
Silas Marner
Sinful Davey
Slavers
Sommersby
Spanish Main, The
Sparrow
Surviving Picasso
Surrogate Mother

Tartuffe
Taste of the Black Earth
Tess
That Hamilton Woman
That Lady
That Night In Varennes
36th Chamber of Shaolin, The
Three Musketeers: The Queen's
   Diamonds, The (Lester)
Three Musketeers, The (Herek)
Three Sisters
Throne of Blood
'Tis Pity She's a Whore
Tom Jones
Torrents of Spring
Total Eclipse
Tournoi, Le
Tous les matins du monde
Treasure Island
Twefth Night

Under Capricorn
Under the Red Robe
Unfinished Piece for
   Mechanical Piano
Utu

Valmont
Vikings, The
Virgin Spring, The

Walk with Love and Death, A
War Lord, The
Washington Square
We Live Again
Where Angels Fear to Tread
Where's Jack?
Wicked Lady, The (Arliss)
Wicked Lady, The (Winner)
Wifemistress
Wilde
William Shakespeare's Romeo
   & Juliet
Wings of the Dove, The
Woodlanders, The
Wolfshead: The Legend of
   Robin Hood
Wuthering Heights (Wyler)
Wuthering Heights
   (Kosminsky)

Young Bess
Young Mr Lincoln
Young Mr Pitt, The
Young Winston

Science Fiction

Abyss, The
Abyss: Special Edition,The
Acción Mutante
Accumulator 1
Akira
Alien
Alien Nation
Alien Resurrection
Aliens
Alien[3]
Alphaville
Amazing Colossal Man, The

Android
Andromeda Strain, The
Arrival, The
August in the Water

Barbarella
Batteries Not Included
Battle Beyond the Stars
Battle for the Planet
   of the Apes
Battlestar Galactica
Beneath the Planet of the Apes

Bermuda Triangle, The
Beware! the Blob
Black Hole, The
Blade Runner
Blade Runner –
  The Director's Cut
Blob, The
Body Snatchers
Body Stealers, The
Born in Flames
Borrower, The
Boy and His Dog, A
Brainstorm
Buck Rogers in the 25th
  Century
Capricorn One
Children of the Damned
Choke Canyon
Close Encounters of the
  Third Kind
Close Encounters of the Third
  Kind (Special Edition)
Communion (Mora)
Conquest of Space
Conquest of the Earth
Conquest of the Planet
  of the Apes
Contact
Crack in the World

Daleks – Invasion Earth
  2150 AD
Damnation Alley
Damned, The (Losey)
Dark Angel
Dark City
Dark Star
D.A.R.Y.L.
Day of the Triffids, The
Day the Earth
  Caught Fire, The
Day the Earth Stood Still, The
Day the World Ended, The
Day Time Ended, The
Deathsport
DeepStar Six
Demon Seed
Destination Moon
Doc Savage –
  the Man of Bronze
Dr Cyclops
Dr Who and the Daleks
Dune

Earth vs the Flying Saucers
Earth vs the Spider
Empire Strikes Back, The
Empire Strikes Back:
  Special Edition, The
Enemy Mine
Escape from the Planet
  of the Apes
ET The Extra-Terrestrial
Event Horizon
Eve of Destruction
Explorers

Fahrenheit 451
Fantastic Planet
Fantastic Voyage
Fifth Element, The
Final Countdown, The
Final Programme, The
Fire in the Sky
Flaming Ears
Flash Gordon
Flesh Gordon
Flight of the Navigator
Forbidden Planet
Forbidden World
Forbin Project, The
Fortress
Freejack
Friendship's Death
Futureworld

Gawin
Ghost in the Shell

Halbe Welt

Hardware
Health Warning
Heavy Metal
Hidden, The
Humanoid, The

Illustrated Man, The
I Married a Monster
  from Outer Space
Incredible Hulk, The
Incredible Shrinking Man, The
Independence Day
Innerspace
In the Belly of the Dragon
Invaders from Mars (Menzies)
Invaders from Mars (Hooper)
Invasion
Invasion of the Body Snatchers
  (Siegel)
Invasion of the Body Snatchers
  (Kaufman)
Invasion of the Saucermen
Invisible Man, The
Invisible Man Returns, The
It Came from Beneath the Sea
It Came from Outer Space
It Conquered the World

Johnny Mnemonic
Journey to the Centre o
  f the Earth
Judge Dredd
Jules Verne's Rocket
  to the Moon

Kamikaze

Laserblast
Last Starfighter, The
Lawnmower Man, The
Lifeforce
Liquid Dreams
Liquid Sky
Logan's Run
Looker

Mac and Me
Mad Max
Mad Max 2
Mad Max
  Beyond Thunderdome
Magnetic Monster, The
Malevil
Man Who Fell to Earth, The
Memories
Metalstorm: the Destruction
  of Jared-Syn
Meteor
Metropolis (Lang)
Metropolis (Lang/Moroder)
Millennium
Mimic
Monolith
Moon 44
Most Dangerous Man Alive

New Barbarians, The
Night Caller
Night of the Big Heat
Nineteen Eighty-Four
No Answer from F.P.1
Not of This Earth

Omega Man, The
Outland

Parasite
Phantasm
Phantasm II
Phase IV
Phenomenon
Philadelphia Experiment, The
Planet of the Apes
Plan 9 from Outer Space
Prayer of the Rollerboys
Projected Man, The
Proteus
Power, The

Quatermass and the Pit
Quatermass Experiment, The

Quatermass II
Queen of Outer Space
Quest for Love
Quiet Earth, The
Quintet

Red Planet Mars
Return of the Jedi
Return of the Jedi:
  Special Edition
Rift, The
Robinson Crusoe on Mars
RoboCop
RoboCop 2
RoboCop 3
Robot
Runaway

Salute of the Jugger, The
Santa Claus Conquers
  the Martians
Saturn 3
Scanners
Scanners II: The New Order
Screamers
Shape of Things to Come, The
Silent Running
Slaughterhouse Five
Solaris
Soylent Green
Spaced Invaders
Spacehunter: Adventures in
  the Forbidden Zone
Space Truckers
Species
Species II
Sphere
Split Second
Starcrash
Stargate
Starman
Starship Troopers
Star Trek – The Motion Picture
Star Trek II: The Wrath of Khan
Star Trek III: The Search for
  Spock
Star Trek V: The Final Frontier
Star Trek VI: The
  Undiscovered Country
Star Trek: Generations
Star Trek: First Contact
Star Wars
Star Wars, Episode IV,
  A New Hope
Strange Invaders
Superman

Superman II
Superman III
Superman IV: The Quest
  for Peace

Teenagers from
  Outer Space
Terminal Man, The
Terminator, The
Terminator 2: Judgment Day
Terminus
TerrorVision
Tetsuo
Tetsuo II: Bodyhammer
Them!
They Live
Thing, The
Thing from Another
  World, The
Things to Come
This Island Earth
THX 1138
Timecop
Time Machine, The
Timescape
Timeslip
Time Travellers, The
Titan Find, The
Total Recall
Trancers
Tremors
Tron
2001: A Space Odyssey
2010
20 Million Miles to Earth

Village of the Damned
Viva la Vie
Voyage Home:
  Star Trek IV, The

War of the Monsters
War of the Satellites
War of the Worlds
Watchers
Weird Science
Welcome to Blood City
Westworld
When Worlds Collide
Who?
Woman in the Moon

X – the Man with X-Ray Eyes
X the Unknown

Zone Troopers

Babysitter, The
Backfire
Background to Danger
Backlash
Bad Blood
Bad Day at Black Rock
Bad Influence
Bad Seed, The
Balance, La
Bande à Part
Basic Instinct
Bayan Ko: My Own Country
Beat the Devil
Beck
Bedlam
Bedroom Window, The
Before and After
Believers, The
Bellman and True
Benefit of the Doubt
Best Revenge
Best Seller
Betrayed
Beverly Hills Cop
Beverly Hills Cop II
Beverly Hills Cop III
Beware, My Lovely
Beyond a Reasonable Doubt
Big Bang Theory
Big Easy, The
Big Fix, The
Big Heat, The
Big Hit, The
Big Man, The
Big Sleep, The (Winner)
Big Trouble
Billion Dollar Brain
Black Christmas
Black Eye
Black Gunn
Blackmail (Hitchcock)
Blackmail (Potter)
Black Marble, The
Black Moon Rising
Blackout (Adams)
Blackout (Ferrara)
Black Rain (Scott)
Black Rainbow
Black Sunday
Black Widow (Johnson)
Black Widow (Rafelson)
Black Windmill, The
Blind Alley
Blind Corner
Blind Date (Losey)
Blind Date (Mastorakis)
Blindfold
Blink
Blood and Wine
Blood Relatives
Blood Ties
Blown Away
Blow Out
Blue Collar
Blue Ice
Blue Knight
Blue Lamp, The
Blue Steel
Blue Sunshine
Blue Thunder
Blue Tiger
B. Must Die
Bob le Flambeur
Body Control
Body Double
Bodyguard, The
Body in the Forest, A
Boiling Point (Harris)
Boomerang (Kazan)
Border, The
Borderline
Boucher, Le
Bound
Boys from Brazil, The
Brainwaves
Brannigan
Brass Target
Breakdown
Breaking Point (Clark)
Breaking Point, The (Curtiz)
Breaking Point, The (Comfort)

Bribe, The
Brides of Fu Manchu
Bride Wore Black, The
Brighton Strangler, The
Bring Me the Head of
    Alfredo Garcia
Brink's Job, The
Broken Mirrors
Brotherhood, The
Brothers and Sisters
Buffet Froid
Bulldog Drummond
Bulldog Drummond
    Comes Back
Bulldog Drummond Escapes
Bullet Train, The
Bullitt
Bunny Lake is Missing
Bureau of Missing Persons
Burglars, The
Burke and Hare
Busting

Cairo Road
Caged
Call Me
Cape Fear (Thompson)
Cape Fear (Scorsese)
Captive
Careful, Soft Shoulder
Carey Treatment, The
Cash on Demand
Cassandra Crossing, The
Cast a Dark Shadow
Castle on the Hudson
Cat Chaser
Chain Reaction, The
Chamber, The
Champagne Murders, The
Charade
Charley Varrick
Charlie Chan and the Curse of
    the Dragon Queen (Donner)
Charlie Chan at the Opera
Chase a Crooked Shadow
Cheap Shots
Chiens, Les
China Moon
China Syndrome, The
Choirboys, The
Circle of Danger
Cisco Pike
City Heat
City of Fear
City of Industry
City on Fire
Clairvoyant, The
Clean, Shaven
Clean Slate
Clear and Present Danger
Client, The
Cloak and Dagger
Closed Circuit
Clouded Yellow, The
Club, The (Wong)
Clue
Cobra (Boisset)
Cohen and Tate
Cold Heaven
Cold Sweat
Colors
Coma
Come Back Charleston Blue
Company Business
Compromising Positions
Compulsion
Confessions of a Nazi Spy
Confidential Agent
Consenting Adults
Conspiracy Theory
Conspirators, The
Contraband
Conversation, The
Coogan's Bluff
Cool Breeze
Cop
Cop au Vin
CopLand
Cops and Robbers
Cop's Honour
Copycat

Cornered
Counsellor, The
Counterfeiters
Courier, The
Crackers
Crack in the Mirror
Crack-Up (St Clair)
Crack-Up (Reis)
Crazy Joe
Crescendo
Crime and Punishment
    (von Sternberg)
Crime and Punishment
    (Kaurismäki)
Crime in the Streets
Crime Story
Crimetime
Crimewave
Criminal. The
Criminal Code, The
Criminal Law
Crimson Kimono, The
Crossfire
Crossroads (Conway)
Cruising
Crying Freeman
Crying Game, The
Cry of the Hunted
Cry Wolf
Custodian, The

Dancing With Crime
Dandy in Aspic, A
Danger by My Side
Dangerously They Live
Dangerous Summer, A
Danger Route
Darker Than Amber
Dark Waters
Dark Wind, The
Day of the Dolphin, The
Day of the Jackal, The
Dead Again
Dead Bang
Deadfall
Dead Heat
Deadly
Deadly Affair, The
Deadly Females, The
Deadly Run
Deadly Strangers
Deadly Trap, The
Dead Calm
Dead of Winter
Dead Pigeon on
    Beethoven Street
Dead Pool, The
Death at Broadcasting House
Death Collector
Death on the Nile
Death Sentence
Death Ship
Deaths in Tokimeki
Deathtrap
Deceived
Deep Cover
Deep Crimson
Defence of the Realm
Delinquent Schoolgirls
Dementia
Desperate Hours
Desperate Measures
Desvio al Paraiso
Detective
Detective, The
Deux Hommes dans Manhattan
Deuxième Souffle, Le
Devil's Advocate, The
Devil's Own, The
Diaboliques, Les
Diabolique
Diagnosis: Murder
Dial M for Murder
Dias Contados
Die Hard
Die Hard 2
Die Hard with a Vengeance
Diggstown
Diplomatic Courier
Dirty Harry
Dirty Weekend

Disappearance, The
Dishonoured
Disparen a Matar
Disparus de Saint-Agil, Les
Diva
Dr M
Dr Mabuse, the Gambler
D.O.A. (Morton/Jankel)
Dog Day Afternoon
$
Domino Principle. The
Donato and Daughter
Don is Dead, The
Don't Look Now
Don't Play With Fire
Doomwatch
Dossier 51, Le
Double Headed Eagle, The
Double Man, The
Double X
Down Three Dark Streets
Dream Demon
Dreamscape
Dressed to Kill
Drive, The
Driver, The
Drôle de Drame
Drowning Pool, The
Duel
Due to an Act of God
Duffy
Dumb Die Fast, the Smart Die
    Slow, The
Du Rififi à Paname
Du Rififi Chez les Hommes

Ecoute Voir...
Eel, The
Eight O'Clock Walk
Electra Glide in Blue
Element of Crime, The
11 Harrowhouse
Emergency
Emergency Call
Empire State
Enchantment, The
Encounter at Raven's Gate
Endangered Species
Endless Night
End of Violence, The
Enfer, L'
Enforcer, The (Windust/Walsh)
Enforcer, The (Fargo)
Enigma
Eraser
Escape (Dean)
Escape from Alcatraz
Espion Lève-toi
Etoile du Nord, L'
Etrange Monsieur Victor, L'
Evil Under the Sun
Executive Action
Executive Decision
Experiment in Terror
Exposé
Exposed
Exquisite Tenderness
Extreme Measures
Extremities
Eye for an Eye
Eyes of a Stranger
Eyes of Laura Mars
Eyewitness (Hough)
Eyewitness (Yates)

Face
Face at the Window, The
Face of Fu Manchu, The
Fade to Black
Fail Safe
Fair Game (Sipes)
Falcon and the Co-eds, The
Falcon and the Snowman, The
Fallen
Fallen Angels
Falling Down
Family Plot
Fan, The (Bianchi)
Fan, The (Scott)
Fanatic
Fantasist, The

Fargo
Fatal Attraction
Fatal Bond
Fear (O'Bannon)
Fear (Foley)
Fear in the Night
Fear is the Key
Fellow Traveller
Femme Infidèle, La
52 Pick-Up
Fille de l'Air, La
Final Analysis
Final Combination
Fingers
Firepower
Firestarter
Firm, The
First Deadly Sin
First Power, The
Five Corners
5 Fingers
Flatliners
Flesh and Fantasy
Flight of the Innocent
Florentine Dagger, The
Flowers in the Attic
Flying Fool, The
Fog Over Frisco
Folle à Tuer
Following
Footsteps in the Fog
Foreign Correspondent
Formula, The
For Them That Trespass
48 HRS
Four Flies on Grey Velvet
Four Just Men, The
Fourteen Hours
Fourth Man, The
Foxy Brown
Framed
Franchise Affair, The
Frantic
Freelance
French Connection, The
French Connection II
Frenzy
Frieda
Friends of Eddie Coyle, The
Frisk
From Dusk Till Dawn
Fruit Machine, The
Fugitive, The (Ford)
Fugitive, The (Davis)
Full Confession
Funeral in Berlin
Funny Money
Further Gesture
Fury
F/X
F/X2

Gambit
Garde a Vue
'Gator Bait
Gauntlet, The
Gaunt Stranger, The
Gentle Gunman, The
Getaway, The (Peckinpah)
Getaway, The (Donaldson)
Get Carter
Get Shorty
Ghosts of the Mississippi
Giro City
Give Us Tomorrow
Gleaming the Cube
Glissements Progressifs du
  Plaisir
Glitter Dome, The
Gloria
God's Army
Gold Coast
Golden Salamander
Gonin
Gonin 2
Gorky Park
Grand Central Murder
Green for Danger
Gridlock'd
Grievous Bodily Harm
Grip of the Strangler

Groundstar Conspiracy, The
Guilty as Sin
Guncrazy

Haine, La
Hana-Bi
Handgun (Garnett)
Handgun (Ransick)
Hand That Rocks
  the Cradle, The
Hanged Man, The
Hard-Boiled
Hard Contract
Hard Men
Hard Rain
Hard to Kill
Harper
Harvest, The
Head Above Water
Hear No Evil
Heart of Midnight
Heat (Mann)
Heatwave
Heaven's Burning
Heaven's Prisoners
He Knows You're Alone
Hell Drivers
Hell Is a City
Hets
Hider in the House
High and Low
Highly Dangerous
Highways by Night
History is Made at Night
Hit List
Holcroft Covenant, The
Hollow Triumph
Home at Seven
Homicide
Homme de Désir, L'
Honeymoon Killers, The
Honorary Consul, The
Hound of the Baskervilles, The
  (Lanfield)
Hound of the Baskervilles, The
  (Fisher)
House of Bamboo
House on Carroll Street, The
Human Factor, The (Dmytryk)
Human Factor, The
  (Preminger)
Hunt for Red October, The

Illustrious Corpses
Impulse (Locke)
In Cold Blood
Innocent Man, An
Innocents With Dirty Hands
Inspecteur Lavardin
Internal Affairs
Internecine Project, The
In the Heat of the Night
In the Line of Fire
Intimate Stranger, The
Intruder, The
Ipcress File, The
I Saw What You Did
I Start Counting
Italian Job, The
I, the Jury
Ivy
I Wake Up Screaming
I Went Down

Jackie Brown
Jack's Wife
Jade
Jaguar
January Man, The
Jennifer 8
Jeopardy
Jerusalem File, The
Jinxed!
Jo
Johnny Allegro
Johnny Angel
Johnny Handsome
Journey Into Fear
Judex
Judgement in Stone, A
Juggernaut

Juice
Jump into the Void
Juror
Just Before Nightfall
Just Cause

Kaleidoscope
Kalifornia
Kansas
Kansas City
Kennel Murder Case, The
Keys to Tulsa
Kid
Kid Glove Killer
Kidnapping of the
  President, The
Killer, The (Woo)
Killer: A Journal of Murder
Killer Inside Me, The
Killer Is on the Phone, The
Killers, The (Siodmak)
Killers, The (Siegel)
Killer's Kiss
Killing of Angel Street, The
Killing Zoe
Kill Me Again
Kill-Off, The
King of Alcatraz
Kings and Desperate Men
Kiss Before Dying, A (Oswald)
Kiss Before Dying, A (Dearden)
Kiss of Death (Schroeder)
Kiss the Girls
Klute
Knife in the Head
Knight Moves
Kremlin Letter, The

Labyrinth of Dreams
LA Confidential
Ladder of Swords
Lady from Shanghai, The
Lady Ice
Lady in Cement
Lady in the Car with Glasses
  and a Gun, The
Lady in the Lake
Lady in White
Lady of Burlesque
Lady on a Train
Lady Vanishes, The
  (Hitchcock)
Lady Vanishes, The (Page)
Lancer Spy
Last Embrace
Last Man Standing
Last of Sheila, The
Last of the Finest, The
Last Rites
Last Seduction, The
Laughing Policeman, The
Lethal Weapon
Lethal Weapon 2
Lethal Weapon 3
Letters to an Unknown Lover
Liar
Liebestraum
Lies
Lifespan
Like a Rolling Stone
Lineup, The
Lipstick
List of Adrian Messenger, The
Little Drummer Girl, The
Little Nikita
Little Odessa
Live Flesh
Lodger, The (Hitchcock)
Lodger, The (Brahm)
Lolly-Madonna XXX
London Belongs to Me
Lone Star
Long Arm, The
Long Goodbye, The
Looking Glass War, The
Loophole
Lost Highway
Lost Moment, The
Love at Large
Love, Cheat & Steal
Lovely Way to Die, A

L.627
Lumière Noire
Lured

M (Lang)
M (Losey)
Madame Claude
Mädchen Rosemarie, Das
Mad Dog Time
Madigan
Mad Monkey, The
Madre Muerta, La
Malice
Malicious
Man Between, The
Manchurian Candidate, The
Man from Majorca, The
Manhunter
Manhunt in Milan
Man in the Road, The
Mani Sulla Città
Manny & lo
Man on Fire
Man on the Roof, The
Man to Respect, A
Man Upstairs, The
Man Who Had His Hair
  Cut Short, The
Man Who Knew
  Too Little, The
Man Who Knew Too Much,
  The (Hitchcock, 1934)
Man Who Knew Too Much,
  The (Hitchcock, 1956)
Man Who Watched Trains
  Go By, The
Man With a Cloak, The
Melancholia
Mercury Rising
Metro
Miami Blues
Midas Run
Midnight Express
Midnight Man, The
Midnight Run
Mighty Quinn, The
Mike's Murder
Ministry of Fear
Miracle Mile
Mirage
Mirror Crack'd, The
Misery
Mission, The (Sayyad)
Mississippi Burning
Miss Pinkerton
Mr Moto's Gamble
Mitchell
Moments
Mona Lisa
Money Movers
Moon in the Gutter, The
Morning After, The
Mortal Thoughts
Moss Rose
Most Wanted
Mother's Boys
Ms .45
Mulholland Falls
Murder
Murder at 1600
Murder by Decree
Murder Is a Murder...
  Is a Murder, A
Murder on the Orient Express
Murphy's Law
Mute Witness
My Name is Julia Ross
Mystery in Mexico

Nada
Naked City, The
Naked Are the Cheaters
Naked Runner, The
Nanny, The
Narrow Margin
Near Room, The
Net, The
Never Talk to Strangers
New Centurions, The
New Jack City
Newman's Law

Next of Kin
Next of Kin, The
Nick Carter – Master Detective
Nick of Time
Night Caller
Nightcomers, The
Night Falls on Manhattan
Night Has Eyes
Nighthawks (Malmuth)
Night Holds Terror, The
Nightmare (Whelan)
Nightmare (Shane)
Nightmare (Francis)
Night Moves
Night Must Fall (Thorpe)
Night Must Fall (Reisz)
Night Nurse
Night of the Demon
Night of the Following
   Day, The
Night of the Hunter, The
Night of the Party, The
Night Train to Munich
Night Watch (Hutton)
Nightwatch (Bornedal)
Night Zoo
Nikita
99 to 44/100% Dead
92 in the Shade
Ninth Configuration, The
Nobody Runs Forever
Nobody Will Speak of Us
   When We're Dead
Noces Rouges, Les
Nocturne
No Man's Land (Werner)
No Mercy
No Orchids for Miss Blandish
Normal Life
North by Northwest
North Dallas Forty
Notorious
November Plan, The
No Way Home
No Way Out (Donaldson)
Nowhere to Run
Nuit de Carrefour, La
Nuits Rouges
Number One (Blair)
Number Seventeen

Obsession (Dmytryk)
Obsession (De Palma)
Obsession, An
October Man, The
Odd Man Out
Odds Against Tomorrow
Offence, The
Off Limits
O.H.M.S.
Once a Thief
Once Upon a Time in America
Once Upon a Time…
   This Morning
On Deadly Ground
One Deadly Summer
One False Move
One Good Cop
One of Those Things
Onion Field, The
Opera
Ordeal by Innocence
Order of Death
Order to Kill
Organization, The
Organized Crime and
   Triad Bureau
Orion's Belt
Outfit, The
Out of Order (Schenkel)
Outside Man, The
Outsider, The
Other, The

Pacific Heights
Package, The
Painted Heart
Paper Mask
Paradine Case, The
Parallax View, The
Paris by Night

Partners
Pasolini, un Delitto Italiano
Patriot Games
Payroll
Pearl of Death, The
Peeping Tom
Pelican Brief, The
Penny Gold
Perfect Friday
Perfect World, A
Permission to Kill
Persecution
Persons Unknown
Petrified Forest, The
Phantom Lady
Phantom Light, The
Phenix City Story, The
Physical Evidence
Pickup on South Street
Pièges
PJ
Playbirds, The
Playmaker, The
Play Misty for Me
Plein Soleil
Point Blank
Point Break
Poison Ivy
Police Story (Graham)
Police Story (Chan)
Power Play
Prayer for the Dying, A
Presumed Innocent
Pretty Maids All in a Row
Prey of the Chameleon
Private Hell 36
Prize of Arms, A
Prize of Peril. The
Prizzi's Honor
Prowler, The (Losey)
Pulp Fiction
Pulse
Puppet on a Chain
Pursuit to Algiers
Pusher

Q & A
Que la Bête Meure
Quiller Memorandum, The

Rage in Harlem, A
Rainmaker, The
Raising Cain
Ransom (Wrede)
Ransom (Howard)
Rape, The
Rear Window
Rebecca
Red Circle, The
Redheads
Red Heat
Red Nightmare
Red Rings of Fear
Red Rock West
Reefer and the Model
Regarde les hommes tomber
Reincarnation of
   Peter Proud, The
Remember My Name
Renegades
Replacement Killers, The
Report to the Commissioner
Resurrection Man
Resurrection of Zachary
   Wheeler, The
Retroactive
Revenge (Scott)
Reward, The
Ricco
Ricochet
Rider on the Rain
Riot in Cell Block 11
Rising Sun
River's Edge
River Wild, The
Road Flower
Robbery
Rock n'Roll Cop
Rogue Cop
Rollercoaster
Rope

Rosary Murders, The
Rough Cut
Rough Shoot
Route de Corinthe, La
Running Hot
Running Man, The (Reed)
Running Scared
Rupture, La
Russia House, The
Russian Roulette
Russicum

Sabotage
Saboteur
Saint in New York, The
St Ives
Sandman, The
Sapphire
Satan Met a Lady
Scarlet Claw, The
Schizo
Scissors
Scorpio
Scorpion, The
Scorta, La
Scoumoune, La
Scream for Help
Seance on a Wet Afternoon
Sea of Love
Second Awakening of Christa
   Klages, The
Second Chance (Maté)
Secret, The (Enrico)
Secret, The (Hui)
Secret Agent, The
Secret Beyond the Door
Secret People
Seins de glace, Les
Sellout, The
Serpent, The
Serpent and the Rainbow, The
Serpico
Set It Off
Seven (Sidaris)
Seven (Fincher)
Seven Days in May
Seven Days to Noon
Seven Sinners (de Courville)
Seventh Sign, The
Shadow of a Doubt
Shadows in the Night
Shakedown
Shallow Grave
Shamus
Shark
Sharky's Machine
Shattered (Leroy)
Shattered (Petersen)
Sheba Baby
Sheriff, Le
Sherlock Holmes and the
   Spider Woman
Shinjuku Triad Society
Ship That Died of Shame, The
Shock to the System, A
Shooting Stars
Shoot to Kill
Show of Force, A
Silence of the Lambs, The
Silencieux, Le
Silent Partner, The
Single White Female
Sirène du Mississipi, La
Sister My Sister
Skin & Bone
Skip Tracer
Skyjacked
Slam Dance
Slaughter
Slaughter's Big Rip-Off
Slayground
Sleepers
Sleeping Car Murder, The
Sleeping Dogs
Sleeping Tiger, The
Sleeping with the Enemy
Sleep, My Love
Sleuth
Slither
Sliver
Slow Attack

Smilla's Feeling for Snow
Sneakers
Sniper, The
Someone to Watch Over Me
Sonatine
Sound of Fury, The
Special Effects
Specialist, The
Specter of the Rose
Speed
Speed 2: Cruise Control
Spellbound
Spider and the Fly, The
Spinnen, Die
Spione
Spy in Black, The
Spy Story
Spy Who Came In From
   the Cold, The
Spy Who Loved Me, The
Squeaker, The
Squeeze, The (Apted)
Stacy's Knights
Star Chamber, The
State of Siege
State Secret
Stepford Wives, The
Stick
Still of the Night
Stone Killer, The
Stoolie, The
Storyville
Straight Out of Brooklyn
Strange Affair, The
Strange Case of Dr Rx, The
Stranger, The (Welles)
Stranger (Nagasaki)
Stranger on the Third Floor
Strangers
Strangers on a Train
Strangler, The
Strapped
Stray Dog
Street of Shadows
Striking Distance
Striptease
Study in Terror, A
Sudden Death
Sudden Fear
Sudden Impact
Suddenly
Sugar Hill
Summerfield
Surveillance
Surviving the Game
Suture

Taffin
TAG, The Assassination Game
Take, The
Taking of Pelham
   One Two Three, The
Tall Target, The
Tango & Cash
Tank Malling
Target (Penn)
Taste of Fear
Tattoo
Taxi!
Telefon
Temptation Harbour
Tenant, The
Ten Days' Wonder
Ten Little Indians
Ten Seconds to Hell
10 to Midnight
Tequila Sunrise
Terror By Night
Terror Train
Testament of Dr Mabuse, The
Tête contre les murs, La
Theft Under the Sun
They Call Me MISTER Tibbs!
They Call That an Accident
They Came to Rob Las Vegas
They Drive By Night (Woods)
They Drive By Night (Walsh)
They're Playing With Fire
They Won't Forget
Thief
Thieves Like Us

Things to Do in Denver
When You're Dead
Thin Man, The
Third Man, The
39 Steps (Hitchcock)
39 Steps (Thomas)
Thirty-Nine Steps, The (Sharp)
This Is My Affair
Thomas Crown Affair, The
1000 Eyes of Dr Mabuse, The
Three Days of the Condor
Three Hours to Kill
301-302
Three the Hard Way
Throwing Down
Thunderheart
Thunder Road
Tiger by the Tail
Tightrope
Time to Kill (Leeds)
Time to Kill, A (Schumacher)
Time Without Pity
To Catch a Thief
Todd Killings, The
To Have and Have Not
Tokyo Drifter
To Live and Die in LA
Tomorrow Never Comes
Tony Rome
Toolbox Murders, The
Topaz
Topkapi
Torn Curtain
Tough Guys Don't Dance
Traces of Red
Trackdown
Traitor Spy
Traveller
Tree of Hands
Trenchcoat
Trespass
Trial by Jury
Trial Run
Trouble in Mind
True Believer
True Confessions
Twilight's Last Gleaming
Two Jakes, The
Two-Minute Warning

Uccello dalle Piume de
Cristallo, L'
Undercover Man
Undercurrent
Underground (Asquith)
Under the Gun
Underworld U.S.A.
Unfaithful, The
Unforgettable
Unlawful Entry
Unsuitable Job for a
Woman, An
Usual Suspects, The

War

Above Us the Waves
Action in the North Atlantic
Albert, RN
All Quiet on the Western Front
(Milestone)
All Quiet on the Western Front
(Mann)
American Guerilla
in the Philippines
Apocalypse Now
Attack!
Austerlitz
Away All Boats

Back Door to Hell
Back to Bataan
Ballad of a Soldier
Bataan
BAT 21
Battleground
Battle of Algiers, The
Battle of Britain

U Turn

Vanishing, The (Sluizer, 1988)
Vanishing, The (Sluizer, 1993)
Vanishing Point
Venom (Haggard)
Verdict, The (Siegel)
Verdict, The (Lumet)
Vérité, La
Vertigo
Vice Squad
Victim
Villain
Violent Cop
Violent Professionals, The
Violent Saturday
Virus
Vivement Dimanche!
V I Warshawski
Voleurs, Les
Voyage

Wait Until Dark
Walk East on Beacon
Walking Stick, The
Wanted Dead or Alive
Warning Shot
War Party
What Ever Happened to
Baby Jane?
What's the Matter
With Helen?
When a Stranger Calls
When Eight Bells Toll
Whip Hand, The
Whistle Blower, The
White Angel
White Dog
White Lightning
White Line Fever
White Man's Burden
White of the Eye
White Sands
Who'll Stop the Rain?
Wicked, Wicked
Wicker Man, The
Wind, The (Mastorakis)
Winged Serpent, The
Winter Kills
Witness
Witness for the Prosecution
Woman Next Door, The
World for Ransom
Wrong Is Right

Year of the Dragon
Year of the Gun
Yellow Dog
Yield to the Night
Young and Innocent
Younger and Younger

Z

Battle of the Bulge
Battle of the River Plate, The
Beach Red
Beast, The
Between Heaven and Hell
Big Red One, The
Bitter Victory
Blue Max, The
Boat, The
Boat, Director's Cut, The
Born on the Fourth of July
Boys in Company C, The
Breaker Morant
Bridge at Remagen, The
Bridge on the River Kwai, The
Bridges at Toko-Ri, The
Bridge Too Far, A
Brylcreem Boys, The
Bullet in the Head

Captive Heart, The
Carve Her Name With Pride

Castle Keep
Casualties of War
Catch 22
Charge of the Light Brigade,
The (Curtiz)
Charge of the Light Brigade,
The (Richardson)
Cockleshell Heroes
Colditz Story, The
Come and See
Confidence
Confirm or Deny
Corvette K-225
Courgae Under Fire
Croix de Bois, Les
Cross of Iron
Cruel Sea, The

Dam Busters, The
Dangerous Moonlight
Dawn Patrol,The (Goulding)
Dawn Patrol, The (Hawks)
Days of Glory
Deer Hunter, The
Deserter and the Nomads, The
Desert Fox, The
Desperate Journey
Destination Gobi
Devil's Brigade, The
Dirty Dozen, The
Dunkirk

84 Charlie Mopic
Empire of the Sun
Enemy Below, The
Era Notte a Roma
Escape
Escape to Athena
Espoir, L'
Every Time We Say Goodbye

Farewell to the King
Fighting Seabees, The
Fighting 69th, The
First of the Few, The
First Yank into Tokyo
Five Graves to Cairo
Fixed Bayonets
Flight of the Intruder
Flying Leathernecks
Force 10 from Navarone
Foreman Went to France,The
49th Parallel
For Whom the Bell Tolls
From Hell to Victory
Full Metal Jacket

Gallipoli
Generation, A
Gettysburg
Girl with the Red Hair, The
Glory
Go Tell the Spartans
Grande Illusion, La
Graveyard of Dreams
Great Escape, The
Green Berets, The
Guadalcanal Diary
Guns of Navarone, The

Halls of Montezuma
Hamburger Hill
Hanna's War
Hannibal Brooks
Heaven & Earth
Hell and High Water
Hellcats of the Navy
Hell is for Heroes
Heroes of Telemark, The
Hill in Korea, A
Hitler's Madman
Hunters, The

Ice Cold in Alex
Ill Met by Moonlight
Immortal Sergeant, The
In Harm's Way
In Which We Serve
Iron Triangle, The
It Happened Here
Ivan's Childhood

Journey's End
Journey Together

Kanal
Kapo
Kelly's Heroes
Key, The
Kings Go Forth

Left Hand of God, The
Libertarias
Lighthorsemen, The
Long Day's Dying, The
Longest Day, The
Lost Patrol, The

Malaya
Memphis Belle
Midnight Clear, A
Midway
Millions Like Us
Miracle in the Rain
Mosquito Squadron
Mrs Miniver
Murphy's War

Naked and the Dead, The
Neige était sale, La
Never So Few
New Lot, The
Night of San Lorenzo, The
Night of the Generals, The
Night Paths
None But the Brave
North Star, The

Objective, Burma!
Occupation in 26 Pictures, The
Odd Angry Shot, The
Odette
One Minute to Zero
One of Our Aircraft Is Missing
One That Got Away, The
1,000 Plane Raid, The
Operation Amsterdam
Operation Crossbow
Operation Daybreak
Orders to Kill
Overlord

Paisà
Paradie Road
Paris After Dark
Password Is Courage, The
Perfect Circle
Perfect Strangers
Platoon
Play Dirty
Pork Chop Hill
Pretty Village, Pretty Flame
Prisoner of the Mountains

Reach for the Sky
Real Glory, The
Red Badge of Courage, The
Regeneration
Return from the River Kwai
Retreat, Hell!
Road to Glory, The

Sahara (Korda)
San Demetrio, London
Sands of Iwo Jima
Sbarco di Anzio, Lo
Sea Chase, The
Sea of Sand
Search, The
Sea Wolves, The
Sergeant York
Silence de la mer, Le
67 Days
Stalingrad
Steel Bayonets, The
Steel Helmet, The
Story of GI Joe, The
Submarine Patrol
Submarine X-1

Tell England
That Summer of White Roses
They Were Expendable

They Were Not Divided
36 Hours
This Above All
This Land is Mine
Three Came Home
Tiara Tahiti
Too Late the Hero
Tora! Tora! Tora!
Torpedo Run
Train, The
Trial on the Road
Twelve O'Clock High
Valley, The
Verboten
Victors, The
Victory
Von Richthofen and Brown

Von Ryan's Express

Walk in the Sun, A
Way Ahead, The
Way to the Stars, The
Welcome to Sarajevo
Went the Day Well?
Westfront 1918
Where Eagles Dare
Wind Cannot Read, The
Wings
Wings of Eagles, The
Wooden Horse, The

Yank in the RAF, A
Yangtse Incident
Young Lions, The

Appendix 15

Westerns

Across the Wide Missouri
Alamo, The
Along Came Jones
Americano, The
Annie Oakley
Apache
Appaloosa, The
At Gunpoint
Autre Homme une Autre
    Chance, Un

Bad Company
Bad Girls
Badlanders, The
Bad Man's River
Ballad of Cable Hogue, The
Ballad of Gregorio Cortez
Ballad of Little Jo, The
Bandolero!
Barbarosa
Beautiful Blonde from
    Bashful Bend, The
Big Country, The
Big Jake
Big Silence, The
Big Sky, The
Big Trail, The
Billy the Kid
Billy Two Hats
Bite the Bullet
Blazing Guns
Blindman
Blood Money
Blood on the Moon
Blood Red
Blood River
Blue
Border Shootout
Boss Nigger
Bravados, The
Breakheart Pass
Brigham Young –
    Frontiersman
Broken Arrow
Broken Lance
Buchanan Rides Alone
Buck and the Preacher
Bugles in the Afternoon
Bullet for the General, A
Burning Hills, The
Butch and Sundance: The
    Early Days
Butch Cassidy and the
    Sundance Kid

Canadians, The
Carson City
Catlow
Cattle Annie and Little Britches
Cattle Queen of Montana
Charge of the Feather River, The
Charley-One-Eye
Charro!
Chato's Land
Cheyenne Autumn
Cheyenne Social Club, The
China 9, Liberty 37
Chisum

Chuka
Cimarron
Cisco Kid and the Lady, The
Colt .45
Comanche Station
Comes a Horseman
Command, The
Companeros
Cowboy
Cowboys, The
Cry Onion
Culpepper Cattle Co., The
Custer of the West

Dakota Incident
Dallas
Dances With Wolves
Dances With Wolves –
    Special Edition
Day of the Evil Gun
Day of the Outlaw
Deadly Companions
Deadly Trackers, The
Dead Man
Deaf Smith & Johnny Ears
Death of a Gunfighter
Desert Trail, The
Devil's Doorway
Dirty Little Billy
Distant Drums
Distant Trumpet, A
Django
Django Kill
Doc
Dodge City
Dragoon Wells Massacre
Drums Along the Mohawk
Duchess and the
    Dirtwater Fox, The
Duel at Diablo
Duel at Silver Creek, The
Duel in the Sun

Eagle's Wing
El Condor
El Dorado (Hawks)
Electric Horseman, The
Escape from Fort Bravo

Far Country, The
Fastest Gun Alive, The
Fistful of Dollars, A
5 Card Stud
Flaming Star
For a Few Dollars More
Fort Apache
40 Graves for 40 Guns
Forty Guns
From Hell to Texas
From Noon Till Three
Furies, The

Geronimo:
    An American Legend
Glory Guys, The
Goin' South
Good Guys and
    the Bad Guys, The

Good, the Bad
    and the Ugly, The
Grayeagle
Great Day in the Morning
Great K & A
    Train Robbery, The
Great Northfield Minnesota
    Raid, The
Great Scout & Cathouse
    Thursday, The
Grey Fox, The
Gunfight, A
Gunfight at the OK Corral, The
Gunfighter, The
Gun Fury

Half-Breed, The
Halliday Brand, The
Hang 'em High
Hannie Caulder
Heartland
Heaven's Gate
Heller in Pink Tights
High Noon
High Plains Drifter
Hired Hand, The
Hondo
Honkers
Horizons West
Horse Soldiers
Hour of the Gun
How the West Was Won

Indian Fighter, The
Iron Horse, The
I Shot Jesse James

Jesse James
Joe Kidd
Johnny Guitar
Junior Bonner

Kentuckian, The
Kid Blue
King and Four Queens, The

Last Challenge, The
Last Command, The
Last Hunt, The
Last of the Mohicans, The
Last Sunset, The
Last Train from Gun Hill
Last Wagon, The
Law and Jake Wade, The
Lawless Street, A
Lawman
Left-Handed Gun, The
Legend of Frenchie King, The
Legend of the
    Lone Ranger, The
Legends of the Fall
Lonely are the Brave
Long Riders, The
Love Me Tender
Lucky Texan, The

Madron
Magnificent Seven, The
Magnificent Seven Ride!, The
Major Dundee
Man Alone, A
Man Called Horse, A
Man Called Noon, The
Man from Colorado, The
Man from Laramie, The
Man in the Wilderness
Man of the West
Man Who Loved
    Cat Dancing, The
Man Who Shot Liberty
    Valance, The
Man Without a Star
Maverick
Mercenario, Il
Misfits, The
Missouri Breaks, The
Mohawk
Monte Walsh
Mule Train
Mustang Country
My Darling Clementine

My Heroes Have
    Always Been Cowboys
My Name is Nobody

Naked Dawn, The
Naked Spur, The
Night Passage

Oklahoma Woman
Once Upon a Time in the West
One-Eyed Jacks
Outlaw, The
Outlaw Josey Wales, The
Ox-Bow Incident, The

Pale Rider
Pocket Money
Pony Soldier
Posse (Douglas)
Posse (Van Peebles)
Proud Ones, The
Pursued

Quantrill's Raiders
Quattro dell'Ave Maria, I
Quick and the Dead, The

Rachel and the Stranger
Raid, The
Ramrod
Rancho Deluxe
Rancho Notorious
Randy Rides Alone
Rare Breed, The
Rawhide
Reason to Live,
    a Reason to Die, A
Red River
Red Sun
Restless Breed, The
Return of a Man
    Called Horse, The
Return of Frank James, The
Return of the Cisco Kid, The
Return to Sabata
Return of the Seven
Revengers, The
Ride in the Whirlwind
Ride Lonesome
Ride in the High Country
Riders of Destiny
Rio Bravo
Rio Conchos
Rio Grande
Rio Lobo
River of No Return
Robin Hood of
    El Dorado, The
Rooster Cogburn
Rough Night in Jericho
Rounders, The
Run for Cover
Run of the Arrow

Sabata
Saddle the Wind
Sam Whiskey
Santa Fe Trail
Santee
Scalphunters, The
Searchers, The
Secrets
Seven Men from Now
7th Cavalry
Shalako
Shane
Sheepman, The
Sheriff of Fractured Jaw, The
She Wore a Yellow Ribbon
Shooting, The
Shootist, The
Silent Tongue
Silverado
Singer Not the Song, The
Smoky
Soldier Blue
South of St Louis
Spikes Gang, The
Stagecoach (Ford)
Stagecoach (Douglas)
Sunchaser, The

Take a Hard Ride
Tall Men, The
Tall T, The
Tell Them Willie Boy is Here
Tennessee's Partner
Tension at Table Rock
Terror in a Texas Town
Texas, Addio
Texas Rangers
There Was a Crooked Man
They Call Him Marcado
They Call Me Trinity
They Died With Their
   Boots On
They Passed This Way
Three Bullets for a Long Gun
Three Godfathers
3.10 to Yuma
Ticket to Tomahawk, A
Time for Dying, A
Tin Star, The
Tombstone
Tom Horn
Town Called Bastard, A
Track of the Cat
Train Robbers, The
Tribute to a Bad Man
Triumphs of a Man
   Called Horse
True Grit
True Story of Jesse James, The
Two Mules for Sister Sara
Two Rode Together

Ulzana's Raid
Unconquered
Undefeated, The
Unforgiven (Eastwood)
Unforgiven, The (Huston)

Valdez il Mezzosangue
Valdez is Coming
Vengeance
Vera Cruz
Villain, The
Viva Villa

Wagon Master
Wanda Nevada
Warlock
War Wagon, The
Way of a Gaucho
Welcome to Hard Times
Western Union
When the Legends Die
White Buffalo, The
White Feather
Wichita
Wild Bill
Wild Bunch, The
Wild Rovers
Will Penny
Winchester '73
Woman Obsessed
Wyatt Earp

Yellow Sky
Young Guns
Young Guns II

Zandy's Bride

Appendices of Major Film-Producing Countries

Australian Films

ABBA The Movie (Swe/Aust)
Adventures of Barry
  McKenzie, The
Adventures of Priscilla Queen
  of the Desert, The
Age of Consent
Alvin Purple
American Roulette (GB/Aust)
Angel Baby
Angst
Annie's Coming Out

Babe
Backlash
Back of Beyond
Backroads
Bedevil
Between Wars
Big Boy Bubby (Aust/It)
Big Steal, The
Black River
Black Robe (Can/Aust)
Bliss
Blood Oath
Blue Fin
BMX Bandits
Body Melt
Boy Who Had Everything, The
Breaker Morant
Brilliant Lies

Cactus
Caddie
Cane Toads – An Unnatural
  History
Captain Johnno
Careful, He Might Hear You
Cars That Ate Paris, The
Castle, The
Cathy's Child
Celia
Chain Reaction, The
Chant of Jimmie
  Blacksmith, The
Clinic, The
Club, The
Coca Cola Kid, The
Country Life
Crocodile Dundee
Crocodile Dundee II
Cry in the Dark, A
Custodian, The

Dance Me to My Song

Dangerous Summer, A
Dark City (US/Aust)
Dawn!
Daydream Believer
Dead Calm
Dead Heart
Deadly
Death in Brunswick
Death of a Soldier
Delinquents, The
Devil's Playground, The
Dogs in Space
Doing Time for Patsy Cline
Don Quixote
Don's Party

Emma's War
Encounter at Raven's Gate
End Play
Everlasting Secret Family, The

Fast Talking
Fatal Bond
Father
FernGully: The Last Rainforest
Fighting Back (Caulfield)
Fistful of Flies
Flirting
Floating Life
For Love or Money
Fortress, The (US/Aust)
Frauds
Fringe Dwellers, The
Frog Dreaming

Gallipoli
Getting of Wisdom, The
Ghosts...of the Civil Dead
Golden Braid
Goodbye, Norma Jean
  (US/Aust)
Good Woman of Bangkok, The
Greenkeeping
Grievous Bodily Harm

Half Life
Hammers Over the Anvil
Harlequin
Heatwave
Heaven's Burning
Heaven Tonight
Hercules Returns
High Tide
Hotel de Love

Hotel Sorrento

Indecent Obsession, An

Just Us

Kangaroo (Burstall)
Killing of Angel Street, The
Kiss or Kill

Last Crop, The (GB/Aust)
Last Days of Chez Nous, The
Last Wave, The
Les Patterson Saves the World
Lightning Jack
Lonely Hearts
Long Weekend
Love and Other Catastrophes
Love in Limbo
Love Letters from Teralba
  Road, The
Lucky Break

Mad Dog Morgan
Mad Max
Mad Max Beyond the
  Thunderdome
Mad Max 2
Malcolm
Malpractice
Man from Hong Kong, The
  (Aust/HK)
Man from Snowy River, The
Manganinnie
Mango Tree
Man of Flowers
Map of the Human Heart
  (GB/Aust/Fr/Can)
Miniskirted Dynamo, The
Mr Reliable (a True Story)
Money Movers
Monkey Grip
Mortgage
Mullaway
Muriel's Wedding
My Brilliant Career
My First Wife
My Life Without Steve

Navigator: A Medieval
  Odyssey, The
Nickel Queen
Norman Loves Rose

Odd Angry Shot, The
Only the Brave
Outback
Over the Hill

Paradise Road (US/Aust)
Patrick
Paws (GB/Aust)
Personal History of the
  Australian Surf, A
Petersen
Phantom, The (US/Aust)
Phar Lap
Piano, The
Picnic at Hanging Rock
Picture Show Man, The
Prejudice
Proof
Puberty Blues
Public Enemy Number One

Punisher, The

Quiet Room, The

Race for the Yankee Zephyr
  (NZ/Aust)
Razorback
Redheads
Return of Captain Invincible
Roadgames
Road to Nhill
Robbery Under Arms
Rollicking Adventures of
  Eliza Fraser, The
Rough Diamonds

Salute of the Jugger, The
Say a Little Prayer
Secrets
Shame
Shark Caller of Kontu, The
Shine (Aust/GB)
Silver City
Sirens (Aust/GB)
Sky Pirates
Slate, Wyn & Me
Southern Cross
Spider and Rose
Spotswood
Stan and George's New Life
Starstruck
Stork
Strictly Ballroom
Strikebound
Summerfield
Sunday Too Far Away
Sweetie

That Eye, the Sky
They're a Weird Mob
  (Aust/GB)
Till There Was You
Tim
Travelling North
True Story of Eskimo Nell,
  The
Turkey Shoot
Turtle Beach
Two Friends

Umbrella Woman, The
Until the End of the World
  (Ger/Fr/Aust)

Vincent: The Life and Death of
  Vincent Van Gogh
Voice of Kurdistan, The
  (GB/Aust)

Walkabout
Well, The
Wendy Cracked a Walnut
We of the Never Never
What Have I Written
Wide Sargasso Sea
Winchester Conspiracy, The
Winner, The (US/Aust)
Winter of Our Dreams
Woman's Tale, A

Year My Voice Broke, The
Year of Living
  Dangerously, The
Young Einstein

Canadian Films

Adjuster, The
Agency
Alien Thunder
Anne Trister (Can/Switz)
Apprenticeship of Duddy
  Kravitz, The
Archangel
Atlantic City (Can/Fr)

Babar: The Movie (Can/Fr)
Bay Boy, The (Can/Fr)

Bear Island (Can/GB)
Beautiful Dreamers
Being at Home with Claude
Best Revenge
Between Friends
Big Meat Eater
Bix
Black Christmas
Black Robe (Can/Aust)
Blood Relatives (Can/Fr)
Breaking Point

Brood, The
Butley (US/GB/Can)
Bye Bye Blues

Calendar (Can/Arm/Ger)
Camilla (Can/GB)
Candy Mountain
  (Switz/Fr/Can)
Care Bears Adventure in
  Wonderland!, The
Careful
Cathy's Curse (Fr/Can)
Changeling, The
Child Under a Leaf
Circle of Two
City on Fire (Can/US)
Class of 1984
Cold Comfort
Comic Book Confidential
Company of Strangers, The
Confessional, The
Crash
Crimes of the Future
Crying Freeman
  (Fr/Can/US/Jap)
Curtis's Crimes

Dancing in the Dark
Dead of Night
Dead Ringers
Death Ship (Can/GB)
Death Weekend
Decline of the American
  Empire, The
Diplomatic Immunity
Disappearance, The (GB/Can)
Distant Thunder (Rosenthal –
  US/Can)
Dogpound Shuffle
Dream Life
Dunston Checks In

Eclipse
Exotica

Family Viewing
Fast Company
Fire
Fortune and Men's Eyes
  (Can/US)
Full Circle (GB/Can)

Galileo (Losey – GB/Can)
Gate, The
Goin' Down the Road
Grey Fox, The

Head On
Heartaches
Heartland Reggae
Highland III – The Sorcerer
  (Can/Fr/GB)
Histoire inventée, Une
Hog Wild
Homme de ma vie, L' (Fr/Can)
Hot Money
Hounds of Notre Dame, The
House

I Love a Man in Uniform
In Celebration (GB/Can)
Incubus
In Praise of Older Women
In the Belly of the Dragon
Intimate Relations (GB/Can)
Iron Eagle II
I've Heard the
  Mermaids Singing

J.A. Martin, Photographer
Janis
Jesus of Montreal (Can/Fr)
Joy (Fr/Can)
Judgement in Stone, A

Kablooak (Fr/Can)
Kanehsatake (Oka) – 270 Years
  of Resistance
Kidnapping of the
  President, The
Kings and Desperate Men

King Solomon's Treasure
Kissed

Last Night
Last Supper, The (Roberts)
Last Temptation of Christ, The
  (US/Can)
Léolo
Leopard in the Snow (GB/Can)
Lilies
Love and Death on Long Island
  (GB/Can)
Love and Human Remains
Luck of Ginger Coffey, The
  (Can/US)
Luther (US/GB/Can)

Maids, The (GB/Can)
Man, a Woman and a Bank, A
Manufacturing Consent: Noam
  Chomsky and the Media
Map of the Human Heart
  (GB/Aust/Fr/Can)
Margaret's Museum (Can/GB)
Marie s'en va-t-en ville
Married Couple, A
Masala
Mask, The
Middle Age Crazy
Mon Oncle Antoine
Montreal Main
Mourir à Tue-Tête
Murder by Decree (Can/GB)
My American Cousin

Naked Lunch (GB/Can)
Neptune Factor, The
Never Talk to Strangers
  (Can/US)
Night Zoo
90 Days
No Skin Off My Ass
Not a Love Story

Outrageous!

Paperback Hero
Paper Wedding, A
Parasite Murders, The
Paris France
Perfectly Normal (GB/Can)
Polygraph, The (Can/Fr/Ger)
Porky's
Porky's II: The Next Day
Porky's Revenge
Power Play (GB/Can)
Punch Me in the Stomach
  (NZ/Can)

Quest for Fire (Can/Fr)

Rabid
Rainbow (GB/Can)
Reason Over Passion
Réjeanne Padavani
Revolving Doors, The

Scanners
Scanners II: The New Order
Screamers (Can/US/Jap)
Screwballs
Screwballs II – Loose Screws
Secret Wedding
  (Arg/Neth/Can)
September Songs: The Music
  of Kurt Weill
Shadow of the Hawk
Shape of Things to Come, The
Shoemaker
Siege
Silent Partner The
Sitting in Limbo
Skip Tracer
Song for Tibet
Soul Investigator
Speaking Parts
Special Day, A (It/Can)
Stepping Razor – Red X
Sunday in the Country
  (Trent)
Super 8½

Swann
Sweet Hereafter , The
Sweet Movie (Fr/Can/WGer)

Tadpole and the Whale
Tales from the Gimli Hospital
Tendresse Ordinaire
Terra-Cotta Warrior, A
(HK/Can)
Terror Train
Terry Fox Story, The
Tête de Normande St-Onge, La
That Cold Day in the Park
Thirty Two Short Films About
Glenn Gould
Ticket to Heaven
Tommy Tricker and the Stamp
Traveller
Tomorrow Never Comes
(Can/GB)
Tribute (US/Can)
True Nature of Bernadette, The
Twilight of the
Ice Nymphs, The

Uncanny, The (GB/Can)
Un©ut
Urinal

Videodrome
Violation of Justine, The
(Fr/It/Can)
Violent Tradition (US/Can)
Violette Nozière (Fr/Can)
Virus (Jap/Can)
Visiting Hours
Volcano

Watchers
Wavelength
Welcome to Blood City
(Can/GB)
When Night Is Falling
White Room (Can/GB)
Why Shoot the Teacher?
Wild Flowers
Winter Tan, A

Zero Patience

Appendix 18

French Films

A Bout de Souffle
Abraham Valley (Fr/Switz)
Accompagnatrice, L'
Aces High (GB/Fr)
Addition, L'
Adieu Bonaparte (Fr/Egypt)
A Double Tour (Fr/It)
Adventures of Pinocchio, The
(GB/Fr/Ger/
Czech Republic/US)
Affaire du Courrier de Lyon, L'
Affiche Rouge, L'
Afraid of the Dark (GB/Fr)
Age d'Or, L'
Agression, L' (Fr/It)
Aigle à Deux Têtes, L'
Ai No Corrida (Jap/Fr)
Air de Famille, Un
A.K. (Fr/Jap)
Albino Aligator (US/Fr)
Alexandre
Alexandria Encore (Egypt/Fr)
Alfredo Alfredo (It/Fr)
Alice in Wonderland
(US/Fr/GB)
All Men Are Mortal
(GB/Neth/Fr)
Alphaville (Fr/It)
Amants, Les
Amants du Pont-Neuf, Les
Amants de Verone, Les
Amarcord (It/Fr)
Amateur (Fr/GB)
Amazons, The (It/Fr)
American Friend, The
(WGer/Fr)
American Stories (Fr/Bel)
American Werewolf in Paris,
An (US/Luxembourg/Fr/GB)
Amour à Mort, L'
Amour Fou, L'
Amour par terre, L'
Amy Foster (GB/US/Fr)
And Now My Love (Fr/It)
And the Ship Sails On (It/Fr)
Angel Dust
Anges du Péché, Les
Annabelle partagée
Année Dernière à Marienbad,
L' (Fr/It)
A Nous la Liberté
A Nous les Petites Anglaises!
Appartement, L (Fr/Sp/It)
Appât, L'
Appel du Silence, L'
Après l'Amour
Arabian Nights (It/Fr)
Argent, L' (L'Herbier)
Argent, L' (Bresson – Switz/Fr)
Argent de Poche, L'
Argent des Autres, L'

Arizona Dreaming
(Fr/Former Yugo)
Armée des Ombres, L' (Fr/It)
Ascenseur pour l'Echafaud
Assassination of Trotsky, The
(Fr/It/GB)
Assassin Habite au 21, L'
Assassin(s)
Asterix and the Big Fight
(Fr/WGer)
Asterix in Britain
Astragale, L' (Fr/WGer)
Atalante, L'
Atlantic City, (Can/Fr)
A Toute Vitesse
Attentat, L' (Fr/It/WGer)
Auberge Rouge, L'
Au Hasard, Balthazar (Fr/Swe)
Au Nom de la Loi
Au Revoir les Enfants
(Fr/WGer)
Austerlitz (Fr/It/Liechtenstein)
Australia (Fr/Bel/Switz)
Autre Homme une Autre
Chance, Un
Aux Yeux du monde
Aveu, L' (Fr/It)
Aviator's Wife, The

Babar: The Movie (Can/Fr)
Baba Yaga (It/Fr)
Bab El-Oued City (Alg/Fr)
Baby of Mâcon, The
(GB/Neth/Fr/Ger)
Bad Man's River (Sp/It/Fr)
Baie des Anges, La
Baisers Volés
Bal, Le (Fr/It/Alg)
Balance, La
Ballon d'Or, Le (Guinea/Fr)
Bande à Part
Barbarella (Fr/It)
Barnabo of the Mountains
(Fr/It/Switz)
Baron Fantôme, Le
Bas-Fonds, Les
Bataille du Rail, La
Battle of the Ten Million, The
(Fr/Bel/Cuba)
Bayan Ko: My Own Country
(Phil/Fr)
Bay Boy, The (Fr/Can)
Bear, The
Beaumarchais
Beau Mariage, Le
Beau Serge, Le
Beauté du Diable, La (Fr/It)
Bee Keeper, The (Fr/Greece)
Before the Rain
(Macedonia/GB/Fr)
Belle (Bel/Fr)

Belle de Jour (Fr/It)
Belle Equipe, La
Belle et la Bête, La
Belle Fille Comme Moi, Une
Belle Noiseuse, La
Belle Noiseuse –
Divertimento, La
Belles de nuit, Les (Fr/It)
Benvenuta (Bel/Fr/It)
Berlin Jerusalem
Bernadette
Bernie
Best Way to Walk, The
Bête, La
Bête Humaine, La
Betty Blue (versions 1 & 2)
Beyond Evil (It/Fr WGer)
Beyond the Clouds (Fr/It/Ger)
Biches, Les (Fr/It)
Bidone, Il (It/Fr)
Big Bang, The (Fr/Bel)
Big Silence, The (Fr/It)
Bilitis
Bird Now (Bel/Fr)
Bisexual (Fr/It)
Bitter Moon (Fr/GB)
Bitter Victory
Black and White in Colour
(Fr/Switz/Ivory C)
Black Moon
Black Orpheus (Fr/It/Braz)
Blackout, The
(Ferrara – US/Fr)
Black Sabbath (It/Fr)
Black Shack Alley
Blaise Pascal (Fr/It)
Blanche
Blood for Dracula (It/Fr)
Blood Relatives (Can/Fr)
Blow-Out (Ferreri – Fr/It)
Blues Under the Skin
Blue Villa, The (Bel/Fr/Switz)
Bob le Flambeur
Bof!
Bohème, La (Fr/It)
Bonheur, Le
Bonheur est dans le Pré, Le
Bonne Année, La (Fr/It)
Bonnes Femmes, Les (Fr/It)
Bonzesse, La
Boomerang (Giovanni – Fr/It)
Borsalino (Fr/It)
Borsalino & Co (Fr/It/WGer)
Bosna!
Both Sides of the Street
Boucher, Le (Fr/It)
Boudu Sauvé des Eaux
Boulangère de Monceau, La
Boule de Suif
Boy from Mercury, The
(GB/Fr/Ire)
Boy Meets Girl
Branches of the Tree (Ind/Fr)
Breaking the Waves
(Den/Swe/Fr/Neth/Nor)
Bride Wore Black, The (Fr/It)
Brigands
Buffet Froid
Burglars, The (Fr/It)
Burnt by the Sun (Rus/Fr)
Business Affair, A
(GB/Fr/Ger/Sp)
Butterfly Effect (Sp/Fr/GB)
Bye Bye Brazil (Braz/Fr)

Cage aux Folles, La (Fr/It)
Cage aux Folles II, La (Fr/It)
Cage aux Folles III: The
Wedding, La (Fr/It)
Calle Mayor (Sp/Fr)
Call of the Wild, The
(GB/WGer/Sp/It/Fr)
Camille Claudel
Camisards, Les
Campana del Infierno, La
(Sp/Fr)
Candy (US/It/Fr)
Candy Mountain
(Switz/Fr/Can)
Canterbury Tales, The (It/Fr)
Capitaine Fracassé, Le

Caporal Epinglé, Le
Captive (GB/Fr)
Captive du Désert, La
Carabiniers, Les (Fr/It)
Caravan to Vaccares (GB/Fr)
Carmen (Rosi – Fr/It)
Carné
Carrière de Suzanne, La
Casanova '70 (It/Fr)
Casque d'Or
Catch Me a Spy (GB/Fr/US)
Catherine and Co. (Fr/It)
Cathy's Curse (Fr/Can)
Cat o'Nine Tails, The
(It/WGer/Fr)
Cavafy (Greece/Fr)
Cecilia, La (It/Fr)
Cela s'appelle l'Aurore (Fr/It)
Celestine, Maid at Your Service
Céline and Julie Go Boating
Cement Garden, The
(GB/Ger/Fr)
Cérémonie, La
César
César and Rosalie (Fr/It/WGer)
Chambre Verte, La
Champagne Murders, The
Chanel Solitaire (Fr/GB)
Chantons sous l'Occupation
Charles and Lucie
Charlotte (Fr/It/WGer)
Chartreuse de Parme, La
Chat, Le
Château de ma mère, Le
Chère Louise (Fr/It)
Cheval d'Orgueil, Le
Chienne, La
Chiens, Les (Fr/Tahiti)
Chinese Box (US/HK/Fr)
Chinese Roulette (WGer/Fr)
Chinoise, La
Chocolat
Choses de la Vie, Les (Fr/It)
Christ Stopped at Eboli (It/Fr)
Chronicle of a Death Foretold
(It/Fr)
Chronique d'un Eté
Cinderella – Italian Style (It/Fr)
Cinema Cinema (Fr/US)
Cinema Paradiso (It/Fr)
Cinema Paradiso: The Special
Edition (It/Fr)
Circle of Deceit (WGer/Fr)
Cité des enfants perdus, La
Citizen Langlois
City of Joy (GB/Fr)
City of Pirates (Fr/Port)
City of Women (It/Fr)
Claire's Knee
Class Relations (WGer/Fr)
Clean Slate
Cléo de 5 à 7 (Fr/It)
Clowns, The (It/Fr/WGer)
Clubbed to Death
(Fr/Port/Neth)
Club de Femmes
Cobra (Boisset – Fr/It)
Cocaine
Coeur en hiver, Un
Coeur qui bat, In
Cold Sweat (Fr/It)
Collectionneuse, La
Colonel Chabert, Le
(Le Hénaff)
Colonel Chabert, Le (Angelo)
Colossus of Rhodes, The
(It/Sp/Fr)
Comedians, The
(US/Bermuda/Fr)
Condamné à Mort s'est
Echappé, Un
Confessional, The
(Can/GB/Fr)
Conformist, The (It/Fr/WGer)
Conte d'été
Convent, The (Port/Fr)
Conversation Piece (It/Fr)
Cook, the Thief, His Wife and
Her Lover, The (GB/Fr)
Cop au Vin
Cop's Honour

Corbeau, Le
Coup de Foudre
Coup de Grâce (WGer/Fr)
Coup pour Coup (WGer/Fr)
Courage Fuyons
Cousin Cousine
Cousins in Love (Fr/WGer)
Crazy Horse of Paris, The
Cri du Coeur, Le
Crime de Monsieur Lange, Le
Crise, La
Croix de Bois, Les
Crying Freeman
  (Fr/Can/US/Jap)
Cyclo
Cyrano de Bergerac

Daens (Bel/Fr/Neth)
Damage (GB/Fr)
Dame aux Camélias, La (Fr/It)
Dames du Bois de Boulgne, Les
Dance of the Wind
  (GB/Fr/Ger/Neth)
Danger: Diabolik (Fr/It)
Danton (Fr/Pol)
Daughters of Darkness
  (Bel/Fr/WGer/It)
Day of the Jackal, The (GB/Fr)
Deadly Run
Deadly Trap, The (Fr/It)
Dear Diary (It/Fr)
Dear Inspector
Death and the Maiden
  (GB/US/Fr)
Death in a French Garden
Death in the Seine (GB/Fr)
Death of Mario Ricci, The
  (Switz/Fr/WGer)
Death Watch (Fr/WGer)
Decameron, The (It/Fr/WGer)
Déjeuner sur l'Herbe, Le
Delicatessen
Demoiselles de Rochefort, Les
Dentellière, La (Fr/Switz/WGer)
Dernières Vacances, Les
Dernier Milliardaire, Le
Dernier Tournant, Le
Dérobade, La
Des Enfants Gâtés
Désert des Tartares, Le
  (Fr/It/WGer)
Des Nouvelles du Bon Dieu
Despair (WGer/Fr)
Destiny
Détective
Deux Anglaises et le
  Continent, Les
Deux Hommes dans Manhattan
Deuxième Souffle, Le
Deux ou Trois Choses que Je
  Sais d'Elle
Diable au Corps, La
Diable Probablement, Le
Diaboliques, Les
Diabolo Menthe
Dialogue des Carmélites, Le
  (Fr/It)
Diary of a Chambermaid, The
  (Buñuel – Fr/It)
Diary of a Country Priest
Dimenticare Venezia (It/Fr)
Discreet Charm of the
  Bourgeoisie, The
Discrète, La
Disparus de Saint-Agil, Les
Diva
Doc's Kingdom (Port/Fr/GB)
Docteur Jekyll et les Femmes
Docteur Petiot
Docteur Popaul (Fr/It)
Dr M (WGer/It/Fr)
Dolce Vita, La (It/Fr)
Doll's House, A (Losey –
  GB/Fr)
Domicile Conjugal (Fr/It)
Don Giovanni (It/Fr/WGer)
Don Juan or If Don Juan
  Were a Woman (Fr/It)
Don Quichotte
Doom Generation, The (Fr/US)
Dossier 51, Le (Fr/WGer)

Dougal and the Blue Cat
Douce
Doulos, Le (Fr/It)
Down the Ancient Stairs (It/Fr)
Downtime (GB/Fr)
Drama of the Rich (It/Fr)
Drifting Clouds (Fin/Ger/Fr)
Drôle de Drame
Du Rififi à Paname
  (Fr/It/WGer)
Du Rififi chez les Hommes
Dust (Bel/Fr)

Eau Froide, L'
Eclipse, The (It/Fr)
Ecoute Voir...
Edith and Marcel
Eighth Day, The (Fr/Bel/GB)
8-Wheel Beast, The (It/Fr)
El Dorado (Saura – Sp/Fr)
Elective Affinities (It/Fr)
Eléna et les Hommes (Fr/It)
Elisa
Emmanuelle
Emmanuelle 2
Emmène-moi
Emmerdeur, L' (Fr/It)
Empire of Passion (Fr/Jap)
En avoir (ou pas)
En Cas de Malheur (Fr/It)
En Compagnie d'Antonin
  Artaud
End of Violence, The
  (US/Fr/Ger)
Enfance nue, L'
Enfant Sauvage, L'
Enfants du Lumière, Les
Enfants du Paradis, Les
Enfants Terribles, Les
Enfer, L'
Enigma (GB/Fr)
Equilibristes, Les
Era Notte a Roma (It/Fr)
Ercole alla conquista di
  Atlantide (It/Fr)
Erendira (Fr/Mex/WGer)
Escalier C
Espion Lève-toi
Espions, Les
Espoir (Fr/Sp)
Et Dieu Créa la Femme
Eternel Retour, L'
Eternity and a Day
  (Greece/Fr/Ger)
Etoile du Nord, L'
Etrange Monsieur Victor, L'
Europa, Europa (Fr/Ger)
Eve (Fr/It)
Everybody's Fine (It/Fr)
Every Little Thing

Fanny (Allégret)
Fantastic Planet (Fr/Czech)
Fantômas contre Fantômas
Fantôme de la Liberté, Le
Fantôme du Moulin Rouge, Le
Farrebique
Fatherland (GB/WGer/Fr)
Faust (Czech Republic/Fr)
Fausto
Faute de l'Abbé Mouret, La
  (Fr/It)
Faute de Soleil
Favourites of the Moon
Favour, the Watch and the
  Very Big Fish, The (Fr/GB)
Fellini-Satyricon (It/Fr)
Fellini's Roma (It/Fr)
Female Vampires
Femme Défendue, La
Femme Douce, Une
Femme du Boulanger, La
Femme entre Chien et Loup,
  Une (Bel/Fr)
Femme est une Femme, Une
Femme française, Une
  (Fr/GB/Ger)
Femme Infidèle, La (Fr/It)
Femme Mariée, Une
F for Fake (Fr/Iran/WGer)
Fiancée du Pirate, La

Fièvre Monte à El Pao, La
  (Fr/Mex)
Fifth Element, The
Fille de D'Artagnan, La
Fille de l'Air, La
Fin du Jour, La
Fiorile (It/Fr/Ger)
First Name: Carmen (Fr/Switz)
First Time with Feeling
  (Fr/WGer)
Five and the Skin (Fr/Phil)
Flame (Zim/Fr/Mamibia)
Flame in My Heart, A
  (Fr/Switz)
Flesh for Frankenstein (It/Fr)
Flic, Un (Fr/It)
Flower of My Secret, The
  (Sp/Fr)
Folle à Tuer (Fr/It)
For Ever Mozart
Fortini/Cani
  (It/Fr/WGer/GB/US)
4 Adventures of Reinette &
  Mirabelle
Four Flies on Grey Velvet
  (It/Fr)
Four Nights of a Dreamer
  (Fr/It)
Fracture du myocarde, La
Franc, Le (Switz/Fr/Senegal)
François Truffaut, Portraits
  Volés
Frantz Fanon: Black Skin,
  White Mask (GB/Fr)
French Cancan
French Mustard
Fresh (US/Fr)
Friends (Fr/Fr)
Friends and Husbands
  (WGer/Fr)
Frisson des Vampires, Le
From Hell to Victory (Fr/It/Sp)
From the Cloud to the
  Resistance (It/Fr/WGer/GB)
Fruits of Passion, The (Fr/Jap)
Full Moon in Paris
Future Is Woman, The
  (It/Fr/WGer)
Future of Emily, The
  (Fr/WGer)

Gabbeh (Iran/Fr)
Gadjo Dilo
Gai Savoir, Le (Fr/WGer)
Gang, Le (Fr/It)
Garde à Vue
Gawin
Gazon maudit
General Amin
Genesis (Fr/Ind/Bel/Switz)
Gens de la rizière, Les
  (Cambodia/Fr)
Germinal (Fr/Bel/It)
Giant of Marathon, The (It/Fr)
Ginger & Fred (Fr/It/WGer)
Girl from Lorraine, A
Girl on a Motorcycle (GB/Fr)
Gito, the Ungrateful
  (Burundi/Switz/Fr)
Glissements Progressifs
  du Plaisir
Gloire de mon père, La
Golden Coach, The (Fr/It)
Golden Eighties (Fr/Bel/Switz)
Goodbye Emmanuelle
Good Morning Babylon
  (It/Fr/US)
Gospel According to St
  Matthew, The (It/Fr)
Goto, l'île d'amour
Goupi-Mains-Rouges
Grand Amour, Le
Grand Chemin, Le
Grande Illusion, La
Grand Jeu, Le
Green Ray, The
Grosse Fatigue
Guerre des Boutons, La
Guerre est Finie, La (Fr/Swe)
Guerre sans nom, La

Gueule d'Amour
Guns for San Sebastian
  (Fr/Mex/It)

Hail, Mary (Fr/Switz)
Haine, La
Hairdresser's Husband, The
Happiness in Twenty Years
Hard Men (GB/Fr)
Harem
He Died with His Eyes Open
Heroes, The (It/Fr/Sp)
Héros très discret, Un
Highlander III – The Sorcerer
  (Can/Fr/GB)
Hiroshima, Mon Amour
  (Fr/Jap)
Histoires Extraordinaires
  (Fr/It)
Hitler, a Film from Germany
  (WGer/GB/Fr)
Ho! (Fr/It)
Homme de Désir, L'
Homme de Marrakesh, l'
  (Fr/It/Sp)
Homme de ma vie, L' (Fr/Can)
Homme de Rio, L' (Fr/It)
Homme et une Femme, Un
Homme qui Dort, Un (Fr/Tun)
Horloger de St Paul, L'
Hors la vie (Fr/It/Bel)
Hôtel de la Plage, L'
Hôtel du Nord
Hôtel du Paradis (GB/Fr)
Hour of the Pig (GB/Fr)
How to Destroy of the
  Reputation of the Greatest
  Secret Agent (Fr/It)
Hunchback of Notre Dame, The
  (Delannoy – Fr/It)
Hussard sur le toit, Le
Hypothesis of the Stolen
  Painting, The

I Am a Dancer
I Am Frigid...Why?
Identification of a Woman
  (It/Fr)
Ile au trésor, L' (Fr/US)
Illustrious Corpses (It/Fr)
I Love You, I Don't
Immoral Tales
Immortal Story, The
Immortelle, L' (Fr/It/Tur)
Improper Conduct
Impudent Girl, An
Indians Are Still Far Away,
  The (Switz/Fr)
India Song
Indochine
Infernal Trio, The (Fr/It/WGer)
Inhumaine, L'
Innocent, The (Visconti – It/Fr)
Innocents with Dirty Hands
  (Fr/It/WGer)
Inspecteur Lavardin
In the French Style (Fr/US)
Inutile Envoyer Photo
Invitation, The (Switz/Fr)
Invitation to Bed
IP5
Irma Vep
It's All True (Fr/US)
I Want to Go Home

Jacquot de Nantes
Jane Eyre (GB/It/Fr/US)
Jean de Florette (Fr/It)
Jeanne Dielman, 23 Quai du
  Commerce, 1080 Bruxelles
  (Bel/Fr)
Jeanne la Pucelle
J'embrasse pas
Jesus of Montreal (Can/Fr)
Je t'aime, Je t'aime
Jetée, La
Jeu de l'oie, Le
Jeune Wether, Le
Jeux Interdits
Jeux Sonts Faits, Les
Jo

Johnny Suede (US/Switz/Fr)
Joli mai, Le
Jonah Who Will Be 25 in the Year 2000
Jour de Fête
Journal de Lady M (Switz/Bel/Sp/Fr)
Jour se Lève, Le
Joy (Fr/Can)
Jules et Jim
Juliet of the Spirits (It/Fr)
Jungle Burger (Fr/Bel)
Just Before Nightfall (Fr/It)

Kabloonak (Fr/Can)
Kafka (US/Fr)
Kamikaze
Kapo (It/Fr)
Katia Ismaïlova (Rus/Fr)
Këita! The Voice of the Griot (Fr/Burkina Faso)
Korczak (Pol/Ger/Fr/GB)

La Baule-les-Pins
Lacho Drom
Lacombe Lucien (Fr/It/WGer)
Lady Chatterley's Lover (GB/Fr)
Lady in the Car with Glasses and a Gun, The
Lady L (Fr/It)
Lancelot du Lac (Fr/It)
Landscape in the Mist (Greece/Fr/It)
Last Battle, The
Last Melodrama, The
Last Metro, The
Last Tango in Paris (Fr/It)
Last Woman, The (Fr/It)
Laughter in the Dark (GB/Fr)
Laura (Hamilton)
Leap into the Void (Fr/It)
Le Cop
Le Cop 2
Lectrice, La
Legend of Frenchie King, The (Fr/It/Sp/GB)
Leon
Leon Morin, Priest (Fr/It)
Lessons in Darkness (Fr/Ger)
Let's Hope It's a Girl (It/Fr)
Letters to an Unknown Lover (GB/Fr)
Letter to Jane
Level Five
Liaisons Dangereuses 1960, Les
Libera Me
Lie, The
Life and Extraordinary Adventures of Private Ivan Chonkin, The (GB/Fr/It/Czech Republic/Rus)
Life and Nothing But
Life Is a Long Quiet River
Life Size (Fr/It/Sp)
Light Years Away (Fr/Switz)
Lion Has Seven Heads, The (Fr/It)
Lisbon Story (Fr/Port)
Little Buddha (Fr/GB)
Live Flesh (Sp/Fr)
Loin des Barbares
Lola Montès (Fr/It)
Lolita (Lyne – Fr/US)
Loulou
Lord of the Dance (Fr/Switz/WGer)
Love etc.
Love in Germany, A (WGer/Fr)
Love in the Afternoon
Love in the Strangest Ways
Love on the Run (Truffaut)
Lover, The (Fr/GB)
L.627
Lucie Aubrac
Lucky Luciano (It/Fr)
Lucky Luke (Fr/Bel)
Ludwig (Fr/It/WGer)
Lumière Noire
Lust and Desire

Madadam Tribu (Fr/Zaire)
Mad Adventures of 'Rabbi' Jacob, The (Fr/It)
Madame Bovary (Renoir)
Madame Bovary (Chabrol)
Madame Butterfly (Fr/Jap/Ger/GB)
Madame Claude
Madame de... (Fr/It)
Madame Rosa
Mademoiselle (GB/Fr)
Mahabharata, Le
Maid for Pleasure
Maison de Jade, La
Maîtresse
Malevil (Fr/WGer)
Malpertuis (Bel/Fr/WGer)
Manèges
Man by the Shore, The
Man in Love, A
Manon des Sources (Fr/It/Switz)
Man on Fire (Fr/It)
Man Who Loved Women, The (Truffaut)
Map of the Human Heart (GB/Aust/Fr/Ger)
Marge, La
Marius
Marius et Jennette
Marquis (Bel/Fr)
Marquise von O..., Die (WGer/Fr)
Marseillaise, La
Marseilles Contract, The (GB/Fr)
Ma Saison Préférée
Mascara (Bel/Neth/Fr/US)
Masculin Féminin (Fr/Swe)
Masques
Massacre in Rome (Fr/It)
Mata-Hari, Agent H.21 (Fr/It)
Mauvais Sang
Ma Vie en Rose (Fr/Bel/GB/Switz)
Ma vie sexuelle (Paul Dedalus' Journey)
Max Mon Amour (Fr/US)
Mayerling
Mazel Tov ou le Mariage
Medea (It/Fr/WGer)
Medusa Touch, The (GB/Fr)
Me Ivan, You Abraham
Mélo
Ménilmontant
Men, Women: User's Manual
Mémoire des apparences
Mépris, Le (Fr/It)
Merci la vie
Merlusse
Mes Petites Amoureuses
Messidor
Métisse
Microcosmos (Fr/Switz/It)
Middle of the World, The (Switz/Fr)
Mignon Has Left (It/Fr)
Million, Le
Milou en mai (Fr/It)
Mina Tannenbaum
Miroir a deux faces, Le (Fr/It)
Misérables, Les (le Chanois)
Misérables, Les (Lelouch)
Mississippi Blues (Fr/US)
Mister Freedom
Mister Frost (Fr/GB)
Moine, Le (Fr/It/WGer)
Moi, Pierre Rivière
Moment d'Egarement, Un
Monde du Silence, Le
Monde sans Pitié, Un
Money Order, The (Fr/Sen)
Mon Homme
Mon Oncle
Mon Oncle d'Amérique
Mon Père, ce héros
Mon Pierre Amour
Monsieur Hire
Montalvo et l'enfant
Montand
Moon in the Gutter, The (Fr/It)

Moonraker (GB/Fr)
Mort en ce Jardin, La (Fr/Mex)
Moses and Aaron (WGer/Fr)
Mother and the Whore, The
Mouchette
Moulin Rouge (US/Fr)
Mouth Agape, The
Mr Arkadin (Sp/Fr)
Mr Klein (Fr/It)
Murder Is a Murder...Is a Murder, A (Fr/It)
Muriel (Fr/It)
Music for the Movies: The Hollywood Sound (US/Jap/Fr)
My Best Friend's Girl
My Girlfriend's Boyfriend
My Name Is Nobody (Fr/It/WGer)
My Night With Maud
Mystère Picasso, Le
Mystery of Alexina, The

Nada (Fr/It)
Name of the Rose, The (WGer/Fr/It)
Nana
Nanou (GB/Fr)
Napoléon
Nathalie Granger
Néa (Fr/WGer)
Neige était sale, La
Nelly & Monsieur Arnaud
Nénette et Boni
News from Home (Fr/Bel)
Nez au Vent, Le
Night and Day
Night Caller (Fr/It)
Night of the Generals, The (GB/Fr)
Night Sun (It/Fr/Ger)
Nikita (Fr/It)
1900 (Fr/It/WGer)
Noce blanche
Noces Rouges, Les (Fr/It)
Noir et Blanc
No Man's Land (Switz/Fr/WGerGB)
Nord
Nosferatu the Vampire (WGer/Fr)
Notre Histoire
Notte, La (It/Fr)
N'oublie pas que tu vas mourir
Nouvelle Vague
November Moon (WGer/Fr)
Nowhere (US/Fr)
Nuit du Carrefour, La
Nuit fantastique, La
Nuits Rouges (Fr/It)
Numéro Deux
Nun and the Devil, The (It/Fr)

Of Great Events and Ordinary People
Old Lady Who Walked in the Sea, The
Olivia
Olivier Olivier
Ombre du Doute, L'
One Deadly Summer
One Man's War (Fr/WGer)
One Sings, The Other Doesn't (Fr/Bel/Cur)
On purge Bébé
Opera do Manlandro (Fr/Braz)
Orgueilleux, Les (Fr/Mex)
Orlando (GB/Rus/Fr/It/Neth)
Orphée
Ostrich Has Two Eggs, The
Out 1: Spectre
Outside Man, The (Fr/It)

Paltoquet, Le
Papa, les Petits Bateaux
Parade (Fr/Swe)
Paradis Perdu
Paranoia (It/Fr)
Parapluies de Cherbourg, Les (Fr/WGer)

Pardon Mon Affaire, Too
Parents Terribles, Les
Parfait Amour!
Parfum d'Yvonne, Le
Paris 1900
Paris Nous Appartient
Paris qui Dort
Paris s'éveille
Paris, Texas (WGer/Fr/GB)
Paris vu par...
Parking
Parsifal (Fr/WGer)
Partie de Campagne, Une
Partie de Plaisir, Une (Fr/It)
Pasolini, un Delitto Italiano (It/Fr)
Passenger, The (It/Fr/Sp)
Passe ton Bac d'Abord
Passion (Fr/Switz)
Passion de Jeanne d'Arc, La
Passione d'Amore (It/Fr)
Pasteur
Patriot Game, The
Paul and Michelle (Fr/GB)
Paulina 1880
Pauline à la Plage
Peau d'Ane
Peau Douce, La
Pépé le Moko
Perceval le Gallois
Père Goriot, Le
Perfect Circle
Péril Jeune, Le
Perles de la Couronne, Les
Permis de Conduire, Le
Pétain
Petite Marchande d'allumettes, La
Petite Voleuse, La
Petit Matin, Le
Petit Price a dit, Le (Fr/Switz)
Petit Soldat, Le
Petit Théâtre de Jean Renoir,Le (Fr/It/WGer)
Peu de Soleil dans l'Eau Froide, Un
Phantom India
Piaf
Pickpocket
Pièges
Pierrot le Fou (Fr/It)
Pigsty (It/Fr)
Pillow Book, The (Neth/Fr/Ger)
Pink Floyd Live at Pompeii (Fr/Bel/WGer)
Pink Telephone, The
Pirates
Plaisir, Le
Playing from Plates (Pol/Fr)
Playtime
Pleins Feux sur l'assassin
Plein Soleil (Fr/It)
Po di Sangui (Fr/Port/Guinea Bissao)
Police
Polygraph, The (Can/Fr/Ger)
Pont du Nord, Le
Porte des Lilas
Portrait of a '60% Perfect' Man: Billy Wilder
Portrait of a Young Girl at the End of the '60s in Brussels
Portraits Chinois (Fr/GB)
Possession (Fr/WGer)
Postino, Il (It/Fr)
Prague (GB/Fr)
Pravda
Préparez Vos Mouchoirs (Fr/Bel)
Présence réelle, La
P..... Respectueuse, La
Prince of Jutland (Fr/GB/Den/Neth/GB)
Princes, Les
Prise de Pouvoir par Louis XIV, La
Private Club
Prize of Peril, The (Fr/Yugo)
Procès de Jeanne d'Arc
Promise, The, The

(Dardenne – Bel/Fr/Lux)
Promise, The
 (von Trotta – Ger/Fr)
Promised Lands
Proprietor, The (Fr/GB/Ger)
Prospero's Books (Neth/Fr/It)
Providence (Fr/Switz)
Pure Formality, A (It/Fr)
Puritan, The
Purple Taxi, The (Fr/It/Eire)
Pussy Talk

Quai des Brumes, Le
Quai des Orfèvres
Quartet (Ivory – GB/Fr)
Quatre Cents Coups, Les
Queimada! (Fr/It)
Que la Bête Meure (Fr/It)
Que la Fête Commence
Querelle (WGer/Fr
Quest for Fire (Can/Fr)

Ramparts of Clay (Fr/Alg)
Ran (Fr/Jap)
Reason to Live, a Reason to
 Die, A (It/Fr/Sp/WGer)
Rebel Nun, The (It/Fr)
Red Circle, The (Fr/It)
Red Desert, The (It/Fr)
Red Sun (Fr/It/Sp)
Regarde les hommes tomber
Règle du Jeu, La
Reine Margot, La (Fr/Ger/It)
Rempart des Béguines, Le
 (Fr/It)
Rendez-vous d'Anna, Les
 (Fr/Bel/WGer)
Rendez-vous de Paris, Les
Requiem pour un Vampire
 (Fr/Ger)
Retour d'Afrique, Le (Switz/Fr)
Retour de Martin Guerre, Le
Return of Sabata (It/Fr/WGer)
Return of the Musketeers, The
 (GB/Fr/Sp)
Reunion (Fr/WGer/GB)
Revolving Doors, The
 (Can/Fr)
Riaba Ma Poule
Rider on the Rain (Fr/It)
Ridicule
Rigolboche
Rise and Fall of a Little Film
 Company from a Novel by
 James Hadley Chase
Roads of Exile, The
 (Fr/Switz/GB)
Road to Salina (Fr/It)
Rocco and His Brothers (It/Fr)
Roi des Aulnes, Les
 (Fr/Ger/GB)
Roman de Renard
Romantic Englishwoman, The
 (GB/Fr)
Romuald et Juliette
Ronde, La
Roseaux Sauvages, Les
Roselyne and the Lions
Rothschild's Violin
 (Fr/Switz/Fin/Hun)
Rouge Baiser (Fr/WGer)
Rough Magic (GB/Fr)
Round Midnight (US/Fr)
Route de Corinthe, La
 (Fr/It/Greece)
Route One/USA (US/Fr/GB/It)
Rupture, La (Fr/It/Bel)

Sacrifice, The (Swe/Fr)
Salaam Bombay! (Ind/Fr/GB)
Saló, o le Centoventi Giornate
 de Sodoma (It/Fr)
Salomé (Fr/It)
Salon Kitty (It/Fr/WGer)
Salut Cousin!
 (Fr/Bel/Alg/Luxembourg)
Same Old Song (Fr/Switz/GB)
Samourai, Le (Fr/It)
Sang d'un Poète, Le
Sans Soleil
Sarraounia (Fr/Burkina Faso)

Sauvage, Le (Fr/It)
Sauve Qui Peut-la Vie
 (Switz/Fr)
Savage Nights
Scene of the Crime, The
Scent of Green Papaya, The
Scoumoune, La (Fr/It)
Season Five (Iran/Fr)
Second Chance (Lelouch)
Second Time, The (It/Fr)
Secret, The (Fr/It)
Secret de Mayerling, Le
Section Spéciale (Fr/It/WGer)
Seins de glace, Les
Sélect Hotel
Semaine de Vacances, Une
S'en fout la mort
Sentinelle, La
Séparation, La
Serpent, The (Fr/It/WGer)
Servante et Maîtresse
Seven Nights in Japan (GB/Fr)
Seven Women for Satan
Sex Shop (Fr/It/WGer)
Shanghai Triad
 (HK/China/Fr)
Shark's Son
Shattered (It/Fr)
Sheriff, Le
Shooting Stars
Sicilian Clan, The
Signe du Lion, Le
Sign of the Gladiator
 (It/Fr/WGer)
Si Jolie Petite Plage, Une
Silence de la mer, Le
Silence est d'Or, Le
Silences of the Palaces, The
 (Fr/Tun)
Silencieux, Le (Fr/It)
Silent Cry, The (GB/WGer/Fr)
Sin Compasión (Peru/Mex/Fr)
Sirène du Mississippi, La (Fr/It)
Si tous les gars du monde…
Sleeping Car Murder, The
Slightly Pregnant Man, The
 (Fr)
Smoking/No Smoking
Snobs (Fr/Switz)
Sodom and Gomorrah (Fr/It)
Soigne ta Droite (Fr/Switz)
Someone Else's America
 (Fr/GB/Ger)
Sommersby (US/Fr)
So there,
Souffle au Coeur, Le
 (Fr/It/WGer)
Soupirant, Le
Souriante Madame Beudet, La
Sous le Soleil de Satan
Sous les Toits de Paris
South, The (Sp/Fr)
Splendor (It/Fr)
Spring into Summer
State of Siege (Fr/It/WGer)
Stavisky… (Fr/It)
Stealing Beauty (It/GB/Fr)
Stepfather
Story of Adèle H., The
Strange Place to Meet, A
Stranger (Ind/Fr)
Subway
Success Is the Best Revenge
 (GB/Fr)
Summer in La Goulette, A
 (Fr/Tun)
Sunday in the Country
Sunflower (It/Fr)
Sur (Arg/Fr)
Swann in Love
Sweet Movie (Fr/Can/WGer)
Symphonie Pastorale, La

Tale of Springtime, A
Tales of Ordinary Madness
 (Fr/It)
Tango
Tango Lesson, The
 (GB/Fr/Arg/Jap/Ger)
Tant qu'on a la Santé
Tartuffe

Tatie Danielle
Tavaszi Zápor (Hun/Fr)
Taxandria (Fr/Bel/Ger)
Taxi Blues (USSR/Fr)
Tenant, The
Ten Days' Wonder
Tenue de Soirée
Terminus (Fr/WGer)
Tess (Fr/GB)
Testament d'Orphée, Le
Tête Contre les Murs, La
That Night in Varennes (Fr/It)
That Obscure Object of Desire
 (Fr/Sp)
Themroc
Thérèse
These Foolish Things
They Call That an Accident
They Came to Rob Las Vegas
 (Sp/Fr/WGer/It)
Thief of Baghdad, The
 (Donner – GB/Fr)
This Sweet Sickness
Thomas l'Imposteur
Those Who Love Me Will Take
 the Train
1000 Eyes of Dr Mabuse, The
 (WGer/Fr/It)
Three Brothers (It/Fr)
Three Colours: Blue
Three Colours: Red
 (Fr/Switz)Pol)
Three Colours: White (Fr/Pol)
Three Crowns of the Sailor
3 Men and a Cradle
Three Sisters (It/Fr/Ger)
Tiger of Eschnapur, The
 (WGer/It/Fr)
Tilaï (Burkina Faso/Switz/Fr)
Tiré à Part
Tirez sur le Pianiste
Tit and the Moon, The (Sp/Fr)
To Kill a Priest (US/Fr)
Tombes du Ciel
Toni
Too Late (Fr/Romania)
To Our Loves
Torrents of Spring (It/Fr)
To Speak the Unspeakable:
 The Message of Elie Wiesel
 (Hun/Fr)
Total Eclipse (Fr/GB/Bel)
Toto the Hero (Bel/Fr/Ger)
Touchez pas au Grisbi (Fr/It)
Tous les matins du monde
Tournoi, Le
Toute une Nuit (Fr/Bel)
Tout Va Bien (Fr/It)
Traffic (Fr/It)
Tragedy of Carmen, The
Train, The (US/Fr/It)
Traitement de Choc (Fr/It)
Trances (Mor/Fr)
Trans-Europ-Express
Trial, The (Welles –
 Fr/It/WGer)
Tristana (Fr/It/Sp)
Trois Vies et une Seule Morte
Trop Belle Pour Toi!
Trop de Bonheur
Trou, Le (Fr/It)
Trou Normand, Le
Truce, The (It/Fr/Ger)
Turtle on Its Back
Twelve Tasks of Asterix, The
23:58
2 x 50 Years of French Cinema
 (GB/Fr)

Ulysses' Gaze (Greece/It/Fr)
Underground (Fr/Ger/Hun)
Un Deux Trois Soleil
Unforgettable Summer, An
 (Fr/Romania)
Unhook the Stars
Uns et les Autres, Les
Until the End of the World
 (Ger/Fr/Aust)
Uranus
Urga (Fr/USSR)
U Turn (US/Fr)

Vacances de M. Hulot, Les
Vagabonde
Valdez il Mezzosangue
 (It/Sp/Fr)
Vallée, La
Valmont (Fr/GB)
Valseuses, Les
Vampires, Les
Van Gogh
Vanishing, The (Neth/Fr)
Veillées d'Armes
Vent d'Est (Fr/It/WGer)
Verdict (Cayatte – Fr/It)
Vérité, La (Fr/It)
Versailles rive gauche
Vertiges (Fr/GB)
Vie à l'Envers, La
Vie de Jésus, La
Vie est à Nous, La
Vie est Belle, La
 (Bel/Fr/Zaire)
Vie est un Roman, La
Vieil Homme et l'Enfant, Le
Vieille Dame Indigne, La
Vie Rêvée des Anges, La
Vincent & Théo (GB/Fr)
Violation of Justine, The
 (Fr/It/Can)
Viol de Vampire, Le
Violette et François
Violette Nozière (Fr/Can)
Violons du Bal, Les
Virgin (Breillat)
Virgin (Karanovic – Yugo/Fr)
Virgin for Saint Tropez, A
 (Fr/It)
Visiteurs, Les
Viva la Muerte (Fr/Tun)
Viva la Vie
Viva Maria! (Fr/It)
Viva Portugal (WGer/Fr)
Vivement Dimanche!
Vivre pour Vivre (Fr/It)
Vivre sa Vie
Vladimir et Rosa
 (Fr/WGer/US)
Voie Lactée, La (Fr/It)
Voleurs, Les
Voyage, The (Arg/Fr)
Voyager (Ger/Fr)
Voyage-Surprise

Wages of Fear, The (Fr/It)
Wall, The
Wanderer, The
War of the Buttons (GB/Fr)
Wedding in Galilee (Bel/Fr)
Weekend (Fr/It)
Western
We Were One Man
What? (Fr/It/WGer)
What Makes David Run?
What's New Pussycat?
 (US/Fr)
When the Cat's Away…
White Fang (It/Fr/Sp)
White Man's Burden (US/Fr)
White Nights
 (Visconti – Fr/It)
Who Are You Polly Maggoo?
William Christie at Les Arts
 Florissants
Will It Snow for Christmas?
Wings of Desire (WGer/Fr)
Winter's Tale, A (Rohmer)
Woman Next Door, The
Woman or Two, A
Writing on the Wall, The
 (Fr/Bel)

Yaaba (Burkina Faso/Fr/Switz)
Yeux sans Visage, Les
Young Ladies of Wilko, The
 (Pol/Fr)
Young Törless (WGer/Fr)
Yoyo

Z (Fr/Alg)
Zazie dans le Métro
Zéro de Conduite
Zouzou

Appendix 19

German Films

Adventures of Baron
  Munchausen, The (Gilliam –
  GB/WGer)
Adventures of Baron
  Munchhausen, The (von
  Baky)
Adventures of Pinocchio
  (GB/Fr/Czech Republic/US)
Adventures of Werner Holt,
  The
Aguirre, Wrath of God
Alice in the Cities
All-Round Reduced Personality
  – Redupers,The
American Friend, The
  (WGer/Fr)
American Soldier, The
Anita: Dances of Vice
Anou Banou or the Daughters
  of Utopia
Army of Lovers or Revolt of
  the Perverts
Artistes at the Top of the Big
  Top: Disorientated
Asphalt Night
Asterix and the Big Fight
  (Fr/WGer)
Asterix Conquers America
Astragale, L' (Fr/WGer)
Attentat, L' (WGer/Fr/It)
Au Revoir les Enfants
  (Fr/WGer)
Autumn Sonata

Baby of Mâcon, The
  (GB/Neth/Fr/Ger)
Bagdad Café
Baker's Bread
Benefit of the Doubt (US/Ger)
Berlin Affair, The (It/WGer)
Berlin Alexanderplatz
Beware of a Holy Whore
Bewegte Mann, Der
Beyond Evil (It/Fr/WGer)
Beyond Silence
Beyond the Clouds (Fr/It/Ger)
Birth of a Nation, The
  (Wyborny)
Bitter Tears of Petra von Kant,
  The
Black Cannon Incident, The
  (China/WGer)
Blind Spot
Bloodline (US/WGer)
Blue Angel, The
Bluebeard's Castle
Blue Exile, The
  (Tur/Ger/Greece)
Boat, The
Bolwieser
Bongo Man
Borsalino & Co (Fr/It/WGer)
Burning Life
Business Affair, A
  (GB/Fr/Ger/Sp)

Cabinet of Dr Caligari, The
Calendar (Can/Arm/Ger)
Call of the Wild, The
  (GB/WGer/Fr/It/Sp)
Capitano, Il (Swe/Fin/Ger/Ded)
Carla's Song (Ger/Sp)
Cassandra Crossing, The
  (GB/It/WGer)
Cat o'Nine Tails, The
  (It/Fr/WGer)
Céleste
Cement Garden, The
  (GB/Ger/Fr)
César and Rosalie (It/Fr/WGer)
Chariots of the Gods
Charlotte (Fr/It/WGer)
Child's Play
Chinese Boxes
Chinese Roulette (WGer/Fr)
Christiane F

Chronicle of Anna Magdalena
  Bach (It/WGer)
Circle of Deceit
City of Angels (US/Ger)
City of Lost Souls
Class Relations (WGer/Fr)
Climax
Clowns, The (It/Fr/WGer)
Cobra Verde
Cold Fever (Ice/Ger/Switz/US)
Colonel Redl (Hun/WGer/Aus)
Coming Out
Companeros (It/Sp/WGer)
Confessions of a Bigamist
  (It/WGer)
Confessions of a Sixth Form
  Girl
Confessions of Winifred
  Wagner, The
Conformist, The (It/Fr/WGer)
Congress Dances
Consequence, The
Count Dracula (Sp/It/WGer)
Coup de Grâce (WGer/Fr)
Coup pour Coup (Fr/WGer)
Cousins in Love (Fr/WGer)
Crimetime (GB/US/Ger)
Criminal
Cross of Iron (GB/WGer)
Cry Onion (It/Sp/WGer)

Damned, The
  (Visconti – It/WGer)
Dance of Love
Dance of the Wind
  (GB/Ger/Fr/Neth)
Daughters of Darkness
  (Bel/Fr/WGer/It)
Dead Pigeon on
  Beethoven Street
Dead Man (US/Ger)
Dear Mother, I'm All Right
Death in the Sun
Death Is My Trade
Death of Maria Malibran, The
Death of Mario Ricci, The
  (Switz/Fr/WGer)
Death Watch (Fr/WGer)
Decameron, The (It/Fr/WGer)
Deep End (WGer/US)
Degree of Murder, A
Dentellière, La
  (Fr/Switz/WGer)
Désert des Tartares, Le
  (Fr/It/WGer)
Despair (WGer/Fr)
Destiny
Devil's Advocate, The
  (Des Teufels Advokat)
Devil's Island (Fridriksson –
  Ice/Nor/Ger/Den)
Diary of a Lost Girl
Dr M (Ger/It/Fr)
Dr Mabuse, The Gambler
Don Giovanni (It/Fr/WGer)
Don't Cry for Me Little Mother
  (WGer/Yug)
Don't Get Me Started (GB/Ger)
Dossier 51, Le (Fr/WGer)
Dreigroschenoper, Die
Drifting Clouds (Fin/Ger/Fr)
Due to an Act of God
Du Rififi à Paname
  (Fr/It/WGer)

Effi Briest
Eika Katappa
End of Violence, The
  (US/Fr/Ger)
Enter the 7 Virgins (HK/WGer)
Erendira (Fr/Mex/WGer)
Erotic Quartet (US/WGer/It)
Erotique (US/Ger/HK)
Escape Route to Marseilles
Eternity and a Day
  (Greece/Fr/Ger)

Europa, Europa (Fr/Ger)
Even Dwarfs Started Small
Exquisite Tenderness (US/Ger)

Faraway, So Close
Farewell, Stranger
Farewell to False Paradise
  (WGer/Tur)
Fata Morgana
Fatherland (GB/WGer/Fr)
Faust
Faustrecht der Freiheit
Fear (It/WGer)
Fear Eats the Soul
Fedora
Female Perversions (US/Ger)
Femme française, Une
  (Fr/GB/Ger)
F for Fake (Fr/Iran/WGer)
Fiorile (It/Fr/Ger)
First Time With Feeling
  (Fr/WGer)
Fistful of Dollars, A
  (It/WGer/Sp)
Fitzcarraldo
Flickering Roads
Flight to Berlin
Forbidden (GB/WGer)
Fortini/Cani
  (It/Fr/WGer/GB/US)
40 Metre Square Germany
Friends and Husbands
  (WGer/Fr)
From Pole to Equator
  (It/WGer)
From the Cloud to the
  Resistance (It/Fr/WGer/GB)
From the Life of the
  Marionettes
Further Gesture, A
  (GB/Ger/Jap/Ire)
Future Is Woman, The
  (It/Fr/WGer)
Future of Emily, The
  (Fr/WGer)

Gai Savoir, Le (Fr/WGer)
Garden of the Finzi-Continis,
  The (It/WGer)
Gathering of Old Men, A
  (US/GB/WGer)
Genuine
Georgette Meunier
German Chainsaw Massacre,
  The
German Sisters, The
Germany in Autumn
Germany, Pale Mother
Germany, Year Zero (It/WGer)
Ghost Chase
Ginger & Fred (It/Fr/WGer)
Girlfriend, The (Arg/WGer)
Girl in a Boot
Gods of the Plague
Golem, The
Gorilla Bathes at Noon
Grass Is Always Greener, The
Guy (GB/Ger)

Handmaid's Tale, The (US/Ger)
Hanussen (Hun/WGer)
Hard Rain
  (US/GB/Jap/Ger/Den)
Heartbreakers, The
Heart of Glass
Heimat
Held for Questioning
Hellhounds of Alaska, The
Hindered (GB/WGer)
Hitler – a Career
Hitler, a Film from Germany
  (WGer/Fr/GB)
Hollow Reed (GB/Ger)
House of Spirits, The
  (Ger/Den/Port)
How Sweet Is Her Valley

I Am My Own Woman
i.d.
I Love You, I'll Kill You
Imposters (US/WGer)

In a Year with 13 Moons
Infernal Trio, The (Fr/It/WGer)
In Georgia
Innocent, The
  (Schlesinger – GB/Ger)
Innocents with Dirty Hands
  (Fr/It/WGer)
Inside Out (GB/WGer)
I Was, I Am, I Shall Be
I Was on Mars

Jeder für sich und Gott gegen
  alle (The Engima of Kaspar
  Hauser)
Joan of Arc of Mongolia
John Heartfield: Photomonteur
Josephine
Joyless Street
Just a Gigolo

Kama Sutra: A Tale of Love
  (Ind/GB/Jap/Ger)
Kämeradschaft (Ger/Fr)
Karl May
Kaspar Hauser
Katzelmacher
Keiner Liebt Mich
King, Queen, Knave (US/WGer)
Knickers Ahoy (WGer/It)
Knife in the Head
Knight Moves (US/Ger)
Komitas
Korczak (Pol/Ger/Fr/GB)
Kühle Wampe

Lacombe Lucien (Fr/WGer/It)
Land of Silence and Darkness
Last Exit to Brooklyn
Last Hole, The
Latin Boys Go to Hell
  (US/Ger/Sp/Jap)
Left-Handed Woman, The
Lessons in Darkness (Fr/Ger)
Letters from the East
  (GB/Ger/Fin/Swe)
Liebelei
Life Is All You Get
Life on a String (China/GB/Ger)
Lightning Over Water
  (WGer/Swe)
Lili Marleen
Lina Braake
Little Angel
Little Godard, A
Little Night Music, A
  (Aus/WGer)
Living Dead, The
Lola
Lola Montès (Fr/WGer)
Lord of the Dance
  (Fr/Switz/WGer)
Lost Honour of Katharina
  Blum, The
Love in Germany, A (Fr/WGer)
Love Is Colder than Death
Ludwig (Fr/It/WGer)
Ludwig – Requiem for a
  Virgin King
Ludwig's Cook

M (Lang)
Madame Butterfly
  (Fr/Jap/Ger/GB)
Madame X
Mädchen in Uniform
Mädchen Rosemarie, Das
Magician of Lublin, The
  (WGer/Isr)
Main Actor, The
Making Up
Malevil (Fr/WGer)
Malou
Malpertuis (Bel/Fr/WGer)
Manhunt in Milan (It/WGer)
Man Like Eva, A
Man to Respect, A (It/WGer)
Man Who Knew Too Little,
  The (US/Ger)
Marquise von O..., Die
  (WGer/Fr)
Marriage of Maria Braun, The

Martha
Mau Mau
Medea (It/Fr/WGer)
Memory of Justice, The
  (GB/US/WGer)
Men
Merchant of Four Seasons, The
Michael Kohlhaas
Mirror, The (WGer/GB)
Mission, The (Sayyad –
  US/WGer)
Moine, Le (Fr/It/WGer)
Moon 44
Moses and Aaron (Fr/WGer)
Motel (US/WGer)
Mother and Son (Rus/Ger)
Mother Küster's Trip to
  Heaven
Mute Witness (GB/Ger/Rus)
My Father Is Coming (Ger/US)
My Mother's Courage
  (Ger/GB/Aus)
My Name Is Nobody
  (It/Fr/WGer)
My Private War
My 20th Century
  (Hun/WGer/Cuba)

Name of the Rose, The
  (WGer/It/Fr)
Nasty Girl, The
Néa (Fr/WGer)
Nela
NeverEnding Story, The
NeverEnding Story II: The
  Next Chapter, The
NeverEnding Story III: Escape
  from Fantasia, The
Nibelungen, Die
Nicht Versöhnt
Nico Icon
Night Paths
Night Sun (It/Fr/Ger)
1900 (It/Fr/WGer)
No Answer from F.P.1
No Man's Land
  (Switz/Fr/WGer/GB)
No Mercy, No Future
Nora Helmer
Nosferatu – eine Symphonie
  des Grauens
Nosferatu the Vampyre
  (WGer/Fr)
Nostradamus (GB/Ger)
Notebook on Cities and Clothes
November Moon (WGer/Fr)

Oberwald Mystery, The
  (It/WGer)
Occasional Work of a
  Female Slave
Odessa File, The (GB/WGer)
One Man's War (Fr/WGer)
1 + 1 = 3
Orchestra Rehearsal (It/WGer)
Othon (WGer/It)
Out of Order
Outside In (GB/WGer)

Palermo or Wolfsburg
  (WGer/It)
Paolozzi Story, The (GB/WGer)
Parapluies de Cherbourg, Les
  (Fr/WGer)
Paris, Texas (WGer/Fr/GB)
Parsifal (WGer/Fr)
Party – Nature Morte, The
Passion of Darkly Noon, The
  (GB/Ger/Bel)
Patriot, The
Pedestrian, The (WGer/Switz)
Peppermint Freedom
Petit Théâtre de Jean Renoir,
  Le (Fr/It/WGer)
Pied Piper
  (Barta – Czech/WGer)
Pink Floyd Live at Pompeii
  (Fr/Bel/WGer)
Platz, Der
Point Is to Change It, The
Polygraph, The (Can/Fr/Ger)

Possession (Fr/WGer)
Poto and Cabengo (WGer/US)
Power of Men Is the Patience of
  Women, The
Prince of Jutland
  (Fr/GB/Den/Neth/Ger)
Prince Valiant (Ger/GB/Ire/US)
Private Popsicle (Isr/WGer)
Promise, The (von Trotta –
  Ger/Fr))
Punk in London

Querelle (WGer/Fr)

Radio On (GB/WGer)
Rainmaker, The (Ger/US)
Raskolnikow
Reason to Live, a Reason to
  Die, A (It/Fr/Sp/WGer)
Rebecca's Daughters (GB/Ger)
Red Rings of Fear (It/Sp/WGer)
Reggae Sunsplash II
Reine Margot, La (Fr/WGer)
Requiem pour un Vampire
  (Fr/Ger)
Reunion (Fr/WGer/GB)
Roi des Aulnes, Le (Fr/Ger/GB)
Rosalie Goes Shopping
Rosa Luxemburg
Rouge Baiser (Fr/WGer)

Salmonberries
Salon Kitty (It/WGer/Fr)
Sandman, The
Sankofa (US/Ger/Ghana/
  Burkina Faso)
Satan's Brew
Scarlet Letter, The (WGer/Sp)
Schizophrenia
Schramm
Schtonk!
Second Awakening of Christa
  Klages, The
Secret Face, The
Secrets of a Soul
Section Spéciale (Fr/It/WGer)
Será Posible el Sur
Serbian Girl, The
Sgt Pepper's Lonely Hearts
  Club Band (US/WGer)
Serpent, The (Fr/It/WGer)
Serpent's Egg, The (WGer//US)
Servicer, The (WGer/US)
Seven Minutes (US/WGer)
71 Fragments of a Chronology
  of Chance (Aus/Ger)
Sex Life in a Convent
Sex Shop (Fr/It/WGer)
Shirin's Wedding
Sign of the Gladiator
  (It/Fr/WGer)
Signs of Life
Silent Cry, The (GB/WGer/Fr)
Singing Ringing Tree, The
Sisters or the Balance of
  Happiness
Slow Attack
Smilla's Feeling for Snow
  (Ger/Den/Swe)
Someone Else's America
  (Fr/GB/Ger)
Something to Believe In
  (GB/Ger)
Song for Beko, A (Ger/Arm)
Souffle au Coeur, Le
  (Fr/It/WGer)
Soufrière, La
South Africa Belongs to Us
  (WGer/SAf)
Spicy Rice (WGer/Switz)
Spinnen, Die
Spione
Spring Symphony
Stalingrad
Stammheim
Stamping Ground
Starke Ferdinand, Der
State of Siege (It/Fr/WGer)
Station Six – Sahara
  (GB/WGer)
Stranger Than Paradise

(US/WGer)
Stroszek
Subjective Factor, The
Succubus
Sudden Fortune of the Good
  People of Kombach, The
Sugarbaby
Summer in the City
Super 8½
Sweet Movie (Fr/Can/WGer)
Swing, The
Swiss Conspiracy, The
  (US/WGer)

Tales from the Vienna Woods
  (Aus/WGer)
Tango Lesson, The
  (GB/Ger/Arg/Jap/Ger)
Taxandria (Fr/Bel/Ger)
Taxi zum Klo
Tenderness of the Wolves
Terminus (Fr/WGer)
Terror 2000
Testament of Dr Mabuse, The
There's No Sex Like Snow Sex
They Came to Rob Las
  Vegas(Sp/Fr/WGer/It)
Third Generation, The
1000 Eyes of Dr Mabuse, The
  (WGer/It/Fr)
3 Women in Love
Three Sisters (It/Fr/Ger)
Tickle in the Heart, A
Tiger of Eschnapur
  (It/Fr/WGer)
Tödliche Maria, Die
Tokyo-Ga (WGer/US)
To the Devil a Daughter
  (GB/WGer)
Toto the Hero (Bel/Fr/Ger)
Trial, The (Welles –
  Fr/It/WGer)
Truce, The (It/Fr/Ger)
Twilight's Last Gleaming
  (US/WGer)

Uccello dalle Piume di
  Cristallo,L' (It/Ger)

Italian Films

Accattone
A Double Tour (Fr/It)
Adventures of Gerard, The
  (GB/It/Switz)
Africa Addio
After the Fox (It/US)
Age of Cosimo de Medici, The
Agony and the Ecstasy, The
  (US/It)
Agression, L' (Fr/It)
Alexander the Great
  (Angelopoulos – Greece/It)
Alfredo Alfredo (It/Fr)
Allegro Non Troppo
Allonsanfan
Alphaville (Fr/It)
Amarcord (It/Fr)
Amazons, The (It/Fr)
Amiche, Le
Amore, L'
Amore Molesto, L'
And Now My Love (Fr/It)
And the Ship Sails On (It/Fr)
Année Dernière à Marienbad,
  L' (Fr/It)
Anticristo, L'
Appartement, L (Fr/Sp/It)
Aprile
Arabian Nights (It/Fr)
Armée des Ombres, L' (Fr/It)
Assassination of Trotsky, The
  (Fr/It/GB)
Attentat, L' (Fr/It/WGer)
Audience, The
Augustine of Hippo
Austerlitz
  (Fr/It/Liechtenstein/Yug)

Underground (Fr/Ger/Hun)
Until the End of the World
  (Ger/Fr/Aust)

Vampyr
Vanessa
Varieté
Vengeance (It/WGer)
Vent d'Est (It/WGer/Fr)
Venus in Furs
Verlorene, Der
Veronika Voss
Virgin Machine
Viva Portugal (WGer/Fr)
Vladimir et Rosa (Fr/WGer/US)
Voyager (Ger/Fr)
Voyage to Cythera
  (Greece/WGer/It/Fr)

Warshots
War Zone
Weber, Die
Westler: East of the Wall
What? (It/Fr/WGer)
Wheels & Deals
Where the Green Ants Dream
Who Is Killing the Great Chefs
  of Europe? (WGer/US)
Wilde (GB/US/Jap/Ger)
Wild Game
Will My Mother Go Back to
  Berlin? (Ger/US)
Wings of Desire (WGer/Fr)
Wise Blood (US/WGer)
Wittstock, Wittstock (Ger/Aus)
Woman in Flames, A
Woyzeck
W.R. – Mysteries of the
  Organism (Yugo/WGer)
Wrong Movement

Year of the Quiet Sun, A
  (Pol/US/WGer)
Yesterday Girl
Younger and Younger
Young Poisoner's Handbook,
  The (GB/Ger)
Young Törless (WGer/Fr)

Avventura, L'
Ay! Carmela (Sp/It)

Baba Yaga (It/Fr)
Bad Boy Bubby (Aust/It)
Bad Man's River (Sp/It/Fr)
Bal, Le (Fr/It/Alg)
Barabbas
Barbarella (Fr/It)
Barnabo of the Mountains
  (Fr/It/Switz)
Battle of Algiers, The (Alg/It)
Beauté du Diable, La (Fr/It)
Before and After Sex
Before the Revolution
Behind Convent Walls
Belle de Jour (Fr/It)
Belles de nuit, Les (Fr/It)
Bellissima
Belly of an Architect, The
  (GB/It)
Benvenuta (Bel/Fr/It)
Berlin Affair, The (It/WGer)
Beyond, The
Beyond Evil (It/Fr/WGer)
Beyond the Clouds (Fr/It/Ger)
Beyond the Door
Bible...In the Beginning, The
  (It/US)
Biches, Les (Fr/It)
Bicycle Thieves
Bidone, Il (It/Fr)
Big Silence, The (Fr/It)
Bisexual (Fr/It)
Bits and Pieces
Bitter Rice
Black Emanuelle

Black Holes
Black Holiday
Black Orpheus (Fr/It/Braz)
Black Sabbath (Fr/It)
Blaise Pascal (Fr/It)
Blazing Guns (It/Sp)
Blindman (US/It)
Blood for Dracula (It/Fr)
Blood Money (HK/It/Sp/US)
Blood River (It/Sp)
Blood Ties
Blow Out (Ferreri – Fr/It)
Blow to the Heart
Blue Belle (GB/It)
Boatman
Boccaccio '70
Bonne Année, La (Fr/It)
Boomerang (Giovanni – Fr/It)
Borsalino (Fr/It)
Borsalino & Co (Fr/It/WGer)
Boucher, Le (Fr/It)
Bread and Chocolate
Bride Wore Black, The (Fr/It)
Brief Vacation, A (It/Sp)
Bronx Warriors
Brother Sun, Sister Moon
(It/GB)
Brutti, sporchi e cattivi
Bullet for the General, A
Burglars, The (Fr/It)
By Nightfall

Cage aux Folles, La (Fr/It)
Cage aux Folles II, La (Fr/It)
Cage aux Folles III: The
Wedding (Fr/It)
Call of the Wild, The
(WGer/GB/Fr/It/Sp)
Caligula (US/It)
Cammina Cammina
Candido Erotico
Candy (US/It/Fr)
Cannibal
Cannibals, The
Canterbury Tales, The (It/Fr)
Carabiniers, Les (Fr/It)
Carmen (Rosi – Fr/It)
Casanova '70 (Fr/It)
Cassandra Crossing, The
(GB/It/WGer)
Catherine and Co (Fr/It)
Cat o' Nine Tails, The
(It/WGer/Fr)
Cecilia, La (It/Fr)
Cela s'Appelle l'Aurore (Fr/It)
César and Rosalie (Fr/It/WGer)
Charlotte (Fr/It/WGer)
Chère Louise (Fr/It)
China Is Near
China 9, Liberty 37
Chi Sei?
Choses de la Vie, Les (Fr/It)
Christ Stopped at Eboli (It/Fr)
Chronicle of a Death Foretold
(It/Fr)
Chronicle of Anna Magdalena
Bach (Fr/WGer)
Cinderella – Italian Style (It/Fr)
Cinema Paradiso (It/Fr)
Cinema Paradiso: The Special
Edition (It/Fr)
Circumstance, The
City of Women (It/Fr)
Cléo de 5 à 7 (Fr/It)
Closed Circuit
Clowns, The (It/Fr/WGer)
Cobra (Boisset – Fr/It)
Cold Sweat (Fr/It)
Colossus of Rhodes, The
(It/Sp/Fr)
Comfort of Strangers, The
(It/GB)
Commare Secca, La
Companeros (It/Sp/WGer)
Confessions of a Bigamist
(WGer/It)
Conformist, The (It/Fr/WGer)
Conquest (It/Sp/Mex)
Conversation Piece (It/Fr)
Coraje del Pueblo, El (Bol/It)
Counsellor, The (It/Sp)

Count Dracula (Sp/It/WGer)
Crazy Joe (US/It)
Creepers
Crime Busters
Cronaca di un amore
Cry Onion (It/Sp/WGer)
Cuba Libre (It/Cuba)
Cyclone, The

Dame aux Camélias, La (Fr/It)
Damned, The
(Visconti – It/WGer)
Danger: Diabolik (It/Fr)
Dark Eyes
Daughters of Darkness
(Bel/Fr/WGer/It)
Day of the Beast, The (Sp/It)
Deadly Trap, The (Fr/It)
Deaf Smith & Johnny Ears
Dear Diary (It/Fr)
Death in Venice
Death of a Cameraman
Decameron, The (It/Fr/WGer)
Demons
Demons 2
Désert des Tartares, Le
(Fr/It/WGer)
Deserter and the Nomads, The
(Czech/It)
Dialogue des Carmélites, Le
(Fr/It)
Diary of a Chambermaid, The
(Buñuel – Fr/It)
Dimenticare Venezia (It/Fr)
Django (It/Sp)
Django Kill (It/Sp)
Docteur Popaul (Fr/It)
Dr M (Ger/It/Fr)
Dolce Vita, La (It/Fr)
Domicile Conjugal (Fr/It)
Don Giovanni (It/Fr/WGer)
Don Juan or If Don Juan Were a
Woman (Fr/It)
Don't Look Now (GB/It)
Doulos, Le (Fr/It)
Down the Ancient Stairs (It/Fr)
Drama of the Rich (It/Fr)
Dramma della Gelosia (It/Sp)
Du Rififi à Paname
(Fr/It/WGer)
During the Summer

Eclipse, The (It/Fr)
8½
8-Wheel Beast, The (It/Fr)
Elective Affinities (It/Fr)
Eléna et les Hommes (Fr/It)
Emanuelle and the Last
Cannibals
Emmerdeur, L' (Fr/It)
En Cas de Malheur (Fr/It)
Era Notte a Roma (It/Fr)
Ercole alla conquista di
Atlantide (It/Fr)
Erotic Quartet (US/WGer/It)
Eve (Fr/It)
Everybody's Fine (It/Fr)

Fair Game
Farinelli Il Castrato (It/Bel)
Faute de l'Abbé Mouret, La
(Fr/It)
Fear (It/WGer)
Fellini-Satyricon (It/Fr)
Fellini's Casanova
Fellini's Roma (It/Fr)
Femme Infidèle, La (Fr/It)
Fiorile (It/Fr/Ger)
Firemen's Ball, The (Czech/It)
Fistful of Dollars, A
(It/WGer/Sp)
Fists in the Pocket
Fit To Be Untied
Flesh for Frankenstein (It/Fr)
Flic, Un (Fr/It)
Flight of the Innocent
Folle à Tuer (Fr/It)
Footman, The
For a Few Dollars More
(It/Sp/WGer)
Forever Mary

Fortini/Cani
(It/Fr/WGer/GB/US)
Four Flies on Grey Velvet
(It/Fr)
Four Nights of a Dreamer
(Fr/It)
Francesco, giullare di Dio
From Hell to Victory (Fr/It/Sp)
From Pole to Equator (It/WGer)
From the Cloud to the
Resistance (It/Fr/WGer/GB)
Fury (It/GB)
Future Is Woman, The
(It/Fr/WGer)

Galileo (Cavani – It/Bulg)
Gang, Le (Fr/It)
Garden of the Finzi-Continis,
The (It/WGer)
Germany, Year Zero (It/WGer)
Germinal (Fr/Bel/It)
Giant of Marathon, The (It/Fr)
Ginger & Fred (Fr/It/WGer)
Giorno della prima di 'Close
Up', Il
Girl from Trieste, The
Giù la Testa
Golden Coach, The (Fr/It)
Goliath and the Barbarians
(It/US)
Good Morning Babylon
(It/Fr/US)
Good, the Bad and the Ugly,
The
Gospel According to St
Matthew, The (It/Fr)
Grazie Zia
Guns for San Sebastian
(Fr/Mex/It)

Heroes, The (Sp/It/Fr)
Histoires Extraordinaires
(Fr/It)
History Lessons
Hitler: the Last Ten Days
(GB/It)
Ho! (Fr/It)
Holocaust 2000 (It/GB)
Homme de Marrakesh, L'
(Fr/It/Sp)
Homme de Rio, L' (Fr/It)
Honey Pot, The (US/It)
Hors la vie (Fr/It/Bel)
House by the Cemetery, The
House of Exorcism, The
House of Smiles
How to Destroy the Reputation
of the World's Greatest
Secret Agent (Fr/It)
Humanoid, The
Hunchback of Notre Dame, The
(Delannoy – Fr/It)

Icicle Thief
Identification of a Woman
(It/Fr)
Illustrious Corpses (It/Fr)
Immortelle, L' (Fr/It/Tur)
Infernal Trio (Fr/It/WGer)
Inferno
Inheritance, The
Inhibitions
Inner Circle, The
Innocent, The (Visconti – It/Fr)
Innocents with Dirty Hands
(Fr/It/WGer)
Intervista
In the Name of the Father
Invincible Barbarian
Island of Mutations
Italy: Year One

Jane Eyre (GB/It/Fr/US)
Jean de Florette (Fr/It)
Just Before Nightfall (Fr/It)

Kapo (It/Fr)
Killer Nun

Lacombe Lucien (Fr/It/WGer)
Lady L (Fr/It)

Lancelot du Lac (Fr/It)
Landscape in the Mist
(Greece/Fr/It)
Last Emperor, The (China/It)
Last Feelings
Last Italian Tango, The
Last Moments
Last Snows of Spring, The
Last Tango in Paris (Fr/It)
Last Woman, The (Fr/It)
Leap Into the Void, (It/Fr)
Legend of Frenchie King, The
(Fr/It/Sp/GB)
Legend of the Holy Drinker,
The
Leon Morin, Priest (Fr/It)
Leopard, The
Let's Hope It's a Girl (It/Fr)
Leviathan (US/It)
Libera
Lies to Live by (Babylon)
Life and the Extraordinary
Adventures of Private Ivan
Chonkin, The
(GB/Fr/It/Czech
Republic/Rus)
Life Is Beautiful
Life Size (Sp/Fr/It)
Lion Has Seven Heads, The
(Fr/It)
Living Dead at the Manchester
Morgue, The (Sp/It)
Living It Up
Lizards, The
Long Live the Lady!
Love in a Women's Prison
Luci del Varietà
Lucky Luciano (It/Fr)
Ludwig (Fr/It/WGer)
Luna, La
Luna e l'Altra

Macaroni
Machine That Kills Bad People,
The
Maciste Contro i Mostri
Mad Adventures of 'Rabbi'
Jacob, The (Fr/It)
Madame de... (Fr/It)
Malizia
Mamma Roma
Manhunt in Milan (It/WGer)
Man Named John, A
Manon des Sources
(Fr/It/Switz)
Man on Fire (Fr/It)
Man to Respect, A (It/WGer)
Maschera del Demonio, La
Mask, The
Massacre in Rome (Fr/It)
Master and Margarita, The
(Yugo/It)
Master of Love
Mata-Hari, Agent H21 (Fr/It)
Maternale
Mattei Affair, The
Medea (Fr/It/WGer)
Mediterraneo
Mépris, Le (Fr/It)
Mercenario, Il (It/Sp)
Microcosmos (Fr/Switz/It)
Mignon Has Left (Fr/It)
Milou en mai (Fr/It)
Miracle in Milan
Miroir a deux faces, Le (Fr/It)
Moine, Le (Fr/It/WGer)
Moment of Truth, The (It/Sp)
Montagna del Dio Cannibale, La
Moon in the Gutter, The (Fr/It)
Moses (It/GB)
Mr Klein (Fr/It)
Murder Is a Murder...Is a
Murder, A (Fr/It)
Muriel (Fr/It)
My First 40 Years
My Name Is Nobody
(It/Fr/WGer)

Nada (Fr/It)
Name of the Rose, The
(Fr/It/WGer)

Nana
Naples Connection, The
Necropolis
Nest of Vipers
New Barbarians, The
Night Caller (Fr/It)
Night of San Lorenzo
Night Porter, The
Night Sun (It/Fr/Ger)
Nikita (Fr/It)
1900 (It/Fr/WGer)
Noces Rouges (Fr/It)
Noi Tre
Notte, La (Fr/It)
Nuits Rouges (Fr/It)
Nun and the Devil, The (It/Fr)

Overwald Mystery, The (It/WGer)
Oedipus Rex
Once Upon a Time in the West
One Hamlet Less
Open Doors
Opera
Operation Crossbow (GB/It)
Orchestra Rehearsal (It/WGer)
Order of Death
Order to Kill (Sp/It/Dom)
Orlando (GB/Rus/Fr/It/Neth)
Ossessione
Otello
Othon (WGer/It)
Outside Man, The (Fr/It)

Padre Padrone
Paisà
Palermo or Wolfsburg (WGer/It)
Paranoia (It/Fr)
Partie de Plaisir, Une (Fr/It)
Partner
Pasolini, un Delito Italiano (It/Fr)
Passenger, The (Fr/It/Sp)
Passione d'Amore (Fr/It)
Paura nella Città dei Morti Viventi
Petit Théâtre de Jean Renoir, Le (Fr/It/WGer)
Petomane, Il
Pierrot le Fou (Fr/It)
Pigsty (It/Fr)
Plein Soleil (Fr/It)
Postino, Il (It/Fr)
Posto, Il
Prince of Homburg, The
Private Vices and Public Virtues (It/Yugo)
Prospero's Books (Neth/Fr/It)
Prostitution Racket, The
Puerto Escondido
Pure Formality, A (It/Fr)
Purple Taxi, The (Fr/It/Ire)

Quattro dell'Ave Maria, I
Queimada!
Que la Bête Meure (Fr/It)

Reason to Live, a Reason to Die, A (It/Fr/Sp/WGer)
Rebel Nun, The (It/Fr)
Recuperanti, I
Red Circle (Fr/It)
Red Desert, The (It/Fr)
Red Rings of Fear (It/Sp/WGer)
Red Sun (Fr/It/Sp)
Reine Margot, La (Fr/Ger/It)
Rempart de Béguines, Le (Fr/It)
Repubblica Nostra
Return of Sabata (Fr/It/WGer)
Rider on the Rain (Fr/It)
Rigoletto
Road to Salina (Fr/It)
Rocco and His Brothers (It/Fr)
Roma, Città Aperta
Romeo and Juliet (GB/It)
Route de Corinthe, La (Fr/It/Greece)
Route One/USA (US/Fr/GB/It)
Rupture, La (Fr/It/Bel)
Russicum

Sabata
Saló, o le Centoventi Giornate di Sodoma (It/Fr)
Salomé (Fr/It)
Salon Kitty (It/Fr/WGer)
Salvatore Giuliano
Samourai, Le (Fr/It)
Santa Sangre
Sauvage, Le (Fr/It)
Savage Man, Savage Beast
Sbarco di Anzio, Lo (Anzio)
Scalawag (US/It)
School
Scorta, La
Scoumoune, La (Fr/It)
Second Time, The (It/Fr)
Secret, The (Fr/It)
Sect, The
Section Spéciale (Fr/It/WGer)
Sellout, The (Fr/It)
Senso
Serpent, The (Fr/It/WGer)
Seven Beauties
Sexorcist, The
Sex Shop (Fr/It/WGer)
Shark's Cave, The (It/Sp)
Shattered (Fr/It)
Sheltering Sky, The (GB/It)
Sicilian Cross
Sign of the Gladiator (It/Fr/WGer)
Signora di Tutti, La
Signora Senza Camelie, La
Silence of the Hams (It/US)
Silencieux, Le
Sirène du Mississipi, La (Fr/It)
Slightly Pregnant Man, The (Fr/It)
Sodom and Gomorrah (Fr/It)
Souffle au Coeur, Le (Fr/It/WGer)
Sparrow
Special Day (It/Can)
Splendor (It/Fr)
State of Seige (Fr/It/WGer)
Stavisky... (Fr/It)
Stealing Beauty (It/GB/Fr)Stolen Children, The
Strada, La
Stromboli, Terra di Dio
Sunflower (It/Fr)
Superargo (It/Sp)
Suspiria
Swept Away...by an Unusual Destiny in the Blue Sea of August

Take a Hard Ride (US/It)
Tales of Ordinary Madness (Fr/It)
Tempter, The (It/GB)
Tenebrae
Tentacles
Terminal Station (It/US)
Texas, Addio (It/Sp)
That Night in Varennes (Fr/It)
Theorem
They Call Me Trinity
They Came to Rob Las Vegas (Sp/Fr/WGer/It)
1000 Eyes of Dr Mabuse, The (WGer/Fr/It)
Three Brothers (It/Fr)
Three Sisters (It/Fr/Ger)
Tiger of Eschnapur, The (WGer/Fr/It)
'Tis Pity She's a Whore
Today It's Me...Tomorrow You
Torrents of Spring
Touchez pas au Grisbi (Fr/It)
Tout Va Bien (Fr/It)
Traffic (Fr/It)
Train, The (US/Fr/It)
Traitement de Choc (Fr/It)
Travelling Light: a Portrait of Lindsay Kemp
Tree of Wooden Clogs, The
Trial, The (Welles – Fr/It/WGer)

Tristana (Sp/Fr/It)
Trou, Le (Fr/It)
Truce, The (It/Fr/Ger)
Turkish Bath – Hamam, The (Sp/It/Tur)

Uccellacci e Uccellini
Uccello dalle Piume di Cristallo, L' (It/WGer)
Ulysses' Gaze (Greece/It/Fr)
Ultrà
Umberto D.
Uncle Tom
Uomo delle stelle, L'

Vaghe Stelle dell'Orsa
Valdez il Mezzosangue (It/Sp/Fr)
Vampires in Venice
Vengeance (It/WGer)
Venial Sin
Vent d'Est (Fr/It/WGer)
Verdict (Fr/It)
Verdugo, El (Sp/It)
Vérité, La (Fr/It)
Viaggio in Italia
Vices in the Family
Violation of Justine (Fr/It/Can)
Violent Professionals, The

Virgin for St Tropez, A (Fr/It)
Visitor, The
Vitelloni, I
Viva Maria! (Fr/It)
Vivre pour Vivre (Fr/It)
Voice of the Moon, The
Voie Lactée, La (Fr/It)
Volere, Volare
Voyage
Voyage to Cythera (Greece/WGer/It/GB)
Wages of Fear, The (Fr/It)
War and Peace (Vidor – US/It)
Watch Out, We're Mad (It/Sp)
Waterloo (It/USSR)
We Don't Want to Talk About It (Arg/It)
Weekend (Fr/It)
We the Living
What? (It/Fr/WGer)
White Fang (It/Sp/Fr)
White Nights (Visconti – Fr/It)
White Sheik, The
Whores, The
Why?
Wifemistress

Zombie Flesh-Eaters

Appendix 21

Japanese Films

About Love, Tokyo
Actor's Revenge, An
Adventures of Milo and Otis, The
Afternoon Breezes
Ai No Corrida (Fr/Jap)
A.K. (Fr/Jap)
Akira
Alone on the Pacific
Angel Dust
Another Lonely Hitman
August in the Water
Autumn Afternoon, An
Autumn Moon (HK/Jap)

Bad Sleep Well, The
Ballad of Narayama, The
Bantsuma: The Life and Times of Tsumasaburo Bando
Bari-Zogon
Beautiful Mystery – Legend of Big Horn
Bent (GB/US/Jap)
Bird People in China, The
Black Rain (Imamura)
Blind Alley
Blood of the Dragon
Boiling Point (Kitano)
Boxer, The (Terayama)
Boy
Branded to Kill
Brother and Sister
Bullet Train, The
Burmese Harp, The

Ceremony, The
Chikamatsu Monogatari
Circus Boys
Comic Magazine
Crazy Family
Crossways
Crying Freeman (Fr/Can/US/Jap)

Dear Summer Sister
Death by Hanging
Deaths in Tokimeki
Dersu Uzala (USSR/Jap)
Destroy All Monsters
Diary of a Shinjuku Thief
Dodes'ka-den
Double Suicide
Drive, The

Early Spring
Ebirah – Terror of the Deep

Eel, The
Eijanaika
Elephant Song
Emmanuelle in Tokyo
Emperor's Naked Army Marches On, The
Empire of Passion (Fr/Jap)
Empress Yang Kwei Fei, The (Jap/HK)
Empty Table, The
Enchantment, The

Family Game
Fighting Elegy
Fire Festival
Fire Within
Fist of the North Star
Five Women Around Utamaro
Flavour of Green Tea Over Rice
Flight from Ashiya (US/Jap)
Flirt (US/GB/Jap)
[Focus]
Four Days of Snow and Blood
Fruits of Passion, The (Fr/Jap)
Further Gesture, A (GB/Ger/Jap/Ire)

Gate of Flesh
Getting Any?
Ghost in the Shell (Jap/GB)
Godzilla 1985
Godzilla vs the Bionic Monster
Godzilla vs the Smog Monster
Gonin
Gonin 2
Gonza the Spearman
Good Men, Good Women (Jap/Tai)
Gunhed

Hair Opera, The
Hana-Bi
Hard Rain (US/GB/Jap/Ger/Den)
Heart, Beating in the Dark
Heaven-6-Box
Hen in the Wind, A
Hidden Fortress, The
High and Low
Hiroshima, Mon Amour (Fr/Jap)
History of Post-War Japan as Told by a Bar Hostess
Hometown
How Old Is the River?

Idiot, The
Ikiru
I Like You, I Like You Very
  Much
Irezumi – Spirit of Tattoo
Iron Maze (US/Jap)
Island, The (Shindo)
I Was Born, But...

Ju Dou (China/Jap)

Kagero-za
Kama Sutra: A Tale of Love
  (Ind/GB/Jap/Ger)
Kamizake Taxi
Kids Return
Kikuchi
Kitami
Kitchen, The
Kuroneko
Kwaidan

Labyrinth of Dreams
Late Spring
Latin Boys Go to Hell
  (US/Ger/Sp/Jap)
Leaving
Life of Chikuzan, The
Life of Oharu, The
Lightning Swords of Death
Like a Rolling Stone
Like Grains of Sand
Lost Sex
Lost World of Sinbad, The
Love Letter
Lower Depths, The

Maborosi
Madadayo
Madame Butterfly
Man Who Left His Will on
  Film, The
March Comes in Like a Lion
MARKS
Memories
Minamata
Minbo Woman – Or the Gentle
  Art of Japanese Extortion
Mishima: A Life in Four
  Chapters (US/Jap)
Mr Baseball (US/Jap)
Moon Has Risen, The
Most Terrible Time of My Life
  (Jap/Tai/China)
Moving
Muddy River
Music for the Movies: The
  Hollywood Sound (US/Fr/Jap)
My Love Has Been Burning
Mystery of Rampo, The
My Sons

None But the Brave (US/Jap)
Nostalgia for Countryland
  (Vietnam/Jap)
Nowhere Man

Obsession, The
Ohayo
Okaeri
Okoge
Ondeko-za on Sado, The
One Generation of Tattoos
Onibaba
Organ
Ososhiki
Outer Way, The

Page of Madness, A
Painted Desert
Pandemonium
Pastoral Hide-and-Seek
Peasants of the Second
  Fortress, The
Promise

Ran (Fr/Jap)
Rashomon
Rebellion
Record of a Tenement
  Gentleman

Red Beard
Remembrance (Nakajima)
Rhapsody in August
Roujin Z

Sadistic City
Saga of Anatahan, The
Sanjuro
Sansho Dayu
Scene at the Sea, A
Screamers (Can/US/Jap)
Seven Samurai
Shall We Dance?
Shin Heike Monogatari
Shinjuku Triad Society
Shogun Assassin (Jap/US)
Skinless Night
Sleeping Man
Some Kinda Love
Sonatine
Son of Godzilla
Space Firebird
Sting of Death, The
Story of the Late
  Chrysanthemums, The
Stranger
Stray Dog
Street of Shame
Sukiyaki
Summer Soldiers
Summer Vacation 1999
Sunless Days (HK/Jap)
Suzaku
Swallowtail
  ButterflySwimming
  Prohibited
Sweet Degeneration (Tai/Jap)
Swimming with Tears

Tango Lesson, The
  (GB/Fr/Arg/Jap/Ger)
Taxing Woman, A
Tetsuo
Tetsuo II: Bodyhammer
This Window Is Yours
Three Resurrected Drunkards
Throne of Blood
Throw Away Your Books,
  Let's Go
  into the Streets
Tokyo Daughter
Tokyo Fist
Tokyo Kyodai
Tokyo Olympiad 1964
Tokyo Story
Tora no O o Fumu Otokotachi
Tora! Tora! Tora! (US/Jap)
To Sleep, So As to Dream
Town of Love and Hope, A
2 Duo

Ugetsu Monogatari

Village of Dreams
Violated Angels
Violent Cop, The
Virus (Jap/Can)
Visions of Light (US/Jap)

War of the Monsters
What's Up Tiger Lily? (US/Jap)
Wicked Reporter, The
Wings of Honeamise
Wilde (GB/US/Jap/Ger)
Without Memory
Wizard of Darkness
Woman of the Dunes
World Apartment Horror
Written Face, The (Switz/Jap)

Yojimbo
Yumeji

Zazie

Actors' Index

Space, regrettably, does not permit the inclusion of a complete index of every performer mentioned in the Guide. The index that follows lists some 270 of the most prominent – or, perhaps, most popular – names from the past century of cinema. Of course, in any selection, deserving candidates have to be left out, and any inclusion or exclusion can always be a source of argument. This index lists only theatrical performances by the actors concerned. Documentaries about any particular actor will be found listed under their names in the General Subject Index.

Adjani, Isabelle *Camille Claudel; Deadly Run (Mortelle Randonnée); Diabolique* (Chechik); *Driver, The; Ishtar; Nosferatu the Vampyre (Nosferatu: Phantom der Nacht); One Deadly Summer (L'Eté Meurtrier); Possession; Quartet* (Ivory); *Reine Margot, La; Story of Adèle H., The (L'Histoire d'Adèle H.); Subway; Tenant, The (Le Locataire); Violette et François.*

Ameche, Don *Cocoon; Cocoon: The Return; Confirm or Deny; Corrina, Corrina; Folks!; Four Sons; Greenwich Village; Harry and the Hendersons (aka Bigfoot and the Hendersons); Heaven Can Wait* (Lubitsch); *Hollywood Cavalcade; Homeward Bound: The Incredible Journey; In Old Chicago; Lillian Russell; Midnight; One in a Million; Oscar; Sleep, My Love; That Night in Rio; Things Change; Trading Places.*

Andrews, Dana *Airport 1975; Ball of Fire; Battle of the Bulge; Best Years of Our Lives, The; Beyond a Reasonable Doubt; Boomerang* (Kazan); *Crack in the World; Daisy Kenyon; Devil's Brigade, The; Edge of Doom (aka Stronger Than Fear); Fallen Angel; Good Guys Wear Black; In Harm's Way; Iron Curtain, The (aka Behind the Iron Curtain); I Want You; Last Tycoon, The; Laura; Loved One, The; My Foolish Heart; Night of the Demon (aka Curse of the Demon); North Star (aka Armored Attack); Ox-Bow Incident, The (aka Strange Incident); Satan Bug, The; State Fair; Swamp Water; Take a Hard Ride; Three Hours to Kill; Tobacco Road; Up in Arms; Walk in the Sun, A; While the City Sleeps.*

Andrews, Julie *Americanization of Emily, The; Darling Lili; Duet for One; Hawaii; Little Miss Marker; Man Who Loved Women, The; Mary Poppins; S.O.B.; Sound of Music, The; Star!; Tamarind Seed, The; '10'; 'That's Life'; Thoroughly Modern Millie; Torn Curtain; Victor/Victoria.*

Arthur, Jean *Devil and Miss Jones, The; Easy Living* (Leisen); *Foreign Affair, A; History Is Made at Night; Lady Takes a Chance, A; Mr Deeds Goes to Town; Mr Smith Goes to Washington; More the Merrier, The; Only Angels Have Wings; Plainsman, The; Shane; Talk of the Town, The; Whole Town's Talking, The (aka Passport to Fame); You Can't Take It With You.*

Astaire, Fred *Band Wagon, The; Barkleys of Broadway, The; Belle of New York, The; Blue Skies; Carefree; Daddy Long Legs; Damsel in Distress, A; Easter Parade; Finian's Rainbow; Flying Down to Rio; Follow the Fleet; Funny Face; Gay Divorcee, The; Ghost Story; Holiday Inn; Midas Run (aka A Run on Gold); On the Beach; Purple Taxi, The (Le Taxi Mauve); Roberta; Royal Wedding (aka Wedding Bells); Shall We Dance?; Silk Stockings; Sky's the Limit, The; Story of Vernon and Irene Castle, The; Swing Time; That's Entertainment!; That's Entertainment Part II; Top Hat; Towering Inferno, The; You'll Never Get Rich; You Were Never Lovelier; Ziegfeld Follies.*

Attenborough, Richard *And Then There Were None (aka Ten Little Indians); Angry Silence, The; Bliss of Mrs Blossom, The; Brannigan; Brighton Rock; Brothers in Law; Chess Players, The (Shatranj ke Khilari); Conduct Unbecoming; Dancing With Crime; Dunkirk; Eight O'Clock Walk; Flight of the Phoenix, The; Great Escape, The; Guinea Pig, The (aka The Outsider); Hamlet*

(Branagh); *Human Factor,
The* (Preminger); *I'm All
Right, Jack; In Which We
Serve; Jet Storm; Journey
Together; Jurrasic Park;
League of Gentlemen, The;
London Belongs to Me (aka
Dulcimer Street); Loot;
Jurassic Park; Magic Box,
The; Magic Christian, The;
Man Upstairs, The; Matter
of Life and Death, A (aka
Stairway to Heaven);
Miracle on 34th Street;
Morning Departure (aka
Operation Disaster); Only
Two Can Play; Only When I
Larf; Private's Progress;
Rosebud; Sand Pebbles, The;
Scamp, The; Seance on a
Wet Afternoon; Sea of
Sand; Shadowlands; Ship
That Died of Shame, The;
10 Rillington Place.*

Audran, Stéphane *And Then
There Were None (aka Ten
Little Indians); Babette's
Feast (Babettes Gaestebud);
Bay Boy, The; Biches, Les
(The Does); Big Red One,
The; Black Bird, The; Blood
Relatives (Liens de Sang); B
Must Die (Hay que Matar a
B); Bonnes Femmes, Les
(The Girls); Boucher, Le
(The Butcher); Cage aux
Folles III: The Wedding, La;
Champagne Murders, The
(Le Scandale); Clean Slate
(Coup de Torchon); Cop au
Vin (Poulet au Vinaigre);
Cousins, Les (The Cousins);
Deadly Run (Mortelle
Randonée); Dead Pigeon on
Beethovenstrasse; Devil's
Advocate, The (Des Teufels
Advokat); Discreet Charm of
the Bourgeoisie, The (Le
Charme Discret de la
Bourgeoisie); Eagle's Wing;
Femme Infidèle, La
(Unfaithful Wife); Just
Before Nightfall (Juste avant
la Nuit); Lady in the Car
with Glasses and a Gun, The
(La Dame dans l'auto avec
des lunettes et un fusil);
Maximum Risk; Murder Is a
Murder...Is a Murder, A (Un
Meurtre est un Meurtre);
Noces Rouges, Les (Blood
Wedding/Red Wedding/
Wedding in Blood); Paris vu
par... (Six in Paris); Rupture,
La; Signe du Lion, Le (The
Sign of Leo); Silver Bears;
Sons (Rockwell); Violette
Nozière.*

Bacall, Lauren *All I Want for
Christmas; Appointment
with Death; Big Sleep, The
(Hawks); Cobweb, The;
Confidential Agent; Dark
Passage; Designing Woman;
Fan, The; Harper (aka The
Moving Target); Health;
How to Marry a Millionaire;
Key Largo; Mirror Has Two
Faces, The; Misery; Mr
North; Murder on the Orient
Express; North West
Frontier (aka Flame Over
India); Sex and the Single
Girl; Shootist, The; To Have
and Have Not; Tree of
Hands; Woman's World;
Written on the Wind; Young
Man with a Horn (aka
Young Man of Music).*

Baker, Stanley *Accident;
Alexander the Great (Rossen);
Blind Date (aka Chance
Meeting); Captain Horatio
Hornblower R.N.; Criminal,
The (aka The Concrete
Jungle); Cruel Sea, The; Eve;
Good Die Young, The; Guns
of Navarone, The; Hill in
Korea, A (aka Hell in Korea);
Hell Drivers; Hell Is a City; In
the French Style; Jet Storm;
Perfect Friday; Prize of Arms,
A; Richard III; Robbery;
Sodom and Gomorrah
(Sodoma e Gomorra);
Where's Jack?; Zulu.*

Bardot, Brigitte *Don Juan or If
Don Juan Were a Woman
(Don Juan 1973 ou si Don
Juan était une Femme); En
Cas de Malheur (La Ragazza
del Peccato/Love Is My
Profession); Et Dieu Créa la
Femme (And God Created
Woman/And Woman...Was
Created); Histoires
Extraordinaires (Spirits of
the Dead/Tales of Mystery);
Legend of Frenchie King,
The (Les Pétroleuses);
Masculin Féminin
(Masculine Feminine);
Mépris, Le (Contempt);
Shalako; Trou Normand, Le
(Crazy for Love); Vérité, La
(The Truth); Viva Maria!*

Bates, Alan *Britannia Hospital;
Butley; Caretaker, The (aka
The Guest); Dr M; Duet for
One; Entertainer, The; Far
From the Madding Crowd;
Fixer, The; Georgy Girl; Go-
Between, The; Grotesque,
The; Hamlet (Zeffirelli);
Hamlet (Branagh); Hands
Up; In Celebration; Kind of
Loving, A; King of Hearts
(Le Roi de Coeur); Mister
Frost; Nijinsky; Nothing But
the Best; Prayer for the
Dying, A; Quartet (Ivory);
Return of the Soldier, The;
Rose, The; Royal Flash;
Running Man, The (Reed);
Secret Friends; Shout, The;
Silent Tongue; Three Sisters
(Olivier); Unmarried
Woman, An; We Think the
World of You; Whistle Down
the Wind; Wicked Lady, The
(Winner); Women in Love;
Zorba the Greek.*

Beatty, Warren *All Fall Down;
Bonnie and Clyde; Bugsy;
Dick Tracy; $ (aka The
Heist); Fortune, The; Heaven
Can Wait (Beatty/Henry);
Ishtar; Kaleidoscope; Lilith;
McCabe and Mrs Miller;
Mickey One; Only Game in
Town, The; Parallax View,
The; Promise Her Anything;
Reds; Roman Spring of Mrs
Stone, The; Shampoo;
Splendor in the Grass.*

Belmondo, Jean-Paul *A Bout de
Souffle (Breathless); A
Double Tour (Leda/Web of
Passion); Borsalino;
Burglars, The (Le Casse);
Casino Royale; Docteur
Popaul (High
Heels/Scoundrel in White);
Doulos, Le (The Finger
Man); Enfants de Lumière,
Les (The Children of*

*Lumière); Femme est une
Femme, Une (A Woman Is a
Woman); Ho! (aka Criminal
Face); Homme de Rio, L'
(That Man from Rio); How
to Destroy the Reputation of
the Greatest Secret Agent (Le
Magnifique); Leon Morin,
Priest (Léon Morin, Prêtre);
Misérables, Les (aka Les
Misérables du vingtième
siècle); Night Caller (Peur sur
la Ville); Pierrot le Fou;
Scoumoune, La (Hit Man/
Scoundrel); Sirène du
Mississipi, La (Mississippi
Mermaid); Stavisky...*

Bennett, Joan *Bulldog
Drummond; Confirm or
Deny; Father of the Bride
(Minnelli); Hollow Triumph
(aka The Scar); Little
Women; Macomber Affair,
The; Man Hunt; Man I
Married, The (aka I Married
a Nazi); Man in the Iron
Mask, The; Man Who Broke
the Bank at Monte Carlo,
The; Reckless Moment, The;
Scarlet Street; Secret Beyond
the Door; Suspiria; There's
Always Tomorrow; We're
No Angels (Curtiz); Woman
in the Window, The; Woman
on the Beach, The.*

Berenger, Tom *At Play in the
Fields of the Lord; Betrayed;
Beyond the Door (Oltre la
Porta); Big Chill, The; Butch
and Sundance: The Early
Days; Chasers; Dogs of War,
The; Eddie and the Cruisers;
Field, The; Gettysburg; In
Praise of Older Women; Last
of the Dogmen; Last Rites;
Looking for Mr Goodbar;
Love at Large; Major
League; Major League II;
Platoon; Sentinel, The;
Shattered; Shoot to Kill (aka
Deadly Pursuit); Sliver;
Sniper; Someone to Watch
Over Me; Substitute, The.*

Bergman, Ingrid *Anastasia;
Arch of Triumph; Autumn
Sonata (Herbstsonate); Bell's
of St Mary's, The;
Casablanca; Dr Jekyll and Mr
Hyde (Fleming); Eléna et les
Hommes (Paris Does
Strange Things); Fear (La
Paura); For Whom the Bell
Tolls; Gaslight (aka The
Murder in Thornton
Square); Indiscreet; Inn of
the Sixth Happiness, The;
Intermezzo (aka Escape to
Happiness); Murder on the
Orient Express; Notorious;
Rage in Heaven; Saratoga
Trunk; Spellbound;
Stromboli, Terra di Dio
(Stromboli); Under
Capricorn; Viaggio in Italia
(Journey to Italy/The Lonely
Woman/Strangers/Voyage to
Italy); Walk in the Spring
Rain, A.*

Bogarde, Dirk *Accident; Blue
Lamp, The; Bridge Too Far,
A; Cast a Dark Shadow;
Damned, The (La Caduta
degli Dei/Götterdämmerung);
Darling; Death in Venice
(Morte a Venezia); Despair;
Doctor in the House; Esther
Waters; Fixer, The; Gentle*

*Gunman, The; High Bright
Sun, The HMS Defiant (aka
Damn the Defiant); Hot
Enough for June; I Could Go
On Singing; Ill Met by
Moonlight (aka Night
Ambush); Justine (Cukor);
King and Country; Libel;
Modesty Blaise; Night
Porter, The (Il Portiere di
Notte); Oh! What a Lovely
War; Once a Jolly Swagman
(aka Maniacs on Wheels);
Our Mother's House;
Password Is Courage, The;
Permission to Kill;
Providence; Quartet (Smart/
French/Crabtree/Annakin);
Serpent, The (Le Serpent);
Servant, The; Simba; Singer
Not the Song, The; Sleeping
Tiger, The; So Long at the
Fair; Song Without End;
Spanish Gardener, The;
These Foolish Things (Daddy
Nostalgie); Victim; Wind
Cannot Read, The.*

Bogart, Humphrey *Across the
Pacific; Action in the North
Atlantic; African Queen,
The; All Through the Night;
Amazing Doctor
Clitterhouse, The; Angels
with Dirty Faces; Barefoot
Contessa, The; Beat the
Devil; Big Shot, The; Big
Sleep, The (Hawks); Brother
Orchid; Bullets or Ballots;
Caine Mutiny, The;
Casablanca; China Clipper;
Conflict; Dark Passage; Dark
Victory; Dead End; Deadline
– USA (aka Deadline); Dead
Reckoning; Desperate Hours,
The; Enforcer, The (aka
Murder, Inc.); Harder They
Fall, The; High Sierra; In a
Lonely Place; In This Our
Life; Invisible Stripes; Key
Largo; Kid Galahad (Curtiz);
Knock on Any Door; Left
Hand of God, The; Love
Lottery, The; Maltese
Falcon, The; Marked
Woman; Passage to
Marseille; Petrified Forest,
The; Return of Doctor X,
The; Roaring Twenties, The;
Sabrina (aka Sabrina Fair);
Sahara (Korda); Stand-In;
Thank Your Lucky Stars;
They Drive By Night (aka
The Road to Frisco) (Walsh);
To Have and Have Not;
Treasure of the Sierra
Madre, The; We're No
Angels (Curtiz).*

Boyer, Charles *Algiers; All
This and Heaven Too; April
Fools, The; Arch of
Triumph; Around the World
in 80 Days; Back Street;
Barefoot in the Park;
Buccaneer, The; Casino
Royale; Cluny Brown;
Cobweb, The; Confidential
Agent; Fanny (Logan); First
Legion, The; Flesh and
Fantasy; Garden of Allah,
The; Gaslight (aka The
Murder in Thornton
Square); History Is Made at
Night; Hold Back the Dawn;
Lost Horizon (Jarrott); Love
Is a Ball (aka All This and
Money Too); Madame de...
(The Earrings of Madame
de...); Mayerling; Stavisky...;
Tovarich.*

Branagh, Kenneth *Dead Again; Hamlet; Henry V; High Season; In the Bleak Midwinter; Looking for Richard; Mary Shelley's Frankenstein; Month in the Country, A; Much Ado About Nothing; Othello; Peter's Friends; Swing Kids.*

Brando, Marlon *Apocalypse Now; Appaloosa, The (aka Southwest to Sonora); Brave, The; Candy; Chase, The; Christopher Columbus: The Discovery; Don Juan DeMarco; Countess from Hong Kong, A; Dry White Season, A; Formula, The; Freshman, The; Fugitive Kind, The; Godfather, The; Guys and Dolls; Island of Dr Moreau, The (Frankenheimer); Julius Caesar; Last Tango in Paris; Men, The; Missouri Breaks, The; Mutiny on the Bounty (Milestone); Nightcomers, The; Night of the Following Day, The; One-Eyed Jacks; On the Waterfront; Queimada! (Burn!); Reflections in a Golden Eye; Sayonara; Streetcar Named Desire, A; Superman; Teahouse of the August Moon, The; Viva Zapata!; Wild One, The; Young Lions, The.*

Bridges, Jeff *Against All Odds; American Heart; American Success Company, The (aka Success); Bad Company; Big Lebowski, The; Blown Away; Cold Feet; Company She Keeps, The; Cutter's Way (aka Cutter and Bone); 8 Million Ways to Die; Fabulous Baker Boys, The; Fat City; Fearless; Fisher King, The; Hearts of the West (aka Hollywood Cowboy); Heaven's Gate; Jagged Edge; King Kong (Guillermin); Kiss Me Goodbye; Last American Hero, The; Last Picture Show, The; Last Unicorn, The; Lolly-Madonna XXX (aka The Lolly-Madonna War); Mirror Has Two Faces, The; Morning After, The; Nadine; Rancho Deluxe; See You in the Morning; Somebody Killed Her Husband; Starman; Stay Hungry; Texasville; Thunderbolt and Lightfoot; Tron; Tucker: The Man and His Dream; Vanishing, The; White Squall; Wild Bill; Winter Kills.*

Bronson, Charles *Apache; Assassination; Borderline; Breakheart Pass; Breakout; Caboblanco; Chato's Land; Cold Sweat (De la Part des Copains); Death Wish; Death Wish II; Death Wish 3; Death Wish 4: The Crackdown; Diplomatic Courier; Dirty Dozen, The; Donato and Daughter; Evil That Men Do, The; From Noon Till Three; Great Escape, The; Guns for San Sebastian (La Bataille de San Sebastian); Hard Times (aka The Streetfighter);*

House of Wax; Indian Runner, The; Kid Galahad (Karlson); Love and Bullets; Machine Gun Kelly; Magnificent Seven, The; Marrying Kind, The; Master of the World; Mechanic, The (aka Killer of Killers); Miss Sadie Thompson; Mr Majestyk; Mob, The (aka Remember That Face); Murphy's Law; Never So Few; Once Upon a Time in the West (C'era una Volta il West); Pat and Mike; Raid on Entebbe; Red Sun (Soleil Rouge); Rider on the Rain (Passager de la Pluie); Run of the Arrow; St Ives; Sandpiper, The; Stone Killer, The; Telefon; 10 to Midnight; This Property Is Condemned; Valdez il Mezzosangue (Chino/The Valdez Horses/Valdez the Halfbreed); Vera Cruz; Villa Rides!; White Buffalo, The.

Brooks, Louise *Beggars of Life; Diary of a Lost Girl (Das Tagebuch einer Verlorenen); Girl in Every Port, A; It's the Old Army Game; Pandora's Box (Die Büchse der Pandora).*

Brynner, Yul *Anastasia; Brothers Karamazov, The (Brooks); Buccaneer, The; Cast a Giant Shadow; Catlow; Double Man, The; Escape from Zahrain; File of the Golden Goose; Flight from Ashiya; Futureworld; King and I, The; Kings of the Sun; Light at the Edge of the World, The; Magic Christian, The; Magnificent Seven, The; Return of the Seven (aka Return of the Magnificent Seven); Romance of a Horsethief; Serpent, The (Le Serpent); Solomon and Sheba; Ten Commandments, The; Testament d'Orphée, Le (Testament of Orpheus); Villa Rides!; Westworld.*

Burton, Richard *Absolution (aka Murder by Confession); Alexander the Great (Rossen); Anne of the Thousand Days; Assassination of Trotsky, The; Bitter Victory (Amère Victoire); Boom; Bramble Bush, The; Candy; Circle of Two (Mankiewicz); Comedians, The; Equus; Exorcist II: The Heretic; Green Grow the Rushes (aka Brandy Ashore); Ice Palace; Klansman, The; Longest Day, The; Look Back in Anger; Massacre in Rome (Rappresaglia); Medusa Touch, The; My Cousin Rachel; Night of the Iguana, The; Nineteen Eighty-Four; Rains of Ranchipur, The; Robe, The; Sandpiper, The; Seawife; Spy Who Came in from the Cold, The; Staircase; Under Milk Wood; Villain; V.I.P.s, The; Wagner; What's New Pussycat?; Where Eagles Dare; Who's Afraid of Virginia Woolf?; Wild Geese, The.*

Buscemi, Steve *Airheads; Barton Fink; Big Lebowski, The; Billy Bathgate; Call Me; Con Air; Desperado; Fargo; Hudsucker Proxy, The; In the Soup; John Carpenter's Escape from L.A.; Kansas City; King of New York; Living in Oblivion; Miller's Crossing; Mystery Train; New York Stories; Parting Glances; Pulp Fiction; Real Blonde, The; Reservoir Dogs; Rising Sun; Slaves of New York; Somebody to Love; Tales from the Darkside: The Movie; Things to Do in Denver When You're Dead; Trees Lounge; Wedding Singer, The; Zandalee.*

Caan, James *Alien Nation; Autre Homme une Autre Chance, Un (Another Man, Another Woman/Another Man, Another Chance); Boy Called Hate, A; Bridge Too Far, A; Chapter Two; Cinderella Liberty; Comes a Horseman; Countdown; Dick Tracy; El Dorado; Eraser; Flesh and Bone; For the Boys; Freebie and the Bean; Funny Lady; Gambler, The; Gardens of Stone; Glory Guys, The; Godfather, The; Harry and Walter Go to New York; Hide in Plain Sight; Honeymoon in Vegas; Irma la Douce; Godfather Part 2, The; Killer Elite, The; Kiss Me Goodbye; Misery; Rain People, The; Red Line 7000; Rollerball; Silent Movie; Slither; Submarine X-!; Thief (aka Violent Streets); Uns et les Autres, Les (Bolero/The Ins and the Outs).*

Cage, Nicolas *Birdy; City of Angels; Con Air; Cotton Club, The; Face/Off; Firebirds (aka Wings of the Apache); Guarding Tess; Honeymoon in Vegas; It Could Happen to You; Kiss of Death (Schroeder); Leaving Las Vegas; Moonstruck; Peggy Sue Got Married; Racing with the Moon; Raising Arizona; Red Rock West; Rock, The; Rumble Fish; Trapped in Paradise; Wild at Heart; Zandalee.*

Cagney, James *Angels With Dirty Faces; Blood on the Sun; Boy Meets Girl (Bacon); Ceiling Zero; Come Fill the Cup; Each Dawn I Die; Fighting 69th, The; Footlight Parade; G-Men; Hard to Handle; Kiss Tomorrow Goodbye; Lady Killer; Lion Is in the Streets, A; Love Me or Leave Me; Mayor of Hell, The; Midsummer Night's Dream, A (Reinhardt/ Dieterle); Mister Roberts; One, Two, Three; Other Men's Women; Picture Snatcher; Public Enemy, The; Ragtime; Roaring Twenties, The; Run for Cover; Taxi!; Torrid Zone; Tribute to a Bad Man; White Heat; Yankee Doodle Dandy.*

Caine, Michael *Alfie; Ashanti; Battle of Britain; Beyond the*

Poseidon Adventure; Billion Dollar Brain; Black Windmill, The; Blame It On Rio; Blood and Wine; Blue Ice; Bridge Too Far, A; Bullseye!; California Suite; Day the Earth Caught Fire, The; Deadfall; Deathtrap; Dirty Rotten Scoundrels; Dressed to Kill; Eagle Has Landed, The; Educating Rita; Fourth Protocol, The; Funeral in Berlin; Gambit; Get Carter; Half Moon Street; Hand, The; Hannah and Her Sisters; Harry and Walter Go to New York; Hill in Korea, A (aka Hell in Korea); Holcroft Covenant, The; Honorary Consul, The (aka Beyond the Limit); Hurry Sundown; Ipcress File, The; Island, The (Ritchie); Italian Job, The; Jaws – The Revenge;Key, The (Reed); Kidnapped; Last Valley, The; Magus, The; Man Who Would Be King, The; Marseille Contract, The; Mona Lisa; Muppet Christmas Carol, The; Noises Off; On Deadly Ground; Peeper; Play Dirty; Pulp; Romantic Englishwoman, The; Shock to the System, A; Silver Bears; Sleuth; Surrender; Swarm, The; Sweet Liberty; Tonite Let's All Make Love in London; Too Late the Hero; Victory (aka Escape to Victory); Water; Whistle Blower, The; Wilby Conspiracy, The; Without a Clue; Wrong Arm of the Law, The; Zee & Co (X, Y and Zee); Zulu.

Carradine, Keith *Almost Perfect Affair, An; Andre; Backfire; Ballad of the Sad Café, The; Choose Me; Cold Feet; Daddy's Dyin' – Who's Got the Will?; Duellists, The; Emperor of the North Pole, The (aka Emperor of the North); Gunfight, A; Hex; Long Riders, The; Maria's Lovers; McCabe and Mrs Miller; Mrs Parker and the Vicious Circle; Moderns, The; Nashville; Old Boyfriends; Pretty Baby; Southern Comfort; Thieves Like Us; Thousand Acres, A; Tie That Binds, The; Trouble in Mind; Welcome to L.A.*

Cassavetes, John *Brass Target; Capone; Crime in the Streets; Dirty Dozen, The; Edge of the City (aka A Man Is Ten Feet Tall); Fury, The; Husbands; Incubus; Killers, The (Siegel); Love Streams; Mikey and Nicky; Minnie and Moskowitz; Night Holds Terror, The; Opening Night; Rosemary's Baby; Saddle the Wind; Shadows; Tempest; Two-Minute Warning; Whose Life Is It Anyway?.*

Chaney, Lon (Sr) *He Who Gets Slapped; Hunchback of Notre Dame, The (Worsley); Phantom of the Opera, The (Julian); Unholy Three, The (Browning); Unholy Three, The (Conway); Unknown, The.*

Chaplin, Charles *Circus, The; City Lights; Countess from Hong Kong, A; Gold Rush, The; Great Dictator, The; Kid, The; King in New York, A; Limelight; Modern Times; Monsieur Verdoux; Show People; Woman of Paris, A.*

Cheung, Leslie *Ashes of Time (Dong Xie Xi Du); Better Tomorrow, A (Yingxiong Bense); Better Tomorrow II, A (Yingxiong Bense II); Chinese Ghost Story, A (Qian Nü Youhun); Chinese Ghost Story II, A; Days of Being Wild (Ahfei Zhenjuang); Farewell My Concubine (Ba Wang Bie Ji); Happy Together (Chunguang Zhaxie); He's a Woman, She's a Man (Jinzhi Yuye); Once a Thief (Zonheng Sihai); Phantom Lover, The (Xin Yeban Gesheng); Rouge (Inji Kau); Temptress Moon (Fengyue).*

Cheung, Maggie *Actress (Ruan Ling Yu); Ashes of Time (Dong Xie Xi Du); As Tears Go By; Chinese Box; Comrades, Almost a Love Story (Tian Mimi); Days of Being Wild (Ahfei Zhenjuang); Full Moon in New York (Ren zai Niu-Yue); Heroic Trio, The (Dongfang San Xia); Iceman Cometh, The (Jidong Qixia); Irma Vep; Moon Warriors; Police Story (Jingcha Gushi); Song of the Exile (Ke Tu Chiu Hen).*

Chow Yun-Fat *Better Tomorrow, A (Yingxiong Bense); Better Tomorrow II, A (Yingxiong Bense II); City on Fire; Full Contact (Xia Dao Gao Fei); Hard-Boiled (Lat Sau San Tam); Killer, The (Diexue Shuang Xiong); Love in a Fallen City (Qingchengzhi Lian); Love Unto Waste (Deiha Tsing); Once a Thief (Zonheng Sihai); Replacement Killers, The; Story of Woo Viet, The (Hu Yue de Gushi).*

Christie, Julie *Afterglow; Billy Liar; Darling; Demon Seed; Doctor Zhivago; Don't Look Now; DragonHeart; Fahrenheit 451; Far from the Madding Crowd; Fast Lady, The; Fools of Fortune; Go-Between, The; Gold Diggers, The; Hamlet (Branagh); Heat and Dust; Heaven Can Wait (Beatty/ Henry); McCabe and Mrs Miller; Memoirs of a Survivor; Miss Mary; Petulia; Power; Return of the Soldier, The; Shampoo; Tonite Let's All Make Love in London; Young Cassidy.*

Clift, Montgomery *Big Lift, The; Freud; From Here to Eternity; Heiress, The; I Confess; Judgment at Nuremberg; Misfits, The; Place in the Sun, A; Raintree County; Red River; Suddenly Last Summer; Terminal Station (Stazione Termini/Indiscretion of an American Wife); Wild River; Young Lions, The.*

Close, Glenn *Air Force One; Big Chill, The; Dangerous Liaisons; Fatal Attraction; House of Spirits, The; Jagged Edge; Hamlet (Zeffirelli); Mary Reilly; Mars Attacks!; Maxie; Meeting Venus; Natural, The; 101 Dalmatians (Herek); Paper, The; Paradise Road; Reversal of Fortune; Stone Boy, The; World According to Garp, The.*

Colbert, Claudette *Arise, My Love; Bluebeard's Eighth Wife; Boom Town; Cleopatra (DeMille); Drums Along the Mohawk; Imitation of Life (Stahl); It Happened One Night; Midnight; Palm Beach Story, The; Phantom President, The; Remember the Day; Sign of the Cross, The; Since You Went Away; Sleep, My Love; Three Came Home; Tovarich; Zaza.*

Colman, Ronald *Around the World in 80 Days; Bulldog Drummond; Double Life, A; Lost Horizon (Capra); Man Who Broke the Bank at Monte Carlo, The; Prisoner of Zenda, The (Cromwell); Raffles; Random Harvest; Talk of the Town, The; Unholy Garden, The.*

Connery, Sean *Anderson Tapes, The; Another Time, Another Place, A; Bridge Too Far, A; Cuba; Diamonds Are Forever; Darby O'Gill and the Little People; Dr No; Damily Business; Fine Madness, A; First Great Train Robbery, The (aka The Great Train Robbery); First Knight; Five Days One Summer; Frightened City, The; From Russia With Love; Goldfinger; Good Man in Africa, A; Hell Drivers; Highlander; Highlander II – The Quickening; Hill, The; Hunt for Red October, The; Indiana Jones and the Last Crusade; Just Cause; Man Who Would Be King, The; Marnie; Medicine Man; Meteor; Molly Maguires, The; Murder on the Orient Express; Name of the Rose, The (Der Name der Rose); Never Say Never Again; Offence, The; Outland; Presidio, The; Ransom; Rising Sun; Robin and Marian; Robin Hood: Prince of Thieves; Rock, The; Russia House, The; Shalako; Sword of the Valiant – The Legend of Gawain and the Green Knight, The; Thunderball; Time Bandits; Untouchables, The; Wind and the Lion, The; Woman of Straw; Wrong Is Right (aka The Man With the Deadly Lens); You Only Live Twice; Zardoz.*

Cooper, Gary *Alice in Wonderland (McLeod); Along Came Jones; Ball of Fire; Beau Geste; Bluebeard's Eighth Wife; City Streets; Cloak and Dagger; Court-Martial of Billy Mitchell, The (aka One Man Mutiny); Dallas; Design for Living; Desire; Distant Drums; Farewell to Arms, A (Borzage); For Whom the Bell Tolls; Fountainhead, The; Friendly Persuasion; High Noon; If I Had a Million; Love in the Afternoon (Wilder); Man of the West; Meet John Doe; Mr Deeds Goes to Town; Morocco; Peter Ibbetson; Plainsman, The; Real Glory, The; Saratoga Trunk; Unconquered; Vera Cruz; Wedding Night, The; Wings.*

Costner, Kevin *Amazing Stories; American Flyers; Bodyguard, The; Bull Durham; Dances with Wolves; Dances with Wolves – Special Edition; Fandango; Field of Dreams; JFK; No Way Out; Perfect World, A; Postman, The; Revenge (Scott); Robin Hood: Prince of Thieves; Silverado; Stacy's Knights; Table for Five; Testament (Littman); Tin Cup; Untouchables, The; War, The; Waterworld; Wyatt Earp.*

Cotten, Joseph *Abominable Dr Phibes, The; Airport '77; Beyond the Forest; Caravans; Citizen Kane; Delicate Balance, A; Duel in the Sun; F for Fake (Vérités et Mensonges); Gaslight (aka The Murder in Thornton Square); Guyana: Crime of the Century (Guyana: El Crimen del Siglo); Halliday Brand, The; Hearse, The; Heaven's Gate; Hush...Hush, Sweet Charlotte; I'll Be Seeing You; Island of Mutations (L'Isola degli Uomini Pesce); Journey into Fear; Last Sunset, The; Love Letters (Dieterle); Lydia; Magnificent Ambersons, The; Man With a Cloak, The; Niagara; Oscar, The; Petulia; Portrait of Jennie; Shadow of a Doubt; Since You Went Away; Soylent Green; Third Man, The; Tora! Tora! Tora!; Touch of Evil; Twilight's Last Gleaming; Under Capricorn.*

Crawford, Joan *Above Suspicion; Autumn Leaves; Gorgeous Hussy, The; Grand Hotel; Humoresque; I Saw What You Did; Johnny Guitar; Karate Killers, The; Love on the Run; Mildred Pierce; Possessed; Rain; Shining Hour, The; Strait-Jacket; Strange Cargo; Sudden Fear; Torch Song; Tramp, Tramp, Tramp; Unknown, The; What Ever Happened to Baby Jane?; When Ladies Meet; Woman's Face, A; Women, The.*

Crosby, Bing *Bells of St Mary's, The; Birth of the Blues; Blue Skies; Connecticut Yankee in King Arthur's Court, A (aka A Yankee in King Arthur's Court); Dixie; Dr Rhythm; Emperor Waltz, The; Going My Way; Here Comes the Groom; Here Come the Waves; High Society; High Time; Holiday Inn; King of Jazz, The; Let's Make Love; Mr Music; Road to Morocco; Road to Utopia; Robin and the 7 Hoods; Son of Paleface; Stagecoach (Douglas); That's Entertainment!.*

Cruise, Tom *All the Right Moves; Born on the Fourth of July; Cocktail; Color of Money, The; Days of Thunder; Far and Away; Few Good Men, A; Firm, The; Interview with the Vampire; Jerry Maguire; Legend; Losin' It; Mission Impossible; Outsiders, The (Coppola); Rain Man; Risky Business; Taps; Top Gun.*

Curtis, Tony *Bad News Bears Go to Japan, The; Boston Strangler, The; Brainwaves; Celluloid Closet, The; Count of Monte-Cristo, The; Criss Corss (Siodmak); Defiant Ones, The; Don't Make Waves; Francis; Insignificance; Kings Go Forth; Last Tycoon, The; Lepke; List of Adrian Messenger, The; Little Miss Marker; Manitou, The; Mirror Crack'd. The; Mister Cory; Naked in New York; Operation Petticoat; Sex and the Single Girl; Sierra; Some Like It Hot; Spartacus; Sweet Smell of Success; Vikings, The; Winchester '73.*

Cushing, Peter *Abominable Snowman, The; Alexander the Great (Rossen); ...And Now the Screaming Starts (aka Fengriffen); Arabian Adventure; Asylum; At the Earth's Core; Beast Must Die, The; Biggles; Black Night, The; Blood Beast Terror, The (aka The Vampire Beast Craves Blood); Brides of Dracula, The; Cash on Demand; Chump at Oxford, A; Creeping Flesh, The; Curse of Frankenstein, The; Daleks – Invasion Earth 2150 A.D.; Dr Phibes Rises Again; Dr Terror's House of Horrors; Dr Who and the Daleks; Dracula (aka Horror of Dracula); Dracula A.D.1972; Fear in the Night; Flesh and the Fiends, The (aka Mania/Psycho Killers/The Fiendish Ghouls); Frankenstein and the Monster from Hell; Frankenstein Created Woman; Frankenstein Must Be Destroyed; From Beyond the Grave; Ghoul, The (Francis); Gorgon, The; Horror Express (Pánico en el Transiberiano); Hound of the Baskervilles, The (Fisher); House of the Long Shadows, The; House That Dripped Blood, The; I, Monster; Incense for the Damned; Legend of the 7 Golden Vampires, The; Legend of the Werewolf; Madhouse (Clark); Mummy, The (Fisher); Night of the Big Heat; No Secrets (aka Touch of the Sun);*

*Nothing But the Night;
Revenge of Frankenstein,
The; Satanic Rites of
Dracula, The (aka Count
Dracula and His Vampire
Bride); Scream and Scream
Again; She; Skull, The; Star
Wars; Sword of the Valiant –
The Legend of Gawain and
the Green Knight, The; Time
Without Pity; Top Secret!;
Torture Garden; Trial by
Combat (aka A Choice of
Weapons/Dirty Knight's
Work); Twins of Evil;
Uncanny, The; Vampire
Lovers, The.*

Darrieux, Danielle *Alexander
the Great (Rossen); Club de
Femmes; Demoiselles de
Rochefort, Les (The Young
Girls of Rochefort); 5
Fingers; Greengage
Summer, The (aka Loss of
Innocence); Madame de...
(The Earrings of Madame
de...); Mayerling; Plaisir, Le
(House of Pleasure); Ronde,
La; Scene of the Crime, The
(Le Lieu du Crime).*

Davis, Bette *All About Eve; All
This and Heaven Too;
Anniversary, The; Beyond
the Forest; Bordertown;
Bunny O'Hare; Bureau of
Missing Persons; Burnt
Offerings; Connecting
Rooms; Dangerous; Dark
Victory; Death on the Nile;
Deception; Fog Over Frisco;
Front Page Woman; Great
Lie, The; Hush...Hush, Sweet
Charlotte; In This Our Life;
It's Love I'm After; Jezebel;
Juarez; Kid Galahad (Curtiz);
Letter, The; Little Foxes,
The; Madame Sin; Man
Who Came to Dinner, The;
Marked Woman; Mr
Skeffington; Nanny, The;
Now, Voyager; Old
Acquaintance; Petrified
Forest, The; Phone Call from
a Stranger; Private Lives of
Elizabeth and Essex, The;
Return from Witch
Mountain; Satan Met a
Lady; Sisters, The; Star,
The; Stolen Life, A; Storm
Center; Thank Your Lucky
Stars; 20,000 Years in Sing
Sing; Watcher in the Woods,
The; Whales of August, The;
What Ever Happened to
Baby Jane?; Wicked
Stepmother.*

Davis, Geena *Accidental Hero;
Accidental Tourist, The;
Angie; Beetlejuice;
CutThroat Island; Earth
Girls are Easy; Fly, The
(Cronenberg); Quick Change;
League of Their Own, A;
Long Kiss Goodnight, The;
Speechless; Thelma &
Louise.*

Day-Lewis, Daniel *Age of
Innocence, The; Bounty,
The; Boxer, The; Crucible,
The; In the Name of the
Father; Last of the
Mohicans, The; My Beautiful
Laundrette; My Left Foot;
Nanou; Room With a View,
A; Stars and Bars;
Unbearable Lightness of
Being, The.*

Dean, James *East of Eden;
Fixed Bayonets; Giant; Has
Anybody Seen My Gal?; Rebel
Without a Cause.*

de Havilland, Olivia
*Adventurers, The;
Adventures of Robin Hood,
The; Airport '77; Anthony
Adverse; Captain Blood;
Charge of the Light Brigade,
The (Curtiz); Dark Mirror,
The; Devotion; Dodge City;
Gone With the Wind; Great
Garrick, The; Heiress, The;
Hold Back the Dawn;
Hush...Hush Sweet Charlotte;
In This Our Life; It's Love
I'm After; Libel; Light in the
Piazza; Midsummer Night's
Dream, A (Reinhardt/
Dieterle); My Cousin Rachel;
Not As a Stranger; Pope
Joan; Private Lives of
Elizabeth and Essex, The;
Santa Fe Trail; Snake Pit,
The; Swarm, The; Thank
Your Lucky Stars; That
Lady; They Died With Their
Boots On.*

Deneuve, Catherine *Agression,
L' (Aggression); April Fools,
The; Argent des Autres, L'
(Other People's Money); Belle
de Jour; Courage Fuyons
(Courage – Let's Run);
Convent, The (O Convento);
Demoiselles de Rochefort,
Les (The Young Girls of
Rochefort); Drama of the
Rich (Fatti di Gente
Perbene); Ecoute Voir... (See
Here My Love); Flic, Un
(Dirty Money); Hunger, The;
Hustle; Indochine; Last
Metro, The (Le Dernier
Métro); Let's Hope It's a Girl
(Speriamo che sia Femmina);
March or Die; Ma Saison
Préférée; Parapluies de
Cherbourg, Les (The
Umbrellas of Cherbourg);
Peau d'Ane (The Magic
Donkey); Repulsion;
Sauvage, Le; Scene of the
Crime, The (Le Lieu du
Crime); Second Chance (Si
c'était à refaire); Sirène du
Mississipi, La (Mississippi
Mermaid); Slightly Pregnant
Man, The (L'Evènement le
plus Important depuis que
l'Homme a Marché sur la
Lune); Strange Place to
Meet, A (Drôle d'Endroit
pour une Rencontre);
Tristana; Voleurs, Les.*

De Niro, Robert *Angel Heart;
Awakenings; Backdraft;
Bloody Mama; Brazil; Bronx
Tale, A; Cape Fear
(Scorsese); Casino; CopLand;
Deer Hunter, The; Falling in
Love; Fan, The (Scott);
Godfather Part II, The;
GoodFellas; Great
Expectations (Cuarón);
Greetings; Guilty by
Suspicion; Heat (Mann); Hi,
Mom!; Jackie Brown;
Jacknife; King of Comedy,
The; Last Tycoon, The; Mad
Dog and Glory; Marvin's
Room; Mary Shelley's
Frankenstein; Mean Streets;
Midnight Run; Mission, The;
Mistress; New York, New
York; Night and the City
(Winkler); 1900 (Novecento);*

*Once Upon a Time in
America; Raging Bull;
Sleepers; Stanley & Iris; Taxi
Driver; This Boy's Life; True
Confessions; Untouchables,
The; Wag the Dog; We're No
Angels (Jordan).*

Depardieu, Gérard *Buffet
Froid; Camille Claudel;
Chiens, Les (The Dogs); Cible
émouvante (Moving Target);
Colonel Chabert, Le (Angelo);
Cyrano de Bergerac; Danton;
1492: Conquest of Paradise;
Germinal; Green Card;
Hamlet (Branagh); Hussard
sur le toit, Le (The
Horseman on the Roof); I
Love You, I Don't (Je t'aime,
moi non plus); I Want to Go
Home (Je veux rentrer à la
maison); Jean de Florette;
Last Metro, The (Le Dernier
Métro); Last Woman, The
(L'Ultima Donna); Left-
Handed Woman, The (Die
linkshändige Frau); Loulou;
Maîtresse; Man in the Iron
Mask, The (Wallace); Merci
la vie (Thank You, Life);
Mon Oncle d'Amérique (My
American Uncle/My Uncle
from America); Mon Père, ce
héros; Moon in the Gutter,
The (La Lune dans le
Caniveau); My Father, the
Hero (Milner); Nathalie
Granger; 1900 (Novecento);
Peu de Soleil dans l'Eau
Froide, Un (Sunlight on Cold
Water); Police; Préparez Vos
Mouchoirs (Get Out Your
Handkerchiefs); Pure
Formality, A (Un Pura
Formalità); Retour de
Martin Guerre, Le (The
Return of Martin Guerre);
Secret Agent, The (aka
Joseph Conrad's The Secret
Agent); Sous le Soleil de
Satan (Under Satan's Sun);
Stavisky...; Strange Place to
Meet, A (Drôle d'Endroit
pour une rencontre);
Tartuffe; Tenue de Soirée
(Evening Dress); This Sweet
Sickness (Dites-lui que Je
l'aime); Tous les matins du
monde; Trop belle pour toi!
(Too Beautiful for You);
Unhook the Stars (Décroches
les étoiles); Uranus;
Valseuses, Les (Going
Places/Making It); Woman
Next Door, The (La Femme
d'à côté); Woman or Two, A
(Une Femme ou Deux).*

Depp, Johnny *Arizona
Dreaming; Benny and Joon;
Brave, The; Cry-Baby; Dead
Man; Don Juan DeMarco;
Donnie Brasco; Edward
Scissorhands; Ed Wood;
Fear and Loathing in Las
Vegas; Nick of Time;
Nightmare on Elm Street, A;
What's Eating Gilbert Grape.*

DeVito, Danny *Batman
Returns; Get Shorty; Hoffa;
Jack the Bear; Jewel of the
Nile, The; Johnny
Dangerously; Junior; LA
Confidential; Mars Attacks!;
My Little Pony; Other
People's Money; Renaissance
Man; Roald Dahl's Matilda;
Romancing the Stone;
Ruthless People; Scalawag;*

*Terms of Endearment;
Throw Momma from the
Train; Tin Men; Twins;
War of the Roses, The; Wise
Guys.*

Dietrich, Marlene *Angel
(Lubitsch); Around the
World in 80 Days; Blonde
Venus; Blue Angel, The
(Der blaue Engel); Desire;
Destry Rides Again; Devil Is
a Woman, The;
Dishonored; Flame of New
Orleans, The; Foreign
Affair, A; Garden of Allah,
The; Judgment at
Nuremberg; Just a Gigolo
(Schöner Gigolo – Armer
Gigolo); Knight Without
Armour; Manpower;
Morocco; No Highway (aka
No Highway in the Sky);
Rancho Notorious; Scarlet
Empress, The; Seven
Sinners; Shanghai Express;
Song of Songs; Stage
Fright; Touch of Evil;
Witness for the Prosecution.*

Donat, Robert *Captain Boycott;
Citadel, The (Vidor); Ghost
Goes West, The; Goodbye,
Mr Chips (Wood); Inn of the
Sixth Happiness, The;
Knight Without Armour;
Lease of Life; Magic Box,
The; New Lot, The; Perfect
Strangers (aka Vacation
from Marriage); Private Life
of Henry VIII, The; 39
Steps, The (Hitchcock);
Young Mr Pitt, The.*

Douglas, Kirk *Ace in the Hole
(aka The Big Carnival);
Arrangement, The; Bad and
the Beautiful, The; Bi Sky,
The; Brotherhood, The; Cast
a Giant Shadow; Catch Me a
Spy (aka To Catch a Spy);
Champion; Cinderella
Liberty; Detective Story;
Final Countdown, The; Fury,
The; Gunfight, A; Gunfight
at the O.K. Corral; Heroes of
Telemark, The; Holocaust
2000 (aka The Children);
Indian Fighter, The; In
Harm's Way; Jacqueline
Susann's Once Is Not
Enough; Last Sunset, The;
Last Train from Gun Hill;
Letter to Three Wives, A;
Light at the Edge of the
World, The; List of Adrian
Messenger, The; Lonely Are
the Brave; Lovely Way to
Die, A (aka A Lovely Way to
Go); Lust for Life; Man from
Snowy River, The; Man to
Respect, A (Un Uomo da
Rispettare); Man Without a
Star; Oscar; Out of the Past
(aka Build My Gallows High);
Paths of Glory; Posse;
Saturn 3; Scalawag; Seven
Days in May; Spartacus;
Strange Love of Martha
Ivers, The; Strangers When
We Meet; There Was a
Crooked Man; Tough Guys;
20,000 Leagues Under the
Sea; Two Weeks in Another
Town; Victory at Entebbe;
Vikings, The; Villain, The
(aka Cactus Jack); War
Wagon, The; Way West,
The; Young Man With a
Horn (aka Young Man of
Music).*

Douglas, Melvyn *Advance to the Rear; Americanization of Emily, The; Angel (Lubitsch); Annie Oakley; As You Desire Me; Being There; Billy Budd; Candidate, The; Captains Courageous; Changeling, The; Ghost Story; Gorgeous Hussy, The; Great Sinner, The; Hud; I Never Sang for My Father; Mr Blandings Builds His Dream House; My Forbidden Past; Ninotchka; Old Dark House, The; Seduction of Joe Tynan, The; Shining Hour, The; Tell Me a Riddle; Tenant, The (Le Locataire); Theodora Goes Wild; Twilight's Last Gleaming; Two-Faced Woman; Vampire Bat, The; Woman's Face, A; Woman's Secret, A.*

Douglas, Michael *American President, The; Basic Instinct; Black Rain (Scott); China Syndrome, The; Chorus Line, A; Coma; Disclosure; Falling Down; Fatal Attraction; Jewel of the Nile, The; Napoleon and Samantha; Romancing the Stone; Shining Through; Star Chamber, The; Wall Street; War of the Roses.*

Dreyfuss, Richard *Addicted to Love; Always (Spielberg); American Graffiti; American President, The; Another Stakeout Apprenticeship of Duddy Kravitz, The; Big Fix, The; Close Encounters of the Third Kind; Close Encounters of the Third Kind – Special Edition; Competition, The; Dillinger (Milius); Down and Out in Beverly Hills; Game, The; Goodbye Girl, The; Inserts; Jaws; Let It Ride; Lost in Yonkers; Mad Dog Time (aka Trigger Happy); Mr Holland's Opus; Moon Over Parador; Night Falls on Manhattan; Nuts; Once Around; Postcards from the Edge; Rosencrantz and Guildenstern Are Dead; Silent Fall; Stakeout; Stand by Me; Tin Men; Victory at Entebbe; What About Bob?; Whose Life Is It Anyway?*

Dunaway, Faye *Albino Alligator; Arizona Dreaming; Arrangement, The; Barfly; Bonnie and Clyde; Burning Secret; Chamber, The; Champ, The; Chinatown; Deadly Trap, The (La Maison sous les Arbres); Doc; Don Juan DeMarco; Dunston Checks In; Eyes of Laura Mars; First Deadly Sin, The; Four Musketeers: The Revenge of Milady, The; Handmaid's Tale, The; Happening, The; Hurry Sundown; Little Big Man; Mommie Dearest; Network; Oklahoma Crude; Ordeal by Innocence; Puzzle of a Downfall Child; Scorchers; Supergirl; Thomas Crown Affair, The; Three Days of the Condor; Three Musketeers: The Queen's Diamonds, The; Towering Inferno, The;*

Voyage of the Damned; Wicked Lady, The (Winner).

Duryea, Dan *Along Came Jones; Ball of Fire; Battle Hymn; Black Angel; Criss Cross; Flight of the Phoenix, The; Lady on a Train; Little Foxes, The; Ministry of Fear; Night Passage; None But the Lonely Heart; Sahara; Scarlet Street; Silver Lode; Winchester '73; Woman in the Window, The; World for Ransom.*

Duvall, Robert *Apocalypse Now; Apostle, The; Badge 373; Betsy, The; Breakout; Bullitt; Chase, The; Colors; Conversation, The; Countdown; Days of Thunder; Deep Impact; Detective, The; Eagle Has Landed, The; Falling Down; Geronimo: An American Legend; Godfather, The; Godfather Part II, The; Greatest, The; Great Northfield Minnesota Raid, The; Great Santini, The; Handmaid's Tale, The; Invasion of the Body Snatchers (Kaufman); Joe Kidd; Killer Elite, The; Lady Ice; Lawman; Lightship, The; M*A*S*H; Natural, The; Network; Newsies (aka The News Boys); Outfit, The; Paper, The; Phenomenon; Rain People, The; Rambling Rose; Revolutionary, The; Scarlet Letter, The; Seven-Per-Cent Solution, The; Show of Force, A; Sling Blade; Something to Talk About; Stone Boy, The; Tender Mercies; Terry Fox Story, The; THX 1138; To Kill a Mockingbird; True Confessions; True Grit; Wrestling Ernest Hemingway.*

Eastwood, Clint *Absolute Power; Any Which Way You Can; Away All Boats; Beguiled, The; Bridges of Madison County, The; Bronco Billy; City Heat; Coogan's Bluff; Dead Pool, The; Dirty Harry; Eiger Sanction, The; Enforcer, The (Fargo); Escape from Alcatraz; Every Which Way But Loose; Firefox; Fistful of Dollars, A (Per un Pugno di Dollari); For a Few Dollars More (Per Qualche Dollari in Più); Gauntlet, The; Good, the Bad and the Ugly, The (Il Buono, il Brutto, il Cattivo); Hang 'em High; Heartbreak Ridge; High Plains Drifter; Honkytonk Man; In the Line of Fire; Joe Kidd; Kelly's Heroes; Magnum Force; Outlaw Josey Wales, The; Paint Your Wagon; Pale Rider; Perfect World, A; Play Misty for Me; Revenge of the Creature; Rookie, The; Sudden Impact; Tarantula; Thunderbolt and Lightfoot; Tightrope; Two Mules for Sister Sara; Unforgiven; Where Eagles Dare; White Hunter, Black Heart; Wild Bill: A Hollywood Maverick.*

Falk, Peter *All the Marbles (aka The California Dolls);*

Big Trouble; Brink's Job, The; Castle Keep; Cheap Detective, The; Cookie; Faraway, So Close (In weiter Ferne, so nah!); Husbands; In-Laws, The; In the Spirit; It's a Mad, Mad, Mad, Mad World; Luv; Mikey and Nicky; Murder by Death; Princess Bride, The; Sbarco di Anzio, Lo (Anzio/The Battle for Anzio); Tune in Tomorrow (aka Aunt Julia and the Scriptwriter); Wind Across the Everglades; Wings of Desire (Der Himmel über Berlin); Woman Under the Influence, A.

Farrow, Mia *Alice (Allen); Another Woman; Avalanche; Broadway Danny Rose; Crimes and Misdemeanors; Dandy in Aspic, A; Death on the Nile; Docteur Popaul (High Heels/ Scoundrel in White); Full Circle (aka The Haunting of Julia); Great Gatsby, The (Clayton); Hannah and Her Sisters; Hurricane; Husbands and Wives; John and Mary; Miami Rhapsody; Midsummer Night's Sex Comedy, A; New York Stories; Purple Rose of Cairo, The; Radio Days; Rosemary's Baby; Secret Ceremony; September; Shadows and Fog; Supergirl; Wedding, A; Widows' Peak; Zelig.*

Fields, WC *Alice in Wonderland (McLeod); Bank Dick, The; David Copperfield; Her Majesty, Love; If I Had a Million; International House; It's a Gift; It's the Old Army Game; Man on the Flying Trapeze, The; My Little Chickadee; Never Give a Sucker an Even Break (aka What a Man!); Old-Fashioned Way, The; Sally of the Sawdust; You Can't Cheat an Honest Man.*

Finch, Peter *Abdication, The; Battle of the River Plate, The (aka Pursuit of the Graf Spee); Bequest to the Nation (aka The Nelson Affair); Dark Avenger, The (aka The Warriors); England Made Me; Far From the Madding Crowd; Father Brown; Flight of the Phoenix, The; Girl with Green Eyes; Heart of the Matter, The; Judith; Legend of Lylah Clare, The; Lost Horizon (Jarrott); Network; Nun's Story, The; Operation Amsterdam; Passage Home; Pumpkin Eater, The; Raid on Entebbe; Simon and Laura; Sins of Rachel Cade, The; Something to Hide; Story of Gilbert and Sullivan, The (aka The Great Gilbert and Sullivan); Sunday, Bloody Sunday; 10:30 P.M. Summer; Town Like Alice, A (aka The Rape of Malaya); Trials of Oscar Wilde, The (aka The Man With the Green Carnation); Train of Events; Windom's Way; Wooden Horse, The.*

Finney, Albert *Annie; Browning Version, The; Charlie Bubbles; Dresser, The; Duellists, The; Entertainer, The; Gumshoe; Looker; Loophole; Man of No Importance, A; Miller's Crossing; Murder on the Orient Express; Night Must Fall (Reisz); Orphans; Playboys, The; Rich in Love; Run of the Country, The; Saturday Night and Sunday Morning; Scrooge; Shoot the Moon; Tom Jones; Two For the Road; Under the Volcano; Victors, The; Washington Square; Wolfen.*

Fishburne, Laurence *Apocalypse Now; Boyz N the Hood; Class Action; Count a Lonely Cadence (aka Stockade); Deep Cover; Event Horizon; Fled; Higher Learning; Just Cause; King of New York; Nightmare on Elm Street 3: Dream Warriors, A; Othello (Parker); Red Heat; Rumble Fish; School Daze; Searching for Bobby Fischer (aka Innocent Moves); Tina: What's Love Got to Do With It (aka What's Love Got to Do With It).*

Flynn, Errol *Adventures of Don Juan (aka The New Adventures of Don Juan); Adventures of Robin Hood, The; Another Dawn; Dark Avenger, The (aka The Warriors); Captain Blood; Charge of the Light Brigade, The (Curtiz); Cry Wolf; Dawn Patrol, The; Desperate Journey; Dive Bomber; Dodge City; Edge of Darkness; Gentleman Jim; Green Light; Kim; Objective, Burma!; Private Lives of Elizabeth and Essex, The; Santa Fe Trail; Sea Hawk, The; Sisters, The; Sun Also Rises, The; Thank Your Lucky Stars; They Died With Their Boots On.*

Fonda, Henry *Advise and Consent; Alpha Caper, The (aka Inside Job); Ash Wednesday; Battle of the Bulge; Best Man, The; Big Hand for the Little Lady, A (aka Big Deal at Dodge City); Big Street, The; Blockade; Boston Strangler, The; Chad Hanna; Cheyenne Social Club, The; City on Fire; Daisy Kenyon; Drums Along the Mohawk; Fail Safe; Fedora; Fort Apache; Fugitive, The (Ford); Grapes of Wrath, The; How the West Was Won; Immortal Sergeant, The; In Harm's Way; Jesse James; Jezebel; Lady Eve, The; Last of the Cowboys, The (aka The Great Smokey Roadblock); Lillian Russell; Longest Day, The; Long Night, The; Madigan; Mad Miss Manton, The; Meteor; Midway (aka Battle of Midway); Mister Roberts; My Darling Clementine; My Name Is Nobody (Mio Nome è Nessuno); Once Upon a Time in the West (C'era una Volta* il West); On Golden Pond; Ox-Bow Incident, The (aka Strange Incident); Return of Frank James, The; Rollercoaster; Rounders, The; Serpent, The (Le Serpent); Sex and the Single Girl; Sometimes a Great Notion (aka Never Give an Inch); Swarm, The; Tentacles (Tentacoli); There Was a Crooked Man; Tin Star, The; Too Late the Hero; 12 Angry Men; Wanda Nevada; War and Peace (Vidor); Warlock (Dmytryk); Welcome to Hard Times (aka Killer on a Horse); Wings of the Morning; Wrong Man, The; Young Mr Lincoln; You Only Live Once; Yours, Mine and Ours.

Fonda, Jane Agnes of God; Any Wednesday (aka Bachelor Girl Apartment); Barbarella; Barefoot in the Park; Blue Bird, The; California Suite; Cat Ballou; Chapman Report, The; Chase, The; China Syndrome, The; Comes a Horseman; Coming Home; Dollmaker, The; Doll's House, A (Losey); Electric Horseman, The; F.T.A.; Fun With Dick and Jane; Histoires Extraordinaires (Spirits of the Dead/Tales of Mystery); Hurry Sundown; Julia; Klute; Morning After, The; Nine to Five; Old Gringo; On Golden Pond; Period of Adjustment; Rollover; Stanley & Iris; Steelyard Blues; They Shoot Horses, Don't They?; Tout Va Bien; Walk on the Wild Side.

Fontaine, Joan Beyond a Reasonable Doubt; Bigamist, The; Born to Be Bad; Casanova's Big Night; Damsel in Distress, A; Emperor Waltz, The; Frenchman's Creek; Gunga Din; Island in the Sun; Ivanhoe; Ivy; Jane Eyre (Stevenson); Letter from an Unknown Woman; Rebecca; Suspicion; This Above All; Women, The.

Ford, Glenn Advance to the Rear; Americano, The; Appointment in Honduras; Big Heat, The; Blackboard Jungle, The; Border Shootout; Cimarron; Cowboy; Day of the Evil Gun; Experiment in Terror (aka The Grip of Fear); Fastest Gun Alive, The; Gazebo, The; Gilda; Human Desire; Last Challenge, The (aka The Pistolero of Red River); Love Is a Ball (aka All This and Money Too); Man from Colorado, The; Midway (aka Battle of Midway); Rounders, The; Santee; Secret of Convict Lake, The; Sheepman, The; Stolen Life, A; Superman; Teahouse of the August Moon, The; 3.10 to Yuma; Torpedo Run; Undercover Man; Virus (Fukkatsu no Hi); White Tower, The.

Ford, Harrison Air Force One; American Graffiti; Blade

Runner; Blade Runner – The Director's Cut; Clear and Present Danger; Devil's Own, The; Empire Strikes Back, The; Emiper Strikes Back: Special Edition, The; Force 10 from Navarone; Frantic; Fugitive, The (Davis); Hanover Street; Heroes; Indiana Jones and the Last Crusade; Indiana Jones and the Temple of Doom; Mosquito Coast, The; Patriot Games; Presumed Innocent; Raiders of the Lost Ark; Regarding Henry; Return of the Jedi; Return of the Jedi: Special Edition; Sabrina Fair; Star Wars; Star Wars, Episode IV, A New Hope; Witness; Working Girl.

Foster, Jodie Accused, The; Bugsy Malone; Candleshoe; Carny; Catchfire; Contact; Five Corners; Foxes; Freaky Friday; Hotel New Hampshire, The; Little Man Tate; Maverick; Napoleon and Samantha; Nell; Shadows and Fog; Siesta; Silence of the Lambs, The; Sommersby; Stealing Home; Taxi Driver; Tom Sawyer.

Freeman, Morgan Amistad; Bonfire of the Vanities, The; Brubaker; Clean and Sober; Deep Impact; Driving Miss Daisy; Glory; Johnny Handsome; Hard Rain; Marie; Kiss the Girls; Moll Flanders; Outbreak; Power of One, The; Robin Hood: Prince of Thieves; Seven (aka Se7en); Shawshank Redemption, The; That Was Then, This Is Now; Unforgiven.

Gabin, Jean Bas-Fonds, Les (The Lower Depths); Belle Equipe, La; Bête Humaine, La (The Human Beast/Judas Was a Woman); Chat, Le (The Cat); Du Rififi à Paname (Rififi in Paris/The Upper Hand); En Cas de Malheur (La Ragazza del Peccato/Love Is My Profession); French Cancan; Grande Illusion, La; Gueule d'Amour; Jour se lève, Le (Daybreak); Misérables, Les; Pépé le Moko; Plaisir, Le (House of Pleasure); Quai des Brumes, Le (Port of Shadows); Sicilian Clan, The (Le Clan des Siciliens); Touchez pas au Grisbi (Grisbi/Honour Among Thieves); Verdict (The Verdict); Zouzou.

Gable, Clark Across the Wide Missouri; After Office Hours; Boom Town; China Seas; Command Decision; Comrade X; Gone With the Wind; Idiot's Delight; It Happened One Night; It Started in Naples; Love on the Run; Manhattan Melodrama; Misfits, The; Mogambo; Mutiny on the Bounty (Lloyd); Night Nurse; Red Dust; San Francisco; Strange Cargo; Tall Men, The; Too Hot to Handle.

Garbo, Greta Anna Christie; Anna Karenina (Brown); As You Desire Me; Camille (Cukor); Flesh and the Devil; Grand Hotel; Joyless Street, The (Die freudlose Gasse); Kiss, The (Feyder); Mata Hari (Fitzmaurice); Ninotchka; Painted Veil, The; Queen Christina; Two-Faced Woman.

Gardner, Ava Barefoot Contessa, The; Bhowani Junction; Bible...In the Beginning, The (La Bibbia); Blue Bird, The; Bribe, The; Cassandra Crossing, The; City on Fire; Earthquake; 55 Days at Peking; Great Sinner, The; Hitler's Madman; Kid Glove Killer; Kidnapping of the President, The; Killers, The (Siodmak); Life and Times of Judge Roy Bean, The; Little Hut, The; Mogambo; My Forbidden Past; Night of the Iguana, The; One Touch of Venus; On the Beach; Pandora and the Flying Dutchman; Permission to Kill; Priest of Love; Sentinel, The; Seven Days in May; Show Boat (Sidney); Snows of Kilimanjaro, The; Sun Also Rises, The; Thank Your Lucky Stars.

Garfield, John Air Force; Body and Soul (Rossen); Breaking Point, The (Curtiz); Dangerously They Live; Force of Evil; Gentleman's Agreement; Humoresque; Juarez; Nobody Lives Forever; Out of the Fog; Postman Always Rings Twice, The (Garnett); Pride of the Marines (aka Forever in Love); Saturday's Children; Sea Wolf, The.

Garland, Judy Babes in Arms; Babes on Broadway; Child Is Waiting, A; Clock, The (aka Under the Clock); Easter Parade; For Me and My Gal; Harvey Girls, The; I Could Go On Singing; In the Good Old Summertime; Judgment at Nuremberg; Little Nellie Kelly; Meet Me in St Louis; Pirate, The; Pigskin Parade; Star Is Born, A (Cukor); Strike Up the Band; Summer Stock (aka If You Feel Like Singing); Wizard of Oz, The; Ziegfeld Follies; Ziegfeld Girl.

Gazzara, Ben Anatomy of a Murder; Big Lebowski, The; Bloodline (aka Sidney Sheldon's Bloodline); Bridge at Remagen, The; Capone; First Knight; Girl from Trieste, The (La Ragazza di Trieste); Happiness; Husbands; Killing of a Chinese Bookie, The; Neptune Factor, The; Opening Night; Road House (Herrington); Saint Jack; Strange One, The (aka End as a Man); Tales of Ordinary Madness (Storie di Ordinaria Follia); They All Laughed; Voyage of the Damned.

Gere, Richard American Gigolo; And the Band Played On; Baby Blue Marine; Bloodbrothers; Breathless; Cotton Club, The; Days of Heaven; Final Analysis; Honorary Consul, The (aka Beyond the Limit); Internal Affairs; Intersection; Jackal, The; King David; Looking for Mr Goodbar; Miles from Home; Mr Jones; No Mercy; Officer and a Gentleman, An; Power; Pretty Woman; Red Corner; Report to the Commissioner (aka Operation Undercover); Rhapsody in August (Hachigatsu no Kyoshikyoku); Sommersby; Yanks.

Gibson, Mel Air America; Bird on a Wire; Bounty, The; Braveheart; Conspiracy Theory; FairyTale – A True Story; Fathers' Day; Forever Young (Miner); Gallipoli; Hamlet (Zeffirelli); Lethal Weapon; Lethal Weapon 2; Lethal Weapon 3; Mad Max; Mad Max 2; Mad Max Beyond Thunderdome; Man Without a Face, The; Maverick; Mrs Soffel; Ransom; River, The (Rydell); Tequila Sunrise; Tim; Year of Living Dangerously, The.

Gielgud, John Aces High; Appointment With Death; Arthur; Arthur 2: On the Rocks; Caligula; Charge of the Light Brigade, The (Richardson); Chariots of Fire; Chimes at Midnight (Campanadas a Medianoche); Conductor, The (Dyrygent); Elephant Man, The; 11 Harrowhouse; Formula, The; Frankenstein: The True Story; Gandhi; Getting It Right; Gold; Good Companions, The; Hamlet (Branagh); Haunted; Human Factor, The (Preminger); Joseph Andrews; Julius Caesar; Lion of the Desert; Looking for Richard; Lost Horizon (Jarrott); Loved One, The; Murder by Decree; Murder on the Orient Express; Oh! What a Lovely War; Plenty; Portrait of a Lady, The; Portrait of the Artist as a Young Man, A; Power of One, The; Priest of Love; Prospero's Books; Providence; Richard III; Saint Joan; Scandalous; Secret Agent, The; Shine; Shining Through; Shoes of the Fisherman, The; Shooting Party, The; Sphinx; TV Dante: Cantos I-VIII, A; Wagner; Whistle Blower, The; Wicked Lady, The (Winner).

Gish, Lillian Birth of a Nation, The (Griffith); Broken Blossoms (Griffith); Cobweb, The; Comedians, The; Duel in the Sun; Hambone and Hillie (aka The Adventures of Hambone and Hillie); Intolerance; Night of the Hunter, The; Orders to Kill; Orphans of the Storm; Portrait of Jennie; Scarlet Letter, The (Sjöström); Sweet

Liberty; Unforgiven, The; Warning Shot; Way Down East; Wedding, A; Whales of August, The; Wind, The.

Goldberg, Whoopi Associate, The; Boys on the Side; Burglar; Celluloid Closet, The; Clara's Heart; Color Purple, The; Corrina, Corrina; Eddie; Fatal Beauty; Ghost; Ghosts of Mississippi (aka Ghosts from the Past); Jumpin' Jack Flash; Lion King, The; Little Rascals, The; Made in America; Moonlight and Valentino; Player, The; Sarafina!; Sister Act; Sister Act 2: Back in the Habit; Soapdish; Star Trek: Generations.

Goldblum, Jeff Adventures of Buckaroo Banzai Across the 8th Dimension, The; Between the Lines; Beyond Therapy; Big Chill, The; California Split; Deep Cover; Earth Girls Are Easy; Favour, the Watch and the Very Big Fish, The (Rue Saint-Sulpice); Fly, The (Cronenberg); Great White Hype, The; Independence Day; Into the Night; Invasion of the Body Snatchers (Kaufman); Jurassic Park; Lost World; Jurassic Park, The; Lush Life; Mad Dog Time (aka Trigger Happy); Mad Monkey, The (El Mono Loco); Mister Frost; Nine Months; Powder; Remember My Name; Right Stuff, The; St Ives; Sentinel, The; Silverado; Tall Guy, The; Thank God It's Friday.

Grable, Betty Beautiful Blonde from Bashful Bend, The; Follow the Fleet; Gay Divorcee, The; How to Be Very, Very Popular; How to Marry a Millionaire; I Wake Up Screaming (aka Hot Spot); Mother Wore Tights; Pigskin Parade; Pin Up Girl; Yank in the RAF, A.

Grahame, Gloria Bad and the Beautiful, The; Big Heat, The; Cobweb, The; Crossfire; Good Die Young, The; Greatest Show on Earth, The; Head Over Heels; Human Desire; In a Lonely Place; It Happened in Brooklyn; It's a Wonderful Life; Macao; Mama's Dirty Girls; Man on a Tightrope; Mansion of the Doomed (aka The Terror of Dr Chaney); Melvin and Howard; Not as a Stranger; Odds Against Tomorrow; Oklahoma!; Sudden Fear; Todd Killings, The; Woman's Secret, A.

Grant, Cary Affair to Remember, An; Alice in Wonderland (McLeod); Arsenic and Old Lace; Awful Truth, The; Bishop's Wife, The; Blonde Venus; Bringing Up Baby; Charade; Crisis; Father Goose; Grass Is Greener, The; Gunga Din; His Girl Friday; Holiday; Houseboat; I'm No Angel; Indiscreet; In Name Only; I

Was a Male War Bride (aka You Can't Sleep Here); Merrily We Go to Hell; Mr Blandings Builds His Dream House; Monkey Business (Hawks); My Favourite Wife; Night and Day; None But the Lonely Heart; North by Northwest; Notorious; Once Upon a Honeymoon; Once Upon a Time; Only Angels Have Wings; Operation Petticoat; Penny Serenade; People Will Talk; Philadelphia Story, The; Pride and the Passion, The; She Done Him Wrong; Suspicion; Sylvia Scarlett; Talk of the Town, The; To Catch a Thief; Topper.

Greenstreet, Sydney Across the Pacific; Background to Danger; Casablanca; Conflict; Conspirators, The; Devotion; In This Our Life; Malaya (aka East of the Rising Sun); Maltese Falcon, The; Mask of Dimitrios, The; Passage to Marseille; Ruthless; They Died With Their Boots On; Verdict, The (Siegel).

Griffith, Melanie Body Double; Bonfire of the Vanities, The; Born Yesterday; Cherry 2000; Close to Eden; Drowning Pool, The; In the Spirit; Lolita (Lyne); Milk Money; Mulholland Falls; Night Moves; Nobody's Fool; Now and Then; One on One; Pacific Heights; Paradise; Roar; Shining Through; Smile; Something Wild; Stormy Monday; Two Much (Loco de amor); Working Girl.

Guinness, Alec Barnacle Bill (aka All at Sea); Bridge on the River Kwai, The; Brother Sun, Sister Moon (Fratello Sole, Sorella Luna); Captain's Paradise, The; Card, The (aka The Promoter); Comedians, The; Cromwell; Doctor Zhivago; Empire Strikes Back, The; Fall of the Roman Empire, The; Father Brown; Great Expectations (Lean); Handful of Dust, A; Hitler: the Last Ten Days; HMS Defiant (aka Damn the Defiant); Horse's Mouth, The; Kafka; Kind Hearts and Coronets; Ladykillers, The; Last Holiday; Lavender Hill Mob, The; Lawrence of Arabia; Little Dorrit; Little Lord Fauntleroy; Lovesick; Man in the White Suit, The; Mudlark, The; Murder by Death; Mute Witness; Oliver Twist (Lean); Our Man in Havana; Passage to India, A; Prisoner, The; Quiller Memorandum, The; Raise the Titanic!; Return of the Jedi; Return of the Jedi: Special Edition; Run for Your Money, A; Scrooge; Star Wars; Star Wars, Episode IV, A New Hope; Tunes of Glory.

Hackman, Gene Absolute Power; All Night Long; Another Woman; Bat 21;

Birdcage, The; Bite the Bullet; Bonnie and Clyde; Bridge Too Far, A; Chamber, The; Cisco Pike; Class Action; Company Business; Conversation, The; Crimson Tide; Domino Principle, The (aka The Domino Killings); Downhill Racer; Eureka; Extreme Measures; Firm, The; French Connection, The; French Connection II; Full Moon in Blue Water; Geronimo: An American Legend; Get Shorty; Gypsy Moths, The; Hawaii; Hoosiers (aka Best Shot); I Never Sang for My Father; Lilith; Loose Cannons; Lucky Lady; March or Die; Marooned; Mississippi Burning; Narrow Margin; Night Moves; No Way Out; Package, The; Poseidon Adventure, The; Postcards from the Edge; Power; Prime Cut; Quick and the Dead, The; Reds; Scarecrow; Split, The; Superman; Superman II; Superman IV: The Quest for Peace; Target; Twice in a Lifetime; Twilight; Uncommon Valor; Under Fire; Unforgiven; Wyatt Earp; Young Frankenstein; Zandy's Bride.

Harlow, Jean China Seas; Dinner at Eight; Hell's Angels; Platinum Blonde; Public Enemy, The; Red Dust.

Harris, Richard Bible...In the Beginning, The (La Bibbia); Bloomfield (aka The Hero); Camelot; Caprice; Cassandra Crossing, The; Cromwell; Deadly Trackers, The; Field, The; Game for Vultures; Golden Rendezvous; Gulliver's Travels; Guns of Navarone, The; Hawaii; Heroes of Telemark, The; Juggernaut; King of the Wind; Long and the Short and the Tall, The; Major Dundee; Man Called Horse, A; Man in the Wilderness; Molly Maguires, The; Mutiny on the Bounty (Milestone); 99 and 44/100% Dead (aka Call Harry Crown); Orca (aka Orca...Killer Whale); Patriot Games; Red Desert, The (Deserto Rosso); Return of a Man Called Horse, The; Robin and Marian; Silent Tongue; Smilla's Feeling for Snow (Fräulein Smillas Gespür für Schnee/aka Smilla's Sense of Snow); Tarzan, The Ape Man; This Is the Sea; This Sporting Life; Triumphs of a Man Called Horse (El Triunfo de un Hombre Llamado Caballo); Trojan Eddie; Unforgiven; Wild Geese, The; Wrestling Ernest Hemingway.

Harrison, Rex Agony and the Ecstasy, The; Anna and the King of Siam; Ashanti; Blithe Spirit; Citadel, The (Vidor); Cleopatra (Mankiewicz); Ghost and Mrs Muir, The; Honey Pot,

The; Major Barbara; Men Are Not Gods; My Fair Lady; Night Train to Munich; Prince and the Pauper, The (aka Crossed Swords); Rake's Progress, The (aka Notorious Gentleman); St Martin's Lane (aka Sidewalks of London); Staircase; Unfaithfully Yours (Sturges).

Hawkins, Jack Adventures of Gerard, The; Angels One Five; Autumn Crocus; Ben-Hur (Wyler); Bridge on the River Kwai, The; Cruel Sea, The; Death at Broadcasting House; Elusive Pimpernel, The; Fallen Idol, The; Home at Seven (aka Murder on Monday); Jane Eyre (Mann); Judith; Kidnapped; Land of the Pharoahs; Lawrence of Arabia; League of Gentlemen, The; Long Arm, The (aka The Third Key); Lord Jim; Mandy (aka Crash of Silence); Masquerade (Dearden); Nicholas and Alexandra; No Highway (aka No Highway in the Sky); Peg of Old Drury; Prisoner, The; Rampage; Shalako; Small Back Room, The; State Secret (aka The Great Manhunt); Theatre of Blood; Waterloo; When Eight Bells Toll; Young Winston; Zulu.

Hayworth, Rita Angels Over Broadway; Blood and Sand (Mamoulian); Cover Girl; Dante's Inferno; Down to Earth; Gilda; Lady from Shanghai, The; Miss Sadie Thompson; Only Angels Have Wings; Pal Joey; Road to Salina (Sur la Route de Salina); You'll Never Get Rich; You Were Never Lovelier.

Hepburn, Audrey Always (Spielberg); Bloodline (aka Sidney Sheldon's Bloodline); Breakfast at Tiffany's; Charade; Funny Face; Lavender Hill Mob, The; Laughter in Paradise; Love in the Afternoon (Wilder); My Fair Lady; Nun's Story, The; Robin and Marian; Roman Holiday; Sabrina (aka Sabrina Fair); Secret People; They All Laughed; Two For the Road; Unforgiven, The; Wait Until Dark; War and Peace (Vidor).

Hepburn, Katharine Adam's Rib; African Queen, The; Alice Adams; Bill of Divorcement, A; Bringing Up Baby; Christopher Strong; Delicate Balance, A; Desk Set (aka His Other Woman); Grace Quigley; Guess Who's Coming to Dinner; Holiday; Keeper of the Flame; Lion in Winter, The; Little Women; Long Day's Journey into Night; Love Among the Ruins; Mary of Scotland; On Golden Pond; Pat and Mike; Philadelphia Story, The; Rooster Cogburn; Spitfire; Stage Door (La Cava); State of the Union (aka The World and His Wife); Suddenly Last Summer; Summertime (aka Summer Madness); Sylvia Scarlett; Undercurrent; Woman of the Year; Woman Rebels, A.

Heston, Charlton Agony and the Ecstasy, The; Airport 1975; Almost an Angel; Antony and Cleopatra; Awakening, The; Beneath the Planet of the Apes; Ben-Hur (Wyler); Big Country, The; Buccaneer, The; Call of the Wild, The; Dark City; Earthquake; El Cid; 55 Days at Peking; Four Musketeers: The Revenge of Milady, The; Gray Lady Down; Greatest Show on Earth, The; Greatest Story Ever Told, The; Gringo in Mañanaland, A; Hamlet (Branagh); In the Mouth of Madness; Khartoum; Last Hard Men, The; Major Dundee; Midway (aka Battle of Midway); Naked Jungle, The; Number One (aka Pro); Omega Man, The; Planet of the Apes; Prince and the Pauper, The (aka Crossed Swords); Ruby Gentry; Skyjacked; Soylent Green; Ten Commandments, The; Three Musketeers: The Queen's Diamonds, The; Tombstone; Touch of Evil; Treasure Island; Two-Minute Warning; War Lord, The; Will Penny.

Hoffman, Dustin Accidental Hero; Agatha; Alfredo Alfredo; All the President's Men; American Buffalo; Billy Bathgate; Death of a Salesman; Dick Tracy; Family Business; Graduate, The; Hook; Ishtar; John and Mary; Kramer vs Kramer; Lenny; Little Big Man; Marathon Man; Midnight Cowboy; Outbreak; Papillon; Rain Man; Sleepers; Sphere; Straight Time; Straw Dogs; Tootsie; Wag the Dog; Who Is Harry Kellerman and Why Is He Saying Those Terrible Things About Me?

Holden, William Ashanti; Blue Knight, The; Born Yesterday; Breezy; Bridge on the River Kwai, The; Bridges at Toko-Ri, The; Casino Royale; Damien – Omen II; Dark Past, The; Devil's Brigade, The; Escape from Fort Bravo; Executive Suite; Fedora; Golden Boy; Horse Soldiers, The; Invisible Stripes; Key, The; Lion, The; Love Is a Many-Splendored Thing; Man from Colorado, The; Moon Is Blue, The; Network; Open Season (Los Cazadores); Our Town; Picnic; Proud and Profane, The; Rachel and the Stranger; Revengers, The; Sabrina (aka Sabrina Fair); Satan Never Sleeps (aka The Devil Never Sleeps); 7th Dawn, The; S.O.B.; Stalag 17; Sunset Boulevard; Toward the Unknown (aka Brink of Hell); Towering Inferno, The; Union Station; When Time Ran Out; Wild Bunch, The; Wild Rovers; World of Suzie Wong, The.

Hope, Bob Beau James; Casanova's Big Night; Cat and the Canary, The (Nugent); Ghost Breakers, The; Global Affair, A; How to Commit Marriage; Muppet Movie, The; My Favourite Blonde; My Favourite Brunette; Never Say Die; Paleface, The; Road to Morocco; Road to Utopia; Son of Paleface.

Hopkins, Anthony All Creatures Great and Small; Amistad; Audrey Rose; August; Bounty, The; Bridge Too Far, A; Change of Seasons, A; Chaplin; Chorus of Disapproval, A; Dawning, The; Desperate Hours; Doll's House, A (Garland); Dracula (aka Bram Stoker's Dracula); Edge, The; 84 Charing Cross Road; Elephant Man, The; Freejack; Good Father, The; Hamlet (Richardson); Howards End; Innocent, The (Schlesinger); International Velvet; Juggernaut; Legends of the Fall; Lion in Winter, The; Looking Glass War, The; Magic; Nixon; Remains of the Day, The; Road to Wellville, The; Shadowlands; Silence of the Lambs, The; Spotswood; Surviving Picasso; Trial, The (Jones); Victory at Entebbe; When Eight Bells Toll; White Bus, The; Young Winston.

Hopper, Dennis American Friend, The (Der Amerikanische Freund); American Way, The (aka Riders of the Storm); Apocalypse Now; Basquiat; Blackout, The; Black Widow (Rafelson); Blood Red; Blue Velvet; Boiling Point (Harris); Carried Away (aka Acts of Love); Catchfire; Chasers; Chattahoochee; Cool Hand Luke; Easy Rider; From Hell to Texas (aka Manhunt); Giant; Glory Stompers, The; Hang 'em High; Hoosiers (aka Best Shot); Indian Runner, The; Kid Blue; Last Movie, The; Mad Dog Morgan (aka Mad Dog); O.C. & Stiggs; Paris Trout; Osterman Weekend, The; Out of the Blue; Rebel Without a Cause; Red Rock West; River's Edge; Rumble Fish; Space truckers; Speed; Super Mario Bros.; Texas Chainsaw Massacre 2, The; Tracks; Trip, The; True Grit; True Romance; Waterworld.

Hoskins, Bob Blue Ice; Brazil; Cotton Club, The; Favour, the Watch and the Very Big Fish, The (Rue Saint-Sulpice); Heart Condition; Honorary Consul, The (aka Beyond the Limit); Hook; Inner Circle, The (Il Proiezionista); Inserts; Lassiter; Lonely Passion of Judith Hearne, The; Long Good Friday, The; Mermaids; Mona Lisa; National Health, The; Nixon; Pink Floyd: The Wall; Prayer for the Dying, A; Raggedy

Rawney, The; Rainbow; Secret Agent, The (aka Joseph Conrad's The Secret Agent); Shattered; Spice World; Super Mario Bros.; Sweet Liberty; TwentyFourSeven; Who Framed Roger Rabbit?

Howard, Leslie First of the Few (aka Spitfire); 49th Parallel; Gentle Sex, The; Gone With the Wind; Intermezzo (aka Escape to Happiness); It's Love I'm After; Petrified Forest, The; Outward Bound; Pimpernel Smith; Pygmalion; Scarlet Pimpernel, The; Secrets (Borzage); Stand-In.

Howard, Trevor Aces High; Battle of Britain; Bawdy Adventures of Tom Jones, The; Brief Encounter; Catch Me a Spy (aka To Catch a Spy); Charge of the Light Brigade, The (Richardson); Clouded Yellow, The; Cockleshell Heroes; Conduct Unbecoming; Count of Monte-Cristo, The; Craze; Dawning, The; Death in the Sun (Der Flüsternde Tod); Doll's House, A (Losey); Dust; 11 Harrowhouse; Father Goose; Foreign Body; Gandhi; Golden Salamander; Green for Danger; Heart of the Matter, The; Hennessy; Hurricane; I See a Dark Stranger (aka The Adventuress); Key, The; Kidnapped; Lady Godiva Rides Again; Light Years Away; Lion, The; Ludwig; Manuela (aka Stowaway Girl); Mary, Queen of Scots; Meteor; Missionary, The; Mutiny on the Bounty (Milestone); Odette; Offence, The; Operation Crossbow; Outcast of the Islands; Passionate Friends, The (aka One Woman's Story); Persecution; Pope Joan; Rollicking Adventures of Eliza Fraser, The (aka A Faithful Narrative of the Capture, Sufferings and Miraculous Escape of Eliza Fraser); Run for the Sun; Ryan's Daughter; Sea Wolves, The; Sir Henry at Rawlinson's End; Slavers; Sons and Lovers; Stevie; Superman; Sword of the Valiant – The Legend of Gawain and the Green Knight, The; Third Man, The; Unholy, The; Von Ryan's Express; Way to the Stars, The; White Mischief; Who?.

Hudson, Rock All That Heaven Allows; Ambassador, The; Avalanche; Battle Hymn; Bend of the River (aka Where the River Bends); Blindfold; Darling Lili; Farewell to Arms, A (Vidor); Gathering of Eagles, A; Giant; Gun Fury; Has Anybody Seen My Gal?; Horizons West; Ice Station Zebra; Last Sunset, The; Magnificent Obsession; Man's Favourite Sport; Mirror Crack'd, The; Pillow Talk; Pretty Maids All in a

Row; Seconds; Send Me No Flowers; Something of Value; Tarnished Angels, The; Undefeated, The; Winchester '73; Written on the Wind.

Huppert, Isabelle Amateur; Après l'Amour; Bedroom Window, The; Cactus; Cérémonie, La (A Judgement in Stone); César and Rosalie (César et Rosalie); Clean Slate (Coup de Torchon); Coup de Foudre (At First Sight/Entre Nous); Dame aux Camélias, La; Dentellière, La (The Lacemaker); Elective Affinities (Le Affinità Elettive); Heaven's Gate; Indians Are Still Far Away, The (Les Indiens Sont Encore Loin); Loulou; Madame Bovary; My Best Friend's Girl (La Femme de Mon Pote); Passion; Rosebud; Sauve Qui Peut – la Vie (Every Man for Himself/Slow Motion); Séparation, La; Valseuses, Les (Going Places/Making It); Violette Nozière.

Hurt, John Alien; Aria; Before Winter Comes; Champions; Contact; Dead Man; Disappearance, The; East of Elephant Rock; Elephant Man, The; Even Cowgirls Get the Blues; Field, The; From the Hip; Ghoul, The (Francis); Heaven's Gate; Hit, The; Jake Speed; King Ralph; Little Malcolm and His Struggle Against the Eunuchs; Lord of the Rings, The; Love and Death on Long Island; Man for All Seasons, A; Midnight Express; Mr Forbush and the Penguins (aka Cry of the Penguins); Monolith; Night Crossing; Nineteen Eighty-Four; Osterman Weekend, The; Partners; Pied Piper, The (Demy); Rob Roy; Rocinante; Roger Corman's Frankenstein Unbound; Scandal; Shout, The; Sinful Davey; Spaceballs; Success is the Best Revenge; 10 Rillington Place; White Mischief; Wild Bill; Windprints.

Hurt, William Accidental Tourist, The; Alice; Altered States; Big Chill, The; Body Heat; Broadcast News; Children of a Lesser God; Dark City; Doctor, The; Eyewitness (aka The Janitor); Gorky Park; I Love You to Death; Jane Eyre; Kiss of the Spider Woman; Loved; Michael; Mr Wonderful; Second Best; Smoke; Time of Destiny, A; Trial by Jury; Until the End of the World (Bis ans Ende der Welt).

Huston, Anjelica Addams Family, The; Addams Family Values; And the Band Played On; Crimes and Misdemeanors; Crossing Guard, The; Dead, The; Enemies, a Love Story; Gardens of Stone; Grifters,

The; Handful of Dust, A; Manhattan Murder Mystery; Mr North; Perez Family, The; Postman Always Rings Twice, The (Rafelson); Prizzi's Honor; Swashbuckler (The Scarlet Buccaneer); Walk with Love and Death, A; Witches, The.

Huston, John Battle for the Planet of the Apes; Bible...In the Beginning, The (La Bibbia); Candy; Cardinal, The; Chinatown; Head On (aka Fatal Attraction); Jaguar Lives; Kremlin Letter, The; Life and Times of Judge Roy Bean, The; Lovesick; Man in the Wilderness; Myra Breckinridge; Tentacles (Tentacoli); Treasure of the Sierra Madre, The; Walk with Love and Death, A; Wind and the Lion, The; Winter Kills; Wise Blood; Young Giants.

Huston, Walter All That Money Can Buy (aka The Devil and Daniel Webster/Daniel and the Devil); American Madness; And Then There Were None (aka Ten Little Niggers); Criminal Code, The; Dragonwyck; Duel in the Sun; Edge of Darkness; Furies, The; Gabriel Over the White House; Great Sinner, The; In This Our Life; Mission to Moscow; North Star; Outlaw, The; Rain; Shanghai Gesture, The; Swamp Water; Treasure of the Sierra Madre, The; Tunnel, The (aka Transatlantic Tunnel); Yankee Doodle Dandy.

Irons, Jeremy Australia; Betrayal; Chinese Box; Chorus of Disapproval, A; Damage; Danny the Champion of the World; Dead Ringers; Die Hard with a Vengeance; French Lieutenant's Woman, The; House of Spirits, The; Kafka; Lolita (Lyne); Man in the Iron Mask, The (Wallace); Mission, The (Joffé); M. Butterfly; Moonlighting; Nijinsky; Reversal of Fortune; Stealing Beauty (Io ballo da sola/Beauté Volée); Swann in Love (Un Amour de Swann); Waterland.

Jackson, Glenda Bequest to the Nation (aka The Nelson Affair); Beyond Therapy; Business As Usual; Class of Miss MacMichael, The; Giro City; Health; Hedda; Hopscotch; House Calls; Incredible Sarah, The; King of the Wind; Lost and Found; Maids, The; Mary, Queen of Scots; Music Lovers, The; Nasty Habits; Persecution and Assassination of Jean-Paul Marat as Performed by the Inmates of the Asylum of Charenton Under the Direction of the Marquis de Sade, The; Rainbow, The; Return of the Soldier, The;

Romantic Englishwoman, The; Salome's Last Dance; Stevie; Sunday, Bloody Sunday; Tempter, The (Il Sorriso del Grande Tentatore); Touch of Class, A; Triple Echo, The; Turtle Diary; Women in Love.

Johnson, Ben Angels in the Outfield (aka Angels); Bite the Bullet; Breakheart Pass; Champions; Cherry 2000; Chisum; Dillinger (Milius); Evening Star; Getaway, The (Peckinpah); Grayeagle; Greatest, The; Hang 'em High; Hunter, The; Hustle; Junior Bonner; Kid Blue; Last Picture Show, The; Major Dundee; Mighty Joe Young; My Heroes Have Always Been Cowboys; One-Eyed Jacks; Rare Breed, The; Radio Flyer; Red Dawn; Rio Grande; Savage Bees, The; Shane; She Wore a Yellow Ribbon; Something Big; Sugarland Express, The; Swarm, The; Terror Train; Three Godfathers; Train Robbers, The; Undefeated, The; Wagon Master; Wild Bunch, The; Will Penny.

Karloff, Boris Bedlam; Before I Hang; Black Cat, The (aka House of Doom); Black Room, The; Black Sabbath (I Tre Volti della Paura); Body Snatcher, The; Boogie Man Will Get You, The; Bride of Frankenstein, The; Charlie Chan at the Opera; Comedy of Terrors, The; Corridors of Blood; Criminal Code, The; Curse of the Crimson Altar (aka The Crimson Cult); Devil Commands, The; Devil's Island (Clemens); Five Star Final; Frankenstein; Ghoul, The (Hunter); Grip of the Strangler (aka The Haunted Strangler); House of Frankenstein; House of Rothschild; Invisible Ray, The; Isle of the Dead; Lost Patrol, The; Lured (aka Personal Column); Mad Genius, The; Mad Monster Party; Man Who Changed His Mind, The (aka The Man Who Lived Again); Mask of Fu Manchu, The; Monster of Terror (aka Die, Monster, Die); Mummy, The (Freund); Old Dark House, The; Raven, The (Friedlander/Landers); Raven, The (Corman); Scarface (Hawks); Secret Life of Walter Mitty; Son of Frankenstein; Sorcerers, The; Strange Door, The; Targets; Terror, The; Unconquered; Walking Dead, The; You'll Find Out.

Keaton, Buster Adventures of Huckleberry Finn, The; Battling Butler; Beach Blanket Bingo; Cameraman, The; College; Film; Funny Thing Happened on the Way to the Forum, A; General, The; Go West (Keaton); In the Good Old Summertime; It's a Mad, Mad, Mad, Mad World; Limelight; Navigator, The; Our Hospitality; Parlor, Bedroom and Bath (aka Romeo in Pyjamas);

Saphead, The; Seven Chances; Sherlock Junior; Spite Marriage; Steamboat Bill, Jr; Sunset Boulevard; Three Ages.

Keaton, Michael Batman; Batman Returns; Beetlejuice; Clean and Sober; Desperate Measures; Dream Team, The; Gung Ho; Jackie Brown; Johnny Dangerously; Mr Mom (aka Mr Mum); Much Ado About Nothing; Multiplicity; My Life; Night Shift; One Good Cop; Pacific Heights; Paper, The; Speechless; Squeeze, The (Young); Touch and Go.

Keitel, Harvey Bad Lieutenant; Bad Timing; Blue Collar; Blue in the Face; Border, The; Buffalo Bill and the Indians, or Sitting Bull's History Lesson; Bugsy; City of Industry; Clockers; CopLand; Death Watch (La Mort en Direct); Duellists, The; Eagle's Wing; Exposed; FairyTale – A True Story; Falling in Love; Fingers; From Dusk Till Dawn; Head Above Water; Imaginary Crimes; January Man, The; Last Temptation of Christ, The; Mean Streets; Men's Club, The; Monkey Trouble; Mortal Thoughts; Mother, Jugs & Speed; Naples Connection, The (Un Complicato Intrigo di Donne, Vicoli e Delitti); Off Beat; Order of Death (aka Corrupt); Piano, The; Point of No Return (aka The Assassin); Pulp Fiction; Reservoir Dogs; Rising Sun; Saturn 3; Sister Act; Smoke; Snake Eyes; Somebody to Love; Taxi Driver; That Night in Varennes (La Nuit de Varennes); Thelma & Louise; Two Jakes, The; Ulysses' Gaze; Welcome to L.A.; Who's That Knocking at My Door? (aka I Call First); Wise Guys; Young Americans.

Kelly, Gene American in Paris, An; Anchors Aweigh; Black Hand, The; Brigadoon; Christmas Holiday; Cover Girl; Demoiselles de Rochefort, Les (The Young Girls of Rochefort); DuBarry Was a Lady; For Me and My Gal; Inherit the Wind; It's Always Fair Weather; Les Girls; Let's Make Love; On the Town; Pirate, The; Singin' in the Rain; Summer Stock (aka If You Feel Like Singing); Take Me Out to the Ball Game (aka Everybody's Cheering); That's Dancing!; That's Entertainment!; That's Entertainment Part II; Viva Knievel!; Xanadu; Ziegfeld Follies.

Kelly, Grace Bridges at Toko-Ri, The; Dial M for Murder; Green Fire; High Noon; High Society; Mogambo; Rear Window; To Catch a Thief.

Kilmer, Val Batman Forever; Doors, The; Heat (Mann); Island of Dr Moreau, The

(Frankenheimer); Kill Me Again; Real Genius; Real McCoy, The; Saint, The; Thunderheart; Tombstone; Top Gun; Top Secret!; True Romance; Willow.

Kinski, Klaus Aguirre, Wrath of God (Aguirre, der Zorn Gottes); Android; Big Silence, The (Il Grande Silenzio); Buddy Buddy; Bullet for the General, A (¿Quién Sabe?); Circus of Fear (aka Psycho-Circus); Cobra Verde; Count Dracula (El Conde Dracula); Fitzcarraldo; For a Few Dollars More (Per Qualche Dollari in più); Fruits of Passion, The (Les Fruits de la Passion); Lifespan; Little Drummer Girl, The; Madame Claude; Nosferatu the Vampyre (Nosferatu: Phantom der Nacht); Operation Thunderbolt; Soldier, The (aka Codename: The Soldier); Time to Love and a Time to Die, A; Titan Find, The (aka Creature); Vampires in Venice (Nosferatu a Venezia); Venom (Sykes); Woyzeck.

Kinski, Nastassja Cat People (Schrader); Exposed; Harem; Hotel New Hampshire, The; Faraway, So Close (In weiter Ferne, so nah!); Fathers' Day; Maria's Lovers; Moon in the Gutter, The (La Lune dans le Caniveau); Night Sun (Il Sole anche di notte); One From the Heart; One Night Stand; Paris, Texas; Revolution; Spring Symphony (Frühlingssinfonie); Terminal Velocity; Tess; Torrents of Spring (Acque di primavera); To the Devil a Daughter; Unfaithfully Yours (Zieff); Wrong Movement (Falsche Bewegung).

Ladd, Alan And Now Tomorrow; Badlanders, The; Black Cat, The (Rogell); Black Knight, The; Blue Dahlia, The; Botany Bay; Glass Key, The; Calcutta; Great Gatsby, The (Nugent); My Favourite Brunette; Santiago (aka The Gun Runner); Shane; This Gun for Hire; Two Years Before the Mast.

Lake, Veronica Blue Dahlia, The; Glass Key, The; I Married a Witch; Ramrod; Sullivan's Travels; This Gun for Hire.

Lamarr, Hedy Algiers; Boom Town; Comrade X; Conspirators, The; Crossroads; Experiment Perilous; I Take This Woman; Lady Without Passport, A; Samson and Delilah; Ziegfeld Girl.

Lancaster, Burt Airport; Apache; Atlantic City (aka Atlantic City U.S.A.); Bird Man of Alcatraz; Brute Force; Buffalo Bill and the Indians, or Sitting Bull's History Lesson; Cassandra Crossing, The; Castle Keep;

Cattle Annie and Little Britches; Child Is Waiting, A; Come Back, Little Sheba; Conversation Piece (Gruppo di Famiglia in un Interno); Crimson Pirate, The; Criss Cross; Elmer Gantry; Executive Action; Field of Dreams; Flame and the Arrow, The; From Here to Eternity; Go Tell the Spartans; Gunfight at the O.K. Corral; Gypsy Moths, The; Island of Dr Moreau, The; Judgment at Nuremberg; Kentuckian, The; Killers, The (Siodmak); Lawman; Leopard, The (Il Gattopardo); List of Adrian Messenger, The; Local Hero; Midnight Man, The; Moses; 1900 (Novecento); Osterman Weekend, The; Professionals, The; Scalphunters, The; Scorpio; Seven Days in May; Sorry, Wrong Number; Sweet Smell of Success; Swimmer, The; Tough Guys; Train, The; Twilight's Last Gleaming; Ulzana's Raid; Unforgiven, The; Valdez Is Coming; Vera Cruz; Victory at Entebbe; Zulu Dawn.

Lange, Jessica All That Jazz; Cape Fear (Scorsese); Blue Sky; Country; Crimes of the Heart; Everybody's All-American (aka When I Fall in Love); Far North; Frances; King Kong (Guillermin); Men Don't Leave; Music Box; Night and the City (Winkler); Postman Always Rings Twice, The (Rafelson); Rob Roy; Sweet Dreams; Thousand Acres, A; Tootsie.

Laughton, Charles Advise and Consent; Arch of Triumph; Barretts of Wimpole Street, The; Big Clock, The; Bribe, The; Hobson's Choice; Hunchback of Notre Dame, The (Dieterle); If I Had a Million; Island of Lost Souls; It Started with Eve; Jamaica Inn; Les Misérables; Mutiny on the Bounty (Lloyd); O. Henry's Full House (aka Full House); Old Dark House, The; Paradine Case, The; Piccadilly; Private Life of Henry VIII, The; Rembrandt; Ruggles of Red Gap; St Martin's Lane (aka Sidewalks of London); Sign of the Cross, The; Spartacus; Strange Door, The; Suspect, The; They Knew What They Wanted; This Land Is Mine; Vessel of Wrath (aka The Beachcomber); Witness for the Prosecution; Young Bess.

Laurel, Stan, and Hardy, Oliver A-Haunting We Will Go; Blockheads; Bonnie Scotland; Chump at Oxford, A; Jitterbugs; Our Relations; Pack Up Your Troubles; Pardon Us; Saps at Sea; Sons of the Desert (aka Fraternally Yours); Way Out West.

Léaud, Jean-Pierre Baisers Volés (Stolen Kisses);

Chinoise, La (La Chinoise, ou plutôt à la Chinoise); Day for Night (La Nuit Américaine); Départ, Le; Détective; Deux Anglaises et le Continent, Les (Anne and Muriel/Two English Girls); Domicile Conjugal (Bed and Board); Gai Savoir, Le; I Hired a Contract Killer; Ile au trésor, L' (Treasure Island); Irma Vep; Last Tango in Paris; Lion Has Seven Heads, The (Der Leone Have Sept Cabecas); Love on the Run (L'Amour en Fuite); Masculin Féminin (Masculine Feminine); Mon Home; Mother and the Whore, The (La Maman et la Putain); Out 1: Spectre; Paris s'éveille (Paris Awakens); Pierrot le Fou; Pigsty (Porcile); Quatre Cents Coups, Les (The 400 Blows); Rise and Fall of a Little Film Company from a ·Novel by James Hadley Chase (Grandeur et Décadence d'un Petit Commerce de Cinéma d'après un roman de JH Chase); Testament d'Orphée, Le (Testament of Orpheus); Vie de Bohème, La (Bohemian Life); Virgin (36 Fillette); Weekend (Week-end).

Lee, Bruce Big Boss, The (Tangshan Daxiong/aka Fists of Fury); Enter the Dragon; Fist of Fury; Marlowe; Way of the Dragon, The.

Lee, Christopher Airport '77; Arabian Adventure; Battle of the River Plate, The (aka Pursuit of the Graf Spee); Bear Island; Beat Girl (aka Wild for Kicks); Bitter Victory (Amère Victoire); Brides of Fu Manchu, The; Caravans; Circus of Fear (aka Psycho-Circus); Corridors of Blood; Count Dracula (El Conde Dracula); Creeping Flesh, The; Curse of Frankenstein, The; Curse of the Crimson Altar (aka The Crimson Cult); Death in the Sun (Der Flüsternde Tod); Death Line (aka Raw Meat); Devil Rides Out, The; Diagnosis: Murder; Diamond Mercenaries, The; Dr Terror's House of Horrors; Dracula (aka Horror of Dracula); Dracula A.D.1972: Dracula Has Risen from the Grave; Dracula, Prince of Darkness; Eye for an Eye, An; Face of Fu Manchu, The; Feast at Midnight, A; Four Musketeers: The Revenge of Milady, The; Funny Man; Gorgon, The; Gremlins 2: The New Batch; Hannie Caulder; Horror Express (Pánico en el Transiberiano); Hound of the Baskervilles (Fisher); House of the Long Shadows, The; House That Dripped Blood, The; I, Monster; Jaguar Lives; Innocents in Paris; Magic Christian, The; Man With the Golden Gun, The; Moulin Rouge; Mummy, The (Fisher); Night of the Big Heat; 1941;

Nothing But the Night; Oblong Box, The; Passage, The; Police Academy &: Mission to Moscow; Private Life of Sherlock Holmes, The; Return from Witch Mountain; Return of Captain Invincible, The; Return of the Musketeers, The; Revenge of the Dead; Satanic Rites of Dracula, The (aka Count Dracula and His Vampire Bride); Scars of Dracula, The; Scott of the Antarctic; Scream and Scream Again; She; Silent Flute, The (aka Circle of Iron); Skull, The; Stupids, The; Taste of Fear (aka Scream of Fear); Taste the Blood of Dracula; That Lady; Three Musketeers: The Queen's Diamonds, The; To the Devil a Daughter; Treasure Island; Two Faces of Dr Jekyll, The (aka House of Fright); Wicker Man, The.

Leigh, Vivien Anna Karenina (Duvivier); Caesar and Cleopatra; Dark Journey; Fire Over England; Gone With the Wind; Roman Spring of Mrs Stone, The; St Martin's Lane (aka Sidewalks of London); Ship of Fools; Streetcar Named Desire, A; That Hamilton Woman (aka Lady Hamilton).

Lemmon, Jack Airport '77; Alex & the Gypsy; Apartment, The; April Fools, The; Avanti!; Buddy Buddy; China Syndrome, The; Cowboy; Dad; Days of Wine and Roses; Fortune Cookie, The (aka Meet Whiplash Willie); Front Page, The (Wilder); Grass Harp, The; Glengarry Glen Ross; Grumpy Old Men; Hamlet (Branagh); Irma la Douce; It Should Happen to You; JFK; Luv; Macaroni (Maccheroni); Missing; Mister Roberts; My Sister Eileen; Odd Couple, The; Out-of-Towners, The; Prisoner of Second Avenue, The; Save the Tiger; Short Cuts; Some Like It Hot; 'That's Life'; Tribute; Wackiest Ship in the Army, The.

Lewis, Jerry Arizona Dreaming; Artists and Models; Bellboy, The; Big Mouth, The; Cinderfella; Cookie; Delicate Delinquent; The; Disorderly Orderly, The; Family Jewels, The; Funny Bones; Geisha Boy, The; Hollywood or Bust; It's Only Money; King of Comedy, The; Ladies' Man, The; Nutty Professor, The (Lewis); Pardners; Patsy, The; Rock-a-Bye Baby; 3 Ring Circus; Which Way to the Front? (aka Ja, Ja, Mein General! But Which Way to the Front?).

Lloyd, Harold Cat's-Paw, The; Feet First; Girl Shy; Kid Brother, The; Movie Crazy; Safety Last; Sin of Harold Diddlebock, The (aka Mad Wednesday); Speedy; Why Worry?.

Lollobrigida, Gina Bad Man's River (El Hombre del Rio Malo); Beat the Devil; Belles de nuit, Les (Beauties of the Night/Night Beauties); Buona Sera, Mrs Campbell; Go Naked in the World; Hunchback of Notre Dame, The (Notre Dame de Paris); King, Queen, Knave (Herzbube); Never So Few; Solomon and Sheba; Woman of Straw.

Lombard, Carole Bolero (Ruggles); Hands Across the Table; In Name Only; Mr and Mrs Smith; My Man Godfrey; Nothing Sacred; Rumba; Supernatural; They Knew What They Wanted; To Be or Not To Be (Lubitsch); True Confession; Twentieth Century.

Loren, Sophia Arabesque; Black Orchid, The; Boccaccio '70; Brass Target; Cassandra Crossing; Cinderella – Italian Style (C'era una Volta); Countess from Hong Kong, A; Desire Under the Elms; El Cid; Fall of the Roman Empire, The; Firepower; Heller in Pink Tights; Houseboat; It Started in Naples; Judith; Key, The; Lady L; Legend of the Lost; Millionairess, The; Operation Crossbow; Pride and the Passion, The; Ready to Wear (aka Prêt-à-Porter); Special Day, A (Una Giornata Particolare); Sunflower (I Girasoli); Verdict (The Verdict).

Lorre, Peter All Through the Night; Arsenic and Old Lace; Background to Danger; Beast With Five Fingers, The; Beat the Devil; Big Circus, The; Black Angel; Boogie Man Will Get You, The; Casablanca; Comedy of Terrors, The; Confidential Agent; Congo Crossing; Conspirators, The; Crack-Up (St Clair); Crime and Punishment (von Sternberg); Face Behind the Mask, The; In This Our Life; Lancer Spy; M (Lang); Mad Love (aka The Hands of Orlac); Maltese Falcon, The; Man Who Knew Too Much, The (1934); Mask of Dimitrios, The; Mr Moto's Gamble; My Favourite Brunette; No Answer from F.P.1 (F.P.1 antwortet nicht); Passage to Marseille; Patsy, The; Raven, The (Corman); Secret Agent, The; Silk Stockings; Strange Cargo; Stranger on the Third Floor, The; Tales of Terror; 20,000 Leagues Under the Sea; Verdict, The (Siegel); Verlorene, Der (The Lost One); You'll Find Out.

Loy, Myrna After the Thin Man; Airport 1975; April Fools, The; Best Years of Our Lives, The; Broadway Bill (aka Strictly Confidential); Cheaper by the Dozen; End, The; From the Terrace; Love in Every Port, A; I Love You Again; Love Crazy; Love Me Tonight;

Manhattan Melodrama; Mask of Fu Manchu, The; Mr Blandings Builds His Dream House; Noah's Ark; Rains Came, The; Senator Was Indiscreet, The; Stamboul Quest; Thin Man, The; Too Hot to Handle.

Lugosi, Bela Abbott and Costello Meet Frankenstein (aka Abbott and Costello Meet the Ghosts); Black Cat, The (aka House of Doom); Black Cat, The (Rogell); Body Snatcher, The; Dark Eyes of London (aka The Human Monster); Dracula (Browning); Frankenstein Meets the Wolf Man; Ghost of Frankenstein, The; Glen or Glenda? (aka I Led Two Lives/I Changed My Sex); International House; Invisible Ray, The; Island of Lost Souls; Mark of the Vampire; Murders in the Rue Morgue (Florey); Ninotchka; Plan 9 from Outer Space; Raven, The (Friedlander/Landers); Return of the Vampire, The; Son of Frankenstein; Voodoo Man; White Zombie; Wolf Man, The; You'll Find Out.

McCrea, Joel Banjo on My Knee; Barbary Coast; Colorado Territory; Come and Get It; Dead End; Foreign Correspondent; Great Moment, The; Lost Squadron, The; More the Merrier, The; Most Dangerous Game, The (aka The Hounds of Zaroff); Mustang Country; Palm Beach Story, The; Primrose Path, The; Ramrod; Ride the High Country (aka Guns in the Afternoon); Rough Shoot (aka Shoot First); South of St Louis; Sullivan's Travels; These Three; They Passed This Way (aka Four Faces West); Unseen, The; Wichita.

MacLaine, Shirley Apartment, The; Around the World in 80 Days; Artists and Models; Ask Any Girl; Being There; Bliss of Mrs Blossom, The; Can-Can; Cannonball Run II; Celluloid Closet, The; Change of Seasons, A; Career; Evening Star, The; Gambit; Guarding Tess; Irma la Douce; Loving Couples; Madame Sousatzka; Mrs Winterbourne; Ocean's 11; Possession of Joel Delaney, The; Robe, The; Sheepman, The; Some Came Running; Steel Magnolias; Sweet Charity; Terms of Endearment; Trouble with Harry, The; Turning Point, The; Two Mules for Sister Sara; Used People; Waiting for the Light; Wrestling Ernest Hemingway.

MacMurray, Fred Above Suspicion; Alice Adams; Apartment, The; At Gunpoint (aka Gunpoint); Caine Mutiny, The; Dive Bomber; Double Indemnity; Hands Across the Table; Happiest Millionaire, The;

Miracle of the Bells, The; Murder, He Says; Rains of Ranchipur, The; Remember the Night; Smoky; Swarm, The; Texas Rangers, The; There's Always Tomorrow; True Confession; Woman's World.

McQueen, Steve Baby the Rain Must Fall; Blob, The (Yeaworth); Bullitt; Cincinnati Kid, The; Enemy of the People, An (Schaefer); Getaway, The (Peckinpah); Great Escape, The; Hell Is for Heroes; Hunter, The; Junior Bonner; Le Mans; Love With the Proper Stranger; Magnificent Seven, The; Never So Few; On Any Sunday; Papillon; Reivers, The; Sand Pebbles, The; Somebody Up There Likes Me; Thomas Crown Affair, The; Tom Horn; Towering Inferno, The.

Magnani, Anna Amore, L'; Bellissima; Fellini's Roma (Roma); Fugitive Kind, The; Golden Coach, The (La Carrozza d'Oro/Le Carrosse d'Or); Mamma Roma; Roma, Città Aperta (Open City/Rome, Open City); Secret of Santa Vittoria, The.

March, Fredric Adventures of Mark Twain, The (Rapper); Affairs of Cellini, The; Alexander the Great, The (Rossen); Anna Karenina (Brown); Anthony Adverse; Barretts of Wimpole Street, The; Best Years of Our Lives, The; Bridges at Toko-Ri, The; Christopher Columbus; Dark Angel, The; Design for Living; Desperate Hours, The; Dr Jekyll and Mr Hyde (Mamoulian); Executive Suite; Hombre; I Married a Witch; Inherit the Wind; Laughter; Les Misérables; Mary of Scotland; Merrily We Go to Hell; Nothing Sacred; Road to Glory, The; Seven Days in May; Sign of the Cross, The; Star Is Born, A (Wellman); Victory (Cromwell); We Live Again; Wild Party, The (Arzner).

Marvin, Lee Attack; Avalanche Express; Bad Day at Black Rock; Big Heat, The; Big Red One, The; Caine Mutiny, The; Cat Ballou; Delta Force, The; Dirty Dozen, The; Donovan's Reef; Duel at Silver Creek, The; Emperor of the North Pole, The (aka Emperor of the North); Gorky Park; Great Scout & Cathouse Thursday, Gun Fury; The; Hell in the Pacific; I Died a Thousand Times; Killers, The (Siegel); Klansman, The; Man Who Shot Liberty Valance, The; Monte Walsh; Not As a Stranger; Paint Your Wagon; Pete Kelly's Blues; Pocket Money; Point Blank; Prime Cut; Professionals, The; Raid, The; Raintree County; Seven Men from Now; Ship of Fools; Shout at the Devil; Spikes Gang, The; Violent Saturday; Wild One, The.

Marx Brothers, Animal Crackers; At the Circus; Big Store, The; Cocoanuts, The; Day at the Races, A; Duck Soup; Go West (Buzzell); Horse Feathers; Love Happy; Monkey Business (McLeod); Mr Music; Night at the Opera, A; Night in Casablanca, A; Room Service.

Mason, James Age of Consent; Autobiography of a Princess; Bad Man's River (El Hombre del Rio Malo); Bells Go Down, The; Bigger Than Life; Bloodline (aka Sidney Sheldon's Bloodline); Blue Max, The; Botany Bay; Boys from Brazil, The; Caught; Child's Play (Lumet); Cold Sweat (De la Part des Copains); Cross of Iron; Dangerous Summer, A; Deadly Affair, The; Desert Fox, The (aka Rommel – Desert Fox); Duffy; 11 Harrowhouse; Escape from Zahrain; Evil Under the Sun; Fall of the Roman Empire, The; Fire Over England; 5 Fingers; Frankenstein: The True Story; Georgy Girl; Great Expectations (Hardy); Hatter's Castle; Heaven Can Wait (Beatty/Henry); Inside Out; Island in the Sun; Journey to the Centre of the Earth; Julius Caesar; Last of Sheila, The; Lolita (Kubrick); Lord Jim; Mackintosh Man, The; Man Between, The; Mandingo; Marseille Contract, The; Murder by Decree; Night Has Eyes, The (aka Terror House); North by Northwest; North Sea Hijack; Odd Man Out; Pandora and the Flying Dutchman; Passage, The; Place of One's Own, A; Prisoner of Zenda, The (Thorpe); Pumpkin Eater, The; Reckless Moment, The; Salem's Lot; Sea Gull, The; Seventh Veil, The; Shooting Party, The; Spring and Port Wine; Star Is Born, A (Cukor); Thunder Rock; Tiara Tahiti; 20,000 Leagues Under the Sea; Verdict, The (Lumet); Voyage of the Damned; Water Babies, The; Wicked Lady, The (Arliss); Yellowbeard.

Mastroianni, Marcello Allonsanfan; Bee Keeper, The (O Melissokomos); Beyond the Door (Oltre la Porta); Blow-Out (La Grande Bouffe); By Nightfall (Verso sera); Casanova '70; City of Women (La Città delle Donne); Dark Eyes (Oci Ciornie); Dolce Vita, La (The Sweet Life); Down the Ancient Stairs (Per le Antiche Scale); Dramma della Gelosia (Jealousy, Italian Style/The Pizza Triangle); 8½ (Otto e Mezzo); Everybody's Fine (Stanno tutti bene); Gabriela; Ginger e Fred (Ginger e Fred); Intervista; Leo the Last; Macaroni (Maccheroni); Massacre in Rome (Rappresaglia); Notte,

La; Ready to Wear (aka Prêt-à-Porter); Slightly Pregnant Man, The (L'Evénement le plus Important depuis que l'Homme a Marché sur la Lune); Soliti Ignoti, I (Big Deal on Madonna Street/Persons Unknown); Special Day, A (Una Giornata Particolare); Splendor; Sunflower (I Girasoli); That Night in Varennes (La Nuit de Varennes); Trois Vies et une Seule Mort (Three Lives and Only One Death); Un Deux Trois Soleil (1, 2, 3, Sun); Used People; We Don't Want to Talk About It (De eso no se Habla); What? (Che?); White Nights (Le Notti Bianche); Wifemistress (Mogliamante).

Matthau, Walter Bad News Bears, The; Bigger Than Life; Buddy Buddy; California Suite; Candy; Casey's Shadow; Charade; Charley Varrick; Couch Trip, The; Dennis the Menace (aka Dennis); Earthquake; Ensign Pulver; Face in the Crowd, A; Fail Safe; First Monday in October; Fortune Cookie, The (aka Meet Whiplash Willie); Front Page, The (Wilder); Grass Harp, The; Grumpy Old Men; Guide for the Married Man, A; Hello, Dolly!; Hopscotch; House Calls; Indian Fighter, The; I Ought to Be in Pictures; JFK; Kentuckian, The; King Creole; Kotch; Laughing Policeman, The (aka An Investigation of Murder); Little Miss Marker; Lonely Are the Brave; Mirage; Movers and Shakers; New Leaf, A; Odd Couple, The; Pete'n'Tillie; Pirates; Plaza Suite; Secret Life of an American Wife, The; Strangers When We Meet; Sunshine Boys, The; Survivors, The; Taking of Pelham One Two Three, The.

Mature, Victor After the Fox (Caccia alla Volpe); Androcles and the Lion; Big Circus, The; Cry of the City; Dangerous Mission; Demetrius and the Gladiators; Easy Living (Tourneur); Every Little Crook and Nanny; Head; I Wake Up Screaming (aka Hot Spot); Kiss of Death (Hathaway); Las Vegas Story, The; Moss Rose; My Darling Clementine; Samson and Delilah; Shanghai Gesture, The; Violent Saturday.

Mifune, Toshiro Bad Sleep Well, The (Warui Yatsu Hodo Yoko Nemuru); Challenge, The; Grand Prix; Hell in the Pacific; Hidden Fortress, The (Kakushi Toride no San-Akunin); High and Low (Tengoku to Jigoku); Idiot, The (Hakuchi); I Live in Fear (Ikimono no Kiroku); The Life of Oharu (Saikaku Ichidai Onna); Lost World of Sinbad, The

(Daitozoku); Lower Depths, The (Donzoko); Midway (aka Battle of Midway); 1941; Paper Tiger; Picture Bride; Rashomon; Rebellion (Joi-Uchi); Red Beard (Akahige); Red Sun (Soleil Rouge); Sanjuro (Tsubaki Sanjuro); Seven Samurai (Shichinin no Samurai); Shogun; Stray Dog (Nora Inu); Throne of Blood (Kumonosu-jo); Yojimbo.

Milland, Ray Aces High; Alias Nick Beal (aka The Contact Man); Arise, My Love; Battlestar Galactica; Beau Geste; Big Clock, The; Bolero (Ruggles); Bugles in the Afternooon; Bulldog Drummond Escapes; Circle of Deceit; Dial M for Murder; Easy Living (Leisen); Escape to Witch Mountain; French Without Tears; Frogs; Game for Vultures; Gold; House in Nightmare Park, The; Kitty; Lady in the Dark; Last Tycoon, The; Lost Weekend, The; Love Story (Hiller); Major and the Minor, The; Man Alone, A; Ministry of Fear; Oliver's Story; Panic in Year Zero; Piccadilly; Premature Burial, The; Rhubarb; River's Edge, The; Slavers; So Evil My Love; Starflight: The Plane That Couldn't Land (aka Starflight One); Swiss Conspiracy, The; Thief, The; Thing With Two Heads, The; Uncanny, The; Uninvited, The; X – The Man with X-Ray Eyes (aka The Man with the X-Ray Eyes).

Mills, John Above Us the Waves; Africa – Texas Style; Bean; Big Blockade, The; Big Sleep, The (Winner); Black Sheep of Whitehall, The; Chuka; Colditz Story, The; Cottage to Let (aka Bombsight Stolen); Deadly Advice; Devil's Advocate, The (Des Teufels Advokat); Dulcima; Dunkirk; Flame in the Streets; Forever England (aka Bound for Glory); Gandhi; Gentle Gunman, The; Ghost Camera, The; Goodbye, Mr Chips (Wood); Great Expectations (Lean); Grotesque, The; Hamlet (Branagh); History of Mr Polly, The; Hobson's Choice; Human Factor, The (Dmytryk); Ice Cold in Alex; In Which We Serve; It's Great to Be Young; I Was Monty's Double; Lady Caroline Lamb; Long Memory, The; Morning Departure (aka Operation Disaster); October Man, The; O.H.M.S. (aka You're in the Army Now); Oh! What a Lovely War; Oklahoma Crude; Operation Crossbow; Rocking Horse Winner, The; Ryan's Daughter (McLaglen); Sahara; Scott of the Antarctic; Singer Not the Song, The; Thirty-Nine Steps, The (Sharp); Tiara Tahiti; Tiger Bay; This Happy Breed; Trial by

Combat (aka A Choice of Weapons/Dirty Knight's Work); Tunes of Glory; War and Peace (Vidor); Waterloo Road; Way to the Stars, The; Who's That Girl; Young Winston; Young Mr Pitt, The; Zulu Dawn.

Mitchum, Robert Agency (aka Mind Games); Ambassador, The; Amsterdam Kill, The; Angel Face; Bandido!; Big Sleep, The (Winner); Big Steal, The (Siegel); Blood on the Moon; Cape Fear (Thompson); Cape Fear (Scorsese); Crossfire; Dead Man; El Dorado; Enemy Below, The; Farewell, My Lovely (Richards); 5 Card Stud; Friends of Eddie Coyle, The; Good Guys and the Bad Guys, The; Grass Is Greener, The; Heaven Knows, Mr Allison; His Kind of Woman; Home from the Hill; Hunters, The; Last Tycoon, The; List of Adrian Messenger, The; Locket, The; Longest Day, The; Lusty Men, The; Macao; Maria's Lovers; Midway (aka Battle of Midway); Mr North; My Forbidden Past; Night of the Hunter, The; Not As a Stranger; One Minute to Zero; Out of the Past (aka Build My Gallows High); Pursued; Rachel and the Stranger; Racket, The; Rampage; River of No Return; Ryan's Daughter; Sbarco di Anzio, Lo (Anzio/The Battle for Anzio); Scrooged; Second Chance (Matè); Secret Ceremony; Story of GI Joe, The; Sundowners, The; That Championship Season; Thunder Road; Track of the Cat; Undercurrent; Villa Rides!; Way West, The; When Strangers Marry (aka Betrayed); Where Danger Lives; Wild Bill: A Hollywood Maverick; Yakuza, The.

Monroe, Marilyn All About Eve; Asphalt Jungle, The; Bus Stop; Clash By Night; Don't Bother to Knock (Baker); Gentlemen Prefer Blondes; How to Marry a Millionaire; Ladies of the Chorus; Let's Make Love; Love Happy; Misfits, The; Monkey Business (Hawks); Niagara; O. Henry's Full House (aka Full House); Prince and the Showgirl, The; River of No Return; Seven Year Itch, The; Some Like It Hot; There's No Business Like Show Business; Ticket to Tomahawk, A.

Montand, Yves Aveu, L' (The Confession); César and Rosalie (César et Rosalie); Grand Prix; Guerre est finie, La (The War Is Over); IP5; Jean de Florette; Let's Make Love; Manon des Sources; Mister Freedom; On a Clear Day You Can See Forever; Portes de la Nuit, Les (Gates of the Night); Red Circle, The (Le Cercle Rouge); Sanctuary; Sauvage, Le;

Sleeping Car Murder, The (Compartiment Tueurs); State of Siege (Etat de Siège); Tout Va Bien; Vivre pour Vivre (Live for Life); Wages of Fear, The (Le Salaire de la Peur); Z.

Moreau, Jeanne Alex in Wonderland; Amants, Les (The Lovers); Ascenseur pour l'Echafaud (Frantic/Lift to the Scaffold); Baie des Anges, La (Bay of Angels); Bride Wore Black, The (La Mariée était en Noir); Chère Louise (Louise); Chimes at Midnight (Campanadas a Medianoche); Dialogue des Carmélites, Le; Diary of a Chambermaid, The (Le Journal d'une Femme de Chambre); Eve; Femme est une Femme, Une (A Woman Is a Woman); Feu Follet, Le (A Time to Live and a Time to Die/The Fire Within/Fox Fire/Will o'the Wisp); Immortal Story, The (Histoire Immortelle); Jules and Jim (Jules et Jim); Last Tycoon, The; Liaisons Dangereuses 1960, Les; Mademoiselle; Map of the Human Heart; Mata-Hari, Agent H.21; Mr Klein; Monte Walsh; Nathalie Granger; Nikita; Notte, La; Old Lady Who Walked in the Sea, The (La Vieille qui Marchait dans la Mer); Paltoquet, Le; Petit Théâtre de Jean Renoir, Le (The Little Theatre of Jean Renoir); Proprietor, The (Le Propriétaire); Querelle; Sailor from Gibraltar, The; Touchez pas au Grisbi (Grisbi/Honour Among Thieves); Train, The; Trial, The (Le Procès); Until the End of the World (Bis ans Ende der Welt); Valseuses, Les (Going Places/Making It); Victors, The; Viva Maria!.

Mui, Anita Au revoir, mon amour (He Rijun Zai Lai); Heroic Trio, The (Dongfang San Xia); Kawashima Yoshiko (Chuandao Fangzi/aka The Last Princess of Manchuria); Moon Warriors; Rouge (Inji Kau); Rumble in the Bronx (Hongfan Qu).

Muni, Paul Black Fury; Bordertown; Good Earth, The; Hi, Nellie!; I Am a Fugitive from a Chain Gang; Juarez; Life of Emile Zola, The; Scarface (Hawks); Song to Remember, A; We Are Not Alone.

Murphy, Eddie Another 48 HRS; Best Defence; Beverly Hills Cop; Beverly Hills Cop II; Beverly Hills Cop III; Boomerang (Hudlin); Coming to America; Distinguished Gentleman, The; 48 HRS; Golden Child, The; Harlem Nights; Metro; Nutty Professor, The (Shadyac); Trading Places; Vampire in Brooklyn.

Newman, Paul Absence of Malice; Blaze; Buffalo Bill

and the Indians, or Sitting Bull's History Lesson; Butch Cassidy and the Sundance Kid; Cat on a Hot Tin Roof; Color of Money, The; Cool Hand Luke; Drowning Pool, The; Exodus; Fat Man and Little Boy (aka Shadow Makers); Fort Apache, the Bronx; From the Terrace; Harper (aka The Moving Target); Harry & Son; Hombre; Hud; Hudsucker Proxy, The; Hustler, The; Lady L; Left-Handed Gun, The; Life and Times of Judge Roy Bean, The; Long, Hot Summer, The; Mackintosh Man, The; Mr and Mrs Bridge; New Kind of Love, A; Nobody's Fool; Pocket Money; Quintet; Rally 'round the Flag, Boys!; Slap Shot; Somebody Up There Likes Me; Sometimes a Great Notion (aka Never Give an Inch); Sting, The; Sweet Bird of Youth; Torn Curtain; Towering Inferno, The; Twilight; Verdict, The (Lumet); When Time Ran Out; WUSA.

Nicholson, Jack As Good As It Gets; Back Door to Hell; Batman; Blood and Wine; Border, The; Broadcast News; Carnal Knowledge; Chinatown; Crossing Guard, The; Easy Rider; Evening Star, The; Few Good Men, A; Five Easy Pieces; Fortune, The; Goin' South; Heartburn; Hell's Angels on Wheels; Hoffa; Ironweed; King of Marvin Gardens, The; Last Detail, The; Last Tycoon, The; Little Shop of Horrors, The (Corman); Man Trouble; Mars Attacks!; Missouri Breaks, The; On a Clear Day You Can See Forever; One Flew Over the Cuckoo's Nest; Passenger, The (Profession: Reporter); Postman Always Rings Twice, The (Rafelson); Prizzi's Honor; Psych-Out; Raven, The (Corman); Rebel Rousers; Reds; Ride in the Whirlwind; Safe Place, A; Shining, The; Shooting, The; Terms of Endearment; Terror, The; Tommy; Two Jakes, The; Witches of Eastwick, The; Wolf.

Niven, David Appointment with Venus (aka Island Rescue); Around the World in 80 Days; Ask Any Girl; Bachelor Mother; Before Winter Comes; Beloved Enemy; Better Late Than Never; Birds and the Bees, The; Bishop's Wife, The; Bluebeard's Eighth Wife; Bonjour Tristesse; Candleshoe; Carringto VC (aka Court Martial); Casino Royale; Charge of the Light Brigade, The (Curtiz); Curse of the Pink Panther; Dawn Patrol, The; Death on the Nile; Elusive Pimpernel, The; Escape to Athena; 55 Days at Peking; First of the Few (aka Spitfire); Four Men and a Prayer; Guns of Darkness; Guns of Navarone, The; Happy Ever After (aka

Tonight's the Night); King, Queen, Knave (Herzbube); Lady L; Little Hut, The; Love Lottery, The; Magnificent Doll; Matter of Life and Death, A (aka Stairway to Heaven); Moon Is Blue, The; Murder by Death; My Man Godfrey (Koster); No Deposit, No Return; Oh, Men! Oh, Women!; Paper Tiger; Pink Panther, The; Please Don't Eat the Daisies; Prisoner of Zenda, The (Cromwell); Real Glory, The; Rough Cut; Sea Wolves, The; Thank You, Jeeves!; Toast of New Orleans, The; Trail of the Pink Panther; Vampira (aka Old Dracula); Way Ahead, The; Wuthering Heights (Wyler).

Noiret, Philippe Alexandre (Alexandre le Bienheureux); Assassination Bureau, The; Attentat, L' (Plot); Blow-Out (La Grande Bouffe); Cinema Paradiso (Nuovo Cinema Paradiso); Cinema Paradiso: The Special Edition; Clean Slate (Coup de Torchon); Dear Inspector (Tendre Poulet); Désert des Tartares, Le; Etoile du Nord, L' (The Northern Star); Fille de D'Artagnan, La (D'Artagnan's Daughter); Grosse Fatigue; Horloger de St Paul, L' (The Clockmaker/The Watchmaker of Saint-Paul); J'embrasse pas (I Don't Kiss); Justine (Cukor); Lady L; Le Cop (Les Ripoux); Le Cop 2 (Ripoux contre ripoux); Let's Hope It's a Girl (Speriamo che sia Femmina); Life and Nothing But (La Vie et Rien d'autre); Masques; Mister Freedom; Murphy's War; Night of the Generals, The; Postino, Il (The Postman); Purple Taxi, The (Le Taxi Mauve); Que la Fête Commence (Let Joy Reign Supreme); Return of the Musketeers, The; 'Round Midnight (Autour de Minuit); Secret, The (Le Secret); Semaine de Vacances, Une (A Week's Holiday); Serpent, The (Le Serpent); Tango; Three Brothers (Tre Fratelli); Time for Loving; Topaz; Uranus; Who Are You Polly Maggoo? (Qui êtes-vous Polly Maggoo?); Who Is Killing the Great Chefs of Europe? (aka Too Many Chefs); Zazie dans le Métro.

Nolte, Nick Affliction; Afterglow; Another 48 HRS; Blue Chips; Cannery Row; Cape Fear (Scorsese); Deep, The; Down and Out in Beverly Hills; Everybody Wins; Extreme Prejudice; Farewell to the King; 48 HRS; Grace Quigley; Heart Beat; I Love Trouble; Jefferson in Paris; Lorenzo's Oil; Mother Night; Mulholland Falls; New York Stories; North Dallas Forty; Prince of Tides, The; Q & A; Teachers; Three Fugitives; Under Fire; Who'll Stop the Rain? (aka Dog Soldiers).

Oates, Warren Badlands; Barquero; Blue Thunder; Border, The; Bring Me the Head of Alfredo Garcia; Brink's Job, The; China 9, Liberty 37; Cockfighter; Dillinger (Milius); Dixie Dynamite; Drum; Hired Hand, The; In the Heat of the Night; Kid Blue; Major Dundee; 1941; 92 in the Shade; Race with the Devil; Return of the Seven (aka Return of the Magnificent Seven); Ride the High Country (aka Guns in the Afternoon); Rise and Fall of Legs Diamond, The; Shooting, The; Sleeping Dogs; Split, The; Stripes; There Was a Crooked Man; Tom Sawyer; Two-Lane Blacktop; U Turn; Welcome to Hard Times (aka Killer on a Horse); White Dawn, The; Wild Bunch, The.

O'Hara, Maureen Battle of the Villa Fiorita, The; Big Jake; Black Swan, The; Dance, Girl, Dance; How Green Was My Valley; Hunchback of Notre Dame, The (Dieterle); Immortal Sergeant, The; Jamaica Inn; Kangaroo (Milestone); Little Romance, A; Long Gray Line, The; Mr Hobbs Takes a Vacation; Only the Lonely; Our Man in Havana; Quiet Man, The; Rare Breed, The; Rio Grande; Sentimental Journey; Sitting Pretty; Spanish Main, The; This Land Is Mine; Wings of Eagles, The; Woman's Secret, A.

Olivier, Laurence Battle of Britain; Beggar's Opera, The; Betsy, The; Bounty, The; Boys from Brazil, The; Bridge Too Far, A; Bunny Lake Is Missing; Carrie (Wyler); Clash of the Titans; Demi-Paradise, The (aka Adventure for Two); Divorce of Lady X, The; Dracula (Badham); Entertainer, The; Fire Over England; 49th Parallel; Hamlet (Olivier); Henry V (Olivier); Jazz Singer, The; Khartoum; Lady Caroline Lamb; Love Among the Ruins; Magic Box, The; Marathon Man; Nicholas and Alexandra; Oh! What a Lovely War; Othello (Burge); Pride and Prejudice; Prince and the Showgirl, The; Rebecca; Richard III; Seven-Per-Cent Solution, The; Shoes of the Fisherman, The; Sleuth; Spartacus; Term of Trial; That Hamilton Woman (aka Lady Hamilton); Three Sisters (Olivier); Wagner; War Requiem; Wild Geese II; Wuthering Heights (Wyler).

O'Toole, Peter Bible...In the Beginning, The (La Bibbia); Caligula; Country Dance (aka Brotherly Love); Creator; FairyTale – A True Story; Goodbye, Mr Chips (Ross); High Spirits; King Ralph; Last Emperor, The; Lawrence of Arabia; Lion in Winter, The; Lord Jim; Man

Friday; Masada (aka The Antagonists); Murphy's War; My Favourite Year; Night of the Generals, The; Power Play; Rebecca's Daughters; Rosebud; Ruling Class, The; Savage Innocents, The; Stunt Man, The; Supergirl; Under Milk Wood; What's New Pussycat?; Wings of Fame; Zulu Dawn.

Pacino, Al ...and justice for all; Author! Author!; Bobby Deerfield; Carlito's Way; City Hall; Cruising; Devil's Advocate, The; Dick Tracy; Dog Day Afternoon; Donnie Brasco; Frankie & Johnny; Glengarry Glen Ross; Godfather, The; Godfather Part II, The; Godfather Part III, The; Heat (Mann); Looking for Richard; Panic in Needle Park, The; Revolution; Scarecrow; Scarface (De Palma); Scent of a Woman; Sea of Love; Serpico.

Palance, Jack Alone in the Dark; Attack!; Austerlitz (aka The Battle of Austerlitz); Bagdad Café (aka Out of Rosenheim); Barabbas (Barabba); Batman; Big Knife, The; Chato's Land; Che!; City Slickers; City Slickers II: The Legend of Curly's Gold; Companeros (Vamos a Matar, Companeros!); Craze; Dracula (Curtis); Hawk the Slayer; Horsemen, The; I Died a Thousand Times; Mépris, Le (Contempt); Mercenario, Il (The Mercenary/A Professional Gun); Monte Walsh; Oklahoma Crude; Panic in the Streets; Professionals, The; Second Chance (Maté); Shane; Shape of Things to Come, The; Sign of the Pagan; Sudden Fear; Tango & Cash; Ten Seconds to Hell; They Came to Rob Las Vegas (Las Vegas 500 Millones); Torture Garden; Welcome to Blood City; Young Guns.

Peck, Gregory Amazing Grace and Chuck (aka Silent Voice); Arabesque; Beloved Infidel; Big Country, The; Billy Two Hats; Boys from Brazil, The; Bravados, The; Cape Fear (Thompson); Captain Horatio Hornblower; Days of Glory; Designing Woman; Duel in the Sun; Gentleman's Agreement; Great Sinner, The; Gunfighter, The; Guns of Navarone, The; How the West Was Won; MacArthur – The Rebel General; Mackenna's Gold; Macomber Affair, The; Marooned; Million Pound Note, The (aka Man With a Million); Mirage; Moby Dick; Old Gringo; Omen, The; On the Beach; Other People's Money; Paradine Case, The; Pork Chop Hill; Roman Holiday; Sea Wolves, The; Snows of Kilimanjaro, The; Spellbound; To Kill a

Mockingbird; Twelve O'Clock High; Yellow Sky; Wild Bill: A Hollwood Maverick.

Penn, Sean At Close Range; Bad Boys; Carlito's Way; Casualties of War; Colors; Crackers; Dead Man Walking; Falcon and the Snowman, The; Fast Times at Ridgemont High (aka Fast Times); Game, The; Judgment in Berlin; Loved; Racing with the Moon; Shanghai Surprise; She's So Lovely; State of Grace; Taps; U Turn; We're No Angels.

Perkins, Anthony Actress, The; Black Hole, The; Catch-22; Champagne Murders, The (Le Scandale); Crimes of Passion; Desire Under the Elms; Edge of Sanity; Friendly Persuasion; In the Deep Woods; Life and Times of Judge Roy Bean, The; Lovin' Molly; Mahogany; Murder on the Orient Express; North Sea Hijack; On the Beach; Phaedra; Pretty Poison; Psycho; Psycho II; Psycho III; Remember My Name; Ten Days' Wonder (La Décade Prodigieuse); Tin Star, The; Trial, The (Le Procès); Winter Kills; WUSA.

Pfeiffer, Michelle Age of Innocence; Batman Returns; Dangerous Liaisons; Dangerous Minds; Fabulous Baker Boys, The; Frankie & Johnny; Grease 2; Into the Night; Ladyhawke; Love Field; Married to the Mob; One Fine Day; Russia House, The; Scarface (De Palma); Sweet Liberty; Tequila Sunrise; Thousand Acres, A; Up Close & Personal; Witches of Eastwick, The; Wolf.

Philipe, Gérard Beauté du Diable, La (Beauty and the Devil); Belles de nuit, Les (Beauties of the Night/Night Beauties); Chartreuse de Parme, La; Diable au corps, Le (Devil in the Flesh); Fièvre Monte à El Pao, La (Republic of Sin); Knave of Hearts (aka Lovers, Happy Lovers!/Monsieur Ripois); Liaisons Dangereuses 1960, Les; Orgueilleux, Les (The Proud Ones); Ronde, La; Si Jolie Petite Plage, Une (Such a Pretty Little Beach).

Piccoli, Michel Adieu Bonaparte (Al-wedaa ya Bonaparte); Atlantic City (aka Atlantic City U.S.A.); Attentat, L' (Plot); Audience, The (L'Udienza); Belle de Jour; Belle Noiseuse, La; Belle Noiseuse – Divertimento, La; Beyond the Door (Oltre la Porta); Blow-Out (La Grande Bouffe); Choses de la Vie, Les (The Things of Life); Danger: Diabolik (Diabolik); Dangerous Moves (La Diagonale du Fou); Death in a French Garden (Péril en la Demeure); Demoiselles de Rochefort, Les (The Young

Girls of Rochefort); Des Enfants Gâtés (Spoiled Children); Diary of a Chambermaid, The (Le Journal d'une Femme de Chambre); Doulos, Le (The Finger Man); Equilibristes, Les (Walking a Tightrope); Espion Lève-toi; Fantôme de la Liberté, Le (The Phantom of Liberty); French Cancan; Guerre est finie, La (The War Is Over); Infernal Trio, The (Le Trio Infernal); Lady L; Last Woman, The (L'Ultima Donna); Leap into the Void (Salto nel Vuoto); Life Size (Tamaño Natural); Masquerade (Dearden); Mauvais Sang (The Night Is Young); Mépris, Le (Contempt); Milou en mai (Milou in May); Mort en ce Jardin, La (Evil Eden); Noces Rouges, Les (Blood Wedding/Red Wedding/Wedding in Blood); Paltoquet, Le; Passion; Prize of Peril, The (Le Prix du Danger); Sleeping Car Murder, The (Compartiment Tueurs); Success Is the Best Revenge; Ten Days' Wonder (La Décade Prodigieuse); Themroc; Topaz; 2 x 50 Years of French Cinema; Viva la Vie; Voie Lactée, La (The Milky Way).

Poitier, Sidney Bedford Incident, The; Blackboard Jungle, The; Buck and the Preacher; Defiant Ones, The; Duel at Diablo; Edge of the City (aka a Man is Ten Feet Tall); Greatest Story Ever Told, The; Guess Who's Coming to Dinner; In the Heat of the Night; Jackal, The; Let's Do It Again; Little Nikita (aka Sleepers); Long Ships; No Way Out (Mankiewicz); Organization, The; Patch of Blue, A; Piece of the Action, A; Shoot to Kill (aka Deadly Pursuit); Sneakers; Something of Value; They Call Me MISTER Tibbs!; To Sir, With Love; Uptown Saturday Night; Warm December, A; Wilby Conspiracy, The; Wild Bill: A Hollywood Maverick.

Powell, Dick Bad and the Beautiful, The; Christmas in July; Cornered; Cry Danger; Dames; Farewell, My Lovely (aka Murder My Sweet); Footlight Parade; 42nd Street; Gold Diggers of 1933; Gold Diggers of 1935; Gold Diggers of 1937; It Happened Tomorrow; Johnny O'Clock; Midsummer Night's Dream, A (Reinhardt/Dieterle); Naughty but Nice; Page Miss Glory; Pitfall; Susan Slept Here; Tall Target, The.

Powell, William After the Thin Man; Crossroads; How to Marry a Millionaire; I Love You Again; Kennel Murder Case, The; Last Command, The (von Sternberg); Life with Father; Love Crazy; Manhattan Melodrama; Mr Peabody and the Mermaid; Mister Roberts; My Man

Godfrey (La Cava); Senator Was Indiscreet, The; Thin Man, The; Ziegfeld Follies.

Power, Tyrone American Guerila in the Philippines; Black Swan, The; Blood and Sand (Mamoulian); Brigham Young – Frontiersman; Diplomatic Courier; In Old Chicago; Jesse James; Long Gray Line, The; Mark of Zorro, The; Nightmare Alley; Pony Soldier; Prince of Foxes; Rains Came, The; Rawhide (aka Desperate Siege); Razor's Edge, The; Rose of Washington Square; Suez; Sun Also Rises, The; Thin Ice (aka Lovely to Look at); This Above All; Untamed; Witness for the Prosecution; Yank in the RAF, A.

Price, Vincent Abominable Dr Phibes, The; Big Circus, The; Bloodbath at the House of Death; Bribe, The; Brigham Young – Frontiersman; Casanova's Big Night; Catchfire; City Under the Sea (aka War Gods of the Deep); Comedy of Terrors, The; Cry of the Banshee; Dangerous Mission; Dr Phibes Rises Again; Dragonwyck; Edward Scissorhands; Eve of St Mark, The; Fly, The (Neumann); Haunted Palace, The; His Kind of Woman; House of the Long Shadows, The; House of Usher, The (aka The Fall of the House of Usher); House of Wax; Invisible Man Returns, The; Las Vegas Story, The; Laura (Preminger); Leave Her to Heaven; Long Night, The; Madhouse (Clark); Mad Magician, The; Masque of the Red Death, The; Master of the World; Monster Club, The; Moss Rose; Oblong Box, The; Percy's Progress; Pit and the Pendulum, The; Private Lives of Elizabeth and Essex, The; Raven, The (Corman); Return of the Fly; Royal Scandal, A; Scream and Scream Again; Song of Bernadette, The; Tales of Terror; Ten Commandments, The; Theatre of Blood; Tingler, The; Tomb of Ligeia, The; Whales of August, The; While the City Sleeps; Wilson; Witchfinder General.

Quinn, Anthony Across 110th Street; Al-Risalah (The Message/Mohammed, Messenger of God); Back to Bataan; Barabbas (Barabba); Black Orchid, The; Black Swan, The; Blood and Sand (Mamoulian); Caravans; City Beneath the Sea; Deaf Smith & Johnny Ears (Los Amigos); Don Is Dead, The; Dream of Kings, A; East of Sumatra; Flap (aka The Last Warrior); Ghost Breakers, The; Gotti; Greek Tycoon, The; Guadalcanal Diary; Guns for San Sebastian (La Bataille de San Sebastian); Guns of Navarone, The; Happening, The; Heller in Pink Tights;

High Risk; High Wind in Jamaica, A; Hunchback of Notre Dame, The (Notre Dame de Paris); Inheritance, The (L'Eredità Ferramonti); Jungle Fever; King of Alcatraz; Last Train from Gun Hill; Last Train from Madrid, The; Lawrence of Arabia; Lion of the Desert; Lust for Life; Magus, The; Marseille Contract, The; Mobsters (aka Mobsters – The Evil Empire); Only the Lonely; Ox-Bow Incident, The (aka Strange Incident); Passage, The; Plainsman, The; Revenge (Scott); River's Edge, The; Road to Morocco; Savage Innocents, The; Secret of Santa Vittoria, The; Shoes of the Fisherman, The; Somebody to Love; Strada, La (The Road); They Died With Their Boots On; Tigers Don't Cry; Viva Zapata!; Walk in the Clouds, A; Walk in the Spring Rain, A; Warlock (Dmytryk); Zorba the Greek.

Rains, Claude Adventures of Robin Hood, The; Anthony Adverse; Caesar and Cleopatra; Casablanca; Clairvoyant, The; Deception; Greatest Story Ever Told, The; Here Comes Mr Jordan; Invisible Man, The; Juarez; Kings Row; Lawrence of Arabia; Lost World, The; Man Who Watched Trains Go By, The (aka Paris Express); Mr Skeffington; Mr Smith Goes to Washington; Notorious; Now, Voyager; Passage to Marseille; Passionate Friends, The (aka One Woman's Story); Phantom of the Opera (Lubin); Saturday's Children; Sea Hawk, The; They Won't Forget; Unsuspected, The; Where Danger Lives; White Tower, The; Wolf Man, The.

Reagan, Ronald Angels Wash Their Faces, The; Boy Meets Girl (Bacon); Cattle Queen of Montana; Gringo in Mañanaland, A; Hellcats of the Navy; Killers, The (Siegel); Kings Row; Naughty but Nice; Santa Fe Trail; Tennessee's Partner.

Redford, Robert All the President's Men; Barefoot in the Park; Bridge Too Far, A; Brubaker; Butch Cassidy and the Sundance Kid; Candidate, The; Chase, The; Downhill Racer; Electric Horseman, The; Great Gatsby, The (Clayton); Great Waldo Pepper, The; Havana; Hot Rock, The (aka How to Steal a Diamond in Four Uneasy Lessons); Indecent Proposal; Inside Daisy Clover; Jeremiah Johnson; Legal Eagles; Natural, The; Out of Africa; Sneakers; Sting, The; Tell Them Willie Boy Is Here; This Property Is Condemned; Three Days of the Condor; Up Close & Personal; Way We Were, The; Wild Bill: A Hollywood Maverick.

Redgrave, Michael Battle of Britain; Big Blockade, The; Browning Version, The; Captive Heart, The; Connecting Rooms; Dam Busters, The; Dead of Night; Go-Between, The; Goodbye, Mr Chips (Ross); Heroes of Telemark, The; Hill, The; Importance of Being Earnest, The; Innocents, The; Lady Vanishes, The (Hitchcock); Law and Disorder; Loneliness of the Long Distance Runner, The; Magic Box, The; Mr Arkadin (aka Confidential Report); Nicholas and Alexandra; Night My Number Came Up, The; Oh Rosalinda!!; Oh! What a Lovely War; Quiet American, The; Secret Agent, The; Secret Beyond the Door; Stars Look Down, The; Thunder Rock; Time Without Pity; Way to the Stars, The; Young Cassidy.

Redgrave, Vanessa Agatha; Ballad of the Sad Café, The; Bear Island; Blow-Up; Bostonians, The; Camelot; Charge of the Light Brigade, The (Richardson); Comrades; Consuming Passions; Deep Impact; Devils, The; House of Spirits, The; Howards End; Isadora; Julia; Little Odessa; Looking for Richard; Mary, Queen of Scots; Mission Impossible; Mrs Dalloway; Month by the Lake, A; Morgan, a Suitable Case for Treatment; Mother's Boys; Murder on the Orient Express; Oh! What a Lovely War; Out of Season; Prick Up Your Ears; Sailor from Gibraltar, The; Sea Gull, The; Seven-Per-Cent Solution, The; Smilla's Feeling for Snow (Fräulein Smillas Gespür für Schnee/aka Smilla's Sense of Snow); Sparrow (Storia di una Capinera); Steaming; Wagner; Wetherby; Wilde; Yanks.

Reggiani, Serge Amants de Vérone, Les (The Lovers of Verona); Armée des Ombres, L' (The Army in the Shadows); Bee Keeper, The (O Melissokomos); Casque d'Or (Golden Marie); Doulos, Le (The Finger Man); I Hired a Contract Killer; Leopard, The (Il Gattopardo); Mauvais Sang (The Night Is Yours); Misérables, Les; Portes de la Nuit, Les (Gates of the Night); Ronde, La; Secret People; Violette et François.

Reynolds, Burt Angel Baby; At Long Last Love; Bean; Best Friends; Best Little Whorehouse in Texas, The; Boogie Nights; Breaking In; Cannonball Run, The; Cannonball Run II; City Heat; Deliverance; End, The; Cop and ½ (aka Cop and a Half); Everything You Always Wanted to Know About Sex, But Were Afraid to Ask; Gator; Hooper; Hustle; Impasse; Longest

Yard, The (aka The Mean Machine); Lucky Lady; Mad Dog Time (aka Trigger Happy); Man Who Loved Cat Dancing, The; Man Who Loved Women, The; Modern Love; Nickelodeon; Paternity; Physical Evidence; Rough Cut; Sam Whiskey; Semi-Tough; Shamus; Shark; Sharky's Machine; Silent Movie; Skulduggery; Smokey and the Bandit; Smokey and the Bandit II (aka Smokey and the Bandit Ride Again); Starting Over; Stick; Striptease; Switching Channels; White Lightning; W.W. and the Dixie Dancekings.

Richardson, Ralph *Alice's Adventures in Wonderland; Anna Karenina* (Duvivier); *Battle of Britain; Bed Sitting Room, The; Bulldog Jack (aka Alias Bulldog Jack); Citadel, The* (Vidor); *Divorce of Lady X, The; Doctor Zhivago; Doll's House, A* (Garland); *Dragonslayer; Exodus; Fallen Idol, The; Four Feathers, The* (Korda); *Frankenstein: The True Story; Ghoul, The* (Hunter); *Give My Regards to Broad Street; Greystoke – The Legend of Tarzan Lord of the Apes; Heiress, The; Home at Seven (aka Murder on Monday); Khartoum; Lady Caroline Lamb; Long Day's Journey Into Night; Looking Glass War, The; Man Who Could Work Miracles, The; Midas Run (aka A Run on Gold); Oh! What a Lovely War; O Lucky Man!; Our Man in Havana; Outcast of the Islands; Richard III; Rollerball; Sound Barrier, The (aka Breaking the Sound Barrier); South Riding; Things to Come; Time Bandits; Wagner; Woman of Straw.*

Robards, Jason *Adventures of Huck Finn; All the President's Men; Any Wednesday (aka Bachelor Girl Apartment); Ballad of Cable Hogue, The; Big Hand for the Little Lady, A (aka Big Deal at Dodge City); Black Rainbow; Boy and His Dog, A; Bright Lights, Big City; Capoblanco; Comes a Horseman; Divorce American Style; Good Mother, The; Hour of the Gun; Hurricane; Isadora; Johnny Got His Gun; Julia; Legend of the Lone Ranger, The; Little Big League; Long Day's Journey Into Night; Melvin and Howard; Murders in the Rue Morgue* (Hessler); *Once Upon a Time in the West (C'era una Volta il West); Paper, The; Parenthood; Pat Garrett and Billy the Kid; Philadelphia; Quick Change; Raise the Titanic; Reunion (L'Ami Retrouvé); St Valentine's Day Massacre, The; Something Wicked This Way Comes; Square Dance; Storyville; Thousand Acres, A; Tora! Tora! Tora!; Trial, The* (Jones).

Robbins, Tim *Bob Roberts; Bull Durham; Cadillac Man; Erik the Viking; Five Corners; The; Howard the Duck (aka Howard...a new breed of hero); Hudsucker Proxy, The; I.Q.; Jacob's Ladder; Jungle Fever; Miss Firecracker; Nothing to Lose; Player, The; Ready to Wear (aka Prêt-à-Porter); Shawshank Redemption, The; Short Cuts; Sure Thing, The; Tapeheads.*

Robinson, Edward G *Amazing Doctor Clitterhouse, The; Barbary Coast; Blackmail (Potter); Brother Orchid; Bullets or Ballots; Cheyenne Autumn; Cincinnati Kid, The; Confessions of a Nazi Spy; Dr Erlich's Magic Bullet; Double Indemnity; Five Star Final; Flesh and Fantasy; Hatchet Man, The (aka The Honourable Mr Wong); Hole in the Head, A; House of Strangers; I Am the Law; Journey Together; Key Largo; Kid Galahad (Curtiz); Last Gangster, The; Little Caesar; Mackenna's Gold; Manpower; Neither By Day Nor By Night; Night Has a Thousand Eyes; Nightmare (Shane); Our Vines Have Tender Grapes; Red House, The; Robin and the 7 Hoods; Sammy Going South (aka A Boy Ten Feet Tall); Scarlet Street; Sea Wolf, The; Slight Case of Murder, A; Song of Norway; Soylent Green; Stranger, The; Ten Commandments, The; Tiger Shark; Two Weeks in Another Town; Whole Town's Talking, The (aka Passport to Fame); Woman in the Window, The.*

Rogers, Ginger *Bachelor Mother; Barkleys of Broadway, The; Black Widow (Johnson); Carefree; Fifth Avenue Girl; Flying Down to Rio; Follow the Fleet; 42nd Street; Gay Divorcee, The; Gold Diggers of 1933; I'll Be Seeing You; Lady in the Dark; Magnificent Doll; Major and the Minor, The; Monkey Business (Hawks); Oh, Men! Oh, Women!; Once Upon a Honeymoon; Primrose Path, The; Roberta; Roxie Hart; Shall We Dance?; Stage Door (La Cava); Story of Vernon and Irene Castle, The; Swing Time; Tender Comrade; Top Hat; Vivacious Lady.*

Russell, Jane *Born Losers, The; Darker Than Amber, The; French Line, The; Gentlemen Prefer Blondes; His Kind of Woman; Hot Blood; Las Vegas Story, The; Macao; Outlaw, The; Paleface, The; Revolt of Mamie Stover, The; Son of Paleface; Tall Men, The.*

Ryan, Robert *About Mrs Leslie; Back from Eternity; Bad Day at Black Rock; Battle of the Bulge; Berlin Express; Beware, My Lovely; Billy Budd; Born to Be Bad; Boy With Green Hair, The;*

Canadians, The; Captain Nemo and the Underwater City; Caught; City Beneath the Sea; Clash By Night; Crossfire; Custer of the West; Day of the Outlaw; Dirty Dozen, The; Escape to Burma; Executive Action; Flying Leathernecks; God's Little Acre; Horizons West; Hour of the Gun; House of Bamboo; Ice Palace (Sherman); I Married a Communist (aka The Woman on Pier 13); Inferno (Baker); King of Kings; Lawman; Lolly-Madonna XXX (aka The Lolly-Madonna War); Longest Day, The; Love Machine, The; Men in War; Naked Spur, The; Odds Against Tomorrow; On Dangerous Ground; Outfit, The; Professionals, The; Proud Ones, The; Racket, The; Sbarco di Anzio, Lo (Anzio/The Battle for Anzio); Set-Up, The; Sky's the Limit, The; Tall Men, The; Tender Comrade; Wild Bunch, The; Woman on the Beach, The.

Sarandon, Susan *Atlantic City (aka Atlantic City U.S.A.); Client, The; Bob Roberts; Bull Durham; Celluloid Closet, The; Compromising Positions; Crash; Dead Man Walking; Dry White Season, A; Front Page, The (Wilder); Great Waldo Pepper, The; Hunger, The; January Man, The; King of the Gypsies; Last of the Cowboys, The (aka The Great Smokey Roadblock); Light Sleeper; Little Women; Lorenzo's Oil; Loving Couples; Lovin' Molly; Other Side of Midnight, The; Pretty Baby; Rocky Horror Picture Show, The; Safe Passage; Sweet Hearts Dance; Tempest; Thelma & Louise; Twilight; White Palace; Who Am I This Time?; Witches of Eastwick, The.*

Scheider, Roy *All That Jazz; Blue Thunder; Cohen and Tate; 52 Pick-up; Fourth War, The; French Connection, The; Jaws; Jaws 2; Klute; Last Embrace; Listen to Me; Loving; Marathon Man; Men's Club, The; Myth of Fingerprints, The; Naked Lunch; Outside Man, The (Un Homme est Mort); Puzzle of a Downfall Child; Romeo Is Bleeding; Russia House, The; Seven-Ups, The; Sorcerer (aka Wages of Fear); Still of the Night; 2010.*

Schneider, Romy *Assassination of Trotsky, The; Bloodline (aka Sidney Sheldon's Bloodline); Bloomfield (aka The Hero); Boccaccio '70; Cardinal, The; César and Rosalie (César et Rosalie); Choses de le Vie, Les (The Things of Life); Death Watch (La Mort en Direct); Garde à Vue (The Inquisitor); Infernal Trio, The (Le Trio Infernal); Innocents with Dirty Hands (Les Innocents*

aux Mains Sales); Ludwig; Otley; Plein Soleil (Delitto in pieno sole/Blazing Sun/Purple Noon); 10:30 P.M. Summer; Trial, The (Le Procès); Victors, The; What's New Pussycat?

Schwarzenegger, Arnold *Batman & Robin; Commando; Conan the Barbarian; Conan the Destroyer; Eraser; Jingle All the Way; Junior; Kindergarten Cop; Last Action Hero, The; Predator; Pumping Iron; Raw Deal; Red Heat; Red Sonja; Running Man, The (Glaser); Stay Hungry; Terminator, The; Terminator 2: Judgment Day; Total Recall; True Lies; Twins; Villain, The (aka Cactus Jack).*

Schygulla, Hanna *Berlin Alexanderplatz; Beware of a Holy Whore (Warnung vor einer heiligen Nutte); Bitter Tears of Petra von Kant, The (Die Bitteren Tränen der Petra von Kant); Blue Exile, The (Mavi Sürgün); Circle of Deceit (Die Fälschung); Dead Again; Delta Force, The; Effi Briest; Friends and Husbands (Heller Wahn); Future Is Woman, The (Il Futuro è Donna); Gods of the Plague (Götter der Pest); Katzelmacher; Lili Marleen; Love in Germany, A (Eine Liebe in Deutschland); Love Is Colder than Death (Liebe ist kälter als der Tod); Marriage of Maria Braun, The (Die Ehe der Maria Braun); Merchant of Four Seasons, The (Händler der vier Jahreszeiten, Der); Passion; That Night in Varennes (La Nuit de Varennes); Third Generation, The (Die Dritte Generation); Wild Game (Wildwechsel); Wrong Movement (Falsche Bewegung).*

Scofield, Paul *Bartleby; Carve Her Name with Pride; Crucible, The; Delicate Balance, A; Hamlet (Zeffirelli); Henry V (Branagh); King Lear (Brook); Man for All Seasons, A; Nineteen Nineteen; Quiz Show; Scorpio; That Lady; Train, The; When the Whales Came.*

Scott, George C *Anatomy of a Murder; Angus; Bank Shot; Beauty and the Beast (Cook); Bible...In the Beginning, The (La Bibbia); Changeling, The; Christmas Carol, A; Day of the Dolphin, The; Dr Strangelove: or, How I Learned to Stop Worrying and Love the Bomb; Exorcist III, The; Firestarter; Flim-Flam Man, The (aka One Born Every Minute); Formula, The; Hardcore (aka The Hardcore Life); Hindenburg, The; Hospital, The; Hustler, The; Islands in the Stream; Jane Eyre*

(Mann); *Last Run, The; List of Adrian Messenger, The; Malice; Movie Movie; New Centurions, The (aka Precinct 45: Los Angeles Police); Oklahoma Crude; Oliver Twist (Donner); Patton (aka Patton: Lust for Glory); Petulia; Prince and the Pauper, The (aka Crossed Swords); Taps; They Might Be Giants.*

Sellers, Peter *After the Fox (Caccia alla Volpe); Alice's Adventures in Wonderland; Battle of the Sexes, The; Being There; Blockhouse, The; Bobo, The; Casino Royale; Dr Strangelove: or, How I Learned to Stop Worrying and Love the Bomb; Down Among the Z Men; Fiendish Plot of Dr Fu Manchu, The; Great McGonagall, The; Heavens Above!; I Love You, Alice B Toklas; I'm All Right, Jack; Ladykillers, The; Lolita (Kubrick); Magic Christian, The; Millionairess, The; Mouse That Roared, The; Murder By Death; Naked Truth, The (aka Your Past Is Showing); Never Let Go; Only Two Can Play; Optimists of Nine Elms, The; Orders are Orders; Party, The; Pink Panther, The; Pink Panther Strikes Again, The; Prisoner of Zenda, The (Quine); Return of the Pink Panther, The; Revenge of the Pink Panther; Shot in the Dark, A; Smallest Show on Earth, The; Soft Beds, Hard Battles; There's a Girl in My Soup; Tom Thumb; Trail of the Pink Panther; Two-Way Stretch; What's New Pussycat?; Wrong Arm of the Law, The.*

Serrault, Michel *Argent des Autres, L' (Other People's Money); Assassin(s); Beaumarchais (Beaumarchais l'insolent); Bonheur est dans le pré, Le; Buffet Froid; Cage aux Folles, La (Birds of a Feather); Cage aux Folles II, La; Cage aux Folles III: The Wedding, La; Deadly Run (Mortelle Randonnée); Diaboliques, Les (Diabolique/The Fiends); Docteur Petiot; Garde à Vue (The Inquisitor); He Died With His Eyes Open (On ne Meurt que 2 Fois); King of Hearts (Le Roi de Coeur); Malevil; Murder Is a Murder...Is a Murder, A (Un Meurtre est un Meurtre); Nelly & Monsieur Arnaud (Nelly and Mister Arnaud); Old Lady Who Walked in the Sea, The (La Vieille qui Marchait dans la Mer); Préparez vos Mouchoirs (Get Out Your Handkerchiefs).*

Seyrig, Delphine *Accident; Année Dernière à Marienbad, L' (Last Year in Marienbad); Baisers Volés (Stolen Kisses); Black Windmill, The; Daughters of Darkness (Le Rouge aux Lèvres); Day of the Jackal,*

The; Discreet Charm of the Bourgeoisie, The (Le Charme Discret de la Bourgeoisie); Doll's House, A (Losey); Golden Eighties; India Song; Jeanne Dielman, 23 Quai du Commerce, 1080 Bruxelles; Joan of Arc of Mongolia; Mister Freedom; Muriel (Muriel, ou le Temps d'un Retour); Peau d'Ane (The Magic Donkey); Voie Lactée, La (The Milky Way); Who Are You Polly Maggoo? (Qui êtes-vous Polly Maggoo?).

Shaw, Robert *Avalanche Express; Battle of Britain; Battle of the Bulge; Birthday Party, The; Black Sunday; Caretaker, The (aka The Guest); Custer of the West; Deep, The; Diamonds; Figures in a Landscape; Force 10 from Navarone; From Russia With Love; Hill in Korea, A (aka Hell in Korea); Hireling, The; Jaws; Luck of Ginger Coffey, The; Man for All Seasons, A; Robin and Marian; Royal Hunt of the Sun, The; Sting, The; Swashbuckler (aka The Scarlet Buccaneer); Taking of Pelham One Two Three, The; Town Called Bastard, A; Young Winston.*

Sheen, Martin *American President, The; Apocalypse Now; Badlands; Believers, The; Beverly Hills Brats; Beyond the Stars (aka Personal Choice); Cassandra Crossing, The; Catch-22; Count a Lonely Cadence (aka Stockade); Da; Dead Zone, The; Eagle's Wing; Enigma; Entertaining Angels: The Dorothy Day Story; Final Countdown, The; Firestarter; Gandhi; Gettysburg; Hear No Evil; In the King of Prussia; Judgment in Berlin; Killing Box, The Loophole; Man, Woman and Child; No Drums, No Bugles; Siesta; Subject Was Roses, The; That Championship Season; Wall Street.*

Signoret, Simone *Against the Wind; Armée des Ombres, L' (The Army in the Shadows); Aveu, L' (The Confession); Casque d'Or (Golden Marie); Chat, Le (The Cat); Deadly Affair, The; Diaboliques, Les (Diabolique/The Fiends); Etoile du Nord, L' (The Northern Star); Madame Rosa (La Vie devant Soi); Manèges (The Wanton); Mort en ce Jardin, La (Evil Eden); Ronde, La; Room at the Top.*

Sim, Alastair *Belles of St Trinian's, The; Blue Muder at St Trinian's; Captain Boycott; Cottage to Let (aka Bombsight Stolen); Escape from the Dark (aka The Littlest Horse Thieves); Folly to Be Wise; Geordie (aka Wee Geordie); Green for Danger; Green Man, The; Happiest Days of Your Life, The; Hue and Cry; Innocents in Paris; Inspector Calls, An; Laughter in Paradise; Left,*

Right and Centre; Let the People Sing; London Belongs to Me (aka Dulcimer Street); Millionairess, The; Royal Flash; Ruling Class, The; School for Scoundrels; Squeaker, The; Stage Fright; Waterloo Road.

Simon, Michel *Atalante, L'; Beauté du Diable, La (Beauty and the Devil); Blanche; Boudu Sauvé des Eaux (Boudu Saved from Drowning); Chienne, La; Disparus de Saint-Agil, Les; Drôle de Drame (Bizarre, Bizarre); Fin du Jour, La (The End of the Day); On Purge Bébé; Passion de Jeanne d'Arc, La (The Passion of Joan of Arc); Quai des Brumes, Le (Port of Shadows); Saadia; Train, The; Vieil Homme et l'Enfant, Le (The Two of Us).*

Sinatra, Frank *Anchors Aweigh; Assault on a Queen; Can-Can; Cannonball Run II; Cast a Giant Shadow; Come Blow Your Horn; Detective, The; Devil at 4 O'Clock, The; First Deadly Sin, The; From Here to Eternity; Guys and Dolls; High Society; Hole in the Head, A; It Happened in Brooklyn; Kings Go Forth; Lady in Cement; List of Adrian Messenger, The; Manchurian Candidate, The; Man With the Golden Arm, The; Miracle of the Bells, The; Naked Runner, The; Never So Few; None But the Brave; Not As a Stranger; Ocean's 11; On the Town; Pal Joey; Pride and the Passion, The; Robin and the 7 Hoods; Some Came Running; Suddenly; Take Me Out to the Ball Game (aka Everybody's Cheering); That's Entertainment!; Tony Rome; Von Ryan's Express; Young at Heart.*

Smith, Maggie *Better Late Than Never; California Suite; Clash of the Titans; Death on the Nile; Evil Under the Sun; First Wives Club, The; Honey Pot, The; Hook; Lonely Passion of Judith Hearne, The; Missionary, The; Murder by Death; Oh! What a Lovely War; Othello (Burge); Prime of Miss Jean Brodie, The; Private Function, A; Pumpkin Eater, The; Quartet (Ivory); Richard III (Loncraine);Room with a View, A; Secret Garden, The; Sister Act; Sister Act II: Back in the Habit; V.I.P.s, The; Washington Square; Young Cassidy.*

Snipes, Wesley *Boiling Point; Demolition Man; Drop Zone; Fan, The; Jungle Fever; King of New York; Major League; Mo' Better Blues; Money Train; Murder at 1600; New Jack City; One Night Stand; Passenger 57; Rising Sun; Streets of Gold; Sugar Hill; To Wong Foo, Thanks For Everything! Julie Newmar;*

U.S. Marshals; Waterdance, The; White Men Can't Jump; Wildcats.

Stallone, Sylvester *Assassins; Capone; Cliffhanger; Cobra (Cosmatos); CopLand; Daylight; Death Race 2000; Demolition Man; Farewell, My Lovely (Richards); First Blood; F.I.S.T.; Judge Dredd; Lock Up; Lords of Flatbush, The; Nighthawks (Malmuth); Oscar; Over the Top; Paradise Alley; Prisoner of Second Avenue, The; Rambo: First Blood, Part II; Rambo III; Rocky; Rocky II; Rocky III; Rocky IV; Rocky V; Specialist, The; Stop! or My Mom Will Shoot; Tango & Cash; Victory (aka Escape to Victory).*

Stanton, Harry Dean *Alien; Black Marble, The; Blue Tiger; Care Bears Movie, The; Christine; Cisco Pike; Cockfighter; Cool Hand Luke; Day of the Evil Gun; Death Watch (La Mort en Direct); Dillinger (Milius); Down Periscope; Escape from New York; Farewell, My Lovely (Richards); Fool for Love; Fourth War, The; Kelly's Heroes; Last Temptation of Christ, The; Man Trouble; Missouri Breaks, The; Mr North; Never Talk to Strangers; 92 in the Shade; Paris, Texas; Pat Garrett and Billy the Kid; Pretty in Pink; Private Benjamin; Rafferty and the Gold Dust Twins; Rancho Deluxe; Rebel Rousers; Red Dawn; Renaldo & Clara; Repo Man; Ride in the Whirlwind; Rose, The; She's So Lovely; Slam Dance; Stars and Bars; Straight Time; Titanic; Twin Peaks: Fire Walk with Me; Twister; What's the Matter With Helen?; Wild at Heart; Wise Blood; Young Doctors in Love; Zandy's Bride.*

Stanwyck, Barbara *All I Desire; Annie Oakley; Baby Face; Ball of Fire; Banjo on My Knee; B.F.'s Daughter; Bitter Tea of General Yen, The; Cattle Queen of Montana; Clash By Night; Crime of Passion; Cry Wolf; Double Indemnity; Escape to Burma; Executive Suite; File on Thelma Jordan, The; Flesh and Fantasy; Forbidden; Forty Guns; Furies, The; Golden Boy; Jeopardy; Lady Eve, The; Lady of Burlesque (aka Striptease Lady); Mad Miss Manton, The; Man With a Cloak, The; Meet John Doe; Miracle Woman, The; Night Nurse; No Man of Her Own; Remember the Night; Sorry, Wrong Number; Stella Dallas; Strange Love of Martha Ivers, The; There's Always Tomorrow; This Is My Affair (aka His Affair); Walk on the Wild Side.*

Steiger, Rod *Al Capone; Amityville Horror, The; Back from Eternity; Ballad of the*

Sad Café, The; Big Knife,
The; Cattle Annie and Little
Britches; Chosen, The;
Court-Martial of Billy
Mitchell, The (aka One Man
Mutiny); Doctor Dolittle;
F.I.S.T.; Giù la Testa (Duck,
You Sucker/A Fistful of
Dynamite/Once Upon a Time
– the Revolution); Happy
Birthday, Wanda June;
Harder They Fall, The;
Hennessy; Heroes, The (Gli
Eroi); Illustrated Man, The;
Incognito; Innocents With
Dirty Hands (Les Innocents
aux Mains Sales); In the
Heat of the Night; January
Man, The; Kindred, The;
Lion of the Desert; Lolly-
Madonna XXX (aka The
Lolly-Madonna War); Love
and Bullets; Loved One, The;
Lucky Luciano; Mani sulla
Città, Le (Hands Over the
City); Man Named John, A
(E Venne un Uomo); Mars
Attacks!; Men of Respect;
Naked Face, The; No Way to
Treat a Lady; Oklahoma!;
On the Waterfront;
Pawnbroker, The; Run of the
Arrow; Specialist, The; That
Summer of White Roses;
Three Into Two Won't Go;
Waterloo; W.C. Fields and
Me.

Stewart, James After the Thin
Man; Airport '77; Anatomy
of a Murder; Bandolero!;
Bend of the River (aka
Where the River Bends); Big
Sleep, The (Winner); Born to
Dance; Broken Arrow; Call
Northside 777; Cheyenne
Autumn; Cheyenne Social
Club, The; Destry Rides
Again; Far Country, The;
Flight of the Phoenix, The;
Glenn Miller Story, The;
Gorgeous Hussy, The;
Greatest Show on Earth,
The; Harvey; How the West
Was Won; It's a Wonderful
Life; Last Gangster, The;
Magic of Lassie, The; Magic
Town; Malaya (aka East of
the Rising Sun); Man from
Laramie, The; Man Who
Knew Too Much, The (1956);
Man Who Shot Liberty
Valance, The; Mr Hobbs
Takes a Vacation; Mr Smith
Goes to Washington; Mortal
Storm, The; Naked Spur,
The; Night Passage; No
Highway (aka No Highway in
the Sky); Philadelphia Story,
The; Rare Breed, The; Rear
Window; Rope; Seventh
Heaven (King); Shootist,
The; Shop Around the
Corner, The; That's
Entertainment!; Two Rode
Together; Vertigo; Vivacious
Lady; Winchester '73; You
Can't Take It With You;
Ziegfeld Girl.

Streep, Meryl Before and After;
Birdges of Madison County,
The; Cry in the Dark, A;
Death Becomes Her; Deer
Hunter, The; Defending
Your Life; Falling in Love;
French Lieutenant's Woman,
The; Heartburn; Ironweed;
House of Spirits, The; Julia;
Kramer vs Kramer;
Manhattan; Marvin's Room;

Out of Africa; Plenty;
Postcards from the Edge;
River Wild, The; Seduction
of Joe Tynan, The; She-
Devil; Silkwood; Sophie's
Choice; Still of the Night.

Sutherland, Donald Alex in
Wonderland; Alien Thunder
(aka Dan Candy's Law);
Backdraft; Bear Island;
Bedford Incident, The;
Benefit of the Doubt; Blood
Relatives (Liens de Sang);
Buffy the Vampire Slayer;
Crackers; Day of the Locust,
The; Disclosure; Dirty Dozen,
The; Disappearance, The; Dr
Terror's House of Horrors;
Don't Look Now; Dry White
Season, A; Eagle Has
Landed, The; Eye of the
Needle; Fallen; Fanatic (aka
Die! Die! My Darling!);
Fellini's Casanova (Il
Casanova di Federico
Fellini); First Great Train
Robbery, The (aka The Great
Train Robbery); F.T.A.;
Heaven Help Us (aka
Catholic Boys); Interlude
(Billington); Invasion of the
Body Snatchers (Kaufman);
JFK; Johnny Got His Gun;
Kelly's Heroes; Kentucky
Fried Movie, The; Klute;
Lady Ice; Little Murders;
Lock Up; Lost Angels (aka
The Road Home); Man, a
Woman and a Bank, A;
M*A*S*H; Murder by
Decree; National Lampoon's
Animal House; 1900
(Novecento); Oedipus the
King; Ordeal by Innocence;
Puppet Masters, The (aka
Robert Heinlein's The Puppet
Masters); Revolution; Rosary
Murders, The; Shadow
Conspiracy; Six Degrees of
Separation; Split, The;
S*P*Y*S; Steelyard Blues;
Time to Kill, A; Younger
and Younger.

Swanson, Gloria Airport 1975;
Queen Kelly; Sadie
Thompson; Sunset
Boulevard.

Taylor, Elizabeth Ash
Wednesday; Blue Bird, The;
Boom; Butterfield 8; Cat on
a Hot Tin Roof; Cleopatra
(Mankiewicz); Comedians,
The; Father of the Bride;
Flintstones, The; Giant;
Ivanhoe; Jane Eyre
(Stevenson); Lassie Come
Home; Last Time I Saw
Paris; Life with Father; Little
Night Music, A; Mirror
Crack'd, The; National
Velvet; Night Watch; Only
Game in Town, The; Place in
the Sun, A; Raintree County;
Reflections in a Golden Eye;
Sandpiper, The; Secret
Ceremony; Suddenly Last
Summer; Sweet Bird of
Youth; That's
Entertainment!; Under Milk
Wood; Victory at Entebbe;
V.I.P.s, The; Who's Afraid of
Virginia Woolf?; Winter
Kills; Zee & Co (X, Y and
Zee).

Taylor, Robert Adventures of
Quentin Durward, The (aka

Quentin Durward); Bataan;
Billy the Kid; Bribe, The;
Broadway Melody of 1936;
Camille (Cukor); Devil's
Doorway; Escape (LeRoy);
Gorgeous Hussy, The;
Ivanhoe; Johnny Eager; Last
Hunt, The; Law and Jake
Wade, The; Party Girl; Quo
Vadis?; Rogue Cop; Saddle
the Wind; This Is My Affair
(aka His Affair); Three
Comrades; Undercurrent;
When Ladies Meet.

Temple, Shirley Adventure in
Baltimore (aka Bachelor
Bait); Captain January;
Dimples; Fort Apache; I'll Be
Seeing You; Littlest Rebel,
The; Since You Went Away.

Tierney, Gene Advise and
Consent; Black Widow
(Johnson); Dragonwyck;
Ghost and Mrs Muir, The;
Heaven Can Wait (Lubitsch);
Iron Curtain, The (aka
Behind the Iron Curtain);
Laura; Leave Her to Heaven;
Left Hand of God, The;
Night and the City (Dassin);
Pleasure Seekers, The;
Razor's Edge, The; Return of
Frank James, The; Secret of
Convict Lake, The; Shanghai
Gesture, The; Tobacco Road;
Way of a Gaucho; Whirlpool.

Tracy, Spencer Actress, The;
Adam's Rib; Bad Day at
Black Rock; Boom Town;
Broken Lance; Captains
Courageous; Dante's
Inferno; Desk Set (aka His
Other Woman); Devil at 4
O'Clock, The; Dr Jekyll and
Mr Hyde (Fleming); Edison
the Man; Father of the
Bride; Fury (Lang); Guess
Who's Coming to Dinner;
Inherit the Wind; I Take
This Woman; It's a Mad,
Mad, Mad, Mad World;
Judgment at Nuremberg;
Keeper of the Flame; Last
Hurrah, The; Malaya (aka
East of the Rising Sun);
Man's Castle; Northwest
Passage; Old Man and the
Sea, The; Pat and Mike;
Power and the Glory, The;
San Francisco; Seventh
Cross, The; State of the
Union (aka The World and
His Wife); 20,000 Years in
Sing Sing; Woman of the
Year.

Travolta, John Blow Out;
Broken Arrow; Carrie;
Devil's Rain, The; Experts,
The; Face/Off; Get Shorty;
Grease; Look Who's Talking;
Look Who's Talking Now;
Look Who's Talking Too;
Michael; Moment by
Moment; Perfect;
Phenomenon; Primary
Colors; Pulp Fiction;
Saturday Night Fever; She's
So Lovely; Shout; Staying
Alive; Two of a Kind; Urban
Cowboy; White Man's
Burden.

Trevor, Claire Amazing Doctor
Clitterhouse, The; Born to
Kill (aka Lady of Deceit);
Cape Town Affair, The;
Crack-Up (Reis); Crossroads;

Dante's Inferno; Dead End;
Farewell, My Lovely (aka
Murder My Sweet); Hard,
Fast and Beautiful; Hoodlum
Empire; Johnny Angel; Key
Largo; Kiss Me Goodbye;
Man Without a Star; Raw
Deal (Mann); Stagecoach
(Ford); Two Weeks in
Another Town.

Trintignant, Jean-Louis
Agression, L' (Aggression);
Argent des Autres, L' (Other
People's Money); Attentat, L'
(Plot); Biches, Les (The
Does); Big Silence, The (Il
Grande Silenzio); Blow to the
Heart (Colpire al Cuore);
Conformist, The (Il
Conformista); Désert des
Tartares, Le; Et Dieu Créa la
Femme (And God Created
Woman/And Woman...Was
Created); Glissements
Progressifs du Plaisir; Héros
très discret, Un (A Self-Made
Hero); Homme et une
Femme, Un (A Man and a
Woman); Liaisons
Dangereuses 1960, Les;
Malevil; Mata Hari, Agent
H.21; Merci la vie (Thank
You, Life); My Night with
Maud (Ma Nuit chez Maud);
Outside Man, The (Un
Homme est Mort); Passione
d'Amore; Pleins Feux sur
l'assassin; Regarde les
hommes tomber (See How
They Fall); Secret, The (Le
Secret); Shattered (Les
Passagers); Si tous les gars
du monde… (Race for Life/If
All the Guys in the World…);
Sleeping Car Murder, The
(Compartiment Tueurs);
That Night in Varennes (La
Nuit de Varennes); Those
Who Love Me Will Take the
Train (Ceux qui m'aiment
prendront le train); Three
Colours: Red (Trois
Couleurs: Rouge); Trans-
Europ-Express; Under Fire;
Violons du Bal, Les; Viva la
Vie; Vivement Dimanche!
(Confidentially Yours/
Finally, Sunday!); Z.

Turner, Kathleen Accidental
Tourist, The; Body Heat;
Crimes of Passion; House of
Cards; Jewel of the Nile; Man
With Two Brains, The;
Moonlight and Valentino;
Naked in New York; Peggy
Sue Got Married; Prizzi's
Honor; Romancing the
Stone; Serial Mom; Simple
Wish, A; Switching
Channels; Undercover Blues;
V I Warshawski; War of the
Roses, The.

Valentino, Rudolph Blood and
Sand (Niblo); Camille
(Smallwood); Cobra, The;
Eagle, The; Isle of Love, The.

Veidt, Conrad Above
Suspicion; All Through the
Night; Cabinet of Dr
Caligari, The (Das Kabinett
des Dr Caligari); Casablanca;
Congress Dances (Der
Kongress tanzt); Contraband
(aka Blackout); Dark
Journey; Escape (LeRoy);
Hands of Orlac, The (Orlacs
Hände); King of the

Damned; Spy in Black, The; Thief of Bagdad, The (Powell/Berger/Whelan/ Korda); Under the Red Robe; Waxworks (Das Wachsfigurenkabinett); Woman's Face, A.

von Stroheim, Erich As You Desire Me; Blind Husbands; Disparus de Saint-Agil, Les; Five Graves to Cairo; Foolish Wives; Grande Illusion, La; Lost Squadron, The; North Star, The (aka Armored Attack); Pièges (Personal Column/ Snares); Sunset Boulevard; Wedding March, The.

von Sydow, Max Ansiktet (The Face/The Magician); Best Intentions, The (Den Goda Viljan); Brass Target; Conan the Barbarian; Death Watch (La Mort en Direct); Désert des Tartares, Le; Dreamscape; Duet for One; Dune; Emigrants, The (Utvandrarna); Exorcist, The; Exorcist II: The Heretic; Father; Flash Gordon; Greatest Story Ever Told, The; Hannah and Her Sisters; Hawaii; Hour of the Wolf (Vargtimmen); Hurricane; Illustrious Corpses (Cadaveri Eccellenti); Judge Dredd; Kiss Before Dying, A (Dearden); Kremlin Letter, The; March or Die; Nattvardsgästerna (The Communicants/Winter Light); Needful Things; Never Say Never Again; Ox, The (Oxen); Passion, A (En Passion); Pelle the Conqueror (Pelle Erobreren); Quiller Memorandum, The; Reward, The; Seventh Seal, The (Det Sjunde Inseglet); Shame, The (Skammen); Silent Touch, The; Steppenwolf; Strange Brew; Three Days of the Condor; Through a Glass Darkly (Sasom i en Spegel); Touch, The; Until the End of the World (Bis ans Ende der Welt); Victory (aka Escape to Victory; Virgin Spring, The (Jungfrukällan); Voyage of the Damned; Wild Strawberries (Smultronstället).

Washington, Denzel Carbon Copy; Courage Under Fire; Crimson Tide; Cry Freedom; Devil in a Blue Dress; Fallen; For Queen and Country; Glory; Heart Condition; Malcolm X; Mighty Quinn, The; Mississippi Masala; Much Ado About Nothing; Mo' Better Blues; Pelican Brief, The; Philadelphia; Power; Preacher's Wife, The; Ricochet; Soldier's Story, A.

Wayne, John Alamo, The; Baby Face; Back to Bataan; Big Jake; Big Trail, The; Brannigan; Cahill – US Marshal; Cast a Giant Shadow; Chisum; Conqueror, The; Cowboys, The; Desret Trail, The; Donovan's Reef; El Dorado; Fighting Seabees, The; Flying Leathernecks; Fort Apache; Greatest Story

Ever Told, The; Green Berets, The; Hatari!; Hondo; Horse Soldiers, The; How the West Was Won; In Harm's Way; Jet Pilot; Lady from Louisiana; Lady Takes a Chance; Legend of the Lost; Longest Day, The; Long Voyage Home, The; Lucky Texan, The; Man Who Shot Liberty Valance, The; McQ; Quiet Man, The; North to Alaska; Randy Rides Alone; Red River; Riders of Destiny; Rio Bravo; Rio Grande; Rio Lobo; Rooster Cogburn; Sands of Iwo Jima; Sea Chase, The; Searchers, The; Seven Sinners; She Wore a Yellow Ribbon; Shootist, The; Stagecoach (Ford); They Were Expendable; Three Godfathers; Train Robbers, The; True Grit; Undefeated, The; War Wagon, The; Wings of Eagles, The.

Welles, Orson Austerlitz (aka The Battle of Austerlitz); Butterfly (Cimber); Casino Royale; Catch-22; Chimes at Midnight (Campanadas a Medianoche); Citizen Kane; Compulsion; Ferry to Hong Kong; F for Fake (Vérités et Mensonges); Hot Money; Immortal Story, The (Histoire Immortelle); Jane Eyre (Stevenson); Journey into Fear; Kremlin Letter, The; Lady from Shanghai, The; Long Hot Summer, The; Macbeth (Welles); Malpertuis; Man for All Seasons, A; Mr Arkadin (aka Confidential Report); Moby Dick; Muppet Movie, The; Oedipus the King; Othello (Welles); Prince of Foxes; Safe Place, A; Sailor from Gibraltar, The; Someone to Love; Stranger, The; Ten Days' Wonder (La Décade Prodigieuse); Third Man, The; Touch of Evil; Trial, The (Le Procès); V.I.P.s, The; Voyage of the Damned; Waterloo.

West, Mae I'm No Angel; Klondike Annie; My Little Chickadee; Myra Breckinridge; Night After Night; She Done Him Wrong.

Whitaker, Forest Bird; Bloodsport; Blown Away; Body Count; Body Snatchers; Consenting Adults; Crying Game, The; Good Morning Vietnam; Jason's Lyric; Johnny Handsome; Lush Life; Phenomenon; Platoon; Rage in Harlem, A; Smoke; Species; Stakeout.

Widmark, Richard Against All Odds; Alamo, The; Bear Island; Bedford Incident, The; Broken Lance; Cheyenne Autumn; Cobweb, The; Coma; Death of a Gunfighter; Destination Gobi; Domino Principle, The (aka The Domino Killings); Don't Bother to Knock (Baker); Flight from Ashiya; Gathering of Old Men, A; Halls of Montezuma; Hanky Panky; Hell and High Water;

How the West Was Won; Judgment at Nuremberg; Kiss of Death (Hathaway); Last Wagon, The; Law and Jake Wade, The; Long Ships, The; National Lampoon Goes to the Movies (aka National Lampoon's Movie Madness); Madigan; Moonshine War, The; Murder on the Orient Express; Night and the City (Dassin); No Way Out (Mankiewicz); Panic in the Streets; Pickup on South Street; Road House (Negulesco); Rollercoaster; Run for the Sun; Sellout, The; Street with No Name, The; Swarm, The; To the Devil a Daughter; Twilight's Last Gleaming; Two Rode Together; Warlock (Dmytryk); Way West, The; When the Legends Die; Who Dares Wins; Yellow Sky.

Williams, Robin Aladdin; Adventures of Baron Munchausen, The (Gilliam); Awakenings; Being Human; Best of Times, The; Birdcage, The; Cadillac Man; Dead Again; Dead Poets Society; Deconstructing Harry; Fathers' Day; Fisher King, The; Flubber; Good Morning Vietnam; Good Will Hunting; Hamlet (Branagh); Hook; Jack; Jumanji; Mrs Doubtfire; Moscow on the Hudson; Nine Months; Popeye; Secret Agent, The (Joseph Conrad's The Secret Agent); Seize the Day; Survivors, The; Toys; World According to Garp, The.

Winger, Debra Betrayed; Black Widow (Rafelson); Cannery Row; Dangerous Woman, A; Everybody Wins; Forget Paris; Leap of Faith; Legal Eagles; Made in Heaven; Mike's Murder; Officer and a Gentleman, An; Shadowlands; Sheltering Sky, The; Slumber Party '57; Terms of Endearment; Thank God It's Friday; Urban Cowboy.

Winters, Shelley Alfie; Big Knife, The; Bloody Mama; Blume in Love; Buona Sera, Mrs Campbell; Chapman Report, The; City on Fire; Cleopatra Jones; Cry of the City; Delta Force, The; Diamonds; Diary of Anne Frank, The; Double Life, A; Elvis (aka Elvis – The Movie); Executive Suite; Fanny Hill; Flap (aka The Last Warrior); Greatest Story Ever Told, The; Great Gatsby, The (Nugent); Harper (aka The Moving Target); Heavy; I Am a Camera; I Died a Thousand Times; King of the Gypsies; Lolita (Kubrick); Mad Room, The; Magician of Lublin, The; Next Stop, Greenwich Village; Night of the Hunter, The; Odds Against Tomorrow; Over the Brooklyn Bridge; Patch of Blue, A; Pete's Dragon; Phone Call from a Stranger; Place in the Sun, A; Portrait

of a Lady, The; Poseidon Adventure, The; Scalphunters, The; Sex Symbol, The; Silence of the Hams, The (Il silenzio dei prosciutti); S.O.B.; Something to Hide; Stepping Out; Tenant, The (Le Locataire); Tentacles (Tentacoli); That Lucky Touch; What's the Matter with Helen?; Wild in the Streets; Winchester '73.

Woods, James Against All Odds; Alex & the Gypsy; Best Seller; Black Marble, The; Boost, The; Casino; Cat's Eye; Chaplin; Choirboys, The; Citizen Cohn; Contact; Cop; Diggstown (aka Midnight Sting); Eyewitness (aka The Janitor); Fast-Walking; Gambler, The; Getaway, The (Donaldson); Ghosts of the Mississippi (aka Ghosts of the Past); Hickey & Boggs; Kicked in the Head; Killer: A Journal of Murder; Night Moves; Nixon; Once Upon a Time in America; Onion Field, The; Raid on Entebbe; Salvador; Specialist, The; Straight Talk; True Believer (aka Fighting Justice); Videodrome.

Directors' Index

Aaron, Paul *Different Story, A; Force of One, A; Maxie.*

Abashidze, Dodo *Ashik Kerib; Legend of the Suram Fortress, The (Legenda Suramskoi Kreposti).*

Abbott, George *Damn Yankees (aka What Lola Wants); Pajama Game, The.*

Abdelsalam, Shadi *Night of Counting the Years, The (El Mumia).*

Abdrashitov, Vadim *Parade of the Planets (Parad Planyet); Plumbum, or a Dangerous Game (Plyumbum, ili opasnaya igra).*

Abel, Robert *Elvis on Tour; Let the Good Times Roll.*

Abey, Dennis *Never Too Young to Rock.*

Abrahams, Jim *Airplane!; Big Business; Hot Shots!; Hot Shots! Part Deux; Ruthless People; Top Secret!; Welcome Home, Roxy Carmichael.*

Abuladze, Tenghiz *Repentance (Monanieba); Wishing Tree, The (Drevo Zhelanya).*

Acevski, Jon *Freddie as F.R.O.7.*

Achbar, Mark *Manufacturing Consent: Noam Chomsky and the Media.*

Achternbusch, Herbert *Last Hole, The (Das letzte Loch).*

Ackerman, Robert Allan *Safe Passage.*

Adams, Catlin *Sticky Fingers.*

Adams, Doug *Blackout (aka The Attic).*

Adelson, Alan *Lodz Ghetto.*

Adidge, Pierre *Elvis on Tour; Mad Dogs and Englishmen.*

Adler, Carine *Under the Skin.*

Adler, Lou *Up In Smoke.*

Adlon, Percy *Bagdad Café (aka Out of Rosenheim); Céleste; Rosalie Goes Shopping; Salmonberries; Sugarbaby (Zuckerbaby); Swing, The (Die Schaukel); Younger and Younger.*

Agland, Phil *Woodlanders, The.*

Agosti, Silvano *Fit to Be Untied (Matti da Slegare).*

Agostini, Philipe *Dialogue des Carmélites, Le.*

Agraz, Carlos Garcia *My Dear Tom Mix.*

Agresti, Alejandro *Buenos Aires Vice Versa; Cross, The (La Cruz); Secret Wedding (Boda Secreta).*

Aguiluz, Tikoy *Boatman (Ang Bangkero).*

Aguirre, Monti *Amazonia: Voices from the Rainforest (Amazonia: Vozes da Floresto).*

Ahearn, Charlie *Wild Style.*

Ahwesh, Peggy *Deadman, The.*

Aitken, Doug *Big Wheels and Sailor.*

Akerman, Chantal (Anne) *American Stories (Histories d'Amérique: Food, Family and Philosophy); Golden Eighties; Jeanne Dielman, 23 Quai du Commerce, 1080 Bruxelles; Je tu il elle (I...You...He...She); News from Home; Night and Day (Nuit et Jour); Portrait of a Young Girl at the End of the '60s in Brussels; Rendez-vous d'Anna, Les (The Meetings of Anna); Toute une Nuit (All Night Long).*

Akkad, Moustapha *Al-Risalah (The Message/Mohammad, Messenger of God); Lion of the Desert.*

Akomfrah, John *Handsworth Songs; Testament; Who Needs a Heart.*

Alaux, Myriam *Animals Film, The.*

Albertini, Adalberto *Black Emanuelle (Emanuelle Nera).*

Albicocco, Jean-Gabriel *Petit Martin, Le (The Virgin and the Soldier); Wanderer, The (Le Grand Meaulnes).*

Alda, Alan *Betsy's Wedding; Four Seasons, The; New Life, A; Sweet Liberty.*

Alderman, Thomas S *Severed Arm, The.*

Aldiss, Will *Stealing Home.*

Aldrich, Robert *All the Marbles (aka The California Dolls); Apache; Attack!; Autumn Leaves; Big Knife, The; Choirboys, The; Dirty Dozen, The; Emperor of the North Pole, The (aka Emperor of the North); Flight of the Phoenix, The; Garment Jungle, The; Hush...Hush, Sweet Charlotte; Hustle; Killing of Sister George, The; Kiss Me Deadly; Last Sunset, The; Legend of Lylah Clare,*

The; Longest Yard, The (aka The Mean Machine); Sodom and Gomorrah (Sodoma e Gomorra); Ten Seconds to Hell; Too Late the Hero; Twilight's Last Gleaming; Ulzana's Raid; Vera Cruz; What Ever Happened to Baby Jane?; World for Ransom.

Alemann, Claudia von Blind Spot (Die Reise nach Lyon); Point Is to Change It, The (Es Kommt drauf an, sie zu Verändern).

Alessandrini, Goffredo We the Living (Noi Vivi).

Alexander, Mike Mairi Mhor.

Alexandrov, Grigori Oktyabr (October/Ten Days That Shook the World).

Algar, James Best of Walt Disney's True Life Adventures, The.

Al Ghosaini, Samir Days in London (Ayam fi London).

Algrant, Dan Naked in New York.

Alk, Howard Janis.

Allanhof, Benjamin What About Me?

Allégret, Marc Blanche Fury; Fanny; Zouzou.

Allégret, Yves Manèges (The Wanton); Orgueilleux, Les (The Proud Ones); Si Jolie Petite Plage, Une (Such a Pretty Little Beach).

Allen, Corey Avalanche; Thunder and Lightning.

Allen, Irwin Beyond the Poseidon Adventure; Lost World, The; Swarm, The.

Allen, Kevin Twin Town.

Allen, Lewis Another Time, Another Place; So Evil My Love; Suddenly; Uninvited, The; Unseen, The.

Allen, Woody Alice; Annie Hall; Another Woman; Bananas; Broadway Danny Rose; Bullets Over Broadway; Crimes and Misdemeanors; Deconstructing Harry; Everyone Says I Love You; Everything You Always Wanted to Know About Sex, But Were Afraid to Ask; Hannah and Her Sisters; Husbands and Wives; Interiors; Love and Death; Manhattan; Manhattan Murder Mystery; Midsummer Night's Sex Comedy, A; Mighty Aphrodite; New York Stories; Purple Rose of Cairo, The; Radio Days; September; Shadows and Fog; Sleeper; Stardust Memories; Take the Money and Run; What's Up Tiger Lily?; Zelig.

Allers, Roger Lion King, The.

Allio, René Camisards, Les; Moi, Pierre Rivière; Vieille Dame indigne, La (The Shameless Old Lady).

Allouache, Merzak Bab El-Oued City; Salut Cousin! (Hey Cousin!).

Almendros, Nestor Improper Conduct (Mauvaise Conduite).

Almereyda, Michael Another Girl, Another Planet; At Sundance; Nadja; Twister.

Almodóvar, Pedro Dark Habits (Entre Tinieblas); Flower of My Secret, The (La Flor di me Secreto/La Fleur de mon secret); High Heels (Tacones Lejanos); Kika; Labyrinth of Passion (Laberinto de Pasiones); Law of Desire, The (La Ley del Deseo); Live Flesh (Carne Trémula/En chair et en os); Matador; Pepi, Luci, Bom... (Pepi, Luci, Bom y otras chicas del montón); Tie Me Up! Tie Me Down! (¡Atame!); What Have I Done to Deserve This? (¿Qué He Hecho Yo para Merecer Esto?); Women on the Verge of a Nervous Breakdown (Mujeres al Borde de un Ataque de Nervios).

Alonzo, John A FM.

Altman, Robert Aria; Beyond Therapy; Brewster McCloud; Buffalo Bill and the Indias, or Sitting Bull's History Lesson; California Split; Come Back to the 5 & Dime Jimmy Dean, Jimmy Dean; Countdown; Fool for Love; Health; Images; James Dean Story, The; Long Goodbye, The; M*A*S*H; McCabe and Mrs Miller; Nashville; O.C. & Stiggs; Perfect Couple, A; Player, The; Popeye; Quintet; Ready to Wear (aka Prêt-à-Porter); Robert Altman's Jazz '34: Remembrances of Kansas City Swing; Kansas City; Secret Honor; Short Cuts; Streamers; That Cold Day in the Park; Thieves Like Us; 3 Women; Vincent & Theo (Vincent et Theo); Wedding, A.

Alvarez, Carlos What Is Democracy? (¿Qué es la Democracia?).

Alves, Joe Jaws 3-D.

Amalou, JK Hard Men.

Amar, Denis Addition, L' (The Patsy).

Amaral, Suzana Hour of the Star (A Hora da Estrela).

Amateau, Rod Drive-In; Seniors, The (aka The Senior).

Amber Films/Amber Production Team Dream On; Eden Valley; In Fading Light; Letters to Katja; Seacoal; T. Dan Smith; Writing in the Sand, The.

Ambrose, Anna Phoelix.

Amelio, Gianni Blow to the Heart (Colpire al Cuore); Open Doors (Porte Aperte); Stolen Children, The (Il Ladro di Bambini).

Amenábar, Alejandro Thesis (Tesis).

Amenta, Pino Heaven Tonight.

Amero, John Blonde Ambition.

Amero, Len Blonde Ambition.

Amiel, Jon Copycat; Queen of Hearts; Man Who Knew Too Little, The; Sommersby; Tune in Tomorrow (aka Aunt Julia and the Scriptwriter).

Amodeo, Rachel What About Me?

Amrohi, Kamal Pakeezah.

Amurri, Franco Flashback; Monkey Trouble.

Amyes, Julian Hill in Korea, A (aka Hell in Korea).

Anders, Allison Four Rooms; Gas Food Lodging; Grace of My Heart; My Crazy Life (Mi Vida Loca).

Andersen, Knut I Was Fifteen (Den Sommeren jeg fylte 15).

Andersen, Thom Eadweard Muybridge, Zoopraxographer.

Anderson, John Murray King of Jazz, The.

Anderson, Laurie Home of the Brave.

Anderson, Lindsay Britannia Hospital; If...; In Celebration; O Lucky Man!; This Sporting Life; Whales of August, The; White Bus, The.

Anderson, Michael Around the World In 80 Days; Chase a Crooked Shadow; Conduct Unbecoming; Dam Busters, The; Doc Savage – The Man of Bronze; Dominique; Flight from Ashiya; Logan's Run; Millennium; Operation Crossbow; Orca (aka Orca...Killer Whale); Pope Joan; Quiller Memorandum, The; Shoes of the Fisherman, The; Yangtse Incident (aka Battle Hell/Escape of The Amethyst).

Anderson, Paul Event Horizon; Mortal Kombat; Shopping.

Anderson, Paul Thomas Boogie Nights; Hard Eight.

Anderson, Steve South Central.

Andonov, Metodi Goat Horn, The (Koziyat Rog).

Andrade, Joaquim Pedro do Macunaima.

Andrea, Dree All Visitors Must Be Announced.

Andreacchio, Mario Captain Johnno.

Andrien, Jean-Jacques Australia.

Ang Lee Eat Drink Man Woman (Yinshi Nan Nü); Ice Storm, The; Pushing Hands (Tui Shou); Sense and Sensibility; Wedding Banquet, The (Xiyan).

Angelo, Yves Colonel Chabert, Le.

Angelopoulos, Theo (Theodore) Alexander the Great (O Megalexandros); Bee Keeper, The (O Melissokomos); Eternity and a Day (Mia Eoniotita Ke Mia Mera); Landscape in the Mist (Topio stin Omichli); Travelling Players, The (O Thiassos); Ulysses' Gaze (To Vlemma Tou Odyssea/aka The Gaze of Ulysses); Voyage to Cythera (Taxidi sta Kithira).

Anger, Kenneth The Anger Magick Lantern Cycle.

Annakin, Ken Battle of the Bulge; Call of the Wild, The; Fast Lady, The; Holiday Camp; Hotel Sahara; Longest Day, The; Loser Takes All; Paper Tiger; Quartet; Trio; Three Men in a Boat; Value for Money; Very Important Person.

Annaud, Jean-Jacques Bear, The (L'Ours); Black and White in Color (La Victoire en Chantant); Lover, The (L'Amant); Name of the Rose, The (Der Name der Rose); Seven Years in Tibet; Quest for Fire.

Annett, Paul Beast Must Die, The.

Anspaugh, David Fresh Horses; Hoosiers (aka Best Shot); Moonlight and Valentino; Rudy.

Anthony, Joseph Career.

Antonelli, John Kerouac.

Antonioni, Michelangelo Amiche, Le (The Girlfriends); Avventura, L' (The Adventure); Beyond the Clouds (Par-delà les Nuages/Al di là nuvole/Jenseits der Wolken); Blow-Up; Cronaca di un Amore (Chronicle of a Love Affair); Eclipse, The (L'Eclisse); Identification of a Woman (Identificazione di una Donna); Oberwald Mystery, The (Il Mistero di Oberwald); Notte, La; Passenger, The (Professione: Reporter); Red Desert, The (Deserto Rosso); Signora senza camelie, La (Camille without Camellias/The Lady without Camellias); Zabriskie Point.

Aoyama, Shinji Obsession, An (Tsumetai Chi).

Appleby, Daniel B *Bound and Gagged: A Love Story.*

Apted, Michael *Agatha; Blink; Bring On the Night; Class Action; Coal Miner's Daughter; Extreme Measures; Gorillas in the Mist; Gorky Park; Nell; P'Tang, Yang, Kipperbang; Squeeze, The; Stardust; Thunderheart; Triple Echo, The.*

Araki, Gregg *Doom Generation, The; Living End, The; Nowhere; Totally F***ed Up.*

Aranda, Vicente *Libertarias; Lovers (Amantes).*

Arau, Alfonso *Like Water for Chocolate (Como Agua para Chocolate); Walk in the Clouds, A.*

Aravindan, G *Bogey Man, The (Kummatty); Masquerade (Marattom); Sometime, Somewhere (Oridathu).*

Arcand, Denys *Decline of the American Empire, The (Le Déclin de l'Empire Américain); Jesus of Montreal (Jésus de Montréal); Love and Human Remains; Réjeanne Padovani.*

Arcelin, Jacques *Bitter Cane.*

Archainbaud, George *Lost Squadron, The.*

Archibugi, Francesca *By Nightfall (Verso Sera); Mignon Has Left (Mignon è partita).*

Ardolino, Emile *Chances Are; Dirty Dancing; Gypsy; Nutcracker, The (aka George Balanchine's The Nutcracker); Sister Act; Three Men and a Little Lady.*

Argento, Dario *Cat o' Nine Tails, The (Il Gatto a Nove Code); Creepers (Phenomena); Four Flies on Grey Velvet (Quattro Mosche di Velluto Grigio); Inferno; Opera (Terror at the Opera); Suspiria; Tenebrae (Sotto gli Occhi dell'Assassino); Uccello dalle Piume di Cristallo, L' (The Bird with the Crystal Plumage/The Gallery Murders).*

Ariç, Nizamettin *Song for Beko, A (Ein Lied für Beko/Klamek ji bo Beko).*

Arioli, Don *Charles Dickens' David Copperfield.*

Aristarain, Adolfo *Place in the World, A.*

Arkin, Alan *Little Murders.*

Arkush, Allan *Deathsport; Hollywood Boulevard; Rock'n'Roll High School.*

Arliss, Leslie *Love Story; Man in Grey, The; Wicked Lady, The; Night Has Eyes, The (aka Terror House).*

Armendáriz, Montxo *Secrets of the Heart (Secretos del corazón); Stories of the Kronen (Historias del Kronen).*

Armitage, George *Grosse Pointe Blank; Miami Blues; Vigilante Force.*

Armiñán, Jaime de *Nest, the (El Nido).*

Armstrong, Gillian *High Tide; Last Days of Chez Nous, The; Little Women; Mrs Soffel; My Brilliant Career; Oscar and Lucinda; Starstruck.*

Arnfred, Morten, *Kingdom, The (Riget); Kingdom II, The (Riget II).*

Arnold, Jack *Black Eye; Boss Nigger (aka The Black Bounty Killer); Creature from the Black Lagoon; Global Affair, A; Incredible Shrinking Man, The; It Came from Outer Space; Marilyn – The Untold Story; Monster on the Campus; Mouse That Roared, The; Revenge of the Creature; Sex Play (aka The Bunny Caper); Swiss Conspiracy, The; Tarantula.*

Arnold, Newt *Bloodsport.*

Aronson, Jerry *Life and Times of Allen Ginsberg, The.*

Arrabal, Fernando *Viva la Muerte.*

Artenstein, Isaac *Break of Dawn.*

Arthur, Karen *Legacy; Mafu Cage, The.*

Arzner, Dorothy *Christopher Strong; Craig's Wife; Dance, Girl, Dance; Merrily We Go to Hell; Nana (aka Lady of the Boulevards); Wild Party, The.*

Ascott, Anthony *Blazing Guns (Uomo avvisato mezzo ammazzato...parola di Spirito Santo).*

Ash *Big Bang Theory, The (aka Bang).*

Ashburne, Derek *Naked Are the Cheaters.*

Ashby, Hal *Being There; Bound for Glory; Coming Home; 8 Million Ways to Die; Harold and Maude; Landlord, The; Last Detail, The; Let's Spend the Night Together (aka Time Is On Our Side); Shampoo.*

Asher, Robert *Early Bird, The; Follow a Star; Intelligence Men, The; Movers and Shakers; On the Beat; Press for Time.*

Asher, William *Beach Blanket Bingo.*

Ashida, Toyoo *Fist of the North Star.*

Ashley, Christopher *Jeffrey.*

Askarian, Don *Komitas.*

Askoldov, Alexander *Commissar, The (Komissar).*

Asquith, Anthony *Browning Version, The; Carrington VC (aka Court Martial); Cottage to Let (aka Bombsight Stolen); Demi-Paradise (aka Adventure for Two); French Without Tears; Guns of Darkness; Importance of Being Earnest, The; Libel; Millionairess, The; Orders to Kill; Pygmalion; Tell England; Underground; V.I.P.s, The; Way to the Stars, The.*

Assayas, Olivier *Eau Froide, L' (Cold Water); Irma Vep; Paris s'éveille (Paris Awakens).*

Asseo, André *Enfants de Lumière, Les (The Children of Lumière).*

Astrakhan, Dimitri *You Are My Only Love.*

Athens, JD *Cannibal Women in the Avocado Jungle of Death (aka Piranha Women in the Avocado Jungle of Death).*

Athié, Francisco *Lolo.*

Atkinson, Jim *Can You Keep It Up for a Week?*

Attenborough, Richard *Bridge Too Far, A; Chaplin; Chorus Line, A; Cry Freedom; Gandhi; In Love and War; Magic; Oh! What a Lovely War; Shadowlands; Young Winston.*

Attias, Daniel *Silver Bullet.*

Attwood, David *Wild West.*

Au, Tony *Au revoir, mon amour (He Rijun Zai Lai).*

Audiard, Jacques *Héros très discret, Un (A Self-Made Hero); Regarde les hommes tomber (See How They Fall).*

Audry, Jacqueline *Olivia.*

Auguiste, Reece *Twilight City.*

August, Bille *Best Intentions, The (Den Goda Viljan); House of Spirits, The; Pelle the Conqueror (Pelle Erobreren); Smilla's Feeling for Snow (Fräulein Smillas Gespür für Schnee/aka Smilla's Sense of Snow).*

Austen, Chris *South Africa Belongs to Us.*

Auster, Paul *Blue in the Face.*

Austin, Michael *Killing Dad; Princess Caraboo.*

Autant-Lara, Claude *Affaire du Courrier de Lyon, L'; Auberge Rouge, L' (The Red Inn); Diable au corps, Le (Devil in the Flesh); Douce; En Cas de Malheur (La*

Ragazza del Peccato/Love Is My Profession).

Auzins, Igor *We of the Never Never.*

Avakian, Aram *Cops and Robbers; 11 Harrowhouse; End of the Road.*

Avary, Roger *Killing Zoe.*

Avati, Pupi *Festival; Noi tre (The Three of Us/We Three).*

Avedis, Howard (Hikmet) *Stepmother, The; They're Playing With Fire.*

Averback, Hy *Chamber of Horrors; I Love You, Alice B Toklas; Where the Boys Are; Where Were You When the Lights Went Out?*

Avildsen, John G *Cry Uncle (aka Super Dick); 8 Seconds; For Keeps (aka Maybe Baby); Formula, The; Karate Kid, The; Karate Kid: Part II, The; Karate Kid Part III, The; Neighbors; Power of One, The; Rocky; Rocky V; Save the Tiger; Slow Dancing in the Big City; Stoolie, The; W.W. and the Dixie Dancekings.*

Avnet, Jon *Fried Green Tomatoes at the Whistle Stop Café; Red Corner; Up Close & Personal; War, The.*

Axel, Gabriel *Babette's Feast (Babettes Gaestebud); Prince of Jutland.*

Axelrod, George *Lord Love a Duck; Secret Life of an American Wife, The.*

Azpurúa, Carlos *Disparen a Matar (Shoot to Kill).*

B, Beth *Salvation! Have You Said Your Prayers Today? (aka Salvation!).*

Babenco, Hector *At Play in the Fields of the Lord; Ironweed; Kiss of the Spider Woman; Pixote (Pixote a lei do mais fraco).*

Bach, Jean *Great Day in Harlem, A.*

Bacon, Lloyd *Action in the North Atlantic; Boy Meets Girl; Brother Orchid; Footlight Parade; 42nd Street; French Line, The; Gold Diggers of 1937; In Caliente; Invisible Stripes; Marked Woman; Miss Pinkerton; Picture Snatcher; Slight Case of Murder, A; You Were Meant for Me.*

Bacsó, Péter *Witness, The (A Tanu).*

Badham, John *American Flyers; Another Stakeout; Bingo Long Travelling All-Stars & Motor Kings, The; Bird on a Wire; Blue Thunder; Dracula; Drop Zone; Hard Way, The; Incognito; Nick of Time; Point of No Return (aka The Assassin); Saturday Night*

Fever; Short Circuit; Stakeout; Sunshine Part II (aka My Sweet Lady); War Games; Whose Life Is It Anyway?

Baer, Max Ode to Billy Joe.

Bae Yong-Kyun Why Did Bohdi-Dharma Leave for the Orient? (Dharmaga tongjoguro kan kkadalgun?).

Bafaloukos, Theodoros Rockers.

Bagdadi, Maroun Fille de l'Air, La; Hors la vie (Out of Life).

Bahr, Fax Hearts of Darkness: A Filmmaker's Apocalypse.

Baigelman, Steven Feeling Minnesota.

Bail, Chuck Choke Canyon (aka On Dangerous Ground); Cleopatra Jones and the Casino of Gold; Gumball Rally, The.

Bailey, John China Moon.

Baily, John Amir.

Baird, Stuart Executive Decision; U.S. Marshals.

Bakari, Imruh Blue Notes and Exiled Voices.

Baker, David Libido.

Baker, Fred Lenny Bruce Without Tears.

Baker, Graham Alien Nation; Final Conflict, The; Impulse.

Baker, Robert S Hellfire Club, The.

Baker, Roy Ward ...And Now the Screaming Starts! (aka Fengriffen); Anniversary, The; Asylum; Dr Jekyll and Sister Hyde; Don't Bother to Knock; Flame in the Streets; Higly Dangerous; Inferno; Legend of the 7 Golden Vampires, The; Monster Club, The; Morning Departure (aka Operation Disaster); Night to Remember, A; October Man, The; One That Got Away, The; Passage Home; Quatermass and the Pit; Scars of Dracula, The; Singer Not the Song, The; Vampire Lovers, The; Vault of Horror.

Bakshi, Ralph Cool World; Fire and Ice; Fritz the Cat; Heavy Traffic; Lord of the Rings, The; Wizards.

Balaban, Bob Last Good Time, The; Parents.

Balasko, Josiane Gazon maudit (French Twist).

Balayan, Roman Dream Flights (Polioty Vo Sne Naiavou).

Balch, Antony Horror Hospital.

Baldi, Ferdinando Blindman; Comin' at Ya!; Texas, Addio

(aka The Avenger); Treasure of the Four Crowns.

Baldwin, Craig Tribulation 99: Alien Anomalies Under America; Sonic Outlaws.

Ballard, Carroll Black Stallion, The; Fly Away Home; Never Cry Wolf; Nutcracker – the Motion Picture; Wind.

Balletbò-Coll, Marta Costa Brava (Family Album).

Balling, Erik One of Those Things (Haendeligt Uheld).

Ballmann, Herbert Girl in a Boot (Einmal Ku'damm und Zurück).

Balshofer, Fred J Isle of Love, The.

Band, Charles Alchemist, The; Metalstorm: The Destruction of Jared-Syn; Parasite; Trancers (aka Future Cop).

Bangura, Roberto Girl with Brains in Her Feet.

Banham, Derek Last Day of Summer.

Banks, Monty Shipyard Sally.

Banno, Yoshimitsu Godzilla vs the Smog Monster (Gojira tai Hedora).

Baran, Jack Destiny Turns on the Radio.

Baratier, Jacques First Time with Feeling (Vous Intéressez-vous à la Chose?).

Barba, Norbert Blue Tiger.

Barbash, Uri Beyond the Walls (Me'Achorei Hasoragim); One of Us (Echad Mi'Shelanu).

Barbera, Joseph Jetsons: The Movie.

Bardem, Juan Antonio Calle Mayor (The Love Maker/Main Street).

Bare, Richard L Wicked, Wicked.

Barkas, Geoffrey Tell England.

Barker, Clive Hellraiser; Lord of Illusions; Nightbreed.

Barker, Mike James Gang, The.

Barnet, Boris House on Trubnaya, The (Dom na Trubnoi).

Barnett, Steve Mindwarp.

Barney, Matthew Cremaster 5.

Barreto, Bruno Carried Away (aka Acts of Love); Doña Flor and Her Two Husbands (Doña Flor e Seus Dois Maridos); Four Days in September (O Que é Isso, Companheiro?); Gabriela; Show of Force, A.

Barrett, Lezli-An Business As Usual.

Barris, Chuck Gong Show Movie, The.

Barron, Arthur Jeremy.

Barron, Steve Adventures of Pinocchio, The; Electric Dreams; Teenage Mutant Ninja Turtles.

Barron, Zelda Secret Places; Shag.

Barroso, Mariano Extasis.

Barry, Ian Chain Reaction, The.

Barta, Jiri Pied Piper, The (Krysar).

Bartel, Paul Cannonball (aka Carquake); Death Race 2000; Eating Raoul; Lust in the Dust; Not for Publication; Private Parts; Scenes from the Class Struggle in Beverly Hills; Secret Cinema.

Bartlett, Hall Jonathan Livingston Seagull.

Barton, Charles T Abbott and Costello Meet Frankenstein (aka Abbott and Costello Meet the Ghosts).

Barua, Jahnu It's a Long Way to the Sea (Hkhagoroloi Bohu Door).

Baser, Tevfik Farewell, Stranger (Lebewohl Fremde); Farwell to False Paradise (Abschied vom Falschen Paradies/Yalanci Cennete Elveda); 40 Metre Square Germany (40 Metrekare Almanya).

Bashore, Juliet Kamikaze Hearts.

Baskin, Richard Sing.

Bass, Jules Mad Monster Party; Last Unicorn, The.

Bass, Saul Phase IV.

Batchelor, Joy Animal Farm.

Battersby, Roy Mr Love.

Battiato, Giacomo Blood Ties (Il Cugino Americano).

Bauer, Evgenij Dying Swan, The (Umirajuseij lebed).

Bauer, Tristan Cortazar.

Bava, Lamberto Demons (Demoni); Demons 2 (Demoni 2).

Bava, Mario Black Sabbath (I Tre Volti della Paura); Danger: Diabolik (Diabolik); Maschera del Demonio, La (Black Sunday/Mask of the Demon/Revenge of the Vampire).

Baxley, Craig R Action Jackson; Dark Angel; Stone Cold.

Baxter, John Crooks' Tour; Let

the People Sing; Love on the Dole.

Bay, Michael Bad Boys; Rock, The.

Bayly, Stephen Coming Up Roses; Just Ask for Diamond.

Beaird, David It Takes Two; Scorchers.

Bean, Robert B Made for Each Other.

Beatt, Cynthia Party – Nature Morte, The.

Beatty, Warren Dick Tracy; Heaven Can Wait; Reds.

Beaudin, Jean Being at Home with Claude; J.A. Martin Photographer (J.A. Martin Photographe).

Beaudine, William Billy the Kid vs. Dracula; Boys Will Be Boys; Old-Fashioned Way, The; Voodoo Man; Windbag the Sailor.

Beaumont, Gabrielle Godsend, The.

Beauvois, Xavier N'oublie pas que tu vas mourir (Don't Forget You're Going to Die); Nord (North).

Beaver, Chris Dark Circle.

Becker, Harold Black Marble, The; Boost, The; City Hall; Malice; Mercury Rising; Onion Field, The; Ragman's Daughter, The; Sea of Love; Taps; Vision Quest (aka Crazy for You).

Becker, Jacques Casque d'Or (Golden Marie); Goupi-Mains-Rouges (It Happened at the Inn); Touchez pas au Grisbi (Grisbi/Honour Among Thieves); Trou, Le (The Hole/The Night Watch).

Becker, Jean Elisa; One Deadly Summer (L'Eté Meurtrier).

Becker, Lutz Double Headed Eagle, The.

Becker, Wolfgang Child's Play (Kinderspiel); Life Is All You Get (Das Leben ist eine Baustelle).

Bedford, Terry Slayground.

Beeman, Greg License to Drive.

Bégéja, Liria Loin des Barbares (Far from the Barbarians).

Behi, Rihda Hyenas' Sun (Soleil des Hyènes).

Beineix, Jean-Jacques Betty Blue (37° 2 le Matin) [versions 1 & 2]; Diva; IP5; Moon in the Gutter, The (La Lune dans le Caniveau); Roselyne and the Lions (Roselyne et les lions).

Belén, Ana How to Be a Woman and Not Die in the Attempt (Como ser mujer y no morir en el intento).

Belikov, Mikhail *When We Were Young (Kak Molody My Byli)*.

Bell, Martin *American Heart; Streetwise*.

Bellamy, Earl *Fire; Speedtrap*.

Bellisario, Donald P *Last Rites*.

Bellocchio, Marco *China Is Near (La Cina è vicina); Fists in the Pocket (I Pugni in Tasca); Fit To Be Untied (Matti da Slegare); In the Name of the Father (Nel Nome del Padre); Leap into the Void (Salto nel Vuoto); Prince of Homburg, The (Il Principe di Homburg)*.

Belmont, Véra *Rouge Baiser*.

Belson, Jerry *Surrender*.

Belvaux, Rémy *Man Bites Dog (C'est arrivé près de chez vous)*.

Bemberg, María Luisa *Camila; I, the Worst of All (Yo, la Peor de Todas); Miss Mary; We Don't Want to Talk About It (De eso no se habla)*.

Ben-Dor Niv, Orna *Because of That War (Biglal Hamilkhama Hahi)*.

Bene, Carmelo *One Hamlet Less (Un Amleto di Meno)*.

Benedek, Laslo *Namu, The Killer Whale; Wild One, The*.

Benedict, Richard *Impasse*.

Benegal, Shyam *Ankur (The Seeling); Ascending Scale (Arohan); Boon, The (Kondura); Role, The (Bhumika); Trikal: Past, Present and Future (Trikal)*.

Benigni, Roberto *Life Is Beautiful (La Vita è Bella)*.

Benjamin, Richard *City Heat; Little Nikita (aka Sleepers); Made in America; Mermaids; Milk Money; Mrs Winterbourne; Money Pit, The; My Favourite Year; My Stepmother Is an Alien; Racing with the Moon*.

Benner, Richard *Outrageous!*

Bennett, Bill *Backlash; Kiss or Kill; Malpractice; Mortgage; Spider and Rose; Two If by Sea (aka Stolen Hearts)*.

Bennett, Compton *Seventh Veil, The; So Little Time*.

Bennett, Edward *Ascendancy; Life Story of Baal, The*.

Bennett, Leroy *Cure Show, The*.

Benson, Robby *Crack in the Mirror; Modern Love*.

Benson, Leon *Sunshine Part II (aka My Sweet Lady)*.

Bentley, Thomas *Old Curiosity Shop, The*.

Benton, Robert *Bad Company; Billy Bathgate; Kramer vs Kramer; Late Show, The; Nadine; Nobody's Fool; Places in the Heart; Still of the Night; Twilight*.

Benveniste, Michael *Flesh Gordon*.

Benz, Obie *Heavy Petting*.

Béraud, Luc *Turtle on Its Back (La Tortue sur la Dos)*.

Bercovici, Luca *Ghoulies*.

Beresford, Bruce *Adventures of Barry McKenzie, The; Aria; Black Robe; Breaker Morant; Club, The; Crimes of the Heart; Don's Party; Driving Miss Daisy; Fringe Dwellers, The; Getting of Wisdom, The; Good Man in Africa, A; Her Alibi; King David; Last Dance; Mister Johnson; Money Movers; Paradise Road; Puberty Blues; Rich in Love; Side by Side; Silent Fall; Tender Mercies*.

Bergenstråhle, Johan *Foreigners (Jag Heter Stelius)*.

Berger, Ludwig *Thief of Bagdad, The*.

Bergman, Andrew *Freshman, The; Honeymoon in Vegas; It Could Happen to You; So Fine; Striptease*.

Bergman, Ingmar *Ansiktet (The Face/The Magician); Autumn Sonata (Herbstsonate); Cries and Whispers (Viskingar och Rop); Devil's Eye, The (Djävulens Oga); Face to Face (Ansikte mot Ansikte); Fanny and Alexander (Fanny och Alexander); From the Life of the Marionettes (Aus dem Leben der Marionetten); Gycklarnas Afton (The Naked Night/Sawdust and Tinsel); Hour of the Wolf (Vargtimmen); Kvinnodröm (Dreams/Journey Into Autumn); Magic Flute, The (Trollflöjten); Nattvardsgästerna (The Communicants/Winter Light); Passion, A (En Passion); Persona; Rite, The (Riten); Scenes from a Marriage (Scener ur ett äktenskap); Serpent's Egg, The (Das Schlangenei); Seventh Seal, The (Det Sjunde Inseglet); Shame, The (Skammen); Silence, The (Tystnaden); Smiles of a Summer Night (Sommarnattens Leende); Sommaren med Monika (Monika/Summer with Monika); Sommarlek (Illicit Interlude/Summer Interlude); Through a Glass Darkly (Sasom i en Spegel); Touch, The; Wild Strawberries (Smultronstället); Virgin Spring, The (Jungfrukällan)*.

Bergon, Serge *Joy*.

Berkeley, Busby *Babes in Arms; Babes on Broadway; For Me and My Gal; Gang's All Here, The (aka The Girls He Left Behind); Gold Diggers of 1935; Strike Up the Band; Take Me Out to the Ball Game (aka Everybody's Cheering)*.

Berkoff, Steven *Decadence*.

Berlanga, Luis Garcia *Life Size; Verdugo, El (The Executioner/Not On Your Life)*.

Berliner, Alain *Ma Vie en Rose*.

Berman, Jonathan *Shvitz, The*.

Berman, Monty *Hellfire Club, The*.

Berman, Ted *Black Cauldron, The; Fox and the Hound, The*.

Bernal, Ishmael *Manila After Dark (aka City After Dark)*.

Bernard, Chris *Letter to Brezhnev, A*.

Bernard, Raymond *Croix de Bois, Les (Wooden Crosses)*.

Bernardin, Alain *Crazy Horse of Paris, The (Crazy Horse de Paris)*.

Bernds, Edward *Quantrill's Raiders; Queen of Outer Space; Return of the Fly*.

Bernhardt, Curtis *Conflict; Devotion; Miss Sadie Thompson; Possessed; Stolen Life, A*.

Bernstein, Walter *Little Miss Marker*.

Berri, Claude *Germinal; Jean de Florette; Lucie Aubrac; Manon des Sources; Mazel Tov ou le mariage (Marry Me! Marry Me!); Moment d'Egarement, Un (In a Wild Moment/One Wild Moment/A Summer Affair); Sex Shop; Uranus; Vieil Homme et l'Enfant, Le (The Two of Us)*.

Berruti, Giulio *Killer Nun (Suor omicidio)*.

Berry, John *Bad News Bears Go to Japan, The; Claudine*.

Bertolucci, Bernardo *Before the Revolution (Prima della Rivoluzione); Commare Secca, La (The Grim Reaper); Conformist, The (Il Conformista); Last Emperor, The; Last Tango in Paris; Little Buddha; Luna, La; 1900 (Novecento); Partner; Sheltering Sky, The; Spider's Stratagem, The (La Strategia del Ragno); Stealing Beauty (Io ballo da sola/Beauté Volée); Tragedy of a Ridiculous Man, The (La Tragedia di un Uomo Ridicolo)*.

Bertuccelli, Jean-Louis *Paulina 1880; Ramparts of Clay (Remparts d'Argile)*.

Berwick Street Film Collective *Ireland: Behind the Wire; Nightcleaners*.

Besson, Luc *Big Blue, The; Fifth Element, The (Le Cinquième Elément); Last Battle, The (Le Dernier Combat); Leon (aka The Professional); Nikita; Subway*.

Beyer, Frank *Held for Questioning (Der Aufenthalt)*.

Bharadwaj, Radha *Closet Land*.

Bhattacharya, Uday *Circle of Gold*.

Bianchi, Edward *Fan, The; Off and Running*.

Biberman, Herbert J *Master Race, The; Salt of the Earth*.

Bicat, Tony *Skinflicker*.

Bierman, Robert *Keep the Aspidistra Flying; Vampire's Kiss*.

Bigelow, Kathryn *Blue Steel; Loveless, The; Near Dark; Point Break; Strange Days*.

Bijl, Jacob *Beck*.

Bill, Tony *Crazy People; Five Corners; Home of Our Own, A; My Bodyguard; Six Weeks; Untamed Heart*.

Billard, Pierre *Enfants de Lumière, Les (The Children of Lumière)*.

Billington, Kevin *Interlude; Light at the Edge of the World, The; Reflections; Rise and Rise of Michael Rimmer, The; Voices*.

Bilson, Bruce *North Avenue Irregulars, The (aka Hill's Angels)*.

Bilson, Danny *Zone Troopers*.

Binder, Mike *Crossing the Bridge*.

Binzer, Roland *Ladies and Gentlemen, the Rolling Stones*.

Birch, Patricia *Grease 2*.

Bird, Antonia *Face; Mad Love; Priest*.

Bird, Stewart *Wobblies, The*.

Birkin, Andrew *Burning Secret; Cement Garden, The*.

Bishop, Larry *Mad Dog Time (aka Trigger Happy)*.

Bishop, Terry *Cover Girl Killer*.

Bistiskas, Alexis *Dawn, The (To Harama)*.

Björkman, Stig *White Wall, The (Den Vita Vüggen)*.

Blaché, Herbert *Saphead, The*.

Black, Cathal *Korea; Pigs*.

Black, Michael *Pictures*.

Black, Noel *Man, a Woman and a Bank, A; Pretty Poison.*

Blackwood, Christian *Motel; Roger Corman: Hollywood's Wild Angel; Signed; Lino Brocka; Tapdancin'.*

Blackwood, Maureen *Passion of Remembrance, The.*

Blair, David *Wax, or The Discovery of Television Among the Bees.*

Blair, Les *Bad Behaviour; Jump the Gun; Number One.*

Blakemore, Michael *Country Life; Personal History of the Australian Surf, A; Privates on Parade.*

Blanc, Christophe *Faute de Soleil (For Want of Sun).*

Blanc, Michel *Grosse Fatigue.*

Blanco, Jorge *Argie.*

Blank, Les *Always for Pleasure; Burden of Dreams; Garlic Is as Good as Ten Mothers.*

Blatty, William Peter *Exorcist III, The; Ninth Configuration, The (aka Twinkle, Twinkle Killer Kane).*

Blier, Bertrand *Buffet Froid; Merci la vie (Thank You Life); Mon Homme; My Best Friend's Girl (La Femme de Mon Pote); Notre Histoire (Our Story/Separate Rooms); Préparez Vos Mouchoirs (Get Out Your Handkerchiefs); Stepfather (Beau-père); Tenue de Soirée (Evening Dress); Trop belle pour toi! (Too Beautiful for You); Un Deux Trois Soleil (1, 2, 3, Sun); Valseuses, Les (Going Places/Making It).*

Bliss, Barry *Fords on Water.*

Blom, Per *Ice Palace, The (Isslottet).*

Bloom, Jeffrey *Bloody Beach; Flowers in the Attic; Dog pound Shuffle (aka Spot).*

Bloomfield, George *Child Under a Leaf (aka Love Child).*

Blum, Chris *Big Time.*

Bluth, Don *All Dogs Go to Heaven; American Tail, An; Anastasia; Land Before Time, The; Pebble and the Penguin, The; Rock-a-Doodle; Secret of NIMH, The; Thumbelina.*

Blystone, John G *Blockheads; Our Hospitality.*

Blyth, Jeff *Cheetah.*

Bobrova, Lidia *In That Land (V toi Stranje).*

Bochner, Hart *High School High.*

Bodrov, Sergei *Freedom Is Paradise (SER); I Wanted to See Angels (Ja Chtela Uwidetj Angelow); Prisoner of the Mountains (Kavkazski Plennik).*

Boetticher, Budd *Buchanan Rides Alone; Bullfighter and the Lady, The; City Beneath the Sea; Comanche Station; East of Sumatra; Horizons West; Ride Lonesome; Rise and Fall of Legs Diamond, The; Seven Men from Now; Tall T, The; Time for Dying, A.*

Bogart, Paul *Broadway Bound; Class of '44; Marlowe; Torch Song Trilogy.*

Bogayevicz, Yurek *Anna; Three of Hearts.*

Bogdanovich, Peter *At Long Last Love; Daisy Miller; Last Picture Show, The; Mask; Nickelodeon; Noises Off; Paper Moon; Saint Jack; Targets; Texasville; They All Laughed; Thing Called Love, The; What's Up Doc?.*

Boger, Chris *Cruel Passion.*

Boisrond, Michel *Catherine and Co (Catherine et Cie),*

Boisset, Yves *Attentat, L' (Plot); Cobra (La Saut de l'Ange); Espion Lève-toi; Folle à Tuer (The Evil Trap); Prize of Peril The (Le Prix du Danger); Purple Taxi, The (Le Taxi Mauve); Sheriff, Le (Le Juge Fayard dit le Sheriff).*

Bokova, Jana *Hôtel du Paradis; Love Is Like a Violin; Militia Battlefield.*

Boldt, Rainer *Due to an Act of God (Im Zeichen des Kreuzes).*

Boleslawski, Richard *Garden of Allah, The; Les Misérables; Painted Veil, The; Rasputin and the Empress; Theodora Goes Wild.*

Böll, Heinrich *Germany in Autumn (Deutschland im Herbst).*

Bollaín, Iciar *Hi, Are You Alone? (Hola, estás sola?).*

Bolognini, Mauro *Dame aux Camélias, La; Down the Ancient Stairs (Per le Antiche Scala); Drama of the Rich (Fatti di Gente Perbene); Inheritance, The (L'Eredità Ferramonti).*

Bolotin, Craig *That Night.*

Bolt, Ben *Arm, The (aka The Big Town).*

Bolt, Robert *Lady Caroline Lamb.*

Bond, Jack *It Couldn't Happen Here.*

Bond III, James *DEF by Temptation.*

Bondarchuk, Sergei *War and Peace (Voina i Mir); Waterloo.*

Bondy, Luc *Josephine (Die Ortliebschen Frauen).*

Bonerz, Peter *Police Academy 6: City Under Siege.*

Bonzel, André *Man Bites Dog (C'est arrivé près de chez vous).*

Boorman, John *Beyond Rangoon; Catch Us If You Can (aka Having a Wild Weekend); Deliverance; Emerald Forest, The; Excalibur; Exorcist II: The Heretic; General, The; Hell in the Pacific; Hope and Glory; Leo the Last; Point Blank; Where the Heart Is; Zardoz.*

Booth, Harry *Go for a Take; Mutiny on the Buses; On the Buses.*

Borau, José Luis *B. Must Die (Hay que Matar a B); Poachers (Furtivos).*

Borden, Lizzie *Born in Flames; Erotique; Working Girls.*

Bordowitz, Gregg *Fast Trip, Long Drop.*

Boris, Robert *Oxford Blues.*

Bork, Miroslav *Consul, The (Konsul).*

Bornedal, Ole *Nightwatch (Nattevagten).*

Boros, Phillip *Grey Fox, The; Mean Season, The.*

Borowczyk, Walerian *Behind Convent Walls (L'Interno di un Convento); Blanche; Bête, La (The Beast); Docteur Jekyll et les Femmes (The Blood of Doctor Jekyll/Doctor Jekyll and Miss Osbourne); Goto, l'île d'amour (Goto, Island of Love); Immoral Tales (Contes Immoraux); Marge, La (The Streetwalker); Story of Sin, The (Dzieje Grzechu).*

Borsos, Phillip *Far from Home: The Adventures of Yellow Dog.*

Borthwick, Dave *Secret Adventures of Tom Thumb, The.*

Borzage, Frank *Desire; Farewell to Arms, A; Green Light; History Is Made at Night; Little Man, What Now?; Magnificent Doll; Man's Castle; Moonrise; Mortal Storm, The; Secrets; 7th Heaven; Shining Hour, The; Spanish Main, The; Strange Cargo; Street Angel; Three Comrades; Till We Meet Again.*

Bose, Tapan K *Indian Story, An.*

Boskovich, John *Without You I'm Nothing.*

Botelho, Joao *Hard Times (Tempos Dificeis, Este Tempo); Other One, The (Conversa Acabada); Portuguese Goodbye, A (Un Adeus Português); Três Palmeiras (Three Palm Trees).*

Bottagisio, Jacqueline *Voice of Kurdistan, The.*

Böttcher, Jürgen *In Georgia (In Georgien).*

Boughédir, Férid *Summer in La Goulette, A (Un été à La Goulette).*

Bouhnik, Laurent *Sélect Hotel.*

Boulting, John *Brighton Rock; Heavens Above!; I'm All Right, Jack; Journey Together; Lucky Jim; Magic Box, The; Private's Progress; Rotten to the Core; Seven Days to Noon.*

Boulting, Roy *Brothers in Law; Desert Victory; French Mistress, A; Guinea Pig, The (aka The Outsider); Pastor Hall; Run for the Sun; Soft Beds, Hard Battles; There's a Girl in My Soup; Thunder Rock; Tunisian Victory.*

Bourguinon, Serge *Reward, The.*

Bowen, Jenny *Street Music.*

Bower, Dallas *Alice In Wonderland.*

Bowers, George *Body and Soul; Hearse, The; My Tutor.*

Bowser, Kenneth *Frank Capra's American Dream.*

Box, Muriel *Beachcomber, The; Happy Family, The (aka Mr Lord Says No); This Other Eden; Simon and Laura.*

Boyd, Don *East of Elephant Rock; Intimate Reflections; Twenty-One.*

Boyd, Joe *Jimi Hendrix.*

Boyer, Jean *Trou Normand, Le (Crazy for Love).*

Boyle, Danny *Shallow Grave; Life Less Ordinary, A; Trainspotting.*

Bozzetto, Bruno *Allegro Non Troppo*

Brabant, Charles *P..... Respectueuse, La (The Respectful Prostitute/The Respectable Prostitute).*

Brabec, FA *King Ubu (Král Ubu).*

Brabin, Charles *Mask of Fu Manchu, The.*

Braddock, Reb *Curdled.*

Bradbury, David *Nicaragua – No Pasarán; Public Enemy Number One.*

Jardin, La (Evil Eden); Nazarin; Olvidados, Los (The Young and the Damned); The Phantom of Liberty (Fantôme de la Liberté, Le); Robinson Crusoe (aka Adventures of Robinson Crusoe); Simon of the Desert (Simón del Desierto); That Obscure Object of Desire (Cet Obscur Objet du Désir); Tristana; Viridiana; Voie Lactée, La (The Milky Way); Young One, The (La Joven).

Burch, Noël Correction, Please or how we got into pictures.

Burge, Stuart Othello.

Burke, Erik Loser.

Burke, Martyn Power Play.

Burnett, Charles Glass Shield, The; Killer of Sheep; My Brother's Wedding; To Sleep with Anger.

Burnley, Fred Neither the Sea Nor the Land.

Burns, Allan Just Between Friends.

Burns, Edward Brothers McMullen, The; She's the One.

Burr, Jeff Leatherface: The Texas Chainsaw Massacre III; Stepfather II, The.

Burrill, Christine Vietnam Journey.

Burroughs, Jackie Winter Tan, A.

Burrowes, Michael Incense for the Damned.

Burrows, James Partners.

Burstall, Tim Alvin Purple; End Play; Kangaroo; Libido; Petersen; Rollicking Adventures of Eliza Fraser, The (aka A Faithful Narrative of the Capture, Sufferings and Miraculous Escape of Eliza Fraser); Stork.

Burton, Norman Lady by Choice.

Burton, Tim Batman; Batman Returns; Beetlejuice; Edward Scissorhands; Ed Wood; Mars Attacks!; Pee-Wee's Big Adventure.

Buscemi, Steve Trees Lounge.

Bussemaker, Jan Bernard Jabula – A Band in Exile.

Bussmann, Tom Whoops Apocalypse.

Bute, Mary Ellen Finnegans Wake (aka Passages from James Joyce's Finnegans Wake).

Butler, David By the Light of the Silvery Moon; Calamity Jane; Captain January; Command, The; Daughter of Rosie O'Grady, The;

Kentucky; Littlest Rebel, The; Lullaby of Broadway; Pigskin Parade; Road to Morocco; Thank Your Lucky Stars; You'll Find Out.

Butler, George Pumping Iron; Pumping Iron II: The Women.

Butler, Robert Blue Knight, The; Turbulence.

Butoy, Hendel Rescuers Down Under, The.

Butterworth, Jez Mojo.

Buttgereit, Jörg Schramm.

Buzzell, Edward At the Circus; Best Foot Forward; Go West.

Byrne, David True Stories.

Byrum, John Heart Beat; Inserts.

Caan, James Hide In Plain Sight.

Cabanne, Christy Mummy's Hand, The.

Cabrera, Sergio Matter of Honour, A (Técnicas de Duelo); Strategy of the Snail, The (La Estratagia del Caracol).

Caccia, Antonia On Our Land.

Cacoyannis, Michael Attila '74; Day the Fish Came Out, The; Zorba the Greek.

Cadena, Jordi Senyora, La.

Caesar, David Greenkeeping.

Cahn, Edward L Invasion of the Saucermen; She Creature, The; Voodoo Woman.

Cain, Christopher Stone Boy, The; That Was Then, This Is Now; Young Guns.

Caiozzi, Silvio Moon in the Mirror, The (La Luna en el Espejo).

Calder, Alexander Dreams That Money Can Buy.

Calenda, Antonia Fury (Il Giorno del Furore).

Callow, Simon Ballad of the Sad Café, The.

Calopresti, Mimmo Second Time, The (La Seconda Volta).

Calparsoro, Daniel Jump into the Void (Salto al Vacio).

Cameron, James Abyss, The; Abyss: Special Edition, The; Aliens; Piranha II: Flying Killers; Terminator, The; Terminator 2: Judgment Day; Titanic; True Lies.

Cameron, Ken Fast Talking; Monkey Grip; Umbrella Woman, The (aka The Good Wife); Winchester Conspiracy.

Cameron, Ray Bloodbath at the House of Death.

Caminito, Augusto Vampires in Venice (Nosferatu a Venezia).

Camino, Jaime Long Holidays of 1936, The (Las Largas Vacaciones del 36).

Cammell, Donald Demon Seed; Performance; White of the Eye.

Camp, Joe Benji.

Campanella, Juan José Boy Who Cried Bitch, The.

Campbell, Dirk I Bought a Vampire Motorcycle.

Campbell, Martin Criminal Law; Lovecraft (aka Cast a Deadly Spell); GoldenEye; No Escape; Three for All.

Campbell, Nicholas Stepping Razor – Red X.

Campion, Anna Loaded.

Campion, Jane Angel at My Table, An; Piano, The; Portrait of a Lady, The; Sweetie; Two Friends.

Campogalliani, Carlo Goliath and the Barbarians (Il Terrore dei Barbari).

Camurati, Carla Carlota Joaquina, Princess of Brazil.

Camus, Marcel Black Orpheus (Orfeu Negro).

Camus, Mario Holy Innocents, The (Los Santos Inocentes); House of Bernarda Alba, The (La Casa de Bernarda Alba).

Cannon, Danny Judge Dredd; Strangers; Young Americans, The.

Capetanos, Leon Servicer, The (Cream – Schwaben-Report).

Capra, Frank American Madness; Arsenic and Old Lace; Bitter Tea of General Yen, The; Broadway Bill (aka Strictly Confidential); Dirigible; Forbidden; Here Comes the Groom; Hole in the Head, A; It Happened One Night; It's a Wonderful Life; Lady for a Day; Lost Horizon; Matinee Idol, The; Meet John Doe; Miracle Woman, The; Mr Deeds Goes to Town; Mr Smith Goes to Washington; Platinum Blonde; Rain or Shine; State of the Union (aka the World and his Wife); Strong Man, The; Tramp, Tramp, Tramp; Tunisian Victory; You Can't Take It With You.

Carax, Léos Amants du Pont-Neuf, Les; Boy Meets Girl; Mauvais Sang (The Night Is Young).

Cardiff, Jack Girl on a Motorcycle (La

Motocyclette/Naked Under Leather); Lion, The; Long Ships, The; Mercenaries, The (aka Dark of the Sun); Mutations, The; Penny Gold; Sons and Lovers; Young Cassidy.

Cardona, René (Sr) Survive! (Supervivientes de los Andes).

Cardona, René (Jr) Guyana: Crime of the Century (Guyana: El Crimen del Siglo); Tintorera.

Cardone, JS Thunder Alley.

Cardos, John 'Bud' Day Time Ended, The; Kingdom of the Spiders; Mutant.

Carle, Gilles True Nature of Bernadette, The (La Vraie Nature de Bernadette); Tête de Normande St-Onge, La.

Carlei, Carlo Flight of the Innocent (La Corsa dell'innocente).

Carlino, Lewis John Class; Great Santini, The; Sailor Who Fell from Grace with the Sea, The.

Carné, Marcel Drôle de Drame (Bizarre, Bizarre); Enfants du Paradis, Les (Children of Paradise); Hôtel du Nord; Jour se lève, Le (Daybreak); Portes de la Nuit, Les (Gates of the Night); Quai des Brumes, Le (Port of Shadows); Visiteurs du Soir, Les (The Devil's Envoys).

Caro, Marc Cité des enfants perdus, La (The City of Lost Children); Delicatessen.

Caron, Glenn Gordon Clean and Sober; Picture Perfect.

Carow, Heiner Coming Out.

Carpenter, John Assault on Precinct 13; Big Trouble in Little China; Body Bags; Christine; Dark Star; Elvis (aka Elvis – The Movie); Escape from New York; Fog, The; Halloween; In the Mouth of Madness; John Carpenter's Escape from L.A.; Memoirs of an Invisible Man; Prince of Darkness; Starman; They Live; Thing, The.

Carpenter, Stephen Kindred, The.

Carradine, David Americana.

Carrera, Carlos No Return Address (Sin Remitente).

Carreras, Michael Blood from the Mummy's Tomb; Curse of the Mummy's Tomb, The; Lost Continent, The; Steel Bayonets, The.

Carson, David Star Trek: Generations.

Carstairs, John Paddy Chiltern Hundreds, The (aka The Amazing Mr Beecham); Dancing With Crime;

Jumping for Joy; Man of the Moment; Trouble in Store.

Carter, Thomas Metro; Swing Kids.

Cartwright, Justin Rosie Dixon, Night Nurse.

Carver, Steve Arena, The; Big Bad Mama; Bulletproof; Capone; Drum; Eye for an Eye, An; Fast Charlie the Moonbeam Rider; Lone Wolf McQuade; Steel.

Casaril, Guy L'Astragale; Piaf (aka Piaf – The Early Years/ The Sparrow of Pigalle); Rempart des Béguines, Le (The Beguines).

Cass, Henry Blood of the Vampire; Glass Mountain, The; Last Holiday.

Cassavetes, John Big Trouble; Child Is Waiting, A; Faces; Gloria; Husbands; Killing of a Chinese Bookie, The; Love Streams; Minnie and Moskowitz; Opening Night, Shadows; Too Late Blues; Woman Under the Influence,A.

Cassavetes, Nick Unhook the Stars (Décroches les étoiles); She's So Lovely.

Cassenti, Frank Affiche Rouge, L'.

Castellari, Enzo G Bronx Warriors (1990 I Guerrieri del Bronx); Cry Onion (Cipolla Colt); New Barbarians, The (I Nuovi Barbari).

Castle, Nick Boy Who Could Fly, The; Dennis the Menace (aka Dennis); Last Starfighter, The; TAG, The Assassination Game; Tap.

Castle, William Americano, The; Homicidal; I Saw What You Did; Macabre; Shanks; Strait-Jacket; Tingler, The; When Strangers Marry (aka Betrayed).

Castro, Rick Hustler White.

Cates, Gilbert Affair, The; Backfire; I Never Sang for My Father; Last Married Couple in America, The; Summer Wishes, Winter Dreams.

Caton-Jones, Michael Doc Hollywood; Jackal, The; Memphis Belle; Rob Roy; Scandal; This Boy's Life.

Cattaneo, Peter The Full Monty.

Caulfield, Michael Fighting Back.

Cavalcanti, Alberto Champagne Charlie; Dead of Night; For Them That Trespass; Nicholas Nickleby; Went the Day Well?

Cavalier, Alain Libera Me; Thérèse.

Cavani, Liliana Berlin Affair, The (Interno Berlinele); Beyond Evil (Al di là Bene e

del Male); Beyond the Door (Oltre la Porta); Cannibals, The (I Cannibali); Galileo; Night Porter, The (Il Portiere di Notte).

Cavara, Paolo Deaf Smith & Johnny Ears (Los Amigos).

Cayatte, André Amants de Verone, Les (The Lovers of Verona); Miroir a deux faces, Le (Lo Specchi a due facce/The Mirror Has Two Faces); Verdict (The Verdict).

Cellan Jones, James Bequest to the Nation (aka The Nelson Affair).

'Cero a la Izquierda' Film Collective El Salvador – Decision to Win (El Salvador – La Decisión de Vencer).

Cervi, Tonino Nest of Vipers (Ritratto di Borghesia in Nero); Today It's Me… Tomorrow You! (Oggi a me…domani a te!).

Cha Chuen-Yee Once Upon a Time in Triad Society (Wangjiao Cha-fit-ren); Once Upon a Time in Triad Society 2 (Qua ba! Cha-fit-ren Bingtuan); Theft Under the Sun (Haoqing Gai Tian).

Chabrol, Claude A Double Tour (Leda/Web of Passion); Beau Serge, Le; Biches, Les (The Does); Blood Relatives (Liens de Sang); Bonnes Femmes, Les (The Girls); Boucher, Le (The Butcher); Cérémonie, La (A Judgement in Stone); Champagne Murders, The (Le Scandale); Cheval d'Orgueil, Le (The Proud Ones); Cop au Vin (Poulet au Vinaigre); Cousins, Les (The Cousins); Dr M; Docteur Popaul (High Heels/Scoundrel in White); Enfer, L' (Torment); Femme Infidèle, La (Unfaithful Wife); Innocents with Dirty Hands (Les Innocents aux Mains Sales); Inspecteur Lavardin; Just Before Nightfall (Juste avant la Nuit); Madame Bovary; Masques; Nada; Noces Rouges, Les (Blood Wedding/Red Wedding/Wedding in Blood); Paris vu par... (Six in Paris); Partie de Plaisir, Une (Love Match); Que la Bête Meure (Killer!); Route de Corinthe, La (The Road to Corinth); Rupture, La; Ten Days' Wonder (La Décade Prodigieuse); Violette Nozière.

Chadha, Gurinder Bhaji on the Beach.

Chaffey, Don Charley-One-Eye; Creatures the World Forgot; Jason and the Argonauts; Jolly Bad Fellow, A; Magic of Lassie, The; Man Upstairs, The; One Million Years B.C.; Persecution; Pete's Dragon; Ride a Wild Pony.

Chahine, Youssef Adieu Bonaparte (Al-wedaa ya

Bonaparte); Alexandria Encore (Eskendereya kaman we kaman); Destiny (Al Massir); Egyptian Story, An (Hadduta Misriya); Saladin (An-Nasr Salah ad-Din).

Chamchoum, FN Georges Lebanon...Why? (Liban...Pourquoi?).

Champion, Gower Bank Shot.

Champion, Gregg Short Time.

Champion, John Mustang Country.

Chan, Evans Journey to Beijing (Bei Zheng).

Chan, Fruit Made in Hong Kong (Xiang-gang Zhizao).

Chan Ho-sun, Peter He's a Woman, She's a Man.

Chan, Jackie Armour of God, The (Long Xiong Hu Di); Police Story (Jingcha Gushi); Project A (A Jihua).

Chan, Joe '92 The Legendary La Rose Noire (Heimeigui dui Heimeigui).

Chan, Peter Comrades, Almost a Love Story (Tian Nimi).

Chan, Philip Front Page (Xin Ban Jin Ba Liang).

Chanan, Michael El Salvador – Portrait of a Liberated Zone.

Chang Cheh Blood Brothers, The (Ci Ma/aka Chinese Vengeance); Chinese Connection, The (Quan Ji/aka Duel of Fists); Golden Swallow (Jin Yanzi); New One-Armed Swordsman, The (Xin Dubi Dao).

Chang, Sylvia Siao Yu (Shaonü Xiao Yu).

Chang Yi Jade Love (Yu Qing sao); This Love of Mine (Wo de Ai).

Chang Yoon-Hyun Contact, The (Cheob Sok).

Chaplin, Charles Circus, The; City Lights; Countess from Hong Kong, A; Gold Rush, The; Great Dictator, The; Kid, The; Limelight; Modern Times; Monsieur Verdoux; Woman of Paris, A.

Chapman, Matthew Hussy; Heart of Midnight; Strangers Kiss.

Chapman, Michael All the Right Moves; Clan of the Cave Bear, The.

Chappell, Peter El Salvador – Portrait of a Liberated Zone.

Chappelle, Joe Halloween: The Curse of Michael Myers.

Charell, Erik Congress Dances (Der Kongress tanzt).

Charlot, André Elstree Calling.

Chatiliez, Etienne Bonheur est dans le pré, Le; Life Is a Long Quiet River (La Vie est un long fleuve tranquile); Tatie Danielle.

Chatri-Chalerm Yukol Song of Chao-Phrya, The (Nong Mia).

Chaudhri, Amin Q Tiger Warsaw.

Chavarri, Jaime To an Unknown God (A un Dios Desconocido).

Chechik, Jeremiah Benny and Joon; Diabolique.

Chelsom, Peter Funny Bones; Hear My Song.

Chenal, Pierre Dernier Tournant, Le.

Cheng Sheng-Fu Silent Thrush, The (Shisheng Huamei).

Chen Kaige Big Parade (Da Yuebing); Farewell My Concubine (Ba Wang Bie Ji); King of the Children (Haizi Wang); Life on a String (Bian Zou Bian Chang); Temptress Moon (Fengyue); Yellow Earth (Huang Tudi).

Chen Yu-Hsun Tropical Fish (Redai Yu).

Cher If These Walls Could Talk.

Chéreau, Patrice Reine Margot, La; Those Who Love Me Will Take the Train (Ceux qui m'aiment prendront le train).

Cherry, John Ernest Saves Christmas.

Cheung, Mabel Yeun-Ting Eight Tales of Gold (Ba Liang Jin).

Chiesa, Alcides Amigomio.

Chiesa, Guido Lies to Live by (Babylon) (Babylon: la paura e la migliore amica dell'uomo).

Chilvers, Colin Moonwalker.

Ching Siu-Tung Chinese Ghost Story, A (Qiannü Youhun); Chinese Ghost Story II, A (Qiannü Youhun zhi Renjian Dao); Swordsman (Xiao'ao Jianghu); Swordsman II (Xiao'ao Jianghu zhi Dongfang Bu Bai); Terra-Cotta Warrior, A (Qin Yong).

Chiodo, Stephen Killer Klowns from Outer Space.

Chionglo, Mel Midnight Dancers (Sibak).

Chomsky, Marvin J Evel Knievel; Tank; Victory at Entebbe.

Chong, Thomas Cheech & Chong's Next Movie (aka High Encounters of the Ultimate Kind).

Chopra, Joyce *Lemon Sisters, The; Smooth Talk.*

Chouikh, Mohamed *Citadel, The (El Kalaa).*

Chouraqui, Elie *Man on Fire; Mon Premier Amour; What Makes David Run? (Qu'est-ce qui fait courir David?).*

Choy, Christine *Best Hotel on Skid Row; Who Killed Vincent Chin?*

Christensen, Benjamin *Witchcraft through the Ages (Häxan).*

Christian, Roger *Nostradamus; Sender, The.*

Christian-Jaque *Boule de Suif; Chartreuse de Parme, La; Disparus de Saint-Agil, Les; Legend of Frenchie King, The (Les Pétroleuses); Perles de la Couronne, Les (The Pearls of the Crown); Rigolboche; Si tous les gars du monde... (Race For Life/If All the Guys in the World...).*

Christopher, Frank *In the Name of the People.*

Chrysanthou, Panicos *Our Wall (Duvarimiz).*

Chu Yuan *Intimate Confessions of a Chinese Courtesan (Ai Nu); Killer, The (Da Sha Shou).*

Chukhrai, Grigori *Ballad of a Soldier (Ballada o Soldate).*

Churchill, Joan *Juvenile Liaison; Juvenile Liaison 2; Lily Tomlin; Soldier Girls; Tattooed Tears.*

Chytilová, Vera *Daisies (Sedmikrásky); Pearls of the Deep (Perlicky na dne).*

Cicero, Nando *Last Italian Tango, The (Ultimo Tango a Zagarol).*

Cimber, Matt *Butterfly.*

Cimino, Michael *Deer Hunter, The; Desperate Hours; Heaven's Gate; Sicilian, The; Sunchaser, The; Thunderbolt and Lightfoot; Year of the Dragon.*

Cinema Action *Film from the Clyde; Miners' Film, The; So That You Can Live.*

Cissé, Souleymane *Brightness (Yeelen); Finyé (The Wind).*

Clair, René *A Nous la Liberté (Freedom for Us); And Then There Were None (aka Ten Little Niggers); Beauté du Diable, La (Beauty and the Devil); Belles de nuit, Les (Beauties of the Night/Night Beauties); Dernier Milliardaire, Le; Fantôme du Moulin Rouge, Le; Flame of New Orleans, The; Ghost Goes West, The; I Married a Witch; It Happened Tomorrow; Million, Le;*

Paris qui Dort (The Crazy Ray); Porte des Lilas (Gate of Lilacs); Silence est d'Or, Le (Man About Town); Sous les Toits de Paris.*

Clark, Bob *Black Christmas; Breaking Point; Christmas Story, A; Dead of Night (aka Deathdream); From the Hip; Loose Cannons; Murder by Decree; Porky's; Porky's II: The Next Day; Tribute; Turk 182!*

Clark, Bruce *Galaxy of Terror; Ski Bum, The.*

Clark, Curtis *Shut Down.*

Clark, Duane *Shaking the Tree.*

Clark, James B *Dog of Flanders, A; Flipper..*

Clark, Jim *Madhouse; Rentadick.*

Clark, Larry *Kids.*

Clark, Louise *Winter Tan, A.*

Clark, Matt *Da.*

Clarke, Alan *Billy the Kid and the Green Baize Vampire; Rita, Sue and Bob Too; Scum.*

Clarke, Frank *Blonde Fist.*

Clarke, James Kenelm *Exposé; Funny Money; Let's Get Laid!*

Clarke, Shirley *Connection, The; Cool World, The; Ornette: Made in America; Portrait of Jason.*

Clavell, James *Last Valley, The; To Sir, With Love; Where's Jack?*

Claxton, William F *Night of the Lepus.*

Clayton, Jack *Great Gatsby, The; Innocents, The; Lonely Passion of Judith Hearne, The; Our Mother's House; Pumpkin Eater, The; Room at the Top; Something Wicked This Way Comes.*

Clayton, Susan *Last Crop, The; Song of the Shirt, The.*

Clegg, Tom *G'Olé!; McVicar; Sweeney 2.*

Clemens, Brian *Captain Kronos Vampire Hunter.*

Clemens, William *Devil's Island; Falcon and the Co-eds, The.*

Clement, Dick *Bullshot; Catch Me a Spy (aka To Catch a Spy); Otley; Porridge; Water.*

Clément, René *Bataille du Rail, La (Battle of the Rails); Jeux Interdits (Forbidden Games/The Secret Game); Knave of Hearts (aka Lovers, Happy Lovers!/Monsieur Ripois); Plein Soleil (Delitto in pieno sole/Blazing Sun/Purple Noon); Rider on the Rain (Passager de la Pluie).*

Clements, Ron *Aladdin; Great Mouse Detective, The (aka Basil the Great Mouse Detective); Hercules; Little Mermaid, The.*

Clifford, Graeme *Frances; Gleaming the Cube; Past Tense; Ruby Cairo.*

Clifton, Peter *London Rock and Roll Show, The; Song Remains the Same, The.*

Climati, Antonio *Savage Man...Savage Beast (Ultima Grida della Savana).*

Cline, Edward F *Bank Dick, The; Ghost Catchers; My Little Chickadee; Never Give a Sucker an Even Break (aka What a Man!).*

Cloos, Hans Peter *Germany in Autumn (Deutschland im Herbst).*

Clouse, Robert *Amsterdam Kill, The; Big Brawl, The; Black Belt Jones; Darker Than Amber; Enter the Dragon; Force: Five; Golden Needles; Gymkata; London Connection, The (aka The Omega Connection); Pack, The; Rats, The (aka Deadly Eyes).*

Clouzot, Henri-Georges *Assassin Habite au 21, L' (The Murderer Lives at Number 21); Corbeau, Le (The Raven); Diaboliques, Les (Diabolique/The Fiends); Espions, Les; Quai des Orfèvres; Mystère Picasso, Le; Vérité, La (The Truth); Wages of Fear, The (Le Salaire de la Peur).*

Clowes, St John L *No Orchids for Miss Blandish.*

Clucher, EB (Enzo Barboni) *Crime Busters (Due Superpiedi quasi Piatti); They Call Me Trinity (Lo Chiamavano Trinità).*

Clunes, Martin *Staggered.*

Clurman, Harold *Deadline at Dawn.*

Clément, René *Deadly Trap, The (La Maison sous les Arbres); Jeux Interdits (Forbidden Games/The Secret Game); Rider on the Rain (Passager de la Pluie).*

Coates, Lewis (Luigi Cozzi) *Starcrash.*

Cobham, David *Tarka the Otter.*

Coccoritti, Gérard *Paris France.*

Cochran, Stacy *Boys; My New Gun.*

Cocteau, Jean *Aigle à Deux Têtes, L' (The Eagle Has Two Heads/Eagle With Two Heads); Belle et la Bête, La (Beauty and the Beast); Orphée (Orpheus); Parents Terribles, Les (The Storm Within); Sang d'un Poète, Le (The Blood of a Poet);*

Testament d'Orphée, Le (Testament of Orpheus).*

Coe, Peter *Lock Up Your Daughters!*

Coe, Wayne *Grim Prairie Tales.*

Coen, Joel *Barton Fink; Big Lebowski, The; Blood Simple; Fargo; Hudsucker Proxy; Miller's Crossing; Raising Arizona.*

Cohen, David *Pleasure Principle, The.*

Cohen, Eli *Summer of Aviya, The (Hakayitz shel Aviya).*

Cohen, Howard R *Saturday the 14th.*

Cohen, Larry *Ambulance, The; Black Caesar (aka The Godfather of Harlem); Bone (aka Dial Rat for Terror/Beverly Hills Nightmare); God Told Me To (aka Demon); Hell Up in Harlem; It Lives Again; It's Alive; Original Gangstas; Private Files of J Edgar Hoover, The; Special Effects; Stuff, The; Wicked Stepmother; Winged Serpent, The (aka Q – The Winged Serpent).*

Cohen Martin B *Rebel Rousers.*

Cohen, Norman *Adolf Hitler – My Part in His Downfall; Confessions from a Holiday Camp; Confessions of a Driving Instructor; Confessions of a Pop Performer; Dad's Army; Stand Up Virgin Soldiers; Till Death Us Do Part.*

Cohen, Rob *Daylight; DragonHeart; Dragon: The Bruce Lee Story; Scandalous.*

Cohen, Tom *Family Business.*

Cohn, Michael *Snow White: A Tale of Terror.*

Coixet, Isabel *Things I Never Told You.*

Cokliss, Harley *Black Moon Rising; Dream Demon; Glitterball, The; That Summer!*

Cole, Henry *Mad Dogs and Englishmen.*

Cole, Sidney *Train of Events.*

Coleman, Graham *Tibet: A Buddhist Trilogy.*

Colizzi, Giuseppe *Blood River (Dio Perdona...Io No!); Quattro dell'Ave Maria, I (Ace High/Revenge in El Paso).*

Colla, Richard A *Battlestar Galactica.*

Collard, Cyril *Savage Nights (Les Nuits Fauves).*

Collectives:
Amber Films/Amber Production Team *Dream On; Eden Valley; In Fading*

Light; Letters to Katja; Seacoal; T. Dan Smith; Writing in the Sand, The.
anon., China Red Detachment of Women (Hung Sik Leung Dje Ching).
Berwick Street Film Collective Ireland: Behind the Wire; Nightcleaners.
'Cero a la Izquierda' Film Collective El Salvador – Decision to Win (El Salvador – La Decisión de Vencer).
Cinema Action Film from the Clyde; Miners' Film, The; So That You Can Live.
Dziga Vertov Group Pravda.
Mariposa Film Group Word Is Out.
Women's Film Workshop We're Alive.

Collier, James FR Cry from the Mountain; Hiding Place, The.

Collins, Arthur Greville Thank You, Jeeves!

Collins, Boon Spirit of the Eagle.

Collins, Lewis D see Lewis Cullen.

Collinson, Peter And Then There Were None (aka Ten Little Indians); House on Garibaldi Street, The; Italian Job, The; Long Day's Dying, The; Man Called Noon, The; Open Season (Los Cazadores); Sellout, The; Spiral Staircase, The; Tigers Don't Cry; Tomorrow Never Comes; Up the Junction.

Colomo, Fernando Butterfly Effect, The (El Efecto Mariposa); Skyline (La Linea del Cielo).

Colpaert, Carl Delusion.

Columbus, Chris Adventures in Babysitting (aka A Night on the Town); Home Alone; Home Alone 2: Lost in New York; Mrs Doubtfire; Nine Months; Only the Lonely.

Comencini, Francesca Annabelle partagée.

Comencini, Luigi Bohème, La.

Comerford, Joe High Boot Benny; Reefer and the Model; Traveller.

Comfort, Lance Bang! You're Dead (aka Game of Danger); Blind Corner; Breaking Point, The (aka The Great Armored Car Swindle); Eight O'Clock Walk; Hatter's Castle; Make Mine a Million; Man in the Road, The; Pit of Darkness; Temptation Harbour.

Comolli, Jean-Louis Cecilia, La.

Compton, Richard Macon County Line.

Concini, Ennio De Hitler: the Last Ten Days.

Condon, Bill Candyman 2: Farewell to the Flesh.

Connell, Merle Test Tube Babies (aka The Pill).

Connelly, Marc Green Pastures, The.

Connolly, Ray James Dean – the First American Teenager.

Connor, Kevin At the Earth's Core; Arabian Adventure; From Beyond the Grave; Land That Time Forgot, The; People That Time Forgot, The; Trial by Combat (aka A Choice of Weapons/Dirty Knight's Work); Warlords of Atlantis.

Conrad, Patrick Mascara.

Conway, Jack Arsene Lupin; Boom Town; Crossroads; Love Crazy; Too Hot to Handle; Unholy Three, The; Viva Villa!

Coninx, Stijn Daens.

Cook, Fielder Beauty and the Beast; Big Hand For the Little Lady, A (aka Big Deal at Dodge City); Patterns (aka Patterns of Power); Seize the Day.

Cooke, Alan Nadia.

Coolidge, Martha Angie; Lost in Yonkers (aka Neil Simon's Lost in Yonkers); Not a Pretty Picture; Rambling Rose; Real Genius; Three Wishes.

Cooney, Ray Not Now, Comrade.

Cooper, Merian C Grass; King Kong.

Cooper, Stuart Disappearance, The; Little Malcolm and His Struggle Against the Eunuchs; Overlord.

Coppola, Francis (Ford) Apocalypse Now; Conversation, The; Cotton Club, The; Dementia 13 (aka The Haunted and the Hunted); Dracula (aka Bram Stoker's Dracula); Gardens of Stone; Finian's Rainbow; Godfather, The; Godfather Part II, The; Godfather Part III, The; Jack; New York Stories; One From the Heart; Outsiders, The; Peggy Sue Got Married; Rainmaker, The (aka John Grisham's The Rainmaker); Rain People, The; Rumble Fish; Tucker: The Man and His Dream; You're a Big Boy Now.

Coraci, Frank Wedding Singer, The.

Corarito, Gregory Delinquent School Girls (aka Sizzlers).

Corbiau, Gérard Farinelli Il Castrato; Music Teacher, The (Le Mâitre de musique).

Corbucci, Sergio Big Silence, The (Il Grande Silenzio); Companeros (Vamos a Matar, Companeros!);

Django; Mercenario, Il (The Mercenary/A Professional Gun); 8-Wheel Beast, The (Il Bestione).

Cordero, Viviana Sensations.

Corman, Roger Bloody Mama; Bucket of Blood, A; Day the World Ended, The; Gas-s-s-s, or it became necessary to destroy the world in order to save it; Haunted Palace, The; House of Usher, The (aka The Fall of the House of Usher); I, Mobster (aka The Mobster); Intruder, The (aka The Stranger); It Conquered the World; Last Woman on Earth, The; Little Shop of Horrors, The; Machine Gun Kelly; Masque of the Red Death, The; Not of This Earth; Oklahoma Woman, The; Pit and the Pendulum, The; Premature Burial, The; Raven, The; Rock All Night; Roger Corman's Frankenstein Unbound; St Valentine's Day Massacre, The; Secret Invasion, The; She Gods of Shark Reef; Sorority Girl; Tales of Terror; Teenage Caveman; Terror, The; Tomb of Ligeia, The; Trip, The; Undead, The; Viking Women and Their Voyage to the Waters of the Great Sea Serpent, The; Von Richthofen and Brown (aka The Red Baron); War of the Satellites; Wasp Woman, The; Wild Angels, The; X – the Man with X-Ray Eyes (aka The Man with The X-Ray Eyes).

Corneau, Alain Enfants de Lumière, Les (The Children of Lumière); Tous les matins du monde.

Cornelius, Henry Genevieve; I Am a Camera; Passport to Pimlico.

Cornell, John Almost an Angel; Crocodile Dundee II.

Cornfield, Hubert Night of the Following Day, The.

Coronado, Celestino Hamlet; Midsummer Night's Dream, A.

Corr, Eugene Desert Bloom.

Correll, Charles In the Deep Woods.

Correll, Richard Ski Patrol.

Corrente, Michael American Buffalo.

Corsicato, Pappi Black Holes, The (I Buchi Neri); Libera.

Corson, Ian Malicious.

Corti, Alex Refusal, The (Die Verweigerung).

Coscarelli, Don Beastmaster, The; Phantasm; Phantasm II.

Cosmatos, George Pan Cassandra Crossing, The; Cobra; Escape to Athena;

Leviathan; Massacre in Rome (Rappresaglia); Rambo: First Blood, Part II; Shadow Conspiracy; Tombstone.

Costa-Gavras Aveu, L' (The Confession); Betrayed; Missing; Music Box; Section Spéciale (Special Section); Sleeping Car Murder, The (Compartiment Tueurs); State of Siege (Etat de Siège); Z.

Costard, Hellmuth Little Godard, A (Der kleine Godard).

Costner, Kevin Dances with Wolves; Dances with Wolves – Special Edition; Postman, The.

Coto, Manny Star Kid.

Cottafavi, Vittorio Ercole alla conquista di Atlantide (Hercules and the Captive Women/Hercules Conquers Atlantis).

Couffer, Jack Darwin Adventure, The; Ring of Bright Water.

Cousteau, Jacques-Yves Monde du Silence, Le (The Silent World).

Couturie, Bill Dear America: Letters Home from Vietnam.

Coward, Noël In Which We Serve.

Cox, Alex Repo Man; Highway Patrolman (El Patrullero); Sid and Nancy; Straight to Hell; Walker; Winner, The.

Cox, Paul Cactus; Golden Braid; Lonely Hearts; Man of Flowers; My First Wife; Vincent: The Life and Death of Vincent Van Gogh; Woman's Tale, A.

Cozarinsky, Edgardo Citizen Langlois; One Man's War (La Guerre d'un Seul Homme); Rothschild's Violin (Le Violon de Rothschild/Rothschildin Viulu).

Crabtree, Arthur Fiend Without a Face; Horrors of the Black Museum; Madonna of the Seven Moons; Quartet.

Crain, William (Bill) Blacula; Midnight Fear.

Crane, Barry Conquest of the Earth.

Crane, Kenneth Monster from Green Hell.

Crane, Peter Assassin; Moments.

Craven, Wes Deadly Blessing; Deadly Friend; Hills Have Eyes, The; Last House on the Left, The (aka Krug and Company/Sex Crime of the Century); Nightmare on Elm Street, A; People Under the

Stairs, The; Scream; Scream 2; Serpent and the Rainbow, The; Shocker; Swamp Thing; Vampire in Brooklyn; Wes Craven's New Nightmare.

Creme, Lol *Lunatic, The.*

Crichton, Charles *Against the Wind; Another Shore; Barnacle Bill (aka All At Sea); Battle of the Sexes, The; Dance Hall; Dead of Night; Divided Heart, The; Fish Called Wanda, A; Hue and Cry; Lavender Hill Mob, The; Law and Disorder; Love Lottery, The; Painted Boats; Titfield Thunderbolt, The; Train of Events.*

Crichton, Michael *Coma; First Great Train Robbery, The (aka The Great Train Robbery); Looker; Physical Evidence; Runaway; Westworld.*

Crisci, Giovanni *Before and After Sex (Prima e Dopo l'Amore...Un Grido d'Allarme).*

Crisp, Donald *Navigator, The.*

Croghan, Emma-Kate *Love and Other Catastrophes.*

Crombie, Donald *Caddie; Cathy's Child; Killing of Angel Street, The; Robbery Under Arms; Rough Diamonds.*

Crome, John *Naked Cell, The.*

Cromwell, John *Algiers; Anna and the King of Siam; Banjo on My Knee; Caged; Company She Keeps, The; Dead Reckoning; Enchanted Cottage, The; Goddess, The; In Name Only; Prisoner of Zenda, The; Racket, The; Since You Went Away; Spitfire; Victory.*

Cronenberg, David *Brood, The; Crash; Crimes of the Future; Dead Ringers; Dead Zone, The; Fast Company; Fly, The; M. Butterfly; Naked Lunch; Parasite Murders, The (aka Shivers/They Came from Within); Rabid; Scanners; Videodrome.*

Crowe, Cameron *Jerry Maguire; Say Anything; Singles.*

Crowe, Christopher *Off Limits (aka Saigon).*

Crumlish, Brian *Tickets for the Zoo.*

Cruze, James *If I Had a Million.*

Crystal, Billy *Forget Paris; Mr Saturday Night.*

Csaky, Mick *How Does It Feel.*

Cuarón, Alfonso *Great Expectations; Little Princess, A.*

Cukor, George *Actress, The; Adam's Rib; Bhowani Junction; Bill of Divorcement,*

A; *Blue Bird, The; Born Yesterday; Camille; Chapman Report, The; David Copperfield; Dinner at Eight; Double Life, A; Gaslight (aka The Murder In Thornton Square); Heller in Pink Tights; Holiday; It Should Happen to You; Justine; Keeper of the Flame; Les Girls; Let's Make Love; Little Women; Love Among the Ruins;. Marrying Kind, The; My Fair Lady; One Hour With You; Pat and Mike; Philadelphia Story, The; Rich and Famous; Star Is Born, A; Sylvia Scarlett; Two-Faced Woman; What Price Hollywood?; Woman's Face, A; Women, The; Zaza.*

Culp, Robert *Hickey & Boggs.*

Cummings, Irving *Hollywood Cavalcade; Lillian Russell; That Night in Rio.*

Cundieff, Rusty *Fear of a Black Hat.*

Cunha, Richard E *She Demons.*

Cunningham, Sean S *Deep Star Six; Friday the 13th; Together (aka Sensual Paradise).*

Curling, Jonathan *Song of the Shirt, The.*

Curran, Peter *No Secrets! (aka Touch of the Sun); Penelope 'Pulls It Off'.*

Curran, William *Love, Cheat & Steal.*

Curteis, Ian *Projected Man, The.*

Curtis, Dan *Burnt Offerings; Dracula.*

Curtis-Hall, Vondie *Gridlock'd.*

Curtiz, Michael *Adventures of Huckleberry Finn, The; Adventures of Robin Hood, The; Angels With Dirty Faces; Best Things in Life Are Free, The; Black Fury; Breaking Point, The; Captain Blood; Casablanca; Charge of the Light Brigade, The; Dive Bomber; Kid Galahad; King Creole; Life with Father; Mad Genius; Mildred Pierce; Mission to Moscow; Mystery of the Wax Museum; Night and Day; Noah's Ark; Passage to Marseille; Private Lives of Elizabeth and Essex, The; Romance on the High Seas (aka It's Magic); Santa Fe Trail; Sea Hawk, The; Sea Wolf, The; 20,000 Years in Sing Sing; Unsuspected, The; Walking Dead, The; We're No Angels; Yankee Doodle Dandy; Young Man With a Horn (aka Young Man of Music).*

Cutts, Graham *Rat, The.*

Czinner, Paul *Catherine the Great.*

Daalder, Renee *Massacre at*

Central High (aka Blackboard Massacre).

Da Costa, Morton *Auntie Mame; Music Man, The.*

Dahl, John (R) *Kill Me Again; Last Seduction, The; Red Rock West; Unforgettable.*

Dalen, Zale R *Hounds of Notre Dame, The; Skip Tracer.*

Dallamano, Massimo *Blue Belle; Venus in Furs (Venus im Pelz).*

Dalrymple, Ian *Esther Waters.*

Dalva, Robert *Black Stallion Returns, The.*

D'Amato, Joe (Aristide Massaccesi) *Emanuelle and the Last Cannibals (Emanuelle e gli Ultimi Cannibali).*

Damiani, Damiano *Amityville II: The Possession; Bullet for the General, A (¿Quién Sabe?); Tempter, The (Il Sorriso del Grande Tenatore).*

Damiano, Gerard *Devil in Miss Jones, The; Memories Within Miss Aggie.*

Damski, Mel *Happy Together; Yellowbeard.*

Dang Nhât Minh *Nostalgia for Countryland (Thuong Nho Dong Que); Return, The (Tro' Vé).*

Daniel, Rod *Beethoven's 2nd; K-9; Like Father, Like Son; Teen Wolf.*

Daniels, Godfrey *Insatiable.*

Danielsson, Tage *Out of an Old Man's Head (I Huvet på en Gammal Gubbe).*

D'Anna, Claude *Salomé.*

Danot, Serge *Dougal and the Blue Cat (Pollux et le Chat Bleu).*

Dansereau, Mireille *Dream Life (La Vie Rêvée).*

Dante, Joe *Amazon Women on the Moon; 'burbs, The; Explorers; Gremlins; Gremlins 2: The New Batch; Hollywood Boulevard; Howling, The; Innerspace; Matinee; Piranha; Twilight Zone – The Movie.*

Danton, Raymond *Psychic Killer.*

D'Antoni, Philip *Seven-Ups, The.*

Darabont, Frank *Shawshank Redemption, The.*

Dardenne, Jean Pierre, *Promise, The (La Promesse).*

Dardenne, Luc, *Promise, The (La Promesse).*

Darling, Joan *First Love.*

Darnborough, Anthony *Astonished Heart, The; So Long at the Fair.*

D'Arrast, Harry D'Abbadie *Laughter; Raffles.*

Dash, Julie *Daughters of the Dust; Illusions.*

Dassin, Jules *Brute Force; Circle of Two; Dream of Passion, A; Du Rififi chez les Hommes (Rififi); Naked City, The; Night and the City, The; Phaedra; 10.30 P.M. Summer; Thieves' Highway; Topkapi.*

Davenport, Harry Bromley *Xtro.*

Daves, Delmer *Badlanders, The; Battle of the Villa Fiorita, The; Broken Arrow; Cowboy; Dark Passage; Demetrius and the Gladiators; Kings Go Forth; Last Wagon, The; Pride of the Marines (aka Forever in Love); Red House, The; 3.10 to Yuma.*

David, Charles *Lady on a Train.*

Davidson, Boaz *Going Steady (Yotz'im Kavna); Last American Virgin, The; Lemon Popsicle (Eskimo Limon); Private Popsicle (Sapiches); Salsa.*

Davidson, John-Paul *Galahad of Everest; Grotesque, The.*

Davidson, Martin *Almost Summer; Eddie and the Cruisers; Hero at Large; Lords of Flatbush, The.*

Davies, Howard *Secret Rapture, The.*

Davies, John *Acceptable Levels; City Farm; Maeve; Ursula and Glenys.*

Davies, Robert *Saturday Night at the Palace.*

Davies, Terence *Distant Voices, Still Lives; Long Day Closes, The; Neon Bible, The; Terence Davies Trilogy, The.*

Davis, Andrew *Above the Law (aka Nico); Code of Silence; Final Terror, The (aka Campsite Massacre); Fugitive, The; Package, The; Steal Big, Steal Little; Under Siege.*

Davis, Desmond *Clash of the Titans; Country Girls, The; Girl with Green Eyes; I Was Happy Here; Ordeal by Innocence.*

Davis, Ossie *Gordon's War.*

Davis, Peter *Hearts and Minds; Paperback Vigilante.*

Davis, Philip *i.d.*

Davis, Redd *Underneath the Arches.*

Davis, Tamra *CB4; Guncrazy.*

Desplechin, Arnaud *Ma vie sexuelle (Paul Dedalus' Journey) (Comment je me suis disputé... ('ma vie sexuelle'))*; Sentinelle, La *(The Sentinel)*.

DeStefano, Lorenzo *Talmage Farlow*.

Deswarte, Benie *Kashima Paradise*.

De Toth, André *Carson City; Dark Waters; Day of the Outlaw; House of Wax; Indian Fighter, The; None Shall Escape; Pitfall; Play Dirty; Ramrod*.

Deutch, Howard *Getting Even With Dad; Pretty in Pink; Some Kind of Wonderful*.

Deval, Jacques *Club de Femmes*.

Devenish, Ross *Boesman and Lena; Marigolds in August*.

Devers, Claire *Noir et Blanc*.

Deville, Michel *Death in a French Garden (Péril en la Demeure); Dossier 51, Le; Lectrice, La; Paltoquet, Le*.

DeVito, Danny *Hoffa; Roald Dahl's Matilda; Throw Momma from the Train; War of the Roses, The*.

DeVito, Ralph *Death Collector*.

Dexter, John *I Want What I Want*.

Dhouailly, Alain *Inutile Envoyer Photo*.

Diaz-Abaya, Marilou *In the Navel of the Sea (Sa Pusod Ng Dagat)*.

Diaz Yanes, Augustin *Nobody Will Speak of Us When We're Dead (Nadie Hablará de Nostras cuando Hayamos Muerto)*.

DiCillo, Tom *Box of Moon Light; Johnny Suede; Living in Oblivion; Real Blonde, The*.

Dick, Kirby *Sick: The Life & Death of Bob Flanagan, Supermasochist*.

Dick, Nigel *Final Combination; P.I. Private Investigations*.

Dickerson, Ernest R *Juice; Surviving the Game; Tales from the Crypt Presents Demon Knight*.

Dickinson, Thorold *Arsenal Stadium Mystery, The; Gaslight; Men of Two Worlds; Next of Kin, The; Queen of Spades, The; Secret People*.

Diegues, Carlos *Bye Bye Brazil; Tieta of Agreste (Tieta do Agreste)*.

Dieterle, William *All That Money Can Buy (aka The Devil and Daniel Webster/Daniel and the Devil); Another Dawn; Dark City; Dr Erlich's Magic Bullet; Blockade; Fog Over Frisco; Her Majesty, Love; Hunchback of Notre Dame, The; I'll Be Seeing You; Juarez; Last Flight, The; Life of Emile Zola, The; Love Letters; Midsummer Night's Dream, A; Portrait of Jennie; Satan Met a Lady; Searching Wind, The*.

Dietl, Helmut *Schtonk!*.

Dignam, Erin *Loved*.

Di Leo, Fernando *Manhunt in Milan (La 'Mala' Ordina)*.

Di Mello, Victor *Giselle*.

Ding, Loni *Color of Honor, The*.

Dingwall, John *Custodian, The*.

Dinner, Michael *Heaven Help Us (aka Catholic Boys); Off Beat*.

Dippé, Mark AZ *Spawn*.

DiSalle, Mark *Kickboxer; Perfect Weapon*.

Di Silvestro, Rino *Love in a Women's Prison (Diario Segreto da un Carcere Femminile)*.

Disney, Walt *Snow White and the Seven Dwarfs*.

Dmytryk, Edward *Back to Bataan; Broken Lance; Caine Mutiny, The; Cornered; Crossfire; Devil Commands, The; Farewell, My Lovely (aka Murder My Sweet); Human Factor, The; Left Hand of God, The; Mirage; Obsession (aka The Hidden Room); Raintree Country; Sbarco di Anzio, Lo (Anzio/The Battle for Anzio); Shalako; Sniper, The; Tender Comrade; Walk on the Wild Side; Warlock; Young Lions, The*.

Dobson, Kevin *Mango Tree, The*.

Dohany, Gael *Occupy!*

Doillon, Jacques *Jeune Werther, Le (Young Werther)*.

Dominici, Paolo (Domenico Paolella) *Nun and the Devil, The (Le Monache di Sant'Arcangelo)*.

Donaldson, Roger *Bounty, The; Cadillac Man; Cocktail; Dante's Peak; Marie; Getaway, The; No Way Out; Sleeping Dogs; Smash Palace; Species; White Sands*.

Donen, Stanley *Arabesque; Bedazzled; Blame It On Rio; Charade; Damn Yankees (aka What Lola Wants); Funny Face; Grass Is Greener, The; Indiscreet; It's Always Fair Weather; Little Prince, The; Lucky Lady; Movie Movie; On the Town; Pajama Game, The; Royal Wedding (aka Wedding Bells); Saturn 3; Seven Brides for Seven Brothers; Singin' in the Rain; Staircase; Two for the Road*.

Donnelly, Dennis *Toolbox Murders, The*.

Donner, Clive *Caretaker, The (aka The Guest); Charlie Chan and the Curse of the Dragon Queen; Christmas Carol, A; Here We Go Round the Mulberry Bush; Luv; Maverick; Nothing But the Best; Nude Bomb, The; Oliver Twist; Stealing Heaven; Thief of Baghdad, The; Vampire (aka Old Dracula); What's New Pussycat?*.

Donner, Jörn *Black on White (Mustaa Valkoisella)*.

Donner, Richard *Assassins; Conspiracy Theory; Goonies, The; Inside Moves; Ladyhawke; Lethal Weapon; Lethal Weapon 2; Lethal Weapon 3; Omen, The; Radio Flyer; Salt & Pepper; Scrooged; Superman; Toy, The*.

Donoghue, Mary Agnes *Paradise*.

Donohue, Jack *Assault on a Queen*.

Donovan, Martin *Apartment Zero*.

Donovan, Paul *Siege*.

Donovan, Terence *Yellow Dog*.

Donskoi, Mark *Childhood of Maxim Gorki, The (Detstvo Gorkovo); Orlovs, The (Suprugi Orlovy)*.

Dore, Mary *Good Fight, The*.

Doring, Jef *Tidikawa and Friends*.

Doring, Su *Tidikawa and Friends*.

Dornhelm, Robert *Children of Theatre Street, The; Cold Feet; Echo Park; Further Gesture, A (aka The Break); Requiem for Dominic; Unfish, The (Der Unfisch)*.

Dorr, John *Luck, Trust & Ketchup: Robert Altman in Carver Country*.

Dörrie, Doris *Keiner Liebt Mich (Nobody Loves Me); Men (Männer)*.

Dos Santos, Nelson Pereira *Barren Lives*.

Douchet, Jean *Paris vu par... (Six in Paris)*.

Douglas, Bill *Comrades; My Childhood/My Ain Folk/My Way Home*.

Douglas, Gordon *Barquero; Charge at Feather River, The; Chuka; Come Fill the Cup; Detective, The; First Yank into Tokyo (aka First Man into Tokyo/Mask of Fury); Follow That Dream; In Like Flint; Kiss Tomorrow Goodbye; Lady in Cement; Rio Conchos; Robin and the 7 Hoods; Santiago (The Gun Runner); Saps at Sea; Skullduggery; Sins of Rachel Cade, The; Slaughter's Big Rip-Off; Stagecoach; Them!; They Call Me MISTER Tibbs!; Tony Rome; Viva Knievall; Young at Heart*.

Douglas, John *Milestones*.

Douglas, Kirk *Posse; Scalawag*.

Douglas, Peter *Tiger's Tale, A*.

Doukas, Bill *Feedback*.

Doukouré, Cheik *Ballon d'Or, Le (The Golden Ball)*.

Dovzhenko, Alexander *Earth (Zemlya)*.

Downey, Robert *Putney Swope*.

Drach, Michel *Violons du Bal, Les*.

Dragojevic, Srdjan *Pretty Village, Pretty Flame (Lepa sela lepo gore)*.

Dragoti, Stan *Dirty Little Billy; Love at First Bite; Mr Mom (aka Mr Mum); Necessary Roughness; She's Out of Control*.

Drake, Jim *Police Academy 4: Citizens on Patrol*.

Drazan, Anthony *Imaginary Crimes*.

Dream, Rinse *Café Flesh*.

Dreifuss, Arthur *Baby Face Morgan*.

Dreyer, Carl Theodor *Day of Wrath (Vredens Dag); Gertrud; Ordet (The Word); Passion de Jeanne d'Arc, La (The Passion of Joan of Arc); Vampyr*.

Drion, Georges *Voice of Kurdistan, The*.

Drury, David *Defence of the Realm; Forever Young*.

Duan Jinchuan *Square, The (Guangchang)*.

DuBoc, Claude *One By One*.

Dubov, Adam *Dead Beat*.

Duchamp, Marcel *Dreams That Money Can Buy*.

Duchemin, Rémy *Fausto*.

Duckworth, Jacqui *Home-Made Melodrama*.

Dudow, Slatan *Kuhle Wampe*.

Duffell, Peter *England Made Me; Experience Preferred But Not Essential; House That Dripped Blood, The; Inside Out; King of the Wind;*

Letters to an Unknown Lover (Les Louves).

Duffy, Martin *Boy from Mercury, The.*

Dugan, Dennis *Happy Gilmore; Problem Child.*

Dugdale, George *Living Doll.*

Dugowson, Martine *Mina Tannenbaum; Portraits Chinois.*

Duguay, Christian *Scanners II: The New Order; Screamers.*

Duigan, John *Flirting; Lawn Dogs; Leading Man, The; Romero; Sirens; Wide Sargasso Sea; Winter of Our Dreams; Year My Voice Broke, The.*

Duke, Bill *Deep Cover; Killing Floor, The; Rage in Harlem, A; Sister Act 2: Back in the Habit.*

Duke, Daryl *Payday; Silent Partner, The.*

Dulac, Germaine *Seashell and the Clergyman, The (La Coquille et le Clergyman; Souriante Madame Beudet, La (The Smiling Madame Beudet).*

Dumaresq, William *Duffer.*

Dumont, Bruno *Vie de Jésus, La (The Life of Jesus).*

Duncan, Patrick *84 Charlie Mopic.*

Dunlop, Frank *Winter's Tale, The.*

Dunne, Griffin *Addicted to Love*

Dunne, Philip *Blindfold; Blue Denim (aka Blue Jeans); Wild in the Country.*

Dunning, George *Yellow Submarine.*

Dunye, Cheryl *Watermelon Woman, The.*

Dupeyron, François *Coeur qui bat, Un (Your Beating Heart); Strange Place to Meet, A (Drôle d'Endroit pour une rencontre).*

Dupont, EA *Piccadilly; Varieté (Variety/Vaudeville).*

Dupontel, Albert *Bernie.*

Durand, Rudy *Tilt.*

Duras, Marguerite *India Song; Nathalie Granger.*

Durham, Duwayne *Homeward Bound: The Incredible Journey.*

Duval, Daniel *Dérobade, La (The Life).*

Duvall, Robert *Angelo My Love; Apostle, The.*

Duvivier, Julien *Anna Karenina; Belle Equipe, La;*

Fin du Jour, La (The End of the Day); Flesh and Fantasy; Great Waltz, The; Lydia; Pépé le Moko.

Dwan, Allan *Angel in Exile; Brewster's Millions; Cattle Queen of Montana; Driftwood; Escape to Burma; Most Dangerous Man Alive; Robin Hood; Restless Breed; River's Edge, The; Sands of Iwo Jima; Silver Lode; Slightly Scarlet; Suez; Tennessee's Partner.*

Dwoskin, Stephen *Ballet Black; Dyn Amo; Further and Particular; Hindered (Behindert); Outside In; Silent Cry, The.*

Dylan, Bob *Renaldo & Clara.*

Dylewska, Jolanta *Warsaw Ghetto Uprising, The.*

Dzhordzhadze, Nana *My English Grandfather (Robinsonada anu Chemi Ingliseli Papa).*

Dziga Vertov Group *Pravda.*

East, John M *Hellcat Mud Wrestlers.*

Eastwood, Clint *Absolute Power; Bird; Bridges of Madison County, The; Breezy; Bronco Billy; Eiger Sanction, The; Firefox; Gauntlet, The: Heartbreak Ridge; High Plains Drifter; Honkytonk Man; Midnight in the Garden of Good and Evil; Outlaw Josey Wales, The; Pale Rider; Perfect World, A; Play Misty for Me; Rookie, The; Sudden Impact; Unforgiven; White Hunter, Black Heart.*

Eberhardt, Thom *Captain Ron; Gross Anatomy (aka A Cut Above); Night of the Comet; Without a Clue.*

Ecaré, Désiré *Faces of Women (Visages de Femmes).*

Edel, Ulrich *Body of Evidence; Christiane F. (Christiane F. wir Kinder vom Bahnhof Zoo); Last Exit to Brooklyn (Letzte Ausfahrt Brooklyn).*

Eder, Harriet *My Private War (Mein Krieg).*

Edmondson, Adrian *More Bad News.*

Edwards, Blake *Blind Date; Breakfast at Tiffany's; Carey Treatment, The; Curse of the Pink Panther; Darling Lili; Days of Wine and Roses; Experiment in Terror (aka The Grip of Fear); Fine Mess, A; High Time; Man Who Loved Women, The; Micki + Maude; Mister Cory; Operation Petticoat; Party, The; Pink Panther, The; Pink Panther Strikes Again, The; Return of the Pink Panther, The; Revenge of the Pink Panther; S.O.B.; Shot in the Dark, A; Skin Deep; Sunset; Switch;*

Tamarind Seed, The; Trail of the Pink Panther; '10'; 'That's Life'; Victor/Victoria; What Did You Do in the War, Daddy?; Wild Rovers.

Edwards, Harry *Tramp, Tramp, Tramp.*

Edwards, Henry *Squibs.*

Edzard, Christine *As You Like It; Biddy; Fool, The; Little Dorrit; Stories from a Flying Trunk.*

Eggleston, Colin *Long Weekend; Sky Pirates.*

Egleson, Jan *Shock to the System, A.*

Egoyan, Atom *Adjuster, The; Calendar; Exotica; Family Viewing; Speaking Parts; Sweet Hereafter, The.*

Eisenman, Rafael *Lake Consequence.*

Eisenstein, Sergei *Alexander Nevsky; Battleship Potemkin (Bronenosets Potyomkin); General Line, The (Staroye i Novoye; aka Old and New); Ivan the Terrible (Ivan Grozny); Oktyabr (October/Ten Days That Shook the World); Strike (Stachka).*

Elçi, Umit *Cockroach, The (Böcek).*

Eldridge, John *Conflict of Wings (aka Fuss Over Feathers); Laxdale Hall (aka Scotch on the Rocks).*

Elek, Judit *To Speak the Unspeakable: The Message of Elie Wiesel (Mondani a mondhatatlant: Elie Wiesel uzenete).*

Elfick, David *Love in Limbo.*

Elgear, Sandra *Voices from the Front.*

Elias, Michael *Lush Life.*

Elliott, Stephan *Adventures of Priscilla Queen of the Desert, The; Frauds.*

Ellis, Arthur *Don't Get Me Started (aka Psychotherapy).*

Else, Jon *Day After Trinity, The.*

Elvey, Maurice *Clairvoyant, The; Dry Rot; Gentle Sex, The; Princess Charming; Tunnel, The (aka Transatlantic Tunnel).*

Emlyn, Endaf *Leaving Lenin (Gadael Lenin); Making of Maps, The; One Full Moon (Un Nos Ola Leuad).*

Emmerich, Roland *Ghost Chase; Godzilla; Independence Day; Moon 44; Stargate; Universal Soldier.*

Enders, Robert *Stevie.*

Endfield, Cyril (Cy) *Hell*

Drivers; Jet Storm; Mysterious Island; Sound of Fury, The (aka Try and Get Me); Zulu.

Engel, Andi *Melancholia.*

English, John *Adventures of Captain Marvel, The (aka The Return of Captain Marvel); Mule Train.*

Englund, Robert *976-Evil.*

Engström, Ingemo *Escape Route to Marseilles (Fluchtweg nach Marseilles).*

Enrico, Robert *Ho! (aka Criminal Face); Secret, The (Le Secret).*

Enright, Ray *Angels Wash Their Faces; China Clipper; Dames; Man Alive; Naughty but Nice; South of St Louis.*

Enyedi, Ildikó *My 20th Century (Az én XX századom).*

Ephron, Nora *Michael; Mixed Nuts; Sleepless in Seattle; This Is My Life.*

Epstein, Marcelo *Body Rock.*

Epstein, Robert (Rob) *Celluloid Closet, The; Common Threads: Stories from the Quilt; Times of Harvey Milk, The.*

Equino, Antonio *Chuquiago.*

Erdöss, Pál *Princess, The (Adj Király Katonát!).*

Erice, Victor *Quince Tree Sun, The (El Sol del Membrillo); South, The (El Sur); Spirit of the Beehive, The (El Espíritu de la Colmena).*

Erkenov, Khusein *100 Days Before the Command (Sto Dnei Do Prikaza…).*

Erman, John *Making It; Stella.*

Erne, Eduarde *Totschweigen (A Wall of Silence).*

Ernst, Max *Dreams That Money Can Buy.*

Erskine, Chester *Androcles and the Lion.*

Eshetu, Theo *Travelling Light: a Portrait of Lindsay Kemp.*

Esteban, Juan *Sensations.*

Estevez, Emilio *Men at Work; Wisdom.*

Etaix, Pierre *Grand Amour, Le; Soupirant, Le (The Suitor); Tant qu'on a la Santé (As Long as You're Healthy); Yoyo.*

Eustache, Jean *Mes Petites Amoureuses; Mother and the Whore, The (La Maman et la Putain).*

Evans, Betsan Morris *Dad Savage.*

Evans, Bruce A *Kuffs.*

Evans, David *Fever Pitch.*

Evans, David Mickey *Sandlot, The (aka The Sandlot Kids).*

Evans, Marc *Gift, The; House of America; Resurrection Man.*

Everett, DS *see* Shebib, Donald.

Export, Valie *Invisible Adversaries (Unsichtbare Gegner).*

Eyre, Richard *Imitation Game, The; Laughterhouse (aka Singleton's Pluck); Loose Connections; Ploughman's Lunch, The.*

Eyres, John *Monolith.*

Faenza, Roberto *Order of Death (aka Corrupt).*

Faiman, Peter *Crocodile Dundee; Dutch (aka Driving Me Crazy).*

Fairfax, Ferdinand *Savage Islands; True Blue.*

Falk, Feliks *And There Was Jazz (Eyl Jazz); Top Dog (Wodzirej).*

Fanaka, Jamaa *Penitentiary.*

Fansten, Jacques *Fracture du myocarde, La (Cross My Heart).*

Faraldo, Claude *Bof!; Themroc.*

Fargo, James *Caravans; Enforcer, The; Every Which Way But Loose; Game for Vultures.*

Farhang, Dariush *Spell, The (Telesm).*

Farrelly, Bobby *Kingpin.*

Farrelly, Peter *Dumb & Dumber; Kingpin.*

Farrina, Corrado *Baba Yaga – The Devil Witch (Baba Yaga).*

Farrow, John *Alias Nick Beal (aka The Contact Man); Back from Eternity; Big Clock, The; Botany Bay; Calcutta; Five Came Back; Full Confession; His Kind of Woman; Hitler Gang, The; Hondo; Night Has a Thousand Eyes; Sea Chase, The; Two Yeas Before the Mast; Where Danger Lives.*

Fassbinder, Rainer Werner *American Soldier, The (Der Amerikanische Soldat); Berlin Alexanderplatz; Beware of a Holy Whore (Warnung vor heiligen Nutte); Bitter Tears of Petra von Kant, The (Die Bitteren Tränen der Petra von Kant); Bolwieser (The Stationmaster's Wife); Chinese Roulette (Chinesisches Roulette); Despair; Effi Briest; Faustrecht der Freiheit (Fox/Fox and His Friends); Fear Eats the Soul (Angst essen Seele auf); Germany in Autumn (Deutschland im Herbst); Gods of the Plague (Götter der Pest); In a Year with 13 Moons (In einem Jahr mit 13 Monden); Katzelmacher; Lili Marleen; Lola; Love Is Colder than Death (Leibe is kälter als der Tod); Marriage of Maria Braun, The (Die Ehe der Maria Braun); Martha; Merchant of Four Seasons, The (Der Händler der vier Jahreszeiten); Mother Küster's Trip to Heaven (Mutter Küsters Fahrt zum Himmel); Nora Helmer; Querelle; Satan's Brew (Satansbraten); Third Generation, The (Die Dritte Generation); Veronika Voss (Die Sehnsucht der Veronika Voss); Wild Game (Wildwechsel).*

Faty Sow, Thierno *Camp Thiaroye (Camp de Thiaroye).*

Favio, Leonardo *Gatica.*

Fei Mu *Spring in a Small Town (Xiao Cheng zhi Chun).*

Feig, Rebecca *Bye-Bye Babushka.*

Feigenbaum, William *Hugo the Hippo.*

Feist, Felix *Donovan's Brain.*

Fejos, Paul (Pál Fejös) *Tavaszi Zápor (Marie – a Hungarian Legend/Marie, légende hongroise/Spring Shower).*

Fekete, Ibolya *Bolshe Vita (Bolse Vita).*

Feldman, John *Alligator Eyes; Dead Funny.*

Fellini, Federico *Amarcord; And the Ship Sails on (E la Nave Va); Bidone, Il (The Swindlers); Boccaccio '70; City of Women (La Città delle Donne); Clowns, The (I Clowns); Dolce Vita, La (The Sweet Life); 8½ (Otto e Mezzo); Fellini-Satyricon; Fellini's Casanova (Il Casanova di Federico Fellini); Fellini's Roma (Roma); Ginger & Fred (Ginger e Fred); Histoires Extraordinaires (Spirits of the Dead/Tales of Mystery); Intervista; Juliet of the Spirits (Giulietta degli Spiriti); Luci del Varietà (Lights of Variety/Variety Lights); Orchestra Rehearsal (Prova d'Orchestra); Strada, La (The Road); Vitelloni, I; Voice of the Moon, The (La Voce della Luna); White Sheik, The (Lo Sceicco Bianco).*

Fenady, Georg *Arnold.*

Fenton, Leslie *Lulu Belle.*

Féret, René *Mystery of Alexina, The (Mystère Alexina).*

Ferguson, Graeme *Love Goddesses, The.*

Ferland, Guy *Babysitter, The; Telling Lies in America.*

Fernández, Emilio *Enamorada (Women in Love); Salón México.*

Ferrara, Abel *Addiction, The; Bad Lieutenant; Blackout, The; Body Snatchers; Cat Chaser; China Girl; Driller Killer, The; Funeral, The; King of New York; Ms.45 (aka Angel of Vengeance); Snake Eyes (aka Dangerous Game).*

Ferrari, Alain *Bosna!*

Ferrer, José *Cockleshell Heroes; I Accuse!*

Ferrer, Mel *Vendetta.*

Ferreri, Marco *Audience, The (L'Udienza); Blow-Out (La Grande Bouffe); Future Is Woman, The (Il Futuro è Donna); House of Smiles (La Casa del Sorriso); Last Woman, The (L'Ultima Donna); Tales of Ordinary Madness (Storie di Ordinaria Follia).*

Fest, Joachim C *Hitler – a Career (Hitler eine Karriere).*

Festa Campanile, Pasquale *Girl from Trieste, The (La Ragazza di Trieste); Il Petomane (The Windbreaker).*

Feuillade, Louis *Vampires, Les.*

Feyder, Jacques *Grand Jeu, Le (Card of Fate); Kermesse Héroique, La (Carnival in Flanders); Kiss, The; Knight Without Armour.*

Field, Connie *Life and Times of Rosie the Riveter, The.*

Figgis, Mike *Browning Version, The; Internal Affairs; Leaving Las Vegas; Liebestraum; Mr Jones; One Night Stand; Stormy Monday.*

Finbow, Colin *Captain Stirrick; Custard Boys, The; Daemon; Dark Enemy; Hard Road; Mister Skeeter; School for Vandals, Swarm in May, A.*

Finch, Nigel *Stonewall.*

Fincher, David *Alien³; Game, The; Seven (aka Se7en).*

Findlay, Seaton *Janis.*

Finkleman, Ken *Airplane II The Sequel.*

Finney, Albert *Charlie Bubbles.*

Fiore, Robert *Pumping Iron.*

Firestone, Cinda *Attica.*

Firstenberg, Sam *American Ninja (aka American Warrior); Ninja III – The Domination.*

Firth, Michael *Sylvia.*

Fischer, Hans Conrad *Nela.*

Fisher, Terence *Astonished Heart, The; Brides of Dracula, The; Curse of Frankenstein, The; Curse of the Werewolf, The; Devil Rides Out, The; Dracula (aka Horror of Dracula); Dracula, Prince of Darkness; Frankenstein and the Monster from Hell; Frankenstein Created Woman; Frankenstein Must Be Destroyed; Gorgon, The; Hound of the Baskervilles, The; Mummy, The; Night of the Big Heat; Phantom of the Opera, The; Revenge of Frankenstein, The; So Long at the Fair; Spaceways; Stranglers of Bombay, The; Two Faces of Dr Jekyll, The.*

Fishman, Bill *Tapeheads.*

Fisk, Jack *Daddy's Dyin' – Who's Got the Will?; Raggedy Man.*

Fitzgerald, Thom *Hanging Garden, The.*

Fitzmaurice, George *As You Desire Me; Mata Hari; One Heavenly Night; Unholy Garden, The.*

Fiveson, Robert S *Parts: The Clonus Horror (aka Clonus).*

Flaherty, Paul *18 Again!; Who's Harry Crumb?*

Flaherty, Robert *Elephant Boy; Louisiana Story; Man of Aran.*

Fleder, Gary *Kiss the Girls; Things to Do in Denver When You're Dead.*

Fleischer, Dave *Betty Boop Follies, The.*

Fleischer, Richard *Amityville 3-D (aka Amityville: The Demon); Armoured Car Robbery; Ashanti; Bandido!; Barabbas (Barabba); Between Heaven and Hell; Boston Strangler, The; Che!; Child of Divorce; Clay Pigeon, The; Compulsion; Conan the Destroyer; Don Is Dead, The; Fantastic Voyage; Incredible Sarah, The; Jazz Singer, The; Last Run, The; Mandingo; Mr Majestyk; Narrow Margin, The; New Centurions, The (aka Precinct 45: Los Angeles Police); Prince and the Pauper, The (aka Crossed Swords); Red Sonja; Soylent Green; Spikes Gang, The; 10 Rillington Place; Tora! Tora! Tora!; 20,000 Leagues Under the Sea; Vikings, The; Violent Saturday.*

Fleischmann, Peter *Hunting Scenes from Bavaria (Jagdszenen aus Niederbayern).*

Fleming, Andrew *Craft, The; Threesome.*

Fleming, Victor *Captains

Courageous; Dr Jekyll and Mr Hyde; Gone With the Wind; Red Dust; Wizard of Oz, The.

Flemyng, Gordon *Daleks – Invasion Earth 2150 A.D.; Dr Who and the Daleks; Split, The.*

Fletcher, Mandie *Deadly Advice.*

Flicker, Florian *Halbe Welt (Half the World).*

Flicker, Theodore J *President's Analyst, The.*

Flitcroft, Kim *Tales from a Hard City.*

Florey, Robert *Beast With Five Fingers, The; Cocoanuts, The; Dangerously They Live; Face Behind the Mask, The; Florentine Dagger, The; King of Alcatraz; Murders in the Rue Morgue.*

Flynn, John *Best Seller; Brainscan; Defiance; Jerusalem File, The; Lock Up; Marilyn – The Untold Story; Outfit, The; Out for Justice.*

Flynn, Tom *Watch It.*

Fok Yiu-Leung, Clarence (aka Clarence Ford) *Before Dawn (Di Ba Zhan); Iceman Cometh, The (Jidong Qixia).*

Foldes, Lawrence D *Young Warriors.*

Foley, James *After Dark, My Sweet; At Close Range; Chamber, The; Fear; Glengarry Glen Ross; Who's That Girl.*

Fonda, Jane *Vietnam Journey.*

Fonda, Peter *Hired Hand, The; Wanda Nevada.*

Fondato, Marcello *Watch Out, We're Mad (Altrimenti ci Arrabbiamo).*

Fong, Allen *Ah Ying (Banbianren); Dancing Bull (Wuniu); Father and Son (Fuzi Qing); Just Like Weather (Meiguo Xin).*

Fong, Eddie *Kawashima Yoshiko (Chuandao Fangzi/aka The Last Princess of Manchuria).*

Fons, Jorge *Jory; Midaq Alley (El Callejon de los Milagros).*

Fonvielle, Lloyd *Dead Can't Lie, The.*

Forbes, Bryan *Better Late Than Never; Deadfall; International Velvet; King Rat; L-Shaped Room, The; Naked Face, The; Raging Moon, The (aka Long Ago, Tomorrow); Seance on a Wet Afternoon; Slipper and the Rose, The; Whisperers, The; Whistle Down the Wind.*

Forcier, André *Histoire inventée, Une (An Imaginary Tale).*

Ford, Clarence see Fok Yiu-Leung.

Ford, Derek *Keep It Up, Jack!.*

Ford, John *Cheyenne Autumn; Donovan's Reef; Drums Along the Mohawk; Fort Apache; Four Men and a Prayer; Fugitive, The; Grapes of Wrath, The; Horse Soldiers, The; How Green Was My Valley; How the West Was Won; Hurricane, The; Informer, The; Iron Horse, The; Judge Priest; Last Hurrah, The; Long Gray Line, The; Long Voyage Home, The; Lost Patrol, The; Man Who Shot Liberty Valance, The; Mary of Scotland; Mister Roberts; Mogambo; My Darling Clementine; Prisoner of Shark Island, The; Quiet Man, The; Rio Grande; Searchers, The; Sergeant Rutledge; Seven Women; She Wore a Yellow Ribbon; Stagecoach; Submarine Patrol; Sun Shines Bright, The; They Were Expendable; Three Godfathers; Tobacco Road; Two Rode Together; Wagon Master; When Willie Comes Marching Home, The (aka Passport to Fame); Wings of Eagles, The; Young Mr Lincoln.*

Ford, Maxim *Live a Life.*

Ford, Philip *Angel in Exile.*

Forde, Eugene *Michael Shayne Private Detective; Shadows in the Night.*

Forde, Walter *Bulldog Jack (aka Alias Bulldog Drummond); Cheer, Boys, Cheer; Chu Chin Chow; Forever England (aka Born for Glory); Four Just Men, The; Gaunt Stranger The (aka The Phantom Strikes); King of the Damned.*

Forder, Timothy *Mystery of Edwin Drood, The.*

Foreman, Carl *Victors, The.*

Forman, Milos *Amadeus; Fireman's Ball, The (Hori, má Panenko); Hair; Lásky Jedné Plavovlásky (A Blonde in Love/Loves of a Blonde); One Flew Over the Cuckoo's Nest; People vs. Larry Flynt, The; Peter and Pavla (Cerny Petr); Ragtime; Taking Off; Valmont; Visions of Eight.*

Forst, Willi *Bel Ami.*

Forsyth, Bill *Being Human; Breaking In; Comfort and Joy; Gregory's Girl; Housekeeping; Local Hero; That Sinking Feeling.*

Fosse, Bob *All That Jazz; Cabaret; Lenny; Star 80; Sweet Charity.*

Foster, Giles *Consuming Passions; Silas Marner; Tree of Hands.*

Foster, Harve *Song of the South.*

Foster, Jodie *Home for the Holidays; Little Man Tate.*

Foster, Lewis R *Dakota Incident; Top of the World.*

Foster, Norman *Journey Into Fear; Rachel and the Stranger.*

Fournier, Claude *Alien Thunder (aka Dan Candy's Law).*

Fowler Jr, Gene *I Married a Monster from Outer Space; I Was a Teenage Werewolf.*

Fowler, Robert *Below the Belt.*

Fox, Dave *Year of the Beaver.*

Fox, Eytan *Song of the Siren (Shirat Ha'Sirena).*

Fraker, William A *Legend of the Lone Ranger, The; Monte Walsh.*

Frakes, Jonathan *Star Trek: First Contact.*

France, Chuck *Jazz in Exile.*

Francis, Freddie *Craze; Creeping Flesh, The; Doctor and the Devils, The; Dr Terror's House of Horrors; Dracula Has Risen from the Grave; Ghoul, The; Legend of the Werewolf; Nightmare; Skull, The; Torture Garden.*

Francis, Karl *Above Us the Earth; Boy Soldier; Giro City; Rebecca's Daughters; Streetlife.*

Franco, Jesús (as Clifford Brown) *Lustful Amazon, The (Maciste contre la Reine des Amazones).*

Franco, Jesús (Jess) *Count Dracula (El Conde Dracula); Female Vampires; Succubus (Necronomicon – Geträumte Sünden).*

Francovich, Allan *On Company Business.*

Franju, Georges *Faute de l'Abbé Mouret, La (The Sin of Father Mouret); Judex; Last Melodrama, The (Le Dernier Mélodrame); Nuits Rouges (Shadowman); Pleins Feux sur l'assassin; Thomas l'Imposteur (Thomas the Imposter); Tête contre les Murs, La (The Keepers); Yeux sans Visage, Les (Eyes Without a Face/The Horror Chamber of Dr Faustus).*

Frank, Christopher *Love in the Strangest Way (Elles n'oublient pas).*

Frank, Hubert *Vanessa*

Frank, Melvin *Buona Sera, Mrs Campbell; Court Jester, The; Duchess and the Dirtwater Fox, The; Knock on Wood; Li'l Abner; Lost and Found; Prisoner of Second Avenue, The; Touch of Class, A; Walk Like a Man.*

Frank, Robert *Candy Mountain; CS Blues; Me and My Brother; Pull My Daisy.*

Frank, TC *Billy Jack; Born Loser, The.*

Frankel, Cyril *Don't Bother to Knock (aka Why Bother to Knock); It's Great to Be Young; Man of Africa; No Time for Tears; Permission to Kill.*

Frankel, David *Miami Rhapsody.*

Frankenheimer, John *All Fall Down; Bird Man of Alcatraz; Black Sunday; Challenge, The; Dead Bang; 52 Pick-up; Fixer, The; Fourth War, The; French Connection II; Grand Prix; Gypsy Moths, The; Holcroft Covenant, The; Horsemen, The; Island of Dr Moreau, The; Manchurian Candidate, The; 99 and 44/100% Dead (aka Call Harry Crown); Prophecy; Seconds; Seven Days in May; Train, The; Year of the Gun; Young Stranger, The.*

Franklin, Carl *Devil in a Blue Dress; One False Move.*

Franklin, Howard *Larger Than Life; Public Eye, The; Quick Change.*

Franklin, Richard *Brilliant Lies; F/X2 (aka F/X2 – The Deadly Art of Illusion); Hotel Sorrento; Link; Patrick; Psycho II; Roadgames; True Story of Eskimo Nell, The (aka Dick Down Under).*

Franklin, Sidney *Barretts of Wimpole Street, The; Dark Angel, The; Good Earth, The.*

Fraser, Harry *Randy Rides Alone.*

Fratzscher, Peter *Asphalt Night (Asphaltnacht).*

Frawley, James *Big Bus, The; Kid Blue, Muppet Move, The.*

Frazer Jones, Peter *George and Mildred.*

Frears, Stephen *Accidental Hero; Bloody Kids; Dangerous Liaisons; Grifters, The; Gumshoe; Hit, The; Mary Reilly; Mr Jolly Lives Next Door; My Beautiful Laundrette; Prick Up Your Ears; St Ann's; Sammy and Rosie Get Laid; Snapper, The; Van, The; Walter (aka Loving Walter).*

Freed, Gregory *Virgin for Saint Tropez, A (Une Vierge pour St Tropez).*

Freedman, Jerrold *Borderline; Kansas City Bomber.*

Freeland, Thornton *Brass Monkey, The (aka Lucky Mascot); Flying Down to Rio.*

Freeman, Joan *Satisfaction; Streetwalkin'.*

Freeman, Morgan *Bopha!*

Freeman, Morgan J *Hurricane Streets.*

Fregonese, Hugo *Apache Drums; Raid, The.*

French, Harold *Encore; Major Barbara; Man Who Watched Trains Go By, The (aka Paris Express); Quartet; Trio.*

Frend, Charles *Big Blockade, The; Cruel Sea, The; Foreman Went to France, The; Johnny Frenchman; Lease of Life; Long Arm, The (aka The Third Key); San Demetrio, London; Run for Your Money, A; Scott of the Antarctic.*

Freund, Karl *Mad Love (aka The Hands of Orlac); Mummy, The.*

Freundlich, Bart *Myth of Fingerprints, The.*

Fricke, Ron *Baraka.*

Fridman, Eugen *Treasure Island (Ostrov Sokrovishch).*

Fridriksson, Fridrik Thór *Children of Nature (Börn Náttúrunnar); Devil's Island (Djöflaeyjan); Cold Fever; Movie Days (Biodagar).*

Friedberg, Rick *Spy Hard.*

Friedenberg, Richard *Adventures of Frontier Fremont, The (aka Spirit of the Wild); Bermuda Triangle, The.*

Friedgen, Bud *That's Entertainment! III.*

Friedkin, William *Birthday Party, The; Blue Chips; Brink's Job, The; Cruising; Exorcist, The; French Connection, The; Guardian, The; Jade; Sorcerer (aka Wages of Fear); To Live and Die in L.A.*

Friedman, Ed *Mighty Mouse in the Great Space Chase; Secret of the Sword, The.*

Friedman, Jeffrey *Celluloid Closet, The; Common Threads: Stories from the Quilt.*

Friedmann, Anthony *Bartleby.*

Frizzell, John *Winter Tan, A.*

Frost, Lee *Dixie Dynamite; Thing with Two Heads, The.*

Frost, Mark *Storyville.*

Fruet, William *Death Weekend (aka The House by the Lake).*

Fucci Thomas A *Don't Call Me Frankie.*

Fuest, Robert *Abominable Dr Phibes, The; And Soon the Darkness; Devil's Rain, The; Dr Phibes Rises Again; Final Programme, The (aka The Last Days of Man on Earth).*

Fujiwara, Ken *Organ.*

Fukasaku, Kinji *Virus (Fukkatsu no Hi).*

Fukuda, Jun *Ebirah – Terror of the Deep (Nankai no Daiketto); Godzilla vs the Bionic Monster (Gojira tai Mekagojira); Son of Godzilla (Gojira no Musuko); War of the Monsters (Gojira Tai Gaigan).*

Fulci, Lucio *Beyond, The (...E Tu Vivrai nel Terrore! L'Aldila); Conquest; House by the Cemetery, The (Quella Villa accanto al Cimitero); Paura nella Città dei Morti Viventi (City of the Living Dead/The Gates of Hell); White Fang (Zanna Bianca); Zombie Flesh-Eaters (Zombi 2).*

Fuller, Samuel *Big Red One, The; Crimson Kimono, The; Dead Pigeon on Beethoven Street (Kressin und die tote Taube in der Beethovenstrasse); Fixed Bayonets; Forty Guns; Hell and High Water; House of Bamboo; I Shot Jesse James; Merrill's Marauders; Naked Kiss, The; Park Row; Pickup on South Street; Run of the Arrow; Shark; Shock Corridor; Steel Helmet, The; Underworld U.S.A; Verboten!; White Dog.*

Fuller, Tex *Prey of the Chameleon.*

Fulton, Keith *Hamster Factor and Other Tales of Twelve Monkeys, The*

Fuqua, Antoine *Replacement Killer, The.*

Furie, Sidney J *Appaloosa, The (aka Southwest to Sonora); Boys in Company C, The; Doctor Blood's Coffin; Entity, The; Gable and Lombard; Hit!; Ipcress File, The; Iron Eagle; Iron Eagle II; Lady Sings the Blues; Lawyer, The; Naked Runner, The; Superman IV: The Quest for Peace; Wonderful Life.*

Furumaya, Tomoyuki *This Window Is Yours (Kono Mado wa Kimi no Mono).*

Gabel, Martin *Lost Moment, The.*

Gabizon, Savi *Lovesick on Nana Street (Hole ahava be'shikun gimel); Shuroo.*

Gábor, Pál *Angi Vera; Horizon (Horizont); Long Ride, The.*

Gabrea, Radu *Man Like Eva, A (Ein Mann wie Eva).*

Gabriel, Mike *Pocahontas; Rescuers Down Under, The.*

Gage, George *Skateboard.*

Gagliardo, Giovanna *Maternale.*

Gainsbourg, Serge *I Love You, I Don't (Je t'aime, moi non plus).*

Gallardo, Cesar *Bamboo Gods and Iron Men.*

Gallo, George *Trapped in Paradise.*

Gance, Abel *Austerlitz (aka The Battle of Austerlitz); Paradis Perdu; Capitaine Fracassé, Le; Napoléon.*

Gans, Christophe *Crying Freeman; Necronomicon (aka H.P. Lovecraft's Necronomicon).*

Gantillon, Bruno *Servante et Maîtresse.*

Garci, José Luis *To Begin Again (Volver a Empezar).*

Gardner, Robert *Clarence and Angel; Forest of Bliss.*

Gárdos, Péter *Whooping Cough (Szamárköhögés).*

Garen, Leo *Hex.*

Garfein, Jack *Strange One, The (aka End As a Man).*

Gargiulo, Maria *Year of My Japanese Cousin, The.*

Gariazzo, Mario *Last Moments (Venditore di Palloncini); Sexorcist, The (L'Ossessa).*

Garland, Patrick *Doll's House, A.*

Garmes, Lee *Angels Over Broadway.*

Garnett, Tay *Bataan; Black Knight, The; Cause for Alarm!; China Seas; Connecticut Yankee in King Arthur's Court, A (aka A Yankee in King Arthur's Court); Joy of Living; One Minute to Zero; Postman Always Rings Twice, The; Seven Sinners; Stand-In.*

Garnett, Tony *Handgun (aka Deep in the Heart); Prostitute.*

Garrett, Oliver HP *Careful, Soft Shoulder.*

Garris, Mick *Critters 2: The Main Course; Sleepwalkers.*

Gasnier, Louis *Reefer Madness.*

Gast, Leon *When We Were Kings.*

Gates, Tudor *Intimate Games.*

Gatlif, Tony *Gadjo Dilo (The Crazy Stranger); Lacho Drom; Princes, Les (The Princes).*

Gatti, Armand *Writing on the Wall, The (Nous Etions Tous des Noms d'Arbres).*

Gaup, Nils *Pathfinder (Veiviseren).*

Gavaldón, Roberto *Otra, La (The Other Sister).*

Gayor, Richard *Alternative Miss World, The.*

Gazdag, Gyula *Hungarian Fairy Tale, A (Hol Volt, Hol nem Volt); Package Tour, The (Társasutazás).*

Geller, Bruce *Harry In Your Pocket; Savage Bees, The.*

Geller, Daniel *Kids of Survival: The Art and Life of Tim Rollins & K.O.S.*

Genée, Heidi *1 + 1 = 3.*

George, George W *James Dean Story, The.*

George, Peter *Surf Nazis Must Die.*

George, Terry *Some Mother's Son.*

Gerard, Francis *Private Life, A.*

Gerber, Paul *Private Pleasures (I Lust och Nöd).*

Gerber, Paul *(as Gerhard Poulsen) Keyhole, The (Noeglehullet).*

Gerhards, Christiane *Viva Portugal.*

Gerima, Haile *Sankofa.*

Gering, Marion *Rumba.*

Germi, Pietro *Alfredo Alfredo.*

Geronimi, Clyde *Lady and the Tramp; One Hundred and One Dalmatians; Peter Pan; Sleeping Beauty.*

Ghatak, Ritwik *Cloud-capped Star (Meghe Dhaka Tara).*

Gherman, Alexei *My Friend Ivan Lapshin (Moi Drug Ivan Lapshin); Trial on the Road (Proverka na Dorogakh); Twenty Days Without War (Dvadtsat Dnei bez Voini).*

Ghose, Goutam *Doll, The (Gudia).*

Giacobetti, Francis *Emmanuelle 2.*

Gianikian, Yervant *From Pole to Equator (Dal Polo all'Equatore).*

Giannaris, Constantine *Caught Looking; North of Vortex.*

Gibbins, Duncan *Eve of Destruction; Fire with Fire.*

Gibson, Alan *Crash!; Crescendo; Dracula A.D. 1972; Satanic Rites of Dracula, The (aka Count Dracula and His Vampire Bride).*

Gibson, Angus *Mandela.*

Gordon, Michael *Pillow Talk; Secret of Convict Lake, The.*

Gordon, Robert *It Came from Beneath the Sea.*

Gordon, Steve *Arthur.*

Gordon, Stuart *Fortress; From Beyond; Pit and the Pendulum, The; Re-Animator; Space Truckers.*

Gordy, Berry *Mahogany.*

Gören, Serif *Yol.*

Goretta, Claude *Death of Mario Ricci, The (La Mort de Mario Ricci); Dentellière, La (The Lacemaker); Girl from Lorraine, A (La Provinciale). Invitation, The (L'Invitation); Roads of Exile, The (Les Chemins de l'Exil).*

Gorin, Jean-Pierre *Letter to Jane; My Crasy Life; Poto and Cabengo; Tout Va Bien; Vladimir et Rosa (Vladimir and Rosa).*

Goritsas, Sotiris *Balkanisator (Valkanisater).*

Gomley, Charles *Heavenly Pursuits.*

Gornich, Michael *Creepshow 2.*

Gorris, Marleen *Antonia's Line (Antonia); Broken Mirrors (Gebroken Spiegels); Mrs Dalloway; Question of Silence, A (De Stilte Rond Christine M).*

Goscinny, René *Lucky Luke; Twelve Tasks of Asterix, The (Les 12 Travaux d'Astérix).*

Gosha, Hideo *Four Days of Snow and Blood (226).*

Goslar, Jürgen *Death in the Sun (Der Flüsternde Tod); Slavers.*

Gosnell, Raja *Home Alone 3.*

Gothár, Péter *Time Stands Still (Megáll az Idó).*

Gottlieb, Carl *Amazon Women on the Moon.*

Gottlieb, Michael *Mannequin; Mr Nanny.*

Gough, Steve *Elenya.*

Gould, Heywood *One Good Cop; Trial by Jury.*

Goulding, Alfred *Chump at Oxford, A; Dick Barton – Special Agent.*

Goulding, Edmund *Dark Victory; Dawn Patrol, The; Everybody Does It; Grand Hotel; Great Lie, The; Nightmare Alley; Razor's Edge, The; We Are Not Alone.*

Gover, Victor M *Curse of the Wraydons, The.*

Graef, Roger *Secret*

Policeman's Ball, The.*

Graeff, Tom *Teenagers from Outer Space (aka The Gargon Terror).*

Graham, Bob *End of August, The.*

Graham, William *Police Story; Return to the Blue Lagoon; Submarine X-1.*

Granier-Deferre, Pierre *Etoile du Nord, L' (The Northern Star); Chat, Le (The Cat).*

Grant, Lee *Staying Together; Tell Me a Riddle.*

Grant, Michael *Head On (aka Fatal Attraction).*

Grasshoff, Alex *Last Dinosaur, The.*

Grau, Jorge *Living Dead at the Manchester Morgue, The (Fin de Semana para los Muertos).*

Gray, F Gary *Friday; Set It Off.*

Gray, James *Little Odessa.*

Gray, John *Glimmer Man, The.*

Gray, Lorraine *With Babies and Banners.*

Grayson, Godfrey *Adventures of PC 49, The.*

Green, Alfred E *Baby Face; Dangerous; Jolson Story, The; Sierra; They Passed This Way (aka Four Faces West).*

Green, David *Buster; Car Trouble; Firebirds (aka Wings of the Apache).*

Green, Guy *Angry Silence, The; Devil's Advocate, The (Des Teufels Advokat); Jacqueline Susann's Once Is Not Enough; Light in the Piazza; Luther; Magus, The; Patch of Blue, A; Sea of Sand; Walk in the Spring Rain, A.*

Green, Jack *Traveller.*

Green, Joseph *Yiddle with His Fiddle (Judel gra na Skrzypkach).*

Green, Walon *Hellstrom Chronicle, The.*

Greenaway, Peter *Baby of Mâcon, The; Belly of an Architect, The; Cook, the Thief, His Wife & Her Lover, The; Death in the Seine; Draughtsman's Contract, The; Drowning by Numbers; Falls, The; Pillow Book, The; Prospero's Books; TV Dante: Cantos I-VIII, A; Walk Through H, A; Zed & Two Noughts, A.*

Greene, David *Count of Monte-Cristo, The; Gray Lady Down; I Start Counting; Madame Sin; People Next Door, The; Strange Affair, The.*

Greengrass, Paul *Resurrected.*

Greenough, George *Crystal Voyager.*

Greenwald, Maggie *Ballad of Little Jo, The; Kill-Off, The.*

Greenwald, Robert *Breaking Up; Hear No Evil; Sweet Hearts Dance; Xanadu.*

Greenwalt, David *Rude Awakening; Secret Admirer.*

Gregg, Colin *Begging the Ring; Lamb; Remembrance; We Think the World of You.*

Greggio, Ezio *Silence of the Hams, The (Il silenzio dei prosciutti).*

Gregor, Manfred (Erwin C Dietrich) *Swedish Massage Parlour (Blutjunge Masseusen).*

Greif, Leslie *Keys to Tulsa.*

Grémillon, Jean *Etrange Monsieur Victor, L'; Gueule d'Amour.*

Gréville, Edmond T *Beat Girl (aka Wild for Kicks); Brief Ecstasy; Noose.*

Grewal, Shani S *Double X.*

Greyson, John *Lilies (Les Feluettes, ou La Répétition d'un drama romantique); Un©ut; Urinal; Zero Patience.*

Gries, Tom *Breakheart Pass; Breakout; Greatest. The; Helter Skelter; Lady Ice; Number One (aka Pro); Will Penny.*

Grieve, Andrew *Letters from the East; On the Black Hill.*

Griffin, Ada Gay *Litany for Survival: The Life and Work of Audre Lorde, A.*

Griffith, Charles B *Eat My Dust!*

Griffith, DW *Birth of a Nation, The; Broken Blossoms; Intolerance; Orphans of the Storm; Sally of the Sawdust; Struggle, The; Way Down East.*

Griffith, Edward H *Sky's the Limit, The.*

Griffiths, Mark *Hardbodies; Running Hot (aka Highway to Hell).*

Grigor, Murray *Big Banana Feet.*

Grigsby, Michael *Living on the Edge.*

Grimaldi, Antonello *Bits and Pieces (Il cielo è sempre più blu).*

Grimaldi, Aurelio *Whores, The (Le Buttane).*

Grimault, Paul *King and Mister Bird, The (Le Roi et l'Oiseau).*

Grimond, Philippe *Asterix and*

the Big Fight (Le Coup de Menhir).*

Grinde, Nick *Before I Hang.*

Grlic, Rajko *That Summer of White Roses.*

Grodecki, Wiktor *Mandragora.*

Grosbard Ulu *Falling in Love; Straight Time; Subject Was Roses, The; True Confessions; Who Is Harry Kellerman and Why Is He Saying Those Terrible Things About Me?*

Grosvenor, Charles *Once Upon a Forest.*

Gross, Yaacov *Yaacov Ben Dov: Father of the Hebrew Film.*

Groussot, Didier *Kamikaze.*

Grune Karl *Pagliacci (aka A Clown Must Laugh); Strasse, Die (The Street).*

Gudmundsson, Agúst *Land and Sons (Land og Symir).*

Guedes, Ann *Bearskin; Rocinante.*

Guedes, Eduardo *Bearskin; Rocinante.*

Guédiguian, Robert *Marius et Jeannette.*

Guercio, James William *Electra Glide in Blue.*

Guerin, José Luis *Train of Shadows (Tren de Sombras).*

Guerra, Ruy *Erendira; Mueda – Memory and Massacre (Mueda – Memoria e Massacre); Opera do Malandro; Sweet Hunters.*

Guerrier, Dominique *Nez au Vent, Le.*

Guest, Christopher *Attack of the 50ft Woman; Big Picture, The.*

Guest, Val *Abominable Snowman, The; Au Pair Girls; Beauty Jungle, The; Boys in Blue, The; Carry On Admiral (aka The Ship Was Loaded); Casino Royale; Confessions of a Window Cleaner; Dance Little Lady; Day the Earth Caught Fire, The; Dentist in the Chair; Diamond Mercenaries, The; Expresso Bongo; Hell Is a City; It's a Wonderful World; Mr Drake's Duck; Quatermass Experiment, The; Quatermass II; When Dinosaurs Ruled the Earth.*

Guilfoyle, Paul *Tess of the Storm Country.*

Guillermin, John *Blue Max, The; Bridge at Remagen, The; Death on the Nile; El Condor; I Was Monty's Double; King Kong; P.J. (aka New Face in Hell); Miss Robin Hood; Never Let Go; Shaft in Africa; Sheena (aka*

Sheena – Queen of the Jungle); Skyjacked; Towering Inferno, The.

Guit, Graham Shooting Stars (Le Ciel est à nous).

Guitry, Sacha Pasteur; Perles de la couronne, Les (The Pearls of the Crown).

Güney, Yilmaz Wall, The (Le Mur).

Gunn, Gilbert Valley of Song (aka Men Are Children Twice).

Gunnarsson, Sturla Diplomatic Immunity.

Guralnick, Robert Mustang... The House that Joe Built.

Gutiérrez, Chus Gypsy Soul (Alma Gitana).

Gutiérrez Alea, Tomás Death of a Bureaucrat (Muerte de un Burocrata); Guantanamera; Last Supper, The (La Ultima Cena); Memories of Underdevelopment (Memorias del Subdesarrollo); Strawberry and Chocolate (Fresa y Chocolate).

Gutiérrez Aragón, Manuel Maravillas.

Gutman, Nathaniel War Zone.

Guttfreund, André Femme Fatale.

Guzman, Patricio Battle of Chile, The (La Batalla de Chile).

Gyarmathy, Livia Escape (Szökés).

Gyles, Anna Benson Swann.

Gyllenhaal, Stephen Dangerous Woman, A; Paris Trout; Waterland.

Haas, Philip Angels and Insects; Music of Chance, The.

Hackford, Taylor Against All Odds; Bound by Honor (aka Blood In Blood Out); Devil's Advocate, The; Dolores Claiborne; Everybody's All-American (aka When I Fall in Love); Hail! Hail! Rock'n'Roll; Officer and a Gentleman, An; White Nights.

Haggard, Piers Fiendish Plot of Dr Fu Manchu, The; Satan's Skin (aka Blood on Satan's Claw). Summer Story, A; Venom.

Hagman, Larry Beware! The Blob (aka Son of Blob).

Hagmann, Stuart Believe in Me.

Hahn, Gerhard Asterix Conquers America (Asterix in Amerika).

Hahn, Steven Starchaster: The Legend of Orin.

Hai, Zafar Perfect Murder, The.

Haines, Fred Steppenwolf.

Haines, Randa Children of a Lesser God; Doctor, The; Wrestling Ernest Hemingway.

Haines, Richard W Class of Nuke 'Em High.

Halas, John Animal Farm.

Hale, William S.O.S. Titanic.

Haley Jr, Jack Love Machine, The; That's Dancing!; That's Entertainment!

Halicki, HB Gone in 60 Seconds.

Halimi, André Chantons sous l'Occupation.

Hall, Alexander Down to Earth; Here Comes Mr Jordan; I Am the Law.

Hall, Peter Akenfield; Homecoming, The; Never Talk to Strangers; Perfect Friday; She's Been Away; Three Into Two Won't Go; Work Is a Four Letter Word.

Hallam, Paul Nighthawks.

Halldorf, Jan What Are You Doing After the Orgy? (Rötmanad).

Hallek, Dee Dee Gringo in Mañanaland, A.

Haller, Daniel Buck Rogers in the 25th Century; Monster of Terror (aka Die, Monster, Die!); Pieces of Dreams; Sunshine Part II (aka My Sweet Lady).

Hallström, Lasse ABBA The Movie; Jag Är Med Barn (Father-to-Be/I'm Expecting); My Life as a Dog (Mit Liv som Hund); Once Around; Something to Talk About; Tva Killar och en Tjej (Happy We/Two Lovers and Their Lass/Two Guys and a Gal); What's Eating Gilbert Grape.

Hallum, Alister News from Nowhere.

Halperin, Victor Supernatural; White Zombie.

Hamer, Robert Dead of Night; Father Brown; It Always Rains on Sunday; Kind Hearts and Coronets; Long Memory, The; Pink String and Sealing Wax; School for Scoundrels; Spider and the Fly, The.

Hamermesh, Mira Loving the Dead.

Hamilton, David Bilitis; Cousins in Love (Tendres Cousines). Laura (Laura, les Ombres de l'Eté).

Hamilton, Guy Battle of Britain; Colditz Story, The;

Diamonds Are Forever; Evil Under the Sun; Force 10 from Navarone; Funeral in Berlin; Goldfinger; Inspector Calls, An; Live and Let Die; Manuela (aka Stowaway Girl); Man With the Golden Gun, The; Mirror Crack'd, The; Remo Williams: The Adventure Begins (aka Remo – Unarmed and Dangerous).

Hamilton, Strathford Proposition, The (Y Fargen); Set Up, The.

Hamm, Nick Martha – Meet Frank, Daniel and Laurence.

Hammer, Robert Don't Answer the Phone!.

Hammerich, Rumle Premonition, The (Svart Lucia).

Hammon, Michael Wheels & Deals.

Hammond, Peter Spring and Port Wine.

Hampton, Christopher Carrington; Secret Agent, The (aka Joseph Conrad's The Secret Agent).

Hancock, John Baby Blue Marine.

Hand, David Bambi.

Handke, Peter Left-Handed Woman, The (Die linkshändige Frau).

Haneke, Michael Benny's Video; Funny Games; 71 Fragments of a Chronology of Chance (71 Fragmente einer Chronologie des Zufalls).

Haney, John Manganinnie.

Hanig, Josh Men's Lives.

Hanks, Tom That Thing You Do!

Hanna, William Jetsons: The Movie.

Hannam, Ken Dawn!; Robbery Under Arms; Summerfield; Sunday Too Far Away.

Hänsel, Marion Dust; Maestro, Il (The Maestro/Double Game/Conductor).

Hanson, Curtis Bad Influence; Bedroom Window, The; Hand That Rocks the Cradle, The; LA Confidential; Losin' It; River Wild, The; Sweet Kill (aka The Arousers).

Hanson, John Northern Lights.

Hara, Kazuo Emperor's Naked Army Marches On, The (Yuki Yukite Shingun).

Harada, Masato Gunhed; Kamikaze Taxi; Leaving (Bounce – Ko Gals); Painted Desert.

Harbutt, Sandy Stone.

Hardy, Joseph Great Expectations.

Hardy, Justin Feast at Midnight, A.

Hardy, Robin Fantasist, The; Wicker Man, The.

Hare, David Designated Mourner, The; Paris by Night; Strapless; Wetherby.

Harel, Philippe Femme Défendue, La (The Forbidden Woman).

Harkin, Margo Hush-a-Bye Baby.

Harlin, Renny Adventures of Ford Fairlane, The; Cliffhanger; CutThroat Island; Die Hard 2; Long Kiss Goodnight, The; Nightmare on Elm Street, 4: The Dream Master, A; Prison.

Harling, Robert Evening Star, The.

Harmon, Robert Gotti; Hitcher, The; Nowhere to Run.

Harries, Andy Lenny Live and Unleashed.

Harrington, Curtis Mata Hari; Ruby; What's the Matter with Helen?.

Harris, Damian Deceived; Rachel Papers, The.

Harris, Frank Killpoint.

Harris, James B Bedford Incident, The; Boiling Point; Cop; Fast-Walking; Some Call It Loving.

Harris, Leslie Just Another Girl on the I.R.T.

Harris, Richard Bloomfield (aka The Hero).

Harris Jr, Wendell B Chameleon Street.

Harrison, John Beautiful Dreamers; Tales from the Darkside: The Movie.

Harrison, Matthew Kicked in the Head; Rhythm Thief.

Harron, Mary I Shot Andy Warhol.

Hart, Harvey Bus Riley's Back in Town; Fortune and Men's Eyes.

Hartford-Davis, Robert Black Gunn; Black Torment, The; Nobody Ordered Love; Take, The.

Hartl, Karl No Answer from F.P.1 (F.P.1 antwortet nicht).

Hartley, Hal Amateur; Flirt; Henry Fool; Simple Men; Surviving Desire; Trust; Unbelievable Truth, The.

Hartman, Rivka Miniskirted Dynamo, The.

Hatta, Kayo Picture Bride.

Harvey, Anthony *Abdication, The; Dutchman; Eagle's Wing; Grace Quigley; Lion in Winter, The; Players; They Might Be Giants.*

Harvey, Herk *Carnival of Souls.*

Harvey, Joan *America – From Hitler to M-X.*

Has, Wojciech *Doll, The (Lalka); Saragossa Manuscript, The (Rekopis Znaleziony w Saragossie).*

Hashiguchi, Ryosuke *Like Grains of Sand (Nagisa no Sindbad).*

Hashimoto, Kohji *Godzilla 1985 (Gojira).*

Haskin, Byron *Conquest of Space; Naked Jungle, The; Power, The; Robinson Crusoe on Mars; Rookery Nook; War of the Worlds.*

Hata, Masanori *Adventures of Milo and Otis, The (Koneko Monogatari).*

Hathaway, Henry *Brigham Young – Frontiersman; Call Northside 777; Dark Corner, The; Desert Fox, The (aka Rommel – Desert Fox); Diplomatic Courier; 5 Card Stud; Fourteen Hours; From Hell to Texas; Hangup; Home in Indiana; House on 92nd Street, The; How the West Was Won; Kiss of Death; Legend of the Lost; Niagara; O. Henry's Full House (aka Full House); North to Alaska; Peter Ibbetson; Rawhide (aka Desperate Siege); Real Glory, The; True Grit; Woman Obsessed.*

Hatton, Maurice *American Roulette; Long Shot; Nelly's Version; Praise Marx and Pass the Ammunition.*

Hauff, Reinhard *Knife in the Head (Messer im Kopf); Main Actor, The (Der Hauptdarsteller); Slow Attack (Endstation Freiheit); Stammheim.*

Hawks, Howard *Air Force; Ball of Fire; Barbary Coast; Big Sky, The; Big Sleep, The; Bringing Up Baby; Ceiling Zero; Come and Get It; Criminal Code, The; Dawn Patrol, The; El Dorado; Gentlemen Prefer Blondes; Girl in Every Port, A; Hatari!; His Girl Friday; I Was a Male War Bride (aka You Can't Sleep Here); Land of the Pharaohs; Man's Favourite Sport?; Monkey Business; O. Henry's Full House (aka Full House); Only Angels Have Wings; Red Line 7000; Red River; Rio Bravo; Rio Lobo; Road to Glory, The; Scarface; Sergeant York; Song Is Born, A; Tiger Shark; To Have and Have Not; Twentieth Century.*

Hay, John *Steal, The.*

Hay, Will *Black Sheep of*

Whitehall, The; *My Learned Friend.*

Hayashi, Kaizo *Circus Boys (Nijusseiki Shonen Dokuhon); Most Terrible Time in My Life, The (Waga Jinsei Saiaku no Toki); To Sleep, So As to Dream.*

Hayden, Tom *Vietnam Journey.*

Haydn, Richard *Mr Music.*

Hayers, Sidney *Circus of Horrors; Conquest of the Earth; Deadly Strangers; Diagnosis: Murder; Night of the Eagle (aka Burn, Witch, Burn!); Payroll; Revenge (aka Inn of the Frightened People); What Changed Charley Farthing?.*

Hayes, John *Mama's Dirty Girls.*

Hayman, David *Hawk, The; Near Room, The; Silent Scream.*

Haynes, Todd *Poison; Safe; Superstar: The Karen Carpenter Story; Velvet Goldmine.*

Hazan, Jack *Bigger Splash, A; Rude Boy.*

He Jianjun *Postman (Youchai).*

He Ping *Red Firecracker, Green Firecracker (Paoda Shuang Deng); Sun Valley (Riguang Xiagu); Swordsman in Double-Flag Town, The (Shuang Qi Zhen Dao Ke).*

He Yi *Red Beads (Xuan Lian).*

Head, John *Jimi Hendrix.*

Heap, Jonathan *Benefit of the Doubt.*

Hebendanz, Johannes *Flickering Roads (Asphaltflimmern).*

Hecht, Ben *Angels Over Broadway; Specter of the Rose.*

Hecht, Dina *Broken Arrow 29.*

Heckerling, Amy *Clueless; Fast Times at Ridgemont High (aka Fast Times); Johnny Dangerously; Look Who's Talking; Look Who's Talking Too.*

Hedden, Roy *Friday the 13th Part VIII: Jason Takes Manhattan.*

Heerman, Victor *Animal Crackers.*

Heffron, Richard T *Fillmore; Futureworld; I, the Jury; Newman's Law; Outlaw Blues; Trackdown.*

Hegedus, Chris *Town Bloody Hall; War Room, The.*

Heifits, Josif *Lady With the Little Dog, The (Dama s Sobachkoi).*

Heinrich, Margarete *Totschweigen (A Wall of Silence).*

Heisler, Stuart *Along Came Jones; Among the Living; Blue Skies; Burning Hills, The; Dallas; Glass Key, The; I Died a Thousand Times; Monster and the Girl, The; Smash-Up, The Story of a Woman; Star, The.*

Hellman, Monte *Back Door to Hell; Beast from Haunted Cave; China 9, Liberty 37; Cockfighter; Ride in the Whirlwind; Shooting, The; Two-Lane Blacktop.*

Hellman, Oliver (Sonia Assonitis) *Tentacles (Tentacoli); Chi Sei? (Beyond the Door/ Devil Within Her).*

Helpern Jr, David *Hollywood on Trial.*

Helpmann, Robert *Don Quixote.*

Hemmings, David *Just a Gigolo (Schöner Gigolo – Armer Gigolo); Race for the Yankee Zephyr; Running Scared.*

Henabery, Joseph *Cobra, The.*

Henderson, Anne *Song for Tibet.*

Henderson, John *Bring Me the Head of Mavis Davis; Loch Ness.*

Hendrickson, Robert *Manson.*

Henenlotter, Frank *Basket Case; Basket Case 2; Brain Damage; Frankenhooker.*

Henkel, Peter *Three Bullets for a Long Gun.*

Henreid, Paul *Ballad in Blue (aka Blues for Lovers).*

Henry, Buck *Heaven Can Wait.*

Henson, Brian *Muppet Christmas Carol, The; Muppet Treasure Island.*

Henson, Jim *Dark Crystal, The; Great Muppet Caper, The; Labyrinth.*

Henzell, Perry *Harder They Come, The.*

Herbst, Helmut *John Heartfield: Photomonteur.*

Herek, Stephen *Bill and Ted's Excellent Adventure; Critters; Don't Tell Mom the Babysitter's Dead; Mighty Ducks, The (aka Champions); Mr Holland's Opus; 101 Dalmatians; Three Musketeers, The.*

Herman, Mark *Blame It on the Bellboy; Brassed Off.*

Hermosillo, Jaime Humberto *Doña Herlinda and Her Son (Doña Herlinda y su Hijo); Homework (La Tarea).*

Hernádi, Tibor *Felix the Cat: The Movie.*

Héroux, Denis *Uncanny, The.*

Herralde, Gonzalo *Race, the Spirit of Franco (Raza, el Espíritu de Franco).*

Herrendoerfer, Christian *Hitler – a Career (Hitler eine Karriere).*

Herrero, Gerardo *Desvio al Paraíso (Shortcut to Paradise); Malena Is a Name from a Tango (Malena es un Nombre de Tango).*

Herrington, Rowdy *Gladiator; Road House; Striking Distance.*

Hershman, Joel *Hold Me, Thrill Me, Kiss Me.*

Herskovitz, Marshall *Jack the Bear.*

Herz, Juraj *Cremator, The (Spalovac Mrtvol).*

Herz, Michael *Toxic Avenger, The; Toxic Avenger Part II, The; War (aka Troma's War).*

Herzfeld, John *2 Days in the Valley; Two of a Kind.*

Herzog, Werner *Aguirre, Wrath of God (Aguirre, der Zorn Gottes); Cobra Verde; Even Dwarfs Started Small (Auch Zwerge haben klein angefangen); Fata Morgana; Fitzcarraldo; Great Ecstasy of Woodcarver Steiner, The (Die Grosse Ekstase des Bildschnitzers Steiner); Heart of Glass (Herz aus Glas); Jeder für sich und Gott gegen alle (The Enigma of Kaspar Hauser/Every Man for Himself and God Against All/The Mystery of Kaspar Hauser); Land of Silence and Darkness (Land des Schweigens und der Dunkelheit); Lessons in Darkness (Lektionen in Finsternis); Nosferatu the Vampyre (Nosferatu: Phantom der Nacht); Signs of Life (Lebenszeichen); Soufrière, La; Stroszek; Where the Green Ants Dream (Wo die grünen Ameisen träumen); Woyzeck.*

Hess, John *Watchers.*

Hessler, Gordon *Cry of the Banshee; Murders in the Rue Morgue; Oblong Box, The; Scream and Scream Again.*

Heston, Charlton *Antony and Cleopatra.*

Heston, Fraser C *Needful Things; Treasure Island.*

Hewitt, Peter *Bill and Ted's Bogus Journey; Borrowers, The.*

Hexter, Russ *Dadetown.*

Heynemann, Laurent *Old Lady Who Walked in the Sea, The (La Vieille qui Marchait dans la Mer).*

Heynowski, Walter *I Was, I Am, I Shall Be (Ich war, ich bin, ich werde sein)*.

Hickenlooper, George *Hearts of Darkness: A Filmmaker's Apocalypse; Killing Box, The; Persons Unknown*.

Hickey, Kieran *Attracta; Exposure*.

Hickox, Anthony *Hellraiser III: Hell on Earth; Prince Valiant (Prinz Eisenherz); Sundown; Waxwork*.

Hickox, Douglas *Brannigan; Entertaining Mr Sloane; Sky Riders; Theatre of Blood; Zulu Dawn*.

Hicks, Scott *Shine*.

Higashi, Yoichi *Village of Dreams (E no Naka no Boku no Mura)*.

Higgins, Colin *Best Little Whorehouse in Texas, The; Foul Play; Nine to Five*.

Higson, Patrick *Big Banana Feet*.

Hill, Claudio Guerin *Campana del Infierno, La (The Bell of Hell/The Bell from Hell)*.

Hill, George Roy *Butch Cassidy and the Sundance Kid; Great Waldo Pepper, The; Hawaii; Little Drummer Girl, The; Little Romance, A; Period of Adjustment; Slap Shot; Slaughterhouse-Five; Sting The; Thoroughly Modern Millie; World According to Garp, The*.

Hill, Jack *Coffy; Foxy Brown*.

Hill, James *Belstone Fox, The; Captain Nemo and the Underwater City; Kitchen, The; Study in Terror, A*.

Hill, Walter *Another 48 HRS; Brewster's Millions; Crossroads; Driver, The; Extreme Prejudice; Geronimo: An American Legend; 48 HRS; Hard Times (aka The Streetfighter); Johnny Handsome; Last Man Standing; Long Riders, The; Red Heat; Southern Comfort; Streets of Fire; Trespass; Warriors, The; Wild Bill*.

Hillcoat, John *Ghosts...of the Civil Dead*.

Hiller, Arthur *Americanization of Emily, The; Author! Author!; Babe, The; Filofax; Hospital, The; In-Laws, The; Love Story; Making Love; Man in the Glass Booth, The; Nightwing; Out-of-Towners, The; Outrageous Fortune; Plaza Suite; Promise Her Anything; See No Evil, Hear No Evil; Silver Streak; Teachers; W.C. Fields and Me*.

Hills, Paul *Boston Kickout*.

Hillyer, Lambert *Dracula's Daughter; Invisible Ray, The*.

Hiroki, Ryuichi *Sadistic City (Ma-o Gai)*.

Hitchcock, Alfred *Aventure Malgache; Birds, The; Blackmail; Bon Voyage; Champagne; Dial M for Murder; Easy Virtue; Elstree Calling; Family Plot; Farmer's Wife, The; Foreign Correspondent; Frenzy; I Confess; Jamaica Inn; Lady Vanishes, The; Lifeboat; Lodger, The; Man Who Knew Too Much, The (1934); Man Who Knew Too Much, The (1956); Manxman, The; Marnie; Mr and Mrs Smith; Murder; North by Northwest; Notorious; Number Seventeen; Paradine Case, The; Psycho; Rear Window; Rebecca; Rich and Strange; Ring, The; Rope; Sabotage; Saboteur; Secret Agent, The; Shadow of a Doubt; Spellbound; Stage Fright; Strangers on a Train; Suspicion; 39 Steps, The; To Catch a Thief; Topaz; Torn Curtain; Trouble with Harry, The; Under Capricorn; Vertigo; Wrong Man, The; Young and Innocent*.

Ho Menghua *Death Kick (Huang Feihong/aka The Master of Kung Fu)*.

Ho Ping *Wolves Cry Under the Moon (Guo Dao Feng Bi)*.

Hobbs, John B *La Passione*.

Hobby, Amy *At Sundance*.

Hoblit, Gregory *Fallen; Primal Fear*.

Hodges, Mike *Black Rainbow; Flash Gordon; Get Carter; Morons from Outer Space; Prayer for the Dying, A; Pulp; Terminal Man, The*.

Hoessli, Andreas *¡Devils Don't Dream! Research on Jacobo Arbenz Guzmán (¡Devils don't dream! Nachforschungen über Jacobo Arbenz Guzmán)*.

Hofbauer, Ernst *Confessions of a Sixth Form Girl (Schulmädchen Report – Was Eltern nicht für möglich halten); Enter the 7 Virgins (Yang Ji/aka Virgins of the Seven Seas)*.

Hoffman, Jerzy *Deluge, The (Potop)*.

Hoffman, Michael *One Fine Day; Privileged; Promised Land; Restless Natives; Restoration; Soapdish; Some Girls (aka Sisters)*.

Hoffs, Tamar Simon *Allnighter, The*.

Hofmann, Nico *Sandman, The (Der Sandmann)*.

Hogan, David *Barb Wire; Most Wanted*.

Hogan, James *Bulldog Drummond Escapes; Last Train from Madrid, The*.

Hogan, PJ *Muriel's Wedding; My Best Friend's Wedding*.

Holcomb, Rod *Donato and Daughter*.

Holden, Lansing C *She*.

Holdt, Jacob *American Pictures (Amerikanske Billeder)*.

Holland, Agnieszka *Europa, Europa; Olivier Olivier; Secret Garden, The; To Kill a Priest; Total Eclipse; Washington Square; Woman on Her Own, A (Kobieta Samotna)*.

Holland, John *Night in Havana: Dizzy Gillespie in Cuba, A*.

Holland, Tom *Child's Play; Fatal Beauty; Fright Night; Stephen King's Thinner*.

Hollander, Eli *Out*.

Holleb, Allan *Candy Stripe Nurses*.

Holloway, Graham *Chasing the Deer*.

Holmes, Ben *Saint in New York, The*.

Holofcener, Nicole *Walking and Talking*.

Holst, Marius *Cross My Heart and Hope to Die (Ti Kniver I Hjertet)*.

Holt, Seth *Blood from the Mummy's Tomb; Danger Route; Nanny, The; Station Six – Sahara; Taste of Fear (aka Scream of Fear)*.

Holzman, Allan *Forbidden World (aka Mutant)*.

Honda, Inoshiro *Destroy All Monsters (Kaiju Soshingeki); Mysterians, The (Chikyu Boeigun)*.

Hondo, Med *Lumière Noire; Sarraounia*.

Hong, Elliott *They Call Me Bruce*.

Hong Sang-Soo *Day a Pig Fell into the Well, The; Power of Kangwon Province, The (Kangwon-do ui Him)*.

Honigmann, Heddy *Au Revoir (Tot Ziens); O Amor Natural*.

Honkasalo, Pirjo *Flame Top (Tulipää)*.

Hook, Harry *Kitchen Toto, The; Last of His Tribe, The; Lord of the Flies*.

Hooker, Ted *Crucible of Terror*.

Hooks, Kevin *Fled; Passenger 57*.

Hooper, Tobe *Body Bags; Death Trap (aka Eaten Alive); Funhouse, The;*

Invaders from Mars; Lifeforce; Mangler, The; Poltergeist; Salem's Lot; Texas Chain Saw Massacre, The; Texas Chainsaw Massacre 2, The*.

Hopkins, Anthony *August*.

Hopkins, Stephen *Blown Away; Ghost and the Darkness, The; Nightmare on Elm Street 5: The Dream Child, A; Predator 2*.

Hopper, Dennis *Chasers; Colors; Easy Rider; Hot Spot, The; Last Movie, The; Out of the Blue*.

Hopper, Dennis (as Alan Smithee) *Catchfire*.

Hopper, Jerry *Madron*.

Hornaday, Jeffrey *Shout*.

Horne, James W *Bonnie Scotland; College; Way Out West*.

Horner Harry *Beware, My Lovely; Red Planet Mars*.

Horton, Peter *Amazon Women on the Moon; Cure, The*.

Horvat, Aleks *Sweethearts*.

Hoskins, Bob *Raggedy Rawney, The; Rainbow*.

Hou Jing *Kung Fu – Girl Fighter (Can Nü Kongshoudao/aka Karate King – On the Waterfront)*.

Hou Xiaoxian (Hou Hsiao-Hsien) *City of Sadness, A (Beiqing Chengshi); Daughter of the Nile (Niluohe Nüer); Dust in the Wind (Lian Lian Feng Chen); Flowers of Shanghai (Hai Shang Hua); Goodbye South, Goodbye (Nanguo Zai Jian, Nanguo); Good Men, Good Women (Haonan Haonü); Puppetmaster, The (Ximeng Rensheng); Summer at Grandpa's, A (Dongdong de Jiaqi); Time to Live and the Time to Die, The (Tongnian Wangshi)*.

Hough, John *Biggles; Brass Target; Dirty Mary, Crazy Larry; Escape to Witch Mountain; Eyewitness; Incubus; Legend of Hell House, The; Return from Witch Mountain; Something to Believe In; Triumphs of a Man Called Horse (El Triunfo de un Hombre Llamado Caballo); Twins of Evil; Watcher in the Woods, The*.

Hough, Johnny *Wolfshead: The Legend of Robin Hood*.

Houston, Bobby *Trust Me*.

Hovde, Ellen *Grey Gardens*.

Howard, Cy *Every Little Crook and Nanny*.

Howard, Leslie *First of the Few*

(aka Spitfire); Gentle Sex,
The; Pimpernel Smith;
Pygmalion.

Howard, Ron Apollo 13;
Backdraft; Cocoon; Far and
Away; Grand Theft Auto;
Gung Ho; Night Shift; Paper,
The; Parenthood; Ransom;
Splash; Willow.

Howard, William K Fire Over
England; Power and the
Glory, The; Squeaker, The.

Howe, JA Kid Brother, The.

Howitt, Peter Sliding Doors.

Hsu Hsiao-Ming Heartbreak
Island (Qunian Dongtian)

Hu Binliu Live in Peace.

Huang Feng Hap-Ki-Do
(Heqidao); Stoner (Tiejin
Gang Da Po Zi Yang Guan)

Huang, George Swimming with
Sharks.

Huang Jianxin Back to Back,
Face to Face; Black Cannon
Incident, The (Heipao
Shijan); Signal Left, Turn
Right (Da Zuo Deng, Xiang
You Zhuan); Stand Up,
Don't Grovel! (Zhanzhiluo,
Bie Paxia!); Surveillance
(Maifu); Wooden Man's
Bride, The (Yan Shen).

Huang Jianzhong Girl of Good
Family, A (Liangjia funü).

Huang Ming-Chuan Bodo
(Baodao Dameng); Man
from Island West, The (Xibu
Lai de Ren).

Hubert Jean-Loup Grand
Chemin, Le.

Hudlin, Reginald Boomerang;
Great White Hype, The;
House Party.

Hudson, Hugh Chariot of Fire;
Greystoke – The Legend of
Tarzan Lord of the Apes;
Lost Angels (aka The Road
Home); Revolution.

Huestis, Marc Sex Is...

Hughes, Albert Dead
Presidents; Menace II
Society.

Hughes, Allen Dead Presidents;
Menace II Society.

Hughes, Bronwen Harriet the
Spy.

Hughes, Carol Missing Link.

Hughes, David Missing Link.

Hughes, Howard Hell's Angels;
Outlaw, The.

Hughes, Ken Brain Machine,
The.

Hughes, John Breakfast Club,
The; Curly Sue; Ferris
Bueller's Day Off; Planes,
Trains and Automobiles;
She's Having a Baby; Sixteen
Candles; Uncle Buck; Weird

Science; What Have I
Written.

Hughes, Ken Alfie Darling;
Casino Royale; Chitty Chitty
Bang Bang; Cromwell;
Internecine Project, The; Joe
Macbeth; Timeslip (aka The
Atomic Man); Trials of
Oscar Wilde, The (aka The
Man With the Green
Carnation).

Hughes, Robert C Hunter's
Blood.

Hughes, Terry Butcher's Wife,
The.

Hui, Ann Ah Kam (A-Jin/aka
The Stuntwoman); Love in a
Fallen City (Qingcheng zhi
Lian); Romance of Book &
Sword, The (Shujian Enchou
Lu); Secret, The (Fengjie);
Song of the Exile (Ketu Qiu
Hen); Spooky Bunch, The
(Zhuang Dao Zheng); Story of
Woo Viet, The (Hu Yue de
Gushi); Summer Snow
(Nüren Sishi).

Huillet, Danièle Class Relations
(Klassenverhältnisse);
Fortini/Cani; From the Cloud
to the Resistance (Nube alla
Resistenza); History Lessons
(Geschichtsunterricht);
Moses and Aaron (Moses
und Aron); Othon (Les Yeux
ne peuvent pas en tout temps
se fermer).

Hulbert, Jack Elstree Calling;
Falling For You.

Hull, Norman Ladder of
Swords.

Hultberg, Ulf Daughter of the
Puma, The.

Humberstone, H Bruce Charlie
Chan at the Opera; Desert
Song, The; Hello, Frisco,
Hello; Iceland (aka Katina);
If I Had a Million; I Wake
Up Screaming (aka Hot
Spot); Pin Up Girl; Sun
Valley Serenade; Wonder
Man.

Hume, Kenneth I've Gotta
Horse.

Humfress, Paul Sebastiane.

Hung, Samo Moon Warriors
(Zhan Shen Chuanshuo);
Wheels on Meals (Kuai-can
Che).

Hunsinger, Tom Boyfriends.

Hunt, Claire Good Wife of
Tokyo, The.

Hunt, Maurice Pagemaster,
The.

Hunt, Paul 40 Graves for 40
Guns (aka The Great
Gundown).

Hunt, Peter Assassination;
Gold; Gulliver's Travels; On
Her Majesty's Secret Service;
1776; Shout at the Devil;
Wild Geese II.

Hunter, Neil Boyfriends.

Hunter, T Hayes Ghoul, The.

Hunter, Tim River's Edge;
Saint of Fort Washington,
The.

Huntington, Lawrence
Franchise Affair, The.

Hur Jin-Ho Christmas in
August (Pal-Wol ui
Christmas).

Huraux, Marc Bird Now.

Hurran, Nick Remember Me?

Hurst, Brian Desmond Black
Tent; Dangerous Moonlight;
Hungry Hill; Simba.

Hussein, Waris Henry VIII and
His Six Wives; Possession of
Joel Delaney, The; Sixth
Happiness, The.

Huston, Danny Mr North.

Huston, John Across the
Pacific; African Queen, The;
Annie; Asphalt Jungle, The;
Beat the Devil; Bible...In the
Beginning, The (La Bibbia);
Casino Royale; Dead, The;
Fat City; Freud; Heaven
Knows, Mr Allison; In This
Our Life; Key Largo;
Kremlin Letter, The; Life
and Times of Judge Roy
Bean, The; List of Adrian
Messenger, The; Mackintosh
Man, The; Maltese Falcon,
The; Man Who Would Be
King, The; Misfits, The;
Moby Dick; Moulin Rouge;
Night of the Iguana, The;
Prizzi's Honor; Red Badge of
Courage, The; Reflections in
a Golden Eye; Sinful Davey;
Treasure of the Sierra
Madre, The; Under the
Volcano; Unforgiven, The;
Victory (aka Escape to
Victory); Walk with Love
and Death, A; Wise Blood.

Hutt, David Nearly Wide
Awake.

Hutt, Robyn Voices from the
Front.

Hutton, Brian G First Deadly
Sin, The; High Road to
China; Kelly's Heroes; Night
Watch; Where Eagles Dare;
Zee & Co (aka X, Y and Zee).

Huyck, Willard Best Defence;
Howard the Duck(aka
Howard...a new breed of
hero).

Hyams, Peter Busting;
Capricorn One; Hanover
Street; Narrow Margin;
Outland; Peeper; Presidio,
The; Relic, The; Running
Scared; Star Chamber, The;
Stay Tuned; Sudden Death;
Timecop; 2010.

Hylkema, Hans Last Date (De
Laatste Sessie).

Hytner, Nicholas Crucible, The;
Madness of King George,
The.

Ibáñez Serrador, Narciso
¿Quién Puede Matar a un

Niño? (Death Is Child's
Play/Island of the
Damned/Would You Kill a
Child?).

Ichaso, Leon Crossover
Dreams; Sugar Dreams.

Ichikawa, Jun Tokyo Kyodai.

Ichikawa, Kon Actor's
Revenge, An (Yukinojo
Henge); Alone on the Pacific
(Taiheiyo Hitoribotchi);
Burmese Harp, The (Biruma
no Tategoto); Tokyo
Olympiad 1964; Visions of
Eight.

Idemoto, Michael Sunsets.

Ihnat, Steve Honkers, The.

Ikoli, Tunde Tunde's Film.

Ilhan, Biket Man in the Street,
The (Sokaktaki Adam).

Imai, Tadashi Brother and
Sister (Ani Imoto/aka Mon
and Ino).

Imamura, Shohei Ballad of
Narayama, The (Narayama
Bushi-ko); Black Rain (Kuroi
Ame); Eel, the (Unagi);
Eijanaika; History of Post-
War Japan as Told by a Bar
Hostess (Nippon Sengo Shi:
Madamu Omboro no
Seikatsu).

Im Kwon-Taek Come, Come,
Come Upward (Aje Aje
Bara-Aje); Festival (Chukje);
Gilsodum; Mandala;
Sopyonje (Seo-Pyon-Jae);
Surrogate Mother (Sibaji);
Taebaek Mountains, The
(Taebaek Sanmaek); Ticket.

Incalcaterra, Daniele
Repubblica Nostra (Our
Republic).

Infascelli, Fiorella Mask, The
(La Maschera).

Ingram, Rex Magician, The.

Ingster, Boris Stranger on the
Third Floor, The.

Iosseliani, Otar Brigands;
Favourites of the Moon (Les
Favoris de la Lune);
Pastorale.

Irmas, Matthew Edie & Pen.

Irvin, John Champions; City of
Industry; Dogs of War,
The; Ghost Story;
Hamburger Hill. Month by
the Lake; Next of Kin; Raw
Deal; Robin Hood; Turtle
Diary; Widows' Peak.

Irving, Judy Dark Circle.

Irving, Stanley Forget-Me-Not
(aka Forever Yours).

Isaka, Satoshi [Focus].

Isasi, Antonio They Came to
Rob Las Vegas.

Ishii, Sogo Angel Dust; August
in the Water (Mizu no Naka
no Hachigatsu); Crazy

Jones, F Richard *Bulldog Drummond.*

Jones, Harmon *Pride of St Louis, The.*

Jones, LQ *Boy and His Dog, A.*

Jones, Michael *My Little Pony.*

Jones, Terry *Erik the Viking; Monty Python and the Holy Grail; Monty Python's Life of Brian; Monty Python's The Meaning of Life; Personal Services; Wind in the Willows, The.*

Jongbloed, Marijke *Fatal Reaction: Singapore.*

Jordá, Joaquín *Body in the Forest, A (Cuerpo en el Bosque).*

Jordan, Glenn *Only When I Laugh (aka It Hurts Only When I Laugh).*

Jordan, Neil *Angel; Butcher Boy, The; Company of Wolves, The; Crying Game, The; High Spirits; Interview With the Vampire; Michael Collins; Miracle, The; Mona Lisa; We're No Angels.*

Josephson, Erland *One and One (En och En).*

Jost, Jon *Angel City; Last Chants for a Slow Dance; Slow Moves; Sure Fire; Uncommon Senses.*

Jouffa, François *Bonzesse, La.*

Jourdain, Pierre *I Am a Dancer (Un Danseur: Rudolph Nureyev).*

Joyce, Paul *Motion and Emotion: The Films of Wim Wenders.*

Judge, Mike *Beavis and Butt-head Do America.*

Julian, Rupert *Merry-Go-Round; Phantom of the Opera, The.*

Julien, Isaac *Frantz Fanon: Black Skin, White Mask; Looking for Langston; Passion of Remembrance, The; Young Soul Rebels.*

July, Serge *Viva Portugal.*

Jurácek, Pavel *Joseph Kilián (Postava k Podpírání).*

Juran, Nathan *Attack of the 50 Foot Woman; Hellcats of the Navy; Jack the Giant Killer; Seventh Voyage of Sinbad, The; 20 Million Miles to Earth.*

Justiniano, Gonzalo *Amnesia; Caluga o Menta.*

Jutra, Claude *Mon Oncle Antoine (My Uncle Antoine).*

Kachivas, Lou *Mighty Mouse in the Great Space Chase; Secret of the Sword, The.*

Kachyna, Karel *Ear, The*

(Ucho); I'm Jumping Over Puddles Again (Uz zase Skácu pres Kaluze).*

Kaczender, George *Agency (aka Mind Games); Chanel Solitaire; In Praise of Older Women.*

Kadár, Ján *Adrift (Hrst Piná Vody); Angel Levine, The; Freedom road; Lies My Father Told Me.*

Kagan, Jeremy Paul *Big Fix, The; By the Sword; Chosen, The; Heroes; Journey of Natty Gann, The; Sting II, The.*

Kahn, Cedric *Trop de Bonheur (Too Much Happiness).*

Kaiserman, Connie *My Little Girl.*

Kal Ng *Soul Investigator, The.*

Kalik, Mikhail *Goodbye, Boys (Do Svidanija, Maltsjiki).*

Kalin, Tom *Swoon.*

Kalvert, Scott *Basketball Diaries, The.*

Kam Kwok-Leung *4 Faces of Eve (4 [Si] Mian Xiawa).*

Kampmann, Steven *Stealing Home.*

Kane, Joseph *Hoodlum Empire.*

Kaneko, Shusuke *Summer Vacation 1999 (Sen-Kyuhayaku-Kyuju-Kyu-Nen no Natsu Yasumi).*

Kaneko, Shu *Necromicon (aka H.P. Lovecraft's Necronomicon).*

Kanevsky, Vitaly *Don't Move, Die and Rise Again! (Zamri, Umri, Voskresni!).*

Kanew, Jeff *Revenge of the Nerds; Tough Guys; V.I. Warshawski.*

Kanievska, Marek *Another Country.*

Kanin, Garson *Bachelor Mother; Great Man Votes, The; My Favourite Wife; They Knew What They Wanted; True Glory, The.*

Kanner, Alexis *Kings and Desperate Men.*

Kanter, Hal *I Married a Woman.*

Kaplan, Jo Ann *Invocation Maya Deren.*

Kaplan, Jonathan *Accused, The; Bad Girls; Heart Like a Wheel; Mr Billion; Over the Edge; Love Field; Project X; Student Teachers, The; Unlawful Entry; White Line Fever.*

Kaplan, Mike *Luck, Trust & Ketchup: Robert Altman in Carver Country.*

Kaplan, Nelly *Charles and

Lucie (Charles et Lucie); Fiancée du Pirate, La (Dirty Mary/A Very Curious Girl); Néa (A Young Emmanuelle); Papa, les Petits Bateaux...*

Kapur, Shekhar *Bandit Queen.*

Karanovic, Srdjan *Virgin (Virgina).*

Karbelnikoff, Michael *F.T.W.; Mobsters (aka Mobsters – The Evil Empire).*

Karel, Russ *Almonds and Raisins.*

Kargl, Gerald *Schizophrenia (aka Angst).*

Karlin, Mark *'33 to '77.*

Karlson, Phil *Ben; Down Memory Lane; Framed; Kid Galahad; Ladies of the Chorus; Phenix City Story, The; Rampage; Walking Tall.*

Karmitz, Marin *Coup pour Coup (Blow for Blow).*

Karson, Eric *Black Eagle.*

Karya, Teguh *Mementos (Doea Tanda Mata); November 1828.*

Karypides, Georges *Dead Liqueur.*

Kasdan, Lawrence *Accidental Tourist, The; Big Chill, The; Body Heat; French Kiss; Grand Canyon; I Love You to Death; Silverado; Wyatt Earp.*

Kassovitz, Mathieu *Assassin(s); Haine, La (Hate); Métisse (Cafe au Lait/Blended).*

Kastle, Leonard *Honeymoon Killers, The.*

Kaszubowski, Jerzy *Road Home, The.*

Katakouzinos, Yorgos *Angelos.*

Kato, Akira *Emanuelle in Tokyo (Tokyo Emmanuelle Fujin).*

Katselas, Milton *Butterflies Are Free; Report to the Commissioner (aka Operation Undercover).*

Katzin, Lee H *Le Mans; What Ever Happened to Aunt Alice?*

Kavur, Omer *Secret Face, The (Gizli Yuz).*

Kaufman, George S *Senator Was Indiscreet, The.*

Kaufman, Lloyd *Toxic Avenger Part II, The; Tromeo & Juliet.*

Kaufman, Philip *Great Northfield Minnesota Raid, The; Henry & June; Invasion of the Body Snatchers; Right Stuff, The; Rising Sun; Unbearable Lightness Being, The; Wanderers, The; White Dawn, The.*

Kaurismäki, Aki *Ariel; Crime and Punishment (Rikos ja Rangaistus); Drifting Clouds (Kauas Pilvet Karkaavat/Au loin s'en vont les nuages); Hamlet Goes Business (Hamlet Liikemaailmassa); I Hired a Contract Killer; Leningrad Cowboys Go America; Match Factory Girl, The (Tulitikkutehtaan Tytto); Take Care of Your Scarf, Tatjana (Pida Huivista Kinni, Tatjana); Total Balalaika Show; Vie de Bohème, La (Bohemian Life).*

Kaurismäki, Mika *Tigrero – A Film That Was Never Made.*

Kavur, Ömer *Night Journey (Gece Yolculugu).*

Kawadri, Anwar *Nutcracker.*

Kawase, Naomi *Suzaku (Moe no Shuzaku).*

Kay, Stephen *Last Time I Committed Suicide, The.*

Kaylor, Robert *Carny; Derby (aka Roller Derby).*

Kazama, Shiori *How Old Is the River? (Fuyu no Kappa).*

Kazan, Elia *America, America (aka The Anatolian Smile); Arrangement, The; Baby Doll; Boomerang; East of Eden; Face in the Crowd, A; Gentleman's Agreement; Last Tycoon, The; Man on a Tightrope; On the Waterfront; Panic in the Streets; Splendor in the Grass; Streetcar Named Desire, A; Viva Zapata!; Wild River.*

Kazan, Nicholas *Dream Lover.*

Kazanski, Gennadi *Snow Queen, The (Snezhnaya Koroleva).*

Kazui, Fran Rubel *Tokyo Pop.*

Keating, David *Last of the High Kings, The.*

Keaton, Buster *Battling Butler; General, The; Go West; Navigator, The; Our Hospitality; Seven Chances; Sherlock Junior; Steamboat Bill, Jr.*

Keaton, Diane *Heaven; Unstrung Heroes.*

Kedzierzawska, Dorota *Crows (Wrony); Devils, Devils (Diably, Diably).*

Keen, Bob *Proteus.*

Keeve, Douglas *Unzipped.*

Keighley, William *Adventures of Robin Hood, The; Bullets or Ballots; Each Dawn I Die; Fighting 69th, The; G-Men; Green Pastures, The; Man Who Came to Dinner, The; Street with No Name, The; Torrid Zone.*

Keiller, Patrick *London; Robinson in Space.*

Keleti, Márton *Loves of Liszt,

The (*Szerelmi Álmok –
Liszt*).

Kellett, Bob *Are You Being
Served?; Don't Just Lie
There, Say Something!;
Spanish Fly.*

Kelljan, Bob *Act of Vengeance
(aka Rape Squad/The
Violator); Count Yorga,
Vampire; Return of Count
Yorga, The.*

Kellman, Barnet *Straight Talk.*

Kellogg, Ray *Green Berets, The.*

Kelly, Gene *Cheyenne Social
Club, The; Guide for the
Married Man, A; Hello,
Dolly!; It's Always Fair
Weather; On The Town;
Singin' in the Rain; That's
Entertainment Part II.*

Kelly, James *Beast in the
Cellar, The (aka Are you
Dying, Young Man?); Night
Hair Child.*

Kelly, Nancy *Thousand Pieces
of Gold, A.*
Kelly, Rory *Sleep With Me.*

Kennedy, Burt *Canadians,
The; Good Guys and the Bad
Guys, The; Hannie Caulder;
Killer Inside Me, The;
Return of the Seven (aka
Return of the Magnificent
Seven); Rounders, The;
Suburban Commando;
Support Your Local
Gunfighter; Support Your
Local Sheriff; Train Robbers,
The; War Wagon, The;
Welcome to Hard Times (aka
Killer on a Horse).*

Kennedy, Chris *Doing Time for
Patsy Cline.*

Kenovic, Ademir *Perfect Circle
(Savresni Krug).*

Kentis, Chris *Grind.*

Kenton, Erle C *Ghost of
Frankenstein, The; House of
Dracula; House of
Frankenstein; Island of Lost
Souls.*

Kernochan, Sarah *Marjoe.*

Kerrigan, Lodge *Clean, Shaven.*

Kershner, Irvin *Empire Strikes
Back, The; Empire Strikes
Back: Special Edition, The;
Eyes of Laura Mars; Fine
Madness, A; Flim-Flam
Man, The (aka One Born
Every Minute); Loving; Luck
of Ginger Coffey, The; Never
Say Never Again; Raid on
Entebbe; Return of a Man
Called Horse, The; RoboCop
2; S*P*Y*S; Up the
Sandbox.*

Kervyn, Emmanuel *Rabid
Grannies.*

Keshishian, Alek *Truth or
Dare (aka In Bed with
Madonna); With Honors.*

Kessler, Bruce *Angels From
Hell.*

Keusch, Erwin *Baker's Bread
(Das Brot des Bäckers).*

Keys, Gary *Memories of Duke.*

Kézdi-Kovács, Zsolt *Forbidden
Relations (Visszaesök); When
Joseph Returns (Ha Megjön
József).*

Khaindrava, Georgi *Graveyard
of Dreams (Ochnebebis
Sasaplao).*

Khleifi, George *You, Me,
Jerusalem.*

Khleifi, Michel *Tale of the
Three Jewels (Conte des trois
diamants); Wedding in Galilee
(Noce en Galilée).*

Khoo, Eric *Mee Pok Man; 12
Storeys.*

Khosa, Rajan *Dance of the
Wind (Wara Mandel).*

Kiarostami, Abbas *And Life
Goes On… (Zendegi Va
Digar Hich…); Close-Up
(Namayeh Nazdik); Taste of
Cherry, The (Ta'm e
Guilass); Through the Olive
Trees (Zir-e darakhtan-e
zeyton/aka Under the Olive
Trees); Where Is My
Friend's House? (Zhaneh-Je
Doost Kojast).*

Kibbee, Roland *Midnight Man,
The.*

Kidron, Beeban *Amy Foster
(aka Swept from the Sea
–The Story of Amy Foster);
Carry Greenham Home; To
Wong Foo, Thanks for
Everything! Julie Newmar;
Used People; Vroom.*

Kiersch, Fritz *Children of the
Corn; Tuff Turf.*

Kieslowski, Krzysztof *Blind
Chance (Przypadek); Camera
Buff (Amator); Dekalog 1: 'I
am the Lord thy God, Thou
shalt have no other God but
me'; Dekalog 2: 'Thou shalt
not take the name of the Lord
thy God in vain'; Dekalog 3:
'Honour the Sabbath Day';
Dekalog 4: 'Honour thy father
and thy mother'; Dekalog 5:
'Thou shalt not kill'; Dekalog
6: 'Thou shalt not commit
adultery'; Dekalog 7: 'Thou
shalt not steal'; Dekalog 8:
'Thou shalt not bear false
witness'; Dekalog 9: 'Thou
shalt not covet thy
neighbour's wife'; Dekalog
10: 'Thou shalt not covet thy
neighbour's goods'; Double
Vie de Véronique, La (The
Double Life of Véronique); No
End (Bez Konca); Scar, The
(Blizna); Short Film About
Killing, A (Krótki Film o
Zabijaniu); Short Film About
Love, A (Krótki Film o
Milosci); Three Colours: Blue
(Trois Couleurs: Bleu); Three
Colours: Red (Trois Couleurs:
Rouge); Three Colours: White
(Trois Couleurs: Blanc).*

Kikoine, Gerard *Buried Alive;
Edge of Sanity.*

Kim Hong-Joon *Jungle Story.*

Kim Ki-Young *Housemaid,
The (Hanyo); Insect Woman,
The (Chung Nyo); Iodo;
Killer Butterfly (Salin
Nabireul Cchotneun Yeoja).*

Kim Ui-Seok *Marriage Story
(Kyolhon Iyagi); That
Woman, That Man (Ke
Yeoja, Ke Namja); Vie en
rose, La (Changmi Bit
Insaeng).*

Kimiai, Masud *Snake Fang
(Dandane Mar).*

Kimmins, Anthony *Captain's
Paradise, The; Come on
George.*

King, Allan *Married Couple, A.*

King, George *Crimes at the
Dark House; Face at the
Window, The.*

King, Henry *Bravados, The;
Beloved Infidel; Black Swan,
The; Carousel; Chad Hanna;
Gunfighter, The; In Old
Chicago; Jesse James; Love Is
a Many-Splendored Thing;
Margie; O. Henry's Full
House (aka Full House);
Prince of Foxes; Remember
the Day; Seventh Heaven;
Snows of Kilimanjaro, The;
Song of Bernadette, The; Sun
Also Rises, The; Twelve
O'Clock High; Untamed; Wait
Till the Sun Shines, Nellie;
Wilson; Yank in the RAF, A.*

King Hu *Fate of Lee Khan,
The (Ying-chun-ge zhi
Fengbo); Legend of the
Mountain (Shan Zhong
Chuanqi); Raining in the
Mountain (Kong Shan Ling
Yu); Swordsman; Touch of
Zen, A (Xia Nü); Valiant
Ones, The (Zhonglie Tu).*

King, Louis *Bulldog
Drummond Comes Back;
Dangerous Mission; Smoky;
Thunderhead, Son of
Flicka.*

King, Rick *Prayer of the
Rollerboys.*

King, Stephen *Maximum
Overdrive.*

King, Zalman *Two Moon
Junction; Wild Orchid.*

Kinugasa, Teinosuke
*Crossways (Jujiro); Page of
Madness, A (Kurutta
Ippeiji).*

Kiral, Erden *Blue Exile, The
(Mavi Sürgün); Mirror, The
(Der Spiegel/ Anya).*

Kirsanoff, Dimitri
Ménilmontant.

Kirsch, Andrea William
*Christie et Les Arts
Florissants ou la Passion du
Baroque.*

Kishon, Ephraim *Sallah.*

Kitakubo, Hiroyuki *Roujin Z
(Rojin Z).*

Kitano, Takeshi *Boiling Point
(3–4x Jugatsu/San tai Yon x
Jugatsu); Getting Any?
(Minna Yatteruka); Hana-Bi;
Kids Return; Scene at the
Sea, A (Ano Natsu, Ichiban
Shizukana Umi); Sonatine;
Violent Cop, The (Sono
Otoko Kyobo ni Tsuki).*

Kizer, RJ *Godzilla 1985 (Gojira).*

Kjaerulff-Schmidt, Palle *Once
There Was a War (Der var
engang en Krig).*

Kjellin, Alf *Midas Run (aka A
Run on Gold).*

Klane, Robert *Thank God It's
Friday.*

Klapisch, Cédric *Air de
Famille, Un; Péril Jeune, Le
(Good Old Daze); When the
Cat's Away… (Chacun
cherche son chat).*

Klein, Bonnie Sherr *Not a Love
Story.*

Klein, Carola *Mirror Phase.*

Klein, James *Union Maids.*

Klein, Rolando *Chac.*

Klein, William *Far from
Vietnam (Loin du Viêt-nam);
Mister Freedom; Who Are
Your Polly Maggoo? (Qui
êtes-vous Polly Maggoo?).*

Kleiser, Randal *Big Top Pee-
Wee; Blue Lagoon, The;
Flight of the Navigator;
Getting It Right; Grandview
U.S.A.; Grease; Honey, I Blew
Up the Kid; It's My Party;
Summer Lovers; White Fang.*

Klier, Michael *Grass Is Always
Greener, The (Uberall ist es
besser, wo wir nicht sind).*

Klimov, Elem *Agony (Agonia);
Come and See (Idi i Smotri);
Farewell (Proshchanie).*

Klinger, Tony *Butterfly Ball,
The.*

Kloetzel, Andre *Savage
Capitalism.*

Kloves, Steve *Fabulous Baker
Boys, The; Flesh and Bone.*

Kluge, Alexander *Artistes at
the Top of the Big Top:
Disorientated (Die Artisten
in der Zirkuskuppel: ratlos);
Germany in Autumn
(Deutschland im Herbst);
Occasional Work of a Female
Slave (Gelegenheitsarbeit
einer Sklavin); Patriot, The
(Die Patriotin); Starke
Ferdinand, Der (Strong-Man
Ferdinand); Yesterday Girl
(Abschied von Gestern).*

Knights, Robert *Dawning, The.*

Knobler, Albert *Happiness in
Twenty Years (Le Bonheur
dans 20 Ans).*

Knowles, Bernard *Jassy; Magic
Bow, The; Perfect Woman,
The; Place of One's Own, A.*

Knudsen, Mette *Take It Like a Man, Ma'am (Ta' det som en Mand, Frue!)*.

Ko, Clifton *Chicken and Duck Talk (Ji Tong ya Jiang)*.

Ko I-cheng *Blue Moon (Lan Yue)*.

Kobayashi, Masaki *Empty Table, The (Shokutaku no Nai ie); Kaseki; Kwaidan; Rebellion (Joi-Uchi)*.

Koch, Howard W *Badge 373*.

Koenigsberg, Paula de *Rate It X*.

Koepp, Volker *Wittstock, Wittstock*.

Koerfer, Thomas *Alzire, or the New Continent (Alzire, oder der neue Kontinent); Death of the Flea Circus Director, The (Der Tod des Flohzirkusdirektors)*.

Koff, David *Black Britannica; Occupied Palestine*.

Kohn, Richard *Lord of the Dance*.

Kokkinos, Anna *Only the Brave*.

Kokkinos, Antonis *End of an Era (Telos Epochis)*.

Kollek, Amos *Goodbye New York*.

Koller, Xavier *Journey of Hope (Reise der Hoffnung)*.

Kolski, Jan Jakub *Johnny Aquarius (Jancio Wodnik); Playing from Plates (Grajacy Z Talerza)*.

Komack, James *Porky's Revenge*.

Konchalovsky, Andrei *Duet for One; Inner Circle, The (Il Proiezionista); Maria's Lovers; Riaba Ma Poule (Ryaba My Chicken); Runaway Train; Shy People; Tango & Cash*.

Konchalovsky, Andrei (as Andrei Mikhalkov-Konchalovsky) *Asya's Happiness (Istoriya Asi Klyachinoi, Kotoraya Lyubila, da nie vshla zamuzh); Nest of Gentlefolk, A (Dvorianskoe Gnezdo)*.

Koning, Olivier *São Paolo, SP*.

Kopple, Barbara *Harlan County, U.S.A.; Wild Man Blues*.

Korda, Alexander *Girl from Maxim's, The; Ideal Husband, An; Marius; Perfect Strangers (aka Vacation from Marriage); Private Life of Henry VIII, The; Rembrandt; That Hamilton Woman (aka Lady Hamilton); Wedding Rehearsal*.

Korda, Zoltan *Drum, The (aka Drums); Elephant Boy;*

Forget-Me-Not (aka Forever Yours); Four Feathers, The; Macomber Affair, The; Sahara; Thief of Bagdad, The.

Koreeda, Hirokazu *Maborosi (Maboroshi no Hikari); Without Memory (Kioku-ga Ushinawareta-toki)*.

Korner, Anthony *Helen, Queen of the Nautch Girls*.

Korine, Harmony *Gummo*.

Korty, John *Alex & The Gypsy; Autobiography of Miss Jane Pittman, The; Ewok Adventure, The (aka Caravan of Courage); Oliver's Story*.

Kosminsky, Peter *Wuthering Heights*.

Koster, Henry *Bishop's Wife, The; Good Morning, Miss Dove; Harvey; It Started with Eve; Man Called Peter, A; Mr Hobbs Takes a Vacation; My Cousin Rachel; My Man Godfrey; No Highway (aka No Highway in the Sky); O. Henry's Full House (aka Full House); One Hundred Men and a Girl; Robe, The*.

Kot, Eric *4 Faces of Eve (4 [Si] Mian Xiawa)*.

Kotani, Tom *Last Dinosaur, The*.

Kotcheff, Ted *Apprenticeship of Duddy Kravitz, The; Billy Two Hats; First Blood; Folks!; Fun with Dick and Jane; Life at the Top; North Dallas Forty; Outback; Shooter, The; Switching Channels; Tiara Tahiti; Uncommon Valor; Weekend at Bernie's; Who Is Killing the Great Chefs of Europe? (aka Too Many Chefs); Winter People*.

Kotler, Beth *Groove on a Stanley Knife*.

Kötting, Andrew *Gallivant*.

Kotulla, Theodor *Death Is My Trade (Aus einem deutschen Leben)*.

Kouf, Jim *Miracles*.

Kouyaté, Dani *Këita! The Voice of the Griot (Këita! L'Héritage du Griot)*.

Kovacs, Steven *'68*.

Kowlaski, Bernard L *Krakatoa – East of Java; Sssssss (aka Sssssnake)*.

Kozintsev, Grigori *Devil's Wheel, The (Chyortovo Koleso); Don Quixote; Hamlet; King Lear (Korol Lir); New Babylon, The (Novyi Vavilon)*.

Kramer, Frank (Gianfranco Parolini) *Sabata (Ehi, Amico … C'è Sabata, hai chiuso!); Return of Sabata (E'Tornato Sabata...Hai Chiuso un'Altra Volta)*.

Kramer, Jerry *Moonwalker*.

Kramer, Robert *Doc's Kingdom; Ice; Milestones; Route One/USA*.

Kramer, Stanley *Defiant Ones, The; Domino Principle, The (aka The Domino Killings); Guess Who's Coming To Dinner; Inherit the Wind; It's a Mad, Mad, Mad, Mad, World; Judgment at Nuremberg; Not As a Stranger; Oklahoma Crude; On the Beach; Pride and the Passion, The; Runner Stumbles, The; Secret of Santa Vittoria, The; Ship of Fools*.

Krawitz, Jan *Little People*.

Krejcik, Jiri *Divine Emma, The (Bozká Ema)*.

Krish, John *Decline and Fall...of a Birdwatcher!; Man Who Had Power Over Women, The*.

Krishen, Pradip *Electric Moon*.

Krishna, Srinivas *Masala*.

Krishnamma, Suri *Man of No Importance, A*.

Krishnan, Tine *Groove on a Stanley Knife*.

Krohn, Bill *It's All True*.

Kroyer, Bill *FernGully: The Last Rainforest*.

Krueger, Lisa *Manny & Lo*.

Kubrick, Stanley *Barry Lyndon; Clockwork Orange, A; Dr Strangelove: or, How I Learned to Stop Worrying and Love the Bomb; Full Metal Jacket; Killer's Kiss; Killing, The; Lolita; Paths of Glory; Shining, The; Spartacus; 2001: A Space Odyssey*.

Kuehn, Andrew J *Terror in the Aisles*.

Kuei Chih-Hung *Enter the 7 Virgins (aka Virgins of the Seven Seas)*.

Kufus, Thomas *My Private War (Mein Krieg)*.

Kuleshov, Lev *By the Law (Dura Lex); Extraordinary Adventures of Mister West in the Land of the Bolsheviks, The (Neobychainiye Priklucheniya Mistera Vesta v Stranye Bolshevikov)*.

Kulik, Buzz *Hunter, The; Shamus: To Find a Man; Villa Rides!; Warning Shot*.

Kumar, Harbance Mickey *Man from Africa and Girl from India*.

Kumashiro, Tatsumi *Like a Rolling Stone (Bo no Kanashimi)*.

Kümel, Harry *Daughters of Darkness (Le Rouge aux Lèvres); Lost Paradise, The*

(Het Verloren Paradijs); Malpertuis; Monsieur Hawarden.

Kunert, Joachim *Adventures of Werner Holt, The (Die Abenteuer des Werner Holt)*.

Kureishi, Hanif *London Kills Me*.

Kurosawa, Akira *Akira Kurosawa's Dreams; Bad Sleep Well, The; Dersu Uzala; Dodes'kaden; Hidden Fortress, The (Kakushi Toride no San-Akunin); High and Low (Tengoku to Jigoku); Idiot, The (Hakuchi); Ikiru (Living/To Live); I Live In Fear (Ikimono no Kiroku); Kagemusha; Lower Depths, The (Donzoko); Madadayo (Not Yet); Noro Inu (Stray Dog); Ran; Rashomon; Red Beard (Akahige); Rhapsody in August (Hachigatsu no Kyoshikyoku); Sanjuro (Tsubaki Sanjuro); Seven Samurai (Shichinin no Samurai); Throne of Blood (Kumonosu-jo); Toro no O o Fumu Otokotachi (The Men Who Tread on the Tiger's Tail/Walkers on the Tiger's Tail); Yojimbo*.

Kurtzman, Robert *Wishmaster*.

Kurys, Diane *Après l'Amour; Coup de Foudre (At First Sight/Entre Nous); Diabolo Menthe (Peppermint Soda); La Baule-les-pins (C'est la Vie); Man in Love, A (Un Homme Amoureux)*.

Kusturica, Emir *Arizona Dreaming; Time of the Gypsies (Dom za Vesanje); Underground; When Father Was Away on Business (Otac na Sluzbenom Putu)*.

Kutz, Kazimierz *Beads of One Rosary, The (Paciorki Jednego Różanca); Converted, The (Zawrócony); Taste of the Black Earth, The (Sól Ziemi Czarnej)*.

Kuzui, Fran Rubel *Buffy the Vampire Slayer*.

Kwak Kyung-Taek *Oksutan (3pm Paradise/Bath House)*.

Kwan, Stanley *Actress (Ruan Ling Yu); Full Moon in New York (Ren zai Niu-Yue); Hold You Tight (Yue Kuai Le, Yue Duoluo); Love Unto Waste (Dixia Qing); Red Rose, White Rose (Hong Meigui Bai Meigui); Rouge (Yanzhi Kou); Still Love You After All (Nian Ni Hao Xi); Yang ± Yin: Gender in Chinese Cinema (Nansheng Nüxiang)*.

Kwapis, Ken *Dunston Checks In; He Said, She Said*.

Kwietniowski, Richard *Love and Death on Long Island*.

Kyrou, Ado *Moine, Le (The Monk)*.

Labib, Jean *Montand.*

LaBruce, Bruce *Hustler White; No Skin Off My Ass, Super 8½.*

LaBute, Neil *In the Company of Men.*

La Cava, Gregory *Affairs of Cellini, The; Fifth Avenue Girl; Gabriel Over the White House; My Man Godfrey; Primrose Path, The; Stage Door.*

Lachman, Harry *Dante's Inferno; Man Who Lived Twice; Our Relations.*

Lafia, John *Child's Play 2; Man's Best Friend.*

Lahiff, Craig *Heaven's Burning.*

Lai, Stan *Peach-Blossom Land, The (Anlian Taohuayuan); Red Lotus Society, The (Feixia A-Da).*

Laine, Edvin *Täällä Pohjantähden alla (Here Beneath the North Star/Akseli and Elina).*

Laing, John *Beyond Reasonable Doubt; Other Halves.*

LaLoggia, Frank *Lady in White.*

Laloux, René *Fantastic Planet (La Planète Sauvage).*

Lam, Ringo *City on Fire (Longhu Fengyun); Burning Paradise (Huoshao Honglian Si); Full Contact (Xia Dao Gao Fei); Maximum Risk.*

Lam, Steffan *Paperback Vigilante.*

Lamb, Jan *4 Faces of Eve (4 [Si] Mian Xiawa).*

Lambert, Mary *Grand Isle; Pet Sematary; Siesta.*

Lamont, Charles *Bowery to Broadway.*

Lamore, Marsh *Mighty Mouse in the Great Space Chase; Secret of the Sword, The.*

Lamy, Benoit *Vie est belle, La.*

Lancaster, Burt *Kentuckian, The; Midnight man, The.*

Landers, Lew *Boogie Man Will Get You, The; Return of the Vampire, The.*

Landers, Lew (as Louis Friendlander) *Raven, The.*

Landis, John *Amazon Women on the Moon; American Werewolf in London, An; Beverly Hills Cop III; Blues Brothers, The; Blues Brothers 2000; Coming to America; Innocent Blood; Into the Night; Kentucky Fried Movie, The; National Lampoon's Animal House; Oscar; Spies Like Us; Stupids, The; Three Amigos!; Trading Places;*

Twilight Zone – The Movie.

Landres, Paul *Go, Johnny, Go!; Return of Dracula, The (aka the Fantastic Disappearing Man).*

Landy, Ruth *Dark Circle.*

Lane, Andrew *Jake Speed.*

Lane, Charles *Sidewalk Stories; True Identity.*

Lane, Rocky *All's Fair.*

Lanfield, Sidney *Hound of the Baskervilles, The; King of Burlesque; My Favourite Blonde; One in a Million; Thin Ice (aka Lovely to Look at); You'll Never Get Rich.*

Lang, Fritz *American Guerilla in the Philippines (aka I Shall Return); Beyond a Reasonable Doubt; Big Heat, The; Blue Gardenia, The; Clash By Night; Cloak and Dagger; Destiny (Der müde Tod); Dr Mabuse, the Gambler (Dr Mabuse, der Spieler); Fury; Hangmen Also Die!; House by the River; Human Desire; M; Man Hunt; Metropolis (1926); Metropolis (1926/1984); Ministry of Fear; Moonfleet; Nibelungen, Die; Rancho Notorious; Return of Frank James, The; Scarlet Street; Secret Beyond the Door; Spinnen, Die (The Spiders); Spione (Spies/The Spy); 1000 Eyes of Dr Mabuse, The (Die Tausend Augen des Dr Mabuse); Testament of Dr Mabuse, The (Das Testament des Dr Mabuse); Tiger of Eschnapur, The (Der Tiger von Eschnapur) [Part I]/ The Indian Tomb (Das Indische Grabmal) [Part II]; Western Union; While the City Sleeps; Woman in the Moon (Frau im Mond); Woman in the Window, The; You and Me; You Only Live Once.*

Lang, Krzysztof *Paper Marriage.*

Lang, Michel *A Nous les Petites Anglaises!; Hôtel de la Plage, L'.*

Lang, Richard *Change of Seasons, A.*

Lang, Samantha *Well, The.*

Lang, Walter *Can-Can; Cheaper by the Dozen; Desk Set (aka His Other Woman); Greenwich Village; King and I, The; Mighy Barnum, The; Mother Wore Tights; Sentimental Journey; Sitting Pretty; State Fair (aka It Happened One Summer); There's No Business Like Show Business; With a Song in My Heart.*

Langer, Carole *Joe Albany...A Jazz Life.*

Langley, Noel *Our Girl Friday (aka The Adventures of Sadie).*

Langton, Simon *Whistle Blower, The.*

Lanza, Anthony M *Glory Stompers, The.*

Lanzac, Frédéric *Le Sexe qui Parle (Pussy Talk).*

Lanzmann, Claude *Shoah.*

Lapine, James *Impromptu.*

Laplaine, José *Macadam Tribu.*

Lara, Gerardo *One Lost Year.*

Larkin, John *Quiet Please, Murder.*

Larrain, Ricardo *Frontera, La.*

Larraz, Joseph/José *Golden Lady, The; Symptoms (aka The Blood Virgin).*

Lasseter, John *Toy Story.*

Lathan, Stan *Beat Street.*

Lattuada, Alberto *Luci del Varietà (Lights of Variety/Variety Lights).*

Lau, Stanley *Young and Dangerous (Guhuozai zhi Ren zai Jianghu); Young and Dangeros 2 (Guhuozai 2 zhi Menglong Guo Jiang); Young and Dangerous 3 (Guhuozai 3 zhi Zhishou Zhetian).*

Lauder, Al *Paolozzi Story, The.*

Laughlin, Tom (Frank Laughlin) *Master Gunfighter, The.*

Laughlin, Michael *Strange Invaders.*

Laughton, Charles *Night of the Hunter, The.*

Lau Kar-Leung (aka Liu Jialiang) *Dirty Ho (Lantou He); 8-Diagram Pole Fighter, The (Wulang Bagua Gun/aka The Invincible Pole Fighters); Executioners from Shaolin (Hong Xiguan); My Young Auntie (Zhangbei); 36th Chamber of Shaolin, The (Shaolin Sanshiliu Fang).*

Lau Kun Wai *Mr Vampire.*

Launder, Frank *Belles of St Trinian's, The; Blue Lagoon, The; Blue Murder at St Trinian's' Bridal Path, The; Captain Boycott; Folly To Be Wise; Geordie (aka Wee Geordie); Happiest Days of Your Life, The; I See a Dark Stranger (aka The Adventuress); Lady Godiva Rides Again; Millions Like Us; Pure Hell of Trinian's, The; Two Thousand Women; Wildcats of St Trinian's, The.*

Laurent, Christine *Vertiges.*

Laurenti, Mariano *Vices in the Family (Vizio de Famiglia).*

Lautner, Georges *Cage aux Folles III: The Wedding, La; Road to Salina (Sur la Route de Salina); Seins de glace,*

Les (Someone Is Bleeding).

Lauzier, Gérard *Mon Père, ce héros.*

Lauzon, Jean-Claude *Léolo; Night Zoo (Un Zoo la Nuit).*

Laven, Arnold *Down Three Dark Streets; Glory Guys, The; Rough Night in Jericho; Sam Whiskey.*

Law, Clara *Autumn Moon (Qiuyue); Erotique; Floating Life.*

Lawrence, Quentin *Cash on Demand.*

Lawrence, Martin *Thin Line Between Love and Hate, A.*

Lawrence, Ray *Bliss.*

Layton, Joe *Richard Pryor Live on the Sunset Strip.*

Lazarus, Ashley *Golden Rendezvous; e'Lollipop.*

Leach, Wilford *Pirates of Penzance, The.*

Leacock, Philip *Brave Don't Cry, The; Spanish Gardener, The.*

Leacock, Richard *Jane.*

Leader, Anton M *Children of the Damned.*

Leahy, Gillian *My Life Without Steve.*

Lean, David *Blithe Spirit; Bridge on the River Kwai, The; Brief Encounter; Doctor Zhivago; Great Expectations; Hobson's Choice; In Which We Serve; Lawrence of Arabia; Madeleine; Major Barbara; Oliver Twist; Passage to India, A; Passionate Friends, The (aka One Woman's Story); Ryan's Daughter; Sound Barrier, The (aka Breaking the Sound Barrier); Summertime (aka Summer Madness); This Happy Breed.*

Lear, Norman *Cold Turkey.*

Le Chanois, Jean-Paul *Misérables, Les.*

Leconte, Patrice *Hairdresser's Husband, The (Le Mari de la coiffeuse); Monsieur Hire; Parfum d'Yvonne, Le; Ridicule; Tango.*

L'Ecuyer, John *Curtis's Charm.*

Leder, Mimi *Deep Impact; Peacemaker, The.*

Leduc, Jacques *Tendresse Ordinaire (Ordinary Tenderness).*

Leduc, Paul *Dollar Mambo; Reed: Insurgent Mexico (Reed: México Insurgente).*

Lee, Bruce *Way of the Dragon, The (Meng Long Guo Jiang/aka Return of the Dragon).*

Lee, Evan *Revenge of the Dead.*

Lee, Jack *Captain's Table, The; Once a Jolly Swagman (aka Maniacs on Wheels); Town Like Alice, A (aka The Rape of Malaya); Wooden Horse, The.*

Lee, Joe *Courier, The.*

Lee Kwang-Mo *Spring in My Hometown (Areumdaun Sijeol).*

Lee Min-Yong *Hot Roof, A (Gyaegotun Nalui Ohu).*

Lee Myung-Se *First Love (Chut Sarang).*

Lee, Rowland V *One Rainy Afternoon; Son of Frankenstein; Zoo in Budapest.*

Lee, Spike *Clockers; Crooklyn; Do the Right Thing; Get on the Bus; Girl 6; Jungle Fever; Malcolm X; Mo' Better Blues; School Daze; She's Gotta Have It.*

Leeds, Herbert I *Cisco Kid and the Lady, The; Return of the Cisco Kid, The; Time to Kill.*

Leenhardt, Roger *Dernières Vacances, Les.*

Leetch, Tom *Return of the Big Cat.*

Lefebvre, Jean-Pierre *Wild Flowers (Les Fleurs Sauvages).*

Léger, Fernand *Dreams That Money Can Buy.*

Legrand, François (Franz Antel) *Confessions of a Bigamist (Warum hab'ich bloss 2 x ja gesagt); Knickers Ahoy (Frau Wirtins tolle Töchterlein).*

Le Grice, Malcolm *Emily – Third Party Speculation.*

Le Hénaff, René *Colonel Chabert, Le.*

Lehmann, Maurice *Affaire du Courrier de Lyon, L'.*

Lehmann, Michael *Airheads; Heathers; Hudson Hawk; Meet the Applegates; Truth About Cats & Dogs, The.*

Lehto, Pekka *Flame Top (Tulipää).*

Leifer, Neil *Yesterday's Hero.*

Leigh, Mike *Bleak Moments; Career Girls; Four Days in July; High Hopes; Life Is Sweet; Naked; Secrets & Lies.*

Leight, Warren *Night We Never Met, The.*

Leisen, Mitchell *Arise, My Love; Bride of Vengeance; Easy Living; Frenchman's Creek; Girl Most Likely, The; Hands Across the Table; Hold Back the Dawn; Kitty; Lady in the Dark; Midnight; Murder at the Vanities; No*

Man of Her Own; Remember the Night.

Leitch, Christopher *Courage Mountain; Teen Wolf Too.*

Leland, David *Big Man, The; Checking Out; Wish You Were Here.*

Lelouch, Claude *And Now My Love (Toute une Vie); Autre Homme une Autre Chance, Un (Another Man, Another Woman/Another Man, Another Chance); Bonne Année, La (Happy New Year); Edith and Marcel (Edith et Marcel); Far from Vietnam (Loin du Viêt-nam); Homme et une Femme, Un (A Man and a Woman); Men, Women: User's Manual (Hommes Femmes Mode d'emploi); Misérables, Les (aka Les Misérables du vingtième siècle); Second Chance (Si c'était à refaire); Uns et les Autres, Les (Bolero/The Ins and the Outs); Visions of Eight; Viva la Vie; Vivre pour Vivre (Live for Life).*

Le Masson, Yann *Kashima Paradise.*

Lemmon, Jack *Kotch.*

Lemoine, Michel *Invitation to Bed (Les Confidences Erotiques d'un Lit Trop Accueillant); Seven Women for Satan (Les Weekends Maléfiques du Comte Zaroff).*

Lemon, Lizzie *UndeRage.*

Lemont, John *And Women Shall Weep; Frightened City, The; Konga.*

Leni, Paul *Cat and the Canary, The; Waxworks (Das Wachsfiguren-kabinett).*

Lenzi, Umberto *Paranoia (Orgasmo).*

Leo, Malcolm *It Came from Hollywood; This Is Elvis.*

Leonard, Brett *Lawnmower Man, The.*

Leonard, Robert Z *After Office Hours; B.F.'s Daughter; Bribe, The; In the Good Old Summertime; New Moon; Pride and Prejudice; When Ladies Meet; Ziegfeld Girl.*

Leone, John *Last of the Cowboys, The (aka The Great Smokey Roadblock).*

Leone, Sergio *Colosuss of Rhodes, The (Il Colosso di Rodi); Fistful of Dollars, A (Per un Pugno di Dollari); For a Few Dollars More (Per Qualche Dollari in Più); Giù la Testa (Duck, You Sucker/A Fistful of Dynamite/Once Upon a Time – the Revolution); Good, the Bad and the Ugly, The (Il Buono, il Brutto, il Cattivo); Once Upon a Time in America; Once Upon a Time in the West (C'era una Volta il West).*

Leonetti, John R *Mortal Kombat 2: Annihilation.*

Lepage, Marquise *Marie s'en va-t-en ville (Marie in the City).*

Lepage, Robert *Confessional, The (Le Confessionnal); Polygraph, The (Le Polygraphe).*

Le Pêcheur, Didier *Des Nouvelles du Bon Dieu (News from the Good Lord).*

Lerner, Irving *City of Fear; Murder by Contract; Royal Hunt of the Sun, The.*

Lerner, Murray *From Mao to Mozart: Isaac Stern in China; Message to Love: The Isle of Wight Festival.*

Lerner, Richard *What Happened to Kerouac?.*

LeRoy, Mervyn *Anthony Adverse; Bad Seed, The; Blossoms in the Dust; Devil at 4 O'Clock, The; Escape; Five Star Final; Gold Diggers of 1933; Gypsy; Hard to Handle; Hi, Nellie!; I Am a Fugitive from a Chain Gang; Johnny Eager; Little Caesar; Madame Curie; Mister Roberts; Page Miss Glory; Quo Vadis?; Random Harvest; They Won't Forget; Toward the Unknown (aka Brink of Hell); Tugboat Annie.*

Leroy, Serge *Shattered (Les Passagers).*

Leslie, Alfred *Pull My Daisy.*

Lessac, Michael *House of Cards.*

Lester, Mark L *Armed and Dangerous; Class of 1984; Commando; Firestarter; Stunts; Truck Stop Women.*

Lester, Richard *Bed Sitting Room, The; Butch and Sundance: The Early Days; Cuba; Finders Keepers; Four Musketeers: The Revenge of Milady, The; Funny Thing Happened on the Way to the Forum, A; Get Back; Hard Day's Night, A; Help!; How I Won the War; It's Trad, Dad!; Juggernaut; Knack...and how to get it, The; Mouse on the Moon, The; Petulia; Ritz, The; Return of the Musketeers, The; Robin and Marian; Royal Flash; Superman II; Superman III; Three Musketeers: The Queen's Diamonds, The.*

Leszczylowski, Michal *Directed by Andrei Tarkovsky (Regi – Andrej Tarkovskij).*

Leterrier, François *Goodbye Emmanuelle.*

Leth, Jørgen *Sunday in Hell, A (En Forårsdag i Helvede).*

Leto, Marco *Black Holiday (La Villeggiatura).*

Lettich, Sheldon *A.W.O.L.;*

Double Impact; Only the Strong.

Letts, Don *Punk Rock Movie, The.*

Leung, Patrick *Task Force (Rexue Zuiqiang).*

Levant, Brian *Beethoven; Flintstones; Jingle All the Way; Problem Child 2.*

Leven, Jeremy *Don Juan DeMarco.*

Levey, Jay *UHF.*

Levey, William A *Slumber Party '57.*

Levin, Henry *Ambushers, The; Bandit of Sherwood Forest, The; Dark Avenger, The (aka Warriors); Journey to the Centre of the Earth; Man from Colorado, The; That Man Bolt.*

Levin, Sid *Let the Good Times Roll.*

Levinson, Barry *Avalon; Bugsy; Diner; Disclosure; Good Morning Vietnam; Jimmy Hollywood; Natural, The; Rain Man; Sleepers; Sphere; Tin Men; Toys; Wag the Dog; Young Sherlock Holmes (Young Sherlock Holmes and the Pyramid of Fear).*

Levitow, Abe *Phantom Tollbooth, The.*

Lévy, Bernard-Henri *Bosna!*

Levy, Dani *I Was on Mars.*

Levy, Don *Herostratus.*

Levy, Gerry *Body Stealers, The (aka Thin Air/Invasion of the Body Stealers).*

Levy, Jacques *Oh! Calcutta!*

Levy, Jefery *S.F.W.*

Levy, Ralph *Do Not Disturb.*

Lewin, Albert *Moon and Sixpence, The; Pandora and the Flying Dutchman; Picture of Dorian Gray, The; Private Affairs of Bel Ami, The; Saadia.*

Lewin, Ben *Favour, the Watch and the Very Big Fish, The (Rue Saint-Sulpice); Lucky Break; Welcome to Britain.*

Lewis, Cullen (Lewis D Collins) *Desert Trail, The.*

Lewis, Everett *Skin & Bone.*

Lewis, George B *Humanoid, The (L'Umanoide).*

Lewis, Herschell Gordon *Color Me Blood Red.*

Lewis, Jerry *Bellboy, The; Big Mouth, The; Family Jewels, The; Ladies' Man, The; Nutty Professor, The; One More Time; Patsy, The; Which Way to the Front? (aka Ja, Ja, Mein General! But Which Way to the Front?).*

Lewis, Jim *Heartland Reggae.*

Lewis, Jonathan *Before Hindsight.*

Lewis, Joseph H *Big Combo, The; Cry of the Hunted; Desperate Search; Gun Crazy (aka Deadly Is the Female); Halliday Brand, The; Lady Without Passport, A; Lawless Street, A; Mad Doctor of Market Street, The; My Name is Julia Ross; Retreat, Hell!; 7th Cavalry; So Dark the Night; Terror in a Texas Town; That Gang of Mine; Undercover Man.*

Lewis, Mark *Cane Toads – An Unnatural History.*

Lewis, Robert Michael *Alpha Caper, The (aka Inside Job).*

L'Herbier, Marcel *Argent, L'; Inhumaine, L'; Nuit fantastique, La (The Fantastic Night).*

Li Hsing *Execution in Autumn (Qiu Jue).*

Li Shaohong *Blush (Hongfen); Family Portrait (Sishi Buhuo); Bloody Morning (Xuese Qingchen).*

Lieberman, Jeff *Blue Sunshine; Squirm.*

Lieberman, Robert *All I Want for Christmas; Fire in the Sky; Table for Five.*

Light, Allie *Dialogues With Madwomen.*

Lim Kwon-Taek *Village in the Mist (Angemaeul).*

Lima, Kevin *Goofy Movie, A.*

Lima Jr, Walter *Oyster and the Wind, The (A ostra e o vento).*

Liman, Doug *Swingers.*

Lin Bing *Legend of Bruce Lee (Xin Siwang Youxi/aka The New Game of Death).*

Lin Cheng-Sheng *Drifting Life, A (Chunhua Menglu); Murmur of Youth (Meili zai Chang-ge); Sweet Degeneration (Fang Lang).*

Lin Ch'ing-Chieh *Student Days (Xuesheng zhi Ai).*

Lindblad, Christian *Ripa Hits the Skids (Ripa Ruostuu).*

Lindblom, Gunnel *Summer Paradise (Paradistorg).*

Lindqvist, Jan *Tupamaros.*

Lindsay, Caleb *Chasing Dreams.*

Lindsay-Hogg, Michael *Frankie Starlight; Guy; Let It Be; Nasty Habits; Object of Beauty.*

Lindström, Jon *Dreaming of Rita (Drömmen om Rita).*

Ling Zifeng *Ripples Across*

Stagnant Water (Sishui Wei Lan).

Link, Caroline *Beyond Silence (Jenseits der Stille).*

Linklater, Richard *Before Sunrise; Dazed and Confused; Slacker; SubUrbia.*

Linson, Art *Where the Buffalo Roam.*

Lion, Mickey *House of Exorcism, The (La Casa dell'Exorcismo).*

Lioret, Philippe *Tombes du Ciel (Lost in Transit).*

Lipmann, Eric *Bisexual (Les Onze Mille Verges).*

Lipscomb, James *Blue Water, White Death.*

Lipsky, Oldrich *Nick Carter in Prague (Adela Jeste Nevecerela).*

Lipstadt, Aaron *Android.*

Lisberger, Steven M *Animalympics, Slipstream; Tron.*

Litten, Peter *Living Doll.*

Litten, Peter Mackenzie *To Die For.*

Littin, Miguel *Alsino and the Condor (Alsino y el Condor); Jackal of Nahueltoro, The (El Chacal de Nahueltoro); Naufragos, Los (Shipwrecked).*

Little, Dwight H *Free Willy 2; Halloween 4: The Return of Michael Myers; Marked for Death; Murder at 1600; Phantom of the Opera; Rapid Fire.*

Littlewood, Joan *Sparrows Can't Sing.*

Littman, Lynne *Testament.*

Litvak, Anatole *All This and Heaven Too; Amazing Doctor Clitterhouse, The; Anastasia; Castle on the Hudson (aka Years Without Days); Confessions of a Nazi Spy; Lady in the Car with Glasses and a Gun, The (La Dame dans l'auto avec des lunettes et un fusil); Long Night, The; Mayerling; Night of the Generals, The; Out of the Fog; Sisters, The; Snake Pit, The; Sorry, Wrong Number; This Above All; Tovarich.*

Livingston, Jennie *Paris Is Burning.*

Li Zuonan *Fist of Fury Part II (Jingwu Men Xuji).*

Liu Jialiang *see* Lau Kar-Leung.

Lizzani, Carlo *Crazy Joe; Prostitution Racket, The (Storie di Vita e Malavita).*

Llobet Gracia, Lorenzo *Life in Shadows (Vida en Sombras).*

Llorca, Pablo *Jardines*

Colgantes (Hanging Gardens).

Llosa, Luis *Anaconda; Sniper; Specialist, The.*

Lloyd, Frank *Blood on the Sun; Cavalcade; Last Command, The; Mutiny on the Bounty.*

Lloyd, Ian FH *Face of Darkness, The.*

Lo Chi-Leung *Viva Erotica! (Seqing Nan Nü).*

Lo Wei *Back Alley Princes (Malu Xiao Yingxiong); Big Boss, The (Tangshan Daxiong/aka Fists of Fury); Fist of Fury (Jingwu Men/aka The Chinese Connection); Kung Fu Girl, The (Tiewa/aka None But the Brave).*

Loach, Ken (Kenneth) *Black Jack; Carla's Song; Fatherland; Family Life; Gamekeeper, The; Hidden Agenda; Kes; Ladybird Ladybird; Land and Freedom; Looks and Smiles; My Name Is Joe; Poor Cow; Raining Stones; Riff-Raff.*

Loader, Jayne *Atomic Café, The.*

Locke, Sondra *Impulse; Ratboy.*

Loden, Barbara *Wanda.*

Loftis, Norman *Small Time.*

Logan, Joshua *Bus Stop; Camelot; Ensign Pulver; Fanny; Paint Your Wagon; Picnic; Sayonara; South Pacific.*

Lombardi, Francisco J *Lion's Den, The (La Boca del Lobo); Sin Compasión (Sans Pitié).*

Lombardo, Lou *Russian Roulette.*

Lommel, Ulli *Brainwaves; Tenderness of the Wolves (Zärtlichkeit der Wölfe).*

Loncraine, Richard *Bellman and True; Brimstone and Treacle; Flame; Full Circle (aka The Haunting of Julia); Missionary, The; Richard III.*

London, Jerry *Shogun.*

Long, Stanley *Adventures of a Private Eye; On the Game.*

Longinotto, Kim *Cross and Passion; Good Wife of Tokyo, The; Theatre Girls; UndeRage.*

Longo, Robert *Johnny Mnemonic.*

Lopez, Temistocles *Chain of Desire.*

López Moctezuma, Juan *House of Madness (La Mansión de la Locura).*

Lophushansky, Konstantin *Letters from a Dead Man (Pisma Myortvovo Chelovyeka).*

Lord, Chip *Motorist.*

Lord, Jean-Claude *Tadpole and the Whale; Visiting Hours.*

Loreau, Dominique *Divine Body (Divine Carcasse).*

Lorre, Peter *Verlorene, Der (The Lost One).*

Losey, Joseph *Accident; Assassination of Trotsky, The; Big Night, The; Blind Date (aka Chance Meeting); Boom; Boy with Green Hair, The; Criminal, The (aka The Concrete Jungle); Damned, The (aka These Are the Damned); Doll's House, A; Don Giovanni; Eve; Figures in a Landscape; Galileo; Go-Between, The; Gypsy and the Gentleman, The; King and Country; Lawless, The (aka The Dividing Line); M; Modesty Blaise; Mr Klein; Prowler, The; Romantic Englishwoman, The; Secret Ceremony; Servant, The; Sleeping Tiger, The; Steaming; Time Without Pity.*

Losey, Joseph (as Joseph Walton) *Intimate Stranger, The (aka Finger of Guilt).*

Lotianou, Emil *Pavlova – A Woman for All Time (aka Anna Pavlova).*

Louise, Fhiona *Cold Light of Day, The.*

Lounguine, Pavel *Taxi Blues.*

Lounsbery, John *Rescuers, The.*

Lourié, Eugène *Beast from 20,000 Fathoms, The; Colossus of New York, The; Gorgo.*

Louvish, Simon *To Live in Freedom.*

Low, Steven *Across the Sea of Time: A New York Adventure.*

Lowenstein, Richard *Dogs in Space; Say a Little Prayer; Strikebound.*

Lowenthal, John *Trials of Alger Hiss, The.*

Lowney, Declan *Time Will Tell.*

Loy, Nanni *Why? (Detenuto in Attesa di Giudizio).*

Lozinski, Pawel *100 Years of Polish Cinema (100 Lat w Kine).*

Lu Wei *Journey to the Western Xia, The (Xi Xia Lu Tiatiao).*

Lubin, Arthur *Footsteps in the Fog; Francis; Phantom of the Opera; Rhubarb.*

Lubitsch, Ernst *Angel; Bluebeard's Eighth Wife; Cluny Brown; Design for Living; Heaven Can Wait; If I Had a Million; Monte Carlo; Ninotchka; One Hour With You; Shop Around the Corner, The; To Be or Not To Be; Trouble in Paradise.*

Lucas, George *American Graffiti; Star Wars; Star Wars, Episode IV, a New Hope; THX 1138.*

Lucas, Kevin *Black River.*

Lucchi, Angela Ricci *From Pole to Equator (Dal Polo all'Equatore).*

Luchetti, Daniele *Footman, The (Il Portaborse); School (la Scuola).*

Lucidi, Maurizio *Sicilian Cross (Gli Esecutori).*

Ludwig, Edward *Fighting Seabees, The; Last Gangster, The.*

Luhrmann, Baz *Strictly Ballroom; William Shakespeare's Romeo & Juliet.*

Lumet, Sidney *Anderson Tapes, The; Bye Bye Braverman; Child's Play; Daniel; Close to Eden; Deadly Affair, The; Deathtrap; Dog Day Afternoon; Equus; Fail Safe; Family Business; Fugitive Kind, The; Group, The; Guilty as Sin; Hill, The; Long Day's Journey Into Night; Lovin' Molly; Morning After, The; Murder on the Orient Express; Network; Night Falls on Manhattan; Offence, The; Pawnbroker, The; Power; Prince of the City; Q&A; Running on Empty; Sea Gull, The; Serpico; 12 Angry Men; Verdict. The; Wiz, The.*

Luna, (JJ) Bigas *Anguish (Angustia); Golden Balls (Huevos de Oro); Jamón Jamón; Tit and the Moon, The (La Teta y la luna/La teta i la lluna/La Lune et le téton).*

Lupino, Ida *Bigamist, The; Hard, Fast and Beautiful; Hitch-hiker, The.*

Lupo, Michele *Man to Respect, A (Un Uomo da Rispettare).*

Luraschi, Tony *Outsider, The.*

Lusk, Don *GoBots: Battle of the Rocklords.*

Luske, Hamilton *Lady and the Tramp; One Hundred and One Dalmatians; Peter Pan; Pinocchio.*

Lussanet, Paul de *Dear Boys (Lieve Jongens).*

Lustig, William *Hit List; Maniac Cop; Maniac Cop 2; Relentless.*

Lynch, David *Blue Velvet; Dune; Elephant Man, The; Eraserhead; Lost Highway; Twin Peaks; Twin Peaks: Fire Walk with Me; Wild at Heart.*

Lynch, Jennifer Chambers *Boxing Helena.*

Lynch, Paul *Prom Night.*

Lynd, Laurie *House.*

Lyne, Adrian *Fatal Attraction; Flashdance; Foxes; Indecent Proposal; Jacob's Ladder; Lolita; 9½Weeks.*

Lynn, Jonathan *Clue; Distinguished Gentleman, The; My Cousin Vinny; Nuns on the Run; Sgt Bilko; Trial and Error.*

Lyon, Danny *Niños Abandonados, Los.*

Lyon, Nelson *Telephone Book, The.*

Lyssy, Rolf *Konfrontation – Assassination in Davos (Konfrontation); Swissmakers, The (Die Schweizermacher).*

Maanouni, Ahmed El *Trances (El Hal).*

Maas, Dick *Amsterdamned; Lift, The (De Lift).*

Maben, Adrian *Pink Floyd Live at Pompeii (Pink Floyd à Pompéi).*

MacAdams, Lewis *What Happened to Kerouac?*

McBride, Jim *Big Easy, The; Breathless; David Holzman's Diary; Great Balls of Fire!; Hot Times; Wrong Man, The.*

Mac Caig, Arthur *Patriot Game, The.*

McCall, Anthony *Sigmund Freud's Dora.*

McCall, Rod *Lewis & Clark & George.*

McCallum, John *Nickel Queen.*

McCarey, Leo *Affair to Remember, An; Awful Truth, The; Bells of St Mary's, The; Duck Soup; Going My Way; Kid from Spain, The; Once Upon a Honeymoon; Rally 'round the Flag, Boys!; Ruggles of Red Gap; Satan Never Sleeps (aka The Devil Never Sleeps).*

McCarey, Raymond *Pack Up Your Troubles.*

MacCarthy, Gerard *Michael Micha.*

McCarthy, Michael *Operation Amsterdam.*

McCarthy, Todd *Visions of Light.*

MacCartney, Sydney *Bridge, The.*

McClatchy, Gregory *Vampire at Midnight.*

McConnell, Mick *Betty's Brood.*

McCormack, Dan *Minotaur.*

McCowan, George *Frogs;*

Magnificent Seven Ridell, The; Shadow of the Hawk; Shape of Things to Come, The.

McCullough Sr, Jim *Aurora Encounter, The*

MacDonald, David *Bad Lord Byron, The; Cairo Road; Christopher Columbus; Crimes at the Dark House; Petticoat Pirates.*

MacDonald, Hettie *Beautiful Thing.*

Macdonald, Kevin *Donald Cammell: The Ultimate Performance.*

Macdonald, Peter *Mo' Money; NeverEnding Story III: Escape from Fantasia, The; Rambo III.*

McDougall, Charles *Arrivederci Millwall.*

McDougall, Don *Spider Man – The Dragon's Challenge.*

MacDougall, Ranald *Go Naked in the World; Subterraneans, The.*

McDowell, Curt *Thundercrack!*

McElwee, Ross *Sherman's March.*

McElwee, Vincent *Herbie Goes Bananas; Herbie Goes to Monte Carlo; Superdad; Treasure of Matecumbe.*

McEveety, Bernard *Napoleon and Samantha.*

McGehee, Scott *Suture.*

McGlynn, Don *Art Pepper: Notes from a Jazz Survivor; Charles Mingus: Triumph of the Underdog.*

McGoohan, Patrick *Catch My Soul.*

McGrath, Douglas *Emma.*

McGrath, John *Blood Red Roses.*

McGrath, Joseph *Bliss of Mrs Blossom, The; Casino Royale; Digby – the Biggest Dog in the World; Great McGonagall, The; Magic Christian, The; Rising Damp; 30 Is a Dangerous Age, Cynthia.*

McGuane, Thomas *92 in the Shade.*

McGuckian, Mary *This Is the Sea.*

McGuire, Don *Delicate Delinquent, The.*

McHenry, Doug *Jason's Lyric.*

Machulski, Juliusz *Sex Mission, The (Seksmisja).*

McIntyre, CJ *Border Shootout.*

Mack, Earle *Children of Theatre Street, The.*

McKellar, Don *Last Night.*

Mackendrick, Alexander *Don't Make Waves; High Wind in Jamaica, A; Ladykillers, The; 'Maggie', The (aka High and Dry); Mandy (aka Crash of Silence); Man in the White Suit, The; Sweet Smell of Success; Sammy Going South (aka A Boy Ten Feet Tall); Whisky Galore! (aka Tight Little Island).*

McKenzie, Brian *Stan and George's New Life.*

MacKenzie, John *Fourth Protocol, The; Honorary Consul, The (aka Beyond the Limit); Innocent, The; Last of the Finest, The (aka Blue Heat); Long Good Friday, The; Made; Ruby; Voyage.*

McKimmie, Jackie *Waiting.*

MacKinnon, Gillies *Conquest of the South Pole; Grass Arena, The; Playboys, The; Regeneration; Simple Twist of Fate, A; Small Faces; Trojan Eddie.*

Mackinnon, Stewart *Justine.*

McLaglen, Andrew V *Ballad of Josie, The; Bandolero!; Cahill – US Marshal; Chisum; Devil's Brigade, The; Last Hard Men, The; Mitchell; North Sea Hijack; Rare Breed, The; Return from the River Kwai; Sahara; Sea Wolves, The; Something Big; Undefeated, The; Way West, The; Wild Geese, The.*

McLaughlin, Sheila *Committed; She Must Be Seeing Things.*

Maclean, Alison *Crush.*

McLean, Steve *Postcards from America.*

McLennan, Don *Mullaway; Slate, Wyn & Me.*

McLeod, Norman Z *Alice in Wonderland; Casanova's Big Night; Horse Feathers; If I Had a Million; It's a Gift; Monkey Business; Paleface, The; Secret Life of Walter Mitty, The; Topper.*

MacMillan, Keith *Culture Club – A Kiss Across the Ocean; Exodus – Bob Marley Live.*

McMullen, Ken *1871; Ghost Dance; Zina.*

McMurchy, Megan *For Love or Money.*

McMurray, Mary *Assam Garden, The.*

McNaught, Bob *Seawife.*

Macnaughton, Ian *And Now for Something Completely Different.*

McNaughton, John *Borrower, The; Henry: Portrait of a Serial Killer; Mad Dog and Glory; Normal Life; Wild Things.*

McTiernan, John *Die Hard; Die Hard with a Vengeance; Hunt for Red October, The; Last Action Hero, The; Medicine Man; Predator.*

Madden, David *Separate Lives.*

Madden, John *Ethan Frome; Mrs Brown.*

Maddin, Guy *Archangel; Careful; Tales from the Gimli Hospital; Twilight of the Ice Nymphs.*

Maeso, José G *Order to Kill (El Clan de los Inmorales).*

Magar, Guy *Retribution; Stepfather III.*

Maggenti, Maria *Incredibly True Adveture of Two Girls in Love, The*

Magnoli, Albert *Purple Rain; Take It Easy.*

Magnuson, John *Lenny Bruce Performance Film, The.*

Magra, Billy *Completely Pogued.*

Mahomo, Nana *Last Grave at Dimbaza.*

Mahoney, Robin *Glastonbury: The Movie.*

Mahurin, Matt *Mugshot.*

Mailer, Norman *Maidstone; Tough Guys Don't Dance.*

Main, Stewart *Desperate Remedies.*

Mainka, Maximiliane *Germany in Autumn (Deutschland im Herbst).*

Mainka-Jellinghaus, Beate *Germany in Autumn (Deutschland im Herbst).*

Mai Tai Kit *Wicked City, The (Yaoshou Dushi).*

Majewski, Lech *Prisoner of Rio.*

Majidi, Majid *Father, The (Pedar).*

Makavejev, Dusan *Coca Cola Kid, The; Gorilla Bathes at Noon; Innocence Unprotected (Nevinost Bez Zastite); Manifesto; Man Is Not a Bird (Covek nije Tica); Montenegro; Sweet Movie; Switchboard Operator, The (Ljubavni Slucaj); W.R. – Mysteries of the Organism (W.R. – Misterije Organizma).*

Makhmalbaf, Mohsen *Gabbeh; Peddler, The (Dastforoush).*

Makhmalbaf, Samira, *Apple, The.*

Makk, Károly *Another Way (Egymásra nézve); Gambler, The; Love (Szerelem); Very Moral Night, A (Egy Erkölcsös Ejszaka).*

Malatesta, Guido *Maciste Contro i Mostri (Colossus of the Stone Age/Fire Monsters Against the Son of Hercules/Land of the Monsters).*

Malick, Terrence *Badlands; Days of Heaven.*

Malle, Louis *Alamo Bay; Amants, Les (The Lovers); ...and the pursuit of happiness; Ascenseur pour l'Échafaud (Frantic/Lift to the Scaffold); Atlantic City (aka Atlantic City U.S.A.); Au Revoir les Enfants; Black Moon; Crackers; Damage; Feu Follet, Le (A Time to Live and a Time to Die/The Fire Within/Fox Fire/Will o'the Wisp); God's Country; Histoires Extraordinaires (Spirits of the Dead/Tales of Mystery); Lacombe Lucien; Milou en mai (Milou in May); Monde du Silence, Le (The Silent World)My Dinner with André; Phantom India (L'Inde Fantôme); Pretty Baby; Souffle au Coeur, Le (Dearest Heart); Vanya on 42nd Street; Viva Maria!; Zazie dans le Métro.*

Malmuth, Bruce *Hard to Kill; Nighthawks.*

Malone, Mark *Killer.*

Malone, William *Titan Find, The (aka Creature).*

Malraux, André *Espoir (Days of Hope/Man's Hope).*

Mambéty, Djibril Diop *Franc, Le; Hyenas (Hyènes).*

Mamet, David *Homicide; House of Games; Oleanna; Things Change.*

Mamin, Yuri *Fountain, The (Fontan).*

Mamoulian, Rouben *Applause; Becky Sharp; Blood and Sand; City Streets; Dry Jekyll and Mr Hyde; Golden Boy; Love Me Tonight; Mark of Zorro, The; Queen Christina; Silk Stockings; Song of Songs; We Live Again.*

Manchevski, Milcho *Before the Rain (Po Dezju).*

Mandel, Robert *F/X (aka F/X – Murder by Illusion); Substitute, The; Touch and Go.*

Mandoki, Luis *Born Yesterday; Gaby – A True Story; When a Man Loves a Woman; White Palace.*

Mangold, James *CopLand; Heavy.*

Mangolte, Babette *Camera: Je, The; Cold Eye, The; What Maisie Knew.*

Mankiewicz, Francis *Revolving Doors, The (Les Portes tournantes).*

Mankiewicz, Joseph L *All About Eve; Barefoot Contessa, The; Cleopatra; Dragonwyck; 5 Fingers; Ghost and Mrs Muir, The;*

Guys and Dolls; Honey Pot, The; House of Strangers; Julius Caesar; Letter to Three Wives. A; No Way Out; People Will Talk; Quiet American, The; Sleuth; Somewhere in the Night; Suddenly Last Summer; There Was a Crooked Man.*

Mankiewicz, Tom *Delirious; Dragnet.*

Mann, Anthony *Bend of the River (aka Where the River Bends); Border Incident; Cimarron; Dandy in Aspic, A; Desperate; Devil's Doorway; El Cid; Fall of the Roman Empire, The; Furies, The; Glenn Miller Story, The; God's Little Acre; Heroes of Telemark, The; Man of the West; Men in War; Naked Spur, The; Raw Deal; Reign of Terror (aka The Black Book); T-Men; Tall Target, The; Tin Star, The; Winchester '73.*

Mann, Daniel *About Mrs Leslie; Butterfield 8; Come Back, Little Sheba; Dream of Kings, A; Judith; Lost in the Stars; Kidnapped; Revengers, The; Teahouse of the August Moon, The.*

Mann, Delbert *All Quiet on the Western Front; Bachelor Party, The; Dark at the Top of the Stairs, The; Desire Under the Elms; Gathering of Eagles, A; Jane Eyre; Marty; Night Crossing; Torn Between Two Lovers.*

Mann, Farhad *Lawnmower Man 2: Beyond Cyberspace.*

Mann, Michael *Heat; Jericho Mile, The; Keep, The; Last of the Mohicans, The; Manhunter; Thief (aka Violent Streets).*

Mann, Ron *Comic Book Confidential.*

Mannas, James *Aggro Seizeman.*

Manning, Michelle *Blue City.*

Manop Udomdej *Dumb Die Fast, Smart Die Slow, The (Galok Bang Tai Cha, Galok Na Tai Gon).*

Manos, Mark *Liquid Dreams.*

Mantello, Joe *Love! Valour! Compassion!*

Manthoulis, Robert *Blues Under the Skin (Le Blues entre les Dents).*

Manuli, Guido *Volere, Volare.*

Marboeuf, Jean *Pétain.*

Marcel, Terry *Hawk the Slayer; Jane and the Lost City.*

March, Alex *Amazing Captain Nemo, The (aka The Return of Captain Nemo).*

Marcheschi, Cork *Survivors, The Blues Today.*

Marconi, David *Harvest, The.*

Marcus, James *Tank Malling.*

Marcus, Mitch *Boy Called Hate, A.*

Marczewski, Wojciech *Escape from the 'Liberty' Cinema (Ucieczka z Kina 'Wolnosc').*

Margolin, François *Lie, The (Mensonge).*

Margolin, Stuart *Glitter Dome, The.*

Margolis, Jeff *Richard Pryor Live in Concert.*

Maria, Guy *Maid for Pleasure (Filles Expertes en Jeux Clandestines).*

Marin, Cheech *Born in East L.A.*

Marin, Edwin L *Colt .45 (aka Thundercloud); Johnny Angel; Nocturne.*

Marino, Gustavo Graef *Johnny 100 Pesos (Johnny Cien Pesos).*

Marinos, Lex *Indecent Obsession, An.*

Mariposa Film Group *Word Is Out.*

Mariscal, Alberto *They Call Him Marcado (Los Marcados).*

Marker, Chris *A.K.; Battle of the Ten Million, The (La Bataille des Dix Millions); Jetée, La (The Jetty/The Pier); Joli mai, Le; Level Five; Sans Soleil (Sunless).*

Markle, Fletcher *Incredible Journey, The; Man With a Cloak, The.*

Markle, Peter *Bat 21; Hot Dog...The Movie; Wagons East!; Youngblood.*

Markov, Ivan *Ghetto.*

Marks, Arthur *Bucktown.*

Marks, George Harrison *Come Play with Me.*

Marquand, Christian *Candy.*

Marquand, Richard *Eye of the Needle; Hearts of Fire; Jagged Edge; Legacy, The; Return of the Jedi; Return of the Jedi: Special Edition.*

Marmorstein, Malcolm *Dead Men Don't Die.*

Marr, Leon *Dancing in the Dark.*

Marre, Jeremy *Roots Rock Reggae.*

Marshall, Frank *Alive; Arachnophobia; Congo.*

Marshall, Fred *Popdown.*

Marshall, Garry *Beaches; Exit to Eden; Flamingo Kid, The; Frankie & Johnny; Nothing* in Common; Overboard; Pretty Woman; Young Doctors in Love.

Marshall, George Advance to the Rear; Blue Dahlia, The; Destry Rides Again; Gazebo, The; Ghost Breakers, The; How the West Was Won; Murder, He Says; Pack Up Your Troubles; Sheepman, The; You Can't Cheat an Honest Man.

Marshall, Noel Roar.

Marshall, Penny Awakenings; Big; Jumpin' Jack Flash; League of Their Own, A; Preacher's Wife, The; Renaissance Man.

Marshall, Stuart Over Our Dead Bodies.

Martin, Darnell I Like It Like That.

Martin, Eugenio Bad Man's River (El Hombre del Río Malo); Horror Express (Pánico en el Transiberiano).

Martin, Kelly Kids in the Hall: Brain Candy.

Martin Lionel C Def Jam's How to Be a Player.

Martin, Richard Limit Up.

Martinez, Rico Desperate.

Martino, Sergio Island of Mutations (L'Isola degli Uomini Pesce); Montagna del Dio Cannibale, La (Prisoner of the Cannibal God/Slave of the Cannibal God); Violent Professionals, The (Milano Trema; La Polizia Vuole Giustizia); The Visitor (Cugini Carnali).

Martinson, Leslie Batman; Fathom; Mrs Pollifax – Spy.

Marton, Andrew Africa – Texas Style; Clarence, the Cross-Eyed Lion; Crack in the World; Green Fire; Longest Day; The.

Martone, Mario Amore Molesto, L'

Marvin, Mike Wraith, The.

Marzynski, Marian Shtetl.

Mason, Christopher Wot! No Art.

Mason, Herbert Back-Room Boy.

Masson, Laetitia En avoir (ou pas).

Massot, Claude Kabloonak.

Massot, Joe Dance Craze; Song Remains the Same, The.

Masters, Quentin Dangerous Summer, A; Stud, The.

Masterson, Peter Blood Red; Full Moon in Blue Water; Trip to Bountiful, The.

Mastorakis, Nico Blind Date; Wind, The (aka The Edge of Terror).

Mastroianni, Armand Cameron's Closet; He Knows You're Alone.

Matalon, Eddy Cathy's Curse (Cauchemars).

Maté, Rudolph Dark Past, The; D.O.A.; Miracle in the Rain; No Sad Songs for Me; Second Chance; Union Station; When Worlds Collide.

Mathias, Sean Bent.

Maticevic, Mladen Ghetto.

Matsuda, Shunsui Bantsuma: The Life and Times of Tsumasaburo Bando (Bantsuma: Bando Tsumasaburo no Shogai).

Matsumoto, Toshio Pandemonium (Shura).

Matthau, Charles Grass Harp, The.

Mattinson, Burny Great Mouse Detective, The (aka Basil the Great Mouse Detective).

Maxwell, Garth Jack Be Nimble.

Maxwell, Paul (Paolo Bianchini) Superargo (Superargo e i Giganti Senza Volto).

Maxwell, Peter Serena; Southern Cross (aka The Highest Honor – A True Story).

Maxwell, Ronald F Gettysburg; Little Darlings.

May, Elaine Heartbreak Kid, The; Ishtar; Mikey and Nicky; New Leaf, A.

May, Joe Invisible Man Returns, The.

Mayberry, Russ Unidentified Flying Oddball, The (aka The Spaceman and King Arthur).

Maybury, John Love Is the Devil.

Mayersberg, Paul Captive.

Mayfield, Les Encino Man (aka California Man); Flubber; Miracle on 34th Street.

Maylam, Tony Burning, The; Hero; Riddle of the Sands, The; Split Second; White Rock.

Mayo, Archie Bordertown; Confirm or Deny; Four Sons; It's Love I'm After; Mayor of Hell, The; Night After Night; Night in Casablanca, A; Orchestra Wives; Petrified Forest, The.

Maysles, Albert Gimme Shelter; Grey Gardens.

Maysles, David Gimme Shelter; Grey Gardens.

Mazursky, Paul Alex in Wonderland; Blume in Love; Bob & Carol & Ted & Alice; Down and Out in Beverly Hills; Enemies, a Love Story; Harry and Tonto; Moon Over Parador; Moscow on the Hudson; Next Stop, Greenwich Village; Scenes from a Mall; Tempest; Unmarried Woman, An; Willie & Phil.

Meadows, Shane Smalltime; TwentyFourSeven.

Meckler, Nancy Alive and Kicking (aka Indian Summer); Sister My Sister.

Medak, Peter Changeling, The; Krays, The; Let Him Have It; Men's Club, The; Odd Job, The; Romeo Is Bleeding; Species II; Zorro the Gay Blade.

Medem, Julio Red Squirrel, The (La Ardilla Roja); Tierra (Earth); Vacas (Cows).

Medford, Don November Plan, The; Organization, The.

Medvedkin, Alexander Happiness (Schaste).

Meerapfel, Jeanine Amigomio; Girlfriend, The (aka La Amiga); Malou.

Megahey, Leslie Hour of the Pig, The.

Megahy, Francis Disappearance of Kevin Johnson, The; Freelance; Real Life; Taffin.

Megginson, RT Pelvis.

Mehrjui, Daryush Cow, The (Gav); Cycle, The (Dayereh Mina).

Mehta, Deepa Camilla; Fire.

Meieran, David Voices from the Front.

Meisel, Myron It's All True.

Mekas, Adolfas Hallelujah the Hills.

Mekas, Jonas Reminiscences of a Journey to Lithuania.

Melchior, Ib Time Travellers, The.

Melendez, Bill Boy Named Charlie Brown, A (aka A Boy Called Charlie Brown); Dick Deadeye, or Duty Done.

Melville, Jean-Pierre Armée des Ombres, L' (The Army in the Shadows); Bob le Flambeur (Bob the Gambler); Deux Hommes dans Manhattan; Deuxième Souffle, Le (Second Breath); Doulos, Le (The Finger Man); Enfants Terribles, Les (The Strange Ones); Flic, Un (Dirty Money); Léon Morin, Priest (Léon Morin, Prêtre); Red Circle, The (Le Cercle Rouge); Samouraï, Le (The Samurai); Silence de la mer, Le.

Menaul, Christopher Feast of July.

Menczel, Judy Angst.

Mendeluk, George Kidnapping of the President, The.

Mendes, Lothar Man Who Could Work Miracles, The.

Menell, Jo Mandela.

Menendez, Ramon Stand and Deliver.

Menges, Chris Second Best; World Apart, A.

Menotti, Gian Carlo Medium, The.

Menshov, Vladimir Moscow Distrusts Tears (Moskva Slezam ne Verit).

Menzel, Jiri Capricious Summer (Rozmarné Leto); Closely Observed Trains (Ostre Sledované Vlaky); Cutting It Short (Postrizini); Larks on a String (Skrivanci na niti); Life and Extraordinary Adventures of Private Ivan Chonkin, The (Zycie i Niezwykłe Przygody Szeregowea i Wana Czonkina); My Sweet Little Village (Vesnicko má Stredisková); Pearls of the Deep (Perlicky na dne); Seclusion Near a Forest (Na samote u lesa); Those Wonderful Movie Cranks (Bájecni Muzi s Klikou).

Menzies, William Cameron Address Unknown; Invaders from Mars; Things To Come; Whip Hand, The.

Merchant, Ismail Courtesans of Bombay, The; In Custody (Hifazaat); Proprietor, The (Le Propriétaire).

Merlet, Agnès Shark's Son (Le Fils du Requin).

Merrick, Laurence Manson.

Mészáros, Márta Adoption (Örökbefogadás); Diary for My Children (Napló Gyermekeimnek); Diary for My Loves (Napló Szerelmeimnek); Nine Months (Kilenc Hónap); Two of Them, The (Ök Ketten).

Metcalf, Andy Unstable Elements – Atomic Stories 1939-85.

Metcalfe, Tim Killer: A Journal of Murder.

Metter, Alan Back to School; Cold Dog Soup; Girls Just Want to Have Fun; Moving; Police Academy 7: Mission to Moscow.

Metzger, Alan Roomates.

Metzger, Radley Cat and the Canary, The; Don't Cry for Me Little Mother; Erotic Quartet.

Meyer, Kevin Perfect Alibi.

Meyer, Muffie *Grey Gardens.*

Meyer, Nicholas *Company Business; Deceivers, The; Star Trek II: The Wrath of Khan; Star Trek VI: The Undiscovered Country; Time After Time; Volunteers.*

Meyer, Russ *Beneath the Valley of the Ultra Vixens; Beyond the Valley of the Dolls; Blacksnake (aka Slaves); Faster, Pussycat! Kill! Kill!; Good Morning...and Goodbye (aka The Lust Seekers); Motor Psycho; Seven Minutes, The; Supervixens; Vixen.*

Michell, Roger *Persuasion.*

Michell, Scott *Innocent Sleep, The.*

Michener, Dave *Great Mouse Detective, The (aka Basil the Great Mouse Detective).*

Middleton, Jonas *Through the Looking Glass.*

Miéville, Anne-Marie *2 x 50 Years of French Cinema.*

Miike, Takashi *Bird People in China, The (Chugoku no Chojin); Shinjuku Triad Society (Shinjuku Kuro Shakai: China Mafia Senso).*

Mikhalkov, Nikita *Burnt by the Sun (Utomlennye solntsem/Soleil trompeur); Dark Eyes (Oci Ciornie); Five Evenings (Pyat Vercherov); Oblomov (Neskolko Dnei iz Zhizni I.I. Oblomova); Private Conservation, A (Bez Svidetelei); Slave of Love, A (Raba Lubvi); Unfinished Piece for Mechanical Piano (Neokonchennaya Pyesa dlya Mekhanicheskogo Pianin); Urga.*

Mikhalkov-Konchalovsky, Andrei *see* Konchalovsky, Andrei.

Mikkelsen, Laila *Little Ida (Liten Ida).*

Miles, Bernard *Chance of a Lifetime, Tawny Pipit.*

Miles, Christopher *Maids, The; Priest of Love; That Lucky Touch; Time for Loving; Virgin and the Gypsy, The.*

Milestone, Hank *From Hell to Victory (De l'Enfer à la Victoire).*

Milestone, Lewis *All Quiet on the Western Front; Arch of Triumph; Edge of Darkness; Front Page, The; Hallelujah, I'm a Bum; Halls of Montezuma; Kangaroo; Les Miserables; Mutiny on the Bounty; North Star, The (aka Armored Attack); Ocean's 11; Of Mice and Men; Pork Chop Hill; Rain; Strange Love of Martha Ivers, The; Walk in the Sun, A.*

Milius, John *Big Wednesday; Conan the Barbarian;*

Dillinger, Farewell to the King; Flight of the Intruder; Red Dawn; Wind and the Lion, The.

Milkina, Sofia *Kreutzer Sonata, The (Kreitzerova Sonata).*

Milland, Ray *Man Alone, A; Panic in Year Zero.*

Millar, Gavin *Danny the Champion of the World; Dreamchild.*

Millar, Stuart *Rooster Cogburn; When the Legends Die.*

Miller, Allan *Small Wonders.*

Miller, Claude *Accompagnatrice, L' (The Accompanist); Best Way to Walk, The (La Meilleure Façon de Marcher); Deadly Run (Mortelle Randonnée); Enfants de Lumière, Les (The Children of Lumière); Garde à Vue (The Inquisitor); Impudent Girl, An (L'Effrontée); Petite Voleuse, La; This Sweet Sickness (Dites-lui que Je l'aime).*

Miller, David *Billy the Kid; Diane; Executive Action; Lonely Are the Brave; Love Happy; Opposite Sex, The; Sudden Fear.*

Miller, George (1) *Andre; Les Patterson Saves the World; Man from Snowy River, The; Over the Hill; NeverEnding Story II: The Next Chapter, The.*

Miller, George (2) *Lorenzo's Oil; Mad Max; Mad Max 2; Mad Max Beyond Thunderdome, The; Twilight Zone – The Movie; Witches of Eastwick, The.*

Miller, Jason *That Championship Season.*

Miller, Kurt *Black Diamond Rush.*

Miller, Michael *Jackson County Jail; National Lampoon's Class Reunion; Silent Rage; Street Girls.*

Miller, Rebecca *Angela.*

Miller, Robert Ellis *Any Wednesday (aka Bachelor Girl Apartment); Baltimore Bullet, The; Buttercup Chain, The; Hawks; Heart Is a Lonely Hunter, The; Reuben, Reuben; Sweet November.*

Mills, Abbott *Jane.*

Mills, Reginald *Tales of Beatrix Potter (aka Peter Rabbit and Tales of Beatrix Potter).*

Milner, Dan *From Hell It Came.*

Milton, Robert *Outward Bound.*

Mimouni, Gilles *Appartement, L'.*

Miner, Steve *Forever Young; Friday the 13th Part 2; House; My Father, the Hero;*

Soul Man; Warlock.

Mingay, David *Rude Boy.*

Minghella, Anthony *English Patient, The; Mr Wonderful; Truly, Madly, Deeply.*

Mingozzi, Gianfranco *Rebel Nun, The (Flavia la Monaca Musulmana).*

Ming-Yuen S Ma *Slanted Vision.*

Minkoff, Ron *Lion King, The.*

Minnelli, Vincente *American in Paris, An; Bad and the Beautiful, The; Band Wagon, The; Bells Are Ringing; Brigadoon; Cabin in the Sky; Cobweb, The; Designing Woman; Father of the Bride; Gigi; Home from the Hill; Kismet; Lust for Life; Meet Me in St Louis; On a Clear Day You Can See Forever; Pirate, The; Sandpiper, The; Some Came Running; Tea and Sympathy; The Clock (aka Under the Clock); Two Weeks in Another Town; Undercurrent; Ziegfeld Follies.*

Mirkin, David *Romy and Michele's High School Reunion.*

Misselwitz, Helke *Little Angel (Engelchen).*

Misumi, Kenji *Lightning Swords of Death (Kozure Ohkami); Shogun Assassin.*

Mita, Merata *Patu.*

Mitchell, Eric *Underground U.S.A.*

Mitchell, Oswald *Asking for Trouble.*

Mitchell, Sollace *Call Me.*

Mitrotti, Roberto *Snatched (aka Little Girl...Big Tease).*

Mitrovic, Zika *67 Days (Uziska Republiksa).*

Mitta, Alexander *Lost in Siberia (Zateriannyi v Sibiri).*

Mitterrand, Frédéric *Madame Butterfly.*

Mizoguchi, Kenji *Chikamatsu Monogatari (The Crucified Lovers); Empress Yang Kwei Fei, The (Yokihi); Five Women Around Utamaro (Utamaro o Meguru Go-nin no Onna); Hometown (Furusato); Life of Oharu, The (Saikaku Ichidai Onna); My Love Has Been Burning (Waga Koi Wa Moenu); Sansho Dayu (Sansho the Bailiff); Shin Heike Monogatari (New Tales of the Taira Clan); Story of the Late Chrysanthemums, The (Zangiku Monogatari); Street of Shame (Akasen Chitai); Ugetsu Monogatari.*

Mizrahi, Moshe *Every Time We*

Say Goodbye; Madame Rosa (La Vie devant Soi); Rachel's Man.

Mochizuki, Rokuro *Another Lonely Hitman (Shin Kanashiki Hitman); Fire Within, The (Onibi); Outer Way, The (Gedo); Skinless Night; Wicked Reporter, The (Gokudo Kisha).*

Mocky, Jean-Pierre *Snobs.*

Moffatt, Tracey *Bedevil.*

Mogeluscu, Miles *Union Maids.*

Moguy, Leonide *Paris After Dark (aka The Night Is Ending).*

Moland, Hans Petter *Last Lieutenant, The (Secondvøitnanten).*

Molina, Josefina *Evening Performance (Función de Noche).*

Molinaro, Edouard *Beaumarchais (Beaumarchais l'insolent); Cage aux Folles, La (Birds of a Feather); Cage aux Folles II, La; Emmerdeur, L' (A Pain in the A**); Just the Way You Are; Pink Telephone, The (Le Téléphone Rose).*

Mollberg, Rauni *Earth Is a Sinful Song (Maa on Syntinen Laulau).*

Mollo, Andrew *It Happened Here; Winstanley.*

Monger, Christopher *Englishman Who Went Up a Hill, But Came Down a Mountain, The; Just Like a Woman; Voice Over; Waiting for the Light.*

Monicelli, Mario *Boccaccio '70; Casanova '70; Let's Hope It's a Girl (Speriamo che sia Femmina); Soliti Ignoti, I (Big Deal on Madonna Street/Persons Unknown).*

Montaldo, Giuliano *Closed Circuit (Circuito Chiuso).*

Monteiro, João César *Recollections of the Yellow House (Recordacões da Casa Amarela).*

Montesi, Jorge *Omen IV: The Awakening.*

Montgomery, Jennifer *Art for Teachers of Children.*

Montgomery, Monty *Loveless, The.*

Montgomery, Robert *Lady in the Lake.*

Moore, Michael (1) *Paradise – Hawaiian Style.*

Moore, Michael (2) *Canadian Bacon; Roger & Me.*

Moore, Richard *Silent Flute, The (aka Circle of Iron).*

Moore, Robert *Chapter Two;*

Cheap Detective, The; Murder by Death.

Moore, Simon *Under Suspicion; Up on the Roof.*

Moore, Tom *'Night Mother.*

Moorhouse, Jocelyn *How to Make an American Quilt; Proof; Thousand Acres, A.*

Mora, Philippe *Brother, Can You Spare a Dime?; Communion; Death of a Soldier; Mad Dog Morgan (aka Mad Dog); Return of Captain Invincible, The; Swastika.*

Morahan, Andy *Highlander III – The Sorcerer.*

Morahan, Christopher *Clockwise; Old Flames; Paper Mask.*

Morais, José Alvaro *Jester, The (O Bobo).*

Moranis, Rick *Strange Brew.*

Moraz, Patricia *Indians Are Still Far Away, The (Les Indiens Sont Encore Loin).*

Mordillat, Gérard *En Compagnie d'Antonin Artaud (My Life and Times with Antonin Artaud).*

Morel, Gaël *A Toute Vitesses (Full Speed).*

More O'Ferrall, George *Angels One Fives; Heart of the Matter, The; Woman for Joe, The.*

Moretti, Nanni *Aprile; Dear Diary (Caro Diario); Giorno della prima di 'Close Up', Il (Day of the Premiere of 'Close Up').*

Mori, Jun *Honey and Venom.*

Morimoto, Koji *Memories.*

Morin, Edgar *Chronique d'un Eté (Chronicle of a Summer).*

Morita, Yoshimitsu *Deaths in Tokimeki (Tokimeki ni Shisu); Family Game (Kazoku Game).*

Morley, Peter *25 Years.*

Morneau, Louis *Retroactive.*

Moroder, Giorgio *Metropolis.*

Morra, Mario *Savage Man...Savage Beast (Ultime Grida della Savana).*

Morris, David Burton *Jersey Girl; Patti Rocks; Purple Haze.*

Morris, Errol *Dark Wind, The; Gates of Heaven; Thin Blue Line, The; Vernon, Florida.*

Morrison, Bruce *Constance; Shaker Run.*

Morrison, Paul *Unstable Elements – Atomic Stories 1939-85.*

Morrissey, Paul *Bike Boy; Blood for Dracula (Dracula Vuole Vivere: Cerca Sangue di Vergine!); Cocaine (Mixed Blood); Flesh; Flesh for Frankenstein (Carne per Frankenstein); Heat; Hound of the Baskervilles, The; Lonesome Cowboys; Trash; Women in Revolt.*

Morse, Hollingsworth *Daughters of Satan.*

Morse, Terry *Young Dillinger.*

Morton, Rocky *D.O.A.; Super Mario Bros.*

Morton, Vincent *Fatal Bond.*

Moshinsky, Elijah *Genghis Cohn.*

Mostow, Jonathan *Breakdown.*

Mottola, Gregg *Daytrippers, The.*

Mourieras, Claude *Montalvo et l'enfant (Montalvo and the Child).*

Mowbray, Malcolm *Don't Tell Her It's Me; Private Function, A.*

Moxey, John *Circus of Fear (aka Psycho-Circus).*

Moyle, Allan *Empire Records; Pump Up the Volume; Times Square.*

Mueller, Kathy *Daydream Believer.*

Mugge, Robert *Black Wax; Sun Ra: A Joyful Noise.*

Mukdasanit, Euthana *Butterfly and Flowers (Peesua lae dokmai); Path of the Brave (Vittee Khon Kla); Tongpan.*

Mulcahy, Russell *Blue Ice; Highlander; Highlander II – The Quickening; Razorback; Reality Bites; Ricochet; Shadow, The.*

Mulligan, Robert *Baby the Rain Must Fall; Blood-brothers; Clara's Heart; Kiss Me Goodbye; Inside Daisy Clover; Love With the Proper Stranger; Man in the Moon, The; Other, The; Pursuit of Happiness, The; Same Time, Next Year; Summer of '42; To Kill a Mockingbird; Up the Down Staircase.*

Mulloy, Phil *In the Forest; Return, The.*

Mulvey, Laura *Crystal Gazing; Penthesilea: Queen of the Amazons; Riddles of the Sphinx.*

Münch, Christopher *Hours and Times, The.*

Mune, Ian *Came a Hot Friday; End of the Golden Weather, The.*

Munro, David I *Knots.*

Munro, Ian *Prejudice.*

Murakami, Jimmy T *Battle Beyond the Stars; When the Wind Blows.*

Muratova, Kira *Asthenic Syndrome, The (Asteniceskij Sindrom).*

Murch, Walter *Return to Oz.*

Murer, Fredi M *Alpine Fire (Höhenfeuer).*

Murlowski, John *Secret Agent Club, The.*

Murnau, FW *City Girl (aka Our Daily Bread); Faust; Last Laugh, The (Der letzte Mann); Nosferatu – eine Symphonie des Grauens; Sunrise; Tabu.*

Murphy, Colleen *Shoemaker.*

Murphy, Eddie *Harlem Nights.*

Murphy, Geoff *Freejack; Goodbye Pork Pie; Quiet Earth, The; Under Siege 2; Utu; Young Guns II.*

Murphy, Pat *Anne Devlin; Maeve.*

Murphy, Richard *Wackiest Ship in the Army, The.*

Murphy, Tab *Last of the Dogmen.*

Murray, Bill *Quick Change.*

Murray, Don *Cross and the Switchblade, The.*

Murray, John B *Libido.*

Murray, Paul *Elstree Calling.*

Musker, John *Aladdin; Great Mouse Detective, The (aka Basil the Great Mouse Detective); Hercules; Little Mermaid, The.*

Musser, Charles *Before the Nickelodeon: The Early Cinema of Edwin S Porter.*

Musso, Jeff *Puritan, The (Le Puritain).*

Mutrux, Floyd *Aloha, Bobby and Rose; American Hot Wax.*

Mweze, Ngangura *Vie est belle, La.*

Mycroft, Walter C *Banana Ridge.*

Myers, Suzanne *Alchemy.*

Myerson, Alan *Police Academy 5: Assignment Miami Beach; Private Lessons; Steelyard Blues.*

Mykkanen, Mafjaana *From Russia with Rock (Sirppi ja Kitara).*

Na'Aman, Rami *Flying Camel, The.*

Naderi, Amir *Runner, The (Dawandeh); Water, Wind, Dust (Ab, Bad, Khak).*

Nag, Shankar *Swamy.*

Nagasaki, Shunichi *Drive, The (Saigo no Drive); Enchantment, The (Yuwakusha); Heart, Beating in the Dark (Yamiutsu Shinzo); Some Kinda Love (Romance); Stranger (Yoru no Stranger – Kyofu!).*

Nair, Mira *Kama Sutra: A Tale of Love; Mississippi Masala; Perez Family, The; Salaam Bombay!*

Nakajima, Takehiro *Okoge; Remembrance (Kyoshu).*

Nakamura, Eric *Sunsets.*

Nakamura, Genji *Beautiful Mystery – Legend of Big Horn (Utsukushiki Nazo: Kyokon Densetu).*

Nakano, Desmond *White Man's Burden.*

Nakata, Toichi *Osaka Story.*

Nalluri, Bharat *Downtime.*

Narizzano, Silvio *Blue; Class of Miss MacMichael, The; Fanatic (aka Die! Die! My Darling!); Georgy Girl; Loot; Why Shoot the Teacher.*

Nasrallah, Yousry *On Boys, Girls and the Veil (Sobyan Wa Banat).*

Nava, Gregory *El Norte; My Family (Mi Familia/aka East LA); Time of Destiny, A.*

Nazareth, HO *Talking History.*

Neal, Peter *Ain't Misbehavin'; Yessongs.*

Neame, Ronald *Card, The (aka The Promoter); Escape from Zahrain; First Monday in October; Foreign Body; Gambit; Golden Salamander; Hopscotch; Horse's Mouth, The; I Could Go On Singing; Meteor; Million Pound Note, The (aka Man With a Million); Odessa File, The; Poseidon Adventure, The; Prime of Miss Jean Brodie, The; Scrooge; Tunes of Glory; Windom's Way.*

Neat, Timothy *Play Me Something.*

Needham, Hal *Cannonball Run, The; Cannonball Run II; Hooper; Smokey and the Bandit; Smokey and the Bandit II (aka Smokey and the Bandit Ride Again); Villain, The (aka Cactus Jack).*

Nee-Owoo, Kwate *Ama.*

Negrin, Alberto *Red Rings of Fear (Enigma Rosso).*

Negulesco, Jean *Conspirators, The; Daddy Long Legs; How to Marry a Millionaire; Humoresque; Mask of Dimitrios, The; Mudlark, The; Nobody Lives Forever; O. Henry's Full House (aka Full House); Phone Call from a Stranger; Pleasure Seekers, The; Rains of Ranchipur,*

The; Road House; Three Came Home; Three Coins in the Fountain; Titanic; Woman's World.

Neill, Roy William *Black Angel; Black Room, The; Frankenstein Meets the Wolf Man; Hoots Mon!; House of Fear, The; Pearl of Death, The; Pursuit to Algiers; Scarlet Claw, The; Sherlock Holmes and the Spider Woman; Terror by Night.*

Neill, Sam *Cinema of Unease.*

Neilson, James *Dr Syn, Alias the Scarecrow; Night Passage; Summer Magic.*

Nelson, David *Last Plane Out.*

Nelson, Gary *Black Hole, The; Freaky Friday; Jimmy the Kid; Santee.*

Nelson, Gene *Kissin' Cousins.*

Nelson, Jessie *Corrina, Corrina.*

Nelson, Ralph *Duel at Diablo; Father Goose; Flight of the Doves; Soldier Blue; Wilby Conspiracy, The.*

Nemec, Jan *Party and the Guest, The (O Slavnosti a Hostech); Pearls of the Deep (Perlicky na dne).*

Nesbitt, Frank *Dulcima.*

Nesher, Avi *Doppelganger: The Evil Within.*

Nesheim, Berit *Other Side of Sunday (Søndagsengler).*

Neufeld Jr, Sigmund *Conquest of the Earth; Incredible Hulk, The.*

Neumann, Kurt *Fly, The; Mohawk.*

Neville, Edgar *Tower of the Seven Hunchbacks, The (La Torre de los Siete Jorobados).*

Newbrook, Peter *Asphyx, The (aka Horror of Death).*

Newby, Chris *Anchoress; Madagascar Skin.*

Newell, Mike *Amazing Grace and Chuck (aka Silent Voice); Awakening, The; Awfully Big Adventure, An; Dance With a Stranger; Donnie Brasco; Enchanted April; Four Weddings and a Funeral; Good Father, The; Into the West; Soursweet.*

Newman, Joseph M *Big Circus, The; King of the Roaring 20's – The Story of Arnold Rothstein (aka The Big Bankroll); Pony Soldier; This Island Earth.*

Newman, Paul *Effect of Gamma Rays on Man-in-the-Moon Marigolds, The; Glass Menagerie, The; Harry & Son; Rachel, Rachel; Sometimes a Great Notion (aka Never Give an Inch).*

Newmeyer, Fred *Girl Shy;*

Safety Last; Why Worry?

Ngabo, Léonce *Gito, the Ungrateful.*

Ng Sze-Yuen *Bloody Fists, The (Dangkou Tan); Bruce Lee: The Man, The Myth (Li Xiaolong Chuanqi/aka Bruce Lee – True Story).*

Nibbelink, Phil *American Tail: Fievel Goes West, An.*

Niblo, Fred *Ben-Hur; Blood and Sand.*

Niccol, Andrew *Gattaca.*

Nichetti, Maurizio *Icicle Thief (Ladri di Saponette); Luna e l'Altra; Volere, Volare.*

Nicholas, Gregor *Broken English.*

Nicholls Jr, George *Adventures of Michael Strogoff, The (aka The Soldier and the Lady/Michael Strogoff); Anne of Green Gables.*

Nichols, Charles A *Charlotte's Web.*

Nichols, Mike *Biloxi Blues; Birdcage, The; Carnal Knowledge; Catch-22; Day of the Dolphin, The; Fortune, The; Graduate, The; Heartburn; Postcards from the Edge; Primary Colors; Regarding Henry; Silkwood; Who's Afraid of Virginia Woolf?; Wolf; Working Girl.*

Nicholson, Jack *Drive, He Said; Goin' South; Two Jakes, The.*

Nicolaidis, Nicos *Singapore Sling.*

Nicolaou, Ted *TerrorVision.*

Nierenberg, George T *No Maps on My Taps.*

Niermans, Edouard *Angel Dust (Poussière d'Ange).*

Nigh, William *Strange Case of Dr Rx, The.*

Nilsson, Bob *Signal 7.*

Nilsson, Rob *Northern Lights.*

Nimibutr, Nonzee *Dang Bireley's and the Young Gangsters (2499 Antapan Krong Muang).*

Nimoy, Leonard *Funny About Love; Good Mother, The; Holy Matrimony; Star Trek III: The Search for Spock; Three Men and a Baby; Voyage Home: Star Trek IV, The.*

Ning Ying *For Fun (Zhao Le).*

Nissimoff, Riki Shelach *Last Winter, The (Hakhoref Ha'Acharon).*

Noble, Adrian *Midsummer Night's Dream, A.*

Noé, Gaspar *Carné.*

Nolan, Christopher *Following.*

Noonan, Chris *Babe.*

Norman, Leslie *Dunkirk; Long and the Short and the Tall, The; Night My Number Came Up, The; X the Unknown.*

Normand, Michael *Dirty Laundry.*

Norton, Bill L (aka BWL Norton/Bill WL Norton) *Baby – Secret of the Lost Legend; Cisco Pike; More American Graffiti; Three for the Road.*

Nosseck, Max *Brighton Strangler, The; Dillinger.*

Nosseck, Noel *Dreamer.*

Nossiter, Jonathan *Sunday.*

Novak, Blaine *Good to Go.*

Novaro, Maria *Danzón; Jardin del Eden, El (The Garden of Eden).*

Noyce, Phillip *Backroads; Blind Fury; Clear and Present Danger; Dead Calm; Heatwave; Newsfront; Patriot Games; Sliver.*

Nuchtern, Simon *New York Nights.*

Nugent, Elliott *Cat and the Canary, The; Great Gatsby, The; My Favourite Brunette; Never Say Die; Up in Arms.*

Nugroho, Garin *...And the Moon Dances (Bulan Tertusuk Ilalang); Letter from an Angel (Surat Untuk Bidadari).*

Nuñez, Victor *Gal Young 'Un; Ruby in Paradise; Ulee's Gold.*

Nunn, Trevor *Hedda; Lady Jane; Twelfth Night.*

Nureyev, Rudolf *Don Quixote.*

Nuridsany, Claude *Microcosmos (Microcosmos: Le Peuple de l'herbe).*

Nutley, Colin *House of Angels (Anglagård).*

Nutter, David *Cease Fire.*

Nuytten, Bruno *Camille Claudel.*

Nyby, Christian *Thing from Another World, The.*

Nykvist, Carl-Gustaf *Women on the Roof, The (Kvinnorna på taket).*

Nykvist, Sven *One and One (En och En); Ox, The (Oxen).*

Nyswaner, Ron *Prince of Pennsylvania, The.*

O'Bannon, Dan *Return of the Living Dead, The.*

O'Bannon, Rockne S *Fear.*

Obitani, Yuri *Hair Opera, The (Mohatsu Kageki).*

Obler, Arch *Arnelo Affair, The; Five.*

Oblowitz, Michael *King Blank; This World, Then the Fireworks.*

Obomsawin, Alanis *Kanehsatake (Oka) – 270 Years of Resistance.*

O'Brien, Jim *Dressmaker, The.*

Obrow, Jeffrey *Kindred, The.*

O'Callaghan, Maurice *Broken Harvest.*

Ockrent, Mike *Dancin' Thru the Dark.*

O'Connell, Maura *Siege.*

O'Connolly, James *Mistress Pamela; Valley of Gwangi, The.*

O'Connor, Pat *Cal; Circle of Friends; Fools of Fortune; Inventing the Abbotts; January Man, The; Month in the Country, A; Stars and Bars.*

O'Connor, William A *Cocaine Fiends, The.*

Odets, Clifford *None But the Lonely Heart.*

Oedekerk, Steve *Ace Ventura – When Nature Calls; Nothing to Lose.*

Ofteringer, Susanne *Nico Icon.*

Ogawa, Shinsuke *Peasants of the Second Fortress, The (Sanrizuka: Daini Toride no Hitobito).*

Ogilvie, George *Mad Max Beyond Thunderdome.*

Ogorodinikov, Valery *Burglar (Vzlomshchik).*

Oguri, Kohei *Muddy River (Doro no Kawa); Sleeping Man (Nemuru Otoko); Sting of Death, The (Shi no Toge).*

O'Hara, Gerry *Bitch, The; Brute, The; Fanny Hill; Leopard in the Snow.*

Okamura, Tensai *Memories.*

Okazaki, Steven *Lisa Theory, The.*

Oken, Tung *Mercedes Mon Amour (Fikrimin Ince Gulu).*

Oki, Hiroyuki *Heaven-6-Box; I Like You, I Like You Very Much (Anata-ga suki desu, dai suki des'); Swimming Prohibited (Yuei Kinishi).*

Ökten, Zeki *Enemy, The (Düsman); Herd, The (Sürü).*

Okuyama, Kazuyoshi *Mystery of Rampo, The (Ranpo).*

Oldman, Gary *Nil by Mouth.*

Olea, Pedro *Fencing Master, The (El Maestro de Esgrima).*

O'Leary, Ronan *Driftwood; Fragments of Isabella.*

Oliansky, Joel *Competition, The.*

Oliphant, Peer *Viva Portugal.*

Oliveira, Manoel de *Abraham Valley (Vale Abraão); Convent, The (O Convento).*

Olivera, Héctor *Funny Dirty Little War, A (No Habrá más Penas ni Olvido).*

Olivier, Laurence *Hamlet; Henry V; Prince and the Showgirl, The; Richard III; Three Sisters.*

Olmi, Ermanno *Cammina Cammina; Circumstance, The (La Circonstanza); During the Summer (Durante l'Estate); Legend of the Holy Drinker, The (La Leggenda del Santo Bevitore); Long Live the Lady! (Lunga Vita alla Signora!); Man Named John, A (E Venne un Uomo); Posto, Il (The Job/The Sound of Trumpets); Recuperanti, I (The Scavengers); Tree of Wooden Clogs, The (L'Albero degli Zoccoli).*

Olofson, Christina *Lines from the Heart (I Rollerna Tre).*

Olsson, Stellan *Close to the Wind (Oss Emellan); Sven Klang's Combo (Sven Klangs Kvintett).*

O'Neil, Lawrence *Throwing Down.*

O'Neil, Robert Vincent *Angel.*

O'Neill, Jevon *Bob's Weekend.*

O'Neill, Ken *Secret Policeman's Third Ball, The.*

O'Neill, Tom *Water and Power.*

Onwurah, Ngozi *Welcome II the Terrordome.*

Ophüls, Marcel *Hotel Terminus: The Life and Times of Klaus Barbie; Memory of Justice, The; Sense of Loss, A; Veillées d'Armes (The Troubles We've Seen).*

Ophüls, Max *Caught; Exile, The; Letter from an Unknown Woman; Liebelei; Lola Montès; Madame de... (The Earrings of Madame de...); Plaisir, Le (House of Pleasure); Reckless Moment, The; Ronde, La; Signora di Tutti, La.*

Orders, Ron *Fly a Flag for Poplar.*

Orentreich, Catherine *Wizard of Waukesha, The.*

Orfini, Mario *Fair Game (Mamba).*

Orme, Stuart *Puppet Masters, The (aka Robert A. Heinlein's The Puppet Masters); Wolves of Willoughby Chase, The.*

Ormeland, Paul *Like It Is.*

Ormrod, Peter *Eat the Peach.*

Ormsby, Alan *Deranged.*

O'Rourke, Dennis *Good Woman of Bangkok, The; Half Life; Shark Callers of Kontu, The.*

Orr, James *Man of the House.*

Ortega, Kenny *Hocus Pocus; Newsies (aka The New Boys).*

Orton, John *Windjammer, The.*

Oshii, Mamoru *Ghost in the Shell (Kokaku Kidotai).*

Oshima, Nagisa *Ai No Corrida (L'Empire des Sens/The Realm of the Senses/In the Realm of the Senses); Boy (Shonen); Ceremony, The (Gishiki); Dear Summer Sister (Natsu no Imoto); Death by Hanging (Koshikei); Diary of a Shinjuku Thief (Shinjuku Dorobo Nikki); Empire of Passion (L'Empire de la Passion/Ai no Borei); Man Who Left His Will on Film, The (Tokyo Senso Sengo Hiwa); Max Mon Amour (Max My Love); Merry Christmas Mr Lawrence; Three Resurrected Drunkards (Kaettekita Yopparai); Town of Love and Hope, A (Ai to Kibo no Machi); Violence at Noon (Hakuchu no Torima).*

O'Sullivan, Thaddeus *December Bride; Nothing Personal.*

Oswald, Gerd *Bunny O'Hare; Crime of Passion; Kiss Before Dying, A; Screaming Mimi.*

Oswald, Richard *Living Dead, The (Unheimliche Geschichten).*

Othenin-Girard, Dominique *Omen IV: The Awakening.*

Otomo, Katsuhiro *Akira; Memories; World Apartment Horror.*

Ott, Thomas *Little People.*

Ottinger, Ulrike *Joan of Arc of Mongolia; Madame X.*

Ouedraogo, Idrissa *Cri du Coeur, Le; Kini & Adams; Samba Traore; Tilaï; Yaaba.*

Oury, Gérard *Mad Adventures of 'Rabbi' Jacob, The (Les Aventures de Rabbi Jacob).*

Ové, Horace *Playing Away; Pressure; Reggae.*

Owen, Cliff *Bawdy Adventures of Tom Jones, The; Magnificent Two, The; Ooh... You Are Awful (aka Get Charlie Tully); Prize of Arms, A; That Riviera Touch; Wrong Arm of the Law, The.*

Owúsu, Kwesi *Ama.*

Oz, Frank *Dark Crystal, The; Dirty Rotten Scoundrels; Housesitter; In & Out; Indian in the Cupboard, The; Little Shop of Horrors; Muppets Take Manhattan, The; What About Bob?*

Ozawa, Shigehiro *Blood of the Dragon (Satsujinken 2); Kung Fu Street Fighter (Gekitotsu! Satsujinken).*

Ozerov, Juri *Visions of Eight.*

Özkan, Yavuz *Two Women (Iki Kadin).*

Ozpetek, Ferzan *Turkish Bath – Hamam, The (Il Bagno Turco – Hamam).*

Ozu, Yasujiro *Autumn Afternoon, An (Samma no aji); Early Spring (Soshun); Flavour of Green Tea Over Rice, The (Ochazuke no aji); Hen in the Wind (Kaze no naka no mendori); I Was Born, But... (Umarete wa Mita Keredo); Late Spring (Banshun); Ohayo (Good Morning); Record of a Tenement Gentleman (Nagaya Shinshiroku); Tokyo Story (Tokyo Monogatari).*

Pabst, Georg Wilhelm *Diary of a Lost Girl (Das Tagebuch einer Verlorenen); Don Quichotte; Dreigroschenoper, Die (The Threepenny Opera); Joyless Street, The (Die freudlose Gasse); Kameradschaft; Love of Jeanne Ney, The (Die Liebe der Jeanne Ney); Pandora's Box (Die Büchse der Pandora); Secrets of a Soul (Geheimnisse einer Seele); Westfront 1918.*

Pachard, Henri *The Devil in Miss Jones Part II.*

Pacino, Al *Looking for Richard.*

Page, Anthony *Absolution (aka Murder by Confession); Forbidden; I Never Promised You a Rose Garden; Inadmissible Evidence; Lady Vanishes, The.*

Pagnol, Marcel *César; Femme du Boulanger, La (The Baker's Wife); Merlusse.*

Pagliero, Marcel *P..... Respectueuse, La (The Respectful Prostitute/The Respectable Prostitute).*

Pajaczkowska, Claire *Sigmund Freud's Dora.*

Pakdivijt, Chalong *S.T.A.B. (aka Thong).*

Pakula, Alan J *All the President's Men; Comes a Horseman; Consenting Adults; Devil's Own, The; Dream Lover; Klute; Orphans; Parallax View, The; Pelican Brief, The; Presumed Innocent; Rollover; See You in the Morning; Sophie's Choice; Starting Over; Sterile Cuckoo, The (aka Pookie).*

Pal, George *Time Machine, The; 7 Faces of Dr Lao; Tom Thumb.*

Palcy, Euzhan *Black Shack Alley (Rue Cases Nègres); Dry White Season, A.*

Palekar, Amol *Square Circle, The (Daayraa); Village Has No Walls, The (Bangarwadi).*

Palmer, John *Ciao! Manhattan.*

Palmer, Tony *Testimony; 200 Motels; Wagner.*

Paltenghi, David *Orders Are Orders.*

Panahi, Jafar *White Balloon, The (Badkonak-E Sefid).*

Panama, Norman *Court Jester, The; How to Commit Marriage; I Will...I Will...For Now; Knock on Wood.*

Pande *Ek Baar Phir (Once Again).*

Panfilov, Gleb *Beginning, The (Nachalo); Theme, The (Tema); Vassa.*

Panh, Rithy *Gens de la rizière, Les (Rice People).*

Papas, Michael *Tomorrow's Warrior (Avrianos Polemistis).*

Papatakis, Nico *Equilibristes, Les (Walking a Tightrope).*

Papousek, Jaroslav *Best Age, The (Nejkrasnejsi Vek).*

Paradjanov, Sergo *Ashik Kerib; Colour of Pomegranates, The (Nran Gouyne); Colour of Pomegranates: Director's Cut, The (Nran Gouyne); Legend of the Suram Fortress, The (Legenda Suramskoi Kreposti); Shadows of Our Forgotten Ancestors (Teni Zanytykh Predkov).*

Paris, Jerry *How Sweet It Is!; Police Academy 2: Their First Assignment; Police Academy 3: Back in Training; Viva Max!*

Park Chon-Won *Our Twisted Hero (Uridleui Ilgureojin Youngung).*

Park Chul-Soo *Farewell My Darling (Haksaeng Bukunshinwi); Push! Push! (San-bu In-gwa); 301-302.*

Park Jae-Ho *Broken Branches (Naeil ui Hyahae Hurunun Kang).*

Park Kwang-Su *Berlin Report; Single Spark, A (Jeon Tae-Il).*

Park, Nick *Close Shave, A.*

Parker, Alan *Angel Heart; Birdy; Bugsy Malone; Come See the Paradise; Commitments, The; Evita; Fame; Midnight Express; Mississippi Burning; Pink Floyd: The Wall; Road to Wellville, The; Shoot the Moon.*

The (Il Ciclone).

Piccoli, Michel *So there, (Alors voilà).*

Picha (Jean-Paul Walravens/Boris Szulzinger) *Big Bang, The (Le Big Bang); Jungle Burger (La Honte de la Jungle).*

Pichel, Irving *And Now Tomorrow; Before Dawn; Destination Moon; Man I Married, The (aka I Married a Nazi); Miracle of the Bells, The; Mr Peabody and the Mermaid; Most Dangerous Game, The (aka The Hounds of Zaroff); Pied Piper, The; She; They Won't Believe Me.*

Pichul, Vasili *Little Vera (Malenkaya Vera).*

Pierce, Charles B *Bootleggers; Evictors, The; Grayeagle; Norseman, The.*

Pierson, Claude *Violation of Justine, The (Justine de Sade).*

Pierson, Frank R *Citizen Cohn; Looking Glass War, The; King of the Gypsies; Star Is Born, A;*

Pieters, Guido *Romantic Agony, The (Vaarwel).*

Pilafian, Peter *Jimi Plays Berkeley.*

Pillsbury, Sam *Free Willy 3: The Rescue; Scarecrow, The; Starlight Hotel: Zandalee.*

Pincus, Ed *Diaries.*

Pinheiro, José *Cop's Honour (Parole de Flic).*

Pinhorn, Maggie *Tunde's Film.*

Pinoteau, Claude *Silencieux, Le (The Man Who Died Twice/The Silent One).*

Pinter, Harold *Butley.*

Pintilié, Lucian *Too Late (Trop Tard); Unforgettable Sumer, An (Eté inoubliable, Un).*

Pintoff, Ernest *Dynamite Chicken; Harvey Middleman, Fireman; Jaguar Lives.*

Piquer-Simon, Juan *Rift, The (La Grieta); Supersonic Man.*

Pirès, Gérard *Agression, L' (Agression).*

Pitts, Rafi *Season Five (Fassloh Padjom/Cinquième saison).*

Platts-Mills, Barney *Bronco Bullfrog; Hero; Private Road.*

Plumb, Hay *Hamlet.*

Po Chih Leong *Ping Pong.*

Podalydès, Bruno *Versailles rive gauche (A Night in Versailles).*

Podeswa, Jeremy *Eclipse.*

Poe, Amos *Subway Riders; Triple Bogey on a Par Five Hole.*

Poelvoorde, Benoît *Man Bites Dog (C'est arrivé près de chez vous).*

Pogostin, S Lee *Hard Contract.*

Poh, Richard (Bu Wancang) *Love and Duty (Lian'ai yu Yiwu).*

Pohland, Hans Jürgen *Stamping Ground (aka Love and Music).*

Poiré, Jean-Marc *Visiteurs, Les.*

Poirier, Anne Claire *Mourir à Tue-Tête (A Scream from Silence).*

Poirier, Léon, *Appel du Silence, L'.*

Poirier, Manuel *Western.*

Poitier, Sidney *Buck and the Preacher; Fast Forward; Hanky Panky; Let's Do It Again; Piece of the Action, A; Stir Crazy; Uptown Saturday Night; Warm December, A.*

Polanski, Roman *Bitter Moon (Lunes de fiel); Chinatown; Cul-de-Sac; Dance of the Vampires (aka The Fearless Vampire Killers); Death and the Maiden; Frantic; Knife in the Water (Noz w Wodzie); Macbeth; Pirates; Repulsion; Rosemary's Baby; Tenant, The (Le Locataire); Tess; What? (Che?).*

Poliakoff, Stephen *Century; Close My Eyes; Hidden City.*

Politi, Edna *Anou Banou or the Daughters of Utopia (Anou Banou oder die Töchter der Utopie).*

Pollack, Barry *Booty Call; Cool Breeze.*

Pollack, Jeff *Above the Rim.*

Pollack, Sydney *Absence of Malice; Bobby Deerfield; Castle Keep; Electric Horseman, The; Firm, The; Havana; Jeremiah Johnson; Out of Africa; Sabrina; Scalphunters, The; They Shoot Horses, Don't They?; This Property Is Condemned; Three Days of the Condor; Tootsie; Way We Were, The; Yakuza, The.*

Pollak, Claire *Cross and Passion; Theatre Girls.*

Pollak, Kay *Elvis! Elvis!*

Pollet, Jean-Daniel *Paris vu par... (Six in Paris).*

Pollock, George *Ten Little Indians.*

Polonsky, Abraham *Force of Evil; Romance of a Horse Thief; Tell Them Willie Boy Is Here.*

Pommer, Erich *Vessel of Wrath (aka The Beachcomber).*

Ponnelle, Jean-Pierre *Rigoletto.*

Pons, Ventura *Actresses (Actrius)*

Pontecorvo, Gillo *Battle of Algiers, The (La Battaglia di Algeri); Kapo; Queimada! (Burn!).*

Pool, Lea *Anne Trister.*

Pope, Angela *Captives; Hollow Reed.*

Pope, Tim *Crow: City of Angels, The; Cure in Orange, The.*

Popkin, Leo *Well, The.*

Post, Ted *Baby, The; Beneath the Planet of the Apes; Go Tell the Spartans; Good Guys Wear Black; Hang 'em High; Harrad Experiment, The; Magnum Force; Whiffs (aka C.A.S.H.).*

Postma, Laurens C *Heaven, Man, Earth.*

Potenza, Anthony *No Nukes.*

Potter, Dennis *Secret Friends.*

Potter, HC *Beloved Enemy; Blackmail; Congo Maisie; Hellzapoppin'; Mr Blandings Builds His Dream House; Story of Vernon and Irene Castle, The.*

Potter, Sally *Gold Diggers, The; Orlando; Tango Lesson, The.*

Potterton, Gerald *Heavy Metal.*

Poulson, Gerry *Under the Doctor.*

Powell, Aubrey *Cure Show, The.*

Powell, Dick *Conqueror, The; Hunters, The; Enemy Below, The.*

Powell, Michael *Age of Consent; Battle of the River Plate, The (aka Pursuit of the Graf Spee); Black Narcissus; Bluebeard's Castle; Canterbury Tale, A; Contraband (aka Blackout); Edge of the World, The; Elusive Pimpernel, The; 49th Parallel; Gone To Earth; Honeymoon (Luna de Miel); I Know Where I'm Going!; Ill Met by Moonlight (aka Night Ambush); Lazybones; Life and Death of Colonel Blimp, The; Love Test, The; Matter of Life and Death, A (aka Stairway to Heaven); Night of the Party, The; Oh Rosalinda!!; One of Our Aircraft Is Missing; Peeping Tom; Phantom Light, The; Queen's Guards, The; Red Shoes, The; Small Back Room, The; Spy in Black, The; Tales of Hoffman, The; They're a Weird Mob; Thief of Bagdad, The.*

Powell, Tristram *American Friends.*

Power, John *Father; Picture Show Man, The.*

Powers, John *I Am a Sex Addict.*

Prado, Guilherme De Almeida *Lady from the Shanghai Cinema, The (A Dama do cine Shanghai).*

Prasad, Udayan *Brothers in Trouble; My Son the Fanatic.*

Preminger, Otto *Advise and Consent; Anatomy of a Murder; Angel Face; Bonjour Tristesse; Bunny Lake is Missing; Cardinal, The; Carmen Jones; Centennial Summer; Court-Martial of Billy Mitchell, The (aka One Man Mutiny); Daisy Kenyon; Exodus; Fallen Angel; Forever Amber; Human Factor, The; Hurry Sundown; In Harm's Way; Laura; Man With the Golden Arm, The; Moon Is Blue, The; River of No Return; Rosebud; Royal Scandal, A; Saint Joan; Such Good Friends; Tell Me That You Love Me, Junie Moon; Whirlpool.*

Pressburger, Emeric *Battle of the River Plate, The (aka Pursuit of the Graf Spee); Black Narcissus; Canterbury Tale, A; Elusive Pimpernel, The; Gone To Earth; I Know Where I'm Going!; Life and Death of Colonel Blimp, The; Matter of Life and Death, A (aka Stairway to Heaven); Oh Rosalinda!!; One of Our Aircraft is Missing; Red Shoes, The; Small Back Room, The; Tales of Hoffman, The.*

Pressman, Michael *Bad News Bears in Breaking Training, The; Boulevard Nights; Great Texas Dynamite Chase, The (aka Dynamite Women); Some Kind of Hero; Teenage Mutant Ninja Turtles II: The Secret of the Ooze.*

Price David F *Dr Jekyll and Ms Hyde.*

Price, Paul (Paolo Poeti) *Inhibitions.*

Price, Will *Rock, Rock, Rock.*

Primus, Barry *Mistress.*

Prince *Prince – Sign o'the Times; Under the Cherry Moon.*

Prince, Harold *Little Night Music, A; Something for Everyone (aka Black Flowers for the Bride).*

Proctor, Elaine *Friends; On the Wire.*

Prosperi, Franco *Africa Addio (Africa Blood and Guts); Uncle Tom (Zio Tom).*

Proud, Peter *Esther Waters.*

Reinhardt, Max *Midsummer Night's Dream, A*.

Reinl, Harald *Chariots of the Gods (Erinnerungen an die Zukunft); Hellhounds of Alaska (Die Blutigen Geier von Alaska)*.

Reis, Irving *Big Street, The; Crack-Up*.

Reisch, Walter *Men Are Not Gods; Song of Scheherazade*.

Reisner, Allen *St Louis Blues*.

Reisner, Charles F *Steamboat Bill, Jr*.

Reisz, Karel *Everybody Wins; French Lieutenant's Woman, The; Gambler, The; Isadora; Morgan, a Suitable Case for Treatment; Night Must Fall; Saturday Night and Sunday Morning; Sweet Dreams; Who'll Stop the Rain? (aka Dog Soldiers)*.

Reitherman, Wolfgang *Aristocats; Jungle Book, The; One Hundred and One Dalmatians; Rescuers, The; Robin Hood; Sword in the Stone, The*.

Reitman, Ivan *Dave; Fathers' Day; Ghostbusters; Ghostbusters II; Junior; Kindergarten Cop; Legal Eagles; Meatballs; Stripes; Twins*.

Reitz, Edgar *Germany in Autumn (Deutschland im Herbst); Heimat (Homeland)*.

Relph, Michael *Desert Mice; Rockets Galore (aka Mad Little Island); Saraband for Dead Lovers*.

René, Norman *Longtime Companion; Prelude to a Kiss*.

Rennie, Howard *Spoor (aka Guns Across the Veldt)*.

Renoir, Jean *Bas-Fonds, Les (The Lower Depths); Boudu Sauvé des Eaux (Boudu Saved from Drowning); Bête Humaine, La (The Human Beast/Judas Was a Woman); Caporal Épinglé, Le (The Elusive Corporal/The Vanishing Corporal); Chienne, La; Crime de Monsieur Lange, Le (The Crime of Monsieur Lange); Diary of a Chambermaid, The; Déjeuner sur l'Herbe, Le (Lunch on the Grass/Picnic on the Grass); Eléna et les Hommes (Paris Does Strange Things); French Cancan; Golden Coach, The (La Carrozza d'Oro/Le Carrosse d'Or); Grande Illusion, La; Madame Bovary; Marseillaise, La; Nana; Nuit du Carrefour, La; On Purge Bébé; Partie de Campagne, Une; Petite Marchande d'allumettes, La (The Little Matchgirl); Petit Théâtre de Jean Renoir, Le (Little Theatre of Jean Renoir, The); River, The; Règle du Jeu, La (The Rules of the Game); Southerner, The; Swamp Water; This Land Is Mine; Toni; Tournoi, Le (The Tournament); Vie est à nous, La (The People of France); Woman on the Beach, The*.

Rényi, Tamás *Valley, The (Volgy)*.

Resnais, Alain *Amour à Mort, L'; Année Dernière à Marienbad, L' (Last Year in Marienbad); Far from Vietnam (Loin du Viêt-nam); Guerre est finie, La (The War Is Over); Hiroshima, Mon Amour; I Want to Go Home (Je Veux Rentrer à la Maison); Je t'aime, Je t'aime; Mon Oncle d'Amérique (My American Uncle/My Uncle from America); Muriel (Muriel, ou le Temps d'un Retour); Mélo; Providence; Same Old Song (On connaît la chanson); Smoking/No Smoking; Stavisky...; Vie est un Roman, La (Life Is a Bed of Roses)*.

Resnikoff, Robert *First Power, The*.

Retes, Gabriel *Bulto, El (Excess Baggage)*.

Rey-Coquais, Cyrille *Georgette Meunier*.

Reynolds, Burt *End, The; 'Gator; Stick; Sharkey's Machine*.

Reynolds, Kevin *Beast, The (aka The Beast of War); Fandango; One Eight Seven; Rapa Nui; Robin Hood: Prince of Thieves; Waterworld*.

Reynolds, Scott *Ugly, The*.

Rezende, Sergio *To the Last Drop (Até a Ultima Gota)*.

Rhodes, Michael Ray *Entertaining Angels: The Dorothy Day Story*.

Rhone, Trevor D *Smile Orange*.

Rich, David Lowell *Airport '80 The Concorde (aka The Concorde – Airport '79); Eye of the Cat; Lovely Way to Die, A (aka A Lovely Way to Go); Sex Symbol, The; That Man Bolt*.

Rich, Matty *Straight Out of Brooklyn*.

Rich, Richard *Black Cauldron, The; Fox and the Hound, The; Swan Princess, The*.

Richard, Jean-Louis *Mata-Hari, Agent H.21*.

Richards, Dick *Culpepper Cattle Co., The; Death Valley; Farewell, My Lovely; Man, Woman and Child; March or Die; Rafferty and the Gold Dust Twins*.

Richards, Julian *Darklands*.

Richardson, Amanda *Carry Greenham Home*.

Richardson, Peter *Eat the Rich; Pope Must Die, The; Supergrass, The*.

Richardson, Ralph *Home at Seven (aka Murder on Monday)*.

Richardson, Tony *Blue Sky; Border, The; Charge of the Light Brigade, The; Dead Cert.; Delicate Balance, A; Entertainer, The; Hamlet; Hotel New Hampshire, The; Joseph Andrews; Laughter in the Dark; Loneliness of the Long Distance Runner, The; Look Back in Anger; Loved One, The; Mademoiselle; Ned Kelly; Sailor from Gibraltar, The; Sanctuary; Taste of Honey, A; Tom Jones*.

Richert, William *American Success Company, The (aka Success); Night in the Life of Jimmy Reardon, A (aka Jimmy Reardon); Winter Kills*.

Richman, Geoff *Fly a Flag for Poplar*.

Richman, Marie *Fly a Flag for Poplar*.

Richmond, Anthony (Teodoro Ricci) *Sharks' Cave, The (Bermude: La Fossa Maledetta)*.

Richter, Hans *Dreams That Money Can Buy*.

Richter, WD *Adventures of Buckaroo Banzai Across the 8th Dimension, The; Late for Dinner*.

Ricker, Bruce *Last of the Blue Devils, The*.

Rickman, Alan *Winter Guest, The*.

Rickman, Tom *River Rat, The*.

Ridley, Philip *Passion of Darkly Noon, The (Die Passion des Darkly Noon); Reflecting Skin, The*.

Riefenstahl, Leni *Olympische Spiele 1936 (Olympiad); Triumph of the Will (Triumph des Willens)*.

Riesner, Charles *Big Store, The*.

Rifkin, Adam *Chase, The*.

Riggs, Marlon T *Tongues Untied*.

Riju, Go *Blind Alley (Mienai); Elephant Song; Zazie*.

Riklis, Eran *Cup Final*.

Rilla, Wolf *Black Rider, The; Blue Peter, The (aka Navy Heroes); Scamp, The; Village of the Damned*.

Riondino, David *Cuba Libre*.

Ripley, Arthur *Thunder Road*.

Ripploh, Frank *Taxi zum Klo*.

Ripstein, Arturo *Deep Crimson (Profundo carmesí/Carmín profond); White Lies (Mentiras Piadosas)*.

Risi, Marco *Forever Mary (Mery per sempre)*.

Rissi, Michael *Soultaker*.

Rissient, Pierre *Five and the Skin (Cinq et la Peau)*.

Ritchie, Michael *Almost Perfect Affair, An; Bad News Bears, The; Candidate, The; Couch Trip, The; Diggstown (aka Midnight Sting); Divine Madness; Downhill Racer; Fletch; Fletch Lives; Golden Child, The; Island, The; Positively True Adventures of the Alleged Texas Cheerleader-Murdering Mom, The; Prime Cut; Semi-Tough; Simple Wish, A; Smile, Survivors, The; Wildcats*.

Rittakol, Bhandit *Once Upon a Time...This Morning (Kala Krangnung Mua Shao Ni)*.

Ritt, Martin *Back Roads; Black Orchid, The; Brotherhood, The; Casey's Shadow; Conrack; Cross Creek; Edge of the City (aka A Man Is Ten Feet Tall); Front, The; Hombre; Hud; Long, Hot Summer, The; Molly Maguires, The; Murphy's Romance; Norma Rae; Nuts; Pete 'n' Tillie; Sounder; Spy Who Came In From the Cold, The; Stanley & Iris*.

Rivette, Jacques *Amour Fou, L'; Amour par terre, L' (Love on the Ground); Belle Noiseuse, La; Belle Noiseuse – Divertimento, La; Céline and Julie Go Boating (Céline et Julie Vont en Bateau: Phantom Ladies over Paris); Jeanne la Pucelle (Joan of Arc); Out 1: Spectre; Paris Nous Appartient (Paris Belongs to Us); Pont du Nord, Le*.

Roach, Hal *Turnabout*.

Roach, Jay *Austin Powers: International Man of Mystery*.

Robbe-Grillet, Alain *Blue Villa, The (Un bruit qui rend fou); Glissements Progressifs du Plaisir; Immortelle, L'; Trans-Europ-Express*.

Robbins, Brian *Good Burger*.

Robbins, Jerome *West Side Story*.

Robbins, Matthew *Batteries Not Included; Bingo; Corvette Summer (aka The Hot One); Dragonslayer; Legend of Billie Jean, The*.

Robbins, Tim *Dead Man Walking; Bob Roberts*.

Roberson, James W *Superstition (aka The Witch).*

Robert, Genevieve *Casual Sex?*

Robert, Yves *Alexandre (Alexandre le Bienheureux); Château de ma mère, Le (My Mother's Castle); Courage Fuyons (Courage – Let's Run); Gloire de mon père, La (My Father's Glory); Guerre des Boutons, La (The War of the Buttons); Pardon Mon Affaire, Too (Nous Irons Tous au Paradis).*

Roberts, Cynthia *Last Supper, The.*

Roberts, John *War of the Buttons; This Boy's Story.*

Roberts, Mel *Intimate with a Stranger.*

Roberts, Stephen *If I Had a Million; Man Who Broke the Bank at Monte Carlo, The.*

Roberts, Steve *Sir Henry at Rawlinson's End.*

Roberts, Will *Men's Lives.*

Robertson, Cliff *J.W. Coop.*

Robertson, Hugh A *Bim; Melinda.*

Robertson, John S *Dr Jekyll and Mr Hyde.*

Robertson, Michael *Back of Beyond.*

Robertson-Pierce, Pamela *Imago – Meret Oppenheim.*

Robins, Herb *Worm Eaters, The.*

Robinson, Bruce *How to Get Ahead in Advertising; Jennifer 8; Withnail & I.*

Robinson, Dave *Take It or Leave It.*

Robinson, John Mark *Kid.*

Robinson, Phil Alden *Field of Dreams; Sneakers; Woo Woo Kid, The.*

Robinson, Richard *Is There Sex After Marriage?.*

Robinson, Todd *Wild Bill: A Hollywood Maverick.*

Robson, Mark *Avalanche Express; Bedlam; Bridges at Toko-Ri, The; Champion; Earthquake, Edge of Doom (aka Stronger Than Fear); From the Terrace; Ghost Ship, The; Happy Birthday, Wanda June; Harder They Fall, The; Inn of the Sixth Happiness, The; Isle of the Dead; I Want You; Little Hut, The; My Foolish Heart; Peyton Place; Seventh Victim, The; Valley of the Dolls; Von Ryan's Express.*

Rocco, Marc *Murder in the First.*

Rocha, Glauber *Antonio das*

Mortes (O Dragão da Maldade contra o Santo Guerreiro); Barravento; Black God, White Devil (Deus e o Diabo na Terra do Sol); Lion has Seven Heads, The (Der Leone Have Sept Cabecas).*

Rochant, Eric *Aux Yeux du monde (Autobus); Monde sans pitié, Un (Tough Life/A World Without Pity).*

Rochat, Eric *Fifth Monkey, The.*

Rockwell, Alexandre *Four Rooms; In the Soup; Somebody to Love; Sons.*

Roddam, Franc *Aria; Bride, The; K2; Lords of Discipline, The; Quadrophenia; War Party.*

Rodley, Chris *Donald Cammell: The Ultimate Performance; Tropical Fish.*

Rodriguez, Robert *Desperado; El Mariachi; Four Rooms; From Dusk till Dawn.*

Roe, Willy *Playbirds, The.*

Roeg, Nicolas *Aria; Bad Timing; Castaway; Cold Heaven; Don't Look Now; Eureka; Insignificance; Man Who Fell to Earth, The; Performance; Sweet Bird of Youth; Track 29; Two Deaths; Walkabout; Witches, The.*

Roemer, Michael *Haunted; Plot Against Harry, The.*

Roffman, Julian *Mask, The (aka The Eyes of Hell).*

Rogell, Albert S *Atlantic Adventure; Black Cat, The.*

Rogers, Maclean *Down Among the Z Men; Gert and Daisy's Weekend.*

Rogosin, Lionel *Come Back Africa.*

Rogozhkin, Alexander *Guard, The (Karaul).*

Rohmer, Eric *Aviator's Wife, The (La Femme de l'Aviateur); Beau Mariage, Le (A Good Marriage); Boulangère de Monceau, La; Carrière de Suzanne, La (Suzanne's Profession); Claire's Knee (Le Genou de Claire); Collectionneuse, La (The Collector); Conte d'été (A Summer's Tale); 4 Adventures of Reinette & Mirabelle (4 Aventures de Reinette & Mirabelle); Full Moon in Paris (Les Nuits de la Pleine Lune); Green Ray, The (Le Rayon Vert); Love in the Afternoon (L'Amour, l'Après-midi); Marquise von O..., Die (The Marquise of O); My Girlfriend's Boyfirend (L'Ami de Mon Amie); My Night with Maud (Ma Nuit chez Maud); Paris vu par... (Six in Paris); Pauline à la Plage (Pauline at the Beach); Perceval le Gallois; Rendez-*

vous de Paris, Les (Rendez-vous in Paris); Signe du Lion, Le (The Sign of Leo); Tale of Springtime, A (Conte de Printemps); Winter's Tale, A (Conte d'hiver).*

Rojas, Orlando *Sometimes I Look at My Life (A Veces Miro Mi Vida).*

Poley, Sutton *How to Steal the World.*

Rolfe, David W *Silent Witness, The.*

Rollin, Jean *Frisson des Vampires, Le (Sex and the Vampire/Vampire Thrills); Requiem pour un Vampire (Requiem for a Vampire/Virgins and Vampires); Viol du Vampire, Le.*

Roman, Phil *Tom and Jerry: The Movie.*

Romanek, Mark *Static.*

Romeo, Roberto *Esperanza & Sardinas.*

Romero, George A *Crazies, The; Creepshow; Dark Half, The; Dawn of the Dead (aka Zombies); Day of the Dead; Jack's Wife (aka Hungry Wives/Season of the Witch); Knightriders; Martin; Monkey Shines; Night of the Living Dead.*

Ronay, Esther *Rapunzel Let Down Your Hair.*

Rondi, Brunello *Master of Love (Racconti Proibiti di Nulla Vestiti).*

Roodt, Darrell James *Dangerous Ground; Jobman; Sarafina!; Stick, The.*

Rooks, Conrad *Siddhartha.*

Ropelewski, Tom *Look Who's Talking Now; Madhouse.*

Rosati, Faliero *Death of a Cameraman (Morte di un Operatore).*

Rose, Bernard *Anna Karenina (aka Leo Tolstoy's Anna Karenina); Candyman; Chicago Joe and the Showgirl; Immortal Beloved; Paperhouse.*

Rose, Les *Hog Wild.*

Rose, Robina *Jigsaw; Nightshift.*

Rosen, Martin *Plague Dogs, The; Season of Dreams (aka Stacking); Watership Down.*

Rosenbaum, Marianne SW *Peppermint Freedom (Peppermint Frieden).*

Rosenberg, Craig *Hotel de Love.*

Rosenberg, Robert *Before Stonewall.*

Rosenberg, Stuart *Amityville Horror, The; April Fools,*

The; Brubaker; Cool Hand Luke; Drowning Pool, The; Laughing Policeman, The (aka An Investigation of Murder); Love and Bullets; My Heroes Have Always Been Cowboys; Pocket Money; Pope of Greenwich Village, The; Voyage of the Damned; WUSA.*

Rosenthal, Rick *American Dreamer; Bad Boys; Distant Thunder; Halloween II.*

Rosi, Francesco *Carmen; Christ Stopped at Eboli (Cristo si è Fermato a Eboli); Chronicle of a Death Foretold (Cronaca di una Morte Annunciata); Cinderella – Italian Style (C'era una Volta); Illustrious Corpses (Cadaveri Eccellenti); Lucky Luciano; Mani sulla Città (Hands Over the City); Mattei Affair, The (Il Caso Mattei); Moment of Truth, The (Il Momento della Verità); Salvatore Giuliano; Three Brothers (Tre Fratelli); Truce, The (La Tregua).*

Rosi, Gianfranco *Boatman.*

Rosman, Mark *House on Sorority Row, The (aka House of Evil).*

Ross, Benjamin *Young Poisoner's Handbook, The.*

Ross, Gaylen *Dealers Among Dealers.*

Ross, Herbert *Boys on the Side; California Suite; Dancers; Footloose; Funny Lady; Goodbye Girl, The; Goodbye, Mr Chips; I Ought to Be in Pictures; Last of Sheila, The; My Blue Heaven; Nijinsky; Owl and the Pussycat, The; Pennies from Heaven; Play It Again, Sam; Protocol; Secret of My Success, The; Seven-Per-Cent Solution, The; Steel Magnolias; Sunshine Boys, The; Turning Point, The; Undercover Blues.*

Rossellini, Roberto *Age of Cosimo de Medici, The (L'Età de Cosimo de'Medici); Amore, L'; Augustine of Hippo (Agostino di Ippone); Blaise Pascal; Era Notte a Roma; Fear (La Paura); Francesco, giullare di Dio (Francis, God's Jester); Germany, Year Zero (Germania, Anno Zero); Italy: Year One (Anno Uno); Machine That Kills Bad People, The (La Macchina Ammazzacattivi); Paisà; Prise de Pouvoir par Louis XIV, La (The Rise to Power of Louis XIV); Roma, Città Aperta (Open City, Rome, Open City); Stromboli, Terra di Dio (Stromboli); Viaggio in Italia (Journey to Italy/The Lonely Woman/Strangers/Voyage to Italy).*

Rossen, Robert *Alexander the Great; All the King's Men; Body and Soul; Hustler, The;*

Island in the Sun; Johnny O'Clock; Lilith.

Rosso, Franco Babylon; Nature of the Beast, The.

Rosson, Richard Corvette K-225 (aka The Nelson Touch).

Roth, Bobby Heartbreakers.

Roth, Joe Coupe de Ville; Streets of Gold.

Rothman, Stephanie Velvet Vampire, The (aka Cemetery Girls/The Waking Hour).

Rothschild, Amalie R Conversations with Willard Van Dyke.

Rouch, Jean Chronique d'un Eté (Chronicle of a Summer); Paris vu par... (Six in Paris).

Rouffio, Jacques Violette et François.

Rouquier, Georges Farrebique.

Rouse, Russell Caper of the Golden Bulls, The (aka Carnival of Thieves); Fastest Gun Alive, The; Oscar, The; Thief, The; Well, The.

Rousselot, Philippe Serpent's Kiss, The.

Rowland, Roy Bugles in the Afternoon; 5000 Fingers of Dr T, The; Our Vines Have Tender Grapes; Rogue Cop; Two Weeks with Love.

Rozema, Patricia I've Heard the Mermaids Singing; When Night Is Falling; White Room.

Rózsa, János Love, Mother (Csók, Anyu); Sunday Daughters (Vasárnapi Szlüok).

Ruane, John Death in Brunswick; That Eye, the Sky.

Rubbo, Michael Tommy Tricker and the Stamp Traveller.

Ruben, Joseph Dreamscape; Good Son, The; Money Train; Sleeping with the Enemy; Stepfather, The; True Believer (aka Fighting Justice).

Ruben, Katt Shea Poison Ivy.

Rubin, Bruce Joel My Life.

Rubinstein, Amnon Heritage, The.

Rudolph, Alan Afterglow; Choose Me; Endangered Species; Equinox; Love at Large; Made in Heaven; Mrs Parker and the Vicious Circle; Moderns, The; Mortal Thoughts; Remember My Name; Return Engagement; Roadie; Songwriter; Trouble in Mind; Welcome to L.A.

Ruggles, Wesley Bolero; I'm No Angel; True Confession.

Ruiz, Raúl City of Pirates (La Ville des Pirates); Hypothesis of the Stolen Painting, The (L'Hypothèse du Tableau Volé); Ile au trésor, L' (Treasure Island); Jeu de l'oie, Le (Snakes and Ladders); Mémoire des apparences (Life Is a Dream); Of Great Events and Ordinary People (De Grands Evénements et des Gens Ordinaires); On Top of the Whale (Het Dak van de Walvis); Présence réelle, La; Three Crowns of the Sailor (Les Trois Couronnes du Matelot); Trois Vies et une Seule Mort (Three Lives and Only One Death).

Rulli, Stefano Fit To Be Untied (Matti da Slegare).

Rupé, Katja Germany in Autumn (Deutschland im Herbst).

Rush, Richard Color of Night; Freebie and the Bean; Getting Straight; Hell's Angels on Wheels; Psych-Out; Stunt Man, The.

Russell, Charles (Chuck) Blob, The; Eraser; Mask, The; Nightmare on Elm Street 3: Dream Warriors, A.

Russell, David O Flirting with Disaster; Spanking the Monkey.

Russell, Ken Altered States; Aria; Billion Dollar Brain; Boy Friend, The; Crimes of Passion; Devils, The; Gothic; Lair of the White Worm, The; Lisztomania; Mahler; Music Lovers, The; Rainbow, The; Salome's Last Dance; Savage Messiah; Tommy; Valentino; Whore; Women in Love.

Russo, Aaron Rude Awakening.

Ryan, Frank Can't Help Singing.

Ryan, Terence Brylcreen Boys, The.

Rydell, Mark Cinderella Liberty; Cowboys, The; Crime of the Century; For the Boys; Fox, The; Harry and Walter Go to New York; Intersection; On Golden Pond; Reivers, The; River, The; Rose, The.

Ryden, Hope Jane.

Rygård, Elisabeth Take It Like a Man, Ma'am (Ta'det som en Mand, Frue!).

Rymer, Judy Cinema of Unease.

Rymer, Michael Angel Baby.

Sábato, Mario To the Heart (Al Corazón).

Sachs, Ira Delta, The.

Sachs, William Incredible Melting Man, The.

Saeta, Eddie Doctor Death: Seeker of Souls.

Safran, Henri Norman Loves Rose.

Sagal, Boris Helicopter Spies, The; Masada (aka The Antagonists); Mosquito Squadron; Omega Man, The; 1,000 Plane Raid, The.

Sagan, Leontine Mädchen in Uniform (Girls in Uniform/Maidens in Uniform).

Sai, Yoichi MARKS (MARKS no Yama).

Saint-Clair, Julien Lust and Desire (Le Désir et la Volupté).

St Clair, Malcolm Crack-Up; Jitterbugs.

St Paul, Stuart Scarlet Tunic, The.

Saks, Gene Barefoot in the Park; Brighton Beach Memoirs; Last of the Red Hot Lovers; Mame; Odd Couple, The.

Sale, Richard Ticket to Tomahawk, A

Salles, Walter Central Do Brasil; Foreign Land.

Salomon, Mikael Far Off Place, A; Hard Rain.

Salva, Victor Powder.

Salvadori, Pierre Apprentis, Les; Cible émouvante (Wild Target).

Salvatores, Gabriele Mediterraneo; Puerto Escondido.

Salwen, Hal Denise Calls Up.

Samperi, Salvatore Grazie Zia (Thank You, Aunt); Malizia; Venial Sin (Peccato Veniale).

Samuels, Stuart Visions of Light.

Sanborn, Keith Deadman, The.

Sander, Helke All-Round Reduced Personality – Redupers, The (Die allseitig reduzierte Persönlichkeit – Redupers); Subjective Factor, The (Der subjektive Faktor).

Sanders, Denis Elvis – That's the Way It Is; Soul to Soul.

Sanders, Jon '36 to '77.

Sanders-Brahms, Helma Future of Emily, The (L'Avenir d'Emilie); Germany, Pale Mother (Deutschland bleiche Mutter); No Mercy, No Future (Die Berührte); Shirin's Wedding (Shirins Hochzeit).

Sandgren, Åke Slingshot, The (Kådisbellan).

Sándor, Pál Daniel Takes a Train (Szerencsés Dániel); Improperly Dressed (Herkulesfürdöi emlék).

Sandrich, Jay Seems Like Old Times.

Sandrich, Mark Carefree; Follow the Fleet; Gay Divorcee, The; Here Come the Waves; Holiday Inn; Shall We Dance?; Top Hat; Woman Rebels, A.

Sane, Kelley Franchesca Page.

Sangster, Jimmy Fear in the Night.

Sanjines, Jorge Bird's Singing, The (Para Recibir el Canto de los Parajos); Blood of the Condor (Yawar Mallku); Coraje del Pueblo, El (The Courage of the People/The Night of San Juan); Secret Nation, The (La Nación Clandestina).

Santell, Alfred Aloma of the South Seas; Beyond the Blue Horizon.

Santiago, Hugo Ecoute Voir... (See Here My Love).

Santini, Derrick In Ismail's Custody.

Santley, Joseph Cocoanuts, The.

Saperstein, David Beyond the Stars (aka Personal Choice).

Sarafian, Deran Back in the USSR; Gunmen; Road Flower; Terminal Velocity.

Sarafian, Richard C Lolly-Madonna XXX (aka The Lolly-Madonna War); Man in the Wilderness; Man Who Loved Cat Dancing, The; Sunburn; Vanishing Point.

Sargent, Joseph Coast to Coast; Forbin Project, The (aka Colossus – The Forbin Project); Jaws – The Revenge; MacArthur – The Rebel General; Nightmares; Sunshine; Sunshine Part II (aka My Sweet Lady); Taking of Pelham One Two Three, The; White Lightning.

Sarin, Vic Cold Comfort.

Sarinana, Fernando Hasta Morir (Until Death).

Sarne, Mike (Michael) Myra Breckinridge; Punk and the Princess, The.

Sarno, Joseph W Butterfly (Broken Butterfly/Baby Tramp).

Sasdy, Peter Countess Dracula; Doomwatch; Hands of the Ripper; I Don't Want to Be Born (aka The Devil Within Her); Lonely Lady, The; Nothing But the Night; Taste the Blood of Dracula; Welcome to Blood City.

Saslavsky, Luis Neige était sale, La (The Stain on the Snow/The Snow Was Black).

Sass, Barbara Tempation (Pokuszenie).

Sathyu, MS *Hot Winds (Garm Hava)*.

Satlof, Ron *Spider-Man Strikes Back*.

Sato, Hisayasu *Kitami (Kurutta Butokai/aka Lunaic Theatre)*.

Sato, Junya *Bullet Train, The (Shinkansen Daibakuha)*.

Sato, Shimako *Tale of a Vampire; Wizard of Darkness (Eko Eko Azaraku)*.

Saunders, Charles *Danger by My Side; Tawny Pipit*.

Saunders, Red *Gift, The*.

Saura, Carlos *Ay! Carmela; Blood Wedding (Bodas de Sangre); Carmen; Caza, La (The Hunt); Cria Cuervos (Raise Ravens); El Dorado; Fast, Fast (Deprisa, Deprisa); Love Bewitched, A (El Amor Brujo); Peppermint Frappé; Sevillanas; Taxi; Tender Hours (Dulces Horas)*.

Sautet, Claude *Choses de la Vie, Les (The Things of Life); César and Rosalie (César et Rosalie); Coeur en hiver, Un (A Heart in Winter); Enfants de Lumière, Les (The Children of Lumière); Nelly & Monsieur Arnaud (Nelly and Mr Arnaud)*.

Saville, Philip *Fellow Traveller; Fruit Machine, The; Oedipus the King; Secrets; Shadey; Those Glory, Glory Days*.

Saville, Victor *Dark Journey; Evensong; Evergreen; First a Girl; Good Companions, The; Hindle Wakes; Kim; Me and Marlborough; South Riding*.

Savini, Tom *Night of the Living Dead*.

Savoca, Nancy *If These Walls Could Talk; True Love*.

Sayles, John *Baby It's You; Brother from Another Planet, The; City of Hope; Eight Men Out; Lianna; Lone Star; Matewan; Passion Fish; Return of the Secaucus Seven; Secret of Roan Inish, The*.

Sayyad, Parviz *Mission, The*.

Schaefer, George *Enemy of the People, An*.

Schaeffer, Eric *My Life's in Turnaround*.

Schaeffer, Francis *Headhunter*.

Schaffner, Franklin J *Best Man, The; Boys from Brazil, The; Double Man, The; Islands in the Stream; Nicholas and Alexandra; Papillon; Patton (aka Patton: Lust for Glory); Planet of the Apes; Sphinx; War Lord, The; Welcome Home; Yes, Giorgio*.

Schamoni, Peter *Spring Symphony (Frühlingssinfonie)*.

Schatzberg, Jerry *Dandy, the All-American Girl (aka Sweet Revenge); Honeysuckle Rose; Panic in Needle Park, The; Puzzle of a Downfall Child; Reunion (L'Ami retrouvé); Scarecrow; Seduction of Joe Tynan, The*.

Scheinman, Andrew *Little Big League*.

Schell, Maximilian *Marlene; Pedestrian, The (Der Fussgänger); Tales from the Vienna Woods (Geschichten aus dem Wiener Wald)*.

Schellerup, Henning *Black Bunch, The (aka Jungle Sex)*.

Schenck, George *Superbeast*.

Schenk, Otto *Dance of Love (Reigen)*.

Schenkel, Carl *Exquisite Tenderness; Knight Moves; Mighty Quinn, The; Out of Order (Abwärts)*.

Schepisi, Fred *Barbarosa; Chant of Jimmie Blacksmith, The; Cry in the Dark, A; Devil's Playground, The; Fierce Creatures; I.Q.; Mr Baseball; Plenty; Roxanne; Russia House, The; Six Degrees of Separation*.

Schertzinger, Victor *Birth of the Blues; Mikado, The*.

Scheumann, Gerhard *I Was, I Am, I Shall Be (Ich war, ich bin, ich werde sein)*.

Schierl, Angela Hans *Flaming Ears*.

Schiller, Greta *Before Stonewall; Paris Was a Woman*.

Schiller, Lawrence *Executioner's Song, The; Marilyn – The Untold Story*.

Schiller, Tom *Nothing Lasts Forever*.

Schipek, Dietmar *Flaming Ears*.

Schirmbeck, Samuel *Viva Portugal*.

Schlamme, Thomas *Miss Firecracker; So I Married an Axe Murderer*.

Schlatter, George *Norman...Is That You?*

Schlesinger, John *Believers, The; Billy Liar!; Colf Comfort Farm; Darling; Day of the Locust, The; Eye for an Eye; Falcon and the Snowman, The; Far From the Madding Crowd; Honky Tonk Freeway; Innocent, The (...und der Himmel steht still); Kind of Loving, A; Madame Sousatzka; Marathon Man; Midnight*

Cowboy; Pacific Heights; Sunday, Bloody Sunday; Visions of Eight; Yanks.

Schlingensief, Christoph *German Chainsaw Massacre, The (Das deutsche Kettensagenmassaker); Terror 2000*.

Schlossberg, Julian *No Nukes*.

Schlöndorff, Volker *Circle of Deceit (Die Fälschung); Coupe de Grâce (Der Fangschuss); Death of a Salesman; Degree of Murder, A (Mord und Totschlag); Gathering of Old Men, A; Germany in Autumn (Deutschland im Herbst); Handmaid's Tale, The; Lost Honour of Katharina Blum, The (Die verlorene Ehre der Katharina Blum); Michael Kohlhaas; Roi des Aulnes, Le (The Erl King); Sudden Fortune of the Good People of Kombach, The (Der plötzliche Reichtum der armen Leute von Kombach); Swann in Love (Un Amour de Swann); Tin Drum, The (Die Blechtrommel); Voyager; Young Törless (Der junge Törless)*.

Schmid, Daniel *Written Face, The (Das Geschriebene Gesicht)*.

Schmidt, Jan *Joseph Kilián (Postava k Podpírání)*.

Schmidt, Richard R *1988: The Remake*.

Schmitz, Oliver *Mapantsula*.

Schnabel, Julie *Basquiat*.

Schneider, Alan *Film*.

Schoedsack, Ernest B *Dr Cyclops; Grass; King Kong; Last Days of Pompeii, The; Mighty Joe Young; Most Dangerous Game, The (aka The Hounds of Zaroff)*.

Schonfeld, Victor *Animals Film, The; Shattered Dreams: Picking Up the Pieces*.

Schorm, Evald *Pearls of the Deep (Perlicky na dne)*.

Schrader, Leonard *Naked Tango*.

Schrader, Paul *Affliction; American Gigolo; Blue Collar; Cat People; Comfort of Strangers, The (Cortesie per gli ospiti); Hardcore (aka The Hardcore Life); Light of Day; Light Sleeper; Mishima: A Life in Four Chapters; Patty Hearst*.

Schrader, Uwe *Mau Mau*.

Schroeder, Barbet *Barfly; Before and After; Desperate Measures; General Amin (Général Idi Amin Dada); Kiss of Death; Maîtresse; Reversal of Fortune; Single White Female; Vallée, La (The Valley)*.

Schroeder, Eberhard *Sex Life in a Convent (Klosterschülerinnen)*.

Schroder, Michael *Out of the Dark*.

Schroeder, Sebastian C *O for Oblomov (O wie Oblomov)*.

Schroeter, Werner *Death of Maria Malibran, The (Der Tod der Maria Malibran); Eika Katappa; Palermo or Wolfsburg (Palermo oder Wolfsburg); Reign of Naples, The (Neapolitanische Geschwister)*.

Schubert, Peter *Germany in Autumn (Deutschland im Herbst)*.

Schulman, Tom *8 Heads in a Duffel Bag*.

Schultz, Carl *Blue Fin; Careful, He Might Hear You; Seventh Sign, The; Travelling North*.

Schultz, Michael *Car Wash; Carbon Copy; Cooley High; Greased Lightning; Krush Groove; Last Dragon, The; Sgt Pepper's Lonely Hearts Club Band*.

Schumacher, Joel *Batman & Robin; Batman Forever; Client, The; Cousins; D.C. Cab (aka Street Fleet); Dying Young; Falling Down; Flatliners; Incredible Shrinking Woman, The; Lost Boys, The; St Elmo's Fire; Time to Kill, A*.

Schunzel, Reinhold *Balalaika*.

Schüppel, Uli M *Platz, Der (The Place)*.

Schuster, Harold *Dragoon Wells Massacre; My Friend Flicka; Wings of the Morning*.

Schütte, Jan *Spicy Rice (Drachenfutter)*.

Schwartz, Douglas N *Your Three Minutes Are Up*.

Schwartz, Robert *Survivors, The Blues Today*.

Schwartz, Stefan *Shooting Fish; Soft Top, Hard Shoulder*.

Schweitert, Stefan *Tickle in the Heart, A*.

Schweitzer, Mikhail *Kreutzer Sonata, The (Kreitzerova Sonata)*.

Sciamma, Alberto *Killer Tongue (La lengua asesina)*.

Schyfter, Guita *Like a Bride (Novia que te Vea)*.

Scoffield, Jon *Max Wall – Funny Man*.

Scola, Ettore *Bal, Le; Brutti, sporchi e cattivi (Ugly, Dirty and Bad/Ugly Dirty and Mean/Down and Dirty); Dramma della Gelosia (Jealousy, Italian Style/The*

Pizza Triangle); Macaroni (Maccheroni); Passione d'Amore; Special Day, A (Una Giornata Particolare); Splendor; That Night in Varennes (La Nuit de Varennes).

Scorsese, Martin After Hours; Age of Innocence, The; Alice Doesn't Live Here Anymore; American Boy; Boxcar Bertha; Cape Fear; Casino; Color of Money, The; GoodFellas; Italianamerican; King of Comedy, The; Kundun; Last Temptation of Christ, The; Last Waltz, The; Mean Streets; New York, New York; New York Stories; Raging Bull; Taxi Driver; Who's That Knocking at My Door? (aka I Call First).

Scott, Campbell Big Night.

Scott, Cynthia Company of Strangers, The.

Scott, James '36 to '77; Adult Fun; Chance, History, Art...; Colin & Platonida; Every Picture Tells a Story.

Scott, Oz Bustin' Loose.

Scott, Peter Graham Bitter Harvest; Cracksman, The.

Scott, Ridley Alien; Black Rain; Blade Runner; Blade Runner – The Director's Cut; Duellists, The; 1492: Conquest of Paradise; G.I. Jane; Legend; Someone to Watch Over Me; Thelma & Louise; White Squall.

Scott, Tony Beverly Hills Cop II; Crimson Tide; Days of Thunder; Fan, The; Hunger, The; Last Boy Scout, The; Revenge; Top Gun; True Romance.

Scribner, George Oliver & Company.

Seacat, Sandra In the Spirit.

Seagal, Steven On Deadly Ground.

Seale, John Till There Was You.

Searle, Francis Emergency.

Sears, Fred F Don't Knock the Rock; Earth vs the Flying Saucers (aka Invasion of the Flying Saucers).

Seaton, George Airport; Big Lift, The; Proud and Profane, The; 36 Hours.

Sebastian, Beverly 'Gator Bait (aka Swamp Bait).

Sebastian, Ferd 'Gator Bait (aka Swamp Bait).

Sébastian, Isabel Both Sides of the Street (La Contre-allée).

Sedgwick, Edward Cameraman, The; Parlor, Bedroom and Bath (aka Romeo in Pyjamas); Spite Marriage; Southern Yankee.

Seed, Paul Affair, The.

Segal, Peter Naked Gun 33⅓: The Final Insult; Tommy Boy.

Sehr, Peter Kaspar Hauser (Verbrechen am Seelenleben eines Menschens); Serbian Girl, The (Das serbische Mädchen).

Seidl, Ulrich Tierische Liebe (Animal Love).

Seidelman, Susan Confessions of a Suburban Girl; Cookie; Desperately Seeking Susan; Making Mr Right; She-Devil; Smithereens.

Seiler, Lewis Guadalcanal Diary; Smiling Ghost, The.

Seiter, William A Broadway; Dimples; If I Had a Million; Lady Takes a Chance; Life Begins in College (aka The Joy Parade); One Touch of Venus; Roberta; Room Service; Sons of the Desert (aka Fraternally Yours); This Is My Affair (aka His Affair); You Were Never Lovelier.

Sekely, Steve Day of the Triffids, The; Hollow Triumph (aka The Scar).

Sekers, Alan Arp Statue, The.

Selick, Henry James and the Giant Peach; Nightmare Before Christmas, The (aka Tim Burton's The Nightmare Before Christmas).

Selignac, Arnaud Gawin.

Sellar, Ian Prague; Venus Peter.

Seltzer, David Lucas; Punchline; Shining Through.

Selznick, Arna Care Bears Movie, The.

Sembene, Ousmane Black Girl (Une Noire de...); Camp Thiaroye (Camp de Thiaroye); Ceddo; Emitaï; Money Order, The (Le Mandat); Xala.

Sen, Aparna 36 Chowringhee Lane.

Sen, Mrinal Genesis (Génésis); In Search of Famine (Aakaler Sandhane); Outsiders, The (Oka Oorie Katha).

Sena, Dominic Kalifornia.

Seresin, Michael Homeboy.

Serious, Yahoo Young Einstein.

Serreau, Coline Crise, La; Romuald et Juliette (Romuald & Juliette); 3 Men and a Cradle (3 Hommes et un Couffin).

Servais, Raoul Taxandria.

Setbon, Philippe Mister Frost.

Sewell, Vernon Blood Beast Terror, The (aka The Vampire Beast Craves

Blood); Burke and Hare; Curse of the Crimson Altar (aka The Crimson Cult).

Sgarro, Nicholas Happy Hooker, The.

Shabazz, Menelik Burning an Illusion; Time and Judgement.

Shadyac, Tom Ace Ventura, Pet Detective; Liar Liar; Nutty Professor, The.

Shafer, Dirk Man of the Year.

Shaffer, Deborah Wobblies, The.

Shah, Hasan Rough Cut and Ready Dubbed.

Shah, Krishna Cinema Cinema.

Shaji Piravi (The Birth).

Shakey, Bernard (Neil Young) Rust Never Sleeps.

Shakhnazarov, Karen Assassin of the Tsar (Tsareubiitsa).

Shane, Maxwell Fear In The Night; Nightmare.

Shanley, John Patrick Joe Versus the Volcano.

Shannon, Frank (MM Tarantini) Invincible Barbarian (Gunan il Vendicatore).

Shapiro, Alan Crush, The; Flipper.

Shapiro, Ken Groove Tube, The.

Shapiro, Susan Rapunzel Let Down Your Hair.

Sharma, Aribam Syam Chosen One, The (Ishanou).

Sharman, Jim Rocky Horror Picture Show, The; Shock Treatment.

Sharp, Don Bear Island; Brides of Fu Manchu, The; Callan; Face of Fu Manchu, The; Four Feathers, The; Hennessy; It's All Happening; Jules Verne's Rocket to the Moon; Kiss of the Vampire (aka Kiss of Evil); Psychomania; Secrets of the Phantom Caves; Thirty-Nine Steps, The.

Sharp, Ian Music Machine, The; Who Dares Wins.

Sharpsteen, Ben Dumbo; Fantasia; Pinocchio.

Shatner, William Star Trek V: The Final Frontier.

Shaughnessy, Alfred Cat Girl; 6.5 Special (aka Calling All Cats).

Shavelson, Melville Beau James; Cast a Giant Shadow; Houseboat; It Started in Naples; Mixed Company; New Kind of Love, A; Yours, Mine and Ours.

Shaw, Dom Rough Cut and Ready Dubbed.

Shaye, Robert Book of Love.

Shbib, Bashar Julia Has Two Lovers.

Shear, Barry Across 110th Street; Deadly Trackers, The; Karate Killers, The; Todd Killings, The; Wild in the Streets.

Shebib, Donald Between Friends; Goin' Down the Road; Heartaches.

Shebib, Donald (as DS Everett) Running Brave.

Sheen, Martin Count a Lonely Cadence (aka Stockade).

Shelton, Ron Blaze; Cobb; Bull Durham; Tin Cup; White Men Can't Jump.

Shengelaya, Eldar Blue Mountains (Golubye Gory Ely Nepravdopodobnaya Istoria).

Shengelaya, Georgy Journey of a Young Composer (Akhalgazrda Kompozitoris Mogzauroba); Pirosmani.

Shen Jiang Return of the Dragon (Qisha Jieaka Infernal Street).

Shepard, Richard Linguini Incident, The.

Shepard, Sam Far North; Silent Tongue.

Shepitko, Larissa Ascent, The (Voskhozhdenie).

Sher, Jack Three Worlds of Gulliver, The.

Sheridan, Jim Boxer, The; Field, The; In the Name of the Father; My Left Foot.

Sheridan, Michael J That's Entertainment! III.

Sherin, Edwin Valdez Is Coming.

Sherman, Gary A Dead and Buried; Vice Squad.

Sherman, Gary Death Line (aka Raw Meat); Poltergeist III; Wanted Dead or Alive.

Sherman, George Big Jake.

Sherman, Lowell She Done Him Wrong.

Sherman, Vincent Adventures of Don Juan (aka The New Adventures of Don Juan); All Through the Night; Garment Jungle, The; Hasty Heart, The; Ice Palace; Mr Skeffington; Old Acquaintance; Return of Doctor X, The; Saturday's Children; Unfaithful, The.

Sherwin, Robert Dirty Laundry.

Sherwood, Bill Parting Glances.

Sherwood, John Creature Walks Among Us, The; Monolith Monsters, The.

Shih Ti Dragon Dies Hard, The (aka The Bruce Lee Story).

Shin, Nelson *Transformers – The Movie, The.*

Shindo, Kaneto *Island, The (Hadaka no Shima); Kuroneko (Yabu no Naka no Kuroneko); Life of Chikuzan, The (Chikuzan Hitori Tabi); Lost Sex (Honno); Onibaba (The Hole).*

Shinoda, Masahiro *Double Suicide (Shinju Ten no Amijima); Gonza the Spearman (Yari no Gonza); Ondeko-za on Sado, The.*

Shinozaki, Makoto *Okaeri.*

Sholder, Jack *Alone in the Dark; Hidden, The; Nightmare on Elm Street Part 2: Freddy's Revenge, A; Renegades.*

Shonteff, Lindsay *Big Zapper; Spy Story.*

Shore, Simon *Henri.*

Shu Kei *Hu-Du-Men (aka Stage Door); Queer Story, A (Jilao Sishi); Sunless Days (Meiyou Taiyang de Rizi).*

Shub, Esther *Fall of the Romanov Dynasty, The.*

Shuker, Gregory *Jane.*

Shumlin, Herman *Confidential Agent.*

Shyer, Charles *Baby Boom; Father of the Bride; Father of the Bride Part II; I Love Trouble; Irreconcilable Differences.*

Siberling, Brad *City of Angels.*

Sichel, Alex *All Over Me.*

Sidaris, Andy *Seven.*

Sidney, George *Anchors Aweigh; Annie Get Your Gun; Bye Bye Birdie; Half a Sixpence; Harvey Girls, The; Holiday in Mexico; Jupiter's Darling; Kiss Me Kate; Pal Joey; Scaramouche; Show Boat; Viva Las Vegas (aka Love in Las Vegas); Young Bess.*

Siegel, David *Suture.*

Siegel, Don *Baby Face Nelson; Beguiled, The; Big Steal, The; Black Windmill, The; Charley Varrick; Coogan's Bluff; Crime in the Streets; Dirty Harry; Duel at Silver Creek, The; Escape from Alcatraz; Flaming Star; Hanged Man, The; Hell Is for Heroes; Hound Dog Man; Invasion of the Body Snatchers; Jinxed!; Killers, The; Lineup, The; Madigan; Private Hell 36; Riot in Cell Block 11; Rough Cut; Shootist, The; Telefon; Two Mules for Sister Sara; Verdict, The.*

Siegel, Don (as Alan Smithee) *Death of a Gunfighter.*

Siegel, Robert J *Line, The.*

Sigel, Thomas *When the Mountains Tremble.*

Signorelli, Jim *Easy Money; Elvira, Mistress of the Dark.*

Silber, Glenn *El Salvador: Another Vietnam.*

Silberg, Joel *Breakin' (aka Breakdance); Lambada; Rappin'.*

Silberling, Brad *Casper.*

Sills, Sam *Good Fight, The.*

Silver, Claudia *Kalamazoo.*

Silver, Joan Micklin *Between the Lines; Big Girls Don't Cry...They Get Even (aka Stepkids); Crossing Delancey; Head Over Heels; Hester Street; Loverboy; Prison Stories: Women on the Inside.*

Silver, Marisa *He Said, She Said; Old Enough; Permanent Record.*

Silver, Scott *Johns.*

Silverstein, Elliot *Car, The; Cat Ballou; Happening, The; Man Called Horse, A.*

Simmons, Anthony *Black Joy; Optimists of Nine Elms, The.*

Simoes, Rui *Deus, Patria e Autoridade (God, Fatherland and Authority); Good People of Portugal, The (Bom Povo Português).*

Simon, Adam *Typewriter, the Writer & the Movie Camera, The.*

Simon, Frank *Queen, The.*

Simon, S Sylvan *Grand Central Murder.*

Simoneau, Yves *In the Belly of Dragon (Dans le Ventre du Dragon); Mother's Boys; Perfectly Normal.*

Sinatra, Frank *None But the Brave.*

Sinclair, Andrew *Under Milk Wood.*

Sinclair, Harry *Topless Women Talk About Their Lives.*

Sinclair, Ingrid *Flame.*

Singer, Bryan J *Public Access; Usual Suspects, The.*

Singleton, John *Boyz N the Hood; Higher Learning; Poetic Justice.*

Singleton, Ralph S *Graveyard Shift.*

Sinise, Gary *Miles from Home; Of Mice and Men.*

Sinkel, Bernhard *Germany in Autumn (Deutschland im Herbst); Lina Braake.*

Sinyor, Gary *Leon the Pig Farmer; Solitaire for 2; Stiff Upper Lips.*

Siodmak, Curt *Magnetic Monster, The.*

Siodmak, Robert *Christmas Holiday; Crimson Pirate, The; Criss Cross; Cry of the City; Custer of the West; Dark Mirror, The; File on Thelma Jordan, The; Great Sinner, The; Killers, The; People on Sunday (Menschen am Sonntag); Phantom Lady; Pièges (Personal Column/ Snares); Son of Dracula; Spiral Staircase, The; Strange Affair of Uncle Harry, The (aka Uncle Harry); Suspect, The.*

Sipes, Andrew *Fair Game.*

Sirk, Douglas *All I Desire; All That Heaven Allows; Battle Hymn; First Legion, The; Has Anybody Seen My Gal?; Hitler's Madman; Imitation of Life; Interlude; Lured (aka Personal Column); Magnificent Obsession; Meet Me at the Fair; Shockproof; Sign of the Pagan; Sleep, My Love; Summer Storm; Take Me to Town; Tarnished Angels, The; There's Always Tomorrow; Time to Love and a Time to Die, A; Written on the Wind.*

Sirk, Douglas (as Detlef Sierck) *Pillars of Society (Stützen der Gesellschaft).*

Sitch, Rob *Castle, The.*

Sjöberg, Alf *Father, The (Fadern); Hets (Frenzy/Torment).*

Sjöman, Vilgot *You're Lying (Ni Ljuger); Till Sex Us Do Part (Troll).*

Sjöström, Victor *He Who Gets Slapped; Outlaw and His Wife, The (Berg-Ejvind och hans Hustru); Scarlet Letter, The; Under the Red Robe; Wind, The.*

Skolimowski, Jerzy *Adventures of Gerard, The; Barrier (Bariera); Deep End; Départ, Le; Hands Up! (Rece do Góry); King, Queen, Knave (Herzbube); Lightship, The; Moonlighting; Shout, The; Success Is The Best Revenge; Torrents of Spring (Acque di Primavera).*

Slesin, Aviva *Directed by William Wyler.*

Sletaune, Pål *Junk Mail (Budbringeren/ Postbudet der vidste for meget).*

Sluizer, George *Crimetime; Vanishing, The (Spoorloos) (1988); Vanishing, The (1993).*

Smallwood, Ray *Camille.*

Smaragdis, Iannis *Cavafy (Cavafis).*

Smart, Ralph *Curtain Up; Quartet.*

Smight, Jack *Airport 1975; Damnation Alley; Frankenstein: The True Story; Harper (aka The Moving Target); Illustrated Man, The; Kaleidoscope; Loving Couples; Midway (aka Battle of Miday); No Way to Treat a Lady; Travelling Executioner, The.*

Smith, Charles Martin *Trick or Treat.*

Smith, Howard *Marjoe.*

Smith, Jack *Flaming Creatures.*

Smith, John N *Dangerous Minds; Sitting in Limbo; Sugartime.*

Smith, Kevin *Chasing Amy; Clerks; Mallrats.*

Smith, Kevin W *Romance and Rejection.*

Smith, Mel *Bean; Radioland Murders; Tall Guy, The.*

Smith, Noella *Hummingbird Tree, The.*

Smith, Peter K *No Surrender; Private Enterprise, A; What Next?*

Smith, Robert *City Farm; Love Child, The; Wild Flowers.*

Smithee, Allen *see Hopper, Dennis; Siegel, Don; Totten, Robert.*

Smyczek, Karle *Just A Little Whistle (Jen si Tak Trochu Pisknout).*

Snoad, Harold *Not Now, Comrade.*

Snow, Michael *Wavelength.*

Soavi, Michele *Sect, The (La Setta).*

Soderbergh, Steven *Kafka; King of the Hill; sex, lies and videotape; Underneath, The.*

Softley, Iain *Backbeat; Hackers; Wings of the Dove, The.*

Sokurov, Aleksandr *Mother and Son (Mat i Syn/ Mutter und Sohn).*

Solanas, Fernando E *Sur; Voyage, The (El Viaje).*

Solas, Humberto *Cantata of Chile (Cantata de Chile); Lucia.*

Solberg, Helena *Carmen Miranda: Bananas Is My Business.*

Sole, Alfred *Communion (aka Holy Terror).*

Solondz, Todd *Happiness; Welcome to the Dollhouse.*

Solt, Andrew *Imagine (aka Imagine: John Lennon); It Came from Hollywood; This Is Elvis.*

Solum, Ola *Orion's Belt (Orions Belte).*

Somai, Shinji *Moving (Ohikkoshi).*

Somer, Yossi *Burning Memory (Resism)*.

Sommers, Stephen *Adventures of Huck Finn; Jungle Book, The (aka Rudyard Kipling's The Jungle Book)*.

Song Neung-Han *No. 3*.

Songsri, Cherd *Puen-Paeng; Scar, The (Prae Kaow)*.

Sonnenfeld, Barry *Addams Family, The; Addams Family Values; For Love or Money (aka The Concierge); Get Shorty*.

Sontag, Susan *Promised Lands*.

Sotirakis, Dimitri *Beverly Hills Brats*.

Sözen, Kadir *Cold Nights (Soguk Geceler)*.

Spacey, Kevin *Albino Alligator*.

Sparr, Robert *Swingin' Summer, A*.

Speck, Wieland *Westler: East of the Wall*.

Speek, Peter *Black Diamond Rush*.

Spence, Richard *Different for Girls*.

Spheeris, Penelope *Beverly Hillbillies, The; Black Sheep; Boys Next Door, The; Decline of Western Civilization, The; Decline of Western Civilization Part II, The: The Metal Years; Dudes; Little Rascals, The; Prison Stories: Women on the Inside; Wayne's World; Wild Side, The (aka Suburbia)*.

Spicer, Bryan *Mighty Morphin Power Rangers: The Movie*.

Spielberg, Steven *Always; Amazing Stories; Amistad; Close Encounters of the Third Kind; Close Encounters of the Third Kind – Special Edition; Color Purple, The; Duel; E.T. The Extra-Terrestrial; Empire of the Sun; Hook; Indiana Jones and the Last Crusade; Indiana Jones and the Temple of Doom; Jaws; Jurassic Park; 1941; Lost World: Jurassic Park, The; Raiders of the Lost Ark; Schindler's List; Sugarland Express, The; Twilight Zone – The Movie*.

Spiers, Bob *Didn't You Kill My Brother?; Spice World*.

Spinosa, Michel *Emmène-moi (Last Chance Hotel)*.

Spoerri, Anselm *Imago – Meret Oppenheim*.

Spottiswoode, Roger *Air America; And the Band Played On; Best of Times, The; Shoot to Kill (aka Deadly Pursuit); Stop! or My Mom Will Shoot; Terror Train;*

Tomorrow Never Dies; Turner & Hooch; Under Fire.

Sprackling, Simon *Funny Man*.

Springer, Brian *Spin*.

Springsteen, RG *Come Next Spring*.

Sprung, Steve *Year of the Beaver*.

Squitieri, Pasquale *Russicum*.

Srour, Heiny *Hour of Liberation – the Struggle in Oman, The (Saat el Tahrir Dakkat Barra Ya Isti'Mar); Leila and the Wolves*.

Stabile, Salvatore *Gravesend*.

Stadler, Heiner *Warshots*.

Stahl, John M *Back Street; Eve of St Mark; Imitation of Life; Immortal Sergeant, The; Leave Her to Heaven; Oh, You Beautiful Doll; Only Yesterday*.

Stallone, Sylvester *Paradise Alley; Rocky II; Rocky III; Rocky IV; Staying Alive*.

Stanley, Richard *Dust Devil; Hardware*.

Starewicz, Wladyslaw *Romand de Renard, Le (The Tale of the Fox)*.

Stark, Graham *Magnificent Seven Deadly Sins, The*.

Starr, Ringo *Born to Boogie*.

Starrett, Jack *Cleopatra Jones; Race with the Devil; Slaughter*.

Steckler, Ray Dennis *Incredibly Strange Creatures Who Stopped Living and Became Mixed-Up Zombies, The*.

Stefani, Francesco *Singing Ringing Tree, The (Das singende klingende Baumchen)*.

Stein, Jeff *Kids Are Alright, The*.

Stein, Paul L *Blossom Time*.

Steinberg, David *Paternity*.

Steinberg, Michael *Bodies, Rest & Motion; Waterdance, The*.

Stelling, Jos *Pointsman, The (De Wisselwachter)*.

Stellman, Martin *For Queen and Country*.

Stebridge, Gerard *Guiltrip*.

Sterling, William *Alice's Adventures in Wonderland*.

Stern, Anthony *Ain't Misbehavin'*.

Stern, Bert *Jazz on a Summer's Day*.

Stern, Daniel *Rookie of the Year*.

Stern, Steven Hillard *BS I Love

You; Devil and Max Devlin, The; Neither By Day Nor By Night.

Stern, Tom *Freaked*.

Stevens, Art *Fox and the Hound, The; Rescuers, The*.

Stevens, David *Clinic, The; Kansas*.

Stevens, Elizabeth *In the Best Interests of the Children*.

Stevens, George *Alice Adams; Annie Oakley; Damsel in Distress, A; Diary of Anne Frank, The; Giant; Greatest Story Every Told, The; Gunga Din; I Remember Mama; More the Merrier, The; Only Game in Town, The; Penny Serenade; Place in the Sun, A; Shane; Swing Time; Talk of the Town, The; Vivacious Lady; Woman of the Year*.

Stevens, Sylvia *Year of the Beaver*.

Stevenson, Robert *Back Street; Bedknobs and Bromsticks; Blackbeard's Ghost; Darby O'Gill and the Little People; Falling For You; Herbie Rides Again; I Married a Communist (aka The Woman on Pier 13); Island at the Top of the World, The; Jane Eyre; King Solomon's Mines; Las Vegas Story, The; Love Bug, The; Man Who Changed His Mind, The (aka The Man Who Lived Again); Mary Poppins; My Forbidden Past; One of Our Dinosaurs Is Missing; Owd Bob; (aka To the Victor) Shaggy D.A., The; That Darn Cat*.

Stewart, Douglas Day *Listen To Me*.

Stewart, Hugh *Tunisian Victory*.

Stewart, Peter (Sam Newfield) *Counterfeiters*.

Stigliano, Roger *Fun Down There*.

Stiller, Ben *Cable Guy; Reality Bites*.

Stillman, Whit *Barcelona; Metropolitan*.

Stöcklin, Tania *Georgette Meunier*.

Stoeffhaas, Jerry *Cheap Shots*.

Stokes, Mark *Joseph Cornell: Worlds in a Box*.

Stoloff, Ben *Affairs of Annabel, The*.

Stone, Alice *She Lives to Ride*.

Stone, Andrew L *Great Waltz, The; Last Voyage, The; Night Holds Terror, The; Password Is Courage, The; Song of Norway; Stormy Weather*.

Stone, Oliver *Born on the Fourth of July; Doors, The;*

Hand, The; Heaven & Earth; JFK; Natural Born Killers; Nixon; Platoon; Salvador; Talk Radio; U Turn; Wall Street.

Stopkewich, Lynne *Kissed*.

Stoppard, Tom *Rosencrantz and Guildenstern Are Dead*.

Storm, Esben *Deadly*.

Stoumen, Louis Clyde *Black Fox*.

Stout, Boris *God's Alcatraz*.

Straub, Jean-Marie *Chronicle of Anna Magdalena Bach (Chronik der Anna Magdalena Bach); Class Relations (Klassenverhältnisse); Fortini/Cani; From the Cloud to the Reistance (Nube alla Resistenza); History Lessons (Geschichtsunterricht); Moses and Aaron (Moses und Aron); Nicht Versöhnt (Not Reconciled); Othon (Les Yeux ne peuvent pas en tout temps se fermer)*.

Strayer, Frank R *Blondie; Vampire Bat, The*.

Streisand, Barbra *Mirror Has Two Faces, The; Prince of Tides, The; Yentl*.

Streitfeld, Susan *Female Perversions*.

Strick, Joseph *Janice; Portrait of the Artist as a Young Man, A; Tropic of Cancer; Ulysses*.

Strick, Wesley *Tie That Binds, The*.

Stuart, Mel *Mean Dog Blues; Wattstax; Willy Wonka and the Chocolate Factory*.

Stuart-Young, Brian *Aggro Seizeman*.

Sturges, John *Bad Day at Black Rock; Eagle Has Landed, The; Escape from Fort Bravo; Great Escape, The; Gunfight at the O.K. Corral; Hour of the Gun; Ice Station Zebra; Jeopardy; Joe Kidd; Last Train from Gun Hill; Law and Jake Wade, The; Magnificent Seven, The; Marooned; McQ; Mystery Street; Never So Few; Old Mand and the Sea, The; Satan Bug, The; Valdez il Mezzosangue (Chino/The Valdez Horses/Valdez the Halfbreed)*.

Sturges, Preston *Beautiful Blonde from Bashful Bend, The; Christmas in July; Great McGinty, The; Great Moment, The; Hail the Conquering Hero; Lady Eve, The; Miracle of Morgan's Creek, The; Palm Beach Story, The; Sin of Harold Diddlebock, The (aka Mad Wednesday); Sullivan's Travels; Unfaithfully Yours*.

Sturridge, Charles *Aria; FairyTale – A True Story;*

Templeman, Conny *Nanou.*

Téno, Jean Marie *Clando (Clandestine).*

Tennant, Andy *Fools Rush In; It Takes Two.*

Tenney, Kevin S *Cellar, The; Night of the Demons.*

Terayama, Shuji *Boxer, The; Fruits of Passion, The (Les Fruits de la Passion); Pastoral Hide-and-Seek (Denen ni Shisu); Throw Away Your Books, Let's Go into the Streets (Sho o Suteyo, Machi e Deyo).*

Teshigahara, Hiroshi *Summer Soldiers; Woman of the Dunes (Suna no Onna).*

Tessari, Duccio *Heroes, The (Gli Eroi).*

Teton, Charles *Dark Summer.*

Tetzlaff, Ted *Johnny Allegro (aka Hounded); Under The Gun; White Tower, The; Window, the.*

Tewkesbury, Joan *Old Boyfriends.*

Tezuka, Osamu *Space Firebird.*

Thacker, David *Broken Glass.*

Theuring, Gerhard *Escape Route to Marseilles (Fluchtweg nach Marseilles).*

Thew, Anna *Hilda Was a Goodlooker.*

Thiago, Paulo *Für Elise.*

Thiele, Rolf *Mädchen Rosemarie, Das (The Girl Rosemarie).*

Thomas, Betty *Brady Bunch Movie, The; Private Parts.*

Thomas, Dave *Experts, The; Strange Brew.*

Thomas, Gerald *Big Job, The; Carry On Columbus; Carry On Sergeant; Iron Maiden, The; Raising the Wind; That's Carry On; Watch Your Stern.*

Thomas, Pascal *Spring into Summer (Pleure Pas la Bouche Pleine).*

Thomas, Ralph *Above Us the Waves; Appointment with Venus (aka Island Rescue); Clouded Yellow, The; Conspiracy of Hearts; Doctor in the House; High Bright Sun, The (aka McGuire Go Home!); The Hot Enough for June; It's a 2' 6" Above the Ground World (aka The Love Ban); Nobody Runs Forever (aka The High Commissioner); Percy; Percy's Progress; Quest for Love; 39 Steps, The; Upstairs and Downstairs; Wind Cannot Read, The.*

Thomas, Ralph L *Terry Fox Story, The; Ticket to Heaven.*

Thome, Rudolf *3 Women in Love (Der Philosoph).*

Thompson, Caroline *Black Beauty.*

Thompson, David *Musicals Great Musicals: The Arthur Freed Unit at MGM.*

Thompson, Ernest *1969.*

Thompson, J Lee *Ambassador, The; Battle for the Planet of the Apes; Before Winter Comes; Caboblanco; Cape Fear; Conquest of the Planet of the Apes; Country Dance (aka Brotherly Love); Death Wish 4: The Crackdown; Evil That Men Do, The; Good Companions, The; Greek Tycoon, The; Guns of Navarone, The; Huckleberry Finn; Ice Cold in Alex; King Solomon's Mines; Kings of the Sun; Mackenna's Gold; Murphy's Law; North West Frontier (aka Flame Over India); No Trees in the Street; Passage, The; Reincarnation of Peter Proud, The; St Ives; 10 to Midnight; Tiger Bay; Weak and the Wicked, The; White Buffalo, The; Woman in a Dressing Gown; Yellow Balloon, The; Yield to the Night.*

Thompson, Marcus *Middleton's Changeling.*

Thomsen, Christian Braad *Ladies on the Rocks (Koks i Kulissen).*

Thomson, Chris *Delinquents, The.*

Thornhill, Michael *Between Wars; Everlasting Secret Family, The.*

Thornley, Jeni *For Love or Money.*

Thornton, Billy Bob *Sling Blade.*

Thoroddsen, Asdis *Ingaló.*

Thorpe, Richard *Above Suspicion; Adventures of Quentin Durward, The (aka Quentin Durward); Black Hand, The; Huckleberry Finn (aka The Adventures of Huckleberry Finn); Ivanhoe; Jailhouse Rock; Last Challenge, The (aka The Pistolero of Red River); Malaya (aka East of the Rising Sun); Night Must Fall; Prisoner of Zenda, The.*

Thorsen, Jens Jorgen *Quiet Days in Clichy (Stille Dage i Clichy).*

Thorsen, Karen *James Baldwin: The Price of the Ticket.*

Thulin, Ingrid *One and One (En och En).*

Thurman, Tom *Warren Oates: Across the Border.*

Tian Zhuangzhuang *Blue Kite, The (Lan Fengzheng); Horse Thief (Daoma Zei).*

Tighe, Fergus *Clash of the Ash.*

Till, Eric *It Shouldn't Happen to a Vet; Walking Stick, The.*

Tillman Jr, George *Soul Food.*

Tillman, Lynne *Committed.*

Ting Shan-Hsi *Blood Reincarnation (Yin-yang Jie).*

Tinling, James *Mr Moto's Gamble.*

Tirl, Jiri *Pistol, The (Pistolen).*

Title, Stacy *Last Supper, The.*

Tlatli, Moufida *Silences of the Palace, The (Saimt el Qusur/Les Silences du Palais).*

To, Johnny *Heroic Trio (Dongfang San Xia).*

Toback, James *Big Bang, The; Exposed; Fingers.*

Todorovsky, Valerii *Katia Ismailova (Podmoskovnye vechera).*

Tognazzi, Ricky *Scorta, La (The Escort); Ultrà (Ultras: Some Lose, Some Die...Some Win).*

Tokar, Norman *Apple Dumpling Gang, The; Candleshoe; Cat From Outer Space, The; Happiest Millionaire, The; No Deposit, No Return; Tiger Walks, A; Where the Red Fern Grows.*

Tolkin, Michael *New Age, The; Rapture, The.*

Tong, Stanley *First Strike (Jingcha Gushi 4 zhi Jiandan Renwu); Rumble in the Bronx (Hongfan Qu).*

Toporoff, Ralph *American Blue Note (aka Fakebook).*

Topper, Burt *Strangler, The.*

Tornatore, Giuseppe *Cinema Paradiso (Nuovo Cinema Paradiso); Cinema Paradiso: The Special Edition; Everybody's Fine (Stanno tutti bene); Pure Formality, A (Una Pura Formalità); Uomo delle stelle, L' (The Starmaker).*

Totten, Robert (as Alan Smithee) *Death of a Gunfighter.*

Toubiana, Serge *François Truffaut, Portraits Volés (François Truffaut, Stolen Portraits).*

Tourneur, Jacques *Anne of the Indies; Appointment in Honduras; Au Nom de la Loi; Berlin Express; Cat People; Circle of Danger; City Under the Sea (aka War Gods of the Deep); Comedy of Terrors, The; Days of Glory; Easy Living; Experiment Perilous; Flame and the Arrow, The; Giant of Marathon, The (La Battaglia di Maratona); Great Day in the Morning; I Walked with a Zombie; Leopard Man, The; Nick Carter – Master Detective; Nightfall; Night of the Demon (aka Curse of the Demon); Out of the Past (aka Build My Gallows High); Way of a Gaucho; Wichita.*

Towne, Robert *Personal Best; Tequila Sunrise.*

Townsend, Robert *BAPS; Eddie Murphy Raw; Five Heartbeats, The; Hollywood Shuffle; Meteor Man, The.*

Toye, Wendy *Teckman Mystery, The.*

Tramont, Jean-Claude *All Night Long.*

Tran Anh Hung *Cyclo (Xich Lo); Scent of Green Papaya, The (L'Odeur de la Papaye Verte/Mui Du Du Xanh).*

Trauberg, Leonid *Devil's Wheel, The (Chyortovo Koleso); New Babylon, The (Novyi Vavilon).*

Trenchard Smith, Brian *BMX Bandits; Frog Dreaming; Man from Hong Kong, The; Turkey Shoot.*

Trent, John *Best Revenge; Middle Age Crazy; Sunday in the Country.*

Tresgot, Annie *Portrait of a '60% Perfect' Man: Billy Wilder (Portrait d'un Homme 'à 60% Parfait': Billy Wilder).*

Treut, Monika *Erotique; My Father Is Coming; Virgin Machine (Die Jungfrauenmaschine).*

Trevelyan, Humphrey *'36 to '77.*

Trevelyan, Philip *Moon and the Sledgehammer, The.*

Trevor, Simon *African Elephant, The (aka King Elephant).*

Triana, Jorge Ali *Time to Die (Tiempo de Morir).*

Trigiani, Adriana *Queens of the Big Time.*

Trikonis, Gus *Touched By Love.*

Trintignant, Nadine *Maison de Jade, La.*

Troche, Rose *Go Fish.*

Troell, Jan *Capitano, Il; Emigrants, The (Utvandrarna); Hurricane; Zandy's Bride (aka For Better, For Worse).*

Trombley, Stephen *Execution Protocol, The.*

Trousdale, Gary *Beauty and the Beast; Hunchback of Notre Dame, The.*

Troyano, Ela *Latin Boys Go to Hell.*

Trueba, David *Good Life, The (La Buena Vida)*.

Trueba, Fernando *Belle Epoque; First Effort (Opera Prima); Mad Monkey, The (El Mono Loco); Two Much (Loco de amor)*.

Truffaut, François *Argent de Poche, L' (Small Change); Baisers Volés (Stolen Kisses); Belle fille comme moi, Une (A Gorgeous Bird Like Me/Such a Gorgeous Kid Like Me); Bride Wore Black, The (La Mariée était en Noir); Chambre Verte, La (The Green Room); Day for Night (La Nuit Américaine); Deux Anglaises et la Continent, Les (Anne and Muriel/Two English Girls); Domicile Conjugal (Bed and Board); Enfant Sauvage, L' (The Wild Child); Fahrenheit 451; Jules and Jim (Jules et Jim); Last Metro, The (Le Dernier Métro); Love on the Run (L'Amour en Fuite); Man Who Loved Women, The (L'Homme qui Aimait les Femmes); Peau Douce, La (Silken Skin/The Soft Skin); Quatre Cents Coups, Les (The 400 Blows); Sirène du Mississipi, La (Mississippi Mermaid); Story of Adèle H., The (L'Histoire d'Adèle H.); Tirez sur le Pianiste (Shoot the Pianist/Shoot the Piano Player); Vivement Dimanche! (Confidentially Yours/Finally, Sunday!); Woman Next Door, The (La Femme d'à côté)*.

Trumbo, Dalton *Johnny Got His Gun*.

Trumbull, Douglas *Brainstorm; Silent Running*.

Tsabadze, Aleko *Stain, The (Laka)*.

Tsai Ming-Liang *Hole, The; My New Friends (Wo Xin Renshi de Pengyou); Rebels of the Neon God (Qing Shaonian Nezha); River, The (Heliu); Vive l'Amour (Aiqing Wansui)*.

Tsiplakova, Elena *In Thee I Trust (Na Tebya Upovayu)*.

Tsuchimoto, Noriaki *Minamata*.

Tsui Hark *Blade, The (Dao); Butterfly Murders, The (Die Bian); Don't Play With Fire (Diyi Leixing Weixian/aka Dangerous Encounter – First Kind); Double Team; Once Upon a Time in China (Huang Feihong); Once Upon a Time in China II (Huang Feihong zhi Er: Nan'r Dang Zi Qiang); Peking Opera Blues (Dao Ma Dan); Shanghai Blues (Shanghai zhi Ye); Swordsman; Zu: Warriors from the Magic Mountain (Shu Shan: Xin Shushan jianxia)*.

Tsukamoto, Shinya *Tetsuo; Tetsuo II: Bodyhammer; Tokyo Fist*.

Tsukerman, Slava *Liquid Sky*.

Tsymbal, Yevgeny *Defence Counsel Sedov*.

Tucci, Stanley *Big Night*.

Tuchner, Michael *Fear Is the Key; Likely Lads, The; Mister Quilp; Trenchcoat; Villain; Wilt*.

Tucker, Anand *Saint-Ex*.

Tucker, Phil *Robot Monster*.

Tuggle, Richard *Tightrope*.

Tu Guangqi *Kung Fu Fighting (Tang Shou Taiquandao/aka Crush)*.

Tully, Montgomery *Battle Beneath the Earth*.

Turell, Saul J *Love Goddesses, The*.

Turgul, Yavuz *Bandit, The (Eskiya)*.

Turk, Ellen Fisher *Split William to Chrysis: Portrait of a Drag Queen*.

Turkiewicz, Sophia *Silver City*.

Turko, Rose-Marie *Scarred*.

Turner, Ann *Celia; Dallas Doll; Hammers Over the Anvil*.

Turner, Martin *Nearly Wide Awake*.

Turner, Paul *Hedd Wyn*.

Turpie, Jonnie *Out of Order*.

Turteltaub, Jon *Cool Runnings; Phenomenon; 3 Ninjas (aka 3 Ninja Kids); While You Were Sleeping*.

Turturro, John *Mac*.

Tuttle, Frank *Dr Rhythm; Roman Scandals; This Gun for Hire*.

Twist, Derek *Green Grow the Rushes (aka Brandy Ashore)*.

Twohy, David N *Arrival, The; Timescape*.

Tykwer, Tom *Tödliche Maria, Die (Deadly Maria)*.

Tyndall, Andrew *Sigmund Freud's Dora*.

Uderzo, Albert *Twelve Tasks of Asterix, The (Les 12 Travaux d'Astérix)*.

Ullmann, Liv *Sofie*.

Ulloa, Juanma *Bajo Madre Muerta, La*.

Ulmer, Edgar G *Black Cat, The (aka House of Doom); Bluebeard, Detour; Light Ahead, The (Fishke der Krumme); Naked Dawn, The; People on Sunday (Menschen am Sonntag); Ruthless*.

Underwood, Ron *City Slickers; Speechless; Tremors*.

Urban Stuart *Preaching to the Perverted*.

Ureles, Jeff *Cheap Shots*.

Uribe, Imanol *Bwana; Dias Contados (Running Out of Time)*.

Usher, Selig *Hot Money*.

Ustinov, Peter *Billy Budd; Lady L; Memed My Hawk; Vice Versa*.

U-Wei Bin Haji Saari *Arsonist, The (Kaki Bakar)*.

Uys, Jamie *Beautiful People; Gods Must Be Crazy, The; Gods Must Be Crazy II, The*.

Vachani, Nilita *When Mother Comes Home for Christmas (Otan Erhtli Mama Gia ta Christougenna)*.

Václav, Petr *Marian*.

Vadim, Roger *And God Created Woman; Barbarella; Charlotte (La Jeune Fille Assassinée); Don Juan or If Don Juan Were a Woman (Don Juan 1973 ou si Don Juan était une Femme); Et Dieu Créa la Femme (And God Created Woman/And Woman…Was Created); Histoires Extraordinaires (Spirits of the Dead/Tales of Mystery); Liaisons Dangereuses 1960, Les; Night Games; Pretty Maids All in a Row*.

Valdez, Luis *Bamba, La*.

Valerii, Tonino *My Name Is Nobody (Mio Nome è Nessuno); Reason to Live, a Reason to Die, A (Una Ragione per Vivere e Una per Morire)*.

Vallois, Phillipe *We Were one Man (Nous Etions un Seul Homme)*.

van Ackeren, Robert *Woman in Flames, A (Die flambierte Frau)*.

Van Damme, Jean-Claude *Quest, The*.

Van Diem, Mike *Karakter (Character)*.

van de Oest, Paula *Another Mother (de Nieuwe Moeder)*.

van de Velde, Jean *All Stars*.

Van Dormael, Jaco *Eighth Day, The (Le Huitième Jour); Toto the Hero (Toto le héros)*.

Van Dyke, WS *After the Thin Man; Bitter Sweet; I Love You Again; I Take This Woman; Journey for Margaret; Love on the Run; Manhattan Melodrama; Naughty Marietta; Rage in Heaven; San Francisco; Thin Man, The*.

Van Horn, Buddy *Any Which Way You Can; Dead Pool, The*.

Van Lamsweerde, Pino *Asterix in Britain (Astérix chez les Brétons)*.

Van Passel, Frank *Manneken Pis*.

Van Peebles, Mario *New Jack City; Panther; Posse*.

Van Peebles, Melvin *Sweet Sweetback's Baadasssss Song; Watermelon Man*.

Van Sant, Gus *Drugstore Cowboy; Even Cowgirls Get the Blues; Good Will Hunting; Mala Noche; My Own Private Idaho; To Die For*.

van Warmerdam, Alex *Abel; Northerners, The (Der Noorderlingen)*.

Vanzina, Carlo *My First 40 Years (I Miei Primi 40 Anni)*.

Varda, Agnès *Bonheur, Le (Happiness); Cléo de 5 à 7 (Cleo from 5 to 7); Far from Vietnam (Loin du Viêt-nam); Jacquot de Nantes; Lions Love; One Sings, the Other Doesn't (L'Une Chante, l'Autre Pas); Vagabonde (Sans Toit ni Loi)*.

Varnel, Marcel *Gasbags; Ghost of St Michael's, The; Good Morning, Boys! (aka Where There's a Will); Oh, Mr Porter!; O-Kay for Sound*.

Vasconcellos, Tete *El Salvador: Another Vietnam*.

Vasquez, Joseph B *Hangin' with the Homeboys*.

Védrès, Nicole *Paris 1900*.

Vega, Pastor *Portrait of Teresa (Retrato de Teresa)*.

Vendramini, Danny *Redheads*.

Verbinski, Gore *MouseHunt*.

Verbong, Ben *Girl with the Red Hair, The (Het Meisje met het Rode Haar); Scorpion, The (De Schorpioen)*.

Verhavert, Roland *Pallieter*.

Verhoeven, Michael *My Mother's Courage (Mutters Courage); Nasty Girl, The (Das schreckliche Mädchen)*.

Verhoeven, Paul *Basic Instinct; Flesh and Blood; Fourth Man, The (De Vierde Man); RoboCop; Showgirls; Spetters; Starship TroopersTotal Recall; Turkish Delight (Turks Fruit)*.

Vermorcken, Chris *I Am Anna Magnani (Io Sono Anna Magnani)*.

Vernay, Robert *Père Goriot, Le; Fantômas contre Fantômas*.

Verneuil, Henri *Burglars, The (La Casse); Guns for San Sebastian (La Bataille de San

Sebastian); Night Caller (Peur sur la Ville); Serpent, The (Le Serpent); Sicilian Clan, The (Le Clan des Siciliens).

Vernon, Richard *Street of Shadows, (aka Shadowman)*.

Vernoux, Marion *Love etc.*

Verona, Stephen F *Boardwalk; Lords of Flatbush, The.*

Verow, Todd *Frisk.*

Vertov, Dziga *Man With a Movie Camera (Chelovek s Kinoapparatom).*

Ve Sota, Bruno *Female Jungle, The.*

Veysset, Sandrine *Will It Snow for Christmas? (Y'aura t'il de la neige à Noël?).*

Vicario, Marco *Wifemistress (Mogliamante).*

Vidor, Charles *Blind Alley; Cover Girl; Farewell to Arms, A; Gilda; Hans Christian Andersen; Ladies in Retirement; Love Me or Leave Me; Mask of Fu Manchu, The; Song Without End; Song to Remember, A.*

Vidor, King *American Romance, An; Beyond the Forest; Big Parade, The; Citadel, The; Comrade X; Crowd, The; Duel in the Sun; Fountainhead, The; Man Without a Star; Northwest Passage; Ruby Gentry; Show People; Solomon and Sheba; Stella Dallas; Texas Rangers, The; War and Peace; Wedding Night, The.*

Vigne, Daniel *Retour de Martin Guerre, Le (The Return of Martin Guerre); Woman or Two, A (Une Femme ou Deux).*

Vigo, Jean *Atalante, L'; Zéro de Conduite (Zero for Conduct).*

Vilo, Camilo *Unholy, The.*

Vilsmaier, Joseph *Stalingrad.*

Vilstrup, Li *Take It Like a Man, Ma'am (Ta'det som en Mand, Frue!).*

Vincent, Christian *Discrète, La; Séparation, La.*

Vincent, Chuck *American Tickler or the Winner of 10 Academy Awards (aka Draws); Bad Blood; In Love (aka Strangers in Love).*

Vinterger, Thomas *Celebration, The (Festen).*

Vinton, Will *Adventures of Mark Twain, The.*

Viola, Al *Mr Forbush and the Penguins (aka Cry of the Penguins).*

Viola, Joe *Hot Box, The.*

Virzi, Paolo *Living It Up (La Bella Vita).*

Visconti, Luchino *Bellissima; Boccaccio '70; Conversation Piece (Gruppo di Famiglia in un Interno); Damned, The (La Caduta degli Dei/Götterdämmerung); Death in Venice (Morte a Venezia); Innocent, The (L'Innocente); Leopard, The (Il Gattopardo); Ludwig; Ossessione; Rocco and His Brothers (Rocco e i Suoi Fratelli); Senso (The Wanton Countess); Vaghe Stelle dell'Orsa (Of a Thousand Delights/Sandra); White Nights (Le Notti Bianche).*

Vitale, Frank *Montreal Main.*

Vitale, Tony *Kiss Me, Guido.*

vom Bruck, Roswitha *Climax (Ich – das Abenteuer heute eine Frau zu sein).*

von Baky, Josef *Adventures of Baron Munchhausen, The (Münchhausen).*

von Fritsch, Gunther *Curse of the Cat People, The.*

von Garnier, Katja *Making Up (Abgeschminkt).*

von Grote, Alexandra *November Moon (Novembermond).*

von Praunheim, Rosa (Holger Mischwitzki) *Anita: Dances of Vice (Anita: Tänze des Lasters); Army of Lovers or Revolt of the Perverts (Armee der Liebenden oder Revolte der Perversen); City of Lost Souls (Stadt der Verlorenen Seelen); I Am My Own Woman (Ich bin meine eigene Frau).*

von Sternberg, Josef *American Tragedy, An; Blonde Venus; Blue Angel, the (Der blaue Engel); Crime and Punishment; Devil Is a Woman, The; Dishonored; Jet Pilot; King Steps Out, The; Last Command, The; Macao; Morocco; Saga of Anatahan, The (Anatahan); Salvation Hunters, The; Scarlet Empress, The; Sergeant Madden; Shanghai Express; Shanghai Gesture, The; Thunderbolt; Underworld.*

von Stroheim, Erich *Blind Husbands; Foolish Wives; Greed; Merry-Go-Round; Merry Widow, The; Queen Kelly; Wedding March, The.*

von Sydow, Max *Katinka (Ved Vejen).*

von Trier, Lars *Breaking the Waves; Element of Crime, The (Forbrydelsens Element); Europa; Idiots, The (Idioterne); Kingdom, The (Riget); Kingdom II, The (Riget II).*

von Trotta, Margarethe *Friends and Husbands (Heller Wahn); German Sisters, The (Die Bleierne Zeit); Lost Honour of Katharina Blum, The (Die verlorene Ehre der Katharina Blum); Promise, The (Das Versprechen/La Promesse); Rosa Luxemburg; Second Awakening of Christa Klages, The (Das zweite Erwachen der Christa Klages); Sisters or the Balance of Happiness (Schwestern oder die Balance des Glücks); Three Sisters (Paura e amore).*

Vorhaus, Bernard *Ghost Camera, The; Lady from Louisiana; Last Journey, The.*

Votocek, Otakar *Wings of Fame.*

Wachowski, Andy *Bound.*

Wachowski, Larry *Bound.*

Wachsman, Daniel *Hamsin.*

Wacks, Jonathan *Mystery Date; Powwow Highway.*

Wadleigh, Michael *Wolfen; Woodstock; Woodstock: The Director's Cut.*

Waggner, George *Man-Made Monster (aka The Electric Man); Red Nightmare; Wolf Man, The.*

Wagner, Jane *Moment by Moment.*

Wainwright, Rupert *Blank Check (aka Blank Cheque).*

Waite, Ralph *On the Nickel.*

Wajda, Andrzej *Ashes and Diamonds (Popiól i Diament); Conductor, The (Dyrygent); Danton; Everything for Sale (Wszystko na Sprzedaz); Generation, A (Pokolenie); Innocent Sorcerers (Niewinni Czarodzieje); Kanal; Korczak; Landscape After a Battle (Krajobraz po Bitwie); Love in Germany, A (Eine Liebe in Deutschland); Man of Iron (Czlowiek z Zelaza); Man of Marble (Czlowiek z Marmur); Miss Nobody (Panna Nikt); Rough Treatment (Bez Znieczulenia); Siberian Lady Macbeth (Sibirska Ledi Magbet); Wedding, The (Wesele); Young Ladies of Wilko, The (Panny z Wilka).*

Wakamatsu, Koji *Violated Angels (Okasareta Byakui).*

Walas, Chris *Fly II, The.*

Waldron, Gy *Moonrunners.*

Waletzky, Joshua *Music for the Movies: Bernard Herrmann; Music for the Movies: The Hollywood Sound.*

Walker, Giles *90 Days.*

Walker, Hal *Road to Utopia.*

Walker, John *Winter Tan, A.*

Walker, Nancy *Can't Stop the Music.*

Walker, Pete *Comeback, The; Frightmare; Home Before Midnight; House of Mortal Sin; House of Whipcord; House of the Long Shadows, The; Schizo; Tiffany Jones.*

Walker, Stuart *Werewolf of London.*

Wallace, Randall *Man in the Iron Mask, The.*

Wallace, Richard *Adventure in Baltimore (aka Bachelor Bait).*

Wallace, Stephen *Blood Oath; Boy Who Had Everything, The; Love Letters from Teralba Road, The; Stir; Turtle Beach.*

Wallace, Tommy Lee *Aloah Summer; Fright Night Part 2; Halloween III; Season of the Witch.*

Waller, Anthony *American Werewolf in Paris, An; Mute Witness.*

Walls, Tom *For Valour; Plunder; Pot Luck; Rookery Nook.*

Walmesley, Howard *Feverhouse.*

Walsh, Aisling *Joyriders.*

Walsh, Raoul *Background to Danger; Big Trail, The; Blackbeard the Pirate; Bowery, The; Captain Horatio Hornblower; Colorado Territory; Desperate Journey; Distant Drums; Distant Trumpet, A; Enforcer, The (aka Murder Inc.); Gentleman Jim; Glory Alley; Gun Fury; High Sierra; King and Four Queens, The; Klondike Annie; Lion Is in the Streets, A; Man I Love, The; Manpower; Naked and the Dead, The; Objective, Burma!; O.H.M.S. (aka You're in the Army Now); Pursued; Regeneration; Revolt of Mamie Stover, The; Roaring Twenties, The; Sadie Thompson; Sheriff of Fractured Jaw, The; Tall Men, The; They Died With Their Boots On; They Drive By Night (aka The Road to Frisco); Thief of Bagdad, The; White Heat.*

Walters, Charles *Ask Any Girl; Barkleys of Broadway, The; Belle of New York, The; Billy Rose's Jumbo (aka Jumbo); Dangerous When Wet; Easter Parade; High Society; Lili; Please Don't Eat the Daisies; Summer Stock (aka If You Feel Like Singing); Torch Song; Unsinkable Molly Brown, The.*

Walton, Fred *Rosary Murders, The; When a Stranger Calls.*

Wam, Svend *Sebastian.*

Wan Jen *Super Citizen Ko (Chaoji Da Guomin).*

Wan Lai-Ming *Uproar in Heaven (Danao Tiangong).*

Wanamaker, Sam *Catlow; File of the Golden Goose, The; Sinbad and the Eye of the Tiger.*

Wang Jin *Girls to Be Married, The (Chujia Nü).*

Wang, Peter *Great Wall Is a Great Wall, The (aka A Great Wall).*

Wang, Wayne *Blue in the Face; Chan Is Missing; Chinese Box; Dim Sum – A Little Bit of Heart; Eat a Bowl of Tea; Joy Luck Club, The; Life Is Cheap...But Toilet Paper Is Expensive; Slam Dance; Smoke.*

Wang Shaudi *Accidental Legend (Fei Tian).*

Wang Tsai-Sheng *Cha-Cha for the Fugitive, A (Gei Taowangzhe de Qiaqia).*

Wang Xiaoshuai *Days, The (Dong-Chun de Rizi).*

Wang Yu *Beach of the War Gods (Zhan Shen Tan); One Armed Boxer (Dubi Quan Wang).*

Ward, David S *Cannery Row; Down Periscope; King Ralph; Major League; Major League II.*

Ward, Donal Lardner *My Life's in Turnaround.*

Ward, Nick *Dakota Road; Look Me in the Eye.*

Ward, Vincent *Map of the Human Heart; Navigator: A Medieval Odyssey, The; Vigil.*

Ware, Clyde *No Drums, No Bugles.*

Wargnier, Régis *Femme française, Une (Eine Französische Frau); Indochine.*

Warhol, Andy *Bike Boy; Blue Movie; Chelsea Girls; Couch; Kitchen; My Hustler.*

Warner, Paul *Fall Time.*

Warren, Charles Marquis *Charro!; Tension at Table Rock.*

Warren, Mark *Come Back Charleston Blue.*

Warren, Norman J *Satan's Slave; Terror.*

Waszynski, Michael *Dybbuk, The.*

Watanable, Fumiki *Bari-Zogon.*

Waters, John *Cry-Baby; Desperate Living; Female Trouble; Hairspray; Mondo Trasho; Pink Flamingos; Polyester; Serial Mom.*

Waters, Mark *House of Yes, The.*

Watkins, Peter *Culloden; Edvard Munch; Privilege;*

Punishment Park.

Watt, Harry *Fiddlers Three; Overlanders, The; Where No Vultures Fly (aka Ivory Hunter).*

Watts, Roy *Hambone and Hillie (aka The Adventures of Hambone and Hillie).*

Wayans, Keenen (Keenan) Ivory *I'm Gonna Git You Sucka; Low Down Dirty Shame, A.*

Wayne, John *Alamo, The; Green Berets, The.*

Webb, Jack *Pete Kelly's Blues.*

Webb, Peter *Give My Regards to Broad Street.*

Webb, Robert D *Beneath the 12-Mile Reef; Cape Town Affair, The; Love Me Tender; Proud Ones, The; White Feather.*

Weber, Billy *Josh and S.A.M.*

Weber, Bruce *Broken Noses; Let's Get Lost.*

Weber, Francis *Three Fugitives.*

Webster, Nicholas *Santa Claus Conquers the Martians.*

Weeks, Andrew *Split William to Chrysis: Portrait of a Drag Queen.*

Weeks, Stephen *Gawain and the Green Knight; I, Monster; Sword of the Valiant – The Legend of Gawain and the Green Knight, The.*

Wegener, Paul *Golem, The (Der Golem, Wie er in die Welt Kam).*

Weil, Samuel *Class of Nuke 'Em High; Toxic Avenger, The; War (aka Troma's War).*

Weiland, Paul *City Slickers II: The Legend of Curly's Gold; Roseanna's Grave (aka For Roseanna).*

Weill, Claudia *Girlfriends.*

Weinstein, Bob *Playing for Keeps.*

Weinstein, Harvey *Playing for Keeps.*

Weinstein, Larry *September Songs: The Music of Kurt Weill.*

Weinstock, Jane *Sigmund Freud's Dora.*

Weir, Peter *Cars That Ate Paris, The; Dead Poets Society; Fearless; Gallipoli; Green Card; Last Wave, The; Mosquito Coast, The; Picnic at Hanging Rock; Truman Show, The; Witness; Year of Living Dangerously, The.*

Weis, Don *I Love Melvin.*

Weis, Gary *80 Blocks from Tiffany's; Jimi Hendrix; Wholly Moses!*

Weisman, David *Ciao! Manhattan.*

Weisman, Sam *Bye Bye Love; D2: The Mighty Ducks; George of the Jungle.*

Weiss, Andrea *Bit of Scarlet, A.*

Weiss, Rob *Amongst Friends.*

Weiss, Robert K *Amazon Women on the Moon.*

Weissbrod, Ellen *Listen Up: The Lives of Quincy Jones.*

Weissman, Aerlyn *Winter Tan, A.*

Weller, Peter *Gold Coast (aka Elmore Leonard's Gold Coast).*

Welles, Orson *Chimes at Midnight (Campanadas a Medianoche); Citizen Kane; F for Fake (Vérités et Mensonges); Immortal Story, The (Histoire Immortelle); Lady from Shanghai, The; Macbeth; Magnificent Ambersons, The; Mr Arkadin (aka Confidential Report); Othello; Stranger, The; Touch of Evil; Trial, The (Le Procès).*

Wellington, David *I Love a Man in Uniform.*

Wellman, William A *Across the Wide Missouri; Battleground; Beau Geste; Beggars of Life; Hatchet Man, The (aka The Honourable Mr Wong); Iron Curtain, The (aka Behind the Iron Curtain); Lady of Burlesque (aka Striptease Lady); Magic Town; Next Voice You Hear...; The Night Nurse; Nothing Sacred; Other Men's Women; Ox-Bow Incident, The; Public Enemy, The; Robin Hood of El Dorado, The; Roxie Hart; Star Is Born, A; Story of GI Joe, The; Track of the Cat; Wings; Yellow Sky.*

Wells, Peter *Desperate Remedies.*

Wells, Simon *American Tail: Fievel Goes West, An; Balto.*

Welz, Peter *Burning Life.*

Wenders, Wim *Alice in the Cities (Alice in den Städten); American Friend, The (Der Amerikanische Freund); End of Violence, The (Am Ende der Gewalt); Faraway, So Close (In weiter Ferne, so nah!); Goalkeeper's Fear of the Penalty, The (Die Angst des Tormanns beim Elfmeter); Hammett; Kings of the Road (Im Lauf der Zeit); Lightning Over Water (aka Nick's Movie); Lisbon Story; Notebook on Cities and Clothes (Aufzeichnungen zu Kleidern und Städten); Paris,*

Texas; Scarlet Letter, The (Der scharlachrote Buchstabe); State of Things, The; Summer in the City; Tokyo-Ga; Until the End of the World (Bis ans Ende der Welt); Wings of Desire (Der Himmel über Berlin); Wrong Movement (Falsche Bewegung).

Wendkos, Paul *Angel Baby; Gidget; Honor Thy Father; Mephisto Waltz, The.*

Wenk, Richard *Vamp.*

Werker, Alfred *A-Haunting We Will Go; Adventures of Sherlock Holmes, The; At Gunpoint (aka Gunpoint); He Walked by Night; House of Rothschild, The; Three Hours to Kill; Walk East on Beacon.*

Werner, Peter *No Man's Land.*

Wertmüller, Lina *Lizards, The (I Basilischi); Naples Connection, The (Un Complicato Intrigo di Donne, Vicoli e Delitti); Seven Beauties (Pasqualino Settebellezze); Swept Away...by an Unusual Destiny in the Blue Sea of August (Travolti da un Insolito Destino nell'Azzurro Mare d'Agosto).*

Wesley, William *Scarecrows.*

West, Robert Jan *Little Sister (Zusje).*

West, Roland *Bat Whispers, The.*

West, Simon *Con Air.*

Weston, Eric *Iron Triangle, The.*

Wetzler, Gwen *Mighty Mouse in the Great Space Chase; Secret of the Sword, The.*

Wexler, Haskell *Latino; Medium Cool; Vietnam Journey.*

Wexler, Mark *Me & My Matchmaker.*

Whale, James *Bride of Frankenstein, The; By Candlelight; Frankenstein; Great Garrick, The; Invisible Man, The; Journey's End; Man in the Iron Mask, The; Old Dark House, The; One More River (aka Over the River); Remember Last Night?; Show Boat.*

Whatham, Claude *All Creatures Great and Small; Buddy's Song; Swallows and Amazons; Sweet William; That'll Be the Day.*

Wheat, Jim *Lies.*

Wheat, Ken *Lies.*

Wheatley, David *Magic Toyshop, The.*

Wheeler, Anne *Bye Bye Blues.*

Whelan, Tim *Action for Slander; Camels Are Coming, The; Divorce of*

Lady X, The; Farewell Again (aka Troopship); Nightmare; St Martin's Lane (aka Sidewalks of London); Thief of Bagdad, The.

Whitaker, Forest Strapped; Waiting to Exhale.

Whitehead, Peter Daddy; Tonite Let's All Make Love in London.

Whitelaw, Alexander Lifespan.

Whitney, Mark Matter of Heart.

Whittaker, Stephen Closing Numbers.

Whorf, Richard It Happened in Brooklyn.

Wicht, David Windprints.

Wichert, Tony Fly a Flag for Poplar.

Wickes, David Silver Dream Racer; Sweeney!

Wicki, Bernhard Longest Day, The.

Wickman, Torgny Anita; Language of Love (Kärlekens Språk); More About the Language of Love (Mera ur Kärlekens Språk).

Widen, Gregory God's Army (aka The Prophecy).

Widerberg, Bo Adalen '31; Elvira Madigan; Joe Hill (aka The Ballad of Joe Hill); Love Lessons (Laererinden/Lust och fägring Stor); Man from Majorca, The (Mannen från Mallorca); Man on the Roof, The (Mannen på Taket); Pram (Barnvagnen); Stubby (Fimpen).

Wiederhorn, Ken Eyes of a Stranger; Return of the Living Dead Part II.

Wieland, Joyce Reason Over Passion (La Raison avant la Passion).

Wiene, Robert Cabinet of Dr Caligari, The (Das Kabinett des Dr Caligari); Genuine; Hands of Orlac, The (Orlacs Hände); Raskolnikow.

Wierzbicki, Krzysztof Krzysztof Kieslowski: I'm So So.

Wilcox, Fred M Forbidden Planet; Lassie Come Home; Secret Garden, The.

Wilcox, Herbert Courtneys of Curzon Street, The (aka The Courtney Affair); Derby Day (aka Four Against Fate); Goodnight Vienna (aka Magic Night); Nell Gwynn; Odette; Peg of Old Drury; Yellow Canary, The.

Wilde, Cornel Beach Red; No Blade of Grass; Sharks' Treasure.

Wilde, Ted Kid Brother, The; Speedy.

Wilder, Billy Ace in the Hole (aka The Big Carnival); Apartment, The; Avanti!; Buddy Buddy; Double Indemnity; Emperor Waltz, The; Fedora; Five Graves to Cairo; Foreign Affair, A; Fortune Cookie, The (aka Meet Whiplash Willie); Front Page, The; Irma la Douce; Kiss Me, Stupid; Lost Weekend, The; Love in the Afternoon; Major and the Minor, The; One, Two, Three; Private Life of Sherlock Holmes, The; Sabrina (aka Sabrina Fair); Seven Year Itch, The; Some Like It Hot; Stalag 17; Sunset Boulevard; Witness for the Prosecution.

Wilder, Gene Adventure of Sherlock Holmes' Smarter Brother, The; Haunted Honeymoon; Woman in Red, The; World's Greatest Lover, The.

Wiley, Ethan House II: The Second Story.

Williams, Linda Maxwell Street Blues.

Williams, Paul November Men, The; Revolutionary, The.

Willing, Nick Photographing Fairies.

Wills, James Elder Big Fella.

Wilson, Jim Head Above Water.

Wilson, Hugh Burglar; First Wives Club, The; Guarding Tess; Police Academy.

Wilson, Jim Stacy's Knights.

Wilson, Richard Al Capone; It's All True.

Wilson, Sandy My American Cousin.

Wincer, Simon D.A.R.Y.L.; Free Willy; Harlequin; Harley Davidson and the Marlboro Man; Lightning Jack; Lighthorsemen, The; Phantom, The; Phar Lap; Quigley Down Under.

Windsor, Chris Big Meat Eater.

Windust, Bretaigne Enforcer, The (aka Murder, Inc.).

Winer, Harry SpaceCamp.

Winer, Lucy Rate It X.

Winham, Francine Rapunzel Let Down Your Hair.

Winkler, Charles Disturbed; You Talkin' to Me?

Winkler, Henry Cop & ½ (aka Cop and a Half); Memories of Me.

Winkler, Irwin Guilty by Suspicion; Net, The; Night and the City.

Winner, Michael Appointment With Death; Big Sleep, The; Bullseye!; Chato's Land; Chorus of Disapproval, A; Death Wish; Death Wish II; Death Wish 3; Dirty Weekend; Firepower; Hanibal Brooks; Lawman; Mechanic, The (aka Killer of Killers); Nightcomers, The; Play It Cool; Scorpio; Scream for Help; Sentinel, The; Stone Killer, The; Wicked Lady, The.

Winslow, Susan All This and World War II.

Winsor, Terry Party Party.

Winston, Stan Gnome Named Gnorm, A (aka Upworld/Adventures of a Gnome Named Gnorm); Pumpkinhead (aka Vengeance, the Demon).

Winter, Alex Freaked.

Winter, Donovan Deadly Females, The; Give Us Tomorrow.

Winterbottom, Michael Butterfly Kiss; Jude; Welcome to Sarajevo.

Wintonick, Peter Manufacturing Consent: Noam Chomsky and the Media.

Wise, Herbert Lovers!, The.

Wise, Kirk Beauty and the Beast; Hunchback of Notre Dame, The.

Wise, Robert Andromeda Strain, The; Audrey Rose; Blood on the Moon; Body Snatcher, The; Born to Kill (aka Lady of Deceit); Destination Gobi; Captive City, The; Curse of the Cat People, The; Day the Earth Stood Still, The; Executive Suite; Haunting, The; Hindenburg, The; I Want to Live!; Mystery in Mexico; Odds Against Tomorrow; Rooftops; Sand Pebbles, The; Set-Up, The; Somebody Up There Likes Me; Sound of Music, The; Star Trek – The Motion Picture; Star!; Tribute to a Bad Man; West Side Story.

Wiseman, Frederick Basic Training; Canal Zone; High School; Hospital; Juvenile Court; Law and Order; Meat; Model; Primate; Sinai Field Mission; Welfare.

Wishman, Doris Deadly Weapons; Double Agent 73.

Witcher, Theodore love jones.

Witney, William Adventures of Captain Marvel, The (aka The Return of Captain Marvel); I Escaped from Devil's Island; Master of the World.

Wohl, Ira Best Boy.

Wolcott, James L Wild Women of Wongo.

Wolf, Fred Mouse and His Child, The; Point, The.

Wolk, Andy Traces of Red.

Wollen, Peter Crystal Gazing; Friendship's Death; Penthesilea; Queen of the Amazons; Riddles of the Sphinx.

Wolman, Dan Nana.

Women's Film Workshop We're Alive.

Wong Kar-Wai As Tears Go By (Wangjiao Jiamen); Chungking Express (Chongqing Senlin); Days of Being Wild (A-Fei Zhengchuan); Fallen Angels (Duoluo Tianshi); Happy Together (Chunguang Zhaxie).

Wong, Kirk (aka Che-Kirk Wong) Ashes of Time (Dong Xie Xi Du); Big Hit, The; Club, The (Wuting); Crime Story (Zhong'an Zu); Health Warning (Da Leitai); Organized Crime and Triad Bureau (Zhong'an Shilu O-ji); Rock n'Roll Cop (Sheng-Gang Yihao Tongji Fan).

Wong-Ho, YN Xenolith.

Woo, John (Wu Yusen) Better Tomorrow, A (Yingxiong Bense); Better Tomorrow II, A (Yingxiong Bense II); Broken Arrow; Bullet in the Head (Diexue Jietou); Face/Off; Hard-Boiled (Lashou Shentan); Hard Target; Just Heroes; Killer, The (Diexue Shuang Xiong); Last Hurrah for Chivalry (Haoxia); Once a Thief (Zongheng Sihai); Violent Tradition.

Wood, Duncan Bargee, The.

Wood Jr, Edward D Glen or Glenda? (aka I Led Two Lives/I Changed My Sex); Night of the Ghouls (aka Revenge of the Dead); Plan 9 from Outer Space.

Wood, Sam Command Decision; Day at the Races, A; Devil and Miss Jones, The; For Whom the Bell Tolls; Goodbye, Mr Chips; Ivy; Kings Row; Night at the Opera, A; Our Town; Saratoga Trunk; Stamboul Quest.

Woodcock, Penny Women in Tropical Places.

Woods, Arthur They Drive By Night.

Wool, Abbe Roadside Prophets.

Woolley, Richard Brothers and Sisters; Telling Tales.

Worsdale, Andrew Shot Down.

Worsley, Wallace Hunchback of Notre Dame, The.

Worth, David Kickboxer.

Worth, Howard Raga.

Worth, Jan *Doll's Eye.*

Wortmann, Sönke *Bewegte Mann, Der (The Most Desired Man/Maybe…Maybe Not).*

Wrede, Caspar *One Day in the Life of Ivan Denisovich; Ransom.*

Wright, Basil *Song of Ceylon.*

Wright, Edgar *Fistful of Fingers, A.*

Wright, Geoffrey *Romper Stomper.*

Wright, Kay *Mighty Mouse in the Great Space Chase.*

Wright, Thomas Lee *Eight-Tray Gangster: The Making of a Crip.*

Wright, Tom *Torchlight.*

Wrye, Donald *Ice Castles.*

Wu Di *Goldfish (Huangjin Yu).*

Wu Ma *Conman and the Kung Fu Kid (Langbei wei Jian/aka Wits to Wits); Deaf and Mute Heroine, The (Longya Jian).*

'Wu Ming' *Frozen (Jidu Hanleng).*

Wu Nianzhen *Borrowed Life, A (Duo-sang); Buddha Bless America (Taiping Tianguo).*

Wu Tian Ming *King of Masks (Bian Lian); Old Well (Lao Jing).*

Wu Yigong *My Memories of Old Beijing (Chengnan Jiushi).*

Wu Yonggang *Goddess, The (Shennu).*

Wu Ziniu *Last Day of Winter, The (Zuihou Yige Dongri).*

Wurlitzer, Rudy *Candy Mountain.*

Wyborny, Klaus *Birth of a Nation, The (Die Geburt der Nation).*

Wyeth, Peter *Twelve Views of Kensal House.*

Wyler, William *Ben-Hur; Best Years of Our Lives, The; Big Country, The; Carrie; Collector, The; Come and Get It; Dead End; Desperate Hours, The; Detective Story; Friendly Persuasion; Funny Girl; Heiress, The; Jezebel; Letter, The; Liberation of L.B. Jones, The; Little Foxes, The; Mrs Miniver; Roman Holiday; These Three; Wuthering Heights.*

Wynn, Bob *Resurrection of Zachary Wheeler, The.*

Wynne-Simmons, Robert *Outcasts, The.*

Wynorski, Jim *Return of the Swamp Thing, The.*

Xhonneux, Henri *Marquis.*

Xia Gang *Concerto of Life.*

Xie Fei *Black Snow (Ben Ming Nian).*

Xie Jin *Hibiscus Town (Furong Zhen); Red Detachment of Women (Hongse Niangzijun); Two Stage Sisters (Wutai Jiemei).*

Yahrhaus, Bill *Vietnam Journey.*

Yakin, Boaz *Fresh.*

Yamada, Yoji *My Sons (Musuko).*

Yamaga, Hiroyuki *Wings of Honneamise, The (Oneamisu No Tsubasa).*

Yanagimachi, Mitsuo *About Love, Tokyo (Ai ni tsuite, Tokyo); Fire Festival (Himatsuri).*

Yang, Edward *Brighter Summer Day, A (Guling Jie Shaonian Sha Ren Shijian); Confucian Confusion, A (Duli Shidai); Mahjong (Majiang); Taipei Story (Qingmei Zhuma); Terroriser, The (Kongbufenzi).*

Yang Fengliang *Ju Dou.*

Yang Jingchen *Shanghai Lil (Hao Ke/aka The Champion).*

Yasar, Secklin *Yellow Smile, The (Sari Tebessum).*

Yates, Pamela *When the Mountains Tremble.*

Yates, Peter *Breaking Away; Bullitt; Deep, The; Dresser, The; Eleni; Eyewitness (aka The Janitor); For Pete's Sake; Friends of Eddie Coyle, The; Hot Rock, The (aka How to Steal a Diamond in Four Uneasy Lessons); House on Carroll Street, The; Innocent Man, An; John and Mary; Krull; Mother, Jugs & Speed; Murphy's War; Robbery; Run of the Country, The; Summer Holiday; Suspect.*

Yazaki, Hitoshi *Afternoon Breezes (Kazetachi no Gogo); March Comes in Like a Lion (Sangatsu no Raion).*

Yeaworth Jr, Irvin S *Blob, The; Dinosaurus!*

Yee Chih-Yen *Lonely Hearts Club (Jimo Fangxin Julebu).*

Yee, Derek (Yee Tung-shing) *C'est la Vie, Ma Cherie (Xin Buliao Qing); Viva Erotica! (Seqing Nan Nü).*

Yilmaz, Atif *Berdel.*

Yim Ho *Buddha's Lock (Tian Pusa); Day the Sun Turned Cold, The (Tianguo Niezi); Homecoming (Si Shui Liu Nian); Kitchen, The (Wo ai Chufang).*

Yim Soon-Rye *Three Friends (Sechinku).*

Yip, Raymond *Portland Street Blues (Hongxing Shisan Mei).*

Yonfang *Bugis Street.*

Yorkin, Bud *Arthur 2: On the Rocks; Come Blow Your Horn; Divorce American Style; Inspector Clouseau; Love Hurts; Twice in a Lifetime.*

Yoshida, Hiroaki *Iron Maze.*

Yoshida, Yoshihige *Promise (Ningen no Yakusoku).*

Young, Neil *see* Shakey, Bernard.

Young, Harold *Scarlet Pimpernel, The.*

Young, Robert *Fierce Creatures; Romance with a Double Bass; Splitting Heirs; Vampire Circus, The; World Is Full of Married Men, The.*

Young, Robert M *Alambrista!; Ballad of Gregorio Cortez, The (aka Gregorio Cortez); Dominick and Eugene (aka Nicky and Geno); Extremities; One-Trick Pony; Rich Kids; Roosters; Saving Grace; Triumph of the Spirit.*

Young, Roger *Gulag; Lassiter; Squeeze, The.*

Young, Terence *Amazons, The (Le Guerriere dal Seno Nuda); Bloodline (aka Sidney Sheldon's Bloodline); Cold Sweat (De la Part des Copains); Dr No; From Russia With Love; Klansman, The; Red Sun (Soleil Rouge); That Lady; They Were Not Divided; Thunderball; Wait Until Dark.*

Yu, Ronny *Phantom Lover, The (Xin Yeban Gesheng); Warriors of Virtue.*

Yuan Kwai *Fong Sai-Yuk (Fang Shiyu).*

Yuan Muzhi *Street Angel (Malu Tianshi).*

Yuen, Corey *No Retreat, No Surrender.*

Yust, Larry *Homebodies.*

Yuzna, Brian *Necronomicon (aka H.P. Lovecraft's Necronomicon); Re-Animator 2; Return of the Living Dead II; Society.*

Zafranovic, Lordan *Occupation in 26 Pictures, The (Okupacija u 26 Slika).*

Zaillian, Steven *Searching for Bobby Fischer (aka Innocent Moves).*

Zaim, Dervis *Somersault in a Coffin (Tabutta Rövasata).*

Zaks, Jerry *Marvin's Room.*

Zampi, Mario *Happy Ever After (aka Tonight's the Night); Laughter in Paradise; Naked Truth, The (aka Your Past Is Showing).*

Zanuck, Darryl F *Longest Day, The.*

Zanuck, Lili Fini *Rush.*

Zanussi, Krzysztof *Constant Factor, The (Constans); Contract, The (Kontrakt); Family Life (Zycie Rodzinne); Illumination (Illuminacja); Life at a Gallop (Cwal); Night Paths (Wege in der Nacht); Silent Touch, The; Year of the Quiet Sun, A (Rok Spokojnego Slonca).*

Zappa, Frank *200 Motels.*

Zarindast, Tony *Guns and the Fury, The.*

Zaritsky, Raul *Maxwell Street Blues.*

Zaslove, Alan *GoBots: Battle of the Rocklords.*

Zauberman, Yolande *Clubbed to Death; Me Ivan, You Abraham (Moi Ivan, Toi Abraham).*

Zeffirelli, Franco *Brother Sun, Sister Moon (Fratello Sole, Sorella Luna); Champ, The; Endless Love; Hamlet; Jane Eyre; Otello; Romeo and Juliet; Sparrow (Storia di una Capinera); Traviata, La.*

Zelnik, Friedrich *Lilac Domino, The; Weber, Die.*

Zeltser, Yuri *Playmaker, The.*

Zemeckis, Robert *Amazing Stories; Back to the Future; Back to the Future Part II; Back to the Future Part III; Contact; Death Becomes Her; Forrest Gump; I Wanna Hold Your Hand; Romancing the Stone; Used Cars; Who Framed Roger Rabbit.*

Zetterling, Mai *Amorosa; Scrubbers; Visions of Eight.*

Zhang Meijun *Dynasty (Qian Dao Wan Li Zhui).*

Zhang Ming *Rainclouds Over Wushan (Wushan Yunyu/aka In Expectation).*

Zhang Nuanxin *Sacrificed Youth (Qingchun Ji).*

Zhang Tielin *Man from China.*

Zhang Yuan *Beijing Bastards (Beijing Zazhong); East Palace, West Palace (Dong Gong Xi Gong); Mama; Sons (Erzi), Square, The (Guangchang).*

Zhang Yimou *Ju Dou; Raise the Red Lantern (Dahong Denglong Gaogao Gua); Red Sorghum; Shanghai Triad (Yao a Yao Yao dao Waipo Qiao); Story of Qiu Ju, The (Qiu Ju da Guansi); To Live (Huozhe).*

Zhang Zeming *Foreign Moon;
Sun and Rain (Taiyang
Yu/aka Sunshine and
Showers); Swan Song
(Juexiang).*

Zheng Changhe *King Boxer
(Tianxia Diyi Quan/aka Five
Fingers of Death).*

Zheng Dongtian *Young
Couples (Yuanyang Iou).*

Zheutlin, Cathy *In the Best
Interests of the Children.*

Zhou Xiaowen *Emperor's
Shadow, The (Qin Song);
Ermo.*

Zhou Youchao *Sweet Grass
(Huang Sha, Qing Cao,
Hong Taiyang).*

Zhuge Qingyun *Shanghai Lil
(Hao Ke/aka The
Champion).*

Zidi, Claude *French Mustard
(La Moutarde Me Monte au
Nez); Le Cop (Les Ripoux);
Le Cop 2 (Ripoux contre
ripoux).*

Zieff, Howard *Dream Team,
The; Hearts of the West (aka
Hollywood Cowboy); House
Calls; Main Event, The; My
Girl; My Girl II; Private
Benjamin; Slither;
Unfaithfully Yours.*

Ziehm, Howard *Flesh Gordon.*

Zielinski, Rafal *Fun;
Screwballs; Screwballs II –
Loose Screws.*

Ziewer, Christian *Dear Mother,
I'm All Right (Liebe Mutter,
mir geht es gut).*

Zimmerman, Vernon *Fade to
Black.*

Zinnemann, Fred *Day of the
Jackal, The; Eyes in the
Night; Five Days One
Summer; From Here to
Eternity; High Noon; Julia;
Kid Glove Killer; Man for All
Seasons, A; Men, The; My
Brother Talks to Horses;
Nun's Story, The; Oklahoma!;
Search, The; Seventh Cross,
The; Sundowners, The.*

Zito, Joseph *Abduction;
Invasion U.S.A.; Missing in
Action; Prowler, The (aka
Rosemary's Killer).*

Zlotoff, Lee David *Spitfire Grill,
The.*

Zonca, Eric *Vie Rêvée des
Anges, La (The Dream Life
of Angels).*

Zucker, David *Airplane!;
Naked Gun, The; Naked
Gun 2½: The Smell of Fear,
The; Ruthless People; Top
Secret!*

Zucker, Jerry *Airplane!; First
Knight; Ghost; Ruthless
People; Top Secret!*

Zuckerman, Francine *Punch
Me in the Stomach.*

Zukor, Lou *Mighty Mouse in
the Great Space Chase.*

Zulawski, Andrzej *Possession;
Third Part of the Night, The
(Trzecia Czesc Nocy).*

Zuniga, Frank *Golden Seal, The.*

Zurlini, Valerio *Désert des
Tartares, Le.*

Zwerin, Charlotte *Gimme
Shelter; Music for the
Movies: Toru Takemitsu;
Thelonious Monk: Straight
No Chaser.*

Zwick, Edward *About Last
Night...; Courage Under Fire;
Glory; Having It All; Leaving
Normal; Legends of the Fall.*

Zwicky, Karl *Paws.*

Zwigoff, Terry *Crumb.*

General Subject Index

Abelard and Heloise, film about, *Stealing Heaven*

Abortion, *Alfie; Blue Denim; Dekalog 2: 'Thou shalt not take the name of the Lord thy God in vain'; Detective Story; Flesh; Hush-a-Bye Baby; If These Walls Could Talk; Love with the Proper Stranger; Making It; A Night in the Life of Jimmy Reardon; Occasional Work of a Female Slave; Patti Rocks; To Find a Man*

Acker, Kathy, film adapted from work, *Variety*

Ackerley, JR, film adapted from work, *We Think the World of You*

Adams, Richard, films adapted from work, *The Plague Dogs; Watership Down*

Adolescence (*see also* **Children and childhood, Runaways, Teenagers and teen movies**)
Aus, *Benny's Video; Fistful of Flies; Only the Brave*
Aust, *Emma's War; Fighting Back; Flirting; The Mango Tree; Mullaway; Two Friends; Walkabout; The Year My Voice Broke*
Bel, *Crazy Love*
Can, *Mon Oncle Antoine; My American Cousin*
China, *In the Heat of the Sun*
Czech, *Peter and Pavla; Valerie and Her Week of Wonders*
Fr, *A Toute Vitesse; The Best Way to Walk; Bonjour Tristesse; Les Dernières Vacances; Le Diable au corps; Diabolo Menthe; Les Enfants Terribles; 4 Adventures of Reinette and Mirabelle; An Impudent Girl; The Lover; Mon Père, ce héros; Montalvo et l'enfant; Nord; Passe Ton Bac d'Abord; Pauline à la Plage; La Petite Voleuse; Mes Petites Amoureuses; Le Petit Matin; Les Quatre Cents Coups; Rouge Baiser; Le Souffle au Coeur; To Our Loves; Virgin* (Breillat); *The Wanderer; Zazie dans le Métro*
GB, *Boston Kickout; Conquest of the South Pole; Experience Preferred But Not Essential; Friends; The Girl with Brains in Her Feet; Gregory's Girl; House of America; The Long Day Closes; The Miracle; Romeo*

and Juliet; Secret Places; Small Faces; Stella Does Tricks; A Summer in La Goulette; Terms of Trial; Wish You Were Here; The Young Poisoner's Handbook
Ger, *Mädchen in Uniform; The Main Actor; Wild Game*
Greece, *End of an Era*
Hun, *The Princess*
Ire, *Hush-a-Bye Baby; Last of the High Kings*
Isr, *Lemon Popsicle*
It, *Fists in the Pocket; Mignon Has Left; Noi Tre; Romeo and Juliet; Stealing Beauty; Venial Sin; The Visitor; I Vitelloni*
Jap, *How Old Is the River?; Love Letter; The Moon Has Risen; Remembrance* (Nakajima)*; This Window Is Yours*
Mex, *Hasta Morir*
Neth, *Spetters*
Nor, *Cross My Heart and Hope to Die; The Ice Palace* (Blom)*; I Was Fifteen; The Other Side of Sunday; Sebastian*
NZ, *An Angel at My Table; The End of the Golden Weather*
Pol, *Miss Nobody; A Short Film About Love*
Sp, *The Good Life*
Swe, *Hets; Love Lessons; Sebastian*
Switz, *The Indians Are Still Far Away*
Tai, *A Brighter Summer Day; Daughter of the Nile*
Tun, *A Summer in La Goulette*
US, *Aloha Summer; Angus; Beautiful Girls; Big Girls Don't Cry...They Get Even; Billy Bathgate; Book of Love; Boyz N the Hood; Brighton Beach Memoirs; Buster and Billie; The Chocolate War; Class of '44; Clueless; Confessions of a Suburban Girl; The Craft; The Delta; Diner; Empire Records; Fire with Fire; Five Corners; Gas Food Lodging; Grandview U.S.A.; Gummo; Heaven Help Us; Heavy Petting; Hopscotch; Housekeeping; Imaginary Crimes; I Never Promised You a Rose Garden; Kicked in the Head; The Last American Virgin; The Last Picture Show; Last Summer; Little Darlings; The Man in the Moon; Manny & Lo; Mermaids; My Bodyguard; My Father, the Hero; My Little Girl; A Night in the Life of Jimmy Reardon; Ode to Billie Joe; Old Enough; Permanent*

Record; The Power of One; Racing with the Moon; Red Sky at Morning; Running on Empty; Square Dance; Staying Together; Summer of '42; Teenage Caveman; This Day and Age; Welcome to the Dollhouse; William Shakespeare's Romeo & Juliet; White Squall; Who's That Knocking at My Door?; The Woo Woo Kid USSR, Goodbye, Boys; Plumbum, or a Dangerous Game; When We Were Young Vietnam, Nostalgia for Countryland Yugo, Time of the Gypsies

Adoption (see also **Orphans**), Adoption; Auntie Mame; L'Enfance nue; Flirting with Disaster; A Global Affair; It Takes Two; Mixed Company; The Official Version; Perfect Circle; Problem Child; Problem Child 2; Santee; Secrets & Lies; A Simple Twist of Fate; The Tie That Binds; The Unforgiven

Advertising, Agency; Boomerang (Hudlin); Christmas in July; Crazy People; A Face in the Crowd; How to Get Ahead in Advertising; Keep the Aspidistra Flying; Nothing in Common; A Shock to the System; Switch; Will Success Spoil Rock Hunter?; A Woman or Two

Afghanistan, in film, The Beast; The Horsemen; Rambo III

Africa, in film (see also individual African nations) colonial life in (see also **Colonialism**), Another Dawn; The Black Bunch; Chocolat; Clean Slate; Cobra Verde; A Good Man in Africa; The Grass Is Singing; La Guerre sans nom; The Heart of the Matter; The Kitchen Toto; Men of Two Worlds; Mister Johnson; No Secrets; Out of Africa; Sammy Going South; The Sheltering Sky; Simba; The Sins of Rachel Cade; White Mischief ethnographic films, Africa Addio; Man of Africa safari films, exploration, etc, Ace Ventura – When Nature Calls; Africa – Texas Style; Clarence, the Cross-Eyed Lion; The Desert Song; A Far Off Place; George of the Jungle; The Gods Must Be Crazy; The Gods Must Be Crazy II; Hatari!; King Solomon's Mines (Stevenson); King Solomon's Mines (Thompson); The Kiss; The Lion; Missing Link; Mogambo; Mountains of the Moon; Roar; The Snows of Kilimanjaro; White Hunter, Black Heart

Afterlife, the (see also **Heaven-can-wait fantasies, Return to life, Undead**), Almost an Angel;

Bad Lord Byron; Bill & Ted's Bogus Journey; Carnival of Souls; Checking Out; Dante's Inferno; Defending Your Life; Flatliners; Heart Condition; Heaven; Made in Heaven; Parking; Soultaker; Static; Truly, Madly, Deeply; Wings of Fame

Age and ageing, The Alpha Caper; An Autumn Afternoon; The Bandit; Batteries Not Included; Bloomfield; Blue Juice; Boardwalk; Branches of the Tree; Charles and Lucie; Children of Nature; Cocoon; Cocoon: The Return; The Company of Strangers; Don Quichotte; Driving Miss Daisy; For Fun; Ginger and Fred; Going in Style; Grumpy Old Men; Guarding Tess; Homebodies; House of Smiles; Ju Dou; Kotch; The Last Good Time; Lina Braake; Love Among the Ruins; Ma Saison Préférée; Middle Age Crazy; My Sons; Number One (Gries); Old Gringo; On Golden Pond; Out of an Old Man's Head; Le Plaisir; Promise; Rooster Cogburn; Roseland; She's Been Away; The Shootist; The Sorcerers; Spider and Rose; The Sunshine Boys; Take It Like a Man, Ma'am; Tatie Danielle; Tell Me a Riddle; 30 Is a Dangerous Age, Cynthia; Three Brothers; Touchez pas au Grisbi; Tough Guys; Travelling North; The Trip to Bountiful; True Grit; Twilight; Umberto D; Unforgiven; Used People; La Vieille Dame indigne; The Whales of August; What Ever Happened to Aunt Alice?; The Whisperers; Wild Strawberries; A Woman's Tale; Wrestling Ernest Hemingway

Age disparity in relationships
older men, younger women, American Friends; Blame It on Rio; The Blue Angel; The Blue Eyes of Yonta; Born Yesterday (Cukor); Born Yesterday (Mandoki); Breezy; Circle of Two; En Cas de Malheur; The Few Seasons; Five Days One Summer; Le Grand Amour; The Greengage Summer; I Know Where I'm Going; The Last Good Time; Laughter; Lolita (Kubrick); Lolita (Lyne); Man of Flowers; Manuela; Nelly & Monsieur Arnaud; The Nest; Noce blanche; Rita, Sue and Bob Too; La Senyora; Susan Slept Here; Three into Two Won't Go; Up Close & Personal; Virgin (Breillat); Voyager
older women, younger men, Les Amants; Boom; Chère Louise; Class; Death in a French Garden; Dekalog 6: 'Thou shalt not commit adultery'; Le Diable au corps; Fear Eats the Soul; The Fugitive Kind; The Graduate; Harold and Maude; La Maison de Jade;

Night Hair Child; The Old Lady Who Walked in the Sea; Real Life; The Roman Spring of Mrs Stone; A Short Film About Love; A Tiger's Tale; Tim; Tune in Tomorrow; White Palace; The Woo Woo Kid

Age reversal/age exchange, Before I Hang; Big, Damn Yankees; 18 Again!; Flight of the Navigator; Freaky Friday; Jack; Like Father, Like Son; The Major and the Minor; Monkey Business (Hawks); Peggy Sue Got Married; The Picture of Dorian Gray; Seconds; Vice Versa (Ustinov); Vice Versa (Gilbert)

Aguirre, Lope de, films about, Aguirre, Wrath of God; El Dorado

AIDS and HIV, The Addiction; Alive and Kicking; And the Band Played On; Being at Home with Claude; Blue; Boys on the Side; Buddies; Casual Sex?; Chain of Desire; Citizen Cohn; Close My Eyes; Closing Numbers; Common Threads: Stories from the Quilt; The Cure; Fast Trip, Long Drop; Grief; It's My Party; Jeffrey; Kids; The Last Supper (Roberts); The Lie; The Living End; Longtime Companion; Love! Valour! Compassion!; My New Friends; N'oublie pas que tu vas mourir; One Night Stand; Over Our Dead Bodies; Philadelphia; Postcards from America; Rock Hudson's Home Movies; Roommates; Roy Cohn/Jack Smith; Savage Nights; Slanted Vision; Stonewall; Strip Jack Naked: Nighthawks II; To Die For; Voices from the Front; Zero Patience

Airships, Dirigible; The Hindenberg

Alain-Fournier, film adapted from work, The Wanderer

The Alamo, films about, The Alamo; The Last Command; Viva Max!

Alaska, in film, By The Law; Cry from the Mountain; The Golden Seal; The Hellhounds of Alaska; Ice Palace; Jet Pilot; K2; Mountain; Road to Utopia; Runaway Train; Salmonberries; Top of the World; When the North Wind Blows; White Fang (Fulci); White Fang (Kleiser)

Albee, Edward, films adapted from work, A Delicate Balace; Who's Afraid of Virginia Woolf?

Alcoholism, Arthur; Arthur 2; On the Rocks; Barfly; The Blackout; Clean and Sober; Come Back, Little Sheba; Come Fill the Cup; Days of Wine and Roses; Dream On; Le Feu Follet; The Grass Arena; The Honorary

Consul; Ironweed; Jacknife; Leaving Las Vegas; The Legend of the Holy Drinker; Liar; The Lost Weekend; The Morning After; My Name Is Joe; On the Nickel; Porte des Lilas; Sir Henry at Rawlinson's End; Skin Deep; The Small Back Room; Smash-Up, The Story of a Woman; Somersault in a Coffin; Special Treatment; The Squeeze; The Struggle; Time Without Pity; Under the Volcano; W.C. Fields and Me; When a Man Loves a Woman

Alcott, Louisa May, film adapted from work, Little Women (Cukor); Little Women (Armstrong)

Aldiss, Brian W, film adapted from work, Roger Corman's Frankenstein Unbound

Algeria, in film, Algiers; L'Attentat; Bab El-Oued City; The Battle of Algiers; The Citadel (Chouikh); La Guerre sans nom; Ramparts of Clay; The Sheltering Sky

Algerian cinema, Bab El-Oued City; The Battle of Algiers; The Citadel (Chouikh); Ramparts of Clay; Salut Cousin!

Ali, Muhammad, film about, The Greatest; When We Were Kings

Allen, Woody film about, Wild Man Blues film adapted from work, Play It Again, Sam

Allende, Isabel, film adapted from work, The House of Spirits

Altman, Robert, in film, Luck, Trust & Ketchup: Robert Altman in Carver Country

Amado, Jorge, films adapted from work, Doña Flor and Her Two Husbands; Tieta of Agreste

Amazonia, see Rain forests

Ambler, Eric, films adapted from work, Background to Danger; Journey into Fear; The Mask of Dimitrios; The October Man; Topkapi

Ambulances, The Ambulance; Mother, Jugs & Speed

America, in film, (see also individual cities and **Blacks in USA, Small town life** and **South, The American**) invaded, The Blob; Bulletproof; Independence Day; Invasion USA; The Mouse That Roared; Prayer of the Rollerboys; The Puppet Masters; Red Dawn; Red Nightmare; Viva Max!; War; The Whip Hand anti-Americanism, Mister Freedom

American Civil War, Advance to the Rear; The Beguiled; Escape from Fort

Ger, *Cross of Iron*
Ire, *Guiltrip*
Isr, *Burning Memory; Private Popsicle*
SAf, *On the Wire; the Stick*
Sen, *Camp Thiaroye*
Tai, *Bodo; Buddha Bless America*
US, *Basic Training; Biloxi Blues; Blue Sky; Canal Zone; Count a Lonely Cadence; A Few Good Men; A Foreign Affair; The Fourth War; From Here to Eternity; F.T.A.; Full Metal Jacket; Gardens of Stone; G.I. Blues; G.I. Jane; A Hill In Korea; The Long Gray Line; The Ninth Configuration; The Package; Private Benjamin; Reflections in a Golden Eye; Renaissance Man; Sergeant York; Sgt Bilko; Soldier Girls; A Soldier's Story; The Strange One; Taps; The Victors; A Walk in the Sun; You'll Never Get Rich*
USSR/Rus, *The Beast; The Life and Extraordinary Adventures of Private Ivan Chonkin; 100 Days Before the Command*

Art and artists
artists in society, *The Affairs of Cellini; Alchemy; Close to the Wind; A Dog of Flanders; The Draughtsman's Contract; The Fountainhead; Good Morning Babylon; The Hair Opera; Heartbreakers; Hour of the Wolf; Kids of Survival: The Art and Life of Tim Rollins & K.O.S.; Love Is the Devil; Loving; News from Nowhere; Right Out of History: The Making of Judy Chicago's Dinner Party; The Sandpiper; Le Sang d'un Poète; La Vie de Bohème; The World of Gilbert & George; Wot! No Art*
graffiti and graffiti artists, *Basquiat*
painters and painting, *The Agony and the Ecstasy; Anne Trister; La Belle Noiseuse; La Belle Noiseuse – Divertimento; A Bigger Splash; Bluebeard; The Bridge; Caravaggio; La Chienne; The Dying Swan; Edvard Munch; Europe After the Rain; Every Picture Tells a Story; Favourites of the Moon; Five Women Around Utamaro; The Horse's Mouth; Imago – Meret Oppenheim; Incognito; Love Is the Devil; Lust for Life; Man from China; The Moon and Sixpence; Moulin Rouge; Le Mystère Picasso; New York Stories; Painters Painting; Pirosmani; The Quince Tree Sun; The Rebel; Rembrandt; Schiele in Prison; Sirens; Sunday in the Country; Surviving Picasso; Trust Me; Van Gogh; Vincent: The Life and Death of Vincent Van Gogh; Venice: Theme and Variation; Vincent & Theo; Yumeji*
sculpture, *A Bucket of Blood; Camille Claudel; Daddy; Joseph Cornell: Worlds in a Box; The Paolozzi Story; Savage Messiah; Song of Songs*

Artaud, Antonin, film about, *En Compagnie d'Antonin Artaud*

Artists' creations coming alive, *Delirious; Genuine; Icicle Thief; Mannequin; Mannequin Two: On the Move; One Touch of Venus*

Art world, *Artists and Models; The Cold Eye; Crack-Up* (Reis)*; Favourites of the Moon; F for Fake; The Golden Salamander; I've Heard the Mermaids Singing; Melancholia; The Moderns; Object of Beauty; Painters Painting; Slaves of New York; Surviving Picasso* art schools, *The Best Age*

Asians in Britain, *Bhaji on the Beach; Foreign Body; Majdhar; My Beautiful Laundrette; A Private Enterprise; Sammy and Rosie Ged Laid; Wild West*

Asians in Canada, *Masala*

Asians in USA, *Lonely in America; Mississippi Masala*

Assassinations, political, *Above the Law; American Roulette; Ashes and Diamonds; Assassin; Assassin of the Tsar; The Assassination of Trotsky; Assassins; L'Attentat; Brass Target; The Conformist; The Day of the Jackal; Executive Action; Four Days of Snow and Blood; Hitler's Madman; In the Line of Fire; The Jackal; JFK; John Carpenter's Escape from L.A.; Konfrontation; The Last Supper* (Title)*; The Manchurian Candidate; Manhunt; Manifesto; Melancholia; Most Wanted; Nick of Time; Nobody Runs Forever; The November Men; Operation Daybreak; The Parallax View; Pasolini, un Delitto Italiano; Patriot Games; The Pelican Brief; Ruby; Rush to Judgment; Russian Roulette; Seven Minutes; The Shooter; State of Siege; Suddenly; TAG, The Assassination Game; The Tall Target; Tigers Don't Cry; The Times of Harvey Milk; Winter Kills; Z*

Astronauts and contemporary space travel, *Apollo 13; Beyond the Stars; Capricorn One; Contact; Countdown; Destination Moon; For All Mankind; Marooned; Moonraker; The Mouse on the Moon; The Right Stuff; Space Camp; Spaceways*

Asylums, see **Mental hospitals and asylums**

Athletics (see also **Olympic Games**)*, Chariots of Fire; Geordie; Jericho Mile; The Loneliness of the Long Distance Runner; Personal Best; Running Brave; True Blue; Superargo*

Attila the Hun, film about, *Sign of the Pagan*

Atwood, Margaret, film adapted from work, *The Handmaid's Tale*

Austen, Jane, films adapted from/based on work, *Clueless; Emma; Jane Austen in Manhattan; Persuasion; Pride and Prejudice; Sense and Sensibility*

Australia, in film
past, *Between Wars; Botany Bay; Caddie; Country Life; For Love or Money; Kangaroo* (Burstall)*; Mad Dog Morgan; Manganinnie; My Brilliant Career; Newsfront; Ned Kelly; The Overlanders; Quigley Down Under; Robbery Under Arms; Silver City; Sirens; Sunday Too Far Away; The Sundowners; We of the Never Never*
contemporary, *The Adventures of Priscilla Queen of the Desert; Backroads; Bad Boy Bubby; Cane Toads – An Unnatural History; Celia; The Club; Crocodile Dundee; Crocodile Dundee II; A Cry in the Dark; Dallas Doll; Dead Heart; Deadly; Death in Brunswick; Doing Time for Patsy Cline; Dogs in Space; Don's Party; Fast Talking; Fatal Bond; First Strike; Floating Life; Geordie; Grievous Bodily Harm; Hammers Over the Anvil; Heaven's Burning; Hotel Sorrento; Kiss or Kill; The Last Crop; Love in Limbo; The Love Letters from Teralba Road; The Man from Snowy River; The Odd Angry Shot; Mr Reliable (a true story); Outback; Over the Hill; A Personal History of the Australian Surf; Public Enemy Number One; The Quiet Room; Redheads; Romper Stomper; Rough Diamonds; Say a Little Prayer; Secrets; Shame; Shine; Spotswood; Strictly Ballroom; That Eye, the Sky; They're a Weird Mob; Walkabout; The Well; What Have I Written?; The Winchester Conspiracy; Winter of Our Dreams; The Year My Voice Broke; Young Einstein*

Australian Aboriginals, *Backlash; Backroads; The Chant of Jimmy Blacksmith; Dead Heart; Deadly; The Fringe Dwellers; The Last Wave; Manganinnie; Quigley Down Under; Walkabout; Where the Green Ants Dream*

Australian cinema, see Appendix 16

Austria, in film, *Bad Timing; Burning Secret; Dishonored; The Divine Emma; Funny Games; Hanussen; The Hotel New Hampshire; The King Steps Out; Mayerling; Oh Rosalinda!; La Ronde; The Sound of Music; Tales from*

the Vienna Woods; The Third Man; Totschweigen; The Unfish; The Wedding March

Austrian cinema, *Benny's Video; Colonel Redl; Funny Games; Halbe Welt; Invisible Adversaries; Hands of Orlac; Invisible Adversaries; My Mother's Courage; The Refusal; Requiem for Dominic; 71 Fragments of a Chronology of Chance; Tierische Liebe; Totschweigen; The Unfish; Wittstock, Wittstock*

Autism, *The Boy Who Could Fly; Jigsaw; La Madre Muerta; Mercury Rising; Rain Man; Silent Fall*

Avant garde cinema, see **Experimental films**

Averroës, film about, *Destiny*

Axelrod, George, films adapted from work, *The Seven Year Itch; Wïlll Success Spoil Rock Hunter?*

Ayckbourn, Alan, films adapted from work, *A Chorus of Disapproval; Smoking/No Smoking; Way Upstream*

`**Aymé,** Marcel, films adapted from work, *The Favour, the Watch and the Very Big Fish; Uranus*

Babies, see **Pregnancy, childbirth and babies**

Babysitting (see also **Nannies, governesses, au pairs**)*, Adventures in Babysitting; The Babysitter; Don't Tell Mom the Babysitter's Dead; Dressed to Kill; Sitting Pretty; Uncle Buck; Unhook the Stars; When a Stranger Calls; When the Cat's Away…*

Bach, JS and Anna Magdalena, *Chronicles of Anna Magdalena Bach*

Bacon, Francis, film about, *Love Is the Devil*

Bader, Douglas, film about, *Reach for the Sky*

Bainbridge, Beryl, films adapted from work, *An Awfully Big Adventure; The Dressmaker; Sweet William*

Baker, Chet, film about, *Let's Get Lost*

Baldacci, Daniel, film adapted from work, *Absolute Power*

Baldwin, James, film about, *James Baldwin: The Price of the Ticket*

Ballard, JG, films adapted from work, *Crash* (Cronenberg)*; Empire of the Sun*

Ballooning, *Night Crossing*

Baltimore, in film, *The Accidental Tourist; Avalon;*

Cry-Baby; Desperate Living; Diner; Female Trouble; Hairspray; Serial Mom; The Tall Target; Tin Men

Balzac, Honoré de, films adapted from work, *La Belle Noiseuse; La Belle Noiseuse – Divertimento; Le Colonel Chabert (Le Hénaff); Le Colonel Chabert (Angelo); Le Père Goriot*

Banks, Lynne Reid, films adapted from work, *The Indian in the Cupboard; The L-Shaped Room*

Banks, Russell, film adapted from work, *Affliction; The Sweet Hereafter*

Barber, Elsie Oaks, film adapted from work, *Angel Baby*

Barker, Clive, films adapted from work, *Candyman; Candyman 2: Farewell to the Flesh; Hellraiser; Hellbound: Hellraiser II; Hellraiser III: Hell on Earth; Nightbreed*

Barmen, *Cocktail*

Barnes, Julian, film based on work, *Love, etc.*

Barnum, PT, film about, *The Mighty Barnum*

Barrie, JM, films adapted from work, *The Admirable Crichton; Hook; Peter Pan* film featuring his work, *An Awfully Big Adventure*

Barry, Philip, films adapted from work, *High Society; Holiday; The Philadelphia Story*

Barstow, Stan, film adapted from work, *A Kind of Loving*

Barth, John, film adapted from work, *End of the Road*

Bartók, Béla, film of opera, *Bluebeard's Castle*

Baseball, *Amazing Grace and Chuck; Angels in the Outfield; The Babe; Brewster's Millions (Hill); Bull Durham; Cobb; Eight Men Out; The Fan (Scott); Field of Dreams; A League of Their Own; Little Big League; Major League; Major League II; Mr Baseball; The Natural; The Pride of St Louis; Rhubarb; Rookie of the Year; The Sandlot; Stealing Home; Take Me Out to the Ball Game*

Basketball, *Above the Rim; The Air Up There; The Basketball Diaries; Blue Chips; Eddie; Hoop Dreams; Hoosiers; One on One; Space Jam; That Championship Season; White Men Can't Jump*

Bates, HE, films adapted from work, *Dulcima; A Month by the Lake; The Triple Echo*

Baum, L Frank, films adapted from work, *Return to Oz; The Wiz; The Wizard of Oz; Zardoz*

Beach movies, *Beach Blanket Bingo; Big Wednesday; Last Summer; A Swingin' Summer; Where the Boys Are*

The Beatles, films of/about (see also **Lennon,** John, and **McCartney,** Paul), *Backbeat; A Hard Day's Night; Help; I Wanna Hold Your Hand; Let It Be; Secrets; Yellow Submarine* musical based on songs, *Sergeant Pepper's Lonely Hearts Club Band*

Beat writers, films about, *A Bucket of Blood; Heart Beat; Kerouac; Last Time I Committed Suicide; The Life and Times of Allen Ginsberg; Whatever Happened to Kerouac?*

Beauty contests, *The Beauty Jungle; The Fireman's Ball; Miss Firecracker; Page Miss Glory; The Positively True Adventures of the Alleged Texas Cheerleader-Murdering Mom; Smile*

Beckett, Samuel, film adapted from work, *Film*

Beethoven, Ludwig van, film about, *Immortal Beloved*

Beiderbecke, Bix, films about, *Bix; Young Man With a Horn*

Belafonte, Harry, film about, *Sometimes I Look at My Life*

Belgian cinema, *American Stories; Anchoress; Australia; Beck; Benvenuta; Bird Now; The Blue Villa; Daens; Daughters of Darkness; Le Départ; Dust; Divine Body; The Eighth Day; L'Etoile du Nord; Farinelli Il Castrato; Une Femme entre Chien et Loup; Germinal; I Am Anna Magnani; Jeanne Dielman, 23 Quai du Commerce, 1080 Bruxelles; Je tu il elle; Le Journal de Lady M; Libertarias; The Lost Paradise; Il Maestro; Malpertuis; Man Bites Dog; The Man Who Had His Hair Cut Short; Manneken Pis; Ma Vie en Rose; The Music Teacher; Pallieter; The Promise (Dardenne/Dardenne); Rendez-vous à Bray; Salut Cousin!; The Sexual Life of the Belgians 1950–1978; Tale of the Three Jewels; Taxandria; Total Eclipse*

Belgium, in film, *Daens; A Dog of Flanders; La Kermesse Héroique; Portrait of a Young Girl at the End of the '60s in Brussels; The Sexual Life of the Belgians 1950–1978; Toute une Nuit*

Bellow, Saul, film adapted from work, *Seize the Day*

Belushi, John, film about, *Wired*

Benchley, Peter, films adapted from work, *The Deep; Island; Jaws*

Benin cinema, *Divine Body*

Bennett, Alan, film adapted from work, *The Madness of King George*

Bennett, Arnold, film adapted from work, *The Card*

Bereavement (see also **Death**), *Le Grand Chemin; Harry and Son; In Country; Komitas; Life and Nothing But; Moonlight and Valentino; Mother Küster's Trip to Heaven; My Girl; My Girl 2; Paradise; Phone Call from a Stranger; A Portuguese Goodbye*

Berendt, John, film based on work, *Midnight in the Garden of Good and Evil*

Berger, John, film adapted from work, *Play Me Something*

Berger, Thomas, films adapted from work, *Little Big Man; Neighbors*

Berkeley, Busby, musicals choreographed by, *Dames; Footlight Parade; For Me and My Gal; 42nd Street; The Gang's All Here; Gold Diggers of 1933; Gold Diggers of 1935; Gold Diggers of 1937; The Kid from Spain; Roman Scandals; Strike Up the Band; Take Me Out to the Ball Game; Two Weeks With Love; Ziegfeld Girl*

Berkoff, Steven, film adapted from work, *Decadence*

Berlin, in film, *Anita: Dances of Vice; Berlin Alexanderplatz; Berlin Jerusalem; The Big Lift; Cabaret; Chinese Boxes; City of Lost Souls; Company Business; Dr M; Dr Mabuse, the Gambler; England Made Me; Enigma; Fatherland; Une Femme française; Flight to Berlin; Flirt; Forbidden; A Foreign Affair; Funeral in Berlin; Germany, Year Zero; Girl in a Boot; Gorilla Bathes at Noon; The Grass Is Always Greener; I Am a Camera; The Innocent (Schlesinger); Judgment in Berlin; Little Angel; The Man Between; No Mercy, No Future; One, Two, Three; Possession; The Quiller Memorandum; Salmonberries; The Serpent's Egg; Taxi zum Klo; Ten Seconds to Hell; Torn Curtain; Verboten; Westler: East of the Wall; Will My Mother Go Back to Berlin?; Wings of Desire*

Berlin, Irving, musicals by, *Annie Get Your Gun; Blue Skies; Carefree; Easter Parade; Follow the Fleet; Holiday Inn; There's No Business Like Show Business; Top Hat*

Bermuda, in film, *The Deep*

Bermuda Triangle, *The Bermuda Triangle; The Sharks' Cave*

Bernhard, Sandra, in performance, *Without You I'm Nothing*

Bernhardt, Sarah, film about, *The Incredible Sarah*

Bernstein, Carl, and Woodward, Bob, film about, *All The President's Men*

Berry, Chuck, in performance, *Hail! Hail! Rock'n'Roll!; Let the Good Times Roll; The London Rock'n'Roll Show*

Bessa-Luis, Augustina, film adapted from work, *Abraham Valley*

Bezzerides, AI, films adapted from work, *They Drive By Night (Walsh); Thieves Highway*

Berlusconi, Silvio, film about, *Repubblica Nostra*

Biblical stories (see also **God, Jesus Christ**), *The Bible...In the Beginning; The Greatest Story Ever Told; King David; King of Kings; Moses; Noah's Ark; Rachel's Man; The Robe; Samson and Delilah; Sodom and Gomorrah; Solomon and Sheba; The Ten Commandments; Wholly Moses!*

Bibliomania, *Quiet Please, Murder*

Bierce, Ambrose, film about, *Old Gringo*

Biggs, Ronald, film about, *Prisoner of Rio*

Bikers, *L'Agression; Akira; Another 48 HRS; The Born Losers; Deathsport; Death Weekend; Easy Rider; Electra Glide in Blue; Evel Knievel; The Glory Stompers; Harley Davidson and the Marlboro Man; Hells Angels on Wheels; Hex; Hog Wild; I Bought a Vampire Motorcyle; I Wanted to See Angels; Knightriders; The Loveless; On Any Sunday; Psychomania; Roadside Prophets; Rebel Rousers; Shame; She Lives to Ride; Stone; Stone Cold; Viva Knievel; Wanda Nevada; Watch Out, We're Mad; The Wild Angels; The Wild One*

Binchy, Maeve, film from work, *Circle of Friends*

Biopics artists/musicians/performers/writers, etc, *Actress; The Adventures of Mark Twain; Amadeus; An Angel at My Table; The Best Things in Life Are Free; Bird; Blossom Time; Bound for Glory; The Buddy Holly Story; Camille Claudel; Carrington; Céleste; Chaplin; Chronicle of Anna Magdalena Bach; Coal*

Miner's Daughter; Committed; The Death of Maria Malibran; The Divine Emma; Dixie; The Doors; The Dragon Dies Hard; Dragon: The Bruce Lee Story; Edith and Marcel; Ed Wood; Elvis – The Movie; Edvard Munch; En Compagnie d'Antonin Artaud; Frances; Funny Girl; Funny Lady; Gable and Lombard; The Glenn Miller Story; Great Balls of Fire!; The Great Waltz (Duvivier); The Great Waltz (Stone); Goodbye Norma Jean; Immortal Beloved; The Incredible Sarah; Isadora; The Jolson Story; Kabloonak; Kafka; Karl May; Lady Sings the Blues; Leadbelly; Lenny; The Life of Chikuzan; The Life of Emile Zola; Lillian Russell; Lola Montès; Love Me or Leave Me; The Loves of Liszt; Lust for Life; The Magic Bow; Mahler; A Man Like Eva; Marilyn – The Untold Story; Marlene; The Mighty Barnum; Mrs Parker and the Vicious Circle; Mommie Dearest; Moulin Rouge; The Music Lovers; My Left Foot; Night and Day; Nijinsky; Oh! You Beautiful Doll; Pavlova – A Woman for All Time; Piaf; Postcards from America; Pirosmani; Prick Up Your Ears; Priest of Love; Puppetmaster; Rhapsody in Blue; Rose of Washington Square; Saint-Ex; St Louis Blues; Savage Messiah; Schiele in Prison; Shine; The Sex Symbol; Song of Norway; A Song to Remember; Spring Symphony; Star; Stevie; Superstar: The Karen Carpenter Story; Sweet Dreams; Testimony; Tina: What's Love Got to Do With It; Tom & Viv; The Tommy Steele Story; Total Eclipse; Valentino; Van Gogh; Vincent & Theo; Wagner; W.C. Fields and Me; Wired; With a Song in My Heart; Yankee Doodle Dandy; Young Cassidy; Young Man with a Horn
politicians/military figures, etc, Agony; Catherine the Great; Che!; Christopher Columbus; Christopher Columbus: The Discovery; Flame Top; Daens; 1492: Conquest of Paradise; The Greek Tycoon; Henry VIII and His Six Wives; Joe Hill; Lawrence of Arabia; MacArthur; Mary of Scotland; Mary Queen of Scots; Michael Collins; Napoléon; Nicholas and Alexandra; Nixon; Patton; Pride of the Marines; The Private Files of J Edgar Hoover; The Private Life of Henry VIII; Reach for the Sky; Reds; The Roads of Exile; Rosa Luxemburg; The Scarlet Empress; That Hamilton Woman; They Died with Their Boots On; Viva Zapata; The Wings of Eagles; Young Mr Lincoln; Young Winston
saints/visionaries/priests,

L'Appel du Silence; Augustine of Hippo; Brother Sun, Sister Moon; Entertaining Angels: The Dorothy Day Story; Kundun; A Man Called Peter; Pastor Hall; Francesco, giullare di Dio; Nostradamus
scientists/doctors, etc, The Darwin Adventure; Dr Ehrlich's Magic Bullet; Edison the Man; Freud; Gorillas in the Mist; The Great Moment; Korczak; Madame Curie; Pasteur
sportsmen/women, The Babe; Cobb; Dawn!; 8 Seconds; Evel Knievel; Greased Lightning; The Greatest; Nadia; The Pride of St Louis; Somebody Up There Likes Me
miscellaneous, Al Capone; The Autobiography of Miss Jane Pittman; Baby Face Nelson; Beyond Evil; Blossoms in the Dust; Born on the Fourth of July; Buster; Capone; Chanel Solitaire; Dillinger (Nosseck); Dillinger (Milius); The Executioner's Song; Gotti; The House of Rothschild; The Inn of the Sixth Happiness; King of the Roaring 20's – The Story of Arnold Rothstein; The Krays; Lucky Luciano; Luther; McVicar; A Man Named John; Ned Kelly; Paperback Vigilante; Patty Hearst; The Rise and Fall of Legs Diamond; Salvatore Giuliano; A Single Spark; Sugartime; Sylvia; The Terry Fox Story; Tucker: The Man and His Dream; Where the Buffalo Roam; Wittgenstein; Young Dillinger

Birds, see **Animals and birds**

Birney, Hoffman, film adapted from work, The Glory Guys

Bisexuality, Basic Instinct; Bisexual; Executioners from Shaolin; Fellini-Satyricon; Labyrinth of Passion; Making Love; A Man Like Eva; The Man Who Had Power over Women; Parking; Skin & Bone; Sunday, Bloody Sunday

Bizet, Georges, films adapted from work, Carmen (DeMille); Carmen (Rosi); Carmen (Saura); Carmen Jones; Dias Contados; First Name: Carmen; The Tragedy of Carmen

Blackmail, Blackmail (Hitchcock); Blackmail (Potter); Boy; Cage of Gold; Crossroads (Conway); The Dumb Die Fast, the Smart Die Slow; Gator; The Gazebo; Intimate Stranger; The Naked Truth; The Night of the Party; One of Those Things; The Private Lesson; Private Lessons; The Reckless Moment; The Suspect; The Swiss Conspiracy; The Unsuspected; Victim; The Woman in the Window; Wrong Is Right

Black marketeering, Dancing with Crime; Tenderness of the Wolves; The Third Man

Blacks in Britain (see also **Asians in Britain**), Ama; Babylon; Blue Notes and Exiled Voices; Burning an Illusion; Flame in the Streets; For Queen and Country; Handsworth Songs; Leo the Last; The Passion of Remembrance; Playing Away; Pressure; Reggae; '36 to '77; Time and Judgement; Tunde's Film; Twilight City; Who Needs a Heart; Young Soul Rebels

Blacks in USA
blaxploitation, Bucktown; Cleopatra Jones; Cleopatra Jones and the Casino of Gold; Coffy; Hell Up in Harlem; Original Gangstas; Penitentiary; Shaft; Shaft in Africa; Shaft's Big Score; Sheba Baby; Slaughter; Slaughter's Big Rip-Off; Superfly; That Man Bolt; Three the Hard Way
parodies of, I'm Gonna Git You Sucka
in Hollywood, BAPS; Hollywood Shuffle; Illusions
in South, Amistad; The Autobiography of Miss Jane Pittman; Cabin in the Sky; Candyman 2: Farewell to the Flesh; The Color Purple; Conrack; Driving Miss Daisy; Drum; Freedom Road, A Gathering of Old Men; Ghosts of Mississippi; Glory; The Green Pastures; Hurry Sundown; In the Heat of the Night; The Intruder; Intruder in the Dust; The Killing Floor; The Klansman; Law and Order; The Liberation of L.B. Jones; Mandingo; Martha & Ethel; Mississippi Blues; Mississippi Burning; A Night in Havana: Dizzy Gillespie in Cuba; Once Upon a Time…When We Were Colored; Paris Trout; La P..... Respectueuse; The Prisoner of Shark Island; The Reivers; Santa Fe Trail; A Soldier's Story; Song of the South; Sounder; Uncle Tom
urban, etc, Above the Rim; Across 110th Street; Action Jackson; Basquiat; Beverly Hills Cop; Beverly Hills Cop II; Beverly Hills Cop III; Blues Under the Skin; Boomerang (Hudlin); Booty Call; Boyz N the Hood; Brewster's Millions (Hill); The Brother from Another Planet; Bustin' Loose; Carmen Jones; Car Wash; Clara's Heart; Claudine; Clockers; Come Back Charleston Blue; Cool Breeze; Cooley High; The Cool World; The Cotton Club; Count a Lonely Cadence; Crooklyn; D.C. Cab; Dead Presidents; Deep Cover; DEF by Temptation; Devil in a Blue Dress; The Distinguished Gentleman; Do the Right Thing; Edge of the City; Fatal Beauty; The Five Heartbeats; Get on the

Bus; Gladiator; The Glass Shield; God's Alcatraz; Good to Go; Gordon's War; Grand Canyon; Hangin' with the Homeboys; Harlem Nights; Hoop Dreams; House Party; James Baldwin: The Price of the Ticket; The Preacher's Wife; Juice; Jungle Fever; Just Another Girl on the I.R.T.; Killer of Sheep; Lady Sings the Blues; The Landlord; Listen Up: The Lives of Quincy Jones; Looking for Langston; love jones; A Low Down Dirty Shame; Mahogany; Malcolm X; Melinda; Menace II Society; The Meteor Man; Mo' Better Blues; Mo' Money; My Brother's Wedding; New Jack City; No Maps on My Taps; Norman...Is That You?; The Nutty Professor (Shadyac); The Organisation; Panther; A Patch of Blue; A Piece of the Action; Poetic Justice; Portrait of Jason; The Price of the Ticket; Putney Swope; A Rage in Harlem; Ragtime; Rappin'; School Daze; Set It Off; Shadows; She's Gotta Have It; Shoot to Kill; Sidewalk Stories; Soul Food; South Central; Straight Out of Brooklyn; Streamers; Sugar Hill; Sun Ra: A Joyful Noise; Sweet Sweetback's Baadasssss Song; Tap; They Call Me MISTER Tibbs!; Tongues Untied; To Sleep with Anger; Uptown Saturday Night; Vampire in Brooklyn; A Warm December; Watermelon Man; The Watermelon Woman; Wattstax; White Men Can't Jump; Who Shot Patakango?; Who's the Man?; The Wiz
in Westerns, Boss Nigger; Buck and the Preacher; Charley-One-Eye; El Condor; Posse; Sergeant Rutledge; Silverado; Take a Hard Ride
women, A Litany for Survival: The Life and Work of Audre Lorde; Waiting to Exhale

Blatty, William Peter, films adapted from work, The Exorcist; The Ninth Configuration; The Exorcist III

Blindness, Afraid of the Dark; Alligator Eyes; Les Amants du Pont-Neuf; Blind Date (Mastorakis); Blind Fury; Blink; Blue; Butterflies Are Free; Cactus; The Dark Angel; Dark Eyes of London; The Day of the Triffids; Eyes in the Night; Faute de Soleil; Ice Castles; An Indian Story; Jennifer 8; The Killer (Woo); Laura (Hamilton); The Life of Chikuzan; Life on a String; The Light Ahead; Love Story (Arliss); Magnificent Obsession; Mansion of the Doomed; The Miracle Worker; A Patch of Blue; Pride of the Marines; Proof; Scent of a

Brothers Karamazov (Brooks); *The Brothers Karamazov* (Pyriev); *The Brothers McMullen; China Is Near; Circus Boys; Coupe de Ville; Crumb; December Bride; Dekalog 10: 'Thou shalt not covet thy neighbour's goods'; Dominick and Eugene; Duel in the Sun; The Emperor's Shadow; The Fabulous Baker Boys; Farinelli Il Castrato; Four Men and a Prayer; From Dusk Till Dawn; The Game; Hell's Angels; A Hole in the Head; Horizons West; House by the River; How Old Is the River?; The Indian Runner; Inventing the Abbotts; Johnny Dangerously; Joseph Cornell: Worlds in a Box; Josh and S.A.M.; Kickboxer; The Kid Brother; The Krays; Legends of the Fall; Lost in Yonkers; Mac; Macadam Tribu; The Mambo Kings; The Man from Laramie; Miles from Home; Mo' Money; Orphans; Pictures; A River Runs Through It; Rocco and His Brothers; Rogue Cop; Rumble Fish; Sabrina* (Pollack); *Sabrina* (Wilder); *Saddle the Wind; Shark's Son; She Gods of Shark Reef; She's the One; Simple Men; Small Faces; Staying Together; Strangers; Sugar Hill; Three Brothers; Trapped in Paradise; True Confessions; Vincent & Theo; Western Union; While You Were Sleeping; Winchester '73; The Witman Boys*

Brothers and sisters, see **Sisters and brothers**

Brown, Christy, film about/adapted from work, *My Left Foot*

Brown, Fredric, film adapted from work, *Screaming Mimi*

Brown, Rosellen, film adapted from work, *Before and After*

Bruce, Lenny film about, *Lenny* in performance, *The Lenny Bruce Performance Film; Lenny Bruce Without Tears*

Bryant, Louise, film about, *Reds*

Buchan, John, films adapted from work, *The 39 Steps* (Hitchcock); *The 39 Steps* (Thomas); *The Thirty-Nine Steps* (Sharp)

Büchner, Georg, films adapted from work, *Woyzeck* (Herzog); *Woyzeck* (Szász)

Buck, Pearl S, film adapted from work, *The Good Earth*

Buddhism, *The Burmese Harp; Buddha's Lock; Burning Paradise; Come, Come, Come Upward; 8-Diagram Pole Fighter; Hwa-om-kyong; The Horse Thief; Kundun; Little Buddha; Lord of the Dance; Mandala; The Outer Way; Tibet: A Buddhist Trilogy; A Tibetan New Year; A Touch of Zen;*

The Valiant Ones; Why Did Bodhi-Dharma Leave for the Orient?

Buddy movies (see also **Friendship**), *Another 48 HRS; Any Which Way You Can; Bengazi; The Best of Times; Le Bonheur est dans le pré; Boom Town; Breaking In; Buddy Buddy; Butch and Sundance: The Early Days; Butch Cassidy and the Sundance Kid; Carny; Catlow; Colors; Enemy Mine; Every Which Way But Loose; Fandango; The First Great Train Robbery; The Fortune; 48 HRS; Freebie and the Bean; A Girl in Every Port; Goodbye Pork Pie; The Great Texas Dynamite Chase; Gunmen; Heartaches; Heart Condition; The In-Laws; K-9; Kuffs; Larger Than Life; The Last Boy Scout; Lethal Weapon; Lethal Weapon 2; Lethal Weapon 3; Mad Dog and Glory; Midnight Cowboy; Midnight Run; Money Train; Renegades; The Rounders; Scarecrow; The Sting; The Sting II; The Sunshine Boys; Tango & Cash; Three Fugitives; Thunderbolt and Lightfoot; Tough Guys; Turner & Hooch; La Vie Revée des Anges; White Men Can't Jump; Your Three Minutes Are Up*

Bukowski, Charles, films adapted from work, *Barfly; Crazy Love; Tales of Ordinary Madness*

Bulgakov, Mikhail, film adapted from work, *The Master and Margarita*

Bulgarian cinema, *Balkanisateur; The Goat Horn*

Bullfighting, *Carmen* (DeMille); *Carmen* (Rosi); *Blood and Sand* (Niblo); *Blood and Sand* (Mamoulian); *The Bobo; Bolero* (Derek); *The Bullfighter and the Lady; The Kid from Spain; Matador; The Moment of Truth; The Sun Also Rises*

Burgess, Anthony, film adapted from work, *A Clockwork Orange*

Burial alive, *The House of Usher; Isle of the Dead; Macabre; The Pit and the Pendulum* (Corman); *The Premature Burial; Tales of Terror*

Burke, James Lee, film adapted from work, *Heaven's Prisoners*

Burke, John, film adapted from work, *The Sorcerers*

Burkina Faso
Burkina Faso cinema, *Këita! The Voice of the Griot; Samba Traore*
Burkina Faso in film, *Këita! The Voice of the Griot; Tilaï; Yaaba*

Burnett, Frances Hodgson, film adapted from work, *Little Lord Fauntleroy; A Little Princess; The Secret Garden* (Holland); *The Secret Garden* (Wilcox)

Burundian cinema, *Gito, the Ungrateful*

Burnett, WR, films adapted from work, *The Asphalt Jungle; The Badlanders; Colorado Territory; Cool Breeze; High Sierra; I Died a Thousand Times; Little Caesar; Nobody Lives Forever; The Whole Town's Talking*

Burroughs, Edgar Rice, films adapted from work, *At the Earth's Core; Greystoke – The Legend of Tarzan, Lord of the Apes; The People That Time Forgot; Tarzan, The Ape Man*

Burroughs, William, film adapted from work, *Naked Lunch* in film, *Kerouac; The Life and Times of Allen Ginsberg*

Bushranger sagas, *Mad Dog Morgan; Ned Kelly; Robbery Under Arms*

Busking, *St Martin's Lane*

Butterworth, Jez, film based on play, *Mojo*

Byatt, AS, film adapted from work, *Angels and Insects*

Byron, Lord, films about, *Bad Lord Byron; Gothic; Haunted Summer; Lady Caroline Lamb; Roger Corman's Frankenstein Unbound*

Cain, James M, films adapted from work, *Butterfly; Le Dernier Tournant; Double Indemnity; Everybody Does It; Interlude* (Sirk); *Interlude* (Billington); *Mildred Pierce; Ossessione; The Postman Always Rings Twice* (Garnett); *The Postman Always Rings Twice* (Rafelson); *Slightly Scarlet*

Cajun music, *Always for Pleasure*

Calderón de la Barca, film adapted from work, *Mémoire des apparences*

Caldwell, Erskine, films adapted from work, *God's Little Acre; Tobacco Road*

Calligraphy, in film, *The Pillow Book*

Cambodia, in film, *The Killing Fields*

Cambodian cinema, *Les Gens de la rizière*

Cameroonian cinema, *Clando*

Camp/trash, *Archangel; Beyond the Valley of the Dolls; Beneath the Valley of the Ultra Vixens; Blacksnake; Candy*

Strip Nurses; Cannibal Women in the Avocado Jungle of Death; Color Me Blood Red; Cry-Baby; Desperate Living; Elvira, Mistress of the Dark; Female Trouble; Faster, Pussycat! Kill! Kill!; The 5,000 Fingers of Dr T; Forbidden World; God Told Me To; Good Morning...and Goodbye; Hairspray; Hold Me, Thrill Me, Kiss Me; The Incredibly Strange Creatures Who Gave Up Living and Became Mixed-Up Zombies; Liquid Sky; Lust in the Dust; Mondo Trasho; Pink Flamingos; Polyester; Slacker; Supervixens; Tales from the Gimli Hospital; Thundercrack!; Tribulation 99: Alien Anomalies Under America; Truckstop Women; Vixen; Wild Women of Wongo

Campbell, John W, films adapted from work, *The Thing; The Thing from Another World*

Camping, *Grim Prairie Tales; She'll Be Wearing Pink Pyjamas*

Canada, in film
past, *The Apprenticeship of Duddy Kravitz; Black Robe; Bye Bye Blues; The Canadians; 49th Parallel; Kabloonak; Lilies; Map of the Human Heart; Margaret's Museum; My American Cousin; Northwest Passage; Why Shoot the Teacher*
contemporary, *Anne Trister; Between Friends; Calendar; Canadian Bacon; Candy Mountain; Cool Runnings; Crossing the Bridge; Dancing in the Dark; The Decline of the American Empire; Desperate Search; Far from Home: The Adventures of Yellow Dog; Fly Away Home; Goin' Down the Road; The Hanging Garden; Homeward Bound: The Incredible Journey; Jesus of Montreal; Kanehsatake (Oka) – 270 Years of Resistance; Love and Human Remains; Masala; Montreal Main; 90 Days; Les Ordres; The Luck of Ginger Coffey; Paperback Hero; A Paper Wedding; Réjeanne Padovani; Shoemaker; Swann; The Sweet Hereafter; La Tête de Normande St-Onge; The True Nature of Bernadette; When Night Is Falling; Why Shoot the Teacher; Woman Obsessed*

Canadian cinema, see Appendix 17

Canals, *Amsterdamned; L'Atalante; The Bargee; Painted Boats*

Cannaughton, Shane, films adapted from work, *The Playboys; The Run of the Country*

Cannibalism, *Alive; Cannibal; Consuming Passions;*

Chayefsky, Paddy, films adapted from work, *Altered States; The Bachelor Party; Marty*

Cheever, John, films adapted from work, *The 5:48; The Swimmer*

Chekhov, Anton, films adapted from work, *August; Black Sabbath; Country Life; Dark Eyes; The Lady with the Little Dog; Romance with a Double Bass; The Sea Gull; Summer Storm; Three Sisters* (Olivier); *Three Sisters* (von Trotta); *Unfinished Piece for Mechanical Piano; Vanya on 42nd Street*

Chess, *Dangerous Moves; The Grass Arena; Knight Moves; Searching for Bobby Fischer*

Chesterton, GK, film adapted from work, *Father Brown*

Chicago, in film, *Bound; Candyman; G-Man; City Streets; Eight Men Out; Gladiator; The Front Page* (Milestone); *The Front Page* (Wilder); *Go Fish; Hoop Dreams; In Old Chicago; Mad Dog and Glory; Next of Kin; Only the Lonely; Robin and the 7 Hoods; Shaking the Tree; Soul Food; Straight Talk; Switching Channels; Underworld; Union Station; The Untouchables; V I Warshawski; While You Were Sleeping*

Child abuse, *Child's Play* (Becker); *M* (Lang); *M* (Losey); *The Offence; L'Ombre du Doute; Tenderness of the Wolves*

Childers, Erskine, film adapted from work, *The Riddle of the Sands*

Child prodigies, *Little Man Tate; Searching for Bobby Fischer*

Children and childhood, in film (see also **Adolescence, Family life, Fathers, Mothers and Pregnancy, childbirth and babies**) Aust, *Captain Johnno; Celia; Frog Dreaming; The Miniskirted Dynamo; The Quiet Room* Bel, *Ma Vie en Rose; Toto the Hero* Braz, *Central Do Brasil; Pixote* Burkina Faso, *Keïta! The Voice of the Griot; Yaaba* Can, *Léolo; Lies My Father Told Me; Tommy Tricker and the Stamp Traveller* Cyprus, *Tomorrow's Warrior* Czech/Czech Rep, *Kolya; The Search* Den, *Once There Was a War* Fr, *L'Argent de Poche; Au Revoir les Enfants; Le Château de ma mère; City of Pirates; L'Enfance nue; La Fracture du myocarde; Fresh; La Gloire de mon père; Le Grand Chemin; La*

Guerre des Boutons; Jacquot de Nantes; Les Jeux Interdits; La Baule-les-pins Gaza Strip, *Tale of the Three Jewels* GB, *Afraid of the Dark; The Amazing Mr Blunden; Bloody Kids; The Borrowers; Bugsy Malone; Burning Secret; Captain Stirrick; Children of the Damned; The Custard Boys; Dance Little Lady; Dark Enemy; Eyewitness* (Hough); *The Fallen Idol; Flight of the Doves; The Full Monty; The Gift; The Go-Between; Hard Road; High Wind in Jamaica; Hope and Glory; Hue and Cry; The Hummingbird Tree; James and the Giant Peach; A Kid for Two Farthings; La Passione; Last Day of Summer; Little Lord Fauntleroy; Lord of the Flies* (Brook); *The Magic Toyshop; Mandy; Mirror Phase; Mister Skeeter; The Mudlark; My Childhood; The Nanny; The Optimists of Nine Elms; Our Mother's House; The Pagemaster; Paperhouse; Queen of Hearts; The Railway Children; The Reflecting Skin; The Scamp; Seance on a Wet Afternoon; This Boy's Story; Tiger Bay; Tree of Hands; Venus Peter; When the Whales Came; The Wolves of Willoughby Chase ; The Yellow Balloon* Ger, *The Blue Bird; Child's Play* (Becker); *Peppermint Freedom; Poto and Cabengo* Greece, *Dead Liqueur; Landscape in the Mist* HK, *Back Alley Princes* Hun, *Whooping Cough* Ind, *Salaam Bombay* Ire, *A Boy from Mercury; War of the Buttons* Iran, *The Apple; The Father; The Runner; Where Is My Friend's House?; The White Balloon* It, *Bellissima; Cinema Paradiso; Cinema Paradiso: The Special Edition; Last Moments; The Last Snows of Spring; The Stolen Children* Jap, *Muddy River; Pastoral Hide and Seek; Summer Vacation 1999 ; Village of Dreams* Latin America (unspecified), *Los Niños Abandonados* Nor, *Little Ida* NZ, *An Angel at My Table* Pol, *Crows* Sp, *Cria Cuervos; ¿Quién Puede Matar a un Niño?; Secrets of the Heart; The South; The Spirit of the Beehive* Swe, *Fanny and Alexander; My Life as a Dog; Stubby; The Slingshot* Tai, *Jade Love; Student Days; Summer at Grandpa's; The Time to Live and the Time to Die* Thai, *Butterfly and Flowers; The Song of Chao-Phrya* Turk, *Cold Nights* US, *The Adventures of Huckleberry Finn; The Adventures of Huck Finn; The Adventures of Tom*

Sawyer; All I Want for Christmas; The Baby; Captain January; Child of Divorce; Child's Play (Holland); *Child's Play 2; A Christmas Story; The Client; Cop & ½; Corrina, Corrina; The Cure; The Curse of the Cat People; Curly Sue; Dennis the Menace; Desperate Search; A Dog of Flanders; Don't Tell Mom the Babysitter's Dead; Driftwood; Empire of the Sun; Escape to Witch Mountain; Explorers; The 5,000 Fingers of Dr T; Flipper* (Clark); *Flipper* (Shapiro); *Flowers in the Attic; Free Willy; Free Willy 2; Free Willy 3: The Rescue; Fresh; Getting Even With Dad; The Goonies; Harriet the Spy; Hide in Plain Sight; Home Alone; Home Alone 2: Lost in New York; Home Alone 3; Honey, I Blew Up the Kid; Honey, I Shrunk the Kids; The Indian in the Cupboard; Jack; Jack the Bear; Josh and S.A.M.; Journey for Margaret; Juvenile Court; The Kid; Kids of Survival: The Art and Life of Tim Rollins & K.O.S.; Kindergarten Cop; King of the Wind; Lawn Dogs; Little Big League; The Little Rascals; Look Who's Talking Now; Look Who's Talking Too; Lord of the Flies* (Hook); *Mac and Me; Manny & Lo; The Mighty Ducks; Monkey Trouble; The Monster Squad; My Girl; My Girl 2; No Deposit, No Return; North; O. Henry's Full House ('The Ransom of Red Chief'); Once Upon a Time…When We Were Colored; Paradise; A Perfect World; Problem Child; Problem Child 2; Return from Witch Mountain; Rich Kids; Ride a Wild Pony; Roald Dahl's Matilda; Rookie of the Year; The Sandlot; A Simple Wish; Stand by Me; Star Kid; Stone Boy; Three Men and a Little Lady; 3 Ninjas; Tom Sawyer; Treasure of Matecumbe; Uncle Buck; Unstrung Heroes; The Witches* USSR and Rus, *Don't Move, Die and Rise Again!; Katok i Skrypka; Micha* non-specific, *The Adventures of Pinocchio*

Chile
Chilean cinema, *Amnesia; Caluga o Menta; La Frontera; The Jackal of Nahueltoro; Johnny 100 Pesos; Los Naufragos; The Moon in the Mirror* Chile in film, *The Battle of Chile; Cantata of Chile; La Frontera; Missing; Los Naufragos*

China, in film
pre-1990, *Accidental Legend; Beach of the War Gods; The Blood Brothers; Burning Paradise; A Chinese Ghost Story; A Chinese Ghost Story II; The Conqueror; Dirty Ho; Dynasty; The Emperor's Shadow; Executioners from*

Shaolin; The Fate of Lee Khan; Flowers of Shanghai; Golden Swallow; Intimate Confessions of a Chinese Courtesan; The Journey to the Western Xia; Love and Duty; Once Upon a Time in China; Once Upon a Time in China II; Peking Opera Blues; The Phantom Lover; Raining in the Mountain; Swordsman; Swordsman II; A Terra-Cotta Warrior; The 36th Chamber of Shaolin; A Touch of Zen; The Valiant Ones early 20th cent, *Actress; Au revoir, mon amour; The Bitter Tea of General Yen; Buddha's Lock; Death Kick; Farewell My Concubine; 55 Days at Peking; The Girls to Be Married; The Good Earth; The Inn of the Sixth Happiness; Ju Dou; King of Masks; Kawashima Yoshiko; Kung Fu Girl; The Last Emperor; The Left Hand of God; My Memories of Old Beijing; My Young Auntie; Raise the Red Lantern; Red Rose, White Rose; Rouge; Satan Never Sleeps; Seven Women; Shanghai Triad; Spring in a Small Town; Street Angel; Sweet Grass; Temptress Moon; To Live; Yellow Earth* post-revolutionary, *Back to Back, Face to Face; The Big Parade* (Chen Kaige); *The Bird People in China; Black Snow; Bloody Morning; Blush; Concerto of Life; The Days; The Day the Sun Turned Cold; East Palace, West Palace; Ermo; Family Portrait; Farewell My Concubine; For Fun; From Mao to Mozart; Frozen; The Goddess; Goldfish; Heartstrings; Hibiscus Town; Hold You Tight; Homecoming; In the Heat of the Sun; Iron & Silk; Journey to Beijing; King of the Children; The Last Day of Winter; Live in Peace; Mama; The Man from Island West; M. Butterfly; Murmur of Youth; My New Friends; Old Well; The Peach-Blossom Land; Portland Street Blues; Postman; Rainclouds Over Wushan; Rapid Fire; Red Corner; Red Detachment of Women* (Collective); *Red Detachment of Women* (Xie Jin); *The Red Lotus Society; The River* (Tsai Ming-Liang); *Rock n'Roll Cop; Sacrificed Youth; Signal Left, Turn Right; Sons; The Square; Stand Up, Don't Grovel!; The Story of Qiu Ju; A Story of Women; Sun and Rain; Sunless Days; Sun Valley; Surveillance; Swan Song; Sweet Degeneration; To Live; Tropical Fish* (Chen Yu-Hsun); *Xiao Wu; Yang ± Yin: Gender in Chinese Cinema; Yangtse Incident; Young Couples* futuristic, *The Hole*

Chinese cinema (see also **Hong Kong cinema, Taiwanese cinema**)
pre-revolutionary, *Love and Duty; Spring in a Small*

Clowns (see also **Circuses**), *The Clowns; Delicatessen; He Who Gets Slapped; Killer Klowns from Outer Space*

Cockfighting, *Cockfighter; Roosters; S'en fout la mort*

Cocteau, Jean, films adapted from work, *L'Aigle à Deux Têtes; Les Enfants Terribles; L'Eternel Retour; Les Dames du Bois de Boulogne; The Oberwald Mystery; Orphée; La Testament d'Orphée; Thomas l'Imposteur*

Cody, William F, film about, *Annie Get Your Gun; Annie Oakley; Buffalo Bill and the Indians*

Coetzee, JM, film adapted from work, *Dust*

Cohan, George M, film about, *Yankee Doodle Dandy*

Cold War, in film espionage, etc, *Avalanche Express; Black Eagle; Catch Me a Spy; Condorman; A Dandy in Aspic; Danger Route; The Deadly Affair; Diplomatic Courier; The Double Man; Enigma; Les Espions; Experts, The; The Falcon and the Snowman; Firestarter; The Fourth Protocol; From Russia with Love; Funeral in Berlin; Gorky Park; The Innocent (MacKenzie); Jumpin' Jack Flash; The Kremlin Letter; The Looking Glass War; The Mackintosh Man; The Man Between; The Manchurian Candidate; Mrs Pollifax – Spy; The Osterman Weekend – Our Man in Havana; The Quiller Memorandum; Rough Shoot; Russian Roulette; Russicum; Scorpio; The Serpent; S.P.Y.S.; The Spy Who Came In From the Cold; The Tamarind Seed; Telefon; Three Days of the Condor; Topaz; Top Secret; Torn Curtain; Walk East on Beacon; The Whistle Blower* other themes, *America – From Hitler to MX; Amazing Grace and Chuck; Atomic Café; The Bedford Incident; Before Winter Comes; Bulletproof; Carry Greenham Home; Defence of the Realm; Dr Strangelove: or, How I Learned to Stop Worrying and Love the Bomb; Fail Safe; The Hunt for Red October; Invasion USA; Judgment in Berlin; Kiss Me Deadly; Man on a Tightrope; Matinee; The Plutonium Circus; Rally 'round the Flag, Boys!; Red Dawn; Red Nightmare; Rockets Galore; Satan Never Sleeps; Seven Days in May; Streets of Gold; Tribulation 99: Alien Anomalies Under America; War Games* post-Cold War, *Company Business; The Fourth War; The Grass Is Always Greener; The Russia House*

Coleman, Ornette, film about, *Ornette: Made in America*

Colette, film adapted from work, *Gigi*

Collard, Cyril, film adapted from work, *Savage Nights*

Colleges and students, in film (see also **Education and school stories** and **Oxbridge**) Arg, *Wake Up, Love* Aust, *Love and Other Catastrophes* Can, *Terror Train* Fr, *Les Cousins; Le Diable, Probablement* GB, *American Friends; Butley; Chariots of Fire; Clockwork Mice; Educating Rita; Intimate Games; Lucky Jim; Night of the Eagle; True Blue; Up on the Roof; Wilt* Hun, *Time Stands Still* Ind, *Piravi* Jap, *Madadayo; Wizard of Darkness* Mali, *Finyé* Pol, *Barrier* SKor, *Black Republic* US, *The Allnighter; Back to School; College; Creator; Dazed and Confused; Dogs; Flubber; The Freshman; Good Will Hunting; Getting Straight; Happy Together; Happy We; Higher Learning; Horse Feathers; How to Be Very, Very Popular; Life Begins in College; Listen to Me; Loverboy; National Lampoon's Animal House; Lucky Star; The Mirror Has Two Faces; Necessary Roughness; The Nutty Professor (Lewis); The Nutty Professor (Shadyac); Oxford Blues; The Paper Chase; Revenge of the Nerds; The Seniors; Son in Law; Sorority Girl; Surviving Desire; Vamp; With Honors; You're a Big Boy Now*

Collins, Jackie, film adapted from work, *The Stud; The World Is Full of Married Men*

Collins, Larry, film adapted from work, *City of Joy*

Collins, Wilkie, films adapted from work, *Crimes at the Dark House; Twin Pawns*

Colombia Colombian cinema, *A Matter of Honour; Amazonia: Voices from the Rainforest; The Strategy of the Snail; Time to Die; What Is Democracy?* Colombia in film, *Chronicle of a Death Foretold; Green Ice; Romancing the Stone*

Colonialism (see also **Africa, Racism**) in Africa, *L'Appel du Silence; The Ghost and the Darkness; La Guerre sans nom; Black and White in Color; Camp Thiaroye; Ceddo; Chocolat; Emitai; Flame; The Four Feathers (Korda); The Four Feathers (Sharp); The Heart of the Matter; The Kitchen Toto; Mister Johnson; Massacre; Mountains of the Moon; Khartoum; Something of Value; Xala; Zulu; Zulu Dawn* in India, *Burra Sahib; Brigand of Kandahar;*

Charulata; Conduct Unbecoming; The Drum; East of Elephant Rock; Elephant Boy; Four Men and a Prayer; Gandhi; Gunga Din; Kim; The Man Who Would Be King; North West Frontier; A Passage to India; The Rains of Ranchipur; The River (Renoir); Trikal: Past Present and Future in Indochina, *Indochine; The Lover* in Indonesia, *November 1828; The Scorpion* in Latin America, *Cobra Verde; The Mission* in Middle East, *The Guns and the Fury* in Pacific, *Hurricane; The Hurricane* in Philippines, *The Real Glory* in West Indies, *Water*

Columbus, Christopher, films about, *Carry On Columbus; Christopher Columbus; Christopher Columbus: The Discovery; 1492: Conquest of Paradise*

Comaneci, Nadia, film about, *Nadia*

Comedians, in performance, *Big Banana Feet; Eddie Murphy Raw; House; The Lenny Bruce Performance Film; Lenny Bruce Without Tears; Lenny Live and Unleashed; Lilly Tomlin; Max Wall – Funny Man; Punch Me in the Stomach; Richard Pryor...Here and Now; Richard Pryor Live in Concert; Richard Pryor Live at Sunset Strip; Roy Cohn/Jack Smith; Without You I'm Nothing*

Comic strip characters, in film, *The Addams Family; Addams Family Values; The Adventures of Captain Marvel; Baba Yaga; Barbarella; Batman (Martinson); Batman (Burton); Batman Forever; Batman Returns; Batman & Robin; Beavis and Butt-head Do America; The Betty Boop Follies; Blondie; A Boy Named Charlie Brown; Buck Rogers in the 25th Century; Conan the Destroyer; Crimewave; The Crow; The Crow: City of Angels; Crying Freeman; Dennis the Menace; Dick Tracy; Doc Savage – the Man of Bronze; Flash Gordon; The Flintstones; George of the Jungle; Howard the Duck; Jake Speed; Jane and the Lost City; Judge Dredd; Lightning Swords of Death; Li'l Abner; Nowhere Man; The Phantom; Popeye; The Rocketeer; Spider-Man; Spider-Man Strikes Back; Spider-Man – the Dragon's Challenge; Supergirl; Superman III; Superman IV: The Quest for Peace; Tales from the Crypt Presents Demon Knight; Tank Girl; Tiffany Jones*

Comics, writers and artists, *Comic Book Confidential; Flaming Ears; Funny Bones;*

The King of Comedy; I Want to Go Home; Soft Top, Hard Shoulder

Communists in Australia, *Celia* in France, *Rouge Baiser; La Vie est à nous* in China, *Homecoming* (Ho) in Czechoslovakia, *L'Aveu; The Ear; Happiness in Twenty Years; Larks on a String; The Unbearable Lightness of Being* in Germany, *Mother Küster's Trip to Heaven; One, Two, Three; Rosa Luxemburg* in Greece, *Eleni* in Estonia, *Letters from the East;* in Hungary, *Silence and Cry; The Witness* in Malaya, *Windom's Way* in Poland, *And There Was Jazz, Blind Chance; A Generation; Man of Iron, Man of Marble; To Kill a Priest* in South Korea, *The Taebeck Mountains* in US, *Fellow Traveller; I Married a Communist; Invasion USA; The Iron Curtain; Pickup on South Street; Reds; Walk East on Beacon* in Vietnam, *The Deer Hunter; The Iron Triangle*

Community/collective action in Australia, *Heatwave* in Britain, *Behind the Rent Strike; Film from the Clyde; Fly a Flag for Poplar; Year of the Beaver* in France, *Des Enfants Gâtés; La Vie est à nous* in Mexico, *El Bruto* in US, *Matewan; The Milagro Beanfield War; Salt of the Earth; Where the Heart Is; Wisdom*

Compilation films comedy, *Ain't Misbehavin; That's Carry On* horror, *It Came from Hollywood; Terror in the Aisles* musicals, *That's Dancing!; That's Entertainment!; That's Entertainment Part II; That's Entertainment! III*

Computers, *Alphaville; The Amateur; Assassins; Blind Date* (Mastorakis); *Brainscan; Demon Seed; Desk Set; Electric Dreams; The Forbin Project; Gunhed; Jumpin Jack Flash; Hackers; The Human Factor* (Dmytryk); *Johnny Mnemonic; Lawnmower Man 2: Beyond Cyberspace; A Man, A Woman and a Bank; The Net; Nightmares; Paws; Sneakers; The Steal; Superman III; The Terminal Man; THX 1138; Tron; 2001: A Space Odyssey; War Games; Weird Science; Welcome to Blood City; Westworld*

Conan Doyle, Arthur, films adapted from/based on work Sherlock Holmes stories, *The Adventure of Sherlock*

Cuban cinema, *Cuba Libre; The Days of Water; Death of a Bureaucrat; Guantanamera; Hello, Hemingway; The Last Supper; Lucia; Memories of Underdevelopment; One Way or Another; Plaff! or Too Afraid of Life; Portrait of Teresa; Sometimes I Look at My Life; Strawberry and Chocolate*

Custer, General GA, in film, *Bugles in the Afternoon; Custer of the West; Little Big Man; Santa Fe Trail; 7th Cavalry; They Died with Their Boots On*

Cycling, *American Flyers; Breaking Away; BMX Bandits; The Fast Lady; A Sunday in Hell*

Cyprus
Cypriot cinema, *Our Wall*
Cyprus in film, *Attila '74; The High Bright Sun; Our Wall; Tomorrow's Warrior*

Czechoslovakia and Czech Republic (see also **Slovakian cinema**)
Czechoslovakian and Czech cinema, *Accumulator 1; The Adventures of Pinocchio; All My Good Countrymen; The Best Age; Capricious Summer; Closely Observed Trains; Conspirators of Pleasure;The Cremator; Cutting It Short; Daisies; The Deserter and the Nomads; The Divine Emma; The Ear; Faust (Svankmajer); The Firemen's Ball; I'm Jumping Over Puddles Again; Joseph Kilián; Just a Little Whistle; King Ubu; Kolya; Larks on a String; Lásky Jedné Plavovlásky (A Blonde in Love); The Life and Extraordinary Adventures of Private Ivan Chonkin; Mandragora; Marian; My Sweet Little Village; Nick Carter in Prague; The Party and the Guests; Pearls of the Deep; Peter and Pavla; The Pied Piper (Krysar); The Ride; Seclusion Near a Forest; Those Wonderful Movie Cranks; Valerie and Her Week of Wonders*
Czechoslovakia and Czech Republic in film, *The Golem; Happiness in Twenty Years; Hot Enough for June; Kafka; Man on a Tightrope; Prague; Pravda; The Shooter; The Trial (Welles); The Trial (Jones); The Unbearable Lightness of Being*

Dadaism, *Dreams That Money Can Buy; Europe After the Rain; John Heartfield, Photomonteur*

Dahl, Roald, film adapted from work, *Danny the Champion of the World; James and the Giant Peach; Roald Dahl's Matilda; The Witches*

Dailey, Robert, film based on work, *Night Falls on Manhattan;*

Daisne, John, film adapted from work, *The Man Who Had His Hair Cut Short*

Dana, Richard Henry, film adapted from work, *Two Years Before The Mast*

Dance and Dancers
ballet, *Alive and Kicking; The Children of Theatre Street; Dance Little Lady; Dancers; Don Quixote; The Dying Swan; Honeymoon; I Am a Dancer; Lives of Performers; The Mad Genius; Nijinsky; Nutcracker; The Nutcracker; Nutcracker – the Motion Picture; Pavlova – A Woman for All Time; The Red Shoes; Slow Dancing in the Big City; Specter of the Rose; Suspiria; Tales of Beatrix Potter; The Turning Point; White Nights (Hackford)*
Chinese ballet, *Red Detachment of Women (Collective)*
other, *Anita: Dances of Vice; Dollar Mambo; Blood Wedding; Body Rock; Bolero; Breakin'; Broadway; Can't Stop the Music; Carmen (Saura); A Cha-Cha for the Fugitive; A Chorus Line; The Courtesans of Bombay; The Cyclone; Dance, Girl, Dance; Dance Hall; Dancing Bull; Danzón; Dirty Dancing; Down to Earth; Driving Me Crazy; Fame; Fast Forward; Flashdance; Girls Just Want to Have Fun; Good to Go; Gypsy Soul; Isadora; Lambada; Lord of the Dance; A Love Bewitched; The Music Machine; No Maps for My Taps; Rooftops; Roseland; Rumba; Saturday Night Fever; Sevillanas; Shall We Dance?; Staying Alive; Strictly Ballroom; Sweet Charity; The Tango Lesson; Tap; Tapdancin'; Thank God It's Friday; They Shoot Horses Don't They?; To the Heart; Travelling Light: a Portrait of Lindsay Kemp; Wild Style*

Danish cinema, see Denmark

D'Annunzio, Gabriele, film adapted from work, *The Innocent (Visconti)*

Dante Alighieri, films adapted from/inspired by work, *A TV Dante: Cantos I–VIII*

Darwin, Charles, and Darwinism, *Angels and Insects;The Darwin Adventure; Inherit the Wind*

Day, Dorothy, film about, *Entertaining Angels: The Dorothy Day Story*

Deafness, *Alpine Fire; Beyond Silence; Captain Johnno; Children of a Lesser God; Hear No Evil; The Heart Is a Lonely Hunter; In the Company of Men; Junk Mail; Land of Silence and*

Darkness; Mandy; The Miracle Worker; Psych-Out; A Scene at the Sea; See No Evil, Hear No Evil; Suspect

Dean, James, films about, *The James Dean Story; James Dean – the First American Teenager*

Death (see also **Corpses** and **Few-months-to-live stories**), *Always (Spielberg); The Asphyx; Because of That War; Bye Bye Braverman; Carnival of Souls; The Comedy of Terrors; The Cremator; Death in the Seine; Destiny; Flatliners; La Fracture du myocarde; Frozen; Gates of Heaven; Grace Quigley; Guantanamera; Ikiru; The Loved One; Maborosi; The Mouth Agape; My Girl; My Girl 2; Nela; Night Shift; Ososhiki; Pearls of the Deep; Savage Man...Savage Beast; Short Time; Sibling Rivalry; Terms of Endearment; These Foolish Things; The Trouble with Harry; Weekend at Bernie's faked/technical, Frozen; Kill Me Again; Mission Impossible; Nikita; Point of No Return; No Man of Her Own*

de Beauvoir, Simone, film adapted from work, *All Men Are Mortal*

Defoe, Daniel, films adapted from work, *Crusoe; Man Friday; Moll Flanders; Robinson Crusoe; Robinson Crusoe on Mars*

Deformity and disfigurement (see also **Mutation**), *The Abominable Dr Phibes; The Affair; Basket Case; Basket Case 2; Circle of Horrors; Darkman; Dr Phibes Rises Again; The Elephant Man; The Enchanted Cottage; The Face Behind a Mask; Freaked; Freaks; House of Wax; How to Get Ahead in Advertising; The Hunchback of Notre Dame (Worsley); The Hunchback of Notre Dame (Dieterle); The Hunchback of Notre Dame (Delannoy); Johnny Got His Gun; Johnny Handsome; Mansion of the Doomed; The Man Without a Face; Mask; The Phantom Lover; The Phantom of the Opera (Julian); Phantom of the Opera (Little); Phantom of the Opera (Lubin); The Phantom of the Opera (Fisher); The Phantom of the Paradise; The Raven (Friedlander); The Severed Arm; A Woman's Face; Les Yeux sans Visage*

Deighton, Len, films adapted from work, *Billion Dollar Brain; Funeral in Berlin; The Ipcress File; Only When I Larf; Spy Story*

Delaney, Shelagh, film adapted from work, *A Taste of Honey*

Delinquents, juvenile, see **Street gangs and juvenile delinquents**

Delivery boys, *Bed of Roses; Loverboy*

Demy, Jacques, film about, *Jacquot de Nantes*

Denmark
Danish cinema, *American Pictures; Babette's Feast; Breaking the Waves; The Celebration; Day of Wrath; The Daughter of the Puma; Devil's Island (Fridriksson); The Element of Crime; Europa; Gertrud; Hard Rain; The House of Spirits; The Idiots; Junk Mail; Katinka; The Kingdom; The Kingdom II; Ladies on the Rocks; Last of the High Kings; Love Lessons; Nightwatch; Once There Was a War; One of Those Things; Ordet; Pelle the Conqueror; Pusher; Smilla's Feeling for Snow; A Sunday in Hell; Take It Like a Man, Ma'am*
Denmark in film, *Babette's Feast; The Celebration; Day of Wrath; Gertrud; Hamlet (Plumb); Hamlet (Kozintsev), Hamlet (Richardson); Hamlet (Zeffirelli); Hamlet (Branagh); The Idiots; Katinka; The Kingdom; The Kingdom II; Ladies on the Rocks; Last of the High Kings; Nightwatch; Once There Was a War; One of Those Things; Ordet; Pelle the Conqueror; Prince of Jutland; Pusher; Smilla's Feeling for Snow; Take It Like a Man, Ma'am*

Dennis, Patrick, film aapted from work, *Auntie Mame*

Depression era, in film
Aust, *Caddie; Careful, He Might Hear You*
Can, *Why Shoot the Teacher*
GB, *The Innocent (MacKenzie); Love on the Dole*
Ger, *Little Man, What Now?*
US, *American Madness; Baby Face Nelson; Billy Bathgate; Black Fury; Bloody Mama; Bonnie and Clyde; Bound for Glory; Brother, Can You Spare A Dime; Each Dawn I Die; Dillinger (Nosseck); Dillinger (Milius); Elmer Gantry; Emperor of the North Pole; Gabriel Over the White House; The Grapes of Wrath; The Grissom Gang; Hard Times (Hill); Hard to Handle; Ironweed; Journey of Natty Gann; Hallelujah, I'm a Bum; Honkytonk Man; King of the Hill; Manhattan Melodrama; Man's Castle; The Mayor of Hell; Miller's Crossing; The Night of the Hunter; Of Mice and Men (Milestone); Of Mice and Men (Sinise); Only Yesterday; Paper Moon; Pennies from Heaven; Places in the Heart; The Rise and Fall of Legs Diamond; The Roaring Twenties; Sounder; Splendor in the Grass; They Shoot Horses, Don't They?; Thieves Like Us; Union*

Women; Prejudice; Prostitute; Reversal of Fortune; Ruby; San Demetrio, Sons; London; Scum; Silkwood; Whore

Dolls, malevolent, *Child's Play* (Holland); *Child's Play 2*

Dominican Republic, in film, *Order to Kill*

Doomsday movies (see also **Nuclear weapons**), *Crack in the World; The Day the Earth Caught Fire; Deep Impact; Dr Strangelove: or, How I Learned to Stop Worrying and Love the Bomb; The Fifth Element; Five; Independence Day; Last Night; Meteor; Millennium; Night of the Comet; The Omega Man; When Worlds Collide*

Dorfman, Ariel, film adapted from work, *Death and the Maiden*

Dostoevsky, Fyodor, films adapted from work, *The Brothers Karamazov* (Brooks); *The Brothers Karamazov* (Pyriev); *Crime and Punishment* (von Sternberg); *Crime and Punishment* (Kaurismäki); *Four Nights of a Dreamer; The Gambler* (Reisz); *The Gambler* (Makk); *The Great Sinner; The Idiot; Une Femme Douce; Raskolnikow; Sin Compasión; White Nights* (Visconti)

Double lives (see also **Impersonation, Multiple personalities)** *The Amazing Doctor Clitterhouse; Back Street* (Stahl); *Back Street* (Stevenson); *The Bigamist; Body Parts; The Captain's Paradise; Confessions of a Bigamist; Deceived; Dr Jekyll and Mr Hyde* (Robertson); *Dr Jekyll and Mr Hyde* (Mamoulian); *Dr Jekyll and Mr Hyde* (Fleming); *Dr Jekyll and Ms Hyde; Dr Jekyll et Les Femmes; Dr Jekyll and Sister Hyde; Edge of Sanity; Europa, Europa; Femme Fatale; Fingers; Grip of the Strangler; I Monster; Lilies; The Man Who Lived Twice; Micki + Maude; Mother Night; Outrageous Fortune; The Secret Life of an American Wife; Separate Lives; That Night in Rio; The Two Faces of Dr Jekyll*

Doubles/doppelgängers (see also **Impersonation**), *L'Affaire du Courrier de Lyon; The Big Mouth; Bill & Ted's Bogus Journey; Bullseye!; The Dark Half; Doppelganger; The Evil Within; La Double Vie de Véronique; Eve of Destruction; Grosse Fatigue; How to Get Ahead in Advertising; I Was Monty's Double; Kagemusha; Love Letter; Luna e l'Altra; The Man in the Iron Mask* (Whale); *The Man in the*

Iron Mask (Wallace); *Mr Klein; Nouvelle Vague; The Nutty Professor* (Lewis); *The Nutty Professor* (Shadyac); *The Prince and the Pauper; The Prisoner of Zenda* (Cromwell); *The Prisoner of Zenda* (Thorpe); *The Prisoner of Zenda* (Quine); *Sliding Doors; Two Much; The Whole Town's Talking*

Douglas, Lloyd C, films adapted from work, *Green Light; Magnificent Obsession; The Robe*

Doyle, Roddy, films adapted from work, *The Commitments; The Snapper*

Dreams, power of, *Akira Kurosawa's Dreams; As in Heaven; Les Belles de nuit; Dream Demon; Dream Lover* (Pakula); *Dreamscape; Dreams That Money Can Buy; Freddy's Dead: The Final Nightmare; Jack's Wife; A Nightmare on Elm Street; A Nightmare on Elm Street Part 2: Freddy's Revenge; A Nightmare on Elm Street, 3: Dream Warriors; A Nightmare on Elm Street, 4: The Dream Master; A Nightmare on Elm Street, 5: The Dream Child; Nostradamus; La Nuit fantastique; Nutcracker – The Motion Picture; Paperhouse; Red Beads; Shocker; Venus Peter; Wes Craven's New Nightmare*

Dreiser, Theodore, films adapted from work, *An American Tragedy; Carrie* (Wyler); *A Place in the Sun*

Dreyfus, Alfred, films about, *I Accuse!; The Life of Emile Zola*

Drivers, learner, *Car Trouble; Confessions of a Driving Instructor; License to Drive; Le Permis de Conduire*

Dropping out, *Alexandre; All Night Long; Bronco Billy; Horizon; Kids; In the Belly of the Dragon; Lost in America; The Rain People; Reefer and the Model; La Tête Contre les Murs; The True Nature of Bernadette; La Vie à l'Envers; A Walk in the Spring Rain*

Drugs extraterrestrial responsibility for, *Dark Angel* fight against, *Best Revenge; Cairo Road; The Camels Are Coming; The Crackdown; Death Wish 4; Deep Cover; Fatal Beauty; Firebirds; A Force of One; Foxy Brown; French Connection; French Connection II; Gordon's War; High Risk; Impulse* (Baker); *K-9; The Last of the Finest; Lethal Weapon; Lethal Weapon 2; L.627; Lucky Luciano; The Marseilles Contract; New Jack City; One False Move; Only the Strong; The Organization; Predator 2; Prince of the City; Puppet on a Chain; Return of the*

Dragon; Running Scared (Hyams); *Shakedown; Sicilian Cross; Stoner; The Super Cops; The Supergrass; Tequila Sunrise; Toy Soldiers; Who'll Stop the Rain?; The Winchester Conspiracy* use, *The Addiction; Altered States; Bad Boys* (Rosenthal); *Bad Boys* (Bay); *Bad Lieutenant; The Basketball Diaries; The Blackout; Boogie Nights; Betty's Brood; Bird; Blood and Concrete; Blue Sunshine; The Boost; Boyz N the Hood; Brain Damage; Bright Lights, Big City; Cheech and Chong's Next Movie; Christiane F.; Ciao Manhattan; Cisco Pike; Clockers; Clean and Sober; Cocaine; The Cocaine Fiends; The Connection; The Courier; Crack in the Mirror; Dark Habits; Drugstore Cowboy; Easy Rider; The Falcon and the Snowman; Fast Talking; Fast, Fast; Friday; Gravesend; Greenkeeping; Gridlock'd; Groove on a Stanley Knife; Harley Davidson and the Marlboro Man; Jackie Brown; Jacob's Ladder; Joe Albany...A Jazz Life; Kids in the Hall: Brain Candy; Killer Nun; Lady Sings the Blues; Let's Get Lost; Light Sleeper; Liquid Dreams; Liquid Sky; Mad Dogs and Englishmen; The Man with the Golden Arm; Marked for Death; Un Monde sans pitié; Naked Lunch; Nico Icon; Nil by Mouth; N'oublie pas que tu vas mourir; Once Upon a Time...This Morning; Panic in Needle Park; The People Next Door; Postcards from the Edge; Pusher; Reefer Madness; Rush; Shooting Stars; Silent Scream; Superfly; Slow Dancing in the Big City; Strangers; Sugar Hill; Throwing Down; Tiger Warsaw; Torchlight; Trainspotting; Trash; Twin Town; Up in Smoke; The Vortex; Wait Until Dark; Where the Buffalo Roam; Wild in the Streets; Wired*

Drummond de Andrade, Carlos, film about, *O Amor Natural*

Dubbing, comic, *What's Up, Tiger Lily?*

Dubois, René-Jean, film adapted from work, *Being at Home with Claude*

Dumas, Alexandre (fils), films adapted from work, *Camille* (Cukor); *Camille* (Smallwood); *La Dame aux Camélias; La Traviata*

Dumas, Alexandre (père), films adapted from work, *The Count of Monte Cristo; The Four Musketeers: The Revenge of Milady; The Man in the Iron Mask* (Whale); *The Man in the Iron Mask* (Wallace); *The Return of the Musketeers; The Three*

Musketeers: The Queen's Diamonds (Lester); *The Three Musketeers* (Herek)

du Maurier, Daphne, films adapted from work, *The Birds; Don't Look Now; Frenchman's Creek; Hungry Hill; Jamaica Inn; My Cousin Rachel; Rebecca*

Dumbness and mutism, *The Big Silence; Jobman; Three Fugitives; Lightning Jack; Mute Witness; The Piano; The Quiet Room*

Duncan, Isadora, film about, *Isadora*

Dunn, Nell, films adapted from work, *Up the Junction; Steaming*

Dunne, John Gregory, film adapted from work, *True Confession*

Duras, Marguerite, films adapted from work, *The Lover; The Sailor from Gibraltar; 10:30 P.M. Summer*

Durrell, Lawrence, film adapted from work, *Justine*

Dürrenmatt, Friedrich, film adapted from work, *Hyenas*

Dwarfs, *Even Dwarfs Started Small; Frankie Stralight; A Gnome Named Gnorm; Horror Hospital; Little People; Time Bandits; The Tin Drum; We Don't Talk About It; The Woman for Joe*

Dylan, Bob, in performance, *Don't Look Back; Renaldo and Clara*

Dyslexia, *La Cérémonie* (Chabrol); *A Judgement in Stone* (Rawi)

Earthquakes, *Earthquake; San Francisco; The Sisters; Superman; Tremors; When Time Ran Out...*

Easter Island, in film, *Rapa Nui*

Eco, Umberto, film adapted from work, *The Name of the Rose*

Ecology (see also **Nature**) cases for, *Akira Kurosawa's Dreams; Amazonia: Voices from the Rainforest; At Play in the Fields of the Lord; Danny the Champion of The World; Day of the Dolphin; Dr M; Doomwatch; The Electric Horseman; The Emerald Forest; Farewell; FernGully: The Last Rainforest; Fire Festival; The Golden Seal; Koyaanisqatsi; Meet the Applegates; Minamata; Montagna del Dio Cannibale; Once Upon a Forest; Powaqqatsi; A River Runs Through It; Savage Capitalism; Tadpole and the Whale; Tieta of Agreste; When the North Wind Blows; Where the Heart Is; Wild*

an Alien; Phenomenon; Return from Witch Mountain; Santa Claus Conquers the Martians; Spaced Invaders; Star Kid; Starman; Suburban Commando; Zone Troopers nasty, The Adventures of Buckaroo Banzai Across the 8th Dimension; Alien Nation; The Arrival; Bad Taste; Beware! The Blob; The Blob; Body Snatchers; The Body Stealers; The Borrower; Conquest of the Earth; Critters; Critters 2: The Main Course; Daleks – Invasion Earth 2150 AD; Dark Angel; Dark City; The Day of the Triffids; Destroy All Monsters; Dr Who and the Daleks; Earth vs the Flying Saucers; The Hidden; I Married a Monster from Outer Space; Independence Day; Invaders from Mars (Menzies); Invaders from Mars (Hooper); Invasion; Invasion of the Body Snatchers (Kaufman); Invasion of the Body Snatchers (Siegel); Invasion of the Saucermen; It Conquered the World; Killer Klowns from Outer Space; Lifeforce; Liquid Sky; Mars Attacks!; The Mysterians; The Night Caller; Night of the Big Heat; Not of This Earth; Parasite; Plan 9 from Outer Space; Predator; Predator 2; The Puppet Masters; Quatermass and the Pit; Quatermass II; Repo Man; Species II; Strange Invasion; Strange Invaders; TerrorVision; They Live; The Thing; The Thing from Another World; Timescape; 20 Million Miles to Earth; Village of the Damned; War of the Satellites; War of the Worlds; X the Unknown; Xtro
both, Highlander; Highlander II – The Quickening; Highlander III – The Sorcerer; Teenagers from Outer Space

Factory farming, Laughterhouse

Fairgrounds, Capricious Summer; Carny; Carousel; Homeboy; Merry-Go-Round; Nightmare Alley; The Ring; Rollercoaster; Something Wicked This Way Comes; Two Moon Junction; The Unholy Three (Browning); The Unholy Three (Conway)

Fairy stories, fairies and goblins, Cinderella; Cinderfella; The Company of Wolves; Darby O'Gill and the Little People; FairyTale – A True Story; A Hungarian Fairy Tale; Labyrinth; The NeverEnding Story; The NeverEnding Story II: The Next Chapter; The NeverEnding Story III: Escape from Fantasia; Photographing Fairies; The Singing Ringing Tree; Snow White: A Tale of Terror; Tom Thumb; Troll; Willow; Wizards

Faith-healing, Leap of Faith; Marjoe; Resurrection

Falklands War, Argie; Arrivederci Millwall; For Queen and Country; The Ploughman's Lunch; Resurrected; Veronico Cruz

Family life (see also **Adolescence, Fathers, Mothers, Children and Childhood**)
Arg, Last Images of the Shipwreck; Miss Mary
Aust, The Last Crop; Mullaway
Bel, Ma Vie en Rose
Cambodia, Les Gens de la rizière
Can, Family Viewing; The Hanging Garden; The Revolving Doors; Wild Flowers (Lefebvre)
Chile, The House of Spirits
China, Live in Peace; Spring in a Small Town; Temptress Moon
Cuba, Plaff! or Too Afraid of Life
Czech, Lásky Jedné Plavovlásky (A Blonde in Love)
Den, The Celebration
Fr, A Double Tour; Un Air de Famille; Le Château de ma mère; Cousin Cousine; La Gloire de mon père; La Baule-les-pins; Life Is a Long Quiet River; Milou en mai; Nord; Numéro Deux; The Ostrich Has Two Eggs; Les Parents Terribles; A Tale of Springtime; Un Deux Trois Soleil; Les Uns et Les Autres; La Vieille Dame indigne; What Makes David Run?
GB, Betty's Brood; The Cement Garden; Distant Voices, Still Lives; Family Life (Loach); Fools of Fortune; Four Days in July; The Homecoming; Ill Fares the Land; In Celebration; The James Gang; The Krays; Ladybird Ladybird; Life Is Sweet; The Long Day Closes; My Left Foot; Nil by Mouth; Queen of Hearts; The Rainbow; Revenge (Hayers); The Secret Rapture; Secrets & Lies; Spring and Port WineThis Happy Breed
Ger, Germany, Pale Mother; Josephine; Rosalie Goes Shopping
Hun, Love, Mother
Ind, The Householder; Journey to Wisdom
Ire, Guiltrip, The Snapper
It, Brutti, sporchi e cattivi; By Nightfall; China Is Near; The Circumstance; Dimenticare Venezia; Everybody's Fine; Fists in the Pocket; Grazie Zia; Mignon Has Left
Jap, Crazy Family; Family Game; Ososhiki; The Moon Has Risen; Ohayo; Tokyo Story
Mex, El Bulto
Neth, Abel
NZ, Once Were Warriors
Pol, Dekalog 7: 'Thou shalt not steal'
SKor, Broken Branches; Farewell My Darling; Gilsodom

Sp, What Have I Done to Deserve This?
Sri Lanka, A Mother Alone
Swe, Fanny and Alexander; The Father; Summer Paradise; Through A Glass Darkly; What Are You Doing After the Orgy?
Tai, A City of Sadness; A Drifting Life
Tur, The Herd
US, The Addams Family; Addams Family Values; Affliction; All I Desire; Among the Living; Avalon; Before and After; Betsy's Wedding; Big Girls Don't Cry...They Get Even; Bloody Mama; The Brady Bunch Movie; Brighton Beach Memoirs; Broadway Bound; The Brothers McMullen; Burnt Offerings; Bye Bye Love; Caught; Cheaper by the Dozen; Communion; Cousins; Crooklyn; Daddy's Dyin' – Who's Got the Will?; The Daytrippers; Death of a Salesman; Desert Bloom; Diaries; Everyone Says I Love You; Family Business (Cohen); Far North; The Flintstones; Fools Rush In; Five Easy Pieces; Fool for Love; Forget Paris; The Glass Menagerie; God's Little Acre; Happiness; Hider in the House; Hollow Reed; Home for the Holidays; Home from the Hill; A Home of Our Own; House of Cards; The House of Yes; How to Make an American Quilt; The Ice Storm; I Remember Mama; King of the Hill; Last Summer in the Hamptons; Life with Father; Little Odessa; Little Women (Cukor); Little Women (Armstrong); Long Day's Journey into Night; The Long Hot Summer; Lost Angels; Lost in Yonkers; Madhouse; The Man in the Moon; Meet the Applegates; Miami Rhapsody; Miss Firecracker; Mr and Mrs Bridge; Mother (Brooks); Mother's Boys; Multiplicity; My Heroes Have Always Been Cowboys; The Myth of Fingerprints; National Lampoon's Vacation; The Next Voice You Hear...; Nothing in Common; One Fine Day; Ordinary People; Parenthood; Parents; Please Don't Eat the Daisies; The Plot Against Harry; The Prince of Pennsylvania; The People Next Door; Radio Flyer; Running on Empty; Safe Passage; See You in the Morning; Some Girls; Something to Talk About; Sometimes a Great Notion; Soul Food; Staying Together; The Stepfather; The Stepfather II; Stepfather III; Striptease; The Stupids; Target (Penn);There's Always Tomorrow; This Boy's Life; Three Wishes; Tiger Warsaw; To Sleep with Anger; Twice in a Lifetime; Twister (Almereyda); Uncle Buck; A Wedding; While You Were Sleeping; Written

on the Wind; You Can't Take It with you; Yours, Mine and Ours
USSR, Vassa

Family member
locked away, Among the Living; The Apple; The Beast in the Cellar; Jane Eyre (Stevenson); Jane Eyre (Mann); Jane Eyre (Zeffirelli); The Man in the Iron Mask (Whale); The Man in the Iron Mask (Wallace); The Oblong Box
long lost, Blackout; Deadly Run; Happy Birthday Wanda June; The Manxman; My Favourite Wife; Olivier Olivier; Le Retour de Martin Guerre; Sunflower; Welcome Home; What Are You Doing After the Orgy?
disappearing, The Vanishing (Sluizer, 1988); The Vanishing (Sluizer, 1993)

Fanon, Frantz, film about, Frantz Fanon: Black Skin, White Mask

Fans, obsessive, The Fan (Scott); The Fan (Bianchi); The King of Comedy; Misery; Wings of Fame

Fante, John, film adapted from work, Full of Life

Farley, Walter, films adapted from work, The Black Stallion; The Black Stallion Returns

Farmer, Frances, films about, Committed; Frances

Fascism (see also **Germany, Politics and politicians, State terror**)
in Britain, Little Malcolm and His Struggle Against the Eunuchs; The Remains of the Day
in Burma, Beyond Rangoon
in Chile, La Frontera
in France, Les Chiens; The Diary of a Chambermaid; Lacombe Lucien
in Italy, The Cannibals; Christ Stopped at Eboli; The Conformist; Down the Ancient Stairs; Garden of the Finzi-Continis; Open Doors; A Special Day
in Japan, Four Days of Snow and Blood
anti-fascism, Fortini/Cani

Fashion & fashion world (see also **Models**); Designing Woman; Fausto; Having It All; Notebook on Cities and Clothes; Ready to Wear; The Real Blonde; Salut Cousin!; Slaves of New York; Unzipped

Fassbinder, Rainer Werner, film about, A Man Like Eva

Fathers (see also **Family life**) and daughters, An Autumn Afternoon; Benefit of the Doubt; Betsy's Wedding; Beyond the Door; Bonjour Tristesse; Broken Blossoms (Griffith); Broken Blossoms (Brahm); Carné; Class Action; Cold Comfort;

Icicle Thief; Intervista;
L'Uomo delle stelle; Volere,
Volare
Jap, *Getting Any?;*
The Hair Opera
Mex, *Homework*
Neth, *Little Sister;*
Wings of Fame
NZ, *Cinema of Unease;*
Topless Women Talk About
Their Lives
Pol, *Camera Buff; Everything*
for Sale; Krzysztof Kieslowski:
I'm So So; 100 Years of
Polish Cinema
Port, *Lisbon Story*
Sp, *The Law of Desire; Life in*
Shadows; The Mad Monkey;
Thesis; Tie Me Up! Tie Me
Down!
Swe, *Directed by Andrei*
Tarkovsky; Lines from the
Heart
Switz, *O for Oblomov*
Tai, *Good Men, Good Women*
Tur, *Night Journey*
US, *An Almost Perfect Affair;*
Alex in Wonderland; At
Sundance; BAPS; The Big
Picture; The Blackout; Boogie
Nights; The Bullfighter and
the Lady; The Celluloid Closet;
Conversations with Willard
Van Dyke; Crimes and
Misdemeanors; Dadetown;
David Holzman's Diary;
Demon Lover; Diary; Directed
by William Wyler; The
Disappearance of Kevin
Johnson; Dragon: The Bruce
Lee Story; Ed Wood; 84
Charlie Mopic; The End of
Violence; Frank Capra's
American Dream; The
Freshman; From the Journals
of Jean Seberg; A Gringo in
Mañanaland; Guy; The
Hamster Factor and Other
Tales of Twelve Monkeys;
Hearts of Darkness: A
Filmmaker's Apocalypse;
Hollywood Cavalcade;
Illusions; In Ismail's Custody;
Inserts; Insdide Daisy Clover;
It's All True; In the Soup;
Irreconcilable Differences; It's
All True; It Should Happen to
You; The Last Movie;
Leaving Las Vegas; Living in
Oblivion; The Lost Squadron;
Luck, Trust & Ketchup:
Robert Altman in Carver
Country; Matinee; Maidstone;
Modern Romance; Mute
Witness; My Life's in
Turnaround; National
Lampoon Goes to the Movies;
Nico Icon; Privilege (Rainer);
The Real Blonde; Robert
Altman's Jazz' 34;
Remembrances of Kansas
City Swing; Roger Corman:
Hollywood's Wild Angel;
S.F.W.; Signed: Lino Brocka;
Snake Eyes; Special Effects;
Stardust Memories; The State
of Things;
Strangers Kiss;
Sullivan's Travels; The
Typewriter, the Rifle & the
Movie Camera; Visions of
Light; Warren Oates: Across
the Border; We Can't Go
Home Again; Wes Craven's
New Nightmare; What About
Me?; White Hunter, Black
Heart; Wild Bill:
A Hollywood Maverick
USSR and Rus, *Man With a*
Movie Camera; Micha;
Mute Witness

Finland
Finnish cinema, *Ariel; Black*
on White; Il Capitano; Crime
and Punishment
(Kaurismäki); *Darkness in*
Tallinn; Drifting Clouds;
Earth Is a Sinful Song;
Flame Top; Hamlet Goes
Business; Leningrad Cowboys
Go America; Letters from the
East; Letters to Katja; The
Match Factory Girl; Ripa
Hits the Skids; Täällä
Pohjantähden alla; Take
Care of Your Scarf, Tatjana;
Total Balalaika Show
Finland in film, *Night on*
Earth

Finney, Charles G, film
adapted from work, *7 Faces*
of Dr Lao

Finney, Jack, films adapted
from work, *Assault on a*
Queen; Invasion of the Body
Snatchers; Maxie

Firefighters, *Backdraft;*
Night of the Big Heat;
Trespass

Fish, etc (see also **Whales**),
Blue Water, White Death; A
Fish Called Wanda; Goldfish;
It Came from Beneath the
Sea; Jaws; Jaws 2; Jaws 3-D;
Jaws – The Revenge; Le
Monde du Silence; Piranha;
Piranha II: Flying Killers;
The Shark Callers of Kontu;
The Sharks' Cave; Tiger
Shark; 20,000 Leagues
Under the Sea; The White
Balloon

Fisher, Carrie, film adapted
from work, *Postcards from*
the Edge

Fishing, *As in Heaven;*
Beneath the 12-Mile Reef;
Blue Fin; Clash By Night; In
Fading Light; Ingaló; Man's
Favourite Sport?; Mystic
Pizza; The Old Man and the
Sea; A River Runs Through
It; Tiger Shark; Venus Peter

Fitzgerald, F Scott
films adapted from work,
The Great Gatsby (Clayton);
The Great Gatsby (Nugent);
The Last Time I Saw Paris;
The Last Tycoon
in film, *Beloved Infidel*

Fitzhugh, Louise, film
adapted from work, *Harriet*
the Spy

Flagg, Fannie, film adapted
from work, *Fried Green*
Tomatoes at the Whistle
Stop Café

Flaherty, Robert, in film,
Kabloonak

Flatulence, *Il Petomane*

Flaubert, Gustave, films
adapted from work,
Abraham Valley; Madame
Bovary (Renoir); *Madame*
Bovary (Chabrol)

Flying
wartime, service, etc, *Aces*
High; Air Force; Battle
Hymn; The Battle of Britain;

The Big Lift; The Blue Max;
The Body Stealers; The
Bridges at Toko-Ri; Broken
Arrow (Woo); *Catch-22;*
Command Decision; Conflict
of Wings; The Court Martial
of Billy Mitchell; The
Dambusters; Dangerous
Moonlight; Dawn Patrol
(Hawks); *Dawn Patrol*
(Goulding); *Desperate*
Journey; Desperate Search;
Dive Bomber; Firebirds;
Flight of the Intruder; Flying
Leathernecks; First of the
Few; A Gathering of Eagles;
The Great Santini; Hell's
Angels; Hot Shots!; The
Hunters; Iron Eagle; Iron
Eagle II; Jet Pilot; Journey
Together; The Lost
Squadron; Memphis Belle;
Moon 44; Mosquito
Squadron; The Night My
Number Came Up; One of
Our Aircraft Is Missing; The
1,000 Plane Raid; Project X;
Reach for the Sky; Top Gun;
Top of the World; Tora!
Tora! Tora!; Toward the
Unknown; Twelve O'Clock
High; Von Richthofen and
Brown; The Way to the
Stars; Wings; The Wings of
Eagles; A Yank in the RAF
non-military, *Air America;*
Air Force One; Airplane;
Airplane II: The Sequel;
Airport; Airport 1975;
Airport '77; Airport '80;
Always (Spielberg); *The*
American Way; Back from
Eternity; Blue Thunder;
Brewster McCloud; Calcutta;
Ceiling Zero; China Clipper;
Con Air; Crack-Up (St Clair);
Christopher Strong; Drop
Zone; La Fille de l'Air; Five
Came Back; Fly Away Home;
The Great Waldo Pepper;
The Gypsy Moths; Jet Storm;
Millennium; No Highway;
Only Angels Have Wings;
Passenger 57; The
Rocketeer; Rosalie Goes
Shopping; Run for the Sun;
Saint-Ex; Sky Pirates; The
Sound Barrier; Starflight:
The Plane That Couldn't
Land; The Tarnished
Angels; Terminal Velocity;
Tombes du Ciel; Too Hot to
Handle; Turbulence

Flynt, Larry, film about, *The*
People vs. Larry Flynt

Folk music, see
Music and musicians,
folk/traditional/world

Fonda, Jane, films about, *Jane;*
Letter to Jane; Vietnam
Journey

Fontane, Theodor, film
adapted from work, *Effi*
Briest

Food (see also **Cooks,**
kitchens, restaurants,
bakeries, etc), *Babette's*
Feast; Baker's Bread; Big
Night; Blow Out (Ferreri);
Chicken and Duck Talk; The
Cook, the Thief, His Wife
and Her Lover; Doña Flor
and Her Two Husbands; Eat
Drink Man Woman; Garlic
Is as Good as Ten Mothers;
Jamón, Jamón; Like Water

for Chocolate; The Scent of
Green Papaya; Soul Food;
Tampopo; Who Is Killing the
Great Chefs of Europe?

Football
American, *All the Right*
Moves; The Best of Times;
Easy Living; Everybody's All-
American; Heaven Can Wait
(Beatty/Henry); *Horse*
Feathers; Jerry Maguire; The
Last Boy Scout; Necessary
Roughness; North Dallas
Forty; Number One (Gries);
Pigskin Parade; Rudy;
Wildcats
Australian rules, *The Club*
post-nuclear rugby, *The*
Salute of the Jugger
rugby league, *This Sporting*
Life
rugby, seven-a-side, *Up 'n'*
Under
rugby union, *Carry Me Back;*
A Run for Your Money
soccer, *All Stars; The*
Arsenal Stadium Mystery; Le
Ballon d'Or; Bloomfield;
Fever Pitch; The Goalkeeper's
Fear of the Penalty; G'Olé!;
Gregory's Girl; Hero
(Maylan); *i.d.; This Boy's*
Story; Those Glory Glory
Days; Stubby; Victory; When
Saturday Comes; Yesterday's
Hero; Young Giants

Football hooligans,
Arrivederci Millwall; Ultrà

Foote, Horton, films adapted
from work, *Baby the Rain*
Must Fall; The Chase; The
Trip to Bountiful

Forbes, Kathryn, film adapted
from work, *I Remember*
Mama

Ford, John (dramatist), film
adapted from work, *'Tis Pity*
She's a Whore

Foreign Legion, French,
A.W.O.L.; Beau Geste; Le
Grand Jeu; Gueule d'Amour;
March or Die; Morocco

Forester, CS, films adapted
from work, *African Queen;*
Captain Horatio Hornblower;
Forever England; The Pride
and the Passion

Forgers and
counterfeiters, *F for Fake;*
Incognito; Johnny Allegro;
Schtonk!; T-Men; To Live
and Die in L.A.

Forster, EM, films adapted
from work, *Howards End;*
Maurice; A Passage to India;
A Room with a View; Where
Angels Fear to Tread

Forsyth, Frederick, films
adapted from work, *The Day*
of the Jackal; The Dogs of
War; The Fourth Protocol;
The Odessa File

Fowles, John, films adapted
form work, *The Collector;*
The French Lieutenant's
Woman; The Magus

Frame, Janet, film
about/adapted from work,
An Angel at My Table

The Terror; Topper; The Tower of the Seven Hunchbacks; Truly, Madly, Deeply; Ugetsu Monogatari; The Uninvited; Yumeji

Gibbons, Stella, film adapted from work, *Cold Comfort Farm*

Gide, André, film adapted from work, *La Symphonie Pastorale*

Gigolos, *American Gigolo; Hold Back the Dawn; Intimate with a Stranger; Just a Gigolo; Loverboy; Masquerade* (Swaim); *Midnight Cowboy; Speaking Parts; Sweet Bird of Youth* (Brooks); *Sweet Bird of Youth* (Roeg)

Gilbert and Sullivan films adapted from operas, *Dick Deadeye, or Duty Done; The Mikado; The Pirates of Penzance;* film about, *The Story of Gilbert and Sullivan*

Gillespie, Dizzy, films about, *A Great Day in Harlem; A Night in Havana: Dizzy Gillespie in Cuba*

Gilliam, Terry, film about, *The Hamster Factor and Other Tales of Twelve Monkeys*

Gilroy, Frank D, films adapted from work, *The Only Game in Town; The Subject Was Roses*

Ginsberg, Allen film about, *The Life and Times of Allen Ginsberg* in film, *Pull My Daisy*

Gipson, Fred, film adapted from work, *Hound Dog Man*

Gladiators, *The Arena; Demetrius and the Gladiators; Spartacus*

Gloag, Julian, film adapted from work, *Our Mother's House*

God portrayed in film (see also **Biblical stories, Jesus Christ**), *Almost an Angel; The Next Voice You Hear...; Oh, God!; Star Trek V: The Final Frontier; Switch; Two of a Kind* message from, *Des Nouvelles du Bon Dieu; Red Planet Mars*

Godden, Rumer, films adapted from work, *The Battle of the Villa Fiorita; Black Narcissus; The Greengage Summer; The River* (Renoir)

Godiva, Lady, in film, *Lady Godiva Rides Again*

Goethe, Johann Wolfgang, films adapted from work, *Elective Affinities; Faust* (Murnau); *Faust* (Svankmajer); *Le Jeune Werther*

Go-Go music, *Good to Go*

Golding, William, films adapted from work, *Lord of the Flies* (Brook); *Lord of the Flies* (Hook)

Goldman, William, films adapted from work, *Magic, Marathon Man; No Way to Treat a Lady; The Princess Bride*

Gold prospecting and gold rushes, *Aguirre, Wrath of God; Back to the Future Part III; By the Law; El Dorado; Eureka; The Gold Rush; Mackenna's Gold; North to Alaska; Road to Utopia; The Robin Hood of El Dorado; Support Your Local Sheriff; A Thousand Pieces of Gold; The Treasure of the Sierra Madre; Way Out West; White Fang* (Fulci); *White Fang* (Kleiser)

Golf, *Caddyshack; Happy Gilmore; Tin Cup; Triple Bogey on a Par Five Hole*

Goncharov, Mikhail, film adapted from work, *Oblomov*

Goodis, David, films adapted from work, *The Burglars; Dark Passage; The Moon in the Gutter; Nightfall; Tirez sur le Pianiste*

The Goons, *Down Among the Z Men*

Gorki, Maxim, films adapted from work, *Les Bas-Fonds; The Childhood of Maxim Gorki; The Lower Depths; Mother* (Pudovkin); *The Orlovs; Vassa*

Gould, Glenn, film about, *Thirty Two Short Films About Glenn Gould*

Graffiti artists, *IP5; Turk 182!; Wild Style*

Graham, Sheilah, film adapted from work, *Beloved Infidel*

Graham, Winston, films adapted from work, *Marnie; The Walking Stick*

Grahame, Kenneth, film adapted from work, *The Wind in the Willows*

Grandparents/grandchildren, *By Nightfall; L'Enfance nue; The Gift; Heartstrings; Lost in Yonkers; Rabid Grannies; The Revolving Doors; A Summer at Grandpa's; Venus Peter*

Grass, Günter, film adapted from work, *The Tin Drum*

Graves, Robert, film adapted form work, *The Shout*

Gray, Simon, films adapted from work, *Butley; Old Flames*

Gray, Spalding, in performance, *Monster in a Box; Swimming to Cambodia*

Graziano, Rocky, film about, *Somebody Up There Likes Me*

Greece, in film Ancient Greece, *Alexander the Great* (Rossen); *The Giant of Marathon* Greek Myths, *The Cannibals; Clash of the Titans; The Colossus of Rhodes; The Dawn; A Dream of Passion, Elektreia; Ercole alla conquista di Atlantide; Hercules; Jason and the Argonauts; Oedipus Rex; Oedipus the King; Orphée; Phaedra; Le Testament d'Orphée; Vaghe Stelle dell'Orsa* Modern Greece, *Alexander the Great* (Angelopoulos); *Balkanisateur; The Bee Keeper; Cavafy; The Day the Fish Came Out; Dead Liqueur; The Dawn; A Era; Escape to Athena; Eternity and a Day; The Guns of Navarone; High Season; Ill Met by Moonlight; Landscape in the Mist; Shirley Valentine; Summer Lovers; The Travelling Players; Ulysses' Gaze; Voyage to Cythera; When Mother Comes Home for Christmas; The Wind* (Mastorakis); *Zorba the Greek*

Greek cinema, *Alexander the Great* (Angelopoulos); *Balkanisateur; The Bee Keeper; The Blue Exile; The Dawn; The Day the Fish Came Out; End of an Era; Eternity and a Day; Dead Liqueur; Singapore Sling; The Travelling Players; Ulysses' Gaze; Voyage to Cythera; When Mother Comes Home for Christmas; Zorba the Greek*

Greene, Graham, films adapted from work, *Brighton Rock; The Comedians; Confidential Agent; England Made Me; The Fallen Idol; The Fugitive* (Ford); *The Heart of the Matter; The Honorary Consul; Loser Takes All; Ministry of Fear; Our Man in Havana; The Quiet American; The Third Man; This Gun for Hire*

Greenwood, Walter, film adapted from work, *Love on the Dole*

Grieg, Edvard, film about, *Song of Norway*

Grimm brothers, films adapted from work, *Rapunzel Let Down Your Hair; Tom Thumb*

Grisham, John, films adapted from work, *The Chamber; The Client; The Firm; The Pelican Brief; The Rainmaker; A Time to Kill*

Grubb, Davis, film adapted from work, *The Night of the Hunter*

Guare, John, film adapted from work, *Six Degrees of Separation*

Guatemala Guatemala in film, *¡Devils Don't Dream! Reserach on Jacobo Arbenz Guzmán; El Norte; When the Mountains Tremble* Guatemalan cinema, *The Daughter of the Puma*

Guaspari-Tzaras, Roberta, film about, *Small Wonders*

Guevara, Che, film about, *Che*

Guinea cinema, *Le Ballon d'Or*

Guinea-Bissau cinema, *The Blue Eyes of Yonta; Po di Sangui*

Gulf War, films about, and aftermath, *Courage Under Fire; Lessons in Darkness; Song of the Siren*

Gun fetishism, *Gun Crazy; Jackie Brown; My New Gun; Taxi Driver; White of the Eye*

Gurley-Brown, Helen, film adapted from work, *Sex and the Single Girl*

Guthrie, Woody, film about, *Bound for Glory*

Guyana Guyanan cinema, *Aggro Seizeman* Guyana in film, *Guyana: Crime of the Century*

Gymnastics, *Nadia; Take It Easy*

Gypsies, travellers, etc, *Devils, Devils; Gadjo Dilo; The Gypsy and the Gentleman; Gypsy Soul; Hot Blood; Into the West; Jassy; King of the Gypsies; Lacho Dom; Marian; Les Princes; The Raggedy Rawney; Stephen King's Thinner; Time of the Gypsies; Traveller; Wings of the Morning*

Haggard, H Rider, films adapted from work, *King Solomon's Mines* (Stevenson); *King Solomon's Mines* (Thompson); *King Solomon's Treasure; She* (Pichel); *She* (Day)

Hailey, Arthur, films adapted from work, *Airport; Airport 1975; Airport '77; Airport '80*

Hair, as fetish, *Golden Braid*

Hairdressers, *Earth Girls Are Easy; The Hairdresser's Husband; Married to the Mob; Mortal Thoughts; Shampoo; Staircase; Three Colours: White; Who's the Man?; Wish You Were Here*

Haiti, in film, *Bitter Cane; The Comedians; The Man by the Shore; The Serpent and the Rainbow; White Zombie*

Hall, Willis, and Waterhouse, Keith, films adapted from work, *Billy Liar; The Long and the Short and the Tall*

Halliday, Brett, film adapted from work, *Michael Shayne Private Detective*

Halliwell, David, film adapted from work, *Little Malcolm and His Struggle Against the Eunuchs*

Hamilton, Lady, film about, *Bequest to the Nation; That Hamilton Woman*

Hamilton, Patrick, films adapted from work, *Gaslight* (Dickinson); *Gaslight* (Cukor); *Hangover Square; Rope*

Hammerstein, Oscar and Kern, Jerome, musicals by, *Centennial Summer; Show Boat* (Whale); *Show Boat* (Sidney) and Rodgers, Richard, musicals by, *Carousel; The King and I; Oklahoma; South Pacific; State Fair*

Hammett, Dashiell, films adapted from work, *The Black Bird; The Glass Key; The Maltese Falcon* (Del Ruth) *The Maltese Falcon* (Huston); *Satan Met a Lady; The Thin Man* film about, *Hammett*

Hamsun, Knut, film adapted from work, *Nearly Wide Awake*

Handy, WC, film about, *St Louis Blues*

Hang gliding, *Sky Riders*

Han Suyin, film adapted from work, *Love Is a Many-Splendored Thing*

Hardy, Thomas, films adapted from work, *Far from the Madding Crowd; Jude; Tess; The Scarlet Tunic; The Woodlanders*

Hare, David, film adapted from work, *Plenty*

Harrer, Heinrich, film based on work, *Seven Years in Tibet*

Harris, Joel Chandler, film adapted from work, *Song of the South*

Harris, Thomas, films adapted from work, *Black Sunday* (Frankenheimer); *Manhunter; The Silence of the Lambs*

Harrison, Jim, films adapted from work, *Carried Away; Legends of the Fall*

Harryhausen, Ray, special effects by, *Clash of the Titans; Earth vs the Flying Saucers; Jason and the Argonauts; One Million Years B.C.; The Seventh Voyage of Sinbad; Sinbad and the Eye of the Tiger; The Three Worlds of Gulliver; The Valley of Gwangi*

Hart, Lorenz, and Rodgers, Richard, musicals by, *Babes in Arms; Billy Rose's Jumbo; Hallelujah, I'm a Bum; Love Me Tonight; Pal Joey*

Hartley, LP, films adapted from work, *The Go-Between; The Hireling*

Hastings, Michael, film adapted from work, *Tom & Viv*

Haunted houses (see also **Ghosts, Unwanted guests**), *The Bat Whispers; Beetlejuice; The Beyond; The Cat and the Canary* (Leni) *The Cat and the Canary* (Nugent); *The Cat and the Canary* (Metzger); *The Ghost Breakers; Ghost Catchers; The Ghost Goes West; Haunted; Haunted Honeymoon; The Haunted Palace; The Haunting Hell Night; High Spirits; House; The House by the Cemetery; House of Fear; House of The Long Shadows; Lady in White; The Legend of Hell House; Maid for Pleasure; Mark of the Vampire; Night of the Demons; The Spell; The Uninvited*

Hauptmann, Gerhart, film adapted from work, *Die Weber*

Hawaii, in film, *Aloha Summer; Blue Hawaii; Frome Here to Eternity; Hawaii; Picture Bride; The Revolt of Mamie Stover, Tora! Tora! Tora!*

Hawthorne, Nathaniel, films adapted from work, *The Scarlet Letter* (Sjöström); *The Scarlet Letter* (Joffe);*The Scarlet Letter* (Wenders)

Hayes, Joseph, film adapted from work, *Desperate Hours* (Cimino); *The Desperate Hours* (Wyler)

Health clubs, *Perfect*

Hearst, Patty, films about, *Abduction; Patty Hearst*

Hearst, William Randolph, film about, *Citizen Kane*

Heartfield, John, film about, *John Heartfield, Photomonteur*

Heaven-can-wait fantasies (see also **Afterlife, Return to life**), *Always* (Spielberg); *Ghost; Heaven Can Wait* (Lubitsch); *Heaven Can Wait* (Beatty); *Here Comes Mr Jordan; It's a Wonderful Life; Jacob's Ladder; Les Jeux sont Faits; A Matter of Life and Death; Le Nez au vent; Switch; Truly, Madly, Deeply; Two of a Kind*

Hecht, Ben, films adapted from work, *The Florentine Dagger; The Front Page* (Milestone); *The Front Page* (Wilder); *His Girl Friday; Twentieth Century*

Hedden, Roger, film adapted from work, *Bodies, Rest & Motion*

Heggen, Thomas, films adapted from work, *Ensign Pulver; Mister Roberts*

Heidi stories, *Courage Mountain; Heidi's Song*

Heists and capers, *American Buffalo; The Asphalt Jungle; The Badlanders; The Caper of the Golden Bulls; Darkness in Tallinn; Du Rififi à Paname; Du Rififi chez les hommes; L'Homme de Marrakesh; Johnny 100 Pesos; The Italian Job; The Killing; The League of Gentlemen; Lewis & Clark & George; Midas Run; Palookaville; A Prize of Arms; Reservoir Dogs; The Set Up; The Spider and the Fly; Topkapi*

Hellman, Lillian film about, *Julia* films adapted from work, *The Little Foxes; The Searching Wind; These Three*

Hemingway, Ernest films adapted from work, *The Breaking Point* (Curtiz); *A Farewell to Arms* (Borzage); *A Farewell to Arms* (Vidor); *For Whom The Bell Tolls; Islands in the Stream; The Killers* (Siodmak); *The Killers* (Siegel); *The Macomber Affair; The Old Man and the Sea; The Snows of Kilimanjaro; The Sun Also Rises; To Have and Have Not* film inspired by life, *In Love and War*

Henley, Beth, films adapted from work, *Crimes of the Heart; Miss Firecracker*

Henry, O, films adapted from work, *The Cisco Kid and the Lady; Dr Rhythm; O. Henry's Full House*

Henry II, King of England, film about, *The Lion in Winter*

Henry VIII, King of England, films about, *Henry VIII and His Six Wives; A Man for All Seasons; The Private Life of Henry VIII*

Herbert, Frank, film adapted from work, *Dune*

Herbert, James, film adapted from his work, *Haunted*

Herbert, Victor, film adapted from work, *Naughty Marietta*

Hermaphroditism, *Fellini-Satyricon; The Final Programme; The Mystery of Alexina; Private Vices & Public Virtues*

Hermits, *Night Sun*

Herriot, James, films adapted from work, *All Creatures Great and Small; It Shouldn't Happen to a Vet*

Hesse, Hermann, films adapted from work, *Siddhartha; Steppenwolf*

Hiaasen, Carl, film adapted from work, *Striptease*

Higgins, George V, film adapted from work, *The Friends of Eddie Coyle*

Higgins, Jack, film adapted from work, *The Eagle Has Landed*

Highsmith, Patricia, films adapted from work, *The American Friend; Plein Soleil; Strangers on a Train; This Sweet Sickness; Throw Momma from the Train*

Highwaymen, *Sinful Davey; Tom Jones; Where's Jack; The Wicked Lady* (Arliss); *The Wicked Lady* (Winner)

Hijacking, *Air Force One; Airport '77; Aux Yeux du monde; Con Air; Die Hard 2; Executive Decision; Jet Storm; Joan of Arc of Mongolia; Judgment in Berlin; Moon 44; Operation Thunderbolt; The Out-of-Towners; Passenger 57; Raid on Entebbe; Runaway Train; Scarecrows; Skyjacked; The Taking of Pelham One Two Three; Under Siege; Victory at Entebbe*

Hilton, James, films adapted from work, *Goodbye, Mr Chips* (Wood); *Goodbye, Mr Chips* (Ross); *Lost Horizon* (Capra); *Lost Horizon* (Jarrott); *Rage in Heaven; Random Harvest; We Are Not Alone*

Himes, Chester, films adapted from work, *Come Back Charleston Blue; A Rage in Harlem*

Hinduism, *The Chosen One; Devi; The Guru; The Home and the World; Hot Winds; Journey to Wisdom; Man from Africa and Girl from India; Siddhartha*

Hinton, SE, films adapted from work, *The Outsiders* (Coppola); *Rumble Fish; That Was Then, This Is Now*

Hispanic Americans, *La Bamba; The Border; Border Incident; Bordertown; Boulevard Nights; Crossover Dreams; El Norte; Hangin' with the Homeboys; Lambada; The Lawless; Mala Noche; The Milagro Beanfield War; My Crazy Life; My Family; The Robin Hood of El Dorado; Rooftops; Running Scared* (Hyams); *Salsa; Salt of the Earth; Stand and Deliver; Touch of Evil; Toy Soldiers; West Side Story*

History and historians, *Talking History*

Hitchhikers, *Alligator Eyes; The Hitcher; The Hitchhiker; Soft Top, Hard Shoulder*

Hitler, Adolf, films about, *Black Fox; Hitler – A Career; Hitler, a Film from Germany; The Hitler Gang; Hitler; The Last Ten Days; Swastika*

Hitler's diaries, *Schtonk!; What Have I Done to Deserve This?*

Hitmen (and women), *Amateur; The American Friend; Another Lonely Hitman; The Assassination Bureau; Assassin(s); The Big Hit; Black Rainbow; Blame It on the Bellboy; B. Must Die; Bring Me the Head of Mavis Davis; Buddy Buddy; Catchfire; The Client; Cohen and Tate; Cible émouvante; Crimes and Misdemeanors; Crying Freeman; The Deadly Females; Deaths in Tokimeki; The Disappearance; 8 Heads in a Duffel Bag; L'Emmerdeur; The Enforcer (Windust/Walsh); The Evil That Men Do; Fallen Angels; Flight of the Innocent; Gonin; Gonin 2; The Green Man; Grosse Pointe Blank; Hard Contract; Hard Men; The Hatchet Man; Hit List; I Hired a Contract Killer; The Internecine Project; Jackie Brown; Killer; The Killer (Woo); Last Man Standing; Leon; The Lineup; Little Odessa; The Long Kiss Goodnight; Mad Dog Time; The Marseille Contract; The Mechanic; Mercury Rising; The Mission (Sayyad); The Most Terrible Time in My Life; Murder by Contract; Nikita; 99 and 44/100% Dead; The Outside Man; Point of No Return; Prizzi's Honor; Pulp Fiction; Red Rock West; The Replacement Killers; Ruby; Le Samouraï; Scorpio; La Scoumoune; The Soldier; Sonatine; Spawn; Sun Valley; The Survivors; Things to Do in Denver When You're Dead; This Gun for Hire; 2 Days in the Valley; U Turn; Wise Guys*

Hoban, Russell, films adapted from work, *The Mouse and His Child; Turtle Diary*

Hochhuth, Rolf, film adapted from work, *A Love in Germany*

Hockney, David film about, *A Bigger Splash* in film, *Tonite Let's All Make Love in London*

Høeg, Peter, film based on work, *Smilla's Feeling for Snow*

Holiday, Billie, film about, *Lady Sings the Blues*

Holiday camps, *The Best Way to Walk; Confessions from a Holiday Camp; Holiday Camp; Meatballs*

Holly, Buddy, film about, *The Buddy Holly Story*

Hollywood and the movie business, in film (see also

Film-makers and film-making) British film industry, *Go for a Take; Nobody Ordered Love; O-Kay for Sound; Orders Are Orders* French film industry, *Day for Night; Irma Vep* Chinese film industry, *Actress* Hollywood: golden age, *The Bad and the Beautiful; Barton Fink; Beloved Infidel; Best Foot Forward; The Big Knife; Boy Meets Girl; Bugsy; The Bullfighter and the Lady; Chaplin; The Day of the Locust; Ed Wood; Fellow Traveller; Frances; Frank Capra's American Dream; Gable and Lombard; The Goddess; Goodbye, Norma Jean; Good Morning Babylon; Guilty by Suspicion; Hearts of the West; Hold Back the Dawn; Hollywood Cavalcade; Hollywood on Trial; Hollywood or Bust; Illusions; In a Lonely Place; It's All True; The James Dean Story; James Dean – The First American Teenager; Lady Killer; The Last Command; The Last Tycoon; The Lost Squadron; Love Goddesses; The Love Lottery; Movie Crazy; Music for the Movies: The Hollywood Sound; Musicals Great Musicals: The Arthur Freed Unit at MGM; Music for the Movies: Bernard Herrmann; Never Give a Sucker an Even Break; Nickelodeon; 1941; The Rocketeer; The Sex Symbol; Show People; Stand-In; The Star; A Star Is Born (Wellman); A Star Is Born (Cukor); Sunset; Sunset Boulevard; Susan Slept Here; Thank Your Lucky Stars; Two Weeks in Another Town; Valentino; The Way We Were; W.C. Fields and Me; Whatever Happened to Baby Jane?; What Price Hollywood?; White Hunter, Black Heart; Wild Bill: A Hollywood Maverick; The Wild Party (Ivory); The World's Greatest Lover; The Young Stranger* Hollywood: contemporary, *Alex in Wonderland; An Almost Perfect Affair; Bert Rigby, You're a Fool; Beyond the Valley of the Dolls; The Big Picture; The Bodyguard; Boogie Nights; Death Becomes Her; The Disappearance of Kevin Johnson; Fedora; F/X; F/X2; Get Shorty; The Hard Way; Hearts of Darkness: A Filmmaker's Apocalypse; Heidi Fleiss – Hollywood Madam; Hollywood Shuffle; Inserts; I Ought to Be in Pictures; Irreconcilable Differences; Jimmy Hollywood; The Ladies' Man; L.A. Story; The Legend of Lylah Clare; Lions Love; The Lonely Lady; A Man in Love; Mistress; Moon Over Parador; Movers and Shakers; Night Games; The Party; The Player; Postcards from the Edge; S.O.B.; Somebody to Love; Star 80; A Star Is Born (Pierson); Sweet Liberty; Swimming to Cambodia; Swimming with*

Sharks; True Identity; Valley of the Dolls; What's the Matter with Helen?; Wired; The Wizard of Speed and Time Indian film industry, *Bombay Talkie; Cinema Cinema; Helen, Queen of the Nautch Girls; The Role; Shakespeare-Wallah* Italian film industry, *Bellissima; La Signora senza camelie* Japanese film industry, *Bantsuma: The Life and Times of Tsumasaburo Bando*

Holocaust, Nazi, see **Germany** and **Jews and Jewish life**

Homosexuality, see **Gays (male) and gay cinema** and **Lesbians and lesbianism**

Honduras, in film, *Appointment in Honduras; Latino*

Hong Kong cinema martial arts, *Ah-Kam; Beach of the War Gods; Beijing Bastards; A Better Tomorrow; A Better Tomorrow II; The Big Boss; The Blade; The Bloody Fists; Burning Paradise; Bruce Lee: The Man, The Myth; Bullet in the Head; The Chinese Connection; The Conman and the Kung Fu Kid; Crime Story; Death Kick; Dirty Ho; Dynasty; 8-Diagram Pole Fighter; The Empress Yang Kwei Fei; Enter the Dragon; Enter the Seven Virgins; Executioners from Shaolin; The Fate of Lee Khan; First Strike; Fist of Fury; Fong Sai-Yuk; Full Contact; Golden Swallow; Hap-Ki-Do; The Heroic Trio; The Iceman Cometh; The Killer (Chu Yuan); King Boxer; King of Kung Fu; Kung Fu Fighting; Kung Fu Gangbusters; The Kung Fu Girl; Kung Fu – The Headcrusher; Last Hurrah for Chivalry; Legend of the 7 Golden Vampires; The Man from Hong Kong; Moon Warriors; My Young Auntie; The New One-Armed Boxer; Once Upon a Time in China; Once Upon a Time in China II; Once Upon a Time in Triad Society; Once Upon a Time in Triad Society 2; Police Story (Chan); Portland Street Blues; Rumble in the Bronx; Shanghai Lil; The Story of Woo Viet; The 36th Chamber of Shaolin; Warriors of Virtue; The Way of the Dragon; Young and Dangerous; Young and Dangerous 2; Young and Dangerous 3; Zu: Warriors from the Magic Mountain* non-martial arts, *Ah-Kam; Ah Ying; Actress; The Armour of God; As Tears Go By; Au revoir, mon amour; Autumn Moon; Back Alley Princes; Back to Back, Face to Face; Before Dawn; The Blood Brothers; The*

Butterfly Murders; C'est la Vie, Ma Cherie; Chinese Box; Chungking Express; Chicken and Duck Talk; A Chinese Ghost Story; A Chinese Ghost Story II; Comrades, Almost a Love Story; City on Fire; The Club (Wong); Dancing Bull; Days of Being Wild; The Day the Sun Turned Cold; The Deaf and Mute Heroine; Don't Play With Fire; Eight Taels of Gold; The Emperor's Shadow; Fallen Angels; Father and Son; Foreign Moon; 4 Faces of Eve; Full Moon in New York; For Fun; Front Page; He's a Woman, She's a Man; Hard-Boiled; Hold You Tight; Homecoming (Ho); Hu-Du-Men; Intimate Confessions of a Chinese Courtesan; Journey to Beijing; Just Heroes; Just Like Weather; Kawashima Yoshiko; The Killer (Woo); King of Masks; Kitchen (Yim Ho); Legend of the Mountain; Love in a Fallen City; Love Unto Waste; Made in Hong Kong; Mr Vampire; '92 The Legendary La Rose Noire; Once a Thief; Organized Crime and Triad Bureau; Peking Opera Blues; The Phantom Lover; A Queer Story; Raining in the Mountain; Red Beads; Red Firecracker, Green Firecracker; Red Rose, White Rose; Ripples Across Stagnant Water; Rock n'Roll Cop; The Romance of Book and Sword; Rouge; The Secret; Shanghai Blues; Shanghai Triad; Signal Left, Turn Right; The Spooky Bunch; Still Love You After All; The Story of Woo Viet; Summer Snow; Sunless Days; Sun Valley; Swordsman; Swordsman II; Task Force; Temptress Moon; A Terra-Cotta Warrior; Theft Under the Sun; To Live; The Valiant Ones; Viva Erotica!; Wheels on Meals; The Wicked City; Xenolith; Yang ± Yin: Gender in Chinese Cinema

Hong Kong, in film, *Autumn Moon; Back Alley Princes; Before Dawn; Blood Reincarnation; Blood Sport; Bullet in the Head; C'est la Vie, Ma Cherie; Chicken and Duck Talk; Chinese Box; Chungking Express; Dancing Bull; Days of Being Wild; Dragon: The Bruce Lee Story; Fallen Angels; Beach of the War Gods; Father and Son; Ferry to Hong Kong; First Strike; Front Page; 4 Faces of Eve; Full Contact; Gambit; Heaven, Man, Earth; Journey to Beijing; Just Heroes; Just Like Weather; The Killer (Woo); Kitchen (Yim Ho); Life Is Cheap...But Toilet Paper Is Expensive; Love in a Fallen City; Made in Hong Kong; Once a Thief; Rouge; Song of the Exile; Still Love You After All; Task Force; That Man Bolt; The World of Suzie Wong*

Hood, Robin, films about, *The Adventures of Robin Hood; The Bandit of Sherwood Forest; Robin and Marian; Robin Hood* (Dwan); *Robin Hood* (Reitherman); *Robin Hood* (Irvin); *Robin Hood – Men in Tights; Robin Hood – Prince of Thieves; Wolfshead – The Legend of Robin Hood*

Hoover, J Edgar, films about/featuring, *Nixon; The Private Files of J Edgar Hoover*

Hornby, Nick, film adapted from work, *Fever Pitch*

Horse racing, *Bite the Bullet; Brighton Rock; Broadway Bill; Casey's Shadow; Champions; A Day at the Races; Dead Cert; Derby Day; Dry Rot; The Grifters; Kentucky; The killing; My Brother Talks to Horses; National Velvet; Phar Lap; The Rainbow Jacket; The Rocking Horse Winner; That Gang of Mine*

Hospital dramas (see also **Doctors and medicine, Illness, Mental hospitals and asylums),** *The Ambulance; Britannia Hospital; The Carey Treatment; Clean and Sober; The Clinic; Coma; The Cycle; Extreme Measures; Feverhouse; The Frighteners; Green for Danger; Halloween II; Halloween 4: The Return of Michael Myers; Hard-Boiled; Hospital; House Calls; An Indecent Obsession; The Kingdom; The Kingdom II; Living Doll; Lorenzo's Oil; Malpractice; M.A.S.H.; The Men; The National Health; Nightwatch; Not as a Stranger; No Time for Tears; The Orlovs; Paper Mask; Red Beard; The Resurrection of Zachary; Wheeler; Rosie Dixon; Night Nurse; Strapless; Such Good Friends; Tales from the Gimli Hospital; They Call That an Accident; Traitement de Choc; Visiting Hours; A Woman's Tale; Young Doctors in Love*

Hostages (see also **Kidnap dramas, Unwanted guests),** *Albino Alligator; Appointment in Honduras; Blind Alley* (Vidor); *Crime Story; The Dark Past; Four Days in September; Jeopardy; Metro; The Night Holds Terror; The Ref; The Rock; S.F.W.; Street Fighter; Toy Soldiers*
political, *La Captive du Désert; The Crying Game; Hors la vie; Hot Shots! Part Deux; A Perfect World; An Unforgettable Summer*

Hotels, *About Mrs Leslie; Barton Fink; The Bellboy; Best Hotel on Skid Row; Blame It on the Bellboy; California Suite; Cat Chaser; Cheap Shots; Club des Femmes; Cocoanuts; Connecting Rooms; Death in Venice; Detective; Don't*

Bother to Knock (Baker); *Dunston Checks In; Electric Moon; For Love or Money; Gold Diggers of 1935; Hotel de Love; Hôtel du Nord; Hôtel du Paradis; The Hotel New Hampshire; Hotel Sahara; L'Île au trésor; International House; The Ladies' Man; London Belongs to Me; Minbo Woman –Or the Gentle Art of Japanese Extortion; The Moon over the Alley; Motel; Mystery Train; Necronomicon; Nelly's Version; Out of Season; Playing for Keeps; Private Parts; Room Service; Sélect Hotel; The Shining; Ski Patrol; Smile Orange; Snake Fang; Street Music; Wicked, Wicked; The Witches; Women in Tropical Places*

Household, Geoffrey, films adapted from work, *Man Hunt; Rough Shoot*

Household appliances, becoming malevolent, *Maximum Overdrive; Pulse; The Refrigerator*

Howard, Leigh, film adapted from work, *Blind Date* (Losey)

Howard, Sidney, film adapted from work, *They Knew What They Wanted*

Hrabal, Bohumil, films adapted from work, *Closely Observed Trains; Pearls of the Deep*

Hughes, Howard, film about, *Melvin and Howard*

Hughes, Thomas, film adapted from work, *Tom Brown's Schooldays*

Hugo, Victor, films adapted from work, *The Hunchback of Notre Dame* (Worsley); *The Hunchback of Notre Dame* (Dieterle); *The Hunchback of Notre Dame* (Delannoy); *The Hunchback of Notre Dame* (Trousdale/Wise); *Les Miserables* (Milestone); *Les Misérables* (Boleslawski) *Les Misérables* (Le Chanois); *Les Misérables* (Lelouch)

Hungarian cinema, *Another Way; Bolshe Vita; Colonel Redl; Confidence; The Confrontation; Daniel Takes a Train; Diary for My Children; Diary for My Loves; Elektreia; Escape; Forbidden Relations; The Gambler* (Makk); *Hanussen; A Hungarian Fairy Tale; Improperly Dressed; Love; Love, Mother; The Loves of Liszt; My 20th Century; My Way Home; Nine Months; The Package Tour; The Princess; The Red and the White; Red Psalm; The Round Up; Silence and Cry; Sunday Daughters; Sweet Emma, Dear Böbe; Tavaszi Zápor; Time Stands Still; The Two of Them; Underground* (Kusturica); *The Valley; A Very Moral Night; When*

Joseph Returns; Whooping Cough; The Witman Boys; The Witness

Hunter, Evan, film adapted from work (see also **McBain,** Ed), *The Blackboard Jungle; Last Summer; Strangers When We Meet*

Hunting, and blood sports, *The Bear; The Belstone Fox; Cockfighter; The Deer Hunter; The Ghost and the Darkness; The Golden Seal; Hard Target; Harry and the Hendersons; The Lost Word: Jurassic Park; The Most Dangerous Game; Murders in the Zoo; Quigley Down Under; Superbeast; White Hunter, Black Heart*

Hurling, *Clash of the Ash*

Hurst, Fannie, films adapted from work, *Back Street* (Stahl); *Back Street* (Stevenson); *Imitation of Life* (Sirk); *Imitation of Life* (Stahl)

Hutterites, in film, *Holy Matrimony*

Huxley, Aldous, film adapted from work, *The Devils*

Hwang, David Henry, film adapted from work, *M. Butterfly*

Hypnosis, *The Cabinet of Dr Caligari; Dead Again; The 5,000 Fingers of Dr T; Heart of Glass; Let's Do It Again; The Magician; Whirlpool*

Hypochondria, *Checking Out; Send Me No Flowers; Why Worry?*

Ibsen, Henrik, films adapted from work, *An Enemy of the People* (Ray); *An Enemy of the People* (Schaefer); *A Doll's House* (Garland); *A Doll's House* (Losey); *Hedda; Nora Helmer*

Ice dramas, *Bear Island; Careful; The Ice Palace* (Blom); *Ice Palace* (Sherman); *Ice Station Zebra; Jeremiah Johnson; Orion's Belt; The Savage Innocents; Scott of the Antarctic; Ski Patrol; The Thing; The Thing from Another World; The White Dawn; White Fang* (Fulci); *White Fang* (Kleiser)

Ice hockey, *The Cutting Edge; D2: The Mighty Ducks; Happy Gilmore; The Hounds of Notre Dame; The Mightly Ducks; Slap Shot; Sudden Death; Touch and Go; Youngblood*

Iceland
Icelandic cinema, *As in Heaven; Children of Nature; Cold Fever; Devil's Island* (Fridriksson); *Ingaló; Land and Sons; Movie Days* Iceland in film, *Devil's Island* (Fridriksson); *The Outlaw and His Wife*

Ice skating, *Iceland; Ice Castles; Lucky Star; One in a Million; Sun Valley Serenade; Thin Ice* (Lanfield); *Thin Ice* (Reid)

Identities confused at birth, *Big Business; Life Is a Long Quiet River; Toto the Hero*

Identity, change of, see **Impersonation**

Illegitimacy, *Asya's Happiness; Better Late than Never; Blanche Fury; Blossoms in the Dust; December Bride; Home from the Hill; How to Commit Marriage; Ju Dou; Man, Woman and Child; The Match Factory Girl; People Will Talk; The Playboys; Tavaszi Zápor; Track 29; Trust; Way Down East; Winter People*

Illiteracy, *Central Do Brasil; The Money Order; Stanley & Iris*

Illness (see also **Doctors and diseases, Few-months-to-live stories, Hospital dramas, Mental illness),** *August in the Water; Awakenings; Le Beau Serge; Cause for Alarm!; Champions; Cléo de 5 à 7; Dad; Dekalog 9: 'Thou shalt not covet thy neighbour's wife'; The Doctor; Don't Tell Her It's Me; Dying Young; An Egyptian Story; Emergency; Emergency Call; The End; The English Patient; Ethan Frome; Folks!; Gattaca; Gawin; Good Morning, Miss Dove; Grazie Zia; The Hole; Ikiru; Kaseki; Last Moments; The Last Snows of Spring; Lorenzo's Oil; Marvin's Room; Men, Women: User's Manual; Mon Premier Amour; Never Say Die; O. Henry's Full House ('The Last Leaf'); On the Beach; Regarding Henry; The Secret Garden* (Holland); *The Secret Garden* (Wilcox); *Sentimental Journey; Sick: The Life & Death of Bob Flanagan, Supermasochist; Si tous les gars du monde…; The Sixth Happiness; Sorry, Wrong Number; Le Souffle au Coeur; Spanking the Monkey; Steel Magnolias; Such Good Friends; Sunshine; Sunshine Part II; Terms of Endearment; These Foolish Things; Tribute; Unnatural Causes: The Agent Orange Story; Unstrung Heroes; The Wind Cannot Read; Without Memory; A Woman's Tale*

Imaginary companions, *Drop Dead Fred; Harvey; Secret Friends; Toto the Hero*

Immigrants and immigration
in Australia, *Captain Johnno; Cathy's Child; Death in Brunswick; Romper Stomper; Silver City; They're a Weird Mob*

Angel; Mementos; November 1828; Vessel of Wrath; Victory; The Year of Living Dangerously

Indonesian cinema, *Letter for an Angel; Mementos; November 1828*

Industry and industrial life, *An American Romance; Australia; The Betsy; Blue Collar; Caprice; Cela s'appelle l'Aurore; Coup pour Coup; Dadetown; The Formula; The Grind; Gung Ho; Highways by Night; I'm All Right, Jack; Iron Maze; Man Is Not a Bird; The Match Factory Girl; Once a Jolly Swagman; The Pajama Game; Roger & Me; Saturday Night and Sunday Morning; The Scar; The Sound Barrier; Spotswood; Stanley & Iris; Tout va bien; Tucker: The Man and His Dream; Woman's World; Work Is a Four Letter Word*

Industrial relations see **Labour relations**

Infertility, *Feelings; Immaculate Conception; Leon the Pig Farmer; Test Tube Babies*

Infidelity (see also **Love stories**)
Aust, *Libido; My First Wife*
Bel, *Une Femme Entre Chien en Loup*
China, *Ju Dou; Flowers of Shanghai; Ripples Across Stagnant Water; Spring in a Small Town*
Fin, *Black on White*
Fr, *A Double Tour; The Aviator's Wife; Les Biches; Le Bonheur; La Chienne; Les Choses de las Vie; Un Coeur qui bat; Courage; Le Dernier Tournant; Fuyons; En Cas de Malheur; La Femme Défendue; Une Femme française; La Femme Infidèle; Une Femme Mariée; Just Before Nightfall; Les Liaisons Dangereuses 1960; Love in the Afternoon* (Rohmer); *Love in the Strangest Way; Madame de...; A Man in Love; Max Mon Amour; Mélo; My Girlfriend's Boyfriend; La Peau Douce; Trop belle pour toi!; Valmont; The Woman Next Door*
GB, *Anna Karenina* (Duvivier); *Betrayal; Brief Ecstasy; Brief Encounter; Closing Numbers; Damage; Diamond Skulls; Do Not Disturb; Don't Bother to Knock* (Frankel); *Hanover Street; The Heart of the Matter; Interlude* (Billington); *Intimate Stranger; Knave of Hearts; Mr Love; Only Two Can Play; The Ring; The Romantic Englishwoman; Sliding Doors; Sparrows Can't Sing; Three into Two Won't Go*
Ger, *Coup de Grâce; Men; The Scarlet Letter* (Wenders); *Varieté; Waterloo Road; Woyzeck* (Herzog)
Hun, *Woyzeck* (Szász)

Ind, *The Home and the World*
It, *The Innocent* (Visconti); *Ossessione*
Jap, *Early Spring*
Pol, *Dekalog 3: 'Honour the Sabbath Day'; Dekalog 9: 'Thou shalt not covet thy neighbour's wife'; Knife in the Water*
Port, *In the White City*
Sp, *Lovers*
Swe, *Love Lessons; Scenes from a Marriage*
Tai, *This Love of Mine*
US, *Afterglow; Alice* (Allen); *All This and Heaven Too; An Almost Perfect Affair; Anna Karenina* (Brown); *Anna Karenina* (Rose); *Almost You; The April Fools; Baby Doll; Big Trouble; Body Heat; The Bramble Bush; Buona Sera, Mrs Campbell; Cat Chase; A Change of Seasons; Clash By Night; Cold Heaven; Consenting Adults; Criss Cross* (Siodmak); *Criss Cross* (Soderbergh); *Crimes and Misdemeanors; Dangerous Liaisons; Dirigible; Dirty Laundry; Do Not Disturb; Double Indemnity; Enemies, Love Story; Fatal Attraction; Feeling Minnesota; Forbidden; Fresh Horses; The Fugitive Kind; Harvey Middleman, Fireman; Having It All; The Honey Pot; Honeysuckle Rose; Human Desire; The Ice Storm; I Love You to Death; Indecent Proposal; Interlude* (Sirk); *Intermezzo; Just Between Friends; Kiss Me, Stupid; Love at Large; Manpower; The Marrying Man; Micki and Maude; Niagara; One Hour With You; One Night Stand; Other Men's Women; Over Her Dead Body; The Painted Veil; Pitfall; Reflections in a Golden Eye; Revenge* (Scott); *Same Time Next Year; The Scarlet Letter* (Joffé); *The Scarlet Letter* (Sjöström); *Scenes from a Mall; sex, lies and videotape; Shattered; She-Devil; Siesta; Skin Deep; Strangers When We Meet; 10.30 P.M. Summer; That's Life; There's Always Tomorrow; They Won't Believe Me; Tin Men; Torn Between Two Lovers; The Touch; Twice in a Lifetime; Two Faced Woman; Undercurrent; The Unfaithful; Unfaithfully Yours* (Sturges); *Unfaithfully Yours* (Zieff); *Vertigo; Where Were You When the Lights Went Out?; The Woman on the Beach; Zaza; Zee & Co*
USSR, *Dark Eyes*

Informers, police, *Le Doulos; The Friends of Eddie Coyle; The Hit; The Informer; Prince of the City; The Stoolie*

Inge, William, films adapted from work, *Come Back, Little Sheba; The Dark at the Top of the Stair; Picnic*

Inheritance, *Better Late than Never; Beyond the Blue Horizon; Brewster's Millions*

(Dwan); *Brewsters's Millions* (Hill); *Cast A Dark Shadow; Chase a Crooked Shadow; Daddy's Dyin' – Who's Got the Will?; Dark Waters; Dial M for Murder; The Field; House of Angels; Howards End; If I Had a Million; The Invitation; It's Only Money; The House in Nightmare Park; Kind Hearts and Coronets; Knickers Ahoy; Lazybones; Little Lord Fauntleroy; Man with a Cloak; Milou en mai; Mr Billion; Mr Deeds Goes to Town; A New Leaf; Night Nurse; Pleins Feux sur l'assassin; Rhubarb; Splitting Heirs; Toys; Le Trou Normand; V I Warshawski; Woman of Straw*

Innocents accused, *L'Affaire du Courrier de Lyon; Along Came Jones; Beyond Reasonable Doubt; The Big Steal* (Siegel); *Blackmail* (Potter); *The Blue Gardenia; Boomerang* (Kazan); *Break of Dawn; Call Northside 777; The Dark Corner; Dark Passage; Deadline at Dawn; Defence Counsel Sedov; El Mariachi; Everybody Wins; For Them That Trespass; Frenzy; Full Confession; Framed; The Fugitive* (Davis); *Fury* (Lang); *'Gator Bait; Her Alibi; I Am a Fugitive from a Chain Gang; I Confess; An Innocent Man; In the Name of the Father* (Sheridan); *Intruder in the Dust; The Invisible Man Returns; I Wake Up Screaming; Human Experiments; Just Cause; Knife in the Head; The Lodger; Lumière Noire; Macon County Line; Madeleine; Murder; Murphy's Law; Mystery Street; Nightfall; Ordeal by Innocence; Orders to Kill; The Ox-Bow Incident; Penitentiary; Physical Evidence; La P.....; Respectueuse; Presumed Innocent; Red Corner; Ride in the Whirlwind; Saboteur; Sergeant Rutledge; Sierra; Silver Lady; Slam Dance; Strangers on a Train; Tango & Cash; Term of Trial; They Drive by Night* (Walsh); *The Thin Blue Line; This Is My Affair; Thunderbolt; Time Without Pity; Tough Guys Don't Dance; True Believer; Under Suspicion; The Walking Dead; Warning Shot; Where Danger Lives; Who's That Girl?; Why?; The Woman in the Window; The Wrong Man* (Hitchcock); *Young and Innocent; The Young One; You Only Live Once*
guilty released, *Criminal Law; Midnight in the Garden of Good and Evil*

Insects, spiders, etc, *Arachnophobia; The Beekeeper; The Butterfly Murders; Earth vs the Spider; The Fly* (Neumann); *The Fly* (Cronenberg); *The Fly II; The Hellstrom Chronicle; Highly Dangerous; Meet the Applegates;*

Microcosmos; Mimic; Naked Lunch; Once Upon a Time; Phase IV; Return of the Fly; The Savage Bees; Starship Troopers; The Swarm; Ticks; Ulee's Gold; Wax, or The Discovery of Television Among the Bees

Insurance investigators, *The Adjuster; Double Indemnity; Frauds; The Killers* (Siodmak); *Mystery in Mexico; Nightfall*

Invalids, see **Illness**

Inventors (see also **Mad scientists**), *Back to the Future, Back to the Future Part II; Back to the Future Part III; Chitty Chitty Bang Bang; Choke Canyon; Darkman; Flubber; Honey, I Blew Up the Kid; Honey, I Shrunk the Kids; The Man in the White Suit; Malcolm; Master of the World; Paris Qui Dort; Short Circuit; Static; The Time Machine; The Time Travellers; Young Einstein*

Invisibility, *Alice* (Allen); *The Invisible Man; The Invisible Man Returns; Memoirs of an Invisible Man*

Iran, in film, *And Life Goes On…; The Apple; Close-Up; The Cow; The Cycle; The Father; Gabbeh; Grass; The Guns and the Fury; Iron Eagle II; Not Without My Daughter; The Peddler; The Runner; Season Five; Snake Fang; A Taste of Cherry; Through the Olive Trees; Where Is My Friend's House?; The White Balloon*

Iranian cinema, *And Life Goes On…; The Apple; Close-Up; The Cow; The Cycle; Gabbeh; The Father; The Peddler; The Runner; Season Five; Snake Fang; The Spell; A Taste of Cherry; Through the Olive Trees; Where Is My Friend's House?; The White Balloon*

Ireland, in film pre-1922, and Irish Republic, *Ailsa; Beloved Enemy; The Bishop's Story; A Boy from Mercury; Broken Harvest; The Brylcreem Boys; The Butcher Boy; Captain Boycott; Circle of Friends; Clash of the Ash; Coilin and Platonida; The Commitments; The Country Girls; The Courier; Da; Darby O'Gill and the Little People; The Dawning; The Dead; Driftwood; Eat the Peach; Exposure; The Fantasist; Far and Away; The Field; Finnegans Wake; Flight of the Doves; Fools of Fortune; Frankie Starlight; A Further Gesture; The General* (Boorman); *Girl with Green Eyes; Guiltrip; Happy Ever After; Hear My Song; High Spirits; Hungry Hill; The Informer; Into the West; I See a Dark Stranger; I Went Down; Joyriders; Korea; Last of the High Kings; The Lonely Passion of Judith Hearne; Man of Aran; A Man of No*

Madame Butterfly modern Japan, *About Love, Tokyo; Angel Dust; An Autumn Afternoon; Bari-Zogon; Black Rain* (Scott); *Boiling Point* (Kitano); *The Boxer* (Terayama); *Boy; Branded to Kill; The Ceremony; Comic Magazine; Crazy Family; Dear Summer Sister; Diary of a Shinjuku Thief; Dodes'ka-Den; The Drive; The Eel; Elephant Song; Fire Festival; The Fire Within; The Flavour of Green Tea Over Rice; Flirt; Gate of Flesh; The Geisha Boy; Gonin; Gonin 2; The Good Wife of Tokyo; The Hair Opera; Hana-Bi; Heaven-6-Box; How Old Is the River?; Ikiru; Irezumi – Spirit of Tattoo; Kids Return; Kamikaze Taxi; Kikuchi; Labyrinth of Dreams; Late Spring; Leaving; Level Five; Like Grains of Sand; Madadayo; The Man Who Left His Will on Film; MARKS; Minamata; Minbo Woman – Or the Gentle Art of Japanese Extortion; Mishima: A Life in Four Chapters; Mr Baseball; Like a Rolling Stone; Maborosi; The Moon Has Risen; My Sons; The Mystery of Rampo; An Obsession; Ohayo; Ondeko-za on Sado; One of Those Things; Organ; Osaka Story; Ososhiki; The Outer Way; The Pillow Book; Record of a Tenement Gentleman; Rhapsody in August; Rising Sun; Sadistic City; Sans Soleil; Shall We Dance?; Skinless Night; Sleeping Man; Stranger; Street of Shame; Sukiyaki; Summer Soldiers; Swimming with Tears; Tampopo; A Taxing Woman; Teenage Mutant Ninja Turtles III; Three Resurrected Drunkards; Thow Away Your Books, Let's Go into the Streets; Sayonara; Shinjuku Triad Society; Sonatine; Some Kinda Love; Suzaku; Swallowtail Butterfly; Swimming Prohibited; Tokyo Drifter; Tokyo Fist; Tokyo-Ga; Tokyo Kyodai; Tokyo Pop; Tokyo Story; A Town of Love and Hope; 2 Duo; Village of Dreams; Violence at Noon; The Wicked Reporter; Wizard of Darkness; World Apartment Horror; Without Memory; The Written Face; The Yakuza; Yellow Dog; Zazie*

Japanese Americans, *The Color of Honor; Come see the Paradise; The Crimson Kimono; Iron Maze; Mr Moto's Gamble; Sunsets*

Japanese cinema, *see* Appendix 21

Japanese music, *The Life of Chikuzan*

Japrisot, Sébastien, films adapted from work, *The Sleeping Car Murder*

Jarry, Alfred, film adapted from work, *King Ubu*

Jazz, in film
documentaries/performance, *Always for Pleasure; Art Pepper: Notes from a Jazz Survivor; Best Foot Forward; Bird Now; Bix; Blue Notes and Exiled Voices; ...But Then, She's Betty Carter; Charles Mingus: Triumph of the Underdog; Dizzy Gillespie in Cuba; A Great Day in Harlem; Jabula – A Band in Exile; Jazz in Exile; Jazz on a Summer's Day; Joe Albany...A Jazz Life; The King of Jazz; Last Date; The Last of the Blue Devils; Let's Get Lost; Listen Up: The Lives of Quincy Jones; Memories of Duke; Mississippi Blues; A Night in Havana; Ornette; Made in America; Sun Ra: A Joyful Noise; Robert Altman's Jazz' 34: Remembrances of Kansas City Swing; Talmage Farlow; Thelonious Monk: Straight No Chaser; Wild Man Blues*
drama/features, *American Blue Note; And There Was Jazz; Bird; Blue Ice; Bye Bye Blues; C'est la Vie, Ma Cherie; The Connection; The Cool World; The Cotton Club; The Glenn Miller Story; It's Trad, Dad!; Jitterbugs; Kansas City; Lady Sings the Blues; Love with the Proper Stranger; Lush Life; The Man with the Golden Arm; Mo' Better Blues; New York, New York; Orchestra Wives; Pete Kelly's Blues; The Revolving Doors; 'Round Midnight; St Louis Blues; Some Call It Loving; A Song Is Born; The Subterraneans; Sun Valley Serenade; Sven Klang's Combo; Swing Kids; Too Late Blues; Young Man With a Horn*

Jefferson Thomas, film about, *Jefferson in Paris*

Jekyll-and-Hyde stories, see **Stevenson,** Robert Louis

Jerome, Jerome K, film adapted from Work, *Three Men in a Boat*

Jessup, Richard, films adapted from work, *The Cincinnati Kid; Chuka*

Jesus Christ, in film (see also **Biblical stories, God**), *God Told Me To; The Gospel According to St Matthew; The Greatest Story Ever Told; Jesus Christ Superstar; Jesus of Montreal; King of Kings; The Last Temptation of Christ; Monty Python's Life of Brian; The Robe*

Jewel prospecting, *Romancing the Stone*

Jews and Jewish life, in film (see also **Israel, Yiddish films**)

in Argentina, *The Girlfriend*
in Australia, *Angst; Norman Loves Rose; Shine*
in Austria, *Colonel Redl*
in Britain, *The Custard Boys; The House of Rothschild; Leon the Pig Farmer*
in Canada, *The Apprenticeship of Duddy Kravitz; Lies My Father Told Me*
in Czechoslovakia *The Golem*
in Denmark, *Sofie*
in France, *Mazel Tov ou le mariage; Mina Tannenbaum; Le Vieil Homme et l'Enfant; What Makes David Run?*
in Germany (pre-Nazi), *Young Törless*
in Italy, *Fortini/Cani; The Garden of the Finzi-Continis*
in Mexico, *Gaby – A True Story; Like a Bride*
in New Zealand *Punch Me in the Stomach*
in Spain, *The Heritage*
and Nazi Holocaust (see also **Germany, War Criminals**), *Angst; Au Revoir les Enfants; Because of That War; Berlin Jerusalem; Broken Glass; Conspiracy of Hearts; Dekalog 8: 'Thou shalt not bear false witness'; The Diary of Anne Frank; Docteur Petiot; Enemies, a Love Story; Europa, Europa; Fragments of Isabella; Genghis Cohn; Hanna's War; The Hiding Place; Judith; Kapo; Korczak; Life Is Beautiful; Lodz Ghetto; Loving the Dead; Madame Rosa; The Man in the Glass Booth; Mr Klein; My Mother's Courage; None Shall Escape; The Package Tour; Reunion; Schindler's List; Shoah; Shtetl; Sophie's Choice; The Summer of Aviya; To Speak the Unspeakable: The Message of Elie Wiesel; Triumph of the Spirit; The Truce; The Warsaw Ghetto Uprising; Voyage of the Damned*
in Romania, *To Speak the Unspeakable: The Message of Elie Wiesel*
in Russia and Poland, *The Commissar; Fiddler on the Roof; The Fixer; The Magician of Lublin; Me Ivan, You Abraham; Rothschild's Violin; Schindler's List; Shtetl; Taxi Blues; The Warsaw Ghetto Uprising; Yentl*
in US, *American Stories; Avalon; Betsy's Wedding; Brighton Beach Memoirs; Broadway Bound; Carbon Copy; The Chosen; Close to Eden; Crossfire; Crossing Delancey; Crimes and Misdemeanors; Dealers Among Dealers; Driving Miss Daisy; Fast Trip, Long Drop; From Here to Eternity; Gentleman's Agreement; Goodbye Columbus; Hester Street; Homicide; Little Odessa; Me & My Matchmaker; Mr Saturday Night; Once Upon a Time in America; Over the Brooklyn Bridge; The Pawnbroker; The Plot Against Harry; Quiz Show; Radio Days; The Shvitz; Tell Me a Riddle; A*

Tickle in the Heart; Used People; Where's Poppa?; White Palace

Jhabvala, Ruth Prawer, film adapted from work, *Heat and Dust*

Joan of Arc, films about, *Jeanne la Pucelle; La Passion de Jeanne d'Arc; Procès de Jeanne d'Arc; Saint Joan*

John XXIII, Pope, film about, *A Man Named John*

Jolson, Al, film about, *The Jolson Story*

Jones, James, films adapted from work, *From Here to Eternity; Some Came Running*

Jonson, Ben, film adapted from work, *The Honey Pot*

Joplin, Janis, film about, *Janis*

Journalism, in film
newsreel, *The Cameraman; Newsfront; Too Hot to Handle*
photojournalism, *Picture Snatcher; Under Fire; Warshots*
print, *Absence of Malice; Ace in the Hole; After Office Hours; All the President's Men; Atlantic Adventure; Between the Lines; The Black Rider; The Bonfire of the Vanities; Call Northside 777; The Captive City; Circle of Deceit; Citizen Kane; Comrade X; Confirm or Deny; Cover Girl Killer; Darklands; The Day the Earth Caught Fire; Deadline – USA; Defence of the Realm; Disparen a Matar; La Dolce Vita; Each Dawn I Die; Eleni; Five Star Final; The Front Page (Milestone); The Front Page (Wilder); Front Page Woman; He Said, She Said; Hi, Nellie!; His Girl Friday; How to Be a Woman and Not Die in the Attempt; I Love Trouble; It Happened Tomorrow; LA Confidential; The Last Plane Out; The Last Train from Madrid; The Lawless; The Mad Miss Manton; The Mean Season; Meet John Doe; The Naked Truth; The Near Room; A New Kind of Love; Newsies; No Orchids for Miss Blandish; Not for Publication; Nothing Sacred; The Paper; The Parallax View; Park Row; The People vs. Larry Flynt; Perfect; Platinum Blonde; Please Don't Eat the Daisies; Prejudice; Press for Time; Public Enemy Number One; Public Eye; Roman Holiday; Rough Treatment; Roxie Hart; Salvador; Schtonk!; The Sisters; Straight Talk; Sweet Smell of Success; Tank Malling; Three O'Clock High; Turtle Beach; Up Your Alley; War Zone; While the City Sleeps; Who'll Stop the Rain?; Woman of the Year; Year of the Gun; The Year of*

Living Dangerously TV; *Broadcast News; The China Syndrome; Comic Magazine; Death of a Cameraman; Extreme Close-Up; Eyes of a Stranger; Eyewitness; Giro City; Open Doors; The Man of Iron; Man of Marble; Switching Channels; Testament* (Akomfrah); *Visiting Hours; Vivre pour Vivre; Windprints*

Joyce, James, films adapted from work, *The Dead; Finnegans Wake; A Portrait of the Artist as a Young Man; Ulysses*

Judges (see also **Courtroom dramas, Lawyers**), *Brothers in Law; Leap into the Void; Open Doors; The Star Chamber; The Sun Shines Bright*

Jung, Carl Gustav, film about, *Matter of Heart*

Jungle dramas (see also **Rain forests**), *Anaconda; Appointment in Honduras; Baby – Secret of the Lost Legend; Back from Eternity; Beyond the Blue Horizon; Cannibal; Cannibal Women in the Avocado Jungle of Death; The Emerald Forest; Escape to Burma; Farewell to the King; Five Came Back; Gorillas in the Mist; Greystoke – The Legend of Tarzan Lord of the Apes; Jumanji; Jungle 2 Jungle; Mogambo; Monster from Green Hell; La Mort en ce Jardin; Predator; Red Dust; Run for the Sun; The 7th Dawn; Sheena; Sorcerer; Tarzan, the Ape Man; Voodoo Woman*

Kafka, Franz films adapted from work, *Class Relations; The Trial* (Welles); *The Trial* (Jones) in film, *Kafka*

Kanga, Firdaus, film based on autobiography, *The Sixth Happiness*

Kanin, Garson, films adapted from work, *Born Yesterday* (Cukor); *Born Yesterday* (Mandoki)

Katzenbach, John, film adapted from work, *Just Cause*

Kazakhstan cinema, *Prisoner of the Mountains*

Kazan, Elia, film adapted from work, *The Arrangement*

Kazantzakis, Nikos, films adapted from work, *The Last Temptation of Christ; Zorba the Greek*

Keane, John B, film adapted from work, *The Field*

Keating, HRF, film adapted from work, *The Perfect Murder*

Kemp, Lindsay, film adapted from work, *Travelling Light: a Portrait of Lindsay Kemp*

Kempinski, Tom, films adapted from work, *Duet for One; Wot! No Art*

Kendrick, Baynard, film adapted from work, *Eyes in the Night*

Keneally, Thomas, film adapted from work, *The Chant of Jimmy Blacksmith; Schindler's List*

Kennaway, James, films adapted from work, *Country Dance; Tunes of Glory*

Kennedy (Onassis), Jacqueline, films about, *The Greek Tycoon; The Grey Gardens*

Kennedy, John F, films about, *Executive Action; In the Line of Fire; JFK; Love Field; Ruby; Rush to Judgment*

Kennedy, Ludovic, films adapted from work, *Crime of the Century; 10 Rillington Place*

Kenya, in film, *The Air Up There; Cheetah; The Ghost and the Darkness; The Kitchen Toto; Out of Africa; Simba; Where No Vultures Fly; White Mischief*

Kern, Jerome musicals by, *Roberta; Swing Time; You Were Never Lovelier* and Hammerstein, Oscar, musicals by, *Centennial Summer; Show Boat* (Whale); *Show Boat* (Sidney)

Kerouac, Jack films about, *Heart Beat; Kerouac; What Happened to Kerouac?* film adapted from work, *The Subterraneans* in film, *Pull My Daisy*

Kesey, Ken films adapted from work, *One Flew Over the Cuckoo's Nest; Sometimes a Great Notion* in film, *The Life and Times of Allen Ginsberg*

Ketcham, Hank, film adapted from comic strip, *Dennis the Menace*

Kieslowski, Krzysztof, film about, *Krzysztof Kieslowski: I'm So So*

Kickboxing, *Kickboxer; Say Anything*

Kidnap dramas, *Abduction; After Dark, My Sweet; Alexander the Great; Baby's Day Out; Beach Blanket Bingo; The Big Lebowski; The Bitter Tea of General Yen; Black Windmill; Captive; Catchfire; The Chase* (Rifkin); *La Cité des enfants perdus; Crime of the Century; Crime Story; Crows; Don't Just Lie There, Say Something!; The Drive; The Everlasting Secret Family; Excess Baggage; The Extraordinary Adventures of*

Mister West in the Land of the Bolsheviks; Fargo; Fille à Tuer; Fog over Frisco; Full Moon in Blue Water; The Grissom Gang; Guarding Tess; The Happening; High and Low; The Honorary Consul; The House on Garibaldi Street; Ill Met by Moonlight; Joan of Arc of Mongolia; Kansas City; Kidnapping the President; King of Comedy; A Life Less Ordinary; Lolly-Madonna XXX; Malpertuis; Manny & Lo; Man on Fire; Mansion of the Doomed; The Man Who Knew Too Much (Hitchcock, 1934); *The Man Who Knew Too Much* (Hitchcock, 1956); *My Name Is Julia Ross; Nada; The Night of the Following Day; No Deposit, No Return; No Orchids for Miss Blandish; O. Henry's Full House ('The Ransom of Red Chief'); Papa, les Petits Bateaux...; Parker; Raising Arizona; Ransom; Rosebud; Ruthless People; School for Vandals; Seance on a Wet Afternoon; The Secret Invasion; Skinflicker; Slow Attack; The Snow Queen; The Sound of Fury; The Squeeze; Streets of Fire; Sudden Death; Tattoo; That Darn Cat; This Alien Earth; Tie Me Up! Tie Me Down!; Tropical Fish* (Chen Yu-Hsun);*Union Station; Venom* (Sykes); *Voodoo Man; White Man's Burden; A Woman or Two; World for Ransom; Who's Harry Crumb?*

King, Carole, film inspired by life of, *Grace of My Heart*

King, Stephen, films adapted from work, *Carrie* (De Palma);*Cat's Eye; Creepshow; Children of the Corn; Christine; Cujo; The Dark Half; The Dead Zone; Dolores Claiborne; Firestarter; Graveyard Shift; The Lawnmower Man; The Mangler; Maximum Overdrive; Misery; Pet Sematary; The Running Man; Salem's Lot; The Shawshank Redemption; Silver Bullet; Sleepwalkers; Tales from the Darkside: The Movie*

King/Queen for a day, *The King of Comedy; Lady for a Day; The Man Who Could Work Miracles; The Prince and the Pauper*

King-Smith, Dick, film adapted from work, *Babe*

Kingsley, Charles, film adapted from work, *The Water Babies*

Kingsley, Sidney, films adapted from work, *Dead End; Detective Story*

Kipling, Rudyard, films adapted from work, *Captains Courageous; Elephant Boy; Gunga Din; The Jungle Book* (Reitherman); *The Jungle Book* (Sommers); *Kim; The Man Who Would Be King*

Kleist, Heinrich von, films adapted from work, *Die Marquise von O...; Michael Kohlhaas; Penthesilea: Queen of the Amazons; The Prince of Homburg*

Kleptomania, *The Locket; Marnie; Slightly Scarlet; Whirlpool*

Kneale, Nigel, films adapted from work, *Halloween III; Quatermass and the Pit; The Quatermass Experiment; Quatermass II*

Knievel, Evil, films about, *Evel Knievel; Viva Knievel*

Koontz, Dean R, films adapted from work, *Shattered; Watchers*

Kopit, Arthur, film adapted from work, *Buffalo Bill and the Indians*

Korczak, Janusz, film about, *Korczak*

Korda, Alexander, films produced by, *Catherine The Great; Dark Journey; The Drum; Elephant Boy; The Elusive Pimpernel; Fire over England; The Four Feathers* (Korda); *The Ghost Goes West; The Girl from Maxim's; That Hamilton Woman; The Man Who Could Work Miracles; The Thief of Bagdad* (Powell/ Berger/Whelan/Korda); *Things to Come; Wedding Rehearsal*

Korea, in film, *Battle Hymn; Black Republic; The Bridges at Toko-Ri; Chilsu and Mansu; Christmas in August; Come, Come, Come Upward; The Contact; The Day a Pig Fell into the Well; Farewell My Darling; Festival* (Im Kwon-Taek); *First Love* (Lee Myung-Se); *Gilsodom; The Housemaid; The Hunters; Hwa-om-kyong; Jungle Story; The Insect Woman; Iodo; Killer Butterfly; Kung Fu Fighting; Lovers in Woomuk-Baemi; Marriage Story; Men in War; No. 3; Oksutan; One Minute to Zero; A Petal; Pork Chop Hill; The Power of Kangwon Province; Push! Push!; Retreat, Hell!; Road to the Racetrack; A Single Spark; Sopyonje; Spring in My Hometown; The Steel Helmet; Surrogate Mother; The Taebeck Mountains; That Woman, That Man; Three Friends; Ticket; Timeless Bottomless Bad Movie; To the Starry Island; To You, From Me; La Vie en rose; Village in the Mist; Why Did Bodhi-Dharma Leave for the Orient?; Wind Echoing in My Being*

Korean Americans, *True Believer*

Korean cinema (South), *Berlin Report; Black Republic; Broken Branches; Chilsu and Mansu;*

Christmas in August; Come, Come, Come Upward; The Contact; The Day a Pig Fell into the Well; Farewell My Darling; Festival (Im Kwon-Taek); First Love (Lee Myung-Se); Gilsodom; A Hot Roof; The Housemaid; Hwa-om-kyong; The Insect Woman; Iodo; Jungle Story; Killer Butterfly; Lovers in Woomuk-Baemi; Mandala; Marriage Story; No. 3; Our Twisted Hero; Oksutan; A Petal; The Power of Kangwon Province; Push! Push!; Road to the Racetrack; A Single Spark; Sopyonje; 301–302; Spring in My Hometown; Surrogate Mother; The Taebeck Mountains; That Woman, That Man; To the Starry Island; To You, From Me; Three Friends; Ticket; Timeless Bottomless Bad Movie; La Vie en rose; Village in the Mist; Why Did Bodhi-Dharma Leave for the Orient?; Wind Echoing in My Being

Korean War, and prelude to, Battle Hymn; The Bridges at Toko-Ri; A Hill In Korea; I Want You; The Hunters; M*A*S*H; One Minute to Zero; Period of Adjustment; Pork Chop Hill; Retreat, Hell!; Sayonara; Spring in My Hometown; The Steel Helmet; The Taebeck Mountains; To the Starry Island

Kotzwinkle, William, film adapted from work, Book of Love

Kundera, Milan, film adapted from work, The Unbearable Lightness of Being

Kurdistan, in film, A Song for Beko; The Voice of Kurdistan

Kurosawa, Akira, films about, A.K.; Akira Kurosawa's Dreams

Labour relations (see also **Industry and industrial life**)
in Australia, Spotswood
in Britain, British Sounds; Business as Usual; Chance of a Lifetime; Comrades; Film from the Clyde; Flame in the Streets; I'm All Right Jack; The Man in the White Suit; '36 to '77; Year of the Beaver
in Chile, The Battle of Chile; Cantata of Chile
in France, Coup pour Coup; Le Crime de Monsieur Lange; Tout Va Bien
in Germany, Dear Mother, I'm All Right
in Philippines, Bayan Ko: My Own Country
in Poland, Man of Iron; Man of Marble
in Russia, Strike
in South Africa, Wheels & Deals
in Sweden, Adalen '31
in US, Black Fury; Blue Collar; Boxcar Bertha; The Devil in Miss Jones; Edge

of the City; F.I.S.T.; The Garment Jungle; The Grapes of Wrath; Gung Ho; Harlan County USA; Hoffa; I Married a Communist; Joe Hill; The Killing Floor; Last Exit to Brooklyn; Matewan; The Molly Maguires; Newsies; The Pajama Game; Roger & Me; Salt of the Earth; So That You Can Live; Stanley & Iris; Union Maids; With Babies and Banners; The Wobblies

Laclos, Choderlos de, films adapted from work, Dangerous Liaisons; Les Liaisons Dangereuses 1960; Valmont

Laing, RD, film adapted from work, Knots

Lamb, Lady Caroline, film about, Lady Caroline Lamb

Langlois, Henri, film about, Citizen Langlois

Laos, in film, Air America

Lapland, in film, Earth Is a Sinful Song; Pathfinder

Las Vegas, in film, Bugsy; Casino; Corvette Summer; The Don Is Dead; Elvis – The Movie; Elvis – That's the Way It Is; Honeymoon in Vegas; Indecent Proposal; The Las Vegas Story; Leaving Las Vegas; Ocean's 11; One from the Heart; The Only Game in Town; Rain Man; Showgirls; Viva Las Vegas

Latin America, unspecified, in film (see also individual countries), B. Must Die; Commando; The Evil That Men Do; La Fievre Monte à el Pao; The Fugitive (Ford); Guns of Darkness; Moon Over Parador; Los Niños Abandonados; Romancing the Stone; Rude Awakening

Latvia, in film, Another Mother

Laundry-press, malevolent, The Mangler

Lawrence, DH
film about, Priest of Love
films adapted from work, The Fox; Kangaroo (Burstall); Lady Chatterley's Lover; The Rainbow; The Rocking Horse Winner; Sons and Lovers; The Virgin and the Gypsy; Women in Love

Lawrence, Gertrude, film about, Star

Lawrence, TE, film about, Lawrence of Arabia

Lawyers (see also **Courtroom dramas, Judges**), Adam's Rib; ...and justice for all; Bird on a Wire; Bordertown; Brothers in Law; Cape Fear (Thompson); Cape Fear (Scorsese); The Chamber; Class Action; The Client;

Criminal Law; Defence Counsel Sedov; The Devil's Advocate (Hackford); Fair Game; The Firm; The Fortune Cookie; The Franchise Affair; From the Hip; Guilty as Sin; The Hour of the Pig; I Am the Law; The Lawyer; Liar Liar; Loved; Mortgage; My Cousin Vinny; Murder in the First; Narrow Margin; Night and the City (Winkler); Night Falls on Manhattan; The Paper Chase; The Paradine Case; The Pelican Brief; Philadelphia; Physical Evidence; Presumed Innocent; Primal Fear; The Rainmaker; Regarding Henry; Reversal of Fortune; Scenes from a Mall; Seems Like Old Times; Shakedown; Shame; The Star Chamber; The Story of Qiu Ju; Suspect; The Sweet Hereafter; They Might Be Giants; True Believer; The Verdict (Lumet); The War of the Roses; Wild Orchid

Lebanon, in film, Circle of Deceit; Cup Final; Hors la vie; Lebanon...Why?; Navy Seals; War Zone

Lebanese cinema, Al-Risalah; Days in London; Hour of Liberation – The Struggle in Oman; Lebanon...Why?; Leila and the Wolves

Le Carré, John, films adapted from work, The Deadly Affair; The Little Drummer Girl; The Looking Glass War; The Russia House; The Spy Who Came In From the Cold

Lee, Bruce, films about, Bruce Lee, The Man, the Myth; The Dragon Dies Hard; Dragon: The Bruce Lee Story

Lee, Harper, film adapted from work, To Kill a Mockingbird

Lee, James, film adapted from work, Career

Le Fanu, Sheridan, films adapted from work, Twins of Evil; The Vampire Lovers, Vampyr

Legends, see **Myths and legends**

Lennon, John, films about, Backbeat; The Hours and Times; Imagine

Lenz, Siegfried, film adapted from work, The Lightship

Leonard, Elmore, films adapted from work, The Ambassador; The Blue Villa; Cat Chaser; 52 Pick Up; Get Shorty; Gold Coast; Hombre; Jackie Brown; The Moonshine War; Stick; The Tall T; 3:10 to Yuma; Valdez Is Coming

Leoncavallo, Ruggiero, film adapted from work, Pagliacci

Leopold and Loeb case, Compulsion; Rope; Swoon

Lerner, Alan J, and Loewe, Frederick, musicals by, Brigadoon; Camelot; The Little Prince; My Fair Lady; Paint Your Wagon

Lermontov, Mikhail, films adapted from work, Ashik Kerib; Fury (Calenda)

Leroux, Gaston, films adapted from work, The Phantom of the Opera (Julian); Phantom of the Opera (Little); Phantom of the Opera (Lubin); The Phantom of the Opera (Fisher); Phantom of the Paradise

Lesbians and lesbianism
Aus, Flaming Ears
Bel, Daughters of Darkness; Je tu il elle
Can, Fire; I've Heard the Mermaids Singing; No Skin Off My Ass; When Night Is Falling
China, Portland Street Blues; Sun and Rain
Fr, L'Astragale; Les Biches; Chanel Solitaire; Club des Femmes; Gazon maudit; November Moon; Olivia; Le Rempart des Béguines
GB, A Bit of Scarlet; Butterfly Kiss; In the Best Interests of the Children; The Killing of Sister George; Home-Made Melodrama; The Pleasure Principle; The Rainbow; Thin Ice (Reid); Wild Flowers (Smith)
Ger, The Berlin Affair; The Bitter Tears of Petra von Kant; Joan of Arc of Mongolia; Mädchen in Uniform; My Father Is Coming; The Second Awakening of Christa Klages; Virgin Machine
HK, Hu-Du-Men
Hun, Another Way
Ind, Fire
It, Love in a Women's Prison
Jap, Afternoon Breezes; he Enchantment
Sp, Costa Brava (Family Album)
Swe, The Silence; The Women on the Roof
Tai, The Silent Thrush
US, Bound; Bound and Gagged: A Love Story; Boys on the Side; Can't Stop the Music; The Color Purple; Daughters of Darkness; Desert Hearts; Desperate Living; A Different Story; Girlfriends; Go Fish; Headhunter; The Incredibly True Adventure of Two Girls in Love; Internal Affairs; Kamikaze Hearts; Lianna; Liquid Sky; A Litany for Survival: The Life and Work of Audre Lorde; MURDER and Murder; She Must Be Seeing Things; Three of Hearts; Two Moon Junction; Without You I'm Nothing; Word Is Out; Zee & Co

Leskov, Nikolai, films adapted from work, Coilin and Platonida; Katia Ismailova; Siberian Lady Macbeth

Tendresse Ordinaire

Fin, *I Hired a Contract Killer*

Fr, *L'Aigle à Deux Têtes; Les Amants de Verone; Les Amants du Pont-Neuf; La Bonne Année; L'Appartement; La Boulangère de Monceau; La Carrière de Suzanne; Casque d'Or; César and Rosalie; Conte d'été; Cyrano de Bergerac; La Dame aux Camélias; Dear Inspector; Delicatessen; Les Demoiselles de Rochefort; Diane; Eléna et les Hommes; Faute de Soleil; Gueule d'Amour; Un Homme et une Femme; Lola; La Maison de Jade; A Man in Love; Marius et Jeannette; Mayerling; Noce blanche; Notre Histoire; Les Parapluies de Cherbourg; Parfait Amour!; Paul and Michelle; Roselyne and the Lions; Le Secret de Mayerling; Le Silence de la mer; A Strange Place to Meet; This Sweet Sickness; A Tale of Springtime; Stealing Heaven; Toute Une Nuit; Trop belle pour toi!; A Winter's Tale*

GB, *Alive and Kicking; American Friends; Anna Karenina* (Duvivier); *Blanche Fury; The Blue Lagoon* (Launder); *Breaking the Waves; Brief Ecstasy; Brief Encounter; The Buttercup Chain; Cal; Dangerous Moonlight; The English Patient; Friends; The Gypsy and the Gentleman; Hussy; I Could Go on Singing; Impromptu; Interlude* (Billington); *Jude; Like It Is; The Love Test; Manuela; Martha – Meet Frank, Daniel and Laurence; Neither the Sea nor the Sand; Pandora and the Flying Dutchman; A Private Life; The Raging Moon; Real Life; Romeo and Juliet; The Scarlet Tunic; Strapless; Sweet William; The Tall Guy; The Tamarind Seed; This Is the Sea; Those Glory, Glory Days; Truly, Madly, Deeply; The Wind Cannot Read; The Wings of the Dove; Yanks*

Ger, *Liebelei; A Love in Germany; The Promise* (von Trotta)

It, *A Brief Vacation; Romeo and Juliet; Stealing Beauty; Terminal Station; Viaggio in Italia; We the Living*

Jap, *A Scene at the Sea; The Story of the Late Chrysanthemums; Summer Vacation 1999*

Mex, *Abismos de pasión; White Lies*

Pol, *The Third Part of the Night; A Year of the Quiet Sun; The Young Ladies of Wilko*

Sp, *Tie Me Up! Tie Me Down!*

Swe, *Elvira Madigan*

Switz, *The Middle of the World*

US, *The Accidental Tourist; Always* (Spielberg); *Anna Karenina* (Brown); *Anna Karenina* (Rose); *Baby, It's You; Big Night; The Black Orchid; The Blue Lagoon* (Kleiser); *Blume in Love; Bobby Deerfield; Bridges of Madison County; Bus Stop;*

By the Light of the Silvery Moon; Camille (Smallwood); *Camille* (Cukor); *Casablanca; Catchfire; The Cobra Cousins; The Dark Angel; Deception; Desert Hearts; Dirigible; Don't Tell Her It's Me; Dying Young; The Eagle; The Emperor Waltz; Endless Love; The English Patient; Everyone Says I Love You; Falling in Love; A Farewell to Arms* (Borzage); *A Farewell to Arms* (Vidor); *First Love* (Darling); *Flesh and the Devil; Forever Young* (Miner); *Frankie & Johnny; The Garden of Allah; Ghost; The Ghost and Mrs Muir; The Grass Is Greener; Green Card; Green Light; Grosse Pointe Blank; Housesitter; I Love You to Death; The Incredibly True Adventure of Two Girls in Love; In Love; In Love and War; Interlude* (Sirk); *Intermezzo; In the Good Old Summertime; I Take This Woman; It Could Happen to You; Jersey Girl; Joe Versus the Volcano; Johnny Suede; Little Man, What Now?; A Little Romance; Love at Large; Love in the Afternoon* (Wilder); *Love Is a Many Splendored Thing; love jones; Made in Heaven; Making Mr Right; Manpower; Man's Castle; Man, Woman and Child; The Marrying Man; Miracle in the Rain; The Mirror Has Two Faces; Moment by Moment; Moonstruck; Neither by Day Nor by Night; Now Voyager; Oliver's Story; Once in Paris...; One from the Heart; One More River; The Only Game in Town; The Other Side of the Mountain; Pat and Mike; Peter Ibbetson; Platinum Blonde; Portrait of Jennie; Prelude to a Kiss; Pretty Woman; A Pyromaniac's Love Story; Random Harvest; Rebecca; Roxanne; Say Anything; 7th Heaven* (Borzage); *Seventh Heaven* (King); *She's So Lovely; The Shining Hour; Sleepless in Seattle; Somewhere in Time; Splendor in the Grass; Starting Over; The Sterile Cuckoo; Summertime; Sunrise; Sunshine; Sunshine Part II; Sure Thing; Surrender; Sweet Hearts Dance; Tabu; They Live by Night; A Time to Love and a Time to Die; Tin Cup; Titanic* (Cameron); *A Touch of Class; Trouble in Mind; True Romance; The Truth About Cats & Dogs; Two Moon Junction; Used People; A Walk in the Spring Rain; A Walk with Love and Death; A Warm December; The Way We Were; We Are Not Alone; We Live Again; The Wedding March; When Harry Met Sally...; While You Were Sleeping; White Palace ; William Shakespeare's Romeo & Juliet*

Yugo, *The Switchboard Operator*

Lowndes, Mrs Belloc, films adapted from work, *The Lodger; Ivy*

Lowry, Malcolm film about, *Volcano* film adapted from work, *Under the Volcano*

Luciano, Lucky, films about, *Lucky Luciano; Marked Woman; Mobsters*

Ludlum, Robert, film adapted from work, *The Osterman Weekend*

Ludwig II of Bavaria, films about, *Ludwig; Ludwig – Requiem for a Virgin King; Ludwig's Cook*

Lumberjacks, *Sometimes a Great Notion*

Luther, Martin, film about, *Luther*

Luxemburg, Rosa, film about, *Rosa Luxemburg*

Lynching (see also **Vigilantes**), *Among the Living; Hang 'em High; Intruder in the Dust; The Lawless; The Ox-Bow Incident; The Sound of Fury*

Lyndon, Barre, film adapted from work, *The Amazing Doctor Clitterhouse*

Lynn, Loretta, film about, *Coal Miner's Daughter*

MacArthur, Charles film about, *Mrs Parker and the Vicious Circle* films adapted from work, *Lulu Belle; The Front Page* (Milestone); *The Front Page* (Wilder); *His Girl Friday; Twentieth Century*

MacArthur, General Douglas, film about, *MacArthur*

McBain, Ed, films adapted from work (see also **Hunter, Evan**), *Blood Relatives; High and Low*

McCabe, Patrick, film based on work, *The Butcher Boy*

McCarthy, Senator Joseph, and McCarthyism, *Chaplin; Citizen Cohn; Comic Book Confidential; The Crucible; Daniel; Fellow Traveller; Force of Evil; For the Boys; The Front; Guilty by Suspicion; Hollywood on Trial; The House on Carroll Street; I.F. Stone's Weekly; I Married a Communist; Insignificance; People Will Talk; Point of Order; Storm Center; Roy Cohn/Jack SmithThe Trials of Alger Hiss; Walk East on Beacon*

McCartney, Paul, in performance (see also **The Beatles**), *Get Back; Give My Regards to Broad Street; Rockshow*

McCoy, Horace, films adapted from work, *Kiss Tomorrow Goodbye; They Shoot Horses, Don't They?*

McCullers, Carson, films adapted from work, *The Ballad of the Sad Café; The Heart Is a Lonely Hunter; The Member of the Wedding; An Impudent Girl; Reflections in a Golden Eye*

McCullough, Colleen, films adapted from work, *An Indecent Obsession; Tim*

McDermott, Alice, film adapted from work, *That Night*

McDonald, Gregory, films adapted from work, *Fletch; Fletch Lives; Running Scared* (Hemmings)

Macdonald, Philip, film adapted from work, *Circle of Danger*

MacDonald, Ross, films adapted from work, *Blue City; The Drowning Pool; Harper; The Moving Target*

Macdonald, Sharman, film adapted from work, *The Winter Guest*

Macedonian cinema, *Before the Rain*

McEwan, Ian, films adapted from work, *The Cement Garden; The Comfort of Strangers; The Innocent* (Schlesinger); *Last Day of Summer*

McGivern, William P, films adapted from work, *The Big Heat; Odds Against Tomorrow; Rogue Cop*

McGrath, John, film adapted from work, *The Bofors Gun*

McGuane, Thomas in film, *Warren Oates: Across the Border* films adapted from work, *Cold Feet; 92 in the Shade*

McIlvanney, William, film adapted from work, *The Big Man*

McInerney, Jay, film adapted from work, *Bright Lights, Big City*

MacInnes, Colin, film adapted from work, *Absolute Beginners*

Mackenzie, Compton, film adapted from work, *Rockets Galore; Whisky Galore!*

Macklin, Robert, film adapted from work, *Storyville*

MacLaverty, Bernard, films adapted from work, *Cal; Lamb*

Maclean, Alistair, films adapted from work, *Bear Island; Breakheart Pass; Caravan to Vaccares; Fear Is the Key; Force 10 from Navarone; Golden Rendezvous; The Guns of Navarone; The Satan Bug; When Eight Bells Toll; Where Eagles Dare*

State of the Union; They Knew What They Wanted; True Love; Turnabout; Vivacious Lady; The War of the Roses; A Wedding; The Wedding Banquet; Who's Afraid of Virginia Woolf?; The Wind (Sjöström); Woman of the Year; Woman's World USSR, The Kreutzer Sonata

Martial arts
Hong Kong, Beach of the War Gods, A Better Tomorrow; A Better Tomorrow II; The Big Boss; The Bloody Fists; Bruce Lee: The Man, the Myth; Burning Paradise; The Chinese Connection; The Conman and the Kung Fu Kid; Death Kick; Dirty Ho; 8-Diagram Pole Fighter; Executioners from Shaolin; The Fate of Lee Khan; First Strike; Fist of Fury; Fong Sai-Yuk; Full Contact; Golden Swallow; Hap-Ki-Do; Intimate Confessions of a Chinese Courtesan; The Killer (Chu Yuan); King Boxer; King of Kung Fu; Kung Fu Fighting; Kung Fu Gangbusters; The Kung Fu Girl; Kung Fu – The Headcrusher; Last Hurrah for Chivalry; Moon Warriors; My Young Auntie; The New One-Armed Boxer; Once Upon a Time in China; Once Upon a Time in China II; Police Story (Chan); Rumble in the Bronx; Stoner; The Story of Woo Viet; The 36th Chamber of Shaolin; The Way of the Dragon; Young and Dangerous; Young and Dangerous 2; Young and Dangerous 3 Hong Kong with other countries, The Dragon Dies Hard; Dynasty; Enter the Dragon; Enter the Seven Virgins; The Legend of the Seven Golden Vampires; The Man from Hong Kong other countries, American Ninja; Best of the Best; Best of the Best 2: The Big Brawl; The Big Zapper; Black Belt Jones; Black Eagle; Blind Fury; Bloodsport; The Challenge; Code of Silence; Double Impact; Dragon: The Bruce Lee Story; Enter the Ninja; An Eye for an Eye; Fist of Fury Part II; Fist of the North Star; Force: Five; A Force of One; The Golden Child; Golden Needles; Good Guys Wear Black; Gymkata; Jaguar Lives; The Karate Kid: Part II; The Karate Kid Part III; Kickboxer; Kung Fu – Girl Fighter; Kung Fu Street Fighter; The Last Dragon; Legend of Bruce Lee; Lone Wolf McQuade; Ninja III – The Domination; No Retreat, No Surrender; Only the Strong; Out for Justice; The Perfect Weapon; The Quest; Rapid Fire; Remo Williams: The Adventure Begins; Return of the Dragon; Road House (Herrington); Rooftops; The Silent Flute; Ten Fingers of Steel; That Man Bolt; Take a Hard Ride; 3 Ninjas; Universal Soldier

Mary Queen of Scots, films about, Mary of Scotland; Mary Queen of Scots

Masters, John, film adapted from work, The Deceivers

Masterson, Whit, films adapted from work, Touch of Evil; Warning Shot

Mata Hari, films about, Mata Hari (Fitzmaurice); Mata Hari (Harrington); Mata Hari – Agent H.21

Matheson, Richard, films adapted from work, The Incredible Shrinking Man; The Legend of Hell House; The Omega Man; Les Seins de glace

Matthiessen, Peter, film adapted from work, At Play in the Fields of the Lord

Maugham, W Somerset, films adapted from work, The Beachcomber; Christmas Holiday; Encore; The Letter; The Magician; Miss Sadie Thompson; The Moon and Sixpence; The Painted Veil; Quartet; Rain; The Razor's Edge; Sadie Thompson; Secret Agent; Trio; The Unfaithful; Vessel of Wrath

Maupassant, Guy de, films adapted from work, Boule de Suif; Golden Braid; Une Partie de Campagne; Le Plaisir; The Private Affairs of Bel Ami

Maxwell, Gavin, film adapted from work, Ring of Bright Water

Mayan civilisation, King of the Sun

Medicine, see **Doctors and medicine, Few-months-to-live stories, Hospital dramas, Illness, Mental hospitals and asylums, Mental illness**

Melville, Herman, films adapted from work, Bartleby; Billy Budd; Moby Dick

Memory
implantation of, Total Recall loss of, Anastasia (Litvak); Anastasia (Bluth/Goldman); As You Desire Me; The Brain Machine; The Brighton Strangler; The Clay Pigeon; Crack-Up (Reis); Crossroads (Conway); Dangerously They Live; Dark City; Dead Again; The Groundstar Conspiracy; Home at Seven; The Lady in the Car with Glasses and a Gun; Libel; The Long Kiss Goodnight; Love Letters (Dieterle); The Man Called Noon; The Man in the Road; March Comes in Like a Lion; Mirage; Mugshot; The October Man; Overboard; Pit of Darkness; The Red Squirrel; Random Harvest; Secret Wedding; Shattered (Petersen); Somewhere in the Night; Spellbound; Sunflower; Without Memory manipulation of, Death and

the Maiden; 36 Hours reflections on, Blue Black Permanent; Ghost Dance; La Jetée; Muriel; The Polygraph; Rendez-vous à Bray; The Revolving Doors; Tender Hours; Wild Strawberries Repressed Memory Syndrome, Never Talk to Strangers

Ménages-à-trois, Alligator Eyes; Annabelle partagée; Bodies, Rest & Motion; Un Coeur en hiver; December Bride; Design for Living; Les Deux Anglaises et le Continent; Les Diaboliques (Clouzot); Diabolique (Chechik); The Fabulous Baker Boys; Gazon Maudit; The Great Lie; Henry & June; Home-Made Melodrama; Homme de Désir; The Last Woman on Earth; Lovers; Lucky Lady; The Lunatic; Making Love; The More the Merrier; The Naked Dawn; The Party – Nature Morte; Prague; Semi-Tough; Splendor; Summerfield; The Talk of the Town; Tenue de Soirée; Threesome; Willie & Phil

Menchú, Rigoberta, film about, When the Mountains Tremble

Menopause, Privilege (Rainer)

Mental handicap (see also **Autism, Disability, Dyslexia**), Benny and Joon; A Child Is Waiting; Dominick and Eugene; The Eighth Day; Jigsaw; Mama; The Man Who Mistook His Wife for a Hat; No Way Home; Touched by Love; Walter

Mental hospitals and asylums, Alone in the Dark; Amorosa; Assassin of the Tsar; Awakenings; Beautiful Dreamers; Bedlam; Blood of the Vampire; The Boy Who Cried Bitch; Chattahoochee; Committed; Cosi Crazy People; Down the Ancient Stairs; The Dream Team; Les Espions; Every Little Thing; The Exorcist III; Fit to Be Untied; King of Hearts; Lies; Nightmare; One Flew Over the Cuckoo's Nest; A Page of Madness; The Persecution and Assassination of Jean-Paul Marat as Performed by the Inmates of the Asylum of Charenton Under the Direction of the Marquis de Sade; Red Beads; Santa Sangre; The Sender; Shining Victory; Shock Corridor; The Snake Pit; La Tête contre les Murs; Walter release from, She's Been Away

Mental illness (see also **Psychiatry, Psychopaths and serial killers**), An Angel at My Table; Benny and Joon; Best Boy; Camille Claudel; Clean, Shaven; Coast to Coast (Sargent); Dementia; Dialogues With

Madwomen; Disturbed; Don't Bother to Knock (Baker); Each Dawn I Die; End of the Road; Experiment Perilous; Face to Face; Family Life (Loach); The Father; Une Femme Douce; The 5,000 Fingers of Dr T; The Florentine Dagger; From Noon till Three; Gaslight (Cukor); Gaslight (Dickinson); The Girl from Trieste; The Grass Is Singing; Hangover Square; Un Homme Qui Dort; The Idiots; Images; I Never Promised You a Rose Garden; Interlude; The Killer Inside Me; King of Hearts; Komitas; Lilith; Love Crazy; Madonna of the Seven Moons; The Mafu Cage; The Man Who Had His Hair Cut Short; The Man Upstairs; Martin; Me and My Brother; Mr Jones; The Nanny; Night Watch; No Mercy, No Future; Nuts; A Page of Madness; A Petal; Possessed; The Pumpkin Eater; Puzzle of a Downfall Child; Rage in Heaven; Regeneration; Repulsion; La Rupture; The Saint of Fort Washington; Screaming Mimi; Shine; Sling Blade; Strait-Jacket; Sybil; La Tête de Normande St-Onge; They Might Be Giants; The Three Faces of Eve; Through a Glass Darkly

Mercenaries, Il Mercenario; Prince of Foxes; Sniper; The Wild Geese; Wild Geese II

Merchant, Ismail, film about, In Ismail's Custody

Mérimée, Prosper, film adapted from work, Vendetta

Mermaids, Mr Peabody and the Mermaid; Splash

Metalious, Grace, film based on work, Peyton Place

Metamorphosis into animals (see also **Mutation**), Cat Girl; Cat People (Tourneur); Cat People (Schrader); The Curse of the Cat People; The She Creature; The Witches

Mexican cinema, Abismos de pasión; Break of Dawn; El Bruto; Chac; The Criminal Life of Archibaldo de la Cruz; Danzón; Deep Crimson; Dollar Mambo; Doña Herlinda and Her Son; El; El Topo; Enamorada; Eréndira; The Exterminating Angel; La Fièvre Monte à El Pao; Hasta Morir; Highway Patrolman; Homework; House of Madness; El Jardín del Eden; Like a Bride; Like Water for Chocolate; Lolo; Midaq Alley; My Dear Tom Mix; Nazarín; No Return Address; Los Olvidados; One Lost Year; La Otra (Gavaldón); Reed: Insurgent Mexico; Robinson Crusoe;

Miniskirted Dynamo; Mommie Dearest; 'Night Mother; No Sad Songs for Me; Not Without My Daughter; The Positively True Adventures of the Alleged Texas Cheerleader-Murdering Mom; Postcards from the Edge; Sailor Beware; Season of Dreams; Secrets & Lies; The Silences of the Palace; Song of the Exile; Steel Magnolias; Stella; Stella Dallas; The Summer of Aviya; Terms of Endearment; This Is My Life; Die Tödliche Maria; Violette Nozière; We Don't Talk About It; Wild at Heart; Wild Flowers (Lefebvre); Wild Flowers (Smith); The Winter Guest; A World Apart
and daughters-in-law, Plaff! or Too Afraid of Life; When Joseph Returns
and sons, Abel; Alice Doesn't Live Here Any More; Bad Blood; Bad Boy Bubby; Because of That War; The Boy Who Cried Bitch; The Boy Who Had Everything; Braindead; Le Château de ma mère; The Day the Sun Turned Cold; The Divided Heart; The Goddess; The Grifters; Killing Dad; The Krays; La Luna; Little Man Tate; Mama; The Manchurian Candidate; The Man I Married; Malizia; Men Don't Leave; Mon Premier Amour; Mother (Brooks);Mother and Son; Mother's Boys; New York Stories; One Full Moon; Only the Lonely; Les Parents Terribles; Persecution; The Real McCoy; The Revolving Doors; The Rockinghorse Winner; Santa Sangre; Some Mother's Son; Le Souffle au Coeur; Spanking the Monkey; Stop! or My Mom Will Shoot; Throw Momma from the Train; Torch Song Trilogy; Track 29; Where's Poppa; White Heat; A Woman on Her Own
both, Bloody Mama; Look Who's Talking; Look Who's Talking Now; Look Who's Talking Too; Mr and Mrs Bridge; Parenthood; Yours, Mine and Ours
surrogate, The Handmaid's Tale; Record of a Tenement Gentleman; Surrogate Mother

Motor sport, Bobby Deerfield; The Cannonball Run; Cannonball Run II; Crash (Gibson); Days of Thunder; Death Race 2,000; Fast Company; Genevieve; Grand Prix; Greased Lightning; Heart Like a Wheel; La Passione; The Last American Hero; Le Mans; Once a Jolly Swagman; One by One; Red Line 7000; Sahara (McLaglen); Shut Down; Silver Dream Racer; Spetters; 23:58; Viva Las Vegas

Mountains and mountaineering, Alive; Careful; Cliffhanger; The Eiger Sanction; The Englishman Who Went Up a Hill, But Came Down a Mountain; Everest; Five Days One Summer; Galahad of Everest; K2; Seven Years in Tibet; The White Tower

Mozambican cinema, Massacre; Shout at the Devil

Mozart, Wolfgang Amadeus films about, Amadeus; Mozart in Love; Noi Tre films of/featuring operas, Con Air; Don Giovanni; The Magic Flute; Vertiges

Multiple personalities (see also **Double lives, Doubles/doppelgängers**), Chameleon Street; Raising Cain; The Secret Life of Walter Mitty; Multiplicty; The Three Faces of Eve; Zelig

Music and musicians, brass bands, Brassed Off; The Music Man

Music and musicians, classical, L'Accompagnatrice; Allegro Non Troppo, Amadeus; Ballad in Blue; Les Belles de nuit; Beyond Silence; Blossom Time; Chronicle of Anna Magdalena Bach; Un Coeur en hiver; The Competition; Concerto of Life; The Conductor; The Confessions of Winifred Wagner; Deception; Duet for One; Fantasia; Fingers; The 5,000 Fingers of Dr T; From Mao to Mozart; The Great Waltz (Duvivier); The Great Waltz (Stone); Immortal Beloved; Hangover Square; Humoresque; Impromptu; Katok i Skrypka; Letter from an Unknown Woman; Lisztomania; Madame Sousatzka; The Magic Bow; Mahler; Meeting Venus; Mélo; The Mephisto Waltz; Music for the Movies: Bernard Herrmann; Music for the Movies: The Hollywood Sound; Music for the Movies: Toru Takemitsu; The Music Lovers; The Music Teacher; The Night Has Eyes; Nocturne; Noi Tre; Oh, You Beautiful Doll; One Hundred Men and a Girl; Orchestra Rehearsal; Parsifai; Pastorale; The Piano; Raising the Wind; Rothschild's Violin; The Seventh Veil; The Silent Touch; Small Wonders; Something to Believe In; Song of Norway; Song of Scheherazade; A Song to Remember; Spring Symphony; Swan Song; Thirty Two Short Films About Glenn Gould; Tous les Matins du monde; Unfaithfully Yours (Zieff); Les Uns et Les Autres; Up on the Roof; William Christie et Les Arts Florissants ou la Passion du Baroque; Wagner

Music and musicians, folk/traditional/world Armenia, Komitas Can, September Song: The Music of Kurt Weill China, The Emperor's Shadow; Life on a String Cuba, The Mambo Kings Ecuador, Sensations Fin, Total Balalaika Show Ger, Fatherland Ind The Courtesans of Bombay, Dance of the Wind; The Doll (Ghose) Jap, Ondeko-za on Sado Kor, Sopyonje Morocco, Trances Scotland, Mairi Mhor US, Baby the Rain Must Fall; Bound for Glory; A Tickle in the Heart; The Weavers; Wasn't That a Time USSR and Rus, Ashik Kerib, Total Balalaika Show Zaire, La Vie est belle

Musicals, music hall and vaudeville, see **Show business**

Musil, Robert, film adapted from work, Young Törless

Mutations (see also **Deformity and disfigurement, Metamorphosis into animals, Shrinking),** Alligator; The Amazing Colossal Man; Attack of the 50 Foot Woman (Juran); Attack of the 50ft Woman (Guest); Attack of the Killer Tomatoes; Basket Case 2; Beneath the Planet of the Apes; Body Parts; The Borrower; Braindead; The Brood; Class of Nuke 'Em High; Crimes of the Future; Damnation Alley; The Day the World Ended; Deathsport; Fiend Without a Face; The Fly (Neumann); The Fly (Cronenberg); The Fly II; Food of the Gods; Forbidden World; From Beyond; The Giant Spider Invasion; Godzilla; I, Monster; The Incredible Hulk; Innerspace; The Invisible Man; The Invisible Man Returns; The Incredible Melting Man; The Invisible Ray; The Island of Dr Moreau (Taylor); The Island of Dr Moreau (Frankenheimer); The Island of Lost Souls; The Island of Mutations; It Came from Beneath the Sea; The Hills Have Eyes; Humanoids from the Deep; Man-Made Monster; The Mask (Russell); Matinee; Mimic; Monkey Shines; Monster from Green Hell; Monster of Terror; Mutant; Mutations; Mysterious Island; Nightbreed; Night of the Lepus; The Omega Man; The People Under the Stairs; The Projected Man; Proteus; The Relic; The Reptile; Return of the Fly; The Return of the Swamp Thing; The Revenge of Frankenstein; The Rift; The She Creature; Son of Godzilla; Species; Swamp Thing; Tarantula; Teenage Mutant Ninja Turtles; Teenage Mutant Ninja Turtles II: The Secret of the Ooze; Teenage Mutant Ninja Turtles III; Terminus; TerrorVision; Them; This Island Earth; The Toxic Avenger; The Toxic Avenger Part II; Quatermass II; Sssssssss; Superbeast; War of the Colossal Beast; The Wasp Woman; Watchers; Who?

Muybridge, Eadweard, film about, Eadweard Muybridge, Zoopraxographer

Myths and legends (see also **Fairies and goblins, Greece),** The Amazons; Ashik Kerib; The Blood Brothers; A Chinese Ghost Story; A Chinese Ghost Story II; Darby O'Gill and the Little People; The Deaf and Mute Heroine; DragonHeart; Erik the Viking; L'Eternal Retour; Excalibur; First Knight; The Fisher King; The Golem; Hero (Platts-Mills); Hercules; The Illustrated Man; Immortal Story; Jason and the Argonauts; Keita! The Voice of the Griot; Lancelot du Lac; The Legend of the Suram Fortress; Le Mahabharata; Die Nibelungen; Onibaba; Pandora and the Flying Dutchman; Parking; Perceval le Gallois; Prince Valiant; The Romantic Agony; The Sword and the Sorceror; The Sword in the Stone; The Sword of the Valiant; Swordsman; Swordsman II; The Swordsman in Double-Flag Town; The Legend of Gawain and the Green Knight; Ugetsu Monogatari; Zu: Warriors from the Magic Mountain; Wishmaster

Nabokov, Vladimir, films adapted from work, Despair; King; Queen, Knave; Laughter in the Dark; Lolita (Kubrick); Lolita (Lyne)

Nagel, James, film adapted from work, In Love and War

Nameless evils, The Blob; Duel; Encounter at Raven's Gate; Event Horizon; The Fog; Forbidden Planet; The Keep; Leviathan; Scarecrows; Secrets of the Phantom Caves; The Seventh Sign; The Skull

Namibia Namibian cinema Flame Namibia in film, Windprints

Nannies, governesses, au pairs, Anna and the King of Siam; Corrina, Corrina; Gaby – A True Story; The Guardian; The Hand That Rocks the Cradle; The Innocents; Jane Eyre (Stevenson); Jane Eyre (Mann); Jane Eyre (Zeffirelli); The King and I; A Little Princess; Martha & Ethel; Miss Mary; Mr Nanny; Mrs Doubtfire; The Nanny; Perfect Alibi; The Unseen; When Mother Comes Home for Christmas

Napoleon I, Emperor of France, films about, Austerlitz; Napoléon; War and Peace (Vidor); War and Peace (Bondarchuk); Waterloo

New Zealand cinema, *An Angel at My Table; Bad Taste; Beyond Reasonable Doubt; Braindead; Broken English; Came a Hot Friday; Carry Me Back; Cinema of Unease; Constance; Crush; Desperate Remedies; The End of the Golden Weather; The Frighteners; Goodbye Pork Pie; Heavenly Creatures; The Lincoln County Incident; Other Halves; Patu; The Piano; Pictures; Punch Me in the Stomach; The Quiet Earth; Race for the Yankee Zephyr; Romper Stomper; Savage Islands; The Scarecrow; Shaker Run; Sleeping Dogs; Smash Palace; Starlight Hotel; Sylvia; Topless Women Talk About Their Lives; Trial Run; The Ugly; Utu; Vigil*

Nexo, Martin Andersen, film adapted from work, *Pelle the Conqueror*

Nicaragua
Nicaraguan cinema, *Alsino and the Condor*
Nicaragua in film, *Carla's Song; The Last Plane Out; Latino; Nicaragua – No Pasarán; Under Fire; Walker*

Nicholas II, Czar of Russia, films about, *The End of St Petersburg; Nicholas and Alexandra*

Nichols, Peter, film adapted from work, *The National Health; Privates on Parade*

Nicholson, William, film adapted from work, *Shadowlands*

Nietzsche, Friedrich, film about, *Beyond Evil*

Nightclubs, see **Show business**

Nilsson, Harry, musical by, *The Point; Popeye*

Nin, Anaïs, film about, *Henry & June*

Nixon, Richard, films about, *All the President's Men; Millhouse; Nixon; Secret Honor; The Trials of Alger Hiss*

Norman, Marsha, film adapted from work, *'Night Mother*

North of England, in film (see also **Liverpool**), *All Creatures Great and Small; Bert Rigby, You're a Fool; Billy Liar; Bob's Weekend; The Boys in Blue; Brassed Off; Come on George; Escape from the Dark; The Full Monty; The Gamekeeper; Get Carter; Groove on a Stanley Knife; Hell Is a City; In Fading Light; The Innocent (MacKenzie); It Shouldn't Happen to a Vet; Juvenile Liaison; Juvenile Liaison 2; A Kind of Loving; Lease of Life; The Likely Lads; Love on the Dole; The Lovers; My Son the Fanatic; The Nature*

of the Beast; The Night Has Eyes; The Old Dark House; Owd Bob; Paper Marriage; Payroll; Raining Stones; Rita, Sue and Bob Too; Room at the Top; Seacoal; South Riding; Spring and Port Wine; The Stars Look Down; A Taste of Honey; T. Dan Smith; This Sporting Life; Up 'n' Under; Up on the Roof; Vroom; Walter; Wetherby; What a Carve Up!; When Saturday Comes; Whistle Down the Wind; The White Bus; Women in Tropical Places; Wuthering Heights (Wyler); Wuthering Heights (Kosminsky); Yanks

Norton, Mary, film based on work, *The Borrowers*

Norway, in film, *Cross My Heart and Hope to Die; Edge of Darkness; Edvard Munch; The Ice Palace (Blom); Junk Mail; The Last Lieutenant; Little Ida; Orion's Belt; The Other Side of Sunday; Sebastian; Song of Norway; Wives; Wives: Ten Years After; Wives III*

Norwegian cinema,
Breaking the Waves; Cross My Heart and Hope to Die; Devil's Island (Fridriksson); Edvard Munch; The Ice Palace (Blom); Junk Mail; I Was Fifteen; The Last Lieutenant; Little Ida; Orion's Belt; The Other Side of Sunday; Pathfinder; Sebastian; Wives; Wives: Ten Years After; Wives III

Nostalgia
for 1900s, *My Brilliant Career*
for 1920s, *Bloodhounds of Broadway; The Boy Friend; The Fortune; Lucky Lady; Thoroughly Modern Millie*
for 1930s, *Borsalino; Borsalino & Co*
for 1940s, *Broadway Bound; Class of 44; Constance; Le Gang; P'Tang, Yang, Kipperbang; Racing with the Moon; Summer of '42*
for 1950s, *Book of Love; Cry-Baby; The Delinquents; Diner; Eddie and the Cruisers; Forever Young; Grease; Grease 2; Hoosiers; The Last Picture Show; Lords of Flatbush; The Man in the Moon; Motorist; Next Stop; Greenwich Village; Radio Days; Slumber Party '57; That'll Be The Day; Tribulation 99: Alien Anomalies Under America; Union City; W.W. and the Dixie Dancekings*
for 1960s, *American Graffiti; Baby, It's You; Coupe de Ville; Dirty Dancing; The Five Heartbeats; The Flamingo Kid; Goin' Steady; Hairspray; Lemon Popsicle; More American Graffiti; Private Popsicle; Shag; The Wanderers; The Year My Voice Broke*
for 1970s, *Shock Treatment; Stardust*
for world of old movies, *The Cheap Detective; Cinema Paradiso; Cinema Paradiso: The Special Edition; Dead*

Men Don't Wear Plaid; Fade to Black; Gumshoe; Movie Movie; Nickelodeon; Splendor; The World's Greatest Lover; Yoyo
for old television, *Down Memory Lane; Dragnet; My Favourite Year; Twilight Zone – The Movie*

Nuclear energy, *Bari-Zogon; The Chain Reaction; The China Syndrome; City of Fear; Class of Nuke 'Em High; Crack in the World; The Damned (Losey); Dark Circle; The Fiend Without a Face; In the King of Prussia; Meet the Applegates; Silkwood; X the Unknown*

Nuclear weapons
development of, *Fat Man and Little Boy; First Yank into Tokyo; The Plutonium Circus*
effects of/threat of, *America – From Hitler to MX; Amazing Grace and Chuck; Atomic Café; The Bedford Incident; Black Rain (Imamura); Blue Sky; Broken Arrow (Woo); Broken Arrow 29; Carry Greenham Home; Crimson Tide; The Day After Trinity; The Day the Earth Caught Fire; The Day the Fish Came Out; Defence of the Realm; Desert Bloom; Dr Strangelove: or, How I Learned to Stop Worrying and Love the Bomb; The Eclipse; Fail Safe; Half Life; Hiroshima, Mon Amour; Home of the Brave; The Hunt for Red October; I Live in Fear; It Came from Beneath the Sea; Kiss Me Deadly; Lost Sex; Miracle Mile; The Peacemaker; Rally 'round the Flag, Boys!; Rhapsody in August; Rockets Galore; Seven Days to Noon; Stargate; Superman IV: The Quest for Peace; Them!; True Lies; Twilight's Last Gleaming; Unstable Elements – Atomic Stories 1939–85; Viva la Vie; War Games; When the Wind Blows*
life after nuclear holocaust, *The Bedsitting Room; The Big Bang; A Boy and His Dog; Buck Rogers in the 25th Century; Café Flesh; Damnation Alley; Dark Enemy; The Day the World Ended; Deathsport; The Deserter and the Nomads; The Falls; Fist of the North Star; The Last Battle; The Last Woman on Earth; Letters from a Dead Man; Lord of the Flies (Brook); Lord of the Flies (Hook); Malevil; Mindwarp; The New Barbarians; On the Beach; Panic in Year Zero; Planet of the Apes; The Quiet Earth; The Sacrifice; The Salute of the Jugger; Surf Nazis Must Die; Testament (Littman)*

Nureyev, Rudolf, in performance, *I Am a Dancer*

O'Barr, James, films adapted from work, *The Crow; The Crow: City of Angels*

O'Brien, Edna, films adapted from work, *The Country Girls; Girl with Green Eyes*

Occult, see **Devil, The Antichrist, Witchcraft, etc**

O'Casey, Sean, film about, *Young Cassidy*

O'Connor, Flannery, film adapted from work, *Wise Blood*

O'Connor, Joseph, film adapted from work, *Ailsa*

Odets, Clifford, films adapted from work, *Clash By Night; Golden Boy*

Offenbach, Jacques, film of opera, *The Tales of Hoffman*

Office life (see also **Boardroom jungle, Work**), *The Apartment; The Associate; The Bachelor Party; The Clock; The Crowd; Desk Set; Glengarry Glen Ross; Nine to Five; The Paper; The Secret of My Success; Stan and George's New Life; Working Girl*

O'Flaherty, Liam, film adapted from work, *The Informer; The Puritan*

O'Hara, John, films adapted from work, *From the Terrace; Pal Joey*

Oil prospecting, *Boom Town; Giant; The Louisiana Story; Oklahoma Crude; Station Six – Sahara; The Two Jakes; When Time Ran Out...*

OK Corral, films featuring, *Doc; Gunfight at the OK Corral; Hour of the Gun; My Darling Clementine; Tombstone; Wyatt Earp*

Olympic Games, and related competitions, in film (see also **Athletics**), *Animalympics; Best of the Best; Chariots of Fire; The Cutting Edge; Geordie; Olympische Spiele 1936; One in a Million; Running Brave; Tokyo Olympiad 1964; Visions of Eight; White Rock*

Oman, in film, *The Hour of Liberation – The Struggle in Oman*

O'Neill, Eugene, films adapted from work, *Desire under the Elms; Long Day's Journey into Night; The Long Voyage Home*

Onstott, Kyle, films adapted from work, *Drum; Mandingo*

Opera and operetta
films of, *Bluebeard's Castle; Bitter Sweet; Black River; La Bohème; Carmen; The Desret Song; Don Giovanni; The King Steps Out; Madame Butterfly; The Magic Flute; The Merry Widow; The Mikado; Otello;*

Pavese, Cesare, film adapted from work, *Le Amiche*

Pavlova, Anna, film about, *Pavlova – A Woman for All Time*

Peace Corps, *Blood of the Condor; The Hotbox; Volunteers*

Peking Opera, see **Opera and operetta**

Pérez Galdos, Benito, film adapted from work, *Tristana*

Pérez Reverte, Arturo, film adapted from work, *The Fencing Master*

Peron, Eva, film about, *Evita; Don't Cry for Me Little Mother*

Peru
Peruvian cinema, *The Lion's Den; Sin Compasión; Todos Somos Estrellas*
Peru in film, *Aguirre, Wrath of God; El Dorado; The Golden Coach; The Last Movie; The Royal Hunt of the Sun; Sin Compasión*

Petrification, *The Monolith Monsters*

Philippines, in film, *American Guerilla in the Philippines; Bayan Ko: My Own Country; In the Navel of the Sea; Jaguar; Kisapmata; Manila by Night; Manila: In the Claws of Darkness; The Real Glory; Signed: Lino Brocka; The Story of Woo Viet*

Philippine cinema, *Bamboo Gods and Iron Men; Bayan Ko: My Own Country; Boatman; In the Navel of the Sea; Jaguar; Kisapmata; Manila by Night; Manila: In the Claws of Darkness; Midnight Dancers*

Photographers and photography, *The All-Round Reduced Personality – Redupers; Baba Yaga; Blow Up; The Bridges of Madison County; Calendar; Comrades; The Favour, the Watch and the Very Big Fish; A Great Day in Harlem; The Indian Fighter; J.A. Martin, Photographer; John Heartfield, Photomonteur; Liebestraum; Mahogany; Model; Model Shop; My Favourite Brunette; Proof; The Public Eye; Skyline; Under Fire; Visions of Light; Who Are You Polly Maggoo?; The Women on the Roof*

Piaf, Edith, films about, *Edith and Marcel; Piaf*

Picasso, Pablo, film about, *Le Mystère Picasso; Surviving Picasso*

Pickpockets, *Harry in Your Pocket; Oliver!; Oliver Twist* (Lean); *Oliver* (Donner); *Pickpocket; Pickup on South Street*

Pilots, see **Flying**

Pimps, *La Balance; Black Gunn; La Chienne; I'm Gonna Git You Sucka; Saint Jack*

Pink Panther films, *Curse of the Pink Panther; The Pink Panther; The Pink Panther Strikes Again; The Return of the Pink Panther; Revenge of the Pink Panther; A Shot in the Dark; Trail of the Pink Panther*

Pinter, Harold, films adapted from work, *Betrayal; The Birthday Party; The Caretaker; The Homecoming*

Pirandello, Luigi, films adapted from work, *As You Desire Me; Kaos*

Pirates, *Blackbeard's Ghost; Blackbeard the Pirate; The Black Pirate; The Black Swan; The Buccaneer; Captain Blood; China Seas; The Crimson Pirate; CutThroat Island; Frenchman's Creek; High Wind in Jamaica; The Island; Madame X; The Pirate; Pirates; Scalawag; The Sea Hawk; The Spanish Main; Swashbuckler; Treasure Island* (Heston); *Treasure Island* (Fridman); *Yellowbeard*

Pirosmani, film about, *Pirosmani*

Plagues (see also **Germ warfare**), *Mauvais Sang; No Blade of Grass; Outbreak; Panic in the Streets; Rabid; The Swarm; 12 Monkeys*

Planet of the Apes films, *Battle for the Planet of the Apes; Beneath the Planet of the Apes; Conquest of the Planet of the Apes; Escape from the Planet of the Apes; Planet of the Apes*

Plastic surgery, *Ash Wednesday; Dark Passage; Death Becomes Her; Doc Hollywood; First Yank into Tokyo; Johnny Handsome; Le Miroir a deux faces; Seconds; Shattered* (Petersen); *Stepfather III; A Woman's Face; Les Yeux sans Visage*

Poachers, *Barnabo of the Mountains; Danny the Champion of the World; Poachers; Where No Vultures Fly*

Poe, Edgar Allan
as character in film, etc, *The Mystery of Rampo; The Spectre of Edgar Allan Poe*
films adapted from work, *The Black Cat; Buried Alive; City Under the Sea; The Haunted Palace; Histoires Extraordinaires; House of Madness; The House of Usher; Masque of the Red Death; Murders in the Rue Morgue* (Florey) *Murders in the Rue Morgue* (Hessler); *The Oblong Box; The Pit and the Pendulum* (Corman); *The Pit and the Pendulum*

(Gordon); *The Premature Burial; The Raven* (Friedlander); *The Raven* (Corman); *Tale of a Vampire; Tales of Terror; The Tomb of Ligeia*

Poland, in film (see also **Polish cinema**), *And There Was Jazz; Ashes and Diamonds; Barrier; Blind Chance; Camera Buff; The Constant Factor; The Consul; The Contract; The Converted; Escape from the 'Liberty' Cinema; A Generation; The Grass Is Always Greener; Interrogation; Johnny Aquarius; Kanal; Kapo; Korczak; Krzysztof Kieslowski: I'm So So; Life at a Gallop; Lodz Ghetto; Loving the Dead; Man of Iron; Man of Marble; Miss Nobody; No End; 100 Years of Polish Cinema; Playing from Plates; The Road Home; Romance of a Horse Thief; Rough Treatment; Schindler's List; Shtetl; The Taste of the Black Earth; Temptation; Three Colours: White; To Be or Not To Be* (Lubitsch); *To Be or Not To Be* (Johnson); *To Kill a Priest; Top Dog; The Scar; The Warsaw Ghetto Uprising; A Woman on Her Own; A Year of the Quiet Sun*

Poles in Britain, *Moonlighting; Success Is the Best Revenge*

Police
Aust, *Deadly; Mr Reliable (a true story)*
Can, *Being at Home with Claude; Urinal*
China, *East Palace, West Palace; Rock n'Roll Cop*
Fr, *Au Nom de la Loi; La Balance; Le Cop; Le Cop 2; L.627; Mister Frost; Police*
GB, *The Adventures of PC 49; Blind Date* (Losey); *The Blue Lamp; Eyewitness* (Hough); *Hell Is a City; Hidden Agenda; i.d.; The Innocent Sleep; Juvenile Liaison; Juvenile Liaison 2; Inspector Clouseau; Ladder of Swords; Nobody Runs Forever; The Offence; The Spider and the Fly; Tank Malling; The Wrong Arm of the Law*
HK, *Before Dawn; Chungking Express; Crime Story; The Killer* (Woo); *Organized Crime and Triad Bureau; Police Story* (Chan); *Rock'n' Roll Cop; Task Force; Theft Under the Sun; The Wicked City*
Ind, *An Indian Story*
Ire, *The Playboys; The Run of the Country*
Isr, *One of Us*
It, *Illustrious Corpses; A Pure Formality; La Scorta; The Stolen Children*
Jap, *Hana-Bi; MARKS; The Most Terrible Time in My Life; An Obsession; The Outer Way; The Violent Cop*
Neth, *Beck; The Rape*
Mex, *Highway Patrolman*

SAf, *Bopha!; A Dry White Season; A Private Life*
Sp, *A Body in the Forest*
Swe, *The Man from Majorca; The Man on the Roof*
US– cops against the system, *Another 48 HRS; Basic Instinct; The Big Heat; Black Rain* (Scott); *Cobra* (Cosmatos); *Coogan's Bluff; Cop; The Custodian; The Dead Pool; Die Hard; Die Hard 2; Die Hard with a Vengeance; Dirty Harry; 8 Million Ways to Die; The Enforcer* (Fargo); *48 HRS; Hard to Kill; The January Man; Kuffs; Lethal Weapon; Lethal Weapon 2; Lethal Weapon 3; A Lovely Way to Die; McQ; Maniac Cop; Maniac Cop 2; Mulholland Falls; Next of Kin; Off Limits; On Dangerous Ground; Out for Justice; Physical Evidence; Prince of the City; The Punisher; Renegades; The Rookie; Serpico; Shakedown; Stone Cold; Tango & Cash; 10 to Midnight; Tightrope; The Violent Professionals; Warning Shot; Year of the Dragon*
– corruption, *Bad Lieutenant; The Captive City; CopLand; Cops and Robbers; Deep Cover; Everybody Wins; The Glass Shield; Harlem Nights; An Innocent Man; Internal Affairs; LA Confidential; The Last of the Finest; Money Train; Order of Death; Q & A; Ransom; Romeo Is Bleeding; Rush; Striking Distance; Touch of Evil; Unlawful Entry*
– futuristic/horrific, *Adrenalin – Fear the Rush; Dark Angel; Demolition Man; Fallen; Judge Dredd; Monolith; Nightbreed; Predator 2; RoboCop; RoboCop 2; RoboCop 3; Seven; Timecop*
– a policeman's lot, *Affliction; The Blue Knight; Bullets or Ballots; Busting; Chasers; The Choirboys; Colors; Cop & ½; The Dark Wind; Dead Bank; The Detective; Detective Story; Devil in a Blue Dress; The Devil's Own; Donato and Daughter; Exit to EdenThe First Power; Fort Apache – The Bronx; The Glimmer Man; The Glitter Dome; A Gnome Named Gnorm; The Hard Way; Heart Condition; Heat* (Mann); *Heaven's Prisoners; Homicide; In the Line of Fire; It Could Happen to You; Jennifer 8; The Killer Inside Me; Kindergarten Cop; K-9; Law and Order; Lone Star; A Low Down Dirty Shame; Miami Blues; The Mob; Mystery Street; National Lampoon's Loaded Weapon 1; The New Centurions; Newman's Law; No Mercy; Normal Life; One False Move; One Good Cop; Only the Lonely; The Onion Field; Police Academy; Policy Academy 2: Their First Assignment; Police Academy 3: Back in Training; Policy Academy 4: Citizens on Patrol; Policy Academy 5: Assignment Miami Beach;*

in US, *Alamo Bay; American Pictures; Amistad; Betrayed; Billy Two Hats; Birth of a Nation; Carbon Copy; The Chamber; Count a Lonely Cadence; The Defiant Ones; The Delta; Do the Right Thing; Dutchman; Freedom Road; Ghosts of Mississippi; The Glass Shield; Glory; Guess Who's Coming to Dinner; The Halliday Brand; Heart Condition; Imitation of Life* (Stahl); *Imitation of Life* (Sirk); *In the Heat of the Night; The Intruder; Intruder in the Dust; Iron Maze; James Baldwin; The Price of the Ticket; The Klansman; The Lawless; The Liberation of L.B. Jones; Lords of Discipline; Mississippi Burning; No Way Out* (Mankiewicz); *Odds Against Tomorrow; Once Upon a Time…When We Were Colored; Paris Trout; The Robin Hood of El Dorado; Running Brave; Sayonara; Sergeant Rutledge; Show Boat* (Whale); *Show Boat* (Sidney); *Soul Man; Thunderheart; A Time to Kill; To Kill a Mockingbird; The Unforgiven; Watermelon Man; The Well; White Dog; The Young One* in Zimbabwe, *The Green Grass Is Singing* reflections on, *Crusoe*

Radicalism/revolutionism,
1960s and after (see also **Sixties counter culture, State terror, Terrorism**)
in Algeria, *Frantz Fanon: Black Skin, White Mask*
in Britain, *Little Malcolm and His Struggle Against the Eunuchs; One Plus One; Praise Marx and Pass the Ammunition; The Revolutionary; Skinflicker*
in France, *Bof!; La Chinoise; Frantz Fanon: Black Skin, White Mask; Le Gai Savoir; Milou en mai; Nada; Themroc; Tout Va Bien; Vent d'Est; Vladimir et Rosa; Weekend*
in Germany, *Germany in Autumn; Melancholia; The Servicer; The Subjective Factor; The Third Generation*
in Italy, *Before the Revolution; China Is Near; Partner*
in Japan, *Diary of a Skinjuku Thief; The Empty Table; The Man Who Left His Will on Film; Throw Away Your Books, Let's Go into the Streets*
in Switzerland, *Charles Dead or Alive; Jonah, Who Will Be 25 in the Year 2000; Le Retour d'Afrique*
in US, *Abduction; Born on the Fourth of July; Drive, He Said; The Enforcer* (Fargo); *Far from Vietnam; Flashback; Getting Straight; Manufacturing Consent: Noam Chomsky and the Media; Medium Cool; 1969; One PM; Patty Hearst; Route One/USA; Rude Awakening; Running on Empty; '68; Underground* (de Antonio)

Radiguet, Raymond, film adapted from work, *Le Diable au corps*

Radio broadcasting, in film, *Airheads; Break of Dawn; Broadway Bound; Citizens Band; Comfort and Joy; The Contact; Death at Broadcasting House; A Face in the Crowd; The Fisher King; FM; Good Morning Vietnam; Grosse Pointe Blank; Once Upon a Honeymoon; Out of Order* (Turpie); *Play Misty for Me; Private Parts; Pump Up the Volume; Radio Days; Radioland Murders; Straight Talk; Talk Radio; The Truth About Cats & Dogs; Tune in Tomorrow; The Unsuspected; Voice Over; WUSA; Young Soul Rebels*

Railways
in Britain, *The First Great Train Robbery; The Last Journey; Oh, Mr Porter!; The Railway Children; Seven Sinners* (de Courville); *Terror by Night; The Titfield Thunderbolt; Train of Events*
in Canada, *Terror Train*
in China, *Shanghai Express*
in Czechoslovakia, *Closely Observed Trains*
in Europe (international), *Avalanche Express; The Cassandra Crossing; The Lady Vanishes* (Hitchcock); *The Lady Vanishes* (Page); *Murder on the Orient Express; Les Rendez-vous d'Anna; Trans-Europ-Express*
in France, *La Bataille du Rail; The Man Who Watched Trains Go By; Subway; Those Who Love Me Will Take the Train; The Train*
in Germany, *Europa; Night Train to Munich*
in India, *North West Frontier*
in Japan, *Angel Dust; The Bullet Train*
in US, *Breakheart Pass; Emperor of the North Pole; Finders Keepers; The General* (Keaton/Bruckman); *Grand Central Murder; The Great K & A Train Robbery; The Great Scout and Cathouse; Thursday; Human Desire; The Iron Horse; Money Train; The Narrow Margin; Narrow Margin; Runaway Train; Silver Streak; Subway Riders; The Taking of Pelham One Two Three; The Tall Target; Tracks; Under Siege 2; Union Station*
in USSR, *Joan of Arc of Mongolia*

Rain forests (see also **Jungle dramas**)
Amazonia, Aguirre, Wrath of God; Amazonia: Voices from the Rainforest; At Play in the Fields of the Lord; Burden of Dreams; El Dorado; The Emerald Forest; Fitzcarraldo; Jungle 2 Jungle; Macunaíma; Medicine Man; The Mission
other, *FernGully: The Last Rainforest; The Shark Callers of Kontu*

Rand, Ayn, films adapted from work, *The Fountainhead; We the Living*

Ransley, Peter, film adapted from work, *The Hawk*

Ransome, Arthur, film adapted from work, *Swallows and Amazons*

Rap films, *Beat Street; Body Rock; D.C. Cab; Fear of a Black Hat; House Party; Juice; Krush Groove; New Jack City; Out of Order* (Turpie); *Rappin; Trespass; Wild Style*

Rape, *The Accused; Act of Vengeance; Bad Lieutenant; La Bête; Bone; Casualties of War; The Everlasting Secret Family; Extremities; Eyes of a Stranger; Handgun* (Garnett); *Hannie Caulder; Humanoids from the Deep; Incubus; Intimate Confessions of a Chinese Courtesan; Jackson County Jail; Kika; Lipstick; Madonna of the Seven Moons; Die Marquise von O…; The Moon in the Gutter; Mourir à Tue-Tête; Ms .45; Not a Pretty Picture; Pepi, Luci, Bom…; A Petal; The Rape; Revenge* (Hayers); *Sanctuary; Shame; Thelma & Louise; Village in the Mist; The Virgin Spring; Voice Over*

Rasputin, Grigori, films about, *Agony; Nicholas and Alexandra; Rasputin and the Empress*

Rastafarians, *Heartland Reggae; Rockers*

Rattigan, Terence, films adapted from work, *Bequest to the Nation; The Browning Version* (Asquith); *The Browning Version* (Figgis); *French Without Tears; The Prince and the Showgirl*

Ray, Nicholas, film about, *Lightning over Water*

Rednecks, hostile, *Death Trap; Deliverance; Easy Rider; The Final Terror; Fighting Mad; Hunter's Blood; Leatherface; The Texas Chainsaw Massacre III; Lolly-Madonna XXX; Murder, He Says; Open Season; Southern Comfort; Tank; The Texas Chainsaw Massacre; The Texas Chainsaw Massacre 2; Walking Tall*

Reed, John, films about, *Reds; Reed: Insurgent Mexico*

Reform schools, etc, *Bad Boys; Buried Alive; Forever Mary; Freedom Is Paradise; The Loneliness of the Long Distance Runner; The Mayor of Hell; Scrubbers; Scum; Shout; Sleepers; Summer School; Tattooed Tears*

Refuse collectors, *Men at Work*

Reggae music, *Bongo Man; Exodus – Bob Marley Live; The Harder They Come; Heartland Reggae; The Lunatic; Reggae; Reggae Sunsplash II; Rockers; Roots Rock Reggae; Stepping Razor – Red X; Time Will Tell*

Reich, Wilhelm, film about, *W.R. – Mysteries of the Organism*

Reincarnation, *The Alchemist; Audrey Rose; The Awakening; Chances Are; Dead Again; I Married a Witch; The Mummy* (Freund); *On a Clear Day You Can See Forever; The Reincarnation of Peter Proud; Rouge; The Wraith*

Religion, Christian (for non-Christian religions see individual listings; see also **Angels and divine manifestations, Biblical stories, God, Jesus Christ, Missionaires**)
Catholicism, *Absolution; The Addiction; The Agony and the Ecstasy; Alive; Anchoress; L'Appel du Silence; L'Auberge Rouge; The Audience; Augustine of Hippo; Bad Lieutenant; The Bells of St Mary's; Bernadette; The Bishop's Story; Black Robe; Brother Orchid; Brother Sun, Sister Moon; Camila; Cammina Cammina; The Cardinal; Child's Play* (Lumet); *The Chocolate War; Communion; Daens; Dekalog 8: 'Thou shalt not bear false witness'; The Devils; The Devil's Playground; Diary of a Country Priest; Edge of Doom; Father Brown; La Faute de l'Abbé Mouret; The Favour, the Watch and the Very Big Fish; The First Legion; The First Power; Foul Play; Four Days in July; The Fourth Man; Francesco, giullare di Dio; The Fugitive* (Ford); *Full Confession; Galileo* (Cavani); *Galileo* (Losey); *The Garden of Allah; The Godfather Part III; God Told Me To; Going My Way; Hail, Mary; The Heart of the Matter; Heaven Help Us; Heavenly Pursuits; The Heritage; House of Mortal Sin; I Confess; In the Name of the Father* (Bellocchio); *It's a 2'6" Above the Ground World; I, the Worst of All; Jeanne la Pucelle; Jesus of Montreal; Juliet of the Spirits; Lamb; The Left Hand of God; The Legend of the Holy Drinker; Leon Morin, Priest; Lilies; A Man for All Seasons; A Man Named John; The Mission; Monsignor; Nazarin; Night Sun; La Passion de Jeanne d'Arc; Paulina 1880; Pieces of Dreams; Pope Joan; The Pope Must Die; Priest; The Prisoner; Queens of the Big Time; The Refusal; La Reine Margot; Repossessed; Romero; The Rosary Murders; The Runner Stumbles; Russicum; Saint Joan; Saving Grace; The*

films, *ABBA – The Movie; Big Time; Black Wax; Born to Boogie; Bring on the Night; Completely Pogued; The Concert for Bangladesh; CS Blues; Culture Club – A Kiss Across the Ocean; The Cure in Orange; The Cure Show; Dance Craze; The Decline of Western Civilization; The Decline of Western Civilization Part II; Divine Madness; Don't Look Back; Eric Clapton and His Rolling Hotel; Exodus – Bob Marley Live; Fillmore; From Russia with Rock; Get Back; Gimme Shelter; Home of the Brave; Imagine; Jimi Hendrix; Jimi Plays Berkeley; The Kids Are Alright; Ladies and Gentlemen, The Rolling Stones; The Last Waltz; Let It Be; Let's Spend the Night Together; Mad Dogs and Englishmen; Message of Love; The Isle of Wight Festival; Monterey Pop; Moonwalker; No Nukes; One Plus One; One-Trick Pony; Pink Floyd Live at Pompeii; Pop Gear; Prince – Sign o' the Times; The Punk Rock Movie; Rockshow; Rough Cut and Ready Dubbed; Rust Never Sleeps; Soft on the Inside; Soigne ta Droite; The Song Remains the Same; Stop Making Sense; Truth or Dare; 200 Motels; U2 Rattle and Hum; Wayne's World II; The Wizard of Waukesha; Woodstock; Woodstock: The Director's Cut; Year of the Horse; Yessongs; Ziggy Stardust and the Spiders from Mars* films about rock/pop world, *The Adventures of Ford Fairlane; Backbeat; Beyond the Valley of the Dolls; Breaking Glass; The Bodyguard; Buddy's Song; Candy Mountain; Catch Us If You Can; The Commitments; Dead Beat; The Doors; Fast Forward; The Five Heartbeats; Four Flies on Grey Velvet; Grace of My Heart; Hairspray; Heartbreakers; Hearts of Fire; Heaven Tonight; Home Before Midnight; It's All Happening; I Wanna Hold Your Hand; Jungle Story; Labyrinth of Passion; Leningrad Cowboys Go America; More Bad News; Parking; Pelvis; Performance; Phantom of the Paradise; Play It Cool; Privilege* (Watkins); *Renaldo and Clara; Roadie; The Rose; Rude Boy; Satisfaction; Singles; 6.5 Special; Smithereens; Spice World; Stardust; Starstruck; Superstar: The Karen Carpenter Story; Take It or Leave It; Tapeheads; This Is Spinal Tap; Thunder Alley; Tina: What's Love Got to Do With It; Tokyo Pop; Trick or Treat; Velvet Goldmine; The Wedding Singer; Welcome to L.A.; Who Is Harry Kellerman and Why Is He Saying Those Terrible Things About Me?; Wild in the Streets; Wild West; The*

Year of My Japanese Cousin; You Light Up My Life; Zazie rock/pop musicals, *All This and World War Two; Body Rock; Breakin'; The Butterfly Ball; Can't Stop the Music; Catch My Soul; Ferry Cross the Mersey; Flame; Flashdance; Girls Just Want to Have Fun; A Hard Day's Night; Head; Help!; It Couldn't Happen Here; The Music Machine; Never Too Young to Rock; Pink Floyd; The Wall; Purple Rain; Quadrophenia; Rock'n'Roll High School; The Rocky Horror Picture Show; Rooftops; Saturday Night Fever; Sergeant Pepper's Lonely Hearts Club Band; Staying Alive; A Swingin' Summer; Thank God It's Friday; Three for All; Times Square; Tommy; Under the Cherry Moon*

Rock'n'roll
original '50s, *Bye Bye Birdie; Don't Knock the Rock; The Girl Can't Help It; Go, Johnny Go!; Idle on Parade; Jailhouse Rock; King Creole; Rock, Rock, Rock* nostalgia, *American Hot Wax; La Bamba; The Buddy Holly Story; Cry-Baby; Eddie and the Cruisers; Elvis; Grease; Grease 2; Great Balls of Fire!; That'll Be the Day; That Thing You Do!* documentaries and concert films, *Elvis on Tour; Elvis – That's the Way It Is; Glastonbury: The Movie; Hail Hail! Rock'n'Roll; Let the Good Times Roll; The London Rock and Roll Show; This Is Elvis*

Rodeos, *8 Seconds; F.T.W.; The Honkers; Junior Bonner; J.W. Coop; The Lusty Men; The Misfits; My Heroes Have Always Been Cowboys; When the Legends Die*

Rodgers, Richard and Hammerstein, Oscar, musicals by, *Carousel; The King and I; Oklahoma; South Pacific* and Hart, Lorenz, musicals by, *Babes in Arms; Billy Rose's Jumbo; Hallelujah, I'm a Bum; Love Me Tonight; Pal Joey*

Rodin, Auguste, film about, *Camille Claudel*

Rohmer, Sax, films adapted from work, *The Bride of Fu Manchu; The Face of Fu Manchu; The Fiendish Plot of Dr Fu Manchu; The Mask of Fu Manchu*

Roller skating, *Derby; Kansas City Bomber; Rollerball; Solarbabies; Xanadu*

The Rolling Stones, films about/in performance, *CS Blues; Gimme Shelter; Ladies and Gentlemen, The Rolling Stones; Let's Spend the Night Together; One Plus One*

Rollins, Tim, film about, *Kids of Survival: The Art and Life of Tim Rollins & K.O.S.*

Romania
Romania in film, *Gadjo Dilo; Requiem for Dominic; Too Late; Two Deaths; An Unforgettable Summer* Romanian cinema, *Too Late; An Unforgettable Summer*

Rome, Ancient, and Roman Empire, *The Arena; Asterix and the Big Fight; Asterix Conquers America; Asterix in Britain; Augustine of Hippo; Barabbas; Ben-Hur* (Niblo); *Ben-Hur* (Wyler); *Caesar and Cleopatra; Caligula; Cleopatra* (DeMille); *Cleopatra* (Mankiewicz); *Demetrius and the Gladiators; The Fall of the Roman Empire; Fellini-Satyricon; Fiddlers Three; A Funny Thing Happened on the Way to the Forum; History Lessons; Julius Caesar; Jupiter's Darling; Mamma Roma; Masada; Quo Vadis?; The Robe; Roman Scandals; Sebastiane; The Sign of the Cross; Sign of the Gladiator; The Sign of the Pagan; Spartacus; Three Ages; The Twelve Tasks of Asterix*

Rome, post-Roman empire, in film
pre-1900, *The Agony and the Ecstasy*
20th cent, *Bellissima; Bits and Pieces; Brutti, sporchi e cattivi; La Dolce Vita; Era Notte a Roma; Fellini's Roma; Ginger and Fred; Il Giorno della prima di 'Close Up'; La Luna; Night on Earth; Roma, Città Aperta; Roman Holiday; The Roman Spring of Mrs Stone; Russicum; School; The Shoes of the Fisherman; Tenebrae; Terminal Station; Three Coins in the Fountain; 20 Million Miles to Earth; Two Weeks in Another Town; The White Sheik; Whoever Says the Truth Will Die*

Rostand, Edmond, films adapted from work, *Cyrano de Bergerac; Roxanne*

Roth, Joseph, film adapted from work, *The Legend of the Holy Drinker*

Roth, Philip, film adapted from work, *Goodbye Columbus*

Rothschild family, film about, *The House of Rothschild*

Rousseau, Jean-Jacques, film about, *The Roads of Exile*

Royalty (see also **British history**)
British, *King Ralph; Royal Wedding; The Mudlark; 25 Years* generic, *Roman Holiday*

Runaways, teenage (see also **Adolescence, Teenagers and teen movies**),

Blackout; A Boy Called Hate; Butterfly (Sarno); *The Delinquents; Foxes; Hardcore; Runners; Mandragora; Marie s'en va-t-en ville; Streetwise; Taking Off; Times Square; Vagabonde; Without a Trace*

Runyon, Damon, films adapted from/based on work, *Bloodhounds of Broadway; Guys and Dolls; Lady for a Day; Lady by Choice; Little Miss Marker; A Slight Case of Murder*

Rural life
in Algeria, *The Citadel* (Chouikh); *Ramparts of Clay* in Australia, *Sunday Too Far Away; We of the Never Never* in Bolivia, *The Secret Nation* in Britain, *Akenfield; All Creatures Great and Small; Cold Comfort Farm; Dakota Road; Danny the Champion of the World; Dulcima; Far From the Madding Crowd; The Farmer's Wife; Gone to Earth; Ill Fares the Land; It Shouldn't Happen to a Vet; On the Black Hill; Requiem for a Village; Tess; Waterland; The Woodlanders* in Burkina Faso, *Tilaï; Yaaba* in Canada, *The Sweet Hereafter; Why Shoot the Teacher* in China, *Bloody Morning; The Girls to Be Married; The Good Earth; Old Well; Raise the Red Lantern; Red Sorghum; Sacrificed Youth; The Story of Qiu Ju; Yellow Earth* in Colombia, *A Matter of Honour* in Czechoslovakia, *All My Good Countrymen; Cutting It Short; Seclusion Near a Forest* in Denmark, *Babette's Feast; Pelle the Conqueror* in Finland, *Earth Is a Sinful Song; Täällä Pohjantähden alla* in France, *Le Beau Serge; Le Cheval d'Orgueil; Farrebique; La Femme du Boulanger; La Fiancée du Pirate; Goupi-Mains-Rouges; Inutile Envoyer Photo; Jean de Florette; Jour de Fête; Madame Bovary* (Renoir); *Madame Bovary* (Chabrol); *Manon des Sources; One Deadly Summer; Spring into Summer; Will It Snow for Christmas?* in Germany, *The Sudden Fortune of the Good People of Kombach* in Iceland, *Land and Sons* in India, *The Bogey Man; The Boon; Genesis; Pather Panchali; The Village Has No Walls* in Iran, *The Cow* in Ireland, *Clash of the Ash; The Field; Fools of Fortune; The Playboys* in Italy, *Christ Stopped at Eboli; The Tree of Wooden Clogs* in Japan, *Peasants of the Second Fortress; Sleeping Man; Village of Dreams* in Netherlands, *Antonia's Line; The Northerners* in New Zealand, *Came a Hot*

Don't Cry; The Bridal Path; Circle of Danger; Geordie; Laxdale Hall; The 'Maggie'; Ring of Bright Water; Rockets Galore; Tunes of Glory; The Wicker Man; X the Unknown
1980s–1990s, Betty's Brood; The Big Man; Blue Black Permanent; Breaking the Waves; Carla's Song; Comfort and Joy; Conquest of the South Pole; Gregory's Girl; Local Hero; Loch Ness; The Near Room; Play Me Something; Restless Natives; Soft Top, Hard Shoulder; Small Faces; So I Married an Axe Murderer; Staggered; That Sinking Feeling; Tickets for the Zoo; Trainspotting; Wild Flowers (Smith); The Winter Guest

Scott, Walter, films adapted from work, The Adventures of Quentin Durward; Ivanhoe

Sea dramas (see also **Submarines, Undersea worlds**)
wartime, service, etc, Above Us the Waves; Action in the North Atlantic; Away All Boats; The Bedford Incident; The Battle of the River Plate; The Battleship Potemkin; Blue Peter; The Boat; The Boat: The Director's Cut; The Bounty; The Bridges at Tokyo-Ri; The Caine Mutiny; Captain Horatio Hornblower; Carry on Admiral; Cockleshell Heroes; Corvette K-225; Crimson Tide; The Cruel Sea; The Enemy Below; Ensign Pulver; Follow the Fleet; Forever England; Gray Lady Down; Hell and High Water; Here Come the Waves; HMS Defiant; The Hunt for Red October; In Harm's Way; In Which We Serve; Islands in the Stream; The Key; Mister Roberts; Morning Departure; Murphy's War; Mutiny on the Bounty (Lloyd); Mutiny on the Bounty (Milestone); Navy Seals; Operation Petticoat; An Officer and a Gentleman; Perfect Strangers; Petticoat Pirates; Remembrance (Gregg); Submarine Patrol; They Were Expendable; Under Siege; The Wackiest Ship in the Army; Watch Your Stern; Yangtse Incident
other, Alone on the Pacific; Amistad; Assault on a Queen; Atlantic Adventure; Beyond the Poseidon Adventure; Blue Black Permanent; Captain Ron; Captains Courageous; The Captain's Table; China Seas; Cinderella Liberty; Dead Calm; The Dove; Edge of the World; Fanny; Ferry to Hong Kong; The Ghost Ship; A Girl in Every Port; Golden Rendezvous; Jaws; Jaws 2; Jaws – The Revenge; Juggernaut; King of Alcatraz; The Last Voyage; Lifeboat; The Long Voyage Home; Lord Jim; The Lost Continent; The Mad Doctor of Market Street; Manuela;

Moby Dick; The Navigator; A Night to Remember; No Answer from F.P.1; The Old Man and the Sea; Orca; Outward Bound; Passage Home; Pirates; The Poseidon Adventure; Raise the Titanic!; Race for the Yankee Zephyr; San Demetrio, London; Saps at Sea; Savage Islands; The Sea Chase; The Sea Wolf; Ship of Fools; The Ship That Died of Shame; Sentimental Journey; Si tous les gars du monde…; S.O.S. Titanic; Three Crowns for the Sailor; Titanic (Negulesco); Titanic (Cameron); Treasure Island (Heston); Treasure Island (Fridman); Triple Bogey on a Par Five Hole; Tugboat Annie; Two Years Before the Mast; The Viking Women and Their Voyage to the Waters of the Great Sea Serpent; Waterworld; Western Approaches; White Squall; Wind; Windbag the Sailor; The Windjammer

Seale, Bobby, film adout, Panther

Searle, Ronald
film based on cartoons, The Belles of St Trinian's; Blue Murder at St Trinian's; The Pure Hell of St Trinian's; The Wildcats of St Trinian's
film designed by, Dick Deadeye, or Duty Done

Segal, Erich, films adapted from work, Love Story; Oliver's Story

Selby Jr, Hubert, film adapted from work, Last Exit to Brooklyn

Senegalese cinema, Black Girl; Camp Thiaroye; Ceddo; Emitai; Le Franc; Hyenas; The Money Order; Xala

Sensory awareness, How Does It Feel?

Serbia
Serbia, film about, Pretty Village, Pretty Flame
Serbian cinema, Ghetto

Serial killers, see **Psychopaths and serial killers**

Sex changes and trans-formations (see also **Hermaphroditism**), The Christine Jorgensen Story; Come Back to the 5 and Dime, Different for Girls; Jimmy Dean, Jimmy Dean; Dr Jekyll and Sister Hyde; Dog Day Afternoon; In a Year with 13 Moons; I Want What I Want; The Law of Desire; Myra Breckenridge; Orlando; Shadey; Swordsman II; The World According to Garp
by divine/supernatural intervention, Switch; Turnabout

Sex films, Anita; Au Pair Girls; La Bête; Bisexual; Black Emanuelle; Blue Belle; Bolero

(Derek); La Bonzesse; Café Flesh; Candido Erotico; Celestine, Maid at Your Service; Climax; Confessions of a Window Cleaner; Cousins in Love; The Crush; Cry Uncle; The Deadly Females; Deadly Weapons; The Devil in Miss Jones; The Devil in Miss Jones II; Double Agent 73; Emanuelle and the Last Cannibals; Emmanuelle; Emmanuelle 2; Emmanuelle in Tokyo; Erotic Quartet; Erotique; Female Perversions; Female Vampires; First Time with Feeling; The Fruits of Passion; Girl on a Motorcycle; Goodbye Emmanuelle; House of Whipcord; How Sweet Is Her Valley; I Am Frigid...Why?; Inhibitions; Insatiable; Invitation to Bed; Is There Sex After Marriage?; Jamón, Jamón; Le Journal de Lady M; Joy; Laura (Hamilton); Love in a Women's Prison; Lust and Desire; Madame Claude; Maid for Pleasure; Oh! Calcutta!; Memories within Miss Aggie; My Tutor; Nana (Wolman); New York Nights; Penelope 'Pulls It Off'; Prison Girls; Private Lessons; Quiet Days in Clichy; Le Rempart de Béguines; Road to Salina; Sadistic City; Sex Play; Sixth Form Girls; Showgirls; Snatched; Street Girls; Student Teachers; Succubus; Super 8½ Swedish Massage Parlour; There's No Sex Like Snow Sex; Thundercrack!; Through the Looking Glass; Tierische Liebe; Till Sex Us Do Part; Together; Turkish Delight; The True Story of Eskimo Nell; Under the Doctor; Vanessa; The Violation of Justine; A Virgin for Saint Tropez; The Virgin Machine; The Visitor; Viva Erotica!

Sex industry (see also **Prostitution**), Boatman; Boogie Nights; Compromising Positions; Dyn Amo; Family Viewing; The Full Monty; Get Carter; The Glitter Dome; Hardcore; Inserts; Kamikaze Hearts; The Keyhole; Out of the Dark; Not a Love Story; The Playbirds; Promise Her Anything; Rate It X; Skinless Night; Star 80; Variety

Sex therapists and sexology, The Chapman Report; Everything You Always Wanted to Know About Sex, But Were Afraid to Ask; The Harrad Experiment; I Am a Sex Addict; I Will...I Will...for Now; Sex and the Single Girl

The Sex Pistols, film about, The Great Rock'n'Roll Swindle; Sid and Nancy

Sexual repression, A Double Tour; The Citadel (Chouikh); Claire's Knee; Cockfighter; Crimes of Passion; The Criminal Life of Archibaldo de la Cruz; Different for Girls; El; Empire of Passion; The

Ice Palace (Blom); Intersection; Man from Africa and Girl from India; Paulina; La Senyora; Tierische Liebe; Tristana; That Obscure Object of Desire; You're a Big Boy Now

Sexuality, explorations of
Aus, Tierische Liebe; The Unfish
Aust, Sirens; The Umbrella Woman
Bel, Je tu il elle; The Sexual Life of the Belgians 1950–1978
Braz, The Oyster and the Wind
Can, Dreamlife; Eclipse; Family Viewing; Head On; In Praise of Older Women; Kissed; Paris France; 90 Days; A Winter Tan

China Yang ± Yin: Gender in Chinese Cinema
Cuba, One Way or Another
Czech, Conspirators of Pleasure
Fr, Les Amants; Amateur; Annabelle partagée; The Best Way to Walk; La Bête; Bitter Moon; Boy Meets Girl (Carax); Charlotte; Un Coeur qui bat; La Collectionneuse; Emmène-moi; A Flame in My Heart; Glissements Progressifs du Plaisir; The Hairdresser's Husband; Immoral Tales; Joy; La Lectrice; The Man Who Loved Women (Truffaut); The Mother and the Whore; Néa; N'oublie pas que tu vas mourir; Le Parfum d'Yvonne; The Pillow Book; Pussy Talk; Requiem pour un Vampire; La Ronde; Sweet Movie; Tango; Les Valseuses; La Vie de Jésus; Virgin (Breillat)
GB, Amateur; The Big Swap; Breaking the Waves; Captives; The Collector; The Cook, the Thief, His Wife and Her Lover; Daddy; Different for Girls; Further and Particular; I Am a Sex Addict; Inserts; Intimate Relations; Justine; Lady Chatterley's Lover; Look Me in the Eye; Middleton's Changeling; Naked; The Pillow Book; The Playmaker; The Pleasure Principle; The Rainbow; Twenty-One; Under the Skin; The Virgin and the Gypsy; Women in Love
Ger, Anita; Dances of Vice; Blue Angel; Dance of Love; My Father Is Coming; 3 Women in Love; A Woman in Flames
HK, Hold You Tight
Hun, The Witman Boys
Ind, Kama Sutra: A Tale of Love
It, The Black Holes; Casanova 70; Fellini-Satyricon; Fellini's Casanova; The Last Woman; Malizia; The Naples Connection; Senso; La Signora di Tutti; Stealing Beauty; What?
Jap, Ai No Corrida; Diary of a Shinjuku Thief; Empire of Passion; The Hair Opera; Heart Beating in the Dark; Irezumi – Spirit of Tattoo; Like Grains of Sand; Woman of the Dunes
Mex, Homework
Neth, Au Revoir; The Pillow Book

Beudet; Le Tournoi; Le s
Vampires
Ger, Diary of a Lost Girl;
Faust (Murnau); The Last
Laugh; Die Nibelungen;
Nosferatu – Eine Symphonie
des Grauens; Pandora's Box;
People on Sunday; Secrets of
a Soul; Die Spinnen; Spione;
Waxworks; Die Weber;
Woman in the Moon
GB, Champagne; The
Farmer's Wife; The Lodger;
The Manxman; Piccadilly;
The Rat; The Ring;
Underground (Asquith)
Jap, Crossways; I Was Born,
But...; A Page of Madness
Swe, The Outlaw and His
Wife; Witchcraft Through the
Ages
US, Beggars of Life; Ben-Hur
(Niblo); The Big Parade
(Vidor); The Birth of a
Nation; Blind Husbands;
Blood and Sand; Broken
Blossoms (Griffith); By the
Law; The Cameraman;
Camille; The Cobra; The
Crowd; Dr Jekyll and Mr Hyde
(Robertson); The Eagle; Easy
Virtue; Flesh and the Devil;
Foolish Wives; The General
(Keaton/Bruckman); A Girl in
Every Port; The Gold Rush;
Go West; The Great K & A
Train Robbery; He Who Gets
Slapped; Intolerance; The Isle
of Love; The Kid Brother;
The Kiss (Feyder); The Last
Command; The Merry-Go-
Round; The Merry Widow;
The Phantom of the Opera;
Sadie Thompson; Safety Last;
Sally of the Sawdust; Salome;
The Salvation Hunters; The
Saphead; The Scarlet Letter
(Sjöström); Spite Marriage;
Steamboat Bill; Seven
Chances; 7th Heaven
(Borzage); Show People;
Sunrise; The Thief of Bagdad
(Walsh); Three Ages; Twin
Pawns; The Unholy Three
(Browning); The Unknown;
Way Down East; The
Wedding March; Why
Worry?; The Wind (Sjöström);
A Woman of Paris
USSR, Battleship Potemkin;
The Devil's Wheel; Earth; The
Dying Swan; The End of St
Petersburg; The Fall of the
Romanov Dynasty;
Happiness; The House on
Trubnaya; The Man with the
Movie Camera; Mother
(Pudovkin); The New
Babylon; Strike
modern silents, Careful; Film;
The Island (Shindo); Sidewalk
Stories; Silent Movie; The
Thief

Sillitoe, Alan, films adapted
from work, The Loneliness of
the Long Distance Runner;
The Ragman's Daughter;
Saturday Night and Sunday
Morning

Simenon, Georges, films
adapted from work, Le Chat;
En Cas de Malheur; L'Etoile
du Nord; L'Horloger de St
Paul; The Man Who
Watched Trains Go By;
Monsieur Hire; La Neige
était sale; La Nuit du
Carrefour; Temptation
Harbour

Simon, Neil, films adapted
from work, Barefoot in the
Park; Biloxi Blues; Brighton
Beach Memoirs; Broadway
Bound; California Suite;
Chapter Two; The Cheap
Detective; Come Blow Your
Horn; The Goodbye Girl;
The Heartbreak Kid; I
Ought to be in Pictures; The
Last of the Red Hot Lovers;
The Marrying Man; The
Odd Couple; Only When I
Laugh; The Out-of-Towners;
Plaza Suite; Seems Like Old
Times

Singapore
Singapore cinema, Bugis
Street; Mee Pok Man; 12
Storeys
Singapore, in film, Bugis
Street; Fatal Reaction:
Singapore; Saint Jack; 12
Storeys; World for Ransom

Singer, Isaac Bashevis, films
adapted from work,
American Stories; Enemies,
a Love Story; The Musician
of Lublin; Yentl

Singles bars, Looking for Mr
Goodbar

Sisters, relationships between
(see also **Brothers, Sisters
and brothers**), Angela;
Careful, He Might Hear You;
Crimes of the Heart; Diabolo
Menthe; Female Perversions;
The German Sisters; Gert
and Daisy's Weekend;
Happiness; Hotel Sorrento;
The House of Bernarda
Alba; In This Our Life; The
Last Days of Chez Nous;
Little Women (Cukor); Little
Women (Armstrong); The
Mafu Cage; The Man I Love;
Marvin's Room; The Moon
Has Risen; My Sister Eileen;
My 20th Century; Nénette et
Boni; sex, lies and videotape;
The Silence; Sisters; The
Sisters; Sisters or the
Balance of Happiness;
Slightly Scarlet; Some Girls;
Sweetie; Three Sisters
(Olivier); Three Sisters (von
Trotta); Under the Skin; The
Whales of August

Sisters and brothers,
relationships between, China
Is Near; Close My Eyes;
Daddy's Dyin' – Who's Got
the Will?; Dead Liqueur; El
Norte; Jack Be Nimble;
Jacknife; Leap into the Void;
The Legend of Billy Jean;
Love Streams; Ma Saison
Préférée; Mullaway; Organ;
The Prince of Tides; Select
Hotel; Speaking Parts; The
Strange Affair of Uncle
Harry; Tokyo Kyodai; Triple
Bogey on a Par Five Hole

Sixties counterculture
(see also **Radicalism/
revolutionism**)
Can, Comic Book
Confidential; The True
Nature of Bernadette
Fr, La Fiancée du Pirate; Girl
on a Motorcycle; La Vallée
GB, Donald Cammell: The
Ultimate Performance; Last
Day of Summer; Petulia;

Tonite Let's All Make Love
in London; The White Bus
Port, Doc's Kingdom
US, Alice's Restaurant;
Between the Lines; The Big
Chill; The Big Fix; The Blues
Brothers; Bob and Carol and
Ted and Alice; BS I Love
You; Bunny O'Hare; Cheech
and Chong's Next Movie;
Chelsea Girls; Ciao
Manhattan; David
Holtzman's Diary; Doc's
Kingdom; Don't Make
Waves; The Doors;
Dynamite Chicken; Easy
Rider; Fritz the Cat; Girl on
a Motorcycle; Gas-s-s-s, or It
Became Necessary to Destroy
the World in Order to Save
It; Getting Straight; The
Graduate; Greetings; The
Guru; Hair; Head; Heavy
Traffic; How to Commit
Marriage; I Love You Alice
B; Toklas; Jimi Plays
Berkeley; Kitchen
(Warhol/Tavel); Lonesome
Cowboys; Manson;
Milestones; Monterey Pop;
1969; Nobody's Fool; The
Nine Lives of Fritz the Cat;
Out; Psych-Out; Purple Haze;
Return Engagement; Return
of the Secaucus Seven; Rude
Awakening; The Sandpiper;
'68; Sunshine; Snshine Part
II; Taking Off; The Trip; We
Can't Go Home Again; Wild
in the Streets; Woodstock;
Woodstock: The Director's
Cut; You're a Big Boy Now
Yugo, W.R. – Mysteries of
the Organism

Sjöwall and Wahlöö, films
adapted from work, The
Laughing Policeman; The
Man from Mallorca; The
Man on the Roof

Skateboarding, Gleaming the
Cube; Skateboard

Skiing, Avalanche; Black
Diamond Rush; Downhill
Racer; The Great Ecstasy of
Woodcarver Steiner; Hot
Dog...The Movie; The Other
Side of the Mountain; The
Ski Bum; Ski Patrol

Slavery
in Africa, Amistad; Cobra
Verde; Sankofa; The Silences
of the Palace
in American South, The
Autobiography of Miss Jane
Pittman; Freedom Road;
Jefferson in Paris;
Mandingo; Slavers; Song of
the South; Uncle Tom
in ancient world, The Arena;
Spartacus
in Caribbean, Blacksnake
in China, Buddha's Lock
white, Harem

Slaughterhouses, Meat

Slovakian cinema, The
Garden

Small town life
in Argentina, A Place in the
World
in Australia, Deadly; Shame
in Canada, The Bay Boy; Bye
Bye Blues; Paperback Hero
in China, Ju Dou
in Czechoslovakia, Capricious

Summer; The Firemen's Ball
in France, Uranus
in Germany, The Nasty Girl
in Italy, Cinema Paradiso;
Cinema Paradiso: The
Special Edition; Splendor; I
Vitelloni
in Japan, The Outer Way
in US, Affliction; All the Right
Moves; Arachnophobia; Baby
Blue Marine; The Best of
Times; Beyond the Forest;
The Blob; Blue Velvet; The
'burbs; Bus Riley's Back in
Town; Citizen's Band; Clash
By Night; Confessions of a
Suburban Girl; Dadetown; A
Dangerous Woman; Doc
Hollywood; Earth vs the
Spider; Edward
Scissorhands; The Experts;
Full Moon in Blue Water;
God's Country; Gremlins;
Groundhog Day; Halloween;
Halloween 4; The Return of
Michael Myers; Halloween:
The Curse of Michael Myers;
Heavy; Henry Fool; The Hot
Spot; The Ice Storm; It's a
Gift; It's a Wonderful Life;
It's the Old Army Game; I
Want You; Kid; Has
Anybody Seen My Gal?; Lady
in White; The Last Picture
Show; The Lawless;
Liebestraum; Lone Star;
Meet Me at the Fair; Meet
the Applegates; Motel;
Murphy's Romance; The
Man on the Flying Trapeze;
Matinee; Mystic Pizza; The
Next Voice You Hear...;
Nobody's Fool; Other Men's
Women; Our Town; Painted
Heart; Parents; Paris Trout;
Peyton Place; Phenomenon;
The Positively True
Adventures of the Alleged
Texas Cheerleader-
Murdering Mom; The Prince
of Pennsylvania; Public
Access; Queens of the Big
Time; Rally 'round the Flag,
Boys!; River's Edge; Rosalie
Goes Shopping; Safe
Passage; Storm Center; The
Sun Shines Bright;
Testament (Littman);
Texasville; These Three; This
Boy's Life; Tremors; True
Stories; Trust; Twin Peaks;
Twin Peaks: Fire Walk With
Me; The Unbelievable Truth;
Vernon Florida; The War;
Welcome Home, Roxy
Carmichael; The Well;
When Willie Comes
Marching Home;
The Wild One

Smiley, Jane, film based on
work, A Thousand Acres

Smith, Dodie, films adapted
from work, Autumn Crocus;
One Hundred and One
Dalmatians
(Reitherman/Luske/Geronimi);
101 Dalmatians (Herek)

Smith, Lady Eleanor, film
adapted from work, The
Man in Grey

Smith, Stevie, film about,
Stevie

Smith, Wilbur, films adapted
from work, Gold; The
Mercenaries; Shout at the
Devil

Bath – Hamam; Train of Shadows; Tristana; Two Much; Vacas; El Verdugo; Viridiana; What Have I Done to Deserve This?; Women on the Verge of a Nervous Breakdown

Spark, Muriel, films adapted from work, *Nasty Habits; The Prime of Miss Jean Brodie*

Spiders, see **Insects, spiders, etc**

Spillane, Mickey, films adapted from work, *I, the Jury; Kiss Me Deadly*

Spiritualism, *Before Dawn; Black Rainbow; Family Plot; The Medium; Nightmare Alley; Supernatural*

Spontaneous combustion, by-product of sex, *Pyrates*

Spots, malevolent, *How to Get Ahead in Advertising*

Spy films
(see also **Bond, James**)
Fr, *Le Dossier 51; Espion Lève-toi; Les Espions; Mata Hari – Agent H.21; La Route de Corinthe; La Sentinelle; The Serpent*
China, *Peking Opera Blues*
GB, *American Roulette; Back-Room Boy; Catch Me a Spy; Confidential Agent; Contraband; Cottage to Let; Crook's Tour; Danger Route; A Dandy in Aspic; Dark Journey; The Deadly Affair; The Double Man; Enigma; Eye of the Needle; Fathom; The Flying Fool; The Four Just Men; The Fourth Protocol; Funeral in Berlin; The Golden Lady; Hidden City; Highly Dangerous; Hot Enough for June; The Human Factor (Preminger); The Ipcress File; The Intelligence Men; I See a Dark Stranger; The Looking Glass War; The Mackintosh Man; The Man Between; The Man in the Road; The Man Who Knew Too Much (1934); Masquerade (Dearden); Mata Hari (Harrington); Modesty Blaise; The Next of Kin; Not Now, Comrade; Otley; Our Man in Havana; The Quiller Memorandum; Rentadick; Rough Shoot; Salt & Pepper; The Secret Agent (Hitchcock); The Secret Agent (Hampton); The Sellout; Spy Hard; The Spy Who Came In From the Cold; The Tamarind Seed; The 39 Steps (Hitchcock); The 39 Steps (Thomas); The Thirty-Nine Steps (Sharp); Timeslip; Traitor Spy; When Eight Bells Toll; The Whistle Blower; The Yellow Canary; Yellow Dog*
Ger, *Dead Pigeon on Beethoven Street*
HK, *Kawashima Yoshiko*
Ire, *Avalanche Express*
It, *Danger: Diabolik; Russiccum; Superargo*
US, *Above Suspicion; Across the Pacific; The Amateru;*

Arabesque; Austin Powers: International Man of Mystery; Background to Danger; Black Eagle; Blindfold; Blue Ice; The Cape Town Affair; Careful, Soft Shoulder; Cloak and Dagger; Company Business; Condorman; Confessions of a Nazi Spy; The Conspirators; Crack-Up (St Clair); Dangerously They Live; Darling Lili; Diplomatic Courier; Dishonoured; The English Patient; The Experts; The Falcon and the Snowman; Firestarter; 5 Fingers; Foreign Correspondent; Gorky Park; The Groundstar Conspiracy; Hanky Panky; Harriet the Spy; The House on 92nd Street; How to Steal the World; The Iron Curtain; Ishtar; Journey into Fear; Jumpin' Jack Flash; The Kremlin Letter; Lancer Spy; The Little Drummer Girl; Little Nikita; Man Hunt; The Man Who Knew Too Much (1956); Mata Hari (Fitzmaurice); Mrs Pollifax – Spy; Midas Run; My Favourite Blonde; Nick Carter – Master Detective; A Night in Casablanca; Nightmare (Whelan); Notorious; The Nude Bomb; Once Upon a Honeymoon; The Osterman Weekend; Permission to Kill; The Russia House; Russian Roulette; Scorpio; Shining Through; Stamboul Quest; TAG, the Assassination Game; Target (Penn);Teen Agent; Telefon; The Thief; This Is My Affair; Three Days of the Condor; Topaz; Top Secret; Torn Curtain; Walk East on Beacon

Squatters, *Pigs*

Sri Lanka
in film, *Song of Ceylon; A Mother Alone; When Mother Comes Home for Christmas*
Sri Lankan cinema, *A Mother Alone*

Stacpoole, H de Vere, films adapted from work, *The Blue Lagoon* (Launder); *The Blue Lagoon* (Kleiser); *Return to the Blue Lagoon*

Stamp-collecting, *Charade; Penny Gold; Tommy Ticker and the Stamp Traveller*

Stark, Richard, films adapted from work (see also **Westlake, Donald E**), *Point Blank; The Outfit; The Split*

State terror (see also **Politics and politicians**)
in Cambodia, *Les Gens de la rizière*
in Canada, *Les Ordres*
in Chile *La Frontera*
in China; *Man from China; Sunless Days*
in Eastern Europe and USSR, *Brigands; Defence Counsel Sedov; The Ear; Escape from the 'Liberty' Cinema; The Inner Circle; Interrogation; Lost in Siberia; No End; The*

Party and the Guests; Pravda; The Prisoner; Requiem for Dominic; Rough Treatment; Whooping Cough; The Witness
in Latin America, *El Coraje del Pueblo; Death and the Maiden; Disparen a Matar; The Evil That Men Do; La Fièvre Monte à el Pao; The Girlfriend; Havana; The Kiss of the Spider Woman; The Lion's Den; Missing; Romero; Secret Wedding; State of Siege; Sur; When the Mountains Tremble*
in South Africa, *Cry Freedom; Mapantsula; A World Apart*
in Taiwan, *Super Citizen Ko*
in Turkey, *The Wall; Yol*
in Western Europe, *Defence of the Realm; Germany in Autumn; Hidden Agenda; Ireland: Behind the Wire; Open Doors; Section Spéciale; Z*
unidentified, *Closet Land*

Steinbeck, John
as movie host, *O. Henry's Full House*
films adapted from work, *Cannery Row, East of Eden; The Grapes of Wrath; Of Mice and Men* (Milestone); *Of Mice and Men* (Sinise)

Stendhal, films adapted from work, *La Chartreuse de Parme; The Nun and the Devil*

Stepmothers, fathers, children, etc, *Big Girls Don't Cry...They Get Even; The Black Orchid; Hollow Reed; Kolya; The Last Gangster; The Lion; Paris s'éveille; The People Under the Stairs; Phaedra; Sons; The Stepfather; The Stepfather II; Stepfather III; The Stepmother; Yours, Mine and Ours; Wicked Stepmother*

Stevenson, Robert Louis, films adapted from work Jekyll-and-Hyde stories, *Dr Jekyll and Mr Hyde* (Robertson); *Dr Jekyll and Mr Hyde* (Mamoulian); *Dr Jekyll and Mr Hyde* (Fleming); *Dr Jekyll and Ms Hyde; Dr Jekyll et Les Femmes; Dr Jekyll and Sister Hyde; Edge of Sanity; Grip of the Strangler; I Monster; Mary Reilly; The Two Faces of Dr Jekyll*
other, *L'Ile au trésor; Kidnapped; Muppet Treasure Island; Scalawag; The Strange Door; Treasure Island* (Heston); *Treasure Island* (Fridman)

Stoker, Bram, films adapted from/inspired by work, *The Awakening; Blood from the Mummy's Tomb; Dracula* (Browning); *Dracula* (Fisher); *Dracula* (Curtis); *Dracula* (Badham); *Dracula* (Coppola); *Dracula A.D. 1972; Dracula: Dead and Loving It; Dracula Has Risen from the Grave; Dracula Prince of Darkness; Dracula's Daughter; The Lair of the White Worm; The Scars of Dracula*

Stone, IF, film about, *I.F. Stone's Weekly*

Stone, Robert, films adapted from work, *Who'll Stop the Rain?; WUSA*

Stoppard, Tom, film adapted from work, *Rosencrantz and Guildenstern Are Dead*

Storey, David, film adapted from work, *This Sporting Life*

Strachey, Lytton, in film, *Carrington*

Strauss, Johann, father and son, films about, *The Great Waltz* (Duvivier); *The Great Waltz* (Stone)

Street gangs and juvenile delinquents (see also **Teenagers and teen movies**)
in Brazil, *Pixote*
in Britain, *Arrivederci Millwall; Brighton Rock; Bronco Bullfrog; A Clockwork Orange; Cosh Boy; Juvenile Liaison; Juvenile Liaison 2; Shopping; Small Faces*
in France, *L'Astragale; L'Eau Froide; L'Enfance nue; La Petite Voleuse; Les Quatre Cents Coups; Shark's Son; Vagabonde*
in Italy, *Ultrà*
in Japan, *Fighting Elegy*
in Korea, *Timeless Bottomless Bad Movie*
in Mexico, *Los Olvidados*
in Spain, *Fast, Fast*
in Taiwan, *A Brighter Summer Day*
in US, *The Angels Wash Their Faces; Assault on Precinct 13; Bad Boys; The Boy Who Cried Bitch; Boyz N the Hood; Bronx Warriors; Colors; Crime in the Streets; The Cross and the Switchblade; Dead End; Death Wish III; Defiance; The Delicate Delinquent; Drugstore Cowboy; Eight-Tray Gangster; The Making of a Crip; 80 Blocks from Tiffany's; Good to Go; Hangin' with the Homeboys; Juice; The Little Rascals; Lords of Flatbush; Lost Angels; Menace II Society; My Crasy Life; Only the Strong; Out of the Blue; The Outsiders* (Coppola); *Prayer of the Rollerboys; Regeneration; Rumble Fish; Streets of Fire; Touch and Go; Tuff Turf; That Gang of Mine; The Wanderers; The Warriors; West Side Story*
in USSR, *Burglar*

Strindberg, August, film adapted from work, *The Father*

Students, see **Colleges and students**

Stuntmen/women, *Ah-Kam; Hooper; The Stunt Man; Stunts*

Styron, William, film adapted from work, *Sophie's Choice*

Round the Mulberry Bush; Out of Order (Turpie); The Rachel Papers; Rita, Sue and Bob Too; Terry on the Fence; That Sinking Feeling; That Summer!; Tickets for the Zoo; TwentyFourSeven; UndeRage Jap, Leaving Sp, Fast, Fast US, All Over Me; All the Right Moves; Amongst Friends; Bill & Ted's Bogus Journey; Bill & Ted's Excellent Adventure; Blue City; Blue Denim; Body Rock; Boulevard Nights; The Boys Next Door; The Breakfast Club; Breakin'; Buffy the Vampire Slayer; Candy; Can't Buy Me Love; Children of the Corn; Class; Class of Nuke 'Em High; Corvette Summer; Courage Mountain; Crossing the Bridge; Cry-Baby; Dirty Dancing; Don't Tell Mom the Babysitter's Dead; Earth vs the Spider; Encino Man; Fast Talking; Fast Times at Ridgemont High; Ferris Bueller's Day Off; The Flamingo Kid; Footloose; For Keeps; Foxes; Friday; Girls Just Want to Have Fun; Gleaming the Cube; Good to Go; Grease; Grease 2; Gremlins; Heathers; House Party; I Know What You Did Last Summer; The Incredibly Strange Creatures Who Stopped Living and Became Mixed-Up Zombies; I Wanna Hold Your Hand; Hurricane Streets; I Was a Teenage Werewolf; Jake Speed; Johnny Suede; The Karate Kid; The Karate Kid II; The Karate Kid III; Kid; Lambada; The Last House on the Left; License to Drive; Little Nikita; Lord Love a Duck; Losin' It; Loverboy; Lucas; Making It; Mallrats; Mobsters; Night of the Comet; Night of the Demons; Nowhere; O.C. & Stiggs; One on One; Out of the Blue; The Outsiders (Coppola); Over the Edge; Pump Up the Volume; Pretty in Pink; Rancho Deluxe; Real Genius; Rebel Without a Cause; Risky Business; Rock'n'Roll High School; Rooftops; Rumble Fish; Say Anything; She's Out of Control; Sing; Sixteen Candles; Society; Some Kind of Wonderful; Some Girls; Son in Law; Teen Agent; Teenagers from Outer Space; Teen Wolf; Teen Wolf II; Telling Lies in America; Thank God It's Friday; That Night; That Was Then, This Is Now; Thunder Alley; Tilt; The Toxic Avenger; The Toxic Avenger Part II; Trick or Treat; Trust; Tuff Turf; Two of a Kind; The Unbelievable Truth; Vision Quest; The Wanderers; WarGames; The Warriors; Waxwork; Wayne's World; Wayne's World II; Weird Science; What's Eating Gilbert Grape; Where the

Boys Are; Wild in the Streets; The Wild One; The Wild Side; Wild Style; Wisdom; Youngblood; Young Guns; Young Guns II; Young Warriors USSR, Burglar; Freedom Is Paradise; Little Vera

Telekinesis, Akira; Cameron's Closet; Carrie (De Palma); Escape to Witch Mountain; Firestarter; The Fury (De Palma); Harlequin; Lord Love a Duck; The Medusa Touch; Patrick; Retribution; Return from Witch Mountain; Time of the Gypsies; Village of the Damned; Xtro

Telepathy (see also **Clairvoyance**), Brainstorm; Eyes of Laura Mars; Fear; Firestarter; The First Power; Manhunter; Powder; Scanners; Scanners II: The New Order; Shadey; The Shining; Shocker; Split Second

Telephones and callers, The Bells Are Ringing; Call Me; Family Viewing; Denise Calls Up; I Saw What You Did; Lola Has Two Lovers; Mouth to Mouth; One Fine Day; Out of Order (Turpie); Out of the Dark; Pillow Talk; Sorry, Wrong Number; The Telephone Book; The Terroriser; Things I Never Told You

Television, in film (see also **Journalism**) life in/satires of, Accidental Hero; The American Way; Broadcast News; The Cable Guy; Comic Magazine; Crimes and Misdemeanors; Crimetime; Dead Men Don't Die; Delirious; Desk Set; A Face in the Crowd; Fellow Traveller; [Focus]; The Gazebo; Ginger and Fred; The Gong Show Movie; Grief; Groundhog Day; High Heels; Icicle Thief; It Should Happen to You; Kamikaze; Kentucky Fried Movie; The Killing of Sister George; L.A. Story; The Love Machine; Meet Mr Lucifer; My Favourite Year; O for Oblomov; Quiz Show; The Sandman; Sion and Laura; Soapdish; Stay Tuned; Stuart Saves His Family; Switching Channels; Tapeheads; Testament (Akomfrah); There's a Girl in My Soup; The Thrill of It All; To Die For; Todos Somos Estrellas; Tootsie; The Truman Show; UHF; Up Close & Personal; Wayne's World; Wayne's World II; Windprints; Wrong Is Right power of, Accumulator 1; Benny's Video; Death Watch; Fahrenheit 451; I Love a Man in Uniform; Liquid Dreams; The Man Who Fell to Earth; Network; The Prize of Peril; Public Access; The Running Man (Glaser); Speaking Parts; TerrorVision; Tout Va Bien; The Truman Show

Tenants/visitors, overstaying their welcome (see also **Unwanted guests**), Apartment Zero; Boudu Sauvé des Eaux; Down and Out in Beverly Hills; Henry: Portrait of a Serial Killer; Madhouse; The More the Merrier; New Year's Day; Pacific Heights; Perfectly Normal; Poison Ivy; Single White Female; To Sleep with Anger; What About Bob?

Tennis, Dial M for Murder; Hard, Fast and Beautiful; Players; School for Scoundrels; Strangers on a Train

Terrorism, and related phenomena, in film (see also **Radicalism/revolutionism, State terror**) in Algeria, The Battle of Algiers in Africa, Death in the Sun; Something of Value in Britain, The Secret Agent (Hampton); Secret People; Seven Days to Noon; Who Dares Wins in Cyprus, The High Bright Sun in France, Nada; Nanou in Germany, The German Sisters; Germany in Autumn; The Third Generation international, Captive; The Cassandra Crossing; Exposed; Golden Rendezvous; The Human Factor (Dmytryk); Kings and Desperate Men; North Sea Hijack; Ransom; That Obscure Object of Desire in Ireland, Cal; The General (Boorman); The Gentle Gunman; Ireland: Behind the Wire; Odd Man Out in Italy, Blow to the Heart; Illustrious Corpses; The Second Time; Three Brothers; The Tragedy of a Ridiculous Man; Year of the Gun in Japan, The Bullet Train in Middle East, The Ambassador; Black Sunday; Hors la vie; Navy Seals; Not Quite Jerusalem; Operation Thunderbolt; Raid on Entebbe; Rosebud; Victory at Entebbe; Wanted Dead or Alive in US, Abduction; Air Force One; Bulletproof; Die Hard; Die Hard 2; Die Hard with a Vengeance; The Enforcer (Windust/Walsh); Executive Action; Face/Off; The Mad Bomber; Nighthawks (Malmuth); Patty Hearst; The Peacemaker; Running on Empty; Toy Soldiers; War

Tevis, Walter, films adapted from work, The Color of Money; The Hustler; The Man Who Fell to Earth

Tey, Josephine, films adapted from work, The Franchise Affair; Young and Innocent

Thackeray, William Makepeace, films adapted from work, Becky Sharp; Barry Lyndon

Thailand Thai cinema, Butterfly and Flowers; Dang Bireley's and the Young Gangsters; The Dumb Dies Fast, the Smart Die Slow; Fun Bar Karaoke; Once Upon a Time…This Morning; Path of the Brave; Puen-Paeng; The Scar; The Song of Chao-Phrya; S.T.A.B.; Tongpan Thailand in film, The Good Woman of Bangkok; Kickboxer

Thanksgiving see **Christmas and Thanksgiving films**

Thatcher's Britain, in film, Arrivederci Millwall; Babylon; Bloody Kids; Britannia Hospital; Business as Usual; Close My Eyes; Coming Up Roses; Crystal Gazing; Dealers; Didn't You Kill My Brother?; Eat the Rich; Empire State; Fords on Water; For Queen and Country; Giro City; High Hopes; How to Get Ahead in Advertising; In Fading Light; The Last of England; Live a Life; Living on the Edge; London; Looks and Smiles; The Love Child; My Beautiful Laundrette; The Nature of the Beast; No Surrender; Out of Order (Turpie); Paris by Night; The Return; Riff-Raff; Rita, Sue and Bob Too; Sammy and Rosie Get Laid; Seacoal; UndeRage; Ursula and Glenys; Women in Tropical Places

Theatre, in film in Africa, Desert Mice in Bosnia For Ever Mozart in Brazil, Bye Bye Brazil in Britain, An Awfully Big Adventure;The Brighton Strangler; A Chorus of Disapproval; Curtain Up; The Dresser; The Good Companions (Saville); The Good Companions (Thompson); The Great Garrick; In the Bleak Midwinter; Looking for Richard; Love Is Like a Violin; Madhouse; Peg of Old Drury; The Punk and the Princess; Sylvia Scarlett; Star; The Tall Guy; Theatre of Blood; Withnail and I in Canada, Une Histoire inventée; Jesus of Montreal in China, The Peach-Blossom Land; Two Stage Sisters in Denmark, Ladies on the Rocks in France, L'Amour par terre; Le Capitaine Fracassé; Les Enfants du Paradis; Every Little Thing; La Fin du Jour; French Can Can; The Incredible Sarah; The Last Melodrama; The Last Metro; Paris Nous Appartient in Germany, Veronika Voss in Greece, The Travelling Players in Hong Kong, Hu-Du-Men in India, Masquerade (Aravindan); Shakespeare-Wallah in Ireland, The Playboys in Italy, Les Amants de

Turkish cinema, *The Bandit; Berdel; The Blue Exile; The Cockroach; Cold Nights; The 80th Step; The Enemy; Farewell to False Paradise; The Herd; The Man in the Street; Mercedes Mon Amour; Night Journey; Somersault in a Coffin; The Turkish Bath – Hamam; Two Women; Yellow Smile*

Turner, Ike and Tina, film about, *Tina: What's Love Got to Do With It*

Twain, Mark
films about, *The Adventures of Mark Twain* (Rapper); *The Adventures of Mark Twain* (Vinton)
films adapted from work, *The Adventures of Huckeberry Finn; The Adventures of Huck Finn; The Adventures of Tom Sawyer; A Connecticut Yankee in King Arthur's Court; The Million Pound Note; The Prince and the Pauper; Tom Sawyer; The Unidentified Flying Oddball*

Twins, *Big Business; The Black Room; The Buttercup Chain; The Dark Mirror; Dead Ringers; Double Impact; Eclipse; Equinox; Hamlet* (Coronado); *Here Come the Waves; Hotel de Love; Malena Is a Name from a Tango; The Man in the Iron Mask* (Whale); *The Man in the Iron Mask* (Wallace); *Maximum Risk; My 20th Century; The Other* (Mulligan); *La Otra* (Gavaldón); *Penny Gold; The Palm Beach Story; Poto and Cabengo; Sisters; Steal Big, Steal Little; A Stolen Life; This World, Then the Fireworks; Twin Pawns; Twins; Twin Town; Village of Dreams*

UFOs (see also **Extra-terrestrials on Earth**), *Chariots of the Gods; Communion; That Eye, the Sky; Some Kinda Love*

Uganda, in film, *Man of Africa*

Uhry, Alfred, film adapted from work, *Driving Miss Daisy*

Undead, the (see also **After-life, Heaven-can-wait fantasies, Return to life**) mummies, *The Awakening; Blood from the Mummy's Tomb; The Curse of the Mummy's Tomb; The Mummy* (Freund); *The Mummy* (Fisher); *The Mummy's Hand; The Mummy's Shroud* zombies, etc, *Army of Darkness; The Medieval Dead; Braindead; Dawn of the Dead; Day of the Dead; Dead Men Don't Die; Dead of Night* (Clark); *Disturbed; Doctor Death; Seeker of Souls; The Evil Dead; Evil Dead II; Face of Darkness; Fantômas contre Fantômas; Ghoulies; Hellbound:*

Hellraiser II; Hellraiser; Hellraiser III: Hell on Earth; The Incredibly Strange Creatures Who Stopped Living and Became Mixed-Up Zombies; In the Mouth of Madness; Isle of the Dead; I Walked with a Zombie; The Killing Box; The Living Dead at the Manchester Morgue; Maniac Cop; Maniac Cop 2; Night of the Creeps; Night of the Ghouls; Night of the Living Dead (Romero); *Night of the Living Dead* (Savini); *Pauranella Città dei Morti Viventi; The Parasite Murders; Phantasm; Phantasm II; The Plague of the Zombies; Re-Animator; Re-Animator 2; The Return of Doctor X; The Return of the Living Dead; Return of the Living Dead Part II; Return of the Living Dead III; Trick or Treat; Voodoo Man; White Zombie; Zombie Flesh-Eaters*

Underground cinema, see **Experimental films**

Undersea worlds, and undersea adventures (see also **Submarines**), *The Abyss; The Abyss: Special Edition; The Big Blue; Captain Nemo and the Underwater City; City Beneath the Sea; City Under the Sea; The Deep; DeepStar Six; Leviathan; The Neptune Factor; The Rift; Shark; The Shark's Cave; Sharks' Treasure; Sphere; 20,000 Leagues Under the Sea; Warlords of Atlantis*

Unemployment
in Britain, *The Big Man; Conquest of the South Pole; The Full Monty; The Innocent* (MacKenzie); *Last Chants for a Slow Dance; Live a Life; Living on the Edge; Looks and Smiles; Love on the Dole; The Nature of the Beast; The Ragman's Daughter; That Sinking Feeling*
in Cuba, *One Way or Another*
in India, *The Adversary*
in Taiwan, *Taipei Story*
in US, *The Boost; Hallelujah, I'm a Bum; The Journey of Natty Gann; Palookaville; Roger & Me; The Survivors; The Toy*

Unions, see **Labour relations**

United Nations, in film, *A Global Affair*

Universities, see **Colleges and students**

Unwanted guests (see also **Tenants/visitors**), *Blind Alley* (Vidor); *The Cellar; The Dark Past; Desperate Hours* (Cimino); *The Desperate Hours* (Wyler); *Funny Games; Hardware; Hider in the House; Malice; MouseHunt; Puerto Escondido; Rawhide; Unlawful Entry; Voyage; Wicked Stepmother*

Updike, John, film adapted from work, *The Witches of Eastwick*

Urban nightmares, *Akira; Angel Dust; Best Hotel on Skid Row; Blade Runner; Blade Runner – The Director's Cut; Bronx Warriors; A Clockwork Orange; Cold Dog Soup; Delicatessen; Dr M; The Driller Killer; Eraserhead; Escape from New York; Exterminator 2; Fort Apache – The Bronx; Ice; John Carpenter's Escape from L.A.; Johnny Mnemonic; Jubilee; Koyannisqatsi; Little Murders; Nightbreed; The Out-of-Towners; Predator 2; Quick Change; RoboCop; RoboCop 2; RoboCop 3; Speed; The Taking of Pelham One Two Three; Tetsuo; Tetsuo II: Bodyhammer; Timecop; Traffic; Welcome II the Terrordome; The Warriors*

Uris, Leon, films adapted from work, *Exodus, Topaz*

Uruguay, in film, *State of Siege; Tupamaros*

Valentino, Rudolph, film about, *Valentino*

Valens, Richie, film about, *La Bamba*

Vampires, *The Addiction; The Alchemist; Blood for Dracula; Brides of Dracula; Buffy the Vampire Slayer; Captain Kronos – Vampire Hunter; Count Dracula; Countess Dracula; Count Yorga, Vampire; Cronos; Dance of the Vampires; Daughters of Darkness; Dead of Night* (Clark); *DEF by Temptation; Discipline of Death; Dracula* (Badham); *Dracula* (Browning); *Dracula* (Fisher); *Dracula* (Coppola); *Dracula A.D. 1972; Dracula: Dead and Loving It; Dracula Has Risen from the Grave; Dracula, Prince of Darkness; Dracula's Daughter; Elvira, Mistress of the Dark; Female Vampires; Fright Night; Fright Night Part 2; Le Frisson des Vampires; I Bought a Vampire Motorcycle; Incense for the Damned; Innocent Blood; Interview With the Vampire; It Conquered the World; Kiss of the Vampire; Legend of the 7 Golden Vampires; Lifeforce; The Lost Boys; Love at First Bite; Mark of the Vampire; Martin; Mr Vampire; The Monster Club; Nadja; Near Dark; Nightwing; Nocturna; Nosferatu – Eine Symphonie des Grauens; Nosferatu the Vampire; Requiem pour un Vampire; The Return of Count Yorga; Return of the Vampire; Salem's Lot; The Satanic Rites of Dracula; The Scars of Dracula; Son of Dracula; Tale of a Vampire; Taste the Blood of Dracula; Twins of Evil; Vamp; Vampira; Vampire at*

Midnight; The Vampire Bat; The Vampire Circus; Vampire in Brooklyn; The Vampire Lovers; Vampires in Venice; Vampyr; The Velvet Vampire; Le Viol du Vampire
imagining oneself to be a vampire, *Vampire's Kiss*
vampire Westerns, *Billy the Kid vs Dracula; Sundown*

Van Druten, John, films adapted from work, *I Am a Camera; Old Acquaintance; Rich and Famous*

Vane, Sutton, film adapted from work, *Outward Bound*

Van Gogh, Vincent, films about, *Lust for Life; Van Gogh; Vincent: The Life and Death of Vincent Van Gogh; Vincent & Theo*

Vargas Llosa, Mario, film adapted from work, *Tune in Tomorrow*

Venereal diseases, *The Clinic*

Venezuelan cinema, *Disparen a Matar*

Venice, in film, *Blame It on the Bellboy; Blume in Love; The Comfort of Strangers; Death in Venice; Don't Look Now; Eve; Everyone Says I Love You; Festival* (Avati); *In Love and War; A Little Romance; Nest of Vipers; Play Me Something; Senso; Summertime; Vampires in Venice; Venice: Theme and Variation; The Wings of the Dove*

Ventriloquism, *Dead of Night; The Doll* (Ghose); *Killing Dad; Knock on Wood; Magic*

Verdi, Giuseppe, films of/featuring operas, *The Adventure of Sherlock Holmes' Smarter Brother; Otello; Rigoletto; La Traviata*

Verlaine, Paul, film about, *Total Eclipse*

Verne, Jules, films adapted from work, *The Adventures of Michael Strogonoff; The Amazing Captain Nemo; Around the World in 80 Days; Captain Nemo and the Underwater City; Journey to the Centre of the Earth; Jules Verne's Rocket to the Moon; The Light at the Edge of the World; Mysterious Island; 20,000 Leagues Under the Sea*

Victoria, Queen of England, in film, *Mrs Brown; The Mudlark*

Vidal, Gore, films adapted from work, *The Best Man; Myra Breckinridge*

Videomakers, *Skinless Night; Tapeheads*

Vienna, in film, *Before Sunrise; Bitter Sweet;*

Goodnight Vienna; Letter from an Unknown Woman; The Third Man

Vietnam
Vietnamese cinema, Cyclo; Nostalgia for Countryland; The Return
Vietnam in film, Cyclo; Nostalgia for Countryland; The Return; The Scent of Green Papaya

Vietnam War, Air America; Apocalypse Now; BAT 21; Born on the Fourth of July; The Boys in Company C; Bullet in the Head; Casualties of War; Dear America: Letters Home from Vietnam; The Deer Hunter; 84 Charlie Mopic; Flight of the Intruder; Full Metal Jacket; Good Morning Vietnam; Go Tell the Spartans; The Green Berets; Hamburger Hill; Heaven & Earth; The Iron Triangle; The Odd Angry Shot; Off Limits; Platoon
aftermath, Cyclo; Turtle Beach
anti-war movement, Far from Vietnam; Letter to Jane; 1969; Rude Awakening; Running on Empty; Vietnam Journey

Vietnam veterans, Accidental Hero; Americana; The American Way; Backfire; The Big Lebowski; Billy Jack; Birdy; Blind Fury; Blue Thunder; Born Losers; Born on the Fourth of July; Ceasefire; Coming Home; Cutter's Way; The Deer Hunter; Desperate Hours (Cimino); The Diamond Mercenaries; The Domino Principle; Don't Play with Fire; Extreme Prejudice; Eyewitness; Firefox; First Blood; The Fourth War; Gardens of Stone; Good Guys Wear Black; Gordon's War; Hearts and Minds; Heroes; Hi, Mom!; In Country; The Indian Runner; Jacknife; Jacob's Ladder; Jason's Lyric; Lethal Weapon; Lethal Weapon 2; Lethal Weapon 3; Missing in Action; Open Season; Rambo: First Blood, Part II; Rambo III; Scent of a Woman; Slaughter; Slaughter's Big Rip-Off; Some Kind of Hero; Summer Soldiers; Taxi Driver; Tracks; Ulee's Gold; Uncommon Valor; Universal Soldier; Unnatural Causes: The Agent Orange Story; Vigilante Force; The War; War; Welcome Home; Who'll Stop the Rain?

Vietnamese in USA, Alamo Bay; Gleaming in the Cuba

Vigilantes, Breaking Point; Cop's Honour; The Crackdown; Death Wish; Death Wish II; Death Wish 3; Death Wish 4: Defiance; Exterminator 2; Eye for an Eye; Falling Down; Fighting Back; Fury (Lang); Gordon's War; Handgun (Garnett); Hero at Large;

Jimmy Hollywood; Law and Disorder; Original Gangstas; The Ox-Bow Incident; Surf Nazis Must Die; Taxi; 10 to Midnight; This Day and Age; Trackdown; Vigilante Force; Young Warriors

Villard, Henry S, film adapted from work, In Love and War

Vikings, Erik the Viking; The Long Ships; The Norseman; The Vikings; The Viking Women and Their Voyage to the Waters of the Great Sea Serpent

Virtual reality, The Lawnmower Man; Lawnmower Man 2: Beyond Cyberspace

Volcanoes, Aloma of the South Seas; Dante's Peak; Krakatoa – East of Java; The Last Days of Pompeii; La Soufrière; Stromboli, Terra di Dio; Volcano

von Arnim, Elizabeth, film adapted from work, Enchanted April

von Bülow, Claus, film about, Reversal of Fortune

von Hoffman, Nicholas, film adapted from work, Citizen Cohn

Vonnegut, Kurt, films adapted from work, Happy Birthday, Wanda June; Mother Night; Slaughterhouse Five; Who Am I This Time?

Voodoo and similar sects, Barravento; The Believers; Curtis's Charm; The Ghost Breakers; Island of Mutation; I Walked with a Zombie; Midnight in the Garden of Good and Evil; Mississippi Burning; The Serpent and the Rainbow; Voodoo Woman; White Zombie; Zombie Flesh-Eaters

Voyeurism, Addicted to Love; Blind Date (Mastorakis); Cheap Shots; Dekalog 6: 'Thou shalt not commit adultery'; Extreme Close-Up; Fetishes; Homework; Jardines Colgantes; Monsieur Hire; Peeping Tom; Rear Window; sex, lies and videotape; A Short Film About Love; Sliver; White Room

Wagner, Richard
film about, Wagner
film of opera, Parsifal

Wagner, Winifred, film about, The Confessions of Winifred Wagner

Wales, in film, August; Boy Soldier; Circle of Danger; Coming Up Roses; Danny Jones; Les Deux Anglaises et le Continent; Darklands; Elenya; The Englishman Who Went Up a Hill, But Came Down a Mountain; Experience Preferred But

Not Essential; Hedd Wyn; House of America; The James Gang; One Full Moon; Only Two Can Play; On the Black Hill; The Phantom Light; The Proposition; Rebecca's Daughters; Second Best; Streetlife; Tiger Bay; Twin Town; Under Milk Wood; Valley of Song

Walker, Alice, film adapted from work, The Color Purple

Walker, Bruce, film adapted from work, Cosh Boy

Walker, David, film adapted from work, Geordie; Operation Amsterdam

Wallace, Edgar, films adapted from work, Before Dawn; Dark Eyes of London; The Gaunt Stranger; The Squeaker

Wallace, William, in film, Braveheart

Waller, Robert James, film from work, The Bridges of Madison County

Walser, Robert, film adapted from work, Institute Benjamenta

Wambaugh, Joseph, films adapted from work, The Black Marble; The Choirboys; The Glitter Dome; The New Centurions; The Onion Field

War criminals (see also **Germany, Jews and Jewish life),** Blood Oath; The Boys from Brazil; Capoblanco; Deadfall; Father; Hotel Terminus: The Life and Times of Klaus Barbie; The House on Carroll Street; The House on Garibaldi Street; Judgment at Nuremberg; The Man in the Glass Booth; The Memory of Justice; Music Box; The Night Porter; None Shall Escape; The Odessa File; The Stranger (Welles)

Warhol, Andy, films about/associated with, Basquiat; Bike Boy; Blood for Dracula; Blue Movie; Chelsea Girls; Couch; Flesh; Heat (Morrissey); I Shot Andy Warhol; Lonesome Cowboys; My Hustler; Nico Icon; Trash; Women in Revolt

Warren, Robert Penn, film adapted from work, All the King's Men

Watergate, All the President's Men; Nasty Habits; Nixon; Paperback Vigilante; Return Engagement; The Werewolf of Washington

Waterhouse, Keith, and Hall, Willis, films adapted from work, Billy Liar; The Long and the Short and the Tall

Waugh, Alec, film adapted from work, Island in the Sun

Waugh, Evelyn, films adapted from work, Decline and Fall...of a Birdwatcher; A Handful of Dust; The Loved One

Waxworks, Chamber of Horrors; Crucible of Terror; House of Wax; Mystery of the Wax Museum; Waxwork

Wedekind, Frank, film adapted from work, Pandora's Box

Weegee, film about, The Public Eye

Weill, Kurt
film about, September Songs: The Music of Kurt Weill
musical by, Lady in the Dark; Lost in the Stars
and Brecht, Bertold, musical by, Die Dreigroschenoper

Weiss, Peter, film adapted from work, The Persecution and Assassination of Jean-Paul Marat as Performed by the Inmates of the Asylum of Charenton under the Direction of the Marquis de Sade

Weldon, Fay, film adapted from work, She-Devil

Wellman, William, film about, Wild Bill: A Hollywood Maverick

Wells, HG
fictional representation, Time After Time
films adapted from/based on work, Empire of the Ants; Food of the Gods; Half a Sixpence; The History of Mr Polly; The Invisible Man; The Island of Dr Moreau (Taylor); The Island of Dr Moreau (Frankenheimer); The Island of Mutations; The Man Who Could Work Miracles; The Passionate Friends; The Shape of Things to Come; Things to Come; Time After Time; The Time Machine; War of the Worlds

Wenders, Wim, film about, Motion and Emotion: The Films of Wim Wenders

Werewolves, An American Werewolf in Paris; The Beast Must Die; The Curse of the Werewolf; Frankenstein Meets the Wolf Man; The Howling; I Was a Teenage Werewolf; The Return of the Vampire; Silver Bullet; Teen Wolf; Teen Wolf II; The Undying Monster; Werewolf of London; The Werewolf of Washington; Wolf; Wolfen; The Wolf Man

Wesker, Arnold, film adapted from work, The Kitchen

West, Morris, films adapted from work, The Devil's Advocate; The Shoes of the Fisherman

West, Nathanael, film adapted from work, The Day of the Locust

Westerns (see Appendix 15 for full listing)
end-of-West, *Comes a Horseman; The Grey Fox; Lonely Are the Brave; The Man Who Shot Liberty Valance; The Misfits; Monte Walsh; Once Upon a Time in the West; Pat Garrett and Billy the Kid; Ride the High Country; The Spikes Gang; The Wild Bunch*
influence of, *My Dear Tom Mix*
schnitzel, *The Hellhounds of Alaska*
spaghetti, *Bad Man's River; The Big Silence; Blazing Guns; Blindman; Blood Money; Blood River; A Bullet for the General; China 9, Liberty 37; Comin' at Ya!; Companeros; Cry Onion; Deaf Smith and Johnny Ears; Django; Django Kill; El Condor; A Fistful of Dollars; A Fistful of Fingers; For a Few Dollars More; The Good, the Bad and the Ugly; Guns for San Sebastian; Il Mercenario; My Name Is Nobody; Once Upon a Time in the West; I Quattro dell'Ave Maria; A Reason to Live, a Reason to Die; Red Sun; Return of Sabata; Sabata; Shalako; Straight to Hell; Take a Hard Ride; Texas, Addio; They Call Me Trinity; Three Bullets for a Long Gun; Today It's Me…Tomorrow You!; A Town Called Bastard; The Triumphs of a Man Called Horse; Valdez il Mezzosangue; Vengeance*

Westlake, Donald E, films adapted from work (see also **Stark, Richard**), *Bank Shot; The Hot Rock; Jimmy the Kid; Two Much; Why Me?*

Whales, *Ace Ventura, Pet Detective; Day of the Dolphin; Flipper* (Clark); *Flipper* (Shapiro); *Free Willy; Free Willy 2; Free Willy 3: The Rescue; Moby Dick; Namu, The Killer Whale; Orca; Tadpole and the Whale; The Unfish; Venus Peter; When the Wales Came*

Wharton, Edith, films adapted from work, *The Age of Innocence; Ethan Frome*

Wharton, William, films adapted from work, *Birdy; A Midnight Clear*

Wheatley, Dennis, films adapted from work, *The Devil Rides Out; The Lost Continent; To the Devil a Daughter*

White, EB, film adapted from work, *Charlotte's Web*

White, TH, film adapted from work, *The Sword in the Stone*

Whitman, Walt, film about, *Beautiful Dreamers*

Wilde, Oscar
films adapted from work, *Black and Silver; Flesh and Fantasy; An Ideal Husband; The Importance of Being Earnest; The Picture of Dorian Gray; Salome* (Bryant); *Salomé* (d'Anna); *Salomé's Last Dance*
his life retold, *A Man of No Importance*
in film, *The Trials of Oscar Wilde; Wilde*

Wilder, Thornton
films adapted from work, *Mr North; Our Town*
work in film, *First Love* (Lee Myung-Se)

Willeford, Charles, films adapted from work, *Cockfighter; Miami Blues*

Williams, Charles, films adapted from work, *Dead Calm; The Hot Spot; Vivement Dimanche*

Williams, Emlyn, films adapted from work, *Night Must Fall* (Thorpe); *Night Must Fall* (Reisz); *Time Without Pity*

Williams, Tennessee, films adapted from work, *Baby Doll; Boom; Cat on a Hot Tin Roof; The Fugitive Kind; The Glass Menagerie; The Night of the Iguana; Noir et Blanc; Period of Adjustment; The Roman Spring of Mrs Stone; A Streetcar Named Desire; Suddenly Last Summer; Summer and Smoke; Sweet Bird of Youth* (Brooks); *Sweet Bird of Youth* (Roeg); *This Property Is Condemned*

Williamson, David, films adapted from work, *Brilliant Lies; The Club; Don't Party; Travelling North*

Williamson, Henry, film adapted from work, *Tarka the Otter*

Willingham, Calder, films adapted from work, *Rambling Rose; The Strange One*

Willis, Ted, film adapted from work, *No Trees in the Street*

Wing, Avra, film adapted from work, *Angie*

Witchcraft, etc (see also **Devil, The, and Antichrist, Magic and magicians**), *Baba Yaga – The Devil Witch; Bedknobs and Broomsticks; The Cellar; The Craft; The Crucible; The Curse of the Crimson Altar; Cry of the Banshee; Daughter of Satan; Day of Wrath; The Devil Rides Out; The Devils; The Devil's Rain; The Face of Darkness; Ghoulies; The Guardian; Halloween III; Halloween: The Curse of Michael Myers; The Haunted Palace; Hello Again; Hex; Hocus Pocus; I Married a Witch; Jack's Wife; The Kiss; The Lair of the White Worm; Maid for Pleasure; The Manitou; La*

Maschera del Demonio; The Mask (Roffman); *The Mask of the Red Death; The Mephisto Waltz; Night of the Demon; Night of the Eagle; Pumpkinhead; Race with the Devil; Rosemary's Baby; Satan's Skin; Satan's Slave; Supergirl; Superstition; Terror; To the Devil a Daughter; To Sleep with Anger; The Undead; The Unholy; Warlock; Wicked Stepmother; Witchcraft Through the Ages; The Witches; The Witches of Eastwick; Witchfinder General; Wizard of Darkness*

Witness-to-crime stories, *Absolute Power; The Bedroom Window; Blow Out* (De Palma); *Body Double; Call Me; Cheap Shots; The Client; Cohen and Tate; Dangerous Mission; The Eyes of Laura Mars; Eyewitness* (Hough); *Eyewitness* (Yates); *Flight of the Innocent; The Fruit Machine; Highways by Night; Lady on a Train; Love and Bullets; The Mad Miss Manton; Monolith; Nadine; Off and Running; Rapid Fire; Rear Window; See No Evil, Hear No Evil; The Sleeping Car Murder; Some Like It Hot; Stop! or My Mom Will Shoot; True Identity; Turner and Hooch; L'Uccello dalle Piume di Cristallo; White Room; The Window; Witness*

Wittgenstein, Ludwig, film about, *Wittgenstein*

Wodehouse, PG, film adapted from work, *Thank You, Jeeves!*

Wolfe, Tom, films adapted from work, *The Bonfire of the Vanities; The Last American Hero; The Right Stuff*

Wolfe, Winifred, film adapted from work, *Ask Any Girl*

Wolff, Tobias, film adapted from work, *This Boy's Life*

Women
and ageing, *Bye-Bye Babushka; The Company of Strangers; The First Wives Club; Good Morning, Miss Dove; MURDER and Murder; Unhook the Stars; La Vieille Dame indigne*
and independence, *All's Fair; Anna Karenina* (Brown); *Anna Karenina* (Duvivier); *Anna Karenina* (Rose); *The Associate; The Ballad of Little Jo; Bandit Queen; Bhaji on the Beach; Blue Steel; Les Bonnes Femmes; Bye Bye Blues; Camilla; Camille Claudel; Century; Christopher Strong; City of Women; Club des Femmes; Confessions of a Suburban Girl; Courage Under Fire; Cross and Passion; Dance, Girl, Dance; Desperately Seeking Susan; Diary of a Mad Housewife; Doll's Eye; The End of August; The*

First Wives Club; Fire; Flowers in the Attic; The Flower of My Secret; Fried Green Tomatoes at the Whistle Stop Café; Full Moon in Paris; Good Morning, Miss Dove; Hi, Are You Alone?; Hindle Wakes; Honey and Venom; How to Make an American Quilt; If These Walls Could Talk; I Like It Like That; Joyriders; Kika; Kiss the Girls; Klute; A League of Their Own; Leaving Normal; The Left-Handed Woman; Lucie Aubrac; Majdhar; The Major and the Minor; Malou; Mama's Dirty Girls; Monkey Grip; MURDER and Murder; My Brilliant Career; My Crazy Life; My Life Without Steve; Mystic Pizza; Nanou; The Net; Nine Months; Norma Rae; 1+1=3; The Opposite Sex; Paris Was a Woman; Patti Rocks; The Prime of Miss Jean Brodie; Privilege (Rainer); *Rachel, Rachel; The Rainbow; Redheads; Right Out of History: The Making of Judy Chicago's Dinner Party; Passion Fish; Salt of the Earth; The Scent of Green Papaya; The Secret of Convict Lake; Set It Off; Shame; She Lives to Ride; Shirley Valentine; Sigmund Freud's Dora; The Silence of the Lambs; Sliding Doors; Strapless; There's Always Tomorrow; Three Colours: Blue; True Lies; Unhook the Stars; Union Maids; An Unmarried Woman; An Unsuitable Job for a Woman; Up the Sandbox; V I Warshawski; Waiting to Exhale; Wanda; The Watermelon Woman; What Have I Written?; The White Wall; Widows Peaks; Wifemistress; The Wild Party* (Arzner); *A Winter Tan; Wives; Wives: Ten Years After; Wives III; A Woman Rebels; Woman to Woman; The Women; Women in Love*
as victim, *The Burning; Calle Mayor; Deceived; La Dentellière; Farewell to False Paradise; Folle à Tuer; 40 Square Metre Germany; Immoral Tales; The Incredible Shrinking Woman; Intimate Confessions of a Chinese Courtesan; Jackson County Jail; Lucia; Die Marquise von O…; The Match Factory Girl; Occasional Work of a Female Slave; The Power of Men Is the Patience of Women; La Signora senza camelie; Sleeping with the Enemy; Stranger; Streetlife; Summer Wishes; Theatre Girls; Thesis; A Thousand Pieces of Gold; We're Alive; Woman in a Dressing Gown; A Woman Under the Influence*
femmes fatales/avengers/destroyers, *Act of Vengeance; Adrenalin – Fear the Rush; Afternoon Breezes; Attack of the Fifty Foot Woman* (Juran); *Attack of the 50ft Woman* (Guest);*

Bayonet; The Story of GI Joe; 36 Hours; The True Glory; Twelve O'Clock High; Verboten; The Victors; A Walk in the Sun; The Way to the Stars; Western Approaches; What Did You Do in the War, Daddy?; Where Eagles Dare; Which Way to the Front?; A Yank in the RAF

World War II: Resistance and life in occupied countries (see also **Germany, Jews and Jewish life**)
in Belgium, *Against the Wind; Une Femme Entre Chien et Loup*
in Burma, *Never So Few*
in China, *Au revoir, mon amour*
in Czechoslovakia, *Closely Observed Trains; The Deserter and the Nomads; Hangmen Also Die; Hitler's Madman; Operation Daybreak*
in Denmark, *Once There Was A War*
in Europe (unidentified), *This Land Is Mine*
in France, *L'Affiche Rouge; L'Armée des Ombres; Au Revoir les Enfants; La Bataille du Rail; Carve Her Name With Pride; Chantons sous l'Occupation; Un Condamné à Mort s'est Echappé; Le Corbeau; Coup de Foudre; Docteur Petiot; Escape Route to Marseille; Hotel Terminus: The Life and Times of Klaus Barbie; Les Jeux Interdits; Julia; Lacombe Lucien; The Last Metro; Leon Morin, Priest; Letters to an Unknown Lover; Lucie Aubrac; November Moon; Odette; One Man's War; Orders to Kill; Paris After Dark; Pétain; Le Petit Matin; Le Roi des Aulnes; Section Spéciale; Le Silence de la mer; Souvenir; Till We Meet Again; The Train; Uranus; Le Vieil Homme et l'Enfant; Les Violons du Bal; We Were One Man*
in Fr West Indies, *The Breaking Point* (Curtiz); *To Have and Have Not*
in Greece, *The Guns of Navarone; Ill Met by Moonlight; Mediterraneo; Signs of Life*
in Hong Kong, *Love in a Fallen City*
in Hungary, *Confidence; Hanna's War; My Mother's Courage; My Way Home*
in Italy, *Era Notte a Roma; From the Cloud to the Resistance; Massacre in Rome; The Night of San Lorenzo; Paisà; Roma, Città Aperta*
in Morocco, *Casablanca*
in the Netherlands, *The Girl With the Red Hair; One of Our Aircraft Is Missing; Operation Amsterdam; Operation Crossbow*
in Norway, *Force 10 from Navarone; The Heroes of Telemark*
in Philippines *American Guerilla in the Philippines*
in Poland, *Ashes and Diamonds; A Generation; Kanal; Korczak; Lodz Ghetto; Night Paths; None Shall Escape; Schindler's List; The Third Part of the Night; To Be or Not To Be* (Lubitsch); *To Be or Not To Be* (Johnson)
in unidentified country *La Neige était sale*
in Yugoslavia, *Innocence Unprotected; The Long Ride; Occupation in 26 Pictures; 67 Days; That Summer of White Roses*

Worms, malevolent, *Squirm; Tremors; The Worm Eaters*

Wouk, Herman, film adapted from work, *The Caine Mutiny*

Wrestling, *Night and the City; The One and Only; Paradise Alley; Vision Quest*
arm wrestling, *Over the Top*
female, *...All the Marbles; Below the Belt; Fetishes; Hellcat Mud Wrestlers*

Writers and writing
in Argentina, *Cortazar; Last Images of the Shipwreck*
in Australia, *Hotel Sorrento; Kangaroo*
in Belgium, *Benvenuta*
in Brazil, *O Amor Natural*
in Britain, *Boom; A Business Affair; Charlie Bubbles; Eve; Gothic; Haunted Summer; Hedd Wyn; Horrors of the Black Museum; Keep the Aspidistra Flying; Love and Death on Long Island; Play Me Something; Prick Up Your Ears; Priest of Love; Prospero's Books; The Pumpkin Eater; Regeneration; The Romantic Englishwoman; Shadowlands; Sleuth; Stevie; Tiré à Part; The Trials of Oscar Wilde; Volcano*
in Canada, *Swann*
in Finland, *Flame Top*
in France, *Beaumarchais; Céleste; La Discrète; En Compagnie d'Antonin Artaud; Impromptu; Les Equilibristes; Jo; The Last Time I Saw Paris; Paris Was a Woman; The Proprietor; Tiré à Part; Total Eclipse; Turtle on Its Back; La Vie de Bohème*
in Germany, *Berlin Jerusalem; Satan's Brew; 3 Women in Love; Wrong Movement*
in Greece, *Cavafy; Zorba the Greek*
in India, *Bombay Talkie; In Custody*
in Ireland, *Girl with Green Eyes; My Left Foot; A Portrait of the Artist as a Young Man; Young Cassidy*
in Italy, *The Footman; Il Postino; Tenebrae; L'Uccello dalle Piume di Cristallo*
in Japan, *Mishima: A Life in Four Chapters; The Mystery of Rampo*
in Malta, *Trenchcoat*
in Mexico, *Gaby – A True Story*
in New Zealand, *An Angel at My Table; Crush*
in Portugal, *The Other One*
in South Korea, *Wind Echoing in My Being*
in Spain, *The Flower of My Secret; Tender Hours*
in Sweden, *Amorosa*
in Switzerland, *La Salamandre*
in US, *The Accidental Tourist; The Adventure of Mark Twain* (Rapper); *The Adventures of Mark Twain* (Vinton); *Another Woman; As Good As It Gets; Author, Author; Barton Fink; Beautiful Dreamers; Beloved Infidel; Best Seller; A Bucket of Blood; Closet Land; Communion; The Dark Half; Deconstructing Harry; Delirious; Equinox; A Fine Madness; The Front; Girl Shy; Hammett; Heartbeat; Henry & June; Henry Fool; Her Alibi; House; House by the River; In a Lonely Place; In the Mouth of Madness; I Remember Mama; James Baldwin; Kerouac; The Price of the Ticket; Julia; Love Streams; Manhattan; Misery; Monster in a Box; Naked Lunch; Never Give a Sucker an Even Break; The Proprietor; Reuben, Reuben; She-Devil; She's Having a Baby; Skin Deep; The Snows of Kilimanjaro; Some Came Running; Sudden Fear; Surrender; Sweet Liberty; Tales of Ordinary Madness; Theodora Goes Wild; Throw Momma from the Train; Tune in Tomorrow; Vampire's Kiss; The Waterdance; The Way We Were; Whatever Happened to Kerouac; When Ladies Meet; Wild in the Country; The Wind* (Mastorakis); *A Winter Tan; The World According to Garp*
in USSR, *Blue Mountains; The Colour of Pomegranates; The Colour of Pomegranates: Director's Cut; The Theme*

Wyndham, John, films adapted from work, *Children of the Damned; The Day of the Triffids; Quest for Love; Village of the Damned*

X-Ray and abnormal vision, *Blind Date* (Mastorakis); *Eyes of Laura Mars; X – the Man with X-Ray Eyes*

Yakuza, in film *Another Lonely Hitman; The Bird People in China; Black Rain* (Scott); *Boiling Point* (Kitano); *Gonin; Golnin 2; Kamizake Taxi; Like a Rolling Stone; Minbo Woman – Or the Gentle Art of Japanese Extortion; One Generation of Tattoos; Organ; The Outer Way; The Punisher; Shinjuku Triad Society; Sonatine; Tokyo Drifter; Violent Cop; The Wicked Reporter; World Apartment Horror; The Yakuza*

The Yeti *The Abominable Snowman*

Yiddish films, *Almonds and Raisins; The Dybbuk; The Light Ahead; Yiddle with His Fiddle;*

Young, Neil, in performance, *Rust Never Sleeps*

Yourcenar, Marguerite, film adapted from work, *Coup de Grâce*

Yugoslavia and Former Yugolslavia, in film, *Innocence Unprotected; Occupation in 26 Pictures; Pretty Village, Pretty Flame; 67 Days; Special Treatment; That Summer of White Roses; Underground* (Kusturica); *Virgin* (Karanovic); *When Father Was Away on Business; W.R. – Mysteries of the Organism*

Yugoslavian and Former Yugoslavian cinema
Arizona Dreaming; Austerlitz; Innocence Unprotected; The Long Ships; Man Is Not a Bird; The Master and Margarita; Occupation in 26 Pictures; Pretty Village, Pretty Flame; Siberian Lady Macbeth; 67 Days; Special Treatment; Time of the Gypsies; Veillées d'Armes; Virgin (Karanovic); *When Father Was Away on Business; W.R. – Mysteries of the Organism*

Zaire/Congo
Zairean cinema, *Macadam Tribu; La Vie est belle*
Zaire/Congo in film, *The Mercenaries; When We Were Kings*

Zangwill, Israel, film adapted from work, *The Verdict* (Siegel)

Zapata, Emiliano, film about, *Viva Zapata!*

Zenobia, Queen of Syria, in film, *Sign of the Gladiator*

Zetterling, Mai, film about, *Lines from the Heart*

Ziegfeld, Florenz, films about, *Ziegfeld Follies; Ziegfeld Girl*

Zimbabwe
Zimbabwean cinema, *Flame; Jit; Kini & Adams*
Zimbabwe in film, *Death in the Sun; Flame; Game for Vultures*

Zola, Emile
film about, *The Life of Emile Zola*
films adapted from work, *L'Argent* (L'Herbier); *La Bête Humaine; La Faute de l'Abbé Mouret; Germinal; Human Desire; Manifesto; Nana* (Arzner); *Nana* (Renoir); *Nana* (Wolman)

Zoos, *Cat People* (Schrader); *Cat People* (Tourneur); *Fierce Creatures; Murders in the Zoo; Roselyne and the Lions; A Zed & Two Noughts; Zoo in Budapest*

Zweig, Stefan, films adapted from work, *Burning Secret; Letter from an Unknown Woman*

Academy & Festival Awards

Academy of Motion Picture Arts and Sciences (Oscars)

1927/28
Picture: *Wings*
Director: Frank Borzage (*7th Heaven*)
Actor: Emil Jannings (*The Last Command, The Way of All Flesh*)
Actress: Janet Gaynor (*7th Heaven, Street Angel, Sunrise*)

1928/29
Picture: *Broadway Melody*
Director: Frank Lloyd (*The Divine Lady, Weary River, Drag*)
Actor: Warner Baxter (*In Old Arizona*)
Actress: Mary Pickford (*Coquette*)

1929/30
Picture: *All Quiet on the Western Front*
Director: Lewis Milestone (*All Quiet on the Western Front*)
Actor: George Arliss (*Disraeli*)
Actress: Norma Shearer (*The Divorcee*)

1930/31
Picture: *Cimarron*
Director: Norman Taurog (*Skippy*)
Actor: Lionel Barrymore (*A Free Soul*)
Actress: Marie Dressler (*Min and Bill*)

1931/32
Picture: *Grand Hotel*
Director: Frank Borzage (*Bad Girl*)
Actor: Wallace Beery (*The Champ*)
Actress: Helen Hayes (*The Sin of Madelon Claudet*)

1932/33
Picture: *Cavalcade*
Director: Frank Lloyd (*Cavalcade*)
Actor: Charles Laughton (*The Private Life of Henry VIII*)
Actress: Katharine Hepburn (*Morning Glory*)

1934
Picture: *It Happened One Night*
Director: Frank Capra (*It Happened One Night*)
Actor: Clark Gable (*It Happened One Night*)
Actress: Claudette Colbert (*It Happened One Night*)

1935
Picture: *Mutiny on the Bounty*
Director: John Ford (*The Informer*)
Actor: Victor McLaglen (*The Informer*)
Actress: Bette Davis (*Dangerous*)

1936
Picture: *The Great Ziegfeld*
Director: Frank Capra (*Mr Deeds Goes to Town*)
Actor: Paul Muni (*The Story of Louis Pasteur*)
Actress: Luise Rainer (*The Great Ziegfeld*)

1937
Picture: *The Life of Emile Zola*
Director: Leo McCarey (*The Awful Truth*)
Actor: Spencer Tracy (*Captains Courageous*)
Actress: Luise Rainer (*The Good Earth*)

1938
Picture: *You Can't Take It With You*
Director: Frank Capra (*You Can't Take It With You*)
Actor: Spencer Tracy (*Boys Town*)
Actress: Bette Davis (*Jezebel*)

1939
Picture: *Gone With the Wind*
Director: Victor Fleming (*Gone With the Wind*)
Actor: Robert Donat (*Goodbye, Mr Chips*)
Actress: Vivien Leigh (*Gone With The Wind*)

1940
Picture: *Rebecca*
Director: John Ford (*The Grapes of Wrath*)
Actor: James Stewart (*The Philadelphia Story*)
Actress: Ginger Rogers (*Kitty Foyle*)

1941
Picture: *How Green Was My Valley*
Director: John Ford (*How Green Was My Valley*)
Actor: Gary Cooper (*Sergeant York*)
Actress: Joan Fontaine (*Suspicion*)

1942
Picture: *Mrs Miniver*
Director: William Wyler (*Mrs Miniver*)
Actor: James Cagney (*Yankee Doodle Dandy*)
Actress: Greer Garson (*Mrs Miniver*)

1943
Picture: *Casablanca*
Director: Michael Curtiz (*Casablanca*)
Actor: Paul Lukas (*Watch on the Rhine*)
Actress: Jennifer Jones (*The Song of Bernadette*)

1944
Picture: *Going My Way*
Director: Leo McCarey (*Going My Way*)
Actor: Bing Crosby (*Going My Way*)
Actress: Ingrid Bergman (*Gaslight*)

1945
Picture: *The Lost Weekend*
Director: Billy Wilder (*The Lost Weekend*)
Actor: Ray Milland (*The Lost Weekend*)
Actress: Joan Crawford (*Mildred Pierce*)

1946
Picture: *The Best Years of Our Lives*
Director: William Wyler (*The Best Years of Our Lives*)
Actor: Fredric March (*The Best Years of Our Lives*)
Actress: Olivia de Havilland (*To Each His Own*)

1947
Picture: *Gentleman's Agreement*
Director: Elia Kazan (*Gentleman's Agreement*)
Actor: Ronald Colman (*A Double Life*)
Actress: Loretta Young (*The Farmer's Daughter*)

1948
Picture: *Hamlet*
Director: John Huston (*The Treasure of the Sierra Madre*)
Actor: Laurence Olivier (*Hamlet*)
Actress: Jane Wyman (*Johnny Belinda*)

1949
Picture: *All the King's Men*
Director: Joseph L Mankiewicz (*A Letter to Three Wives*)
Actor: Broderick Crawford (*All the King's Men*)
Actress: Olivia de Havilland (*The Heiress*)

1950
Picture: *All About Eve*
Director: Joseph L Mankiewicz (*All About Eve*)
Actor: José Ferrer (*Cyrano de Bergerac*)
Actress: Judy Holliday (*Born Yesterday*)

1951
Picture: *An American in Paris*
Director: George Stevens (*A Place in the Sun*)
Actor: Humphrey Bogart (*The African Queen*)
Actress: Vivien Leigh (*A Streetcar Named Desire*)

1952
Picture: *The Greatest Show on Earth*
Director: John Ford (*The Quiet Man*)
Actor: Gary Cooper (*High Noon*)
Actress: Shirley Booth (*Come Back Little Sheba*)

1953
Picture: *From Here to Eternity*
Director: Fred Zinnemann (*From Here to Eternity*)
Actor: William Holden (*Stalag 17*)
Actress: Audrey Hepburn (*Roman Holiday*)

1954
Picture: *On the Waterfront*
Director: Elia Kazan (*On the Waterfront*)
Actor: Marlon Brando (*On the Waterfront*)
Actress: Grace Kelly (*The Country Girl*)

1955
Picture: *Marty*
Director: Delbert Mann (*Marty*)
Actor: Ernest Borgnine (*Marty*)
Actress: Anna Magnani (*The Rose Tattoo*)

1956
Picture: *Around the World in Eighty Days*
Director: George Stevens (*Giant*)
Actor: Yul Brynner (*The King and I*)
Actress: Ingrid Bergman (*Anastasia*)

1957
Picture: *The Bridge on the River Kwai*
Director: David Lean (*The Bridge on the River Kwai*)
Actor: Alec Guinness (*The Bridge on the River Kwai*)
Actress: Joanne Woodward (*The Three Faces of Eve*)

1958
Picture: *Gigi*
Director: Vincente Minnelli (*Gigi*)
Actor: David Niven (*Separate Tables*)
Actress: Susan Hayward (*I Want To Live*)

1959
Picture: *Ben-Hur*
Director: William Wyler (*Ben-Hur*)
Actor: Charlton Heston (*Ben-Hur*)
Actress: Simone Signoret (*Room at the Top*)

1960
Picture: *The Apartment*
Director: Billy Wilder (*The Apartment*)
Actor: Burt Lancaster (*Elmer Gantry*)
Actress: Elizabeth Taylor (*Butterfield 8*)

1961
Picture: *West Side Story*
Director: Jerome Robbins, Robert Wise (*West Side Story*)
Actor: Maximilian Schell (*Judgment at Nuremberg*)
Actress: Sophia Loren (*Two Women*)

1962
Picture: *Lawrence of Arabia*
Director: David Lean (*Lawrence of Arabia*)
Actor: Gregory Peck (*To Kill a Mockingbird*)
Actress: Anne Bancroft (*The Miracle Worker*)

1963
Picture: *Tom Jones*
Director: Tony Richardson (*Tom Jones*)
Actor: Sidney Poitier (*Lilies of the Field*)
Actress: Patricia Neal (*Hud*)

1964
Picture: *My Fair Lady*
Director: George Cukor (*My Fair Lady*)
Actor: Rex Harrison (*My Fair Lady*)
Actress: Julie Andrews (*Mary Poppins*)

1965
Picture: *The Sound of Music*
Director: Roben Wise (*The Sound of Music*)
Actor: Lee Marvin (*Cat Ballou*)
Actress: Julie Christie (*Darling*)

1966
Picture: *A Man for All Seasons*
Director: Fred Zinnemann (*A Man for All Seasons*)
Actor: Paul Scofield (*A Man for All Seasons*)
Actress: Elizabeth Taylor (*Who's Afraid of Virginia Woolf?*)

1967
Picture: *In the Heat of the Night*
Director: Mike Nichols (*The Graduate*)
Actor: Rod Steiger (*In the Heat of the Night*)
Actress: Katharine Hepburn (*Guess Who's Coming to Dinner*)

1968
Picture: *Oliver!*
Director: Carol Reed (*Oliver!*)
Actor: Cliff Robertson (*Charly*)
Actress: Katharine Hepburn (*The Lion in Winter*)

1969
Picture: *Midnight Cowboy*
Director: John Schlesinger (*Midnight Cowboy*)
Actor: John Wayne (*True Grit*)
Actress: Maggie Smith (*The Prime of Miss Jean Brodie*)

1970
Picture: *Patton*
Director: Franklin J Schaffner (*Patton*)
Actor: George C Scott (*Patton*)
Actress: Glenda Jackson (*Women in Love*)

1971
Picture: *The French Connection*
Director: William Friedkin (*The French Connection*)
Actor: Gene Hackman (*The French Connection*)
Actress: Jane Fonda (*Klute*)

1972
Picture: *The Godfather*
Director: Bob Fosse (*Cabaret*)
Actor: Marlon Brando (*The Godfather*)
Actress: Liza Minnelli (*Cabaret*)

1973
Picture: *The Sting*
Director: George Roy Hill (*The Sting*)
Actor: Jack Lemmon (*Save the Tiger*)
Actress: Glenda Jackson (*A Touch of Class*)

1974
Picture: *The Godfather Part II*
Director: Francis Ford Coppola (*The Godfather Part II*)
Actor: Art Carney (*Harry and Tonto*)
Actress: Ellen Burstyn (*Alice Doesn't Live Here Anymore*)

1975
Picture: *One Flew Over the Cuckoo's Nest*
Director: Milos Forman (*One Flew Over the Cuckoo's Nest*)
Actor: Jack Nicholson (*One Flew Over the Cuckoo's Nest*)
Actress: Louise Fletcher (*One Flew Over the Cuckoo's Nest*)

1976
Picture: *Rocky*
Director: John G Avildsen (*Rocky*)
Actor: Peter Finch (*Network*)
Actress: Faye Dunaway (*Network*)

1977
Picture: *Annie Hall*
Director: Woody Allen (*Annie Hall*)
Actor: Richard Dreyfuss (*The Goodbye Girl*)
Actress: Diane Keaton (*Annie Hall*)

1978
Picture: *The Deer Hunter*
Director: Michael Cimino (*The Deer Hunter*)
Actor: Jon Voight (*Coming Home*)
Actress: Jane Fonda (*Coming Home*)

1979
Picture: *Kramer vs Kramer*
Director: Robert Benton (*Kramer vs Kramer*)
Actor: Dustin Hoffman (*Kramer vs Kramer*)
Actress: Sally Field (*Norma Rae*)

1980
Picture: *Ordinary People*
Director: Robert Redford (*Ordinary People*)
Actor: Robert De Niro (*Raging Bull*)
Actress: Sissy Spacek (*Coal Miner's Daughter*)

1981
Picture: *Chariots of Fire*
Director: Warren Beatty (*Reds*)
Actor: Henry Fonda (*On Golden Pond*)
Actress: Katharine Hepburn (*On Golden Pond*)

1982
Picture: *Gandhi*
Director: Richard Attenborough (*Gandhi*)
Actor: Ben Kingsley (*Gandhi*)
Actress: Meryl Streep (*Sophie's Choice*)

1983
Picture: *Terms of Endearment*
Director: James L Brooks (*Terms of Endearment*)
Actor: Robert Duvall (*Tender Mercies*)
Actress: Shirley MacLaine (*Terms of Endearment*)

1984
Picture: *Amadeus*
Director: Milos Forman (*Amadeus*)
Actor: F Murray Abraham (*Amadeus*)
Actress: Sally Field (*Places in the Heart*)

1985
Picture: *Out of Africa*
Director: Sydney Pollack (*Out of Africa*)
Actor: William Hurt (*Kiss of the Spider Woman*)
Actress: Geraldine Page (*The Trip to Bountiful*)

1986
Picture: *Platoon*
Director: Oliver Stone (*Platoon*)
Actor: Paul Newman (*The Color of Money*)
Actress: Marlee Matlin (*Children of a Lesser God*)

1987
Picture: *The Last Emperor*
Director: Bernardo Bertolucci (*The Last Emperor*)
Actor: Michael Douglas (*Wall Street*)
Actress: Cher (*Moonstruck*)

1988
Picture: *Rain Man*
Director: Barry Levinson (*Rain Man*)
Actor: Dustin Hoffman (*Rain Man*)
Actress: Jodie Foster (*The Accused*)

1989
Picture: *Driving Miss Daisy*
Director: Oliver Stone (*Born on the Fourth of July*)
Actor: Daniel Day Lewis (*My Left Foot*)
Actress: Jessica Tandy (*Driving Miss Daisy*)

1990
Picture: *Dances with Wolves*
Director: Kevin Costner (*Dances with Wolves*)
Actor: Jeremy Irons (*Reversal of Fortune*)
Actress: Kathy Bates (*Misery*)

1991
Picture: *The Silence of the Lambs*
Director: Jonathan Demme (*The Silence of the Lambs*)
Actor: Anthony Hopkins (*The Silence of the Lambs*)
Actress: Jodie Foster (*The Silence of the Lambs*)

1992
Picture: *Unforgiven*
Director: Clint Eastwood (*Unforgiven*)
Actor: Al Pacino (*Scent of a Woman*)
Actress: Emma Thompson (*Howards End*)

1993
Picture: *Schindler's List*
Director: Steven Spielberg (*Schindler's List*)
Actor: Tom Hanks (*Philadelphia*)
Actress: Holly Hunter (*The Piano*)

1994
Picture: *Forrest Gump*
Director: Robert Zemeckis (*Forrest Gump*)
Actor: Tom Hanks (*Forrest Gump*)
Actress: Jessica Lange (*Blue Sky*)

1995
Picture: *Braveheart*
Director: Mel Gibson (*Braveheart*)
Actor: Nicolas Cage (*Leaving Las Vegas*)
Actress: Susan Sarandon (*Dead Man Walking*)

1996
Picture: *The English Patient*
Director: Anthony Minghella (*The English Patient*)
Actor: Geoffrey Rush (*Shine*)
Actress: Frances McDormand (*Fargo*)

1997
Best Picture: *Titanic*
Best Director: James Cameron (*Titanic*)
Best Actor: Jack Nicholson (*As Good As It Gets*)
Best Actress: Helen Hunt (*As Good As It Gets*)
Best Supporting Actor: Robin Williams (*Good Will Hunting*)
Best Supporting Actress: Kim Basinger (*LA Confidential*)
Best Foreign Film: *Karakter* (Netherlands)
Best Original Screenplay: Ben Affleck, Matt Damon (*Good Will Hunting*)
Best Adapted Screenplay: Brian Helgeland, Curtis Hanson (*LA Confidential*)
Best Editing: *Titanic*
Best Art Direction: *Titanic*
Best Visual Effects: *Titanic*
Best Dramatic Score: *Titanic*
Best Musical Score: *The Full Monty*
Best Original Song: 'My Heart Will Go On' (*Titanic*)
Best Costume: *Titanic*

British Academy of Film and Television Arts (BAFTA Awards)

1948
Film: *The Best Years of Our Lives*

1949
Film: *Hamlet*

1950
Film: *Bicycle Thieves*

1951
Film: *All About Eve*

1952
Film: *La Ronde*

1953
Film: *The Sound Barrier*
Actor: Ralph Richardson (*The Sound Barrier*)
Actress: Vivien Leigh (*A Streetcar Named Desire*)

1954
Film: *Jeux Interdits*
Actor: John Gielgud (*Julius Caesar*)
Actress: Audrey Hepburn (*Roman Holiday*)

1955
Film: *The Wages of Fear*
Actor: Kenneth More (*Doctor in the House*)
Actress: Yvonne Mitchell (*The Divided Heart*)

1956
Film: *Richard III*
Actor: Laurence Olivier (*Richard III*)
Actress: Katie Johnson (*The Ladykillers*)
Actress: Betsy Blair (*Marty*)

1957
Film: *Gervaise*
Actor: Peter Finch (*A Town Like Alice*)
Actress: Virginia McKenna (*A Town Like Alice*)

1958
Film: *The Bridge on the River Kwai*
Actor: Alec Guinness (*The Bridge on the River Kwai*)
Actress: Heather Sears (*The Story of Esther Costello*)

1959
Film: *Room at the Top*
Actor: Trevor Howard (*The Key*)
Actress: Irene Worth (*Orders to Kill*)

1960
Film: *Ben-Hur*
Actor: Peter Sellers (*I'm All Right, Jack*)
Actress: Audrey Hepburn (*The Nun's Story*)

1961
Film: *The Apartment*
Actor: Peter Finch (*The Trials of Oscar Wilde*)
Actress: Rachel Roberts (*Saturday Night and Sunday Morning*)

1962
Film: *Ballad of a Soldier*
Actor: Peter Finch (*No Love for Johnnie*)
Actress: Dora Bryan (*A Taste of Honey*)

1963
Film: *Lawrence of Arabia*
Actor: Peter O'Toole (*Lawrence of Arabia*)
Actress: Leslie Caron (*The L-Shaped Room*)

1964
Film: *Tom Jones*
Actor: Dirk Bogarde (*The Servant*)
Actress: Rachel Roberts (*This Sporting Life*)

1965
Film: *Dr Strangelove: or, How I Learned to Stop Worrying and Love the Bomb*
Actor: Richard Attenborough (*Seance on A Wet Afternoon, Guns at Batasi*)
Actress: Audrey Hepburn (*Charade*)

1966
Film: *My Fair Lady*
Actor: Dirk Bogarde (*Darling*)
Actress: Julie Christie (*Darling*)

1967
Film: *Who's Afraid of Virginia Woolf?*
Actor: Richard Burton (*Who's Afraid of Virginia Woolf?, The Spy Who Came in from the Cold*)
Actress: Elizabeth Taylor (*Who's Afraid of Virginia Woolf?*)

1968
Film: *A Man for All Seasons*
Actor: Paul Scofield (*A Man for All Seasons*)
Actress: Edith Evans (*The Whisperers*)

1969
Film: *The Graduate*
Actor: Spencer Tracy (*Guess Who's Coming To Dinner*)
Actress: Katharine Hepburn (*Guess Who's Coming To Dinner, The Lion in Winter*)

1970
Film: *Midnight Cowboy*
Actor: Dustin Hoffman (*Midnight Cowboy*)
Actress: Maggie Smith (*The Prime of Miss Jean Brodie*)

1971
Film: *Butch Cassidy and the Sundance Kid*
Actor: Robert Redford (*Butch Cassidy and the Sundance Kid*)
Actress: Katharine Ross (*Butch Cassidy and the Sundance Kid, Tell Them Willie Boy Is Here, Downhill Racer*)

1972
Film: *Sunday, Bloody Sunday*
Actor: Peter Finch (*Sunday, Bloody Sunday*)
Actress: Glenda Jackson (*Sunday, Bloody Sunday*)

1973
Film: *Cabaret*
Actor: Gene Hackman (*The French Connection, The Poseidon Adventure*)
Actress: Liza Minnelli (*Cabaret*)

1974
Film: *Day for Night*
Actor: Walter Matthau (*Pete 'n' Tillie*)
Actress: Stéphane Audran (*The Discreet Charm of the Bourgeoisie*)

1975
Film: *Lacombe Lucien*
Actor: Jack Nicholson (*Chinatown, The Last Detail*)
Actress: Joanne Woodward (*Summer Wishes, Winter Dreams*)

1976
Film: *Alice Doesn't Live Here Anymore*
Actor: Al Pacino (*The Godfather Part II, Dog Day Afternoon*)
Actress: Ellen Burstyn (*Alice Doesn't Live Here Anymore*)

1977
Film: *One Flew Over the Cuckoo's Nest*
Actor: Jack Nicholson (*One Flew Over the Cuckoo's Nest*)
Actress: Louise Fletcher (*One Flew Over The Cuckoo's Nest*)

1978
Film: *Annie Hall*
Actor: Peter Finch (*Network*)
Actress: Diane Keaton (*Annie Hall*)

1979
Film: *Julia*
Actor: Richard Dreyfuss (*The Goodbye Girl*)
Actress: Jane Fonda (*Julia*)

1980
Film: *Manhattan*
Actor: Jack Lemmon (*The China Syndrome*)
Actress: Jane Fonda (*The China Syndrome*)

1981
Film: *The Elephant Man*
Actor: John Hurt (*The Elephant Man*)
Actress: Judy Davis (*My Brilliant Career*)

1982
Film: *Chariots of Fire*
Actor: Burt Lancaster (*Atlantic City*)
Actress: Meryl Streep (*The French Lieutenant's Woman*)

1983
Film: *Gandhi*
Actor: Ben Kingsley (*Gandhi*)
Actress: Katharine Hepburn (*On Golden Pond*)

1984
Film: *Educating Rita*
Actor: Michael Caine (*Educating Rita*)
Actor: Dustin Hoffman (*Tootsie*)
Actress: Julie Walters (*Educating Rita*)

1985
Film: *The Killing Fields*
Actor: Haing S Ngor (*The Killing Fields*)
Actress: Maggie Smith (*A Private Function*)

1986
Film: *The Purple Rose of Cairo*
Actor: William Hurt (*Kiss of the Spider Woman*)
Actress: Peggy Ashcroft (*A Passage to India*)

1987
Film: *A Room with a View*
Actor: Bob Hoskins (*Mona Lisa*)
Actress: Maggie Smith (*A Room with a View*)

1988
Film: *Jean de Florette*
Actor: Sean Connery (*The Name of the Rose*)
Actress: Anne Bancroft (*84 Charing Cross Road*)

1989
Film: *The Last Emperor*

Actor: John Cleese (*A Fish Called Wanda*)
Actress: Maggie Smith (*The Lonely Passion of Judith Hearne*)

1990
Film: *Dead Poets Society*
Actor: Daniel Day Lewis (*My Left Foot*)
Actress: Pauline Collins (*Shirley Valentine*)

1991
Film: *GoodFellas*
Actor: Philippe Noiret (*Cinema Paradiso*)
Actress: Jessica Tandy (*Driving Miss Daisy*)

1992
Film: *The Commitments*
Actor: Anthony Hopkins (*The Silence of the Lambs*)
Actress: Jodie Foster (*The Silence of the Lambs*)

1993
Film: *Howards End*
Actor: Robert Downey Jr (*Chaplin*)
Actress: Emma Thompson (*Howards End*)

1994
Film: *Schindler's List*
Actor: Anthony Hopkins (*The Remains of the Day*)
Actress: Holly Hunter (*The Piano*)

1995
Film: *Four Weddings and a Funeral*
Actor: Hugh Grant (*Four Weddings and a Funeral*)
Actress: Susan Sarandon (*The Client*)

1996
Film: *Sense and Sensibility*
Actor: Nigel Hawthorne (*The Madness of King George*)
Actress: Emma Thompson (*Sense and Sensibility*)

1997
Film: *The English Patient*
Actor: Geoffrey Rush (*Shine*)
Actress: Brenda Blethyn (*Secrets & Lies*)

1998
Best Film: *The Full Monty*
Best Director: Baz Luhrmann (*William Shakespeare's Romeo & Juliet*)
Best Actor: Robert Carlyle (*The Full Monty*)
Best Actress: Judi Dench (*Mrs Brown*)
Best Original Screenplay: Gary Oldman (*Nil by Mouth*)
Best Adapted Screenplay: Craig Pearce, Baz Luhrmann (*William Shakespeare's Romeo & Juliet*)
Best Supporting Actor: Tom Wilkinson (*The Full Monty*)
Best Supporting Actress: Sigourney Weaver (*The Ice Storm*)
Best Foreign Film: *L'Appartement*

Cannes Film Festival

1946
Director: René Clément (*La Bataille du Rail*)
Director: Mikhail Romm (*Chelovyek No. 217*)
Actor: Ray Milland (*The Lost Weekend*)
Actress: Michèle Morgan (*La Symphonie Pastorale*)

1949
Director: René Clément (*Au-delà des Grilles*)
Actor: Edward G Robinson (*House of Strangers*)
Actress: Isa Miranda (*Au-delà des Grilles*)

1951
Director: Luis Buñuel (*Los Olvidados*)
Actor: Michael Redgrave (*The Browning Version*)
Actress: Bette Davis (*All About Eve*)

1952
Director: Christian-Jaque (*Fanfan la Tulipe*)
Actor: Marlon Brando (*Viva Zapata!*)
Actress: Lee Grant (*Detective Story*)

1953
Actor: Charles Vanel (*The Wages of Fear*)
Actress: Shirley Booth (*Come Back Little Sheba*)

1955
Palme d'Or: *Marty*
Director: Sergei Vasiliev (*Heroes of Shipka*)
Director: Jules Dassin (*Du Rififi Chez les Hommes*)

1956
Palme d'Or: *Le Monde du Silence*
Director: Sergei Yutkevich (*Othello*)

1957
Palme d'Or: *Friendly Persuasion*
Director: Robert Bresson (*Un Condamné à Mort s'est Echappé*)
Actor: John Kitzmiller (*Dolina Miru*)
Actress: Giulietta Masina (*Le Notti di Cabiria*)

1958
Palme d'Or: *The Cranes Are Flying*
Director: Ingmar Bergman (*So Close to Life*)
Actor: Paul Newman (*The Long Hot Summer*)
Actress: Ingrid Thulin, Eva Dahlbeck and Barbro Hiort af Ornäs (*So Close to Life*)

1959
Palme d'Or: *Black Orpheus*
Director: François Truffaut (*Les Quatre Cents Coups*)
Actor: Bradford Dillman, Dean Stockwell, Orson Welles (*Compulsion*)
Best Actress: Simone Signoret (*Room at the Top*)

1960
Palme d'Or: *La Dolce Vita*
Actress: Melina Mercouri (*Never on Sunday*)
Actress: Jeanne Moreau (*Moderato Cantabile*)

1961
Palme d'Or: *Une Aussi Longue Absence*
Palme d'Or: *Viridiana*
Director: Yulia Solntseva (*Povest Plamennykh Let*)
Actor: Anthony Perkins (*Aimez-Vous Brahms?*)
Actress: Sophia Loren (*Two Women*)

1962
Palme d'Or: *O Pagador de Promessas*

1963
Palme d'Or: *The Leopard*
Actor: Richard Harris (*This Sporting Life*)
Actress: Marina Vlady (*Queen Bee*)

1964
Actor: Saro Urzi (*Seduced and Abandoned*)
Actor: Antál Pager (*Pacsirta*)
Actress: Anne Bancroft (*The Pumpkin Eater*)
Actress: Barbara Barrie (*One Potato, Two Potato*)

1965
Director: Liviu Ciulei (*The Lost Forest*)
Best Actor: Terence Stamp (*The Collector*)
Best Actress: Samantha Eggar (*The Collector*)

1966
Director: Sergei Yutkevich (*Portrait of Lenin*)
Actor: Per Oscarsson (*The Hunger*)
Actress: Vanessa Redgrave (*Morgan, a Suitable Case for Treatment*)

1969
Director : Glauber Rocha (*Antonio das Mortes*)
Director: Vojtech Jasny (*All Good Citizens*)
Actor: Jean-Louis Trintignant (*Z*)
Actress: Vanessa Redgrave (*Isadora*)

1970
Director: John Boorman (*Leo the Last*)
Actor: Marcello Mastroianni (*Jealousy – Italian Style*)
Actress: Ottavia Piccolo (*Metello*)

1971
Actor: Riccardo Cucciolla (*Sacco & Vanzetti*)
Actress: Kitty Winn (*Panic in Needle Park*)

1972
Director: Miklós Jancsó (*Red Psalm*)
Actor: Jean Yanne (*We Will Not Grow Old Together*)
Actress: Susannah York (*Images*)

1973
Actor: Giancarlo Giannini (*Love and Anarchy*)
Actress: Joanne Woodward (*The Effect of Gamma Rays on Man-in-the-Moon Marigolds*)

1974
Actor: Jack Nicholson (*The Last Detail*)
Actress: Marie-José Nat (*Les Violons du Bal*)

1975
Palme d'Or: *Ahdat Sanawouach El-Djamr*
Director: Costa-Gavras (*Section Spéciale*)
Director: Michel Brault (*Les Ordres*)
Actor: Vittorio Gassman (*Profumo di Donna*)
Actress: Valerie Perrine (*Lenny*)

1976
Palme d'Or: *Taxi Driver*
Director: Ettore Scola (*Brutti, sporchi e cattivi*)
Actor: José Luis Gómez (*Pascual Duarte*)
Actress: Dominique Sanda (*The Inheritance*)
Actress: Mari Töröcsik (*Deryne, Hol Van?*)

1977
Palme d'Or: *Padre Padrone*
Actor: Fernando Rey (*Elisa, Vida Mia*)
Actress: Shelley Duvall (*3 Women*)
Actress: Monique Mercure (*J.A. Martin, Photographer*)

1978
Palme d'Or: *The Tree of Wooden Clogs*
Director: Nagisa Oshima (*Empire of Passion*)
Actor: Jon Voight (*Coming Home*)
Actress: Jill Clayburgh (*An Unmarried Woman*)
Actress: Isabelle Huppert (*Violette Nozière*)

1979
Palme d'Or: *Apocalypse Now*
Palme d'Or: *The Tin Drum*
Director: Terrence Malick (*Days of Heaven*)
Actor: Jack Lemmon (*The China Syndrome*)
Actress: Sally Field (*Norma Rae*)

1980
Palme d'Or: *Kagemusha*
Palme d'Or: *All That Jazz*
Actor: Michel Piccoli (*Leap into the Void*)
Actress: Anouk Aimée (*Leap into the Void*)

1981
Palme d'Or: *Man of Iron*
Actor: Ugo Tognazzi (*The Tragedy of a Ridiculous Man*)
Actress: Isabelle Adjani (*Possession, Quartet*)

1982
Palme d'Or: *Yol*
Palme d'Or: *Missing*
Director: Werner Herzog (*Fitzcarraldo*)
Actor: Jack Lemmon (*Missing*)
Actress: Jadwiga Jankowska-Cieslak (*Egymára Nézve*)

1983
Palme d'Or: *The Ballad of Narayama*
Actor: Gian Maria Volonté (*The Death of Mario Ricci*)
Actress: Hanna Schygulla (*Storia di Piera*)

1984
Palme d'Or: *Paris, Texas*
Director: Bertrand Tavernier (*Sunday in the Country*)
Actor: Francisco Rabal and Alfredo Landa (*Los Santos Inocentes*)
Actress: Helen Mirren (*Cal*)

1985
Palme d'Or: *When Father Was Away on Business*
Director: André Téchiné (*Rendez-vous*)
Actor: William Hurt (*Kiss of the Spider Woman*)
Actress: Norma Aleandro (*The Official Version*)

1986
Palme d'Or: *The Mission*
Director: Martin Scorsese (*After Hours*)
Actor: Bob Hoskins (*Mona Lisa*)
Actress: Barbara Sukowa (*Rosa Luxemburg*)
Actress: Fernanda Torres (*Eu Sei Que Vou Te Amar*)

1987
Palme d'Or: *Under Satan's Sun*
Director: Wim Wenders (*Wings of Desire*)
Actor: Marcello Mastroianni (*Dark Eyes*)
Actress: Barbara Hershey (*Shy People*)

1988
Palme d'Or: *Pelle the Conqueror*
Director: Fernando Solanas (*Sur*)
Actor: Forest Whitaker (*Bird*)
Actress: Barbara Hershey, Jodhi May and Linda Mvusi (*A World Apart*)

1989
Palme d'Or: *sex, lies and videotape*
Director: Emir Kusturica (*Time of the Gypsies*)
Actor: James Spader (*sex, lies and videotape*)
Actress: Meryl Streep (*A Cry in the Dark*)

1990
Palme d'Or: *Wild at Heart*
Director: Pavel Lounguine (*Taxi Blues*)
Actor: Gérard Depardieu (*Cyrano de Bergerac*)
Actress: Krystyna Janda (*The Interrogation*)

1991
Palme d'Or: *Barton Fink*
Director: Joel Coen and Ethan Coen (*Barton Fink*)
Actor: John Turturro (*Barton Fink*)
Actress: Irène Jacob (*The Double Life of Véronique*)

1992
Palme d'Or: *Intentions*
Director: Robert Altman (*The Player*)
Actor: Tim Robbins (*The Player*)
Actress: Pernilla Ostergran (*Den Goda Viljan*)

1993
Palme d'Or: *Farewell My Concubine*
Palme d'Or: *The Piano*
Director: Mike Leigh (*Naked*)
Actor: David Thewlis (*Naked*)
Actress: Holly Hunter (*The Piano*)

1994
Palme d'Or: *Pulp Fiction*
Director: Nanni Moretti (*Dear Diary*)
Actor: Ge You (*To Live*)
Actress: Virna Lisi (*La Reine Margot*)

1995
Palme d'Or: *Underground*
Director: Mathieu Kassovitz (*La Haine*)
Actor: Jonathan Pryce (*Carrington*)
Actress: Helen Mirren (*The Madness of King George*)

1996
Palme d'Or: *Secrets & Lies*
Director: Joel Coen (*Fargo*)
Actor: Daniel Auteuil (*The Eighth Day*)
Actor: Pascal Duquenne (*The Eighth Day*)
Actress: Brenda Blethyn (*Secrets & Lies*)

1997
Palme d'Or: *A Taste of Cherry* (*Ta'me-gilas*) (Abbas Kiarostami)
Palme d'Or: *Unagi* (Shohei Imamura)
Best Director: Wong Kar-Wai (*Happy Together*)
Best Actor: Sean Penn (*She's So Lovely*)
Best Actress: Kathy Burke (*Nil by Mouth*)

1998
Palme d'Or: *Eternity and a Day* (*Mia Eoniotita Ke Mia Mera*) (Theo Angelopoulos)
Best Director: John Boorman (*The General*)
Best Actor: Peter Mullan (*My Name Is Joe*)
Best Actress: Elodie Bouchez (*La Vie Rêvée des Anges*)
Best Actress: Natacha Régnier (*La Vie Rêvée des Anges*)
Best Script: Hal Hartley (*Henry Fool*)
Grand Jury Prix: *La Vita è Bella* (Roberto Benigni)
Jury Prize: *Class Trip* (Claude Miller)
Jury Prize: *Festen* (Thomas Vinterberg)
Best Artistic Contribution: *Velvet Goldmine* (*Todd Haynes*)

Berlin Film Festival

1956
Golden Bear: *Invitation to the Dance*
Actor: Burt Lancaster (*Trapeze*)
Actress: Elsa Martinelli (*Donatella*)

1957
Golden Bear: *12 Angry Men*
Director: Mario Monicelli (*Padri e Figli…*)
Actor: Pedro Infante (*Tizoc*)
Actress: Yvonne Mitchell (*Woman in a Dressing Gown*)

1958
Golden Bear: *Wild Strawberries*
Director: Tadashi Imai (*Jun-Ai Monogatari*)
Actor: Sidney Poitier (*The Defiant Ones*)
Actress: Anna Magnani (*Wild Is the Wind*)

1959
Golden Bear: *Les Cousins*
Director: Akira Kurosawa (*The Hidden Fortress*)
Actor: Jean Gabin (*Archimède le Clochard*)
Actress: Shirley MacLaine (*Ask Any Girl*)

1960
Golden Bear: *El Lazarillo de Tormes*
Director: Jean-Luc Godard (*A Bout de Souffle*)
Actor: Fredric March (*Inherit the Wind*)
Actress: Juliette Mayniel (*Kirmes*)

1961
Golden Bear: *La Notte*
Director: Bernhard Wicki (*Das Wunder des Malachias*)
Actor: Peter Finch (*No Love for Johnnie*)
Actress: Anna Karina (*Une Femme est une Femme*)

1962
Golden Bear: *A Kind of Loving*
Director: Francesco Rosi (*Salvatore Giuliano*)
Actor: James Stewart (*Mr Hobbs Takes a Vacation*)
Actress: Viveca Lindfors and Rita Gam (*No Exit*)

1963
Golden Bear: *Bushido – Samurai Saga*
Golden Bear: *The Devil*
Director: Nikos Koundouros (*Mikres Aphrodites*)
Actor: Sidney Poitier (*Lilies of the Field*)
Actress: Bibi Andersson (*The Swedish Mistress*)

1964
Golden Bear: *Waterless Summer*
Director: Satyajit Ray (*Mahanagar*)
Actress: Sachiko Hidari (*The Insect Woman, She and He*)

1965
Golden Bear: *Alphaville*
Director: Satyajit Ray (*Charulata*)
Actor: Lee Marvin (*Cat Ballou*)
Actress: Madhur Jaffrey (*Shakespeare Wallah*)

1966
Golden Bear: *Cul-de-Sac*
Director: Carlos Saura (*La Caza*)
Actor: Jean-Pierre Léaud (*Masculin Féminin*)
Actress: Lola Albright (*Lord Love a Duck*)

1967
Golden Bear: *Le Départ*
Director: Zivojin Pavlovic (*Budenje Pacova*)
Actor: Michel Simon (*Le Vieil Homme et l'Enfant*)
Actress: Edith Evans (*The Whisperers*)

1968
Golden Bear: *Who Saw Him Die?*
Director: Carlos Saura (*Peppermint Frappé*)
Actor: Jean-Louis Trintignant (*L'Homme qui Ment*)
Actress: Stéphane Audran (*Les Biches*)

1969
Golden Bear: *Rani Radovi*

1971
Golden Bear: *The Garden of the Finzi-Continis*
Actor: Jean Gabin (*Le Chat*)
Actress: Simone Signoret (*Le Chat*)
Actress: Shirley MacLaine (*Desperate Characters*)

1972
Golden Bear: *The Canterbury Tales*
Director: Jean-Pierre Blanc (*La Vieille Fille*)
Actor: Alberto Sordi (*Why?*)
Actress: Elizabeth Taylor (*Hammersmith Is Out*)

1973
Golden Bear: *Distant Thunder*

1974
Golden Bear: *The Apprenticeship of Duddy Kravitz*

1975
Golden Bear: *Örökbefogadas*
Director: Sergei Solovyov (*Sto Dnei Posle Detstva*)
Actor: Vlastimil Brodsky (*Jakob der Lügner*)
Actress: Kinuyo Tanaka (*Sandakan Hachibanshokan Bohkyo*)

1976
Director: Mario Monicelli (*Caro Michele*)
Actor: Gerd Olschewski (*Verlorenes Leben*)

1977
Golden Bear: *Voskhozhdenie*
Director: Manuel Gutiérrez Aragón (*Camada Negra*)
Actor: Fernando Fernán Gómez (*El Anácoreta*)
Actress: Lily Tomlin (*The Late Show*)

1978
Golden Bear: *Las Truchas*
Golden Bear: *Las Palabras de Max*
Director: Georgi Dyulgerov (*Avantazh*)
Actor: Craig Russell (*Outrageous*)
Actress: Gena Rowlands (*Opening Night*)

1979
Golden Bear: *David*
Director: Astrid Henning-Jensen (*Vinterboern*)
Actor: Michele Placido (*Ernesto*)
Actress: Hanna Schygulla (*The Marriage of Maria Braun*)

1980
Golden Bear: *Palermo oder Wolfsburg*
Golden Bear: *Heartland*

1981
Golden Bear: *Fast, Fast*
Director: Markus Imhoof (*Das Boot Ist Voll*)
Actor: Anatoli Solonitsyn (*Twenty-Six Days in the Life of Dostoevsky*)
Actor: Jack Lemmon (*Tribute*)
Actress: Barbara Grabowska (*Fever*)

1982
Golden Bear: *Veronika Voss*
Director: Mario Monicelli (*Il Marchese del Grillo*)
Actor: Michel Piccoli (*Une Etrange Affaire*)
Actor: Stellan Skarsgård (*A Simple-Minded Murderer*)
Actress: Katrin Sass (*Bürgschaft für ein Jahr*)

1983
Golden Bear: *Ascendancy*
Golden Bear: *La Colmena*
Director: Eric Rohmer (*Pauline à la Plage*)
Actor: Bruce Dern (*That Championship Season*)
Actress: Evgenia Glushenko (*Love by Request*)

1984
Golden Bear: *Love Streams*
Actor: Albert Finney (*The Dresser*)
Actress: Inna Churikova (*Wartime Romance*)
Actress: Monica Vitti (*Flirt*)

1985
Golden Bear: *Wetherby*
Golden Bear: *Die Frau und der Fremde*
Director: Robert Benton (*Places in the Heart*)
Actor: Fernando Fernán Gómez (*Stico*)
Actress: Jo Kennedy (*Wrong World*)

1986
Golden Bear: *Stammheim*
Director: Giorgi Shengelaja (*Journey of a Young Composer*)
Actor: Tuncel Kurtiz (*The Smile of the Lamb*)
Actress: Charlotte Valandrey (*Rouge Baiser*)
Actress: Marcélia Cartaxo (*Hour of the Star*)

1987
Golden Bear: *The Theme*
Director: Oliver Stone (*Platoon*)
Actor: Gian Maria Volonté (*The Moro Affair*)
Actress: Ana Beatriz Nogueira (*Vera*)

1988
Golden Bear: *Red Sorghum*
Director: Norman Jewison (*Moonstruck*)
Actor: Jörg Posse (*Bear Ye One Another's Burdens*)
Actor: Manfred Möck (*Bear Ye One Another's Burdens*)
Actress: Holly Hunter (*Broadcast News*)

1989
Golden Bear: *Rain Man*
Director: Dusan Hanák (*I Love, You Love*)
Actor: Gene Hackman (*Mississippi Burning*)
Actress: Isabelle Adjani (*Camille Claudel*)

1990
Golden Bear: *Music Box*
Director: Michael Verhoeven (*The Nasty Girl*)
Actor: Iain Glen (*Silent Scream*)
Joint Performance: Jessica Tandy and Morgan Freeman (*Driving Miss Daisy*)

1991
Golden Bear: *House of Smiles*
Silver Bear: Jonathan Demme (*The Silence of the Lambs*)
Silver Bear: Ricky Tognazzi (*Ultrà*)
Silver Bear: Maynard Eziashi (*Mister Johnson*)
Actress: Victoria Abril (*Amantes*)

1992
Golden Bear: *Grand Canyon*
Director: Jan Troell (*Il Capitano*)
Actor: Armin Mueller-Stahl (*Utz*)
Actress: Maggie Cheung (*Actress*)

1993
Golden Bear: *Hsi Yen*
Golden Bear: *Xian Hunnü*
Director: Andrew Birkin (*The Cement Garden*)
Actor: Denzel Washington (*Malcolm X*)
Actress: Michelle Pfeiffer (*Love Field*)

1994
Golden Bear: *In the Name of the Father*
Director: Krzysztof Kieslowski (*Three Colours: White*)
Actor: Tom Hanks (*Philadelphia*)
Actress: Chrissy Rock (*Ladybird Ladybird*)

1995
Golden Bear: *The Bait*
Director: Richard Linklater (*Before Sunrise*)
Actor: Paul Newman (*Nobody's Fool*)
Actress: Josephine Siao (*Nuiyan, Seisap*)

1996
Golden Bear: *Sense and Sensibility*
Director: Richard Loncraine (*Richard III*)
Director: Ho Yim (*The Day the Sun Turned Cold*)
Actor: Sean Penn (*Dead Man Walking*)
Actress: Anouk Grinberg (*Mon Homme*)

1997
Golden Bear: *The People vs. Larry Flynt*
Special Jury Prize: *He Liu* (Tsai Ming-Liang)
Best Director: Eric Heumann (*Port Djema*)
Best Actor: Leonardo DiCaprio (*William Shakespeare's Romeo & Juliet*)
Best Actress: Juliette Binoche (*The English Patient*)

1998
Golden Bear: *Central Do Brasil* (Walter Salles)
Special Jury Prize: *Wag the Dog* (Barry Levinson)
Best Director: Neil Jordan (*The Butcher Boy*)

Best Actor: Samuel L Jackson (*Jackie Brown*)
Best Actress: Fernanda Montenegro (*Central Do Brasil*)

Venice Film Festival

1934
Foreign Film: *Man of Aran*
Italian Film: *Teresa Confalonieri*
Actor: Wallace Beery (*Viva Villa!*)
Actress: Katharine Hepburn (*Little Women*)

1935
Foreign Film: *Anna Karenina*
Italian Film: *Casta Diva*
Director: King Vidor (*The Wedding Night*)
Actor: Pierre Blanchar (*Crime and Punishment*)
Actress: Paula Wessely (*Episode*)

1936
Foreign Film: *The Emperor of California*
Italian Film: *Squadrone Bianco*
Director: Jacques Feyder (*La Kermesse Heroique*)
Actor: Paul Muni (*The Story of Louis Pasteur*)
Actress: Annabella (*Veille d'Armes*)

1937
Foreign Film: *Un Carnet de Bal*
Italian Film: *Scipione l'Africano*
Director: Robert Flaherty and Koltan Korda (*Elephant Boy*)
Italian Director: Mario Camerini (*Il Signor Max*)
Actor: Emil Jannings (*Der Herrscher*)
Actress: Bette Davis (*Kid Galahad, Marked Woman*)

1938
Foreign Film: *Olympische Spiele 1936*
Italian Film: *Luciano serra Pilota*
Actor: Leslie Howard (*Pygmalion*)
Actress: Norma Shearer (*Marie Antoinette*)

1940
Foreign Film: *Der Postmeister*
Italian Film: *L'Assedio dell'Alcazar*

1941
Foreign Film: *Ohm Krüger*
Italian Film: *La Corona di Ferro*
Actor: Ermete Zacconi (*Don Buonaparte*)
Actress: Luise Ullrich (*Annelie*)

1947
Grand Prix: *Sirena*
Director: Henri-Georges Clouzot (*Quai des Orfèvres*)
Actor: Pierre Fresnay (*Monsieur Vincent*)
Actress: Anna Magnani (*Angelina*)

1948
Grand Prix: *Hamlet*
Director: GW Pabst (*Der Prozess*)
Actor: Ernst Deutsch (*Der Prozess*)
Actress: Jean Simmons (*Hamlet*)

1949
Director: Augusto Genina (*Cielo sulla Palude*)
Actor: Joseph Cotten (*The Portrait of Jennie*)
Actress: Olivia de Havilland (*The Snake Pit*)

1950
Actor: Sam Jaffe (*The Asphalt Jungle*)
Actress: Eleanor Parker (*Caged*)

1951
Golden Lion: *Rashomon*
Actor: Jean Gabin (*La Nuit est mon Royaume*)
Actress: Vivien Leigh (*A Streetcar Named Desire*)

1952
Golden Lion: *Jeux Interdits*
Actor: Fredric March (*Death of a Salesman*)

1953
Actor: Henri Vilbert (*Le Bon Dieu sans Confession*)
Actress: Lilli Palmer (*The Fourposter*)

1954
Golden Lion: *Romeo and Juliet*
Actor: Jean Gabin (*L'Air de Paris, Touchez pas au Grisbi*)

1956
Actor: Bourvil (*La Traversée de Paris*)
Actress: Maria Schell (*Gervaise*)

1957
Golden Lion: *Aparajito*
Actor: Anthony Franciosa (*A Hatful of Rain*)
Actress: Dzidra Ritenbergs (*Malva*)

1958
Golden Lion: *The Rickshaw Man*
Actor: Alec Guinness (*The Horse's Mouth*)
Actress: Sophia Loren (*The Black Orchid*)

1959
Golden Lion: *Il Generale della Rovere*
Golden Lion: *The Great War*
Actor: James Stewart (*Anatomy of a Murder*)
Actress: Madeleine Robinson (*A Double Tour*)

1960
Golden Lion: *Le Passage du Rhin*
Actor: John Mills (*Tunes of Glory*)
Actress: Shirley MacLaine (*The Apartment*)

1962
Golden Lion: *Family Diary*
Actor: Burt Lancaster (*Birdman of Alcatraz*)
Actress: Emmanuelle Riva (*Thérèse Desqueyroux*)

1963
Golden Lion: *Hands over the City*
Actor: Albert Finney (*Tom Jones*)
Actress: Delphine Seyrig (*Muriel*)

1964
Golden Lion: *The Red Desert*
Actor: Tom Courtenay (*King and Country*)
Actress: Harriet Andersson (*To Love*)

1965
Golden Lion: *Vaghe Stelle dell'Orsa*
Actor: Toshiro Mifune (*Red Beard*)
Actress: ? (*Trois Chambres à Manhattan*)

1967
Golden Lion: *Belle de Jour*
Actor: Ljubisa Samardzic (*Morning*)
Actress: Shirley Knight (*Dutchman*)

1968
Golden Lion: *Artistes at the Top of the Big Top: Disorientated*
Actor: John Marley (*Faces*)
Actress: Laura Betti (*Theorem*)

1980
Golden Lion: *Atlantic City*
Golden Lion: *Gloria*

1981
Golden Lion: *The German Sisters*

1982
Golden Lion: *The State of Things*

1983
Golden Lion: *Prénom Carmen*
Actor: The cast of *Streamers*
Actress: Darling Legitimus (*Black Shack Alley*)

1984
Golden Lion: *A Year of the Quiet Sun*
Actress: Pascale Ogier (*Full Moon in Paris*)
Actor: Naseeruddin Shah (*The Crossing*)

1985
Golden Lion: *Vagabonde*
Actor: Gérard Depardieu (*Police*)

1986
Golden Lion: *The Green Ray*
Actor: Carlo Delle Piane (*Regalo di Natale*)
Actress: Valeria Golino (*Storia d'Amore*)

1987
Golden Lion: *Au Revoir les Enfants*
Actor: Hugh Grant and James Wilby (*Maurice*)
Actor: Kang Soo-Yeon (*The Surrogate Woman*)

1988
Golden Lion: *The Legend of the Holy Drinker*
Director: Theo Angelopoulos
Actor: Don Ameche and Joe Mantegna (*Things Change*)
Actress: Isabelle Huppert (*Une Affaire de Femmes*)
Actress: Shirley MacLaine (*Madame Sousatzka*)

1989
Golden Lion: *City of Sadness*
Actor: Marcello Mastroianni and Massimo Troisi (*What Time Is It?*)
Actress: Peggy Ashcroft and Geraldine James (*She's Been Away*)

1990
Golden Lion: *Rosencrantz and Guildenstern Are Dead*
Direction: Martin Scorsese (*GoodFellas*)
Actor: Oleg Borisov (*The Final Testimony*)
Actress: Gloria Munchmeyer (*The Moon in the Mirror*)

1991
Golden Lion: *Urga*
Actor: River Phoenix (*My Own Private Idaho*)
Actress: Tilda Swinton (*Edward II*)

1992
Golden Lion: *The Story of Qiu Ju*
Actor: Jack Lemmon (*Glengarry Glen Ross*)
Actress: Gong Li (*The Story of Qiu Ju*)

1994
Golden Lion: *Before the Rain*
Golden Lion: *Aiqing Wansui*
Actor: Xia Yu (*Yangguang Canlan de Rizi*)
Actress: Maria de Medeiros (*Três Irmãos*)

1995
Golden Lion: *Cyclo*
Actor: George Götz (*Der Totmacher*)
Actress: Sandrine Bonnaire and Isabelle Huppert (*La Cérémonie*)

1996
Golden Lion: *Michael Collins*
Best Actor: Liam Neeson (*Michael Collins*)
Best Actress: Victoire Thivisol (*Ponette*)

1997
Golden Lion: *Hana-Bi*
Best Actor: Wesley Snipes (*One Night Stand*)
Best Actress: Robin Tunney (*Niagara*)
Special Jury Prize: *Ovosodo* (Paolo Virzi)
Best Screenplay: Gilles Taurand, Anne Fontaine (*Nettoyage à Sec*)
Best Photography: Emmanel Machuel (*Ossos*)
Best Music: Graeme Revell (*Chinese Box*)
Gold Medal of the President of the Senate: Pavel Chukhrai (*Vor*)